READER'S DIGEST
ILLUSTRATED
ENCYCLOPEDIC
DICTIONARY

READER'S DIGEST ILLUSTRATED ENCYCLOPEDIC DICTIONARY
A Reader's Digest book adapted
and developed from the lexical databases of the
Houghton Mifflin Company of Boston, Massachusetts,
with permission.

Lexical Databases, Copyright © 1987 by
Houghton Mifflin Company of Boston

The acknowledgments that appear on pages 1917–1920 are
hereby made a part of this copyright page.

READER'S DIGEST ILLUSTRATED ENCYCLOPEDIC DICTIONARY
First edition, Copyright © 1987
The Reader's Digest Association, Inc.
Pleasantville, New York

Library of Congress Cataloging in Publication Data

Reader's Digest illustrated encyclopedic dictionary.

1. Encyclopedias and dictionaries.   I. Reader's
Digest Association.
AG5.R37   1987   031   87 - 9650
ISBN 0 - 89577 - 269 - 8 (set)
ISBN 0 - 89577 - 267 - 1 (v. 1)
ISBN 0 - 89577 - 268 - X (v. 2)

READER'S DIGEST and the Pegasus logo are registered
trademarks of The Reader's Digest Association, Inc.

Printed in the United States of America
Fifth Printing, March 1993

READER'S DIGEST
ILLUSTRATED
ENCYCLOPEDIC
DICTIONARY

Volume One
A-K

The Reader's Digest Association, Inc.

Pleasantville, New York • Montreal

READER'S DIGEST ILLUSTRATED
ENCYCLOPEDIC DICTIONARY

Reader's Digest

EDITOR
David Rattray

ART EDITOR
Richard J. Berenson

ART ASSOCIATE
Morris Karol

EDITORIAL ASSISTANT
Vita Gardner

PICTURE EDITOR
Robert J. Woodward

CONTRIBUTING EDITOR
Madeleine Walker

CONTRIBUTING PICTURE RESEARCHER
Mary Leverty

CONTRIBUTING COPY EDITOR
Marsha Lutch Lloyd

READER'S DIGEST GENERAL BOOKS
Editorial Director: John A. Pope, Jr.
Managing Editor: Jane Polley
Art Director: David Trooper
Group Editors: Norman B. Mack
Susan J. Wernert

Houghton Mifflin

COORDINATING EDITOR
Pamela B. DeVinne

EDITORS
Kaethe Ellis, Susan M. Innes, David A. Jost,
James P. Marciano

CONTRIBUTING EDITORS
Walter M. Havighurst, Ramona Michaelis,
Trudy Nelson, Anne D. Steinhardt

PRODUCTION MANAGER
Christopher Leonesio

PRODUCTION COORDINATOR
Donna L. Muise

EDITORIAL PRODUCTION ASSISTANTS
Patricia McTiernan, Margaret Anne Miles

ART ASSISTANT
Tom Flynn

EDITORIAL DEPARTMENT SECRETARY
Cara Murray

COMPOSITION KEYBOARDING
Brenda Bregoli-Sturtevant, Celester Jackson,
Ron Perkins, Tracy Weiner

— PREFACE —

The English language was born fifteen hundred years ago when the Saxon invaders of the Roman province of Britain started raising children in their new homeland. Children are the inventors of language. In the earliest centuries of its existence, English remained almost identical with the Saxon dialects spoken by the settlers' forebears in what is now Germany and Denmark, across the North Sea. From A.D. 793 to 1066, England was invaded again and again by Norsemen, and for two centuries much of northern Britain was under Danish rule. Our language has retained a slightly Scandinavian flavor ever since. Following the Conquest of 1066, by French-speaking Normans, English as we know it came into being, a peculiar Germanic tongue whose vocabulary is more than two-thirds French in origin. With the Age of Exploration came the British Empire (a term coined by Queen Elizabeth's astrologer John Dee) and the language expanded in many different directions at once. Thousands of new words for new concepts and things flowed in from Latin and Greek. The vocabularies of politics, commerce, and the arts soaked up words from French, Italian, Spanish, Dutch, and other languages. At the same time, English-speaking settlers put down roots in new countries all over the globe, and within a few generations there were as many new dialects of English as there were British colonies. By the end of the 20th century, World English has already become the most important language on the planet, and North American its leading dialect. The day is at hand when everyone on earth will know at least some North American, regardless of his or her home language.

A language serving so many different communities and fields represents a body of information too vast for any one person to master. Hence the need for dictionaries. Everybody needs one nowadays. It was established some years ago that there are more dictionaries than television sets in North America. The basic purpose served by a dictionary is to furnish a word's correct spelling and syllabication, meaning, and pronunciation. In a language as vast as World English, spellings, meanings, and pronunciations fluctuate almost as rapidly as the ebb and flow of the events they mirror. As North American English becomes Number One in science, industry, and politics worldwide, people are coming to expect the dictionary to provide authoritative information about not only words but the objects and ideas they denote. This has led to a need for a new type of dictionary, one that provides all that traditional dictionaries give, and then some. In the present work we have accounted for more than 200,000 meanings coming from all of the many varieties of English, with special emphasis on North American but extensive coverage of all the rest. We continued to add important new words to the text up until the last days before the book went to press. In addition to such traditional features as word origins, usage notes, illustrative quotations, and synonyms, we have added the most extensive biographical and geographic coverage ever provided in a dictionary, together with several hundred illustrated feature articles, and 2,300 four-color pictures. Each of the pictures was chosen for its information value, the better to identify, visualize, or understand the item in question.

There is another feature that, although intangible, looms larger than all of the foregoing put together, and that is the element of due proportion and measure that we have brought to the writing of this book. Dictionary writing, like medicine, is partly a science, mostly an art. Estimates vary as to the actual number of words present in the language at any given time. Some authorities fix this at around 340,000 live items. Yet many of these are so trivial or so ephemeral that they do not really belong in a reference book. The dictionary writer, in attempting to meet the need for all-round usefulness, must rely heavily on intuition, judgment, guesswork. In a dictionary with additional encyclopedic material, the editor has to make strong-minded choices, to include or to exclude, every step of the way. At the same time, by our choice of quotations as well as our own use of English in the articles, definitions, and captions you will read in the following pages, we have tried to keep the focus on the book's highest object, which is the thing of rare beauty that is our language. According to the Book of Proverbs, "A word fitly spoken is like apples of gold in a setting of silver." It is to help our readers find many such words that we offer the present book.

—The Editor

HOW TO USE THIS DICTIONARY

FINDING THE WORD YOU WANT

All the entries in this Dictionary are listed in strict alphabetical order, letter by letter. This applies equally to hyphenated entries and entries that consist of two or more words:

> **run·ny** (rŭn′ē) *adj.*
> **Run·ny·mede** (rŭn′ē-mēd′).
> **run off** *intr.v.*
> **run-off** (rŭn′ôf′, -ŏf′) *n.*
> **run-of-the-mill** (rŭn′əv-*th*ə-mĭl′) *adj.*

Single letters, word parts, and abbreviations are also listed in alphabetical order:

> **i, I** (ī) *n., pl.* **i's** or **I's**.
> **I** (ī) *pron.*
> **i–¹.** Variant of **y-**.
> **i–².** Variant of **in-** (not).
> **IA** Iowa (used with a Zip Code).
> **i.a.** in absentia.

When an entry word contains a number, it is listed (in numerical order, where necessary) before a word that has a letter in the same position:

> **u·ra·ni·um** (yŏŏ-rā′nē-əm) *n.*
> **uranium 235** *n.*
> **uranium 238** *n.*
> **uranium dioxide** *n.*

However, when an entry begins with a number, it is listed as though it were spelled out in full:

> **two-fold** (tŏŏ′fōld′, -fōld′) *adj.* **1.** Having two components . . . .
> **2, 4, 5-T** (tŏŏ′fôr′fīv′tē′) *n.* **Trichlorophenoxyacetic acid** *(see).*
> **two-hand·ed** (tŏŏ′hăn′dĭd) *adj.* **1.** Requiring the use of two hands at once: *a two-handed sledgehammer* . . . .

Words that have the same spelling but different etymologies are listed separately and distinguished by raised numbers:

> **bay¹** (bā) *n.* **1.** *Abbr.* **b., B.** A body of water partly enclosed by land, but having a wide outlet to the sea. . . . [Middle English *baye,* from Old French *baie,* from Old Spanish *bahia,* perhaps from Iberian.]
> **bay²** *n.* **1.** *Architecture.* A part of a building or other structure . . . [Middle English, from Old French *baee,* an opening, from *baer,* to gape, from Medieval Latin *batāre,* to yawn, gape.]

Proper names
Mac- and **Mc-** entries are also listed in strict alphabetical order—that is, **Mc** is not listed as if it were spelled **Mac:**

> **Ma·cau·lay** (mə-kô′lē), **Thomas Babington, Ist Baron**
> **Mba·bane** (əm-bä-bän′).
> **Mc·Cau·ley** (mə-kô′lē), **Mary Ludwig Hays**

Towns and cities named after saints appear at **Saint** or **St.**, following conventional spelling. Biographies of saints appear at the name of the saint: for example, Saint Paul is entered at **Paul.**

Names of people and places are alphabetized up to the first period, by surname or distinguishing proper name:

> **Wash·ing·ton¹** (wŏsh′ĭng-tən, wôsh′-).
> **Washington².**
> **Washington, Booker Taliaferro** (1856–1915).
> **Washington, George** (1732–1799).
> **Washington, Martha Dandridge Custis** (1731–1802).
> **Washington, Mount.**

Fictional and legendary characters are entered with the forename or title first, if this is how they are best known:

> **Don Qui·xo·te**
> **Rob·in Hood**

Fixed phrases
Fixed phrases of two or more words whose meaning cannot be worked out from the literal sense of the individual words are entered under the key word (usually the first noun). For example, **throw the book at** will be listed under **book; hand over fist** is listed under **hand.** The only exceptions to this rule are phrases that function as nouns, such as **green thumb** or **cold feet.** These are listed in their alphabetical place.

Fixed verb phrases with a special meaning, such as **come across** (to meet) or **put down** (to rebuke), will either be listed under the verb or, if they can be used in several ways—as adjectives or nouns, for example, will be entered separately.

Inflections
Inflections are grammatically different forms of a word, such as the plural of a noun, the past tense of a verb, or the comparative degree of an adjective. Inflections are shown in shortened form, unless the entry has only one syllable or the first syllable is a vowel standing alone:

> **ear·ly** (ûr′lē) *adj.* **-lier, -liest.**
> **o·bey** (ō-bā′) *v.* **obeyed, obeying, obeys.**

Plurals
Plural forms of nouns are shown when these are irregular (that is, when the plural is not formed simply by adding *-s* or *-es*) and when more than one plural is possible:

> **ra·di·us** (rā′dē-əs) *n., pl.* **-dii** (-dē-ī′) or **-uses.**
> **car·go** (kär′gō) *n., pl.* **-goes** or **-gos.**

In cases where it is difficult to tell whether a word takes a singular or a plural verb, the Dictionary indicates what construction to use:

> **ge·net·ics** (jə-nĕt′ĭks) *n.* **1.** *Used with a singular verb.* The biology of heredity; . . . **2.** *Used with a singular or plural verb.* The genetic constitution of an individual, group, or class.

Verbs
The principal parts of all verbs, whether regular or irregular, are shown following the base form, in the order past tense, past participle (if different), present participle, 3rd person singular present tense:

> **al·ter** (ôl′tər) *v.* **-tered, -tering, -ters.**

Adjectives and adverbs
The comparative and superlative forms of all adjectives and adverbs are shown following the base form, in the order comparative, superlative:

> **air·y** (âr′ē) *adj.* **-ier, -iest.**

Alternate forms of entry words

The first form given is always the preferred one. When a word has an alternate but still acceptable written form, this is shown after the entry word in one of two positions.

When an alternate form of a word is so close to the preferred spelling that it shares the same pronunciation, it is shown immediately after the entry word and before the pronunciation:

> **me·di·e·val, me·di·ae·val** (mē′dē-ē′vəl, mĕ-dē′vəl) *adj.*

Alternate British or chiefly British spellings of common words are shown like this:

> **col·or** (kŭl′ər) *n.* Also *chiefly British* **col·our.**

When an alternate form of a word is different enough in spelling to require a pronunciation of its own, this is shown after the part of speech:

> **bi·o·log·i·cal** (bī′ə-lŏj′ĭ-kəl) *adj.* Also **bi·o·log·ic** (-lŏj′ĭk).

Alternate forms that need qualifying, for example because they are found in a particular variety of English or apply only to specific senses of a word, are also shown in this way:

> **where·so·ev·er** (hwâr′sō-ĕv′ər, wâr′-) *conj.* Also *poetic* **where·so·e'er** (-âr′).
> **di·van** . . . *n.* Also **di·wan** (dĭ-wän′) (for senses 2, 5).

Alternate forms that fall more than ten places away from their preferred form in the alphabetical list are entered as follows:

> **foetus.** Variant of **fetus.**

Definitions

When an entry word has several meanings, these are listed with the central meaning shown first:

> **fell**[1] (fĕl) *tr.v.* **felled, felling, fells. 1.** To cause to fall; cut or knock down: *fell a tree; fell an opponent.* **2.** To sew or finish (a seam) with the raw edges flattened, turned under, and stitched down.

The different meanings of a word are indicated by numbers, or, in the case of closely related meanings, by lower-case letters. Any italic label, such as *Informal, Chemistry,* or *Southwestern U.S.,* that comes before the first definition number of a word applies to all the numbered meanings of that word. However, if it follows a letter or number, it applies to the definition(s) covered by that letter or number:

> **ear·ful** (îr′fŏŏl′) *n. Informal.* **1.** A quantity of information or gossip. **2.** A severe reprimand.
> **ef·flo·resce** (ĕf′lə-rĕs′) *intr.v.* **-resced, -rescing, -resces. 1.** To blossom; flower; bloom. **2.** *Chemistry.* **a.** To become a powder by losing water of crystallization. **b.** To become covered with a powdery deposit, as by evaporation.

In the example at **earful,** the label *Informal* applies to senses **1** and **2.** In the example at **effloresce,** the label *Chemistry* applies to senses **2a** and **2b.**

Cross-references

Cross-references, usually shown in **boldface** print, direct you to another entry word in the dictionary where further information will be found.

GUIDANCE ON THE USE OF WORDS

Some words or uses of a word are associated with a particular context—for example, a geographic area or a special style of speech or writing. Such specialized uses are marked by a range of italic labels.

Historical labels

Archaic indicates that a word is no longer in common use and will be found only in certain contexts, such as poetry or legal texts. Occasionally a modern author might use such words to give an old-fashioned "feel" to a piece of writing. *Obsolete* indicates that there is no evidence of a word or meaning being used since 1714, other than for literary effect.

Geographic labels

Words, spellings, or meanings that occur in specific areas of the English-speaking world are labeled accordingly:

> **bushed** (bŏŏsht) *adj.* . . . **2.** *Chiefly Australian & Canadian.* Lost or confused.

Regional indicates that an expression is commonly used in one area and little used—even if known—in other areas. Such expressions bear area labels, such as *Southwestern U.S.* and *New England.* Often an expression may be common to several areas and yet not be used in American speech in general. These expressions are labeled *Regional:* for example, the use of **fair**[1] as a verb in *The weather will fair today.*

Field labels

Many definitions are labeled according to the field of knowledge with which they are concerned. These labels are merely an aid to orientation; they are not to be interpreted as stating that the sense is not used outside the special field, only that the sense being defined is of primary concern within that field. Such labels are especially useful when a word has many senses; for example, senses 5, 7, 8, 9, 10, 11, and 13 of **base**[1] are labeled *Sports, Military, Architecture, Heraldry, Linguistics, Mathematics,* and *Chemistry,* respectively.

Stylistic labels

Informal indicates that a word or meaning is typically used by speakers addressing one another directly on familiar terms, as in a casual conversation. Informal terms are often mildly humorous or euphemistic in tone, for example, *creepy* or *funny bone.*

Slang indicates a closer degree of familiarity between speakers, or between reader and author, than *Informal.* Slang words are often associated with "in-groups" within the community, such as servicemen. The distinguishing feature of slang is the striving for rhetorical effect through the use of extravagant and often facetious figures of speech. Slang is usually transitory and either dies out or is incorporated into the standard vocabulary as its rhetorical aspect is lost.

Nonstandard indicates that a word or meaning is in widespread use but is regarded as incorrect by most educated speakers of English. For example, the use of *disinterested* to mean "uninterested" is labeled *Nonstandard.* Controversial uses and those on which guidance may be helpful are dealt with more fully in usage notes.

Short notes describing a particular attitude on the part of the user will be found after some words or meanings. "Used derogatorily," for example, indicates that the speaker wishes to show contempt or disapproval. "Considered offensive" indicates that a word or meaning might cause offense, even when the speaker intends none.

Foreign-language labels are used at some expressions from other languages which, though fairly common, are still felt by the native speaker as not belonging to English. Such words are represented in italic type by many publications. The language from which they come is indicated in the Dictionary by a label:

> **ad in·ter·im** (ăd ĭn'tər-əm) *adv. Abbr.* **ad int.** *Latin.* In the meantime; meanwhile. —**ad in·ter·im** *adj.*

Many terms that appear to be foreign have been incorporated into the vocabulary of a special field such as law or medicine. These are given the label of the field rather than a language label. Thus the entry:

> **no·lo con·ten·de·re** (nō'lō kən-tĕn'də-rē') *n. Law.* A plea made by the defendant . . . . [Latin, "I do not wish to contend."]

Usage notes

Occasionally the use of a word or phrase may require extended discussion. The paragraphs labeled *Usage* following many of the entries in this Dictionary supply information on the conventions observed by most users of the language. They identify areas of controversy over the meaning or grammatical use of a word so that the reader can see what the linguistic "state of play" is in contemporary English and make confident decisions in speaking and writing. The usage notes never tell a reader what to do or how to react; they simply present the alternatives. It is enough to know in what circumstances a usage is preferred, or avoided—for example, in formal writing, or in very informal speech. What was frowned upon a generation ago may be widely accepted today; but the reader who understands what the norms are will at least know when they are being disregarded.

GUIDE TO PRONUNCIATION

All pronunciations are shown in parentheses following the entry word or any alternate form of it. If part of an entry has already appeared separately elsewhere in the Dictionary, its pronunciation is not repeated. Similarly, entry words followed by raised numbers, indicating that they have the same spelling but a different origin, are assumed to have the same pronunciation, unless otherwise indicated.

Pronunciation Symbols

The set of symbols used in this Dictionary is designed to enable the reader to reproduce a satisfactory pronunciation with no more than a quick reference to the key.

A shorter form of the key below appears in the margins at intervals throughout the Dictionary.

Spellings	Symbols	Spellings	Symbols
pat	ă	noise	oi
pay	ā	out	ou
care	âr	book	ŏŏ
father, are	ä	boot	ōō
bib	b	pop	p
church	ch	roar	r
deed, milled	d	sauce	s
pet	ĕ	ship, dish	sh
be	ē	tight, stopped	t
fife, phase, rough	f	thin, path	th
gag	g	this, bathe	*th*
hat	h	cut	ŭ
which	hw	fur, term, firm,	ûr
pit	ĭ	word, heard	
pie, by	ī	valve	v
pier	îr	with, which	w
judge	j	yes	y
kick, cat, pique	k	zebra, xylem,	z
lid, needle	l (nēd'l)	size	
mum	m	vision, pleasure,	zh
no, sudden	n (sŭd'n)	garage	
thing	ng	about, item,	ə
pot, horrid	ŏ	edible, gallop,	
toe, hoarse	ō	circus, peaceful	
caught, paw, for	ô	butter	ər

Foreign		Stress Marks	
French ami	à	Primary stress: '	
French feu,	œ	**in·cite'** (ĭn-sīt')	
German schön			
French tu,	ü	Secondary stress: '	
German über		**in'sight'** (ĭn'sīt')	
German ich,	KH		
Scottish loch			
French bon	N		
French Compiègne	y' (kôn-pyĕn'y')		

Alternate pronunciations

All pronunciations given are acceptable in all circumstances. When more than one is given, the first is assumed to be the most common, but the difference in frequency may be insignificant.

Americans do not all speak alike; nevertheless, they can understand one another, at least on the level of speech sounds. For most words a single set of symbols can represent the pronunciation found in each regional variety of American English, provided the symbols are planned to enable the reader to reproduce a satisfactory pronunciation. When a single pronunciation is given in this Dictionary, the reader will supply those features of his own regional speech that are suggested by his reading of the key. The policy of this Dictionary is to record pronunciations used in educated speech. In every community, educated speech is accepted and understood by everyone, including those who do not themselves use it.

To save space, where alternate pronunciations are given, only that part of the word that varies from the standard form is repeated:

> **glo·ri·fi·ca·tion** (glôr'ə-fĭ-kā'shən, glōr'-) *n.*

Explanatory Notes

ə: this nonalphabetical symbol is called a *schwa*. The symbol is used in the Dictionary to represent a reduced vowel, that is, a vowel that receives the weakest level of stress (which can be thought of as no stress) within a word and that therefore nearly always has a different quality than it would have if it were stressed, as in **telegraph** (tĕl'ə-grăf') and **telegraphy** (tə-lĕg'rə-fē). Vowels are never reduced to a single vowel sound; the schwa sound varies, sometimes according to the vowel it is representing and often according to the sounds surrounding it.

âr, îr, ûr: these symbols represent vowels that have been altered by the *r* that follows. This situation can be understood by considering the words **Mary, merry,** and **marry.** In some regional varieties of American English, all three words are pronounced alike (mĕr'ē). However, in many individual American speech patterns, the three words are distinguished. It is this pattern that the Dictionary represents, thus: **Mary** (mâr'ē), **merry** (mĕr'ē), **marry** (măr'ē). However, in some words all three pronunciations are heard, grading indistinctly one into another. For these words the Dictionary represents only (â), for example, **care** (kâr), **dairy** (dâr'ē).

In words such as **hear, beer,** and **dear,** the vowel could be represented by (ē) were it not for the effect of the following *r*, which makes it approach (ĭ) in sound. In this Dictionary a special symbol (îr) is used for this combination, as in **beer** (bîr).

The symbol (ûr), used in **her** (hûr), **fur** (fûr), etc., has a regular regional variant that is not separately recorded. In one pattern the effect of the *r* is heard simultaneously with the vowel; in the other, some, but not all, such syllables are heard with a vowel like (ŭ) before the onset of the *r*.

ôr, ōr, ŏr: there are regional differences in the distinctions among various pronunciations of the syllable *-or-*. In pairs such as **horse, hoarse,** the vowel varies between (ô) and (ō). In this Dictionary these vowels are represented as follows: **horse** (hôrs), **hoarse** (hôrs, hōrs). Other words for which both forms are shown include **more** (môr, mōr), **glory** (glôr'ē, glōr'-). Another group of words with variation in the pronunciation of *-or-* syllables includes words such as **forest** and **horrid,** in which the pronunciation of *o* before *r* varies between (ô) and (ŏ). In these words the (ôr) pronunciation is given first: **forest** (fôr'ĭst, fŏr'-), **horrid** (hôr'ĭd, hŏr'-).

Syllabic Consonants

Two consonants are often represented as complete syllables. These are *l* and *n* (called *syllabics*) when they occur after stressed syllables ending in or followed by *d* or *t* in such words as **cradle** (krād'l), **rattle** (răt'l), **redden** (rĕd'n), **cotton** (kŏt'n), and **midden** (mĭd'n). Syllabic *n* is not shown following *-nd-* or *-nt-*, as in **abandon** (ə-băn'dən) and **mountain** (moun'tən); but syllabic *l* is shown in that position: **spindle** (spĭnd'l).

Stress

In this Dictionary, *stress,* the relative degree of loudness with which the syllables of a word (or phrase) are spoken, is indicated in three different ways. An unmarked syllable has the weakest stress in the word. The strongest, or *primary,* stress is marked with a bold mark ('). An intermediate level of stress, here called *secondary,* is marked with a similar but lighter mark (').

Words of one syllable show no stress mark, since there is no other stress level to which the syllable is compared.

Syllabication

All entry words of more than one syllable, as well as their alternate and derived forms, are divided into syllables by centered dots that show where the word can be hyphenated. No syllable dots are shown for words that have already appeared as separate entries.

Pronunciations are also syllabicated for the sake of clarity, although the syllabication of the phonetic form does not necessarily match the syllabication of the graphic form of the entry word. The former follows phonological rules; the latter represents the established practice of printers and editors in breaking words at the end of a line.

THE ORIGINS OF WORDS

The text in square brackets at the end of the entry gives the etymology, or historical derivation, of the entry word, except in the instances mentioned below. If a word is native to the language, the etymology normally traces its history back to the earlier stages of English—Old English (A.D. 450–1100) and Middle English (1100–1500). If the word is derived from a foreign language, the etymology usually traces it back to its earliest written form in the language of its origin:

> **ef·fi·gy** (ĕf'ə-jē) . . . [Middle English *effigie,* from Latin *effigiēs,* likeness, image, from *effingere,* to form, portray : *ex-,* out of + *fingere,* to fashion, shape.]

The etymologies are intended to be easily readable and therefore no special abbreviations have been used. The languages mentioned in the derivations (Old French, Old High German, Old Norse, for example), which are frequently earlier forms of modern languages, are all defined in the body of the Dictionary. So too are technical terms such as "back-formation," "unattested," "akin," and "folk etymology."

Source words are usually printed in *italics.* They are omitted altogether, however, if identical to the entry word or to the source word listed just before. Where the source word is itself an entry in the Dictionary, it is usually printed in SMALL CAPITALS; this alerts the reader to the fact that there is further information at that entry (either in its definition or in its etymology):

> **frank·in·cense** . . . [Middle English *frank encens,* from Old French *franc encens* : *franc,* free, superior, FRANK + *encens,* INCENSE.]

A cross-reference in **bold** type indicates that the reader should consult the etymology of this word, where more information will be found:

> **dis·crete** . . . [Middle English, from Latin *discrētus,* separate. See **discreet.**]

Many words are combinations of other words or word parts. This is shown in a number of ways, as in the example of **frankincense** above, or in simpler cases:

> **pul·sar** . . . [From *puls*ating s*tar.*]
> **mel·a·nous** . . . [MELAN(O)- + -OUS.]

In the cases of some words, the combination is so obvious that the etymology can be omitted entirely—for example, at **evergreen** (ever + green) or **eventuality** (eventual + ity). (The only other class of words usually not given an etymology is that of proper nouns, including trademarks.)

Some words, by contrast, have uncertain origins. If evidence is lacking or highly unreliable, the etymology will be limited to the simple explanation "origin obscure," often preceded by a century date to indicate when the word first appeared in written form in English:

> **flunk** . . . [19th century : origin obscure.]

In the case of a source word which is in turn of unknown origin, the obelisk or dagger symbol † is printed after it:

> **Men·sa**[1] . . . [Latin *mēnsa*†, table.]

A special effort has been made to include in the etymologies information that explains the origin and changes in meaning of certain words and phrases. Such etymologies may trace a word or phrase back to a Biblical allusion, a name of a person or place, or a historical incident, for example:

> **mav·er·ick** . . . [After Samuel A. *Maverick* (1803–70), Texas cattleman who did not brand his calves.]
> **quark** . . . [From a line in James Joyce's *Finnegans Wake,* "Three quarks for Muster Mark!"]

READING THE ENTRIES

The examples numbered below are a guide to the symbols and terms used in creating the entries in this Dictionary. They summarize and illustrate the information given on the preceding pages and act as a quick source of reference for the reader. Each example is printed in blue to make it stand out from the surrounding text and given a number that is keyed to the explanatory notes alongside.

KEY

1 **Entry word.**

2 Parentheses enclose **pronunciation.**

3 Words made up of **two or more elements** are entered separately.

4 Main **inflected forms** of verb.

5 **Cross-reference** to entry word with **Synonym list.**

6 **Usage note** comments on problems of spelling, grammar, style, or meaning.

7 **Cross-reference** to entry word with **Usage note.**

8 **Note** in entry indicates limitations of **usage.**

9 Italic label indicates **part of speech.**

10 **Alternate spelling** with same pronunciation as entry word.

11 **Boldface dots** divide entry word into **syllables.**

12 **Irregular plural** of entry word.

13 Parentheses enclose **object of verb.**

14 **Alternate spelling** entered separately.

15 **Cross-reference** to related entry word.

16 **Brackets** enclose **etymology.**

17 **Example phrase** shows word used in context.

18 **Numbers** distinguish entry words with the **same spelling but different origins.**

19 Italic label indicates **usage level** of word or sense.

20 **Alternate spelling** of entry word with different pronunciation.

21 **Cross-reference** to etymology of another entry word.

22 **Derived forms** made up of the entry word and a word part that is entered elsewhere.

23 Italic label indicates **geographic area** of use.

---

1 **cli·ma·tol·o·gy** (klī′mə-tŏl′ə-jē) *n.* The meteorological study of climate. [CLIMAT(E) + -LOGY.] —**cli·ma·to·log·ic** (klī′mə-tə-lŏj′ĭk), **cli·ma·to·log·i·cal** *adj.* —**cli·ma·tol·o·gist** (klī′mə-tŏl′ə-jĭst) *n.*

2 **cli·max** (klī′măks′) *n.* **1. a.** The point of greatest intensity, excitement, or interest in any series or progression of events; the culmination. **b.** Such a point in a literary or dramatic work. **2.** An orgasm. **3.** *Rhetoric.* **a.** A series of statements or ideas in an ascending order of force or intensity. **b.** The final statement in such a series. **4.** The stage in ecological development or evolution in which the community of organisms becomes stable. —See Synonyms at **summit.** ~*v.* **climaxed, -maxing, -maxes.** —*intr.* To reach a climax. —*tr.* To bring to a climax. [Latin, rhetorical climax, from Greek *klimax,* ladder.]

3 **climax community** *n. Ecology.* The mature or stabilized stage in a successional series of communities, usually associated with maximum complexity, when dominant species are completely adapted to environmental conditions, as in tropical rain forests.

4 **climb** (klīm) *v.* **climbed** or *archaic* **clomb** (klŏm), **climbing, climbs.** —*tr.* To move up or mount, especially by using the hands and feet; ascend. —*intr.* **1.** To rise to a higher position; move upward: *The sun climbed in the sky.* **2.** To rise slowly or with effort in rank, status, or fortune. **3.** To slant or slope upward. **4.** To grow in an upward direction, as some plants do, by twining about or clinging to another object for support. 5 **5.** To move in a specified direction by or as if by clambering: *climbed out of the window.* —See Synonyms at **rise.** ~*n.* **1.** An act of climbing; an ascent. **2.** A place to be climbed. [Climb, clomb; Middle English *climben, clomb,* Old English *climban, clamb* (or *clomb*).] —**climb·a·ble** *adj.*

6 *Usage:* Both *up* and *down* are used with this verb in standard English. *Climb up* has been said to contain an unnecessary element, in that climbing implies ascent. By the same token, *climb down* is said to be self-contradictory, but both uses are well established.

climb down *intr.v.* **1.** To move downward by using the limbs. **2.** To retreat in an argument or dispute; back down. —*tr.v.* To descend by using the limbs. 7 —See Usage note at **climb.**

climb·er (klī′mər) *n.* **1.** Something or someone that climbs; especially, a person who climbs mountains. **2.** *Informal.* A person seeking to gain a higher social or professional position. 8 Used derogatorily. **3.** A plant that grows upward by clinging to or twining about something.

9 **climbing irons** *pl.n.* Iron bars with spikes or spurs attached, which are strapped to a shoe or boot and used in climbing telegraph poles, trees, or ice slopes.

clime (klīm) *n. Poetic.* Climate or region. [Middle English, region of the earth, zone, from Late Latin *clīma,* CLIMATE.]

–clinal *suffix.* Indicates a slope or inclination; for example, **anti·clinal, synclinal.** [-CLINE + -AL.]

10 **cli·mo·graph** (klī′mə-grăf′, -gräf′) *n. Meteorology.* A graph in which one climatic feature at a location is plotted against another, for example temperature against humidity. Also called "climagram," "climogram." [CLIMATE + 12 GRAPH.]

clin-. Variant of **clino-.**

11 **cli·nan·dri·um** (klī-năn′drē-əm) *n., pl.* **-dria** (-drē-ə). *Botany.* A hollow containing the anther in the upper part of the column of an orchid. [New Latin, "stamen bed" : CLIN(O)- + *-andrium,* "stamen," from Greek *anēr* (stem *andr-*), man.]

clinch (klĭnch) *v.* **clinched, clinching, clinches.** —*tr.* **1.** To fix or 13 secure (a nail or bolt, for example) by bending down or flattening the end that has been driven through something. **2.** To fasten together in this way. **3.** To settle definitely and conclusively; make final. **4.** *Nautical.* To fasten with a clinch. —*intr.* **1.** In boxing and wrestling, to hold the opponent's body with one or both arms to prevent or hinder his movements. **2.** *Informal.* To embrace. ~*n.* **1.** The act of clinching. **2.** Something that clinches, such as a clinched nail or clamp. **3.** The clinched part of a nail, bolt, rivet, or the like. **4.** In boxing and wrestling, the act or an instance of clinching. **5.** *Nautical.* A knot in a rope made by a half hitch with the end of the rope fastened back by seizing. Also called "clench." **6.** *Informal.* An amorous or romantic embrace. [Variant of CLENCH.]

clinch·er (klĭnch′ər) *n.* **1.** One that clinches; specifically, a tool for clinching nails or bolts. **2.** *Informal.* A decisive point, fact, or remark, as in an argument.

14 **clincher-built.** Variant of **clinker-built.**

cline (klīn) *n. Ecology.* A continuous variation in form within members of a species or population, resulting from gradual changes or transitions in the environment over a wide range. **2.** Loosely, a

continuum. [Greek *klinein,* to slope, lean.]

–cline *suffix.* Indicates slope; for example, **anticline, syncline.** [Greek *klinein,* to slope.]

cling (klĭng) *intr.v.* **clung** (klŭng), **clinging, clings. 1.** To hold fast or adhere to something, as by grasping, sticking, or entwining. **2. a.** To stay near; remain close. **b.** To resist separation. **3.** To hold on, often stubbornly; remain attached: *cling to old-fashioned ideas.* [Cling, clung (past tense), clung (past participle); Middle English *clingen, clong* (past singular), *clungen* (past plural), *clungen,* Old English *clingan, clang, clungon, clungen.*] —**cling·er** *n.*

15 **cling·stone** (klĭng′stōn′) *n.* A fruit, especially a peach, having pulp that adheres partially to the stone. Compare **freestone.** —**cling·stone** *adj.*

cling·y (klĭng′ē) *adj.* **-gier, -giest.** Tending to cling: *a clingy dress.*

16 **clin·ic** (klĭn′ĭk) *n.* **1.** An establishment, often a department of a hospital specializing in a particular branch of medicine, devoted to the treatment and care of outpatients. **2.** A medical establishment run by several specialists working cooperatively. **3.** A private hospital or nursing home. **4.** A group meeting or seminar devoted to the study of problems in a particular field, or offering to teach certain skills to those who attend: *a tennis clinic.* [French *clinique,* originally "a bedridden person," from Greek *klinikē,* medical treatment at sickbed, from *klinikos,* "of a bed," doctor who visits bedridden persons, from *klinē,* bed.]

–clinic *suffix.* Indicates: **1.** Inclination or slope; for example, **isoclinic. 2.** A specified number of oblique axial intersections; for example, **triclinic.** [-CLINE + -IC.]

17 **clin·i·cal** (klĭn′ĭ-kəl) *adj.* **1.** Pertaining to or connected with a clinic. **2.** Of or pertaining to direct observation and treatment of patients: *a clinical lecture.* **3.** Analytical; highly objective; rigorously scientific: *clinical details.* **4.** Suggestive of a hospital or clinic; austere; antiseptic: *a clinical style of decor.* ~*n.* A class in which medical students are instructed in the examination and treatment of patients at the bedside. —**clin·i·cal·ly** *adv.*

cli·ni·cian (klĭ-nĭsh′ən) *n.* A doctor, psychologist, or psychiatrist specializing in clinical studies or practice. [French *clinicien,* from *clinique,* CLINIC.]

18 **clink**[1] (klĭngk) *n.* A soft, sharp, ringing sound. ~*v.* **clinked, clinking, clinks.** —*intr.* To make a clink. —*tr.* To cause to clink. [Middle English, from Middle Dutch *klinken.*]

clink[2] *n. Slang.* Prison. [16th century (as *the Clink,* name of former prison near London) : origin obscure.]

clink·er (klĭng′kər) *n.* **1.** The incombustible residue, fused into irregular lumps, that remains after the combustion of coal. **2.** A partially vitrified brick or a mass of bricks fused together. **3.** An extremely hard burned brick. **4.** Vitrified matter expelled by a volcano. **5.** *Slang.* A conspicuous mistake or failure. ~*intr.v.* **clinkered, -ering, -ers.** To form clinker while burning. [Earlier *clincart, klincard,* from obsolete Dutch *klinckaerd,* "one that clinks" (from its clinking sound when struck), from Middle Dutch *klinken, clinken,* CLINK.]

20 **clink·er-built** (klĭng′kər-bĭlt′) *adj.* Also **clinch·er-built** (klĭn′chər-). Built with overlapping planks or boards. Said of ships or boats. Compare **carvel-built.** [From *clinker,* a fastening or clinching with nails, from Middle English *clinken,* probably variant of *clenchen,* 21 CLENCH.]

clino-, clin- *prefix.* Indicates slope or slant; for example, **clinometer, clinandrium.** [New Latin, from Greek *klinein,* to slope, and *klinē,* bed.]

22 **cli·nom·e·ter** (klī-nŏm′ə-tər, klĭ-) *n.* An instrument for measuring the angle of an incline, as of an embankment. Also called "inclinometer." [CLINO- + -METER.] —**cli·no·met·ric** (klī′nə-mĕt′rĭk), **cli·no·met·ri·cal** *adj.* —**cli·nom·e·try** (klī-nŏm′ə-trē) *n.*

clin·quant (klĭng′kənt; *French* klăn-kän′) *adj. Archaic.* Adorned with gold or silver. ~*n. Archaic.* Imitation gold leaf; tinsel. [French, "glistening," from *clinquer,* to glitter, clink, from Middle Dutch *clinken,* CLINK.]

cli·o·met·rics (klī′ə-mĕt′rĭks) *n. Used with a singular verb.* The use of statistics in the study of history. —**cli·o·met·ric** *adj.*

23 **clip**[1] (klĭp) *tr.v.* **clipped, clipping, clips. 1.** To cut off or cut out with or as if with scissors or shears: *clip an article from a newspaper; clipped three seconds off the record.* **2.** To make shorter by cutting; trim. **3.** To cut off the edge of: *clip a coin.* **4. a.** To cut short (a word or words) by leaving out letters or syllables. **b.** To enunciate with clarity and precision: *clip one's speech.* **5.** *British.* To punch a hole in (a ticket). **6.** *Informal.* To hit with a sharp blow. **7.** *Slang.* To cheat or overcharge.

LIST OF ABBREVIATIONS USED IN ENTRIES

Abbr.	abbreviation	A.T.C.; F.O.	n.	noun	marble; lawn mower.
adj.	adjective	lovable; red.	pl.n.	plural noun	environs; cattle.
adv.	adverb	merrily; moreover.	prep.	preposition	with; despite.
comb. form	combining form	all-; -in.	pron.	pronoun	she; myself.
conj.	conjunction	and; inasmuch as.	tr.v.	transitive verb	hire; repatriate.
interj.	interjection	hi; ouch.	v.	verb (transitive and intransitive)	grow; advertise.
intr.v.	intransitive verb	emigrate; subside.			

gha·ri·al (gä′rē-əl) n. A reptile, the **gavial** (see).

ghar·ry, ghar·ri (găr′ē, gär′ē) n., pl. **-ries.** A small horse-drawn carriage in India. [Hindi *gārī*.]

ghast·ly (găst′lē, gäst′-) adj. **-lier, -liest. 1.** Terrifying; dreadful: *a ghastly accident.* **2.** Having a deathlike pallor: *"amid the dim and ghastly glare of a snowy night"* (Washington Irving). **3.** Extremely unpleasant or bad: *a ghastly little book.* ~adv. Dreadfully; horribly. [Middle English *gastlich*, Old English *gāstlīc*, spiritual, ghostly, ghastly, from *gāst*, soul, ghost.] —**ghast·li·ness** n.
> *Synonyms:* grim, grisly, gruesome, lurid, macabre.

ghat, ghaut (gôt, gät) n. In India: **1.** A mountain pass. **2.** A mountain chain. **3.** A flight of steps down to the bank of a river. **4.** An area beside a river, used for bathing. [Hindi *ghāt*, from Sanskrit *ghaṭṭa*, perhaps from *ghṛṣṭa*, rubbed.]

Ghats (gôts, gäts). Two coastal mountain ranges in India, forming the edges of the Deccan plateau. The Western Ghats extend approximately 1,500 kilometers (932 miles) along the west coast and rise to 2,698 meters (8,852 feet) at Anai Mudi. The Eastern Ghats extend approximately 1,400 kilometers (880 miles) along the east coast, rising to 2,637 meters (8,651 feet) at Doda Betta.

gha·zi (gä′zē) n., pl. **-zies. 1.** A Muslim warrior who has fought successfully against infidels. Often used as a title of honor. **2.** A high-ranking Turkish warrior. [Arabic *ghāzi*, participle of *ghazā*, he made war.]

Ghazzah. See **Gaza.**

ghee (gē) n. Clarified butter from the butterfat of buffalo or other milk. It is used in cooking, especially in India and neighboring countries. [Hindi *ghī*, from Sanskrit *ghṛta*, present participle of *ghṛ†*, to sprinkle.]

Ghent (gĕnt). *Flemish* **Gent** (gĕnt); *French* **Gand** (gäɴ). A city and port in northwest-central Belgium, the capital of East Flanders.

ghe·rao (gə-rou′) n. In India, a coercive tactic adopted during industrial disputes whereby workers surround an employer and detain him on his own premises until he agrees to their demands. ~tr.v. **gheraoed, -raoing, -raoes.** To coerce (an employer) by using this technique. [Bengali, to surround, from Indic *gher-* (unattested), causative of *ghir-* (unattested), "to go around," from Dravidian.]

gher·kin (gûr′kĭn) n. **1.** A small cucumber, especially one used for pickling. **2.** A tropical American vine, *Cucumis anguria*, bearing prickly, edible fruit. **3.** The fruit of this vine. [Dutch *agurk(je)*, from Low German *agurke*, from Lithuanian *agurkas*, from Polish *ogorek*, *ogurek*, from Medieval Greek *angourion*, probably from Greek *agouros*, youth, "unripe," from *aōros* : *a-*, not + *ōros*, time.]

ghet·to (gĕt′ō) n., pl. **-tos** or **-toes. 1.** A slum section of a city occupied predominantly by members of a minority group who live there because of social or economic pressure. **2.** A section or quarter in a European city to which Jews were formerly restricted. **3.** An area occupied by a group, institution, or the like, with a distinctive, and often exclusive, specified common trait: *a cultural ghetto.* [Italian *ghetto†*.]

Ghib·el·line (gĭb′ə-lēn′, -lĭn′, -lĭn) n. Any of the members of the aristocratic political faction who fought during the Middle Ages for German imperial control of Italy, in opposition to the Guelphs, who favored papal control. Compare **Guelph.** [Italian *Ghibellino*, from Middle High German *Waiblingen*, name of a Hohenstaufen estate.]

Ghi·ber·ti (gē-bĕr′tē), **Lorenzo** (c.1378–1455). Italian goldsmith and sculptor. He is best known for his series of bronze panels for the doors of the baptistry of Florence Cathedral, depicting scenes from the New and Old Testaments.

ghilgai. Variant of **gilgai.**

ghil·lie (gĭl′ē) n., pl. **-lies. 1.** A low-cut sports shoe with fringed laces, originally worn by the Scots. **2.** Variant of **gillie.** [Scottish Gaelic *gille*, boy, servant, GILLIE.]

ghost (gōst) n. **1.** The spirit of a dead person, supposed to haunt living persons or former habitats; a specter; a phantom; a wraith. **2.** *Archaic.* The animus or soul as opposed to the body. **3.** A returning or haunting memory or image. **4.** A slight trace or vestige of something; a hint; a semblance: *a ghost of a smile; a ghost of a chance.* **5.** A faint, false secondary image, such as: **a.** A displaced image in a mirror caused by reflection from the front of the glass. **b.** A displaced image in a photograph caused by the optical system of the camera. **c.** A secondary image on a television or radar screen caused by reflected waves. **d.** A false spectral line caused by imperfections in the diffraction grating. **6.** *Printing.* A variation in or unevenness of color intensity on a surface intended to be solidly tinted, as the result of irregular distribution of ink. **7.** *Obsolete.* The Holy Ghost. **8.** *Informal.* A ghostwriter. **9.** A nonexistent publication listed in bibliographies. In this sense, also called "ghost edition." **10.** A ghost word. —**give up the ghost.** To die. ~v. **ghosted, ghosting, ghosts.** —*intr. Informal.* To work as a ghostwriter. —*tr.* **1.** To haunt. **2.** *Informal.* To write (a work) as a ghostwriter. [Middle English *gost, gast*, Old English *gāst*, from Germanic.]

ghost crab n. Any of several light-colored burrowing crabs of the genus *Ocypoda*, frequenting the tide line along sandy shores.

ghost dance n. Either of two religious dances practiced chiefly by certain North American Indians of the southwestern United States and California during the latter half of the 19th century to invoke a return of their former condition.

ghost gum n. Any of various Australian eucalyptus trees with a smooth, whitish trunk and branches.

ghost·ly (gōst′lē) adj. **-lier, -liest. 1.** Pertaining to or resembling a ghost or apparition; spectral; eerie. **2.** Pertaining to the spirit or to religion; spiritual. —**ghost·li·ness** n.

ghost town n. A town, especially a boom town of the West, that has now been completely abandoned.

ghost word n. A word that has come into a language through the perpetuation of a misreading of a manuscript, a typographical error, or a misunderstanding. For example, in *Ye Olde Sweete Shoppe, Ye* is a ghost word, the *y* having been a misreading of the runic letter thorn.

ghost·write (gōst′rīt′) v. **-wrote** (-rōt′), **-written** (-rĭt′n), **-writing, -writes.** —*intr.* To work as a ghostwriter. —*tr.* To write (something) as a ghostwriter.

ghost·writ·er (gōst′rī′tər) n. A person who is hired to write for another person who then takes credit of authorship. Also informally called "ghost."

ghoul (gōōl) n. **1.** One who delights in what is revolting, macabre, or loathsome. **2.** A grave robber. **3. a.** A malevolent ghost. **b.** An evil spirit or demon in Muslim folklore supposed to plunder graves and feed on corpses. [Arabic *ghūl*, from *ghāla*, he took suddenly.] —**ghoul·ish** adj. —**ghoul·ish·ly** adv. —**ghoul·ish·ness** n.

GHQ, G.H.Q. general headquarters.

ghyll. Variant of **gill** (stream or ravine).

gi gill (liquid measure).

Gi gilbert (unit of magnetomotive force).

GI (jē′ī′) n., pl. **GIs** or **GI's.** A serviceman in or ex-serviceman of any of the U.S. armed forces. ~adj. **1.** Pertaining to or characteristic of a GI. **2.** In conformity to or accordance with U.S. military regulations or procedures. **3.** Issued by an official U.S. military supply department. [Abbreviation of *general issue* or *government issue*.]

GI 1. general issue. **2.** Government Issue.

G.I. Government Issue.

Gia·co·met·ti (jä′kō-mĕt′ē), **Alberto** (1901–66). Swiss painter and sculptor. From 1922 to 1935 he experimented with cubism but later evolved a distinctive, elongated style of representing the human figure.

gi·ant (jī′ənt) n. **1. a.** A person or thing of extraordinary size or strength. **b.** A person of outstanding importance or achievement: *He is a giant in his field.* **2. a.** *Greek Mythology.* Any of a race of manlike beings of enormous strength and stature who warred with the Olympians, by whom they were finally destroyed. **b.** Any similar being in folklore or myth. ~adj. Of immense size; gigantic; huge. [Middle English *geant*, from Old French, from Vulgar Latin *gangante* (unattested), from Latin *gigās* (stem *gigant-*), from Greek *gigas†*.]

giant anteater n. See **anteater.**

giant axon n. A **giant fiber** (see).

giant chromosome n. A chromosome consisting of many parallel strands of chromatids that have failed to separate after duplication. Giant chromosomes, which occur in the salivary glands of *Drosophila* and other insects, are used to study gene activity.

gi·ant·ess (jī′ən-tĭs) n. A female giant.

giant fiber n. *Zoology.* A nerve fiber with a very large diameter found in many invertebrate animals that is capable of rapid conduction of impulses. Also called "giant axon."

giant hogweed n., pl. **giant hogweeds** or collectively **giant hogweed.** A very tall plant, *Heracleum mantegazzianum*, with clusters of small white flowers, found especially on waste ground.

gi·ant·ism (jī′ən-tĭz′əm) n. **1.** The condition of being a giant. **2.** *Pathology.* **Gigantism** (see).

a, A (ā) *n., pl.* **a's** or **A's.** 1. The first letter of the modern English alphabet. See feature at **alphabet.** 2. Any of the speech sounds represented by this letter. 3. Anything shaped like the letter A. 4. A The best or highest in quality, class, or rank: *grade A milk.* 5. A The highest mark awarded for academic work. 6. A a. The sixth tone in the scale of C major. b. The key or a scale in which A is the tonic. c. A written or printed note representing A. d. A string, key, or pipe tuned to the pitch of A. 7. A A human blood type of the ABO group. See **ABO.**

a, A, a., A. *Note:* As an abbreviation or symbol, *a* may be a small or a capital letter, with or without a period. Established forms or those generally preferred precede the definition. When no form is given, all four forms are in general use in that sense. 1. a. about. 2. A. academician; academy. 3. a acceleration. 4. A, a., A. acre. 5. a. acreage. 6. a. acting. 7. a. adjective. 8. a. afternoon. 9. A. alto. 10. a., A. amateur. 11. A. America; American. 12. A ammeter. 13. A ampere. 14. a. anonymous. 15. a., A. answer. 16. a. anterior. 17. a, A. are (measurement). 18. A area. 19. a *Physics.* atto-. 20. a before. [Latin *ante*] 21. a. in the year. [Latin *annō*] 22. *Physics.* A Helmholtz function. 23. a. year. [Latin *annus*] 24. The first in a series.

a¹ (ə; *emphatic* ā). Indefinite article functioning as an adjective. 1. Used before nouns and noun phrases that denote a single, but unspecified, person or thing: *a region; a man.* 2. Used before plural nouns modified by *few, good many,* or *great many: a few donations.* 3. One kind of: *birds of a feather.* 4. Any: *a broken leg soon mends; not a drop to drink.* 5. Used before mass nouns to indicate: a. A particular type of: *a good education.* b. A unit of: *a beer.* 6. Used before nouns that indicate a state or action, to denote a single instance: *had a long wait; cut prices at a stroke.* 7. One like: *a Casanova.* 8. A certain: *A Mrs. Brown just called.* 9. A type of: *Chianti is a wine.* 10. A work of art by: *It's a Picasso.* See **an.** [Middle English *a(n),* from Old English *an, ān,* one.]

Usage: The general rule of thumb is that *a* is used before words beginning with a consonant, and *an* before those beginning with a vowel, but difficulties may arise over abbreviations and words beginning with *u* and *h.* In all such cases it is the *sound* of the letters that determines which form is used, so it is *an M.B.A., a union, an umbrella, a hair, an heir.*

In a few cases, *a* or *an* are used almost interchangeably. When *h* is in an unstressed syllable at the beginning of a word, *an* is sometimes used (*an hotel*) but it sounds old-fashioned. In rapid speech, however, the *h* may be so reduced in strength that the use of *an* sounds quite natural, so that variation occurs between *a habitual worry* and *an habitual worry.*

a² (ə). Indefinite article functioning as a preposition. In every; to each; per: *once a month; 50 cents a pound.* [Middle English *a, o,* reduced forms of *an, on,* in, at, ON.]

a³ (ə, ă) *v. Regional.* Have: *He'd a come if he could.* [Middle English *a, ha,* reduced forms of *haven, habben,* to HAVE.]

a-¹ *prefix.* Indicates without, not, or opposite to; for example, **amoral, acotyledon.** [Greek *a-, an-,* not.]

a-² *prefix.* Indicates: 1. On or in; for example, **aboard, abed.** 2. In the act of; for example, *a-fishing, a-going.* 3. In a specified state or manner; for example, **aloud, asleep.**

a-³ Indicates: 1. Up, out, or away; for example, **arise, awake.** 2. Intensified action; for example, **abide, amaze.** [Middle English *a-,* up, out, away, Old English *ā-,* reduced form of *ar-, or-,* from Germanic.]

a-⁴. Indicates of or from; for example, **anew, afresh.** [Middle English *a-, o-,* reduced form of OF.]

Å angstrom.

A-1, A-one (ā'wŭn') *adj.* 1. *Informal.* Excellent; splendid. 2. Having a hull and equipment in top condition. Said of a ship. [The symbol used by Lloyd's Register of Shipping to designate ships in first-class condition.]

A1C airman first class.

aa *Pharmacology.* ana (in prescriptions).

AA 1. Alcoholics Anonymous. 2. antiaircraft.

AAA American Automobile Association.

Aa·chen (ä'κнən). *French* Aix-la-Cha·pelle (ĕks'lȧ-shȧ-pĕl'). City in North Rhine-Westphalia, Germany, near the Dutch and Belgian borders. Charlemagne made it the northern capital of his empire, and from 936 to 1531 many Holy Roman Emperors were crowned in its cathedral. It is now an important industrial and manufacturing center.

Aalborg. See Ålborg.

Aalesund. See Ålesund.

Aal·to (äl'tō), Alvar (1898–1976). Finnish architect whose work is noted for the use of contrasting materials, such as pine boarding with rough concrete. One of his finest buildings is the Paimio Tuberculosis Sanatorium, Finland (1929–33).

A & M 1. agricultural and mechanical. 2. ancient and modern.

A. & R. artists and repertory (or repertoire).

aard·vark (ärd'värk') *n.* A burrowing mammal, *Orycteropus afer,* of southern Africa, having a stocky, hairy body, large ears, a long, tubular snout, and powerful digging claws for excavating ant and termite nests. Also called "ant bear." [Obsolete Afrikaans, "earth-pig" : *aarde,* earth, from Dutch, from Middle Dutch *aerde* + *vark,* pig, from Middle Dutch *varken,* little pig; akin to FARROW (litter of pigs).]

aard·wolf (ärd'wŏolf') *n., pl.* -wolves (-wŏolvz'). A hyenalike mammal, *Proteles cristatus,* of southern and eastern Africa, having gray fur with black stripes, and feeding mainly on termites and insect larvae. [Afrikaans, "earth-wolf" : *aarde,* earth (see **aardvark**) + *wolf,* WOLF.]

Aarhus. See Århus.

Aar·on (âr'ən, ăr'-). The original high priest of the Hebrew nation, the elder brother of Moses. Exodus 28:1-4; 40:12-13.

Aaron's rod *n.* 1. Any of several flowering plants having tall, erect stems; especially, *Thermopsis caroliniana,* of the southeastern United States, having compound leaves and erect clusters of yellow flowers. 2. A common Eurasian plant, *Verbascum thapsus,* with whitish downy leaves and erect clusters of yellow flowers. See **mullein.** 3. *Architecture.* A rod-shaped molding decorated with a design of leaves, scrolls, or a twined serpent. [After the rod of the high priest Aaron, which blossomed and produced almonds (Numbers 17:8).]

Ab. Variant of **Av.**

ab-¹ *prefix.* Indicates a position or quality off, outside of, opposite to, or removed from another specified position or quality; for example, **abomasum, aboral, abnormal.** [Latin, from *ab,* away from. In Latin compounds, *ab-* becomes *a-* before *m, p,* and *v; au-* before *f;* and *abs-* before *t.*]

ab-² *prefix.* Indicates a centimeter-gram-second electromagnetic unit of measurement; for example, **abcoulomb.** [Short for ABSOLUTE.]

AB A human blood type of the ABO group. See **ABO.**

a.b. able-bodied seaman.

A.B. 1. able-bodied seaman. 2. Bachelor of Arts. [Latin *Artium Baccalaureus*]

a·ba, ab·ba (ə-bä') *n.* 1. A light fabric woven from the hair of camels or goats. 2. A loose-fitting sleeveless garment of this fabric worn by Arabs. [Arabic *'abā'.*]

ABA 1. American Bankers Association. 2. Also **A.B.A.** American Bar association. 3. American Booksellers Association.

ab·a·ca (ăb'ə-kä') *n.* A Philippine plant, *Musa textilis,* related to the banana. Its leafstalks are the source of **Manila hemp** *(see).* [Spanish *abacá,* from Tagalog *abaká.*]

a·back (ə-băk') *adv.* 1. *Nautical.* Facing into a headwind in such a way that the sails are pressed against the mast. 2. *Archaic.* Back; backward. [Middle English *abak,* Old English *on bæc* : ON + *bæc,* BACK.]

ab·a·cus (ăb'ə-kəs) *n., pl.* -cuses or -ci (-sī'). 1. A manual calculating device consisting of a frame holding parallel rods strung with movable counters. 2. A slab on the top of the capital of a column. [Latin *abacus,* from Greek *abax* (stem *abak-*), slab, mathematical

aardvark *The aardvark of southern Africa (whose name comes from the Afrikaans for "earth pig") feeds on insects, breaking up termite nests with its powerful front claws and gathering up the insects with its 45-centimeter-long (18-inch) tongue. It is the sole member of the scientific order* Tubilidentata—*so called because the aardvark's teeth are a mass of small tubes, quite unlike those of any other mammal.*

aardwolf *A small member of the hyena family, the aardwolf lives in the dry plains of southern and eastern Africa. It has a weak jaw with small teeth and lives chiefly on termites and insect larvae.*

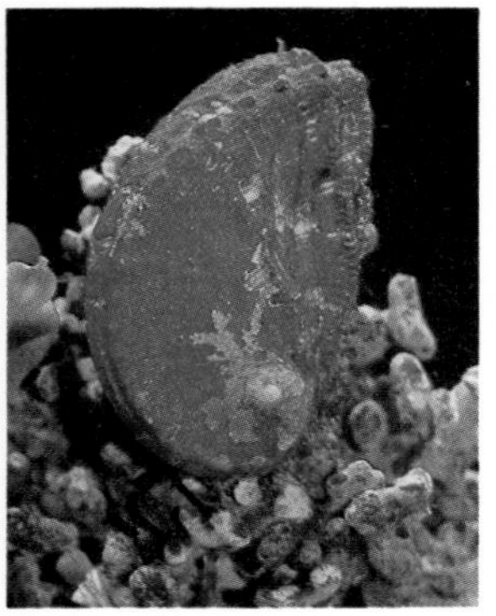

abalone *Found in warm seas, the abalone is a marine snail prized both for its tasty flesh and for its shell that provides mother-of-pearl. This is a small tropical abalone.*

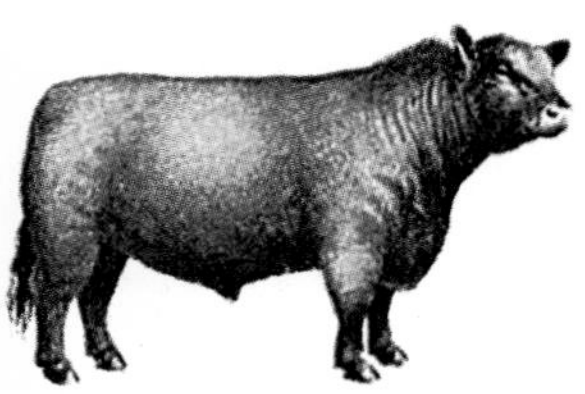

Aberdeen Angus *A stocky Scottish breed of cattle that grows quickly and produces high-quality beef.*

PRONUNCIATION KEY

ă, pat; ā, pay; âr, care;
ä, father, are; b, bib;
ch, church; d, deed; ĕ, pet;
ē, be; f, fife; g, gag; h, hat;
hw, which; ĭ, pit; ī, pie;
îr, pier; j, judge; k, kick;
l, lid, needle; m, mum;
n, no, sudden; ng, thing;
ŏ, pot; ō, toe; ô, paw, for;
oi, noise; ou, out; o͝o, book;
o͞o, boot; p, pop; r, roar;
s, sauce; sh, ship, dish;
t, tight; th, thin, path;
th, this, bathe; ŭ, cut; ûr, fur;
v, valve; w, with; y, yes;
z, zebra, size; zh, vision;
ə, about, item, edible, gallop, circus, peaceful

IN FOREIGN WORDS:

à, *Fr.* ami; œ, *Fr.* feu, *Ger.* schön; ü, *Fr.* tu, *Ger.* über; KH, *Ger.* ich, *Scot.* loch; N, *Fr.* bon; y', *Fr.* Compiègne

STRESS MARKS:

Primary stress: ′
in·cite′ (ĭn-sīt′)
Secondary stress: ′
in′sight′ (ĭn′sīt′)

table, originally a drawing board covered with dust, from Hebrew *'ābhāq,* dust.]

Ab·a·dan (ä′bə-dän′, ăb′ə-dăn′). City in southwest Iran, on Abadan Island in the Shatt al Arab. A major oil-refining and oil-exporting center, it was severely damaged in the 1980 war with Iraq.

a·baft (ə-băft′, ə-bäft′) *adv. Nautical.* Toward the stern.
~*prep. Nautical.* Behind: *abaft the mainmast.* [Middle English *o(n) baft* : ON + *baft,* from Old English *beæftan,* behind : *be,* at, BY + *æftan,* behind.]

ab·a·lo·ne (ăb′ə-lō′nē) *n.* Any of the various large, edible marine gastropod mollusks of the genus *Haliotis,* having an ear-shaped shell with a row of holes and a colorful, pearly interior often used for making ornaments. [American Spanish *abulón*†.]

ab·amp (ăb′ămp′) *n.* An abampere.

ab·am·pere (ăb-ăm′pîr′) *n.* A centimeter-gram-second electromagnetic unit of current, equal to the current that produces a force of two dynes per centimeter of length on each of two infinitely long straight parallel wires one centimeter apart. It is equal to ten amperes. [AB- (absolute) + AMPERE.]

a·ban·don (ə-băn′dən) *tr.v.* **-doned, -doning, -dons. 1.** To forsake; desert: *abandon one's child.* **2.** To leave or leave behind; withdraw from: *abandon ship.* **3.** To surrender one's claim or right to. **4.** To give up completely and irrevocably; relinquish: *abandon hope.* **5.** To end prematurely: *abandon play because of rain.* **6.** To yield (oneself) completely and without restraint, as to emotion. **7.** To relinquish (property) to an insurer in order to make a full claim in case of damage or partial loss.
~*n.* A complete surrender of inhibitions. [Middle English *abandounen,* from Old French *abandoner,* from *(metre) a bandon,* "(to put) in one's power" : *a,* to, at, from Latin *ad,* to + *bandon,* power, from *ban,* jurisdiction, power, from Frankish *ban* (unattested); akin to Old English *gebann,* proclamation, BANNS.] **—a·ban·don·ment** *n.*

a·ban·doned (ə-băn′dənd) *adj.* **1.** Forsaken; deserted. **2.** Completely uninhibited. **3.** Shameless; immoral.

a·base (ə-bās′) *tr.v.* **abased, abasing, abases.** To lower in rank, prestige, or esteem; humble; humiliate. —See Synonyms at **degrade.** [Middle English *abassen,* from Old French *abaissier,* from Vulgar Latin *abbassiāre* (unattested) : *ad-,* to + *bassiāre* (unattested), to lower, from Late Latin *bassus,* low.] **—a·base·ment** *n.*

a·bash (ə-băsh′) *tr.v.* **abashed, abashing, abashes.** To make ashamed or uneasy; disconcert. [Middle English *abaisen, abashen,* to gape with surprise, be dumbfounded, from Norman French *abaiss-,* variant of Old French *e(s)bass-,* present stem of *e(s)bahir* : *es-,* from Latin *ex-,* out of + *baer,* to gape, from Latin *batāre* (unattested), to yawn, gape.] **—a·bash·ment** *n.*

a·bate (ə-bāt′) *v.* **abated, abating, abates.** —*tr.* **1.** To reduce in amount, degree, or intensity; lessen. **2.** To deduct from an amount; subtract. **3.** *Law.* **a.** To put an end to: *abate a nuisance.* **b.** To make void: *abate a writ.* —*intr.* **1.** To subside: *The storm abated.* **2.** *Law.* To become void. —See Synonyms at **decrease.** [Middle English *abaten,* from Old French *abatre,* to beat down, from Vulgar Latin *abbattuere* (unattested) : *ad-,* at, to (used here to express completed action) + *battuere*†, to beat.]

a·bate·ment (ə-bāt′mənt) *n.* **1.** Diminution in degree or intensity; moderation. **2.** The amount abated; reduction. **3.** *Law.* The act of abating; elimination or annulment.

ab·at·toir (ăb′ə-twär′) *n.* A slaughterhouse. [19th century : French, from *abattre,* to fell. See **abate.**]

ab·ax·i·al (ăb-ăk′sē-əl) *adj.* Facing away from the axis. Said of the lower surface of leaves. Compare **adaxial.**

abba. Variant of **aba.**

Ab·ba (ăb′ə) *n.* **1.** In the New Testament, God. Mark 14:36. **2. abba.** Father. Used as a title of honor in several Eastern churches. [Middle English, from Late Latin, from Greek, from Aramaic *abbā,* father.]

ab·ba·cy (ăb′ə-sē) *n., pl.* **-cies.** The office, term, or jurisdiction of an abbot. [Middle English *abbatie,* from Late Latin *abbātia,* from *abbās* (stem *abbāt-*), ABBOT.]

Ab·bas·sid (ə-băs′ĭd, ăb′ə-sĭd). Also **Ab·bas·side** (-īd). Arabic dynasty (750–1258) that expanded the Moslem Empire to cover much of Asia Minor, North Africa, and parts of Spain. It took its name from al-Abbas (*c.* 566–652), uncle of the prophet Mohammed, and its authority was based chiefly on the religious prestige enjoyed by the prophet's descendants. **—Ab·bas·sid, Ab·bas·side** *adj. & n.*

ab·ba·tial (ə-bā′shəl) *adj.* Of or pertaining to an abbey, abbot, or abbess. [Middle English *abbacyal,* from Late Latin *abbātiālis,* from *abbās* (stem *abbāt-*), ABBOT.]

ab·bé (ăb′ā, ă-bā′) *n., pl.* **abbés.** In France, originally the superior of an abbey, now any priest. Used especially as a title. [French, from Old French, from Late Latin *abbās,* ABBOT.]

ab·bess (ăb′ĭs) *n., pl.* **-besses.** The female superior of a convent of nuns. [Middle English *abbesse,* from Old French, from Late Latin *abbātissa,* from *abbās* (stem *abbāt-*), ABBOT.]

Ab·be·vil·li·an (ăb′ə-vĭl′ē-ən) *adj.* Of or designating the earliest Paleolithic archaeological sites in Europe, characterized by bifacial stone hand axes. Formerly called "Chellian." [After *Abbeville,* France, site of the archaeological finds.]

ab·bey (ăb′ē) *n., pl.* **-beys. 1.** A monastery or convent. **2.** A church that is or once was part of an abbey. [Middle English, from Old French *abaie,* from Late Latin *abbātia,* from *abbās,* ABBOT.]

ab·bot (ăb′ət) *n.* The superior of a monastery. [Middle English *abbod,* Old English *abbod, abbad,* from Late Latin *abbās* (stem *abbāt-*), from Late Greek *abbās,* from Aramaic *abbā,* father, ABBA.]

abbr., abbrev. abbreviation.

ab·bre·vi·ate (ə-brē′vē-āt′) *tr.v.* **-ated, -ating, -ates. 1.** To make shorter by removing or leaving out parts. **2.** To reduce (a word or phrase) to a shorter form intended to represent the full form. [Middle English *abbreviaten,* from Late Latin *abbreviāre,* to shorten : *ab-,* off, or *ad-,* toward + *brevis,* short.] **—ab·brev·i·at·or** *n.*

ab·bre·vi·a·tion (ə-brē′vē-ā′shən) *n. Abbr.* **abbr., abbrev. 1.** The act or product of abbreviating. **2.** A shortened form of a word or phrase used chiefly in writing to represent the complete form; for example, *Mass.* for Massachusetts. Compare **contraction.**

ABC[1] (ā′bē′sē′) *n., pl.* **ABC's. 1.** *Usually* **ABC's.** The alphabet. **2. ABC's.** The rudiments of reading and writing. **3.** An alphabetical guidebook or instruction manual.

ABC[2] **1.** American Broadcasting Company. **2.** atomic, biological, and chemical. **3.** Australian Broadcasting Commission.

ab·cou·lomb (ăb-ko͞o′lŏm′, -lōm′) *n.* A centimeter-gram-second electromagnetic unit of charge, equal to the charge passing in one second through any cross section of a conductor carrying a steady current of one abampere. It is equal to ten coulombs. [AB- (absolute) + COULOMB.]

ab·di·cate (ăb′dĭ-kāt′) *v.* **-cated, -cating, -cates.** —*tr.* To relinquish (power or responsibility) formally. —*intr.* To relinquish formally high office or responsibility. Used especially of a monarch. [Latin *abdicāre,* to disclaim : *ab-,* away from + *dicāre,* to proclaim.] **—ab·di·ca·ble** (ăb′dĭ-kə-bəl) *adj.* **—ab·di·ca·tion** (ăb′dĭ-kā′shən) *n.* **—ab·di·ca·tor** (ăb′dĭ-kā′tər) *n.*

ab·do·men (ăb′də-mən, ăb-dō′mən) *n.* **1.** The part of the body in vertebrates that lies between the thorax and the pelvis, and that encloses the viscera; the belly. **2.** In arthropods, the major posterior part of the body. [16th century : Latin *abdōmen*†, belly.] **—ab·do·mi·nal** (ăb-dŏm′ə-nəl) *adj.* **—ab·dom·i·nal·ly** *adv.*

ab·du·cens nerve (ăb-do͞o′sənz, -dyo͞o′-) *n.* Either of the 6th pair of cranial nerves, which supply one of the eye muscles. [Latin *abdūcens,* "leading away," present participle of *abdūcere,* to ABDUCT.]

ab·duct (ăb-dŭkt′) *tr.v.* **-ducted, -ducting, -ducts. 1.** To carry off (a person) by force; kidnap. **2.** *Physiology.* To draw away from the median line of a bone or muscle or from an adjacent part or limb. [Latin *abdūcere* (past participle *abductus*) : *ab-,* away + *dūcere,* to lead.] **—ab·duc·tion** *n.* **—ab·duc·tor** *n.*

Ab·dul Rah·man (ăb′do͝ol räKH′mən), **Tunku** (1903–73). Malaysian statesman who negotiated the independence of Malaya from Britain in 1957 and helped establish the Federation of Malaysia in 1963. He was the first prime minister of Malaya (1957–63) and of Malaysia (1963–70).

a·beam (ə-bēm′) *adv.* At right angles to the keel of a ship or length of an aircraft or directly opposite the middle of its side. [A- (in the direction of) + BEAM (keel).]

a·be·ce·dar·i·an (ā′bē-sē-dâr′ē-ən) *n.* Also **a·be·ce·da·ry** (ā′bē-sē′-də-rē). **1.** One who teaches or studies the alphabet. **2.** One who is just learning; a novice.
~*adj.* Arranged alphabetically. [Middle English, from Medieval Latin *abecedārium,* alphabet, from Late Latin *abecedārius,* pertaining to the alphabet, from the first four letters.]

a·bed (ə-bĕd′) *adv.* In bed.

A·bed·ne·go (ə-bĕd′nĭ-gō′). One of the three young men, the others being Meshach and Shadrach, who came unharmed out of the fiery furnace in Babylon. Daniel 3:12–30.

A·bel (ā′bəl). The second son of Adam and Eve, slain by his elder brother, Cain. Genesis 4:2. [Middle English, from Late Latin, from Greek, from Hebrew *Hebhel,* akin to Assyrian *ablu,* son.]

Ab·e·lard (ăb′ə-lärd′), **Peter** (1079–1142). *French* **Pierre A·bé·lard** (à-bā-làr′). French philosopher and theologian whose application of the principles of ancient Greek logic to the doctrines of the medieval Catholic Church led him into great controversy and charges of heresy. In Paris he secretly married one of his pupils, Héloise, after she bore him a child. Héloise's family had Abelard castrated; she became a nun and he became a monk.

a·bele (ə-bēl′) *n.* A tree, the **white poplar** *(see).* [16th century : Dutch *abeel,* from Old French *abel, aubel,* from Medieval Latin *albellus,* diminutive of Latin *albus,* white.]

a·be·li·a (ə-bē′lē-ə) *n.* Any of various shrubs of the genus *Abelia,* having tubular red, pink, or white flowers and widely grown as garden ornamentals.

A·be·li·an group (ə-bē′lē-ən, ə-bēl′yən) *n. Algebra.* A **commutative group** *(see).* [After Niels Henrik *Abel* (1802–29), Norwegian mathematician.]

a·bel·mosk (ā′bəl-mŏsk′) *n.* A hairy plant, *Hibiscus abelmoschus,* of tropical Asia, having large yellow flowers and musk-scented seeds that are used in perfumery. Also called "musk mallow." [New Latin *Abelmoschus,* from Arabic *ḥabb-al-musk* (vulgar pronunciation *ḥabb-el-mosk*), "grain of musk" : *ḥabb,* grain + *mosk,* MUSK.]

Ab·er·deen (ab′ər-dēn′). City, port, and administrative center of Grampian Region, northeast Scotland, on the North Sea coast at the mouth of the Dee River. Granted a royal charter in 1176, it has a 14th-century cathedral and a university formed by the amalgamation in 1860 of its two ancient colleges, King's College (founded 1494) and Marischal College (founded 1593). It is known as the "Granite City" because the local stone is used in many of its buildings. Aberdeen is the third-largest fishing port in Britain and the main town servicing the North Sea oil industry.

Aberdeen An·gus (ăng′gəs) *n.* Any of a breed of black, hornless beef cattle that originated in Scotland.

ISLANDS OF CIVILIZATION

Abbeys preserved Europe's intellectual and artistic traditions in the Middle Ages

Abbeys have their roots in the early religious communities of the Middle East and Greece. The first European abbey, however, was built in 529 on the rugged peak of Monte Cassino, Italy, by St. Benedict, founder of Western monasticism. The abbot—from Aramaic *abba* ("father")—was seen both as the representative of Christ and as the monastery's temporal authority. The name abbey was given to a monastic community under an abbot or abbess, but it was used loosely for other religious foundations—and often as another word for monastery.

The monastic life was attractively secure when, outside, governments were weak and life unruly. In Christian Western Europe 100 abbeys were founded in the 7th century and 100 more by 750. For six centuries, abbeys were islands of civilization all over Europe. A large abbey could serve a considerable area as an administrative, intellectual, and spiritual center. Some could house 1,000 people—several hundred monks, servants, and guests. Many became extremely wealthy and were famed for their splendid buildings.

In Britain, as a consequence of his break with the papacy and his need for additional income, Henry VIII dissolved the monasteries (1536–40). Most abbeys were destroyed, leaving only some abbey churches such as Westminster Abbey. Several have been restored, but few new ones have been built.

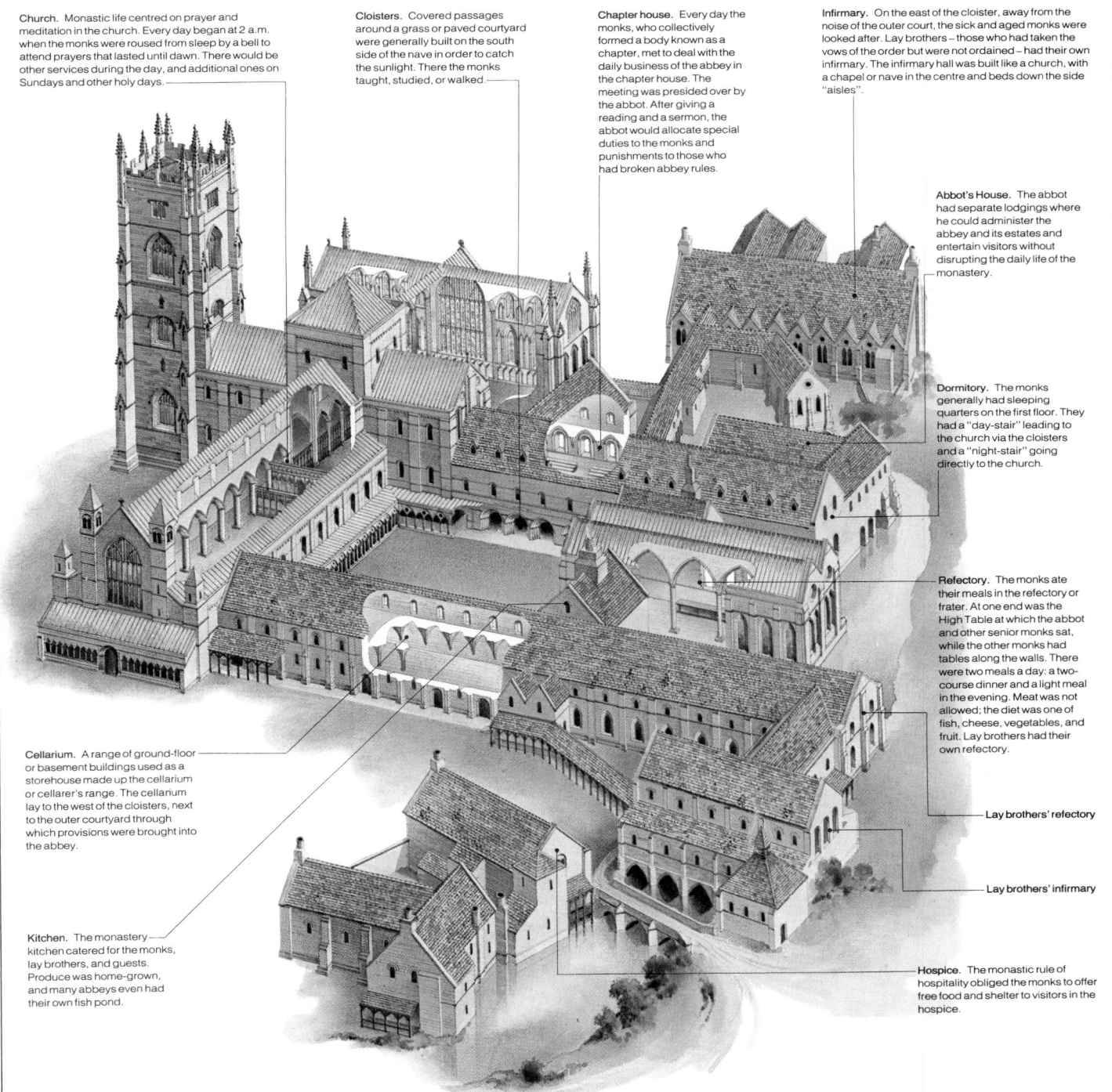

Church. Monastic life centred on prayer and meditation in the church. Every day began at 2 a.m. when the monks were roused from sleep by a bell to attend prayers that lasted until dawn. There would be other services during the day, and additional ones on Sundays and other holy days.

Cloisters. Covered passages around a grass or paved courtyard were generally built on the south side of the nave in order to catch the sunlight. There the monks taught, studied, or walked.

Chapter house. Every day the monks, who collectively formed a body known as a chapter, met to deal with the daily business of the abbey in the chapter house. The meeting was presided over by the abbot. After giving a reading and a sermon, the abbot would allocate special duties to the monks and punishments to those who had broken abbey rules.

Infirmary. On the east of the cloister, away from the noise of the outer court, the sick and aged monks were looked after. Lay brothers – those who had taken the vows of the order but were not ordained – had their own infirmary. The infirmary hall was built like a church, with a chapel or nave in the centre and beds down the side "aisles".

Abbot's House. The abbot had separate lodgings where he could administer the abbey and its estates and entertain visitors without disrupting the daily life of the monastery.

Dormitory. The monks generally had sleeping quarters on the first floor. They had a "day-stair" leading to the church via the cloisters and a "night-stair" going directly to the church.

Refectory. The monks ate their meals in the refectory or frater. At one end was the High Table at which the abbot and other senior monks sat, while the other monks had tables along the walls. There were two meals a day: a two-course dinner and a light meal in the evening. Meat was not allowed; the diet was one of fish, cheese, vegetables, and fruit. Lay brothers had their own refectory.

Cellarium. A range of ground-floor or basement buildings used as a storehouse made up the cellarium or cellarer's range. The cellarium lay to the west of the cloisters, next to the outer courtyard through which provisions were brought into the abbey.

Kitchen. The monastery kitchen catered for the monks, lay brothers, and guests. Produce was home-grown, and many abbeys even had their own fish pond.

Lay brothers' refectory

Lay brothers' infirmary

Hospice. The monastic rule of hospitality obliged the monks to offer free food and shelter to visitors in the hospice.

Ab·er·deen·shire (ăb′ər-dēn′shĭr′). Former county of northeast Scotland. Since 1975 it has been part of Grampian Region.

Aberdeen terrier *n.* The **Scottish terrier** *(see).*

ab·er·rant (ă-bĕr′ənt) *adj.* **1.** Deviating from the proper or expected course. **2.** Deviating from what is normal; untrue to type. **—ab·er·rance, ab·er·ran·cy** *n.*

ab·er·ra·tion (ăb′ə-rā′shən) *n.* **1.** A deviation from the proper or expected course. **2.** A departure from the normal or typical. **3.** An abnormal alteration in one's mental state; a lapse in mental capacities. **4.** *Optics.* **a.** A defect of focus, such as blurring or distortion, in an image. **b.** A physical defect in an optical element, as in a mirror or lens, that causes such an imperfection. See **chromatic aberration, spherical aberration, astigmatism, coma.** **5.** The apparent displacement of the position of a celestial body in the direction of motion of an observer on Earth, caused by the motion of the Earth. [Latin *aberrātiō,* diversion, from *aberrāre,* to go astray : *ab-,* from + *errāre,* to stray.]

a·bet (ə-bĕt′) *tr.v.* **abetted, abetting, abets.** To encourage and assist; especially, to incite to a criminal act. [Middle English *abetten,* from Old French *abeter,* to entice : *a-,* from Latin *ad-,* to + *beter,* to bait, from Germanic.] **—a·bet·ment** *n.* **—a·bet·ter, a·bet·tor** *n.*

ab ex·tra (ăb ĕk′strə) *adv. Latin.* From without.

a·bey·ance (ə-bā′əns) *n.* **1.** The condition of being temporarily set aside or suspended. **2.** *Law.* A condition of undetermined ownership, as of an estate that has not yet been assigned. [Norman French *abeiance,* variant of Old French *abeance,* desire, from *abaer,* "to gape at," yearn for : *a-,* from Latin *ad-,* to + *baer,* to gape (see **abash**).] **—a·bey·ant** *adj.*

ab·far·ad (ăb-făr′ăd′, -əd) *n.* A centimeter-gram-second electromagnetic unit of capacitance, equal to the capacitance of a capacitor having a charge of one abcoulomb and a potential difference of one abvolt. It is equal to 10^9 farads. [AB- (absolute) + FARAD.]

ab·hen·ry (ăb-hĕn′rē) *n., pl.* **-ries.** A centimeter-gram-second electromagnetic unit of inductance, equal to the inductance resulting from a current variation of one abampere per second that produces an induced electromotive force of one abvolt. It is equal to 10^{-9} henry. [AB- (absolute) + HENRY.]

ab·hor (ăb-hôr′) *tr.v.* **-horred, -horring, -hors.** **1.** To regard with horror or loathing; abominate. **2.** To reject vehemently; shun. [Middle English *abhorren,* from Latin *abhorrēre,* to shrink from : *ab-,* from + *horrēre,* to shudder, bristle.] **—ab·hor·rence** *n.* **—ab·hor·rer** *n.*

ab·hor·rent (ăb-hôr′ənt, -hŏr′-) *adj.* **1.** Disgusting; loathsome; repellent. **2.** In opposition; completely contrary: *Carelessness was abhorrent to his nature.* **—ab·hor·rent·ly** *adv.*

A·bib (ä-vēv′) *n.* In the ancient Hebrew calendar, an earlier name for the month of **Nisan** *(see).* [Hebrew *'ābhībh,* "(month of) fresh barley," "spring."]

a·bide (ə-bīd′) *v.* **abode** (ə-bōd′) or **abided, abiding, abides.** *—tr.* **1.** To put up with; tolerate: *can't abide hypocrisy.* **2.** To withstand; persevere under: *abide the horrors of war.* **3.** *Archaic.* To wait patiently for: *"I will abide the coming of my Lord"* (Tennyson). *—intr.* **1.** To remain in one place or state. **2.** To continue; endure: *"Who can abide in the fierceness of his anger?"* (Cotton Mather). **3.** *Archaic.* To dwell or sojourn. —See Synonyms at **bear.** **—abide by.** **1.** To conform to; comply with. **2.** To accept the consequences of; rest satisfied with. [Middle English *abiden,* Old English *ābīdan* : *a-* (intensive) + *bīdan,* to remain, await.] **—a·bid·ance** *n.*

a·bid·ing (ə-bī′dĭng) *adj.* Lasting; enduring: *an abiding devotion.* **—a·bi·ding·ly** *adv.*

Ab·i·djan (ăb′ĭ-jän′). The capital of the Ivory Coast, on the Gulf of Guinea. It lies on an enclosed lagoon and is the country's leading port and industrial center.

ab·i·et·ic acid (ăb′ē-ĕt′ĭk) *n.* A yellowish resinous powder, $C_{19}H_{29}COOH$, occurring naturally in rosin and used in lacquers, varnishes, and soaps. [19th century : from Latin *abiēs*† (stem *abiēt-*), fir (the acid occurs in its resin).]

ab·i·gail (ăb′ə-gāl′) *n. Archaic.* A lady's maid. [From the name of a serving maid in *The Scornful Lady* (*c.* 1613), play by Beaumont and Fletcher.]

Ab·i·gail (ăb′ə-gāl′). The wife of David. I Samuel 25:14–44. [Hebrew *Abhīgayil,* "my father is joy."]

Ab·i·lene[1] (ăb′ə-lēn′). A city in central Kansas, west of Topeka. It was originally a boisterous cow town and terminus of the Abilene trail, a cattle-driving route from Texas to Kansas. Dwight D. Eisenhower lived in Abilene during his youth; the Eisenhower Center includes his family homestead, a museum, a library, and his grave.

Abilene[2]. A city in west-central Texas. Originally a shipping center for cattle, Abilene is now the financial, commercial, and educational center of a large part of western Texas.

a·bil·i·ty (ə-bĭl′ə-tē) *n., pl.* **-ties.** **1.** The quality of being able to do something; the fact of having the requisite means, skill, strength, mental capacity, or legal power. **2.** A natural or acquired skill or talent. [Middle English *abilite,* from Old French *habilite,* from Latin *habilitās,* from *habilis,* ABLE.]

Synonyms: *aptitude, capacity, competence, skill, talent.*

-ability, -ibility *suffix.* Indicates: **1.** Ability to undergo the specified action or process: for example, **wearability.** **2.** Possession of a specified quality; for example, **variability.** [-ABLE + -ITY or -IBLE + -ITY.]

ab in·i·ti·o (ăb′ ĭ-nĭsh′ē-ō) *adv. Latin.* From the beginning.

ab in·tra (ăb′ ĭn′trə) *adv. Latin.* From within.

a·bi·o·gen·e·sis (ā′bī-ō-jĕn′ə-sĭs, ăb′ē-ō-) *n.* The hypothetical development of living organisms from nonliving matter as is assumed to have occurred in the origin of life on earth. Also called "autogenesis." See **primordial soup, spontaneous generation.** [A- (without) + BIO- + -GENESIS.] **—a·bi·o·ge·net·ic** (ā′bī-ō-jə-nĕt′ĭk) *adj.*

a·bi·ot·ic (ā′bī-ŏt′ĭk) *adj.* Devoid of life; inanimate. Said especially of environments or environmental factors.

ab·ject (ăb′jĕkt′, ăb-jĕkt′) *adj.* **1.** Of the most contemptible kind: *an abject liar.* **2.** Of the most miserable kind; wretched: *abject poverty.* **3.** Humble and often ingratiating in manner; servile. —See Synonyms at **mean** (ignoble). [Middle English, "rejected," from Latin *abjectus,* cast away, from the past participle of *abjicere,* to cast away : *ab-,* away from + *jacere,* to throw.] **—ab·jec·tion** *n.* **—ab·ject·ly** *adv.*

ab·jure (ăb-jŏŏr′) *tr.v.* **-jured, -juring, -jures.** **1. a.** To repudiate or recant solemnly. **b.** To renounce under oath; forswear. **2.** To abstain from; give up. [Middle English *abjuren,* from Old French *abjurer,* from Latin *abjūrāre* : *ab-,* away + *jūrāre,* to swear.] **—ab·ju·ra·tion** *n.* **—ab·jur·er** *n.*

abl. ablative.

ab·late (ă-blāt′) *tr.v.* **-lated, -lating, -lates.** To remove by ablation. [Back-formation from ABLATION.]

ab·la·tion (ă-blā′shən) *n.* **1.** Surgical excision or amputation of any part of the body. **2.** The totality of erosive processes by which a glacier or ice sheet is reduced. **3.** *Aerospace.* The dissipation of heat generated by atmospheric friction, especially in the atmospheric reentry of a spacecraft or missile, by means of a melting **heat shield** *(see).* [Late Latin *ablātiō,* from *ablātus,* removed (past participle of *auferre,* to carry away) : *ab-,* away from + *-lātus,* carried.]

ab·la·tive (ăb′lə-tĭv) *n. Abbr.* **abl.** **1.** The grammatical case in certain Indo-European languages, such as Latin, that denotes separation, direction away from, and sometimes manner or agency. **2.** A form or construction in this case. [Middle English, from Old French *ablatif,* from Latin *ablātīvus,* "expressing removal," from *ablātus,* removed. See **ablation.**] **—ab·la·tive** *adj.*

ablative absolute *n.* In Latin grammar, an adverbial phrase syntactically independent from the rest of the sentence and containing two main constituents, both in the ablative case. It is usually used to express cause, circumstance, or time; for example, in the sentence *Regibus expulsis, leges respublica condit (The kings having been expelled, the republic sets up laws),* the phrase *Regibus expulsis* is the ablative absolute.

ab·la·tor (ă-blā′tər) *n.* A **heat shield** *(see).* [ABLAT(ION) + -OR.]

ab·laut (äb′lout′, äp′-) *n. Linguistics.* A patterned change in root vowels of verb forms, characteristic of Indo-European languages, indicating alteration of tense, aspect, or function; for example, *ring, rang, rung.* Also called "gradation," "vowel gradation." Compare **umlaut.** [German *Ablaut,* "off sound" : *ab,* off, away from, from Old High German *aba* + *Laut,* sound, from Middle High German *lūt,* from Old High German *hlūt.*]

a·blaze (ə-blāz′) *adj.* **1.** On fire. **2.** Radiant; aglow.

a·ble (ā′bəl) *adj.* **abler, ablest.** **1.** Having sufficient ability or resources. **2. a.** Capable; competent: *an able administrator.* **b.** Talented; gifted. **3.** Legally qualified: *able to inherit.* [Middle English, from Old French, from Latin *habilis,* manageable, apt, expert, from *habēre,* to hold, handle.]

-able, -ible *suffix.* Indicates: **1.** Able to undergo the specified action; for example, **debatable, drinkable, collapsible.** **2.** Having or sharing a specified quality; for example, **knowledgeable, comfortable, fashionable.** **3.** Causing or deserving; for example, **honorable, objectionable.** [Middle English, from Old French, from Latin *-ābilis, -ībilis,* forms (with different vowel stems) of the passive adjectival suffix *-bilis.*]

a·ble-bod·ied (ā′bəl-bŏd′ēd) *adj.* Physically strong and healthy.

able-bodied seaman *n. Abbr.* **a.b., A.B.** A merchant seaman certified for all seaman's duties. Also called "able seaman."

a·bloom (ə-blōōm′) *adj.* In bloom; flowering. **—a·bloom** *adv.*

ab·lu·tion (ə-blōō′shən) *n.* **1.** A washing or cleansing of the body, especially as part of a religious ceremony. **2.** The liquid used in such cleansing. **3. ablutions.** The act of washing oneself. Usually used humorously. [Middle English, from Latin *ablūtiō,* from *abluere,* to wash away : *ab-,* away from + *luere,* to wash, from *lavere,* variant of *lavāre,* to wash.] **—ab·lu·tion·ar·y** *adj.*

a·bly (ā′blē) *adv.* In an able manner; capably.

ABM antiballistic missile.

abn airborne.

Ab·na·ki (ăb-nä′kē) *n., pl.* **-kis** or collectively **Abnaki** (for senses 1, 2). **1.** A tribe of North American Indians of Maine, New Brunswick, and southern Quebec. **2.** A member of the Abnaki. **3.** The Algonquian language of the Abnaki.

ab·ne·gate (ăb′nĭ-gāt′) *tr.v.* **-gated, -gating, -gates.** To deny to oneself; give up; renounce. [Latin *abnegāre,* to refuse, reject : *ab-,* away from + *negāre,* to deny.]

ab·ne·ga·tion (ăb′nĭ-gā′shən) *n.* **1.** Renunciation. **2.** Self-denial or self-sacrifice; self-abnegation.

ab·nor·mal (ăb-nôr′məl) *adj.* **1.** Not normal; untypical; irregular. **2.** Peculiar; deviant. [Latin *abnormis,* departing from normal : *ab-,* away from + *norma,* rule, norm.] **—ab·nor·mal·ly** *adv.*

ab·nor·mal·i·ty (ăb′nôr-măl′ə-tē) *n., pl.* **-ties.** **1.** The condition of not being normal. **2.** An abnormal phenomenon; an irregularity. **3.** A physical defect or deformity.

abnormal psychology *n.* The study of behavioral abnormalities and mental disorders in human beings.

ABO (ā-bē′ō′) *n.* A classification of human blood types according to their compatibility in transfusion, which depends on the presence or

PRONUNCIATION KEY

ă, pat; ā, pay; âr, care; ä, father, are; b, bib; ch, church; d, deed; ĕ, pet; ē, be; f, fife; g, gag; h, hat; hw, which; ĭ, pit; ī, pie; îr, pier; j, judge; k, kick; l, lid, needle; m, mum; n, no, sudden; ng, thing; ŏ, pot; ō, toe; ô, paw, for; oi, noise; ou, out; ŏŏ, book; ōō, boot; p, pop; r, roar; s, sauce; sh, ship, dish; t, tight; th, thin, path; *th,* this, bathe; ŭ, cut; ûr, fur; v, valve; w, with; y, yes; z, zebra, size; zh, vision; ə, about, item, edible, gallop, circus, peaceful

IN FOREIGN WORDS:

à, *Fr.* ami; œ, *Fr.* feu, *Ger.* schön; ü, *Fr.* tu, *Ger.* über; KH, *Ger.* ich, *Scot.* loch; N, *Fr.* bon; y′, *Fr.* Compiègne

STRESS MARKS:

Primary stress: ′ **in·cite′** (ĭn-sīt′)
Secondary stress: ′ **in′sight′** (ĭn′sīt′)

absence of either of two antigens, A and B. Blood types are classified as A, B, AB, or O.

a·board (ə-bôrd′, ə-bōrd′) *adv.* On or onto a ship, train, airplane, or other passenger vehicle.
~*prep.* On, in, onto, or into (a ship, train, or the like). [Middle English : A- (on) + BOARD.]

a·bode (ə-bōd′). Past tense and past participle of **abide.**
~*n.* A dwelling place or home. [Middle English *abod,* from *abiden,* ABIDE.]

ab·ohm (ăb-ōm′) *n.* A centimeter-gram-second electromagnetic unit of resistance equal to 10^{-9} ohm. [AB- (absolute) + OHM.]

a·bol·ish (ə-bŏl′ ĭsh) *tr.v.* **-ished, -ishing, -ishes.** To do away with (an institution or practice, for example); put an end to. [Middle English *abolysshen,* from Old French *abolire* (present stem *aboliss-*), from Latin *abolēre,* to destroy.] **—a·bol·ish·a·ble** *adj.* **—a·bol·ish·er** *n.* **—a·bol·ish·ment** *n.*
Synonyms: *eradicate, extirpate.*

ab·o·li·tion (ăb′ə-lĭsh′ən) *n.* **1.** An act of abolishing or state of being abolished; annulment; extinction. **2.** *Sometimes* **Abolition.** The ending of slavery and the slave trade, especially in the United States. [Latin *abolitiō,* from *abolitus,* past participle of *abolēre,* ABOLISH.] **—ab·o·li·tion·ar·y** *adj.*

ab·o·li·tion·ist (ăb′ə-lĭsh′ə-nĭst) *n.* **1.** One who wishes to abolish a law, institution, or the like. **2.** *Sometimes* **Abolitionist.** A supporter of the abolition of slavery, especially in the United States during the period before the Civil War. **—ab·o·li·tion·ism** *n.*

ab·o·ma·sum (ăb′ō-mā′səm) *n., pl.* **-sa** (-sə). The fourth division of the stomach in ruminant animals, in which true digestion takes place. [New Latin : AB- (away from) + OMASUM.] **—ab·o·ma·sal** *adj.*

A-bomb (ā′bŏm′) *n.* An **atomic bomb** *(see).*

a·bom·i·na·ble (ə-bŏm′ə-nə-bəl) *adj.* **1.** Detestable; loathsome. **2. a.** Thoroughly unpleasant. **b.** Of extremely poor quality. [Middle English, from Old French, from Latin *abōminābilis,* from *abōminārī,* to ABOMINATE.] **—a·bom·i·na·bly** *adv.*

abominable snowman *n.* A legendary humanlike animal reportedly inhabiting the high Himalayas. Also called "yeti." [Translation of Tibetan *metohkangmi* : *metoh,* abominable + *kangmi,* snowman.]

a·bom·i·nate (ə-bŏm′ə-nāt′) *tr.v.* **-nated, -nating, -nates.** To detest; abhor. [Latin *abōminārī,* "to shun as a bad omen" : *ab-,* away from + *ōmen* (stem *ōmin-*), omen.] **—a·bom·i·na·tor** *n.*

a·bom·i·na·tion (ə-bŏm′ə-nā′shən) *n.* **1.** Something or someone that causes great revulsion or abhorrence. **2.** An intense dislike or loathing for someone or something.

ab·o·ral (ă-bôr′əl, -bōr′-) *adj. Biology.* Opposite to or away from the mouth. [AB- (away from) + ORAL.] **—ab·o·ral·ly** *adv.*

ab·o·rig·i·nal (ăb′ə-rĭj′ə-nəl) *adj.* **1.** Native; indigenous: *The Indians are among the aboriginal inhabitants of South America.* **2.** Of or pertaining to aborigines.
~*n.* **1.** An aborigine. **2. Aboriginal.** An Australian Aborigine. **—ab·o·rig·i·nal·ly** *adv.*

ab·o·rig·i·ne (ăb′ə-rĭj′ə-nē′) *n.* **1.** An indigenous inhabitant of a region. **2. Aborigine.** A member of the indigenous dark-skinned people of Australia. **3. Aborigine.** Any of the languages of this people. **4. aborigines.** The plants and animals native to a geographical area. [Latin *Aborīginēs,* pre-Roman tribes inhabiting Latium, probably an alteration of some tribal name, reshaped by folk etymology as if derived from *ab orīgine,* "from the beginning."]

a·born·ing (ə-bôr′nĭng, ə-bōr′-) *adv.* While coming into being or getting under way: *The project almost died aborning.* [A- (in the act of) + BORN + -ING.]

a·bort (ə-bôrt′) *v.* **aborted, aborting, aborts.** *—intr.* **1. a.** To miscarry. Used of a pregnant mammal. **b.** To be expelled prematurely from the womb. Used of a fetus. **2.** To cease organic growth before full development or maturation. **3.** To end prematurely; especially, to terminate an operation involving a missile or a space vehicle before completion. *—tr.* **1. a.** To cause the abortion of (a fetus). **b.** To terminate prematurely the pregnancy of. **2.** To interfere with or terminate the normal development of. **3.** To bring to an end prematurely or before scheduled completion: *Equipment failure forced us to abort the space mission.* [Latin *abortāre,* frequentative of *aborīrī* (past participle *abortus*), to die, disappear, miscarry : *ab,* off, away, hence, badly + *orīrī,* to arise, appear, be born.]

a·bor·ti·cide (ə-bôr′tə-sīd′) *n.* **1.** The destruction of a fetus within the womb. **2.** The drug used in this process. [ABORT + -CIDE.]

a·bor·ti·fa·cient (ə-bôr′tə-fā′shənt) *adj.* Causing abortion.
~*n.* Anything used to induce abortion. [ABORT(ION) + -FACIENT.]

a·bor·tion (ə-bôr′shən) *n.* **1.** The premature expulsion of a fetus from the womb, which may be either spontaneous (a miscarriage) or induced. Compare **stillbirth. 2.** An operation to remove a fetus from the womb. **3.** Cessation of normal growth, especially of an organ, prior to full development or maturation. **4.** An aborted organism. **5.** Anything malformed or incompletely developed. **6.** An action or plan that has not been carried to a successful conclusion.

a·bor·tion·ist (ə-bôr′shən-ĭst) *n.* One who performs abortions.

a·bor·tive (ə-bôr′tĭv) *adj.* **1.** Failing to accomplish an intended objective; fruitless. **2.** Partially or imperfectly developed. **3.** Causing abortion; abortifacient. **—a·bor·tive·ly** *adv.*

aboulia. Variant of **abulia.**

a·bound (ə-bound′) *intr.v.* **abounded, abounding, abounds. 1.** To be present in great numbers or large amount. **2.** To have a large number or amount; teem: *The rivers here abound in game fish. Her letters abound with playful humor.* [Middle English *abounden,* from Old French *abonder,* from Latin *abundāre,* to overflow : *ab-,* away from + *undāre,* to flow, from *unda,* wave.]

a·bout (ə-bout′) *adv. Abbr.* **a. 1.** Approximately; roughly. **2.** Nearly; almost. **3.** To a reversed position or direction: *She turned about and retraced her steps.* **4.** In no particular direction; with no particular destination: *wandering about.* **5. a.** All around; on every side. **b.** In various places; here and there: *scattered about; lying about.* **6.** In the area or vicinity. **7.** In succession; one after another: *Turn about is fair play.* **8.** Prevailing; current: *There's a lot of flu about.* **9.** *Informal.* In an extreme degree. Used ironically as an understatement: *About time.* **10.** Into existence; so as to occur: *How did it come about? Bring it about.*
~*prep.* **1.** On all sides of; surrounding. **2.** In the vicinity of; around: *somewhere about 110°.* **3.** In and around; here and there in; through. **4.** Almost the same as; close to; near. **5.** In reference to; relating to. **6.** On, attached to, or in the possession or character of: *He has his wits about him; an air of caution about her.* **7.** On the verge of doing something. Used with an infinitive: *The chorus is about to sing.* **8.** Willing or prepared. Used in the negative and with an infinitive to indicate determination: *I'm not about to give up now.* **9.** Involved with or engaged in: *going about his work cheerfully; make me a cup while you're about it.*
~*adj.* Out of bed, after sleep or illness: *up and about.* [Middle English *about,* Old English *abūtan, onbūtan* : ON + *būtan,* outside of.]
Usage: *about, around, round.* These terms are sometimes interchangeable, as adverbs and prepositions. However, *around* either specifies or suggests complete encirclement of something, whereas *about* and *round* are less exact and indicate, more or less, semiencirclement: *The children gathered about* (or *round*) *the fire place; then they danced around the table.* • The construction *not about to,* or a variant with *about* and a negative, is used to emphasize intention or express determination. The construction is principally appropriate to informal speech or writing.

a·bout-face (ə-bout′fās′) *n.* **1.** A reversal of orientation, accomplished by a pivotal movement from a stationary position; a movement resulting in the body facing the opposite direction. **2.** A change to an opposite opinion or point of view.
~*intr.v.* **about-faced, -facing, -faces. 1.** To make an about-face. **2.** To reverse direction.

a·bout-turn (ə-bout′tûrn′) *n. Chiefly British.* An about-face.

a·bove (ə-bŭv′) *adv.* **1.** Overhead; on high: *the clouds above.* **2.** In heaven; heavenward. **3.** Upstairs: *a table in the dining room above.* **4.** In a higher place. **5.** On the top or upper side. **6.** Beyond a given amount or figure: *designed for children of 12 and above.* **7.** Upstream: *the rapids above.* **8.** In an earlier part of the text: *figures quoted above.* Also used in combination: *the above-mentioned figures.* **9.** In or to a higher rank or position: *promoted to the grade above.*
~*prep.* **1.** Over; higher than: *situated above the treeline.* **2. a.** Superior to; of more importance than: *placed his country above his family ties.* **b.** Of higher rank or status than. **3. a.** Beyond the level or reach of: *above suspicion.* **b.** Beyond the grasp or understanding of: *The political discussion was above me.* **4.** In preference to. **5.** Too honorable to engage in: *above petty intrigue.* **6.** Greater than, as in weight, price, age, temperature, or pitch: *above the age of 65; a shot heard above the music.* **7.** North of: *Canada is directly above the United States.* **8.** Upstream from. **—above all.** Most of all. **—above and beyond.** In addition to.
~*n.* Something that is above: *as the above should make clear.*
~*adj.* Appearing earlier in the same text: *flaws in the above interpretation.* [Middle English *aboven, abuven,* Old English *abufan* : A- (on) + *bufan,* above.]
Usage: *The above, cf. above,* and other such uses, are common in business and legal writing, but they are often considered awkward or stilted and are usually avoided in popular writing.

a·bove·board (ə-bŭv′ bôrd′, -bōrd′) *adv.* Without deceit or trickery.
~*adj.* Honest; not concealed: *an open and aboveboard agreement.* [Originally a gambling term, "above the gambling table, not changing cards under the table."]

a·bove·ground (ə-bŭv′ground′) *adj.* **1.** Located on or above the surface of the ground: *an aboveground nuclear explosion.* **2.** Not hidden or secret; open. **3.** Using conventional standards, means, or procedures: *the aboveground press.*

ab o·vo (ăb ō′vō) *adv. Latin.* From the start. [Literally, "from the egg."]

abp., Abp. archbishop.

abr. abridged; abridgment.

ab·ra·ca·dab·ra (ăb′rə-kə-dăb′rə) *n.* **1.** A word held to possess supernatural powers to ward off disease or disaster. **2.** A formula spoken by conjurors when performing a trick. **3.** Jargon; mumbo jumbo; gibberish. [Late Latin, from Late Greek *abrasadabra,* a magic word used by a Gnostic sect, probably derived from *Abraxas,* name of a Gnostic deity.]

a·brade (ə-brād′) *tr.v.* **abraded, abrading, abrades. 1.** To rub off or wear away by or as if by friction. **2.** *Geology.* To wear away as a result of corrosion. [Latin *abrādere,* to scrape off : *ab-,* off + *rādere,* to scrape.] **—a·bra·dant** *adj. & n.* **—a·brad·er** *n.*

A·bra·ham (ā′brə-hăm′). The first patriarch and progenitor of the Hebrew people; father of Isaac. Genesis 11–25. [Middle English, from Late Latin, from Late Greek, from Hebrew *Abhrāhām,* "father of a multitude," altered from *Abram,* "high father."]

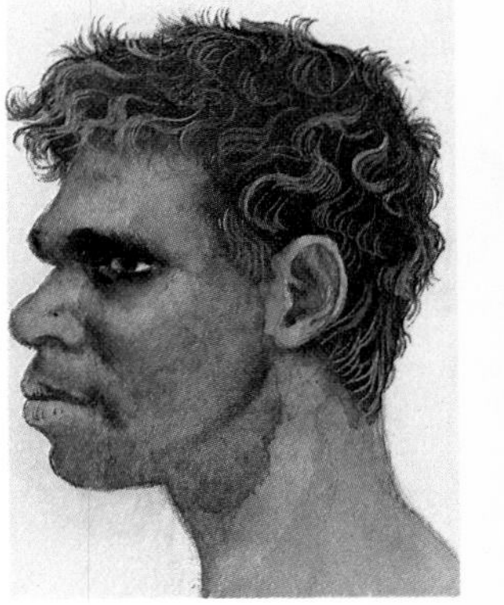

Aborigine *The only surviving members of the Australoid race, Aborigines are thought to have reached Australia from Asia about 40,000 years ago. By tradition they are nomadic hunters, but since the arrival of Europeans in the 18th century, their numbers have declined —from about 300,000 to a total now of about 200,000—and most have settled in towns.*

Abraham, Plains of. A plateau near Quebec, where the British under Gen. James Wolfe defeated the French under Gen. Louis Montcalm in 1759 and effectively won Canada for Britain.

a·bran·chi·ate (ā-brăng′kē-ĭt, -āt′) *adj. Zoology.* Having no gills. [A- (without) + Greek *brankhia*, gills. See **branchia**.]

ab·ra·sion (ə-brā′zhən) *n.* **1.** The process of wearing down or rubbing away by means of friction. **2.** A scraped or worn area; a graze. [Medieval Latin *abrāsiō*, from Latin *abrādere*, to ABRADE.]

ab·ra·sive (ə-brā′sĭv, -zĭv) *adj.* **1.** Causing abrasion; harsh; rough. **2.** Harsh in manner; rude.
~*n.* A substance that abrades, especially emery, pumice, or similar material, used to clean or smooth surfaces..

ab·re·act (ăb′rē-ăkt′) *tr.v.* **-acted, -acting, -acts.** *Psychology.* To release repressed emotions by abreaction. [Translation of German *abreagieren* : AB- (away from) + *reagieren*, to react.]

ab·re·ac·tion (ăb′rē-ăk′shən) *n. Psychology.* The release of the tension resulting from conflict or from repressed emotion, achieved either unconsciously or through conscious examination and the acting out, in imagination, words, or action, of the situation causing the conflict.

a·breast (ə-brĕst′) *adv.* **1.** Side by side. **2.** Up to date; aware: *abreast of the news.* [Middle English *abrest* : A- (on) + BREAST.]

a·bridge (ə-brĭj′) *tr.v.* **abridged, abridging, abridges.** **1.** To reduce the length of (a written text); condense. **2.** To cut short. **3.** To limit or curtail (freedom or rights). [Middle English *abregen*, from Old French *abregier*, from Late Latin *abbreviāre*, to ABBREVIATE.] —**a·bridg·er** *n.*

a·bridg·ment (ə-brĭj′mənt) *n.* Also *chiefly British* **a·bridge·ment.** *Abbr.* **abr.** **1. a.** The action of abridging. **b.** The state of being abridged. **2.** A condensation of a book, play, or the like; an abridged version.

a·broad (ə-brôd′) *adv.* **1.** Out of one's own country. **2.** In a foreign country or countries. **3.** Away from one's place of residence; outdoors. **4.** On the move; at large; circulating. **5.** Broadly; widely. **6.** *Archaic.* Not on target; astray; in error.
~*n.* A foreign country; foreign countries collectively: *a student from abroad.* [Middle English *abro(o)d*, "broadly, widely scattered" : A- (on, in) + *brood*, BROAD.]

ab·ro·gate (ăb′rō-gāt′, -rə-) *tr.v.* **-gated, -gating, -gates.** To abolish or annul by authority. —See Synonyms at **nullify**. [Latin *abrogāre* : *ab-*, away + *rogāre*, to ask, propose.] —**ab·ro·ga·tion** *n.* —**ab·ro·ga·tor** *n.*

a·brupt (ə-brŭpt′) *adj.* **1.** Unexpectedly sudden. **2.** Curt; brusque. **3.** Touching on one subject after another with sudden transitions: *abrupt, nervous prose.* **4.** Steeply inclined. **5.** *Biology.* Appearing to be cut or broken off short; truncate. [Latin *abruptus*, past participle of *abrumpere*, to break off : *ab-*, off + *rumpere*, to break.] —**a·brupt·ly** *adv.* —**a·brupt·ness** *n.*

A·bruz·zi (ä-brōōt′tsē). Also **A·bruz·zo** (-tsō). Region of central Italy, bordering on the Adriatic in the east. It is mountainous, containing the highest peak in the Apennines, Monte Corno (2,914 meters; 9,560 feet), and is fairly poor, with small-scale agriculture and industry. Its capital is L'Aquila.

abs absolute temperature.

abs. **1.** absence; absent. **2.** absolute; absolutely. **3.** abstract.

Ab·sa·lom (ăb′sə-ləm). In the Old Testament, David's favorite son, killed when rebelling against his father. II Samuel 13–39.

ab·scess (ăb′sĕs′) *n.* A localized collection of pus in any part of the body, surrounded by an inflamed area and often caused by bacterial infection.
~*intr.v.* **abscessed, -scessing, -scesses.** To form an abscess. [Latin *abscĕssus*, "a going away (of bad humors)," hence, collection of pus, from *abscēdere*, to go away : *abs-, ab-*, away from + *cēdere*, to go.]

ab·scise (ăb-sīz′) *v.* **-scised, -scising, -scises.** —*tr.* To remove; cut off. —*intr.* To be shed by abscission. [Latin *abscindere* (past participle *abscissus*) : *abs-, ab-*, away + *scindere*, to cut.]

ab·scis·sa (ăb-sĭs′ə) *n., pl.* **-sas** or **-scissae** (-sĭs′ē′). *Mathematics.* The coordinate representing the distance of a point from the *y*–axis in a plane Cartesian coordinate system, measured along a line parallel to the *x*–axis. Compare **ordinate.** [New Latin *(linea) abscissa*, "cut-off (line)," from Latin *abscissus*, past participle of *abscindere*, to cut off, ABSCISE.]

ab·scis·sion (ăb-sĭzh′ən) *n.* **1.** The act of cutting off. **2.** The process by which plant parts, such as leaves and flowers, are shed. A layer of cells forms at the base of the plant part and then disintegrates, causing the part to become separated.

ab·scond (ăb-skŏnd′) *intr.v.* **-sconded, -sconding, -sconds.** To leave quickly and secretly and hide oneself, especially in order to escape imprisonment, arrest, or prosecution. [Latin *abscondere* : *abs-, ab-*, away + *condere*, to hide.] —**ab·scond·er** *n.*

ab·seil (ăp′zīl′) *intr.v.* **-seiled, -seiling, -seils.** **1.** In mountaineering and caving, to descend a steep or vertical rock face using a rope attached above and secured around the body. **2.** To descend from a helicopter by means of a rope.
~*n.* An instance of abseiling. [German *abseilen*, to descend by means of a rope : *ab-*, down + *Seil*, rope.]

ab·sence (ăb′səns) *n. Abbr.* **abs.** **1.** The state of being away. **2.** The time during which one is away. **3.** Lack: *an absence of corroborating evidence.* **4.** Inattention; abstraction: *absence of mind.*

ab·sent (ăb′sənt) *adj. Abbr.* **abs.** **1.** Missing or not present. **2.** Not existent; lacking. **3.** Inattentive.
~*tr.v.* (ăb-sĕnt′) **absented, -senting, -sents.** **1.** To keep (oneself)

away. **2.** To withdraw (oneself). [Middle English, from Old French, from Latin *absēns*, present participle of *abesse*, to be away : *abs-, ab-*, away from + *esse*, to be.] —**ab·sent·ly** *adv.*

ab·sen·tee (ăb′sən-tē′) *n.* One who is absent.
~*adj.* **1.** Habitually absent or not in residence: *absentee landlords.* **2.** Of or pertaining to one that is absent: *an absentee vote.*

ab·sen·tee·ism (ăb′sən-tē′ ĭz′əm) *n.* Habitual failure to appear, especially for work.

ab·sent·mind·ed (ăb′sənt-mīn′dĭd) *adj.* Heedless of one's immediate surroundings or activity, especially because of preoccupation with unrelated matters; inattentive and forgetful. —See Synonyms at **abstracted, forgetful.** —**ab·sent·mind·ed·ly** *adv.* —**ab·sent·mind·ed·ness** *n.*

ab·sinthe, ab·sinth (ăb′sĭnth) *n.* **1.** A pale-green liqueur that has a high alcoholic content and is flavored with aniseed and wormwood or a wormwood substitute. **2.** A plant, **wormwood** *(see).* [French, from Latin *absinthium*, wormwood, from Greek *apsinthion*, of Mediterranean origin.]

ab·so·lute (ăb′sə-lōōt′) *adj. Abbr.* **abs.** **1.** Perfect in quality or nature; complete: *an absolute vacuum.* **2.** Not mixed; pure; unadulterated: *absolute alcohol.* **3. a.** Not limited by restrictions or exceptions; unconditional: *absolute freedom.* **b.** Unqualified in extent or degree; total: *an absolute pardon.* **4.** Not limited by constitutional provisions or other restraints: *an absolute monarch.* **5.** Unrelated and independent of anything else: *an absolute value.* **6.** Not to be doubted or questioned; positive; certain: *absolute truth.* **7.** *Grammar.* **a.** Designating a construction in a sentence that is syntactically independent of the main clause. For example, in *Their ship having sailed, we went home,* the construction *Their ship having sailed* is an absolute phrase. **b.** Pertaining to or characterizing a transitive verb when its object is implied but not stated; for example, *inspires* in *We have a teacher who inspires.* **c.** Pertaining to or characterizing an adjective or pronoun that stands alone, the noun it modifies being implied but not stated; for example, *Theirs* and *best* in *Theirs were the best.* **8.** *Physics.* **a.** Pertaining to measurements or units of measurement derived from fundamental relationships of space, mass, and time. **b.** Pertaining to absolute temperature. **c.** Indicating a pressure measurement that is not relative to atmospheric pressure. Compare **gauge.** **9.** *Law.* Complete and unconditional; having no encumbrances; final.
~*n.* Something that is absolute. —**the Absolute.** *Philosophy.* **1.** Something regarded as the ultimate basis of all thought and being. **2.** Something regarded as independent of and unrelated to anything else. **3.** In the philosophy of Hegel, the ultimate condition toward which everything is moving. [Middle English *absolut*, from Latin *absolūtus*, completed, unfettered, unconditional, from the past participle of *absolvere*, to free from, complete : *ab-*, away from + *solvere*, to loose.] —**ab·so·lute·ness** *n.*

absolute alcohol *n.* Ethyl alcohol containing no more than one percent of water by weight.

absolute ceiling *n.* The maximum altitude above sea level at which an aircraft or missile can maintain horizontal flight under standard atmospheric conditions.

absolute humidity *n.* The humidity of a gas, especially air, expressed as the mass of water vapor in grams per cubic meter of gas. Compare **relative humidity.**

ab·so·lute·ly (ăb′sə-lōōt′lē, ăb′sə-lōōt′ lē) *adv. Abbr.* **abs.** **1.** Definitely and completely; positively; unquestionably. **2.** *Grammar.* In an absolute manner: *The verbs in "Man proposes, God disposes" are used absolutely.*
~*interj.* Used to express complete agreement.

absolute magnitude *n. Astronomy.* A measure of the brightness of a star or other astronomical body equal to the apparent magnitude it would have if it were 10 parsecs or 32.6 light-years from the Earth.

absolute majority *n.* A majority of over 50 percent of a total, as of votes cast or seats obtained. Compare **relative majority.**

absolute music *n.* Instrumental music designed not to represent images or actions but to have an intellectual and emotional content that depends solely on its rhythmic, melodic, and contrapuntal structures. Compare **program music.**

absolute permeability *n.* The **magnetic constant** *(see).*

absolute permittivity *n.* See **permittivity.**

absolute pitch *n.* **1.** The precise pitch of an isolated tone, as established by its rate of vibration measured on a standard scale. **2.** The ability to identify the pitch of any tone heard, or to reproduce a tone without reference to another previously sounded. Also called "perfect pitch." Compare **relative pitch.**

absolute scale *n.* A scale of temperature with absolute zero as the minimum and scale units equal in magnitude to centigrade degrees. It is equivalent to the **thermodynamic scale** *(see).*

absolute temperature *n. Abbr.* **abs** Temperature measured or calculated on the absolute scale.

absolute value *n. Mathematics.* **1.** The numerical value or magnitude of a quantity, as of a vector or of a negative integer, without regard to its sign. **2.** The modulus of a complex number, equal to the square root of the sum of the squares of the real and imaginary parts of the number.

absolute zero *n. Physics.* The temperature at which substances possess minimal energy, equal to $-273.15°C$ or $-459.67°F.$

ab·so·lu·tion (ăb′sə-lōō′shən) *n.* **1.** Forgiveness; release from obligation or punishment. **2.** *Roman Catholic Church.* **a.** The formal remission of sin imparted by a priest as part of the sacrament of penance. **b.** The specific words spoken by a priest in granting this remission.

ab·so·lut·ism (ăb′sə-lo͞o′tĭz′əm) *n.* **1.** A system of government in which all power is vested in a monarch or dictator. **2.** The political theory reflecting this system. **—ab·so·lut·ist** *n. & adj.*

ab·solve (ăb-zŏlv′, -sŏlv′) *tr.v.* **-solved, -solving, -solves. 1.** To pronounce free of blame or guilt. **2.** To relieve of a requirement or obligation. **3. a.** To grant a remission of sin to. **b.** To pardon or remit (a sin). [Middle English *absolven,* from Latin *absolvere,* to free from : *ab-,* away from + *solvere,* to loose, free.] **—ab·solv·a·ble** *adj.* **—ab·solv·er** *n.*

ab·sorb (ăb-sôrb′, -zôrb′) *v.* **-sorbed, -sorbing, -sorbs.** *—tr.* **1.** To take in through or as if through pores or interstices; soak in or up. **2.** To occupy the full attention, interest, or time of; engross. **3. a.** To take in so as to make part of an existing whole; incorporate. **b.** To take into the mind; assimilate. **4.** To receive (the impact of a projectile) without recoil. **5.** To defray (costs). **6.** To take in and use up (marketable goods): *The market could not absorb the increased sugar production.* **7.** *Physiology.* **a.** To assimilate (the products of digestion). **b.** To take up (gases and fluids) through surface tissues. **8.** *Chemistry.* To take in (a gas or liquid) and hold by means of physical forces. Compare **adsorb. 9.** *Physics.* To receive (electromagnetic radiation, for example) and retain fully, without reflection or transmission. *—intr.* To cause or undergo absorption: *The sponge was too dry to absorb well.* [Old French *absorber,* from Latin *absorbēre* : *ab-,* away from + *sorbēre,* to suck.] **—ab·sorb·a·bil·i·ty** *n.* **—ab·sorb·a·ble** *adj.* **—ab·sorb·er** *n.*

ab·sorbed (ăb-sôrbd′, -zôrbd′) *adj.* Engrossed. —See Synonyms at **abstracted. —ab·sorb·ed·ly** (ăb-sôr′bĭd-lē, -zôr′-) *adv.*

absorbed dose *n. Physics.* A **dose** *(see).*

ab·sor·be·fa·cient (ăb-sôr′bə-fā′shənt, -zôr′-) *adj.* Inducing or causing absorption.

∼n. A medicine that induces absorption. [ABSORB + -FACIENT.]

ab·sorb·ent (ăb-sôr′bənt, -zôr′-) *adj.* Capable of absorbing something: *absorbent cloth.*

∼n. A substance having this capability. **—ab·sorb·en·cy** *n.*

absorbent cotton *n.* Loose cotton that is sterilized, pressed into wads, and used as an absorbent or protective material, as in dressing wounds. Also called "cotton wool."

ab·sorb·ing (ăb-sôr′bĭng, -zôr′-) *adj.* Fully occupying one's time or attention; engrossing. **—ab·sorb·ing·ly** *adv.*

ab·sorp·tance (ăb-sôrp′təns, -zôrp′-) *n.* The ratio of the absorbed flux of incident radiation to the incident flux for a given body or surface. Compare **reflectance, transmittance.** [ABSORPT(ION) + -ANCE.]

ab·sorp·tion (ăb-sôrp′shən, -zôrp′-) *n.* **1.** The act or process of absorbing or the state of being absorbed. **2.** A state of mental concentration. [Latin *absorptiō,* from *absorbēre,* to ABSORB.] **—ab·sorp·tive** *adj.*

absorption nebula *n. Astronomy.* A dark **nebula** *(see).*

absorption spectrum *n. Physics.* The spectrum of dark lines or bands observed when radiation traverses an absorbing medium. Compare **emission spectrum.**

ab·sorp·tiv·i·ty (ăb′sôrp-tĭv′ĭ-tē, -zôrp-) *n.* The absorptance of a body per unit of radiation path length, measured under conditions in which the surfaces of the sample do not influence the amount of absorption.

ab·stain (ăb-stān′) *intr.v.* **-stained, -staining, -stains. 1.** To do without or refrain by one's own choice: *abstain from alcohol.* **2.** To withhold one's vote. [Middle English *absteinen, abstenen,* from Old French *abstenir,* from Latin *abstinēre,* to hold (oneself) back : *abs-, ab-,* away from + *tenēre,* to hold.] **—ab·stain·er** *n.*

ab·ste·mi·ous (ăb-stē′mē-əs) *adj.* **1.** Sparing or restrained, especially in one's consumption of food and alcohol. **2.** Restricted to bare necessities; marked by moderation; sparing: *an abstemious household.* [Latin *abstēmius* : *abs-, ab-,* away from + *-tēmus,* from *tēmētum*†, alcoholic drink, mead, wine.] **—ab·ste·mi·ous·ly** *adv.* **—ab·ste·mi·ous·ness** *n.*

ab·sten·tion (ăb-stĕn′shən) *n.* **1.** The act or habit of abstaining. **2. a.** A deliberate act of refraining from voting. **b.** One who abstains from voting. [Late Latin *abstentiō* (stem *abstentiōn-*), from Latin *abstinēre,* to ABSTAIN.]

ab·ster·gent (ăb-stûr′jənt) *adj.* Scouring or cleansing.

∼n. A scouring agent.

ab·sti·nence (ăb′stə-nəns) *n.* **1. a.** Denial of the appetites; abstention. **b.** Abstention from alcoholic drinks. **2.** *Roman Catholic Church.* Abstention from certain foods, especially meat, on days of penitential observance. [Middle English, from Old French, from Latin *abstinentia,* from *abstinēns,* present participle of *abstinēre,* to ABSTAIN.] **—ab·sti·nent** *adj.* **—ab·sti·nent·ly** *adv.*

Synonyms: *continence, self-denial, temperance.*

ab·stract (ăb-străkt′, ăb′străkt′) *adj. Abbr.* **abs., abstr. 1.** Considered apart from concrete existence or specific objects and actions. **2.** Theoretical; not applied or practical. **3.** Not easily understood; abstruse. **4.** Thought of or stated without reference to a specific instance. **5.** Designating a genre of art that does not represent scenes or objects naturalistically, but in which the intellectual and emotional content depends solely on intrinsic form.

∼n. (ăb′străkt′) *Abbr.* **abs., abstr. 1.** A statement summarizing the important points of a given text. **2.** The concentrated essence of a larger whole. **3.** Something abstract, such as a term. **4.** An abstract work of art. **—in the abstract.** Apart from actual substance or experience; in theory rather than in reality.

∼tr.v. (ăb-străkt′, ăb′străkt′) **abstracted, -stracting, -stracts. 1.** To take away; remove. **2.** To remove without permission; steal. **3.** To consider theoretically; think of (a quality or attribute) without reference to a particular example or object. **4.** To detach or disengage (thoughts or the attention). **5.** To summarize. [Middle English, from Latin *abstractus,* "removed from (concrete reality)," past participle of *abstrahere,* to pull away, remove : *abs-, ab-,* away from + *trahere,* to pull.] *n.* **—ab·stract·ly** *adv.* **—ab·stract·ness** *n.* **—ab·strac·tor, ab·stract·er** *n.*

ab·stract·ed (ăb-străk′tĭd) *adj.* **1.** Removed or separated from something; apart. **2.** Lost or deep in thought; preoccupied; meditative. —See Synonyms at **forgetful. —ab·stract·ed·ly** *adv.* **—ab·stract·ed·ness** *n.*

Synonyms: *absent-minded, absorbed.*

abstract expressionism *n.* A school of painting that flourished after World War II until the early 1960's, characterized by the active and free application of the paint to the canvas, as by splattering, and its nonrepresentational design.

ab·strac·tion (ăb-străk′shən) *n.* **1.** The act or process of abstracting: *the abstraction of metal from ore.* **2. a.** The act or process of separating the inherent qualities or properties from the actual physical object or concept to which they belong. **b.** A product of this process; a general idea or word expressing a quality: *Beautiful things are concrete, but beauty is an abstraction.* **3.** Preoccupation. **4.** An abstract work of art.

ab·strac·tion·ism (ăb-străk′shə-nĭz′əm) *n.* The theory and practice of abstract art. **—ab·strac·tion·ist** *n. & adj.*

abstract noun *n.* A noun that refers to a quality rather than a thing or to an abstract idea as opposed to a material object. Compare **concrete noun.**

abstract of title *n. Law.* A statement of the history of an unregistered piece of land, for the purpose of establishing ownership.

ab·struse (ăb-stro͞os′) *adj.* Difficult to understand because intellectually complicated or somewhat obscure. [Latin *abstrūsus,* past participle of *abstrūdere,* to hide : *abs-, ab-,* away + *trūdere,* to push.] **—ab·struse·ly** *adv.* **—ab·struse·ness** *n.*

ab·surd (ăb-sûrd′, ăb-zûrd′) *adj.* **1.** Foolishly incongruous or unreasonable; ridiculous. **2.** Reflecting or dealing with the absurd. —See Synonyms at **foolish.**

∼n. Sometimes **Absurd.** A 20th-century philosophical concept, embodied in many modern novels and plays, emphasizing the cruelty, ludicrousness, and ultimate futility of human life. Preceded by *the.* [French *absurde,* from Latin *absurdus.*] **—ab·surd·ism** *n.* **—ab·surd·ist** *n. & adj.* **—ab·surd·i·ty, ab·surd·ness** *n.* **—ab·surd·ly** *adv.*

A·bu-Bekr (ä′bo͞o-bĕk′ər) (573–634). First caliph of the Muslim Empire, who ruled from 632. He made Islam a political and military force throughout Arabia after the death of his son-in-law, the prophet Muhammad.

A·bu Dha·bi (ä′bo͞o dä′bē). Sheikdom and town in eastern Arabia on the Persian Gulf. The town is the capital of the United Arab Emirates. With enormous oil revenues, the sheikdom is one of the richest states in the world in terms of per capita income.

A·bu·ja (ä-bo͞o′jə). Capital of Nigeria. It formally became the seat of government in 1991. The plan to build Abuja in the center of the nation as a replacement for the capital Lagos was proposed in 1976.

a·bu·li·a, a·bou·li·a (ə-bo͞o′ lē-ə) *n. Psychology.* Loss or impairment of the ability to decide or act independently. [New Latin, from Greek *aboulia,* irresolution : *a-,* without + *boulē,* will.] **—a·bu·lic** *adj.*

a·bun·dance (ə-bŭn′dəns) *n.* Also **a·bun·dan·cy** (-dən-sē). **1.** A great quantity; a plentiful amount. **2.** Fullness to overflowing: *"My thoughts . . . are from the abundance of my heart"* (Thomas De Quincey). **3.** Affluence; wealth. **4.** *Chemistry.* The relative amount of a substance in a particular environment, especially the proportion of a particular element or mineral in the earth's crust, usually expressed in parts per million or as a percentage. **5.** *Physics.* The ratio of the number of atoms of a given isotope to the total number of atoms of the element in a given sample, especially the proportion in a naturally occurring sample.

a·bun·dant (ə-bŭn′dənt) *adj.* **1.** In plentiful supply; more than sufficient; ample. **2.** Amply supplied; abounding. Used with *in.* [Middle English *abundaunt,* from Old French *abundant,* from Latin *abundāns* (stem *abundant-*), present participle of *abundāre,* to ABOUND.] **—a·bun·dant·ly** *adv.*

ab ur·be con·di·ta (ăb ûr′bē kŏn′dĭ-tə). *Abbr.* **A.U.C.** *Latin.* From the founding of the city. Used to indicate the date in ancient Rome, the base year being 753 B.C.

a·buse (ə-byo͞oz′) *tr.v.* **abused, abusing, abuses. 1.** To use wrongly or improperly; misuse. **2.** To hurt or injure by maltreatment. **3.** To speak to in a contemptuous, coarse, or insulting way; revile.

∼n. (ə-byo͞os′). **1.** Misuse. **2.** A corrupt practice or custom. **3.** Maltreatment: *child abuse.* **4.** Insulting or coarse language. [Middle English *abusen,* from Old French *abuser,* from *abus,* improper use, from Latin *abūsus,* a using up, past participle of *abūtī,* to use up, make (improper) use of : *ab-,* away + *ūtī,* to USE.] **—a·bus·er** *n.*

Synonyms: *ill-treat, maltreat, mistreat, misuse.*

A·bu Sim·bel (ä′bo͞o sĭm′bəl). Village in southern Egypt on the Nile River and the site of the massive temples constructed by Ramses II *c.* 1250 B.C. The temples were raised over 60 meters (200 feet) in order to escape the rising waters of Lake Nasser, caused by the completion of the Aswan High Dam in 1966.

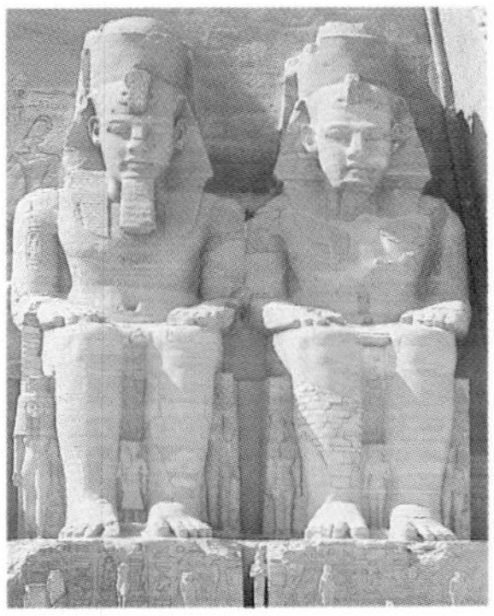

Abu Simbel *Giant statues of the Egyptian pharaoh Ramses II guard the temple complex he built in the Nile Valley near the village of Abu Simbel. Statues and temples were raised 61 meters (200 feet) above their original site in the 1960's to rescue them from the lake formed by the Aswan High Dam.*

a·bu·sive (ə-byo͞o′sĭv, -zĭv) *adj.* **1.** Of, pertaining to, or characterized by abuse. **2.** Marked by or using insulting or contemptuous language. —**a·bu·sive·ly** *adv.* —**a·bu·sive·ness** *n.*

a·but (ə-bŭt′) *v.* **abutted, abutting, abuts.** —*intr.* To touch at one end or side; lie adjacent. Used with *on,* *upon,* or *against.* —*tr.* To border upon; be next to. [Middle English *abutten,* from Old French *abouter,* to border on : *a,* to + *bout,* end.]

a·bu·ti·lon (ə-byo͞o′tə-lŏn′) *n.* Any of various shrubs or plants of the genus *Abutilon;* especially, the **flowering maple** *(see).* [New Latin, from Arabic *aubūṭīlūn.*]

a·but·ment (ə-bŭt′mənt) *n.* **1.** The act or process of abutting. **2. a.** That on which something abuts. **b.** The point of contact of two abutting objects or parts. **3.** *Architecture.* That element which shares a common boundary or surface with its neighbor. **4.** *Engineering.* **a.** A structure that supports an arch or the end of a bridge. **b.** A structure that anchors the cables of a suspension bridge.

a·but·tal (ə-bŭt′l) *n.* **1.** An abutment. **2. abuttals.** *Law.* The parts, especially of a piece of land, that abut against other property; boundaries.

ab·volt (ăb′vōlt′, ăb-vōlt′) *n. Abbr.* **abv.** A centimeter-gram-second electromagnetic unit of potential difference or electromotive force, equal to the potential difference between two points such that one erg of work must be performed to move a one-abcoulomb charge from one of the points to the other. It is equal to 10^{-8} of a volt. [AB- (absolute) + VOLT.]

ab·watt (ăb′wŏt′, ăb-wŏt′) *n. Abbr.* **abw.** A centimeter-gram-second electromagnetic unit of power, equal to the power dissipated by a current of one abampere flowing between two points with a potential difference of one abvolt. It is equal to 10^{-7} watt. [AB (absolute) + WATT.]

a·bysm (ə-bĭz′əm) *n.* An abyss. [Middle English *abi(s)me,* from Old French, from Late Latin *abyssus,* ABYSS.]

a·bys·mal (ə-bĭz′məl) *adj.* **1.** Unfathomable; very great: *abysmal ignorance.* **2.** Of or resembling an abyss. **3.** *Informal.* Extremely poor in quality. —**a·bys·mal·ly** *adv.*

a·byss (ə-bĭs′) *n.* **1. a.** A very steep gorge or deep crack in a mountain or on the earth. **b.** An unfathomable chasm; a yawning gulf. **2.** Any immeasurably great depth or void. **3. a.** Primeval chaos. **b.** The bottomless pit; hell. [Late Latin *abyssus,* from Greek *abussos (limnē),* "bottomless (lake)" : *a-,* not + *bussos,* bottom.]

a·bys·sal (ə-bĭs′əl) *adj.* **1.** Abysmal. **2.** Of or pertaining to the depths of the oceans, usually below 1,000 fathoms: *abyssal plain.*

Ab·ys·sin·i·a (ăb′ə-sĭn′ē-ə). See **Ethiopia.**

Ab·ys·sin·i·an (ăb′ə-sĭn′ē-ən) *adj.* Of or pertaining to Ethiopia or its inhabitants.
~*n.* An inhabitant of Ethiopia.

Abyssinian cat *n.* A short-haired cat of a breed developed from Near Eastern stocks, having a reddish-brown coat tipped with small black markings.

ac alternating current.

Ac The symbol for the element actinium.

a.c. *Medicine.* before meals. [New Latin *ante cibum*]

A.C. **1.** Air Corps. **2.** aircraftman. **3.** alternating current. **4.** appellation controlée. **5.** athletic club. **6.** before Christ. [New Latin *ante Christum*] **7.** Companion of the Order of Australia.

a/c, A/C **1.** account; account current. **2.** air conditioning.

a·ca·cia (ə-kā′shə) *n.* **1.** Any of various chiefly tropical trees of the genus *Acacia,* having compound leaves and small yellow or white flowers. Some species yield gums having a wide variety of uses. **2.** A related tree, the **locust** *(see).* **3.** A substance, **gum arabic** *(see).* [Latin, from Greek *akakia,* probably from Egyptian.]

acad. academic; academy.

ac·a·deme (ăk′ə-dēm′) *n.* **1.** *Sometimes* **Academe.** The world of scholarship and higher education; scholarly or academic life or its associated environment. **2.** *Archaic.* A place of learning; a university. **3.** *Archaic.* A scholar, teacher, or pedant. [Pseudo-Greek form of Greek *Akadēmia,* ACADEMY.]

ac·a·de·mi·a (ăk′ə-dē′mē-ə) *n.* The academic world; academe. [New Latin, from Latin *Academia,* ACADEMY.]

ac·a·dem·ic (ăk′ə-dĕm′ĭk) *adj. Abbr.* **acad. 1.** Of, pertaining to, or characteristic of a university, college, or other institution of learning. **2.** Scholarly to the point of being impractical or unaware of the outside world. **3.** Pertaining to or based on formal education, as in the humanities or sciences, rather than on practical or vocational training: *an education geared to children with academic ability.* **4.** Formalistic; conventional: *academic painters.* **5.** Merely theoretical; speculative: *"I took an academic interest in the thought of stealing the car"* (John Knowles). **6. Academic.** Of or pertaining to the Academy and philosophy of Plato.
~*n.* A member of a university or college; especially, a university teacher. —**ac·a·dem·i·cal·ly** *adv.*

academic freedom *n.* Liberty to pursue, discuss, and teach knowledge without hindrance or censorship.

ac·a·de·mi·cian (ăk′ə-də-mĭsh′ən) *n. Abbr.* **A.** A member of an academy or society of the arts or sciences.

ac·a·dem·i·cism (ăk′ə-dĕm′ə-sĭz′əm) *n.* Also **a·cad·e·mism** (ə-kăd′ə-mĭz′əm). Traditional formalism; conventionalism, especially in art.

A·ca·dé·mie Fran·çaise (à-kà-dā-mē′ frän-sĕz′) *n. French.* An association of 40 French intellectuals, scholars, and writers founded by Cardinal Richelieu in 1635, whose role is to pronounce on the correct usage of the French language.

a·cad·e·my (ə-kăd′ə-mē) *n., pl.* **-mies.** *Abbr.* **A., acad. 1.** An associ-ation of artists or scholars. **2.** A school for special instruction: *a naval academy.* **3. a.** A secondary school, especially a private one. **b.** In Scotland, a grammar school. **4. Academy. a.** The grove near Athens where Plato taught. **b.** The philosophy of Plato. **c.** The disciples of Plato. [Latin *Academia,* from Greek *Akadēmia,* the Platonic school of philosophy, from *Akadēmia, Akadēmeia,* name of the place in Athens where Plato taught, after *Akadēmos,* legendary Attic hero.]

Academy Award *n.* Any of the golden statuettes awarded annually by the Academy of Motion Picture Arts and Sciences for achievement in motion pictures. Also called "Oscar."

A·ca·di·a (ə-kā′dē-ə). *French* **A·ca·die** (à-kà-dē′). Region and former French colony in eastern Canada, encompassing Nova Scotia, Cape Breton Island, Prince Edward Island, New Brunswick, and part of Maine. Nova Scotia was ceded to Britain in 1713, and many of its inhabitants migrated or were deported (1755) to the southern colonies, including Louisiana, where their descendants came to be called Cajuns (from "Acadians"). The rest of Acadia, excluding Maine, came under British rule in 1763.

A·ca·di·an (ə-kā′dē-ən) *adj.* Of or pertaining to Acadia or its inhabitants.
~*n.* Any of the early French settlers of Acadia or their descendants. See **Cajun.**

Acadia National Park. A scenic recreation area on Mount Desert Island off the coast of southern Maine. The rugged terrain includes glacier-scoured areas and a wave-eroded coastline.

a·ca·jou (ă-kə-zho͞o′) *n.* Mahogany. [French, cashew, from Portuguese *(a)caju,* from Tupi, mahogany, probably by confusion with Tupi *agapú.*]

acantho-, acanth- *prefix.* Indicates thorns; for example, **acantho-cephalan.** [New Latin, from Greek *akanthos,* thorn plant, from *akantha,* thorn : *ak-,* sharp + *antha,* of Mediterranean origin.]

a·can·tho·ceph·a·lan (ə-kăn′thō-sĕf′ə-lən) *n.* Any of various parasitic worms of the phylum Acanthocephala, having a proboscis armed with hooked spines. [New Latin *Acanthocephala,* "thornheads" (from the spiky proboscis) : ACANTHO- + *-cephala,* neuter plural of *-cephalus,* -CEPHALOUS.]

a·can·thoid (ə-kăn′thoid′) *adj.* Resembling a thorn or spine. [ACANTH(O)- + -OID.]

ac·an·thop·ter·yg·i·an (ăk′ən-thŏp′tə-rĭj′ē-ən) *n.* Any fish of the superorder Acanthopterygii, which includes fishes having spiny fins, such as bass, perch, and mackerel. Compare **malacopterygian.** [New Latin *Acanthopterygii* : ACANTHO- + Greek *pterugion,* diminutive of *pterux,* wing, fin, from *pteron,* feather, wing.] —**ac·an·thop·ter·yg·i·an** *adj.*

a·can·thus (ə-kăn′thəs) *n., pl.* **-thuses** or **-thi** (-thī′). **1.** Any of various plants of the genus *Acanthus,* native to the Mediterranean region, having large, segmented, thistlelike leaves. **2.** An architectural ornament patterned after the leaves of the acanthus, used especially on capitals of Corinthian columns. [New Latin, from Greek *akanthos,* thorn plant, from *akantha,* thorn. See **acantho-.**] —**a·can·thine** (ə-kăn′thĕn′) *adj.*

a cap·pel·la (ä kə-pĕl′ə) *adv. Music.* Without instrumental accompaniment. [Italian, "in the manner of the chapel (or choir)."] —**a cap·pel·la** *adj.*

a ca·pric·cio (ä kə-prēt′chō) *adv. Music.* At whatever tempo and with whatever expression the performer or conductor desires. Used as a direction. [Italian, "capriciously."]

A·ca·pul·co (de Juá·rez) (ä′kə-po͞ol′kō də hwär′əs). A city of southern Mexico on the Pacific Ocean. Acapulco is a fashionable resort and has a fine natural harbor surrounded by cliffs and promontories.

ac·a·ri·a·sis (ăk′ə-rī′ə-sĭs) *n.* Infestation with mites or ticks. [New Latin : ACAR(ID) + -IASIS.]

a·car·i·cide (ə-kăr′ə-sīd′) *n.* A substance lethal to ticks and mites; a miticide. [ACARI(D) + -CIDE.] —**a·car·i·ci·dal** *adj.*

ac·a·rid (ăk′ə-rĭd) *n.* Any arachnid of the order Acarina, which includes the mites and ticks. [New Latin *Acaridae* (family), from *Acarus* (genus), from Greek *akari†,* a kind of mite.] —**ac·a·rid** *adj.*

ac·a·roid resin (ăk′ə-roid′) *n.* A gum obtained from various Australian grass trees, and used in varnishes, lacquers, and paper. Also called "acaroid gum," "gum accroides." [New Latin *acaroides,* from Greek *akari,* a kind of mite that bred in wax or resin. See **acarid.**]

a·car·pous (ā-kär′pəs) *adj. Botany.* Producing no fruit; sterile. [A- (not) + -CARPOUS.]

ac·a·rus (ăk′ə-rəs) *n., pl.* **-ri** (-rī′). A mite, especially one of the genus *Acarus.* [New Latin *Acarus.* See **acarid.**]

ac·a·tal·ec·tic (ā′kăt′ə-lĕk′tĭk) *adj.* Designating a line of verse having the required number of syllables in the last foot.
~*n.* An acatalectic line. [Late Latin *acatalēcticus,* from Greek *akatalēktikos* : *a-,* not + *katalēktikos,* CATALECTIC.]

a·cau·date (ā-kô′dāt′) *adj. Zoology.* Having no tail. [A- (not) + CAUDATE.]

a·cau·les·cent (ā′kô-lĕs′ənt) *adj. Botany.* Stemless, or nearly so. [A- (not) + CAULESCENT.]

acc. 1. acceptance. **2.** accompanied. **3.** account; accountant. **4.** accusative. **5.** according to.

Accad. See **Akkad.**

Accadian. Variant of **Akkadian.**

ac·cede (ăk-sēd′) *intr.v.* **-ceded, -ceding, -cedes. 1.** To give one's assent; agree. Often used with *to.* **2.** To take up or come into an office or high-ranking position. Used with *to: accede to the throne.*

Abyssinian cat *A short-haired breed, the Abyssinian is a domestic cat thought to be closely related to the sacred species of ancient Egypt.*

3. To become a party, as to an agreement. Used with *to*: *accede to a treaty.* —See Synonyms at **assent.** [Middle English *acceden,* from Latin *accēdere,* to go near, agree : *ad-,* to + *cēdere,* to go.] —**ac·ced·ence** (ăk-sē′dəns) *n.* —**ac·ced·er** *n.*

ac·cel·er·an·do (ä-chĕl′ə-rän′dō) *adj. Music.* Gradually accelerating or quickening in time. Used as a direction. [Italian, from Latin *accelerandum,* gerund of *accelerāre,* to ACCELERATE.] —**ac·cel·er·an·do** *n. & adv.*

ac·cel·er·ate (ăk-sĕl′ə-rāt′) *v.* **-ated, -ating, -ates.** —*tr.* **1.** To increase the speed of. **2.** To cause to occur sooner than expected or usual: *Hard work accelerated her promotion.* **3.** *Physics.* To cause a change of velocity in. —*intr.* **1.** To move or act faster. **2.** *Physics.* To change in velocity. —See Synonyms at **speed.** [Latin *accelerāre* : *ad-* (intensive) + *celerāre,* to hasten, from *celer,* swift.] —**ac·cel·er·a·tive** (ăk-sĕl′ə-rā′tĭv) *adj.*

ac·cel·er·a·tion (ăk-sĕl′ə-rā′shən) *n.* **1. a.** The act of accelerating. **b.** The state of being accelerated. **2. a.** *Physics. Symbol* **a** The rate of change of velocity with respect to time. **b.** Broadly, the ability to increase speed: *a car with good acceleration.*

acceleration of free fall *n. Symbol* **g** The acceleration of freely falling bodies under the influence of terrestrial gravity in a vacuum. The standard value is 9.80665 meters per second per second (approximately 32 feet per second per second) at sea level. Also called "acceleration due to gravity" or "acceleration of gravity."

ac·cel·er·a·tor (ăk-sĕl′ə-rā′tər) *n.* **1.** A device that controls the speed of a motor vehicle, especially by means of a pedal regulating the fuel intake to the engine. **2.** A substance that increases the speed of a chemical reaction. **3.** *Physics.* Any device, such as a cyclotron or linear accelerator, that accelerates charged subatomic particles or nuclei to energies useful for research. In this sense, also called "particle accelerator," "atom smasher."

ac·cel·er·om·e·ter (ăk-sĕl′ə-rŏm′ə-tər) *n.* Any of various devices used to measure acceleration. [ACCELER(ATION) + -METER.]

ac·cent (ăk′sĕnt′) *n.* **1.** *Linguistics.* The relative prominence given to a particular syllable of a word by greater intensity *(stress accent),* or by variation or modulation of pitch or tone *(pitch accent).* **2.** Vocal prominence or emphasis given to a particular syllable, word, or phrase. **3.** A characteristic pronunciation, especially: **a.** One that is typical of a particular regional or social group. **b.** One determined by the phonetic habits of the speaker's native language carried over to his use of another language. **4.** A mark or symbol used in printing and writing for any of various purposes, as: **a.** A mark used in certain languages to indicate the vocal quality to be given to a particular letter: *an acute accent.* **b.** A mark used to indicate the stressed syllables of a spoken word. **c.** A mark used to indicate an unusual or unexpected stress pattern, especially in poetry; for example, *venturèd, Délilàh.* **5.** Rhythmically significant stress in a line of verse. **6.** *Music.* **a.** Special stress given to a musical note within a phrase. **b.** A mark representing this stress. **c.** The rhythmical pattern of a piece of music based on the primary beat in each bar. **7.** *Mathematics.* **a.** A mark, or one of several marks, used as a superscript to distinguish variables represented by the same symbol; for example, x', x''. **b.** A mark used as a superscript to indicate the first derivative of a variable. **c.** Any of various marks used as a superscript to indicate a unit. See **prime. 8.** A distinctive character or quality: *a modern building but with a classical accent.* **9.** A strongly contrasting detail. **10.** Particular emphasis: *a mechanics course with the accent on practical experience.*
~*tr.v.* (ăk′sĕnt′, ăk-sĕnt′) **accented, -centing, -cents. 1.** To stress or emphasize the pronunciation of. **2.** To mark with a written or printed accent. **3.** To draw attention to; accentuate: *"the effect of appropriate drapery in accenting feminine graces"* (Edward Bellamy). [Middle English, from Old French, from Latin *accentus,* accentuation, originally "song added to (speech)" (translation of Greek *prosōidia,* PROSODY) : *ad-,* to + *cantus,* song, from the past participle of *canere,* to sing.]

ac·cen·tor (ăk-sĕn′tər) *n.* Any of various sparrowlike songbirds of the family Prunellidae, most of which frequent mountainous regions. [Late Latin, "one who sings with another" : Latin *ad-,* to + *cantor,* singer, from *cantus,* song (see **accent**).]

ac·cen·tu·al (ăk-sĕn′cho͞o-əl) *adj.* **1.** Of or pertaining to accent. **2.** Designating verse rhythm based on stress accents rather than on the number of syllables. —**ac·cen·tu·al·ly** *adv.*

ac·cen·tu·ate (ăk-sĕn′cho͞o-āt′) *tr.v.* **-ated, -ating, -ates. 1.** To give greater prominence or emphasis to; heighten or emphasize. **2.** To mark or pronounce with a stress or accent. [Medieval Latin *accentuāre,* from Latin *accentus,* ACCENT.] —**ac·cen·tu·a·tion** *n.*

ac·cept (ăk-sĕpt′) *v.* **-cepted, -cepting, -cepts.** —*tr.* **1.** To take or receive (something offered) willingly. **2.** To receive as adequate, satisfactory, or admissible: *accepted his excuse.* **3.** To admit, as to a group or place: *accepted in the best circles.* **4.** To regard with favor or approval. **5. a.** To regard as usual, proper, or right. **b.** To regard as true; believe in: *accept a witness's version of what happened.* **6. a.** To bear up under resignedly or patiently: *accept one's fate.* **b.** To submit to without argument. **7. a.** To respond to affirmatively: *accept an invitation.* **b.** To take upon oneself (a duty or responsibility, for example); undertake. **8.** To be able to hold (something applied or inserted): *This wood will not accept oil paints.* **9.** *Commerce.* To consent to pay (a bill, for example), as by a signed agreement. —*intr.* To receive or agree to something willingly. —See Synonyms at **assent.** [Middle English *accepten,* from Old French *accepter,* from Latin *acceptāre,* frequentative of *accipere* (past participle *acceptus*), to receive, "take to oneself" : *ad-,* to + *capere,* to take.]

ac·cept·a·ble (ăk-sĕp′tə-bəl) *adj.* **1.** Satisfactory; adequate. **2.** Welcome; gratifying: *a most acceptable gift.* **3.** Tolerable. —**ac·cept·a·bil·i·ty, ac·cept·a·ble·ness** *n.* —**ac·cept·a·bly** *adv.*

ac·cep·tance (ăk-sĕp′təns) *n. Abbr.* **acc. 1.** The act or process of accepting. **2.** The state or condition of being accepted or acceptable. **3.** Favorable reception; approval. **4.** Belief in something; agreement; assent. **5.** *Commerce.* **a.** A formal indication by a party of willingness to pay a bill of exchange when it falls due, as by writing the word *accepted* and affixing his signature across the face of the document. **b.** The bill itself when so endorsed. **6.** *Law.* Assent by one party, through conduct or the spoken word, to the terms and conditions of offer of another so that a contract becomes legally binding between them.

ac·cep·tant (ăk-sĕp′tənt) *adj.* Accepting willingly.

ac·cep·ta·tion (ăk′sĕp-tā′shən) *n.* **1.** The usual or accepted meaning, as of a word or expression. **2.** *Archaic.* **a.** Favorable reception. **b.** Belief or assent.

ac·cept·ed (ăk-sĕp′tĭd) *adj.* Generally approved, believed, or recognized.

ac·cep·tor, ac·cept·er (ăk-sĕp′tər) *n.* **1.** *Commerce.* One who formally accepts a bill of exchange. **2.** *Physics.* An impurity that accepts electrons in a semiconductor, thus increasing the p-type semiconductivity. Compare **donor. 3.** *Chemistry.* An atom, molecule, or group that can accept a pair of electrons in forming a coordinate bond. Compare **donor. 4.** *Electronics.* A resonant circuit with the inductance and capacitance in series, which produces a large current at a particular frequency. Compare **rejector.**

ac·cess (ăk′sĕs′) *n.* **1.** A means of approaching or entering; a passage or entrance. **2.** The right or ability to enter, approach, or make use of. **3.** The state or quality of being approachable or reachable: *easy of access.* **4.** A sudden onset or outburst: *an access of rage.*
~*tr.v.* **accessed, -cessing, -cesses. 1.** To retrieve from a computor's storage files: *to access data.* **2.** To obtain access to; reach. [Middle English, from Old French *acces,* arrival, from Latin *accessus,* from the past participle of *accēdere,* to arrive : *ad-,* to + *cēdere,* to come.]

ac·ces·si·ble (ăk-sĕs′ə-bəl) *adj.* **1.** Easily reached or entered. **2.** Easily obtained. **3.** Easily understood or appreciated: *a very accessible writer.* **4.** Susceptible; open: *accessible to flattery.* —**ac·ces·si·bil·i·ty, ac·ces·si·ble·ness** *n.* —**ac·ces·si·bly** *adv.*

ac·ces·sion (ăk-sĕsh′ən) *n.* **1.** The attainment of rank or high office. **2. a.** Increase by means of something added. **b.** An addition or acquisition; especially, a library book added to an existing collection. **3.** *Law.* **a.** The addition to or increase in value of property by means of improvements or natural growth. **b.** The right of a proprietor to ownership of such addition or increase. **4.** Agreement; assent. **5.** The act of formally accepting or becoming a party to a treaty or agreement: *Britain's accession to the Treaty of Rome.* **6.** Access; admittance. **7.** A sudden outburst; an access.
~*tr.v.* **accessioned, -sioning, -sions.** To record as acquired. —**ac·ces·sion·al** *adj.*

ac·ces·so·rize (ăk-sĕs′ə-rīz′) *tr.v.* **-rized, -rizing, -rizes.** To provide with accessories.

ac·ces·so·ry (ăk-sĕs′ər-ē) *n., pl.* **-ries.** Also **ac·ces·sa·ry** (for sense 2). **1.** Something supplementary; an adjunct, as: **a.** A small, minor, or decorative item of clothing, such as a belt or scarf. **b.** A minor or additional part, device, or attachment, as for a motor vehicle. **2. a.** One who incites or aids another in the commission of a crime, but is not present at the time of the crime. Used in the phrase *accessory before the fact.* **b.** One who aids a criminal after the commission of a crime, but was not present at the time of the crime. Used in the phrase *accessory after the fact.* —See Synonyms at **appendage.**
~*adj.* Also **ac·ces·sa·ry** (for sense 2). **1.** Having a secondary, supplementary, or subordinate function. **2.** Serving to aid or abet a criminal either before or after the commission of the crime, without being present at the time the crime was committed. [Middle English *accessorie,* from Medieval Latin *accessōrius,* from *accessor,* helper, accessory, subordinate, from Latin *accessus,* ACCESS.] —**ac·ces·so·ri·al** (ăk′sə-sôr′ē-əl, -sōr′-) *adj.* —**ac·ces·so·ri·ly** *adv.* —**ac·ces·so·ri·ness** *n.*

accessory fruit *n.* A **pseudocarp** *(see).*

accessory nerve *n.* Either of the 11th pair of cranial nerves, which supply certain muscles in the neck and, with the vagus nerve, supply the internal laryngeal muscles.

ac·ciac·ca·tu·ra (ä-chä′kə-to͝or′ə) *n., pl.* **-ture** (-to͝or′ā) or **-turas** (-to͝or′əz). *Music.* A short grace note, usually immediately below a principal note, sounded immediately before or at the same time in order to add sustained dissonance. Compare **appoggiatura.** [Italian *acciaccatura,* "crushing sound," from *acciaccare*†, to crush.]

ac·ci·dence (ăk′sə-dəns, -dĕns′) *n.* The part of grammar that deals with the inflections of words. [Latin *accidentia,* accidental or supplementary things, hence, inflections, from *accidere,* to happen (see **accident**).]

ac·ci·dent (ăk′sə-dənt, -dĕnt′) *n.* **1.** An unexpected and undesirable event, especially one resulting in damage, injury, or death; a mishap. **2.** Anything that occurs unexpectedly or unintentionally: *By a happy accident, I met him at the bus stop.* **3.** A property or attribute that is not essential to our conception of the nature of something. **4.** Any incidental or nonessential feature; an adjunct or accessory. **5.** Fortune; chance: *rich by accident of birth.* **6.** *Geology.* An irregu-

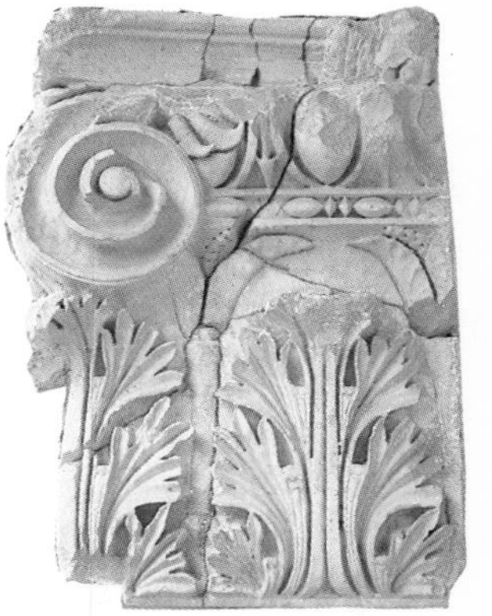

acanthus *Greek and, later, Roman architects used acanthus-leaf designs to decorate Corinthian columns.*

PRONUNCIATION KEY

ă, pat; ā, pay; âr, care;
ä, father, are; b, bib;
ch, church; d, deed; ĕ, pet;
ē, be; f, fife; g, gag; h, hat;
hw, which; ĭ, pit; ī, pie;
îr, pier; j, judge; k, kick;
l, lid, needle; m, mum;
n, no, sudden; ng, thing;
ŏ, pot; ō, toe; ô, paw, for;
oi, noise; ou, out; o͝o, book;
o͞o, boot; p, pop; r, roar;
s, sauce; sh, ship, dish;
t, tight; th, thin, path;
th, this, bathe; ŭ, cut; ûr, fur;
v, valve; w, with; y, yes;
z, zebra, size; zh, vision;
ə, about, item, edible,
gallop, circus, peaceful

IN FOREIGN WORDS:

à, *Fr.* ami; œ, *Fr.* feu, *Ger.* schön; ü, *Fr.* tu, *Ger.* über;
KH, *Ger.* ich, *Scot.* loch;
N, *Fr.* bon; y′, *Fr.* Compiègne

STRESS MARKS:

Primary stress: ′
in·cite′ (ĭn-sīt′)
Secondary stress: ′
in′sight′ (ĭn′sīt′)

lar or unusual natural formation. [Middle English, from Old French, from Latin *(rēs) accidēns* (stem *accident-*), "(a thing) happening," from *accidere,* to fall upon, happen : *ad-,* to + *cadere,* to fall.]

ac·ci·den·tal (ăk'sə-dĕn'təl) *adj.* **1.** Occurring unexpectedly and unintentionally: *a verdict of accidental death.* **2.** Of or characterizing a nonessential property or attribute; supplementary; incidental. **3.** *Music.* Of or designating a sharp, flat, or natural not indicated in the key signature.

∼*n.* **1.** A factor or attribute that is not essential. **2.** *Music.* An accidental note or the symbol indicating this. **—ac·ci·den·tal·ly** *adv.*

accident insurance *n.* Insurance against injury or death because of accident.

ac·ci·dent-prone (ăk'sə-dənt-prōn') *adj.* Especially liable to suffer an accident or injury.

ac·ci·die (ăk'sə-dē) *n.* Also **a·ce·di·a** (ə-sē'dē-ə). Spiritual torpor; apathy. [Late Latin, from Greek *akēdia, akēdeia,* indifference, apathy : *a-,* not + *kēdos,* care.]

ac·cip·i·ter (ăk-sĭp'ə-tər) *n.* Any hawk of the genus *Accipiter,* characterized by short wings and a long tail. [Latin, hawk.] **—ac·cip·i·trine** (ăk-sĭp'ə-trīn', -trĭn) *adj.*

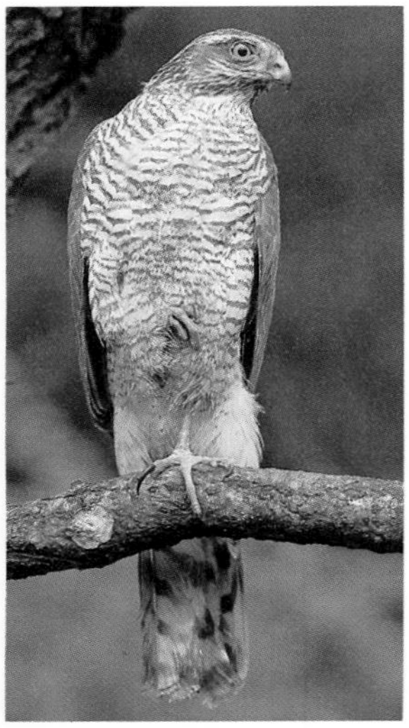

accipiter *This is a worldwide genus containing more than 40 species of hawk.*

ac·claim (ə-klām') *v.* **-claimed, -claiming, -claims.** *—tr.* **1.** To greet, especially publicly, with enthusiastic praise or approval. **2.** To acknowledge or declare with enthusiastic and unanimous approval: *acclaimed as the best play in town.* *—intr.* To shout approval. —See Synonyms at **praise.**

∼*n.* Enthusiastic applause or approval. [Latin *acclāmāre,* to shout at : *ad-,* to + *clāmāre,* to shout.] **—ac·claim·er** *n.*

ac·cla·ma·tion (ăk'lə-mā'shən) *n.* **1.** The act of acclaiming or being acclaimed. **2.** A public expression of enthusiastic approval or praise. **3.** An expression of overwhelming or unanimous assent, as by cheers or shouts, taken as a vote of approval without a formal ballot: *The president was renominated by acclamation.* **—ac·clam·a·to·ry** (ə-klăm'ə-tôr'ē, -tōr'ē) *adj.*

ac·cli·mate (ə-klī'mĭt, ăk'lə-māt') *v.* **-mated, -mating, -mates.** *—tr.* To accustom (something or someone) to a new environment or situation; adapt; acclimatize. *—intr.* To become accustomed to a new environment. [French *acclimater* : *ac-,* from Latin *ad,* to + *climate,* CLIMATE.]

ac·cli·ma·tion (ăk'lə-mā'shən) *n.* **1.** Acclimatization. **2.** The adaptation of an organism to its immediate natural climatic environment. Compare **acclimatization.**

ac·cli·ma·ti·za·tion (ə-klī'mə-tə-zā'shən) *n.* **1.** The process of acclimatizing or the state of being acclimatized. **2.** The climatic adaptation, often over several generations, of an organism that has been moved to a new environment. Compare **acclimation.**

ac·cli·ma·tize (ə-klī'mə-tīz') *v.* **-tized, -tizing, -tizes.** *—tr.* To acclimate (someone or something). *—intr.* To acclimate. **—ac·cli·ma·tiz·a·ble** *adj.* **—ac·cli·ma·tiz·er** *n.*

ac·cliv·i·ty (ə-klĭv'ə-tē) *n., pl.* **-ties.** An upward slope. Compare **declivity.** [Latin *acclīvitās,* from *acclīvis,* uphill : *ad-,* to + *clīvus,* slope.]

ac·co·lade (ăk'ə-lād', ăk'ə-läd') *n.* **1.** An expression of praise or approval: *critics' accolades.* **2.** An award or honor: *the highest accolade of the literary world.* **3.** The ceremonial bestowal of knighthood, as by a tap on the shoulder with the flat of a sword or, formerly, by an embrace. [French, from Provençal *acolada,* an embrace, from *acolar,* to embrace, from Vulgar Latin *accollāre* (unattested), to hug around the neck : *ad-,* to + *collum,* neck.]

ac·com·mo·date (ə-kŏm'ə-dāt') *v.* **-dated, -dating, -dates.** *—tr.* **1.** To do a favor or service for; oblige. **2.** To furnish or supply with something needed; especially, to provide with lodging or housing. **3. a.** To contain comfortably or have space for. **b.** To admit the inclusion of: *The party accommodates a wide range of moderate views.* **4.** To adapt, adjust, or make fit. Often used with *to.* **5.** To bring into harmony or agreement; settle; reconcile. *—intr.* To become adjusted, as the eye to focusing on objects at a distance. —See Synonyms at **contain.** [Latin *accommodāre,* to make fit : *ad-,* to + *commodus,* fit, "conforming with the (right) measure" : *con-,* with + *modus,* measure.] **—ac·com·mo·da·tive** *adj.*

ac·com·mo·dat·ing (ə-kŏm'ə-dā'tĭng) *adj.* Helpful and obliging. **—ac·com·mo·dat·ing·ly** *adv.*

ac·com·mo·da·tion (ə-kŏm'ə-dā'shən) *n.* **1.** The act of accommodating or the state of being accommodated; adaptation, adjustment, or reconciliation. **2.** Anything that meets a need; a convenience. **3. accommodations. a.** Space for living or staying; lodgings. **b.** A seat or compartment on a public vehicle. **4.** An arrangement by which opposing views are settled; a compromise. **5.** *Physiology.* Adaptation or adjustment in an organism, organ, or part, as takes place in the lens of the eye to permit retinal focus of images of objects at different distances. **6.** *Commerce.* A loan or other financial favor.

accommodation bill *n.* A bill of exchange endorsed by a guarantor to ensure the credit of the drawer.

accommodation ladder *n. Nautical.* A portable ladder or stairway hung from the side of a ship.

ac·com·pa·ni·ment (ə-kŭm'pə-nē-mənt, ə-kŭmp'nē-) *n.* **1.** Something that accompanies; a concomitant. **2.** Something added for embellishment, completeness, or symmetry; a complement. **3.** *Music.* A vocal or instrumental part that supports a solo part.

ac·com·pa·nist (ə-kŭm'pə-nĭst, ə-kŭmp'nĭst) *n. Music.* A performer, such as a pianist, who plays an accompaniment.

ac·com·pa·ny (ə-kŭm'pə-nē, ə-kŭmp'nē) *v.* **-nied, -nying, -nies.** *—tr.* **1.** To go along with; join in company. **2.** To supplement; add to: *the caption accompanying an illustration.* **3.** To coexist or occur with. **4.** To perform a musical accompaniment to or for. *—intr.* To play a musical accompaniment. [Middle English *accompanien,* from Old French *accompagner* : *ac-,* from Latin *ad-,* to + *compain(g),* companion, from Late Latin *compāniō,* COMPANION.]

Synonyms: *chaperone, conduct, escort.*

ac·com·plice (ə-kŏm'plĭs) *n.* One who aids or abets another in wrongdoing, especially in a criminal act. —See Synonyms at **partner.** [Middle English, from *a complice,* a COMPLICE (influenced by ACCOMPLISH).]

ac·com·plish (ə-kŏm'plĭsh) *tr.v.* **-plished, -plishing, -plishes. 1.** To succeed in doing; achieve. **2.** To reach the end of; complete; finish. —See Synonyms at **perform, reach.** [Middle English *accomplissen,* from Old French *accomplir* (present stem *accompliss-*), to complete : *ac-,* from Latin *ad-,* to + *complir,* to complete, from Latin *complēre,* "to fill up," to finish : *com-* (intensive) + *plēre,* to fill.] **—ac·com·plish·a·ble** *adj.* **—ac·com·plish·er** *n.*

ac·com·plished (ə-kŏm'plĭsht) *adj.* **1.** Skilled; proficient, especially through training and practice. **2.** Sophisticated; having many social accomplishments.

ac·com·plish·ment (ə-kŏm'plĭsh-mənt) *n.* **1.** The act of accomplishing or the state of being accomplished; completion. **2.** Something completed successfully; an achievement. **3.** A quality or faculty that contributes to a person's social poise; a social skill. **4.** Any talent or skill.

ac·cord (ə-kôrd') *v.* **-corded, -cording, -cords.** *—tr.* **1.** To cause to conform or agree; bring into harmony. **2.** To grant or bestow: *I accord you my blessing.* *—intr.* To be consistent, in agreement, or in harmony. —See Synonyms at **agree.**

∼*n.* **1.** Agreement, harmony, or conformity. Used especially in the phrase *in accord with.* **2.** A settlement or compromise between conflicting opinions; especially, a settlement of points at issue between nations; a treaty. **—of one's own accord.** Voluntarily. **—with one accord.** Unanimously. [Middle English *acorden,* from Old French *acorder,* from Vulgar Latin *accordāre* (unattested), "to be heart-to-heart with" : Latin *ad-,* to + *cor* (stem *cord-*), heart.]

ac·cord·ance (ə-kôr'dəns) *n.* **1.** Agreement; conformity. Used especially in the phrase *in accordance with.* **2.** The act of granting.

ac·cord·ant (ə-kôr'dənt) *adj.* In agreement or harmony; corresponding; consonant. Usually used with *with.* **—ac·cord·ant·ly** *adv.*

ac·cord·ing as (ə-kôr'dĭng) *conj.* **1.** Consistently with the way in which; to the extent. **2.** Depending on whether.

ac·cord·ing·ly (ə-kôr'dĭng-lē) *adv.* **1.** In a way that corresponds or accords with what the circumstances imply or demand; appropriately. **2.** Consequently.

according to *prep. Abbr.* **acc. 1.** In accordance with. **2.** In proportion to. **3.** In the report of; as stated or shown by.

ac·cor·di·on (ə-kôr'dē-ən) *n.* A portable musical instrument with a small keyboard and free metal reeds that sound when air is forced past them by pleated bellows operated by the player. See **piano accordion.** [German *Akkordion,* from *Akkord,* agreement, "harmony," from French *accord,* from Old French *acorder,* to ACCORD.] **—ac·cor·di·on·ist** *n.*

ac·cost (ə-kôst', ə-kŏst') *tr.v.* **-costed, -costing, -costs. 1.** To approach and speak to, especially boldly or accusingly. **2.** To solicit sexually. [Old French *accoster,* from Vulgar Latin *accostāre* (unattested), to come alongside someone : Latin *ad-,* near + *costa,* side, rib.]

ac·couche·ment (ȧ-ko͞osh-mäN') *n.* A confinement; childbirth.

ac·cou·cheur (ȧ-ko͞o-shœr') *n. Feminine* **ac·cou·cheuse** (ȧ-ko͞o-shœz'). A midwife or obstetrician. [French, "one attending at the bedside" : *ac-,* at + *coucheur,* from *couche,* bed.]

ac·count (ə-kount') *n.* **1.** A written or oral narration or description: *an eyewitness account of the accident.* **2.** An explanatory statement or report; especially, a statement explaining and justifying one's conduct: *called to give an account of his behavior.* **3.** A demonstration or exposition, as of one's qualities or abilities: *gave a good account of herself at the interview.* **4.** A particular version, report, or stated opinion: *by all accounts a formidable character.* **5.** Worth, standing, or importance: *a man of some account.* **6.** Consideration; notice: *taking into account the level of inflation.* **7.** Profit; advantage: *turned her talents to good account.* **8.** A precise list or enumeration of monetary transactions. **9.** *Abbr.* **a/c, A/C, acct., acc.** *Finance.* **a.** A business relationship involving the exchange of money or credit: *a bank account.* **b.** The client or customer involved in such a relationship. **c.** The amount of money held by a depositor in a bank. **d.** A statement recording all transactions relating to an account during a particular period and showing the current balance. **—call to account. 1.** To hold answerable. **2.** To reprimand. **—on account. 1.** On credit. **2.** In part payment. **—on account of. 1.** Because of. **2.** For the sake of: *Don't wait on account of me.* **3.** *Regional.* Because. **—on no account.** Under no circumstances. **—on one's own account. 1.** On one's own behalf. **2.** At one's own risk.

∼*tr.v.* **accounted, -counting, -counts.** To consider or esteem: "*Your honor is accounted a merciful man*" (Shakespeare). **—account for. 1.** To provide a reckoning of (people or funds, for example): *Six survivors have been accounted for.* **2.** To provide an explanation or justification for: *They couldn't account for the thumping noise in the cellar.* **3.** To be the explanation or cause of. **4.** To kill, capture, or disable. [Middle English, from Old French *acont,* *acompt,* from *acunter, acompter,* "to count up to," reckon : *ac-,* from Latin *ad-,* to + *cunter, compter,* to COUNT (compute).]

ac·count·a·ble (ə-koun'tə-bəl) *adj.* **1.** Liable to be called to account for one's conduct; answerable. Used with *to* or *for.* **2.** Capable of being explained. —**ac·count·a·bil·i·ty, ac·count·a·ble·ness** *n.* —**ac·count·a·bly** *adv.*

ac·count·an·cy (ə-koun'tən-sē) *n.* The practice, profession, or business of an accountant.

ac·count·ant (ə-koun'tənt) *n. Abbr.* **acc.** One who keeps, audits, and inspects the financial records of individuals or business concerns and prepares financial reports and tax returns.

account executive *n.* An employee of an advertising firm who manages the account of one or more clients.

ac·count·ing (ə-koun'tĭng) *n.* The principles and methods involved in keeping a financial record of business transactions and in preparing statements concerning the assets, liabilities, and operating results of a business.

ac·cou·ter (ə-kōō'tər) *tr.v.* **-tered, -tering, -ters.** Also *chiefly British* **ac·cou·tre** (-tər) **-tred, -tring, -tres.** To equip or attire, especially with a particular type of outfit or uniform. Usually used in the passive. [French *accoutrer,* from Old French *acoustrer,* from Vulgar Latin *acconsūtūrāre* (unattested), to equip (with clothes) : Latin *ad-,* to + *consūtūra* (unattested), sewing, clothes, from Latin *consuere,* to sew together : *con-,* together + *suere,* to sew.]

ac·cou·ter·ment (ə-kōō'tər-mənt) Also *chiefly British* **ac·cou·tre·ment** (-tər-mənt, -trə-mənt) *n.* **1.** The act of accoutering. **2. accouterments.** Equipment, adornments, or accessories; especially, the equipment other than arms and uniform issued to a soldier. **3. accouterments.** The outward forms whereby a thing may be recognized; trappings.

Ac·cra (ə-krä', ăk'rə). The capital of Ghana, located on the Gulf of Guinea. It was originally the capital of an ancient Ga kingdom and became the capital of the Gold Coast, a British colony, in 1876. It developed into the country's economic center after the completion in 1923 of a railway to the mining and agricultural regions inland.

ac·cred·it (ə-krĕd'ĭt) *tr.v.* **-ited, -iting, -its. 1. a.** To ascribe or attribute to someone. **b.** To credit (someone) with something. **2. a.** To supply with credentials or authority; authorize. **b.** To appoint as an ambassador or envoy. **3.** To recognize or certify as meeting a prescribed standard. [French *accréditer,* from *(mettre) à crédit,* "(to put) to CREDIT."] —**ac·cred·it·ed** *adj.*

ac·cred·i·ta·tion (ə-krĕd'ə-tā'shən) *n.* The act of accrediting or the condition of being accredited; especially, the granting of approval to an institution of learning by an official reviewing body after the school has met specific requirements.

ac·crete (ə-krēt') *v.* **-creted, -creting, -cretes. —***tr.* To attract or attach (additional elements) so as to cause increased growth. *—intr.* **1.** To grow together; fuse. **2.** To become attached, so as to cause increased growth. Used with *to.* [Back-formation from ACCRETION.]

ac·cre·tion (ə-krē'shən) *n.* **1.** Growth or increase in size by the gradual addition, fusion, or inclusion of external elements; specifically, the process by which an astronomical body increases in size or mass as a result of gravitationally attracting less dense material surrounding or adjoining it. **2.** Something added externally to promote such growth or increase. **3.** *Biology.* **a.** Any growing together of plant or animal tissues that are normally separate. **b.** A build-up of foreign matter in a cavity. **4.** *Geology.* A slow build-up of material, such as deposition of a water-borne sediment. **5.** *Law.* **a.** An increase of land through a process of natural growth, as by alluvial deposit. **b.** An increase in the share of a property when a joint owner or beneficiary dies or fails to take up his share. [Latin *accrēscere* (past participle *accrētus*), to ACCRUE.] —**ac·cre·tion·ar·y, ac·cre·tive** *adj.*

accretion theory *n.* The theory that the continents have increased in size during geological time as continental drift has moved the landmasses about the globe, building up new mountain ranges.

ac·crue (ə-krōō') *intr.v.* **-crued, -cruing, -crues. 1.** To come to someone or something as a gain or addition. **2.** To increase or accumulate, as by natural growth or as interest on capital. **3.** *Law.* To become enforceable or permanent. Used of a right. [Middle English *acrewen,* probably from Old French *accreue,* growth, from the past participle of *accreistre,* to increase, from Latin *accrēscere* : *ad-,* to + *crēscere,* to grow.] —**ac·cru·al, ac·crue·ment** *n.*

acct. account.

ac·cul·tur·ate (ə-kŭl'chə-rāt') *v.* **-ated, -ating, -ates. —***tr.* To cause to change by the process of acculturation. *—intr.* To change or be modified by acculturation.

ac·cul·tur·a·tion (ə-kŭl'chə-rā'shən) *n.* The modification of the culture of an individual or group through prolonged contact with a different culture; especially, the modification of a primitive culture through contact with an advanced culture. [AD- (toward) + CULTUR(E) + -ATION.]

ac·cum·bent (ə-kŭm'bənt) *adj. Botany.* Resting against another part. Said especially of cotyledons. [Latin *accumbēns,* (stem *accumbent-*), present participle of *accumbere,* to recline : *ad-,* near to + *-cumbere,* to recline.] —**ac·cum·ben·cy** *n.*

ac·cu·mu·late (ə-kyōōm'yə-lāt') *v.* **-lated, -lating, -lates. —***tr.* To amass or gather; pile up; collect. *—intr.* To grow or increase; mount up. —See Synonyms at **gather.** [Latin *accumulāre* : *ad-,* in addition + *cumulāre,* to pile up, from *cumulus,* a heap.] —**ac·cu·mu·la·ble** *adj.*

ac·cu·mu·la·tion (ə-kyōōm'yə-lā'shən) *n.* **1.** The act or process of accumulating; amassing or growing, as into a heap or large amount.

2. A mass or quantity that has accumulated or been accumulated. **3.** The growth of capital by retention of interest or profit.

ac·cu·mu·la·tive (ə-kyōōm'yə-lā'tĭv, -lə-tĭv) *adj.* **1.** Characterized by or showing the effects of accumulation; cumulative. **2.** Having a tendency to amass material or wealth; acquisitive. —**ac·cu·mu·la·tive·ly** *adv.* —**ac·cu·mu·la·tive·ness** *n.*

ac·cu·mu·la·tor (ə-kyōōm'yə-lā'tər) *n.* **1.** Someone or something that accumulates. **2.** A register or electrical circuit in a calculator or computer that stores figures for computation. **3.** *Chiefly British.* A **storage battery** *(see),* especially one used in a motor vehicle. **4.** *British.* A kind of bet, a **parlay** *(see).*

ac·cu·ra·cy (ăk'yər-ə-sē) *n.* Exactness; correctness.

ac·cu·rate (ăk'yər-ĭt) *adj.* **1. a.** Having no errors; correct. **b.** Marked by or showing careful attention to what is true or correct. **2.** Deviating only slightly or within acceptable limits from a standard. [Latin *accūrātus,* done with care, past participle of *accūrāre,* to attend to carefully : *ad-,* to + *cūrāre,* to care for, attend to, from *cūra,* care.] —**ac·cu·rate·ly** *adv.* —**ac·cu·rate·ness** *n.*

ac·curs·ed (ə-kûr'sĭd, ə-kûrst') *adj.* Also **ac·curst** (ə-kûrst'). **1.** Under a curse; doomed. **2.** Abominable; hateful. [Middle English *acursed,* from *acursen,* to curse, Old English *ācursian* : *ā-* (intensive) + *cursian,* to curse, from *curs,* CURSE.] —**ac·curs·ed·ly** *adv.* —**ac·curs·ed·ness** *n.*

ac·cu·sal (ə-kyōō'zəl) *n.* An accusation.

ac·cu·sa·tion (ăk'yōō-zā'shən) *n.* **1.** The act of accusing or the fact of being accused. **2.** An allegation. **3.** *Law.* A formal charge brought before a court against a person, stating that he is guilty of some punishable offense.

ac·cu·sa·tive (ə-kyōō'zə-tĭv) *adj. Abbr.* **acc.** Of, pertaining to, or designating the case of a noun, pronoun, adjective, or participle that is the direct object of a verb or the object of certain prepositions. *~n.* The accusative case. [Middle English, from Latin *(casus) accūsātīvus,* "(case) indicating accusation" (mistranslation of Greek *aitiatikos ptōsis,* "case of causation"), from *accūsāre,* to ACCUSE.] —**ac·cu·sa·tive·ly** *adv.*

ac·cu·sa·to·ri·al (ə-kyōō'zə-tôr'ē-əl, -tōr'ē-əl) *adj.* Of or designating a procedure of criminal justice in which the judge assesses the validity of an accusation as argued by a prosecutor. Compare **inquisitorial.**

ac·cu·sa·to·ry (ə-kyōō'zə-tôr'ē, -tōr'ē) *adj.* Containing or implying an accusation.

ac·cuse (ə-kyōōz') *tr.v.* **-cused, -cusing, -cuses. —***tr.* **1.** To charge with a shortcoming or error; blame. **2.** To bring charges against (someone) for a crime or offense. Used with *of.* *~intr.* To make an accusation. [Middle English *acusen,* from Old French *acuser,* from Latin *accūsāre,* to accuse, "call to account" : *ad-,* to + *causa,* CAUSE.] —**ac·cus·er** *n.* —**ac·cus·ing·ly** *adv.*

ac·cused (ə-kyōōzd') *n., pl.* **accused.** *Law.* The defendant in a criminal case. Preceded by *the.*

ac·cus·tom (ə-kŭs'təm) *tr.v.* **-tomed, -toming, -toms.** To familiarize, as by constant practice, use, or habit. Often used reflexively. [Middle English *accustomen,* from Old French *aco(u)stumer* : *a-,* from Latin *ad-,* to + *costume,* CUSTOM.]

ac·cus·tomed (ə-kŭs'təmd) *adj.* **1.** Usual, characteristic, or normal: *sitting in her accustomed place.* **2.** In the habit of; used. Used with *to: accustomed to sleeping late.* —See Synonyms at **usual.**

ace (ās) *n.* **1. a.** A single pip or spot on a playing card, die, or domino. **b.** A playing card, die, or domino having one spot or pip. **2.** In racket games: **a.** A serve which one's opponent is unable to reach. **b.** Any serve which one's opponent fails to return. **3.** In golf, a hole in one stroke. **4.** A military aircraft pilot who has destroyed five or more enemy aircraft. **5.** *Informal.* A person with great skill in a particular activity. —**within an ace of.** Very close to: *within an ace of victory.* *~adj. Informal.* **1.** Highly skilled; expert. **2.** *Informal.* Of the highest quality; really good. *~tr.v.* **aced, acing, aces. 1.** In racket games, to serve an ace against. **2.** *Slang.* To receive a grade of A on: *She aced the exam.* [Middle English *aas,* from Old French *as,* from Latin *ās,* unit. See **as** (Roman coin).]

-acean *suffix.* Indicates an animal belonging to a taxonomic class or order; for example, **cetacean.** [New Latin *-acea* and *-aceae,* neuter and feminine plural of *-aceus,* -ACEOUS.]

acedia. Variant of **accidie.**

A·cel·da·ma¹ (ə-sĕl'də-mə). The potter's field near Jerusalem purchased by the priests as a burying ground for strangers with the reward that Judas had received for betraying Jesus and later had returned to them. Matthew 27:7. [Greek *Akeldama,* from Aramaic *ḥāqēl dĕmā,* "field of blood."]

Aceldama² *n.* Any place with dreadful associations.

a·cel·lu·lar (ā-sĕl'yə-lər) *adj. Biology.* Containing no cells; not made up of cells.

a·cen·tric (ā-sĕn'trĭk) *adj.* **1.** Having no center. **2.** Not centered; placed off-center. [A- (not) + CENTRIC.]

-aceous *suffix.* Indicates: **1.** Of or pertaining to; for example, **sebaceous. 2.** Resembling or of the nature of; for example, **farinaceous. 3.** Belonging to a taxonomic category, especially a botanical family; for example, **orchidaceous.** [New Latin *-aceus,* from Latin *-āceus,* "of a special kind or group," originally an extension of an adjectival suffix *-āx,* (stem *-āc-*).]

a·ceph·a·lous (ā-sĕf'ə-ləs) *adj.* **1.** *Zoology.* Headless or lacking a clearly defined head. **2.** Having no leader: *an acephalous tribe.*

[Medieval Latin *acephalus,* headless, from Greek *akephalos* : *a-* (not) + -CEPHALOUS.]

ac·e·rate (ăs'ə-rāt') *adj.* Also **ac·e·rat·ed** (-rā'tĭd). *Biology.* Pointed at one end; needle-shaped. [Latin *ācer,* sharp.]

ac·er·bate (ăs'ər-bāt) *tr.v.* **-bated, -bating, -bates.** To vex; annoy. [Latin *acerbāre,* to make sour, from *acerbus,* ACERBIC.]

a·cerb·ic (ə-sûr'bĭk) *adj.* Also **a·cerb** (ə-sûrb'). **1.** Sour; bitter; astringent. **2.** Harsh in manner or speech; cutting. [Latin *acerbus,* sharp, bitter.]

a·cer·bi·ty (ə-sûr'bə-tē) *n., pl.* **-ties. 1.** Sourness of taste. **2.** Acrimony; sharpness of speech or manner. **3.** An instance of this.

ac·e·rose (ăs'ə-rōs') *adj. Botany.* Slender and sharp-pointed, as a pine needle is. [Incorrect use (by Linnaeus as if from Latin *ācer,* sharp, ACERATE) of Latin *acerōsus,* from *acus* (stem *acer-*), chaff.]

acet. acetone.

acet. a. acetic acid.

ac·e·tab·u·lum (ăs'ə-tăb'yə-ləm) *n., pl.* **-la** (-lə). **1.** *Anatomy.* The cup-shaped cavity in the hipbone into which the head of the thighbone fits. **2.** *Zoology.* A sucker, such as that of an octopus or cuttlefish. [Latin *acetābulum,* vinegar cup, from *acētum,* vinegar; akin to *ācer,* sharp.] **—ac·e·tab·u·lar** *adj.*

ac·e·tal (ăs'ə-tăl) *n.* **1.** A colorless, flammable, volatile liquid, CH₃CH(OC₂H₅)₂, used in cosmetics and as a solvent. **2.** Any of the class of compounds formed from aldehydes combined with alcohols. [German *Azetal* : ACET(O)- + AL(COHOL).]

ac·et·al·de·hyde (ăs'ĭt-ăl'də-hīd') *n.* A colorless, flammable liquid, CH₃CHO, used to manufacture acetic acid, perfumes, and drugs. Also called "aldehyde." [ACET(O)- + ALDEHYDE.]

a·cet·a·mide (ə-sĕt'ə-mīd', ăs'ĭt-ăm'īd') *n.* Also **a·cet·a·mid** (ə-sĕt'-ə-mĭd, ăs'ĭt-ăm'ĭd). The crystalline amide of acetic acid, CH₃CONH₂, used as a wetting agent and in lacquers and explosives. Also called "ethanamide." [German *Azetamid* : ACET(O)- + AMIDE.]

ac·et·an·i·lide (ăs'ĭt-ăn'ə-lĭd') *n.* Also **ac·et·an·i·lid** (-lĭd). A white crystalline compound, C₆H₅NH(COCH₃), used medicinally to relieve pain and reduce fever. [ACET(O)- + ANIL(INE) + -IDE.]

ac·e·tate (ăs'ə-tāt) *n.* **1.** A salt or ester of acetic acid. **2.** Cellulose acetate or any of various products, especially fibers and fabrics, derived from it. [ACET(O)- + -ATE.] **—ac·e·tat·ed** *adj.*

a·ce·tic (ə-sē'tĭk) *adj.* Of, pertaining to, or containing acetic acid or vinegar. [Latin *acētum,* vinegar, akin to *ācer,* sharp.]

acetic acid *n. Abbr.* **acet. a.** A clear, colorless organic acid, CH₃COOH, with a distinctive pungent odor, widely used as a solvent and in industry. It is the characteristic ingredient of vinegar. Also called "ethanoic acid" and, when at least 99.8 percent pure, "glacial acetic acid."

acetic anhydride *n.* An organic liquid, (CH₃CO)₂O, with a pungent odor, combining with water to produce acetic acid and used as an acetylating agent.

a·cet·i·fy (ə-sĕt'ə-fī') *v.* **-fied, -fying, -fies.** *—tr.* To convert (a neutral liquid) to acetic acid or vinegar. *—intr.* To become acetic; turn into acetic acid or vinegar. [ACET(O)- + -FY.] **—a·cet·i·fi·ca·tion** *n.* **—a·cet·i·fi·er** *n.*

aceto-, acet- *prefix.* Indicates the presence of acetic acid or the acetyl radical; for example, **acetophenetidin, acetify.** [Latin *acētum,* vinegar.]

ac·e·to·a·ce·tic acid (ăs'ə-tō-ə-sē'tĭk, ə-sē'tō-) *n.* A syrupy, colorless acid, CH₃COCH₂COOH, excreted in the urine and found in abnormal quantities in the urine of diabetics.

ac·e·tone (ăs'ə-tōn') *n. Abbr.* **acet.** A colorless, volatile, extremely flammable liquid, CH₃COCH₃, widely used as an organic solvent and, in especially pure grades, to clean and dry electronic component materials. Also called "propanone." [German *Azeton* : ACET(O)- + -ONE.] **—a·ce·ton·ic** (ăs'ə-tŏn'ĭk) *adj.*

acetone body *n. Biochemistry.* A **ketone body** *(see).*

ac·e·to·phe·net·i·din (ăs'ə-tō-fə-nĕt'ə-dĭn) *n.* A white powder or crystalline solid, CH₃CONHC₆H₄OC₂H₅, used in medicine to reduce fever and relieve pain. Also called "phenacetin." [ACETO- + PHEN(O)- + ET(HYL) + -ID(E) + -IN.]

ac·e·tous (ăs'ə-təs, ə-sē'təs) *adj.* Also **ac·e·tose** (ăs'ə-tōs'). **1.** Of, pertaining to, or producing acetic acid or vinegar. **2.** Having an acetic taste; sour-tasting. [Late Latin *acētōsus,* vinegary, from *acētum,* vinegar.]

a·ce·tum (ə-sē'təm) *n.* An acetic acid solution of a drug. [Latin *acētum,* akin to *ācer,* sharp.]

ac·e·tyl (ăs'ə-tĭl, ə-sĕt'l) *n.* The acetic acid radical CH₃CO. [ACET(O)- + -YL.] **—ac·e·tyl·ic** (ăs'ə-tĭl'ĭk) *adj.*

a·cet·y·late (ə-sĕt'l-āt') *v.* **-lated, -lating, -lates.** *—tr.* To introduce an acetyl group into (an organic molecule), using a reagent such as acetic anhydride. *—intr.* To undergo introduction of an acetyl group. **—a·cet·y·la·tion** *n.*

ac·e·tyl·cho·line (ăs'ə-tĭl-kō'lēn', ə-sĕt'l-) *n.* A white crystalline compound, C₇H₁₇NO₃, released at some nerve endings when a nerve impulse is transmitted from one nerve fiber to another. [ACETYL + CHOLINE.]

ac·e·tyl·cho·lin·es·ter·ase (ăs'ə-tĭl-kō'lə-nĕs'tə-rās') *n.* An enzyme, **cholinesterase** *(see).*

a·cet·y·lene (ə-sĕt'l-ēn', -ən) *n.* A colorless, highly flammable or explosive gas, C₂H₂, used for metal welding and cutting and as an illuminant. Also called "ethyne." [ACETYL + -ENE.] **—a·cet·y·len·ic** *adj.*

acetylene series *n.* A series of unsaturated aliphatic hydrocarbons, each containing a triple carbon bond, having chemical properties

acorn *The fruit of the oak was once an important food used for raising pigs. In England's New Forest, farmers still exercise the ancient right of pannage, when pigs are let loose to feed on the acorns that fall in the autumn.*

resembling acetylene and having the general formula CₙH₂ₙ₋₂, acetylene being the simplest member. Also called "alkyne series."

a·ce·tyl·sal·i·cyl·ic acid (ə-sĕt'l-săl'ə-sĭl'ĭk) *n.* A common drug, **aspirin** *(see).*

ace·y·deuc·y (ā'sē-dōō'sē, -dyōō'sē) *n.* A variation of backgammon. [ACE + DEUCE.]

A·chae·a (ə-kē'ə). Also **A·cha·ia** (ə-kī'ə, ə-kā'ə). *Greek* **A·khaï·a** (ə-kī'ə, ə-kā'ə). A region of ancient Greece occupying the north part of the Peloponnese on the Gulf of Corinth. The cities of the region banded together in the early 3rd century B.C. to form the Achaean League, which defeated Sparta but was eventually beaten by the Romans. Rome annexed Achaea in 146 B.C. and later gave the name to a Roman province comprising all of Greece south of Thessaly. The name Achaea is now used for a modern prefecture in the northern Peloponnese, whose capital is Patras.

A·chae·an (ə-kē'ən) *n.* Also **A·cha·ian** (ə-kī'ən). **1.** A native or inhabitant of Achaea. **2.** A Greek, especially of the Mycenaean era. **—A·chae·an** *adj.*

A·chae·me·nid (ə-kē'mə-nĭd, ə-kĕm'ə-) *n.* A member of the ruling dynasty of Persia from the time of Cyrus the Great to the death of Darius III (559–330 B.C.). [Greek *Akhaimenidēs,* from *Akhaimenēs,* founder of the dynasty.] **—A·chae·me·nid** *adj.*

A·cha·tes (ə-kā'tēz) *n.* A loyal friend. [After *Achates,* the faithful companion of Aeneas, in Virgil's epic poem the *Aeneid.*]

ache (āk) *intr.v.* **ached, aching, aches. 1.** To suffer, or cause one to suffer, a dull, sustained pain. **2.** *Informal.* To yearn painfully. *~n.* A dull, steady pain. [Middle English *aken,* Old English *acan.*]

A·che·be (ə-chē'bā), **Chinua** (1930–). Nigerian Ibo novelist and poet, whose writings deal with the conflict arising when traditional African society faces Western culture. His works include the novels *Things Fall Apart* (1958) and *A Man of the People* (1966).

a·chene (ə-kēn') *n. Botany.* A dry, thin-walled, one-seeded fruit, such as that of the buttercup and dandelion, that does not split open when ripe. [New Latin *achēnium,* "one that does not yawn or split open" : A- (not) + Greek *khainein,* to yawn.] **—a·che·ni·al** (ə-kē'nē-əl) *adj.*

A·cher·nar (ā'kər-när') *n.* A star in the constellation Eridanus that is one of the brightest stars in the sky and is 114 light-years from Earth. [Arabic *ākhir al-nahr,* "the end of the river" (referring to the star's position in Eridanus).]

Ach·e·ron (ăk'ə-rŏn') *n. Greek Mythology.* **1.** The river of woe over which Charon ferried the souls of the dead to Hades. **2.** The underworld; Hades.

Ach·e·son (ăch'ə-sən), **Dean Gooderham** (1893–1971). U.S. lawyer and statesman. He was secretary of state under President Harry S Truman and later became a presidential adviser. He promoted the Marshall Plan and helped establish NATO.

A·cheu·li·an, A·cheu·le·an (ə-shōō'lē-ən) *adj. Archaeology.* Of or designating a stage of culture of the European Lower Paleolithic Age, about 250,000 years ago, characterized by symmetrical stone hand axes. [French *acheuléen,* after St. *Acheul,* village in northern France and site of the archaeological finds from which the culture was classified.]

à che·val (ä shə-väl') *adv.* Positioned so as to straddle a line on a gambling table between two numbers or cards. Used especially in roulette. [French, "on horseback."]

a·chieve (ə-chēv') *v.* **achieved, achieving, achieves.** *—tr.* **1.** To accomplish; succeed in doing. **2.** To attain or get as a result of one's efforts, skill, or perseverance: *We inched up the rock face until we achieved the ledge. —intr.* To attain a satisfactory standard: *schoolchildren who fail to achieve.* —See Synonyms at **perform, reach.** [Middle English *acheven,* from Old French *achever,* "to bring to a head," from *a chef,* "to a head" : *a,* to, from Latin *ad-* + *chef,* head, from Latin *caput.*] **—a·chiev·a·ble** *adj.* **—a·chiev·er** *n.*

a·chieve·ment (ə-chēv'mənt) *n.* **1.** The act of accomplishing, attaining, or finishing something. **2.** Something that has been accomplished successfully, especially by means of skill, practice, or perseverance. **3.** *Heraldry.* A coat of arms.

A·chil·les (ə-kĭl'ēz). *Greek Legend.* The greatest of the Greek warriors at the siege of Troy, who killed the Trojan Hector and was himself later killed by Paris. He was the son of Peleus and Thetis.

Achilles' heel *n.* A small but significant weakness; a vulnerable point. [From Achilles' being vulnerable only in the heel.]

Achilles' tendon *n.* The large tendon running from the heel bone to the calf muscle of the leg.

Ach·ill Island (ăk'ĭl). A rugged and mountainous island in the Republic of Ireland off the west coast of County Mayo. With an area of 148 square kilometers (57 square miles), it is the largest offshore Irish island.

a·chi·o·te (ä'chē-ō'tē) *n.* The seeds of the **annatto** *(see)* or a preparation made from them, used to flavor and impart a yellow or reddish color to various foods. [Spanish, from Nahuatl (Aztec) *achi(y)otl.*]

Achitophel. See **Ahithophel.**

ach·la·myd·e·ous (ăk'lə-mĭd'ē-əs) *adj. Botany.* Having no floral envelope; without calyx or corolla. [A- (not) + CHLAMYDEOUS.]

a·chon·drite (ā-kŏn'drīt') *n.* A stony meteorite that contains no **chondrules** *(see).* **—a·chon·drit·ic** (ā'kŏn-drĭt'ĭk) *adj.*

a·chon·dro·pla·si·a (ā-kŏn'drō-plā'zhē-ə) *n.* Abnormal development of cartilage at the ends of the long bones, resulting in congenital dwarfism. [A- (not) + CHONDRO- + -PLASIA.] **—a·chon·dro·plas·tic** (ā-kŏn'drō-plăs'tĭk) *adj.*

ach·ro·mat·ic (ăk'rə-măt'ĭk) *adj.* **1.** Free from color; having no hue. Said of neutral colors like gray, black, and white. **2.** *Optics.* Refracting light without spectral color separation. **3.** *Biology.* Not readily absorbing color from standard dyes. **4.** *Music.* Having only the diatonic tones of the scale. [Greek *akhrōmatos,* colorless : *a-,* not, without + *khrōma,* color.] —**ach·ro·mat·i·cal·ly** *adv.* —**a·chro·ma·tism** (ā-krō'mə-tĭz'əm), **a·chro·ma·tic·i·ty** (ā-kro'mə-tĭs'ə-tē) *n.*

achromatic lens *n.* A combination of lenses to produce images free of chromatic aberrations.

a·chro·ma·tize (ā-krō'mə-tīz') *tr.v.* **-tized, -tizing, -tizes.** To make achromatic; rid of color.

a·chro·ma·tous (ā-krō'mə-təs) *adj.* **1.** Without color. **2.** With less color than is usual or needed. [Greek *akhrōmatos,* ACHROMATIC.]

a·chro·mic (ā-krō'mĭk) *adj.* Also **a·chro·mous** (ā-krō'məs). Colorless. [A- (not) + CHROMIC.]

a·cic·u·la (ə-sĭk'yə-lə) *n., pl.* **-lae** (-lē'). A needlelike object or part, such as a bristle, spine, or crystal. [New Latin, from Latin *acicula,* hairpin, diminutive of *acus,* needle.] —**a·cic·u·lar, a·cic·u·late** (ə-sĭk'yə-lĭt, -lāt'), **a·cic·u·lat·ed** *adj.*

ac·id (ăs'ĭd) *n.* **1.** *Chemistry.* **a.** Any of a large class of substances, the aqueous solutions of which can turn litmus indicators red, can react with and dissolve certain metals to form salts, can react with bases or alkalis to form salts, or have a sour taste. **b.** A substance that ionizes in solution to give the positive ion of the solvent. **c.** A substance capable of giving up a proton. **d.** Any molecule or ion that can combine with another by forming a covalent bond with two electrons of the other. In this sense, also called "Lewis acid." **2.** A substance with a sour taste. **3.** *Slang.* A hallucinogen, **LSD** *(see).* **4.** A sarcastic, bitter, or scornful quality: *a letter oozing with acid.*
~*adj.* **1.** *Chemistry.* **a.** Of or pertaining to an acid. **b.** Having a high concentration of acid. **2.** Having a sour taste. **3.** Having or indicative of a biting, sharp, or unkind nature; caustic: *an acid wit.* **4.** *Geology.* Designating an igneous rock containing more than 66 percent silica. **5.** Designating soil having a pH value below 7.2. [Latin *acidus,* sharp, sour, from *acēre,* to be sour, akin to *ācer,* sharp.] —**ac·id·ly** *adv.* —**ac·id·ness** *n.*

ac·id-fast (ăs'ĭd-făst', -fäst') *adj.* Not readily decolorized by acid. Said of stained tissues and microorganisms. —**ac·id-fast·ness** *n.*

a·cid-head (ăs'ĭd-hĕd) *n. Slang.* A person who habitually uses the drug LSD.

a·cid·ic (ə-sĭd'ĭk) *adj.* **1.** Acid. **2.** Tending to form an acid.

a·cid·i·fy (ə-sĭd'ə-fī') *v.* **-fied, -fying, -fies.** —*tr.* To make acid. —*intr.* To become acid. —**a·cid·i·fi·a·ble** *adj.* —**a·cid·i·fi·ca·tion** (ə-sĭd'ə-fĭ-kā'shən) *n.* —**a·cid·i·fi·er** *n.*

ac·i·dim·e·ter (ăs'ĭ-dĭm'ə-tər) *n.* A hydrometer used to determine the relative density of acid solutions. Also called "acidometer." —**ac·i·di·met·ric** (ăs'ĭ-dĭ-mĕt'rĭk) *adj.* —**ac·i·dim·e·try** *n.*

a·cid·i·ty (ə-sĭd'ə-tē) *n.* **1.** The state, quality, or degree of being acid. **2.** *Medicine.* Excessive acidity, **hyperacidity** *(see).*

ac·i·do·phil·ic (ăs'ĭ-dō-fĭl'ĭk) *adj. Microbiology.* **1.** Growing well in an acid medium. **2.** Easily stained with acid dyes. [ACID + -PHILIC.] —**a·cid·o·phil** (ə-sĭd'ə-fĭl'), **a·cid·o·phile** (ə-sĭd'ə-fīl') *n.*

ac·i·doph·i·lus milk (ăs'ĭ-dŏf'ə-ləs) *n.* Milk containing bacterial cultures that thrive in dilute acid, often used in treating gastrointestinal disorders. [New Latin *acidophilus,* "acid-loving" : Latin *acidus,* ACID + -PHILOUS.]

ac·i·do·sis (ăs'ĭ-dō'sĭs) *n.* A condition of pathologically high acidity of the blood and body tissues. —**ac·i·dot·ic** (ăs'ĭ-dŏt'ĭk) *adj.*

acid precipitation *n.* Precipitation having an abnormally high sulfuric and nitric acid content caused by industrial pollution.

acid rain *n.* Acid precipitation falling as rain.

acid rock *n.* A type of rock music supposedly inspired by the drug LSD, characterized by freely improvised instrumental passages.

acid salt *n.* A salt of a polybasic acid in which one or more acid hydrogen atoms have not been replaced by positive ions, as in sodium bicarbonate ($NaHCO_3$).

acid test *n.* A rigorous or decisive test of worth or quality. [From the test of gold in nitric acid.]

a·cid·u·late (ə-sĭj'ə-lāt') *tr.v.* **-lated, -lating, -lates.** To make slightly acid. [ACIDUL(OUS) + -ATE.] —**a·cid·u·la·tion** *n.*

a·cid·u·lous (ə-sĭj'ə-ləs) *adj.* **1.** Rather sour in taste. **2.** Sour in feeling or manner; biting; caustic. [Latin *acidulus,* sourish, diminutive of *acidus,* sour, ACID.]

acid value *n.* The amount of free acid in a fat, oil, or the like, expressed as the number of milligrams of potassium hydroxide necessary to neutralize the free acid in one gram of the substance.

ac·i·er·ate (ăs'ē-ə-rāt') *tr.v.* **-ated, -ating, -ates.** To convert (iron) into steel. [French *acier,* steel, from Latin *aciēs,* sharpness, from *ācer,* sharp + -ATE.] —**ac·i·er·a·tion** (ăs'ē-ə-rā'shən) *n.*

ac·i·nac·i·form (ăs'ĭ-năs'ə-fôrm') *adj. Botany.* Resembling a scimitar in shape: *acinaciform leaves.* [Latin *acinācēs,* short saber, from Greek *akinakēs,* from Iranian + -FORM.]

ac·i·nar (ăs'ĭ-nər) *adj. Anatomy.* Of or pertaining to an acinus.

a·cin·i·form (ə-sĭn'ə-fôrm') *adj.* Having the shape of a cluster of grapes or of a berry such as the raspberry. [ACIN(US) + -FORM.]

ac·i·nous (ăs'ĭ-nəs) *adj.* Consisting of small lobules or acini.

ac·i·nus (ăs'ĭ-nəs) *n., pl.* **-ni** (-nī'). **1.** *Botany.* Any of the small divisions or drupelets of an aggregate fruit such as the raspberry. **2.** The stone or seed of a grape or berry. **3.** *Anatomy.* Any of the small saclike dilations composing a compound gland. [New Latin, from Latin *acinus,* berry (especially a grape), probably of Mediterranean origin.]

-acious *suffix.* Indicates a tendency toward or abundance of something; for example, **fallacious.** [French *-acieux,* from Latin *-ācius* and *-āx* (stem *-āc-*), adjectival suffixes.]

-acity *suffix.* Indicates a quality or state of being; for example, **tenacity.** [French *acité,* from Latin *-ācitās,* from *-āx* (stem *-āc-*), -ACIOUS.]

ack-ack (ăk'ăk') *n. Military Slang.* **1.** An antiaircraft gun. **2.** Antiaircraft fire. Also used adjectivally: *an ack-ack gun.* [British telephonic code for *AA,* abbreviation for ANTIAIRCRAFT.]

ackee. Variant of **akee.**

ac·knowl·edge (ăk-nŏl'ĭj) *tr.v.* **-edged, -edging, -edges. 1.** To admit or accept the existence, reality, or fact of: *acknowledge one's mistakes.* **2.** To accept as valid or as having authority. **3. a.** To express recognition of. **b.** To express thanks or gratitude for. **4.** To report the receipt of. **5.** *Law.* To accept or certify as legally binding: *acknowledge a deed.* [Middle English, blend of *acknowen,* to recognize, acknowledge, Old English *oncnāwan* : *on,* ON + *cnāwan,* to KNOW and KNOWLEDGE.] —**ac·knowl·edge·a·ble** *adj.*
Synonyms: *admit, avow, concede, confess, own.*

ac·knowl·edg·ment, ac·knowl·edge·ment (ăk-nŏl'ĭj-mənt) *n.* **1.** The act of admitting, or accepting responsibility for, something. **2.** Recognition of someone's or something's existence, validity, authority, or right. **3.** An answer or response in return for something done. **4. a.** An expression or token of appreciation or thanks. **b. acknowledgments.** An author's expression of thanks, at the beginning or end of a book, to those who have helped him. **5.** A formal declaration made to authoritative witnesses to ensure legal validity.

a·clin·ic (ā-klĭn'ĭk) *adj. Geology.* Having no inclination or dip. [Greek *aklinēs,* not inclining to either side : *a-,* not + *klinein,* to lean.]

aclinic line *n.* The **magnetic equator** *(see).*

ACLU American Civil Liberties Union.

ac·me (ăk'mē) *n.* The highest point of attainment; the peak. —See Synonyms at **summit.** [Greek *akmē,* point, summit.]

ac·ne (ăk'nē) *n.* An inflammatory disease of the sebaceous glands, characterized by pimples on the face, neck, and upper torso, that is common in adolescents. [New Latin, misreading of Greek *akmē,* eruption on the face, point, ACME.]

ac·node (ăk'nōd') *n. Mathematics.* A point with coordinates that satisfy the equation of a curve, but that does not lie on the curve. Also called "isolated point." [Latin *acus,* needle + NODE (comparing the isolated point to a needle prick).]

a·cock (ə-kŏk') *adj.* In a cocked position. —**a·cock** *adv.*

ac·o·lyte (ăk'ə-līt') *n.* **1.** One who assists a priest in the performance of a religious service or ceremony; especially, in the Roman Catholic Church, an altar server who carries a candle. **2.** An attendant or follower. [Middle English *acolite,* from Old French, from Medieval Latin *acolytus,* variant of *acoluthus,* from Greek *akolouthos,* follower, following. See **anacoluthon.**]

A·con·ca·gua, Mount (ä'kōn-kä'gwä). A mountain in the Andes in western Argentina, near the Chilean border. It rises to 6,960 meters (22,835 feet), and until recent surveys revealed Ojos del Salado to be higher, it was regarded as the highest peak in the Western Hemisphere.

ac·o·nite (ăk'ə-nīt') *n.* **1.** Any plant of the genus *Aconitum,* such as **monkshood. 2.** The dried, poisonous root of monkshood, *A. napellus,* sometimes used in medicine to relieve pain or to reduce fever. [Latin *aconītum,* from Greek *akoniton,* possibly from *akonitos,* "dustless," unconquerable (with reference to the deadly properties of the plant) : *a-,* without + *-konitos,* "dusty," from *koniein,* to raise dust, struggle, from *konis,* dust.]

Açôres. See **Azores.**

a·corn (ā'kôrn', ā'kərn) *n.* The fruit of the oak tree, consisting of a thick-walled nut usually set in a woody, cuplike base. [Middle English, variant of *akern,* from Old English *æcern.*]

acorn barnacle *n.* A barnacle, such as *Balanus balanoides,* that lives attached to rocks and has a conical shell.

acorn tube *n.* A small, acorn-shaped vacuum tube used in very high frequency devices. Also *chiefly British* "acorn valve."

acorn worm *n.* Any of the wormlike marine animals with an acorn-shaped proboscis that belong to the genus *Balanoglossus* or related genera.

a·cot·y·le·don (ā'kŏt-ə-lēd'n) *n. Botany.* A plant having no cotyledons, or seed leaves, such as a moss or fern. —**a·cot·y·le·don·ous** (ā'kŏt-ə-lēd'ə-nəs) *adj.*

a·cous·tic (ə-kōō'stĭk) *adj.* Also **a·cous·ti·cal** (-stĭ-kəl). **1.** Of or pertaining to sound, the sense of hearing, or the science of sound. **2. a.** Designed to carry, absorb, or control sound: *an acoustic delay line.* **b.** Designating a device that is operated by sound waves: *an acoustic mine.* **c.** Designating a device that is designed to assist hearing: *an acoustic aid.* **3.** Not using electronic amplification. Said of a musical instrument, especially a guitar. [Greek *akoustikos,* pertaining to hearing, from *akouein,* to hear.] —**a·cous·ti·cal·ly** *adv.*

ac·ous·ti·cian (ăk'ōō-stĭsh'ən) *n.* A specialist in acoustics.

acoustic nerve *n.* Either of the eighth pair of cranial nerves, each consisting of a *cochlear nerve,* which conducts acoustic stimuli to the brain, and a *vestibular nerve,* which conducts stimuli related to bodily equilibrium to the brain. Also called "auditory nerve," "vestibulocochlear nerve."

a·cous·tics (ə-kōō'stĭks) *n.* Also **a·cous·tic** (-tĭk) (for sense 2).

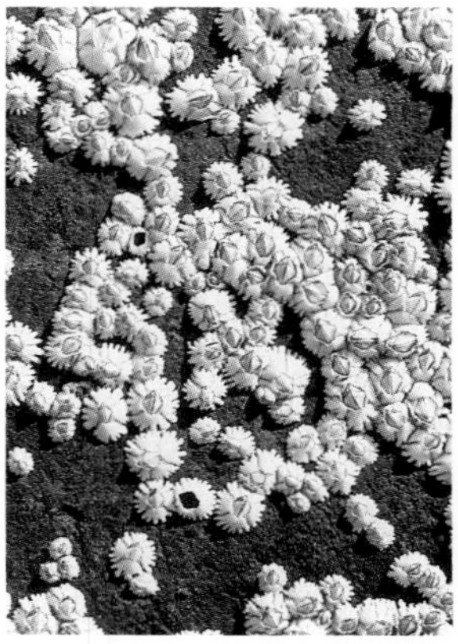

acorn barnacle *As a larva, the acorn barnacle has no bony shell. It floats freely in the sea until it lands on a suitable rock; then it uses a cement gland in its head to fix itself permanently to the spot. Once settled, it grows a shell with a hinged lid, which it opens at high tide to feed.*

PRONUNCIATION KEY

ă, pat; ā, pay; âr, care;
ä, father, are; b, bib;
ch, church; d, deed; ĕ, pet;
ē, be; f, fife; g, gag; h, hat;
hw, which; ĭ, pit; ī, pie;
îr, pier; j, judge; k, kick;
l, lid, needle; m, mum;
n, no, sudden; ng, thing;
ŏ, pot; ō, toe; ô, paw, for;
oi, noise; ou, out; ŏŏ, book;
ōō, boot; p, pop; r, roar;
s, sauce; sh, ship, dish;
t, tight; th, thin, path;
th, this, bathe; ŭ, cut; ûr, fur;
v, valve; w, with; y, yes;
z, zebra, size; zh, vision;
ə, about, item, edible,
gallop, circus, peaceful

IN FOREIGN WORDS:

à, *Fr.* ami; œ, *Fr.* feu, *Ger.* schön; ü, *Fr.* tu, *Ger.* über; KH, *Ger.* ich, *Scot.* loch; N, *Fr.* bon; y', *Fr.* Compiègne

STRESS MARKS:

Primary stress: '
in·cite' (ĭn-sīt')
Secondary stress: '
in'sight' (ĭn'sīt')

1. *Used with a singular verb.* The scientific study of sound, especially of its production, perception, and interaction with materials and other forms of radiation. **2.** *Used with a plural verb.* The quality and fidelity of the sound experienced in a particular room, auditorium, or other enclosed space: *a hall with poor acoustics.*

ac·quaint (ə-kwānt') *tr.v.* **-quainted, -quainting, -quaints. 1.** To make familiar. Used reflexively and with *with: acquaint oneself with the rules of the game.* **2.** To inform. Used with *with: acquaint someone with one's plans.* **3.** To cause to know personally. Used in the passive and with *with: I see you're already acquainted with each other.* [Middle English *aqueynten, acointen,* from Old French *acointer,* from Medieval Latin *accognitāre,* from Latin *accognitus,* past participle of *accognōscere,* to know perfectly : *ad-* (intensive) + *cognōscere,* to know : *co-, com-,* completely + *gnōscere,* to know.]

ac·quain·tance (ə-kwān'təns) *n.* **1.** Knowledge of or information about someone or something, especially when based on direct experience. **2.** Knowledge of a person acquired by a relationship less intimate than friendship. **3.** A person whom one knows, but who is not a close friend. **—ac·quain·tance·ship** *n.*

ac·qui·esce (ăk'wē-ĕs') *intr.v.* **-esced, -escing, -esces.** To accept, consent, or comply passively or without protest. Often used with *in: acquiesce in a ruling.* **—See Synonyms at assent.** [Latin *acquiēscere,* to remain at rest, agree tacitly : *ad-,* at, to + *quiēscere,* to rest, from *quiēs,* rest, QUIET.]

ac·qui·es·cence (ăk'wē-ĕs'əns) *n.* **1.** Passive assent or agreement without protest. **2.** The state of acquiescing or a tendency to acquiesce. **3.** *Law.* Failure to object to something such as an infringement of a right, taken as signifying acceptance or consent. **—ac·qui·es·cent** *adj.* **—ac·qui·es·cent·ly** *adv.*

ac·quire (ə-kwīr') *tr.v.* **-quired, -quiring, -quires. 1.** To gain possession of. **2.** To get, especially by one's own efforts or qualities: *acquire a reputation for honesty.* **3.** To locate (an object in the atmosphere or in space) for the purpose of tracking: *acquire a target.* [Middle English *acqueren,* from Old French *acquerre,* from Latin *acquīrere,* to add to, get : *ad-,* in addition to + *quaerere,* to seek, obtain.]

acquired characteristic (ə-kwīrd') *n.* A nonhereditary change in an organ caused by use or disuse or by environmental factors.

acquired immune deficiency syndrome *n.* **AIDS** *(see).*

acquired taste *n.* Something that initially seems unpleasant, but for which one develops a liking.

ac·quire·ment (ə-kwīr'mənt) *n.* **1.** The act of acquiring. **2.** An attainment, such as a skill or social accomplishment.

ac·qui·si·tion (ăk'wə-zĭsh'ən) *n.* **1.** The act of acquiring. **2.** Something or someone acquired, especially as an addition to an established category or group. **3.** *Aerospace.* The process of locating a satellite, guided missile, or moving target so that its track or orbit can be determined. [Middle English *acquisicioun,* from Latin *acquīsītiō* (stem *acquīsītiōn-),* from *acquīrere,* to ACQUIRE.]

ac·quis·i·tive (ə-kwĭz'ə-tĭv) *adj.* **1.** Eager to acquire material possessions. **2.** Tending to acquire and retain ideas or information: *an acquisitive mind.* **—ac·quis·i·tive·ly** *adv.* **—ac·quis·i·tive·ness** *n.*

ac·quit (ə-kwĭt') *tr.v.* **-quitted, -quitting, -quits. 1.** To clear of a criminal charge; declare to be not guilty. **2.** To release or discharge from duty or obligation. **3.** To conduct (oneself) in a specified way: *In her first formal speech she acquitted herself well.* [Middle English *acquiten,* from Old French *aquiter,* from Vulgar Latin *acquitāre* (unattested), "to bring to rest," set free : *ad-,* to + *quitāre, quiētāre* (unattested), to put to rest, set free, from *quiēs,* QUIET.] **—ac·quit·ter** *n.*

ac·quit·tal (ə-kwĭt'l) *n.* The judgment of a jury or judge that a person is not guilty of a crime as charged.

ac·quit·tance (ə-kwĭt'əns) *n.* A written release from an obligation or debt.

a·cre (ā'kər) *n.* **1.** *Abbr.* **A, a., A.** A unit of area used in land measurement and equal to 4840 square yards or 4046.86 square meters or 0.4047 hectares. **2. acres.** Property in the form of land. **3.** *Usually* **acres.** *Informal.* A wide expanse of space: *acres of room.* [Middle English *acre,* Old English *æcer,* field, acre; akin to Latin *ager,* field.]

A·cre (ä'kər, ā'kər, ä'krə). *Hebrew* **Ak·ko** (ăk'ō). *Arabic* **Ak·ka** (ăk'ə). Town and port in northern Israel on the Bay of Haifa. During the Crusades it changed hands many times between Christians and Arabs. It finally fell to the Saracens in 1291 and became part of the Ottoman Empire in the 16th century. During World War I it was won by the British and became part of the Palestinian protectorate. Acre was ceded to the Arabs in the UN partition of Palestine (1948), but was captured by Israel shortly afterward.

a·cre·age (ā'kər-ĭj, ā'krĭj) *n.* Area of land in acres.

a·cred (ā'kərd) *adj.* Comprising or possessing many acres of land. Used chiefly in combination: *a many-acred estate.*

ac·rid (ăk'rĭd) *adj.* **1.** Harsh and irritating to the taste or smell. **2.** Bitterly caustic in language or tone. [From Latin *ācer* (stem *ācr-),* sharp, bitter (probably influenced by ACID).] **—a·crid·i·ty** (ə-krĭd'ə-tē), **ac·rid·ness** *n.* **—ac·rid·ly** *adv.*

ac·ri·dine (ăk'rĭ-dēn', -dĭn) *n.* A coal tar derivative, $C_{13}H_9N$, that has a strongly irritating odor and is used in the manufacture of dyes and synthetics.

ac·ri·fla·vine (ăk'rĭ-flā'vēn') *n.* A brown or orange powder, $C_{14}H_{14}N_3Cl$, derived from acridine and used as an antiseptic. [AC-RI(DINE) + FLAVIN.]

ac·ri·mo·ni·ous (ăk'rĭ-mō'nē-əs) *adj.* Bitter and caustic in speech,

tone, or manner; rancorous. **—ac·ri·mo·ni·ous·ly** *adv.* **—ac·ri·mo·ni·ous·ness** *n.*

ac·ri·mo·ny (ăk'rĭ-mō'nē) *n.* Bitterness or ill-natured animosity, especially in speech or manner. [Latin *ācrimōnia,* sharpness, from *ācer,* sharp.]

acro– *prefix.* Indicates: **1.** A height or summit; for example, **acrophobia. 2.** An outer end, tip, or point; for example, **acrogen. 3.** An extremity of the body; for example, **acromegaly.** [Greek *akros,* topmost, extreme.]

ac·ro·bat (ăk'rə-băt') *n.* **1.** A performer, as in a circus, who is skilled in feats of agility and balance. **2.** One adept at quick changes of position, political stance, or the like. [French *acrobate,* from Greek *akrobatēs,* "one who walks on tiptoe," from *akrobatein,* to walk on tiptoe : ACRO- + *bat-,* stem of *bainein,* to walk.] **—ac·ro·bat·ic** (ăk'rə-băt'ĭk) *adj.* **—ac·ro·bat·i·cal·ly** *adv.*

ac·ro·bat·ics (ăk'rə-băt'ĭks) *n.* **1.** *Used with a singular verb.* The art of an acrobat. **2.** *Used with a plural verb.* The feats performed by an acrobat. **3.** *Used with a plural verb.* Any manifestation of spectacular mental or physical agility.

ac·ro·car·pous (ăk'rō-kär'pəs) *adj. Botany.* Having the spore-bearing capsule at the end or top of a leafy stem or stalk, as in many mosses. [New Latin *acrocarpus,* from Greek *akrokarpos,* bearing fruit at the top : ACRO- + -CARPOUS.]

ac·ro·cy·a·no·sis (ăk'rō-sī'ə-nō'sĭs) *n.* Slow circulation of the blood through the small vessels in the skin, resulting in bluish-purple discoloration of the hands and feet.

ac·ro·dont (ăk'rə-dŏnt') *adj. Zoology.* Having or designating teeth that lack roots and are fused to the bony ridge of the jaw, as in certain reptiles. [ACR(O)- + -ODONT.]

ac·ro·drome (ăk'rə-drōm') *adj.* Also **a·crod·ro·mous** (ə-krŏd'rə-məs). Designating a pattern of leaf venation in which there are two or more main veins, each terminating at the leaf tip. [ACRO- + -DROMOUS.]

ac·ro·gen (ăk'rə-jən) *n.* A flowerless plant, such as a fern or moss, in which all growth proceeds from the tip. [ACRO- + -GEN.] **—ac·ro·gen·ic** (ăk'rə-jĕn'ĭk), **a·crog·e·nous** (ə-krŏj'ə-nəs) *adj.* **—a·crog·e·nous·ly** *adv.*

a·cro·le·in (ə-krō'lē-ĭn) *n.* A colorless, flammable, poisonous liquid, CH_2:CHCHO, having an acrid odor and vapors dangerous to the eyes. Also called "propenal." [ACR(ID) + OLEIN.]

ac·ro·meg·a·ly (ăk'rō-mĕg'ə-lē) *n.* Pathological enlargement of the bones of the hands, feet, and face, resulting from excess production of growth hormone by the pituitary gland. [French *acromégalie,* "enlargement of extremities" : ACRO- + Greek *megal-,* stem of *megas,* big.] **—ac·ro·me·gal·ic** (ăk'rō-mĭ-găl'ĭk) *n. & adj.*

ac·ro·nym (ăk'rə-nĭm') *n.* A word formed from the initial letters of a name, such as *NATO,* from *North Atlantic Treaty Organization,* or by combining initial letters or parts of a series of words, such as *radar,* from *radio detecting and ranging.* [ACR(O)- + -ONYM.] **—ac·ro·nym·ic** (ăk'rə-nĭm'ĭk), **a·cron·y·mous** (ə-krŏn'ə-məs) *adj.*

a·crop·e·tal (ə-krŏp'ə-təl) *adj. Botany.* Developing upward toward the apex from the base, as certain forms of inflorescence do. [ACRO- + -PETAL.] **—a·crop·e·tal·ly** *adv.*

ac·ro·pho·bi·a (ăk'rə-fō'bē-ə) *n.* Abnormally intense fear of being in high places. [ACRO- + -PHOBIA.] **—ac·ro·pho·bic** *adj.*

a·crop·o·lis (ə-krŏp'ə-lĭs) *n.* **1.** The fortified citadel of an ancient Greek city. **2. the Acropolis.** The citadel of Athens, which is the site of the Parthenon. [Greek *akropolis,* "upper city" citadel : ACRO- + *polis,* city.]

ac·ro·some (ăk'rə-sōm') *n.* A structure in the head of a sperm that contains enzymes to break down the egg wall and allow fertilization. [ACRO- + -SOME (body).]

ac·ro·spire (ăk'rə-spīr') *n. Botany.* The first sprout from a germinating grain seed. [Variant (influenced by ACRO-) of dialectal *akerspire,* "ear-sprout" : *aker,* ear of grain, ultimately from Old English *æhher, ēar* + Middle English *spire,* Old English *spīr.*]

a·cross (ə-krôs', ə-krŏs') *prep.* **1.** On or at the other side of: *across the road.* **2.** So as to cross; over; through: *draw lines across the paper.* **3.** From one side to the other: *a bridge across a river.* **4.** Extending throughout: *across all social classes.* *—adv.* **1.** From one side to the other: *The bridge swayed when he ran across.* **2.** On or to the opposite side: *We came across by ferry.* [Middle English *acros, on croice,* from Old French *a croix, en croix,* "in the form of a CROSS," hence "transversely."]

a·cross-the-board (ə-krôs'thə-bôrd', -bōrd', ə-krŏs'-) *adj.* **1.** Affecting all categories or members, especially in an occupation or industry: *an across-the-board wage increase.* **2.** Wagering equal amounts on the same contestant to win, place, or show: *an across-the-board bet in horse racing.*

a·cros·tic (ə-krôs'tĭk, ə-krŏs'-) *n.* A poem or series of lines in which certain letters, usually the first in each line, form a name, motto, or message when read in sequence. [French *acrostiche,* from Old French, from Greek *akrostikhis,* "end-line" : ACRO- + *stikhos,* line of verse.] **—a·cros·tic** *adj.* **—a·cros·ti·cal·ly** *adv.*

ac·ry·late resin (ăk'rĭ-lāt') *n.* Any of a class of acrylic resins used in emulsion paints, adhesives, plastics, and textile and paper finishes. Also called "acrylate."

a·cryl·ic (ə-krĭl'ĭk) *adj.* Based on or relating to acrylic acid. *—n.* **1.** Acrylic fiber. **2.** Acrylic resin. **3.** Acrylic paint. [ACR(O-LEIN) + -YL + -IC.]

acrylic acid *n.* An easily polymerized, colorless, corrosive liquid, H_2C:CHCOOH, used as a monomer for acrylate resins. Also called "propenoic acid."

~*n., pl.* **adagios.** **1.** *Music.* A composition or movement played in this tempo. **2.** In ballet, a section of a pas de deux, in which the ballerina and her partner perform steps requiring lyricism and great skill in lifting, balancing, and turning. [Italian *adagio,* "at ease" : *ad-,* at, from Latin, at, toward + *agio,* ease, from Old Provençal *aize,* from Vulgar Latin *adjacēs* (unattested), variant of Latin *adjacēns,* convenient, ADJACENT.] **—a·da·gi·o** *adj.*

Ad·am[1] (ăd′əm). **1.** The first man and progenitor of mankind, according to the Bible. Genesis 2:7. **2.** The unregenerate side of human nature: *the old Adam.* **—not know someone from Adam.** To be completely ignorant of the identity of. [Late Latin, from Hebrew *ādām,* "man," from *adāmāh,* earth.] **—A·dam·ic** (ə-dăm′ĭk) *adj.*

Adam[2] *adj.* In, pertaining to, or characteristic of the neoclassical style of furniture and architecture originated by Robert and James Adam: *an Adam fireplace.*

Adam (ăd′əm), **Robert** (1728–92). British architect. Adam built in a delicate classical style, a development of the Palladian tradition, and was equally outstanding as an interior designer. In 1763 he went into partnership in London with his brother **James** (1730–94).

ad·a·mant (ăd′ə-mənt, -mănt′) *n.* **1.** A stone of uncertain identity formerly believed to be unbreakable. **2.** Any substance of exceptional hardness and resilience.
~*adj.* **1.** Unshakably firm in purpose or opinion; unyielding. **2.** Adamantine. —See Synonyms at **inflexible.** [Middle English *adama(u)nt,* diamond, magnet, from Old French *adamaunt,* from Latin *adamās* (stem *adamant-*), from Greek *adamas,* hard metal, steel, diamond, possibly, "unbreakable" : *a-* not + *daman,* to tame, break down.] **—ad·a·mant·ly** *adv.*

ad·a·man·tine (ăd′ə-măn′tēn′, -tĭn, -tīn′) *adj.* **1.** Made of or resembling adamant. **2.** Having the hardness or luster of a diamond. **3.** Unyielding; inflexible.

Ad·am·ite (ăd′ə-mīt′) *n.* A descendant of Adam; a human being.

Ad·ams (ăd′əmz), **Abigail** (1744–1818). U.S. letter writer and first lady (1797–1801) as the wife of President John Adams. During frequent separations caused by the Revolutionary War, she wrote constantly to her husband, providing a vivid picture of her life and times in Massachusetts.

Adams, Ansel (1902–84). U.S. photographer. The American wilderness, from Death Valley to the Sierra Nevada, was the raw material for his magnificent photographs. Adams also worked tirelessly for the preservation of wilderness areas in the United States.

Adams, John (1735–1826). First vice president (1789–97) and second president (1797–1801) of the United States. Adams played a leading part in the American Revolution, shaping the Constitution and helping draft the Declaration of Independence.

Adams, John Couch (1819–92). British astronomer who was the first to predict the position of Neptune. Adams calculated the position of the new planet, purely mathematically, in 1845. However the planet was not discovered until Urbain Leverrier's independent prediction had been made and confirmed in 1846.

Adams, John Quincy (1767–1848). Sixth president of the United States (1825–29) and son of John Adams. As secretary of state (1817–25) he helped formulate the Monroe Doctrine. He later became an active campaigner against slavery.

Adam's apple *n.* The projection of the largest laryngeal cartilage at the front of the throat, especially in men. [Translation of Hebrew *tappūah hāādām.*]

ad·ams·ite (ăd′əmz-īt′) *n. Symbol* **DM** A yellow crystalline compound, $(C_6H_4)_2(NH)AsCl$, used dispersed in air as a poison gas. [After Roger *Adams* (1889–1971), U.S. chemist.]

Adam's needle *n.* A plant, the **Spanish bayonet** *(see).* [From the spines on its leaves and with allusion to Genesis 3:7: " . . . they sewed fig leaves together, and made themselves aprons."]

a·dapt (ə-dăpt′) *v.* **adapted, adapting, adapts.** *—tr.* **1.** To adjust to a new environment or situation. **2.** To modify for a different use or purpose: *adapt a stage play for the radio.* *—intr.* To become adapted. [Latin *adaptāre,* to fit to : *ad-* to + *aptāre,* to fit, from *aptus,* APT.]

a·dapt·a·ble (ə-dăp′tə-bəl) *adj.* Capable of adapting or of being adapted. —See Synonyms at **flexible.** **—a·dapt·a·bil·i·ty** (ə-dăp′tə-bĭl′ə-tē), **a·dapt·a·ble·ness** *n.*

ad·ap·ta·tion (ăd′ăp-tā′shən) *n.* **1. a.** The act or process of adapting. **b.** The state of being adapted. **2.** Something that has adapted or been adapted so as to suit a new or special use or situation: *a new adaptation for radio.* **3.** An adjustment or process of adjustment, often hereditary, by which a species or individual improves its condition in relationship to its environment. **4.** The responsive alteration of a sense organ to repeated stimuli of a particular type. **—ad·ap·ta·tion·al** *adj.* **—ad·ap·ta·tion·al·ly** *adv.*

a·dapt·er, a·dap·tor (ə-dăp′tər) *n.* **1.** One that adapts. **2.** A device used to connect an electrical plug of one type into a supply point having a different fitting. **3.** A device that enables several electrical plugs to be fitted into one supply point. **4.** Any device that enables one part of an apparatus or machine to be fitted into another part having a different size or fitting.

a·dap·tive (ə-dăp′tĭv) *adj.* Tending toward, fit for, or having a capacity for adaptation. **—a·dap·tive·ly** *adv.* **—a·dap·tive·ness** *n.*

adaptive radiation *n.* The evolution of one relatively unspecialized species into several related species characterized by different specializations that fit them for life in various environments. See feature, next page.

A·dar (ä-där′) *n.* The sixth month of the year in the Hebrew calendar. See feature at **calendar.** [Hebrew *Adhār,* from Akkadian *ad(d)aru,* "the dark or cloudy month," from *adāru,* to be dark.]

Adar She·ni (shā-nē′) *n.* An intercalary Hebrew month, **Veadar** *(see).* [Hebrew *Adhār shēnī,* "second Adar."]

ad·ax·i·al (ăd-ăk′sē-əl) *adj.* Facing toward the axis. Said of the upper surface of leaves. Compare **abaxial.**

ADC, a.d.c., A.D.C. aide-de-camp.

add (ăd) *v.* **added, adding, adds.** *—tr.* **1.** To join or unite so as to increase in size, quantity, or scope. **2.** To combine (a column of figures, for example) to form a total. Often used with *up.* **3.** To say or write further. **4.** To provide as an additional feature or quality; impart: *Wine can add zest to a meal.* *—intr.* **1.** To create or constitute an addition. Used with *to.* **2.** To find a sum in arithmetic. **—add up.** *Informal.* **1.** To come to a correct or desired total: *His figures don't add up.* **2.** To be reasonable, plausible, or consistent; make sense. **—add up to.** *Informal.* To mean; amount to. [Middle English *adden,* from Latin *addere,* to add, "to put to": *ad-,* to + *-dere,* to put, from *dare,* to give.] **—add·a·ble, add·i·ble** *adj.*

Ad·dams (ăd′əmz), **Charles** (1912–88). U.S. cartoonist. Addams is known for the macabre humor and gothic settings of his cartoons, many of which appeared in *The New Yorker.*

Addams, Jane (1860–1935). U.S. social reformer. In 1889 she opened Hull House, a settlement house in a slum neighborhood of Chicago offering adult-education courses and activities for the poor and foreign-born of the area. Addams became a leader of the pacifist movement in the early 1900's and was awarded a Nobel Peace Prize in 1931.

ad·dax (ăd′ăks′) *n.* An antelope, *Addax nasomaculatus,* of northern Africa having long, spirally twisted horns. [Latin *addāx,* of African origin.]

add·ed value (ăd′ĭd) *n. Economics.* The increase in the value of goods occurring in the process of production. It is measured as the difference between the producer's total revenue and the cost to him of raw materials.

ad·dend (ăd′ĕnd′, ə-dĕnd′) *n.* Any of a set of numbers to be added. [Shortened from ADDENDUM.]

ad·den·dum (ə-dĕn′dəm) *n., pl.* **-da** (-də). Something added or to be added; especially, a supplement, appendix, or list of matter wrongly omitted from a publication. [Latin, neuter of *addendus,* gerundive of *addere,* to ADD.]

ad·der (ăd′ər) *n.* **1.** Any of various venomous snakes of the family Viperidae, especially the common viper, *Vipera berus,* of Eurasia. **2.** Any of several similar snakes, such as the **hognose snake** *(see),* or puff adder, of North America. [Middle English *addre,* from *an addre,* mistaken from *a naddre,* Old English *nǣdre,* snake.]

ad·der's-tongue (ăd′ərz-tŭng′) *n.* **1.** Any of several ferns of the genus *Ophioglossum*; especially, *O. vulgatum,* of the Northern Hemisphere, having a single sterile, leaflike frond, and a spore-bearing stalk. **2.** Any of various plants of the genus *Erythronium,* such as the **dogtooth violet** *(see).* [From the spike sticking out from the base of the frond of the fern, suggesting a snake's tongue.]

ad·dict (ə-dĭkt′) *tr.v.* **-dicted, -dicting, -dicts.** **1.** To cause to become physiologically or psychologically dependent, especially on a drug. Usually used in the passive and with *to.* **2.** To devote (oneself) excessively or compulsively.
~*n.* (ăd′ĭkt). **1.** One who is addicted, especially to a drug. **2.** *Informal.* A devotee: *a TV addict.* [Latin *addīctus,* "given over," one awarded to another as a slave, past participle of *addīcere,* to award to : *ad-,* to + *dīcere,* to say, pronounce, adjudge.] **—ad·dic·tion** *n.* **—ad·dic·tive** *adj.*

Ad·dis Ab·a·ba (ăd′ĭs ăb′ə-bə). Capital and largest city of Ethiopia, located in the center of the country on a plateau more than 2,440 meters (8,000 feet) above sea level. It became the capital in 1889. Captured by the Italians in 1936 and made the capital of Italian East Africa, it was liberated by the Allies in 1941 and returned to Ethiopia.

Ad·di·son (ăd′ə-sən), **Joseph** (1672–1719). British essayist, poet, and Whig politician. He is best known for his witty, elegant essays, which were mainly contributed to two periodicals: Richard Steele's *Tatler,* and the *Spectator,* founded by Steele and Addison.

Addison's disease *n.* A disease caused by failure of the adrenal cortex to function and marked by a bronzelike skin pigmentation, anemia, and prostration. [After Thomas *Addison* (1793–1860), British physician who discovered it.]

ad·di·tion (ə-dĭsh′ən) *n.* **1.** The act or process of adding. **2. a.** The result of adding. **b.** Something or someone added. **3.** The process of combining numbers so as to find their sum. **4.** A part added to a building; an extension. —See Synonyms at **appendage.** **—in addition.** Besides; also. **—in addition to.** Over and above; as well as. —See Usage note at **together.**

ad·di·tion·al (ə-dĭsh′ə-nəl) *adj.* In addition; added; extra.

ad·di·tion·al·ly (ə-dĭsh′ə-nə-lē) *adv.* Furthermore; in addition. —See Synonyms at **also.**

ad·di·tive (ăd′ə-tĭv) *adj.* **1.** Marked by, produced by, or involving addition. **2.** Designating any of certain colors of wavelengths that may be mixed with one another to produce other colors. Compare **subtractive.** See **primary color.**
~*n.* A substance added in small amounts to something else, especially a food or drink, to improve, strengthen, or otherwise alter it.

ad·dle (ăd′l) *v.* **-dled, -dling, -dles.** *—tr.* To muddle; confuse: *His brain is addled by too much drink.* *—intr.* **1.** To become rotten. Used of an egg. **2.** To become confused.
~*adj.* Mixed-up; confused. Usually used in combination: *addle-*

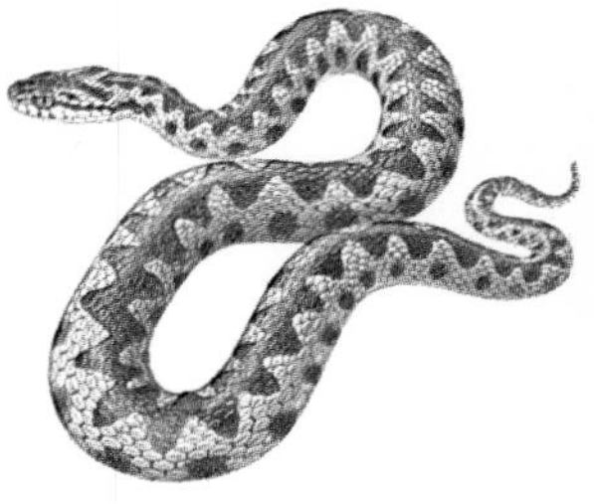

adder *The family of venomous snakes known commonly as adders, or vipers, includes some that are extremely dangerous to man—among them the puff adders of Africa. The common adder of Europe and Asia,* Vipera berus *(above), will not, however, attack man unless provoked; and its bite is very rarely fatal. The death adder of Australia is a member of the cobra family and is not related to adders; it is so named only because it superficially resembles them.*

PRONUNCIATION KEY

ă, **pat**; ā, **pay**; âr, **care**;
ä, **father, are**; b, **bib**;
ch, **church**; d, **deed**; ĕ, **pet**;
ē, **be**; f, **fife**; g, **gag**; h, **hat**;
hw, **which**; ĭ, **pit**; ī, **pie**;
îr, **pier**; j, **judge**; k, **kick**;
l, **lid, needle**; m, **mum**;
n, **no, sudden**; ng, **thing**;
ŏ, **pot**; ō, **toe**; ô, **paw, for**;
oi, **noise**; ou, **out**; ŏŏ, **book**;
ōō, **boot**; p, **pop**; r, **roar**;
s, **sauce**; sh, **ship, dish**;
t, **tight**; th, **thin, path**;
th, **this, bathe**; ŭ, **cut**; ûr, **fur**;
v, **valve**; w, **with**; y, **yes**;
z, **zebra, size**; zh, **vision**;
ə, **about, item, edible, gallop, circus, peaceful**

IN FOREIGN WORDS:

à, *Fr.* **ami**; œ, *Fr.* **feu**, *Ger.* **schön**; ü, *Fr.* **tu**, *Ger.* **über**; KH, *Ger.* **ich**, *Scot.* **loch**; N, *Fr.* **bon**; y', *Fr.* **Compiègne**

STRESS MARKS:

Primary stress: ′
in·cite′ (ĭn-sīt′)
Secondary stress: ′
in′sight′ (ĭn′sīt′)

adaptive radiation

EVOLUTION OF NEW SPECIES BY ADAPTATION
How various animal and plant species evolve

Living beings are always more or less like their parents, but never exactly like them. Because of this, according to the Darwinian theory of evolution, species change over thousands of generations. In any species, those members best adapted to their environment survive and breed, and their progeny tend to inherit the characteristics that best fit them to survive. The species becomes even better adapted through the generations and in time may change so much that it is a new species.

Sometimes the changes involve a single line of evolving plants or animals—as in man's line of descent from apelike ancestors to modern human beings. More often, however, one species in the past has become the ancestor of various related kinds, all alike in some ways but each adapted to survive in slightly different ways.

This fanning-out process is called adaptive radiation.

All the cat family come from the same ancestors and hunt in broadly the same way, but large cats such as lions can hunt large prey, and smaller cats hunt smaller prey. Large cats, such as lions, tigers, and leopards, have evolved different camouflage so they can hunt in different places.

Some of the most striking examples occur when one kind of animal becomes cut off in one part of the world. Charles Darwin observed an example on the Galápagos Islands in the Pacific Ocean, where 13 species of finch had adapted to the different local environments on the various islands. The marsupials, or pouched mammals, of Australia, which nowadays lead very varied lives, are another example.

AUSTRALIAN MARSUPIALS *Cut off in Australia, the common ancestor of the marsupials produced generations of young that adapted to various environments and eventually diversified into different species. The hairy-nosed wombat has strong legs for burrowing and the fat-tailed mouse anticipates shortages by storing fat in its tail. Long hind legs give the red kangaroo speed in its search for sparse food,* *and the bush-tailed opossum can hang from branches with its clawless hind digit. The pointed muzzle of the long-nosed bandicoot helps it to root for worms. The numbat has powerful claws to dig up ants' nests and a long, sticky tongue to mop up the ants. The marsupial mole has a horny shield to protect its nose as it burrows in the harsh desert.*

---

brained. [Middle English *adel,* rotten, putrid, Old English *adela,* filth, urine; akin to Middle Low German *adele†.*]

ad·dress (ə-drĕs′) *tr.v.* **-dressed, -dressing, -dresses. 1.** To speak to; especially, to use a certain form in speaking to: *I addressed her by her first name.* **2.** To make a formal speech to. **3.** To direct (a spoken or written comment) to the attention of. Used with *to: Please address your remarks to the chairman.* **4.** To mark (a letter, parcel, or the like) with the name of the person and place to which it is to be delivered. **5. a.** To direct (oneself) in speech. Used with *to.* **b.** To direct the efforts or attention of (oneself): *address oneself to a task.* **c.** To direct one's efforts or attention to (a problem, for example). **6.** To consign (a ship or its cargo) to an agent or factor. **7.** To adjust and aim a golf club or billiard cue when preparing to strike (a ball).
~*n.* (ə-drĕs′; *also* ăd′rĕs *for senses 3,4,7*). **1.** A formal spoken or written communication: *polite forms of address.* **2.** A formal speech. **3.** The location at which a particular organization or person may be found or reached. **4.** Information giving details of this, written on a letter, parcel, or the like. **5.** Skillfulness, adroitness, or tact in handling a situation. **6.** The act of consigning a ship or its cargo, as to an agent or factor. **7.** *Computer Science.* A number used in information storage or retrieval that is assigned to a specific memory location. **8.** *Usually* **addresses.** Courteous attention; wooing. Used chiefly in the phrase *pay one's addresses.* **9.** Manner or bearing of a person, especially in conversation. [Middle English *addressen,* from Old French *addresser,* from Vulgar Latin *addrictiāre* (unattested), to straighten, direct oneself toward : *ad-,* + *directiāre* (unattested), to straighten, from Latin *dīrectus,* DIRECT.] —**ad·dress·er, ad·dres·sor** *n.*

ad·dress·a·ble (ə-drĕs′ə-bəl) *adj.* Accessible through an address, as in a computer memory.

ad·dress·ee (ăd′rĕs-ē′, ə-drĕs′ē′) *n.* One to whom something, such as a letter, is addressed.

Ad·dress·o·graph (ə-drĕs′ə-grăf′) *n.* A trademark for a machine that prints addresses on letters.

ad·duce (ə-dōōs′, ə-dyōōs′, ă-) *tr.v.* **-duced, -ducing, -duces.** To cite as an example, explanation, or means of proof; bring forward for consideration. [Latin *addūcere,* to bring to (someone) : *ad-,* toward + *dūcere,* to lead.] —**ad·duce·a·ble, ad·duc·i·ble** *adj.*

ad·du·cent (ə-dōō′sənt, ə-dyōō′-, ă-) *adj. Physiology.* Drawing toward or together; adducting. Said of a muscle.

ad·duct (ə-dŭkt′, ă-) *tr.v.* **-ducted, -ducting, -ducts.** To pull or draw (a limb) toward the main axis. Used of a muscle. [Back-formation from ADDUCTOR.] —**ad·duc·tion** *n.* —**ad·duc·tive** *adj.*

ad·duc·tor (ə-dŭk′tər, ă-) *n.* A muscle that adducts. [Latin *adductor,* "a bringer toward," from *addūcere,* to ADDUCE.]

–ade *suffix.* Indicates a sweetened drink of; for example, **lemonade.** [French *-ade,* from Provençal, Portuguese, and Spanish *-ada* and Italian *-ata,* all from Latin *-āta,* feminine of *-ātus,* "furnished with," past participial ending of verbs in *-āre.*]

Ad·e·laide (ăd′ə-lād′). Capital of South Australia, on the Torrens River in the southeast of the state. The products of its manufacturing industries include textiles, cars, and electronics, and it exports agricultural goods.

A·dé·lie Land (ə-dā′lē). Also **Adélie Coast.** Region of Antarctica on the coast of Wilkes Land, claimed by the French.

Adélie penguin *n.* A common Antarctic penguin, *Pygoscelis adeliae,* of medium size, with white underparts and black back and head. It lives and breeds in large exposed rookeries.

–adelphous *suffix. Botany.* Indicates stamens united by their filaments to form a specified number of groups; for example, **diadelphous.** [New Latin *-adelphus,* "having the stamens grouped together (in a 'brotherhood')," from Greek *adelphos,* brother.]

a·demp·tion (ə-dĕmp′shən) *n. Law.* The invalidation of a bequest, especially as a result of some action by the testator during his lifetime, such as the disposal of the property in question. [Latin *ademptiō,* a taking away, from *adimere* (past participle *ademptus*), to take to (oneself), take away : *ad-,* toward + *emere,* to buy, "take."]

A·den (ăd′n, ād′n). Capital and chief port of South Yemen on the Gulf of Aden, the western arm of the Arabian Sea. It has always been one of the chief ports of southern Arabia. It was annexed by Britain in 1839, and became a major trading and refueling station after the opening of the Suez Canal in 1869. Aden is the country's industrial and commercial center.

A·den·au·er (ăd′n-ou′ər, ād′n-), **Konrad** (1876–1967). German statesman and first chancellor of the Federal Republic of Germany. In 1946 Adenauer, a former Rhineland politician who had been twice imprisoned by the Nazis, became leader of the Christian

Democratic Union (CDU), which won the first West German elections in 1949. Under Adenauer West Germany embarked on a program of economic reconstruction and gained membership in NATO and the European Economic Community.

ad·en·ec·to·my (ăd′n-ĕk′tə-mē) *n., pl.* **-mies.** Surgical excision of a gland. [ADEN(O)- + -ECTOMY.]

ad·e·nine (ăd′n-ēn′, -ĭn) *n. Biochemistry.* A purine derivative, $C_5H_5N_5$, that is a constituent of nucleic acid in the pancreas, spleen, and other organs. [ADEN(O)- + -INE.]

ad·e·ni·tis (ăd′n-ī′tĭs) *n.* Inflammation of a lymph node or gland. [ADEN(O)- + -ITIS.]

adeno-, aden– *prefix.* Indicates a gland or glands; for example, **adenocarcinoma.** [New Latin, from Greek *adēn*, gland.]

ad·e·no·car·ci·no·ma (ăd′n-ō-kär′sə-nō′mə) *n., pl.* **-mata** (-mə-tə) or **-mas.** A malignant tumor originating in glandular tissue. **—ad·e·no·car·ci·nom·a·tous** (ăd′n-ō-kär′sə-nōm′ə-təs, -nō′mə-təs) *adj.*

ad·e·no·hy·poph·y·sis (ăd′n-ō-hī-pŏf′ĭ-sĭs) *n.* The front section of the pituitary gland. Compare **neurohypophysis.**

ad·e·noid (ăd′n-oid′) *adj.* Also **ad·e·noi·dal** (ăd′n-oid′l). 1. Glandlike; glandular. 2. Of or pertaining to the adenoids.

ad·e·noi·dal (ăd′n-oid′l) *adj.* 1. Variant of **adenoid.** 2. a. Having a nasal or constricted tone: *an adenoidal singer.* b. Breathing through the mouth; open-mouthed.

ad·e·noids (ăd′n-oidz′) *pl.n.* Lymphoid tissue growths in the nose above the throat that when swollen may obstruct nasal breathing, induce postnasal discharge, and make speech difficult. [Greek *adenoeidēs* : ADEN(O)- + -OID.]

ad·e·no·ma (ăd′n-ō′mə) *n., pl.* **-mata** (-mə-tə) or **-mas.** An epithelial tumor of glandular origin and structure that is usually benign or of low-grade malignancy. [ADEN(O)- + -OMA.] **—ad·e·nom·a·tous** (ăd′n-ōm′ə-təs) *adj.*

a·den·o·sine (ə-dĕn′ə-sēn′) *n.* An organic compound, $C_{10}H_{13}N_5O_4$, that is a structural component of nucleic acids. [Blend of ADENINE and RIBOSE.]

adenosine diphosphate *n.* **ADP** (see).

adenosine monophosphate *n.* **AMP** (see).

adenosine triphosphate *n.* **ATP** (see).

ad·e·no·vi·rus (ăd′n-ō-vī′rəs) *n.* Any of a group of viruses that cause respiratory infections producing symptoms like those of the common cold.

a·dept (ə-dĕpt′) *adj.* Highly skilled; expert. —See Synonyms at **proficient.**
~*n.* (ăd′ĕpt′). One who is thoroughly proficient or highly skilled; an expert. [Latin *adeptus*, "having attained (knowledge or skill)," past participle of *adipīscī*, to attain : *ad-*, toward + *apīscī*, to reach for.] **—a·dept·ly** *adv.* **—a·dept·ness** *n.*

ad·e·quate (ăd′ĭ-kwĭt) *adj.* 1. a. Sufficient for a particular purpose or need. b. Able to satisfy a requirement or standard; suitable. c. Having the necessary qualities to meet the demands of a situation: *proved adequate to the task.* 2. Barely satisfactory or sufficient. [Latin *adaequatus*, past participle of *adaequāre*, to make equal to : *ad-*, toward + *aequāre*, to make equal, from *aequus*, EQUAL.] **—ad·e·qua·cy** (ăd′ĭ-kwə-sē), **ad·e·quate·ness** *n.* **—ad·e·quate·ly** *adv.*
Usage: The prepositions *to* and *for* following this word are becoming interchangeable. *To* is generally recommended in contexts such as *adequate to his needs, adequate to the task,* but *for* is increasingly common: *There was adequate food for our purposes.*

ad·here (ăd-hîr′) *intr.v.* **-hered, -hering, -heres.** 1. To stick fast or together by or as if by grasping, suction, or being glued. Often used with *to.* 2. To be devoted as a follower or supporter. Used with *to.* 3. To follow closely or strictly. Used with *to: adhere to a plan.* [Latin *adhaerēre*, to stick to : *ad*, toward + *haerēre*, to stick.]

ad·her·ence (ăd-hîr′əns) *n.* 1. The act or state of adhering; adhesion. 2. Fidelity or attachment, as to a party, cause, or set of rules.

ad·her·ent (ăd-hîr′ənt) *adj.* 1. Sticking or holding fast; attached. 2. *Botany.* Growing or fused together; adnate.
~*n.* A supporter, as of a cause, idea, or individual. **—ad·her·ent·ly** *adv.*

ad·he·sion (ăd-hē′zhən) *n.* 1. a. The act or state of sticking together. b. Firm physical contact between surfaces: *the wallpaper's adhesion to the wall.* 2. Loyalty or attachment; adherence. 3. Assent or agreement, especially to join or associate oneself. 4. The physical attraction or joining together of two substances; especially, the molecular attraction of dissimilar substances. Compare **cohesion.** 2. *Biology & Medicine.* An abnormal joining together of two organic parts. [Latin *adhaesiō*, from *adhaerēre*, to ADHERE.]

ad·he·sive (ăd-hē′sĭv) *adj.* 1. Tending to adhere; sticky. 2. Gummed so as to adhere.
~*n.* An adhesive substance, such as paste or glue. **—ad·he·sive·ly** *adv.* **—ad·he·sive·ness** *n.*

ad hoc (ăd hŏk′) *adj. Latin.* For a specific purpose, case, or situation: *an ad hoc committee.* [Latin, "toward this."] **—ad hoc** *adv.*

ad hom·i·nem (ăd hŏm′ĭ-nĕm) *adj. Latin.* 1. Appealing to personal interests, prejudices, or emotions rather than to reason: *an argument ad hominem.* 2. Attacking an opponent personally, rather than answering the opponent's arguments. [Latin, "to the man."] **—ad hom·i·nem** *adv.*

ad·i·a·bat·ic (ăd′ē-ə-băt′ĭk, ā′dī-ə-) *adj. Physics.* Of, pertaining to, or designating a reversible thermodynamic process executed at constant entropy; loosely, occurring without gain or loss of heat. [Greek *adiabatos*, "impassable (to heat)" : *a-*, not + *diabatos*, passable, from *diabainein*, to go through : *dia*, through + *bainein*, to go.]

a·dieu (ə-dyōō′, ə-dōō′) *interj.* Good-by; farewell.
~*n., pl.* **adieus** or **adieux** (ə-dyōōz′, ə-dōōz′). A farewell. [Middle English, from Old French, from *a dieu*, "(I commend you) to God" : *a,* to, from Latin *ad* + *dieu*, God, from Latin *deus*, god.]

ad in·fi·ni·tum (ăd ĭn′fə-nī′təm) *adv. Abbr.* **ad inf.** *Latin.* To infinity; endlessly.

ad in·ter·im (ăd ĭn′tər-əm) *adv. Abbr.* **ad int.** *Latin.* In the meantime; meanwhile. **—ad in·ter·im** *adj.*

a·di·os (ä′dē-ōs′, ăd′ē-ōs′) *interj.* Good-by; farewell. [Spanish, translation of French *adieu*, ADIEU.]

ad·i·pose (ăd′ə-pōs′) *adj.* Of or related to animal fat; fatty.
~*n.* The fat found in adipose tissue. [New Latin *adiposus*, from Latin *adeps*† (stem *adip-*), fat.] **—ad·i·pose·ness, ad·i·pos·i·ty** (ăd′-ə-pŏs′ə-tē) *n.*

adipose fin *n.* An additional dorsal fin in certain fishes, such as the salmon, consisting mostly of fatty tissue and usually without supporting rays.

adipose tissue *n.* Connective tissue in the body that contains stored cellular fat.

Ad·i·ron·dack Mountains (ăd′ə-rŏn′dăk′). Also **Ad·i·ron·dacks** (-dăks). Group of mountains in eastern New York State. The highest peak is Mt. Marcy (1,628 meters; 5,344 feet). The region's lakes and forests attract many tourists, and there are also numerous winter sports resorts, including Lake Placid, site of the Winter Olympic Games of 1932 and 1980.

ad·it (ăd′ĭt) *n.* A horizontal, or near horizontal, passage cut in a hill slope for mining or drainage purposes. [Latin *aditus*, access, from the past participle of *adīre*, to approach : *ad-*, toward + *īre*, to go.]

A·di·va·si (ä′dĭ-vä′sē) *n., pl.* **-sis** or collectively **Adivasi.** A member of any of the aboriginal peoples of India.

adj. 1. adjective. 2. adjourned. 3. adjutant.

ad·ja·cent (ə-jā′sənt) *adj.* 1. Lying or being close in space or time. 2. Having a common border; contiguous or adjoining. [Middle English, from Latin *adjacēns* (stem *adjacent-*), present participle of *adjacēre*, to lie near : *ad-*, near to + *jacēre*, to lie, "be thrown down," intransitive of *jacere*, to lay, throw.] **—ad·ja·cen·cy** *n.* **—ad·ja·cent·ly** *adv.*

adjacent angle *n.* Either of two angles having a common side and a common vertex and lying on opposite sides of the common side.

ad·jec·tive (ăj′ĭk-tĭv) *n. Abbr.* **adj., a.** 1. A part of speech comprising a class of words that modify a noun or other substantive by limiting, qualifying, or specifying. 2. A word belonging to this class, such as *nice* in *a nice house.* 3. A word used as an adjective, such as *brick* in *a brick house.*
~*adj.* 1. Pertaining to or functioning as an adjective. 2. Dependent; subordinate. 3. *Law.* Concerned with court procedure as opposed to legal principles. Compare **substantive.** 4. Requiring the use of a mordant to make permanent: *adjective dyes.* [Middle English, from Old French *adjectif*, from Latin *adjectīvus*, "attributive," from *adjectus*, "attributed," added, from *adjicere*, to throw to, add : *ad-*, to + *jacere*, to throw.] **—ad·jec·ti·val** (ăj′ĭk-tī′vəl) *adj.* **—ad·jec·ti·val·ly** *adv.*

ad·join (ə-join′) *v.* **-joined, -joining, -joins.** —*tr.* 1. To be next to; be contiguous to. 2. To attach; append. Used with *to.* —*intr.* To be nearby or contiguous: *in the adjoining room.* [Middle English *adjoinen*, from Old French *ajoindre*, from Latin *adjungere*, to join to : *ad-*, to + *jungere*, to join.]

ad·journ (ə-jûrn′) *v.* **-journed, -journing, -journs.** —*tr.* To break off (especially a meeting or court session) until a later time. —*intr.* 1. To suspend transfer or proceedings to another time or place. 2. To move from one place to another. Often used humorously: *We adjourned to the living room.* [Middle English *adjournen*, from Old French *ajourner*, "to put off to an appointed day" : *a-*, to, from Latin *ad-* + *jour*, day, from Late Latin *diurnum*, day, from *diurnus*, daily, from *diēs*, day.] **—ad·journ·ment** *n.*

adjt. adjutant.

ad·judge (ə-jŭj′) *tr.v.* **-judged, -judging, -judges.** 1. To determine or settle by judicial procedure; adjudicate. 2. To order or pronounce judicially; rule. 3. To award (costs or damages, for example) by law. 4. To consider or pronounce to be; deem. [Middle English *ajugen*, from Old French *ajuger*, from Latin *adjūdicāre*, to ADJUDICATE.]

ad·ju·di·cate (ə-jōō′dĭ-kāt′) *v.* **-cated, -cating, -cates.** —*tr.* 1. To hear and settle (a case) by judicial procedure. 2. To pronounce judicially; adjudge: *was adjudicated a bankrupt.* —*intr.* To act as a judge. Usually used with *on* or *upon.* [Latin *adjūdicāre*, to award (judicially) : *ad-*, to + *jūdicāre*, to be a judge, from *jūdex*, a judge.] **—ad·ju·di·ca·tion** (ə-jōō′dĭ-kā′shən) *n.* **—ad·ju·di·ca·tive** (ə-jōō′-dĭ-kā′tĭv, -kə-tĭv) *adj.* **—ad·ju·di·ca·tor** *n.*

ad·junct (ăj′ŭngkt′) *n.* 1. Something attached to another thing but in a subordinate or incidental relation. 2. A person associated with another in a subordinate or auxiliary capacity; a helper; an assistant. 3. A word or words added to clarify or modify other words in a sentence, but not grammatically essential to the sentence. 4. *Logic.* A nonessential attribute of a thing. —See Synonyms at **appendage.**
~*adj.* Added or connected in a subordinate or auxiliary capacity: *an adjunct clause.* [Latin *adjunctum*, from *adjunctus*, past participle of *adjungere*, to ADJOIN.] **—ad·junc·tion** (ə-jŭngk′shən) *n.* **—ad·junc·tive** (ə-jŭngk′tĭv) *adj.*

ad·ju·ra·tion (ăj′ŏŏ-rā′shən) *n.* An earnest or solemn appeal. —**ad·jur·a·to·ry** (ə-jŏŏr′ə-tôr′ē, -tōr′ē) *adj.*

ad·jure (ə-jŏŏr′) *tr.v.* **-jured, -juring, -jures. 1.** To command or enjoin solemnly, as under oath or penalty. **2.** To appeal to or entreat earnestly. [Middle English *adjuren*, from Latin *adjūrāre*, to swear to : *ad-*, to + *jūrāre*, to swear.] —**ad·jur·er**, **ad·ju·ror** *n.*

ad·just (ə-jŭst′) *v.* **-justed, -justing, -justs.** —*tr.* **1.** To change so as to match or fit; cause to correspond. **2.** To adapt; change so as to harmonize with new conditions. **3.** To regulate so as to make accurate or efficient. **4.** To decide how much is to be paid on (an insurance claim). —*intr.* To adapt oneself, as to changed conditions; become suited or fit. [Obsolete French *adjuster*, from Old French *ajoster*, from Vulgar Latin *adjuxtāre* (unattested), to put close to : Latin *ad-*, near to + *juxtā*, close by, near.] —**ad·just·a·ble** *adj.* —**ad·just·a·bly** *adv.* —**ad·just·er**, **ad·jus·tor** *n.* —**ad·jus·tive** *adj.*

ad·just·ment (ə-jŭst′mənt) *n.* **1.** The act of adjusting or state of being adjusted. **2.** A slight alteration or modification. **3.** A means for adjusting. **4.** The settlement of a debt or claim.

ad·ju·tant (ăj′ŏŏ-tənt) *n.* **1.** *Abbr.* **adj., adjt.** *Military.* A staff officer who helps a commanding officer with and is responsible for administrative work. **2.** An assistant. **3.** A stork, the **marabou** *(see).* [Latin *adjūtāns* (stem *adjūtant-*), present participle of *adjūtāre*, to assist, AID.] —**ad·ju·tan·cy**, **ad·ju·tant·ship** *n.*

adjutant general *n., pl.* **adjutants general.** *Abbr.* **A.G., AG** *Military.* **1.** An adjutant of a military unit having a general staff. **2.** An officer in charge of the National Guard of one of the states of the United States. **3. Adjutant General.** The chief administrative officer, a major general, of the U.S. Army.

adjutant stork *n.* The **marabou** *(see).* [Alluding to the military stiffness of its posture and gait.]

ad·ju·vant (ăj′ə-vənt) *adj.* Helping or contributing.
~*n.* One that aids; specifically, an ingredient that increases the effectiveness of a medicine.

Ad·ler (ăd′lər), **Alfred** (1870–1937). Austrian physician and psychiatrist. Originally a follower of Sigmund Freud, Adler broke away in 1911. He rejected Freud's emphasis on sexuality and held that much behavior arises from subconscious efforts to compensate for feelings of inferiority and that neurosis results from overcompensation. —**Ad·le·ri·an** (ăd-lîr′ē-ən) *adj. & n.*

ad lib (ăd lĭb′) *adv.* **1.** Without preparation; spontaneously. **2.** Without limit; freely. —See Synonyms at **extemporaneous.**

ad-lib (ăd-lĭb′) *v.* **-libbed, -libbing, -libs.** *Informal.* —*tr.* To improvise and deliver without rehearsal (words, music, or the like). —*intr.* To improvise a speech, lines, or the like; extemporize.
~*n.* Words, music, or actions ad-libbed.
~*adj.* Spoken or performed spontaneously; impromptu. [Shortened from AD LIBITUM.] —**ad-lib·ber** *n.*

ad lib·i·tum (ăd lĭb′ə-təm) *adv. Abbr.* **ad lib., ad libit.** *Music.* Without limit or restriction; performed as desired. Used as a direction. Compare **obbligato.** [Latin, "to the desire."]

ad li·tem (ăd lī′təm) *adv. Law.* For a lawsuit or action. Said of a guardian appointed for such a purpose.

ad loc (ăd lŏk′) *adv.* To (or at) the place already mentioned. [Latin *ad locum.*]

Adm. admiral; admiralty.

ad·man (ăd′măn′) *n., pl.* **-men** (-mĕn′). *Informal.* A man employed in the advertising business.

ad·meas·ure (ăd-mĕzh′ər) *tr.v.* **-ured, -uring, -ures.** To divide and distribute proportionally; apportion. [Middle English *amesuren*, from Old French *amesurer*, to measure out to.] —**ad·meas·ure·ment** *n.* —**ad·meas·ur·er** *n.*

Ad·me·tus (ăd-mē′təs) *Greek Mythology.* A king of Thessaly and the husband of Alcestis.

admin. administration; administrator.

ad·min·is·ter (ăd-mĭn′ĭs-tər) *v.* **-tered, -tering, -ters.** —*tr.* **1.** To have charge of; direct; manage (the affairs of a person, business, government, or the like). **2. a.** To give or perform in a formal or ritualistic way: *administer the last rites.* **b.** To apply or give as a remedy: *administer a sedative.* **3.** To dispense; put into operation: *administer justice.* **4.** To manage or dispose of (trusts and estates) under a will or an official appointment. **5.** To impose, offer, or tender (an oath, for example). —*intr.* **1.** To act as an administrator. **2.** To attend to the needs of others; minister. Used with *to: administering to their pleasure.* [Middle English *administren*, from Old French *administrer*, from Latin *administrāre*, to be an aid to : *ad-*, to + *ministrāre*, to serve, from *minister*, servant.] —**ad·min·is·tra·ble** *adj.* —**ad·min·is·trant** (ăd-mĭn′ĭs-trənt) *adj. & n.*

ad·min·is·trate (ăd-mĭn′ĭs-trāt′) *tr.v.* **-trated, -trating, -trates.** To administer; be in charge of the affairs of.

ad·min·is·tra·tion (ăd-mĭn′ĭs-trā′shən) *n. Abbr.* **admin. 1.** The management of affairs, especially in government or business. **2.** The people who make up the managing body of any institution, public or private. **3.** *Often* **Administration.** The executive branch of government or its term of office: *a member of the Reagan administration.* **4.** *Law.* The management and disposal of a trust or estate. **5.** The dispensing, applying, or tendering of something, such as an oath, sacrament, or medicine. —**ad·min·is·tra·tive** (ăd-mĭn′ĭ-strā′tĭv, -strə-tĭv) *adj.* —**ad·min·is·tra·tive·ly** *adv.*

ad·min·is·tra·tor (ăd-mĭn′ĭs-trā′tər) *n. Abbr.* **admin. 1.** One who administers, especially public or business affairs. **2.** *Law.* A person appointed to administer an estate.

ad·mi·ra·ble (ăd′mər-ə-bəl) *adj.* Deserving admiration; excellent. —**ad·mi·ra·ble·ness** *n.* —**ad·mi·ra·bly** *adv.*

ad·mi·ral (ăd′mər-əl) *n.* **1.** The commander in chief of a navy or fleet. **2.** *Abbr.* **Adm.** In the U.S., British, or Canadian Navy: **a.** An officer holding the next-to-highest rank, who commands a whole fleet. **b.** An **Admiral of the Fleet,** a **rear admiral,** or a **vice admiral** *(all of which see).* **3.** The ship carrying an admiral; a flagship. **4.** Any of various brightly colored butterflies of the genera *Limenitis* and *Vanessa.* [Middle English *a(d)miral,* from Medieval Latin *a(d)mīrālis* (reshaped as if from *admīrārī,* to admire), from Old French *amiral,* from Arabic *'amīr-al-,* "commander of" : *'amīr,* commander, EMIR + *al,* the.]

Admiral of the Fleet *n.* In the U.S., British, or Canadian navy, the officer holding the highest rank, equivalent to field marshal or general of the army. Also called "Admiral," "Fleet Admiral."

ad·mi·ral·ty (ăd′mər-əl-tē) *n., pl.* **-ties.** *Abbr.* **Adm. 1. a.** A court exercising jurisdiction over all maritime causes. **b.** Maritime law. **2. Admiralty.** The British government department that controls naval affairs.

Ad·mi·ral·ty Islands (ăd′mər-əl-tē). Group of 40 volcanic islands in the southwest Pacific Ocean. The islands lie in the Bismarck Archipelago, and are part of Papua New Guinea. Lorengau, the administrative center and chief port, is on Manus, the largest island.

ad·mi·ra·tion (ăd′mə-rā′shən) *n.* **1. a.** A feeling of pleasure and approval. **b.** A feeling of disinterested and pleased respect. **2.** An object of wonder; a marvel: *His success made him the admiration of all his friends.* **3.** *Archaic.* Wonder. —See Synonyms at **regard.**

ad·mire (ăd-mīr′) *tr.v.* **-mired, -miring, -mires. 1.** To look at with pleasure and approval: *stood in front of the mirror admiring himself.* **2.** To have a high opinion of; regard with respect. **3.** *Archaic.* To marvel or wonder at. [Latin *admīrārī,* to wonder at : *ad-,* to, at + *mīrārī,* to wonder, from *mīrus,* wonderful.] —**ad·mir·ing** *adj.* —**ad·mir·ing·ly** *adv.*

ad·mir·er (ăd-mīr′ər) *n.* One who admires; especially, a man who is attracted to a particular woman.

ad·mis·si·ble (ăd-mĭs′ə-bəl) *adj.* **1.** Capable of being accepted; allowable. Said especially of evidence in a court case. **2.** Qualified or permitted to enter. —**ad·mis·si·bil·i·ty** (ăd-mĭs′ə-bĭl′ə-tē), **ad·mis·si·ble·ness** *n.* —**ad·mis·si·bly** *adv.*

ad·mis·sion (ăd-mĭsh′ən) *n.* **1. a.** The act of admitting or allowing to enter. **b.** The state of being allowed to enter. **2.** The right to enter; access. **3.** The cost of entering; entrance fee. **4.** The act or process of acceptance and entry into a position or situation; appointment. **5.** A confession of crime or wrongdoing. **6.** A voluntary acknowledgment that something is true. —See Usage note at **admittance.** [Middle English *admissioun,* from Latin *admissiō* (stem *admissiōn-*), from *admittere* (past participle *admissus*), to ADMIT.] —**ad·mis·sive** (ăd-mĭs′ĭv) *adj.*

ad·mit (ăd-mĭt′) *v.* **-mitted, -mitting, -mits.** —*tr.* **1.** To permit to enter. **2.** To serve as an authorization of entrance: *This ticket admits the whole group.* **3.** To permit to join or exercise certain rights, functions, or privileges. **4.** To have room for; be able to accommodate. **5.** To allow the possibility of; permit. **6.** To acknowledge; confess: *admit the truth.* **7.** To grant as true or valid, as for the sake of argument; concede. **8.** To acknowledge as being lawful or valid. —*intr.* **1.** To allow the possibility; permit. Used with *of.* **2.** To allow entrance; afford access. Used with *to: This door admits to the main hall.* —See Synonyms at **acknowledge.** [Middle English *admitten,* from Latin *admittere,* to send in to : *ad-,* to + *mittere,* to send.]

ad·mit·tance (ăd-mĭt′əns) *n.* **1.** The act of admitting or entering. **2.** Permission to enter; the power or right of entrance. **3.** *Electricity.* The reciprocal of impedance. It is the ratio of a voltage to a current, is measured in siemens, and may be expressed as a complex quantity, the real part of which is conductance and the imaginary part susceptance.

Usage: Admittance applies largely to physical entry to a specific place (*admittance to the jury room*). In the corresponding sense of entry, *admission* is used figuratively (*admission of evidence to the court record*) or, when physical entry is involved, in the additional sense of right or privilege of participation (*admission to a club; price of admission to a theater*).

ad·mit·ted·ly (ăd-mĭt′ĭd-lē) *adv.* By general admission; granted that: *admittedly the quality is poor.*

ad·mix·ture (ăd-mĭks′chər) *n.* **1. a.** The act of mingling or mixing. **b.** The state of being mingled or mixed. **2.** That which is mingled or mixed; a mixture. **3.** Anything added in mixing; an ingredient. [From Latin *admixtus,* past participle of *admiscēre,* to mix into : *ad,* to + *miscēre,* to mix.]

ad·mon·ish (ăd-mŏn′ĭsh) *tr.v.* **-ished, -ishing, -ishes. 1.** To reprove mildly or kindly, but firmly. **2.** To counsel against something; caution; warn. **3.** To remind or advise about something forgotten or disregarded, by means of a warning, reproof, or exhortation. —See Synonyms at **warn.** [Middle English *admonissen,* back-formation from *admonesten* (the stem *admonest-* was mistaken for a past participle), from Old French *admonester,* from Vulgar Latin *admonestāre* (unattested), variant of Latin *admonēre,* to bring to (someone's) mind : *ad-,* to + *monēre,* to remind, advise.] —**ad·mon·ish·ing·ly** *adv.* —**ad·mon·ish·er** *n.* —**ad·mon·ish·ment** *n.*

Synonyms: rebuke, reprimand, reproach, reprove.

ad·mo·ni·tion (ăd′mə-nĭsh′ən) *n.* **1.** A mild rebuke or warning. **2.** Cautionary advice. [Middle English *admonicioun,* from Old

French *amonition,* from Latin *admonitiō* (stem *admonitiōn-*), from *admonēre,* to ADMONISH.]

ad·mon·i·to·ry (ăd-mŏn′ə-tôr′ē, -tōr′ē) *adj.* Cautionary.

ad·nate (ăd′nāt′) *adj. Biology.* Joined to or fused with another part or organ. Said of parts not usually united. [Latin *adnātus,* past participle of *adnāscī, agnāscī,* to be born in addition to. See **agnate.**] **—ad·na·tion** (ăd-nā′shən) *n.*

ad nau·se·am (ăd nô′zē-əm) *adv. Latin.* To a sickening or tedious degree.

ad·noun (ăd′noun′) *n. Grammar.* An adjective used as a noun, as in *the bold and the brave.* [AD- (additional) + NOUN (by analogy with ADVERB).] **—ad·nom·i·nal** (ăd-nŏm′ə-nəl) *adj.*

a·do (ə-do͞o′) *n.* Bustle; fuss; trouble; bother. [Middle English, from the phrase *at do,* "to do" : *at,* from Old Norse *at* (used with infinitive), to + *don,* to DO.]

a·do·be (ə-dō′bē) *n.* **1. a.** Clay or loess, probably wind-blown in origin, found in the deserts of the southwestern United States and Mexico. **b.** A sun-dried brick made from this or a similar material. **2.** A structure built with such bricks. [Spanish *adobe,* from Arabic *aṭṭōba, al-tōba,* "the brick."] **—a·do·be** *adj.*

ad·o·les·cence (ăd′l-ĕs′əns) *n.* **1.** The period of physical and psychological development from the onset of puberty to maturity. **2.** The condition of a person during that period.

ad·o·les·cent (ăd′l-ĕs′ənt) *adj.* **1.** Of, pertaining to, or undergoing adolescence. **2.** Immature in attitude or behavior; puerile: *adolescent dreams.*
~*n.* An adolescent person. —See Synonyms at **young.** [Middle English, from Old French, from Latin *adolēscēns* (stem *adolēscent-*), present participle of *adolēscere,* to grow up : *ad-,* toward + *alēscere,* to grow, "be nourished," inceptive of *alere,* to nourish.]

Ad·o·nai (ăd′ō-nī′). *Hebrew.* Lord. Used in Judaism as a spoken substitute for the name of God. See **Tetragrammaton.** [Hebrew *adōnāi,* "my lord(s)," from Phoenician *adōn,* lord.]

A·don·ic (ə-dŏn′ĭk, ə-dō′nĭk) *adj.* **1.** Of or designating a verse measure consisting of a dactyl followed by a spondee or trochee. **2.** Of or pertaining to Adonis.
~*n.* An Adonic verse. [This meter was said to have been first used in verses lamenting Adonis's death.]

A·don·is[1] (ə-dŏn′ĭs, ə-dō′nĭs). *Greek Mythology.* A youth loved by Aphrodite for his striking beauty. [Greek *Adōnis,* from Phoenician *adōn,* lord. See also **Adonai.**]

Adonis[2] *n.* A young man of great physical beauty.

a·dopt (ə-dŏpt′) *tr.v.* **adopted, adopting, adopts. 1.** To take into one's family through legal means and bring up as one's own child. **2.** To select and bring into a new relationship, as a friend, heir, or citizen, for example. **3.** To take and follow (a course of action, for example) by choice or assent: *adopt a new technique.* **4.** To take up and use (an idea or word, for example) as one's own. **5.** To take on or assume: *"He adopted the important air of a herald in red and gold"* (Stephen Crane). **6.** To vote to accept: *adopt a resolution.* **7.** To choose as a standard or required textbook or reference book in a school course. [Latin *adoptāre,* to choose for oneself : *ad-,* to + *optāre,* to choose, desire.] **—a·dopt·a·ble** *adj.* **—a·dopt·er** *n.* **—a·dop·tion** *n.*

a·dopt·ed (ə-dŏp′tĭd) *adj.* Related by adoption: *an adopted child.*

a·dop·tive (ə-dŏp′tĭv) *adj.* **1.** Related by adoption: *an adoptive parent.* **2.** Tending to adopt. **—a·dop·tive·ly** *adv.*

a·dor·a·ble (ə-dôr′ə-bəl, ə-dōr′-) *adj.* **1.** Delightful; lovable; charming. **2.** *Archaic.* Worthy of or eliciting worship. **—a·dor·a·bil·i·ty** (ə-dôr′ə-bĭl′ĭ-tē), **a·dor·a·ble·ness** *n.* **—a·dor·a·bly** *adv.*

ad·o·ra·tion (ăd′ə-rā′shən) *n.* **1.** The act of worship. **2.** Profound love or regard.

a·dore (ə-dôr′, ə-dōr′) *tr.v.* **adored, adoring, adores. 1.** To worship with divine honors. **2.** To love deeply. **3.** *Informal.* To like very much: *He adores being tickled.* —See Synonyms at **revere.** [Middle English *adoren,* from Old French *adorer,* from Latin *adōrāre,* to pray to : *ad-,* to + *ōrāre,* to speak, pray.] **—a·dor·er** *n.* **—a·dor·ing·ly** *adv.*

a·dorn (ə-dôrn′) *tr.v.* **adorned, adorning, adorns. 1.** To be a decoration to; lend beauty to: *"the pale mimosas that adorned the favourite promenade"* (Ronald Firbank). **2.** To decorate; furnish with ornaments. **3.** To add luster or distinction to. [Middle English *adornen,* from Old French *adorner,* from Latin *adornāre,* to put ornaments on : *ad-,* to + *ornāre,* to furnish, deck.] **—a·dorn·er** *n.* **—a·dorn·ment** *n.*

ADP *n.* An organic compound, $C_{10}H_{15}N_5O_{10}P_2$, that is formed when ATP undergoes hydrolysis of the terminal phosphate bond and releases its energy. [*A*denosine *d*i*p*hosphate.]

A.D.P. automatic data processing.

ad rem (ăd rĕm′) *adj. Latin.* To the point; pertinent. **—ad rem** *adv.*

ad·re·nal (ə-drē′nəl) *adj.* **1.** At, near, or on the kidneys. **2.** Of or pertaining to the adrenal glands or their secretions.
~*n.* An adrenal gland. [AD- (toward, near) + RENAL.]

adrenal cortex *n.* The three-zoned center of the adrenal glands.

adrenal gland *n.* Either of two small dissimilarly shaped endocrine glands, one located above each kidney, consisting of the cortex, which secretes corticosteroid hormones, and the medulla, which secretes epinephrine. Also called "suprarenal gland."

a·dren·a·lin (ə-drĕn′əl-ĭn) *n.* Also **ad·ren·a·line. 1.** A secretion of the adrenal glands, **epinephrine** *(see).* **2.** Broadly, a substance that is supposed to cause heightened emotion and a sudden increase in physical strength, as during fear or anger. [ADRENAL + -INE.]

ad·re·ner·gic (ăd′rə-nûr′jĭk) *adj.* Of, pertaining to, or having chemical activity like that of epinephrine. Said of certain nerve fibers. [ADREN(ALINE) + Greek *ergon,* work, action.]

ad·re·no·cor·ti·co·trop·ic (ə-drē′nō-kôr′tĭ-kō-trŏp′ĭk, -trō′pĭk) *adj.* Also **ad·re·no·cor·ti·co·troph·ic** (-trŏf′ĭk, -trō′fĭk). Stimulating or otherwise acting upon the cortex of the adrenal gland. [ADREN(AL) + CORTICO- + -TROPIC.]

adrenocorticotropic hormone *n.* A hormone, **ACTH** *(see).*

A·dri·an (ā′drē-ən), **Edgar Douglas, 1st Baron** (1889–1977). British physiologist. His research on nerve cells led to major advances in the understanding of the nervous and muscular systems. He won the 1932 Nobel Prize for physiology and medicine.

Adrian IV, born Nicholas Breakspear (*c.* 1100–1159). Also **Ha·dri·an IV** (hā′drē-ən). Pope (1154–59); the only English pope.

Adrianople. See **Edirne.**

A·dri·at·ic (ā′drē-ăt′ĭk) *adj.* Of or pertaining to the Adriatic Sea or to the peoples inhabiting its islands and coasts.

Adriatic Sea. A northern arm of the Mediterranean, between Italy and the Balkan Peninsula. It is *c.* 800 kilometers (500 miles) long, from the Gulf of Venice in the north to the Strait of Otranto.

a·drift (ə-drĭft′) *adv.* **1.** Without anchor or steering; drifting. **2.** Purposelessly; aimlessly. **3.** Wrong; not according to plan: *His schemes went badly adrift.* **4.** *Chiefly British Informal.* Unfastened or unattached: *Your shoelace has come adrift.* **—a·drift** *adj.*

a·droit (ə-droit′) *adj.* **1.** Dexterous; deft. **2.** Resourceful and quick-thinking under pressure. —See Synonyms at **dexterous.** [French, from *à droit,* "rightly" : *à,* to, at, from Latin *ad-* + *droit,* right, from Latin *dīrectus,* DIRECT.] **—a·droit·ly** *adv.* **—a·droit·ness** *n.*

ad·sci·ti·tious (ăd′sĭ-tĭsh′əs) *adj.* Not inherent or essential; added as a supplementary part. [From Latin *adscītus,* derived, assumed, past participle of *adscīscere,* to approve, arrogate to oneself : *ad-,* to + *scīscere,* to seek to know, assume, inceptive of *scīre,* to know.]

ad·sorb (ăd-sôrb′, -zôrb′) *tr.v.* **-sorbed, -sorbing, -sorbs.** To take up by adsorption. Compare **absorb.** [AD- + Latin *sorbēre,* to drink in, suck.]

ad·sor·bate (ăd-sôr′bĭt, -zôr′-) *n.* An adsorbed substance.

ad·sor·bent (ăd-sôr′bənt, -zôr′-) *adj.* Capable of adsorption.
~*n.* An adsorbent material, such as activated carbon.

ad·sorp·tion (ăd-sôrp′shən, -zôrp′-) *n.* The assimilation of gas, vapor, or dissolved matter by the surface of a solid. [ADSORB + -TION.] **—ad·sorp·tive** *adj.*

adsuki bean. Variant of **adzuki bean.**

ad·u·lar·i·a (ăj′o͞o-lâr′ē-ə) *n. Mineralogy.* A variety of **orthoclase** *(see).* [Italian, from French *adulaire,* after *Adula,* mountain group in Switzerland.]

ad·u·late (ăj′o͞o-lāt′) *tr.v.* **-lated, -lating, -lates.** To praise excessively or fawningly. [Back-formation from ADULATION.] **—ad·u·la·tor** *n.* **—ad·u·la·to·ry** (ăj′o͞o-lə-tôr′ē, -tōr′ē) *adj.*

ad·u·la·tion (ăj′o͞o-lā′shən) *n.* Excessive praise or flattery. [Middle English *adulacioun,* from Old French *adulation,* from Latin *adulātiō,* from *adulārī,* to flatter.]

a·dult (ə-dŭlt′, ăd′ŭlt) *n.* **1.** One who has attained maturity or legal age. **2.** A fully grown, mature organism, such as an insect that has completed its final stage of metamorphosis.
~*adj.* **1.** Fully developed and mature. **2.** Pertaining to, befitting, or intended for mature persons: *adult education.* **3.** Sexually explicit; pornographic. Used euphemistically: *adult films.* [Latin *adultus,* past participle of *adolescere,* to grow up. See **adolescent.**] **—a·dult·hood** *n.*

a·dul·ter·ant (ə-dŭl′tər-ənt) *n.* A substance that adulterates.
~*adj.* Adulterating.

a·dul·ter·ate (ə-dŭl′tə-rāt′) *tr.v.* **-ated, -ating, -ates.** To make impure, spurious, or inferior by adding extraneous or improper ingredients.
~*adj.* **1.** Spurious; adulterated; corrupt: *"prefer the adulterate enjoyments of the town to the genuine pleasures of a country"* (Smollett). **2.** Adulterous. [Latin *adulterāre,* to pollute, commit adultery.] **—a·dul·ter·a·tion** (ə-dŭl′tə-rā′shən) *n.* **—a·dul·ter·a·tor** *n.*

a·dul·ter·er (ə-dŭl′tər-ər) *n.* A person, especially a man, who commits adultery.

a·dul·ter·ess (ə-dŭl′trĭs, ə-dŭl′tər-ĭs) *n.* A woman who commits adultery.

a·dul·ter·ine (ə-dŭl′tə-rīn′, -rīn) *adj.* **1.** Characterized by adulteration; spurious; fake. **2.** Unauthorized by law; illegal. **3.** Born of adultery: *adulterine offspring.* [Latin *adulterīnus* from *adulterāre,* to commit adultery, ADULTERATE.]

a·dul·ter·ous (ə-dŭl′tər-əs, -trəs) *adj.* Characterized by, inclined to, or having committed adultery. **—a·dul·ter·ous·ly** *adv.*

a·dul·ter·y (ə-dŭl′tər-ē, -trē) *n., pl.* **-ries.** Voluntary sexual intercourse between a married person and a partner other than the lawful husband or wife. [Middle English *adulterie, a(d)vouterie,* from Old French *avoutrie, avoutire,* from Latin *adulterium,* from *adulter,* adulterer, from *adulterāre,* to ADULTERATE.]

ad·um·bral (ăd-ŭm′brəl) *adj.* In shadow. [AD- (in) + Latin *umbra,* shadow.]

ad·um·brate (ăd′əm-brāt′, ə-dŭm′-) *tr.v.* **-brated, -brating, -brates. 1.** To give a sketchy outline of. **2.** To prefigure indistinctly; foreshadow. **3.** To disclose partially or guardedly. **4.** To overshadow; obscure. [Latin *adumbrāre,* to overshadow : *ad-,* to + *umbra,* shadow.] **—ad·um·bra·tion** (ăd′əm-brā′shən) *n.* **—ad·um·bra·tive** (ə-dŭm′brə-tĭv) *adj.* **—ad·um·bra·tive·ly** *adv.*

a·dust (ə-dŭst′) *adj.* **1.** Burnt; scorched. **2.** Melancholy; gloomy. [Middle English, from Latin *adūstus,* from the past participle of *adūrere,* to set fire to : *ad-,* to + *ūrere,* to burn.]

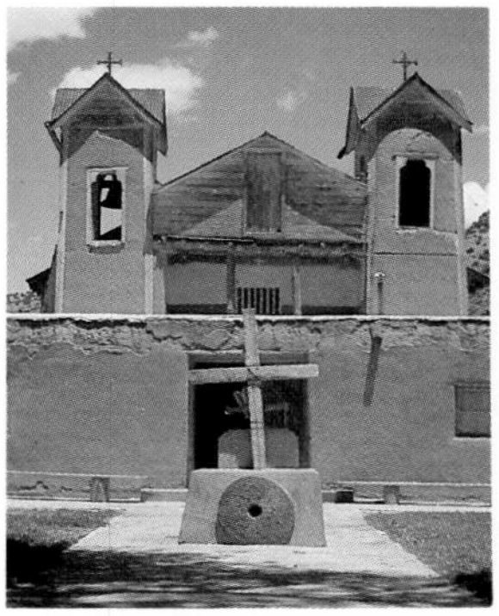

adobe *An adobe church in New Mexico built of sun-dried bricks that are made from a mixture of clay and straw.*

PRONUNCIATION KEY

ă, pat; ā, pay; âr, care;
ä, father, are; b, bib;
ch, church; d, deed; ĕ, pet;
ē, be; f, fife; g, gag; h, hat;
hw, which; ĭ, pit; ī, pie;
îr, pier; j, judge; k, kick;
l, lid, needle; m, mum;
n, no, sudden; ng, thing;
ŏ, pot; ō, toe; ô, paw, for;
oi, noise; ou, out; o͝o, book;
o͞o, boot; p, pop; r, roar;
s, sauce; sh, ship, dish;
t, tight; th, thin, path;
th, this, bathe; ŭ, cut; ûr, fur;
v, valve; w, with; y, yes;
z, zebra, size; zh, vision;
ə, about, item, edible, gallop, circus, peaceful

IN FOREIGN WORDS:

à, *Fr.* ami; œ, *Fr.* feu, *Ger.* schön; ü, *Fr.* tu, *Ger.* über; KH, *Ger.* ich, *Scot.* loch; N, *Fr.* bon; y′, *Fr.* Compiègne

STRESS MARKS:

Primary stress: ′
in·cite′ (ĭn-sīt′)
Secondary stress: ′
in′sight′ (ĭn′sīt′)

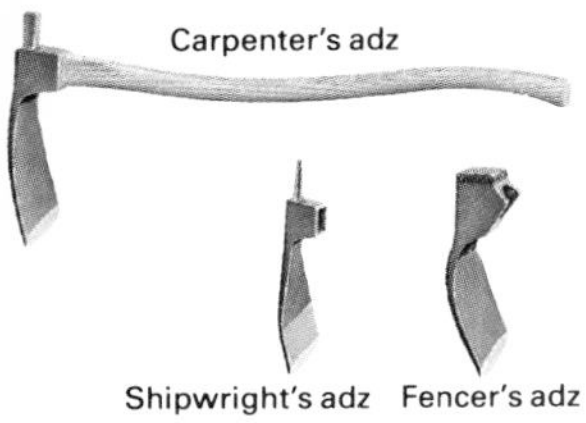
Carpenter's adz
Shipwright's adz
Fencer's adz

adz *A carpenter's cutting tool on a handle. The adz is a forerunner of the plane, and has been in common use for more than 5,000 years.*

adv. adverb; adverbial.

ad va·lo·rem (ăd və-lôr′əm, -lōr′-) *adj. Latin. Abbr.* **a.v., ad val.** In proportion to the value: *ad valorem duties on imported goods.* **—ad va·lo·rem** *adv.*

ad·vance (ăd-văns′, -väns′) *v.* **-vanced, -vancing, -vances.** *—tr.* **1.** To move or bring forward in position. **2.** To put forward; propose; suggest. **3.** To aid the growth or progress of; further. **4.** To raise in rank; promote. **5.** To cause to occur sooner; hasten. **6.** To raise in amount or rate; increase. **7.** To pay (money or interest) before legally due. **8.** To supply or lend, especially on credit. *—intr.* **1.** To go or move forward or onward. **2.** To make progress; improve; grow. **3.** To rise in rank, position, or value.
∼n. **1.** The act or process of moving or going forward. **2.** Improvement; progress. **3.** A rise or increase of price or value. **4. advances.** Personal approaches made to secure acquaintance, favor, or an agreement; overtures. **5. a.** The furnishing of funds or goods on credit. **b.** The funds or goods so furnished; a loan. **6.** A payment of money before legally or normally due. **—in advance. 1.** In front. **2.** Ahead of time; beforehand; early. Often used with *of.*
∼adj. **1.** Made or given ahead of time; prior. **2.** Going before; in front; forward. [Middle English *advancen,* from Old French *avancier,* from Vulgar Latin *abantiāre* (unattested), from Latin *abante,* "from before" : *ab-,* away from + *ante,* before.] **—ad·vance·ment** *n.* **—ad·vanc·er** *n.*
Synonyms: *forward, further, promote.*

ad·vanced (ăd-vănst′, -vänst′) *adj.* **1. a.** Far on in development or progress: *The child is very advanced for her age.* **b.** Far on in life: *advanced in years.* **2.** Ahead of contemporary thought or practice: *advanced ideas.* **3.** At a high level of difficulty: *advanced mathematics.*

advanced gas-cooled reactor *n. Abbr.* **A.G.R.** A type of nuclear reactor in which the coolant is gaseous carbon dioxide, the moderator is graphite, and the fuel is ceramic uranium dioxide in a stainless-steel casing.

advance guard *n. Military.* A detachment of troops sent ahead of the main force to reconnoiter and provide protection.

ad·van·tage (ăd-văn′tĭj, ăd-vän′-) *n.* **1.** A factor favorable or conducive to success. **2.** Benefit or profit; gain. **3.** A position of relative superiority: *has the advantage.* **4.** In racket games, the first point scored after deuce, or the resulting score. In this sense, also called "ad," "vantage." **—take advantage of. 1.** To put to good use; avail oneself of. **2.** To profit selfishly by; exploit. **3.** To seduce. Used euphemistically. **—to advantage.** So as to produce a good or favorable effect: *She uses her husky voice to advantage.*
∼tr.v. **advantaged, -taging, -tages.** To afford profit or gain to; benefit. [Middle English *avantage,* from Old French, "the condition of being ahead," from *avant,* before, from Latin *abante,* (from) before. See **advance.**]

ad·van·ta·geous (ăd′văn-tā′jəs, ăd′vən-) *adj.* Affording benefit or gain; profitable; useful. **—ad·van·ta·geous·ly** *adv.* **—ad·van·ta·geous·ness** *n.*

ad·vec·tion (ăd-vĕk′shən) *n. Meteorology.* The transfer of heat or water vapor by horizontally moving air. [Latin *advectiō* (stem *advectiōn-*), conveyance, from *advehere* (past participle *advectus*), to carry to : *ad-,* to + *vehere,* to carry.]

ad·vent (ăd′vĕnt′) *n.* The coming or arrival, especially of something expected or momentous: *"a melodious tinkle of strings announced the advent of the minstrels"* (Ronald Firbank). [Middle English, from Latin *adventus,* from the past participle of *advenīre,* to come to.]

Advent *n.* **1.** The birth of Christ. **2.** See **Second Coming. 3.** The period including four Sundays before Christmas, the first of which is called Advent Sunday.

Ad·vent·ist (ăd′vĕn-tĭst) *n.* A member of any of several Christian denominations that believe Christ's second coming and the end of the world are near at hand. See **Seventh-Day Adventist. —Ad·vent·ism** *n.*

ad·ven·ti·ti·a (ăd′vĕn-tĭsh′ē-ə) *n.* The outermost covering of an organ, especially of a blood vessel. [New Latin, from Latin *adventīcius,* ADVENTITIOUS.]

ad·ven·ti·tious (ăd′vĕn-tĭsh′əs) *adj.* **1.** Acquired by accident; added by chance; not inherent: *adventitious scribblings in the margins of a manuscript.* **2.** *Biology.* Appearing in an unusual place or in an irregular or sporadic manner: *adventitious shoots.* [Latin *adventīcius,* "arriving (from outside)," from *adventus,* arrival, ADVENT.] **—ad·ven·ti·tious·ly** *adv.* **—ad·ven·ti·tious·ness** *n.*

ad·ven·tive (ăd-vĕn′tĭv) *adj. Biology.* Not native to, and not fully established in, a new habitat or environment; locally or temporarily naturalized: *an adventive weed.*
∼n. Biology. An adventive organism. [Latin *adventus,* arrival, ADVENT.] **—ad·ven·tive·ly** *adv.*

Advent Sunday *n.* The first of the four Sundays of Advent; the Sunday nearest to the last day of November.

ad·ven·ture (ăd-vĕn′chər) *n.* **1.** An undertaking of a hazardous nature; a risky enterprise: *Fording the stream was an adventure.* **2.** An unusual experience or course of events marked by excitement and suspense. **3.** Participation in hazardous or exciting experiences: *a wandering life, full of adventure.* **4.** A financial speculation or business venture.
∼v. **adventured, -turing, -tures.** *—tr.* To venture upon; risk; dare. *—intr.* **1.** To take risks; engage in hazardous activities. **2.** To dare to enter or embark. Used with *on* or *upon.* [Middle English *aventure,* from Old French, from Vulgar Latin *(rēs) adventūra* (unattested), "(a thing) that will happen," from Latin *adventūrus,* future participle of *advenīre,* to arrive. See **advent.**]

ad·ven·tur·er (ăd-vĕn′chər-ər) *n.* **1.** One who adventures. **2.** A mercenary soldier. **3.** A heavy speculator. **4.** One who seeks wealth and social position by unscrupulous means.

ad·ven·ture·some (ăd-vĕn′chər-səm) *adj.* Daring; venturesome. **—ad·ven·ture·some·ly** *adv.* **—ad·ven·ture·some·ness** *n.*

ad·ven·tur·ess (ăd-vĕn′chər-ĭs) *n.* A woman who seeks social and financial advancement by dubious means.

ad·ven·tur·ism (ăd-vĕn′chə-rĭz′əm) *n.* Recklessness in political or financial activities. **—ad·ven·tur·ist** *n. & adj.*

ad·ven·tur·ous (ăd-vĕn′chər-əs) *adj.* **1.** Inclined to undertake new and daring enterprises or activities; bold; daring: *trails for adventurous hikers.* **2.** Hazardous; risky. —See Synonyms at **reckless. —ad·ven·tur·ous·ly** *adv.* **—ad·ven·tur·ous·ness** *n.*

ad·verb (ăd′vûrb′) *n. Abbr.* **adv. 1.** A part of speech comprising a class of words that modify a verb, adjective, whole sentence, or other adverb. **2.** A word belonging to this class, such as *rapidly* in *He runs rapidly.* [Middle English, from Old French *adverbe,* from Latin *adverbium* (translation of Greek *epirrhēma,* "added word") : *ad-,* additional + *verbum,* word.]

ad·ver·bi·al (ăd-vûr′bē-əl) *adj.* Of, pertaining to, or used as an adverb: *an adverbial phrase.*
∼n. **1.** An adverb. **2.** A word, phrase, or clause functioning as an adverb. *Nicely* and *in a nice way* can both be adverbials. **—ad·ver·bi·al·ly** *adv.*

ad ver·bum (ăd vûr′bəm) *adv. Latin.* Word for word; verbatim.

ad·ver·sar·i·al (ăd′vər-sâr′ē-əl) *adj.* Involving, or considered to involve, adversaries or strongly opposed interests: *an adversarial relationship.*

ad·ver·sar·y (ăd′vər-sĕr′ē) *n., pl.* **-ies.** An opponent; an enemy. **—the Adversary.** The Devil. [Middle English *adversarie,* from Latin *adversārius,* opponent, from *adversus,* ADVERSE.]

ad·ver·sa·tive (ăd-vûr′sə-tĭv) *adj. Grammar.* Expressing antithesis or opposition. Said of words and clauses.
∼n. An adversative word, such as *however* or *but.* [Latin *adversātivus,* from *adversārī,* to be opposed to, from *adversus,* ADVERSE.] **—ad·ver·sa·tive·ly** *adv.*

ad·verse (ăd-vûrs′, ăd′vûrs′) *adj.* **1.** Antagonistic in design or effect; hostile; opposed: *adverse criticism.* **2.** Contrary to one's interests or welfare; unfavorable; unpropitious: *adverse circumstances.* **3.** In an opposite or opposing direction or position: *adverse winds.* **4.** *Botany.* Facing the axis or main stem. —See Synonyms at **contrary.** [Middle English, from Old French *advers,* from Latin *adversus,* past participle of *advertere,* to turn toward (with hostility).] **—ad·verse·ly** *adv.* **—ad·verse·ness** *n.*

adverse possession *n. Law.* Occupation of a property in a way that threatens the rights of the owner.

ad·ver·si·ty (ăd-vûr′sə-tē) *n., pl.* **-ties. 1.** A state of hardship, suffering, or affliction; misfortune. **2.** A calamitous event. —See Synonyms at **misfortune.**

ad·vert[1] (ăd-vûrt′) *intr.v.* **-verted, -verting, -verts.** To call attention; refer: *advert to a problem.* [Middle English *a(d)verten,* from Old French *a(d)vertir,* from Vulgar Latin *advertīre* (unattested), from Latin *advertere,* to turn toward. See **adverse.**] **—ad·vert·ence, ad·vert·en·cy** *n.* **—ad·vert·ent** *adj.* **—ad·vert·ent·ly** *adv.*

ad·vert[2] (ăd′vûrt′) *n. Chiefly British Informal.* An advertisement.

ad·ver·tise (ăd′vər-tīz′) *v.* **-tised, -tising, -tises.** *—tr.* **1. a.** To make public announcement of: *advertise a vacancy.* **b.** To cause to be generally or publicly known: *Roosevelt did not conceal his disability, but he did not advertise it.* **2.** To proclaim publicly the qualities or advantages of (a product or service, for example) so as to increase sales. **3.** *Archaic.* To warn or notify. *—intr.* **1.** To call the attention of the public to a product, service, or the like: *The store advertises on television.* **2.** To ask in a public notice, as in a newspaper; make a public request. Often used with *for*: *I'm advertising for a new roommate.* [Middle English *a(d)vertisen,* from Old French *a(d)vertir* (present participle *advertissant*), TO ADVERT.] **—ad·ver·tis·er** *n.*

ad·ver·tise·ment (ăd′vər-tīz′mənt, ăd-vûr′tĭs-, -tĭz-) *n. Abbr.* **advt.** Any public notice, such as a poster, newspaper display, television, film, or radio announcement, designed to sell a product, publicize a vacancy or service, influence opinion, or the like.

ad·ver·tis·ing (ăd′vər-tī′zĭng) *n.* **1.** The action of attracting public attention, as to a product or business. **2.** The business of preparing and distributing advertisements for publication or broadcast. **3.** Printed or broadcast advertisements collectively.

ad·vice (ăd-vīs′) *n.* **1.** Opinion from one not immediately concerned as to what could or should be done in a given situation; counsel. **2.** *Often* **advices.** Information or a report, especially when communicated from a distance: *advices from an ambassador.* **3.** A formal notice regarding a financial transaction: *a stock-purchase advice.* [Middle English *a(d)vise,* from Old French *a(d)vis,* opinion, from Vulgar Latin *advīsum* (unattested), opinion, probably from some such phrase as *ad (meum) vīsum,* "according to (my) view" : *ad,* to + *vīsum,* view, from the neuter past participle of *vidēre,* to see.]

ad·vis·a·ble (ăd-vī′zə-bəl) *adj.* Worthy of being recommended or suggested; prudent; expedient. **—ad·vis·a·bil·i·ty** (ăd-vī′zə-bĭl′ə-tē), **ad·vis·a·ble·ness** *n.* **—ad·vis·a·bly** *adv.*

ad·vise (ăd-vīz′) *v.* **-vised, -vising, -vises.** *—tr.* **1.** To offer advice to; counsel: *aides who advise the president.* **2.** To recommend by way of advice; suggest: *My broker advised caution.* **3.** To inform; notify: *advise a person of a decision.* *—intr.* **1.** To offer or be able to give advice. **2.** To consult; take counsel. Used with *with*: *You should*

PRONUNCIATION KEY

ă, pat; ā, pay; âr, care;
ä, father, are; b, bib;
ch, church; d, deed; ĕ, pet;
ē, be; f, fife; g, gag; h, hat;
hw, which; ĭ, pit; ī, pie;
îr, pier; j, judge; k, kick;
l, lid, needle; m, mum;
n, no, sudden; ng, thing;
ŏ, pot; ō, toe; ô, paw, for;
oi, noise; ou, out; o͝o, book;
o͞o, boot; p, pop; r, roar;
s, sauce; sh, ship, dish;
t, tight; th, thin, path;
th, this, bathe; ŭ, cut; ûr, fur;
v, valve; w, with; y, yes;
z, zebra, size; zh, vision;
ə, about, item, edible, gallop, circus, peaceful

IN FOREIGN WORDS:

à, *Fr.* ami; œ, *Fr.* feu, *Ger.* schön; ü, *Fr.* tu, *Ger.* über; KH, *Ger.* ich, *Scot.* loch; N, *Fr.* bon; y′, *Fr.* Compiègne

STRESS MARKS:

Primary stress: ′
in·cite′ (ĭn-sīt′)
Secondary stress: ′
in′sight′ (ĭn′sīt′)

advise with your associates before making a decision. [Middle English *a(d)visen,* from Old French *a(d)viser,* from Vulgar Latin *advīsāre* (unattested), to observe (influenced by Latin *advīsum,* ADVICE) : Latin *ad-,* to, at + *vīsere,* desiderative of *vidēre* (past participle *vīsus*), to see.] **—ad•vi•so•ry** *adj.*

Usage: In the sense of "inform" or "notify," the use of *advise* is usually restricted to business correspondence.

ad•vised (ăd-vīzd′) *adj.* Considered; thought out. Used chiefly in the combinations *well-advised* and *ill-advised.* **—ad•vis•ed•ly** (ăd-vī′zĭd-lē) *adv.*

ad•vise•ment (ăd-vīz′mənt) *n.* **1.** Careful consideration. **2.** Consultation.

ad•vis•er, ad•vi•sor (ăd-vī′zər) *n.* A person who offers advice, especially in an official or professional capacity.

ad•vo•caat, ad•vo•kaat (ăd′vō-kät′) *n.* A sweet, thick, yellow Dutch liqueur made of raw egg yolks and brandy. [Dutch, shortened from *advocaatenborrel,* from *advocaat,* ADVOCATE (noun) + *borrel,* drink.]

ad•vo•ca•cy (ăd′və-kə-sē) *n.* Active support, as of a cause.

ad•vo•cate (ăd′və-kāt′) *tr.v.* **-cated, -cating, -cates.** To speak in favor of; recommend. —See Synonyms at **support.**

~n. (ăd′və-kĭt, -kāt′). **1.** A person who argues for a cause or idea; a supporter or defender. **2.** A person who pleads on another's behalf; an intercessor. **3.** *Law.* In Scotland and South Africa, a **barrister** *(see).* —See Usage note at **lawyer.** [Middle English *a(d)vocat,* a lawyer, from Old French, from Latin *advocātus,* "one summoned (to give evidence)," from *advocāre,* to call or summon to : *ad,* to + *vocāre,* to call.] **—ad•vo•ca•to•ry** (ăd-vŏk′ə-tôr′ē, -tōr′ē) *adj.*

ad•vow•son (ăd-vou′zən) *n.* In English ecclesiastical law, the right to nominate the successor to a vacant benefice. [Middle English *avoweson, advounson,* from Norman French *a(d)voeson,* variant of Old French *avoueson,* from Medieval Latin *advocātiō,* presentation, summoning, from Latin *advocāre,* to summon, ADVOCATE.]

advt. advertisement.

ad•y•na•mi•a (ăd′ə-nā′mē-ə, ā′dī-năm′ē-ə) *n.* Loss of energy or strength, especially after illness; feebleness or debility. [A- (not) + Greek *dunamis,* power, from *dunasthai,* to be able.] **—ad•y•nam•ic** (ăd′ə-năm′ĭk, ā′dī-năm′ĭk) *adj.*

ad•y•tum (ăd′ə-təm) *n., pl.* **-ta** (-tə). The sanctum in an ancient temple. [Latin, from Greek *aduton,* neuter of *adutos,* not to be entered : *a-,* not + *duein†,* to enter, sink.]

adz, adze (ădz) *n.* An axlike tool with an arched blade at right angles to the handle, used for dressing wood. [Middle English *adse,* Old English *adesa†.*]

ad•zu•ki bean (ăd-zōō′kē) *n.* Also **ad•su•ki bean** (ăd-sōō′kē, -zōō′-). A plant, *Phaseolus angularis,* with yellow flowers and pods bearing edible seeds, widely cultivated as a food crop in the Orient. [Japanese *azuki,* "red bean."]

A.E.A. Actor's Equity Association.

A.E. and P. Ambassador Extraordinary and Plenipotentiary.

AEC, A.E.C. Atomic Energy Commission.

ae•ci•o•spore (ē′sē-ō-spôr′, -spōr′). Also **ae•cid•i•o•spore** (ē-sĭd′-ē-ō-spôr′, -spōr) *n. Botany.* A rust spore, formed in a chainlike series in an aecium. [*Aecium* + *spore.*]

ae•ci•um (ē′sē-əm, ē′shē-əm) *n., pl.* **-cia** (-sē-ə, -shē-ə). Also **ae•cid•i•um** (ē-sĭd′ē-əm), *pl.* **-ia** (-ē-ə). *Botany.* A cuplike structure in rust fungi, containing chains of aeciospores. [New Latin, from Greek *aikia,* injury (rust fungi are destructive), from *aikēs,* unseemly.] **—ae•ci•al** (ē′sē-əl, -shē-əl) *adj.*

a•e•des (ā-ē′dēz) *n., pl.* **aedes.** Any mosquito of the genus *Aedes,* such as *A. aegypti,* which transmits yellow fever and dengue. [New Latin *Aedes,* from Greek *aēdēs,* unpleasant : *a-,* not + *ēdos,* pleasant.]

ae•dile (ē′dīl′) *n.* In ancient Rome, an elected official who was responsible for public works and games and for the supervision of markets, the grain supply, and the water supply. [Latin *aedīlis,* "(one) concerned with buildings," from *aedēs,* house.]

Ae•ge•an (ĭ-jē′ən) *adj.* **1.** Of or pertaining to the Aegean Sea. **2.** Of, pertaining to, or designating the prehistoric civilization that flourished in the Aegean area in the Bronze Age.

Aegean Sea. A northeastern arm of the Mediterranean between Greece and Turkey. It is roughly 630 kilometers (380 miles) long and 300 kilometers (186 miles) wide and contains numerous, mainly Greek islands. The **Aegean Islands** include the Cyclades, the Dodecanese, and the Sporades.

Ae•gi•na (ē-jī′nə). *Greek* **Ai•gi•na** (ā′gĭn-ə). Greek town and island in the Aegean, near Athens. It was a prosperous and important city-state in the 5th century B.C., but declined in importance after defeat by the Athenians, who expelled its inhabitants.

Ae•gir (ăg′ər). *Norse Mythology.* The god of the sea.

ae•gis (ē′jĭs) *n.* Also **e•gis. 1.** *Greek Mythology.* The shield of Zeus, lent by him to Athena. **2.** Protection or sponsorship: *a conference held under the aegis of the World Health Organization.* Compare **auspices.** [Latin, from Greek *aigis* (often depicted as a goatskin, and associated by folk etymology with *aix,* stem *aig-,* goat).]

Ae•gis•thus (ē-jĭs′thəs). In Greek legend, the son of Thyestes and lover of Clytemnestra.

Ael•fric (ăl′frĭk), also called "Grammaticus" (*c.* 955–*c.* 1020). English abbot and writer. He is considered to be the greatest prose writer of Anglo-Saxon times. His prolific output included *Homilies* (the first Christian texts written in English), *Lives of the Saints,* a Latin grammar, and translations of Latin religious literature.

-aemia. Variant of **-emia.**

Ae•ne•as (ĭ-nē′əs). In classical legend, a Trojan prince, the son of Anchises and Aphrodite, who, as recounted in the Aeneid, escaped the sack of Troy and after an arduous sea voyage settled in Italy, where his descendants eventually founded Rome.

Ae•ne•id (ĭ-nē′ĭd) *n.* An epic poem in Latin by Virgil, telling of the adventures of Aeneas after the destruction of Troy.

a•e•ne•ous (ā-ē′nē-əs) *adj.* Having a brassy or golden-green color. [Latin *aeneus, aenus,* of bronze or copper, from *aes,* bronze, copper.]

Ae•o•li•an (ē-ō′lē-ən) *adj.* **1.** Of or pertaining to Aeolus, god of the winds. **2.** *Music.* Of or designating a mode represented by the white notes of the scale of A on the piano keyboard. **3. aeolian.** Of or caused by the action of the wind. Said of erosion.

~n. **1.** A member of one of the major Greek tribes that settled in central Greece and on the west coast of Asia Minor. **2.** Aeolic.

Aeolian harp *n.* A musical instrument consisting of an open box with strings stretched across it that sound when wind passes over them. Also called "wind harp."

Aeolian Islands. See **Lipari Islands.**

Ae•ol•ic (ē-ŏl′ĭk) *n.* One of the four main dialects of ancient Greek, spoken in Thessaly, Boeotia, and in the coastal region of Asia Minor north of Ionia. Compare **Arcado-Cyprian, Attic-Ionic, Doric.**

ae•ol•i•pile (ē-ŏl′ə-pīl′) *n.* A prototype steam turbine invented *c.* 100 B.C., consisting of a hollow sphere fitted with projecting angled exhaust jets and mounted to permit free rotation about the steam inlet axis. [Latin *aeolipila,* from Greek *aiolipulē,* "wind-vent" : *Aiolos,* AEOLUS + *pulē,* gate.]

Ae•o•lus (ē′ə-ləs). *Greek Mythology.* The god of the winds. [Latin, from Greek *Aiolos,* from *aiolos†,* quick-moving.]

aeon. Variant of **eon.**

aer•ate (âr′āt′) *tr.v.* **-ated, -ating, -ates. 1.** To charge (liquid) with a gas, especially carbon dioxide. **2.** To expose to the circulation of air for purification. **3.** To supply (blood) with oxygen. [AER(O)- + -ATE.] **—aer•a•tion** (âr-ā′shən) *n.*

aer•a•tor (âr′ā′tər) *n.* A device for aerating liquids.

aer•i•al (âr′ē-əl, ā-ĭr′ē-əl) *adj.* **1.** Existing or functioning in the air: *an aerial telephone cable.* **2.** Reaching high into the air; lofty. **3.** Light and airy; insubstantial; imaginary. **4.** Of, by, or from aircraft: *an aerial photograph.* **5.** *Botany.* Borne in the air rather than underground or under water: *aerial roots.*

~n. (âr′ē-əl). *Electronics.* An **antenna** *(see).* [Latin *āerius,* from Greek *aērios,* from *aēr,* air.]

aer•i•al•ist (âr′ē-əl-ĭst) *n.* An acrobat who performs on a tightrope, trapeze, or similar apparatus.

aerial ladder *n.* A ladder that can be extended to reach high places, especially one mounted on a fire engine.

aer•ie (âr′ē, ăr′ē, ĭr′ē) *n.* Also **aer•y, eyr•ie. 1.** The nest of an eagle or other predatory bird, built on a crag or other high place. **2.** A room, house, or fortification built on a height. [Medieval Latin *aeria, aerea,* from Old French *aire, aere,* from Latin *ārea,* open field, threshing floor, bird's nest (possibly influenced by Latin *ager,* native place, acre).]

aero-, aer- *prefix.* Indicates: **1.** Air, gas, or the atmosphere; for example, **aerate, aerosphere. 2.** Aircraft; for example, **aeromedicine.** [Middle English, from Old French, from Latin, from Greek, from *aēr,* air.]

aer•o•bal•lis•tics (âr′ō-bə-lĭs′tĭks) *n. Used with a singular verb.* The ballistics of missiles and other projectiles in the atmosphere.

aer•o•bat•ics (âr′ō-băt′ĭks) *n. Used with a singular or plural verb.* The performance of stunts, such as rolls and loops, in an airplane or glider. [AERO- + (ACRO)BATICS.]

aer•obe (âr′ōb′) *n.* An organism, such as a bacterium, requiring molecular oxygen or air to live. [French *aérobie,* "air-life" : AERO- + Greek *bios,* life.]

aer•o•bic (â-rō′bĭk) *adj.* **1.** Of or indicating a process, such as respiration, dependent on molecular oxygen or air. **2.** Of or pertaining to aerobes. **3.** Of or pertaining to aerobics. **—aer•o•bic•al•ly** *adv.*

aer•o•bics (â-rō′bĭks) *n. Used with a singular verb.* A system of vigorous physical exercises, sometimes combined with dance routines, designed to speed up the breathing and stimulate blood circulation. [AERO- + Greek *bios,* life + -ICS.]

aer•o•bi•ol•o•gy (âr′ō-bī-ŏl′ə-jē) *n.* The study of airborne microorganisms, pollen, spores, and the like, especially those causing disease.

aer•o•bi•o•sis (âr′ō-bī-ō′sĭs) *n.* Life in the presence of molecular oxygen or air. [AERO- + -BIOSIS.]

aerodrome. *Chiefly British.* Variant of **airdrome.**

aer•o•dy•nam•ic (âr′ō-dī-năm′ĭk) *adj.* **1.** Of or pertaining to aerodynamics. **2.** Embodying aerodynamic principles; streamlined: *the car's sleek aerodynamic lines.*

aer•o•dy•nam•ics (âr′ō-dī-năm′ĭks) *n. Used with a singular verb.* The dynamics of gases, especially of atmospheric interactions with moving objects. See feature, next page.

aer•o•dyne (âr′ə-dīn′) *n.* Any heavier-than-air aircraft that derives its lift chiefly from motion. [AERO- + *-dyne,* from Greek *dunamis,* power, from *dunasthai,* to be able.]

aer•o•em•bo•lism (âr′ō-ĕm′bə-lĭz′əm) *n.* The presence of nitrogen bubbles in the blood and tissues caused by a sudden reduction in atmospheric pressure, as occurs in decompression sickness.

aer•o engine (âr′ō) *n.* An engine used to power an aircraft.

aerofoil. *Chiefly British.* Variant of **airfoil.**

aer•o•gram, aer•o•gramme (âr′ə-grăm′) *n.* An airmail letter written on a standard, lightweight form that folds into the shape of an envelope and can be sent at a low postage rate. Also called "air letter." [AERO- + -GRAM.]

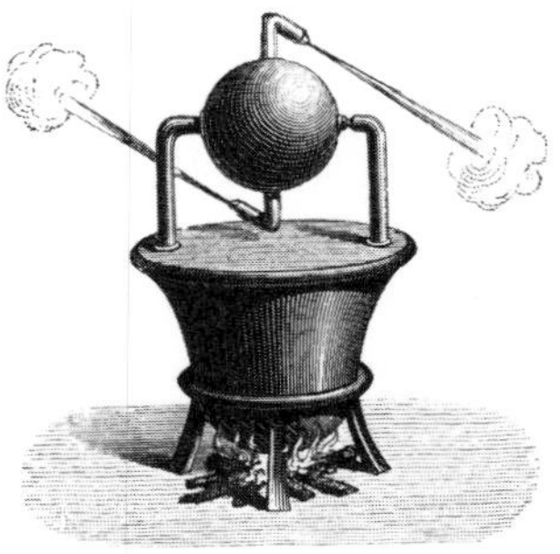

aeolipile *The Greek engineer Hero of Alexandria invented this simple form of steam turbine in 100 B.C. A closed caldron produced steam that passed into a hollow ball and then escaped through narrow, bent pipes, causing the ball to rotate. It was not until the 1600's, however, that the idea of using steam for power was really exploited.*

aerodynamics

BASICS OF FLIGHT
How control, thrust, and lift keep an airplane in the air

When, on December 17, 1903, the Wright brothers in Kitty Hawk, North Carolina, made the first powered flight in an airplane, Wilbur Wright acknowledged his debt to a British engineer of 100 years before.

The work done by Sir George Cayley between 1799 and 1809 laid the foundations of modern aerodynamics. Models and gliders designed by him proved that heavier-than-air flight was possible. Cayley also estab-

lished the principles that govern the flight of airplanes: that an aircraft needs a lifting force to raise it into the air, a system of control, and a means of propulsion.

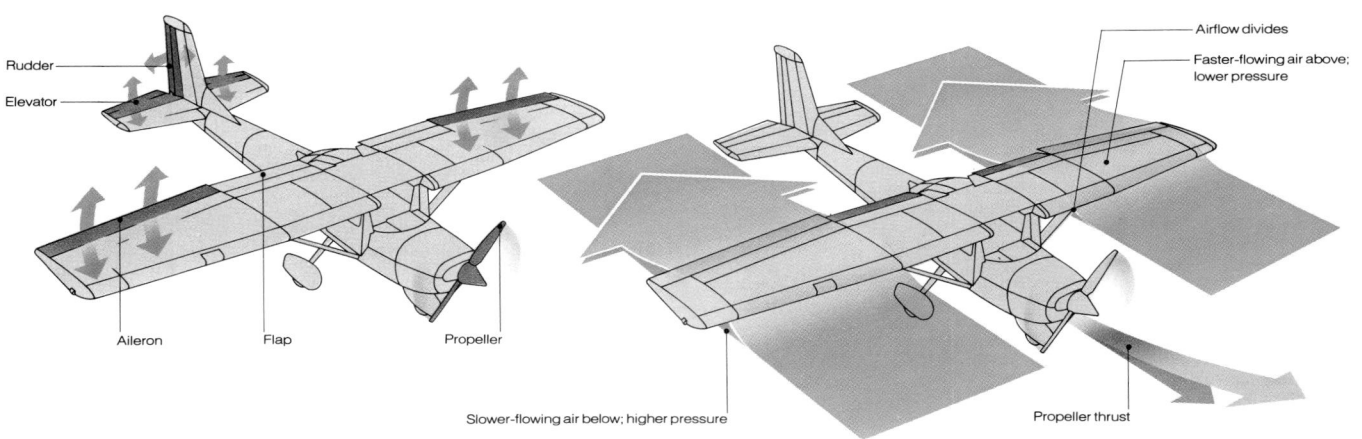

CONTROL AND THRUST *On a simple, light aircraft, a propeller powered by an internal-combustion engine provides thrust through the air. The moving control surfaces consist of ailerons and flaps on the wings and a rudder and elevators on the tail.*

LIFT *Air passing over the curved top surface of the wing has farther to go, and therefore travels faster, than the air passing under the flatter, bottom surface. The pressure of the slower-moving air under the wing is greater, and the wings lift.*

---

aer·o·lite (âr′ə-līt′) *n.* A chiefly silicious meteorite. [AERO- + -LITE.] —**aer·o·lit·ic** (âr′ə-lĭt′ĭk) *adj.*

aer·ol·o·gy (âr-ŏl′ə-jē) *n.* Total atmospheric meteorology as opposed to surface-based study; climatology. [AERO- + -LOGY.] —**aer·o·log·ic** (âr′ə-lŏj′ĭk), **aer·o·log·i·cal** *adj.* —**aer·ol·o·gist** (âr-ŏl′ə-jĭst) *n.*

aer·o·me·chan·ics (âr′ō-mĭ-kăn′ĭks) *n. Used with a singular verb.* The science of the motion and equilibrium of air and other gases, comprising aerodynamics and aerostatics. —**aer·o·me·chan·i·cal** *adj.* —**aer·o·me·chan·i·cal·ly** *adv.*

aer·o·med·i·cine (âr′ō-mĕd′ə-sĭn) *n.* The medical study and treatment of disturbances, disorders, and diseases resulting from or associated with atmospheric flight. Compare **aviation medicine.** —**aer·o·med·i·cal** *adj.*

aer·o·me·te·or·o·graph (âr′ō-mē′tē-ôr′ə-grăf′, -grăf′) *n.* An aircraft instrument for simultaneously recording temperature, atmospheric pressure, and humidity.

aer·om·e·ter (âr-ŏm′ə-tər) *n.* A device for determining the weight and density of air or other gas.

aer·o·naut (âr′ə-nôt′) *n.* A pilot or navigator of a balloon or lighter-than-air craft. [French *aéronaute* : AERO- (air) + Greek *nautēs,* sailor. See **nautical.**]

aer·o·nau·tics (âr′ə-nô′tĭks) *n. Used with a singular verb.* **1.** The science of aircraft design and construction. **2.** The theory and practice of aircraft navigation. —**aer·o·nau·tic, aer·o·nau·ti·cal** *adj.*

aer·on·o·my (âr-ŏn′ə-mē) *n.* The study of the upper atmosphere, especially of regions of ionized gas. [AERO- + -NOMY.]

aer·o·pause (âr′ə-pôz′) *n.* The region of the atmosphere above which aircraft cannot fly. [AERO- + -PAUSE.]

aer·o·pha·gia (âr′ə-fā′jə) *n.* The abnormal, spasmodic swallowing of air, especially as a symptom of hysteria.

aer·o·pho·bi·a (âr′ə-fō′bē-ə) *n.* The abnormal fear of air or of drafts.

aer·o·phyte (âr′ə-fīt′) *n. Botany.* An epiphyte *(see).*

aeroplane. *Chiefly British.* Variant of **airplane.**

aer·o·sol (âr′ə-sôl′, -sŏl′, -sōl′) *n.* **1.** A gaseous suspension of fine solid or liquid particles. **2. a.** A substance, such as a detergent, insecticide, or paint, packaged under pressure with a gaseous propellant for release as an aerosol. **b.** A container from which an aerosol is released; an aerosol bomb. [AERO- + SOL(UTION).]

aerosol bomb *n.* A usually hand-held container or dispenser from which an aerosol is released.

aer·o·space (âr′ō-spās′) *adj.* **1.** Of or designating Earth's atmosphere and the space beyond. **2.** Of or pertaining to the science or technology of flight. —**aer·o·space** *n.*

aerospace vehicle *n.* A vehicle capable of flight both within and outside Earth's atmosphere.

aer·o·sphere (âr′ō-sfîr′) *n.* The lower portion of the atmosphere in which both unmanned and manned flight is possible; the troposphere and stratosphere.

aer·o·stat (âr′ō-stăt′) *n.* An aircraft, especially a balloon or dirigi-

ble, deriving its lift from the buoyancy of surrounding air rather than from aerodynamic motion. [French *aérostat* : AERO- + -STAT.] —**aer·o·stat·ic** (âr′ō-stăt′ĭk), **aer·o·stat·i·cal** *adj.*

aer·o·stat·ics (âr′ō-stăt′ĭks) *n. Used with a singular verb.* The science of gases in equilibrium and of the equilibrium of balloons or aircraft under changing atmospheric flight conditions.

aer·o·ther·mo·dy·nam·ics (âr′ō-thûr′mō-dī-năm′ĭks) *n. Used with a singular verb.* The study of the thermodynamics of gases, especially at high relative velocities.

ae·ru·go (ĭ-rōō′gō) *n.* Verdigris *(see).* [Latin *aerūgō,* from *aes* (stem *aer-*), copper, bronze.]

aer·y[1] (âr′ē, ā′ə-rē) *adj. Poetic.* Ethereal; insubstantial.

aery[2] Variant of **aerie.**

Aes·chy·lus (ĕs′kə-ləs, ēs′-) (*c.* 525–456 B.C.). Greek dramatist. He wrote some 90 plays, of which 7 complete tragedies survive. His best-known work is the trilogy of the *Oresteia* (458 B.C.): *Agamemnon, Choephori,* and *Eumenides.* His plays are concerned with the justice of the gods and are based on tales from mythology and history.

Aes·cu·la·pi·an (ĕs′kyōō-lā′pē-ən) *adj.* Of or pertaining to the healing art; medical: *the Aesculapian art.*

Aes·cu·la·pi·us (ĕs′kyōō-lā′pē-əs). The Roman god of medicine and healing; identified with the Greek god Asclepius.

Ae·sir (ā′sîr, ē′sîr) *pl.n.* The gods of Norse mythology. [Old Norse, plural of *āss,* a god.]

Ae·sop (ē′sŏp′, ē′səp) (6th century B.C.). Supposed author of *Aesop's Fables.* Nothing is known for certain about his life, but he is said to have been Greek and born a slave and to have been deformed. The fables are moral tales, originating in folklore, with animal protagonists. Among the best-known are "The Tortoise and the Hare" and "The Fox and the Grapes."

Ae·so·pi·an (ē-sō′pē-ən) *adj.* Also **Ae·sop·ic** (ē-sŏp′ĭk). **1.** In the manner of Aesop's animal fables. **2.** Expressed allegorically or obliquely so as to elude political censorship.

aes·thete, es·thete (ĕs′thēt′) *n.* A person who has, or affects to have, a sensitive appreciation of the beautiful, especially in art. [Back-formation from AESTHETIC.]

aes·thet·ic, es·thet·ic (ĕs-thĕt′ĭk) *adj.* **1.** Of or pertaining to aesthetics. **2.** Of or concerning the criticism of taste or the appreciation of the beautiful. **3.** Having or showing a well-developed sense of beauty. [French *esthétique,* from German *ästhetisch,* from New Latin *aestheticus,* from Greek *aisthētikos,* pertaining to sense perception, from *aisthēta,* perceptible things, from *aisthenasthai,* to perceive.] —**aes·thet·i·cal·ly** *adv.*

aes·the·ti·cian, es·the·ti·cian (ĕs′thə-tĭsh′ən) *n.* A specialist in aesthetics or the theory of beauty.

aes·thet·i·cism, es·thet·i·cism (ĕs-thĕt′ə-sĭz′əm) *n.* **1.** The pursuit of the sensuously beautiful; devotion to beauty and refined taste. Sometimes used derogatorily to characterize an excessive or affected appreciation of beauty. **2. a.** The belief that beauty is the basic principle from which all other principles, especially moral principles, are derived. **b.** The belief that art and artists should be judged according to aesthetic considerations alone.

aes·thet·ics, es·thet·ics (ĕs-thĕt′ĭks) *n. Used with a singular verb.* The branch of philosophy dealing with the nature and perception of the beautiful.

aes·ti·val, es·ti·val (ĕs′tə-vəl, ĕs-tī′-) *adj.* Of or appearing in summer. [Middle English *estival*, from Old French, from Latin *aestivālis*, from *aestīvus*, from *aestās*, summer.]

aes·ti·vate, es·ti·vate (ĕs′tə-vāt′) *intr.v.* **-vated, -vating, -vates.** To pass the summer, especially in a state of dormancy, as lungfish and some other animals do. Compare **hibernate.** [Latin *aestīvāre*, from *aestīvus*, AESTIVAL.]

aes·ti·va·tion, es·ti·va·tion (ĕs′tə-vā′shən) *n.* **1.** *Zoology.* A state of dormancy or torpor during the summer or periods of drought. Compare **hibernation. 2.** *Botany.* The arrangement of petals, sepals, and other floral organs in the unopened bud.

ae·ta·tis su·ae (ē-tā′tĭs sōō′ē). *Abbr.* **aetat., aet.** *Latin.* Of his (or her) age.

Aethelred. See **Ethelred.**

Aethelstan. See **Athelstan.**

ae·ther (ē′thər) *n.* **1. Aether.** *Greek Mythology.* The poetic personification of the clear upper air breathed by the Olympians. **2.** Variant of **ether** (sense 3).

aethereal. Variant of **ethereal.**

aetiology. Variant of **etiology.**

AF, A.F. 1. air force. **2.** Anglo-French. **3.** audio frequency.

Af. Africa; African.

a.f. audio frequency.

a·far (ə-fär′) *adv.* At or to a distance; far away. [Middle English *afer*, from *on fer*, at a distance, and *of fer*, from a distance, from *fer*, FAR.]

Afars and Issas, French Territory of the. See **Djibouti.**

AFB air force base.

a·feard, a·feared (ə-fîrd′) *adj. Regional & Archaic.* Afraid; frightened: *"Be not afeared; the isle is full of noises"* (Shakespeare). [Middle English *afered*, Old English *āfǣred*, past participle of *āfǣran*, to frighten : *ā-*, intensive prefix + *fǣran*, to frighten, from *fǣr*, fear.]

af·fa·ble (ăf′ə-bəl) *adj.* Easy to speak to; approachable; amiable. [Old French, from Latin *affābilis*, from *affāri*, to speak to : *ad-*, to + *fārī*, to speak.] **—af·fa·bil·i·ty** *n.* **—af·fa·bly** *adv.*

af·fair (ə-fâr′) *n.* **1.** Anything that has been done or is to be done or dealt with. **2. affairs. a.** Personal or business concerns in general: *a man of affairs.* **b.** Matters or events of public interest: *affairs of state.* **3.** Any object or contrivance: *Our first car was a ramshackle affair.* **4.** A private matter; a personal concern. **5.** A matter causing scandal and controversy: *the Dreyfus affair.* **6.** A sexual relationship, usually of limited duration, between two people who are not married to one another. [Middle English *afere*, from Old French *afaire*, from the phrase *a faire*, "to do" : *a*, to, from Latin *ad-* + *faire*, to do, from Latin *facere*.]

af·faire d'hon·neur (à-fâr′ dô-nœr′) *n. French.* A matter in which honor is at stake; a duel.

af·fect¹ (ə-fĕkt′) *tr.v.* **-fected, -fecting, -fects. 1.** To have an effect on; bring about a change in. **2.** To touch or move the emotions of. **3.** To have an adverse effect on; especially, to attack or infect. Used of disease, pain, or the like. **4.** To allot or assign. Used only in the passive.
~ *n.* (ăf′ĕkt′). *Psychology.* **1.** A feeling or emotion as distinguished from cognition, thought, or action. **2.** A strong feeling having active consequences. [Latin *afficere* (past participle *affectus*), to do something to, exert influence on : *ad-*, to + *facere*, to do.]
Synonyms: impress, influence, move, strike, touch.
Usage: Affect and effect have no senses in common; therefore the tendency to confuse the words must be guarded against closely. As verbs, *affect* (the more common) is used principally in the senses of influence (*how smoking affects health*) and pretense or imitation (*affecting nonchalance to hide fear*), whereas *effect* applies only to accomplishment or execution (*reductions designed to effect economy; means adopted to effect an end*). As nouns, the terms can be kept straight by remembering that *affect* is now confined to psychology.

af·fect² (ə-fĕkt′) *tr.v.* **-fected, -fecting, -fects. 1.** To simulate in order to make some desired impression; pretend to feel: *affect indifference.* **2.** To imitate; assume: *affect an American accent.* **3. a.** To display a preference for. **b.** *Archaic.* To fancy; love. **c.** To tend to by nature; tend to assume: *affect crystalline form.* [Middle English *affecter*, from Latin *affectāre*, to strive after, frequentative of *afficere* (past participle *affectus*), to AFFECT.] **—af·fect·er** *n.*

af·fec·ta·tion (ăf′ĕk-tā′shən) *n.* **1.** A pretense or false display. **2.** Any artificial behavior adopted to impress others. [Latin *affectātiō* (stem *affectātiōn-*), from *affectāre*, to strive after, AFFECT.]

af·fect·ed¹ (ə-fĕk′tĭd) *adj.* Emotionally stirred or moved.

affected² *adj.* **1.** Assumed or simulated to impress others. **2.** Speaking or behaving in an artificial or insincere way to make a particular impression. **3.** Disposed or inclined. Used with *to* or *toward*: *was well affected to their cause.* **4.** Fancied; taken up: *a book much affected by experts in the subject.* **—af·fect·ed·ly** *adv.* **—af·fect·ed·ness** *n.*

af·fect·ing (ə-fĕk′tĭng) *adj.* Full of pathos; touching; moving: *an affecting sight.* —See Synonyms at **moving. —af·fect·ing·ly** *adv.*

af·fec·tion (ə-fĕk′shən) *n.* **1.** A fond or tender feeling toward another. **2.** Often **affections.** Feeling or emotion. **3.** Any pathological condition of the mind or body. **4.** The act of affecting or state of being affected. **5.** Mental disposition or tendency. —See Syn-

onyms at **love.** [Middle English *affecioun*, from Old French *affection*, from Latin *affectiō* (stem *affectiōn-*), (friendly) disposition, from *afficere*, to AFFECT.] **—af·fec·tion·al** *adj.* **—af·fec·tion·al·ly** *adv.*

af·fec·tion·ate (ə-fĕk′shə-nĭt) *adj.* **1.** Having or showing fond feelings or affection; loving; tender. **2.** *Archaic.* Strongly or favorably disposed. Used with *to.* **—af·fec·tion·ate·ly** *adv.* **—af·fec·tion·ate·ness** *n.*

af·fec·tive (ə-fĕk′tĭv) *adj.* **1.** *Psychology.* Pertaining to or resulting from emotions or feelings rather than from thought. **2.** Pertaining to or arousing affection or emotion; emotional. **—af·fec·tiv·i·ty** (ăf′-ĕk-tĭv′ə-tē) *n.*

af·fen·pin·scher (ăf′ən-pĭn′chər, ä′fən-) *n.* Any of a breed of small dogs of European origin, having dark, wiry, shaggy hair and a tufted muzzle. [German *Affenpinscher*, "monkey-terrier" (so called because its face resembles a monkey's) : *Affe*, monkey, APE + *Pinscher*, terrier (see **Doberman pinscher**).]

af·fer·ent (ăf′ər-ənt) *adj.* Directed toward a central organ or section, as are nerves that conduct impulses from the periphery of the body inward to the brain or spinal cord. Compare **efferent.** [Latin *afferēns* (stem *afferent-*), present participle of *afferre*, to bring toward : *ad-*, toward + *ferre*, to bring.]

af·fet·tu·o·so (ăf′fĕt-tŏo-ō′zō) *adv. Music.* With tender or passionate feeling. Used as a direction. [Italian.] **—af·fet·tu·o·so** *adj.*

af·fi·ance (ə-fī′əns) *tr.v.* **-anced, -ancing, -ances.** To promise (oneself or another) in marriage; betroth. [Middle English *affiaunce*, from Old French *affiance*, "trust," from *affier*, to trust to, from Medieval Latin *affīdāre* : Latin *ad-*, to + *fīdāre*, variant of Latin *fīdere*, to trust.]

af·fi·ant (ə-fī′ənt) *n. Law.* One who makes an affidavit. [Old French, present participle of *affier*, to trust to. See **affiance.**]

af·fi·da·vit (ăf′ə-dā′vĭt) *n. Law.* A written declaration made under oath before a notary public or other authorized officer. [Medieval Latin *affīdāvit*, "he has pledged," from *affīdāre*, to trust to. See **affiance.**]

af·fil·i·ate (ə-fĭl′ē-āt′) *v.* **-ated, -ating, -ates.** **—***tr.* **1.** To adopt as an associate or subsidiary member or branch of a group or larger organization: *an affiliated member; a union affiliated with the AFL-CIO.* **2.** To associate (oneself) as a subordinate or subsidiary. Used with *with.* **3.** *Law.* To impute the paternity of (an illegitimate child). Used with *upon* or *to.* **—***intr.* To associate or connect oneself: *We decided to affiliate.*
~ *n.* (ə-fĭl′ē-ĭt). A person or organization associated with another in a subordinate relationship. [Medieval Latin *affīliāre*, "to take to oneself as a son" : *ad-*, to + *fīlius*, son.] **—af·fil·i·a·tion** (ə-fĭl′ē-ā′-shən) *n.*

af·fine (ə-fīn′) *adj.* **1.** Of or pertaining to a mathematical transformation of coordinates that is equivalent to a translation, contraction, or expansion with respect to a fixed origin and fixed coordinate system. **2.** Of or pertaining to the geometry of affine transformations. [Old French *affin*, AFFINED.]

af·fined (ə-fīnd′) *adj.* Joined by kinship or affinity. [French *affiné*, from Old French *affin*, closely related, from Latin *affīnis*, neighboring, allied by marriage : *ad-*, near to + *fīnis*, border.]

af·fin·i·ty (ə-fĭn′ə-tē) *n., pl.* **-ties. 1.** A natural personal attraction or liking: *A good swimmer, she always seemed to have an affinity to water.* **2.** Relationship by marriage or adoption rather than by blood. **3.** An inherent similarity between organisms or things: *The language has some affinities with Russian.* **4.** A chemical or physical attraction or attractive force. —See Synonyms at **likeness.** [Middle English *affinite*, from Old French *afinite*, from Latin *affīnitās*, from *affīnis*, AFFINED.]

af·firm (ə-fûrm′) *v.* **-firmed, -firming, -firms.** **—***tr.* **1.** To declare positively or firmly; maintain the truth or existence of, especially in response to a question or doubt: *affirmed his innocence of the accusations.* **2.** To ratify or confirm. **—***intr. Law.* To declare solemnly and formally to tell the truth, but without taking an oath: *Witnesses may swear or affirm.* —See Synonyms at **assert.** [Middle English *affermen*, from Old French *afermer*, from Latin *affirmāre*, "to give firmness to," strengthen, assert : *ad-*, to + *firmāre*, to make firm, from *firmus*, firm.] **—af·firm·a·ble** *adj.* **—af·firm·a·bly** *adv.* **—af·firm·ant** *adj. & n.* **—af·firm·er** *n.*

af·fir·ma·tion (ăf′ər-mā′shən) *n.* **1.** The act of affirming or state of being affirmed. **2.** *Law.* A solemn and formal declaration to tell the truth, as made by a person who conscientiously objects to taking an oath. **3.** Any formal or solemn declaration.

af·firm·a·tive (ə-fûr′mə-tĭv) *adj.* **1.** Responding with the word *yes* or any other expression of agreement or consent: *an affirmative reply.* **2.** Asserting that something is true as represented; confirming. **3.** *Logic.* Designating a proposition in which the predicate states something about the subject to be true; for example, *Apples have seeds* is an affirmative proposition.
~ *n.* **1.** A word or phrase showing agreement or assent: *My request was answered in the affirmative.* **2.** The side in a debate that upholds a proposition.
~ *interj.* Used, especially in a military context, in place of *yes* to express confirmation or consent. Compare **negative. —af·firm·a·tive·ly** *adv.*
Usage: The expressions *in the affirmative* and *in the negative,* as in *she answered in the affirmative,* are generally regarded as pompous. *She answered yes* would be more acceptable even at the most formal levels of style.

affirmative action *n.* Action taken to provide opportunities, as in admissions or employment, for members of groups suffering from the effects of past or present discrimination. Also used adjectivally: *an affirmative-action employer.*

af·fix (ə-fĭks′) *tr.v.* **-fixed, -fixing, -fixes. 1.** To secure (an object) to another; attach: *affix a label to a parcel.* **2.** To impute; attribute: *affix blame for the error to him.* **3.** To place at the end; append: *affix a postscript.*
~*n.* (ăf′ĭks). **1.** Something that is attached, joined, or added. **2.** *Grammar.* A word element, such as a prefix or suffix, that can only occur attached to a base, stem, or root. [Medieval Latin *affīxāre* : Latin *ad-*, to + *fīxāre*, to fix, frequentative of *fīgere* (past participle *fīxus*), to fasten.] —**af·fix·er** *n.*

af·fla·tus (ə-flā′təs) *n.* A creative impulse; an inspiration. Used chiefly in the phrase *divine afflatus.* [Latin *afflātus*, inspiration, past participle of *afflāre*, to breathe on : *ad-*, toward + *flāre*, to blow.]

af·flict (ə-flĭkt′) *tr.v.* **-flicted, -flicting, -flicts.** To inflict physical or mental suffering upon; cause great distress to. [Middle English *afflicten*, from Latin *affligere* (past participle *afflīctus*), to dash against : *ad-*, to + *flīgere*, to strike.] —**af·flic·ter** *n.* —**af·flic·tive** *adj.* —**af·flic·tive·ly** *adv.*

af·flic·tion (ə-flĭk′shən) *n.* A condition or cause of pain, suffering, or distress, such as disease or grief.

af·flu·ence (ăf′lōō-əns) *n.* **1.** A plentiful supply of material goods; the state of being affluent; wealth. **2.** An abundance.

af·flu·ent (ăf′lōō-ənt) *adj.* **1.** Amply supplied with material goods and comforts; wealthy: *the affluent society.* **2.** Copious; abundant. **3.** Flowing freely.
~*n.* A stream or river that flows into another or other body of water; a tributary. [Middle English, from Old French, from Latin *affluēns* (stem *affluent-*), present participle of *affluere*, to flow to : *ad-*, toward + *fluere*, to flow.] —**af·flu·ent·ly** *adv.*

af·flux (ăf′lŭks′) *n.* A flowing toward a particular area: *an afflux of blood to the head.* [Medieval Latin *affluxus*, from Latin, past participle of *affluere*, to flow to. See **affluent.**]

af·ford (ə-fôrd′, ə-fōrd′) *tr.v.* **-forded, -fording, -fords. 1.** To have the financial means for; be able to meet the expense of. Preceded by *can* or *be able.* **2.** To be able to spare or give up. Preceded by *can* or *be able.* **3.** To be able to do or bear (something) without incurring serious loss, difficulty, or criticism. Preceded by *can* or *be able: He can afford to take a tolerant attitude.* **4.** To provide or give: *The balcony affords a marvelous view.* [Middle English *aforthen*, Old English *geforthian*, to further, achieve, carry out, from *forthian*, to promote, from *forth*, forward.] —**af·ford·a·ble** *adj.*

af·for·est (ə-fôr′ĭst, ə-fŏr′-) *tr.v.* **-ested, -esting, -ests.** To convert (open land) into forest. [Medieval Latin *afforestāre* : *ad-*, to + *forestāre*, from Late Latin *forestis*, FOREST.] —**af·for·es·ta·tion** (ə-fôr′ĭs-tā′shən, ə-fŏr′-) *n.*

af·fran·chise (ə-frăn′chīz′) *tr.v.* **-chised, -chising, -chises.** To free from servitude; liberate from obligation or liabilities. [15th century : alteration of Old French *affranchis* (stem *affranchiss-*), to free, from *franchis*, to free.] —**af·fran·chise·ment** *n.*

af·fray (ə-frā′) *n. Law.* A public quarrel or brawl noisy enough to disturb those not involved. —See Synonyms at **conflict.**
~*tr.v.* **affrayed, -fraying, -frays.** *Archaic.* To frighten. [Middle English, from Old French *effray, esfrei*, from *affreer, esfreer*, to fight in public, from Vulgar Latin *exfridāre* (unattested), "to break the peace" : Latin *ex*, out of + Frankish *frithuz* (unattested), peace.]

af·fri·cate (ăf′rĭ-kĭt) *n. Phonetics.* A speech sound produced when the breath stream is completely stopped and then released at articulation; for example, the *t* plus *sh* sound in *churn* or *clutch* or the *j* sound in *judge.* Also called "affricative." [Latin (*vox*) *affricāta*, "rubbed" (sound), feminine past participle of *affricāre*, to rub against : *ad-*, to + *fricāre*, to rub.] —**af·fri·cate** (ăf′rĭ-kāt′) *v.* —**af·fri·ca·tion** (ăf′rĭ-kā′shən) *n.* —**af·fric·a·tive** *adj. & n.*

af·fric·a·tive (ə-frĭk′ə-tĭv) *adj.* Of, pertaining to, or forming an affricate.
~*n.* An **affricate** (see).

af·fright (ə-frīt′) *tr.v.* **-frighted, -frighting, -frights.** *Archaic.* To frighten; terrify.
~*n. Archaic.* **1.** Terror. **2.** A cause of terror. —**af·fright·ment** *n.*

af·front (ə-frŭnt′) *tr.v.* **-fronted, -fronting, -fronts. 1.** To slight or insult openly; cause offense to. **2.** *Archaic.* To meet face to face defiantly; confront. —See Synonyms at **offend.**
~*n.* **1.** An open or intentional slight or insult. **2.** Anything that causes offense. [Middle English *affronten*, from Old French *afronter*, from Vulgar Latin *affrontāre* (unattested) : Latin *ad-*, to + *frōns* (stem *front-*), forehead, FRONT.]

af·fu·sion (ə-fyōō′zhən) *n.* A pouring on of water, especially as in baptism. [Latin *affūsiō* (stem *affūsiōn-*), from *affūsus*, past participle of *affundere*, to pour on : *ad-*, to + *fundere*, to pour.]

Af·ghan (ăf′găn′, -gən) *n.* **1.** A native or inhabitant of Afghanistan or a person of Afghan descent. **2.** A major language of Afghanistan, **Pashto** (*see*). **3. afghan.** A coverlet of wool, knitted or crocheted in colorful geometric designs. **4. afghan.** A type of sheepskin or goatskin coat, usually decorated with embroidery. —**Af·ghan** *adj.*

Afghan hound *n.* A large, slender dog of an ancient breed, having long, thick hair, a pointed muzzle, and drooping ears.

af·ghan·i (ăf-găn′ē) *n.* The basic monetary unit of Afghanistan, equal to 100 puls. See feature at **currency.**

Af·ghan·i·stan (ăf-găn′ĭ-stăn′). Arid, landlocked state of west-central Asia, dominated by mountains radiating from the Hindu Kush. Only 10 percent is cultivable, yet normally 85 percent of workers are in farming, mostly at subsistence level. The country is rich in minerals, but only gas and coal are exploited to any extent. Dried fruit, gas, skins, cotton, and wool are the main exports, and the country is famed for its carpets. Afghanistan lies astride ancient invasion routes and is ethnically diverse as a result. Most people are Muslim, and less than 8 percent are literate. The area was part of the Persian Empire and was later conquered by Alexander the Great. It fell to the Arabs, who introduced Islam (8th century), and later to Genghis Khan (1220) and Tamerlane (14th century). The country was part of the Mogul Empire (16th century), until an Afghan chief revolted and founded the present state (1747). This buffer state between Russia and British India survived to win complete independence (1919) and was proclaimed a republic (1973). A military coup (1978) led to an unpopular regime dependent on the U.S.S.R. and to Soviet occupation of the country (1979–89). Area, 647,497 square kilometers (249,934 square miles). Population, 16,600,000. Capital, Kabul.

a·fi·ci·o·na·do (ə-fē′sē-ə-nä′dō, ə-fĭs′ē-ə-) *n., pl.* **-dos. 1.** An enthusiastic admirer or follower; a devotee. **2.** A devotee of bullfighting. [Spanish, from the past participle of *aficionar*, to incite affection, from *aficion*, from Latin *affectiō*, AFFECTION.]

a·field (ə-fēld′) *adv.* Off the usual or desired track; away from one's home or usual environment. Used chiefly in the phrase *far afield.*

a·fire (ə-fīr′) *adj.* **1.** On fire. **2.** Intensely interested and involved: *He was afire with enthusiasm about the new project.* —**a·fire** *adv.*

a·flame (ə-flām′) *adj.* **1.** On fire; flaming. **2.** Keenly excited and interested: *aflame with a desire to learn.* —**a·flame** *adv.*

af·la·tox·in (ăf′lə-tŏk′sĭn) *n.* A poison, produced by the fungus *Aspergillus flavus*, growing on peanuts and cereals, that is thought to cause certain cancers. [*A*(*spergillus*) *fla*(*vus*) + TOXIN.]

AFL-CIO, A.F.L.-C.I.O. The American Federation of Labor and Congress of Industrial Organizations.

a·float (ə-flōt′) *adj.* **1.** Floating. **2.** On a boat or ship away from the shore; at sea. **3.** In circulation; being spread about: *All sorts of rumors were afloat.* **4.** Awash; flooded. **5.** Drifting about; moving without guidance. **6.** Out of debt. —**a·float** *adv.*

a·flut·ter (ə-flŭt′ər) *adj.* In a flutter; nervous and excited.

a·foot (ə-fŏŏt′) *adj.* **1.** Being prepared or carried out; astir: *some nasty business afoot.* **2.** Walking; on foot. —**a·foot** *adv.*

a·fore (ə-fôr′, ə-fōr′) *adv.* **1.** *Archaic & Regional.* Before. **2.** *Nautical.* In front.
~*prep.* **1.** *Archaic.* Before. **2.** *Nautical.* In front of.
~*conj. Archaic.* Before. [Middle English *afor(e)n*, Old English *onforan* : ON + *foran*, dative of *for*, FORE.]

a·fore·men·tioned (ə-fôr′měn′shənd, ə-fōr′-) *adj.* Mentioned previously or before. Used especially in legal documents.
~*n., pl.* **aforementioned.** The person mentioned already. Preceded by *the.*

a·fore·said (ə-fôr′sĕd′, ə-fōr′-) *adj.* Spoken of or referred to earlier.
~*n., pl.* **aforesaid.** The person, thing, or fact already stated or referred to. Preceded by *the.*

a·fore·thought (ə-fôr′thôt′, ə-fōr′) *adj.* Planned or intended beforehand; premeditated. Used chiefly in the legal phrase *malice aforethought.*

a·fore·time (ə-fôr′tīm′, ə-fōr′-) *adv. Archaic.* At a former or past time; previously. —**a·fore·time** *adj.*

a for·ti·o·ri (ä fôr′shē-ôr′ē, ā fōr′shē-ō′rī′) *adv.* With greater reason; all the more: *If there are to be cuts in the education budget, then a fortiori there should be cuts in the defense budget.*

a·foul (ə-foul′) *adv.* In or into a condition of entanglement, conflict, or collision. —**run** (or **fall**) **afoul of.** To become entangled with; come into collision with. —**a·foul** *adj.*

afp alpha-fetoprotein.

Afr. Africa; African.

a·fraid (ə-frād′) *adj.* **1.** Filled with fear; frightened or apprehensive: *afraid of snakes.* **2.** Disinclined; averse: *not afraid of work.* **3.** Filled with regret. Used especially as a polite way of lessening the force of

AFGHANISTAN

TURKMENISTAN   UZB.   TAJIKISTAN   CHINA
Amu Darya (Oxus)
BACTRIA
Mazar-i-Sharif   •Baghlan
Hindu Kush
6059m
5143m   GANDHARA
Paropamisus Mts   Bāmī-Baba   Paghman   Khyber
Hari   •Herat   Bamiyan   Pass
Rud   KABUL   Jalalabad
IRAN   AFGHANISTAN   Gardez•   INDIA
Farah   •Farah
Rud
Dasht-i-   •Kandahar   PAKISTAN
Margo
Helmand   Indus
Km 0   200   400   600
Miles 0   100   200   300

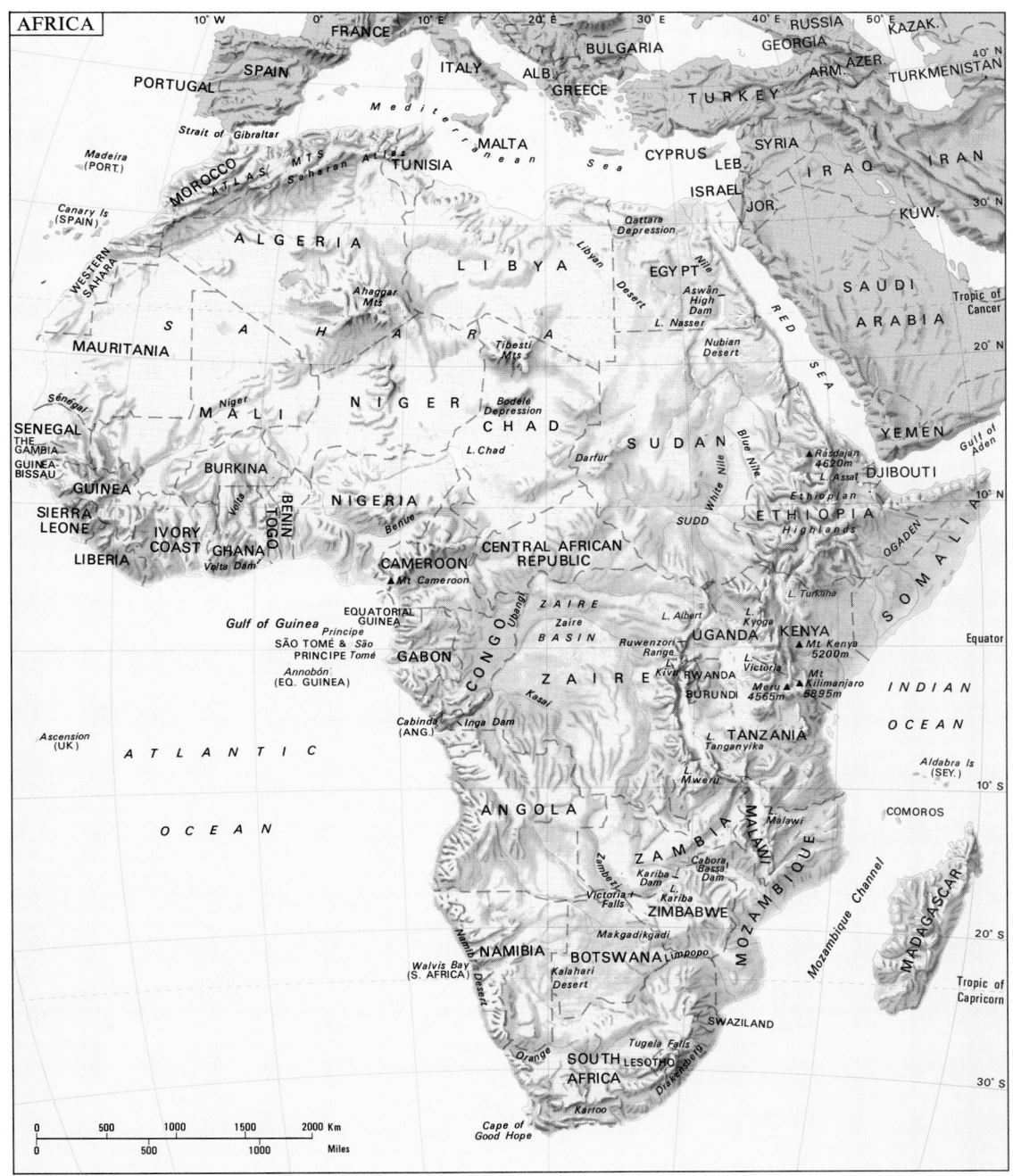

AFRICA

an unpleasant statement: *I'm afraid that I disagree with you.* [Middle English *af(f)raied,* past participle of *affraien,* to frighten, from Old French *affreer,* to AFFRAY.]

af·reet, af·rit (ăf′rēt′, ə-frēt′) *n. Arabic Mythology.* A powerful evil spirit or gigantic and monstrous demon. [Arabic *'ifrīt,* probably from Persian *āfrīda,* "a created being," from *āfrīdan,* to create.]

a·fresh (ə-frĕsh′) *adv.* Anew; again; from the beginning: *start afresh.*

Af·ri·ca (ăf′rĭ-kə). *Abbr.* **Af., Afr.** The second-largest continent after Asia, consisting mostly of high, monotonous plateaus, which drop dramatically to narrow coastal plains. It has a very short coastline for its area and has few inlets with deep harbors. Africa has few fold mountains: only the Atlas ranges in the northeast, part of the great Alpine-Himalayan system, and the older, smoother Cape ranges in the far south. Some ranges, such as the rugged Drakensberg and Ruwenzori, are the edges of tilted plateaus, while the others are generally of volcanic origin. The Great Rift Valley slashes through the continent from the mouth of the Zambezi to Djibouti and continues in the Red Sea. The valley encloses Lakes Malawi and Turkana, while Lakes Tanganyika and Mobutu Sese Seko lie in an arm to the west. Africa's largest lake, Victoria, lies in a shallow depression between the two arms of the valley. Africa's longest rivers, the Nile, Zaire (Congo), and Niger, are among the 10 longest in the world. Many rivers leave the plateaus by spectacular falls, such as

those on the Tugela River in South Africa, and these provide great potential for hydroelectric schemes. There are also vast areas of inland drainage, with no outlet to the sea, the Chad and Makgadikgadi depressions being two of them. Two thirds of the continent lies within the Tropics, and though temperatures are much modified by altitude, Africa is the hottest continent. It is also one of the driest: one third of it has less than 250 millimeters (10 inches) of rain a year. The Sahara, covering 25 percent of the total area, and the Namib and Kalahari deserts are among the world's harshest. Savannas, increasingly dry as they near the deserts, cover another 40 percent of the land. Soils in Africa are often poor, but rich chernozems (black earths) cover much of the East African highlands, and the alluvium of the great river valleys provides good soils. Soil erosion, frequently the result of overgrazing by livestock, is a problem in many countries. Arable land covers less than 7.5 percent of the continent, yet farming provides a living for some 75 percent of its people, the highest proportion of any continent. Africa's great strength lies in its vast and varied mineral reserves. It has 30 percent of the Western world's known mineral resources apart from oil, and already produces more than 10 percent of the world's oil. Many African countries, especially those with fewer natural resources, are finding tourism an increasingly valuable source of foreign exchange. The continent's sunny climate, warm seas, sandy

African marigold *An annual plant native to Mexico.*

African violets Saintpaulias, *or African violets, are native to tropical Africa, but they are now grown as popular houseplants around the world. Varieties exist in a range of colors from white to dark blue.*

agama *The red-headed agama (above) is one member of this desert-dwelling family of lizards.*

beaches, and scenery are a good base for development, while another asset is its remarkably varied wildlife, in many places preserved in national park and game reserves. Area, 30,334,562 square kilometers (11,712,252 square miles).

Af·ri·can (ăf′rĭ-kən) *adj. Abbr.* **Afr., Af.** Of or pertaining to Africa, or any of its peoples, languages, fauna, or the like.
~*n.* **1.** A native or inhabitant of Africa. **2.** A member of any of the indigenous peoples of Africa.

Af·ri·can·der, Af·ri·kan·der (ăf′rĭ-kăn′dər) *n.* **1.** Any of a breed of cattle with a humped back and large, spreading horns, originally developed in South Africa. **2.** *Obsolete.* An Afrikaner. [Afrikaans *Afrikaander,* alteration (influenced by *Hollander*) of Dutch *Afrikaner.*] **—Af·ri·can·der, Af·ri·kan·der** *adj.*

Af·ri·can·ism (ăf′rĭ-kə-nĭz′əm) *n.* A characteristically African feature; especially, a word or expression from an African language when used in a non-African language.

Af·ri·can·ist (ăf′rĭ-kən-ĭst) *n.* A specialist in African affairs, culture, or languages.

Af·ri·can·ize (ăf′rĭ-kən-īz′) *tr.v.* **-ized, -izing, -izes.** To make African; especially, to transfer to African control or give a specifically African character to. **—Af·ri·can·i·za·tion** (ăf′rĭ-kən-ĭ-zā′shən) *n.*

African lily *n.* A plant, *Agapanthus africanus,* native to southern Africa, having rounded clusters of blue, violet, or white flowers.

African mahogany *n.* **1.** Any of several African trees of the genus *Khaya;* especially, *K. ivorensis,* having wood similar to that of true mahogany. **2.** The wood of this tree, used for furniture, musical instruments, and boat interiors. **3.** Any of various other African woods resembling true mahogany.

African marigold *n.* A widely cultivated plant, *Tagetes erecta,* native to Mexico, having finely divided foliage and showy, rounded, orange or yellow flowers.

African National Congress *n. Abbr.* **A.N.C.** A South African resistance movement favoring majority rule. It was banned in South Africa until 1990.

African trypanosomiasis *n.* **Sleeping sickness** *(see).*

African violet *n.* Any of several plants of the genus *Saintpaulia,* native to tropical East Africa and widely cultivated as house plants; especially, *S. ionantha,* having violet, white, or pink flowers. Also called "saintpaulia."

Af·ri·kaans (ăf′rĭ-käns′, -känz′) *n.* A language developed from 17th-century Dutch among the Afrikaners. It shares with English official-language status in the Republic of South Africa. Also called "Taal," formerly "Cape Dutch." **—Af·ri·kaans** *adj.*

Afrikander. Variant of **Africander.**

Af·ri·kan·er (ăf′rĭ-kä′nər) *n.* An Afrikaans-speaking descendant of the Dutch settlers of South Africa. **—Af·ri·kan·er** *adj.*

Af·ri·kan·er·dom (ăf′rĭ-kä′nər-dəm) *n.* The sense of solidarity among Afrikaners; loyalty to and pride in the cultural and political values of the Afrikaner people and their pioneer origins.

Af·ro (ăf′rō) *n., pl.* **-ros.** A hairstyle in which the hair is shaped into a round frizzy mass.
~*adj.* **1.** Of or for an Afro. **2.** Directly or indirectly African in style. [Perhaps short for AFRO-AMERICAN.]

Afro– *prefix.* Indicates Africa or African or African and; for example, **Afro-American.** [Latin *Āfr-,* stem of *Āfer,* an African.]

Af·ro-A·mer·i·can (ăf′rō-ə-mĕr′ə-kən) *adj.* Of or pertaining to American blacks of African ancestry, their history, or their culture.
~*n.* An American black of African ancestry.

Af·ro-A·si·at·ic (ăf′rō-ā′zhē-ăt′ĭk) *n.* A family of languages of southwestern Asia and northern Africa. Also called "Hamito-Semitic," "Semito-Hamitic." **—Af·ro-A·si·at·ic** *adj.*

af·ror·mo·si·a (ăf′rôr-mō′zē-ə, -mō′zhə) *n.* **1.** Any of several North and West African trees of the genus *Pericopsis.* **2.** The hard teaklike wood of this tree. [AFRO- + *Ormosia* (genus name), from Greek *hormos,* necklace, alluding to the use of its berries in making necklaces.]

aft (ăft, äft) *adv.* At, in, toward, or close to the stern of a vessel or the back of an aircraft. [Probably shortening of ABAFT.] **—aft** *adj.*

aft. afternoon.

af·ter (ăf′tər, äf′-) *prep.* **1.** Following in place or order: *D comes after C.* **2.** Following in time; subsequent to: *Come after dinner.* **3.** Following continually: *week after week of cold weather.* **4.** In quest or pursuit of: *The police are after them.* **5. a.** Considering; bearing in mind: *After the way he treated her, I'm not surprised she left.* **b.** In spite of: *After all my work, the job still wasn't finished on time.* **6.** Concerning: *He asked after you.* **7.** Next to or lower than in order or importance: *Football is his favorite sport after bicycling.* **8.** In the style of; in imitation of: *a painting after the style of Picasso.* **9.** With the same name as; in honor or memory of: *named after her mother.* **10.** Past the hour of; past: *It's ten after three.* **11.** According to the nature or desires of; in accordance with: *a person after my own heart.* **—after all.** **1.** When everything is considered. **2.** Eventually; ultimately.
~*adv.* **1.** Behind; in the rear. **2.** At a later time; afterward.
~*adj.* **1.** Subsequent in time or place; later; following: *in after years.* Often used in combination: *afterglow.* **2.** *Nautical.* Nearer the stern of a vessel; further aft.
~*conj.* Following or subsequent to the time that: *I saw her after I arrived.* [Middle English *after,* Old English *æfter.*]

af·ter·birth (ăf′tər-bûrth′, äf-) *n.* The placenta and fetal membranes expelled from the uterus after birth of the offspring. Also called "secundines."

af·ter·burn·er (ăf′tər-bûr′nər, äf′-) *n.* **1.** A device for increasing the thrust of a jet engine by burning additional fuel with the uncombined oxygen in the exhaust gases. **2.** A device for removing or neutralizing harmful gases in the exhaust of an internal-combustion engine, especially as fitted to a car.

af·ter·care (ăf′tər-kâr′, äf′-) *n.* Treatment or special care given to someone after discharge from an institution, such as a hospital.

af·ter·damp (ăf′tər-dămp′, äf′-) *n.* An asphyxiating mixture of gases, primarily nitrogen and carbon dioxide, left in a mine after a fire or explosion.

af·ter·deck (ăf′tər-dĕk′, äf′-) *n. Nautical.* The part of a deck lying between the middle and stern of a ship.

af·ter·ef·fect (ăf′tər-ə-fĕkt′, äf′-) *n. Often* **aftereffects.** An effect that follows some time after its cause or after an initial effect.

af·ter·glow (ăf′tər-glō′, äf′-) *n.* **1.** The light emitted or remaining after removal of a source of illumination, as: **a.** The atmospheric glow after sunset. **b.** The glow of an incandescent metal as it cools. **c.** Emission from a phosphor after removal of excitation. **2.** The comfortable feeling following a pleasant experience. **3.** A lingering pleasant impression, as of past happiness or success.

af·ter·heat (ăf′tər-hēt′, äf′-) *n.* The heat produced in a nuclear reactor after it has been shut down, as a result of residual radioactivity in the fuel elements.

af·ter-hours (ăf′tər-ourz′, äf′-) *adj.* **1.** Occurring or done after closing time or after the normal working period. **2.** Open after a legal or established closing time: *an after-hours club.*

af·ter·im·age (ăf′tər-ĭm′ĭj, äf′-) *n.* A visual image that persists after a visual stimulus ceases. Also called "photogene."

af·ter·life (ăf′tər-līf′, äf′-) *n.* **1.** A life believed to follow death. **2.** The part of one's life that follows a particular event.

af·ter·math (ăf′tər-măth′, äf′-) *n.* **1.** A resulting state or period, especially following a disaster or misfortune: *in the aftermath of the explosion.* **2.** A second growth or crop of grass in one season. [AFTER + obsolete *math,* mowing, Middle English *math* (unattested), Old English *mǣth.*]

af·ter·noon (ăf′tər-no͞on′, äf′-) *n.* **1.** *Abbr.* **a., aft.** The part of the day from noon until evening. **2.** The closing part: *in the afternoon of one's life.*
~*adj.* Of or occurring in the afternoon.

af·ter·noons (ăf′tər-no͞onz′, äf′-) *adv. Informal.* Regularly in the afternoon; on any afternoon.

af·ter·pains (ăf′tər-pānz′, äf′-) *pl.n.* The cramps or pains following childbirth, resulting from the contraction of the uterus.

af·ters (ăf′tərz, äf′-) *n. British Informal.* Dessert.

af·ter·sen·sa·tion (ăf′tər-sĕn-sā′shən, äf′-) *n.* A sensory impression, such as an afterimage or aftertaste, that persists or recurs after removal of a stimulus.

af·ter·shave lotion (ăf′tər-shāv′, äf′-) *n.* An astringent lotion, usually scented, applied to the face after shaving. Also called "aftershave."

af·ter·shock (ăf′tər-shŏk′, äf′-) *n.* A relatively small earthquake following a large-magnitude earthquake, occurring fairly close to the focus, and probably caused by mechanical readjustment in the earth's mantle following the release of energy by the main shock.

af·ter·taste (ăf′tər-tāst′, äf′-) *n.* **1.** A taste that remains in the mouth after the substance causing it is no longer present. **2.** A usually unpleasant feeling that remains after an event or experience.

af·ter·thought (ăf′tər-thôt′, äf′-) *n.* **1.** An idea, response, or explanation that occurs to one after an event or decision. **2.** A later addition to something completed: *The last paragraph was a bit of an afterthought.*

af·ter·time (ăf′tər-tīm′, äf′-) *n.* The time to come; the future.

af·ter·ward (ăf′tər-wərd, äf′-) *adv.* Also **af·ter·wards** (-wərdz). At a later time; subsequently.

af·ter·word (ăf′tər-wûrd′, äf′-) *n.* Something added to the end of a literary work, such as an epilogue.

Ag The symbol for the element silver. [Latin *argentum.*]

A.G., AG **1.** adjutant general. **2.** attorney general.

a·ga, a·gha (ä′gə) *n.* A high-ranking official of the Ottoman Empire. [Turkish *ağa,* "lord."]

A·ga·dir (ä′gə-dîr′, ăg′ə-). Port in southwest Morocco. In 1911 it was the scene of an international crisis known as the Agadir Incident, when Britain forcibly protested at the sending by Germany of a gunboat to Agadir. War was averted owing to French arbitration. In 1960 earthquakes virtually destroyed the town, killing over 10,000 of its inhabitants.

a·gain (ə-gĕn′) *adv.* **1.** Once more; another time; anew. **2.** Back to a previous place, position, or state: *He left home, but went back again.* **3.** Furthermore; moreover. **4.** On the other hand: *He might go, and again he might not.* **—again and again.** Repeatedly; frequently. **—as much again.** **1.** The same amount again. **2.** Twice as much. [Middle English *again, ayen,* Old English *ongēan,* in return, toward, against, from Germanic : ON + *gagin* (unattested), straight.]

a·gainst (ə-gĕnst′) *prep.* **1.** In a direction or course opposite to: *row against the current.* **2.** So as to come into forcible contact with: *waves dashing against the shore.* **3.** In contact with so as to rest or press on: *He leaned against the tree.* **4.** In opposition or resistance to: *the war against crime; 10 votes for and 12 against.* **5.** Contrary to: *against my better judgment; against all the odds.* **6.** In contrast or comparison with the setting or background of: *dark colors against a fair skin.* **7.** In preparation for; in anticipation of: *food stored against winter.* **8.** As a defense or safeguard from, or from the effects of: *protection against the cold; insurance against fire and theft.* **9.** Unfavorable or disadvantageous to: *Her age is against her.* [Middle English *against, ayenst,* alteration of *ayenes, againes,* from *again, ayen,* against. See **again.**]

A·ga Khan (ä'gə kän') *n.* A hereditary title of the religious and spiritual leader of the sect of Ismaili Muslims.

Aga Khan III (1877–1957). The title of Aga Sultan Sir Mahomed Shah, leader (imam) of the Ismaili Muslim sect. He represented India at the League of Nations in the 1930's, becoming president of the League in 1937. He appointed his grandson, **Aga Khan IV** (formerly Prince Karim; 1936–) to be his successor as imam, in preference to his son (the prince's father), Prince Aly Khan.

a·gal (ə-gäl') *n.* A cord worn wound around the head by many desert Arabs that keeps the kaffiyeh (headdress) in place. [Arabic *'īgal,* cord, rope.]

ag·a·ma (ăg'ə-mə) *n.* Any of various small, long-tailed, insect-eating lizards of the family Agamidae, found in Old World tropics. [Carib.]

Ag·a·mem·non (ăg'ə-mĕm'nŏn'). *Greek Mythology.* The king of Mycenae, leader of the Greeks against Troy, husband of Clytemnestra, and father of Orestes, Electra, and Iphigenia.

a·ga·mete (ā'gə-mēt', ā-găm'ēt') *n. Biology.* A single-celled organism that reproduces asexually.

a·gam·ic (ā-găm'ĭk) *adj.* Also **ag·a·mous** (ăg'ə-məs). *Biology.* Occurring or reproducing without the union of male and female cells; asexual or parthenogenetic. [Late Latin *agamus,* unmarried, from Greek *agamos* : *a-,* not + -GAMOUS.] **—a·gam·i·cal·ly** *adv.*

ag·a·mo·gen·e·sis (ăg'ə-mō-jĕn'ə-sĭs, ā'găm-ō-) *n. Biology.* Asexual reproduction, as by budding, cell division, or parthenogenesis. [AGAM(IC) + GENESIS.] **—ag·a·mo·ge·net·ic** (ăg'ə-mō-jə-nĕt'ĭk) *adj.*

A·ga·na (ə-gä'nyə). Capital of Guam, on the west coast of the island. It was almost completely destroyed in World War II. U.S. military bases on the island are important to Agana's economy.

ag·a·pan·thus (ăg'ə-păn'thəs) *n.* Any plant of the genus *Agapanthus,* which includes the **African lily** *(see).* [New Latin : Greek *agapē,* love, AGAPE + *anthos,* flower.]

a·gape¹ (ə-gāp', ə-găp') *adv.* In a state of wonder or amazement, often with the mouth wide open. **—a·gape** *adj.*

a·ga·pe² (ä'gə-pā') *n., pl.* **-pae** (-pē'). **1.** Christian love. **2.** In the early Christian Church, the **love feast** *(see)* accompanied by a celebration of the Eucharist. [Greek *agapē*†, love.]

a·gar (ā'gär, ä'gär) *n.* Also **a·gar-a·gar** (ā'gär'ā'gär, ä'gär'ä'gär). A mucilaginous material prepared from certain marine algae and used as a base for bacterial culture media, as a laxative, and for thickening certain foods. [Malay, "jelly, gelatin."]

ag·a·ric (ăg'ə-rĭk, ə-găr'ĭk) *n.* **1.** Any fungus of the family Agaricaceae, including the common cultivated mushroom, *Agaricus campestris,* and the **fly agaric** *(see).* **2.** The dried fruiting body of the fungus *Fomes laricis,* formerly used in medicine. [Latin *agaricum,* from Greek *agarikon,* perhaps after *Agaria,* city in Sarmatia.]

Ag·as·siz (ăg'ə-sē), **(Jean) Louis Rodolphe** (1807–73). Swiss-born U.S. naturalist and geologist. He won fame for his pioneering studies of fossil fishes, and was the first man to recognize from geological evidence that ice ages had once occurred in the Northern Hemisphere.

ag·ate (ăg'ĭt) *n.* **1.** A fine-grained quartz, a variety of chalcedony, with color banding or irregular clouding. **2.** A child's marble made of this material or a glass imitation of it. **3.** A tool with agate parts, such as a bookbinder's burnisher. **4.** A printer's type size, approximately 5½ points. [Old French, from Latin *achātēs,* from Greek *akhātēs*†.]

a·ga·ve (ə-gä'vē, ə-gä'-) *n.* Any of numerous fleshy-leaved tropical American plants of the genus *Agave,* which includes the **century plant** *(see).* Some species yield valuable fibers. [New Latin, "noble (plant)" (probably so named because of its height), from Greek *agauē,* feminine of *agauos*†, noble.]

age (āj) *n.* **1.** The period or amount of time during which someone or something has existed. **2.** An advanced stage of life or existence; the state of being old. **3.** That time in life when a person becomes eligible or entitled to do something, such as being qualified to assume certain civil and personal rights and responsibilities. Used chiefly in the phrases *of age* and *under age.* **4.** Any of the various stages of life: *at an awkward age.* **5.** *Sometimes* **Age.** Any period in history or geology designated by a specified characteristic: *the atomic age; the Stone Age.* **6.** A generation: *future ages.* **7.** *Often* **ages.** *Informal.* A very long time: *We waited an age. They left ages ago.* **8.** *Psychology.* See **mental age.** **—come of age. 1.** To reach the age at which one is considered legally an adult. **2.** To reach a state of maturity.

~v. **aged, aging, ages** or *chiefly British* **aged, ageing, ages.** *—tr.* To cause to grow or seem older or more mature. *—intr.* **1.** To become old. **2.** To show signs of old age. **3.** To mature with age. Used especially of alcoholic drinks. [Middle English, from Old French *age, aage,* from Vulgar Latin *aetāticum* (unattested), from Latin *aetās* (stem *aetāt-*), age.] **—ag·er** *n.*

-age *suffix.* Indicates: **1.** Collectively; for example, **acreage, baggage. 2.** Relation to or connection with; for example, **parentage. 3.** Result, action, or process; for example, **passage, spillage. 4.** Condition or position; for example, **vagabondage, marriage. 5.** Charge or fee; for example, **postage, cartage. 6.** Residence or place; for example, **vicarage, orphanage. 7.** Rate; for example, **mileage.** [Middle English, from Old French, from Late Latin *-āticum,* from the neuter of *-āticus* : Latin *-ātus,* -ATE + -IC.]

a·ged (ā'jĭd *for senses 1,4;* ājd *for senses 2,3, and occasionally for other senses*) *adj.* **1.** Old; advanced in years. **2.** Of the age of: *aged three.* **3.** Having undergone the process of aging; matured. **4.** *Geology.* Near the base level of erosion. —See Synonyms at **old. —a·ged·ness** *n.*

A·gee (ā'jē), **James** (1909–55). U.S. writer. His most influential work, done in collaboration with the photographer Walker Evans, was *Let Us Now Praise Famous Men* (1941), a harrowing documentary account of the lives of Alabama sharecroppers during the Depression.

age group *n.* All the people of a particular age or between two particular ages, considered as a group.

age·ing. *Chiefly British.* Variant of **aging.**

age·ism (ā'jĭz'əm) *n.* Unfair discrimination based on age, especially against middle-aged and elderly people. **—age·ist** *adj. & n.*

age·less (āj'lĭs) *adj.* **1.** Never seeming to grow old. **2.** Existing forever; eternal. **—age·less·ly** *adv.* **—age·less·ness** *n.*

a·gen·cy (ā'jən-sē) *n., pl.* **-cies. 1.** Action; operation; power: *Rust occurs through the agency of moisture in the air.* **2. a.** A business or service authorized to act for others: *an employment agency.* **b.** The office or premises from which such a business operates. **3.** An organization set up by a government department or international body. [Latin *agentia,* from *agēns,* acting, AGENT.]

a·gen·da (ə-jĕn'də) *n.* A list of things to be done, especially the program for a meeting. [Latin, plural of *agendum,* neuter gerundive of *agere,* to do.]

a·gen·e·sis (ā-jĕn'ə-sĭs) *n.* Also **ag·e·ne·sia** (ăj'ə-nē'zhə). *Biology.* Failure of an organism, organ, or part to develop.

a·gent (ā'jənt) *n.* **1.** One that acts or has the power or authority to act. **2. a.** One who acts for or as the representative of another: *an actor's agent.* **b.** A sales representative: *an insurance agent.* **3.** A means by which something is done or caused; an instrument. **4.** A force or substance that causes changes: *a chemical agent.* [Middle English, from Latin *agēns* (stem *agent-*), present participle of *agere,* to act, drive, do.] **—a·gen·tial** (ā-jĕn'shəl) *adj.*

Agent Orange *n.* A powerful toxic herbicide containing the chemical 2,4,5-T, used as a defoliant. [After the color of the identifying stripe on the barrels containing the herbicide.]

a·gent pro·vo·ca·teur (ȧ-zhäN' prô-vô-kȧ-tœr') *n., pl.* **agents provocateurs** (*pronounced as singular*). A person employed to associate with individuals or groups suspected of seditious or other criminal activities and to incite them to commit illegal acts so as to incur punishment. [French, "provocative agent."]

age of consent *n. Law.* The age at which a person may choose to have sexual intercourse.

Age of Reason *n.* The period of the **Enlightenment** *(see),* especially in Britain, France, and the United States. Preceded by *the.*

age-old (āj'ōld') *adj.* Very old or of long standing.

ag·e·ra·tum (ăj'ə-rā'təm) *n.* **1.** Any of various plants of the genus *Ageratum;* especially, *A. houstonianum,* a commonly cultivated species having clusters of usually violet-blue flowers. **2.** Loosely, any of several other plants having similar flower clusters. [New Latin *Ageratum,* from Latin *agēraton,* from Greek, neuter of *agēratos,* ageless : *a-,* not + *-gēratos,* from *gēras,* old age.]

ag·gie (ăg'ē) *n.* A playing marble. [AG(ATE) + -IE.]

ag·gior·na·men·to (äd-jôr'nä-mĕn'tō) *n., pl.* **-ti** (-tē). *Italian.* The process or an instance of modernizing an institution or organization.

ag·glom·er·ate (ə-glŏm'ə-rāt') *v.* **-ated, -ating, -ates.** *—tr.* To form or collect into a rounded mass. *—intr.* To take the shape of a rounded mass.

~adj. (ə-glŏm'ər-ĭt). Gathered into a rounded mass.

~n. (ə-glŏm'ər-ĭt). **1.** A confused or jumbled mass of things clustered together; a heap. **2.** A volcanic rock consisting of angular and rounded fragments fused together. [Latin *agglomerāre* : *ad-,* to + *glomerāre,* to wind into a ball, from *glomus* (stem *glomer-*), ball.] **—ag·glom·er·a·tive** (ə-glŏm'ər-ə-tĭv, -ə-rā'tĭv) *adj.* **—ag·glom·er·a·tor** (ə-glŏm'ə-rā'tər) *n.*

ag·glom·er·a·tion (ə-glŏm'ə-rā'shən) *n.* **1.** The action of agglomerating or the state of being agglomerated. **2.** A confused or jumbled mass; an agglomerate.

ag·glu·ti·nate (ə-glo͞ot'n-āt') *v.* **-nated, -nating, -nates.** *—tr.* **1.** To join together by causing adhesion, as with glue. **2.** *Linguistics.* To form (words) by combining words, or words and word elements. **3.** *Physiology.* To cause (red blood cells or microorganisms) to clump together. *—intr.* **1.** To join together into a group or mass. **2.** *Linguistics.* To form words by agglutination. **3.** To undergo agglutination. [Latin *agglūtināre* : *ad-,* to + *glūtināre,* to glue, from *glūten,* glue.] **—ag·glu·ti·nant** *adj. & n.*

ag·glu·ti·na·tion (ə-glo͞ot'n-ā'shən) *n.* **1.** The process of agglutinating; adhesion of distinct parts. **2.** A mass formed in this manner. **3.** *Linguistics.* The process of forming words by combining component units that retain their original forms and meanings with little change, as in the formation of *houseboat* from *house* and *boat.*

ag·glu·ti·na·tive (ə-glo͞ot'n-ā'tĭv) *adj.* **1.** Tending toward, concerning, or characteristic of agglutination. **2.** *Linguistics.* Designating a language, such as Turkish, in which words are formed primarily by means of agglutination.

ag·glu·ti·nin (ə-glo͞ot'n-ĭn) *n.* An antibody that induces agglutination in blood cells or microorganisms. [AGGLUTIN(ATION) + -IN.]

ag·grade (ə-grād') *tr.v.* **-graded, -grading, -grades.** To fill and raise the level of (the bed of a stream or a beach, for example) by depositing sediment. [AD- (toward) + GRADE.] **—ag·gra·da·tion** (ăg'rə-dā'shən) *n.* **—ag·gra·da·tion·al** *adj.*

ag·gran·dize (ə-grăn'dīz', ăg'rən-dīz') *tr.v.* **-dized, -dizing, -dizes.**

Agamemnon *A golden death mask, known as the Agamemnon mask after the legendary king who led the Greeks in the siege of Troy. The mask, dating from about the 16th century* B.C., *is now in the National Museum, Athens.*

agave *Members of this genus of tropical plant are used in the manufacture of the Mexican drink tequila.*

ageratum *An American tropical plant now widely cultivated.*

1. To increase the scope of; enlarge; extend. 2. To make greater in power, influence, stature, or reputation. 3. To make (something) seem greater; exaggerate. [French *aggrandir* (present stem *aggrandiss-*) : *a*, to, from Latin *ad-* + *grandir,* to grow larger, from Latin *grandīre,* from *grandis,* great, GRAND.] **—ag·gran·dize·ment** *n.* **—ag·gran·diz·er** *n.*

ag·gra·vate (ăg′rə-vāt′) *tr.v.* **-vated, -vating, -vates.** 1. To make worse or more serious: *Sunlight can aggravate certain skin conditions.* 2. *Informal.* To annoy or exasperate; provoke; irritate. [Latin *aggravāre,* to make heavier : *ad-,* in addition to + *gravāre,* to burden, from *gravis,* heavy.] **—ag·gra·vat·ing** *adj.* **—ag·gra·va·tor** *n.*

Usage: The word *aggravate* is widely used to mean "to irritate," as in *The mechanic's surliness aggravated me no end.* But many still insist that the word should be used only to mean "to make worse," in referring to a situation or condition, as in: *The plight of the small farmer has been aggravated by the drought. Kim's bad luck was aggravated by his refusal to get sufficient rest.*

ag·gra·va·tion (ăg′rə-vā′shən) *n.* 1. The action of aggravating. 2. The state of being aggravated. 3. A thing that irritates or makes worse or more troublesome. 4. *Informal.* Exasperation; bother.

ag·gre·gate (ăg′rə-gĭt′) *adj.* 1. Gathered together so as to make a whole; total. 2. *Botany.* Crowded or massed into a dense cluster. 3. *Geology.* Consisting of a mixture of mineral or rock fragments separable by mechanical means. Said of rock.

~n. 1. Any total or whole considered with reference to its constituent parts; a group of distinct particulars massed together; a gross amount: *"an empire is the aggregate of many states under one common head"* (Edmund Burke). 2. The mineral materials, such as sand or stone, used in making concrete. **—in the aggregate.** Considered collectively or as a whole.

~tr.v. (ăg′rə-gāt′) **aggregated, -gating, -gates.** 1. To gather into a mass, sum, or whole. 2. To total; add up to. [Middle English *aggregat,* from Latin *aggregātus,* past participle of *aggregāre,* to add to (the flock), attach to : *ad-,* to + *gregāre,* to herd, from *grex* (stem *greg-*), flock.] **—ag·gre·gate·ly** *adv.* **—ag·gre·ga·tion** (ăg′rə-gā′shən) *n.* **—ag·gre·ga·tive** (ăg′rə-gā′tĭv, ăg′rə-gə-tĭv) *adj.* **—ag·gre·ga·tor** *n.*

aggregate fruit *n.* A fruit, such as a raspberry or blackberry, consisting of a cluster of drupelets formed from the ovaries of a single flower.

ag·gress (ə-grĕs′) *v.* **-gressed, -gressing, -gresses.** *—intr.* To start an attack or a quarrel. *—tr.* To commit an act of aggression against. [Latin *aggredī* (past participle *aggressus*), to approach (with hostility), attack : *ad-,* toward + *gradī,* to step, go.]

ag·gres·sion (ə-grĕsh′ən) *n.* 1. The act or an instance of commencing an attack, invasion, or quarrel; an assault. 2. The habit or practice of launching attacks. 3. *Psychology.* Hostile action or behavior.

ag·gres·sive (ə-grĕs′ĭv) *adj.* 1. Inclined to provoke argument or hostility; belligerent. 2. Assertive; bold; forceful: *an aggressive salesman.* **—ag·gres·sive·ly** *adv.* **—ag·gres·sive·ness** *n.*

ag·grieve (ə-grēv′) *tr.v.* **-grieved, -grieving, -grieves.** 1. To distress or afflict. 2. To injure unjustly; give reason for just complaint. [Middle English *agreven,* from Old French *agrever,* from Latin *aggravāre,* to make heavier, AGGRAVATE.]

ag·grieved (ə-grēvd′) *adj.* 1. Hurt or offended, especially because of wrongful or unfair treatment. 2. *Law.* Treated unjustly by a decision of the court or other legal authority. **—ag·griev·ed·ly** (ə-grē′vĭd-lē) *adv.* **—ag·griev·ed·ness** *n.*

agha. Variant of **aga.**

a·ghast (ə-găst′, ə-gäst′) *adj.* Shocked, as by something horrible; appalled: *stood aghast at the sight.* [Middle English *agast,* past participle of *agasten,* to frighten : *a-* (intensive) + *gasten,* to frighten, Old English *gæstan,* from *gāst,* ghost.]

ag·ile (ăj′əl, ăj′īl) *adj.* 1. Able to move in a quick and easy fashion; active. 2. Mentally alert. —See Synonyms at **nimble.** [Middle English, from Old French, from Latin *agilis,* easily moved, light, nimble, from *agere,* to drive.] **—ag·ile·ly** *adv.* **—ag·ile·ness, a·gil·i·ty** (ə-jĭl′ə-tē) *n.*

a·gin (ə-gĭn′) *prep. Regional.* Against.

A·gin·court (ăj′ĭn-kôrt′). *French* **A·zin·court** (ȧ-zăN-ko͝or′). Village in northern France, scene of a decisive battle that took place in 1415 when an English army led by Henry V defeated a much larger French force. The victory, largely due to the superiority of the English archers, left nearly 6,000 French dead while the English losses were few.

ag·ing (ā′jĭng) *n.* Also *chiefly British* **age·ing.** 1. The process of becoming old or mature. 2. Any artificial process for imparting the characteristics and properties of age.

ag·i·o (ăj′ē-ō) *n., pl.* **-os.** *Finance.* 1. A premium paid for changing one kind of money into another. 2. An allowance or premium for the difference in value between two currencies being exchanged. 3. Agiotage. [Italian *ag(g)io,* alteration of dialectal *lajjē,* from Medieval Greek *allagion,* exchange, from *allagē,* change, from *allos,* other.]

ag·i·o·tage (ăj′ē-ə-tĭj, äzh′ə-täzh′) *n. Finance.* 1. The business of brokerage; speculation in stocks and shares. 2. Exchange transactions, especially of currencies. [French, from *agioter,* to practice stockjobbing, from *agio,* stockbroking, from Italian *aggio,* AGIO.]

a·gist (ə-jĭst′) *tr.v.* **agisted, agisting, agists.** *Law.* To feed and take care of (cattle or horses belonging to others) in return for payment. [Middle English *agisten,* to pasture, from Old French *agister,* "to provide lodging for" : *a-,* from Latin *ad-,* to + *gister,* to lodge, from Vulgar Latin *jacitāre* (unattested), to make lie down, frequentative of Latin *jacēre,* to lie, intransitive of *jacere,* to throw.] **—a·gist·ment** *n.*

ag·i·tate (ăj′ə-tāt′) *v.* **-tated, -tating, -tates.** *—tr.* 1. To move with violence or sudden forcefulness: *a storm agitating the ocean.* 2. To excite or trouble; disturb: *Signs of the approaching storm agitated the birds.* 3. To arouse interest in (a cause, for example) by the written or spoken word; discuss; debate. 4. *Archaic.* To ponder over; consider. *—intr.* To stir up public interest in a cause: *agitate for better working conditions.* [Latin *agitāre,* frequentative of *agere,* to do, drive.] **—ag·i·tat·ed·ly** *adv.*

ag·i·ta·tion (ăj′ə-tā′shən) *n.* 1. The act of agitating. 2. The state of being agitated; disturbance; commotion. 3. Extreme emotional disturbance. 4. The stirring up of public interest, especially in favor of political or social change. **—ag·i·ta·tion·al** *adj.*

a·gi·ta·to (ä′jē-tä′tō) *adv. Music.* Agitated; fast and stirring. Used as a direction. [Italian, from Latin *agitātus,* past participle of *agitāre,* to AGITATE.] **—a·gi·ta·to** *adj.*

ag·i·ta·tor (ăj′ə-tā′tər) *n.* 1. A person who agitates, especially one who engages in political agitation. 2. A machine for stirring or shaking. **—ag·i·ta·to·ri·al** (ăj′ə-tə-tôr′ē-əl, -tōr′ē-əl) *adj.*

a·git·prop (ăj′ĭt-prŏp′) *n.* Political agitation and propaganda, especially in aid of left-wing or radical causes. [Shortened from Russian *Agitpropbyuro,* a Communist Party propaganda department, from *agitatsya-propaganda,* agitation-propaganda.] **—a·git·prop** *adj.*

A·gla·ia (ə-glā′ə, ə-glī′ə). *Greek Mythology.* One of the three **Graces** *(see).* [Greek, personification of *aglaia,* splendor, from *aglaos,* bright, splendid.]

a·gleam (ə-glēm′) *adj.* Brightly shining. **—a·gleam** *adv.*

ag·let (ăg′lĭt) *n.* Also **ai·glet** (ā′glĭt) 1. A tag or metal sheath on the end of a lace, cord, or ribbon to facilitate its passing through eyelet holes. 2. A similar device used as an ornament. [Middle English, from Old French *aguillette,* diminutive of *aguille,* needle, from Late Latin *acūcula,* pin, pine needle, diminutive of Latin *acus,* needle.]

a·gley (ə-glā′, ə-glī′) *adv.* Also **a·glee** (ə-glē′). *Scottish.* Off to the wrong direction; awry: *"The best laid schemes o' mice an' men/ Gang aft agley"* (Robert Burns). [Scottish, "squintingly" : *a-,* on + *gley,* to squint, from Middle English (Scottish dialect) *gleyen*†.]

a·glim·mer (ə-glĭm′ər) *adj.* Lighting up faintly; glimmering. **—a·glim·mer** *adv.*

a·glit·ter (ə-glĭt′ər) *adj.* Glittering; sparkling. **—a·glit·ter** *adv.*

a·glow (ə-glō′) *adj.* Glowing; in a glow. **—a·glow** *adv.*

ag·ma (ăg′mə) *n.* A phonetic symbol, **eng** *(see).*

ag·mi·nate (ăg′mə-nĭt, -nāt′) *adj.* Also **ag·mi·nat·ed** (-nā′tĭd). Gathered in clusters. [Latin *agmen* (stem *agmin-*), moving multitude, troop.]

ag·nail (ăg′nāl′) *n.* 1. A hangnail. 2. A painful sore or swelling around a fingernail or toenail; a whitlow. [Middle English *agnail,* Old English *angnægl,* "painful prick in the flesh" : *ang-,* painful + *nægl,* (iron) nail.]

ag·nate (ăg′nāt′) *adj.* 1. Related on or descended from the father's or male side. 2. From a common source; akin.

~n. A relative on the male or father's side only. [Middle English, from Latin *agnātus,* "born in addition," past participle of *agnāsci,* to be born in addition to : *ad-,* in addition + *nāscī, gnāscī,* to be born.] **—ag·nat·ic** (ăg-năt′ĭk) *adj.* **—ag·nat·i·cal·ly** *adv.* **—ag·na·tion** *n.*

Ag·ni (ŭg′nē). *Hinduism.* The Vedic god of fire and guardian of man. [Sanskrit *agniḥ,* fire.]

ag·no·men (ăg-nō′mən) *n., pl.* **-nomina** (-nŏm′ə-nə). 1. An additional cognomen given to an ancient Roman, often in honor of military victories, as Publius Cornelius Scipio *Africanus.* 2. A nickname. [Latin *agnōmen* : *ad-,* additional + *(g)nōmen,* name.]

Ag·non (ăg′nôn′), **Shmuel Yosef,** born Samuel Czaczkes (1888–1970). Israeli novelist. Born in Galicia (now in the U.S.S.R.), he moved to Palestine in 1907. His dramatic and influential novels, written in Hebrew, include *A Guest for the Night* (1938) and *The Day Before Yesterday* (1945). He was awarded the Nobel Prize for literature in 1966.

ag·nos·tic (ăg-nŏs′tĭk) *n.* Someone who doubts the existence or knowability of God but does not deny the possibility that God exists.

~adj. 1. Pertaining to agnostics. 2. Uncertain or uncommitted on any particular question at issue. [19th century : A- (not) + GNOSTIC (coined by T.H. Huxley as a description of his own views, as opposed to those of Victorian "gnostics," who believed that there were immaterial or spiritual phenomena).] **—ag·nos·ti·cal·ly** *adv.*

ag·nos·ti·cism (ăg-nŏs′tə-sĭz′əm) *n.* The philosophical view that it is impossible to know whether or not God exists; doubt as to the existence or knowability of God.

Ag·nus De·i (ăg′nəs dē′ī, äg′no͞os dā′ē) *n.* 1. The Lamb of God, an emblem of Christ, derived from John 1:29 and Isaiah 53:7. 2. A representation of this. 3. A wax disk stamped with this emblem and blessed by the pope. 4. **a.** A threefold prayer said or sung shortly after the Eucharistic Prayer in the Mass. **b.** A musical setting of the Latin text of this prayer. [Latin.]

a·go (ə-gō′) *adj.* Gone by; past: *two years ago.*

~adv. In the past: *It happened long ago.* [Middle English *ago(n),* past participle of *agon,* to go away, be past, Old English *āgān* : *ā-* (intensive) + *gān,* to go.]

a·gog (ə-gŏg′) *adv.* In a state of keen anticipation; highly excited: *The court was all agog to hear the verdict.* [Middle English, from Old French *en gogues,* "in merriments," from *gogue,* merriment, probably imitative of hubbub.] **—a·gog** *adj.*

agouti *A burrowing rodent native to South and Central America, the agouti is a fast runner about the size of a rabbit.*

PRONUNCIATION KEY

ă, pat; ā, pay; âr, care;
ä, father, are; b, bib;
ch, church; d, deed; ĕ, pet;
ē, be; f, fife; g, gag; h, hat;
hw, which; ĭ, pit; ī, pie;
îr, pier; j, judge; k, kick;
l, lid, needle; m, mum;
n, no, sudden; ng, thing;
ŏ, pot; ō, toe; ô, paw, for;
oi, noise; ou, out; o͝o, book;
o͞o, boot; p, pop; r, roar;
s, sauce; sh, ship, dish;
t, tight; th, thin, path;
th, this, bathe; ŭ, cut; ûr, fur;
v, valve; w, with; y, yes;
z, zebra, size; zh, vision;
ə, about, item, edible,
gallop, circus, peaceful

IN FOREIGN WORDS:

ȧ, *Fr.* ami; œ, *Fr.* feu, *Ger.* schön; ü, *Fr.* tu, *Ger.* über;
KH, *Ger.* ich, *Scot.* loch;
N, *Fr.* bon; y', *Fr.* Compiègne

STRESS MARKS:

Primary stress: ′
in·cite′ (ĭn-sīt′)
Secondary stress: ′
in′sight′ (ĭn′sīt′)

á go·go, á go-go (ä gō-gō′) *adj. Informal.* Unlimited; galore: *champagne á gogo.* [French, "in a joyful manner," from *gogo,* probably reduplication of the first syllable of *gogue,* merriment, from Old French. See **agog.**] **—á go·go** *adv.*

-agogue, -agog *suffix.* Indicates: **1.** A leader or inciter of; for example, **demagogue. 2.** *Medicine.* Something that stimulates the flow of; for example, **emmenagogue.** [Late Latin *-agōgus,* from Greek *-agōgos,* from *agōgos,* leading, drawing forth, from *agein,* to lead.]

a·gone (ə-gôn′, ə-gŏn′) *adj. Archaic.* Gone; gone by; past. [Middle English *agon,* AGO.] **—a·gone** *adv.*

a·gon·ic (ā-gŏn′ĭk, ə-gŏn′-) *adj.* Having no angle. [Greek *agōnos* : *a-,* not + *gōnia,* angle.]

agonic line *n.* An imaginary line on the earth's surface connecting points where the magnetic declination is zero.

ag·o·nist (ăg′ə-nĭst) *n. Physiology.* A muscle whose contraction effects movement of a part of the body. It is opposed by contraction in another muscle, the **antagonist** *(see).* [Back-formation from ANTAGONIST.]

ag·o·nis·tic (ăg′ə-nĭs′tĭk) *adj.* **1.** Striving to overcome in argument; competitive; combative. **2.** Straining to achieve effect. **3.** Of or pertaining to contests, originally those of the ancient Greeks. [Late Latin *agōnisticus,* from Greek *agōnistikos,* from *agōnistēs,* contestant, from *agōn,* contest.] **—ag·o·nis·ti·cal·ly** *adv.*

ag·o·nize (ăg′ə-nīz′) *v.* **-nized, -nizing, -nizes.** *—intr.* **1.** To be in extreme pain or suffer great anguish. **2.** To make a prolonged or intense mental effort: *We agonized over the decision all night. —tr.* To cause great pain or anguish to. [Old French *agoniser,* from Late Latin *agōnizāre,* from Greek *agōnizesthai,* to contend for a prize, to struggle, from *agōnia,* contest, AGONY.] **—ag·o·niz·ing·ly** *adv.*

ag·o·ny (ăg′ə-nē) *n., pl.* **-nies. 1.** The suffering of intense physical or mental pain. **2.** A sudden or intense emotion of a particular sort: *an agony of doubt.* **3.** A violent or intense struggle. **—last agony** or **agonies.** The struggle that precedes death. [Middle English *agonie,* from Old French, from Late Latin *agōnia,* from Greek, contest, anguish, from *agōn,* contest, from *agein,* to drive.]

agony column *n. Informal.* **1.** A newspaper column containing advertisements chiefly about missing relatives or friends. **2.** *British.* A newspaper or magazine feature that prints letters from troubled readers together with a columnist's replies and advice.

ag·o·ra[1] (ăg′ə-rə) *n., pl.* **-rae** (-rē′, -rī′) or **-ras. 1.** A marketplace in ancient Greece, customarily used for holding meetings of the people's assembly. **2.** The assembly itself. [Greek *agora,* from *ageirein,* to assemble.]

a·go·ra[2] (ä′gə-rä′) *n., pl.* **-rot** or **-roth** (-rōt′). An Israeli monetary unit equal to 1/100 of the shekel of Israel. See feature at **currency.** [Hebrew *'agōrāh,* from *āgōr,* to collect.]

ag·o·ra·pho·bi·a (ăg′ə-rə-fō′bē-ə) *n.* Abnormal fear of open spaces or of going out in public. [New Latin : Greek *agora,* open space, AGORA + -PHOBIA.] **—ag·o·ra·pho·bic** (ăg′ə-rə-fō′bĭk, -fŏb′ĭk) *adj.*

a·gou·ti (ə-gōō′tē) *n., pl.* **-tis** or **-ties.** Any of several burrowing rodents of the genus *Dasyprocta,* of tropical America, having grizzled brownish or dark-gray fur. [French, from Spanish *agutí,* from Guarani *acutí.*]

agr. agricultural; agriculture.

A.G.R. advanced gas-cooled reactor.

A·gra (ä′grə). City in north-central India in Uttar Pradesh on the Jumna River. It was a capital of the Mogul Empire in the 16th and 17th centuries. The Taj Mahal was built here by Shah Jahan. Modern Agra is an important commercial city whose products include carpets and glassware.

a·graffe (ə-grăf′) *n.* **1.** A hook-and-loop clasp on armor and clothing. **2.** In stonemasonry, a cramp iron for holding stones together. [French *agrafe,* from Old French *agrafer,* to hook on to : *a-,* to, from Latin *ad-* + *grafer,* to hook, from *grafe,* hook, from Old High German *krāpfo.*]

a·gran·u·lo·cy·to·sis (ā-grăn′yə-lō-sī-tō′sĭs) *n.* A drug-induced disease marked by high fever, lesions of the mucous membranes, and a marked decrease in granular white blood corpuscles. [New Latin : A- (not) + GRANULE + -CYT(E) + -OSIS.]

a·gra·pha (ăg′rə-fə) *pl.n. Often* **Agrapha.** The sayings of Jesus not recorded in the Gospels. [Greek, "things unwritten," neuter plural of *agraphos,* unwritten : *a-,* not + *graphein,* to write.]

a·graph·i·a (ā-grăf′ē-ə) *n. Pathology.* Acquired inability to write, caused by disease of the parietal lobe of the brain. [New Latin : A- (not) + Greek *graphein,* to write.] **—a·graph·ic** *adj.*

a·grar·i·an (ə-grâr′ē-ən) *adj.* **1.** Relating to or concerning the land and its ownership, cultivation, and tenure. **2.** Pertaining to agricultural or rural matters.
~n. A person who favors equitable distribution of land. [From Latin *agrārius,* from *ager* (stem *agri-*), land, field.]

a·grar·i·an·ism (ə-grâr′ē-ə-nĭz′əm) *n.* A movement for equitable distribution of land and for agrarian reform.

a·gree (ə-grē′) *v.* **agreed, agreeing, agrees.** *—intr.* **1.** To grant consent; be willing. Used with the infinitive: *He agreed to accompany us.* **2.** To correspond; be in accord: *The copy agrees with the original.* **3.** To be of one opinion. Often used with *with.* **4.** To come to an understanding or to terms. Used with *about, upon,* or *on*: *Is it possible to agree on such great problems?* **5.** To be beneficial to the constitution or health. Used with *with*: *Spicy food does not agree with him.* **6.** *Grammar.* To correspond in gender, number, case, or person. *—tr.* **1.** To grant or concede: *He agreed that we should go.* **2.** *Chiefly British.* To come to an understanding or settlement regarding: *agree terms.* —See Synonyms at **assent.** [Middle English *agreen,* from Old French *agreer,* from Vulgar Latin *aggrātāre* (unattested), to be pleasing to : *ad-,* to + *grātus,* pleasing, beloved, agreeable.]
Synonyms: *accord, coincide, conform, correspond, harmonize.*

a·gree·a·ble (ə-grē′ə-bəl) *adj.* **1.** Pleasing; pleasant; to one's liking: *an agreeable painting.* **2.** Ready to consent or submit: *They needed a lift, and I was agreeable.* **—a·gree·a·bil·i·ty, a·gree·a·ble·ness** *n.* **—a·gree·a·bly** *adv.*

a·greed (ə-grēd′) *adj.* **1.** Determined by common consent: *the agreed meeting place.* **2.** Of one opinion: *Both parties were agreed.* **3.** Allowed; granted. Used as an interjection.

a·greed-val·ue policy (ə-grēd′văl′yōō) *n.* An insurance policy requiring the insurer to pay the insured the full face value of the policy in the event of total loss, regardless of the actual value of the property lost. Also called "valued policy."

a·gree·ment (ə-grē′mənt) *n.* **1.** The act of agreeing. **2.** The state of being agreed; concord; harmony. **3.** An arrangement between parties regarding a course of action; a covenant; a treaty. **4.** *Law.* **a.** A properly executed and legally binding contract. **b.** The writing or document embodying this. **5.** *Grammar.* Correspondence in gender, number, case, or person between words.

a·gres·tal (ə-grĕs′təl) *adj. Botany.* Growing wild, especially in cultivated areas. [From Latin *agrestis,* rural, from *ager* (stem *agr-*), field, land.]

a·gres·tic (ə-grĕs′tĭk) *adj.* Also **a·gres·ti·cal** (-tĭ-kəl). **1.** Rural; rustic. **2.** Unpolished; crude.

ag·ri·busi·ness (ăg′rə-bĭz′nĭs) *n.* Farming engaged in as a large-scale business, including the production, processing, and distribution of farm products and the manufacture of farm machinery, equipment, and supplies. [AGRI(CULTURE) + BUSINESS.]

agric. agriculture; agriculturist.

A·gric·o·la (ə-grĭk′ə-lə), **Georgius,** born Georg Bauer (1494–1555). German mineralogist. In his book *De Re Metallica,* published in 1556, he dealt with mineralogy, geology, and mining, and produced the first systematic and scientific description of minerals and ores.

Agricola, Gnaeus Julius (c. A.D. 40–93). Roman general and conqueror of Britain. A consul in *c.* 71, he was governor of Britain (*c.* 78–85). An enlightened ruler, he circumnavigated the mainland and pacified most of the island, subduing northern Wales and advancing far into Scotland.

ag·ri·cul·ture (ăg′rĭ-kŭl′chər) *n. Abbr.* **agr., agric.** The science or occupation of cultivating the soil, producing crops, and raising livestock; farming. [Latin *agricultūra,* originally *agrī cultūra,* "cultivation of land" : *agrī,* genitive of *ager,* land + *cultūra,* cultivation, CULTURE.] **—ag·ri·cul·tur·al** (ăg′rĭ-kŭl′chə-rəl) *adj.* **—ag·ri·cul·tur·al·ly** *adv.* **—ag·ri·cul·tur·ist** (ăg′rĭ-kŭl′chə-rĭst), **ag·ri·cul·tur·al·ist** *n.*

Agri Dagi. See **Ararat, Mount.**

ag·ri·mo·ny (ăg′rə-mō′nē) *n., pl.* **-nies. 1.** Any of various plants of the genus *Agrimonia,* having compound leaves, long clusters of small yellow flowers, and bristly fruits. **2.** Any of several other plants, such as the **hemp agrimony** *(see).* [Middle English *agrimonie,* from Old French *aigremoine,* from Latin *agrimōnia,* alteration of *argemōnia,* from Greek *argemōnē, argemōnia,* poppy, perhaps from Hebrew *'argāmān,* red-purple.]

ag·ri·ol·o·gy (ăg′rē-ŏl′ə-jē) *n.* The study of primitive cultures. [Greek *agrios,* wild, from *agros,* open field + -LOGY.] **—ag·ri·o·log·i·cal** (ăg′rē-ə-lŏj′ĭ-kəl) *adj.*

A·grip·pa (ə-grĭp′ə), **Marcus Vipsanius** (63–12 B.C.). Roman general and statesman, the adviser of the emperor Augustus, whose daughter Julia he married. He was in command of the fleet that defeated the forces of Mark Antony and Cleopatra at Actium.

Ag·rip·pi·na (ăg′rə-pī′nə, -pē′-), known as "the Elder" (*c.* 13 B.C.–A.D. 33). Roman matron, daughter of Agrippa, granddaughter of Augustus, and mother of the emperor Caligula. She accompanied her husband, Germanicus Caesar, on all his campaigns and was famous for her courage. After Germanicus's death Tiberius banished her to the island of Pandataria, where she died of starvation.

Agrippina, known as "the Younger" (*c.* A.D. 15–59). Roman empress, daughter of Agrippina the Elder and mother of the emperor Nero. She was known for her ambition and ruthlessness, and it is thought that she murdered her third husband, her uncle the emperor Claudius. She managed to place Nero on the throne and exerted considerable power through her son. Eventually they quarreled, and Nero had her murdered.

agro- *prefix.* Indicates field, earth, or soil; for example, **agronomy.** [Greek *agros,* open field.]

ag·ro·bi·ol·o·gy (ăg′rō-bī-ŏl′ə-jē) *n.* The science of plant and animal growth and nutrition as related to soil variation and crop yield. **—ag·ro·bi·o·log·ic** (ăg′rō-bī′ə-lŏj′ĭk), **ag·ro·bi·o·log·i·cal** *adj.* **—ag·ro·bi·o·log·i·cal·ly** *adv.* **—ag·ro·bi·ol·o·gist** (ăg′rō-bī-ŏl′ə-jĭst) *n.*

a·grol·o·gy (ə-grŏl′ə-jē) *n.* The applied science of soils in relation to crops. Compare **pedology.** [AGRO- + -LOGY.] **—ag·ro·log·ic** (ăg′rə-lŏj′ĭk), **ag·ro·log·i·cal** *adj.* **—ag·ro·log·i·cal·ly** *adv.* **—a·grol·o·gist** (ə-grŏl′ə-jĭst) *n.*

ag·ro·nom·ics (ăg′rə-nŏm′ĭks) *n. Used with a singular verb.* Agronomy.

a·gron·o·my (ə-grŏn′ə-mē) *n.* The application of the various soil and plant sciences to soil management and the raising of crops; scientific agriculture. [French *agronomie* : AGRO- + -NOMY.] **—ag·ro·nom·ic** (ăg′rə-nŏm′ĭk), **ag·ro·nom·i·cal** *adj.* **—a·gron·o·mist** (ə-grŏn′ə-mĭst) *n.*

ag·ros·tol·o·gy (ăg′rə-stŏl′ə-jē) *n.* The botanical study of grasses.

agrimony *This common European wildflower,* Agrimonia eupatoria, *has had many uses in the past—from curing snakebites to producing a dye for wool. An infusion from its leaves is still used as a tonic.*

[Greek *agrōstis,* a kind of wild grass, from *agros,* field + -LOGY.]

a·ground (ə-ground′) *adv.* On the ground or bottom; stranded, as in shallow water: *The ship ran aground.* **—a·ground** *adj.*

a·gue (ā′gyo͞o) *n.* **1.** An attack of malarial fever, with alternate fever and chills. **2.** A recurrent chill or fit of shivering. [Middle English, from Old French *ague,* from Medieval Latin *(fēbris) acūta,* "sharp (fever)," feminine of *acūtus,* sharp, past participle of *acuere,* to sharpen, from *acus,* needle.] **—a·gu·ish** (ā′gyo͞o-ĭsh) *adj.* **—a·gu·ish·ly** *adv.* **—a·gu·ish·ness** *n.*

a·gue·weed (ā′gyo͞o-wēd′) *n.* **1.** A plant, *Gentiana quinquefolia,* of eastern North America, having clusters of pale blue-violet or white flowers. **2.** A plant, **boneset** *(see).*

A·gul·has, Cape (ə-gŭl′əs). Headland in South Africa, the most southerly point of Africa. Its meridian (longitude 20° E) marks the division between the Atlantic and Indian oceans.

ah (ä) *interj.* Used to express various emotions, such as surprise, delight, pain, satisfaction, or regret. See **ooh.** [Middle English *a(h),* from Old French.]

A.H. in the year of the Hegira. Used to indicate the date in the Muslim world, the base year being A.D. 622. [Latin *anno Hegirae*]

a·ha (ä-hä′) *interj.* Used to express surprise, triumph, or pleasure. [Middle English : AH + HA.]

A·hab (ā′hăb′). A king of Israel in the 9th century B.C., husband of Jezebel. I Kings 16:29.

A·has·u·e·rus (ə-hăz′yo͞o-ē′rəs). A king of ancient Persia, often identified with Xerxes; the husband of Esther. Esther 1:1.

a·head (ə-hĕd′) *adv.* **1.** At or to the front or leading position. **2.** Before in space or in time; in advance. **3.** Onward; forward. **—ahead of.** In front of. **—get ahead.** To attain success. **—a·head** *adj.*

a·hem (ə-hĕm′) *interj.* Used to attract attention or to express doubt or warning. [Imitative. See **hem².**]

a·him·sa (ə-hĭm′sä′) *n.* An Indian doctrine of nonviolence, expressing belief in the sacredness of all living creatures and the possibility of reincarnation. It is strictly practiced by the Jains and subscribed to by Buddhists and Hindus. [Sanskrit *ahiṁsā,* noninjury : *a-,* without + *hiṁsā,* injury, from *hiṁsati,* he injures.]

a·his·tor·i·cal (ā′hĭ-stôr′ĭ-kəl, ā′hĭ-stŏr′-) *adj.* Also **a·his·tor·ic** (ā′-hĭ-stôr′ĭk, -stŏr′ĭk). Not historical; unrelated to history.

A·hith·o·phel (ə-hĭth′ə-fĕl). Also in Douay Bible **A·chit·o·phel** (ə-kĭt′-). A counselor of David, who became an adviser to Absalom in his rebellion and hanged himself when his advice was disregarded.

Ah·ma·da·bad, Ah·me·da·bad (ä′məd-ə-bäd′). Capital of Gujarat state, India. Founded in 1412 as the capital of the former Gujarat kingdom, it is the largest town of Gujarat as well as being the state's cultural and commercial center. Ahmadabad's textile industry is one of the largest in India.

-aholic. Variant of **-holic.**

a·hoy (ə-hoi′) *interj. Nautical.* Used to hail a ship or person, or to attract attention. [AH + HOY (interjection).]

A.H.Q. army headquarters.

Ah·ri·man (ä′rĭ-mən) *n.* In Zoroastrianism, the spirit of evil, understood by some as the arch rival of **Ormazd** *(see).* [Persian *Ahrīman,* probably from Avestan *aṅra mainyu,* "the evil spirit" : *aṅra,* evil, hostile, probably from Iranian root *ans-*†, to hate + *mainyu,* spirit.]

A·hu·ra Maz·da (ä-ho͝or′ə măz′də). **Ormazd** *(see).*

Ah·ve·nan·maa (äKH′vĕ-năn-mä′). Also **Å·land Islands** (ō′län). Province of Finland, comprising about 80 inhabited islands and 6,000 uninhabited islets in the Baltic Sea between Finland and Sweden at the entrance to the Gulf of Bothnia. Ahvenanmaa, the largest island, is the site of the capital, Maarianhamina.

ai (ī) *n., pl.* **ais.** See **sloth** (sense 2a). [Portuguese, from Tupi *ai, hai.*]

A.I. **1.** artificial insemination. **2.** artificial intelligence.

ai·a (ī′ə) *n. South African.* **1.** A child's nursemaid or nanny, especially a native woman. **2.** *Informal.* An old native woman. [Portuguese, nurse. Compare **ayah.**]

aid (ād) *v.* **aided, aiding, aids.** *—intr.* To help; assist. *—tr.* To give help or assistance to. —See Synonyms at **help.**

~n. **1.** The act or result of helping; assistance; cooperation. **2. a.** One that helps; an assistant or helper. **b.** A device that helps: *a hearing aid; a teaching aid.* **3. Foreign aid** *(see).* **4.** An aide-de-camp or aide. **5.** In medieval England: **a.** Any of several revenues or subsidies paid to the king. **b.** A money payment to a feudal lord by a vassal. [Middle English *eyden, aiden,* from Old French *aider,* from Latin *adjūtāre,* frequentative of *adjuvāre,* to give aid to, help : *ad,* to + *juvāre*†, to help.] **—aid·er** *n.*

A.I.D. **1.** acute infectious disease. **2.** Agency for International Development. **3.** artificial insemination by donor.

Ai·dan (ā′dən), **Saint** (*c.* A.D. 600–51). Irish monk. From the monastery at Iona he was sent as a missionary to Northumbria in 635. He founded a famous monastery at (Holy Island) Lindisfarne and became its first bishop.

aide (ād) *n.* **1.** An aide-de-camp. **2.** An assistant; a helper: *a president's aide.* [French, from *aider,* to help, AID.]

aide-de-camp (ād′də-kămp′) *n., pl.* **aides-de-camp** (ādz′-). *Abbr.* **ADC, a.d.c., A.D.C.** A naval or military officer acting as secretary and confidential assistant to a superior officer of general or flag rank. [French, "camp assistant."]

aide-mé·moire (ād′mĕm-wär′) *n., pl.* **aides-mé·moire** (ādz′-). A statement in summary form, usually of the terms of an agreement, to be used in drafting a formal document. [French, "help memory."]

AIDS (ādz) *n.* An abnormal, ultimately fatal condition of the body's immune system, in which the body's defenses against disease are permanently weakened. [*A*cquired *I*mmune *D*eficiency *S*yndrome.]

Aigina. See **Aegina.**

aiglet. Variant of **aglet.**

ai·grette, ai·gret (ā-grĕt′, ā′grĕt) *n.* **1.** An ornamental tuft of upright plumes, especially the tail feathers of an egret. **2.** An ornament or item of jewelry, such as a spray of gems, resembling such a tuft. [French. See **egret.**]

ai·guille (ā-gwēl′) *n.* **1.** A sharp, pointed mountain peak. **2.** A needle-shaped drill for boring holes in rock or masonry. [French, "needle," from Old French, AGLET.]

ai·guil·lette (ā′gwĭ-lĕt′) *n.* An ornamental cord or braid worn on the shoulder of a military uniform. [French, AGLET.]

A.I.H. artificial insemination by husband.

Ai·ken (ā′kən), **Charles Avery** (1872–1965). U.S. painter and graphic artist. He is noted for his watercolors of flowers and landscapes. Aiken also originated the technique of making prints from plaster blocks.

Aiken, Conrad Potter (1889–1973). U.S. poet, novelist, and critic. He won a Pulitzer Prize for his *Selected Poems* in 1930. Among his most famous works is *Collected Poems* (1953), which earned him the recognition he had long been denied.

ai·ki·do (ī′kē-dō′, ī-kē′dō) *n.* A 20th-century Japanese martial art similar to judo.

ail (āl) *v.* **ailed, ailing, ails.** *—intr.* **1.** To feel ill or have pain; be unwell. **2.** To be in a weak or unsound condition: *The economy is ailing.* *—tr.* To cause pain; make ill or uneasy; trouble: *What ails you?* [Middle English *eilen,* Old English *eglan,* to trouble, from *egle,* troublesome.]

ailanthus *This tree,* Ailanthus altissima, *was introduced to the Western world in the 1750's. It was given the name "tree of heaven" because its branches are said to reach toward Paradise, but the name rightly belongs to the related species* Ailanthus moluccana.

ai·lan·thus (ā-lăn′thəs) *n.* A deciduous tree, *Ailanthus altissima,* native to China and widely grown for ornament, especially in urban areas. It has compound leaves and clusters of small greenish flowers with a strong odor. Also called "tree of heaven." [New Latin, from Amboinese (an Indonesian language) *ai lanto,* "tree (of) heaven"; Latin form influenced by Greek *anthos,* flower.]

ai·le·ron (ā′lə-rŏn′) *n.* A movable control surface on the trailing edge of an airplane wing. [French, diminutive of *aile,* wing, from Old French, from Latin *āla.*]

ail·ment (āl′mənt) *n.* A physical or mental disorder; especially, a mild illness.

ai·lu·ro·phile (ā-lo͝or′ə-fīl′) *n.* A person who loves cats. [Greek *ailouros,* cat + -PHILE.]

ai·lu·ro·phobe (ā-lo͝or′ə-fōb′) *n.* A person with an intense fear or dislike of cats. [Greek *ailouros,* cat + -PHOBE.]

aim (ām) *v.* **aimed, aiming, aims.** *—tr.* To direct (a weapon, remark, or blow, for example) at someone or something. *—intr.* **1.** To direct a weapon. **2. a.** To direct one's efforts toward something; strive: *aim at perfection.* **b.** To intend; propose; plan. Used with *for* or with an infinitive: *We are aiming for an early start. We aim to get to the bottom of this.*

~n. **1.** The act of aiming or pointing. **2.** The sighting or line of fire of something aimed: *take aim.* **3.** A purpose; an intention; a plan. —See Synonyms at **intention.** [Middle English *aimen,* to guess, aim, from Old French *aesmer,* to guess at : *a-,* at, to, from Latin *ad-* + *esmer,* to guess, from Latin *aestimāre,* to ESTIMATE.]

aim·less (ām′lĭs) *adj.* Without direction or purpose. **—aim·less·ly** *adv.* **—aim·less·ness** *n.*

ain¹ (ān) *adj. Scottish.* Own.

ain². Variant of **ayin.**

ain't (ānt). *Nonstandard.* Contraction of *am not.* Also extended in use to mean *are not, is not, has not,* and *have not.*

Usage: Although widely used in colloquial speech, *ain't* is considered nonstandard by educated speakers. It should always be avoided in writing or formal speech, unless you are deliberately trying to create a humorous effect or using a fixed phrase like *Things ain't what they used to be. Aren't I* (as in *aren't I coming too?*) has sometimes also been attacked on the grounds that it misleadingly suggests a corresponding form *I are.* But the full form, *am I not,* is so formal that in many contexts it may be considered ridiculously stilted, and *aren't I* is therefore a quite acceptable usage in educated English. The form *amn't I* has some currency in regional English, but is considered nonstandard.

Ai·nu (ī′no͞o) *n., pl.* **-nus** or collectively **Ainu.** **1.** A member of an aboriginal Caucasian people inhabiting the northernmost islands of Japan. **2.** The language of this people. [Ainu, "man."]

aï·o·li (ī-ō′lē) *n.* Garlic-flavored mayonnaise. [French, from *ail,* garlic.]

air (âr) *n.* **1. a.** A colorless, odorless, tasteless, gaseous mixture, mainly nitrogen (approximately 78 percent) and oxygen (approximately 21 percent) with lesser amounts of argon, carbon dioxide, neon, helium, and other gases. **b.** This mixture with varying amounts of moisture, low-altitude pollutants, and particulate matter, enveloping Earth; the atmosphere. **c.** The air or atmosphere in an enclosed space: *The air in the conference room is invariably half cigar smoke.* **d.** In ancient thought, one of the four elements. **2. a.** The sky; the firmament. **b.** The space above the ground: *leaped into the air.* **3.** An atmospheric movement; a breeze; a wind. **4.** The sky as a medium of transport or conveyance: *sent it by air.* **5.** Utterance; public expression: *give air to one's grievances.* **6.** A peculiar or characteristic impression; an appearance or aura: *an air of excitement.* **7.** Personal bearing, appearance, or manner; mien: *He has an air of gentility.* —See Synonyms at **bearing.** **8. airs.** Affectations; haughty manner: *She gives herself airs.* **9.** *Music.* A

melody or tune, especially: **a.** The soprano or treble part in a harmonized composition. **b.** A solo for voice or instrument, with or without accompaniment. **10.** *Archaic.* Breath. **—clear the air.** To dispel emotional differences and tensions. **—in the air. 1.** In circulation; prevalent. **2.** Uncertain; not settled; being thought out or formulated. **—on the air.** Broadcast, or being broadcast, on radio or television. **—take the air.** To go outdoors for fresh air; take a short walk or ride. **—up in the air.** Not decided; uncertain. **—walk on air.** To feel elated or extremely happy.
~*tr.v.* **aired, airing, airs. 1.** To expose (a room or laundry, for example) to air or warmth, in order to dry, cool, or freshen; ventilate. **2.** To give public utterance to; circulate: *air one's grievances.* **—See** Synonyms at **vent.** [Blend of senses of several origins: 1. Atmosphere: Middle English *eir, ayr,* from Old French *air,* from Latin *āēr,* from Greek *aēr,* breath, atmospheric air; 2. Manner, appearance: French *air,* from Old French *aire,* nature, quality, originally "place of origin," from Latin *ager,* place, field, and Latin *ārea,* open space, threshing floor, AREA; 3. Melody: Italian *aria,* ARIA. In English these senses have interacted inextricably, with the first prevailing.]
AIR 1. artist in residence. **2.** All India Radio.
air bag *n.* A safety device designed for use in cars, consisting of a large bag that inflates upon collision and prevents passengers from pitching forward.
air base *n.* A base of operations for military aircraft.
air battery *n.* A rechargeable battery in which the current is produced as a result of oxidation of a metal.
air bearing *n.* A device that uses compressed air to separate working parts, for example of a dental drill, to reduce noise level.
air bed *n.* An inflatable mattress, especially one used for supporting patients with extensive burns.
air bladder *n. Biology.* **1.** An air-filled structure near the spinal column in many fishes, which functions to maintain buoyancy or, in some species, as an aid in respiration or hearing. Also called "swim bladder." **2.** Any air-filled saclike structure, such as one of the dilated parts of the thallus in certain seaweeds.
air·boat (âr′bōt′) *n.* A **swamp boat** (see).
air·borne (âr′bôrn′, -bōrn′) *adj.* Abbr. **abn 1.** Carried by or through the air: *airborne pollen.* **2.** Transported in aircraft: *airborne troops.* **3.** Flying; in flight.
air brake *n.* A brake operated by compressed air.
air brick *n.* A brick with holes running through it, built into a wall as a means of ventilation.
air bridge *n.* A transport link by aircraft between two distant points.
air·brush (âr′brŭsh′) *n.* An atomizer using compressed air to spray paint or other liquids on a surface.
~*tr.v* **airbrushed, -brushing, -brushes.** To paint or coat (a surface) using an airbrush.
air·burst (âr′bûrst′) *n.* An explosion of a bomb or shell in the atmosphere.
air·bus (âr′bŭs′) *n.* A usually wide-bodied jet airplane carrying a large number of passengers over relatively short distances.
air chamber *n.* **1.** Any enclosure filled with air for a special purpose. **2.** Such a compartment, especially in a hydraulic system, in which air elastically compresses and expands to regulate the flow of a fluid.
air command *n.* A unit of the U.S. Air Force that is larger than an air force.
air·con·di·tion (âr′kən-dĭsh′ən) *tr.v.* **-tioned, -tioning, -tions.** To provide with or ventilate by air conditioning. **—air·con·di·tioned** *adj.*
air conditioning *n.* **1.** *Abbr.* **a/c, A/C** A system or apparatus for controlling, especially lowering, the temperature and humidity of a building or vehicle. **2.** The condition so produced. **—air conditioner** *n.*
air·cool (âr′kōōl′) *tr.v.* **-cooled, -cooling, -cools.** To cool (an engine, for example) by a flow of air.
air corridor *n.* An air route established by international agreement, along which aircraft are allowed to fly.
air cover *n.* **1.** Protection for ground operations provided by military aircraft. **2.** The aircraft so employed.
air·craft (âr′krăft′, -kräft′) *n., pl.* **aircraft.** Any machine or device, such as an airplane, helicopter, glider, or balloon, capable of flight in the air, by means of buoyancy or aerodynamic forces.
aircraft carrier *n.* A large naval ship designed as a mobile air base at sea, having a long flat deck to serve as a landing strip.
air·craft·man (âr′krăft′mən, -kräft′mən) *n., pl.* **-men** (-mĭn). *Abbr.* **A.C.** A serviceman of the lowest rank in the British Royal Air Force.
air·craft·wom·an (âr′krăft′wŏom′ən, -kräft′wŏom′ən) *n., pl.* **-women** (-wĭm′ĭn) *Abbr.* **A.C.W.** A servicewoman of the lowest rank in the British Women's Royal Air Force.
air cushion *n.* **1.** An inflatable cushion. **2.** The downward flow of air that lifts and supports a hovercraft. **3.** An **air spring** (see).
air·cush·ion vehicle (âr′kŏosh′ən) *n.* A vehicle supported by a cushion of air, a **Hovercraft** (see).
air division *n.* A unit of the U.S. Air Force larger than a wing and smaller than an air force.
air door *n.* A strong current of warm air directed upward and used instead of a conventional door to prevent heat loss from a building. Also called "air curtain."
air·drome (âr′drōm′) *n.* Also *chiefly British* **aer·o·drome** (âr′ə-drōm′). **1.** An airport. **2.** A landing field. **3.** An airplane hangar.

[Earlier *aerodrome* : AERO- + -DROME.]
air-drop (âr′drŏp′) *n.* A delivery, as of supplies or troops, by parachute from aircraft in flight.
~*tr.v.* **airdropped, -dropping, -drops.** To drop (supplies or troops, for example) from an aircraft.
air-dry (âr′drī′) *tr.v.* **-dried, -drying, -dries.** To dry by exposure to the air.
~*adj.* Sufficiently dry so that further exposure to air will not evaporate moisture.
Aire·dale (âr′dāl′) *n.* A large terrier of a breed developed in England, having a wiry tan coat marked with black. Also called "Airedale terrier." [After *Airedale,* a valley in Yorkshire, England.]
air embolism *n. Pathology.* Obstruction of blood flow from the heart by the presence of air in the circulation, resulting from surgery, injury, or the like.
air·field (âr′fēld′) *n.* An area with hard-surfaced runways where aircraft can take off and land, but usually smaller than an airport and without its facilities for travelers.
air·flow (âr′flō′) *n.* The air currents caused by the motion of an object such as an airplane or motor vehicle.
air·foil (âr′foil′) *n.* Also *chiefly British* **aer·o·foil** (âr′ə-foil′). An aircraft part or surface, such as a wing, propeller blade, or rudder, the shape and orientation of which control stability, direction, lift, thrust, or propulsion.
air force *n. Abbr.* **AF, A.F. 1.** The aviation branch of a country's armed forces. **2.** A unit of the U.S. Air Force larger than an air division and smaller than an air command.
air·frame (âr′frām′) *n.* An aircraft body excluding its engine.
air freight *n.* **1.** A system of transporting freight by air. **2.** The amount charged for this service. **—air-freight** *v.*
air gas *n.* A manufactured fuel gas, **producer gas** (see).
air·glow (âr′glō′) *n.* A faint photochemical light in the upper atmosphere, observable in regions of low and middle latitude. Compare **aurora.**
air gun *n.* A gun discharged by compressed air.
air·head (âr′hĕd′) *n.* An area of hostile or enemy-controlled territory secured by paratroops.
air hole *n.* **1.** A hole or opening through which gas or air may pass. **2.** An opening in the frozen surface of a body of water. **3.** *Aviation.* An **air pocket** (see).
air hostess *n.* A stewardess on an aircraft.
air·i·ly (âr′ə-lē) *adv.* **1.** In a light spirit; gaily; jauntily. **2.** In a light manner; delicately; gently.
air·i·ness (âr′ē-nĭs) *n.* **1.** The quality or state of being light or airy. **2.** Delicacy. **3.** Gaiety; jauntiness.
air·ing (âr′ĭng) *n.* **1.** Exposure to fresh or warm air for ventilation or drying. **2.** Public disclosure or discussion: *giving the whole subject an airing.*
air lane *n.* A regular route of travel for aircraft; an airway.
air layering *n.* A method of plant propagation in which a twig or shoot attached to the parent plant is wrapped in moist sphagnum moss or polyethylene plastic so that it will form roots and can later be removed and replanted.
air·less (âr′lĭs) *adj.* **1.** Without air. **2.** Lacking fresh air; stuffy. **3.** Without a breeze or wind; still. **—air·less·ness** *n.*
air letter *n.* **1.** An airmail letter. **2.** An **aerogram** (see).
air·lift (âr′lĭft′) *n.* An operation by which passengers, troops, or supplies are transported by air when surface routes are blocked.
~*tr.v.* **airlifted, -lifting, -lifts.** To transport by air, as when ground routes are blocked.
air·line (âr′līn′) *n.* **1.** A system for the scheduled transport of passengers and freight by air. **2.** A business organization providing such a system of air transport. **3.** An air route. **4.** The shortest distance between two geographical points; a direct line.
air·lin·er (âr′lī′nər) *n.* A large airplane designed for carrying passengers.
air lock *n.* **1.** An airtight chamber, usually located between two regions of unequal pressure, in which air pressure can be regulated so as to allow access or communication between the regions while maintaining their pressure difference. **2.** A bubble or pocket of air or vapor, as in a pipe, that stops the normal flow of fluid through the conducting path.
air mail, air·mail (âr′māl′) *n.* **1.** The system of conveying mail by aircraft. **2.** Mail conveyed by aircraft. **—air·mail** *adj.*
air·mail (âr′māl′) *tr.v.* **-mailed, -mailing, -mails.** To send (a letter, for example) by airmail.
air·man (âr′mən) *n., pl.* **-men** (-mĭn). A pilot, navigator, or member of any technical profession dealing primarily with aircraft, especially one serving in an air force.
air mass *n. Meteorology.* A large body of air with only small horizontal variations of temperature, pressure, and moisture content.
air mile *n.* A unit of distance in air navigation. See **nautical mile.**
air piracy *n.* The hijacking of an airplane in flight. **—air pirate** *n.*
air·plane (âr′plān′) *n.* Also *chiefly British* **ae·ro·plane** (âr′ə-plān′). A winged flying vehicle that is heavier than air and is powered by jet engines or propellers. [French *aéroplane,* from Late Greek *aeroplanos,* wandering in the air : AERO- + *-planos,* wandering, from *planasthai,* to wander.]
air plant *n. Botany.* An **epiphyte** (see).
air pocket *n.* A downward air current that causes an aircraft to lose altitude abruptly. Also called "air hole."
air·port (âr′pôrt′, -pōrt′) *n.* A tract of leveled land where aircraft can take off and land, especially one equipped with hard-surfaced land-

ing strips, a control tower, hangars, facilities for passengers and cargo, and usually a customhouse.

air pump *n.* A piece of equipment for compressing, removing, or forcing a flow of air.

air raid *n.* An attack by hostile military aircraft, especially when armed with bombs. —**air-raid** (âr'rād') *adj.*

air rifle *n.* A low-powered rifle using manually compressed air to fire small pellets.

air sac *n. Biology.* An air-filled space, such as one of the spaces in a bird's body that forms a connection between the lungs and the bone cavities, or a dilation in the trachea of many insects.

air scoop *n.* An air inlet on an aircraft, designed to take in air for ventilation or pressure.

air·screw (âr'skrōō') *n. British.* The propeller of an airplane.

air-sea rescue (âr'sē') *n.* Rescue at sea, carried out by aircraft.

air·ship (âr'shĭp') *n.* A self-propelled lighter-than-air craft with directional control surfaces; a dirigible.

air·sick·ness (âr'sĭk'nĭs) *n.* Nausea resulting from nervous tension or changes in pressure or motion in an aircraft. —**air·sick** *adj.*

air sock *n.* A windsock (see).

air·space (âr'spās') *n.* The portion of the atmosphere above a particular land area; especially, the air above a nation or other political subdivision, considered to be under its jurisdiction.

air speed *n.* Speed, especially of an aircraft, relative to the air.

air spray *n.* 1. A device for spraying liquids using compressed air; an aerosol. 2. The liquid sprayed by such a device.

air spring *n.* An enclosed volume of air which, by its resilience, acts as a spring or shock absorber. Also called "air cushion."

air·stream (âr'strēm') *n.* 1. The current of air passing over a surface. 2. A wind, especially at high altitude.

air·strip (âr'strĭp') *n.* A cleared area serving as an airfield; a landing strip.

airt (ärt) *n. Scottish.* Any of the points on the compass; a direction, especially of the wind. [Middle English *art,* from Scottish Gaelic *aird,* probably from Old Irish *aird†.*]

air terminal *n.* See **terminal** (sense 4b).

air·tight (âr'tīt') *adj.* 1. Impermeable to air or other gas. 2. Having no weak points; sound: *an airtight excuse.*

air time *n.* 1. The period of time during which a radio or television station broadcasts. 2. An amount of broadcasting time allocated or available for a particular purpose.

air-to-air missile (âr'tə-âr') *n.* A missile, usually guided, designed to be fired from aircraft at aircraft.

air-to-surface missile (âr'tə-sûr'fĭs) *n.* A missile, usually guided, designed to be fired from aircraft at targets on the ground. Also called "air-to-ground missile."

air-traf·fic control (âr'trăf'ĭk) *n. Abbr.* **A.T.C.** 1. A system of directing aircraft movements in which the required speed, direction, and altitude of each aircraft in a given area is communicated by radio to its pilot. 2. The people operating this system. —**air-traf·fic control·ler** *n.*

air·waves (âr'wāvz') *pl.n.* The medium used for the transmission of radio and television signals: *a new program coming to you over the airwaves.*

air·way (âr'wā') *n.* 1. A passageway for a current of air, as to the lungs or to a mine. 2. A designated route of passage for an aircraft; an air lane.

air·wom·an (âr'wŏŏm'ən) *n., pl.* **-women** (-wĭm'ĭn). A female airman.

air·wor·thy (âr'wûr'thē) *adj.* Prepared and in fit condition to fly. Said of aircraft. —**air·wor·thi·ness** *n.*

air·y (âr'ē) *adj.* **-ier, -iest.** 1. Having the constitution or nature of air. 2. High in the air; lofty; towering. 3. a. Open to the air; breezy; full of fresh air. b. Spacious; uncluttered. 4. Resembling air; immaterial: *an airy apparition.* 5. Insubstantial; irrational; unrealistic: *airy political views.* 6. Light as air; graceful or delicate: *an airy veil.* 7. Nonchalant or breezy in manner.

air·y-fair·y (âr'ē-fâr'ē) *adj.* 1. Extremely light and delicate; insubstantial. 2. *Informal.* Unrealistic; fanciful: *airy-fairy notions.*

Aisha. See **Ayesha.**

aisle (īl) *n.* 1. A part of a church divided laterally from the nave by a row of pillars or columns. 2. A passageway between rows of seats, such as in a church or auditorium. —**rolling in the aisles.** *Informal.* Overwhelmed by laughter. [Middle English *eile* (influenced by *ile,* *isle,* ISLE), from Old French *ele, aile,* wing of a building, from Latin *āla,* wing.]

ait. Variant of **eyot.**

aitch (āch) *n.* The letter h. [Obsolete *ache,* from French *hache,* probably from Vulgar Latin *hacca†* (unattested), of obscure origin.]

aitch·bone (āch'bōn') *n.* 1. The rump bone in cattle. 2. The cut of meat containing this bone. [Middle English *hachboon,* from phrase *an hach boon,* originally *a nachebon* : *nache, nage,* buttock, from Old French, from Late Latin *natica,* from Latin *natis,* buttock + *bon,* BONE.]

Aix-en-Pro·vence (ĕks'äN-prô-väNs'). City and spa in Bouches-du-Rhône department, southeast France. It has been the capital of Provence since the 12th century and is an important cultural center.

Aix-la-Chapelle. See **Aachen.**

a·jar¹ (ə-jär') *adv.* Partially opened. Said of doors and windows: *Please leave the door ajar.* [Middle English *on char,* "in the act of turning" : ON + *char,* a turn, Old English *cierr* (see **char**).] —**a·jar** *adj.*

ajar² *adv.* Not harmonious; jarring: *ajar with the times.* [A- (on, in

the act of) + JAR (discord).] —**a·jar** *adj.*

A·jax¹ (ā'jăks). *Greek Mythology.* A Greek warrior of great stature and prowess who fought against Troy; son of Telamon of Salamis.

Ajax². *Greek Mythology.* A Greek warrior of small stature and arrogant character who fought against Troy; son of Ileus of Locris.

AK Alaska (used with a Zip Code).

AK 47 *n.* A type of rifle, a **Kalashnikov** (see).

a.k.a. also known as.

Ak·bar (ăk'bär'), known as "the Great" (1542–1605). The greatest of India's Mogul emperors, who reigned from 1556. His conquests added most of northern India to the Mogul Empire.

ak·ee, ack·ee (ăk'ē, ă-kē') *n.* 1. A tropical tree, *Blighia sapida,* native to Africa and cultivated in the West Indies, having fragrant flowers and capsules containing black seeds. 2. The edible aril surrounding these seeds, used in tropical cooking. [Native name in Liberia.]

Akhaïa. See **Achaea.**

A·khe·na·ton (ä'kə-nä'tən) (died *c.* 1360 B.C.). Also **Ikh·na·ton** (ĭk-), **A·men·ho·tep IV** (ä'mən-hō'tĕp). King of Egypt, who reigned from *c.* 1379–*c.* 1360 B.C. Originally named Amenhotep IV, he changed his name on rejecting the old gods and initiating the worship of the sun god Aten (Aton). He built a new capital at Tell-el-Amarna.

Akh·ma·to·va (äkH-mät'ə-və, äkH'-, -mä'tə-), **Anna,** pen name of Anna Andreevna Gorenko (1889–1966). Russian poet. Her intense and lyrical poems, often dealing with tragic love, have established her as one of the foremost 20th-century Russian poets.

a·kim·bo (ə-kĭm'bō) *adj.* With the hands on the hips and the elbows bowed outward. Used chiefly in the phrase *with arms akimbo.* [Middle English *in kenebowe,* "in keen bow," "in a sharp curve," probably from Old Norse *i keng boginn* (unattested), "bent like a bow" : *keng,* accusative of *kengr†,* a curve, hook + *boginn,* accusative of *bogi,* a bow.] —**a·kim·bo** *adv.*

a·kin (ə-kĭn') *adj.* 1. Of the same kin; related. 2. Having a similar quality or character; analogous. Often used with *to.* 3. *Linguistics.* Related in origin; cognate. Said of languages or of words in different languages derived from the same source. [A- (of) + KIN.]

Akka. See **Acre.**

Ak·kad or **Ac·cad** (ăk'ăd', ä'käd'). Ancient region of central Mesopotamia, now in Iraq. The Akkadian empire flourished from *c.* 2340 B.C. to *c.* 2240 B.C., especially under Sargon, who ruled from his capital of Agade (or Akkad).

Ak·ka·di·an, Ac·ca·di·an (ə-kā'dē-ən) *n.* 1. A native or inhabitant of Akkad. 2. The Semitic language spoken in ancient Akkad.

~*adj.* Of, pertaining to, or relating to the Akkadians or their Semitic language.

Akko. See **Acre.**

Ak·ron (ăk'rən). City in northeastern Ohio. It became known as the rubber capital of the world in the early 20th century.

Ak·sum or **Ax·um** (äk'sōōm). Town in northern Ethiopia that was the center of the northern Ethiopian empire from the 1st to the 8th centuries A.D. Its kings were converted to Christianity in the 4th century. According to tradition, the Ark of the Covenant was brought here from Jerusalem and placed in the Church of St. Mary of Zion, where the emperors of Ethiopia were crowned.

–al¹ *suffix.* Indicates a relation to or connection with; for example, **adjectival.** [Middle English *-al, -el,* from Old French, from Latin *-ālis.*]

–al² *suffix.* Indicates the act or process of doing or experiencing the action specified; for example, **denial, arrival.** [Middle English *-aille,* from Old French, from Latin *-ālia,* substantive neuter plural of *-ālis,* adjectival suffix.]

–al³ *suffix. Chemistry.* Indicates an aldehyde, an organic compound; for example, **ethanal, butanal.** [*Al*dehyde.]

Al The symbol for the element aluminum.

AL 1. Alabama (used with a Zip Code). 2. American League. 3. American Legion.

al. alcohol; alcoholic.

à la (ä'lä, ä'lə, ăl'ə) *prep.* Also **a la.** In the style or manner of; in accordance with: *mushrooms à la grecque; a poem à la Ogden Nash.* [French, short for *à la mode de,* "in the manner of."]

a·la (ä'lə) *n., pl.* **alae** (ä'lē). *Biology.* A winglike structure or part, such as the flattened part of certain bones, the membranous border of some seeds, or one of the side petals of certain flowers, such as the sweet pea. [Latin *āla,* wing]

Ala. Alabama.

a.l.a. all letters answered.

Al·a·bam·a (ăl'ə-băm'ə). State in the southeastern United States. It was admitted as the 22nd state in 1819. Montgomery is the capital and Birmingham the largest city. Alabama is still a major cotton-growing state, but since World War II mining and manufacturing have accounted for the largest share of the state's income. Products include coal, oil, steel, chemicals, and textiles. —**Al·a·bam·i·an** (ăl'ə-bā'mē-ən), **Al·a·bam·an** *adj. & n.*

al·a·bas·ter (ăl'ə-băs'tər, -bäs'tər) *n.* 1. A dense, translucent, white or tinted, fine-grained gypsum, often used in sculpture. 2. A variety of hard calcite, translucent and sometimes banded. 3. Pale yellowish pink to yellowish gray.

~*adj.* Also **al·a·bas·trine** (ăl'ə-băs'trĭn, -băs'trīn). Of or similar to alabaster; smooth and white. [Middle English *alabastre,* from Old French, from Latin *alabaster,* from Greek *alabast(r)os,* perhaps of Egyptian origin.]

à la carte (ä'lä kärt', ăl'ə) *adj.* Having a separate price for each item. Said of a menu or part of a menu. Compare **prix fixe, table d'hôte.**

Ajax *During the sack of Troy, according to Greek legend, the Greek hero Ajax, son of Ileus of Lochis, raped the priestess Cassandra on the altar of the goddess Athena. On this vase, dating from about 450 B.C., the naked priestess clasps the goddess's statue for protection as Ajax grabs her hair.*

[French, "by the menu."] —**à la carte** *adv.*

a·lack (ə-lăk′) *interj.* Also **a·lack·a·day** (ə-lăk′ə-dā′). *Archaic.* Used to express sorrow, regret, or alarm. [Middle English *alacke,* "ah, (what) loss!" : probably *a, ah,* AH + LACK, by analogy with *alas.*]

a·lac·ri·ty (ə-lăk′rə-tē) *n.* **1.** Cheerful willingness; eagerness. **2.** Lively action; sprightliness. [Latin *alacritās,* from *alacer* (stem *alacr-*), lively, eager.] —**a·lac·ri·tous** *adj.*

A·lad·din (ə-lăd′n). In the *Arabian Nights,* a boy who acquires a magic lamp and a magic ring with which he can summon two genies to fulfill any desire.

A·lain-Four·nier (ä′lăN-fōor-nyā′), pen name of Henri Alban Fournier (1886–1914). French novelist. He is principally remembered for his novel *Le Grand Meaulnes* (1913), translated into English as *The Lost Domain.* He was killed in battle in World War I.

à la king (ä′ lä kĭng′, ăl′ə) *adj.* Prepared in a cream sauce with green pepper and mushrooms: *chicken à la king.*

Alamannian, Alamannic. Variants of **Alemannic.**

Alamein. See El Alamein.

Al·a·mo (ăl′ə-mō′). A chapel built in 1744 as part of the Mission of San Antonio de Valero at San Antonio, Texas. During the Texas Revolution against Mexican rule some 182 revolutionaries were besieged here from February 24 to March 6, 1836, by Gen. Santa Anna and an army of thousands. All the insurgents, including Davy Crockett, William B. Travis, and Jim Bowie, were killed.

à la mode (ä′ lä mōd′, ăl′ə) *adj.* **1.** According to or in style or fashion; fashionable. **2. a.** Served with ice cream. **b.** Braised with vegetables and served in a rich, brown sauce. [French, "in the fashion."]

a·la·mode (ä′lə-mōd′, ăl′ə-mōd′) *n.* A lustrous plain-weave silk fabric, used especially for head coverings and scarfs. [From À LA MODE.]

Al·a·mo·gor·do (ăl′ə-mə-gôr′dō). A town in southern New Mexico. The first atomic bomb was exploded at the White Sands Missile Range, 97 kilometers (60 miles) northwest of the city, in a test on July 16, 1945.

Al·an·brooke (ăl′ən-brook′), **Alan Francis Brooke, 1st Viscount** (1883–1963). British field marshal. During World War II he was commander in chief of the home forces from 1940 to 1941 and chief of the Imperial General Staff from 1941 to 1946.

Åland Islands. See Ahvenanmaa.

al·a·nine (ăl′ə-nēn′) *n.* An amino acid, CH₃CH(NH₂)COOH, a constituent of most proteins. [German *Alanin* : AL(DEHYDE) + *-an* (euphonic infix) + *-IN(E)*.]

a·lar (ā′lər) *adj.* **1.** Of, pertaining to, or having wings or alae. **2.** Shaped like or resembling a wing. **3.** *Anatomy.* Pertaining to the armpit; axillary. [Latin *ālāris,* from *āla,* wing.]

Al·a·ric (ăl′ə-rĭk) (c. A.D. 370–410). King of the Visigoths. In 395 he invaded and plundered Greece, and from 400 onward he attacked Italy, capturing Rome in 410.

a·larm (ə-lärm′) *n.* **1.** A sudden fear caused by an awareness of danger; fright. **2.** A warning of approaching or existing danger. **3.** An electrical or mechanical device that serves to warn of danger, fire, or the like by means of a sound or signal. **4. a.** The sounding mechanism of an alarm clock. **b.** An alarm clock. **5.** *Archaic.* A call to arms. **6.** *Fencing.* A stamp on the ground with the advancing foot. —See Synonyms at **fear.** ~*tr.v.* **alarmed, alarming, alarms. 1.** To fill with alarm or apprehension. **2.** To warn of approaching or existing danger. —See Synonyms at **frighten.** [Middle English *alarme,* from Old French, from Old Italian *allarme,* from *all'arme,* "to arms!" : *alla,* to, from Latin *ad illam,* to that, from *ille,* that + *arme,* arms, from Latin *arma.*] —**a·larm·a·ble** *adj.* —**a·larm·ing·ly** *adv.*

alarm bird *n.* Any of various Australian birds, such as the kookaburra, having a characteristic loud cry.

alarm clock *n.* A clock that can be set to sound a bell or buzzer at any desired hour, especially to wake a person up. Also called "alarm."

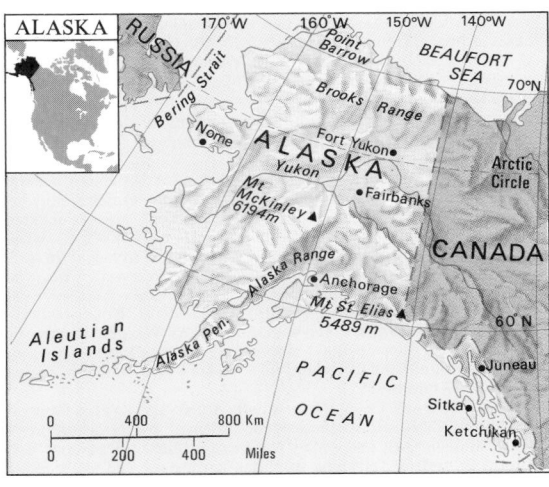

a·larm·ist (ə-lär′mĭst) *n.* A person who needlessly alarms or attempts to alarm himself or others, as by inventing or spreading frightening rumors and prophesying political or social calamities. —**a·larm·ism** *n.* —**a·larm·ist** *adj.*

a·lar·um (ə-lär′əm, ə-lär′-) *n. Archaic.* **1.** An alarm, especially a call to arms. **2.** A clamorous confusion onstage, especially in Elizabethan drama. Used chiefly in the phrase *alarums and excursions.* [Middle English *alarom, alarme,* ALARM.]

a·lar·y (ā′lər-ē) *adj.* **1.** Of or pertaining to wings. **2.** Resembling a wing; wing-shaped. [Latin *ālārius,* from *āla,* wing.]

a·las (ə-lăs′, ə-läs′) *interj.* An exclamation expressing regret, grief, compassion, or alarm. [Middle English, from Old French : *a,* AH + *las,* wretched, from Latin *lassus,* weary.]

Alas. Alaska.

a·las·ka (ə-lăs′kə) *n.* **1.** A kind of heavy-duty rubberized overshoe. **2. a.** A heavy dress and coat fabric of cotton and wool. **b.** A yarn made of cotton and wool. [After ALASKA.]

A·las·ka (ə-lăs′kə). Largest state in the United States, situated in the extreme northwest of North America, and separated from the rest of the country by Canada. It has a total area of 1,530,694 square kilometers (591,004 square miles) but fewer people than any other mainland territory, and was admitted as the 49th state in 1959. Alaska is mostly mountainous, and much of it is frozen all year. Gold was once mined extensively, but platinum and coal mining are now more important. Mining, oil, and natural gas are the most valuable industries. Fishing and timber are also important. Its capital is now Juneau but may be moved to Willow, near the largest city, Anchorage. —**A·las·kan** *adj. & n.*

Alaskan malamute *n.* A dog, the malamute *(see).*

a·las·tor (ə-lăs′tôr) *n. Often* **Alastor.** An avenging deity or spirit, frequently evoked in Greek tragedy; a masculine personification of Nemesis. [Greek *alastōr,* "unforgetting one," from *alastos,* unforgettable : *a-,* not + *lathein, lanthanesthai* (stem *las-*), to forget.]

a·late (ā′lāt′) *adj.* Also **a·lat·ed** (ā′lā′tĭd). *Biology.* Having thin, winglike extensions or parts; winged. [Latin *ālātus,* from *āla,* wing.]

Al-'Ayzariyah. See Bethany.

alb (ălb) *n.* A long white linen robe with tapered sleeves worn by a priest, especially during Mass. [Middle English *albe, aube,* Old English *albe,* from Medieval Latin *(vestis) alba,* "white (garment)," from Latin *albus,* white.]

Alb. Albania; Albanian.

Al·ba·ce·te (ăl′bə-sā′tē). Province of southeast-central Spain. The provincial capital, Albacete, was the site of battles between Moors and Christians in 1145 and 1146.

al·ba·core (ăl′bə-kôr′, -kōr′) *n., pl.* **-cores** or collectively **albacore.** A large marine fish, *Thunnus alalunga,* of warm seas, having edible flesh that is a major source for canned tuna. [Portuguese *albacor,* from Arabic *al-bakrah* : *al,* the + *bakr,* young camel.]

Al·ban (ôl′bən), **Saint** (died *c.* A.D. 304). First Christian martyr in Britain. A soldier in the Roman army in Britain, he was executed for having given shelter to a Christian priest, who converted him to Christianity. In 793 an abbey was founded on the site of his martyrdom, and the town of St. Albans grew around it.

Al·ba·ni·a (ăl-bā′nē-ə, -bān′yə, ôl-) *Abbr.* **Alb.** *Albanian* **Shqip·e·ri** (shkyĭp-ə-rē′). Country lying on the Adriatic Sea. Most of the country is either mountainous or swampy. It is fast developing its rich mineral resources, hydroelectric potential, and manufacturing, but farming remains the major occupation. After more than four centuries of Turkish rule, Albania proclaimed its independence in 1912, and that independence was guaranteed by the Allied powers after World War I. The country became a republic in 1925. In 1944 the Communist Party gained control, and Albania became a satellite of the U.S.S.R. It declared itself the first atheist state, abolishing all public worship in 1967. In 1961 it broke with the Soviets and in 1968 withdrew from the Warsaw Pact. After 1961 it was closely tied, diplomatically and commercially, with China, but relations between the two countries deteriorated after the death of Mao Ze-dong in 1976. In 1990 Albania moved toward political, eco-

alabaster Tree of Jesse, *a medieval carving in alabaster at the Victoria and Albert Museum, London. Alabaster is a type of gypsum—the mineral from which plaster of Paris is made.*

nomic, and social reforms. Area 28,748 square kilometers (11,097 square miles). Population, 3,200,000. Capital, Tirana.

Al·ba·ni·an (ăl-bā′nē-ən, -bān′yən, ôl-) *adj. Abbr.* **Alb.** Of or pertaining to Albania, its inhabitants, or its language.
— *n.* **1.** A native or inhabitant of Albania. **2.** The Indo-European language of Albania.

Al·ba·ny (ôl′bə-nē). Capital city, since 1797, of the state of New York, on the west bank of the Hudson River at the head of deep-water navigation. A major urban-renewal project in the downtown area was initiated in the 1960's.

al·ba·ta (ăl-bā′tə) *n.* A metallic alloy, **nickel silver** (see). [Latin *albata,* "clothed in white," from *albus,* white.]

al·ba·tross (ăl′bə-trôs′, -trŏs′) *n., pl.* **-trosses** or collectively **albatross. 1.** Any of various large, web-footed birds of the family Diomedeidae, chiefly of the oceans of the Southern Hemisphere, having a hooked beak and long, narrow wings. The wandering albatross, *Diomedea irrorata,* has the largest wingspan of any bird. **2.** An obvious handicap, constant burden, or heavy cross to bear. [Alteration (influenced by Latin *albus,* white) of Portuguese *alcatraz,* pelican, from Arabic *al-ghaṭṭās : al,* the + *ghaṭṭās,* white-tailed sea eagle. Sense 2 is a reference to S.T. Coleridge's Ancient Mariner, who sinned by killing an albatross and who had to wear it around his neck in penance.]

Al Bayda. See **Zawiyat al Bayda.**

al·be·do (ăl-bē′dō) *n., pl.* **-dos.** The fraction of incident electromagnetic radiation reflected by a surface. [Late Latin *albēdō,* whiteness, from Latin *albus,* white.]

Al·bee (ăl′bē), **Edward (Franklin)** (1928–). U.S. playwright. His most successful play has been *Who's Afraid of Virginia Woolf?* (1962), a savage and comic play about a power struggle between an academic couple. He won Pulitzer Prizes for two later plays, *A Delicate Balance* (1967) and *Seascape* (1975).

al·be·it (ôl-bē′ĭt, ăl-) *conj.* Although; even though; notwithstanding. [Middle English *al be it,* "let it be entirely (that)" : *al,* ALL + *be,* subjunctive of *been,* to BE + IT.]

Al·bé·niz (ăl-bā′nĕth, -nĕs), **Isaac Manuel Francisco** (1860–1909). Spanish composer and concert pianist. He used traditional folk songs and is known for his piano music, especially *Iberia.*

Al·bert I (ăl′bərt) (1875–1934). King of the Belgians (1909–34). During World War I he was commander in chief of the Belgian army and led the Belgian and French forces that reconquered Belgium in 1918.

Albert, Lake. See **Mobutu (Sese Seko) Lake.**

Albert, Prince (1819–1861). Prince Consort and husband of Queen Victoria. He was a strong influence on the queen and an active patron of the arts, sciences, and industry.

Al·ber·ta (ăl-bûr′tə). Province in western Canada. The capital and largest city is Edmonton. Wheat and cattle farming were the basis of the province's economy until the discovery of petroleum and natural gas in the early 1960's.

Al·ber·ti (ăl-bâr′tē), **Leon Battista** (1404–72). Italian Renaissance architect. Among the buildings that he designed are the churches of Santa Maria Novella in Florence (built 1446–51) and Sant' Andrea in Mantua (1472–94). Alberti was also an accomplished painter, musician, and writer.

Al·ber·tus Mag·nus (ăl-bûr′təs măg′nəs), **Saint,** born Albert, Count von Bollstadt (*c.* 1206–80). German theologian, scholastic philosopher, and scientist. He taught at various German schools, then at Paris (1245) and Cologne (1248–54), where Thomas Aquinas was one of his students. His reputation as an alchemist stemmed from his extensive knowledge of chemistry and physical sciences. He was beatified in 1622 and canonized in 1932.

al·bes·cent (ăl-bĕs′ənt) *adj.* Becoming white or moderately white; whitish. [Latin *albēscēns* (stem *albescent-*), from *albescere,* to become white, from *albus,* white.]

Al·bi (ăl-bē′). Capital of Tarn department in the Languedoc region of southern France, on the Tarn River. It was the center of the heresy of the Albigenses in the 12th and 13th centuries.

Al·bi·gen·ses (ăl′bə-jĕn′sēz′) *pl.n.* The members of a Catharist religious sect that flourished in southern France in the 12th and 13th centuries, and was eradicated by the Inquisition under Pope Innocent III, following the Albigensian Crusade. See **Catharism.** [Medieval Latin, inhabitants of *Albiga,* ALBI (where the sect was dominant).] —**Al·bi·gen·si·an** (ăl′bə-jĕn′sē-ən, -jĕn′shən) *adj.* —**Al·bi·gen·si·an·ism** *n.*

al·bin·ism (ăl′bə-nĭz′əm) *n.* **1.** Absence of normal pigmentation in a person, animal, or plant. **2.** The condition of being an albino. [French *albinisme,* from German *Albinismus,* from ALBINO.] —**al·bin·ic** (ăl-bĭn′ĭk), **al·bin·is·tic** (ăl′bə-nĭs′tĭk) *adj.*

al·bi·no (ăl-bī′nō) *n., pl.* **-nos.** An organism lacking normal pigmentation; especially, a person having abnormally pale skin, very light hair, and lacking normal eye coloring, or an animal, such as a rabbit, having white hair or fur and red eyes. [Portuguese, from *albo,* white, from Latin *albus* (originally applied to black Africans having albinism).]

Al·bi·no·ni (ăl′bə-nō′nē), **Tomaso** (1671–1750). Italian violinist and composer, court musician to the Duke of Mantua. He wrote about 50 operas and was the first composer to write concertos for solo violin.

Al·bi·on (ăl′bē-ən) *Archaic & Literary.* England or Great Britain. [Latin *Albiōn,* from Celtic *alb-* (unattested), high. See also **Alps.**]

al·bite (ăl′bīt′) *n.* A widely distributed white feldspar, NaAlSi₃O₈, one of the common rock-forming plagioclase group. [Swedish *albit,*

alder *The alder tree likes damp soil and, like clover, can fix nitrogen from the air.*

from Latin *albus,* white.] —**al·bit·ic** (ăl-bĭt′ĭk), **al·bit·i·cal** *adj.*

Ål·borg, Aal·borg (ôl′bôrg′). City and port in northern Jutland, Denmark, on the Lim Fjord.

al·bum (ăl′bəm) *n.* **1.** A book or binder with blank pages for the insertion and preservation of stamps, photographs, keepsakes, autographs, or the like. **2. a.** A long-playing phonograph record, usually of popular music. **b.** A set of phonograph records stored together in sleeves in one booklike holder. **3.** A collection of miscellaneous musical compositions. **4.** A tall, handsomely printed book, especially popular in the 19th century, often having a profusion of illustrations and short, sentimental texts. [Latin, blank tablet, neuter of *albus,* white.]

al·bu·men (ăl-byōō′mĭn) *n.* **1.** The white of an egg, consisting of a mixture of proteins (albumins). **2.** The material stored in a plant seed; the endosperm. **3.** Variant of **albumin.** [Latin *albūmen,* from *albus,* white.]

al·bu·min, al·bu·men (ăl-byōō′mən) *n.* Any of several simple, water-soluble proteins that are coagulated by heat and are found in egg white, blood serum, milk, various animal tissues, and many plant juices and tissues. [ALBUM(EN) + -IN.]

al·bu·mi·noid (ăl-byōō′mə-noid′) *adj.* Also **al·bu·mi·noi·dal** (-byōō′-mə-noi′dəl). Resembling albumin.
— *n. Biochemistry.* **Scleroprotein** (see).

al·bu·mi·nous (ăl-byōō′mə-nəs) *adj.* Of, like, or containing albumin.

al·bu·mi·nu·ri·a (ăl-byōō′mə-nŏŏr′ē-ə, -nyŏŏr′ē-ə) *n.* The presence of albumin and other serum proteins in the urine, sometimes indicative of kidney disease. Also called "proteinuria." [ALBUMIN + -URIA.] —**al·bu·mi·nu·ric** (ăl-byōō′mə-nŏŏr′ĭk, -nyŏŏr′ĭk) *adj.*

al·bu·mose (ăl′byə-mōs′, -mōz′) *n.* Any of a class of albuminous substances formed by enzymatic action on proteins during digestion. [French : *album(ine),* ALBUM(IN) + -OSE.]

Al·bu·quer·que (ăl′bə-kûr′kē). A town in the United States, on the upper Rio Grande. It is the largest city in New Mexico.

al·bur·num (ăl-bûr′nəm) *n. Botany.* **Sapwood** (see). [Latin, from *albus,* white.]

alc. alcohol; alcoholic.

Al·ca·ic (ăl-kā′ĭk) *adj.* Of or designating a verse form used in Greek and Latin poetry, consisting of strophes having four lines each containing four feet.
— *n. Often* **Alcaics.** Verse composed in Alcaic strophes. [Late Latin *Alcaicus,* from Greek *Alkaïkos,* "of Alcaeus" (*fl.* 600 B.C.), Greek lyric poet.]

al·cai·de, al·cay·de (ăl-kī′dē) *n.* In former times, the commander or governor of a fortress in Spain, Portugal, or Latin America. [Spanish, from Arabic *al-qā'id,* the commander, from *qād,* to command.]

al·cal·de (ăl-kăl′dē) *n.* The mayor or chief judicial official of a Spanish or Latin-American town. [Spanish, from Arabic *al-qāḍī : al,* the + *qāḍī,* judge, from *qaḍā,* to judge.]

Al·ca·traz (ăl′kə-trăz′). A rocky island in San Francisco Bay, California. The island served as a federal prison until 1963.

al·caz·ar (ăl-kăz′ər, ăl′kə-zär′) *n.* A Spanish palace or fortress, originally one built by the Moors. [Spanish *alcázar,* from Arabic *al-qaṣr : al,* the + *qaṣr,* castle, from Latin *castra,* fort, plural of *castrum,* camp.]

Al·cá·zar de San Juan (ăl′kə-zär′ də săn wän′). Town of Roman origin in the Ciudad Real province of central Spain. It was the center of the order of San Juan from the 14th to the 16th century.

Al·ces·tis (ăl-sĕs′tĭs). *Greek Mythology.* The wife of King Admetus of Thessaly. She agreed to die in place of her husband and was later rescued from Hades by Hercules.

al·che·mist (ăl′kə-mĭst) *n.* A practitioner of alchemy. —**al·che·mis·tic, al·che·mis·ti·cal** (ăl′kə-mĭs′tĭ-kəl) *adj.*

al·che·mize (ăl′kə-mīz′) *tr.v.* **-mized, -mizing, -mizes.** To transform by or as if by alchemy; transmute.

al·che·my (ăl′kə-mē) *n.* **1.** In medieval Europe, a philosophy and branch of science that sought to find a way of turning base metals into gold, a universal cure, and the elixir of life. **2.** Any seemingly magical power or process of transmuting. —See Synonyms at **magic.** [Middle English, from Old French *alquemie,* from Medieval Latin *alchymia,* from Arabic *al-kīmiyā',* "the art of transmutation" : *al,* the + *kīmiyā',* from Greek *khēm(e)ia,* "art of transmutation (of metals)."] —**al·chem·i·cal** (ăl-kĕm′ĭ-kəl), **al·chem·ic** *adj.* —**al·chem·i·cal·ly** *adv.*

al·che·rin·ga (ăl′chə-rĭng′gə) *n.* Also **al·che·ra** (ăl′chə-rə). In Australian Aboriginal mythology, the **Dreamtime** *(see).* [Native Australian.]

Al·ci·bi·a·des (ăl′sĭ-bī′ə-dēz′) (*c.* 450–404 B.C.). Athenian general and politician. He was brought up by his uncle, Pericles, and became a protégé of Socrates. His brilliant political career foundered during the Peloponnesian War against Sparta (431–404 B.C.), when he commanded a disastrous military attack on Syracuse in 415.

Alc·me·ne (ălk-mē′nē). *Greek Mythology.* Amphitryon's wife, who gave birth to Hercules after being seduced by Zeus.

Al·cock (ôl′kŏk), **Sir John William** (1892–1919). British aviator. On June 14, 1919, together with Sir Arthur Whitten Brown, he made the first nonstop flight across the Atlantic Ocean. They flew from Newfoundland to Ireland in a Vickers-Vimy bomber, taking 16 hours 27 minutes.

al·co·hol (ăl′kə-hôl′) *n.* **1.** *Abbr.* **al., alc.** A colorless volatile flammable liquid, C₂H₅OH, synthesized or obtained by fermentation of sugars and starches, and widely used, either pure or denatured, as a solvent or in drugs, cleaning solutions, explosives, and intoxicating beverages. Also called "ethanol," "ethyl alcohol," "grain alcohol." **2.** Intoxicating drink containing alcohol. **3.** Any of a series of compounds that contain a hydroxyl group bound to a hydrocarbon group. Simple examples are methanol (CH_3OH) and butanol (C_4H_9OH). [New Latin *alcohol (vini)*, spirit (of wine), from Medieval Latin *alcohol*, fine powder of antimony used to tint the eyelids, any powder obtained by sublimation, quintessence, from Arabic *al-koḥl, al-kuḥl,* : *al,* the + *koḥl, kuḥl,* KOHL.]

al·co·hol·ic (ăl′kə-hôl′ĭk, -hôl′ĭk) *adj. Abbr.* **alc., alc. 1.** Of, pertaining to, or resulting from alcohol. **2.** Containing or preserved in alcohol. **3.** Suffering from alcoholism.
~*n.* A person who drinks habitually and to excess, and is unable to stop doing so; a sufferer from alcoholism.

al·co·hol·ic·i·ty (ăl′kə-hôl-ĭs′ə-tē) *n.* Alcoholic content.

Alcoholics Anonymous *n. Abbr.* **A.A.** A fellowship of alcoholics who wish to stop drinking and stay sober.

al·co·hol·ism (ăl′kə-hôl-ĭz′əm) *n.* **1.** Habitual excessive consumption of alcohol. **2.** A chronic pathological condition resulting from this, chiefly affecting the nervous and gastroenteric systems and characterized by mental disturbance, muscular incoordination, and eventually cirrhosis of the liver.

al·co·hol·ize (ăl′kə-hôl-īz′) *tr.v.* **-ized, -izing, -izes.** To make alcoholic; saturate, mix, or treat with alcohol. —**al·co·hol·i·za·tion** *n.*

al·co·hol·om·e·ter (ăl′kə-hôl-ŏm′ə-tər) *n.* A hydrometer for determining the percentage of alcohol in liquids.

alcohol thermometer *n.* A simple glass thermometer containing alcohol colored with a red dye, used instead of a mercury thermometer for measuring lower temperatures.

Al·co·ran, Al·ko·ran (ăl′kô-răn′, -rän′) *n.* The sacred book of the Muslims, the **Koran** (*see*).

Al·cott (ôl′kət, -kŏt′), **Louisa May** (1832–88). U.S. novelist. Her most famous work, *Little Women* (1868–69), was a largely autobiographical account of herself and her family.

al·cove (ăl′kōv′) *n.* **1. a.** A recessed or partly enclosed area connected to or forming part of a room. **b.** Any arched niche or recess, as in a wall. **2.** A secluded bower or similar enclosed structure in a garden. [French *alcôve*, from Spanish *alcoba*, from Arabic *al-qubbah*, "the vault."]

Al·cuin (ăl′kwĭn) (735–804). English scholar and theologian. In 781 he became an adviser to Charlemagne, whose court became the center of the revival of learning and the arts that came to be known as the Carolingian Renaissance.

Al·cy·o·ne (ăl-sī′ə-nē) *n.* **1.** *Astronomy.* The brightest star in the Pleiades, in the constellation Taurus. **2.** *Greek Mythology.* One of the **Pleiades** (*see*).

Ald. alderman.

Al·dab·ra (ăl-dăb′rə). Group of four coral islands in the Indian Ocean north of Madagascar, famous for its giant tortoises and other wildlife. Formerly British, it joined the Seychelles in 1976.

Al·deb·a·ran (ăl-dĕb′ə-rən) *n.* A double star in the constellation Taurus, one of the brightest stars in the sky, 68 light-years from Earth. [Middle English, from Medieval Latin *Aldebaran*, from Arabic *al-dabarān*, "the follower (of the Pleiades)" : *al,* the + *dabarān,* following, from *dabar,* to follow.]

al·de·hyde (ăl′də-hīd′) *n.* **1.** Any of a class of highly reactive organic chemical compounds obtained by oxidation of primary alcohols, characterized by the common group CHO (the **aldehyde group**), and used in the manufacture of resins, dyes, and organic acids. Examples are formaldehyde (HCHO) and butanal (C_3H_7CHO). **2.** Such a compound, **acetaldehyde** (*see*). [German *Aldehyd*, from New Latin, abbreviation of *al(cohol) dehyd(rogenatum)*, "dehydrogenized alcohol."]

al den·te (ăl dĕn′tē) *adj.* Cooked so as to be still slightly firm. Said of pasta. [Italian, "to the tooth."] —**al den·te** *adv.*

al·der (ôl′dər) *n.* **1.** Any of various deciduous shrubs or trees of the genus *Alnus*, growing in cool, moist places, and having toothed rounded leaves, woody cones, and reddish wood used in underwater construction and cabinet work. **2.** Any of several similar shrubs or trees. [Middle English *alder*, Old English *aler, alor*; akin to Old Norse *ölr*, Latin *alnus*.]

alder fly *n.* Any insect of the group Sialoidea, related to the lacewings, found near water and having large wings.

al·der·man (ôl′dər-mən) *n., pl.* **-men** (-mĭn). **1.** *Abbr.* **Ald., Aldm.** In many town and city governments, a member of the municipal legislative body. **2.** *Abbr.* **Ald., Aldm.** In England and Wales before 1974, a member of the higher branch of a municipal or borough council, elected by the councilors themselves. **3.** In Anglo-Saxon England: **a.** A high-ranking noble. **b.** The chief officer of a shire. [Middle English *alderman*, guild official, Old English *(e)aldormann*, viceroy : *(e)aldor*, chief, "elder," from *(e)ald*, old + MAN.] —**al·der·man·cy** *n.* —**al·der·man·ic** (ôl′dər-măn′ĭk) *adj.*

Al·der·ney¹ (ôl′dər-nē) Northernmost island of the larger Channel Islands. It was part of the domain of Normandy from the 11th century, but is today included in the bailiwick of Guernsey, although it is self-governing.

Alderney² *n., pl.* **-neys.** One of a breed of small dairy cattle originally bred in the Channel Islands.

Al·dine (ôl′dīn′, -dēn′) *adj.* Of, pertaining to, or published by the press of Aldus **Manutius** (*see*) and his family.

Aldm. alderman.

aldo- *prefix.* Indicates the presence of an aldehyde group; for example, **aldohexose, aldopentose.** [From ALDEHYDE.]

al·do·hex·ose (ăl′dō-hĕk′sōs, -sōz) *n.* An aldose sugar that has six carbon atoms in its molecules.

al·dol (ăl′dôl′, -dŏl′) *n.* **1.** A thick colorless to pale-yellow liquid, $CH_3CH(OH)CH_2CHO$, obtained from acetaldehyde and used to make perfumes and in ore flotation. **2.** Any of a class of organic chemical compounds that have a hydroxyl group and an aldehyde group in their molecules on adjacent carbon atoms.

al·do·pent·ose (ăl′dō-pĕn′tōs, -tōz) *n.* An aldose sugar that has five carbon atoms in its molecules.

al·dose (ăl′dōs′, -dōz′) *n. Chemistry.* Any of a class of monosaccharide sugars containing an aldehyde group. Compare **ketose.** Also called "aldose sugar."

al·dos·te·rone (ăl-dŏs′tə-rōn′) *n.* A steroid hormone, secreted by the adrenal cortex, that regulates salt and water balance by its action on the kidneys.

al·dox·ime (ăl-dŏk′sēm′) *n.* A chemical compound formed by reaction of an aldehyde with hydroxylamine and having the characteristic group ·CHNON or :CNOH in its molecules.

al·drin (ôl′drĭn) *n.* A brownish-white crystalline pesticide. [After Kurt *Alder* (1902–58), German chemist.]

Aldus Manutius. See **Manutius.**

ale (āl) *n.* A fermented alcoholic drink containing malt and formerly made without hops, similar to but often heavier than beer. [Middle English *ale*, Old English *alu, ealu.*]

a·le·a·to·ry (ā′lē-ə-tôr′ē, -tōr′ē) *adj.* **1.** Dependent upon chance or luck. **2.** Using or consisting of elements chosen at random or arrived at by chance. Said of musical or other artistic compositions. [Latin *āleātōrius*, from *āleātor*, gambler, from *ālea†*, dice.]

A·lec·to (ə-lĕk′tō). *Greek Mythology.* One of the **Furies** (*see*).

a·lee (ə-lē′) *adv. Nautical.* At, on, or to the leeward side. Compare **aweather.**

al·e·gar (ăl′ə-gər, ā′lə-) *n.* Vinegar produced by the fermentation of ale; malt vinegar. [Middle English : ALE + (VINE)GAR.]

ale·house (āl′hous′) *n.* **1.** In former times, a place where ale was sold and drunk. **2.** *British Informal.* A pub.

Aleichem, Sholem. See **Sholem Aleichem.**

Al·e·man·ni (ăl′ə-măn′ī) *pl.n.* A group of Germanic tribes that settled in Alsace and nearby areas during the 4th century A.D. [Latin, from Germanic *Alamanniz* (unattested); akin to Gothic *alamannam* (dative plural), mankind : probably ALL + MAN.]

Al·e·man·nic, Al·a·man·nic (ăl′ə-măn′ĭk) *n.* The High German dialect of the Alemanni, forms of which are now spoken in Alsace and parts of southern Germany and Switzerland.
~*adj.* Also **Al·e·man·ni·an, Al·a·man·ni·an** (ăl′ə-măn′ē-ən). Of or pertaining to the Alemanni or their language.

a·lem·bic (ə-lĕm′bĭk) *n.* **1.** An apparatus formerly used for distilling. **2.** Something that purifies or transforms by a process comparable to distillation. [Middle English, from Old French *alambic*, from Medieval Latin *alambicum*, from Arabic *al-anbīq* : *al,* the + *anbīg,* still, from Greek *ambix†* (stem *ambik-*), cup.]

Al·en·çon (ăl-äN-sôN′). Capital of Orne department, in Normandy, northwestern France. It is famous for "point d'Alençon" lace.

a·leph, a·lef (ä′lĭf) *n.* The first letter of the Hebrew alphabet. See feature at **alphabet.** [Hebrew *āleph,* "ox"; akin to ALPHA.]

a·leph-null (ä′lĭf-nŭl′) *n. Mathematics.* The first **transfinite number** (*see*). Also called "aleph-zero." [ALEPH (symbol for transfinite number) + NULL (smallest possible entity).]

A·lep·po (ə-lĕp′ō). *Arabic* **Ha·leb** (hä-lĕb′). City in northwest Syria, which was probably first settled as long ago as 6000 B.C. It was once a major station on the caravan route across Syria to Baghdad, and was a center of Christianity in the Middle East.

a·lert (ə-lûrt′) *adj.* **1.** Vigilantly attentive; watchful: *alert to danger.* **2.** Mentally responsive and perceptive; quick. **3.** Brisk; lively.
~*n.* **1.** A warning signal of attack or danger; especially, a siren warning of an air raid. **2.** The period of time during which such a warning is in effect. —**on the alert.** Watchful and prepared for danger or emergency.
~*tr.v.* **alerted, alerting, alerts.** To notify or cause to be aware of approaching or potential danger; warn: *a campaign alerting people to the dangers of smoking.* [French *alerte*, from Italian *all'erta*, "on the watch" : *alla,* at the, from Latin *ad illam,* from *ille,* that + *erta,* watch, from *(torre)erta,* watchtower, "high (tower)," from Latin *ērectus,* raised, ERECT.]

Å·le·sund, Aa·le·sund (ô′lə-sōōn′). Fishing port and town in Norway, dating from the 9th century. It is the headquarters for cod and halibut trawling and of the Arctic sealing fleet.

Al·etsch Glacier (ăl′ĭch). Glacier in the Bernese Alps. It occupies 171 square kilometers (66 square miles) and is the largest glacier in Europe.

a·leu·rone, a·leu·ron (ə-lōōr′ōn′, ăl′yə-rōn′) *n.* A protein consisting of minute granules, forming the outermost layer of the endosperm in cereal grains. [German *Aleuron*, from Greek *aleuron,* flour.] —**al·eu·ron·ic** (ăl′yə-rŏn′ĭk) *adj.*

A·leut (ə-lōōt′, ăl′ē-ōōt′) *n., pl.* **Aleuts** or collectively **Aleut.** Also **A·leu·tian** (for sense 1). **1.** A member of the Eskimo people inhabiting the Aleutian Islands. **2.** A subfamily of the Eskimo-Aleut family of languages, spoken in the Aleutian Islands. [Russian *aleút,* probably from Chukchi *aliuit,* "beyond the shore."]

A·leu·tian (ə-lōō′shən) *adj.* Of or pertaining to the Aleuts, their language, or their culture.
~*n.* **1.** Variant of **Aleut** (sense 1). **2. Aleutians.** The Aleutian Islands.

Aleutian Islands. Also **Aleutians.** Archipelago of volcanic islands

alder fly *An insect often found in spring near ponds and muddy streams. It is related to the lacewing fly. Alder flies, which are poor fliers, get their name because they breed on waterside plants, including alder trees.*

alexanders *This member of the parsley family is a native of Macedonia but is now common on roadsides and wasteland throughout Europe and much of North America. Its name is a reference to its country of origin—the home of the Greek conqueror Alexander the Great.*

Alexander the Great *A silver coin showing the head of the fourth-century* B.C. *Macedonian conqueror. The coin was minted either on the Greek island of Rhodes or in Alexandria, Egypt—both parts of Alexander's vast empire.*

PRONUNCIATION KEY

ă, pat; ā, pay; âr, care; ä, father, are; b, bib; ch, church; d, deed; ĕ, pet; ē, be; f, fife; g, gag; h, hat; hw, which; ĭ, pit; ī, pie; îr, pier; j, judge; k, kick; l, lid, needle; m, mum; n, no, sudden; ng, thing; ŏ, pot; ō, toe; ô, paw, for; oi, noise; ou, out; o͝o, book; o͞o, boot; p, pop; r, roar; s, sauce; sh, ship, dish; t, tight; th, thin, path; *th*, this, bathe; ŭ, cut; ûr, fur; v, valve; w, with; y, yes; z, zebra, size; zh, vision; ə, about, item, edible, gallop, circus, peaceful

IN FOREIGN WORDS:

à, *Fr.* ami; œ, *Fr.* feu, *Ger.* schön; ü, *Fr.* tu, *Ger.* über; KH, *Ger.* ich, *Scot.* loch; N, *Fr.* bon; y', *Fr.* Compiègne

STRESS MARKS:

Primary stress: ′
in·cite′ (ĭn-sīt′)
Secondary stress: ′
in′sight′ (ĭn′sīt′)

extending westward for nearly 2,000 kilometers (1,250 miles) from the tip of the Alaska Peninsula. There are radar stations (part of the Distant Early Warning Line) and military bases on the islands, which are of vital strategic importance because of their proximity to the U.S.S.R.

ale·wife[1] (āl′wīf′) *n., pl.* **-wives** (-wīvz′). A fish, *Alosa* (or *Pomolobus*) *pseudoharengus,* closely related to the herrings, of North American Atlantic waters and some inland lakes. Also called "oldwife." [Alteration (by association with ALEWIFE, alehouse keeper, "pot-bellied woman") of obsolete *allowes* (plural), probably from French *alose,* shad, from Gaulish Latin *alōsa*†.]

alewife[2] *n., pl.* **-wives.** Formerly, a woman who kept an alehouse.

Al·ex·an·der I (ăl′ĭg-zăn′dər, -zän′-) (1777–1825). Czar of Russia. He came to the throne in 1801 when his father, Paul I, was murdered. His plans to liberalize his country's government were delayed by prolonged wars with Napoleon, until eventually he was converted to rigid conservatism.

Alexander II (1818–81). Czar of Russia. Considered the ablest and most liberal of the Romanov dynasty, he came to the throne in 1855 and immediately began a program of political, educational, and military reforms. In 1861 he emancipated Russia's 10 million male serfs and their families, an act that won him the title "Czar liberator." He was assassinated by a member of a revolutionary party.

Alexander III (1845–94). Czar of Russia. He came to the throne after the assassination of his father, the liberal Alexander II, and immediately abandoned all reforms, reaffirming his "faith in the principle of autocracy." He pursued extreme reactionary policies, persecuted Jews and reformers, increased repressive police powers, and let the education system decline.

Alexander VI, born Rodrigo Borgia (*c.*1431–1503). Pope (1492–1503). On achieving the papacy (through bribery), he is said to have commented, "God has given us the papacy. Let us enjoy it." He used papal wealth and power for the advancement of his illegitimate children, and together with his son, Cesare Borgia, he embarked on the conquest of central Italy for the benefit of his family and himself. He was also a great patron of the arts.

Alexander Nev·sky (nĕv′skē, nĕf′-) (1220–63). Russian hero and saint, Prince of Novgorod (1236) and Grand Duke of Kiev and Novgorod (1246) and Vladimir (1252). He is famous for defeating the Swedes in 1240 in a battle near the Neva River (thus acquiring the name Nevsky). In 1242 he won a victory against the Teutonic Knights on the frozen waters of Lake Peipus.

Alexander of Tu·nis (to͞o′nĭs, tyo͞o′-), **Harold Alexander, 1st Earl** (1891–1969). British field marshal. In World War II he oversaw the evacuation of the British forces from Dunkirk and Burma. He directed the campaign that brought about the Allied victory in North Africa (1943), and then led the successful invasions of Sicily and Italy (1944–45), ending the war as Allied supreme commander in the Mediterranean. He was governor general of Canada (1946–52) and British minister of defense (1952–54).

al·ex·an·ders (ăl′ĭg-zăn′dərz, -zän′dərz) *pl.n.* An umbelliferous plant, *Smyrnium olusatrum,* native to southern Europe, whose stems were formerly eaten like celery. [Middle English, from Old French from Medieval Latin *alexandrum,* perhaps alteration (through association with *Alexander* the Great) of Latin *holus atrum,* "black vegetable" : *holus,* vegetable + *atrum,* neuter of *ater,* black.]

Alexander the Great (356–323 B.C.). King of Macedonia and conqueror of an empire that covered much of Asia. He was the son of the founder of the Macedonian Empire, Philip II, and the pupil of Aristotle. Alexander ascended the throne after the murder of his father in 336 B.C. He forcibly united the warring Greek states and in 334 invaded the Persian Empire with some 35,000 men, defeating its king, Darius III, at Issus. Within four years Alexander had conquered Asia Minor, Syria, Egypt (where he founded Alexandria), Babylonia, and Persia itself. He then invaded northern India and defeated the Indian king, Porus, in 327. A mutiny in his army prevented his advancing to the Ganges, and he returned reluctantly to Babylon, where he died of a fever.

Al·ex·an·dra[1] (ăl′ĭg-zăn′drə, -zän′-) (1844–1925). Queen consort of Edward VII. The eldest daughter of King Christian IX of Denmark, she married Edward in 1863, when he was the prince of Wales.

Alexandra[2] (1872–1918). Last czarina of Russia. A German princess and the granddaughter of Queen Victoria, she married Nicholas II in 1894. During World War I she was in charge of the government and, under the influence of the monk Rasputin, ruled disastrously. After the Revolution in 1917 she and her family were imprisoned and later shot.

Al·ex·an·dri·a (ăl′ĭg-zăn′drē-ə, -zän′-). Egypt's leading port, standing at the western tip of the Nile Delta on the Mediterranean Sea. It was founded by Alexander the Great in 332 B.C. and became a repository of Jewish, Arab, and Hellenistic culture, famous for its two royal libraries. Its pharos (lighthouse) was one of the Seven Wonders of the Ancient World. Early Christianity flourished there, and Alexandria remains the seat of the patriarch of the Eastern Orthodox Church. It was captured by the Arabs in A.D. 642 and soon after was replaced by Cairo as the capital of Egypt.

Al·ex·an·dri·an (ăl′ĭg-zăn′drē-ən, -zän′drē-ən) *adj.* **1.** Of or pertaining to Alexander the Great. **2.** Of or pertaining to Alexandria in Egypt. **3.** Of, characteristic of, or designating the learned school of Hellenistic literature, science, and philosophy that flourished in Alexandria in the last three centuries B.C. **4.** Characterized by the careful study or imitation of earlier forms and masterpieces, rather than by originality. Said of writers and literary works. **5.** Of or designating the school of early Christian philosophy and theology of Alexandria.
∼*n.* **1.** A native or inhabitant of Alexandria, Egypt, especially of Hellenistic times. **2.** A scholar, writer, or theologian of the Alexandrian school.

al·ex·an·drine (ăl′ĭg-zăn′drĭn, -zän′-) *n. Often* **Alexandrine. 1.** The commonest French verse form, consisting of a line of twelve syllables with a caesura usually falling after the sixth syllable. **2.** A line of English verse composed in iambic hexameter, usually with a caesura after the third foot. [French *alexandrin,* from Old French, from *Alexandre,* title of a romance about Alexander the Great, written in this meter.] **—al·ex·an·drine, Al·ex·an·drine** *adj.*

al·ex·an·drite (ăl′ĭg-zăn′drīt′, -zän′drīt′) *n.* A greenish mineral that appears red in artificial light, used as a gemstone. It is a form of chrysoberyl. [German *Alexandrit,* named in honor of Czar ALEXANDER I.]

a·lex·i·a (ə-lĕk′sē-ə) *n.* A disorder in which cerebral lesions cause loss of the ability to read. Also called "word blindness." Compare **dyslexia.** [New Latin : A- (without) + Greek *lexis,* speech, from *legein,* to speak.]

a·lex·in (ə-lĕk′sĭn) *n.* Also **a·lex·ine** (ə-lĕk′sēn). A blood component, **complement** *(see).* [German *Alexin,* "protection (from bacteria)," from Greek *alexein,* to protect, ward off.]

a·lex·i·phar·mic (ə-lĕk′sĭ-fär′mĭk) *adj.* Preventing or resisting effects of poison or infection; antidotal; prophylactic.
∼*n.* An antidote. [Obsolete *alexipharmac,* from French *alexipharmaque,* from Greek *alexipharmakos* : *alexein,* to ward off + *pharmakon,* poison (see **pharmaco-**).]

al·fal·fa (ăl-făl′fə) *n.* A plant, *Medicago sativa,* native to Eurasia, having compound leaves with three leaflets, and clusters of small purple flowers. It is widely cultivated for forage and is used as a commercial source of chlorophyll. Also called "lucerne." [Spanish, from Arabic *al-fasfaṣah,* best fodder.]

Al Fatah *n.* See **Fatah.**

al·fil·a·ri·a, al·fil·e·ri·a (ăl-fĭl′ə-rē′ə) *n.* A plant, *Erodium cicutarium,* native to Europe but widely naturalized in North America, having finely divided leaves and small pink or purplish flowers. Also called "filaree," "pin clover." [American Spanish *alfilerillo,* from Spanish, diminutive of *alfiler,* a pin, from Arabic *al-khilāl,* thorn, pin.]

Al·fred the Great (ăl′frĭd) (849–99). King of Wessex. He became ruler of Wessex in 871 and conducted several wars against the Danes, driving them from Wessex. Alfred built Britain's first navy, reorganized Wessex's army, and set up a complex of fortified earthworks. He was also an able administrator and drew up a legal code and encouraged scholarship.

al·fres·co (ăl-frĕs′kō) *adv.* In the fresh air; outdoors: *Let's eat alfresco.*
∼*adj.* Taking place outdoors; outdoor: *an alfresco meal.* [Italian, "in the fresh (air)" : *a il,* in the + *fresco,* fresh, FRESCO.]

Al Furāt. See **Euphrates.**

Al Fustat. See **Cairo.**

Alf·vén wave (ălf-vān′) *n. Physics.* A transverse wave propagated through a plasma, such as the matter in a star, under the influence of magnetohydrodynamic forces. [After Hannes Olof Gösta *Alfvén* (1908–), Swedish astrophysicist.]

Alg. Algeria.

al·gae (ăl′jē) *pl.n. Singular* **al·ga** (ăl′gə). Primitive, chiefly aquatic, one-celled or multicellular plants that lack true stems, roots, and leaves but contain chlorophyll. Included among the algae are kelps and other seaweeds, and the diatoms. [Latin *algae,* plural of *alga*†, seaweed.] **—al·gal** (ăl′gəl) *adj.*

al·gar·ro·ba (ăl′gə-rō′bə) *n.* **1.** A tree, the **mesquite** *(see).* **2.** A tree, the **carob** *(see).* **3.** The edible pod of either of these trees. [Spanish, from Arabic *al-kharrūbah* : *al,* the + *kharrūbah,* CAROB.]

Al·gar·ve (äl-gär′və, ăl-). Former kingdom and province of southernmost Portugal, now the district of Faro. Farming and fishing are the main occupations, and it is also noted for cork.

al·ge·bra (ăl′jə-brə) *n.* **1.** A generalization of arithmetic in which symbols, usually letters of the alphabet, represent numbers and are related by operations that hold for all numbers in the set. **2.** A set of entities (such as matrices, propositions, or vectors) together with operations for combining these entities to give other members of the set. See **algebraic structure.** [Medieval Latin, from Arabic *al-jebr, al-jabr,* "the (science of) reuniting" (referring to the solving of algebraic equations) : *al,* the + *jabr,* reunification, bone-setting.] **—al·ge·bra·ist** (ăl′jə-brā′ĭst) *n.*

al·ge·bra·ic (ăl′jə-brā′ĭk) *adj.* **1.** Of, pertaining to, or involving algebra. **2.** Designating an expression, equation, or function in which only numbers, letters, and arithmetical operations are contained or used. **3.** Indicating or restricted to a finite number of algebraic operations. **—al·ge·bra·i·cal·ly** *adv.*

algebraic logic *n.* A method of presenting a problem for a calculator or computer with the operations entered in the order in which they would be written out.

algebraic number *n.* **1.** Any positive or negative number. **2.** A number that is a root of a polynomial equation with rational coefficients.

algebraic operation *n.* Addition, subtraction, multiplication, division, exponentiation, root extraction, or any finite combination of these operations.

algebraic structure *n.* The general set of operations and relationships in an algebra, considered independently of the particular mathematical entities used.

algebraic sum *n.* The sum of algebraic quantities produced by arithmetic addition, in which negative quantities are added by the subtraction of corresponding positive quantities. For example, the algebraic sum of 6 and −2 is 4.

Al·ge·ci·ras (ăl′jə-sîr′əs). Port and tourist center in southern Spain, situated on the Mediterranean Sea across the bay from Gibraltar.

Al·ger (ăl-zhā′). *English* **Al·giers** (ăl-jîrz′). Capital of Algeria and an ancient Mediterranean port. It was taken by the French (1830), and during World War II was the seat of the French government in exile and headquarters of the Allied forces in North Africa.

Al·ger (ăl′jər), **Horatio** (1832–99). U.S. author. His first successful novel was *Ragged Dick* (1867). He wrote more than a hundred books based on the formula that a poor boy—with hard work, honesty, gumption, and a little (or a lot) of luck—could become rich and famous.

Al·ge·ri·a (ăl-jîr′ē-ə). *Abbr.* **Alg.** *French* **Al·gé·rie** (ál′zhə-rē′). Country in northwest Africa bordering on the Mediterranean Sea, the second-largest country in Africa, after Sudan. Arab armies conquered Algeria in the 7th century, and the north fell to the Ottoman Turks in 1519. The French invaded the country in 1830, and in 1871 the north became three departments of France. Algeria gained its independence, after a long terrorist and guerrilla campaign, in 1962. The country has two distinct regions: the northern cultivated region of the Mediterranean littoral and the Atlas Mts. (about 15 percent of the country), and the arid wastes of the Sahara in the south. Algeria has extensive deposits of oil and natural gas, which account for 90 percent of its exports. Area, 2,381,741 square kilometers (919,352 square miles). Population, 25,000,000. Capital, Alger (Algiers). **—Al·ge·ri·an** *adj. & n.*

-algia *n. suffix.* Indicates pain or a painful condition; for example, **neuralgia.** [Greek, from *algos†*, pain.]

al·gi·cide (ăl′jə-sīd′) *n.* A chemical used to kill algae in water.

al·gid (ăl′jĭd) *adj.* Chilly; clammy. Said especially of the skin. [Latin *algidus*, from *algēre†*, to be cold.] **—al·gid·i·ty** *n.*

Algiers. See **Alger.**

al·gin (ăl′jĭn) *n.* A gelatinous substance consisting of alginic acid or its salts or esters, obtained from certain algae, especially the giant kelp, and used as an emulsifier, a thickener for foods, and a fabric dressing. [ALG(AE) + -IN.]

al·gi·nate (ăl′jə-nāt′) *n.* A salt or ester of alginic acid.

al·gin·ic acid (ăl-jĭn′ĭk) *n.* A gelatinous substance obtained from certain seaweeds. See **algin.**

algo- *prefix.* Indicates pain; for example, **algolagnia.** [Greek, from *algos†*, pain.]

al·goid (ăl′goid′) *adj.* Of or resembling algae.

Al·gol (ăl′gŏl′, ăl′gôl′) *n.* A double, eclipsing, variable star in the constellation Perseus, almost as bright as Polaris. [Arabic *al ghūl*, "the ghoul" : *al*, the + *ghūl*, GHOUL.]

AL·GOL (ăl′gŏl′, ăl′gôl′) *n.* An arithmetical language by which numerical procedures may be precisely presented to a computer in a standard form. [*Algorithmic Oriented Language.*]

al·go·lag·ni·a (ăl′gō-lăg′nē-ə) *n.* Sexual gratification derived from inflicting or experiencing pain. See **masochism, sadism.** [New Latin : ALGO- + Greek *lagneia*, lust, from *lagnos*, lustful.] **—al·go·lag·ni·ac** *n. & adj.*

al·gol·o·gy (ăl-gŏl′ə-jē) *n.* The study of algae. [ALG(AE) + -LOGY.] **—al·go·log·i·cal** (ăl′gə-lŏj′ĭ-kəl) *adj.* **—al·gol·o·gist** (ăl-gŏl′ə-jĭst) *n.*

al·gom·e·ter (ăl-gŏm′ə-tər) *n.* An apparatus for determining sensitivity to pain caused by pressure. [ALGO- + -METER.] **—al·go·met·ric** (ăl′gə-mĕt′rĭk), **al·go·met·ri·cal** *adj.* **—al·gom·e·try** (ăl-gŏm′ə-trē) *n.*

Al·gon·ki·an (ăl-gŏng′kē-ən) *n., pl.* **-ans** or collectively **Algonkian** (for sense 2). **1.** *Geology.* In Canada, the late **Proterozoic** (*see*). **2.** Variant of **Algonquian.** [After the rock formations in the Great Lakes district, homeland of the Algonquin Indians.]

Al·gon·qui·an (ăl-gŏng′kwē-ən, -kē-ən) *n., pl.* **-ans** or collectively **Algonquian** (for sense 2). Also **Al·gon·ki·an** (-kē-ən). **1.** A principal family of about 50 North American Indian languages spoken in an area stretching from the Atlantic to the Rocky Mountains, and from Labrador in the north to North Carolina and Tennessee in the south, and used by such tribes as the Ojibwa, Delaware, Cree, Fox, Blackfoot, Illinois, and Shawnee. **2.** A member of a tribe using a language of this family. [From ALGONQUIN.] **—Al·gon·qui·an, Al·gon·ki·an** *adj.*

Al·gon·quin (ăl-gŏng′kwĭn, -kĭn) *n., pl.* **-quins** or collectively **Algonquin** (for sense 1). Also **Al·gon·kin** (-kĭn) **1.** A member of any of several Algonquian-speaking North American Indian tribes formerly inhabiting the region along the Ottawa River and near the northern tributaries of the St. Lawrence River. See **Ottawa.** **2.** The Algonquian language of these tribes. [Canadian French, from earlier *Algoumequins†* (plural).]

al·go·pho·bi·a (ăl′gō-fō′bē-ə) *n.* Abnormal fear of pain. [New Latin : ALGO- + -PHOBIA.]

al·go·rism (ăl′gə-rĭz′əm) *n.* **1.** The Arabic system of numbers; the decimal system. **2.** Variant of **algorithm.** [Middle English *algorisme*, from Old French, from Medieval Latin *algorismus*, after Muhammad ibn-Musa AL-KHWARIZMI.]

al·go·rithm (ăl′gə-rĭth′əm) *n.* Also **al·go·rism** (-rĭz′əm). *Mathematics.* Any mechanical or recursive computational procedure. [Variant (influenced by ARITHMETIC) of ALGORISM.] **—al·go·rith·mic** (ăl′gə-rĭth′mĭk) *adj.*

algorithmic language *n.* An arithmetical language presenting numerical procedures to a computer in a standard form.

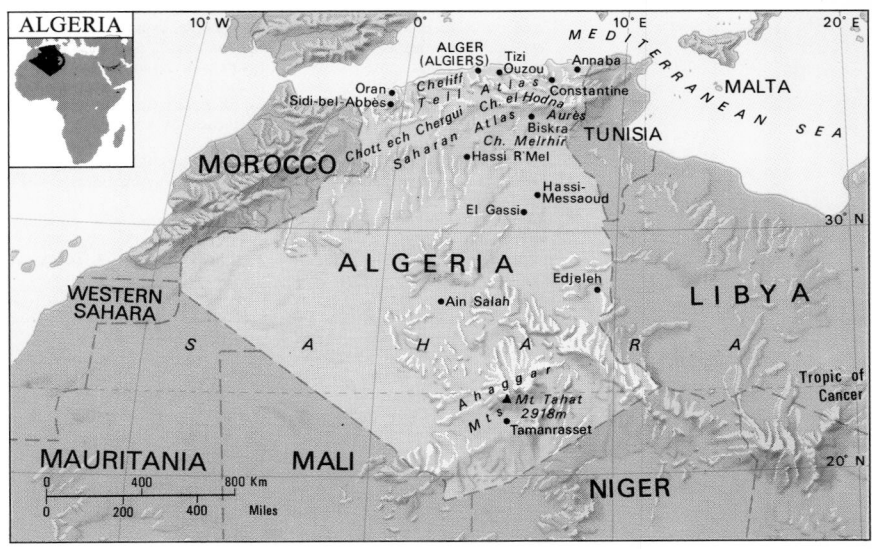

ALGERIA

Al·ham·bra, the (ăl-hăm′brə). Citadel and palace, overlooking Granada in southern Spain. It was built by the Moorish kings in the 13th and 14th centuries and is the best example of Moorish architecture in Spain.

A·li (ä′lē) (c. 600–61). Fourth caliph of Islam (656–61). He was the cousin and son-in-law (by his marriage to Fatima) of the prophet Muhammad and one of the first converts to Islam. His reign was marred by conflict between his supporters and rivals, and after his assassination, Islam came to be divided into Sunnites and Shiites, the Shiites holding that Ali and his descendants had the only valid claim to the caliphate.

A·li (ä-lē′), **Muhammad,** originally Cassius Marcellus Clay (1942–). U.S. boxer. He won the world heavyweight championship in 1964. He became a Black Muslim, changed his name, and refused military service in 1967. For this last action he was stripped of his title. He regained the championship by defeating George Foreman in 1974, losing it briefly in 1978 and regaining it again that year.

a·li·as (ā′lē-əs, āl′yəs) *n., pl.* **-ases.** An assumed name. *~adv.* Otherwise named or known as: *Johnson, alias Rogers.* [Latin *aliās*, otherwise, from *alius*, other.]

A·li Ba·ba (ä′lē bä′bə). In the *Arabian Nights,* a poor woodcutter who gains entrance to the treasure cave of the forty thieves by saying the magic words "Open, Sesame!"

al·i·bi (ăl′ə-bī′) *n., pl.* **-bis.** **1.** *Law.* **a.** A form of defense whereby a defendant attempts to prove that he was elsewhere when the crime in question was committed. **b.** The evidence supporting this. **2.** *Informal.* An excuse. *~tr.v.* **alibied, -biing, -bis.** *Informal.* To provide an excuse or alibi for. [Latin *alibī*, elsewhere : *alius*, other + *ubī*, where.]

al·i·ble (ăl′ə-bəl) *adj.* Having nutrients; nourishing. [Latin, *alibilis*, from *alere*, to nourish.]

A·li·can·te (ä′lē-kän′tē). Mediterranean port and tourist resort in the Valencia region of southeastern Spain. It is the capital of Alicante province.

Al·ice-band (ăl′ĭs-bănd′) *n.* A firm, U-shaped headband worn over the crown and tucked behind the ears. [After the headband worn by Alice in Sir John Tenniel's (1820–1914) illustrations of *Through the Looking-Glass.*]

Al·ice-in-Won·der·land (ăl′ĭs-ĭn-wŭn′dər-lănd′) *adj.* Absurd; fantastic. [After the fantastic logic and events of Wonderland in Lewis Carroll's book.]

Al·ice Springs (ăl′ĭs). Town in Northern Territory, Australia, lying almost at the midpoint of the continent. It is a center for tourism and transport.

al·i·cy·clic (ăl′ĭ-sī′klĭk, -sĭk′lĭk) *adj.* Of, pertaining to, or designating chemical compounds having both aliphatic and cyclic characteristics or structures. Examples of alicyclic compounds include cyclohexane and sucrose. [German *alicyclisch* : ALI(PHATIC) + CYCLIC.]

al·i·dade (ăl′ə-dād′) *n.* Also **al·i·dad** (-dăd). **1.** A surveying instrument consisting of a rule with sights at each end, used on a plane table to draw lines of sight onto distant objects. Also called "sight rule." **2.** A similar rule with a telescope mounted parallel to it. **3.** The index of a graduated surveying instrument such as an astrolabe. [French, from Medieval Latin *allidada*, from Arabic *al-'idāda*, "the revolving radius of a circle," from *'aḍud*, humerus.]

a·li·en (ā′lē-ən, āl′yən) *adj.* **1.** Owing political allegiance to a country other than the one in which one is resident; foreign: *a large alien population.* **2. a.** Belonging to, characteristic of, or derived from another place, society, or person; not one's own; unfamiliar; strange: *the problems of adjusting to an alien culture.* **b.** Belonging or pertaining to another planet or world: *an alien spaceship.* **3.** Inconsistent or incompatible; repugnant. Used with *to*: *Lying is alien to his nature.* **—See Synonyms at extrinsic.**

Ali Baba *In the* Arabian Nights *story, the 40 thieves conceal themselves in large oil jars at Ali Baba's house, planning to kill him because he knows the secret of their magic cave. But, as this 19th-century illustration shows, Ali and his servant Morgiana discover their hiding place, and Morgiana kills the thieves by pouring boiling oil over them.*

~*n.* **1.** A foreign resident of a country who has not been naturalized. **2.** A member of another family, people, region, or the like; especially, a being from another planet or world. **3.** A person who is excluded from some group; an outsider. **4.** *Ecology.* A plant native to one region but naturalized in another. ~*tr.v.* **aliened, -ening, -ens.** *Law.* To alienate (property). [Middle English, from Old French, from Latin *aliēnus,* belonging to another, from *alius,* other.]

a·li·en·a·ble (āl′yə-nə-bəl, ā′lē-ə-) *adj. Law.* Capable of being transferred to the ownership of another. Said typically of property. —**a·li·en·a·bil·i·ty** *n.*

a·li·en·age (āl′yə-nĭj, ā′lē-ə-) *n.* The state or condition of being alien or an alien.

a·li·en·ate (āl′yə-nāt′, ā′lē-ə-) *tr.v.* **-ated, -ating, -ates. 1.** To cause (someone previously friendly or affectionate) to become unfriendly or indifferent; estrange. **2.** To dissociate or isolate (oneself). **3.** To cause to be transferred; turn away: *"he succeeded . . . in alienating the affections of my only ward"* (Oscar Wilde). **4.** *Law.* To transfer (property) to the ownership of another. [Latin *aliēnāre,* from *aliēnus,* ALIEN.] —**a·li·en·a·tor** *n.*

a·li·en·at·ed (āl′yə-nā′tĭd, ā′lē-ə-) *adj. Psychology.* **1.** Suffering from alienation. **2.** Loosely, out of sympathy with one's immediate social environment.

a·li·en·a·tion (āl′yə-nā′shən, ā′lē-ə-) *n.* **1.** The condition of being an outsider; a state of isolation. **2.** *Psychology.* A state of estrangement between the self and the objective world, or between different parts of the personality. **3.** The act of alienating, as: **a.** Estrangement; disaffection: *"In the decades after 1795 there was a profound alienation between classes in Britain"* (E.P. Thompson). **b.** *Law.* The transference of property, or the title to it, to another. **4.** In Marxist theory, the sense of loss of personal identity and worth caused in workers by the fragmentation of labor, mechanization, and lack of control over the means of production. **5.** In the theater, the distancing of the audience from the action of the play by dramatic devices: *Brecht's alienation effects.* [Sense 4: translation of German *Entäusserung.* Sense 5: short for *alienation effect,* translation of German *Verfremdungseffekt.*]

a·li·en·ee (āl′yə-nē′, ā′lē-ə-nē′) *n. Law.* A person to whom ownership of property is transferred.

a·li·en·ist (āl′yə-nĭst, ā′lē-ə-nĭst) *n.* **1.** *Archaic.* A doctor specializing in mental illness. **2.** *Law.* A psychiatrist who has been accepted by a court as an expert on the mental competence of principals or witnesses appearing before it. [French *aliéniste,* from *aliéné,* insane, from Latin *aliēnātus,* "estranged," past participle of *aliēnāre,* to ALIENATE.]

a·li·en·or (āl′yə-nôr′, ā′lē-ə-) *n. Law.* A person who transfers ownership of property to another.

a·lif (ä′lĭf) *n.* The first letter of the Arabic alphabet. See feature at **alphabet.** [Arabic.]

a·li·form (ā′lə-fôrm′, ăl′ə-) *adj.* Shaped like a wing; alar. [Latin *āla,* wing + -FORM.]

a·light[1] (ə-līt′) *intr.v.* **alighted** or **alit** (ə-lĭt′), **alighting, alights. 1.** To come down and settle, as after flight. Used with *on* or *upon: a bird alighting on a branch.* **2. a.** To get out of (a vehicle, for example). **b.** To dismount. Used with *from.* **3.** To come upon by chance. Used with *on* or *upon: His gaze alighted on an old vase.* [Middle English *ali(g)hten,* Old English *ālīhtan : ā-* (intensive) + *līhtan,* to dismount, lighten, from *līht,* LIGHT (adjective).]

a·light[2] *adj.* **1.** Burning. **2.** Lighted; lit up. Used after the noun: *Her face was alight with intelligence.* [Middle English *alight,* Old English *ālīht,* past participle of *ālīhtan,* to light up : *a-* + *līhtan,* to light, from *līht,* LIGHT.] —**a·light** *adv.*

a·lign (ə-līn′) *v.* **aligned, aligning, aligns.** —*tr.* **1.** To arrange in a line. **2.** To ally (oneself, for example) with one side of an argument, cause, policy, or the like. **3.** To bring (two or more parts of a machine, for example) into correct relation with one another. —*intr.* To fall into line or position. [French *aligner,* from Old French : *a-,* from Latin *ad-,* to + *ligne,* LINE.] —**a·lign·er** *n.*

a·lign·ment (ə-līn′mənt) *n.* **1.** Arrangement or position in a straight line. **2.** A ground plan, as of a railway. **3.** The act of aligning or the condition of being aligned: *In the new political alignment; all parties opposed the government.* **4.** The correct or proper adjustment or positioning of related parts, as of a machine.

alignment chart *n. Mathematics.* A nomogram (see).

a·like (ə-līk′) *adj.* Having a close resemblance; similar. Usually used after the noun: *His sons are alike.* ~*adv.* In the same way or manner, or to the same degree: *They dress and walk alike.* [Middle English *ilik,* Old English *gelīc* : *ge-* (collective prefix) + *līc,* form.] —**a·like·ness** *n.*

al·i·ment (ăl′ə-mənt) *n. Formal.* **1.** Food; nourishment. **2.** Something that supports or sustains. **3.** In Scots law, alimony or maintenance. ~*tr.v.* (ăl′ə-mĕnt′) **alimented, -menting, -ments.** *Formal.* To supply with food or other sustenance. [Middle English, from Latin *alimentum,* from *alere,* to nourish.] —**al·i·men·tal** (ăl′ə-mĕn′təl) *adj.* —**al·i·men·tal·ly** *adv.*

al·i·men·ta·ry (ăl′ə-mĕn′trē, -tə-rē) *adj.* **1.** Of or pertaining to food or nutrition. **2.** Providing nourishment.

alimentary canal *n.* The mucous-membrane-lined tube of the digestive system, extending from the mouth to the anus and including the esophagus, stomach, and intestines.

al·i·men·ta·tion (ăl′ə-mĕn-tā′shən) *n.* **1.** The act or process of giving or receiving nourishment. **2.** Support; sustenance.

al·i·mo·ny (ăl′ə-mō′nē) *n., pl.* **-nies. 1.** *Law.* An allowance for support made under court order and usually given by one spouse to the other after divorce or legal separation. **2.** Sustenance; support. [Latin *alimōnia,* nutriment, support, from *alere,* to nourish.]

al·i·phat·ic (ăl′ə-făt′ĭk) *adj.* Of, pertaining to, or designating organic chemical compounds with reactions characteristic of compounds with open chains of carbon atoms rather than the closed chains of aromatic (see) compounds. See **alicyclic.** [From Greek *aleiphar* (stem *aleiphat-*), oil, from *aleiphein,* to anoint.]

al·i·quant (ăl′ə-kwənt) *adj.* Of, pertaining to, or designating a number or quantity that is not an exact factor or divisor of some other number or quantity. [New Latin *aliquantus,* from Latin, "a certain quantity" : *alius,* some + *quantus,* how much.]

al·i·quot (ăl′ə-kwŏt′, -kwət) *adj.* **1.** *Mathematics.* Of, pertaining to,

---

alien message

MESSAGES AIMED AT THE STARS
Man's attempts to communicate with alien civilizations

The first deliberate messages from Earth to alien civilizations have already been sent. Two identical "letters," in the form of engraved metal plaques, were fixed to the Pioneer 10 and 11 spacecraft that were launched by the United States in the early 1970's. Neither probe was aimed at any particular star. So both could drift through the emptiness of interstellar space, unnoticed but untarnished, for millions of years—until long after every 20th-century artifact on Earth has crumbled to dust.

Even if the letters are found by beings from another planet, a reply will take some time. Although scientists calculate that our own galaxy alone may contain as many as a million Earth-type planets—or about one for every 100,000 of its stars—the distances they are from Earth are so vast that even a reply sent at the speed of light could take many thousands of years to reach us.

A second message, which took only three minutes to transmit but which will take 24,000 years to arrive, was sent in 1974. It was a powerful radio signal beamed from the 305-meter-wide (1,000-foot) radio telescope at Arecibo, Puerto Rico. The message was aimed at a cluster of 300,000 stars known as M13 in the constellation of Hercules, 24,000 light-years away. The signal consists of 1,679 on-off pulses that make up a strip of pictograms carefully designed to show the basic details of terrestrial life. Even the total number of pulses was chosen to avoid ambiguity; 1,679 can be arranged into a rectangular pattern in only one way—as 73 rows of 23 pulses each.

Because humans have only recently learned to send messages to the stars, and because interstellar communications are so slow, any message that reaches Earth *from* outer space in the near future will almost certainly have come from a civilization far in advance of our own. Despite years of listening, however, astronomers have yet to hear any intelligible signal.

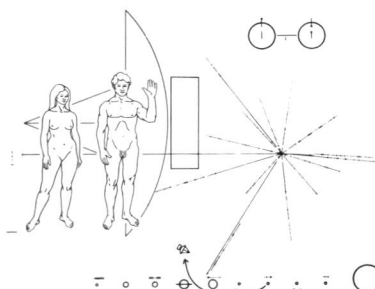

PEACE FROM EARTH *Plaques on the Pioneer space probes show two human figures drawn to scale against an outline of the craft—with the man holding up his hand in greeting. On the right are representations of the universe's basic building block, the hydrogen atom, the sun's position in relation to various radio sources, and the probe's journey from Earth.*

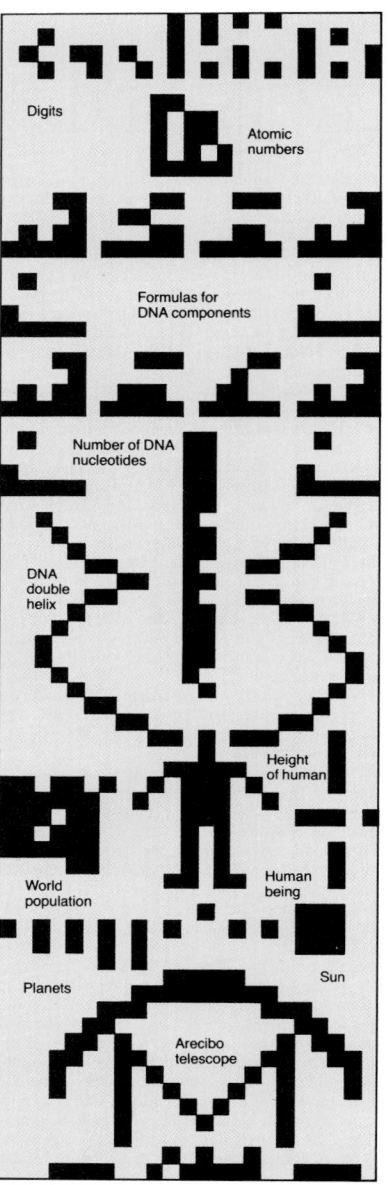

Digits · Atomic numbers · Formulas for DNA components · Number of DNA nucleotides · DNA double helix · Height of human · World population · Human being · Planets · Sun · Arecibo telescope

OVER AND OUT *The pictogram message that was flashed to the stars from Puerto Rico. It includes details about terrestrial arithmetic and atomic numbers, and the chemicals on which all life on earth is based. The message also contains simple pictures of a human figure, with an indication of its size, and of the giant Arecibo radio telescope itself.*

or designating an exact divisor or factor of a quantity, especially of an integer. **2.** Contained exactly or an exact number of times. [French *(partie) aliquote,* aliquot (part), from Medieval Latin *(pars) aliquotae,* from Latin *aliquot,* some, several : *alius,* some, other + *quot,* how many.]

a·lit. Alternate past tense of **alight.**

a·li·un·de (ā'lē-ŭn'dē, ăl'ē-) *adv. Law.* From another source; from elsewhere: *evidence aliunde.* [Latin, from elsewhere : *alius,* other + *unde,* whence.]

a·live (ə-līv') *adj.* **1.** Having life; in a living state. **2.** In existence or operation; not extinct or inactive: *keep love alive.* **3.** In a state of animation; full of life; lively: *Her performance was splendidly alive.* **4.** Now living. Used as an intensive, usually with a superlative: *the strongest man alive.* **5.** Aware; sensitive: *alive to the moods of others.* **6.** Swarming: *The square was alive with happy people.* —See Synonyms at **living.** —**alive and kicking.** Lively; active. —**look alive.** To be alert. Used in the imperative. [Middle English *alive, on live,* Old English *on līfe* : ON + *līfe,* dative of *līf,* LIFE.] —**a·live·ness** *n.*

a·liz·a·rin (ə-lĭz'ə-rĭn) *n.* Also **a·liz·a·rine** (-rĭn, -rēn'). An orange-red compound, $C_{14}H_8O_4$, used as a dyestuff. [French *alizarine,* from *alizari,* madder, from Spanish, from Arabic *al-'aṣārah,* the juice pressed out : *al,* the + *'aṣara,* he pressed.]

al·ka·hest (ăl'kə-hĕst') *n.* The hypothetical universal solvent once sought by alchemists. [Medieval Latin *alchahest,* probably coined as a pseudo-Arabic word by Paracelsus.]

al·ka·les·cent (ăl'kə-lĕs'ənt) *adj.* Becoming alkaline; slightly alkaline. [ALKAL(I) + -ESCENT.] —**al·ka·les·cence, al·ka·les·cen·cy** *n.*

al·ka·li (ăl'kə-lī') *n., pl.* **-lis** or **-lies. 1.** *Chemistry.* A soluble base such as ammonia or a hydroxide or carbonate of an alkali metal, the aqueous solution of which is bitter, slippery, and caustic. **2.** Any of various soluble mineral salts found in natural water and arid soils. [Middle English *alcaly,* from Medieval Latin *alcali,* from Arabic *al-qalīy,* the ashes (of saltwort), from *qalay,* to fry.]

al·ka·li·fy (ăl'kə-lə-fī', ăl-kăl'ə-fī') *v.* **-fied, -fying, -fies.** —*tr.* To make alkaline; alkalize. —*intr.* To become alkaline.

alkali metal *n.* Any of a group of soft, white, low-density, low-melting, highly reactive metallic elements, including lithium, sodium, potassium, rubidium, cesium, and francium. The alkali metals constitute Group I of the periodic table of the elements.

al·ka·lim·e·ter (ăl'kə-lĭm'ə-tər) *n.* **1.** An apparatus for measuring alkalinity. **2.** An apparatus for measuring the amount of carbon dioxide evolved from a solid. —**al·ka·lim·e·try** (ăl'kə-lĭm'ə-trē) *n.*

al·ka·line (ăl'kə-lĭn, -līn') *adj.* **1.** Of, relating to, containing, or having the nature of an alkali. **2.** Designating a soil having a pH greater than 7.

alkaline earth *n.* **1.** An oxide of an alkaline-earth metal. **2.** Loosely, an alkaline-earth metal. —**al·ka·line-earth** *adj.*

alkaline-earth metal *n.* Any of a group of silvery, fairly reactive metallic elements, especially calcium, strontium, and barium, but generally including beryllium, magnesium, and radium. The alkaline-earth metals constitute Group II of the periodic table of the elements.

al·ka·lin·i·ty (ăl'kə-lĭn'ĭ-tē) *n.* The alkali concentration or alkaline quality of an alkali-containing substance or solution.

al·ka·lize (ăl'kə-līz') *v.* **-lized, -lizing, -lizes.** Also **al·ka·lin·ize** (-lĭn-īz'), **-ized, -izing, -izes.** —*tr.* To make alkaline. —*intr.* To become an alkali. —**al·ka·li·za·tion** *n.*

al·ka·loid (ăl'kə-loid') *n.* Any of various physiologically active nitrogen-containing organic bases derived from plants, including nicotine, quinine, cocaine, atropine, and morphine. [German : ALKAL(I) + -OID.] —**al·ka·loi·dal** (ăl'kə-loid'l) *adj.*

al·ka·lo·sis (ăl'kə-lō'sĭs) *n.* Pathologically high alkali content in the blood and tissues. [New Latin : ALKAL(I) + -OSIS.]

al·kane series (ăl'kān') *n. Chemistry.* The **paraffin** series *(see).* [ALK(YL) + -ANE.]

al·ka·net (ăl'kə-nĕt') *n.* **1. a.** A European plant, *Alkanna tinctoria,* the roots of which yield a red dye. **b.** The root of this plant, or a dye prepared from it. **2.** Any of several hairy plants of the genus *Anchusa,* native to the Old World, having clusters of blue flowers. Also called "bugloss." [Middle English, from Spanish *alcaneta,* diminutive of *alcana,* henna, from Medieval Latin *alchanna,* from Arabic *al-hinnā',* the HENNA.]

al-Kartum, Al Khartum. See **Khartoum.**

al·kene (ăl'kēn') *n.* Any of a class of unsaturated aliphatic hydrocarbons that contain at least one double carbon-carbon bond in their molecules. The simplest alkenes have only one double bond and form a series (the *alkene series*) with the general formula C_nH_{2n}. The first members of the series are ethene ($CH_2{:}CH_2$), propene ($CH_3CH_2{:}CH_2$), and butene ($C_2H_5CH_2{:}CH_2$). Also called "olefine." [ALK(YL) + -ENE.]

Al Khalil. See **Hebron.**

al-Khwa·riz·mi (ăl'KHwä-rēz'mē), **Muhammad ibn-Musa** (*c.* 780–*c.* 850). Arab mathematician. His work introduced the Hindu system of notation into Arabic mathematics, and a 10th-century Latin translation of it introduced this system, now known as "Arabic numerals," to Western mathematics. The word "algebra" comes from the title of al-Khwarizmi's treatise on it, and the word for the calculating procedure he discussed, "algorism" (algorithm), is derived from his name.

al·kie, al·ky (ăl'kē) *n., pl.* **-kies.** *Slang.* An alcoholic.

Alkoran. Variant of **Alcoran,** the **Koran** *(see).*

al·kox·ide (ăl-kŏk'sīd') *n. Chemistry.* Any of a class of chemical compounds that are salts formed by removing a hydrogen atom from the hydroxyl group of an alcohol. Sodium methoxide, $NaOCH_3$, is a simple example. [ALK(YL) + OX(Y)- + -IDE.]

al·kyd resin (ăl'kĭd) *n.* A widely used durable synthetic resin derived from glycerol and phthalic anhydride. Also called "alkyd." [Blend of ALKYL and ACID.]

al·kyl (ăl'kəl) *n. Chemistry.* A monovalent radical, such as ethyl or propyl, having the general formula C_nH_{2n+1}. [German : ALC(OHOL) + -YL.]

al·kyl·a·tion (ăl'kə-lā'shən) *n. Chemistry.* Any process in which an alkyl group is added to or substituted in a molecule, as in the reaction of alkenes with alkanes to make high-octane fuels.

al·kyl·ben·zene (ăl'kəl-bĕn'zēn') *n. Chemistry.* Any of a class of hydrocarbons with molecules that have an alkyl group joined to a benzene ring. Toluene ($C_6H_5{\cdot}CH_3$) is the simplest example.

al·kyne series (ăl'kīn') *n.* A series of hydrocarbons, the **acetylene series** *(see).* [ALKY(L) + -(I)NE.]

all (ôl) *adj.* **1.** The total entity or extent of: *All Europe was threatened.* **2.** The entire or total number, amount, or quantity of: *All animals are alike in some respects.* Often used after a pronoun: *I like them all.* **3.** Every one of a group or class: *All the staff were present.* **4.** The greatest possible: *in all honesty.* **5. a.** Many: *all sorts of books.* **b.** Every. Used in the phrase *all manner of.* **6.** Any whatsoever: *beyond all doubt.* **7.** Nothing but; only: *He was all skin and bones.*

~*pron.* **1.** Each and every one: *Education for all.* **2. a.** Each and every thing: *Ten ships sailed and all have now docked.* **b.** Everything collectively: *He remembered all he saw.*

~*n.* **1.** Everything one has: *She gave her all.* **2.** The whole number; totality. —**all and sundry.** Everyone without restriction. —**all in all. 1.** With everything being taken into account. **2.** Of the highest importance. —**at all. 1. a.** To some or any extent: *He can't walk at all.* **b.** Whatever: *He did no work at all.* Used as an intensive in negative sentences. **2. a.** Ever: *Do you see him at all now?* **b.** To any extent; in any way: *Does he feel better at all?* Used in questions to suggest some doubt in the speaker's mind. —**for all.** To the limited extent that: *for all I care.* —**in all.** Including everyone or everything: *That makes twelve packages in all.*

~*adv.* **1.** Wholly; entirely; completely: *This is all wrong.* **2.** *Informal.* Very; thoroughly: *The coat was all dirty.* **3.** Each; apiece: *a score of five all.* **4.** Exclusively: *The cake is all for you.* **5. a.** To a great extent or degree: *happens all too often.* **b.** To such an extent: *all the more reason not to trust him.* —**all about.** Mainly or exclusively concerned with: *This book is all about trout fishing.* —**all along.** Over a period of time; consistently: *I hoped all along that he'd come.* —**all but.** Nearly; almost: *He all but fainted.* —**all in.** *Informal.* Tired; exhausted. —**all of.** Not less than: *It's all of ten miles.* —**all that.** Particularly. Used in the negative: *It wasn't all that difficult.* —**all there.** *Informal.* Mentally competent or alert. —**all the same. 1.** Nevertheless. **2.** Of little importance: *It's all the same to me.* [Middle English *al(le),* Old English *all, eall.*]

Usage: *All* can occur with either a singular or plural verb, according to whether an uncountable or a countable noun respectively is present or understood. *All is not lost, all human life is there, all (members) were present,* are equally correct. The use of *of* before the definite article in such phrases is optional: *all (of) the members;* it is often preferred in American English and omitted in British English, especially in writing.

all–[1] *comb. form.* Indicates: **1.** Wholly or entirely; for example, **all-night, all-wool. 2.** Extremely; very; for example, **all-important. 3.** Representing the whole of; for example, **all-American. 4.** Every kind of; for example, **all-weather.**

all–[2]. Variant of **allo-.**

al·la bre·ve (ä'lə brĕv'ā) *adv. Music.* In duple or quadruple time with the half note being the unit of time. [Italian, "according to the breve."] —**al·la bre·ve** *adj.*

Al·lah (ăl'ə, ä'lə) *n.* Almighty God, the Supreme Being. Name of God used in Islam. [Arabic *Allāh* : *al,* the + *Ilāh,* god.]

Al·la·ha·bad (ăl'ə-hə-băd', -bäd'). City in Uttar Pradesh, northern India, at the confluence of the Ganges and Jumna rivers. It was an important center of the movement for Indian national independence.

al·la·man·da, al·la·man·de (ăl'ə-măn'də) *n.* Any of several woody vines of the genus *Allamanda,* native to tropical America, having showy, funnel-shaped yellow flowers. [After Jean N.S. *Allamand* (1713–87), Swiss scientist.]

all-A·mer·i·can (ôl'ə-mĕr'ĭ-kən) *adj.* **1.** Representative of the best of its kind in the United States. **2.** *Sports.* Chosen as the best amateur in the United States at a particular position or event: *an all-American halfback.* **3.** Composed of Americans or American materials exclusively. **4.** Entirely within the territorial limits of the United States. **5.** Of all the Americas.

~*n. Often* **All-American.** An all-American athlete.

al·lan·ite (ăl'ə-nīt') *n.* A rare brown mineral found in certain igneous rocks, consisting of an aluminosilicate of calcium, iron, and several lanthanoid elements. [After T. *Allan* (1777–1833), British mineralogist.]

al·lan·toid (ə-lăn'toid) *adj.* Also **al·lan·toi·dal** (ăl'ən-toid'l). **1.** Of or having an allantois. **2.** *Botany.* Shaped like a sausage.

~*n.* The allantois. [French *allantoïde,* from Old French, from Greek *allantoeidēs (humēn),* "the sausage-shaped (membrane)" : *allantos*†, sausage + -OID.]

al·lan·to·is (ə-lăn'tō-ĭs) *n., pl.* **allantoides** (ăl'ən-tō'ə-dēz). A membranous sac that develops from the hindgut in the embryos of mam-

alkanet *An upright, hairy plant with tiny blue flowers that look like birds' eyes. It has spread all over southern Europe and eastern North America. Egyptian women made henna, a red dye for hair and nails, from it.*

PRONUNCIATION KEY

ă, pat; ā, pay; âr, care;
ä, father, are; b, bib;
ch, church; d, deed; ĕ, pet;
ē, be; f, fife; g, gag; h, hat;
hw, which; ĭ, pit; ī, pie;
îr, pier; j, judge; k, kick;
l, lid, needle; m, mum;
n, no, sudden; ng, thing;
ŏ, pot; ō, toe; ô, paw, for;
oi, noise; ou, out; ŏŏ, book;
ōō, boot; p, pop; r, roar;
s, sauce; sh, ship, dish;
t, tight; th, thin, path;
th, this, bathe; ŭ, cut; ûr, fur;
v, valve; w, with; y, yes;
z, zebra, size; zh, vision;
ə, about, item, edible,
gallop, circus, peaceful

IN FOREIGN WORDS:

à, *Fr.* ami; œ, *Fr.* feu, *Ger.* schön; ü, *Fr.* tu, *Ger.* über; KH, *Ger.* ich, *Scot.* loch; N, *Fr.* bon; y', *Fr.* Compiègne

STRESS MARKS:

Primary stress: '
in·cite' (ĭn-sīt')
Secondary stress: '
in'sight' (ĭn'sīt')

mals, birds, and reptiles. In mammals it takes part in the formation of the umbilical cord and the placenta. [New Latin, from Greek *allantoeidēs*, ALLANTOID.] **—al·lan·to·ic** (ăl'ən-tō'ĭk) *adj.*

al·lar·gan·do (ä'lär-gän'dō) *adv. Music.* To be performed more slowly. Used as a direction. [Italian, from *allargare*, to make slow, widen, ultimately from Latin *largus*, abundant, LARGE.]

all-a·round (ôl'ə-round') *adj.* Also **all-round** (ôl'round'). **1.** Comprehensive in extent or depth: *a program of all-around vocational training.* **2.** Able to do many or all things well; versatile: *an all-around athlete.*

al·lay (ə-lā') *tr.v.* **-layed, -laying, -lays. 1.** To lessen or relieve (pain or grief, for example); reduce the intensity of. **2.** To calm or pacify (fear, for example); set at rest. —See Synonyms at **relieve.** [Middle English *alaien*, Old English *ālecgan* : *ā-*, away, aside + *lecgan*, to lay.] **—al·lay·er** *n.*

all clear *n.* **1.** A signal, usually by siren, that an air raid is over. **2.** An indication of the absence of immediate obstacles or impending danger. **3.** Official approval to proceed: *We need the all clear from the boss.*

al·le·ga·tion (ăl'ə-gā'shən) *n.* **1.** The act of alleging. **2.** A statement offered without proof, especially regarding the wrongdoings of another; a mere assertion. **3.** *Law.* A statement, charge, or claim put forward by a party to be proved or supported with evidence. [Middle English, from Latin *allēgātiō* (stem *allēgātiōn-*), from *allēgāre*, to dispatch, adduce: *ad-*, toward + *lēgāre*, to charge.]

al·lege (ə-lĕj') *tr.v.* **-leged, -leging, -leges. 1.** To assert to be true; affirm; declare. **2.** To assert without proof. **3.** To bring forward (a plea or excuse, for example) in support or denial of a claim or accusation. **4.** *Archaic.* To cite or quote, as in confirmation. —See Synonyms at **assert.** [Middle English *alleg(g)en*, from Norman French *alegier*, Old French *esligier*, from Vulgar Latin *exlītigare* (unattested), to clear of charges in lawsuit: *ex-*, out of + *lītīgāre*, to LITIGATE.] **—al·leg·er** *n.*

al·leged (ə-lĕjd', ə-lĕj'ĭd) *adj.* Claimed to exist or to be as described but without proof; merely supposed: *the alleged theft.* **—al·leg·ed·ly** (ə-lĕj'ĭd-lē) *adv.*

Al·le·ghe·ny Mountains (ăl'ə-gā'nē). Also **Al·le·ghe·nies** (-nēz). Mountain range forming the western part of the Appalachian Mts. in the eastern United States. The range stretches some 800 kilometers (500 miles) through Pennsylvania, Maryland, Virginia, and West Virginia and rises to 1,480 meters (4,860 feet) at Spruce Knob in West Virginia.

al·le·giance (ə-lē'jəns) *n.* **1.** Loyalty, or the obligation of loyalty, as to a nation, sovereign, or cause. **2.** The obligations of a vassal to his overlord. —See Synonyms at **fidelity.** [Middle English *allegeaunce*, from Old French *ligeance*, from *li(e)ge*, LIEGE.] **—al·le·giant** *adj.*

al·le·gor·i·cal (ăl'ə-gôr'ĭ-kəl, -gŏr'ĭ-kəl) *adj.* Also **al·le·gor·ic** (ăl'ə-gôr'ĭk, -gŏr'ĭk). Pertaining to, characteristic of, or having the nature of allegory. **—al·le·gor·i·cal·ly** *adv.*

al·le·go·rize (ăl'ə-gô-rīz', -gə-rīz') *v.* **-rized, -rizing, -rizes.** —*tr.* **1.** To express as, or in the form of, an allegory. **2.** To interpret allegorically. —*intr.* To use or make allegory. **—al·le·go·ri·za·tion** (ăl'ə-gə-rə-zā'shən) *n.* **—al·le·go·riz·er** *n.*

al·le·go·ry (ăl'ə-gôr'ē, -gōr'ē) *n., pl.* **-ries. 1.** The representation of a subject in a story, play, or picture, using the people or events portrayed to illustrate deeper or more general truths: *The story of the Holy Grail is an allegory of man's spiritual quest.* **2.** An instance of such representation. **3.** Any symbolic representation. [Middle English *allegorie*, from Old French, from Latin *allēgoria*, from Greek, from *allēgorein*, to speak figuratively, "speak in other terms" : *allos*, other + *agoreuein*, to speak (in public), from *agora*, an assembly.] **—al·le·go·rist** *n.*

al·le·gret·to (ăl'ə-grĕt'ō, ä'lə-) *adv. Music.* In quick tempo; slower than allegro but faster than andante. Used as a direction. ~*n., pl.* **allegrettos.** *Music.* A movement or passage in this tempo. [Italian, diminutive of ALLEGRO.] **—al·le·gret·to** *adj.*

al·le·gro (ə-lĕg'rō, ə-lā'grō) *adv. Music.* In rapid tempo; faster than allegretto but slower than presto. Used as a direction. ~*n., pl.* **allegros.** *Music.* A movement or passage in this tempo. [Italian, "lively," from Latin *alacer*, brisk.] **—al·le·gro** *adj.*

al·lele (ə-lēl') *n.* Any of the alternative forms of a gene, which occupy the same relative position on homologous chromosomes. Also called "allelomorph." [German *Allel*, short for ALLELOMORPH.] **—al·le·lic** (ə-lē'lĭk, ə-lĕl'ĭk) *adj.*

al·le·lo·morph (ə-lē'lə-môrf', ə-lĕl'ə-) *n.* An allele. [Greek *allēlōn*, reciprocally, from *allos*, another + -MORPH.] **—al·le·lo·mor·phic** (ə-lē'lə-môr'fĭk) *adj.* **—al·le·lo·mor·phism** (ə-lē'lə-môr'fĭz'əm) *n.*

al·le·lu·ia (ăl'ə-lōō'yə) *interj.* Used as a Christian expression of praise to God or of thanksgiving. ~*n., pl.* **alleluias. 1.** A part of the Catholic Mass beginning and ending with this word. **2.** A musical setting of this. [Middle English, from Medieval Latin *allēlūja*, from Late Greek *allēlouia*, from Hebrew *hallelūyāh*, HALLELUJAH.]

al·le·mande (ăl'ə-mănd', ăl'ə-mänd') *n.* **1. a.** A lively, late 18th-century dance in ¾ time. **b.** A movement in square dancing and country dancing. **2.** *Music.* The first movement of a 17th- or 18th-century classical suite. [French, feminine of *allemand*, German, from Latin *Alemannus*, singular of ALEMANNI.]

Al·len (ăl'ən), **Ethan** (1738–89). U.S. Revolutionary soldier. He commanded the Green Mountain Boys, who helped capture Fort Ticonderoga from the British (1775).

Allen, Fred, born John Florence Sullivan (1894–1956). U.S. humorist. Allen was noted for his work in vaudeville, radio, and early television and for his dry humor and deadpan delivery.

Allen, Woody, born Allen Stewart Konigsberg (1935–). U.S. film director, comic actor, and writer. His films include *Play It Again Sam* (1972), *Sleeper* (1973), *Annie Hall* (1977, two Academy Awards), and *Manhattan* (1979).

---

allegory

UNIVERSAL THEMES IN WORDS AND PICTURES

Great art that shimmers with layers of meaning

Since ancient times, artists have used allegory to express abstract themes vividly. In Greek and Roman frescoes, for instance, bulls are often more than just animals; they symbolize fertility or virility as well. In medieval religious paintings, a dove may be a mark of divine favor or a symbol of peace.

Many allegories have been literary rather than pictorial. John Bunyan's *The Pilgrim's Progress* (published in 1678) traces the hero's journey through places such as Vanity Fair and the Slough of Despond in order to illustrate the Christian's search for salvation. Jonathan Swift's book, *Gulliver's Travels* (1726) is both an adventure story and a bitter satire on the follies of mankind. And George Orwell's *Animal Farm* (1945) hides an attack on the leadership of the international Communist movement and the U.S.S.R. beneath a simple tale about a revolt by farm animals. So close is the parallel that figures such as Marx, Lenin, Trotsky, and Stalin can be identified among the animals.

LOVE CONQUERS ALL *In this allegorical painting,* Mars and Venus, *by the 15th-century Italian painter Sandro Botticelli, Mars, symbolizing war, is soothed into a peaceful sleep by the Roman goddess of love—illustrating the Christian belief that violence should be overcome by gentleness. The painting was designed to commemorate a marriage.*

Al·len·de (ä-yĕn′dā), **Salvador** (1908–73). Chilean statesman, president of Chile (1970–1973) and the first democratically elected Marxist head of government. He attempted to achieve socialism by gradual peaceful change, including land reform and nationalization, but many measures, especially the nationalization of foreign investments, were controversial, and financial credit was withdrawn from the Chilean economy. Right-wing opposition to Allende in Chile was encouraged by U.S. intervention, and his government was overthrown by a military coup in 1973, in which he was killed.

al·ler·gen (ăl′ər-jən) *n.* A substance that causes an allergy. [German *Allergen* : *Allergie,* ALLER(GY) + -GEN.] **—al·ler·gen·ic** (ăl′ər-jĕn′ĭk) *adj.*

al·ler·gic (ə-lûr′jĭk) *adj.* **1.** Characteristic of or concerning allergy. **2.** Having an allergy. **3.** *Informal.* Having a dislike; averse. Used with *to*: *allergic to work.*

al·ler·gist (ăl′ər-jĭst) *n.* A doctor specializing in allergies.

al·ler·gy (ăl′ər-jē) *n., pl.* **-gies. 1.** Excessive sensitivity to some environmental factor or substance, such as pollens, particular foods, dust, or microorganisms, causing an adverse physical reaction. **2.** *Informal.* A dislike; an aversion. [German *Allergie,* "altered reaction" : ALL(O)- + Greek *ergon,* work, effect.]

al·le·thrin (ăl′ə-thrĭn′) *n.* A synthetic amber liquid insecticide, similar to pyrethrin. [ALL(YL) + (PYR)ETHRIN.]

al·le·vi·ate (ə-lē′vē-āt′) *tr.v.* **-ated, -ating, -ates.** To make more bearable; reduce (pain or grief, for example). —See Synonyms at **relieve.** [Late Latin *alleviāre,* to lighten : Latin *ad-,* toward + *levis,* light.] **—al·le·vi·a·tion** (ə-lē′vē-ā′shən) *n.* **—al·le·vi·a·tor** *n.*

al·le·vi·a·tive (ə-lē′vē-ā′tĭv) *adj.* Also **al·le·vi·a·to·ry** (ə-lē′vē-ə-tôr′ē, -tōr′ē). Promoting alleviation.

al·ley[1] (ăl′ē) *n., pl.* **-leys. 1.** A narrow street or passageway between or behind buildings. **2.** A path between flowerbeds or trees in a garden or park. **3.** A **bowling alley** *(see).* **4.** Either of the parallel lanes at the sides of a tennis court, reserved for use in doubles play. **—up one's alley.** *Slang.* Compatible with one's interests or qualifications. [Middle English *aley,* from Old French *alee,* from the feminine past participle of *aler,* to go, from Latin *ambulāre,* to walk.]

alley[2] *n., pl.* **-leys.** A large playing marble; often used as the shooter. [Short for ALABASTER.]

Al·leyn (ăl′ən, -ĕn′, -ān′), **Edward** (1566–1626). English actor, one of the finest of the Elizabethan stage. Alleyn created the leading roles in Marlowe's *Tamburlaine* and *Doctor Faustus.*

al·ley·way (ăl′ē-wā′) *n.* A narrow passage between buildings.

All Fools' Day *n.* April 1, **April Fools' Day** *(see).*

all fours *pl.n.* **1.** All four limbs of an animal or person: *A baby crawls on all fours.* **2.** *Used with a singular verb.* A card game, **seven-up** *(see).*

all hail *interj. Archaic.* All health. Used as a greeting.

All·hal·low·mas (ôl′hăl′ō-məs) *n.* Also **All·hal·lows** (ôl′hăl′ōz). *Archaic.* **All Saints' Day** *(see).*

all-heal (ôl′hēl′) *n.* Any of several plants reputed to have healing powers, such as **valerian** and **self-heal** *(both of which see).*

al·li·a·ceous (ăl′ē-ā′shəs) *adj. Botany.* **1.** Belonging to the same genus (*Allium*) as onions and garlic. **2.** Tasting or smelling of onions or garlic. [Latin *allium*†, garlic + -ACEOUS.]

al·li·ance (ə-lī′əns) *n.* **1. a.** A formal pact of union joining nations or parties in a common cause. **b.** The nations or parties so conjoined. **2.** The act of allying or the state of being allied. **3.** Any union or relationship based on kinship, marriage, or common interest. **4.** A sharing or affinity of qualities or characteristics. **5.** *Botany.* A subclass of related plant families. [Middle English *alliaunce,* from Old French *aliance,* from *alier,* to ALLY.]

al·lied (ə-līd′, ăl′īd′) *adj.* **1.** Joined, especially in a pact; united. **2.** Of a similar nature; related: *allied studies.* **3. Allied.** Of or pertaining to the Allies.

Al·lies (ăl′īz′, ə-līz′) *pl.n.* **1.** In World War I, the nations allied against the Central Powers of Europe. They were France, Great Britain, and initially Russia, and later many others, including the United States. **2.** In World War II, the nations, primarily the United Kingdom, the U.S.S.R., and the United States, allied against the Axis powers.

al·li·ga·tor (ăl′ə-gā′tər) *n.* **1.** Either of two large, amphibious reptiles, *Alligator mississipiensis,* of the southeastern United States, or *A. sinensis,* of China, having sharp teeth and powerful jaws, and differing from crocodiles in having a broader, shorter snout. **2.** Loosely, any crocodilian reptile. **3.** Leather made from the hide of an alligator. **4.** A tool or machine having strong, adjustable toothed jaws for gripping or crushing. [Obsolete *alagarto,* from Spanish *el lagarto* : *el,* the, from Latin *ille,* that + *lagarto,* lizard, from Latin *lacertus,* LIZARD.]

alligator pear *n.* A tree, the **avocado** *(see),* or its fruit. [Folk etymology, variant of AVOCADO (the trees are said to grow in places infested by alligators).]

all-im·por·tant (ôl′ĭm-pôr′tənt) *adj.* Of vital importance.

all-in·clu·sive (ôl′ĭn-klōō′sĭv) *adj.* Including everything; comprehensive.

Al·ling·ham (ăl′ĭng-əm), **Margery Louise** (1904–66). British detective-story writer. She created a popular fictional detective in the deceptively mild Albert Campion and wrote a number of ingenious and later serious thrillers including *The Crime at Black Dudley* (1928), *Flowers for The Judge* (1936), *Tiger in The Smoke* (1952), and *The China Governess* (1963).

all-in wrestling (ôl′ĭn′) *n.* Professional wrestling with few restrictions on holds. **—all-in wrestler** *n.*

al·lit·er·ate (ə-lĭt′ə-rāt′) *v.* **-ated, -ating, -ates.** *—intr.* **1.** To use alliteration in speech or writing. **2.** To have or contain alliteration. *—tr.* To form or arrange with alliteration. [Back-formation from ALLITERATION.] **—al·lit·er·a·tor** *n.*

al·lit·er·a·tion (ə-lĭt′ə-rā′shən) *n.* The occurrence in a phrase or line of speech or writing of two or more words having the same initial sound; for example, *wailing in the winter wind.* [New Latin *alliterātiō* (stem *alliterātiōn-*) : Latin *ad-,* to + *littera,* LETTER.]

al·lit·er·a·tive (ə-lĭt′ə-rā′tĭv, -ər-ə-tĭv) *adj.* Of or characterized by alliteration. **—al·lit·er·a·tive·ly** *adv.* **—al·lit·er·a·tive·ness** *n.*

al·li·um (ăl′ē-əm) *n.* Any of various plants of the genus *Allium,* characterized by their pungent odor, and including the onion, leek, chive, garlic, and shallot. [New Latin *Allium,* from Latin *allium, ālium*†, garlic.]

all-night (ôl′nīt′) *adj.* **1.** Continuing throughout the night. **2.** Open all night: *an all-night diner.*

allo–, all– *prefix.* Indicates divergence, opposition, or difference; for example, **allopathy.** [Greek, other, altered, from *allos,* other.]

al·lo·bar (ăl′ə-bär′) *n. Physics.* A mixture of isotopes differing in composition from the natural isotopic composition of the element. [ALLO- + Greek *baros,* weight]

al·lo·cate (ăl′ə-kāt′) *tr.v.* **-cated, -cating, -cates. 1.** To designate for a special purpose; set apart: *allocate funds to clean up toxic chemical dumps.* **2.** To distribute as a share; apportion; allot. **3.** To determine the location of; locate. —See Synonyms at **assign.** [Medieval Latin *allocāre,* to place to : Latin *ad-,* toward + *locāre,* to place, from *locus,* place, LOCUS.] **—al·lo·ca·ble** (ăl′ə-kə-bəl) *adj.*

al·lo·ca·tion (ăl′ə-kā′shən) *n.* **1.** The act of allocating or the state of being allocated. **2.** A portion or share that has been allocated.

al·lo·chem (ăl′ə-kĕm′) *n. Geology.* A discrete particle, such as a fossil, oolite, or intraclast, found in a limestone. [ALLO- + CHEM(ICAL), referring to rocks, such as limestones, deposited from solution].

al·lo·cu·tion (ăl′ə-kyōō′shən) *n.* A formal and authoritative speech or address. [Latin *allocūtiō,* from *alloqui* (past participle *allocūtus*), to speak to : *ad-,* to + *loquī,* to speak.]

al·lo·di·um, a·lo·di·um (ə-lō′dē-əm) *n., pl.* **-dia** (-dē-ə). Land held in absolute ownership, and without obligation or service to any feudal overlord. [Medieval Latin *allodium,* from Frankish *al-ōd-* (unattested), "complete property" : *al-,* ALL + *ōd-* (unattested), property.] **—al·lo·di·al** *adj.* **—al·lo·di·al·ly** *adv.*

al·log·a·my (ə-lŏg′ə-mē) *n. Botany.* **Cross-fertilization** *(see).* [ALLO- + -GAMY.] **—al·log·a·mous** *adj.*

al·lo·graph (ăl′ə-grăf′, -gräf′) *n.* **1.** Writing, especially a signature, made by one person on behalf of another. **2.** Any of several ways of representing a sound in writing, or of writing a letter of the alphabet. [ALLO- + -GRAPH.]

al·lom·er·ism (ə-lŏm′ə-rĭz′əm) *n.* Similarity in crystalline form in substances that have different chemical compositions. [ALLO- + Greek *meros,* part.] **—al·lom·er·ous** *adj.*

al·lom·e·try (ə-lŏm′ə-trē) *n. Biology.* The study of the change in proportion of various parts of an organism as a consequence of growth. [ALLO- + -METRY.] **—al·lo·met·ric** (ăl′ə-mĕt′rĭk) *adj.*

al·lo·morph (ăl′ə-môrf′) *n.* **1.** *Mineralogy.* A **paramorph** *(see).* **2.** *Linguistics.* Any of the variant forms of a morpheme; for example, the phonetic *s* of *cats, z* of *dogs,* and *iz* of *horses* are allomorphs of the English morpheme *s.* [ALLO- + -MORPH.] **—al·lo·mor·phic** (ăl′ə-môr′fĭk) *adj.* **—al·lo·mor·phism** *n.*

al·lo·path (ăl′ə-păth′) *n.* Also **al·lop·a·thist** (ə-lŏp′ə-thĭst). A person who practices allopathy.

al·lop·a·thy (ə-lŏp′ə-thē) *n.* Medical treatment by orthodox means, using drugs that alleviate the symptoms of the disease. Compare **homeopathy.** [German *Allopathie* : ALLO- + -PATHY.] **—al·lo·path·ic** (ăl′ə-păth′ĭk) *adj.* **—al·lo·path·i·cal·ly** *adv.*

al·lo·pat·ric (ăl′ə-păt′rĭk) *adj. Ecology.* Occurring in separate, widely differing areas. Compare **sympatric.** [From ALLO- + Greek *patra,* fatherland, from *patēr,* father.] **—al·lo·pat·ri·cal·ly** *adv.*

al·lo·phane (ăl′ə-fān′) *n.* An amorphous clay mineral, essentially hydrous aluminum silicate. [Greek *allophanēs,* "appearing otherwise" : ALLO- + -PHANE.]

al·lo·phone (ăl′ə-fōn′) *n. Linguistics.* Any of the variant forms of a phoneme; for example, the aspirated *p* of *pit* and the unaspirated *p* of *spit* are allophones of the English phoneme *p.* [ALLO- + -PHONE.] **—al·lo·phon·ic** (ăl′ə-fŏn′ĭk) *adj.*

al·lo·pu·ri·nol (ăl′ō-pyŏŏr′ə-nôl′) *n.* A drug, $C_5H_4N_4O$, used in the treatment of gout, that acts by reducing the amount of uric acid in the blood and tissues. [ALLO- + PURIN(E) + -OL.]

all-or-none (ôl′ər-nŭn′) *adj.* Designating a physiological response, especially a nerve impulse, that will only occur if the stimulus that elicits it is above a certain threshold value. Above this threshold the response is maximal.

all-or-noth·ing (ôl′ər-nûth′ĭng) *adj.* Depending upon or prepared to accept only complete success: *He had an all-or-nothing approach to the venture.*

al·lot (ə-lŏt′) *tr.v.* **-lotted, -lotting, -lots. 1.** To distribute; apportion. **2.** To give or assign; allocate: *allot three weeks to a project.* —See Synonyms at **assign.** [Middle English *alotten,* from Old French *aloter* : *a-,* from Latin *ad-,* to + *lot,* a portion, lot, from Frankish *lot* (unattested).] **—al·lot·tee** *n.* **—al·lot·ter** *n.*

al·lot·ment (ə-lŏt′mənt) *n.* **1.** The act of allotting. **2.** That which is allotted. **3.** A portion of a serviceman's pay set aside for a member of his family or for insurance.

al·lo·trope (ăl′ə-trōp′) *n.* Any of the different crystalline or molecu-

allium *This species of wild garlic,* Allium ursinum, *known as ramson, or bear's garlic, flavors the milk of any cow that eats it. The* Allium *genus contains about 280 species, including numerous garden flowers and all the onion family.*

PRONUNCIATION KEY

ă, pat; ā, pay; âr, care;
ä, father, are; b, bib;
ch, church; d, deed; ĕ, pet;
ē, be; f, fife; g, gag; h, hat;
hw, which; ĭ, pit; ī, pie;
îr, pier; j, judge; k, kick;
l, lid, needle; m, mum;
n, no, sudden; ng, thing;
ŏ, pot; ō, toe; ô, paw, for;
oi, noise; ou, out; ŏŏ, book;
ōō, boot; p, pop; r, roar;
s, sauce; sh, ship, dish;
t, tight; th, thin, path;
th, this, bathe; ŭ, cut; ûr, fur;
v, valve; w, with; y, yes;
z, zebra, size; zh, vision;
ə, about, item, edible,
gallop, circus, peaceful

IN FOREIGN WORDS:

à, *Fr.* ami; œ, *Fr.* feu, *Ger.* schön; ü, *Fr.* tu, *Ger.* über; KH, *Ger.* ich, *Scot.* loch; N, *Fr.* bon; y′, *Fr.* Compiègne

STRESS MARKS:

Primary stress: ′
in·cite′ (ĭn-sīt′)
Secondary stress: ′
in′sight′ (ĭn′sīt′)

lar forms of an element that displays allotropy. [Back-formation from ALLOTROPY.]

al·lot·ro·py (ə-lŏt′rə-pē) *n.* The existence, especially in the solid state, of two or more crystalline or molecular structural forms of an element. Diamond and graphite, for example, are allotropic forms of carbon. [ALLO- + -TROPY.] —**al·lo·trop·ic** (ăl′ə-trŏp′ĭk), **al·lo·trop·i·cal** *adj.* —**al·lo·trop·i·cal·ly** *adv.*

all′ ot·ta·va (äl ō-tä′və). *adv. Music.* Symbol **va** To be played an octave higher or lower than written. [Italian, "at the octave."] —**all′ ot·ta·va** *adj.*

all out *adv.* With maximum effort, determination, or strength: *She went all out to win the contest.*

all-out (ôl′out′) *adj.* Using all one's resources; holding nothing in reserve: *an all-out effort.*

all over *adv.* **1.** In every possible place; everywhere. **2.** *Informal.* Typically; in every respect: *He refused to back down—that's him all over.*

all-o·ver (ôl′ō′vər) *adj.* Covering an entire surface.

al·low (ə-lou′) *v.* **-lowed, -low·ing, -lows.** —*tr.* **1.** To raise or constitute no objection, restraint, or bar to; let happen or be done; permit: *Do the rules allow a recount?* **2.** To acknowledge or admit; concede: *allow the legality of a claim.* **3.** To permit to have. **4.** To make provision for: *allow time for a coffee break.* **5.** To permit the presence of: *No pets allowed.* **6.** To provide (the needed amount): *allow funds in case of emergency.* **7.** To grant as a discount or in exchange: *They allowed me twenty dollars on my old typewriter.* —*intr.* **1.** To make an allowance or provision. Used with *for: allow for bad weather.* **2.** To permit or accommodate; be susceptible. Used with *of: a clause allowing of several interpretations.* [Middle English *allowen,* from Old French *al(l)ouer,* to permit, approve, a blend of: (a) Medieval Latin *allocāre,* to assign, ALLOCATE, and (b) Latin *allaudāre,* to give praise to : *ad-,* to + *laudāre,* to praise, LAUD.]

al·low·a·ble (ə-lou′ə-bəl) *adj.* That may be allowed; permissible.

al·low·ance (ə-lou′əns) *n.* **1.** The act of allowing. **2.** A regular provision of money, food, or the like, as to a dependent. **3.** Money provided for a particular purpose: *a clothing allowance.* **4.** A price reduction granted as in exchange for used merchandise; a discount. **5.** A consideration for something that might happen: *an allowance for breakage.* **6.** allowances. A taking into account of modifying factors or extenuating circumstances: *make allowances for his age.* **7.** An allowed difference in dimension of closely mating machine parts.
~*tr.v.* **allowanced, -ancing, -ances.** **1.** To restrict to an allowance. **2.** To put on an allowance.

al·low·ed·ly (ə-lou′ĭd-lē) *adv.* By general admission; admittedly.

al·loy (ăl′oi′, ə-loi′) *n.* **1.** A macroscopically homogeneous mixture or solid solution of two or more metals or of a metal with an element such as carbon, with the atoms of one replacing or occupying interstitial positions between atoms of the other. **2.** Anything added that lowers value or purity.
~*tr.v.* (ə-loi′, ăl′oi′) **alloyed, -loying, -loys.** **1.** To combine (metals) to form an alloy. **2.** To lower the purity or value of (a metal) by mixing with an inferior metal. **3.** To debase or reduce in purity by the addition of an inferior element. [Old French *aloi,* from *aloier, aleier,* to alloy, to bind, from Latin *alligāre,* to bind to, ALLY.]

al·loyed junction (ə-loid′, ăl′oid′) *n. Electronics.* A semiconductor junction formed by alloying a metal contact with a wafer of semiconducting material.

alloy steel *n.* Any of various types of steel that contain large amounts of other metals, such as chromium, vanadium, or tungsten, used for special purposes. Compare **carbon steel.**

all-pur·pose (ôl′pûr′pəs) *adj.* Fulfilling many different functions; capable of being used in various ways: *an all-purpose vehicle.*

all right *adj.* **1.** Satisfactory; as desired; average. **2.** Correct. **3.** Not injured or sick. **4.** Permissible: *Is it all right to leave now?*
~*adv.* **1.** To one's satisfaction. **2.** Safely. **3.** Very well; yes. Used to express agreement or concession. **4.** Without a doubt: *He's a fool, all right!*
Usage: It is still not acceptable to write *all right* as a single word, *alright,* despite the parallel to words like *already* and *altogether* and despite the fact that in casual speech the expression is often pronounced as if it were one word.

all-right (ôl′rīt′) *adj. Slang.* **1.** Dependable; honorable: *He's an all-right guy.* **2.** Good; excellent: *an all-right movie.*

all-round. Variant of **all-around.**

all-round·er (ôl′roun′dər) *n. Chiefly British.* A person who has many talents or abilities, especially in sport.

All Saints' Day *n.* November 1, a church festival in honor of all saints.

all-seed (ôl′sēd′) *n. Botany.* Any of several plants having many seeds, such as knotgrass (*see*).

All Souls' Day *n.* November 2, observed by the Roman Catholic Church as a day of prayer for souls in purgatory.

all-spice (ôl′spīs′) *n.* **1.** A tropical American tree, *Pimenta officinalis,* having small white flowers and aromatic berries. **2.** The dried berries of this tree, used whole or ground as a spice. Also called "pimento." [ALL + SPICE, after its supposed flavor of nutmeg, cloves, and cinnamon.]

all-star (ôl′stär′) *adj.* Made up wholly of star performers: *a play with an all-star cast.*
~*n. Sports.* A player chosen for an all-star team.

all-time (ôl′tīm′) *adj. Informal.* Of all time: *one of the all-time greats of football.*

all told *adv.* In all; altogether; with everything or everyone considered: *over 50 deaths all told.*

al·lude (ə-lōōd′) *intr.v.* **-luded, -luding, -ludes.** To make an indirect reference; refer, without identifying specifically. Used with *to: When he said he had received expert help, the speaker was alluding to his wife.* [Latin *allūdere,* to play with, jest at : *ad-,* to + *lūdere,* to play, from *lūdus,* game.]

al·lure (ə-lōōr′) *tr. v.* **-lured, -luring, -lures.** To entice with something desirable; tempt.
~*n.* The power to entice or tempt; fascination; strong attraction. [Middle English *aluren,* from Old French *aleurrer : a-,* to + *leurrer,* to lure, from *loirre, leurre,* LURE.] —**al·lure·ment** *n.* —**al·lur·er** *n.*

al·lur·ing (ə-lōōr′ĭng) *adj.* Tempting, enticing, or fascinating. —**al·lur·ing·ly** *adv.*

al·lu·sion (ə-lōō′zhən) *n.* **1.** The act of alluding **2.** An indirect, but pointed or meaningful, reference. [Late Latin *allūsiō* (stem *allūsiōn-*), a playing with, from Latin *allūdere* (past participle *allūsus*), to play with, ALLUDE.]

al·lu·sive (ə-lōō′sĭv) *adj.* Containing or making allusions; suggestive. —**al·lu·sive·ly** *adv.* —**al·lu·sive·ness** *n.*

al·lu·vi·al (ə-lōō′vē-əl) *adj.* **1.** Of, pertaining to, or composed of alluvium. **2.** Found in alluvium: *alluvial gold.*

alluvial fan *n.* A fan-shaped accumulation of alluvium deposited at the mouth of a ravine. Also called "alluvial cone."

alluvial plain *n.* A plain resulting from the deposit of alluvium.

al·lu·vi·on (ə-lōō′vē-ən) *n.* **1.** Alluvium. **2.** The flow of water against a shore or bank. **3.** Inundation by water; flooding. **4.** *Law.* The formation of new land, especially along a river bed, by deposited alluvium. Compare **avulsion.** [Latin *alluviō* (stem *alluviōn-*), from *alluere,* to wash against : *ad-,* to + *lavere,* to wash.]

al·lu·vi·um (ə-lōō′vē-əm) *n., pl.* **-viums** or **-via** (-vē-ə) Any sediment deposited by flowing water, as in a river bed, flood plain, or delta. Also called "alluvion." [Latin, from the neuter of *alluvius,* alluvial, from *alluere,* to wash against. See **alluvion.**]

all-weath·er (ôl′wĕth′ər) *adj.* Suitable for or usable in any kind of weather: *all-weather garments.*

al·ly¹ (ə-lī′, ăl′ī′) *v.* **-lied, -lying, -lies.** —*tr.* **1.** To unite or connect in a formal relationship or bond, as by treaty, marriage, or other arrangement. Used with *to* or *with: The United States allies itself with Great Britain.* **2.** To connect or associate. Used chiefly in the passive. —*intr.* To enter into an alliance.
~*n.* (ăl′ī′, ə-lī′) *pl.* **allies.** **1.** One that is united with another in some formal or personal relationship. See **Allies.** **2.** A close associate or supporter. **3.** *Biology.* A plant or animal species or other group that is related to another such group. —See Synonyms at **partner.** [Middle English *al(l)ien,* from Old French *alier,* from Latin *alligāre,* to bind to : *ad-,* to + *ligāre,* to bind.]

ally². Variant of **alley** (a marble).

al·lyl (ăl′ĭl) *n.* The univalent organic radical $CH_2{:}CHCH_2$. [Latin *allium†,* garlic + -YL (so called because it was first obtained from garlic).] —**al·lyl·ic** (ə-lĭl′ĭk) *adj.*

allyl alcohol *n.* A colorless, poisonous, flammable liquid, $CH_2{:}CHCH_2OH$, used in poison gas, resins, plastics, and herbicides.

allyl resin *n.* Any of a class of synthetic resins derived from allyl alcohol esters and dibasic acids, and used as laminating adhesives and in varnishes and molding compounds.

almacantar. Variant of **almucantar.**

Al Madinah. See **Medina.**

Al·ma·gest (ăl′mə-jĕst′) *n.* **1.** A comprehensive work on astronomy and geography compiled by Ptolemy about A.D. 150. **2.** *Sometimes* **almagest.** In medieval science, any similar work concerned with astronomy or alchemy. [Middle English *almageste,* from Old French, from Arabic *al-majisti : al,* the + Greek *megistē (suntaxis),* greatest (collection), feminine of *megistos,* superlative of *megas,* great.]

al·ma ma·ter, Al·ma Ma·ter (ăl′mə mä′tər, ăl′mə) *n.* **1.** The school, college, or university that one has attended. **2.** The anthem or school song of an institution of higher learning. [Latin, "cherishing or fostering mother."]

al·ma·nac (ôl′mə-năk, ăl′-) *n.* **1.** An annual publication including calendars with weather forecasts, astronomical information, tide tables, and other related tabular information. **2.** An annual publication composed of various lists, charts, and tables of useful information in many unrelated fields. [Middle English *almenak,* from Medieval Latin (Roger Bacon) *almanac(h)†.*]

Al Manamah. See **Manama.**

al·man·dine (ăl′mən-dēn′) *n.* Also **al·man·dite** (-dīt′). A deep violet-red garnet, essentially $Fe_3Al_2(SiO_4)_3$, found in metamorphic rocks and used as a gemstone. [Variant of earlier *alabandine,* from Middle English *alabandina,* from Late Latin (*gemma*) *alabandīna,* "(gem) of *Alabanda,*" town in Caria, ancient district of Asia Minor, famous for jewelry.]

Al·ma-Tad·e·ma (ăl′mə-tăd′ə-mə), **Sir Lawrence** (1836–1912). Dutch-born British painter. He is famous for his grand romantic paintings set in classical Greece and Rome and ancient Egypt.

al·me·mar (ăl-mē′mär) *n. Judaism.* A kind of pulpit, a *bema (see).* [Hebrew *almēmār,* from Arabic *al-minbar,* the pulpit.]

Al·me·rí·a (ăl′mä-rē′ä). Seaport on the Gulf of Almería in the Mediterranean and the capital of Almería province in the Andalusia region of Spain.

al·might·y (ôl-mī'tē) *adj.* **1.** All-powerful; omnipotent: *almighty God.* **2.** *Informal.* Great. Used as an intensive: *an almighty din.* ~*n.* **the Almighty.** God. ~*adv. Slang.* Extremely: *almighty scared.* [Middle English *almighty,* Old English *ealmihtig* : *eall,* ALL + *mihtig,* from *miht,* MIGHT.] —**al·might·i·ly** *adv.*

al·mond (ä'mənd, ăm'ənd, äl'mənd, ăl'-) *n.* **1.** A small tree, *Prunus amygdalus,* native to the Mediterranean region, having pink flowers and fruit containing an edible nut. **2.** The nut itself, ellipsoid in shape, and having a soft yellowish-brown shell. **3.** Something having the oval, pointed shape of an almond. **4.** Pale tan. [Middle English *almande,* from Old French, from Late Latin *amandula,* corruption of Latin *amygdala,* from Greek *amugdalē†.*] —**al·mond** *adj.*

al·mon·er (ăl'mə-nər, ä'mə-) *n.* **1.** One who distributes alms, as for a church or royal family. **2.** *British.* Formerly, a social worker in a hospital. [Middle English *a(u)moner,* from Norman French, from Old French *aumosnier,* from *amosne,* alms, from Vulgar Latin *alemosina* (unattested), from Late Latin *eleēmosyna,* ALMS.]

al·mon·ry (ăl'mən-rē, ä'mən-) *n., pl.* **-ries.** The house of an almoner; a place at which alms are distributed.

Al·mo·ra·vides (ăl-môr'ə-vīdz', -mŏr'-). Also **Al·mo·ra·vids** (-vĭdz'). A Berber dynasty and Muslim sect, based in the western Sahara, that conquered northwestern Africa and much of Spain in the 11th and 12th centuries. [Arabic *al-murābitūn,* "holy ones," from *murābit,* holy-man.]

al·most (ôl'mōst', ôl-mōst') *adv.* Slightly short of; not quite; all but; very nearly. [Middle English *almost,* Old English *(e)almæst,* completely, for the most part : *eall,* ALL + *mæst,* MOST.]

alms (ämz) *pl.n.* Money or goods given to the poor as charity. [Middle English *almes, almesse,* from Old English *ælmesse,* from Common Germanic *alemosina* (unattested), alteration (through influence of Latin *alimōnia;* see **alimony**) of Late Latin *eleēmosyna,* from Greek *eleēmosunē,* pity, from *eleēmōn,* pitiful, from *eleos†,* pity.]

alms·house (ämz'hous') *n.* **1.** A poorhouse. **2.** *British.* A house founded and supported by a charity to provide accommodation for the poor and elderly.

alms·man (ämz'mən) *n., pl.* **-men** (-mĭn). One dependent on alms for support.

al·mu·can·tar (ăl'myŏŏ-kăn'tər) *n.* Also **al·ma·can·tar** (ăl'mə-kăn'tər). *Astronomy.* **1.** A circle on the celestial sphere that is parallel to the horizontal plane. **2.** An instrument for measuring azimuth and altitude. [Middle English, from Medieval Latin *almucantarath,* from Arabic *almukantarāt,* the sundial.]

al·ni·co (ăl'nĭ-kō') *n.* Any of a class of hard, strong alloys of aluminum, cobalt, copper, iron, nickel, and sometimes niobium or tantalum, used to make strong permanent magnets. [*Al*uminium *ni*ckel *co*balt.]

alodium. Variant of **allodium.**

al·oe (ăl'ō) *n.* Any of various plants of the genus *Aloe,* mostly native to southern Africa, having fleshy, spiny-toothed leaves and red or yellow flowers. [Middle English *aloe,* Old English *aluwe,* from Latin *aloē,* from Greek, probably of Oriental origin.] —**al·o·et·ic** (ăl'ō-ĕt'ĭk) *adj.*

al·oes (ăl'ōz) *n.* Used with a singular verb. **1.** A cathartic drug derived from the aloe, **bitter aloes** (see). **2.** The fragrant wood of a tree, *Aquilaria agallocha,* of tropical Asia. In this sense, also called "aloes wood," "eaglewood."

a·loft (ə-lôft', ə-lŏft') *adv.* **1.** In or into a high place; high or higher up. **2.** *Nautical.* In or toward the upper rigging. ~*prep.* On top of: *A strange flag was flying aloft the main mast.* [Middle English, from Old Norse *ā lopt* : *ā,* on, in + *lopt,* air, sky.]

a·lo·ha (ä-lō'hä') *interj.* Used in Hawaii to express greeting or farewell. [Hawaiian, "love."]

al·o·in (ăl'ō-ĭn) *n.* A bitter crystalline compound obtained from the aloe and used as a laxative. [ALO(E) + -IN.]

a·lone (ə-lōn') *adj.* **1.** Apart from others; single; solitary. **2. a.** Excluding anything or anyone else; with nothing further; only: *Man cannot live by bread alone.* **b.** Taking no one or nothing else into account: *The price alone should have made you suspicious.* **3.** Unique or by oneself in a particular position, belief, or ability: *I wasn't alone in opposing his plan.* —**go it alone.** *Informal.* To take action independently of others. —**leave alone.** *Informal.* To refrain from tampering or interfering with. —**let alone.** Not to speak of or think of; even less: *I haven't a minute to spare, let alone an hour.* [Middle English, from *al one* : ALL + ONE.] —**a·lone** *adv.* —**a·lone·ness** *n.*

a·long (ə-lông', ə-lŏng') *adv.* **1.** With a progressive onward motion; forward: *walking along at a brisk pace.* **2.** In association; together. Usually used with *with.* **3.** As company; as a companion: *Bring your son along.* **4.** In a line; from one to another: *Read the note, and pass it along.* —**be along.** *Informal.* To come; arrive at a place: *Our guests should be along very soon.* —**get along.** **1.** To manage successfully; survive. **2.** To be compatible; agree: *Do the cat and dog get along?* ~*prep.* **1.** Over or through the length of: *running along the road.* **2.** In a line with; following the length or path of: *trees growing along the river.* [Middle English *along,* Old English *andlang,* "extending opposite" : *and-,* against, facing + *lang,* extending, LONG.]

a·long·shore (ə-lông'shôr', -shōr', ə-lŏng'-) *adv.* Along, near, or by the shore, either on land or in the water.

a·long·side (ə-lông'sīd', ə-lŏng'-) *adv.* Along, near, at, or to the side of something, especially a ship.

~*prep.* By the side of; side by side with.

a·loof (ə-lōōf') *adj.* Distant, especially in one's relations with other people; reserved. ~*adv.* At a distance, but within view; apart; withdrawn. [From obsolete *aloufe!* (nautical use), "(steer the ship) up into the wind!" : A- (to) + *loufe,* LUFF.] —**a·loof·ly** *adv.* —**a·loof·ness** *n.*

a·lo·pe·ci·a (ăl'ə-pē'shē-ə, -pē'shə) *n.* Loss of hair; baldness. [Latin *alopēcia,* mange of fox, baldness, from Greek *alōpekia,* from *alōpēx,* fox.] —**a·lo·pe·cic** (ăl'ə-pē'sĭk) *adj.*

a·loud (ə-loud') *adv.* **1.** Louder than a whisper; audibly: *afraid to say it aloud.* **2.** With the voice; not silently: *Read aloud.*

Al·o·y·si·us (ăl'ō-ĭsh'ē-əs, -ĭsh'əs), **Saint,** born Luigi Gonzaga (1568-91). Italian Jesuit, patron saint of youth; canonized in 1726.

alp (ălp) *n.* **1.** A shoulder high on a mountain side; especially, a gentle, grassy slope above a valley, often used as summer pasture. **2.** A high mountain peak, especially one of the **Alps** (see).

al·pac·a (ăl-păk'ə) *n.* **1.** A domesticated South American mammal, *Lama pacos,* related to the llama, and having fine, long wool. **2. a.** The silky wool of this animal. **b.** Cloth made from this wool. **3.** A glossy cotton or rayon and wool fabric, usually black. [Spanish, from Aymara *alpaco,* from *packo,* reddish brown.]

al·pen·glow (ăl'pən-glō') *n.* A rosy glow appearing around snow-covered mountain peaks at sunrise or dusk on a clear day. [Partial translation of German *Alpenglühen* : *Alpen,* ALPS + *glühen,* to glow.]

al·pen·horn (ăl'pən-hôrn') *n.* Also **alp·horn** (ălp'hôrn'). A curved wooden horn, sometimes as long as 20 feet, used especially formerly by herdsmen in the Alps to call cows to pasture. [German *Alpenhorn* : *Alpen,* ALPS + *Horn,* HORN]

al·pen·stock (ăl'pən-stŏk') *n.* A long staff with an iron point, used by mountain climbers. [German *Alpenstock* : *Alpen,* ALPS + *Stock,* a staff, from Old High German *stoc.*]

al·pes·trine (ăl-pěs'trĭn) *adj. Botany.* Growing at high altitudes; alpine or subalpine. [Medieval Latin *alpestris,* mountainous, from *Alpes,* the ALPS.]

al·pha (ăl'fə) *n.* **1.** The first letter in the Greek alphabet, written A, α. Transliterated in English as *A, a.* See feature at **alphabet.** **2.** The first of anything; beginning. **3.** *Astronomy.* The brightest or main star in a constellation. **4.** *Physics.* **a.** An alpha particle. **b.** An alpha ray. ~*adj. Chemistry.* Closest to the functional group of atoms in a molecule. [Middle English, from Latin, from Greek, from a Phoenician word akin to Hebrew *āleph,* ALEPH.]

alpha and omega *n.* **1.** The first and the last: "*I am Alpha and Omega, the beginning and the ending, saith the Lord*" (Revelation 1:8). **2.** The most important part of something.

Alpha A·quil·ae (ə-kwĭl'ē) *n.* A star, **Altair** (see).

al·pha·bet (ăl'fə-bĕt', -bət) *n.* **1.** The set of letters in which a language or group of languages is written, arranged in the order fixed by custom. **2.** Any system of characters or symbols representing sounds, words, or things: *the semaphore alphabet.* **3.** The basic or elementary principles of anything; rudiments. [Latin *alphabētum,* from Greek *alphabētos* : ALPHA + BETA.] See feature, next page.

al·pha·bet·i·cal (ăl'fə-bĕt'ĭ-kəl) *adj.* Also **al·pha·bet·ic** (-bĕt'ĭk). **1.** Arranged in the customary order of the letters of an alphabet. **2.** Of, pertaining to, or expressed by an alphabet. —**al·pha·bet·i·cal·ly** *adv.*

al·pha·bet·ize (ăl'fə-bə-tīz') *tr.v.* **-ized, -izing, -izes. 1.** To arrange in or put into alphabetical order. **2.** To express by or supply with an alphabet. —**al·pha·bet·i·za·tion** (ăl'fə-bĕt'ə-zā'shən) *n.* —**al·pha·bet·iz·er** *n.*

Alpha Cen·tau·ri (sĕn-tôr'ē) *n.* A double star in Centaurus, the brightest in the constellation, 4.4 light-years from Earth.

Alpha Cru·cis (krōō'sĭs) *n.* A double star in the constellation Crux, approximately 230 light-years from Earth.

alpha decay *n. Physics.* A form of radioactive decay in which an unstable nucleus emits an alpha particle, transforming into a lighter nucleus.

al·pha-fe·to·pro·tein (ăl'fə-fē'tō-prō'tēn) *n. Abbr.* **afp** A protein formed in the fetus and present in the amniotic fluid surrounding it in the womb. Its presence in high levels is used as a prenatal diagnostic test for such abnormal conditions as spina bifida. See **amniocentesis.**

Alpha Le·o·nis (lē-ō'nĭs) *n.* A star, **Regulus** (see).

al·pha·nu·mer·ic (ăl'fə-nŏŏ-mĕr'ĭk, -nyŏŏ-mĕr'ĭk) *adj.* Also **al·pha·mer·ic** (ăl'fə-mĕr'ĭk). **1. a.** Consisting of alphabetical and numerical symbols. **b.** Consisting of such symbols and also of punctuation marks, mathematical symbols, and other conventional symbols used in computer work. **2.** Of, pertaining to, or employing an alphanumeric code or system.

alpha particle *n. Symbol* α A positively charged composite particle consisting of two protons and two neutrons; a helium-atom nucleus.

alpha privative *n.* The Greek negative prefix *a-* (*an-* before vowels). See **a-** (negative prefix).

alpha ray *n.* A narrow stream of alpha particles.

alpha rhythm *n.* One of the electroencephalographic waveforms found in recordings of the electrical activity of the adult brain, characterized by 8 to 12 smooth, regular oscillations per second in subjects at rest. Also called "alpha wave." Compare **beta rhythm.**

al·pho·sis (ăl-fō'sĭs) *n. Pathology.* Lack of skin pigment, as in albinism. [New Latin : Greek *alphos,* kind of leprosy + -OSIS.]

al·pine (ăl'pīn') *adj.* **1.** Of or pertaining to high mountains.

aloe *A colorful plant native to Africa. There are at least 275 species of aloe, but new types are still being discovered. This one grows wild in the Namib Desert of Namibia.*

ABC's OF WRITTEN COMMUNICATION

Letters of the alphabet replaced symbolic pictures

The alphabet developed from ancient writing systems in which each word was represented by a picture (pictography), as in Egyptian hieroglyphics, or later by a symbol (ideography), as in Chinese. In these systems many thousands of symbols had to be learned.

Around 2000 B.C., systems developed in the Middle East in which each symbol stood for a syllable of the spoken language. A syllabary, as it was called, was much simpler to learn than a pictographic system because it contained far fewer symbols. The Japanese began using a syllable script known as *kana* as late as A.D. 800, and it is still in use.

The alphabet made written language even easier to learn, especially as successive developments reduced the number of letters needed in most languages to between 20 and 40. The number of letters used depends upon the number of sounds the alphabet was devised to represent.

The first alphabet was the North Semitic, which emerged about 1700 B.C. at the eastern end of the Mediterranean. From this alphabet stemmed the Hebrew, the Arabic, and the Phoenician, which was introduced into Europe by the Greeks about 1000 B.C. The Greeks modified the Phoenician, standardizing the direction of the written lines to read from left to right, rather than in various different directions. They also added symbols for vowel sounds.

All Western alphabets evolved from the Greek. First came the Etruscan in central Italy about 800 B.C. This led to the Latin or Roman, and the subsequent variations of it that suited the language of different countries, including English. In eastern Europe, the Cyrillic alphabet, from which developed the Bulgarian, and then the Russian, Ukrainian, and Serbian, was devised from the Greek in the 9th century A.D. by St. Cyril, a Greek missionary.

In the chart below, the transliteration column shows the Roman (English) equivalent of the Hebrew, Arabic, Greek, and Cyrillic letters.

ROMAN	GREEK			CYRILLIC (Russian)		HEBREW			ARABIC		
form	form	name	transliteration	form	transliteration	form	name	transliteration	form	name	transliteration
A a	Αα	alpha	a	А а	a	א	'aleph, 'alef	'	ا	'alif	'
B b	Ββ	beta	b	Б б	b	ב	bēth	b(bh)	ب	bā	b
C c	Γγ	gamma	g	В в	v	ג	gimel	g(gh)	ت	tā	t
D d	Δδ	delta	d	Г г	g	ד	dāleth	d(dh)	ث	thā	th
E e	Εε	epsilon	e	Д д	d	ה	hē	h	ج	jim	j
F f	Ζζ	zēta	z	Е е	e	ו	vav waw	w	ح	ḥā	ḥ
G g	Ηη	ēta	ē	Ё ё	yo	ז	zayin	z	خ	khā	kh
H h	Θθ	thēta	th	Ж ж	zh	ח	ḥeth	ḥ	د	dāl	d
I i	Ιι	iota	i	З з	z	ט	ṭeth	ṭ	ذ	dhāl	dh
J j	Κκ	kappa	k	И и, Й й	i, ĭ	י	yod, yodh	y	ر	rā	r
K k	Λλ	lambda	l	К к	k	כ ך	kāph	k(kh)	ز	zāy	z
L l	Μμ	mu	m	Л л	l	ל	lāmedh	l	س	sin	s
M m	Νν	nu	n	М м	m	מ ם	mēm	m	ش	shin	sh
N n	Ξξ	xi	x	Н н	n	נ ן	nūn	n	ص	ṣād	ṣ
O o	Οο	omicron	o	О о	o	ס	samekh	s	ض	ḍād	ḍ
P p	Ππ	pi	p	П п	p	ע	'ayin	'	ط	ṭā	ṭ
Q q	Ρρ	rhō	r, rh	Р р	r	פ ף	pē	p(ph)	ظ	ẓā	ẓ
R r	Σσς	sigma	s	С с	s	צ ץ	sade, ṣadhe	ṣ	ع	'ayn	'
S s	Ττ	tau	t	Т т	t	ק	qōph	q	غ	ghayn	gh
T t	Υυ	upsilon	u	У у	u	ר	rēsh	r	ف	fā	f
U u	Φφ	phi	ph	Ф ф	f	ש	sin	s	ق	qāf	q
V v	Χχ	chi khi	kh	Х х	kh	שׁ	shin	sh	ك	kāf	k
W w	Ψψ	psi	ps	Ц ц	ts	ת	tāv, tāw	t(th)	ل	lām	l
X x	Ωω	ōmega	ō	Ч ч	ch				م	mim	m
Y y				Ш ш	sh				ن	nūn	n
Z z				Щ щ	shch				ه	hā	h
				Ъ ъ	'				و	wāw	w
				Ь ь	'				ى	yā	y
				Ы ы	y						
				Э э	e						
				Ю ю	yu						
				Я я	ya						

2. a. *Biology.* Living or growing on mountains above the treeline. **b.** *Botany.* Small enough to be suitable for growing in a rock garden. **3.** Intended for or concerned with mountaineering. **4. Alpine. a.** Of, pertaining to, or characteristic of the Alps or their inhabitants. **b.** Of or pertaining to a subdivision of the Caucasian race predominant around the Alps. **5.** *Geology.* Of, pertaining to, or designating the last great mountain-building period. It began in mid-Tertiary times and resulted in the main fold-mountain ranges of Europe and Asia, including the Alps. **6. Alpine.** Of or designating downhill and slalom skiing events. Compare **Nordic.** —*n. Botany.* An alpine plant. [Latin *Alpīnus,* of the ALPS.]

alpine azalea *n.* A low-growing, shrubby plant, *Loiseleuria procumbens,* of northern regions, having small evergreen leaves and clusters of small pink or white flowers.

al·pin·ist (ăl′pĭ-nĭst) *n. Sometimes* **Alpinist.** A mountain climber. —**al·pin·ism** *n.*

Alps (ălps). A major mountain system consisting of a great arc of fold mountains, which runs for *c.* 800 kilometers (500 miles) from the north shore of the Ligurian Sea through southeast France, northern Italy, Switzerland, Germany, and Austria into northwest Yugoslavia. The highest peak, Mont Blanc, in Haute-Savoie, France, rises to 4,807 meters (15,771 feet).

Al Qahira. See **Cairo.**

Al Quds. See **Jerusalem.**

al·read·y (ôl-rĕd′ē) *adv.* **1.** By a specified or implied time: *already dead when they found him.* **2.** As early or soon as this: *Is he back already?* **3.** Before; previously: *I've already asked her and don't feel like asking again.* **4.** *Slang.* For goodness' sake! Used as an intensive to show irritation: *That's enough already!* [Middle English *al redy* : ALL + READY.]

Usage: The use of *already* with the simple past tense is common in informal speech: *I already got it, he already went.* In formal English, however, only the *have* form of the verb is acceptable: *He has already gone.*

al·right (ôl-rīt′) *adv. Nonstandard.* All right. —See Usage note at **all right.**

Al·sace (ăl-săs′, -sās′). Region of eastern France, lying on the German border. Annexed by Germany, along with Lorraine, after the Franco-Prussian War of 1870, it was returned to France by the Treaty of Versailles (1919).

Al·sa·tian (ăl-sā′shən) *adj.* Of or pertaining to Alsace, its inhabitants, or their culture. —*n.* **1.** A native or inhabitant of Alsace. **2.** *Chiefly British.* A dog, a German shepherd (*see*).

al·sike clover (ăl′sĭk′, -sīk′) *n.* A plant, *Trifolium hybridum,* native to Eurasia and widely cultivated for forage, having compound leaves and pink or whitish flowers. [After *Alsike,* town in Sweden, where it was first found.]

al·so (ôl′sō) *adv.* Besides; in addition; too. [Middle English *also,* from Old English *(e)alswā,* even so, altogether thus : *(e)al-,* all + *swā,* so.]

Synonyms: additionally, besides, furthermore, moreover, too.

Usage: The use of *also* as a connective word, in the sense of "and," should be avoided in formal written English. *He studied French and German, also Russian and Greek* is a poorly constructed sentence, which would be better in the form *He studied French and German and also Russian and Greek.*

Al·sop (ôl′səp, ŏl′-), **Joseph Wright, Jr.** (1910–89) and **Stewart Johonnot Oliver** (1914–74). U.S. journalists. Known for their astute reporting of politics and the Washington scene, the Alsop brothers wrote many articles, columns, and books. From 1946 to 1958 they collaborated on the column "Matter of Fact."

al·so-ran (ôl′sō-răn′) *n.* **1.** A horse or dog that fails to finish in the first three, or sometimes four, places in a race. **2.** *Informal.* One that is defeated in a race, election, or other competition; a loser or failure.

alt (ălt) *n. Music.* The first octave above the treble staff. Used chiefly in the phrase *in alt.* [Latin *altus,* high, deep.]

alt. altitude.

Al·tai Mountains (ăl′tī). Central Asian mountain range. It lies mostly in Kazakhstan and Russia, but spreads into western China and Mongolia. Belukha, the highest peak in Russia, rises to 4,506 meters (14,783 feet).

Al·ta·ic (ăl-tā′ĭk) *n.* A language family of Europe and Asia, including Turkic, Tungus, Mongolian, and possibly Korean. [After the ALTAI MOUNTAINS, where the languages originated.] —**Al·ta·ic** *adj.*

Al·tair (ăl-târ′, -tīr′) *n.* A very bright, double, variable star in the constellation Aquila, approximately 15.7 light-years from Earth. Also called "Alpha Aquilae." [Arabic *al-tā'ir,* "the star."]

Al·ta·mi·ra (ăl′tə-mîr′ə). Caves lying 21 kilometers (13 miles) southwest of Santander in northern Spain, containing magnificent Stone Age wall paintings discovered in 1879.

al·tar (ôl′tər) *n.* **1.** An elevated place or structure upon which sacrifices are offered or incense burned, or before which religious ceremonies are enacted. **2.** In Christian churches, a table or similar structure upon which the Eucharist is celebrated. —**lead to the altar.** To marry. [Middle English *alter,* Old English *altar,* from Late Latin *altare,* "high place," from Latin *altus,* high.]

altar boy An attendant who assists a priest in the performance of a religious service, especially in the Roman Catholic Church; an acolyte.

al·tar·piece (ôl′tər-pēs′) *n.* A painting, carving, or the like placed above and behind an altar.

alt·az·i·muth (ălt-ăz′ə-məth) *n.* A mounting for astronomical telescopes that permits both horizontal (azimuth) rotation and vertical (altitude) rotation. [ALT(ITUDE) + AZIMUTH.]

Alt·dorf (ält′dôrf′, ält′-). Town in central Switzerland, the capital of Uri canton, home of the legendary hero William Tell. A bronze statue erected in 1895 marks the spot where Tell is supposed to have shot an apple, with his crossbow, off the head of his son.

Alt·dor·fer (ält′dôr′fər, ält′-) **Albrecht** (*c.* 1480–1538). German painter. He is often regarded as the first true landscape painter as many of his scenes contain no figures or only insignificant ones.

al·ter (ôl′tər) *v.* **-tered, -tering, -ters.** —*tr.* **1.** To modify or make different, usually without changing the fundamental nature of. **2.** To adjust or remake (a garment) for a better fit. **3.** To castrate or spay. —*intr.* To change or become different. —See Synonyms at **change.** [Middle English *alteren,* from Old French *alterer,* from Medieval Latin *alterāre,* from Latin *alter,* other.] —**al·ter·a·bil·i·ty** (ôl′tər-ə-bĭl′ə-tē), **al·ter·a·ble·ness** *n.* —**al·ter·a·ble** *adj.* —**al·ter·a·bly** *adv.*

al·ter·a·tion (ôl′tə-rā′shən) *n.* **1.** The act or procedure of altering. **2.** The condition resulting from altering; a modification; a change.

al·ter·a·tive (ôl′tə-rā′tĭv) *adj.* **1.** Tending to alter or produce alteration. **2.** *Medicine.* Tending to restore normal health. —*n.* Also **al·ter·ant** (ôl′tər-ənt). An alterative treatment or medicine.

al·ter·cate (ôl′tər-kāt′) *intr.v.* **-cated, -cating, -cates.** To argue or dispute vehemently. [Latin *altercārī,* to have differences with another, from *alter,* another.]

al·ter·ca·tion (ôl′tər-kā′shən) *n.* A heated and noisy quarrel.

al·ter e·go (ôl′tər ē′gō) *n.* **1.** Another side of oneself; a second self. **2.** An intimate or inseparable friend; a constant companion. [Latin, "other I."]

al·ter·nate (ôl′tər-nāt′, ăl′-) *v.* **-nated, -nating, -nates.** —*intr.* **1.** To occur in successive turns. Usually used with *with: The rainy season alternates with the dry season.* **2.** To pass from one state, action, or place to a second, back to the first, and so on repeatedly. Usually used with *between: alternate between optimism and pessimism.* **3.** To change direction regularly. Used of an electric current or voltage. —*tr.* **1.** To do or perform by turns. **2.** To cause to follow in turns; interchange regularly. —*adj.* (ôl′tər-nĭt, ăl′-). **1.** Happening or following in turns; succeeding each other continuously: *alternate rain and sunshine.* **2.** Every other one of a series: *on alternate days.* **3.** In place of another; substitute: *an alternate plan.* **4.** *Botany.* **a.** Growing at alternating intervals on either side of a stem. Said especially of leaves. Compare **opposite. b.** Arranged alternately between other parts, as stamens are between petals. —*n.* (ôl′tər-nĭt, ăl′-). A person acting in the place of another; a substitute. [Latin *alternāre,* from *alternus,* by turns, interchangeable, from *alter,* other.] —**al·ter·nate·ness** *n.*

alternate angle *n. Geometry.* An angle on one side of a **transversal** (*see*) that cuts two lines, having one of the intersected lines as a side.

al·ter·nate·ly (ôl′tər-nĭt-lē, ăl′-) *adv.* In alternate order or place; by turns.

al·ter·nat·ing current (ôl′tər-nā′tĭng, ăl′-) *n. Abbr.* **ac, A.C.** An electric current that reverses direction in a circuit at regular intervals, especially one that varies sinusoidally.

al·ter·na·tion (ôl′tər-nā′shən, ăl′-) *n.* Successive changes from one state to another and back again.

alternation of generations *n.* The occurrence within the life cycle of many plants and certain animals of alternating sexual and asexual reproductive forms. Also called "digenesis," "heterogenesis," "metagenesis," "xenogenesis."

al·ter·na·tive (ôl-tûr′nə-tĭv, ăl-) *n.* **1.** The possibility or necessity of choosing only one of two or more things, courses of action, or the like: *You have the alternative of paying a fine or going to prison.* **2.** Either or any of the things from which one is to be chosen: *Is there any alternative to taking the train?* —See Synonyms at **choice.** —*adj.* **1.** Offering or necessitating a choice between two or more things or courses; constituting an alternative. **2.** *Grammar.* Indicating that the words or phrases connected are alternatives: *an alternative conjunction.* **3.** Different from or opposed to conventional and established types: *alternative medicine; the alternative press.* —**al·ter·na·tive·ly** *adv.*

Usage: Alternative is widely used to denote simply "one of a set of possible courses of action," but many traditionalists continue to insist that its use be restricted to situations in which only two possible choices present themselves. In this stricter sense, *alternative* is incompatible with all numerals (*there are three alternatives*), and the use of *two,* in particular, is held to be redundant (*the two alternatives are life and death* would be unacceptable to traditionalists). Similarly, traditionalists reject as unacceptable sentences like *there is no other alternative* on the grounds that it is equivalent to the simpler *there is no alternative.*

al·ter·na·tor (ôl′tər-nā′tər, ăl′-) *n.* An electric generator that produces alternating current.

al·the·a, al·thae·a (ăl-thē′ə) *n.* **1.** Any plant of the genus *Althaea,* which includes the hollyhock. **2.** A shrub, the **rose of Sharon** (*see*). [Latin, marsh mallows, from Greek *althaia,* "healer," from *althein,* to heal.]

Al·thing (ăl′thĭng, ôl′-) *n.* The Icelandic parliament. [Icelandic, from Old Norse *althingi,* assembly of all. See **all, thing.**]

alt·horn (ălt′hôrn′) *n.* A brass instrument that sometimes replaces the French horn. Also called "alto horn." [German *Althorn* : *alt,*

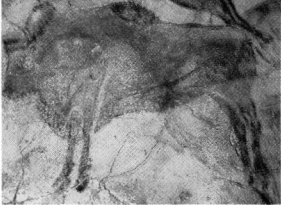

Altamira *Detail of one of the Stone Age wall paintings found in 1879 by a 12-year-old boy in a cave in northern Spain. The paintings, which date from about 12,000 B.C., are now known by the name of the nearby village.*

alyssum *A plant once believed to be a cure for rabies. The species shown here is* Alyssum saxatile, *an evergreen that flowers in the Northern Hemisphere from April to June.*

amaranth *A genus of plants grown for their tassellike flowers. This species is love-lies-bleeding,* Amaranthus caudatus.

alto, from Italian *alto,* ALTO + *Horn,* HORN.]

al·though (ôl-*thō*′) *conj.* Regardless of the fact that; even though. [Middle English : *al,* ALL + THOUGH.]

Usage: *Although* and *though* are often interchangeable: *I came to work, (al)though I was ill; (Al)though I was ill, I came to work. Though* is more colloquial and tends to occur when the clause it introduces is in second position in the sentence. *Although* is preferred with clauses in first position. Note that *though* has a certain mobility in some constructions *(Angry though I was. . .),* which does not extend to *although.*

al·tim·e·ter (ăl-tĭm′ə-tər) *n.* An instrument for determining altitude, used especially in aircraft and commonly based on sensing of pressure changes with altitude or on determination of the frequency delay in a radio signal reflected from the ground. [Latin *altus,* high + -METER.] **—al·tim·e·try** (ăl-tĭm′ə-trē) *n.*

al·ti·plan·a·tion (ăl′tĭ-plə-nā′shən) *n. Geology.* The process in which terraces are formed in rock on a hillside by weathering. [Latin *altus,* high + PLANATION.]

al·ti·pla·no (äl′tē-plä′nō) *n.* A high plateau, as in the Andes of Bolivia, Peru, and Argentina. [American Spanish, from Latin *altus,* high + Latin *planum,* plain.]

al·tis·si·mo (ăl-tĭs′ə-mō′) *adj. Music.* **1.** Of the highest pitch. **2.** Of or in the octave G to F, two octaves above the treble staff. [Italian, "highest," superlative of *alto,* high, from Latin *altus,* high.] **—al·tis·si·mo** *n. & adv.*

al·ti·tude (ăl′tə-to͞od′, -tyo͞od′) *n. Abbr.* **alt. 1.** The height of a thing above a particular level, especially above sea level or above the earth's surface. Also called "elevation." **2.** *Often* **altitudes.** A high location or area: *the difficulty of breathing at high altitudes.* **3.** *Astronomy.* The angular distance of a celestial object above the horizon. **4.** *Geometry.* The perpendicular distance from the base of a geometric figure or solid to the opposite vertex, parallel side, or parallel surface. **5.** A high position or rank. [Middle English, from Latin *altitūdō,* from *altus,* high.] **—al·ti·tud·i·nal** (ăl′tə-to͞od′n-əl, -tyo͞od′n-əl) *adj.*

altitude sickness *n.* Illness with symptoms such as nausea, breathlessness, and exhaustion, caused by oxygen deficiency, as encountered at high altitudes. Also called "mountain sickness."

al·to (ăl′tō) *n., pl.* **-tos.** *Abbr.* **A.** *Music.* **1.** A low, female singing voice; a contralto. **2.** A high male singing voice; a countertenor. **3.** The range between soprano and tenor. **4.** A singer whose voice lies within this range. **5.** An instrument that plays notes within this range, such as an alto saxophone. **6.** A vocal or instrumental part written for such a voice or instrument.
~*adj.* Pertaining to or playing notes within this range. [Italian, "high," from Latin *altus,* high.]

alto clef *n.* The C clef that places middle C on the third line of the staff.

al·to·cu·mu·lus (ăl′tō-kyo͞o′myə-ləs) *n.* A cloud formation of rounded, fleecy, white or gray masses arranged in bands or waves, occurring at 6,000 to 20,000 feet. [Latin *altus,* high + CUMULUS.]

al·to·geth·er (ôl′tə-gĕ*th*′ər, ôl′tə-gĕ*th*′ər) *adv.* **1.** Entirely; completely; utterly. **2.** With all included or counted; in all; all told: *Altogether 100 people were there.* **3.** On the whole; with everything considered: *Altogether, I'm sorry it happened.* **—in the altogether.** *Informal.* Naked; nude. [Middle English *al togeder* : *al,* ALL + TOGETHER.]

Usage: *Altogether* should be distinguished from *all together. All together* is used of a group to indicate that its members performed or underwent an action collectively: *The nations stood all together. The prisoners were herded all together. All together* can be used only if it is possible to rephrase the sentence so that *all* and *together* may be separated by other words: *The books lay all together in a heap. All the books lay together in a heap.*

al·to-re·lie·vo (ăl′tō-rĭ-lē′vō) *n., pl.* **-vos.** Also *Italian* **al·to-ri·lie·vo** (äl′tō-rē-lyā′vō), *pl.* **-vi** (-vē). **High relief** *(see).* [Italian *alto rilievo,* "high relief."]

al·to·stra·tus (ăl′tō-strā′təs, -străt′əs) *n.* An extended cloud formation of bluish or gray sheets or layers occurring at 6,000 to 20,000 feet. [Latin *altus,* high + STRATUS.]

al·tri·cial (ăl-trĭsh′əl) *adj.* Of or characterizing birds that are helpless and naked when hatched, such as young pigeons. Compare **precocial.** [Latin *altricēs,* plural of *altrix,* feminine of *altōr,* nourisher, from *alere,* to nourish.]

al·tru·ism (ăl′tro͞o-ĭz′əm) *n.* **1.** Concern for the welfare of others, as opposed to egoism; selflessness. **2.** *Zoology.* Instinctive cooperative behavior by an animal that apparently protects or benefits other members of its species, and its species in general, rather than itself. [Italian *altrui,* others, from Latin *alteri,* plural of *alter,* other.] **—al·tru·ist** *n.* **—al·tru·is·tic** (ăl′tro͞o-ĭs′tĭk) *adj.* **—al·tru·is·ti·cal·ly** *adv.*

al·u·del (ăl′yə-dĕl′) *n. Chemistry.* A pear-shaped glass apparatus, open at both ends, formerly used to collect condensed mercury and other liquids. [Middle English *alutel,* from Old French *aludel,* from Spanish, from Arabic *al-'uthāl,* the vessel.]

al·u·la (ăl′yə-lə) *n., pl.* **-lae** (-lē′). **1.** The feathers attached to the part of a bird's wing corresponding to the thumb. Also called "bastard wing." **2.** A small lobe near the base of the wing in certain insects. [New Latin, diminutive of Latin *āla,* wing.] **—al·u·lar** (ăl′yə-lər) *adj.*

al·um (ăl′əm) *n.* Any of various double sulfates of a trivalent metal such as aluminum, chromium, or iron, and a univalent metal or radical such as potassium, sodium, or ammonium; especially, potassium aluminum sulfate *(potash alum,* $K_2SO_4 \cdot Al_2(SO_4)_3 \cdot 12H_2O$), which is widely used as a mordant and size for paper and, medicinally, as an astringent and styptic. See **chrome alum.** [Middle English, from Old French, from Latin *alūmen*†.]

a·lu·mi·na (ə-lo͞o′mə-nə) *n.* Any of several forms of aluminum oxide, Al_2O_3, occurring naturally as corundum, in a hydrated form in bauxite, and with various impurities as ruby, sapphire, and emery. It is used in aluminum production, in abrasives, refractories, ceramics, and electrical insulation, and as an absorbent material. [New Latin, from Latin *alūmen* (stem *alūmin-*), ALUM.]

a·lu·min·ate (ə-lo͞o′mə-nāt′, -nĭt) *n.* A chemical compound containing the negative ion AlO_2^-.

a·lu·mi·nif·er·ous (ə-lo͞o′mə-nĭf′ər-əs) *adj.* Containing or yielding aluminum, alumina, or alum. [Latin *alūmen* (stem *alūmin-*), ALUM + -FEROUS.]

a·lu·min·ize (ə-lo͞o′mə-nīz′) *tr.v.* **-ized, -izing, -izes.** To coat or cover with aluminum or aluminum paint.

a·lu·min·o·sil·i·cate (ə-lo͞o′mə-nō-sĭl′ə-kāt′) *n.* Any of a large number of complex inorganic crystalline substances or glasses, consisting of silicate compounds in which some of the silicon atoms have been replaced by aluminum atoms. Many are found naturally in rocks and minerals. [ALUMIN(UM) + SILICATE.]

a·lu·mi·no·ther·my (ə-lo͞o′mə-nō-thûr′mē) *n. Chemistry.* The reduction of metal oxides to metals using aluminum powder, a process that produces great heat and that is used in welding and in incendiary devices.

a·lu·mi·nous (ə-lo͞o′mə-nəs) *adj.* Of, pertaining to, or containing aluminum or alum.

a·lu·mi·num (ə-lo͞o′mə-nəm) *n.* Also *chiefly British* **al·u·min·i·um** (ăl′yə-mĭn′ē-əm). *Symbol* **Al** A silvery-white, ductile metallic element, the most abundant in the earth's crust, but found only in combination, chiefly in bauxite. It is used to form many hard, light, corrosion-resistant alloys. Atomic number 13, atomic weight 26.98, melting point 660.2°C, boiling point 2,467°C, specific gravity 2.69, valence 3. [New Latin, earlier *alumium* : ALUMINA + -IUM.]

aluminum foil *n.* Aluminum in the form of a very thin sheet, used chiefly as a protective wrapping for foodstuffs. Also called "foil."

aluminum oxide *n.* A white crystalline compound, Al_2O_3, occurring naturally as **alumina** *(see).*

aluminum sulfate *n.* A white crystalline compound, $Al_2(SO_4)_3$, used chiefly in papermaking, water purification, sanitation, and tanning.

a·lum·na (ə-lŭm′nə) *n., pl.* **-nae** (-nē′). A female graduate or former student of a school, college, or university. [Latin, feminine of *alumnus.*]

a·lum·nus (ə-lŭm′nəs) *n., pl.* **-ni** (-nī′). A male graduate or former student of a school, college, or university. [Latin *alumnus,* a pupil, foster son, from *alere,* to nourish.]

al·um·root (ăl′əm-ro͞ot′, -ro͝ot′) *n.* Any of various North American plants of the genus *Heuchera,* having clusters of small white, reddish, or green flowers and astringent roots.

A·lun·dum (ə-lŭn′dəm) *n.* A trademark for a hard, artificial abrasive of fused alumina, used in making oilstones and grinding wheels.

al·u·nite (ăl′yə-nīt′) *n.* A gray mineral, chiefly $KAl_3(SO_4)_2(OH)_6$, used in making alum and fertilizer. Also called "alumstone." [French, from *alun,* ALUM.]

al·ve·o·lar (ăl-vē′ə-lər) *adj.* **1.** Of or pertaining to an alveolus. **2.** *Anatomy.* **a.** Pertaining to the section of the jaw containing the tooth sockets. **b.** Pertaining to the alveoli of the lungs. **3.** *Phonetics.* Formed with the tip of the tongue touching or near the hard ridge behind the upper teeth, as the English *t, d,* and *s.*
~*n. Phonetics.* An alveolar consonant or sound. [French *avéolaire,* from *alvéole,* ALVEOLUS.]

al·ve·o·late (ăl-vē′ə-lĭt) *adj.* Having alveoli; deeply pitted; honeycombed. [Latin *alveolātus,* hollowed, from ALVEOLUS.] **—al·ve·o·la·tion** (ăl-vē′ə-lā′shən) *n.*

al·ve·o·lus (ăl-vē′ə-ləs) *n., pl.* **-li** (-lī′). **1.** A small cavity or pit, such as a honeycomb cell. **2.** A tooth socket in the jawbone. **3.** An air sac of the lungs, at the end of a bronchiole, through which exchange of respiratory gases takes place. [Latin, small cavity, diminutive of *alveus,* a cavity, hollow, from *alvus,* a hollow, belly.]

al·ways (ôl′wāz, -wĭz) *adv.* **1.** On every occasion; every time: *always leaves at six.* **2.** Ceaselessly; forever: *friends always.* **3.** Continually; repeatedly: *He's always fiddling with his car.* **4.** In every instance: *Cats always have whiskers.* **5.** As a possibility; as a last resort: *You could always just refuse.* [Middle English *alwayes,* adverbial genitive of *alwei,* Old English *ealne weg,* "along all the way" : *ealne,* accusative of *eall,* ALL + *weg,* WAY.]

al·ys·sum (ə-lĭs′əm) *n.* **1.** Any of various plants of the genus *Alyssum,* having dense clusters of yellow or white flowers. Also called "madwort." **2.** See **sweet alyssum.** [New Latin, from Greek *alusson,* madwort (believed to cure rabies), from neuter of *alussos,* curing rabies : *a-,* not + *lussa,* rabies, madness.]

Alz·heim·er's disease (älts′hī′mərz, ălts′-) *n.* A degenerative disease of the brain, often occurring in middle age, causing progressive loss of mental faculties. Also called "presenile dementia." [After Alois *Alzheimer* (1864–1915), German doctor.]

am (ăm; *unstressed* əm). The first person singular, present indicative of **be.**

am, AM amplitude modulation.

Am The symbol for the element americium.

Am. America; American.

a.m. ante meridiem

A.M. 1. ante meridiem. **2.** in the year of the world. [Latin *anno mundi*] **3.** Master of Arts. [Latin *Artium Magister*]

a·mah, a·ma (ä′mə, ä′mä) *n.* In the Orient, a maidservant who looks after children; especially, a wet nurse. [Portuguese *ama,* wet nurse, from Medieval Latin *amma,* from Latin *amma* (unattested), mother.]

a·main (ə-mān′) *adv. Archaic & Poetic.* **1.** With strength and intensity. **2.** With speed or haste. **3.** Greatly; exceedingly. [A- (on, by) + MAIN (strength).]

Am·a·lek·ite (ăm′ə-lĕk-īt′, ə-măl′ə-kīt′) *n.* A member of an ancient nomadic tribe reputedly descended from Esau's grandson Amalek and hostile to the Israelites. Genesis 36:12–16. Exodus 17:13. I Samuel 15:7. [Hebrew *'Ămālēqī,* after *'Ămālēq,* Amalek.]

a·mal·gam (ə-măl′gəm) *n.* **1.** Any of various alloys of mercury with other metals, such as tin or silver: *dental amalgam.* **2.** Any combination or mixture of diverse elements. [Middle English *amalgame,* from Old French, from Medieval Latin *amalgama*†.]

a·mal·ga·mate (ə-măl′gə-māt′) *v.* **-mated, -mating, -mates.** —*tr.* **1.** To mix so as to make a unified whole; blend; unite; combine. **2.** To mix or alloy (a metal) with mercury. —*intr.* **1.** To combine, unite, or consolidate. **2.** To form an amalgam with mercury. Used of metals. —See Synonyms at **mix.** —**a·mal·ga·ma·tive** (ə-măl′gə-mā′tĭv, -mə-tĭv) *adj.* —**a·mal·ga·ma·tor** *n.*

a·mal·ga·ma·tion (ə-măl′gə-mā′shən) *n.* **1.** The act of or condition resulting from amalgamating. **2.** A merger, as of several companies. **3.** *Chemistry.* The dissolving of a metal in mercury to form an alloy.

a·mand·la (ə-mänd′lə) *interj. South African.* Power. Used as a slogan by supporters of Black Power. [Zulu.]

am·a·ni·ta (ăm′ə-nī′tə, -nē′tə) *n.* Any of various mushrooms of the genus *Amanita,* most of which are extremely poisonous. See **death cup, fly agaric.** [From Greek *amanitai*† (plural), a type of fungus.]

a·man·ta·dine (ə-măn′tə-dēn′) *n.* An antiviral drug, $C_{10}H_{17}NHCl$, used in the treatment of influenza and Parkinson's disease. [Alteration (through influence of *amine*) of *adamantane,* an organic compound, from ADAMANT.]

a·man·u·en·sis (ə-măn′yo͞o-ĕn′sĭs) *n., pl.* **-ses** (-sēz). **1.** One employed to take dictation or to copy manuscript. **2.** A personal assistant to a writer. [Latin *āmanuensis,* from *(servus) ā manū,* "(slave) at hand(writing)" : *ab-,* by + *manus,* hand.]

am·a·ranth (ăm′ə-rănth) *n.* **1.** Any of various plants of the genus *Amaranthus,* having clusters of small greenish, red, or purplish flowers. See **pigweed, tumbleweed, love-lies-bleeding.** **2.** *Poetic.* An imaginary flower that never fades. **3.** Deep reddish purple. [New Latin *amaranthus,* variant (influenced by *-anthus,* flower) of Latin *amarantus,* from Greek *amarantos,* unfading : *a-,* not + *marainein,* to waste, wither.]

am·a·ran·thine (ăm′ə-răn′thĭn, -thīn′) *adj.* **1.** Of, pertaining to, or resembling the amaranth. **2.** Eternally beautiful; unfading; everlasting. **3.** Deep purple in color.

am·a·relle (ăm′ə-rĕl′) *n.* A variety of sour cherry having pale-red fruit. [German *Amarelle,* from Medieval Latin *amarellum,* from Latin *amārus,* bitter.]

am·a·ret·to (ăm′ə-rĕt′ō) *n.* An almond-flavored Italian liqueur. [Italian, "bitter," from *amaro,* bitter; referring to bitter almonds, on which the liqueur is based.]

Am·a·ril·lo (ăm′ə-rĭl′ō). A city of northern Texas. It is a commercial, banking, and industrial center of the Texas Panhandle. The discovery of gas (1918) and oil (1921) spurred the city's growth.

am·a·ryl·lis (ăm′ə-rĭl′ĭs) *n.* **1.** A bulbous plant, *Amaryllis belladonna,* native to southern Africa, having large, lilylike reddish or white flowers. Also called "belladonna lily." **2.** Any of several related or similar plants. [After AMARYLLIS.]

Amaryllis. A shepherdess who appears in the pastoral poetry of Virgil and other classical writers. [Latin girl's name, from Greek *Amarullis.*]

a·mass (ə-măs′) *tr.v.* **amassed, amassing, amasses.** **1.** To pile or gather up in a mass. **2.** To collect for oneself; accumulate, especially for one's own pleasure or profit. —See Synonyms at **gather.** [Old French *amasser* : *a-,* to, from Latin *ad-* + *masser,* to gather together, from *masse,* a MASS.] —**a·mass·a·ble** *adj.* —**a·mass·er** *n.* —**a·mass·ment** *n.*

am·a·teur (ăm′ə-tûr′, -tər, -ə-cho͝or′, -chər, -tyo͝or′) *n.* **1.** A person who engages in any art, science, study, or sporting activity as a pastime rather than as a profession. **2.** *Abbr.* **a., A.** A sportsman or sportswoman who has never participated in competition for money or a livelihood. **3.** One lacking professional skill or judgment in a certain area, as in art.
~*adj.* **1.** *Abbr.* **a., A.** Pertaining to or performed by an amateur or amateurs. **2.** *Abbr.* **a., A.** Made up of amateurs: *an amateur orchestra.* **3.** Not professional; unskillful. [French, from Latin *amātōr,* a lover, from *amāre,* to love.] —**am·a·teur·ism** *n.*

am·a·teur·ish (ăm′ə-tûr′ĭsh, -cho͝or′ĭsh, -tyo͝or′ĭsh) *adj.* Characteristic of an amateur; not professional; unskillful. —**am·a·teur·ish·ly** *adv.* —**am·a·teur·ish·ness** *n.*

A·ma·ti[1] (ä-mä′tē). A family of violin makers in Cremona, Italy, in the 16th and 17th centuries. They include **Andrea Amati** (*c.* 1505–75) who established the early design for the modern violin. His grandson **Nicolò Amati** (1596–1684) was the most famous craftsman and was also the teacher of Stradivari and Guarneri.

Amati[2] *n.* A violin, cello, or similar instrument made by Nicolò Amati or any of the members of his family.

am·a·tive (ăm′ə-tĭv) *adj.* Amorous. [Medieval Latin *amātīvus,* from Latin *amāre,* to love.] —**am·a·tive·ness** *n.*

am·a·tol (ăm′ə-tôl′, -tōl′) *n.* A highly explosive mixture of ammonium nitrate and trinitrotoluene. [*Am*monium + trinitro*tol*uene.]

am·a·to·ry (ăm′ə-tôr′ē, -tōr′ē) *adj.* Also **am·a·to·ri·al** (ăm′ə-tôr′ē-əl, -tōr′ē-əl). Of, pertaining to, or expressive of love, especially sexual love: *amatory verse.* [Latin *amātōrius,* from *amātōr,* a lover, from *amāre,* to love.]

am·au·ro·sis (ăm′ô-rō′sĭs) *n.* Partial or complete blindness, especially when not associated with disease of the eye. [Greek *amaurōsis,* from *amauroun,* to darken, from *(a)mauros*†, dark.] —**am·au·rot·ic** (ăm′ô-rŏt′ĭk) *adj.*

a·maze (ə-māz′) *tr.v.* **amazed, amazing, amazes.** **1.** To affect with surprise or great wonder; astonish. **2.** *Obsolete.* To bewilder. —See Synonyms at **surprise.**
~*n. Archaic & Poetic.* Amazement; wonder. [Middle English *amasen,* Old English *āmasian*†, to bewilder. See **maze.**] —**a·maz·ed·ly** (ə-mā′zĭd-lē) *adv.*

a·maze·ment (ə-māz′mənt) *n.* **1.** A state of extreme surprise or wonder; astonishment. **2.** *Obsolete.* Bewilderment; perplexity.

a·maz·ing (ə-mā′zĭng) *adj.* Causing amazement; greatly surprising; wonderful. —**a·maz·ing·ly** *adv.*

Am·a·zon[1] (ăm′ə-zŏn′, -zən) *n.* **1.** *Greek Mythology.* A member of a nation of female warriors reputed to have lived in Scythia, near the Black Sea. **2.** *Often* **amazon.** Any tall, vigorous, athletic woman. [Middle English, from Latin *Amāzon,* from Greek. Probably of non-Indo-European origin but interpreted by the Greeks as *a-,* without + *mazos,* breast (from the belief that the Amazons removed their right breasts in order to make it easier to use their bows.] —**Am·a·zo·ni·an** (ăm′ə-zō′nē-ən) *adj.*

Amazon[2]. *Portuguese* **Ri·o Am·a·zo·nas** (rē′o͞o ăm′ə-zō′nəs). River formed by the confluence of the Ucayali and Marañón rivers, it flows 6,570 kilometers (4,082 miles) from northern Peru across northern Brazil into the Atlantic Ocean. It carries so great a volume of water (more than any other river) that fresh water is to be found in the ocean some 320 kilometers (200 miles) from its mouth. Its vast basin covers an area of more than 6,475,000 square kilometers (2,500,000 square miles). It is the second-longest river in the world, after the Nile. —**Am·a·zo·ni·an** (ăm′ə-zō′nē-ən) *adj.*

Amazon ant *n.* Any of several small red ants of the genus *Polyergus,* that take over and enslave the young ants of other species. [After the legend that the Amazons raised captured children.]

am·a·zon·ite (ăm′ə-zən-īt′) *n.* A blue-green variety of microcline, often used as a semiprecious stone. Also called "amazon stone." [After the AMAZON River, near which it is found.]

amb., Amb. ambassador.

am·bas·sa·dor (ăm-băs′ə-dər, -dôr′) *n. Abbr.* **amb., Amb.** **1.** A diplomatic official of the highest rank appointed and accredited as representative in residence by one government to another. Called in full "ambassador extraordinary and plenipotentiary." **2.** Any of various diplomatic officials of the highest rank. **3.** A diplomatic official heading his or her country's permanent mission to certain international organizations, such as the United Nations. **4.** Any authorized messenger or representative. **5.** One who stands for or represents a particular belief, set of values, or culture: *an ambassador for change.* [Middle English *ambassadour,* from Old French *ambassadeur,* from Old Italian *ambasciator,* from Vulgar Latin *ambactiātor* (unattested), from Medieval Latin *ambactia,* mission, from Germanic *ambakhtaz* (unattested), from Latin *ambactus,* vassal, probably from Celtic.] —**am·bas·sa·do·ri·al** (ăm-băs′ə-dôr′ē-əl, -dōr′ē-əl) *adj.* —**am·bas·sa·dor·ship** *n.*

am·bas·sa·dress (ăm-băs′ə-drĭs) *n.* **1.** The wife of an ambassador. **2.** A female ambassador or representative.

am·ber (ăm′bər) *n.* **1.** A hard, translucent, brownish-yellow fossil resin, found chiefly along the shores of the Baltic Sea, and used for making jewelry and other ornamental objects. **2.** Medium to dark or deep orange yellow. **3.** An amber-toned stage light used to simulate sunlight. [Middle English *ambre,* from Old French, from Medieval Latin *ambra, ambar,* from Arabic *'anbar,* ambergris, amber.] —**am·ber** *adj.*

am·ber·gris (ăm′bər-grĭs′, -grēs′) *n.* A waxy, grayish substance, mainly cholesterol, formed in the intestines of sperm whales and found floating at sea or washed ashore. It is used as a fixative in perfumes. [Middle English *ambregris,* from Old French *ambre gris* : AMBER + *gris,* gray, from Frankish *gris* (unattested).]

am·ber·oid (ăm′bə-roid′) *n.* Also **am·broid** (ăm′broid′). A synthetic form of amber made by melting together small pieces of amber and other resins under pressure.

ambi- *prefix.* Indicates both; for example, **ambiversion.** [Latin, round, on both sides.]

am·bi·ance, am·bi·ence (ăm′bē-əns, äN-byäNs′) *n.* **1.** The atmosphere or character of a place: *a strange ambiance.* **2.** A pleasant or congenial atmosphere or environment: *a restaurant lacking in ambiance.* [French, from *ambiant,* surrounding, from Latin *ambiēns,* AMBIENT.]

am·bi·dex·trous (ăm′bĭ-dĕk′strəs) *adj.* **1.** Able to use both hands with equal facility. **2.** Unusually dexterous or adroit, especially in more than one activity; versatile. **3.** Deceptive; hypocritical. [Late Latin *ambidexter* : Latin *ambi-,* AMBI- + *dexter,* right-handed.] —**am·bi·dex·ter** (ăm′bĭ-dĕk′stər) *n. & adj.* —**am·bi·dex·ter·i·ty** (ăm′bĭ-dĕk-stĕr′ə-tē) *n.* —**am·bi·dex·trous·ly** *adv.*

am·bi·ent (ăm′bē-ənt) *adj.* Surrounding; designating or pertaining to the immediate environment: *the ambient temperature.* [Latin *ambiēns* (stem *ambient-*), present participle of *ambīre,* to go round : *ambi-,* round + *īre,* to go.]

am·bi·gu·i·ty (ăm′bĭ-gyo͞o′ə-tē) *n., pl.* **-ties.** **1.** The state of being ambiguous. **2.** Something ambiguous.

amaryllis *A plant named after a shepherdess in classical pastoral poetry. It is a native of southern Africa.*

Amazons *A portrayal of these legendary women warriors in battle. The relief is part of the decoration of a chariot made in Ionia—a Greek colony in present-day Turkey—in the sixth century B.C.*

PRONUNCIATION KEY

ă, pat; ā, pay; âr, care;
ä, father, are; b, **bib**;
ch, **church**; d, **deed**; ĕ, pet;
ē, be; f, **fife**; g, **gag**; h, **hat**;
hw, **which**; ĭ, pit; ī, pie;
îr, **pier**; j, **judge**; k, **kick**;
l, lid, needle; m, **mum**;
n, no, sudden; ng, **thing**;
ŏ, pot; ō, **toe**; ô, **paw**, for;
oi, noise; ou, **out**; o͝o, **book**;
o͞o, **boot**; p, **pop**; r, **roar**;
s, **sauce**; sh, **ship**, **dish**;
t, **tight**; th, **thin**, **path**;
th, **this**, bathe; ŭ, cut; ûr, **fur**;
v, valve; w, **with**; y, **yes**;
z, **zebra**, size; zh, vision;
ə, about, item, edible, gallop, circus, peaceful

IN FOREIGN WORDS:

à, *Fr.* ami; œ, *Fr.* feu, *Ger.* schön; ü, *Fr.* tu, *Ger.* über;
KH, *Ger.* ich, *Scot.* loch;
N, *Fr.* bon; y′, *Fr.* Compiègne

STRESS MARKS:

Primary stress: ′
in·cite′ (ĭn-sīt′)
Secondary stress: ′
in′sight′ (ĭn′sīt′)

am·big·u·ous (ăm-bĭg'yo͞o-əs) *adj.* **1.** Open to more than one interpretation. **2.** Doubtful or uncertain. [Latin *ambiguus,* uncertain, "going about," from *ambigere,* to wander about : *ambi-,* around + *agere,* to drive, lead.] **—am·big·u·ous·ly** *adv.* **—am·big·u·ous·ness** *n.*

am·bit (ăm'bĭt) *n.* **1.** The external boundary of something; a circuit. **2.** The sphere or scope of something. [Middle English, from Latin *ambitus,* a going round, from *ambīre* (past participle *ambitus*), to go round. See **ambient.**]

am·bi·tion (ăm-bĭsh'ən) *n.* **1.** An eager or strong desire to achieve success, distinction, fortune, or the like; will to succeed. **2.** A strong desire to achieve a particular end. **3.** The object or goal desired. [Middle English *ambicioun,* from Old French *ambition,* from Latin *ambitiō* (stem *ambitiōn-*), a going round (for votes), from *ambīre,* to go round. See **ambient.**]

am·bi·tious (ăm-bĭsh'əs) *adj.* **1.** Full of, characterized by, or motivated by ambition. **2.** Greatly desirous; eager. Used with *of* or an infinitive: *"I am not ambitious of ridicule"* (Edmund Burke). **3.** Showing or requiring much skill, ambition, or effort; challenging: *an ambitious plan.* **—am·bi·tious·ly** *adv.* **—am·bi·tious·ness** *n.*

ambulacrum *The underside of a starfish's arms—the part of the body known as the ambulacrum—is covered with the trunklike appendages shown here. The appendages are the animal's feet.*

am·biv·a·lence (ăm-bĭv'ə-ləns) *n.* Also **am·biv·a·len·cy** (-lən-sē). The simultaneous existence in a person's mind of mutually conflicting feelings or thoughts toward or about something or someone. [German *Ambivalenz* (coined by Freud) : AMBI- + VALENCE]. **—am·biv·a·lent** (ăm-bĭv'ə-lənt) *adj.* **—am·biv·a·lent·ly** *adv.*

am·bi·ver·sion (ăm'bĭ-vûr'zhən, -shən) *n. Psychology.* The condition of showing both introversion and extroversion. [AMBI- + (INTRO)VERSION or (EXTRO)VERSION.] **—am·bi·vert** (ăm'bĭ-vərt) *n.*

am·ble (ăm'bəl) *intr.v.* **-bled, -bling, -bles. 1.** To move along smoothly by lifting first both legs on one side and then both on the other. Used of horses and other animals. **2.** To walk slowly; move with a leisurely gait. **3.** To ride an ambling horse.
~*n.* **1.** An ambling gait, especially that of a horse. **2.** An unhurried pace. **3.** A leisurely walk. [Middle English *amblen,* from Old French *ambler,* from Latin *ambulāre,* to AMBULATE.] **—am·bler** *n.*

Am·bler (ăm'blər), **Eric** (1909–). British novelist. He has written many successful thrillers, including *The Mask of Dimitrios* (1939), *A Passage of Arms* (1959), and *Send No More Roses* (1977).

am·blyg·o·nite (ăm-blĭg'ə-nīt') *n.* A white or creamy white mineral with composition $(Li,Na)Al(PO_4)(F,OH)$. It is an important source of lithium. [German *Amblygonit,* "the stone with obtuse angles (in its crystals)" : Greek *amblugōnios,* having obtuse angles : *amblus,* blunt + *gōnia,* angle + -ITE.]

am·bly·o·pi·a (ăm'blē-ō'pē-ə) *n.* Dimness of vision without apparent physical defect or disease of the eye. [New Latin, from Greek *ambluōpia* : *amblus,* blunt, dim + -OPIA.] **—am·bly·op·ic** (ăm'blē-ō'pĭk, -ŏp'ĭk) *adj.*

am·bo (ăm'bō) *n., pl.* **-bos** or **ambones** (ăm-bō'nēz). Either of the two pulpits or raised stands in early Christian churches from which parts of the service were chanted or read. [Medieval Latin, from Greek *ambōn*†, pulpit, a raised edge or rim.]

am·boy·na, am·boi·na (ăm-boi'nə) *n.* The reddish-brown, curly-grained wood of a tree, *Pterocarpus indicus,* of southeastern Asia, used for decorative cabinetwork. [After *Amboina* in the Moluccas, Indonesia.]

ambroid. Variant of **amberoid.**

Am·brose (ăm'brōz'), **Saint** (*c.* A.D. 340–397). Bishop of Milan and leader of the early Christian Church. He was influential in imposing orthodoxy on the early Church and strengthening the power of the Church against the state.

am·bro·si·a (ăm-brō'zhə, -zhē-ə) *n.* **1.** *Greek & Roman Mythology.* The food of the gods, thought to impart immortality. Compare **nectar. 2.** Anything with an especially delicious flavor or fragrance. **3. Beebread** *(see).* [Latin, from Greek, "immortality," from *ambrotos,* immortal : *a-,* not + *mbrotos,* archaic form of *brotos,* mortal.] **—am·bro·si·al, am·bro·si·an** *adj.*

ambrosia beetle *n.* Any of various small bark beetles that tunnel into solid wood and feed on fungi. [After *ambrosia fungus,* on which the beetles feed.]

Am·bro·si·an chant (ăm-brō'zē-ən) *n.* A type of liturgical chant, supposedly introduced by St. Ambrose and used to the present day in the Cathedral of Milan.

am·bro·type (ăm'brō-tīp') *n.* In early photography, a positive picture produced by backing a glass negative with black paper or paint. [Greek *ambro(tos),* immortal (see **ambrosia**) + -TYPE.]

am·bry (ăm'brē) *n., pl.* **-bries.** Also **aum·bry** (ôm'brē). **1.** In churches, a niche near the altar for keeping sacred vessels and vestments. **2.** *Archaic.* A small storeroom or cupboard. [Middle English *aumry,* from Old French *almarie, aumaire,* from Medieval Latin *almārium,* store, from Latin *armārium,* from *arma,* tools, ARMS.]

ambs·ace (āmz'ās') *n.* **1.** Double aces, the lowest throw at dice. **2.** Misfortune; bad luck. **3.** The smallest amount or most worthless thing possible. [Middle English *ambes as,* from Old French, from Latin *ambās ās,* "both aces" : *ambās,* feminine accusative of *ambō,* both + *ās,* a unit (see **ace**).]

am·bu·la·crum (ăm'byə-lā'krəm) *n., pl.* **-cra** (-krə). *Zoology.* One of the five radial areas on the undersurface of the starfish and similar echinoderms, on which the tube feet are borne. [New Latin, from Latin *ambulācrum,* avenue (hence the row of pores for protrusion of the tube feet), from *ambulāre,* to AMBULATE.]

am·bu·lance (ăm'byə-ləns) *n.* A vehicle specially equipped to transport the sick or injured. [French, from *(hôpital) ambulant,* itinerant (hospital), from Latin *ambulāns* (stem *ambulant-*), present participle of *ambulāre,* to AMBULATE.]

ambulance chaser *n. Slang.* **1.** A lawyer or a lawyer's agent who obtains clients by persuading accident victims to sue for damages. **2.** A lawyer avid for clients.

am·bu·lant (ăm'byə-lənt) *adj.* Moving or walking about; shifting from place to place. [French. See **ambulance.**]

am·bu·late (ăm'byə-lāt') *intr.v.* **-lated, -lating, -lates.** To walk from place to place; move about. [Latin *ambulāre,* to go about, walk : *ambi-,* around, about + *-ul-, -el-* (unattested), to go.] **—am·bu·la·tion** *n.*

am·bu·la·to·ry (ăm'byə-lə-tôr'ē, -tōr'ē) *adj.* **1.** Of, pertaining to, or adapted for walking. **2.** Capable of walking; not bedridden. **3.** Moving about; not stationary. **4.** *Law.* Capable of being changed or revoked, as a will during the life of the testator.
~*n., pl.* **ambulatories. 1.** An aisle around the east end of a church. **2.** A covered place for walking, as in a cloister.

am·bus·cade (ăm'bə-skād') *n.* An ambush.
~*tr.v.* **ambuscaded, -cading, -cades.** To ambush. [Old French *embuscade,* from Old Italian *imboscata,* feminine past participle of *imboscare,* to ambush, from Vulgar Latin *imboscāre* (unattested), to AMBUSH.] **—am·bus·cad·er** *n.*

am·bush (ăm'bo͝osh') *n.* **1.** A lying in wait to attack by surprise. **2.** A surprise attack made from a concealed position. **3. a.** Those in hiding to make such an attack. **b.** Their hiding place. **4.** Any hidden peril or trap.
~*tr.v.* **ambushed, -bushing, -bushes.** To attack from a concealed position. [Middle English *embushen,* to ambush, from Old French *embuschier,* from Vulgar Latin *imboscāre* (unattested), "to hide in the bushes" : *in,* in + *boscus* (unattested), bush, from Germanic.] **—am·bush·er** *n.*

A.M.D.G. To the greater glory of God. Used as the motto of the Jesuits. [Latin *ad majorem Dei gloriam.*]

ameba. Variant of **amoeba.**

ameer. Variant of **emir.**

a·me·li·o·rate (ə-mēl'yə-rāt') *v.* **-rated, -rating, -rates.** —*tr.* To make better; improve. —*intr.* To become better. [French *améliorer,* to improve, from Old French *ameillorer* : *a-,* to, from Latin *ad-* + *meillor,* better, from Latin *melior,* better.] **—a·me·li·o·ra·ble** (ə-mēl'yə-rə-bəl) *adj.* **—a·me·li·o·ra·tive** (ə-mēl'yə-rā'tĭv, -rə-tĭv) *adj.* **—a·me·li·o·ra·tor** *n.*

a·me·li·o·ra·tion (ə-mēl'yə-rā'shən) *n.* **1.** The act of ameliorating or the state of being ameliorated. **2.** Something resulting from amelioration; an improvement. **3.** *Linguistics.* A change in the meaning of a word to a more favorable sense. For example, the word *shrewd* has undergone amelioration from its earlier senses of "mischievous" and "dangerous." Also called "melioration."

a·men (ā-mĕn', ä-) *interj.* Used at the end of a prayer or a statement to express concurrence, ratification, or approval.
~*n.* **1.** An utterance of this interjection. **2.** Any expression of conviction or assent. [Middle English *amen,* Old English *amen,* from Late Latin, from Greek, from Hebrew *āmēn,* certainly, verily.]

A·men, A·mon (ä'mən, ăm'ən). *Egyptian Mythology.* The god of life and reproduction, represented as a man with a ram's head. Sometimes identified with **Amen-Ra** *(see).*

a·me·na·ble (ə-mē'nə-bəl, ə-mĕn'ə-) *adj.* **1.** Willing to follow advice or suggestion; tractable; responsive. **2.** Responsible to authority; accountable. **3.** Open or liable to testing, criticism, or judgment. —See Synonyms at **obedient.** [Norman French (legal use), from French *amener,* to lead, bring, from Old French : *a-,* to, from Latin *ad-* + *mener,* to lead, from Latin *mināre,* to drive (cattle), from *minārī,* "to shout at," threaten, from *minae,* threats.] **—a·me·na·bil·i·ty** (ə-mē'nə-bĭl'ə-tē, ə-mĕn'ə-), **a·me·na·ble·ness** *n.* **—a·me·na·bly** *adv.*

a·mend (ə-mĕnd') *v.* **amended, amending, amends.** —*tr.* **1.** To remove the faults or errors of; correct; rectify. **2.** To improve; better. **3.** To alter formally (a legislative measure, for example) by adding, deleting, or rephrasing. —*intr.* To improve one's conduct; reform. —See Synonyms at **correct.** [Middle English *amenden,* from Old French *amender,* alteration of Latin *ēmendāre,* to free from faults : *ex-,* removal, out of + *menda, mendum,* defect, fault.] **—a·mend·a·ble** *adj.* **—a·mend·er** *n.*

a·mend·a·to·ry (ə-mĕn'də-tôr'ē, -tōr'ē) *adj.* Serving or tending to amend; constituting an amendment.

a·mend·ment (ə-mĕnd'mənt) *n.* **1.** The act or process of amending. **2.** A correction, alteration, or improvement. **3.** An alteration formally proposed for or made in a legislative measure.

a·mends (ə-mĕndz') *pl.n.* Reparation or compensation made as satisfaction for insult or injury. Used chiefly in the phrase *make amends.* —See Synonyms at **reparation.** [Middle English *amendes,* from Old French, plural of *amende,* reparation, from *amender,* to AMEND.]

Amenhotep IV. See **Akhenaton.**

a·men·i·ty (ə-mĕn'ə-tē, ə-mē'nə-) *n., pl.* **-ties. 1.** Pleasantness; agreeableness. **2.** A feature or facility that increases physical or material comfort: *recreational amenities.* **3. amenities.** Social courtesies; pleasantries; civilities. [Middle English *amenite,* from Old French, from Latin *amoenitās,* from *amoenus*†, pleasant, delightful.]

a·men·or·rhe·a, a·men·or·rhoe·a (ā-mĕn'ə-rē'ə) *n.* Abnormal suppression or absence of menstruation. [New Latin : A- (not) + Greek *mēn,* month + -RRHEA.]

Amen-Ra (ä'mən-rä') The chief national god of ancient Egypt during the period of Theban domination, regarded as the sun god.

am·ent¹ (ăm′ənt, ā′mənt) *n. Botany.* A **catkin** *(see).* [New Latin *amentum,* from Latin *ammentum,* a thong, strap.] **—am·en·ta·ceous** (ăm′ən-tā′shəs, ā′mən-) *adj.* **—am·en·tif·er·ous** (ăm′ən-tĭf′ər-əs, ā′mən-) *adj.*

a·ment² (ā′mənt, ā′mĕnt′) *n. Psychology.* A mentally deficient or feeble-minded person. [Latin *āmēns* (stem *āment-*) : *ā-,* out of, away from + *mēns,* mind.]

a·men·tia (ā-mĕn′shə) *n. Psychology.* Subnormal mental development; feeble-mindedness. [Latin *āmentia,* from *āmēns,* AMENT.]

Amer. America; American.

A·mer·a·sian (ăm′ə-rā′zhən, -shən) *n.* A person of mixed American and Asian descent. **—Amer·a·sian** *adj.*

a·merce (ə-mûrs′) *tr.v.* **amerced, amercing, amerces. 1.** To punish by a fine imposed arbitrarily at the discretion of the court. **2.** To punish by imposing any arbitrary penalty. [Middle English *amercien,* from Norman French *amercier,* from *a merci,* at the mercy of : *a-,* to, from Latin *ad-* + *merci,* mercy, from Latin *mercēs,* wages.] **—a·merce·ment** *n.* **—a·merc·er** *n.*

A·mer·i·ca (ə-mĕr′ə-kə). *Abbr.* **A., Am., Amer. 1.** The United States of America. **2.** North America, Central America, and South America together. In this sense, also called "the Americas." [After *Americus* Vespucius (Latinized form of Amerigo VESPUCCI).]

A·mer·i·can (ə-mĕr′ə-kən) *adj. Abbr.* **A., Am., Amer. 1.** Of, relating to, belonging to, or characteristic of the United States of America, its language, people, culture, government, or history. **2.** Of or pertaining to the Americas. **3.** Of or pertaining to the American Indians. **4.** Indigenous to the Americas. Often used with plant and animal names: *American elm; American elk.* ~*n. Abbr.* **A., Am., Amer. 1.** A native or inhabitant of America. **2.** A citizen of the United States. **3.** American English.

A·mer·i·ca·na (ə-mĕr′ə-kä′nə, -kä′nə, -kä′nə) *pl.n.* **1.** Objects relating to American history, folklore, or geography. **2.** A collection of such objects. [AMERIC(A) + -ANA.]

American Beauty *n.* A type of rose bearing large, long-stemmed, purplish-red flowers.

American dream *n.* **1.** The democratic and egalitarian ideals espoused by Americans. **2.** The material affluence that the United States traditionally offers its inhabitants.

American eagle *n.* The **bald eagle** *(see),* especially as it appears on the Great Seal of the United States.

American elk *n.* The **wapiti** *(see).*

American English *n.* The English language as used in the United States. Also called "American."

American Federation of Labor *n. Abbr.* **AFL, A.F.L., A.F.** of L. A federation of U.S. labor unions organized in 1886, and merged with the Congress of Industrial Organizations in 1955.

American Indian *n.* A member of any of the aboriginal peoples of North America (except the Innuit, or Eskimos), South America, and Central America, considered to belong to the Mongoloid ethnic division of the human species.

A·mer·i·can·ism (ə-mĕr′ə-kə-nĭz′əm) *n.* **1.** A custom, trait, or tradition originating in or peculiar to the United States. **2.** A usage of language characteristic of American English. **3.** Allegiance to the United States and its values and institutions.

A·mer·i·can·ist (ə-mĕr′ə-kə-nĭst) *n.* **1.** A specialist in some facet of America, such as its history or geology. **2.** An anthropologist specializing in the study of American aboriginal culture.

A·mer·i·can·ize (ə-mĕr′ə-kə-nīz′) *v.* **-ized, -izing, -izes.** *—tr.* To cause to become American in character, spirit, or form. *—intr.* To become American in character, spirit, or form. **—A·mer·i·can·i·za·tion** (ə-mĕr′ə-kə-nə-zā′shən, -nī-zā′shən) *n.*

American plan *n.* A system of hotel tariffs in which a guest pays a fixed daily rate for room, meals, and service. Compare **European plan.**

American Revolution *n.* The war fought between Great Britain and her colonies in North America (1775–83) by which the colonies won independence. Also called "Revolutionary War" and, in Great Britain, "War of American Independence." See feature, next page.

American robin *n.* See **robin** (sense 1).

American sable *n.* See **sable** (sense 2).

American Sa·mo·a (sə-mō′ə). Also **Eastern Samoa.** An unincorporated territory of the United States comprising the seven easternmost islands of the Samoan archipelago, lying in the South Pacific Ocean *c.* 1,000 kilometers (620 miles) northeast of Fiji. The islands are administered by the U.S. Department of the Interior. The capital is Pago Pago on Tutuila, the main island.

American Spanish *n.* The variety of Spanish spoken in the Americas.

American Standard Version *n. Abbr.* **ASV, ARV** A revised version of the Authorized Version of the Bible published in the United States in 1901. Also called "American Revised Version."

Americas, the. The landmasses and islands between the main bodies of the Atlantic and Pacific oceans, also known as the New World or Western Hemisphere. With some 28 percent of the world's land, the Americas approach Asia in size, but have only just over a quarter of Asia's population. They stretch for more than 15,300 kilometers (*c.* 9,500 miles), through more degrees of latitude than any other continent. Two areas with roughly the same north-south extent result from a division at the Isthmus of Panama: North America (Panama and all lands and islands to the north) and South America (as above). These in turn can be divided into North America (Mexico and lands to the north); South America (as above); and Central America. A cultural division can be made into North America (or

Anglo-America) and Latin America (all lands south of the United States); virtually all of Latin America was for 300 years part of either the Spanish or Portuguese empires. The region of Pre-Columbian civilization of Central America (southern Mexico, Belize, Guatemala, western Honduras, and El Salvador) is sometimes called Middle America.

America's Cup *n.* An international yachting trophy awarded to the winner of a yacht race between a selected challenger and a selected American yacht. It was first won by the yacht *America* in 1851.

a·mer·i·ci·um (ăm′ə-rĭsh′ē-əm) *n. Symbol* **Am** A white metallic transuranic element of the actinide series, having isotopes with mass numbers from 237 to 246 and half-lives from 25 minutes to 7,950 years. Its longest-lived isotopes, Am-241 and Am-243, are alpha-ray emitters used as radiation sources in research. Atomic number 95, specific gravity 13.67, valences 3, 4, 5, 6. [New Latin, from AMERICA (where it was first produced).]

Amerigo Vespucci. See **Vespucci.**

Am·er·in·di·an (ăm′ə-rĭn′dē-ən) *n.* Also **Am·er·ind** (ăm′ə-rĭnd′). An American Indian or an Eskimo. [AMER(ICAN) + INDIAN.] **—Am·er·in·di·an, Am·er·ind·ic** *adj.*

am·e·thyst (ăm′ə-thĭst) *n.* **1.** A purple or violet form of transparent quartz used as a gemstone. **2.** A purple variety of corundum, used as a gemstone. Also called "oriental amethyst." **3.** Moderate to reddish purple. [Middle English *ametist,* from Old French *ametiste,* from Latin *amethystus,* from Greek *amethustos,* amethyst, "anti-intoxicant" (amethyst was thought to be a remedy for intoxication) : *a-,* not + *methuskein,* to intoxicate, from *methuein,* to be drunk, from *methu,* wine.] **—am·e·thys·tine** (ăm′ə-thĭs′tĭn, -tīn′) *adj.*

amethystine python *n.* The largest Australian python, *Liasis amethystinus.* Also called "rock python."

am·e·tro·pi·a (ăm-ə-trō′pē-ə) *n.* Any eye abnormality, such as near sightedness, farsightedness, or astigmatism, resulting from faulty refraction. [New Latin : Greek *ametros,* beyond measure, disproportionate : *a-,* without + *metron,* measure + -OPIA.]

Am·har·ic (ăm-hăr′ĭk, äm-hä′rĭk) *n.* A southern Semitic language, the official language in Ethiopia. **—Am·har·ic** *adj.*

a·mi·a·ble (ā′mē-ə-bəl) *adj.* **1.** Friendly and likable; good-natured; agreeable. **2.** Cordial; congenial. [Middle English, from Old French, from Late Latin *amīcābilis,* AMICABLE.] **—a·mi·a·bil·i·ty** (ā′mē-ə-bĭl′ə-tē), **ami·a·ble·ness** *n.* **—a·mi·a·bly** *adv.*

am·i·an·thus (ăm′ē-ăn′thəs) *n.* Also **am·i·an·tus** (-təs). An asbestos with fine, silky fibers. [Latin *amiantus,* from Greek *amiantos* (*lithos*), "unpolluted (stone)" : *a-,* not + *miainein,* to pollute, defile.]

am·i·ca·ble (ăm′ĭ-kə-bəl) *adj.* Characterized by or showing friendliness; especially, made in a spirit of good will and without rancor: *an amicable settlement of their dispute.* [Middle English, from Late Latin *amīcābilis,* from Latin *amīcus,* friend.] **—am·i·ca·bil·i·ty** (ăm′ĭ-kə-bĭl′ə-tē), **am·i·ca·ble·ness** *n.* **—am·i·ca·bly** *adv.*

am·ice (ăm′ĭs) *n.* In Christian churches, a liturgical vestment consisting of an oblong piece of white linen worn round the neck and shoulders and partly under the alb. [Middle English *amyse,* perhaps from Old French *amis,* plural of *amit,* amice, from Latin *amictus,* mantle, "(a garment) thrown around one," from *amicīre,* to throw round : *ambi-,* round + *jacere,* to throw.]

A·mi·ci (ä-mē′chē), **Giovanni Battista** (1786–1863). Italian astronomer. He is noted for his improvements in designing scientific instruments, especially telescopes and microscopes, and particularly for his development of the achromatic lens.

a·mi·cus cu·ri·ae (ə-mē′kəs kyōōr′ē-ī′) *n.,pl.* **amici curiae** (ə-mē′kē kyōōr′ē-ī′). *Law.* A person invited to advise a court on a matter of law in a case to which he is not a party. [Latin, "friend of the court."]

a·mid (ə-mĭd′) *prep.* Also **a·midst** (ə-mĭdst′). Surrounded by, in the middle of, or in the course of. **—See Synonyms at among.** [Middle English *amidde,* Old English *onmiddan* : ON + *middan,* dative singular of *midd(e),* middle.]

am·ide (ăm′īd′, -ĭd) *n.* **1.** An organic compound, such as acetamide, containing the $CONH_2$ group. **2.** A compound with a metal replacing hydrogen in ammonia, such as *sodium amide,* $NaNH_2$. [AM(MONIA) + -IDE.] **—a·mid·ic** (ə-mĭd′ĭk) *adj.*

am·i·dol (ăm′ĭ-dôl′, -dōl′) *n.* A colorless crystalline compound $(NH_2)_2C_6H_3OH \cdot 2HCl$, used as a photographic developer. [German *Amidol* (trademark) : *amide* + *phenol.*]

a·mid·ships (ə-mĭd′shĭps) *adv.* Also **a·mid·ship** (-shĭp′). *Nautical.* To, near to, or in the middle of a ship

A·mi·ens (ăm′ē-ənz, ả-myăN). City in northern France dating from pre-Roman times. Situated in the Somme valley north of Paris, it is the principal city and capital of the Somme department. It has been a center of textile manufacturing since the Middle Ages, and its fine Gothic cathedral is the largest church in France.

a·mi·go (ə-mē′gō) *n., pl.* **-gos.** A friend. [Spanish, from Latin *amīcus,* friend.]

A·min Da·da (ä-mēn′ dä-dä′), **Idi** (*c.* 1925–). President of Uganda from 1971 to 1979. He became commander in chief of the Ugandan army in 1966, and in 1971 led the military coup that overthrew President Milton Obote. In 1972 he ordered the expulsion of Uganda's 80,000-strong Asian community. Thereafter his rule became increasingly brutal and repressive, and in 1979 he fled the country after being deposed in a Tanzanian-backed coup.

Amindivi Islands. See **Lakshadweep.**

a·mine (ə-mēn′, ăm′ēn′) *n.* Any of a group of organic compounds of nitrogen, such as ethylamine, $C_2H_5NH_2$, that may be considered ammonia derivatives in which one or more hydrogen atoms has

amethyst *The ancient Greeks wore amulets made of this semiprecious stone, believing that it could prevent drunkenness, dispel sleep, sharpen the intellect, and act as an antidote to poison.*

THE BIRTH OF A GREAT NATION

How Puritan ideals from the Old World inspired revolution in the New

When Britain drove the French from Canada (1763) the writ of empire ran from Labrador to the Gulf of Mexico. Troops and administrators were needed to control the land, and King George III imposed a succession of new taxes on the 13 American colonies to help pay the costs.

The colonists resisted. They were independent people, struggling to open virgin lands and steeped in the Puritan principles of self-help. From England's own traditions they inherited a belief that governments derived their power from the consent of the governed, that liberty was a natural right. The colonists demanded "No taxation without representation" and refused to buy British imports that were taxed, a move that halved British trade to America by 1769. Parliament at length dropped the duties, but kept a tax on tea as a token of English supremacy. It was a provocative gesture: in 1773 colonists dressed as Indians held what history would call the Boston Tea Party, boarding a newly arrived ship and hurling 342 chests of tea into the harbor.

An angry Parliament reacted by closing Boston harbor and sending more troops. As tensions mounted, citizens formed militias and began drilling and stockpiling weapons. On the morning of April 19, 1775, British soldiers sent to seize arms were faced by local militiamen across the green at Lexington, Massachusetts. Shots were fired, and the conflict began. Early in 1776 Parliament blockaded the colonies and hired German mercenaries to help quell the uprising.

Outcry followed in America. A committee appointed by the Continental Congress issued a declaration, written chiefly by Thomas Jefferson. "We hold these truths to be self-evident," it stated, "that all men are created equal, that they are endowed by their Creator with certain inalienable rights, that among these are life, liberty, and the pursuit of happiness." Congress unanimously approved the Declaration of Independence at Philadelphia on July 4, 1776.

The war itself dragged on until, in 1781, 7,000 British soldiers surrendered to General Washington at Yorktown, Virginia. The rebels had won, and in 1783 Parliament accepted the inevitable—eight years after the skirmish at Lexington, Britain formally recognized the United States of America.

MEN OF IDEAS *Pictured on a snuffbox lid are Benjamin Franklin (1706–90), right, with the philosophers Voltaire (1694–1778), left, and Rousseau (1712–78). Franklin persuaded the French to back the American colonists.*

LEADERS OF THE EMPIRE *An 18th-century print shows George III (1760–1820) with the elder Pitt (left) and James Wolfe, the minister and general who won Canada from the French (1763). A major part of their American empire was soon to be in revolt against the English king.*

THE VOICE OF INDEPENDENCE *Thomas Jefferson (1743–1826) insisted that Parliament should have no authority in America. His pen wrote the echoing words that among man's rights were: "Life, liberty, and the pursuit of happiness."*

FIRST PRESIDENT *George Washington (1732–99) commanded the colonial troops throughout the Revolutionary War. In 1789 he answered his country's call once more—and became the first President of the United States.*

BUNKER HILL (1775) *British troops fought all day to move the Patriot farmers from a promontory overlooking Boston. The fierce resistance of the colonists set the pattern for the long war.*

BIRTH OF A NATION *Thomas Jefferson and his committee laid the Declaration of Independence before Congress in the State House, Philadelphia, on July 4, 1776. A young brigade major, John Trumbull, painted the historic moment from sketches made at the scene. To the right of Jefferson is Benjamin Franklin, to the left are John Adams, Roger Sherman, and Robert Livingston. Their words, unanimously accepted by Congress, summed up the new ideas of liberty and equality, and set the 13 colonies on a course of freedom from the British empire.*

been replaced by a hydrocarbon radical. [AM(MONIUM) + -INE.]

–amine *suffix.* Indicates an amine; for example, **methylamine.**

a·mi·no (ə-mē′nō, ăm′ə-nō′) *adj.* Pertaining to or consisting of an amine or other chemical compound containing NH_2 combined with a nonacid organic radical. [Independent use of AMINO-.]

amino– *prefix.* Indicates replacement of one of the hydrogen atoms in ammonia by a nonacid organic radical; for example, **aminophenol.** [From AMINE.]

amino acid *n.* Any organic compound containing both an amino group (NH_2) and a carboxyl group (COOH). Amino acids are essential components of proteins.

a·mi·no·ac·i·de·mi·a (ə-mē′nō-ăs′ĭ-dē′mē-ə, ăm′ə-nō-) *n.* A condition marked by excess amino acids in the blood.

a·mi·no·ac·i·du·ri·a (ə-mē′nō-ăs′ĭ-dŏŏr′ē-ə, -dyŏŏr′-, ăm′ə-nō-) *n.* A condition marked by excess amino acids in the urine.

a·mi·no·ben·zo·ic acid (ə-mē′nō-bĕn-zō′ĭk, ăm′ə-nō-) *n.* Any of three benzoic acid derivatives, $NH_2C_6H_4COOH$, especially the yellowish para form, which is part of the vitamin B complex.

a·mi·no·phe·nol (ə-mē′nō-fē′nôl′, -nōl′, ăm′ə-nō-) *n.* One of three organic compounds with composition $C_6H_4NH_2OH$, used as photographic developers and dye intermediates.

a·mi·no·py·rine (ə-mē′nō-pī′rēn′, ăm′ə-nō-) *n.* A colorless crystalline compound, $C_{13}H_{17}N_3O$, used to reduce fever and relieve pain. [AMINO- + (ANTI)PYRINE.]

amir. Variant of **emir.**

A·mis (ā′mĭs), **Kingsley** (1922–). British novelist, poet, and critic. His first novel, *Lucky Jim* (1954), a satire on provincial university life, became an immediate popular success. His other works include *Jake's Thing* (1978), *The Green Man* (1969), *The Riverside Villas Murder* (1973), and *Russian Hide-and-Seek* (1980).

A·mish (ä′mĭsh, ăm′ĭsh, ā′mĭsh) *pl.n.* An orthodox U.S. Anabaptist sect that separated from the Mennonites in the late 17th century. [German *amisch,* after Jacob Amman, 17th-century Swiss Mennonite bishop.]
—adj. Of or pertaining to this sect or its members.

a·miss (ə-mĭs′) *adj.* Out of proper order, wrong, or out of place in the circumstances: *What is amiss?*
—adv. In an improper, erroneous, or defective way. **—take amiss.** To misunderstand; feel offended by. [Middle English *a mis* : A- (on, at) + *mis,* a mistake, from *missen,* to MISS.]

a·mi·to·sis (ā′mī-tō′sĭs) *n. Biology.* Cell division characterized by simple nuclear cleavage without the formation of chromosomes. [New Latin : A- (not) + MITOSIS.] **—a·mi·tot·ic** (ā′mī-tŏt′ĭk) *adj.* **—a·mi·tot·i·cal·ly** *adv.*

am·i·ty (ăm′ə-tē) *n., pl.* **-ties.** Peaceful and cordial relations, especially between nations; friendship. [Middle English *amite,* from Old French *amitie,* from Medieval Latin *amīcitās,* from Latin *amīcus,* friend.]

Am·man (ə-män′, ə-măn′). The capital and by far the largest and most modern city of Jordan, on the Jabbok (Zarga) River in the north of the country. Since 1948 remains from the Chalcolithic period (c. 4000 B.C.–c. 3000 B.C.) have been unearthed on the site.

am·me·ter (ăm′mē′tər) *n. Abbr.* **A** An instrument that measures electric current. [AM(PERE) + -METER.]

am·mine (ăm′mēn′, ă-mēn′) *n.* Any of a class of chemical compounds, such as aniline, derived from replacement of hydrogen atoms in ammonia by univalent hydrocarbon radicals. [AMM(ONIA) + -INE.] **—am·mi·no** (ă-mē′nō) *adj.*

am·mo (ăm′ō) *n. Informal.* Ammunition.

am·mo·cete (ăm′ə-sēt′) *n.* The blind, wormlike larva of the lamprey. [New Latin *Ammocoetes* (former genus name), "ones that lie in sand" : Greek *ammos,* sand + *koitē,* bed, from *keisthai,* to lie.]

am·mo·nia (ə-mōn′yə) *n.* **1.** A colorless, pungent gas, NH_3, extensively used to manufacture fertilizers and a wide variety of nitrogen-containing organic and inorganic chemicals. **2.** A solution of ammonia in water, **ammonium hydroxide** *(see).* [New Latin, from Latin *(sal) ammōniācus,* "(salt) of Amen," from Greek *ammōniakos,* from *Ammōn,* AMEN (it was originally obtained from a region near the temple of Amen, in Libya).]

am·mo·ni·ac[1] (ə-mō′nē-ăk′) *adj.* Also **am·mo·ni·a·cal** (ăm′ə-nī′ə-kəl). Of, containing, or similar to ammonia.

ammoniac[2] *n.* A strong-smelling gum resin from the stems of a plant, *Dorema ammoniacum,* of northern Asia, formerly used in medicine as an expectorant and stimulant. Also called "gum ammoniac." [Middle English *ammonyak,* from Latin *ammōniacum,* from Greek *ammōniakon,* neuter of *ammōniakos,* of Amen. See **ammonia.**]

am·mo·ni·ate (ə-mō′nē-āt′) *tr.v.* **-ated, -ating, -ates.** To treat or combine with ammonia.
—n. A compound that contains ammonia. **—am·mo·ni·a·tion** *n.*

ammonia water *n. Chemistry.* Ammonium hydroxide.

am·mon·i·fi·ca·tion (ə-mŏn′ə-fĭ-kā′shən, ə-mō′nə-) *n.* **1.** Impregnation with ammonia or an ammonium compound. **2.** The generation of ammonia or ammonium compounds by the action of bacteria on nitrogenous organic matter in soil.

am·mon·i·fy (ə-mŏn′ə-fī′, ə-mō′nə-) *v.* **-fied, -fying, -fies.** **—tr.** To subject to ammonification. **—intr.** To undergo ammonification. [AMMONI(A) + -FY.] **—am·mo·ni·fi·er** *n.*

am·mon·ite[1] (ăm′ə-nīt′) *n.* **1.** The coiled, flat, chambered shell of any of various extinct cephalopod mollusks of the subclass Ammonoidea, found as fossils in Mesozoic formations. **2.** Any mollusk of the subclass Ammonoidea. [New Latin *Ammonītēs,* from Latin *(cornus) Ammōnis,* "(horn) of Amen" (because it resembles the horns of Amen), from *Ammōnis,* genitive of *Ammōn,* AMEN.]

ammonite[2] *n.* **1.** An explosive mixture of ammonium nitrate and a small quantity of TNT or a similar substance. **2.** A nitrogenous fertilizer made from animal wastes. [*Ammonium* + *nitrate.*]

Am·mo·nite (ăm′ə-nīt′) *n.* A member of a Semitic people living east of the river Jordan, mentioned frequently in the Old Testament. [Late Latin *Ammonītēs,* the Ammonites, from Hebrew *'Ammōn,* city or people of Amman, from Canaanite *'am-,* "folk."]

am·mo·ni·um (ə-mō′nē-əm) *n.* The chemical ion NH_4^+. [New Latin : AMMON(IA) + -IUM.]

ammonium carbonate *n.* A white powder with composition $(NH_4)HCO_3 \cdot (NH_4)CO_2NH_2$, used in baking powders, smelling salts, and fire-extinguishing compounds. Also called "sal volatile."

ammonium chloride *n.* A slightly hygroscopic white crystalline compound, NH_4Cl, used in dry cells, as a soldering flux, as an expectorant, and in various industrial applications. Also called "sal ammoniac."

ammonium hydroxide *n.* A colorless basic aqueous solution of ammonia, NH_4OH, used as a household cleanser and to manufacture a wide variety of products including textiles, rayon, rubber, fertilizers, and plastics. Also called "ammonia water."

ammonium nitrate *n.* A colorless crystalline salt, NH_4NO_3, used in fertilizers, explosives, and solid rocket propellants.

ammonium sulfate *n.* A brownish-gray to white crystalline salt, $(NH_4)_2SO_4$, used in fertilizers and water purification.

am·mu·ni·tion (ăm′yə-nĭsh′ən) *n.* **1. a.** Bullets, shells, or the like, along with their fuses and primers, that can be fired from guns or otherwise propelled. **b.** Any nuclear, biological, chemical, or explosive material used in warfare. **2.** Any means of attack or defense, such as facts that can be used in an argument. [Obsolete French *amunition,* from phrase *l'amunition,* misinterpretation of *la munition,* the MUNITION.]

am·ne·si·a (ăm-nē′zhə) *n.* Partial or total loss of memory, especially through shock, psychological disturbance, brain damage, or illness. [New Latin, from Greek *amnēsia* : *a-,* not + *mnasthai,* to remember.] **—am·ne·si·ac** (ăm-nē′zē-ăk′, -zhē-ăk′) *n. & adj.* **—am·nes·tic** (ăm-nĕs′tĭk) *adj.*

am·nes·ty (ăm′nəs-tē) *n., pl.* **-ties. 1.** A general pardon granted by a government, especially to people guilty of political offenses. **2.** A period during which this is in force. **3.** A period of immunity during which penalties for past infringements are waived.
—tr.v. **amnestied, -tying, -ties.** To grant an amnesty to. [Greek *amnēstia,* "forgetfulness," from *amnēstos,* forgotten : *a-,* not + *mnasthai,* to remember.]

Amnesty International *n.* An organization that investigates violations of human rights and campaigns for the release of prisoners of conscience and the humane treatment of political prisoners.

am·ni·o·cen·te·sis (ăm′nē-ō-sĕn-tē′sĭs) *n., pl* **-ses** (-sēz′). The withdrawal of a sample of amniotic fluid from a pregnant woman, usually for the diagnosis of genetic or developmental disorders in the fetus. [AMNION + Greek *kentesis,* a puncturing, from *kentein,* to prick.]

am·ni·og·ra·phy (ăm′nē-ŏg′rə-fē) *n.* Radiography of the amnion in order to examine the placenta and umbilical cord. [AMNIO(N) + -GRAPHY.]

am·ni·on (ăm′nē-ən, -ŏn′) *n., pl.* **-ons** or **-ni·a** (-nē-ə). A thin, tough, membranous sac that contains a watery fluid in which the embryo of a mammal, bird, or reptile is suspended. It is the inner of two embryonic membranes. Compare **chorion.** [New Latin, from Greek *amnion,* caul, diminutive of *amnos,* lamb.] **—am·ni·ot·ic** (ăm′nē-ŏt′ĭk), **am·ni·on·ic** (ăm′nē-ŏn′ĭk) *adj.*

am·ni·os·co·py (ăm′nē-ŏs′kə-pē) *n., pl.* **-pies.** Examination of the interior of the amniotic sac by means of an instrument passed through the wall of the abdomen. [AMNIO(N) + -SCOPY.] **—am·ni·o·scope** (ăm′nē-ə-skōp′) *n.*

am·n't (ăm′ənt) *Chiefly Regional.* Contraction of am not. **—See** Usage note at **ain't.**

a·moe·ba, a·me·ba (ə-mē′bə) *n., pl.* **-bas** or **-bae** (-bē). Any of various protozoans of the genus *Amoeba* and related genera, occurring in water, soil, and as internal animal parasites, characteristically having an indefinite, changeable form and moving by means of pseudopodia. [New Latin, from Greek *amoibē,* change, from *ameibein,* to change.] **—a·moe·bic** (ə-mē′bĭk) *adj.*

am·oe·bae·an, am·oe·be·an (ăm′ē-bē′ən) *adj.* Alternately answering, as dialogue. [Late Latin *amoebaeus,* from Greek *amoibaios,* from *amoibē,* change. See **amoeba.**]

am·oe·bi·a·sis, am·e·bi·a·sis (ăm′ə-bī′ə-sĭs) *n., pl.* **-ses** (-sēz′). An infection caused by amoebas, especially by *Entamoeba histolytica.* [New Latin : AMOEB(A) + -IASIS.]

amoebic dysentery *n.* An infectious, inflammatory disease of the colon, caused by *Entamoeba histolytica* and resulting in severe pain and diarrhea.

a·moe·bo·cyte (ə-mē′bə-sīt′) *n.* Any cell, such as a leucocyte, having amoebic form. [AMOEB(A) + -CYTE.]

a·moe·boid (ə-mē′boid′) *adj.* Of or resembling an amoeba, especially in changeable form and means of locomotion.

amok. Variant of **amuck.**

a·mo·le (ə-mō′lē) *n.* **1.** Any of several plants, chiefly of southwestern North America, with parts, as roots or bulbs, used as soap. **2.** The parts of an amole used as soap. [Spanish, from Nahuatl *amol(li).*]

Amon. Variant of **Amen.**

a·mong (ə-mŭng′) *prep.* Also **a·mongst** (ə-mŭngst′). **1.** In the midst

ammonite *The fossil remains of a number of types of extinct shellfish are known as ammonites. This ammonite, dating from perhaps 200 million years ago, was found in West Germany.*

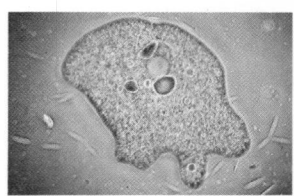
amoeba *The microscopic amoeba is the simplest form of animal life. It reproduces by splitting in two.*

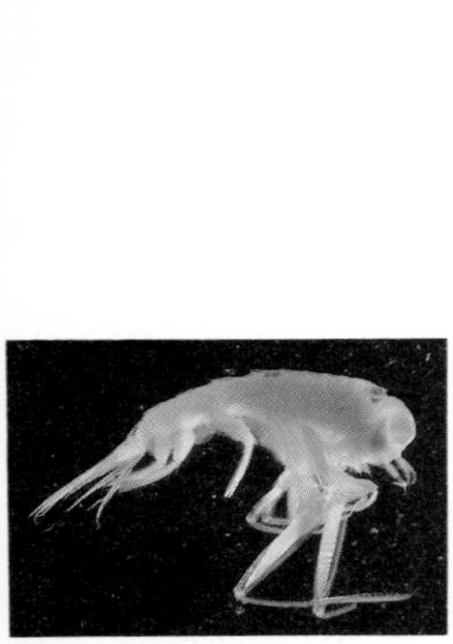

amphipod *There are over 4,000 species of this tiny crustacean: the smallest are microscopic, the largest little more than 25 millimeters (1 inch) long. They form the main diet of many fish. This is* Parathemisto gudichaudi, *an amphipod species that lives several hundred meters below sea level.*

PRONUNCIATION KEY

ă, pat; ā, pay; âr, care;
ä, father, are; b, **bib**;
ch, **church**; d, **deed**; ĕ, pet;
ē, be; f, **fife**; g, **gag**; h, **hat**;
hw, **which**; ĭ, pit; ī, pie;
îr, pier; j, **judge**; k, **kick**;
l, **lid**, needle; m, **mum**;
n, no, sudden; ng, thing;
ŏ, pot; ō, toe; ô, paw, for;
oi, noise; ou, out; o͝o, book;
o͞o, boot; p, **pop**; r, roar;
s, sauce; sh, ship, dish;
t, **tight**; th, thin, path;
th, this, bathe; ŭ, cut; ûr, fur;
v, valve; w, with; y, yes;
z, zebra, size; zh, vision;
ə, about, item, edible, gallop, circus, peaceful

IN FOREIGN WORDS:

à, *Fr.* ami; œ, *Fr.* feu, *Ger.* schön; ü, *Fr.* tu, *Ger.* über;
KH, *Ger.* ich, *Scot.* loch;
N, *Fr.* bon; y', *Fr.* Compiègne

STRESS MARKS:

Primary stress: ′
in·cite′ (ĭn-sīt′)
Secondary stress: ′
in′sight′ (ĭn′sīt′)

of; surrounded by. **2.** In the group, number, or class of: *among the fastest runners in the country; among other things.* **3.** In the company of; in association with: *traveling among a group of tourists.* **4.** With or by many or most of: *a custom popular among the Greeks.* **5.** By the joint action of: *Among us, we will get the job done.* **6.** With portions to each of: *Distribute this among them.* **7.** Each with the other of; between one another in a group of: *Don't fight among yourselves.* [Middle English *among,* Old English *on gemang* : *on,* in, ON + *gemang,* a crowd.]

a·mon·til·la·do (ə-mŏn′tə-lä′dō) *n., pl.* **-dos.** A fairly pale medium-dry sherry. [Spanish *(vino) amontillado,* "(wine) made in Montilla" : *a-,* to, from Latin *ad-* + *Montilla,* Spanish town.]

a·mor·al (ā-môr′əl, ā-mŏr′-) *adj.* **1.** Not admitting of moral distinctions or judgments; outside the sphere of morality; nonmoral. **2.** Lacking moral judgment or sensibility; unable to distinguish between right and wrong. [A- (not) + MORAL.] **—a·mo·ral·i·ty** (ā′mô-răl′ə-tē, -mə-), **a·mor·al·ism** *n.* **—a·mor·al·ly** *adv.*

am·o·ret·to (ăm′ə-rĕt′ō, ä′mə-) *n., pl.* **-retti** (-rĕt′ē) or **-tos.** A cupid. [Italian, diminutive of *Amore,* Cupid, from Latin *Amor,* from *amor,* love, from *amāre,* to love.]

am·o·rist (ăm′ə-rĭst) *n.* One who is dedicated to or writes about love. [From Latin *amor,* love.]

Am·o·rite (ăm′ə-rīt′) *n.* A member of a people inhabiting Canaan before the Israelites, mentioned frequently in the Old Testament. [Hebrew *Emōrī.*]

a·mo·ro·so (ä′mə-rō′sō, ăm′ə-) *adv. Music.* In a loving manner; tenderly. Used as a direction. [Italian, "amorous."] **—am·o·ro·so** *adj.*

am·o·rous (ăm′ər-əs) *adj.* **1.** Strongly attracted to love, especially sexual love. **2.** Indicative of love: *an amorous glance.* **3.** Of or concerned with love: *an amorous poem.* **4.** In love; enamored. Sometimes used with *of.* [Middle English, from Old French, from Medieval Latin *amōrōsus,* from Latin *amor,* love.] **—am·or·ous·ly** *adv.* **—am·or·ous·ness** *n.*

a·mor·phism (ə-môr′fĭz′əm) *n.* The state or quality of being amorphous, especially with respect to lack of crystalline structure.

a·mor·phous (ə-môr′fəs) *adj.* **1.** Without definite form; lacking a specific shape. **2.** Of no particular type or character; formless; indeterminate. **3.** Lacking distinct crystalline structure. [Greek *amorphos* : A- (without) + -MORPHOUS.] **—a·mor·phous·ly** *adv.* **—a·mor·phous·ness** *n.*

am·or·ti·za·tion (ăm′ər-tə-zā′shən, ə-môr′tə-) *n.* **1. a.** The act or process of amortizing or the condition of being amortized. **b.** The money set aside for this purpose. **2.** In reckoning the yield of a bond bought at a premium, the periodic subtraction from its current yield of a proportionate share of the premium between the purchase date and the maturity date.

am·or·tize (ăm′ər-tīz′, ə-môr′tīz′) *tr.v.* **-tized, -tizing, -tizes. 1.** *Finance.* To liquidate (a debt) by installment payments or payment into a sinking fund. **2.** *Accounting.* **a.** To reduce gradually the book value of (an asset) over a period equal to its projected useful life. **b.** To provide for the cost of replacing (an asset) by periodic payments into a sinking fund. **3.** *Law.* To transfer (property) in mortmain. [Middle English *amortisen,* from Old French *amortir* (present stem *amortiss-*), from Vulgar Latin *admortīre* (unattested), to deaden : *ad-,* to + *mortus* (unattested), dead, from Latin *mors* (stem *mort-*), death.] **—am·or·tiz·a·ble** *adj.*

a·mor·tize·ment (ə-môr′tĭz-mənt) *n.* Amortization.

A·mos[1] (ā′məs). A Hebrew prophet of the 8th century B.C.

Amos[2] *n.* A book of the Old Testament containing the prophecies of Amos.

a·mount (ə-mount′) *n. Abbr.* **amt. 1.** The total figure or quantity; a sum or aggregate: *could only raise half the amount needed.* **2.** A quantity or supply: *attracted a tremendous amount of interest.* **3.** A principal plus its interest, as in a loan. **4.** The overall effect or meaning; import.
~*intr.v.* **amounted, amounting, amounts. 1.** To add up in number or quantity: *The total purchase amounts to ten dollars.* **2.** To be equivalent or tantamount: *accusations amounting to an indictment.* [Middle English *amounten,* to rise, from Old French *amonter,* from *amont,* upward, "to the mountain" : *a-,* to, from Latin *ad-* + *mont,* mountain, from Latin *mōns* (stem *mont-*).]

a·mour (ə-mo͝or′) *n.* A love affair, especially an illicit one: *His latest amours were in all the gossip columns.* [Middle English, from Old French, from Old Provençal *amor,* from Latin *amor,* love, from *amāre,* to love.]

a·mour-pro·pre (ə-mo͝or′prôp′rə) *n.* Self-esteem. [French, "self-love."]

Amoy. See **Xiamen.**

amp (ămp) *n.* **1.** An ampere. **2.** *Informal.* An amplifier.

AMP (ā′ĕm-pē′) *n.* A mononucleotide, $C_{10}H_{14}N_5O_7P$, found in animal cells, that is reversibly convertible to ADP and ATP. [*A*denosine *m*ono*p*hosphate.]

am·pe·lop·sis (ăm′pə-lŏp′sĭs) *n.* Any of several woody vines of the genus *Ampelopsis,* having small greenish or yellowish flowers and occurring in warm regions of Asia and America. [New Latin *Ampelopsis* : Greek *ampelos,* grapevine, + -OPSIS.]

am·per·age (ăm′pər-ĭj, ăm′pîr′-) *n.* The strength of an electric current expressed in amperes.

am·pere (ăm′pîr′) *n. Abbr.* **A 1.** A unit of electric current in the meter-kilogram-second system. It is the steady current that when flowing in straight parallel wires of infinite length and negligible cross section, separated by a distance of one meter in free space, produces a force between the wires of 2×10^{-7} newtons per meter of length. One ampere is equal to one coulomb per second. **2.** A former unit of electric current, the international ampere, equal to 0.999835 ampere. Also shortened to "amp." [After André-Marie AMPÈRE.]

Am·père (ăm′pîr′), **André-Marie** (1775–1836). French physicist and mathematician. He formulated Ampère's law, a mathematical description of the magnetic field produced by a current-carrying conductor. The SI unit of electric current is named after him.

am·pere-hour (ăm′pîr-our′) *n.* The electric charge transferred past a specific circuit point by a current of one ampere in one hour.

am·pere-turn (ăm′pîr-tûrn′) *n.* A unit of magnetomotive force equal to the magnetomotive force around a path linking one turn of a conducting loop carrying a current of one ampere.

am·per·sand (ăm′pər-sănd′) *n.* The character or sign (&) representing *and.* [From *and per se and,* "& by itself (equals) *and,*" phrase formerly used to explain the character.]

am·phet·a·mine (ăm-fĕt′ə-mēn′, -mĭn) *n.* **1.** A colorless volatile liquid, $C_9H_{13}N$, used primarily as a central nervous system stimulant. **2.** A phosphate or sulfate of amphetamine used as a central nervous system stimulant. [*A*lpha *m*ethyl *ph*enyl *et*hyl *amine.*]

amphi– *prefix.* Indicates: **1.** On both sides; on both ends; of both kinds; both; for example, **amphibious. 2.** Around; on all sides; for example, **amphithecium.** [Latin, from Greek, from *amphi,* around, on both sides, on all sides.]

am·phi·ar·thro·sis (ăm′fē-är-thrō′sĭs) *n., pl.* **-ses** (-sēz′). A relatively immobile joint between bony surfaces connected by ligaments or elastic cartilage.

am·phib·i·an (am-fĭb′ē-ən) *n.* **1.** Any of various cold-blooded, smooth-skinned, vertebrate organisms of the class Amphibia, such as a frog, toad, or salamander, characteristically hatching as aquatic larvae that breathe by means of gills and metamorphosing to an adult form having air-breathing lungs. **2.** Any amphibious organism. **3.** An aircraft that can take off and land either on land or on water. **4.** A vehicle that can move over land and on water.
~*adj.* Of or pertaining to an amphibian, especially one of the Amphibia. [New Latin *Amphibia,* plural of *amphibium,* an amphibian, from Greek *amphibion,* neuter of *amphibios,* AMPHIBIOUS.]

am·phi·bi·ot·ic (ăm′fĭ-bī-ŏt′ĭk) *adj.* Living in water during an early stage of development and on land during the adult stage.

am·phib·i·ous (ăm-fĭb′ē-əs) *adj.* **1.** Living or able to live both on land and in water. **2. a.** Able or trained to operate on both land and water: *amphibious troops.* **b.** Involving operations on both land and water: *an amphibious invasion.* **3.** Of a mixed or twofold nature. [Greek *amphibios,* "living a double life" : AMPHI- + *bios,* life.] **—am·phib·i·ous·ly** *adv.* **—am·phib·i·ous·ness** *n.*

am·phi·bole (ăm′fĭ-bōl′) *n.* Any of a large group of structurally similar hydrated double silicate minerals including hornblende and several types of asbestos, containing various combinations of sodium, calcium, magnesium, iron, and aluminum. [French, from Late Latin *amphibolus,* ambiguous (from its many varieties), from Greek *amphibolos,* doubtful, from *amphiballein,* to throw around, doubt : AMPHI- + *ballein,* to throw.] **—am·phi·bol·ic** (ăm′fĭ-bŏl′ĭk) *adj.*

am·phib·o·lite (ăm-fĭb′ə-līt′) *n.* A metamorphic rock composed chiefly of amphibole with some plagioclase and quartz. [AMPHIBOL(E) + -ITE.]

am·phi·bol·o·gy (ăm′fĭ-bŏl′ə-jē) *n., pl.* **-gies.** Also **am·phib·o·ly** (ăm-fĭb′ə-lē) *pl.* **-lies. 1.** Ambiguity arising from a grammatical construction that can be understood in more than one way. **2.** A statement, as *flying planes can be dangerous,* containing amphibology. [Middle English *amphibologie,* from Late Latin *amphibologia,* from *amphibolia,* from Greek *amphibolia,* from *amphibolos,* ambiguous. See **amphibole.**] **—am·phib·o·log·i·cal** (ăm-fĭb′ə-lŏj′ĭ-kəl) *adj.* **—am·phib·o·log·i·cal·ly** *adv.*

am·phib·o·lous (ăm-fĭb′ə-ləs) *adj.* Having two meanings; ambiguous; equivocal. [Greek *amphibolos.* See **amphibole.**]

am·phi·brach (ăm′fə-brăk′) *n.* A trisyllabic metrical foot having one accented or long syllable between two unaccented or short syllables, as in the word *remember.* [Latin *amphibrachys,* from Greek *amphibrakhus* : *amphi–,* on both sides + *brakhus,* short.]

am·phi·coe·lous, am·phi·ce·lous (ăm′fĭ-sē′ləs) *adj.* Concave on both ends or sides, as the vertebrae of most fishes are. [Late Greek *amphikoilos* : AMPHI- + *koilos,* hollow.]

am·phic·ty·o·ny (ăm-fĭk′tē-ə-nē) *n., pl.* **-nies.** In ancient Greece, a group of neighboring states associated for a common religious or political purpose, especially the protection and maintenance of a common religious center or shrine, such as the one at Delphi. [Greek *amphiktuonia,* from *amphiktuones,* neighbors : AMPHI- + *ktizein,* to found.] **—am·phic·ty·on·ic** (ăm-fĭk′tē-ŏn′ĭk) *adj.*

am·phi·mix·is (ăm′fĭ-mĭk′sĭs) *n.* True sexual reproduction, with fusion of sperm and egg nuclei. Compare **apomixis.** [New Latin : AMPHI- + Greek *mixis,* a mingling, from *mignunai,* to mingle.] **—am·phi·mic·tic** (ăm′fĭ-mĭk′tĭk) *adj.*

am·phi·ox·us (ăm′fē-ŏk′səs) *n.* A primitive chordate organism, the **lancelet** *(see).* [New Latin, "sharp at both ends" : AMPHI- + Greek *oxus,* sharp.]

am·phi·pod (ăm′fĭ-pŏd′) *n.* Any of numerous small crustaceans of the order Amphipoda, which includes the beach fleas. [New Latin *Amphipoda,* "having feet on both sides" : AMPHI- + -POD.]

am·phip·ro·style (ăm-fĭp′rə-stīl′, ăm′fĭ-prō′-) *adj.* Having a prostyle or set of columns at each end, but none along the sides. Said especially of an ancient temple. [Latin *amphiprostylos,* from Greek *am-*

phiprostulos, "with pillars in front and behind" : AMPHI- + *prostulos,* with pillars in front (see **prostyle**).] —**am·phi·pro·style** *n.*

am·phis·bae·na (ăm'fĭs-bē'nə) *n.* **1.** A mythological serpent having a head at each end of its body. **2.** A wormlike burrowing lizard of the genus *Amphisbaena.* [Latin, from Greek *amphisbaina,* "one that goes in both directions" : *amphis,* both ways, + *bainein,* to go.] —**am·phis·bae·nic** *adj.*

am·phi·sty·lar (ăm'fĭ-stī'lər) *adj. Architecture.* Having columns at both front and back or on each side. [AMPHI- + Greek *stulos,* a pillar.]

am·phi·the·a·ter (ăm'fə-thē'ə-tər) *n.* Also *chiefly British* **am·phi·the·a·tre.** **1.** An oval or round structure having tiers of seats rising gradually outward from an open space or arena at the center. **2.** A public place where contests are held; an arena. **3.** A level area surrounded by upward sloping ground. **4.** An upper, sloping gallery in a theater. [Latin *amphitheatrum,* from Greek *amphitheatron* : AMPHI- + THEATER.] —**am·phi·the·at·ric** (ăm'fə-thē-ăt'rĭk), **am·phi·the·at·ri·cal** *adj.* —**am·phi·the·at·ri·cal·ly** *adv.*

am·phi·the·ci·um (ăm'fĭ-thē'shē-əm, -sē-əm) *n., pl.* **-ci·a** (-shē-ə, -sē-ə). *Botany.* The outer layer of cells of the spore-containing capsule of a moss. [New Latin : AMPHI- + Greek *thēkion,* diminutive of *thēkē,* a case.]

am·phit·ri·chous (ăm-fĭt'rĭ-kəs) *adj.* Having a flagellum or flagella at both ends, as certain microorganisms do. [AMPHI- + -TRICHOUS.]

Am·phi·tri·te (ăm'fĭ-trī'tē). *Greek Mythology.* The goddess of the sea, wife of Poseidon, and one of the Nereids.

am·phit·ro·pous (ăm-fĭt'rə-pəs) *adj. Botany.* Partly inverted, so that the point of attachment is near the middle. Said of an ovule. [AMPHI- + -TROPOUS.]

am·pho·ra (ăm'fər-ə) *n., pl.* **-rae** (-rē) or **-ras.** A large two-handled jar with a narrow neck, used by the ancient Greeks and Romans to carry wine or oil. [Latin *amphora,* from Greek *amphoreus, amphiphoreus* : AMPHI- + *phoreus,* a bearer, from *pherein,* to bear.] —**am·pho·ral** (ăm'fər-əl) *adj.*

am·pho·ter·ic (ăm'fə-tĕr'ĭk) *adj. Chemistry.* Capable of reacting either as an acid or a base. [Greek *amphoteros,* either of two, from *amphō,* both.]

am·pi·cil·lin (ăm'pə-sĭl'ĭn) *n.* An antibiotic given orally or by injection primarily to treat a variety of infections of the urinary, respiratory, and intestinal tracts. [AM(INO-) + P(EN)ICILLIN.]

am·ple (ăm'pəl) *adj.* **-pler, -plest.** **1.** Large in extent or capacity; spacious: *an ample living room.* **2.** Large in degree, scope, or amount: *a family of ample means.* **3.** Rather stout; portly: *an ample figure.* **4.** Enough or more than enough for a particular need or purpose. [Middle English, from Old French, from Latin *amplus†,* wide, ample.] —**am·ple·ness** *n.*

am·plex·i·caul (ăm-plĕk'sĭ-kôl') *adj. Botany.* Having a base that clasps or encircles the stem, as some leaves do. [New Latin *amplexicaulis,* embracing stem : Latin *amplexus,* past participle of *amplectī,* to wind around : AM(BI)- + *plectere,* to plait + *caulis,* stem.]

am·pli·fi·ca·tion (ăm'plə-fĭ-kā'shən) *n.* **1.** The act or result of amplifying; especially, the process of expanding a statement, narrative, or the like, as for clarification or rhetorical effect. **2. a.** Material used to amplify a statement. **b.** A statement so amplified. **3.** *Physics.* **a.** The process of increasing the magnitude of a variable quantity, especially of a voltage or current, without altering any other quality. **b.** The result of such a process.

am·pli·fi·er (ăm'plə-fī'ər) *n.* **1.** One that amplifies, enlarges, or extends. **2.** Any of various electronic devices or circuits that increase the current or voltage of a signal fed into them; for example, an audio-frequency amplifier that feeds the loudspeakers in a radio, record-player, or the like.

am·pli·fy (ăm'plə-fī') *v.* **-fied, -fying, -fies.** —*tr.* **1.** To enlarge (a statement or idea, for example) by adding material that clarifies, illustrates, or otherwise expands. **2.** To extend, enhance, or increase, as in scope or importance. **3.** *Physics.* To produce amplification of. —*intr.* To write or discourse at greater length on what has been written or said. [Middle English *amplifien,* from Old French *amplifier,* from Latin *amplificāre* : *amplus,* AMPLE + *facere,* to make.]

am·pli·tude (ăm'plə-tood', -tyood') *n.* **1.** Greatness of size or extent; magnitude. **2.** Fullness of scope; breadth or range, as of mind. **3.** *Astronomy.* The angular distance along the horizon from true east or west to the intersection of the vertical circle of a celestial body with the horizon. **4.** *Physics.* The maximum value of a periodically varying quantity. **5.** *Mathematics.* **a.** The maximum ordinate value of a periodic curve. **b.** The angle made with the positive horizontal axis by the vector representation of a complex number. In this sense, also called "argument." [Latin *amplitūdō,* from *amplus,* AMPLE.]

amplitude modulation *n. Abbr.* **AM, am** The encoding of a carrier wave by variation of its amplitude in accordance with an input signal. Compare **frequency modulation.**

am·ply (ăm'plē) *adv.* In an ample manner; largely; liberally; sufficiently.

am·poule, am·pule (ăm'pool, -pyool) *n.* A small glass tube, sealed after filling and used chiefly as a container for a hypodermic injection solution. [French, from Old French, from Latin *ampulla,* AMPULLA.]

am·pul·la (ăm-pool'ə, -pŭl'ə) *n., pl.* **-pullae** (-pool'ē, -pŭl'ē). **1.** A nearly round bottle with two handles used by the ancient Romans for wine, oil, or perfume. **2. a.** A container used for wine or water at the Eucharist. **b.** A vessel for consecrated wine or holy oil.

3. *Anatomy.* A small dilation in a canal or duct, especially in the semicircular canal of the ear. [Latin, diminutive of *amp(h)ora,* AMPHORA.] —**am·pul·lar** *adj.*

am·pul·la·ceous (ăm'poo-lā'shəs) *adj.* Resembling an ampulla; bladder-shaped. [Latin *ampullāceus* : AMPULL(A) + -ACEOUS.]

am·pu·tate (ăm'pyoo-tāt') *tr.v.* **-tated, -tating, -tates.** To cut off (a bodily part, usually a limb), especially by surgery. [Latin *amputāre,* to cut around : AM(BI)- + *putāre,* to cut.] —**am·pu·ta·tion** *n.*

am·pu·tee (ăm'pyoo-tē') *n.* A person who has had one or more limbs removed by amputation.

am·ri·ta, am·ree·ta (ŭm-rē'tə) *n. Hindu Mythology.* **1.** The ambrosia, prepared by the gods, that bestows immortality. **2.** The immortality achieved by drinking this ambrosia. [Sanskrit *amṛta,* "deathless" : *a-,* without + *mṛta,* death.]

Am·rit·sar (ŭm-rĭt'sər). The administrative center and largest city in the Punjab, northwestern India, on the border with Pakistan. Founded in 1577 by the fourth guru of the Sikhs, Ram Das, it has remained the center of the Sikh faith. In 1919 it was the scene of a massacre in which hundreds of Indian nationalists were killed by British-led troops.

Am·ster·dam (ăm'stər-dăm'). The capital and largest city of the Netherlands, in North Holland province. It lies on the Ij, an arm of the Ijsselmeer, and is linked to the North Sea by a ship canal. The city has one of the world's most important stock exchanges and is a major center of the diamond-cutting industry. Among its many museums, the Rijksmuseum, which houses a large collection of Dutch paintings, is outstanding.

amt. amount.

amu *Physics.* atomic mass unit.

a·muck (ə-mŭk') *adv.* Also **a·mok** (ə-mŭk', ə-mŏk'). **1.** In a frenzy to do violence or kill. **2.** In a wild, frantic, or uncontrollable manner. Used in the phrase *run amok.* [Malay *amok,* furious attack.]

A·mu Dar·ya (ä'moo där'yə). Ancient name **Ox·us** (ŏk'səs). A river that rises in the Pamir Mts. of central Asia and flows *c.* 2,580 kilometers (1,600 miles) northwest to the Aral Sea.

am·u·let (ăm'yə-lĭt) *n.* An object worn, especially around the neck, as a charm against evil or injury. [Latin *amulētum†.*]

A·mund·sen (ä'mən-sən), **Roald** (1872–1928). Norwegian explorer. He was the first to navigate the Northwest Passage (1903–06), and he fixed the position of the North Magnetic Pole. He became the first person to reach the South Pole in 1911, 34 days ahead of Robert Falcon Scott. With the Italian explorer Umberto Nobile he was the first to make a flight over the North Pole. Amundsen died on a flight to the Arctic to search for Nobile, whose airship had crashed.

A·mur (ä-moor'). *Chinese* **Hei·long Ji·ang** (hä'loong' jē-äng'). One of the principal waterways of Asia. It is formed by the confluence of the Shilka and Argun on the northern border of Manchuria and flows some 2,900 kilometers (1,800 miles) to the Sea of Japan. For more than 1,600 kilometers (1,000 miles) it serves as the border between China and Russia.

a·muse (ə-myooz') *tr.v.* **amused, amusing, amuses.** **1.** To occupy in an agreeable, pleasing, or entertaining fashion. **2.** To cause to laugh or smile by giving pleasure. [Old French *amuser,* "to cause to idle away time" : *a,* to, from Latin *ad-* + *muser,* to idle, MUSE.] —**a·mus·er** *n.*

a·muse·ment (ə-myooz'mənt) *n.* **1.** The pleasurable occupation of time or the attention; diversion; entertainment: *sang for the amusement of her guests.* **2.** The state of being amused, entertained, or pleased. **3.** Something that amuses.

amusement park *n.* A commercially operated enterprise that offers various forms of entertainment, as rides on a merry-go-round, and often has stands where refreshments are sold.

a·mus·ing (ə-myoo'zĭng) *adj.* **1.** Entertaining or pleasing. **2.** Arousing laughter. —**a·mus·ing·ly** *adv.* —**a·mus·ing·ness** *n.*

a·myg·dale (ə-mĭg'dāl) *n.* An amygdule. [Greek *amugdalē,* ALMOND.]

a·myg·da·loid (ə-mĭg'də-loid) *n.* A volcanic rock containing many amygdules.
~*adj.* Also **a·myg·da·loi·dal** (ə-mĭg'də-loid'l) (for sense 2). **1.** Almond-shaped. **2.** *Geology.* Resembling amygdaloid. [Latin *amygdala,* ALMOND + -OID.]

a·myg·dule (ə-mĭg'dool) *n.* A small gas bubble in lavar or other igneous rock that has filled with secondary minerals such as zeolite, calcite, or quartz. [Latin *amygdala,* ALMOND (from its shape) + (NOD)ULE.]

am·yl (ăm'əl) *n.* Any univalent organic radical with the formula C_5H_{11}. See **pentyl.** [Latin *amylum,* starch, AMYLUM.]

am·y·la·ceous (ăm'ə-lā'shəs) *adj.* Of, pertaining to, or resembling starch; starchy. [AMYL(O)- + -ACEOUS.]

amyl acetate *n.* An organic compound, $CH_3COOC_5H_{11}$, used commercially in isomeric mixtures as a flavoring agent, as a paint and lacquer solvent, and in the preparation of penicillin. Also called "banana oil," "pear oil."

amyl alcohol *n.* Any of eight isomers of the composition $C_5H_{11}OH$, one of which, $CH_3CH_2CH(CH_3)CH_2OH$, is the principal constituent of fusel oil.

am·y·lase (ăm'ə-lās', -lāz') *n.* Any of various enzymes that convert starch or glycogen to sugar. [AMYL(O)- + -ASE.]

am·yl·ene (ăm'ə-lēn) *n. Chemistry.* Pentene (see).

amyl nitrite *n.* The nitrous acid ester of isoamyl alcohol, $(CH_3)_2CHCH_2CH_2NO_2$, used in medicine as a vasodilator, mainly in the treatment of angina pectoris.

amphitheater *This amphitheater in Athens, built in the second century A.D., can seat 5,000 spectators. It is still used for music festivals and for performances of ancient Greek plays.*

amylo–, amyl– *prefix.* Indicates starch; for example, **amylolysis, amylase.** [Latin *amylum,* starch, AMYLUM.]

am·y·loid (ăm'ə-loid') *n.* **1.** A starchlike substance. **2.** *Pathology.* A hard starchlike protein deposited in tissues in certain degenerative diseases. [AMYL(O)- + -OID.] —**am·y·loid** *adj.*

am·y·lol·y·sis (ăm'ə-lŏl'ə-sĭs) *n.* The enzymatic conversion of starch to sugars. [AMYLO- + -LYSIS.] —**am·y·lo·lyt·ic** (ăm'ə-lō-lĭt'ĭk) *adj.*

am·y·lo·pec·tin (ăm'ə-lō-pĕk'tĭn) *n.* The major and insoluble portion of starch. Compare **amylose.**

am·y·lop·sin (ăm'ə-lŏp'sĭn) *n.* The starch-digesting amylase produced by the pancreas. [AMYLO- + (TRY)PSIN.]

am·y·lose (ăm'ə-lōs', -lōz') *n.* The relatively soluble portion of starch. Compare **amylopectin.** [AMYL(O)- + -OSE.]

am·y·lum (ăm'ə-ləm) *n.* Starch. [Latin, from Greek *amulon,* starch, the finest flour, from neuter of *amulos,* "not ground in a mill": A- (not) + *mulē,* mill.]

a·my·o·to·ni·a (ā-mī'ə-tō'nē-ə) *n.* Lack of muscle tone. [New Latin : A- (without) + MYO- + -TONIA.]

an¹ (ăn, ən). The indefinite article, a form of *a* used before words beginning with a vowel or with an unpronounced *h*: *They saw an elephant. The work took an hour.* —See Usage note at **a.** [Middle English *an,* Old English *an,* one.]

an², an' (ăn, ən) *conj. Archaic.* And if; if. [Middle English *an,* Old English *an,* short for AND.]

An *Physics.* actinon.

an– *prefix.* Indicates not or without; for example, **anaerobe, anosmia.** [Greek *an-,* not, without, lacking.]

–an¹ *suffix.* Indicates: **1.** Pertaining to, belonging to, or resembling; for example, **American, Mexican. 2.** Believing in or adhering to; for example, **Anglican, Darwinian.** [Latin *-ānus,* adjectival suffix.]

–an² *suffix. Chemistry.* Indicates: **1.** A heterocyclic compound; for example, **furan. 2.** An anhydride of a carbohydrate; for example, **dextran.** [Latin *-ānus,* adjectival suffix.]

an. **1.** before. [Latin *ante*] **2.** in the year. [Latin *annō*]

an·a¹ (ăn'ə, ä'nə) *n., pl.* **ana** or **anas. 1.** A collection of a person's memorable sayings. **2.** A collection of anecdotes and other information relating to or illustrating the character of a person or place. [Independent use of -ANA.]

an·a² (ăn'ə) *adv. Abbr.* **aa** *Pharmacology.* Both in the same quantity; of each. Used to refer to ingredients in prescriptions. [Middle English, from Medieval Latin, from Greek, to the amount of, literally "up."]

ana– *prefix.* Indicates: **1.** Upward progression; for example, **anabolism, anaphase. 2.** Reversion; for example, **anaplasia. 3.** Renewal or intensification; for example, **anaphylaxis.** [In borrowed Greek compounds, *ana-* indicates: **1.** Upward, as in **anabasis. 2.** According to, as in **analogy. 3.** Back, as in **anabiosis. 4.** Backward, reversed, as in **anachronism. 5.** Again, anew, as in **anaphora.** Greek, from *ana,* up, throughout, according to.]

–ana, –iana *suffix.* Indicates a collection of assorted material, as facts, anecdotes, objects, and pictures, relating to or illustrating the character of a specified place, person, topic, or period; for example, **Victoriana.** [New Latin, from Latin *-āna,* "the things pertaining to," neuter plural of *-ānus,* -AN.]

an·a·bae·na (ăn'ə-bē'nə) *n.* Any of various freshwater algae of the genus *Anabaena,* sometimes occurring in drinking water and causing a bad taste and odor. [New Latin *Anabaena,* from Greek *anabainein,* to go up (from their periodic rise to the surface) : *ana-,* up + *bainein,* to go.]

an·a·ban·tid (ăn'ə-băn'tĭd) *n.* Any of various tropical freshwater fishes of the family Anabantidae, which includes the **Siamese fighting fish** *(see).* [New Latin *Anabantidae : Anabas* (stem *Anabant-*), type genus, from Greek *anabas,* aorist participle of *anabainein,* to go up + -IDAE.]

An·a·bap·tist (ăn'ə-băp'tĭst) *n.* A member of one of the radical movements of the Reformation that insisted that only adult baptism was valid and held that true Christians should not bear arms, use force, or hold government office. [New Latin *anabaptista,* "one who is rebaptized," from Late Greek *anabaptizein,* to baptize again : Greek *ana-,* again + *baptizein,* to baptize, from *baptein,* to dip.] —**An·a·bap·tism** *n.* —**An·a·bap·tist** *adj.*

an·a·bas (ăn'ə-băs') *n.* Any member of the genus *Anabas,* which includes freshwater fishes of Africa and Asia, resembling perch. [New Latin *Anabas.* See **anabantid.**]

a·nab·a·sis (ə-năb'ə-sĭs) *n., pl.* **-ses** (-sēz'). A large-scale military advance; specifically, the expedition across Asia Minor (401 B.C.) made by Greek mercenaries led by Cyrus the Younger of Persia, as described by Xenophon. [Greek, a going up or forward, from *anabainein,* to go up. See **anabaena.**]

an·a·bat·ic (ăn'ə-băt'ĭk) *adj.* Of, pertaining to, or designating rising wind currents. [Late Greek *anabatikos,* from Greek, rising, from *anabainein,* to go up. See **anabaena.**]

an·a·bi·o·sis (ăn'ə-bī-ō'sĭs) *n.* A restoring to life from a deathlike condition; resuscitation. [New Latin, from Greek *anabiōsis,* from *anabioun,* to come back to life : *ana-,* back + *bioun,* to live, from *bios,* life.]

an·a·bi·ot·ic (ăn'ə-bī-ŏt'ĭk) *adj.* In a state resembling death, but capable of resuscitation.

an·a·bol·ic (ăn'ə-bŏl'ĭk) *adj.* Of, pertaining to, or characterized by anabolism.

anabolic steroid *n.* Any of a group of synthetic sex hormones used to increase muscle size and strength, as in debilitated underweight patients and in athletes.

an·a·bo·lism (ə-năb'ə-lĭz'əm) *n.* The metabolic process by which simple substances are synthesized into the complex materials of living tissue; constructive metabolism. Compare **catabolism.** [ANA- + (META)BOLISM.]

an·a·bo·lite (ə-năb'ə-līt') *n.* A product of anabolism. —**a·nab·o·lit·ic** (ə-năb'ə-lĭt'ĭk) *adj.*

a·nach·ro·nism (ə-năk'rə-nĭz'əm) *n.* **1.** The representation of something as existing or happening at other than its proper or historical time. **2. a.** Anything out of its proper time. **b.** Someone or something no longer appropriate to or in harmony with the time. [French *anachronisme,* from Greek *anakhronismos,* from *anakhronizein,* to be an anachronism : *ana-,* backward, reversed + *khronizein,* to belong to a particular time, from *khronos,* time (see **chronic**).] —**a·nach·ro·nis·tic** (ə-năk'rə-nĭs'tĭk), **a·nach·ro·nous** (ə-năk'rə-nəs) *adj.* —**a·nach·ro·nis·ti·cal·ly, a·nach·ro·nous·ly** *adv.*

an·a·cli·nal (ăn'ə-klī'nəl) *adj.* Designating valleys and similar formations that progress in an opposite direction to the dip of surrounding rock strata. [ANA- + -CLINAL.]

an·a·cli·sis (ăn'ə-klī'sĭs) *n.* Psychological dependence on others. [New Latin, from Greek *anaklisis,* a leaning back, from *anaklinein,* to lean on.] —**an·a·clit·ic** (ăn'ə-klĭt'ĭk) *adj.*

an·a·co·lu·thon (ăn'ə-kə-lōō'thŏn') *n., pl.* **-thons** or **-tha** (-thə). A statement characterized by an abrupt change to a second grammatical construction inconsistent with the first, sometimes used for rhetorical effect; for example, *I warned him that if he continues to drink, what will become of him?* [Late Latin, from Greek *anakolouthon,* inconsistent, from *anakolouthos,* inconsistent : *an-,* not + *akolouthos,* following : *a-,* together + *keleuthos†,* path.] —**an·a·co·lu·thic** *adj.*

an·a·con·da (ăn'ə-kŏn'də) *n.* **1.** A large, nonvenomous, arboreal snake, *Eunectes murinus,* of South America, that constricts its prey. **2.** Any of several similar or related snakes. [Unexplained alteration of Sinhalese *henakandayā,* whip snake (originally applied to a snake of Sri Lanka) : *hena,* lightning + *kanda,* stem.]

A·nac·re·on (ə-năk'rē-ən, -ŏn') (c. 572–c. 488 B.C.). Greek poet, noted for his songs praising love and wine.

A·nac·re·on·tic (ə-năk'rē-ŏn'tĭk) *adj.* Characteristic of or in the style of the poems of Anacreon; specifically, convivial or amatory.

an·a·cru·sis (ăn'ə-krōō'sĭs) *n.* **1.** One or more unstressed syllables at the beginning of a line of verse, before the reckoning of the normal meter begins. **2.** *Music.* An upbeat. [New Latin, from Greek *anakrousis,* the beginning of a tune, from *anakrouein,* to strike up: ANA- + *krouein,* to strike.]

an·a·dem (ăn'ə-dĕm') *n. Poetic.* A wreath or garland for the head. [Latin *anadēma,* from Greek, from *anadein,* to bind up : ANA- + *dein,* to bind.]

an·a·di·plo·sis (ăn'ə-dĭ-plō'sĭs) *n., pl.* **-ses** (-sēz'). Rhetorical repetition at the beginning of a phrase of the word or words with which the previous phrase ended; for example, *ruined his reputation—his reputation that had taken so long to establish.* [Latin *anadiplōsis,* from Greek, from *anadiploun,* to reduplicate.]

a·nad·ro·mous (ə-năd'rə-məs) *adj.* Migrating up rivers from the sea to breed in fresh water, as salmon do. Compare **catadromous.** [Greek *anadromos,* running up : ANA- + *dromos,* a running.]

anaemia. Variant of **anemia.**

an·aer·obe (ăn'ə-rōb', ăn-âr'ōb') *n.* A microorganism, such as a bacterium, able to live in the absence of free oxygen.

an·aer·o·bic (ăn'ə-rō'bĭk, ăn-âr-ō'-) *adj.* **1.** Of or designating a process, such as respiration, that does not require free oxygen. **2.** Of or pertaining to anaerobes. —**an·aer·o·bi·cal·ly** *adv.*

anaesthesia. Variant of **anesthesia.**

an·a·glyph (ăn'ə-glĭf) *n.* **1.** An ornament carved in low relief. **2.** A photographic process whereby two superimposed images of an object, usually in red and green, produce a three-dimensional effect when viewed through red and green lenses. [Greek *anagluphos,* wrought in low relief, from *anagluphein,* to carve in relief : *ana-,* up + *gluphein,* to carve.] —**an·a·glyph·ic** (ăn'ə-glĭf'ĭk) *adj.*

an·a·go·ge, an·a·go·gy (ăn'ə-gō'jē) *n.* A mystical interpretation of a word, passage, or text; specifically, scriptural exegesis that detects hidden spiritual allusions or meanings. [Late Latin *anagōgē,* from Late Greek, spiritual uplift, from *anagein,* to uplift, lead up : ANA- + *agein,* to lead.] —**an·a·gog·ic** (ăn'ə-gŏj'ĭk), **an·a·gog·i·cal** *adj.* —**an·a·gog·i·cal·ly** *adv.*

an·a·gram (ăn'ə-grăm') *n.* A word or phrase formed by reordering the letters of another word or phrase: *"Pear" is an anagram of "reap."* [French *anagramme,* from New Latin *anagramma* : ANA- + -GRAM.] —**an·a·gram·mat·ic** (ăn'ə-grə-măt'ĭk) *adj.* —**an·a·gram·mat·i·cal·ly** *adv.*

an·a·gram·ma·tize (ăn'ə-grăm'ə-tīz') *tr.v.* **-tized, -tiz·ing, -tizes.** To make an anagram of.

a·nal (ā'nəl) *adj.* **1.** Of, pertaining to, or near the anus. **2.** *Psychoanalysis.* Of, pertaining to, or designating: **a.** The stage of psychosexual development of the infant in which gratification is derived from sensations associated with the anus. **b.** Personality traits originating during toilet training and distinguished as **anal-expulsive** or **anal-retentive** *(both of which see).* Compare **genital, oral.** [New Latin *analis,* from Latin *ānus,* ANUS.]

anal. **1.** analogous; analogy. **2.** analysis; analytic.

a·nal·cime (ə-năl'sēm') *n. Mineralogy.* A white or colorless zeolite, found in some dolerites and basalts. [French, from Greek *analkimos,* weak (from its weak electric power) : AN- (not) + *alkimos,* strong, from *alkē,* strength.]

a·nal·cite (ə-năl'sīt') *n.* Analcime.

an·a·lects (ăn′ə-lĕkts′) *pl.n.* Also **an·a·lec·ta** (ăn′ə-lĕk′tə). Selections or parts of a literary work or group of works. [Latin *analecta,* from Greek *analekta,* neuter plural of *analektos,* select, from *analegein,* to gather : *ana-,* up + *legein,* to gather.] —**an·a·lec·tic** (ăn′ə-lĕk′tĭk) *adj.*

an·a·lem·ma (ăn′ə-lĕm′ə) *n.* A graduated scale, in the shape of a figure eight, indicating the sun's declination and the equation of time for every day of the year, usually found on sundials and globes. [Latin, a sundial, from Greek *analēmma,* a support, from *analambanein,* to take up, restore. See **analeptic.**] —**an·a·lem·mat·ic** (ăn′ə-lĕ-măt′ĭk) *adj.*

an·a·lep·tic (ăn′ə-lĕp′tĭk) *adj.* Restorative or stimulating. ~*n.* An analeptic medication. [Greek *analēptikos,* from *analambanein,* to take up, restore : *ana-,* up + *lambanein,* to take.]

a·nal-ex·pul·sive (ā′nəl-ĭk-spŭl′sĭv) *adj. Psychoanalysis.* Of, designating, or exhibiting personality traits such as conceit, suspicion, ambition, and generosity, originating in habits, attitudes, or values associated with infantile pleasure in the expulsion of feces.

anal fin *n.* An unpaired fin in fishes, located on the ventral median line between the tail and the anus.

an·al·ge·si·a (ăn′əl-jē′zē-ə, -zhə) *n. Medicine.* Insensibility to pain without loss of consciousness. [New Latin, from Greek *analgēsia,* want of feeling : AN- (not) + *algēsia,* sense of pain, from *algein,* to feel pain, from *algos,* pain.]

an·al·ge·sic (ăn′əl-jē′zĭk, -sĭk) *n.* A drug or other substance that reduces or eliminates pain. ~*adj.* Of or causing analgesia.

a·nal·i·ty (ā-năl′ə-tē) *n., pl.* **-ties.** *Psychoanalysis.* The quality or state of being anal.

an·a·log (ăn′ə-lôg′, -lŏg′) *adj.* **1.** Of, pertaining to, or constituting an analogue. **2.** Designating a watch or clock in which the time is indicated by means of hands moving around a dial in the traditional manner. **3.** Designating a means of recording sound in which the changes to the recording medium are continuous and analogous to the changes in the wave form of the sound. ~*n.* Variant of **analogue.** Compare **digital.**

analog computer *n.* A computer in which numerical data are represented by analogous physical magnitudes or electrical signals. Compare **digital computer.**

analog data *pl.n. Used with a singular or plural verb.* Data presented or collected in continuous form, as temperature variation or voltage measurement.

an·a·log·i·cal (ăn′ə-lŏj′ĭ-kəl) *adj.* Also **an·a·log·ic** (-lŏj′ĭk) Of, pertaining to, consisting of, or based upon an analogy. —**an·a·log·i·cal·ly** *adv.*

a·nal·o·gist (ə-năl′ə-jĭst) *n.* One who looks for or reasons from analogies.

a·nal·o·gize (ə-năl′ə-jīz′) *v.* **-gized, -gizing, -gizes.** —*tr.* To make an analogy to. —*intr.* To think or reason by analogy.

a·nal·o·gous (ə-năl′ə-gəs) *adj. Abbr.* **anal. 1.** Similar or alike in a way that permits the drawing of an analogy; comparable in certain respects. **2.** *Biology.* Similar in function but not in evolutionary origin, as the gills of a fish and the lungs of a mammal. Compare **homologous.** [Latin *analogus,* from Greek *analogos,* proportionate, resembling : *ana-,* according to + *logos,* proportion, word, from *legein,* to speak.] —**a·nal·o·gous·ly** *adv.* —**a·nal·o·gous·ness** *n.*

an·a·logue, an·a·log (ăn′ə-lôg′, -lŏg′) *n.* **1.** Something that bears an analogy to something else. **2.** *Biology.* An organ or structure that is similar in function to one in another kind of organism, but is of dissimilar evolutionary origin. **3.** *Chemistry.* A structural derivative of a parent compound. [French, from Greek *analogos,* ANALOGOUS.]

a·nal·o·gy (ə-năl′ə-jē) *n., pl.* **-gies.** *Abbr.* **anal. 1. a.** Correspondence in some respects between things otherwise dissimilar. **b.** A statement illustrating such correspondence: *to draw an analogy.* **2.** A form of logical inference, or an instance of it, based on the assumption that if two things are known to be alike in some respects, then they will be alike in other respects. **3.** *Biology.* Correspondence in function or position but not in evolutionary origin. **4.** *Linguistics.* The creation of new forms on the model of known ones: *A child might say "teached" instead of "taught" by analogy with "reached."* —See Synonyms at **likeness.** [Latin *analogia,* from Greek, from *analogos,* ANALOGOUS.]

an·al·pha·bet·ic (ăn′ăl′fə-bĕt′ĭk) *adj.* **1.** Not alphabetical. **2.** Unable to read; illiterate. ~*n.* A person who cannot read; an illiterate.

a·nal·re·ten·tive (ā′nəl-rĭ-tĕn′tĭv) *adj. Psychoanalysis.* Of, designating, or exhibiting personality traits such as meticulousness, avarice, and obstinacy, originating in habits, attitudes, or values associated with infantile pleasure in the retention of feces.

a·nal·y·sand (ə-năl′ə-sănd′) *n.* A person who is being psychoanalyzed. [From ANALYZE (by analogy with MULTIPLICAND).]

analyse. *Chiefly British.* Variant of **analyze.**

a·nal·y·sis (ə-năl′ə-sĭs) *n., pl.* **-ses** (-sēz′). *Abbr.* **anal. 1.** The breaking down of a complex intellectual or substantial whole, as for example, an argument or a set of statistics, into its constituent elements in order to examine its nature, significance, and interrelationships. Compare **synthesis. 2.** A statement of the results of such a study. **3.** *Chemistry.* **a.** Separation of a substance into constituents or the determination of its composition. **b.** The stated findings of such separation or determination. **4.** *Mathematics.* **a.** Methodology principally involving algebra and calculus as opposed to synthetic geometry, group theory, and number theory. **b.** The method

of proof in which a known truth is sought as a consequence of reasoning from the thing to be proved. **5.** Psychoanalysis. —**in the last** (or **final**) **analysis.** When everything has been taken into account; in the end. [Medieval Latin, from Greek *analusis,* a loosening, from *analuein,* to undo : *ana-,* back + *luein,* to loosen, free.]

analysis si·tus (sī′təs) *n.* Formerly, **topology** (see). [New Latin, "analysis of region."]

an·a·lyst (ăn′ə-lĭst) *n.* **1.** One who analyzes. **2.** A psychoanalyst. **3.** A systems analyst.

an·a·lyt·ic (ăn′ə-lĭt′ĭk) *adj.* Also **an·a·lyt·i·cal** (-ĭ-kəl). *Abbr.* **anal. 1.** Of, pertaining to, or based on analysis: *adopted an analytic approach to the problem.* **2.** Showing an ability to analyze and reason from a perception of the parts and interrelations of a subject; skilled in analysis: *an analytic mind.* **3.** *Linguistics.* Characteristically expressing grammatical distinctions by using two or more words instead of an inflected form: *English is analytic in its use of the comparative "more beautiful" instead of "beautifuler."* **4.** *Philosophy.* Designating a statement or proposition whose truth depends entirely on the meaning of the words of which it is composed rather than any fact about the world. In this sense, compare **synthetic.** —**an·a·lyt·i·cal·ly** *adv.*

analytical balance *n.* A balance for chemical analysis.

analytical reagent *n.* A chemical of high purity containing known amounts of contaminants and therefore suitable for use in a quantitative analysis.

analytic geometry *n.* The analysis of geometric structures and properties principally by algebraic operations on variables defined in terms of position coordinates. Also called "coordinate geometry."

an·a·lyt·ics (ăn′ə-lĭt′ĭks) *n. Used with a singular verb.* The branch of logic dealing with analysis.

an·a·lyze (ăn′ə-līz′) *tr.v.* **-lyzed, -lyzing, -lyzes. 1.** To separate into constituent elements or basic principles so as to elucidate the interrelation of the parts and the nature or significance of the whole; examine methodically. **2.** To make a chemical or mathematical analysis of. **3.** To psychoanalyze. [French *analyser,* from *analyse,* ANALYSIS.] —**an·a·lyz·a·ble** *adj.* —**an·a·lyz·er** *n.*

Anam. See **Annam.**

an·am·ne·sis (ăn′ăm-nē′sĭs) *n., pl.* **-ses** (-sēz′). **1.** *Psychology.* A recalling to memory; recollection. **2.** *Medicine.* The complete case history of a patient. **3.** *Often* **Anamnesis.** That part of the Eucharist which recalls Christ's passion. [New Latin, from Greek *anamnēsis,* from *anamimnēskein,* to recall to memory : *ana-,* back + *mimnēskein,* to call to mind.] —**an·am·nes·tic** (ăn′ăm-nĕs′tĭk) *adj.* —**an·am·nes·ti·cal·ly** *adv.*

an·a·mor·phic (ăn′ə-môr′fĭk) *adj.* Having, producing, or designating different optical magnification along mutually perpendicular radii: *an anamorphic lens.* [ANA- + -MORPHIC.]

an·a·mor·pho·sis (ăn′ə-môr′fə-sĭs, -môr-fō′sĭs) *n., pl.* **-ses** (-sēz′). *Optics.* An image distorted so that it can be viewed without distortion only from a special angle or with a special instrument. [Medieval Greek *anamorphōsis,* "a forming anew," from Late Greek *anamorphoun,* to transform : *ana-,* again + *morphoun,* to form, from *morphē,* form.]

A·nan·da (ə-nän′də, ä′nən-də) (5th–4th century B.C.). Favorite disciple of Buddha. He was the Buddha's first cousin and is known as the "beloved disciple."

an·an·drous (ăn-ăn′drəs) *adj. Botany.* Having no stamens. [Greek *anandros,* "without a man" : AN- + *anēr* (stem *andr-*), man.]

an·an·thous (ăn-ăn′thəs) *adj. Botany.* Lacking flowers. Said of some angiosperms. [AN- + -ANTHOUS.]

an·a·pest, an·a·paest (ăn′ə-pĕst′) *n.* **1.** A metrical foot composed of two short syllables followed by one long one, written (˘˘ˉ). **2.** A line of verse in this meter: " 'Twas the night before Christmas and all through the house" (Clement Moore). [Latin *anapaestus,* from Greek *anapaistos,* "struck back" (an anapest being a dactyl reversed) : *ana-,* back + *paiein,* to strike.] —**an·a·pest·ic** *adj.*

an·a·phase (ăn′ə-fāz′) *n. Biology.* The stage of mitosis in which the daughter chromosomes move toward the poles of the nuclear spindle. [ANA- + PHASE.]

a·naph·o·ra (ə-năf′ər-ə) *n.* **1.** The deliberate repetition in rhetoric of a word or phrase at the beginning of several successive verses, clauses, or paragraphs. **2.** Reference to an antecedent by the use of a grammatical substitute, as a pronoun. [Late Latin, from Greek *anaphora,* repetition, from *anapherein,* to repeat : *ana-,* again + *pherein,* to carry.]

an·a·phor·ic (ăn′ə-fôr′ĭk, -fōr′ĭk) *adj. Grammar.* Referring to an antecedent: *the anaphoric pronoun "one" in "May I have another one?"*

an·aph·ro·dis·i·a (ăn-ăf′rə-dĭz′ē-ə, -dĭzh′ə) *n.* Absence or decline of sexual desire. [AN- + Greek *aphrodisia,* sexual desire (see **aphrodisiac**).] —**an·aph·ro·dis·i·ac** (ăn-ăf′rə-dĭz′ē-ăk′) *adj. & n.*

an·a·phy·lac·toid (ăn′ə-fə-lăk′toid′) *adj. Pathology.* **1.** Of or pertaining to an anaphylactic reaction that occurs without causing antibodies. **2.** Of or pertaining to a toxic reaction caused in an unsensitized person by an excessive dose of a substance that causes anaphylaxis in a sensitized person.

an·a·phy·lax·is (ăn′ə-fə-lăk′sĭs) *n.* Hypersensitivity to a foreign substance induced by a small preliminary or sensitizing injection of the substance. [New Latin : ANA- + (PRO)PHYLAXIS.] —**an·a·phy·lac·tic** (ăn′ə-fə-lăk′tĭk) *adj.* —**an·a·phy·lac·ti·cal·ly** *adv.*

an·a·pla·si·a (ăn′ə-plā′zhə) *n. Biology.* Reversion of cells or tissues to a more primitive or less differentiated form. [ANA- + -PLASIA.]

an·a·plas·tic (ăn′ə-plăs′tĭk) *adj.* **1.** Pertaining to or involving the restoration of a lost or absent part, as by plastic surgery. **2.** Of or pertaining to anaplasia of cells.

an·a·plas·ty (ăn′ə-plăs′tē) *n.* Plastic surgery. [French *anaplastie*, from Greek *anaplasis*, remodeling, from *anaplassein*, to form anew : ANA- + *plassein*, to mold.]

an·arch (ăn′ärk′) *n.* A leader or advocate of anarchy.

an·ar·chic (ăn-är′kĭk) *adj.* Also **an·ar·chi·cal** (-kĭ-kəl). **1.** Of, like, or promoting anarchy. **2.** Lacking order or control; chaotic. —**an·ar·chi·cal·ly** *adv.*

an·ar·chism (ăn′ər-kĭz′əm) *n.* **1.** The theory that all forms of government are oppressive and undesirable, and should be abolished and replaced by voluntary cooperation. **2.** Active resistance and terrorism against the state, as used by some anarchists. **3.** Rejection of all forms of coercive control and authority.

an·ar·chist (ăn′ər-kĭst) *n.* **1.** An advocate of anarchism. **2.** One who actively promotes anarchism or anarchy, as by the use of terrorism, to destabilize the existing order.

an·ar·chis·tic (ăn′ər-kĭs′tĭk) *adj.* Of, pertaining to, or tending toward anarchism.

anarcho– *prefix.* Indicates anarchistic tendencies or anarchism; for example, **anarcho-syndicalism.** [Medieval Latin, from Greek *anarkhos*, without a ruler. See **anarchy.**]

an·ar·cho-syn·di·cal·ism (ăn-är′kō-sĭn′dĭ-kə-lĭz′əm) *n.* A revolutionary doctrine, **syndicalism** *(see).* [ANARCHO- + SYNDICALISM.]

an·ar·chy (ăn′ər-kē) *n., pl.* **-chies. 1.** Absence of any form of political authority. **2.** Political disorder and confusion. **3.** Any state of disorder or confusion, especially when caused by absence of a recognized authority or cohesive principle: *classroom anarchy.* [Greek *anarkhia*, from *anarkhos*, without a ruler : AN- + *arkhos*, ruler, -ARCH.]

an·ar·thri·a (ăn-är′thrē-ə) *n.* Loss of the ability to speak. [New Latin, from Greek *anarthros*, not articulated. See **anarthrous.**] —**an·arth·ric** (ăn-är′thrĭk) *adj.*

an·ar·throus (ăn-är′thrəs) *adj. Zoology.* Lacking joints; unjointed. [Greek *anarthros*, not articulated : AN- (without) + *arthron*, joint, article.]

an·a·sar·ca (ăn′ə-sär′kə) *n.* A general accumulation of serum in the subcutaneous connective tissue, resulting in swelling of the trunk and legs. [New Latin, from Greek *ana sarka*, "throughout the body" : *ana*, throughout + *sarka*, accusative of *sarx*, flesh.] —**an·a·sar·cous** (ăn′ə-sär′kəs) *adj.*

An·a·sta·si·a (ăn′ə-stā′zhə), **Grand Duchess** (1901–*c.* 1918). Youngest daughter of the last czar of Russia, Nicholas II. She is thought to have been killed with the rest of her family after the Russian Revolution, but several women have since claimed to be her without conclusive proof, most notably (from 1920) a woman known as Anna Anderson.

an·as·tig·mat (ăn-ăs′tĭg-măt′) *n.* A compound lens corrected for astigmatism and for at least one off-axis zone in the image plane. [AN- (not) + ASTIGMAT(IC).]

an·as·tig·mat·ic (ăn-ăs′tĭg-măt′ĭk) *adj.* **1.** Not astigmatic. Said of a lens that forms an accurate point image of a point object. **2.** Of or designating a compound lens in which the separate components compensate for the astigmatism of each. [AN- + ASTIGMATIC.]

a·nas·to·mose (ə-năs′tə-mōz′, -mōs′) *v.* **-mosed, -mosing, -moses.** —*tr.* To join by anastomosis. —*intr.* To become connected by anastomosis. [Back-formation from ANASTOMOSIS.]

a·nas·to·mo·sis (ə-năs′tə-mō′sĭs) *n., pl.* **-ses** (-sēz′). **1.** The union or connection of branches, as of rivers, veins of leaves, or blood vessels. **2.** A surgical connection of separate or severed hollow organs to form a continuous channel. [New Latin, from Greek *anastomōsis*, an outlet, opening, from *anastomoun*, to furnish with a mouth : *ana*-, up + *stoma*, a mouth, opening.] —**a·nas·to·mot·ic** (ə-năs′tə-mŏt′ĭk) *adj.*

a·nas·tro·phe (ə-năs′trə-fē) *n.* Inversion, as for rhetorical effect, of the normal syntactic order of words; for example, *to market went she.* [Greek *anastrophē*, a turning upside down, from *anastrephein*, to turn upside down : *ana*-, back + *strephein*, to turn.]

anat. anatomical; anatomy.

an·a·tase (ăn′ə-tās′, -tāz′) *n.* A rare blue or light-yellow to black mineral consisting of titanium dioxide in tetragonal form. Formerly called "octahedrite." [French, from Greek *anatasis*, extension (from its long crystals), from *anateinein*, to extend, stretch up : *ana*-, up + *teinein*, to stretch.]

a·nath·e·ma (ə-năth′ə-mə) *n., pl.* **-mas. 1.** Someone or something cursed, reviled, shunned, or detested: *Fascism was anathema to her.* **2.** A formal ecclesiastical pronouncement of damnation; a denunciation or excommunication. **3.** Any vehement denunciation; an imprecation; a curse. [Late Latin, a curse, a person cursed, an offering, from Greek *anathēma*, votive offering, from *anatithenai*, to dedicate : *ana*-, up + *tithenai*, to put.]

a·nath·e·ma·tize (ə-năth′ə-mə-tīz′) *tr.v.* **-tized, -tizing, -tizes.** To proclaim an anathema on; denounce or curse. —**a·nath·e·ma·ti·za·tion** (ə-năth′ə-mə-tĭ-zā′shən) *n.*

An·a·to·li·a (ăn′ə-tō′lē-ə). Also **A·sia Mi·nor** (ā′zhə mī′nər, ā′shə). The Asian part of Turkey. In ancient times it was the great meeting place of Oriental and Occidental commerce. The region was slowly conquered by the Ottoman Turks in the 14th and 15th centuries and remained part of the Ottoman Empire until the republic of Turkey was established.

An·a·to·li·an (ăn′ə-tō′lē-ən, -tōl′yən) *n.* **1.** A native or inhabitant of Anatolia. **2.** Any of a family of extinct Indo-European languages of ancient Anatolia. —**An·a·to·li·an** *adj.*

an·a·tom·i·cal (ăn′ə-tŏm′ĭ-kəl) *adj.* Also **an·a·tom·ic** (-tŏm′ĭk). *Abbr.* **anat.** **1.** Of or pertaining to anatomy. **2.** Of or pertaining to dissection. **3.** Structural as opposed to functional. —**an·a·tom·i·cal·ly** *adv.*

a·nat·o·mist (ə-năt′ə-mĭst) *n.* An expert in or student of anatomy.

a·nat·o·mize (ə-năt′ə-mīz′) *tr.v.* **-mized, -mizing, -mizes. 1.** To dissect. **2.** To analyze in minute detail. —**a·nat·o·mi·za·tion** (ə-năt′ə-mī-zā′shən) *n.*

a·nat·o·my (ə-năt′ə-mē) *n., pl.* **-mies.** *Abbr.* **anat. 1.** The structure of a plant or animal, or of any of its parts. **2.** The science of the shape and structure of organisms and their parts. **3.** A treatise on this science. **4.** The dissection of a plant or animal to disclose the various parts, their positions, structure, and interrelation. **5.** Any detailed examination or analysis: *The psychologist wrote a book entitled "The Anatomy of Depression."* **6.** The human body. [Middle English *anatomie*, from Old French, from Late Latin *anatomia*, from Greek *anatomē*, dissection, from *anatemnein*, to dissect : *ana*-, up + *temnein*, to cut.]

a·nat·ro·pous (ə-năt′rə-pəs) *adj. Botany.* Inverted so that the micropyle is next to the hilum, and the embryonic root is at the other end. Said of an ovule. [ANA- + -TROPOUS.]

anatto. Variant of **annatto.**

An·ax·ag·o·ras (ăn′ăk-săg′ə-rəs) (*c.* 500–428 B.C.). Greek philosopher. Born in Clazomenae, Asia Minor (now in Turkey), he moved to Athens, where he gained the friendship of Pericles. He taught that the universe was composed of an infinite number of elements and gave the true explanation of solar eclipses.

A·nax·i·man·der (ə-năk′sə-măn′dər) (*c.*611–*c.*547 B.C.). Greek philosopher and astronomer from Miletus, Asia Minor (now in Turkey). One of the earliest thinkers to speculate on the origin of the universe, he held that it arose out of the separation of opposite qualities from one primordial substance and that animal life had evolved from the sea.

An·ax·im·e·nes (ăn′ăk-sĭm′ə-nēz′) (*c.* 570–*c.* 500 B.C.). Greek philosopher from Miletus, Asia Minor (now in Turkey). He held that the fundamental matter of the universe was air or vapor and that all other substances were derived from it by condensation, compression, or rarefaction.

an·bur·y (ăn′bĕr′ē) *n.* **1.** A soft tumor afflicting horses and oxen. **2.** A disease of root crops, such as turnips, in which the roots are swollen or distorted. [16th century : perhaps from *ang*-, "painful" (as in Old English *angnægl*, AGNAIL) + *-bury*, BERRY (referring to the reddish tumor).]

anc. ancient.

-ance, -ancy *suffix.* Indicates an action, quality, or condition; for example, **riddance, compliancy.** [Middle English *-ance, -aunce*, from Old French *-ance*, from Latin *-antia*, abstract noun suffix of *-ant-*, stem of *-āns*, present participle ending, -ANT.]

an·ces·tor (ăn′sĕs′tər) *n.* **1.** Any person from whom one is descended, especially if more remote than a grandparent; a forebear. **2.** An early or original type of a later person or thing; a precursor: *The clavichord is one of the ancestors of the modern piano.* **3.** *Biology.* The actual or hypothetical organism or stock from which later kinds have evolved. [Middle English *ancestre, ancessour*, from Old French *ancestre, ancessor*, from Latin *antecessor*, "one that goes before," from *antecessus*, past participle of *antecēdere*, to go before : ANTE- + *cēdere*, to go.]

an·ces·tral (ăn-sĕs′trəl) *adj.* Of, pertaining to, evolved from, or inherited from an ancestor or ancestors: *The family lived on the ancestral farm.* —**an·ces·tral·ly** *adv.*

an·ces·tress (ăn′sĕs′trĭs) *n.* A female ancestor.

an·ces·try (ăn′sĕs′trē) *n., pl.* **-tries. 1.** Ancestral descent or lineage. **2.** Ancestors collectively. [Middle English *ancestrie*, from Old French *ancesserie*, from *ancessour*, ANCESTOR.]

An·chi·ses (ăng-kī′sēz′, ăn-). *Greek and Roman Mythology.* The father of Aeneas, rescued by his son from the ruins of Troy.

an·chor (ăng′kər) *n.* **1.** A heavy, usually metal, object attached to a vessel by a cable and cast overboard to keep the vessel in place, usually by flukes that grip the bottom. **2.** Something used to keep an object firmly in position. **3.** Someone or something providing security or stability. **4.** *Radio & Television.* An anchorperson. —*adj.* anchor. Anchored.
~*v.* anchored, -choring, -chors. —*tr.* **1.** To hold fast by or as if by an anchor. **2.** To act as the anchorperson of (a news broadcast, for example). —*intr.* To drop anchor or lie at anchor. Used of a ship. [Middle English *anker*, Old English *ancer, ancor*, from Latin *anc(h)ora*, from Greek *ankura*.]

an·chor·age (ăng′kər-ĭj) *n.* **1.** A place for anchoring. **2.** A fee charged for the privilege of anchoring. **3. a.** The act of anchoring. **b.** The condition of being at anchor. **4.** Something that provides stability or support.

An·chor·age (ăng′kər-ĭj). Chief port and largest city of Alaska. It is situated on Cook Inlet in the southern part of the state, and was founded in 1915 as the headquarters for the building of the Alaska Railway.

an·cho·ress (ăng′kər-ĭs) *n.* A female anchorite.

an·cho·rite (ăng′kə-rīt′) *n.* Also **an·cho·ret** (-rĕt). A person who has retired into seclusion, usually for religious reasons; a hermit; a recluse. [Middle English, from Medieval Latin *anchorīta*, variant of Late Latin *anchorēta*, from Late Greek *anakhōrētēs*, "one who withdraws (from the world)," from *anakhōrein*, to withdraw : Greek *ana-*, back + *khōrein,* to make room.] **—an·cho·rit·ic** (ăng′kə-rĭt′-ĭk) *adj.*

an·chor·man (ăng′kər-măn′) *n., pl.* **-men** (-mĕn′). **1.** One who plays a crucial part in providing strength, stability, or cohesion. **2.** The runner, usually the strongest in a team, who performs the last stage of a relay race. **3.** The presenter or coordinator of a broadcast involving several different contributors or correspondents.

an·chor·per·son (ăng′kər-pûr′sən) *n.* An anchorman or anchorwoman.

anchor ring *n. Mathematics.* A torus *(see).*

an·chor·wom·an (ăng′kər-wŏŏm′ən) *n., pl.* **-women** (-wĭm′ĭn). A woman who presents or coordinates a broadcast involving several different contributors or correspondents.

an·cho·vy (ăn′chō′vē, ăn-chō′vē) *n., pl.* **-vies** or collectively **anchovy.** Any of various small, herringlike marine fishes of the family Engraulidae. Several species, especially *Engraulis encrasicholus,* are widely used as food fish. [Spanish *anchova, anchoa,* perhaps from Basque *anchu.*]

anchovy pear *n.* **1.** A tropical American tree, *Grias cauliflora,* that bears edible fruit similar in taste to the mango. **2.** The fruit of the anchovy pear. [The fruit is so called after its use, like anchovies, as a first course or hors d'oeuvre.]

an·chu·sa (ăng-kyŏŏ′sə-, -zə) *n.* Any plant of the genus *Anchusa.* See **bugloss.** [New Latin *Anchusa,* from Latin *anchūsa,* a plant used as a cosmetic, from Greek *ankhousa†,* alkanet.]

anchylose. Variant of **ankylose.**

an·cien ré·gime (äN-syăN′ rā-zhēm′) *n.* **1.** The political and social system existing in France before the Revolution of 1789. **2.** Any system or regime that has been superseded. [French, "old regime."]

an·cient¹ (ān′shənt) *adj. Abbr.* **anc. 1.** Having lived or existed for a long time; very old. **2.** Of, existing in, or occurring in times long past; especially, belonging to the historical period prior to the fall of the Western Roman Empire (A.D. 476). —See Synonyms at **old.** ~*n.* **1.** A person who lived in ancient times, especially one belonging to any of the classical civilizations of antiquity. **2. ancients.** The ancient Greek and Roman authors. **3.** A very old person. [Middle English *ancien,* from Old French, from Vulgar Latin *anteānus* (unattested), "going before," from Latin *ante,* before.] **—an·cient·ness** *n.*

an·cient² *n. Obsolete.* **1.** An ensign; a flag. **2.** A flag-bearer or lieutenant. [Variant of ENSIGN.]

Ancient Greek *n.* The Greek language of historical antiquity, from its first documentation in the 14th century B.C. until the time of the late Roman Empire, divided into two principal dialect areas, **East Greek** and **West Greek** (*both of which see*).

ancient history *n.* **1.** The history of ancient times. **2.** *Informal.* Common knowledge, especially of a recent event that has lost its original impact or importance.

ancient light *n.* A window whose light has long been enjoyed and according to common law may not be obstructed by an adjacent owner.

an·cient·ly (ān′shənt-lē) *adv.* In ancient times.

an·cil·lar·y (ăn′sə-lĕr′ē) *adj.* **1.** Of secondary importance; subordinate: *"For Degas, sculpture was never more than ancillary to his painting"* (Herbert Read). **2.** Helping; auxiliary: *She was a member of the ancillary staff in the hospital.* ~*n., pl.* **ancillaries.** One who works in a subordinate or auxiliary capacity. [Latin *ancillāris,* servile, from *ancilla,* maidservant, feminine diminutive of *anculus,* servant.]

an·cip·i·tal (ăn-sĭp′ə-təl) *adj.* Flattened and two-edged, as certain plant stems are. [From Latin *anceps* (stem *ancipit-*), two-headed : AMBI- + *caput,* head.]

an·con (ăng′kŏn′) *n., pl.* **ancones** (ăng-kō′nēz). A projecting bracket used in classical architecture to carry the upper elements of a cornice; a console. [Latin *ancōn,* from Greek *ankōn,* elbow, bend of the arm.] **—an·co·nal** (ăng-kō′nəl) *adj.*

An·co·na (ăng-kō′nə). Adriatic port and capital of the province of the same name in central Italy.

-ancy. Variant of **-ance.**

an·cy·lo·sto·mi·a·sis (ăn′sə-lō-stō-mī′ə-sĭs, ăng′kə-lō-) *n.* A disease caused by hookworm infestation of the intestine and marked by progressive anemia. Also called "hookworm disease." [New Latin : *Ancylostoma,* hookworm (genus), "hook-mouth" : Greek *ankulos,* crooked + *stoma,* mouth + -IASIS.]

Ancyra. See **Ankara.**

and (ənd, an; *stressed* ănd) *conj.* **1.** Together with or along with; also; in addition; as well as. Used to connect words, phrases, or clauses, especially those having the same grammatical function: *trials and tribulations; a long and happy life.* **2. a.** Added to; plus: *Two and two make four.* **b.** Prepared, served, eaten, or drunk with as a unit: *bread and butter; gin and tonic.* **3.** As a result. Used to express an actual or likely consequence: *She felt tired and went to bed. One more remark like that and I'll knock your block off.* **4.** Next in time; then: *paid the bill and left.* **5.** *Informal.* Used instead of *to* after verbs such as *go, come,* or *try: try and find it; come and see.* **6.** Used, especially in news broadcasting, to initiate discussion of an announced topic: *The Middle East—and Egypt has announced . . .* **7.** Used as a connection between identical words to express repetition, continuation, or progression: *rolled over and over; waited and waited; getting hotter and hotter.* **8.** Used to express a contrast in quality between things of the same basic type: *There are cameras and cameras.* **9.** Used, especially after *good* and *nice,* to give adverbial force to the words preceding it: *nice and warm.* **10.** Used to

introduce a comment or parenthetic remark: *Here's our meal—and not a minute too early! After that—and this is the funny part — he fell into the pool.* **11.** *Archaic.* If: *and it please you.* [Middle English *and,* Old English *and, ond.*]

Usage: Although frowned upon by some, the use of *and* to begin a sentence has a long and respectable history: *"And it came to pass in those days"* (Luke 2:1).

AND (ănd) *n. Computer Science.* A logic operator equivalent to the sentential connective "and." [From AND.]

An·da·lu·sia (ăn′də-lōō′zhə). *Spanish* **An·da·lu·cí·a** (än′dä-lōō-thē′ə). The largest region in Spain, covering much of the south of the country. It was the last part of Spain to be reconquered from the Moors in the 15th century and contains some magnificent Moorish architecture, including the historic towns of Seville, Granada, and Córdoba. **—An·da·lu·sian** *n. & adj.*

an·da·lu·site (ăn′də-lōō′sīt′) *n.* A mineral consisting of aluminum silicate, Al_2SiO_5, usually found in prisms of various colors. [French *andalousite,* discovered in ANDALUSIA.]

An·da·man and Nic·o·bar Islands (ăn′də-mən; nĭk′ə-bär′). Indian possessions in the Bay of Bengal. The Andamans comprise more than 200 small islands, the Nicobars 19. Port Blair on South Andaman Island is the capital.

An·da·man·ese (ăn′də-mə-nēz′, -nēs′) *n., pl.* **Andamanese. 1.** A member of a Negrito people native to the Andaman Islands. **2.** The agglutinative language of this people, not known to be connected with any other language family. **—An·da·man·ese** *adj.*

an·dan·te (än-dän′tā, ăn-dăn′tē) *adv. Music.* In a moderate tempo; faster than adagio, but slower than allegretto. Used as a direction: *performed andante.* ~*n. Music.* A movement or passage in a moderate tempo. [Italian, "walking," present participle of *andare,* to walk, from Vulgar Latin *ambitāre* (unattested), from Latin *ambulāre,* to AMBULATE.] **—an·dan·te** *adj.*

an·dan·ti·no (än′dän-tē′nō, ăn′dăn-) *adv. Music.* In a tempo slightly faster than andante. Used as a direction. ~*n., pl.* **andantinos.** *Music.* A movement or passage in this tempo. [Italian, diminutive of ANDANTE.] **—an·dan·ti·no** *adj.*

An·de·an (ăn′dē-ən, ăn-dē′ən) *adj.* Of, pertaining to, or resembling the Andes or their inhabitants.

An·der·sen (än′dər-sən), **Hans Christian** (1805–75). Danish writer, famous chiefly for his fairy tales. The son of a poor shoemaker, he made his reputation with the publication in 1835 of his first collection of fairy tales, *Eventyr* ("Tales Told for Children").

An·der·son (än′dər-sən), **Carl David** (1905–91). U.S. physicist. In 1936 he was awarded the Nobel Prize for his discovery of the positively charged particle, the positron (1932).

Anderson, Marian (1902–). U.S. contralto singer. She was most famous for her interpretation of Negro spirituals and was the first black singer to perform at the Metropolitan Opera in New York, making her debut in 1955.

Anderson, Maxwell (1888–1959). U.S. playwright. Many of his dramas, including *Winterset* (1935), were written in verse. He also cowrote *What Price Glory?* (1924) and *Knickerbocker Holiday* (1938).

Anderson, Sherwood (1876–1941). U.S. author of novels and short stories. Most of his often autobiographical works detail the frustrations of life in small Midwestern towns. Anderson's best-known work is *Winesburg, Ohio* (1919), a collection of interrelated short stories and sketches.

An·des (ăn′dēz). Mountain system running along the Pacific coast of South America for 8,000 kilometers (5,000 miles), loftier than any other mountain range in the world except the Himalayas. Its maximum width is 480 kilometers (300 miles), and its highest peak, Ojos del Salado on the Chile-Argentina border (7,084 meters; 23,241 feet), is the highest mountain in the Western Hemisphere.

an·de·site (ăn′dĭ-zīt′) *n.* A fine-grained volcanic rock containing plagioclase and feldspar. [German *Andesit,* from the ANDES.]

AND gate *n. Computer Science.* A logic circuit with two or more input wires that emits a signal only if all input wires receive coincident signals. See **OR gate.** [So called because the emission of the signal is comparable to the use of the conjunction *and* in logic.]

An·dhra Pra·desh (än′drə prə-dāsh′). State in southeastern India, bordering on the Bay of Bengal. It was created in 1956 from the Telegu-speaking regions of Madras and Hyderabad. The capital is Hyderabad.

and·i·ron (ănd′ī′ərn) *n.* Either of a pair of metal supports for holding up logs in a fireplace. Also called "firedog." [Middle English *aundiren,* variant of Old French *andier,* firedog, from Gaulish *andero-* (unattested), young bull (andirons were often decorated with heads of animals at the top).]

and/or (ănd′ôr′) *conj.* Used to indicate that either *and* or *or* may be used to connect words, phrases, or clauses, depending upon what meaning is intended.

Usage: *And/or* is mainly used in legal, commercial, and technical contexts, where it is a succinct way of setting forth three distinct and exclusive possibilities: either of two things considered separately, or the two in combination (that is, one or the other or both). Thus, *an offense punishable by a fine and/or imprisonment* means "either by a fine, or by imprisonment, or both."

An·dor·ra (ăn-dôr′ə, -dōr′ə). Tiny, independent state high in the eastern Pyrenees on the Franco-Spanish border. It is an ancient coprincipality and still pays nominal dues to the president of France and the Spanish bishop of Urgel. Area, 453 square kilome-

Andes *Aerial view of the northernmost section of the mountains that stretch the length of South America. Here, in Colombia, the Andes are a cordillera—a series of parallel ranges—more than 320 kilometers (200 miles) wide and rising to more than 2,700 meters (9,000 feet).*

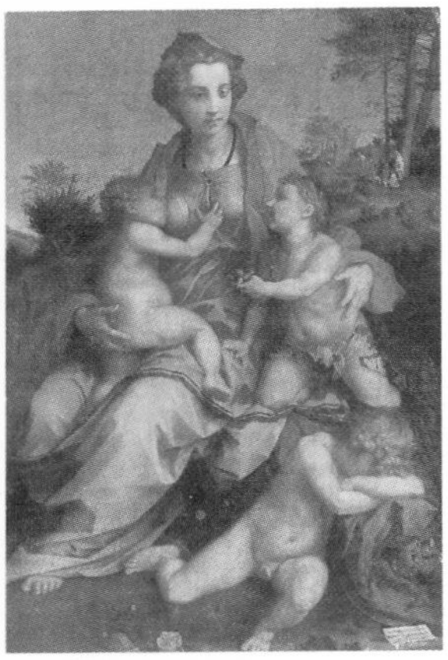

Andrea del Sarto painting *A symbolic portrait of Charity by the Florentine painter. The canvas is now in the Louvre, Paris.*

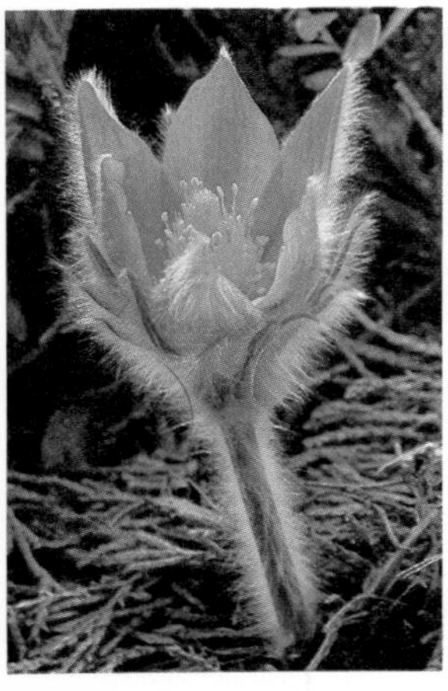

anemone *There are 150 species in the* Anemone *genus varying in color between white, yellow, purple, and red. This is* Anemone patens.

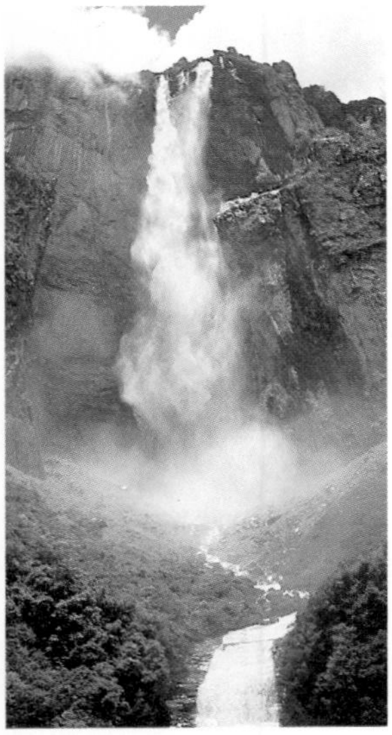

Angel Fall *The highest uninterrupted waterfall in the world lies in the Guiana Highlands of southeast Venezuela, where a river cascades over the edge of the Auyán-Tapuí plateau.*

ters (175 square miles). Population, 47,000. Capital, Andorra la Vella. See map at **France.**

an·dra·dite (ăn-drä'dīt', ăn'drə-dīt') *n.* A green to brown or black calcium-iron garnet, $Ca_3Fe_2(SiO_4)_3$, used as a gem. [After José B. de *Andrada* e Silva (1763–1838), Brazilian geologist.]

An·dre·a del Sar·to (än-drā'ä dĕl sär'tō), born Andrea d'Agnolo (1486–1530). Florentine painter. He painted chiefly religious subjects in the classical manner of Raphael and is best known for the fresco cycle of the life of John the Baptist in the Chiostro dello Scalzo, Florence.

An·drew (ăn'dro͞o'). One of the Apostles, the brother of Simon called Peter. [Middle English, from Latin *Andreas,* from Greek, probably from *andreios,* manly, from *anēr* (stem *andr-*), man.]

andro–, andr– *prefix.* Indicates: **1.** The male sex or masculine; for example, **androgen. 2.** *Botany.* Stamen or anther; for example, **androecium.** [Greek, from *anēr* (stem *andr-*), man.]

an·droe·ci·um (ăn-drē'shē-əm, -shəm) *n., pl.* **-cia** (-shē-ə, -shə). The stamens of a flower considered collectively. [New Latin : ANDR(O)- + Greek *oikion,* residence, diminutive of *oikos,* house.] **—an·droe·cial** (ăn-drē'shəl) *adj.*

an·dro·gen (ăn'drə-jən) *n.* Any of the steroid hormones that develop and maintain masculine characteristics, such as the growth of facial hair. Compare **estrogen.** [ANDRO- + -GEN.] **—an·dro·gen·ic** (ăn'drə-jĕn'ĭk) *adj.*

an·drog·y·nous (ăn-drŏj'ə-nəs) *adj.* **1.** Having both female and male characteristics. **2.** *Botany.* Composed of staminate and pistillate flowers. Said of the flower spikes of certain sedges. [Latin *androgynus,* from Greek *androgunos* : ANDRO- + -GYNOUS.] **—an·drog·y·ny** (ăn-drŏj'ə-nē) *n.*

an·droid (ăn'droid') *adj.* Possessing human features.
~n. In science fiction, a synthetic person created from biological materials, as distinguished from a robot. Also called "humanoid." [Late Greek *androeidēs,* manlike : ANDR(O)- + -OID.]

An·drom·a·che (ăn-drŏm'ə-kē). *Greek Mythology.* The faithful wife of Hector, captured by the Greeks at the fall of Troy.

An·drom·e·da[1] (ăn-drŏm'ə-də). *Greek Mythology.* The daughter of Cepheus and Cassiopeia, who married Perseus after he had rescued her from a sea monster.

Andromeda[2] *n.* A constellation in the Northern Hemisphere near Lacerta and Perseus.

An·dro·pov (ăn-drŏp'ŏf, -ŏv), **Yuri Vladimirovich** (1914–84). General secretary of the Communist Party of the U.S.S.R (1982) after the death of Leonid Brezhnev; president (1983). Andropov was Soviet ambassador to Hungary in 1956 when that country was invaded by the U.S.S.R. From 1967 until May of 1982 he was chairman of the K.G.B., the Soviet security police, leaving that post just six months before achieving the country's most important political appointment.

An·dros[1] (ăn'drəs). Largest of the Bahama Islands. Andros is in the western group of islands and is the only island in the Bahamas that is traversed by streams.

An·dros[2] (ăn'drəs, -drŏs). Greek island in the Aegean Sea. It is the northernmost of the Cyclades. Andros was colonized by Athens in the 5th century B.C. and later came under the control of Macedonia, Rome, Venice, and Turkey. In 1829 it became part of Greece.

An·dros (ăn'drəs, -drŏs), **Sir Edmund** (1637–1714). British colonial administrator. As governor of the Dominion of New England his autocratic manner and vigorous enforcement of unpopular laws angered the colonists, and in 1689 the people of Boston revolted and threw Andros into jail. He soon after returned to England.

an·dros·ter·one (ăn-drŏs'tə-rōn') *n.* A male sex hormone excreted in urine and synthetically produced from cholesterol. [ANDRO- + STER(OL) + -ONE.]

-androus *suffix. Botany.* Indicates a specified number or type of stamens; for example, **monandrous.** [New Latin *-andrus,* from Greek *-andros,* "having men," from *anēr* (stem *andr-*), man.]

-andry *suffix.* Indicates the state or custom of having a specified number of husbands; for example, **monandry.** [Greek *anēr* (stem *andr-*), man.]

-ane *suffix. Chemistry.* Indicates a saturated hydrocarbon; for example, **hexane, propane.** [Variant of -ENE, -INE, or -ONE.]

a·near (ə-nîr) *adv. Archaic.* **1.** Near. **2.** Nearly; almost.
~tr.v. **aneared, anearing, anears.** *Archaic.* To approach: *"The castle tonight . . . anears its fall"* (Elizabeth Barrett Browning). **—a·near** *prep.*

an·ec·dot·age (ăn'ĭk-dō'tĭj) *n.* **1.** Anecdotes collectively. **2.** Garrulous old age or senility. Used humorously. [Sense 2 is a blend of ANECDOTE and DOTAGE.]

an·ec·dot·al (ăn'ĭk-dōt'l) *adj.* Characterized by, containing, or given to telling anecdotes.

an·ec·dote (ăn'ĭk-dōt') *n.* A short account of some interesting, biographical, or humorous incident. [French, from Greek *anekdota,* "things unpublished," from *anekdotos,* unpublished : AN- (not) + *ekdotos,* given out, from *ekdidonai,* to give out : *ek-,* out + *didonai,* to give.] **—an·ec·dot·ist** (ăn'ĭk-dō'tĭst), **an·ec·dot·al·ist** (ăn'ĭk-dōt'l-ĭst) *n.*

an·ec·dot·ic (ăn'ĭk-dŏt'ĭk) *adj.* Also **an·ec·dot·i·cal** (-ĭ-kəl). **1.** Anecdotal. **2.** Full of or given to telling anecdotes.

an·e·cho·ic (ăn'ĕ-kō'ĭk) *adj.* Neither having nor producing echoes: *an anechoic chamber.* [AN- (not) + ECHOIC.]

a·ne·mi·a, a·nae·mi·a (ə-nē'mē-ə) *n.* A pathological deficiency in the oxygen-carrying material of the blood, measured in unit volume concentrations of hemoglobin, red blood cell volume, and red blood cell number.

a·ne·mic, a·nae·mic (ə-nē'mĭk) *adj.* **1.** Of, relating to, or suffering from anemia. **2.** Listless and weak; pallid. **3.** Lacking in vigor.

anemo– *prefix.* Indicates wind; for example, **anemology.** [Greek *anemos,* wind.]

a·nem·o·chore (ə-nĕm'ə-kôr', -kōr') *n.* A plant, such as the dandelion, having seeds, spores, or similar reproductive parts that are dispersed by the wind. [ANEMO- + -CHORE.]

a·nem·o·graph (ə-nĕm'ə-grăf', -gräf') *n.* A recording anemometer. [ANEMO- + -GRAPH.] **—a·nem·o·graph·ic** *adj.*

an·e·mog·ra·phy (ăn'ə-mŏg'rə-fē) *n.* The science of recording wind direction and force. [ANEMO- + -GRAPHY.]

an·e·mol·o·gy (ăn'ə-mŏl'ə-jē) *n.* The scientific study of winds. [ANEMO- + -LOGY.]

an·e·mom·e·ter (ăn'ə-mŏm'ə-tər) *n.* An instrument for measuring and indicating wind force and speed. [ANEMO- + -METER.] **—an·e·mo·met·ric** (ăn'ə-mə-mĕt'rik), **an·e·mo·met·ri·cal** *adj.*

an·e·mom·e·try (ăn'ə-mŏm'ə-trē) *n.* The determination of wind force and velocity. [ANEMO- + -METRY.]

a·nem·o·ne (ə-nĕm'ə-nē) *n.* **1.** Any of various plants of the genus *Anemone,* of the North Temperate Zone, having white, yellow, purple, or red cup-shaped flowers. Some species are also called "windflower." See **pasqueflower, wood anemone. 2.** A marine invertebrate, the **sea anemone** *(see).* [Latin *anemōnē,* from Greek, perhaps from Semitic.]

anemone fish *n.* Any of various small, brightly colored marine fishes of the genus *Amphiprion,* found near sea anemones.

an·e·moph·i·lous (ăn'ə-mŏf'ə-ləs) *adj.* Pollinated by wind-dispersed pollen. [ANEMO- + -PHILOUS.] **—an·e·moph·i·ly** *n.*

an·en·ceph·al·y (ăn'ĕn-sĕf'ə-lē) *n.* Congenital absence of part or all of the brain. [AN- + *-encephaly* : ENCEPHAL(O)- + -Y (state or condition).] **—an·en·ce·phal·ic** (ăn-ĕn'sə-făl'ĭk) *adj.*

a·nent (ə-nĕnt') *prep. Archaic & Scottish.* Regarding; concerning. [Middle English *anent, onevent,* Old English *onemn, on efen,* alongside, together : ON + *efen,* EVEN.]

an·er·oid (ăn'ə-roid') *adj.* Not using fluid. [French *anéroïde* : A- (not) + Greek *nēron,* water.]

aneroid barometer *n.* A barometer in which variations of atmospheric pressure are measured by the relative bulges of a thin elastic metal disc covering a partially evacuated chamber, the movements being magnified by a train of levers to move a needle over a calibrated scale.

an·es·the·sia, an·aes·the·sia (ăn'ĭs-thē'zhə) *n.* **1.** Total or partial loss of sensation, especially tactile sensibility induced by disease or an anesthetic. **2.** Artificially induced unconsciousness or local or general insensibility to pain. [New Latin from Greek *anaisthēsia,* lack of sensation : AN- + *aisthēsis,* feeling.]

an·es·the·si·ol·o·gy, an·aes·the·si·ol·o·gy (ăn'ĭs-thē'zē-ŏl'ə-jē) *n.* The medical study and application of anesthetics.

an·es·thet·ic, an·aes·thet·ic (ăn'ĭs-thĕt'ĭk) *adj.* **1.** Relating to or resembling anesthesia. **2.** Causing anesthesia. **3.** Insensitive.
~n. An agent that causes unconsciousness or insensitivity to pain.

a·nes·the·tist, a·naes·the·tist (ə-nĕs'thĭ-tĭst) *n.* A person, usually a physician, trained to administer anesthetics.

a·nes·the·tize, a·naes·the·tize (ə-nĕs'thĭ-tīz') *tr.v.* **-tized, -tizing, tizes.** To induce anesthesia in.

an·es·trus (ăn-ĕs'trəs) *n.* An interval of sexual dormancy between two periods of estrus.

Aneto, Pico de. See **Pico de Aneto.**

an·eu·rysm, an·eu·rism (ăn'yə-rĭz'əm) *n.* A pathological blood-filled dilatation of a blood vessel. [Greek *aneurusma,* from *aneurunein,* to dilate : *ana-,* "throughout" + *eurunein,* to dilate, widen, from *eurus,* wide.] **—an·eu·rys·mal** (ăn'yə-rĭz'məl) *adj.*

a·new (ə-no͞o', ə-nyo͞o') *adv.* **1.** Again. **2.** In a new and different way, form, or manner. [Middle English *anewe, of newe,* Old English *of nīwe* : OF + *nīwe,* NEW.]

an·frac·tu·os·i·ty (ăn-frăk'cho͞o-ŏs'ə-tē) *n., pl.* **-ties. 1.** The state or quality of being anfractuous. **2.** Something anfractuous, such as a winding passage or a complicated process.

an·frac·tu·ous (ăn-frăk'cho͞o-əs) *adj.* Full of twists and turns; winding; tortuous. [French *anfractueux,* from Late Latin *anfractuōsus,* from Latin *anfractus,* a winding : *an-,* from AMBI- + *fractus,* past participle of *frangere,* to break.]

an·ga·ry (ăng'gə-rē) *n. International Law.* The right of a belligerent state to seize, use, or destroy the property of a neutral, provided that full compensation is made. [Late Latin *angaria,* enforced service to a lord, from Greek *angareia,* impressment for public service, from *angaros,* mounted courier, perhaps of Persian origin.]

an·gel (ān'jəl) *n.* **1.** *Theology.* **a.** An immortal, spiritual being attendant upon God, conventionally represented as a winged being of human form. **b.** In medieval angelology, one of nine orders of spiritual beings (listed from the highest to lowest in rank): seraphim, cherubim, thrones, dominations or dominions, virtues, powers, principalities, archangels, and angels. **2.** A guardian spirit or guiding influence. **3.** A sweet-tempered or kind person, especially a child or a woman. **4.** *Christian Science.* God's thoughts passing to man. **5.** *Informal.* A financial backer of an enterprise, especially a dramatic production. [Middle English, from Old French *angele,* from Late Latin *angelus,* from Greek *angelos* (translation of Hebrew *mal'ākh*), messenger, perhaps of Persian origin.]

An·gel Fall (ān'jəl). The highest waterfall in the world, with a drop of 980 meters (3,215 feet). Set among the dense forests of southeastern Venezuela, it was discovered in 1935 and named after James Angel, a U.S. pilot who crashed nearby in 1937.

an·gel·fish (ăn′jəl-fĭsh′) *n., pl.* **-fishes** or collectively **angelfish.** **1.** Any of several brightly colored fishes of the family Chaetodontidae, of warm seas, having laterally compressed bodies. **2.** A freshwater fish, *Pterophyllum scalare,* native to rivers of South America, having a laterally compressed, usually striped body. Also called "scalare." [After its fancied resemblance to the brilliance of an angel and, in some species, alluding to its fins as an angel's wings.]

angel food cake *n.* Also **angel cake.** A white, almond-flavored sponge cake.

an·gel·ic (ăn-jĕl′ĭk) *adj.* Also **an·gel·i·cal** (-ĭ-kəl). **1.** Of or consisting of angels: *angelic hosts.* **2.** Suggestive of or resembling an angel, as in innocence, kindness, or beauty. **—an·gel·i·cal·ly** *adv.*

an·gel·i·ca (ăn-jĕl′ĭ-kə) *n.* **1.** Any of various plants of the genus *Angelica,* having compound leaves and clusters of small white or greenish flowers; especially, *A. archangelica,* whose aromatic seeds, leaves, stems, and roots are used in medicine and as flavoring. **2.** The candied stem of this plant, used especially for decorating cakes and sweet dishes. [New Latin, from Medieval Latin *(herba) angelica,* "angelic (herb)," from Late Latin, feminine of *angelicus,* from Greek *angelikos,* from *angelos,* messenger. See **angel.**]

An·gel·i·co (ăn-jĕl′ĭ-kō), **Fra** (1387–1455). Florentine painter, famous for his frescos of religious subjects. His real name was Guido di Pietro, which he changed when he became a Dominican monk. His best-known work is the cycle of 35 paintings that decorates the sanctuary of the Church of SS. Annunziata.

an·gel·ol·o·gy (ăn′jə-lŏl′ə-jē) *n.* The branch of theology having to do with angels. [ANGEL + -LOGY.]

angel shark *n.* Any of several raylike sharks of the genus *Squatina,* having a broad, flat head and body.

An·ge·lus, an·ge·lus (ăn′jə-ləs) *n. Roman Catholic Church.* **1.** A devotional prayer at morning, noon, and night to commemorate the Annunciation. **2.** A bell rung as a summons to recite this prayer. [Medieval Latin, *"Angelus (Domini . . .),"* "The Angel (of the Lord)" (the beginning of the liturgy commemorating the Incarnation), from *angelus,* ANGEL.]

an·ger (ăng′gər) *n.* A feeling of extreme displeasure, hostility, indignation, or exasperation toward someone or something.
∼*v.* **angered, -gering, -gers.** *—tr.* To make angry; enrage. *—intr.* To become angry. [Middle English, from Old Norse *angr,* grief.]
Synonyms: *fury, indignation, ire, rage, resentment, wrath.*

an·ger·ly (ăng′gər-lē) *adv. Archaic.* In an angry manner; angrily.

An·gers (än-zhā′). Town of pre-Roman origin, the capital of Maine-et-Loire department in western France. Formerly the capital of Anjou, it boasts a rich heritage of medieval architecture.

An·ge·vin (ăn′jə-vĭn) *adj.* **1.** Of or pertaining to Anjou. **2.** Of or pertaining to the ruling house of Anjou, especially as represented by the Plantagenet kings of England, from Henry II, the son of Geoffrey, Count of Anjou, to Richard II (1154–1399). [French, from Old French, from Medieval Latin *Andegavīnus,* from *Andegavia,* ANJOU.] **—An·ge·vin** *n.*

an·gi·na (ăn-jī′nə) *n.* **1.** Any disease, such as croup or diphtheria, in which spasmodic and painful suffocation or spasms occur. **2.** Angina pectoris. [Latin, quinsy, from Greek *ankhonē,* a strangling.] **—an·gi·nal** *adj.*

angina pec·to·ris (pĕk′tər-ĭs) *n.* Severe paroxysmal pain in the chest characterized by feelings of suffocation and apprehension and caused by a momentary lack of adequate blood supply to the heart. [New Latin, "angina of the chest."]

angio-, angi- *prefix.* Indicates: **1.** Blood or lymph vessel; for example, **angiography. 2.** Seed vessel; for example, **angiosperm.** [Greek *angeion,* vessel, diminutive of *angos*†, vessel.]

an·gi·og·ra·phy (ăn′jē-ŏg′rə-fē) *n.* The x-ray examination of blood vessels after the injection of a radiopaque dye. **—an·gi·o·gra·phic** (ăn′jē-ə-grăf′ĭk) *adj.*

an·gi·ol·o·gy (ăn′jē-ŏl′ə-jē) *n.* The study of blood and lymph vessels.

an·gi·o·ma (ăn′jē-ō′mə) *n., pl.* **-mas** or **-mata** (-mə-tə). A tumor composed of lymph and blood vessels. [ANGIO- + -OMA.] **—an·gi·om·a·tous** (ăn′jē-ŏm′ə-təs) *adj.*

an·gi·o·sperm (ăn′jē-ə-spûrm′) *n. Botany.* Any plant of the class Angiospermae, characterized by having seeds enclosed in an ovary; a flowering plant. **—an·gi·o·sper·mous** (ăn′jē-ə-spûr′məs) *adj.*

an·gi·o·ten·sin (ăn′jē-ō-tĕn′sĭn) *n.* A protein in the blood that causes constriction of blood vessels and stimulates secretion of the hormone aldosterone from the adrenal cortex. [ANGIO- + TENS(ION) + -IN.]

Ang·kor (ăng′kôr′). Major archaeological site in northwestern Kampuchea (Cambodia), the capital of the Khmer empire from the 9th to the 15th century. The ruins include two major Hindu temple complexes, Angkor Wat (12th century) and Angkor Thom (13th century).

Angl. Anglican.

an·gle¹ (ăng′gəl) *intr.v.* **-gled, -gling, -gles. 1.** To fish with a hook and line. **2.** To try to get something by deceitful or indirect means. Used with *for*: *angle for an invitation.*
∼*n. Obsolete.* A fishhook or fishing tackle. [Middle English *anglen,* from *angel,* a fishhook, Old English *angul, ongul.*]

angle² *n.* **1.** *Geometry.* **a.** The figure formed by two lines diverging from a common point. **b.** The figure formed by two planes diverging from a common line. **c.** The rotation required to superimpose either of two such lines or planes on the other. **d.** The space between such lines or surfaces. **e.** A **solid angle** *(see).* **2.** An angular or projecting corner, as of a building. **3. a.** The place, position, or direction from which an object is presented to view. **b.** *Informal.* A particular aspect of a complex whole, viewed separately: *He deals with the advertising angle.* **c.** *Informal.* A particular viewpoint: *From his angle, it's a disaster.* **4.** *Slang.* A scheme; a devious method.
∼*v.* **angled, -gling, -gles.** *—tr.* **1.** To move or turn at an angle. **2.** To aim or hit (a ball, for example) at an angle. **3.** *Informal.* To impart a particular bias or point of view to (a story or report, for example). *—intr.* To move or proceed by angles: *The path angled through the woods.* [Middle English, from Old French, from Latin *angulus,* angle, corner.]

An·gle (ăng′gəl) *n.* A member of a Germanic people that migrated to England from southern Denmark in the 5th century A.D., founded the kingdoms of Northumbria, East Anglia, and Mercia, and together with the Jutes and Saxons formed the Anglo-Saxon peoples. [Latin *Anglī, Anglii* (plural), from Germanic; related to Old English *angul,* fishhook; perhaps alluding to the shape of the original homeland, the Angul district of Schleswig.]

angle bracket *n.* Either of the punctuation marks, < >, used to enclose written or printed material, or to indicate an integral in quantum mechanics.

angle iron *n.* A length of steel or iron having an L-shaped cross-section, used as part of a structural framework.

angle of attack *n.* **1.** The acute angle between the chord of an airfoil and a line representing the undisturbed relative airflow. **2.** Any other acute angle between two reference lines designating the cant of an airfoil relative to the oncoming air.

angle of incidence *n.* **1.** *Physics.* The angle formed by the path of a body or of radiation incident on a surface and a perpendicular to the surface at the point of impact. **2.** *Aviation.* The angle of attack.

angle of reflection *n.* The acute angle formed by the path of a reflected body or reflected radiation with a perpendicular to the surface at the point of reflection.

angle of refraction *n.* The acute angle formed by the path of refracted radiation with a perpendicular to the refracting surface at the point of refraction.

angle of repose *n.* The maximum angle to the horizontal that a pile of rocks, soil, or the like can sustain without sliding.

angle of view *n.* The angle included by two lines drawn from opposite extreme corners of an image to the center of a lens.

angle of yaw *n.* The angle between an aircraft's longitudinal axis and its line of travel, as seen from above.

angle plate *n.* **1.** A right-angled metal bracket, used on the face plate of a lathe to hold pieces being worked. **2.** A flat steel plate in the shape of a right-angled triangle, used to strengthen frameworks, connect structural members, and the like.

an·gler (ăng′glər) *n.* **1.** A fisherman who uses a hook. **2.** An anglerfish.

an·gler·fish (ăng′glər-fĭsh′) *n., pl.* **-fishes** or collectively **anglerfish.** Any of various marine fishes of the order Lophiiformes (or Pediculati), having a long dorsal fin ray that is suspended over the mouth and serves as a lure to attract prey.

An·gle·sey (ăng′gəl-sē). Island separated from the northwestern mainland of Wales by the Menai Strait. Formerly a separate county, it has been part of the new county of Gwynedd since 1974.

angle shades *n. Used with a singular verb.* A common European moth, *Phlogophora meticulosa,* that resembles a withered leaf when the wings are folded. [From the angular markings of the wings.]

an·gle·site (ăng′glə-sīt′) *n.* A lead sulphate mineral, occurring in white or tinted crystals. [After ANGLESEY, where it was first found.]

an·gle·worm (ăng′gəl-wûrm′) *n.* A worm, such as an earthworm, used as bait in fishing.

An·gli·a (ăng′glē-ə). The medieval Latin name for England. [Latin, from *Anglī,* the ANGLE(S).]

An·gli·an (ăng′glē-ən) *n.* **1.** An Angle. **2.** The Old English dialects of Northumbrian and Mercian.
∼*adj.* Of or pertaining to the Angles.

An·gli·can (ăng′glĭ-kən) *adj. Abbr.* **Angl.** Of, pertaining to, or characteristic of the Church of England or any of the churches related to it in origin and communion, such as the Protestant Episcopal Church.
∼*n.* A member of the Church of England or of any of the churches related to it. [Medieval Latin *Anglicānus,* from *Anglicus,* English, from Latin *Anglī,* ANGLE(S.)]

Anglican Communion *n.* The Church of England and those Episcopal churches, chiefly in English-speaking countries, that share with it substantially the same doctrine and are in communion with the Archbishop of Canterbury. Also called "Anglican Church."

An·gli·can·ism (ăng′glĭ-kə-nĭz′əm) *n.* The doctrine, system, and practice of the Anglicans.

An·gli·ce (ăng′glə-sē) *adv.* In the English form: *Firenze, Anglice Florence.* [Medieval Latin *Anglicē,* adverb of *Anglicus,* English, from Latin *Anglī,* the ANGLE(S).]

An·gli·cism (ăng′glə-sĭz′əm) *n. Often* **anglicism. 1.** A word, phrase, or idiom peculiar to the English language, especially as it is spoken in England. **2.** Attachment to or admiration of English customs or values.

An·gli·cize, an·gli·cize (ăng′glə-sīz′) *v.* **-cized, -cizing, -cizes.** *—tr.* To make English in form, idiom, style, or character. *—intr.* To become Anglicized. **—An·gli·ci·za·tion** (ăng′glə-sĭ-zā′shən) *n.*

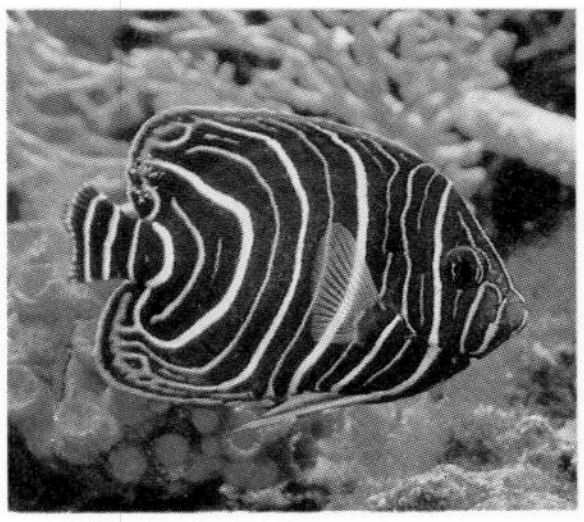

angelfish *These small, brilliantly colored fish are found mainly on coral reefs in the Indian Ocean and the Pacific.*

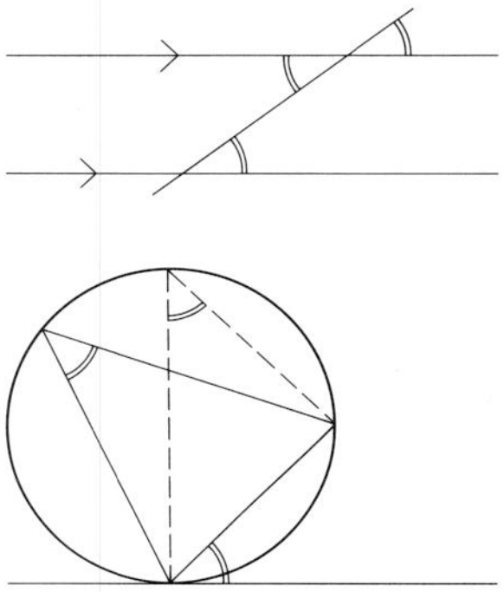

angle *Angles are formed whenever lines or planes cross each other or diverge from a common point. In each of these drawings, all the marked angles are equal.*

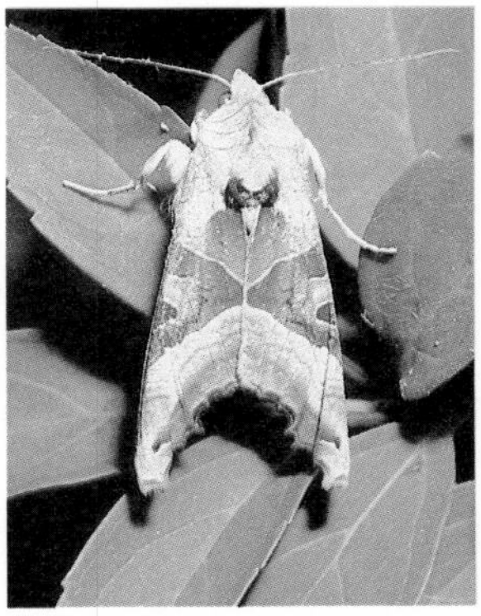

angle shades moth *When this common moth folds its wings, it resembles a withered leaf.*

an·gling (ăng′glĭng) *n.* The act, process, or art of fishing with a hook and line and usually a rod.

An·glo (ăng′glō) *n., pl.* **-glos.** *Informal.* An Anglo-American, especially a white resident of the United States who is not of Latin descent. [Short for ANGLO-AMERICAN.] **—An·glo** *adj.*

Anglo– *prefix.* Indicates: **1.** English or England; for example, **Anglophile. 2.** Involving the English or British and; for example, *Anglo-Israeli relations.* [New Latin, from Medieval Latin *Anglī,* the English people, from Latin, the ANGLE(s).]

An·glo·A·mer·i·can (ăng′glō-ə-mĕr′ə-kən) *n.* An American, especially a resident of the United States, whose language, ancestry, and culture are English. **—An·glo·A·mer·i·can** *adj.*

An·glo·Cath·o·lic (ăng′glō-kăth′lĭk, -kăth′ə-lĭk) *n.* A member of the Anglican Communion who inclines toward the Roman Catholic Church in matters of ritual and worship. **—An·glo·Cath·o·lic** *adj.* **—An·glo·Ca·thol·i·cism** (ăn′glō-kə-thŏl′ə-sĭz′əm) *n.*

An·glo·French (ăng′glō-frĕnch′) *n. Abbr.* **AF, A.F.** Norman French *(see).* Also called "Anglo-Norman." **—An·glo·French** *adj.*

An·glo·In·di·an (ăng′glō-ĭn′dē-ən) *n.* **1.** A person of British and Indian descent. **2.** A person of British origin living in India during British rule. **3.** The dialect of English used in India. **—An·glo·In·di·an** *adj.*

An·glo·I·rish (ăng′glō-ī′rĭsh) *pl.n.* Inhabitants of Ireland of English origin. Preceded by *the.* **—An·glo·Ir·ish** *adj.*

An·glo·Nor·man (ăng′glō-nôr′mən) *n.* **1.** Any of the Norman people who settled in England after 1066, or a descendant of these settlers. **2.** *Abbr.* **AN, A.N.** The Norman-French language spoken by these people. **—An·glo·Nor·man** *adj.*

An·glo·phile (ăng′glə-fīl′) *n.* An admirer of England and English customs or manners. **—An·glo·phile** *adj.* **—An·glo·phil·i·a** (ăng′glə-fīl′ē-ə) *n.*

An·glo·phobe (ăng′glə-fōb′) *n.* One who has an aversion to England and English customs or manners. **—An·glo·phobe** *adj.* **—An·glo·pho·bi·a** (ăng′glə-fō′bē-ə) *n.*

An·glo·phone (ăng′glə-fōn′) *adj.* **1.** Of, pertaining to, or being an English-speaking individual, especially in a country where two or more languages are spoken. Compare **Francophone. —An·glo·phone** *n.*

An·glo·Sax·on (ăng′glō-săk′sən) *n. Abbr.* **AS, A.S., AS. 1.** A member of one of the Germanic peoples (Angles, Saxons, and Jutes) who settled in Britain in the 5th and 6th centuries A.D. **2.** Any of the descendants of these peoples who were dominant in England until the Norman Conquest of 1066. **3. a. Old English** *(see).* **b.** Plain, unadorned English. **4.** Any person of English ancestry. **—An·glo·Sax·on** *adj.*

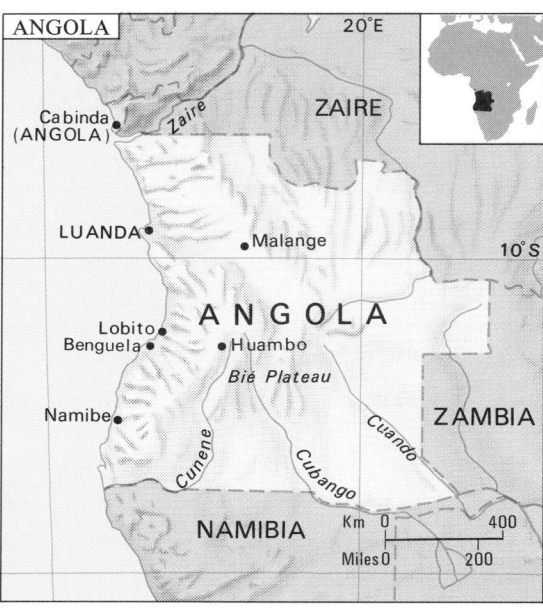

An·go·la (ăng-gō′lə). Country in southwest Africa. formerly **Portuguese West Africa,** it gained its independence in 1975 after a long guerrilla war. A civil war then ensued between the three former independence groups: the National Front for the Liberation of Angola (FNLA), the National Union for the Total Independence of Angola (UNITA), and the People's Movement for the Liberation of Angola (MPLA). The Cuban-backed MPLA eventually gained control over most of the country. The country has great hydroelectric potential and considerable mineral resources. Coffee, oil, diamonds, and iron ore are the chief exports. Area, 1,246,700 square kilometers (481,226 square miles). Population, 10,000,000. Capital, Luanda. **—An·go·lan** *n. & adj.*

An·go·ra¹ (ăng-gôr′ə, -gōr′ə) *n.* **1.** *Often* **angora. a.** The hair of the Angora goat. **b.** The fine, light hair of the Angora rabbit, some-

times blended with wool in fabrics. **c.** A yarn or fabric made from either of these fibers. **2.** An Angora cat. **3.** An Angora goat. **4.** An Angora rabbit. [From ANGORA (Ankara), name given first to the goat and its wool.]

Angora². See Ankara.

Angora cat *n.* A long-haired domestic cat similar to the Persian cat.

Angora goat *n.* Any of a breed of domestic goats having long, silky hair.

Angora rabbit *n.* Any of a breed of domestic rabbits having long, soft, usually white hair.

an·gos·tu·ra bark (ăng′gə-stŏŏr′ə, -styŏŏr′ə) *n.* The bitter, aromatic bark of either of two Brazilian trees, *Galipea officinalis* or *Cusparia trifoliata,* used as a tonic. [From *Angostura,* former name of Ciudad Bolívar.]

Angostura bitters *pl.n.* A trademark for a tonic used to flavor alcoholic drinks. [After ANGOSTURA BARK.]

an·gry (ăng′grē) *adj.* **-grier, -griest. 1.** Feeling or showing anger; incensed or enraged. **2.** Indicative of or resulting from anger: *an angry silence.* **3.** Having a menacing aspect; seeming to threaten: *angry clouds.* **4.** Inflamed: *an angry sore.* [Middle English, from ANGER.] **—an·gri·ly** (ăng′grə-lē) *adv.* **—an·gri·ness** *n.*

angry young man *n.* **1.** Any of a group of British writers of the 1950's whose works are characterized by vigorous social protest. **2.** Any young man with strongly felt radical or anti-Establishment views. [Perhaps from *Angry Young Man* (1951), an autobiography by L. A. Paul (1901–), British journalist.]

angst (ängkst) *n.* A feeling of anxiety. [German *Angst,* from Middle High German *angest,* from Old High German *angust.*]

ang·strom, Ång·ström (ăng′strəm) *n. Symbol* **Å** A unit of length that is equal to one hundred-millionth (10⁻⁸) of a centimeter, used especially to specify radiation wavelengths. Also called "angstrom unit." [After Anders Jonas ÅNGSTRÖM.]

Ång·ström (ăng′strəm, ông′-), **Anders Jonas** (1814–74). Swedish physicist. He was a founder of the science of spectroscopy, and the angstrom unit of measurement is named after him. He laid the foundations of modern spectral analysis and discovered by investigating the solar spectrum that there is hydrogen in the sun's atmosphere.

An·guil·la (ăng-gwĭl′ə, ăn-). One of the Leeward Islands in the Caribbean Sea, discovered by Columbus in 1493. A British colony ruled from St. Kitts since the 17th century, it was linked with St. Kitts-Nevis as a British associated state in 1962. The Anguillans sought independence from Britain and St. Kitts in 1967 and again in 1969, when British troops and London police quelled their revolt. The island finally became a separate self-governing dependency in 1980. **—An·guil·lan** *adj. & n.*

an·guil·li·form (ăng-gwĭl′ə-fôrm′) *adj.* Having the elongated shape of an eel. [New Latin *anguilla,* from Latin, eel, diminutive of *anguis,* snake + -FORM.]

an·guine (ăng′gwĭn) *adj.* Of, pertaining to, or resembling a snake; snakelike. [Latin *anguīnus,* from *anguis,* snake.]

an·guish (ăng′gwĭsh) *n.* Extreme pain, especially mental pain; torment; torture. **~v. anguished, -guishing, -guishes. —tr.** To cause to suffer or feel anguish. **—intr.** To suffer or feel anguish. [Middle English *anguisshe,* from Old French *anguisse,* from Latin *angustia,* straightness, narrowness, from *angustus,* narrow.]

an·guished (ăng′gwĭsht) *adj.* Filled with or expressing anguish: *an anguished cry.*

an·gu·lar (ăng′gyə-lər) *adj.* **1.** Having, forming, or consisting of an angle or angles. **2.** Measured by an angle or degrees of an arc. **3.** Bony and lean; gaunt. **4.** Lacking grace or smoothness in movement or manner; awkward: *an angular gait.* [Latin *angulāris* : *angulus,* ANGLE + -*āris,* -AR.] **—an·gu·lar·ly** *adv.* **—an·gu·lar·ness** *n.*

angular acceleration *n. Physics.* The rate of change of angular velocity with respect to time.

an·gu·lar·i·ty (ăng′gyə-lăr′ə-tē) *n., pl.* **-ties. 1.** The state or quality of being angular. **2. angularities.** Angular forms, outlines, or corners.

angular momentum *n. Physics.* **1.** The vector product of the position vector and linear momentum of a particle in motion relative to an axis. **2.** The sum of such products, one for each component particle of an extended body, expressible as the product of the angular velocity and the moment of inertia of the body. Also called "moment of momentum."

angular velocity *n. Physics.* A vector quantity describing rotational motion, the magnitude of which is the time rate of change of angle, and the direction of which is along the axis of rotation.

an·gu·late (ăng′gyə-lĭt, -lāt′) *adj.* Also **an·gu·lat·ed** (-lā′tĭd). Having angles or an angular shape. **~v.** (-lāt′) **angulated, -lating, -lates. —tr.** To cause to become angular. **—intr.** To become angular. [Latin *angulātus,* past participle of *angulāre,* to make angular, from *angulus,* ANGLE.] **—an·gu·late·ly** *adv.*

an·gu·la·tion (ăng′gyə-lā′shən) *n.* **1.** The formation of angles. **2.** An angular part, position, or formation. **3.** The measurement of angles.

an·hin·ga (ăn-hĭng′gə) *n.* A bird, the **water turkey** *(see).* [Portuguese, from Tupi.]

an·hy·dride (ăn-hī′drīd) *n.* **1.** A chemical compound formed from another by the removal of water. **2.** A compound that forms an acid or a base when water is added to it. **3.** An organic compound containing two carboxyl groups from which a single water molecule has been removed, leaving the group -CO·O·CO-. [ANHYDR(OUS) + -IDE.]

an·hy·drite (ăn-hī′drīt′) n. A white to grayish or reddish mineral of anhydrous calcium sulfate, CaSO₄, occurring as layers in gypsum deposits. [ANHYDR(OUS) + -ITE.]

an·hy·drous (ăn-hī′drəs) adj. Without water, especially water of crystallization. [Greek anudros, waterless : an-, without + hudōr, water.]

an·i·con·ic (ăn′ī-kŏn′ĭk) adj. Not in human or animal form. Said of mythical symbols, portrayals of gods, or the like. [AN- (not) + ICONIC.]

an·il (ăn′ĭl) n. 1. The indigo plant. 2. The blue dye obtained from the indigo plant. [French, from Portuguese, from Arabic an-nīl, the indigo plant, from Persian nīl, indigo.]

an·ile (ăn′īl, ā′nīl′) adj. Feeble and frail like an old woman. [Latin anīlis, from anus, old woman.] —a·nil·i·ty (ă-nĭl′ə-tē) n.

an·i·line, an·i·lin (ăn′ə-lĭn) n. A colorless, oily, poisonous benzene derivative, C₆H₅NH₂, used in the manufacture of rubber, dyes, resins, pharmaceuticals, and varnishes. ~adj. Derived from aniline. [German Anilin : ANIL + -INE.]

aniline dye n. Any of numerous synthetic dyes, originally those derived from aniline.

an·i·ma (ăn′ə-mə) n. 1. The soul. 2. In the psychology of Carl Jung: **a.** The soul, or true inner self. Compare **persona**. **b.** The feminine inner personality, as present in the unconscious of the male. Compare **animus**. [Latin, feminine of animus, mind, ANIMUS.]

an·i·mad·ver·sion (ăn′ə-măd-vûr′zhən, -shən) n. 1. Hostile criticism. 2. A considered and usually censorious or critical remark. Used with on or upon. [Latin animadversiō, from animadvertere, to ANIMADVERT.]

an·i·mad·vert (ăn′ə-măd-vûrt′) intr.v. -verted, -verting, -verts. To remark or comment critically, usually with strong disapproval or censure. Used with on or upon. [Latin animadvertere, to direct the mind to, censure : animus, mind + advertere, to turn toward : ad-, to + vertere, to turn.]

an·i·mal (ăn′ə-məl) n. 1. Any organism of the kingdom Animalia, distinguished from plants by certain typical characteristics, such as the power of locomotion, fixed structure and limited growth, nonrigid cell walls, specialized sense organs and rapid response to stimuli, and nonphotosynthetic metabolism. 2. Any such organism other than a human being; especially, a mammal. 3. A person of inhuman character or behavior; someone who is bestial or brutish. 4. A person considered in terms of a characteristic quality or interest: *Her husband is the complete domestic animal.* 5. Animality: *Drinking releases the animal in him.* ~adj. 1. Of, pertaining to, or characteristic of animals. 2. Produced by or derived from animals: *animal fat.* 3. Pertaining to the sensual or physical as distinct from the spiritual nature of human beings. [Latin, an animal, from animālis, living, from anima, feminine of animus, breath, soul.]

animal cracker n. A small cookie baked in the shape of an animal.

an·i·mal·cule (ăn′ə-măl′kyōōl) n. Also **an·i·mal·cu·lum** (-kyə-ləm) pl. **-cula** (-kyə-lə). 1. A microscopic or minute organism usually regarded as an animal, as an amoeba or paramecium. 2. Archaic. A tiny animal, such as a mosquito. [New Latin animalculum, diminutive of ANIMAL.] —an·i·mal·cu·lar (ăn′ə-măl′kyə-lər) adj.

animal heat n. The heat generated in an animal's body.

animal husbandry n. The care and breeding of domestic animals such as cattle, pigs, sheep, and horses.

an·i·mal·ism (ăn′ə-mə-lĭz′əm) n. 1. A state of sound health resulting from the full satisfaction of physical drives. 2. A state of brutish indifference to all but the physical appetites. 3. The doctrine that human beings are purely animal with no spiritual nature. —an·i·mal·ist n. —an·i·mal·is·tic (ăn′ə-mə-lĭs′tĭk) adj.

an·i·mal·i·ty (ăn′ə-măl′ə-tē) n. 1. The characteristics or nature of an animal. 2. Animals collectively; the animal kingdom. 3. The animal as distinct from the spiritual nature of mankind.

an·i·mal·ize (ăn′ə-mə-līz′) tr.v. -ized, -izing, -izes. 1. To make coarse and brutal. 2. To endow (a deity) with the attributes, especially the form, of an animal. —an·i·mal·i·za·tion n.

animal kingdom n. The category of living organisms that includes all animals. Compare **mineral kingdom, plant kingdom**.

animal magnetism n. 1. Magnetic personal presence. 2. Sensuality. 3. Hypnotism or mesmerism.

animal spirits pl.n. Buoyancy that results from good physical health and vitality.

animal starch n. **Glycogen** (see).

an·i·mate (ăn′ə-māt′) tr.v. -mated, -mating, -mates. 1. To give life to; fill with life. 2. To impart interest or zest to; enliven. 3. To fill with spirit, courage, or resolution; encourage. 4. To impart motion or activity to. 5. To make, design, or produce (a film, for example) by means of animation. ~adj. (-mĭt). 1. Possessing life; living. 2. Lively; vivacious. [Latin animāre, to fill with breath, from anima, breath, soul. See **animal**.]

an·i·mat·ed (ăn′ə-mā′tĭd) adj. 1. Filled with life, activity, vigor, or spirit; enlivened: *an animated discussion.* 2. Made or designed so as to seem alive and moving: *an animated doll.* 3. Involving or using animation: *an animated film.* —an·i·mat·ed·ly adv.

animated cartoon n. A motion picture involving the animation of cartoon figures. Also called "cartoon."

animated oat n. A grass, *Avena sterilis*, of the Mediterranean region, having seeds that move or twist in response to changes in moisture.

an·i·ma·tion (ăn′ə-mā′shən) n. 1. The act, process, or result of animating. 2. The condition or quality of being animate; liveliness;

spirit; vitality. 3. **a.** An optical illusion of continuous movement achieved by the rapid succession of separate, still, but gradually varying images, utilized for entertainment in animated cartoons, for example. **b.** The art or process of achieving this illusion.

a·ni·ma·to (ä′nə-mä′tō, ä′nə-) adv. Music. In an animate or lively manner. Used as a direction. [Italian, from Latin animātus, past participle of animāre, to ANIMATE.] —a·ni·ma·to adj.

an·i·ma·tor, an·i·mat·er (ăn′ə-mā′tər) n. 1. One that animates. 2. An artist or technician who produces an animated cartoon.

an·i·mism (ăn′ə-mĭz′əm) n. 1. Any of various cultural beliefs whereby natural phenomena and things animate and inanimate are held to possess individual innate souls. 2. Any belief in spiritual beings or spiritual forces. 3. The hypothesis, first advanced by Pythagoras and Plato, of an immaterial force animating the universe. 4. An 18th-century doctrine that viewed the soul as the vital principle and source of both the normal and the abnormal phenomena of life. [German Animismus, from Latin anima, breath, soul. See **animal**.] —an·i·mist n. —an·i·mis·tic (ăn′ə-mĭs′tĭk) adj.

an·i·mos·i·ty (ăn′ə-mŏs′ə-tē) n., pl. **-ties**. Active hostility or open enmity. [Middle English animosite, from Old French, from Late Latin animōsitās, vehemence, spirit, from Latin animōsus, bold, spirited, from animus, soul, mind.]

an·i·mus (ăn′ə-məs) n. 1. An animating motive; an intention or purpose. 2. A feeling of animosity; bitter hostility or hatred. 3. In the psychology of Carl Jung, the masculine inner personality, as present in the unconscious of the female. Compare **anima**. [Latin, mind, soul.]

an·i·on (ăn′ī′ən) n. A negatively charged ion that migrates to an anode, as in electrolysis. Compare **cation**. [Greek, "that which goes up" (i.e., toward the anode), neuter present participle of anienai, to go up : an(a)-, up + ienai, to go.] —an·i·on·ic (ăn′ī-ŏn′ĭk) adj.

an·ise (ăn′ĭs) n. 1. A plant, *Pimpinella anisum*, native to the Mediterranean region, having clusters of small yellowish-white flowers and licorice-flavored seeds. 2. Aniseed. [Middle English anis, from Old French, from Latin anīsum, from Greek anison†.]

an·i·seed (ăn′ī-sēd′) n. The licorice-flavored seed of the anise plant, used in medicine and as flavoring. [Middle English anis seed : ANISE + SEED.]

an·i·sei·ko·ni·a (ăn-ī′sī-kō′nē-ə) n. An ocular defect in which the perception of image, shape, and size differ in each eye. [New Latin : ANIS(O)- + Greek eikōn, image.] —an·i·sei·kon·ic (ăn-ī′sī-kŏn′ĭk) adj.

an·i·sette (ăn′ə-sĕt′, -zĕt′) n. An anise-flavored liqueur. [French, diminutive of anis, ANISE.]

aniso– prefix. Indicates not equal or alike; for example, **anisomerous**. [New Latin, from Greek anisos, unequal : AN-, not + isos, equal (see **iso-**).]

an·i·sog·a·my (ăn′ī-sŏg′ə-mē) n. Biology. A union between markedly different gametes. [ANISO- + -GAMY.] —an·i·sog·a·mous (ăn′-ī-sŏg′ə-məs) adj.

an·i·sole (ăn′ə-sōl′) n. A colorless liquid, C₆H₅OCH₃, used as a solvent, vermicide, and flavoring. [ANIS(E) + -OLE.]

an·i·som·er·ous (ăn′ī-sŏm′ər-əs) adj. Botany. Having or designating floral whorls that have unequal numbers of parts. [ANISO- + -MEROUS.]

an·i·so·met·ric (ăn-ī′sə-mĕt′rĭk) adj. 1. Not isometric. 2. Denoting a crystal that has unequal axes. [French anisométrique : AN- (not) + ISOMETRIC.]

an·i·so·me·tro·pi·a (ăn-ī′sə-mə-trō′pē-ə) n. Pathology. Difference in the refractive power of the eyes. [New Latin : Greek anisometros : AN- (not) + isometros, ISOMETR(IC) + -OPIA.]

an·i·so·trop·ic (ăn-ī′sə-trŏp′ĭk) adj. 1. Not isotropic. 2. Physics. Having properties that differ according to the direction of measurement. [AN- (not) + ISOTROPIC.] —an·i·so·trop·i·cal·ly adv. —an·i·sot·ro·pism (ăn′ī-sŏt′rə-pīz′əm), an·i·sot·ro·py (ăn′ī-sŏt′rə-pē) n.

An·jou (ăn′jōō). Ancient region of western France, ruled by the powerful counts of Anjou in the early Middle Ages. From their line came Geoffrey Plantagenet (1131–51), Count of Anjou and the father of the English king Henry II. See **Angevin**.

An·ka·ra (ăng′kə-rə, äng′-) In ancient times known as **An·cy·ra** (ăn-sī′rə), later **An·go·ra** (ăng-gôr′ə, -gōr′ə). The capital and second-largest city of Turkey, lying 900 meters (3,000 feet) above sea level in the west-central part of the country.

an·ker·ite (ăng′kə-rīt′) n. A dolomitelike mineral in which iron partially replaces magnesium. [German Ankerit, after M.J. Anker (died 1843), Austrian mineralogist.]

ankh (ăngk) n. An **ansate cross** (see). [Egyptian 'nh, soul, life.]

an·kle (ăng′kəl) n. 1. The joint, consisting of the talus bone and related structures, that connects the foot with the leg. 2. The slender section of the leg immediately above the foot. [Middle English ankel and anclowe, respectively from Old Norse ankula (unattested) and Old English anclēow.]

an·kle·bone (ăng′kəl-bōn′) n. The **talus** (see).

an·klet (ăng′klĭt) n. 1. An ornament worn around the ankle. 2. A sock that reaches just above the ankle. [ANKL(E) + -LET.]

an·ky·lose, an·chy·lose (ăng′kə-lōs′, -lōz′) v. -losed, -losing, -loses. —tr. To join or consolidate by ankylosis. —intr. To become joined or consolidated by ankylosis. [Back-formation from ANKYLOSIS.]

an·ky·lo·sis, an·chy·lo·sis (ăng′kə-lō′sĭs) n. 1. Anatomy. The consolidation of bones or their parts forming a single unit. 2. Pathology. The stiffening of a joint as the result of abnormal bone fusion, surgery, or growth of fibrous tissue within the joint. [New Latin,

annual ring *A section through a larch tree showing a ring for each year's growth. The rings' markings are created by fast growth in spring, followed by slow growth in summer and no growth in winter.*

PRONUNCIATION KEY

ă, pat; ā, pay; âr, care;
ä, father, are; b, **bib**;
ch, **church**; d, **deed**; ĕ, pet;
ē, be; f, **fife**; g, **gag**; h, **hat**;
hw, **which**; ĭ, pit; ī, pie;
îr, **pier**; j, **judge**; k, **kick**;
l, **lid**, need**le**; m, **mum**;
n, **no**, sudden; ng, thi**ng**;
ŏ, pot; ō, toe; ô, paw, for;
oi, noise; ou, **out**; o͝o, **book**;
o͞o, **boot**; p, **pop**; r, **roar**;
s, **sauce**; sh, **ship**, **dish**;
t, **tight**; th, **thin**, **path**;
th, **this**, ba**the**; ŭ, cut; ûr, **fur**;
v, **valve**; w, **with**; y, **yes**;
z, **zebra**, **size**; zh, vi**sion**;
ə, **about**, item, edible,
gallop, circus, peaceful

IN FOREIGN WORDS:

à, *Fr.* ami; œ, *Fr.* **feu**, *Ger.* **schön**; ü, *Fr.* **tu**, *Ger.* **über**; KH, *Ger.* **ich**, *Scot.* **loch**; N, *Fr.* **bon**; y', *Fr.* Compiègne

STRESS MARKS:

Primary stress: ′
in·cite′ (ĭn-sīt′)
Secondary stress: ′
in′sight′ (ĭn′sīt′)

from Greek *ankulōsis,* stiffening of the joints, from *ankuloun,* to bend, from *ankulos,* bent, curved, crooked.] —**an·ky·lot·ic** (ăng′kə-lŏt′ĭk) *adj.*

an·lace (ăn′lĭs, -lās′) *n.* A two-edged medieval dagger. [Middle English *anlas, anelas*†.]

an·la·ge (ăn′lä′gə) *n., pl.* **-gen** (-gən) or **-ges.** **1.** *Embryology.* The initial cell structure from which an embryonic part or organ develops; a primordium. **2.** A fundamental principle; a foundation. [German *Anlage,* from Middle High German *anlāge,* a request, a laying on : *ane-,* on, from Old High German *ana* + *lāge,* act of laying, from Old High German *āga.*]

ann. 1. annals. **2.** annual. **3.** annuity.

an·na (ä′nə) *n.* **1.** A former monetary unit of India, Burma, and Pakistan, equal to 1/16 of a rupee. **2.** A copper coin worth one anna. [Hindi *ānā,* from Sanskrit *áṇu*-†, small.]

an·na·berg·ite (ăn′nə-bûr′gīt′) *n.* A rare mineral consisting of hydrated nickel arsenate, $Ni_3(AsO_4)_2{\cdot}8H_2O$. Also called "nickel bloom." [After *Annaberg,* Saxony, where it was discovered.]

An·na Com·ne·na (ăn′ə kŏm-nē′nə) (1083–*c.*1148). Byzantine princess and historian, daughter of the emperor Alexis I Comnenus. She wrote the *Alexiad,* a history of her father's reign, one of the great works of medieval historical literature.

an·nal·ist (ăn′ə-lĭst) *n.* One who writes annals; a historian. [French *annaliste,* from Old French, from *annales,* annals, from Latin *annālēs,* ANNALS.] —**an·nal·is·tic** *adj.*

an·nals (ăn′əlz) *pl.n. Abbr.* **ann. 1.** A chronological record of the events of successive years. **2.** Any descriptive account or record; a history. **3.** A periodical journal compiling the records and reports of a particular learned field, society, or the like. [Latin *(librī) annālēs,* "yearly (books)," from *annālis,* yearly, from *annus,* year.]

An·nam or **A·nam** (ă-năm′, ăn′ăm′). Former kingdom, lying in central Vietnam. Originally centered on the Red River valley, it was ruled by China from 111 B.C. until A.D. 939 and came under French influence in the 19th century. Its capital was Hué.

An·na·mese (ăn′ə-mēz′, -mēs′) *n., pl.* **Annamese** (for sense 1). Also **An·na·mite** (ăn′ə-mīt′). **1.** A native or inhabitant of Annam. **2.** Formerly, the Vietnamese language. —**An·na·mese** *adj.*

An·nap·o·lis (ə-năp′ə-lĭs). Capital of the state of Maryland, on the Atlantic seaboard. It was the site of the Annapolis Convention of 1786, which led to the drafting of the Constitution in 1787. It is the seat of the U.S. Naval Academy.

An·na·pur·na (ăn′ə-po͝or′nə, -pûr′-). Himalayan mountain in north-central Nepal. Annapurna I, one of the world's highest peaks, rises to 8,078 meters (26,503 feet) and was scaled by French mountaineers in 1950.

an·nates (ăn′āts′) *pl.n. Roman Catholic Church.* A full year's revenue formerly paid to the pope by a bishop or other ecclesiastic on first being appointed. [French, plural of *annate,* from Medieval Latin *annāta,* a year's revenue, from Latin *annus,* year, + *-āta,* "product of" (past participial ending forming nouns).]

an·nat·to, a·nat·to (ə-nä′tō) *n., pl.* **-tos.** Also **ar·nat·to** (är-nä′tō). **1.** A small tropical American tree, *Bixa orellana,* having red or pinkish flowers and seeds used in cooking. See **achiote. 2.** A yellowish-red dye obtained from the pulp of annatto seeds. [Cariban (the name of the tree).]

Anne (ăn), **(Elizabeth Alice Louise)** (1950–). British princess, second child and only daughter of Elizabeth II. She has represented Great Britain in equestrian events at the Olympic Games.

Anne, Queen (1665–1714). Queen of England, Scotland, and Ireland from 1702, the last monarch of the Stuart line. She was the second daughter of James II and came to the throne on the death of William III. She was the last English monarch to exercise the royal veto over legislation, in 1707.

an·neal (ə-nēl′) *tr.v.* **-nealed, -nealing, -neals. 1.** To subject (glass or metal) to a process of heating and slow cooling in order to toughen and reduce brittleness. **2.** To temper. **3.** To strengthen (the will or determination, for example).
∼*n.* An act of or treatment by annealing. [Middle English *anelen,* Old English *onǣlan* : ON + *ǣlan,* to set fire to, from *āl,* fire.]

an·ne·lid (ăn′ə-lĭd) *adj.* Also **an·nel·i·dan** (ə-nĕl′ə-dən). Of or belonging to the phylum Annelida, which includes the earthworms, leeches, and other worms having cylindrical segmented bodies.
∼*n.* Also **an·nel·i·dan.** An annelid worm. [New Latin *Annelida,* from French *annélide* : *annelés,* ringed, from *anneler,* to encircle, from Old French *annel,* ring, from Latin *annellus,* diminutive of *ānulus,* small ring + -IDE.]

Anne of Cleves (klēvz) (1515–57). Fourth wife of Henry VIII of England, sister of the German Protestant prince William, Duke of Cleves. She married Henry in January 1540, but the marriage was never consummated and they were divorced in July 1540.

an·nex (ə-nĕks′, ăn′ĕks′) *tr.v.* **-nexed, -nexing, -nexes. 1.** To add or join; append or attach, especially to something larger or more significant. **2.** To incorporate (territory) into an existing state, country, or empire. **3.** To add or attach, as an attribute, condition, or consequence. **4.** To take possession of without permission.
∼*n.* (ăn′ĕks′, -ĭks). **1.** An auxiliary building added on to, or situated near, a larger one. **2.** An addition to a record or document; an appendix or addendum. [Middle English *annexen,* from Old French *annexer,* from Latin *annectere* (past participle *annexus*), to bind to : *ad-,* to + *nectere,* to tie.] —**an·nex·a·ble** *adj.*

an·nex·a·tion (ăn′ĕk-sā′shən) *n.* **1.** The act or process of annexing. **2.** The condition of being annexed. **3.** Something that has been annexed. —**an·nex·a·tion·al** *adj.* —**an·nex·a·tion·ism** *n.* —**an·nex·a·tion·ist** *n. & adj.*

annexe. *Chiefly British.* Variant of **annex.**

An·nie Oak·ley (ăn′ē ōk′lē) *n. Slang.* A complimentary ticket of admittance; a free ticket or pass. [After *Annie Oakley* (1860–1926), American sharpshooter, from the association of the punched ticket with one of her bullet-riddled targets.]

an·ni·hi·late (ə-nī′ə-lāt′) *v.* **-lated, -lating, -lates.** —*tr.* **1.** To destroy completely; wipe out; reduce to nonexistence. **2.** To nullify or render void; abolish. **3.** *Informal.* To overwhelm completely; render helpless or ineffective. —*intr. Physics.* To participate in annihilation, as an electron and a positron do. [Late Latin *annihilāre,* to reduce to nothing : Latin *ad-,* to + *nihil,* nothing.] —**an·ni·hi·la·ble** (ə-nī′ə-lə-bəl) *adj.* —**an·ni·hi·la·tive** (ə-nī′ə-lā′tĭv, -lə-tĭv), **an·ni·hi·la·to·ry** (ə-nī′ə-lə-tôr′ē, -tōr′ē) *adj.* —**an·ni·hi·la·tor** *n.*

an·ni·hi·la·tion (ə-nī′ə-lā′shən) *n.* **1.** The act or process of annihilating. **2.** The condition or result of having been annihilated; utter destruction. **3.** *Theology.* The destruction of the soul at the death of the body. **4.** *Physics.* The phenomenon in which a particle and an antiparticle, such as an electron and a positron, disappear with a resultant release of energy approximately equivalent to the sum of their masses.

an·ni·hi·la·tion·ism (ə-nī′ə-lā′shə-nĭz′əm) *n. Theology.* The doctrine that the souls of the wicked are destroyed at death.

an·ni·ver·sa·ry (ăn′ə-vûr′sə-rē) *n., pl.* **-ries. 1.** The annual recurrence of the date on which a notable event took place in some preceding year: *a wedding anniversary.* **2.** A commemorative celebration on this date. [Middle English *anniversarie,* from Medieval Latin *(diēs) anniversāria,* "anniversary (day)," from Latin *anniversārius,* "returning yearly" : *annus,* year + *versus,* past participle of *vertere,* to turn.] —**an·ni·ver·sa·ry** *adj.*

an·no Dom·i·ni (ăn′ō dŏm′ə-nī′, dŏm′ə-nē) *adv. Abbr.* **A.D.** In a specified year of the Christian era: *He died A.D. 961.* —See Usage note at **A.D.** [Latin, "in the year of the Lord."]

an·no·tate (ăn′ə-tāt′) *v.* **-tated, -tating, -tates.** —*tr.* To provide (a literary work) with critical commentary or explanatory notes; gloss. —*intr.* To gloss a text. [Latin *annotāre,* to note down : *ad-,* to + *notāre,* to mark, from *nota,* a mark, note.] —**an·no·ta·tive** *adj.* —**an·no·ta·tor** *n.*

an·no·ta·tion (ăn′ə-tā′shən) *n.* **1.** The act or process of annotating. **2.** A critical or explanatory note; a commentary.

an·nounce (ə-nouns′) *v.* **-nounced, -nouncing, -nounces.** —*tr.* **1.** To bring to public notice; declare or proclaim officially or formally. **2.** To proclaim the presence, readiness, or arrival of: *announce a visitor.* **3.** To make known in advance; serve to indicate: *The footsteps announced the presence of an unexpected visitor.* —*intr.* To serve as a broadcasting announcer. [Middle English *announcen,* from Old French *annoncer,* from Latin *annuntiāre* : *ad-,* to + *nuntiāre,* to announce, from *nuntius,* messenger.]

an·nounce·ment (ə-nouns′mənt) *n.* **1.** The act of announcing. **2.** Something that has been announced. **3.** A printed or published statement or notice, as in a newspaper.

an·nounc·er (ə-noun′sər) *n.* **1.** Someone who announces. **2.** One who provides program continuity and delivers news bulletins on television or radio.

an·noy (ə-noi′) *v.* **-noyed, -noying, -noys.** —*tr.* **1.** To bother or irritate; anger slightly. **2.** To injure or harm; molest. —*intr.* To behave in an annoying manner.
∼*n. Archaic.* Something that annoys. [Middle English *anoien,* from Old French *anoier, enuier,* from Late Latin *inodiāre,* to make odious, from Latin *in odiō,* "in hatred," odious : *in,* in + *odiō,* ablative of *odium,* hatred.] —**an·noy·er** *n.* —**an·noy·ing·ly** *adv.*
Synonyms: *bother, irk, irritate, provoke, vex.*

an·noy·ance (ə-noi′əns) *n.* **1.** Something that annoys; a nuisance. **2.** The act of annoying. **3.** Vexation; irritation.

an·nu·al (ăn′yo͞o-əl) *adj. Abbr.* **ann. 1.** Recurring, done, or performed every year; yearly. **2.** Of or pertaining to the year; determined by a year's time: *an annual income.* **3.** *Botany.* Living and growing for only one year or season. Compare **perennial, biennial.**
∼*n.* **1. a.** A periodical published yearly; a yearbook. **b.** A special issue, as of a children's comic book, published yearly. **2.** A plant that lives and grows for only one year or season. [Middle English *annuel,* from Old French, from Late Latin *annuālis,* from Latin *annus,* year.] —**an·nu·al·ly** *adv.*

annual parallax *n. Astronomy.* **Parallax** *(see)* in a celestial body caused by motion of the earth around the sun, defined by the angle subtended at the celestial body by the earth's radius. Also called "heliocentric parallax."

annual ring *n.* Any of the concentric layers of wood, especially in a tree trunk, indicating a year's growth in temperate climates and seasonal growth in regions of wet and dry seasons. Also called "growth ring."

an·nu·i·tant (ə-no͞o′ə-tənt, ə-nyo͞o′-) *n.* A person who receives or is qualified to receive an annuity.

an·nu·i·ty (ə-no͞o′ə-tē, ə-nyo͞o′-) *n., pl.* **-ties.** *Abbr.* **ann. 1. a.** The annual payment of an allowance or income. **b.** The sum of money involved in such a payment. **2.** The right to receive or the obligation to make an annuity. **3. a.** The interest or dividends paid annually on an investment of money. **b.** The investment made. [Middle English *annuite,* from Old French, from Medieval Latin *annuitās,* yearly payment, from Latin *annuus,* yearly, from *annus,* year.]

an·nul (ə-nŭl′) *tr.v.* **-nulled, -nulling, -nuls. 1.** To make or declare void or invalid; nullify or cancel (a marriage or a law, for example).

2. To obliterate the existence or effect of; annihilate. —See Synonyms at **nullify.** [Middle English *annullen,* from Old French *annuller,* from Late Latin *annullāre,* to make into nothing : Latin *ad-,* to + *nullus,* none, null.] —**an·nul·la·ble** *adj.*

an·nu·lar (ăn′yə-lər) *adj.* Forming or shaped like a ring. [Old French *annulaire,* from Latin *annulāris, ānulāris,* from *annulus, ānulus,* ring.] —**an·nu·lar·i·ty** (ăn′yə-lăr′ə-tē) *n.* —**an·nu·lar·ly** *adv.*

annular eclipse *n.* A solar eclipse in which the moon covers all but a bright ring around the circumference of the sun.

annular ligament *n.* A ligament or fibrous band that encircles a part of the body, such as the ankle or wrist.

an·nu·late (ăn′yə-lĭt, -lāt) *adj.* Also **an·nu·lat·ed** (-lā′tĭd). Having or consisting of rings or ringlike segments. [Latin *annulātus, ānulātus,* from *annulus, ānulus,* ring. See **annulet.**] —**an·nu·late·ly** *adv.*

an·nu·la·tion (ăn′yə-lā′shən) *n.* **1.** The act or process of forming rings. **2.** A ringlike structure or segment.

an·nu·let (ăn′yə-lĭt) *n.* **1.** *Architecture.* A ringlike molding around the capital of a pillar. **2.** *Heraldry.* A ring shape. **3.** A small ring. [Diminutive formation from Latin *annulus, ānulus,* ring.]

an·nul·ment (ə-nŭl′mənt) *n.* **1.** The act of annulling. **2.** A retrospective as well as prospective invalidation, especially of an unconsummated marriage.

an·nu·lus (ăn′yə-ləs) *n., pl.* **-luses** or **-li** (-lī′). **1.** A ringlike figure, part, structure, or marking. **2.** *Geometry.* The figure bounded by and containing the area between two concentric circles. [Latin *annulus, ānulus,* ring.]

an·nun·ci·ate (ə-nŭn′sē-āt′) *tr.v.* **-ated, -ating, -ates.** To announce; proclaim. [Latin *annuntiāre,* to ANNOUNCE.] —**an·nun·ci·a·to·ry** (ə-nŭn′sē-ə-tôr′ē, -tōr′ē) *adj.*

an·nun·ci·a·tion *n.* **1.** The act of announcing. **2.** The angel Gabriel's announcement of the Incarnation to the Virgin Mary. Luke 1:26–38. **3. Annunciation.** The festival, on March 25, in celebration of this event.

Annunciation lily *n.* The **Madonna lily** *(see).* [From its frequent depiction in paintings of the Annunciation.]

an·nun·ci·a·tor (ə-nŭn′sē-ā′tər) *n.* **1.** An electrical signaling device used in hotels or offices to indicate the source of calls on a switchboard. **2.** A signaling device indicating the position of a train.

an·nus mi·rab·i·lis (ăn′əs mĭ-răb′ə-lĭs) *n.* **1.** A remarkable or fateful year. **2.** The year 1666, memorable for the Great Fire of London and the English victory over the Dutch. [New Latin, "wondrous year," originally designating the year 1588 in a forecast of its disasters.]

a·no·a (ə-nō′ə) *n.* A small buffalo, *Anoa depressicornis,* of Celebes and the Philippines, having short, pointed horns. [Native name in Celebes.]

an·ode (ăn′ōd′) *n.* **1.** Any positively charged electrode, as of an electrolytic cell or electron tube. **2.** The negatively charged terminal of a primary cell or of a storage battery that is supplying current. [Greek *anodos,* a way up (i.e., from the positive pole into the electrolyte) : *ana-,* up + *hodos,* road, way.] —**an·od·al** (ăn-ō′dəl), **an·od·ic** (ăn-ŏd′ĭk) *adj.*

an·o·dize (ăn′ə-dīz′) *tr.v.* **-dized, -dizing, -dizes.** To coat (a metallic surface) electrolytically with a protective oxide. [ANOD(E) + -IZE.] —**an·o·di·za·tion** *n.*

an·o·dyne (ăn′ə-dīn′) *adj.* **1.** Able to soothe or relieve pain. **2.** Relaxing; soothing. **3.** Watered-down; insipid; innocuous: *anodyne references to progress and freedom.*
∼*n.* **1.** A medicine that relieves pain. **2.** Anything that soothes or comforts. [Latin *anōdynus,* from Greek *anōdunos,* free from pain : AN- (without) + *odunē,* pain.] —**an·o·dyn·ic** (ăn′ə-dĭn′ĭk) *adj.*

an·o·e·sis (ăn′ō-ē′sĭs) *n. Psychology.* A state of consciousness involving sensation but not thought. [A- (without) + Greek *noēsis,* thought, understanding.] —**an·o·et·ic** (ăn′ō-ĕt′ĭk) *adj.*

a·noint (ə-noint′) *tr.v.* **anointed, anointing, anoints. 1.** To apply oil, ointment, or a similar substance to. **2.** To put oil on as a sign of sanctification or consecration in a religious ceremony. [Middle English *anointen,* from Old French *enoindre* (past participle *enoint*), from Latin *inunguere* : *in-,* upon + *unguere,* to smear, anoint.] —**a·noint·er** *n.* —**a·noint·ment** *n.*

a·no·le (ə-nō′lē) *n.* Any of various chiefly tropical New World lizards of the genus *Anolis,* characterized by a distensible throat flap and the ability to change color. Also called "chameleon." [New Latin *Anolis,* from French *anolis,* anole, from Cariban *anoli.*]

a·nom·a·lis·tic (ə-nŏm′ə-lĭs′tĭk) *adj.* Also **a·nom·a·lis·ti·cal** (-tĭ-kəl). Of or pertaining to the astronomical anomaly.

anomalistic month *n.* A month measured as the interval between two successive passages of the moon through perigee and equal to 27.55455 mean solar days.

anomalistic year *n.* A year measured as the interval between two successive passages of the earth through perihelion and equal to 365.25964 mean solar days.

a·nom·a·lous (ə-nŏm′ə-ləs) *adj.* Deviating from the normal or common order, form, or rule; abnormal, deviant, or irregular. [Late Latin *anōmalos,* from Greek, uneven, irregular : AN- (not) + *homalos,* even, from *homos,* same.] —**a·nom·a·lous·ly** *adv.* —**a·nom·a·lous·ness** *n.*

a·nom·a·ly (ə-nŏm′ə-lē) *n., pl.* **-lies. 1.** Deviation from the normal or common order, form, or rule; abnormality. **2.** Anything anomalous, irregular, or abnormal. **3.** *Astronomy.* **a.** The angular deviation, as observed from the sun, of a planet from its perihelion. **b.** The angular deviation of a satellite from its perigee. [Latin *anōmalia,* from Greek *anōmalia.* See **anomalous.**]

an·o·mie, an·o·my (ăn′ə-mē) *n.* **1.** The absence of the social consensus necessary for governing a society. **2.** The state of alienation experienced by an individual or class in such a situation. **3.** Disorientation of the personality resulting in unsocial behavior. [Greek *anomia,* lawlessness, from *anomos,* without law : A- (without) + *nomos,* law.] —**a·nom·ic** (ə-nŏm′ĭk, -nō′mĭk) *adj.*

a·non (ə-nŏn′) *adv.* **1.** In a short time; soon. **2.** At another time; again. **3.** *Archaic.* At once; immediately: *"The same is he that heareth the word, and anon with joy receiveth it"* (Matthew 13:20). [Middle English *anon, onon,* from Old English *on ān,* "in one," at once : *on,* in, ON + *ān,* one.]

anon. anonymous.

an·o·nym (ăn′ə-nĭm′) *n.* **1.** An anonymous publication or person. **2.** A pseudonym. [French *anonyme,* noun use of adjective, ANONYMOUS.]

an·o·nym·i·ty (ăn′ə-nĭm′ə-tē) *n., pl.* **-ties. 1.** The state or quality of being anonymous. **2.** One that is anonymous.

a·non·y·mous (ə-nŏn′ə-məs) *adj. Abbr.* **a., anon. 1.** Having an unknown name. **2.** Of unknown or undeclared authorship, origin, or agency: *an anonymous donation.* **3.** Inconspicuous; lacking in individuality. [Late Latin *anōnymus,* from Greek *anōnumos,* nameless : AN- (without) + *onoma,* name.] —**a·non·y·mous·ly** *adv.* —**a·non·y·mous·ness** *n.*

a·noph·e·les (ə-nŏf′ə-lēz′) *n.* Any of various mosquitoes of the genus *Anopheles,* many of which carry the malaria parasite and transmit the disease to humans by their bite. [New Latin *Anopheles,* "the hurtful ones," from Greek *anōphelēs,* useless, hurtful : AN- (without) + *ophelos,* advantage.] —**a·noph·e·line** (ə-nŏf′ə-līn′) *adj.* & *n.*

anopheles *Larvae of an anopheles mosquito. Adult females carry and transmit malaria to humans.*

an·o·rak (ăn′ə-răk′) *n.* A padded waterproof and windproof jacket with a hood. [Eskimo (Greenland) *ánorâq.*]

an·o·rec·tic (ăn′ə-rĕk′tĭk) *adj.* Also **an·o·rex·ic** (-rĕk′sĭk). **1.** Marked by anorexia. **2.** Suppressing or causing loss of appetite.
∼*n.* **1.** One that is anorectic. **2.** An anorectic drug. [Greek *anorektos* : AN- (without) + *oregein,* to reach out for.]

an·o·rex·i·a (ăn′ə-rĕk′sē-ə) *n.* **1.** Loss of appetite. **2.** Anorexia nervosa. [Late Latin *anorexia,* from Greek : AN- (without) + *orexis,* a longing, from *oregein,* to reach out for.]

anorexia ner·vo·sa (nûr-vō′sə, -zə) *n.* An illness thought to be psychological in origin in which the patient, usually a young woman, refuses to eat over a long period. Compare **bulimia nervosa.** [New Latin, " nervous anorexia."]

anorexic. Variant of **anorectic.**

an·or·thite (ăn-ôr′thīt′) *n.* A plagioclase feldspar with high calcium oxide content, occurring in igneous rocks. [French : AN- (not) + Greek *orthos,* straight (from its oblique crystals) + -ITE.] —**an·or·thit·ic** (ăn′ôr-thĭt′ĭk) *adj.*

an·or·tho·site (ăn-ôr′thə-sīt′) *n.* A plutonic rock, chiefly plagioclase. [French *anorthose* (see **anorthite**) + -ITE.]

an·os·mi·a (ăn-ŏz′mē-ə) *n.* Loss of the sense of smell. [New Latin : AN- (without) + Greek *osmē,* smell + -IA.] —**an·os·mic** *adj.*

an·oth·er (ə-nŭth′ər) *adj.* **1.** Distinctly different from the first: *That's another matter.* **2.** Some other; any other: *in another country; Come again another day.* **3. a.** Additional; one more: *Take another cake.* **b.** Reminiscent of the specified phenomenon: *another Hitler; another Babylon.*
∼*pron.* **1.** A different one. **2.** One of the same kind. **3.** An additional one. [Middle English *an other.*]

A·nou·ilh (ä-no͞o-ē′), **Jean** (1910–87). French dramatist. Many of his plays written during the Nazi occupation of France were derived from classical tradition, for example, *Eurydice* (1942) and *Antigone* (1944). Two of the best-received of his postwar plays were *Ring Around the Moon* (1948) and *Becket*(1959).

an·ov·u·lant (ăn-ŏv′yə-lənt) *n.* A drug that prevents ovulation. [AN- (not) + OVUL(ATION) + -ANT.] —**an·ov·u·lant** *adj.*

an·ov·u·la·to·ry (ăn-ŏv′yə-lə-tôr′ē, -tōr′ē) Of, pertaining to, or characterized by the failure or suppression of ovulation. [AN- (without) + OVUL(ATION) + -ORY.]

an·ox·e·mi·a (ăn′ŏk-sē′mē-ə) *n.* An abnormally low concentration of oxygen in the blood. [New Latin : AN- (without) + OX(Y)- + -EMIA.] —**an·ox·e·mic** *adj.*

an·ox·i·a (ă-nŏk′sē-ə) *n.* **1.** Absence or lack of oxygen. **2.** The condition resulting from a deficiency in the supply of oxygen to the tissues; especially, **hypoxia** *(see).* [AN- (without) + OX(Y)- + -IA.] —**an·ox·ic** *adj.*

ans. answer.

an·sate (ăn′sāt′) *adj.* Also **an·sat·ed** (-sā′tĭd). Having a handle or a part resembling a handle. [Latin *ānsātus,* from *ānsa,* handle.]

ansate cross *n.* A cross shaped like a T with a loop at the top used, especially in Egyptian art, as a symbol of life. Also called "ankh," "crux ansata."

ansate cross *Detail of a 15th-century* B.C. *Egyptian relief, showing an ankh, or ansate cross, the symbol of life, being carried by the pharaoh Tuthmosis III.*

An·schluss (än′shlo͝os′) *n. Often* **anschluss.** A union; specifically, the political union of Nazi Germany and Austria in 1938. [German, from *anschliessen,* to join: *an-* to, up + *schliessen,* to close.]

An·selm (ăn′sĕlm′), **Saint** (*c.*1033–1109). Italian theologian and philosopher and archbishop of Canterbury from 1093 until his death. In his *Proslogion* the argument for the existence of God marks him as one of the founders of Scholasticism.

an·ser·ine (ăn′sə-rīn′) *adj.* Also **an·ser·ous** (-sər-əs) (for sense 3). **1.** Of, belonging to, or pertaining to the subfamily Anserinae, which includes geese, swans, and certain ducks. **2.** Resembling a goose; gooselike. **3.** Stupid; silly; foolish. [New Latin *Anserinae,* from Latin *ānserīnus,* gooselike: *ānser,* goose + *-īnus,* -INE.]

an·swer (ăn′sər) *n. Abbr.* **ans., a., A. 1.** A spoken or written reply, as

to a question, request, statement, accusation, or letter. **2. a.** A solution or result, as to a problem. **b.** The correct response or solution. **3.** An act in response or retaliation. **4.** *Law.* A defendant's defense against charges filed against him. **5.** *Music.* A phrase in a fugue similar to the subject but in a different voice. **6.** A counterpart; an equivalent: *America's answer to the royal family.*
  ~*v.* **answered, -swering, -swers.** —*intr.* **1.** To respond in words or action. Used with *to.* **2. a.** To be liable or accountable. Used with *for.* **b.** To atone; make amends. Used with *for.* **3.** To serve the purpose; suffice; do: *use three words where one would answer.* **4.** To correspond; match. Used with *to: answering to the description.* —*tr.* **1. a.** To reply to. **b.** To say in reply. **2.** To respond correctly to; solve. **3.** To fulfill the demands of; serve: *"my fortune has answered my desires"* (Izaak Walton). **4.** To conform or correspond to. **5.** To be responsible for; meet; discharge (a claim or debt, for example). **6.** To offer an explanation or justification for (an accusation, charge, or the like). **7.** To attend to a signal or summons from: *answer the phone.* —**answer back.** To give a rude or defiant reply instead of showing politeness or deference. [Middle English answer(e), Old English andswaru.] —**an·swer·er** *n.*
  Synonyms: *reply, respond, retort.*

an·swer·a·ble (ăn′sər-ə-bəl) *adj.* **1.** Responsible; accountable; liable. Used with *for* or *to: Members of Congress are answerable to their constituents.* **2.** Able to be answered. **3.** *Archaic.* Corresponding; suitable. Used with *to.* —See Synonyms at **responsible.** —**an·swer·a·bil·i·ty, an·swer·a·ble·ness** *n.* —**an·swer·a·bly** *adv.*

answering machine *n.* A machine that can be plugged into a telephone line to record any message a caller may wish to leave.

answering service *n.* A commercial service that deals with telephone calls and telephone messages for its clients.

ant (ănt) *n.* Any of various social insects of the family Formicidae, characteristically having wings only in the males and fertile females, and living in colonies that have a complex social organization. [Middle English *ante, amete,* Old English *æmette.*]

ant–. Variant of **anti–.**

ant *There are some 10,000 species of this insect worldwide, all living in colonies consisting of a queen ant and up to 500,000 worker ants. Shown here are the winged queen and a worker of the species, Lasius flavus.*

ant

HALF A MILLION SOCIAL INSECTS WORKING IN HARMONY

Specialist roles for ants in an efficiently run society

Man is not the only animal to herd livestock, grow crops—or enslave others of his own kind. Ants do all these things as well. Many ant species breed sap-sucking aphids in their nests. The ants drive the aphids out to pasture on nearby plants, then "milk" them by licking off the sweet honeydew they exude. South American leaf-cutter ants spread a compost of chewed leaves inside their nest as a bed on which they grow fungus for food.

A species of ant native to Europe and North America, and known to scientists as *Formica sanguinea,* raids the nests of other ants to capture slaves. The hunters carry off pupae—ants in the dormant stage between larva and adult. When the captives emerge as adults, they are put to work extending the nest, caring for the young, and collecting food for their captors.

Most ants live in nests in highly organized colonies of up to half a million insects. Each colony has a single queen to lay all the eggs, and a few winged males whose only function is to fertilize the queen and on its one marriage flight; then they die. The rest of the colony consists of wingless and sterile female ants, which act as workers and soldiers.

A few species, such as the army ants of South America and the driver ants of Africa, have no permanent homes. They remain endlessly on the march in columns of up to 1,500,000 ants, eating anything in their path. Once, a tethered horse was reduced to a skeleton in three hours.

READY FOR SEWING *Weaver ants of Southeast Asia and Australia make their nests by sewing together leaves with silk. It is produced by ant larvae that they carry in their mouths. Here workers, each able to carry three times its own weight, maneuver two leaves into position.*

–ant *suffix.* Indicates performing, promoting, or causing a specified state or action; for example, **deodorant.** [Middle English, from Old French, from Latin *-āns* (stem *-ant-*), present participial ending of first conjugation verbs.]

ant. **1.** antenna. **2.** antonym.

an·ta (ăn′tə) *n., pl.* **-tae** (-tē). *Architecture.* **1.** A thickening of the projecting end of the lateral wall of a Greek temple. **2.** A pier that constitutes one boundary of the porch. [Latin *antae* (plural), door jamb.]

ant·ac·id (ănt-ăs′ĭd) *adj.* Correcting acidity; neutralizing acids.
  ~*n.* A substance, as medicinal remedy, that neutralizes acid, especially in the stomach. [ANT(I)- + ACID.]

An·tae·us (ăn-tē′əs) *n.* Greek Mythology. A giant, invincible while touching the ground, who was lifted into the air by Hercules and crushed to death.

an·tag·o·nism (ăn-tăg′ə-nĭz′əm) *n.* **1.** Active, and often mutual, resistance, opposition, or hostility. **2.** The condition of being an opposing principle, force, or factor. **3.** The opposing action of two muscles such that the contraction of one is accompanied by the relaxation of the other. **4.** The interaction of two substances, such as drugs or hormones, such that one partly or wholly inhibits the action of the other. [French *antagonisme.* See ANTAGONIST, -ISM.]

an·tag·o·nist (ăn-tăg′ə-nĭst) *n.* **1.** One who opposes and actively competes with another; an adversary. **2.** *Anatomy.* A muscle whose action opposes that of another muscle. Compare **agonist. 3.** *Pharmacology.* A drug that counteracts or neutralizes another drug. [French *antagoniste,* from Late Latin *antagonista,* from Greek *antagōnistēs* : *antagōnizesthai,* to struggle against (see **antagonize**) + *-istes,* -IST.] —See Synonyms at **opponent.**

an·tag·o·nis·tic (ăn-tăg′ə-nĭs′tĭk) *adj.* Arising from or characterized by antagonism. —**an·tag·o·nis·ti·cal·ly** *adv.*

an·tag·o·nize (ăn-tăg′ə-nīz′) *tr.v.* **-nized, -nizing, -nizes. 1.** To incur or provoke the dislike or hostility of. **2.** To counteract. [Greek *antagōnizesthai,* to struggle against : *anti-,* against + *agōnizesthai,* to struggle, from *agōn,* contest (see **agony**).]

Antakya. See **Antioch.**

An·ta·nan·a·ri·vo (ăn′tə-năn′ə-rē′vō). Formerly **Ta·nan·a·rive** (tə-năn′ə-rēv′). The capital of Madagascar. It is the largest city in the country and was founded in the early 17th century as a walled citadel.

Ant·arc·tic (ănt-ärk′tĭk, -är′tĭk) *adj.* Of or pertaining to the regions surrounding the South Pole.
  ~*n.* **the Antarctic.** Antarctica and its surrounding waters. [Middle English *Antartik,* from Medieval Latin *Antarticus,* from Latin *antarcticus,* southern, from Greek *antarktikos* : *anti-,* opposite + ARCTIC.]

Ant·arc·ti·ca (ănt-ärk′tĭ-kə, -är′tĭ-kə). The coldest, stormiest, and driest continent, lying over the South Pole. It has 9 percent of the world's land, *c.* 13,209,000 square kilometers (5,100,000 square miles), 95 percent of it covered by an ice sheet more than 3 kilometers (1.9 miles) thick in places, making up 90 percent of the world's permanent ice and snow. Temperatures average –50°C (–58°F) at the pole, and the world's lowest recorded temperature, –88.2°C (–126.9°F), occurred near Vostok. Antarctica's rocks are believed to contain coal, gas, metal ore, and oil deposits, but their extraction through the constantly moving ice sheet would be extremely difficult. The surrounding seas are a potentially rich source of food. There is no permanent population in Antarctica, but many countries have made territorial claims in the continent; these have been held in abeyance in the interests of international cooperation for exploration and scientific research. The Antarctic Treaty of 1959 forbids any military use of the area.

Antarctic Circle *n.* A parallel of latitude 66°32′ south, along which the sun does not set on one day of the year, around December 22.

An·tar·es (ăn-târ′ēz, -tăr′ēz) *n.* A double and variable star, the brightest in the southern sky, about 424 light-years from Earth in the constellation Scorpius. [Greek *antarēs,* "opposing Mars" (that is, rivaling Mars in color) : ANTI- + ARES.]

ant bear *n.* **1.** An anteater. **2.** An **aardvark** (*see*).

ant cow *n.* An aphid that yields a honeylike substance on which ants feed.

an·te (ăn′tē) *n.* **1.** In poker, the stake that each player must put into the pool before receiving his hand, or before receiving new cards. **2.** An amount paid or to be paid in advance, especially as one's share in a financial venture.
  ~*tr.v.* **anted** or **-teed, -teing, -tes.** In poker, to put (one's stake) into the pool. Often used with *up.* [Latin *ante,* before.]

ante– *prefix.* Indicates: **1.** In front of; for example, **anteroom. 2.** Previous to; for example, **antenatal.** [Latin, from *ante,* before, in front of, previous to.]

ant·eat·er (ănt′ē′tər) *n.* **1.** Any of several tropical American mammals of the family Myrmecophagidae, that lack teeth and feed on ants and termites; especially, *Myrmecophaga tridactyla,* having a long, narrow snout, a long, sticky tongue, and a long, shaggy-haired tail. This species is also called "giant anteater" and sometimes "ant bear." **2.** Any of several other animals that feed on ants, such as the echidna, the pangolin, and the aardvark.

an·te·bel·lum (ăn′tē-bĕl′əm) *adj.* Belonging to the period prior to a war, especially the American Civil War. [Latin *ante bellum,* before the war.]

an·te·cede (ăn′tə-sēd′) *tr.v.* **-ceded, -ceding, -cedes.** To go before in rank, place, or time; precede. [Latin *antecēdere* : ANTE- + *cēdere,* to go.]

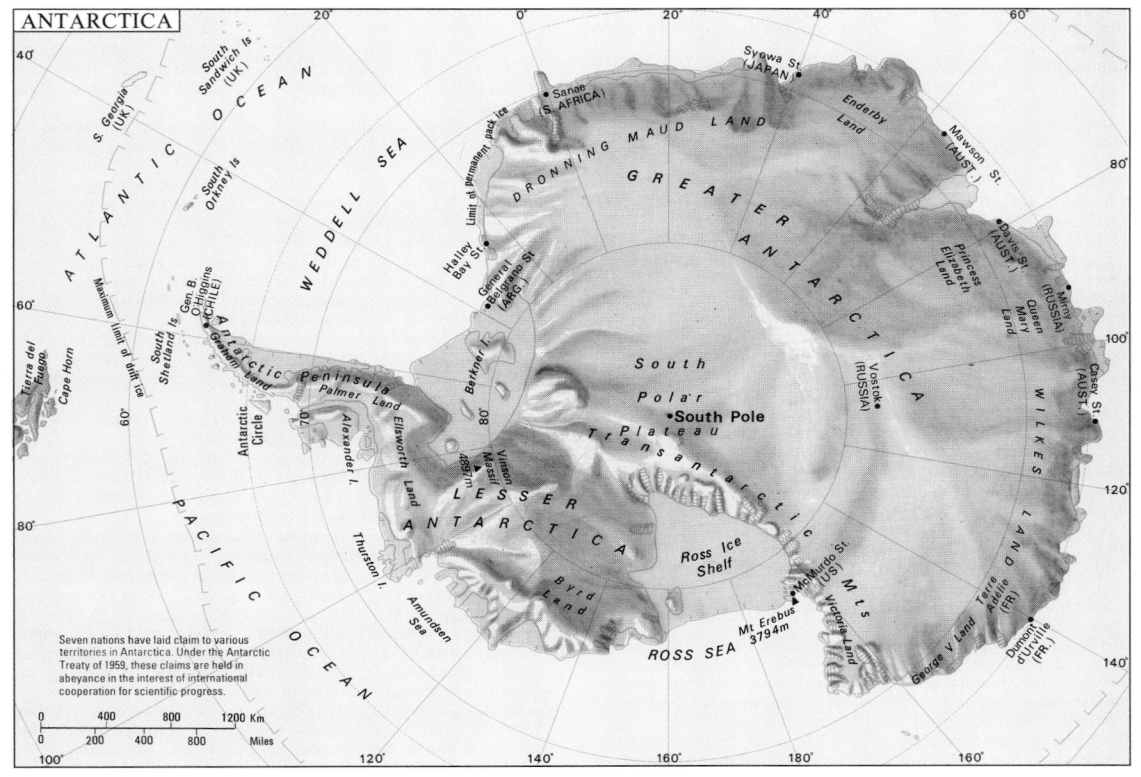

ANTARCTICA

Seven nations have laid claim to various territories in Antarctica. Under the Antarctic Treaty of 1959, these claims are held in abeyance in the interest of international cooperation for scientific progress.

Antarctica *The continent around the South Pole is largely covered by a vast ice sheet that in places extends over the sea, ending in spectacular ice cliffs like these.*

an·te·ce·dence (ăn′tə-sēd′ns) *n.* Precedence.

an·te·ce·dent (ăn′tə-sēd′nt) *adj.* Going before; preceding; prior. ~*n.* **1.** An occurrence or circumstance that precedes another, often having a causal relationship with what follows. **2. antecedents.** One's ancestors, ancestry, or past life. **3.** *Grammar.* The word, phrase, or clause to which a relative pronoun refers. **4.** *Mathematics.* The first term of a ratio. **5.** *Logic.* The first proposition or premise within a conditional proposition. —**an·te·ce·dent·ly** *adv.*

an·te·cham·ber (ăn′tē-chām′bər) *n.* A smaller room serving as an entrance into a larger room; an anteroom. [French *antichambre* : *anti-,* before + *chambre,* room, CHAMBER.]

an·te·cha·pel (ăn′tē-chăp′əl) *n.* An inner porch or vestibule at the western end of a chapel.

an·te·choir (ăn′tē-kwīr′) *n.* A place in front of the choir reserved for the clergy and choir members.

an·te·date (ăn′tī-dāt′) *tr.v.* **-dated, -dating, -dates. 1.** To be of an earlier date than; precede in time. **2.** To give a date earlier than the actual date to (a document, manuscript, or the like), especially in order to deceive: *antedate a check.* **3.** To assign a date to (a historical period or event) that is earlier than previously thought. **4.** *Archaic.* To bring about sooner than expected. ~*n.* A date given to an event or a document that is earlier than the actual date.

an·te·di·lu·vi·an (ăn′tī-də-loo′vē-ən) *adj.* **1.** Occurring or belonging to the era before the Flood. Genesis 7, 8. **2. a.** Very old; antiquated. **b.** Old-fashioned; extremely conservative. ~*n.* **1.** A person or thing existing before the Flood. **2.** A very old person. [From ANTE- + Latin *diluvium,* flood (see **diluvial**).]

an·te·fix (ăn′tī-fīks′) *n., pl.* **-fixes** or **antefixa** (ăn′tī-fīk′sə). *Architecture.* An upright ornament along the eaves of a tiled roof to conceal the joints between the rows of tiles. [Latin *antefixus,* "fastened before" (the joints) : *ante-,* before + *fixus,* past participle of *fīgere,* to fasten.] —**an·te·fix·al** *adj.*

an·te·lope (ăn′tə-lōp′) *n., pl.* **-lopes** or collectively **antelope. 1.** Any of various slender, swift-running, long-horned ruminants of the family Bovidae, of Africa and Asia. **2.** An animal that resembles a true antelope, such as the **pronghorn** (*see*). **3.** Leather made from the hide of an antelope. [Middle English, from Old French *antelop,* a fabulous oriental beast, from Medieval Latin *anthalopus,* from Late Greek *antholops*†.]

an·te·me·rid·i·an (ăn′tē-mə-rĭd′ē-ən) *adj.* Of, pertaining to, or taking place in the morning. [Latin *antemerīdiānus* : *ante-,* before + *merīdiānus,* MERIDIAN.]

an·te me·rid·i·em (ăn′tē mə-rĭd′ē-əm) *adv. Abbr.* **a.m., A.M.** Before noon. Used chiefly in the abbreviated form to specify the hour: *10:30* A.M. [Latin : *ante-,* before + *merīdiēs,* midday, noon (see **meridian**).]

an·te mor·tem (ăn′tē môr′təm) *adj. Latin.* Before death.

an·te·na·tal (ăn′tē-nāt′l) *adj.* Of, pertaining to, or occurring before birth; prenatal.

an·ten·na (ăn-tĕn′ə) *n., pl.* **-tennae** (-tĕn′ē) (for sense 1) or **-nas** (for sense 2). **1.** One of the paired, flexible, jointed sensory appendages on the head of an insect, myriapod, or crustacean. **2.** *Abbr.* **ant.** A metallic apparatus for sending and receiving electromagnetic waves. In this sense, also called "aerial." [Medieval Latin, from Latin *antemna, antenna*†, sail yard.] —**an·ten·nal** *adj.*

an·ten·nule (ăn-tĕn′yool) *n. Zoology.* A small antenna, especially either of the first pair in crustaceans. [French, diminutive of *antenne,* ANTENNA.]

an·te·pen·di·um (ăn′tē-pĕn′dē-əm) *n., pl.* **-dia** (-dē-ə). **1.** A hanging for the front of an altar. **2.** A pulpit cloth. [Medieval Latin : Latin *ante-,* in front of + *pendēre,* to hang.]

an·te·pe·nult (ăn′tē-pē′nŭlt′, -pĭ-nŭlt′) *n.* The third syllable from the end in a word; for example, *te* is the antepenult of the word *antepenult.* [Late Latin *antepaenultima,* feminine of *antepaenultimus,* ANTEPENULTIMATE.]

an·te·pe·nul·ti·mate (ăn′tē-pĭ-nŭl′tə-mĭt) *adj.* Third from the end in a series. ~*n.* An antepenult. [Late Latin *antepaenultimus* : Latin ANTE- + *paenultimus,* PENULT.]

an·te·post (ăn′tē-pōst′) *adj. Chiefly British.* **1.** Made before the runners' numbers are posted on the board. Said of a racing bet. **2.** Occurring in or pertaining to the period before a horse race.

an·te·ri·or (ăn-tîr′ē-ər) *adj.* **1.** Placed in front; located forward. **2.** Prior in time; earlier. **3.** *Zoology.* **a.** Of, pertaining to, or located near the head in lower animals. **b.** Of or pertaining to the front of the body in higher animals and man; ventral. **c.** Located on or near the front of the body or of an organ. **4.** *Botany.* In front of and facing away from the axis or stem. Said of part of a flower or leaf. Compare **posterior.** [Latin, comparative of *ante,* before.] —**an·te·ri·or·i·ty** (ăn-tîr′ē-ôr′ə-tē) *n.* —**an·te·ri·or·ly** *adv.*

an·te·room (ăn′tē-room′, -room′) *n.* A room that leads into a larger room and that is often used as a waiting room.

ant·he·li·on (ănt-hē′lē-ən, ăn-thē′-) *n., pl.* **-lia** (-lē-ə) or **-ons.** A luminous, white, halolike area occasionally seen in the sky opposite the Sun on the **parhelic circle** (*see*). [Greek *anthēlion,* from *anthēlios,* opposite the sun : *ant(i)-,* opposite + *hēlios,* sun.]

ant·hel·min·tic (ănt′hĕl-mĭn′tĭk, ăn′thĕl-) *adj.* Also **ant·hel·min·thic** (-thĭk). Acting to expel or destroy intestinal worms. ~*n.* An anthelmintic remedy; a vermifuge. [ANT(I)- + Greek *helmins* (stem *helminth-*), worm.]

an·them (ăn′thəm) *n.* **1.** A song of praise or loyalty, as to a nation. **2.** A choral composition, often set to words from the Bible. **3.** A religious chant sung in alternation as part of a church service. [Middle English *antem, antefn,* Old English *antefn,* antiphonal song, from Medieval Latin *antiphōna,* from Late Greek, "sung responses," neuter plural of *antiphōnos,* singing in response : *anti-,* opposite + *phōnē,* voice.]

an·the·mi·on (ăn-thē′mē-ən) *n., pl.* **-mia** (-mē-ə). A pattern of honeysuckle, lotus, or palm leaves in a radiating cluster, used especially as a motif in ancient Greek art and architecture. [Greek, diminutive of *anthemon,* name of a plant, from *anthos,* flower.]

an·ther (ăn′thər) *n. Botany.* The organ that forms the upper end of a stamen, and that produces and discharges pollen. [New Latin

anteater *Using its tubular snout, the giant anteater (above) probes inside an ant colony or termite mound before capturing the insects on its long, sticky tongue. It has powerful front claws that can rip open a rock-hard anthill, and its stomach contains special grit to crush the insects' shells.*

anthera, from Medieval Latin *anthĕra*, pollen, from Latin, medicine composed of flowers, from Greek *anthĕros*, flowery, from *anthos*, flower.] —**an·ther·al** *adj.*

an·ther·id·i·um (ăn'thə-rĭd'ē-əm) *n., pl.* **-ia** (-ē-ə). *Botany.* An organ that produces male gametes in the algae, fungi, mosses, and ferns. Compare **archegonium.** [New Latin : *anthera*, ANTHER + -IDIUM.] —**an·ther·id·i·al** *adj.*

an·ther·o·zo·id (ăn'thər-ə-zō'ĭd) *n. Botany.* A male sex cell produced by an antheridium. [ANTHER + ZO(O)ID.]

an·the·sis (ăn-thē'sĭs) *n. Botany.* The blooming or time of full bloom of a plant. [New Latin, from Greek *anthēsis*, from *anthein*, to bloom, from *anthos*, flower.]

ant·hill (ănt'hĭl') *n.* 1. A mound formed by ants or termites in digging or building a nest. 2. Anything suggestive of this, such as a teeming city or an overcrowded building.

antho– *prefix. Botany.* Indicates a plant or flower; for example, **anthocyanin.** [Greek *anthos*, blossom, flower.]

an·tho·cy·a·nin (ăn'thō-sī'ə-nĭn) *n.* Any of a class of water-soluble pigments, found in the sap of certain plants, that impart red, purple, or blue coloring to flowers, fruits, and autumn leaves. [ANTHO- + CYANIN(E).]

an·tho·di·um (ăn-thō'dē-əm) *n., pl.* **-dia** (-dē-ə). *Botany.* The flower head of composite plants, such as the aster, thistle, and golden rod. [New Latin, from Greek *anthōdēs*, flowerlike : ANTHO- + -OID.]

an·thol·o·gize (ăn-thŏl'ə-jīz') *tr.v.* **-gized, -gizing, -gizes.** To compile or include in an anthology.

an·thol·o·gy (ăn-thŏl'ə-jē) *n., pl.* **-gies.** 1. A collection of literary pieces, such as poems, short stories, or plays, usually suggesting a common theme. 2. Any collection of works of art, such as paintings, based on a specific period, theme, or subject. [New Latin *anthologia*, from Medieval Greek, from Greek, "flower gathering," a collection : ANTHO- + -LOGY.] —**an·tho·log·i·cal** (ăn'thə-lŏj'ĭ-kəl) *adj.* —**an·thol·o·gist** *n.*

An·tho·ny (ăn'thə-nē, -tə-), **Saint** (*c.* A.D. 250–350). Egyptian hermit and monk, known as St. Anthony of Egypt and St. Anthony the Abbot. He forsook a wealthy inheritance and went into the desert to become a hermit. Although he established no order, he is considered to be the founder of Christian monasticism.

Anthony, Susan Brownell (1820–1906). U.S. feminist leader and suffragette. She played a major part in getting the first legislation passed giving married women legal rights over their children, property, and wages. In 1869, with Elizabeth Stanton, she founded the National American Woman Suffrage Association.

Anthony of Pad·u·a (păj'ōō-ə), **Saint** (1195–1231). Portuguese friar, the most celebrated follower of St. Francis of Assisi. He gained a reputation as a miracle worker before his death in Padua.

–anthous *suffix.* Indicates a flower; for example, **ananthous.** [New Latin *-anthus*, from Greek *anthos*, flower.]

an·tho·zo·an (ăn'thə-zō'ən) *n.* Any of various marine organisms of the class Anthozoa, growing singly or in colonies, and including the corals and sea anemones. Also called "actinozoan." [New Latin *Anthozoa*, "flowerlike organisms" : ANTHO- + -ZOA.] —**an·tho·zo·an, an·tho·zo·ic** *adj.*

an·thra·cene (ăn'thrə-sēn') *n.* A crystalline hydrocarbon, $C_6H_4(CH)_2C_6H_4$, extracted from coal tar and used in the manufacture of dyes and organic chemicals. [Greek *anthrax* (stem *anthrak-*), ANTHRAX + -ENE.]

an·thra·cite (ăn'thrə-sīt') *n.* A hard coal containing more than 85 percent carbon and little volatile matter, that burns with a clean flame. Also called "hard coal." [Greek *anthrakitēs*, a kind of coal, from ANTHRAX.] —**an·thra·cit·ic** (ăn'thrə-sĭt'ĭk) *adj.*

an·thrac·nose (ăn-thrăk'nōs') *n.* Any of several diseases of plants caused by fungi and characterized by black spots on the leaves, twigs, or fruit. [French : Greek *anthrax*, charcoal, carbuncle, ANTHRAX + Greek *nosos*, disease.]

an·thrax (ăn'thrăks') *n.* 1. *Pathology.* An infectious, often fatal disease of warm-blooded animals, especially of cattle and sheep, caused by the bacterium *Bacillus anthracis*. It is transmissible to man, capable of affecting various organs, and especially characterized by malignant ulcers. 2. A lesion caused by this disease. [Latin, virulent ulcer, from Greek *anthrax†*, charcoal, carbuncle, pustule.]

anthrop. anthropological; anthropology.

an·throp·ic (ăn-thrŏp'ĭk) *adj.* Also **an·throp·i·cal** (-ĭ-kəl). Of or pertaining to humans or the era of human life. [Greek *anthrōpikos*, from *anthrōpos*, human being.]

anthropo–, anthrop– *prefix.* Indicates man or human; for example, **anthropoid, anthroposophy.** [From Greek *anthrōpos*, human being.]

an·thro·po·cen·tric (ăn'thrə-pə-sĕn'trĭk) *adj.* 1. Regarding the human race as the central fact of the universe. 2. Interpreting reality exclusively in terms of human values and experience. —**an·thro·po·cen·tric·i·ty** (ăn'thrə-pə-pō-sĕn-trĭs'ə-tē), **an·thro·po·cen·trism** (-sĕn'trĭz'əm) *n.*

an·thro·po·gen·e·sis (ăn'thrə-pə-jĕn'ə-sĭs) *n.* The scientific study of the origin of man. [New Latin : ANTHROPO- + -GENESIS.] —**an·thro·po·ge·net·ic** (ăn'thrə-pō-jə-nĕt'ĭk) *adj.*

an·thro·po·gen·ic (ăn'thrə-pə-jĕn'ĭk) *adj.* Of, pertaining to, or originating as a result of human activity. [ANTHROPO- + -GENIC.]

an·thro·po·ge·og·ra·phy (ăn'thrə-pō-jē-ŏg'rə-fē) *n.* The science of the geographical distribution of human communities.

an·thro·poid (ăn'thrə-poid') *adj.* 1. Resembling man, as the tailless semi-erect apes of the family Pongidae, which includes gorillas, chimpanzees, orangutans, and gibbons. 2. Resembling or charac-

teristic of an ape; apelike. 3. Shaped like a human being: *an anthropoid sarcophagus.*

~*n.* 1. Any member of the family Pongidae. 2. A person resembling an ape in appearance, behavior, or intelligence. [Greek *anthrōpoeidēs* : ANTHROP(O)- + -OID.] —**an·thro·poid·al** (ăn'thrə-poid'l) *adj.*

an·thro·pol·o·gy (ăn'thrə-pŏl'ə-jē) *n. Abbr.* **anthrop., anthropol.** The scientific study of the origin and of the physical, social, and cultural development and behavior of mankind. [New Latin *anthropologia* : ANTHROPO- + -LOGY.] —**an·thro·po·log·ic** (ăn'-thrə-pə-lŏj'ĭk), **an·thro·po·log·i·cal** *adj.* —**an·thro·po·log·i·cal·ly** *adv.* —**an·thro·pol·o·gist** *n.*

an·thro·pom·e·try (ăn'thrə-pŏm'ə-trē) *n.* The study of or technique for measuring the various sizes and proportions of the human body, for use in anthropological classification and comparison. [ANTHROPO- + -METRY.] —**an·thro·po·met·ric** (ăn'thrə-pə-mĕt'rĭk), **an·thro·po·met·ri·cal** *adj.* —**an·thro·pom·e·trist** *n.*

an·thro·po·mor·phism (ăn'thrə-pə-môr'fĭz'əm) *n.* The attribution of human form, motivation, characteristics, or behavior to inanimate objects, animals, gods, or natural phenomena. —**an·thro·po·mor·phic** *adj.*

an·thro·po·mor·phize (ăn'thrə-pə-môr'fīz') *tr.v.* **-phized, -phizing, -phizes.** To ascribe human characteristics to.

an·thro·po·mor·phous (ăn'thrə-pə-môr'fəs) *adj.* 1. Having or suggesting human form and appearance. 2. Of or pertaining to anthropomorphism. [Greek *anthrōpomorphos* : ANTHROPO- + -MORPHOUS.] —**an·thro·po·mor·phous·ly** *adv.*

an·thro·pop·a·thism (ăn'thrə-pŏp'ə-thĭz'əm) *n.* The attribution of human feelings to nonhuman beings, such as gods, animals, inanimate objects, or natural phenomena. [From Greek *anthrōpopathēs*, with human feelings : ANTHROPO- + *pathos*, feeling (see -pathy).]

an·thro·poph·a·gus (ăn'thrə-pŏf'ə-gəs) *n., pl.* **-gi** (-jī'). An eater of human flesh; cannibal. [Latin *anthrōpophagus*, from Greek *anthrō-pophagos*, man-eating : ANTHROPO- + -PHAGOUS.] —**an·thro·po·phag·ic** (ăn'thrə-pə-făj'ĭk), **an·thro·poph·a·gous** (-pŏf'ə-gəs) *adj.* —**an·thro·poph·a·gy** (ăn'thrə-pŏf'ə-jē) *n.*

an·thro·pos·o·phy (ăn'thrə-pŏs'ə-fē) *n.* A 20th-century religious system of thought derived from theosophy by Rudolph Steiner, that centers on human beings rather than God and concentrates on the development of all the human faculties. [ANTHROPO- + -SOPHY.] —**an·thro·po·soph·ic** (ăn'thrə-pə-sŏf'ĭk) *adj.* —**an·thro·pos·o·phist** (-pŏs'ə-fĭst) *n.*

–anthropus *suffix.* Indicates man; for example, **pithecanthropus.** [New Latin, from Greek *anthrōpos*, human being.]

an·thur·i·um (ăn-thŏor'ē-əm) *n.* Any of various tropical American plants of the genus *Anthurium*, many of which are cultivated as potted plants for their showy foliage. [New Latin *Anthurium*, "flower-tail" : ANTH(O)- + Greek *oura*, tail.]

an·ti (ăn'tī', ăn'tē) *n., pl.* **-tis.** *Informal.* A person who is opposed, as to a policy or proposal. [Noun use of ANTI-.] —**an·ti** *adj.*

anti–, ant– *prefix.* Indicates: 1. **a.** Opposition to; for example, **antismoking, antiabortion.** **b.** Hostility toward; for example, **anti-Semitic, antiwoman.** 2. Opposite to, especially in character; for example, **anticlimax, antihero.** 3. Reciprocal correspondence to; for example, **antilogarithm.** 4. Converse operation to; for example, **anticyclone, anticlockwise.** 5. Action against or prevention of; for example, **antifreeze, antidepressant.** *Note:* Many compounds other than those entered here may be formed with *anti-*. In forming compounds, *anti-* is normally joined to the following element without a space or hyphen: *antibody*. However, if the second element begins with a capital letter, it is separated with a hyphen: *anti-British*. It is also preferable to use the hyphen if the second element begins with *i*: *anti-intellectual*. The hyphen may always be used to aid clarity, as in nonce coinages: *anti-antivivisection*, or when the compound brings together three or more vowels: *anti-aesthetic*. [In borrowed Greek compounds *anti-* indicates : 1. Over against, opposite, as in **antichrist.** 2. Against, opposite, as in **antipathy.** 3. Responding to, as in **antiphon.** 4. Instead of, as in **antonomasia.** 5. Mirroring, counterfeiting, as in **antirrhinum.** Greek, from *anti*, opposite, against.]

an·ti·a·bor·tion (ăn'tē-ə-bôr'shən, ăn'tī-) *adj.* Opposed to abortion. —**an·ti·a·bor·tion·ist** *n.*

an·ti·air·craft (ăn'tē-âr'krăft', -kräft', ăn'tī-) *adj. Abbr.* **AA** Defensive, especially from a surface position, against aircraft or missile attack.

~*n.* An antiaircraft weapon.

an·ti·al·ler·gic (ăn'tē-ə-lûr'jĭk, ăn'tī-) *adj.* Also **an·ti·al·ler·gen·ic** (-ăl'ər-jĕn'ĭk). Preventing or relieving allergies.

an·ti·bal·lis·tic missile (ăn'tē-bə-lĭs'tĭk, ăn'tī-) *n. Abbr.* **ABM** A defensive missile designed to intercept and destroy a ballistic missile in flight.

an·ti·bar·y·on (ăn'tē-băr'ē-ŏn', ăn'tī-) *n.* The antiparticle of the **baryon** *(see).*

An·tibes (än-tēb'). Fashionable resort on the French Riviera, lying across the Bay of Angels from Nice. It is the center of one of Europe's largest flower-producing regions and is noted for the collection of Picasso's paintings in the Grimaldi Museum.

an·ti·bi·o·sis (ăn'tē-bī-ō'sĭs, ăn'tī-) *n.* An association between two or more organisms, particularly microorganisms, that is injurious to one of them. [New Latin : ANTI- + -BIOSIS.]

an·ti·bi·ot·ic (ăn'tē-bī-ŏt'ĭk, ăn'tī-) *n.* Any of various substances, such as penicillin and streptomycin, produced by certain fungi, bacteria, and similar organisms, that are effective in inhibiting the

anthurium *The bright waxy flowers of this tropical American plant have made it a popular potted plant around the world. This species,* Anthurium scherzerianum, *comes from Guatemala.*

growth of or destroying microorganisms and are widely used in the prevention and treatment of diseases. —*adj.* **1.** Of or pertaining to antibiotics. **2.** Of or pertaining to antibiosis. [New Latin *antibioticus* : ANTI- + BIOTIC.] —**an·ti·bi·ot·i·cal·ly** *adv.*

an·ti·bod·y (ăn′tĭ-bŏd′ē) *n., pl.* **-ies. 1.** Any of various proteins in the blood that are generated in reaction to the invasion of foreign substances, which they neutralize, thus producing immunity against infections. **2.** An object composed of antimatter. [20th century : translation of German *Antikörper* : ANTI- + *Körper*, body.]

an·tic (ăn′tĭk) *n.* **1.** *Often* **antics.** A ludicrous or extravagant act or gesture; a caper; a prank. **2.** *Archaic.* A clown; a jester. —*adj. Archaic.* Ludicrous; odd; fantastic. [Italian *antico*, "grotesque," "ancient" (originally with reference to fantastic sculptures found in ancient Roman ruins, hence, anything fantastic or grotesque), from Latin *antiquus*, ANTIQUE.]

an·ti·cat·a·lyst (ăn′tē-kăt′l-ĭst, ăn′tī-) *n.* **1.** A substance that retards or arrests a chemical reaction. **2.** A substance that reduces or destroys the effectiveness of a catalyst. Also called "inhibitor."

an·ti·cath·ode (ăn′tē-kăth′ōd′, ăn′tī-) *n.* An electrode that is the target in a cathode-ray tube, especially in an x-ray tube.

an·ti·chlor (ăn′tĭ-klôr′, -klōr′) *n.* A substance, such as sodium thiosulfate, used to neutralize the excess chlorine or hypochlorite left after bleaching textiles, fiber, or paper pulp. [ANTI- + CHLOR(INE).] —**anti·chlo·ristic** (ăn′tĭ-klô-rĭs′tĭk) *adj.*

an·ti·cho·lin·er·gic (ăn′tē-kō′lə-nûr′jĭk, ăn′tī-) *adj.* Opposing or antagonistic to the physiological action of parasympathetic or other cholinergic nerve fibers. —**an·ti·cho·lin·er·gic** *n.*

an·ti·cho·lin·es·ter·ase (ăn′tē-kō′lə-nĕs′tə-rās′, -rāz′, ăn′tī-) *n.* Any substance that inhibits the activity of **cholinesterase** (*see*).

an·ti·christ (ăn′tĭ-krīst′) *n.* **1.** An enemy of Christ or Christianity. **2. Antichrist.** The great antagonist who was expected by the early Church to take over the world but to be conquered forever by Christ at the Second Coming. **3.** A false Christ. [Middle English *Antecrist*, from Old French, from Late Latin *Antichrīstus*, from Greek *Antikhristos* (I John 2:18) : ANTI- + *Khristos*, CHRIST.]

an·tic·i·pant (ăn-tĭs′ə-pənt) *adj.* **1.** Coming or acting in advance. **2.** Expectant. —*n.* One who anticipates.

an·tic·i·pate (ăn-tĭs′ə-pāt′) *tr.v.* **-pated, -pating, -pates. 1.** To sense or realize beforehand; foresee. **2.** To look forward to as likely or certain; expect. **3.** To act in advance so as to prevent or counter; forestall. **4.** To foresee and fulfill or satisfy in advance. **5.** To cause to happen in advance; accelerate; precipitate. **6.** To consider prematurely; bring up before the proper time. **7.** To use in advance, as income not yet available. **8.** To pay (a debt) before it is due. —See Synonyms at **expect.** [Latin *anticipāre*, to take before : *ante-*, before + *capere*, to take.] —**an·tic·i·pa·tor** *n.* —**an·tic·i·pa·to·ry** (ăn-tĭs′ə-pə-tôr′ē, -tōr′ē) *adj.*

Usage: Some traditionalists hold that *anticipate* should not be used simply as a synonym for *expect.* They would restrict its use to senses in which it suggests some advance action, either to fulfill (*anticipate my desires*) or to forestall (*anticipate her opponent's next move*). Others accept its use in the senses of "to feel or realize beforehand" and "to look forward to" (often with the implication of foretasting pleasure): *He is anticipating a visit with his son.*

an·tic·i·pa·tion (ăn-tĭs′ə-pā′shən) *n.* **1.** The act of anticipating. **2.** The act or state of looking forward to something. **3.** Foreknowledge; intuition; premonition. **4.** *Law.* The use or assignment of funds from a trust fund before legitimately available for use. **5.** *Music.* The introduction of a note or notes of a new chord before the previous chord is resolved.

an·ti·cler·i·cal (ăn′tĭ-klĕr′ĭ-kəl, ăn′tī-) *adj.* Opposed to the influence and power of the clergy, especially in political affairs. —**an·ti·cler·i·cal** *n.* —**an·ti·cler·i·cal·ism** *n.*

an·ti·cli·max (ăn′tĭ-klī′măks′) *n.* **1.** A decline viewed in disappointing contrast with a previous rise: *the anticlimax of a brilliant career.* **2.** Something trivial or commonplace coming to conclude a series of significant events. **3.** *Rhetoric.* **a.** A sudden descent from the impressive or significant to the ludicrous or inconsequential. **b.** An instance of this; for example, *For God, for country, and for my dog.* —**an·ti·cli·mac·tic** (ăn′tĭ-klī-măk′tĭk) *adj.*

an·ti·cli·nal (ăn′tĭ-klī′nəl) *adj.* Sloping downward in opposite directions, as an anticline. [ANTI- + -CLINAL.]

an·ti·cline (ăn′tĭ-klīn′) *n. Geology.* A fold with strata sloping downward on both sides from a common crest. [ANTI- + -CLINE.]

an·ti·clock·wise (ăn′tĭ-klŏk′wīz′) *adv. Chiefly British.* Counterclockwise. —**an·ti·clock·wise** *adj.*

an·ti·co·ag·u·lant (ăn′tĭ-kō-ăg′yə-lənt, ăn′tī-) *n.* A substance that suppresses or counteracts coagulation, especially of the blood. —*adj.* Acting as an anticoagulant.

an·ti·co·in·ci·dence circuit (ăn′tē-kō-ĭn′sə-dəns, ăn′tī-) *n.* A specific binary logic element designed to provide input signals to a device according to fixed rules.

an·ti·con·vul·sant (ăn′tē-kən-vŭl′sənt, ăn′tī-) *n.* A drug that reduces or prevents convulsions. —**an·ti·con·vul·sant, an·ti·con·vul·sive** (ăn′tē-kən-vŭl′sĭv, ăn′tī-) *adj.*

an·ti·cy·clone (ăn′tĭ-sī′klōn′) *n.* An extensive system of winds spiraling outward from a high-pressure center, circling clockwise in the Northern Hemisphere and counterclockwise in the Southern Hemisphere. —**an·ti·cy·clon·ic** (ăn′tĭ-sī-klŏn′ĭk) *adj.*

an·ti·de·pres·sant (ăn′tē-dĭ-prĕs′ənt, ăn′tī-) *adj.* Any drug that relieves the symptoms of depression. —**an·ti·de·pres·sant, an·ti·de·pres·sive** (ăn′tē-dĭ-prĕs′ĭv, ăn′tī-) *adj.*

an·ti·di·u·ret·ic hormone (ăn′tē-dī′ə-rĕt′ĭk, ăn′tī-) *n.* A hormone, vasopressin (*see*).

an·ti·dote (ăn′tĭ-dōt′) *n.* **1.** A remedy or other agent to counteract or neutralize the effects of a poison. **2.** Anything that relieves or counteracts an unwanted condition. [Latin *antidotum*, from Greek *antidoton*, from *antididonai*, to give as a remedy against : ANTI- + *didonai*, to give.] —**an·ti·dot·al** (ăn′tī-dōt′l) *adj.*

an·ti·e·lec·tron (ăn′tē-ĭ-lĕk′trŏn′, ăn′tī-) *n.* A positron (*see*).

an·ti·en·zyme (ăn′tē-ĕn′zīm′, ăn′tī-) *n.* A substance that neutralizes or counteracts an enzyme. —**an·ti·en·zy·mat·ic** (ăn′tē-ĕn′zī-măt′ĭk, ăn′tī-), **an·ti·en·zy·mic** (-ĕn-zī′mĭk) *adj.*

An·tie·tam (ăn-tē′təm). Town in northern Maryland, emptying into the Potomac River. The bloody and inconclusive Battle of Antietam (or Sharpsburg, as it was called by the Confederates) was fought on its banks on September 17, 1862.

an·ti·feb·rile (ăn′tē-fĕb′rəl, -fē′brəl, -brīl′, ăn′tī-) *adj.* Able to reduce fever; antipyretic. —*n.* An antifebrile drug or agent.

an·ti·fer·ro·mag·ne·tism (ăn′tē-fĕr′ō-măg′nə-tĭz′əm, ăn′tī-) *n. Physics.* The property of certain substances that have relative permeabilities resembling paramagnetic substances but behave as ferromagnetic substances when their temperature is changed.

an·ti·foul·ing (ăn′tē-fou′lĭng, ăn′tī-) *adj.* Designed to prevent build-up on surfaces, clogging of valves, and the like.

antifouling paint *n.* A paint applied to ships' bottoms to prevent the growth of barnacles and other marine organisms.

an·ti·freeze (ăn′tĭ-frēz′) *n.* A substance, often a liquid such as ethylene glycol or alcohol, mixed with another liquid to lower the freezing point of the latter; especially, the liquid added to the cooling water of an internal-combustion engine to prevent freezing.

an·ti·gen (ăn′tĭ-jən) *n.* Any substance that, when introduced into the body, stimulates the production of an antibody. [ANTI- + -GEN.] —**an·ti·gen·ic** (ăn′tĭ-jĕn′ĭk) *adj.* —**an·ti·gen·i·cal·ly** *adv.* —**an·ti·ge·nic·i·ty** (ăn′tĭ-jə-nĭs′ə-tē) *n.*

An·tig·o·ne (ăn-tĭg′ə-nē). *Greek Mythology.* The daughter of Oedipus and Jocasta, who performed funeral rites over the body of her brother Polynices in defiance of her uncle Creon.

An·tig·o·nus I (ăn-tĭg′ə-nəs) (382–301 B.C.). King of Macedonia (after 306 B.C.). He was one of Alexander the Great's generals, and after Alexander's death he warred against other eastern governors in an attempt to gain sole control of Asia. He was killed in battle during his unsuccessful invasion of Egypt.

an·ti·grav·i·ty (ăn′tē-grăv′ə-tē, ăn′tī-) *n.* The effect of reducing or canceling a gravitational field. —*adj.* Canceling or reducing gravity or protecting against its effect.

An·ti·gua and Bar·bu·da (ăn-tē′gə, -gwə; bär-bōō′də). State in the Leeward Islands of the Caribbean comprising Antigua, Barbuda, and Redonda (uninhabited). Antigua was reached by Columbus (1493) and was colonized by the British (1632). Barbuda was annexed to Antigua in 1860. The territory was a British associated state from 1967 until independence in 1981. Antigua is a communications and business center for the Caribbean area. Formerly dependent on sugar, the economy now relies on tourism and cotton. Area, 422 square kilometers (171 square miles). Population, 76,000. Capital, St. John's. —See map at **Latin America.** —**An·ti·guan** *adj. & n.*

an·ti·ha·la·tion backing (ăn′tē-hā-lā′shən, ăn′tī-). A backing applied to a photographic film, consisting of a dye or pigment that absorbs light, to prevent halation that would otherwise occur as a result of light being reflected back into the emulsion.

an·ti·he·ro (ăn′tē-hîr′ō, ăn′tī-) *n.* A main character in a dramatic or literary work who is characterized by a lack of traditional heroic qualities.

an·ti·his·ta·mine (ăn′tē-hĭs′tə-mēn′, -mĭn, ăn′tī-) *n.* Any of various drugs used to reduce physiological effects associated with histamine production in allergies and colds. —**an·ti·his·ta·min·ic** (ăn′tē-hĭs′tə-mĭn′ĭk, ăn′tī-) *adj.*

an·ti·knock (ăn′tĭ-nŏk′, ăn′tī-) *n.* A substance, such as tetraethyl lead, added to gasoline to reduce engine knock.

An·ti-Leb·a·non Mountains (ăn′tĭ-lĕb′ə-nən). Range of mountains on the Lebanon-Syria border. The highest peak, Mt. Hermon, rises to 2,814 meters (9,232 feet).

an·ti·lep·ton (ăn′tē-lĕp′tŏn′, ăn′tī-) *n. Physics.* The antiparticle of any **lepton** (*see*).

An·til·les (ăn-tĭl′ēz). Two groups of islands in the West Indies. The Greater Antilles include Cuba, Hispaniola (Haiti and the Dominican Republic), Jamaica, and Puerto Rico; the Lesser Antilles include the Leeward Islands, the Windward Islands, the Netherlands Antilles, Trinidad and Tobago, and Barbados.

an·ti·log·a·rithm (ăn′tē-lô′gə-rĭth′əm, ăn′tē-lŏg′ə-, ăn′tī-) *n.* The number for which a given logarithm stands; for example, where log x equals y, the x is the antilogarithm of y. Also called "antilog." See **logarithm.** —**an·ti·log·a·rith·mic** *adj.*

an·ti·ma·cas·sar (ăn′tē-mə-kăs′ər, ăn′tī-) *n.* A protective or decorative covering for the backs of chairs and sofas. [ANTI- + MACASSAR (OIL).]

an·ti·mag·net·ic (ăn′tē-măg-nĕt′ĭk, ăn′tī-) *adj.* Impervious to the effect of a magnetic field; magnetization-resistant. Said especially of watch movements.

an·ti·ma·lar·i·al (ăn′tē-mə-lâr′ē-əl, ăn′tī-) *adj.* Effective against malaria. —*n.* An antimalarial drug.

an·ti·mat·ter (ăn'tĭ-măt'ər) n. A hypothetical form of matter consisting of antiparticles and having positron-surrounded nuclei composed of antiprotons and antineutrons. See **antiparticle**.

an·ti·mere (ăn'tĭ-mîr') n. Biology. A part or division corresponding to an opposite or similar part in an organism characterized by bilateral or radial symmetry. [ANTI- + -MERE.]

an·ti·mi·cro·bi·al (ăn'tē-mī-krō'bē-əl) adj. Capable of destroying or suppressing the growth of microorganisms.
—n. An antimicrobial agent.

an·ti·mis·sile (ăn'tē-mĭs'əl, ăn'tī-) n. A missile designed to intercept and destroy another missile in flight.

an·ti·mo·ni·al (ăn'tə-mō'nē-əl) adj. Of or containing antimony.
—n. A medicine with antimony as an ingredient.

an·ti·mo·ny (ăn'tə-mō'nē) n. Symbol **Sb** A metallic element having four allotropic forms the most common of which is a hard, extremely brittle, lustrous, silver-white, crystalline material. It is used in a wide variety of alloys, especially with lead in battery plates, and in the manufacture of flame-proofing compounds, paints, semiconductor devices, and ceramic products. Atomic number 51, atomic weight 121.75, melting point 630.5°C, boiling point 1,380°C, specific gravity 6.684, valences 3, 5. [Middle English, from Medieval Latin antimonium†.]

antimony glance n. An antimony ore, **stibnite** (see).

an·ti·ne·o·plas·tic (ăn'tē-nē'ō-plăs'tĭk, ăn'tī-) adj. Inhibiting the growth or spread of malignant tumors.

an·ti·neu·tri·no (ăn'tē-nōō-trē'nō, -nyōō-trē'nō, ăn'tī-) n., pl. -nos. Physics. The **antiparticle** (see) of the neutrino.

an·ti·neu·tron (ăn'tē-nōō'trŏn', -nyōō'trŏn', ăn'tī-) n. Physics. The **antiparticle** (see) of the neutron.

ant·ing (ăn'tĭng) n. The placing or rubbing by some birds of ants in their plumage, possibly to repel parasites.

an·ti·node (ăn'tĭ-nōd') n. Physics. The region or point of maximum amplitude between adjacent **nodes** (see).

an·ti·no·mi·an (ăn'tĭ-nō'mē-ən) n. Theology. A member of a Christian sect holding that faith alone is sufficient for salvation and that it is not necessary to obey any moral law.
—adj. 1. Of or pertaining to such a sect or doctrine. 2. Opposed to universal applicability of moral laws. [From Medieval Latin antinomus, from Greek : ANTI- + nomos, law.] —an·ti·no·mi·an·ism n.

an·tin·o·my (ăn-tĭn'ə-mē) n., pl. -mies. 1. Opposition or contradiction, especially between two laws or rules. 2. Contradiction between propositions that seem equally necessary and reasonable; a paradox. [Latin antinomia, from Greek : ANTI- + nomos, law.]

an·ti·nu·cle·on (ăn'tē-nōō'klē-ŏn', -nyōō'klē-ŏn', ăn'tī-) n. Physics. The **antiparticle** (see) of a nucleon.

An·ti·och (ăn'tē-ŏk'). Turkish **An·ta·kya** (ăn-täk'yə). Ancient city in southeastern Turkey, lying on the Orontes River near its mouth on the Mediterranean. St. Paul preached here and followers of Christ first adopted the name "Christian" here.

An·ti·o·chus (ăn-tī'ō-kəs). A Seleucid dynasty ruling in Syria (280–64 B.C.). Its most important member was **Antiochus III**, known as "the Great" (242–187; ruled 223–187). He conquered much of Asia Minor, but was forced to yield his territories after he was defeated by the Romans (190).

an·ti·ox·i·dant (ăn'tē-ŏk'sə-dənt, ăn'tī-) n. A chemical compound or substance that inhibits oxidation. —an·ti·ox·i·dant adj.

an·ti·par·al·lel (ăn'tē-păr'ə-lĕl', ăn'tī-) adj. 1. Physics. Parallel but rotating or pointing in opposite directions: antiparallel spin. 2. Mathematics. **a.** Designating two parallel lines that cut another pair of parallel lines in such a way that the interior opposite angles of the quadrilateral so formed are supplementary. **b.** Having the same magnitude but opposite senses. Said of vectors. Compare **parallel**.

an·ti·par·ti·cle (ăn'tē-pär'tĭ-kəl, ăn'tī-) n. A subatomic particle, such as a positron, antiproton, or antineutron, having the same mass, average lifetime, spin, magnitude of magnetic moment, and magnitude of electric charge as the particle to which it corresponds, but having the opposite sign of electric charge, opposite intrinsic parity, and opposite direction of magnetic moment. See **annihilation**.

an·ti·pas·to (ăn'tē-pä'stō, ăn'tē-păs'tō) n., pl. -tos or -ti (-tē). An appetizer; an hors d'oeuvre. [Italian : ANTI- (before) + pasto, food, from Latin pastus, past participle of pascere, to feed.]

An·tip·a·ter (ăn-tĭp'ə-tər) (c. 398–319 B.C.). Macedonian general and ruler. He acted as regent of Macedonia from 334 to 323 during Alexander the Great's Asian campaign and again from 321 to 319 for the mentally deficient Philip III and the infant Alexander IV. After his death the centralized unity of the Macedonian empire quickly disintegrated.

an·tip·a·thet·ic (ăn-tĭp'ə-thĕt'ĭk) adj. Also **an·tip·a·thet·i·cal** (-ĭ-kəl). 1. Having an inherent feeling of aversion, repugnance, or opposition. Often used with to: antipathetic to new ideas. 2. Causing a feeling of antipathy. —an·tip·a·thet·i·cal·ly adv.

an·tip·a·thy (ăn-tĭp'ə-thē) n., pl. -thies. 1. A strong feeling of aversion or opposition. 2. The object of this feeling. [Latin antipathia, from Greek antipatheia, from antipathēs, of opposite feelings : ANTI- (opposite) + pathos, feeling (see -pathy).]

an·ti·pe·ri·od·ic (ăn'tē-pîr'ē-ŏd'ĭk, ăn'tī-) adj. Preventing regular recurrence of disease or fever.
—n. An antiperiodic drug.

an·ti·per·i·stal·sis (ăn'tē-pĕr'ə-stôl'sĭs, -stăl'sĭs, ăn'tī-) n. Physiology. Contractions of the alimentary canal that push food back toward the mouth. Compare **peristalsis**.

an·ti·per·son·nel (ăn'tē-pûr'sə-nĕl', ăn'tī-) adj. Military. Designed to inflict casualties on the military personnel or civilian population of an enemy country rather than on equipment or arms.

an·ti·per·spi·rant (ăn'tē-pûr'spər-ənt, ăn'tī-) n. A preparation applied to the skin to reduce or prevent perspiration.

an·ti·phlo·gis·tic (ăn'tē-flə-jĭs'tĭk, ăn'tī-) adj. Reducing inflammation. —an·ti·phlo·gis·tic n.

an·ti·phon (ăn'tə-fŏn', -fən) n. 1. A plainsong setting of words, usually from the Bible, sung as a response as part of a liturgy. 2. A plainsong setting of a short liturgical text chanted or sung as a response before or after a psalm, psalm verse, or canticle. 3. A response; an answer: a resounding antiphon of dissent. [Late Latin antiphona, from Greek antiphōna, sung responses, ANTHEM.]

an·tiph·o·nal (ăn-tĭf'ə-nəl) adj. 1. Pertaining to or resembling an antiphon. 2. Sung or played as a response or in alternation (as in antiphony).
—n. Variant of **antiphonary**. —an·tiph·o·nal·ly adv.

an·tiph·o·nar·y (ăn-tĭf'ə-nĕr'ē) n., pl. -ies. Also **an·tiph·o·nal** (-nəl). A bound collection of antiphons, especially of the responsive choral parts of the divine office.

an·tiph·o·ny (ăn-tĭf'ə-nē) n., pl. -nies. 1. Responsive or antiphonal singing or chanting. 2. A composition that is sung in alternation or responsively; an antiphon. 3. A musical or other sound effect that answers or echoes another.

an·tiph·ra·sis (ăn-tĭf'rə-sĭs) n., pl. -ses (-sēz'). The use of a word in a sense contrary to its normal or accepted meaning for ironic or humorous effect; for example, He is just a mere baby of thirty years. [Late Latin, from Greek, from antiphrazein, "to speak by using the opposite sense": anti-, opposite + phrazein, to speak.]

an·tip·o·dal (ăn-tĭp'ə-dəl) adj. 1. Of, pertaining to, or situated on the opposite side or opposite sides of the earth. 2. Diametrically opposed; exactly opposite.

an·ti·pode (ăn'tĭ-pōd') n. A direct or exact opposite or contrary. [Back-formation from ANTIPODES.]

an·tip·o·des (ăn-tĭp'ə-dēz') pl.n. 1. Any two places or regions that are on opposite sides of the Earth. 2. Often **Antipodes**. Australia and New Zealand. [Middle English, from Latin, from Greek, plural of antipous (stem antipod-), with the feet opposite : ANTI- + pous, foot.] —an·tip·o·de·an (ăn-tĭp'ə-dē'ən) n. & adj.

an·ti·pope (ăn'tī-pōp') n. A person claiming to be or elected pope in opposition to the one considered to have been chosen by church law. [Middle English, from Old French antipape, from Medieval Latin antipāpa : ANTI- + pāpa, POPE.]

an·ti·pro·ton (ăn'tē-prō'tŏn', ăn'tī-) n. Physics. The **antiparticle** (see) of the proton.

an·ti·py·ret·ic (ăn'tē-pī-rĕt'ĭk) adj. Reducing or tending to reduce fever.
—n. Medication that reduces fever. —an·ti·py·re·sis (ăn'tē-pī-rē'sĭs) n.

an·ti·py·rine (ăn'tē-pī'rēn') n. A white powder, $C_{11}H_{12}N_2O$, used to reduce fever and relieve pain. [German Antipyrin (trademark) : ANTI- + PYR(O)- + -INE.]

antiq. 1. antiquarian; antiquary. 2. antiquity.

an·ti·quar·i·an (ăn'tĭ-kwâr'ē-ən) adj. Abbr. **antiq.** 1. Of or pertaining to antiquaries or the study of antiquities. 2. Dealing in or having to do with old or rare books.
—n. An antiquary. —an·ti·quar·i·an·ism n.

an·ti·quar·y (ăn'tə-kwĕr'ē) n., pl. -ies. Abbr. **antiq.** A student of, collector of, or dealer in antiquities or antiques. [Latin antīquārius, from adjective, of antiquity, from antīquus, ANTIQUE.]

an·ti·quate (ăn'tə-kwāt') tr.v. -quated, -quating, -quates. 1. To make obsolete or old-fashioned. 2. To give an antique appearance to. [Latin antiquāre, to leave in its ancient state, from antīquus, ANTIQUE.] —an·ti·qua·tion n.

an·ti·quat·ed (ăn'tə-kwā'tĭd) adj. 1. So old as to be no longer useful or applicable; outmoded; obsolete: antiquated laws. 2. Very old; aged. —an·ti·quat·ed·ness n.

an·tique (ăn-tēk') adj. 1. Belonging to, made in, or typical of an earlier period. 2. Of or belonging to ancient times; especially, of, from, or characteristic of ancient Greece or Rome. 3. Of or dealing in antiques. 4. Old-fashioned. —See Synonyms at **old**.
—n. 1. An object having special value because of its age; especially, a piece of furniture or other work of art valued for its workmanship, beauty, and age. 2. The style or manner of ancient times, especially that of ancient Greek or Roman art. Preceded by the: an admirer of the antique.
—tr.v. antiqued, -tiquing, -tiques. To give the appearance of an antique to. [French, from Latin antīquus, ancient, former.] —an·tique·ly adv. —an·tique·ness n. —an·tiqu·er n.

an·tiq·ui·ty (ăn-tĭk'wə-tē) n., pl. -ties. Abbr. **antiq.** 1. Often **Antiquity**. Ancient times, especially the times preceding the Middle Ages. 2. The people of ancient times. 3. The quality of being old or ancient; considerable age: a carving of great antiquity. 4. Often **antiquities**. Something belonging to or dating from a time long past.

an·ti·ra·chit·ic (ăn'tē-rə-kĭt'ĭk, ăn'tī-) adj. Curing or preventing rickets.
—n. An antirachitic drug or food.

an·tir·rhi·num (ăn'tə-rī'nəm) n. Any plant of the genus Antirrhinum, such as a **snapdragon** (see). [New Latin, from Greek antirrhinon, "plant having snoutlike flowers" : anti-, counterfeiting + rhis† (stem rhin-), nose (see **rhino-**).]

an·ti·scor·bu·tic (ăn'tē-skôr-byōō'tĭk, ăn'tī-) adj. Curing or preventing scurvy.
—n. A food or drug that cures or prevents scurvy.

antler Found on the heads of most species of deer, antlers are normally confined to the male and are used during the breeding season in contests between rivals. Made of bone, they are shed at the end of each mating season and regrow with more spikes every year. The antlers of the barren ground caribou (above) can have a spread of up to 1.2 meters (4 feet).

---

an·ti·Sem·ite (ăn′tē-sĕm′īt′, ăn′tī-) *n.* A person who is hostile toward or prejudiced against Jews. —**an·ti·Se·mit·ic** (ăn′tē-sə-mĭt′ĭk, ăn′tī-) *adj.* —**an·ti·Sem·i·tism** *n.*

an·ti·sep·sis (ăn′tə-sĕp′sĭs) *n.* The destruction of microorganisms that cause disease, fermentation, or putrefaction. Compare **asepsis.**

an·ti·sep·tic (ăn′tə-sĕp′tĭk) *adj.* **1.** Of, pertaining to, or designating antisepsis. **2.** Capable of producing antisepsis. **3.** Thoroughly clean. **4.** *Informal.* Devoid of enlivening or enriching qualities; austere; clinical.
~*n.* An antiseptic drug or agent. —**an·ti·sep·ti·cal·ly** *adv.*

an·ti·se·rum (ăn′tē-sîr′əm, ăn′tī-) *n., pl.* **-rums** or **-ra** (-rə). Human or animal serum containing antibodies against at least one antigen, used to treat or provide immunity to an infection.

an·ti·slav·er·y (ăn′tē-slā′və-rē, -slāv′rē, ăn′tī-) *adj.* Opposed to or against slavery.

an·ti·so·cial (ăn′tē-sō′shəl, ăn′tī-) *adj.* **1.** Shunning the society of others; unsociable. **2.** Upsetting or offensive to other people: *antisocial behavior.* **3.** Opposed to or interfering with the social order or the general welfare of society. —**an·ti·so·cial·ly** *adv.*

an·ti·spas·mod·ic (ăn′tē-spăz-mŏd′ĭk, ăn′tī-) *adj.* Easing or preventing spasms.
~*n.* An antispasmodic drug.

an·ti·stat·ic (ăn′tē-stăt′ĭk, ăn′tī-) *adj.* Preventing or inhibiting the build-up of static electricity.

an·tis·tro·phe (ăn-tĭs′trə-fē) *n.* **1.** In ancient Greek choral poetry or drama, the movement following and in the same meter as the strophe, sung while the chorus moves in the opposite direction from that of the strophe. **2.** The second stanza, and those like it, in a poem consisting of alternating stanzas in contrasting metric form. [Late Latin, from Greek *antistrophē* : ANTI- + STROPHE.] —**an·ti·stroph·ic** (ăn′tĭ-strŏf′ĭk) *adj.* —**an·ti·stroph·i·cal·ly** *adv.*

an·ti·sub·ma·rine (ăn′tē-sŭb′mə-rēn′, -sŭb′mə-rēn′, ăn′tī-) *adj. Abbr.* **AS** Directed against enemy submarines.

an·ti·tank (ăn′tē-tăngk′, ăn′tī-) *adj. Abbr.* **AT** Designed or used for combat against tanks or other armored vehicles.

an·tith·e·sis (ăn-tĭth′ə-sĭs) *n., pl.* **-ses** (-sēz′). **1.** Direct contrast; opposition. **2.** The direct or exact opposite: *Despair is the antithesis of hope.* **3. a.** The juxtaposition of sharply contrasting ideas in balanced or parallel words, phrases, or grammatical structures; for example, *They died that we might live.* **b.** The second and contrasting part of such a juxtaposition. **4.** In Hegelian philosophy, the second stage of the dialectic process. [Late Latin, from Greek, opposition, from *antitithenai*, to oppose : ANTI- + *tithenai*, to set, place.]

an·ti·thet·i·cal (ăn′tə-thĕt′ĭ-kəl) *adj.* Also **an·ti·thet·ic** (-ĭk). **1.** Pertaining to, of the nature of, or including antithesis. **2.** Directly opposed in every respect. —See Synonyms at **opposite.** [Late Latin *antitheticus,* from Greek *antithetikos,* from *antitithenai,* to oppose. See **antithesis.**] —**an·ti·thet·i·cal·ly** *adv.*

an·ti·tox·ic (ăn′tī-tŏk′sĭk) *adj.* **1.** Counteracting a toxin or poison. **2.** Of, pertaining to, or constituting an antitoxin.

an·ti·tox·in (ăn′tī-tŏk′sĭn) *n.* **1.** An antibody formed in response to and capable of neutralizing a poison of biological origin. **2.** An animal serum containing such antibodies.

an·ti·trades (ăn′tī-trādz′, ăn′tī-) *pl.n.* The westerly winds above the trade winds of the tropics, which become the westerly winds of the middle latitudes.

an·ti·trust (ăn′tē-trŭst′, ăn′tī-) *adj.* Opposing or concerned with the regulation of trusts, cartels, or similar business monopolies.

an·ti·tus·sive (ăn′tē-tŭs′ĭv, ăn′tī-) *adj.* Capable of relieving coughing.
~*n.* An antitussive drug.

an·ti·type (ăn′tī-tīp′) *n.* One that is foreshadowed or represented by a symbol or earlier type, such as a figure in the New Testament who has a counterpart in the Old Testament. [Medieval Latin *antitypus,* from Greek *antitupos,* "opposite to the die" (hence, anything resembling the impression made by a die or stamp) : *anti-,* opposite + *tupos,* die (see **type**).] —**an·ti·typ·i·cal** (ăn′tī-tĭp′ĭ-kəl) *adj.*

an·ti·ven·in (ăn′tē-vĕn′ĭn, ăn′tī-) *n.* **1.** An antitoxin active against a particular venom. **2.** An antiserum containing such an antitoxin. [ANTI- + VEN(OM) + -IN.]

ant·ler (ănt′lər) *n.* Either of a pair of hard, bony, deciduous growths, usually elongated and branched, that characteristically grow on the heads of male deer and related animals. [Middle English *aunteler,* from Old French *antoillier,* from Vulgar Latin *anteoculāris* (unattested), "before the eyes" : ANTE- + Latin *oculus,* eye.] —**ant·lered** (ănt′lərd) *adj.*

Ant·li·a (ănt′lē-ə) *n.* A constellation in the Southern Hemisphere near Hydra and Vela. [Latin *antlia,* pump, from Greek *antlia, antlos,* bucket.]

ant lion *n.* Any insect of the family Myrmeleontidae, of which the adults resemble dragonflies; especially, the larva of such an insect, which digs holes to trap ants and other insects for food. Also called "doodlebug."

An·to·ne·scu (ăn′tə-nĕs′kōō), **Ion** (1882–1946). Romanian marshal and prime minister. He was chief of staff of the Romanian army and was appointed prime minister with unlimited powers on September 5, 1940, by King Carol II. For the rest of World War II Antonescu acted as Hitler's puppet and connived at violent pogroms against the Jews. He was executed for his war crimes in 1946.

An·to·nine Wall (ăn′tə-nīn′). A defensive Roman frontier in Scotland that stretched for *c.* 58 kilometers (36 miles) between the Clyde and the Firth of Forth. It was built in A.D. 142 on the orders of the

emperor Antoninus Pius. Small traces of the wall remain.

An·to·ni·o·ni (ăn-tō′nē-ō′nē), **Michelangelo** (1912–). Italian film director. He developed a highly visual style in which realism was subordinated to a metaphorical treatment of subject. Among his most famous films are *L'Avventura* (1959), *The Red Desert* (1964), *Blow-up* (1966), and *Zabriskie Point* (1969).

Antonius, Marcus. See Mark Antony.

an·to·no·ma·sia (ăn-tə-nō-mā′zhə) *n.* **1.** The substitution of a title or epithet for a proper name, as in calling a king "His Majesty." **2.** The substitution of a personal name for a common noun to designate a member of a group or class, as in calling a libertine "a Don Juan." [Latin, from Greek, from *antonomazein,* to name instead : *ant(i)-,* instead of + *onomazein,* to name, from *onoma,* name.] —**an·ton·o·mas·tic** (ăn-tŏn′ə-măs′tĭk) *adj.*

an·to·nym (ăn′tə-nĭm′) *n. Abbr.* **ant.** A word having a meaning opposite to that of another word; for example, *light* is an antonym of *dark.* Compare **synonym.** [ANT(I)- + -ONYM.] —**an·ton·y·mous** (ăn-tŏn′ə-məs) *adj.* —**an·ton·y·my** (ăn-tŏn′ə-mē) *n.*

an·tre (ăn′tər) *n. Chiefly Poetic.* A cavern or cave. [French, from Latin *antrum,* cave. See **antrum.**]

An·trim (ăn′trĭm). A predominantly agricultural county in northeastern Northern Ireland. Its county town is Belfast.

an·trorse (ăn′trôs′) *adj. Biology.* Directed forward and upward. [New Latin *antrorsus* : perhaps blend of ANTERIOR and DEXTRORSE.] —**an·trorse·ly** *adv.*

an·trum (ăn′trəm) *n., pl.* **-tra** (-trə). A cavity, usually in bone; especially, either of the sinuses in the upper jaw opening into the nose. [Late Latin, cavity in the body, from Latin, cave, from Greek *antron.*]

Ant·wer·pen (änt′vĕr′pən). *French* **An·vers** (äN-vâr′); *English* **Antwerp** (ănt′wûrp′). One of Europe's busiest ports, lying on the Scheldt River in northern Belgium. It was a trading center as early as the 8th century, and the world's first stock exchange was founded here in 1460. It has been one of the leading centers of the diamond industry since the 15th century.

A·nu·bis (ə-nōō′bĭs, ə-nyōō′-). *Egyptian Mythology.* A jackal-headed god, son of Osiris, who conducted the dead to judgment.

A·nu·ra·dha·pu·ra (ə-nə-rä′də-pōōr′ə). Market town in northern Sri Lanka and the capital of North Central province. It was founded in the 5th century B.C. and became the capital of the Sinhalese kingdom and a major center of Buddhism.

a·nu·ran (ə-nōōr′ən, ə-nyōōr′-) *adj.* Of or belonging to the Anura, an order of amphibians containing the frogs and toads; salientian. ~*n.* A frog or toad. Also called "salientian." [New Latin *Anura* : AN- (without) + Greek *oura,* tail.]

an·u·re·sis (ăn′yə-rē′sĭs) *n.* Inability to urinate. [AN- (without) + Greek *ouresis,* urination, from *ourein,* to urinate, from *ouran,* urine.] —**an·u·ret·ic** (ăn′yə-rĕt′ĭk) *adj.*

a·nu·ri·a (ə-nōōr′ē-ə, ə-nyōōr′-) *n.* The pathological condition characterized by failure of the kidneys to produce urine. [New Latin : AN- (not) + -URIA.] —**a·nu·ric** *adj.*

a·nu·rous (ə-nōōr′əs, ə-nyōōr′-) *adj.* Having no tail; tailless. [AN- + -UROUS.]

a·nus (ā′nəs) *n., pl.* **anuses.** The excretory opening at the end of the alimentary canal. [Latin *ānus,* ring.]

Anvers. See **Antwerpen.**

an·vil (ăn′vĭl) *n.* **1.** A heavy block of iron or steel with a smooth, flat top on which metals are shaped by hammering. **2.** A part of a tool or device that resembles an anvil in shape or function, such as: **a.** The lower part of a telegraph key. **b.** The fixed jaw in a set of calipers, against which the object to be measured is placed. **3.** *Anatomy.* A bone, the **incus** *(see).* [Middle English *anvil(t), anvelt,* Old English *anfealt, anfilt* : *an- + -fealt,* "beaten."]

anx·i·e·ty (ăng-zī′ə-tē) *n., pl.* **-ties. 1.** A state of uneasiness and distress about future uncertainties; apprehension; worry. **2.** A cause of such uneasiness; a worry. **3.** *Psychiatry.* Intense fear or dread lacking an unambiguous cause or a specific threat. **4.** Eagerness: *his anxiety to go home.* [Latin *anxietās* (stem *anxietāt-*), from *anxius,* ANXIOUS.]

   Synonyms: concern, solicitude, worry.

anx·ious (ăngk′shəs, ăng′shəs) *adj.* **1.** Worried and strained about some uncertain event or matter; uneasy. **2.** Attended with, showing, or causing such worry; full of anxieties: *This is an anxious time for her.* **3.** Eagerly or earnestly desirous. Used with *to: The child was anxious to please the teacher.* —See Synonyms at **eager.** [Latin *anxius,* from *angere,* to torment, choke.] —**anx·ious·ly** *adv.* —**anx·ious·ness** *n.*

an·y (ĕn′ē) *adj.* **1. a.** One or some, taken at random from three or more; a, an, or some: *Any book will do. Pick any four numbers.* **b.** Each and every: *Any child knows that.* **c.** The whole amount; all: *We will turn over any profit to charity.* **2. a.** Some, regardless of quantity, number, or extent: *Did you buy any butter?* **b.** Even the smallest amount or quantity: *Don't make any noise!* **c.** Unlimited in extent, amount, or number: *any amount of luck; any number of books.* **3.** Of an ordinary or indeterminate kind. Used in negative statements, often with *just: Edwin can't wear just any tie.* **4.** No matter how large or small: *not at any price.*
~*pron.* **1.** Any one or ones among three or more. **2.** Any quantity or part; some. **3.** Anybody; any person.
~*adv.* **1.** To any degree or extent. Used with comparative forms: *Is he any better now?* **2.** *Informal.* At all: *The medicine didn't help any.* [Middle English *any, eny,* Old English *ænig.*]

   Usage: Any may be used with either a singular or a plural verb:

Anubis *A bronze statuette of the jackal-headed Egyptian god, probably made during the Ptolemaic period (323–30 B.C.).*

Any of these books would be suitable implies "any *one* of . . ."; *Are any available?* implies "some." In negative constructions, *any* is the accepted usage. *I haven't any money* does not have a corresponding form *I haven't some money.* There is, however, a more formal alternative, *I have no money.*

An·yang (än′yäng′). Agricultural trading center in Henan province, northeast China. It was the capital of the Shang dynasty *c.* 1711–1066 B.C.

an·y·bod·y (ĕn′ē-bŏd′ē, -bŭd′ē, bə-dē) *pron.* Any person, no matter who.
~*n., pl.* **anybodies.** A person of some consequence: *everybody who is anybody.*

an·y·how (ăn′ē-hou′) *adv.* **1.** In any case; at any rate. **2.** Carelessly; neglectfully.

an·y·more (ĕn′ē-môr′, -mōr′) *adv.* Any longer; from now on. Used in negative and interrogative constructions: *The store doesn't accept credit cards anymore.*

an·y·one (ĕn′ē-wŭn′, -wən) *pron.* Any person, no matter who; any body: *Anyone who disagrees with this editorial can write a letter to the editor.*

Usage: A controversy arises over the appropriate pronoun to use in certain types of sentence where *anyone* is the subject: *Anyone can do what — wants.* The use of the traditionally neutral pronoun *he* in this context may be misleading if females are involved, and in recent years has attracted criticism as being sexist. On the other hand, the use of *she* sounds odd and possibly insulting, and to use *he or she* is extremely awkward. For such reasons, the use of *they, their,* or the like, long-attested but widely condemned, has taken on a new respectability as an idiomatic solution to the problem. The traditional grammarian, however, would wish the singular sense of *anyone* to be matched by a singular pronoun and verb, and this principle is still the safest one to follow in formal speech or writing.

aphid *Greenfly (top) and blackfly are both aphids—soft-bodied insects that feed on the sap of plants and often act as carriers of plant diseases. Many species are milked by ants for their honeydew, a sugary secretion exuded by the aphids' bodies.*

an·y·place (ĕn′ē-plās′) *adv.* Anywhere.

an·y·road (ĕn′ē-rōd′) *adv. British Regional.* Anyway.

an·y·thing (ăn′ē-thĭng′) *pron.* Any object, act, occurrence, or matter whatever.
~*adv.* To any degree or extent; at all: *The movie wasn't anything like we'd expected.* **—anything but.** By no means; not at all. **—like anything.** *Informal.* Used as an intensive: *She screamed like anything.* **—or anything.** *Informal.* Something similar: *Did he argue or anything?*

an·y·time (ĕn′ē-tīm′) *adv.* At any time.

an·y·way (ĕn′ē-wā′) *adv.* **1.** Nevertheless; at any rate; in any case. **2.** In any manner or by any means whatever. **3.** Carelessly; neglectfully.

an·y·ways (ĕn′ē-wāz′) *adv. Nonstandard.* Anyway.

an·y·where (ăn′ē-hwâr′) *adv.* **1.** To, in, or at any place. **2.** To any extent or degree; at all: *We aren't anywhere near being finished.* **—anywhere from** (or **between**). Any quantity, degree, time, or the like between given bounds: *It could last anywhere from 20 minutes to an hour.* **—get anywhere.** To succeed to any degree: *I don't see how he can get anywhere with his attitude.* **—get nowhere.** To fail to succeed: *I got nowhere with my proposal.*

an·y·wise (ĕn′ē-wīz′) *adv.* In any way or manner. [Old English *on ǣnige wīsan,* in any wise.]

An·zac (ăn′zăk′) *n.* **1.** A soldier in the Australian and New Zealand Army Corps formed in World War I. **2.** Any soldier from New Zealand or Australia. **—An·zac** *adj.*

A-OK, A-O·kay (ā′ō-kā′) *adj.* Functioning perfectly; excellent; fine. [From the phrase *all systems o.k.*]

Aorangi. See Mount **Cook.**

a·o·rist (ā′ər-ĭst) *n.* A verb tense originally used in classical Greek. It usually denotes past action without indicating completion, continuation, or repetition of this action. [Greek *(khronos) aoristos,* "the indefinite (tense)" : A- (not) + *horistos,* definable, from *horizein,* to delimit, from *horos*†, boundary, limit.] **—a·o·rist, a·o·ris·tic** *adj.* **—a·o·ris·ti·cal·ly** *adv.*

Aphrodite *The* Venus de Milo, *as it is known, is a statue of the Greek goddess Aphrodite, dating from about 100* B.C. *It was found on the Greek island of Milos and is in the Louvre, Paris.*

a·or·ta (ā-ôr′tə) *n., pl.* **-tas** or **-tae** (-tē). *Anatomy.* The main trunk of the systemic arteries, carrying oxygenated blood from the left side of the heart to the arteries of all limbs and organs except the lungs. [New Latin, from Greek *aortē,* aorta, "appendices (of the heart)," from *aeirein,* to raise up.] **—a·or·tic** (ā-ôr′tĭk), **a·or·tal** (ā-ôr′tl) *adj.*

aortic arch *n.* The section of the aorta that passes over the top of the heart and back down to the fourth thoracic vertebra.

Aotearoa. See **New Zealand.**

a·ou·dad (ä′o͞o-dăd′, ou′dăd′) *n.* A wild sheep, *Ammotragus lervia,* of northern Africa, having long, curved horns and a beardlike growth of hair on the neck and chest. Also called "Barbary sheep." [French, from Berber *audad.*]

ap. apothecary.

a.p. **1.** additional premium. **2.** author's proof.

A.P. Associated Press.

a·pace (ə-pās′) *adv.* At a rapid pace; rapidly; swiftly. [Middle English *apas, apace,* step by step, from Old French *a pas* : *a,* to, from Latin *ad* + *pas,* step, PACE.]

a·pache (ə-păsh′) *n., pl.* **apaches** (ə-păsh′). A member of the Parisian underworld. [French, from (English) APACHE (alluding to the tribe's warlike or violent character).]

A·pach·e (ə-păch′ē) *n., pl. -es* or collectively **Apache** (for sense 1). **1.** A member of a formerly nomadic tribe of North American Indians inhabiting the southwestern United States and northern Mexico. **2.** Any of the Athapascan languages of the Apache. [Spanish, probably from Zuñi *Apachu,* enemy.]

apanage. Variant of **appanage.**

ap·a·re·jo (ŏp′ə-rā′hō, -rā′ō) *n., pl.* **-jos.** *Southwestern U.S.* A packsaddle made of a stuffed leather pad. [Mexican Spanish, from Spanish, equipment, from *aparejar,* to prepare.]

a·part (ə-pärt′) *adv.* **1. a.** In pieces. **b.** To pieces. **2. a.** Separately or at a distance in time, place, or position: *Over the years, they grew apart.* **b.** To one side; aside. **3.** One from another: *It's easy to confuse the two pictures if you see them apart.* **4.** Independently or separately in consideration or thought. **5.** Out of consideration or set aside; aside: *These few problems apart, it's all going well.* **—apart from.** **1.** With the exception of. **2.** Besides: *Apart from me, there are four others.*
~*adj.* Having individualizing features or characteristics. Used after the noun: *a race apart.* [Middle English, from Old French *a part,* to the side : *a,* to + PART.]

a·part·heid (ə-pärt′hīt′, -hāt′) *n.* **1.** An official policy of racial segregation practiced in the Republic of South Africa with a view to promoting and maintaining white ascendancy. **2.** A condition of separateness; separation or segregation. [Afrikaans, "apartness" : *apart,* separate, from French *à part,* APART + *-heid,* -HOOD.]

a·part·ment (ə-pärt′mənt) *n. Abbr.* **apt. 1.** A room or suite of rooms designed for housekeeping and generally located in a building occupied by more than one household. **2.** A building that comprises a number of apartments. **3.** A room. [French *appartement,* from Italian *appartemento,* from *appartare,* to separate, from *a parte,* APART.]

apartment house *n.* A building divided into apartments. Also called "apartment building."

ap·as·tron (ă-păs′trən, -trŏn′) *n., pl.* **-tra** (-trə). *Astronomy.* The point in an orbit around a star that is farthest from the star; especially, this point in the orbit of one star around another in a binary system. [New Latin, from Greek : *ap(o)-,* away from + *astron,* star.]

ap·a·tet·ic (ăp′ə-tĕt′ĭk) *adj. Zoology.* Pertaining to or designating coloration serving as natural camouflage to an animal. [Greek *apatētikos,* deceptive, from *apateuein,* to cheat, from *apatē*†, deceit, fraud.]

ap·a·thet·ic (ăp′ə-thĕt′ĭk) *adj.* **1.** Feeling or showing little or no emotion. **2.** Uninterested; indifferent; listless. —See Synonyms at **indifferent.** [Blend of APATHY and PATHETIC.] **—ap·a·thet·i·cal·ly** *adv.*

ap·a·thy (ăp′ə-thē) *n.* **1.** Lack of emotion or feeling. **2.** Lack of interest or absence of response, especially to what is generally found exciting, interesting, or moving; indifference. [Greek *apatheia,* from *apathēs,* without feeling : A- (without) + *pathos,* feeling.]

ap·a·tite (ăp′ə-tīt′) *n.* A natural, variously colored form of calcium fluoride phosphate, $Ca_5F(PO_4)_3$, with chlorine, hydroxyl, or carbonate sometimes replacing the fluoride. It is a source of phosphorus compounds and is used in the manufacture of fertilizers. [German *Apatit,* "the deceptive stone" (often mistaken for other minerals), from Greek *apatē,* deceit. See **apatetic.**]

ape (āp) *n.* **1.** Any of various large, tailless Old World primates of the family Pongidae, including the chimpanzee, gorilla, gibbon, and orang-utan. **2.** Broadly, any monkey. **3.** A mimic or imitator. **4.** *Informal.* A large, clumsy, coarse person.
~*tr.v.* **aped, aping, apes.** To mimic. —See Synonyms at **imitate.** [Middle English *ape,* Old English *apa,* from Germanic *apan-* (unattested).]

a·peak (ə-pēk′) *adv. Nautical.* In a vertical or almost vertical position or direction. [Earlier *apike* : A- + PIKE (peak).]

A·pel·les (ə-pĕl′ēz) (*fl.* 4th century B.C.). Greek painter. He was court painter to Philip II of Macedon and Alexander the Great and was considered the greatest painter of his time. No copies of his paintings exist.

ape-man (āp′măn′) *n., pl.* **-men** (-mĕn′). Loosely, any of several extinct primates considered intermediate between apes and modern man.

Ap·en·nines (ăp′ə-nīnz′). Mountain system running about 1,350 kilometers (840 miles) along the length of peninsular Italy. It has two active volcanoes, Vesuvius and Etna. The highest peak, at 2,914 meters (9,560 feet), is Monte Corno.

a·per·çu (ä′pĕr-sü′) *n., pl.* **-çus** (-sü′). A brief outline; summary. [Past participle of *apercevoir,* to PERCEIVE.]

a·pe·ri·ent (ə-pîr′ē-ənt) *adj.* Gently purgative; laxative.
~*n.* A mild laxative. [Latin *aperiēns* (stem *aperient-*), present participle of *aperīre,* to uncover, open.]

a·pe·ri·od·ic (ā′pîr′ē-ŏd′ĭk) *adj.* **1.** Not occurring at regular intervals; irregular. **2.** *Electronics.* Of or designating a circuit that is not capable of resonance at the frequency used. **—a·pe·ri·od·i·cal·ly** *adv.* **—a·pe·ri·o·dic·i·ty** (ā′pîr′ē-ə-dĭs′ə-tē) *n.*

a·pé·ri·tif (ä-pĕr′ə-tēf′) *n.* An alcoholic drink taken to stimulate the appetite before a meal. [French, from Old French *aperitif,* from Medieval Latin *aperitīvus,* from Latin *aperīre,* to open.]

ap·er·ture (ăp′ər-cho͝or′, -chər) *n.* **1.** A hole, gap, slit, or other opening; an orifice. **2.** *Optics.* **a.** A usually adjustable opening in an optical instrument that limits the amount of light passing through a lens or onto a mirror. **b.** The effective diameter of a lens or mirror divided by its focal length. See **f-number. 3.** The diameter of a radio telescope. [Latin *apertūra,* from *apertus,* open, from the past participle of *aperīre,* to open.] **—ap·er·tur·al** *adj.*

aperture card *n.* A punched card upon which some portion of a microfilmed document is mounted.

a·pet·al·ous (ā-pĕt′l-əs) *adj. Botany.* Having no petals. **—a·pet·al·y** (ā-pĕt′l-ē) *n.*

a·pex (ā′pĕks′) *n., pl.* **apexes** or **apices** (ā′pə-sēz′, ăp′ə-) **1.** The highest point of something; the vertex. **2.** The culmination, as of an activity or effort. **3.** The pointed end of something; the tip. **3.** *Astronomy.* A point on the celestial sphere toward which the solar system moves relative to neighboring stars. —See Synonyms at **summit.** [Latin *apex*, point, summit, top.]

A·PEX, A·pex (ā′pĕks′) *n.* A system of discount air fares available on bookings paid for in advance of a minimum stipulated period. [*A*dvance *P*urchase *Ex*cursion.]

a·phaer·e·sis, a·pher·e·sis (ə-fĕr′ə-sĭs) *n., pl.* **-ses** (-sēz′). The loss of one or more letters or sounds from the beginning of a word, as in *round* for *around* or *most* for *almost.* [Late Latin, from Greek *aphairesis*, a taking away, from *aphairein*, to take away from : *ap(o)-*, away from + *hairein†*, to take.] —**aph·ae·ret·ic** (ăf′ə-rĕt′ĭk) *adj.*

a·pha·gi·a (ə-fā′jē-ə, -jə) *n.* Inability to swallow. [New Latin : A- (not) + -PHAGIA.]

aph·a·nite (ăf′ə-nīt′) *n.* Any igneous rock with constituents so fine that they cannot be seen by the naked eye. [French : Greek *aphanēs*, unseen : A- (not) + *phainesthai*, to be seen, from *phainein*, to see + -ITE.] —**aph·a·nit·ic** (ăf′ə-nĭt′ĭk) *adj.* —**aph·a·nit·ism** *n.*

a·pha·sia (ə-fā′zhə) *n.* Partial or total loss of the ability to use or articulate words, usually resulting from brain damage. [New Latin, from Greek : A- (without) + -PHASIA.] —**a·pha·si·ac** (ə-fā′zē-ăk′) *n.* —**a·pha·sic** (ə-fā′zĭk) *adj.* &. *n.*

a·phe·li·on (ə-fē′lē-ən, ə-fēl′yən, ə-fēl′yən) *n., pl.* **-lia** (-lē-ə). The point on the orbit of a planet or comet that is farthest from the sun. Compare **perihelion.** [New Latin, variant of *aphelium* : Greek *ap(o)-*, away from + *hēlios*, Sun.]

a·phe·li·o·trop·ic (ə-fē′lē-ə-trŏp′ĭk) *adj. Biology.* Turning away from the sun, as roots do. [AP(O)- (away from) + HELIOTROPIC.] —**a·phe·li·o·trop·i·cal·ly** *adv.* —**a·phe·li·ot·ro·pism** (ə-fē′lē-ŏt′rə-pĭz′əm) *n.*

aph·e·sis (ăf′ə-sĭs) *n, pl.* **-ses** (-sēz). The loss of a short unstressed vowel from the beginning of a word; for example, *squire* for *esquire.* [New Latin, from Greek *aphesis*, a letting go, from *aphienai*, to let go : *ap(o)-*, away + *hienai*, to send.] —**a·phet·ic** (ə-fĕt′ĭk) *adj.* —**a·phet·i·cal·ly** *adv.*

a·phid (ā′fĭd, ăf′ĭd) *n.* Any of various small, soft-bodied insects of the family Aphididae, such as greenflies, that feed by sucking sap from plants. Also called "plant louse." [From New Latin *aphis* (stem *aphid-*), APHIS.] —**a·phid·i·an** (ə-fĭd′ē-ən) *adj.* &. *n.*

aphid lion. The larva of any of several insects of the family Chrysopidae, such as the lacewing, that feed on aphids.

a·phis (ā′fĭs, ăf′ĭs) *n., pl.* **aphides** (ā′fə-dēz′, ăf′ə-). An aphid, especially one of the genus *Aphis.* [New Latin *Aphis* (coined by Linnaeus), of obscure origin but perhaps due to a misreading of Greek *koris*, bug.]

a·pho·ni·a (ā-fō′nē-ə) *n.* Voicelessness or loss of speech as a result of disease or injury to the organs of speech. [New Latin, from Greek *aphōnia*, voicelessness, from *aphōnos*, voiceless : A- (without) + *phōnē*, voice.]

a·phon·ic (ā-fŏn′ĭk, ā-fō′nĭk) *adj.* **1.** *Pathology.* Affected with or having aphonia. **2.** *Phonetics.* Voiceless.

aph·o·rism (ăf′ə-rĭz′əm) *n.* A pithy statement of a truth or opinion; a maxim; an adage. —See Synonyms at **saying.** [Old French *aphorisme*, from Greek *aphorismos*, a delimitation, from *aphorizein*, to mark off by boundaries : *ap(o)-*, off, away from + *horizein*, to limit, from *horos†*, boundary, limit.] —**aph·o·ris·tic** (ăf′ə-rĭs′tĭk) *adj.* —**aph·o·rist** *n.* —**aph·o·ris·ti·cal·ly** *adv.*

aph·o·rize (ăf′ə-rīz′) *intr.v.* **-rized, -rizing, -rizes.** To express oneself, as in speaking, in or as if in aphorisms.

a·pho·tic (ā-fō′tĭk) *adj.* **1.** Without light. **2.** Of or designating the ocean zone below the level at which photosynthesis can occur (about 200 meters or 656 feet). [A- (not) + PHOTIC.]

aph·ro·dis·i·ac (ăf′rə-dĭz′ē-ăk′) *adj.* Stimulating or intensifying sexual desire.
~*n.* Anything having aphrodisiac properties, such as a drug or food. [Greek *aphrodisiakos*, from *aphrodisia*, aphrodisiac pleasures, from *aphrodisios*, of Aphrodite.]

Aph·ro·di·te (ăf′rə-dī′tē) *Greek Mythology.* The goddess of love and beauty, identified with the Roman goddess Venus. Also called "Cytherea."

a·phyl·lous (ā-fĭl′əs) *adj. Botany.* Having or bearing no leaves. [Greek *aphullos* : A- (not) + -PHYLLOUS.] —**a·phyl·ly** (ā′fĭl′ē) *n.*

A·pi·a (ä-pē′ä). Capital and only port of Western Samoa, on the northern coast of Upolu Island. Vailima, the former home of Robert Louis Stevenson, is the residence of the head of state.

a·pi·an (ā′pē-ən) *adj.* Of or pertaining to bees. [Latin *apiānus*, from *apis†*, bee.]

a·pi·ar·i·an (ā′pē-âr′ē-ən) *adj.* Of or pertaining to bees or to the breeding and care of bees.
~*n.* An apiarist.

a·pi·a·rist (ā′pē-ər-ĭst, ā′pē-ĕr′ĭst) *n.* A beekeeper.

a·pi·ar·y (ā′pē-ĕr′ē) *n., pl.* **-ies.** A place containing a number of beehives, in which bees are kept and raised, usually for their honey. [Latin *apiārium*, beehive, from *apis†*, bee.]

ap·i·cal (ăp′ĭ-kəl, ā′pĭ-) *adj.* **1.** Of, pertaining to, located at, or constituting the apex. **2.** *Phonetics.* Of or designating consonants articulated with the tip of the tongue, as *t, d,* and *s.* [New Latin *apicalis*, from Latin *apex* (stem *apic-*), APEX.]

apices. Alternate plural of **apex.**

a·pic·u·late (ə-pĭk′yə-lĭt) *adj. Botany.* Ending with a sharp, abrupt tip: *an apiculate leaf.* [From New Latin *apiculus*, a sharp point, diminutive of Latin *apex* (stem *apic-*), APEX.]

a·pi·cul·ture (ā′pĭ-kŭl′chər) *n.* The breeding and care of bees. [Latin *apis†*, bee + CULTURE.] —**a·pi·cul·tur·al** *adj.* —**a·pi·cul·tur·ist** *n.*

a·piece (ə-pēs′) *adv.* To or for each one; each: *Give them an apple apiece.* [Middle English *a pece* : A + PIECE.]

A·pis (ā′pĭs) *n.* A sacred bull of the ancient Egyptians.

ap·ish (ā′pĭsh) *adj.* **1.** Slavishly or foolishly imitative. **2.** Silly; foolish. [AP(E) + -ISH.] —**ap·ish·ly** *adv.* —**ap·ish·ness** *n.*

a·piv·o·rous (ā-pĭv′ə-rəs) *adj.* Feeding on bees. [Latin *apis†*, bee + -VOROUS.]

APL (ā′pē-ĕl) *n.* A computer programming language designed for use at remote terminals. [*A P*rogramming *L*anguage.]

a·pla·cen·tal (ā′plə-sĕn′təl) *adj.* Having no placenta. Said of marsupials and monotremes. [A- (not) + PLACENT(A) + -AL.]

ap·la·nat·ic (ăp′lə-năt′ĭk) *adj.* Of, pertaining to, or designating optical systems that correct for spherical aberration and coma. [Greek *aplanētos*, unable to go astray : A- (not) + *planētos, planēs*, wandering, from *planasthai*, to wander.]

a·plan·o·spore (ā-plăn′ə-spôr′, -spōr′) *n.* A nonmotile, asexual spore characteristic of the green algae. [A- (not) + Greek *planos*, wandering + SPORE.]

a·pla·sia (ə-plā′zhə) *n.* Defective development or congenital absence of tissue, of an organ, or of an organ part. [New Latin : A- (not) + -PLASIA.]

a·plas·tic (ā-plăs′tĭk) *adj.* **1.** Lacking form. **2.** *Pathology.* Of, relating to, or characterized by aplasia: *aplastic anemia.* [A- (not) + -PLASTIC.]

a·plen·ty (ə-plĕn′tē) *adj.* Being in abundance. Used after the noun: *goods aplenty.*
~*adv.* **1.** In abundance. **2.** To an extreme degree.

ap·lite (ăp′līt′) *n.* Also **hap·lite** (hăp′-). A fine-grained, light-colored granitic rock consisting primarily of orthoclase and quartz. [German *Aplit* : Greek *haplous*, single, simple (see **haploid**) + -ITE.] —**ap·lit·ic** (ā-plĭt′ĭk) *adj.*

a·plomb (ə-plŏm′, ə-plŭm′) *n.* Self-confidence; poise; assurance. [French, uprightness, from Old French *a plomb,* perpendicularly, according to the plummet : *a,* to + *plomb,* plummet, lead weight, from Latin *plumbum,* lead.]

ap·ne·a, ap·noe·a (ăp′nē-ə) *n.* Temporary suspension of respiration. [New Latin, from Greek *apnoia,* absence of respiration : A- (without) + *pnoē,* breathing, from *pnein,* to breathe.] —**ap·ne·ic, ap·noe·ic** (ăp-nē′ĭk) *adj.*

apo-, ap- *prefix.* Indicates: **1.** Being away from; for example, **aphelion. 2.** Lack of; for example, **apogamy. 3.** Separation of; for example, **apocarpous. 4.** *Geology.* Derived from; for example, **apophysis. 5.** *Chemistry.* Derived from; for example **apomorphine.** [In borrowed Greek compounds, *apo-* indicates: **1.** Away from, as in **apogee. 2.** Away, off, as in **apothecary. 3.** Return, as in **apodosis. 4.** Intensive action, as in **aposiopesis. 5.** Keeping off, defense, as in **apology. 6.** Change from an existing state, as in **apotheosis. 7.** Reversal, as in **Apocalypse.** Greek *apo-,* from *apo,* away from, off.]

Apoc. 1. Apocalypse. **2.** Apocrypha; Apocryphal.

A·poc·a·lypse (ə-pŏk′ə-lĭps′) *n.* **1.** *Abbr.* **Apoc.** The last book of the New Testament, **Revelation** *(see).* **2.** apocalypse. A prophetic disclosure or revelation; especially, a vision of the end of the world. **3.** apocalypse. An event marked by violent destruction and upheaval. [Middle English *Apocalipse,* from Late Latin *Apocalypsis,* from Greek *apokalupsis,* revelation, from *apokaluptein,* to uncover : *apo-,* reversal + *kaluptein,* to cover.]

a·poc·a·lyp·tic (ə-pŏk′ə-lĭp′tĭk) *adj.* Also **a·poc·a·lyp·ti·cal** (-tĭ-kəl). **1.** Of or pertaining to a prophetic disclosure or revelation. **2.** Portending violent disaster or ultimate doom. **3.** Suggesting the end of the world: *an apocalyptic spectacle.* —**a·poc·a·lyp·ti·cal·ly** *adv.*

ap·o·carp (ăp′ə-kärp′) *n. Botany.* An apocarpous fruit. [Back-formation from APOCARPOUS.]

ap·o·car·pous (ăp′ə-kär′pəs) *adj. Botany.* Having distinctly separated carpels. [APO- + -CARPOUS.] —**ap·o·car·py** (ăp′ə-kär′pē) *n.*

ap·o·ca·tas·ta·sis (ăp′ō-kə-tăs′tə-sĭs) *n. Theology.* The doctrine of Universalism *(see).* [Latin, from Greek, restoration, from *apokathistanai,* to re-establish, "set back down" : *apo-,* back + *kata-,* down + *histanai,* (cause to) stand.]

ap·o·chro·mat·ic (ăp′ō-krō-măt′ĭk) *adj. Optics.* Corrected for both chromatic and spherical aberration. —**ap·o·chro·ma·tism** (ăp′ə-krō′mə-tĭz′əm) *n.*

a·poc·o·pe (ə-pŏk′ə-pē) *n.* A cutting off or omitting of the last sound or syllable of a word; for example, *goin'* for *going.* [Latin *apocopē,* from Greek *apokopē,* from *apokoptein,* to cut off : *apo-,* off + *koptein,* to cut.]

ap·o·crine (ăp′ə-krĭn, -krīn′, -krēn′) *adj.* Of, pertaining to, or designating a gland that loses part of its cytoplasm in secretion. Compare **holocrine, merocrine.** [APO- + Greek *krinein,* to separate.]

A·poc·ry·pha (ə-pŏk′rə-fə) *n.* Used with a singular or plural verb. *Abbr.* **Apoc. 1.** The 14 books of the Septuagint included in the Vulgate but considered uncanonical by Protestants. Eleven of these books are accepted in the Roman Catholic canon, and appear in the Douay Bible. **2.** Various early Christian writings proposed as additions to the New Testament, but rejected by the major canons. **3.** apocrypha. Any writings of questionable authorship or authenticity. [Middle English *Apocripha,* from Medieval Latin *scripta apocrypha,* hidden writings (that is, hidden and excluded from the canon because spurious); from Late Latin *apocryphus,* hidden, from

Apis *A bronze statuette of this sacred bull that was worshiped by ancient Egyptians. The statuette, found at Memphis, Egypt, dates from the fourth century* B.C.

Greek *apokruphos*, from *apokruptein*, to hide away : *apo-*, away + *kruptein*, to hide.]

a·poc·ry·phal (ə-pŏk′rə-fəl) *adj.* **1.** Of questionable authorship or authenticity. **2.** False; counterfeit. **3.** Apocryphal. *Abbr.* **Apoc.** Of or pertaining to the Apocrypha. —**a·poc·ry·phal·ly** *adv.*

ap·o·cyn·thi·on (ăp′ə-sĭn′thē-ən) *n.* The point at which a spacecraft launched from earth into orbit around the moon is most distant from the moon. Compare **pericynthion.** [APO- (away) + *cynthion*, from CYNTHIA (goddess of the moon).]

ap·o·dal (ăp′ə-dəl) *adj. Zoology.* Having no limbs, feet, or footlike appendages. [From Greek *apous* (stem *apod-*) : A- (without) + *pous*, foot.]

ap·o·dic·tic (ăp′ə-dĭk′tĭk) *adj.* Clearly proven or demonstrated; incontestable. [Latin *apodicticus*, from Greek *apodeiktikos*, from *apodeiknunai*, to point out or away from : *apo-*, away from + *deiknunai*, to show.]

a·pod·o·sis (ə-pŏd′ə-sĭs) *n.*, *pl.* **-ses** (-sēz′). *Grammar.* The clause stating the conclusion or consequence of a conditional sentence. Compare **protasis.** [New Latin, from Greek, response (to the protasis), "a giving back," from *apodidonai*, give up or back : *apo-*, back + *didonai*, to give.]

ap·o·dous (ăp′ə-dəs) *adj.* Apodal.

ap·o·en·zyme (ăp′ō-ĕn′zīm′) *n.* An inactive enzyme that needs to be combined with a **coenzyme** (*see*) to become functional.

a·pog·a·my (ə-pŏg′ə-mē) *n. Botany.* In ferns, the production of the sporophyte directly from a cell of the gametophyte, without the formation of gametes. Compare **apospory.** [APO- (away from) + -GAMY.] —**ap·o·gam·ic** (ăp′ə-găm′ĭk), **a·pog·a·mous** (ə-pŏg′ə-məs) *adj.*

ap·o·gee (ăp′ə-jē) *n.* **1.** The point in the orbit of the moon or of an artificial satellite most distant from the earth. Compare **perigee.** **2.** The farthest or highest point; the apex. [French *apogée*, from New Latin *apogaeum*, from Greek *apogaion*, neuter of *apogaios*, "away from the earth" : *apo-*, away from + *gaia, gē*, earth.] —**ap·o·ge·an** (ăp′ə-jē′ən) *adj.*

a·po·lit·i·cal (ā′pə-lĭt′ĭ-kəl) *adj.* Having no association with or interest in politics. —**a·po·lit·i·cal·ly** *adv.*

A·pol·li·naire (ä′pô-lē-nâr′), **Guillaume,** born Wilhelm Apollinaris de Kostrowitzky (1880–1918). French poet and leading figure in avant-garde literary and painting circles.

a·pol·lo (ə-pŏl′ō) *n.*, *pl.* **-los.** A young man of great physical beauty. [After APOLLO (the god).]

A·pol·lo¹ (ə-pŏl′lo). *Greek & Roman Mythology.* The god of the sun, prophecy, music, medicine, and poetry.

Apollo² *n.* Any of a series of 17 U.S. spacecraft designed to land people on the moon. The first 10 Apollo craft were used to test various aspects of the program, the first moon landing (July, 1969) being achieved by Apollo 11. The remaining members of the series also made manned moon landings, except Apollo 13, which was safely aborted. [After APOLLO (the god).]

Ap·ol·lo·ni·an (ăp′ə-lō′nē-ən) *adj.* **1.** Of or pertaining to Apollo or his cult. **2.** *Often* **apollonian.** In the philosophy of Nietzsche, characteristic of or embodying the theoretical, rational, calm, harmonious qualities of human nature. Compare **dionysian.** **3. apollonian.** Noble; dignified; serene. —**Ap·ol·lo·ni·an** *n.*

Ap·ol·lo·ni·us of Per·ga (ăp′ə-lō′nē-əs, pûr′gə) (*c.* 262 B.C.–*c.* 190 B.C.). Greek mathematician. He was the first to define, in his work on conic sections, the curves called the parabola, hyperbola, and ellipse.

Apollonius of Rhodes (rōdz). Greek poet of the late 3rd and early 2nd centuries B.C. His epic *Argonautica* recounts the adventures of the Argonauts. Apollonius was also librarian at Alexandria.

a·pol·o·get·ic (ə-pŏl′ə-jĕt′ĭk) *adj.* **1.** Making an apology or excuse. **2.** Conveying self-recrimination and regret: *an apologetic smile.* **3.** Explaining or defending in speech or writing.
~*n.* A formal defense or apology. —**a·pol·o·get·i·cal·ly** *adv.*

a·pol·o·get·ics (ə-pŏl′ə-jĕt′ĭks) *n.* *Used with a singular verb.* The branch of theology that deals with the defense and proof of Christianity.

ap·o·lo·gi·a (ăp′ə-lō′jē-ə, -jə) *n.* A formal defense or justification. [Latin, APOLOGY.]

a·pol·o·gist (ə-pŏl′ə-jĭst) *n.* A person who argues in defense or justification of another person or cause.

a·pol·o·gize (ə-pŏl′ə-jīz′) *intr.v.* **-gized, -gizing, -gizes. 1.** To make excuse for or regretful acknowledgment of a fault or offense. **2.** To make a formal defense or justification in speech or writing. —**a·pol·o·giz·er** *n.*

ap·o·logue (ăp′ə-lôg′, -lŏg′) *n.* A moral fable. [French *apologue*, from Latin *apologus*, from Greek *apologos*, fable : *apo-*, away, off + *logos*, discourse.]

a·pol·o·gy (ə-pŏl′ə-jē) *n.*, *pl.* **-gies. 1.** A statement, either written or verbal, expressing regret or asking pardon for a fault or offense. **2.** A formal justification or defense. **3.** An inferior substitute: *a poor apology for a dinner.* [French *apologie*, from Late Latin *apologia*, from Greek *apologiā*, speech in defense : *apo-*, defense + *logos*, discourse, speech.]

ap·o·lune (ăp′ə-lōōn′) *n.* The point at which a spacecraft launched from the moon into lunar orbit is farthest from the moon. Also called "aposelene." Compare **perilune, apocynthion.** [APO- (away from) + *lune*, from Latin *lūna*, moon.]

ap·o·mict (ăp′ə-mĭkt′) *n. Biology.* An organism, especially a plant, that is the result of apomixis. [APO- + Greek *miktos*, mixed, from *mignunai*, to mix.]

ap·o·mix·is (ăp′ə-mĭk′sĭs) *n.* An asexual reproductive process in which a new individual is produced from a female cell or cells other than the egg cell, often in a manner that mimics sexual reproduction. [New Latin : APO- + Greek *mixis*, a mingling, from *mignunai*, to mix.]

ap·o·mor·phine (ăp′ə-môr′fēn′) *n.* A poisonous white crystalline alkaloid, $C_{17}H_{17}NO_2$, derived from morphine and used medicinally as an emetic, expectorant, and hypnotic.

ap·o·neu·ro·sis (ăp′ə-nōō-rō′sĭs, ăp′ə-nyōō-) *n.*, *pl.* **-ses** (-sēz′). A sheetlike membrane, resembling a flattened tendon, that forms the end of certain muscles and connects them to bones. [New Latin, from Greek *aponeurōsis*, from *aponeurousthai*, to become a nerve : *apo-* (change) + *neuron*, nerve.] —**ap·o·neu·rot·ic** (ăp′ə-nōō-rŏt′ĭk, ăp′ə-nyōō-) *adj.*

apophthegm. Variant of **apothegm.**

a·poph·y·ge (ə-pŏf′ə-jē) *n. Architecture.* The curvature at the top and bottom of the shaft of a column. [Greek *apophugē*, "escape" : *apo-*, away + *phugē*, flight.]

a·poph·yl·lite (ə-pŏf′ə-līt′, ăp′ə-fĭl′īt′) *n.* A white, pale-pink, or pale-green crystalline mineral, essentially $KCa_4FSi_4O_{10}\cdot 8H_2O$. [APO- + PHYLLITE.]

a·poph·y·sis (ə-pŏf′ə-sĭs) *n.*, *pl.* **-ses** (-sēz′) **1.** *Biology.* A swelling, projection, or outgrowth of an organ or part. **2.** *Geology.* A branch from a dike or vein. [New Latin, from Greek *apophusis*, side-shoot : *apo-*, off, away + *phusis*, growth, from *phuein*, to grow.] —**a·poph·y·sate** (ə-pŏf′ə-sāt′), **a·poph·y·se·al** (ə-pŏf′ə-sē′əl) *adj.*

ap·o·plec·tic (ăp′ə-plĕk′tĭk) *adj.* **1.** Of, resembling, or causing apoplexy. **2.** Having or exhibiting symptoms of apoplexy. **3.** *Informal.* **a.** Of a sort to cause apoplexy: *We found him in an apoplectic fury.* **b.** Extremely annoyed. —**ap·o·plec·ti·cal·ly** *adv.*

ap·o·plex·y (ăp′ə-plĕk′sē) *n.* Sudden loss of muscular control, with diminution or loss of sensation and consciousness, resulting from rupture or blocking of a blood vessel in the brain; a stroke. [Middle English *apoplexie*, from Old French, from Late Latin *apoplēxia*, from Greek, from *apoplēssein*, to cripple by a stroke : *apo-* (intensive) + *plēssein*, to strike.]

a·port (ə-pôrt′, ə-pōrt′) *adv. Nautical.* On or toward the port, or left, side.

ap·o·se·le·ne (ăp′ō-sə-lē′nē) *n.* An **apolune** (*see*). [APO- (away from) + Greek *selēnē*, moon.]

ap·o·se·mat·ic coloration (ăp′ə-sə-măt′ĭk) *n.* **Warning coloration** (*see*). [APO- (away from) + SEMATIC.]

ap·o·si·o·pe·sis (ăp′ə-sī′ə-pē′sĭs) *n.*, *pl.* **-ses** (-sēz′). A sudden and dramatic breaking off in the middle of a sentence, as though the speaker were unwilling or unable to continue, often done for rhetorical effect. [Late Latin *aposiōpēsis*, from Greek, a becoming silent, from *aposiōpān*, to maintain silence : *apo-* (intensifier) + *siōpān*, to be silent, from *siōpē*, silence.] —**ap·o·si·o·pet·ic** (ăp′ə-sī′ə-pĕt′ĭk) *adj.*

ap·o·spor·y (ăp′ə-spôr′ē, -spōr′ē, ə-pŏs′pə-rē) *n. Botany.* In mosses and ferns, the development of the gametophyte directly from a cell of the sporophyte, without spore formation. Compare **apogamy.** [APO- (away from) + SPOR(E) + -Y (state).]

a·pos·ta·sy (ə-pŏs′tə-sē) *n.*, *pl.* **-sies.** An abandonment of one's religious faith or of any cause or principle to which one was attached. [Middle English *apostasie*, from Late Latin *apostasia*, from Greek, desertion, revolt, from *apostanai*, "to stand away from," rebel : *apo-*, away from + *stanai*, to stand.]

a·pos·tate (ə-pŏs′tāt′, -tĭt) *n.* One who is guilty of apostasy. [Middle English, from Late Latin *apostata*, from Greek *apostatēs*, deserter, rebel, from *apostanai*, to rebel. See **apostasy.**] —**a·pos·tate** *adj.*

a·pos·ta·tize (ə-pŏs′tə-tīz′) *intr.v.* **-tized, -tizing, -tizes.** To give up or abandon one's faith, political party, or cause.

a pos·te·ri·o·ri (ä′ pŏ-stîr′ē-ôr′ē, -ōr′ē, -ôr′ī′, -ōr′ī′, ä′ pŏ-stîr′ī′) *adj. Logic.* Of, pertaining to, or designating arguments, propositions, or knowledge derived from reasoning from facts or particulars to general principles, or from effects to causes; inductive; empirical. Compare **a priori.** [Latin, "from the subsequent."] —**a pos·te·ri·o·ri** *adv.*

a·pos·tle (ə-pŏs′əl) *n.* **1.** *Usually* **Apostle.** Any of the twelve disciples chosen by Christ to preach His gospel. Luke 6:13–16. **2.** A missionary of the early Christian Church. **3.** A leader of the first Christian mission to a country or region. **4.** Any of the twelve members of the Mormon administrative council. **5.** One who leads or advocates a new cause. [Middle English *apostel, apostle*, Old English *apostol*, from Late Latin *apostolus*, from Greek *apostolos*, messenger, envoy, from *apostellein*, to send away from : *apo-*, away from + *stellein*, to place.]

Apostles' Creed *n.* A Christian creed traditionally ascribed to the twelve Apostles.

Apostle spoon, apostle spoon *n.* A spoon, usually of silver, with a handle ending in the figure of an Apostle.

ap·os·tol·ic (ăp′ə-stŏl′ĭk) *adj.* **1.** Of, pertaining to, or contemporary with the Apostles. **2.** Of, pertaining to, or conforming to the faith, teaching, or practice of the Apostles. **3.** Of or pertaining to the pope as successor to Saint Peter.

Apostolic Father *n.* A church father who received personal instruction from the twelve Apostles or from their disciples.

apostolic see *n.* **1.** A bishopric founded, according to tradition, by one of the Apostles. **2. Apostolic See.** The See of Rome founded, according to tradition, by the Apostle Peter.

apostolic succession *n.* The doctrine that authority in the Christian Church is derived from the Apostles through an unbroken succession of bishops.

a·pos·tro·phe¹ (ə-pŏs′trə-fē) *n.* The superscript sign (') used in punctuation to indicate the omission of a letter or letters from a word, the omission of a number or numbers, as from a date, the possessive case, and certain plurals, especially those of numbers and letters. [French, from Old French, from Late Latin *apostrophus,* from Greek *(prosōidia) apostrophos,* "(accent of) turning away," sign of elision, from *apostrephein,* to turn away : *apo-,* away + *strephein,* to turn.] **—ap·os·troph·ic** (ăp′ə-strŏf′ĭk) *adj.*

apostrophe² *n.* A digression in discourse; especially, a rhetorical device by which a speaker or writer breaks off to address an absent or imaginary person. [Latin *apostrophē,* from Greek, from *apostrephein,* to turn away. See apostrophe (sign).] **—ap·os·troph·ic** (ăp′ə-strŏf′ĭk) *adj.*

a·pos·tro·phize (ə-pŏs′trə-fīz′) *v.* **-phized, -phizing, -phizes.** *—tr.* To address by apostrophe. *—intr.* To speak or write in apostrophe.

apothecaries' measure *n.* A system of liquid volume measure used in pharmacy.

apothecaries' weight *n.* A system of weights used in pharmacy and based on an ounce equal to 480 grains and a pound equal to 12 ounces.

a·poth·e·car·y (ə-pŏth′ə-kĕr′ē) *n., pl.* **-ries.** *Abbr.* **ap.** One who prepares and sells drugs and medicines; a pharmacist. [Middle English, from Medieval Latin *apothecārius,* from Late Latin, from Latin *apothēca,* storehouse, from Greek *apothēkē,* from *apotithenai,* to put away : *apo-,* away + *tithenai,* to put.]

ap·o·the·ci·um (ăp′ə-thē′shē-əm, -sē-əm) *n., pl.* **-cia** (-shē-ə, -sē-ə). An open disk-shaped or cup-shaped fruiting body in certain fungi that is lined with a layer bearing spores. [New Latin, from Latin *apothēca,* storehouse (see apothecary).] **—ap·o·the·cial** (ăp′ə-thē′shəl) *adj.*

ap·o·thegm (ăp′ə-thĕm′) *n.* A terse and witty instructive saying; maxim. [Greek *apophthegma,* a pointed saying, from *apophthengesthai,* to speak out plainly : *apo-,* away from + *phthengesthai,* to speak; akin to *phthongos,* sound (see diphthong).] **—ap·o·theg·mat·ic** (ăp′ə-thĕg-măt′ĭk) *adj.* **—ap·o·theg·mat·i·cal·ly** *adv.*

ap·o·them (ăp′ə-thĕm′) *n. Geometry.* In a regular polygon, the perpendicular distance from the center to any of the sides. [APO-, away from + Greek *thema,* position, THEME.]

a·poth·e·o·sis (ə-pŏth′ē-ō′sĭs, ăp′ə-thē′ə-sĭs) *n., pl.* **-ses** (-sēz′). **1.** Exaltation to divine rank or stature; deification. **2.** An exalted or glorified ideal. **3.** The culmination or highest development; the quintessence. [Late Latin *apotheōsis,* from Greek *apotheōsis,* from *apotheoun,* to deify : *apo-* (change) + *theos,* god.]

ap·o·the·o·size (ăp′ə-thē′ə-sīz′, ə-pŏth′ē-ə-sīz′) *tr.v.* **-sized, -sizing, -sizes.** To glorify, exalt, or deify.

ap·o·tro·pa·ic (ăp′ə-trō-pā′ĭk) *adj.* Having the power to avert or purpose of averting evil: *an apotropaic ritual.* [Greek *apotropaios,* from *apotrepein,* to turn away : *apo-* away + *trepein,* to turn.] **—ap·o·tro·pa·i·cal·ly** *adv.*

app. **1.** apparatus. **2.** appendix. **3.** applied. **4.** appoint; appointed.

Ap·pa·la·chi·a (ăp′ə-lā′chē-ə, -chə, -lăch′ē-ə, -lăch′ə). The region including the Appalachian Mountains. In popular usage, Appalachia is often thought to include only the isolated mountain regions of western Virginia and West Virginia. The people living in these areas have long been among the poorest in the United States.

Ap·pa·la·chi·an (ăp′ə-lā′chən, -lā′chē-ən, -lăch′ən) *adj.* Of, from, or pertaining to the Appalachian Mountains, the Appalachian mountain region, or the inhabitants of the region and their culture.

Appalachian Mountains. Also **Ap·pa·la·chi·ans** (-ənz). Mountain range in eastern North America, stretching from Newfoundland to Alabama. It includes the Alleghenies, Blue Ridge, and Cumberland mountains. The highest peak, Mt. Mitchell (2,037 meters; 6,684 feet), is in North Carolina.

Appalachian Trail. A network of mountain trails covering 3,300 kilometers (2,050 miles). It extends from Mt. Katahdin in central Maine to Springer Mt. in northern Georgia and is the longest continuous hiking path in the world.

ap·pall (ə-pôl′) *tr.v.* **-palled, -palling, -palls.** To fill with consternation, dismay, or horror. [Middle English *ap(p)allen,* from Old French *apalir,* to grow pale : *a-,* to, from Latin *ad-,* to + *palir,* from Latin *pallescere,* from *pallēre,* to be pale.]

ap·pall·ing (ə-pô′lĭng) *adj.* **1.** Causing dismay; frightful; horrifying. **2.** *Informal.* Very bad; terrible: *The child had really appalling manners.* **—ap·pall·ing·ly** *adv.*

ap·pa·loo·sa (ăp′ə-lōō′sə) *n.* A horse of a breed developed in northwestern North America, characteristically having a spotted rump. [Probably after the *Paloose* Indians, who bred the horse.]

ap·pa·nage, ap·a·nage (ăp′ə-nĭj) *n.* **1.** Land or some other source of revenue given by a king for the maintenance of a member of the ruling family. **2.** A perquisite. **3.** A natural or rightful attribute or adjunct. [French *apanage,* from Old French, from *apaner,* to make provisions for, from Medieval Latin *appānāre* : Latin *ad-,* to + *pānis,* bread.]

ap·pa·rat (ăp′ə-răt′, ä′pə-rät′) *n.* The organization and administrative apparatus of a political party, especially that of the Communist Party in the former U.S.S.R. and some other Communist countries. [Russian, from German, APPARATUS.]

ap·pa·rat·chik (ä′pə-rä′chĭk) *n., pl.* **-chiks** or **-chiki** (-chĭ-kē). **1.** One who belongs to a Communist apparat. **2.** An official, as a bureaucrat, who is slavishly devoted to the organization for which he

works or to his superiors. [Russian : APPARAT + *-chik,* suffix indicating agent, adherent, member.]

ap·pa·ra·tus (ăp′ə-rā′təs, -răt′əs) *n., pl.* **apparatus** or **-tuses.** *Abbr.* **app.** **1.** The totality of things provided or necessary for the accomplishment of a particular task or purpose. **2.** A machine, instrument, or other piece of equipment with a specific function. **3.** *Physiology.* A group of organs having a collective function: *the respiratory apparatus.* **4.** A political, bureaucratic, or other organizational system. **5.** A set of principles or standards, as for judging or testing. [Latin *apparātus,* from the past participle of *apparāre,* to prepare : *ad-,* to + *parāre,* to make ready.]

apparatus crit·i·cus (krĭt′ĭ-kəs) *n.* **1.** Reference materials used in literary research. **2.** Special appendixes, notes, or glossaries in an edition of a text. Also called "critical apparatus." [New Latin, "critical apparatus."]

ap·par·el (ə-păr′əl) *n.* **1.** Clothing, especially outer garments; attire. **2.** Something that covers or adorns. **3.** The equipment of a vessel, especially a sailing ship. ~*tr.v.* **appareled, -eling, -els.** Also *Chiefly British* **-elled, -elling, -els.** **1.** To clothe; dress. **2.** To adorn; embellish. [Middle English *appareil,* from Old French *apareil,* preparation, furnishings, from *apareillier,* to prepare, from Vulgar Latin *appariculāre* (unattested), from Latin *apparāre* : *ad-,* to + *parāre,* to make ready.]

ap·par·ent (ə-păr′ənt, ə-pâr′-) *adj.* **1.** Readily seen; open to view; visible. **2.** Readily understood or perceived; plain or obvious: *His pleasure was apparent to everyone.* **3.** Appearing as such but not necessarily so; seeming: *an apparent advantage.* —See Synonyms at **evident.** [Middle English, from Old French *aparent,* present participle of *aparoir,* to APPEAR.] **—ap·par·ent·ness** *n.*

apparent horizon *n.* See **horizon** (sense 1).

ap·par·ent·ly (ə-păr′ənt-lē, ə-pâr′-) *adv.* **1.** So far as one can tell; evidently. **2.** According to the information one has: *Apparently they're going to cut the interest rate.* **3.** Seemingly but perhaps not actually.

apparent magnitude *n. Astronomy.* **Magnitude** *(see).*

apparent time *n.* Local time *(see).*

ap·pa·ri·tion (ăp′ə-rĭsh′ən) *n.* **1.** A ghostly figure; a specter. **2.** A sudden or unusual sight. **3.** The act of appearing; appearance. [Middle English *apparicioun,* from Old French *apparition,* from Late Latin *apparitiō* (stem *apparitiōn-*), appearance, epiphany (translation of Greek *epiphaneia,* from Latin *appārēre,* to APPEAR.] **—ap·pa·ri·tion·al** *adj.*

ap·par·i·tor (ə-păr′ə-tər) *n.* An official who was formerly sent to carry out the orders of an ecclesiastical or civil court. [Latin, from *appārēre,* to serve, APPEAR (as a servant).]

ap·pas·sio·na·to (ə-păsh′ə-nä′tō) *adv. Music.* In an impassioned manner. Used as a direction. [Italian, "impassioned," past participle of *appassionare,* to inspire with passion : *ap-* (intensive) + *passionare,* from *passione,* from Late Latin *passiō,* PASSION.] **—ap·pas·sio·na·to** *adj.*

ap·peal (ə-pēl′) *n.* **1.** An earnest or urgent request, entreaty, or supplication. **2.** A resort or application to some higher authority, as for sanction, corroboration, or a decision: *an appeal to reason.* **3.** The power of attracting interest or of arousing sympathy: *For her the great appeal of crossword puzzles was the intellectual challenge.* **4.** *Law.* **a.** The transfer of a case from a lower to a higher court for a new hearing. **b.** A request for a new hearing. **c.** A case so transferred. **5.** A campaign to raise funds or resources, usually for a charitable cause: *launched an appeal on behalf of the refugees.* ~*v.* **appealed, -pealing, -peals.** *—intr.* **1.** To make an earnest or urgent request, as for help or sympathy. **2.** To resort or have recourse to some higher authority, as for sanction, corroboration, or a decision. **3.** To be attractive or interesting. **4.** *Law.* To make or apply for an appeal. *—tr. Law.* To transfer or apply to transfer (a case) to a higher court for rehearing. [Middle English *appelen, apelen,* from Old French *apeler,* from Latin *appellāre,* to apply to, entreat, address.] **—ap·peal·a·ble** *adj.* **—ap·peal·er** *n.* **—ap·peal·ing·ly** *adv.*

ap·pear (ə-pîr′) *intr.v.* **-peared, -pearing, -pears.** **1.** To come into view; become visible: *A plane appeared in the sky.* **2.** To come into existence: *New strains of viruses appear periodically.* **3.** To seem or look to be: *They appeared unhappy.* **4.** To seem likely: *It appears they will be late.* **5.** To come before the public; be presented or published. **6.** To present oneself formally; especially, in law, to present oneself before a court as defendant, plaintiff, or counsel. [Middle English *apperen, aperen,* from Old French *aparoir,* from Latin *appārēre* : *ad-,* toward + *pārēre†,* to show.]

ap·pear·ance (ə-pîr′əns) *n.* **1.** The act or an instance of appearing. **2.** An act or instance of being present: *put in an appearance.* **3.** The outward aspect of someone or something. **4.** Something that appears; a phenomenon. **5.** An apparition. **6.** A pretense or semblance; a false show. **7.** **appearances.** Outward indications: *Appearances can be deceptive.*

ap·pease (ə-pēz′) *tr.v.* **-peased, -peasing, -peases.** **1.** To bring peace to; soothe. **2.** To placate or conciliate by yielding to the demands of. **3.** To satisfy or relieve: *appease thirst.* —See Synonyms at **pacify.** [Middle English *appesen, apesen,* from Old French *apaisier* : *ap-,* to + *pais,* peace, from Latin *pāx.*] **—ap·peas·a·ble** *adj.* **—ap·peas·a·bly** *adv.* **—ap·peas·er** *n.*

ap·pease·ment (ə-pēz′mənt) *n.* **1. a.** The act of appeasing. **b.** The condition of being appeased. **2.** The policy of granting concessions to potential enemies with the aim of maintaining peace.

ap·pel (ə-pĕl′) *n. Fencing.* **1.** A quick stamp of the foot used as a feint to produce an opening. **2.** A blow with a weapon to produce an opening. [French, a call, challenge, from *appeler,* to call, from Old French *apeler,* to APPEAL.]

ap·pel·lant (ə-pĕl′ənt) *adj.* Of or pertaining to an appeal; appellate. ~*n.* One who appeals a court decision.

ap·pel·late (ə-pĕl′ĭt) *adj.* Having the power to hear appeals and to reverse court decisions: *an appellate court.* [Latin *appellātus,* past participle of *appellāre,* to APPEAL.]

ap·pel·la·tion (ăp′ə-lā′shən) **1.** A name, title, or epithet. **2.** The act of naming. [Middle English *appellacioun,* from Latin *appellātiō* (stem *appellātiōn-*), from *appellāre,* to APPEAL.]

ap·pel·la·tion con·trô·lée (á′pĕ-lá′syôn kôn′trō-lā′) *n. Abbr.* **A.C.** *French.* A designation awarded to wines of high quality that are produced in limited amounts from specific regions. ["Certified name."]

ap·pel·la·tive (ə-pĕl′ə-tĭv) *adj.* **1.** Of or relating to the assignment of names. **2.** *Grammar.* Used to designate a class; common: *appellative nouns.* ~*n.* A name or descriptive epithet. [Middle English, from Late Latin *appellātīvus,* from *appellāre,* to call by name, APPEAL.] —**ap·pel·la·tive·ly** *adv.*

ap·pel·lee (ăp′ə-lē′) *n. Law.* One against whom an appeal has been taken. [Old French *apele,* from *apeler,* to APPEAL.]

ap·pend (ə-pĕnd′) *tr.v.* **-pended, -pending, -pends. 1.** To add as a supplement. **2.** To attach; fix. Used with *to.* [Latin *appendere : ad-,* to + *pendere,* to hang.]

ap·pend·age (ə-pĕn′dĭj) *n.* **1.** Something appended, especially something of lesser importance. **2.** *Biology.* Any part or organ that is joined to an axis or trunk, such as an arthropod limb.

> **Synonyms:** *accessory, addition, adjunct, attachment.*

ap·pen·dant (ə-pĕn′dənt) *adj.* **1.** Hanging attached; suspended. **2.** Accompanying; attendant: *faith and its appendant hope.* **3.** *Law.* Belonging as a subsidiary right. ~*n.* **1.** Something attached or added. **2.** *Law.* A subsidiary right.

ap·pen·dec·to·my (ăp′ən-dĕk′tə-mē) *n., pl.* **-mies.** The surgical removal of the vermiform appendix. [Latin *appendix* (stem *appendic-*) + -ECTOMY.]

ap·pen·di·ci·tis (ə-pĕn′də-sī′tĭs) *n.* Inflammation of the vermiform appendix. [APPENDIX + -ITIS.]

ap·pen·dic·u·lar (ăp′ən-dĭk′yə-lər) *adj.* **1.** Of, pertaining to, or consisting of an appendage or appendages. **2.** Of or pertaining to the vermiform appendix. **3.** *Biology.* Of or pertaining to limbs: *appen-* *dicular skeleton.* [Latin *appendicula,* diminutive of *appendix* (stem *appendic-*), APPENDIX.]

ap·pen·dix (ə-pĕn′dĭks) *n., pl.* **-dixes** or **-dices** (-də-sēz′) *Abbr.* **app. 1. a.** An appendage. **b.** A collection of supplementary material at the end of a book. **2.** The **vermiform appendix** (see). [Latin *appendix,* appendage, from *appendere,* to APPEND.]

> *Usage:* In its medical sense, the plural is *appendixes.* In the sense of "supplementary material at the end of a book," formal usage still prefers *appendices.*

ap·per·ceive (ăp′ər-sēv′) *tr.v.* **-ceived, -ceiving, -ceives. 1.** To be conscious of perceiving. **2.** *Psychology.* To perceive in terms of past perceptions. [Middle English *apperceiven, aperceiven,* from Old French *aperceivre : a-,* toward + *perceivre,* to PERCEIVE.]

ap·per·cep·tion (ăp′ər-sĕp′shən) *n.* **1.** Conscious perception with full awareness. **2.** *Psychology.* The process of understanding by which newly observed qualities of something are related to past experience. —**ap·per·cep·tive** (ăp′ər-sĕp′tĭv) *adj.*

Ap·pert (á-pâr′), **Nicolas** (c. 1749–1841). French inventor of preserving food by enclosing it in sealed jars.

ap·per·tain (ăp′ər-tān′) *intr.v.* **-tained, -taining, -tains.** To belong as a function or part; pertain properly. Used with *to.* [Middle English *apperteinen,* from Old French *apartenir,* from Vulgar Latin *appartenere* (unattested), variant of Late Latin *appertinēre,* to PERTAIN.]

ap·pe·stat (ăp′ə-stăt′) *n.* The mechanism in the hypothalamus of the brain that controls appetite. [APPE(TITE) + -STAT.]

ap·pe·tence (ăp′ə-təns) *n.* Also **ap·pe·ten·cy** (-tən-sē) *pl.* **-cies. 1.** A strong craving or desire. **2.** A tendency or proclivity; a propensity. [Latin *appetentia,* from *appetēns* (stem *appetent-*), present participle of *appetere,* to strive after, desire eagerly. See **appetite.**]

ap·pe·tite (ăp′ə-tīt′) *n.* **1.** A desire for food or drink. **2.** Any physical craving or desire. **3.** A strong wish or urge: *Some students have a great appetite for learning.* [Middle English *appetit, apetit,* from Old French *apetit,* from Latin *appetītus,* from *appetere,* to strive after, desire eagerly : *ad-,* toward + *petere,* to seek.] —**ap·pe·ti·tive** (ăp′ə-tī′tĭv, ə-pĕt′ə-tĭv) *adj.*

ap·pe·tiz·er (ăp′ə-tī′zər) *n.* **1.** A food or drink served before a meal, or before the main course of a meal, to stimulate the appetite. **2.** Something that stimulates the senses or arouses expectations.

ap·pe·tiz·ing (ăp′ə-tī′zĭng) *adj.* Stimulating or appealing to the appetite.

Ap·pi·an Way (ăp′ē-ən) *n.* Roman road connecting Rome and Capua, and later extended to Brundisium (Brindisi), some 589 kilo-

---

apple

THE STONE-AGE FRUIT THAT BECAME PART OF POPULAR LEGEND

A symbol of fruitfulness and a charm for lovers—but not in the Garden of Eden

The apple has been eaten by man since at least the New Stone Age—nearly 6,000 years ago—when it grew wild in Europe and western Asia. So great was its appeal that it entered into mythology as a symbol of fruitfulness and has been thought of as a love charm, a means to perpetual youth, and a medicine. But despite popular belief it is not mentioned in the Bible as the fruit Eve ate in the Garden of Eden. The Book of Genesis refers only to "the fruit of the tree which is in the midst of the garden."

Today's apple, of which there are several thousand varieties, has been developed, frequently by grafting, from the wild apple to produce strains that are resistant to disease and have particular flavors and colors.

Apples may be divided into two main groups, the sweetest for eating, and sharper varieties for cooking and for making alcoholic drinks such as cider and apple brandy (calvados or applejack).

Chenango Strawberry apple ripens early.

Rhode Island Greening, a cooking apple, dates from colonial days.

Winesap is an old favorite cider apple.

Rome Beauty is a large apple used for cooking.

Grimes Golden is a richly flavored winter apple.

Jonathan apple is good for eating and cooking.

Roxbury Russet ripens late and gains sweetness in storage.

Spitzenburg was the favorite apple of Thomas Jefferson.

York Imperial, an excellent keeper, comes from eastern Pennsylvania.

meters (366 miles). It was inaugurated in 312 B.C. by the censor Appius Claudius Caecus.

appl. applied.

ap·plaud (ə-plôd′) v. **-plauded, -plauding, -plauds.** —*intr.* To express approval, especially by clapping the hands. —*tr.* **1.** To express approval of, especially by clapping the hands. **2.** To praise; approve. [Latin *applaudere,* to clap at : *ad-,* to + *plaudere†,* to clap.] —**ap·plaud·er** n.

ap·plause (ə-plôz′) n. Publicly expressed approval, especially when shown by the clapping of hands. [Medieval Latin *applausus,* from Latin, past participle of *applaudere,* to APPLAUD.]

ap·ple (ăp′əl) n. **1. a.** A tree, *Pyrus malus,* of temperate regions, having fragrant pink or white flowers and edible fruit. **b.** The firm, rounded fruit of this tree, having skin that is red, yellow, or green. **2. a.** Any of several trees or plants having fruit resembling the apple, such as the **custard apple** *(see).* **b.** The fruit of any of these trees or plants. **3.** The hard wood of an apple tree. —**apple of one's eye.** A precious or much-loved person or thing: *My granddaughter is the apple of my eye.* [Middle English *appel,* Old English *æppel.*]

ap·ple·cart (ăp′əl-kärt′) n. A cart loaded with apples. —**upset the applecart.** To spoil a plan or scheme.

apple green n. Moderate to vivid yellowish green. —**ap·ple-green** (ăp′əl-grēn′) adj.

ap·ple·jack (ăp′əl-jăk′) n. Brandy distilled from cider. [APPLE + JACK (fellow, chap).]

ap·ple-pie bed (ăp′əl-pī′) n. A bed which has been made with one of the sheets folded double as a joke, so that one cannot lie down. [Perhaps alteration of French *nappe pliée,* folded sheet.]

apple-pie order n. *Informal.* Excellent order: *The guests left their room in apple-pie order.*

ap·ple-pol·ish (ăp′əl-pŏl′ĭsh) intr.v. **-ished, -ishing, -ishes.** *Informal.* To seek favor by toadying. —**ap·ple-pol·ish·er** n.

ap·ple sauce (ăp′əl-sôs′) n. **1.** Apples stewed to a pulp, sweetened, and sometimes spiced. **2.** *Slang.* Foolishness; nonsense.

Appleseed, Johnny. See John **Chapman.**

Ap·ple·ton layer (ăp′əl-tən) n. The **F** layer *(see)* of the ionosphere. [After Sir Edward *Appleton* (1892–1965), British physicist.]

ap·pli·ance (ə-plī′əns) n. **1.** A device or instrument; especially, one operated by electricity and designed for household use, such as a refrigerator or vacuum cleaner. **2.** An attachment or accessory; especially, one that adapts a tool for a different use. —See Synonyms at **tool.** [From APPLY.]

ap·pli·ca·ble (ăp′lĭ-kə-bəl, ə-plĭk′ə-) adj. **1.** Capable of being applied; appropriate. **2.** In force; effective: *New rates are applicable from Monday.* —**ap·pli·ca·bil·i·ty** n. —**ap·pli·ca·bly** adv.

ap·pli·cant (ăp′lĭ-kənt) n. One who applies, as for a job. [Latin *applicāns* (stem *applicant-*), present participle of *applicāre,* to APPLY.]

ap·pli·ca·tion (ăp′lĭ-kā′shən) n. **1.** The act of applying or putting something on. **2.** Anything that is applied, such as a cosmetic or curative agent. **3.** The act of putting something to a special use or purpose. **4. a.** A method of applying or using; a specific use: *industrial applications.* **b.** The capacity of being usable; relevance: *The theory has no application in this case.* **5.** Attention, diligence, or effort. **6. a.** A formal request, as for employment or admission. **b.** A written statement making such a request. **c.** The printed form upon which such a statement is often made: *fill out an application.* [Middle English *applicacioun,* from Latin *applicātiō* (stem *applicātiōn-*), from *applicāre,* to APPLY.]

ap·pli·ca·tive (ăp′lĭ-kā′tĭv, ə-plĭk′ə-) adj. **1.** Characterized by actual application to something. **2.** Of practical use; applicatory. —**ap·pli·ca·tive·ly** adv.

ap·pli·ca·tor (ăp′lĭ-kā′tər) n. An instrument for applying something, such as a medicament or glue.

ap·pli·ca·to·ry (ăp′lĭ-kə-tôr′ē, -tōr′ē, ə-plĭk′ə-) adj. Of practical value; useful.

ap·plied (ə-plīd′) adj. *Abbr.* **app., appl.** Intended to have practical consequences; capable of being put to practical use: *applied physics.* Compare **theoretical.**

ap·pli·qué (ăp′lĭ-kā′) n. A decoration or ornament, as in needlework, made by cutting pieces of one material and applying them to the surface of another.
~adj. Of or like appliqué.
~tr.v. **appliquéd, -quéing, -qués.** To decorate with appliqué work. [French, past participle of *appliquer,* to put on, apply, from Latin *applicāre,* to APPLY.]

ap·ply (ə-plī′) v. **-plied, -plying, -plies.** —*tr.* **1.** To bring near to or into contact with something; put on or onto: *apply the glue to both surfaces.* **2.** To put to or adapt for a special use: *This principle is applied in glass manufacture.* **3.** To use (an epithet, for example) with reference to a particular person or thing. Used with *to.* **4.** To devote (oneself or one's efforts) to something. **5.** To bring into operation: *applied the brakes.* —*intr.* **1.** To be pertinent or relevant. **2.** To request or seek employment, acceptance, or admission. Used with *for* or *to.* [Middle English *applien, aplien,* from Old French *aplier,* from Latin *applicāre,* to join to, apply to : *ad-,* to + *plicāre,* to fold together.]

ap·pog·gia·tu·ra (ə-pŏj′ə-tŏŏr′ə) n. *Music.* A grace note of varying length, usually one step above or below the note it precedes. Compare **acciaccatura.** [Italian, "a supporting," from *appoggiare,* to lean on, from Vulgar Latin *appodiāre* (unattested) : Latin *ad-,* to +

podium, balcony, from Greek *podion,* small foot, base, diminutive of *pous* (stem *pod-*), foot.]

ap·point (ə-point′) v. **-pointed, -pointing, -points.** *Abbr.* **app., appt. 1.** To select or designate to fill an office or position. **2.** To fix or set by authority or by mutual agreement. **3.** To order, require, or enjoin with authority; prescribe. **4.** To furnish; equip. Used chiefly in the passive and in combination: *a well-appointed apartment.* **5.** *Law.* To direct the disposition of (property) to a person or persons in exercise of a power granted for this purpose by a preceding deed. [Middle English *appointen, apointen,* from Old French *apointier,* to arrange, from *(rendre) à point,* "(to bring) to a point" : *a-,* to + POINT.] —**ap·point·ee** (ə-poin′tē′, ăp′oin-tē′) n.

ap·point·ive (ə-poin′tĭv) adj. Pertaining to or filled by appointment: *an appointive office.*

ap·point·ment (ə-point′mənt) n. **1.** The act of appointing or state of being appointed, as to an office or position. **2.** The office or position to which a person has been appointed. **3.** An arrangement to do something or meet someone at a particular time and place. **4.** *Usually* **appointments.** Fittings or equipment. **5.** *Law.* The act of directing the disposition of property by virtue of a power granted under a preceding deed.

ap·poin·tor (ə-poin′tər, ə-poin′tôr′) n. *Law.* One who executes a power of appointment of property.

Ap·po·mat·tox (ăp′ə-măt′əks). Town in central Virginia where the Civil War came to a close. The Confederate general Robert E. Lee surrendered to the Union general Ulysses S. Grant here on April 9, 1865.

ap·port (ə-pôrt′, ə-pōrt′) n. **1.** In spiritualism, the act of conjuring up or transporting a material object. **2.** The object so transported. [Middle English, a bringing, from Old French *aport,* from Medieval Latin *apportum,* offering, contribution, from Latin *apportāre* : *ad-,* near to + *portāre,* to carry.]

ap·por·tion (ə-pôr′shən, ə-pōr′-) tr.v. **-tioned, -tioning, -tions.** To divide and assign according to some plan or proportion; allot; partition. —See Synonyms at **assign.** [French *apportionner* : *a-,* to + *portionner,* to divide into portions, from PORTION.]

ap·por·tion·ment (ə-pôr′shən-mənt, ə-pōr′-) n. **1. a.** The act of apportioning or the condition of being apportioned. **b.** An amount apportioned. **2.** The proportional distribution of the number of members of the U.S. House of Representatives on the basis of the population of each state.

ap·pose (ă-pōz′) tr.v. **-posed, -posing, -poses. 1.** To put or apply (one thing) to another. **2.** To arrange (things) near to each other or side by side. [Back-formation from APPOSITION (by analogy with COMPOSE, COMPOSITION).]

ap·po·site (ăp′ə-zĭt) adj. Fitting; suitable; appropriate. —See Synonyms at **relevant.** [Latin *appositus,* "situated near," past participle of *appōnere,* to place near to, apply to. See **apposition.**] —**ap·po·site·ly** adv. —**ap·po·site·ness** n.

ap·po·si·tion (ăp′ə-zĭsh′ən) n. **1.** *Grammar.* **a.** A construction in which one noun or noun phrase is placed after another to explain it, both having the same function in the sentence. In the sentence *Copley, the famous painter, was born in Boston, Copley* and *the famous painter* are in apposition. **b.** The relationship between such nouns or noun phrases. **2.** A placing side by side or next to other. **3.** *Biology.* The growth in thickness of a cell wall by deposition of successive layers of material. [Middle English *apposicioun,* from Medieval Latin *appositiō* (stem *appositiōn-*), from Latin *appōnere* (past participle *appositus*), to place near to, apply to : *ad-,* near to + *pōnere,* to put.] —**ap·po·si·tion·al** adj. —**ap·po·si·tion·al·ly** adv.

ap·pos·i·tive (ə-pŏz′ə-tĭv) adj. Of, pertaining to, or being in apposition.
~n. A word or phrase that is in apposition. [From APPOSITION.] —**ap·pos·i·tive·ly** adv.

ap·prais·al (ə-prā′zəl) n. **1.** The act of appraising. **2.** An account or evaluation of the merits and defects of someone or something. **3.** An expert or official valuation of something, as for taxation.

ap·praise (ə-prāz′) tr.v. **-praised, -praising, -praises. 1.** To evaluate the importance or worth of, especially in an official capacity. **2.** To estimate the quality, amount, size, and other features of; judge. —See Synonyms at **estimate.** [Middle English *appreisen,* partly from *preise,* value, PRAISE, partly from Old French *aprisier,* from Late Latin *appretiāre,* to set a value on : *ad-,* to + *pretiāre,* to value, from Latin *pretium,* price.] —**ap·prais·a·ble** adj. —**ap·praise·ment** n. —**ap·prais·er** n.

ap·pre·ci·a·ble (ə-prē′shə-bəl) adj. Capable of being noticed, estimated, or measured; noticeable. —See Synonyms at **perceptible.** —**ap·pre·ci·a·bly** adv.

ap·pre·ci·ate (ə-prē′shē-āt′) v. **-ated, -ating, -ates.** —*tr.* **1.** To be fully aware of or sensitive to; realize: *He doesn't appreciate the difficulties involved.* **2.** To recognize the quality, significance, or magnitude of; value: *appreciated their freedom.* **3.** To be thankful or show gratitude for. **4.** To enjoy and understand critically or emotionally: *appreciates fine wines.* **5.** To raise in value or price. —*intr.* To go up in value or price: *Their art collection appreciates every year.* [Late Latin *appretiāre,* to set a value on : *ad-,* to + *pretiāre,* to value, from *pretium,* price.] —**ap·pre·ci·a·tor** n.
Synonyms: cherish, esteem, prize, treasure, value.

ap·pre·ci·a·tion (ə-prē′shē-ā′shən) n. **1.** Gratefulness; gratitude. **2.** Awareness or delicate perception, especially of aesthetic qualities or values: *an appreciation of Manet's brushwork.* **3.** An assessment of the true nature of someone or something: *a fair appreciation of* *the economic situation.* **4.** A usually favorable expression of criticism. **5.** A rise in value or price.

ap·pre·cia·tive (ə-prē′shə-tĭv, -shē-ā′tĭv) *adj.* Capable of or showing appreciation. **—ap·pre·cia·tive·ly** *adv.*

ap·pre·hend (ăp′rĭ-hĕnd′) *v.* **-hended, -hending, -hends.** *—tr.* **1.** To take into custody; arrest. **2.** To grasp mentally; understand. **3.** To look forward to fearfully; anticipate with anxiety. *—intr.* To understand. [Middle English *apprehenden,* from Latin *apprehendere,* to lay hold of, seize : *ad-,* to + *prehendere,* to seize.]
Synonyms: *comprehend, grasp, understand.*

ap·pre·hen·si·ble (ăp′rĭ-hĕn′sə-bəl) *adj.* Capable of being apprehended or understood. **—ap·pre·hen·si·bly** *adv.*

ap·pre·hen·sion (ăp′rĭ-hĕn′shən) *n.* **1.** A fearful or uneasy anticipation of the future. **2.** A seizing or capturing; an arrest. **3.** The ability to apprehend or understand; understanding. **4.** An opinion or estimate. [Middle English *apprehensioun,* from Late Latin *apprehensiō* (stem *apprehensiōn-*), from *apprehendere* (past participle *apprehensus*), APPREHEND.]
Synonyms: *foreboding, misgiving, presentiment.*

ap·pre·hen·sive (ăp′rĭ-hĕn′sĭv) *adj.* **1.** Anxious or fearful about the future; uneasy. **2.** Capable of understanding; quick to apprehend. **3.** Aware; cognizant. **—ap·pre·hen·sive·ly** *adv.* **—ap·pre·hen·sive·ness** *n.*

apricot *Although the apricot is native to central Asia and China, it is widely cultivated in other parts of the world for canning and jam making.*

ap·pren·tice (ə-prĕn′tĭs) *n.* **1.** One bound by legal agreement to work for another for a given length of time in return for instruction in a trade, art, or business. **2.** A person who is learning a trade or occupation, especially as a member of a labor union. **3.** A beginner; a learner.
~*tr.v.* **apprenticed, -ticing, -tices.** To place or take on as an apprentice; bind by indenture. [Middle English *aprentis,* from Old French, from *aprendre,* to learn, from Latin *appre(he)ndere,* to APPREHEND.] **—ap·pren·tice·ship** *n.*

ap·pressed (ə-prĕst′) *adj.* Lying flat or pressed closely against something, as leaves on a stem. [Latin *appressus,* past participle of *apprimere,* to press to : *ad-,* to + *premere,* to press.]

ap·prise (ə-prīz′) *tr.v.* **-prised, -prising, -prises.** To cause to know; make aware; inform. Used with *of.* [French *apprendre* (past participle *appris*), to cause to learn, inform, from Old French *aprendre,* to learn, from Latin *appre(he)ndere,* to APPREHEND.]

ap·proach (ə-prōch′) *v.* **-proached, -proaching, -proaches.** *—intr.* To come near or nearer in space, time, or magnitude. *—tr.* **1.** To come near or nearer to. **2.** To come close to in appearance, quality, condition, or other characteristics; approximate: *Her talent approaches genius.* **3.** To make a proposal to; make overtures to. **4.** To begin to deal with or work on. **5.** To bring or draw closer: *The scientist approached the microscope to the slide.*
~*n.* **1.** The act of coming or drawing near. **2.** A fairly close resemblance; an approximation. **3.** A way or means of reaching someone or a destination; an access: *All approaches to the town are blocked.* **4.** The method used in dealing with or accomplishing something: *We took a logical approach to the problem.* **5.** *Often* **approaches.** An advance or overture made by one person to another. **6.** In golf, the stroke following the drive from the tee with which the player tries to get the ball onto the putting green. **7.** The last stage in an aircraft's flight before it lands: *We are now commencing the approach to the airport.* **8. approaches.** *Military.* Works such as trenches or bulwarks for the protection of troops besieging a fortified position. [Middle English *aprochen,* from Old French *aprochier,* from Late Latin *appropiāre,* to go nearer to : *ad-,* to + *propius,* nearer, from *prope,* near.]

ap·proach·a·ble (ə-prō′chə-bəl) *adj.* **1.** Capable of being approached or reached; accessible. **2.** Easily approached; receptive to overtures; friendly. **—ap·proach·a·bil·i·ty** *n.*

ap·pro·bate (ăp′rə-bāt′) *tr.v.* **-bated, -bating, -bates.** To give permission or approval for; sanction or authorize. [Middle English *approbaten,* from Latin *approbāre,* to APPROVE.] **—ap·pro·ba·tive** (ăp′rə-bā′tĭv, ə-prō′bə-tĭv), **ap·pro·ba·to·ry** (ə-prō′bə-tôr′ē, -tōr′ē) *adj.*

ap·pro·ba·tion (ăp′rə-bā′shən) *n.* **1.** Praise; commendation. **2.** Official approval. —See Synonyms at **regard.**

ap·pro·pri·a·ble (ə-prō′prē-ə-bəl) *adj.* Capable of being appropriated.

ap·pro·pri·ate (ə-prō′prē-ĭt) *adj.* Suitable for a particular person, condition, occasion, or place; proper or fitting: *A book would be an appropriate gift.* —See Synonyms at **fit.**
~*tr.v.* (ə-prō′prē-āt′) **appropriated, -ating, -ates. 1.** To set apart for a specific use. **2.** To take possession of or make use of exclusively for oneself, often without permission. [Middle English *appropriaten,* from Late Latin *appropriāre* (past participle *appropriātus*), to make one's own : Latin *ad-,* to + *proprius,* own.] **—ap·pro·pri·ate·ly** *adv.* **—ap·pro·pri·ate·ness** *n.* **—ap·pro·pri·a·tive** (ə-prō′prē-ā′tĭv, -ə-tĭv) *adj.* **—ap·pro·pri·a·tor** *n.*

ap·pro·pri·a·tion (ə-prō′prē-ā′shən) *n.* **1.** The act of appropriating for a specific use or purpose. **2.** The act of appropriating to oneself. **3.** Public funds set aside for a specific purpose.

ap·prov·al (ə-pro͞o′vəl) *n.* **1.** The act or an instance of approving. **2.** Commendation; favorable regard; good opinion. **—on approval.** For examination or trial by a potential customer without the obligation to buy.

ap·prove (ə-pro͞ov′) *v.* **-proved, -proving, -proves.** *—tr.* **1.** To confirm or consent to officially; sanction; ratify: *approve the proposals.* **2.** To view with approval; commend. **3.** *Obs.* To prove or demonstrate: *"the letter he spoke of which approves him an intelligent party"* (Shakespeare). *—intr.* To feel, voice, or demonstrate approval. Usually used with *of: approve of capital punishment.* [Middle English *approven,* from Old French *aprover,* from Latin *approbāre,* to make good, admit as good : *ad-,* to + *probus,* good.] **—ap·prov·a·ble** *adj.* **—ap·prov·ing·ly** *adv.*
Synonyms: *certify, endorse, ratify, sanction.*

approved school *n. Chiefly British.* Formerly, a school for young offenders. Compare **community home.**

approx. approximate; approximately.

ap·prox·i·mate (ə-prŏk′sə-mĭt) *adj. Abbr.* **approx. 1.** Almost exact, correct, complete, or perfect. **2.** Very similar; closely resembling. **3.** Close together; near.
~*v.* (ə-prŏk′sə-māt′) **approximated, -mating, -mates.** *—tr.* **1.** To come close to; be nearly the same as. **2.** To cause to approach; bring near. *—intr.* To come near or close in degree, nature, quality, or other characteristics. [Late Latin *approximātus,* past participle of *approximāre,* to come near to : Latin *ad-,* to + *proximāre,* to come near, from *proximus,* nearest.]

ap·prox·i·mate·ly (ə-prŏk′sə-mĭt-lē) *adv.* Almost but not exactly; about: *It's approximately two o'clock.*

ap·prox·i·ma·tion (ə-prŏk′sə-mā′shən) *n.* **1.** The act, process, or result of approximating. **2.** A nearly accurate account, calculation, or estimate: *an approximation of the facts.* **3.** *Mathematics.* An inexact result or relationship, adequate for a given purpose. **—ap·prox·i·ma·tive** (ə-prŏk′sə-mā′tĭv, -mə-tĭv) *adj.* **—ap·prox·i·ma·tive·ly** *adv.*

appt. appoint; appointed.

ap·pulse (ə-pŭls′, ă-pŭls′) *n.* An apparent close approach of two celestial bodies in which no occultation or eclipse occurs. [Latin *appulsus,* approach, from past participle of *appellere,* to drive toward : *ad-,* toward + *pellere,* to drive.]

ap·pur·te·nance (ə-pûrt′n-əns) *n.* **1.** Something added to another more important thing; an appendage; an accessory. **2. appurtenances.** Equipment, such as clothing or tools, used for a specific purpose or task; gear. **3.** *Law.* A right, privilege, or minor property that is considered as accompanying the principal property for purposes such as passage of title, conveyance, or inheritance. [Middle English *appurtenaunce,* from Norman-French *apurtenance,* variant of Old French *apertenance,* from Vulgar Latin *appertinentia* (unattested), from Late Latin *appertinēre,* to APPERTAIN.]

ap·pur·te·nant (ə-pûrt′n-ənt) *adj.* **1.** *Law.* Constituting an appurtenance. **2.** Belonging, accessory, or relating.

Apr. April.

a·prax·i·a (ā-prăk′sē-ə) *n.* The inability to perform coordinated movements as a result of lesions in the cerebral cortex. [New Latin, from Greek, inaction : *a-,* without + Greek *praxis,* action, from *prassein,* to do.] **—a·prac·tic** (ā-prăk′tĭk) *adj.*

a·près- *comb. form.* Indicates a time following a specified period or activity; for example, **après-ski.** [French, "after."]

a·près-ski (ä′prā-skē′, ăp′rā-) *n.* Social activities in the afternoon or evening at a ski resort. **—a·près-ski** *adj.*

a·pri·cot (ăp′rĭ-kŏt′, ā′prĭ-) *n.* **1.** A tree, *Prunus armeniaca,* native to western Asia and Africa, widely cultivated for its edible fruit. **2.** The juicy, yellow-orange peachlike fruit of this tree. **3.** Moderate, light, or strong orange to orange yellow. [Earlier *abrecock,* perhaps from obsolete Catalan *abercoc,* from Arabic *al-birqūq,* "the apricot," from Late Greek *praikokion,* from Latin *(prūnum) praecoquum,* "early-ripening (plum)," from *praecoquere,* to ripen early : *prae-,* before + *coquere,* to ripen, cook.] **—a·pri·cot** *adj.*

A·pril (ā′prəl) *n. Abbr.* **Apr.** The fourth month of the year according to the Gregorian calendar. April has 30 days. See feature at **calendar.** [Middle English, from Latin *aprīlis,* perhaps "month of Venus," from Etruscan *apru,* from Greek *Aphrō,* short form of *Aphroditē,* APHRODITE.]

April fool *n.* The victim of a trick played on April Fools' Day.

April Fools' Day *n.* April 1, marked as a day for playing practical jokes. Also called "All Fools' Day."

a pri·o·ri (ä′ prē-ôr′ē, -ōr′ē, ā′ prī-ôr′ī, -ōr′ī) *adj.* **1.** *Logic.* Pertaining to or proceeding from a known or assumed cause or general principle to a necessarily related effect or conclusion; deductive. **2. a.** Based on reason alone; not provable empirically. **b.** Based on a hypothesis or convention rather than on experiment or experience. **3.** Claimed as true without examination; not supported by factual study. Compare **a posteriori.** [Latin, "from the previous (causes or hypotheses)."] **—a·pri·or·i·ty** (ä′prē-ôr′ə-tē, ā′prī-) *n.*

a·pron (ā′prən) *n.* **1.** A garment worn over all or part of the front of the body to protect one's clothes or as a decorative part of a costume. **2.** Anything resembling an apron in appearance or function. **3.** The hard-surfaced area in front of and around airport hangars and terminal buildings. **4.** The part of a stage in a theater extending in front of the curtain. **5. a.** A platform of planking or other material at the entrance to a dock. **b.** A covering or structure along the shoreline of a body of water for protection against erosion. **c.** A platform serving a similar purpose below a dam or in a sluiceway. **6.** A continuous conveyor belt. **7.** *Geology.* An area covered by sand and gravel deposited at the front of a glacial moraine. **8.** A panel, board, or the like between a windowsill and a board. **9.** A metal plate that protects a machine operator, gunner, or the like from pieces of flying debris. **—tied to someone's apron strings.** Dominated by, controlled by, or dependent on another person, usually a wife or mother.
~*tr.v.* **aproned, aproning, aprons.** To cover, protect, or provide with an apron; put an apron or aprons on. [Middle English *(an) apron,* originally *(a) napron,* from Old French *naperon,* diminutive

PRONUNCIATION KEY

ă, pat; ā, pay; âr, care;
ä, father, are; b, bib;
ch, church; d, deed; ĕ, pet;
ē, be; f, fife; g, gag; h, hat;
hw, which; ĭ, pit; ī, pie;
îr, pier; j, judge; k, kick;
l, lid, needle; m, mum;
n, no, sudden; ng, thing;
ŏ, pot; ō, toe; ô, paw, for;
oi, noise; ou, out; o͝o, book;
o͞o, boot; p, pop; r, roar;
s, sauce; sh, ship, dish;
t, tight; th, thin, path;
th, this, bathe; ŭ, cut; ûr, fur;
v, valve; w, with; y, yes;
z, zebra, size; zh, vision;
ə, about, item, edible,
gallop, circus, peaceful

IN FOREIGN WORDS:

à, *Fr.* ami; œ, *Fr.* feu, *Ger.* schön; ü, *Fr.* tu, *Ger.* über; KH, *Ger.* ich, *Scot.* loch; N, *Fr.* bon; y', *Fr.* Compiègne

STRESS MARKS:

Primary stress: ′
in·cite′ (ĭn-sīt′)
Secondary stress: ′
in′sight′ (ĭn′sīt′)

of *nape,* tablecloth, from Latin *mappa,* napkin.]
apron stage *n.* A part of the Elizabethan stage that extends into the area occupied by the audience.
ap·ro·pos (ăp′rə-pō′) *adj.* Appropriate; pertinent; opportune.
~*adv.* **1.** Pertinently; relevantly; opportunely. **2.** By the way; incidentally. Used to introduce a remark.
~*prep.* Also **apropos of.** Speaking of; with reference to. [French *à propos,* "to the purpose."]
a·pro·tic (ā-prō′tĭk) *adj. Chemistry.* Having no protons; not producing or accepting hydrogen ions. Used of substances or solutions that are not hydrogen acids or hydroxide bases. [A- (without) + PROT(ON) + -IC.]
apse (ăps) *n.* **1.** *Architecture.* A semicircular or polygonal, usually domed, projection of a building, especially at the altar or east end of a church. Also called "apsis." **2.** *Astronomy.* An orbital position, **apsis** *(see).* [Medieval Latin *apsis, absis.* See **apsis.**] —**ap·si·dal** (ăp′sə-dəl) *adj.*
ap·sis (ăp′sĭs) *n., pl.* **-sides** (-sə-dēz′) **1.** *Astronomy.* The point of greatest or least distance of a celestial body from a center of attraction. Also called "apse." **2.** *Architecture.* An apse. [Medieval Latin *apsis,* architectural apse, from Latin, arch, vault, orbit, from Greek *apsis, hapsis,* "a fastening together," from *haptein*†, to fasten.]
apt (ăpt) *adj.* **1.** Exactly suitable; appropriate: *That was an apt reply.* **2.** Likely: *The handle is apt to break off.* **3.** Having a tendency; inclined: *He is apt to stammer when he is excited.* **4.** Quick to learn or understand. —See Synonyms at **fit, relevant.** [Middle English, from Latin *aptus,* fit, suited, from the past participle of *apere,* to fasten.] —**apt·ly** *adv.* —**apt·ness** *n.*
APT (ā′pē-tē′) *n.* A computer programming language designed for use with computer-controlled machine tools. [*A*utomatically *Pro*grammed *T*ool.]
apt. apartment.
ap·ter·al (ăp′tər-əl) *adj. Architecture.* Having no columns along the sides. [Greek *apteros,* wingless, APTEROUS.]
ap·ter·ous (ăp′tər-əs) *adj.* **1.** *Zoology.* Having no wings: *an apterous insect.* **2.** *Botany.* Having no winglike parts or extensions. [Greek *apteros,* wingless : *a-,* without + -PTEROUS.]
ap·ter·yg·i·al (ăp′tə-rĭj′ē-əl) *adj. Zoology.* Without wings or fins. [A- (without) + Greek *pterux* (stem *pterug-*), wing, fin.]
ap·ter·yx (ăp′tə-rĭks) *n.* A bird, the **kiwi** *(see).* [New Latin : A- (without) + Greek *pterux,* wing, from *pteron,* feather, wing.]
ap·ti·tude (ăp′tə-to͞od′, -tyo͞od′) *n.* **1.** A natural or acquired talent, skill, or ability: *an aptitude for sculpture.* **2.** Quickness in learning and understanding; intelligence. **3.** The state or quality of being fitting; aptness. —See Synonyms at **ability.** [Middle English, from Late Latin *aptitūdō,* fitness, from *aptus,* APT.]
aptitude test *n.* A standardized test designed to measure the ability of an individual to develop skills or acquire knowledge.
A·pu·lei·us (ăp′yə-lē′əs), **Lucius,** also known as "Apuleius of Madaura" (A.D. *c.* 125–*c.* 180). Roman philosopher and satirist, born in Numidia. His most famous work, *The Golden Ass,* or *Metamorphoses,* is the story of a man who is changed into an ass.
A·pu·lia (ə-po͞ol′yə). *Italian* **Pu·glia** (po͞o′lyä). A farming region, chiefly low-lying, in southeast Italy. Its southern portion forms the heel of the Italian "boot." Bari is the chief city.
A·pus (ā′pəs) *n.* A constellation in the Southern Hemisphere near Musca and Pavo. [New Latin, from Latin *apus,* the swallow, from Greek *apous,* the swift, "footless" (probably because the swift is seldom seen perching) : *a-,* without + *pous,* foot.]
a·py·ret·ic (ā′pī-rĕt′ĭk) *adj.* Without fever. [A- (without) + Greek *puretos,* fever.]
aq. aqueous.
A·qa·ba (ä′kə-bə, ăk′ə-). Jordan's only seaport, located at the head of the Gulf of Aqaba, an arm of the Red Sea between the Sinai Peninsula and Saudi Arabia.
aq·ua (ăk′wə, ä′kwə) *n., pl.* **aquae** (ăk′wē, ä′kwī′) or **-uas. 1.** *Pharmacology.* Liquid; solution, especially in water. **2.** The color aquamarine. [Latin, water.] —**aq·ua** *adj.*
aqua- *prefix.* Indicates water; for example, **aquarium, aquanaut.** [Latin.]
aq·ua·cade (ăk′wə-kād′, ä′kwə-) *n.* A water show with swimmers and divers. [AQUA + (CAVAL)CADE.]
aq·ua·cul·ture (ăk′wə-kŭl′chər, ä′kwə-) *n.* The farming of sea organisms, as shellfish, for human use.
Aq·ua·dag (ăk′wə-dăg′, ä′kwə-) *n.* A trademark for a colloidal suspension of graphite in water, used as a lubricant and conducting coating.
aqua fortis *n.* Also **aq·ua·for·tis** (ăk′wə-fôr′tĭs, ä′kwə-). *Chemistry.* **Nitric acid** *(see).* [New Latin, "strong water."]
Aqua Lung *n.* A trademark for an underwater breathing apparatus.
aq·ua·ma·rine (ăk′wə-mə-rēn′, ä′kwə-) *n.* **1.** A transparent blue-green variety of beryl, used as a gemstone. **2.** Pale blue to light greenish blue. [New Latin *aqua marīna,* from Latin, sea water : *aqua,* AQUA- + *marīnus,* of the sea, MARINE.] —**aq·ua·ma·rine** *adj.*
aq·ua·naut (ăk′wə-nôt′, ä′kwə-) *n.* A person trained to live in underwater installations and conduct or assist in scientific research. [AQUA- + Greek *nautēs,* sailor.]
aq·ua·plane (ăk′wə-plān′, ä′kwə-) *n.* A board on which a person rides in a standing position while it is pulled over the water by a motorboat.
~*intr.v.* **aquaplaned, -planing, -planes.** To ride on an aquaplane. [AQUA- + PLANE (surface).]
aqua re·gi·a (rē′jē-ə, -jə) *n.* A corrosive, fuming mixture of concentrated hydrochloric and nitric acids, used for testing metals and dissolving platinum and gold. Also called "nitrohydrochloric acid." [New Latin, "royal water" (because it dissolves gold and platinum, which were known as the "noble metals").]
aq·ua·relle (ăk′wə-rĕl′, ä′kwə-) *n.* A drawing in transparent water colors. [French, from obsolete Italian *acquarella,* water color, from *acqua,* water, from Latin *aqua.*] —**aq·ua·rel·list** *n.*
a·quar·ist (ə-kwâr′ĭst) *n.* One who keeps an aquarium.
a·quar·i·um (ə-kwâr′ē-əm) *n., pl.* **-ums** or **-ia** (-ē-ə). **1.** A tank, bowl, or other water-filled enclosure in which living aquatic animals and plants are kept. **2.** A place for the public exhibition of such animals and plants. [19th century : noun use of Latin *aquārius,* of water, from *aqua,* water, formed by analogy with *vivarium.*]
A·quar·i·us (ə-kwâr′ē-əs) *n.* **1.** A constellation in the equatorial region of the Southern Hemisphere near Pisces and Aquila. **2. a.** The 11th sign of the **zodiac** *(see).* Also called the "Water Bearer." **b.** One born under this sign. [Latin *aquārius,* from *aqua,* water.] —**A·quar·i·an** (ə-kwâr′ē-ən) *n. & adj.*
a·quat·ic (ə-kwŏt′ĭk, ə-kwăt′-) *adj.* **1.** Living or growing in or on the water. **2.** Taking place in or on the water.
~*n.* **1.** An aquatic organism. **2. aquatics.** Aquatic sports. [Old French *aquatique,* from Latin *aquāticus,* from *aqua,* water.]
aq·ua·tint (ăk′wə-tĭnt′, ä′kwə-) *n.* **1.** A process of etching capable of producing several tones by varying the etching time of different areas of a copper plate so that the resulting print resembles the flat tints of an ink or wash drawing. **2.** An etching made in this way.
~*tr.v.* **aquatinted, -tinting, -tints.** To etch in aquatint. [French *aquatinte,* from Italian *acqua tinta,* "tinted water," water color, hence aquatint (which imitates water color) : *acqua,* water + *tinta,* tinted, from Latin *tincta,* feminine of *tinctus,* dyed (see **tint**).]
a·qua·vit (ä′kwə-vēt′) *n.* A strong, clear Scandinavian liquor distilled from potato or grain mash and flavored with caraway seed. [Swedish, Danish, and Norwegian *akvavit,* from Medieval Latin *aqua vītae,* "water of life."]
aqua vi·tae (vī′tē) *n.* **1.** Whiskey, brandy, or other strong liquor. **2.** Alcohol. [Middle English *aquavite,* from Medieval Latin *aqua vītae,* "water of life," originally an alchemist's term for alcohol or spirits.]

aqueduct *The Pont du Gard was built by the Romans in the first century to carry water across a valley in Provence, France.*

aq·ue·duct (ăk′wə-dŭkt′) *n.* **1.** A manmade channel designed to transport water over long distances, usually by gravity. **2.** An elevated structure supporting a channel or canal passing over a river or low ground. **3.** *Anatomy.* A channel or passage carrying fluid in the body. [Latin *aquae ductus* : *aquae,* genitive of *aqua,* water + DUCT.] See feature, next page.
a·que·ous (ā′kwē-əs, ăk′wē-) *adj. Abbr.* **aq. 1.** Pertaining to, similar to, containing, or dissolved in water; watery. **2.** *Geology.* Formed from matter deposited by water, as are certain sedimentary rocks. [Medieval Latin *aqueus,* from Latin *aqua,* water.]
aqueous humor *n.* A clear, lymphlike fluid in the chamber of the eye between the cornea and the lens. Compare **vitreous humor.**
aqui- *prefix.* Indicates water; for example, **aquiculture.** [Latin, from *aqua,* water.]
aq·ui·cul·ture (ăk′wĭ-kŭl′chər, ä′kwĭ-) *n.* A method of cultivation, **hydroponics** *(see).* —**aq·ui·cul·tur·al** *adj.*
aq·ui·fer (ăk′wə-fər, ä′kwə-) *n.* A water-bearing rock, rock formation, or group of formations. [AQUI- + -FER.] —**a·quif·er·ous** (ə-kwĭf′ər-əs) *adj.*
Aq·ui·la (ăk′wə-lə) *n.* A constellation in the Northern Hemisphere and the Milky Way near Aquarius and Serpens Cauda. [Latin *aquila,* EAGLE.]
aq·ui·le·gi·a (ăk′wə-lē′jē-ə, -jə) *n.* A plant, the **columbine** *(see).* [New Latin, from Medieval Latin *aquilēgia, aquilēja*†, columbine.]
aq·ui·line (ăk′wə-līn′, -lĭn) *adj.* **1.** Of or similar to an eagle. **2.** Curved or hooked like an eagle's beak: *an aquiline nose.* [Latin *aquilīnus,* from *aquila,* eagle. See **eagle.**]
A·qui·nas (ə-kwī′nəs), **Saint Thomas** (*c.* 1225–74). Italian Doctor of the Church, theologian, and philosopher, the outstanding representative of the medieval system of thought known as Scholasticism. By far the most influential example of Aquinas's application of Aristotelian methods to Christian theology is *Summa Theologica* (1267–73).
Aq·ui·taine (ăk′wə-tān′). Region of southwest France, stretching north from the Pyrenees to the Garonne River. It formed the Roman province of Aquitania and was subsequently part of the Visigothic and Frankish kingdoms.
a·quiv·er (ə-qwĭv′ər) *adj.* Marked by quivering: *all aquiver with anticipation.*
Ar 1. The symbol for the element argon. **2.** The symbol for an aromatic group in an organic compound.
AR Arkansas (used with a Zip Code).
-ar[1] *suffix.* Indicates like, pertaining to, or of the nature of; for example, **titular, polar, spectacular.** [Middle English *-ar, -er,* from Old French *-er,* from Latin *-āris,* dissimulated alteration (after bases ending in *l*) of *-ālis,* -AL.]
-ar[2] *suffix.* Indicates someone performing or involved with a specified occupation; for example, **bursar, burglar.** [Middle English variant of **-er**[1].]
Ar. 1. Arabia; Arabian. **2.** Arabic. **3.** Aramaic.
A·ra (âr′ə) *n.* A constellation in the Southern Hemisphere near the constellations Norma and Telescopium. [Latin *āra,* altar.]

Arab *A light-framed horse with a deep chest and great stamina. All thoroughbred racehorses are descended from Arab stallions.*

Ar·ab (ăr′əb) *n.* **1.** A native or inhabitant of Arabia. **2.** A member of a Semitic people originally from Arabia, but later widely scattered throughout the Middle East, North Africa, and the Arabian Penin-

aqueduct

MOVING WATER BY AQUEDUCT
Bridges and channels transporting water to cities

The first aqueducts were built in the Middle East before 700 B.C., but it was the Romans who took water supply most seriously, making it a deliberate part of their public health policy. Several Roman aqueducts can still be seen: for example at Nîmes in France, at Segovia in Spain, and in Rome. It is a tribute to the engineering skills of the Romans that many of the aqueducts of today are based on the principles they pioneered. California has the most advanced system of aqueducts in the world, because the bulk of the water supply comes from the north while most of the demand is in the south.

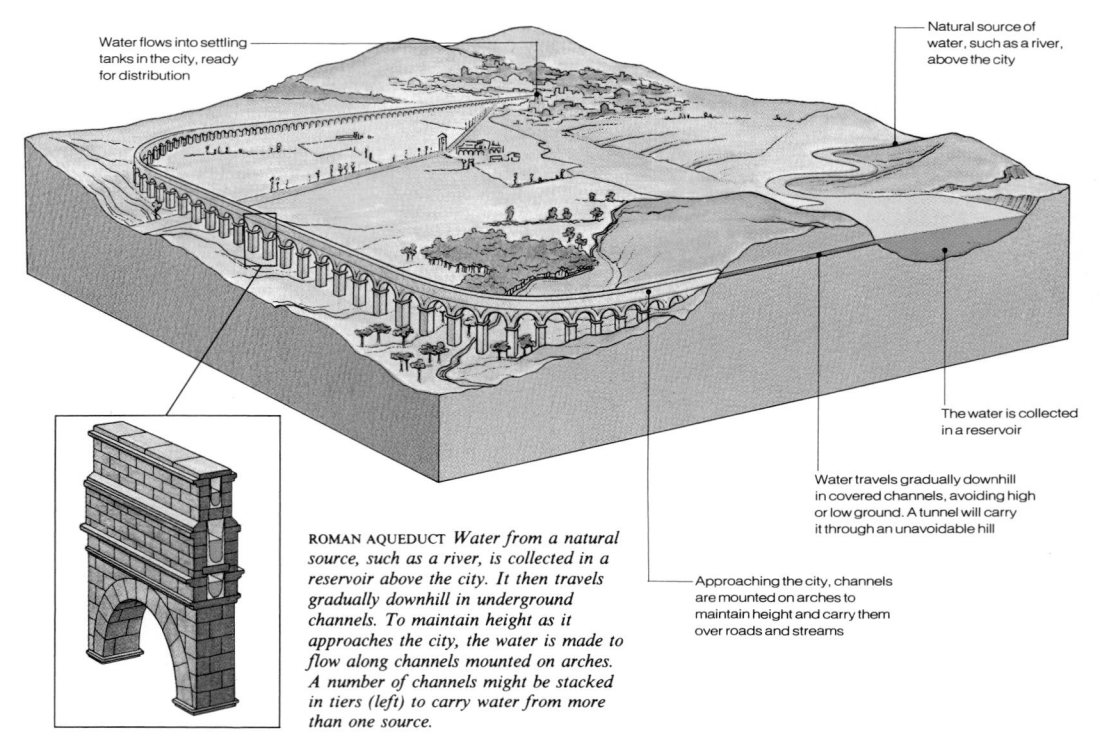

Water flows into settling tanks in the city, ready for distribution

Natural source of water, such as a river, above the city

The water is collected in a reservoir

Water travels gradually downhill in covered channels, avoiding high or low ground. A tunnel will carry it through an unavoidable hill

Approaching the city, channels are mounted on arches to maintain height and carry them over roads and streams

ROMAN AQUEDUCT *Water from a natural source, such as a river, is collected in a reservoir above the city. It then travels gradually downhill in underground channels. To maintain height as it approaches the city, the water is made to flow along channels mounted on arches. A number of channels might be stacked in tiers (left) to carry water from more than one source.*

sula. **3.** A horse of a swift, graceful breed native to Arabia, used mainly for riding. **4.** A street Arab; waif.
~*adj.* Of or pertaining to the Arabs or Arabia. [Middle English, from Old French *Arabe,* from Greek *Arabs, Araps,* from Arabic *'arab.*]
Arab. 1. Arabia; Arabian. **2.** Arabic.
ar·a·besque (ăr′ə-bĕsk′) *n.* **1.** A complex and ornate design with intertwined flowers, leaves, and geometrical figures. **2.** A ballet position in which the dancer stands on one leg, with the other leg extended backward and the arms stretched out.
~*adj.* Pertaining to, resembling, or formed as an arabesque. [French, from Italian *arabesco,* "made or done in Arabic fashion."]
A·ra·bi·a (ə-rā′bē-ə). *Abbr.* **Ar., Arab.** Peninsula in southwest Asia, including Saudi Arabia and its adjoining states to the south and east. It is estimated to have about a third of the world's petroleum reserves.
A·ra·bi·an (ə-rā′bē-ən) *adj. Abbr.* **Ar., Arab.** Of or pertaining to Arabia or the Arabs; Arab.
~*n.* **1.** A native or inhabitant of Arabia. **2.** A horse of a breed native to Arabia; an Arab.
Arabian camel *n.* The **dromedary** *(see).*
Arabian Nights *n.* A collection of oriental stories of love and adventure dating from the 10th century A.D. and including the stories of Aladdin and Sinbad. Also called the "Thousand and One Nights."
~*adj.* Sumptuous and exotic: *an Arabian Nights costume.*
Arabian Sea. The northwestern part of the Indian Ocean, bounded by eastern Africa, Arabia, and western India.
Ar·a·bic (ăr′ə-bĭk) *adj.* Of or pertaining to Arabia, the Arabs, their language, or their culture.
~*n. Abbr.* **Ar., Arab. 1.** The Southwest Semitic language of the Arabs, which is now (in a variety of dialects) the prevailing language of the Arabian peninsula and most of the Middle East and North Africa. **2.** The literary language of the Koran, as employed in formal usage in Arabic-speaking countries; classical Arabic.
Arabic numeral *n.* One of the numerical symbols 1, 2, 3, 4, 5, 6, 7, 8, 9, and 0. Compare **Roman numeral.**
a·rab·i·nose (ə-răb′ə-nōs′, -nōz′) *n.* A pentose sugar, $C_5H_{10}O_5$, found in plant gums, pectins, and mucilages, especially of certain conifers. It is used in bacteriology as a constituent of culture media.

[*Arabin,* from (GUM) ARAB(IC) + -IN + -OSE.]
Ar·ab·ist (ăr′ə-bĭst) *n.* **1.** A specialist in the Arabic language or culture, or in the politics of the Arab world. **2.** A supporter of Arab interests.
ar·a·ble (ăr′ə-bəl) *adj.* Fit for the cultivation of crops.
~*n.* Arable land. [Middle English, from Old French, from Latin *arābilis,* from *arāre,* to plough.]
Arab League *n.* An association of independent Arab nations formed in 1945 by Iraq, Jordan, Lebanon, Saudi Arabia, Egypt, Syria, and Yemen. There are now 22 members, including the Palestine Liberation Organization.
Ar·a·by (ăr′ə-bē). *Poetic.* Arabia.
a·ra·ceous (ə-rā′shəs) *adj. Botany.* Aroid. [New Latin *Araceae* (family), from Latin *arum,* ARUM.]
A·rach·ne (ə-răk′nē). *Greek Mythology.* A maiden who was transformed into a spider by Athena for beating her in a weaving contest. [Latin *Arachnē,* from Greek *Arakhnē,* from *arakhnē†,* spider.]
a·rach·nid (ə-răk′nĭd) *n.* Any of various arthropods of the class Arachnida, such as a spider, scorpion, tick, or mite, characteristically having four pairs of legs, simple eyes, and no antennae. Also called "arachnoid." [New Latin *Arachnida,* from Greek *arakhnē,* spider, ARACHNE.] —**a·rach·ni·dan** (ə-răk′nə-dən) *adj. & n.*
a·rach·noid (ə-răk′noid′) *n.* **1.** The middle of the three delicate membranes covering the spinal cord and brain, lying between the pia mater and the dura mater. **2.** An arachnid.
~*adj.* **1.** Of or pertaining to the arachnoid membrane. **2.** Of, pertaining to, or resembling the arachnids. **3.** Covered with or consisting of thin, soft, entangled hairs like the threads of a cobweb. [New Latin *arachnoides,* from Greek *arakhnoeidēs,* cobweblike : *arakhnē,* spider, ARACHNE + -OID.]
Ar·a·fat (âr′ə-făt′), **Yasir** (1929–). Leader of Al Fatah and of the Palestine Liberation Organization (PLO). In 1974 Arab leaders endorsed him as the spokesman for all Palestinians, but in recent years his influence has diminished as more militant terrorist groups have sought to gain control.
Ar·a·gon (ăr′ə-gŏn′). *Spanish* **Ar·a·gón** (ä′rä-gōn′). Region of northeast Spain. It became an independent kingdom (1035) and united with Castile (1479) to form the nucleus of modern Spain.
A·ra·gon (är-ə-gôN′), **Louis** (1897–1982). French poet and novelist,

one of the founders of literary surrealism. In 1919 he helped found the surrealist journal *Littérature.*

Ar·a·go·nese (ăr'ə-gə-nēz', -nēs) *adj.* Of or pertaining to Aragon, its inhabitants, their language, or their culture.
—*n., pl.* **Aragonese.** A native or inhabitant of Aragon.

a·rag·o·nite (ə-răg'ə-nīt', ăr'ə-gə-) *n.* An orthorhombic mineral form of calcium carbonate, dimorphous with calcite. [After ARAGON, where it was first found.]

A·ral Sea (ăr'əl). The fourth-largest inland body of water in the world, covering some 68,682 square kilometers (26,518 square miles) in the southern U.S.S.R.

Ar·am (ăr'əm). A Biblical name for ancient Syria.

Aram, Eugene (1704–59). English philologist. Largely self-taught, Aram was the first man to demonstrate that the Celtic languages belong to the Indo-European group. In 1759 he was executed for the murder, 14 years earlier, of his friend Daniel Clark.

Ar·a·ma·ic (ăr'ə-mā'ĭk) *n.* A Northwest Semitic language used as the commercial lingua franca for nearly all of southwestern Asia after about 300 B.C. and still spoken in parts of Syria and Lebanon. Compare **Biblical Aramaic.** —**Ar·a·ma·ic** *adj.*

Ar·a·me·an, Ar·a·mae·an (ăr'ə-mē'ən) *adj.* Of or pertaining to Aram, its inhabitants, language, or culture.
—*n.* **1.** A native or inhabitant of Aram. **2.** The Aramaic language.

Ar·an (ăr'ən) *adj.* Knitted from undyed wool in an elaborate cable-stitch pattern that originated in the Aran Islands off the west coast of Ireland: *an Aran sweater.*

ar·a·pai·ma (ăr'ə-pī'mə) *n.* A large South American freshwater food fish, *Arapaima gigas,* sometimes attaining a length of 15 feet. Also called "pirarucu." [Spanish and Portuguese, from Tupi.]

Ar·a·rat, Mount (ăr'ə-răt'). Turkish **A·gri Da·gi** (ä'rē dä-ē'). Massif in eastern Turkey. Great Ararat (5,165 meters; 16,945 feet) is its highest peak and is traditionally regarded as the resting place of Noah's Ark.

ar·a·ro·ba (ăr'ə-rō'bə) *n.* **1.** A Brazilian tree, *Andira araroba,* having yellowish wood from which a medicinal powder is obtained. **2.** The powder itself, found in cavities in the wood. In this sense, also called "Goa powder." See **chrysarobin.** [Portuguese, probably from Tupi : *arara,* parrot + *yba,* tree.]

Ar·au·ca·ni·an (ăr'ô-kā'nē-ən) *n.* Also **A·rau·can** (ə-rô'kən). **1.** A South American Indian language family spoken in Chile and the western pampas of Argentina. **2.** A member of any of the Araucanian-speaking peoples. —**Ar·au·ca·ni·an** *adj.*

ar·au·car·i·a (ăr'ô-kâr'ē-ə) *n.* Any of several evergreen trees of the coniferous genus *Araucaria.* See **bunya, monkey puzzle.** [New Latin *Araucaria,* from Spanish *Araucano,* (tree) of *Araucania,* region of Chile.]

Ar·a·wak (ăr'ə-wäk') *n., pl.* **-waks** or collectively **Arawak. 1.** An Indian people now living chiefly in certain regions of the Guianas. **2.** A member of the Arawak. **3.** The Arawakan language of the Arawak.

Ar·a·wa·kan (ăr'ə-wä'kən) *n., pl.* **-kans** or collectively **Arawakan. 1.** A member of a group of Indian people living in a wide area of South America including Venezuela, Colombia, the Guianas, Peru, Bolivia, Paraguay, and the Amazon basin of Brazil. **2.** A language family that consists of the languages spoken by the Arawakan peoples.

ar·ba·lest (ăr'bə-lĭst) *n.* Also **ar·be·list.** A medieval weapon designed on the crossbow principle and used for firing arrows, stones, balls, and other missiles. [Middle English *arbelast, arblast,* Old English *arblast,* from Old French *arbaleste,* from Late Latin *arcuballista* : Latin *arcus,* bow + BALLISTA.] —**ar·ba·lest·er** *n.*

ar·bi·ter (ăr'bĭ-tər) *n.* **1.** One chosen or appointed to judge or decide a disputed issue; an arbitrator. **2.** One who has the power to judge or ordain at will. **3.** One who has the authority to make influential judgments: *an arbiter of taste.* —See Synonyms at **judge.** [Middle English *arbitre,* from Old French, from Latin *arbiter†,* judge.]

ar·bi·tra·ble (ăr'bĭ-trə-bəl) *adj.* Subject to arbitration; capable of being referred to an arbitrator.

ar·bi·trage (ăr'bĭ-träzh') *n.* The purchase of securities, commodities, or the like, on one market for immediate resale on another in order to profit from a price discrepancy. [French, arbitration, from *arbitrer,* to ARBITRATE.]

ar·bit·ra·ment (ăr-bĭt'rə-mənt) *n.* **1.** The act of arbitrating. **2.** The judgment or award made by an arbitrator. [Middle English, from Old French *arbitrement,* from *arbitrer,* to ARBITRATE.]

ar·bi·trar·y (ăr'bĭ-trĕr'ē) *adj.* **1.** Determined by chance, whim, or impulse, not by reason or law. **2.** Based on or subject to individual judgment or discretion. **3.** Established by a court or judge rather than by a specific law or statute; discretionary. **4.** Not limited by law; absolute; despotic: *the arbitrary power of a dictator.* —See Synonyms at **dictatorial.** [Middle English, from Latin *arbitrārius,* from *arbiter,* ARBITER.] —**ar·bi·trar·i·ly** (ăr'bĭ-trâr'ə-lē) *adv.* —**ar·bi·trar·i·ness** *n.*

ar·bi·trate (ăr'bĭ-trāt') *v.* **-trated, -trating, -trates.** —*tr.* **1.** To judge or decide as or in the manner of an arbitrator. **2.** To submit to settlement or judgment by arbitration. —*intr.* **1.** To serve as an arbitrator or arbiter. **2.** To refer a dispute to arbitration. [Latin *arbitrārī* (past participial stem *arbitrāt-*), from *arbiter,* ARBITER.]

ar·bi·tra·tion (ăr'bĭ-trā'shən) *n.* The process by which the parties to a dispute submit their differences to the judgment of an impartial party appointed by mutual consent or statutory provision. —See Synonyms at **mediation.**

ar·bi·tra·tor (ăr'bĭ-trā'tər) *n.* **1.** A person chosen to settle the issue between parties engaged in a dispute or controversy. **2.** One having the ability or power to make authoritative decisions; an arbiter. —See Synonyms at **judge.**

ar·bor¹ (ăr'bər) *n.* **1.** A shady garden shelter or bower, often made of rustic work or latticework, on which climbing plants, as vines or roses, are grown. **2.** *Obsolete.* An orchard or garden.

arbor² *n.* **1.** An axis or shaft supporting a rotating part on a lathe. **2.** A rotating shaft fitted with a device for holding work while it is being machined. **3.** An axle or spindle of a wheel, as in a watch or a clock. **4.** *Archaic.* A tree. [French *arbre* (in a Latinized respelling), axle, axis, tree, from Latin *arbor†,* tree.]

Arbor Day *n.* In the United States, Canada, Australia, and New Zealand, a day set apart annually for the community planting of trees.

ar·bo·re·al (är-bôr'ē-əl, är-bōr'-) *adj.* **1.** Of, pertaining to, or resembling a tree. **2.** Living in trees: *Some monkeys are arboreal animals.* —**ar·bo·re·al·ly** *adv.*

ar·bo·re·ous (är-bôr'ē-əs, är-bōr'-) *adj.* **1.** Having many trees; wooded. **2.** Resembling or characteristic of a tree; treelike.

ar·bo·res·cent (är'bə-rĕs'ənt) *adj.* Having the form or characteristics of a tree; treelike. [Latin *arborēscēns* (stem *arborescent-*), present participle of *arborēscere,* to grow to be a tree, from *arbor†,* tree.] —**ar·bo·res·cence** *n.*

ar·bo·re·tum (är'bə-rē'təm) *n., pl.* **-tums** or **-ta** (-tə). A place where many different species and varieties of trees and shrubs are grown for scientific study and public exhibition. [New Latin, from Latin *arborētum,* a place where trees are grown, from *arbor†,* tree. See **arbor** (shaft).]

ar·bo·ri·cul·ture (är'bər-ĭ-kŭl'chər, är-bôr'ĭ-, är-bōr'ĭ-) *n.* The cultivation of trees for ornament or for the production of timber. [Latin *arbor†,* tree + *-culture,* by analogy with *agriculture.*] —**ar·bo·ri·cul·tur·al** *adj.* —**ar·bo·ri·cul·tur·ist** *n.*

ar·bor·ist (är'bər-ĭst) *n.* One who specializes in the cultivation and care of trees.

ar·bor·i·za·tion (är'bər-ə-zā'shən) *n.* **1.** A treelike shape or arrangement, as in certain minerals or fossils. See **dendrite. 2.** The formation of such a shape or arrangement.

ar·bo·rize (är'bə-rīz') *intr.v.* **-rized, -rizing, -rizes.** To have or form many branches.

ar·bor·vi·tae, arbor vi·tae (är'bər-vī'tē) *n.* **1. a.** Any of several evergreen shrubs and trees of the genus *Thuja,* having tiny, scalelike leaves and egg-shaped cones. **b.** A similar tree of the genus *Thujopsis.* **2.** *Anatomy.* The white matter of the cerebellum seen in cross section, having the appearance of a tree. [New Latin *arbor vitae,* "tree of life," referring to the tree's remaining green all year.]

arbour. *Chiefly British.* Variant of **arbor.**

ar·bo·vi·rus (är'bə-vī'rəs) *n.* Any of various viruses that are transmitted by arthropods, especially insects, and cause such diseases as encephalitis and yellow fever. [*Ar*thropod-*bo*rne *virus.*]

Ar·buth·not (är-bŭth'nət, är'bəth-nŏt'), **John** (1667–1735). Scottish physician and essayist. His five anti-Whig pamphlets, published as *The History of John Bull* (1712), were satirical pieces that introduced the character of John Bull to English tradition.

ar·bu·tus (är-byōō'təs) *n.* **1.** Any of several broad-leaved evergreen trees of the genus *Arbutus,* having clusters of white or pinkish flowers, especially the **strawberry tree** (see). **2.** A plant, **trailing arbutus** (see). [New Latin *Arbutus,* from Latin *arbūtus†,* strawberry tree, referring to the appearance of its berries.]

arc (ärk) *n.* **1.** Anything shaped like a bow, curve, or arch. **2.** In geometry, a segment of a curve. **3.** *Electricity.* A luminous discharge of electric current crossing a gap between two electrodes.
—*adj.* *Mathematics.* Designating an inverse trigonometric function: *the arc sine of a quantity.*
—*intr.v.* **arced** (ärkt) or **arcked, arcing** (är'kĭng) or **arcking, arcs.** To form an arc. [Middle English *ark,* Old English *arc,* from Latin *arcus,* bow, arc.]

ar·cade (är-kād') *n.* **1.** *Architecture.* **a.** A series of arches supported by columns, piers, or pillars. **b.** An arched, roofed building or part of a building. **2.** A roofed passageway or lane, especially one with shops on either side. [French, from Italian *arcata,* from *arco,* arch, from Vulgar Latin *arca* (unattested). See **arch.**]

Ar·ca·di·a (är-kā'dē-ə) *n.* **1.** A mountainous region of ancient Greece whose inhabitants, isolated from the rest of the world, lived a simple, pastoral life. **2.** A place or region thought to epitomize rustic contentment and simplicity.

Ar·ca·di·an (är-kā'dē-ən) *adj.* **1.** Of, pertaining to, or characteristic of Arcadia. **2.** *Often* **arcadian.** Rustic, peaceful, and simple; pastoral. —See Synonyms at **rural.**
—*n.* **1.** A native of Arcadia. **2.** *Often* **arcadian.** A person who leads or prefers a simple, rural life. **3.** The Ancient Greek dialect of Arcadia, belonging to Arcado-Cyprian.

Ar·ca·do-Cyp·ri·an (är-kā'dō-sĭp'rē-ən) *n.* One of the four main dialects of ancient Greek, comprising Arcadian, Pamphylian, and Cypriot. Compare **Aeolic, Attic-Ionic, Doric.** —**Ar·ca·do-Cyp·ri·an** *adj.*

Ar·ca·dy (är'kə-dē) *n.* *Poetic.* Arcadia.

ar·cane (är-kān') *adj.* Known or understood only by those having special, secret knowledge; esoteric. [Latin *arcānus,* closed, secret, from *arcēre,* to close up, shut, from *arca,* chest.]

ar·ca·num (är-kā'nəm) *n., pl.* **-na** (-nə). **1.** A profound secret; a mystery. **2.** The reputed great secret of nature that alchemists sought to find. **3.** An elixir. [Latin *arcānum,* a mystery, secret, from the neuter of *arcānus,* closed, secret, ARCANE.]

archaeopteryx *The long-extinct archaeopteryx, one of the earliest flying animals, lived about 150 million years ago. This is the fossilized imprint of its body, with the shape of the wings visible as feathery lines radiating from the skeleton.*

arc·bou·tant (ȧr'boo-tän') *n., pl.* **arcs-boutants** (ȧr'boo-tän'). *French.* A flying buttress (see).

arch[1] (ärch) *n.* **1.** A curved structure, especially of masonry, forming the upper edge of an opening or a support, as in a bridge or doorway. **2.** Any similar structure, such as a monument. **3.** Anything curved like an arch. **4.** *Anatomy.* Any of various arch-shaped structures, especially the structure in the foot formed by the tarsal and metatarsal bones. **5.** One of the three basic patterns by which fingerprints are classified, consisting of numerous curved ridges one above the other. Compare **loop, whorl.**
~*v.* **arched, arching, arches.** —*tr.* **1.** To supply with an arch. **2.** To cause to form an arch or similar curve: *arch one's eyebrows.* **3.** To span: *"the rude bridge that arched the flood"* (Emerson). —*intr.* **1.** To form an arch or archlike curve: *Elm trees arched over the road.* **2.** To move in a course shaped like an arch: *The football arched over the goal post.* [Middle English *arche,* from Old French, from Vulgar Latin *arca* (unattested), plural noun from Latin *arcus,* bow, ARC.]

arch[2] *adj.* **1.** Chief; principal. Used before the noun: *an arch-thief.* **2.** Mischievous; roguish: *an arch glance.* [From ARCH-.] —**arch·ly** *adv.* —**arch·ness** *n.*

arch– *prefix.* Indicates: **1.** Highest rank or chief status; for example, **archduke, archbishop. 2.** Ultimate of a kind; for example, **archfiend.** [Middle English *arche-, arch-,* from Old English *ærce-, arce-, erce-,* and Old French *arch(e)-,* both from Latin *arch(i)-,* from Greek *arkh(i)-,* from *arkhos,* chief, ruler, from *arkhein†,* to begin, rule.]

–arch *suffix.* Indicates a ruler or leader; for example, **monarch, matriarch.** [Middle English *-arche,* from Old French, from Late Latin *-archa,* from Latin *-archēs,* from Greek *-arkhēs,* from *arkhos,* ruler, from *arkhein†,* to rule.]

arch. **1.** archaic; archaism. **2.** archery. **3.** archipelago. **4.** architect; architectural; architecture.

Arch. archbishop.

Archaean. Variant of **Archean.**

archaeo–, archeo– *prefix.* Indicates ancient times or an early condition; for example, **archaeology, archaeopteryx.** [New Latin, from Greek *arkhaio-,* from *arkhaios,* ancient, from *arkhē,* beginning, from *arkhein†,* to begin.]

ar·chae·o·as·tron·o·my (är'kē-ō-ə-strŏn'ə-mē) *n.* The study of megalithic sites and other ancient structures with a view to showing that they were built to align with or predict astronomical observations. —**ar·chae·o·as·tron·o·mer** *n.*

ar·chae·ol·o·gy, ar·che·ol·o·gy (är'kē-ŏl'ə-jē) *n.* The systematic recovery by scientific methods and study of material evidence, such as graves, buildings, tools, and pottery, of man's life, culture, and history in former times. [French *archéologie,* from Late Latin *archaeologia,* "the study of antiquity," from Greek *arkhaiologia :* ARCHAEO- + -LOGY.] —**ar·chae·o·log·i·cal** (är'kē-ə-lŏj'ĭ-kəl), **ar·chae·o·log·ic** *adj.* —**ar·chae·olo·gist** *n.*

ar·chae·o·mag·net·ism (är'kē-ō-măg'nə-tĭz'əm) *n.* A technique used in archaeology for dating clay objects by measuring the extent to which they have been magnetized by the earth's magnetic field. —**ar·chae·o·mag·net·ic** (är'kē-ō-măg-nĕt'ĭk) *adj.*

ar·chae·op·ter·yx (är'kē-ŏp'tər-ĭks) *n.* An extinct primitive bird of the genus *Archaeopteryx,* of the Jurassic period, having wings, feathers, and a long tail, and representing a transitional form between reptiles and birds. [New Latin, "ancient bird" : ARCHAEO- + Greek *pterux,* bird, wing, from *pteron,* feather, wing.]

ar·chae·o·zo·ol·o·gy (är'kē-ō-zō-ŏl'ə-jē) *n.* The scientific study of ancient animal remains, especially fossilized bones, as evidence of early domestication, the hunting habits of a given culture, climatic changes, and the like.

ar·cha·ic (är-kā'ĭk) *adj. Abbr.* **arch.** **1.** Belonging to a much earlier time; ancient: *archaic sculpture.* **2.** No longer current or applicable; antiquated: *archaic laws.* **3.** Of, pertaining to, or characteristic of words and language that were once common but are now used chiefly to suggest an earlier style or period. —See Synonyms at **old.** [French *archaïque,* from Greek *arkhaikos,* from *arkhaios,* ancient, from *arkhē,* beginning, from *arkhein†,* to begin.] —**ar·cha·i·cal·ly** *adv.*

archaic smile *n.* A representation of the human mouth with slightly upturned corners, characteristic of early Greek sculpture.

ar·cha·ism (är'kē-ĭz'əm, är'kā-) *n. Abbr.* **arch.** **1.** An archaic word or expression. **2.** An archaic style or quality. **3.** The imitation of archaic styles, as in literature or art. [New Latin *archaeismus,* from Greek *arkhaïsmos,* from *arkhaios,* ancient, ARCHAIC.] —**ar·cha·ist** *n.* —**ar·cha·is·tic** (är'kē-ĭs'tĭk, är'kā-) *adj.*

ar·cha·ize (är'kē-īz', är'kā-) *v.* **-ized, -izing, -izes.** —*tr.* To impart an archaic quality or character to. —*intr.* To use archaisms. [Greek *arkhaïzein,* from *arkhaios,* ancient, ARCHAIC.] —**ar·cha·iz·er** *n.*

arch·an·gel (ärk'ān'jəl) *n. Theology.* **1.** A celestial being next in rank above an angel. **2. archangels.** The eighth of the nine orders of angels. See **angel.** [Middle English, from Norman-French *archangele,* from Late Latin *archangelus,* from Greek *arkhangelos :* ARCH- + ANGEL.] —**arch·an·gel·ic** (ärk'ān-jĕl'ĭk) *adj.*

Archangel. See Arkhangelsk.

arch·bish·op (ärch-bĭsh'əp) *n. Abbr.* **abp., Abp., Arch., Archbp.** A bishop of the highest rank, heading an archdiocese or province. [Middle English *erchebishop, archebishop,* Old English *ærcebiscop, arcebiscop,* from Late Latin *archiepiscopus,* from Late Greek *arkhiepiskopos :* ARCH- + *episkopos,* BISHOP.]

arch

THE GROWTH OF THE ARCH
How a simple skill transformed construction

The arch is a curved or pointed span joining the walls on either side of an opening. The Egyptians made small ones from 4000 B.C., but it was the Roman development of the arch that revolutionized architecture. They built their arches over wooden frames, extending the span to more than 30 meters (90 feet) high and wide. With buttressed walls, buildings became huge, airy, and spectacular.

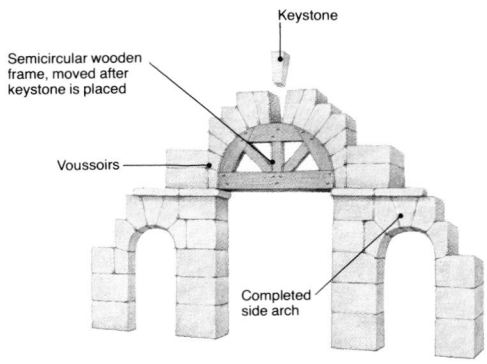

THE SEMICIRCULAR ARCH *Made from wedge-shaped masonry blocks called voussoirs, and built over a frame. A keystone, dropped into place, locks the voussoirs in place.*

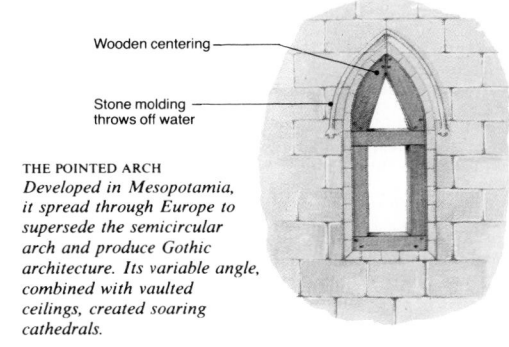

THE POINTED ARCH *Developed in Mesopotamia, it spread through Europe to supersede the semicircular arch and produce Gothic architecture. Its variable angle, combined with vaulted ceilings, created soaring cathedrals.*

THE SEGMENTAL ARCH *A shallow, less than semicircular curve gives a wide base. It was common in Europe from the 16th century for bridge building.*

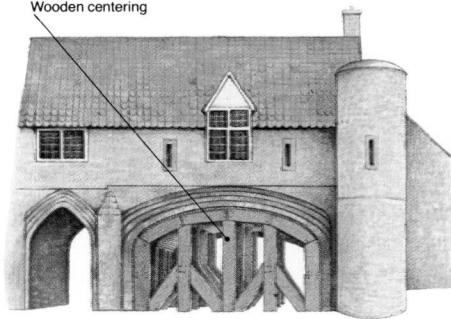

THE ELLIPTICAL ARCH *A half-oval curve gave a low rise-to-span ratio. It used less stone and its very shallow curve was ideal for bridges.*

arch·bish·op·ric (ärch-bĭsh′ə-prĭk) *n.* **1.** The rank, office, or term of an archbishop. **2.** The jurisdiction of an archbishop.

arch·dea·con (ärch-dē′kən) *n.* A clergyman, chiefly in the Anglican Church, in charge of temporal and other affairs in a diocese, with powers delegated from the bishop. [Middle English *archedeken,* Old English *ærcediakon,* from Late Latin *archidiāconus,* from Late Greek *arkhidiakonos* : ARCH- + DEACON.]

arch·dea·con·ry (ärch-dē′kən-rē) *n., pl.* **-ries.** The office, jurisdiction, residence, or district of an archdeacon.

arch·di·o·cese (ärch-dī′ə-sĭs, -sēs′, -sēz′) *n.* A diocese under an archbishop's jurisdiction. **—arch·di·oc·e·san** (ärch′dī-ŏs′ə-sən) *adj.*

arch·du·cal (ärch-do͞o′kəl, -dyo͞o′kəl) *adj.* Of or pertaining to an archduke or an archduchy.

arch·duch·ess (ärch-dŭch′ĭs) *n.* **1.** The wife or widow of an archduke. **2.** A woman having a rank equivalent to that of an archduke; especially, an Austrian princess.

arch·duch·y (ärch-dŭch′ē) *n., pl.* **-ies.** The territory over which an archduke or an archduchess has authority.

arch·duke (ärch-do͞ok′, -dyo͞ok′) *n.* In certain royal families, especially that of imperial Austria, a nobleman having a rank equivalent to that of a sovereign prince.

Ar·che·an (är-kē′ən) *adj. Geology.* Of, pertaining to, or designating the oldest rocks of the Precambrian era, predominantly igneous in composition.

arched (ärcht) *adj.* **1.** Forming an arch or a curve like that of an arch. **2.** Provided, made, or covered with an arch or arches.

ar·che·go·ni·um (är′kə-gō′nē-əm) *n., pl.* **-nia** (-nē-ə). *Botany.* A multicellular female sex organ of mosses, ferns, and conifers, which produces a single gamete. Compare **antheridium.** [New Latin, diminutive of Greek *arkhegonos,* primal parent : ARCH- (chief) + *-gonos,* race.] **—ar·che·go·ni·al** *adj.* **—ar·che·go·ni·ate** (är′kə-gō′nē-ĭt) *adj.*

arch·en·e·my (ärch-ĕn′ə-mē) *n., pl.* **-mies.** **1.** A chief or principal enemy. **2.** *Often* **Archenemy.** The devil; Satan.

arch·en·ter·on (är-kĕn′tə-rŏn′, -rən) *n.* The embryonic digestive tract, essentially a cavity in the gastrula. [New Latin : ARCH- + ENTERON.] **—arch·en·ter·ic** (är′kĕn-tĕr′ĭk) *adj.*

archeo–. Variant of **archaeo-.**

archeology. Variant of **archaeology.**

arch·er (är′chər) *n.* **1.** One who engages in archery. **2. Archer.** The constellation and sign of the zodiac **Sagittarius** *(see).* [Middle English, from Old French *archier,* from Late Latin *arcārius,* alteration of *arcuārius,* "of a bow," from Latin *arcus,* bow, ARC.]

Ar·cher (är′chər), **Frederick Scott** (1813–57). British photographer. He invented the wet collodion process, by which more than one photograph could be printed from a glass negative.

Archer, Thomas (*c.* 1668–1743). English baroque architect. Among the churches he designed are St. John's, Smith Square, London, and St. Paul's, Deptford.

arch·er·fish (är′chər-fĭsh′) *n., pl.* **-fishes** or collectively **archerfish.** Any of several small freshwater Indo-Australian fishes of the family Toxotidae, capable of capturing insects by squirting water at them.

arch·er·y (är′chə-rē) *n. Abbr.* **arch.** **1.** The art, sport, or skill of shooting with a bow and arrows. **2.** The equipment of an archer. **3.** A troop or body of archers.

ar·che·spore (är′kə-spôr′, -spōr′) *n.* Also **ar·che·spo·ri·um** (är′kə-spôr′ē-əm, -spōr′ē-əm) *pl.* **-sporia** (-spôr′ē-ə, -spōr′ē-ə). *Botany.* A cell or mass of cells producing spores in a sporangium. [New Latin *archesporium* : ARCH- + *spora,* SPORE.] **—ar·che·spo·ri·al** *adj.*

ar·che·type (är′kə-tīp′) *n.* **1.** An original model or type after which other similar things are patterned; a prototype. **2.** A perfect or typical example. **3.** In the psychology of C. G. Jung, an inherited idea in the individual unconscious that is thought to derive from the collective experience of mankind as a whole. —See Synonyms at **ideal.** [Latin *archetypum,* from Greek *arkhetupon,* neuter of *arkhetupos,* "first-molded" : ARCH- + *tupos,* mold, stamp, TYPE.] **—ar·che·typ·al** (är′kə-tī′pəl), **ar·che·typ·i·cal** (-tĭp′ĭ-kəl) *adj.* **—ar·che·typ·i·cal·ly** *adv.*

arch·fiend (ärch-fēnd′) *n.* **1.** A chief or foremost fiend. **2.** *Often* **Archfiend.** The devil; Satan.

ar·chi·di·ac·o·nal (är′kĭ-dī-ăk′ə-nəl) *adj.* Of or pertaining to an archdeacon, his duties, or his office. [From Late Latin *archidiāconus,* ARCHDEACON.]

ar·chi·di·ac·o·nate (är′kĭ-dī-ăk′ə-nĭt) *n.* The office or status of an archdeacon. [Medieval Latin *archidiācōnātus,* from Late Latin *archidiāconus,* ARCHDEACON.]

ar·chi·e·pis·co·pal (är′kē-ĭ-pĭs′kə-pəl) *adj.* Of or pertaining to an archbishop or an archbishopric. [Medieval Latin *archiepiscopālis,* from Late Latin *archiepiscopus,* ARCHBISHOP.]

ar·chi·e·pis·co·pate (är′kē-ĭ-pĭs′kə-pĭt, -pāt′) *n.* The rank, office, or term of an archbishop. [Medieval Latin *archiepiscopātus,* from Late Latin *archiepiscopus,* ARCHBISHOP.]

archil. Variant of **orchil.**

Ar·chi·lo·chi·an (är′kĭ-lō′kē-ən) *adj.* Of, pertaining to, or characteristic of Archilochus, Greek satiric poet of the 7th century B.C., or of the verse form invented by him.

ar·chi·mage (är′kə-māj′) *n.* A great magician or chief wizard. [Late Greek *arkhimagos* : ARCH- + *magos,* magician. See **magi.**]

ar·chi·man·drite (är′kə-măn′drīt′) *n.* In the Eastern Orthodox Church: **1.** A cleric ranking below a bishop. **2.** The head of a monastery or group of monasteries. [Late Latin *archimandrītēs, archimandrīta,* from Late Greek *arkhimandritēs* : ARCH- + *mandra*†, monastery, from Greek, enclosure, cattle pen.]

Ar·chi·me·de·an (är′kə-mē′dē-ən, -mĭ-dē′ən) *adj.* Of or pertaining to Archimedes or his inventions.

Archimedean screw *n.* An ancient apparatus for raising water, consisting of either a spiral tube around an inclined axis or an inclined tube containing a tight-fitting, broad-threaded screw. Also called "Archimedes' screw."

Ar·chi·me·des (är′kə-mē′dēz) (*c.* 287–212 B.C.). Greek mathematician and inventor from Syracuse. He is considered, with Karl F. Gauss and Isaac Newton, one of the three greatest mathematicians of all time. He discovered and analyzed the principle of the lever and invented the Archimedean screw for raising water. His most famous discovery, the principle of buoyancy, is said to have come to him when he observed the amount of water his body displaced in his bath. In his excitement he ran naked through the streets shouting "Eureka!" ("I have found it"). When Syracuse fell to the Romans, he was killed, it is said, while drawing geometric figures in the sand.

Archimedes' principle *n.* The principle that the apparent loss in the weight of a body immersed in a fluid is equal to the weight of the fluid displaced.

ar·chine, ar·shin (är-shēn′) *n.* A Russian unit of linear measure equivalent to 28 inches. [Russian *arshin,* of Turkic origin; akin to Turkish and Kazan Tatar *aršyn,* an ell.]

ar·chi·pel·a·go (är′kə-pĕl′ə-gō′) *n., pl.* **-goes** or **-gos.** *Abbr.* **arch.** **1.** A large group of islands. **2.** A sea containing many groups of islands, such as the Aegean. [From *Archipelago,* the Aegean Sea, from Italian *Arcipelago,* "the Chief Sea" (a misinterpretation of Greek *Aigaion pelagos,* the Aegean Sea) : ARCH- + Greek *pelagos,* sea.] **—ar·chi·pe·lag·ic** (är′kə-pə-lăj′ĭk) *adj.*

archit. architecture.

ar·chi·tect (är′kə-tĕkt′) *n. Abbr.* **arch.** **1.** One who designs and supervises the construction of buildings or other large structures, such as ships. **2.** Any planner or deviser: *the architect of European unity.* [French *architecte,* from Latin *architectus,* from Greek *arkhitektōn,* master builder : ARCH- + *tektōn,* builder, craftsman.]

ar·chi·tec·ton·ic (är′kə-tĕk-tŏn′ĭk) *adj.* **1.** Of or pertaining to architecture or design. **2.** Having qualities characteristic of architecture; designed and structured. **3.** *Philosophy.* Of or pertaining to the scientific systematization of knowledge. [Latin *architectōnicus,* architectural, from Greek *arkhitektōnikos,* from *arkhitektōn,* ARCHITECT.] **—ar·chi·tec·ton·i·cal·ly** *adv.*

ar·chi·tec·ton·ics (är′kə-tĕk-tŏn′ĭks) *n. Used with a singular verb.* **1.** The science of architecture. **2.** Structural design, as in a musical work. **3.** *Philosophy.* The scientific systematization of knowledge.

ar·chi·tec·ture (är′kə-tĕk′chər) *n. Abbr.* **arch., archit.** **1.** The art and science of designing and erecting buildings. **2.** A structure or structures collectively. **3.** A particular style and method of design and construction: *Byzantine architecture.* **4.** The planning or design evidenced in any structure or arrangement: *the architecture of nature.* [French, from Latin *architectūra,* from *architectus,* ARCHITECT.] **—ar·chi·tec·tur·al** *adj.* **—ar·chi·tec·tur·al·ly** *adv.*

ar·chi·trave (är′kə-trāv′) *n. Architecture.* **1.** The lowermost part of an entablature, resting directly on top of a column as in classical architecture. Also called "epistyle." **2.** The molding around a door or window. [Old French, from Old Italian, "chief beam" : ARCH- + *trave,* beam, from Latin *trabs.*]

ar·chi·val (är-kī′vəl) *adj.* Of, pertaining to, or kept in archives.

archival standards *pl.n.* Standards set by the U.S. Bureau of Standards to assure permanence of microfilm images.

ar·chive (är′kīv′) *n. Often* **archives.** **1.** An organized body of records pertaining to an organization, institution, or the like. **2.** A place in which such records are preserved. **3.** Any repository of evidence or information: *the archives of the mind.* [French *archive,* from Late Latin *archī(v)um,* from Greek *arkheion,* public office (plural *arkheia,* public records, archives), from *arkhē,* beginning, hence first place, government, from *arkhein*†, to begin.]

ar·chi·vist (är′kə-vĭst, är′kī′-) *n.* One who is in charge of archives.

ar·chi·volt (är′kə-vōlt′) *n.* Also **ar·chi·vault** (-vôlt′). *Architecture.* A decorative molding carried around an arched wall opening. [Italian *archivolto* : *arco,* arch, from Latin *arcus,* ARC + *volta,* VAULT.]

ar·chon (är′kŏn′, -kən) *n.* **1.** Any of the nine principal governing officials of ancient Athens. **2.** Any of various officials of the Byzantine Empire. **3.** *Often* **Archon.** In certain Gnostic systems, any of several powers believed to be superior to the angels. [Latin *archōn,* from Greek *arkhōn,* "ruler," from the present participle of *arkhein*†, to rule.] **—ar·chon·ship** *n.*

arch·priest (ärch-prēst′) *n.* Formerly, a priest holding first rank among the members of a cathedral chapter, acting as chief assistant to a bishop. Now used only as a title of honor. [Middle English *archeprest,* from Old French *archeprestre,* from Late Latin *archipresbyter* : ARCHI- + *presbyter,* PRIEST.] **—arch·priest·hood, arch·priest·ship** *n.*

arch·way (ärch′wā′) *n.* **1.** A passageway under an arch. **2.** An arch covering or enclosing an entrance or passageway.

–archy *suffix.* Indicates rule or government; for example, **oligarchy.** [Middle English *-archie,* from Old French, from Latin *-archia,* from Greek *-arkhia,* from *-arkhēs,* -ARCH.]

ar·ci·form (är′sə-fôrm′) *adj.* Formed like an arc. [Latin *arci-,* from *arcus,* bow, ARC + -FORM.]

arc jet *n.* An arc-jet engine.

arc-jet engine (ärk′jĕt′) *n.* A rocket engine that operates by heating the propellant gas with an electric arc.

arcked. Alternate past tense and past participle of **arc.**

archaic smile *This enigmatic expression, typical of early Greek sculpture, appears here on a statue of the goddess Persephone carved in about 510 B.C.*

archerfish *A freshwater fish of Southeast Asia that catches insects by shooting them down from overhanging foliage with a jet of water. An adult archerfish can hit its prey with remarkable accuracy over a distance of up to about 90 centimeters (3 feet).*

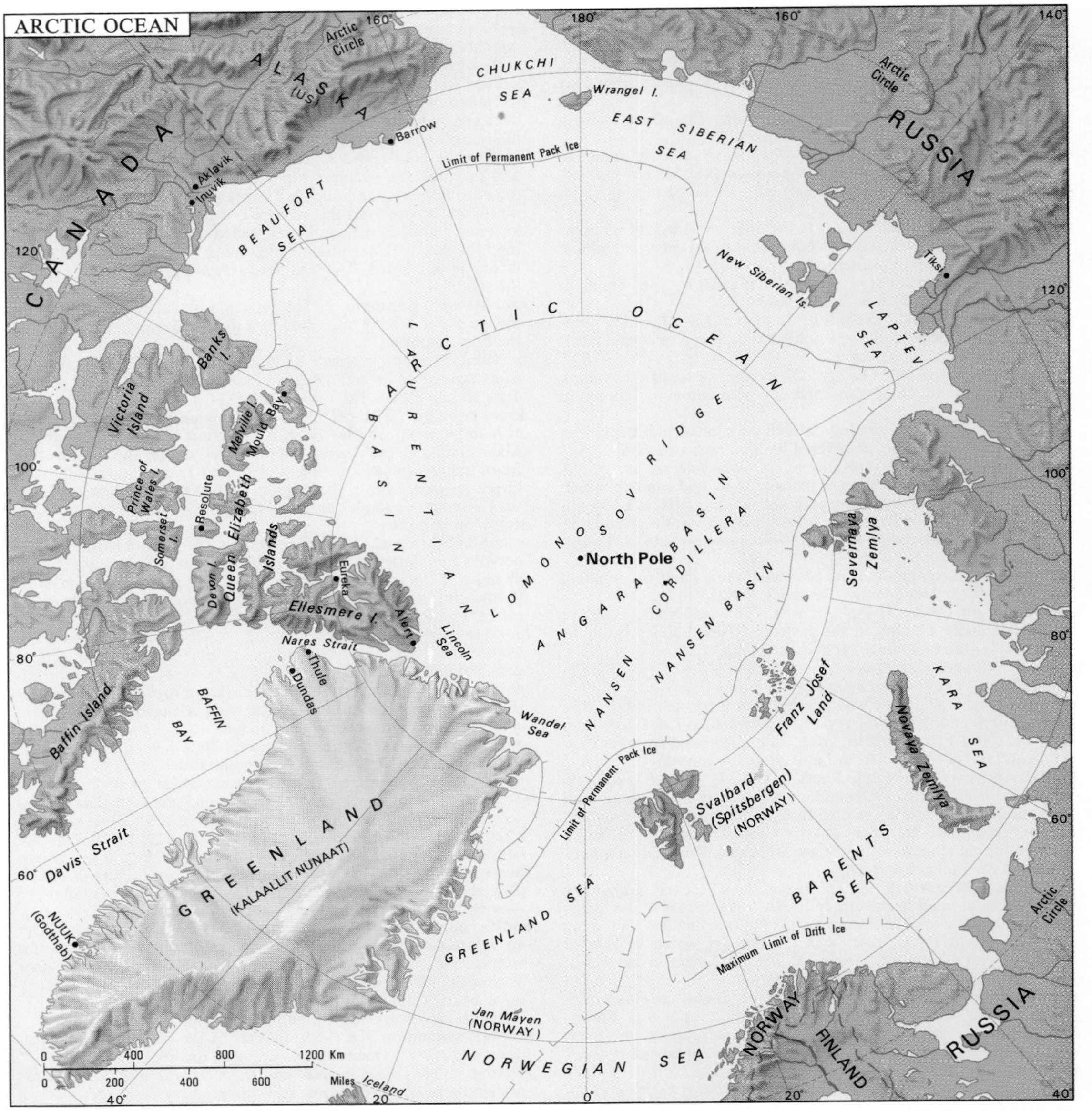

ARCTIC OCEAN

[Map of the Arctic Ocean showing ALASKA (U.S.), CANADA, CHUKCHI SEA, Wrangel I., EAST SIBERIAN SEA, RUSSIA, LAPTEV SEA, New Siberian Is., BEAUFORT SEA, Barrow, Limit of Permanent Pack Ice, Aklavik, Inuvik, Banks I., Victoria Island, ARCTIC OCEAN, LOMONOSOV RIDGE, ANGARA BASIN, NANSEN CORDILLERA, NANSEN BASIN, North Pole, Severnaya Zemlya, KARA SEA, Prince of Wales I., Somerset I., Devon I., Queen Elizabeth Islands, Melville I., Mould Bay, Resolute, LAURENTIAN BASIN, Eureka, Ellesmere I., Alert, Lincoln Sea, Nares Strait, Thule, Dundas, Novaya Zemlya, BAFFIN BAY, Baffin Island, GREENLAND (KALAALLIT NUNAAT), Wandel Sea, Limit of Permanent Pack Ice, Franz Josef Land, Svalbard (Spitsbergen) (NORWAY), BARENTS SEA, Davis Strait, NUUK (Godthåb), Maximum Limit of Drift Ice, GREENLAND SEA, NORWAY, FINLAND, RUSSIA, Jan Mayen (NORWAY), NORWEGIAN SEA, Iceland; scale 0 400 800 1200 Km, 0 200 400 600 Miles]

arcking. Alternate present participle of **arc.**

arc lamp *n.* A lamp in which the light is produced by an electric arc between two closely spaced electrodes. Often carbon electrodes are used to produce an intense white light.

arc·tic (ärk′tĭk, är′tĭk) *adj.* **1.** *Usually* **Arctic.** Of, pertaining to, or characteristic of a geographical area extending from the North Pole to the northern timberline. **2. a.** Characteristic of the North Pole or polar regions; extremely cold. **b.** Suitable for very cold conditions: *arctic clothing.*
~*n.* A warm, waterproof overshoe. [Middle English *artik,* from Latin *ar(c)ticus,* from Greek *arktikos,* from *arktos,* bear, hence the northern constellation Ursa Major, the Great Bear, hence "north."] —**arc·ti·cal·ly** *adv.*

Arc·tic, the (ärk′tĭk, är′tĭk). Northernmost area of the earth, centered on the North Pole.

Arctic Archipelago. A group of more than 50 large islands in the Arctic Ocean between North America and Greenland. The islands are part of the Northwest Territories, Canada.

Arctic Circle *n.* A parallel of latitude 66°33′ north, along which the sun does not set on one day in the year, around June 21.

Arctic Current. See **Labrador Current.**

arctic fox *n.* A fox, *Alopex lagopus,* inhabiting arctic regions, having fur that is white or light-gray in winter and brown or blue-gray in summer. Also called "blue fox."

Arctic Ocean. The world's smallest ocean, covering some 14,000,-000 square kilometers (5,500,000 square miles) over the North Pole. It is covered by pack ice throughout the year, and its main outlet is the East Greenland Current, which takes icebergs far into the Atlantic Ocean.

arctic tern *n.* A tern, *Sterna paradisaea,* that breeds in the Arctic and migrates to the Antarctic, southern Africa, and South America.

Arc·to·gae·a (ärk′tə-jē′ə) *n.* The zoogeographical region that includes the Palaearctic, Nearctic, Ethiopian, and Oriental regions. Compare **Notogaea.** [New Latin, "north earth," from Greek *arktos,* bear, Ursa Major, north + *gaia,* earth.] —**Arc·to·gae·an** *adj.*

Arc·tu·rus (ärk-toor′əs, -tyoor′əs) *n.* The brightest star in the constellation Boötes, approximately 36 light-years from earth. [Middle English *Artur, Arcturus,* from Latin *Arcturus,* from Greek *Arktouros,* "guardian of the Bear" (from its position behind the tail of Ursa Major) : *arktos,* bear + *ouros,* a guard.] —**Arc·tu·ri·an** *adj.*

ar·cu·ate (är′kyoo-ĭt, -āt′) *adj.* Also **ar·cu·at·ed** (-ā′tĭd). Having the form of a bow; curved; arched: *arcuate veins in a leaf; arcuate horns.* [Latin *arcuātus,* past participle of *arcuāre,* to bend like a bow, from *arcus,* bow.] —**ar·cu·ate·ly** *adv.*

ar·cu·a·tion (är′kyoo-ā′shən) *n.* **1.** The process of curving or the state of being curved. **2.** *Architecture.* The use of arches or vaults in building.

ar·cus se·ni·lis (är′kəs sə-nī′lĭs) *n.* A narrow, opaque circle around the cornea of the eye, often seen in old people. [Latin, "senile bow."]

arc-weld (ärk′wĕld′) *tr.v.* **-welded, -welding, -welds.** To weld by means of heat produced by an electric arc between an electrode and the part being welded. —**arc-weld·ing** *n.*

ard (ärd) *n.* A primitive plow, used in prehistoric times and now in some less developed countries. [Middle English, from Old Norse *arthr,* plow, from Latin *arātrum.*]

–ard, –art *suffix.* Indicates: **1.** One who does something to excess; for example, **drunkard, braggart. 2.** One who is characterized by a particular, especially an undesirable, quality; for example, **sluggard.** [Middle English, from Old French from Germanic *-hart, -hard,* "bold, hardy," often in proper names such as *Raynard, Gerhart.*]

arctic fox *Found throughout the tundra regions of the Northern Hemisphere, the arctic fox has a very thick coat, rounded ears, and furred feet. It feeds on small birds, rodents, and carrion left by polar bears.*

ar·deb (är'dĕb') n. A unit of dry measure in several countries of the Near East, usually equal to 5.6 U.S. bushels but with variations in different localities. [Colloquial Arabic *ardabb,* from Greek *artabē,* probably from Egyptian.]

ar·den·cy (är'dən-sē) n. The state or quality of being ardent.

Ar·dennes (är-dĕnz'). Wooded plateau in southeastern Belgium, extending into France and Luxembourg.

ar·dent (är'dənt) adj. **1. a.** Expressing or characterized by warmth of passion, emotion, or desire. **b.** Displaying or characterized by strong enthusiasm or devotion; fervent; zealous: *"an impassioned age, so ardent and serious in its pursuit of art"* (Walter Pater). **2.** Glowing; flashing; fierce: *ardent eyes.* **3.** Hot as fire; burning: *an ardent sun.* [Middle English *ardaunt,* from Old French *ardant,* from Latin *ardēns* (stem *ardent-*), present participle of *ardēre,* to burn.] **—ar·dent·ly** adv.

ardent spirits pl.n. Strong alcoholic drinks, such as whiskey.

ar·dor (är'dər) n. Also *chiefly British* **ar·dour. 1. a.** Great warmth or intensity, as of emotion, passion, or desire. **b.** Fervent enthusiasm or devotion; zeal: *"the dazzling conquest of Mexico gave a new impulse to the ardor of discovery"* (William H. Prescott). **2.** Intense heat, as of fire. [Middle English *ardour,* from Old French, from Latin *ardor,* from *ardēre,* to burn.]

ar·du·ous (är'jŏō-əs) adj. **1.** Demanding great care, effort, or exertion; strenuous. **2.** Testing severely the powers of endurance; full of hardships: *a long, arduous journey.* **3.** Hard to climb or surmount; steep: *an arduous path.* **—See Synonyms at burdensome, hard.** [Latin *arduus,* high, steep, difficult.] **—ar·du·ous·ly** adv. **—ar·du·ous·ness** n.

are[1] (är). Present tense, indicative plural, and second person singular of **be.**

are[2] (âr, är) n. Abbr. **a, a.** A metric unit of area equal to 100 square meters. [French, from Latin *ārea,* AREA.]

ar·e·a (âr'ē-ə) n. **1.** A flat, open, or unoccupied piece of ground. **2.** A part of the earth's surface; a region. **3.** A distinct spatial extent; a part, section, or locality having a particular function or characteristic quality: *a residential area; a room with a living area and a dining area.* **4.** A field of study or activity: *the whole area of finance.* **5.** Abbr. **A** The measure of a planar region or of the surface of a solid. **6.** A section of computer storage set aside for a particular purpose. [Latin *ārea†,* open field.] **—ar·e·al** adj.

    Synonyms: *district, locality, region, zone.*

Area Code, area code n. A number, often with three digits, assigned to a telephone area, as in the United States and Canada, used when placing a call to another area.

a·re·ca (ə-rē'kə, ăr'ī-kə) n. Any of various tall palms of the genus *Areca,* of southeast Asia, having white flowers and red or orange egg-shaped nuts. See **betel palm.** [New Latin *Areca,* from Portuguese *areca,* from Malayalam *aṭekka, aṭakka.*]

a·re·na (ə-rē'nə) n. **1.** The area in the center of an ancient Roman amphitheater where contests and other spectacles were held. **2.** Any similar place: *a boxing arena.* **3.** A sphere or field of conflict, interest, or activity: *the political arena.* [Latin *(h)arēna,* sand, arena covered with sand, perhaps from Etruscan.]

ar·e·na·ceous (ăr'ə-nā'shəs) adj. **1.** Sandlike in appearance or qualities: *arenaceous limestone.* **2.** Growing in sandy areas. [Latin *(h)arēnaceus* : *(h)arēna,* sand, ARENA + -ACEOUS.]

arena stage n. The stage of a theater-in-the-round.

arena theater n. A theater-in-the-round *(see).*

ar·ene (ăr'ēn') n. *Chemistry.* An aromatic hydrocarbon or a derivative of an aromatic hydrocarbon. [AR(OMATIC) + -ENE.]

ar·e·nic·o·lous (ăr'ə-nĭk'ə-ləs) adj. Growing or living in sand. [Latin *(h)arēna,* sand, ARENA + -COLOUS.]

aren't (ärnt, är'ənt). Contraction of *are not.*

a·re·o·la (ə-rē'ə-lə) n., pl. **-lae** (-lē') or **-las.** Also **a·re·ole** (âr'ē-ōl'). **1.** *Biology.* A small space or interstice, such as an area bounded by small veins in a leaf or an insect's wing. **2.** *Anatomy.* A small, dark-colored area around a center portion, as about a nipple or part of the iris of the eye. [New Latin, from Latin *āreola,* diminutive of *ārea,* open place, AREA.] **—a·re·o·lar, a·re·o·late** adj.

Ar·e·op·a·gus (ăr'ē-ŏp'ə-gəs) n. The highest council of ancient Athens. [Greek *Areios pagos,* Ares' hill.] **—Ar·e·op·a·gite** (ăr'ē-ŏp'ə-jīt', -gīt') n. **—Ar·e·op·a·git·ic** (ăr'ē-ŏp'ə-jĭt'ĭk) adj.

Ar·es (âr'ēz'). *Greek Mythology.* The god of war, identified with the Roman god Mars. [Greek *Arēs†,* god of war, the planet Mars.]

a·rête (ə-rāt') n. A sharp, narrow mountain ridge or spur. [French *arête,* fishbone, spiny ridge, from Old French *areste,* from Latin *arista†,* fishbone, spine, beard of grain.]

ar·e·thu·sa (ăr'ə-thōō'zə, -sə) n. Any of several orchids of the genus *Arethusa,* especially *A. bulbosa,* of eastern North America, having a solitary rose-purple flower fringed with yellow. [After the nymph ARETHUSA.]

Ar·e·thu·sa (ăr'ə-thōō'zə, -sə). *Greek Mythology.* A nymph who was turned into a spring so as to avoid the attentions of the river god Alpheus. [Latin, from Greek *Arethousa.*]

A·re·ti·no (ä'rā-tē'nō), **Pietro** (1492-1556). Italian writer and satirist. He wrote five comedies, but was best known for his satirical attacks on the wealthy and powerful, which, together with a collection of lewd poems, *Sonnetti Lussuriosi* (1524), compelled him to flee Rome in 1527. For the rest of his life he lived in Venice, amassing wealth by writing satires or by being paid not to write them.

arg. argent.

Arg. Argentina.

argal. Variant of **argol.**

ar·ga·li (är'gə-lē) n., pl. **-lis** or collectively **argali.** A large wild sheep, *Ovis ammon,* of mountainous regions of central and northern Asia, the male of which has massive, spirally curved horns. [Mongolian *argali,* mountain goat.]

Ar·gand diagram (är'gänd', -gänd') n. *Mathematics.* A diagram in which complex numbers are represented in a coordinate system with two perpendicular axes determining the real and imaginary parts of the number. The number $x + iy$ is the point (x, y) or the directed line segment from the origin to the point (x, y). [After Jean-Robert *Argand* (1768-1822), French mathematician.]

ar·gent (är'jənt) n. **1.** *Poetic.* Silver or anything resembling it. **2.** *Abbr.* **arg.** *Heraldry.* The metal silver, represented by the color white. [Middle English, from Old French, from Latin *argentum.*] **—argent** adj.

ar·gen·tic (är-jĕn'tĭk) adj. Of or containing silver. Said especially of chemical compounds containing silver having a valence of 2 or 3. [Latin *argentum,* silver + -IC.]

ar·gen·tif·er·ous (är'jən-tĭf'ər-əs) adj. Bearing or producing silver. [ARGENT + -FEROUS.]

Ar·gen·ti·na (är'jən-tē'nə) Abbr. **Arg.** Country of South America. It was a Spanish colony from 1620 until independence was proclaimed in 1816. Since 1929 the military have intervened in the government several times, most notably in 1943, a move that paved the way for the rise of Col. Juan Perón (president 1945-55, 1973-74). He was succeeded by his third wife, Isabel, who was deposed by the military (1976). In 1982 Argentinian forces occupied South Georgia and the Falkland Islands, which the country claims, but were expelled by a British task force. Argentina is among the most developed Latin-American countries and was the most prosperous until the recent political instability. The fertile pampas and sheep ranches of Patagonia provide most of its exports: meat, cere-

ard *A farmer using an ard in Morocco. The ard is a primitive type of plowshare, having no moldboard or other device for turning the soil.*

[Map of Argentina showing cities including Salta, San Miguel de Tucumán, Santiago del Estero, San Juan, Córdoba, Paraná, Santa Fé, Rosario, Mendoza, Aconcagua 6960m, Buenos Aires, La Plata, Bahía Blanca, Mar del Plata, Comodoro Rivadavia, Deseado, Esquel, Lake Traful, Nahuel Huapí Nat. Park, Bahía Grande, and neighboring countries Brazil, Paraguay, Uruguay, Chile, with features including Tropic of Capricorn, Chaco, Gran Chaco, Pilcomayo, Paraná, Salado, Colorado, Negro, Gulf of San Matías, Pampas, Río de la Plata, Iguazú Falls, Corrientes, Entre Ríos, Patagonia, Atlantic Ocean, Falkland Is (UK), Stanley, Str. of Magellan, Tierra del Fuego. Scale: Km 0–400, Miles 0–200. 60°W, 30°S, 40°S, 50°S.]

als, hides and skins, wool, and linseed oil. It has few mineral resources, but does produce most of its own oil. Area, 2,776,889 square kilometers (1,072,157 square miles). Population, 32,300,000. Capital, Buenos Aires. [Spanish *(Tierra) Argentina,* "silvery (land)," (with reference to the rivers and lakes), from Latin, feminine of *argentīnus,* silvery, ARGENTINE.] —**Ar·gen·tine** (är′jən-tēn′, -tīn′), **Ar·gen·tin·ian** (är′jən-tĭn′ē-ən) *n. & adj.*

ar·gen·tine (är′jən-tīn′, -tēn′) *adj.* Silvery.
~*n.* **1.** Any of various silvery metals. **2.** Any of several small, silvery marine fishes of the family Argentinidae. [French *argentin,* from Latin *argentīnus,* from *argentum,* silver, ARGENT.]

ar·gen·tite (är′jən-tīt′) *n.* A valuable silver ore, Ag_2S, with a lustrous, lead-gray color. [Latin *argentum,* silver, ARGENT + -ITE.]

ar·gen·tous (är-jĕn′təs) *adj.* Of or containing silver. Said especially of chemical compounds containing silver with a valence of 1. [Latin *argentum,* silver + -OUS.]

ar·gil (är′jĭl) *n.* Clay, especially that used by potters. [Middle English *argil, argilla,* from Latin *argilla,* from Greek *argillos.*]

ar·gil·la·ceous (är′jə-lā′shəs) *adj.* Containing, made of, or resembling clay; clayey. [Latin *argillāceus* : *argilla,* ARGIL + -ACEOUS.]

ar·gil·lite (är′jə-līt′) *n.* A metamorphic rock, intermediate between shale and slate, that does not possess true slaty cleavage. [Latin *argilla,* ARGIL + -ITE.] —**ar·gil·lit·ic** (är′jə-lĭt′ĭk) *adj.*

ar·gi·nine (är′jə-nēn′) *n.* An essential amino acid, $C_6H_{14}N_4O_2$, obtained from plant and animal protein or the digestive action of bacteria. [German *Arginin* : perhaps Greek *arginoeis,* bright, white + -INE.]

Ar·give (är′jīv′, -gīv′) *adj.* **1.** Of or pertaining to Argos. **2.** Of or pertaining to the Greeks or Greece.
~*n.* A Greek, especially an inhabitant of Argos.

argle-bargle. Variant of **argy-bargy.**

Ar·go (är′gō) *n.* **1.** *Greek Mythology.* The ship in which Jason sailed in search of the Golden Fleece. **2.** A constellation in the Southern Hemisphere, now known by the names of its four smaller parts, **Carina, Puppis, Pyxis,** and **Vela** *(all of which see).*

ar·gol, ar·gal (är′gəl) *n.* Crude tartar deposited on casks as a by-product of winemaking. [Middle English *argoile,* from Norman-French *argoil*†.]

ar·gon (är′gŏn′) *n. Symbol* **Ar** A colorless, odorless, inert gaseous element constituting approximately one percent of the earth's atmosphere, from which it is commercially obtained by fractionation of liquid air for use in electric lamps, fluorescent tubes, electronic valves, and as an inert gas shield in arc-welding. Atomic number 18, atomic weight 39.94, melting point −189.4°C, boiling point −185.9°C. [Greek, neuter of *argos,* inert, idle, "not working" : *a-,* without + *ergon,* work.]

ar·go·naut (är′gə-nôt′) *n.* A mollusk, the **paper nautilus** *(see).* [New Latin *Argonauta* (genus name), from Latin, ARGONAUT.]

Ar·go·naut (är′gə-nôt′) *n. Greek Mythology.* One who sailed with Jason on the *Argo* in search of the Golden Fleece. [Latin *Argonauta,* from Greek *Argonautēs* : *Argō,* name of Jason's ship + *nautēs,* sailor, from *naus,* ship.] —**Ar·go·nau·tic** (är′gə-nô′tĭk) *adj.*

Ar·gonne (är-gŏn′, är′gŏn′). Wooded, hilly region of eastern France, forming a natural barrier between the districts of Champagne and Lorraine. It was a major battleground throughout World War I.

Ar·gos (är′gŏs′, -gəs). A city of ancient Greece, in the northeastern Peloponnese. Occupied from the early Bronze Age, it is possibly Greece's oldest city. Argos was one of the strongest cities of ancient Greece until the rise of Sparta and later flourished as a trade center under Roman control.

ar·go·sy (är′gə-sē) *n., pl.* **-sies.** **1.** A large merchant ship. **2.** A fleet of such ships. [Earlier *argose, ragusye,* from Italian *ragusea,* vessel of *Ragusa,* former name of the port of Dubrovnik, Yugoslavia.]

ar·got (är′gō, -gət) *n.* A specialized vocabulary or set of idioms used by a particular class or group; especially, the jargon of the underworld. [French *argot*†.] —**ar·got·ic** (är-gŏt′ĭk) *adj.*

ar·gu·a·ble (är′gyo͞o-ə-bəl) *adj.* **1.** Open to argument; questionable. **2.** That can be supported by argument. —See Synonyms at **doubtful.** —**ar·gu·a·bly** *adv.*

ar·gue (är′gyo͞o) *v.* **-gued, -guing, -gues.** —*tr.* **1.** To put forward reasons for or against; debate. **2.** To prove or attempt to prove by reasoning; maintain in argument; contend. **3.** To give evidence of; indicate: *"similarities can always be used to argue descent"* (Isaac Asimov). **4.** To persuade or influence, as by presenting reasons: *He argued me into going.* —*intr.* **1.** To put forward reasons for or against an opinion, procedure, proposal, or the like. **2.** To quarrel; engage in a dispute. —See Synonyms at **discuss.** [Middle English *arguen,* from Old French *arguer,* to blame, argue against, from Latin *arguere,* to make clear, assert, prove.] —**ar·gu·er** *n.*
***Synonyms:** bicker, haggle, quarrel, squabble, wrangle.*

ar·gu·fy (är′gyə-fī′) *v.* **-fied, -fying, -fies.** *Regional.* —*tr.* To argue over. —*intr.* To argue stubbornly; wrangle. —**ar·gu·fi·er** *n.*

ar·gu·ment (är′gyə-mənt) *n.* **1. a.** A discussion in which reasons are put forward in support of or against an opinion, procedure, proposal, or the like; a debate. **b.** A quarrel; a contention. **2. a.** A course of reasoning aimed at demonstrating the truth or falsehood of something. **b.** A fact or statement advanced in support of or against a plan of action, suggestion, proposal, or the like. **3.** A summary or short statement of the plot or subject of a literary work. **4.** *Logic.* The minor premise in a syllogism. **5.** *Mathematics.* **a.** The independent variable of a function. **b.** The **amplitude** *(see)* of a complex number. [Middle English, from Old French, from Latin *argūmentum,* from *arguere,* to ARGUE.]
***Synonyms:** controversy, dispute, wrangling.*

ar·gu·men·ta·tion (är′gyə-mĕn-tā′shən) *n.* **1.** The act or process of presenting and elaborating an argument. **2.** Deductive reasoning in debate. **3.** A debate.

ar·gu·men·ta·tive (är′gyə-mĕn′tə-tĭv) *adj.* **1.** Given to excessive arguing; disputatious. **2.** Of or characterized by argument; controversial: *an argumentative discourse.* —**ar·gu·men·ta·tive·ly** *adv.* —**ar·gu·men·ta·tive·ness** *n.*

ar·gu·men·tum (är′gyə-mĕn′təm) *n., pl.* **-ta** (-tə). *Logic.* An argument, proof, or appeal to reason in support or refutation of a proposition. [Latin, "argument."]

argumentum ad hom·i·nem (ăd hŏm′ə-nĕm′) *n.* An argument appealing to personal prejudices and emotions rather than to logic or reason. [Latin, "argument to the man."]

Ar·gus (är′gəs). *Greek Mythology.* A giant with a hundred eyes who was made guardian of Io and later slain by Hermes.

Ar·gus-eyed (är′gəs-īd′) *adj.* Extremely observant; vigilant.

argus pheasant *n.* A large bird, *Argusianus argus,* having long tail feathers marked with brilliantly colored eyelike spots. [After the eyelike markings, imagined to resemble the numerous eyes of Argus.]

ar·gy-bar·gy (är′jē-bär′jē) *n.* Also **ar·gle-bar·gle** (är′gəl-bär′gəl). *Chiefly British Informal.* Quarreling; bickering. [19th century : Scottish, variant of *argle-bargle,* reduplication of *argue,* altered through confusion with or perhaps through influence of *haggle.*] —**ar·gy-bar·gy** *v.*

ar·gyle, ar·gyll (är′gīl′) *n.* **1.** A geometric knitting pattern of varicolored, diamond-shaped areas on a solid color background. **2.** A sock knit in an argyle pattern. [After Campbell of *Argyle* (Argyll), the clan whose tartan was adapted for this pattern.]

Ar·gyll (är-gīl′, är′gīl′). Also **Ar·gyll·shire** (-shĭr). Former county in west-central Scotland, since 1975 divided between Highland and Strathclyde regions.

ar·hat (är′hət) *n.* A Buddhist monk who has reached the state of nirvana. [Sanskrit, "(one) deserving respect," from *arhati,* "he deserves."]

År·hus (ôr′ho͞os′). Commercial and industrial city, on Århus Bay in Jutland, Denmark. It is Denmark's second-largest city and one of its oldest. Until 1948 its name was spelled "Aarhus."

a·ri·a (är′ē-ə) *n. Music.* **1.** An air; a melody. **2.** A solo vocal piece with instrumental accompaniment, as in an opera or oratorio. [Italian *aria,* melody, "(atmospheric) air," from Latin *āera,* accusative of *āēr,* air, from Greek *aēr.*]

Ar·i·ad·ne (ăr′ē-ăd′nē). *Greek Mythology.* The daughter of Minos and Pasiphae who gave Theseus the thread with which to find his way out of the Minotaur's labyrinth.

Ar·i·an[1] (ăr′ē-ən, âr′-) *adj.* Of or pertaining to Arius or Arianism.
~*n.* A believer in Arianism.

Arian[2]**.** Variant of **Aryan.**

-arian *suffix.* Indicates: **1.** Sect; for example, **Unitarian.** **2.** Belief, advocacy; for example, **authoritarian, vegetarian.** [Latin *-ārius,* -ARY + -AN.]

Ar·i·an·ism (ăr′ē-ə-nĭz′əm, âr′-) *n. Theology.* The doctrines of Arius, denying that Jesus was of the same substance as God and holding instead that he was only the highest of created beings.

ar·id (ăr′ĭd) *adj.* **1.** Very dry; lacking sufficient rainfall to support agriculture; parched. **2.** Lacking interest or feeling; lifeless; dull. [French *aride,* from Latin *āridus,* from *ārēre,* to be dry or parched.] —**a·rid·i·ty** (ə-rĭd′ə-tē), **ar·id·ness** *n.* —**ar·id·ly** *adv.*

ar·i·el (ăr′ē-əl, âr′-) *n.* A gazelle, *Gazella arabica* (or *dama*), native to Arabia. [Arabic *'aryal,* stag.]

Ar·ies (âr′ēz′, âr′ē-ēz′, ăr′-) *n.* **1.** A constellation in the Northern Hemisphere near Taurus and Pisces. **2. a.** The first sign of the **zodiac** *(see).* Also called the "Ram." **b.** One born under this sign. [Latin *ariēs,* ram.]

a·ri·et·ta (ăr′ē-ĕt′ə) *n.* Also **a·ri·ette** (-ĕt′). A short aria. [Italian, diminutive of ARIA.]

a·right (ə-rīt′) *adv.* Properly; correctly. [Middle English *aright,* Old English *ariht, on riht* : A- (on) + *riht,* RIGHT (noun).]

ar·il (ăr′əl) *n. Botany.* An outer covering or appendage of some seeds, arising at or near the hilum. It is often fleshy or brightly colored, as in the yew. [New Latin *arillus,* from Medieval Latin *arillus*†, raisin, grape seed.] —**ar·il·late** (ăr′ə-lāt′) *adj.*

ar·il·lode (ăr′ə-lōd′) *n. Botany.* An appendage or covering that resembles an aril but arises from the micropyle rather than the hilum. [New Latin *arillus,* ARIL + -ODE (like).]

a·rio·so (ä-ryō′sō) *adv. Music.* In the style of an aria. Used as a direction.
~*n., pl.* **ariosos.** A piece of recitative sung in this style, rather than the usual declamatory style. [Italian, from ARIA.] —**a·rio·so** *adj.*

A·ri·os·to (ä′rē-ô′stō), **Ludovico** (1474–1533). Italian poet and dramatist. He is chiefly remembered for his epic comic masterpiece, *Orlando Furioso,* published in its final form in 1532.

a·rise (ə-rīz′) *intr.v.* **arose** (ə-rōz′), **arisen** (ə-rĭz′ən), **arising, arises.** **1.** To get up, as from a sitting or prone position. **2.** To move upward; ascend. **3.** To come into being; originate. **4.** To result, issue, or proceed. Used with *from.* **5.** To become apparent. [Middle English *arisen,* Old English *ārīsan* : A- (up) + *rīsan,* RISE.]

a·ris·ta (ə-rĭs′tə) *n., pl.* **-tae** (-tē). A bristlelike part, such as the awns of grasses or the antennae of certain insects. [New Latin, from Latin *arista*†, beard of grain, spine.] —**a·ris·tate** *adj.*

Ar·is·tar·chus of Sa·mos (ăr′ĭs-tär′kəs; sā′mŏs) *(fl.* 270 B.C.). Greek

aril *The waxy red aril, or coating, of nutmeg seeds is used to make mace, an aromatic spice. The seeds grow inside a fleshy fruit that splits open when ripe.*

PRONUNCIATION KEY

ă, pat; ā, pay; âr, care;
ä, father, are; b, bib;
ch, church; d, deed; ĕ, pet;
ē, be; f, fife; g, gag; h, hat;
hw, which; ĭ, pit; ī, pie;
îr, pier; j, judge; k, kick;
l, lid, needle; m, mum;
n, no, sudden; ng, thing;
ŏ, pot; ō, toe; ô, paw, for;
oi, noise; ou, out; o͝o, book;
o͞o, boot; p, pop; r, roar;
s, sauce; sh, ship, dish;
t, tight; th, thin, path;
th, this, bathe; ŭ, cut; ûr, fur;
v, valve; w, with; y, yes;
z, zebra, size; zh, vision;
ə, about, item, edible,
gallop, circus, peaceful

IN FOREIGN WORDS:

à, *Fr.* ami; œ, *Fr.* feu, *Ger.* schön; ü, *Fr.* tu, *Ger.* über; KH, *Ger.* ich, *Scot.* loch; N, *Fr.* bon; y', *Fr.* Compiègne

STRESS MARKS:

Primary stress: ′
in·cite′ (ĭn-sīt′)
Secondary stress: ′
in′sight′ (ĭn′sīt′)

astronomer of the Alexandrian school. He was one of the first men to propose that the sun was the center of the universe and that the earth moves around it.

ar·is·toc·ra·cy (ăr′ĭs-tŏk′rə-sē) *n., pl.* **-cies. 1.** A hereditary privileged ruling class or nobility. **2.** Government by the nobility or by a privileged minority or upper class. **3.** A state or country having this form of government. **4.** *Rare.* **a.** Government by the best citizens. **b.** A state having such government. **5.** Any group or class considered to be superior. [Old French *aristocratie,* from Late Latin *aristocratia,* from Greek *aristokratia,* "rule by the best (citizens)" : *aristos,* best + -CRACY.]

a·ris·to·crat (ə-rĭs′tə-krăt′, ăr′ĭs-tə-) *n.* **1.** A member of the nobility or aristocracy. **2.** A person having the tastes, opinions, manners, and other characteristics of an upper class. **3.** A person who advocates government by an aristocracy. **4.** One that is superior in a specified field: *The aristocrat of pianos.* [French *aristocrate,* from *aristocratie,* ARISTOCRACY.] **—a·ris·to·crat·ic, a·ris·to·crat·i·cal** *adj.* **—a·ris·to·crat·i·cal·ly** *adv.*

Ar·is·toph·a·nes (ăr′ĭs-tŏf′ə-nēz′) (*c.* 448–*c.* 387 B.C.). Greek comic poet and dramatist, considered the greatest of ancient writers of satirical comedy. Among his surviving plays are *The Clouds* (423), *Lysistrata* (411), and *The Frogs* (405).

Ar·is·to·te·li·an (ăr′ĭs-tə-tē′lē-ən, -tēl′yən) *adj.* Of or pertaining to Aristotle or his philosophy.
~n. A follower of Aristotle or his teachings.

Aristotelian logic *n.* Aristotle's deductive method of logic and the logical system based on this, especially the theory of the syllogism.

Ar·is·tot·le (ăr′ĭs-tŏt′l) (384–322 B.C.). Greek ethical, metaphysical, and political philosopher, who wrote on most branches of learning, including physics and biology, and whose influence extended for more than a thousand years. From 367 to 347 he studied under Plato; from 342 to *c.* 339 he was tutor to Alexander the Great. He returned to Athens and opened a school, the Lyceum, in 335. The most important of his surviving works are the six-volume treatise on logic, *Organon,* the *Physics,* the *Nicomachean Ethics,* and the *Politics.* The fundamental propositions of Aristotle's system of thought were that theory should follow upon the empirical observation of nature and things and that logic, based upon the syllogism, was the essential method of all rational inquiry.

a·rith·me·tic (ə-rĭth′mə-tĭk) *n.* **1.** The mathematics of integers under simple operations such as addition, subtraction, multiplication, division, involution, and evolution. **2.** Counting or problem-solving involving arithmetic operations.
~adj. **ar·ith·met·ic** (ăr′ĭth-mĕt′ĭk). Also **ar·ith·met·i·cal** (-ĭ-kəl). Of or pertaining to arithmetic. [Middle English *ar(i)smet(r)yk, arithmet(r)ik,* from Old French *ar(i)smetique,* from Latin *arithmētica,* from Greek *arithmētikē (tekhnē),* "(the art) of counting," from the feminine of *arithmētikos,* of counting, from *arithmein,* to count, from *arithmos,* number.] **—ar·ith·met·i·cal·ly** *adv.*

a·rith·me·ti·cian (ə-rĭth′mə-tĭsh′ən) *n.* An arithmetic expert.

ar·ith·met·ic mean (ăr′ĭth-mĕt′ĭk) *n.* The number obtained by dividing the sum of a set of quantities by the number of quantities in the set. Also called "average," "mean."

ar·ith·met·ic progression (ăr′ĭth-mĕt′ĭk) *n.* A sequence, such as the odd integers 1, 3, 5, 7, . . . , in which each term after the first is formed by adding a constant to each preceding term.

ar·ith·met·ic series (ăr′ĭth-mĕt′ĭk) *n.* A series in which the terms form an arithmetic progression, as in $1 + 3 + 5 + \ldots$.

-arium *suffix.* Indicates a place or housing for; for example, **planetarium, terrarium.** [Latin, from the neuter of *-ārius,* -ARY.]

A·ri·us (ə-rī′əs, âr′ē-əs) (*c.* 250–336). Christian priest of Alexandria, whose teaching gave rise to the Arianism heresy.

A·ri·zo·na (ăr′ə-zō′nə). A state in the southwestern United States. The capital and largest city is Phoenix. The state includes the Grand Canyon, the Painted Desert, and the Petrified Forest National Park. It joined the Union in 1912.

Ar·ju·na (ăr′jo͞o-nə). *Hinduism.* The prince in the **Bhagavad-Gita** *(see)* to whom Krishna, disguised as a charioteer, expounds the whole nature of being, including the nature of God and the means by which human beings can come to know him.

ark (ärk) *n.* **1. Ark.** The chest containing the Ten Commandments written on stone tablets which represented to the Hebrews a sacred symbol of God's presence and was carried by them during their desert wanderings. Numbers 10:35. Also called "Ark of the Covenant." **2.** The **Holy Ark** *(see).* **3.** The boat built by Noah in readiness for the Flood. Genesis 6–9. **4.** Any large, commodious boat. **5.** A place of shelter or refuge. [Middle English *ark,* Old English *arc, aerc, earc,* from Common Germanic *ark-* (unattested), from Latin *arca,* chest, box, coffer.]

Ar·kan·sas (är′kən-sô′). A state in the central-southwestern United States. The capital and largest city is Little Rock. Most of its eastern border is formed by the Mississippi River. It joined the Union in 1836.

Ar·khan·gelsk (är-kăn′gĕlsk, -KHän′-). *English* **Arch·an·gel** (ärk′ān′jəl). City and major timber port of Russia, in the northwest on the Northern Dvina River.

ar·kose (är-kōz′) *n.* Coarse-grained sandstone containing at least 25 percent feldspar as well as quartz. [French.]

Ark·wright (ärk′rīt), **Sir Richard** (1732–92). British inventor. He patented his invention, a machine for spinning called a water frame, in 1769. He also established cotton mills that were among the earliest examples of the new factory system.

Arles (ärlz). City and port on the Rhône delta in Provence in southern France. It was one of the leading cities in the Western Roman Empire (a Roman arena is still used for bullfights and plays) and the capital of a medieval kingdom.

arm¹ (ärm) *n.* **1.** Either of the upper limbs of the human body connecting the hand and wrist to the shoulder. **2.** A part similar to an arm, such as the forelimb of an animal, a branch of a tree, or a long part projecting from a central support in a machine. **3.** Anything designed to cover or support the human arm, such as a sleeve on an article of clothing or a projecting support on a chair or sofa. **4.** Anything branching out from a large mass: *an arm of the sea.* **5.** An administrative or functional branch, as of an organization. **6.** Power; authority: *the long arm of the law.* **7.** *Mathematics.* Either of the two straight lines that form an angle. **8.** *Physics.* Any of the resistors forming a Wheatstone bridge or similar circuit. **—arm in arm.** With arms linked one through the other. **—at arm's length.** At a distance; not on friendly or intimate terms. **—twist someone's arm.** To coerce or put pressure on someone. **—with open arms.** Cordially; hospitably. [Middle English *arm,* Old English *arm, earm.*]

arm² *n.* **1.** A weapon, especially a firearm. **2.** A branch of a military force, such as the infantry, cavalry, or air force.
~v. **armed, arming, arms.** *—intr.* **1.** To supply or equip oneself with weapons. **2.** To prepare oneself for or as if for warfare. *—tr.* **1.** To equip with weapons. **2.** To prepare for war; fortify. **3.** To provide with anything that strengthens, increases efficiency, or prepares. **4.** *Military.* To prepare (a bomb, for example) for detonation, as by releasing a safety device. [Back-formation from ARMS (plural).] **—arm·er** *n.*

ar·ma·da (är-mä′də, -mā′də) *n.* **1.** A fleet of warships. **2.** Any large mobile force. **3. Armada.** The **Spanish Armada** *(see).* [Spanish, from Medieval Latin *armāta,* army, fleet, from Latin *armātus,* past participle of *armāre,* to arm, from *arma,* arms.]

ar·ma·dil·lo (är′mə-dĭl′ō) *n., pl.* **-los.** Any of several omnivorous, burrowing mammals of the family Dasypodidae, of southern North America and Central and South America, having a covering of armorlike, jointed, bony plates. [Spanish, diminutive of *armado,* armor-plated, past participle of *armar,* to arm, from Latin *armāre,* from *arma,* arms.]

Ar·ma·ged·don (är′mə-gĕd′n) *n.* **1.** The scene of a final battle between the forces of good and evil, prophesied in the Bible to occur at the end of the world. Revelation 16:16. **2.** Any great conflict causing widespread destruction. [Late Latin *Armagedōn,* from Greek, from Hebrew *har megiddōn,* the mountain region of *Megiddo,* site of several great battles in the Old Testament.]

Ar·magh (är-mä′). A market town in the county of Armagh, in the south of Northern Ireland. It is the seat of both the Roman Catholic and Protestant primates of Ireland.

Ar·ma·gnac (är′mən-yăk′) *n.* A dry brandy of superior quality made in the department of Gers in southwestern France. [After *Armagnac,* former name of the region.]

ar·ma·ment (är′mə-mənt) *n.* **1.** The weapons and supplies of war with which a military unit is equipped. **2.** *Often* **armaments.** All the military forces and war equipment of a country. **3.** A military force equipped for war. **4.** The process of arming for war. [Late Latin *armāmentum* (singular), from Latin *armāmenta* (plural), implements, equipment, from *arma,* tools, ARMS.]

ar·ma·men·tar·i·um (är′mə-mĕn-târ′ē-əm) *n., pl.* **-taria** (-târ′ē-ə). **1.** The complete equipment of a physician or medical institution, including medicines, supplies, and instruments. **2.** All the articles used in a field of activity; paraphernalia. [Latin, store of weapons. See **armament, -arium.**]

ar·ma·ture (är′mə-cho͝or′) *n.* **1.** *Electricity.* **a.** The rotating part of a dynamo consisting essentially of copper wire wound around an iron core. **b.** The moving part of an electromagnetic device such as a relay, buzzer, or loud-speaker. **c.** A piece of soft iron connecting the poles of a magnet. **2.** *Biology.* The protective covering or structure of an animal or plant. **3.** A framework serving as a supporting core for clay sculpture. **4.** *Archaic.* Armor. [Latin *armātūra,* equipment, from *armāre,* to arm, from *arma,* weapons, tools.]

arm·band (ärm′bănd′) *n.* A strip of material worn around the upper arm for identification or as a sign of mourning.

arm·chair (ärm′châr′) *n.* A chair, usually upholstered, with supports at the sides for the arms or elbows.
~adj. Remote from active involvement; purely theoretical: *an armchair warrior.*

armed (ärmd) *adj.* **1.** Equipped with weapons. **2.** Having or characterized by an arm or arms of a specified kind or number. Usually used in combination: *strong-armed.* **3.** Ready to face adversity.

armed forces *pl.n.* The military forces of a country or countries. Also called "armed services."

Ar·me·ni·a (är-mē′nē-ə, -mēn′yə). **1.** Republic lying on the southern flanks of the Caucasus Mts. Formerly a constituent republic of the U.S.S.R., it became part of the Commonwealth of Independent States in 1991. Area, 29,946 square kilometers (11,506 square miles). Population, 3,350,000. Capital, Yerevan. **2.** Ancient Asian kingdom centered on Mt. Ararat and now divided between Turkey, Iran, and the republic of Armenia. Established in the 8th century B.C., it became the world's first country to make Christianity the state religion (A.D. 303). It was partitioned between Persia and the Eastern Roman Empire (A.D. 387), and thereafter endured many conquerors. Between 1894 and 1915 the Turks massacred most of the Armenians because they were Christians.

Ar·me·ni·an (är-mē′nē-ən, -mēn′yən) *n.* **1.** A native or inhabitant of

Arjuna *The legendary Indian hero, with a red quiver slung across him, fires an arrow in battle. His charioteer is the blue-skinned Hindu god Krishna.*

armadillo *All species of armadillo are protected by small plates of bone covered with horny skin. They are found in southern North America and Central and South America. This is a Brazilian armadillo that grows to about 45 centimeters (18 inches) long; some species can reach a length of 90 centimeters (3 feet).*

armor

PROTECTIVE COVERING FOR COMBAT

The continuing struggle to provide a defense against new arms technology

Armor made of rigid plates was originally worn by the Greeks in about 700 B.C. Several other types, including scale armor (overlapping metal plates attached to fabric) and mail (interlocking metal rings) were widely used by soldiers of the Roman Empire. In 11th-century Europe, mail was the predominant armor; whalebone, wax-hardened leather (cuir bouilli), or metal plates came into use as additional protection from the end of the 13th century.

Mail was the most used form of armor in early medieval Europe because it was readily available. From the 14th century, plate armor was used increasingly, perhaps to give greater protection against the longbow and the halberd. In turn, weapon design changed in response to the new plate armor—swords, for example, were more pointed to penetrate the gaps between plates, or stronger to smash through the plates.

The great period of the suit (or harness) of armor was the 15th century. By the early 16th century, magnificent custom-made suits, often elaborately etched and gilded, proclaimed the wealth and status of the wearer, and horse armor was sometimes made to match the rider's suit. Apart from the chamfron to cover a horse's head, armor for horses was never widely used.

The average weight of full armor was about 22.7 kilograms (50 pounds)—no more than the weight of the equipment carried by a modern soldier. The popular belief that a knight had to be hoisted into his saddle with a crane is a myth; the main source of discomfort was heat.

During the 14th and 15th centuries jousts and tournaments became popular as a sport, rather than a military exercise, and specially reinforced armor was designed for combatants.

With the growing ascendancy of the infantry and firearms, full armor became obsolete. Light armor consisting of a cuirass (back and breast plate) and a helmet continued to be worn by certain cavalry units until the 20th century. During World War I there was a renewed need for head protection, this time from gas as well as bullets. In World War II gas masks and helmets were issued in vast numbers and bullet-resistant vests were made from a form of scale armor.

Today the term "armored" usually refers to vehicles and aircraft, but the armed forces, the police, and bomb-disposal units all depend on equipment such as flame-resistant headgear and body suits, gas masks, and riot shields. Bulletproof vests have fiber-glass inserts over which impact-absorbing ceramic plates fit.

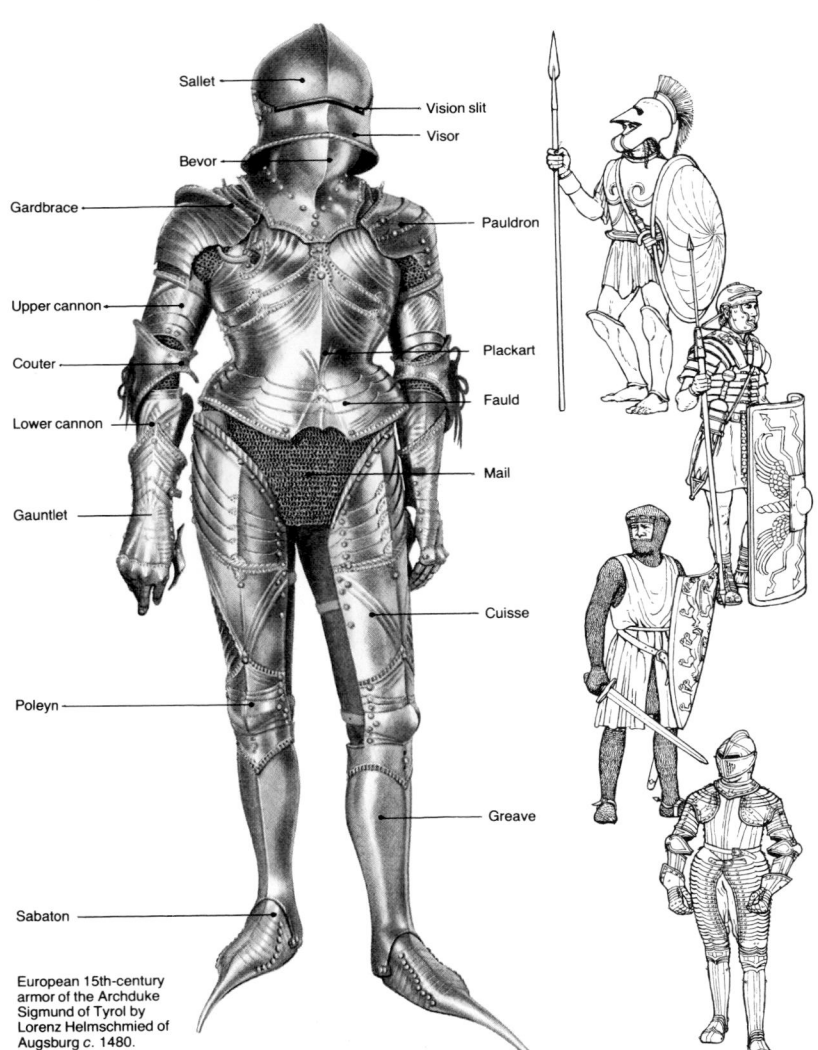

Sallet
Vision slit
Visor
Bevor
Gardbrace
Pauldron
Upper cannon
Plackart
Couter
Fauld
Lower cannon
Mail
Gauntlet
Cuisse
Poleyn
Greave
Sabaton

European 15th-century armor of the Archduke Sigmund of Tyrol by Lorenz Helmschmied of Augsburg c. 1480.

Armenia. **2.** The Indo-European language of the Armenians. —**Ar·me·ni·an** *adj.*

Armenian Church *n.* The independent church of the Armenians, founded in about A.D. 300 and similar to the Eastern Orthodox Church in its practices and doctrines.

ar·met (är′mĕt) *n.* A medieval light helmet with a neck guard and movable visor. [Old French *armet*, partly from *arme*, singular of *armes*, ARMS, and partly from Old Spanish *almete*, from Old French *helmet*, HELMET.]

arm·ful (ärm′fŏŏl′) *n., pl.* **-fuls.** As much as one or both arms can hold.

arm·hole (ärm′hōl′) *n.* An opening for the arm in a garment.

ar·mi·ger (är′mĭ-jər) *n.* **1.** An armorbearer for a knight; a squire. **2.** A person entitled to heraldic arms. [Latin *armiger* : *arma*, ARMS + *gerere*, to carry.]

ar·mil·lar·y sphere (är′mə-lĕr′ē, är-mĭl′ə-rē) *n.* An astronomical model with solid rings, all circles of a single sphere, used to display relationships among the principal circles on the celestial sphere. [Old French *armillaire*, from Medieval Latin *armilla*, ring, from Latin, arm ring, from *armus*, arm.]

Ar·min·i·an·ism (är-mĭn′ē-ən-ĭz′əm) *n.* The doctrine of Jacobus Arminius and his followers, opposing the Calvinist doctrine of absolute predestination and holding that salvation is possible for all. It was the basis of the Methodist position of John and Charles Wesley. —**Ar·min·i·an** *adj. & n.*

Ar·min·i·us (är-mĭn′ē-əs), **Jacobus** (1560–1609). Theologian of the Dutch Reformed Church. His opposition to the strict predestinarianism of John Calvin became known as Arminianism and had a wide influence throughout Europe.

ar·mip·o·tent (är-mĭp′ə-tənt) *adj. Archaic.* Mighty in arms or battle. [Middle English, from Latin *armipotēns* : *arma*, ARMS + *potēns* (stem *potent-*), POTENT.] —**ar·mip·o·tence** *n.*

ar·mi·stice (är′mə-stĭs) *n.* A temporary cessation or suspension of hostilities by mutual consent; a truce. [French, from New Latin *armistitium* : Latin *arma*, ARMS + *-stitium*, "stoppage."]

Armistice Day *n.* November 11, celebrated as the anniversary of the armistice of World War I in 1918. It has been called **Veterans Day** *(see)* since 1954.

arm·let (ärm′lĭt) *n.* **1.** A band or bracelet worn on the arm for ornament or identification. **2.** A small arm, as of the sea.

ar·moire (ärm-wär′, är′mər) *n.* A large, ornate cabinet or wardrobe. [Old French, variant of *armaire*, from Latin *armārium*, closet, from *arma*, weapons, tools.]

ar·mor (är′mər) *n. Also British* **ar·mour.** **1.** A defensive covering, such as chain mail, leather, or metal plates, worn as protection against weapons. **2.** Any tough protective covering, such as the bony scales or plates covering certain animals, or metal plates on tanks or warships. **3.** Anything serving as a safeguard or protection. **4.** The armored vehicles of an army collectively. ~*tr.v.* **armored, -moring, -mors.** To cover with armor. [Middle English *armure*, from Old French, from Latin *armātūra*, equipment, from *armāre*, to arm, from *arma*, ARMS.]

ar·mor·bear·er (är′mər-bâr′ər) *n.* One who carries the arms or armor of a warrior.

ar·mor·clad (är′mər-klăd′) *adj.* Wearing or covered with armor.

ar·mored (är′mərd) *adj.* **1.** Clad with armor or a protective covering, such as scales. **2.** Equipped with armored vehicles, as a military unit.

armored car *n.* **1.** A light, armored, military vehicle usually having a mounted machine gun and used especially for reconnaissance. **2.** A light armored van used for transporting money or valuables.

ar·mor·er (är′mər-ər) *n.* **1.** One who makes or repairs armor. **2.** A manufacturer of weapons. **3.** *Military.* A serviceman in charge of maintenance and repair of the small arms of a unit.

ar·mo·ri·al (är-môr′ē-əl, är-mōr′-) *adj.* Of or pertaining to heraldry or heraldic arms. ~*n.* A book containing coats of arms. [From *armory*, a rare word for heraldry + -AL.]

Ar·mor·i·ca (är-môr′ə-kə, -mōr′-). A literary name for Brittany.

Ar·mor·i·can (är-môr′ĭ-kən) *adj. Also* **Ar·mor·ic** (är-môr′ĭk). **1.** Of or pertaining to Armorica or the people or language of Amorica. **2.** *Geology.* Hercynian. ~*n. Also* **Ar·mor·ic.** **1.** A native or inhabitant of Armorica. **2.** The language of Armorica; Breton.

armor plate *n.* Hard steel plate used to cover warships, vehicles, and fortifications. —**ar·mor·plat·ed** *adj.*

ar·mor·y (är′mər-ē) *n., pl.* **-ies.** **1.** A storehouse for arms; an arsenal. **2.** A building for storing arms and military equipment, especially one serving as a headquarters for military reserve personnel. **3.** An arms factory. [Middle English *armourie*, from *armure*, ARMOUR.]

ar·mour. *British.* Variant of **armor.**

arm·pit (ärm′pĭt′) *n.* The hollow under the arm at the shoulder.

arm·rest (ärm′rĕst′) *n.* A support for the arm, as on a piece of furniture or the inner surface of the door of a vehicle.

arms (ärmz) *pl.n.* **1.** Weapons. **2.** Warfare. **3.** Heraldic bearings. **4.** Insignia, as of a state, official, family, or organization. —**bear arms against.** To attack with arms; wage war on. —**in** (or **under**) **arms.** Armed. —**lay down one's arms.** To surrender. —**order arms.** *Military.* To bring a rifle vertically against the right side of the body with the butt touching the ground. —**shoulder arms.** *Military.* To hold a rifle in a sloping position with the barrel over the shoulder and the butt in the hand. —**up in arms.** Aroused to anger and ready to protest. [Middle English *armes*, from Old

French, from Latin *arma,* weapons, tools.]
arms race *n.* A continuous build-up of weapons and forces by two or more competing nations in order to maintain equality or superiority of military power.
Arm·strong (ärm′strông′), **Louis** (1900–71). U.S. jazz musician, popularly known as "Satchmo." He was born in New Orleans. In 1922 he joined King Oliver's band in Chicago and quickly rose to national fame as both a trumpeter and a singer.
Armstrong, Neil Alden (1930–). U.S. astronaut and first man to walk on the moon. In July, 1969, he commanded Apollo XI on its mission to the moon, and on July 20 he set the lunar module *Eagle* down on the surface. Millions of people watched a live television transmission of his first steps on the moon.
ar·my (är′mē) *n., pl.* **-mies. 1.** A large body of men organized and trained for warfare on land. **2.** The entire military land forces of a country. **3.** A tactical and administrative military unit consisting of a headquarters, two or more army corps, and auxiliary forces. **4.** Any large group of people organized for a specific cause. **5.** A large multitude, as of people or animals. —See Synonyms at **multitude.** [Middle English *armee,* from Old French, from Medieval Latin *armāta,* army, fleet, from Latin *armātus,* past participle of *armāre,* to arm, from *arma,* arms.]
army ant *n.* Any of various chiefly tropical New World ants of the subfamily Dorylinae, forming large colonies that move from place to place. Also called "legionary ant."
ar·my·worm (är′mē-wûrm′) *n.* Any of various insect larvae that travel in large groups, destroying crops; especially, the caterpillar of a New World moth, *Leucania* (or *Pseudaletia*) *unipuncta.*
arnatto. Variant of **annatto.**
Arne (ärn), **Thomas Augustine** (1710–78). British composer. Largely self-taught, he wrote songs, oratorios, and operas. The song "Rule, Britannia" comes from his opera *Alfred* (1740).
Arn·hem (ärn′hĕm′, är′nəm). Industrial town and port on the Lower Rhine River in the eastern Netherlands. It was the site of a major defeat inflicted upon British airborne troops in September 1944.
Arnhem Land. Northernmost part of Northern Territory in Australia, site of the largest of the country's 17 aboriginal reservations.
ar·ni·ca (är′nĭ-kə) *n.* **1.** Any of various alpine or arctic plants of the genus *Arnica,* having bright-yellow, rayed flowers. **2.** A tincture of the dried flower heads of *A. montana,* used for sprains and bruises. [18th century : New Latin *Arnica*†.]
Ar·no (är′nō). River of central Italy. It rises in the Apennines and flows some 240 kilometers (150 miles) to the Ligurian Sea. In 1966 it flooded, causing severe damage to art treasures in Florence.
Ar·no (är′nō), **Peter,** born Curtis Arnoux Peters (1904–68). U.S. cartoonist. His drawings, with their urbane, satirical observations on the foibles of café and high society, were a noted feature of *The New Yorker* from 1925 on.
Ar·nold (är′nəld), **Benedict** (1741–1801). Revolutionary soldier and traitor. Arnold was appointed commander of West Point in 1780. Troubled by debts and embittered by what he considered unfair treatment by the Continental Congress, he offered to surrender the fort to the British for 20,000 pounds. The British go-between, Maj. John André, was captured while carrying papers implicating Arnold, and the plot was foiled. Arnold fled, first to New York and later to England (1781).
Arnold, Matthew (1822–88). British poet, critic, and essayist. His famous poem "Dover Beach" (1867) expressed his personal moral and religious doubts. He is most widely known for his classic study *Culture and Anarchy* (1869), a trenchant polemic against the materialism of Victorian society.
ar·oid (ăr′oid′, âr′-) *adj.* Also **a·ra·ceous** (ə-rā′shəs). Of or belonging to the Araceae, a family of plants that includes the arums and callas.
∼*n.* Any of various plants of the family Araceae.
a·roint (ə-roint′) *tr.v.* **arointed, arointing, aroints.** *Archaic.* Begone: *"Aroint thee, witch!"* (Shakespeare). [Origin unknown.]
a·ro·ma (ə-rō′mə) *n.* **1.** A pleasant, characteristic odor, as of a plant, spice, or food. **2.** A distinctive, intangible quality; an aura. —See Synonyms at **smell.** [Latin *arōma,* from Greek *arōma*†, aromatic herb or spice.]
ar·o·mat·ic (ăr′ə-măt′ĭk) *adj.* **1.** Having an aroma; fragrant, sweet-smelling, or spicy. **2.** *Chemistry.* Of, pertaining to, or containing the 6-carbon ring characteristic of the benzene series and related organic groups. Compare **aliphatic.**
∼*n.* An aromatic plant or substance. [Middle English, from Old French *aromatique,* from Late Latin *arōmaticus,* from Greek *arōmatikos* : AROMA (stem *arōmat-*) + -IC.] **—ar·o·mat·i·cal·ly** *adv.*
ar·o·ma·tic·i·ty (ăr′ə-mə-tĭs′ə-tē, ə-rō′mə-) *n.* **1.** Aromatic quality or character. **2.** The characteristic structure or properties of the aromatic chemical compounds.
a·ro·ma·tize (ə-rō′mə-tīz′) *v.* **-tized, -tizing, -tizes.** —*tr.* **1.** To make aromatic or fragrant. **2.** *Chemistry.* To change (a compound) into an aromatic compound. —*intr.* To become aromatic. Used of chemical compounds. **—a·ro·ma·ti·za·tion** *n.*
arose. Past tense of **arise.**
a·round (ə-round′) *adv.* **1.** In all directions from a specific point: *famous for miles around.* **2.** On or to all sides or in all directions; about: *looked around in vain.* **3.** Along a circuit: *passed the plate around.* **4.** In or toward the opposite direction, position, or attitude; round: *swung around at the noise.* **5.** From one place to another; here and there; about: *wander around.* **6.** *Informal.* Close at hand; nearby: *He waited around all day.* **7.** In circumference: *a pole three feet around.* **8.** In existence; about: *There is at least one around somewhere.* **9.** *Informal.* To a specific place: *when you come around again.* **—get around.** *Informal.* **1.** To avoid and so overcome (a problem, for example). **2.** To have wide knowledge of worldly matters. **—get around to.** *Informal.* To find time or occasion to give one's attention to.
∼*prep.* **1.** On all sides of: *the world around us.* **2.** So as to enclose, surround, or envelop. **3.** About the circumference or periphery of: *a path around the lake.* **4.** About the central point of: *the earth's motion around the sun.* **5.** In or to a place or places within or near: *driving around the countryside.* **6.** On or to the other side of: *the house around the corner.* **7.** Approximately; about: *around 20 guests.* **8.** So as to get past or avoid: *a way around the problem.* —See Usage note at **about.** [Middle English : A- (on) + ROUND (noun).]
a·rous·al (ə-rou′zəl) *n.* The act of arousing or state of being aroused.
a·rouse (ə-rouz′) *tr.v.* **aroused, arousing, arouses. 1.** To awaken from or as if from sleep. **2.** To excite or stimulate. —See Synonyms at **provoke.** [16th century : A- (intensive) + ROUSE, by analogy with *rise, arise, wake, awake,* and the like.] **—a·rous·er** *n.*
Arp (ärp), **Jean** or **Hans** (1887–1966). French sculptor and painter. Arp was an experimental artist who produced abstract works in a variety of forms, including collages, full rounded sculptures, painted wood reliefs, and painted cutouts.
ar·peg·gi·o (är-pĕj′ē-ō, -pĕj′ō) *n., pl.* **-os.** *Music.* **1.** The playing of the notes of a chord in rapid succession rather than simultaneously. **2.** A chord played or sung in this manner. [Italian *arpeggio,* "chord played as on a harp," from *arpeggiare,* to play the harp, from *arpa,* harp, from Germanic *harpon-* (unattested), HARP.] **—ar·peg·gi·oed** *adj.*
ar·pent (är-päɴ′) *n.* An old French unit of land measurement approximately equivalent to an acre. [French, from Old French, from Vulgar Latin *arependis* (unattested), variant of Latin *arepennis,* half acre, of Gaulish origin; related to Old Irish *airchenn* (a land measure).]
arquebus. Variant of **harquebus.**
arr. 1. arrival; arrive; arrived. **2.** arranged (by).
ar·rack (ăr′ək, ə-răk′) *n.* A strong, alcoholic drink of the Middle and Far East, usually distilled from rice or molasses. [Arabic *'araq,* sweet juice, liquor, as in *'araq at-tamr,* fermented juice of the date.]
ar·raign (ə-rān′) *tr.v.* **-raigned, -raigning, -raigns. 1.** *Law.* To call before a court to answer to an indictment. **2.** To call to account; charge; accuse. [Middle English *arreinen,* from Old French *araisnier,* from Vulgar Latin *adrationāre* (unattested), "to call to account" : *ad-,* to + Latin *ratiō,* reason, from *rērī* (past participle *ratus*), to think, reckon.] **—ar·raign·er** *n.*
ar·raign·ment (ə-rān′mənt) *n.* The act or procedure of arraigning or being arraigned; especially, the formal summoning of a prisoner in a law court to answer to an indictment.
Ar·ran (ăr′ən). A granite island at the mouth of the Firth of Clyde in western Scotland.
ar·range (ə-rānj′) *v.* **-ranged, -ranging, -ranges.** —*tr.* **1.** To put into a deliberate order or relation; dispose: *arrange flowers in a vase.* **2.** To plan or prepare for: *arrange a picnic.* **3.** To agree about; settle: *arrange the date of the marriage.* **4.** *Music.* To rescore (music) for other instruments or voices, or for another style of performance. —*intr.* **1.** To come to an agreement: *arranged to meet on Sunday.* **2.** To make preparations; plan: *arranged for a trip south.* [Middle English *arangen, arengen,* from Old French *arangier, arengier* : *a-,* from *ad,* to + *rengier,* to put in a line, from *renc, reng,* line, row, from Frankish *hring* (unattested), circle, ring.] **—ar·rang·er** *n.*
ar·range·ment (ə-rānj′mənt) *n.* **1.** The act or process of arranging. **2.** The condition, manner, or result of being arranged; disposal; order. **3.** Something that has been arranged. **4.** A collection or set of things that have been arranged: *a floral arrangement.* **5.** *Often* **arrangements.** A provision or plan made in preparation for some undertaking. **6.** An agreement; settlement; disposition: *an arrangement to share the rent.* **7.** *Music.* **a.** An adaptation of a composition for other voices or instruments, or to another style or level of difficulty. **b.** A composition so adapted.
ar·rant (ăr′ənt) *adj.* Notorious; unmitigated; thoroughgoing: *an arrant knave.* [14th century : variant of ERRANT, wandering; pejorative sense developed through frequent use in phrases such as *arrant* (i.e., vagabond) *thief.*] **—ar·rant·ly** *adv.*
ar·ras (ăr′əs) *n.* **1.** A tapestry. **2.** A wall hanging, especially of tapestry. [Middle English, from Norman-French *(drap de) Arras,* (cloth of) ARRAS.]
Ar·ras (ăr′əs). Administrative center of Pas-de-Calais department on the Scarpe River of northern France. It was a famous woolen and tapestry center in the Middle Ages.
ar·ray (ə-rā′) *tr.v.* **-rayed, -raying, -rays. 1.** To arrange or draw up (troops, for example) in battle order. **2.** To deck in finery; adorn.
∼*n.* **1.** An orderly arrangement, especially of troops. **2.** An impressive display of numerous persons or objects. **3.** Splendid attire; finery. **4.** *Mathematics.* **a.** A rectangular arrangement of quantities in rows and columns, as in a matrix or determinant. **b.** Numerical data linearly ordered by magnitude. **5.** *Law.* A list of the jurors impaneled to try a case. **6.** *Electronics.* A regular arrangement of antennas used for radar or radio astronomy. —See Synonyms at **multitude.** [Middle English *arayen, arrayen,* from Old French *areer, arayer,* from Vulgar Latin *arrēdāre* (unattested), to arrange : *ad,* towards + *rēdāre* (unattested), to provide, from Germanic.]

armillary sphere *This piece of astronomical equipment was made in Florence in 1554 and is now in the Science Museum, London. The movable rings of the sphere were used to display the supposed relationships between the principal celestial bodies.*

armorial bearing *This coat of arms is in the form known as quartering of six. The top left section is inherited from the father; the others are the coats of arms of families to which the first is related by marriage.*

arrowhead *A freshwater plant of wide distribution with arrowhead-shaped leaves. Some species have edible tubers.*

PRONUNCIATION KEY

ă, pat; ā, pay; âr, care;
ä, father, are; b, bib;
ch, church; d, deed; ĕ, pet;
ē, be; f, fife; g, gag; h, hat;
hw, which; ĭ, pit; ī, pie;
îr, pier; j, judge; k, kick;
l, lid, needle; m, mum;
n, no, sudden; ng, thing;
ŏ, pot; ō, toe; ô, paw, for;
oi, noise; ou, out; o͝o, book;
o͞o, boot; p, pop; r, roar;
s, sauce; sh, ship, dish;
t, tight; th, thin, path;
th, this, bathe; ŭ, cut; ûr, fur;
v, valve; w, with; y, yes;
z, zebra, size; zh, vision;
ə, about, item, edible,
gallop, circus, peaceful

IN FOREIGN WORDS:

à, *Fr.* ami; œ, *Fr.* feu, *Ger.* schön; ü, *Fr.* tu, *Ger.* über; KH, *Ger.* ich, *Scot.* loch; N, *Fr.* bon; y', *Fr.* Compiègne

STRESS MARKS:

Primary stress: ′
in·cite′ (ĭn-sīt′)
Secondary stress: ′
in′sight′ (ĭn′sīt′)

ar·ray·al (ə-rā′əl) *n.* **1.** The act or process of arraying. **2.** Something arrayed; an array.

ar·rear (ə-rîr′) *n.* **1.** *Usually* **arrears.** An unpaid and overdue debt, or an unfulfilled obligation. **2.** *Usually* **arrears.** The state of being behind in fulfilling contractual obligations or payments. Used with *in*: *in arrears on his rent.* [Middle English *ar(r)ere,* behind, from Old French *arriere, arrere,* from Late Latin *ad retrō,* backward : *ad-,* toward + *retrō,* backward, behind.]

ar·rear·age (ə-rîr′ĭj) *n.* **1.** The state of being in arrears. **2.** An amount owed in payment. **3.** *Rare.* Something held in reserve.

ar·rest (ə-rĕst′) *tr.v.* **-rested, -resting, -rests. 1.** To prevent the motion, progress, growth, or spread of; stop or check. **2.** To seize and hold under authority of the law. **3.** To capture and hold briefly (the attention, for example); engage.
~*n.* **1. a.** The act of arresting. **b.** The state of being arrested. **2.** A device for arresting motion, especially of a moving part. **—under arrest.** Detained in legal custody. [Middle English *aresten,* from Old French *arester,* from Vulgar Latin *arrestāre* (unattested), to cause to stop : Latin *ad-,* to + *restāre,* to stop, stay behind : *re-,* back + *stāre,* to stand.] **—ar·rest·er** *n.* **—ar·rest·ment** *n.*

ar·rest·a·ble (ə-rĕs′tə-bəl) *adj.* Liable to incur or lead to arrest if committed: *an arrestable offense.*

ar·rest·ing (ə-rĕs′tĭng) *adj.* Attracting and holding the attention; striking. **—ar·rest·ing·ly** *adv.*

arrest of judgment *n. Law.* **1.** A request by the accused before being sentenced that judgment be postponed owing to some irregularity. **2.** The suspension of judgment by a court if an indictment does not disclose an offense known to law.

Ar·rhe·ni·us (ə-rē′nē-əs, ə-rā′-), **Svante August** (1859–1927). Swedish chemist, a pioneer of modern physical chemistry. His research into the aqueous solutions of bases and acids led to the discovery, called the Arrhenius theory, of electrolytes, for which he was awarded the Nobel Prize in chemistry in 1903.

ar·rhyth·mi·a (ə-rĭ*th*′mē-ə) *n.* Any irregularity in the force or rhythm of the heartbeat. [New Latin, from Greek, from *arrhuthmos,* unrhythmical : *a-,* not + *rhuthmos,* RHYTHM.]

ar·rhyth·mic (ə-rĭ*th*′mĭk) *adj.* Also **ar·rhyth·mi·cal** (-mĭ-kəl). **1.** Lacking rhythm or regularity of rhythm. **2.** *Pathology.* Characterized by arrhythmia. **—ar·rhyth·mi·cal·ly** *adv.*

ar·ri·ère-ban (ăr′ē-âr-bän′, -băn′) *n.* **1.** In medieval France, a royal proclamation by which vassals were summoned to military service. **2.** The vassals so summoned. [French, from Old French *arriereban,* alteration of *arban, herban,* from Old High German *heriban* : *heri,* army + *ban,* proclamation.]

ar·ri·ère-pen·sée (ăr′ē-âr-päN-sā′) *n.* An intention or a thought which is not disclosed, often because of an ulterior motive. [French, "behind thought."]

ar·ris (ăr′ĭs) *n., pl.* **arris** or **-rises.** *Architecture.* The sharp edge or ridge formed by two surfaces meeting at an angle, as in a molding. [Old French *areste* (modified), ridge, ARÊTE.]

ar·ri·val (ə-rī′vəl) *n. Abbr.* **arr. 1.** The act of arriving. **2.** One that arrives or has arrived. Also used adjectivally: *the arrival lounge at the airport.* **3.** The reaching of a goal or objective as a result of some process or effort.

ar·rive (ə-rīv′) *intr.v.* **-rived, -riving, -rives. 1.** To reach a destination; come to a particular place. **2.** To reach a goal or object through some process or effort. Usually used with *at*: *arrive at a decision.* **3.** To come at length; take place: *The day of crisis has arrived.* **4.** *Informal.* To achieve success or recognition. **5.** *Informal.* To be born. [Middle English *ariven,* from Old French *ariver,* from Vulgar Latin, *arripāre* (unattested), to land, come to shore : Latin *ad-,* to + *rīpa,* shore.] **—ar·riv·er** *n.*

ar·ri·ve·der·ci (ə-rē′və-dâr′chē) *interj. Italian.* Goodbye.

ar·ri·viste (ä-rē-vēst′) *n., pl.* **-vistes** (-vēst′). A social climber or opportunist; an upstart. [French, from *arriver,* to ARRIVE.]

ar·ro·ba (ə-rō′bə) *n.* **1.** An old unit of weight in Spanish-speaking countries equal to about 25 pounds. **2.** An old unit of weight in Portuguese-speaking countries equal to about 32 pounds. **3.** A liquid measure used in Spanish-speaking countries, having varying value, but approximately equal to 16 liters (17 quarts) when used to measure wine. [Spanish and Portuguese, from Arabic *ar-rub',* the quarter (of a quintal).]

ar·ro·gance (ăr′ə-gəns) *n.* The state or quality of being arrogant; insolent pride; haughtiness.

ar·ro·gant (ăr′ə-gənt) *adj.* **1.** Excessively convinced of one's own importance; haughty. **2.** Characterized by or arising from haughty self-importance. —See Synonyms at **proud.** [Middle English, from Latin *arrogāns* (stem *arrogant-*), present participle of *arrogāre,* ARROGATE.] **—ar·ro·gant·ly** *adv.*

ar·ro·gate (ăr′ə-gāt′) *tr.v.* **-gated, -gating, -gates. 1.** To appropriate presumptuously; claim or assume without right. **2.** To attribute to another without justification. [Latin *arrogāre,* to claim for oneself : *ad-,* to + *rogāre,* to ask.] **—ar·ro·ga·tion** *n.* **—ar·ro·ga·tive** (ăr′ə-gā′tĭv) *adj.* **—ar·ro·ga·tor** (ăr′ə-gā′tər) *n.*

ar·ron·disse·ment (ȧ-rôN-dēs-mäN′) *n. French.* **1.** The chief administrative subdivision of a department in France. **2.** A municipal subdivision of some large French cities. [French, from *arrondir,* to make round, round out, from *rond,* ROUND.]

ar·row (ăr′ō) *n.* **1.** A straight, thin shaft, shot from a bow and usually made of light wood with a pointed head at one end and flight-stabilizing feathers at the other. **2.** Anything similar in form, function, or speed, such as a sign or symbol used to indicate direction. [Middle English *arewe, arwe,* Old English *arwe, earh.*]

ar·row·head (ăr′ō-hĕd′) *n.* **1.** The pointed, removable striking tip of an arrow. **2.** Something shaped like an arrowhead, such as a mark indicating a limit on a drawing. **3.** Any aquatic or marsh plant of the genus *Sagittaria,* especially *S. sagittifolia,* having arrowhead-shaped leaves and purple-spotted white flowers.

ar·row·root (ăr′ō-ro͞ot′, -ro͝ot′) *n.* **1.** A tropical American plant, *Maranta arundinacea,* having roots that yield an edible starch. **2.** The edible starch from this plant and from certain plants of the genera *Manihot, Curcuma,* and *Tacca.* [After the use of the root by the American Indians to absorb poison from arrow wounds.]

ar·row·wood (ăr′ō-wo͝od′) *n.* Any of several small shrubs of the genus *Viburnum,* having straight tough stems formerly used by American Indians to make arrows.

arrow worm *n.* Any of various small, transparent marine worms of the phylum Chaetognatha, having prehensile bristles on each side of the mouth.

ar·roy·o (ə-roi′ō) *n., pl.* **-os.** *Southwestern U.S.* **1.** A deep gully cut by a stream; a dry ravine. **2.** A brook or creek. [Spanish, from Vulgar Latin *arrugium* (unattested), variant of Latin *arrugia*†, mineshaft.]

ar·se·nal (är′sə-nəl) *n.* **1.** An establishment for the storing, manufacturing, or repairing of arms, ammunition, and other war materiel. **2.** A stock of weapons. **3.** A collection or storehouse: *an arsenal of debating points.* [Italian *arsenale, arzanale,* originally, naval dockyard, from Arabic *dār-aṣ-ṣinā'ah* : *dār,* house + *aṣ-,* variant of *al-,* the + *ṣinā'ah,* manufacture, from *ṣana'a,* he made.]

ar·se·nate (är′sə-nĭt, -nāt′) *n.* A salt or ester of arsenic acid.

ar·se·nic (är′sə-nĭk) *n.* **1.** *Symbol* **As** A highly poisonous metallic element having three allotropic forms, yellow, black, or gray, of which the brittle, crystalline gray form is the most common. Arsenic and its compounds are used in insecticides, weed killers, solid-state doping agents, and various alloys. Atomic number 33, atomic weight 74.922, valence 3 or 5. Gray arsenic melts at 817°C (at 28 atm pressure), sublimes at 613°C, and has a specific gravity of 5.73. **2.** Arsenic trioxide.
~*adj.* **ar·sen·ic** (är-sĕn′ĭk). Of or containing arsenic. Used especially of chemical compounds containing arsenic with a valence of 5. [Middle English, from Old French, from Latin *arsenicum, arrenicum,* from Greek *arsenikon, arrhenikon,* yellow orpiment, alteration (influenced by *arsenikos, arrhenikos,* male, virile) of Syriac *zarnīkā,* from Iranian; akin to Avestan *zarniya,* gold.]

ar·sen·ic acid (är-sĕn′ĭk) *n.* A poisonous, white, translucent crystalline compound, H_3AsO_4, used to manufacture arsenates.

ar·sen·i·cal (är-sĕn′ĭ-kəl) *adj.* Of or containing arsenic.
~*n.* A drug or preparation containing arsenic.

arsenical nickel *n.* A nickel ore, **niccolite** *(see).*

ar·se·nic trioxide (är′sə-nĭk) *n.* A poisonous, white powder, As_2O_3, used in insecticides, rat poison, and weed killers. Also loosely called "arsenic."

ar·se·nide (är′sə-nīd′) *n.* A compound of arsenic with a more electropositive element. [ARSEN(IC) + -IDE.]

ar·se·ni·ous (är-sē′nē-əs) *adj.* Of or containing arsenic. Used especially of chemical compounds containing arsenic with a valence of 3.

ar·se·no·py·rite (är′sə-nō-pī′rīt′) *n.* A silver-white to gray arsenic ore, essentially FeAsS. Also called "mispickel." [ARSEN(IC) + PYRITE.]

arshin. Variant of **archine.**

ar·sine (är-sēn′, är′sēn′) *n.* A colorless, flammable, very poisonous gas, AsH_3, used as a military poison gas, as a solid-state doping agent, and in organic synthesis. [ARS(ENIC) + -INE.]

ar·sis (är′sĭs) *n., pl.* **-ses** (-sēz′). **1.** Originally, the unaccented or shorter part of a foot of verse. **2.** In modern usage, the accented or longer part of a foot of verse. **3.** *Music.* The upbeat, or unaccented part, of a measure. Compare **thesis.** [Late Latin, accented syllable, "raising of the voice," from Greek, unaccented syllable, "raising of the foot in beating time," from *aeirein,* to lift.]

ar·son (är′sən) *n.* The crime of maliciously burning property belonging to someone else, or of burning one's own property for some improper or illegal purpose, as to collect insurance. [Norman French (legal use), from Old French, from Medieval Latin *arsiō* (stem *arsion-*), act of burning, from Latin *ardēre* (past participle *arsus*), to burn.] **—ar·son·ist** *n.*

ars·phen·a·mine (ärs-fĕn′ə-mēn′) *n.* A yellow hygroscopic arsenical powder, $C_{12}H_{12}N_2O_2As \cdot 2HCl \cdot 2H_2O$, formerly used to treat syphilis. A trademark is "Salvarsan." [ARS(ENIC) + PHEN(YL) + AMINE.]

art[1] (ärt) *n.* **1.** Human effort to imitate, supplement, alter, or counteract the work of nature. **2.** The conscious production or arrangement of sounds, colors, forms, words, movements, or other elements in a manner that affects the sense of beauty; especially, the production of the beautiful in a graphic or plastic medium, for example, painting and sculpture. **3.** The product of these activities; human works of beauty, collectively. Also used adjectivally: *an art exhibition.* **4.** High quality of conception or execution, as found in works of beauty; aesthetic value. **5.** Any field or category of art, such as music, ballet, or literature. **6. arts.** Nonscientific branches of learning, for example, languages or philosophy. **7. a.** A system of principles and methods employed in the performance of a set of activities: *the art of building.* **b.** A trade or craft that applies such a system of principles and methods: *pursuing the baker's art.* **8.** Any skill or faculty, whether acquired by study and practice or based on intuition: *the art of conversation.* **9. a.** *Usually* **arts.** Artful devices; stratagems; tricks. **b.** Artfulness; contrivance; cunning. **10.** *Print-*

ing. Illustrative material as distinguished from text. **—get something down to a fine art.** To become skilled at doing something through constant repetition or practice. [Middle English, from Old French, from Latin *ars* (stem *art-*).]

art². *Archaic.* Second person singular, present indicative of **be.** Used with *thou.*

–art. Variant of **-ard.**

art. 1. article. 2. artificial. 3. artillery.

Ar·taud (är-tō'), **Antonin** (1896–1948). French poet and dramatist. His view that the theater ought to harrow and disquiet the audience was put forward in two treatises, *Manifesto of the Theater of Cruelty* (1932) and *The Theater and its Double* (1938). His own plays were unsuccessful, but his theories had a great influence on the generation of dramatists of the absurd.

art de·co (dĕk'ō) *n. Sometimes* **Art Deco.** A style of decoration and architecture popular in the 1920's and 1930's, characterized by bold geometrical and rectilinear shapes and the use of man-made materials, such as plastic and steel. [Shortened from French *arts décoratifs,* decorative arts.]

artefact. Variant of **artifact.**

ar·tel (är-tĕl') *n.* A cooperative enterprise of industrial or agricultural workers in the U.S.S.R. [Russian *artel',* from Italian *artieri,* plural of *artiere,* artisan, from *arte,* art, work, from Latin *ars* (stem *art-*).]

Ar·te·mis (är'tə-mĭs). *Greek Mythology.* The virgin goddess of the hunt and the moon, and twin sister of Apollo. Identified with the Roman goddess Diana.

ar·te·mis·i·a (är'tə-mĭzh'ē-ə, -mĭz'ē-ə) *n.* Any of various plants of the genus *Artemisia,* which includes sagebrush and wormwood. [Middle English, from Latin, from Greek, "plant sacred to Artemis," from ARTEMIS.]

ar·te·ri·al (är-tîr'ē-əl) *adj.* 1. Of, like, or in an artery or arteries. 2. Of or designating the blood in the arteries that has absorbed oxygen in the lungs and is bright red. 3. Of or designating a route in a transport or communications system carrying a main flow and having many branches. **—ar·te·ri·al·ly** *adv.*

ar·te·ri·al·ize (är-tîr'ē-əl-īz') *tr.v.* **-ized, -izing, -izes.** To convert (venous blood) into arterial blood by absorption of oxygen in the lungs. **—ar·te·ri·al·i·za·tion** *n.*

arterio-, arter– *prefix.* Indicates an artery or the arteries; for example, **arteriosclerosis.** [Greek *artērio-,* from *artēria,* ARTERY.]

ar·te·ri·og·ra·phy (är-tîr'ē-ŏg'rə-fē) *n.* The x-ray examination of an artery that has been injected with a radiopaque substance. **—ar·te·ri·o·gram** (är-tîr'ē-ə-grăm') *n.* **—ar·te·ri·o·graph·ic** *adj.*

ar·te·ri·ole (är-tîr'ē-ōl') *n. Anatomy.* One of the small terminal branches of an artery that subdivides into capillaries. [New Latin *arteriola,* diminutive of Latin *artēria,* ARTERY.] **—ar·te·ri·o·lar** (är-tîr'ē-ō'lär', -lər) *adj.*

ar·te·ri·o·scle·ro·sis (är-tîr'ē-ō-sklə-rō'sĭs) *n.* A chronic disease in which thickening and hardening of arterial walls interferes with blood circulation. Also called "hardening of the arteries." [ARTERIO- + SCLEROSIS.] **—ar·te·ri·o·scle·rot·ic** (är-tîr'ē-ō-sklə-rŏt'ĭk) *adj.*

ar·te·ri·o·ve·nous (är-tîr'ē-ō-vē'nəs) *adj.* Of, pertaining to, or connecting the arteries and veins.

ar·te·ri·tis (är'tə-rī'tĭs) *n.* Inflammation of an artery. [ARTER(IO)- + -ITIS.]

ar·ter·y (är'tər-ē) *n., pl.* **-ies.** 1. *Anatomy.* Any of a branching system of muscular tubes that carry blood away from the heart. 2. A major route in a transportation or communications system, which local routes join. [Middle English *arterie,* from Latin *artēria,* from Greek; probably related to *airein,* to raise.]

ar·te·sian well (är-tē'zhən) *n.* A well drilled through impermeable strata to reach water capable of rising to the surface by internal hydrostatic pressure. [French *(puit) artésien,* (well) of Artois (former French province), where such wells were first drilled.]

art form *n.* Any activity that can be considered as a medium of artistic expression.

art·ful (ärt'fəl) *adj.* 1. Deceitful or tricky; cunning; crafty. 2. Having or showing skill, especially in finding the means to an end; clever; ingenious. 3. Exhibiting art or technical skill. 4. *Archaic.* Artificial. —See Synonyms at **sly.** **—art·ful·ly** *adv.* **—art·ful·ness** *n.*

Artful Dodger *n.* A person who manages to escape from difficulties, usually in an ingenious and engaging way. [After the young pickpocket in Dickens's novel *Oliver Twist* (1838).]

ar·thral·gia (är-thrăl'jə, -jē-ə) *n.* Pain in a joint. [ARTHR(O)- + -ALGIA.] **—ar·thral·gic** *adj.*

ar·thri·tis (är-thrī'tĭs) *n.* Inflammation of a joint or joints, producing pain and stiffness. See **osteoarthritis, rheumatoid arthritis.** [Latin, from Greek: ARTHR(O)- + -ITIS.] **—ar·thrit·ic** (är-thrĭt'ĭk) *adj. & n.*

arthro-, arthr– *prefix.* Indicates joint; for example, **arthropod, arthritis.** [Greek *arthron.*]

ar·thro·mere (är'thrə-mîr') *n.* One of the body segments of an arthropod. [ARTHRO- + -MERE.] **—ar·thro·mer·ic** (är'thrə-měr'ĭk, -mîr'ĭk) *adj.*

ar·throp·a·thy (är-thrŏp'ə-thē) *n.* Any disease of a joint. [ARTHRO- + -PATHY.]

ar·thro·pod (är'thrə-pŏd') *n.* Any of numerous invertebrate organisms of the phylum Arthropoda, which includes the insects, crustaceans, arachnids, millipedes, and centipedes, having a horny, segmented external covering and jointed limbs. [New Latin *Ar-*

thropoda : ARTHRO- + -POD.] **—ar·throp·o·dous** (är-thrŏp'ə-dəs), **ar·throp·o·dal** *adj.*

ar·thro·sis (är-thrō'sĭs) *n., pl.* **-ses** (-sēz'). 1. A connection or joint between bones. 2. A degenerative process in a joint. [New Latin, from Greek *anthrosis:* ARTHR(O)- + -OSIS.]

ar·thro·spore (är'thrə-spôr', -spōr') *n. Botany.* A sporelike cell characteristic of segmented filamentous fungi or certain algae. [ARTHRO- + SPORE.] **—ar·thro·spor·ic, ar·thro·spor·ous** *adj.*

---

art deco

MASS-MARKET MODERNISM
Bright colors, bold designs, and manmade material

Art deco sprang, like jazz, from the mood of its age. It was confident and brash and a powerful reaction against the ornateness and tradition in art that existed before World War I. The name came from a Paris exhibition of decorative arts in 1925. The influences were cubism and the Fauvists—the bold colorists led by Matisse. The style was simple and geometric, inspired by tribal art and Egyptian motifs uncovered in 1922 in Tutankhamen's tomb. The materials, popularized by the avant-garde designers at the Bauhaus in Dessau, Germany, were manmade—glass, plastic, metal—and the products were unashamedly for a mass market.

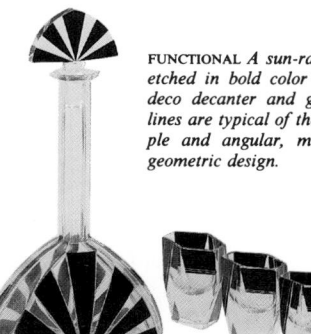

FUNCTIONAL *A sun-ray pattern is etched in bold color on this art deco decanter and glasses. The lines are typical of the style, simple and angular, matching the geometric design.*

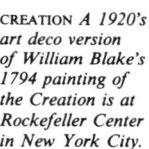

CREATION *A 1920's art deco version of William Blake's 1794 painting of the Creation is at Rockefeller Center in New York City.*

A FIGURINE REVOLUTION *Bold geometric designs gave a new look to 1920's figurines, as in Gerdago's ivory dancer (1925).*

MASS PRODUCTION *A major influence was the need for items that could be mass-produced. This lady's cigarette case, in enamel on silver, is an example.*

AMBITIOUS SWIRLS *Gunta Stolzl, one of the trend-setting Bauhaus group, whose original ideas gave such impetus to the art deco movement, wove this tapestry (1927–29). Its geometric shapes form complex swirls of striking colors.*

Arthurian legend

THE KING FROM CAMELOT

How the legend of Arthur and the Round Table grew through the centuries

Most modern historians agree that the British hero Arthur did exist, but he may not have been a king. He was probably a cavalry chieftain who defeated invading Saxons in the 6th century. The tales of his prowess spread. He was first written about in the 10th-century Welsh chronicles, *Annales Cambriae*. Stories of Arthur were embroidered by Geoffrey of Monmouth in his 12th-century *History of the Kings of Britain*.

Geoffrey makes Arthur a great king who won many famous victories and held court at Camelot. The site of Camelot is uncertain but may have been Cadbury Castle, near Yeovil, Somerset. Called to fight in Rome, Arthur left his nephew Modred to guard the kingdom, but

Modred betrayed his trust and abducted Arthur's queen, Guinevere. When Arthur returned he defeated Modred in battle but was mortally wounded. He was taken to the sacred Isle of Avalon to be healed.

Breton minstrels brought the story of Arthur to Europe. Local legends were added to it and French writers worked in new themes, including the Round Table, a means of avoiding disputes over precedence among the knights. Also added were the stories of Sir Lancelot and Guinevere and of the Holy Grail, the chalice from the Last Supper in which Christ's blood was preserved. The legend of Arthur ends with the prediction that he will one day return and rule England.

EXCALIBUR *Magic played a great part in the legends of King Arthur. This 13th-century French illumination shows Arthur proving his right to the kingdom by pulling the sword Excalibur from an anvil when others had failed.*

HOLY GRAIL *The legend combined with religious themes in the 12th century. A woman bears the Grail, which Galahad set out to find.*

MAGIC ARM *As Arthur dies, Bedivere throws Excalibur into a lake, to be caught by a mysterious arm.*

Ar·thur (är′thər). Legendary British king of the 6th century A.D., whose court was at Camelot.

Arthur, Chester Alan (1830–86). 21st U.S. president (1881–85). Known as a staunch defender of the spoils system, Arthur became vice president in 1881. He became president on September 19, 1881, after James A. Garfield's assassination, and to everyone's surprise supported the 1883 Pendleton Act that created the Civil Service Commission to regulate federal appointments.

Ar·thu·ri·an (är-thŏor′ē-ən) *adj.* Of or pertaining to King Arthur and his Knights of the Round Table: *Arthurian legends.*

ar·ti·choke (är′tə-chōk′) *n.* **1.** A thistlelike plant, *Cynara scolymus,* having a large flower head with numerous fleshy, scalelike bracts. **2.** The unopened flower head of this plant, cooked and eaten as a vegetable. Also called "globe artichoke." **3.** The **Jerusalem artichoke** (see). [Italian (northern dialect) *articiocco, arciciocco,* alteration of *arcicioffo,* from Old Spanish *alcarchofa,* from Arabic *al-kharshūf,* the artichoke.]

ar·ti·cle (är′tĭ-kəl) *n. Abbr.* **art. 1.** An individual thing belonging to a class; an item: *an article of clothing.* **2.** A piece of material goods or property. **3.** A particular section or item of a series in a document, such as a contract, constitution, or creed: *the Articles of Confederation.* **4.** A nonfictional literary composition that forms an independent part of a publication, as of a newspaper, magazine, or reference work. **5.** *Grammar.* Any of a class of words used to signal nouns and to specify their application. In English, the articles are *a* and *an* (indefinite articles) and *the* (definite article). **6.** A specific part or detail; a particular.
—*tr.v.* **articled, -cling, -cles. 1.** To bind, as for a period of training or apprenticeship, by articles set forth in a contract: *an articled clerk.* **2.** *Archaic.* To make specific or formal charges against; accuse. [Middle English, from Old French, from Latin *articulus,* small joint, division, part, diminutive of *artus,* joint.]

article of faith *n.* **1.** A belief that is an essential part of a church's creed. **2.** Any deeply held conviction.

articles of association *pl.n.* **1.** The set of rules by which a registered company is administered. **2.** The document in which these rules are set down, which must by law be open to public inspection.

Articles of Confederation *pl.n.* The first constitution of the United States, adopted by the original 13 states in 1781 and lasting until 1788 when the present Constitution was ratified.

ar·tic·u·lar (är-tĭk′yə-lər) *adj.* Of or pertaining to a joint or joints. [Middle English *articuler,* from Latin *articulāris,* from *articulus,* small joint, ARTICLE.] —**ar·tic·u·lar·ly** *adv.*

ar·tic·u·late (är-tĭk′yə-lĭt) *adj.* **1.** Capable of, speaking in, or characterized by clear, expressive language. **2.** Spoken in or divided into clear and distinct words or syllables. **3.** Endowed with the power of speech. **4.** *Biology.* Having joints or segments.
—*v.* (är-tĭk′yə-lāt′) **articulated, -lating, -lates.** —*tr.* **1.** To utter (a speech sound or sounds) by moving the necessary organs of speech. **2.** To pronounce distinctly and carefully; enunciate. **3.** To express in coherent verbal form; give words to (an emotion, for example). **4.** To unite by means of a joint or joints. —*intr.* **1.** To utter a speech sound or sounds. **2.** To speak clearly and distinctly. **3.** To form a joint; be jointed. [Latin *articulātus,* jointed, distinct, past participle of *articulāre,* to divide into joints, utter distinctly, from *articulus,* small joint, ARTICLE.] —**ar·tic·u·late·ly** *adv.* —**ar·tic·u·late·ness** *n.*

ar·tic·u·la·tion (är-tĭk′yə-lā′shən) *n.* **1.** The act or process of speaking. **2.** *Phonetics.* **a.** The movements of speech organs employed in producing a particular speech sound. **b.** Any speech sound, especially a consonant. **3. a.** A jointing together or an instance of being jointed together. **b.** The method or manner of jointing. **4.** *Zoology.* **a.** A joint between bones, or between movable parts of an outside shell. **b.** The manner in which jointed parts are connected. **5.** *Botany.* **a.** A joint between two separable parts, such as a leaf and a stem. **b.** A node, or a space on a stem between two nodes. —See Synonyms at **diction.** —**ar·tic·u·la·tive** (är-tĭk′yə-lə-tĭv, -lā′tĭv), **ar·tic·u·la·to·ry** (är-tĭk′yə-lə-tôr′ē, -tōr′ē) *adj.*

ar·tic·u·la·tor (är-tĭk′yə-lā′tər) *n.* **1.** A person or thing that articulates. **2.** *Phonetics.* An organ used in producing speech sounds, such as the tongue, lips, hard palate, or glottis.

ar·ti·fact (är′tə-făkt′) *n.* Also **ar·te·fact. 1.** An object produced or shaped by human workmanship; especially, a simple tool, weapon, or ornament of archaeological or historical interest. **2.** *Biology.* A structure or substance not normally present, but produced by some external agency or action; especially, a structure seen in a microscopic specimen after fixation that is not present in the living tissue. [Latin *arte,* by skill, ablative or *ars,* ART + *factum,* something made, from past participle of *facere,* to make.]

ar·ti·fice (är′tə-fĭs) *n.* **1.** A crafty expedient; an artful device or stratagem. **2.** Subtle but base deception; trickery. **3.** Ingenuity; cleverness; skill. [French, from Old French, craftsmanship, from Latin *artificium,* from *artifex,* craftsman : *ars* (stem *art-*), ART + *-fex,* -maker, from *facere,* to make.]
      Synonyms: *dodge, feint, finesse, guile, maneuver, ruse, stratagem, subterfuge, trick, wile.*

ar·tif·i·cer (är-tĭf′ə-sər) *n.* **1.** A skilled worker; a craftsman. **2.** One that contrives, devises, or constructs something: *"The labyrinth . . . was built by Daedalus, a most skilled artificer"* (Thomas Bulfinch).

ar·ti·fi·cial (är′tə-fĭsh′əl) *adj. Abbr.* **art. 1.** Made by man, rather than occurring in nature. **2.** Made in imitation of something natural. **3.** Feigned; pretended. **4.** Affected; forced. [Middle English, from Old French, from Latin *artificiālis,* from *artificium,* ARTIFICE.]

—ar·ti·fi·ci·al·i·ty (är′tə-físh′ē-ăl′ə-tē) n. —ar·ti·fi·cial·ly adv.
Synonyms: counterfeit, ersatz, simulated, synthetic.

artificial cinnabar n. Chemistry. **Mercuric sulfide** (see).

artificial horizon n. **1.** A gyroscopic instrument displaying a line on a flight indicator that lies within the horizontal plane, and about which the pitching and banking movements of an airplane are shown. **2.** A level reflecting surface, such as a dish of mercury, used with a sextant on land to establish a horizontal reference in a navigational or astronomical instrument.

artificial insemination n. Abbr. **A.I.** The introduction of semen into the female reproductive organs by means other than sexual contact.

artificial intelligence n. Abbr. **A.I.** The branch of computer science concerned with ways of programming and designing computers to mimic human mechanisms of reasoning.

artificial kidney n. A **kidney machine** (see).

artificial respiration n. Any of various methods for restoring normal breathing in an asphyxiated but living person, usually through rhythmic forcing of air into and out of the lungs by means of mouth-to-mouth breathing or manual pressure on the chest.

artificial satellite n. Aerospace. A man-made **satellite** (see).

artificial silk n. Rayon (see).

ar·til·ler·ist (är-tĭl′ər-ĭst) n. An artilleryman; a gunner.

ar·til·ler·y (är-tĭl′ər-ē) n. Abbr. **art., arty. 1.** Large-caliber firing weapons, such as howitzers, cannons, and missile launchers on suitable mounts, which are served by crews. **2.** Troops armed with such guns. **3.** The branch of an armed force that specializes in the use of large, mounted guns. **4.** The science of the use of guns; gunnery. **5.** Catapults, crossbows, slings, and similar devices for discharging missiles. [Middle English artil(le)rie, from Old French artillerie, from artillier, alteration (influenced by art, ART) of atillier, to fortify, arm, from Latin apticulāre (unattested), from aptāre, to fit, adapt, from aptus, fitting, APT.]

ar·til·ler·y·man (är-tĭl′ər-ē-mən) n., pl. **-men** (-mĭn). A soldier in the artillery.

ar·ti·o·dac·tyl (är′tē-ō-dăk′təl) n. Any of various hoofed mammals of the order Artiodactyla, which includes cattle, deer, camels, and hippopotamuses, having an even number of toes, either two or four, on each foot. [New Latin Artiodactyla, "the even-toed ones" : Greek artios, even, matching + DACTYL.] —ar·ti·o·dac·tyl, ar·ti·o·dac·ty·lous adj.

ar·ti·san (är′tə-zən, -sən) n. A skilled manual worker; a craftsman. [Old French, from Italian artigiano, from Vulgar Latin artitiānus (unattested), a skilled laborer, from Latin artītus, skilled in arts, from artīre, to instruct in the arts, from ars (stem art-), ART.]

art·ist (är′tĭst) n. **1.** One who creates works of art; especially, a painter or sculptor. **2.** Anyone whose work shows skill, imagination, or other artistic qualities. **3.** An artiste. **4.** Slang. One who is adept at, or keen on, a particular activity: a con artist. [Old French artiste, from Italian artista, one skilled in the arts, from arte, ART.]

ar·tiste (är-tēst′) n. A public performer or entertainer, especially a singer or dancer. [French, from Old French, ARTIST.]

ar·tis·tic (är-tĭs′tĭk) adj. **1.** Of, relating to, or befitting art or artists. **2.** Appreciative of or sensitive to art or beauty. —ar·tis·ti·cal·ly adv.

art·ist·ry (är′tĭs-trē) n. Artistic ability, quality, or workmanship.

art·less (ärt′lĭs) adj. **1.** Without guile, cunning, or deceit; ingenuous; naive. **2.** Free of artificiality; natural; simple. **3.** Lacking art or skill; crude. **4.** Uncultured; ignorant. —art·less·ly adv. —art·less·ness n.

art nou·veau (ärt nōō-vō′) n. Sometimes **Art Nouveau.** A style of decoration and architecture first current in the 1890's, characterized particularly by depiction of leaves and flowers in sinuous, flowing lines. [French, "new art."]

art·sy-craft·sy (ärt′sē-krăft′sē, -kräft′-) adj. Also **art·y-craft·y** (är′tē-krăf′tē, -kräf′-). Informal. **1.** Decorative rather than useful or comfortable: artsy-craftsy furniture. **2.** Pretentiously or self-consciously artistic.

art·work (ärt′wûrk′) n. **1.** Work in the graphic or plastic arts; especially, small handmade decorative or artistic objects. **2.** Printing. The illustrative and decorative matter in a publication, as opposed to the text.

art·y (är′tē) adj. **-ier, -iest.** Also **art·sy** (ärt′sē). Informal. Showy or affected in trying to appear artistic. —art·i·ly adv. —art·i·ness n.

A·ru·ba (ə-rōō′bə). A self-governing island of the Netherlands, in the Leeward Islands off the coast of Venezuela. Tourism and the refining of Venezuelan oil are the major industries.

ar·um (âr′əm) n. **1.** Any of various plants of the genus Arum, such as the cuckoopint, having arrow-shaped leaves and small flowers on a spadix surrounded by or enclosed within a spathe. **2.** Any of several similar or related plants, such as the **calla** (see). In this sense, also called "arum lily." [New Latin Arum, from Latin arum, cuckoopint, from Greek aron†.]

a·run·di·na·ceous (ə-rŭn′də-nā′shəs) adj. Of, pertaining to, or resembling a reed; reedlike. [Latin arundināceus, from (h)arundō†, reed.]

aruspex. Variant of haruspex.

-ary suffix. Indicates of, engaged in, or connected with; for example, **functionary, parliamentary, reactionary.** [Middle English -arie, from Old French -arie, -aire, from Latin -ārius, -āria, -ārium, noun suffixes, from -ārius, adjective suffix.]

Ar·y·an (âr′ē-ən) n. Also **Ar·i·an. 1.** A member of the prehistoric people that spoke Proto-Indo-European. **2.** A member of any of the peoples descended from this people; especially, any speaker of an Indic or Iranian language. **3.** Proto-Indo-European, or a language

---

art nouveau

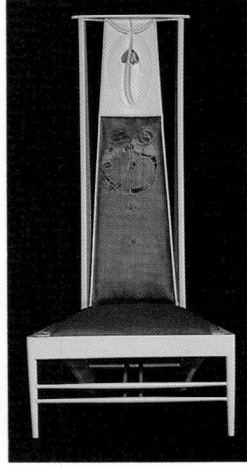

THE "NEW ART" OF 1900
A style of flowing lines and ornamental motifs

Art nouveau, and its successor art deco, were both modernist trends that reacted against the emphasis in 19th-century art on history and tradition.

The new style aimed to produce designs of high esthetic quality suitable for machine production. It was characterized by organic forms based on flowers and the human body.

The leading exponents included the English illustrator Aubrey Beardsley (1872–98); the Scottish architect and designer Charles Rennie Mackintosh (1868–1928); the Belgian architect and designer Victor Horta (1861–1947); the Spanish architect Antonio Gaudi (1852–1926); the Austrian artist Gustav Klimt (1868–1910); and the French glassmakers René Lalique (1860–1945) and Emile Gallé (1846–1904).

FRENCH The wrought-iron railings at the entrance to the Louvre metro station in Paris were designed by Hector Guimard (1867–1942).

ENGLISH A silver box made for the English store Liberty & Co. about 1900. It is an art nouveau version of a traditional Celtic design.

SCOTTISH A tall-backed chair, designed in 1902. Its white-painted woodwork and flower pattern is typical of Charles Rennie Mackintosh's work.

SPANISH Casa Battló in Barcelona (1905) was designed by the architect Antonio Gaudí. Although Gaudí developed his own style, the curving lines are characteristically art nouveau.

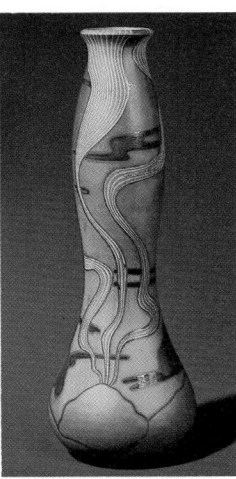

HUNGARIAN An elongated, curved, glazed stoneware vase designed by the Hungarian artist Jozsef Rippl-Rónai (1861–1927) about 1890.

ENGLISH The flowing pattern of leaves and flowers is typical of the textile and wallpaper designs of William Morris (1834–96).

AUSTRIAN Gustav Klimt was a leading art nouveau painter. In Salome (1909) elaborate patterns and gold leaf enhance the sensuality of the skin.

or language group descended from it, especially Indo-Aryan. **4.** In Nazi ideology, a Caucasian gentile, especially of Nordic type.
~adj. Of or pertaining to Aryans or their culture or language. [Sanskrit *ārya* (adjective and noun), noble, Aryan.]

ar·yl (ăr′əl) *n. Chemistry.* **1.** A radical or group derived from an aromatic hydrocarbon by removal of a hydrogen atom, for example, the phenyl group C_6H_5. **2.** An organometallic compound in which a metal atom is directly bound to an aryl group. [AR(OMATIC) + -YL.]

ar·y·te·noid (ăr′ə-tē′noid′, ə-rĭt′n-oid′) *adj. Anatomy.* **1.** Of, pertaining to, or designating either of two small cartilages attached to the back of the larynx and to the vocal cords. **2.** Of, pertaining to, or designating any of three small muscles of the larynx.
~n. An arytenoid cartilage or muscle. [New Latin *arytaenoides*, from Greek *(khondros) arutainoeidēs*, "the ladle-shaped (cartilage)" : *arutaina*, ladle, from *arueint*, to draw water + -OID.] —**ar·y·te·noi·dal** *adj.*

as¹ (ăz; *weak form* əz) *adv.* **1.** To the same extent or degree: *just as smart; twice as wide.* **2.** For instance: *large carnivores, as the bear or lion.* **3.** Considered in the specified way: *workers as distinct from management.*
~conj. **1.** To the same degree or quantity that. Often used as the consequent in correlative constructions: *as sweet as sugar; not so bad as you suggest.* **2.** In the same manner or way that: *Think as I think; treat him as you would a friend.* **3.** At the same time that; while: *As we were leaving, it began to snow.* **4.** For the reason that; since; because: *could not call as we had no phone.* **5.** Though: *Unaccustomed as I am to public speaking.* **6.** With the result that: *so changed as to be unrecognizable.* **7.** *Informal.* That: *I don't know as I can.* —**as far as.** To the extent that: *She is right, as far as I know.* —**as from** (or **of**). Starting from a specified time. —**as if** (or **though**). In the same way that it would be if. —**as is.** *Informal.* Just the way it is; without making changes.
~pron. **1.** A fact that: *He is a fool, as everyone knows.* **2.** Which also; so too: *Jean comes from California, as does her husband.* **3.** *Regional.* Who or which: *Those as want to can come with us.*
~prep. In the role, capacity, or function of: *acting as a mediator.* —**as for.** With regard to; concerning: *As for me, I prefer walking.* [Middle English *as* (adverb and conjunction), reduced form of Old English *alswā, ealswā, aelswā,* just as, likewise, ALSO.]

Usage: In positive comparisons, the double use of *as* is required: *He's as tall as I am.* In negative comparisons, traditional grammar prescribes *so . . . as* (*He's not so tall as I am*), but *as . . . as* is still widely used. Several *as* constructions are potentially ambiguous. A sentence such as *He came as I was leaving* could be interpreted to mean either "He came at the same time as I left" or "He came because I was leaving." In consequence, many speakers prefer *because* to *as* in such contexts. A similar ambiguous case is *He likes her as much as Jim,* which could mean "as much as he likes Jim" or "as much as Jim likes her." This prompts some speakers to use *I* in place of *me* in such sentences as: *He likes her as much as I (do), He likes her as much as (he likes) me.* See also **like, than.**

as² (ăs) *n., pl.* **asses** (ăs′ēz′, ăs′ĭz). **1.** An ancient Roman copper coin of low value, a quarter of a **sesterce** *(see).* **2.** A unit of weight in ancient Rome equal to about one troy pound. [Latin *ās,* a whole, unit, copper coin, perhaps from Etruscan.]

As The symbol for the element arsenic.

AS **1.** Anglo-Saxon. **2.** antisubmarine.

As. Asia; Asian.

AS., A.S. Anglo-Saxon.

ASA, A.S.A. American Standards Association (used in photography, preceded by a number, as a measurement of film speed).

as·a·fet·i·da, as·a·foet·i·da (ăs′ə-fĕt′ə-də) *n.* A yellow-brown, bitter, unpleasantly pungent resinous material obtained from the roots of several plants of the genus *Ferula,* used as a spice in oriental cuisine, and formerly used in medicine. [Middle English *asa-fetida,* from Medieval Latin *asafoetida* : *asa,* gum, from Persian *azāt,* mastic + Latin *foetida,* feminine of *foetidus,* FETID.]

a.s.a.p., asap As soon as possible.

as·a·ra·bac·ca (ăs′ə-rə-băk′ə) *n.* A creeping, perennial plant, *Asarum europaeum,* with shiny, kidney-shaped leaves and dull, purple flowers. [Alteration of obsolete *asarabacara,* from Spanish *asarabácara* : *ásaro,* ASARUM + *bácara,* clary, from Latin *baccaris,* plant with aromatic roots, from Greek *bakkaris.*]

as·a·rum (ăs′ə-rəm) *n.* The dried, strong-scented roots of the wild ginger, formerly used in medicine and as a flavoring agent. [New Latin, from Latin, wild spikenard, from Greek *asaront.*]

as·bes·tos (ăs-bĕs′təs, ăz-) *n. Abbr.* **asb.** Any of the fibrous variety of four distinct incombustible, chemical-resistant silicate minerals, used for fireproofing, electrical insulation, building materials, brake linings, and chemical filters. See **chrysotile, crocidolite.**
~adj. Of, made of, or containing asbestos. [17th century : Middle English *asbeston,* a mythical stone with unquenchable heat, from Old French, from Latin, from Greek, from *asbestos,* inextinguishable : A- (not) + *sbennunai,* to extinguish.] —**as·bes·tine** (ăs-bĕs′tĭn, -tēn′), **as·bes·tic** *adj.*

as·bes·to·sis (ăs′bĕs-tō′sĭs, ăz′-) *n.* A lung disease caused by prolonged inhalation of asbestos particles, characterized by breathlessness. [New Latin : ASBEST(OS) + -OSIS.]

as·ca·ri·a·sis (ăs′kə-rī′ə-sĭs) *n.* Infestation with nematode worms of the species *Ascaris lumbricoides,* usually in the intestines, but also in the liver, lungs, or stomach. [New Latin : Late Latin *ascaris,* ASCARID + -IASIS.]

as·ca·rid (ăs′kə-rĭd) *n.* Any of various nematode worms of the fam-

ily Ascaridae, such as the common intestinal parasite *Ascaris lumbricoides.* [Late Latin *ascaris* (stem *ascarid-*), intestinal worm, from Greek *askarist.*]

as·cend (ə-sĕnd′) *v.* **-cended, -cending, -cends.** *—intr.* **1.** To go or move upward; rise. **2.** To rise gradually. **3.** To slope upward. *—tr.* **1.** To move upward upon or along; climb. **2.** To succeed to. Used in the phrase *ascend the throne.* —See Synonyms at **rise.** [Middle English *ascenden,* from Latin *ascendere* : *ad-,* towards + *scandere,* to climb.] —**as·cend·a·ble, as·cend·i·ble** *adj.*

as·cen·dan·cy (ə-sĕn′dən-sē) *n.* Also **as·cen·den·cy** (-dəns), **as·cen·dance, as·cen·dence** (-dəns). The state of being in the ascendant; superiority or decisive advantage.

as·cen·dant (ə-sĕn′dənt) *adj.* Also **as·cen·dent. 1.** Inclining or moving upward; ascending; rising. **2.** Dominant in position or influence; superior.
~n. **1.** The position or state of being dominant or in a position of decisive advantage: *in the ascendant.* **2.** *Astrology.* The section of the zodiac that rises in the east at the time of a particular event, such as a person's birth. **3.** *Rare.* An ancestor.

as·cend·er (ə-sĕn′dər) *n.* **1.** One that ascends. **2.** *Printing.* **a.** The part of certain lower-case letters that extends above most other lower-case letters. **b.** Any letter containing such a part, as *d, f,* or *k.*

as·cend·ing (ə-sĕn′dĭng) *adj.* Moving, going, or growing upward: *a tree with ascending branches.* —**as·cend·ing·ly** *adv.*

as·cen·sion (ə-sĕn′shən) *n.* **1.** The act or process of ascending; ascent. **2.** *Astronomy.* The rising of a star above the horizon. —**the Ascension.** The ascent of Christ into heaven, celebrated on Ascension Day, the 40th day after Easter. Acts 1:9. [Middle English *ascencion,* from Latin *ascensiō* (stem *ascension-*), from *ascendere,* ASCEND.] —**as·cen·sion·al** *adj.*

As·cen·sion (ə-sĕn′shən). Island in the South Atlantic Ocean, 1,130 kilometers (700 miles) northwest of St. Helena. Britain made it a dependency of St. Helena in 1922. Rocky and barren, it has an airstrip and a U.S. tracking station.

as·cent (ə-sĕnt′) *n.* **1.** The act or process of ascending. **2.** An advancement, especially in social status. **3.** An upward slope or incline. **4.** A going back in time or genealogical succession. [17th century (Shakespeare and the King James Bible); from ASCEND (by analogy with DESCEND, DESCENT).]

as·cer·tain (ăs′ər-tān′) *tr.v.* **-tained, -taining, -tains. 1.** To discover through examination or experimentation; find out for certain. **2.** *Archaic.* To make definite. [Middle English *ascertainen,* from Old French *acertainer, acertener* : *a-,* from Latin *ad-,* to + *certain,* CERTAIN.] —**as·cer·tain·a·ble** *adj.* —**as·cer·tain·a·ble·ness** *n.* —**as·cer·tain·a·bly** *adv.* —**as·cer·tain·ment** *n.*

as·cet·ic (ə-sĕt′ĭk) *n.* A person who renounces material comforts and leads a life of austere self-discipline, especially as an act of religious devotion.
~adj. Also **as·cet·i·cal** (ə-sĕt′ĭ-kəl). Pertaining to or characteristic of an ascetic; self-denying; austere. —See Synonyms at **severe.** [Greek *askētikos,* from *askētēs,* hermit, "one who exercises (self-discipline)", from *askeint,* to exercise.] —**as·cet·i·cal·ly** *adv.*

as·cet·i·cism (ə-sĕt′ə-sĭz′əm) *n.* **1.** Ascetic practice or discipline. **2.** A doctrine or theory supporting this practice, such as the belief that the ascetic life releases the soul from bondage to the body and permits union with the divine.

Asch (äsh), **Sholem** or **Shalom** (1880–1957). Polish writer who wrote in modern Yiddish. A prolific novelist, his most controversial works were those in which he sought to reconcile Judaism and Christianity: *The Nazarene* (1939), *The Apostle* (1943), *Mary* (1949), and *The Prophet* (1955). He lived in the United States from 1909 until 1956, then in Israel until his death.

As·cham (ăs′kəm), **Roger** (1515–68). English humanist scholar. Latin secretary to Edward VI, Mary I, and Elizabeth I, his historical importance rests largely on his advocacy of the use of the vernacular in literature.

as·cid·i·an (ə-sĭd′ē-ən) *n.* Any of various saclike marine animals of the class Ascidiacea, which includes the sea squirts.
~adj. Of or belonging to the Ascidiacea. [New Latin *Ascidia* (genus name), from Greek *askidion,* little wineskin, from *askost,* wineskin. See **ascus.**]

as·cid·i·um (ə-sĭd′ē-əm) *n., pl.* **-ia** (-ē-ə). *Botany.* A sac-shaped or bottle-shaped part or organ, such as a leaf of a pitcher plant. [New Latin, from Greek *askidion,* little wineskin, from *askost,* wineskin. See **ascus.**]

as·ci·tes (ə-sī′tēz) *n.* An abnormal accumulation of serous fluid in the abdominal cavity. [Middle English *aschytes,* from Late Latin *ascītēs,* from Greek *askītēs,* from *askost,* bag, belly. See **ascus.**] —**as·cit·ic** (ə-sĭt′ĭk), **as·cit·i·cal** *adj.*

As·cle·pi·us (ə-sklē′pē-əs). *Greek Mythology.* Apollo's son, the god of medicine, identified with the Roman god Aesculapius.

asco- *prefix.* Indicates a saclike or bladderlike part; for example, **ascospore.** [New Latin, from Greek *askost,* bag, bladder. See **ascus.**]

as·co·carp (ăs′kə-kärp′) *n. Botany.* A globular structure containing the spore sacs of ascomycetous fungi. [ASCO- + -CARP.] —**as·co·car·pous** *adj.*

as·co·go·ni·um (ăs′kə-gō′nē-əm) *n., pl.* **-nia** (-nē-ə). *Botany.* A female reproductive structure of certain fungi. [New Latin : ASCO- + -GONIUM.] —**as·co·go·ni·al** *adj.*

as·co·my·cete (ăs′kō-mī′sēt′, -mĭ-sēt′) *n. Botany.* Any of numerous fungi that produce spores in a saclike structure, or ascus. [New

Latin *Ascomycetes* : ASCO- + -MYCETE.] —**as·co·my·ce·tous** (ăs'-kō-mī-sē'təs) *adj.*

a·scor·bic acid (ə-skôr'bĭk) *n.* A white, crystalline vitamin, $C_6H_8O_6$, found in citrus fruits, tomatoes, potatoes, and leafy green vegetables. It is used to prevent scurvy. Also called "vitamin C." [A- (not) + SCORB(UT)IC.]

as·co·spore (ăs'kə-spôr', -spōr') *n. Botany.* A sexual spore formed in an ascus. —**as·co·spo·rous** (ăs'kə-spôr'əs, -spōr'-), **as·co·spo·ric** (ăs'kə-spôr'ĭk, -spōr'-) *adj.*

as·cot (ăs'kət, -kŏt') *n.* A kind of scarf or necktie, knotted so that its broad ends are laid flat upon each other. [After *Ascot*, Berkshire, where it was probably first worn.]

As·cot (ăs'kət) A village in Berkshire, in southern England. The Royal Ascot meeting, a week of horse races on Ascot Heath, was begun by Queen Anne in 1711.

as·cribe (ə-skrīb') *tr.v.* **-cribed, -crib·ing, -cribes.** **1.** To attribute to a specified cause, source, author: *The Iliad is ascribed to Homer.* **2.** To assign as a quality or characteristic. —See Synonyms at **attribute.** [Middle English *ascriben,* from Latin *ascrībere,* to add to in writing : *ad-,* in addition + *scrībere,* to write.] —**as·crib·a·ble** *adj.*

as·crip·tion (ə-skrĭp'shən) *n.* **1.** The act of ascribing. **2.** A statement that ascribes. [Latin *ascrīptiō,* from *ascrībere,* ASCRIBE.]

as·cus (ăs'kəs) *n., pl.* **asci** (ăs'ī, -kī') *Botany.* A saclike structure in certain fungi, containing ascospores. [New Latin, from Greek *askos†,* wineskin, bag, bladder, belly.]

as·dic (ăz'dĭk) *n.* A sonar device used in antisubmarine warfare. [*A*nti-*S*ubmarine *D*etection *I*nvestigation *C*ommittee.]

-ase *suffix. Chemistry.* Indicates an enzyme; for example, **amylase.** [Diast*ase.*]

a·sea (ə-sē') *adv.* Toward or on the sea; at sea.

ASEAN Association of Southeast Asian Nations.

a·seis·mic (ā-sīz'mĭk) *adj.* Having no earthquakes: *an aseismic region.*

a·sep·sis (ā-sĕp'sĭs) *n.* The state of being free of pathogenic organisms. Compare **antisepsis.** [A- (without) + SEPSIS.]

a·sep·tic (ā-sĕp'tĭk) *adj.* **1.** Of or pertaining to asepsis. **2.** Lacking animation or emotion: *an aseptic smile.* [A- (not) + SEPTIC.]

a·sex·u·al (ā-sĕk'shōo-əl) *adj.* **1.** Having no evident sex or sex organs; sexless. **2.** Pertaining to or characterizing reproduction involving a single individual, and without male or female gametes, as in binary fission or budding. **3.** Having no apparent interest in or desire for sex. [A- (not) + SEXUAL.] —**a·sex·u·al·i·ty** (ā-sĕk'shōo-ăl'ə-tē) *n.* —**a·sex·u·al·ly** *adv.*

As·gard (ăs'gärd, äz'-). Also **As·garth** (-gärth), **As·gar·dhr** (-gär'thr'). *Norse Mythology.* The heavenly residence of the gods and slain heroes of war.

asgmt. assignment.

ash¹ (ăsh) *n.* **1.** The soft, powdery, grayish-white to black residue left over when something is burnt. **2.** *Geology.* Pulverized particulate matter ejected by volcanic eruption. **3. ashes.** Ruins: *Bombs reduced the town to ashes.* **4. ashes.** Human remains, especially after cremation. [Middle English *asshe,* Old English *asce, æsce.*]

ash² *n.* **1.** Any of various trees of the genus *Fraxinus;* especially, *F. excelsior,* having compound leaves, clusters of small greenish flowers, and winged seeds. **2.** The durable, close-grained, elastic wood of any of these trees. Compare **mountain ash.** [Middle English *asshe,* Old English *æsc.*]

ash³ *n.* The alphabetical digraph (æ) used especially in Old English. [Old English *æsc,* the name of the letter in the runic alphabet.]

a·shamed (ə-shāmd') *adj.* **1.** Feeling shame or guilt. **2.** Reluctant through fear of resulting humiliation or shame: *Don't be ashamed to ask for help.* **3.** Feeling inferior, inadequate, or embarrassed: *ashamed of her torn coat.* [Middle English, Old English *āscamod,* past participle of *āscamian,* to feel shame : *ā-,* intensive + *scamian,* to be ashamed.] —**a·sham·ed·ly** (ə-shā'mĭd-lē) *adv.* —**a·sham·ed·ness** (ə-shā'mĭd-nĭs) *n.*

A·shan·ti¹ (ə-shăn'tē, -shän'-) An ancient powerful kingdom of the Ashanti people of Africa. It was annexed to the British Gold Coast colony in 1901, and is now an administrative region of Ghana, with Kumasi as the capital.

Ashanti² *n., pl.* **-tis** or collectively **Ashanti.** **1.** An inhabitant of Ashanti. **2.** A dialect of **Twi** *(see),* spoken by the Ashantis.

ash blonde *adj.* Very fair or pale blonde.

ash can *n.* A large metal receptacle for trash.

Ashe (ăsh), **Arthur Robert** (1943-). American tennis player. He was the first black to win the United States championship (1968) and the Wimbledon championship (1975). He also won the Australian championship (1970).

ash·en¹ (ăsh'ən) *adj.* **1.** Consisting of ashes. **2.** Resembling ashes in color; very pale: *Her face was ashen with grief.*

ashen² *adj.* Of, pertaining to, or made from the wood of the ash tree.

Ash·er¹ (ăsh'ər). A son of Jacob. Genesis 49:20.

Asher² *n.* The tribe of Israel descended from Asher.

ash·et (ăsh'ĭt) *n. Scottish.* A large plate or serving dish. [French *assiette,* a seating of guests at dinner, hence, course, dish, from Old French *assedita* (unattested), a sitting, seating, from Latin *assiditus,* past participle of *assidēre,* to sit by, from *ad-* at, by + *sedēre,* to sit.]

Ash·ke·lon or **Ash·qe·lon** (ăsh'kə-lŏn'). Site of an ancient city in southwestern Israel. Herod greatly enlarged the city and built fine public buildings, many of which have been excavated in the 20th century. It was destroyed by Saladin in 1270.

Ash·ke·na·zi (ăsh'kə-nä'zē) *n., pl.* **-nazim** (-nä'zīm). A central or eastern European Jew, generally Yiddish-speaking. Compare **Sephardi.** —**Ash·ke·na·zic** *adj.*

Ash·ke·na·zy (ăsh'kə-nä'zē), **Vladimir Davidovich** (1937-). Russian-born pianist and conductor. He is noted especially for his interpretations of the 19th-century masters. He took Icelandic nationality in 1972.

ash-key (ăsh'kē') *n.* The winged seed of the ash tree. [After its keylike shape.]

Ash·kha·bad (ăsh'kə-băd', -bäd'). The capital of Turkmenistan, situated in a fertile oasis. After an earthquake in 1948 the city had to be almost entirely rebuilt.

ash·lar, ash·ler (ăsh'lər) *n.* **1.** A squared block of building stone. **2.** Masonry of such stones. **3.** A thin, dressed rectangle of stone for facing walls. In this sense, also called "ashlar veneer." [Middle English *asheler,* from Old French *aisselier,* beam, from Latin *axilla,* diminutive of *axis,* board, plank, probably variant of *assis,* akin to *assert,* beam.]

ash-leaved maple (ăsh'lēvd') *n.* A tree, the **box-elder** *(see).*

Ash·ley (ăsh'lē), **Laura** (1925-85). British designer. Ashley's designs for clothing, fabrics, linens, and household appurtenances evoked the English countryside and the Welsh retreat where she established a studio and school.

a·shore (ə-shôr', ə-shōr') *adv.* **1.** Toward or on the shore. **2.** On land; aground.

ash·plant (ăsh'plănt') *n.* A staff or walking stick made from an ash sapling.

Ashqelon. See **Ashkelon.**

ash·ram (ăsh'rəm, -räm') *n.* **1.** A Hindu religious retreat or hermitage. **2.** Loosely, the meeting place of any eastern religious community. [Sanskrit *āśrama,* from *ā,* toward + *śrama,* religious training.]

Ash Sham. See **Damascus.**

Ash·ton (ăsh'tən), **Sir Frederick William Mallandaine** (1904-89). British dancer and choreographer, born in Ecuador. He joined the Vic-Wells (later Royal) Ballet in 1935 and made his name as a mime and character dancer. His ballets include *The Dream* (1964) and *A Month in the Country* (1976). He was director of the Royal Ballet from 1963 to 1970.

Ash·to·reth (ăsh'tə-rĕth'). The ancient Syrian and Phoenician goddess of sexual love and fertility. Identified with Astarte.

ash·tray (ăsh'trā') *n.* A receptacle for tobacco ashes.

A·shur¹ (ä'shōor'). Town on the banks of the Tigris River, in northern Iraq. It was the religious capital of Assyria in ancient times, when it was known as Qal'at Shargat. The town was destroyed by the Babylonians in 614 B.C.

A·shur² (ä'shōor'). Also **As·shur, As·sur, A·sur.** *Assyrian Mythology.* The principal deity and god of war and empire.

Ash Wednesday *n.* The seventh Wednesday before Easter and the first day of Lent, on which Roman Catholics customarily have ashes placed on the forehead as a sign of penitence.

ash·y (ăsh'ē) *adj.* **-i·er, -i·est.** **1.** Pertaining to, resembling, or covered with ashes. **2.** Ashen; pale.

A·sia (ā'zhə, ā'shə). *Abbr.* **As.** The largest of the continents, making up about 33 percent of the earth's land area. It has an even greater proportion of the world's people: roughly three out of every five humans live in Asia. This great landmass both physically and culturally falls into five broad subcontinents. North Asia comprises the part of Russia east of the Ural Mts. The Far East is made up of the temperate and subtropical parts in the east, where most people are of Mongoloid origin. The hot, dry lands of the west, whose inhabitants are of Semitic stock, many of whom are Moslems, make up the Middle East. The generally humid tropical lands of the south can be divided into two: Middle South Asia is the subcontinent of India (including Pakistan, Bangladesh, and Sri Lanka), with largely Dravidian and Indo-Aryan people; Southeast Asia, the remainder of the continent, has great ethnic and cultural diversity, many of its people being derived from other parts of Asia in historic times. See map, next page.

Asia Minor. See **Anatolia.**

A·sian (ā'zhən, ā'shən) *adj. Abbr.* **As.** Of or pertaining to Asia or its people.
~*n.* **1.** A native or inhabitant of Asia. **2.** *British.* A person of Indian, Pakistani, or Bangladeshi extraction.

A·si·at·ic (ā'zhē-ăt'ĭk) *adj.* Asian. —**A·si·at·ic** *n.*

a·side (ə-sīd') *adv.* **1.** On or to one side: *stand aside.* **2.** Out of one's thoughts or mind; away from consideration: *Put doubts aside.* **3.** In reserve: *put a little money aside.* **4.** Apart; dispensed with: *all joking aside.* —**aside from.** Excluding; excepting.
~*n.* **1.** A piece of dialogue that other actors on stage are supposed by dramatic convention not to hear. **2.** A remark made in an undertone, not intended to be heard by anyone present. **3.** A parenthetical departure; a digression.

as·i·nine (ăs'ə-nīn') *adj.* **1.** Of or resembling an ass. **2.** Utterly stupid: *an asinine remark.* [Latin *asinīnus,* from *asinus,* ass.] —**as·i·nine·ly** *adv.* —**as·i·nin·i·ty** (ăs'ə-nĭn'ə-tē) *n.*

Asiut. See **Asyut.**

ask (ăsk, äsk) *v.* **asked, asking, asks.** —*tr.* **1.** To put a question to. **2.** To seek information about; inquire about. **3.** To make a request of or for: *asked her forgiveness.* **4. a.** To require or call for. **b.** To expect or demand: *ask too much of a child; How much are they asking for their home?* **5.** To invite. —*intr.* **1.** To inquire. Used with *about.* **2.** To make a request. Often used with *for.* —**ask after.** To inquire about the health or well-being of. —**ask for.** *Informal.* To

ash *In pre-Christian times the ash tree was worshiped by northern peoples as a symbol of the life-force. Its strong, straight-grained wood is commonly used for oars, ax shafts, and tool handles.*

ASIA

[Map of Asia with labels: EUROPE, ARCTIC OCEAN, Barents Sea, Novaya Zemlya, Severnaya Zemlya, New Siberian Is, East Siberian Sea, Laptev Sea, Kolyma Range, Kamchatka, Bering Sea, L. Onega, L. Ladoga, URALS, Ob, West Siberian Plain, Irtysh, Yenisey, Central Siberian Plateau, Lena, Sea of Okhotsk, Sakhalin, RUSSIA, Black Sea, TURKEY, Anatolia, Taurus, Armenia, ASIA MINOR, CYP, LEB, SYRIA, IRAQ, ISRAEL, JORDAN, EGYPT, Mesopotamia, Tigris, Euphrates, KUW, Caspian Sea, Elburz Mts, Dasht-e-Lut, IRAN, Aral Sea, KAZAKHSTAN, L Balkhash, Kyzyl Kum, Kara Kum, TURKMENISTAN, UZBEKISTAN, TAJIK, KYRGY, Issyk Kul, Tien Shan, Altai, L Baikal, Yenisey, MONGOLIA, GOBI, Manchuria, NORTH KOREA, Japan, SOUTH KOREA, JAPAN, Honshu, Shikoku, Kyushu, Huang Hai (Yellow Sea), Hokkaido, SAUDI ARABIA, BAH, QATAR, U.A.E., OMAN, YEMEN, Red Sea, Gulf of Aden, SOMALIA, AFGHANISTAN, Hindu Kush, Pamirs, Kashmir, Nanga Parbat 8126m, K2 8611m, Kunlun Shan, Taklimakan Shamo, TIBET, HIMALAYA, Dhaulagiri 8172m, Annapurna 8078m, Makalu 8481m, Kangchenjunge 8585m, NEPAL, Mt Everest 8848m, BHUTAN, Ganges, CHINA, Qin Ling Shan, Chang Jiang (Yangtze), Huang He (Yellow River), East China Sea, Yunnan Plateau, Xi Jiang, Wuyi Shan, TAIWAN, Ryukyu Is, PACIFIC OCEAN, Tropic of Cancer, PAKISTAN, Baluchistan, Thar, Indus, INDIA, W Ghats, Gersoppa Falls, ARABIAN SEA, BURMA, Irrawaddy, Salween, Chao Phraya, Mekong, Mien Tung, THAILAND, LAOS, VIETNAM, CAM., Gulf of Thailand, Hainan, South China Sea, HONG KONG (UK), Macau, Luzon, PHILIPPINES, Mindanao, Mt Apo 2954m, BAY OF BENGAL, Andaman Is (IND), Nicobar Is (IND), SRI LANKA, THE MALDIVES, Lakshadweep (IND), SEYCHELLES, INDIAN OCEAN, Mt Kinabulu 4101m, Sabah, BRUNEI, Sarawak, MALAYSIA, SINGAPORE, BORNEO, Kalimantan, Sumatra, Str of Malacca, Kerinci 3805m, Krakatoa, Java Sea, Java, Bali, Sulawesi (Celebes), Celebes Sea, Banda Sea, Sulu Sea, Palawan, Makassar Strait, INDONESIA, Timor, Timor Sea, IRIAN JAYA, NEW GUINEA, Pk Jaya 5030m, Equator, AUSTRALIA, Chagos Arch. (UK), Diego Garcia. Scale: 0 800 1600 Km, 0 500 1000 Miles]

asparagus *The young shoots of Asparagus officinalis, a member of the lily family, have been a delicacy for at least 2,000 years.*

act in a manner that provokes (trouble, punishment, or the like): *He's really asking for it.* [Middle English *asken, axen,* Old English *āscian, ācsian.*] —**ask·er** *n.*

    Synonyms: examine, inquire. interrogate, query, question.

a·skance (ə-skăns′) *adv.* Also **a·skant** (ə-skănt′). **1.** With a sideways or oblique glance. **2.** With disapproval, suspicion, or distrust. [Earlier *a scanche, a sca(u)nce, a sconce,* obliquely, of unknown origin.]

a·ska·ri (ə-skä′rē) *n.* In parts of Africa, a native soldier or watchman, formerly one in the service of colonial authorities. [Arabic '*askarī,* soldier.]

a·skew (ə-skyōō′) *adj.* Crooked; oblique.
  ~*adv.* To one side; obliquely; awry. [16th century : A- (on) + SKEW.]

a·slant (ə-slănt′, ə-slänt′) *adj.* Oblique; slanting.
  ~*adv.* At a slant; obliquely.
  ~*prep.* Obliquely over or across; athwart. [A- (on) + SLANT.]

a·sleep (ə-slēp′) *adj.* **1.** Sleeping. **2.** Inactive; dormant. **3.** Numb: *My leg is asleep.* **4.** Dead. Used euphemistically.
  ~*adv.* Into a state of sleep. [A- (on) + SLEEP, replacing Middle English *o slepe,* from Old English *on slǽpe.*]

a·slope (ə-slōp′) *adv.* At a slope or slant.
  ~*adj.* Sloping.

As·ma·ra (ăz-mä′rə). The capital of the province of Eritrea in northern Ethiopia.

As·mo·de·us (ăz′mə-dē′əs). In Jewish demonology, king of the demons. [Latin *Asmodaeus,* from Greek *Asmodaios,* from Middle He-

brew *Ashməday,* from Avestan *Aēsma-daēva,* "spirit of anger" : *aēsma-,* anger + *daēva-,* demon.]

A·so, Mount (ä′sō). Also **A·so·san** (ä′sō-sän′). A volcanic mountain in central Kyushu in Japan. It has one of the largest craters in the world, containing five volcanic cones. The highest peak is Takadake (1,593 meters; 5,225 feet). One peak, Naka-dake, is active.

a·so·cial (ā-sō′shəl) *adj.* **1.** Avoiding the society of others; not gregarious. **2.** Inconsiderate of others; self-centered.

asp¹ (ăsp) *n.* **1.** A viper, *Vipera aspis,* of southern Europe, with a brown skin marked with black stripes. **2.** The venomous snake that killed Cleopatra, probably the Egyptian cobra, *Naja haje.* **3.** The **horned viper** (*see*). [Middle English *aspis,* from Latin, from Greek *aspis†.*]

asp² *n. Rare.* A tree, the aspen. [See aspen.]

Aspadana. See Isfahan.

as·par·a·gine (ə-spăr′ə-jēn′) *n.* A nonessential amino acid, $C_4H_8N_2O_3$, found mainly in asparagus, potatoes, and beetroot. [AS-PARAG(US) + -INE.]

as·par·a·gus (ə-spăr′ə-gəs) *n.* Any of several plants of the genus *Asparagus,* native to Eurasia, having small scales or needlelike branchlets rather than true leaves; especially, the widely cultivated species *A. officinalis,* the young shoots of which are cooked and eaten as a vegetable. [Latin, from Greek *asparagos, aspharagos†.*]

asparagus beetle *n.* A small, spotted beetle, *Crioceris asparagi,* that infests and damages asparagus plants.

asparagus fern *n.* An ornamental asparagus plant, *Asparagus plumosus,* native to southern Africa, having fernlike foliage.

as·par·tic acid (ə-spär′tĭk) *n.* Also **as·pa·rag·ic acid** (ăs′pə-răj′ĭk). A nonessential amino acid, $C_4H_7NO_4$, found especially in young sugar cane and sugar beet. [*Aspartic,* irregularly from ASPARAGUS (because it is obtained by hydrolysis of a crystalline amino acid found in asparagus) + ACID.]

A.S.P.C.A. American Society for the Prevention of Cruelty to Animals.

as·pect (ăs′pĕkt′) *n.* **1.** Appearance to the eye, especially when seen from a specific view. **2. a.** An angle or viewpoint of an idea or problem: *study the case from every possible aspect.* **b.** A particular feature or element of a problem or idea: *a different aspect of the same problem.* **3.** A particular facial expression, mien, or air: *a matron of grim aspect.* **4.** A position facing or commanding a given direction; an exposure. **5.** A side or surface facing in a particular direction: *the ventral aspect of the body.* **6.** *Astronomy.* The relative positions of two celestial bodies. **7.** *Astrology.* The configuration of the stars or planets in relation to one another or to the subject. **8.** *Grammar.* A category of the verb denoting primarily the relation of the action to the passage of time, especially in reference to completion, duration, or repetition. Compare **mood. 9.** *Archaic.* A gaze; a look. [Middle English, from Latin *aspectus,* a view, past participle of *aspicere,* look at : *ad-,* at + *specere,* to look.]

aspect ratio *n.* **1.** The width-to-height ratio of a television image. It is 4:3 in most countries. **2.** The width-to-length ratio of the conductivity channel in an integrated circuit.

a·spec·tu·al (ă-spĕk′cho͞o-əl) *adj. Grammar.* Of or pertaining to the aspect of a verb.

as·pen (ăs′pən) *n.* Any of several trees of the genus *Populus,* having leaves that flutter readily on the breeze because of their flattened leafstalks. *P. Tremuloides,* of North America, is often called "quaking aspen."
~*adj.* **1.** Of or relating to an aspen. **2.** Shivering or trembling like the leaves of an aspen. [Middle English *aspen,* "of an aspen" (adjective misinterpreted as a noun), replacing *aspe,* an aspen, Old English *æspe,* of Germanic origin.]

As·pen (ăs′pən). A city of west-central Colorado, in the Sawatch range of the Rocky Mts. It was founded *c.* 1879 by silver prospectors and is now a popular ski resort.

as·per·ate (ăs′pə-rāt′) *tr.v.* **-ated, -ating, -ates.** To make uneven; roughen. [Latin *asperāre,* from *asper*†, rough.]

as·per·ges (ə-spûr′jēz) *n. Roman Catholic Church.* A short rite, preceding the High Mass on Sundays, that consists of sprinkling the congregation with holy water. [Latin *asperges me, Domine,* "thou wilt sprinkle me, Lord", first words of the rite, from *aspergere,* to sprinkle, ASPERSE.]

as·per·gil·lo·sis (ăs-pûr′jĭ-lō′sĭs) *n.* An infectious disease of the mucous membranes, lungs, and other parts of the body, caused by certain fungi of the genus *Aspergillus.* [New Latin : ASPERGILL(US) + -OSIS.]

as·per·gil·lum (ăs′pər-jĭl′əm) *n., pl.* **-la** (-lə) or **-lums.** Also **as·per·gill** (-jĭl). *Roman Catholic Church.* A brush, perforated container, or other instrument used for sprinkling holy water. [New Latin *aspergillum,* sprinkler, from Latin *aspergere,* to sprinkle on, ASPERSE.]

as·per·gil·lus (ăs′pər-jĭl′əs) *n., pl.* **-gilli** (-jĭl′ī′). Any of various fungi of the genus *Aspergillus,* which includes many common molds. [New Latin, from *aspergillum,* ASPERGILLUM, from its resemblance to an aspergillum brush.]

as·per·i·ty (ă-spĕr′ə-tē) *n. pl.* **-ties. 1.** Roughness or harshness, as of surface, weather, or sound: *the asperity of the climate.* **2.** Ill temper; irritability. [Latin *asperitās,* from *asper*†, rough.]

as·perse (ə-spûrs′) *tr.v.* **-persed, -persing, -perses. 1.** To spread false charges against; defame; slander. **2.** *Rare.* To sprinkle with water or dust. [Latin *aspergere* (past participle *aspersus*), to sprinkle on, spatter : *ad-,* to + *spargere,* to strew, scatter.] **—as·pers·er, as·per·sor** *n.* **—as·per·sive** *adj.* **—as·per·sive·ly** *adv.*

as·per·sion (ə-spûr′zhən, -shən) *n.* **1.** A calumnious report or remark; slander. Often used in the phrase *cast aspersions on.* **2.** The act of defaming or slandering. **3.** *Rare.* A sprinkling; especially, a baptism by sprinkling.

as·phalt (ăs′fôlt′) *n.* Also **as·phal·tum** (ăs-fôl′təm), **as·phal·tus** (-təs). **1.** A brownish-black solid or semisolid mixture of bitumens obtained from native deposits or as a petroleum by-product, used in paving, roofing, and waterproofing. Also called "mineral pitch." **2.** Mixed asphalt and crushed stone gravel or sand, used for paving or roofing.
~*tr.v.* **asphalted, -phalting, -phalts.** To pave or coat with asphalt. [Middle English, *asp(h)alt, aspaltoun,* from Late Latin *asphaltus,* from Greek *asphaltos, asphalton,* bitumen, pitch, origin obscure.] **—as·phal·tic** (ăs-fôl′tĭk) *adj.*

as·phal·tite (ăs′fôl-tīt′) *n.* A solid, dark-colored complex of hydrocarbons, found in natural veins and deposits.

a·spher·ic (ā-sfîr′ĭk, ā-sfĕr′-) *adj.* Also **a·spher·i·cal** (-ĭ-kəl). Not spherical. Said of lenses and mirrors designed with parabaloidal or other surfaces in order to reduce aberrations.

as·pho·del (ăs′fə-dĕl′) *n.* **1.** An unidentified flower of classical legend, said to resemble the narcissus and to cover the Elysian Fields. **2.** Any of several plants of the genus *Asphodeline* or the genus *Asphodelus,* of the Mediterranean region, having clusters of white or yellow flowers. See **bog asphodel.** [Latin *asphodelus,* from Greek *asphodelos*†.]

as·phyx·i·a (ăs-fĭk′sē-ə) *n.* Unconsciousness or death ocurring when oxygen is prevented from reaching the tissues; suffocation. [New Latin, from Greek *asphuxia,* stopping of the pulse : *a-,* not + *sphuxis,* heartbeat, pulsation, from *sphuzein*†, to throb.] **—as·phyx·i·al** *adj.*

as·phyx·i·ant (ăs-fĭk′sē-ənt) *adj.* Inducing or tending to induce asphyxia.
~*n.* A substance or condition that causes asphyxia.

as·phyx·i·ate (ăs-fĭk′sē-āt′) *v.* **-ated, -ating, -ates.** —*tr.* To cause asphyxia in; smother. —*intr.* To undergo asphyxia; suffocate. **—as·phyx·i·a·tion** *n.* **—as·phyx·i·a·tor** *n.*

as·pic¹ (ăs′pĭk) *n.* A clear jelly made of stock and gelatin and used to make a meat, fish, or vegetable mold or as a garnish in cookery. [French *(sauce)* or *(ragoût) à l'aspic,* from *aspic,* ASPIC (snake), from the fancied resemblance of the different colors of the jelly to those of the snake.]

aspic² *n. Poetic & Archaic.* The asp, a poisonous snake. [Old French, from *aspe,* from Latin *aspis,* ASP (snake).]

aspic³ *n.* A species of lavender, *Lavandula spica,* that yields a fragrant oil used in perfumery. [French, from Old French, from Old Provençal *espic,* spike (of a grain such as barley), from Latin *spīca,* spike.]

as·pi·dis·tra (ăs′pə-dĭs′trə) *n.* Any of several Asian plants of the genus *Aspidistra;* especially, *A. lurida,* having long, tough, evergreen leaves and small brownish flowers. This species is widely cultivated as a house plant. [New Latin *Aspidistra* : Greek *aspis*† (stem *aspid-*), shield (referring to the shape of the leaves) + *-istra,* after *Tupistra* (a genus of the lily family).]

as·pi·rant (ăs′pər-ənt, ə-spīr′ənt) *n.* One who aspires, especially after advancement, honors, or a high position.
~*adj.* **1.** Aspiring after recognition or distinction: *aspirant poets.* **2.** *Poetic.* Rising; ascending.

as·pi·rate (ăs′pə-rāt′) *tr.v.* **-rated, -rating, -rates. 1.** *Phonetics.* **a.** To pronounce (a vowel or word) with the initial release of breath associated with English *h,* as in *hurry.* **b.** To follow (a consonant, especially a stop consonant) with a puff of breath that is clearly audible before the next sound begins, as in English *p, t,* and *k* before vowels. **2.** *Medicine.* To remove (fluids or gases) from the body by means of an aspirator.
~*n.* (ăs′pər-ĭt). *Phonetics.* **1.** The speech sound represented by the English *h.* **2.** Any speech sound followed by a puff of breath.
~*adj.* (ăs′pər-ĭt). *Phonetics.* Aspirated. Said of a speech sound. [Latin *aspīrāre,* to breathe upon, aspirate : *ad-,* to + *spīrāre,* to breathe.]

as·pi·ra·tion (ăs′pə-rā′shən) *n.* **1.** Expulsion of breath in speech. **2.** *Phonetics.* **a.** The pronunciation of an aspirate. **b.** The puff of air accompanying the release of a stop consonant. **3.** *Medicine.* Removal of fluids or gases from the body with an aspirator. **4. a.** A strong desire for high achievement. **b.** An object of such desire; an ambition.

as·pi·ra·tor (ăs′pə-rā′tər) *n.* **1.** Any device that removes liquids or gases from a space by suction, especially one used medically to evacuate a bodily cavity. **2.** A suction pump used to create a partial vacuum.

as·pir·a·to·ry (ə-spīr′ə-tôr′ē, -tōr′ē) *adj.* Of, concerning, or suited for breathing or suction.

as·pire (ə-spīr′) *intr.v.* **-pired, -piring, -pires. 1.** To have a great ambition or ultimate goal: *aspired to stardom.* **2.** To strive toward an end; aim. **3.** *Archaic.* To rise upward; soar. [Middle English *aspiren,* from Old French *aspirer,* from Latin *aspīrāre,* to breathe upon, desire, ASPIRATE.] **—as·pir·er** *n.* **—as·pir·ing·ly** *adv.*

as·pi·rin (ăs′pər-ĭn, -prĭn) *n.* **1.** A white crystalline compound, $CH_3COOC_6H_4COOH$, commonly used in tablet form to relieve pain, fever, and inflammation. Also called "acetylsalicylic acid." **2.** A tablet of aspirin. [German, from AC(ETYL) + *spir(aeic acid),* old name for salicylic acid, from SPIRAEA + -IN.]

as·pir·ing (ə-spīr′ĭng) *adj.* Aiming for recognition or distinction: *an aspiring young lawyer.*

a·squint (ə-skwĭnt′) *adv.* With a sidelong glance. [Middle English : perhaps A- (on) + Dutch *schuinte*†, a slope, slant, from *schuin,* sideways, slanting.] **—a·squint** *adj.*

As·quith (ăs′kwĭth), **Herbert Henry, 1st Earl of Oxford and Asquith** (1852–1928). British Liberal politician, prime minister (1908–16). His government passed the Parliament Act of 1911 and took away the power of veto from the House of Lords. It also introduced unemployment insurance and old-age pensions. In 1915 he formed a coalition government with the Conservatives and a year later was forced to resign in favor of Lloyd George. He remained leader of the Liberal Party until 1926.

ass (ăs) *n., pl.* **asses** (ăs′ĭz). **1.** Any of several hoofed mammals of the genus *Equus;* especially, *E. asinus* of Africa and *E. hemionus* of Asia, resembling and closely related to the horses and zebras but having longer ears. See **donkey, onager. 2.** A stupid person, especially one who is vain and self-important. [Middle English *asse,* Old English *assa,* from Old Celtic *as(s)in* (unattested), from Latin *asinus.*]

assagai. Variant of **assegai.**

as·sai¹ (ä-sī′) *n.* **1.** Any of several palm trees of the genus *Euterpe,* of tropical South America, having edible, fleshy purple fruit. **2.** A beverage made from this fruit. [Brazilian Portuguese *assaí,* from Tupi *assahi.*]

assai² *adv. Music.* Very. Used in directions: *allegro assai.* [Italian, "enough," from Vulgar Latin *ad satis* (unattested), "to the point of sufficiency." See **assets.**]

as·sail (ə-sāl′) *tr.v.* **-sailed, -sailing, -sails. 1.** To attack with or as if with violent blows; assault. **2.** To attack verbally, as with ridicule

aspen *The constant rustling of the aspen's leaves—caused by the slenderness of the stalks that hold them to the tree—was formerly thought to indicate someone's secret grief or guilt. Another theory was that the tree trembled because it had provided the wood for Christ's cross.*

aspidistra *An east Asian plant popular as an indoor evergreen in Victorian Britain. It was able to thrive in the extremes of temperature and dim light often found in Victorian homes.*

or censure. **3.** To trouble: *She was assailed by doubts.* —See Synonyms at **attack.** [Middle English *asailen,* from Old French *asaillir,* from Medieval Latin *assalīre* from Latin *assilīre,* to jump on : *ad-,* to + *salīre,* to leap.] **—as·sail·a·ble** *adj.* **—as·sail·a·ble·ness** *n.* **—as·sail·er** *n.* **—as·sail·ment** *n.*

as·sail·ant (ə-sā′lənt) *n.* A person who assails another.

As·sam (ə-săm′, ăs′əm). A state in the far northeast of India, almost isolated from the rest of the country by Bangladesh. The capital is Shillong. It is a tea-growing region, but also has important oil reserves and refineries.

As·sa·mese (ăs′ə-mēz′, -mēs′) *adj.* Of or pertaining to Assam, its people, or their language.
~*n., pl.* **Assamese. 1.** A native or inhabitant of Assam. **2.** The Indo-European Indic language of the Assamese.

as·sas·sin (ə-săs′ĭn) *n.* **1.** A murderer, especially one who carries out a plot to kill a prominent public figure. **2. Assassin.** A member of a secret order of Muslim fanatics who terrorized and killed Christian Crusaders. [French, from Medieval Latin *assassīnus,* from Arabic *ḥashshāshīn,* plural of *ḥashshāsh,* "hashish eater," (originally referring to members of an Ismaili sect who took the drug before attacking their enemies), from *ḥashīsh,* HASHISH.]

as·sas·si·nate (ə-săs′ə-nāt′) *tr.v.* **-nated, -nating, -nates. 1.** To murder (a prominent person). **2.** To injure or destroy treacherously: *assassinated her good name.* **—as·sas·si·na·tive** *adj.* **—as·sas·si·na·tor** (ə-săs′ə-nā′tər) *n.*

as·sas·si·na·tion (ə-săs′ə-nā′shən) *n.* **1.** Murder, especially of a prominent person. **2.** Malicious injury, especially of a person's good reputation: *character assassination.*

assassin bug *n.* Any of various predatory insects of the large family Reduviidae, having short, curved, powerful beaks adapted for sucking blood and capable of inflicting a painful bite on humans. Some species transmit disease. See **kissing bug.**

as·sault (ə-sôlt′) *n.* **1.** A violent attack, either physical or verbal. **2.** *Military.* **a.** An attack upon a fortified area or place. **b.** The concluding stage of an attack in which there is close combat with the enemy. **3.** *Law.* An unlawful attempt or threat to injure another physically. **4.** Rape.
~*tr.v.* **assaulted, -saulting, -saults.** To make an assault on. —See Synonyms at **attack.** [Middle English *assaut,* from Old French *asaut, assaut,* from Vulgar Latin *assaltus* (unattested), variant of Latin *assultus,* past participle of *assilīre,* ASSAIL.] **—as·sault·er** *n.*

assault and battery *n. Law.* The threat to make a physical attack on someone and the carrying out of the threat.

assault course *n.* **1.** A military exercise in which troops are made to go over a course of physical obstacles. **2.** Any procedure presenting a series of difficulties.

as·say (ăs′ā′, ă-sā′) *n.* **1. a.** The qualitative or quantitative analysis of a substance, especially of an ore or drug. **b.** A substance to be so analyzed. **c.** The result of such an analysis. **2.** Any analysis or examination. **3.** *Obsolete.* An attempt; an essay.
~*v.* (ă-sā′, ăs′ā′) **assayed, -saying, -says.** —*tr.* **1.** To subject to chemical analysis; make an assay of. **2.** To examine by trial or experiment; put to a test: *assay one's ability.* **3.** To evaluate; assess. **4.** To attempt; try. —*intr.* To be shown by analysis as having a certain proportion, usually of a precious metal. —See Synonyms at **estimate.** [Middle English, from Old French *assai, essai,* trial, ESSAY.] **—as·say·a·ble** *adj.* **—as·say·er** *n.*

assay office *n.* An office or laboratory in which ore is analyzed to determine the proportion of precious metal it contains.

as·se·gai, as·sa·gai (ăs′ə-gī′) *n.* **1.** A light spear or javelin used by southern African tribesmen. **2.** A tree, *Curtisia faginea,* of southern Africa, the wood of which is used for making spears.

as·sem·blage (ə-sĕm′blĭj) *n.* **1. a.** The act of assembling. **b.** The state of being assembled. **2.** A collection of people or things. **3.** A fitting together of parts, as of a machine. **4.** A sculpture consisting of an arrangement of miscellaneous objects, such as scraps of metal, cloth, or string.

as·sem·ble (ə-sĕm′bəl) *v.* **-bled, -bling, -bles.** —*tr.* **1.** To bring or gather together into a group or whole. **2.** To fit or join together the parts of. **3.** *Computer Science.* To run an assembler program on (data). —*intr.* **1.** To gather together; congregate. **2.** To be capable of undergoing assembly: *The kit assembles into a bookcase.* —See Synonyms at **gather.** [Middle English *assemblen,* from Old French *assembler,* from Vulgar Latin *assimulāre* (unattested), to bring together : Latin *ad-,* to + *simul,* together, at the same time.] **—as·sem·bler** *n.*

as·sem·bler (ə-sĕm′blər) *n.* **1.** A person or device that assembles something. **2.** *Computer Science.* A program that converts input data into machine code. Compare **compiler.**

as·sem·bly (ə-sĕm′blē) *n., pl.* **-blies.** *Abbr.* **assy. 1. a.** The act of assembling. **b.** The state of being assembled. **2.** A group of persons gathered together for a common purpose, usually legislative, religious, educational, or social. **3. Assembly.** In certain U.S. states, the lower house of the legislature. **4. a.** The putting together of manufactured parts to make a completed product, such as a machine or electronic circuit. **b.** A set of parts so assembled. **5.** *Military.* The signal calling troops to form ranks.

assembly language *n. Computer Science.* A programming language that is a close approximation of machine code.

assembly line *n.* A line of factory workers and equipment on which the product being assembled passes consecutively from operation to operation until completed. Also called "production line." **—as·sem·bly-line** *adj.*

as·sem·bly·man (ə-sĕm′blē-mən) *n., pl.* **-men** (-mĭn). A member of a legislative assembly.

Assembly of God *n.* A Pentecostal congregation founded in the United States in 1914.

assembly time *n. Computer Science.* The time required for an assembler to translate symbolic language into machine code.

as·sent (ə-sĕnt′) *intr.v.* **-sented, -senting, -sents.** To express agreement; concur. Used with *to: assent to his plan.*
~*n.* **1.** Agreement, as to a proposal; compliance. **2.** Acquiescence; consent. [Middle English *assenten,* from Old French *assenter,* from Latin *assentārī,* frequentative of *assentīre,* "to join in feeling," agree with : *ad-,* toward + *sentīre,* to feel, think.] **—as·sent·er, as·sen·tor** (ə-sĕn′tər) *n.* **—as·sent·ing·ly** *adv.* **—as·sent·ive** *adj.* **—as·sent·ive·ness** *n.*

Synonyms: *accede, accept, acquiesce, agree, concur, consent, subscribe.*

as·sen·ta·tion (ăs′ĕn-tā′shən) *n.* Ill-considered or servile agreement with another's opinions.

as·sert (ə-sûrt′) *tr.v.* **-serted, -serting, -serts. 1.** To state or express positively or forcefully; affirm. **2.** To defend or maintain (one's rights, for example). **3.** To put (oneself) forward, forcefully or boldly. [Latin *asserere,* "to join to oneself," maintain, claim : *ad-,* to + *serere,* to join.] **—as·sert·a·ble, as·sert·i·ble** *adj.* **—as·sert·er, as·ser·tor** (ə-sûr′tər) *n.*

Synonyms: *affirm, allege, asseverate, aver, avow, declare.*

as·ser·tion (ə-sûr′shən) *n.* **1.** The act of asserting or declaring. **2.** A declaration stated positively but with no support or attempt at proof. **—as·ser·tion·al** *adj.*

as·ser·tive (ə-sûr′tĭv) *adj.* Inclined to bold or confident assertion; aggressive. **—as·ser·tive·ly** *adv.* **—as·ser·tive·ness** *n.*

assertiveness training *n.* A method of training individuals to behave in a boldly self-confident manner.

as·ser·to·ry (ə-sûr′tər-ē) *adj.* Asserting or affirming.

as·ses¹. Plural of **as** (Roman coin).

ass·es². Plural of **ass.**

as·sess (ə-sĕs′) *tr.v.* **-sessed, -sessing, -sesses. 1.** To estimate the value of (property) for taxation. **2.** To set or determine the amount of (a tax, fine, or other payment). **3.** To charge (a person or property) with a tax, fine, or other special payment. **4.** To evaluate; appraise. —See Synonyms at **estimate.** [Middle English *assessen,* from Old French *assesser,* from Latin *assidere* (past participle *assessus*), "to sit beside," be an assistant judge (hence, Medieval Latin, to tax) : *ad-,* near to + *sedēre,* to sit.] **—as·sess·a·ble** *adj.*

as·sess·ment (ə-sĕs′mənt) *n.* **1.** The act of assessing. **2.** An account of an act of assessing. **3.** An amount assessed, as for taxation or costing purposes. **4.** An evaluation; an appraisal.

as·ses·sor (ə-sĕs′ər) *n.* **1.** An official who makes assessments, as for taxation. **2.** An assistant to a judge, selected for his special knowledge of a particular area. **3.** Any adviser or assistant. **—as·ses·so·ri·al** (ăs′ə-sôr′ē-əl, -sōr′-) *adj.*

as·set (ăs′ĕt′) *n.* **1.** A useful or valuable quality, person, or thing. **2.** A valuable item that is owned. [Back-formation from ASSETS.]

as·sets (ăs′ĕts′) *pl.n.* **1.** *Accounting.* The entries on a balance sheet showing all of a person's or enterprise's properties and claims against others that may be applied, directly or indirectly, to cover liabilities. Assets include the value of tangible things, such as cash and stock, and that of intangibles, such as a trademark or goodwill. **2.** The entire property owned by a person, especially a dead person or a bankrupt, which can be used to settle debts. [Norman French *asetz* (legal use), from Old French *asez,* "enough (to satisfy creditors)," from Vulgar Latin *ad satis* (unattested), "to the point of sufficiency," enough : Latin *ad-,* to + *satis,* sufficient.]

Synonyms: *belongings, effects, property, possessions.*

as·sev·er·ate (ə-sĕv′ə-rāt′) *tr.v.* **-ated, -ating, -ates.** To declare seriously or positively; affirm. —See Synonyms at **assert.** [Latin *assevērāre,* to assert earnestly : *ad-,* to + *sevērus,* earnest, serious.] **—as·sev·er·a·tion** *n.*

as·sib·i·late (ə-sĭb′ə-lāt′) *tr.v.* **-lated, -lating, -lates.** *Phonetics.* To make sibilant; pronounce with a hissing sound. [AD- (in addition to) + SIBILATE.] **—as·sib·i·la·tion** *n.*

as·si·du·i·ty (ăs′ə-dōō′ə-tē, -dyōō′ə-tē) *n., pl.* **-ties. 1.** Close and constant application; unflagging effort; diligence. **2. assiduities.** Constant personal attentions; solicitude.

as·sid·u·ous (ə-sĭj′ōō-əs) *adj.* **1.** Constant in application or attention; diligent; devoted: *an assiduous churchgoer.* **2.** Unceasing; persistent. —See Synonyms at **busy.** [Latin *assiduus,* from *assidēre,* to sit beside, attend to : *ad-,* near to + *sedēre,* to sit.] **—as·sid·u·ous·ly** *adv.* **—as·sid·u·ous·ness** *n.*

as·sign (ə-sīn′) *tr.v.* **-signed, -signing, -signs. 1.** To set apart or fix for a particular purpose; designate. **2.** To select for a duty or office; appoint. **3.** To give out as a task; allot. **4.** To ascribe; attribute. **5.** *Law.* To transfer (property, rights, or interests). **6.** *Military.* To place (a unit or personnel) integrally into a particular organization. Compare **attach.** —See Synonyms at **attribute, commit.**
~*n. Law.* An assignee. [Middle English *assignen,* from Old French *assigner,* from Latin *assignāre,* to mark out : *ad-,* to + *signāre,* to mark, from *signum,* sign.] **—as·sign·a·bil·i·ty** *n.* **—as·sign·a·ble** *adj.* **—as·sign·a·bly** *adv.* **—as·sign·er** *n.*

Synonyms: *allocate, allot, apportion.*

as·sig·nat (ăs′ĭg-năt′; *French* à-sē-nyà′) *n.* Any of the notes of the paper currency issued in France (1789–96) by the revolutionary government on the security of confiscated lands. [French, from

Latin *assignātum,* "something assigned," past participle of *assignāre,* ASSIGN.]

as·sig·na·tion (ăs'ĭg-nā'shən) *n.* **1.** The act of assigning. **2.** Something assigned; an assignment. **3.** An appointment for a meeting between lovers; a tryst.

as·sign·ee (ə-sī'nē', ăs'ĭ-nē') *n. Law.* **1.** A person to whom a transfer of property, rights, or interest is made. **2.** One appointed to act for another; a deputy; an agent.

as·sign·ment (ə-sīn'mənt) *n. Abbr.* **asgmt. 1.** The act of assigning. **2.** Something assigned, such as a task. **3.** A position or post of duty to which one is assigned. **4.** *Law.* **a.** The transfer of a claim, right, interest, or property. **b.** The document or deed by which this transfer is made. **c.** That which is transferred. —See Synonyms at **task.**

as·sign·or (ə-sī'nôr', ə-sī'nər, ăs'ə-nôr') *n. Law.* A person who makes an assignment.

as·sim·i·la·ble (ə-sĭm'ə-lə-bəl) *adj.* Capable of being assimilated. —**as·sim·i·la·bil·i·ty** *n.*

as·sim·i·late (ə-sĭm'ə-lāt') *v.* **-lated, -lating, -lates.** —*tr.* **1.** *Biology.* **a.** To consume and incorporate into the body; digest. **b.** To transform (digested food) into living tissue; metabolize constructively. **2.** To absorb and incorporate (knowledge, for example). **3.** To cause to belong or become integrated: *Can the community assimilate these newcomers?* **4.** To make similar; cause to assume a resemblance. **5.** *Linguistics.* To alter (a sound) by assimilation. —*intr.* To become assimilated. [Middle English *assimilaten,* from Latin *assimilāre, assimulāre,* to make similar to : *ad-,* to + *simulāre, similāre,* to simulate, from *similis,* similar.] —**as·sim·i·la·tor** *n.*

as·sim·i·la·tion (ə-sĭm'ə-lā'shən) *n.* **1. a.** The act or process of assimilating. **b.** The condition or process of being assimilated. **2.** *Biology.* The process by which the molecules of digested food are incorporated into living tissue; constructive metabolism. **3.** *Linguistics.* The process by which a sound is modified to make it resemble an adjacent sound. For example, the prefix *in-,* as in *intolerable,* becomes *im-* in *impossible* by assimilation. **4.** The process whereby a group, especially a minority or immigrant group, gradually adopts the characteristics of another culture.

as·sim·i·la·tive (ə-sĭm'ə-lā'tĭv, -lə-tĭv) *adj.* Also **as·sim·i·la·to·ry** (-lə-tôr'ē, -tōr'ē). Marked by or causing assimilation.

As·si·si (ə-sē'zē, -sē). Town in the Umbrian region of central Italy, lying on the slopes of the Apennines. St. Francis of Assisi was born here in 1182 and the convent built immediately after his canonization in 1228 still stands.

as·sist (ə-sĭst') *v.* **-sisted, -sisting, -sists.** —*tr.* **1.** To aid; help. **2.** To aid in a professional capacity: *assist a surgeon in an operation.* —*intr.* **1.** To give aid or support. **2.** To be present; attend. Usually used with *at.* —See Synonyms at **help.** ~*n.* **1.** An act of giving aid; help. **2. a.** In baseball, a handling of the ball that enables a runner to be put out. **b.** In ice hockey, a pass of the puck to the teammate scoring a goal. [Middle English *assisten,* from Old French *assister,* from Latin *assistere,* to stand beside, help : *ad-,* near to + *sistere,* to stand.] —**as·sist·er** *n.*

as·sis·tance (ə-sĭs'təns) *n.* **1.** The act of assisting. **2.** Aid.

as·sis·tant (ə-sĭs'tənt) *n. Abbr.* **asst. 1.** One that assists; a helper; especially, a professional aide. **2.** A person serving customers in a shop. ~*adj. Abbr.* **asst. 1.** Holding an auxiliary position; subordinate. **2.** Giving aid; auxiliary.

assistant professor *n.* A college teacher who ranks above an instructor and below an associate professor.

as·sis·tant·ship (ə-sĭs'tənt-shĭp') *n.* An academic position that carries a stipend and usually involves part-time teaching or research, given to a qualified graduate student.

Assiut. See Asyut.

as·size (ə-sīz') *n.* **1.** *English History* **a.** A session of a legislative or judicial body or court. **b.** A decree, verdict, or edict rendered at such a session. **2. assizes. a.** Any of the periodic court sessions formerly held in each of the counties of England and Wales for the trial of civil or criminal cases. Its functions are now carried out by the High Court and Crown Court. **b.** The time or place of such sessions. [Middle English *assise,* from Old French, feminine of *assis,* past participle of *as(s)eeir,* to seat, from Vulgar Latin *assedēre* (unattested), from Latin *assidēre,* to sit beside, be an assistant judge. See **assiduous.**]

assn. association.

assoc. associate; association.

as·so·ci·a·ble (ə-sō'shē-ə-bəl, -shə-bəl) *adj.* Capable of being associated. —**as·so·ci·a·bil·i·ty, as·so·ci·a·ble·ness** *n.*

as·so·ci·ate (ə-sō'shē-āt', -sē-āt') *v.* **-ated, -ating, -ates.** —*tr.* **1.** To bring into company with another; join in a relationship. **2.** To connect or join together; combine; link. **3.** To connect in the mind or imagination: *I always associate the Lake District with Wordsworth.* —*intr.* **1.** To join in or form a league, union, or association. **2.** To keep company. —See Synonyms at **join.** ~*n.* (ə-sō'shē-ĭt, -sē-ĭt, -shē-āt', -sē-āt') *Abbr.* **assoc. 1.** A person united with another or others in some action, enterprise, or business; a partner; a colleague. **2.** A companion; a comrade. **3.** Anything that habitually accompanies or is associated with another; an attendant circumstance. **4.** A member of an institution or society who is granted only partial status or privileges. —See Synonyms at **partner.** ~*adj.* (ə-sō'shē-ĭt, -sē-ĭt, -shē-āt', -sē-āt'). *Abbr.* **assoc. 1.** Joined with another or others and having equal or nearly equal status: *an associate editor.* **2.** Having partial status or privileges: *an associate*

member of the club. **3.** Following or accompanying; concomitant. [Middle English *associaten,* from Latin *associāre,* to join to : *ad-,* to + *sociāre,* to join, from *socius,* companion.]

associate professor *n.* A college or university teacher who ranks below a full professor and above an assistant professor.

as·so·ci·a·tion (ə-sō'sē-ā'shən, -shē-) *n.* **1.** The act of associating. **2.** The state of being associated. **3.** *Abbr.* **assn., assoc.** An organized body of people who have some interest, activity, or purpose in common; a society. **4.** A mental connection or relation between thoughts, feelings, ideas, or sensations. **5.** *Chemistry.* Any of various processes of chemical combination, such as hydration, solvation, or complex-ion formation, depending on relatively weak chemical bonding. **6.** *Ecology.* A large community of organisms in a specific area with one or two dominant species. —**as·so·ci·a·tion·al** *adj.*

association football *n. Chiefly British.* The official name for **soccer** (see).

as·so·ci·a·tion·ism (ə-sō'sē-ā'shən-ĭz'əm, -shē-) *n.* The psychological theory that association is the basic principle of all mental activity. —**as·so·ci·a·tion·ist** *n. & adj.*

Association of Southeast Asian Nations. *Abbr.* **ASEAN** A group formed in 1967 to stimulate economic growth in Southeast Asia. Its members are Brunei, Indonesia, Malaysia, the Philippines, Singapore, and Thailand.

as·so·ci·a·tive (ə-sō'shē-ā'tĭv, -sē-ā'tĭv, -shə-tĭv) *adj.* **1.** Of, characterized by, resulting from, or causing association. **2.** *Mathematics.* Independent of the grouping of elements. Said of mathematical operations: *If $a + (b + c) = (a + b) + c$, the operation indicated by + is associative.* —**as·so·ci·a·tive·ly** *adv.*

as·soil (ə-soil') *tr.v.* **-soiled, -soiling, -soils.** *Rare.* **1.** To absolve or pardon. **2.** To atone for. [Middle English *assoilen,* from Norman French *as(s)oiler,* from Old French *assoldre* (stem *assoil-*), from Latin *absolvere,* to set free from : *ab-,* away from + *solvere,* to loosen, set free.]

as·so·nance (ăs'ə-nəns) *n.* **1.** Resemblance in sound, especially in the vowel sounds of words. **2.** A partial rhyme in which the accented vowel sounds correspond but the consonants differ, as in *brave* and *vain.* **3.** Rough similarity; approximate agreement. [French, from Latin *assonāns,* present participle of *assonāre,* to sound in response to : *ad-,* to + *sonāre,* to sound.] —**as·so·nant** *adj. & n.*

as·sort (ə-sôrt') *v.* **-sorted, -sorting, -sorts.** —*tr.* **1.** To separate into groups according to kinds; classify. **2.** To supply with a variety of goods. —*intr.* **1.** To fall into a class; match. Often used with *with.* **2.** To associate; consort. Used with *with.* [Old French *assorter : a-,* from Latin *ad-,* to + *sorte,* kind, from Vulgar Latin *sorta* (unattested), kind, from Latin *sors* (stem *sort-*), chance, fortune, lot.] —**as·sort·a·tive** (ə-sôr'tə-tĭv) *adj.* —**as·sort·er** *n.*

as·sort·ed (ə-sôr'tĭd) *adj.* **1.** Consisting of a number of different kinds; various. **2.** Placed in classes; classified. **3.** Suited or matched. Often used in combination: *well-assorted; ill-assorted.* —See Synonyms at **miscellaneous.**

as·sort·ment (ə-sôrt'mənt) *n.* **1.** The act of assorting; separation into classes. **2.** A collection of various things; a variety.

Assouan, Assuan. See Aswan.

asst. assistant.

as·suage (ə-swāj') *tr. v.* **-suaged, -suaging, -suages. 1.** To make less severe or burdensome; ease: *assuage her grief.* **2.** To satisfy; appease, as thirst. **3.** To pacify or calm. —See Synonyms at **relieve.** [Middle English *aswagen,* from Old French *assouagier,* from Vulgar Latin *assuāviāre* (unattested), to sweeten : *ad-,* to + *suāvis,* sweet.] —**as·suage·ment** *n.* —**as·suag·er** *n.*

as·sua·sive (ə-swā'sĭv, -zĭv) *adj.* Soothing. [AD- + -*suasive,* as in PERSUASIVE but influenced by ASSUAGE.]

as·sume (ə-sōōm') *tr.v.* **-sumed, -suming, -sumes. 1.** To put on; don (a garment, for example). **2.** To take upon oneself; undertake: *assume responsibility.* **3. a.** To appropriate or usurp. **b.** To invest oneself formally with: *assume the presidency.* **4.** To take on; adopt: *"the god assumes a human form"* (John Ruskin). **5.** To feign; affect: *assume interest.* **6.** To take for granted; suppose. **7.** *Theology.* To receive, as into heaven. —See Synonyms at **presume.** [Middle English *assumen,* from Latin *assūmere,* to take to oneself; adopt : *ad-,* to + *sūmere,* to take.] —**as·sum·a·ble** *adj.* —**as·sum·a·bly** *adv.* —**as·sum·er** *n.*

as·sumed (ə-sōōmd') *adj.* **1.** Pretended; adopted; fictitious: *an assumed name.* **2.** Taken for granted. —**as·sum·ed·ly** (ə-sōō'mĭd-lē) *adv.*

as·sum·ing (ə-sōō'mĭng) *adj.* Presumptuous or arrogant. ~*conj.* Accepting as provisionally true, for the sake of argument; supposing: *Assuming you miss the train, how will you get there?* —**as·sum·ing·ly** *adv.*

as·sump·sit (ə-sŭmp'sĭt) *n. Law.* **1.** An agreement or promise not under seal; a contract. **2.** A legal action to enforce or recover damages for a breach of such an agreement. [New Latin, "he undertook," from *assūmere,* to undertake, ASSUME.]

as·sump·tion (ə-sŭmp'shən) *n.* **1.** The act of assuming. **2.** A statement accepted or supposed to be true without proof or demonstration. **3.** Presumption or arrogance. **4.** *Logic.* A minor premise. **5. Assumption. a.** *Theology.* The bodily taking up of the Virgin Mary into heaven. **b.** A church feast on August 15 celebrating this event. [Middle English, from Latin *assumptiō* (stem *assumptiōn-*), a taking up, adoption, from *assūmere,* ASSUME.]

as·sump·tive (ə-sŭmp'tĭv) *adj.* **1.** Of or characterized by assumption: *assumptive facts.* **2.** Taken for granted. **3.** Presumptuous; assuming. **—as·sump·tive·ly** *adv.*

as·sur·ance (ə-shŏŏr′əns) *n.* **1. a.** The act of assuring. **b.** The state of being assured. **2.** A statement or indication that inspires confidence. **3. a.** Freedom from doubt; certainty. **b.** Self-confidence. **4.** Boldness; audacity. **5.** *Chiefly British.* Insurance making provision for events that are certain rather than probable, especially for death. **—See Synonyms at certainty.**

as·sure (ə-shŏŏr′) *tr.v.* **-sured, -sur·ing, -sures. 1.** To inform confidently, with a view to removing doubt. **2.** To cause to feel sure; convince. **3.** To give confidence to; reassure. **4.** To make certain; ensure: *This will assure the success of our enterprise.* **5.** To make safe or secure. **6.** To insure, especially against death. [Middle English *assuren,* from Old French *assurer,* from Medieval Latin *assēcūrāre,* to make sure : Latin *ad-,* to + *sēcūrus,* SECURE.] **—as·sur·a·ble** *adj.* **—as·sur·er** *n.*

as·sured (ə-shŏŏrd′) *adj.* **1.** Undoubted; guaranteed; made certain. **2.** Confident; bold. **3.** Insured, especially against death. **—See Synonyms at sure.**
~ *n., pl.* **assured. 1.** A person whose life is insured. **2.** A person who stands to benefit from a life insurance policy. **—as·sur·ed·ly** (ə-shŏŏr′ĭd-lē) *adv.* **—as·sur·ed·ness** *n.*

as·sur·gent (ə-sûr′jənt) *adj.* **1.** Rising or tending to rise. **2.** *Botany.* Slanting or curving upward; ascending. [Latin *assurgēns* (stem, *assurgent-*), present participle of *assurgere,* to rise up to : *ad-,* to + *surgere,* to SURGE.] **—as·sur·gen·cy** *n.*

assy. assembly.

Assyr. Assyrian.

As·syr·i·a (ə-sîr′ē-ə). An ancient civilization of western Asia, which began to develop at the beginning of the 3rd millennium B.C. around the city of Ashur on the upper Tigris River. The zenith of the Assyrian Empire was reached between the 9th and 7th centuries B.C. when it was extended from the Mediterranean across Arabia and Armenia. Its capital, Nineveh, fell in 612 B.C. to the Medes and Babylonians.

As·syr·i·an (ə-sîr′ē-ən) *adj.* Of or pertaining to Assyria, its people, their language or culture.
~ *n.* **1.** A native or inhabitant of Assyria. **2.** *Abbr.* **Assyr.** The Semitic language of Assyria.

As·syr·i·ol·o·gy (ə-sîr′ē-ŏl′ə-jē) *n.* The study of the ancient civilization of Assyria. **—As·syr·i·ol·o·gist** *n.*

a·sta·ble (ā-stā′bəl) *adj.* **1.** Not stable. **2.** *Electronics.* Designating or pertaining to a component or circuit that can exist in two distinct states.

As·taire (ə-stâr′), **Fred,** born Frederick Austerlitz (1899–1987). U.S. dancer and actor. His first film with Ginger Rogers, *Flying Down to Rio* (1933), marked the start of one of Hollywood's most famous partnerships. Among his other films are *Top Hat* (1935), *Easter Parade* (1948), and *Daddy Long Legs* (1955). In 1949 he was awarded a special Academy Award.

As·tar·te (ə-stär′tē). *Phoenician Mythology.* The goddess of love and fertility. [Latin *Astartē,* from Greek, from Phoenician *'strt,* akin to Hebrew *'Ashtoreth.*]

a·sta·sia (ə-stā′zhə) *n.* Inability to stand because of poor muscular coordination. [New Latin, from Greek instability, from *astatos,* unstable : *a-,* not + *statos,* standing.]

a·stat·ic (ā-stăt′ĭk) *adj.* **1.** Unsteady; unstable. **2.** *Physics.* Pertaining to or designating a device having two magnetic coils to compensate for the earth's magnetic field: *an astatic galvanometer.* **—a·stat·i·cal·ly** *adv.* **—a·stat·i·cism** (ā-stăt′ə-sĭz′əm) *n.*

as·ta·tine (ăs′tə-tēn′) *n. Symbol* **At** A highly unstable radioactive element that resembles iodine in solution and accumulates in the thyroid gland. Its longest lived isotope is At 210, having a half-life of 8.3 hours, used in medicine as a radioactive tracer. Atomic number 85, valences probably 1, 3, 5, and 7. [Greek *astatos,* unstable : *a-,* not + *statos,* standing + -INE.]

as·ter (ăs′tər) *n.* **1.** Any of various tall, perennial plants of the genus *Aster,* having rayed, daisylike flowers ranging in color from white to bluish purple or pink. See **Michaelmas daisy. 2.** The China aster *(see).* **3.** *Biology.* A star-shaped structure appearing in the cytoplasm of the cell and associated with the centrosome during mitosis. [New Latin, from Latin *astēr,* star, from Greek.]

-aster *suffix.* Indicates inferiority or fraudulence; for example, *poetaster.* [Middle English, from Latin, suffix denoting either smallness or partial resemblance (often pejorative).]

as·te·ri·at·ed (ă-stîr′ē-ā′tĭd) *adj. Mineralogy.* Exhibiting asterism. [Greek *asterios,* starry, from *astēr,* star.]

as·ter·isk (ăs′tə-rĭsk′) *n.* **1.** A star-shaped figure (*) used in printing to indicate an omission or a reference to a footnote. **2.** *Linguistics.* This sign used to indicate an unattested form or entity.
~ *tr.v.* **asterisked, -isking, -isks.** To indicate by means of an asterisk; mark with an asterisk. [Late Latin *asteriscus,* from Greek *asteriskos,* little star, asterisk, diminutive of *astēr,* star.]

as·ter·ism (ăs′tə-rĭz′əm) *n.* **1.** Three asterisks in triangular form used to call attention to a following passage. **2.** *Astronomy.* **a.** A cluster of stars. **b.** A constellation. **3.** In mineralogy, a six-rayed starlike figure observed in some crystal structures using reflected or transmitted light. [Greek *asterismos,* from *asterizein,* to arrange in constellations, from *astēr,* star.] **—as·ter·is·mal** *adj.*

a·stern (ə-stûrn′) *adv. Nautical.* **1.** Behind a vessel. **2.** Toward the rear of a vessel. **3.** To the rear; backward. [17th century : A- (toward) + STERN, formed by analogy with *ahead.*] **—a·stern** *adj.*

a·ster·nal (ā-stûr′nəl) *adj. Anatomy.* **1.** Not connected to the sternum. **2.** Lacking a sternum.

as·ter·oid (ăs′tə-roid′) *n.* **1.** *Astronomy.* Any of numerous celestial bodies with characteristic diameters between one and several hundred miles and orbits lying in a zone, the *asteroid belt,* chiefly between Mars and Jupiter. Also called "minor planet," "planetoid." **2.** *Zoology.* Star-shaped.
~ *adj.* Also **as·ter·oi·dal** (ăs′tə-roid′l). Star-shaped. [Greek *asteroeidēs,* like a star : *astēr,* star + -OID.]

Asterope. Variant of **Sterope.**

as·the·ni·a (ăs-thē′nē-ə) *n.* Also **as·the·ny** (ăs′thə-nē). *Pathology.* Loss or lack of strength; weakness. [New Latin, from Greek *asthenia,* from *asthenēs,* weak : *a-,* without + *sthenos†,* strength.]

as·then·ic (ăs-thĕn′ĭk) *adj.* **1.** Of or having a slender, long-limbed physique. **2.** Of or having asthenia.
~ *n.* A slender, long-limbed person. **—as·then·i·cal** *adj.*

as·the·no·pi·a (ăs′thə-nō′pē-ə) *n.* Eyestrain, especially with headache and dimming of the vision. [New Latin, ASTHEN(IA) + -OPIA.] **—as·the·nop·ic** (ăs′thə-nŏp′ĭk) *adj.*

as·then·o·sphere (ăs-thĕn′ə-sfîr′) *n.* A deformable zone in the earth's mantle lying between the lithosphere and the mesosphere (a depth of between 30 and 150 miles). [Greek *asthenēs,* weak (see **asthenia**) + SPHERE.]

asth·ma (ăz′mə) *n.* A chronic respiratory disease, often allergic in origin and marked by labored breathing, a sense of chest constriction, and coughing or gasping. [Middle English *asma,* from Medieval Latin, from Greek *asthma†.*] **—asth·mat·ic** (ăz-măt′ĭk) *adj. & n.* **—asth·mat·i·cal·ly** *adv.*

As·ti (ä′stē). Town in the Piedmont region of northwest Italy, famous for its sparkling white wine, Asti Spumante.

as·tig·mat·ic (ăs′tĭg-măt′ĭk) *adj.* **1.** Of or having astigmatism. **2.** Correcting astigmatism. **—as·tig·mat·i·cal·ly** *adv.*

a·stig·ma·tism (ə-stĭg′mə-tĭz′əm) *n.* **1.** A refractive defect of a lens that prevents focusing of sharp, distinct images. It occurs when the lens has different curvatures in two different directions. **2.** Faulty vision caused by such defects in the lens of the eye. [A- (without) + Greek *stigma* (stem *stigmat-*), spot, (tattoo) mark, "focus," from *stizein,* to tattoo.]

a·stil·be (ə-stĭl′bē) *n.* Any plant of the genus *Astilbe,* cultivated as garden plants for their ornamental pink or white plumelike flower clusters. [New Latin : A- (not) + Greek *stilbē,* from *stilbos,* glittering, with reference to the small, inconspicuous individual flowers.]

a·stir (ə-stûr′) *adj.* **1.** Moving about. **2.** Out of bed; awake. [Scottish *asteer* : A- (on) + *steer,* variant of STIR (noun).]

a·stom·a·tous (ā-stŏm′ə-təs, ā-stō′mə-) *adj.* Also **as·tom·ous** (ăs′tə-məs), **a·stom·a·tal** (ā-stŏm′ə-təl, ā-stō′mə-). *Biology.* Having no mouth or stomata.

As·ton (ăs′tən), **Francis William** (1877–1945). British physicist and chemist. In 1922 he was awarded the Nobel Prize in chemistry for the development of the mass spectrograph, which led to the discovery of a number of isotopes of nonradioactive elements and the accurate determination of atomic weights of elements.

a·ston·ied (ə-stŏn′ēd) *adj. Archaic.* Bewildered; dazed. [Middle English *aston(y)ed,* past participle of *astonen,* ASTONISH.]

a·ston·ish (ə-stŏn′ĭsh) *tr.v.* **-ished, -ishing, -ishes.** To fill with sudden wonder or amazement; surprise greatly. **—See Synonyms at surprise.** [Extension (with verbal suffix *-ish,* as in ABOLISH, FINISH) of obsolete *astony,* Middle English *astonen, astonien,* from Old French *estoner,* from Vulgar Latin *extonāre* (unattested), to strike with thunder, stun : Latin *ex-,* out of + *tonāre,* to thunder.] **—a·ston·ish·ing·ly** *adv.*

a·ston·ish·ment (ə-stŏn′ĭsh-mənt) *n.* **1.** Great surprise or amazement. **2.** A cause of amazement; a marvel.

As·tor (ăs′tər), **John Jacob** (1763–1848). U.S. fur trader and land investor. He founded the fortune of the Astors, one of the United States' wealthiest families.

Astor, Nancy Witcher Langhorne, Viscountess (1879–1964). British Conservative politician, born in the United States. Her second husband was **Waldorf Astor, 2nd Viscount Astor** (1879–1952), the great-great-grandson of John Jacob Astor. When he succeeded to the peerage in 1919, she was elected to his old seat of Plymouth and thus became the first woman to sit in the House of Commons. She held the seat until 1945.

a·stound (ə-stound′) *tr.v.* **astounded, astounding, astounds.** To strike with sudden wonder. **—See Synonyms at surprise.** [Originally the past participle of obsolete *astone,* to amaze, from Middle English *astonen,* ASTONISH.] **—a·stound·ing·ly** *adv.*

a·strad·dle (ə-străd′l) *adv.* In a straddling position; astride.
~ *prep.* So as to straddle; astride.

As·trae·a (ă-strē′ə). *Greek Mythology.* The goddess of justice. [New Latin, from Greek *astraios,* starry, from *astēr,* star.]

as·tra·gal (ăs′trə-gəl) *n. Architecture.* A narrow, convex molding, often having the form of beading. [Latin *astragalos,* from Greek *astragalos,* ankle bone (from the shape of the molding).]

as·trag·a·lus (ə-străg′ə-ləs) *n., pl.* **-li** (-lī′). A bone, the *talus (see).* [New Latin, from Greek *astragalos.*] **—as·trag·a·lar** *adj.*

as·tra·khan, as·tra·chan (ăs′trə-kăn′, -kən) *n.* **1.** The curly or wavy fur made from the wool of young lambs from the region of Astrakhan. **2.** A fabric with a curly, looped pile that is made to resemble this fur.

As·tra·khan (ăs′trə-kăn, -kən). City on the delta islands of the Volga, in southwest Russia. The city was taken from the Tatars by Ivan the Terrible in 1556.

as·tral (ăs′trəl) *adj.* **1.** Of, pertaining to, consisting of, emanating from, or resembling the stars. **2.** *Biology.* Pertaining to or shaped like an aster; star-shaped. **3.** In theosophy, consisting of or pertaining to a substance from which a higher, nonphysical body is made; mystical. [Late Latin *astrālis,* from Latin *astrum,* star, from Greek *astron.*] —**as·tral·ly** *adv.*

as·tra·pho·bi·a (ăs′trə-fō′bē-ə) *n.* Fear of lightning and thunder. [New Latin : Greek *astrapē,* lightning + -PHOBIA.]

a·stray (ə-strā′) *adv.* **1.** Away from the correct path or direction. **2.** Away from the right or good; toward evil or wrong ways. **3.** In the manner of one that strays: *My glasses have gone astray.* [Middle English *astray, astraie,* from Old French *estraie,* past participle of *estraier,* to STRAY.] —**a·stray** *adj.*

as·trict (ə-strĭkt′) *tr.v.* **-tricted, -tricting, -tricts.** To bind, especially by moral or legal obligations. [Latin *astrictus,* past participle of *astringere,* to bind fast, ASTRINGE.] —**as·tric·tion** *n.*

as·tric·tive (ə-strĭk′tĭv) *adj.* Astringent. ~*n.* An astringent. —**as·tric·tive·ly** *adv.* —**as·tric·tive·ness** *n.*

a·stride (ə-strīd′) *adv.* **1.** With the legs separated so that one is on each side: *rode the horse astride.* **2.** With the legs wide apart. ~*prep.* **1.** Upon or over and with a leg on each side of. **2.** With a part on each side of; spanning or bridging.

as·tringe (ə-strĭnj′) *tr.v.* **-tringed, -tringing, -tringes.** To draw together; constrict. [Latin *astringere,* to bind together : *ad-,* to + *stringere,* to bind.]

as·trin·gent (ə-strĭn′jənt) *adj.* **1.** Tending to draw together or constrict tissue; contracting; styptic. **2.** Harsh; severe: *an astringent wit.* **3.** Sharp-tasting; acidic. ~*n.* **1.** An astringent substance or drug, such as alum, used to constrict soft tissue and reduce superficial bleeding. **2.** An astringent cosmetic preparation; especially, a lotion for toning up the complexion. —**as·trin·gen·cy** *n.* —**as·trin·gent·ly** *adv.*

as·tri·on·ics (ăs′trē-ŏn′ĭks) *n. Used with a singular verb.* Electronics used in astronautics. [Irregularly from ASTRO(NAUTICS) + (ELECTR)ONICS.]

astro-, astr– *prefix.* Indicates: **1.** Star or star-shaped; for example, **astrocyte. 2.** Outer space; for example, **astronautics. 3.** Astronomical; for example, **astrophysics.** [Middle English, from Old French, from Latin, from Greek *astron,* star.]

as·tro·bi·ol·o·gy (ăs′trō-bī-ŏl′ə-jē) *n.* Exobiology (*see*).

as·tro·bleme (ăs′trō-blēm′) *n.* An ancient crater on the earth's surface formed by the impact of a meteorite. [ASTRO- + Greek *blēma,* a shot, wound.]

as·tro·chem·is·try (ăs′trō-kĕm′ĭs-trē) *n.* The study of the composition and reactions of substances present in celestial objects and interstellar matter.

as·tro·com·pass (ăs′trō-kŭm′pəs, -kŏm′-) *n.* A navigational instrument for determining direction relative to a fixed star.

as·tro·cyte (ăs′trə-sīt′) *n.* A star-shaped cell, especially a neuroglial cell. [ASTRO- + -CYTE.]

as·tro·cy·to·ma (ăs′trō-sī-tō′mə) *n., pl.* **-mas** or **-mata** (-mə-tə). A malignant brain tumor composed of astrocytes. [ASTROCYT(E) + -OMA.]

as·tro·dome (ăs′trə-dōm′) *n.* **1.** A transparent dome on the top of an aircraft, through which celestial observations are made for navigation. **2. Astrodome.** An enclosed stadium, used mainly for sports events, with a translucent dome.

as·tro·dy·nam·ics (ăs′trō-dī-năm′ĭks) *n. Used with a singular verb.* The dynamics of celestial bodies.

as·tro·ge·ol·o·gy (ăs′trō-jē-ŏl′ə-jē) *n.* The study of the structure, composition, and formation of rocks and minerals on other planets.

as·troid (ăs′troid′) *n. Geometry.* A type of plane curve; a hypocycloid that has four cusps. [ASTRO- + -OID (referring to its starlike shape).]

astrol. astrologer; astrological; astrology.

as·tro·labe (ăs′trə-lāb′) *n.* A medieval instrument consisting of a graduated vertical circle with a movable arm, used to determine the altitude of the sun or other celestial bodies for astronomical or navigational purposes. [Middle English, from Old French, from Medieval Latin *astrolabium,* from Greek *(organon) astrolabon,* "(instrument) for taking the stars" : ASTRO- + *lambanein,* to take.]

as·trol·o·gy (ə-strŏl′ə-jē) *n. Abbr.* **astrol.** The study of the positions and aspects of heavenly bodies with a view to assessing or predicting their supposed influence on human characteristics and the course of human affairs. [Middle English *astrologie,* from Old French, from Latin *astrologia,* from Greek, from *astrologos,* astronomer, (later) astrologer : ASTRO- + -LOGY.] —**as·trol·o·ger, as·trol·o·gist** *n.* —**as·tro·log·ic** (ăs′trə-lŏj′ĭk), **as·tro·log·i·cal** *adj.* —**as·tro·log·i·cal·ly** *adv.*

as·trom·e·try (ə-strŏm′ə-trē) *n.* The scientific measurement of the positions and movements of celestial bodies. —**as·tro·met·ric** (ăs′trə-mĕt′rĭk), **as·tro·met·ri·cal** *adj.*

astron. astronomer; astronomical; astronomy.

as·tro·naut (ăs′trə-nôt′) *n.* A person trained to pilot, navigate, or otherwise participate in the flight of a spacecraft. [ASTRO- + Greek *nautēs,* sailor, from *naus,* ship.]

as·tro·nau·tics (ăs′trə-nô′tĭks) *n. Used with a singular verb.* The science and technology of space flight. [ASTRO- + Latin *nautica,* neuter plural of *nauticus,* NAUTICAL.] —**as·tro·nau·tic, as·tro·nau·ti·cal** *adj.* —**as·tro·nau·ti·cal·ly** *adv.*

as·tro·nav·i·ga·tion (ăs′trō-năv′ə-gā′shən) *n.* **1.** Navigation of outer space, as in spacecraft. **2. Celestial navigation** (*see*). —**as·tro·nav·i·ga·tor** *n.*

as·tron·o·mer (ə-strŏn′ə-mər) *n. Abbr.* **astron.** A scientist specializing in astronomy. [Middle English, from Late Latin *astronomus,* from Greek *astronomos,* "star-arranger" : ASTRO- + -*nomos,* from *nemein,* to arrange (see -**nomy**).]

as·tro·nom·i·cal (ăs′trə-nŏm′ĭ-kəl) *adj.* Also **as·tro·nom·ic** (-nŏm′ĭk). **1.** *Abbr.* **astron.** Of or pertaining to astronomy. **2.** Inconceivably large; immense. —**as·tro·nom·i·cal·ly** *adv.*

astronomical telescope *n.* A reflecting or refracting telescope designed for astronomical observation. Compare **terrestrial telescope.**

astronomical unit *n. Abbr.* **A.U.** A unit of length used in measuring astronomical distances, equal to the distance of the earth from the sun, approximately 93 million miles.

astronomical year *n.* A tropical year (*see*).

as·tron·o·my (ə-strŏn′ə-mē) *n. Abbr.* **astron.** The scientific study of the universe beyond the earth, especially the observation, calculation, and theoretical interpretation of the positions, dimensions, distribution, motion, composition, and evolution of celestial bodies and phenomena. [Middle English *astronomie,* from Old French, from Latin *astronomia,* from Greek, from *astronomos,* ASTRONOMER.]

as·tro·pho·tog·ra·phy (ăs′trō-fə-tŏg′rə-fē) *n.* Astronomical photography. —**as·tro·pho·to·graph·ic** (ăs′trō-fō′tə-grăf′ĭk) *adj.*

as·tro·phys·ics (ăs′trō-fĭz′ĭks) *n. Used with a singular verb.* The branch of astronomy concerned with the theoretical physics of celestial bodies and phenomena. —**as·tro·phys·i·cal** *adj.* —**as·tro·phys·i·cist** *n.*

as·tro·sphere (ăs′trō-sfîr′) *n. Biology.* **1.** The central portion of a cell aster; the centrosphere. **2.** The entire cell aster with the exception of the centrosome. [ASTRO- + -SPHERE.]

As·tro·Turf (ăs′trō-tûrf′) *n.* A trademark for an artificial grasslike surfacing material made of nylon and vinyl, used especially on sports fields.

As·tu·ri·as (ə-stŏor′ē-əs, ə-styŏor′-). Region and old kingdom (established in 718) in northern Spain, coinciding with the present-day province of Oviedo. The 9th-century shrine at Santiago de Compostela remains a spiritual center of Christian Spain. —**As·tu·ri·an** *n. & adj.*

Asturias, Miguel Angel (1899–1974). Guatemalan novelist, poet, and diplomat. In 1923 he settled in Paris and came under the influence of André Breton. *Men of Corn* (1949) is usually considered to be his best novel. He received the Nobel Prize for literature (1967).

as·tute (ə-stōot′, ə-styōot′) *adj.* Keen in judgment. —See Synonyms at **shrewd.** [Latin *astūtus,* from *astus,* craft.] —**as·tute·ly** *adv.* —**as·tute·ness** *n.*

As·ty·a·nax (ə-stī′ə-năks′). *Greek Mythology.* The young son of Hector and Andromache, flung from the walls of Troy by the conquering Greeks.

a·sty·lar (ā-stī′lər) *adj.* Not having columns or pilasters. [A- (without) + Greek *stulos,* pillar.]

A·sun·ción (ə-sōōn-syŏn′). Chief port, industrial center, and capital of Paraguay, on the Paraguay River.

a·sun·der (ə-sŭn′dər) *adv.* **1.** Into separate parts or pieces. **2.** Apart from each other, either in position or direction. [Middle English *asonder,* Old English *onsundran, onsundrum* : *on,* on + *sundran, sundrum,* singly, separately, from *sunder,* apart, separate.] —**a·sun·der** *adj.*

Asur. Variant of **Ashur.**

A·swan (ăs′wän, ăs-wän′). Also **As·souan** or **As·suan.** City in southern Egypt, on the Nile River. It was an important station in the trade between ancient Egypt and the Sudan.

Aswan High Dam. Dam built on the Nile River *c.* 11 kilometers (7 miles) south of Aswan, opened in 1971. The building costs were largely supplied by the U.S.S.R. The dam is 114 meters (375 feet) high and 3,600 meters (11,800 feet) long. Its reservoir, Lake Nasser, is one of the largest artificial lakes in the world.

a·syl·lab·ic (ā′sĭ-lăb′ĭk) *adj.* Not syllabic.

a·sy·lum (ə-sī′ləm) *n.* **1.** A place offering protection or safety. **2.** Formerly, a temple or church affording sanctuary for criminals or debtors. **3.** Protection and immunity from extradition granted by a government to a political refugee from another country. **4.** Formerly, an institution for the care of the severely handicapped and especially the mentally ill. —See Synonyms at **shelter.** [Middle English *asilum,* from Latin *asylum,* from Greek *asulon,* sanctuary, from *asulos,* inviolable : *a-,* without + *sulon†,* right of seizure.]

a·sym·met·ric (ā′sĭ-mĕt′rĭk) *adj.* Also **a·sym·met·ri·cal** (-mĕt′rī-kəl). *Abbr.* **asym.** Not symmetrical. —**a·sym·met·ri·cal·ly** *adv.*

asymmetric atom *n. Chemistry.* An atom that is attached to four different groups in a molecule, such that the compound exhibits optical isomerism.

a·sym·me·try (ā-sĭm′ə-trē) *n.* Lack of symmetry or balance. [Greek *asummetria* : *a-,* without + *summetria,* SYMMETRY.]

a·symp·to·mat·ic (ā′sĭmp-tə-măt′ĭk) *adj.* Neither causing nor exhibiting symptoms. —**a·symp·to·mat·i·cal·ly** *adv.*

as·ymp·tote (ăs′ĭm-tōt′, -ĭmp-) *n. Mathematics.* **1.** A straight line that approaches a curve so that the perpendicular distance from a moving point on the curve to the line approaches zero as the point moves an infinite distance from the origin. **2.** A plane that approaches a curved surface at infinite distance from the origin. [New Latin *asymptota,* from Greek *(grammē) asumptōtos,* "(a line) not falling together" : *a-,* not + *sumptōtos,* from *sumpiptein,* to fall together : *sun-,* together + *piptein,* to fall.] —**as·ymp·tot·ic** (ăs′ĭm-tŏt′ĭk, -ĭmp-), **as·ymp·tot·i·cal** *adj.* —**as·ymp·tot·i·cal·ly** *adv.*

Atahualpa *When taken prisoner by Francisco Pizarro, the Inca Atahualpa offered as ransom to fill a room of 169 cubic meters (5,984 cubic feet) halfway up with gold, and to fill the entire room twice over with silver. Despite the vast amount of Inca treasure collected—some 6,080 kilograms (13,420 pounds) of gold and 11,790 kilograms (26,000 pounds) of silver—Atahualpa was garroted by the Spaniards.*

a·syn·chro·nism (ā-sĭng′krə-nĭz′əm) *n.* Also **a·syn·chro·ny** (-krə-nē). Lack of synchronism.

a·syn·chro·nous (ā-sĭng′krə-nəs) *adj.* Not synchronous. **—a·syn·chro·nous·ly** *adv.*

a·syn·de·ton (ə-sĭn′də-tŏn′) *n., pl.* **-tons** or **-ta** (-tə). The omission of conjunctions from constructions in which they would normally be used; for example: *He wrote, he drew, he painted.* Compare **parataxis.** [Late Latin, from Greek *asundeton,* from *asundetos,* "without conjunctions," unconnected : *ā-,* not + *sundetos,* bound together, from *sundein,* to bind together : *sun-,* together + *dein,* to bind.] **—as·yn·det·ic** (ăs′ĭn-dĕt′ĭk) *adj.* **—as·yn·det·i·cal·ly** *adv.*

a·syn·tac·tic (ā′sĭn-tăk′tĭk) *adj.* Not syntactic.

As·yut or **As·iut** or **As·siut** (ăs-yo͞ot′). An industrial city in central Egypt, on the Nile River.

at[1] (at, *weak form* ət) *prep.* **1. a.** In the location of: *at the market.* **b.** In the position of: *at the center of the page.* **2.** To or toward the direction of: *Look at him.* **3.** Present in; attending: *at the dance.* **4.** In the duration of; during: *at night.* **5.** In the state or condition of: *at peace with one's conscience; at liberty.* **6.** In the manner of: *at a run.* **7.** To the extent or amount of: *at thirty cents a pound.* **8.** On the exact or approximate moment of: *at three o'clock.* **9.** Because of: *rejoice at a victory.* **10.** Engaged in: *at war.* **11.** According to: *at one's discretion.* **12.** Dependent upon: *at the mercy of the court.* **13.** Maintaining or in accordance with a given rate, speed, or degree: *driving at 55 miles per hour.* [Middle English *at, atte,* Old English *æt.*]

at[2] (ät) *n., pl.* **at.** A monetary unit equal to 1/100 of the kip of Laos. [Thai.]

aT *Physics.* attotesla.

At The symbol for the element astatine.

AT antitank.

At·a·brine (ăt′ə-brĭn, -brēn′). A trademark for a yellow, bitter, crystalline compound, quinacrine hydrochloride, used primarily as an antimalarial drug.

A·ta·ca·ma Desert (ăt′ə-kăm′ə). Arid region of northwestern Chile. It is one of the world's driest areas, much of it having no recorded rainfall. It has some nitrate and copper reserves.

a·tac·tic (ā-tăk′tĭk) *adj. Chemistry.* Of or pertaining to a polymer with a nonregular arrangement of groups along its chain. Compare **stereospecific.** [A- (not) + -TACTIC.]

ataghan. Variant of **yataghan.**

A·ta·hual·pa or **A·ta·huall·pa** (ăt′ə-wäl′pə). Also **A·ta·ba·li·pa** (-bä′lə-pə). (*c.* 1502–33). The last Inca to rule Peru, captured and executed by the Spaniards.

At·a·lan·ta (ăt′ə-lăn′tə). *Greek Mythology.* A maiden who agreed to marry any man who could outrun her, and who was defeated by Hippomenes when he dropped three golden apples that she paused to pick up.

at·a·man (ăt′ə-măn′) *n., pl.* **-mans.** A Cossack chief. [Russian, from Polish *hetman,* from German *Hauptmann,* captain, from Middle High German *houbetman,* from Old High German *houbitman* : *houbit,* head + *man,* man.]

at·a·rac·tic (ăt′ə-răk′tĭk) *adj.* Also **at·a·rax·ic** (-răk′sĭk). Pertaining to or producing calmness and peace of mind.
~*n.* Also **at·a·rax·ic.** A drug that reduces nervous tension; a tranquilizer. [Greek *ataraktos,* undisturbed : *a-,* not + *taraktos,* disturbed, from *tarattein,* to disturb.]

at·a·rax·i·a (ăt′ə-răk′sē-ə) *n.* Peace of mind; emotional tranquillity. [Greek *ataraxia,* from *ataraktos,* ATARACTIC.]

A·ta·türk (ăt′ə-tûrk′), **Kemal,** born Mustafa Kemal (1881–1938). Turkish national leader, the founder of modern Turkey. In 1919 he organized the Turkish Nationalist Party and set up a rival government to the Ottoman sultan at Ankara. In 1923, after a civil war, he was elected the first president of the Turkish republic, a position that he held until his death. His rule was marked by westernization and internal reform. The name "Atatürk" means "Father of the Turks."

a·tav·ic (ə-tăv′ĭk) *adj.* Of or concerning a remote ancestor.

at·a·vism (ăt′ə-vĭz′əm) *n.* **1.** The reappearance of a characteristic in an organism after several generations of absence, caused by a recessive gene or complementary genes. **2.** An individual or part displaying atavism. Also loosely called "reversion," "throwback." **3.** Reversion to a primitive or earlier state of behavior. [French *atavisme,* from Latin *atavus,* ancestor, great-great-great-grandfather : *atta,* father + *avus,* grandfather.] **—at·a·vist** *n.* **—at·a·vis·tic** (ăt′ə-vĭs′tĭk) *adj.* **—at·a·vis·ti·cal·ly** *adv.*

a·tax·i·a (ə-tăk′sē-ə, ā-) *n.* Also **a·tax·y** (ə-tăk′sē, ā-). Loss or lack of muscular coordination. [Greek *ataxia,* from *ataktos,* disorderly : *a-,* not + *taktos,* ordered, from *tattein,* to arrange.]

a·tax·ic (ə-tăk′sĭk, ā-) *adj.* Of or pertaining to ataxia.
~*n.* An individual exhibiting symptoms of ataxia.

A.T.C. Air Traffic Control.

ate. Past tense of **eat.**

-ate[1] *suffix.* Indicates: **1.** Possessing; for example, **nervate, affectionate. 2.** Shaped like; for example, **lyrate. 3.** Having the general characteristics of; for example, **Latinate.** [Middle English *-at,* from Old French, from Latin *-ātus,* ending of the past participle of verbs in *-āre* (first conjugation). It thus appears in: **1.** Participial adjectives; for example, **ornate. 2.** Nouns converted from adjectives, either in Latin or in English; for example, **associate. 3.** Verbs originally formed from the corresponding nouns and adjectives in *-ate;* for example, **aggregate, conjugate;** and subsequently, by analogy with these, adopted directly from Latin, taking participial form but infinitive sense; for example, **desiccate, eradicate.**]

-ate[2] *suffix.* Indicates: **1.** The product of a specified process; for example, **distillate. 2.** *Chemistry.* **a.** The salt of an oxygen acid; for example, **nitrate, sulfate. b.** The ester of an oxygen acid or carboxylic acid; for example, **acetate, stearate.** [Special use of -ATE[1].]

-ate[3] *suffix.* Indicates: **1.** Rank or status; for example, **magistrate. 2.** A group of people performing a specified function or holding a specified office; for example, **electorate.** [Latin *-ātus,* an abstract suffix made up of the *-āt-* of *-ātus,* participial ending (-ATE[1]) and the feminine *-us* of fourth declension nouns. It originally designated the collective status of a group, as in **senate,** later the power of a specific type of ruler, as in **triumvirate.**]

-ate[4] *suffix.* Indicates: **1.** To cause to become; for example, **activate. 2.** To supply or impregnate with; for example, **oxygenate.** [Abstracted from verbs of Latin origin ending in *-ate.* See **-ate**[1].]

at·el·ier (ăt′l-yā′) *n.* A workshop or artist's studio. [French, from Old French *astelier,* woodpile, hence carpenter's shop, from *astele,* splinter, shaving, chip, from Late Latin *astella,* variant of Latin *astula, assula,* diminutive of *assis,* board, plank, probably variant of *axis.* See **ashlar.**]

a tem·po (ä tĕm′pō) *adv. Music.* In normal time; resuming the original tempo. Used as a direction. [Italian, "in time."]

a·tem·po·ral (ā-tĕm′pər-əl) *adj.* Independent of time; timeless.

A·ten, A·ton (ä′tən). *Egyptian Mythology.* A sun god, regarded during the reign of Akhenaton as the only god.

Ath·a·bas·ka or **Ath·a·bas·ca** (ăth′ə-băs′kə). River in northern Alberta in Canada, rising in the Rockies and flowing 1,230 kilometers (765 miles) northeast into Lake Athabaska.

Ath·a·na·sian (ăth′ə-nā′zhən) *adj.* Of or pertaining to Athanasius.
~*n.* A follower of Athanasius and his teachings.

Athanasian creed *n.* A Christian creed or profession of faith dating from about A.D. 425, expounding the doctrine of the Trinity. [After St. ATHANASIUS.]

Ath·a·na·si·us (ăth′ə-nā′shəs), **Saint** (A.D. *c.* 297–373). Doctor of the Christian Church and patriarch of Alexandria (328–373). He played an important part at the First Council of Nicaea in the debate against Arianism. He was formerly thought to be the author of the Athanasian creed.

Ath·a·pas·can (ăth′ə-păs′kən) *n.* Also **Ath·a·bas·can** (-băs′kən). **1.** A North American Indian language stock, including languages of Alaska and northwest Canada, of the coast of Oregon and California, and the Navaho and Apache languages of the southwestern United States. **2.** A member of an Athapascan-speaking people.
~*adj.* Of or designating this language stock. [From the name of Lake *Athabaska* in western Canada, Northern Cree *athapaskaaw,* "there is scattered grass."]

a·the·ism (ā′thē-ĭz′əm) *n.* **1.** Disbelief in or denial of the existence of God. Compare **agnosticism. 2.** Godlessness; wickedness. **3.** The doctrine that there is no deity. [Old French *atheisme,* from *athee,* atheist, from Greek *atheos,* godless : *a-,* without + *theos,* god.]

A·the·ist (ā′thē-ĭst) *n.* One who denies the existence of God.

a·the·is·tic (ā′thē-ĭs′tĭk) *adj.* Also **a·the·is·ti·cal** (-tĭ-kəl). **1.** Pertaining to or characteristic of atheism or atheists. **2.** Inclined to atheism. **—a·the·is·ti·cal·ly** *adv.*

ath·e·ling, aeth·e·ling (ăth′ə-lĭng, ăth′-) *n.* An Anglo-Saxon nobleman or prince. [Middle English *atheling,* Old English *ætheling,* prince : *æthel,* noble + *-ing,* descendant of.]

Ath·el·stan, Aeth·el·stan (ăth′əl-stən′) (895–940). King of Mercia and Wessex, the first Saxon ruler to establish his authority over all of England. He was elected king of Mercia in *c.* 924 and a year later was crowned king of the whole country.

a·the·mat·ic (ā′thē-măt′ĭk) *adj.* **1.** *Music.* Not based on themes. **2.** *Linguistics.* Designating a verb that has no vowel between the stem and the ending.

A·the·na (ə-thē′nə). Also **A·the·ne** (-nē). *Greek Mythology.* The goddess of wisdom and the arts. Identified with the Roman goddess Minerva. Also called "Pallas Athena."

ath·e·ne·um, ath·e·nae·um (ăth′ə-nē′əm) *n.* **1.** An institution, such as a literary club or scientific academy, for the promotion of learning. **2.** A library, reading room, or similar place. [Late Latin *Athēnaeum,* a Roman school of art, after Greek *Athēnaion,* the temple of Athena at Athens, where philosophy was taught, from *Athēnē,* ATHENA.]

Ath·ens (ăth′ənz). *Greek* **A·thi·ne, A·thi·nai** (ə-thē′nī′). Capital and industrial center of Greece, in the east of the country near the Saronic Gulf. At the time of the Persian Wars (500–499 B.C.) it was the most powerful Greek city state and the cradle of democracy. The zenith of its cultural achievements and imperial power was reached during the time of Pericles (443–429 B.C.), when Socrates, Sophocles, Aeschylus, and Euripides all flourished. It became the capital of modern Greece when the country won its independence from Turkey in 1834.

a·ther·man·cy (ə-thûr′mən-sē, ā-) *n. Physics.* The inability of substances to transmit infrared radiation. [Greek *athermantos,* not heated : A-(not) + *thermantos,* from *thermē,* heat.] **—a·ther·man·ous** *adj.*

ath·er·o·ma (ăth′ə-rō′mə) *n., pl.* **-mas** or **-mata** (-mə-tə). *Pathology.* **1.** A deposit or degenerative accumulation of pulpy, acellular, lipid-containing materials, especially in arterial walls. **2.** A form of arteriosclerosis characterized by such deposits. [New Latin, from Latin, from Greek *athērōma,* a cyst full of gruellike pus, from *athēra,* gruel, from *athēr*†, beard of grain.] **—ath·er·o·ma·to·sis** (ăth′ə-rō-mə-tō′sĭs) *n.* **—ath·er·o·ma·tous** (ăth′ə-rō′mə-təs) *adj.*

ath·er·o·scle·ro·sis (ăth′ə-rō-sklə-rō′sĭs) n. Pathology. A disease in which fatty deposits form in the arteries and obstruct the blood flow; atheromatous arteriosclerosis; atheroma. [atheroma + sclerosis.] —**ath·er·o·scle·rot·ic** (ăth′ə-rō-sklə-rŏt′ĭk) adj.

a·thirst (ə-thûrst′) adj. 1. Strongly desirous; eager. Usually used with for: athirst for freedom 2. Archaic. Thirsty.

ath·lete (ăth′lēt′) n. 1. One who takes part in competitive sports, especially track and field events. 2. A person possessing the natural prerequisites for sports competition, such as strength, speed, agility, and endurance. [Middle English, from Latin athlēta, from Greek athlētēs, contestant, from athlein, to contend for an award, from athlon†, award, prize.]

athlete's foot n. A chronic fungal infection of the skin of the foot, usually causing itching, blisters, and cracking.

ath·let·ic (ăth-lĕt′ĭk) adj. 1. Of, pertaining to, or befitting athletics or athletes. 2. Physically strong; muscular. 3. Physically active and agile. —**ath·let·i·cal·ly** adv. —**ath·let·i·cism** (ăth-lĕt′ə-sĭz′əm) n.

ath·let·ics (ăth-lĕt′ĭks) n. 1. Used with a plural verb. **a.** Physical activities, such as competitive sports or games. **b.** Track and field sporting events. 2. Used with a singular verb. The principles or practice of athletic exercises and training.

athletic supporter n. A **jockstrap** (see).

ath·o·dyd (ăth′ə-dĭd) n. A simple jet engine. See **ramjet, pulsejet.** [Aerothermodynamic duct.]

at-home (ət-hōm′) n. An informal reception at one's home.

-athon, -thon suffix. Indicates a prolonged or strenuous event or activity, often involving financial sponsorship; for example, **telethon, talkathon.** [Abstracted from MARATHON.]

Ath·os, Mount (ăth′ŏs, ā′thŏs). A mountain peak, rising to 2,030 meters (6,660 feet) at the southern tip of the Athos Peninsula in northeast Greece. It is the site of the virtually independent group of 20 monasteries of the Order of St. Basil of the Eastern Orthodox Church. In 1927 Mount Athos was granted the status of a theocratic republic under the suzerainty of Greece.

a·thwart (ə-thwôrt′) adv. 1. From side to side; crosswise; transversely. 2. So as to thwart or obstruct; perversely. ~prep. 1. From one side to the other of; across. 2. Contrary to; against. 3. Nautical. Across the course, line, or length of. [Middle English, a- (on) + THWART (side).]

a·tilt (ə-tĭlt′) adv. 1. In a tilted position; inclined upward. 2. As if tilting with a lance: "Break a lance, and run atilt at death" (Shakespeare). —**a·tilt** adj.

-ation suffix. Indicates: 1. Action or process of; for example, **strangulation, negotiation.** 2. State, condition, or quality of; for example, **isolation, moderation.** 3. Result or product of; for example, **dramatization, civilization.** [Middle English -acioun, from Old French -ation, from Latin -ātiō (stem -ātiōn-), abstract noun suffix, from -ātus. See -ate¹, -ion.]

-ative suffix. Indicates relation, nature, or tendency; for example, **authoritative, illustrative, formative.** [Middle English, from Old French -atif, from Latin -ātīvus, from -ātus. See -ate¹, -ive.]

Atkins, Tommy. See **Tommy Atkins.**

Atl. Atlantic.

At·lan·ta (ăt-lăn′tə). The capital of Georgia, in the northwest part of the state. It was founded in 1837, but had to be almost entirely rebuilt after being burned during the Civil War on November 15, 1864, just before Gen. William Tecumseh Sherman began his "march to the sea" from the town. Today it is the largest city in Georgia and the cultural and business center of the state.

At·lan·te·an (ăt′lăn-tē′ən, ăt-lăn′tē-ən) adj. 1. Of, pertaining to, or resembling Atlas. 2. Of or pertaining to Atlantis. [Latin Atlanteus : Atlas (stem Atlant-), ATLAS + -AN.]

at·lan·tes. Architecture. Plural of **atlas** (sense 4).

At·lan·tic (ăt-lăn′tĭk) adj. 1. Abbr. **Atl.** Of, in, near, upon, or pertaining to the Atlantic Ocean. 2. Of or pertaining to Atlas or to the Atlas Mountains. ~n. The Atlantic Ocean. [Latin (mare) Atlanticum, from Greek (pelagos) Atlantikos, "(the sea) of Atlas" (the sea lying beyond the Atlas Mountains), from Atlas (stem Atlant-), ATLAS.]

Atlantic Charter n. A declaration of the aims of the Allied Nations concerning a postwar settlement in World War II, made jointly by Churchill and Roosevelt after a meeting at sea in August 1941.

Atlantic City. A resort and convention city on the Atlantic coast of New Jersey. The city thrives almost exclusively on tourism and legalized gambling, introduced in 1978.

Atlantic Ocean. The world's second-largest ocean, with an area of 82,217,000 square kilometers (31,744,000 square miles). Its average depth is 3,660 meters (12,000 feet). It is divided into two great basins, the North Atlantic and the South Atlantic, the former with clockwise-flowing currents, the latter with counterclockwise currents. Down the center of the ocean, running for 16,000 kilometers (10,000 miles) is the Mid-Atlantic Ridge. See map, next page.

Atlantic salmon n. A food fish, Salmo salar, of northern Atlantic waters. See **salmon.**

At·lan·tis (ăt-lăn′tĭs). Legendary island in the Atlantic west of Gibraltar, said by Plato to have sunk beneath the sea.

at·las (ăt′ləs) n., pl. **atlases** or **atlantes** (ăt-lăn′tēz) (for sense 4).) 1. A bound collection of maps. 2. Any volume of tables, charts, or plates that systematically illustrate a subject: anatomical atlas. 3. A large size of drawing paper, measuring 26 by 33 or 34 inches. 4. Plural **atlantes.** Architecture. A figure of a man used as a masonry column on a building to support an entablature. 5. Anatomy. The top or first cervical vertebra of the neck, which supports the skull.

[From representations of the Titan ATLAS upholding the heavens, common in 16th-century books of maps.]

At·las (ăt′ləs). Greek Mythology. A giant, one of the Titans, who was condemned to support the heavens upon his shoulders for rebelling against the gods. [Latin, from Greek Atlas (stem Atlant-); the name was subsequently applied to the Atlas Mts. in northwest Africa and then to the sea nearby (Atlantis, Atlantic).]

Atlas Mountains. Series of fold mountain ranges extending from Morocco through Algeria into Tunisia. They form a climatic barrier between the Mediterranean lowlands and the Sahara. The highest peak is Jebel Toubkal (4,165 meters; 13,665 feet).

atm. atmosphere; atmospheric.

at·man (ät′mən) n. Hinduism. 1. The individual soul; the principle of life. 2. **Atman.** The universal soul, from which all individual souls arise; Brahma. [Sanskrit ātman, breath, spirit, soul.]

atmo- prefix. Indicates the presence of or relation to vapor; for example, **atmosphere.** [New Latin, from Greek atmos, vapor, breath.]

at·mol·y·sis (ăt-mŏl′ə-sĭs) n., pl. **-ses** (-sēz). The separation of a mixture of gases, each with different diffusibility, by diffusion through a porous material. [ATMO- + -LYSIS.]

at·mom·e·ter (ăt-mŏm′ə-tər) n. An instrument that measures the rate of water evaporation. [ATMO- + -METER.] —**at·mo·met·ric** (ăt′mō-mĕt′rĭk) adj. —**at·mom·e·try** n.

atmos. atmosphere; atmospheric.

at·mos·phere (ăt′mə-sfîr′) n. 1. Abbr. **atm., atmos.** The gaseous mass or envelope surrounding a celestial body, especially that surrounding the earth, and retained by the body's gravitational field. 2. The quality of the air or climate in a specific place: a very smoky atmosphere. 3. Abbr. **atm** Physics. A unit of pressure equal to 1.01325 × 10⁵ newtons per square meter at sea level. 4. A psychological environment: He grew up in an atmosphere of austerity. 5. The predominant tone or mood of a work of art. 6. **a.** A pervading quality, effect, or mood, especially as associated with a particular place: a dark old house with a depressing atmosphere. **b.** A distinctively exotic or romantic quality or effect: a Greek restaurant with lots of atmosphere. [New Latin atmosphaera, "sphere of vapor" : ATMO- + -SPHERE.] See feature, page 117.

at·mos·pher·ic (ăt′mə-sfîr′ĭk, -sfĕr′ĭk) adj. Also **at·mos·pher·i·cal.** Abbr. **atm., atmos.** 1. Of, pertaining to, or existing in the atmosphere. 2. Produced by, dependent on, or coming from the atmosphere. —**at·mos·pher·i·cal·ly** adv.

atmospheric pressure n. The pressure exerted by the atmosphere. At sea level it has a mean value of 1.01325 × 10⁵ newtons per square meter (760 mmHg) but reduces with increasing altitude.

at·mos·pher·ics (ăt′mə-sfîr′ĭks, -sfĕr′ĭks) n. Used with a singular verb. 1. Electromagnetic radiation produced by natural phenomena such as lightning. 2. Radio interference produced by such radiation. Also called "spherics."

a·toll (ă′tôl′, ā′tôl′, ā′-) n. A ringlike coral reef that nearly or entirely encloses a lagoon. [Malayalam atoḷu, "reef," native name for the Maldive Islands.]

at·om (ăt′əm) n. 1. Anything considered an irreducible constituent of a specified system. 2. The irreducible, indestructible material unit of ancient **atomism** (see). 3. Physics & Chemistry. A unit of matter, the smallest unit of an element, consisting of a dense, central, positively charged **nucleus** (see) surrounded by a system of electrons, equal in number to the number of nuclear protons, the entire structure having an approximate diameter of 10⁻⁸ centimeter and characteristically remaining undivided in chemical reactions except for limited removal, transfer, or exchange of outer electrons. 4. This unit regarded as a source of nuclear energy. [Middle English attome, attomus, from Latin atomus, from Greek atomos, indivisible : a-, not + temnein, to cut. See -tome, -tomy.]

a·tom·ic (ə-tŏm′ĭk) adj. 1. Of or relating to an atom or atoms. 2. Of or employing atomic energy: an atomic submarine. 3. Very small; infinitesimal. —**a·tom·i·cal·ly** adv.

atomic age n. Also **Atomic Age.** The current era as characterized by the discovery, technological applications, and sociopolitical consequences of atomic energy.

atomic bomb n. A **nuclear bomb** (see).

atomic clock n. An extremely precise timekeeping device regulated in correspondence with a characteristic invariant frequency of an atomic or molecular system.

atomic energy n. Nuclear energy (see).

atomic heat n. The product of an element's atomic weight and its specific heat capacity.

at·o·mic·i·ty (ăt′ə-mĭs′ə-tē) n. 1. The state of being composed of atoms. 2. Chemistry. **a.** The number of atoms in a molecule. **b.** Valence.

atomic mass n. The mass of an atomic system or constituent, usually expressed in atomic mass units.

atomic mass unit n. Abbr. **amu** A unit of mass equal to ¹/₁₂ the mass of the carbon isotope with mass number 12, approximately 1.6604 × 10⁻²⁴ gram.

atomic number n. Symbol **Z** The number of protons in an atomic nucleus. Also called "proton number."

atomic pile n. A **nuclear reactor** (see).

atomic power n. Nuclear power (see).

atomic reactor n. A **nuclear reactor** (see).

atomic theory n. 1. The physical theory of the structure, properties, and behavior of the atom. 2. Atomism.

Athena The Greek goddess of wisdom. This Roman statuette dates from 130 A.D. and is in the Athens National Museum.

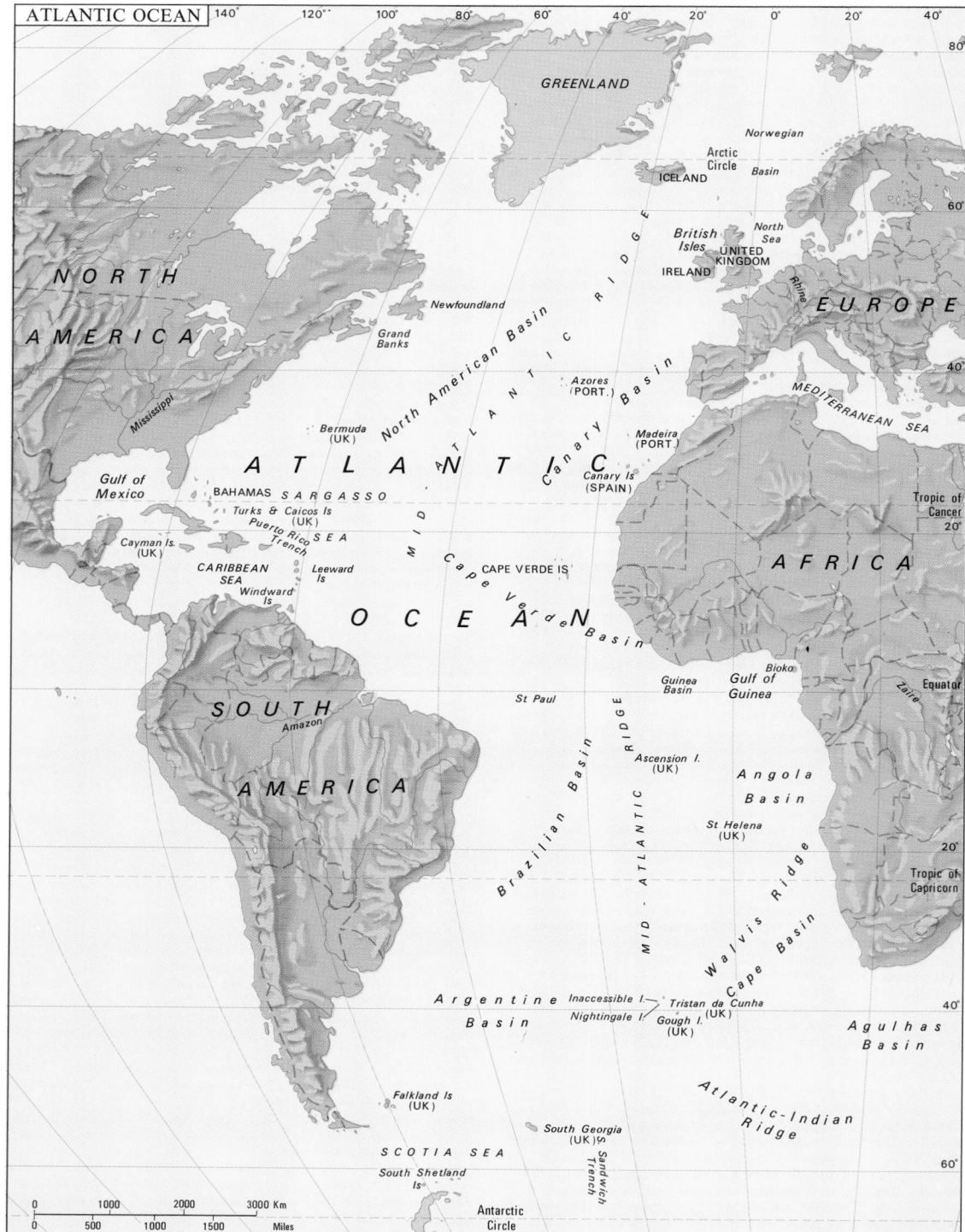

atomic volume _n._ The ratio of an element's atomic weight to its density.

atomic weight _n. Abbr._ **at wt** The average weight of an atom of an element, usually expressed relative to one atom of the carbon isotope taken to have a standard weight of 12. Also called "relative atomic mass."

at·om·ism (ăt´əm-ĭz´əm) _n._ **1.** The ancient theory of Democritus, Epicurus, and Lucretius, according to which simple, indivisible, and indestructible atoms are the basic components of the entire universe. **2.** In sociology, any theory according to which social institutions and processes arise solely from the acts of individual men. **3.** In political theory: **a.** The division or tendency to divide into subclasses, groups, or units of a given society. **b.** Such a tendency accompanied by or arising from a strong subjective individualism. —**at·om·ist** _n._ —**at·om·is·tic, at·om·is·ti·cal** _adj._ —**at·om·is·ti·cal·ly** _adv._

at·om·ize (ăt´əm-īz´) _tr.v._ **-ized, izing, -izes. 1.** To reduce or separate into atoms. **2. a.** To reduce (a liquid) to a spray. **b.** To spray (a liquid) in this form. **3.** To subject to bombardment with atomic weapons. **4.** To reduce to individual parts or units; fragment. —**at·om·i·za·tion** _n._

at·om·iz·er (ăt´əm-ī´zər) _n._ A device for producing a fine spray, especially of perfume or medicine.

atom smasher _n._ An atomic particle **accelerator** _(see)._

at·o·my[1] (ăt´ə-mē) _n., pl._ **-mies.** _Archaic._ **1.** A tiny particle. **2.** A tiny being: "_Drawn with a team of little atomies_" (Shakespeare). [Latin _atomī,_ plural of _atomus,_ ATOM.]

atomy[2] _n., pl._ **-mies.** _Archaic._ A skeleton or a gaunt person. [From ANATOMY, misinterpreted as _an atomy._]

Aton. Variant of **Aten.**

a·to·nal (ā-tō´nəl) _adj._ _Music._ Lacking a tonal center or established key. Compare **serial, twelve-tone.** —**a·to·nal·ism** *n.* —**a·to·nal·ly** *adv.*

a·to·nal·i·ty (ā′tō-nǎl′ə-tē) *n. Music.* **1.** The lack of a tonal center or key in musical composition, or the deliberate disregarding of it, especially as an alternative to the diatonic system. **2.** The theory of atonal composition.

a·tone (ə-tōn′) *v.* **atoned, atoning, atones.** —*intr.* **1.** To make amends, as for a sin or fault. Used with *for.* **2.** *Archaic.* To agree. —*tr. Archaic.* **1.** To expiate. **2.** To reconcile or harmonize. **3.** To conciliate; appease. [Middle English *atonen,* to be reconciled, from *at one,* of one mind, in accord : AT + ONE.] —**a·ton·a·ble, a·tone·a·ble** *adj.* —**a·ton·er** *n.*

a·tone·ment (ə-tōn′mənt) *n.* **1.** Amends or reparation made for an injury or wrong; expiation; recompense. **2.** In the Hebrew scriptures, man's reconciliation with God after having transgressed the covenant. **3. Atonement.** *Theology.* **a.** The redemptive life, suffering, and death of Christ. **b.** The reconciliation of God and man thus brought about by Christ. **4.** *Christian Science.* The radical obedience and purification, exemplified in the life of Jesus, by which humanity finds man's oneness with God. **5.** *Archaic.* Reconciliation; concord.

a·ton·ic (ā-tŏn′ĭk) *adj.* **1.** Not accented: *atonic words and syllables.* **2.** *Pathology.* Pertaining to, caused by, or characterized by atony. —*n.* A word, syllable, or sound that is unaccented. [French *atonique,* from Greek *atonos.* See atony.] —**a·to·nic·i·ty** (ăt′ə-nĭs′ə-tē, ā′tō-) *n.*

at·o·ny (ăt′ə-nē) *n.* **1.** *Pathology.* **1.** Insufficient muscular tone. **2.** *Phonetics.* Lack of accent or stress. [Late Latin *atonia,* from Greek, from *atonos,* not stretched : *a-,* without + *tonos,* a stretching, TONE.]

a·top (ə-tŏp′) *adv. Archaic.* On or at the top. —*prep.* On top of. —**a·top** *adj.*

–ator *suffix.* Indicates one that acts or does; for example, **aviator, radiator.** [Middle English *-atour,* from Old French, from Latin *-ātor* : *-ātus,* -ATE + -OR.]

–atory *suffix.* Indicates pertinence to, characteristic of, result of, or effect of; for example, **placatory, perspiratory, amendatory.** [Middle English, from Latin *-ātōrius* : *-ātus,* -ATE + *-ōrius,* -ORY.]

ATP *n. Biochemistry.* A nucleotide, $C_{10}H_{16}N_5O_{13}P_3$, occurring in plant and animal cells, that is a major energy source for vital processes. The energy is released when ATP is converted to ADP. [*a*denosine *t*riphosphate.]

at·ra·bil·ious (ăt′rə-bĭl′yəs) *adj.* Also **at·ra·bil·i·ar** (-bĭl′ē-ər). **1.** Inclined to melancholy; gloomy. **2.** Having a peevish disposition; surly. [Latin *ātra bīlis,* black bile (translation of Greek *melankhōlia,* MELANCHOLY) : *ātra,* feminine of *āter,* black + *bīlis,* BILE.] —**at·ra·bil·ious·ness** *n.*

A·treus (ā′trōōs′, ā′trē-əs). *Greek Mythology.* A king of Mycenae, father of Agamemnon and Menelaus.

a·tri·o·ven·tric·u·lar (ā′trē-ō-vĕn-trĭk′yə-lər) *adj. Anatomy.* Pertaining to the atria and the ventricles of the heart. [New Latin *atrio-,* heart chamber, ATRIUM + VENTRICULAR.]

a·trip (ə-trĭp′) *adj. Nautical.* Just clear of the bottom; aweigh. Said of an anchor. [A- (on) + TRIP (to raise an anchor).] —**a·trip** *adv.*

a·tri·um (ā′trē-əm) *n., pl.* **atria** (ā′trē-ə) or **-ums. 1.** An open central court, especially in an ancient Roman house. **2.** A body cavity or chamber; especially, either of the two upper chambers of the heart, from which the blood passes to the ventricles. Also called "auricle." **3.** A court in front of a church, often surrounded by colonnades. [Latin *ātrium;* akin to *āter,* black, blackened (by fire), perhaps with reference to the part of a Roman house blackened by smoke from the hearth.] —**a·tri·al** (ā′trē-əl) *adj.*

a·tro·cious (ə-trō′shəs) *adj.* **1.** Extremely evil or cruel; monstrous: *an atrocious crime.* **2.** Exceptionally bad; terrible: *atrocious decor; atrocious behavior.* [Latin *ātrōx* (stem *atrōc-*), "dark-looking," horrible, cruel; akin to *āter,* black.] —**a·tro·cious·ly** *adv.* —**a·tro·cious·ness** *n.*

a·troc·i·ty (ə-trŏs′ə-tē) *n., pl.* **-ties. 1.** Atrocious condition, quality, or behavior; monstrousness; vileness. **2. a.** An atrocious action, situation, or object; an outrage. **b. atrocities.** Savage or brutal acts committed in wartime.

at·ro·phy (ăt′rə-fē) *n., pl.* **-phies. 1.** *Pathology.* The emaciation or wasting of tissues, organs, or the entire body. **2.** Any wasting away or diminution: *moral atrophy.* —*v.* **atrophied, -phying, -phies.** —*tr.* To cause to waste away. —*intr.* To waste away; wither. [Late Latin *atrophia,* from Greek, from *atrophos,* ill-nourished : *a-,* without + *trophē,* nourishment, from *trephein,* to feed.] —**a·tro·phic** (ā-trō′fĭk) *adj.*

at·ro·pine (ăt′rə-pēn′) *n.* An extremely poisonous, bitter, crystalline alkaloid, $C_{17}H_{23}NO_3$, obtained from belladonna and related plants. It is used in medicine to dilate the pupil of the eye and as an antispasmodic. [New Latin *Atropa,* genus of belladonna, deadly nightshade, from Greek *atropos,* unchangeable, inflexible. See Atropos.]

At·ro·pos (ăt′rə-pŏs′, -pəs). *Greek Mythology.* One of the three **Fates** (*see*). She cuts the thread of life. [Greek, from *atropos,* inexorable, inflexible : *a-,* not + *trop-,* stem of *trepein,* to turn.]

A.T.S. 1. American Temperance Society. **2.** Army Transport Service.

at·ta·boy (ăt′ə-boi′) *interj.* Used to express encouragement or approval.

at·tach (ə-tăch′) *v.* **-tached, -taching, -taches.** —*tr.* **1.** To fasten on or affix to; connect or join. **2.** To connect as an adjunct or associ-

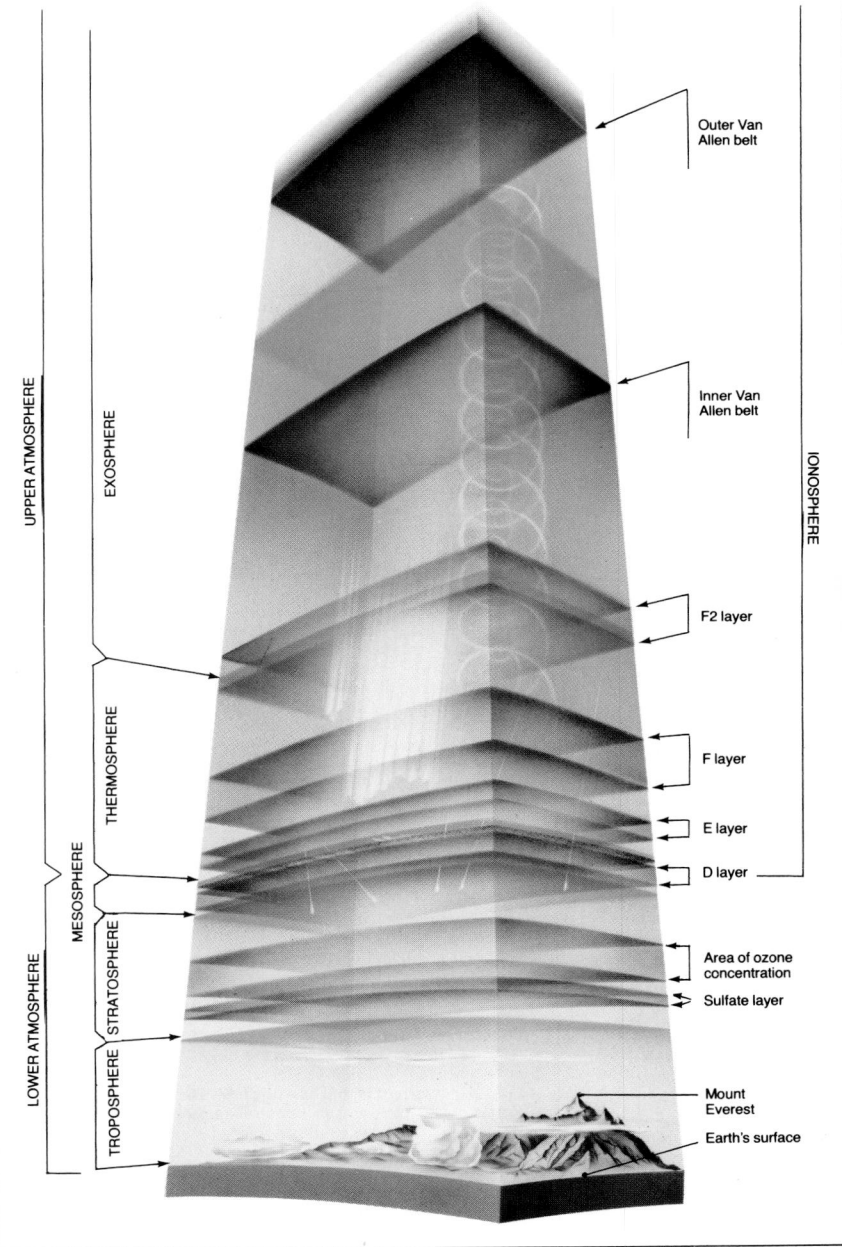

OUR MULTILAYERED ATMOSPHERE
A barrier of gases protecting Earth from space

The atmosphere is a mixture of gases encircling Earth and held by Earth's gravity. This invisible mixture of nitrogen, oxygen, argon, carbon dioxide, and water vapor protects the planet from harmful radiation and makes life on Earth possible. The atmosphere's density decreases with height, but not at a uniform rate. Above about 90 kilometers (55 miles) the air is extremely rarefied but it extends thousands of miles above Earth.

Different layers of atmosphere are distinguished by their temperatures. The troposphere extends 18 kilometers (11 miles) above Earth. It is warmed by solar rays reradiated from Earth's surface. This causes convection currents that bring changes in the weather. Temperature in the troposphere decreases with height to -60°C (-76°F), but in the stratosphere it rises to near freezing point. The stratosphere extends to 50 kilometers (30 miles). It contains ozone, which absorbs ultraviolet rays from the sun. In the mesosphere, which extends to 80 kilometers (50 miles) above Earth, temperature drops to -113°C (-173°F). These three layers form the lower atmosphere. In the rarefied upper atmosphere, temperature rises, reaching 227°C (441°F) even at night where thermosphere and exosphere meet 450 kilometers (280 miles) above Earth.

The upper atmosphere absorbs much harmful radiation and in doing so produces electrically charged particles—ions. In this region, called the ionosphere, layers of greater ion concentration—the D, E, and F layers—exist, although they vary daily or seasonally. Man uses them to bounce radio waves around the earth. Farther out in the ionosphere are two Van Allen belts, zones of radiation concentration.

Outer Van Allen belt

Inner Van Allen belt

IONOSPHERE

UPPER ATMOSPHERE

EXOSPHERE

F2 layer

THERMOSPHERE

F layer

E layer

D layer

MESOSPHERE

Area of ozone concentration

Sulfate layer

LOWER ATMOSPHERE

STRATOSPHERE

Mount Everest

TROPOSPHERE

Earth's surface

ated part. **3.** To affix or append; add, as a signature. **4.** To ascribe or assign: *I attach no significance to the threat.* **5.** To bind by personal ties, as of affection or loyalty. Usually used in the passive with *to*: *He's very attached to his mother.* **6.** To appoint officially. **7.** *Military.* To assign (personnel) to a unit on a temporary basis. Compare **assign. 8.** *Law.* To seize (persons or property) by legal writ. **9.** *Law.* To order the withholding of payment of (a debt) because a third party holds judgment for money against the creditor. **10.** To cause (oneself) to be part of or associated with a particular group. —*intr.* **1.** To become attached; adhere. **2.** To be an integral part of something: *Misery attaches to such a way of life.* [Middle English *attachen,* from Old French *attacher, estachier,* to fasten (with a stake), from *estache,* STAKE.] **—at·tach·a·ble** *adj.* **—at·tach·er** *n.*

at·ta·ché (ăt′ə-shā′, ə-tă′shā′) *n.* A person officially assigned to the staff of a diplomatic mission to serve in some particular capacity: *a cultural attaché.* [French, "one attached (to a diplomatic mission)," past participle of *attacher,* ATTACH.]

attaché case *n.* A briefcase resembling a small suitcase, with hinges and flat sides, used for carrying papers.

at·tached (ə-tăcht′) *adj.* Married, engaged, or committed to a serious romantic relationship.

at·tach·ment (ə-tăch′mənt) *n.* **1.** The act of attaching or the condition of being attached. **2.** Something that serves to attach one thing to another; a tie, band, or fastening. **3.** Fond regard; affection. **4.** A supplementary part; an accessory: *an attachment for a blender.* **5.** *Law.* **a.** The legal seizure of a person or property. **b.** The writ ordering such a seizure. **6.** *Law.* The procedure by which debts are attached. —See Synonyms at **appendage.**

at·tack (ə-tăk′) *v.* **-tacked, -tacking, -tacks.** —*tr.* **1.** To set upon with violent force; begin hostilities against or conflict with. **2.** To bombard with hostile criticism. **3.** To start work on with purpose and vigor: *attack a problem.* **4.** To begin to affect harmfully: *a disease that attacks crops.* —*intr.* **1.** To make an attack; launch an assault. **2.** To play offensively or take the initiative in a sport or game.

∼*n.* **1.** The act of attacking; an assault. **2.** A hostile criticism. **3.** An occurrence of or seizure by a disease or medical condition, especially one whose main symptoms recur at intervals: *an attack of asthma.* **4.** The act of setting to work on any task or undertaking: *made an attack on the problem.* **5.** *Music.* **a.** The manner in which a passage or phrase is begun. **b.** Force and incisiveness in performing. **6.** *Sports.* The offensive players, or the positions taken up by them, in a game between two teams. [French *attaquer,* from Old French, from Old Italian *attaccare,* variant of *estaccare* (unattested), to attach, join (battle), from *stacca* (unattested), STAKE.] **—at·tack·er** *n.*

Synonyms: *assail, assault, beset, bombard, storm.*

at·tain (ə-tān′) *v.* **-tained, -taining, -tains.** —*tr.* **1.** To gain, reach, or accomplish by mental or physical effort. **2.** To arrive at, as in time: *attain a ripe old age.* —*intr.* To succeed in gaining or reaching something; arrive at. Usually used with *to*: *He attained to the highest office in the land.* —See Synonyms at **reach.** [Middle English *atteignen,* from Norman-French, from Old French *ataindre* (stem *ataign-*), to reach to, from Vulgar Latin *attangere* (unattested), from Latin *attingere* : *ad-,* to + *tangere,* to touch.] **—at·tain·a·ble** *adj.* **—at·tain·a·bil·i·ty, at·tain·a·ble·ness** *n.*

at·tain·der (ə-tān′dər) *n.* **1.** The loss of all civil rights following a sentence of death or outlawry for a capital offense. See **bill of attainder. 2.** *Obsolete.* Dishonor. [Middle English *attendre,* conviction, from Norman French, noun use of *ateindre,* from Old French *ataindre,* to ATTAIN.]

at·tain·ment (ə-tān′mənt) *n.* **1.** The act of attaining. **2.** Something that is attained; an accomplishment or acquisition.

at·taint (ə-tānt′) *tr.v.* **-tainted, -tainting, -taints. 1.** *Law.* To condemn by a sentence of attainder. **2.** *Archaic.* To impart stigma to; disgrace. **3.** *Obsolete.* To accuse or prove guilty. Used with *of.*

∼*n.* **1.** Attainder. **2.** *Archaic.* A disgrace; a stigma. [Middle English *attaynten,* from Old French *ataint,* past participle of *ataindre,* to convict, originally, to ATTAIN (sense development influenced by TAINT).]

at·tar (ăt′ər) *n.* Also **ot·tar** (ŏt′ər), **ot·to** (ŏt′ō). A fragrant essential oil or perfume obtained from the petals of flowers, especially certain species of roses *(attar of roses).* [Persian *'attār,* perfumed, from *'iṭr,* perfume, from Arabic.]

at·tempt (ə-tĕmpt′) *tr.v.* **-tempted, -tempting, -tempts. 1.** To endeavor to do or achieve; try. **2.** To try to climb (a mountain). **3.** *Archaic.* To tempt. **4.** *Archaic.* To attack.

∼*n.* **1. a.** An effort or try. **b.** A try at conquering or winning something: *an attempt on the world record.* **2.** An attack; an assault: *an attempt on one's life.* **3.** The result of an attempt, especially when unsuccessful. [Middle English *attempten,* from Old French *attempter,* from Latin *attemptāre* : *ad-,* to + *temptāre,* to try, TEMPT.] **—at·tempt·a·ble** *adj.* **—at·tempt·er** *n.*

At·ten·bor·ough (ăt′ən-bûr′ə, -bər-ə), **Sir Richard** (1923–). British film actor, director, and producer. He produced two films, including *The L-Shaped Room* (1962). Films he has directed include *Oh What a Lovely War!* (1968) and *Ghandi* (1982). He was knighted in 1976.

at·tend (ə-tĕnd′) *v.* **-tended, -tending, -tends.** —*tr.* **1.** To be present at; go to: *attend medical school; attend lectures.* **2.** To accompany as a circumstance or follow as a result: *The speech was attended by wild applause.* **3.** To accompany as an attendant or servant; wait upon. **4.** To take care or charge of (a sick person, for example). **5.** To listen to; heed: *Attend my warning.* **6.** *Archaic.* To wait for; expect. —*intr.* **1.** To be present. **2.** To pay attention; heed. Used with *to.* **3.** To remain ready to serve; wait. Used with *on* or *upon*: *We attend upon your wishes.* **4.** To apply or direct oneself. Used with *to*: *Please attend to the matter at once.* **5.** To deal with the needs of; take care of. Used with *to*: *attend to a patient.* [Middle English *attenden,* from Old French *atendre,* from Latin *attendere,* to stretch toward, direct attention to : *ad-,* toward + *tendere,* to stretch.] **—at·tend·er** *n.*

at·ten·dance (ə-tĕn′dəns) *n.* **1.** The act of attending. **2.** The persons or number of persons who are present, as at a class.

at·ten·dant (ə-tĕn′dənt) *n.* **1.** One who attends; especially, one who waits on another. **2.** One who is present, as at a class. **3.** An accompanying thing or circumstance; a consequence or concomitant. **4.** One who is employed to provide a service, as to a customer: *flight attendant.*

∼*adj.* Accompanying or consequent: *attendant circumstances.* **—at·ten·dant·ly** *adv.*

at·ten·tion (ə-tĕn′shən) *n. Abbr.* **attn. 1.** Concentration of the mental powers upon an object; a close or careful observing or listening. **2.** The ability or power to concentrate mentally. **3. a.** Observation; notice: *Your suggestion has come to our attention.* **b.** Consideration with a view to deciding on a course of action: *an injury requiring prompt attention.* **4.** Respectful consideration: *attention to the feelings of others.* **5.** *Usually* **attentions.** An act of courtesy, consideration, or gallantry indicating romantic interest. **6.** *Military.* **a.** A posture assumed by a soldier, with the body erect, eyes to the front, arms at the sides, and heels together. **b.** A command to assume this position. [Middle English *attencioun,* from Latin *attentiō* (stem *attentiōn-*), from *attendere,* ATTEND.] **—at·ten·tion·al** *adj.*

at·ten·tive (ə-tĕn′tĭv) *adj.* **1.** Paying attention; observant; listening. **2.** Courteous or devoted; considerate; thoughtful. **—at·ten·tive·ly** *adv.* **—at·ten·tive·ness** *n.*

at·ten·u·ate (ə-tĕn′yo͞o-āt′) *v.* **-ated, -ating, -ates.** —*tr.* **1.** To make slender, fine, or small. **2.** To reduce in strength, force, value, or amount; weaken. **3.** To lessen in density; dilute or rarefy (a liquid or gas). **4.** *Bacteriology.* To make (a pathogenic microorganism) less virulent, as by treating with heat or chemicals. —*intr.* To become thin, weak, fine, or reduced in power.

∼*adj.* (ə-tĕn′yo͞o-ĭt) **1.** Thinned; diluted; weakened. **2.** *Botany.* Gradually tapering to a point; slender and pointed. [Latin *attenuāre,* to make thin : *ad-,* to + *tenuāre,* to make thin, from *tenuis,* thin.] **—at·ten·u·a·ble** *adj.*

at·ten·u·a·tion (ə-tĕn′yo͞o-ā′shən) *n.* **1.** An act or instance of attenuating or the state of being attenuated. **2.** *Physics.* **a.** The loss in energy of radiation, sound, or the like, as it passes through matter, primarily as a result of absorption or scattering. **b.** The power loss suffered by an electric current passing through a circuit.

at·ten·u·a·tor (ə-tĕn′yo͞o-ā′tər) *n.* Any device or object that causes attenuation; especially, a device that reduces the power of a wave, signal, or the like, without causing distortion.

at·test (ə-tĕst′) *v.* **-tested, -testing, -tests.** —*tr.* **1.** To affirm to be correct, true, or genuine; corroborate. **2.** To certify by signature or oath; affirm officially. **3.** To supply evidence or proof of: *His vast holdings attest his wealth.* **4.** To constitute documentary or other material proof of the former existence of. Used especially in archaeology and historical linguistics. **5.** To put under oath. —*intr.* To bear witness; give testimony. Used with *to*: *I attest to his good faith.*

∼*n. Archaic.* An act of attesting. [French *attester,* from Old French, from Latin *attestārī* : *ad-,* to + *testārī,* to be a witness, from *testis,* witness.] **—at·test·ant** (ə-tĕs′tənt) *n.* **—at·tes·ta·tion** (ăt′ĕs-tā′shən, ăt′ə-stā′-) *n.* **—at·test·er, at·tes·tor** (ə-tĕs′tər) *n.*

at·tic (ăt′ĭk) *n.* **1.** A story or room directly below the roof of a house. **2.** *Architecture.* A low wall or story above the cornice of a classical façade. [French *attique,* "attic story," a top story above or enclosed by columns in an Attic style.]

At·tic (ăt′ĭk) *adj.* **1.** Of, pertaining to, or characteristic of ancient Attica, Athens, or the Athenians. **2.** *Sometimes* **attic.** Characterized by classical purity and simplicity.

∼*n.* The ancient Greek dialect of Athens, in which the bulk of classical Greek literature is written, belonging to Attic-Ionic.

At·ti·ca (ăt′ĭ-kə). Region of ancient Greece, occupying the area around Athens. According to Greek legend, there were four Attic tribes, unified into a single community by Theseus.

At·tic-I·on·ic (ăt′ĭk-ī-ŏn′ĭk) *n.* One of the four main dialects of ancient Greek, spoken in Attica and Ionia. Compare **Aeolic, Arcado-Cyprian, Doric.**

At·ti·cism (ăt′ə-sĭz′əm) *n.* **1.** Something characteristic of the Attic Greek language. **2.** An expression or style of expression characterized by simplicity, conciseness, and elegance.

Attic salt *n.* Dry, delicate, pointed wit. Also called "Attic wit."

At·ti·la (ăt′ə-lə, ə-tĭl′ə), also known as "Attila the Hun," "the Scourge of God" (died A.D. 453). Leader of the Huns and the most notorious of the barbarian invaders of the Roman Empire. After 441 he attacked the empire repeatedly from the east, gaining much territory, but was checked at Constantinople (443), in Gaul (451), and in Italy (452).

at·tire (ə-tīr′) *tr.v.* **-tired, -tiring, -tires.** To dress, especially in elaborate or splendid garments; clothe.

∼*n.* **1.** Clothing, especially of an elaborate or special kind: *formal attire.* **2.** *Heraldry.* The antlers of a deer. [Middle English *attiren,* from Old French *atirier,* to arrange into ranks, put in order : *a-,* from Latin *ad-,* to + *tire,* order, rank (see **tier**).]

PRONUNCIATION KEY

ă, pat; ā, pay; âr, care;
ä, father, are; b, bib;
ch, church; d, deed; ĕ, pet;
ē, be; f, fife; g, gag; h, hat;
hw, which; ĭ, pit; ī, pie;
îr, pier; j, judge; k, kick;
l, lid, needle; m, mum;
n, no, sudden; ng, thing;
ŏ, pot; ō, toe; ô, paw, for;
oi, noise; ou, out; o͝o, book;
o͞o, boot; p, pop; r, roar;
s, sauce; sh, ship, dish;
t, tight; th, thin, path;
th, this, bathe; ŭ, cut; ûr, fur;
v, valve; w, with; y, yes;
z, zebra, size; zh, vision;
ə, about, item, edible,
gallop, circus, peaceful

IN FOREIGN WORDS:

à, *Fr.* ami; œ, *Fr.* feu, *Ger.* schön; ü, *Fr.* tu, *Ger.* über; KH, *Ger.* ich, *Scot.* loch; N, *Fr.* bon; y′, *Fr.* Compiègne

STRESS MARKS:

Primary stress: ′
in·cite′ (ĭn-sīt′)
Secondary stress: ′
in′sight′ (ĭn′sīt′)

at·ti·tude (ăt′ə-tōōd′, -tyōōd′) n. 1. A position of the body or manner of carrying oneself, indicative of a mood or condition: "men . . . sprawled alone or in heaps, in the careless attitudes of death" (John Reed). 2. A state of mind or feeling with regard to some matter. 3. A way of behaving; disposition. 4. Aeronautics. The orientation of an aircraft's axes relative to some reference line or plane, such as the horizon. 5. Aerospace. The orientation of a spacecraft relative to its direction of motion. 6. A ballet position in which a dancer stands on one leg with the other leg raised and bent backward. [French, from Italian attitudine, disposition, from Late Latin aptitūdō, faculty, fitness, from Latin aptus, fit, APT.] —at·ti·tu·di·nal (ăt′ə-tōōd′n-əl, -tyōōd′-) adj.

at·ti·tu·di·nize (ăt′ə-tōōd′n-īz′, -tyōōd′-) intr.v. -nized, -nizing, -nizes. To assume an affected attitude.

Att·lee (ăt′lē), **Clement Richard Attlee, 1st Earl** (1883–1967). British politician. In 1935 he became leader of the Labour Party. He was deputy prime minister in Churchill's wartime coalition government (1940–45). As prime minister from 1945 to 1951 he presided over the establishment of the National Health Service, the expansion of public ownership of industry, and the granting of independence to India. He received his peerage in 1955.

attn. attention.

atto– prefix. Symbol **a** Indicates one quintillionth (10⁻¹⁸); for example, **attotesla.** [Danish or Norwegian atten, eighteen, from Old Norse āttjān.]

at·torn (ə-tûrn′) intr.v. -torned, -torning, -torns. Law. To acknowledge a new owner as landlord. [Middle English attournen, from Old French atorner, to turn to, assign to : a-, from Latin ad-, to + torner, to turn, from Latin tornāre, to TURN.] —at·torn·ment n.

at·tor·ney (ə-tûr′nē) n., pl. -neys. Abbr. **atty.** A person legally appointed or empowered to act for another; especially an attorney at law. —See Usage note at lawyer. [Middle English attourney, from Old French atorne, "one appointed," past participle of atorner, to appoint, ATTORN.] —at·tor·ney·ship n.

attorney at law n. One who is qualified to represent clients in a court of law and to advise them on legal matters; a lawyer.

attorney general n., pl. **attorneys general.** 1. The chief law officer and legal counsel of the government of a state or nation. 2. In some states, a public prosecutor.

Attorney General n., pl. **Attorneys General.** Abbr. **A.G., Atty. Gen.** The chief law officer and legal counsel of the government of the United States, who is also a Cabinet member and head of the Department of Justice.

at·to·tes·la (ăt′ō-tĕs′lə) n. Abbr. **aT** Physics. One quintillionth (10⁻¹⁸) of a tesla.

at·tract (ə-trăkt′) v. -tracted, -tracting, -tracts. —tr. 1. To cause to draw near or adhere. 2. To draw or direct to oneself by some quality or action: attract attention. 3. To evoke interest or admiration in; allure. —intr. To possess or use the power of attraction; be magnetic or alluring. [Middle English attracten, from Latin attrahere (past participle attractus) : ad-, toward + trahere, to draw.] —at·tract·a·ble adj. —at·trac·tor, at·tract·er (ə-trăk′tər) n.

at·tract·ant (ə-trăk′tənt) n. A substance that attracts, especially a chemical produced by insects and other animals to attract opposite-sexed members of the same species. See pheromone.

at·trac·tion (ə-trăk′shən) n. 1. The act of attracting. 2. The quality or power of attracting; allure; charm. 3. A feature, characteristic, or factor that attracts: Money was not the least of her attractions. 4. A public spectacle or entertainment. 5. A force that causes one body to attract another body with which it is not in contact: gravitational attraction; magnetic attraction.

at·trac·tive (ə-trăk′tĭv) adj. 1. Having the power to attract. 2. Pleasing to the eye or mind; appealing. 3. Personally engaging; charming. —at·trac·tive·ly adv. —at·trac·tive·ness n.

at·trib·ute (ə-trĭb′yət, -yōōt′) —tr.v. -uted, -uting, -utes. To regard or assign as belonging to or resulting from someone or something; ascribe: attribute a painting to Rembrandt; attributed his downfall to greed.
~n. (ăt′rə-byōōt′). 1. A quality or characteristic belonging to a person or thing; a distinctive feature: Travel has lost the attributes of privilege and fashion" (John Cheever). 2. An object associated with and serving to identify a character, person, or office: Lightning bolts are the attribute of Zeus. 3. Grammar. An adjective or a phrase used as an adjective. —See Synonyms at quality. [Latin attribūtum, "quality belonging to something," noun use of past participle of attribuēre : ad-, to + tribuēre, to allot, grant (see tribute).] —at·trib·ut·a·ble adj. —at·trib·ut·er, at·trib·u·tor (ə-trĭb′yə-tər) n.
Synonyms: ascribe, assign, credit, impute.

at·tri·bu·tion (ăt′rə-byōō′shən) n. 1. The act of attributing. 2. Something that is ascribed; an attribute.

at·trib·u·tive (ə-trĭb′yə-tĭv) adj. 1. Grammar. Pertaining to or designating an adjective or a word or phrase used adjectivally that is joined directly to the noun it modifies without a linking verb. For example, in the sentence The young girl is ill, young is an attributive adjective. Compare predicative. 2. Of or having the nature of an attribution or attribute. 3. Of an attributed origin: an attributive Rubens.
~n. Grammar. An attributive adjective or adjectival phrase. —at·trib·u·tive·ly adv. —at·trib·u·tive·ness n.

at·trit·ed (ə-trī′tĭd) adj. Worn down by attrition. [Latin attrītus, from past participle of atterere, to rub away. See attrition.]

at·tri·tion (ə-trĭsh′ən) n. 1. A rubbing away or wearing down by friction, especially of rock particles during transport by wind or water. 2. The act or result of gradually wearing down and exhausting an opponent by constant stress and harassment: a war of attrition. 3. A gradual reduction in membership or personnel through retirement, resignation, or death. 4. Theology. Repentance for sin motivated by fear of punishment rather than by love of God. In this sense, compare contrition. [Middle English attricioun, from Medieval Latin attrītiō (stem attrītiōn-), "chastisement," from Latin, a rubbing against, from atterere, to rub against : ad-, against + terere, to rub.]

at·tune (ə-tōōn′, -tyōōn′) tr.v. -tuned, -tuning, -tunes. 1. To bring into harmony. 2. To accustom to a special perception; make aware: an ear attuned to dissonance. 3. To tune (an instrument). [16th century : AD- (to) + TUNE.]

atty. attorney.

Atty. Gen. attorney general.

a·twit·ter (ə-twĭt′ər) adj. In a state of nervous excitement.

At·wood (ăt′wōōd′), **Margaret** (1939–). Canadian writer. Her works include a collection of poems, The Circle Game (1966), and the novels The Edible Woman (1969) and Lady Oracle (1976).

at wt atomic weight.

a·typ·i·cal (ā-tĭp′ĭ-kəl) adj. Also **a·typ·ic** (ā-tĭp′ĭk). Not typical; varying from the type. —a·typ·i·cal·ly adv.

Au The symbol for the element gold. [Latin aurum.]

A.U. astronomical unit.

au·bade (ō-bäd′) n. 1. A musical composition intended to be played or sung at dawn or early in the morning. 2. A poem appropriate to this time of day. [French, from Old French, from Old Provençal auba, alba, dawn, from Vulgar Latin alba (unattested), feminine of Latin albus, white.]

au·ber·gine (ō′bər-zhēēn′) n. 1. A vegetable, the eggplant (see). 2. Blackish purple. [French, from Catalan alberginia, from Arabic al-bādindjān, from Persian bādin-gān, from Sanskrit vātimgana.]

Au·brey (ô′brē), **John** (1626–97). English antiquarian and writer. His work, Brief Lives (published in the 19th century), contains brilliant sketches of his contemporaries.

Aubrey hole n. Any of the 56 holes that form the outer ring of the circle at Stonehenge. [After John AUBREY.]

au·brie·tia, au·bre·tia (ō-brē′shə) n. Any trailing plant of the genus Aubrietia, having purple or red flowers and widely cultivated in gardens. [New Latin, after Claude Aubriet, 18th-century French painter of animals and flowers, in whose honor it was named.]

au·burn (ô′bərn) n. Moderate reddish brown to brown. [Middle English aborne, blond, from Old French auborne, alborne, from Medieval Latin alburnus, whitish, from Latin albus, white.] —au·burn adj.

Au·bus·son (ō-bōō-sôN′). Town in Creuse department in central France. It has been famous for its manufacture of carpets and tapestries since the 16th century.

A.U.C. ab urbe condita.

Auck·land (ôk′lənd). The largest city and chief port of New Zealand, on an isthmus in the northern part of North Island. It was the capital until 1865.

au cou·rant (ō kōō-räN′) adj. Informed on current affairs; up-to-date. [French, "in the current."]

auc·tion (ôk′shən) n. 1. A public sale in which property or items of merchandise are sold to the highest bidder. 2. The bidding in the game of bridge.
~tr.v. auctioned, -tioning, -tions. To sell at or by an auction. Often used with off. [Latin auctiō (stem auctiōn-), (a sale by) increase (of bids), from augēre, to increase.]

auction bridge n. A variety of the game of bridge in which tricks made in excess of the contract are scored toward game. Compare contract bridge.

auc·tion·eer (ôk′shə-nîr′) n. A person who conducts an auction and controls the bidding.
~tr.v. auctioneered, -eering, -eers. To act as an auctioneer.

auctioneer bird n. A small Australian black-headed bird, Orthonyx spaldingi, that lives in mountain scrub and has a loud call. Also called "chowchilla."

auc·to·ri·al (ôk-tôr′ē-əl, -tōr′-) adj. Of or pertaining to an author. [Latin auctor, AUTHOR + -IAL.]

au·da·cious (ô-dā′shəs) adj. 1. Fearlessly daring; bold. 2. Lacking restraint or tact; arrogantly insolent. —See Synonyms at brave, reckless. [Latin audāx (stem audāc-), bold, from audēre, to dare, "be eager," from avidus, AVID.] —au·da·cious·ly adv. —au·da·cious·ness n.

au·dac·i·ty (ô-dăs′ə-tē) n., pl. -ties. 1. Boldness; daring. 2. Unrestrained impudence; presumption. 3. An instance of boldness or presumption. —See Synonyms at temerity.

Au·den (ôd′n), **Wystan Hugh** (1907–73). British poet. In the 1930's he was a member of the literary circle that included Christopher Isherwood, with whom he wrote several verse dramas. He immigrated to the United States in 1939 and became a citizen (1946).

au·di·bil·i·ty (ô′də-bĭl′ə-tē) n. The capacity to be heard.

au·di·ble (ô′də-bəl) adj. Capable of being heard. [Late Latin audībilis, from Latin audīre, to hear.] —au·di·ble·ness n. —au·di·bly adv.

au·di·ence (ô′dē-əns) n. 1. A gathering of spectators or listeners, as at a concert, play, or film. 2. The readers, hearers, or viewers reached by a book, radio broadcast, or television program. 3. A formal meeting or conference, as with a king or pope. 4. An opportunity to be heard or to express one's views. 5. The act of hearing or attending. [Middle English, from Old French, from Latin audi-

aubrietia A perennial plant that thrives in limy soil and is commonly grown in rock gardens and borders. Aubrietia deltoidea, shown here, is a native of southern Europe and Asia Minor.

Audubon painting *The pictures of the 19th-century American naturalist John James Audubon form a detailed record of birds such as this red-billed blue magpie.*

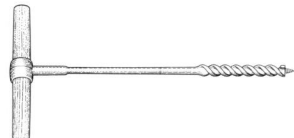

auger *A tool used to make holes in wood. The screw at the end pulls the tool into the wood when the auger is turned.*

entia, from *audiēns* (stem *audient-*), present participle of *audīre,* to hear.]

au·di·ent (ô′dē-ənt) *adj.* Hearing; listening. [Latin *audiēns* (stem *audient-*), present participle of *audīre,* to hear.]

au·dile (ô′dīl′) *adj. Psychology.* Capable of learning chiefly from auditory, rather than tactile or visual, stimuli.
~*n.* An audile person. [Latin *audīre,* to hear, by analogy with *tactile*]

au·di·o (ô′dē-ō′) *adj.* **1.** Of or pertaining to audible sound. **2. a.** Of or pertaining to the broadcasting of sound. **b.** Of or pertaining to the high-fidelity reproduction of sound.
~*n.* **1.** The audio part of television equipment. **2.** Audio broadcasting or reception. **3.** Audible sound. Compare **video.** [Independent use of AUDIO-.]

audio– *prefix.* Indicates sound or hearing; for example, **audiometer.** [Latin *audīre,* to hear.]

audio frequency *n. Abbr.* **a.f., A.F., AF** A frequency in a range, usually between 15 hertz and 20,000 hertz, characteristic of signals audible to the normal human ear.

au·di·o·lin·gual (ô′dē-ō-lĭng′gwəl) *adj.* Designating an approach to language learning that involves speaking and listening rather than reading and writing.

au·di·ol·o·gy (ô′dē-ŏl′ə-jē) *n.* The scientific study of hearing; especially, the study and treatment of hearing defects. —**au·di·o·log·i·cal** (ô′dē-ō-lŏj′ĭ-kəl) *adj.* —**au·di·ol·o·gist** *n.*

au·di·om·e·ter (ô′dē-ŏm′ə-tər) *n. Medicine.* An instrument for measuring hearing thresholds for pure tones of normally audible frequencies. —**au·di·o·met·ric** (ô′dē-ō-mĕt′rĭk) *adj.* —**au·di·om·e·try** *n.*

au·di·o·phile (ô′dē-ō-fīl′) *n.* One who has a great interest in high-fidelity sound reproduction.

au·di·o·tape (ô′dē-ō-tāp′) *n.* A sound tape recording, as opposed to a videotape.

au·di·o·typ·ist (ô′dē-ō-tī′pĭst) *n.* One who types directly from tape recordings as opposed to written material. Compare **copy typist.** —**au·di·o·typ·ing** *n.*

au·di·o·vis·u·al (ô′dē-ō-vĭzh′ōō-əl) *adj. Abbr.* **A.V. 1.** Both audible and visible. **2.** Of or pertaining to educational materials, such as sound filmstrips, that present information in audible and visible form.

audio-visual aids *pl.n.* Also **audio-visuals.** Educational materials that present information in audible and visible form.

au·dit (ô′dĭt) *n.* **1.** An examination of records or accounts to check their accuracy. **2.** An adjustment or correction of accounts. **3.** An examined and verified account. **4.** *Rare.* An audience or hearing.
~*v.* **audited, -diting, -dits.** —*tr.* **1.** To examine, verify, or correct (accounts, records, or claims). **2.** To register for and attend (a college course) without receiving academic credit. —*intr.* To examine accounts. [Middle English, from Latin *audītus,* a hearing, from the past participle of *audīre,* to hear.]

au·di·tion (ô-dĭsh′ən) *n.* **1.** The act or sense of hearing. **2.** A presentation of something heard; a hearing. **3.** A trial performance, as by an actor or musician, to demonstrate ability or skill.
~*v.* **auditioned, -tioning, -tions.** —*tr.* To test in an audition. —*intr.* To perform or be tested in an audition. [Latin *audītiō* (stem *audītiōn-*), from *audīre,* to hear. See **audit.**]

au·di·tive (ô′də-tĭv) *adj.* Auditory.

au·di·tor (ô′də-tər) *n.* **1.** One who hears; a listener. **2.** One who audits accounts. **3.** One who audits a course of study. [Middle English *auditour,* from Old French *auditeur,* from Latin *audītor,* hearer (in Medieval Latin, also one who audits accounts), from *audīre,* to hear.]

au·di·to·ri·um (ô′də-tôr′ē-əm, -tōr′-) *n., pl.* **-toriums** or **-toria** (-tôr′ē-ə, -tōr′-). **1.** The part of a theater, school, or other public building where an audience sits. **2.** A large building for public meetings or artistic performances. [Latin *audītōrium,* from *audīre,* to hear.]

au·di·to·ry (ô′də-tôr′ē, -tōr′ē) *adj.* Of or pertaining to the sense, the organs, or the experience of hearing. [Late Latin *audītōrius,* from Latin *audīre,* to hear.]

auditory nerve *n. Anatomy.* The **acoustic nerve** *(see).*

Au·du·bon (ô′də-bŏn′, -bən), **John James** (1785–1851). American naturalist and painter, born in Haiti. He was the first ornithologist to ring birds so as to discover their migratory habits. His *Birds of America* (1827–38) is a classic of both naturalism and art.

au fait (o fě′) *adj. French.* **1.** Skilled or knowledgeable; expert. **2.** Conversant or familiar. Often used with *with.* [Literally, "to the point."]

Auf·klä·rung (ouf′klä′rōōng) *n. German.* The Enlightenment.

au fond (o fôN′) *adv. French.* Basically; essentially. [Literally, "at the bottom."]

auf Wie·der·seh·en (ouf vē′dər-zā′ən) *interj. German.* Until we see one another again; farewell.

Aug. August.

Au·ge·an Stables (ô-jē′ən) *pl.n.* **1.** *Greek Mythology.* The stables of King Augeas that had not been cleaned for thirty years and which Hercules had to clean as one of his twelve labors. **2.** A place or state of extreme filth or corruption. [After *Augeas,* king of Elis in Greek mythology.]

au·gend (ô′jĕnd′) *n. Mathematics.* A quantity to which another quantity, the addend, is added. [Latin *augendum,* "the thing to be increased," gerundive of *augēre,* to increase.]

au·ger (ô′gər) *n.* **1.** A tool with a corkscrew-shaped bit, for boring holes in wood. **2.** A large tool for boring into the earth. [Middle

English *an auger,* originally *a nauger,* Old English *nafogār,* "tool for piercing wheel hubs."]

Au·ger effect (ō-zhā′) *n. Physics.* The emission of an electron instead of a photon by an excited ion when a vacancy in an inner electron shell is filled. [After Pierre *Auger* (born 1899), French physicist.]

aught¹ (ôt) *pron.* Also *regional* **ought. 1.** All: *For aught we know he may have changed his name.* **2.** *Archaic.* Anything whatever; any least part.
~*adv.* Also *regional* **ought.** At all; in any respect. [Middle English *aught, ought,* Old English *āuht, āwiht,* "ever a thing," anything.]

aught² (ôt) *n.* Also **ought. 1.** A cipher; the symbol 0; zero. **2.** *Archaic.* Nothing. [From *an aught,* originally *a* NAUGHT.]

au·gite (ô′jīt′) *n.* A dark-green to black pyroxene mineral that contains aluminum, iron, and magnesium. [Latin *augītēs,* a precious stone, from Greek *augītēs,* from *augē,* ray, brightness.]

aug·ment (ôg-mĕnt′). *v.* **-mented, -menting, -ments.** —*tr.* **1.** To make greater, as in size, extent, or quantity; enlarge; increase: *He augmented his salary by writing..* **2.** *Music.* To increase (a perfect or major interval) by a semitone. Compare **diminish.** —*intr.* To become greater; enlarge. —See Synonyms at **increase.**
~*n.* (ôg′mĕnt′). A morphological indication of past tense in Greek and Sanskrit verbs, consisting of the prefixing of a vowel or the lengthening of the initial vowel. [Middle English *augmenten,* from Old French *augmenter,* from Late Latin *augmentāre,* from *augmentum,* increase, from Latin *augēre,* to increase.] —**aug·ment·a·ble** *adj.*

aug·men·ta·tion (ôg′mĕn-tā′shən) *n.* **1. a.** The act or process of augmenting. **b.** The condition of being augmented. **2.** Something that enlarges or increases; an addition. **3.** *Music.* The repetition of a theme in notes of usually double the value of those originally assigned to it. Compare **diminution.**

aug·men·ta·tive (ôg-mĕn′tə-tĭv) *adj.* Also **aug·men·tive** (ôg-mĕn′tĭv). **1.** Having the tendency or ability to augment. **2.** Designating a word or affix that produces an increase in size or intensity when added to another word, such as *super-* in *superstar.* Compare **diminutive.**
~*n.* Also **aug·men·tive.** An augmentative word or affix.

aug·men·ted (ôg-mĕn′tĭd) *adj. Music.* Increased from the corresponding major or perfect interval by a semitone. Said of an interval.

au gra·tin (ō grät′n, grăt′n; *French* ō grà-tăN′) *adj.* Covered with breadcrumbs and sometimes grated cheese and browned in an oven or under a broiler: *cauliflower au gratin.* [French, "with the crust (of bread crumbs)."] —**au gra·tin** *adv.*

Augs·burg (ougz′bûrg′, ôgz′-). Industrial city in Bavaria in Germany, on the Lech River. It was the home of the great banking families of Fugger and Welser.

au·gur (ô′gər) *n.* **1.** One of a group of religious officials of ancient Rome who foretold events by observing and interpreting signs and omens. **2.** A seer or prophet; a soothsayer.
~*v.* **augured, -guring, -gurs.** —*tr.* **1.** To predict or prognosticate, as from signs or omens. **2.** To serve as an omen of; betoken. —*intr.* **1.** To conjecture or foretell from signs or omens. **2.** To be a sign or omen. Used in the phrase *augur ill* or *well.* —See Synonyms at **foretell.** [Latin *augur, auger : au-,* perhaps from *avis,* bird + *gerere,* to do, perform (with reference to observing birds' flight or examining their viscera as a means of divination). See **auspice.**] —**au·gu·ral** (ô′gyə-rəl) *adj.*

au·gu·ry (ô′gyə-rē) *n., pl.* **-ries. 1.** The art, ability, or practice of auguring; divination. **2.** The rite performed by an augur. **3.** A sign or omen; an indication. [Middle English *augurie,* from Old French, from Latin *augurium,* from *augur,* AUGUR.]

au·gust (ô-gŭst′) *adj.* **1.** Inspiring awe or admiration; majestic. **2.** Venerable for reasons of age or high rank. —See Synonyms at **grand.** [Latin *augustus,* venerable, magnificent.] —**au·gust·ly** *adv.* —**au·gust·ness** *n.*

Au·gust (ô′gəst) *n. Abbr.* **Aug.** The eighth month of the year according to the Gregorian calendar. August has 31 days. See feature at **calendar.** [Middle English *August,* Old English *August,* from Latin *(mensis) Augustus,* (month) of Augustus, after the emperor AUGUSTUS.]

Au·gus·ta (ô-gŭs′tə). The capital of Maine, in the southwestern part of the state on the Kennebec River. A trading post was established here in the early 17th century.

Au·gus·tan (ô-gŭs′tən) *adj.* **1.** Pertaining to or characteristic of the emperor Augustus or his reign or times. **2.** Pertaining to or characteristic of any era resembling the reign of Augustus, as in classicism and refinement.
~*n.* A writer in an Augustan age.

Augustan age *n.* **1.** The golden age of Latin literature during the reign of Augustus (27 B.C.–A.D. 14), to which Horace, Livy, and Ovid belonged. **2.** A similar period of great literary achievement, as during the 18th century in England.

Au·gus·tine of Can·ter·bur·y (ô-gə-stēn′, ô-gŭs′tĭn; kăn′tər-bĕr′ē), **Saint** (died *c.* 605). Founder of the Christian Church in southern Britain and first archbishop of Canterbury. A Benedictine prior, he was appointed by Pope Gregory I to lead an evangelizing mission to Britain in 597. He was received by King Ethelbert of Kent, who gave him land at Canterbury. Ethelbert adopted the Christian faith, and in 598 Augustine was ordained as bishop of the English at Arles.

Augustine of Hip·po (hĭp′ō), **Saint** (A.D. 354–430). Latin Father and Doctor of the Church. Raised as a Christian, he abandoned the faith for Manichaeism after studying in Carthage. He later came under the influence of St. Ambrose, Bishop of Milan, and in 387 was baptized as a Christian. In 391 he was chosen by the Christians of Hippo (in present-day Algeria) to be their priest. He remained in Hippo for the rest of his life, becoming bishop *c.* 395. His *Confessions* (*c.* 400) and *The City of God* (after 412) are eloquent and moving testaments of Christian piety and belief.

Au·gus·tin·i·an (ô'gə-stĭn'ē-ən) *adj.* **1.** Pertaining to St. Augustine of Hippo or his doctrines. **2.** Designating or belonging to any of several orders following or influenced by the rule of St. Augustine. ~*n.* **1.** A follower of the principles and doctrines of St. Augustine of Hippo. **2.** A monk or friar belonging to an Augustinian orders. **—Au·gus·tin·i·an·ism.**

Au·gus·tus (ô-gŭs'təs) *n.* **1.** A title of the Roman emperors. **2.** After Hadrian, the title of the senior emperor as distinct from his junior colleague, the **Caesar** *(see).* [Latin *Augustus,* AUGUST, "Imperial Majesty," adopted by Octavian as a personal title when he acquired supreme power.]

Augustus, born Gaius Octavius, later "Gaius Julius Caesar Octavianus." Known as Octavian (63 B.C.–A.D. 14). First Roman emperor, the grand-nephew of Julius Caesar. Named by Caesar as his heir, Octavian became leader of the faction against Mark Antony. In 43 B.C. he, Mark Antony, and Lepidus formed the Second Triumvirate, whose armies defeated Brutus and Cassius at Philippi in 42. Antony's intrigues with Cleopatra led to the appointment of Octavian as general in 31. Following the defeat of Antony and Cleopatra at Actium in the same year, Octavian controlled all the lands of the empire. In 29 the senate named him *imperator,* or emperor, and in 27 gave him the honorary title Augustus. He subsequently devoted himself to consolidating Caesar's conquests, restoring civilian rule in Rome, building roads, and reforming the taxation system.

au jus (ō zhōō') *adj.* Served with the natural juices or gravy: *roast beef au jus.* [French, "with juice."]

auk (ôk) *n., pl.* **auks** or collectively **auk.** Any of several sea birds of the family Alcidae, of northern regions, having a squat body, short wings, and black and white plumage, such as the **razorbill** *(see).* See **great auk, little auk.** [Norwegian *alk, alka,* from Old Norse *ālka.*]

auk·let (ôk'lĭt) *n.* Any of various small auks of the genus *Aethia* and related genera, of northern Pacific coasts and waters.

au lait (ō lā') *adj.* Cooked or served with milk. [French, "with milk."]

auld (ôld) *adj. Scottish.* Old.

auld lang syne (ôld lăng zīn') *n.* The good old days long past. [Scottish, "old long since" : AULD + LANGSYNE.]

au·lic (ô'lĭk) *adj. Archaic.* Pertaining to a royal court; courtly. [French *aulique,* from Latin *aulicus,* from Greek *aulikos,* from *aulē,* court.]

Aulic Council *n.* The emperor's privy council in the Holy Roman Empire from 1498, when it was established by Maximilian I, until the dissolution of the Empire in 1806.

aumbry. Variant of **ambry.**

au na·tu·rel (ō nā-tü-rel') *adj.* **1.** In a natural state; nude. **2.** Cooked simply. Said of food. [French, "in the natural."]

aunt (ănt, änt) *n.* **1.** The sister of one's father or mother. **2.** The wife of one's uncle. [Middle English *aunte,* from Norman French, from Old French *ante,* from Latin *amita,* paternal aunt.]

aunt·ie, aunt·y (ăn'tē, än'-) *n.* Variant of **aunt.** Used as a familiar form of address.

Aunt Sally *n., pl.* **Aunt Sallies.** *British.* **1.** A fairground game in which sticks or balls are thrown at a wooden dummy. **2. a.** Someone or something that is the object of insults or derision. **b.** Any easy target of criticism; a scapegoat. [After the fairground dummy, usually the head of an old woman smoking a clay pipe.]

au pair (ō pâr') *n.* Also **au pair girl.** A foreign girl who lives with a family, doing housework and looking after the children in exchange for room and board.
~*intr.v.* **au paired, au pairing, au pairs.** To work as an au pair. [French, "on equal basis," by exchange of services rather than money.]

au·ra (ôr'ə) *n., pl.* **-ras** or **aurae** (ôr'ē). **1.** An invisible breath or emanation. **2.** A distinctive air or quality that characterizes a person or thing: *an aura of nobility.* **3.** An emanation of light said to surround a person and to be visible to those claiming psychic powers. **4.** A subjective sensation, as of a cold breeze or flashes of light, preceding the onset of an attack in certain nervous disorders, especially epilepsy. [Middle English, from Latin, from Greek, : "breath, breeze," akin to *aēr,* AIR.]

au·ral[1] (ôr'əl) *adj.* Of, pertaining to, or perceived by the ear.
~*n.* An aural examination in music. [Latin *auris,* ear + -AL.]

aural[2] (ôr'əl) *adj.* Characterized by or pertaining to an aura.

au·rar. Plural of **eyrir.**

au·re·ate (ôr'ē-ĭt) *adj.* **1.** Of a golden color; gilded. **2.** Speaking in or characterized by a florid and pompous style. [Middle English *aureat,* from Medieval Latin *aureātus,* from Latin *aureus,* golden, from *aurum,* gold.] **—au·re·ate·ly** *adv.* **—au·re·ate·ness** *n.*

Au·re·li·an (ô-rēl'yən). Latin name, "Lucius Domitius Aurelianus." (A.D. *c.* 215–75). Roman emperor (270–75). In a series of victories he held the barbarians in check beyond the Rhine and regained Britain, Gaul, Spain, Syria, and Egypt for the empire.

au·re·ole (ôr'ē-ōl') *n.* Also **au·re·o·la** (ô-rē'ə-lə). **1.** A circle of light or radiance surrounding the head or body of a representation of a deity or holy person; a halo. **2.** A bright, circumferential region around a luminous celestial body, such as the sun or moon, especially when observed through a haze or fog. **3.** *Geology.* A zone around an intrusion which has been altered by the heat and chemicals generated during the intrusion of the magma. [Middle English *aureole, auriole,* from Old French *auriole,* from Medieval Latin *(corōna) aureola,* golden (crown), from Latin *aureolus,* golden, from *aurum,* gold.]

Au·re·o·my·cin (ôr'ē-ō-mī'sĭn) *n.* A trademark for **chlortetracycline** *(see).*

au·re·us (ôr'ē-əs) *n., pl.* **aurei** (ôr'ē-ī'). A gold coin of the late Roman Republic and of the Roman Empire.

au re·voir (ō rə-vwär') *interj. French.* Until we meet again; good-by.

au·ric (ôr'ĭk) *adj.* Of, pertaining to, derived from, or containing gold, especially with valence 3. [Latin *aurum,* gold.]

au·ri·cle (ôr'ĭ-kəl) *n.* Also **au·ric·u·la** (ô-rĭk'yə-lə) *pl.* **-lae** (-lē') or **-las. 1.** *Anatomy.* **a.** The external part of the ear; the pinna. **b.** An **atrium** *(see)* of the heart. **2.** *Biology.* Any earlike part, process, or appendage, especially at the base of an organ. [Latin *auricula,* diminutive of *auris,* ear.] **—au·ri·cled** (ôr'ĭ-kəld) *adj.*

au·ric·u·la (ô-rĭk'yə-lə) *n., pl.* **-las** or **-lae** (-lē'). **1.** A species of primrose, *Primula auricula,* native to the Alps but widely cultivated, having clusters of variously colored flowers. Also called "bear's-ear." **2.** Variant of **auricle.** [New Latin, "little ear" (from the shape of the leaves), from Latin, AURICLE.]

au·ric·u·lar (ô-rĭk'yə-lər) *adj.* **1.** Of or pertaining to the sense or organs of hearing. **2.** Perceived by or spoken into the ear: *an auricular confession.* **3.** Having the shape of an ear. **4.** Of or pertaining to an auricle of the heart.
~*n.* **auriculars.** The feathers covering the opening of the ear in some birds, such as owls. [Late Latin *auriculāris,* from *auricula,* AURICLE.] **—au·ric·u·lar·ly** *adv.*

au·ric·u·late (ô-rĭk'yə-lĭt, -lāt') *adj.* Also **au·ric·u·lat·ed** (-lā'tĭd). **1.** Having ears or earlike parts or extensions: *an auriculate leaf.* **2.** Having the shape of an ear. [Latin *auricula,* AURICLE.] **—au·ric·u·late·ly** *adv.*

au·rif·er·ous (ô-rĭf'ər-əs) *adj.* Containing gold; gold-bearing. Said of rocks or gravels. [Latin *aurifer* : *aurum,* gold + -FER.]

au·ri·form (ôr'ə-fôrm') *adj.* Ear-shaped. [Latin *auris,* ear + -FORM.]

Au·ri·ga (ô-rī'gə) *n.* A constellation in the Northern Hemisphere near Lynx and Perseus. Also called the "Charioteer." [Latin *aurīga,* charioteer.]

Au·rig·na·cian (ôr'ĭg-nā'shən, ôr'ēn-yā'shən) *adj. Sometimes* **aurignacian.** *Archaeology.* Of or relating to the Old World Upper Paleolithic culture between Mousterian and Solutrean, associated with Cro-Magnon man, and characterized by artifacts such as figures of stone and bone, paintings on the walls of caves, and the use of dress and adornment. [After *Aurignac,* commune in the French Pyrenees, near which such artifacts were found.]

au·rochs (ou'rŏks', ô'-) *n.* **1.** An extinct bovine mammal, *Bos taurus primigenius,* of northern Africa, Europe, and western Asia, believed to be the forerunner of domestic cattle. Also called "urus." **2.** Loosely, the European bison, or wisent. [German, from Old High German *ūrohso* : *ūro,* bison, from Germanic *ūrus* (unattested) + *ohso,* ox.]

au·ro·ra (ô-rôr'ə, ô-rōr'ə) *n., pl.* **-ras** or **aurorae** (ô-rôr'ē, ô-rōr'ē). **1.** High-altitude, many-colored, flashing luminosity, visible in night skies of polar and sometimes temperate zones, and thought to be caused by the capture of charged particles, especially ones of solar origin, by the earth's magnetic field. Compare **airglow. 2.** *Poetic.* The dawn. **3.** *Rare.* An early part or stage; a beginning. [Latin *aurōra,* dawn.]

Au·ro·ra (ô-rôr'ə, ô-rōr'ə). *Roman Mythology.* The goddess of the dawn, identified with the Greek goddess Eos.

aurora aus·tra·lis (ô-strā'lĭs) *n.* Aurora occurring in southern regions. Also called "southern lights." [New Latin : AURORA + AUSTRAL.]

aurora bo·re·al·is (bôr'ē-ăl'ĭs, bōr'-) *n.* Aurora occurring in northern regions. Also called "northern lights." [New Latin : AURORA + BOREAL.]

au·ro·ral (ô-rôr'əl, ô-rōr'-) *adj.* Also *poetic* **au·ro·re·an** (ô-rôr'ē-ən, ô-rōr'-) (for sense 1). **1.** Pertaining to or resembling the dawn. **2.** *Meteorology.* Pertaining to, caused by, or like an aurora. **—au·ro·ral·ly** *adv.*

au·rous (ôr'əs) *adj.* Of or pertaining to gold, especially with valence 1. [Late Latin *aurōsus,* from Latin *aurum,* gold.]

au·rum (ôr'əm) *n. Symbol* **Au** The element gold. [Latin, gold.]

Aus. 1. Australia; Australian. **2.** Austria; Austrian.

Auschwitz. See **Oświęcim.**

aus·cul·tate (ô'skəl-tāt') *tr.v.* **-tated, -tating, -tates.** *Medicine.* To examine by auscultation. [Back-formation from AUSCULTATION.] **—aus·cul·ta·tive** *adj.* **—aus·cul·ta·to·ry** (ô-skŭl'tə-tôr'ē, -tōr'ē) *adj.*

aus·cul·ta·tion (ô'skəl-tā'shən) *n.* **1.** *Medicine.* Diagnostic monitoring with a stethoscope or other instrument of sounds within the body. **2.** The act of listening. [Latin *auscultātiō* (stem *auscultātiōn-*), from *auscultāre,* to listen to.]

aus·form (ôs'fôrm') *tr.v.* **-formed, -forming, -forms.** To subject (a metal, especially steel) to deformation, quenching, and tempering while it is in the austenite temperature range, in order to improve its wear properties. [*Aus*tenitic de*form.*]

Aus·gleich (ous'glĭKH') *n., pl.* **-gleiche** (-glī'KHə). *German.* Compromise; agreement; specifically, the treaty between Hungary and Austria in 1867 organizing their dual monarchy.

Augustus *Bronze head portraying Rome's first emperor. The head is part of a 2,000-year-old Roman statue found at Merowe in the Sudan.*

aurochs *The earliest cattle in Europe to be domesticated, aurochs were large, brown or black, and had horns measuring as much as 1 meter (3 feet) from tip to tip. They are thought to have become extinct in 1627.*

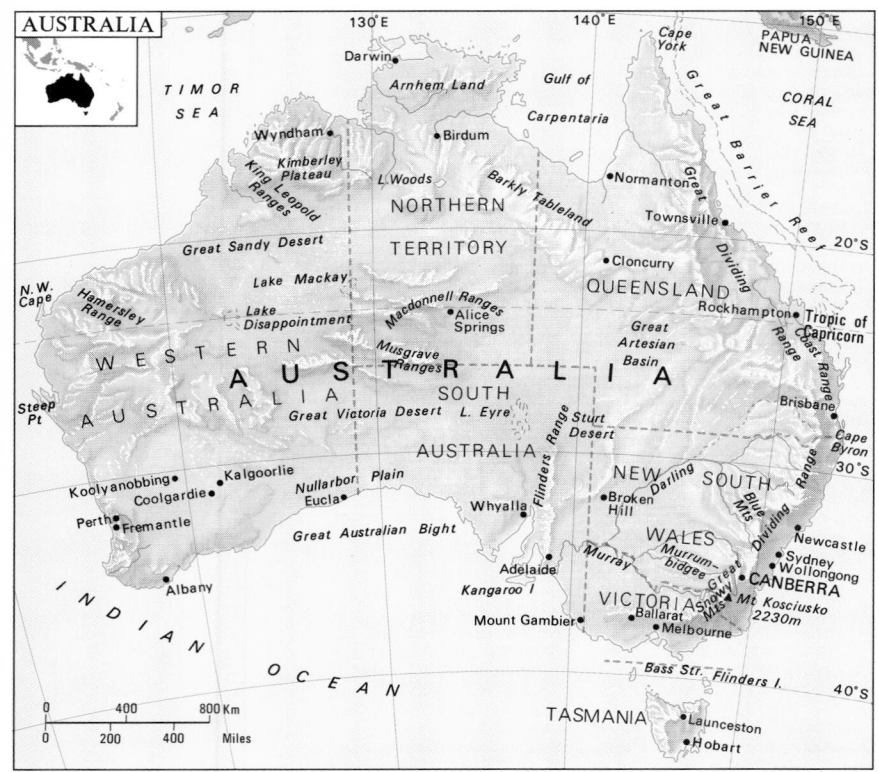

AUSTRALIA

AUSTRIA

---

aus·pex (ô'spĕks') *n., pl.* **auspices** (ô'spə-sēz'). An augur of ancient Rome, especially one who interpreted omens taken from the actions of birds. [Latin. See **auspice**.]

aus·pi·cate (ô'spĭ-kāt') *tr.v.* **-cated, -cating, -cates.** *Rare.* To begin or inaugurate with a ceremony designed to bring good luck. [Latin *auspicārī*, from *auspex*, bird augur. See **auspice**.]

aus·pice (ô'spĭs) *n., pl.* **auspices** (ô'spə-sēz'). **1.** *Usually* **auspices.** Protection or support; patronage. Used in the phrase *under the auspices of.* Compare **aegis. 2.** A portent, omen, or augury, especially when observed in the actions of birds. **3.** Observation of and divination from the actions of birds. [Latin *auspicium*, bird divination, from *auspex* (stem *auspic-*), a bird augur : *au-*, from *avis*, bird + *-spex*, from *specere*, to look.]

aus·pi·cious (ô-spĭsh'əs) *adj.* **1.** Attended by favorable circumstances; promising. **2.** Marked by success; fortunate; prosperous. —See Synonyms at **favorable.** —**aus·pi·cious·ly** *adv.* —**aus·pi·cious·ness** *n.*

Aus·sie (ô'sē) *n. Slang.* An Australian. —**Aus·sie** *adj.*

Aust. 1. Australia; Australian. **2.** Austria; Austrian.

Aus·ten (ôs'tən), **Jane** (1775–1817). English novelist. Although her subject matter and personal experience may have been limited, her novels, which include *Sense and Sensibility* (1811), *Pride and Prejudice* (1813), *Mansfield Park* (1814), and *Emma* (1816), are notable for their incisive social satire, irony, and wit and for their fine observation of manners and morality.

aus·ten·ite (ôs'tə-nīt') *n.* **1.** A nonmagnetic solid solution of ferric carbide or carbon in iron, used in making corrosive-resistant steel. **2.** Any solid solution based on the gamma phase of iron, especially when stabilized by the addition of nickel. [After Sir William Roberts-*Austen* (1843–1902), British metallurgist.]

aus·ten·it·ic (ôs'tə-nĭt'ĭk) *adj.* Designating a form of steel that con-

---

tains sufficient nickel, nickel and chromium, or manganese to maintain the structure of austenite: *austenitic stainless steel.*

Aus·ter (ôs'tər) *n. Poetic.* The south wind. [Latin *auster†*, south wind, the south.]

aus·tere (ô-stîr') *adj.* **1.** Severe or stern in disposition or appearance; somber; grave: *"an austere man that never laughed or smiled"* (Alan Paton). **2.** Strict or severe in moral discipline; ascetic. **3.** Without adornment or ornamentation; simple; bare. **4.** *Archaic.* Bitter or sour to the taste. —See Synonyms at **severe.** [Middle English, from Old French, from Latin *austērus*, from Greek *austēros*, harsh, rough, severe.] —**aus·tere·ly** *adv.* —**aus·tere·ness** *n.*

aus·ter·i·ty (ô-stĕr'ə-tē) *n., pl.* **-ties. 1.** The quality of being austere. **2.** Severely simple living conditions, especially as an economic policy: *wartime austerity.* **3.** *Usually* **austerities.** An ascetic habit or practice: *Hermits were renowned for their austerities.*

Aus·ter·litz (ô'stər-lĭts'). A town in Moravia, in southern Czechoslovakia. Nearby, Napoleon won a brilliant victory (December 2, 1805) over the Russian and Austrian armies under Czar Alexander I and Emperor Francis II. Tolstoy described the battle in his *War and Peace.*

Aus·tin (ôs'tən) *adj.* Augustinian. Now used only in the phrase *Austin Friars.* [Shortening of *Augustine.*]

Austin. The capital of Texas, in the south-central part of the state, on the Colorado River. It is the commercial center of a large ranching, poultry, dairy, cotton, and grain area, with diversified manufactures. The main campus of the University of Texas is in Austin.

Austin, Stephen Fuller (1793–1836). Colonizer and political leader in Texas. He founded a colony in the area in 1822. Although he originally worked to make Texas a state of Mexico, he helped the Texas settlers gain their independence in 1836.

aus·tral (ôs'trəl) *adj.* **1.** Of, pertaining to, or coming from the south: *austral winds.* **2. Austral.** Australian; Australasian. [Middle English, from Latin *austrālis*, from *auster†*, south, **AUSTER**.]

Aus·tral·a·sia (ôs'trəl-ā'zhə, -shə). An imprecise term referring to lands in the Pacific Ocean. The name is used in a broad sense to include the Malay Archipelago, Micronesia, Polynesia, and Melanesia in addition to New Zealand, the island of New Guinea, and Australia. It is used more commonly to refer simply to Australia and New Zealand and their dependencies (or former dependencies), such as Papua New Guinea. —**Aus·tral·a·sian** *n. & adj.*

Aus·tra·lia (ô-strāl'yə). *Abbr.* **Aus., Aust.** Island commonwealth lying between the Indian and Pacific oceans. Nearly half of it is desert or dry scrub. About 85 percent of its people live in towns, and nearly 20 percent of its workers are in manufacturing, the chief products being steel, aluminum, vehicles, textiles, and machinery. However, minerals, wool, beef, and sugar are still the main exports. The population, about 75 percent of British or Irish descent, includes some 140,000 aborigines. Dutch navigators were the first Europeans to sight Australia (1606), and Capt. James Cook claimed the east coast for Britain (1770). The first colony, a penal settlement, was established at Sydney Cove (1788), and by 1850 there were colonies at what are now the other six state capitals. Discovery of gold in New South Wales and Victoria (1851) stimulated their growth, and in 1901 the Commonwealth of Australia, a federation of six former colonies (Tasmania, Victoria, South Australia, Western Australia, Queensland, and New South Wales), was born. Northern Territory came under federal control, and the Capital Territory was created in 1911. Australia became a dominion within the Commonwealth in 1931. Since 1945 traditional ties with Europe have weakened. Australia signed the ANZUS Pact (1952) and was a member of SEATO (1954–77); some Australians now favor a republican government. Area, 7,686,848 square kilometers (2,967,123 square miles). Population, 16,900,000. Capital, Canberra.

Australia Day *n.* In Australia, the national holiday held on January 26 or the first Monday following it to commemorate the landing of the British in 1788.

Aus·tra·lian (ô-strāl'yən) *n.* **1.** A native or citizen of the Commonwealth of Australia. **2.** An aborigine of Australia. **3.** Any of the languages of the Australian aborigines. **4.** English as it is spoken by Australians.

~*adj.* **1.** Of or pertaining to Australia or its inhabitants and their languages or cultures. **2.** *Ecology.* Of or designating the zoogeographic region that includes Australia, the islands adjacent to it, and New Guinea.

Australian Alps (ălps). A chain of mountain ranges forming a segment of the Great Dividing Range, occupying the southeastern corner of Australia.

Australian Antarctic Territory. A territory claimed by Australia, including all the islands and lands south of latitude 60° and between longitudes 160° and 45° east, except for Adélie Land.

Australian ballot *n.* A printed ballot that bears the names of all candidates and the texts of propositions and is distributed to the voter at the polls to be marked in secret.

Australian Capital Territory. *Abbr.* **A.C.T.** Formerly **Federal Capital Territory.** The name for the separate administrative unit enclosed by New South Wales in Australia, comprising the national capital, Canberra, and land around it. The territory has an area of 2,430 square kilometers (940 square miles).

Australian crawl *n.* A swimming stroke, a variation of the **crawl** *(see)* executed with an eight-beat flutter kick to each stroke.

Australian Rules *n. Used with a singular verb.* In Australia, a variety of football played on an oval field between teams of 18 players.

Australian terrier *n.* A small dog of a breed developed in Australia, having a coarse blackish coat with tan markings.

Aus·tra·loid (ôs'trə-loid') *adj.* Of or pertaining to an ethnic group including the Australian aborigines. [AUSTRAL(IAN) + -OID.] —**Aus·tra·loid** *n.*

aus·tra·lo·pith·e·cine (ô-strā'lō-pĭth'ə-sīn') *n.* Any of several extinct humanlike primates of the genera *Australopithecus* and *Paranthropus* or *Zinjanthropus,* known chiefly from late Pliocene and Pleistocene fossil remains found in southern and eastern Africa.
~*adj.* Of, pertaining to, or characteristic of the australopithecines. [New Latin *Australopithecus,* "southern ape" : AUSTRAL + New Latin *pithēcus,* ape, from Greek *pithēkos* (see **pithecanthropus**).]

Aus·tra·sia (ô-strā'zhə, -shə). The eastern portion of the Frankish kingdom from the 6th to the 8th century, consisting of parts of eastern France, western Germany, and the Netherlands. It was eventually absorbed by the empire of the Carolingian kings. —**Aus·tra·sian** *adj.*

Aus·tri·a (ô'strē-ə). *Abbr.* **Aus., Aust.** *German* **Ös·ter·reich** (œs'tə-rīKH). Landlocked Alpine republic in Central Europe. A former territory of Rome and of Charlemagne's empire, it came under the Habsburgs (1246), who were also Holy Roman Emperors (1438–1806). Under the statesman Prince Metternich, the arbiter of Europe, the Habsburgs built a vast multinational empire, which was a bulwark against the Turks. However, discontent grew within the empire. The Hungarians forced the dual monarchy of Austria-Hungary on Francis Joseph I (1867), and the assassination of the empire's heir, Archduke Francis Ferdinand, in Sarajevo (1914) unleashed World War I. In 1919 Austria was defeated, reduced to its German-speaking area, and became a republic. After suffering economic collapse, it was annexed by Hitler (1938). After World War II the Allies occupied the country until 1955, when a federal republic, obligated to remain neutral, was set up. Austria has reserves of oil, gas, lignite, and iron ore. It exports iron and steel, machinery, wooden goods, timber from its vast forests, and livestock products. Tourism is a major industry. Area, 83,849 square kilometers (32,366 square miles). Population, 7,600,000. Capital, Vienna. —**Aus·tri·an** *n. & adj.*

Aus·tri·a-Hun·ga·ry (ôs'trē-ə-hŭng'gə-rē). Two states ruled (1867–1918) by the Hapsburgs, one as emperors of Austria (Austria, Bohemia, Moravia, Austrian Poland, Austrian Silesia, and Slovenia), the other as kings of Hungary (Hungary, Transylvania, Croatia, and lands along the Dalmatian coast).

Austro–¹ *prefix.* Indicates southern; for example, **Austro-Asiatic.** [Latin *auster*†, the south, AUSTER.]

Austro–² *prefix.* Indicates Austrian; for example, **Austro-Hungarian.**

Aus·tro-A·si·at·ic, Aus·tro·a·si·at·ic (ôs'trō-ā'zhē-ăt'ĭk) *n.* A family of languages of southeastern Asia, believed to have once been dominant in northeastern India and Indochina. —**Austro-Asiatic** *adj.*

Aus·tro-Hun·gar·i·an (ôs'trō-hŭng-gâr'ē-ən) *adj.* Of or pertaining to Austria-Hungary.

Aus·tro·ne·sia (ôs'trō-nē'zhə, -shə). The islands in the Pacific Ocean, including Indonesia, Melanesia, Micronesia, and Polynesia.

Aus·tro·ne·sian (ôs'trō-nē'zhən, -shən) *adj.* Of or pertaining to Austronesia, its peoples, or their languages.
~*n.* A family of languages spoken in Austronesia, including the Indonesian, Melanesian, Micronesian, and Polynesian subfamilies. Also called "Malayo-Polynesian."

aut–. Variant of **auto–.**

au·ta·coid, au·to·coid (ô'tə-koid') *n.* An organic substance, such as a hormone, formed by the cells of an organ and secreted into the blood or lymph to act on the cells of other parts of the organism. [AUT(O)- + Greek *akos,* cure.]

au·tar·chy (ô'tär'kē) *n., pl.* **-chies. 1.** Absolute rule or power; autocracy. **2.** A country under such rule. **3.** Variant of **autarky.** [Greek *autarkhia,* from *autarkhos,* self-governing : AUT(O)- + -ARCH.] —**au·tar·chic** (ô-tär'kĭk), **au·tar·chi·cal** *adj.*

au·tar·ky (ô'tär'kē) *n., pl.* **-kies. 1.** A policy of national self-sufficiency and nonreliance on imports or economic aid. **2.** A self-sufficient region or country. [Greek *autarkeia,* self-sufficiency, from *autarkēs,* self-sufficient : AUT(O)- + *arkein,* to suffice.] —**au·tar·kic** (ô-tär'kĭk), **au·tar·ki·cal** *adj.*

au·te·col·o·gy (ô'tĭ-kŏl'ə-jē) *n.* The ecology of a species or an individual organism. Compare **synecology.** [AUT(O)- + ECOLOGY.]

auth. 1. authentic. **2.** author. **3.** authorized. **4.** authority.

au·then·tic (ô-thĕn'tĭk) *adj. Abbr.* **auth. 1. a.** Conforming to fact and therefore worthy of trust, reliance, or belief: *authentic records.* **b.** Having an undisputed origin; genuine: *an authentic Chippendale chair.* **2.** *Law.* Executed with due process of law: *an authentic deed.* **3.** *Music.* **a.** Designating a medieval mode having a range from its final note to the octave above it. **b.** Designating a cadence with the dominant chord immediately preceding the tonic chord. Compare **plagal.** —See Synonyms at **real.** [Middle English *autentik,* from Old French *autentique,* from Late Latin *authenticus,* from Greek *authentikos,* genuine, authoritative, from *authentēs*†, perpetrator, author.] —**au·then·ti·cal·ly** *adj.*

au·then·ti·cate (ô-thĕn'tĭ-kāt') *tr.v.* **-cated, -cating, -cates. 1.** To establish as worthy of belief: *authenticate a story.* **2.** To confirm as genuine; prove or verify the origin of: *authenticate a painting.* **3.** To invest (a deed, for example) with legal validity. —See Synonyms at **confirm.** —**au·then·ti·ca·tion** *n.* —**au·then·ti·ca·tor** (ô-thĕn'tĭ-kā'tər) *n.*

au·then·tic·i·ty (ô'thĕn-tĭs'ə-tē) *n.* The condition or quality of being authentic, trustworthy, or genuine. —See Synonyms at **truth.**

au·thor (ô'thər) *n.* **1.** *Abbr.* **auth. a.** The original writer of a literary work, as a book, essay, or article. **b.** One who practices writing as a profession. **c.** An author's works collectively: *reading my favorite author.* **2.** The beginner, originator, or creator of anything: *the author of the universe; the author of a theory.*
~*tr.v.* **authored, -thoring, -thors. 1.** To be the author of; write. **2.** To originate; create: *author a new fashion.* [Middle English *autour,* from Old French *autor,* from Latin *auctor,* creator, from *augēre* (past participle *auctus*), to create, increase.] —**au·thor·i·al** (ô-thôr'ē-əl, ô-thōr'-) *adj.*

au·thor·ess (ô'thər-ĭs) *n.* A female author. Sometimes considered disparaging.

au·thor·i·tar·i·an (ə-thôr'ə-târ'ē-ən, ə-thŏr'-, ô-) *adj.* **1.** Characterized by or favoring absolute obedience to authority, as against individual freedom. **2.** Favoring strong government powers.
~*n.* One who believes in or practices authoritarian policies or methods. —**au·thor·i·tar·i·an·ism** *n.*

au·thor·i·ta·tive (ə-thôr'ə-tā'tĭv, ə-thŏr'-, ô-) *adj.* **1.** Having or arising from proper authority; official: *authoritative sources.* **2.** Having a commanding air; wielding authority: *an authoritative voice.* —**au·thor·i·ta·tive·ly** *adv.* —**au·thor·i·ta·tive·ness** *n.*

au·thor·i·ty (ə-thôr'ə-tē, ə-thŏr'-, ô-) *n., pl.* **-ties.** *Abbr.* **auth. 1.** The right or power to act, command, enforce laws, exact obedience, determine, or judge. **2. a.** A person or group invested with this right or power. **b. authorities.** Government officials having this right or power. Preceded by *the.* **3.** Power delegated to others; authorization: *You have my authority to decide.* **4.** *Often* **Authority.** A public agency or corporation with administrative powers limited to a specified field: *the Transit Authority.* **5. a.** An accepted source of expert information or advice: *This book is an authority on civil law.* **b.** A quotation or citation from such a source used in defense or support of one's actions, opinions, or the like. **6.** An expert in a given field: *an authority on plants.* **7.** Power to influence or persuade resulting from knowledge or experience: *write with authority.* **8.** A claim to be accepted or believed: *on the authority of the press.* **9.** An authoritative statement or decision that provides adequate grounds for a course of action or that may be taken as a precedent. [Middle English *autorite, auctorite,* from Old French *auctorite,* from Latin *auctōritās* (stem *auctōritāt-*), from *auctor,* AUTHOR.]

au·thor·i·za·tion (ô'thər-ə-zā'shən) *n.* **1.** The act of conferring authority; permission. **2.** Written permission. **3.** Legal power, right, or sanction.

au·thor·ize (ô'thə-rīz') *tr.v.* **-ized, -izing, -izes. 1.** To grant authority or power to. **2.** To approve or give permission for; sanction: *authorize a highway project.* **3.** To be sufficient grounds for; justify. [Middle English *autorisen,* from Old French *autoriser,* from Medieval Latin *auctorizāre,* from Latin *auctor,* AUTHOR.] —**au·thor·iz·er** *n.*

au·thor·ized (ô'thə-rīzd') *adj. Abbr.* **auth. 1.** Invested with authority; authoritative. **2.** Having official permission. **3.** Sanctioned by law or command.

Authorized Version *n. Abbr.* **A.V.** The **King James Bible** *(see).*

au·thor·ship (ô'thər-shĭp') *n.* **1.** The profession or occupation of writing. **2.** A source or origin, as of a book or idea.

au·tism (ô'tĭz'əm) *n.* A condition of abnormal subjectivity marked by absorption in self-centered thought and behavior and an inability to communicate or to relate to other people. Also called "infantile autism." [New Latin *autismus* : AUT(O)- + -ISM.] —**au·tis·tic** (ô-tĭs'tĭk) *adj.*

au·to (ô'tō) *n., pl.* **-tos.** *Informal.* An automobile.

auto–, aut– *prefix.* Indicates: **1.** Acting or directed from within; for example, **autogenesis, autism. 2.** Self; same; for example, **autobiography. 3.** Indicates self-propelled; automotive; for example, **autogiro.** [Greek, from *autos*†, self.]

auto. 1. automatic. **2.** automotive.

au·to·an·ti·bod·y (ô'tō-ăn'tē-bŏd'ē) *n., pl.* **-ies.** An antibody that acts against cells of the organism in which it is formed. See **autoimmune.**

au·to·bahn (ou'tō-bän') *n., pl.* **-bahns** or **-bahnen** (-bä'nən). A German expressway. [German *Autobahn* : AUTO- (automobile) + *Bahn,* road, from Middle High German *ban, bane.*]

au·to·bi·og·ra·phy (ô'tō-bī-ŏg'rə-fē, -bē-) *n., pl.* **-phies. 1.** The written story of one's own life; memoirs. **2.** Such writings as a literary form. —**au·to·bi·og·ra·pher** *n.* —**au·to·bi·o·graph·ic** (ô'tō-bī'ə-grăf'ĭk), **au·to·bi·o·graph·i·cal** *adj.* —**au·to·bi·o·graph·i·cal·ly** *adv.*

au·to·ca·tal·y·sis (ô'tō-kə-tăl'ə-sĭs) *n., pl.* **-ses** (-sēz'). Catalysis of a chemical reaction by one of the products of the reaction.

au·to·ceph·a·lous (ô'tō-sĕf'ə-ləs) *adj.* Independent of outside authority; having its own head. Said especially of Eastern Christian churches. [Late Greek *autokephalos* : *auto-,* self + *kephalē,* head.]

au·to·chrome (ô'tə-krōm') *n.* A photographic plate once used in three-color photography. [French : AUTO- + -CHROME.]

au·toch·thon (ô-tŏk'thən) *n., pl.* **-thons** or **-thones** (-thə-nēz'). **1. autochthons** or **autochthones.** The earliest known or aboriginal inhabitants of a particular place. **2.** *Ecology.* Any indigenous plant or animal. [Greek *autokhthōn,* "one sprung from the land itself," indigenous : AUTO- + *khthōn,* earth.]

au·toch·tho·nous (ô-tŏk'thə-nəs) *adj.* Also **au·toch·tho·nal** (ô-tŏk'thə-nəl), **au·toch·thon·ic** (ô'tŏk-thŏn'ĭk). Native to a particular place; aboriginal; indigenous. —**au·toch·thon·ism** (ô-tŏk'thə-nĭz'əm), **au·toch·tho·ny** *n.* —**au·toch·tho·nous·ly** *adv.*

au·to·clave (ô'tō-klāv') *n.* A strong, pressurized, steam-heated vessel, used to establish special conditions for chemical reactions, for sterilization, and for cooking.

PRONUNCIATION KEY

ă, pat; ā, pay; âr, care;
ä, father, are; b, bib;
ch, church; d, deed; ĕ, pet;
ē, be; f, fife; g, gag; h, hat;
hw, which; ĭ, pit; ī, pie;
îr, pier; j, judge; k, kick;
l, lid, needle; m, mum;
n, no, sudden; ng, thing;
ŏ, pot; ō, toe; ô, paw, for;
oi, noise; ou, out; ŏŏ, book;
ōō, boot; p, pop; r, roar;
s, sauce; sh, ship, dish;
t, tight; th, thin, path;
th, this, bathe; ŭ, cut; ûr, fur;
v, valve; w, with; y, yes;
z, zebra, size; zh, vision;
ə, about, item, edible,
gallop, circus, peaceful

IN FOREIGN WORDS:

à, *Fr.* ami; œ, *Fr.* feu, *Ger.* schön; ü, *Fr.* tu, *Ger.* über; KH, *Ger.* ich, *Scot.* loch; N, *Fr.* bon; y', *Fr.* Compiègne

STRESS MARKS:

Primary stress: '
in·cite' (ĭn-sīt')
Secondary stress: '
in'sight' (ĭn'sīt')

~*tr.v.* **autoclaved, -claving, -claves.** To process in an autoclave. [French, "self-locking" : AUTO- + Latin *clāvis*, key.]

autocoid. Variant of **autacoid.**

au·toc·ra·cy (ô-tŏk'rə-sē) *n., pl.* **-cies.** 1. Government by a single person having unlimited power; despotism. 2. A country or state having this form of government. [From AUTOCRAT.]

au·to·crat (ô'tə-krăt') *n.* 1. A ruler having absolute or unrestricted power; a despot. 2. Any arrogant and domineering person. [French *autocrate,* from Greek *autokratēs,* ruling by oneself : AUTO- + -CRAT.] —**au·to·crat·ic, au·to·crat·i·cal** *adj.* —**au·to·crat·i·cal·ly** *adv.*

au·to·cross (ô'tō-krôs') *n. Chiefly British.* A form of automobile racing, with races held on a rough grass track.

au·to·da·fé (ou'tō-də-fā', ô'tō-) *n., pl.* **au·tos-da-fé** (ou'tōz-, ô'tōz-). 1. The public announcement of the sentences imposed on persons tried by the Inquisition. 2. The public execution of these sentences by the secular authorities, especially the burning of condemned heretics at the stake. [Portuguese *auto da fé,* "act of the faith" : *auto,* act, from Latin *āctus,* ACT + *da,* of the + *fé,* faith, from Latin *fidēs.*]

au·to·di·dact (ô'tō-dī'dăkt') *n.* A person who is self-taught. [Greek *autodidaktos,* self-taught : AUTO- + *didaktos,* taught (see **didactic**).] —**au·to·di·dac·tic** (ô'tō-dī-dăk'tĭk) *adj.*

au·to·dyne (ô'tə-dīn') *n.* A heterodyne radio device in which one valve serves as both oscillator and detector. [AUTO- + (HETERO)-DYNE.] —**au·to·dyne** *adj.*

au·toe·cious (ô-tē'shəs) *adj. Biology.* Completing all stages of a life cycle on the same host. Said especially of certain rust fungi. Compare **heteroecious.** [AUT(O)- + -*oecious,* from Greek *oikos,* house.] —**au·toe·cism** (ô-tē'sĭz'əm) *n.*

au·to·er·o·tism (ô'tō-ĕr'ə-tĭz'əm) *n.* Also **au·to·e·rot·i·cism** (ô'tō-ĭ-rŏt'ə-sĭz'əm). Self-arousal and self-satisfaction of sexual desire, as by masturbation. —**au·to·e·rot·ic** (ô'tō-ĭ-rŏt'ĭk) *adj.*

au·tog·a·my (ô-tŏg'ə-mē) *n.* 1. *Botany.* Fertilization of a flower by its own pollen; self-fertilization. 2. *Biology.* The union of nuclei within and arising from a single cell, as in certain protozoans. [AUTO- + -GAMY.] —**au·tog·a·mous** (ô-tŏg'ə-məs) *adj.*

au·to·gen·e·sis (ô'tō-jĕn'ə-sĭs) *n.* Also **au·tog·e·ny** (ô-tŏj'ə-nē). *Biology.* Abiogenesis (see). —**au·to·ge·net·ic** (ô'tō-jə-nĕt'ĭk) *adj.* —**au·to·ge·net·i·cal·ly** *adv.*

au·tog·e·nous (ô-tŏj'ə-nəs) *adj.* Also **au·to·gen·ic** (ô'tə-jĕn'ĭk). Self-generated; self-produced. [Greek *autogenēs,* self-producing : AUTO- + -GENOUS.] —**au·tog·e·nous·ly** *adv.*

au·to·gi·ro, au·to·gy·ro (ô'tō-jī'rō) *n., pl.* **-ros.** An aircraft powered by a conventional propeller and supported in flight by a freewheeling horizontal rotor mounted above the fuselage that provides lift. [AUTO- + Greek *guros,* circle.]

au·to·graft (ô'tō-grăft', -grăft') *n. Medicine.* A tissue graft obtained from the body of the recipient.

au·to·graph (ô'tə-grăf', -grăf') *n.* 1. A person's own signature or handwriting. 2. A manuscript in the author's handwriting. ~*tr.v.* **autographed, -graphing, -graphs.** 1. To write one's name or signature on or in; sign. 2. To write in one's own handwriting. ~*adj.* 1. Written in a person's own handwriting. 2. Containing signatures or autographs. [Latin *autographum,* from Greek *autographon,* autograph manuscript, from *autographos,* written by oneself : AUTO- + -GRAPH.] —**au·to·graph·ic, au·to·graph·i·cal** *adj.* —**au·to·graph·i·cal·ly** *adv.*

au·tog·ra·phy (ô-tŏg'rə-fē) *n.* 1. The writing of something in one's own handwriting. 2. Autographs collectively.

au·to·harp (ô'tō-härp') *n.* A musical instrument, similar to a zither, on which a desired chord can be selected by depressing a particular damper. [Originally a trademark : AUTO- (self) + HARP.]

au·to·hyp·no·sis (ô'tō-hĭp-nō'sĭs) *n.* 1. The act or process of hypnotizing oneself. 2. A self-induced hypnotic state. —**au·to·hyp·not·ic** (ô'tō-hĭp-nŏt'ĭk) *adj.*

au·to·im·mune (ô'tō-ĭ-myōon') *adj.* Of, relating to, or caused by the action of antibodies against the body's own tissues: *an autoimmune disease.* —**au·to·im·mu·ni·ty** *n.* —**au·to·im·mu·ni·za·tion** (ô'tō-ĭm'yə-nə-zā'shən) *n.*

au·to·in·fec·tion (ô'tō-ĭn-fĕk'shən) *n.* Infection, as with recurrent boils, caused by germs or viruses persisting on or in the body.

au·to·in·oc·u·la·tion (ô'tō-ĭn-ŏk'yə-lā'shən) *n.* 1. Inoculation with a vaccine made from microorganisms derived from the recipient. 2. A secondary infection caused by a disease already in the body.

au·to·in·tox·i·ca·tion (ô'tō-ĭn-tŏk'sə-kā'shən) *n.* Self-poisoning caused by endogenous microorganisms, metabolic wastes, or other toxins in the body. Also called "autotoxemia."

au·to·i·on·i·za·tion (ô'tō-ī'ə-nə-zā'shən) *n. Physics.* A process in which an excited atom or molecule emits an electron rather than a photon when it decays. See **Auger effect.**

au·to·load·ing (ô'tō-lō'dĭng) *adj.* **Semiautomatic** (see).

au·tol·y·sate (ô-tŏl'ə-sāt', -zāt') *n. Biochemistry.* An end product of autolysis.

au·tol·y·sin (ô-tŏl'ə-sĭn, ô'tə-lī'sĭn) *n. Biochemistry.* A substance that causes autolysis. [AUTOLYS(IS) + -IN.]

au·tol·y·sis (ô-tŏl'ə-sĭs) *n. Biochemistry.* The destruction of tissues or cells of an organism by self-produced enzymes. [AUTO- + -LYSIS.] —**au·to·lyt·ic** (ô'tə-lĭt'ĭk) *adj.*

au·to·mak·er (ô'tō-mā'kər) *n.* A manufacturer of automobiles.

au·to·mat (ô'tə-măt') *n.* A restaurant in which the customers obtain food from closed compartments by inserting coins in a slot. [From trademark *Automat,* from AUTOMATIC.]

au·to·mate (ô'tə-māt') *v.* **-mated, -mating, -mates.** —*tr.* 1. To convert (a process, factory, or machine) to automation. 2. To control or operate by automation. —*intr.* To convert to or make use of automation. [Back-formation from AUTOMATIC.]

au·to·mat·ic (ô'tə-măt'ĭk) *adj. Abbr.* **auto.** 1. a. Acting or operating in a manner essentially independent of external influence or control; self-moving. b. Self-regulating. 2. Lacking volition, intention, or conscious planning; involuntary; reflex. 3. Occurring as a matter of course or routine: *automatic weekly inspections.* 4. Having an automatic transmission. Said of a motor vehicle. 5. Capable of firing continuously until ammunition is exhausted. Said of firearms. Compare **semiautomatic.** —See Synonyms at **spontaneous.** ~*n.* 1. An automatic firearm, especially an automatic pistol. 2. An automatic machine, vehicle, or device. [Greek *automatos,* acting by itself, spontaneous of one's own will : AUTO- + -*matos,* willing.] —**au·to·mat·i·cal·ly** *adv.*

au·tom·a·tic·i·ty (ô-tŏm'ə-tĭs'ə-tē) *n.* 1. The state of being automatic. 2. Automatic action.

automatic pilot *n.* An aircraft control mechanism that automatically maintains altitude, preset course, and steadiness. Also called "autopilot," "robot pilot."

automatic pistol *n.* A pistol that can be fired automatically or semiautomatically.

automatic rifle *n.* A light machine gun that can be fired automatically or semiautomatically, normally the latter.

automatic transmission *n.* A device in a motor vehicle that enables gear changes to be operated mechanically rather than manually according to car or engine speed.

au·to·ma·tion (ô'tə-mā'shən) *n.* 1. Automatically controlled operation of a process, equipment, or a system. 2. The act or process of conversion to such operation. 3. The totality of mechanical and electronic techniques and equipment used to achieve such operation. 4. The condition of being automatically controlled or operated. [AUTOM(ATIC) + -ATION.] —**au·to·ma·tive** *adj.*

au·tom·a·tism (ô-tŏm'ə-tĭz'əm) *n.* 1. a. The state or quality of being automatic. b. Automatic mechanical action. 2. *Philosophy.* The theory that all living organisms are automatons. 3. *Physiology.* a. The automatic operation of organs and cells, such as the beating of the heart. b. Performance of an act without conscious control, as in the operation of the reflexes. 4. The effort at suspension of consciousness made by certain surrealist writers and artists in order to express subconscious ideas and feelings. [French *automatisme* : *automate,* AUTOMATON + -*isme,* -ISM.] —**au·tom·a·tist** *n.*

au·tom·a·tize (ô-tŏm'ə-tīz') *tr.v.* **-tized, -tizing, -tizes.** To make automatic.

au·tom·a·ton (ô-tŏm'ə-tən, -tŏn') *n., pl.* **-tons** or **-ta** (-tə). 1. See **robot** (sense 2). 2. One that behaves in an automatic or mechanical fashion. [Latin, self-operating machine, from Greek *automaton,* neuter of *automatos,* AUTOMATIC.] —**au·tom·a·tous** *adj.*

au·to·mo·bile (ô'tō-mō-bēl', -mō'bēl', ô'tə-mō-bēl') *n.* A self-propelled passenger vehicle that usually has four wheels and an internal-combustion engine, used for land transport. [French : AUTO- + MOBILE.] —**au·to·mo·bil·ist** *n.*

au·to·mo·tive (ô'tə-mō'tĭv) *adj. Abbr.* **auto.** 1. Self-moving; self-propelling. 2. Of or pertaining to self-propelled vehicles.

au·to·net·ics (ô'tə-nĕt'ĭks) *n. Used with a singular verb.* The study of automatic guidance and control systems. [AUTO- + -*netics,* as in CYBERNETICS.]

au·to·nom·ic (ô'tə-nŏm'ĭk) *adj.* 1. Of, relating to, or controlled by the autonomic nervous system. 2. Resulting from internal causes; self-generated; spontaneous. —**au·to·nom·i·cal·ly** *adv.*

autonomic nervous system *n.* The division of the vertebrate nervous system that regulates involuntary action, as of the intestines, heart, and glands, and consists of the **sympathetic nervous system** and the **parasympathetic nervous system** *(both of which see).*

au·ton·o·mous (ô-tŏn'ə-məs) *adj.* 1. a. Independent. b. Self-contained. 2. a. Independent of the laws of another state or government; self-governing. b. Of or pertaining to an autonomy. 3. Autonomic. [Greek *autonomos,* self-ruling : AUTO- + *nomos,* law.] —**au·ton·o·mous·ly** *adv.*

au·ton·o·my (ô-tŏn'ə-mē) *n., pl.* **-mies.** 1. The condition or quality of being self-governing. 2. Self-government or the right of self-government; self-determination; independence. 3. A self-governing state, community, or group. 4. A condition of moral or personal independence. [Greek *autonomia,* from *autonomos,* AUTONOMOUS.] —**au·ton·o·mist** *n.*

au·to·phyte (ô'tə-fīt') *n. Botany.* An autotrophic plant. [AUTO- + -PHYTE.] —**au·to·phyt·ic** (ô'tə-fĭt'ĭk) *adj.*

au·to·pi·lot (ô'tō-pī'lət) *n.* An **automatic pilot** *(see).*

au·to·plas·ty (ô'tō-plăs'tē) *n.* Surgical repair or replacement with tissue taken from another part of the patient's body. [AUTO- + -PLASTY.] —**au·to·plas·tic** *adj.* —**au·to·plas·ti·cal·ly** *adv.*

au·top·sy (ô'tŏp'sē, ô'təp-) *n., pl.* **-sies.** The examination and dissection of a dead body to determine the cause of death. Also called "necropsy," "post-mortem." [New Latin *autopsia,* from Greek, a seeing for oneself : AUT(O)- + Greek *opsis,* sight.] —**au·top·sy** *v.*

au·to·ra·di·og·ra·phy (ô'tō-rā'dē-ŏg'rə-fē) *n.* A process for producing an image of the amount and distribution of radioactive material in an object by means of direct exposure of a photographic plate to radiation emitted by the object. Also called "radioautography." —**au·to·ra·di·o·graph** (ô'tō-rā'dē-ə-grăf', -grăf') *n.* —**au·to·ra·di·o·graph·ic** *adj.*

au·to·ro·ta·tion (ô′tō-rō-tā′shən) *n.* Rotation of the blades of a helicopter in free unpowered descent.

au·to·some (ô′tə-sōm′) *n.* Any chromosome that is not a sex chromosome. [AUTO- + (CHROMO)SOME.] **—au·to·so·mal** *adj.*

au·to·sug·ges·tion (ô′tō-səg-jĕs′chən) *n. Psychology.* The process by which a person induces self-acceptance of an opinion, belief, or plan of action. **—au·to·sug·gest** *v.* **—au·to·sug·gest·i·bil·i·ty** *n.* **—au·to·sug·gest·i·ble** *adj.* **—au·to·sug·ges·tive** *adj.*

au·tot·o·mize (ô-tŏt′ə-mīz′) *v.* **-mized, -mizing, -mizes.** *—tr.* To cause the autotomy of (a body part). *—intr.* To undergo autotomy.

au·tot·o·my (ô-tŏt′ə-mē) *n. Zoology.* The spontaneous casting off of a body part, such as the tail of certain lizards, for self-protection. **—au·to·tom·ic** (ô′tə-tŏm′ĭk) *adj.*

au·to·tox·e·mi·a (ô′tō-tŏk-sē′mē-ə) *n.* Also **au·to·tox·i·co·sis** (ô′-tō-tŏk′sĭ-kō′sĭs). **Autointoxication** *(see).*

au·to·tox·in (ô′tō-tŏk′sĭn) *n.* A poison that acts on the organism in which it is generated. **—au·to·tox·ic** *adj.*

au·to·trans·form·er (ô′tō-trăns-fôr′mər) *n.* An electrical transformer in which the primary and secondary coils have some or all windings in common.

au·to·troph (ô′tə-trŏf′, -trōf′) *n. Biology.* An autotrophic organism, such as a green plant. [Back-formation from AUTOTROPHIC.]

au·to·tro·phic (ô′tə-trō′fĭk, -trŏf′ĭk) *adj. Biology.* Designating or characterizing plants or certain microorganisms capable of manufacturing their own food from inorganic materials, as in photosynthesis. **—au·to·tro·phi·cal·ly** *adv.* **—au·tot·ro·phy** (ô-tŏt′rə-fē) *n.*

aut·ox·i·da·tion (ôt-ŏk′sə-dā′shən) *n. Chemistry.* **1.** An oxidation reaction that involves atmospheric oxygen as the oxidizing agent. **2.** An oxidation reaction that is induced by a second reaction taking place in the system.

au·tumn (ô′təm) *n.* **1.** The season of the year between summer and winter, strictly lasting from the autumnal equinox to the winter solstice and considered to be from September to November in the Northern Hemisphere and from March to May in the Southern Hemisphere. Also called "fall." **2.** A time or period of maturity verging on decline: *in the autumn of one's life.* [Middle English *autumpne,* from Old French *automne,* from Latin *autumnus,* perhaps of Etruscan origin.] **—au·tum·nal** (ô-tŭm′nəl) *adj.* **—au·tum·nal·ly** *adv.*

autumnal equinox *n.* **1.** The **equinox** *(see)* of September 22 or 23 in the Northern Hemisphere, or March 21 or 22 in the Southern Hemisphere, when the sun crosses the celestial equator going toward the equator, marking the start of autumn. **2.** *Astronomy.* The point in Virgo on the celestial sphere at which the celestial equator and the ecliptic intersect. Compare **vernal equinox.**

autumn crocus *n.* A plant, *Colchicum autumnale,* native to Europe and northern Africa, having pink or purplish flowers that bloom in the autumn. Also called "meadow saffron."

au·tun·ite (ō-tŭn′īt′, ô′tən-īt′) *n.* A yellowish fluorescent, minor ore of uranium with composition $Ca(UO_2)_2(PO_4)_2 \cdot 10\text{-}12H_2O$. [After *Autun,* France, where it was discovered.]

Au·vergne (ō-vârn′). A mainly agricultural region and former province of central France.

aux. auxiliary.

aux·e·sis (ôg-zē′sĭs, ôk-sē′-) *n. Biology.* An increase in the size of a cell or tissue without cell division. [Greek *auxēsis,* growth, from *auxanein,* to grow, increase.]

aux·il·ia·ry (ôg-zĭl′yər-ē, -zĭl′ər-ē) *adj. Abbr.* **aux. 1.** Giving assistance or support; aiding; helping. **2.** Subsidiary; supplementary; additional. **3.** Held in or used as a reserve: *auxiliary troops.* **4.** *Nautical.* Equipped with a motor to supplement the sails.
~*n., pl.* **auxiliaries. 1.** One that assists or helps; an assistant. **2.** A group or organization that assists or is supplementary to a larger one. **3. auxiliaries.** Foreign troops serving a country in wartime. **4.** An auxiliary verb. **5.** *Nautical.* A sailing vessel equipped with a motor. **6.** *Naval.* A vessel for use in other than combat services, such as a supply ship. [Latin *auxiliārius,* from *auxilium,* help.]

auxiliary verb *n. Grammar.* A verb that accompanies particular forms of the main verb of a clause to form a phrasal unit expressing the tense, mood, voice, or aspect of the main verb. *Have, may, can, must,* and *will* are some auxiliary verbs, as in *He will come.*

aux·in (ôk′sĭn) *n.* Any of several plant hormones, or similar synthetic substances, that affect growth by increasing cell elongation. [Greek *auxein,* to grow + -IN] **—aux·in·ic** *adj.*

aux·o·chrome (ôk′sə-krōm) *n.* A group of atoms that produces or intensifies the color of a dye. [*auxo-* (increasing), from Greek *auxein,* to grow + -CHROME.]

Av (ôv, äb) *n.* Also **Ab** (äb, ôv). The 11th month of the year on the Hebrew calendar, usually coinciding with August. See feature at **calendar.** [Hebrew *ābh,* from Akkadian *abu.*]

av. 1. avenue. **2.** average. **3.** avoirdupois.

Av. avenue.

a.v. ad valorem.

A.V. 1. audio-visual. **2.** Authorized Version.

a·vail (ə-vāl′) *v.* **availed, availing, avails.** *—tr.* To be of use or advantage to; assist; help. *—intr.* To be of use value, or advantage; serve. **—avail oneself of.** To make use of.
~*n.* Use, benefit, or advantage. Now used chiefly in the phrase *to* or *of no avail.* [Middle English *availen* : A- (intensive) + *vailen,* to avail, from Old French *valoir* (stem *vail-*), to be worth, from Latin *valēre,* to be strong, be worth.] **—a·vail·ing·ly** *adv.*

a·vail·a·ble (ə-vā′lə-bəl) *adj.* **1.** Accessible for use; obtainable. **2.** At the disposal of an employer, visitor, or the like. **—a·vail·a·bil·i·ty,** **a·vail·a·ble·ness** *n.* **—a·vail·a·bly** *adv.*

av·a·lanche (ăv′ə-lănch′, -länch′) *n.* **1.** A fall or slide of a large mass of snow, rock, or other material down a mountainside. **2.** Something resembling such an overwhelming fall or slide.
~*v.* **avalanched, -lanching, -lanches.** *—intr.* To fall, as an avalanche. *—tr.* To overwhelm. [French, from Swiss French *avalantse,* altered (through influence of *avaler,* to descend) from Savoyard *lavantse,* from Vulgar Latin (unattested) *labanca*†.]

avalanche lily *n.* A plant, *Erythronium montanum,* of western North America, having nodding white flowers. [So called because it grows near the snow line and blooms when the snow begins to melt.]

Av·a·lon (ăv′ə-lŏn′). *Celtic Mythology.* An island paradise in the western seas where King Arthur and other heroes went at death.

a·vant-garde (ä′vänt-gärd′; *French* à-väN-gàrd′) *n.* A group, as of writers and artists, regarded as pre-eminent in the invention and application of new styles and techniques in a given field.
~*adj.* **1.** Of or belonging to the avant-garde, as in the arts. **2.** Ahead of the times. [French, VANGUARD.]

av·a·rice (ăv′ə-rĭs) *n.* An extreme desire to amass wealth; greed; cupidity. [Middle English, from Old French, from Latin *avāritia,* from *avārus,* greedy, from *avēre*†, to desire.]

av·a·ri·cious (ăv′ə-rĭsh′əs) *adj.* Immoderately fond of accumulating wealth. **—av·a·ri·cious·ly** *adv.* **—av·a·ri·cious·ness** *n.*

a·vast (ə-văst′, ə-väst′) *interj.* Used as a nautical command to stop: *Avast heaving there.* [Shortened from Dutch *houd vast,* "hold fast" : *houd,* imperative of *houden,* to hold, + *vast,* fast.]

av·a·tar (ăv′ə-tär′) *n.* **1. a.** One regarded as the incarnation or embodiment of some known model or category. **b.** An entity regarded as an extreme or notably complete manifestation of its kind; exemplar; archetype. **2.** In Hindu mythology, the descent to earth of a deity in human or animal form. Used as a generic term for the incarnations of Vishnu. [Sanskrit *avatāra,* descent, from *avatarati,* he descends : *ava,* down + *tarati,* he crosses.]

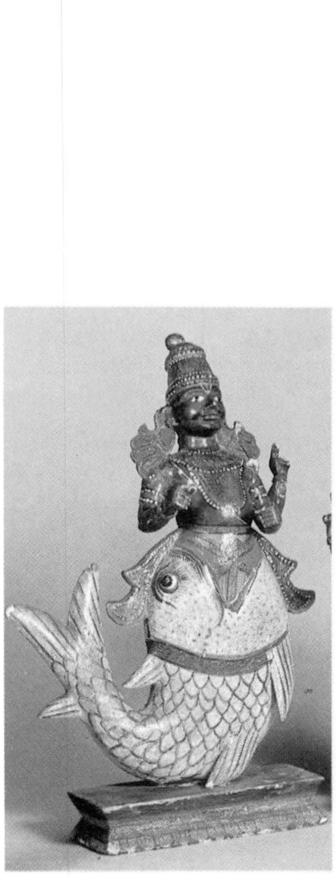

avatar *A representation of one of the incarnations, or avatars, of the Hindu god Vishnu. The carving is in the Horniman Museum, London.*

a·vaunt (ə-vônt′, ə-vänt′) *interj. Archaic.* Used as a command to be gone. [Middle English, from Old French *avant,* "forward," "go away!" See **vanguard.**]

avdp. avoirdupois.

A·ve (ä′vā) *n., pl.* **Aves.** The Ave Maria.

ave., Ave. avenue.

Ave·bur·y (āv′bə-rē, -brē). A village on the Marlborough Downs, Wiltshire, in southern England. It is situated on one of the most important prehistoric sites in Europe, lying within a Neolithic ring of upright stones older and larger than those at Stonehenge.

A·ve Ma·ri·a (ä′vā mə-rē′ə). *n.* **1.** A Roman Catholic prayer, based on the greetings of Gabriel and Elizabeth to the Virgin Mary. Luke 1:28, 42. Also called "Ave," "Hail Mary." **2. a.** A recitation of this prayer. **b.** The hour when it is customarily said. **3.** One of the small beads on a rosary used to count recitations of this prayer. [Middle English, from Medieval Latin, "Hail Mary!"]

a·venge (ə-vĕnj′) *v.* **avenged, avenging, avenges.** *—tr.* **1.** To take revenge or exact satisfaction for (a wrong or injury). **2.** To take vengeance on behalf of. *—intr.* To take vengeance. [Middle English *avengen* : *a-,* from Latin *ad-,* to + *vengen,* to revenge, from Old French *vengier,* from Latin *vindicāre,* from *vindex* (stem *vindic-*), protector, avenger.] **—a·veng·er** *n.* **—a·veng·ing·ly** *adv.*

a·vens (ăv′ĭnz) *n., pl.* **-enses** orcollectively **avens. 1.** Any of various plants of the genus *Geum,* having irregularly shaped leaves, white, yellow, or reddish flowers, and plumed seed clusters. **2.** Any of several related plants of the genus *Dryas,* of mountainous and arctic regions. [Middle English *avence,* from Old French, from Medieval Latin *avencia*†.]

Av·en·tine (ăv′ən-tīn′, -tēn′). One of the seven hills of Rome.

a·ven·tu·rine (ə-vĕn′chə-rēn′, -rĭn) *n.* Also **a·ven·tu·rin** (ə-vĕn′-chə-rĭn). **1.** An opaque or semitranslucent brown glass flecked with small metallic particles, often of copper or chromic oxide. **2.** Any of several varieties of quartz or feldspar flecked with particles of mica, hematite, or other materials. Also called "sunstone." [French, from *aventure,* accident, ADVENTURE; so called because of its accidental discovery.] **—a·ven·tu·rine** *adj.*

av·e·nue (ăv′ə-nōō′, -nyōō′) *n. Abbr.* **av., Av., ave., Ave. 1. a.** A wide street or thoroughfare. **b.** Any path resembling such a thoroughfare. **2. a.** A road, normally lined with trees. **b.** *Chiefly British.* A drive or road, usually tree-lined, leading to a country house. **3.** An opening or means of approach to a given place, activity, or goal: *new avenues of trade.* [French, from Old French, approach, avenue, feminine past participle of *avenir,* to approach, arrive, from Latin *advenīre,* to come to : *ad-,* to + *venīre,* to come.]

a·ver (ə-vûr′) *tr.v.* **averred, averring, avers. 1.** To declare in a positive manner; affirm. **2.** *Law.* To assert formally as a fact; justify or prove (a plea). —See Synonyms at **assert.** [Middle English *averren,* from Old French *averer,* from Medieval Latin *adverāre,* to assert as true : *ad-,* to + *vērus,* true.] **—a·ver·ment** *n.* **—a·ver·ra·ble** *adj.*

av·er·age (ăv′rĭj, ăv′ər-ĭj) *n. Abbr.* **av., avg. 1.** Something such as an amount, degree, or standard that is considered typical, normal, or representative. **2.** *Mathematics.* **a.** A number that typifies a set of numbers of which it is a function. **b.** The **arithmetic mean** *(see).* **3.** A ratio, relative proportion, or degree indicating position or achievement: *a goal average; batting averages.* **4.** *Law.* **a.** The incurrence of and loss due to damage at sea to a ship or cargo. **b.** The equitable distribution of such a loss among concerned parties. **c.** Any charges incurred through such a loss. **—on the average.** As a mean rate, amount, or the like.
~*adj.* **1.** Of, pertaining to, or constituting a mathematical average.

PRONUNCIATION KEY

ă, pat; ā, pay; âr, care;
ä, father, are; b, bib;
ch, church; d, deed; ĕ, pet;
ē, be; f, fife; g, gag; h, hat;
hw, which; ĭ, pit; ī, pie;
îr, pier; j, judge; k, kick;
l, lid, needle; m, mum;
n, no, sudden; ng, thing;
ŏ, pot; ō, toe; ô, paw, for;
oi, noise; ou, out; ŏŏ, book;
ōō, boot; p, pop; r, roar;
s, sauce; sh, ship, dish;
t, tight; th, thin, path;
th, this, bathe; ŭ, cut; ûr, fur;
v, valve; w, with; y, yes;
z, zebra, size; zh, vision;
ə, about, item, edible, gallop, circus, peaceful

IN FOREIGN WORDS:

à, *Fr.* ami; œ, *Fr.* feu, *Ger.* schön; ü, *Fr.* tu, *Ger.* über; KH, *Ger.* ich, *Scot.* loch; N, *Fr.* bon; y′, *Fr.* Compiègne

STRESS MARKS:

Primary stress: ′
in·cite′ (ĭn-sīt′)
Secondary stress: ′
in′sight′ (ĭn′sīt′)

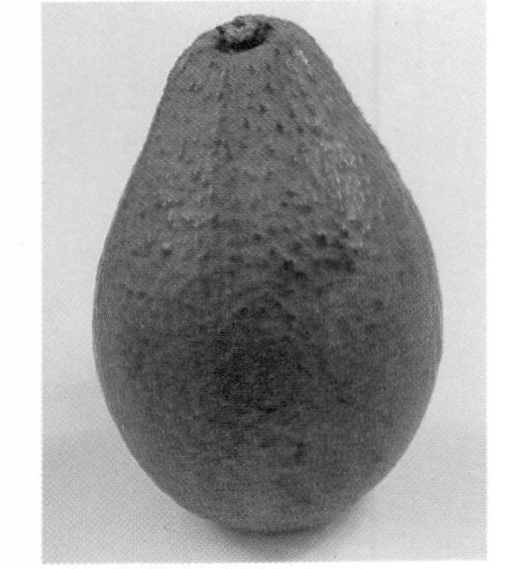

avocado *Avocado trees, which are native to the Americas, are now grown in other parts of the world for their pear-shaped fruit that are rich in protein, fats, and vitamins.*

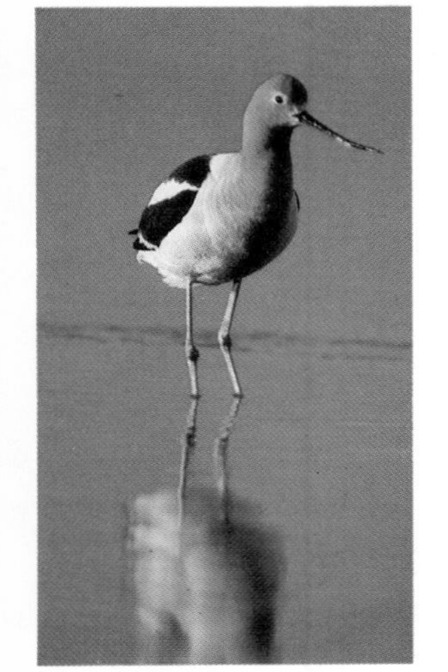

avocet *The upturned bills of this worldwide group of wading birds act as scoops. By sweeping them through the water, avocets collect the small crustaceans that form the major part of their diet.*

2. Typical; usual. **3.** *Law.* Assessed in compliance with the laws of average.
~v. **averaged, -aging, -ages.** *—tr.* **1.** To calculate the average of; especially, to calculate the arithmetic mean of (a set of numbers, quantities, or the like). **2.** To accomplish or obtain an average of: *average three hours work a day.* **3.** To distribute proportionately. *—intr.* **1.** To be or amount to an average. **2.** To buy or sell more goods or shares to obtain more than an average price. **—average out. 1.** *Informal.* To attain an average eventually. **2.** To work out so as to attain an average. [Alteration (by *-age,* as in *damage*) of obsolete *averie,* financial loss on damaged shipping, hence such loss shared equitably among investors, hence numerical average, from Old French *avarie,* damage to shipping, from Old Italian *avaria,* from Arabic *'awārīyah,* damaged goods, from *'awar,* fault, blemish.]
Synonyms: *fair, indifferent, mediocre, medium, middling, run-of-the-mill, so-so, tolerable.*

A·ver·ro·ës (ə-vĕr′ō-ēz′, ăv′ə-rō′ēz), (1126–98). *Arabic* **ibn-Rushd** (ĭb′ən-ro͝osht′). Spanish-Arabian philosopher. He attempted to bring together the Islamic and Greek traditions of thought.

a·verse (ə-vûrs′) *adj.* **1.** Opposed; reluctant; disinclined. Usually used with *to.* **2.** *Botany.* Turned away from the central stem or axis: *averse leaves.* [Latin *āversus,* past participle of *āvertere,* AVERT.] **—a·verse·ly** *adv.* **—a·verse·ness** *n.*

a·ver·sion (ə-vûr′zhən, -shən) *n.* **1.** Intense dislike. Used with *to.* **2.** A feeling of extreme repugnance. **3.** A greatly disliked person or thing: *a pet aversion.*

aversion therapy *n.* A form of therapy designed to overcome an addiction or a harmful habit by associating it, in the mind of the patient, with something unpleasant, such as vomiting.

a·vert (ə-vûrt′) *tr.v.* **averted, averting, averts. 1.** To turn away: *avert one's eyes.* **2.** To ward off or prevent: *avert disaster.* [Middle English *averten,* from Old French *avertir,* from Vulgar Latin *āvertīre* (unattested), variant of Latin *āvertere* : *ab-,* away from + *vertere,* to turn.] **—a·vert·ed·ly** *adv.* **—a·vert·i·ble, a·vert·a·ble** *adj.*

Av·e·ry (ā′vər-ē), **Oswald Theodore** (1877–1955). Canadian-born bacteriologist. In 1944 he isolated and identified DNA.

A·ves·ta (ə-vĕs′tə) *n.* The sacred writings of the Zoroastrian religion, the **Zend-Avesta** *(see).* [Middle Persian *apastāk*†, text.]

A·ves·tan (ə-vĕs′tən) *n.* The dialect of Old Iranian, in which the Avesta was written. Also called "Zend."
~adj. Of or pertaining to the Avesta or to the language in which it was written.

avg. average.

av·go·lem·o·no (ăv′gō-lĕm′ə-nō) *n.* A Greek chicken soup or sauce made with eggs and lemons. [Modern Greek *avgolemono* : *avgon,* egg + *lemonion,* lemon.]

a·vi·an (ā′vē-ən) *adj. Zoology.* Of, pertaining to, or characteristic of birds. [Latin *avis,* bird.]

a·vi·ar·y (ā′vē-ĕr′ē) *n., pl.* **-ies.** A large enclosure built to house live birds. [Latin *aviārium,* from *avis,* bird.] **—a·vi·a·rist** *n.*

a·vi·a·tion (ā′vē-ā′shən, ăv′ē-) *n. Abbr.* **avn. 1.** The operation of aircraft. **2.** The production of aircraft. **3.** Military aircraft. [French, from Latin *avis,* bird.] **—a·vi·ate** *v.*

aviation medicine *n.* The branch of medicine comprising **aeromedicine** and **space medicine** *(both of which see).*

a·vi·a·tor (ā′vē-ā′tər, ăv′ē-) *n.* One who operates an aircraft; pilot. [French *aviateur,* from *aviation,* AVIATION.]

a·vi·a·trix (ā′vē-ā′trĭks, ăv′ē-) *n., pl.* **-trixes.** A woman who operates an aircraft.

Av·i·cen·na (ăv′ə-sĕn′ə), (980–1037). *Arabic* **ibn-Si·na** (ĭb′ən-sē′nə). Persian philosopher and physician. His most famous work was the *Canon of Medicine.*

a·vi·cul·ture (ā′vĭ-kŭl′chər, ăv′ĭ-) *n.* The raising or keeping of birds. [Latin *avis,* bird + CULTURE.] **—a·vi·cul·tur·ist** *n.*

av·id (ăv′ĭd) *adj.* **1. a.** Eager. Often used with *of* or *for*: *avid for adventure.* **b.** Greedy. **2.** Enthusiastic; ardent: *an avid sportsman.* —See Synonyms at **eager.** [French *avide,* from Latin *avidus,* from *avēre,* to long for. See **avarice.**] **—av·id·ly** *adv.*

av·i·din (ăv′ə-dĭn) *n.* A protein in egg albumin, capable of inactivating biotin, consequently causing a deficiency of this vitamin in the consumer. [AVID + -IN, from its affinity for biotin.]

a·vid·i·ty (ə-vĭd′ə-tē) *n.* **1. a.** Eagerness. **b.** Greed. **2.** *Chemistry.* **a.** The dissociation-dependent strength of an acid or base. **b.** Degree of **affinity** *(see).*

a·vi·fau·na (ā′və-fô′nə, ăv′ə-) *n.* All the birds of a specific region. [New Latin : Latin *avis,* bird + FAUNA.] **—a·vi·fau·nal** *adj.*

A·vi·gnon (ȧ-vē-nyôN′). Industrial city in Vaucluse department in southeastern France, on the Rhône River. It was the seat of several antipopes from 1378 to 1408 and still contains the papal palace, one of the greatest of medieval fortress-castles.

A·vi·la (ä′və-lə). Capital of the province of the same name, in central Spain, on the upper Adaja River.

a·vi·on·ics (ā′vē-ŏn′ĭks, ăv′ē-) *n. Used with a singular verb.* The science and technology of electronics applied to aeronautics and astronautics. [AVI(ATION) + (ELECTR)ONICS.] **—a·vi·on·ic** *adj.*

a·vir·u·lent (ā-vĭr′yə-lənt, ā-vĭr′ə-lənt) *adj. Medicine.* Not infectious or virulent.

a·vi·ta·min·o·sis (ā-vī′tə-mĭn-ō′sĭs) *n.* Any disease caused by deficiency of vitamins. [A- (without) + VITAMIN + -OSIS.]

av·i·zan·dum (ăv′ə-zăn′dəm) *n. British.* **1.** In Scots law, a judge's decision to delay giving judgment for a certain time. **2.** The period of this delay. [Medieval Latin, "a being considered," gerund of *avisare,* to consider. See **advise.**]

avn. aviation.

av·o·ca·do (ăv′ə-kä′dō) *n., pl.* **-dos. 1.** A tropical American tree, *Persea americana,* cultivated for its edible fruit. **2.** The oval or pear-shaped fruit of this tree, having leathery green or blackish skin, a large seed, and bland, greenish-yellow pulp. Also called "alligator pear." **3.** A dull green. [Spanish *aguacate,* from Nahuatl *ahuacatl,* "testicle" (from the shape of the fruit).]

av·o·ca·tion (ăv′ō-kā′shən) *n.* **1.** An activity engaged in, usually for enjoyment, in addition to one's regular work or profession; hobby. **2.** *Archaic.* One's regular work or profession. [Latin *āvocātiō* (stem *āvocātiōn-*), a calling away, diversion, from *āvocāre,* to call away : *ab-,* away + *vocāre,* to call.]

av·o·cet (ăv′ə-sĕt′) *n.* Any of several long-legged shore birds of the genus *Recurvirostra,* having a long, slender, upturned beak. [French *avocette,* from Italian *avosetta*†.]

a·vo·di·re (ăv′ə-də-rā′, -dī-rā′) *n.* **1.** A tree, *Turreanthus africana,* of western Africa, having light-colored wood with a clearly marked grain. **2.** The wood of this tree, used in cabinetwork. [French *avodiré*†.]

A·vo·ga·dro number (ä′və-gä′drō, ăv′ə-) *n.* Also **Avogadro's number.** *Abbr.* **N** The number of molecules in one mole of a substance, approximately 6.0225 × 10^{23}. Also called "Avogadro constant." [After Amedeo *Avogadro* (1776–1856), Italian physicist.]

Avogadro's law *n.* The principle that equal volumes of different gases under identical conditions of pressure and temperature contain the same number of molecules. Also called "Avogadro's hypothesis." [After Amedeo *Avogadro.*]

a·void (ə-void′) *tr.v.* **avoided, avoiding, avoids. 1.** To keep away from; stay clear of; shun. **2.** To prevent from happening. **3.** *Law.* To annul or make void (a contract or deed). —See Synonyms at **escape.** [Middle English *avoiden,* from Norman-French *avoider,* from Old French *esvuidier,* "to empty out," hence, to leave : *es-,* from Latin *ex-,* out + *vuidier,* to empty, from *vuide,* VOID.] **—a·void·a·ble** *adj.* **—a·void·a·bly** *adv.* **—a·void·er** *n.*

a·void·ance (ə-void′əns) *n.* **1.** The act of avoiding or shunning something. **2.** *Law.* A making void; an annulment. **3.** *Anthropology.* The custom, common among many primitive tribes, by which a member of a family may not meet or speak to another member.

av·oir·du·pois (ăv′ər-də-poiz′) *n. Abbr.* **av., avdp., avoir. 1.** Avoirdupois weight. **2.** *Informal.* Weight; heaviness. Said of a person. [Middle English *avoir de pois,* "commodities sold by weight," from Old French *aver de peis* : *aver,* property, from *aver, aveir,* to possess, have, from Latin *habēre,* to have + *de,* of, from Latin *dē* + *pois, peis,* weight, from *peser,* to weigh, POISE.]

avoirdupois weight *n.* A system of weights and measures, formerly used in most English-speaking countries, based on a pound containing 16 ounces or 7,000 grains and equal to 453.59 grams.

A·von[1] (ā′vŏn, ā′vən). Also **Upper Avon.** English river that rises near Naseby, Northamptonshire, and flows 155 kilometers (96 miles) through Stratford-upon-Avon to the Severn River near Tewkesbury, Gloucestershire.

Avon[2]. Also **Lower Avon.** English river that rises near Tetbury, Gloucestershire, and flows some 121 kilometers (75 miles) through Bath and Bristol to the Severn estuary at Avonmouth.

Avon[3]. A county in southwest England, created in 1974 and comprising Bath, Bristol, and areas formerly in Somerset and Gloucestershire. Its administrative center is Bristol.

a·vouch (ə-vouch′) *tr.v.* **avouched, avouching, avouches. 1.** To take responsibility for; guarantee. **2.** To assert positively; affirm. **3.** To acknowledge one's responsibility for; confess; avow. [Middle English *avouchen,* from Old French *avochier,* from Latin *advocāre,* to call on (as adviser) : *ad-,* to + *vocāre,* to call.]

a·vow (ə-vou′) *tr.v.* **avowed, avowing, avows.** To acknowledge openly; confess: *avow guilt.* —See Synonyms at **acknowledge, assert.** [Middle English *avowen,* from Old French *avouer,* from Latin *advocāre,* to call on (as adviser), appeal to. See **avouch.**] **—a·vow·a·ble** *adj.* **—a·vow·a·bly** *adv.* **—a·vow·er** *n.*

a·vow·al (ə-vou′əl) *n.* An admission or acknowledgment.

a·vowed (ə-voud′) *adj.* Frankly acknowledged; confessed: *an avowed rebel.* **—a·vow·ed·ly** (ə-vou′ĭd-lē) *adv.*

a·vul·sion (ə-vŭl′shən) *n.* **1.** A ripping off or forcible separation, as of a part of the body by injury. **2.** A part removed in this way. **3.** *Law.* The removal of soil from one property to another by the movement of floodwater, a shift in the course of a boundary stream, or encroachment by the sea. In this sense, compare **alluvion.**

a·vun·cu·lar (ə-vŭng′kyə-lər) *adj.* **1.** Of, pertaining to, or resembling an uncle, especially a benevolent uncle. **2.** Benevolent; kindly and friendly. [Latin *avunculus,* maternal uncle.]

a·vun·cu·late (ə-vŭng′kyə-lĭt) *n.* Customs regulating relations between a maternal uncle and his nephew in certain societies and concerning various duties and rights, especially of inheritance. [Latin *avunculus,* maternal uncle + -ATE (group, rank).]

A·WACS, A·wacs (ā′wăks′) *n.* A defense system of aircraft equipped with radar used by the U.S. Air Force to detect enemy bombers. [*A*irborne *W*arning *A*nd *C*ontrol *S*ystem.]

a·wait (ə-wāt′) *v.* **awaited, awaiting, awaits.** *—tr.* **1.** To wait for. **2.** To be in store for. *—intr.* To wait. —See Synonyms at **expect.** [Middle English *awaiten,* from Old North French *awaitier,* watch for, wait for: *a-,* to + *waitier,* to watch, WAIT.]

a·wake (ə-wāk′) *v.* **awoke** (ə-wōk′) or *rare* **awaked, awaked** or **awoken** (ə-wō′kən) or *rare* **awoke, awaking, awakes.** *—tr.* **1.** To rouse from sleep; waken. **2.** To stir up or excite (memories or fears, for example). *—intr.* **1.** To wake up. **2.** To become alert. **3.** To be-

come aware or cognizant. Often used with *to*: *They awoke to reality.* —See Usage note at **wake**.
~*adj.* **1.** Not asleep. **2.** Alert; vigilant; watchful. [Middle English *awaken, awakien,* Old English *awacan, awacian* : A- (intensive) + *wacan, wacian,* to be awake, WAKE.]

a·wak·en (ə-wā′kən) *v.* **-ened, -ening, -ens.** —*tr.* To cause to wake up. —*intr.* To wake up; awake. —See Usage note at **wake**. [Middle English *awak(e)nen,* Old English *āwæcnan, āwæcnian* : A- (on) + *wæcnan, wæcnian,* to WAKE.]

a·wak·en·ing (ə-wā′kən-ĭng) *adj.* **1.** Waking up. **2.** Rousing; exciting.
~*n.* **1.** The act of waking; an emergence from sleep. **2.** A stirring up; a rousing of attention, awareness, or interest.

a·ward (ə-wôrd′) *tr.v.* **awarded, awarding, awards. 1.** To grant as merited or due. **2.** To declare as legally due: *awarded damages.* **3.** To bestow for performance or quality: *award a prize.*
~*n.* **1.** A decision, especially one made by a judge or arbitrator. **2.** Something awarded, such as a medal or a sum of money. [Middle English *awarden,* from Norman French *awarder,* variant of Old North French *eswarder,* to judge after careful observation : *es-,* from Latin *ex-,* out + *warder,* to observe, keep, judge, from Germanic.] **—a·ward·ee** (ə-wôr-dē′) *n.* **—a·ward·a·ble** *adj.* **—a·ward·er** *n.*

a·ware (ə-wâr′) *adj.* **1.** Conscious; cognizant. Often used with *of*: *aware of their limitations.* **2.** Well-informed; knowledgeable: *politically aware.* **3.** *Informal.* Sensitive and perceptive: *an aware person.* [Middle English *awar, iwar,* Old English *gewær.*] **—a·ware·ness** *n.*

a·wash (ə-wŏsh′, ə-wôsh′) *adj.* **1.** Level with or washed by waves. **2.** Flooded. **3.** Floating on waves. **—a·wash** *adv.*

a·way (ə-wā′) *adv.* **1. a.** From a particular place or position; off. **b.** To or at another place or position. **2.** At a distance. **3.** In a different direction; aside: *He glanced away.* **4.** Out of existence: *The music faded away.* **5.** From one's possession or notice: *He gave the money away.* **6.** Continuously; persistently: *He worked away at his job.* **7.** Immediately: *Fire away!* **8.** *Informal.* In a penal or mental institution: *put away for robbery.* **9.** So as to pass a period of time in a specified activity: *danced the night away.* **10.** At or on an opponent's playing field or location: *playing away on Saturday.* **—away with. 1.** Take away. **2.** Go away: *Away with you!* **—do away with. 1.** To get rid of. **2.** To murder.
~*adj.* **1.** Absent. **2.** At a distance: *He is miles away.* **3. a.** Played on an opponent's playing field or location. **b.** Of, pertaining to, or occurring at an away match or game: *six away goals.*
~*interj.* Used as an order of dismissal. [Middle English *away, on way,* from Old English *aweg, oweg, onweg,* "on the way (from)" : *a-, on,* ON + *weg,* WAY.]

awe (ô) *n.* **1. a.** An emotion of mingled reverence, dread, and wonder inspired by something majestic or sublime. **b.** Respect, tinged with fear, for authority. **2.** *Archaic.* The power to inspire reverence or fear. —*tr.v.* **awed, awing** or **aweing, awes.** To inspire with awe. [Middle English *awe, age, aghe,* from Old Norse *agi.*]

a·wea·ry (ə-wîr′ē) *adj. Poetic.* Tired; weary.

a·weath·er (ə-wĕth′ər) *adv. Nautical.* To windward. Compare **alee**.

a·weigh (ə-wā′) *adj. Nautical.* Hanging just clear of the bottom. Said of an anchor. [A- (on) + WEIGH.]

awe-in·spir·ing (ô′ĭn-spī′rĭng) *adj.* Causing great admiration or wonder; spellbinding.

awe·some (ô′səm) *adj.* **1.** Inspiring awe. **2.** Expressing or characterized by awe. **—awe·some·ly** *adv.* **—awe·some·ness** *n.*

awe-strick·en (ô′strĭk′ən) *adj.* Also **awe-struck** (-strŭk′). Full of awe.

aw·ful (ô′fəl) *adj.* **1.** Extremely bad or unpleasant; terrible; horrible. **2.** Dreadful; appalling; fearsome. **3.** Used as an intensive: *an awful fool; an awful lot of people.* [Middle English *awful, aweful* : AWE + -FUL.] **—aw·ful·ness** *n.*

aw·ful·ly (ô′fə-lē, ô′flē) *adv.* **1.** In an extremely unpleasant manner; horribly. **2.** Used as an intensive: *He's awfully late.*

a·while (ə-hwīl′) *adv.* For a short time.
Usage: *Awhile,* an adverb, is never preceded by a preposition such as *for,* but the two-word form *a while* may be preceded by a preposition. In writing, each of the following is acceptable: *stay awhile; stay for a while; stay a while* (but not *stay for awhile*).

awk·ward (ôk′wərd) *adj.* **1.** Not graceful; ungainly. **2.** Not dexterous; clumsy; unskillful. **3.** Hard to handle; unwieldy: *an awkward bundle.* **4.** Difficult or dangerous: *an awkward climb.* **5.** Inconvenient; uncomfortable: *an awkward pose.* **6.** Causing embarrassment; trying: *an awkward predicament.* **7.** Embarrased; ill-at-ease: *I felt awkward.* **8.** Difficult to cope with; contrary; perverse. [Middle English *awkeward,* "in the wrong direction," awry : *awke,* backhanded, perverse, wrong, from Old Norse *afugr,* turned backwards + -WARD.] **—awk·ward·ly** *adv.* **—awk·ward·ness** *n.*
Synonyms: *awkward, bungling, clumsy, gauche, inept, maladroit, ungainly.*

awkward age *n.* The period between childhood and adulthood; adolescence.

awl (ôl) *n.* A pointed tool for making holes, as in wood or leather. [Middle English *aule, al,* Old English *æl.*]

awl·wort (ôl′wûrt′, -wôrt′) *n.* A small aquatic plant, *Subularia aquatica,* of the Northern Hemisphere, having narrow, pointed leaves and minute white flowers. [From the shape of its leaves.]

awn (ôn) *n. Botany.* A slender, bristlelike terminal part, such as those found on the spikelets of many grasses. [Middle English *awne, agene,* from Old Norse *ögn*; akin to Gothic *ahana,* chaff.]

awn·ing (ô′nĭng) *n.* A rooflike structure, as of canvas, stretched over a frame as a shelter from the weather. [17th century (nautical use) : origin obscure.]

a·woke. A past tense of **awake**.

a·wok·en. A past participle of **awake**.

A·WOL, a·wol (ā′wôl′) *adj.* Absent without leave, especially from the military service.
~*n.* One that is AWOL. **—A·WOL** *adv.*

a·wry (ə-rī′) *adv.* **1.** Turned or twisted to one side; askew. **2.** Away from the correct course; amiss; wrong. [Middle English *awrie, on wry* : ON + *wry,* twisted, WRY.] **—a·wry** *adj.*

ax, axe (ăks) *n., pl.* **axes. 1.** A tool having a head with a sharp cutting edge mounted on a handle, used for felling, chopping, or splitting trees and wood. **2.** Any similar tool or weapon, such as a battle-ax. **3.** Anything that acts drastically to remove or reduce something: *The ax fell on the research program.* **—get the ax.** To be fired from one's job. **—have an ax to grind.** To pursue a private, selfish, or subjective aim.
~*tr.v.* **axed, axing, axes. 1.** To work on with an ax. **2. a.** To cancel (a project, for example). **b.** To reduce substantially (manpower or expenditure, for example). **c.** To dismiss from employment. [Middle English *ax, axe,* Old English *æx, aces.*]

ax. axiom.

ax·el (ăk′səl) *n.* A jump in figure skating involving one and a half turns in the air. [After *Axel* Paulsen (died 1938), Norwegian skater.]

a·xen·ic (ā-zĕn′ĭk, ā-zē′nĭk) *adj. Biology.* Free of symbionts or parasites; uncontaminated. Said of cultures or culture media. [A- (without) + XEN(O)- + -IC.]

ax·es. 1. Plural of **axis**. **2.** Plural of **ax**.

ax·i·al (ăk′sē-əl) *adj.* **1.** Pertaining to or forming an axis. **2.** Located on, around, or in the direction of an axis. [AXI(S) + -AL.] **—ax·i·al·ly** *adv.*

ax·il (ăk′sĭl) *n.* The angle between the upper surface of a leafstalk, flower stalk, branch, or similar part, and the stem or axis from which it arises. [Latin *axilla,* armpit, AXILLA.]

ax·il·la (ăk-sĭl′ə) *n., pl.* **axillae** (ăk-sĭl′ē). The armpit, or an analogous part such as the underside of a bird's wing. [Latin *axilla,* armpit.]

ax·il·lar (ăk-sĭl′ər, ăk′sə-lər) *adj.* Axillary.
~*n.* One of the feathers in the axilla of a bird's wing.

ax·il·lar·y (ăk′sə-lĕr′ē) *adj.* **1.** *Anatomy.* Of, relating to, or near the armpit. **2.** *Botany.* Of, pertaining to, or located in an axil: *axillary buds.*
~*n., pl.* **axillaries.** An axillar.

ax·i·ol·o·gist (ăk′sē-ŏl′ə-jĭst) *n.* An expert in or student of axiology.

ax·i·ol·o·gy (ăk′sē-ŏl′ə-jē) *n. Philosophy.* The study of the nature of values and value judgments. [Greek *axios,* worth + -LOGY.] **—ax·i·o·log·i·cal** (ăk′sē-ə-lŏj′ĭ-kəl) *adj.* **—ax·i·o·log·i·cal·ly** *adv.*

ax·i·om (ăk′sē-əm) *n.* **1.** A self-evident or universally recognized truth; a maxim. **2.** An established rule, principle, or law. **3.** *Abbr.* **ax.** *Mathematics & Logic.* A statement or proposition requiring no proof, as: **a.** An undemonstrated proposition concerning an undefined set of elements, properties, functions, and relationships; a postulate. **b.** A self-evident, self-consistent, or accepted principle. [Latin *axiōma,* from Greek, "that which is thought fitting or worthy," from *axioun,* to think worthy, from *axios,* worthy.]

ax·i·o·mat·ic (ăk′sē-ə-măt′ĭk) *adj.* Also **ax·i·o·mat·i·cal** (-ĭ-kəl). **1.** Of, pertaining to, or resembling an axiom; self-evident. **2.** Based on logical axioms: *axiomatic method; axiomatic set theory.* **3.** Containing axioms; aphoristic. **—ax·i·o·mat·i·cal·ly** *adv.*

ax·is (ăk′sĭs) *n., pl.* **axes** (ăk′sēz′). **1.** A straight line about which a body or geometrical object rotates or may be conceived to rotate. **2.** *Mathematics.* **a.** A line, half-line, or line segment serving to orient a space or object, especially a line about which the object is symmetrical. **b.** A reference line from which distances or angles are measured in a coordinate system. **3.** A center line to which parts of a structure or body may be referred. **4.** *Fine Arts.* An imaginary line to which elements of the work are referred for measurement or symmetry. **5.** *Anatomy.* **a.** The second cervical vertebra, on which the head turns. **b.** Any of various central structures, such as the spinal column. **c.** An imaginary line through the center of the body or one of its parts, used as a positional referent. **6.** *Botany.* The main stem or central part about which organs or plant parts such as branches are arranged. **—the Axis** or **the Axis powers.** The alliance of Germany and Italy (1936), later including Japan and other nations, that opposed the Allies in World War II. [Latin *axis,* hub, axis, axle.]

axis deer *n.* A deer, *Axis axis,* of central Asia, having a brown coat with white spots. Also called "chital." [Latin *axis*†, given by Pliny as the Indian name of an unidentified animal.]

ax·le (ăk′səl) *n.* **1.** A supporting shaft or bar upon which a wheel or wheels revolve. **2.** The spindle of an axletree. **3.** Either end of an axletree. [Middle English *axil, axel,* from Old Norse *öxull.*]

ax·le·tree (ăk′səl-trē′) *n.* A crossbar or rod supporting a vehicle, as a drawn cart, and having terminal spindles on which the wheels revolve.

ax·man (ăks′mən) *n., pl.* **-men** (-mĭn). A man who wields an ax; especially a worker who fells trees or chops logs.

Ax·min·ster (ăks′mĭn′stər) *n.* A kind of carpet with a long, soft cut-wool pile, formerly handmade in Axminster, England.

ax·o·lotl (ăk′sə-lŏt′l) *n.* Any of several western North American and Mexican salamanders of the genus *Ambystoma,* especially *A. mexicanum.* [Nahuatl : *atl,* water + *xolotl,* servant, spirit.]

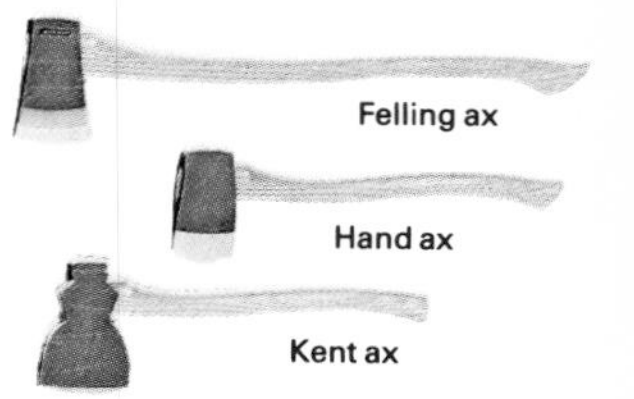

ax *One of mankind's oldest tools and weapons. The first axes, chipped from stone or flint and with no handles, were in use more than 600,000 years ago. The three modern types shown here are a felling ax (top), a hand ax (center), and a Kent ax.*

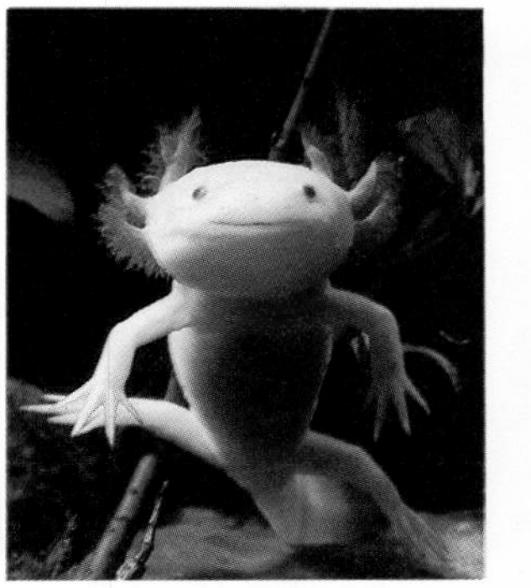

axolotl *Most animals become capable of breeding only when they are adult. This rare Mexican amphibian, however—a type of salamander—usually mates and gives birth to a new generation while it is still in its larval form (above).*

PRONUNCIATION KEY

ă, pat; ā, pay; âr, care;
ä, father, are; b, bib;
ch, church; d, deed; ĕ, pet;
ē, be; f, fife; g, gag; h, hat;
hw, which; ĭ, pit; ī, pie;
îr, pier; j, judge; k, kick;
l, lid, needle; m, mum;
n, no, sudden; ng, thing;
ŏ, pot; ō, toe; ô, paw, for;
oi, noise; ou, out; o͝o, book;
o͞o, boot; p, pop; r, roar;
s, sauce; sh, ship, dish;
t, tight; th, thin, path;
th, this, bathe; ŭ, cut; ûr, fur;
v, valve; w, with; y, yes;
z, zebra, size; zh, vision;
ə, about, item, edible, gallop, circus, peaceful

IN FOREIGN WORDS:

à, *Fr.* ami; œ, *Fr.* feu, *Ger.* schön; ü, *Fr.* tu, *Ger.* über; KH, *Ger.* ich, *Scot.* loch; N, *Fr.* bon; y′, *Fr.* Compiègne

STRESS MARKS:

Primary stress: ′
in·cite′ (ĭn-sīt′)
Secondary stress: ′
in′sight′ (ĭn′sīt′)

Ayers Rock *The biggest single rock in the world lies in the Ayers Rock–Mount Olga National Park in the south of Australia's Northern Territory. Made largely of sandstone, it is some 6 kilometers (4 miles) long by 2.4 kilometers (1.5 miles) wide and rises to 348 meters (1,143 feet) above the surrounding desert. The feature is named after Henry Ayers, a former governor of South Australia.*

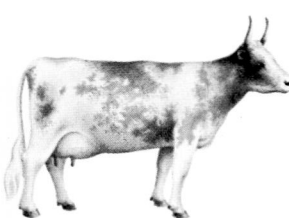

Ayrshire *A sturdy breed of dairy cow from Scotland. It produces milk with a high butterfat content and makes good beef when crossed with the beef shorthorn.*

ax·on (ăk′sŏn′) *n.* Also **ax·one** (ăk′sōn′). The long unbranched process extending from the cell body of a nerve cell that generally conducts impulses away from the nerve cell. Also called "neuraxon." [New Latin, from Greek *axōn*, axis.]

Axum. See **Aksum.**

a·yah (ä′yə, ä′ə, ī′ə) *n.* A native maid or nurse in India. [Hindi *āyā*, from Portuguese *aia*, nursemaid, from Latin *avia*, grandmother.]

a·ya·tol·lah (ī′ə-tō′lə, -tōl′ə) *n.* In the Shiite branch of Islam, a religious leader of the highest rank. [Arabic *āyatollāh*, sign of God.]

aye[1], **ay** (ī) *n.* A vote or voter voting in favor of a proposal. —*adv.* Yes; yea. [16th century : probably the same word as the pronoun *I*, used as an affirmative answer.]

aye[2], **ay** (ā) *adv. Regional & Poetic.* Always; ever. [Middle English *ay, ei*, from Old Norse *ei*.]

aye-aye (ī′ī′) *n.* A small, nocturnal, arboreal mammal, *Daubentonia madagascariensis*, of Madagascar, related to the lemurs. [French, from Malagasay *aiay*, probably imitative of its cry.]

Ayer (âr), **Sir Alfred Jules** (1910–89). British philosopher. His book *Language, Truth and Logic* (1936) was the first and most influential exposition of logical positivism in English.

A·yers Rock (ā′ərz) The largest monolith in the world, situated in the southwestern part of Northern Territory in Australia.

Ay·e·sha or **A·i·sha** (ä-ē′shə) (611–78). The third and favorite wife of Muhammad, the founder of Islam. She led an unsuccessful revolt against Muhammad's successor, Ali.

a·yin, a·in (ä′yĭn) *n.* The 16th letter of the Hebrew alphabet. See feature at **alphabet.** [Hebrew *'ayin*.]

Ay·ma·ra (ī′mä-rä′) *n., pl.* **-ras** or collectively **Aymara** (for sense 1). **1.** A member of an Indian people inhabiting Bolivia and Peru. **2.** A language family including that spoken by the Aymara people. —**Ay·ma·ran** *adj. & n.*

Ayr·shire[1] (âr′shîr, -shər). Formerly, a county in southwest Scotland, since 1975 part of Strathclyde Region.

Ayrshire[2] *n.* Any of a breed of brown and white dairy cattle originating in Ayrshire in the late 18th century.

A·yub Khan (ä′yŏŏb kän′), **Mohammad** (1907–74). Pakistani army commander and politician. He seized the presidency by a military coup in 1958. In 1965 he was confirmed in the presidency by a national election. He resigned in 1969.

A·yur·ve·da (ä′yŏŏr-vā′də, -vē′də) *n.* The ancient Hindu science of health and medicine, consisting of the following branches: removal of foreign substances and bodies from the body; cure of diseases by sharp instruments; cure of diseases affecting the whole body; treatment of mental illnesses supposed to be caused by demoniacal influence; treatment of children's diseases; and the doctrines of antidotes, elixirs, and aphrodisiacs. [Sanskrit : *āyur*, life + *veda*, knowledge.]

AZ Arizona (used with a Zip Code).

az. azimuth.

a·zal·e·a (ə-zāl′yə) *n.* Any of a group of deciduous or evergreen shrubs, part of the genus *Rhododendron*, of the North Temperate Zone, many of which are cultivated for their showy, variously colored flowers. [New Latin, "the dry plant" (growing in dry soil), from Greek, feminine of *azaleos*, dry.]

a·zan (ä-zän′) *n.* The Muslim summons to prayer, called by the muezzin from a minaret of a mosque five times a day. [Arabic *adhān*, from *adhina*, to proclaim. See **muezzin.**]

A·za·ña y Dí·az (ə-zän′yə̆ ē dē′əz), **Manuel** (1880–1940). Spanish writer and politician. He was prime minister from 1931 to 1933 and again in 1936. In May 1936 he was elected president. He fled to France in 1939 after the Nationalist victory in the civil war.

A·za·ni·a (ə-zä́n-yə, -ḗ-ə). South Africa. Used by black African nationalists. [Latin *Azania*, Africa, probably from Arabic *Zanj*, a dark-skinned African.]

az·a·thi·o·prine (ăz′ə-thī′ə-prēn′) *n.* A drug that suppresses the body's immune response, used mainly to assist the survival of organ transplants. [*Aza-*, variant of AZO- + THIO- + P(U)RINE.]

A·za·zel (ə-zā′zəl, ăz′ə-zĕl′). In ancient Hebrew tradition, the rebel leader of the angels who seduced mankind. [Hebrew *'azāzēl*, "removal," hence scapegoat (ritually "sent" into the wilderness) : *'ez*, goat + *'azl*, to go.]

a·zed·a·rach (ə-zĕd′ə-răk′) *n.* **1.** A tree, the **chinaberry** (*see*). **2.** The astringent bark of this tree, formerly used as an emetic. [French *azedarac*, from Persian *āzād-dirakht* : *āzād*, free + *dirakht*, tree.]

a·ze·o·trope (ə-zē′ə-trōp′) *n.* A mixture of two or more liquids that, at a given pressure and temperature, boils without change of composition (the composition of the vapor is the same as that of the boiling liquid). [A- (not, without) + Greek *zeō*, (infinitive *zein*, boil) + -TROPE.] —**a·ze·o·trop·ic** *adj.*

A·zer·bai·jan (ăz′ər-bī-jän′, ä′zər-). Republic in Transcaucasia. It was formed from territory ceded by Persia to Russia in 1813 and 1828. A former constituent republic of the U.S.S.R., it became part of the Commonwealth of Independent States in 1991. Area, 86,600 square kilometers (33,400 square miles). Population, 7,140,000. Capital, Baku.

A·zer·bai·ja·ni (ä′zər-bī-jä′nē, ăz′ər-) *n., pl.* **-nis** or collectively **Azerbaijani. 1.** A native or inhabitant of Azerbaijan S.S.R. **2.** The Turkic language of Azerbaijanis.

a·zide (ā′zīd′) *n. Chemistry.* **1.** An inorganic compound containing the negative ion N_3^-. **2.** An organic compound containing the group $-N_3$. **3.** The group or radical N_3. [AZO- + -IDE.]

A·zil·ian (ə-zĭl′yən) *adj. Archaeology.* Of or denoting a western Eu-

ropean culture, especially of France and Spain, following the Magdalenian era and preceding the Neolithic. [After Le Mas d'Azil, village in the French Pyrenees, where such artifacts were found.]

az·i·muth (ăz′ə-məth) *n. Abbr.* **az. 1.** The horizontal angular distance from a fixed reference direction to a position, object, or object referent, as to a great circle intersecting a celestial body, usually measured clockwise in degrees along the horizon from a point due south. **2.** *Military.* The lateral deviation of a projectile or bomb. [Middle English, from Old French *azimut*, from Arabic *as-sumūt*, plural of *as-samt*, "the way," compass bearing, from Latin *semita*†, path.] —**az·i·muth·al** (ăz′ə-mŭth′əl) *adj.* —**az·i·muth·al·ly** *adv.*

azimuthal equidistant projection *n.* A map projection of the earth designed so that a straight line from a given point on the map to any other point gives the shortest distance between the two points.

Azincourt. See **Agincourt.**

az·ine (ăz′ēn′, ā′zēn′) *n.* A six-membered heterocyclic compound, such as pyridine, containing one or more atoms of nitrogen in the ring. [AZ(O)- + -INE.]

azine dye *n.* Any of various dyes derived from **phenazine** (*see*).

az·o (ăz′ō) *adj. Chemistry.* Containing a nitrogen group. [From AZO-.]

azo-, az- *prefix. Chemistry.* Indicates the presence of a nitrogen group, especially one attached at both ends in a covalent bond to other groups; for example, **azobenzene, azole.** [French *azote*, nitrogen, "lifeless" (unlike the life-sustaining oxygen) : A- (not) + Greek *zōē*, life.]

az·o·ben·zene (ăz′ō-bĕn′zĕn, -bĕn-zēn′) *n.* A yellow or orange crystalline compound, $C_6H_5N_2C_6H_5$, used in the manufacture of dyes and as a fumigant.

Aztec

MYSTIC WARRIORS OF ANCIENT MEXICO
Aztecs practiced mass human sacrifice

The Aztecs were warrior nomads who settled on a lake island in Central America in the 14th century. The island grew into Tenochtitlán, a great, waterbound city of about 200,000 people supported by intensive agriculture, markets, and tribute from subject peoples in the countryside. The Aztecs believed that their world was protected by a god, Huitzilopochtli, who fought darkness each night so the sun would rise next day. To give the god strength, they sacrificed human beings, cutting the hearts from living victims, usually criminals or prisoners of war. In 1519 the Spanish conquistador, Hernando Cortés, landed in Mexico with 600 soldiers, overthrew the Aztec king, Montezuma, and claimed the country as a Spanish colony.

GIFTS TO A GOD *In a 16th-century Indian painting of an Aztec human sacrifice, one priest holds a victim's legs while another cuts out the still-beating heart. An earlier victim is being dragged away.*

AZTEC IMAGE *The stone carving of an Aztec god is probably of Huitzilopochtli himself. His image was usually decorated with skulls, stylized earrings, and open hands, apparently receiving a skull as an offering. At the dedication of his temple in Tenochtitlán (1487), it took four days to sacrifice the 20,000 victims.*

azo dye *n.* Any of various red, brown, or yellow acidic or basic dyes containing the azo groups.

a·zo·ic (ă-zō′ĭk, ə-) *adj.* Of or pertaining to geological periods that precede the appearance of life. [A- (not) + -ZOIC.]

az·ole (ăz′ōl′, ā′zōl′) *n.* **1.** Any organic compound having a five-membered heterocyclic ring. **2. Pyrrole** *(see).* [AZ(O)- (because it contains atoms of nitrogen) + -OLE.]

a·zon·ic (ā-zŏn′ĭk) *adj.* Not restricted to any particular zone or region; not local. [A- (not) + ZONE + -IC.]

A·zores (ā′zôrz, ə-zôrz′). *Portuguese* **A·çô·res** (ä-sŏ′rĭs). Group of nine volcanic islands in the Atlantic Ocean, forming three administrative districts of Portugal. Lying some 1,190 kilometers (740 miles) west of mainland Portugal, they were settled by the Portuguese in the mid-15th century. The islanders live by fishing, farming, and tourism. Ponta Delgada on São Miguel Island is the capital.

az·o·te·mi·a (ăz′ə-tē′mē-ə) *n.* Uremia *(see).* [New Latin : French *azote,* nitrogen (see **azo-**) + NAEMIA.] —**az·o·te·mic** *adj.*

az·oth (ăz′ŏth′, -ōth′) *n. Alchemy.* **1.** Mercury. **2.** Paracelsus's universal remedy. [Arabic *az-zā′ūq,* the mercury.]

a·zo·to·bac·ter (ā-zō′tō-băk′tər, ə-) *n.* Any of various nitrogen-fixing bacteria of the family Azotobacteraceae. [New Latin : French *azote,* nitrogen (see **azo-**) + BACTER(IA).]

az·o·tu·ri·a (ăz′ə-tŏŏr′ē-ə, -tyŏŏr′-) *n.* Increase of nitrogenous substances, especially urea, in the urine. [New Latin : French *azote,* nitrogen (see **azo-**) + -URIA.]

Az·ov, Sea of (ăz′ôf′). The northern arm of the Black Sea, between Ukraine and Russia. The shallow sea, maximum depth *c.*15 meters (50 feet), has important fisheries. It is connected with the Black Sea by Kerch Strait.

Az·ra·el (ăz′rā-ĕl′). The angel who separates the soul from the body at death in Moslem and Jewish legend. [Arabic *Azrā′īl,* from Hebrew *'Āzar′ēl,* "God has helped."]

Az·tec (ăz′tĕk′) *n.* **1.** A member of an Indian people of Central Mexico who established a great empire that was overthrown by Cortés in the 16th century. **2.** The language of this people, Nahuatl. ~*adj.* Also **Az·tec·an** (ăz′tĕk′ən). Of the Aztecs, their language, culture, or empire. [Spanish *Azteca,* from Nahuatl *Aztecatl* (plural *Azteca*) : *Azt(a)lan,* the supposed place of origin of the people, "near the crane"; *aztatl* (plural *azta*), crane + *tlan,* near + *-tecatl,* suffix denoting origin.]

az·ure (ăzh′ər) *n.* **1. a.** Light purplish blue, like a summer sky. **b.** *Heraldry.* The color blue. **2.** An azure pigment. **3.** *Poetic.* The blue sky. [Middle English, from Old French *azur* from Old Spanish *azul, azur,* from Arabic *allāzaward,* lapis lazuli, from Persian *lāzhuward,* LAPIS LAZULI.] —**az·ure** *adj.*

az·u·rite (ăzh′ə-rīt′) *n.* An azure-blue vitreous mineral of basic copper carbonate, $2CuCO_3 \cdot Cu(OH)_2$, used as a copper ore and as a gemstone. [French : Old French *azur,* AZURE + -ITE.]

az·y·gous (ăz′ĭ-gəs) *adj. Biology.* Occurring singly; unpaired. [New Latin *azygos,* from Greek *azugos,* unwedded, unpaired : *a-,* without + *zugon,* yoke.]

azalea *Gardeners all over the world cultivate this hardy shrub, which is related to the rhododendron and belongs to the heath family.*

Ba *The symbol of the soul or life after death in ancient Egyptian religion. It was portrayed by a bird with a human head.*

baboon *Members of the monkey family, baboons are native to the drier areas of Arabia and Africa and live mainly on the ground, in troops of up to 150 animals. They feed on vegetation, insects, and small animals.*

b, B (bē) *n., pl.* **b's** or **B's. 1.** The second letter of the modern English alphabet. See feature at **alphabet. 2.** Any of the speech sounds represented by this letter. **3. B** A human blood type of the ABO group. See **ABO. 4.** The second in a series. **5.** The second best or highest in quality or rank: *grade B meat; a mark of B on an English theme.* **6. B** *Music.* **a.** The seventh tone in the scale of C major, or the second tone in the relative minor scale. **b.** The key or a scale in which B is the tonic. **c.** A written or printed note representing this tone. **d.** A string, key, or pipe tuned to the pitch of this tone. **7. B** Something second-rate; especially, something that is the inferior or secondary item of a pair. Often used adjectivally: *a B film; the B side of a record.* **8. B** A fairly soft pencil or pencil-lead. Often used adjectivally: *a B pencil.*

b, B, b., B. *Note:* As an abbreviation or symbol, *b* may be a small or a capital letter, with or without a period. Established forms or those generally preferred precede the definition. When no form is given, all four forms are in general use in that sense. **1. B.** bachelor. **2. B.** bacillus. **3. b** *Physics.* barn. **4. B** baryon number. **5. b., B.** base. **6. b., B.** *Music.* basso. **7. B.** Baumé scale. **8. b., B.** bay. **9. B.** Bible. **10. B** *Chess.* bishop. **11. b., B.** bolivar. **12. b., B.** book. **13. b., B.** born. **14. B** The symbol for the element boron. **15. b** *Cricket.* bowled. **16. b., B.** breadth. **17. B.** British. **18. b., B.** brother. **19. B.** brotherhood.

B- *Military.* bomber: *a B-52.*

Ba¹ The symbol for the element barium.

Ba² (bä) *n.* In ancient Egyptian religion, the soul or life after death represented as a bird with a human head. [Egyptian.]

B.A. 1. Bachelor of Arts. **2.** British Academy. **3.** British Association (for the Advancement of Science).

baa (bă, bä) *intr.v.* **baaed, baaing, baas.** To make a bleating sound, as a sheep does.
~*n.* The bleat of a sheep. [Imitative.]

Baa·der-Mein·hof Gang (bä′dər-mīn′hôf′) *n.* A West German revolutionary group, also known as the Red Army Faction, committed to the destruction of capitalism through acts of terrorism and violence. The group's original leading members, Andreas Baader (1943–77) and Ulrike Meinhof (1934–76), both died in prison.

Ba·al (bā′əl) *n., pl.* **-alim** (-ə-lĭm). **1. a.** Any of various local fertility and nature gods of the ancient Semitic peoples, considered to be false idols by the Hebrews. **b.** The chief god of the Phoenicians and Canaanites. **2.** *Sometimes* **baal.** Any false god or idol. [Hebrew *bá'al,* owner, master, lord.] **—Ba·al·ism** *n.*

Ba'al·bek, Baal-bek (băl′bĕk′, bä′əl-). Village in east Lebanon, site of an ancient Phoenician city, probably devoted to Baal. It is now a tourist center famous for its extensive Roman ruins.

Baal Shem Tov (bäl′ shĕm′ tōv′), original name Israel ben Eliezer (*c.* 1700–60). Polish-born Jewish religious leader and mystic and founder of Chassidism. His name means "Master of the Holy Name."

baas (bäs) *n., pl.* **baas.** *South African.* **1.** A master or boss. **2.** Sir; master. Used as a term of address, chiefly by black South Africans to whites. [Afrikaans, from Dutch *baas,* master or captain.]

baas·skap (bäs′käp) *n. South African.* The condition of mastery or overlordship; especially, the political supremacy of South African whites over blacks. [Afrikaans, from Dutch : *baas,* master + *-skap,* -SHIP.]

Bab (băb), **the,** title of Ali Muhammad of Shiraz (*c.* 1819–50). Persian founder of Babism and one of the three central figures of the Bahai faith, who proclaimed himself as the Bab (or "Gateway") to the truth.

Bab. Babylonia; Babylonian.

ba·ba (bä′bə) *n.* A sponge cake leavened with yeast, sometimes made with raisins and usually flavored with rum. Also called "rum baba." [French, from Polish, "old woman."]

Babar. See **Baber.**

ba·bas·su (bä′bə-sōō′) *n.* A Brazilian palm tree, *Orbignya martiana* (or *O. speciosa*), bearing hard nuts that yield an oil similar to coconut oil. [Brazilian Portuguese *babaçu,* probably a native name.]

Bab·bage (băb′ĭj), **Charles** (1792–1871). British mathematician and inventor. He designed a computer that was based on principles like those used in modern computers. Input data was stored on punched cards.

bab·bitt (băb′ĭt) *tr.v.* **-bitted, -bitting, -bitts.** To line or face with Babbitt (metal).

Bab·bitt¹ (băb′ĭt) *n.* A member of the American middle class whose attachment to its ideals is such as to make him a model of narrow-mindedness and self-satisfaction. Used disparagingly. [After George F. *Babbitt,* main character in Sinclair Lewis's novel *Babbitt* (1922).] **—Bab·bitt·ry** *n.*

Babbitt² *n.* A trademark for a soft, silvery antifriction alloy composed of tin with small amounts of copper and antimony. [After Isaac *Babbitt* (1799–1862), U.S. inventor.]

bab·ble (băb′əl) *v.* **-bled, -bling, -bles. —***intr.* **1.** To utter an incoherent or meaningless confusion of words or sounds: "*the telescreen was still babbling away about pig iron and the overfulfillment of the Ninth Three-Year Plan*" (George Orwell). **2.** To talk foolishly or idly; chatter. **3.** To make a continuous low, murmuring sound, as flowing water does. **—***tr.* **1.** To utter in a rapid, indistinct voice. **2.** To blurt out impulsively; disclose without careful consideration. **~***n.* **1.** Inarticulate or meaningless talk or sounds. **2.** Idle or foolish talk; chatter; prattle. **3.** A continuous murmuring sound. **4.** Jargon, especially that characteristic of a particular field of interest or activity. Used in combination: *psychobabble; Eurobabble.* [Middle English *babelen,* of imitative origin.]

bab·bler¹ (băb′lər) *n.* **1.** One who babbles. **2.** A small songbird of the Old World family Timaliidae, occurring especially in Southeast Asia and having a loud babbling cry.

babbler² *n. Australian Slang.* A cook at a camp or sheep ranch. [From *babbling brook,* rhyming slang for *cook.*]

babe (bāb) *n.* **1.** *Archaic.* A baby; an infant. **2.** *Slang.* An innocent or naive person. **3.** *Slang.* A term of familiar address, usually used to a girl or young woman. [Middle English *babe,* imitative of a baby's sounds.]

ba·bel (bā′bəl, băb′əl) *n. Often* **Babel. 1.** A confusion of sounds, voices, or languages: "*in the babel of two hundred voices he would forget himself*" (Joseph Conrad). **2.** A scene of noise and confusion. **—**See Synonyms at **noise.** [After BABEL.]

Ba·bel (bā′bəl, băb′əl). A city (now thought to be Babylon) in Shinar where, according to Genesis 11:1–9, an attempt to construct a tower to reach heaven incurred the wrath of God, who interrupted the work by making the builders unable to understand one another's language. [Hebrew *Bābhél,* from Akkadian *Bāb-ilu,* "gate of God."]

Ba·ber or **Ba·bar** or **Ba·bur** (bä′bər), original name Zahir ud-Din Muhammad (1483–1530). Mongol conqueror of India. A descendant of Genghis Khan and Tamerlane, he made periodic raids into India from 1519 to 1524. After he occupied Delhi and Agra (1526), he established the Mogul dynasty, which ruled India until 1857.

Ba·bi (bä′bē) *n.* **1.** Babism. **2.** A follower of the Bab.

bab·i·ru·sa, bab·i·rus·sa, bab·i·rous·sa (băb′ə-rōō′sə, bä′bə-) *n.* A hairless wild pig, *Babyrousa babyrussa,* of the East Indies, having four long, upward-curving tusks in the male. [Malay *bābīrūsa* : *bābī,* hog + *rūsa,* deer.]

Bab·ism (bä′bĭz′əm) *n.* The beliefs and practices of a 19th-century Persian religious sect, founded about 1844 by the **Bab** *(see),* in which polygamy, concubinage, begging, trading in slaves, and the use of alcohol or drugs were forbidden. Also called "Babi."

bab·ka (băb′kə) *n.* A coffee cake flavored with orange rind, rum, almonds, and raisins. [Polish, "little old woman," diminutive of *baba,* old woman.]

ba·boon (bă-bōōn′) *n.* **1.** Any of several chiefly African omnivorous monkeys of the genus *Papio* (or *Chaeropithecus*) and related genera, having an elongated, doglike muzzle and large teeth. See **gelada, hamadryas. 2.** *Slang.* A large, clumsy, often coarse person. [Middle English *baboyne,* from Old French *babuin,* gaping figure, baboon, perhaps a blend of *babine,* pendulous lip, and *baboue,* grimace.]

ba·bu, ba·boo (bä′bōō) *n.* **1.** A form of address in Hindi equivalent or similar to *Mister,* placed before a man's full name or after his first name. **2. a.** A Hindu clerk possessing a prerequisite degree of literacy in English. Considered offensive. **b.** A native of India who has acquired some superficial education in English. Used derogatorily. [Hindi *bābū,* "father."]

Babur. See **Baber.**

ba·bush·ka (bə-bo͞osh′kə) *n.* A woman's headscarf, folded triangularly and tied under the chin. [Russian, "grandmother," diminutive of *baba,* old woman.]

ba·by (bā′bē) *n., pl.* **-bies. 1.** A newborn or very young boy or girl; an infant. **2.** The youngest member of a family or group. **3.** A newborn or very young animal. **4.** An adult or young person who acts like an infant. **5.** *Slang.* **a.** A girlfriend or boyfriend. **b.** A term of familiar address, usually used to a woman or girl. **6.** *Slang.* An object of personal concern or interest: *The project was his baby.*
~*adj.* **1.** Of or pertaining to a baby or babies. **2.** Infantile; childish. **3.** Small in comparison with others of the same kind.
~*tr.v.* **babied, -bying, -bies.** To treat oversolicitously; coddle. —See Synonyms at **pamper.** [Middle English *babie,* imitative.] **—ba·by·hood** *n.*

baby blue *n.* Very light to very pale greenish or purplish blue. **—ba·by-blue** *adj.*

ba·by-blue-eyes (bā′bē-blo͞o′īz′) *n. Used with a singular or plural verb.* A low-growing plant, *Nemophila menziesii,* of California, having bell-shaped blue flowers.

baby carriage *n.* A small four-wheeled carriage for an infant. Also called "baby buggy," "buggy."

baby face *n. Slang.* **1.** A plump, smooth face like a baby's. **2.** An adult having a baby face. **—ba·by-faced** *adj.*

baby grand *n.* A small grand piano.

ba·by·ish (bā′bē-ĭsh) *adj.* **1.** Like a baby; childlike. **2.** Childish; immature. **—ba·by·ish·ly** *adj.* **—ba·by·ish·ness** *n.*

Bab·y·lon¹ (băb′ə-lən, -lŏn′). City in ancient Mesopotamia, some 88 kilometers (55 miles) south of modern Baghdad. Founded in the 2nd millennium B.C., it flourished as Hammurabi's capital. It was virtually destroyed by the Assyrians under Sennacherib (*c.* 689 B.C.), but rose again, achieving vast wealth as the capital of a neo-Babylonian empire. Nebuchadnezzar II rebuilt the city, and his Hanging Gardens were one of the Seven Wonders of the World. Babylon fell to Cyrus the Great (538 B.C.) and became a minor center of the Persian Empire.

Babylon² *n.* **1.** A place of great luxury and corruption. **2.** A place of captivity or exile. **3.** In Rastafarian ideology, the corrupt and materialistic values of the West. See **Zion.** [After BABYLON.]

Bab·y·lo·ni·a (băb′ə-lō′nē-ə). *Abbr.* **Bab.** Empire of ancient Mesopotamia. Created in the 2nd millennium B.C., it rose to greatness under Hammurabi. It then fell to successive invaders and eventually to the Assyrians (*c.* 722 B.C.). A native king established a neo-Babylonian empire (*c.* 625 B.C.), and under Nebuchadnezzar II this was expanded to include Mesopotamia and Palestine. The empire declined after his death and fell to the Persians (538 B.C.).

Bab·y·lo·ni·an (băb′ə-lō′nē-ən) *adj. Abbr.* **Bab. 1.** Of or pertaining to ancient Babylonia or Babylon, their people, culture, or language. **2.** Characterized by a luxurious, pleasure-seeking, and immoral way of life.
~*n. Abbr.* **Bab. 1.** A native or inhabitant of ancient Babylon or Babylonia. **2.** The Semitic language of the Babylonians, a form of Akkadian.

Babylonian captivity *n.* **1.** The deportation of the Jews to Babylonia and their period of exile there, initiated by Nebuchadnezzar II in 597 B.C. and formally terminated by Cyrus in 538 B.C. Also called "Babylonian exile." **2.** The period (1309–78) when the French popes resided at Avignon rather than Rome.

ba·by's-breath, ba·bies'-breath (bā′bēz-brĕth′) *n.* **1.** Any plant of the genus *Gypsophila;* especially, *G. paniculatum,* having numerous small white flowers in branching clusters. **2.** Any of several other plants with small, pleasantly scented flowers.

baby sitter *n.* A person who looks after one or more children while the parents are out, especially in the evening. **—ba·by-sit** *v.*

baby talk *n.* **1.** The early speech of a very young child. **2.** The infantile speech of an adult imitating a very young child.

ba·by-tears (bā′bē-tîrz′) *n.* Also **ba·by's-tears** (bā′bēz-tîrz′). *Used with a singular or plural verb.* A creeping plant, *Helxine soleirolii,* native to Corsica, having numerous very small leaves and minute green flowers.

baby tooth *n.* A **milk tooth** *(see).*

Ba·car·di (bə-kär′dē) *n.* **1.** A trademark for a brand of rum originally distilled in Cuba. **2.** A cocktail made with this rum, containing lime or lemon juice and sugar or grenadine.

bac·ca·lau·re·ate (băk′ə-lôr′ē-ĭt) *n.* **1.** The university degree of **Bachelor** *(see).* **2.** A farewell address in the form of a sermon delivered to a graduating class. [Medieval Latin *baccalaureātus,* from *baccalaureus,* variant (influenced by *bacca lauri,* "laurel berry") of *baccalārius,* BACHELOR.]

bac·ca·rat (bä′kə-rä′, băk′ə-) *n.* A card game in which two or more players bet against a dealer and the winner is the player holding two or three cards totaling closest to nine. [French *baccara*†.]

bac·cate (băk′āt′) *adj.* **1.** Bearing berries. **2.** Resembling a berry in texture or form. [Latin *baccatus,* "having berries," from *bāca, bacca,* berry, perhaps akin to BACCHUS.]

Bac·chae (băk′ē) *pl.n.* The priestesses and female followers of Bacchus. [Latin, from Greek *Bakkhai,* plural of *Bakkhē,* priest of BACCHUS.]

bac·cha·nal (băk′ə-năl′, -näl′, băk′ə-nəl) *n.* **1.** A participant in the Bacchanalia. **2.** *Sometimes* **bacchanals.** The Bacchanalia. **3.** Any drunken or riotous celebration. **4.** A reveler.
~*adj.* Bacchanalian. [Latin *bacchānālis,* of BACCHUS.]

Bac·cha·na·li·a (băk′ə-nāl′yə, -nā′lē-ə) *n., pl.* **Bacchanalia. 1.** The ancient Roman festival in honor of Bacchus. **2. bacchanalia.** A riotous or drunken festivity; a revel. [Latin *bacchānālia,* neuter plural of *bacchānālis,* BACCHANAL.]

bac·cha·na·lian (băk′ə-nāl′yən, -nā′lē-ən) *adj.* **1.** Of or pertaining to the Bacchanalia. **2.** Characterized by riotous, drunken revelry; orgiastic.
~*n.* A drunken reveler; a bacchanal.

bac·chant (bə-kănt′, -känt′, băk′ənt) *n., pl.* **-chants** or **-chantes** (-kăn′tēz, -kän′tēz, -kănts′, -känts′). **1.** A priest or votary of Bacchus. **2.** A boisterous reveler.
~*adj.* **1.** Wine-loving. **2.** Riotous; carousing. [Latin *bacchāns* (stem *bacchant-*), present participle of *bacchārī,* to celebrate the festival of Bacchus, from Greek *bakkhān,* from *Bakkhos,* BACCHUS.]

bac·chante (bə-kăn′tē, -kän′tē, -kănt′, -känt′) *n.* **1.** A priestess or female votary of Bacchus. **2.** A female participant in a drunken or orgiastic revel. [French, from Latin *bacchāns,* BACCHANT.]

Bac·chic (băk′ĭk) *adj.* **1.** Of or pertaining to Bacchus. **2. bacchic.** Drunken and carousing; bacchanalian.

Bac·chus (băk′əs). The god of grape-growing, wine, and pleasure, often identified with Dionysus. [Latin, from Greek *Bakkhos.*]

bac·cif·er·ous (băk-sĭf′ər-əs) *adj. Botany.* Bearing berries. [Latin *baccifer* : *bacca,* berry + -FEROUS.]

bac·ci·form (băk′sə-fôrm′) *adj.* Having the shape of a berry. [Latin *bacca,* berry + -FORM.]

bac·cy (băk′ē) *n. Chiefly British Informal.* Tobacco.

bach¹ (băch) *intr.v.* **bached, baching, baches.** Also **batch.** *Slang.* To live alone and keep house for oneself, especially in a makeshift fashion. Used especially in the expression *bach it.* [Short for BACHELOR.]

bach² (băch) *n. New Zealand.* A small cottage or beach house. [Short for BACHELOR.]

Bach (bäKH), **Johann Sebastian** (1685–1750). German composer and musician. Among his religious works are over 200 cantatas, the *St. Matthew Passion* (1729), and the Mass in B minor (1733–38). His many orchestral pieces include the six *Brandenburg Concertos* (1721), and he wrote numerous compositions for the keyboard, including *The Well-Tempered Clavier* (1722, 1744) and the *Goldberg Variations* (1742). Of those of his 20 children who became musicians, two are especially renowned. **Carl Philipp Emanuel Bach** (1714–88) played an important part in the development of the symphony; **Johann Christian Bach** (1735–82) became music master to the British royal family and is sometimes known as the English or London Bach. See feature, next page.

Bachan. See **Batjan.**

bach·e·lor (băch′ə-lər, băch′lər) *n.* **1.** An unmarried man. **2.** In feudal times, a young knight in the service of another knight. Also called "bachelor-at-arms." See **knight bachelor. 3. Bachelor.** *Abbr.* **B. a.** A college or university degree signifying completion of the undergraduate curriculum and graduation. **b.** A person who holds such a degree. **4.** A young male fur seal who is kept from the breeding territory by older males. In this sense, also called "bachelor seal." [Middle English *bacheler,* from Old French, squire, from Vulgar Latin *baccalārius*†.] **—bach·e·lor·dom** *n.* **—bach·e·lor·hood** *n.* **—bach·e·lor·ship** *n.*

Bachelor of Arts *n. Abbr.* **B.A., A.B. 1.** An academic degree conferred by a college or university upon a person who has completed his or her undergraduate studies, usually in the arts or humanities. Compare **Master of Arts, Doctor of Philosophy. 2.** A person who has received this degree.

Bachelor of Science *n. Abbr.* **B.S., B.Sc., S.B. 1.** An academic degree conferred by a college or university upon a person who has completed his or her undergraduate studies in the sciences or some social sciences. Compare **Master of Science, Doctor of Philosophy. 2.** A person who has received this degree.

bach·e·lor's-but·ton (băch′ə-lərz-bŭt′n, băch′lərz-) *n.* **1.** A plant, the **cornflower** *(see).* **2.** The common European daisy. See **daisy. 3.** Any of various plants of the daisy family having buttonlike flower heads.

Bach trumpet (bäKH) *n.* A small modern trumpet designed to simplify the playing of the high trumpet parts found in the works of J.S. Bach and similar composers.

ba·cil·lar·y (băs′ə-lĕr′ē, bə-sĭl′ə-rē) *adj.* Also **ba·cil·lar** (bə-sĭl′ər, băs′ə-lər). **1.** Of, pertaining to, or caused by bacilli. **2.** Rod-shaped. From BACILLUS.]

ba·cil·li·form (bə-sĭl′ə-fôrm) *adj.* Rod-shaped.

ba·cil·lus (bə-sĭl′əs) *n., pl.* **-li** (-ī′). **1.** *Abbr.* **B.** Any rod-shaped bacterium. Compare **coccus, spirillum. 2.** Any of various rod-shaped, aerobic bacteria of the genus *Bacillus,* often occurring in chainlike formations. —See Usage note at **germ.** [New Latin, from Late Latin, diminutive of Latin *baculum,* rod, stick.]

bac·i·tra·cin (băs′ə-trā′sĭn) *n.* An antibiotic obtained from the bacterium *Bacillus subtilis* and usually used externally to treat skin infections. [BACI(LLUS) + Margaret *Tracy,* an American child in whose blood it was first isolated in 1945 + -IN.]

back¹ (băk) *n.* **1. a.** The region of the vertebrate body located nearest the spine, in man consisting of the rear area from the neck to the pelvis. **b.** The analogous dorsal region in other animals, such as insects. **2. a.** The backbone or spine. **b.** The surface of the human

Babylon *A replica of a tower that once stood in the ancient Mesopotamian capital. The tower is dedicated to Ishtar, the Babylonian goddess of love and fertility.*

Bacchae *A follower of the wine god Bacchus beats a hand drum in a marble frieze from a first-century Roman villa.*

Bach

THE GREATEST OF A MUSICAL FAMILY

Heredity, faith, and craft were elements in Bach's musical genius

For Johann Sebastian Bach (1685–1750), the composing and playing of music was an art whose "aim and final reason . . . should be none else but the Glory of God and the recreation of the mind." That principle infuses not only Bach's religious works such as the Passions, the many Cantatas, and the B-minor Mass, but also his secular music, including the Well-tempered Clavier, the Art of Fugue, and other works created to teach keyboard students.

Bach occupied about midpoint in a family line that produced successful musicians for over 200 years. Of his 20 children from two marriages (his first wife having died in 1720), Wilhelm Friedemann (1710–84), Carl Philipp Emanuel (1714–88), Johann Christoph Friedrich (1732–95), and Johann Christian (1735–82) became admired composers. In a distinguished if unspectacular career that took him never farther than 200 miles from his birthplace at Eisenach, Bach held a number of musical posts culminating in the position of musical director at St. Thomas Church, Leipzig.

BACH IN HIS SIXTIES *The authenticity of Bach portraits has been much debated among scholars, but this painting by Elias Gottlob Haussmann almost certainly shows Bach as he looked in 1746. He is holding a copy of his six-part canon BWV 1076.*

body, or any part of it, or any part of the body of an animal, that is located on the side facing away from the front: *the back of the leg.* **3. a.** The part, area, or surface farthest from the front. **b.** The upper or convex side of something: *the back of one's hand.* **4.** The part opposite to or behind that adapted for use or view. **5.** The reverse or underside, as of a coin or sheet of paper. **6. a.** A part that supports or strengthens from the rear: *the back of a chair.* **b.** Something that covers the back; for example, that part of a garment that covers the back. **7. a.** The part of a book where the pages are stitched together into the binding. **b.** The binding itself. **8. a.** In certain games, such as football or hockey, a player taking a position behind the front line of players. **b.** The position of such a player. **—at the back of one's mind.** In one's memory or subconscious. **—back to front.** The wrong way round; reversed. **—behind someone's back.** Without someone's knowledge or approval. **—get off someone's back.** *Informal.* To cease pestering or scolding someone. **—get (or put) someone's back up.** *Informal.* To annoy or antagonize. **—in back of.** At the rear of; behind. **—on one's back.** Incapacitated or helpless; bedridden. **—put one's back into.** To put great effort into. **—stab in the back.** To attack or betray (a friend or colleague). **—the back of beyond.** A very remote, insignificant, and inaccessible place. **—turn one's back on. 1.** To ignore the plight of; forsake. **2.** To turn away from; renounce. **—with one's back to the wall.** In a desperate position from which one cannot retreat.
~v. **backed, backing, backs.** *—tr.* **1.** To cause to move backward or in a reverse direction. **2.** To furnish or strengthen with a back, backing, or lining. **3. a.** To provide with support, assistance, or encouragement. **b.** To provide a musical backing for. **4.** To bring forward evidence in support of; substantiate. Often used with *up*: *backing up an argument with facts.* **5.** To bet on. **6.** To form the back or background of. **7.** To endorse by signing on the back of. *—intr.* **1.** To move backward. **2.** To shift counterclockwise in direction, as from south to southeast. Used of the wind. Compare **veer.** **3.** To have the back facing in a particular direction: *the house backs onto the park.* **—back and fill. 1.** To maneuver a sailing vessel in a narrow channel by alternately filling and spilling the sails. **2.** To vacillate in one's actions or decisions. **—back down.** To withdraw from a position, opinion, or commitment; abandon a former stand. **—back off.** To retreat or draw away. **—back out.** To withdraw from an enterprise, commitment, or plan, especially before completion: *He announced he was backing out of the project.*
~adj. **1.** Located at the rear. **2.** Distant from a center of activity; remote. **3.** Of a past date; not current. **4.** Owing or due from an earlier time; in arrears. **5.** Moving in a backward direction. **6.** *Phonetics.* Articulated with the tongue pulled to the rear of the mouth. *~adv.* **1.** At, to, or toward the rear or back; backward. **2.** In, to, or toward a former location. **3.** In, to, or toward a former condition. **4.** In, to, or toward a past time. **5.** Away; at a distance: *Stand back!* **6.** In reserve or concealment. **7.** In check. **8.** In return. **9.** In retort.

—back and forth. From one place to another and back again; to and fro. **—go back on. 1.** To fail to keep (a promise or commitment). **2.** To betray or desert (a person). [Middle English *bak*, Old English *bæc*, from Germanic *bakam* (unattested).]
back² *n.* A shallow vat or tub used chiefly by brewers. [Dutch *bak*, from French *bac*, from Old French, from Vulgar Latin *bacca* (unattested), a water vessel, perhaps from Celtic.]
back·ache (băk′āk′) *n.* A usually persistent ache or pain in the lower back.
back·bench·er (băk′bĕn′chər) *n. Chiefly British.* **1.** Any of the Members of Parliament, who sit on the rear benches of the House of Commons but are not ministers or shadow ministers. Also called "bencher." See **front bench, crossbench. 2.** One occupying an equivalent position in a similar legislative body.
back·bite (băk′bīt′) *v.* **-bit** (-bĭt′), **-bitten** (-bĭt′n) or *informal* **-bit, -biting, -bites.** *—tr.* To slander the character or reputation of (an absent person). *—intr.* To speak spitefully or slanderously of a person in his absence. **—back·bit·er** *n.*
back·blocks (băk′blŏks′) *pl.n. Australian.* A remote and sparsely populated area, especially in the interior of Australia. **—back·block·er** *n.*
back·board (băk′bôrd′, -bōrd′) *n.* **1.** A board that can be worn, or one that can be placed under the mattress of a bed, to support the back. **2.** *Basketball.* The elevated, vertical board from which the basket projects.
back·bone (băk′bōn′) *n.* **1.** The vertebrate spine or spinal column. **2.** Anything that resembles a backbone in appearance or position, such as the keel of a ship. **3.** A main support or major sustaining factor: *"Doubt and the Land League were the backbone of the conflict with England"* (Sean O'Faolain). **4.** Strength of character; fortitude; determination. **5.** The main ridge of a mountain range or the main range of mountains in a region. **—See Synonyms at courage. —back·boned** *adj.*
back·break·ing (băk′brā′kĭng) *adj.* Demanding great physical exertion; exhausting; arduous. **—back·break·er** *n.*
back·chat (băk′chăt′) *n. Chiefly British.* Back talk.
back·cloth (băk′klôth′, -klŏth′) *n. Chiefly British.* **1.** A large, usually painted, cloth forming the background to a stage set. **2.** A setting or background.
back·comb (băk′kōm′) *v.* **-combed, -combing, -combs.** *—tr.* To comb (the hair) from the ends toward the roots to give fullness. *—intr.* To backcomb the hair.
back country *n.* A remote, sparsely populated area.
back·court (băk′kôrt′, -kōrt′) *n.* **1.** In tennis and other racket games, the part of a court between the service line and the base line. **2.** In other games, such as handball or basketball, the part of the playing area farthest from the goal or target wall.
back·cross (băk′krôs′, -krŏs′) *v.* **-crossed, -crossing, -crosses.** *Genetics. —tr.* To mate (a first-generation hybrid) with a parent or member of the parental stock. *—intr.* To breed or cross in this way.
~n. Genetics. The act or result of backcrossing.
back·date (băk′dāt′) *tr.v.* **-dated, -dating, -dates.** To make retroactive by assigning an earlier date to: *The June pay raise was backdated to January.*
back door *n.* **1.** A door to a building other than the front or main door. **2.** An unfair, covert, or underhand method used to obtain a promotion, job, or the like: *He got into the company through the back door.*
back·door (băk′dôr′, -dōr′) *adj.* Done or formed secretly or surreptitiously; clandestine.
back·drop (băk′drŏp′) *n.* **1.** A painted curtain or screen forming the background to a stage set. **2.** The setting, as of a historical event.
backed (băkt) *adj.* Having or furnished with a back or backing. Usually used in combination: *a low-backed chair.*
back end *n. British Informal.* Autumn.
back·er (băk′ər) *n.* **1.** One who supports, gives aid to, or invests in a person, group, or enterprise. **2.** One who bets on a contestant.
back·field (băk′fēld′) *n.* **1.** *Football.* The players stationed behind the line of scrimmage. **2.** The area occupied by these players.
back·fill (băk′fĭl′) *tr.v.* **-filled, -filling, -fills.** To refill (an excavated ditch).
back·fire (băk′fīr′) *n.* **1.** An explosion of prematurely ignited fuel or of unburned exhaust gases in an internal-combustion engine. **2.** A fire started purposely in the path of an oncoming fire so that the latter will be extinguished on reaching an area that has already been burned out. **3.** An explosion of ammunition in the breech of a gun. *~intr.v.* **backfired, -firing, -fires. 1.** To explode in or make the sound of a backfire. **2.** To start or employ a backfire. **3.** To produce an unexpected and undesired result: *His plot backfired on him.*
back·for·ma·tion (băk′fôr-mā′shən) *n. Linguistics.* **1.** A new word created by removing from an existing word what is mistakenly thought to be an affix, as *laze* from *lazy* or *edit* from *editor.* **2.** The process of forming words in this way.
back·gam·mon (băk′găm′ən) *n.* A game for two persons, played on a specially marked board with pieces whose moves are determined by throws of dice. [BACK (referring to the movement of the pieces) + GAMMON (a type of victory in the game).]
back·ground (băk′ground′) *n.* **1.** The ground located behind closer areas. **2. a.** The space in pictorial representation, usually appearing as if in the distance, arranged to provide relief for the principal objects. **b.** The general scene or surface against or upon which designs, patterns, figures, or the like are seen or represented. **3.** An

area or position of relative obscurity or unimportance. **4.** The underlying or supporting causes of or the contributory circumstances connected with an occurrence or development; the context in which something occurs. **5. a.** A person's experience, training, and education, often in a specified area. **b.** A person's social class, personal history, or family circumstances. **6. a.** Music or sounds heard as accompaniment to dialogue or action in a dramatic performance, film, or broadcast. **b.** Subdued music played in a public place, such as a restaurant or airport, to create atmosphere. **7.** Radiation at a constant low level at any specific location, usually due to traces of naturally occurring radioactive elements and cosmic rays. Also called "background radiation." **8.** Noise or interference, usually at a constant level, that is picked up by electronic devices. —**background** adj.

back·ground·er (băk′groun′dər) n. Slang. An informal meeting at which an official provides background information, as to news reporters, about a governmental issue.

back·hand (băk′hănd′) n. **1.** In sports such as tennis and table tennis, a stroke or motion, as of a racket, made with the back of the hand facing outward and the arm typically held across the body. Compare **forehand.** **2.** Handwriting characterized by letters that slant to the left. ~adj. Backhanded. ~adv. With a backhanded stroke or motion. ~tr.v. **backhanded, -handing, -hands.** To perform, hit, or catch backhand.

back·hand·ed (băk′hăn′dĭd) adj. **1.** Made with the back of the hand or with the back of the hand facing outward and moving away from the body. **2.** Slanting toward the left. **3.** Containing a disguised insult or rebuke: a backhanded compliment. **4.** Twisted or formed in a direction opposite to the normal one: backhanded rope. —**backhand·ed·ly** adv. —**back·hand·ed·ness** n.

back·hand·er (băk′hăn′dər) n. **1.** A backhanded stroke or hit. **2.** British Informal. A bribe. **3.** An indirect verbal attack.

back·hoe (băk′hō′) n. A machine used in excavating, having a digging device attached to a hinged extension that draws it toward the operator with a motion like that used in hoeing.

back·ing (băk′ĭng) n. **1.** Material that provides support or strength from the back. **2.** Support or aid; endorsement. **3.** Those who provide aid or support. **4.** A musical accompaniment for a performer.

back·lash (băk′lăsh′) n. **1.** A strongly adverse, usually delayed, reaction to some prior development that has been construed as a threat, as in the context of morality or social or race relations. **2.** A sudden or violent backward whipping motion. **3.** A snarl in the part of a fishing line wound round the reel. **4.** The play resulting from loose connections between gears or other mechanical elements, which is most evident on reversal of movement.

back·less (băk′lĭs) adj. Having no back; especially, of a dress, cut to the waist or very low at the back.

back·list (băk′lĭst′) n. A publisher's list of older titles kept in print.

back·log (băk′lôg′, -lŏg′) n. **1.** An accumulation, especially of unfinished work or unfilled orders. **2.** A reserve supply or source. **3.** A large log placed at the back of a fire to support other logs and maintain heat.

back matter n. Printing. End matter (see).

back number n. **1.** An out-of-date periodical or newspaper. **2.** Informal. An out-of-date or old-fashioned person or thing.

back·pack (băk′păk′) n. **1.** A knapsack, often mounted on a lightweight frame, that is worn on the back to carry camping supplies. **2.** A piece of equipment made for use while being carried on the back. ~v. **backpacked, -packing, -packs.** —intr. To hike while carrying supplies in a backpack. —tr. To carry in a backpack. —**backpack·er** n.

back·ped·al (băk′pĕd′l) intr.v. **-aled, -aling, -als** or chiefly British **-alled, -alling.** **1.** To turn the pedals backward, as on a bicycle. **2.** To withdraw from or qualify a previous commitment, stance, opinion, or the like. **3.** In boxing, to go backward.

back projection n. The projection of a film onto a screen from behind the screen, often used as a background for a scene being filmed from the front.

back·rest (băk′rĕst′) n. A support or rest for the back.

back·room (băk′rōōm′, -rŏŏm′) adj. Of or pertaining to a planning department or scientific laboratory in which confidential work, often governmental and military, is carried out and from which indirect influence is often exercised. —**back room** n.

backroom boy n. Chiefly British Informal. A person engaged in backroom work.

back·rush (băk′rŭsh′) n. The seaward return of water after the landward motion of a wave.

back·saw (băk′sô′) n. A saw that is reinforced by a metal band along its back edge.

back·scat·ter (băk′skăt′ər) n. The deflection of waves or particles through angles greater than 90° by electromagnetic or nuclear forces. Also called "backscattering."

back·scratch·er (băk′skrăch′ər) n. **1.** A long-handled implement made of wood or plastic, used to scratch one's own back. **2.** Informal. One involved in the giving and receiving of favors for personal gain, often in an underhand way, as in politics or business. —**backscratch·ing** n.

back seat n. **1.** A seat in the back, especially of a vehicle or an auditorium. **2.** Informal. A subordinate position. Used chiefly in the phrase take a back seat.

back-seat driver (băk′sēt′) n. Informal. **1.** A passenger in a car who constantly advises, corrects, or nags the driver. **2.** Any person who persists in giving unsolicited advice.

back·set (băk′sĕt′) n. **1.** A setback; reversal. **2.** An eddy or countercurrent in water.

backsheesh, backshish. Variants of **baksheesh.**

back·side (băk′sīd′) n. **1.** The back or rear part of something. **2.** Informal. The buttocks; rump.

back·sight (băk′sīt′) n. **1.** In surveying, a reading taken facing backward to a previous position. **2.** Chiefly British. The sight on a rifle nearer the stock.

back·slap·ping (băk′slăp′ĭng) adj. Excessively hearty. —**back·slap·ping** n.

back·slide (băk′slīd′) intr.v. **-slid** (-slĭd′), **-slid** or **-slidden** (-slĭd′n), **-sliding, -slides.** To revert to a bad habit, sin, wrongdoing, or the like. —**back·slid·er** n.

back·space (băk′spās′) intr.v. **-spaced, -spacing, -spaces.** To move the carriage of a typewriter back one or more spaces by striking the key used for this purpose. ~n. The key on a typewriter used for backspacing. Also called "backspacer," "backspace key."

back·spin (băk′spĭn′) n. A spin that tends to retard, arrest, or reverse the linear motion of an object, especially of a ball.

back·stage (băk′stāj′) adv. **1.** In or toward the dressing rooms, wings, or other areas behind the performing area in a theater. **2.** In or toward a place closed to public view; privately. ~adj. (băk′stāj′). **1.** Occurring or situated behind the performing area of a theater. **2.** Not open or known to the public; private or concealed.

back·stairs (băk′stârz′) n. A secondary staircase at the back of a house especially one formerly used by servants. ~adj. Also **back·stair** (-stâr′). **1.** Furtive; clandestine. **2.** Scandalous.

back·stay (băk′stā′) n. **1.** A rope or shroud extending from the top of the mast aft to the ship's side or stern to help support the mast. **2.** A support at or for the back of something.

back·stitch (băk′stĭch′) n. A stitch made by inserting the needle at the midpoint of the preceding stitch, so that each stitch overlaps another by half its length. —**back·stitch** v.

back·stop (băk′stŏp′) n. **1.** A screen or fence used to prevent a ball from being thrown or hit far out of a playing area, as in baseball or tennis. **2.** Baseball. A catcher. **3.** A device that prevents excessive backward movement, as of a machine part. ~tr.v. **backstopped, -stopping, -stops. 1.** To serve as a backstop for. **2. a.** To support. **b.** To substitute for (another) in an emergency.

back straight n. Chiefly British. The backstretch.

back·street (băk′strēt′) n. A minor or side street, especially one away from a main thoroughfare. ~adj. **1.** Situated on or pertaining to a backstreet. **2.** Operating or performed illegally or secretly: a backstreet abortion.

back·stretch (băk′strĕch′) n. The part of an oval racecourse farthest from the spectators and opposite the homestretch, usually a straightaway.

back·stroke (băk′strōk′) n. **1.** A swimming stroke that resembles an inverted crawl. It is executed with the swimmer on his back, using a flutter kick, and moving his arms in backward circular strokes. **2.** A backhanded stroke. **3.** A stroke or motion made in return or as a recoil.

back·swim·mer (băk′swĭm′ər) n. Any of various insects of the family Notonectidae that swim or float on their backs.

back·sword (băk′sôrd′, -sōrd′) n. **1.** A sword with only one cutting edge. **2.** A stick used in fencing practice, a singlestick (see). **3.** One who fights with a backsword.

back talk n. Impudent contradiction; an insolent retort.

back-to-back (băk′tə-băk′) adj. **1.** Facing away from each other. **2.** British. Having the backs facing or adjoining. Said of rows of houses. **3.** Informal. In succession: two films back-to-back. ~n. British. A back-to-back house. —**back-to-back** adv.

back·track (băk′trăk′) intr.v. **-tracked, -tracking, -tracks. 1.** To go back over the course by which one has come. **2.** To reverse one's position or policy.

back up tr.v. **1.** To support or help, especially through reinforcement, confirmation, or safeguards. **2.** Printing. To print the reverse side of (a sheet). **3.** Computer Science. To provide a duplicate copy of (a data file). —intr.v. To accumulate.

back·up (băk′ŭp′) n. **1. a.** A reserve supply, as of provisions. **b.** One kept in reserve, as a safeguard or substitute, for example. **2. a.** Support or backing. **b.** A background accompaniment, as for a musical performer. **3.** Computer Science. A copy of a data file made and kept in case of computer failure. **4.** An overflow caused by clogged plumbing. ~adj. **1.** Kept in reserve; standby: a back-up pilot. **2.** Supporting; auxiliary.

back·veld (băk′fĕlt′, -vĕlt′) n. South African. A remote, rural, thinly populated area. [Afrikaans backvelt, "back field."] —**back·veld** adj. —**back·veld·er** n.

back·ward (băk′wərd) adj. **1. a.** Directed or facing toward the back or rear. **b.** Directed toward the beginning or start. **c.** Directed toward the past; regressive. **2. a.** Done with the back leading or first: a backward somersault. **b.** Done or arranged in reverse or in a manner contrary to the usual. **3.** Unwilling to act; reluctant; shy. **4.** Behind others in progress or development.

bacteria

THE EARLIEST FORMS OF LIFE ON EARTH

Without microscopic bacteria, plants and animals could not survive

Bacteria are some of the simplest of all organisms. Traces have been found in rocks as much as 3,100 million years old; they probably represent the earliest stages of the development of life on earth.

Bacteria originated in the ocean, and today are found in greatest abundance in seas, lakes, and other moist environments.

Although many bacteria cause disease, others perform functions that are essential to life. Some bacteria break down the vast range of organic matter in the soil; without them the soil would become sterile and grow nothing. Others turn nitrogen from the air into a form that can be used as plant food. There are also bacteria that break down waste products in the gut of the host animal.

 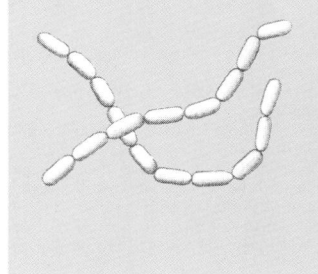 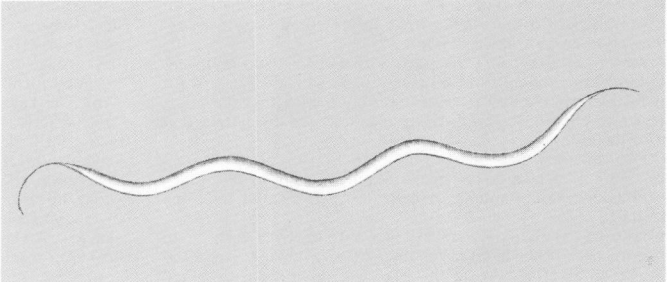

BACTERIA SHAPES *Bacteria occur in enormous numbers. Most of them reproduce by cell division—one cell dividing into two new ones. In this way a single bacterial cell can produce 16 million progeny in 24 hours. There are three main shapes, illustrated from left to right: spherical (coccus), rodlike (bacillus), and spiral (spirillum).*

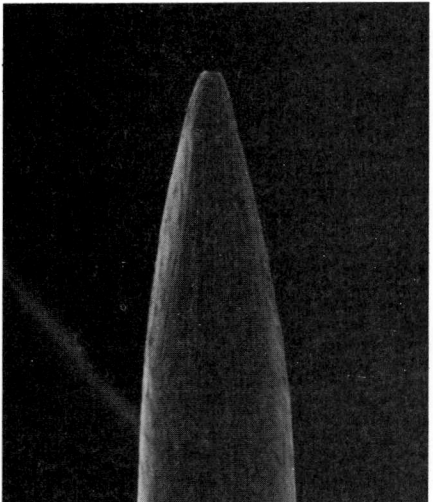 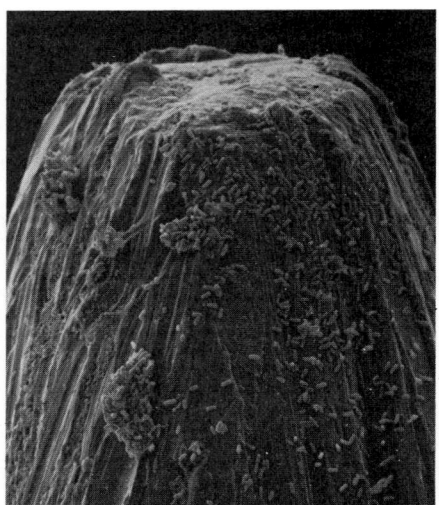 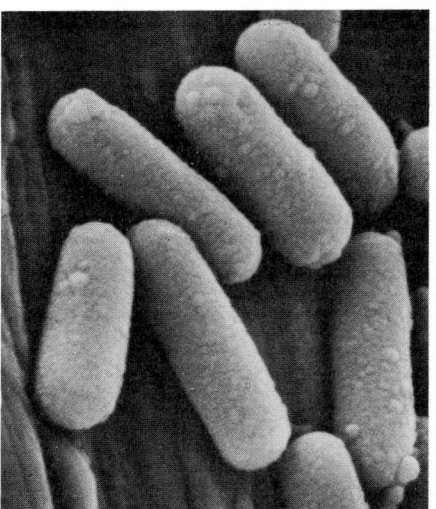

BACTERIA SIZES *Bacteria are tiny, ranging from about 0.0001 to 0.0005 millimeter in length. They are so profuse that a single drop of saliva may contain millions of them, and a gram of garden soil billions. These bacteria on the point of a pin have been magnified (left to right) 50, 1,250, and 31,250 times.*

Bactrian camel *This largely domesticated two-humped camel is used throughout central Asia for riding and to supply meat, hides, wool, and some milk. Unlike the single-humped dromedary, Bactrian camels can survive in cold desert regions as well as hot ones.*

~*adv.* Also **back·wards. 1.** To or toward the back or rear. **2.** With the back leading. **3.** In a manner or order contrary to the usual or expected; in reverse. **4.** To, toward, or into the past. —**back·ward·ly** *adv.* —**back·ward·ness** *n.*

back·wash (băk′wŏsh′, -wôsh′) *n.* **1.** Water moved backward, as by the action of oars or a motor. **2.** A backward flow of air, as from the propeller of an aircraft. **3.** A flow of water back down a beach after a wave has broken. **4.** A condition resulting from some disturbing or irregular event; an aftermath.

back·wa·ter (băk′wô′tər, -wŏt′ər) *n.* **1.** Water held or pushed back by or as if by a dam or current; especially, a body of stagnant or still water thus formed. **2.** A place or situation regarded as stagnant or backward: *a cultural backwater.*

back·woods (băk′wŏŏdz′, -wŏŏdz′) *pl.n.* **1.** Heavily wooded, uncultivated areas. **2.** Any remote, thinly populated, and backward area. —**back·woods** *adj.*

back·woods·man (băk′wŏŏdz′mən, -wŏŏdz′mən) *n., pl.* **-men** (-mĭn). **1.** One who lives or was brought up in a backwoods area, especially one who is unfamiliar with the customs of urban life; a rustic. **2.** *British.* A peer who rarely or never attends the House of Lords.

back yard, back·yard (băk′yärd′) *n.* **1.** A yard at the rear of a house. **2.** A region or sphere of special concern, especially one that is geographically close: *a war in America's back yard.*

ba·con (bā′kən) *n.* The salted and often smoked meat from the back and sides of a pig. —**bring home the bacon.** *Informal.* **1.** To provide food and other necessities. **2.** To make good; succeed. —**save one's bacon.** To escape harm or loss. [Middle English *bacon, ba-* *koun,* from Old French *bacon, bacun,* from Frankish *bako* (unattested), ham, from Germanic *bakkon* (unattested), perhaps akin to *bakam* (unattested), BACK.]

Ba·con (bā′kən), **Francis** (1910–92). British painter. He was best known for his disturbing portraits in which subjects are distorted and invested with feelings of terror.

Bacon, Francis, 1st Baron Verulam, Viscount St. Albans (1561–1626). English philosopher, politician, and Lord Chancellor. His many influential writings include *The Advancement of Learning* (1605) and the *Novum Organum* (1620), in which he put forward a new theory of scientific knowledge based on observation and experiment that came to be known as the inductive method.

Bacon, Roger (*c.* 1214–94). English scientist, encyclopedist, philosopher, alchemist, and Franciscan monk; for these diverse skills he was called *Doctor Mirabilis* ("Admirable Doctor").

Ba·co·ni·an (bā-kō′nē-ən) *adj.* Of, pertaining to, or characteristic of the works or thought of the philosopher Francis Bacon.

~*n.* **1.** A follower of the doctrines of Francis Bacon. **2.** One who believes that Francis Bacon wrote Shakespeare's plays.

bact. bacteria; bacterial.

bac·te·re·mi·a (băk′tə-rē′mē-ə) *n.* The presence of viable bacteria in the blood. [New Latin : BACTER(IO)- + -EMIA.] —**bac·te·re·mic** *adj.* —**bac·te·re·mi·cal·ly** *adv.*

bac·te·ri·a (băk-tîr′ē-ə) *pl.n. Singular* **-rium** (-əm). *Abbr.* **bact.** Microorganisms, usually single-celled, constituting the class Schizomycetes, occurring in a wide variety of forms. Most bacteria are either free-living saprophytes, bringing about decomposition, or parasites, many of which cause disease. —See Usage note at **germ.** [New

Latin, plural of *bacterium,* from Greek *baktērion,* diminutive of *baktron,* rod.] **—bac·te·ri·al** *adj.* **—bac·te·ri·al·ly** *adv.*

bac·te·ri·cide (băk-tîr′ə-sīd′) *n.* A substance that destroys bacteria. [BACTERI(O)- + -CIDE.] **—bac·te·ri·ci·dal** *adj.*

bac·te·rin (băk′tə-rĭn) *n.* A vaccine prepared from dead bacteria. [BACTER(IO) + -IN.]

bacterio-, bacteri-, bacter- *prefix.* Indicates bacteria, bacterial activity, or relationship to bacteria; for example, **bacteriophage, bactericide, bacteroid.** [From BACTERIA.]

bac·te·ri·ol·o·gy (băk-tîr′ē-ŏl′ə-jē) *n. Abbr.* **bacteriol.** The study of bacteria, especially in relation to medicine and agriculture. [BACTERIO- + -LOGY.] **—bac·te·ri·o·log·i·cal** (băk-tîr′ē-ə-lŏj′ĭ-kəl), **bac·te·ri·o·log·ic** *adj.* **—bac·te·ri·o·log·i·cal·ly** *adv.* **—bac·te·ri·ol·o·gist** *n.*

bac·te·ri·ol·y·sis (băk-tîr′ē-ŏl′ə-sĭs) *n.* The dissolution of bacteria, especially by the action of specific antibodies. [New Latin : BACTERIO- + -LYSIS.] **—bac·te·ri·o·lyt·ic** (băk-tîr′ē-ə-lĭt′ĭk) *adj.*

bac·te·ri·o·phage (băk-tîr′ē-ə-fāj′) *n.* A virus that is parasitic on and destroys bacteria. Also called "phage." [BACTERIO- + -PHAGE.] **—bac·te·ri·o·phag·ic, bac·te·ri·oph·a·gous** (băk-tîr′ē-ŏf′ə-gəs) *adj.* **—bac·te·ri·o·phag·i·cal·ly** *adv.*

bac·te·ri·o·sta·sis (băk-tîr′ē-ō-stā′sĭs) *n.* The arresting or inhibition of bacterial growth and reproduction, usually by the action of drugs. [New Latin : BACTERIO- + -STASIS.] **—bac·te·ri·o·stat·ic** (băk-tîr′ē-ō-stăt′ĭk) *adj.* **—bac·te·ri·o·stat·i·cal·ly** *adv.*

bac·te·ri·um. Singular of **bacteria.**

bac·te·roid (băk′tə-roid′) *adj.* Also **bac·te·roi·dal** (băk′tə-roid′l). Resembling bacteria in appearance or action.
~*n.* Any of various irregularly shaped bacteria, such as those occurring on the roots of leguminous plants. [BACTER(IO)- + -OID.]

Bac·tri·an camel (băk′trē-ən) *n.* A two-humped camel, *Camelus bactrianus,* native to central and southwestern Asia and used as a beast of burden. Compare **dromedary.**

bac·u·li·form (băk′yə-lə-fôrm′, bə-kyōō′lə-) *adj.* Rod-shaped. [Latin *baculum,* stick, staff + -FORM.]

bad¹ (băd) *adj.* **worse** (wûrs), **worst** (wûrst). **1.** Inferior; poor in quality. **2.** Evil; wicked; sinful. **3.** Misbehaving; disobedient; naughty. **4.** Disagreeable; unpleasant; disturbing: *bad news.* **5.** Unfavorable: *bad reviews.* **6.** Rotten; spoiled; decomposed. **7.** Harmful in effect; detrimental: *bad habits.* **8.** Not able to be recovered or discharged: *a bad debt.* **9. a.** Faulty or incorrect: *bad grammar.* **b.** Incompetent: *bad at sums.* **10.** Not valid or genuine: *a bad check.* **11.** Severe; violent; intense: *a bad cold.* **12.** In poor health; in pain; ill. **13.** Sorry; regretful; unhappy: *Don't feel bad about it.* **14.** *Slang.* Very good; excellent. **—in bad.** *Informal.* In trouble or disfavor. **—not half** (or **so**) **bad.** *Informal.* Rather good; acceptable.
~*n.* Wickedness: *go to the bad.*
~*adv. Informal.* Badly. [Middle English *badde,* perhaps from Old English *bæddel,* effeminate man, hermaphrodite.] **—bad·ness** *n.*

bad² *Archaic.* A past tense of **bid.**

bad blood *n.* Bitterness; animosity.

bad·der·locks (băd′ər-lŏks′) *n. Used with a singular or plural verb.* An edible seaweed, *Alaria esculenta,* having long, yellowish-green fronds. [18th century : origin obscure.]

bad·dy, bad·die (băd′ē) *n., pl.* **-dies.** *Informal.* A criminal or villain, especially as portrayed in a film, play, or book.

bade. A past tense of **bid.**

Ba·den¹ (bäd′n). Also **Ba·den bei Wien** (bī vēn′). Spa town in Lower Austria, near Vienna, at the foot of the Wienerwald.

Baden². Health resort in Aargau canton, northern Switzerland, famous for its hot springs.

Baden³. Former state in southwestern West Germany. Bounded by the Main and Rhine rivers, it is now part of Baden-Württemberg.

Ba·den-Ba·den (bäd′n-bäd′n). Fashionable spa town in Baden-Württemberg, Germany. Its hot springs have been known since Roman times.

Ba·den-Pow·ell (bäd′n-pō′əl), **Robert Stephenson Smyth, 1st Baron** (1857–1941). British general, founder of the Boy Scout movement. As a soldier he is famous for his heroic defense of Mafeking during the Boer War.

Ba·den-Würt·tem·berg (bäd′n-vûrt′əm-bĕrg′). State of southern Germany. It was formed (1952) by the amalgamation of Baden and Württemberg. Stuttgart is its capital.

bad faith *n.* A dishonest and deceiving attitude.

badge (băj) *n.* **1.** A small metal disk worn on clothing, bearing a design, slogan, or the like. **2.** A device or emblem worn as an insignia of rank, office, or membership in an organization or as an award or honor. **3.** Any characteristic mark or symbol. **—See** Synonyms at **sign.** [Middle English *bag(g)e†.*]

badg·er (băj′ər) *n.* **1.** Any of several large carnivorous, burrowing animals of the family Mustelidae, such as *Meles meles,* of Eurasia, or *Taxidea taxus,* of North America, typically having black and white stripes on the head, short legs, long claws on the front feet, and a heavy, silvery grizzled coat. **2.** The fur or hair of a badger. **3.** Any of several mammals related to or resembling the badger, uch as the **honey badger** *(see),* or, in Australia, the wombat or the bandicoot.
~*tr.v.* **badgered, -ering, -ers.** To harass persistently; pester. **—See** Synonyms at **harass.** [16th century : perhaps BADGE (from the white mark on its forehead).]

bad·i·nage (băd′ə-näzh′) *n.* Light, playful banter; flippant repartee. [French, from *badin,* fool, joker, from Provençal, from *badar,* to gape, from Vulgar Latin *batāre* (unattested).]

bad·lands (băd′lăndz′) *pl.n.* An area of barren land characterized by roughly eroded ridges, peaks, and plateaus.

Bad·lands (băd′lăndz′). A heavily eroded arid region of southwestern South Dakota, characterized by gullies and sharply indented ridges. It is now a national monument.

Badlands *This arid, heavily eroded plateau in South Dakota, also known as the Big Badlands, got its name because explorers found it difficult to cross. The area has given its name to similar regions around the world.*

---

badger

THE UNDERGROUND LIFE OF THE BADGER

The fastidious housekeeper that hunts by night

During the day most badgers in Europe live in groups in a set—a labyrinth of underground tunnels and chambers that penetrates up to 18 meters (20 yards) into woodland hillside and that they keep scrupulously clean. It is only at night that they emerge to search for bedding and food, which includes earthworms, insects, small mammals, snails, and berries. Sometimes they leave a trail of scent behind them so that they can find their way back home.

There are eight species of badger, six of which are found only in south and southeast Asia. The Eurasian badger, which is found from western Europe to China, has a silver-gray body with bold black-and-white stripes on its head. The American badger, which is widespread in North America, is a smaller animal with a gray body, a single white stripe from its muzzle to its shoulders, and black patches on its cheeks. It is found in the western part of North America, usually in open, dry country. For most of the time it lives alone. It burrows rapidly with its powerful claws and can defend itself fiercely from an attacker if cornered.

EURASIAN BADGER *This species of badger is some 900 millimeters (35 inches) long, with strong claws for burrowing.*

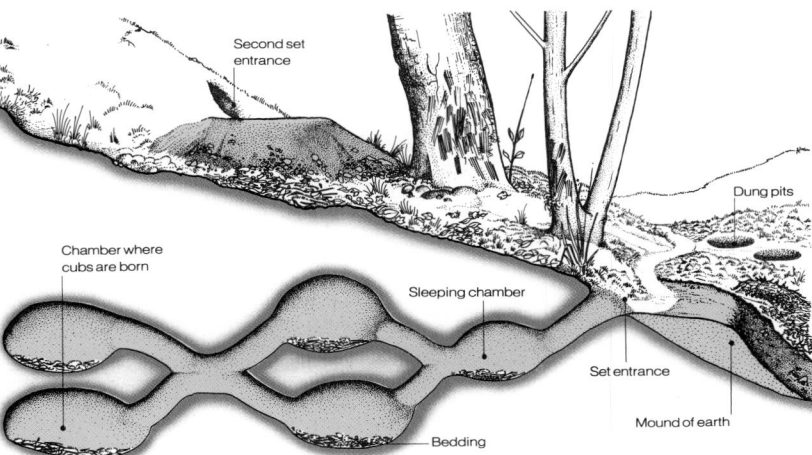

BADGER'S SET *The badger digs a deep set at the base of a tree, building up a mound of earth at the entrance. It sharpens its claws against the tree.*

Second set entrance

Chamber where cubs are born

Sleeping chamber

Dung pits

Set entrance

Mound of earth

Bedding

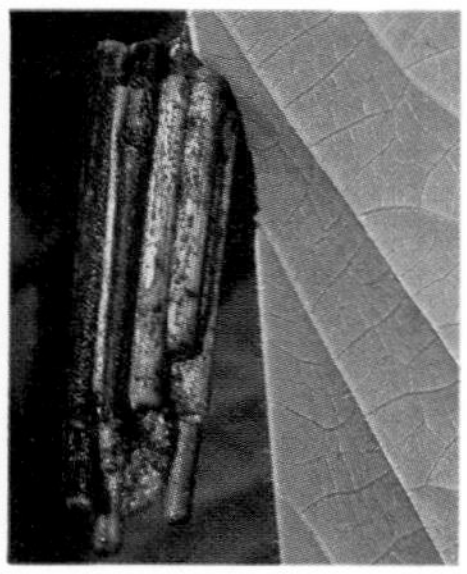

bagworm The caterpillar of the bagworm builds a case, or bag (above), of twigs, leaves, or fiber in which it lies while it changes from caterpillar to adult. The female remains in the bag until she has been fertilized by the winged male, then lays her eggs in it before dying.

bad·ly (băd′lē) *adv.* **worse, worst. 1.** In a bad manner. **2.** Very much; greatly.

bad·min·ton (băd′mĭn′tən) *n.* **1.** A game played by volleying a shuttlecock back and forth over a high, narrow net by means of a light, long-handled racket. **2.** *Chiefly British.* A drink usually made with claret, soda water, and sugar and served cold. [After BADMINTON.]

Bad·min·ton (băd′mĭn′tən). A village in Avon, England, in the Cotswolds. Annual horse trials are held on the grounds of Badminton House (built 1682), the country seat of the dukes of Beaufort. The game of badminton is reputed to have originated here.

bad·mouth (băd′mouth′, -mouth′) *tr.v.* **-mouthed, -mouthing, -mouths.** *Slang.* To criticize or disparage, often spitefully or unfairly; run down.

bad news *n. Used with a singular verb. Slang.* A troublesome or undesirable person, thing, or situation.

Baeda. See **Bede.**

Bae·de·ker (bā′dĭ-kər) *n.* **1.** Any of a series of guidebooks to Europe and the Middle East produced by the German publisher Karl Baedeker (1801–59) or his company. **2.** Any guidebook.

Baeke·land (bāk′lənd′), **Leo Hendrick** (1863–1944). Belgian-born U.S. chemist and inventor. He invented the first plastic that hardens permanently on heating and does not soften when reheated, which he called **Bakelite** *(see).* He also invented the first commercially successful photographic printing paper.

Baer (bâr), **Karl Ernst von** (1792–1876). Estonian-born German zoologist. He made pioneering researches in the mammalian reproductive system, discovering the mammalian egg, and is considered to be one of the founders of the science of embryology.

Ba·ez (bī′ĕz′, bī-ĕz′), **Joan** (1941–). U.S. folk singer and political activist.

Baf·fin (băf′ĭn), **William** (1584–1622). English navigator. While searching for the Northwest Passage (1615–16), he discovered Baffin Bay and explored the northern part of Baffin Island.

Baffin Island. Formerly **Baffin Land.** The largest island in the Canadian Arctic Archipelago, and at 476,068 square kilometers (183,810 square miles) the fifth-largest island in the world.

baf·fle (băf′əl) *tr.v.* **-fled, -fling, -fles. 1.** To foil; thwart; frustrate: *The police were baffled by the lack of clues.* **2.** To perplex to the point of helplessness; bewilder. **3.** To impede the force or movement of; interfere with. —See Synonyms at **puzzle.**
—*n.* Any structure used to impede, regulate, or alter the flow of a fluid or to control the emission or distribution of sound. Also called "baffle plate." [Perhaps obscurely related to French *bafouer,* to hoodwink, deceive, from Old French *beffer*†, ridicule.] **—baf·fle·ment** *n.* **—baf·fler** *n.*

baf·fling (băf′lĭng) *adj.* **1.** Of a nature that defies solution or understanding; bewildering. **2.** *Nautical.* Shifting in direction and tending to impede or interfere with progress. Said of winds.

bag (băg) *n.* **1.** A container in the form of a sack or pouch, made from a flexible material, such as paper, cloth, plastic, or leather. **2.** A woman's handbag. **3.** A suitcase, satchel, or other piece of hand luggage. **4.** An organic sac or pouch, such as the udder of a cow. **5.** Something resembling a bag or pouch. **6.** *Nautical.* The bulging part of a sail. **7. a.** The amount held in a bag; bagful. **b.** *British.* Any of various units of dry measure. **8.** The amount of game killed or permitted to be killed in a single day during one shooting expedition, or by one member of a shoot. **9.** *Informal.* A collection of persons or things: *His friends were a mixed bag.* **10.** *Baseball.* A base. **11.** *Slang.* An area of interest, activity or skill: *Cooking is not my bag.* **12.** *Slang.* An unpleasant or unattractive woman: *a disagreeable old bag.* **13.** A small amount of heroin, marijuana, or some other drug wrapped in paper. **—bag and baggage.** With all one's belongings; completely: *He moved out bag and baggage.* **—holding the bag.** *Informal.* Having full responsibility or blame thrust upon one. **—in the bag.** *Slang.* Assured of successful outcome; virtually accomplished or won.
—*v.* **bagged, bagging, bags.** —*tr.* **1.** To put into a bag. **2.** To cause to bulge like a bag. **3.** To capture or kill (game). **4.** *Informal.* **a.** To gain possession of; capture or steal. **b.** *British Informal.* To reserve the right to do or have. Used especially by children: *Bags I. Bags that piece of cake.* **5.** *Australian Slang.* To disparage; belittle. —*intr.* **1.** To hang or bulge loosely. **2.** To swell out. [Middle English *bagge,* from Old Norse *baggi*†.]

ba·gasse (bə-găs′) *n.* The dry pulp remaining from sugar cane or sugar beet after the juice has been extracted, used for making paper and as a fuel. [French, from Spanish *bagazo,* dregs, from *baga,* pod, husk, from Latin *băca, bacca,* berry.]

bag·a·telle (băg′ə-təl′) *n.* **1.** An unimportant or insignificant thing; a trifle. **2.** A short piece of light verse or music. **3.** A game played on an oblong table with a cue and balls. [French, from Italian *bagatella,* diminutive formation perhaps from Latin *băca, bacca,* berry.]

Bagdad. See **Baghdad.**

Bage·hot (băj′ət), **Walter** (1826–77). British economist, journalist, political theorist, and literary critic. He wrote *The English Constitution* (1867), an analysis of the comparative powers of the British organs of government.

ba·gel, bei·gel (bā′gəl) *n.* A ring-shaped roll with a tough, chewy texture, made from plain yeast dough that is dropped briefly into nearly boiling water and then baked. [Yiddish *beygel,* ultimately from Middle High German *bouc,* ring, bracelet, from Old High German *boug.*]

bag·ful (băg′fo͝ol′) *n., pl.* **-fuls** or **bagsful.** The amount held by or contained in a bag.

bag·gage (băg′ĭj) *n.* **1.** The trunks, bags, and suitcases in which one carries one's belongings while traveling; luggage. **2.** The movable equipment and supplies of an army; impedimenta. **3.** *Informal.* A badly behaved, impudent, or saucy girl or woman. **4.** A set of ideas, beliefs, theories, or the like, especially when out-of-date or redundant. [Middle English *bagage,* from Old French, from *bague*†, bundle, pack.]

bag·ging (băg′ĭng) *n.* Coarse material used for making bags.

bag·gy (băg′ē) *adj.* **-gier, -giest.** Bulging or hanging loosely: *baggy trousers.* **—bag·gi·ly** *adv.* **—bag·gi·ness** *n.*

Bagh·dad or **Bag·dad** (băg′dăd′). The capital of Iraq since 1920, reputed to be the fabled city of the *Arabian Nights.* Situated on the Tigris River near the center of the country, it was built by the Abbassid caliph al-Mansur (8th century) on the site of an old Babylonian town. Modern Baghdad is an important industrial, commercial, and cultural center in the Arab world.

bag lady *n.* A homeless woman, especially one in a big city, who carries all her possessions in a shopping bag.

bag·man (băg′mən) *n., pl.* **-men** (-mĭn). **1.** *Slang.* A person who collects money for racketeers. **2.** *British.* A traveling salesman. **3.** *Australian.* A tramp; a swagman.

bagn·io (băn′yō) *n., pl.* **-ios. 1.** A brothel. **2.** *Obsolete.* A prison for slaves in the Orient. **3.** *Obsolete.* A public bathhouse in Italy or Turkey. [Italian *bagno,* "bath," from Latin *balneum,* from Greek *balaneion*†.]

bag of bones *n. Informal.* A very thin person or animal.

bag·pipe (băg′pīp′) *n.* Often **bagpipes.** A musical instrument having a flexible bag inflated either by being blown into through a tube with valves or by bellows, a double-reed melody pipe, and from one to four drone pipes. **—bag·pip·er** *n.*

ba·guette (bă-gĕt′) *n.* Also **ba·guet** (for senses 1, 2, 3). **1.** A gem cut into the form of a narrow rectangle. **2.** The form of such a gem. **3.** *Architecture.* A narrow, convex molding. **4.** A long, stick-shaped loaf of French bread. [French, "small rod," from Italian *bacchetta,* diminutive of *bacchio,* rod, from Latin *baculum,* stick, staff.]

bag·worm (băg′wûrm′) *n.* The larva of any of several moths of the family Psychidae, that encloses itself in a characteristic fibrous case, and that feeds upon and destroys tree foliage.

bah (bä, bă) *interj.* Used to express impatient rejection or contempt. [Probably from French (imitative).]

ba·ha·dur (bə-hô′do͝or, -hä′do͝or) *n.* A Hindu title of respect. Often used with the names of army officers. [Hindi *bahādur,* hero, from Persian *bahādur*†, brave.]

Ba·ha·i (bä-hä′ē, -hī′) *adj.* Of, pertaining to, or designating a religion founded in 1863 by the Iranian religious leader Bahaullah (1817–92), developed from **Babism** *(see),* and emphasizing the spiritual unity of all mankind.
—*n.* A teacher of or believer in the Bahai faith. [Persian *bahā'ī,* "of glory," from *Bahā' u'llāh,* Bahaullah, "Glory of God."] **—Ba·ha·ism** (bə-hä′ĭz′əm, -hī′ĭz′əm) *n.* **—Ba·ha·ist** *adj.* & *n.*

Ba·ha·mas (bə-hä′məz). Also **Ba·ha·ma Islands** (-mə). Island state in the Atlantic Ocean, comprising some 700 islands and islets and numerous cays. Columbus made his first landfall here in 1492. The islands became a British colony (1717), internally self-governing (1964), and independent within the Commonwealth (1973). Tourism, including gambling, provides more than 60 percent of state revenues. Agriculture, fishing, and small industries are developing, but 80 percent of food requirements are still imported. Some 80 percent of the people are black descendants of slaves. Area, 13,935 square kilometers (5,379 square miles). Population, 500,000. Capital, Nassau, on New Providence Island. See map at **Cuba.** **—Ba·ha·mi·an** (bə-hā′mē-ən) *adj.* & *n.*

Ba·ha·sa Indonesia (bä-hä′sə) *n.* The Malay language that is the official language of Indonesia.

Bahasa Malaysia *n.* Also **Bahasa Malay.** The Malay language that is the official language of Malaysia.

Ba·hi·a (bä-ē′ə, bə-hē′ə). State of northeast Brazil. Its capital is Salvador (also called Bahia).

Bahía de Cochinos. See **Bay of Pigs.**

Bah·rain or **Bah·rein** (bä-rān′). Arab country comprising a group of low, sandy islands off eastern Arabia. It was the first Arabian state to strike oil (1932), but this is now running out. However, oil revenues have created a welfare state and new industries, including oil refining (of imported and home-produced oil) and ship repairing. Bahrain is also a banking, communications, and tax-free entrepôt center for the Persian Gulf region. Area, 622 square kilometers (240 square miles). Population, 516,000. Capital, Manama, on Bahrain Island. See map at **Gulf States.**

Bahr el Azraq. See **Blue Nile.**

Bahret Lut. See **Dead Sea.**

baht (bät) *n., pl.* **bahts** or **baht. 1.** The basic monetary unit of Thailand, equal to 100 satangs. See feature at **currency. 2.** A note worth one baht. [Thai *bāt.*]

ba·hu·vri·hi (bä′ho͞o-vrē′hē) *adj.* Designating a word made up of two elements, the first of which describes a feature of the second; for example, *graybeard.* Compare **dvandva.** [Sanskrit "having much rice," a compound made in this way.] **—ba·hu·vri·hi** *n.*

Bai·kal or **Bay·kal, Lake** (bī-kôl′, -käl′). The world's deepest lake, located in Siberia in Russia. Its maximum depth is 1,742 meters (5,714 feet), and it covers 31,492 square kilometers (12,159 square miles).

bail¹ (bāl) *n*. **1.** Security, usually a sum of money, exchanged for the release of an arrested person, as a guarantee of his appearance for trial. **2.** Release from imprisonment provided by the payment of such security. **3.** The person who provides such security. —**jump bail.** To fail to appear in court when required after having been allowed bail. —**stand** (or **go**) **bail for.** To supply bail for; act as security for. ~*tr.v.* **bailed, bailing, bails. 1.** To secure the release of (a person) by providing bail. Often used with *out*. **2.** To release (a person) for whom bail has been paid. **3.** To deliver or transfer (property) to another for a special purpose, but without permanent transference of ownership. [Middle English *baile*, "custody," from Old French *bail*, from *baillier*, to take charge of, carry, from Latin *bājulāre*, from *bājulus*†, carrier.] —**bail·er** *n*.

bail² *v*. **bailed, bailing, bails.** Also *chiefly British* **bale.** —*tr.* **1.** To remove (water) from a boat by repeatedly filling a container and emptying it over the side. **2.** To empty (a boat) of water by this means. Usually used with *out*. —*intr*. To empty a boat of water by scooping or dipping. ~*n*. Also *chiefly British* **bale.** A container used for bailing. [Middle English *baille*, bucket, from Old French *baille*, probably from Vulgar Latin *bājula* (unattested), "carrier (of water)," from Latin *bājulus*, carrier. See **bail** (security).] —**bail·er** *n*.

bail³, bale (bāl) *n*. **1.** The arched, hooplike handle of a pail, kettle, or similar container. **2.** An arch or hoop, such as those used to support the top of a covered wagon. **3.** *Australian & New Zealand.* A frame used to secure the head of a cow while it is being milked. —**bail up.** *Australian & New Zealand.* To secure (a cow) in a bail. [Middle English *baile*, handle, probably from Old Norse *beygla*, bow, from *beygja* to bend.]

bail⁴ *n*. **1.** *Cricket.* One of the two small bars of wood placed across the top of the stumps to form the wicket. **2.** A pole or bar used to separate horses in an open stable. **3.** The hinged bar on a typewriter holding the paper against the platen. —**bail up.** *Australian.* **1.** To hold up in order to rob. **2.** To accost in order to speak to. [Middle English, from Old French *bail(e)*, enclosed court, from *bailler*† to enclose.]

bail·a·ble (bā′lə-bəl) *adj*. **1.** Eligible for bail. **2.** Allowing or admitting of bail: *a bailable offense.*

Baile Átha Cliath. See **Dublin.**

bail·ee (bā-lē′) *n*. A person to whom property is bailed.

bai·ley (bā′lē) *n., pl.* **-leys.** The outer wall of a castle or the space enclosed by it. [Middle English *bailly, baile*, variant of BAIL (in cricket).]

Bailey bridge *n*. A temporary steel bridge that can be assembled rapidly from prefabricated parts. [Designed by Sir Donald *Bailey* (1901–85), British engineer.]

bail·ie (bā′lē) *n*. A Scottish municipal magistrate, elected by town councilors. [Middle English *bailli*, from Old French, variant of *baillif*, BAILIFF.]

bail·iff (bā′lĭf) *n*. **1.** A court attendant entrusted with a variety of duties, such as the custody of prisoners under arraignment, the protection of jurors, and the maintenance of order in a courtroom during a trial. **2.** An official who assists a British sheriff and who has the power to execute writs, processes, and arrests. **3.** *Chiefly British.* An agent who administers an estate on behalf of a landowner; a steward. [Middle English *baillif*, from Old French, from Medieval Latin *bājulīvus*, from Latin *bājulus*, carrier, "person in charge." See **bail** (security).]

bail·i·wick (bā′lĭ-wĭk′) *n*. **1.** The office or district of a bailiff. **2.** A person's specific area of interest, skill, or authority. [Middle English *bailliwik* : BAILIE + WICK.]

bail·ment (bāl′mənt) *n. Law.* **1.** The process of providing bail for an accused person. **2.** The act of delivering goods or personal property to another in trust.

bail·or (bā′lər, bā-lôr′) *n. Law.* A person who bails property to another.

bail out *intr.v.* **1.** To parachute from an aircraft. **2.** *Slang.* To abandon a project or enterprise. —*tr.v. Informal.* To extricate (another) from a difficult situation.

bail-out (bāl′out′) *n*. A rescue from financial difficulties.

bails·man (bālz′mən) *n., pl.* **-men** (-mĭn). *Law.* One who provides bail or security for another.

Bai·ly's beads (bā′lēz) *pl. n.* Bright spots of sunlight that appear briefly around the edge of the moon's disk immediately before and after the central phase in a solar eclipse, caused by the sun's shining through lunar valleys. [After Francis *Baily* (1774–1844), British astronomer.]

bain-ma·rie (băn′mə-rē′) *n., pl.* **bains-ma·rie** (băn′mə-rē′). A device consisting of a large pan containing hot water in which smaller pans may be set to cook the contents slowly or keep them warm. [French, from Medieval Latin *balneum Mariae*, "bath of Mary" (mistranslation of Medieval Greek *kaminos Marias*, "furnace of Mary"), after *Mary*, sister of Moses and an alleged alchemist.]

Bai·ram (bī-räm′, bī′räm′) *n*. Either of two Muslim festivals occurring after Ramadan: *Lesser Bairam* occurs at the end of Ramadan and lasts for 3 days; *Greater Bairam* occurs 70 days later and lasts for 4 days. [Turkish *bayrām*.]

Baird (bârd), **John Logie** (1888–1946). British electrical engineer noted for his pioneering work in the field of television and in the use of radar and fiber optics.

bairn (bârn) *n. Scottish.* A child. [Middle English *barn*, Old English *bearn*.]

Bairns·fa·ther (bärnz′fä′thər), **Charles Bruce** (1888–1959). British cartoonist and author, famous for his World War I cartoon character "Old Bill."

bait¹ (bāt) *n*. **1.** Food or other lure placed on a hook or in a trap and used in the catching of fish, birds, or other animals. **2.** Any enticement; a temptation. **3.** *Chiefly British.* **a.** A stop for food or rest during a journey or a break from work. **b.** The food or drink consumed during such a break. ~*v*. **baited, baiting, baits.** —*tr.* **1.** To place food or other lure in or on (a trap or fishing hook). **2.** To lure or entice, especially by trickery or strategy. **3.** To set dogs upon (a chained animal, for example) for sport. **4.** To attack or torment, especially with persistent insult, criticism, or ridicule. **5.** To tease. **6.** *Archaic.* To feed (an animal) on a journey. —*intr. Archaic.* To stop for food or rest during a journey. —See Synonyms at **harass.** [Middle English, partly from Old Norse *beita*, to hunt with dogs, harass, and partly from Old Norse *beita* (a separate word), pasture, food, fish bait.] —**bait·er** *n*.

bait². *Falconry.* Variant of **bate.**

bai·za (bī′zä) *n*. A monetary unit of Oman equal to ¹/₁,₀₀₀ of the rial-omani. See feature at **currency.** [Arabic, from Hindi *paisā*.]

baize (bāz) *n*. A cotton or woolen material resembling felt, often bright green in color, and used chiefly as a cover for gaming and billiard tables. [French *baie* (plural *baies*), from *bai*, BAY (probably its original color).]

Baja California. See **Lower California.**

bake (bāk) *v*. **baked, baking, bakes.** —*tr.* **1. a.** To cook with continuous, even, dry heat, especially in an oven. **b.** To make by baking: *bake a cake; bake bread.* **2.** To harden, dry, or otherwise affect by subjecting to heat in or as if in an oven. —*intr.* **1.** To cook food, primarily bread, cakes, or pastry, by baking. **2.** To become cooked by baking. **3.** To become hard, dry, or otherwise affected by exposure to steady, dry heat. **4.** *Informal.* To feel very hot. ~*n*. **1. a.** The act or process of baking. **b.** The amount baked. **2.** A social gathering at which food is baked and served. Sometimes used in combination: *a clambake.* [Middle English *baken*, Old English *bacan*.]

baked Alaska *n*. A dessert consisting of ice cream covered with meringue, which is baked for a short time at a high temperature.

Ba·ke·lite (bā′kə-līt′) *n*. A trademark for any of a group of thermosetting plastics having high chemical and electrical resistance and used in a variety of manufactured articles. [After Leo BAEKELAND.]

bak·er (bā′kər) *n*. **1.** One who bakes and sells bread, cakes, or the like. **2.** A portable oven.

Bak·er, Mount (bā′kər). Peak, 3,287 meters (10,778 feet) high, in northwestern Washington, in the Cascade Range just south of the Canadian border.

baker's dozen *n*. A group of 13; one dozen plus one. [After the former custom among bakers of adding an extra roll to every dozen purchased as a safeguard against the possibility that 12 rolls might weigh light.]

Bak·ers·field (bā′kərz-fēld′). A city in south-central California, at the southern end of the fertile San Joaquin Valley. It is an oil, mining, and agricultural center. Gold was discovered in the region in 1855 and petroleum in 1899.

bak·er·y (bā′kə-rē) *n., pl.* **-ies. 1.** A place where products such as bread, cake, and pastries are baked. Also called "bakehouse." **2.** A shop where baked goods are sold. In this sense, also called "bakeshop."

bak·ing (bā′kĭng) *n*. **1.** The act or process of baking. **2.** The amount baked. ~*adj. Informal.* Extremely hot. ~*adv.* Used as an intensive: *baking hot.*

baking powder *n*. Any of various powdered mixtures of sodium bicarbonate, starch, and at least one slightly acidic compound such as cream of tartar, used as a raising agent in baking.

baking soda *n*. A chemical compound, **sodium bicarbonate** (see).

ba·kla·va (bä′klə-vä′) *n*. A dessert made of paper-thin layers of pastry, chopped nuts, and honey. [Turkish.]

bak·sheesh (băk′shēsh′) *n*. Also **bak·shish, back·sheesh, back·shish.** In Turkey, Egypt, India, and other Eastern countries, a tip, gratuity, or charitable gift. [Persian *bakhshīsh*, from *bakhshīdan*, to give.]

Bakst (bäkst), **Léon** (c. 1866–1924). Russian artist noted for his work in modernizing theater design. His best-known works were for ballets produced by Sergei Diaghilev in Paris.

Ba·ku (bä-kōo′). Capital city of Azerbaijan, on the Caspian Sea. Since the 1870's it has been a center of oil production.

Ba·ku·nin (bə-kōo′nĭn, bä-), **Mikhail Aleksandrovich** (1814–76). Russian anarchist and political theorist. Imprisoned in Russia for his revolutionary activities and exiled to Siberia, he escaped to London (1861). After many arguments with Marx, his brand of anarchism took final shape as the antithesis of Marx's communism.

BAL¹ (bāl) *n*. A colorless, oily, viscous liquid, $C_3H_5(SH)_2(OH)$, used as an antidote for poisoning caused by lewisite, organic arsenic compounds, and heavy metals including mercury and gold. [B(RITISH) + A(NTI-) + L(EWISITE).]

BAL² *n. Computer Science.* A low-level assembly language. [B(ASIC) A(SSEMBLY) L(ANGUAGE).]

bal. balance.

bal·a·cla·va (băl′ə-klä′və) *n*. Sometimes **Balaclava. 1.** A woolen hood almost completely covering the head and neck. **2.** A similar hood often covering the shoulders as well, worn by soldiers and sailors, and originally worn by soldiers fighting in the Crimean

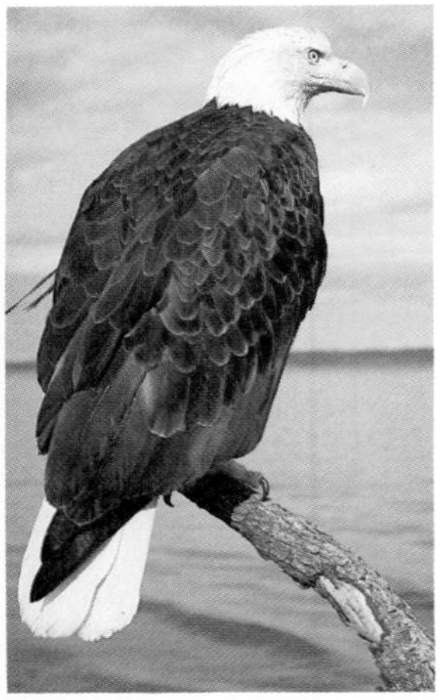

bald eagle *In their spectacular courtship display, a pair of bald eagles may plummet through the air with their claws locked together, breaking apart just before they reach the ground. The bald eagle, which nests near water, is native to North America and is the national emblem of the United States. It is classified as an endangered species.*

War. Also called "balaclava helmet." [After BALAKLAVA.]

Ba·la·kla·va (băl′ə-klä′və). A small port in southern Crimea in Ukraine, now part of Sevastopol. It is famous for the battle between Russian troops and Turkish and British troops (1854) in the Crimean War, during which the British Light Brigade made a hopeless charge against heavy Russian guns.

bal·a·lai·ka (băl′ə-lī′kə) *n.* A Russian musical instrument with a triangular body and three strings. [Russian.]

bal·ance (băl′əns) *n. Abbr.* **bal.** **1. a.** A weighing device typically consisting of a rigid beam, horizontally suspended by a low-friction support at its center, with identical weighing pans hung at either end, one of which holds an unknown weight while the effective weight in the other is changed by known amounts until the beam is level and motionless. Also called "beam balance." **b.** Any of various other weighing devices, such as a **spring balance** *(see).* **2.** A critical state in which the outcome is still to be determined: *lives hanging in the balance.* **3.** A stable state characterized by cancellation of all forces, weights, or the like by equal opposing ones. **4.** A state of bodily equilibrium. **5.** A stable mental or psychological state; emotional equilibrium. **6.** A harmonious or satisfying arrangement or proportion of parts or elements, as in a design or composition. **7. a.** An influence or force tending to produce equilibrium; a counterpoise. **b.** A control or mechanism for achieving balance; specifically, a control balancing the average sound level from a high-fidelity system. **8.** The difference in magnitude between opposing forces, weights, or influences, representing the excess held by one side over another: *The balance of control lies with the parents.* **9. a.** Equality of totals in the debit and credit sides of an account. **b.** The difference between such totals, either on the credit or the debit side of an account. **10.** *Informal.* Anything that remains or is left over. **11.** *Chemistry.* Equality of the number, kinds, and net electric charge of reacting species on each side of a chemical equation. **12.** *Mathematics.* Equality with respect to the net number of reduced symbolic quantities on each side of an equation. **13.** A **balance wheel** *(see).* **14.** A dance movement first toward and then away from one's partner. **15. Balance.** *Astronomy.* A constellation and sign of the zodiac, **Libra** *(see).* —See Synonyms at **proportion, remainder.** **—on balance.** All things considered. **—strike a balance.** To achieve a state or position between extremes.

∼*v.* **balanced, -ancing, -ances.** —*tr.* **1.** To weigh or poise in or as if in a balance. **2.** To compare as if weighing in the mind. **3.** To bring into or maintain in a state of equilibrium. **4.** To act as an equalizing weight or force to; offset; counterbalance. **5. a.** To calculate the difference between the debits and credits of (an account). **b.** To reconcile or equalize the sums of the debits and credits of (an account). **c.** To settle by paying what is owed. **6.** To bring into or keep in equal or satisfying proportion or harmony. **7.** *Mathematics.* To bring (an equation) into mathematical balance. **8.** *Chemistry.* To bring (a chemical equation) into chemical balance. **9.** To move toward and then away from (one's dance partner). —*intr.* **1.** To be in or come into equilibrium. **2.** To be equal or equivalent. **3.** To sway or waver as if losing or regaining equilibrium. **4.** To be in or come into a state of balance. Used of a chemical or mathematical equation. **5.** To move toward and then away from one's dance partner. [Middle English, from Old French, from Vulgar Latin *bilancia* (unattested), scales, from Late Latin *(lībra) bilanx* (stem *bilanc-*), (a balance) having two scales : Latin *bi-*, double + *lanx*†, scale, plate, pan.]

balance of nature *n.* The state of stability achieved by plant and animal communities in their natural environment by means of such interactions as adaptation and competition.

balance of payments *n.* A systematic recording of a nation's total payments to foreign countries and international institutions, including the price of imports and the outflow of capital and gold, and its total receipts from abroad, including the price of exports and the inflow of capital and gold.

balance of power *n.* **1.** A distribution of power between nations, often by means of alliance and counteralliance, whereby no one nation is able to dominate or conquer the others. **2.** Any similar distribution of power.

balance of terror *n.* A balance of power between nations, especially the Eastern and Western blocs, maintained by an equivalent distribution of nuclear weapons.

balance of trade *n.* The difference in value between the total exports and imports of a nation.

bal·anc·er (băl′ən-sər) *n.* **1.** One that balances. **2.** A rudimentary insect wing, a **halter** *(see).*

balance sheet *n. Abbr.* **B.S.** A statement of the assets and liabilities of a business, association, or individual at a given date.

balance wheel *n.* A wheel that regulates rate of movement in machine parts; especially, a wheel that swings back and forth against a hair spring in a watch or small clock. Also called "balance."

Bal·an·chine (băl′ən-chēn′), **George,** born Georgy Melitonovich Balanchivadze (1904–83). Russian-born U.S. ballet dancer, choreographer, and director. In 1948 he was appointed artistic director of the New York City Ballet. He choreographed over 100 ballets, including *Firebird* (1950) and *Don Quixote* (1965).

Ba·la·ra·ma (bŭl′ə-rä′mə). *Hinduism.* See **Rama.**

bal·as (băl′əs) *n.* A rose-red to orange spinel, used as a semiprecious gem. [Middle English, from Old French *balais,* from Medieval Latin *balascus,* from Arabic *bálakhsh,* from Persian *Badhakhshān,* a region in northeastern Iran, where the gem is found.]

ba·la·ta (bə-lä′tə) *n.* **1.** A tropical American tree, *Manilkara bidentata,* that yields a latexlike sap. **2.** A tough, nonelastic gum obtained from this sap and used for golf-ball covers, industrial belting, and gaskets. [American Spanish, from Cariban.]

Ba·la·ton, Lake (băl′ə-tŏn′). The largest lake in Central Europe, situated in western Hungary. It has an area of 600 square kilometers (230 square miles) and many lakeside resorts.

bal·bo·a (băl-bō′ə) *n.* **1.** The basic monetary unit of Panama, equal to 100 centesimos. See feature at **currency.** **2.** A coin worth one balboa. [After Vasco Núñez de BALBOA.]

Bal·bo·a (băl-bō′ə), **Vasco Núñez de** (1475–1519). Spanish explorer. While serving as governor of Darién on the Isthmus of Panama, he heard stories of a great body of water to the south. He set out with an exploring party on September 1, 1513, and on September 25 first sighted the Pacific Ocean, which he called El Mar del Sur (the South Sea).

bal·brig·gan (băl-brĭg′ən) *n.* **1.** A knitted unbleached cotton fabric, often used in the manufacture of underwear. **2.** *Usually* **balbriggans.** Underwear made of this fabric. [After *Balbriggan,* Irish seaport where it was first manufactured.]

bal·co·ny (băl′kə-nē) *n., pl.* **-nies.** **1.** A platform that projects from the wall of a building and is surrounded by a railing, balustrade, or parapet. **2.** A gallery that projects over the main floor in a theater or auditorium. [Italian *balcone,* from Germanic *balkon* (unattested).]

bald (bôld) *adj.* **balder, baldest.** **1.** Having little or no hair on the top of the head. **2.** Lacking natural or usual covering: *a bald spot on the lawn.* **3.** Having the tread worn away through use. Said of a tire. **4.** Having white feathers or markings on the head: *a bald eagle.* **5.** Lacking ornament; bare; unadorned. **6.** Undisguised; blunt: *a bald statement.* [Middle English *ballede,* perhaps Old English *bællede* (unattested), from *ball-* (unattested), "white patch."] **—bald·ly** *adv.* **—bald·ness** *n.*

bal·da·chin, bal·da·quin (bôl′də-kĭn, băl′-) *n.* Also **bal·da·chi·no** (băl′də-kē′nō). **1.** A rich fabric of silk and gold brocade. **2.** A canopy of fabric carried in church processions or placed over an altar, throne, or dais. **3.** *Architecture.* A stone or marble structure built in the form of a canopy, especially over the altar of a church. [Italian *baldacchino,* from Old Italian, from *Baldacco,* BAGHDAD, famous in the Middle Ages for its brocades.]

bald cypress *n.* A cone-bearing but deciduous tree, *Taxodium distichum,* of the southeastern United States, growing in swamps and damp ground.

bald eagle *n.* A North American eagle, *Haliaeetus leucocephalus,* having a dark body and a white head and tail. It appears on the national emblem of the United States. Also called "American eagle."

Bal·der (bôl′dər). *Norse Mythology.* The god of peace and light, son of Odin and Frigg, renowned for his goodness and beauty.

bal·der·dash (bôl′dər-dăsh′) *n.* Nonsense. [16th century ("froth," "mixture of drinks") : origin obscure.]

bald-faced (bôld′fāst′) *adj.* **1.** Having a white face or face markings. **2.** Brash; undisguised.

bald·head (bôld′hĕd′) *n.* **1.** A person whose head is bald. **2.** Any of several birds having white markings on the head.

bald·head·ed (bôld′hĕd′ĭd) *adj.* Having a bald head.

balding (bôl′dĭng) *adj.* Becoming bald.

bald·pate (bôld′pāt′) *n.* **1.** A baldheaded person. **2.** An American duck, the **widgeon** *(see).*

bal·dric (bôl′drĭk) *n.* A belt, usually of ornamented leather, worn over one shoulder and across the chest to support a sword or bugle. [Middle English *baud(e)rik,* from Old French *baldrei, baudrei*†.]

Bald·win (bôld′wĭn), **James Arthur** (1924–87). U.S. author and dramatist whose first novel, *Go Tell It on the Mountain* (1953), was based on his early experiences of religion and deprivation in Harlem, New York City.

Baldwin, Stanley, 1st Earl Baldwin of Bewdley (1867–1947). British Conservative prime minister (1923–29; 1935–37). As prime minister, he responded to the General Strike of 1926 with an anti-union bill, the Trade Disputes Act of 1927, and was at the political center of the events leading to Edward VIII's abdication.

bale¹ (bāl) *n. Abbr.* **bl.** A large bound package or bundle of raw or processed material.

∼*tr.v.* **baled, baling, bales.** To wrap or form into bales. [Middle English, probably from Old French, from Germanic.] **—bal·er** *n.*

bale² *n. Poetic.* **1.** Evil influence. **2.** Mental suffering; anguish. [Middle English *bale,* Old English *bealu,* from Germanic.]

bale³. Variant of **bail** (to empty a boat).

bale⁴. Variant of **bail** (hoop or hooplike device).

Bâle. See **Basel.**

Bal·e·ar·ic Islands (băl′ē-ăr′ĭk). *Spanish* **Is·las Ba·le·a·res** (ēz′läz bä′lā-ä′rās). Archipelago in the Mediterranean, off the east coast of Spain. A Spanish province, it includes the islands of Mallorca (Majorca), Menorca (Minorca), Ibiza, and Formentera. Because of the islands' mild climate, the principal local industry is tourism.

ba·leen (bə-lēn′) *n.* **Whalebone** *(see).* [Middle English *balene,* whale, baleen, from Old French *baleine,* from Latin *balaena,* whale.]

bale·ful (bāl′fəl) *adj.* **1.** Harmful or malignant in intent or effect. **2.** Portending evil; dire. **—bale·ful·ly** *adv.* **—bale·ful·ness** *n.*

Usage: *Baleful* and *baneful* overlap in meaning, but *baleful* usually applies to that which menaces or foreshadows evil: *a baleful look. Baneful* is used most often of that which is actually harmful or destructive: *the baneful effects of pollution.*

PRONUNCIATION KEY

ă, pat; ā, pay; âr, care;
ä, father, are; b, bib;
ch, church; d, deed; ĕ, pet;
ē, be; f, fife; g, gag; h, hat;
hw, which; ĭ, pit; ī, pie;
îr, pier; j, judge; k, kick;
l, lid, needle; m, mum;
n, no, sudden; ng, thing;
ŏ, pot; ō, toe; ô, paw, for;
oi, noise; ou, out; ŏŏ, book;
ōō, boot; p, pop; r, roar;
s, sauce; sh, ship, dish;
t, tight; th, thin, path;
th, this, bathe; ŭ, cut; ûr, fur;
v, valve; w, with; y, yes;
z, zebra, size; zh, vision;
ə, about, item, edible, gallop, circus, peaceful

IN FOREIGN WORDS:

à, *Fr.* ami; œ, *Fr.* feu, *Ger.* schön; ü, *Fr.* tu, *Ger.* über;
KH, *Ger.* ich, *Scot.* loch;
N, *Fr.* bon; y′, *Fr.* Compiègne

STRESS MARKS:

Primary stress: ′
in·cite′ (ĭn-sīt′)
Secondary stress: ′
in′sight′ (ĭn′sīt′)

Ba·len·ci·a·ga (bə-lĕn'sē-ä'gə), **Cristóbal** (1895–1972). Spanish fashion designer. He settled in Paris in 1937 and became noted for his stark, elegant designs.

Bal·four (băl'fo͝or'), **Arthur James, 1st Earl** (1848–1930). British Conservative prime minister (1902–05). He served as foreign secretary in Lloyd George's cabinet from 1916 to 1919.

Balfour Declaration *n.* A statement by A.J. Balfour on November 2, 1917, that Britain would support the establishment of a national home for Jews in Palestine, on condition that the rights of existing non-Jewish communities there would be safeguarded.

Ba·li (bä'lē). Indonesian island east of Java. Mountainous and volcanic with a tropical climate and fertile soil, it is sometimes called the "Jewel of the East." The Balinese are renowned for the delicacy of their arts and crafts. Bali resisted the spread of Islam through Indonesia in the 16th and 17th centuries and has been Hindu since the 7th century A.D.

Ba·li·nese (bä'lə-nēz', -nēs') *adj.* Of or pertaining to Bali, its people, culture, or language.
~*n.* **1.** A native or inhabitant of Bali. **2.** The Indonesian language spoken in Bali.

Baliol, John de. See **Balliol.**

balk (bôk) *v.* **balked, balking, balks.** Also **baulk.** --*intr.* **1.** To stop short and refuse to go on. **2.** To refuse obstinately or show great reluctance; shrink. Used with *at*: *He balked at the very idea of compromise.* **3.** *Sports.* To make an incomplete or misleading move, especially an illegal one. —*tr.* **1.** To put obstacles in the way of; check or thwart. **2.** *Archaic.* To allow to go by; miss: *balk an opportunity.* —See Synonyms at **frustrate, hinder.**
~*n.* Also **baulk. 1.** A hindrance, check, or defeat. **2.** A blunder or failure. **3. a.** In baseball, an illegal move; especially, a false move made by the pitcher to throw the ball when there are runners on base. **b.** In various other sports, an incomplete or misleading move. **4. a.** An unplowed strip of land. **b.** A ridge between furrows. **5.** A wooden beam or rafter. **6.** On a billiard table, the space between the cushion and the balk line. [Old English *balc,* ridge, hindrance, from Old Norse *bálkr,* partition, from Germanic *balkuz* (unattested).] **—balk·er** *n.*

Bal·kan (bôl'kən) *adj.* Of or pertaining to the Balkans or their inhabitants.

Bal·kan·ize (bôl'kə-nīz') *tr.v.* **-ized, -izing, -izes.** *Sometimes* **balkanize.** To divide (a region or territory) into small, often mutually hostile, units. [From the division of the Balkan countries by the Great Powers in the early 20th century.] **—Bal·kan·i·za·tion** *n.*

Bal·kans (bôl'kənz). Also **Balkan Peninsula.** Region of southeast Europe. Formerly part of the Roman and Byzantine empires, it broke into rival states, which, with the exception of Montenegro, fell to the Ottoman Turks by 1500. Nationalist movements arose, and by 1908 Greece, Romania, Bulgaria, Serbia, and Montenegro were independent; but Bosnia, Croatia, Dalmatia, and Hercegovina were part of Austria-Hungary, and Macedonia, Albania, and Thrace were still Turkish. The First Balkan War (1912–13) resulted in independence for Albania and the division of Macedonia between Bulgaria, Greece, Montenegro, and Serbia. The Second Balkan War (1913) and World War I, largely the result of Austrian pressure on Serbia, led to the emergence of Yugoslavia, comprising Serbia, Montenegro, Bosnia and Hercegovina, Dalmatia, Slovenia, and part of Macedonia. In 1992, Croatia, Slovenia, Bosnia and Hercegovina, and Macedonia withdrew from Yugoslavia.

Bal·kis (băl'kĭs). The Queen of Sheba in the Koran.

balk line *n.* On a billiard table, a line drawn parallel to one end, from behind which a player makes the opening shot.

balk·y (bô'kē) *adj.* **-ier, -iest.** Given to stopping at obstacles, real or imagined. Said especially of horses.

ball[1] (bôl) *n.* **1. a.** A spherical or almost spherical body. **b.** Anything approximately spherical: *a ball of flame.* **2. a.** Any of various rounded movable objects used in sports and games. **b.** A game, especially baseball, played with such an object. **3. a.** *Sports.* A ball moving, thrown, hit, or kicked in a particular manner: *a low ball.* **b.** *Cricket.* One delivery of the ball by the bowler. **4. a.** A solid projectile of spherical or pointed shape, such as that shot from a cannon. **b.** Projectiles of this kind collectively. **5.** A rounded part or protuberance, especially of the body: *the ball of the foot.* **6.** *Mathematics.* A three-dimensional region formed by the set of points that are less than a fixed distance from a given point; the interior of a sphere. **—keep the ball rolling.** To make sure that a project, event, or the like continues. **—on the ball.** *Slang.* Alert, competent, or efficient. **—play ball. 1.** To begin or resume a ball game or other activity. **2.** *Informal.* To cooperate. **—set** (or **start**) **the ball rolling.** *Informal.* To get something under way.
~*v.* **balled, balling, balls.** —*tr.* To form into a ball. —*intr.* To become formed into a ball. [Middle English *bal,* from Old Norse *böllr,* from Germanic *balluz* (unattested).]

ball[2] *n.* A formal gathering for social dancing. **—have a ball.** *Informal.* To have a very enjoyable time. [French *bal,* from Old French, from *baller,* to dance, from Late Latin *ballāre,* from Greek *ballizein.*]

Ball (bôl), **John** (died 1381). English priest and rebel who became one of the leaders of the Peasants' Revolt (1381) and was executed after the failure of the revolt.

Ball, Lucille (1911–1989). U.S. comedienne. After a moderately successful career as a model and film actress, she premiered in the television series "I Love Lucy" in 1951. It was a hit show for six seasons and still appears around the world in syndication. A fine comedienne who ranged from slapstick to pathos, Ball appeared in several other television series, musical comedies, and motion pictures.

bal·lad (băl'əd) *n.* **1.** A narrative peom, often of folk origin and intended to be sung, consisting of simple stanzas and usually having a recurrent refrain. **2.** The music for such a poem. **3.** A popular song of a romantic or sentimental nature, in which the same melody is used for each stanza. [Middle English *balade,* from Old French *ballade,* from Provençal *balada,* piece to be accompanied by dancing, from *balar,* to dance, from Late Latin *ballāre.* See **ball** (dance).]

bal·lade (bə-läd', bă-) *n.* **1.** *Prosody.* A verse form usually consisting of three stanzas of eight or ten lines each, with the same concluding line in each stanza, and an envoy, or brief final stanza, ending with the same last line as that of the preceding stanzas. **2.** A musical composition, usually for the piano, having the romantic or dramatic quality of a ballad. [Earlier form of BALLAD.]

bal·lad·eer (băl'ə-dîr') *n.* One who sings ballads.

bal·lad·ist (băl'ə-dĭst') *n.* A singer or writer of ballads.

bal·lad·ry (băl'ə-drē) *n.* Ballads collectively.

ballad stanza *n.* A four-line stanza often used in ballads, rhyming in the second and fourth lines, and having four metrical feet in the first and third lines, and three in the second and fourth.

ball-and-sock·et joint (bôl'ən-sŏk'ĭt) *n.* **1.** A joint consisting of a spherical knob or knoblike part fitted into a socket so that some degree of motion is possible in nearly any direction. **2.** *Anatomy.* A freely movable joint, such as the hip or shoulder joint, in which the rounded head of a long bone fits into a rounded cavity.

bal·last (băl'əst) *n.* **1.** Any heavy material placed in the hold of a ship or the gondola of a balloon to enhance stability. **2.** Coarse gravel or crushed rock laid to form a bed for roads or railroads. **3.** That which gives stability, especially to character. **4.** *Electronics.* A circuit element, such as a resistor, used to stabilize or maintain the current in a circuit.
~*tr.v.* **ballasted, -lasting, -lasts. 1.** To stabilize or provide with ballast. **2.** To fill (a road or railroad bed) with ballast. [Perhaps from Old Swedish or Old Danish *barlast,* "bare load" (cargo carried only for its weight) : *bar,* bare + *last,* load.]

ball bearing *n.* **1.** A friction-reducing bearing, consisting essentially of a ring-shaped track containing freely revolving hard metal balls against which a rotating shaft or other part turns, either in direct contact with the balls or with a second matched ring. **2.** A hard ball used in such a bearing.

ball boy *n.* In tennis, a court attendant who collects the ball when it is out of play.

ball cock *n.* A self-regulating device controlling the supply of water in a tank, cistern, or toilet by means of a floating hollow ball connected to a valve that opens or closes with a change in water level.

bal·le·ri·na (băl'ə-rē'nə) *n.* **1.** A principal female dancer in a corps de ballet. **2.** Any female ballet dancer. Compare **prima ballerina.** [Italian, from *ballare,* to dance. See **ball** (dance).]

bal·let (bă-lā', băl'ā') *n.* **1.** An artistic dance form characterized by grace and precision of movement and an elaborate formal technique. Sometimes preceded by *the.* **2.** A theatrical presentation of group or solo dancing to a musical accompaniment, usually in costume and with scenic effects, and conveying a story, theme, or atmosphere. **3.** A musical composition written or used for ballet. **4.** A company or group that performs ballet. [French, from Italian *balletto,* diminutive of *ballo,* a dance. See **ball** (dance).] **—bal·let·ic** (bă-lĕt'ĭk) *adj.*

bal·let·o·mane (bă-lĕt'ə-măn') *n.* An ardent admirer of the ballet. [Blend of BALLET and MANIA.] **—bal·let·o·ma·ni·a** (bă-lĕt'ə-mā'nē-ə, -mān'yə) *n.*

ball·flow·er (bôl'flou'ər) *n.* *Architecture.* An ornament in the form of a ball cupped in the petals of a circular flower.

ball game *n.* **1.** A game played with a ball. **2.** *Informal.* A state of affairs; business: *This makes the election a whole new ball game.*

ball girl *n.* In tennis, a court attendant who collects the ball when it is out of play.

Bal·liol or **Bal·iol** (bāl'yəl, bā'lē-əl), **John de** (1249–1315). Scottish king, given the Scottish crown (1292) by Edward I of England, who acted as arbitrator in the contest for the throne. Balliol rose against English domination (1295), but was defeated by the English (1296) and fled to France.

bal·lis·ta (bə-lĭs'tə) *n., pl.* **-tae** (-tē'). A military engine used in ancient and medieval warfare to hurl heavy projectiles. [Latin, from Greek *ballein,* to throw.]

bal·lis·tic (bə-lĭs'tĭk) *adj.* **1.** Of or pertaining to ballistics. **2.** Of or pertaining to projectiles, their motion, or their effects. **3.** Of, pertaining to, or designating a measuring instrument that relies on a short impulse or current pulse to cause a movement, the magnitude of which is related to the quantity to be measured: *a ballistic galvanometer.* [From BALLISTA.] **—bal·list·i·cal·ly** *adv.*

ballistic missile *n.* A projectile that assumes a free-falling trajectory after an internally guided, self-powered ascent. Compare **guided missile.**

bal·lis·tics (bə-lĭs'tĭks) *n.* *Used with a singular verb.* **1. a.** The study of the dynamics of projectiles. **b.** The study of the flight characteristics of projectiles. **2. a.** The study of the functioning of firearms. **b.** The study of the firing, flight, and effect of ammunition. **—bal·lis·ti·cian** (băl'ĭ-stĭsh'ən) *n.*

ball lightning *n.* A rare form of atmospheric lightning in which the electrical discharge occurs as a slow-moving, luminous sphere of ionized gas. Also called "fireball."

ball of fire *n.* *Informal.* A lively, dynamic person.

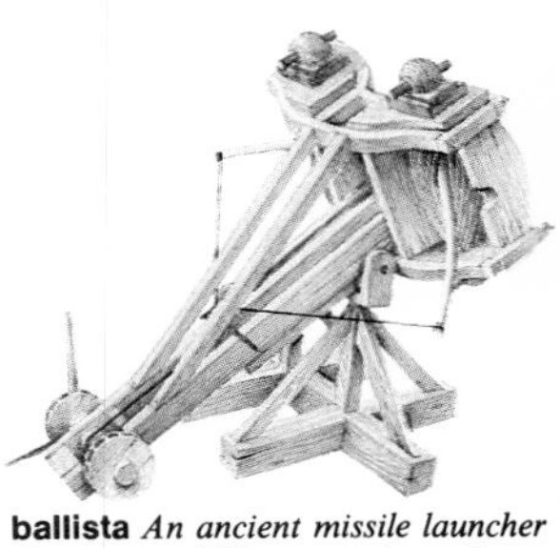

ballista *An ancient missile launcher that operated like a crossbow: the two arms were pulled back, then released to fire the missile.*

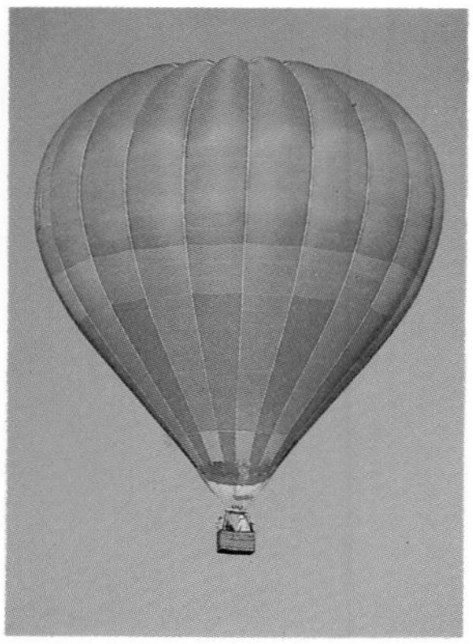

balloon *The earliest 18th-century balloons were filled with air, heated by burning wood or straw. In this modern hot-air balloon, however, the air is heated by a gas burner. Other balloons are inflated with gases that are lighter than air: hydrogen or, more usually, helium.*

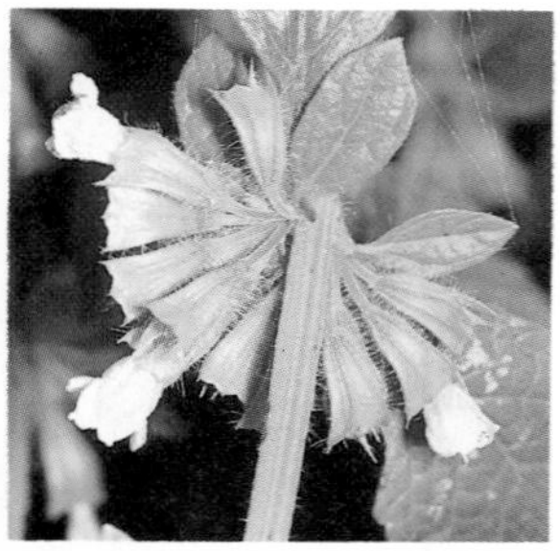

balm Melissa officinalis, *or balm, is a fragrant perennial herb native to Europe. The stems and lemon-scented leaves have long been used for medicinal purposes, and today the plant is sometimes used as a mild stimulant or tonic.*

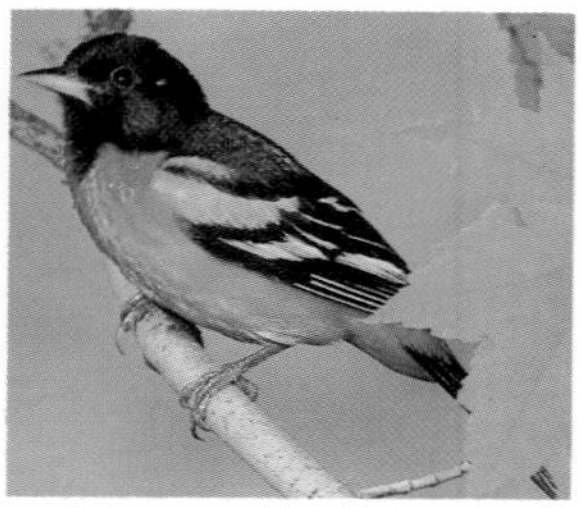

Baltimore oriole *The most common oriole in North America east of the Rockies. Migrating flocks of Baltimore orioles sometimes raid orchards, causing considerable damage to fruit crops.*

bal·lo·net (băl′ə-nā′) *n.* One of several small auxiliary gasbags placed inside a balloon or a nonrigid airship that can be inflated or deflated during flight to control and maintain shape and buoyancy. [French *ballonnet,* diminutive of *ballon,* BALLOON.]

bal·loon (bə-lo͞on′) *n.* **1.** A spherical or pear-shaped, flexible, nonporous bag inflated with a gas lighter than air, such as helium, that causes it to rise and float in the atmosphere; especially, such a bag with sufficient capacity to lift a suspended gondola. See **barrage balloon, hot-air balloon. 2.** A small brightly colored, inflatable rubber bag used as a toy or decoration. **3.** A rounded or irregularly shaped outline containing the words a character in a cartoon is represented as saying.
∼*v.* **ballooned, -looning, -loons.** —*intr.* **1.** To ascend or ride in a balloon. **2.** To expand or swell out like a balloon. —*tr.* To cause to expand by or as if by inflating. [French *ballon,* from Italian *ballone,* augmentative of *balla,* BALL.] **—bal·loon·ist** *n.*

balloon flower *n.* A plant, *Platycodon grandiflorum,* native to Asia, cultivated for its showy, blue, bell-shaped flowers.

balloon sail *n.* A comparatively large foresail, used when going before the wind in races to supplement or replace a jib.

balloon tire *n.* A pneumatic tire with a wide tread, inflated to low pressure, and now used chiefly on trucks.

balloon vine *n.* An ornamental tropical climbing plant, *Cardiospermum halicacabum,* with balloonlike seed capsules.

bal·lot (băl′ət) *n.* **1.** A written or printed paper or ticket used to cast or register a vote, especially a secret vote. **2.** The act, process, or system of voting, especially by the use of secret ballots or voting machines. **3.** A list of candidates running for office; ticket. **4.** The total of all votes cast in an election. **5.** The right to vote; the franchise. **6.** Formerly, a small ball used to register a vote.
∼*v.* **balloted, -loting, -lots.** —*intr.* **1.** To cast a ballot; vote. **2.** To draw lots. —*tr.* To obtain a vote from: *The union balloted its membership.* [Italian *ballotta,* small ball or pebble used for voting, diminutive of *balla,* BALL.] **—bal·lot·er** *n.*

ballot box *n.* **1.** A box in which a voter places his or her completed ballot. **2.** The process or system of secret voting; the ballot: *The government's popularity will be tested at the ballot box.*

bal·lotte·ment (bə-lŏt′mənt) *n.* A technique for detecting or examining a floating object in the body, as: **1.** The use of a finger to push sharply against the uterus and detect the presence or position of a fetus by its return impact. **2.** A test for a floating kidney in which the kidney is moved by alternating external digital pressures. [French, a tossing, from *balloter,* to toss, from *ballotte,* diminutive of *balle,* BALL.]

ball·park (bôl′pärk′) *n.* A park or stadium in which ball games are played. **—in the ballpark.** *Informal.* Within the proper range; approximately right.
∼*adj. Informal.* Approximate: *a ballpark figure.*

ball-peen hammer (bôl′pēn′) *n.* A hammer having one end of the head hemispherical.

ball·play·er (bôl′plā′ər) *n.* One who plays baseball.

ball-point pen (bôl′point′) *n.* A pen having as its writing point a small ball bearing that transfers ink stored in a cartridge onto a writing surface. Also called "ball point."

ball·room (bôl′ro͞om′, -ro͝om′) *n.* A large room for dancing.

ballroom dancing *n.* Formal, social dancing with conventional rhythms and steps, such as the waltz and foxtrot.

ball valve *n.* A valve regulated by the position of a free-floating ball that moves in response to fluid or mechanical pressure. It is often used as a one-way valve.

bal·ly·hoo (băl′ē-ho͞o′) *n., pl.* **-hoos.** *Informal.* **1.** Sensational or clamorous advertising. **2.** Noisy shouting or uproar.
∼*tr.v.* **ballyhooed, -hooing, -hoos.** *Informal.* To advertise by sensational methods; publicize exaggeratedly. [20th century (U.S.) : origin obscure.]

ballyrag. Variant of **bullyrag.**

balm (bäm) *n.* **1.** An aromatic, oily resin exuded by various chiefly tropical trees and shrubs and used in medicine. **2.** Any tree or shrub yielding such a substance, such as the balm of Gilead. **3.** Any aromatic ointment, oil, unguent, or similar substance. **4.** An aromatic herb, *Melissa officinalis,* native to Europe, having clusters of small, fragrant white flowers. Also called "lemon balm." **5.** Any of several similar aromatic plants. **6.** A pleasing, aromatic fragrance. **7.** Something that soothes, heals, or comforts. [Middle English *baume, basme,* from Old French *basme,* from Latin *balsamum,* BALSAM.]

bal·ma·caan (băl′mə-kăn′) *n.* A loose, full overcoat with raglan sleeves, originally made of rough, woolen cloth. [After *Balmacaan,* an estate near Inverness, Scotland.]

balm of Gil·e·ad (gĭl′ē-əd, -ăd′) *n.* **1.** An aromatic evergreen tree of the genus *Commiphora;* especially, *C. opobalsamum,* of Africa and Asia Minor. **2.** A fragrant resin obtained from this tree. **3.** A North American deciduous tree, *Populus candicans,* having broad, heart-shaped leaves. **4.** A fragrant resin obtained from the **balsam fir** *(see).*

Bal·mor·al[1] (băl-môr′əl, -mŏr′əl) *n.* **1.** A brimless Scottish cap with a flat, round top. **2.** *Sometimes* **balmoral.** A heavy, laced walking shoe. [After BALMORAL Castle.]

Balmoral[2]**.** A castle in Grampian Region, close to the Dee River. It is the private residence of the British monarch in Scotland.

balm·y (bä′mē) *adj.* **-ier, -iest. 1.** Having the quality or fragrance of balm. **2.** Mild and pleasant: *a balmy breeze.* **3.** *Slang.* Eccentric in behavior. [Sense 3, variant of BARMY.] **—balm·i·ly** *adv.* **—balm·i·ness** *n.*

bal·ne·al (băl′nē-əl) *adj.* Of or pertaining to baths or bathing. [From Latin *balneum,* bath, from Greek *balaneion*†, bath.]

bal·ne·ol·o·gy (băl′nē-ŏl′ə-jē) *n.* The therapeutic use of mineral baths. [Latin *balneum,* bath (see **balneal**) + -LOGY.]

ba·lo·ney, bo·lo·ney (bə-lō′nē) *n.* **1.** Variant of **bologna. 2.** *Slang.* Nonsense. [Perhaps from BOLOGNA (sausage).]

bal·sa (bôl′sə) *n.* **1.** A tree, *Ochroma lagopus,* of tropical America, having wood that is unusually light in weight. **2.** The wood of this tree. **3.** A raft consisting of a frame fastened to buoyant cylinders of wood or metal. [Spanish *balsa*†, raft.]

bal·sam (bôl′səm) *n.* **1.** An oily or gummy oleoresin, usually containing benzoic or cinnamic acids, obtained from the exudations of various trees and shrubs, and used as a base for cough syrups, other medications, and perfumes. See **balsam of Peru, balsam of Tolu, Canada balsam. 2.** Any similar substance, especially a fragrant ointment used as medication. **3.** Any of various trees yielding an aromatic, resinous substance; especially, the **balsam fir** *(see).* **4.** Any of several plants of the genus *Impatiens;* especially, *I. balsamina,* cultivated for its double flowers of various colors. [Latin *balsamum,* from Greek *balsamon,* from Hebrew *bāśām,* "spice."]

balsam apple *n.* A tropical vine, *Momordica balsamina,* native to the Old World, having yellow flowers and warty, orange fruit.

balsam fir *n.* A small, evergreen tree, *Abies balsamea,* of northeastern North America. It yields Canada balsam. Also called "balsam," "Canada balsam."

bal·sam·ic (bôl-săm′ĭk) *adj.* **1.** Of, pertaining to, or resembling balsam. **2.** Containing or yielding balsam.

bal·sam·if·er·ous (bôl′sə-mĭf′ər-əs) *adj.* Yielding balsam.

balsam of Peru *n.* The aromatic resin of a tropical American tree, *Myroxylon pereirae,* used to make perfume and other products.

balsam of To·lu (tə-lo͞o′) *n.* The aromatic resin of a tropical American tree, *Myroxylon toluiferum,* used in cough remedies and in the manufacture of perfumes. Also called "tolu."

balsam pear *n.* A tropical vine, *Momordica charantia,* native to the Old World, having yellow-orange fruit.

balsam poplar *n.* A North American tree, *Populus balsamifera,* having large buds coated with a gummy, fragrant resin. Also called "tacamahac."

Balt (bôlt) *n.* A member of the Baltic-speaking people inhabiting the southeastern shores of the Baltic Sea and formerly occupying a wide area bounded by Gdańsk, Riga, Moscow, and Kiev.

Bal·tha·zar[1] (băl-thă′zər, -thăz′ər, bôl′thə-zär′, băl′-). Also **Bal·tha·sar.** One of the three Magi who traveled to see the infant Jesus.

Balthazar[2] *n.* A wine bottle that holds as much as 16 standard bottles. [Probably after BALTHAZAR (the Magus).]

Bal·ti (bŭl′tē) *n.* A Tibeto-Burman language of the people of northern Kashmir.

Bal·tic (bôl′tĭk) *adj.* **1.** Of or pertaining to the Baltic Sea, or to the Baltic States and their inhabitants or cultures. **2.** Of or designating a group of languages of the Indo-European family, consisting of Lithuanian, Lettish, and Old Prussian. See **Balto-Slavic.**
∼*n.* The Baltic language group.

Baltic Sea. Arm of the Atlantic Ocean bounded by Denmark, Sweden, Finland, Estonia, Latvia, Lithuania, Russia, Poland, and Germany. It opens to the North Sea by channels between Denmark and Sweden. It is relatively shallow, with very low salinity, and can freeze for three to five months of the year.

Baltic States. The republics of Estonia, Latvia, and Lithuania, on the eastern coast of the Baltic Sea. Beginning in the 18th century they were subject to Russian rule. They achieved independence between World War I and World War II, were then incorporated into the U.S.S.R., and in 1991 regained independence.

Bal·ti·more (bôl′tə-môr′, -mōr′). Industrial city, seaport, and cultural center in northern Maryland. Situated at the mouth of the Patapsco River, it has been a busy port and shipbuilding center since the 18th century. In 1827 it was the starting point of the first public railway.

Baltimore oriole *n.* An American songbird, *Icterus galbula,* of which the male has bright-orange, black, and white plumage. [After George Calvert, 1st Baron *Baltimore* (1605–75); (the colors of the male are the same as those in Lord Baltimore's coat of arms).]

Bal·to-Sla·vic (bôl′tō-slä′vĭk, -slăv′ĭk) *n.* A subfamily of the Indo-European language family, composed of the Baltic group and the Slavic group.

Ba·lu·chi (bə-lo͞o′chē) *n., pl.* **-chis** or collectively **Baluchi. 1.** A native or inhabitant of Baluchistan. **2.** The Iranian language of the Baluchi people. **—Ba·lu·chi** *adj.*

Ba·lu·chi·stan (bə-lo͞o′chĭ-stăn′, -stän′). Province in Pakistan, bordering on Iran and Afghanistan. An arid and mountainous region, its inhabitants are mostly Muslim Baluchi and Pathan nomads. Quetta is the capital.

ba·lu·chi·ther·i·um (bə-lo͞o′chĭ-thîr′ē-əm) *n., pl.* **-ther·i·a** (-thîr′ē-ə). An extinct, rhinoceroslike mammal of the genus *Baluchitherium,* of the Oligocene and Miocene epochs, which was one of the largest land mammals ever to have lived. [New Latin.]

bal·un (băl′ən) *n.* An electrical device for coupling an aerial to a transmission line. [*bal*anced + *un*balanced (impedance).]

bal·us·ter (băl′ə-stər) *n.* One of the posts or supports of a handrail, as on a bannister. [French *balustre,* from Italian *balaustro,* from *balaustra,* flower of the pomegranate (from the shape of the post), from Latin *balaustium,* from Greek *balaustion*†.]

bal·us·trade (băl′ə-strād′) *n.* A rail and the row of posts that support it, as along the edge of a staircase. [French, from Italian *balaustrata,* from *balaustro,* BALUSTER.]
Bal·zac (bôl′zăk′, băl′-), **Honoré de** (1799–1850). French author. Often considered the greatest French novelist and the founder of the realist school of fiction, Balzac portrayed French society in a series of works known collectively as *La Comédie Humaine.*
Bam·a·ko (băm′ə-kō). Port on the Niger River and the capital of Mali in West Africa.
Bam·ba·ra (bäm-bä′rä) *n., pl.* **-ras** or collectively **Bambara. 1.** A member of a Negroid people of the upper Niger River valley. **2.** The Mande language of this people.
bam·bi·no (băm-bē′nō, bäm-) *n., pl.* **-nos** or **-ni** (-nē). **1.** Used as an affectionate term for a child or baby. **2.** A representation of the infant Jesus. [Italian, diminutive of *bambo,* child.]
bam·boo (băm-bo͞o′) *n., pl.* **-boos. 1.** Any of various mostly tropical grasses of the subfamily Bambusoideae, having hard-walled stems with ringed joints. **2.** The hollow woody stems of these plants, used in building, making furniture and utensils, and in certain crafts. **3.** Any of various tall, bamboolike grasses such as those of the genera *Arundinaria* and *Dendrocalamus.* [Earlier *bamboos* (misunderstood as plural), from Dutch *bamboes,* unexplained variant of Portuguese *mambu,* from Malay.] **—bam·boo** *adj.*
Bamboo Curtain *n.* A political and especially an ideological barrier existing between the People's Republic of China and other major powers, such as the United States and the U.S.S.R., especially during the leadership of Mao Ze-dong. [Formed by analogy with IRON CURTAIN.]
bam·boo·zle (băm-bo͞o′zəl) *tr.v.* **-zled, -zling, -zles.** *Informal.* **1.** To trick or deceive by elaborate misinformation; hoax. **2.** To mystify or confuse. —See Synonyms at **deceive.** [Probably a cant variant of *bumbazzle,* from *bombace,* padding, BOMBAST.] **—bam·boo·zle·ment** *n.*
ban[1] (băn) *tr.v.* **banned, banning, bans. 1.** To prohibit, especially by official decree. **2.** *Archaic.* To heap curses upon; execrate. **3.** *South African.* To deprive (a person suspected of illegal political activity) of the right of free movement and association with others.
~*n.* **1.** A prohibition, especially one imposed by law or official decree. **2.** *Archaic.* An excommunication or condemnation by church officials. **3.** In feudal times, a summons to arms. **4.** *Archaic.* Censure through public opinion. **5.** *Archaic.* A curse or imprecation. [Middle English *bannen,* to summon, banish, curse, partly from Old English *bannan,* to summon, proclaim, and partly from Old Norse *banna,* to prohibit, curse, both ultimately from Germanic *bannan* (unattested).]
ban[2] (bän) *n., pl.* **bani** (bä′nē). A monetary unit equal to 1/100 of the leu of Romania. See feature at **currency.** [Romanian, from Serbo-Croatian *bān,* lord, from Turkish; akin to *bayan,* rich.]
ba·nal (bə-näl′, -năl′, bā′nəl) *adj.* Lacking originality, depth, and inspiration; trite and drearily predictable: *a banal love story.* See Synonyms at **trite.** [French, commonplace, from Old French, common to everyone, shared (as by tenants in a feudal jurisdiction), from *ban,* summons to military service, from Frankish *ban* (unattested).] **—ba·nal·i·ty** (bə-năl′ə-tē, bā-) *n.* **—ba·nal·ly** *adv.*
ba·nan·a (bə-năn′ə) *n.* **1.** Any of several treelike tropical or subtropical plants of the genus *Musa;* especially, *M. sapientum,* having long, broad leaves and hanging clusters of edible fruit. **2.** The crescent-shaped fruit of any of these plants, having white, pulpy flesh and thick, easily removed yellow, green, or reddish skin. [Portuguese and Spanish, from a native name in Guinea.]
banana oil *n.* **1.** A liquid mixture of nitrocellulose and amyl acetate, or a similar solvent, having a bananalike odor. **2.** An organic compound, **amyl acetate** *(see).* **3.** *Slang.* Insincere flattery.
banana republic *n. Informal.* A small country, especially in Central America, often economically dependent on a single crop, such as bananas, and regarded as politically unstable.
ba·na·nas (bə-năn′əz) *adj. Slang.* Crazy; wild. Often used in the phrase *go bananas.* [20th century : origin obscure.]
banana split *n.* A dessert consisting of a banana cut lengthwise and served with ice cream, syrup, fruit, nuts, and whipped cream.
ba·nau·sic (bə-nô′sĭk) *adj.* Materialistic and practical, especially to the point of being dull or pedestrian. [Greek *banausikos,* suitable for artisans, from *baunos,* forge.]
ban·co (băng′kō, bäng′-) *n., pl.* **-cos.** A bet in certain gambling games for the entire amount the banker offers to accept.
~*interj.* Used to announce a banco. [Italian *banco, banca,* BANK (financial establishment).]
band[1] (bănd) *n.* **1.** A thin strip of flexible material used to encircle and bind one object or to hold a number of objects together: *a rubber band.* **2.** A narrow strip of fabric used to trim, finish, or reinforce articles of clothing. Often used in combination: *a waistband.* **3.** Any strip or stripe that contrasts with its surroundings in color, texture, or material. **4. a.** A neckband or collar. **b. bands.** The two strips hanging from the front of a collar as part of the dress of certain clergymen, scholars, and lawyers. **c.** A high collar popular in the 16th and 17th centuries. **5.** *Architecture.* A flat strip along a wall. **6.** *Biology.* Any chromatically or functionally differentiated strip or stripe in or on an organism. **7.** *Physics.* **a.** A range of some physical variable, as of radiation wavelength or frequency, between well-defined limits; especially, a range of emitted or absorbed wavelengths in a spectrum. **b.** A restricted range of very closely spaced electron energy levels in solids, the distribution and nature of which determine the electrical properties of a material. **8.** The cords across the back of a book, to which the quires or sheets are attached. **9.** A track on a phonograph record. **10.** *Computer Science.* The recording area on a magnetic disk or drum.
~*tr.v.* **banded, banding, bands. 1.** To tie, bind, or encircle with a band. **2.** To mark with a band or bands. [Middle English, from Old French *bande,* bond, tie, link, from Germanic.]
band[2] *n.* **1. a.** A group of people, especially when joined together for a common purpose: *a band of robbers.* **b.** A group of animals, as a flock or herd. **2.** A group of musicians who play together, especially: **a.** One not including stringed instruments. **b.** One playing popular music, such as jazz or rock. **3.** *Anthropology.* A self-sufficient subdivision of a tribe.
~*v.* **banded, banding, bands.** —*tr.* To assemble or unite in a group. —*intr.* To form a group; unite. Often used with *together: to band together to oppose legislation.* [Middle English, from Old French *bande,* a troop, from Medieval Latin *banda,* from Germanic.]
band[3] *n. Archaic.* **1.** *Usually* **bands.** A physical restraint; a manacle or fetter. **2.** A moral or legal restraint; a bond. [Middle English, from Old Norse.]
Ban·da (băn′də), **Hastings Kamuzu** (*c.* 1906–). African statesman. He practiced medicine in the United Kingdom during World War II and then in the United States. In 1958 he returned to Malawi (then Nyasaland) to lead the fight for independence from the British, which was achieved in 1964. He became prime minister and then president in 1966, when Malawi was declared a republic. In 1970 he was made president for life.
band·age (băn′dĭj) *n.* A strip of fabric or other material used as a protective covering for a wound or other injury.
~*tr.v.* **bandaged, -aging, -ages.** To apply a bandage to. [French, from *bande,* BAND (strip).] **—band·ag·er** *n.*
Band-Aid (bănd′ād′) *n.* A trademark for a small adhesive plaster with a gauze pad in the center, used on minor wounds.
ban·dan·na, ban·dan·a (băn-dăn′ə) *n.* A large handkerchief or scarf, usually brightly colored. [Probably from Portuguese *bandana,* from Hindi *bāndhnū,* a dyeing process in which the cloth is tied at various points, from *bāndhnā,* to tie, from Sanskrit *bandhnāti.*]
Ban·da·ra·na·i·ke (băn′də-rə-nī′ə-kə), **Sirimavo Ratwatte Dias** (1916–). The world's first woman prime minister. She succeeded her husband, S.W.R.D. Bandaranaike, to the presidency of the Sri Lanka Freedom Party after his assassination. She served as prime minister from 1960 until 1965 and from 1970 to 1977.
Bandaranaike, Solomon West Ridgeway Dias (1899–1959). Sri Lankan statesman who was prime minister of what was then Ceylon (1956–59). He was assassinated by a Buddhist monk.
Ban·dar Se·ri Be·ga·wan (bän′där sĕr′ē bə-gä′wən). Formerly **Bru·nei Town** (bro͞o-nī′). Capital of Brunei. Situated near the mouth of the Brunei River, it is partly built on piles.
b. & b. bed and breakfast.
band·box (bănd′bŏks′) *n.* A lightweight, rounded box originally designed to hold collars but now used for any small articles of dress. **—as if one came out of a bandbox.** Extremely smart and neat.
ban·deau (băn-dō′) *n., pl.* **-deaux** (-dōz′) or **-deaus.** A narrow band for the hair; a fillet. [French, from Old French *bandel,* diminutive of *bande,* BAND (strip).]
ban·de·ril·la (băn′də-rē′ə, -rēl′yə) *n.* In bullfighting, a decorated barbed dart that is thrust into the bull's neck or shoulder muscles by a banderillero. [Spanish, diminutive of *bandera,* banner, from Vulgar Latin *bandāria* (unattested), BANNER.]
ban·de·ril·le·ro (băn′də-rē-âr′ō, -rēl-yâr′ō) *n., pl.* **-ros.** In bullfighting, one who implants the banderillas. [Spanish, from BANDERILLA.]
ban·de·role, ban·de·rol (băn′də-rōl′) *n.* Also **ban·ne·rol** (băn′ə-rōl′). **1.** A narrow forked flag or streamer attached to a staff or lance or flown from a masthead. **2.** *Art & Architecture.* A representation of a ribbon or scroll bearing an inscription. **3.** A square flag, sometimes carried at a funeral and placed over a tomb. [French, from Italian *banderuola,* diminutive of *bandiera,* banner, from Vulgar Latin *bandāria* (unattested), BANNER.]
ban·di·coot (băn′dĭ-ko͞ot′) *n.* **1.** Any of several ratlike marsupials of the family Peramelidae, of Australia and adjacent islands, having a long, tapering snout and long hind legs. **2.** Any of several large rats of the genera *Bandicota* and *Nesokia,* of southeastern Asia. In this sense, now usually called "bandicoot rat" and sometimes "mole-rat." [Telegu *pandikokku* : *pandi,* pig + *kokku,* rat.]
ban·dit (băn′dĭt) *n., pl.* **-dits** or **banditti** (băn-dĭt′ē). A robber; especially, an outlaw who belongs to a gang. [Italian *bandito,* from the past participle of *bandire,* to BAN.] **—ban·dit·ry** *n.*
band leader *n.* One who conducts a band, especially a large band that plays popular dance music.
band·mas·ter (bănd′măs′tər, -mäs′-) *n.* One who conducts a band, especially a military or brass band.
ban·dog (băn′dôg′, -dŏg′) *n.* A dog formerly kept chained up as a watchdog or because of its ferocious nature. [Middle English *band-dogge* : BAND (fetter) + DOG.]
ban·do·leer, ban·do·lier (băn′də-lîr′) *n.* A belt fitted with small pockets or loops for carrying cartridges and worn across the chest by soldiers. [French *bandoulière,* from Spanish *bandolera,* from *banda,* sash, probably from Germanic.]
ban·dore (băn′dôr′, -dōr′) *n.* A 16th-century stringed, bass musical instrument resembling the lute. Also called "pandore." [Portuguese *bandurra,* from Late Latin *pandūra,* a three-stringed lute, from Greek *pandoura.*]

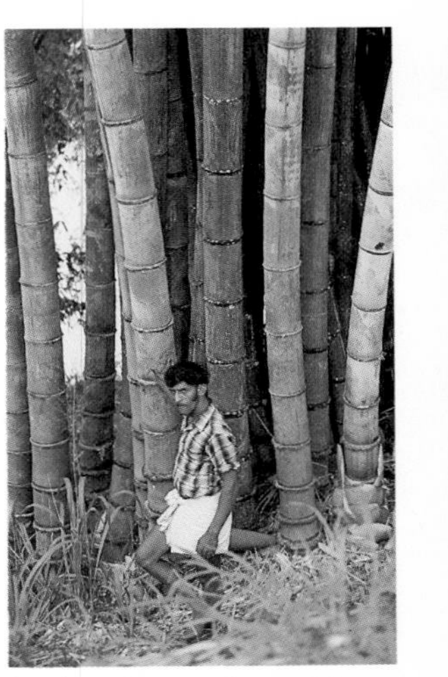

bamboo *A group of perennial grasses found in tropical and subtropical regions of the Eastern and Western hemispheres. Bamboo grows rapidly and there are approximately 200 different species. Giant varieties, like the one shown here, are used to build houses and even road bridges. Split bamboo is woven into mats, baskets, and hats.*

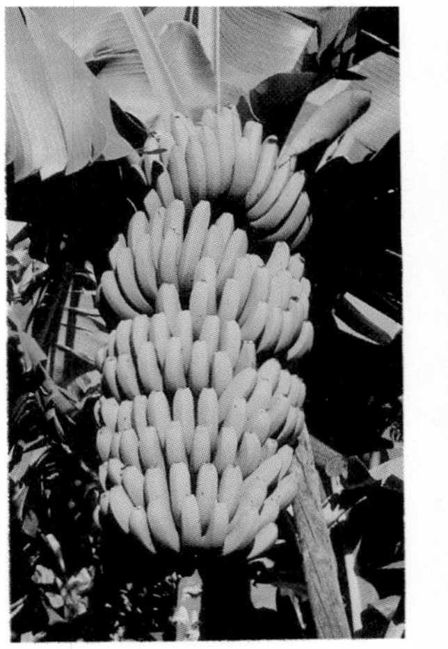

banana *Originating in southwest Asia, bananas are now an important commercial crop grown in tropical and subtropical climates around the world.*

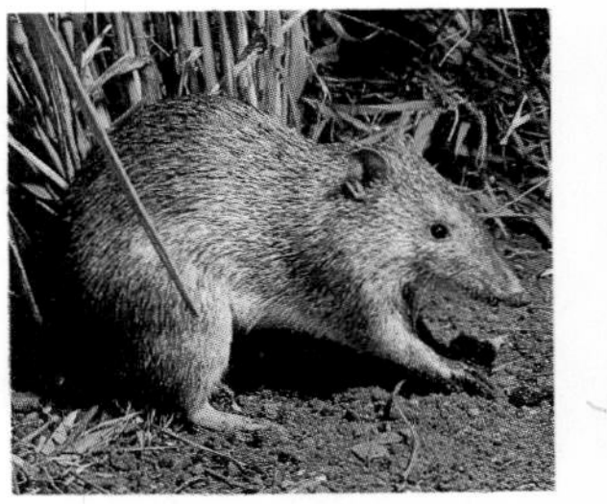

bandicoot *These marsupials are found in Australia and New Guinea. The female carries her young in a pouch on her belly. Largely nocturnal, bandicoots feed mostly on insects and mice, although some species are vegetarian, and others prey on a number of small mammals and lizards.*

band-pass filter (bănd′păs′) *n. Electronics.* A filter that blocks all signals but those within a selected frequency range.

band saw *n.* A power saw consisting essentially of a toothed metal band coupled to and continuously driven round the circumferences of two wheels.

band shell *n.* A bandstand equipped at the rear with a concave, almost hemispheric wall that serves as a sounding board.

bands·man (băndz′mən) *n., pl.* **-men** (-mĭn). A musician who plays an instrument in a band, especially a military or brass band.

band spectrum *n.* A molecular spectrum in which a number of bands of closely spaced lines occur as a result of emission or absorption of radiation.

band·stand (bănd′stănd′) *n.* A platform for a band or orchestra, usually outdoors and having a roof.

Ban·dung (bän′dŏng′). City in Indonesia, in western Java. The Bandung Conference (1955) was attended by representatives of 29 African and Asian countries opposed to colonialism.

band·wag·on (bănd′wăg′ən) *n.* **1.** An elaborately decorated wagon used to transport musicians in a parade. **2.** *Informal.* A cause or party that attracts increasing numbers of adherents. **—climb (or jump) on the bandwagon.** *Informal.* To support or shift one's support to a party, cause, or enterprise that appears likely to win or succeed.

band·width (bănd′wĭdth′) *n. Electronics.* **1.** The frequency range used by a transmitted signal on either side of the carrier frequency. **2.** The range of frequencies over which an amplifier gives a power amplification that falls within a stipulated fraction of the maximum value.

ban·dy¹ (băn′dē) *tr.v.* **bandied, bandying, bandies. 1.** To toss, throw, or strike back and forth: *"A sunrise breeze bandied the curtains"* (Truman Capote). **2.** To exchange (words or blows). **3.** To discuss in a casual or frivolous manner. **4.** To pass round or along indiscriminately. [Perhaps from French *bander*, to form sides (as for a game), oppose oneself against, from BAND (group).]

bandy² *adj.* Bowed or bent in an outward curve: *bandy legs.* **~***n., pl.* **bandies.** *Chiefly British.* **1.** An early form of hockey. **2.** A stick, bent at one end, used in playing this game. [Adjective sense from noun (hockey stick), obscurely related to BANDY (toss, throw).]

ban·dy-leg·ged (băn′dē-lĕg′ĭd) *adj.* Having **bowlegs** (*see*); bowlegged. [From BANDY (curved stick).]

bane (bān) *n.* **1.** Someone or something that is a nuisance or cause of distress: *the bane of one's life.* **2.** *Poetic.* Fatal injury or ruin. **3.** A cause of death, destruction, or ruin. **4.** A deadly poison. Used in combination: *henbane; wolf's-bane.* [Middle English *bane*, Old English *bana*, slayer, cause of death or destruction, ruin.]

bane·ber·ry (bān′bĕr′ē) *n., pl.* **-ries. 1.** Any plant of the genus *Actaea*, especially *A. spicata*, having clusters of white flowers and red or white poisonous berries. **2.** A berry of any of these plants.

bane·ful (bān′fəl) *adj.* **1.** Full of venom or harm. **2.** Destructive; pernicious: *"Criticism is really, in itself, a baneful and injurious employment"* (Matthew Arnold). **—See Usage note at baleful.**

Banff (bămf). A town in southwestern Alberta, Canada, in the Rocky Mts. near Lake Louise. It is a famous winter resort and tourist center.

bang¹ (băng) *n.* **1.** The sudden loud noise of an explosion. **2.** A sudden loud impact or thump. **3.** *Informal.* A sudden burst of action. **4.** *Slang.* A sense of excitement; a thrill. **—with a bang.** With notable success.

~*v.* **banged, banging, bangs. —***tr.* **1.** To hit noisily; strike heavily and repeatedly: *banging the table with his fist.* **2.** To close suddenly and loudly; slam. **3.** To handle noisily or violently: *bang the dishes in the sink.* **4.** To hit sharply: *I've banged my elbow. —intr.* **1.** To make a sudden loud noise. **2.** To crash noisily against something. **3.** To strike with a sudden loud noise.

~*adv.* **1.** With a bang. **2.** Exactly; precisely: *bang on time.* **3.** Suddenly; completely: *If we make one mistake, bang go our hopes of winning.* **—bang on.** *Informal.* Exactly right: *That answer was bang on.* [16th century : perhaps from Scandinavian, akin to Old Norse *bang*, a hammering.]

bang² *n. Often* **bangs.** Hair cut in a fringe straight across the forehead.

~*tr.v.* **banged, banging, bangs.** To cut (hair) straight across the forehead. [Perhaps ultimately from Old Norse *banga*, to cut off.]

bang³. Variant of **bhang.**

Ban·ga·lore (băng′gə-lôr′, -lōr′). Capital city of Karnataka state in south India, 290 kilometers (180 miles) west of Madras.

bangalore torpedo *n.* A piece of metal pipe filled with an explosive, used primarily to clear a path through barbed wire or to detonate land mines. [After BANGALORE, where it was first used.]

bang·er (băng′ər) *n. Chiefly British.* **1.** A firework that explodes with a sudden loud noise. **2.** *Informal.* A sausage. [Sense 2: probably from the sputtering sound made in cooking.]

Bangkok. See **Krung Thep.**

Ban·gla·desh (băng′lə-dĕsh′, băng′-). Formerly **East Pak·i·stan** (păk′ĭ-stăn′). Muslim country of south Asia, lying mostly in the fertile Ganges-Brahmaputra delta. Formerly part of Bengal, it became East Pakistan on Indian independence (1947), but Calcutta, Bengal's chief port and industrial center for its jute, became part of India. Disastrously weakened economically, East Pakistan was neglected by the government in West Pakistan. Unrest erupted into a savage civil war (1971), and independent Bangladesh was born. Sheik Mujibur Rahman, the East Bengali leader, was released from prison in West Pakistan to form the country's first government

baneberry *The poisonous fruit of* Actaea spicata, *a European bush found in limestone woodlands, gets its common name from the old English word* bane, *meaning* "poison."

(1972) but was killed in a military coup (1975). A countercoup installed another military regime, and Gen. Ziaur Rahman took over the government the same year. He was elected president (1978) but was assassinated (1981). A bloodless military coup (1982) was led by Gen. Hussein Ershad, who became president (1983). Despite some industrialization and advances that have made more than 75 percent of the land cultivable, political instability, droughts, floods, and cyclones have kept Bangladesh a poor country dependent on foreign aid. Area, 143,998 square kilometers (55,583 square miles). Population, 115,600,000. Capital, Dacca. **—Bang·la·desh·i** *adj. & n.*

ban·gle (băng′gəl) *n.* **1.** A rigid bracelet or anklet, especially one with no clasp. **2.** An ornament hung from a bracelet, necklace, or the like. [Hindi *baṅgrī†*, glass bracelet.]

Ban·gor (băng′gôr, -gər). A river port of southern Maine, on the Penobscot River. It is the gateway to an extensive resort and lumbering region.

bang·tail (băng′tāl′) *n.* **1.** An animal's tail that has been cut straight across and short. **2.** An animal, especially a horse, with such a tail. [Probably BANG (cut) + TAIL.]

Ban·gui (bäng-gē′). Capital of the Central African Republic. Situated on the Ubangi River, it is the chief port of the country and also handles goods for Chad.

bang up *tr.v.* **1.** To cause damage or injury to. **2.** *Chiefly British.* To raise; increase: *bang up a price.*

bang-up (băng′ŭp′) *adj. Slang.* Excellent: *a bang-up job.*

Bang·we·u·lu, Lake (băng′wə-ŏŏ′lŏŏ). A shallow lake bordered by swamps, on a plateau in northeast Zambia. It was discovered by David Livingstone in 1868.

ba·ni. Plural of **ban** (currency).

ban·i·an (băn′yən) *n.* **1.** A member of a Hindu merchant or trader caste, whose members eat no meat. **2.** A loose shirt, jacket, or gown worn in India. **3.** Variant of **banyan.** [Portuguese, from Gujarati *vāṇiyo*, from Sanskrit *vāṇija*, merchant.]

ban·ish (băn′ĭsh) *tr.v.* **-ished, -ishing, -ishes. 1.** To force to leave a country or place by official decree; exile. **2.** To drive away; expel: *He banished all doubts from his mind.* [Middle English *banishen*, from Old French *banir* (present stem *baniss-*), from Vulgar Latin *bannīre* (unattested), from Germanic *bannjan* (unattested), to BAN.] **—ban·ish·er** *n.* **—ban·ish·ment** *n.*
 Synonyms: *deport, exile, expatriate, extradite, transport.*

ban·is·ter, ban·nis·ter (băn′ĭ-stər) *n.* **1.** *Usually* **banisters.** The handrail or balustrade of a staircase. **2.** A baluster. [From earlier *barrister*, variant BALUSTER.]

ban·jo (băn′jō) *n., pl.* **-jos** or **-joes.** A fretted stringed musical instrument, having a long narrow neck and a hollow circular body with a stretched diaphragm of vellum upon which the bridge rests. [Probably of African origin.] **—ban·jo·ist** *n.*

banjo clock *n.* A wall clock of a type made in the United States in the 19th century, resembling a banjo in shape.

Ban·jul (băn-jŏŏl′). Formerly **Bath·urst** (băth′ərst). Capital of Gambia, in West Africa. Situated at the mouth of the Gambia River, it is a port and the country's only sizable town.

bank¹ (băngk) *n.* **1.** Any piled-up mass, as of snow or clouds; a mound; a ridge. **2.** A steep natural incline. **3.** An artificial embankment, especially one built on a bend in a road to help vehicles to

corner safely. **4. a.** *Often* **banks.** The slope of land adjoining a body of water, especially adjoining a lake, river, or sea. **b.** A part of a town situated on one side of a river flowing through it: *the Left Bank.* **5.** *Often* **banks.** A large elevated area of a sea floor. **6.** The cushion of a billiard or pool table. **7.** *Aviation.* The lateral tilt of an aircraft when turning. —See Usage note at **shoal.**
~*v.* **banked, banking, banks.** —*tr.* **1.** To border or protect with a ridge or embankment. Often used with *up.* **2.** To pile up; amass. Often used with *up*: *bank up earth along a wall.* **3.** To cover (a fire) with ashes or fresh fuel to ensure continued low burning. Often used with *up.* **4.** To construct with a slope rising to the outside edge. Often used with *up.* **5.** *Aviation.* To tilt (an aircraft) laterally in flight. **6.** In billiard games, to strike (a ball) so that it rebounds from the table's cushion. —*intr.* **1.** To take the form of or rise in a bank or banks. **2.** *Aviation.* To tilt an aircraft laterally when turning. **3.** To round a sloping embankment, especially at speed. [Middle English *banke,* probably from Old Danish *banke,* sandbank, from Germanic *bankon* (unattested).]

bank² *n. Abbr.* **bk. 1.** A business establishment or organization authorized to perform one or more of the following services: receive and safeguard money and other valuables; lend money at interest; negotiate bills of exchange, such as checks and drafts; purchase and exchange foreign currency; issue currency. **2.** The offices or building in which such an establishment, or a branch of such an organization, is located. **3. a.** The funds owned by a gambling establishment. **b.** The funds held by a dealer or banker in some gambling games. **4. a.** The reserve pieces, cards, chips, or play money, from which the players may draw, in games such as poker or dominoes. **b.** The player holding this stock. **5.** A supply or stock held in reserve: *a blood bank.* **6.** Any place of safekeeping or storage. **7.** *Obsolete.* A moneychanger's table or place of business.
~*v.* **banked, banking, banks.** —*tr.* To deposit (money) in a bank. —*intr.* **1.** To transact business with a bank; especially, to maintain a bank account. **2.** To operate a bank. **3.** To hold the bank in some gambling games. **4.** *Informal.* To depend or rely. Used with *on* or *upon.* —See Synonyms at **rely.** [French *banque,* from Italian *banca,* bench, moneychanger's table, from Germanic *bank* (unattested), BENCH.]

bank³ *n.* **1.** A set of similar or matched things arranged in a row: *a bank of desks.* **2.** A row of keys on a keyboard. **3.** *Nautical.* **a.** A bench for rowers in a galley. **b.** A row of oars in a galley. **4.** The lines of type under a newspaper headline. **5.** *Printing.* A slanting table on which type matter in galleys or sheets is stored or corrected before being made up in pages. **6.** A row of fixed electrical contacts forming part of an automatic switching unit in a telephone circuit.
~*tr.v.* **banked, banking, banks.** To arrange or set up in a row: *"Every street was banked with purple-blooming trees"* (Doris Lessing). [Middle English *bank,* from Old French *banc,* from Germanic *bank* (unattested), BENCH.]

bank·a·ble (băng′kə-bəl) *adj.* **1.** Acceptable to or at a bank. **2.** *Informal.* Guaranteed to bring profit: *a bankable movie star.*

bank acceptance *n.* A draft or bill of exchange drawn upon and accepted by a bank. Also called "banker's acceptance."

bank account *n.* **1.** An agreement between a bank and a customer whereby money is deposited with the bank and can be added to or withdrawn. **2.** The amount the customer deposits with the bank.

bank annuities *pl.n. Chiefly British.* **Consols** *(see).*

bank barn *n.* A barn built into a hillside as protection against cold, with a back entrance at the second-floor level.

bank·book (băngk′bo͝ok′) *n.* A book held by a person having a deposit account at a bank, in which deposits and withdrawals are recorded by the bank. Also called "passbook."

bank·card (băngk′kärd′) *n.* A credit card issued by a bank.

bank discount *n.* The interest on a loan, computed in advance, and deducted at the time the loan is made.

bank·er¹ (băng′kər) *n.* **1.** A person who owns or manages a bank. **2.** The player in charge of the bank in games such as poker or dominoes.

banker² *n.* A person or boat engaged in cod fishing on the Newfoundland banks.

banker³ *n.* A workbench used by masons and sculptors.

Bank·head (băngk′hĕd′), **Tallulah** (1903–68). U.S. actress. Noted as much for her extravagant lifestyle as for her performances on stage and screen, she did, however, win acclaim for her appearances in plays such as *The Little Foxes* by Lillian Hellman (1939).

bank holiday *n.* **1.** A weekday on which banks are legally closed. **2.** *British.* One of five days regarded as legal holidays, when banks are ordered to remain closed.

bank·ing (băng′kĭng) *n. Abbr.* **bkg.** The business of a bank or the occupation of a banker.

bank manager *n.* The person in charge of a local branch of a bank.

bank·note (băngk′nōt′) *n.* A note issued by an authorized bank representing its promise to pay a specific sum to the bearer on demand and acceptable as money. Also called "bank bill."

bank paper *n.* **1.** Banknotes. **2.** Securities, drafts, bills of exchange, and other commercial paper acceptable by a bank.

bank rate *n.* The rate of discount established by a country's central bank or banks.

bank·roll (băngk′rōl′) *n.* **1.** A roll of paper money. **2.** *Informal.* A person's ready cash.
~*tr.v.* **bankrolled, -rolling, -rolls.** *Slang.* To provide financial backing for (a business enterprise, for example).

bank·rupt (băngk′rŭpt′, -rəpt) *n. Abbr.* **bkpt. 1.** *Law.* An individual or corporate debtor, who, after a voluntary petition to the court or one invoked by creditors, is judged legally insolvent. His remaining property is then administered for his creditors or distributed among them in accordance with the law. **2.** Any person unable to pay his creditors in full. **3.** One who is or has become devoid of some resource or quality: *an intellectual bankrupt.*
~*adj.* **1.** Subject to legal procedure because of insolvency; legally declared a bankrupt. **2.** Financially ruined; impoverished. **3.** Completely lacking in some quality; destitute: *morally bankrupt.*
~*tr.v.* **bankrupted, -rupting, -rupts.** To cause to become bankrupt. [16th century : from Italian *banca rotta,* "broken bench," symbol of an insolvent moneychanger : *banca,* moneychanger's bench + *rotta,* past participle of *rompere,* to break (assimilated to Latin *rupta*).] —**bank·rupt·cy** *n.*

bankrupt worm *n.* A roundworm of the genus *Trichostrongylus* that causes gastroenteritis in sheep and cattle. [So called because it can bring bankruptcy to cattle raisers.]

Banks (băngks), **Sir Joseph** (1743–1820). British botanist and explorer. His most famous expedition was the circumnavigation of the world with Captain James Cook on the *Endeavour* (1768–71). He discovered and catalogued many species of animal and plant life, especially from Australia, and promoted the introduction of crop plants from their native regions to other parts of the world.

bank·si·a (băngk′sē-ə) *n.* Any shrub or tree of the Australian genus *Banksia,* whose flowers are borne on densely packed spikes that form cylindrical heads.

bank statement *n.* A statement showing the transactions and current balance of a bank account, especially one that is sent on a regular basis to the holder of the account.

ban·ner (băn′ər) *n.* **1.** A strip of cloth, either hung overhead or carried between poles, bearing a message or slogan. **2.** A piece of cloth attached to a staff and used as a standard by a monarch, knight, or military commander. **3. a.** The flag of a nation, state, army, or sovereign. **b.** An ensign bearing a motto, emblem, or legend, as of a society or trade union. **4.** A headline spanning the width of a newspaper page. Also called "banner headline." **5.** A principle, ideal, or slogan: *The Party is campaigning under the banner of democracy.*
~*adj.* Outstanding; superior. [Middle English *banere,* from Norman-French, from Old French *baniere,* from Vulgar Latin *bandāria* (unattested), from Late Latin *bandum,* standard, from Germanic.]

banner cloud *n.* A type of cloud that forms in clear skies on the side of a mountain peak sheltered from the wind, as air rising to pass over the peak cools.

ban·ner·et¹, ban·ner·ette (băn′ər-ĭt, -ə-rĕt′) *n.* A small banner. [Middle English *baneret,* from Old French *banerete,* diminutive of *baniere,* BANNER.]

ban·ner·et² *n.* **1.** A feudal knight entitled to lead men into battle under his own standard. **2.** This knight's rank between knight bachelor and baron. Also called "knight banneret." [Middle English *baneret,* from Old French, "bannered," from *baniere,* BANNER.]

bannerol. Variant of **banderole.**

bannister. Variant of **banister.**

Ban·nis·ter (băn′ə-stər), **Sir Roger Gilbert** (1929–). British middle-distance runner, the first man to break the four-minute mile barrier (May 6, 1954) with a time of 3 minutes 59.4 seconds. He was British mile champion (1951, 1953, and 1954) and European 1,500-meters champion and record holder.

ban·nock (băn′ək) *n.* Also **bon·nock** (bŏn′ək). *Scottish & British Regional.* A griddlecake, usually unleavened, made of oatmeal, barley, or wheat flour and sometimes containing dried fruit. [Middle English *bannok,* Old English *bannuc,* perhaps from Celtic.]

Ban·nock·burn (băn′ək-bûrn′, băn′ək-bûrn′). Small town now in Central Region, Scotland, on the Bannock River, a tributary of the Forth River. It is the site of the battle (1314) where the Scots, under Robert the Bruce, won a famous victory over the English, under Edward II.

banns, bans (bănz) *pl.n.* A spoken or published announcement in a church of an intended marriage, usually read out on three successive Sundays. [Middle English *banes,* plural of *bane, ban,* proclamation, BAN.]

ban·quet (băng′kwĭt) *n.* **1.** An elaborate and sumptuous meal. **2.** A ceremonial dinner honoring a particular guest or occasion.
~*v.* **banqueted, -queting, -quets.** —*tr.* To entertain at a banquet. —*intr.* To partake of a banquet; feast. [Old French, diminutive of *banc,* bench, from Germanic.] —**ban·quet·er** *n.*

ban·quette (băng-kĕt′) *n.* **1.** *Military.* A platform lining a trench or parapet wall where soldiers may stand when firing. **2.** *Southern U.S.* A sidewalk. **3.** A long upholstered bench, either placed against or built into a wall. **4.** Any ledge or shelf, as on a buffet. [French, from Italian *banchetta,* diminutive of *banca,* bench, from Germanic.]

ban·shee, ban·shie (băn′shē) *n.* A female spirit in Gaelic folklore believed to presage a death in the family by wailing outside the house. [Irish Gaelic *bean sídhe,* "woman of the fairies," from Old Irish *ben síde* : *ben,* woman + *síde*†, fairy folk.]

ban·tam (băn′təm) *n.* **1.** Any of various breeds of small domestic fowl. **2.** A small but aggressive person.
~*adj.* **1.** Diminutive; miniature. **2.** Spirited or aggressive. [From the belief that the fowl were native to *Bantam,* village in Java.]

ban·tam·weight (băn′təm-wāt′) *n.* A boxer weighing between 112 and 118 pounds.

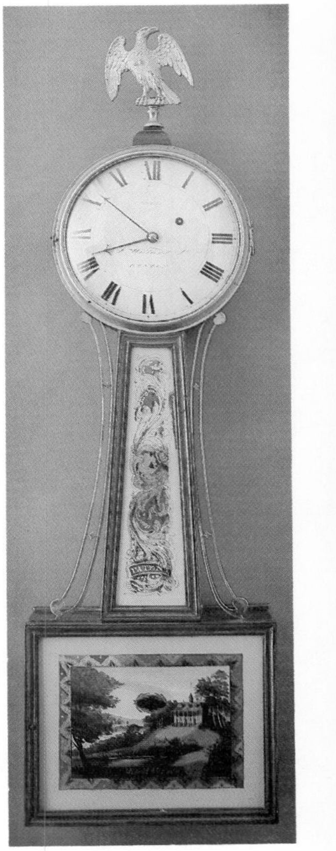

banjo clock *A 19th-century American clock design named for its resemblance to the musical instrument. The case accommodates a small falling weight. The example illustrated was made in 1841.*

ban·ter (băn′tər) *n.* Good-humored teasing or playful repartee.
~v. **bantered, -tering, -ters.** *—tr.* To tease or mock gently. *—intr.* To exchange mildly teasing remarks. [17th century : origin obscure.] **—ban·ter·er** *n.* **—ban·ter·ing·ly** *adv.*

Ban·ting (băn′tĭng), **Sir Frederick Grant** (1891–1941). Canadian physiologist. In 1921, in collaboration with Charles H. Best, he discovered a technique for isolating the hormone insulin from pancreatic tissue and thus discovered a treatment for diabetics. He was awarded the Nobel Prize (1923) jointly with his professor at Toronto University, John J.R. Macleod, but gave half of his share of the prize to Best.

bant·ling (bănt′lĭng) *n. Archaic.* A young child; a brat. [16th century : perhaps a variant of German *Bänkling,* bastard, from *Bank,* bench (i.e., "a child begotten on a bench"), from Old High German *banc.*]

Ban·try Bay (băn′trē). Atlantic inlet on the southwest coast of County Cork, Republic of Ireland.

Ban·tu (băn′to͞o) *n., pl.* **Bantus** or collectively **Bantu. 1.** A member of any of several Negroid tribes of central and southern Africa. **2.** A family of languages spoken by the Bantu, including Kongo, Luba, Kikuyu, Luganda, Nyanja, Swahili, and Zulu.
~adj. Of or pertaining to any of the Bantu peoples or their languages.

Ban·tu·stan (băn′to͞o-stän′) *n. South African.* A **homeland** *(see).*

banx·ring (băngks′rĭng′) *n.* A small squirrellike animal from Java. Also called "tree-shrew." [Javanese.]

ban·yan, ban·ian (băn′yən) *n.* A tree, *Ficus benghalensis,* of tropical India and the East Indies, having large, oval leaves, reddish fruit, and many aerial roots that develop into additional trunks. Compare **peepul.** [Originally name applied to one such tree near Bandar Abbas, Iran, beneath which Hindu banians had built a pagoda.]

ban·zai (bän-zī′) *n.* A Japanese battle cry, patriotic cheer, or greeting. [Japanese, "(may you live) ten thousand years," from Chinese *wàn sùi* : *wàn,* ten thousand + *sùi,* year.]

banzai attack *n.* A desperate, suicidal attack, as practiced by Japanese troops in World War II. Also called "banzai charge."

ba·o·bab (bā′ō-băb′, bä′-) *n.* A tree, *Adansonia digitata,* of tropical Africa, having an extremely thick trunk, large, pendulous white flowers, and hard-shelled, fleshy fruit called "monkey bread." [New Latin (16th century) : probably a native Central African name.]

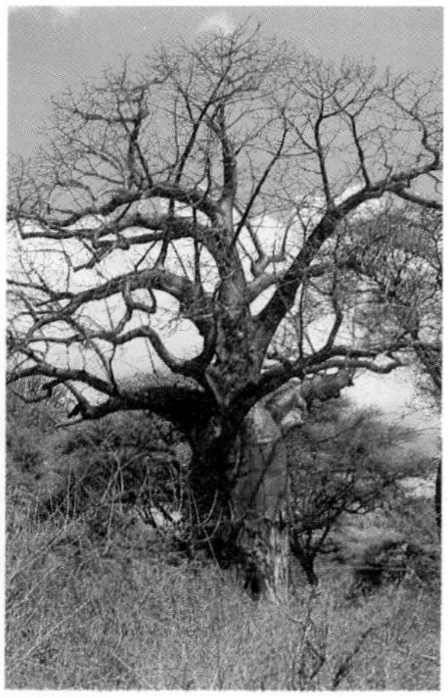

baobab *An African member,* Adansonia digitata, *of a family of tropical flowering trees. The thick, barrel-shaped trunk acts as a water reservoir, enabling the tree to survive long droughts.*

bap., bapt. 1. baptism. **2.** baptized.

Bap., Bapt. Baptist.

bap·tism (băp′tĭz′əm) *n. Abbr.* **bap., bapt. 1.** A Christian sacrament, symbolic of spiritual regeneration, in which, as a result of immersion or sprinkling with water, accompanied by the recital of a form of words, the recipient is considered cleansed of original sin, given a name, and admitted into Christianity or a specific Christian church. **2.** Any ceremony, trial, or experience by which one is initiated, purified, or given a name. **3.** *Christian Science.* A submergence in Spirit or purification by Spirit. [Middle English *bapteme,* from Old French *bapteme, baptesme,* from Late Latin *baptisma,* from Greek, from *baptizein,* to BAPTIZE.] **—bap·tis·mal** (băp-tĭz′məl) *adj.* **—bap·tis·mal·ly** *adv.*

baptism of fire *n.* **1.** A soldier's first experience of actual combat conditions. **2.** Any severe ordeal experienced for the first time.

Bap·tist (băp′tĭst) *n. Abbr.* **Bap., Bapt. 1.** A member of any of various Protestant denominations believing that the sacrament of baptism should be given only to adult members upon a profession of faith and usually by immersion. **2. baptist.** One who baptizes. **—the Baptist.** John the Baptist. **—Bap·tist** *adj.*

bap·tis·ter·y, bap·tis·try (băp′tĭs-trē) *n., pl.* **-ies. 1.** A part of a church, or a separate building, where baptisms take place. **2.** A font used for baptism. **3.** A tank for baptizing by total immersion used in Baptist churches.

bap·tize (băp-tīz′, băp′tīz′) *v.* **-tized, tizing, -tizes.** *—tr.* **1.** To dip or immerse (a person) in water or to sprinkle water on (a person) during a baptismal ceremony. **2. a.** To cleanse or purify. **b.** To initiate. **3.** To give a first or Christian name to; christen. *—intr.* To administer baptism. [Middle English *baptizen,* from Old French *baptiser,* from Late Latin *baptizāre,* from Greek *baptizein,* from *baptein,* to dip.] **—bap·tiz·er** *n.*

bar[1] (bär) *n.* **1.** A relatively long, straight, rigid piece of any solid material used, for example, as a support, barrier, or structural or mechanical member, or to fasten something. **2. a.** A solid oblong block of a substance, such as soap or candy. **b.** A rectangular block of a precious metal. **c.** A unit of quantity based on such a block. **3.** Anything that impedes or prevents; an obstacle. **4.** A sandbar. **5.** A stripe or band, such as one formed by light or color. **6.** *British.* The heating element in an electric fire. **7.** *Heraldry.* A pair of horizontal parallel lines drawn across a shield. **8.** *Law.* **a.** The nullifying, defeating, or preventing of a claim or action. **b.** The process by which this is done. **9.** The railing in a courtroom enclosing the part of the room where the judges and lawyers sit, witnesses are heard, and prisoners are tried. **10. a.** Lawyers collectively. Preceded by *the.* **b.** The legal profession collectively. Preceded by *the.* **11. a.** A particular system of law courts. **b.** Any tribunal or place of judgment. **12.** *Music.* **a.** A vertical line dividing a staff into equal measures. Also *British* "bar line." **b.** A measure. **c.** A **double bar** *(see).* **13. a.** A counter at which alcoholic drinks and sometimes meals or snacks are served. **b.** An establishment or room containing such a counter. **14. a.** A counter where goods or services of a specified kind are sold or provided: *a hat bar.* **b.** An establishment or room containing such a counter: *a snack bar.* **15.** *British.* An insignia added to a military decoration indicating that it has been awarded a second time. **16.** Variant of **barre. —behind bars.** In prison. —See Synonyms at **obstacle.** —See Usage note at **shoal.**
~tr.v. **barred, barring, bars. 1.** To fasten securely with a bar. **2.** To keep in or out with or as if with bars. **3.** To obstruct or impede; block. **4.** To exclude. **5.** To mark with bars or stripes. **6.** *Music.* To indicate measures in (a piece of music) by using bars. **7.** *Law.* To stop (an action or claim) by legal objection. —See Synonyms at **hinder.**
~prep. Excluding; except for; barring: *That was his best performance, bar none.* [Middle English *barre,* from Old French, from Vulgar Latin (unattested) *barra*†.]

bar[2] *n.* A unit of pressure equal to 10^5 newtons per square meter or 0.98697 standard atmosphere. [German, from Greek *baros,* weight.]

BAR Browning automatic rifle.

bar. 1. barometer; barometric. **2.** barrel.

Ba·rab·bas (bə-răb′əs). A condemned thief whose release was demanded of Pilate by the multitude instead of that of Jesus. Matthew 27:15–26.

Ba·ra·ka (bə-rä′kə), **Imamu Amiri,** born (Everett) LeRoi Jones (1934–). U.S. playwright and poet. He is a leading black nationalist politician and founder of the Black Community Development and Defense Organization (1968).

bar·a·the·a (băr′ə-thē′ə) *n.* A soft fabric of silk and cotton or silk and wool. [19th century : origin obscure.]

barb[1] (bärb) *n.* **1.** A sharp point projecting in reverse direction to the main point of a weapon or tool, as on an arrow, fishhook, or spear. **2.** A cutting or biting remark. **3.** *Botany.* A hooked bristle or hairlike projection. **4.** *Ornithology.* Any of the many parallel filaments projecting from the main shaft of a feather. **5.** Any of various Old World freshwater fishes of the genus *Barbus* (or *Puntius*) and related genera, many of which are popular in home aquariums. **6.** Any of the small folds of mucous membrane below the tongue of horses and cattle. **7.** A white linen covering for a woman's head, throat, and chin, worn in medieval times; nowadays worn by certain orders of nuns. **8.** *Obsolete.* A beard.
~tr.v. **barbed, barbing, barbs.** To provide or furnish with a barb or barbs. [Middle English *barbe,* beard, beardlike appendage, from Old French, from Latin *barba,* beard.]

barb[2] *n.* **1.** A hardy racehorse of a breed that originated in northern Africa. **2.** Any of a breed of domestic pigeons having dark plumage. **3.** *Australian.* A type of sheepdog, a black **kelpie** *(see).* [French *barbe,* Barbary horse, from Italian *barbero,* BARBARY.]

barb[3] *n. Slang.* A barbiturate.

Bar·ba·dos (bär-bā′dōs, -dəs). Prosperous West Indian island, the most easterly of the Antilles. It was probably first visited by the Portuguese, who named it Los Barbados ("bearded") because of its numerous bearded fig trees. The British first landed in 1605 and began colonizing it in 1627. The island was a British colony until 1966 when it became independent within the Commonwealth. The economy is based on sugar and tourism. It is densely populated, and over 80 percent of the people are black descendants of African slaves. Area, 431 square kilometers (166 square miles). Population, 255,000. Capital, Bridgetown. See map at **Trinidad and Tobago.**

Barbados gooseberry *n.* A cactus, the **blade-apple** *(see).*

bar·bar·i·an (bär-bâr′ē-ən) *n.* **1.** Originally, a foreigner; especially, one not Greek or Roman and therefore regarded as uncivilized. **2.** One belonging to a people or tribe considered to have a primitive civilization. **3.** A fierce, brutal, or cruel person. **4.** An insensitive, uncultured person; a boor.
~adj. Characteristic of or resembling a barbarian; rough and uncivilized. [French *barbarien,* from Latin *barbaria,* foreign country, from *barbarus,* BARBAROUS.] **—bar·bar·i·an·ism** *n.*

bar·bar·ic (bär-băr′ĭk) *adj.* **1.** Of, pertaining to, or characteristic of a barbarian or barbarians. **2.** Marked by crudeness or wildness of taste, style, or manner. **3.** Extremely cruel and inhuman.

bar·ba·rism (bär′bə-rĭz′əm) *n.* **1.** An instance, act, trait, or custom characterized by brutality or coarseness. **2. a.** The use of words or forms considered incorrect or nonstandard in a language. **b.** A specific word or form so used. **3.** Anything that offends against accepted standards of taste or manners. [Old French *barbarisme,* from Latin *barbarismus,* from Greek *barbarismos,* foreign or incorrect speech, from *barbaros,* foreign, BARBAROUS.]
Usage: *Barbarism* applies to an uncivilized condition generally, with emphasis on crudity of taste, and to crudity of expression in particular. *Barbarity* primarily denotes grossly cruel behavior.

bar·bar·i·ty (bär-băr′ə-tē) *n., pl.* **-ties. 1.** Harsh or cruel conduct. **2.** An inhuman, brutal act. **3.** Crudity; coarseness. —See Usage note at **barbarism.**

bar·ba·rize (bär′bər-īz′) *v.* **-ized, -izing, -izes.** *—tr.* To make crude or barbarous; corrupt. *—intr.* To become barbarous.

Barbarossa. See **Frederick I.**

bar·ba·rous (bär′bər-əs) *adj.* **1.** Primitive in culture and customs; uncivilized. **2.** Characterized by savagery; cruel; brutal. **3.** Lacking refinement or culture; coarse; boorish. **4.** Of, pertaining to, or designating language that violates classical or accepted usage standards. —See Synonyms at **cruel.** [Latin *barbarus,* from Greek *barbaros,* non-Greek, foreign, rude.] **—bar·ba·rous·ly** *adv.* **—bar·ba·rous·ness** *n.*

Bar·ba·ry (bär′bə-rē). A region of the North African coast from Egypt to the Atlantic Ocean. It takes its name from the Berbers, inhabitants of the area since the 2nd millennium B.C. It fell to the

Arabs (7th century A.D.), who introduced Islam. Between the 16th and 19th centuries, it was notorious for its pirates.

Barbary ape *n.* A tailless monkey, *Macaca sylvanus,* of Gibraltar and northern Africa. A species of macaque, it is the only monkey found wild in Europe. Also called "magot."

Barbary sheep *n.* The aoudad *(see).*

bar·bas·co (bär-băs′kō) *n., pl.* **-cos.** Any of several tropical American trees of the genus *Lonchocarpus,* used locally as the source of a poison for killing fish. [American Spanish, from Spanish, perhaps from Latin *verbascum†,* a plant, mullein.]

bar·bate (bär′bāt) *adj. Biology.* Having a beard, or tufted hairs resembling a beard. [Latin *barbātus,* from *barba,* beard.]

bar·be·cue (bär′bĭ-kyoō′) *n.* **1. a.** A pit or outdoor fireplace for cooking meat or other food. **b.** A grill or similar apparatus used for cooking food outdoors. **2.** Meat or other food cooked over an open fire or on a spit. **3.** A social gathering, usually held outdoors, at which food is prepared on a barbecue.
—*tr.v.* **barbecued, -cuing, -cues.** To roast or grill over hot charcoal or an open fire. [American Spanish *barbacoa,* from Haitian Creole, framework of sticks set on posts, from Taino.]

barbed (bärbd) *adj.* **1.** Having a barb or barbs. **2.** Piercing or stinging: *a barbed statement.*

barbed wire *n.* Twisted strands of fencing wire with barbs at regular intervals. Also called "barbwire."

bar·bel (bär′bəl) *n.* **1.** Any of the slender, whiskerlike sensory organs on the head of certain fishes, such as catfish. **2.** Any of several Old World freshwater fish of the genus *Barbus,* resembling the carp but with a longer snout. [Middle English, from Old French, from Late Latin *barbellus,* diminutive of *barbus,* barbel (the fish), from Latin *barba,* beard (from its beardlike fleshy filaments).]

bar·bell (bär′běl′) *n.* A bar with adjustable weights at each end, used in weightlifting.

bar·bel·late (bär′bə-lāt′) *adj.* Having minute, hooked bristles or hairs. [From New Latin *barbella,* short stiff hair, diminutive of Latin *barbula,* little beard, diminutive of *barba,* beard.]

bar·ber (bär′bər) *n.* One whose business is to cut hair and to shave or trim beards.
—*tr.v.* **barbered, -bering, -bers.** **1.** To cut the hair of. **2.** To shave or trim the beard of. [Middle English *barbour,* from Old French *barbeor,* from Medieval Latin *barbātor,* from *barba,* beard, from Latin.]

Bar·ber (bär′bər), **Samuel** (1910–81). U.S. composer. A musical prodigy, he wrote his first opera at the age of six. Barber's 1956 opera *Vanessa,* with a libretto by Gian-Carlo Menotti, won a Pulitzer Prize.

bar·ber·ry (bär′běr′ē) *n., pl.* **-ries.** A shrub of the genus *Berberis,* having small leaves, clusters of yellow flowers, and small orange or red berries. [Variant (influenced by BERRY) of Middle English *barbere,* from Old French *berberis†.*]

bar·ber·shop (bär′bər-shŏp′) *n.* The place of business of a barber.
—*adj. Informal.* Of or designating male voices singing sentimental songs in close, usually four-part, harmony: *a barbershop quartet.*

barber's itch *n.* Any of various infections of the skin beneath a beard, especially ringworm. Not in technical usage.

bar·bet (bär′bĭt) *n.* Any of various tropical birds of the family Capitonidae, having a broad bill bristled at the base and brightly colored plumage, and related to the toucans. [French, from Latin *barbātus,* BARBATE.]

bar·bette (bär-bĕt′) *n.* **1.** A platform or mound within a fort high enough to permit firing of guns over the parapet. **2.** An armored protective cylinder around a revolving turret on a warship. [French, diminutive of *barbe,* beard.]

bar·bi·can (bär′bĭ-kən) *n.* A tower or other fortification on the approach to a castle or town, especially one at a gate or drawbridge. [Middle English, from Old French *barbacane†.*]

bar·bi·cel (bär′bə-sĕl′) *n. Ornithology.* Any of the minute projections that fringe the edges of the barbules of feathers and interlock with those on adjacent barbules. [New Latin *barbicella,* diminutive of Latin *barba,* beard.]

bar·bi·tal (bär′bə-tôl′) *n.* A barbiturate drug, $C_8H_{12}N_2O_3$, used as a sedative or to induce sleep. [BARBIT(URIC ACID) + (VERON)AL.]

bar·bi·tu·rate (bär-bĭch′ər-ĭt, -ə-rāt′) *n.* **1.** A salt or ester of barbituric acid. **2.** Any of a group of barbituric acid derivatives used as sedatives or to induce sleep. Prolonged use may lead to dependence. [BARBITUR(IC ACID) + -ATE.]

bar·bi·tu·ric acid (bär′bə-toōr′ĭk, -tyoōr′ĭk) *n.* An organic acid, $C_4H_4N_2O_3$, used in the manufacture of barbiturates and some plastics. [Partial translation of German *Barbitursäure* : *Barbitur,* perhaps from the name *Barbara* + UR(IC) + *Säure,* ACID.]

Bar·bi·zon school (bär′bə-zŏn′) *n.* A 19th-century group of landscape painters in France, including Corot, Daubigny, Millet, and Rousseau. [After *Barbizon,* a small village near Paris, where they worked.]

Barbuda. See **Antigua and Barbuda.**

bar·bule (bär′byoōl) *n. Biology.* A small barb or pointed projection; especially, any of the small projections fringing the edges of the barbs of feathers. [Latin *barbula,* diminutive of *barba,* beard.]

Bar·busse (bär-büs′), **Henri** (1873–1935). French novelist and journalist who came to fame with the publication of his novel *Under Fire* (1916), based on his experiences in World War I. His disillusionment led him first to pacifism and later to communism.

barb·wire (bärb′wīr′) *n.* **Barbed wire** *(see).*

Bar·ca (bär′kə). The name of a prominent family of ancient Car-thage, whose members included Hannibal and other Carthaginian generals.

bar·ca·role, bar·ca·rolle (bär′kə-rōl′) *n.* **1.** A Venetian gondolier's song, with a rhythm suggestive of rowing. **2.** A musical composition imitating this. [French, from Italian *barcaruola,* from *barca-ruolo,* gondolier, from *barca,* barge, from Late Latin *barca,* BARK (ship).]

Bar·ce·lo·na (bär′sə-lō′nə). Capital of Barcelona province, in Catalonia, northeast Spain, on the Mediterranean coast. Founded by the Carthaginians, it prospered under the Romans and the Visigoths. It was captured by the Moors (713) and by Charlemagne (801). With the incorporation of Catalonia into Spain, the city grew as the center of Catalan separatist, anarcho-syndicalist, and socialist movements. In the Civil War (1936–39) it was the seat of the Republican government. Barcelona is a major cultural center and an enclave of Catalan art and literature. It is the largest port in Spain and a leading commercial and industrial center.

B.Arch. Bachelor of Architecture.

bar·chan, bar·chane, bar·khan (bär-kän′) *n.* A type of crescent-shaped sand dune, concave on the side sheltered from the prevailing wind. [Russian *barkhan,* from Kirghiz.]

bar chart *n.* A bar graph *(see).*

bar code *n.* A code in the form of vertical lines and numbers printed on a book or item of merchandise, for example, so that it can be identified by an optical scanner.

bar-code (bär′kōd′) *tr. v.* **-coded, -coding, -codes.** To provide with a bar code.

bard¹ (bärd) *n.* **1.** Any of an ancient Celtic order of singing poets who composed and recited verses on the legends and history of their people. **2.** Any poet, especially an exalted national poet. —See Synonyms at **poet.** [Middle English, from Gaelic and Irish *bárd* and Welsh *bardd.*] —**bard·ic** *adj.*

bard², barde (bärd) *n.* Any piece of armor used to protect or ornament a horse.
—*tr.v.* **barded, barding, bards.** To equip (a horse) with bards. [Old French *barde,* probably from Old Italian *barda,* from Arabic *barda'ah,* stuffed packsaddle.]

Bard of Avon. William Shakespeare, so called because he was born and buried at Stratford-on-Avon.

bar·dol·a·try (bär-dŏl′ə-trē) *n.* Inordinate admiration of Shakespeare and his works. Usually used facetiously. [BARD (Shakespeare) + -LATRY.] —**bar·dol·a·ter** *n.*

Bar·dot (bär-dō′), **Brigitte** (1934–). French actress and model. Among her best-known films are *And God Created Woman* (1956) and *Shaloko* (1968).

bare¹ (bâr) *adj.* **barer, barest.** **1.** Without the usual or appropriate covering or clothing; naked: *a bare chest.* **2.** Exposed to view; unconcealed: *laid bare the secret agreements.* **3.** Lacking the usual furnishings, equipment, or decoration: *walls bare of pictures.* **4.** Without addition, adornment, or qualification; simple; plain: *the bare facts.* **5.** Just sufficient; mere: *the bare necessities of life.* **6.** Empty: *a bare cupboard.* **7.** *Obsolete.* Bareheaded. —See Synonyms at **empty.**
—*tr.v.* **bared, baring, bares.** **1.** To make bare; strip of covering. **2.** To expose; reveal: *The dog bared its teeth.* —See Synonyms at **strip.** [Middle English *bare,* Old English *bær,* from Germanic *bazaz* (unattested).] —**bare·ness** *n.*

bare². *Archaic.* Past tense of **bear** (to carry).

bare·back (bâr′băk) *adj.* Also **bare·backed** (-băkt′). On a horse or pony, with no saddle: *a bareback rider.* —**bare·back** *adv.*

bare·faced (bâr′fāst′) *adj.* **1. a.** Having no covering over the face. **b.** Having no beard. **2.** Unconcealed; without disguise. **3.** Presumptuous and shameless; brazen: *a barefaced lie.* —See Synonyms at **shameless.** —**bare·fac·ed·ly** (bâr′fā′sĭd-lē, -fāst′lē) *adv.* —**bare·fac·ed·ness** *n.*

bare·foot (bâr′foōt′) *adj.* Also **bare·foot·ed** (-foōt′ĭd). Wearing nothing on the feet. —**bare·foot** *adv.*

barefoot doctor *n.* A medical worker, especially in rural areas of developing countries, who carries out such tasks as treating simple injuries and ailments, or assisting at childbirth.

ba·rege, ba·rège (bə-rĕzh′) *n.* A sheer fabric woven of silk or cotton and wool, used for women's apparel. [French *barège,* first made in *Barèges,* southwestern France.]

bare·hand·ed (bâr′hăn′dĭd) *adj.* **1.** Having no covering on the hands. **2.** With the hands alone; unaided by tools or weapons. —**bare·hand·ed** *adv.*

bare·head·ed (bâr′hĕd′ĭd) *adj.* Having no head covering. —**bare·head·ed** *adv.*

bare·legged (bâr′lĕg′ĭd, -lĕgd′) *adj.* Having the legs uncovered. —**bare·leg·ged** *adv.*

bare·ly (bâr′lē) *adv.* **1.** By a very little; hardly; only just. **2.** Meagerly; scantily. **3.** *Archaic.* Without disguise; openly.

Bar·en·boim (bär′ən-boim′), **Daniel** (1942–). Israeli pianist and conductor. He married (1967) the cellist Jacqueline du Pré and was musical director of the Orchestre de Paris (1975–89).

Bar·ents (bär′ənts), **Willem** (c. 1550–97). Dutch navigator. Barents commanded expeditions (1594, 1595, 1596–97) to find the Northeast Passage. He discovered Spitsbergen on his third voyage and died after being trapped in the ice off Novaya Zemlya. The accuracy of his charts and meteorological data guaranteed his reputation as one of the most important Arctic explorers.

Barents Sea. Shallow section of the Arctic Ocean lying between Svalbard and Novaya Zemlya. The North Atlantic Current keeps

Barbary ape *The Moors—who occupied Gibraltar for most of the period between A.D. 711 and 1462—are thought to have introduced these small apes to the Rock from their native North Africa. The apes are now the only wild monkeys in Europe. Legend has it that when they leave the Rock, the British will follow.*

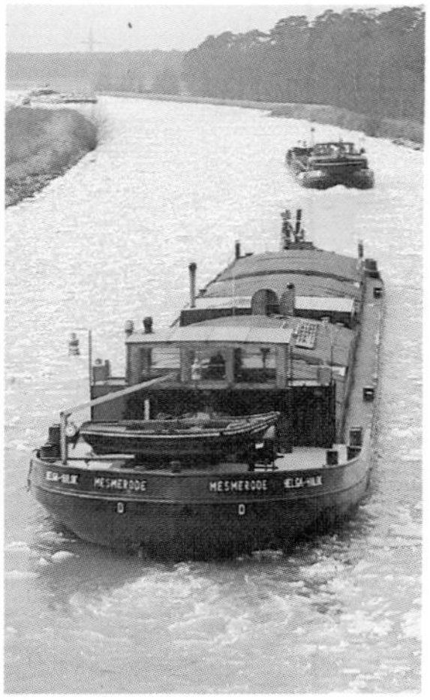

barge *A large flat-bottomed boat for carrying freight. This one is on a canal in Holland.*

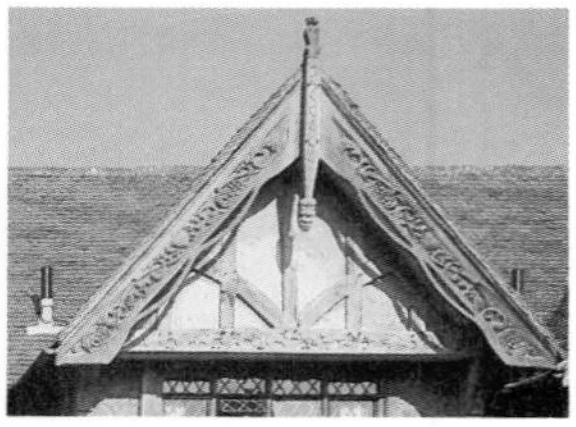

bargeboard *Bargeboards are built against the edge of a gable roof and usually decorated with ornate carving. This Tudor example is at Rottingdean in Sussex, England.*

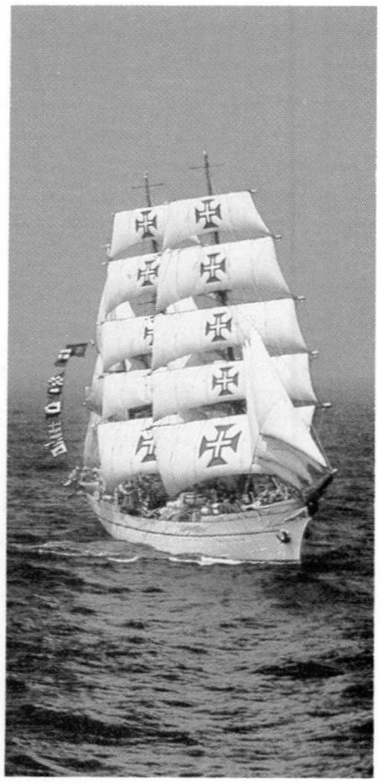

bark *The Portuguese naval training ship* Sagres II *(above) is a modern bark. It has three masts: the forward two are square-rigged; the stern, or mizzenmast, has a fore-and-aft rig.*

its southern ports ice-free all the year. The sea floor is potentially rich in oil and gas; this and the desire of the U.S.S.R. to command the shipping lanes to the strategic ice-free port of Murmansk have led to disputes over the Norwegian-Soviet border across the sea.

bar·fly (bär′flī′) *n., pl.* **-flies.** *Slang.* One who frequents bars.

bar·gain (bär′gĭn) *n.* **1.** An agreement or deal made between parties, especially one involving the sale and purchase of goods or services. **2.** The terms or conditions of such an agreement: *He met his part of the bargain by handing over the goods.* **3.** The property acquired or services rendered as a result of such an agreement. **4.** Something offered or acquired at a price advantageous to the buyer. **—into the bargain.** Over and above what is expected. **—strike a bargain.** To agree on the terms of a transaction.
~*v.* **bargained, -gaining, -gains.** —*intr.* **1.** To negotiate the terms of a sale, exchange, or other agreement. **2.** To arrive at an agreement. —*tr.* To exchange or trade: *He bargained his watch for a meal.* **—bargain away.** To give up or lose (something of value, such as rights or freedom) without getting anything substantial in return. **—bargain for.** To expect; count on: *got more than she'd bargained for.* **—bargain on.** To rely on. [Middle English *bargaynen,* from Old French *bargaignier,* haggle in the market, probably from Germanic.] **—bar·gain·er** *n.*

bargaining chip *n.* Also *chiefly British* **bargaining counter.** Something offered by one side in negotiations to try to get concessions from the other side.

barge (bärj) *n.* **1.** A long, large boat, usually flat-bottomed, used chiefly on inland waterways for transporting freight. It may have its own power or be towed by other craft. **2.** A large pleasure boat used for parties, pageants, or formal ceremonies. **3.** *Slang.* Any old or unwieldy boat or ship. **4.** *Naval.* A power boat reserved for the use of a flag officer.
~*v.* **barged, barging, barges.** —*tr.* To carry by barge. —*intr. Informal.* **1.** To move about clumsily. **2.** To collide. Used with *into.* **3.** To enter or interrupt rudely and abruptly; intrude. Used with *in* or *into.* [Middle English, from Old French *barge,* perhaps from Medieval Latin *barica* (unattested), from Greek *baris,* BARK (ship).]

barge·board (bärj′bôrd′, -bōrd′) *n. Architecture.* A board, often ornately carved, attached along the projecting edge of a gable roof. [*Barge,* perhaps akin to Medieval Latin *bargus,* gallows.]

bar·gee (bär-jē′) *n. British.* A bargeman.

barge·man (bärj′mən) *n., pl.* **-men** (-mĭn). The master or a crew member of a barge.

barge·pole (bärj′pōl′) *n.* A stout pole used for guiding and pushing a barge.

bar graph *n.* A graph consisting of parallel, usually vertical, bars or rectangles with lengths proportional to specific quantities in a set of data. Also called "bar chart."

Ba·ri (bä′rē). Seaport in Italy, on the Adriatic Sea. Once the Roman colony of Barium, it was held successively by Goths, Lombards, Byzantines, Normans, and Venetians and became part of the kingdom of Naples (1557).

ba·ril·la (bə-rēl′yə, -rē′yə) *n.* **1.** Either of two Old World plants, *Salsola kali* or *S. soda,* or a similar plant, *Halogeton soda,* that were formerly burned to obtain a form of sodium carbonate. **2.** The sodium carbonate thus obtained. [Spanish *barrilla*†.]

bar·ite (bâr′īt′) *n.* A colorless crystalline mineral of barium sulfate that is the chief source of barium chemicals. Also called "barytes," "heavy spar." [Greek *barutēs,* weight, from *barus,* heavy.]

bar·i·tone (bâr′ə-tōn′) *n.* Also **bar·y·tone. 1.** A male singer or voice having a range higher than a bass and lower than a tenor. **2.** A part written for a baritone. **3.** A brass wind instrument with a similar range.
~*adj.* **1.** Of, pertaining to, or having the range of a baritone. **2.** Having the second-lowest range in a family of instruments: *the baritone saxophone.* [Italian *baritono,* from Greek *barutonos,* deep sounding : *barus,* heavy, + *tonos,* pitch, TONE.]

bar·i·um (bâr′ē-əm, băr′-) *n. Symbol* **Ba** A soft, silvery-white, alkaline-earth metal, used to deoxidize copper, in various alloys, and in rat poison. Atomic number 56, atomic weight 137.34, melting point 725°C, boiling point 1,140°C, specific gravity 3.50, valence 2. [BAR(YTA) + -IUM.] **—bar·ic** *adj.*

barium enema *n.* A preparation of barium sulfate infused into the rectum in order to reveal the large intestine by x-ray.

barium hydroxide *n.* A white, poisonous, crystalline compound, $Ba(OH)_2$, used in the extraction of beet sugar. Also called "baryta."

barium meal *n.* A preparation of barium sulfate swallowed before x-ray examination of the stomach and small intestine.

barium oxide *n.* A white soluble powder, BaO, used as a dehydrating agent and in the manufacture of certain types of glass. Also called "baryta."

barium sulfate *n.* A fine white powder, $BaSO_4$, used as a pigment, as a filler for textiles, rubbers, and plastics, and as an indicator in x-ray photography of the digestive tract. Also called "baryta."

barium yellow *n.* **1.** A pigment made of barium chromate, $BaCrO_4$. **2.** Light or moderate greenish yellow to brilliant yellow.

bark¹ (bärk) *n.* **1.** The characteristic harsh, abrupt, usually gruff sound of a dog and certain other animals. **2.** Any similar sound, such as a gunshot or cough.
~*v.* **barked, barking, barks.** —*intr.* **1.** To utter a bark. **2.** *Informal.* To cough. **3.** To speak sharply; snap: *He barked at his assistant.* **4.** *Informal.* To work as a barker. —*tr.* To utter sharply in a loud, harsh voice. [Middle English *berken,* to bark, Old English *beorcan.*]

bark² *n.* **1.** The protective outer covering of the woody stems, branches, and main trunks of trees and other woody plants, consisting of dead cells. **2.** A specific kind of bark used for a special purpose, as in tanning or medicine.
~*tr.v.* **barked, barking, barks. 1.** To remove bark from (a tree or log). **2.** To rub off the skin of; bruise. **3.** To tan, dye, or treat medically using bark. [Middle English *barke,* from Old Norse *börkr,* from North Germanic *barkuz* (unattested).]

bark³ *n.* Also **barque** (bärk). **1.** A sailing ship with from three to five masts, all of them square-rigged except the after mast, which is fore-and-aft rigged. Compare **barkentine. 2.** *Poetic.* Any boat, especially a small sailing vessel. [Middle English *barke,* boat, from Old French *barque,* probably from Italian *barca,* from Late Latin, small boat, bark, barge, from Greek *baris,* Egyptian barge, akin to Coptic *bari,* barge.]

bark beetle *n.* Any of various small beetles of the family Scolytidae that damage trees by boring along the surface of the wood beneath the bark.

bar·ken·tine (bär′kən-tēn′) *n.* Also **bar·quen·tine.** A sailing ship with from three to five masts of which only the foremast is square-rigged, the other masts being fore-and-aft rigged. Compare **bark.** [Probably blend of BARK (boat) and BRIGANTINE.]

bark·er¹ (bär′kər) *n.* **1.** An animal or person making a barking sound. **2.** *Informal.* An employee who stands before the entrance to a show and attracts customers with loud, colorful sales talk.

barker² *n.* A person or machine that removes bark from trees or prepares it for tanning.

barkhan. Variant of **barchan.**

Bark·hau·sen effect (bärk′hou′zən) *n.* A phenomenon exhibited by ferromagnetic materials, in which the process of magnetization and demagnetization proceeds in discrete jumps. [First described by Heinrich *Barkhausen* (1881–1956), German physicist.]

barking deer *n.* The **muntjac** *(see).*

bark·y (bär′kē) *adj.* **-ier, -iest.** Covered with, containing, or resembling bark.

bar·ley (bär′lē) *n.* **1.** A widely cultivated cereal grass of the genus *Hordeum*; especially, *H. vulgare,* bearing bearded flower spikes with edible seeds. **2.** The grain of this plant, used as food and in making beer, ale, and whiskey. See **pearl barley.** [Middle English *barrlig,* originally "of barley," Old English *bærlic,* from *bære, bere,* barley.]

bar·ley·corn (bär′lē-kôrn′) *n.* **1.** The seed or grain of barley. **2.** Formerly, a unit of measure equal to the width of a grain of barley, or approximately 1/3 inch.

Barleycorn, John. See **John Barleycorn.**

barley sugar *n.* A clear, hard candy made by boiling down sugar, formerly with an extract of barley added.

barley water *n.* A drink prepared by boiling pearl barley in water, to which lemon juice is often added.

barley wine *n.* A very strong beer.

bar line *n. British.* A vertical line dividing a musical staff into equal measures; a bar.

barm (bärm) *n.* The yeasty foam that rises to the surface of fermenting malt liquors. [Middle English *berme,* Old English *beorma.*]

bar·maid (bär′mād′) *n.* A woman who serves drinks in a bar.

bar·man (bär′mən) *n., pl.* **-men** (-mĭn). *Chiefly British.* A bartender.

Bar·me·ci·dal (bär′mə-sīd′l) *adj.* Also **Bar·me·cide** (bär′mə-sīd′). Plentiful or abundant in appearance only; illusory: *a Barmecide feast.* [From *Barmecide,* name of an 8th-century noble Persian family, one of whom served a beggar an imaginary feast in the *Arabian Nights.*]

bar mitz·vah, bar miz·vah (bär mĭts′və) *n. Judaism.* **1.** A thirteen-year-old Jewish male, considered an adult and thenceforth responsible for his moral and religious duties. **2.** The ceremony conferring and celebrating this status.
~*tr.v.* **bar mitzvahed, -vahing, -vahs.** To admit to the status of bar mitzvah. [Hebrew, "son of commandment."]

barm·y (bär′mē) *adj.* **-ier, -iest. 1.** Full of barm; frothy; foamy. **2.** *British Informal.* Slightly mad; foolish.

barn (bärn) *n.* **1.** A large farm building used for storing grain, hay, and other farm products, and for sheltering livestock. **2.** Any building that resembles a barn in being uncomfortably large and bare. **3.** A large shed for the housing of railroad cars, trucks, or other vehicles. **4.** *Physics. Symbol* **b** A unit of area equal to 10^{-24} square centimeter, used to express nuclear cross sections. [Middle English *bern,* from Old English *bern, berern* : *bere,* BARLEY + *ern, ærn,* house, from Germanic *razn-* (unattested) (see **ransack**).]

bar·na·cle (bär′nə-kəl) *n.* **1.** Any of various marine crustaceans of the order Cirripedia that, in the adult stage, form a hard shell from which feathery food-catching appendages protrude and which remain attached to a submerged surface, thus fouling ship bottoms. See **acorn barnacle, goose barnacle. 2.** Formerly, the barnacle goose. [Middle English *bernak, bernacle,* barnacle goose, from Medieval Latin *bernaca, bernecat*†, barnacle, barnacle goose (from the belief that the geese were produced from the shellfish that supposedly clung to trees).] **—bar·na·cled** *adj.*

barnacle goose *n.* A waterfowl, *Branta leucopsis,* of northern Europe and Greenland, having black, white, and gray plumage.

Bar·nard (bär′nərd, bär-närd′), **Christiaan Neethling** (1923–). South African surgeon noted for pioneering heart transplant operations. He performed the world's first heart transplant (December 3, 1967) at the Groote Schuur Hospital, Cape Town. The recipient was Louis Washkansky, who died of pneumonia 18 days after the operation.

Bar·nard (bär′nərd), **Edward Emerson** (1857–1923). U.S. astronomer. He is noted for his discovery of Jupiter's fifth satellite (1892) and for his discovery of Barnard's star (1916).

Barnard's star *n.* A star in the constellation Ophiuchus, 6 light-years from the sun and the second-nearest star system to the sun. It has an extremely large proper motion, which indicates the presence of an orbiting system of planets.

barn dance *n.* **1.** A social gathering, usually held in a barn, with music and square dancing. **2.** *Chiefly British.* A kind of country dance.

barn door *n.* **1.** The door of a barn. **2.** A target so large that it is hard to miss.

bar·ney (bär′nē) *n. British.* A noisy quarrel.
~*intr.v.* **barneyed, -neying, -neys.** To quarrel noisily. [19th century : origin obscure.]

barn owl *n.* A long-legged owl, *Tyto alba,* having light-brown and white plumage and a heart-shaped face, and often frequenting barns and other buildings.

barn·storm (bärn′stôrm′) *v.* **-stormed, -storming, -storms.** —*intr.* **1.** To travel about the country making political speeches, especially in an election campaign. **2.** To tour rural areas presenting theatrical performances, often in makeshift theaters. **3.** To tour rural areas giving exhibitions of stunt flying, especially in the early days of aviation. —*tr.* To travel through in order to go barnstorming. **—barn·storm·er** *n.*

barn swallow *n.* A widely distributed bird, *Hirundo rustica,* having a deeply forked tail, a dark-blue back, and tan underparts. [The bird often builds its nest in the eaves of barns.]

Bar·num (bär′nəm), **P(hineas) T(aylor)** (1810–91). U.S. showman who first popularized "freak shows" in 1842. Among his exhibits were Chang and Eng, the original Siamese twins. His circus was established in 1871 and in 1881 merged with that of his great rival, James A. Bailey.

barn·yard (bärn′yärd′) *n.* The area of ground surrounding a barn, often enclosed by a fence; a farmyard.
~*adj.* **1.** Of or pertaining to a barnyard: *a barnyard fence.* **2.** Rustic; earthy: *barnyard humor.*

baro– *prefix.* Indicates weight or pressure; for example, **barometer.** [From Greek *baros,* weight.]

Ba·ro·da (bə-rō′də). City in southeast Gujarat state, India. Once the capital of the princely state of Baroda, it is distinguished by many fine public buildings, palaces, and Hindu temples.

bar·o·gram (băr′ə-grăm′) *n.* A graphic record produced by a barograph. [BARO- + -GRAM.]

bar·o·graph (băr′ə-grăf′, -gräf′) *n.* A self-recording barometer. [BARO- + -GRAPH.] **—bar·o·graph·ic** *adj.*

ba·rom·e·ter (bə-rŏm′ə-tər) *n.* **1.** *Abbr.* **bar.** An instrument for measuring atmospheric pressure, used in weather forecasting and in determining altitude. The main types are the **aneroid barometer** and the **mercury barometer** *(both of which see).* **2.** Anything that gives notice of fluctuations; an indicator: *This election will be a barometer of the government's popularity.* [BARO- + -METER.] **—bar·o·met·ric** (băr′ə-mĕt′rĭk), **bar·o·met·ri·cal** *adj.* **—bar·o·met·ri·cal·ly** *adv.* **—ba·rom·e·try** *n.*

barometric gradient *n.* A **pressure gradient** *(see).*

bar·on (băr′ən) *n.* **1.** Formerly: **a.** A feudal tenant holding his rights and title directly from the king or another feudal superior. **b.** A lord or nobleman; a peer. **2.** A member of the lowest rank of nobility in Great Britain, certain European countries, and Japan. **3.** *Abbr.* **Bn., bn.** The rank or title of such a nobleman. **4.** A man with great and coercive power in a specified sphere of commercial activity; a magnate. **5.** A cut of beef consisting of a double sirloin. Also called "baron of beef." [Middle English, from Norman French, from Old French, accusative of *ber,* from Medieval Latin *barō*† (stem *barōn-*), man, warrior.]

bar·on·age (băr′ə-nĭj) *n.* **1.** The rank, title, or dignity of a baron. **2.** A list of barons. **3.** All of the peers of a kingdom.

bar·on·ess (băr′ə-nĭs) *n.* **1.** The wife or widow of a baron. **2.** A woman holding a barony in her own right.

bar·on·et (băr′ə-nĭt, băr′ə-nĕt′) *n.* **1.** A British hereditary title of honor, ranking next below a baron, held by commoners. **2.** *Abbr.* **Bart., Bt.** The bearer of such a title. [Middle English, diminutive of BARON.]

bar·on·et·age (băr′ə-nĭt-ĭj, -nĕt′ĭj) *n.* **1.** The rank or dignity of a baronet. **2.** A list of baronets. **3.** Baronets collectively.

bar·on·et·cy (băr′ə-nĭt-sē, -nĕt′sē) *n., pl.* **-cies.** The dignity or rank of a baronet.

ba·rong (bă-rông′, -rŏng′) *n.* A large, broad-bladed knife used by the Moros of the Philippines. [Native Philippine name, probably akin to Malay PARANG.]

ba·ro·ni·al (bə-rō′nē-əl) *adj.* **1.** Of or pertaining to a baron or barony. **2.** Suited for or befitting a baron; stately; grand.

bar·o·ny (băr′ə-nē) *n., pl.* **-nies. 1.** The domain of a baron. **2.** The rank or dignity of a baron. **3.** In Ireland, a division of a county. **4.** In Scotland, a large estate.

ba·roque (bə-rōk′) *adj.* **1.** *Often* **Baroque. a.** Of, pertaining to, or designating a style in art and architecture developed in Europe from the late 16th to the early 18th centuries, typified by elaborate and ornate scrolls, curves, and other symmetrical ornamentation. **b.** Of, pertaining to, or designating music of this period, characterized especially by chromaticism and elaborate ornamentation. **2.** Ornate or flamboyant in style; richly ornamented. **3.** Irregular in shape: *baroque pearls.*
~*n.* **1.** *Often* **Baroque.** The baroque style in art, architecture, and music. **2.** The period during which baroque styles flourished, from the late 16th to the early 18th centuries. **3.** Any elaborate or ornate style. [French (originally used of pearls), from Portuguese *barroco*†, and Spanish *barrueco*†; (in architecture), from Italian *barroco*†.] See feature, next page.

bar·o·re·cep·tor (băr′ə-rĭ-sĕp′tər) *n. Physiology.* A group of nerve endings, found in the walls of various blood vessels and the heart, that is sensitive to changes in blood pressure.

bar·o·scope (băr′ə-skōp′) *n.* Any instrument or device for estimating atmospheric pressure; especially, a manometer with one leg open to the atmosphere. [BARO- + -SCOPE.]

bar·o·stat (băr′ə-stăt) *n.* **1.** Any device for maintaining a constant pressure, as in the cabin of an airplane. **2.** A device used on gas turbines that regulates the input and output pressures of the fuel-metering equipment, in order to compensate for variations of atmospheric pressure. [BARO- + -STAT.]

Ba·rot·se·land (bə-rŏt′sē-lănd′). A former kingdom in central Africa, now Western province, Zambia, inhabited by the Lozi people. Under their chief, Lewanika (died 1916), the kingdom became part of the protectorate of Northern Rhodesia; and when Zambia became independent (1964), Barotseland tried unsuccessfully to become a separate kingdom.

ba·rouche (bə-ro͞osh′) *n.* A four-wheeled carriage with a collapsible top, two double seats inside opposite each other, and a box seat outside in front for the driver. [German *Barutsche,* from Italian *baroccio,* earlier *biroccio* (unattested), from Late Latin *birotium,* two-wheeled, from Latin *birotus* : BI- + *rota,* wheel.]

barque. Variant of **bark** (ship).

barquentine. Variant of **barkentine.**

bar·rack[1] (băr′ĭk) *tr.v.* **-racked, -racking, -racks.** To house in barracks.

barrack[2] *v.* **-racked, -racking, -racks.** —*intr.* **1.** *British.* To jeer or shout at a player, speaker, or team. **2.** *Australian.* To shout support for a team. Used with *for.* —*tr. British.* To shout against; jeer at. [From native Australian *borak,* banter, chaff.] **—bar·rack·er** *n.*

bar·racks (băr′ĭks) *n., pl.* **barracks.** *Used with a singular or plural verb.* **1. a.** *Abbr.* **bks.** A building or group of buildings used to house soldiers. **b.** A post or station of the state police. **2.** Any large building used for temporary accommodation. **3.** Any unadorned or unattractive building. [From French *baraque,* from Italian *baracca,* soldier's tent, from Spanish *barraca,* mud hut, perhaps from Catalan *barraca*†.]

barracks bag *n.* A soldier's cloth bag, usually with a drawstring, for the storage of clothing or laundry in the barracks.

bar·ra·coon (băr′ə-ko͞on′) *n.* Formerly, a barracks in which slaves and convicts were temporarily confined. [Spanish *barracón,* augmentative of *barraca,* hut. See **barracks.**]

bar·ra·cu·da (băr′ə-ko͞o′də) *n., pl.* **-das** or collectively **barracuda.** Any of various voracious, mostly tropical, marine fishes of the genus *Sphyraena;* especially, *S. barracuda,* having a long, narrow body and projecting jaws with fanglike teeth. [American Spanish *barracuda*†.]

bar·rage[1] (băr′ĭj) *n.* An artificial obstruction in a watercourse, used especially to promote irrigation or prevent flooding. [French, from *barrer,* BAR.]

bar·rage[2] (bə-räzh′) *n.* **1.** A heavy curtain of artillery fire often placed in front of friendly troops to screen and protect them. **2.** Any rapid, concentrated discharge of missiles, or heavy, blanket bombardment. **3.** An overwhelming, concentrated outpouring, as of words or blows: *a barrage of questions.* **4.** A deciding bout in fencing.
~*tr.v.* **barraged, -raging, -rages.** To direct a barrage at. [French, from *(tir de) barrage,* barrier (fire), from BARRAGE (barrier).]

barrage balloon *n.* A balloon anchored singly or as one of a series, supporting cables or nets in order to hinder the passage of low-flying enemy aircraft.

bar·ra·mun·da (băr′ə-mŭn′də) *n., pl.* **-das** or collectively **barramunda.** Also **bar·ra·mun·di** (-mŭn′dē) *pl.* **-dis** or collectively **barramundi.** Any of several Australian food fishes, such as the river fish *Scleropages leichhardtdii,* or the lungfish *Neoceratodus forsteri.* [From a native Australian name.]

bar·ran·ca (bə-răng′kə) *n. Southwestern U.S.* A deep ravine or gorge. [Spanish, probably from Iberian.]

Bar·ran·quil·la (băr′ən-kē′ə, -yə). A large seaport in northern Colombia, on the Magdalena River near its mouth on the Caribbean Sea.

bar·ra·tor, bar·ra·ter (băr′ə-tər) *n. Law.* One who commits barratry. [Middle English, from Norman-French *baratour,* from Old French *barateor,* swindler, from *barater,* to cheat, BARTER.]

bar·ra·try (băr′ə-trē) *n., pl.* **-tries. 1.** *Law.* Formerly, the offense of exciting or stirring up quarrels or groundless lawsuits. **2.** *Maritime Law.* An unlawful breach of duty on the part of a ship's master or crew that is to the prejudice or disadvantage of the ship's owner. **3.** The sale or purchase of positions in the church or state. [Middle English *barratrie,* the purchase of church offices, from Old French *barateric,* deception, from *barater,* to cheat, BARTER.] **—bar·ra·trous** *adj.* **—bar·ra·trous·ly** *adv.*

Bar·rault (bȧ-rō′), **Jean Louis** (1910–). French actor, director, and producer. He was producer-director with the Comédie Française (1940–46) and director of the Theâtre de France (1959–68). His film credits include *La Symphonie Fantastique* (1942) and *Les Enfants du Paradis* (1944).

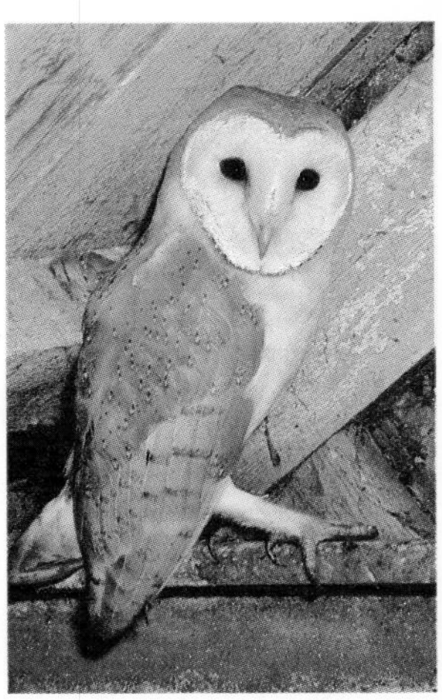

barn owl *The barn owl, which often nests in old barns, has extremely sensitive hearing and, with its silent flight, can hunt rodents by sound alone, even in complete darkness.*

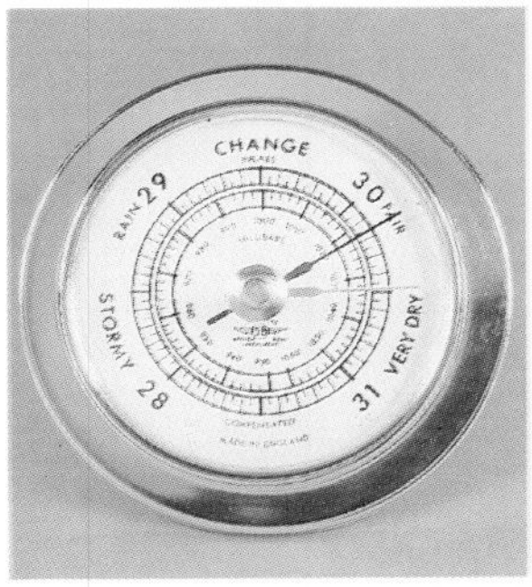

barometer *A modern aneroid barometer. Barometers are used to measure changes in air pressure as an aid to weather forecasting.*

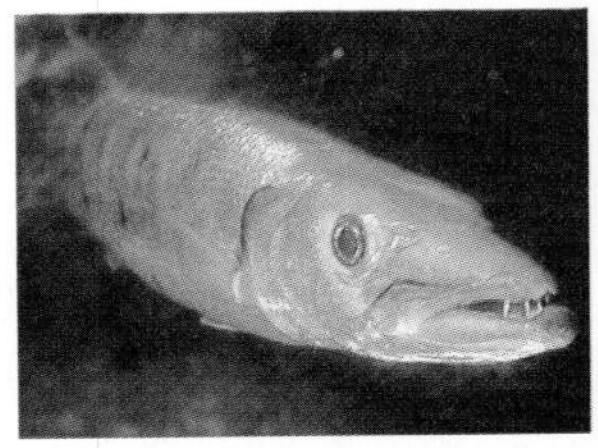

barracuda *A fierce predator of tropical and sometimes temperate waters. It can grow to nearly 2.5 meters (8 feet) long and weigh about 18 kilograms (40 pounds).*

baroque

THE ART OF 17TH-CENTURY ROMAN CATHOLIC EUROPE

An extravagant style of painting, sculpture, and architecture

The baroque was predominantly a style of Roman Catholic Europe, reaching its finest expression in mid-17th-century Rome.

The style is characterized by the subordination of the various parts of a building, sculpture, or painting to an overall dramatic, three-dimensional, even theat-rical effect. Lines are curved and bold, decoration is elaborate, and composition makes a direct appeal to the emotions.

The outstanding exponents of the baroque in Rome were the sculptor and architect Gianlorenzo Bernini (1598–1680), the architect Francesco Borromini (1599–1667), and the painter Michelangelo da Cara-vaggio (c. 1565–1610). Under the auspices of the Jesu-its, the baroque style spread to the German-speaking countries and to the Spanish Netherlands, where the Flemish painter Peter Paul Rubens (1577–1640) reigned supreme.

RELIGIOUS RAPTURE *The Ecstasy of St. Teresa, a group by Bernini, stands in a side chapel of Santa Maria della Vittoria in Rome. The swirling drapery and the ecstatic central figure portray an intense religious experience.*

RELIGIOUS DRAMA *The vault of a chapel completed about 1700 in San Carlo ai Catinari in Rome is an exuberant example of how Antonio Gherardi (1644–1702) combined sculpture and architecture into one overwhelming and dramatic whole.*

RELIGIOUS REALISM *In religious paintings such as* The Supper at Emmaus, *Caravaggio pioneered a new style of intense realism and dramatic use of light and shade.*

barre, bar (bär) *n.* A bar fixed to a wall in a studio to aid ballet dancers when practicing. [French.]

bar·ré (bä-rā′) *n. Music.* A technique, used by guitar and lute play-ers, of laying the forefinger over some or all of the strings and so changing the pitch. [French, "barred."]

barred owl *n.* A North American owl, *Strix varia,* having barred, brownish plumage, a streaked belly, and a strident, hooting cry.

bar·rel (băr′əl) *n.* **1.** A large, nearly cylindrical container, tradition-ally made of wooden staves bound together with hoops, and having a flat top and bottom of equal diameter and, usually, sides that bulge outward in the middle. **2.** The quantity that a barrel with a given or standard capacity will hold. **3.** *Abbr.* **bar., bbl, bbl., bl.** Any of various units of volume or capacity. In the U.S. Customary Sys-tem it varies, as a liquid measure, from 31 to 42 gallons as estab-lished by law or usage. **4.** The metal, cylindrical part of a firearm through which the bullet travels. **5.** A cylinder that contains a mov-able piston. **6.** The drum of a capstan. **7.** The cylinder within the mechanism of a timepiece that contains the mainspring. **8.** The cy-lindrical part or hollow shaft of any of various other instruments and mechanisms. **9.** The ink container of a fountain pen. **10.** *Infor-mal.* A large quantity: *a barrel of fun.* **—over a barrel.** Helpless; defenseless. **—scrape the (bottom of the) barrel.** To use one's last and poorest resources.
~v. **barreled** or **barrelled, -reling** or **-relling, -rels.** *—tr.* To put or pack in a barrel or barrels. *—intr. Informal.* To move at high speed. Usually used with *along.* [Middle English *barel,* from Old French *baril,* probably from *barre,* BAR (rod).]

barrel chair *n.* A large, upholstered chair having a high, rounded back resembling a half-barrel.

bar·rel-chest·ed (băr′əl-chĕs′tĭd) *adj.* Having a very large out-ward-curving chest.

bar·rel·house (băr′əl-hous′) *n.* **1.** A disreputable, old-time saloon or bawdyhouse. **2.** An early style of jazz characterized by free group improvization and an accented two-beat rhythm.

barrel organ *n.* A portable musical instrument operated by the action of a revolving barrel with pegs or pins that open air valves leading from a bellows to a series of pipes.

barrel roll *n.* A flight maneuver in which an aircraft makes a complete rotation on its longitudinal axis while approximately maintaining its original direction.

barrel vault *n. Architecture.* A simple vault with a continuous semicircular section.

bar·ren (băr′ən) *adj.* **1. a.** Not producing offspring; childless or fruitless. **b.** Incapable of producing offspring; infertile; sterile. **2.** Lacking vegetation, especially useful vegetation; unproductive. **3.** Unproductive of results or gains; unprofitable. **4.** Devoid; lacking: *writing barren of insight.* **5.** Lacking in liveliness or interest. —See Synonyms at **empty, sterile.**
∼*n. Usually* **barrens.** A tract of unproductive land, often with a scrubby growth of trees: *the pine barrens of New Jersey.* [Middle English *barein(e),* from Norman French, from Old French *baraigne, barhaine*†.] —**bar·ren·ly** *adv.* —**bar·ren·ness** *n.*

bar·ren·wort (băr′ən-wərt) *n.* A European perennial herbaceous plant, *Epimedium alpinum,* with clusters of red and yellow flowers. [From the belief that it caused sterility.]

bar·ret (băr′ĭt) *n.* A flat cap; especially, a **biretta** *(see).* [French, *barrette,* from Italian *barretta, berretta,* BIRETTA.]

bar·rette (bə-rĕt′, bä-) *n.* A small clasp used by women for holding the hair in place. Also *British* "hair-slide." [French, diminutive of *barre,* BAR.]

bar·ri·cade (băr′ə-kād′, băr′ə-kād′) *n.* **1.** A structure set up across a road, as a means of defense or to obstruct passage. **2.** Anything acting to obstruct passage; a barrier. —See Synonyms at **bulwark.**
∼*tr.v.* **barricaded, -cading, -cades. 1.** To close off or block with a barricade. **2.** To keep in or out by means of a barricade. [French, from *barrique,* barrel (the earliest barricades were made of earth-filled barrels), from Spanish *barrica,* from *barril,* akin to Old French *baril,* BARREL.] —**bar·ri·cad·er** *n.*

Bar·rie (băr′ē), **Sir James Matthew** (1860–1937). Scottish novelist and dramatist. His first novel, *The Little Minister* (1891), was an immediate success. With *The Little White Bird* (1902), he began the Peter Pan cycle, which was continued with the play *Peter Pan* (1904), *Peter Pan in Kensington Gardens* (1906), and *Peter Pan and Wendy* (1908). His later plays include *What Every Woman Knows* (1908) and *Dear Brutus* (1917). He was made a baronet (1913).

bar·ri·er (băr′ē-ər) *n.* **1.** A fence, wall, or other structure built to prevent or control access or passage. **2.** Anything, material or immaterial, that acts to obstruct or prevent passage. **3.** A boundary or limit. **4.** Anything that separates or holds apart: *social barriers.* **5.** A movable gate that keeps racehorses in line before the start of a race. **6. barriers.** The palisades or fences enclosing the lists of a medieval tournament. **7.** *Geology.* An **ice barrier** *(see).* —See Synonyms at **obstacle.** [Middle English; from Norman French *barrere,* from Old French *barriere,* probably from *barre,* BAR.]

barrier beach *n.* A long, narrow bar of sand built up parallel to a coastline by wave action, and exposed at high tide. Also called "barrier island."

barrier reef *n.* A long, narrow ridge of coral or rock parallel to and relatively near a coastline, separated from the coastline by a lagoon too deep for coral growth.

bar·ring (bär′ĭng) *prep.* Unless (something) occurs; excepting: *Barring strong headwinds, the plane will arrive on time.*

bar·ri·o (bä′ryō) *n., pl.* **-os. 1.** An enclave, ward, or urban district in a Latin-American country or in the Philippines. **2.** A chiefly Spanish-speaking community or neighborhood, especially in a U.S. city. [Spanish, from Arabic *barrī,* of an open area, from *barr,* open area, open country, outside.]

bar·ris·ter (băr′ĭ-stər) *n. Chiefly British.* A lawyer admitted to plead at the bar in the superior courts. Compare **advocate, solicitor.** —See Usage note at **lawyer.** [16th century : from BAR (railing) + *-rister,* perhaps by analogy with *minister.*]

bar·room (bär′ro͞om′, -ro͝om′) *n.* A room or building in which alcoholic beverages are sold at a counter or bar.

bar·row[1] (băr′ō) *n.* **1. a.** A flat, rectangular tray or cart, having handles at each end. **b.** The load carried on such a tray. **2.** A **wheelbarrow** *(see).* [Middle English *bar(o)we,* Old English *bearwe,* basket, wheelbarrow.]

barrow[2] *n. Archaeology.* A large mound of earth or stones placed over a burial site. Also called "mound." [Middle English *borewe, burgh,* Old English *beorg,* from Germanic *bergaz* (unattested).]

barrow[3] *n.* A pig that has been castrated before reaching sexual maturity. [Middle English *barow,* Old English *bearg, barg.*]

Bar·ry (băr′ē). Port in South Glamorgan, on the Bristol Channel in southern Wales. Barry Island, a popular holiday resort, is joined to the mainland south of Barry.

Bar·ry·more (băr′ĭ-môr′, -mōr′). Family of U.S. actors. **Lionel** (1878–1954) first appeared on stage at age six. Among his films were *Free Soul* (1931), for which he won an Oscar, and the Dr. Kildare series. His sister, **Ethel** (1879–1959), appeared mainly in the theater but also made motion pictures, including the Oscar-winning *None but the Lonely Heart* (1944). Their younger brother, **John** (1882–1942), was known as "the Great Profile." He appeared on stage as Hamlet and Richard III and in many popular motion pictures, including *Dinner at Eight* (1933).

bar sinister *n.* **1.** A heraldic bend or baton sinister held to signify bastardy. Not in technical usage. **2.** A hint or proof of illegitimate birth.

Bart. baronet.

bar·tend·er (bär′tĕn′dər) *n.* One who mixes and serves alcoholic drinks at a bar. Also *especially British* "barman."

bar·ter (bär′tər) *v.* **-tered, -tering, -ters.** —*intr.* **1.** To trade goods or services without the exchange of money. **2.** To haggle or bargain. —*tr.* To exchange (goods or services) without using money: *He bartered his watch for food.*
∼*n.* **1.** The act or practice of bartering. **2.** Any exchange, as of agreements or concessions by two or more sides; a bargaining. **3.** Something that is bartered. [Middle English *barteren,* probably from Old French *barater,* to barter, cheat, perhaps from Vulgar Latin *prattāre* (unattested), cheat, do, from Greek *prattein,* to do, manage.] —**bar·ter·er** *n.*

Barth (bärt), **Karl** (1886–1968). Swiss Protestant theologian, who advocated a return to the principles of the Reformation and the teachings of the Bible. In his books *Epistle to the Romans* (1918) and *Church Dogmatics,* which he started in 1932 and completed in 1962, he emphasized the sovereignty of God and the inherent sinfulness of mankind.

Barthes (bärt), **Roland** (1915–80). French philosopher and social critic. He wrote on structuralism, modern linguistics, and semiology—the science of signs or sign language, which he extended to clothing, sports, and fashions in general.

Bar·thol·di (bär-thŏl′dē, -tôl′dē), **Frédéric Auguste** (1834–1904). French sculptor. He is best known for his monumental figure of *Liberty Enlightening the World,* the Statue of Liberty in New York Harbor, presented to the United States by France and dedicated in 1886. The statue was extensively restored in preparation for a gala July 4, 1986, centennial celebration.

Bar·thol·o·mew (bär-thŏl′ə-myo͞o′), **Saint,** sometimes called "Nathanael." One of the Twelve Apostles. Mark 3:18.

bar·ti·zan, bar·ti·san (bär′tə-zən, bär′tə-zăn′) *n. Architecture.* A small, overhanging turret on a wall or tower. [Spurious architectural term (coined by Sir Walter Scott), from Scottish *bartisane,* corruption of *bratticing,* from BRATTICE.] —**bar·ti·zaned** *adj.*

Bart·lett (bärt′lĭt) *n.* A widely grown English variety of pear having large, juicy, yellow fruit. [Named after Enoch *Bartlett* (1779–1860), U.S. merchant who cultivated and popularized it.]

Bar·tók (bär′tôk), **Béla** (1881–1945). Hungarian pianist and composer. In 1940 he took up residence in the United States. His compositions blend elements of Eastern European folk music with dissonant harmonies. In addition to three piano concertos, he composed the music for the opera *Duke Bluebeard's Castle* (1911) and for the ballet *The Miraculous Mandarin* (1919). His most popular work is the *Concerto for Orchestra* (1943).

Bar·ton (bärt′n), **Clara,** in full Clarissa Harlowe Barton (1821–1912). U.S. founder of the American Red Cross. She first did battlefield relief work during the Civil War. The U.S. branch of the Red Cross was organized in 1881.

Bar·uch (bâr′ək, bə-ro͞ok′) *n.* A book of the Old Testament Apocrypha.

Ba·ruch (bə-ro͞ok′), **Bernard Mannes** (1870–1965). U.S. financier and statesman. He accumulated a large fortune on Wall Street and after 1916 devoted much of his time to governmental advisory commissions. Baruch was widely known as a confidant and adviser of every president from Woodrow Wilson to John F. Kennedy.

bar·y·cen·ter (băr′ə-sĕn′tər) *n. Physics.* **Center of mass** *(see).* [Greek *barus,* heavy + CENTER.]

bar·y·on (băr′ē-ŏn′) *n.* Any of a family of subatomic particles, including the nucleon and hyperon multiplets, that participate in strong interactions, have half-integral spins, and are generally more massive than mesons. [Greek *barus,* heavy + -ON.] —**bar·y·on·ic** *adj.*

baryon number *n. Symbol* **B** A conserved quantum number equal to the difference between the number of baryons and the number of antibaryons in a system of subatomic particles.

Ba·rysh·ni·kov (bə-rĭsh′nĭ-kôf′), **Mikhail** (1948–). Russian-born U.S. dancer and choreographer. Until his defection in 1974 Baryshnikov danced with the Kirov Ballet in Leningrad. In the United States he has danced with the American Ballet Theater, appeared on television and in motion pictures, and choreographed numerous works, including the classic *Nutcracker.*

ba·ry·ta (bə-rī′tə) *n.* **1. Barium hydroxide** *(see).* **2. Barium oxide** *(see).* **3. Barium sulfate** *(see).* [From BARYTES + *-a,* as in *soda,* etc.]

ba·ry·tes (bə-rī′tēz) *n.* A mineral, **barite** *(see).*

barytone. Variant of **baritone.**

bas·al (bā′səl, -zəl) *adj.* **1.** Pertaining to, located at, or forming a base. **2.** Of primary importance; basic. —**bas·al·ly** *adv.*

basal complex *n.* The part of the earth's crust that lies below any sedimentary rock or sediment and extends down to the Moho; it is usually Precambrian in age. Also called "basement complex."

basal ganglia *pl.n.* Several masses of gray matter situated deep within the brain that are concerned with the unconscious control of voluntary movements.

basal metabolic rate *n. Abbr.* **BMR** The rate at which energy is used by an organism at complete rest, expressed in terms of heat production per unit of body surface area per day.

basal metabolism *n.* The least amount of energy required to maintain vital functions, such as respiration and digestion, in an organism at complete rest.

ba·salt (bə-sôlt′, bā′sôlt′) *n.* **1.** A hard, fine-grained, dense, dark

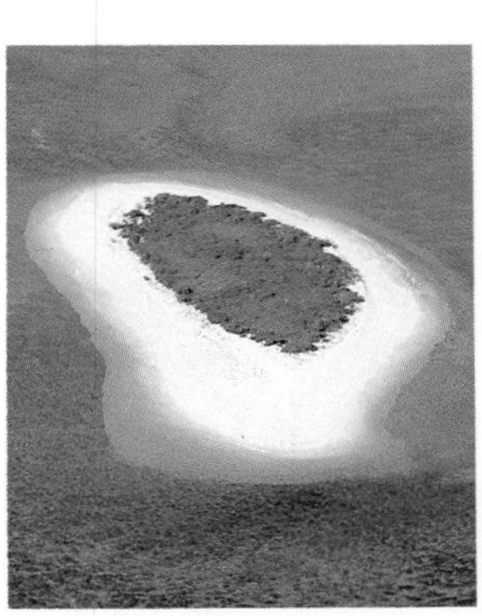

barrier reef *The Great Barrier Reef—the largest barrier reef in the world and the largest structure built by any living creature—runs for more than 1,900 kilometers (1,180 miles) off the coast of Queensland, northeast Australia, and is up to 160 kilometers (100 miles) wide. Formed by coral polyps, the ridge is made up of more than 2,500 separate reefs, some of which, as here, are topped by coral islands.*

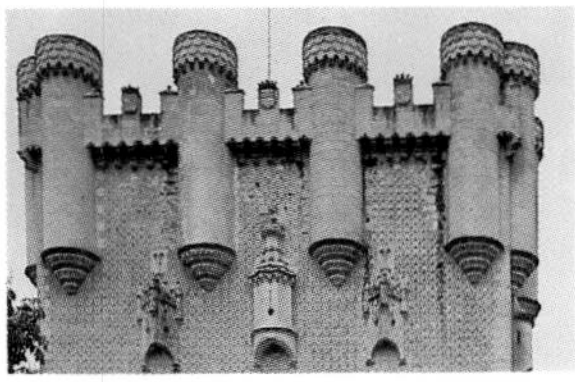

bartizan *Overhanging turrets, or bartizans, jut from the walls of the Alcazar castle at Segovia in southern Spain.*

PRONUNCIATION KEY

ă, pat; ā, pay; âr, **care;**
ä, father, are; b, **bib;**
ch, **church;** d, **deed;** ĕ, **pet;**
ē, be; f, **fife;** g, **gag;** h, **hat;**
hw, **which;** ĭ, **pit;** ī, **pie;**
îr, **pier;** j, **judge;** k, **kick;**
l, **lid, needle;** m, **mum;**
n, **no, sudden;** ng, **thing;**
ŏ, **pot;** ō, **toe;** ô, **paw, for;**
oi, **noise;** ou, **out;** o͝o, **book;**
o͞o, **boot;** p, **pop;** r, **roar;**
s, **sauce;** sh, **ship, dish;**
t, **tight;** th, **thin, path;**
th, **this, bathe;** ŭ, **cut;** ûr, **fur;**
v, **valve;** w, **with;** y, **yes;**
z, **zebra, size;** zh, **vision;**
ə, **about, item, edible, gallop, circus, peaceful**

IN FOREIGN WORDS:

à, *Fr.* **ami;** œ, *Fr.* **feu,** *Ger.* **schön;** ü, *Fr.* **tu,** *Ger.* **über;**
KH, *Ger.* **ich,** *Scot.* **loch;**
N, *Fr.* **bon;** y′, *Fr.* **Compiègne**

STRESS MARKS:

Primary stress: ′
in·cite′ (ĭn-sīt′)
Secondary stress: ′
in′sight′ (ĭn′sīt′)

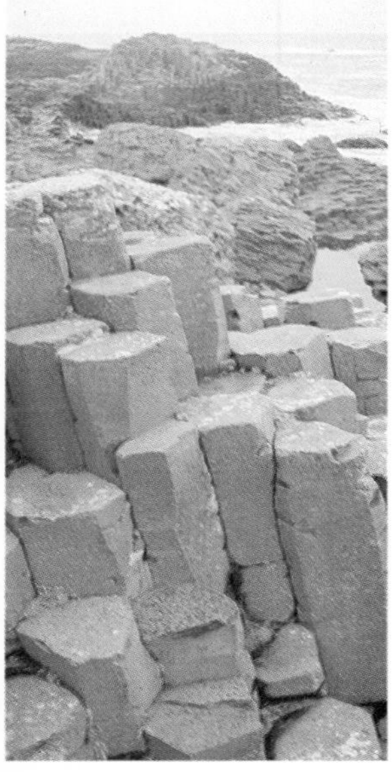

basalt *A common volcanic rock formed from the molten magma of the earth's interior. As it cools, it cracks along natural planes of cleavage, often forming hexagonal columns like these at the Giant's Causeway in Northern Ireland.*

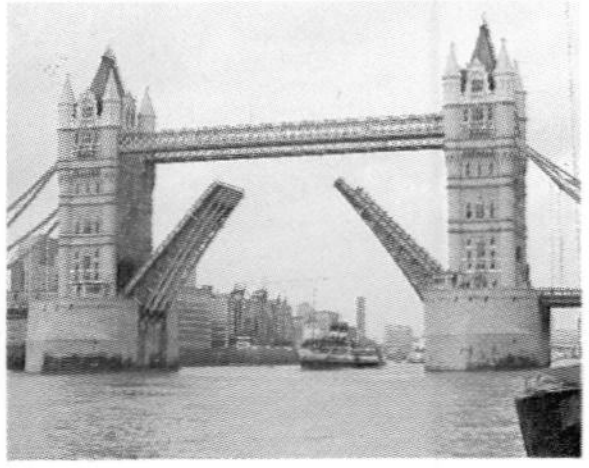

bascule *The roadway of Tower Bridge in London is an example of this kind of counterbalanced apparatus.*

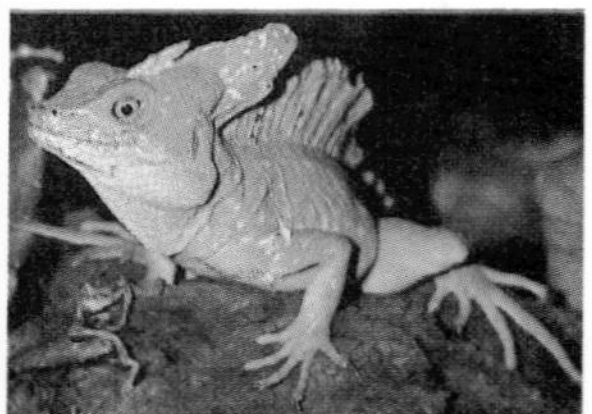

basilisk *A lizard found near Central American rivers and streams. It can run for short distances along the surface of the water on its hind legs, balancing itself upright with its long tail. Its prominent crest, which can be raised like a cockscomb, has caused it to be named after a mythical creature that was reared by a serpent from a rooster's egg.*

volcanic rock composed chiefly of plagioclase, augite, and magnetite and often having a glassy appearance. **2.** A kind of black, unglazed pottery. In this sense, also called "basaltware." [Earlier *basaltes,* from Latin *basaltēs,* manuscript error for *basanītēs (lapis),* touchstone, from Greek *basanitēs,* from *basanos,* from Egyptian *bakhan.*] **—ba·sal·tic** *adj.*

B.A.Sc. **1.** Bachelor of Agricultural Science. **2.** Bachelor of Applied Science.

bas·cule (băs′kyo͞ol) *n.* **1.** A device counterbalanced so that when one end is lowered, the other is raised. **2.** A bridge that incorporates such a device. **3.** A road, forming part of a bridge, that can be raised and lowered. [French, seesaw, from earlier *basse cule,* variant (influenced by *basse,* low) of earlier *bacule* : *bat(t)re,* to beat, BATTER + *cul,* buttocks, from Latin *cūlus.*]

base¹ (bās) *n. Abbr.* **b., B. 1. a.** The lowest or supporting part or layer; a foundation. **b.** An infrastructure: *the nation's industrial base.* **2.** The fundamental principle or underlying concept of a system or theory. **3.** The fundamental ingredient from which a mixture is prepared; a chief constituent: *a paint with an oil base.* **4.** The fact, observation, or premise from which a measurement, study, or reasoning process is begun. **5.** *Sports.* **a.** A goal, starting point, or safety area. **b.** In baseball, any of the four corners of the infield, marked by a bag or plate, which players must pass in order to score. **6.** A center of organization, supply, or activity; a headquarters. **7.** *Military.* **a.** A fortified center of operations. **b.** A supply center for a large force. **8.** *Architecture.* The lowest part of a structure, considered as a separate architectural unit: *the base of a column.* **9.** *Heraldry.* The lower part of a shield. **10.** *Linguistics.* **a.** A morpheme or morphemes regarded as a form to which affixes or other bases may be added; a root or stem. For example, in the words *filled* and *refill, fill* is the base. **b. Base component** *(see).* **11.** *Mathematics.* **a.** The side or face of a geometric figure or solid to which an altitude is drawn or is considered to be drawn. **b.** The number that is raised to various powers to generate the principal counting units of a number system. **c.** The number raised to the logarithm of a designated number in order to produce that designated number. **12.** A line used as a reference for measurement or calculations. **13.** *Chemistry.* **a.** Any of a large class of compounds, including the hydroxides and oxides of metals, that have a bitter taste and are slippery in solution, and have the ability to turn litmus blue and to react with acids to form salts. **b.** A molecular or ionic substance capable of combining with a proton to form a new substance. **c.** A substance that provides a pair of electrons for a coordinate bond with an acid. Also called "Lewis base." **14.** *Biology.* **a.** The region of a part or organ, such as a leaf, that is closest to its point of attachment. **b.** The point of attachment of such an organ. **15.** *Electronics.* **a.** The region in a transistor between the emitter and the collector. **b.** The electrode attached to this region.

∼adj. **1.** Forming or serving as a base. **2.** Situated at or near the base or bottom.

∼tr.v. **based, basing, bases. 1.** To provide with a base: *a mixture based on alcohol; a firm based in San Francisco.* **2.** To provide an intellectual basis for; establish. Used with *on* or *upon.* **3.** To provide the imaginative basis or central idea for: *The play was based on a novel by Dickens.* [Middle English, from Old French, from Latin *basis,* pedestal, base, from Greek.]

Synonyms: *basis, foundation, grounds.*

Usage: *Base* and *basis* both have the written plural *bases,* but the pronunciation differs. The plural form of *base* is (bā′sĭz); the plural of *basis,* (bā′sēz′). *Base* is mainly used literally and refers to the lowest or supporting part or layer of something. It is occasionally used figuratively, as in *the industrial base of the economy. Basis* is nearly always used figuratively to mean foundation, as in the *basis of an argument.*

base² *adj.* **baser, basest. 1.** Having or proceeding from low moral standards; treacherous; contemptible. **2.** Inferior in quality or value; shabby. **3.** Not precious; common: *a base metal.* **4.** Valueless, or greatly depreciated in value; debased: *base currency.* **5.** Corrupted by extraneous elements: *base Latin.* **6. a.** *Archaic.* Of low birth, rank, or position. **b.** Characteristic of a person of low station; servile; menial. **7.** *Obsolete.* Short in stature. —See Synonyms at **mean** (ignoble). [Middle English *bas,* low, inferior, from Old French, from Late Latin *bassus,* fat, low.] **—base·ly** *adv.* **—base·ness** *n.*

base·ball (bās′bôl′) *n.* **1.** A game played with a wooden bat and hard ball by two opposing teams of nine players, each team batting and fielding alternately, the players batting having to run a course of four bases laid out in a diamond pattern in order to score. **2.** The ball used in this game.

base·board (bās′bôrd′, -bōrd′) *n.* **1.** A molding that conceals the joint between an interior wall and a floor. Also *chiefly British* "skirting board." **2.** Any board or plate that serves as a base of something.

base·born (bās′bôrn′) *adj. Archaic.* **1.** Of humble birth. **2.** Born of unmarried parents; illegitimate. **3.** Ignoble; contemptible.

base·burn·er (bās′bûr′nər) *n.* A stove or furnace that automatically replenishes consumed coal or other fuel from above.

base component *n.* In transformational grammar, a set of rules specifying the deep structure of the language. Also called "base."

base hit *n. Baseball.* A hit by which the batter reaches base safely, without an error or force play being made.

Ba·sel (bä′zəl) or **Basle** (bäl). *French* **Bâle** (bäl). City in Switzerland, the capital of Basel canton. It lies on the Rhine River, at the meeting point of the French, German, and Swiss borders. It is a major business and industrial center.

basela. Variant of **bonsella.**

base·less (bās′lĭs) *adj.* Having no basis or foundation.

base level *n.* The lowest level to which a land surface can be reduced by the action of running water.

base·line (bās′līn′) *n.* **1.** A line or imaginary level used as a base for measurement or comparison, as in surveying. **2.** In tennis and badminton, a line bounding each end of a court, marking the limits of play. **3.** In baseball, a path between successive bases.

base·ment (bās′mənt) *n.* **1.** The substructure or foundation of a building. **2.** The lowest habitable story of a building, usually below ground level. Often used adjectivally: *a basement flat.* [Probably from Dutch (obsolete), perhaps from Italian *basamento,* foundation (of a column), from *basare,* to BASE.]

basement complex *n.* A **basal complex** *(see).*

base metal *n.* Any relatively common, inexpensive metal, such as iron or copper, as distinguished from a precious metal, such as gold or silver.

ba·sen·ji (bə-sĕn′jē) *n., pl.* **-jis.** A small dog of a breed originally from Africa, having a short, smooth coat, and not uttering the barking sound characteristic of most dogs. [Bantu.]

base point *n. Heraldry.* The lowest point on a shield.

base rate *n. British.* The rate of interest offered by clearing banks, used as a basis for lending rates.

ba·ses¹. Plural of **basis.** —See Usage note at **base.**

bas·es². Plural of **base.** —See Usage note at **base.**

bash (băsh) *tr.v.* **bashed, bashing, bashes.** *Informal.* To strike or smash with a heavy and crushing blow. Often used with *in.* **—bash into.** *Informal.* To crash into; collide with.

∼n. **1.** *Informal.* A heavy, crushing blow. **2.** *British Informal.* An attempt; a try. **3.** *Slang.* A celebration; a party. [17th century : imitative, perhaps a blend of BANG + *-sh,* as in SMASH or CRASH.]

ba·shaw (bə-shô′) *n. Obsolete.* A **pasha** *(see).*

bash·ful (băsh′fəl) *adj.* **1.** Inclined to shrink from notice through shyness; diffident; self-conscious. **2.** Characterized by, showing, or resulting from social shyness or self-consciousness. —See Synonyms at **shy.** [Middle English *baschen,* short for *abashen,* to ABASH + -FUL.] **—bash·ful·ly** *adv.* **—bash·ful·ness** *n.*

bash·i-ba·zouk (băsh′ē-bə-zo͞ok′) *n.* A member of the Turkish irregulars, a 19th-century cavalry troop noted for its brutality. [Turkish *başıbozuk,* irregular soldier : *baş,* head + *bozuk,* depraved, out of order.]

Bash·kir (băsh′kîr) *n., pl.* **-kirs** or collectively **Bashkir. 1.** A member of a Mongoloid people living in the Bashkir A.S.S.R. **2.** The Turkic language of this people.

Bashkir Autonomous Soviet Socialist Republic. Also **Bash·kir·i·a** (băsh-kîr′ē-ə). An administrative division in eastern European U.S.S.R. in the southwest Urals. It has large mineral deposits and its main agricultural crop is grain. The capital and main administrative and industrial center is Ufa.

basi-, baso- *prefix.* Indicates: **1.** The base or lower part; for example, **basipetal. 2.** A chemical base; for example, **basophil.** [Latin *basis,* BASIS.]

ba·sic (bā′sĭk) *adj.* **1. a.** Of, pertaining to, or constituting a basis; underlying; fundamental. **b.** Simple; unadorned; without extras: *a basic salary.* **2.** *Chemistry.* **a.** Producing, resulting from, or pertaining to a base. **b.** Containing a base, especially in excess of acid. **3.** *Geology.* Containing little silica. Said of igneous rocks. **4.** *Metallurgy.* Of, designating, or produced by a steel-making process in which the furnace is lined with a basic material, such as magnesium oxide. The lining combines with acidic impurities in the ore to form basic slag.

BASIC *n. Computer Science.* A simple high-level computer-programming language. [*B*eginner's *A*ll-purpose *S*ymbolic *I*nstruction *C*ode.]

ba·si·cal·ly (bā′sĭk-lē) *adv.* Fundamentally; essentially.

Basic English *n.* A simplified, copyrighted form of English with a vocabulary of 850 English words and a short list of words in international use, intended to provide a basis for an auxiliary language and for the introductory teaching of English. [Coined by C.K. OGDEN to represent *B*ritish *A*merican *S*cientific *I*nternational *C*ommercial.]

ba·sic·i·ty (bā-sĭs′ə-tē) *n. Chemistry.* The quality or degree of being a base.

basic oxide *n.* A metallic oxide that is a base or that forms a hydroxide if combined with water.

basic process *n.* A method of steel production that uses a furnace lined with a basic refractory material.

basic rock *n.* A dark-colored igneous rock containing less than 52 percent silica bound up in its feldspar and rich in iron and magnesium.

ba·sics (bā′sĭks) *pl.n.* Fundamental or rudimentary principles or practices: *back to basics.*

basic salt *n.* A salt formed from a base by replacement of only part of the hydroxide or oxide content, as in basic lead carbonate, $2PbCO_3 \cdot Pb(OH)_2$.

basic slag *n.* Furnace slag containing a sufficiently high proportion of calcium phosphate to make it useful as a fertilizer. It is produced during the course of basic-process steel making.

basic training *n.* The initial period of training of a recruit in the armed forces.

ba·sid·i·o·my·cete (bə-sĭd′ē-ō-mī′sēt′, -mī-sēt′) *n.* Any fungus of the class Basidiomycetes, which includes the mushrooms, puffballs, and other fungi that produce spores on a basidium. [New Latin *Basidiomycetes* : BASIDI(UM) + -MYCETE.] **—ba·sid·i·o·my·ce·tous** (bə-sĭd′ē-ō-mī-sē′təs) *adj.*

ba·sid·i·o·spore (bə-sĭd′ē-ō-spôr′, -spōr′) *n.* A spore formed on a basidium. [BASIDI(UM) + SPORE.]

ba·sid·i·um (bə-sĭd′ē-əm) *n., pl.* **-ia** (-ē-ə) A club-shaped structure characteristic of basidiomycetous fungi, which produces sexual spores, usually four, at the tips. [New Latin, from Greek *basidion,* diminutive of BASIS.] **—ba·sid·i·al** *adj.*

Ba·sie (bā′sē) **Count,** born William Basie (1904–84). U.S. jazz musician noted for his "big band" sound. One of the great jazz pianists, he was influenced by Harlem ragtime music.

ba·si·fy (bā′sə-fī′) *tr.v.* **-fied, -fying, -fies.** *Chemistry.* To make basic. [BAS(E) + -FY.] **—ba·si·fi·ca·tion** *n.* **—ba·si·fi·er** *n.*

bas·il (băz′əl, bā′zəl) *n.* **1.** An herb, *Ocimum basilicum,* native to the Old World, having spikes of small white flowers and aromatic leaves used as seasoning. Also called "sweet basil." **2.** A related plant, *Calamintha vulgaris,* native to Europe, having dense clusters of small pink or purplish flowers. This species is also called "wild basil." [Middle English *basile,* from Old French, from Medieval Latin *basilicum,* from Greek *basilikon,* "royal," from *basileus*†, king.]

Bas·il (băz′əl, bā′zəl), **Saint,** called "the Great" (*c.* A.D. 330–*c.* 379). Bishop of Caesarea in Cappadocia (from 370) who is credited with the authorship of the liturgy of St. Basil, which is still used on certain days in the Eastern Orthodox Church. He was one of the chief opponents of the heresy of Arianism.

bas·i·lar (băs′ə-lər) *adj.* Also **bas·i·lar·y** (-lĕr′ē). Pertaining to or located at or near the base, especially the base of the skull. [New Latin *basilaris,* from Latin *basis,* BASE (bottom).]

ba·sil·ic (bə-sĭl′ĭk) *adj.* Also **ba·sil·i·cal** (-ĭ-kəl,) **ba·sil·i·can** (-kən). Of or pertaining to a basilica.

ba·sil·i·ca (bə-sĭl′ĭ-kə) *n.* **1.** Any of various oblong buildings of ancient Rome having two rows of columns dividing the interior into a nave and two side aisles, used as a court or place of assembly. **2.** A building of this kind or design used as a Christian church. **3.** *Roman Catholic Church.* **a.** Any of several ancient churches in Rome. **b.** A church or cathedral accorded certain special ceremonial rights. [Latin, from Greek *basilikē (stoa),* "royal (portico, court)," from *basileus*†, king.]

bas·i·lisk (băs′ə-lĭsk′, băz′-) *n.* **1.** A legendary serpent or dragon with lethal breath and glance. Compare **cockatrice. 2.** Any of various tropical American lizards of the genus *Basiliscus,* having an erectile crest at the back of the head. [Middle English, from Latin *basiliscus,* from Greek *basiliskos,* "princelet," diminutive of *basileus*† king; the serpent was believed to have a mark resembling a crown on its head.]

ba·sin (bā′sən) *n.* **1.** An open, rounded vessel with sides that narrow toward the base, used especially for holding or mixing liquids. **2.** The amount such a vessel will hold. **3.** A washbasin; a sink. **4. a.** An artificially enclosed area of a river or harbor, so designed that the water level remains unaffected by tidal changes. **b.** A small enclosed or partly enclosed body of water. **5.** A region drained by a single river system. Also called "river basin." **6.** A vast depression on the earth's surface, filled by an ocean. Also called "ocean basin." **7.** *Geology.* **a.** A tract of land in which the rock strata are tilted toward a common center. **b.** Any bowl-shaped depression in the surface of the land. [Middle English *ba(s)cin,* from Old French *bacin,* from Late Latin *bacchinus* (unattested), from Vulgar Latin *bacca* (unattested), water vessel, BACK (vat).]

bas·i·net (băs′ə-nĕt′, băs′ə-nĭt) *n.* A light, round, close-fitting medieval helmet, often with a visor. [Middle English *bacinet,* from Old French, diminutive of *bacin,* BASIN.]

ba·sip·e·tal (bā-sĭp′ə-təl) *adj. Botany.* Developing or growing in order from the top toward the base. Said of certain leaves and flowers. Compare **acropetal.** [BASI- + -PETAL.] **—ba·sip·e·tal·ly** *adv.*

ba·sis (bā′sĭs) *n., pl.* **-ses** (-sēz′). **1.** A foundation upon which something rests. **2.** The chief or most stable component of anything; a fundamental ingredient. **3.** A principle; a criterion. —See Synonyms and Usage note at **base.** [Latin, pedestal, foot, base, from Greek.]

bask (băsk, bäsk) *intr.v.* **basked, basking, basks. 1.** To expose oneself pleasantly to warmth. **2.** To thrive in the presence of a pleasant or advantageous influence. [Middle English *basken,* probably from Scandinavian; akin to Norwegian dialectal *baska,* to splash in the water, and Old Norse *batha,* to BATHE.]

bas·ket (băs′kĭt) *n.* **1. a.** A container made of interwoven material, such as rushes, twigs, or strips of wood, often having a handle. **b.** The amount a basket will hold. **2.** Something resembling a basket in shape or function, such as the container suspended from a hot-air balloon. **3.** *Basketball.* **a.** Either of the two goals, each consisting of a metal hoop from which an open-bottomed circular net is suspended. **b.** The score, normally worth two points, made by throwing the ball through the basket. [Middle English, from Norman French and Old French *basket*†.]

bas·ket·ball (băs′kĭt-bôl′) *n.* **1.** A game played between two teams of five players each, the object being to throw the ball through an elevated basket on the opponent's side of the rectangular court. **2.** The round, inflated ball used in this game.

basket chair *n.* A chair made of wickerwork or cane.

basket hilt *n.* A sword hilt with a basket-shaped guard serving to cover and protect the hand.

bas·ket·ry (băs′kĭt-rē) *n.* **1.** The craft or process of making baskets. **2.** Baskets collectively.

basket star *n.* Any of various marine organisms of the class Ophiuroidea, related to the starfishes, and having slender, many-branched arms. Also called "basket fish."

basket weave *n.* A textile weave consisting of double threads interlaced to produce a checkered pattern similar to that of a woven basket.

basking shark *n.* A very large shark, *Cetorhinus maximus,* that feeds on plankton and often floats near the surface of the water.

Basle. See **Basel.**

bas mitzvah, bas mizvah. Variants of **bat mitzvah.**

baso–. Variant of **basi-.**

ba·so·phil (bā′so-fĭl) *n.* A cell, especially a white blood cell, having granules that exhibit an affinity for basic dyes. [BASO- + -PHIL(E).] **—ba·so·phil·ic, ba·soph·i·lous** (bə-sŏf′ə-ləs) *adj.*

Ba·so·tho (bə-so͞o′to͞o, -sō′tō) *n, pl.* **-thos** or collectively **Basotho.** A member of an African people, a **Mosotho** *(see).*

basque (băsk) *n.* A woman's close-fitting bodice. [French, variant (influenced by *basquine,* petticoat) of earlier *baste,* from Provençal *basta,* perhaps from Germanic.]

Basque (băsk) *n.* **1.** A member of a people of unknown origin inhabiting the western Pyrenees in France and Spain. **2.** The language of the Basques, of no known relationship to any other language. [French, from Latin *Vascō* † (stem *Vascōn-*), whence also GASCON.] **—Basque** *adj.*

Bas·ra (băs′rə, bŭs′-). Iraq's only port, on the Shatt al Arab in the southeast of the country.

bas-re·lief (bä′rĭ-lēf′) *n. Sculpture.* Relief that projects very little from the background. Also called "basso-relievo," "low relief." [French, from Italian *bassorilievo,* low relief : *basso,* low, BASE + *rilievo,* RELIEF.]

bass¹ (băs) *n., pl.* **basses** or collectively **bass. 1.** Any of several North American freshwater fishes of the family Centrarchidae, related to but larger than the sunfishes. See **largemouth bass** and **smallmouth bass. 2.** Any of various marine fishes of the family Serranidae, such as the **sea bass** and the **striped bass** *(both of which see).* [Middle English, from dialect *barse,* from Old English *bærs.*]

bass² (bās) *n.* **1.** A low-pitched tone. **2.** The notes in the lowest register of a musical instrument. **3.** The lowest part in vocal or instrumental part music. **4.** A male singing voice of the lowest range. **5.** A man who has such a singing voice. **6.** A musical instrument that produces notes in a low register; especially, a **double bass** *(see)* or a **bass guitar** *(see).* **7.** The response to the low-frequency notes of an audio-frequency amplifier, especially in a record player or tape recorder.
~*adj.* **1.** Having a deep tone; low in pitch. **2.** Being the largest and having lowest range of a family of instruments: *a bass recorder.*

bass³ (băs) *n.* A fibrous plant product, **bast** *(see).* [Variant of BAST.]

Bas·sa·no (bə-sä′nō), **Jacopo,** also known as Giacomo da Ponte (1510–92). Italian painter of the Venetian school. He is one of the earliest known artists to depict rustic life in both secular and religious scenes.

bass clef (bās) *n.* A musical clef that designates F below middle C as being on the fourth line above the bottom of the staff. Also called "F clef."

bass drum (bās) *n.* A large drum having a cylindrical body and two drumheads, both of which can be struck to produce a low, resonant sound.

bas·set (băs′ĭt) *n.* A dog, the **basset hound** *(see).* [French, Old French, from *basset,* short and low, from *bas,* BASE.]

basset horn *n.* An alto clarinet in F, having a range of three and a half octaves and sounding notes a fifth lower than they are written. [German *Bassetthorn,* part translation of French *cor de bassette,* from Italian *corno di bassetto* : *corno,* horn + *di,* of + *bassetto,* diminutive of BASSO.]

basset hound *n.* A short-haired dog of a breed originating in France, having a long body, short, crooked forelegs, and long, drooping ears.

bass fiddle (bās) *n. Informal.* A **double bass** *(see).*

bass guitar (bās) *n.* An electric guitar that has the same pitch as a double bass. Also called "bass."

bass horn (bās) *n.* A tuba *(see).*

bas·si·net (băs′ə-nĕt′) *n.* An oblong basket, often resting on legs, used as a crib for an infant. [French, small basin, from Old French *bacinet,* diminutive of *bacin,* BASIN.]

bass·ist (bā′sĭst) *n.* **1.** A person who plays a double bass. **2.** A person who plays a bass guitar.

bas·so (băs′ō, bä′sō) *n., pl.* **-sos** or **-si** (-sē). *Abbr.* **b., B.** A bass singer, especially an operatic bass. [Italian, from Late Latin *bassus,* fat, short, low.]

basso continuo *n.* A **continuo** *(see).* [Italian, "continuous bass."]

bas·soon (bə-so͞on′, bă-) *n.* A low-pitched woodwind instrument with a double reed, having a long wooden body attached to a lateral tube that leads to the mouthpiece. [French *basson,* from Italian *bassone,* augmentative of *basso,* BASS.] **—bas·soon·ist** *n.*

basso os·ti·na·to (ŏs′tĭ-nä′tō) *n.* A **ground bass** *(see).* [Italian, "persistent bass."]

basso pro·fun·do (prə-fŭn′dō, prō-fo͞on′dō) *n., pl.* **basso profundos** or **bassi profundi** (-dē) *Music.* **1.** A bass voice of the lowest range. **2.** A singer having such a voice. [Italian, "deep bass."]

bas·so-re·lie·vo (băs′ō-rĭ-lē′vō) *n., pl.* **-vos.** Also *Italian* **bas·so-ri·**

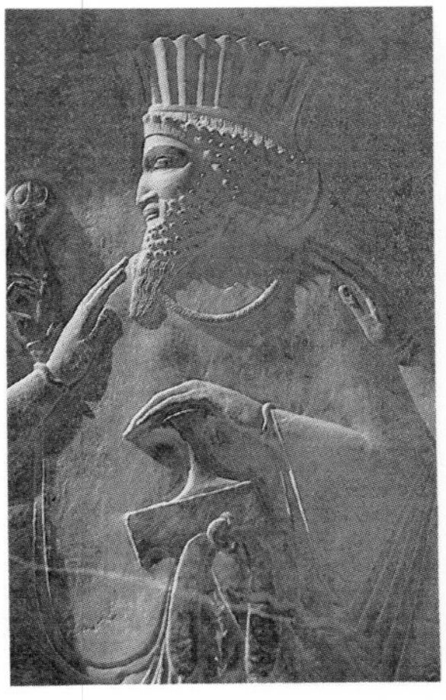

bas-relief *A detail of a bas-relief carving on a wall in Persepolis, Iran.*

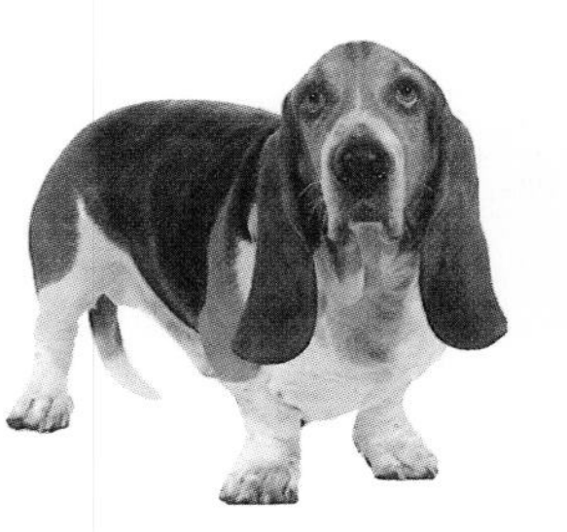

basset hound *Descended from bloodhound stock, the basset has an excellent sense of smell and is used for hunting hares, rabbits, and pheasants.*

PRONUNCIATION KEY

ă, pat; ā, pay; âr, care;
ä, father, are; b, bib;
ch, church; d, deed; ĕ, pet;
ē, be; f, fife; g, gag; h, hat;
hw, which; ĭ, pit; ī, pie;
îr, pier; j, judge; k, kick;
l, lid, needle; m, mum;
n, no, sudden; ng, thing;
ŏ, pot; ō, toe; ô, paw, for;
oi, noise; ou, out; o͝o, book;
o͞o, boot; p, pop; r, roar;
s, sauce; sh, ship, dish;
t, tight; th, thin, path;
th, this, bathe; ŭ, cut; ûr, fur;
v, valve; w, with; y, yes;
z, zebra, size; zh, vision;
ə, about, item, edible, gallop, circus, peaceful

IN FOREIGN WORDS:

à, *Fr.* ami; œ, *Fr.* feu, *Ger.* schön; ü, *Fr.* tu, *Ger.* über; KH, *Ger.* ich, *Scot.* loch; N, *Fr.* bon; y′, *Fr.* Compiègne

STRESS MARKS:

Primary stress: ′
in·cite′ (ĭn-sīt′)
Secondary stress: ′
in′sight′ (ĭn′sīt′)

lie·vo (bä′sō-rē-lyâ′vō) pl. **-vi** (-vē). Sculpture. **Bas-relief** (see). [Italian, BAS-RELIEF.]

bass saxophone (bās) n. A large saxophone with a low range, usually supported on a stand while being played.

Bass Strait (bās). A channel separating mainland Australia from Tasmania. It is 240 kilometers (150 miles) at its widest point and 290 kilometers (180 miles) long.

bass viol (bās) n. Music. **1.** A **double bass** (see). **2.** A **viola da gamba** (see).

bass·wood (băs′wŏŏd′) n. **1.** Any of several linden trees of eastern North America; especially, Tilia americana, having clusters of fragrant yellowish flowers. **2.** The soft, light-colored wood of any of these trees.

bast (băst) n. Botany. **1.** The fibrous or somewhat woody outer layer of the stems of certain plants, such as flax, hemp, and ramie, used to make cordage and textiles. Also called "bass." **2.** A plant tissue, **phloem** (see). [Middle English baste, Old English bæst, from Common Germanic bastaz (unattested).]

bas·tard (băs′tərd) n. **1.** An illegitimate child. **2.** Slang. **a.** A mean, disagreeable, or obnoxious person. Used derogatorily. **b.** A person, especially a man. Used familiarly or humorously: lucky bastard. **c.** A tedious or difficult task or problem. **3.** Any product of irregular, inferior, or dubious origin. ~adj. **1.** Born of unwed parents; illegitimate. **2.** Not genuine; spurious. **3.** Of inferior breed or kind. **4.** Resembling a known kind or species, but not truly such: bastard toadflax. [Middle English, from Old French, perhaps (fils de) bast, "packsaddle (son)," from Medieval Latin bastum, packsaddle, perhaps from Vulgar Latin bastāre (unattested), to carry, from Greek bastazein†, to lift, bear.] —**bas·tard·ly** adj.

bas·tard·ize (băs′tər-dīz′) tr.v. **-ized, -izing, -izes.** To debase; corrupt. —**bas·tard·i·za·tion** n.

bastard toadflax n. Any plant of the genus Comandra; especially, C. umbellata, of eastern North America, having rounded clusters of small greenish flowers.

bastard wing n. Ornithology. An **alula** (see).

bas·tard·y (băs′tər-dē) n. The condition of being of illegitimate birth; illegitimacy.

baste¹ (bāst) tr.v. **basted, basting, bastes.** To sew loosely with large running stitches so as to hold together temporarily; tack. [Middle English basten, from Old French bastir, from Common Germanic bastjan (unattested), to sew with bast, from bastaz (unattested), BAST.]

baste² tr.v. **basted, basting, bastes.** To pour pan drippings or sauce over (meat) while cooking. [16th century : origin obscure.]

baste³ tr.v. **basted, basting, bastes. 1.** To beat vigorously; thrash. **2.** To berate. [Perhaps ultimately from Old Norse beysta, to thrash, strike.]

Bas·ti·a (bäs′tē-ə, bäs′-). Port on the northeast coast of Corsica, France, and the largest city on the island.

bas·tille, bas·tile (băs-tēl′) n. **1.** A prison. **2.** A fortress. [Middle English, from Old French, variant of bastide, from Provençal bastida, from the past participle of bastir, to build.]

Bas·tille (băs-tēl′). A fortress in Paris used as a prison until captured on July 14, 1789, at the outset of the French Revolution.

bas·ti·na·do (băs′tə-nā′dō, -nä′dō) n., pl. **-does.** Also **bas·ti·nade** (-tə-nād′, -näd′). **1.** A beating with a stick or cudgel, especially on the soles of the feet. **2.** A stick or cudgel. ~tr.v. **bastinadoed, -doing, -does.** Also **bas·ti·nade, -naded, -nading, -nades.** To subject to a beating, especially on the soles of the feet. [Spanish bastonada, from baston, stick, BATON.]

bast·ing (bā′stĭng) n. **1.** The act of sewing together loosely. **2.** The thread used to baste. **3. bastings.** The loose stitches used to baste material; tacking.

bas·ti·on (băs′chən, băs′tē-ən) n. **1.** A projecting part of a rampart or other fortification. **2.** Any well-fortified or defended position. **3.** A person, place, or institution regarded as a defender or stronghold of a belief, cause, or the like. —See Synonyms at **bulwark.** [French, from earlier bastillon, from Old French bastille, BASTILLE.]

bast·naes·ite, bast·nas·ite (băst′nə-sīt′) n. A yellowish to reddish-brown mineral, a fluorocarbonate of several lanthanide elements, used as a rare-earth ore. [Swedish bastnäsit, after Bastnäs, Sweden, where it was discovered.]

Ba·su·to (bə-sōō′tō) n., pl **-tos** or collectively **Basuto. 1.** A **Mosotho** (see). **2.** The dialect of **Sotho** (see) spoken in Lesotho. In both senses, not in current usage.

Basutoland. See **Lesotho.**

bat¹ (băt) n. **1.** A stout wooden stick or club; a cudgel. **2.** A blow, as with a stick. **3. a.** Baseball. A rounded wooden club, wider and heavier at the hitting end and tapering at the handle, used to strike the ball. **b.** Cricket. A wooden club having a broad, flat-surfaced hitting end and a narrow handle. **c.** The club or racket used in other games, such as table tennis. **d.** Either of a pair of sticks with flat round ends used to guide taxiing aircraft. **4.** Cricket. A batsman. **5.** Slang. A binge; a spree. —**at bat.** Baseball & Cricket. Taking one's turn batting. —**go to bat for.** Informal. To support or defend. —**(right) off the bat.** Informal. Without hesitation; immediately. ~v. **batted, batting, bats.** —tr. **1.** To hit with, or as if with, a club or bat. **2.** Baseball. To have (some specified score) as a batting average. **3.** Informal. To discuss or consider at length. Usually used with around. —intr. **1.** Baseball. **a.** To use a bat. **b.** To have a turn at bat. **2.** Slang. To go from place to place; wander. [Middle English bat, late Old English batt, cudgel, club, probably from Old French batte, club, from battre, to beat.]

bat² n. **1.** Any of various nocturnal flying mammals of the order Chiroptera, having membranous wings that extend from the forelimbs to the hind limbs or tail. The order is subdivided into the **fruit bats** and the **insectivorous bats** (both of which see). **2.** Slang. A small-minded, nagging person, usually a woman. Used chiefly in the phrase old bat. —**have bats in the belfry.** Slang. To be eccentric; have foolish or crazy ideas. [16th-century variant of Middle English bakke, from Scandinavian; akin to Middle Swedish -bakka, from Old Norse -blaka in ledhrblaka, "leather-flapper," bat.]

bat³ tr.v. **batted, batting, bats.** To wink or flutter: to bat one's eyelashes. —**not bat an eye.** To evince no sign of surprise or emotion. [Probably a variant of BATE (flap).]

bat. battalion.

Ba·taan (bə-tăn′, -tän′). A mountainous, jungle-covered peninsula of western Luzon, the Philippines. In World War II it was the scene of defensive action by U.S. and Filipino troops who resisted the Japanese advance for three months (1942).

Batavia. See **Jakarta.**

batch¹ (băch) n. **1.** The amount of loaves, cakes, or the like produced at one baking. **2.** The quantity of something produced as the result of one operation: a batch of cement. **3.** The quantity of material needed for one operation: a batch of dough. **4.** Any group of persons or things treated or regarded as a set: He was working on a second batch of inquiries. [Middle English bacche, Old English bæcce (unattested), from bacan, to BAKE.]

batch². Variant of **bach** (to live alone).

batch processing n. Computer Science. A system in which data is accumulated and processed together as a single unit. Compare **time-sharing.**

bate¹ (bāt) tr.v. **bated, bating, bates. 1.** To lessen the force of; hold back: with bated breath. **2.** To take away; subtract. [Middle English baten, variant of abaten, to ABATE.]

bate² intr.v. **bated, bating, bates.** Also **bait.** Falconry. To flap the

---

bat

THE MAMMAL THAT CAN FLY

How some bat species "see" in the dark

Bats are the only mammals that fly. There are nearly 950 species, which can be grouped according to what they eat. Fruit bats, which often have wingspans of up to 1.5 meters (5 feet), feed on fruit and nectar; some species of insect-eating bats feed on flowers, birds, lizards, or fish, as well as insects; and vampire bats live on blood that they obtain by making a small incision in a sleeping animal.

Most bats are nocturnal and navigate by echolocation, sending out sounds and sensing the shape and location of an object from the echoes. However, fruit bats—a large number among the bat species—do not use echolocation.

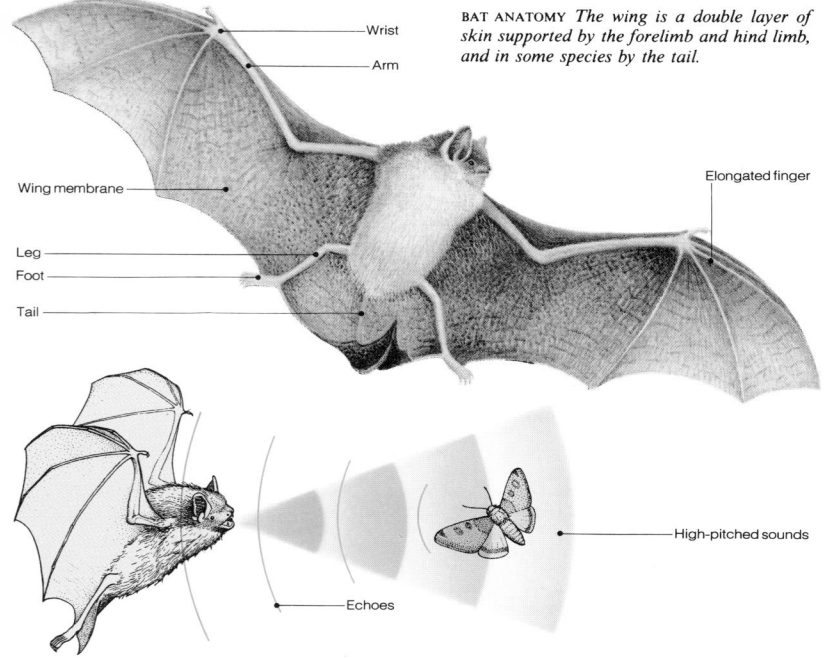

BAT ANATOMY *The wing is a double layer of skin supported by the forelimb and hind limb, and in some species by the tail.*

Wrist
Arm
Wing membrane
Leg
Foot
Tail
Elongated finger
High-pitched sounds
Echoes

ECHOLOCATION *To find food and navigate at night, a bat emits high-pitched sounds. Echoes are reflected from prey such as moths, or from obstacles, and are picked up by the bat.*

wings wildly, as if in impatience. [Middle English *baten,* from Old French *bat(t)re,* to beat, BATTER.]

ba·teau (bă-tō′) *n., pl.* **-teaux** (-tōz′). A light, flat-bottomed boat, used especially in Louisiana and Canada. [Canadian French, from French, from Old French *batel,* from Old English *bāt,* BOAT.]

Bates (bāts), **Henry Walter** (1825–92). British naturalist and explorer who gave his name to Batesian mimicry, a phenomenon he discovered in the Amazon valley.

Bates, Herbert Ernest (1905–74). British novelist and short-story writer. During World War II he served with the Royal Air Force and, as "Flying Officer X," wrote many short stories based on his experiences. He also wrote war novels under his own name, the best known of which is *Fair Stood the Wind for France* (1944). His other novels include *The Darling Buds of May* (1958) and *A Moment in Time* (1964).

Bates·i·an mimicry (bāt′sē-ən) *n.* A defense mechanism that confers a degree of protection against predators on an otherwise defenseless species of animal, in which the harmless species bears a strong resemblance to another species that is dangerous or unpalatable to its predators. Also called "protective coloring."

Bate·son (bāt′sən), **William** (1861–1926). British biologist, one of the founders of the science of genetics.

bat·fish (băt′fĭsh′) *n., pl.* **-fishes** or collectively **batfish.** Any of various marine fishes of the family Ogcocephalidae, having a flattened body and fleshy pectoral and pelvic fins, and living on the sea floor.

bat·fowl (băt′foul′) *intr.v.* **-fowled, -fowling, -fowls.** To catch roosting birds at night by blinding them with a light. [BAT (club) + FOWL, later associated with BAT (animal) and the use of a blinding light.]

bath[1] (băth, bäth) *n., pl.* **baths** (bă*th*z, băths, bä*th*z, bäths). **1.** The act of washing, dipping, or immersing the body in water. **2.** The water used for bathing. **3.** *Chiefly British.* A bathtub. **4.** A liquid, or a liquid and its container, used to regulate the temperature of, soak, or otherwise act upon an immersed object. **5.** A bathroom. **6.** *Usually* **baths.** A public building with facilities for swimming and, sometimes, for washing. **7.** *Often* **baths.** A resort providing therapeutic baths; a spa. [Middle English *bath,* Old English *bæth.*]

bath[2] (băth) *n.* An ancient Hebrew unit of liquid measure, equal to approximately 10 U.S. gallons. [Hebrew.]

Bath (băth, bäth). City in Avon, on the Lower Avon River in southwest England. Its Roman baths are considered to be among the best of the Roman remains in Britain. It was a fashionable spa town in the 18th century and has many elegant Georgian buildings.

Bath brick *n.* Fine calcareous and siliceous silt pressed into blocks and used for scouring and polishing metal. [After BATH.]

Bath chair *n. Sometimes* **bath chair.** A hooded wheelchair used especially by invalids, as at a spa. [After BATH, where it was first used.]

bathe (bā*th*) *v.* **bathed, bathing, bathes.** —*intr.* **1.** To take a bath; wash oneself. **2.** To go swimming. **3.** To become immersed in or as if in liquid. —*tr.* **1.** To immerse in liquid. **2.** To wash or wet. **3.** To apply a liquid to for soothing or healing purposes. **4.** To suffuse: *The garden was bathed in sunlight.* [Middle English *bathen,* Old English *bathian.*] —**bath·er** *n.*

ba·thet·ic (bə-thĕt′ĭk) *adj.* Characterized by bathos. [Probably a blend of BATHOS and PATHETIC.] —**ba·thet·i·cal·ly** *adv.*

bath·house (băth′hous′, bäth′-) *n.* **1.** A building equipped for bathing. **2.** A building with dressing rooms for swimmers.

bathing beauty *n.* An attractive young woman in a bathing suit, especially one who is a contestant in a beauty contest.

bathing machine *n.* In former times, a small hut on wheels that could be moved to the edge of the sea, and in which bathers changed their clothes.

bathing suit *n.* A garment worn for swimming; a swimsuit. Also *chiefly British* "bathing costume."

bath·mat (băth′măt′, bäth′-) *n.* A washable mat used in front of a bathtub.

batho–. Variant of **bathy-.**

bath·o·lith (băth′ə-lĭth′) *n.* Also **bath·o·lite** (-līt′). A large irregularly shaped body of igneous rock that has melted and intruded surrounding strata at great depths, and usually covering more than 100 square kilometers (40 square miles). [German : BATHO- + -LITH.] —**bath·o·lith·ic** *adj.*

ba·thom·e·ter (bə-thŏm′ə-tər) *n.* An instrument used to measure the depth of water. [BATHO- + -METER.]

bath·o·pho·bi·a (băth′ə-fō′bē-ə) *n.* An abnormal fear of depths.

ba·thos (bā′thŏs′) *n.* **1. a.** A ludicrously abrupt transition from an elevated or inspired to a commonplace style. **b.** An anticlimax. **c.** The lowest point; a nadir. **2. a.** Insincere or grossly sentimental pathos. **b.** Extreme triteness or dullness. —See Usage note at **pathos.** [Greek, depth, from *bathus,* deep.]

bath·robe (băth′rōb′, bäth′-) *n.* A loose-fitting robe worn before and after bathing and for lounging; a dressing gown.

bath·room (băth′ro͞om′, -ro͝om′, bäth′-) *n.* A room equipped for taking a bath or shower and usually also containing a washbasin and toilet.

bath salts *pl.n.* Crystals for scenting or softening bath water.

Bath·she·ba (băth-shē′bə, băth′shĭ-bə). The wife of Uriah and later of David and, by David, the mother of Solomon. II Samuel 11–12.

bath·tub (băth′tŭb′, bäth′-) *n.* An oblong tub for bathing. Also *chiefly British* "bath."

Bath·urst[1] (băth′ərst). City in New South Wales, Australia, on the Macquarie River. It was the scene of a gold rush in 1851.

Bathurst[2]. See **Banjul.**

bathy–, batho– *prefix.* Indicates deepness or some relationship to depth; for example, **bathyscaph, bathometer.** [From Greek *bathus,* deep, and *bathos,* depth, from *bathus.*]

bath·y·al (băth′ē-əl) *adj.* Of, pertaining to, or designating a zone on the continental slope between 200 and 2,000 meters (650 and 6,550 feet) below sea level. [BATHY- + -AL.]

ba·thym·e·try (bə-thĭm′ə-trē) *n.* The measurement of the depth of large bodies of water. [French *bathymétrie* : BATHY- + -METRY.] —**bath·y·met·ric** (băth′ə-mĕt′rĭk) **bath·y·met·ri·cal** *adj.* —**bath·y·met·ri·cal·ly** *adv.*

bath·y·pe·lag·ic (băth′ə-pə-lăj′ĭk) *adj.* Of, relating to, or living in the depths of the ocean, especially below 2,000 feet.

bath·y·scaph (băth′ĭ-skăf′) *n.* Also **bath·y·scaphe** (-skăf, -skāf′). A free-diving, self-contained, deep-sea research vessel, consisting essentially of a large flotation hull with a manned observation capsule fixed to its underside. [BATHY- + Greek *skaphē,* basin, light boat.]

bath·y·sphere (băth′ĭ-sfîr′) *n.* A reinforced, spherical deep-diving chamber, manned, and lowered by cable.

bath·y·ther·mo·graph (băth′ə-thûr′mə-grăf′, -gräf′) *n.* An instrument that records water temperature as a function of depth.

ba·tik, bat·tik (bə-tēk′, băt′ĭk) *n.* **1.** A method of dyeing print into a fabric in which the parts of the cloth not intended to be dyed are covered with removable wax. **2.** The print that is dyed into cloth by this method. **3.** The cloth so dyed. [Malay, from Javanese, "painted."] —**ba·tik** *adj.*

Ba·tis·ta y Zal·dí·var (bə-tēs′tə ē zäl-dē′vär), **Fulgencio** (1901–73). Cuban president (1940–44; 1954–58). His repressive and authoritarian style of government proved unpopular, and, on New Year's Day, 1959, he was ousted by a revolutionary movement led by Fidel Castro.

ba·tiste (bə-tēst′, bă-) *n.* A fine, plain-woven fabric made from various fibers and used especially for clothing. [Earlier *baptist cloth* (translation of French *toile de Batiste*), first made by *Baptiste* of Cambrai (13th century).]

Ba·tjan, Ba·chan (bä′chän). A large island, 2,367 square kilometers (914 square miles) in area, in the Moluccas, Indonesia, lying southwest of Halmahera Island.

bat·man (băt′mən) *n., pl.* **-men** (-mĭn). In the British armed forces, a soldier who is an officer's personal servant. [Obsolete *bat,* packsaddle, from Middle English *batt,* from Old French *ba(s)t,* from (unattested), a carrying, perhaps from Vulgar Latin *bastum* (unattested), a carrying, perhaps from *bastāre* (unattested), to carry (see **bastard**) + MAN.]

bat mitz·vah, bat miz·vah (bät mĭts′və) *n.* Also **bas mitz·vah** (bäs), **bas miz·vah.** *Judaism.* **1.** A Jewish girl, usually between twelve and fourteen years, considered an adult and thenceforth responsible for her moral and religious duties. **2.** In some congregations, the ceremony marking the arrival of a girl's religious commitment. See **bar mitzvah.** [Hebrew *baṭ mitzvāh,* "daughter of commandment."]

ba·ton (bə-tŏn′, băt′n) *n.* **1.** A short staff carried by some public and military officials as a symbol of office. **2.** A slender wooden stick or rod used by a conductor to direct an orchestra or band. **3.** The hollow metal rod with heavy rubber tips twirled by a drum major or majorette. **4.** *British.* A short thick stick used by the police as a weapon. **5.** *Heraldry.* A shortened narrow **bend** *(see)* on a coat of arms, often signifying bastardy. [French *bâton,* from Old French *baston,* from Vulgar Latin *baston-* (unattested), from Late Latin *bastum,* stick.]

Bat·on Rouge (băt′n ro͞ozh′). Capital of Louisiana. Situated on the Mississippi River at the head of oceangoing navigation, it is also a major industrial and commercial center.

bat·o·pho·bi·a (băt′ə-fō′bē-ə) *n.* An abnormal fear of being near an object of great height, such as a skyscraper or mountain. [Gk. *batos,* passable + -PHOBIA.]

ba·tra·chi·an (bə-trā′kē-ən) *adj.* Of or pertaining to frogs and toads. ~*n.* A frog or toad. [New Latin *Batrachia* (former order name, now Salienta), from Greek *batrakhos*†, frog.]

bats (băts) *adj. Slang.* Eccentric; insane.

bats·man (băts′mən) *n., pl.* **-men** (-mĭn). **1.** *Baseball & Cricket.* A batter. **2.** *Aeronautics.* A ground official who signals to landing aircraft with a pair of bats.

batt (băt) *n.* A mass of cotton fibers, **batting** *(see).*

batt. battalion.

bat·tal·i·on (bə-tăl′yən) *n. Abbr.* **bat., batt., bn., Bn. 1.** A tactical military unit, typically consisting of a headquarters company and four infantry companies, or a headquarters battery and four artillery batteries. **2.** An indefinite number of military troops. **3.** *Often* **battalions.** A large group or number. [French *battaillon,* from Italian *battaglione,* augmentative of *battaglia,* troop, BATTLE.]

bat·ten[1] (băt′n) *intr.v.* **-tened, -tening, -tens. 1. a.** To become fat. **b.** To feed gluttonously; gorge oneself. **2.** To thrive and prosper, especially at another's expense: *slum landlords who batten on the poor.* [Ultimately from Old Norse *batna,* to improve.]

batten[2] *n.* **1.** A strip of wood used in building to support tiles, slates, laths, or the like. **2.** A narrow strip of wood, used for flooring. **3.** Any of several flexible strips of wood placed in pockets at the outer edge of a sail to keep it flat.
~*tr.v.* **battened, -tening, -tens. 1.** To furnish with battens: *batten a sail.* **2.** To fasten or make secure with battens. Usually used with *up* or *down: batten down the hatches.* [French *bâton,* BATON.]

Bat·ten (băt′n), **Jean** (1909–82). New Zealand aviator and the first

bat *The only flying mammals, most bats—such as the long-eared bat shown here—find their way by listening to the echoes of their high-pitched squeaks bouncing off objects in their path. They feed on insects, which they catch on the wing at night. Fruit bats, however, feed largely on fruit and have large eyes to help them see at night. During the day, bats roost in caves and dark buildings, usually hanging upside down to sleep.*

PRONUNCIATION KEY

ă, pat; ā, pay; âr, care;
ä, father, are; b, bib;
ch, church; d, deed; ĕ, pet;
ē, be; f, fife; g, gag; h, hat;
hw, which; ĭ, pit; ī, pie;
îr, pier; j, judge; k, kick;
l, lid, needle; m, mum;
n, no, sudden; ng, thing;
ŏ, pot; ō, toe; ô, paw, for;
oi, noise; ou, out; o͝o, book;
o͞o, boot; p, pop; r, roar;
s, sauce; sh, ship, dish;
t, tight; th, thin, path;
th, this, bathe; ŭ, cut; ûr, fur;
v, valve; w, with; y, yes;
z, zebra, size; zh, vision;
ə, about, item, edible,
gallop, circus, peaceful

IN FOREIGN WORDS:

ä, *Fr.* ami; œ, *Fr.* feu, *Ger.* schön; ü, *Fr.* tu, *Ger.* über;
KH, *Ger.* ich, *Scot.* loch;
N, *Fr.* bon; y′, *Fr.* Compiègne

STRESS MARKS:

Primary stress: ′
in·cite′ (ĭn-sīt′)
Secondary stress: ′
in′sight′ (ĭn′sīt′)

woman to make a solo flight from England across the South Atlantic Ocean to South America (1935).

bat·ter¹ (băt′ər) v. **-tered, -tering, -ters.** —tr. **1. a.** To hit heavily and repeatedly with violent blows. **b.** To subject a child or woman to persistent violence or psychological cruelty. Used chiefly in the phrases *battered baby* and *battered wife.* **2.** To damage by heavy wear. —intr. To pound repeatedly with heavy blows. —n. Printing. **1.** A damaged area on the face of type or on a plate. **2.** The defect in print resulting from such damaged type. [Middle English *bateren,* from Norman-French, from Old French *bat(t)re,* to beat, from Latin *battuere.*]

bat·ter² n. A thick, beaten liquid mixture, as of flour, milk, and eggs, used in cooking. [Middle English *bater,* from Norman-French *batour,* from Old French *bateūre,* akin to BATTER (beat).]

battery

PORTABLE STOREHOUSE OF POWER

How electricity can be made by chemical reaction

A battery cell contains two plates of dissimilar metals (called electrodes) immersed in acid, alkaline, or salt solution (the electrolyte). When a wire is connected to the two electrodes, a chemical reaction between electrolyte and electrode causes free electrons to move along the wire. The movement is electric current. This was discovered by the Italian physicist Alessandro Volta in 1800. It is the basis of all batteries, which are portable sources of electricity. The wet battery, as used in motor cars, consists of lead plates immersed in sulfuric acid. The dry battery, as used in a flashlight, has electrodes of zinc and carbon in a damp paste of chemicals.

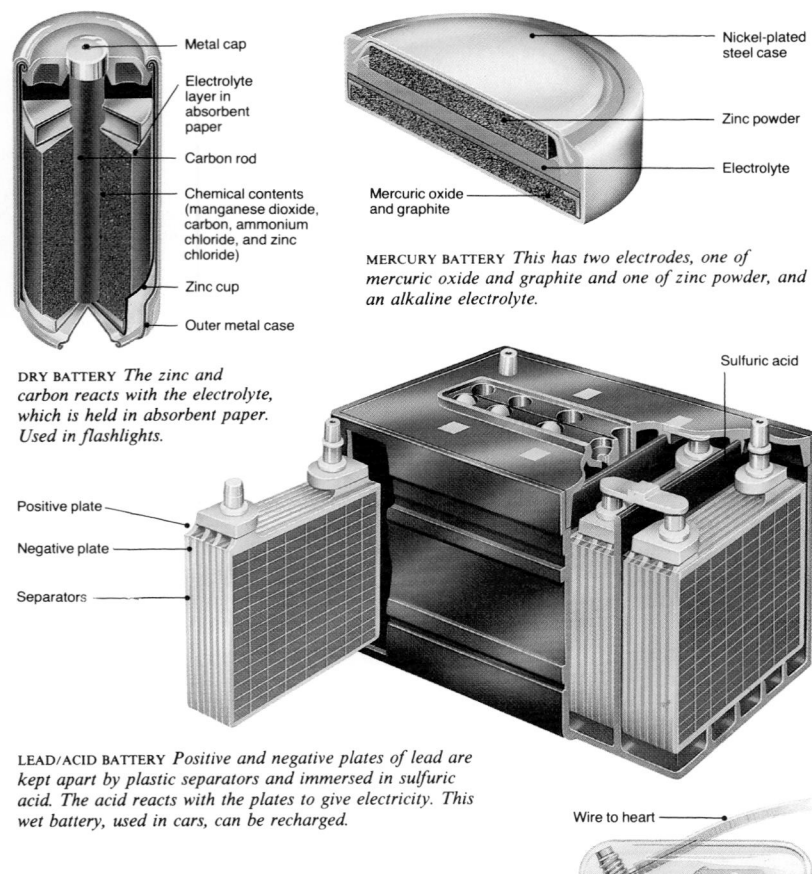

Metal cap
Electrolyte layer in absorbent paper
Carbon rod
Chemical contents (manganese dioxide, carbon, ammonium chloride, and zinc chloride)
Zinc cup
Outer metal case

DRY BATTERY *The zinc and carbon reacts with the electrolyte, which is held in absorbent paper. Used in flashlights.*

Nickel-plated steel case
Zinc powder
Electrolyte
Mercuric oxide and graphite

MERCURY BATTERY *This has two electrodes, one of mercuric oxide and graphite and one of zinc powder, and an alkaline electrolyte.*

Sulfuric acid
Positive plate
Negative plate
Separators

LEAD/ACID BATTERY *Positive and negative plates of lead are kept apart by plastic separators and immersed in sulfuric acid. The acid reacts with the plates to give electricity. This wet battery, used in cars, can be recharged.*

LITHIUM BATTERY *Power is created by a reaction between an iodine complex, the lithium, and an electrolyte of a thin layer of lithium iodide. This type of battery is quite small and light. It is used to provide the electricity in some heart pacemakers.*

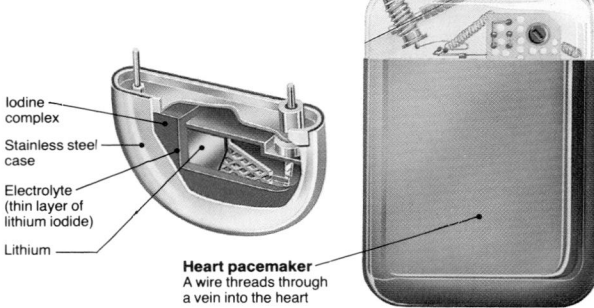

Wire to heart
Iodine complex
Stainless steel case
Electrolyte (thin layer of lithium iodide)
Lithium
Heart pacemaker A wire threads through a vein into the heart

batter³ n. A slope, as of the outer side of a wall, that recedes from bottom to top. —tr.v. **battered, -tering, -ters.** To construct so as to slope thus. [Middle English *batter†.*]

batter⁴ n. Baseball & Cricket. The player whose turn it is to bat.

bat·ter·ing-ram (băt′ər-ĭng-răm′) n. Also **battering ram. 1.** A heavy beam used in ancient warfare to batter down walls and gates. **2.** Any device resembling this or used for similar purposes.

Bat·ter·sea (băt′ər-sē). Part of the Greater London borough of Wandsworth, on the south bank of the Thames River. The river at Battersea is crossed by three of London's most famous bridges, the Albert (built 1873), the Battersea (1890), and the Chelsea (1937).

bat·ter·y (băt′ə-rē) n., pl. **-ies. 1.** A number of **primary cells** *(see)* connected together to provide a source of electric current. **2.** One or more primary cells connected together in which the electrolyte is in the form of a paste. Also *chiefly British* "dry battery." **3.** One or more **secondary cells** *(see)* connected together as a source of electric current; especially, the device used for this purpose in a motor vehicle. Also *chiefly British* "accumulator." **4. a.** A beating or pounding. **b.** Law. The unlawful beating of another person. Compare **assault and battery. 5. a.** An emplacement for one or more pieces of artillery. **b.** A set of guns or other heavy artillery, as on a warship. **c.** Abbr. **btry.** The basic tactical artillery unit, corresponding to the company in the infantry. **6.** An array or grouping of like things to be used together. **7.** The pitcher and catcher on a baseball team. **8.** The percussion section of an orchestra. **9.** A system of keeping poultry confined in cages in order to produce high yields of eggs. Often used adjectivally: *battery hens.* [French *batterie,* from *battre,* from Old French *bat(t)re,* to BATTER.]

Bat·ter·y, the (băt′ə-rē) Also **Battery Park.** A park at the southern tip of Manhattan Island on the upper end of New York Bay in New York City. Coastal artillery was mounted here during Colonial and Revolutionary times.

battik. Variant of **batik.**

bat·ting (băt′ĭng) n. **1.** The action of one who bats. **2.** Cotton or wool fiber wadded together and used for stuffing furniture and mattresses. Also called "batt," "cotton batting." [Sense 2, from the beating of raw cotton or wool to clean it.]

bat·tle (băt′l) n. **1.** A large-scale combat between armed forces. **2.** Armed fighting; combat. **3.** Any intense competition; a struggle. —v. **battled, -tling, -tles.** —intr. To engage in or as if in battle. —tr. To fight against; force: *He battled his way through the crowd.* —**give battle.** To begin fighting. [Middle English *bataille,* from Old French, from Vulgar Latin *battālia* (unattested), from Late Latin *battuālia,* fighting and fencing exercises, from Latin *battuere,* to BATTER.]

Bat·tle (băt′l). Town in East Sussex, England. The Battle of Hastings was fought (1066) on a ridge, called Senlae, to the southeast. William the Conqueror built an abbey to commemorate his victory over the Saxon king, Harold II.

bat·tle-ax, bat·tle-axe (băt′l-ăks′) n., pl. **-axes. 1.** A heavy broadheaded ax, formerly used as a weapon. **2.** Slang. An overbearing woman; a virago.

battle cruiser n. A warship with less heavy armor than a battleship, and with the speed of a cruiser.

battle cry n. **1.** A shout uttered by troops in battle. **2.** A slogan used by the proponents of a cause.

bat·tle-dore (băt′l-dôr′, -dōr′) n. **1.** An early form of badminton played with a flat wooden racket and a shuttlecock. Also called "battledore and shuttlecock." **2.** The racket used in this game. [Middle English *batildore,* perhaps from Old Provençal *batedor,* a beater, from *bat(t)re,* to beat, BATTER.]

battle fatigue n. **Combat fatigue** *(see).*

bat·tle-field (băt′l-fēld′) n. A field or area where an actual or figurative battle is fought. Also called "battleground."

bat·tle-front (băt′l-frŭnt′) n. The area where opponents meet or clash in battle: *a contest that was fought on political and military battlefronts.*

bat·tle-ment (băt′l-mənt) n. Usually **battlements.** A parapet built on top of a wall, with indentations for defense or decoration. [Middle English *batelment,* from Old French *bataillier,* to provide with battlements, from *batailles,* battlements, plural of *bataille,* BATTLE.] —**bat·tle-ment·ed** adj.

battle royal n., pl. **battles royal. 1.** A battle in which numerous combatants participate. **2.** A fight to the finish. **3.** An intense altercation.

bat·tle-ship (băt′l-shĭp′) n. Any of a class of warships of the largest size, carrying the greatest number of guns and batteries and clad with the heaviest armor.

battleship gray n. Medium gray.

bat·tle-wag·on (băt′l-wăg′ən) n. Slang. A battleship.

bat·tue (bă-tōō′, -tyōō′; French bá-tü′) n. **1.** The driving of wild game from cover by beaters toward waiting hunters. **2.** A hunt employing this procedure. **3.** Wholesale massacre, as of a defenseless crowd. [French, from the feminine past participle of *bat(t)re,* to beat, BATTER.]

bat·ty (băt′ē) adj. **-tier, -tiest.** Slang. Eccentric; crazy.

bau·ble (bô′bəl) n. **1.** A small, showy ornament or trinket, such as a Christmas tree decoration. **2.** A baton surmounted with a grotesquely carved head, carried by a court jester as a mock scepter of his office. [Middle English *babel, babulle,* from Old French *babel, baubel†,* plaything.]

baud (bôd) n. **1.** A unit for the speed of telegraphic or telephonic transmission equal to a transmission speed of one unit element per second. **2.** *Computer Science.* A unit of speed in data transmission, as one bit per second for binary signals. [After J. M. E. *Baudot* (1845–1903), French engineer and inventor of a telegraph system.]

Baude·laire (bōd-lâr′), **Charles** (1821–67). French poet and literary, art, and music critic. He discovered Edgar Allan Poe and translated many of his works. Baudelaire published an autobiographical novel, *La Fanfarlo* (1847), and his only volume of poetry, *Les Fleurs du Mal* (1857, revised 1861).

Bau·douin I (bō-dwăɴ′) (1930–). King of Belgium. He ascended to the throne in 1951, succeeding his father, Leopold III. He married Fabiola de Mora y Aragon in 1960.

Bau·haus (bou′hous′). An institute founded in 1919 by Walter Gropius in Weimar, Germany, for the study of art, design, and architecture and noted for its development of a style of functional architecture and its experimental use of building materials. It was closed by the Nazis in 1933. [German, "architecture house."]

bau·hin·i·a (bô-hĭn′ē-ə) *n.* Any plant of the leguminous genus *Bauhinia,* consisting of woody climbers with flattened stems and showy flowers, widely cultivated for ornament. [After Jean (1541–1613) and Gaspard (1560–1624) *Bauhin,* Swiss physicians and botanists.]

baulk. Variant of **balk.**

Baum (bäm, bôm), **L(yman) Frank** (1856–1919). U.S. novelist famous for writing *The Wonderful Wizard of Oz* (1900).

Bau·mé scale (bō-mā′) *n. Abbr.* **Bé, B.** A hydrometer scale in which 1 degree Baumé is equivalent to $145(1 - v)$ for liquids heavier than water and $140v - 130$ for liquids lighter than water, where *v* is the reciprocal of the relative density of the liquid at 60°F. [After Antoine *Baumé* (1728–1804), French pharmacist, inventor of a hydrometer.]

baum marten (boum) *n.* The fur of any of several Eurasian martens. [Partial translation of German *Baummarder*: *Baum,* tree, from Old High German *boum* + MARTEN.]

baux·ite (bôk′sīt′) *n.* The principal ore of aluminum. It is composed mainly of aluminum hydroxide, with some iron hydroxide, and forms as a result of leaching of the soil in tropical conditions. It is used as an abrasive and catalyst. Compare **laterite.** [French, first found at Les *Baux,* southern France.]

Bav. Bavaria; Bavarian.

Ba·va·ri·a (bə-vâr′ē-ə). *German* **Bay·ern** (bī′ərn). A large state in Germany, lying in the extreme south. The Bavarian Alps contain Germany's highest peak, the Zugspitze (2,963 meters; 9,721 feet). Beer, grain, salt, graphite, lignite, and iron ore are the region's chief products. The capital is Munich.

Ba·var·i·an (bə-vâr′ē-ən) *n. Abbr.* **Bav. 1.** A native or inhabitant of Bavaria. **2.** The High German dialect spoken in Bavaria and Austria. **—Ba·var·i·an** *adj.*

baw·bee, bau·bee (bô′bē′) *n. Scottish Informal.* A halfpenny. [After Alexander Orok of *Sillebawby,* 16th-century Scottish master of the mint.]

bawd (bôd) *n.* **1.** A woman who keeps a brothel; a madam. **2.** A prostitute. [Middle English *bawde,* probably from Old French *baude, baud,* lively, bold, from Old High German *bald,* bold.]

bawd·ry (bô′drē) *n.* Obscene or coarse language on the subject of sex. [Middle English *bawdery,* from BAWD.]

bawd·y (bô′dē) *adj.* **-ier, -iest.** Humorously coarse; vulgar; lewd. **—bawd·i·ly** *adv.* **—bawd·i·ness** *n.*

bawd·y·house (bô′dē-hous′) *n.* A house of prostitution.

bawl (bôl) *v.* **bawled, bawling, bawls.** *—intr.* **1.** To cry loudly, as from pain or annoyance; howl. **2.** To cry out loudly and vehemently; shout. *—tr.* To utter in a loud, vehement voice. **—bawl out.** *Informal.* To reprimand or scold in a loud voice.
~n. A loud, extended outcry; a wail. [Middle English *baulen,* probably from Scandinavian, of imitative origin, akin to Icelandic *baula,* to low.] **—bawl·er** *n.*

bay[1] (bā) *n.* **1.** *Abbr.* **b., B.** A body of water partly enclosed by land, but having a wide outlet to the sea. **2.** A broad stretch of low land between hills. **3.** An arm of prairie partly enclosed by woodland. [Middle English *baye,* from Old French *baie,* from Old Spanish *bahia,* perhaps from Iberian.]

bay[2] *n.* **1.** *Architecture.* A part of a building or other structure marked off by vertical elements. **2. a.** A **bay window** *(see).* **b.** Any opening or recess in a wall. **3.** An extension of a building; a wing. **4.** A compartment in a barn, used for storing hay or grain. **5.** A ship's sickbay. **6.** A compartment in an aircraft: *the bomb bay.* **7.** *British.* A dead end in a railway station marking the termination of a line, with a platform surrounding it on three sides. [Middle English, from Old French *baee,* an opening, from *baer,* to gape, from Medieval Latin *batāre,* to yawn, gape.]

bay[3] *adj.* Reddish-brown: *a bay colt.*
~n. **1.** A reddish-brown color. **2.** An animal, especially a horse, of this color. [Middle English, from Old French *bai,* from Latin *badius.*]

bay[4] *n.* **1.** A deep, prolonged barking, especially of hounds closing in on prey. **2.** The position of one cornered by pursuers and forced to turn and fight at close quarters. **3.** The position of someone or something checked or kept at a safe distance.
~v. **bayed, baying, bays.** *—intr.* To utter a deep, prolonged bark or howl. *—tr.* **1.** To pursue or challenge with barking: *"I had rather be a dog, and bay the moon"* (Shakespeare). **2.** To express by barking. **3.** To bring to bay: *"too big for the dogs which tried to bay it"* (William Faulkner). [Middle English *baien,* short for *abaien,* from Old French *abaiier, abayer,* from Vulgar Latin *abbaiāre* (unattested).]

bay[5] *n.* **1.** The true laurel, *Laurus nobilis,* native to the Mediterranean area, having stiff, glossy, aromatic leaves. See **bay leaf.** Also called "bay laurel," "bay tree," "laurel." **2.** Any of several similar trees or shrubs, such as the **sweet bay** *(see).* **3.** *Usually* **bays.** A crown or wreath made of the leaves and branches of the bay or similar plants, conferred or awarded in classical times as a sign of honor. **4. bays.** Renown; honor. [Middle English *baye,* laurel berry, from Old French *baie,* from Latin *bāca,* berry.]

ba·ya·dere (bī′ə-dîr′, -dâr′) *n.* A fabric with vividly contrasting horizontal stripes. [French *bayadère,* Hindu dancing girl, from Portuguese *bailadeira,* from *bailar,* to dance.]

Ba·yard (bā′ərd, bī′-, bä-yär′), **Pierre de Terrail, Seigneur de** (*c.* 1473–1524). French soldier known for his fearlessness and chivalry.

bay·ber·ry (bā′bĕr′ē) *n., pl.* **-ries. 1.** Any of several aromatic shrubs or small trees of the genus *Myrica;* especially, *M. pensylvanica,* of eastern North America, bearing gray, waxy berries. **2.** A tropical American tree, *Pimenta acris,* yielding an oil used in making bay rum. Also called "bay rum tree." **3.** The fruit of any of these trees or shrubs.

Bayern. See **Bavaria.**

Bayes·i·an (bā′zē-ən) *adj.* Of or designating a method or theory for reassessing the probability of a proposition in the light of new relevant information. [After Thomas *Bayes* (1701–61), British mathematician.]

Ba·yeux (bä-yōō′, bā-). Small town in northwestern France, in the Calvados department of Normandy. It was the first French town (June 8, 1944) to be liberated from Nazi occupation by the Allies in World War II.

Bayeux tapestry *n.* An 11th- or 12th-century tapestry, 50 centimeters (20 inches) wide by 70.5 meters (231 feet) long, embroidered with scenes depicting the Norman Conquest of England, and preserved in the town of Bayeux.

Baykal. See **Baikal, Lake.**

Bayle (bāl), **Pierre** (1647–1706). French philosopher, a forerunner of the 18th-century philosophes. Although he was brought up as a Calvinist, he devoted his writings to the cause of religious tolerance and skeptical subversion of Christian belief. His most famous work was the *Dictionnaire Historique et Critique* (1697).

bay leaf *n.* The dried, aromatic leaf of the bay, *Laurus nobilis,* or of the bayberry, *Pimenta acris,* used as seasoning in cooking.

Bay·lis (bā′lĭs), **Lilian Mary** (1874–1937). English theater manager. She became manager of the Old Vic, London (1912), and created a theater for the production of Shakespeare's plays. In 1931 she assumed the management of the Sadler's Wells theater and transformed it into a center for opera and ballet.

bay lynx *n.* The **bobcat** *(see).*

Bay of Pigs (pĭgz). *Spanish* **Ba·hí·a de Co·chin·os** (bä-hē′ə dā kə-chē′nōs). Bay on the southern coast of Cuba, the site of the unsuccessful Bay of Pigs invasion of April 17, 1961, when a force of about 1,500 U.S.-trained troops, rebels against the regime of Fidel Castro, landed here from Guatemala.

bay·o·net (bā′ə-nĭt, -nĕt′, bā′ə-nĕt′) *n.* A knife or spike adapted to fit the muzzle end of a rifle and used in close combat.
~tr.v. **bayoneted** or **bayonetted, -neting** or **-netting, -nets.** To stab or prod with a bayonet. [French *baïonnette,* first manufactured at BAYONNE, France.]

bayonet fitting *n. Chiefly British.* A method of fastening two cylindrical parts together, similar to the original method of attaching a bayonet to a rifle. It is used in fitting light bulbs into holders, two pins on the bulb cap engaging with two L-shaped slots on the holder.

Ba·yonne (bā-ōn′, bä-yôn). Port in the Pyrénées-Atlantique department of France, now joined with the resort of Biarritz. The town gave its name to the bayonet, which was first used by local Basques in the 17th century.

bay·ou (bī′ōō, bī′ō) *n., pl.* **-ous.** *Southern U.S.* A marshy, sluggish body of water tributary to a lake or river. [Louisiana French, from Choctaw *bayuk.*]

Bay·reuth (bī-roit′). Industrial city of Bavaria, in southern Germany. Richard Wagner lived here from 1872 to 1883, and the Festival Theater, devoted to the performance of his operas, was opened in 1876.

bay rum *n.* An aromatic liquid obtained by distilling the leaves of the bayberry tree, *Pimenta acris,* with rum, and now also synthesized from alcohol, water, and various oils.

bay rum tree *n.* See **bayberry** (sense 1).

Bay Street *n.* The controlling financial interests of Canada. [After the main street of the financial district of Toronto.]

bay tree *n.* **1.** A tree, the **bay** *(see).* **2.** The **California laurel** *(see).*

bay window *n.* **1.** A large window or series of windows projecting from the wall of a building and forming a recess within. Also called "bay." **2.** *Slang.* A protruding belly; paunch.

bay·wood (bā′wŏŏd′) *n.* The wood of a tropical American mahogany, *Swietenia macrophylla.* [After the Bay of Campeche, Mexico.]

ba·zaar, ba·zar (bə-zär′) *n.* **1.** An Oriental market, usually consisting of an area of streets lined with shops and stalls. **2.** A shop or part of a store for the sale of miscellaneous articles. **3.** A fair at which miscellaneous articles are sold, usually for charitable purposes. [Earlier *bazarro, bazar,* probably from Italian *bazarro,* from Turkish, from Persian *bāzār,* from Middle Persian *bāchār,* from Old Persian *abēcharish*†.]

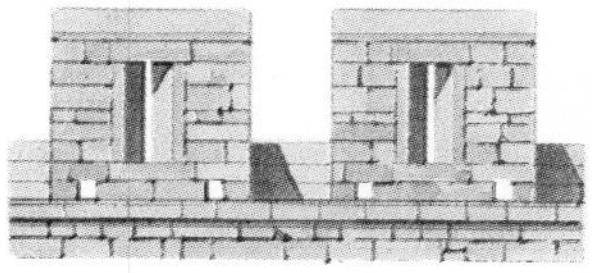

battlement *Archers shot arrows through the open sections in castle walls, known as embrasures, and hid behind the solid sections (merlons). Slits in the merlons enabled the archers to see out.*

bay *The sacred tree of the god Apollo. In ancient Rome, a garland of its leaves was the highest honor bestowed on a warrior.*

beagle *The stamina of this breed—along with its acute sense of smell—has made it popular as a hunting dog. It is often used in packs to hunt hares.*

ba·zoo·ka (bə-zōō′kə) *n.* A portable military weapon consisting of a long, metal, smoothbore tube for firing small, armor-piercing, explosive rockets at short range. [After the *bazooka,* a crude wind instrument made of pipes, invented by Bob Burns (1896–1956), U.S. comedian.]

bb, b.b. ball bearing.

BB (bē′bē) *n.* A standard size of lead shot that measures about .46 cm (or 0.18 in.) in diameter. [Perhaps from the letter *b.*]

B.B.A. Bachelor of Business Administration.

BBB, B.B.B. Better Business Bureau.

BBC, B.B.C. British Broadcasting Corporation.

BB gun *n.* A small air rifle firing BB shot.

bbl, bbl. barrel (of oil).

B.C. **1.** Bachelor of Chemistry. **2.** Bachelor of Commerce. **3.** before Christ (usually small capitals, B.C.). —See Usage note at **A.D. 4.** British Columbia.

B.C.E. **1.** Bachelor of Chemical Engineering. **2.** Bachelor of Civil Engineering.

B cell *n.* A lymphocyte derived from bone marrow that takes part in the immune response. [*Bone-marrow-derived* + CELL.]

BCG Bacillus Calmette-Guérin (a strain of tuberculosis bacillus used in a vaccine against the disease).

B.Ch.E. Bachelor of Chemical Engineering.

B.C.L. **1.** Bachelor of Common Law. **2.** Bachelor of Civil Law.

B.C.S. **1.** Bachelor of Chemical Science. **2.** Bachelor of Commercial Science.

bd. **1.** board. **2.** bond. **3.** *Bookbinding.* bound.

B.D. **1.** Bachelor of Divinity. **2.** bank draft. **3.** bills discounted.

bdel·li·um (dĕl′ē-əm) *n.* **1.** An aromatic gum resin similar to myrrh, produced by various trees of the genus *Commiphora,* of western Asia and Africa. **2.** A substance mentioned in the Bible, variously interpreted to be carbuncle, rock crystal, pearl, or gum resin. Numbers 11:7. [Latin, from Greek *bdellion,* probably from Hebrew *bədōlaḥ.*]

bd. ft. board foot.

bds. bound in boards.

B.D.S. Bachelor of Dental Surgery.

be (bē) *v.*

	1st person	2nd person	3rd person
Present Tense			
singular	**am** (ăm)	**are** (är)†	**is** (ĭz)
plural	**are**	**are**	**are**

†*Archaic 2nd person singular* **art** (ärt)

	1st person	2nd person	3rd person
Past Tense			
singular	**was** (wŭz; wŏz)	**were** (wûr)‡	**was**
plural	**were**	**were**	**were**

‡*Archaic 2nd person singular* **wast** (wŏst) *or* **wert** (wûrt)

Present Participle: **being** (bē′ing)   Present Subjunctive: **be**
Past Participle: **been** (bĭn)   Past Subjunctive: **were**

Used as an auxiliary verb in certain constructions, as: **a.** With the past participle of a transitive verb to form the passive voice: *The competition is held annually. Our club may be disbanded for lack of funds.* **b.** With the present participle of a verb to express a continuing action: *We are working to improve housing conditions.* **c.** With the present participle or the infinitive of a verb, to express intention, obligation, or future action: *All visitors are to leave by 10:00 p.m. The finals are to be held in London.* **d.** *Archaic.* With the past participle of certain intransitive verbs to form the perfect tense: *Christ is risen from the dead.* —*intr.* **1.** To exist in actuality; have reality or life: *I think, therefore I am.* **2.** To exist in a specified place; stay; reside: *"Oh, to be in England,/ Now that April's there"* (Robert Browning). **3.** To occupy a specified position: *The food is on the table.* **4.** To take place; occur: *Her party was last week.* **5.** To go. Used chiefly in the past and perfect tenses: *Have you ever been to Italy?* **6.** *Archaic.* To belong; befall. Used in the subjunctive: *Peace be unto you.* **7.** Used as a copula linking a subject and a predicate nominative, adjective, or pronoun, in such senses as: **a.** To equal in meaning or identity: *"To be a Christian was to be a Roman"* (James Bryce). **b.** To signify; indicate: *A is excellent, C is passable, F is failing.* **c.** To belong to a specified class or group: *A human is a primate.* **d.** To have or show a specified essential quality or characteristic: *She is courageous. All men are mortal.* **e.** To have or show a specified quality or characteristic at a particular time: *I'm busy just now.* **f.** To represent or embody the essential character of; symbolize: *She is the liberal party.* [1. Be; been: Middle English *be(e)n; be(o)n,* Old English *bēon; bēon,* to come to be. 2. Am; art; is; are (singular and plural): Middle English *am; art, eart; is; are* (singular), *aren* (plural); Old English *eam, eom; eart; is; (e)aron* (plural only), from Germanic *es-* (unattested) and *ar-* (unattested). 3. Was; were: Middle English *wes, was; ware, were* (singular), *weren, were* (plural); Old English *wæs; wǣre* (singular), *wǣron* (plural), from Germanic *wes-* (unattested).]

Usage: When pronouns follow a form of the verb *to be,* the nominative is traditionally required, on the grounds that the pronoun denotes the same entity as the subject. Thus, the rules require *it is I, that must be she,* and so forth. The rules create problems, however, when the pronoun after *to be* denotes an entity that is also understood to be the object of some other verb or preposition. Shall we say *it is I she loves* or *it is me she loves?* There is no strict rule, but given the natural tendency to use objective forms like *me* rather than nominatives like *I* in undecided cases, the use of *me* is entirely defensible here. It should also be noted that the use of the nominative following *to be* sounds stilted when the verb has been contracted. Nevertheless, a purist would say *it's I* rather than *it's me,* or *that's they* rather than *that's them.*

be– *prefix.* Indicates: **1.** A complete or profuse covering or affecting; for example, **becloud, besmear. 2.** A thorough or excessive degree; for example, **bewilder. 3.** An action that causes a condition to exist; for example, **besot, befriend.** [Middle English *be-,* Old English, weak form of *bī-,* BY. In Middle English *be-* indicates: **1.** Thoroughly, as in **beloved, betray. 2.** On all sides, as in **besiege. 3.** About, over, in relation to, as in **betroth, bequest.** Old English *be-, bi-* indicates: **1.** About, over, as in **bethink. 2.** On all sides, as in **beset. 3.** Away, away from, as in **benumb.**]

Be The symbol for the element beryllium.

Bé Baumé scale.

B.E. **1.** Bachelor of Education. **2.** Bachelor of Engineering. **3.** Bank of England. **4.** Board of Education.

B/E **1.** bill of entry. **2.** bill of exchange.

beach (bēch) *n.* **1.** The shore of a body of water. **2.** The sand or pebbles on a shore. **3.** The accumulation of shingle, sand, and rocks on the coast between the lowest level reached by spring tides and the highest point attained by storm waves.

~*tr.v.* **beached, beaching, beaches.** To haul or drive (a boat for example) ashore. [16th century : origin obscure.]

beach buggy *n.* A car usually open and fitted with balloon tires, used for driving on beaches and sand.

beach·comb·er (bēch′kō′mər) *n.* **1.** One who collects flotsam and jetsam from beaches and port areas; especially, a vagrant who makes a living in this way. **2.** A long wave rolling in toward a beach. [Sense 2, from COMB, in the sense "to break with foam."]

beach flea *n.* Any of various small, jumping crustaceans of the family Talitridae, living on sandy beaches at or near the tide line. Also called "sand hopper."

beach·head (bēch′hĕd′) *n.* **1.** A position on an enemy shoreline captured by advance troops of an invading force. **2.** A first achievement that opens the way for further development.

beach-la-mar (bēch′lə-mär′) *n.* A dialect, **bêche-de-mer** *(see).* [Alteration of Portuguese *bicho do mar.*]

beach pea *n.* Either of two similar North American plants, *Lathyrus maritimus,* of the Atlantic coast, or *L. littoralis,* of the Pacific coast, having purplish flowers and sprawling stems.

beach plum *n.* A seacoast shrub, *Prunus maritima,* of northeastern North America, having white flowers and edible plumlike fruit.

beach wormwood *n.* A seacoast plant, *Artemisia stelleriana,* originally native to Asia but now widespread, covered with dense, white down and having small yellow flowers. Also called "dusty miller."

bea·con (bē′kən) *n.* **1. a.** A signal fire lit on a hill or other high place; especially, one used to warn of an enemy's approach. **b.** *Chiefly British.* A hill suitable for such a fire. **2.** A lighthouse or other signaling or guiding device on a coast. **3.** A radio transmitter that emits a characteristic signal as a warning or guide. **4.** Anything that warns or guides.

~*v.* **beaconed, -coning, -cons.** —*tr.* To provide a beacon for. —*intr.* To serve as a beacon. [Middle English *beken,* sign, standard, Old English *bēacen.*]

bead (bēd) *n.* **1.** A small, ball-shaped piece of glass, metal, wood, or other material pierced for stringing or threading. **2. beads. a.** A necklace made of such pieces. **b.** A rosary. **3.** Any small, round object, especially: **a.** A small drop of moisture. **b.** A bubble of gas in a liquid. **c.** A small knob of metal on the muzzle of a rifle or gun, used for sighting. **4.** *Architecture.* A strip of stone or wood, with one molded edge placed flush against a wall, door, or window frame. Also called "bead butt." **5.** *Chemistry.* A borax bead *(see).* **6.** *Metallurgy.* A small blob of metal from a welding rod applied to the material to be welded in order to test the nature of the weld. —**count** (or **say** or **tell**) **one's beads.** To pray with a rosary.

~*v.* **beaded, beading, beads.** —*tr.* To ornament or cover with beads. —*intr.* To collect into beads. [Middle English *bede,* bead, prayer, prayer bead, bead, Old English *gebed,* prayer, from Germanic *bedh-* (unattested).]

bead·ing (bē′dĭng) *n.* **1.** Beads or material used for beads. **2.** Ornamentation with beads. **3.** *Architecture.* A narrow, half-rounded molding. **4.** Any narrow strip of trimming. **5.** A narrow piece of openwork lace through which ribbon may be run. **6.** Bubbles or froth, as on the rim of a glass.

bea·dle (bēd′l) *n.* **1.** Formerly, a minor parish official in an English church, whose duties included keeping order and ushering during services. **2.** An official at certain English universities who supervises and walks before processions. **3.** *Judaism.* A **shammes** *(see).* [Middle English *bedele, bidel,* herald, messenger, beadle, from Old French *bedel* (of Germanic origin), replacing Old English *bydel.*]

bea·dle·dom (bēd′l-dəm) *n.* Petty bureaucratic officiousness.

bead test *Chemistry.* A test to identify the component elements of a substance. See borax bead.

bead·work (bēd′wûrk′) *n.* **1.** Decorative work in beads. **2.** *Architecture.* Beaded molding.

bead·y (bē′dē) *adj.* **-ier, -iest. 1.** Small, round, and shiny: *beady eyes.* **2.** Decorated or covered with beads.

bea·gle (bē′gəl) *n.* Any of a breed of small hounds having short legs, drooping ears, and a smooth coat with white, black, and tan markings. [Middle English *begle,* perhaps from Old French *bee-gueule,* noisy person : probably *beer,* to gape, from (unattested) Vulgar Latin *batāre* (see **bay,** opening) + *gueule,* throat, from Latin *gula.*]

beak (bēk) *n.* **1.** The horny, projecting structure forming the mandibles of a bird; a bill. **2.** A part or organ resembling this, as in some turtles, insects, or fish. **3.** Any hard, cone-shaped, or pointed structure or part. **4.** *Informal.* A person's nose. **5.** *British Slang.* **a.** A schoolmaster. **b.** A judge. [Middle English *bec, bek,* from Old French *bec,* from Latin *beccus,* from Gaulish.]

beak·er (bē′kər) *n.* **1. a.** A large drinking cup with a wide mouth. **b.** The contents of such a cup. **2.** An open glass cylinder with a pouring lip, used as a standard laboratory container or vessel for mixing and heating. [Middle English *biker, beker,* from Old Norse *bikarr,* probably from Vulgar Latin *bicārium* (unattested), perhaps from Greek *bikos,* drinking-jar.]

Beaker Folk *pl.n.* An ancient people inhabiting Europe in the Bronze Age, whose artifacts, especially metal beakers, have been found in their round burial barrows. Also called "Beaker People."

be-all and end-all (bē′ôl′ ənd ĕnd′ôl′) *n.* The chief aim or consideration, to the exclusion of all others. [From Shakespeare's *Macbeth* (1605), Act I, scene 7, in which Macbeth considers the murder of Duncan: ". . . this blow/Might be the be-all and the end-all. . . ."]

beam (bēm) *n.* **1.** A squared-off log or large, oblong piece of timber, metal, or stone, used especially in construction. **2.** *Nautical.* **a.** The breadth of a ship at the widest point. **b.** A transverse structural member of the framing of a vessel, used to support a deck and to brace the sides against stress. **c.** The shank of an anchor. **3.** A steel tube or wooden roller with flanged ends on which the warp is wound in a loom. **4.** An oscillating lever connected to an engine piston rod and used to transmit power to the crankshaft. **5.** The bar of a balance, from which weighing pans are suspended. **6.** Either of the main stems of a deer's antlers. **7.** The main horizontal bar on a plow to which the share, colter, and handles, if any, are attached. **8. a.** A ray of light or other electromagnetic radiation. **b.** A group of particles traveling together in close parallel trajectories. **9.** A radio beam (see). **—broad in the beam.** Wide-hipped; fat. **—off the beam. 1.** Not following the radio beam. Said of an aircraft. **2.** *Informal.* Not on the right track; mistaken. *~v.* **beamed, beaming, beams.** *—tr.* **1.** To emit or transmit: *beaming the message.* **2.** To express by means of a broad or radiant smile. *—intr.* **1.** To radiate light; shine. **2.** To smile expansively. [Middle English *beme, beem,* Old English *bēam,* tree, beam.]

beam compass *n.* A form of compass used for drawing large circles. It consists of a horizontal beam along which two vertical legs slide, one fitted with a pin to act as a center and the other with a pen or pencil. Not in technical usage. Also called "trammel."

beam-ends (bēm′ĕndz′) *pl.n.* The ends of a ship's beams. **—on the beam-ends.** Listing so far over that the beams are nearly vertical and there is danger of capsizing. **—on one's beam-ends.** *Informal.* Having no money at all.

beam hole *n.* A hole through a nuclear-reactor shield enabling a beam of radiation to be used for experimental purposes.

beam rider *n.* A guided missile that steers itself along the axis of a scanned beam of microwave radiation. **—beam riding** *n.*

beam·y (bē′mē) *adj.* **-ier, -iest. 1.** Broad at the beam. Said of a ship. **2.** Emitting beams, as of light; radiant.

bean (bēn) *n.* **1.** Any of several plants of the genus *Phaseolus,* having compound leaves, white or yellow flowers, and seed-bearing pods. See **lima bean, string bean. 2.** The edible seed or pod of any of these plants. **3.** Any of several related plants bearing similar pods and seeds. See **broad bean. 4.** Any of various other seeds or pods resembling beans, such as the coffee bean or the vanilla bean. **5. beans.** *Slang.* A small amount: *I don't know beans about the stock market.* **6.** *Slang.* The head. **7.** *British Slang.* A fellow; a chap: *old bean.* **—full of beans.** *Informal.* Very lively; energetic. **—spill the beans.** *Informal.* To disclose what was not meant to be disclosed. [Middle English *ben(e),* Old English *bēan.*]

bean·bag (bēn′băg′) *n.* A small bag filled with dried beans and used for throwing in games.

bean ball *n.* A baseball pitch aimed at the batter's head.

bean caper *n.* A plant of the genus *Zygophyllum;* especially, *Z. fabago,* a shrub of the Middle East, bearing edible buds used as capers.

bean curd *n.* A soft soybean cheese of the Orient. Also called "tofu." [Translation of Chinese (Mandarin) *dou⁴ fu³: dou⁴,* bean + *fu³,* curdled.]

bean·feast (bēn′fēst′) *n. British Informal.* **1.** An annual dinner given by a firm for its employees. **2.** A party or celebration. [19th century : beans and bacon were always served at such annual dinners.]

bean·ie (bē′nē) *n.* A small brimless cap.

bean·o (bē′nō) *n.* A form of bingo, especially one using beans as markers. [Perhaps blend of BINGO and BEAN.]

bean·pole (bēn′pōl′) *n.* **1.** A thin pole used to support bean plants. **2.** *Slang.* A very tall, thin person.

bean sprout *n.* A young, tender shoot of certain beans, such as the soybean or the mung bean, used in Chinese cooking.

bean·stalk (bēn′stôk′) *n.* The stem of a bean plant.

bean tree *n.* Any of various trees, such as the catalpa, that bear beanlike fruit.

bear[1] (bâr) *v.* **bore** (bôr, bōr) or *archaic* **bare** (bâr), **borne** (bôrn, bōrn) (for all senses) or **born** (for sense 11 only), **bearing, bears.** *—tr.* **1.** To support; hold up: *bore him on her shoulders.* **2.** To carry

THE MANY SHAPES OF BEAKS

How birds have adapted to the demands of their diets

The shape of a bird's beak depends on its feeding habits. Scavengers, such as gulls and crows, have all-purpose beaks so that they can feed on a wide range of animals and plants. The diets of some birds, however, have become very specialized in order to avoid competition for food, and their beaks have adapted to the demands of these specialized diets.

WIGEON *Wide beak shears grass and plants.*

OYSTERCATCHER *Beak can pry open the shell of prey.*

WOODPECKER *Tapering beak chisels into bark for insects.*

WOODCOCK *Long, thin beak probes for worms in soft earth.*

SWIFT *Wide beak for catching insects on the wing.*

HUMMINGBIRD *Long, narrow beak for collecting nectar.*

MERGANSER *Serrated beak for gripping slippery fish.*

HERON *Long, daggerlike beak for seizing fish.*

PUFFIN *Large, triangular beak can hold several fish.*

AVOCET *Long, upcurved beak skims food from water surface.*

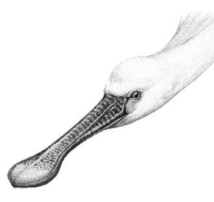

SPOONBILL *Spatulate beak sifts food from the shallows.*

PELICAN *Pouch beneath long, pointed beak holds fish.*

COCKATOO *Hooked beak for cracking nuts.*

TOUCAN *Huge, brightly colored beak reaches for fruit.*

MACAW *Hooked beak for cracking nuts.*

GOLDEN EAGLE *Strong, hooked beak for tearing flesh.*

OWL *Short, hooked beak for catching prey.*

PETREL *Narrow, hooked beak for catching fish.*

bearberry Arctostaphylos uva-ursi, *the bearberry, is an evergreen shrub that bears small white or pink flowers and red berries. It grows on wetlands and bogs in the cooler regions of the Northern Hemisphere.*

bearded reedling *A native of Europe and Asia, the bearded reedling is a member of the babbler family and lives in reedbeds on lakes and marshes. It is also called the bearded tit. The bird gets its name because the male (above) has a "beard" of black feathers beneath its beak.*

Beardsley lithograph *This study of Isolde (Iseult)—the Irish princess in the tragic Arthurian love story* Tristan and Isolde*—was first published in* The Studio, *an art magazine, in October 1895.*

on one's person; convey. **3.** To carry as if in the mind; maintain: *bearing love for others.* **4.** To transmit at large; bring: *bearing glad tidings.* **5.** To have as a visible characteristic; show: *bearing a scar on his right arm.* **6.** To have as a visible quality or form; exhibit: *"A thousand different shapes it bears"* (Abraham Cowley). **7.** To conduct or carry (oneself) in a particular way. **8.** To be accountable for; assume. **9.** To tolerate; endure: *couldn't bear her husband.* **10.** To be capable of undergoing; admit of: *doesn't bear thinking about.* **11.** To give birth to. —See Usage note below. **12.** To produce; yield. **13.** To offer; render: *bearing witness.* **14.** To move by steady pressure; push: *"boats against the current, borne back ceaselessly into the past"* (F. Scott Fitzgerald). —*intr.* **1.** To yield a product; produce. **2.** To withstand stress, difficulty, or attrition. Often used with *up.* **3.** To have relevance; apply. Used with *on.* **4.** To turn or proceed in a specified direction: *"I bore right, to avoid the Beduin"* (T.E. Lawrence). —See Synonyms at **convey.** —**bear down on** (or **upon**). **1.** To come toward in an aggressive or threatening way. **2.** To exert pressure or weight on. —**bear out.** To prove right or justified; confirm: *The results bear out her claims.* —**bear up.** To withstand stress or difficulty. —**bear with.** To be patient or tolerant with. [Bear, bore, borne; Middle English *beren, bare, boren,* Old English *beran, bær, boren.*]

Synonyms: *abide, endure, stand, suffer, tolerate.*

Usage: In its literal sense the past participle *born* is used only of mammals and only with *to be: The baby was born.* It may also be used figuratively: *A star is born. Borne,* said of the act of birth, refers only to the mother's role, but it can be used actively or passively: *She has borne three children. Three children were borne by her* (but *born to her*). In all other senses of *bear* the past participle is *borne*: *The soil has borne abundant crops. Such a burden cannot be borne by anyone.*

bear² *n.* **1.** Any of various usually omnivorous mammals of the family Ursidae, having a shaggy coat, strong claws, and a short tail, and walking with the entire lower surface of the foot touching the ground. See **black bear, brown bear, grizzly bear, polar bear.** **2.** Any of various animals resembling a bear in some respect, such as the **koala** *(see).* **3.** A person who is awkward, clumsy, or ill-mannered. **4. Bear.** *Astronomy.* Either of two constellations, **Ursa Major** or **Ursa Minor** *(both of which see).* **5.** *Stock Market.* An investor or concern that sells securities or commodities in the expectation that prices will fall. Compare **bull.**

~*v.* **beared, bearing, bears.** —*tr.* To engage in speculative selling so as to lower the price of (stocks and shares) or prices in (a market). —*intr.* To fall in price. Compare **bull.**

~*adj.* Characterized by falling prices: *a bear market.* Compare **bull.** [Middle English *bere,* Old English *bera.* Stock market senses, 18th century : originally probably *bearskin jobber,* alluding to the proverb, *To sell the bear's skin before one has caught the bear.*]

bear·a·ble (bâr'ə-bəl) *adj.* Capable of being borne; endurable; tolerable. —**bear·a·bly** *adv.*

bear-bait·ing (bâr'bā'tĭng) *n.* The former sport of setting dogs to attack or torment a chained bear.

bear·ber·ry (bâr'bĕr'ē) *n., pl.* **-ries.** A trailing shrub, *Arctostaphylos uva-ursi,* of the Northern Hemisphere, having small evergreen leaves, white or pink flowers, and red berries. Also called "kinnikinnick" and sometimes "crowberry."

beard (bîrd) *n.* **1. a.** The hair on the chin, cheeks, and throat of a man: *three days' growth of beard.* **b.** This hair allowed to grow and cover the skin: *a foot-long beard.* **2.** Any similar hairy or hairlike growth such as that on or near the face of certain mammals. **3.** A tuft or group of bristles on certain plants, especially cereals; an awn. **4.** The barb or hook of a fishhook, arrow, or the like. **5.** The gills of an oyster. **6.** *Printing.* The part of a piece of type between the face and the shoulder; the neck.

~*tr.v.* **bearded, bearding, beards. 1.** To furnish with a beard. **2.** To grasp by the beard. **3.** To confront boldly: *beard the lion in his den.* [Middle English *berd,* Old English *beard.*]

bearded iris *n.* Any of many varieties of iris having beardlike growths at the bases of the three lower, recurved petals.

bearded reedling *n.* A small Eurasian marsh bird, *Panurus biarmicus,* having black, mustachelike markings in the male. Also called "bearded tit," "reedling."

bearded vulture *n.* A bird, the **lammergeier** *(see).*

beard·less (bîrd'lĭs) *adj.* **1. a.** Having no beard. **b.** Having the beard shaved off; clean-shaven. **2. a.** Not old enough to have a beard. **b.** Immature; inexperienced. —**beard·less·ness** *n.*

Beards·ley (bîrdz'lē), **Aubrey Vincent** (1872–98). British illustrator. His flowing designs, characteristic of the art nouveau style, are usually figurative ink drawings done in black and white, contrasting areas of elaborate intricacy with stark white spaces and dense black shadows. Works that he illustrated include Wilde's *Salome,* Pope's *Rape of the Lock,* and Ben Jonson's *Volpone.*

bear·er (bâr'ər) *n.* **1.** One that carries or supports. **2. a.** A porter. **b.** *British.* A domestic or personal servant, especially in India. **3.** A person who presents for payment a check or other redeemable note. **4.** A **pallbearer** *(see).* **5.** Any fruit-bearing plant.

bear garden *n.* **1.** Formerly, a place where bears were confined and exhibited, as for bearbaiting. **2.** A place or scene of tumult.

bear grass *n.* **1.** A tall plant, *Xerophyllum tenax,* of northwestern North America, having narrow, grasslike leaves and white flowers in a large terminal cluster. **2.** Any of several similar or related plants, especially any of several species of yucca.

bear hug *n.* A very tight, enveloping hug or embrace.

bear·ing (bâr'ĭng) *n.* **1.** The manner in which a person carries or conducts himself; deportment. **2.** *Engineering.* **a.** Any part that supports another part or structure. **b.** A device that supports, guides, and reduces the friction of motion between fixed and moving machine parts. **3.** Anything that bears weight or acts as a support. **4.** The part of an architectural arch or beam that rests on a support. **5. a.** The act or period of producing fruit or offspring. **b.** The quantity produced; the yield. **6.** Direction, especially angular direction measured from one position to another using geographical or celestial reference lines. **7.** *Usually* **bearings.** The position or situation of a person or object relative to the surroundings. **8.** Relevance; relationship; connection: *This has no bearing on the subject.* **9.** *Heraldry.* A charge or device on a field.

Synonyms: *air, carriage, demeanor, manner, mien, presence.*

bearing rein *n.* A rein for a horse, a **checkrein** *(see).*

bear·ish (bâr'ĭsh) *adj.* **1.** Like a bear; clumsy, boorish, or surly. **2.** Causing, expecting, or characterized by falling stock-market prices. Compare **bullish.** —**bear·ish·ly** *adv.* —**bear·ish·ness** *n.*

bé·ar·naise sauce (bā-är-nāz') *n.* A sauce made from butter, egg yolks, lemon juice or vinegar, and flavored with tarragon, shallots, and chervil. Also called "sauce béarnaise." [French *béarnaise,* feminine of *béarnais,* of Béarn, region in southwestern France.]

bear's-ear (bârz'îr') *n.* A plant, the **auricula** *(see).*

bear·skin (bâr'skĭn') *n.* **1.** Something, such as a rug, made from the skin of a bear. **2.** A tall military headdress made of black fur. —**bear·skin** *adj.*

beast (bēst) *n.* **1.** Any animal except a human; especially, any large, four-footed animal. **2.** The qualities of an animal; animal nature. **3.** A brutal or vile person. [Middle English *beste,* from Old French, from Latin *bēstia*†.]

beast·ly (bēst'lē) *adj.* **-lier, -liest. 1.** Of or like a beast; bestial. **2.** *Informal.* Disagreeable; nasty; abominable.

~*adv. Chiefly British Informal.* Used as an intensive: *It's beastly cold outside.* —**beast·li·ness** *n.*

beast of burden *n.* An animal used for transporting loads.

beast of prey *n.* An animal that kills and eats other animals.

beat (bēt) *v.* **beat, beaten** (bēt'n) or **beat, beating, beats.** —*tr.* **1. a.** To strike or hit repeatedly. **b.** To strike (a drum, for example) in order to produce a noise. **2.** To punish by hitting or whipping; flog. **3.** To pound or strike against repeatedly: *waves beating the shore.* **4.** To shape or break by repeated blows; forge. **5.** To make flat by pounding or trampling. **6.** To mix rapidly with an instrument to a frothy consistency: *beat two eggs in a bowl.* **7.** To flap (wings, for example). **8.** To sound (a signal), as on a drum. **9.** To mark or count (time or rhythm) with the hands or with a baton. **10.** To disturb (bushes, for example) in order to drive out game for shooting. **11.** To defeat or subdue. **12.** *Informal.* To excel or surpass. **13.** *Informal.* To avoid or counter the effects of; circumvent: *beat the traffic.* **14.** To precede or arrive in advance of; forestall: *They beat us to it.* **15.** *Slang.* To perplex or baffle. —*intr.* **1.** To inflict repeated blows. **2.** To throb or pulsate rhythmically. **3.** *Physics.* **a.** To cause beating by superposing waves of different frequencies. **b.** To undergo beating. Said of waves of alternating electrical signals. **4.** To emit sound when struck: *The gong beat thunderously.* **5.** To sound a signal, as on a drum. **6.** To admit of rapid whipping to a froth. **7.** To hunt through woods or undergrowth to drive out game. **8.** *Nautical.* To progress against the wind by tacking. —See Synonyms at **defeat, pulsate.** —**beat about** (or **around**) **the bush.** To approach a subject in a roundabout manner. —**beat a retreat.** To flee or withdraw. —**beat back.** To force to retreat or withdraw. —**beat down.** To force or persuade (a seller) to accept a lower price. —**beat it.** *Slang.* To get going; go away. Usually used in the imperative. —**beat off.** To drive away. —**beat up.** *Informal.* To give a thorough beating to; thrash.

~*n.* **1.** A stroke or blow, especially one that produces a sound or acts as a signal. **2.** A periodic pulsation or throb. **3.** *Physics.* An amplitude pulse produced by beating. **4.** *Music.* **a.** A regular and rhythmical unit of time. **b.** The pulse given to a piece of music by the recurrence of this unit. **c.** The gesture given by a conductor or the symbol representing this unit of time. **5.** The measured and rhythmical sound of verse; meter. **6.** The area regularly covered by a policeman, sentry, or newspaper reporter. **7.** A process of disturbing the undergrowth to drive out game when shooting. **8.** A member of the **beat generation** *(see).* **9.** *Slang.* The reporting of a news item obtained ahead of one's competitors. —See Synonyms at **rhythm.**

~*adj. Informal.* Worn-out; exhausted. [Beat, beat, beaten; Middle English *beten, bette, beten,* Old English *bēatan, bēot, bēaten.*]

beat·en (bēt'n) *adj.* **1.** Defeated; completely baffled. **2.** Made thin or formed by hammering. **3.** Worn by many footsteps; very traveled: *a beaten path.* **4.** Exhausted; worn-out. —**off the beaten track** (or **path**). **1.** In a remote, out-of-the-way place. **2.** Not well-known; unusual.

beat·er (bē'tər) *n.* **1.** One that beats, especially an instrument for beating: *a carpet beater.* **2.** A person who drives wild game from under cover for a hunter.

beat generation *n.* In the 1950's, a group of young Americans, including Jack Kerouac, Allen Ginsberg, and William Burroughs, who expressed disillusionment with Western values and turned for inspiration to Eastern religion, trying experimental literary forms and adopting a bohemian lifestyle. [Perhaps from BEATEN (exhausted).]

be·a·tif·ic (bē'ə-tĭf'ĭk) *adj.* Showing or producing exalted joy or

bearing

HOW MACHINERY IS KEPT MOVING SAFELY AND SMOOTHLY

The modern use of an old device to minimize friction between moving parts

When, in ancient Egypt and Mesopotamia, building blocks were hauled over logs, the logs were acting as bearings as they rolled. Today's bearings fulfill a similar function: they cut down the friction between two parts of a mechanism, at least one of which is moving. By minimizing friction, they ease movement and reduce wear.

Bearings are now essential components of all kinds of modern machinery. They can be classified according to their shape. The three most common types are journal bearings, roller bearings, and ball bearings. The journal bearing is the simplest, the oldest, and still the most commonly used of the three. It originated in about 1000 B.C. among the Celts of France and Germany who fitted a wooden insert between the wheel hub and axle of a cart.

The idea of the roller bearing was also put to use by the Celts—as wooden rollers fitted inside a sleeve on a hub. Ball bearings first came into general use in the bicycle in 1868.

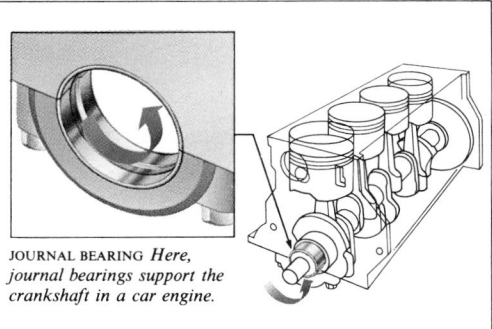

JOURNAL BEARING *Here, journal bearings support the crankshaft in a car engine.*

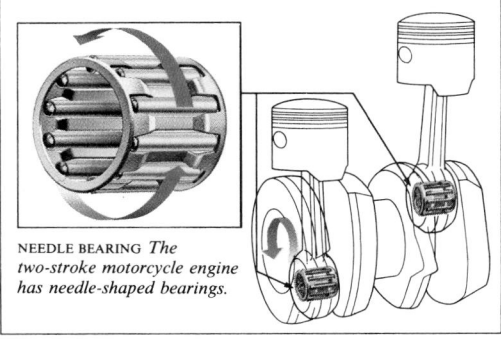

NEEDLE BEARING *The two-stroke motorcycle engine has needle-shaped bearings.*

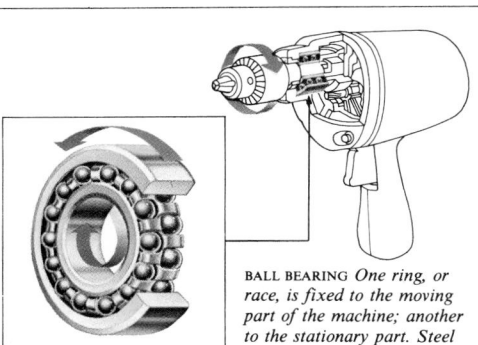

BALL BEARING *One ring, or race, is fixed to the moving part of the machine; another to the stationary part. Steel balls are packed in between.*

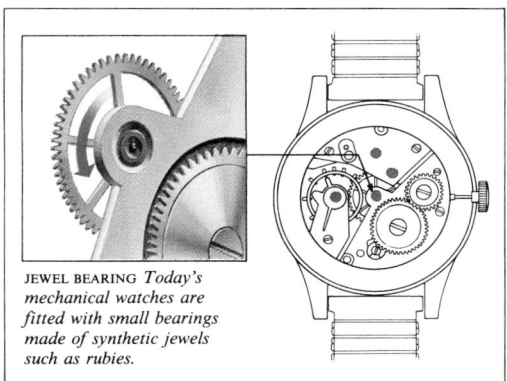

JEWEL BEARING *Today's mechanical watches are fitted with small bearings made of synthetic jewels such as rubies.*

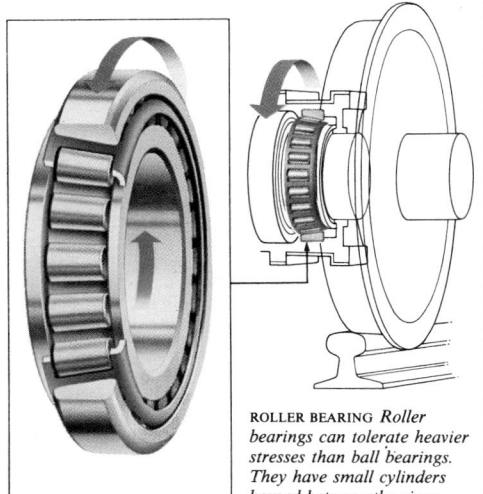

ROLLER BEARING *Roller bearings can tolerate heavier stresses than ball bearings. They have small cylinders housed between the rings.*

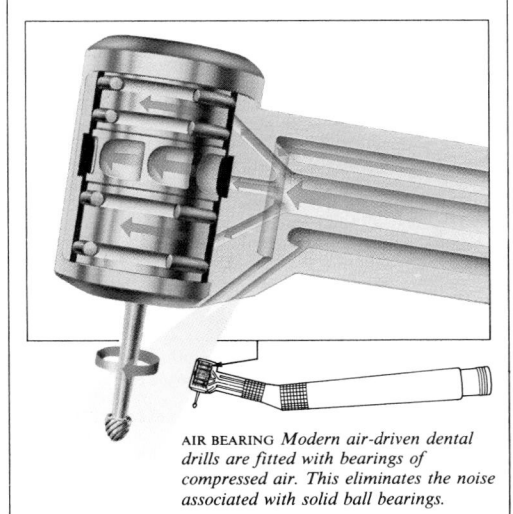

AIR BEARING *Modern air-driven dental drills are fitted with bearings of compressed air. This eliminates the noise associated with solid ball bearings.*

bearskin *Tall fur hat that is part of the ceremonial dress of the British Guards regiments. First used by the Grenadier Guards in the 18th century, it is seen here worn by a soldier of the Scots Guards.*

blessedness: *a beatific smile.* [Late Latin *beātificus* : Latin *beātus,* blessed, from the past participle of *beāre,* to make happy + *facere,* to do.] —**be·a·tif·i·cal·ly** *adv.*
be·at·i·fy (bē-ăt′ə-fī) *tr.v.* **-fied, -fying, -fies. 1.** To make blessedly happy. **2.** *Roman Catholic Church.* To proclaim (a deceased person)

to be one of the blessed and thus worthy of public religious honor, usually prior to canonization. **3.** To exalt above all others. [Late Latin *beātificāre,* from *beātificus,* BEATIFIC.] —**be·at·i·fi·ca·tion** *n.*
beat·ing (bē′tĭng) *n.* **1.** Punishment by whipping, flogging, or thrashing. **2.** A defeat. **3.** A throbbing or pulsation, as of the heart.

4. *Physics.* The periodic alternation of amplitude maxima and minima produced by interference between two waves of different frequency.

be·at·i·tude (bē-ăt′ə-tōōd′, -tyōōd′) *n.* **1.** Supreme blessedness or happiness. **2. Beatitude.** Any of the nine declarations of blessedness made by Jesus in the Sermon on the Mount. Matthew 5:3–11. [Latin *beātitūdo,* from *beātus,* blessed. See **beatific.**]

Beat·les (bēt′əlz), **the.** English pop group, comprising John Lennon, Ringo Starr, Paul McCartney, and George Harrison. They were all born in Liverpool and began performing together in Liverpool clubs in 1960. They first gained international fame in 1962, with records such as "Love Me Do" and "Please Please Me." For the next eight years they were the most famous pop group in the world. The group disbanded in 1970.

beat·nik (bēt′nĭk) *n.* **1.** A member of the **beat generation** *(see).* **2.** Especially in the 1950's, a person whose dress and behavior showed pointed, often exaggerated, disregard for conventional norms. [BEAT + -NIK.]

Bea·ton (bēt′n), **Sir Cecil Walter Hardy** (1904–80). English photographer, internationally famous for his portraits of celebrities. He also designed many theatrical productions, including *My Fair Lady* (stage, 1956; film, 1964).

Be·a·trix (bē′ə-trĭks′), in full Beatrix Wilhelmina Armgard (1938–). Queen of the Netherlands. She became queen in April 1980 after the abdication of her mother, Juliana.

beau (bō) *n., pl.* **beaus** (bōz) or **beaux. 1.** The sweetheart of a woman or girl. **2.** A man excessively interested in fine clothes and social etiquette; a dandy. [French, fine, handsome, from Latin *bellus,* pretty, handsome, fine.]

Beau Brum·mell (bō brŭm′əl) *n.* A dandy; fop. [After George Bryan *("Beau")* BRUMMELL.]

Beau·fort scale (bō′fərt) *n.* A scale on which successive ranges of wind velocities are assigned code numbers from 0 to 12 or from 0 to 17, corresponding to names from *calm* to *hurricane.* [After Sir Francis *Beaufort* (1774–1857), British admiral.]

Beaufort Sea. Sea in the Arctic Ocean, lying between Point Barrow, Alaska, and the Canadian Arctic Archipelago. It is never free of pack ice.

beau geste (bō zhĕst′) *n., pl.* **beaux gestes** (bō zhĕst′) or **beau gestes** (bō zhĕst′). **1.** A gracious gesture. **2.** A gesture noble in form but meaningless in substance. [French, "beautiful gesture."]

Beau·har·nais (bō-är-nā′), **Alexandre, Vicomte de** (1760–94). French general, who fought on the side of the Colonists in the American Revolution and then in France in the Revolutionary army. He was guillotined during the Reign of Terror.

Beauharnais, Joséphine de. See **Joséphine.**

beau i·de·al (bō ī-dē′əl) *n., pl.* **beau ideals. 1.** The concept of perfect beauty. **2.** An idealized type or model. [French *beau idéal,* "ideal beauty."]

Beau·jo·lais¹ (bō′zhə-lā′). Hilly region of east-central France, lying west of the Saône River between Mâcon and Lyon. It is one of the most famous wine districts in France.

Beau·jo·lais² (bō′zhə-lā′) *n. Often* **beaujolais.** A light red or white wine from central France.

Beau·mar·chais (bō-mär-shā′), **Pierre Augustin Caron de** (1732–99). French dramatist. His two most famous plays, both rich in subversive innuendo against feudal privileges, served as the basis for Rossini's *The Barber of Seville* and Mozart's *The Marriage of Figaro.*

beau monde (bō mŏnd′; *French* bō môNd′) *n., pl.* **beaux mondes** (bō mônd′) or **beau mondes** (bō môndz′). Fashionable society. [French, "beautiful world."]

Beau·mont (bō′mŏnt), **Francis** (1584–1616). English dramatist who collaborated with John Fletcher from c. 1606 until c. 1616. Their most famous joint work was *The Maid's Tragedy* (1611). Beaumont is credited with the sole authorship of *The Woman Hater* (1607) and *The Knight of the Burning Pestle* (c. 1607).

Beaune (bōn). Small town in Côte-d'Or department in southeastern France. The center of the Burgundy wine industry, its vineyards date from the period of Roman occupation.

Beau·re·gard (bō′rə-gärd′), **Pierre Gustave Toutant de** (1818–93). Confederate army officer in the Civil War. He gave the order to fire on Fort Sumter and fought at the first Battle of Bull Run (1861) and the Battle of Shiloh (1862).

beaut (byōōt) *n. Slang.* Something outstanding of its kind. [Short for BEAUTY.]

beau·te·ous (byōō′tē-əs, -tyəs) *adj.* Beautiful, especially to the sight. —**beau·te·ous·ly** *adv.* —**beau·te·ous·ness** *n.*

beau·ti·cian (byōō-tĭsh′ən) *n.* One skilled in cosmetic treatment, especially one working in a beauty salon. [BEAUT(Y) + -ICIAN.]

beau·ti·ful (byōō′tə-fəl) *adj.* **1.** Pleasing to the senses. **2.** Pleasing to the mind: *a beautiful irony.* **3.** Excellent. **4.** Desirable; of great worth: *Small is beautiful.*
—*n.* Beauty, as an aesthetic or philosophical principle. Preceded by *the.* —**beau·ti·ful·ly** *adv.* —**beau·ti·ful·ness** *n.*
　　Synonyms: comely, fair, handsome, lovely, pretty.

beautiful people *pl.n.* People who are prominent and fashionable, especially in international society.

beau·ti·fy (byōō′tə-fī) *v.* **-fied, -fying, -fies.** —*tr.* To make beautiful; adorn. —*intr.* To become beautiful. [BEAUT(Y) + -FY.] —**beau·ti·fi·ca·tion** *n.* —**beau·ti·fi·er** *n.*

beau·ty (byōō′tē) *n., pl.* **-ties. 1.** A quality that appeals to the senses or the mind through harmony of form or color, excellence of art-

istry or craftsmanship, truthfulness, originality, or some other, often unspecifiable, property. **2.** Appearance or sound that arouses a strong, contemplative delight; loveliness: *a woman who has preserved her youthful beauty.* **3.** A person or thing that arouses such delight; especially, a woman widely regarded as beautiful. **4.** A part, characteristic, or attribute that arouses such delight; a specific excellence or grace. **5.** The feature that is most effective, gratifying, or telling: *The beauty of the venture is that we stand to lose nothing.* **6.** *Informal.* An outstanding or conspicuous example. [Middle English *beau(l)te,* from Old French *bealte, beaute,* from Vulgar Latin *bellitās* (unattested), from Latin *bellus,* pretty, handsome, fine.]

beau·ty·ber·ry (byōō′tē-bĕr′ē) *n., pl.* **-ries.** Any shrub of the genus *Callicarpa,* having glistening, purplish, berrylike fruit. *C. americana,* of southeastern North America, is also called "Bermuda mulberry," "French mulberry."

beauty contest *n.* A competition in which a number of girls or women are judged on the basis of appearance.

beauty queen *n.* A girl or woman who has won a beauty contest or who enters such contests.

beauty salon *n.* An establishment providing services that include hair treatment, manicures, facials, and the like. Also called "beauty parlor," "beauty shop."

beauty sleep *n.* Sleep, especially in the hours before midnight, supposed to preserve a youthful appearance.

beauty spot *n.* **1.** Formerly, a small black mark glued on a woman's face or shoulders to accentuate the fairness of her skin. Also called "patch." **2.** A mole or freckle. **3.** A place of outstanding natural beauty.

Beau·vais (bō-vā′). Town in the Oise department in northern France. Its world-famous tapestry works, established as a royal factory in the 17th century, was destroyed in World War II. The Cathedral of St. Pierre, intended to be the largest in Christendom, was never completed, but its Gothic choir remains the loftiest (48 meters; 157 feet) in the world.

Beau·voir (bō-vwär′), **Simone de** (1908–86). French writer and feminist thinker. For many years the lover of Jean Paul Sartre, she devoted much of her writing to the exploration of existentialist themes. Her best-known works are the feminist treatise *The Second Sex* (1949–50), her autobiography, and a study of different cultures' treatment of old age, *The Coming of Age* (1970).

beaux. Alternative plural of **beau.**

beaux-arts (bō-zàr′) *pl.n. French.* The fine arts.

bea·ver¹ (bē′vər) *n.* **1.** A large, amphibious rodent of the genus *Castor,* of Eurasia and North America, having thick brown fur, webbed hind feet, a paddlelike, hairless tail, and chisellike front teeth adapted for gnawing bark and felling trees used to build dams. **2.** The fur of a beaver. **3. a.** A full beard. **b.** A bearded man. **4.** A top hat, originally made of the beaver's underfur. **5.** A napped wool fabric, similar to felt, used for outer garments. **6.** Grayish brown to light or dark grayish yellowish brown.
—*intr.v.* **beavered, -vering, -vers.** *Chiefly British.* To work with determination. Used with *away.* [Middle English *bever,* Old English *be(o)for.*]

beaver² *n.* **1.** A movable piece of medieval armor attached to a helmet or breastplate to protect the mouth and chin. **2.** The visor on a helmet. [Middle English *baviere,* from Old French *baviere, bib,* from *baver,* to slaver, from *beve,* saliva, from (unattested) Vulgar Latin *baba* (imitative).]

bea·ver·board (bē′vər-bôrd′, -bōrd′) *n.* A light, semirigid building material of compressed wood pulp, used for walls and partitions. [From the former trademark *Beaverboard.*]

Bea·ver·brook (bē′vər-brŏŏk′), **William Maxwell Aitken, 1st Baron** (1879–1964). British press baron, financier, and politician, born in Canada. He came to England in 1910, was elected to Parliament, and remained in the House of Commons until 1917, when he was given a peerage. He gained control of the *Daily Express* in 1916 and the *Evening Standard* in 1923. He was minister of aircraft production (1940–41), of war production (1942), and lord privy seal (1943–45). His writings include *Politicians and the War, 1914–1916* (1928, 1932), and *Men and Power: 1917–1918* (1956).

be·bop (bē′bŏp′) *n.* A type of music, **bop** *(see).* [Imitative of a two-beat phrase in this music.]

be·calm (bĭ-käm′) *tr.v.* **-calmed, -calming, -calms. 1.** To render (a ship) motionless for lack of wind. **2.** To make calm or still; soothe.

be·came. Past tense of **become.**

be·cause (bĭ-kôz′, -kŭz′) *conj.* **1.** For the reason that; since. **2.** *Nonstandard.* The fact that: *Because you're here doesn't mean that I'm ready.* —**because of.** By reason of; on account of. [Middle English *bi cause* : *bi,* BY + CAUSE.]
　　Usage: In clauses introduced by *The reason that . . .* or *The reason is . . . ,* the use of *because* is common but superfluous. In a sentence like *The reason why you're tired is because you went to bed late* the notion of "cause" is expressed twice; it is sufficient to say *The reason you're tired is that you went to bed late,* or, more simply, *You're tired because you went to bed late.*

bec·ca·fi·co (bĕk′ə-fē′kō) *n., pl.* **-cos.** Any small songbird or warbler of various genera, eaten as a delicacy in Italy. [Italian, "figpecker" : *beccare,* to peck, from *becco,* beak, from *beccus,* BEAK + *fico,* fig, from Latin *fīcus,* FIG.]

bé·cha·mel sauce (bā′shə-mĕl′) *n.* A white sauce, made from butter, flour, milk or cream, and seasonings. Also called "sauce béchamel." [French *sauce béchamelle,* after Louis de *Béchamel,* steward of Louis XIV, who invented it.]

beaver

THE DAM BUILDERS
How the work of beavers helps to improve the environment

At one time beavers were valued only for their fur. Today, they are legally protected in most countries. North American beavers are recognized as natural conservationists; for the dams they build help to control the flow of mountain streams, preventing soil erosion and creating new homes for plants and animals.

Beavers, which are found mainly in North America and in the forests of northern Europe and Asia, are rodents—gnawing animals. They have powerful jaws and chisellike front teeth that enable them to gnaw on bark and vegetation for food and to fell trees for their dams.

The ponds that form above the dams become natural moats, keeping predators away from the wooden lodges that the beavers build. Dozens of animals may work together to construct a dam from wood, stones, mud, and weeds. The result can be huge: frequently 200 meters (about 650 feet) long and 4 meters (13 feet) high, and even up to 550 meters (1,800 feet) long.

Food store   Ventilated roof   Living area   Dam

BEAVERS' LODGE *Protected by the lake that forms behind their dam, beavers build dens called lodges, just above the water. Each lodge may be occupied by a family of up to ten animals—the parents and two litters of young—and several families may share the same lake, all helping to maintain or enlarge a single dam. The animals, who can stay submerged for up to 15 minutes, enter and leave the lodges through underwater passages.*

PADDLE AND RUDDER *The beaver's webbed feet serve as paddles, and its broad tail as a rudder. An adult can be 1 meter (3 feet 3 inches) long and weigh up to 15 kilograms (about 33 pounds).*

be·chance (bĭ-chăns′, -chäns′) *v.* **-chanced, -chancing, -chances.** *Rare.* —*intr.* To happen; chance. —*tr.* To befall; happen to.
bêche-de-mer (bĕsh′də-mâr′) *n., pl.* **bêches-de-mer** (bĕsh′də-mâr′). **1.** A marine animal, the **trepang** *(see),* or a food prepared from it. **2.** A lingua franca that combines Malay and English, spoken in the southwest Pacific. In this sense, also called "beach-la-mar." [French, from earlier *biche de mer,* from Portuguese *bicho do mar,* "sea worm" : *bicho,* worm, from Late Latin *bēstulus,* diminutive of Latin *bēstia,* BEAST + *mar,* sea, from Latin *mare.* The designation of the language is probably from the use of trepang as an important trade item in this area.]
Bech·u·a·na (bĕch′ōō-ä′nə) *n., pl.* **-nas** or collectively **Bechuana.** **1.** A former name for a member of a Bantu people inhabiting Botswana in south-central Africa. **2.** A language, **Tswana** *(see).*
Bechuanaland. See **Botswana.**
beck[1] (bĕk) *n.* A gesture of beckoning or summons. —**at someone's beck and call.** Having to carry out someone's every wish. [Middle English, from *beknen,* to BECKON.]
beck[2] *n. British.* A small brook. [Middle English, from Old Norse *bekkr.*]
beck·et (bĕk′ĭt) *n. Nautical.* A device, such as a looped rope, hook and eye, strap, or grommet, for holding or fastening loose ropes, spars, or oars in position. [18th century : origin obscure.]
Beck·et (bĕk′ĭt), **Saint Thomas,** also known as "Thomas à Becket" (c. 1118–70). English cleric. He entered the household of Theobald, archbishop of Canterbury, in c. 1142 and was appointed archdeacon of Canterbury in 1154. In the same year Henry II made him his chancellor. Appointed archbishop of Canterbury in 1162, he fell into disfavor with Henry by becoming the spokesman for the Church. Charged in 1164 with misappropriating crown funds as chancellor, Becket fled the country and remained in exile for six years. He returned in 1170 and immediately became embroiled in the controversy surrounding Henry's illegal appointment of his eldest son as archbishop of York. At Henry's behest, four knights of the royal household murdered Becket in Canterbury Cathedral on December 29. He was canonized in 1173.
Beck·ett (bĕk′ĭt), **Samuel** (1906–89). Irish playwright, novelist and critic. He settled in Paris in 1937, and many of his works were written in both French and English. His first novel, *Murphy* (1938), was followed by *Watt* (1942) and *Malone Dies* (1951), and *Molloy* (1951). He is known to a wider audience for his plays in the style of the theater of the absurd, especially *Waiting for Godot* (1952), *Endgame* (1957), *Krapp's Last Tape* (1959), and *Happy Days* (1961). In 1969 he won the Nobel Prize for literature.

Beck·mann (bĕk′män), **Max** (1884–1950). German painter and printmaker. Beckmann developed an expressionist manner under the influence of Edvard Munch, and in the 1920's he came to his most lasting style, the painting of brutal, often grotesque, large figurative canvases. Persecuted by the Nazis, he fled to Amsterdam in 1937 and in 1947 settled in the United States, where he died.
Beck·mann thermometer (bĕk′mən, -män) *n.* A mercury thermometer with a small adjustable range, used in scientific experiments for the accurate measurement of small temperature changes. [After Ernst *Beckmann* (1853–1923), German chemist.]
beck·on (bĕk′ən) *v.* **-oned, -oning, -ons.** —*tr.* **1.** To signal or summon (another), as by nodding or waving. **2.** To attract as if with gestures; invite: *"a lovely, sunny country that seemed to beckon them on to the Emerald City"* (L. Frank Baum). —*intr.* **1.** To make a summoning or signaling gesture. **2.** To be attractive or enticing. ~*n.* A gesture or motion of summons. [Middle English *bekmen,* Old English *bēcnan, bīecnan.*] —**beck·on·er** *n.* —**beck·on·ing·ly** *adv.*
be·cloud (bĭ-kloud′) *tr.v.* **-clouded, -clouding, -clouds.** **1.** To darken with clouds. **2.** To confuse; obscure.
be·come (bĭ-kŭm′) *v.* **-came** (-kām′), **-come, -coming, -comes.** —*intr.* To grow or come to be: *After two months together, the relationship was becoming predictable.* —*tr.* **1.** To be appropriate or suitable to: *"it would not become me . . . to interfere with parties"* (Jonathan Swift). **2.** To show to advantage; look good with or on. —**become of.** To be the fate or subsequent condition of; happen to. [Middle English *becomen,* Old English *becuman* : BE- + COME.]
be·com·ing (bĭ-kŭm′ĭng) *adj.* **1.** Appropriate; suitable; proper. **2.** Pleasing or attractive to the eye. —**be·com·ing·ly** *adv.* —**be·com·ing·ness** *n.*
Bec·que·rel (bĕ-krĕl′, bĕk′ə-rĕl′), **Antoine Henri** (1852–1908). French physicist, grandson of **Antoine César Becquerel** (1788–1878), one of the first investigators of electrochemistry, and son of **Alexandre Edmond Becquerel** (1820–91), the inventor of the phosphoroscope. Principally devoted to the study of the effect of the earth's magnetism on the atmosphere, he discovered radioactivity in uranium (1896) and shared the Nobel Prize for physics (1903) with Marie and Pierre Curie.
bed (bĕd) *n.* **1. a.** A piece of furniture for reclining and sleeping, typically consisting of a flat, rectangular frame, a mattress resting on springs, and bedclothes. **b.** A bedstead. **c.** A mattress or a mattress with bedclothes. **2. a.** Rest or sleep. **b.** Any place or surface upon which one may rest or sleep. **c.** A place where one may sleep for the night; a lodging. **3. a.** Sexual intercourse. **b.** A situation of

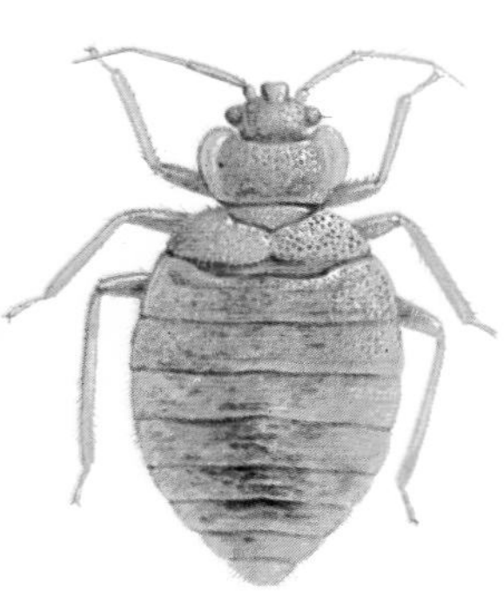

bedbug *This blood-sucking insect—which is 4-6 millimeters (1/4 inch) long—is so named because it feeds at night, sometimes on sleeping humans. It is not common nowadays in most developed countries.*

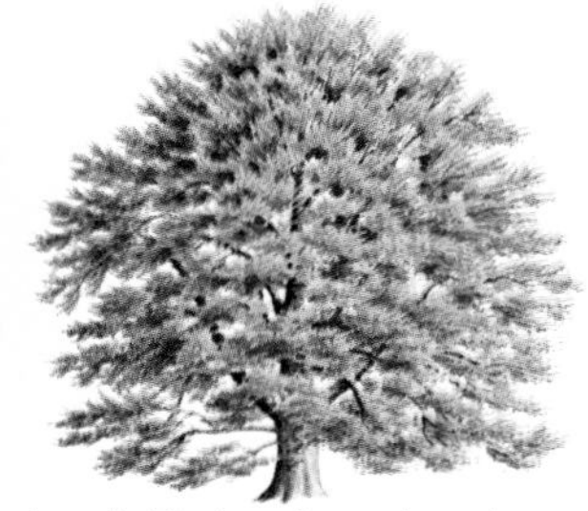

beech *The knot-free and supple, fine-grained wood of this tree is ideal for making chairs. The prickly fruit are known as mast.*

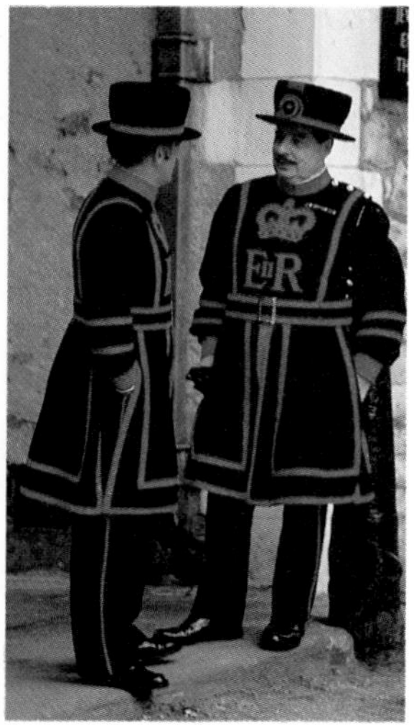

beefeater *Yeomen warders of the Tower of London in their day uniform. First formed as a royal bodyguard for the coronation of Henry VII in 1485, the yeomen are thought to have acquired their nickname from an envious reference to their generous rations.*

sexual intimacy. **4. a.** A small plot of cultivated or planted land: *a flower bed.* **b.** Part of a river or sea bed used for cultivation, especially of oysters. **5.** The bottom of a watercourse or other body of water. **6.** A supporting, underlying, or securing part, especially: **a.** A layer of food on which another kind of food rests: *lobster on a bed of rice.* **b.** A foundation of crushed rock or a similar substance for a road or railway; roadbed. **c.** A layer of mortar upon which stones or bricks are laid. **d.** The flat underside of something, as of a brick. **e.** The heavy table of a printing press in which the type form is placed. **7.** *Geology.* **a.** A rock mass of large horizontal extent bounded, especially above, by physically different material. **b.** A deposit, as of ore or lava, parallel to the local stratification. Compare **mass, vein.** —**put** (or **go**) **to bed.** In journalism, to send or go to press; have or be printed.
~*v.* **bedded, bedding, beds.** —*tr.* **1.** To provide with a bed or sleeping place. **2.** To put to bed. **3.** To embed. **4.** To make a bed for; spread litter for. Usually used with *down*: *She bedded down the sheep under a lean-to.* **5.** To plant in a prepared bed of soil. **6.** To lay flat or arrange in layers. **7.** To have sexual intercourse with. —*intr.* **1.** To go to bed. Usually used with *down.* **2.** To form layers or strata. [Middle English *bed(e),* Old English *bed(d).*]

B.Ed. Bachelor of Education.

bed and board *n.* Sleeping accommodation and meals.

bed and breakfast *n. Abbr.* **b. & b. 1.** Overnight accommodation and breakfast. **2.** A guest house or private house providing this. —**bed-and-breakfast** *adj.*

be·daub (bĭ-dôb′) *tr.v.* **-daubed, -daubing, -daubs. 1.** To smear; soil. **2.** To ornament in a vulgar and showy fashion.

be·daz·zle (bĭ-dăz′əl) *tr.v.* **-zled, -zling, -zles.** To dazzle so completely as to confuse or blind. —**be·daz·zle·ment** *n.*

bed·bug, bed bug (bĕd′bŭg′) *n.* A wingless, bloodsucking insect of the genus *Cimex*; especially, *C. lectularius,* that has a flat, reddish body and a disagreeable odor and that often infests dirty human dwellings.

bed·cham·ber (bĕd′chām′bər) *n.* A bedroom.

bed·clothes (bĕd′klōz′, -klō*thz*′) *pl.n.* Coverings, such as sheets and blankets, used on a bed.

bed·ding (bĕd′ĭng) *n.* **1.** Bedclothes. **2.** Straw or similar material for animals to sleep on. **3.** Something that forms a foundation or bottom layer. **4.** *Geology.* Stratification or layering of rocks.

Bede (bēd), **Saint.** Also **Bae·da** (bē′də). (*c.* 673–735). Anglo-Saxon Benedictine monk and scholar known as the "the Venerable Bede." His theological works gained him the title of Doctor of the Church, the only Englishman so honored. He is best known for his *Historia Ecclesiastica Gentis Anglorum (Ecclesiastical History of the English Nation),* a record of the spread of Christianity and Anglo-Saxon culture in Britain. He was canonized in 1899.

be·deck (bĭ-dĕk′) *tr.v.* **-decked, -decking, -decks.** To deck out or adorn in a showy fashion; cover with decorations.

bedes·man (bēdz′mən) *n., pl.* **-men** (-mĭn). Formerly, an almsman. [Variant of *beadsman,* an almsman who had promised to pray (or say the rosary) for his benefactor.]

be·dev·il (bĭ-dĕv′əl) *tr.v.* **-iled, -iling, -ils** or *chiefly British* **-illed, -illing. 1.** To torment devilishly; plague; harass. **2.** To worry, annoy, or frustrate. **3.** To possess as with a devil; bewitch. **4.** To spoil; ruin. —**be·dev·il·ment** *n.*

be·dew (bĭ-do͞o′, -dyo͞o′) *tr.v.* **-dewed, -dewing, -dews.** To wet with or as if with dew.

bed·fel·low (bĕd′fĕl′ō) *n.* **1.** A person with whom one shares a bed; a bedmate. **2.** A temporary associate, collaborator, or ally.

Bed·ford (bĕd′fərd). Town in central England, on the Great Ouse River. The county town of Bedfordshire, it was the site of a British victory over the Saxons in 571.

Bedford cord *n.* A heavy cotton or woolen fabric in a ribbed weave with wide or narrow raised cords, similar to corduroy. [After BEDFORD, where it was made.]

Bed·ford·shire (bĕd′fərd-shîr, -shər). County in central England, most of it lying in the fertile valley of the Great Ouse River. Its county town is Bedford.

be·dight (bĭ-dīt′) *tr.v.* **-dight, -dight** or **-dighted, -dighting, -dights.** *Archaic.* To dress or adorn. [Middle English *bedighten* : *be-,* thoroughly + DIGHT.]

be·dim (bĭ-dĭm′) *tr.v.* **-dimmed, -dimming, -dims.** To make dim.

be·di·zen (bĭ-dī′zən, -dĭz′ən) *tr.v.* **-zened, -zening, -zens.** To dress or ornament vulgarly or tastelessly. [BE- + DIZEN.] —**be·di·zen·ment** *n.*

bed jacket *n.* A jacket worn when sitting up in bed.

bed·lam (bĕd′ləm) *n.* **1.** Any place or scene of noisy uproar and confusion. **2.** *Archaic.* A lunatic asylum; madhouse. [Middle English *Bedlem, Bethlem,* Hospital of St. Mary of *Bethlehem,* in south-eastern London, which was an asylum at one time.]

bed linen *n.* The sheets and pillowcases used on a bed.

Bed·ling·ton terrier (bĕd′lĭng-tən) *n.* A dog of a breed developed in England, having long legs and a woolly grayish or brownish coat. [After *Bedlington,* northeastern England.]

bed·mate (bĕd′māt′) *n.* One with whom a bed is shared.

bed molding *n. Architecture.* **1.** The molding between the corona and frieze of an entablature. **2.** Any molding below a projection.

bed of roses *n.* A state of idyllic comfort or luxury.

Bed·ou·in, Bed·u·in (bĕd′o͞o-ĭn) *n., pl.* **-ins** or collectively **Bedouin** or **Beduin.** An Arab of any of the nomadic tribes of the deserts of North Africa, Arabia, Jordan, and Syria. [Middle English *Bedoin,* from Old French *beduin,* from Arabic *badāwīn,* desert dwellers, plural of *badāwī,* from *badw,* desert.] —**Bed·ou·in** *adj.*

bed·pan (bĕd′păn′) *n.* **1.** A metal, glass, or plastic receptacle for the excreta of people who are bedridden. **2.** A **warming pan** *(see).*

bed·plate (bĕd′plāt′) *n.* A metal plate, frame, or platform serving as a base or support for a machine.

bed·post (bĕd′pōst′) *n.* Any of the four vertical posts at the corners of some beds.

be·drag·gled (bĭ-drăg′əld) *adj.* Wet, limp, and untidy. Said of the hair, clothes, or appearance.

bed·rid·den (bĕd′rĭd′n) *adj.* Confined to one's bed because of illness or infirmity. [Middle English *bedreden, bedrede,* Old English *bedrida,* from noun, "one who is bedridden" : BED + *rīda,* a rider, from *rīdan,* to RIDE.]

bed·rock (bĕd′rŏk′) *n.* **1.** The solid rock that underlies all soil, sand, clay, gravel, and loose material on the earth's surface. **2.** The lowest or bottom level. **3.** Fundamental principles.

bed·roll (bĕd′rōl′) *n.* A portable roll of bedding used especially by campers and others who sleep outdoors. Compare **sleeping bag.**

bed·room (bĕd′ro͞om′, -ro͝om′) *n.* A room for sleeping in.

bed·side (bĕd′sīd′) *n.* The space alongside a bed, especially the bed of a sick person.
~*adj.* Near a bed: *a bedside table.*

bedside manner *n.* The attitude and conduct of a doctor in the presence of a patient, intended to inspire confidence and allay fears.

bed·sit·ter (bĕd′sĭt′ər) *n. Chiefly British.* An **efficiency apartment** *(see).* Also called "bedsit," "bed-sitting room."

bed·sore (bĕd′sôr′, -sōr′) *n.* A pressure-induced ulceration of the skin with necrosis and sometimes deep muscular infection, occurring during long confinement in bed. Also called "decubitus ulcer," "pressure sore."

bed·spread (bĕd′sprĕd′) *n.* A usually decorative bed covering.

bed·spring (bĕd′sprĭng′) *n.* **1.** The network of springs supporting the mattress of a bed. **2.** Any of these springs.

bed·stead (bĕd′stĕd′) *n.* The frame of a bed, which supports the mattress.

bed·straw (bĕd′strô′) *n.* Any of various plants of the genus *Galium,* such as *G. verum* (lady's bedstraw), having whorled leaves, small white or yellow flowers, and prickly burrs. [After its former use as a mattress stuffing.]

bed·time (bĕd′tīm′) *n.* The time when one goes or should go to bed.

Beduin. Variant of **Bedouin.**

bed-wet·ting (bĕd′-wĕt′ĭng) *n.* Urinating in bed, especially when considered as a condition that may require medical or psychiatric treatment; nocturnal **enuresis** *(see).* —**bed-wet·ter** *n.*

bee[1] (bē) *n.* **1.** Any of various winged, hairy-bodied, usually stinging insects of the order Hymenoptera, including many solitary species, such as the **mason bee** and **leaf-cutter bee** *(both of which see),* as well as the social members of the family Apidae. They are characterized by structures for sucking nectar and gathering pollen from flowers. See **bumblebee, honeybee. 2.** A social gathering where people combine work, competition, and amusement: *a spelling bee.* [Middle English *bee,* Old English *bēo.*]

bee[2] *n.* A **bee block** *(see).* [Middle English *bege,* a ring of metal, Old English *bēag.*]

Bee·be (bē′bē), **(Charles) William** (1879–1962). U.S. naturalist and author. From 1919 on he was director of the New York Zoological Society's department of tropical research. In 1934 he made a record descent into the ocean in a bathysphere he had helped design.

bee block *n. Nautical.* A piece of hardwood on either side of a bowsprit through which forestays are reeved. Also called "bee."

bee·bread (bē′brĕd′) *n.* A brownish substance consisting of a mixture of pollen and nectar, fed by bees to their larvae. Also called "ambrosia."

beech (bēch) *n.* **1.** Any tree of the genus *Fagus,* characterized by smooth, light-colored bark and edible nuts partly enclosed in a prickly husk, especially, *F. grandifolia,* of eastern North America, and *F. sylvatica,* of Europe. **2.** Any tree of the genus *Nothofagus,* of the Southern Hemisphere, similar to the northern beeches but with evergreen leaves. **3.** The wood of any of these trees. [Middle English *beche,* Old English *bēce.*] —**beech** *adj.*

Bee·cham (bē′chəm), **Sir Thomas** (1879–1961). British symphony conductor. He founded the London Philharmonic (1932) and the Royal Philharmonic (1946) orchestras and did much to popularize the works of Frederick Delius.

beech·drops (bēch′drŏps′) *n., pl.* **beechdrops.** A leafless plant, *Epifagus virginiana,* of eastern North America, that has brownish or purplish flowers and is parasitic on the roots of the beech tree.

Bee·cher (bē′chər), **Henry Ward** (1813–87). U.S. clergyman and reformer. He was well known for his opposition to slavery, his passionate sermons, and his unorthodox private life.

Beecher, Lyman (1775–1863). U.S. clergyman and reformer. He was a fiery preacher, a strong abolitionist, and patriarch of a remarkable family that included Henry Ward Beecher and Harriet Beecher Stowe.

beech marten *n.* A **stone marten** *(see).*

beech mast *n.* The nuts of the beech tree; beechnuts.

beech·nut (bēch′nŭt′) *n.* The small, triangular nut of the beech tree, which provides food for livestock.

bee-eat·er (bē′ē′tər) *n.* Any of various chiefly tropical Old World birds of the family Meropidae, having brightly colored plumage and a downward-curving bill, and feeding chiefly on bees.

beef (bēf) *n., pl.* **beeves** (bēvz) or **beefs** (only form for sense 4).

1. The flesh of a slaughtered full-grown bull, ox, or cow. **2.** A full-grown bull, ox, or cow, especially one intended for use as meat. **3.** *Informal.* Human muscle; brawn. **4.** *Slang.* A complaint. ~*intr.v.* **beefed, beefing, beefs.** *Slang.* To complain. —**beef up.** *Slang.* To reinforce; build up; fill out. [Middle English *boef, beef, beef, ox,* from Old French *boef,* from Latin *bōs* (stem *bov-*), ox.] —**beef** *adj.*

beef bour·gui·gnon (bōōr′gē-nyôn′) *n.* Also *French* **boeuf bour·gui·gnon** (bœf′bōōr-gē-nyôn′). Braised cubes of beef simmered in a seasoned sauce with red wine, mushrooms, carrots, and onions. [Partial translation of French *boeuf bourguignon,* beef Burgundy style, from *Bourgogne,* BURGUNDY.]

beef·burg·er (bēf′bûr′gər) *n.* A hamburger.

beef·cake (bēf′kāk′) *n. Slang.* **1.** A photograph, as in an advertisement, of a scantily clothed man showing off his muscular physique. **2.** Such photographs collectively. **3.** Men who appear, or look as though they might appear, in such photographs. Compare **cheesecake.** [BEEF + (CHEESE)CAKE.]

beef cattle *pl.n.* Cows, bulls, or oxen bred and raised for meat.

beef·eat·er (bēf′ē′tər) *n.* A yeoman of the royal guard in England or a yeoman warder of the Tower of London, wearing a characteristic red and gold or red and black uniform. [17th century : popular term for a well-fed servant.]

bee fly *n.* Any of various flies of the family Bombyliidae, resembling bees and having larvae that are parasitic on the young of bees, wasps, and other insects.

beef·steak (bēf′stāk′) *n.* A thick slice of beef, as from the loin or the hindquarters, suitable for grilling or frying.

beefsteak fungus *n.* An edible fungus, *Fistularia hepatica,* growing on decaying wood and having a large, irregularly shaped reddish cap.

beef stro·ga·noff (strô′gə-nôf′, -nŏf′, strō-gän′ôf) *n.* Thinly sliced beef fillet sautéed and served with mushrooms and sour cream. [After Count Paul *Stroganoff,* 19th-century Russian diplomat.]

beef tea *n.* Broth made from beef extract or by boiling pieces of lean beef, often used as a restorative and for invalids.

beef Wellington *n.* Roast fillet of beef, covered with paté de foie gras and pastry, and baked. [After the 1st Duke of WELLINGTON.]

beef·wood (bēf′wŏŏd′) *n.* Any of various trees of the genus *Casuarina,* mostly native to Australia, having small, scalelike leaves and flowers and very hard wood. Also called "she-oak." [Perhaps from its reddish color.]

beef·y (bē′fē) *adj.* **-ier, -iest. 1.** Resembling beef. **2.** Muscular in build; heavy; brawny. —**beef·i·ness** *n.*

bee·hive (bē′hīv′) *n.* **1.** A hive, either natural or manmade, for bees. **2.** Any place teeming with activity. **3.** A hairstyle in which the hair is backcombed and piled on top of the head.

bee·keep·er (bē′kē′pər) *n.* One who keeps bees; apiarist.

bee·line (bē′līn′) *n.* A fast, direct course. Used chiefly in the phrase *make a beeline for.* [From the belief that a pollen-laden bee flies straight back to its hive.]

Be·el·ze·bub (bē-ĕl′zĭ-bŭb′). **1.** The Devil. **2.** In Milton's *Paradise Lost,* the chief of the fallen angels, next to Satan in power. [Late Latin, from Greek *Beelzeboub,* from Hebrew *bá'al zəbūb,* "lord of flies," god of the Ekronites (II Kings 1:2) : *bá'al,* lord + *zəbūb,* fly.]

bee moth *n.* A pyralid moth, such as *Galleria mellonella,* that lays its eggs in beehives, where the larvae feed on the honeycombs and the young bees. Also called "wax moth."

been. Past participle of **be.**

been·to, bin·tu (bĭn′tōō) *n. British Informal.* An African or Asian who has lived in Britain for part of his life, especially one who has received his education there, and has since returned to his country of origin. Used in various African and Asian countries. [From *been to* (Britain).] —**been·to** *adj.*

bee orchid *n.* A European orchid, *Ophrys apifera,* having a flower that resembles a bumblebee.

beep (bēp) *n.* A high-pitched sound such as that emitted by a car horn or some types of electrical apparatus. ~*v.* **beeped, beeping, beeps.** —*intr.* To make a beep. —*tr.* To cause to make a beep. [Imitative.]

beep·er (bē′pər) *n.* **1.** One that beeps. **2.** A small portable electronic device that emits a beeping signal when the person carrying it is being paged.

beer (bîr) *n.* **1.** A fermented alcoholic beverage brewed from malt and flavored with hops. **2.** Any of various drinks made from extracts of roots and plants. **3.** A glass or mug of such a drink. [Middle English *ber(e),* Old English *bēor,* from a West Germanic word, from Late Latin *biber,* a drink, from Latin *bibere,* to drink.]

beer and skittles *n. Slang.* Easygoing existence.

beer belly *n.* A person's stomach that is excessively large from the regular consumption of beer or some other alcoholic beverage.

Beer·bohm (bîr′bōm′), **Sir (Henry) Max(imilian)** (1872–1956). English caricaturist and writer, called by George Bernard Shaw "the incomparable Max." He was the half-brother of the actor-producer Sir Herbert Beerbohm Tree. His first satirical essays, *The Works of Max Beerbohm,* and his first caricatures, *Caricatures of Twenty-five Gentlemen,* both appeared in 1896. His only novel, *Zuleika Dobson,* an Oxford fantasy, was published in 1911. After 1910 he lived, apart from the World War II years, in Rapallo, Italy. He was knighted in 1939.

Beer·she·ba (bîr-shē′bə). *Hebrew* **Be·'er She·va'** (bîr shē′və). Town in southern Israel. It was famous in Biblical times as the abode of Isaac and Jacob and as the place where Abraham made his cov-

---

bee

INSIDE A BEEHIVE

A rigid caste system separates queen, drone, and worker

Most of the 12,000 species of bees in the world are solitary insects, coming together only to mate. Honeybees, on the other hand, live in highly organized colonies—sometimes in hives provided for them by beekeepers. Each colony contains, on average, a single queen—a fertile female who lives for between four and five years—a few dozen drones, or male bees, and about 60,000 worker bees—sterile females.

The workers, who rarely live more than a few months, collect nectar for the hive's winter food store of honey, build honeycombs from wax produced by their bodies, and bring pollen to the hive to feed the young larvae. In a good summer, a single colony can produce 30 kilograms (66 pounds) of honey.

The drones have to be fed by the workers because they are unable to feed themselves. The drones' only function is to fertilize a young queen before she takes over a colony from a dead or aging queen, or flies off with half the workers (known as swarming) to found a new one. Fertilization takes place in midair during a mating flight by the queen. The five or six drones who succeed in mating with the queen die soon afterward. The remainder survive till the end of summer; then they are driven out of the colony by the workers to die.

From this single flight, the queen receives all the sperm she needs for a lifetime of egg laying. Thereafter, between early spring and late autumn each year, she lays eggs at the rate of about one a minute—up to 1,500 a day. Depending on the population balance of the colony, these eggs are either fertilized with the sperm she has stored in her body—and develop into females as workers or queens—or they are laid unfertilized and hatch into male drones. Eggs that will grow into queens are identical at first to the eggs of the workers, but are laid in a special large cell, called a queen cell. The larvae that hatch there are fed extra amounts of royal jelly by the workers, who secrete the milky substance in their saliva.

As long as the existing queen remains healthy, she produces from glands on her head a pheromone known as queen substance that has the effect of calming the workers and preventing them from raising new queens. But when she sickens or dies, the pheromone supply is cut off, and the workers immediately start to rear new queens to replace her.

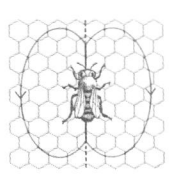  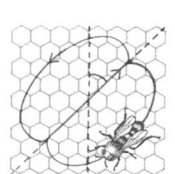 

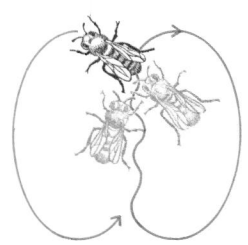

DANCE OF THE BEE *Worker bees foraging for food pass on news of their finds to others in the colony by means of a sophisticated dance. The dance, which is usually done on the vertical face of a honeycomb, follows a figure-eight pattern. The crucial part is the straight run between the two loops. If the bee dances directly upward, it means the food is in the direction of the sun. If the run is off to either side of the vertical, it means the food is at the same angle right or left of the sun. The bee also wags its body to indicate the food's distance, while other workers follow the dancer, apparently to help them memorize the information.*

---

enant with the Philistines. The city is still, as it has been for centuries, a watering place and market center for the nomadic Bedouins of the Negev.

beer·y (bîr′ē) *adj.* **-ier, -iest. 1.** Smelling or tasting of beer. **2.** Affected or produced by beer.

bee's knees *n. Used with a singular verb. Chiefly British Informal.* A person or thing considered to be marvelous. Preceded by *the.*

beest·ings (bē′stĭngz) *n. Used with a singular or plural verb.* The first milk given by a cow or other mammal after parturition; colostrum. [Middle English *bestynge* (singular), Old English *bēsting* (untested), from *bēost,* beestings, akin to Middle Dutch *biest,* Old High German *biost†.*]

bees·wax (bēz′wăks′) *n.* **1.** The yellowish to dark-brown wax secreted by the honeybee for making honeycombs. **2.** Commercial wax obtained by processing and purifying the crude wax of the honeybee, used in making candles, crayons, and polishes. ~*tr.v.* **beeswaxed, -waxing, -waxes.** To polish with this wax. [From *bee's wax.*]

bees·wing (bēz′wĭng′) *n.* **1.** A thin crust of tartar scales that sometimes forms on old port or other old wines. **2.** Wine affected by this crust. [From *bee's wing.*]

beet (bēt) *n.* **1.** Any of several widely cultivated plants of the genus *Beta;* especially, *B. vulgaris,* having leaves sometimes eaten as greens and a thickened, fleshy root. See **sugar beet. 2.** The bulbous root of this plant, characteristically dark red in color, eaten as a vegetable. Also *chiefly British* "beetroot." [Middle English *bete,* Old English *bēte,* from Latin *bēta†.*]

Bee·tho·ven (bā′tō-vən), **Ludwig van** (1770–1827). German composer. He was an outstanding representative of the transition from the classical to the romantic era of musical composition. He was born in Bonn, but settled in Vienna (1792). In 1801 his hearing began to fail and by 1819 he was deaf. He wrote music of all genres,

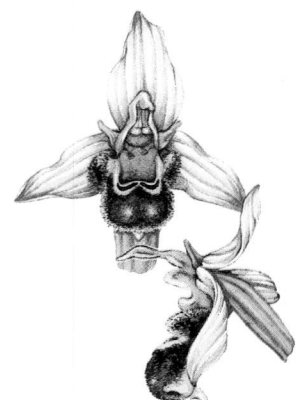

bee orchid *The flower of this plant appears to have a female bumblebee resting on it. The ruse attracts male bumblebees, which try to mate with the female and in doing so pollinate the flower.*

including 9 symphonies, 5 piano concertos, 1 violin concerto, 32 piano sonatas, 10 violin sonatas, 5 cello sonatas, 2 Masses, and 1 opera, *Fidelio.*

bee·tle¹ (bēt'l) *n.* **1.** Any of numerous insects of the order Coleoptera, having biting mouth parts and front wings modified to form horny wing covers that overlie the membranous rear wings when at rest. **2.** Loosely, any insect resembling a beetle.
~*intr.v.* **beetled, -tling, -tles.** To hurry off; scuttle. Usually used with *off.* [Middle English *bityl,* Old English *bitula, biter,* from *bītan,* to BITE.]

beetle² *adj.* Jutting; overhanging: *beetle brows.*
~*intr.v.* **beetled, -tling, -tles.** To overhang. [Middle English *bitel-* (*brouwed*), origin obscure.]

beetle³ *n.* **1.** A heavy mallet with a large wooden head. **2.** A small wooden household mallet. **3.** A heavy wooden club used in stamping and finishing handmade linen. **4.** A cloth-finishing machine that stamps cloth with revolving wooden hammers.
~*tr.v.* **beetled, -tling, -tles.** **1.** To pound with a beetle. **2.** To stamp and finish (cloth) with a beetle. [Middle English *betel,* Old English *bētel,* from Germanic *bautilaz* (unattested), from *bautan* (unattested), to BEAT.]

bee·tle-browed (bēt'l-broud') *adj.* Having projecting and shaggy eyebrows.

beet·root (bēt'rōōt', -rŏŏt') *n. British.* The beet.

beet sugar *n.* The sugar that is obtained from sugar beets.

beeves. A plural of **beef.**

be·fall (bĭ-fôl') *v.* **-fell** (-fĕl'), **-fallen** (-fôl'ən), **-falling, -falls.** —*intr.* To come to pass; happen. —*tr.* To happen to: *"There shall no evil befall thee"* (Psalms 91:10). —See Synonyms at **happen.**

be·fit (bĭ-fĭt') *tr.v.* **-fitted, -fitting, -fits.** To be suitable to or appropriate for.

be·fit·ting (bĭ-fĭt'ĭng) *adj.* Appropriate; suitable; proper. —**be·fit·ting·ly** *adv.*

be·fog (bĭ-fôg', -fŏg') *tr.v.* **-fogged, -fogging, -fogs.** **1.** To cover or obscure with or as if with fog; make foggy. **2.** To cause confusion in; muddle.

be·fool (bĭ-fōōl') *tr.v.* **-fooled, -fooling, -fools.** **1.** To make a fool of; hoodwink; trick; deceive. **2.** To treat as a fool.

be·fore (bĭ-fôr', -fōr') *adv.* **1.** In front; ahead; in advance. **2.** In the past; previously.
~*prep.* **1.** In front of; ahead of. **2.** Prior to. **3.** Awaiting: *Your happiness lies before you.* **4.** In or into the presence of: *She ordered the man to be brought before her.* **5.** Under the consideration or jurisdiction of: *the case before the court.* **6.** In preference to; sooner than. **7.** In advance of, or in precedence to, as in rank, condition, or development: *The princess is before him in the line of succession.*
~*conj.* **1.** In advance of the time when: *before he went.* **2.** Rather than; sooner than: *She would die before she would betray her cause.* [Middle English *before(n),* Old English *beforan,* from Germanic : *bi-* (unattested), BY + *forana* (unattested), from the front.]

be·fore·hand (bĭ-fôr'hănd', bĭ-fōr'-) *adv.* In anticipation; in advance; early: *We arrived beforehand.* —**be·fore·hand** *adj.*

be·fore·time (bĭ-fôr'tīm', bĭ-fōr'-) *adv. Rare.* Formerly.

be·foul (bĭ-foul') *tr.v.* **-fouled, -fouling, -fouls.** **1.** To make dirty; soil. **2.** To speak badly of; cast aspersions upon.

be·friend (bĭ-frĕnd') *tr.v.* **-friended, -friending, -friends.** **1.** To make friends with; initiate friendship with. **2.** To act as a friend to; aid; assist.

be·fud·dle (bĭ-fŭd'l) *tr.v.* **-dled, -dling, -dles.** **1.** To confuse; perplex. **2.** To stupefy with or as if with alcoholic drink.

beg¹ (bĕg) *v.* **begged, begging, begs.** —*tr.* **1.** To ask for as charity. **2.** To ask earnestly for, or of; entreat. **3.** To leave (a point) unresolved. —*intr.* **1.** To solicit alms. **2.** To make a humble or urgent plea. —**beg off.** To seek release from (a penalty or obligation). —**go begging.** To be unclaimed or unwanted. [Middle English *beggen†.*]

Synonyms: beseech, crave, entreat, implore, importune.

beg² (bĕg, bāg) *n.* A governor or other official of the Ottoman Empire or Mogul Empire; bey. [Ottoman Turkish, BEY.]

be·gan. Past tense of **begin.**

be·get (bĭ-gĕt') *tr.v.* **-got** (-gŏt') or *rare* **-gat** (-găt'), **-gotten** (-gŏt'n) or **-got, -getting, -gets.** **1.** To father; sire. **2.** To cause to exist. [Middle English *begeten,* to acquire, procreate, Old English *begietan.*] —**be·get·ter** *n.*

beg·gar (bĕg'ər) *n.* **1.** One who solicits alms. **2.** One who has no money; an impoverished person; a pauper. **3.** A rascal; rogue: *lucky beggar.* —**beggars can't be choosers.** People who have nothing must accept what is offered.
~*tr.v.* **-gared, -garing, -gars.** **1.** To impoverish; make a beggar of. **2.** To exhaust the resources of: *His beauty beggars all description.* [Middle English *begger(e), beggar(e),* from *beggen,* to BEG.]

beg·gar·ly (bĕg'ər-lē) *adj.* Of or pertaining to a beggar; very poor or meager: *a beggarly pension.* —**beg·gar·li·ness** *n.*

beg·gar-my-neigh·bor (bĕg'ər-mĭ-nā'bər) *n.* A simple card game of chance in which, by means of face cards, one must capture all one's opponents' cards.
~*adj.* Helping oneself at the expense of others: *a beggar-my-neighbor policy.*

beg·gar's-lice (bĕg'ərz-līs') *pl.n.* **1.** *Used with a singular or plural verb.* Any of several plants bearing small, prickly fruit that cling readily to clothing or the fur of animals, such as the **stickseed** (*see*). **2.** The seeds of such a plant.

beg·gar-ticks (bĕg'ər-tĭks') *pl.n.* **1.** *Used with a singular or plural*

verb. Any of several plants having seeds that cling to clothing, often by means of barbed bristles; especially, the **bur marigold** and the **tick trefoil** (*both of which see*). **2.** The seeds of any of these plants.

beg·gar·y (bĕg'ə-rē) *n.* **1.** Extreme poverty; penury. **2.** The state or condition of being a beggar. **3.** Beggars collectively.

be·gin (bĭ-gĭn') *v.* **-gan** (-găn'), **-gun** (-gŭn'), **-ginning, -gins.** —*intr.* **1.** To start; commence. **2.** To come into being: *when life began.* —*tr.* **1.** To start to do; commence. **2.** To be the cause or origin of: *It was her obstinacy that began the quarrel.* **3.** To show some likelihood of or capacity for: *doesn't begin to tackle the problem.* —**to begin with.** As a start; in the first place. [Begin, began, begun; Middle English *beginnen, bigan, begun,* Old English *beginnan, began, begunnen,* from West Germanic *bi-ginnan* (unattested) : *bi-,* BE- + *-ginnan* (unattested), origin obscure.]

Synonyms: commence, inaugurate, initiate, start.

Be·gin (bā'gĭn), **Menachem** (1913–92). Israeli politician, born in Brest in Belarus. He was sent to a labor camp in Siberia in 1941 for Zionist activities. Released in 1942, he went to Palestine, where he joined the Zionist underground movement, Irgun, which was campaigning for an independent Jewish state, and became its leader (1943–48). He helped found the Herut (Freedom) Party (1948), became its leader, and was elected to the Knesset. He became joint chairman of the newly founded Likud Party (1973), led it to electoral victory, and became prime minister (1977–83). He shared the Nobel Peace Prize with Anwar el-Sadat (1978).

be·gin·ner (bĭ-gĭn'ər) *n.* **1.** One who begins something. **2.** One who is just starting to learn or do something; novice.

be·gin·ning (bĭ-gĭn'ĭng) *n.* **1.** The act or process of bringing, or being brought, into being; start; commencement. **2.** The time when something begins or is begun: *"In the beginning God created the heaven and the earth"* (Genesis 1:1). **3.** The place where something begins or is begun: *at the beginning of the road.* **4.** The source or origin of something: *"The fear of the Lord is the beginning of wisdom"* (Psalms 111:10). **5.** The first part: *the beginning of the play.* **6.** *Often* **beginnings.** The early or rudimentary phase: *the beginnings of history; the beginnings of an agreement.*

be·gird (bĭ-gûrd') *tr.v.* **-girt** (-gûrt') or **-girded, -girt, -girding, -girds.** To gird or encircle; surround.

be·gone (bĭ-gôn', -gŏn') *interj.* Used as an order of dismissal. [Middle English : BE (imperative) + GONE.]

be·go·nia (bĭ-gōn'yə) *n.* Any of various plants of the genus *Begonia,* mostly native to the tropics but widely cultivated, having leaves that are often brightly colored or veined and irregular, waxy flowers of various colors. [New Latin, after Michel *Bégon* (1638–1710), French governor in the West Indies and patron of science.]

be·gor·ra (bĭ-gôr'ə) *interj.* Used to express surprise, alarm, or the like. It is used only humorously, as a supposed characteristic of Irish speakers. [Euphemistic for *by God!*]

be·got. Past tense and alternative past participle of **beget.**

be·got·ten. Past participle of **beget.**

be·grime (bĭ-grīm') *tr.v.* **-grimed, -griming, -grimes.** To smear or soil with dirt or grime.

be·grudge (bĭ-grŭj') *tr.v.* **-grudged, -grudging, -grudges.** **1. a.** To envy the possession or enjoyment of: *She begrudged his youth.* **b.** To envy for a possession: *She begrudged him his youth.* **2.** To give with reluctance.

be·guile (bĭ-gīl') *tr.v.* **-guiled, -guiling, -guiles.** **1.** To deceive by guile; delude: *"The serpent beguiled me and I did eat"* (Genesis 3:13). **2. a.** To take away from by guile; cheat. Used with *of* or *out of.* **b.** To divert; distract the attention of: *"to beguile you from the grief of a loss so overwhelming"* (Lincoln). **3.** To attract strongly; fascinate. **4.** To cause to vanish unnoticed or without pain: *"The history of a soldier's wound beguiles the pain of it"* (Lawrence Sterne). —See Synonyms at **deceive, lure.** [BE- + GUILE (verb).] —**be·guile·ment** *n.* —**be·guil·er** *n.*

be·guine (bĭ-gēn') *n.* **1.** A ballroom dance in the rhythm of a bolero based on a dance originating in Martinique and St. Lucia. **2.** The music for this dance. [American French *béguine,* from French *béguin,* hood, flirtation (as in *avoir un béguin pour quelqu'un,* "to be sweet on someone"), probably from Old French *Beguine,* BEGUINE.]

Beg·uine (bĕg'ēn') *n.* A member of any of several Roman Catholic lay sisterhoods existing in the Netherlands since the 12th century. [Old French *Beguine,* perhaps after Lambert le *Bègue* (Lambert the Stammerer), priest of Liège who founded the community.]

be·gum (bē'gəm) *n.* A Muslim lady of high rank. [Urdu *begam,* from Ottoman Turkish *begim,* possessive of *beg,* BEY.]

be·gun. Past participle of **begin.**

be·half (bĭ-hăf', -häf') *n.* Interest, support, or benefit. Used chiefly in the phrases *in behalf of* and *on behalf of.* —See Usage note below. [Middle English *(on min) behalfe,* "on my side" : *be,* BY + *half,* side, HALF.]

Usage: *In behalf of* and *on behalf of* have distinct senses. *In behalf of* means "in the interest of" or "for the benefit of": *We raised money in behalf of the orphans. We acted in their behalf. On behalf of* means "as the agent of" or "on the part of": *The guardian sued on behalf of the minor child. On whose behalf did he act?*

Be·han (bē'ən), **Brendan** (1923–64). Irish writer. He joined the I.R.A. in 1937, was arrested in England in 1940, and was sentenced to three years in a reform school. The years there were described in *The Borstal Boy* (1958). In 1942 he was convicted in Dublin of attempted murder and sentenced to 14 years' imprisonment. He was released in 1946. His prison years provided the experience for his most famous play, *The Quare Fellow* (1954). His later works include *Brendan Behan's Island* (1962) and *Confessions of an Irish Rebel* (1965).

be·have (bĭ-hāv′) *v.* **-haved, -having, -haves.** *—intr.* **1.** To act, react, function, or perform in a particular way. **2. a.** To conduct oneself in a specified way. **b.** To conduct oneself in a proper way. *—tr.* **1.** To conduct (oneself) properly. **2.** To conduct (oneself) in a specified way. [Middle English *behaven*, to hold oneself in a certain way : *be-*, thoroughly + *haven*, to HAVE.]

be·hav·ior (bĭ-hāv′yər) *n.* Also *chiefly British* **be·hav·iour. 1.** The manner in which one behaves; deportment; demeanor. **2.** The actions or reactions of persons or things under specified circumstances. **—be·hav·ior·al** *adj.* **—be·hav·ior·al·ly** *adv.*

behavioral science *n.* A science, such as sociology, psychology, or anthropology, that seeks to discover general truths about human social behavior. **—behavioral scientist** *n.*

be·hav·ior·ism (bĭ-hāv′yə-rĭz′əm) *n.* The psychological school holding that objectively observable organismic behavior constitutes the only valid scientific basis for psychological data and investigation and stressing the role of environment as a determinant of human and animal behavior. **—be·hav·ior·ist** *n.* **—be·hav·ior·is·tic** *adj.*

behavior therapy *n. Psychology.* Any method of treating psychological disorders that involves the patient's learning new patterns of behavior. It includes **aversion therapy** (*see*).

be·head (bĭ-hĕd′) *tr.v.* **-headed, -heading, -heads.** To separate the head from; decapitate. [Middle English *beheveden*, Old English *behēafdian* : *be-*, away from + *hēafdian*, to behead, from *hēafod*, HEAD.]

be·he·moth (bĭ-hē′məth, bē′ə-mŏth′) *n.* **1.** A huge animal, possibly the hippopotamus. Job 40:15-24. **2.** An enormous, or enormously powerful, person or thing. [Hebrew *bəhēmōth*, intensive plural ("great beasts") of *bəhēmāh*, beast.]

be·hest (bĭ-hĕst′) *n.* An order or authoritative command; a request or bidding. Used chiefly in the phrase *at the behest of.* [Middle English *behest*, promise, command, Old English *behǣs.*]

be·hind (bĭ-hīnd′) *adv.* **1.** In, to, or toward the rear: *He walked behind.* **2.** In a place or condition that has been passed or left: *He left his gloves behind.* **3.** In arrears; late: *fell behind in her payments.* **4.** Below the standard level; in an inferior position: *fall behind in class.* **5.** Slow: *His watch is running behind.* **6.** *Rare.* In reserve; yet to come: *There is no more behind.* ~*prep.* **1.** At the back of or in the rear of: *She sat behind him.* **2.** On the farther side of; beyond: *behind the door.* **3.** In a place or time that has been passed or left by: *Their worries are behind them.* **4.** After (a set time); later than: *The project was behind schedule.* **5.** Inferior to; less advanced than: *behind us in technology.* **6.** Hidden or concealed by: *behind the scenes.* **7.** Serving to support: *He had the army behind him.* ~*n. Informal.* The buttocks. [Middle English *bihinden*, Old English *behindan, bihindan* : *bi-*, BY + *hindan*, from behind.]

be·hind·hand (bĭ-hīnd′hănd′) *adv.* **1.** In arrears. **2.** Behind time; slow. **3.** In a backward state. **—behind·hand** *adj.*

Behn (bĕn), **Aphra** (1640-89). English writer, the first Englishwoman to make a professional career in letters. Her poetry is largely forgotten, but *Oroonoko* (1688) retains its place in English literary history as one of the earliest English novels.

be·hold (bĭ-hōld′) *tr.v.* **-held** (-hĕld′), **-holding, -holds.** To gaze at; look upon. **—See Synonyms at see.** ~*interj.* Used to express amazement or draw attention. [Middle English *beholden*, Old English *behealdan*, to possess, hold, observe.]

be·hold·en (bĭ-hōl′dən) *adj.* Obliged; indebted. [Middle English *beholden*, bound by obligation, Old English *behealden*, past participle of *behealdan*, to hold, BEHOLD.]

be·hoof (bĭ-hōōf′) *n. Rare.* Benefit; advantage; use. [Middle English *behove*, Old English *behōf.*]

be·hoove (bĭ-hōōv′) *tr. v.* **-hooved, -hooving, -hooves.** To be necessary or proper for. Used impersonally: *It behooves us to consider the question carefully.* [Middle English *behoven*, Old English *behōfian*, to require, be needful or fitting.]

Beh·ring (bâr′ĭng), **Emil (Adolph) von** (1854-1917). German bacteriologist. He is most famous for his work in serum therapy. For his demonstrations of serum immunization against diphtheria and tetanus he received the Nobel Prize in physiology and medicine in 1901. Behring coined the word "antitoxin."

Behring, Vitus. See **Bering.**

Bei·der·becke (bī′dər-bĕk′), **Bix,** born Leon Bismark Beiderbecke (1903-31). U.S. jazz musician. He was a self-taught pianist and cornet player and was the first white jazz musician to be recognized as a luminary of the jazz world by black musicians.

beige (bāzh) *n.* **1.** Light grayish brown, or yellowish brown to grayish yellow. **2.** A soft fabric of unbleached and originally undyed wool. [French, from Old French *bege†.*] **—beige** *adj.*

beigel. Variant of **bagel.**

Bei·jing (bā′jĭng′). Also **Pe·king** (pē′kĭng′, pā′-). Formerly (1928-49) **Pei·ping** (pā′pĭng′). Capital and second-largest city of China. It is a major cultural, communications, and industrial center. Founded by the Zhou as a frontier town on the North China Plain (*c.* 700 B.C.), the city was Kublai Khan's capital of Khanbalik (1264-67). The Ming made it their capital (1421), and it remained China's capital until 1912. Foreign troops occupied the city in 1860 and during the Boxer Rebellion (1900-01), and thereafter foreign garrisons were stationed in it. The city changed hands many times in the civil war following the formation of the Chinese Republic (1911-12). The Communists took Beijing (1949) and made it China's capital once

more. In it is preserved the Inner or Tatar City containing the Imperial or Forbidden City.

be·ing (bē′ĭng) *n.* **1. a.** Existence or a state of existence. **b.** A condition of particular existence. **2.** An object, idea, or symbol that exists, is thought to exist, or is represented as existing. **3.** A person: *"The artist after all is a solitary being"* (Virginia Woolf). **4.** One's basic or essential nature. **5.** *Philosophy.* **a.** That which can be conceived as existing. **b.** Absolute existence in its perfect and unqualified state; the essence of existence.

Bei·ra (bā′rə). Port in Mozambique, at the mouth of the Pungoe River. It is a beach resort and railway terminal, handling trade for Zimbabwe and Malawi.

Bei·rut or **Bey·routh** (bā-rōōt′). Capital and chief port of Lebanon. Founded by the Phoenicians, it was an important Greek and Roman trade center. It fell to the Arabs (635) and was much fought over during the Crusades. The Ottoman Turks took the city and later allowed the Druses to control it. The French captured Beirut (1918), and it became Lebanon's capital (1920). The city prospered as the chief financial and trade center of the Middle East, but from 1958 was severely damaged in the country's factional strife, in which the Syrians intervened (1976). It became a stronghold of the PLO and suffered at the hands of the Israelis until most of the PLO was evacuated (1982). Serious factional fighting resumed in 1983.

Be·ja (bā′jə) *n., pl.* **Beja. 1.** A member of a pastoral people living as nomads in the area between the Nile and the Red Sea. **2.** The Cushitic language of this people.

be·ja·bers (bē-jā′bərz) *interj.* Used to express surprise, alarm, or the like. [Euphemistic for *By Jesus!*]

Bé·jart (bā-zhär′), **Maurice,** born Maurice Jean de Berger (1927-). French dancer and choreographer. In 1954 he formed *Les Ballets de l'Etoile*, later renamed the *Ballet Théâtre de Paris.*

be·jew·el (bĭ-jōō′əl) *v.* **-eled, eling, els** or *chiefly British* **-elled, -elling.** To adorn with or as if with jewels.

bel (bĕl) *n.* A unit used for comparing two levels of power, voltage, current, or sound intensity equal to the logarithm to the base 10 of the ratio of the two levels. See **decibel.** [After Alexander Graham BELL.]

Bel (bĕl). *Babylonian Mythology.* The god of heaven and earth.

be·la·bor (bĭ-lā′bər) *tr.v.* **-bored, -boring, -bors. 1.** To beat, hit, or whip; attack with blows. **2.** To attack verbally. **3.** To go over repeatedly or for an absurd amount of time: *to belabor a point.*

be·lah (bē′lə) *n.* Any of various types of Australian tree, especially the casuarina. [From a native Australian name.]

Belarus. See **Byelorussia.**

Be·las·co (bə-lăs′kō), **David,** known as "the bishop of Broadway" (1853-1931). U.S. playwright, producer, and director, famous for his realistic stage settings and innovative lighting effects. Among his productions were *Madame Butterfly* (1900), *The Girl of the Golden West* (1905), and *Laugh, Clown, Laugh* (1923).

be·lat·ed (bĭ-lā′tĭd) *adj.* Tardy; after the appropriate time: *a belated birthday card.* [Past participle of obsolete *belate*, to delay : BE- + LATE.] **—be·lat·ed·ly** *adv.* **—be·lat·ed·ness** *n.*

Be·lau (bə-lou′). Also **Pa·lau** (pə-) or **Be·lew** (bə-lōō′). Four volcanic islands and numerous islets in the Caroline Islands, in the west Pacific Ocean. When the group opted to become part of the Federated States of Micronesia (1978), Belau broke away. The republic is in "free association" with the United States, which will be responsible for its defense until 1996. The people, largely Micronesian, live by fishing and farming. Area, 465 square kilometers (179 square miles). Population, 10,000 (1977). Capital, Koror. See map at **Pacific Ocean.**

be·lay (bĭ-lā′) *v.* **-layed, -laying, -lays.** *—tr.* **1.** *Nautical.* To secure or make fast (a rope) by winding on a cleat or pin. **2.** To secure (a mountain climber) at the end of a length of rope. *—intr.* **1.** To be made secure. **2.** *Nautical.* To stop. Used in the imperative. ~*n.* In mountain climbing, the securing of a rope on a rock or other projection. [Middle English *beleggen*, to beset, surround, Old English *belecgan*, to cover, surround. Current senses (from 16th century), from Dutch *beleggen.*]

be·lay·ing pin (bĭ-lā′ĭng) *n. Nautical.* A short, removable wooden or metal pin, fitted in a hole in the rail of a boat, and used for securing running gear.

bel can·to (bĕl kän′tō) *n.* A style of operatic singing characterized by rich tonal lyricism and brilliant display of vocal technique. [Italian, "beautiful singing."]

belch (bĕlch) *v.* **belched, belching, belches.** *—intr.* **1.** To expel gas noisily from the stomach through the mouth; eruct. **2.** To expel the contents violently; erupt: *The volcano belched with a roar.* **3.** To issue spasmodically; gush forth. *—tr.* **1.** To expel (gas) noisily from the stomach through the mouth; eruct. **2.** To eject violently from within: *The volcano belched hot lava.* ~*n.* A belching; an eructation. [Middle English *belchen*, perhaps Old English *bealcan* or *b(i)elcan* (unattested).] **—belch·er** *n.*

bel·dam, bel·dame (bĕl′dəm) *n.* An old woman, especially one who is loathsome or ugly. [Middle English, grandmother : Old French *bel-*, prefix indicating respect, from BELLE + DAME.]

be·lea·guer (bĭ-lē′gər) *tr.v.* **-guered, -guering, -guers. 1.** To besiege by surrounding with troops. **2.** To harass; plague; beset. [Dutch *belegeren* : *be-* + *leger*, camp, from Middle Dutch.] **—be·lea·guer·er** *n.* **—be·lea·guer·ment** *n.*

Be·lém (bə-lĕm′). Formerly **Pa·rá** (pə-rä′). Seaport on the Pará River in northern Brazil. It is a communications and market center for much of the Amazon basin.

bel·em·nite (bĕl'əm-nīt') *n.* A pointed, cigar-shaped fossil, the internal shell of any of various extinct cephalopods related to the cuttlefish. Also called "thunderstone." [New Latin *belemnites,* from Greek *belemnon,* dart; from the superstitious belief that such fossils were thunderbolts.]

bel esprit (bĕl'ĕs-prē') *n., pl.* **beaux esprits** (bōz' ĕs-prē'). *French.* A witty and intelligent person. ["Fine mind."]

Be·lew. See **Belau.**

Bel·fast (bĕl'făst', bĕl-făst'). Capital and largest city of Northern Ireland. Because of its large natural harbor on Belfast Lough, it has enjoyed a substantial trade and was a flourishing shipbuilding center. In the 19th century it was also one of the great linen centers of the world.

bel·fry (bĕl'frē) *n., pl.* **-fries.** **1.** A tower or steeple in which one or more bells are hung. **2.** The part of a tower or steeple in which the bells are hung. [Middle English *berfrey* (altered through influence of *bell*), portable siege tower, bell tower, from Old French *berfrei,* from Germanic, probably from *bergan* (unattested), protect + *frithuz* (unattested), shelter.] **—bel·fried** *adj.*

Belg. Belgian; Belgium.

Bel·gae (bĕl'jē, -jē') *pl.n.* An ancient Gallic people who formerly inhabited what is now Belgium and northern France.

Bel·gian (bĕl'jən) *n. Abbr.* **Belg.** A native or inhabitant of Belgium. See **Fleming, Walloon.** **—Bel·gian** *adj.*

Belgian Congo. See **Zaire.**

Belgian hare *n.* A large, reddish-brown rabbit of a domestic breed developed in England from Belgian stock.

Bel·gic (bĕl'jĭk) *adj.* Of or pertaining to Belgium or the Belgians, to the Netherlands, or to the Belgae.

Bel·gium (bĕl'jəm). *Abbr.* **Belg.** Kingdom of northwest Europe, whose strategic position made it the "cockpit of Europe." It was a Roman province and later part of Charlemagne's empire. United under the dukes of Burgundy (14th century), it fell to the Habsburgs (1477) and passed to Spain. Napoleon occupied the country (1797), and after the Battle of Waterloo (1815), it became part of the United Netherlands. Belgium won its independence (1830), and its neutrality was guaranteed by the Great Powers (1839), but this was violated by Germany in both world wars. Belgium joined the Benelux Union (1948) and was a founding member of the EEC. The country is culturally divided into Dutch-speaking Flanders to the north of Brussels and French-speaking Wallonia to the south. Apart from coal, Belgium has few raw materials, yet it is one of the world's most industrialized countries, with over half its workers in manufacturing. Following land improvements, more than half its area is farmed intensively. Engineering goods, textiles, chemicals, glass, and foodstuffs are the main products and exports. Area, 30,513 square kilometers (11,781 square miles). Population, 9,800,000. Capital, Brussels.

Bel·grade (bĕl'grād', -grād, bĕl'grād'). *Serbo-Croatian* **Be·o·grad** (bā'ə-grăd'). The capital and largest city of Yugoslavia, lying at the confluence of the Danube and Sava rivers. Founded as a Celtic fortress (3rd century B.C.), it became (12th century) the capital of Serbia, which fell to the Ottoman Turks (1521). A major Turkish stronghold, garrisoned until 1867, Belgrade was made the capital of independent Serbia (1882) and (1918) of the Kingdom of the Serbs, Croats, and Slovenes (which became Yugoslavia in 1929).

Bel·gra·vi·a (bĕl-grā'vē-ə). Fashionable residential district in south-western London, England. It is named after Belgrave Square, which is included in the district.

Be·li·al (bē'lē-əl, bēl'yəl). A satanic personification of wickedness and ungodliness alluded to in the New Testament. II Corinthians 6:15. [Hebrew *bəlīyya'al,* "uselessness" : *bəlīy,* without + *ya'al,* use.]

be·lie (bĭ-lī') *tr.v.* **-lied, -lying, -lies.** **1.** To misrepresent or picture falsely; disguise: *"He spoke roughly in order to belie his air of gentility"* (James Joyce). **2.** To show to be false: *Their laughter belied their grief.* **3.** To disappoint or leave unfulfilled. **4.** *Archaic.* To tell lies about; slander; defame. [Middle English *belien,* Old English *belēogan.*] **—be·li·er** *n.*

be·lief (bĭ-lēf') *n.* **1.** The mental act, condition, or habit of placing trust or confidence in a person or thing. **2.** Mental acceptance or conviction in the truth or existence of something. **3.** Something believed or accepted as true; especially, a particular tenet, or a body of tenets, accepted by a group of people. —See Synonyms at **opinion.** [Middle English *beleve,* Old English *bileafe, gelēafa.*]

be·lieve (bĭ-lēv') *v.* **-lieved, -lieving, -lieves.** *—tr.* **1.** To accept as true or real. **2.** To credit with truthfulness; trust. **3.** To expect or suppose; think: *I believe that he will come shortly.* *—intr.* **1.** To have faith, especially religious faith. **2.** To have faith or confidence; trust. Used with *in: I believe in his ability.* **3.** To have confidence in the truth, value, or existence of something. Used with *in: Her gardener did not believe in artificial fertilizers.* [Middle English *bileven, beleven,* Old English *belēfan, gelēfan,* from Germanic *galaubjan* (unattested), hold dear; akin to **lief.**] **—be·liev·a·ble** *adj.* **—be·liev·er** *n.*

be·like (bĭ-līk') *adv. Archaic.* Perhaps; probably.

be·lit·tle (bĭ-lĭt'l) *tr.v.* **-tled, -tling, -tles.** **1.** To represent or speak of as small or unimportant; disparage. **2.** To cause to seem less or little. —See Synonyms at **decry.** **—be·lit·tle·ment** *n.* **—be·lit·tler** *n.*

Be·lize[1] (bə-lēz'). Formerly **British Hon·du·ras** (hŏn-dŏŏr'əs, -dyŏŏr'-). Low-lying country of the Central American mainland. Nearly half of it is forested, and British loggers in search of hardwoods were the first outsiders to settle here (17th century). The territory was made a British colony (1884), became internally self-governing (1964), and changed its name to Belize (1973). Belize gained independence within the Commonwealth (1981). Fish, forest products, sugar, and citrus fruits are the main products and exports. Agriculture is being expanded, but this has been hampered by devastating hurricanes and floods. Area, 22,965 square kilometers (8,867 square miles). Population, 187,000. Capital, Belmopan. See map at **Central American States.**

Belize[2]. Port and the largest city of Belize. It was the capital until 1970, when it was replaced by Belmopan.

bell[1] (bĕl) *n.* **1.** A hollow, metal instrument, usually cup-shaped with a flared opening and having a clapper suspended inside. It emits a metallic tone when struck. **2.** A device consisting of an electromagnetically operated hammer that repeatedly strikes a hemispherical metal disk to make a ringing sound as a signal. **3.** Something shaped like a bell, as: **a.** The round, flared mouth of some musical wind instruments. **b.** The corolla of a flower. **c.** A hollow, usually inverted vessel, such as a diving bell. **4.** *Nautical.* **a.** A stroke on a bell to mark the half-hour intervals. **b.** The time indicated by the striking of a bell, divided into half hours. **—ring a bell.** To remind one of something previously known or experienced.
—v. **belled, belling, bells.** *—tr.* **1.** To put a bell on. **2.** To shape or cause to flare like a bell. *—intr.* To flare like a bell. [Middle English *belle,* Old English *belle,* perhaps akin to **BELL[2].**]

bell[2] *n.* The bellowing or baying cry of certain animals, such as a deer in rut or a beagle on the hunt.
—intr.v. **belled, belling, bells.** To bellow; bay. [Middle English *bellen,* to bay, Old English *bellan.*]

Bell (bĕl), **Alexander Graham** (1847–1922). U.S. inventor, born in Edinburgh. He went to Canada in 1870 and settled in New England shortly afterward. He was the inventor of the telephone, the first electrical transmission of speech by his apparatus taking place in 1876. The Bell Telephone Company was founded in 1877. He also invented the audiometer, an early hearing aid, and flat and cylindrical wax recorders for phonographs.

bel·la·don·na (bĕl'ə-dŏn'ə) *n.* **1.** A poisonous Eurasian plant, *Atropa belladonna,* having purplish-red, bell-shaped flowers and small black poisonous berries. Also called "deadly nightshade." **2.** An atropine powder or tincture derived from the leaves and roots of the belladonna and used to treat asthma, colic, and hyperacidity. [Italian, "fair lady" (supposedly from its use in cosmetics).]

belladonna lily *n.* A plant, the **amaryllis** (see).

Bel·la·trix (bĕ-lā'trĭks) *n.* A giant star, the third brightest in the constellation Orion.

Bel·lay (bə-lā'), **Joachim du** (1524–60). French poet. One of the founders of a group of poets known as the Pléiade, du Bellay wrote sonnets, satires on literary conventions and pretensions, and a manifesto of the Pléiade's poetic principles.

bell·bird (bĕl'bûrd') *n.* **1.** Any of various tropical American birds of the genus *Procnias,* family Cotingidae, having a characteristic bell-like call. **2.** A New Zealand honeyeater, *Anthornis melanura.*

bell·bot·toms (bĕl'bŏt'əmz) *pl.n.* Trousers with legs that flare out at the bottom. **—bell·bot·tom, bell·bot·tomed** *adj.*

bell·boy (bĕl'boi') *n.* A boy or man employed by a hotel to carry luggage, run errands, and the like. Also called "bellhop."

bell buoy *n.* A buoy fitted with a warning bell that is activated by the movement of the waves.

Bellerophon *A Greek terra cotta, made in Melos about 450 B.C., shows the legendary Greek hero on the winged horse Pegasus battling with the Chimera. The Chimera was part lion, part goat, and part dragon and is usually portrayed as a lion with a goat's head on its back.*

BELGIUM

NORTH SEA

NETHERLANDS

GERMANY

FRANCE

LUXEMBOURG

belle (bĕl) *n.* **1.** An attractive and much-admired girl or woman. **2.** The most attractive girl or woman at a specified place: *the belle of the ball.* [French, "beautiful," from Latin *bella,* feminine of *bellus,* handsome, pretty.]

belle é·poque (bĕl ā-pŏk′) *n.* The period preceding World War I. [French, "fine period."]

Bel·ler·o·phon (bə-lĕr′ə-fŏn′). *Greek Mythology.* The Corinthian hero who, with the aid of the winged horse Pegasus, slew the Chimera.

belles-let·tres (bĕl-lĕt′rə) *pl.n. Used with a singular verb.* Literature regarded for its aesthetic value rather than for its didactic or informative content. [French, "fine letters" (literature).] **—bel·let·rism** *n.* **—bel·let·rist** *n.* **—bel·le·tris·tic** (bĕl′ə-trĭs′tĭk) *adj.*

bell·flow·er (bĕl′flou′ər) *n.* Any of various plants of the genus *Campanula,* characteristically having blue, bell-shaped flowers. See **harebell, bluebell.**

bell·hop (bĕl′hŏp′) *n.* A **bellboy** *(see).*

bel·li·cose (bĕl′ĭ-kōs′) *adj.* Warlike in manner or temperament; pugnacious. [Middle English, from Latin *bellicōsus,* from *bellicus,* of war, from *bellum,* earlier *duellum,* war.] **—bel·li·cose·ly** *adv.* **—bel·li·cos·i·ty** (bĕl′ĭ-kŏs′ə-tē), **bel·li·cose·ness** *n.*

bel·lig·er·en·cy (bə-lĭj′ər-ən-sē) *n.* The state of being at war or engaged in a warlike conflict.

bel·lig·er·ent (bə-lĭj′ər-ənt) *adj.* **1.** Given to or marked by hostile or aggressive behavior. **2.** Of, pertaining to, or engaged in warfare: *the belligerent powers.*
~n. A person or state engaging in warfare. [Latin *belligerāns* (stem *belligerant-*), present participle of *belligerāre,* to wage war, from *belliger,* waging war : *bellum,* war + *gerere,* to bear, carry.] **—bel·lig·er·ence** *n.* **—bel·lig·er·ent·ly** *adv.*
Synonyms: *contentious, pugnacious, quarrelsome.*

Bel·li·ni (bə-lē′nē), **Gentile** (*c.* 1429–1507). Venetian painter of the Renaissance, son of Jacopo and brother of Giovanni.

Bellini, Giovanni (*c.* 1430–1516). Venetian painter of the Renaissance, son of Jacopo and brother of Gentile, the most illustrious of the family. His *Madonna with Saints,* an altarpiece for the church of Frari, Venice, was praised by John Ruskin as one of the three most beautiful paintings in the world. His coloring and atmospheric landscapes had a great influence, especially through his pupil Titian, on the development of the Venetian school.

Bellini, Jacopo (*c.* 1400–1470). Venetian painter of the Renaissance, father of the painters Gentile and Giovanni. Most of his famous paintings have been lost, including the *Crucifixion* for the cathedral at Verona.

bell jar *n.* A cylindrical glass vessel with a rounded top and an open base used to protect and display fragile objects or to establish a controlled atmosphere or environment in scientific experiments.

bell magpie *n.* A bird, the **currawong** *(see).*

bell·man (bĕl′mən) *n., pl.* **-men** (-mĭn). A **town crier** *(see).*

bell metal *n.* An alloy of tin and copper with small amounts of zinc and lead, used to make bells.

bell-mouthed (bĕl′mouthd′, -moutht′) *adj.* Having a flaring, bell-shaped mouth, as a flask might.

Bel·loc (bĕl′ŏk′, -ək), **Hilaire,** born Joseph Hilary Pierre Belloc (1870–1953). British writer and politician, born in France. He became a British citizen in 1902 and was a Liberal M.P. (1906–10). He is famous chiefly for his droll verse, especially *The Bad Child's Book of Beasts* (1896).

bel·low (bĕl′ō) *v.* **-lowed, -lowing, -lows.** *—intr.* **1.** To roar, as a bull does. **2.** To shout in a deep voice. *—tr.* To utter in a loud and powerful voice.
~n. **1.** The roar of a bull, elephant, or other large animal. **2.** A very loud utterance; a shout. **3.** The sound of artillery, thunder, or the like. [Middle English *belwen,* Old English *belgan* (unattested).]

Bel·low (bĕl′ō), **Saul** (1915–). U.S. novelist, born in Quebec, Canada. His novels include *Dangling Man* (1944), *The Adventures of Augie March* (1953), and his most famous one, *Herzog* (1964). He won the Nobel Prize in 1976.

bel·lows (bĕl′ōz, -əz) *n. Used with a singular or plural verb.* **1.** An apparatus for producing a strong current of air, as for sounding a pipe organ or increasing the draft to a fire. It consists of a flexible, valved air chamber that is contracted and expanded by pumping to force the air through a nozzle. **2.** Something resembling a bellows, such as the pleated windbag of an accordion. [Middle English *belwes, belows,* plural of *belu, below,* probably from Old English *belga,* plural of *bel(i)g, bælig,* bag, bellows. See **belly.**]

bell pepper *n.* **1.** A pepper plant, *Capsicum frutescens grossum,* cultivated for its edible fruit. **2.** The mild-flavored, bell-shaped fruit of this plant, usually red when ripe but often eaten when green. Also called "sweet pepper."

bell pull *n.* A sash, cord, or handle that is pulled to ring a bell.

bell-ring·er (bĕl′rĭng′ər) *n.* **1.** One who rings church bells, especially on ceremonial occasions. **2.** One who plays musical handbells.

bells of Ireland *n. Used with a singular or plural verb.* A plant, the **shellflower** *(see).*

bell·weth·er (bĕl′wĕth′ər) *n.* **1.** A male sheep, usually castrated, with a bell hung from its neck, that leads a flock of sheep. **2.** One that is followed, such as a leader. **3.** One that acts as a standard or representative.

bel·ly (bĕl′ē) *n., pl.* **-lies. 1.** The part of the body of mammals between the rib cage and the pelvis that contains the intestines; the abdomen. **2.** The underside of the body of certain other vertebrates, such as snakes, amphibians, and fish. **3. a.** The stomach. **b.** Appetite for food; gluttony. **4.** Any part that bulges or protrudes: *the belly of a sail.* **5.** The deep, hollow interior of something: *a ship's belly.* **6.** The bulging part of a muscle. **7.** The front part of the body of a stringed musical instrument. In this sense, also called "table." **8.** The womb; the uterus. *—v.* **bellied, -lying, -lies.** *—intr.* To swell out; bulge: *"mud-colored clouds bellied downwards from the sky"* (Thomas Hardy).
~tr. To cause to bulge. [Middle English *bely, baly,* Old English *bel(i)g, bæl(i)g,* bag, purse, bellows.]

bel·ly·ache (bĕl′ē-āk′) *n. Informal.* An ache or pain in the stomach or abdomen.
~intr.v. **bellyached, -aching, -aches.** *Slang.* To grumble or complain, especially in a whining manner. **—bel·ly·ach·er** *n.*

bel·ly·band (bĕl′ē-bănd′) *n.* **1.** A band passed around the belly of an animal to secure something, such as a saddle. **2.** An encircling cloth band for holding in the protruding navel of a baby.

bel·ly·but·ton (bĕl′ē-bŭt′n) *n. Informal.* The **navel** *(see).*

belly dance *n.* A dance performed by women, originally in the Middle East, in which the hips and naked abdomen jerk and undulate. **—bel·ly-dance** *v.* **—belly dancer** *n.*

belly flop *n.* A dive in which the front of the body hits against the surface of the water. **—belly-flop** *v.*

bel·ly·ful (bĕl′ē-fo͝ol′) *n. Informal.* An amount that satisfies or exceeds what one desires or can endure.

belly landing *n.* A landing of an aircraft onto the underside of its fuselage, without the use of its undercarriage.

belly laugh *n.* A deep, unrestrained laugh.

Bel·mo·pan (bĕl′mə-păn′). Capital of Belize since 1970. After the former capital, Belize City, was devastated by Hurricane Hattie and its storm wave (1961), it was decided to build a new capital on higher ground 80 kilometers (50 miles) inland.

Be·lo Ho·ri·zon·te (bā′lō hôr′ĭ-zŏn′tē). City in eastern Brazil. An important manufacturing and marketing center, it was the first of Brazil's planned cities, built 1895–97.

be·long (bĭ-lông′, -lŏng′) *intr.v.* **-longed, -longing, -longs. 1.** To be the property or concern of. Used with *to: "the earth belongs to the living"* (Thomas Jefferson). **2.** To be part of or in natural association with something. **3.** To be a member of an organization. Used with *to: belong to a club.* **4.** To have a proper or suitable place: *Those clothes belong in the drawer.* **5.** *Informal.* To be socially acceptable: *made her feel she belonged.* [Middle English *belongen* : *be-,* thoroughly + *longen,* to suit (see **long,** to yearn).]

be·long·ing (bĭ-lông′ĭng, bĭ-lŏng′-) *n.* **1. belongings.** Personal possessions; effects. **2.** Close and secure relationship: *a sense of belonging.* —See Synonyms at **assets.**

Be·lo·rus·sia (bĕl′ō-rŭsh′ə). Also **Bye·lo·rus·sia** (byĕl′-). Former name of **Be·la·rus** (byĕl′ə-ro͞os′, bĕl′-); also **Bye·la·rus** (byĕl′ə-ro͞os′). Republic in eastern Europe. The eastern part of Belarus joined with other Soviet republics to form the U.S.S.R. in 1922. Western Belarus was transferred from Poland in 1939. In 1991 the republic became independent. Area, 207,600 square kilometers (80,100 square miles). Population, 10,370,000. Capital, Minsk.

Be·lo·rus·sian (bĕl′ō-rŭsh′ən) *adj.* Also **Bye·lo·rus·sian** (byĕl′-). Former term for **Be·la·rus·sian** (byĕl′ə-rŭsh′ən, bĕl′-). Of or pertaining to Belarus, its people, or their language.
~n. Former term for Belarussian. **1.** A native or inhabitant of Belarus. **2.** The Slavonic language of the Belarussians.

be·lov·ed (bĭ-lŭv′ĭd, -lŭvd′) *adj.* Held in great affection.
~n. One that is loved. [Middle English, past participle of *beloven,* to love thoroughly : *be-,* thoroughly + *loven,* to LOVE.]

be·low (bĭ-lō′) *adv.* **1.** In or to a lower place; beneath. **2. a.** On or to a lower floor; downstairs. **b.** *Nautical.* On or to a lower deck. **3.** Farther down or on, as on a page. **4.** In or to hell or Hades. **5.** On earth. **6.** In a lower rank or class.
~prep. **1.** Lower than; beneath. **2.** Unworthy of or unsuitable to the rank or dignity of. **3.** Downstream of. **4.** South of. [Middle English *bilooghe* : *bi,* BY + *loogh, lowe,* LOW.]
Usage: *below, under, beneath, underneath. Below,* in its principal physical sense, denotes only position lower than a given point of reference. *Under* specifies position directly below, lower than the point of reference and in approximately vertical line with it. *Below* is also used to indicate direction and distance in a horizontal plane: *a town on the Hudson below Albany. Beneath* may have the basic sense of *below* or, more often, of *under. Underneath* combines the basic sense of *under* with that of at least partial concealment. Figuratively, *below* indicates deficiency or lesser status in a general way: *below normal; below one's rank. Under* indicates specific deficiency or explicitly subordinate relationship: *under legal age; serve under a captain. Beneath* applies to deficiency in moral or social senses: *beneath ordinary decency; beneath one's level.*

Beloye More. See **White Sea.**

Bel·shaz·zar (bĕl-shăz′ər). The son of Nebuchadnezzar II and the last king of Babylon, who was warned of his downfall and death by the handwriting on the wall. Daniel 5.

belt (bĕlt) *n.* **1.** A band of leather, cloth, or other flexible material, worn round the waist to support clothing, secure tools or weapons, or serve as decoration. **2.** *Sports.* A belt worn as a mark of distinction: *won a black belt in judo.* **3.** A **seat belt** *(see).* **4.** A strip of armor surrounding a warship at the water line. **5.** A continuous band of a flexible material for transferring motion or power or conveying materials from one wheel or shaft to another. See **conveyor belt, fan belt. 6. a.** An encircling route or highway. **b.** A **belt line** *(see).* **7.** A geographical, sociological, or meteorological region,

bellflower *There are about 300 varieties of bellflower, including the harebell shown here, which is the "bluebell of Scotland."*

bell jar *An open-ended glass cover used as a display case for fragile objects and in scientific experiments. Antoine Lavoisier (1743–94) used the bell jar shown here to investigate combustion, by which he discovered the presence of oxygen in the air.*

especially an elongated one, that is distinctive in some specific way. **8.** A narrow channel. **9.** *Slang.* A powerful blow; a punch. **—below the belt. 1.** *Boxing.* In the area below the waistline, where a blow is foul. **2.** *Informal.* Not according to the rules; unfair. **—tighten one's belt.** To become more thrifty and frugal.
~v. **belted, belting, belts.** *—tr.* **1.** To encircle; gird. **2.** To attach with or as if with a belt. **3.** To mark with or as if with a belt. **4.** To strike with a belt. **5.** *Slang.* To strike forcefully; punch. **6.** *Slang.* To sing in a loud and forceful manner. Often used with *out*: *belt out a note.* *—intr. Slang.* To run, ride, or drive very quickly. [Middle English *belt,* Old English *belt,* from Common Germanic *baltjaz* (unattested), from Latin *balteus,* probably from Etruscan.]

Bel·tane (bĕl'tān', -tĭn) *n.* **1.** May Day in the old Scottish calendar. **2.** The ancient Celtic May Day celebration. [Middle English *beltane,* from Scottish Gaelic *bealltainn,* probably from Old Celtic *belote(p)nia* (unattested).]

belt drive *n.* A mechanism for transmitting power between drive shafts by means of a belt connecting pulleys on a shaft. Compare **direct drive.**

belt highway *n.* A highway that skirts an urban area.

belt·ing (bĕl'tĭng) *n.* **1.** Belts collectively. **2.** The material used to make belts. **3.** *Informal.* A physical beating.

belt line *n.* A transportation line, as of trains, trolleys, or buses, that makes a complete circuit of an urban area.

be·lu·ga (bə-lo͞o'gə) *n.* **1.** The **white whale** *(see).* **2.** A sturgeon, *Huso huso,* of the Black and Caspian seas, whose roe is used for caviar. Also called "beluga sturgeon." [Russian *byeluga,* sturgeon, and *byelukha,* white whale : *byelii,* white + *-uga, -ukha,* augmentative suffix.]

bel·ve·dere (bĕl'və-dîr') *n.* A structure, such as a summerhouse or an open roofed gallery, situated so as to command a fine view. [Italian, "beautiful view."]

be·ma (bē'mə) *n., pl.* **-mata** (-mə-tə). Also **bi·mah** (bē'mə), *pl.* **-mahs. 1.** *Judaism.* The platform from which services are conducted in a synagogue. Also called "almemar." **2.** *Eastern Orthodox Church.* The enclosed area about the altar; the sanctuary. [Late Latin *bēma,* from Greek, platform.]

beluga *The beluga, or white whale, is found along coasts in the Arctic and the far north. Adults are about 4 meters (13 feet) long.*

Bem·ba (bĕm'bə) *n. pl.* **-bas** or collectively **Bemba. 1.** A member of a south-central African people, living mainly in Zambia. **2.** The language of this people.

Be·mel·mans (bē'məl-mənz, bĕm'əl-), **Ludwig** (1898–1962). U.S. artist and author. Born in Austria, he immigrated to New York in 1914. His experiences in the restaurant and hotel business form the basis for many of his whimsical short stories and novels, often illustrated with his own drawings and water colors.

be·mire (bĭ-mīr') *tr.v.* **-mired, -miring, -mires. 1.** To soil with mud. **2.** To bog down in mud. Usually used in the passive.

be·moan (bĭ-mōn') *v.* **-moaned, -moaning, -moans.** *—tr.* **1.** To lament; mourn over. **2.** To express pity or grief for. *—intr.* To mourn; lament.

be·muse (bĭ-myo͞oz') *tr.v.* **-mused, -musing, -muses.** To confuse or stupefy.

be·mused (bĭ-myo͞ozd') *adj.* **1.** Confused; bewildered. **2.** Deep in thought; engrossed.

ben¹ (bĕn) *n. Scottish.* The inner room or parlor of a house.
~adv. Scottish. Inside; within.
~adj. Scottish. Inner.
~prep. Scottish. Within. [Middle English *ben, binne(n),* within, Old English *binnan* : *be,* BY + *innan,* within.]

ben² *n. Scottish.* A mountain peak. Used in names of mountains: *Ben Nevis.* [Scottish Gaelic *beann,* peak, height.]

ben³ *n.* Any of several Asiatic trees of the genus *Moringa,* bearing winged seeds that yield an oil used in perfumes and cosmetics. [Dialectal Arabic *bēn,* from Arabic *bān.*]

Ben·a·dryl (bĕn'ə-drĭl) *n.* A trademark for diphenhydramine, an antihistamine drug used mainly to treat allergy symptoms and, in combination with a hypnotic, to induce sleep.

Benares. See **Varanasi.**

Ben Bel·la (bĕn bĕl'ə), **Ahmed** (1919–). Algerian revolutionary leader and politician. He was the leader of the terrorist wing of the Algerian nationalist movement against France after World War II, and he helped found the National Liberation Front (1954). When Algeria gained its independence (1962), he became its first prime minister, after serving six years in prison. He was elected Algeria's first president (1963) but was ousted by a coup (1965).

bench (bĕnch) *n.* **1.** A long seat, usually made of wood or stone and without a back, for two or more persons. **2.** A thwart in a boat. **3. a.** The seat for judges in a courtroom. **b.** The office or position of a judge. **4.** The judge or judges composing a court. **5. a.** A seat occupied by persons in some official capacity. **b.** The office of the persons occupying such a seat. **6.** A strong worktable, such as one used in carpentry. **7.** A platform on which animals, especially dogs, are exhibited. **8.** *Sports.* **a.** The place where the players on a team sit while they are not participating in the game. **b.** The reserve players on a team. **9.** *Geology.* **a.** A level, narrow stretch of land interrupting a slope. **b.** A level elevation of land along a shore or coast, especially one marking a former shoreline. **10.** The working platform in a quarry or a mine.
~adj. Used in work done at a bench: *a bench plane.*
~tr.v. **benched, benching, benches. 1.** To furnish with a bench or benches. **2.** To seat on a bench, especially in a judicial capacity. **3.** To show (dogs) in a bench show. **4.** To keep out of or remove from a game. [Middle English *bench,* Old English *benc.*]

bench·er (bĕn'chər) *n. British.* **1.** A member of the inner or higher bar who acts as a governor of one of the Inns of Court. **2.** A **backbencher** *(see).*

Bench·ley (bĕnch'lē), **Robert Charles** (1889–1945). U.S. actor, film director, drama critic, and comic essayist. He is best remembered for his essays, represented in *The Benchley Roundup* (1954).

bench mark *n.* **1.** *Abbr.* **B.M.** A surveyor's mark made on some stationary object of previously determined position and elevation, and used as a reference point in tidal observations and surveys. **2.** A standard or reference point against which something is measured; a touchstone.

bench warrant *n. Law.* A warrant issued by a judge or court, ordering the arrest of an offender.

bend¹ (bĕnd) *v.* **bent** (bĕnt) or *rare* **bended, bending, bends.** *—tr.* **1.** To bring (a bow, for example) into tension by pulling or exerting pressure. **2. a.** To cause to assume a curved or angular shape. **b.** To force to assume a different shape or direction. **3.** To cause to swerve from a straight line; turn; deflect. **4.** To turn or direct (one's eyes or attention, for example): *"And to my cries . . . Thine ear with favor bend"* (Milton). **5.** To influence coercively; subdue. **6.** To decide; resolve. Used in the passive, with *on*: *He was bent on leaving.* **7.** To apply (the mind) closely; concentrate. **8.** *Nautical.* To fasten: *bend a mainsail onto the boom.* *—intr.* **1. a.** To turn or be altered from straightness or from an initial shape or position: *Wire bends easily.* **b.** To assume a curved, crooked, or angular form or direction: *The saplings bent in the wind.* **2.** To take a new direction; swerve. **3.** To incline the body; stoop. **4.** To bow in submission; yield. **5.** To apply oneself closely; concentrate. Used with *to.* **—bend over backward.** *Informal.* To make a considerable effort.
~n. **1.** The act or fact of bending. **2.** The state of being bent. **3.** Something bent; a curve; crook. **4.** *Nautical.* **a. bends.** The thick planks in a ship's side; the wales. **b.** A knot that joins a rope to a rope or another object. **—round the bend.** *Chiefly British Informal.* Mad or eccentric; dotty. **—the bends. Caisson disease** *(see).* [Bend, bent, bent; Middle English *benden, bente* and *bende, bente* and *bende,* Old English *bendan, bende, bended.*]

bend² *n. Heraldry.* A band passing from the upper dexter corner of the escutcheon to the lower sinister corner. [Middle English *bend,* Old English *bend,* ribbon, band.]

Ben Day *n.* Also **ben·day** (bĕn-dā'), **Ben·day, ben·day. 1.** A method of adding a tone to a printed image by imposing a transparent sheet of dots or other patterns on the image at some stage of a photographic reproduction process. **2.** A screen or pattern used in this process. [After Benjamin *Day* (1838–1916), New York printer.]

bend·er (bĕn'dər) *n.* **1.** One that bends. **2.** *Slang.* A drinking spree.

bend sinister *n. Heraldry.* A band passing from the upper sinister corner of the escutcheon to the lower dexter corner.

be·neath (bĭ-nēth') *adv.* **1.** In a lower place; below. **2.** Underneath.
~prep. **1.** Below; under. **2.** Covered by: *The earth lay beneath a blanket of snow.* **3.** Under the power or influence of. **4.** Lower than in rank or station; inferior to: *An earl is beneath a duke.* **5.** Unworthy of; unbefitting: *It is beneath him to beg.* —See Usage note at **below.** [Middle English *benethe(n),* Old English *binithan* : *bi,* BY + *nithan, neothan,* from below, BELOW.]

Ben·e·dic·i·te (bĕn'ə-dĭs'ə-tē) *n.* **1.** A canticle, used in various Christian churches, beginning *"Benedicite, omnia opera Domini Domino"* ("All ye works of the Lord, bless the Lord"). **2. benedicite.** An invocation of a blessing, especially before meals. [Middle English, from Latin, imperative of *benedīcere,* to bless.]

ben·e·dict (bĕn'ə-dĭkt') *n.* Also **ben·e·dick** (-dĭk'). A confirmed bachelor who has recently married. [After *Benedick,* a character in Shakespeare's *Much Ado About Nothing* (1598–99).]

Ben·e·dict (bĕn'ə-dĭkt'), **Saint** (*c.*480–*c.*543). Italian monk, founder of the Benedictine order, known from his birthplace as "Benedict of Nursia." After studying in Rome, he lived as a hermit in Subiaco, then moved to Monte Cassino, where he founded the first Benedictine monastery and established the principles of the order and of western monasticism in general in the book *The Rule of St. Benedict.*

Ben·e·dic·tine (bĕn'ə-dĭk'tĭn, -tēn') *adj.* Of or pertaining to St. Benedict of Nursia or his monastic order.
~n. (bĕn'ə-dĭk'tĭn, -tēn' *for sense 1*; bĕn'ə-dĭk'tēn' *for sense 2).* **1.** A monk or nun belonging to the order founded by St. Benedict. **2.** A trademark for a liqueur made originally by Benedictine monks.

ben·e·dic·tion (bĕn'ə-dĭk'shən) *n.* **1.** A blessing or the act of blessing. **2.** An invocation of divine blessing, usually at the end of a service. **3. Benediction.** *Roman Catholic Church.* A short service consisting of prayers, the singing of a Eucharistic hymn, and the blessing of the congregation with the Host. Also called "Benediction of the Blessed Sacrament." **4.** The state of blessedness. [Middle English *benediccioun,* from Old French *benediction,* from Latin *benedictiō* (stem *benedictiōn-*), from *benedictus,* blessed, from *benedīcere,* to bless : *bene,* well + *dīcere,* to say.] **—ben·e·dic·tive, ben·e·dic·to·ry** *adj.*

Benedict's solution *n.* A solution of potassium, sodium tartrates, copper sulfate, and sodium carbonate, used to detect the presence of reducing sugars, especially in urine. [After S.R. *Benedict* (1884–1936), U.S. chemist.]

Ben·e·dic·tus (bĕn'ə-dĭk'təs) *n.* **1.** A short canticle that begins, *"Benedictus qui venit in nomine Domini"* ("Blessed is he that cometh in the name of the Lord"). Matthew 21:9. **2.** A canticle starting *"Benedictus Dominus Deus Israel"* ("Blessed be the Lord God of Israel"). Luke 1:68. **3.** A musical setting of either of these canticles.

[Latin, "blessed." See **benediction.**]

ben·e·fac·tion (bĕn′ə-făk′shən) n. 1. The act of conferring help or a benefit. 2. A charitable gift or deed. [Late Latin *benefactiō* (stem *benefactiōn-*), from *benefactus*, past participle of *beneficere*, to do well : Latin *bene*, well + *facere*, to do.]

ben·e·fac·tor (bĕn′ə-făk′tər) n. One who gives financial or other aid. [Late Latin, from *benefactiō*, BENEFACTION.]

ben·e·fac·tress (bĕn′ə-făk′trĭs) n. A female benefactor.

be·nef·ic (bə-nĕf′ĭk) adj. Exerting a beneficent influence; beneficent. [Latin *beneficus*. See **beneficence.**]

ben·e·fice (bĕn′ə-fĭs) n. 1. a. A church office, such as a rectory, endowed with fixed capital assets. b. The revenue from such assets. 2. A piece of land granted in feudal tenure to a vassal. ~tr.v. beneficed, -ficing, -fices. To endow or provide with a benefice. [Middle English, from Old French, from Medieval Latin *beneficium*, from Latin, favor, benefit, from *beneficus*, beneficent. See **beneficence.**]

be·nef·i·cence (bə-nĕf′ə-səns) n. 1. The quality of charity or kindness: *nature's beneficence.* 2. A charitable act or gift. [French, from Latin *beneficentia*, from *beneficus*, beneficent, generous : *bene*, well + *facere*, to do.]

be·nef·i·cent (bə-nĕf′ə-sənt) adj. 1. Characterized by or performing acts of kindness or charity: "*even cruel savage brutes . . . have at times . . . beneficent impulses*" (W.H. Hudson). 2. Conferring benefit; beneficial. —**be·nef·i·cent·ly** adv.

ben·e·fi·cial (bĕn′ə-fĭsh′əl) adj. 1. Promoting a favorable result; enhancing or having the right to receive proceeds or other advantages: *a beneficial interest in sales.* [From BENEFICE, in the obsolete sense "benefit."] —**ben·e·fi·cial·ly** adv. —**ben·e·fi·cial·ness** n.

ben·e·fi·ci·ar·y (bĕn′ə-fĭsh′ē-ĕr-ē, -fĭsh′ə-rē) n., pl. -ies. 1. One who receives a benefit. 2. *Law.* The recipient of funds, property, or other benefits from an insurance policy, will, or similar settlement. 3. The holder of an ecclesiastical benefice. ~adj. Pertaining to or holding a feudal benefice. [Latin *beneficiārius*, of a favor, from *beneficium*, favor, BENEFICE.]

ben·e·fit (bĕn′ə-fĭt) n. 1. Anything that promotes or enhances well-being; an advantage. 2. A payment or series of payments made, for example by the government or by an insurance company, to one in need: *unemployment benefits.* 3. A public entertainment, performance, or social event held to raise funds for a person or cause. 4. *Archaic.* An act of charity; a kindly deed. ~v. benefited, -fiting, -fits. —tr. To be helpful or advantageous to. —intr. To gain advantage; profit. Used with *from.* [Middle English *benfet*, from Norman French, from Latin *benefactum*, benefit, good deed, from *bene facere*, to do well : *bene*, well + *facere*, to do.]

benefit of clergy n. 1. The exemption from trial or punishment except by church court given to the clergy in the Middle Ages. 2. The church's official approval. Used euphemistically: *cohabiting without benefit of clergy.*

benefit of the doubt n. A favorable judgment granted in the absence of full evidence.

benefit society n. An association that guarantees its members financial aid in times of need, as by hospitalization insurance, by the collection of dues. Also called "benefit association."

Be·ne·lux (bĕn′ə-lŭks). Economic union established (1948) by Belgium, the Netherlands, and Luxembourg. It came into effect (1960) as the world's first completely free international market for goods and labor.

Be·neš (bĕn′ĕsh), **Eduard** (1884–1948). Czechoslovakian politician. He served under Tomáš Masaryk as foreign minister (1918–35) and succeeded him as president. He resigned from the presidency after the Munich Agreement (1938). He was again elected president (1946), but after the imposition of a Soviet-style constitution, he once more resigned. He died soon afterward.

Be·nét (bĭ-nā′), **Stephen Vincent** (1898–1943). U.S. poet and short-story writer. He is remembered chiefly for his long narrative poem of the Civil War, *John Brown's Body* (1928).

be·nev·o·lence (bə-nĕv′ə-ləns) n. 1. An inclination or tendency to perform charitable acts; goodwill. 2. A kindly act. 3. In medieval England, a compulsory tax or payment exacted by some sovereigns without the consent of Parliament.

be·nev·o·lent (bə-nĕv′ə-lənt) adj. 1. Characterized by benevolence; kindly. 2. Of or concerned with charity: *a benevolent fund.* —See Synonyms at **kind.** [Middle English, from Latin *benevolēns* (stem *benevolent-*), wishing well : *bene*, well + *volēns*, present participle of *velle*, to wish.] —**be·nev·o·lent·ly** adv.

B. Eng. Bachelor of Engineering.

Ben·gal (bĕn-gôl′, bĕng-). Region of eastern India and Bangladesh, a state of India before the partition into India and Pakistan (1947). The western part became the Indian state of West Bengal, whose capital is Calcutta. The eastern part became East Pakistan (1947) and Bangladesh (1971).

Bengal, Bay of. Large bay in the Indian Ocean, bordered by Sri Lanka and India on the west, Bangladesh on the north, and Burma and Thailand on the east.

Ben·ga·li (bĕn-gô′lē, bĕng-gô′-) n. 1. An inhabitant of Bengal. 2. The modern Indic language spoken in Bengal. It is the official language of Bangladesh and the main language of the Indian state of West Bengal. ~adj. Of or characteristic of Bengal, its inhabitants, or its language.

ben·ga·line (bĕng′gə-lēn′, bĕng′gə-lēn′) n. A fabric having a cross-wise ribbed effect, made of silk, wool, or synthetic fibers. [French, after its similarity to a fabric made in BENGAL.]

Bengal light n. A type of firework that burns with a brilliant, sustained blue light, formerly used for signaling. [First made in and exported from BENGAL.]

Ben·gha·zi or **Ben·ga·si** (bĕn-gä′zē). Town in northeastern Libya, on the Mediterranean coast. It is the second-largest town in the country and the most important port. From 1951 to 1972 the city shared the status of being the nation's capital with Tripoli.

Ben·guel·a (bĕn-gĕl′ə, -gwĕl′ə, bĕng-). Seaport of Angola. It gives its name to the Benguela Current, a cold current flowing northward along the west coast of southern Africa.

Ben-Gur·i·on (bĕn-goŏr′ē-ən), **David,** born David Grün (1886–1973). Israeli politician, born in Poland. He settled in Palestine (1906) and became an active member of the Zionist campaign for an independent Jewish nation. He founded the Mapai Party in 1930. After World War II he led the resistance movement against the British, and when Israel was created (1948), he became prime minister. He held the office until 1953 and was again prime minister (1955–63).

be·night·ed (bĭ-nī′tĭd) adj. 1. In moral or intellectual darkness; unenlightened; ignorant. 2. Overtaken by darkness or night. —**be·night·ed·ly** adv. —**be·night·ed·ness** n.

be·nign (bĭ-nīn′) adj. 1. Of a kind disposition. 2. Manifesting gentleness and mildness. Often said of weather. 3. Tending to promote well-being; beneficial. 4. *Pathology.* Not malignant: *a benign tumor.* Compare **malignant.** —See Synonyms at **favorable, kind.** [Middle English *benigne*, from Old French, from Latin *benīgnus*, "well-born" : *bene*, well + *-GENOUS.*] —**be·nign·ly** adv.

be·nig·nant (bĭ-nĭg′nənt) adj. 1. Favorable; beneficial. 2. Kind and gracious. —**be·nig·nant·ly** adv.

be·nig·ni·ty (bĭ-nĭg′nə-tē) n., pl. -ties. Also **be·nig·nan·cy** (-nən-sē). 1. The quality or condition of being benign. 2. A kindly or gracious act.

Be·nin¹ (bə-nĭn′, -nēn′). Formerly (until 1975) **Da·ho·mey** (də-hō′mē). Republic of West Africa. Formerly several ancient African kingdoms colonized by France, it gained its independence (1960). It is one of the smallest countries in Africa and, despite rich reserves of offshore petroleum, chromite, and iron ore, is one of the poorest and least industrially developed, largely because of political instability. The mainstays of the economy are palm products, cotton, and coffee. Area, 112,522 square kilometers (43,484 square miles). Population, 4,600,000. Capital, Porto Novo. See map at **West African States.**

Benin² or **Benin City.** Port in southeastern Nigeria, on the Benin River. It is the center of Nigeria's rubber industry. From the 14th to the 17th century it was the capital of the African kingdom of Benin, noted for its bronze works of art.

ben·i·son (bĕn′ə-zən, -sən) n. A blessing or benediction. [Middle English *benes(u)n*, from Old French *beneisson*, from Latin *benedictiō*, BENEDICTION.]

ben·ja·min (bĕn′jə-mən) n. A resin, benzoin (see). Also called "gum benjamin." [Variant (influenced by the name) of earlier *benjoin*, BENZOIN.]

Ben·ja·min¹ (bĕn′jə-mən). The youngest son of Jacob and Rachel, favorite son of Jacob. Genesis 35:18. [Hebrew, "son of the right hand" : *bēn*, son + *yāmīn*, right hand.]

Benjamin² n. The tribe of Israel descended from Benjamin. —**Ben·ja·mite** (bĕn′jə-mīt) adj. & n.

benjamin bush n. The **spicebush** (see).

ben·ne, or **ben·ni** (bĕn′ē) n. A plant, the *sesame* (see), or its seeds or oil. [Of African origin, akin to Mandingo *bēne.*]

ben·net (bĕn′ĭt) n. See **herb bennet.**

Ben·nett (bĕn′ĭt), **(Enoch) Arnold** (1867–1931). English novelist and dramatist. Most of his novels are set in the "Five Towns" of the Midlands pottery district. Influenced by the French realist writers, Bennett specialized in a sympathetic depiction of everyday life among the lower middle classes. His novels include *The Old Wives' Tale* (1908) and the *Clayhanger* trilogy (1910–16).

Ben Ne·vis (bĕn nĕ′vĭs, nĕv′ĭs). Highest mountain in Great Britain, rising to 1,343 meters (4,406 feet), in the Lochaber district of the Scottish Highlands.

ben·ny (bĕn′ē) n., pl. -nies. *Slang.* An amphetamine tablet. [From BENZEDRINE.]

Ben·ny (bĕn′ē), **Jack,** born Benjamin Kubelsky (1894–1974). He enjoyed a long career in vaudeville, motion pictures, radio, and television. Known for his famous delayed delivery, complete with arched eyebrow and bemused stare, he built many routines on his so-called reputation as a miser, his never-changing age of thirty-nine, and his supposed lack of skill as a violinist.

bent¹ (bĕnt). Past tense and past participle of **bend.** ~adj. 1. Deviating from a straight line; crooked. 2. On a fixed course of action; determined. Used with *on*: "*I perceived he was bent on refusing my mediation*" (Emily Brontë). 3. *Chiefly British Slang.* **a.** Corrupt; dishonest. **b.** Homosexual. 4. *Archaic.* Heading toward; on the way to. ~n. 1. The state of being crooked. 2. An individual tendency, disposition, or inclination: "*The natural bent of my mind was to science*" (Thomas Paine). 3. The limit of endurance. Used chiefly in the phrase *to the top of one's bent.* 4. A structural member or framework used for strengthening a bridge or trestle transversely.

bent² n. 1. Any of several grasses of the genus *Agrostis*, some species of which are used in lawn mixtures and for hay. Also called "bent

Benin *A sculpted head, depicting a queen of the Benin, a West African people. Cast in bronze, it dates probably from the 16th century.*

grass." **2.** The stiff stalk of various grasses. **3.** *Rare.* A moor; a heath. [Middle English *bent,* grassy plain, Old English *beonet-* (attested in place names), from West Germanic *binut-* (unattested).]

Ben·tham (bĕn′thəm), **Jeremy** (1748–1832). English political theorist and philosopher. He was one of the first Englishmen to systematically analyze law and legislation, and he laid the foundations of the ethical system known as utilitarianism.

Ben·tham·ism (bĕn′thə-mĭz′əm) *n.* The utilitarian philosophy of Jeremy Bentham. See **utilitarianism.** —**Ben·tham·ite** *n. & adj.*

ben·tho·graph (bĕn′thə-grăf′, -gräf′) *n.* A steel sphere containing cameras and lights, designed to be lowered to great depths for underwater exploration.

ben·thos (bĕn′thŏs′) *n.* **1.** The bottom of the sea or of a lake, especially at considerable depths. **2.** The organisms living on sea or lake bottoms. [Greek, depth of the sea.] —**ben·thic** (bĕn′thĭk), **ben·thal** (bĕn′thəl), **ben·thon·ic** (bĕn-thŏn′ĭk) *adj.*

Ben·tinck (bĕn′tĭngk), **Lord William Henry Cavendish** (1774–1839). English colonial statesman. As the first governor general of British India (1828–35) he suppressed suttee, the burning of widows on their husbands' graves.

Bent·ley (bĕnt′lē), **Edmund Clerihew** (1875–1956). British man of letters. His detective story *Trent's Last Case* (1913) is a classic, but he is famous chiefly for inventing the short verse biography called a "clerihew."

Ben·ton (bĕnt′n), **Thomas Hart** (1889–1975). U.S. painter. His paintings and murals, executed in a flat, realistic style known as regionalism, portrayed everyday life in the Midwest and South. He won wide acclaim for his paintings of American farm life and his murals, such as *The History of Missouri* in the state capitol at Jefferson City.

ben·ton·ite (bĕn′tə-nīt′) *n.* Either of two principally aluminum silicate clays, containing some magnesium and iron, distinguished by sodium or calcium content with corresponding high or low swelling capacity, and used in cements, adhesives, fillers, and as a drilling mud in oil wells. [After Fort *Benton,* north-central Montana.] —**ben·ton·it·ic** (bĕn′tə-nĭt′ĭk) *adj.*

bent·wood (bĕnt′wŏŏd′) *n.* Wood that has been steamed until pliable and then bent into shape.
~ *adj.* Of or designating a style of furniture made of wood so treated.

be·numb (bĭ-nŭm′) *tr.v.* **-numbed, -numbing, -numbs. 1.** To make numb, especially by cold. **2.** To make inactive; stupefy. [Middle English *benomen,* past participle of *benimen,* to take away, Old English *beniman : be-,* away + *niman,* to take.] —**be·numb·ment** *n.*

Benz (bĕnz, bĕnts), **Karl Friedrich** (1844–1929). German engineer. He is credited with manufacturing the first car to be driven by an internal-combustion engine, patented in 1886. His company merged with the Daimler Motor Company (1926) to become Daimler-Benz AG, the makers of the famous Mercedes Benz automobile.

benz-. Variant of **benzo-.**

benz·al·de·hyde (bĕn-zăl′də-hīd′) *n.* A colorless or yellowish, strongly reactive, volatile oil, C_6H_5CHO, used as a solvent, flavoring, and in perfumery. [German *Benzaldehyd : benzoin + aldehyde.*]

Ben·ze·drine (bĕn′zə-drēn′) *n.* A trademark for a brand of **amphetamine** (*see*).

ben·zene (bĕn′zēn′, bĕn-zēn′) *n.* A clear, colorless, highly refractive, flammable liquid, C_6H_6, derived from petroleum and used to manufacture a wide variety of chemical products including detergents, insecticides, and motor fuels. In nontechnical usage, also called "benzol." [BENZ(OIN) + -ENE.]

benzene hexachloride *n.* **Hexachlorocyclohexane** (*see*).

benzene ring *n.* The hexagonal ring structure in the benzene molecule and its substitutional derivatives, each vertex of which is occupied and distinguished by a carbon atom. Also called "benzene nucleus."

benzene series *n.* A series of chemically related aromatic hydrocarbons containing the benzene ring, the simplest member of which is benzene.

ben·zi·dine (bĕn′zə-dēn′) *n.* A yellowish, white, or reddish-gray aromatic amine, $NH_2C_6H_4NH_2$, crystalline powder, $C_{12}H_{12}N_2$, used in the manufacture of dyes and to detect bloodstains.

benzine (bĕn′zēn′, bĕn-zēn′) *n.* A mixture of hydrocarbons, **ligroin** (*see*). [German *Benzin* : BENZ(OIN) + -INE.]

benzo- or **benz-** *prefix.* Indicates benzene or benzoic acid: for example, **benzophenone.** [From BENZOIN.]

ben·zo·ate (bĕn′zō-at′) *n.* A salt or ester of benzoic acid.

benzoate of soda *n. Chemistry.* **Sodium benzoate** (*see*).

ben·zo·caine (bĕn′zə-kān′) *n.* A white, odorless, tasteless crystalline ester, $C_9H_{11}NO_2$, used as a local anesthetic.

ben·zo·di·az·e·pine (bĕn′zō-dī-ăz′ə-pēn′) *n.* Any of several chemical compounds used as sedatives and muscle relaxants. [BENZO- + DIAZEP(AM) + -INE.]

ben·zo·ic acid (bĕn-zō′ĭk) *n.* A white crystalline acid, C_6H_5COOH, used to season tobacco and in perfumes, dentifrices, and germicides.

ben·zo·in (bĕn′zō-ĭn, -zoin′) *n.* **1.** Any of several resins containing benzoic acid, obtained as a gum from various trees of the genus *Styrax* and used in ointments, perfumes, and medicine. Also called "benjamin," "gum benzoin." **2.** Any of various aromatic shrubs and trees of the genus *Lindera,* which includes the **spicebush** (*see*). **3.** A white or yellowish crystalline compound, $C_{14}H_{12}O_2$, derived from benzaldehyde and used as an antiseptic. [Earlier *benjoin,*

from French, from New Latin *benzoe,* from Arabic *lubān jāwī,* "frankincense of Java."]

ben·zol (bĕn′zôl′, -zōl′) *n.* **Benzene** (*see*). Not in technical usage.

ben·zo·phe·none (bĕn′zō-fĭ-nōn′, -fē′nōn′) *n.* A white crystalline compound, $(C_6H_5)_2CO$, used in perfumery and in medicine. Also called "diphenylketone."

ben·zo·py·rene (bĕn′zō-pī′rēn′) *n.* A yellow, crystalline, aromatic hydrocarbon, $C_{20}H_{12}$, that is a carcinogen found in coal tar and cigarette smoke.

ben·zo·yl (bĕn′zō-ĭl′) *n.* The univalent radical C_6H_5CO derived from benzoic acid.

benzoyl peroxide *n.* A flammable, white, granular solid, $(C_6H_5CO)_2O_2$, used as a bleaching agent for flour, fats, waxes, and oils, as a polymerization catalyst, and in pharmaceuticals.

ben·zyl (bĕn′zĭl, -zēl′) *n.* The univalent radical $C_6H_5CH_2$ derived from toluene.

Beograd. See **Belgrade.**

Be·o·wulf (bā′ə-wŏŏlf′). The hero of an anonymous Old English epic poem believed to have been composed in northern England in the early 8th century.

be·queath (bĭ-kwēth′, -kwēth′) *tr.v.* **-queathed, -queathing, -queaths. 1.** *Law.* To give or leave (property) by will. **2.** To pass on or hand down: *His mother bequeathed to him a love of paintings.* [Middle English *bequethen,* Old English *becwethan,* to say, bequeath *: be-,* about, over + *cwethan,* to say, speak.] —**be·queath·al** *n.* —**be·queath·er** *n.* —**be·queath·ment** *n.*

be·quest (bĭ-kwĕst′) *n.* **1.** The act of bequeathing. **2.** That which is bequeathed; a legacy. [Middle English *: be-,* about + *-quiste,* a decree, Old English *-cwiss.*]

be·rate (bĭ-rāt′) *tr.v.* **-rated, -rating, -rates.** To rebuke or scold harshly. —See Synonyms at **scold.** [BE- + RATE (verb).]

Ber·ber (bûr′bər) *n.* **1.** A member of one of several Muslim tribes of North Africa. **2.** The branch of the Afro-Asiatic languages spoken by these tribes. —**Ber·ber** *adj.*

Ber·be·ra (bûr′bĕr-ə). Port on the Gulf of Aden in northern Somalia. The town was captured from the Egyptians by Britain (1884); from then until 1941 it was the capital of British Somaliland.

ber·ber·ine (bûr′bə-rēn′) *n.* A bitter-tasting yellow alkaloid, $C_{20}H_{19}NO_5$, obtained from the root of a North American plant, *Hydrastis canadensis,* from the barberry, and from other plants, and used in medicine as a tonic. [German *Berberin* : New Latin *Berberis* (genus), from Old French *berberis,* BARBERRY + *-in,* -INE.]

ber·ber·is (bûr′bə-rəs) *n.* Any shrub of the genus *Berberis,* many species of which are grown in gardens for their ornamental foliage, flowers, or berries. See **barberry.** [19th century : Medieval Latin *barbaris,* barberry.]

ber·ceuse (bĕr-sœz′) *n., pl.* **-ceuses** (*pronounced as singular*). **1.** A cradlesong or lullaby. **2.** A musical composition with a soothing accompaniment, usually in moderate $^6/_8$ time. [French, from *bercer,* to rock.]

Berch·tes·ga·den (bĕrкн′təs-gäd′n). Town in the eastern Bavarian Alps of Germany. It lies in a deep valley, surrounded on three sides by Austrian territory. The chalets and air-raid shelters of Hitler, Goering, and other Nazi leaders are on the Obersalzberg peak overlooking the town.

be·reave (bĭ-rēv′) *tr.v* **-reaved** or **-reft** (-rĕft′), **-reaving, -reaves. 1.** To deprive, as of life or hope: *"To a man bereft of the sense of purpose"* (G. Wilson Knight). **2.** To leave desolate, especially by the death of a loved one: *"cry aloud for the man who is dead, for the woman and children bereaved"* (Alan Paton). [Middle English *bireven,* Old English *berēafian.*] —**be·reave·ment** *n.* —**be·reav·er** *n.*

be·reft (bĭ-rĕft′). Past participle of **bereave.**
~ *adj.* **1. a.** Deprived of something: *bereft of his dignity.* **b.** Lacking something needed or expected: *a dictionary bereft of pictures.* **2.** Suffering the death of a loved one; bereaved.

Ber·e·ni·ce's Hair (bĕr′ə-nī′sēz) *n.* **Coma Berenices** (*see*).

Ber·en·son (bĕr′ən-sən), **Bernard** (1865–1959). U.S. art critic and historian, born in Lithuania. He is most famous for his writings on the Italian Renaissance, especially the comprehensive *Italian Painters of the Renaissance* (1894–1907).

be·ret (bə-rā′) *n.* A round, visorless cloth cap, worn originally by men in the Basque country. [French *béret,* from Old Gascon *barret,* cap, from Late Latin *birrus†,* hooded cape.]

beretta. Variant of **biretta.**

berg (bûrg) *n.* **1.** An iceberg (*see*). **2.** *South African.* A mountain.

Berg (bĕrкн), **Alban** (1885–1935). Austrian composer. A pupil of Arnold Schoenberg, he adopted his atonal manner and, with Anton von Webern and Schoenberg, formed the "Second Viennese School" of composers. He is best known for his two operas, *Wozzeck* (1925) and *Lulu* (1937), for the chamber *Lyric Suite* (1926), and his last completed work, the *Violin Concerto* (1936).

Ber·ga·mo (bĕr-gä′mō). Industrial city in the Lombardy region of northern Italy, lying in the foothills of the Alps between the Brembo and Serio rivers.

ber·ga·mot (bûr′gə-mŏt′) *n.* **1.** A small, spiny tree, *Citrus aurantium bergamia,* bearing sour, pear-shaped fruit, the rind of which yields an aromatic oil. Also called "bergamot orange." **2.** The oil itself, used in perfumery. Also called "bergamot oil." **3.** Any of several plants of the genus *Monarda;* especially the **wild bergamot** (*see*). [French *bergamote,* from Italian *bergamotta,* probably from Turkish *beg-armûdī,* "bey's pear."]

Ber·gen[1] (bûr′gən, bĕr′-). Norway's second-largest city, built on Bergen Fiord in the southwest of the country. Founded (*c.* 1070) by

King Olaf III, it was the capital of Norway in the 12th and 13th centuries and is now the center of the country's oil industry.

Bergen². See Mons.

Bergerac, Cyrano de. See Cyrano de Bergerac.

Ber·gi·us process (bûr'gē-əs) *n.* A process for the manufacture of diesel oil and gasoline from coal by hydrogenation of finely powdered coal with a catalyst at high temperatures. [After Friedrich *Bergius* (1884–1949), German chemist.]

Berg·man (bûrg'mən), **(Ernst) Ingmar** (1918–). Swedish film director. *Smiles of a Summer Night* (1955) announced the main elements of his highly distinctive style: a slow pace, laconic dialogue, and the heavy use of symbolism to explore the psychological states of his characters. Most critics consider his finest achievement to be his studies of psychosis, such as *The Silence* (1963) and *Persona* (1966).

Bergman, Ingrid (1915–82). Swedish film and stage actress, who gained international fame in the Hollywood version of *Intermezzo* (1939). Thereafter she retained her place as one of the great international film stars. She won an Academy Award for best actress in *Gaslight* (1944), *Anastasia* (1956), and *Murder on the Orient Express* (1974). She was awarded an Emmy for her portrayal of Golda Meir in *A Woman Called Golda* (1982).

berg·schrund (bĕrg'shrŏont') *n. Geology.* A crevasse at the head of a glacier that separates the moving ice from stationary ice adhering to the valley walls. [German *Bergschrund* : *Berg,* mountain from Old High German *bĕrg* + *Schrunde,* crack, from Old High German *scrunta.*]

Berg·son (bĕrg'sən), **Henri** (1859–1941). French philosopher. The central item in Bergson's philosophy is the opposition between the life force and the material world. He also assigned an important role to intuition, as opposed to the rational intelligence, in man's perception of reality. Among his best-known works are *Time and Free Will* (1889), *Creative Evolution* (1907), and *The Creative Mind* (1934).

Berg·so·ni·an (bĕrg-sō'nē-ən) *adj.* Of or pertaining to Henri Bergson or to his philosophy. —**Berg·so·ni·an** *n.*

Berg·son·ism (bĕrg'sə-nĭz'əm) *n.* Bergson's philosophy, which asserts that the flow of time as personally experienced is free and unrestricted rather than measured as on a clock and contends that all living forms arise from a persisting natural force, the **élan vital** *(see).*

berg wind *n.* A hot wind that blows from the plateau in South Africa down to the coast. [Afrikaans, "hill wind."]

be·rhyme (bĭ-rīm') *tr.v.* **-rhymed, -rhyming, -rhymes. 1.** To celebrate in verse. **2.** To lampoon in verse.

Be·ri·a (bĕr'ē-ə), **Lavrenti Pavlovich** (1899–1953). Soviet politician, born in Georgia. In 1946 he became a member of the Politburo and, on Stalin's death (1953), was appointed first deputy premier under Malenkov. In July 1953 he was arrested with six others, convicted of conspiracy, and executed.

ber·i·ber·i (bĕr'ē-bĕr'ē) *n.* A thiamine (vitamin B₁) deficiency disease of the peripheral nervous system, endemic in eastern and southern Asia, and characterized by partial paralysis of the extremities, emaciation, and anemia. [Singhalese, reduplication of *beri,* weakness.]

Ber·ing (bâr'ĭng), **Vitus.** Also **Beh·ring.** (1680–1741). Danish navigator in the employ of Russia. On the first voyage (1725) he explored the northern coast of Siberia. In 1728 he set out from Kamchatka Peninsula and traversed the Bering Strait, proving (though he did not realize it at the time) that Asia and North America are separate continents.

Bering Sea. Part of the North Pacific Ocean, lying north of the Aleutian Islands and connected to the Arctic Ocean by the Bering Strait.

Bering Strait. A narrow stretch of water (90 kilometers; 56 miles wide), separating Alaska from Siberia and connecting the Arctic Ocean and the Bering Sea. It is believed that in prehistoric times the strait formed a land bridge by which the original inhabitants of North America arrived from Asia.

Bering time *n.* The time in western Alaska and the Aleutian Islands, which lie in the 11th time zone west of Greenwich, England. [After the BERING SEA.]

Berke·le·ian (bär'klē-ən, bûr'–) *adj.* Of or pertaining to George Berkeley or his philosophy. —**Berke·le·ian** *n.*

Berke·le·ian·ism (bär'klē-ə-nĭz'əm, bûr'–) *n.* The philosophy of George Berkeley, holding that material objects have no existence independent of a mind perceiving them and that the uniform and continuous nature of the universe must be maintained by a divine mind always perceiving everything.

Berke·ley¹ (bûrk'lē). A city of western California, located on San Francisco Bay. Americans purchased the site from a Spanish family in 1853. The settlement, first called Oceanview, was renamed Berkeley in 1866. A large campus of the University of California is in Berkeley.

Berkeley². A suburb of St. Louis in eastern Missouri. The first International Air Meet in the United States was held here in 1910.

Berke·ley (bûrk'lē), **Busby,** born William Berkeley Enos (1895–1976). U.S. dance director. His trademark, lavish dance routines with precisely synchronized chorus lines, first appeared in *The Gold Diggers* series (1933–37) and *Footlight Parade* (1933).

Berke·ley (bärk'lē), **George** (1685–1753). Irish philosopher and clergyman. His important treatises are the *Essay Towards a New Theory of Vision* (1709) and the *Treatise Concerning the Principles of Human Knowledge* (1710). The basic tenet of his philosophy, directed against the materialism of Thomas Hobbes, was that to be is to perceive or to be perceived.

ber·ke·li·um (bər-kē'lē-əm, bûrk'lē-əm) *n. Symbol* **Bk** A synthetic transuranic element having 9 isotopes with mass numbers from 243 to 250 and half-lives from 3 hours to 1,380 years. Atomic number 97, valences 3, 4. [New Latin, after BERKELEY, California.]

Berk·shire¹ (bärk'shîr, –shər). Also **Berks** (bärks). A chiefly agricultural county in south-central England, lying in the Thames basin. The county town is Reading.

Berk·shire² (bûrk'shîr, –shər) *n.* A pig of a domestic breed that originated in Berkshire, England, having a black body with white feet and face.

Berk·shire Hills (bûrk'shîr, –shər). Also **Berk·shires.** A range of wooded hills in western Massachusetts. The highest elevation is Mt. Greylock (1,065 meters; 3,491 feet). There are many resorts, state parks, and forests in the area.

ber·ley, bur·ley (bûr'lē) *n. Australian.* **1.** Ground bait for angling. **2.** *Slang.* Nonsense.

ber·lin (bər-lĭn') *n.* **1.** A light wool used in tapestry or for making clothing, especially gloves. Also called "Berlin wool." **2.** Also **ber·line.** A four-wheeled covered carriage with a seat behind. **3.** Also **ber·line.** A limousine with a glass window between the front and rear seats. [After BERLIN.]

Ber·lin (bûr-lĭn'). City in Germany on the Spree and Havel rivers. It was the capital of Prussia, and from 1871 the capital of the German empire. In 1949 the city was divided into West Berlin, belonging to West Germany, and East Berlin, belonging to East Germany and becoming its capital. The East German government erected the Berlin Wall between the two parts of the city in 1961. The wall began to be dismantled in 1989, and with the unification of Germany (1990) Berlin became its capital.

Berlin, Irving, born Israel Baline (1888–1989) in Russia. U.S. composer. Although he never learned to read music or play the piano, except in the key of F sharp, he became the most versatile and successful of 20th-century popular songwriters. He wrote more than 1,500 songs. His first major success was "Alexander's Ragtime Band" (1911). Among his famous musical comedies are *Top Hat* (1935), and *Annie Get Your Gun* (1946).

berline. Variant of **berlin** (senses 2, 3).

Ber·li·oz (bĕr'lē-ōz'; *French* bĕr-lyōz'), **(Louis) Hector** (1803–69). French composer, the leading representative of the romantic movement in French music. An early work, the *Symphonie Fantastique* (1830), is notable for its freedom from classical form and expansive scoring for a very large orchestra. His other most famous works are the symphonies *Harold in Italy* (first performed 1834) and *Romeo and Juliet* (1839), the operas *Benvenuto Cellini* (1838) and *The Trojans* (1855, 1858), the "concert opera" *The Damnation of Faust* (1846), and the oratorio *The Childhood of Christ* (1854).

berm, berme (bûrm) *n.* **1. a.** A narrow ledge or shelf, as along a slope. **b.** A shoulder of a road. **2.** A ledge between the parapet and the moat in a fortification. [French *berme,* from Dutch *berm,* slope, edge of a dike or dam, from Middle Dutch *berme,* perhaps akin to Old Norse *barmr,* brim.]

Ber·mu·da (bər-myōō'də). A self-governing British colony in the North Atlantic Ocean, comprising about 300 coral islands, some 20 of which are inhabited. The capital, Hamilton, is on the largest of the islands, called Bermuda or Great Bermuda. Bermuda has been a British colony since 1609 and relies on tourism.

Bermuda grass *n.* A grass, *Cynodon dactylon,* that has wiry, creeping rootstocks and is used for lawns and pasturage in warm regions. Also called "scutch grass," "wiregrass."

Bermuda lily *n.* A plant, the **Easter lily** *(see).*

Bermuda mulberry *n.* The **beautyberry** *(see).*

Bermuda rig *n.* A fore-and-aft rig, distinguished by a tall triangular mainsail, widely used on cruising and racing vessels. Also called "Marconi rig." —**Ber·mu·da-rigged** *adj.*

Bermuda shorts *pl.n.* Shorts that end slightly above the knees. Also called "Bermudas."

Bermuda Triangle. Area of the North Atlantic Ocean remarkable for the number of ships and airplanes that have disappeared without explanation in its waters. The triangle lies approximately in the area between latitude 25° to 40°N and longitude 55° to 85°W, between Bermuda, Puerto Rico, and Florida.

Bern (bûrn, bĕrn). Also **Berne.** The capital of Switzerland, situated on the Aar River in the west-central part of the country. The city joined the Swiss Confederation (1353) and became its capital (1848). Bern is also the name of the canton that surrounds the city.

Ber·na·dette (bûr'nə-dĕt'), **Saint,** born Marie Bernarde Soubirous (1844–79). French girl whose visions of the Virgin Mary at a grotto near her birthplace, Lourdes, led to the establishment of a shrine there. She had her first visions when she was 14 (1858). She was canonized in 1933.

Bernadotte, Jean Baptiste Jules. See **Charles XIV.**

Ber·nard·ine (bûr'nər-dīn, –dēn') *adj.* **1.** Of or pertaining to St. Bernard of Clairvaux. **2.** Of or pertaining to the Cistercians, the order of monks reformed by St. Bernard in 1115. ~*n.* A member of a Cistercian order.

Ber·nard of Clair·vaux (bər-närd' əv klâr-vō'), **Saint.** (*c.* 1090–1153). French mystic and Doctor of the Church. He entered the Cistercian order (1112) and was sent to establish a monastery (1115) at Clairvaux, where he remained abbot for the rest of his life. He is sometimes called the second founder of the Cistercian broth-

Berkshire *Developed in the Thames Valley of England in the 19th century, the traditional Berkshire pig is now becoming rare. It is a small pork-producing pig that has been crossed with other breeds as bacon has become more important commercially.*

Bernini

MASTERPIECES IN MARBLE

A sculptor and architect who left his imprint on Rome

Gianlorenzo Bernini (1598–1680) was the son of a sculptor who worked in Rome for Pope Paul V. Gianlorenzo began sculpting as a boy and attracted a patron in the pope's nephew, Cardinal Scipione Borghese, for whom he made *Aeneas and Anchises* (1618–19), *The Rape of Proserpina* (1621–22), and *David* (1623). These established him as an unmatched master, and his reputation became international. His greatest achievements are to be seen in Rome, in tombs, busts, statues, buildings, and fountains.

Bernini was a splendid sculptor in white marble, but his use of polychrome marble, on its own or combined with gilded bronze, is outstanding. He used the combination in the tomb of Pope Urban VIII (1628–47) and of Pope Alexander VII (1671–78). Characteristic of his style are swirling movement in draperies and ecstatic gestures and facial expressions.

His architecture includes St. Peter's Piazza, much work in St. Peter's Basilica, and several churches, including St. Andrea al Quirinale (1658–70). His busts, among them one of Louis XIV (at Versailles), are the finest pieces of baroque portrait sculpture. The most notable of his fountains are the Triton, the Moro, and the Four Rivers.

Perhaps Bernini's most characteristic masterpiece is the chapel he created (1645–52) for the Cornaro family in the church of Santa Maria della Vittoria. Saint Theresa and the angel are flanked by members of the Cornaro family. The group combines white and colored marble, gilded bronze, and natural light filtering from a window behind the figures.

A MOMENT CAUGHT FOREVER Apollo and Daphne *(1622–24), in the Borghese Museum, Rome, shows Bernini's unrivaled skill in portraying movement in pose, drapery, and gesture.*

erhood. His simple devotion to the Virgin Mary and the infant Christ make him a precursor of the movement known as the *devotio moderna.* His most influential writings, apart from his sermons (more than 300 of which survive), were *On the Steps of Humility and Pride* (c. 1125) and *On the Love of God* (c. 1127).

Bern·hardt (bûrn′härt′, bĕrn′-), **Sarah,** born Henriette Rosine Bernard, known as "the Divine Sarah" (1844–1923). French actress, one of the most renowned in the history of the theater. She made her debut at the Comédie Française (1862), but her great reputation did not begin until her appearance there as *Phèdre* (1874). In 1912 she appeared in two films, *La Dame aux Camélias* and *Queen Elizabeth.* She continued acting all over the world even after her leg was amputated (1915).

Ber·ni·ni (bĕr-nē′nē), **Giovanni Lorenzo** or **Gianlorenzo** (1598–1680). Italian sculptor, painter, and architect, the outstanding representative of the Italian baroque. He was appointed architect to St. Peter's in Rome (1629) and made the great ornate baldachin over the high altar and the *Cathedra Petri* monument enshrining St. Peter's throne. He later decorated the apse of St. Peter's with a group of the Fathers of the Church, designed the colonnade around the piazza at the front of the church, and created the royal staircase in the Vatican.

Ber·noul·li (bər-n̄oo′lē), **Daniel** (1700–82). Swiss physician, mathematician, and physicist, son of Jean. He was one of the first natural philosophers who could properly be called a mathematical physicist. He anticipated the law of the conservation of energy and did important pioneering work in the molecular theory of gases; he also contributed to probability theory and the theory of differential equations. He is best known for his formulation of **Bernoulli's law,** which appears in *Hydrodynamica* (1738).

Bernoulli, Jacques or **Jakob** (1654–1705). Swiss mathematician, brother of Jean. He was professor of natural philosophy at Basel (1687–1705). He is one of the most important founders of the theory of ordinary calculus and the calculus of variations. He was the first user of the word "integral," in his solution to the problem of the isochronal curve.

Bernoulli, Jean or **Johann** (1667–1748). Swiss mathematician, brother of Jacques and father of Daniel. He succeeded his brother as professor of natural philosophy at the University at Basel. He is important for his development of integral and exponential calculus.

Bernoulli distribution *n. Statistics.* The **binomial distribution** *(see).* [After Jacques BERNOULLI.]

Bernoulli effect *n.* The phenomenon of internal pressure reduction with increased stream velocity in a fluid. [After Daniel BERNOULLI.]

Bernoulli's law *n.* **1.** *Statistics.* The probability theorem stating that for a very large number of independent repeated Bernoulli trials the observed relative frequency of successes will approximate the probability of success on each trial. Also called "law of large numbers." **2.** *Physics.* The relationship between internal fluid pressure and fluid velocity, essentially a statement of the conservation of energy, that has as a consequence the Bernoulli effect. Also called "Bernoulli's theorem." [Statistics law, after Jacques BERNOULLI; physics law, after Daniel BERNOULLI.]

Bernoulli trial *n. Statistics.* An experiment having just two possible results, usually denoted *success* and *failure,* with the property that the occurrence of one excludes the occurrence of the other in any given trial. [After Jacques BERNOULLI.]

Bern·stein (bûrn′stīn′), **Leonard** (1918–90). U.S. symphony conductor, composer, pianist, and teacher. He was the permanent conductor of the New York Philharmonic (1958–70). He wrote a number of choral and symphonic works, but is best known for his musical comedies, including *On the Town* (1944) and *West Side Story* (1957).

Ber·ra (bĕr′ə), **Yogi,** born Lawrence Peter Berra (1925–). U.S. baseball player and manager. Considered one of the best catchers in the history of baseball, Berra played for the New York Yankees from 1946 to 1963. In 1972 he was elected to the Baseball Hall of Fame.

berretta. Variant of **biretta.**

ber·ry (bĕr′ē) *n., pl.* **-ries. 1.** Any of various usually fleshy, edible fruits, such as the strawberry, blackberry, or raspberry. **2.** *Botany.* A fleshy fruit, such as the grape, date, or tomato, that usually has two or more seeds and does not split open when ripe. **3.** Any of various seeds or dried kernels, such as that of the coffee plant. **4.** The small, dark egg of certain crustaceans or fishes.
~*intr.v.* **berried, -rying, -ries. 1.** To hunt for or gather berries. **2.** To produce or bear berries. [Middle English *berye,* Old English *beri(g)e.*]

Ber·ry (bĕr′ē), **Chuck,** born Charles Edward Anderson Berry (1926–). U.S. popular songwriter and singer. He was one of the first singers in the 1950's to evolve the rock 'n' roll style.

ber·seem (bər-sēm′) *n.* A clover, *Trifolium alexandrinum,* native to northern Africa and southwestern Asia, and grown for soil improvement in dry regions of southwestern North America. Also called "Egyptian clover." [Arabic *barsīm, birsīm,* from Coptic *bersīm.*]

ber·serk (bər-sûrk′, -zûrk′) *adj.* **1.** Destructively or frenetically violent. **2.** Deranged.
~*n.* A berserker. —**ber·serk** *adv.*

ber·serk·er (bər-sûr′kər, -zûr′-) *n.* A fierce ancient Norse warrior who fought in battle with frenzied violence and fury. [Icelandic *berserkr,* "bear's skin" : *björn* (stem *ber-*), a bear + *serkr,* shirt, SARK.]

berth (bûrth) *n.* **1.** A usually built-in bed or bunk in a ship or railroad sleeping car. **2.** *Nautical.* A space at a wharf for a ship to dock or anchor. **3.** *Nautical.* Enough space for a ship to maneuver; sea room. **4.** A position of employment, especially on a ship. **—give a wide berth to.** To stay at a substantial distance from; avoid. *~v.* **berthed, berthing, berths.** *—tr.* **1.** To bring (a ship) to a berth. **2.** To provide (a ship) with a berth. **3.** To provide a bunk for, as on a ship or train. *—intr.* To come to a berth; dock. [Probably BEAR (verb, in nautical sense, "to sail in a certain direction") + -TH (noun suffix expressing result).]

ber·tha (bûr′thə) *n.* A wide, deep collar, often of lace, that covers the shoulders of a low-necked dress. [French *berthe,* after Queen *Bertha,* mother of Charlemagne.]

Ber·til·lon system (bûr′tə-lŏn′; *French* bĕr-tē-yôN′) *n.* A former system for identifying persons, especially criminal, by means of a record of various body measurements, coloring, markings, and the like. [After Alphonse *Bertillon* (1853-1914), French criminologist.]

Ber·wick·shire (bĕr′wĭk-shĭr, -shər) *n.* A former county of Scotland, since 1975 included in Borders Region.

ber·yl (bĕr′əl) *n.* A mineral, essentially aluminum beryllium silicate, $Be_3Al_2Si_6O_{18}$, occurring in hexagonal prisms. It is the chief source of beryllium and is used as a gem. [Middle English, from Old French, from Latin *bēryllus,* from Greek *bērullos,* perhaps of Dravidian origin.] **—beryl·line** (bĕr′ə-lĭn, -līn′) *adj.*

be·ryl·li·um (bə-rĭl′ē-əm) *n.* *Symbol* **Be** A lightweight, corrosion-resistant, rigid, steel-gray metallic element used as an aerospace structural material, as a moderator and reflector in nuclear reactors, and in a copper alloy used for springs, electrical contacts, and nonsparking tools. Atomic number 4, atomic weight 9.0122, melting point 1,287°C, boiling point 2,970°C, specific gravity 1.848, valence 2. [New Latin, from BERYL.]

Ber·ze·li·us (bər-zā′lē-əs, -zĕ′-), **Jöns Jakob, Baron** (1779-1848). Swedish chemist, one of the most important founders of modern chemistry. He made enormous contributions to the development of the science in atomic weights (he published a table of these in 1828), electrochemical theory (by his experiments in electrolysis of various solutions), and the discovery of the elements selenium and thorium and the isolation of silicon. He coined the words "isomerism," "allotropy," and "protein." His most important publication was the *Theory of Chemical Proportions and the Chemical Action of Electricity* (1814).

Bes (bĕs). *Egyptian Mythology.* A god of music and revelry.

Be·san·çon (bə-zän-sôN′). Industrial city in eastern France, on the Doubs River. It is famous for watches and clocks.

Bes·ant (bĕz′ənt), **Annie,** born Annie Wood (1847-1933). English freethinker and theosophist. In 1889 she became a disciple of Helena Blavatsky and for the rest of her life devoted herself to theosophy. She later became the founder-president of the India Home Rule League (1916) and president of the Indian National Congress (1917).

be·seech (bĭ-sēch′) *tr.v.* **-sought** (-sôt′) or **-seeched, -seeching, -seeches. 1.** To address an earnest or urgent request to; implore. **2.** To request earnestly; beg for. —See Synonyms at **beg.** [Middle English *besechen,* to seek : *be-,* thoroughly + *sechen, seken,* to SEEK.] **—be·seech·er** *n.* **—be·seech·ing·ly** *adv.*

be·seem (bĭ-sēm′) *tr.v.* **-seemed, -seeming, -seems.** *Archaic.* To be appropriate for; befit. [Middle English *besemen,* to seem, appear to do well : *be-,* thoroughly + *semen,* to SEEM.]

be·set (bĭ-sĕt′) *tr.v.* **-set, -setting, -sets. 1.** To attack from all sides. **2.** To trouble persistently; harass: *beset by doubts.* **3.** To surround; hem in. **4.** To stud, as with jewels. —See Synonyms at **attack.** [Middle English *besetten,* Old English *besettan : be-,* on all sides + SET (place).] **—be·set·ment** *n.*

be·set·ting (bĭ-sĕt′ĭng) *adj.* Constantly troubling or attacking.

be·shrew (bĭ-shrōō′) *tr.v.* **-shrewed, -shrewing, -shrews.** *Archaic.* To invoke evil upon; curse. [Middle English *beshrewen,* to corrupt, curse : *be-,* thoroughly + *shrewen,* to curse, from *shrewe,* SHREW.]

be·side (bĭ-sīd′) *prep.* **1.** Next to; at or by the side of. **2.** In comparison with. **3.** Except for. —See Usage note at **besides. 4.** Wide of; unrelated to: *beside the point.* **—beside oneself.** Out of one's senses with excitement, grief, rage, or the like; extremely agitated. *~adv.* In addition to. [Middle English *biside,* Old English *be sīdan : be,* BY + *sīdan,* dative of *sīde,* SIDE.]

be·sides (bĭ-sīdz′) *adv.* **1.** In addition; also; over and above. **2.** Moreover; furthermore. **3.** Otherwise; else. —See Synonyms at **also.** *~prep.* **1.** In addition to. **2.** Except for. [Middle English *bisides,* adverbial genitive of *biside,* BESIDE.]

> *Usage:* In modern usage, the senses *in addition to* and *except for* are conveyed more often by *besides* than *beside.* Thus: *He had few friends besides us.*

be·siege (bĭ-sēj′) *tr.v.* **-sieged, -sieging, -sieges. 1.** To surround with aggressive intent in order to compel surrender; lay siege to. **2.** To crowd round; hem in. **3.** To harass or importune, as with requests. [Middle English *besegen : be-,* on all sides + *sege,* SIEGE.] **—be·siege·ment** *n.* **—be·sieg·er** *n.*

be·smear (bĭ-smîr′) *tr.v.* **-smeared, -smearing, -smears. 1.** To smear over. **2.** To tarnish; defile.

be·smirch (bĭ-smûrch′) *tr.v.* **-smirched, -smirching, -smirches. 1.** To make dirty; soil. **2.** To dim the purity or luster of (someone's reputation, for example); tarnish; dishonor. **—be·smirch·er** *n.* **—be·smirch·ment** *n.*

be·som (bē′zəm) *n.* **1.** A bundle of twigs attached to a handle and used as a broom. **2.** In curling, the broom used to sweep the ice from the path of a curling stone. **3.** *Rare.* The broom plant. *~tr. v.* **besomed, -soming, -soms.** To sweep using a besom. [Middle English *besem,* Old English *bes(e)ma,* from West Germanic *besmo-* (unattested).]

be·sot·ted (bĭ-sŏt′ĭd) *adj.* **1.** Muddled or stupefied, especially with liquor. **2.** Infatuated.

be·sought. Past tense and past participle of **beseech.**

be·span·gle (bĭ-spăng′gəl) *tr.v.* **-spangled, -spangling, -spangles.** To ornament or cover with spangles.

be·spat·ter (bĭ-spăt′ər) *tr.v.* **-tered, -tering, -ters. 1.** To spatter or soil thoroughly, as with mud. **2.** To cast aspersions on; defame.

be·speak (bĭ-spēk′) *tr.v.* **-spoke** (-spōk′) or *archaic* **-spake** (-spāk′), **-spoken** (-spō′kən) or **-spoke, -speaking, -speaks. 1.** To be or give a sign of; indicate; signify. **2.** *Archaic.* To speak to; address. **3.** To engage or claim in advance; reserve. **4.** To foretell; portend.

be·spec·ta·cled (bĭ-spĕk′tə-kəld) *adj.* Wearing eyeglasses.

be·spoke (bĭ-spōk′) *adj.* Also **be·spo·ken** (bĭ-spō′kən). *Chiefly British.* **1.** Made-to-order. Usually said of clothing. **2.** Dealing in custom-made articles: *a bespoke tailor.*

be·spread (bĭ-sprĕd′) *tr.v.* **-spread, -spreading, -spreads.** To cover or spread over, usually thickly.

be·sprent (bĭ-sprĕnt′) *adj.* *Poetic.* Besprinkled. [Middle English *bespreynt,* past participle of *besprengen,* to besprinkle, Old English *besprengan : be-,* around, over + *sprengan,* to scatter, burst.]

be·sprin·kle (bĭ-sprĭng′kəl) *tr.v.* **-kled, -kling, -kles.** To sprinkle over, as with water. [Middle English *besprengelen,* frequentative of *besprengen,* to besprinkle. See **besprent.**]

Bes·sa·ra·bi·a (bĕs′ə-rā′bē-ə). Historic region in Moldova and western Ukraine. Russia gained the area (1812), but it declared itself the independent republic of Moldavia (1918) and voted for union with Romania. Romania was forced formally to cede it to the U.S.S.R. (1940).

Bes·sel equation (bĕs′əl) *n.* The differential equation, $x^2 f''(x) + xf'(x) + (x^2 - n^2)f(x) = 0$. [After Friedrich Wilhelm *Bessel* (1784-1846), German astronomer and mathematician.]

Bessel function *n.* Any of the solutions of the Bessel equation, having many applications in mathematical physics, including the representation of current density and magnetic field strength, and in problems of heat conduction.

Bes·se·mer (bĕs′ə-mər), **Sir Henry** (1813-98). British engineer and inventor. Over his lifetime he patented more than 100 inventions. He is most famous for inventing the **Bessemer process.** He was knighted in 1879.

Bessemer converter *n.* A large pear-shaped container in which molten pig iron is converted to steel by the Bessemer process. [After Sir Henry BESSEMER.]

Bessemer process *n.* A method for making steel by blasting compressed air through molten iron, burning out excess carbon and other impurities. [After Sir Henry BESSEMER.]

best (bĕst) **1.** Superlative of **good. 2.** Superlative of **well.** *~adj.* **1.** Surpassing all others in quality; most excellent. **2.** Most satisfactory, suitable, or useful; most desirable or attractive: *the best solution.* **3.** Greatest; largest: *It took the best part of a week.* *~adv.* **1.** In the best way; most creditably, attractively, or advantageously. **2.** To the greatest degree or extent; most: *"He was certainly the best hated man in the ship"* (Somerset Maugham). **—had best.** Should; ought to; would be wisest to. *~n.* **1.** That which is best among several. Preceded by *the.* **2.** The best person or persons. Preceded by *the.* **3.** The best condition or quality: *look your best.* **4.** One's best clothing. **5.** The best effort one can make: *doing his best.* **6.** One's warmest wishes or regards: *Give them my best.* **—at best. 1.** When interpreted most favorably. **2.** Under the most favorable conditions. **—for the best.** For the ultimate good. **—get (or have) the best of.** To defeat, surpass, or outwit. **—make the best of.** To do as well as possible under unfavorable conditions. *~tr.v.* **bested, besting, bests.** To prevail over; surpass; defeat: *"I'm a rough customer, I expect, but I know when I'm bested"* (Nathanael West). [Middle English *best,* Old English *bet(e)st.*]

Best (bĕst), **Charles Herbert** (1899-1978). Canadian physician and physiologist, famous for collaborating with John J.R. MacLeod and Sir Frederick Banting in the extraction of the hormone insulin from a dog's pancreas (1921) and the subsequent demonstration that it could be used to arrest the progress of diabetes mellitus, then a fatal disease.

be·stead (bĭ-stĕd′) *tr.v.* **-steaded** or **-stead, -steading, -steads.** *Archaic.* To be of service to; avail; aid. *~adj.* *Archaic.* Placed; located. [BE- + STEAD (to help).]

bes·tial (bĕs′chəl, bĕst′yəl) *adj.* **1.** Of or pertaining to an animal. **2.** Having the qualities of or behaving in the manner of a brute; savage; depraved. **3.** Subhuman in intelligence. [Middle English, from Old French, from Late Latin *bēstiālis,* from Latin *bēstia,* BEAST.] **—bes·tial·ly** *adv.*

bes·ti·al·i·ty (bĕs′chē-ăl′ə-tē, bĕs′tē-ăl′-) *n., pl.* **-ties. 1.** The quality of being bestial; animal nature. **2.** An action or conduct marked by repugnant carnality or brutality. **3.** Sexual relations between a human being and an animal; sodomy.

bes·tial·ize (bĕs′chə-līz′, bĕst′yə-) *tr.v.* **-ized, -izing, -izes.** To make bestial; brutalize.

bes·ti·ar·y (bĕs′chē-ĕr′ē, bĕs′tē-) *n., pl.* **-ies. 1.** A medieval collection of allegorical fables about the habits and traits of animals, each fable followed by an interpretation of its moral significance. **2.** A modern version of such a collection. [Medieval Latin *bēstiārium*, from Latin *bēstia*, BEAST.]

be•stir (bĭ-stûr′) *tr.v.* **-stirred, -stirring, -stirs.** To cause to become active; rouse. Usually used reflexively: *She bestirred herself and went for a walk.*

best man *n.* The bridegroom's chief attendant at a wedding.

be•stow (bĭ-stō′) *tr.v.* **-stowed, -stowing, -stows. 1.** To present as a gift or honor; confer. Used with *on* or *upon.* **2.** To give in marriage. **3.** To apply; use: *"On Hester Prynne's story . . . I bestowed much thought"* (Nathaniel Hawthorne). **4.** *Archaic.* To store; house. [Middle English *bestowen* : *be-* (intensive) + STOW.] **—be•stow•able** *adj.* **—be•stow•al, be•stow•ment** *n.*

be•strew (bĭ-strōō′) *tr.v.* **-strewed, -strewed** or **-strewn** (-strōōn′), **-strewing, -strews. 1.** To strew (a surface) with things so as to cover it. **2.** To scatter or cast things profusely on a surface. **3.** To lie scattered over or about.

be•stride (bĭ-strīd′) *tr.v* **-strode** (-strōd′), **-stridden** (-strĭd′n), **-striding, -strides. 1.** To sit or stand on with the legs widely spread; straddle. **2.** To step over. [Middle English *bestriden,* Old English *bestrīdan* : *be-*, over + *strīdan,* to STRIDE.]

best seller *n.* A book or other product that is among those sold in the largest numbers. **—best-sell•ing** (bĕst′sĕl′ĭng) *adj.*

bet (bĕt) *n.* **1.** An agreement between two parties such that the one proved wrong about an uncertain outcome will forfeit a stipulated thing or sum to the other; a wager. **2.** The fact, event, or outcome on which a wager is made. **3.** The object or amount risked in a wager; the stake. **4. a.** A plan or course of action: *Your best bet is to leave now.* **b.** *Informal.* A view; opinion: *My bet is that she won't come.* **—hedge one's bets. 1.** To protect oneself from possible loss by betting on more than one outcome. **2.** To guard against risk; cover oneself.
~*v.* **bet** or *rare* **betted, betting, bets.** —*tr.* **1.** To stake (an object or amount, for example) in a bet. **2.** To make a bet with. **3.** To make a bet on (a contestant or an outcome). **4.** To predict confidently. —*intr.* To make or place a bet. **—you bet.** *Informal.* Surely. [16th century : perhaps short for ABET in the sense of "instigation."]

be•ta (bā′tə, bē′-) *n.* **1.** The second letter in the Greek alphabet, written Β, β. Transliterated in English as *B, b,* and sometimes, for Modern Greek words, as *V, v.* See feature at **alphabet. 2.** The second item in a series or system of classification. **3.** *Chiefly British.* A second-class mark for an examination, essay, or the like. **4.** *Physics.* **a.** A **beta particle** *(see).* **b.** A **beta ray** *(see).* [Greek *bēta,* from Hebrew *bēth,* BETH.]

beta blocker *n.* Any of a group of drugs that slow down the action of the heart by blocking the action of nerve endings called *beta-receptors.* They are used to treat abnormal heart conditions and high blood pressure.

be•ta•ine (bē′tə-ēn′) *n.* A sweet, crystalline alkaloid, $C_5H_{11}NO_2$, occurring in sugar beets and other plants and formerly used in treatment of muscular degeneration. [Latin *bēta,* BEET + -INE.]

be•take (bĭ-tāk′) *tr.v.* **-took** (-tŏŏk′), **-taken, -taking, -takes. 1.** To cause (oneself) to go or move. **2.** *Archaic.* To commit or apply (oneself) to something: *He betook himself to fasting.*

Be•tan•court (bĕ-tän-kŏŏr′), **Romulo** (1908–81). Venezuelan politician. He founded the National Democratic Party (1935), later renamed Democratic Action. He spent several years in exile, but served twice as president.

beta particle *n.* A high-speed electron or positron, especially one emitted in radioactive decay.

beta ray *n.* A stream of beta particles, especially of electrons.

beta rhythm *n.* The waveform occurring in electroencephalograms of the adult brain, characteristically having a frequency from 18 to 30 cycles per second and associated with an alert waking state. Also called "beta wave." Compare **alpha rhythm.**

be•ta•tron (bā′tə-trŏn′, bē′-) *n.* A fixed-radius magnetic induction electron **accelerator** *(see)* capable of accelerating electrons to energies of a few million to a few hundred million electron volts. [BETA + -TRON.]

be•tel (bēt′l) *n.* A climbing Asiatic plant, *Piper betle,* the leaves of which are chewed with the betel nut, especially in southeastern Asia, to induce both stimulating and narcotic effects. [Portuguese *betel, betle,* from Malayalam *veṭṭila.*]

Be•tel•geuse, Be•tel•geux (bēt′l-jōōz′, bĕt′l-joez′) *n.* A bright-red intrinsic-variable star, about 600 light years from Earth, in the constellation Orion. [French *Bételgeuse,* from Arabic *bīt al-jauzā′,* "shoulder of the Giant (Orion)."]

betel nut *n.* Also **be•tel•nut** (bēt′l-nŭt′). The seed of the fruit of the betel palm, chewed, together with betel leaves and lime, by many people of southeastern Asia.

betel palm *n.* A palm tree, *Areca catechu,* of tropical Asia, having featherlike leaves and orange or scarlet fruit. See **betel nut.**

bête noire (bĕt nwär′) *n., pl.* **bêtes noires** *(pronounced as singular).* Someone or something that one especially dislikes or avoids. [French, "black beast."]

beth (bĕt) *n.* The second letter of the Hebrew alphabet. See feature at **alphabet.** [Hebrew *bēth,* "house."]

Beth•a•ny (bĕth′ə-nē). *Arabic* **Al-′Ay•zar•i•yah** (äl-ī′zə-rē′ə, -yə). Small village at the southeastern foot of the Mount of Olives, in the Israeli-occupied West Bank. The miracle of Lazarus's resurrection took place here (the Arabic name means "Lazarus").

Be•the (bā′tə), **Hans Albrecht** (1906–). American physicist, born in Germany. His chief work has been the study of nuclear reactions in stars, especially that by which hydrogen is converted to helium. He was awarded the Nobel Prize in physics (1967).

beth•el (bĕth′əl, bĕ′thĕl′) *n.* **1.** A hallowed or holy place. **2.** A chapel for seamen. **3.** *Chiefly British.* A Nonconformist chapel. [Hebrew *bēth ′Ēl,* "house of God."]

Beth•el (bĕth′əl). A town of Biblical Palestine, about 18 kilometers (11 miles) north of Jerusalem. Genesis 28:19.

Be•thes•da (bə′thĕz′də). An urban center in west-central Maryland, forming a residential suburb of Washington, D.C. The National Institutes of Health, the National Cancer Institute, and the Naval Medical Center are located in Bethesda.

be•think (bĭ-thĭngk′) *v.* **-thought** (-thôt′), **-thinking, -thinks.** —*tr.* **1.** *Archaic.* To reflect upon; think about; consider. **2.** To remind (oneself); remember. —*intr. Archaic.* To meditate; ponder. [Middle English *bethinken,* Old English *bethencan* : *be-*, about + *thencan,* to THINK.]

Beth•le•hem (bĕth′lĭ-hĕm, -lē-əm). Small market town in the Judaean Hills, south of Jerusalem, in the Israeli-occupied West Bank. Traditionally held to be the birthplace of Christ, it was the home and probably the birthplace of David, who was annointed King of Israel by Samuel here.

Be•thune (bĭ-thōōn′), **Mary McLeod** (1875–1955). U.S. educator. Noted for her work on behalf of education for blacks and improved racial relations, she served as an adviser on minority affairs for President Franklin D. Roosevelt. In 1945 she was an observer with the U.S. delegation to the first United Nations meeting in San Francisco.

be•tide (bĭ-tīd′) *v.* **-tided, -tiding, -tides.** —*tr.* To happen to: *Woe betide you if you harm his son.* —*intr.* To take place; befall. —See Synonyms at **happen.** [Middle English *betiden* : *be-*, thoroughly + *tiden,* to happen, Old English *tīdan.*]

be•times (bĭ-tīmz′) *adv.* **1.** Early; in good time: *He awoke betimes.* **2.** *Archaic.* Quickly; soon. [Middle English, adverbial genitive of *betime* : *be,* BY + TIME.]

bê•tise (bā-tēz′) *n., pl.* **bêtises** *(pronounced as singular).* **1.** A foolish or gauche remark or action. **2.** Folly; ignorance. [French.]

Bet•je•man (bĕch′ə-mən), **Sir John** (1906–84). British poet laureate (1972–84). He produced many collections of poems, including a verse autobiography, *Summoned by Bells* (1960), and wrote extensively on Victorian architecture.

be•to•ken (bĭ-tō′kən) *tr.v.* **-kened, -kening, -kens.** To give a sign or portent of: *Those clouds betoken snow.* —See Synonyms at **foretell.** [Middle English *betokenen,* Old English *bitācnian* (unattested).] **—be•to•ken•er** *n.*

bet•o•ny (bĕt′ə-nē) *n., pl.* **-nies. 1.** Any of several plants of the genus *Stachys*; especially, *S. officinalis,* native to Eurasia, having a spike of reddish-purple flowers. **2.** A plant, the **lousewort** *(see).* [Middle English *betone,* from Old French *betoine,* from Latin *bētonica, vettonica,* probably after the *Vettones,* an ancient Iberian tribe.]

be•took. Past tense of **betake.**

be•tray (bĭ-trā′) *tr.v.* **-trayed, -traying, -trays. 1.** To give aid or information to an enemy of; commit treason against or be a traitor to: *betray one's nation.* **2.** To be disloyal or faithless to. **3.** To divulge in a breach of confidence: *"A servant . . . betrayed their presence . . . to the Germans"* (William Styron). **4.** To make known unintentionally: *"Only the young have the right to betray their ignorance"* (Henry Adams). **5.** To show unintentionally; reveal; indicate: *His shaking hands betrayed his nervousness.* **6.** To deceive; lead astray. **7.** *Archaic.* To seduce and forsake (a woman). —See Synonyms at **reveal, deceive.** [Middle English *betrayen* : *be-*, thoroughly + *trayen,* to betray, from Old French *trair,* from Latin *trādere* : *trāns-*, over + *dare,* to give.] **—be•tray•al, be•tray•ment** *n.* **—be•tray•er** *n.*

be•troth (bĭ-trōth′, -trôth′) *tr.v.* **-trothed, -trothing, -troths. 1.** To promise to give in marriage. **2.** To promise to marry.

be•troth•al (bĭ-trō′*th*əl, -trô′thəl) *n.* Also **be•troth•ment** (bĭ-trō*th*′mənt, -trôth′-). **1.** The act of becoming betrothed or of betrothing. **2.** A mutual promise to marry; an engagement.

be•trothed (bĭ-trō*th*d′, -trôtht′) *adj.* Engaged to be married.
~*n., pl.* **betrothed.** A person who is engaged to be married.

bet•ter¹ (bĕt′ər). **1.** Comparative of **good. 2.** Comparative of **well.**
~*adj.* **1.** Greater in excellence or higher in quality. **2.** More useful, suitable, or desirable. **3.** Larger; greater: *the better part of a summer.* **4.** Healthier than before. **—better off.** In a better or wealthier condition.
~*adv.* **1.** In a more useful, suitable, or desirable way. **2.** To a greater or higher extent or degree. **3.** More: *better than a year.* **—go one better.** To outdo or improve upon someone or something. **—had better.** Ought to; would be wise to. **—think better of.** To change one's mind about (a course of action) after reconsideration.
~*n.* **1.** Something more useful, excellent, desirable, or suitable. Usually used with *the.* **2.** *Usually* **betters.** One's superiors, especially in social standing, competence, or intelligence. **—for the better.** Resulting in an improvement. **—for better for worse.** Whatever happens subsequently; despite any future setbacks. **—get** (or **have**) **the better of. 1.** To overcome; defeat. **2.** To gain an advantage over.
~*v.* **bettered, -tering, -ters.** —*tr.* **1.** To improve. Often used reflexively. **2.** To surpass or exceed. —*intr.* To become better. —See Synonyms at **improve.** [Middle English *bettre,* Old English *betera.*]

bet•ter², bet•tor (bĕt′ər) *n.* One who bets.

better half *n.* A spouse. Used humorously.

bet•ter•ment (bĕt′ər-mənt) *n.* **1.** An improvement. **2.** *Usually* **betterments.** *Law.* Any improvement, excluding mere repairs, that adds to the value of real property.

PRONUNCIATION KEY

ă, pat; ā, pay; âr, care;
ä, father, are; b, bib;
ch, church; d, deed; ĕ, pet;
ē, be; f, fife; g, gag; h, hat;
hw, which; ĭ, pit; ī, pie;
îr, pier; j, judge; k, kick;
l, lid, needle; m, mum;
n, no, sudden; ng, thing;
ŏ, pot; ō, toe; ô, paw, for;
oi, noise; ou, out; ŏŏ, book;
ōō, boot; p, pop; r, roar;
s, sauce; sh, ship, dish;
t, tight; th, thin, path;
th, this, bathe; ŭ, cut; ûr, fur;
v, valve; w, with; y, yes;
z, zebra, size; zh, vision;
ə, about, item, edible,
gallop, circus, peaceful

IN FOREIGN WORDS:

à, *Fr.* ami; œ, *Fr.* feu, *Ger.* schön; ü, *Fr.* tu, *Ger.* über; KH, *Ger.* ich, *Scot.* loch; N, *Fr.* bon; y′, *Fr.* Compiègne

STRESS MARKS:

Primary stress: ′
in•cite′ (ĭn-sīt′)
Secondary stress: ′
in′sight′ (ĭn′sīt′)

betting shop *n. Chiefly British.* Licensed premises where bets may be placed; a bookmaker's shop.

be·tween (bǐ-twēn′) *prep.* **1.** Intermediate in the space separating two places or things. **2.** Intermediate to two times, quantities, or degrees: *between 11:00 and 12:00.* **3.** At a point in relation to two specified points, such that a perpendicular from the first point can be dropped to the line joining the two other points. **4.** Connecting spatially: *a path between the house and the road.* **5.** Connecting in reciprocal action or effort: *an agreement between workers and management.* **6.** By the combined efforts of: *Between them, they succeeded.* **7.** In the combined possession of: *They had three dollars between them.* **8.** Either one or the other of: *choose between riding and walking.* **—between you and me.** In strictest confidence. *~adv.* In an intermediate space, position, or time; in the interim. **—in between.** In an intermediate position or situation. [Middle English *betwene,* Old English *betwēonum.*]

be·tween·times (bǐ-twēn′tīmz′) *adv.* In the interval; between other acts.

be·twixt (bǐ-twǐkst′) *adv. Archaic & Poetic.* Between. *~prep. Archaic & Poetic.* Between. **—betwixt and between.** In an intermediate or indecisive state; in a middle position; neither wholly one nor the other. [Middle English *betwix(te),* Old English *betwēohs, betwihs.*]

Beu·lah (byōo′lə). **1.** In the Old Testament, the land of Israel. Isaiah 62:4. **2.** The land of peace described in Bunyan's *Pilgrim's Progress.*

BeV *Physics.* Billion electron volts. The abbreviation **GeV** (gigaelectron volts) is preferred in standard international usage.

Bev·an (běv′ən), **Aneurin,** known as "Nye" (1897–1960). British politician. A coal miner and trade unionist, he was a Labour member of Parliament (1929–60). As minister of health (1945–51) he was the chief architect of the National Health Service.

bev·el (běv′əl) *n.* **1.** The angle or inclination of a line or surface that meets another at any angle other than 90 degrees. **2.** A rule with an adjustable arm, used to measure or draw angles or to fix a surface at an angle. In this sense, also called "bevel square." *~adj.* Inclined at an angle; slanted. *~v.* **beveled, -eling, -els.** Also *chiefly British* **-elled, -elling.** *—tr.* To cut at an inclination that forms an angle other than a right angle. *—intr.* To be inclined; slope. [Old French *bevel* (unattested), from *baif,* open-mouthed, from *bayer,* to gape. See **bay** (space).]

bevel gear *n.* Either of a pair of gears with teeth surfaces cut so that the gear shafts are not parallel.

bev·er·age (běv′rǐj, běv′ə-rǐj) *n.* Any of various liquid refreshments, usually excluding water. [Middle English *beverege,* from Old French *bevrage,* from Vulgar Latin *biberāticum* (unattested), from Latin *bibere,* to drink.]

Bev·er·ly Hills (běv′ər-lē). City in California, completely surrounded by greater Los Angeles. It adjoins Hollywood and is famous as the residential area of wealthy stars of show business.

Bev·in (běv′ĭn), **Ernest** (1881–1951). British trade unionist and politician. Bevin became secretary of the dock workers' union (1911) which became the Transport and General Workers' Union (1921). He entered Parliament (1940) and joined Churchill's war cabinet as minister of labor and national service. As foreign secretary (1945–51) he played an important part in the establishment of NATO.

bev·y (běv′ē) *n., pl.* **-ies. 1.** A group of animals or birds, especially larks or quail. **2.** A group, especially of girls. [15th century : origin obscure.]

be·wail (bǐ-wāl′) *v.* **-wailed, -wailing, -wails.** *—tr.* To express sorrow or regret over; cry or complain about. *—intr.* To wail or lament. **—be·wail′er** *n.* **—be·wail′ment** *n.*

be·ware (bǐ-wâr′) *v.* **-wared, -waring, -wares.** *—tr.* To be on guard against; be cautious of. Used chiefly in the imperative or infinitive. *—intr.* To be wary or careful. Used chiefly in the imperative or infinitive, sometimes with *of.* [Middle English *be war* : BE (imperative) + *war(e),* WARY.]

Bew·ick (byōo′ĭk), **Thomas** (1753–1828). English illustrator and wood engraver whose best-known work is his *History of British Birds* (1797–1804).

be·wil·der (bǐ-wǐl′dər) *tr.v.* **-dered, -dering, -ders. 1.** To confuse or befuddle, especially with numerous conflicting situations, objects, or statements. **2.** *Rare.* To cause to become lost. —See Synonyms at **puzzle.** [BE- + archaic *wilder,* to stray, probably from WILDERNESS.] **—be·wil′der·ing·ly** *adv.*

be·wil·der·ment (bǐ-wǐl′dər-mənt) *n.* **1.** The condition of being bewildered. **2.** A situation of perplexity or confusion.

be·witch (bǐ-wǐch′) *tr.v.* **-witched, -witching, -witches. 1.** To place under one's power by magic; cast a spell over. **2.** To captivate completely; fascinate. [Middle English *bewicchen* : *be-,* thoroughly + *wicchen,* to bewitch, Old English *wiccian.*] **—be·witch′er** *n.* **—be·witch′ing·ly** *adv.* **—be·witch·ment** *n.*

be·wray (bǐ-rā′) *tr.v.* **-wrayed, -wraying, -wrays.** *Archaic.* To disclose, especially inadvertently; betray. [Middle English *bewreien* : *be-,* thoroughly + *wreien,* to accuse, Old English *wrēgan,* from Germanic *wrōgian* (unattested).]

bey (bā) *n.* **1.** A provincial governor in the Ottoman Empire. **2.** A native ruler of the former kingdom of Tunis. **3. a.** A Turkish title of honor and respect. **b.** A Turkish form of address equivalent to *Mr.* [Turkish, prince, lord, gentleman, from Ottoman Turkish *beg.*]

be·yond (bē-ŏnd′) *prep.* **1.** Farther away than; on the far side of. **2.** After a specified time; later than. **3. a.** Past or outside the limits, reach, or scope of. **b.** Not comprehensible to: *It's beyond me.* **4.** In addition to; besides. *~adv.* Farther along; to the farther side. *~n. Sometimes* **Beyond.** That which is outside the scope of human experience; especially, life after death: *the Great Beyond.* [Middle English *beyonde,* Old English *begeondan* : *be,* BY + *geondan,* farther, from *geond,* YONDER.]

Beyrouth. See **Beirut.**

bez·ant, bez·zant (běz′ənt, bə-zănt′) *n.* Also **byz·ant** (bǐz′ənt, bī-zănt′). **1.** A gold coin issued in Byzantium; a solidus. **2.** *Architecture.* A flat disk, used as an ornament. **3.** *Heraldry.* A round gold mark. [Middle English *besant,* from Old French, from Latin *Bȳzantius,* of BYZANTIUM.]

bez·el, bez·il (běz′əl) *n.* **1.** A slanting surface or bevel on the edge of various cutting tools. **2.** The upper, faceted portion of a cut gem, above the girdle. **3.** A groove or flange designed to hold the beveled edge of a watch crystal or a gem. [Probably from Old French *besel†* (unattested).]

be·zique (bə-zēk′) *n.* **1.** A card game similar to whist for two players, played with two packs of cards with all of the cards from two to six removed. **2.** The highest-scoring combination in this game, that of queen of spades and knave of diamonds. [French *bésigue†.*]

be·zoar (bē′zôr′, -zōr′) *n.* A hard gastric or intestinal mass, found chiefly in ruminants and once considered an antidote to poison. [Middle English *bezear,* from Old French *bezar,* from Arabic *bā-zahr,* from Persian *pād-zahr* : *pād,* protecting against, + *zahr,* poison, from (unattested) Old Persian *jathra.*]

bf, bf. boldface.

b.f. 1. boldface. **2.** *Accounting.* brought forward.

B/F *Accounting.* brought forward.

B.F.A. Bachelor of Fine Arts.

Bha·ga·vad-Gi·ta (bä′gə-väd-gē′tə) *n.* A sacred Hindu text that is incorporated into the *Mahabharata,* an ancient Sanskrit epic. It takes the form of a philosophical dialogue in which Krishna, disguised as a charioteer, explains to the prince Arjuna the whole nature of being. [Sanskrit *Bhagavad-gītā,* "Song of the Blessed One" : *Bhágaḥ,* god of wealth, "the allotter," from *bhájati,* apportion, enjoy + *gītā,* a song.]

bha·ji·a (bä′jē-ə) *n.* Also **bha·gi** (bä′jē). An Indian savory consisting of a vegetable deep-fried in gram flour batter. [Hindi.]

bhak·ti (bŭk′tē) *n. Hinduism.* The devotional way of achieving salvation, open to all irrespective of sex or caste. [Sanskrit, "portion," from *bhajati,* he allocates.]

bhang (băng) *n.* **1.** A plant, hemp *(see).* **2.** Any of several narcotics made from hemp. [Hindi *bhāng,* from Sanskrit *bhangā†,* hemp.]

bha·ra·ta na·tyam (bŭr′ə-tə nät′yəm) *n.* Also **bha·ra·ta na·tya** (-yə). A traditional Hindu dance, formerly performed as a religious ceremony, involving pantomime and song. [Sanskrit, "Bharata's dancing" : *Bharata,* supposed author of a classical treatise on dance and drama + *nātyam,* dancing, dramatic art.]

bhin·di (bǐn′dē) *n.* Okra, as used in Indian dishes. [Hindi.]

Bho·pal (bō-päl′). The capital city of Madhya Pradesh state in central India. A major railway junction and trade center, it is the site of the 19th-century Táj-ul-Masjid, the largest mosque in India.

bhp, b.hp. brake horsepower.

Bhu·tan (bōo-tăn′, -tän′). Isolated kingdom in the eastern Himalayas. Although independent, its foreign affairs have been directed by Great Britain (1910–49) and since then by India. The country's eight fertile valleys opening onto the plains of India support more than 95 percent of its people. The main sources of foreign exchange are tourism and exports of timber, postage stamps, fruit, and handicrafts. Less than 5 percent of the people are literate. Area, 47,000 square kilometers (18,142 square miles). Population, 1,500,000. Capital, Thimphu. See map at **India.**

Bhu·tan·ese (bōo′tə-nēz′, -nēs′) *n., pl.* **Bhutanese.** Also **Bhu·ta·ni** (bōo-tä′nē), *pl.* **-nis** or collectively **Bhutani. 1.** A native or inhabitant of Bhutan. **2.** The Sino-Tibetan language spoken in Bhutan. *~adj.* Of or characteristic of Bhutan, its people, or their language or culture.

Bhut·to (bōo′tō), **Zulfikar Ali** (1928–79). Pakistani politician. In 1963 he was appointed foreign minister, quarreled with the government over the peace terms with India (1965), and formed his own opposition party, the Pakistan People's Party (1967). In 1971 he became president of Pakistan and subsequently prime minister (1973). In 1977 he won a massive victory at the polls; but his opponents claimed that he had rigged the elections, and in July he was deposed by an army coup. Two years later he was executed for alleged crimes against the state.

Bi The symbol for the element bismuth.

bi–¹. Variant of **bio-.**

bi–², bin– *prefix.* Indicates: **1.** Two; for example, **binocular. 2. a.** Appearance or occurrence in intervals of two; for example, **bicentennial. b.** Appearance or occurrence twice during; for example, **biannual. 3.** Occurrence on both sides or directions; for example, **biconcave, bilateral. 4.** *Chemistry.* **a.** An acid salt, in which only part of the hydrogen of the acid has been replaced; for example, **sodium bicarbonate. b.** An organic compound containing a double radical; for example, **biphenyl.** [Latin *bi-, bin-,* from *bis,* twice.]

Usage: **Bimonthly** and **biweekly** mean "once every two months" and "once every two weeks." For "twice a month" and "twice a week," the words *semimonthly* and *semiweekly* should be used. But

bezant *An example of this Byzantine gold coin, with a portrait of Justinian I, who ruled in Constantinople* A.D.527–65.

there is a great deal of confusion over the distinction, and a writer is well advised to substitute expressions like "every two months" or "twice a month" where possible. However, used as nouns to denote "a publication that appears every two months," the words with *bi-* are unavoidable.

Bi·a·fra (bē-ä′frə, -ăf′rə). Former region of eastern Nigeria, chiefly peopled by the Ibo. It seceded as Biafra (1967–70), reverting only after a savage civil war. It now forms the federal states of Anambra, Imo, and Cross River. —**Bi·af·ran** *adj. & n.*

Biafra, Bight of. The eastern arm of the Gulf of Guinea on the west coast of Africa, stretching from the Niger delta to northern Gabon.

Bia·ly·stok (bē-ä′lĭ-stŏk′). Industrial and railway city in northeast Poland. Nearly half of the city's population was killed during the Nazi occupation (1941–44).

bi·an·nu·al (bī-ăn′yōō-əl) *adj.* Happening twice each year; semiannual. —**bi·an·nu·al·ly** *adv.*

Usage: There is confusion between this word and *biennial. Biannual* means "twice a year"; *biennial* means "once in two years" or "lasting for two years."

Bi·ar·ritz (bē′ə-rĭts′). Seaside resort and spa in southwestern France, on the Bay of Biscay. It is a fashionable gambling resort.

bi·as (bī′əs) *n.* **1.** A line cutting diagonally across the grain of fabric: *cut cloth on the bias.* **2. a.** Preference or inclination that inhibits impartial judgment; prejudice. **b.** A particular instance of this. **3. a.** A weight or irregularity in a ball that causes it to swerve, as in lawn bowling. **b.** The tendency of such a ball to swerve. **4.** The fixed voltage applied to an electrode, in a valve, transistor, or electronic circuit. **5.** *Statistics.* **a.** An influence that distorts the true expected value of a statistic. **b.** A distortion in findings from an oversight in investigation.
~*adj.* Slanting or diagonal; oblique: *a bias fold.*
~*adv.* Obliquely; aslant.
~*tr.v.* **biased** or **biassed, biasing** or **biassing, biases** or **biasses.** **1.** To cause to have a prejudiced view; prejudice or influence. **2.** To apply a small voltage to (an electrode). [French, from Old French *biais,* oblique, from Old Provençal, perhaps from Greek *epikarsios†,* oblique.]

Usage: Bias has generally been defined as "uninformed or unintentional inclination"; as such it may operate either for or against someone or something. Recently *bias* has been used in the sense of "adverse action or discrimination": *Congress included a provision in the Civil Rights Act of 1964 banning racial bias in employment.*

bias binding *n.* A strip of material cut across the grain of a fabric used to strengthen hems, finish edges, or the like.

bi·ath·lete (bī-ăth′lēt′) *n.* One who takes part in a biathlon.

bi·ath·lon (bī-ăth′lŏn, -lŏn′) *n.* An athletic competition that combines events in cross-country skiing and rifle-shooting. [BI- + Greek *athlon,* contest.]

bi·au·ric·u·lar (bī′ô-rĭk′yə-lər) *adj.* Also **bi·au·ric·u·late** (-lĭt, -lāt′). Possessing two auricles.

bi·ax·i·al (bī-ăk′sē-əl) *adj.* Having two axes. Used especially of crystals that have two optic axes. —**bi·ax·i·al·i·ty** (bī-ak′sē-ăl′ə-tē) *n.* —**bi·ax·i·al·ly** *adv.*

bib (bĭb) *n.* **1.** A piece of cloth or plastic worn under the chin by small children, to protect the clothing during meals. **2.** The part of an apron, smock, or pair of overalls worn over the chest. **3.** A European food fish, *Gadus luscus,* related to the cod, with a barbel on its lower jaw. Also called "pout," "whiting pout."
~*v.* **bibbed, bibbing, bibs.** —*tr.* To drink; imbibe. —*intr.* To indulge in drinking; tipple. [Middle English *bibben,* to tipple, drink, perhaps from Latin *bibere.*]

Bib. Bible; Biblical.

bib and tucker *n.* *Informal.* Clothing; an outfit. Usually used in the phrase *one's best bib and tucker.*

bibb (bĭb) *n.* **1.** A bracket on the mast of a ship to support the trestletrees. **2.** A bibcock *(see).* [Variant of BIB (napkin).]

bib·ber (bĭb′ər) *n.* A tippler; a drinker: *a wine-bibber.* [From BIB (to drink).]

bib·cock (bĭb′kŏk′) *n.* A tap with a nozzle that is bent downward. Also called "bibb." [BIB (napkin) + COCK.]

bi·be·lot (bĭb′lō; *French* bē-blō′). A trinket or small decorative curio. [French, from Old French *beubelet,* from a reduplication of *bel,* beautiful, from Latin *bellus,* handsome, fine.]

bibl., Bibl. Biblical.

Bi·ble (bī′bəl) *n. Abbr.* **B., Bib.** **1.** The sacred book of Christianity, a collection of ancient writings including the books of both the Old Testament and the New Testament, and, in the Roman Catholic Bible, the deuterocanonical books. See **Old Testament, New Testament, Apocrypha, King James Bible, Revised Version, Revised Standard Version, Douay Bible, Vulgate, New English Bible, Jerusalem Bible. 2.** The Old Testament, the sacred book of Judaism. See **Hebrew Scriptures. 3. bible.** Any book or collection of writings constituting the guiding text of a religion, political movement, or individual lifestyle. **4. bible.** Any book considered authoritative in its field. [Middle English, from Old French, from Medieval Latin *biblia,* from Greek *(ta) biblia,* "(the) books," plural of *biblion,* book, originally a diminutive of *biblos, bublos,* papyrus, scroll, book, after *Bublos,* Phoenician port from which the Egyptian papyrus was exported to Greece.]

Bible Belt *n.* Those sections of the United States, especially in the South and Middle West, where Protestant fundamentalism prevails. [Coined by H.L. MENCKEN, *c.* 1925.]

Bible paper *n.* A thin, strong, opaque printing paper used for Bi-

bib *An embroidered chestpiece, or bib, on a Palestinian dress from Bethlehem.*

bles and reference books. Also called "India paper."

Bible thumper *n. Informal.* A person who enthusiastically, dogmatically, and often aggressively expounds and refers to the Bible or religion. —**Bible-thumping** *n. & adj.*

Bib·li·cal (bĭb′lĭ-kəl) *adj. Sometimes* **biblical.** *Abbr.* **Bib., Bibl., bibl. 1.** Of, pertaining to, or contained in the Bible. **2.** In keeping with the nature of the Bible, especially: **a.** Suggestive of the personages or times depicted in the Bible. **b.** Suggestive of the prose or narrative style of the King James Bible. [Obsolete *biblic,* probably from Medieval Latin *biblicus,* from *biblia,* BIBLE.] —**Bib·li·cal·ly** *adv.*

Biblical Aramaic *n.* A form of Aramaic that was the original language of the non-Hebrew portions of the Old Testament, such as certain passages in Ezra, Daniel, and Jeremiah. Also called "Chaldee." Compare **Aramaic.**

Bib·li·cist (bĭb′lə-sĭst) *n.* Also **Bib·list** (bĭb′lĭst). **1.** An expert on the Bible. **2.** A person who interprets the Bible literally. **3.** One who emphasizes the authority of the Bible rather than tradition. [From obsolete *biblic,* BIBLICAL.] —**Bib·li·cism** *n.*

biblio– *prefix.* Indicates books; for example, **bibliomania.** [Greek *biblion,* book. See **Bible.**]

bib·li·o·film (bĭb′lē-ō-fĭlm′) *n.* A type of microfilm used especially to photograph the pages of books.

bibliog. bibliographer; bibliography.

bib·li·og·ra·pher (bĭb′lē-ŏg′rə-fər) *n.* Also **bib·li·o·graph** (bĭb′lē-ə-grăf′, -grăf′). *Abbr.* **bibliog. 1.** An expert in the description and cataloguing of printed matter. **2.** One who compiles a bibliography.

bib·li·og·ra·phy (bĭb′lē-ŏg′rə-fē) *n., pl.* **-phies.** *Abbr.* **bibliog. 1. a.** A list of the works of a particular author or publisher, or of sources of information in print on a particular subject. **b.** A list of sources used as reference for the writing of a book, thesis, or the like. **2. a.** The description and identification of the editions, dates of issue, authorship, and typography of books or other written material. **b.** A compilation of such information. [French *bibliographie,* from New Latin *bibliographia* : BIBLIO- + -GRAPHY.] —**bib·li·o·graph·ic** (bĭb′lē-ə-grăf′ĭk), **bib·li·o·graph·i·cal** *adj.* —**bib·li·o·graph·i·cal·ly** *adv.*

bib·li·ol·a·try (bĭb′lē-ŏl′ə-trē) *n.* **1.** Excessive adherence to a literal interpretation of the Bible. **2.** Extreme devotion to or concern with books. [BIBLIO- + -LATRY.] —**bib·li·ol·a·ter** *n.* —**bib·li·ol·a·trous** *adj.*

bib·li·o·man·cy (bĭb′lē-ō-măn′sē) *n., pl.* **-cies.** Divination by interpretation of a passage chosen at random from a book, especially the Bible. [BIBLIO- + -MANCY.]

bib·li·o·ma·ni·a (bĭb′lē-ō-mā′nē-ə, -mān′yə) *n.* An exaggerated liking for acquiring and owning books. [BIBLIO- + -MANIA.] —**bib·li·o·ma·ni·ac** *n. & adj.* —**bib·li·o·ma·ni·a·cal** (bĭb′lē-ō-mə-nī′ə-kəl) *adj.*

bib·li·o·phile (bĭb′lē-ə-fīl′) *n.* Also **bib·li·o·phil** (-fīl′), **bib·li·oph·i·list** (bĭb′lē-ŏf′ə-lĭst). **1.** One who loves books. **2.** A book collector. [French : BIBLIO- + -PHILE.] —**bib·li·o·phil·ic** (bĭb′lē-ə-fīl′ĭk) *adj.* —**bib·li·oph·i·lism** (bĭb′lē-ŏf′ə-lĭz′əm), **bib·li·oph·i·ly** *n.* —**bib·li·oph·i·lis·tic** (bĭb′lē-ŏf′ə-lĭs′tĭk) *adj.*

bib·li·o·pole (bĭb′lē-ə-pōl′) *n.* Also **bib·li·op·o·list** (bĭb′lē-ŏp′ə-lĭst). A person who deals in rare books. [Latin *bibliopōla,* from Greek *bibliopōlēs* : BIBLIO- + *pōlēs,* seller, from *pōlein,* to sell.] —**bib·li·o·pol·ic** (bĭb′lē-ə-pōl′ĭk) *adj.* —**bib·li·op·o·ly** (bĭb′lē-ŏp′ə-lē) *n.*

bib·li·o·the·ca (bĭb′lē-ə-thē′kə) *n.* **1.** A book collection; a library. **2.** A catalogue of books. [Latin *bibliothēca,* from Greek *bibliothēkē,* "case for books" : BIBLIO- + *thēkē,* receptacle, case.] —**bib·li·o·the·cal** *adj.*

Biblist. Variant of **Biblicist.**

bib·u·lous (bĭb′yə-ləs) *adj.* Given to or marked by convivial drinking. [Latin *bibulus,* from *bibere,* to drink.] —**bib·u·lous·ly** *adv.* —**bib·u·lous·ness** *n.*

bi·cam·er·al (bī-kăm′ər-əl) *adj.* Composed of two houses, chambers, or branches: *a bicameral legislature.* [BI- + Late Latin *camera,* room, CHAMBER.] —**bi·cam·er·al·ism** *n.*

bi·cap·su·lar (bī-kăp′sə-lər, -syōō-lər) *adj. Botany.* **1.** Having two capsules. **2.** Having a capsule with two locules.

bi·carb (bī-kärb′) *n. Informal.* **Sodium bicarbonate** *(see).*

bi·car·bon·ate (bī-kär′bə-nāt′, -nĭt) *n.* The radical group HCO_3 or a compound, such as sodium bicarbonate, containing it. Also called "hydrogen carbonate."

bicarbonate of soda *n.* **Sodium bicarbonate** *(see).*

bice blue *n.* Moderate blue, the color of azurite. [Partial translation of French *azur bis,* "dark blue" : AZURE + *bis,* brown, tawny, from Old French *bis†.*]

bice green *n.* Moderate yellow green, the color of malachite. [See **bice blue.**]

bi·cen·ten·a·ry (bī′sĕn-tĕn′ĕr′ē, -ə-rē) *n., pl.* **-ries.** *Chiefly British.* A bicentennial. —**bi·cen·ten·a·ry** *adj.*

bi·cen·ten·ni·al (bī′sĕn-tĕn′ē-əl) *adj.* **1.** Happening once every 200 years. **2.** Lasting for 200 years. **3.** Pertaining to a 200th anniversary.
~*n.* A 200th anniversary or its celebration.

bi·cen·tric (bī-sĕn′trĭk) *adj.* Having two centers. —**bi·cen·tric·i·ty** (bī-sĕn-trĭs′ə-tē) *n.*

bi·ceph·a·lous (bī-sĕf′ə-ləs) *adj.* Two-headed.

bi·ceps (bī′sĕps′) *n., pl.* **biceps** or **-cepses** (-sĕp′sĭz). Any muscle having two heads or points of origin, especially: **a.** The large muscle at the front of the upper arm that flexes the elbow joint. **b.** The large muscle at the back of the thigh that flexes the knee joint.

[New Latin, from Latin, "two-headed" : BI- + -ceps, from caput, head.]

bi·chlo·ride (bī-klôr′īd′, -klōr′-) n. Chemistry. **Dichloride** (see).

bi·chro·mate (bī-krō′māt′, -mīt). Chemistry. **A dichromate** (see).

bi·cip·i·tal (bī-sĭp′ə-təl) adj. Of or pertaining to the biceps. [New Latin biceps (stem bicipit-), BICEPS.]

bick·er (bĭk′ər) intr.v. -ered, -ering, -ers. 1. To engage in a petty quarrel; squabble. 2. Poetic. To flicker; glisten; quiver. —See Synonyms at **argue**. ~n. A petty quarrel; a tiff. [Middle English bikerent, to attack.] —**bick·er·er** n.

bi·col·or (bī′kŭl′ər) adj. Also **bi·col·ored** (bī′kŭl′ərd). Having two colors.

bi·con·cave (bī′kŏn-kāv′, bī-kŏn′kāv′) adj. Concave on both sides or surfaces. —**bi·con·cav·i·ty** (bī′kŏn-kāv′ə-tē) n.

bi·con·di·tion·al (bī′kən-dĭsh′ən-əl) n. Logic. 1. A statement containing two propositions related in such a way that one can be true only if the other is true, and false only if the other is false. 2. The relation that exists between two such propositions. Compare **equivalence**. —**bi·con·di·tion·al** adj.

bi·con·vex (bī′kŏn-vĕks′, bī-kŏn′vĕks′) adj. Convex on both sides or surfaces. —**bi·con·vex·i·ty** n.

bi·corn (bī′kôrn′) adj. Also **bi·cor·nu·ate** (bī-kôr′nyōō-ĭt, -āt′). 1. Having two horns or two horn-shaped parts. 2. Shaped like a crescent. [Latin bicornis : BI- + cornū, HORN.]

bi·cor·po·ral (bī-kôr′pər-əl) adj. Also **bi·cor·po·re·al** (bī′kôr-pôr′ē-əl, -pōr′ē-əl). Having two distinct bodies or main parts.

bi·cul·tur·al (bī-kŭl′chər-əl) adj. Of or relating to two separate cultures in one community. —**bi·cul·tur·al·ism** n.

bi·cus·pid (bī-kŭs′pĭd) adj. Also **bi·cus·pi·date** (-pə-dāt′). Having two points or cusps, as the crescent moon or the **mitral valve** (see) of the heart do. ~n. A bicuspid tooth, especially a **premolar** (see). [New Latin bicuspis (stem bicuspid-) : BI- + Latin cuspis, point, CUSP.]

bi·cy·cle (bī′sĭk′əl, -sī-kəl) n. A vehicle, usually designed for one person, consisting of a metal frame mounted upon two wire-spoked wheels with narrow rubber tires, one behind the other. It has a seat, handlebars for steering, brakes, and two pedals or a small motor by which it is driven. ~intr.v. **bicycled, -cling, -cles**. To ride or travel on a bicycle. [French : BI- + Greek kuklos, circle, wheel.] —**bi·cy·clist** n.

bicycle pump n. A portable hand pump for inflating bicycle tires.

bi·cy·clic (bī-sī′klĭk, -sĭk′lĭk) adj. Also **bi·cy·cli·cal** (-sī′klĭ-kəl, -sĭk′lĭ-kəl). 1. Consisting of or having two cycles. 2. Botany. Composed of or arranged in two distinct whorls, as are the petals or stamens of a flower. 3. Chemistry. Consisting of or having molecules containing two fused rings.

bid (bĭd) v. For transitive senses 1, 2, 3: **bade** (băd, bād) or archaic **bad** (băd), **bidden** (bĭd′n) or **bid, bidding, bids**. For remaining senses: **bid, bade, bid, bidding, bids**. —tr. **1. a**. To direct; command. **b**. To enjoin politely. **2**. To utter (a greeting or salutation). **3**. To invite to attend; summon. **4**. Card Games. To state one's intention to take (tricks of a certain number or suit): bid four hearts. **5**. To offer or propose (an amount) as a price. —intr. **1**. To make an offer to pay or accept a specified price. **2**. To seek to win or attain something; strive: a bid for the party leadership. —See Synonyms at **command**. —**bid defiance**. To refuse to submit; offer resistance. —**bid fair**. To appear likely; seem. Note: In these phrases the past tense and past participle is **bid**. ~n. **1. a**. An offer or proposal of a price, as for an item at an auction or for a contract. **b**. The amount offered or proposed. **2**. An invitation, especially one offering membership in a group or club. **3**. Card Games. **a**. The act of bidding. **b**. The number of tricks or points declared. **c**. The trump or no-trump declared. **d**. The turn of a player to bid. **4**. A serious attempt to gain something; a striving: a bid for the party leadership. [Bid, bade, bidden; from two verbs: 1. Middle English bidden, ask, beseech, demand, command, bad, beden, Old English biddan, bæd (plural bǣdon), (ge)beden. 2. Middle English beden, to offer, present, proclaim, command (last sense adopted from bidden), bead, boden, Old English bēodan, bēad (plural budon), (ge)boden.] —**bid·der** n.

b.i.d. Medicine. twice a day. [Latin bis in die]

bi·dar·ka (bĭ-där′kə) n. A hide-covered canoe used by Eskimos of Alaska. [Russian baidarka, diminutive of baidarat.]

bid·da·ble (bĭd′ə-bəl) adj. **1**. Worth bidding on. Said of a hand or suit in cards. **2**. Docile; tractable. —**bid·da·bil·i·ty** n.

bid·den. A past participle of **bid**.

bid·ding (bĭd′ĭng) n. **1**. A demand that something be done; a command. **2**. A request to appear; a summons. **3. a**. The act of making bids, as at an auction or in playing cards. **b**. The bids collectively. —**at the bidding of**. At the service of; on the command of. —**do the bidding of**. To follow the orders of.

bid·dy¹ (bĭd′ē) n., pl. -dies. A hen; a fowl. [Perhaps imitative of a call used for hens.]

biddy² n., pl. -dies. Slang. A garrulous or interfering old woman. [Pet form of Bridget, a feminine name.]

bide (bīd) v. **bided** or **bode** (bōd), **bided, biding, bides**. —intr. **1**. To stay in some condition or state; remain the same: "England shall bide till Judgement Tide" (Rudyard Kipling). **2. a**. To wait or tarry: bide for a while. **b**. To stay: bide at home. **c**. To be left; remain: "Waters stink soon, if in one place they bide" (John Donne). —tr. To await. Used only in the phrase bide one's time. [Bide,

bode; Middle English biden, bod (past singular), Old English bīdan, bād.]

bi·den·tate (bī-dĕn′tāt′) adj. **1**. Biology. Having two teeth or two toothlike projecting parts. **2**. Chemistry. Designating a ligand that can coordinate at two separate positions to the same atom or ion.

bi·det (bē-dā′) n. A basinlike fixture designed to be straddled for washing the genitals and the posterior parts. [French, "small horse," possibly from Old French bidert, to trot.]

Bie·der·mei·er (bē′dər-mī′ər) adj. **1**. Of, pertaining to, or designating a type of German furniture of the first half of the 19th century, modeled after Empire styles. **2**. Staid and conventional; philistine. [After Gottlieb Biedermeier, the imaginary humdrum author of poems written by L. Eichroth (1827–92), German poet.]

Biel (bēl). French **Bienne** (byĕn). Town in Bern canton in northwest Switzerland, renowned for its clocks.

Bie·le·feld (bē′lə-fĕlt′). Major industrial city in North Rhine-Westphalia in Germany, long famous as a linen center.

bi·en·ni·al (bī-ĕn′ē-əl) adj. **1**. Lasting or living for two years. **2**. Happening every second year. **3**. Botany. Having a normal life cycle of two years. Compare **annual, perennial**. ~n. **1**. An event that occurs once every two years. **2**. A plant that normally requires two years to reach maturity, producing leaves in the first year, blooming and producing fruit in its second year, and then dying. —See Usage note at **biannual**. [From BIENNIUM.] —**bi·en·ni·al·ly** adv.

bi·en·ni·um (bī-ĕn′ē-əm) n., pl. **-ums** or **-ennia** (-ĕn′ē-ə). A two-year period. [Latin : BI- + annus, year.]

bier (bîr) n. A stand on which a corpse, or a coffin containing a corpse, is placed to lie in state or to be carried to the grave. [Middle English bere, Old English bēr, bær.]

Bierce (bîrs), **Ambrose Gwinnett** (1842–c. 1914). U.S. writer. His scathing wit and fascination with the supernatural influenced many of his works, including The Fiend's Delight (1872), Can Such Things Be? (1893), and The Devil's Dictionary (1906). He disappeared in Mexico and is thought to have died there in a battle.

bi·fa·cial (bī-fā′shəl) adj. **1**. Having two faces, fronts, or façades. **2**. Botany. Having upper and lower surfaces that are distinct and dissimilar. Said of leaves. **3**. Having two opposing surfaces that are alike.

biff (bĭf) tr.v. **biffed, biffing, biffs**. Slang. To strike or punch. ~n. Slang. A blow or cuff. [Imitative.]

bi·fid (bī′fĭd) adj. Biology. Divided or cleft into two parts or lobes. [Latin bifidus : BI- + -FID.] —**bi·fid·i·ty** n. —**bi·fid·ly** adv.

bi·fi·lar (bī-fī′lər) adj. Physics. Fitted with or involving the use of two threads or wires, as in certain types of electrical measuring instruments or resistors. [BI- + FILAR.] —**bi·fi·lar·ly** adv.

bi·flag·el·late (bī-flăj′ə-lĭt, -lāt′) adj. Biology. Having two flagella: a biflagellate protozoan.

bi·fo·cal (bī-fō′kəl) adj. **1**. Having two different focal lengths. **2**. Correcting for both near and distant vision.

bi·fo·cals (bī-fō′kəlz) pl.n. Spectacles with bifocal lenses, used for both near and distant vision.

bi·fo·li·ate (bī-fō′lē-ĭt, -āt′) adj. Having two leaves.

bi·fo·li·o·late (bī-fō′lē-ə-lāt′, -lĭt) adj. Having two leaflets.

bi·fo·rate (bī-fôr′āt′, -fōr′āt′, bī′fə-rāt′) adj. Biology. Having two openings or perforations. [BI- + Latin forātus, past participle of forāre, to pierce, bore.]

bi·forked (bī′fôrkt′) adj. Divided into two branches; bifurcate.

bi·form (bī′fôrm′) adj. Also **bi·formed** (-fôrmd′). Having a combination of features or qualities of two distinct forms, as a sphinx does.

bi·fur·cate (bī′fər-kāt′, bī-fûr′kāt′) v. **-cated, -cating, -cates**. —tr. To divide or separate into two parts or branches. —intr. To separate into two parts; fork. —adj. (bī′fər-kāt′, -kĭt, bī-fûr-kāt′, -kĭt). Also **bi·fur·cat·ed** (-kā′tĭd). Forked or divided into two parts. [Medieval Latin bifurcātus (adjective), from Latin bifurcus, two-forked : BI- + furca, forked stake (see **fork**).] —**bi·fur·cate·ly** adv. —**bi·fur·ca·tion** n.

big (bĭg) adj. **bigger, biggest**. **1**. Of considerable size, number, quantity, magnitude, or extent; large. **2. a**. Obsolete. Of great force or violence: "Farewell the plumed troop and the big wars" (Shakespeare). **b**. Having great intensity; great; strong. **3**. Grown-up. **4**. Elder. **5**. Pregnant. Used with with: big with child. **6**. Filled up; brimming over. **7**. Having or exercising considerable authority, control, or influence. **8**. Conspicuous in position, wealth, or importance; prominent; influential. **9**. Of great significance; important; momentous. **10**. Loud and firm; resounding. **11**. Bountiful; generous; kindly. **12**. Informal. **a**. Self-important; boastful; pompous. **b**. Ambitious: big ideas. —**big on**. Informal. Enthusiastic about: big on women's rights. ~adv. Slang. **1. a**. Pompously; pretentiously; boastfully: "Toad talked big about all he was going to do in the days to come" (Kenneth Grahame). **b**. Ambitiously: think big. **2**. With considerable success; in an outstanding manner: His speech went down big at the conference. [Middle English big, byg, strong, stout, full-grown, probably of Scandinavian origin.] —**big·gish** adj. —**big·ness** n.

big·a·mous (bĭg′ə-məs) adj. **1**. Involving bigamy. **2**. Guilty of bigamy. —**big·a·mous·ly** adv.

big·a·my (bĭg′ə-mē) n., pl. **-mies**. Law. The criminal offense of marrying one person while still legally married to another. [Middle English bigamie, from Old French, from bigame, bigamous, from Late Latin bigamus : BI- + -GAMOUS.] —**big·a·mist** n.

Big Apple n. New York. Used as a nickname, preceded by the.

big·ar·reau (bĭg′ə-rō′) n. Any of several varieties of sweet cherry

bilberry *The bilberry's berrylike flowers appear in early summer, and the blue-gray edible berries in autumn. The bilberry grows on poor soil in northern temperate mountainous areas.*

with firm, often light-colored flesh. [French, from *bigarrer,* to variegate : BI- + Old French *garre*†, variegated.]
big band *n.* A large dance or jazz band.
big-bang theory (bĭg′băng′) *n.* A theory that the universe originated as a small, very dense mass that exploded, throwing out matter in all directions, from which galaxies and stars formed. The theory accounts for the **expanding universe** and the **microwave background** *(both of which see).* Compare **steady-state theory.**
Big Ben *n.* **1.** The bell in the clock tower of the Houses of Parliament in London. **2. a.** The clock itself. **b.** Loosely, the clock tower.
Big Bend. A section of the Columbia River in east-central Washington where the river is forced by lava beds to make a big bend westward before resuming its southerly course.
Big Bend National Park. A park in western Texas on the Mexican border, located in a triangle formed by the Rio Grande. The river and its deep canyons, the desert plain, and the Chisos Mts. offer sharp contrasts in wilderness scenery.
Big Bertha *n.* A large cannon used by the Germans in World War I. [Translation of German *dicke Bertha,* "fat Bertha," after *Bertha* Krupp von Bohlen und Halbach (1886–1957), proprietress of the Krupp Works, where the cannon was made.]
big brother *n.* **1.** An older brother or someone with whom one has a similar protective relationship. **2. Big Brother.** A vague, threatening figure representing the all-seeing, omnipresent power of an authoritarian government. [Sense 2, after *Big Brother,* a character in George Orwell's novel *1984* (1949).]
big business *n.* **1.** Commercial operations on a large scale, especially when regarded as powerful or manipulative. **2.** Any activity or undertaking regarded as commercially successful.
big deal *n. Informal.* An impressive achievement or proposition. ~*interj. Informal.* Used ironically to express contempt.
Big Dipper *n.* A cluster of seven stars in the constellation Ursa Major, four forming the bowl and three the handle of a dipper-shaped configuration. Also called the "Plow," the "Wain," the "Wagon."
bi·gem·i·nal (bī-jĕm′ə-nəl) *adj.* Occurring in pairs; twinned. [Late Latin *bigeminus,* doubled : BI- + Latin *geminus,* paired, double, twin.]
big·eye (bĭg′ī′) *n.* Any of several tropical or subtropical marine fishes of the family Priacanthidae, having large eyes and reddish scales.
big game *n.* **1.** Large animals or fish hunted or caught for sport. **2.** *Slang.* An important objective. **—big-game** (bĭg′gām′) *adj.*
big·gie (bĭg′ē) *n. Informal.* **1.** A bigwig; big wheel. **2.** Something, as a corporation, that is considered big or important.
big gun *n. Slang.* An important person; a bigwig.
big·head (bĭg′hĕd′) *n.* **1.** *Informal.* Conceit; egotism. **2.** Any of various diseases of animals characterized by swelling of the head. **—big·head·ed** (bĭg′hĕd′ĭd) *adj.* **—big·head·ed·ness** *n.*
big·heart·ed (bĭg′här′tĭd) *adj.* Generous; charitable. **—big·heart·ed·ly** *adv.* **—big·heart·ed·ness** *n.*
big·horn (bĭg′hôrn′) *n.* A wild sheep, *Ovis canadensis,* of the mountains of western North America, having massive, curved horns in the male. Also called "mountain sheep," "Rocky Mountain sheep."
Big·horn (bĭg′hôrn′). A river rising in west-central Wyoming and flowing *c.* 742 kilometers (461 miles) northward to join the Yellowstone River in southern Montana.
bight (bīt) *n.* **1. a.** A loop in a rope. **b.** The middle or slack part of an extended rope. **2.** A bend or curve, especially in a shoreline. **3.** A wide bay formed by such a bend or curve.
~*tr.v.* **bighted, bighting, bights.** To tie in or secure with a bight of a rope. [Middle English *byght,* bend, bay, armpit, Old English *byht,* bend, angle.]
big league *n.* **1.** A major league. **2.** Big time. **—big leaguer** *n.*
big-league (bĭg′lēg′) *adj.* **Major-league** *(see).*
big·mouth (bĭg′mouth′) *n. Slang.* A loud-mouthed or gossipy person. **—big·mouthed** (bĭg′mou*th*d′, -moutht′) *adj.*
big·no·ni·a (bĭg-nō′nē-ə) *n.* A tropical American plant of the genus *Bignonia*; especially, the **cross-vine** *(see).* [New Latin, after the Abbé Jean-Paul *Bignon* (1662–1743), librarian to Louis XV.]
big·ot (bĭg′ət) *n.* A person of strong conviction or prejudice, especially in matters of religion, race, or politics, who is intolerant of those who feel differently. [French, from Old French *bigot*†, a pejorative term for the Normans.] **—big·ot·ed** *adj.* **—big·ot·ed·ly** *adv.* **—big·ot·ed·ness** *n.*
big·ot·ry (bĭg′ə-trē) *n.* The attitude, state of mind, or behavior characteristic of a bigot; intolerance.
big shot *n. Slang.* An important, powerful, or influential person.
big stick *n. Informal.* A display or threat of force.
big-tick·et (bĭg′tĭk′ĭt) *adj. Informal.* Having a high price.
big time *n. Slang.* The most prestigious level of attainment in a competitive field. **—big-time** (bĭg′tīm′) *adj.* **—big-tim·er** *n.*
big top *n. Informal.* **1.** The main tent of a circus. **2.** The circus.
big tree *n.* The **giant sequoia** *(see).*
big wheel *n. Slang.* A person of importance.
big·wig (bĭg′wĭg′) *n. Informal.* An important person; a dignitary.
Bi·har (bĭ-här′). State in east-central India, crossed by the Ganges. Patna is the capital. Buddha passed his early years in Bihar, and the town of Buddh Gaya is a leading Buddhist center.
Bi·ha·ri (bē-hä′rē) *n.* **1.** A native or inhabitant of Bihar. **2.** The Indic language spoken in northeastern India. **—Bi·ha·ri** *adj.*
bi·jou (bē′zho͞o′) *n., pl.* **-joux** (-zho͞oz′). **1.** A small, exquisitely wrought trinket. **2.** Any charming, delicately made thing. [French, from Breton *bizou,* ring with a stone, from *biz*†, finger.]
bi·jou·te·rie (bē-zho͞o′tə-rē) *n.* **1.** Jewelry and trinkets. **2.** A collection of jewelry or trinkets. [French, from BIJOU.]
bike (bīk) *n.* **1.** A bicycle. **2.** A motorcycle. **3.** A motorbike. ~*intr.v.* **biked, biking, bikes.** To ride a bike. [Short for BICYCLE.]
bi·ker (bī′kər) *n.* A motorcyclist, especially one who belongs to a motorcycle gang.
bi·ki·ni (bĭ-kē′nē) *n.* A brief two-piece bathing suit worn by women. [French, after BIKINI Atoll (referring to the "atomic" impact of the first bikinis).]
Bi·ki·ni (bĭ-kē′nē). Atoll in the west-central Pacific Ocean, part of the Ralik, or western, chain of the Marshall Islands, now a commonwealth of the United States. The area was used by the U.S. government to test nuclear bombs (1946–58).
Bi·ko (bē′kō), **Steve,** born Bantu Stephen Biko (1947–77). Black South African political leader, honorary president of the Black People's Convention. In 1969 he cofounded the radical "Black Consciousness" movement, the South African Students' Organization. He was expelled from the University of Natal (1973) and joined the Black Community Program to rally black opposition to the Nationalist regime. He spent several periods in police detention and died in September 1977, six days after being arrested.
bi·la·bi·al (bī-lā′bē-əl) *adj.* **1.** *Phonetics.* Pronounced or articulated with both lips. Said of certain consonants, such as *b, p,* and *m.* **2.** Pertaining to or having a pair of lips.
~*n. Phonetics.* A bilabial sound or consonant. **—bi·la·bi·al·ly** *adv.*
bi·la·bi·ate (bī-lā′bē-ĭt, -āt′) *adj. Botany.* Having two lips. Said of a flower or corolla.
bil·an·der (bĭl′ən-dər, bī′lən-) *n.* A small two-masted sailing vessel, used especially on canals in the Low Countries. [Dutch *bijlander,* "ship that sails by the land" : *bij,* by + *land,* land.]
bi·lat·er·al (bī-lăt′ər-əl) *adj.* **1.** Of, pertaining to, or having two sides; two-sided. **2.** Having two symmetrical sides. **3.** Affecting or undertaken by two sides equally; binding on both parties. **4.** Occurring on one of two sides after affecting the other: *bilateral recurrence of breast cancer.* **5.** Pertaining to descent through both the paternal and maternal lines. Compare **unilateral.** **—bi·lat·er·al·ism, bi·lat·er·al·ness** *n.* **—bi·lat·er·al·ly** *adv.*
bilateral symmetry *n.* The arrangement of the parts of an organism or organ in such a way that it can be divided into two halves that are mirror images of each other along only one plane. Compare **radial symmetry.**
Bil·ba·o (bĭl-bä′ō). Major port of Spain, on the Nervión River near the Bay of Biscay. It is the largest city of the three Basque provinces and the center of a heavily industrialized, iron-producing region.
bil·ber·ry (bĭl′bĕr′ē) *n., pl.* **-ries.** **1.** Any of several shrubby or woody plants of the genus *Vaccinium,* having edible blue or blackish berries. The European species, *V. myrtillus,* is also called "whortleberry." **2.** The fruit of any of these plants. [Probably from Scandinavian, akin to Danish *böllebaer* : *bolle,* ball, round roll + *baer,* berry.]
bil·bo (bĭl′bō) *n., pl.* **-boes** or **-bos.** A kind of well-tempered sword, used in former times. [After BILBAO, famous for its ironworks.]
bil·boes (bĭl′bōz) *pl.n.* An iron bar with sliding fetters, formerly used to shackle the feet of prisoners. [16th century : origin obscure.]
Bil·dungs·ro·man (bĭl′dŭngs-rō-män′, -dŭngz-) *n.* A novel concerning the hero's early life and development. [German, "education novel."]
bile (bīl) *n.* **1.** *Physiology.* A bitter, alkaline, brownish-yellow or greenish-yellow liquid that is secreted by the liver, stored in the gall bladder, and discharged into the duodenum, where it aids in digestion, chiefly by emulsifying fats so that they can be more easily absorbed. Bile contains the pigments bilirubin and biliverdin. **2.** Bitterness of temper; irascibility; ill humor; spleen. **3.** In medieval physiology, either of two humors: *black bile,* thought to cause melancholy or *yellow bile,* thought to cause anger. [French, from Latin *bīlis,* from Old Latin *bis(t)lis* (unattested), perhaps from Celtic.]
bile acid *n.* Any of the liver-generated steroid acids that appear in the bile as sodium salts.
bile duct *n.* Any of the ducts that drain bile from the liver. They join to form the *common bile duct,* which opens into the duodenum.
bile salt *n.* **1.** Any of the sodium salts found in the bile. **2.** A mixture of ox-gall salts used medicinally as a hepatic stimulant or laxative.
bilge (bĭlj) *n.* **1.** The lowest inner part of a ship's hull. **2.** Water that collects in this part. Also called "bilge water." **3.** The bulge of a barrel or cask. **4.** *Slang.* Stupid talk; nonsense.
~*v.* **bilged, bilging, bilges.** —*intr.* **1.** To spring a leak in the bilge. **2.** To bulge or swell. —*tr.* To break open the bilge of. [Probably variant of BULGE.] **—bilg·y** *adj.*
bilge keel *n.* Either of two beams or fins fastened lengthwise along the outside of a ship's bilge to inhibit heavy rolling.
bil·har·zi·a·sis (bĭl′här-zī′ə-sĭs) *n.* A disease, **schistosomiasis** *(see).* [New Latin : *Bilharzia,* schistosomes discovered by T. *Bilharz* (1825–62), German parasitologist + -IASIS.]
bil·i·ar·y (bĭl′ē-ĕr′ē) *adj.* Of or pertaining to bile or to bile ducts: *biliary colic.*
biliary cirrhosis *n.* Progressive inflammatory disease of the liver caused by bile-duct obstruction.
bi·lin·e·ar (bī-lĭn′ē-ər) *adj. Mathematics.* Linear with respect to each of two variables or positions.
bi·lin·gual (bī-lĭng′gwəl) *adj.* **1.** Able to speak two languages with

PRONUNCIATION KEY

ă, pat; ā, pay; âr, care;
ä, father, are; b, bib;
ch, church; d, deed; ĕ, pet;
ē, be; f, fife; g, gag; h, hat;
hw, which; ĭ, pit; ī, pie;
îr, pier; j, judge; k, kick;
l, lid, needle; m, mum;
n, no, sudden; ng, thing;
ŏ, pot; ō, toe; ô, paw, for;
oi, noise; ou, out; o͝o, book;
o͞o, boot; p, pop; r, roar;
s, sauce; sh, ship, dish;
t, tight; th, thin, path;
th, this, bathe; ŭ, cut; ûr, fur;
v, valve; w, with; y, yes;
z, zebra, size; zh, vision;
ə, about, item, edible, gallop, circus, peaceful

IN FOREIGN WORDS:

à, *Fr.* ami; œ, *Fr.* feu, *Ger.* schön; ü, *Fr.* tu, *Ger.* über; KH, *Ger.* ich, *Scot.* loch; N, *Fr.* bon; y′, *Fr.* Compiègne

STRESS MARKS:

Primary stress: ′
in·cite′ (ĭn-sīt′)
Secondary stress: ′
in′sight′ (ĭn′sīt′)

equal skill. **2.** Written or expressed in two languages. **3.** In which two languages are used equally: *a bilingual city.*
~n. A bilingual person. [Latin *bilinguis* : BI- + *lingua,* tongue.] **—bi·lin·gual·ly** *adv.*

bi·lin·gual·ism (bī-lĭng′gwə-lĭz′əm) *n.* Habitual use of two languages, especially in speaking.

bil·ious (bĭl′yəs) *adj.* **1.** Of, pertaining to, or containing bile; biliary. **2.** Pertaining to, characterized by, or experiencing gastric distress, especially nausea and vomiting, caused by sluggishness of the liver or gallbladder. **3.** Reminiscent of bile, especially in color; sickly. **4.** Of a peevish disposition; sour-tempered; irascible. **—bil·ious·ly** *adv.* **—bil·ious·ness** *n.*

bil·i·ru·bin (bĭl′ə-rōō′bĭn, bĭ′lə-) *n.* A reddish-yellow organic compound, $C_{33}H_{36}O_6N_4$, occurring in bile and derived from hemoglobin during normal and pathological destruction of erythrocytes. [Latin *bīlis,* BILE + *ruber,* red.]

-bility *suffix.* Indicates quality or state of being; for example, **capability, visibility.** [Middle English *-bilite,* from Old French, from Latin *-bilitās,* from *-bilis,* adjective suffix. See **-able.**]

bil·i·ver·din (bĭl′ə-vûr′dĭn) *n.* A green compound, $C_{33}H_{34}O_6N_4$, occurring in bile, sometimes formed by oxidation of bilirubin. [Swedish : *bili-,* from Latin *bīlis,* BILE + obsolete French *verd,* green, from Latin *viridis,* from *virēre,* to be green.]

bilk (bĭlk) *tr.v.* **bilked, bilking, bilks. 1.** To defraud, cheat, or swindle. Often used with *out of.* **2.** To evade payment of. **3.** To balk or frustrate. **4.** To elude.
~n. **1.** One who cheats. **2.** A hoax or swindle. [Perhaps an alteration of BALK (to refuse to go farther), originally used in cribbage, "to deprive an opponent of his score."] **—bilk·er** *n.*

bill¹ (bĭl) *n.* **1.** An itemized statement of money owed for goods or services supplied. **2.** A statement or list of particulars, such as a playbill or menu. **3.** The entertainment offered by a theater. **4.** An advertising poster or similar public notice. **5.** A piece of legal paper money; a banknote. **6.** A bill of exchange *(see)* or a similar commercial note. **7.** A draft of a proposed law presented for approval to a legislative body. **8.** *Law.* A bill of indictment *(see).* **—fill** (or **fit**) **the bill.** *Informal.* To be quite satisfactory; meet all necessary requirements. **—foot the bill.** *Informal.* To pay the complete cost of. *~tr.v.* **billed, billing, bills. 1.** To present a statement of costs or charges to. **2.** To enter on a statement of costs or a particularized list. **3.** To advertise, announce, or schedule, either by public notice or as part of a program. [Middle English *bille,* from Norman French, from Medieval Latin *billa,* variant of *bulla,* seal affixed to a document, document, from Latin, bubble, ball, amulet.]

bill² *n.* **1.** The beak of a bird. **2.** A beaklike mouth-part, such as that of a turtle. **3.** The visor of a cap. **4.** The tip of the fluke of an anchor.
~intr.v. **billed, billing, bills.** To touch beaks together. **—bill and coo.** To kiss and murmur amorously. [Middle English *bile.*]

bill³ *n.* **1.** A pruning implement, a billhook *(see).* **2.** A halberd or similar weapon with a hooked blade and a long handle. [Middle English *bil,* Old English *bil.*]

bil·la·bong (bĭl′ə-bông′, -bŏng) *n. Australian.* **1.** A dead-end channel extending from the main stream of a river. **2.** A stream bed filled with water only in the rainy season. **3.** A stagnant pool or backwater. [Native Australian name : *billa,* river, water + *bong,* dead.]

bill·board (bĭl′bôrd′, -bōrd′) *n.* **1.** A structure for the display of advertisements in public places or alongside highways. Also *chiefly British* "hoarding." **2.** *Broadcasting.* The opening listing of title, sponsors, products, talent, and the like, designed to stimulate audience interest in the program to follow.

bill·er (bĭl′ər) *n.* **1.** A clerk who makes out bills. **2.** A machine for making out bills.

bil·let¹ (bĭl′ĭt) *n.* **1.** A lodging for troops in a nonmilitary building. **2.** A written order directing that such quarters be provided. **3.** Any assigned quarters. **4.** *Informal.* A position of employment; a job. *~v.* **billeted, -leting, -lets.** *—tr.* **1.** To quarter (soldiers), especially in nonmilitary buildings. **2.** To serve (a person) with an order to provide such quarters. **3.** To assign lodging to. *—intr.* To be quartered; lodge. [Middle English *bylett,* from Old French *billette, bullette,* diminutives of *bulle,* document, from Medieval Latin *bulla,* document, BILL.]

billet² *n.* **1.** A short, thick piece of firewood. **2.** *Architecture.* One of a series of square or log-shaped decorations forming part of a molding. **3.** A bar of iron or steel in an intermediate stage of manufacture. **4. a.** The part of a harness strap that passes through a buckle. **b.** A loop or pocket for securing the tongue of a harness strap. [Middle English, from Old French *billette, billot,* diminutive of *bille,* log, block, tree trunk, from Medieval Latin *billus, billa,* branch, trunk, probably from Celtic; akin to Irish *bile†,* sacred tree, large tree.]

bil·let-doux (bĭl′ā-dōō′, bĭl′ē-) *n., pl.* **billets-doux** (-dōōz′). A love letter. [French : *billet,* short note, from Old French *billette, bullette,* short note, BILLET¹ + *doux,* sweet.]

bill·fish (bĭl′fĭsh′) *n., pl.* **-fishes** or collectively **billfish. 1.** Any of various fishes of the family Istiophoridae, such as a marlin or sailfish, having an elongated, swordlike or spearlike snout and upper jaw. **2.** Any of various other fishes having long, pointed jaws.

bill·fold (bĭl′fōld′) *n.* A folding pocket-sized case for carrying money and personal documents; a wallet.

bill·head (bĭl′hĕd′) *n.* A sheet of paper with a business name and address printed at the top, used for making out bills.

bill·hook (bĭl′hŏŏk′) *n.* An implement with a curved blade attached to a handle, used especially for clearing brush and for rough pruning. Also called "bill."

bil·liard (bĭl′yərd) *adj.* Of, pertaining to, or used in billiards.
~n. A shot in billiards; a carom.

bil·liards (bĭl′yərdz) *n. Used with a singular verb.* **1.** A game played on a rectangular, cloth-covered table with raised, cushioned edges, in which a long, tapering cue is used to hit three small, hard balls against one another or the side cushions of the table. **2.** Any of several similar games, such as one played on a table with pockets. Compare **pool, snooker.** [French *billard,* bent stick, billiard cue, from Old French, from *bille,* log. See **billet** (stick).]

bill·ing (bĭl′ĭng) *n.* **1.** The relative importance of performers as indicated by the position and type size in which their names are listed on programs, theater billboards, or advertisements. **2. a.** Advertising. **b.** *Often* **billings.** The total amount of business done in a specific period, as by a company.

Bil·lings (bĭl′ĭngz). A city in southern Montana, on the Yellowstone River. Founded in 1882 by the Northern Pacific Railroad, Billings today is a trade and manufacturing center for the surrounding area. Yellowstone National Park is nearby.

Billings, Josh. See Henry Wheeler **Shaw.**

bil·lings·gate (bĭl′ĭngz-gāt′; *British* bĭl′ĭngz-gĭt) *n.* Foul-mouthed abuse. [With allusion to scurrilous fishmongers at BILLINGSGATE.]

Billingsgate. Formerly, the oldest market in London, situated at the north end of London Bridge until it moved to West India Dock (1982). It had been principally a fish market since the 16th century.

bil·lion (bĭl′yən) *n., pl.* **billion** (for senses 1 and 2), or **-lions** (for sense 3). **1.** The cardinal number represented by 1 followed by 9 zeros, usually written 10^9. Also *British* "milliard." **2.** *Chiefly British.* The cardinal number represented by 1 followed by 12 zeros, usually written 10^{12}. **3.** An indefinitely large number. [French : BI- + (M)ILLION.] **—bil·lion** *adj.*

bil·lion·aire (bĭl′yə-nâr′) *n.* A person whose wealth amounts to at least a billion dollars, pounds, or comparable monetary units. [*billion* + *millionaire.*]

bil·lionth (bĭl′yənth) *n.* **1.** The ordinal number one billion in a series. **2.** One of a billion equal parts. **—bil·lionth** *adj. & adv.*

bill of attainder *n.* A former legislative act, last used in the 18th century, pronouncing a person guilty of a crime, usually treason, without trial and subjecting that person to **attainder** *(see).*

bill of exchange *n. Abbr.* **B/E** A written order directing that a specified sum of money be paid to a specified person on a specified date. Also called "bill."

bill of fare *n.* A menu.

bill of health *n.* A certificate stating whether or not there is infectious disease aboard a ship or in its port of departure, and given to the ship's master for presentation at the next port of arrival. **—clean bill of health.** *Informal.* A statement that someone or something is in a satisfactory condition.

bill of indictment *n. Law.* A written statement charging someone with a crime, formerly presented to a grand jury to be ratified. Also called "bill."

bill of lading *n. Abbr.* **B/L** A document listing and acknowledging receipt of goods for shipment.

bill of rights *n.* **1.** A formal summary of those rights and liberties considered essential to a people or group of people. **2. Bill of Rights.** The first ten amendments to the Constitution of the United States. **3. Bill of Rights.** A declaration of rights restricting the power of the Crown, enacted by the English Parliament in 1689.

bill of sale *n. Abbr.* **b.s.** A document that attests a transference of the ownership of personal property.

bil·lon (bĭl′ən) *n.* **1.** An alloy of gold or silver with a greater proportion of another metal such as tin or copper, used in making coins. **2.** An alloy of silver with a high percentage of copper, used in making medals and tokens. [French, from Old French, ingot, from *bille,* log. See **billet** (stick).]

bil·low (bĭl′ō) *n.* **1.** A large wave or ocean swell. **2.** A great swell or surge, as of smoke or sound.
~v. **billowed, -lowing, -lows.** *—intr.* **1.** To surge or roll in or as if in billows. **2.** To swell out: *The sails billowed in the wind.* *—tr.* **1.** To cause to swell or rise in billows. [Old Norse *bylgja.*] **—bil·low·i·ness** *n.* **—bil·low·y** *adj.*

bill-post·er (bĭl′pōs′tər) *n.* One who posts notices, posters, or advertisements. Also called "billsticker." **—bill-post·ing** *n.*

bil·ly¹ (bĭl′ē) *n., pl.* **-lies.** *Informal.* A billy club *(see).* [Probably from the name *Billy,* pet form of William.]

billy² *n., pl.* **-lies.** *Australian.* A metal pot or kettle used in camp cooking. [Short for *billycan* : *billa,* a native Australian word for water + CAN (container).]

billy club *n.* A short wooden club, especially a policeman's club.

bil·ly·cock (bĭl′ē-kŏk′) *n. British.* A man's felt hat with a low crown, similar to a derby. [Possibly after *Billy* or William *Coke,* nephew of Thomas William Coke, Earl of Leicester (1752–1842), for whom the first billycock was made.]

billy goat *n. Informal.* A male goat. Compare **nanny goat.**

Bil·ly the Kid (bĭl′ē). See William H. **Bonney.**

bi·lo·bate (bī-lō′bāt′) *adj.* Also **bi·lo·bat·ed** (-bā′tĭd), **bi·lobed** (bī′lōbd′). Divided into or having two lobes.

bi·loc·u·lar (bī-lŏk′yə-lər) *adj.* Also **bi·loc·u·late** (-lĭt, -lāt′). *Biology.* Divided into or containing two chambers, cavities, or cells. [BI- + LOCULUS.]

Bi·lox·i¹ (bə-lŭk′sē, -lŏk′sē) *n., pl.* **-is** or collectively **Biloxi.** One of a tribe of Siouan-speaking North American Indians originally inhabiting the area of the lower Mississippi River.

Biloxi². A city in southeastern Mississippi, on a peninsula between Biloxi Bay and Mississippi Sound, on the Gulf of Mexico. It is a popular resort, and its industries include fishing, boatbuilding, shrimp and oyster packing, and the manufacture of small appliances. Old Biloxi was first settled by the French in 1699.

bil·sted (bĭl'stĕd') *n.* A tree, the **sweet gum** *(see).* [Origin obscure.]

bil·tong (bĭl'tŏng', -tông') *n. South African.* Narrow strips of meat, salted and dried in the sun. [Afrikaans : *bil,* buttock + *tong,* tongue.]

bimah. Variant of **bema.**

bi·man·u·al (bī-măn'yōō-əl) *adj.* Using or requiring the use of both hands. —**bi·man·u·al·ly** *adv.*

bi·max·il·lar·y (bī-măk'sə-lĕr'ē) *adj.* Pertaining to the two halves of the maxilla.

bi·mes·tri·al (bī-mĕs'trē-əl) *adj.* Bimonthly. [Latin *bimē(n)stris* : BI- + *mēnsis,* month.]

bi·me·tal·lic (bī'mə-tăl'ĭk) *adj.* **1.** Consisting of two metals. **2.** Of, based on, or employing the principles of bimetallism.

bimetallic strip *n.* A strip consisting of two metals welded together, each metal having a different coefficient of expansion, so that a change of temperature causes the strip to buckle. Bimetallic strips are used in switches, thermostats, and the like.

bi·met·al·lism (bī-mĕt'l-ĭz'əm) *n.* **1.** The use of gold and silver as the monetary standard of currency and value. **2.** The doctrine advocating such a standard. —**bi·met·al·list** *n.*

Bi·mi·nis (bĭm'ə-nēz). A group of small islands in the Straits of Florida, in the northwestern section of the Bahamas. According to legend, the Biminis are the site of the Fountain of Youth sought by Juan Ponce de León.

bi·mod·al (bī-mōd'l) *adj.* Having two distinct statistical modes. —**bi·mo·dal·i·ty** (bī'mō-dăl'ə-tē) *n.*

bi·mo·lec·u·lar (bī'mə-lĕk'yə-lər) *adj.* Pertaining to, consisting of, or affecting two molecules.

bi·month·ly (bī-mŭnth'lē) *adj.* **1.** Happening every two months. **2.** Happening twice a month; semimonthly.
—*adv.* **1.** Once every two months. **2.** Twice a month; semimonthly. —*n., pl.* **bimonthlies.** A publication issued bimonthly. —See Usage note at **bi-.**

bi·morph (bī'môrf') *n.* Also **bimorph cell.** *Electronics.* A cell consisting of two piezoelectric crystals cemented together so that a voltage applied to the cell causes one crystal to expand and the other to contract or so that a mechanical deformation of the cell causes a voltage to be generated. Bimorphs are used in microphones, vibration detectors, record player pickups, and the like.

bi·mor·phe·mic (bī'môr-fē'mĭk) *adj.* Consisting of two morphemes.

bi·mo·tored (bī-mō'tərd) *adj.* Possessing, especially powered by, two motors.

bin (bĭn) *n.* **1.** A storage receptacle or container. **2.** *Slang.* A **loony bin** *(see).* **3.** A storage rack containing one kind of wine.
—*tr.v.* **binned, binning, bins.** To place or store in a bin. [Middle English *binne,* Old English *binn, binne,* basket, crib.]

bin-. Variant of **bi-.**

bi·nal (bī'nəl) *adj.* Twofold; double. [New Latin *binalis,* twin, from Latin *bini,* two by two.]

bi·na·ry (bī'nə-rē) *adj.* **1.** Characterized by or composed of two different parts; twofold; double. **2.** *Chemistry.* Consisting of or containing only molecules consisting of just two kinds of atoms. **3.** Of, designating, or belonging to a number system that has 2 as its base. **4.** Of or pertaining to an alloy consisting of two components. **5.** *Music.* Having two subjects or themes.
—*n., pl.* **binaries.** An entity consisting of two distinct parts, especially a **binary star** *(see).* [Late Latin *bīnārius,* from *bīnī,* two by two.]

binary code *n. Computer Science.* A code consisting of a unique group of bits, each having two possible values, used to represent each of a set of numbers or letters.

binary coded decimal *n. Abbr.* **BCD** A number in binary code expressed in groups of four bits, each group representing one digit of the decimal number.

binary digit *n.* Either of the digits 0 or 1 used to express a number in the binary notation.

binary fission *n.* **Fission** *(see),* especially of a cell or of an atomic nucleus, that results in just two approximately equal products.

binary measure *n. Music.* A measure of two beats to the bar.

binary notation *n. British.* The **binary numeration system** *(see).*

binary numeration system *n.* A system of numeration, based on 2, in which the numerals are represented as sums of powers of 2 and in which all numerals can be written using the symbols 0 and 1. The system is used in computers, as the digits 0 and 1 can be represented by an electrical system in the "off" and "on" states.

binary operation *n.* An operation, such as addition, that is applied to two elements of a set to produce a single element of the set.

binary star *n.* A stellar system consisting of two stars orbiting about a common center of mass and often appearing as a single visual or telescopic object. Also called "binary," "double star."

bi·nate (bī'nāt') *adj. Botany.* Consisting of two parts or divisions; growing in pairs: *a binate leaf.* [Latin *bīnī,* two by two.] —**bi·nate·ly** *adv.*

bi·na·tion·al (bī-năsh'ə-nəl) *adj.* Of, relating to, or involving two nations.

bin·au·ral (bī-nôr'əl, bĭn-ôr'əl) *adj.* **1.** Having or related to two ears;

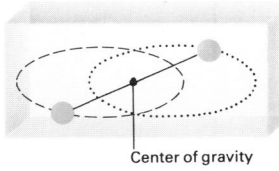
Center of gravity

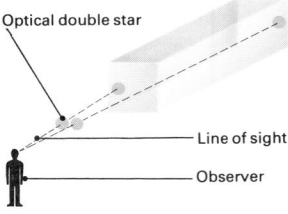
Optical double star

Line of sight
Observer

binary star *Many stars are in pairs, revolving around a common center of gravity, and appearing from earth to be a single star (upper illustration). An optical double star is a pair that are actually very far from each other, but lie in almost the same line of sight (lower illustration).*

hearing with both ears. **2.** Of or pertaining to sound transmission from two sources, which may vary acoustically, as in tone or pitch, relative to a listener. Compare **stereophonic.**
—*n.* Binaural sound recording or transmission. [BIN- + AURAL.]

bind (bīnd) *v.* **bound** (bound), **binding, binds.** —*tr.* **1.** To tie or secure, as with a rope or cord. **2.** To fasten or wrap by encircling with a belt, girdle, or the like. **3.** To bandage. Often used with *up: bind up a wound.* **4.** To hold or restrain with or as if with bonds. **5.** To compel, obligate, or unite, as with a sense of moral duty. **6.** *Law.* To place under legal obligation by contract or oath. **7.** To make certain or irrevocable: *bind a bargain.* **8.** To hold or employ as an apprentice; indenture. Often used with *out* or *over.* **9.** To cause to cohere or stick together in a mass. **10.** To enclose and fasten (a book) between covers. **11.** To furnish with an edge or border for reinforcement or ornamentation. **12.** To constipate. **13.** *Chemistry.* To cause to form a chemical bond. —*intr.* **1.** To tie up or fasten anything. **2.** To be tight and uncomfortable. **3.** To become stiff, compact, or solid; cohere; jam. **4.** To be obligatory or compulsory. **5.** *Chemistry.* To form a chemical bond. —**bind off.** In knitting, to cast off (stitches). —**bind over.** *Law.* To hold on bail or place under bond.
—*n.* **1. a.** Something that binds. **b.** The act of binding. **c.** The state of being bound. **2.** *Informal.* A difficult situation or dilemma. **3.** *Music.* A **tie** *(see).* **4.** A twining plant, **bine** *(see).* [Bind, bound, bound; Middle English *binden, bond, b(o)unden,* Old English *bindan, band* (plural *bundon), bunden.*]

bind·er (bīn'dər) *n.* **1.** One who binds books by trade; a bookbinder. **2.** Something used to tie or fasten, such as a cord, rope, or band. **3.** A notebook cover with rings or clamps for holding sheets of paper. **4.** A material used to ensure uniform consistency, solidification, or adhesion to a surface, as the eggs in batter or the gum in paint. **5. a.** An attachment on a reaping machine that ties grain in bundles. **b.** A machine for reaping and tying grain. **6.** *Law.* A payment or written statement making an agreement legally binding until the completion of a formal contract, especially an insurance contract. **7.** A beam or steel girder supporting floor joists.

bind·er·y (bīn'də-rē) *n., pl.* **-ies.** A place where books are bound.

bind-i-eye (bīn'dē-ī') *n.* Any small Australian perennial herb of the genus *Calotis,* having burrlike fruit. [20th century : origin obscure.]

bind·ing (bīn'dĭng) *n.* **1.** The action or process of one that binds. **2.** Something that binds or is used as a binder. **3.** The cover that holds together the pages of a book. **4.** A strip sewn or attached over or along the edge of something for protection, reinforcement, or ornamentation.
—*adj.* **1.** Serving to bind. **2.** Uncomfortably tight and confining. **3.** Having the power to hold to an agreement or commitment; obligatory. —**bind·ing·ly** *adv.* —**bind·ing·ness** *n.*

binding energy *n. Symbol* E_B **1.** The net energy required to decompose a system, especially an atomic nucleus, into its constituent particles. Also called "mass defect." **2.** The net energy required to remove a particle from a system, especially to remove an electron from its orbit in an atom or molecule. See **ionization potential.**

bin·dle·stiff (bīnd'l-stĭf') *n. Slang.* A migrant worker or hobo who carries his own bedroll. [*Bindle,* alteration of BUNDLE + STIFF.]

bind·weed (bīnd'wēd') *n.* **1.** Any of several trailing or twining plants of the genera *Convolvulus* and *Calystegia,* having pink or white trumpet-shaped flowers. **2.** Any of various similar trailing or twining plants.

bine (bīn) *n.* **1.** The flexible stem of any of various climbing and twining plants, such as the hop, woodbine, or bindweed. **2.** Any of these plants. [Variant of dialectal *bind,* clinging vine, Middle English *bynde,* from BIND.]

Bi·net-Si·mon scale (bĭ-nā'sī'mən) *n.* A scale evaluating mental ability through a series of early psychological tests of childhood intelligence. Also called "Binet Scale," "Binet-Simon test." See **Stanford-Binet scale.** [After Alfred *Binet* (1857-1911) and Théodore *Simon* (1873-1961), French psychologists.]

Bing (bĭng), **Sir Rudolph** (1902-). Opera impresario, born in Austria, but a naturalized British citizen after 1946. He was the general manager of the Glyndebourne opera festival (1934-49) and gained international recognition for his work at the Metropolitan Opera in New York, where he was the general manager (1950-72).

binge (bĭnj) *n. Slang.* **1.** A drunken spree or revel. **2.** A burst of self-indulgence in something, especially after a period of restraint.
—*intr.v.* **binged, binging, binges.** *Informal.* To be uncontrolled and self-indulgent, especially by overeating. [British dialectal *binge†,* to fill a boat with water, to drink heavily.]

bin·go (bĭng'gō) *n.* A game of chance in which players place markers on a pattern of numbered squares according to numbers drawn and announced by a caller. Compare **lotto, keno.**
—*interj.* **1.** Used by a player to announce a win. **2.** Used to express pleasurable surprise or unexpected satisfaction. [Originally the winner's exclamation, from *bing,* ringing sound, sound expressing surprise (imitative).]

bin·man (bĭn'mən) *n., pl.* **-men** (-mĭn). *British.* A trash or garbage collector.

bin·na·cle (bĭn'ə-kəl) *n.* The nonmagnetic stand on which a ship's compass case is supported. [Earlier *bittacle,* from Middle English *bitakle,* from Spanish *bitácula* or Portuguese *bitácola,* from Latin *habitáculum,* little house, from *habitáre,* to dwell, abide, from *habēre,* to have.]

bin·oc·u·lar (bə-nŏk'yə-lər, bī-) *adj.* **1.** Pertaining to, used by, or

COUNTING IN "DOUBLING UP"

A mathematical "language" for the computer

Human beings count in tens (the decimal system) because we have ten fingers and thumbs. A computer, however, "thinks" in terms of just two possibilities and so counts in twos. Either a signal is passing a point in the computer's circuitry or it is not. The binary system, or counting in twos, is just as convenient for computer design as the decimal system is for humans.

In the familiar decimal system, with hundreds, tens, units, and so on, moving a number one place to the left has the effect of multiplying its value by 10. Thus, 357 in the decimal system means 3 hundreds + 5 tens + 7 units. The binary system uses only two symbols, 0 and 1, and moving a number one place to the left has the effect of doubling its value.

In the binary system all numbers are composed of successive doublings of the numbers 1 and 0. The value of 0 can, of course, be doubled an infinite number of times and it will still be 0. The value of 1, as it is doubled, becomes: 2, 4, 8, 16, 32, 64, 128, 256, and so on. So the three-figure number 357 is written in the binary system as 101100101. This is because it is made up of 256 + 0 + 64 + 32 + 0 + 0 + 4 + 0 + 1. The chart below explains why this is so:

Binary scale	256	128	64	32	16	8	4	2	1	
Binary numbers:	1	0	1	1	0	0	1	0	1	
Decimal equivalent:	256	0	+ 64	+ 32	0	0	+ 4	0	+ 1	= 357

The first ten binary numbers are:

Binary numbers	1	10	11	100	101	110	111	1000	1001	1010
Decimal equivalent	1	2	3	4	5	6	7	8	9	10
Explanation	1	2 + 0	2 + 1	4 + 0 + 0	4 + 0 + 1	4 + 2 + 0	4 + 2 + 1	8 + 0 + 0 + 0	8 + 0 + 0 + 1	8 + 0 + 2 + 0

Fractions are represented by figures to the right of the "binary point," which is similar to the decimal point, except that it halves the value of each number to the right, instead of dividing it by 10 as happens in the decimal system.

Clearly the number of digits employed in the binary codes makes the system too cumbersome for anything but the simplest calculations in mental arithmetic. But, when the system is applied to computers, the difficulties raised by the length of the sequences are far outweighed by the ease of handling just two signals, which can be represented in electromagnetic terms by the presence or absence of a pulse. For this reason, digital computers—those built to process purely numerical information—all work with the binary system.

Modern computers can store and integrate millions of "bits" (*bi*nary dig*its*), and since the pulses travel at the speed of light, they can perform millions of calculations per second.

---

involving both eyes at the same time. **2.** Having two eyes arranged to produce stereoscopic vision.
~*n.* Often **binoculars.** An optical device, especially a pair of field glasses, designed for use by both eyes at once. [BIN- + OCULAR.] —**bin·oc·u·lar·i·ty** *n.* —**bin·oc·u·lar·ly** *adv.*
binocular vision *n.* The ability of both eyes to focus on the same object at the same time, possessed by primates (including man) and predators (such as owls).
bi·no·mi·al (bī-nō′mē-əl) *adj.* Consisting of or pertaining to two names or terms.
~*n.* **1.** *Mathematics.* An expression consisting of two terms connected by a plus or minus sign; a polynomial in two terms. **2.** A taxonomic name in **binomial nomenclature** (*see*). [New Latin *binōmium* : BI- + Greek *nomos,* portion, part.] —**bi·no·mi·al·ly** *adv.*
binomial distribution *n. Statistics.* The frequency distribution of the probability of a specified number of successes in an arbitrary number of repeated independent Bernoulli trials. Also called "Bernoulli distribution."
binomial nomenclature *n.* A system of naming plants and animals by a double name, the first of which is the name of the genus and the second that of the species within the genus; for example, *Odobenus rosmarus,* the walrus.
binomial theorem *n.* A mathematical theorem that specifies the expansion of a binomial to any power without requiring the explicit multiplication of the binomial terms. If n is a positive integer, $(x+a)^n = x^n + (n/1!) ax^{n-1} + [n(n-1)/2!]a^2x^{n-2} + \ldots a^n$.
binto. Variant of **beento.**
bin·tu·rong (bĭn′tyə-rŏng) *n.* An arboreal mammal, *Arctictis binturong,* of Southeast Asia, closely related to the palm civets. It has shaggy hair and a prehensile tail. [Malay.]
bi·nu·cle·ate (bī-nōō′klē-ĭt, -āt′, bī-nyōō′-) *adj.* Also **bi·nu·cle·ar** (-ər), **bi·nu·cle·at·ed** (-ā′tĭd). Having two nuclei.
Bin·yon (bĭn′yən), **Laurence** (1869–1943). English poet and art critic. His most valuable pieces of art criticism and history were on Oriental subjects. He is best known for his poem "For the Fallen," from which the quatrain beginning "They shall grow not old" is traditionally recited at services honoring the war dead.
bio-, bi- *prefix.* Indicates: **1.** Life or living organisms; for example, **biocide, bionics. 2.** Biology; for example, **biophysics.** [Greek, from *bios,* life, mode of life.]
bi·o·as·say, bi·o·as·say (bī′ō-ăs′ā′, -ă-sā′) *n.* Evaluation of the activity of a drug, hormone, or other substance by comparison of its effect with that of a standard on a test organism. —**bi·o·as·say** *v.*
bi·o·as·tro·nau·tics (bī′ō-ăs′trə-nô′tĭks) *n. Used with a singular verb.* The study of the biological and medical effects of space flight.
bi·o·cat·a·lyst (bī′ō-kăt′l-ĭst) *n.* A substance, especially an enzyme, that initiates or modifies the rate of a biological process. —**bi·o·cat·a·lyt·ic** (bī′ō-kăt′l-ĭt′ĭk) *adj.*
biochemical oxygen demand *n. Abbr.* **BOD** The amount of oxygen required to meet the metabolic needs of microorganisms in a sample of water in a given period of time, used as a measure of the organic pollution of water. Also called "biological oxygen demand."
bi·o·chem·is·try (bī′ō-kěm′ĭ-strē) *n.* The chemistry of biological substances and processes. —**bi·o·chem·i·cal** *adj.* —**bi·o·chem·i·cal·ly** *adv.* —**bi·o·chem·ist** *n.*
bi·o·cide (bī′ə-sīd′) *n.* A substance, such as a pesticide or an antibiotic, that is capable of destroying living organisms. [BIO- + -CIDE.] —**bi·o·ci·dal** *adj.*
bi·o·cli·ma·tol·o·gy (bī′ō-klī′mə-tŏl′ə-jē) *n.* The study of the effects of climatic conditions on organic life.
bi·o·de·grad·a·ble (bī′ō-dĭ-grā′də-bəl) *adj.* Capable of being decomposed by natural biological processes: *a biodegradable detergent.*
bi·o·en·er·get·ics (bī′ō-ĕn-ər-jĕt′ĭks) *n. Used with a singular verb.* The study of energy relationships between organisms, particularly the cycle of energy in a natural community. —**bi·o·en·er·get·ic** *adj.*
bi·o·en·gi·neer·ing (bī′ō-ĕn′jə-nîr′ĭng) *n.* **1.** The design and manufacture of aids or replacements for defective or missing organs, such as artificial limbs, heart pacemakers, and hearing aids. **2.** The design, manufacture, and use of equipment for industrial biosynthetic processes, such as fermentation.
bi·o·feed·back (bī′ō-fēd′băk′) *n.* A technique whereby one seeks consciously to regulate a bodily function thought to be involuntary, such as heartbeat or blood pressure, by using an instrument to monitor the function and to signal changes in it.
bi·o·fla·vo·noid (bī′ō-flā′və-noid′) *n.* Any of a group of biologically active substances found widely in plants and functioning in the maintenance of the walls of small blood vessels. Also called "vitamin P." [BIO- + FLAVON(E) + -OID.]
biog. biographer; biographical; biography.
bi·o·gas (bī′ō-gǎs′) *n.* A mixture of methane and carbon dioxide produced through bacterial action.
bi·o·gen·e·sis (bī′ō-jěn′ə-sĭs) *n.* Also **bi·og·e·ny** (bī-ŏj′ə-nē). **1.** The doctrine that living organisms develop only from other living organisms and not from nonliving matter. Compare **abiogenesis. 2.** The generation of living organisms from other living organisms. —**bi·o·ge·net·ic, bi·o·ge·net·i·cal, bi·og·e·nous** *adj.* —**bi·o·ge·net·i·cal·ly** *adv.*
bi·o·gen·ic (bī′ō-jěn′ĭk) *adj.* Developing or produced by living organisms. —**bi·o·gen·ic·al·ly** *adv.*
bi·o·ge·og·ra·phy (bī′ō-jē-ŏg′rə-fē) *n.* The biological study of the

geographical distribution of plants and animals. **—bi·o·ge·o·graph·ic, bi·o·ge·o·graph·i·cal** *adj.*

bi·og·ra·pher (bī-ŏg′rə-fər, bē-) *n. Abbr.* **biog.** One who writes a biography.

bi·o·graph·i·cal (bī′ə-grăf′ĭ-kəl) *adj.* Also **bi·o·graph·ic** (-grăf′ĭk). *Abbr.* **biog.** 1. Containing, consisting of, or pertaining to the facts or events in a person's life. 2. Of or pertaining to biography as a literary form. **—bi·o·graph·i·cal·ly** *adv.*

bi·og·ra·phy (bī-ŏg′rə-fē, bē-) *n., pl.* **-phies.** *Abbr.* **biog.** 1. An account of a person's life written by another; a life history. 2. Such writings as a literary form. [New Latin *biographia,* from Medieval Greek : BIO- + -GRAPHY.]

biol. biological; biology.

bi·o·log·i·cal (bī′ə-lŏj′ĭ-kəl) *adj.* Also **bi·o·log·ic** (-lŏj′ĭk). *Abbr.* **biol.** 1. Of or pertaining to biology. 2. Of, pertaining to, caused by, or affecting life or living organisms. ~*n. Pharmacology.* A drug derived from a biological source. **—bi·o·log·i·cal·ly** *adv.*

biological clock *n.* An intrinsic biological mechanism responsible for the periodicity or other time-dependent aspects of certain classes of behavior in living organisms.

biological control *n.* The control of pests using other organisms, usually their natural predators, parasites, or diseases.

biological oxygen demand *n.* Biochemical oxygen demand *(see).*

biological warfare *n.* Warfare in which disease-producing microorganisms or organic biocides are used to destroy livestock, crops, or human life.

bi·ol·o·gy (bī-ŏl′ə-jē) *n. Abbr.* **biol.** 1. The science of life and life processes, including the study of structure, functioning, growth, origin, evolution, ecology, and distribution of living organisms. 2. The life processes or characteristic phenomena of any group or category of living organisms. 3. The plant and animal life of a specific region or place. [German *Biologie* : BIO- + -LOGY.] **—bi·ol·o·gist** *n.*

bi·o·lu·mi·nes·cence (bī′ō-lōō′mə-nĕs′əns) *n.* The emission of visible light by living organisms such as the firefly, various fish, fungi, bacteria, and other organisms. It is the result of the biochemical oxidation of the compound luciferin. Compare **fluorescence, phosphorescence. —bi·o·lu·mi·nes·cent** *adj.*

bi·ol·y·sis (bī-ŏl′ə-sĭs) *n.* Death caused or accompanied by lysis. [New Latin : BIO- + -LYSIS.] **—bi·o·lyt·ic** (bī′ə-lĭt′ĭk) *adj.*

bi·o·mass (bī′ō-măs′) *n.* The total mass of living matter within a given volume of environment.

bi·ome (bī′ōm′) *n. Ecology.* A community of living organisms of a single major ecological region, such as a desert or tropical forest. [BI(O)- + -OME.]

bi·om·e·try (bī-ŏm′ĭ-trē) *n.* Also **bi·o·met·rics** (bī′ō-mĕt′rĭks). *Used with a singular verb.* The statistical study of biological data. **—bi·o·met·ric, bi·o·met·ri·cal** *adj.* **—bi·o·met·ri·cal·ly** *adv.*

bi·o·morph (bī′ō-môrf′) *n.* In art and sculpture, a form representing a living object. [BIO- + -MORPH.] **—bi·o·morph·ic, bi·o·morph·i·cal** *adj.*

bi·on·ic (bī-ŏn′ĭk) *adj.* 1. Of or pertaining to bionics. 2. In science fiction, having certain functions carried out by electronic equipment instead of by the normal physiological processes.

bi·on·ics (bī-ŏn′ĭks) *n. Used with a singular verb.* The application of biological principles to the study and design of engineering systems, especially electronic systems. [BI(O)- + (ELECTR)ONICS.]

bi·o·nom·ics (bī′ə-nŏm′ĭks) *n. Used with a singular verb.* **Ecology** *(see).* [French *bionomique,* pertaining to ecology, from *bionomie,* ecology : BIO- + -NOMY.] **—bi·o·nom·ic, bi·o·nom·i·cal** *adj.* **—bi·o·nom·i·cal·ly** *adv.*

bi·ont (bī′ŏnt′) *n.* A living organism. **—bi·on·tic** (bī-ŏn′tĭk) *adj.*

bi·o·phys·ics (bī′ō-fĭz′ĭks) *n. Used with a singular verb.* The physics of biological processes. **—bi·o·phys·i·cal** *adj.* **—bi·o·phys·i·cal·ly** *adv.* **—bi·o·phys·i·cist** *n.*

bi·o·plasm (bī′ō-plăz′əm) *n.* Living protoplasm, especially as distinguished from its nonliving content. [BIO- + -PLASM.]

bi·op·sy (bī′ŏp′sē) *n., pl.* **-sies.** The examination of tissues removed from the body as an aid to medical diagnosis. [French *biopsie* : BI(O)- + -OPSY.] **—bi·op·sic** *adj.*

bi·o·rhythm (bī′ō-rĭth′əm) *n.* A phenomenon found to a greater or lesser extent in most organisms whereby patterns of growth, behavior, or the like exhibit a natural periodic cycle in response to environmental changes or to various internal control mechanisms. **—bi·o·rhyth·mic** *adj.*

bi·o·scope (bī′ə-skōp′) *n.* 1. An early film projector, used about 1900. 2. *South African.* A cinema. [BIO- + -SCOPE.]

–biosis *suffix.* Indicates a specific way of living; for example, **symbiosis.** [New Latin, from Greek *biōsis,* way of life, from *bioun,* to live, from *bios,* mode of life.]

bi·o·sphere (bī′ə-sfīr′) *n.* The totality of regions of the earth that support self-sustaining and self-regulating ecological systems. [BIO- + -SPHERE.]

bi·o·sta·tis·tics (bī′ō-stə-tĭs′tĭks) *n. Used with a singular verb.* Statistical techniques used in studies of health and social welfare.

bi·o·syn·the·sis (bī′ō-sĭn′thə-sĭs) *n., pl.* **-ses** (-sēz′). The production of complex substances from simple ones by or with living organisms. **—bi·o·syn·thet·ic** *adj.* **—bi·o·syn·thet·i·cal·ly** *adv.*

bi·o·ta (bī-ō′tə) *n.* The animal and plant life of a particular region considered as a total ecological entity. [New Latin, from Greek *biotē,* way of life, from *bios,* life.]

bi·o·tech·nol·o·gy (bī′ō-tĕk-nŏl′ə-jē) *n.* 1. The manipulation of the physiology of microorganisms, especially bacteria, usually by genetic techniques, to produce useful chemicals on an industrial scale. See **genetic engineering.** 2. **Ergonomics** *(see).*

bi·ot·ic (bī-ŏt′ĭk) *adj.* Pertaining to life or specific life conditions. [Greek *biōtikos,* from *bios,* mode of life.]

biotic potential *n.* 1. The likelihood of survival of a specific organism in a specific environment, especially in an unfavorable environment. 2. The growth rate of a population that maintains a stable age distribution.

bi·o·tin (bī′ə-tĭn) *n.* A colorless crystalline vitamin, $C_{10}H_{16}N_2O_3S$, part of the vitamin B complex found in large quantities in liver, egg

birch *Druids believed the birch had powers of purification, so its twigs were used to drive out spirits. Echoes of this belief still survive in one of the wood's traditional uses: as the source of the twiggy house-cleaning brooms known as besoms.*

---

biological clock

RHYTHMS OF LIFE
Internal clocks keep us in step with the sun

Nearly all plants and animals have built-in biorhythms: regular cycles of activity, such as the annual blooming of some plants, the daily dawn chorus of birds, or the 28-day cycle of menstruation in women. Many of these changes follow a circadian, or 24-hour pattern. In humans, the most obvious examples are sleeping and eating; but there are also less noticeable daily variations in body temperature, pulse rate, blood pressure, and speed of cell growth.

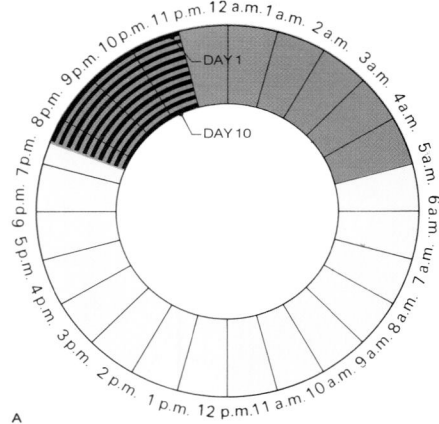

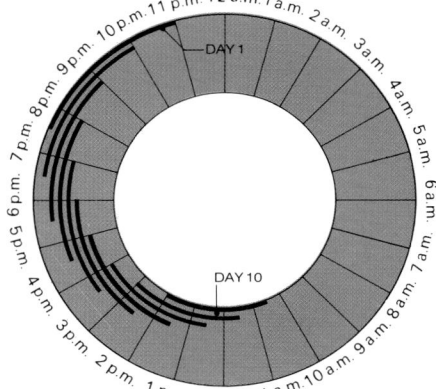

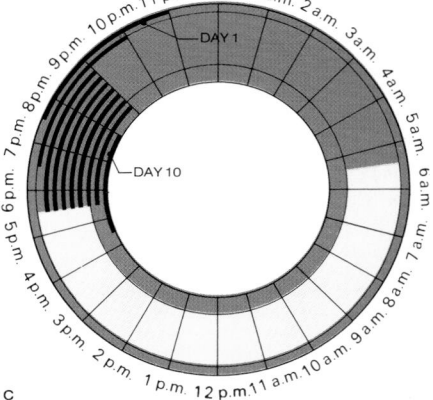

Activity each day

Dark   Light

THE EFFECT OF DARKNESS *Diagram A shows the normal evening activity period of a nocturnal animal. If the animal is confined in total darkness (B), that 3-hour period drifts forward by about an hour each day as the animal slips into a 23-hour routine. If, on the other hand, the same animal is put into an environment where day and night are both 12 hours long (C), the activity period drifts at first, then synchronizes with the new cycle. If the cycle is changed a second time, the activity period will drift again.*

yolk, milk, and yeast. [Greek *biotos,* life, from *bios,* life, mode of life + -IN.]

bi·o·tite (bī′ə-tīt′) *n.* A dark-brown to black mica, $K(Mg, Fe)_3AlSi_3O_{10}(OHF)_2$, found in igneous and metamorphic rocks. [German *Biotit,* after Jean Baptiste *Biot* (1774–1862), French physicist.] **—bi·o·tit·ic** (bī′ə-tĭt′ĭk) *adj.*

bi·o·tope (bī′ə-tōp′) *n.* A limited ecological region or niche, such as a dung heap, in which the environment is suitable for certain forms of life. [BIO- + Greek *topos,* place (see **topic**).]

bi·o·type (bī′ə-tīp′) *n.* A group of organisms having identical genetic but varying physical characteristics. **—bi·o·typ·ic** *adj.*

bip·a·rous (bĭp′ər-əs) *adj.* **1.** *Biology.* Producing two offspring in a single birth. **2.** *Botany.* Having two axes or branches. Said of certain flower clusters. [BI- + -PAROUS.]

bi·par·ti·san (bī-pär′tə-zən) *adj.* Consisting of or supported by members of two parties, especially two major political parties. **—bi·par·ti·san·ism** *n.* **—bi·par·ti·san·ship** *n.*

bi·par·tite (bī-pär′tīt′) *adj.* Also **bi·part·ed** (-pär′tĭd). **1.** Having or consisting of two parts. **2.** Having two corresponding parts, one for each party: *a bipartite treaty.* **3.** *Botany.* Divided into two, almost to the base. Said of certain leaves. [Latin *bipartītus,* past participle of *bipartīre,* to divide into two parts : BI- + *partīre,* to part, from *pars* (stem *part-*), a share, part.] **—bi·par·tite·ly** *adv.* **—bi·par·ti·tion** (bī′pär-tĭsh′ən) *n.*

bi·ped (bī′pĕd′) *n.* An animal with two feet.
~adj. Also **bi·ped·al** (bī-pĕd′l). Having two feet; two-footed. [Latin *bipēs,* "two-footed" : BI- + -PED.]

bi·pet·al·ous (bī-pĕt′l-əs) *adj. Botany.* Having two petals; dipetalous.

bi·phen·yl (bī-fĕn′əl, -fē′nəl) *n.* A colorless crystalline compound, $C_6H_5C_6H_5$, used as a heat-transfer agent, in fungicides, and in organic synthesis. Also called "diphenyl."

bi·pin·nate (bī-pĭn′āt′) *adj. Botany.* Having opposite leaflets that are subdivided into opposite leaflets. Said of compound leaves. **—bi·pin·nate·ly** *adv.*

bi·plane (bī′plān′) *n.* An early aircraft distinguished by single or paired wings fixed at two different levels, especially one above and one below the fuselage. Compare **monoplane.**

bi·pod (bī′pŏd′) *n.* A stand having two legs, as for the support of an instrument or a weapon. [BI- + -POD.]

bi·po·lar (bī-pō′lər) *adj.* **1.** Pertaining to or having two poles. **2.** Relating to or involving both of Earth's poles. **3.** Having or expressing two opposite or contradictory ideas or qualities. **—bi·po·lar·i·ty** (bī′pō-lăr′ə-tē) *n.*

bi·pro·pel·lant (bī′prə-pĕl′ənt) *n.* A two-component rocket propellant, such as liquid hydrogen and liquid oxygen, combined as fuel and oxidizer. Also called "dipropellant."

bi·quad·rat·ic (bī′kwŏ-drăt′ĭk) *adj. Mathematics.* Of or pertaining to the fourth degree.
~n. Mathematics. An algebraic equation of the fourth degree.

bi·quar·ter·ly (bī-kwôr′tər-lē) *adj.* Happening or appearing twice during each three-month period of a year.

bi·ra·cial (bī-rā′shəl) *adj.* Of, for, or consisting of members of two races. **—bi·ra·cial·ism** *n.*

bi·ra·di·al (bī-rā′dē-əl) *adj. Biology.* Both bilaterally and radially symmetrical.

bi·ra·mous (bī-rā′məs) *adj. Biology.* Having two branches, as in an arthropod appendage.

birch (bûrch) *n.* **1.** Any of several deciduous trees of the genus *Betula,* common in the Northern Hemisphere, and having white, yellowish, or gray bark that can be separated from the wood in sheets. **2.** The hard, close-grained wood of any of these trees. **3.** A rod or bundle of twigs from a birch tree, used to administer a whipping.
~tr.v. **birched, birching, birches.** To whip (someone) with or as if with birch twigs or a birch rod. [Middle English *birche,* Old English *birce, beorc(e).*] **—birch** *adj.*

Birch·er (bûr′chər) *n.* Also **Birch·ite** (bûr′chīt′), **Birch·ist** (bûr′chĭst). **1.** A member of the **John Birch Society** *(see).* **2.** A supporter of its doctrines and activities. **—Birch·ism** *n.*

bird (bûrd) *n.* **1.** Any member of the class Aves, which includes warm-blooded, egg-laying feathered vertebrates with forelimbs modified to form wings. **2.** A bird hunted as game. **3.** *Slang.* A rocket or guided missile. **4.** A target, a **clay pigeon** *(see).* **5.** The feather-tipped object used in playing badminton, a **shuttlecock** *(see).* **6.** *Slang.* One who is odd or remarkable. **7.** *British Slang.* A young woman. **8.** *Slang.* A sound of disapproval or derision. Used chiefly in the expressions *give someone the bird; get the bird.* **9.** *British Slang.* A prison sentence; imprisonment. Used chiefly in the phrase *do bird.* **—a bird in the hand.** A certainty; something achieved. **—for the birds.** *Slang.* Objectionable or worthless. **—the birds and the bees.** Human reproduction and sexuality, as explained to children. Often used humorously. [Middle English *byrd, bryd,* young bird, Old English *brid*†. Sense 8, short for *birdtime,* rhyming slang for *time.*] See feature, next page.

bird·bath (bûrd′băth′) *n.* A garden trough or basin filled with water in which birds may bathe.

bird·brain (bûrd′brān′) *n. Slang.* A silly, frivolous person. **—bird-brained** *adj.*

bird·cage (bûrd′kāj′) *n.* A cage for birds.

bird·call (bûrd′kôl′) *n.* **1.** The song of a bird. **2. a.** An imitation of the song of a bird. **b.** A small device for producing this.

bird cherry *n.* A cherry tree, *Prunus padus,* native to Eurasia, having clusters of white flowers and small black fruit.

bird colonel *n. Slang.* A full colonel. [From the eagle insignia worn by a full colonel.]

bird dog *n.* **1.** A dog used to hunt game birds; gun dog. **2.** *Slang.* One who seeks out something for another.

bird-dog (bûrd′dôg′, -dŏg′) *v.* **-dogged, -dog·ging, -dogs.** *—intr.* To watch closely. *—tr.* To seek out; follow.

bird·farm (bûrd′färm′) *n. Slang.* An aircraft carrier.

bird-foot violet (bûrd′fo͝ot′) *n.* Also **bird's-foot violet** (bûrdz′-). A North American violet, *Viola pedata,* having blue flowers and leaves divided into narrow lobes.

bird·house (bûrd′hous′) *n.* **1.** An aviary. **2.** A small box made as a nesting place for birds.

bird·ie (bûr′dē) *n.* **1.** *Informal.* A small bird. **2.** *Golf.* One stroke under par for any hole. **3.** A **shuttlecock** *(see).*

bird·lime (bûrd′līm′) *n.* **1.** A sticky substance smeared on branches to capture small birds. **2.** Something that captures and ensnares.
~tr.v. **birdlimed, -liming, -limes.** **1.** To smear with birdlime. **2.** To catch with birdlime.

bird louse *n.* A **louse** *(see).*

bird·man (bûrd′mən) *n., pl.* **-men** (-mĭn). **1.** A person who is interested in birds; ornithologist. **2.** *Slang.* An aviator.

bird of paradise *n.* Any of various birds of the family Paradisaeidae, native to New Guinea and adjacent areas, usually having brilliant plumage and long tail feathers in the male.

bird-of-par·a·dise flower *n.* (bûrd′əv-pâr′ə-dīs′) *n.* A perennial plant, *Strelitzia reginae,* having purple bracts and large orange or yellow flowers with blue tongues. [After its stalks of colorful flowers resembling birds of paradise.]

bird of passage *n.* A migratory bird or a transient person.

bird of prey *n.* Any of various predatory carnivorous birds, such as the eagle or hawk, having powerful claws and a strong bill.

bird pepper *n.* **1.** A tropical plant, *Capsicum frutescens,* that is the probable ancestor of the mild peppers and many of the hot peppers. **2.** The narrow, extremely pungent fruit of this plant.

bird·seed (bûrd′sēd′) *n.* A mixture of various kinds of seeds used for feeding birds, especially caged birds.

bird's-eye (bûrdz′ī′) *adj.* **1.** Dappled or patterned with spots thought to resemble birds' eyes: *bird's-eye maple.* **2.** Seen from high above or from a remote distance: *a bird's-eye view.*
~n. **1.** Any of various plants having small, brightly colored flowers, such as the bird's-eye primrose or the bird's-eye speedwell. **2. a.** A fabric woven with a pattern of small diamonds, each having a dot in the center. **b.** The pattern of such a fabric.

bird's-eye primrose *n.* A plant, *Primula farinosa,* native to Eurasia, having clusters of small, purplish, yellow-throated flowers.

bird's-eye speedwell *n.* A weak-stemmed plant, *Veronica chamaedrys,* native to Eurasia, having small, bright-blue flowers.

bird's-foot (bûrdz′fo͝ot′) *n., pl.* **bird's-foots.** **1.** A European plant, *Ornithopus perpusillus,* with small whitish flowers and curved pods. **2.** Any of various other plants that have flowers, leaves, or pods resembling a bird's foot or claw.

bird's-foot fern *n.* A fern, *Pellaea mucronata,* native to California, having fronds with wiry leaves grouped to resemble a bird's foot.

bird's-foot trefoil *n.* A sprawling plant, *Lotus corniculatus,* having yellow flowers and seed pods resembling the claws of a bird.

bird's-nest fungus (bûrdz′nĕst′) *n.* Any of various fungi of the family Nidulariaceae, having a cuplike fruiting body containing several round, egglike structures that enclose the spores.

bird's-nest orchid *n.* A brown parasitic orchid, *Neottia nidus-avis,* that grows in woods in Europe and Asia and has thick intertwining roots.

bird's-nest soup *n.* A Chinese soup made from a gelatinous coating on the nests of certain swifts native to the Orient. [Translation of Chinese (Mandarin) *yen⁴ wo¹ t'ang¹* : *yen⁴,* the swallow or swift + *wo¹,* nest + *t'ang¹,* soup.]

birds of a feather *pl.n.* People who are alike in some way. Used chiefly in the saying *Birds of a feather flock together.*

bird·song (bûrd′sông′, -sŏng′) *n.* **1.** The singing of birds. **2.** A bird's cry or call.

bird spider *n.* Any spider of the tropical American family Aviculariidae, which is large and hairy and preys on birds.

bird watcher *n.* A person who observes and identifies birds in their natural surroundings. **—bird watch·ing** *n.*

bird·y·back (bûr′dē-băk′) *n.* The transporting of loaded truck trailers by airplane. [BIRD + -Y + (PIGGY)BACK.]

bi·re·frin·gence (bī′rī-frĭn′jəns) *n.* The resolution or splitting of a light wave into two waves with mutually perpendicular vibration directions by an optically anisotropic medium such as a crystal of calcite, topaz, or quartz. Also called "double refraction." **—bi·re·frin·gent** *adj.*

bi·reme (bī′rēm′) *n.* An ancient galley equipped with two tiers of oars on each side. [Latin *birēmis* : BI- + *rēmus,* oar.]

bi·ret·ta, be·ret·ta (bə-rĕt′ə) *n.* Also **ber·ret·ta, bir·ret·ta.** A stiff square cap that is worn by Roman Catholic clergy and is black for a priest, purple for a bishop, and red for a cardinal. Also called "barret." [Italian *berretta* or Spanish *birreta,* from Medieval Latin *birretum,* cap, from Late Latin *birrus,* hooded cloak. See **beret.**]

Birk·beck (bûr′bĕk, bûrk′-), **George** (1776–1841). British educational reformer. His lectures to workingmen in Glasgow (1800–04) led to the establishment of the first Mechanics' Institute in Britain (1823). He was one of the founders of London University (1827).

Bir·ken·head (bûr′kən-hĕd′). Industrial port in Merseyside in northwest England, on the Mersey River, opposite Liverpool.

bird of paradise *Count Raggi's bird of paradise,* Paradisaea raggiana *(above), was discovered in New Guinea in 1873. It was named after the Marquis Francis Raggi, a French amateur ornithologist.*

bird of paradise flower *A native of southern Africa, this exotic plant resembles the plumed head of a bird of paradise, found in the forests of New Guinea and northern Australia. The species shown here is* Strelitzia reginae.

bird's-nest orchid *In European woodlands this orchid feeds on decaying leaves. Its tangled roots, looking like an untidy bird's nest, give the plant its name.*

bird

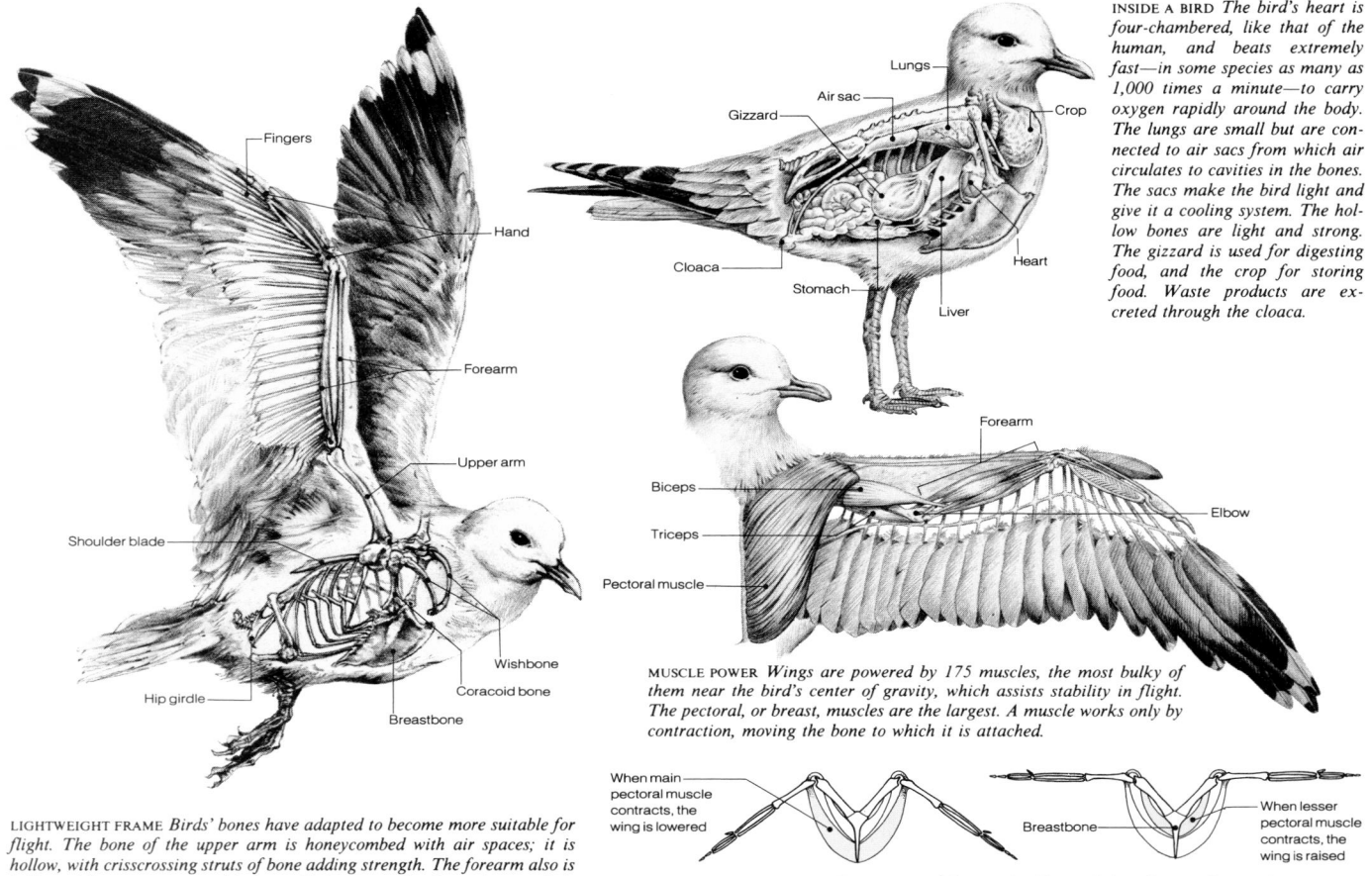

BUILT FOR FLIGHT

How adaptations of anatomy have made birds masters of the air

Birds had feathers before they could fly, but it was feathers that made flight possible. The earliest known ancestor of the birds, called archaeopteryx, lived 150 million years ago and was a halfway stage between reptile and bird. Its feathers were modified scales use-

ful in temperature control. The nearest it came to flight may have been weak flapping that helped it to glide between trees. Birds may have come to fly by chance, perhaps by flapping their forelimbs while running on their hind legs or leaping from tree to tree.

Birds have evolved into some 8,600 species, most of which have thrived by mastery of the air. A bird has become perfectly adapted for flight. As well as feathers, which maintain lift, it has light bones, big breast muscles, and a fast-beating heart.

INSIDE A BIRD *The bird's heart is four-chambered, like that of the human, and beats extremely fast—in some species as many as 1,000 times a minute—to carry oxygen rapidly around the body. The lungs are small but are connected to air sacs from which air circulates to cavities in the bones. The sacs make the bird light and give it a cooling system. The hollow bones are light and strong. The gizzard is used for digesting food, and the crop for storing food. Waste products are excreted through the cloaca.*

LIGHTWEIGHT FRAME *Birds' bones have adapted to become more suitable for flight. The bone of the upper arm is honeycombed with air spaces; it is hollow, with crisscrossing struts of bone adding strength. The forearm also is hollow and has a similarly light but strong structure. The wishbone and coracoid bones act as bracing struts when the wings are spread in flight. The powered muscles for flight are attached to the breastbone and to the wings.*

MUSCLE POWER *Wings are powered by 175 muscles, the most bulky of them near the bird's center of gravity, which assists stability in flight. The pectoral, or breast, muscles are the largest. A muscle works only by contraction, moving the bone to which it is attached.*

USING THE MUSCLES IN FLIGHT *Contraction of the main pectoral muscle produces the downward wing beat, the chief power stroke. The wing is raised by contraction of the lesser pectoral mus-*

cle. This is below the arm bone it has to raise; the lifting is managed by a "rope and pulley" attachment connected to the upper surface of the bone.

Birkenhead, Frederick Edwin Smith, 1st Earl of (1872–1930). British lawyer and politician. He was solicitor general (1915), attorney general (1915–19), Lord Chancellor (1919–22), and secretary of state for India (1924–28).

bir·kie (bûr′kē) *adj. Scottish.* Cheeky and lively; cocky. [Perhaps from Scandinavian; compare Old Norse *berkja,* to bark, boast.]

birl¹ (bûrl) *v.* **birled, birling, birls.** —*tr.* To cause (a floating log) to spin rapidly by rotating with the feet. —*intr.* To whirr; hum. ~*n.* A whirring noise; hum. [Blend of BIRR and WHIRL.]

birl², birle (bûrl) *tr.v.* **birled, birling, birls** or **birles.** *Scottish.* To pour out (drink). [Old English *byrelian;* akin to *byrele,* cup-bearer.]

birl·ing (bûr′lĭng) *n.* A game of skill, originating among lumberjacks, in which two competitors try to balance on a floating log while spinning it with their feet. Also called "logrolling." [From BIRL (spin around).]

Bir·ming·ham¹ (bûr′mĭng-əm). City in the West Midlands in England, the second-largest city in the United Kingdom and center of the automobile industry. It owes its leading industrial position partly to the fact that it lies equidistant from London, Bristol, Manchester, and Liverpool and partly to its proximity to large deposits of iron and coal.

Bir·ming·ham² (bûr′mĭng-hăm′). The largest city in Alabama. It is the center of a mining and industrial region.

Birobidzhan. See **Jewish Autonomous Region.**

birr¹ (bûr) *n.* A whirring sound. ~*intr.v.* **birred, birring, birrs.** To make this sound. [Middle English

bir(re), byrr, strong wind, onrush, from Old Norse byrr, favorable wind.]

birr² *n.* The basic monetary unit of Ethiopia, equal to 100 cents. See feature at **currency.** [Amharic.]

birretta. Variant of **biretta.**

birth (bûrth) *n.* **1.** The beginning of existence; the fact of being born. **2.** Any beginning or origin. **3. a.** The act of bearing young; parturition. **b.** The passage of a child or other young mammal from the uterus. **4.** Ancestry; parentage: *a man of noble birth.* **5.** Origin; lineage: *a Southerner by birth.* —**give birth to.** To bring forth. ~*tr.v.* **birthed, birthing, births.** *Chiefly Regional.* **1.** To deliver (a baby). **2.** To bear (a child). [Middle English *birth,* from Old Norse *byrth.*]

birth canal *n.* The cavity of the uterus and the vagina traversed by the fetus during birth.

birth certificate *n.* An official record of a person's parentage and the date, time, and place of birth.

birth control *n.* **1.** Voluntary limitation or control of conception, especially by planned use of contraceptive techniques. **2.** Contraceptive materials.

birth·day (bûrth′dā′) *n.* **1.** The day of one's birth. **2.** The anniversary of one's birth.

Birthday honors *pl.n. British.* Decorations or titles conferred on the sovereign's official birthday.

birthday suit *n. Informal.* A state of complete nakedness. Used humorously.

birth·ing (bûr′thĭng) *adj.* Pertaining to or used during the act of giving birth: *a bad birthing position.* **—birth·ing** *n.*

birth·mark (bûrth′märk′) *n.* A mole, mark, or blemish present on the body from birth; nevus.

birth·place (bûrth′plās′) *n. Abbr.* **b.pl.** The place where someone is born or where something originates.

birth·rate (bûrth′rāt′) *n.* The number of live births in a specified population per unit time, especially per thousand of the population per year. Also called "natality."

birth·right (bûrth′rīt′) *n.* **1.** Any privilege granted a person by virtue of birth. **2.** Any special privilege accorded the first-born. **—See** Synonyms at **right.**

birth·stone (bûrth′stōn′) *n.* A jewel associated with a specific month and thought to bring good luck to a person born in that month.

birth trauma *n.* **1.** An injury sustained by an infant during birth. **2.** An emotional shock sustained by an infant during birth.

birth·wort (bûrth′wûrt′, -wôrt′) *n.* Any of several climbing plants of the genus *Aristolochia,* such as the European species *A. clematitis,* having reddish or brownish, usually unpleasantly scented flowers. [Formerly given to women in childbirth.]

bis (bĭs) *adv.* Twice; again; encore. Used chiefly as a direction in music. [French, from Latin, twice.]

BIS, B.I.S. **1.** Bank for International Settlements. **2.** British Information Service.

Bis·cay, Bay of (bĭs′kā). The section of the Atlantic Ocean east of a line running roughly from Ushant Island, off Brittany, to Cape Ortegal in northwestern Spain.

biscay green *n.* A moderate yellow green color.

bis·cuit (bĭs′kĭt) *n., pl.* **-cuits** or **biscuit. 1.** A small cake of shortened bread leavened with baking powder or soda. **2.** *British.* A thin, crisp cracker of unleavened bread. **3.** Pale brown; beige. **4.** *Ceramics.* Pottery that has been fired once but not glazed. Also called "bisque." **—take the biscuit.** *British Informal.* To be the most surprising or outstanding instance of something ever encountered. [Middle English *besquite,* from Old French *bescoit, bescuit,* from (unattested) Medieval Latin *biscoctus (panis),* "twice-cooked (bread)" : Latin *bis-,* BI- + *coctus,* past participle of *coquere,* to cook.]

bise (bēz) *n.* A cold, dry, northerly wind that blows in Switzerland and the adjacent areas of France and Italy. [Middle English, from Old French, from Germanic; akin to Old Swedish *bisa,* whirlwind.]

bi·sect (bī′sĕkt′, bī-sĕkt′) *v.* **-sected, -secting, -sects.** *—tr.* To cut or divide into two equal parts. *—intr.* To split; fork: *The road bisects at the junction.* [BI- + -SECT.] **—bi·sec·tion** *n.* **—bi·sec·tion·al** *adj.* **—bi·sec·tion·al·ly** *adv.*

bi·sec·tor (bī′sĕk′tər, bī-sĕk′-) *n.* Anything that bisects, especially a straight line or plane that bisects an angle.

bi·ser·rate (bī-sĕr′āt′) *adj. Biology.* **1.** Having serrations that are themselves serrated; doubly serrate: *biserrate leaves.* **2.** Serrated on both sides: *biserrate antennae.*

bi·sex·u·al (bī-sĕk′sho͞o-əl) *adj.* **1.** Of or pertaining to both sexes. **2.** Having both male and female organs; hermaphroditic. Said of some plants and animals. **3.** Sexually attracted to members of both sexes.
~n. **1.** A bisexual organism; a hermaphrodite. **2.** A person who is sexually attracted to members of both sexes. **—bi·sex·u·al·ism, bi·sex·u·al·i·ty** *n.* **—bi·sex·u·al·ly** *adv.*

bish·op (bĭsh′əp) *n.* **1.** *Abbr.* **bp.** A high-ranking Christian clergyman, in modern churches usually in charge of a diocese and having the power to confirm and ordain, and in some churches regarded as having received the highest ordination in unbroken succession from the apostles. **2.** *Abbr.* **B** A miter-shaped chessman that can move diagonally across any number of unoccupied spaces of the same color linked in a straight line. **3.** Mulled port spiced with oranges, sugar, and cloves. [Middle English *bisshop,* Old English *biscop, bisceop,* from Vulgar Latin *biscopus* (unattested), variant of Late Latin *episcopus,* from Greek *episkopos,* guardian, overseer : *epi-,* on, over + *skopos,* one who watches.]

bish·op·ric (bĭsh′əp-rĭk) *n.* **1.** The office or rank of a bishop. **2.** The diocese of a bishop. [Middle English *bisshopriche, bisshoprike,* Old English *bisceoprīce* : BISHOP + *rīce,* realm.]

bishop's weed *n.* A plant, the **ground elder** *(see).*

Bis·marck (bĭz′märk′). The capital of North Dakota, on the Missouri River in the south-central part of the state. Bismarck was originally a camp for the men who were building the Northern Pacific Railroad. [It was named after Prince Otto von BISMARCK in the hope of attracting German investment in the railroad.]

Bismarck, Prince Otto Eduard Leopold von (1815–98). German politician, known as the "Iron Chancellor." In 1862 he became prime minister of Prussia and was largely responsible for the successful war against Austria (1866) and the creation of the North German Confederation, excluding Austria (1867). After the Franco-Prussian War (1870–71) he became chancellor of the new German empire. His chancellorship (1871–90) was notable for a complex series of foreign alliances and for his sweeping social reforms, introduced in the mid-1880's, by which he sought to stem the advance of German socialism.

Bismarck Archipelago. Group of volcanic islands in the southwest Pacific Ocean, now part of Papua New Guinea. The largest island is New Britain.

bis·muth (bĭz′məth) *n. Symbol* **Bi** A white, crystalline, brittle, highly diamagnetic metallic element used in alloys to form sharp castings for objects sensitive to high temperatures and in various low-melting alloys for fire-safety devices. Atomic number 83, atomic weight 208.980, melting point 271.3°C, boiling point 1,560°C, specific gravity 9.747, valences 3, 5. [New Latin *bisemutum,* Latinization of German *Wismut*†.] **—bis·muth·al, bis·muth·ic** *adj.*

bis·muth·in·ite (bĭz-mŭth′ə-nīt′) *n.* A gray, natural form of bismuth sulfide that occurs in veins associated with tin, copper, lead, and other ores, and is used as a source of bismuth. Also called "bismuth glance."

bis·na·ga (bĭs-nä′gə) *n.* Any of several spiny, globe-shaped or barrel-shaped cacti of the southwestern United States and Mexico. [Spanish *biznaga,* alteration of *vitznauac,* from Nahuatl *huitznahuac* : *huitztli,* spine + *nahuac,* around.]

bi·son (bī′sən, -zən) *n., pl.* **bison. 1.** A hoofed mammal, *Bison bison,* of western North America, having a dark-brown coat, a shaggy mane, and short, curved horns. Also called "buffalo." **2.** A similar, somewhat smaller animal, *B. bonasus,* of Europe. In this sense, also called "wisent." [Latin *bisōn,* from Germanic.]

bisque[1] (bĭsk) *n.* **1. a.** A thick, rich soup made from meat, fish, or shellfish. **b.** A thick cream soup made of vegetables that have been puréed. **2.** Ice cream mixed with crushed macaroons or nuts. [French *bisque*†.]

bisque[2] *n.* **1.** *Ceramics.* **Biscuit** *(see).* **2.** Pale orange yellow to yellowish gray. [From BISCUIT.]

bisque[3] *n.* An advantage allowed an inferior player in certain games; especially, a free point taken when desired in a tennis set. [French *bisque*†.]

Bis·sau (bĭ-sou′). Capital, largest city, and chief port of Guinea-Bissau in West Africa.

bis·sex·tile (bī-sĕks′tĭl, -tīl′, bĭ-) *adj.* **1.** Of or pertaining to a leap year. **2.** Of or pertaining to the extra day falling in a leap year. *~n.* A leap year. [Late Latin *bissextilis,* from Latin *bissextus,* intercalary day in the Julian calendar, which followed February 24, the sixth day before the calends of March : *bis,* twice, BI- + *sextus,* sixth.]

bi·sta·ble (bī-stā′bəl) *adj.* Having two stable states: *a bistable circuit.*

bis·ter, bis·tre (bĭs′tər) *n.* **1.** A water-soluble, yellowish-brown pigment made from soot obtained from beech or other wood. **2.** Grayish to yellowish brown. [French *bistre*†.] **—bis·ter, bis·tered** *adj.*

bis·tort (bĭs′tôrt′) *n.* Any of several plants of the genus *Polygonum,* especially: **1.** A Eurasian plant, *P. bistorta,* having pointed clusters of small, pinkish flowers. **2.** A similar plant, *P. bistortoides,* of the mountains of western North America, having oval clusters of pink or white flowers. [Old French *bistorte,* "twice-twisted" : Latin *bis,* twice, BI- + *tortus,* past participle of Latin *torquēre,* to twist.]

bis·tou·ry (bĭs′tə-rē) *n., pl.* **-ries.** A long, narrow surgical knife for minor incisions. [French *bistouri,* from Old French *bistorie, bistorit,* dagger, from Italian (northern dialect) *bistorino* (unattested), variant of *pistorino,* "of Pistoia," from *Pistoja,* Pistoia, Italy (where sharp knives were made).]

bis·tro (bē′strō, bĭs′trō) *n., pl.* **-tros.** A small bar, restaurant, or nightclub. [French *bistro*†.]

bi·sul·cate (bī-sŭl′kāt′) *adj.* Cleft or cloven, as a hoof. [BI- + SULCATE.]

bi·sul·fate (bī-sŭl′fāt′) *n. Chemistry.* The inorganic acid group HSO_4 or any compound containing it.

bi·sul·fide (bī-sŭl′fīd′) *n. Chemistry.* A **disulfide** *(see).*

bi·sul·fite (bī-sŭl′fīt′) *n. Chemistry.* The inorganic acid group HSO_3 or any compound containing it.

bit[1] (bĭt) *n.* **1.** A small piece, portion, or amount. **2.** A brief amount of time; moment. **3. a.** An entertainment routine given regularly by a performer; act. **b.** A short scene or episode in a play, movie, or the like. **4.** A **bit part** *(see).* **5.** *Informal.* **a.** A particular kind of action, situation, or behavior: *She did the whole bit.* **b.** A matter being considered: *What's this bit about inflation?* **6.** *Informal.* An amount equal to one eighth of a dollar. Used only in multiples of two. **7.** *British.* Formerly, a small coin: *a threepenny bit.* **—a bit.** Somewhat; to some extent. **—a bit of. 1.** Some. **2.** In some way; to some degree: *a bit of a bore.* **—a bit of all right.** *British Informal.* An attractive thing or person, especially a woman. **—bit by bit.** Little by little; gradually. **—do one's bit.** To make one's contribution; do one's share. **—every bit as.** Quite as; to the same degree as. **—to bits. 1.** Into small pieces or fragments. **2.** To distraction: *thrilled to bits.* [Middle English *bit,* Old English *bita,* piece bitten off, morsel.]

bit[2] *n.* **1.** The sharp part of a tool, such as the blade of a knife, plane, or the like. **2.** A pointed and threaded tool for drilling and boring that is secured in a brace, bitstock, or drill press. **3.** The part of a key that enters the lock and engages the bolt or tumblers. **4.** The metal mouthpiece of a bridle, serving to control, curb, and direct an animal. See **bridle. 5.** Anything that controls, guides, or curbs. **6.** The gripping end of a pair of pincers. **7.** The copper end of a soldering iron. **—take the bit in one's teeth.** To start up and proceed uncontrollably.
~tr.v. **bitted, bitting, bits. 1.** To place a bit in the mouth of (a horse). **2.** To check or control, as if with a bit. **3.** To make or grind a bit on (a key). [Middle English *bitt,* cutting edge, mouthpiece of a bridle, Old English *bite,* a sting, bite.]

bit[3] *n. Computer Science.* **1.** A single character of a language having just two characters, such as either of the binary digits 0 or 1. **2.** A unit of information equivalent to the choice of either of two equally likely states of an information-containing system. **3.** A unit of in-

bison *The bison—known as the buffalo in its native North America—was hunted almost to extinction with the coming of frontiersmen to the prairies. "Buffalo Bill" Cody alone shot 3,000 in one year. Their population dropped from about 40 million in 1830 to less than 1,000 in 1894, when they became a protected species in the United States.*

PRONUNCIATION KEY

ă, **pat**; ā, **pay**; âr, **care**;
ä, **father**, **are**; b, **bib**;
ch, **church**; d, **deed**; ĕ, **pet**;
ē, **be**; f, **fife**; g, **gag**; h, **hat**;
hw, **which**; ĭ, **pit**; ī, **pie**;
îr, **pier**; j, **judge**; k, **kick**;
l, **lid**, **needle**; m, **mum**;
n, **no**, **sudden**; ng, **thing**;
ŏ, **pot**; ō, **toe**; ô, **paw**, **for**;
oi, **noise**; ou, **out**; o͝o, **book**;
o͞o, **boot**; p, **pop**; r, **roar**;
s, **sauce**; sh, **ship**, **dish**;
t, **tight**; th, **thin**, **path**;
th, **this**, **bathe**; ŭ, **cut**; ûr, **fur**;
v, **valve**; w, **with**; y, **yes**;
z, **zebra**, **size**; zh, **vision**;
ə, **about**, **item**, **edible**, **gallop**, **circus**, **peaceful**

IN FOREIGN WORDS:

à, *Fr.* **ami**; œ, *Fr.* **feu**, *Ger.* **schön**; ü, *Fr.* **tu**, *Ger.* **über**;
KH, *Ger.* **ich**, *Scot.* **loch**;
N, *Fr.* **bon**; y', *Fr.* **Compiègne**

STRESS MARKS:

Primary stress: ′ **in·cite′** (ĭn-sīt′)
Secondary stress: ′ **in′sight′** (ĭn′sīt′)

bittern *The courting male bittern makes a loud booming call—and the bird's name is thought to derive from the Latin term* butitaurus, *meaning "bird that bellows like an ox."*

bittersweet *The common name for woody nightshade—*Solanum dulcamara. *Bittersweet grows in woods, hedges, and on sand dunes. Its poisonous, glossy red berries (above) taste first bitter, then sweet.*

blackbird *Evolution originally fitted blackbirds to live in woodland clearings, but many have adapted to living in gardens as well, so that they are now one of the commonest songbirds. This is a male bird; females have light brown plumage.*

formation storage capacity, as of a computer memory. [BI(NARY) (DIGI)T.]

bit⁴. Past tense and alternate past participle of **bite.**

bi·tar·trate (bī-tär′trāt′) *n. Chemistry.* The tartrate of an acid.

bitch (bĭch) *n.* **1.** A female dog or other canine animal. **2.** *Slang.* A spiteful woman. Used derogatorily. **3.** *Slang.* A complaint. **4.** *Slang.* A difficult or confounding problem.
~*intr.v.* **bitched, bitching, bitches.** *Slang.* **1.** To talk spitefully. **2.** To complain; grumble. **3.** To botch; bungle. Used with *up.* [Middle English *bicche,* Old English *bicce,* female dog, from Germanic *bekjōn-* (unattested).]

bitch·y (bĭch′ē) *adj.* **-ier, -iest.** *Slang.* Malicious, spiteful, or ill-tempered. **—bitch·i·ly** *adv.* **—bitch·i·ness** *n.*

bite (bīt) *v.* **bit** (bĭt), **bitten** (bĭt′n), **biting, bites.** —*tr.* **1.** To cut, grip, or tear with or as if with the teeth. **2.** To pierce the skin of with the teeth, fangs, or stinger. **3.** To cut into with a sharp instrument, such as a knife or drilling bit. **4.** To grip, grab, or seize. **5.** To eat into; corrode. **6.** To cause to sting or smart. **7.** *Informal.* To irritate. —*intr.* **1.** To grip, cut into, or injure something with or as if with the teeth. **2.** To have a stinging effect or a sharp taste. **3.** To have the desired, usually unpleasant, effect: *The new tax is really beginning to bite.* **4.** To take or swallow bait. **5.** To be taken in by a ploy or deception. **—bite the dust. 1.** To fall dead, especially in combat. **2.** To be badly defeated. **3.** To become useless.
~*n.* **1.** The act of biting. **2.** A wound or injury resulting from biting. **3.** A stinging or smarting sensation. **4.** An incisive, penetrating quality. **5.** An amount of food taken into the mouth at one time; mouthful. **6.** *Informal.* A light meal or snack. **7.** An attempt by a fish to take the bait on an angler's line. **8. a.** A secure grip or hold applied by a tool or machine upon a working surface. **b.** A surface, as on a file, applying such a grip. **9.** *Dentistry.* The angle at which the upper and lower teeth meet when they come into contact. **10.** The corrosive action of acid upon an etcher's metal plate. **—put the bite on.** *Slang.* To borrow money from. [Bite, bit, bitten; Middle English *biten, bot* (past plural *biten*), *biten,* Old English *bītan, bāt* (past plural *biton*), *biten.*] **—bit·er** *n.*

Bi·thy·ni·a (bĭ-thĭn′ē-ə). An ancient country in Asia Minor, in northwestern present-day Turkey. Originally inhabited by Thracians, by the end of the 1st century B.C. it had been absorbed into the Roman Empire.

bit·ing (bī′tĭng) *adj.* **1.** Causing a stinging sensation. **2.** Incisive; caustic. —See Synonyms at **incisive. —bit·ing·ly** *adv.*

bit part *n.* A small role in a play or film, having only a few spoken lines.

bit·stock (bĭt′stŏk′) *n.* A brace or handle in which a drilling or boring bit is secured.

bitt (bĭt) *n.* Either of a pair of vertical posts set on the deck of a ship and used to secure cables.
~*tr.v.* **bitted, bitting, bitts.** To wind (a cable) around a bitt. [Middle English, probably of Low German origin, akin to Low German and Dutch *beting.*]

bit·ten. Past participle of **bite.**

bit·ter (bĭt′ər) *adj.* **-terer, -terest. 1.** Having or being a taste that is sharp, acrid, and unpleasant. **2.** Causing sharp pain to the body or discomfort to the mind; harsh. **3.** Difficult or distasteful to accept or admit: *the bitter truth.* **4.** Exhibiting or proceeding from strong animosity: *bitter foes.* **5.** Marked by resentfulness or rancor: *a bitter old man.*
~*n. British.* A sharp-tasting beer made with hops.
~*v.* **bittered, -tering, -ters.** —*tr.* To make bitter. —*intr.* To become bitter. [Middle English *bitter,* Old English *biter.*] **—bit·ter·ly** *adv.* **—bit·ter·ness** *n.*

bitter almond *n.* A variety of the common almond, *Prunus amygdalus amara,* having bitter kernels that yield a highly poisonous oil, which is used for flavoring when the prussic acid in it has been removed.

bitter aloes *pl.n. Used with a singular verb.* A cathartic drug derived from the juice of the fleshy leaves of a tropical plant, *Aloe barbadensis.* See **aloe.**

bitter apple *n.* A plant, the **colocynth** *(see),* or its fruit.

bitter end *n.* **1.** *Nautical.* The end of a rope or cable that is wound around a bitt. **2.** A final, painful, or difficult conclusion; the absolute end.

bit·ter·ling (bĭt′ər-lĭng) *n.* A small colorful freshwater fish, *Rhodeus sericeus,* related to the carp and often kept in aquariums. [German: BITTER + -LING.]

bit·tern¹ (bĭt′ərn) *n.* Any of several wading birds of the genera *Botaurus* and *Ixobrychus,* having mottled, brownish plumage, and notable for its deep, resonant cry. [Middle English *botor, bitter,* from Old French *butor,* from Vulgar Latin *būtitaurus* (unattested), perhaps "bird (that bellows like) an ox" (after its booming call) : Latin *būtiō,* bittern + *taurus,* ox, bull.]

bittern² *n.* The solution of bromides, magnesium, and calcium salts remaining after sodium chloride has been crystallized out of sea water. [From BITTER.]

bit·ter·nut (bĭt′ər-nŭt′) *n.* A hickory tree, *Carya cordiformis,* of eastern North America, having nuts with bitter kernels.

bitter orange *n.* The **Seville orange** *(see).*

bitter principle *n. Pharmacology.* Any of a large number of bitter substances, frequently of vegetable origin.

bit·ter·root (bĭt′ər-ro͞ot′, -ro͝ot′) *n.* A plant, *Lewisia rediviva,* of western North America, having showy pink or white flowers and a starchy, edible root.

bit·ters (bĭt′ərz) *pl.n.* A bitter, usually alcoholic liquid made with herbs or roots and used in cocktails or as a tonic.

bit·ter·sweet (bĭt′ər-swēt′) *n.* **1.** A North American woody vine, *Celastrus scandens,* having orange or yellowish fruits that split open to expose seeds enclosed in fleshy scarlet arils. **2.** A sprawling vine, *Solanum dulcamara,* native to Eurasia, having purple flowers and poisonous scarlet berries. Also called "woody nightshade."
~*adj.* **1.** Bitter and sweet at the same time. **2.** Producing a mixture of pain and pleasure.

bit·ter·weed (bĭt′ər-wēd′) *n.* Any of various plants that yield or contain a bitter principle, such as the **ragweed** *(see),* or plants of the genus *Picris.*

bit·ter·wood (bĭt′ər-wo͝od′) *n.* **1.** The wood of the tree *Quassia amara.* See **quassia. 2.** Any of various other trees from whose bitter wood a substitute for quassia is obtained.

bi·tu·men (bĭ-to͞o′mən, bī-tyo͞o′-) *n.* Any of various mixtures of hydrocarbons, occurring naturally or obtained by distillation from coal or petroleum, found in asphalt and tar, and used for surfacing roads and for waterproofing. [Middle English *bithumen,* from Latin *bitūmen,* probably from Gaulish *bet* (unattested).] **—bi·tu·mi·noid** *adj.*

bi·tu·mi·nize (bĭ-to͞o′mə-nīz′, bĭ-tyo͞o′-) *tr.v.* **-nized, -nizing, -nizes.** To treat with bitumen. **—bi·tu·mi·ni·za·tion** *n.*

bi·tu·mi·nous (bĭ-to͞o′mə-nəs, bĭ-tyo͞o′-, bī-) *adj.* **1.** Like or containing bitumen. **2.** Of or pertaining to bituminous coal.

bituminous coal *n.* A mineral coal that burns with a smoky, yellow flame, yielding volatile bituminous constituents. Also called "soft coal."

bi·va·lent (bī-vā′lənt) *adj.* **1.** *Chemistry.* Having a valence of 2; divalent. **2.** *Genetics.* Composed of two homologous chromosomes or two sets of such chromosomes.
~*n. Genetics.* A pair of homologous chromosomes associated together during meiosis. **—bi·va·lence, bi·va·len·cy** *n.*

bi·valve (bī′vălv′) *n.* Any mollusk of the class Bivalvia (or Pelecypoda), having a shell consisting of two dorsally hinged valves. Bivalves include oysters, cockles, clams, scallops, and mussels. Also called "lamellibranch," "pelecypod."
~*adj.* Also **bi·val·vate** (-văl′vāt′), **bi·val·vu·lar** (-văl′vyə-lər) (for sense 2). **1.** Having a two-valved shell. **2.** Consisting of two similar separable parts.

biv·ou·ac (bĭv′o͞o-ăk, bĭv′wăk) *n.* A temporary encampment made by soldiers in the field.
~*intr.v.* **bivouacked, -acking, -acks** or **-acs.** To encamp in a bivouac. [French, earlier *biwacht,* probably from Swiss German *beiwacht,* "supplementary night watch," from German *Beiwache, Beiwacht* : *bei,* by, at + *Wache,* watch.]

bi·week·ly (bī-wēk′lē) *adj.* **1.** Happening every two weeks. **2.** Happening twice a week; semiweekly.
~*n., pl.* **biweeklies.** A publication issued every two weeks.
~*adv.* **1.** Every two weeks. **2.** Twice a week; semiweekly.

bi·year·ly (bī-yîr′lē) *adj.* **1.** Biennial. **2.** Biannual. **—bi·year·ly** *adv.*

bi·zarre (bĭ-zär′) *adj.* Strikingly unconventional and far-fetched in style or appearance; odd; grotesque. —See Synonyms at **fantastic.** [French, originally "handsome," "brave," from Spanish *bizarro,* from Basque *bizar,* beard ("bearded," hence "spirited").] **—bi·zarre·ly** *adv.* **—bi·zarre·ness** *n.*

Bi·zet (bē-zā′), **Georges,** born Alexandre César Léopold Bizet (1838–75). French composer. His reputation rests chiefly on the opera *Carmen* (1873–74) and the *Arlésienne* suite.

Bk The symbol for the element berkelium.

bk. 1. bank. **2.** book.

bkg. banking.

bkpg. bookkeeping.

bkpt. bankrupt.

bks. 1. barracks. **2.** books.

bl. 1. bale. **2.** barrel. **3.** black. **4.** blue.

B.L. 1. Bachelor of Laws. **2.** Bachelor of Letters; Bachelor of Literature.

B/L bill of lading.

B.L.A. Bachelor of Liberal Arts.

blab (blăb) *v.* **blabbed, blabbing, blabs.** —*tr.* To reveal (a secret), especially through indiscretion. —*intr.* **1.** To talk of secret matters. **2.** To chatter indiscreetly.
~*n.* **1.** A person who blabs. **2.** Lengthy chatter. [Middle English *blabben,* akin to *blabberen,* to BLABBER.] **—blab·by** *adj.*

blab·ber (blăb′ər) *intr.v.* **-bered, -bering, -bers.** To chatter.
~*n.* **1.** Idle chatter. **2.** One who blabs. [Middle English *blabberen,* from an imitative Germanic root *blab-* (unattested).]

blab·ber·mouth (blăb′ər-mouth′) *n., pl.* **-mouths** (-mouthz). *Slang.* One who chatters indiscreetly and at length.

black (blăk) *n. Abbr.* **bl., blk. 1.** An achromatic color value of minimum lightness or maximum darkness; one extreme of the neutral gray series, the opposite being white. Although strictly a response to zero stimulation of the retina, the perception of black appears to depend on contrast with surrounding color stimuli. **2.** Clothing of this color, especially for mourning. **3.** *Often* **Black. a.** Any member of a Negroid people. **b.** Loosely, any member of a dark-skinned ethnic group. **4.** The black-colored chess or checker pieces, or the player using them. **—in the black.** On the credit side of a ledger; prosperous.
~*adj.* **blacker, blackest.** *Abbr.* **bl., blk. 1.** Being of the darkest achromatic visual value; producing or reflecting comparatively little light and having no predominant hue. **2.** Having no light whatso-

ever: *a black cave.* **3.** *Often* **Black. a.** Belonging to a Negroid group. **b.** Loosely, belonging to an ethnic group having dark skin. **4.** Dark in color or having parts that are dark in color. Used with animal and plant names: *black bass; black birch.* **5.** Soiled, as from soot. **6.** Evil; sinister: *black deeds.* **7.** Cheerless and depressing; gloomy. **8.** Angered; sullen; threatening: *a black look.* **9.** Attended with disaster; calamitous. **10.** Of or designating a form of humor dealing with the abnormal and grotesque aspects of life and society and evoking a sense of the comedy of human despair and failure. **11.** Indicating or incurring censure or dishonor: *a black record of environmental pollution.* **12.** Wearing black clothing: *the black knight.* **13.** Served without milk or cream. Said of coffee. **14.** Evading the attention of the tax authorities; illegal: *the black market.* **15.** Purporting to originate from one's own side, when in fact being enemy propaganda: *black radio.* **16.** *British.* Boycotted or not approved by a trade union: *black labor.*

~*tr.v.* **blacked, blacking, blacks. 1.** To make black or dirty; soil. **2.** To put black dye, paint, or polish on. **3.** To bruise (an eye) with a blow. **4.** *British.* To refuse to have anything to do with (a cargo, for example) because of trade union objections. [Middle English *blak,* Old English *blæc.*] **—black•ly** *adv.* **—black•ness** *n.*

Usage: The preferred term for a person today is *black* rather than *Negro.* Another acceptable term is *Afro-American.* The noun and the adjective *black* are usually but not invariably lower-cased: *"Together, blacks and whites can move our country beyond racism"* (Whitney Young, Jr.).

Black (blăk), **Joseph** (1728–99). Scottish chemist and physicist. He rediscovered what was then called "fixed air" (carbon dioxide) and formulated the concepts of latent heat and specific heat.

black alder *n.* **1.** A deciduous holly, *Ilex verticillata,* of eastern North America, bearing bright-scarlet berries. **2.** A tree, *Alnus glutinosa,* native to Eurasia, having dark bark.

black•a•moor (blăk'ə-mo͝or') *n.* Any dark-skinned person; especially, a North African. [Earlier *black More* : BLACK + MOOR.]

black-and-blue (blăk'ən-blo͞o') *adj.* Discolored from coagulation of blood below the surface of the skin.

Black and Tan *n.* An auxiliary member of the Royal Irish Constabulary, mostly British ex-servicemen, specially recruited to suppress the Sinn Fein rebellion of 1920–21. [After the color of the uniform.]

black-and-tan terrier (blăk'ən-tăn') *n.* A **Manchester terrier** *(see).*

black and white *n.* **1.** Print or writing: *Be sure to get the agreement in black and white.* **2.** Tones of black and white. **3.** A picture or photograph in tones of black and white.

black-and-white (blăk'ən-hwīt', -wīt') *adj.* **1.** Pertaining or restricted to film or photography in tones of black and white: *a black-and-white television set.* **2.** Presenting exaggeratedly simplistic ideas, usually polarized in moral terms.

black art *n.* **Black magic** *(see).*

black•ball (blăk'bôl') *n.* **1.** A small, black ball used as a negative ballot. **2.** A negative vote that blocks the admission of an applicant to an organization.

~*tr.v.* **blackballed, -balling, -balls. 1.** To vote against; especially, to veto the admission of. **2.** To exclude from a social group; ostracize. [From the small black ball dropped into a ballot box to represent an adverse vote.] **—black•ball•er** *n.*

black bass *n.* Any of several North American freshwater game fishes of the genus *Micropterus.*

black bear *n.* Either of two black or dark-brown bears, *Ursus* (or *Euarctos*) *americanus,* of North America, or *Selenarctos thibetanus,* of Asia. The Asian species has a pale V-shaped chest marking.

Blackbeard. See Edward **Teach.**

black belt *n.* **1. a.** The rank of expert in a system of self-defense such as judo or karate. **b.** The black-colored sash that symbolizes this rank. **c.** A person who holds this rank. **2.** A region of rich, black soil. **3.** An area with a predominantly black population.

black•ber•ry (blăk'bĕr'ē, -bər-ē) *n., pl.* **-ries. 1.** Any of several woody plants of the genus *Rubus,* having canelike, usually thorny stems and black, glossy, edible berries. Also called "bramble." See **black raspberry, dewberry, loganberry. 2.** The fruit of any of these plants.

blackberry lily *n.* A plant, *Belamcanda chinensis,* having spotted orange flowers and a seed cluster that resembles a blackberry.

black bile *n.* One of the four **humors** *(see)* of medieval physiology, supposed to cause melancholia.

black bindweed *n.* A vine, *Polygonum convolvulus,* native to Europe and naturalized as a weed in North America.

black birch *n.* A North American tree, *Betula lenta,* having dark, brownish bark and twigs and leaves that yield an aromatic oil.

black•bird (blăk'bûrd') *n.* **1.** Any of various New World birds of the family Icteridae, having black or predominantly black plumage in the male. **2.** A common Eurasian bird, *Turdus merula,* of the thrush family, of which the male is black with a yellow bill and the female is brown. See **cowbird, grackle, redwing.**

black•board (blăk'bôrd', -bōrd') *n.* A panel with a black or sometimes colored surface for writing on with chalk, used especially in schools; chalkboard.

blackboard jungle *n.* **1.** A school with a reputation for violence by pupils. **2.** The phenomenon of aggression and violence in schools. [From the title of a book (1954) by Evan Hunter, popularized as a film.]

black•bod•y (blăk'bŏd'ē) *n., pl.* **-ies.** *Physics.* A theoretically perfect absorber of all incident radiation.

blackbody radiation *n.* The thermal radiation emitted by a blackbody at a given temperature. The total amount of radiation emitted is given by the **Stefan-Boltzmann law** and the spectral energy distribution by **Planck's formula** *(both of which see).*

black book *n.* A record of people liable to punishment. **—in someone's black book.** In disfavor with someone.

black box *n.* **1.** A device or theoretical construct, especially an electric circuit, with known or specified performance characteristics but unknown or unspecified constituents and means of operation. **2.** A **flight recorder** *(see).* **3.** Any device used for automatically recording the details of a journey. See **tachograph.**

black bread *n.* Coarse rye bread.

black bryony *n.* A climbing European plant, *Tamus communis,* having small, greenish flowers and poisonous red berries.

black•buck (blăk'bŭk') *n.* An antelope, *Antilope cervicapra,* of India, of which the male has a dark back and spiral horns. Also called "sasin."

Black•burn (blăk'bərn). Industrial town in northwest England, in the central Lancashire coal field. It is located on the Leeds-Liverpool canal.

black•cap (blăk'kăp') *n.* **1.** The **black raspberry** *(see).* **2.** A small European bird, *Sylvia atricapilla,* of which the male is gray with a black crown. **3.** Any of various other black-crowned birds.

black•cock (blăk'kŏk') *n.* The male of the **black grouse** *(see).*

black cohosh *n.* A tall plant, *Cimicifuga racemosa,* of eastern North America, having long clusters of small, whitish flowers.

black crappie *n.* An edible North American fish, *Pomoxis nigromaculatus,* having dark, mottled coloring.

black currant *n.* **1.** A widely cultivated Eurasian shrub, *Ribes nigrum,* producing clusters of small edible black berries. **2.** The fruit of this shrub.

black•damp (blăk'dămp') *n.* A gas composed of a mixture of carbon dioxide and nitrogen, found in mines after fires and explosions of combustible gases. Also called "chokedamp."

Black Death *n.* A form of plague that was pandemic throughout Europe and much of Asia during periods in the 14th century. [From the dark splotches it causes on the skin.]

black diamond *n.* **1.** A variety of diamond, **carbonado** *(see).* **2. black diamonds.** Coal.

black dog *n.* A melancholy state or mood; depression. Usually preceded by *the.*

black earth *n.* A type of soil, **chernozem** *(see).* **—black-earth** *adj.*

black•en (blăk'ən) *v.* **-ened, -ening, -ens.** —*tr.* **1.** To make black. **2.** To stain (someone's reputation, for example); defame. —*intr.* To become black or dark. **—black•en•er** *n.*

Black•ett (blăk'ĭt), **Patrick Maynard Stuart, Baron** (1897–1974). British physicist. For his contributions to the study of cosmic radiation, he was awarded the Nobel Prize for physics (1948).

black eye *n.* **1.** A bruised discoloration of the flesh surrounding the eye, resulting from a blow. **2.** A heavy defeat; bad setback.

black-eyed pea (blăk'īd') *n.* The edible seed of the **cowpea** *(see).*

black-eyed Susan *n.* **1.** Any of several North American plants of the genus *Rudbeckia*; especially, *R. hirta,* having hairy stems and leaves, and flowers with orange-yellow rays and dark-brown centers. **2.** A vine, *Thunbergia alata,* native to tropical Africa, having white or orange-yellow flowers with purple throats.

black•face (blăk'fās') *n.* **1.** Make-up for a conventionalized comic travesty of blacks, as in a minstrel show. **2.** An actor in a minstrel show. **3.** *Printing.* Boldface type. **4.** *British.* A black-faced sheep.

black•fish (blăk'fĭsh') *n., pl.* **-fishes** or collectively **blackfish. 1.** Any of various dark-colored fishes, such as: **a.** A freshwater fish, *Dallia pectoralis,* of far northern regions. **b.** The **tautog** *(see).* **2.** The **pilot whale** *(see).* **3.** A female salmon that has recently spawned. Compare **redfish.**

black flag *n.* The flag used by pirates, the **Jolly Roger** *(see).*

black fly *n.* Any of various small, dark-colored, bloodsucking flies of the family Simuliidae. Also called "buffalo gnat."

black•fly (blăk'flī') *n., pl.* **-flies** or collectively **blackfly.** A black aphid, *Aphis fabae,* that feeds in large masses on bean plants, spinach, dock, and the like.

Black•foot (blăk'fo͝ot') *n., pl.* **-feet** or collectively **Blackfoot. 1.** Any of three tribes of Algonquian-speaking Indians formerly inhabiting the regions of Montana, Alberta, and Saskatchewan. **2.** A member of one of these tribes. **3.** The Algonquian language spoken by these peoples. [Translation of Blackfoot *Siksika*; said to be so named because the soles of their moccasins were black from walking across burned prairie.] **—Black•foot** *adj.*

black-foot•ed ferret (blăk'fo͝ot'ĭd) *n.* A weasellike mammal, *Mustela nigripes,* of central North America, related to the polecat and having yellowish fur and dark feet. Also called "ferret."

Black Forest. See **Schwarzwald.**

Black Friar *n.* A Dominican friar. [After the black mantles worn by the Dominican friars.]

black frost *n.* A condition in which the air temperature falls below the freezing point without frost forming, causing blackening and internal damage in vegetation.

black gold *n.* Crude oil.

black grouse *n.* A Eurasian game bird, *Lyrurus tetrix.* of which the black male is called "blackcock," the mottled female is called "greyhen," and for which the collective plural is "black game."

black•guard (blăg'ərd, -ärd) *n.* **1.** A scoundrel. **2.** A scurrilous person.

~*adj.* Of or like a blackguard; foulmouthed.

black currant *The cultivated fruit of this shrub is rich in vitamin C and is used mainly in soft drinks and for making jam.*

blackface *Once a Scottish breed, the blackface is now widespread. Kept mainly for meat, the sheep does not yield a heavy fleece, but the wool is long and flowing.*

black grouse *A male black grouse, or blackcock, fans its tail as part of its courtship display. In the mating season, these northern European game birds gather at communal mating grounds known as leks, often returning to the same site year after year. Females have brown plumage.*

~*v.* **blackguarded, -guarding, -guards.** —*tr.* To abuse or revile. —*intr.* To behave like a blackguard. [Originally, the kitchen workers and menials of a noble household or of an army.] —**black·guard·ism** *n.* —**black·guard·ly** *adj. & adv.*

Black Hand *n.* A secret society organized for acts of terrorism and blackmail, composed mainly of Sicilians active in the United States in the early 20th century. Compare **Mafia.**

Black Hawk (blăk'hôk'), original name Makataimeshekiakiak (1767–1838). U.S. Indian leader. Resenting an 1804 treaty that ceded all of his tribe's lands east of the Mississippi River to the United States, he led 1,000 Fox and Sauk Indians in the Black Hawk War. His autobiography is a classic statement of Indian indignation toward white intrusion.

black·head (blăk'hĕd') *n.* **1.** A plug of dried fatty matter capped with blackened dust and epithelial debris that clogs a pore of the skin. Also called "comedo." **2.** *Veterinary Medicine.* An infectious, often fatal, liver and intestinal disease of turkeys and some wildfowl. Also called "infectious enterohepatitis." **3.** Any of various birds with dark head markings.

black·heart (blăk'härt') *n.* **1.** A disease of potatoes and other plants, in which the inner tissues darken. **2.** Abnormal blackening of the stems in woody plants, probably caused by extreme cold. **3.** A variety of dark-skinned purple-fleshed cherry.

black·heart·ed (blăk'här'tĭd) *adj.* Evil by nature; wicked.

Black·heath (blăk'hēth'). District and former village in southeast Greater London in England, in the boroughs of Greenwich and Lewisham. Its common was used as a rallying-point by Wat Tyler and Jack Cade for attacks on London in the rebellions of 1381 and 1450.

Black Hills. Rugged mountains of southwest South Dakota and northeast Wyoming. Harney Peak (2,209 meters; 7,242 feet) is the highest peak. The region is rich in mineral resources.

black hole *n.* A region in space caused by a star collapsing under its own gravitational force to such an extent that its gravitational field prevents any matter, light, or other electromagnetic radiation leaving the region. See **singularity, white hole.**

Black Hole of Calcutta *n.* **1.** A small dungeon at Calcutta, India, in which 123 of the 146 British prisoners confined there on June 20, 1756, died of suffocation. **2. black hole of Calcutta.** An uncomfortable, confined space.

black horehound *n.* A strong-smelling plant, *Ballota nigra,* native to Europe, having clusters of purple flowers.

black humor *n.* The humor of the morbid and the absurd, especially as a literary genre.

black·ing (blăk'ĭng) *n.* **1. Lamp black** *(see).* **2.** A black paste or liquid used as shoe polish.

black·ish (blăk'ĭsh) *adj.* Somewhat black. —**black·ish·ly** *adv.*

black·jack[1] (blăk'jăk') *n.* A small leather-covered bludgeon with a short, flexible shaft or strap, used as a hand weapon. ~*tr.v.* **blackjacked, -jacking, -jacks. 1.** To hit with a blackjack. **2.** To coerce by threats. [BLACK + JACK (tool).]

blackjack[2] *n.* An oak tree, *Quercus marilandica,* of the southeastern United States, having blackish bark. Also called "blackjack oak." [BLACK + JACK (tool).]

blackjack[3] *n.* A card game in which the object is to accumulate cards with a total count nearer to 21 than that of the dealer. Also called "twenty-one." [BLACK + JACK (knave in cards).]

blackjack[4] *n.* A tankard made of tarred or waxed leather. [BLACK + Middle English *jakke,* leather coat, container, from Old French *jacque* (see **jacket**).]

blackjack[5] *n.* Sphalerite or zinc sulfide ore. [BLACK + JACK (impertinent, worthless person); miners' term for this worthless mixture in lead ore.]

black lead *n.* **Graphite** *(see).*

black·leg (blăk'lĕg') *n.* **1.** *Veterinary Medicine.* An infectious, usually fatal, gas gangrene affecting the heavily muscled upper parts of the legs of sheep and cattle. **2.** A bacterial or fungous plant disease that causes the stems of plants to turn black. **3.** One who cheats in gambling, especially a professional gambler; cardsharp. **4.** *British.* A strikebreaker; scab.

black letter *n. Printing.* **1.** A heavy typeface having very broad counters and thick, ornamental serifs. Also called "gothic," "church text," "Old English." **2.** Loosely, any heavy, black typeface. —**black-let·ter** *adj.*

black light *n.* Invisible ultraviolet or infrared radiation.

black·list (blăk'lĭst') *n.* A list of persons or organizations to be disapproved of, boycotted, or suspected of disloyalty. ~*tr.v.* **blacklisted, -listing, -lists.** To place (a name) on a blacklist.

black lung *n.* A disease suffered by coal miners involving chronic inflammation of the lungs as a result of inhaling coal dust.

black magic *n.* Magic as practiced in league with the Devil; witchcraft. Also called "black art." —See Synonyms at **magic.**

black·mail (blăk'māl') *n.* **1.** Extortion by the threat of exposure or criminal prosecution. **2.** Money extorted in this manner. **3.** Tribute formerly paid to freebooters along the Scottish border for protection against pillage. ~*tr.v.* **blackmailed, -mailing, -mails. 1.** To extort money or something of value from (a person) by means of blackmail. **2.** To coerce or influence the behavior of by means of blackmail. [BLACK + *mail,* tribute, Middle English *maill, male,* Old English *māl,* agreement, from Old Norse *māl,* speech, agreement.] —**black·mail·er** *n.*

Black Ma·ri·a (mə-rī'ə) *n.* A police van, used especially for transporting offenders.

black mark *n.* A sign of disapprobation, discredit, or the like.

black market *n.* **1.** The illicit trade in goods or currencies in violation of price controls, rationing, or other restrictions. **2.** A place where such trade takes place.

black-mar·ket (blăk'mär'kĭt) *tr.v.* **-keted, -keting, -kets.** To trade (goods) on a black market. —**black marketer, black marketeer** *n.*

black mass *n.* A travesty of the Roman Catholic Mass practiced by Satanists.

black measles *n.* A severe form of measles, characterized by a dark rash due to subcutaneous bleeding.

black medic, black medick *n.* A cloverlike plant, *Medicago lupulina,* native to Europe, having compound leaves, small yellow flower heads, and black pods. Also called "nonesuch."

Black·more (blăk'mōr', -môr'), **Richard Doddridge** (1825–1900). British novelist and poet. He wrote several volumes of verse and published 15 novels, but he is remembered now only for his historical romance *Lorna Doone* (1869).

Black Muslim *n.* A member of the **Nation of Islam** *(see).*

black mustard *n.* A plant, *Brassica nigra,* native to Eurasia, having clusters of yellow flowers. Its pungent seeds, ground to a powder, are a source of the condiment mustard.

black-necked stork *n.* The **jabiru** *(see).*

black nightshade *n.* A plant, the **deadly nightshade** *(see).*

black oak *n.* A deciduous tree, *Quercus velutina,* of eastern North America, having hard, durable wood. Also called "quercitron."

black out *tr.v.* **1.** To cause or produce the blacking out of (a city, theater, or radio station, for example). **2.** To suppress or delete for political reasons or by censorship. —*intr.v.* To undergo a blackout; especially, to suffer a temporary loss of consciousness, memory, or vision.

---

black hole

THE INVISIBLE GIANTS
Stars so dense that not even light can escape their pull

When a star dies, its nuclear fuel exhausted, it cools and contracts dramatically. In a star the size of our sun, this contraction eventually produces a dense dwarf star, a thimbleful of whose matter would weigh about 10 tons. But in a very large star—several times as massive as the sun —many physicists believe that there is no limit to the contraction. The star collapses under the pull of its gravity until nothing, not even light, can escape. It becomes a black hole.

By their very nature, black holes cannot be seen directly. But their presence can be deduced from their effect on nearby material. What may be the first known black hole was found in the 1970's about 6,000 light-years away in the constellation of Cygnus the Swan. The area around the hole is known as Cyg X-1; it gives off strong x-rays—the result, astronomers believe, of material being compressed and heated just before it is sucked in.

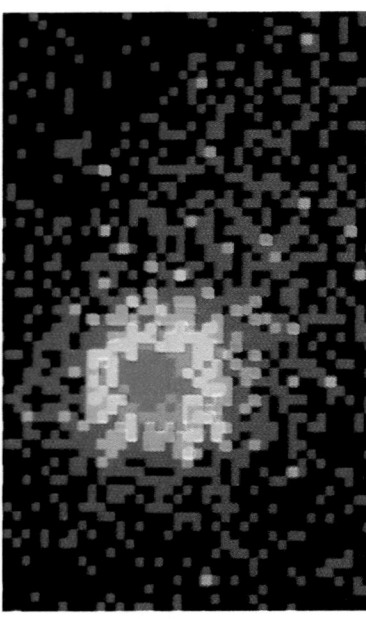

CYG X-1 *A color-coded impression (above) of the x-rays given off by Cyg X-1. They suggest that a giant star has an invisible companion, possibly a black hole, about 15 times as massive as the sun. A black hole cannot yet be described, but some theorists envisage one as a gravitational "well" or funnel (right) pouring matter from our universe into another as yet unknown.*

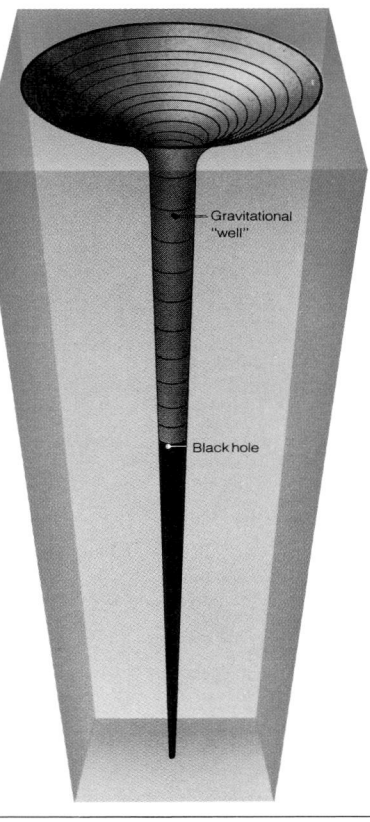

Gravitational "well"

Black hole

black·out (blăk′out′) *n.* **1.** The extinguishing or concealing of lights that might be visible to enemy aircraft during an air raid at night. Compare **dim-out. 2.** A temporary loss of electric power. **3.** In the theater, the sudden extinguishing of all stage lights to indicate passage of time, or to mark the end of an act or a scene. **4.** A temporary loss of consciousness or vision. **5.** A suppression or stoppage, as of news for political reasons. **6.** A temporary loss or stoppage of radio or television communication or broadcasting caused by a technical fault, a strike, or the like.

Black Panther *n.* A member of a militant organization of black Americans.

black pepper *n.* See **pepper.**

black·poll (blăk′pōl′) *n.* A North American warbler, *Dendroica striata,* of which the male has a black cap.

black poplar *n.* An ornamental poplar tree, *Populus nigra,* native to Eurasia, having spreading branches and pointed, triangular leaves. See **Lombardy poplar.**

Black Power *n.* A movement among black Americans emphasizing racial pride and social equality through the creation of black political and cultural institutions.

Black Prince. See **Edward, Prince of Wales.**

black pudding *n. Chiefly British.* **Blood pudding** *(see).*

black raspberry *n.* **1.** A prickly shrub, *Rubus occidentalis,* of eastern North America, bearing black fruit. **2.** The fruit of this plant. Also called "blackcap."

black rat *n.* A type of **rat** *(see).*

Black Rod *n.* A British official, the chief usher of various institutions, including the House of Lords.

black rot *n.* Any of various plant diseases, particularly affecting fruits and vegetables, caused by fungi or bacteria and resulting in darkening of the leaves and decay.

Black Sash *n.* A movement in South Africa of women against apartheid.

Black Sea. A sea lying between Europe and Asia. It is connected to the Mediterranean Sea by the Bosporus, the Sea of Marmara, and Dardanelles. The Ukrainian Black Sea port of Odessa, frozen for three months, is kept open all year by icebreakers.

black sheep *n.* **1.** A sheep with black fleece. **2.** A person considered undesirable or disgraceful by his family or peer group.

Black Shirt *n.* A member of a fascist party organization, especially Mussolini's Italian Fascist party. [After the black shirts of Italian Fascist uniforms.]

black·smith (blăk′smĭth′) *n.* **1.** One who forges and shapes iron with an anvil and hammer. **2.** One who makes, repairs, and fits horseshoes. [Middle English *blaksmith,* "a worker in black metal" (iron).] **—black·smith·ing** *n.*

black·snake (blăk′snāk′) *n.* **1.** Any of various dark-colored, nonvenomous snakes, such as the black racer, *Coluber constrictor,* or the black rat snake, *Elaphe obsoleta,* of North America. **2.** *Western U.S.* A long, tapering, braided rawhide or leather whip with a snapper on the end. **3.** Any of various venomous black snakes, such as the Australian species *Pseudechis porphyriacus.*

black spot *n.* Any of various plant diseases caused by fungi or bacteria and resulting in small black spots on the leaves.

black spruce *n.* An evergreen tree, *Picea mariana,* of northern North America, growing mostly in bogs. Sometimes called "spruce pine."

Black·stone (blăk′stən, -stōn′), **Sir William** (1723–80). British jurist. His enduring fame rests on his monumental four-volume *Commentaries on the Laws of England* (1765–69), the most comprehensive single treatment of the body of English law.

black·strap (blăk′străp′) *n.* A dark, very thick molasses used in the manufacture of industrial alcohol, and as an ingredient in cattle feed. Also called "blackstrap molasses."

black-tailed deer (blăk′tāld′) *n.* Also **black·tail deer** (blăk′tāl′). The **mule deer** *(see).*

black tea *n.* A dark tea, the leaf of which is fully fermented or oxidized before drying. Compare **green tea, oolong.**

black·thorn (blăk′thôrn′) *n.* A thorny Eurasian shrub, *Prunus spinosa,* having clusters of white flowers and bluish-black, plumlike fruit. Also called "sloe."

black tie *n.* **1.** A black bow tie worn with a dinner jacket. **2.** Semiformal evening wear for men, typically requiring a black dinner jacket. Compare **white tie. —black-tie** *adj.*

black·top (blăk′tŏp′) *n.* A bituminous material, such as asphalt, used to pave roads.
~*tr.v.* **blacktopped, -topping, -tops.** To pave with blacktop.

black velvet *n.* A drink consisting of stout and champagne.

black vomit *n.* **1.** A vomit consisting of bloody matter. **2.** Severe yellow fever with symptomatic regurgitation of such vomit.

black vulture *n.* A carrion-eating bird, *Coragyps atratus,* of central North America and South America, having black plumage and a bald, black head.

black walnut *n.* **1.** A deciduous walnut tree, *Juglans nigra,* of eastern North America, having dark, hard wood and edible nuts. **2.** The grained wood of this tree, used for cabinetwork.

Black Watch *n.* **1.** A Highland regiment of the British Army, the men of which wear uniforms of a dark-blue and dark-green tartan. **2.** *Often* **black watch.** The tartan of the Black Watch.

black·wa·ter fever (blăk′wô′tər, -wŏt′ər) *n.* A severe, frequently fatal malaria with symptomatic excretion of blood in the urine caused by destruction of red blood cells.

black widow *n.* A New World spider, *Latrodectus mactans,* of which the extremely venomous female is black with red markings. [From the fact that the female eats its mate.]

blad·der (blăd′ər) *n.* **1.** *Anatomy.* Any of various distensible membranous sacs found in most animals, especially the **urinary bladder** *(see).* **2.** Anything resembling such a sac: *the bladder of a football.* **3.** *Botany.* An inflated, hollow structure, such as the air sac in certain seaweeds. **4.** *Pathology.* A blister, pustule, or cyst filled with fluid or air. [Middle English *bladdre,* Old English *blǣdre.*]

bladder campion *n.* A plant, *Silene cucubalus,* native to Europe, having white flowers and an inflated calyx.

blad·der·nose (blăd′ər-nōz′) *n.* An aquatic mammal, the **hooded seal** *(see).*

blad·der-nut (blăd′ər-nŭt′) *n.* Any of several shrubs or small trees of the genus *Staphylea,* of the North Temperate Zone, having small, whitish flowers and inflated seed pods.

bladder worm *n.* The bladderlike, encysted larva of the tapeworm.

blad·der·wort (blăd′ər-wûrt′, -wôrt′) *n.* Any of various aquatic plants of the genus *Utricularia,* having violet or yellow flowers, and, in most species, small bladders that trap minute aquatic animals.

bladder wrack *n.* A rockweed, *Fucus vesiculosus,* having forked, brownish-green fronds with air-filled bladders.

blade (blād) *n.* **1.** The flat-edged cutting part of a sharpened tool or weapon. **2. a.** A sword. **b.** A swordsman. **3.** A dashing young man. **4.** Any flat, thin structural member or section, such as the flat part of an oar or propeller. **5.** *Anatomy.* The **scapula** *(see).* **6.** *Botany.* **a.** The leaf of a grass or similar plant. **b.** The expanded, usually green part of a leaf, as distinguished from the leafstalk. **7.** The upper surface of the tongue, just behind the tip. [Middle English *blade,* Old English *blæd,* leaf, blade.] **—blad·ed** *adj.*

blade-ap·ple (blăd′ăp′əl) *n.* A spiny, vinelike, tropical American cactus, *Pereskia aculeata,* having true leaves, white flowers, and pulpy yellow fruit. Also called "Barbados gooseberry."

blah (blä) *n. Slang.* **1.** Worthless nonsense; drivel. **2. blahs.** A general feeling of physical or psychological discomfort or dissatisfaction.
~*adj.* Dull and uninteresting. [Imitative.]

blain (blān) *n.* A skin sore; blister; blotch. [Middle English *blein, blain,* an inflammatory swelling, Old English *blegen.*]

Blake (blāk), **Robert** (1599–1657). English admiral who was on the Parliamentarian side in the English Civil War. He pursued Prince Rupert to the Mediterranean (1650) and virtually destroyed the Royalist fleet there.

Blake, William (1757–1827). British poet and painter. He trained as an engraver and illustrated his own poems. Both his poems and his paintings have a mystical, visionary quality. His first important volumes of poetry were the childlike *Songs of Innocence* (1789) and *Songs of Experience* (1794). In these and his later, prophetic volumes, such as *The Marriage of Heaven and Hell* (*c.* 1790), Blake railed against both cruelty and injustice and made a plea for the freedom of the human spirit.

blame (blām) *tr.v.* **blamed, blaming, blames. 1.** To hold responsible; accuse. **2.** To find fault with; censure. **3.** To place responsibility for (something) on a person or thing: *blamed the accident on the cyclist.* —See Synonyms at **criticize.**
~*n.* **1.** The responsibility for a fault or error. **2.** Censure; condemnation. **—be to blame.** To be guilty or responsible. Used with *for.* [Middle English *blamen,* from Old French *blamer,* earlier *blasmer,* from Vulgar Latin *blastēmāre* (unattested), alteration of Late Latin *blasphēmāre,* to reproach, BLASPHEME.] **—blam·a·ble, blame·a·ble** *adj.* **—blam·er** *n.*

blame·ful (blām′fəl) *adj.* Deserving of blame; blameworthy. **—blame·ful·ly** *adv.* **—blame·ful·ness** *n.*

blame·less (blām′lĭs) *adj.* Free from blame or guilt; innocent. **—blame·less·ly** *adv.* **—blame·less·ness** *n.*

blame·wor·thy (blām′wûr′*thē*) *adj.* Deserving of blame; reprehensible. **—blame·wor·thi·ness** *n.*

Blanc (bläN), **Louis** (1811–82). Spanish-born French politician and political theorist. His lasting importance rests on his writings, especially the *Organization of Work* (1839), one of the most influential of early socialist treatises.

Blanc, Mont. See **Mont Blanc.**

blanc fixe (blăngk′fĭks′) *n.* Powdered barium sulfate used as a white base for water-color pigments. [French, "fixed white."]

blanch (blănch, blänch) *v.* **blanched, blanching, blanches.** Also **blench** (blĕnch). —*tr.* **1.** To take color from; bleach. **2.** To whiten (a growing food plant, such as celery) by covering to cut off direct light. **3.** To whiten (a metal) by soaking in acid or by coating with tin. **4. a.** To loosen the skin of (almonds, for example) by scalding. **b.** To boil (food) briefly to remove strong or bitter flavors or to kill enzymes prior to freezing. **5.** To cause to turn pale. —*intr.* To turn white or become pale as through shock or illness. [Middle English *blaunchen,* from Old French *blanchir,* from *blanche,* feminine of *blanc,* white, from Vulgar Latin *blancus* (unattested), from Germanic.] **—blanch·er** *n.*

blanc·mange (blə-mänj′; *French* bläN-mäNzh′) *n.* A flavored and sweetened milk pudding, thickened with cornstarch and set with gelatin in a mold. [Middle English *blancmanger,* dish of chopped chicken or fish with rice, from Old French, "white food" : *blanc,* white (see **blanch**) + *manger,* food, from *mangier,* to eat (see **mange**).]

bland (blănd) *adj.* **blander, blandest. 1.** Characterized by a moderate, undisturbing, or tranquil quality: **a.** Pleasant in manner; ingratiating. **b.** Free of irritation; soothing: *a bland diet.* **c.** Mild; balmy.

black widow *The black widow spider is so called because the female sometimes devours the male after mating. She is recognizable by her red mottling and is seen here with an egg sac. Black widow spiders are highly venomous, but their bite is seldom fatal to humans.*

bladder campion *This plant grows from 22 centimeters (9 inches) to 60 centimeters (2 feet) high and has white—and very occasionally pink—flowers. A native of Europe, it is widely naturalized in the United States and blooms from June to August.*

2. Lacking a distinctive character; mediocre. [Latin *blandus,* caressing, flattering, "soft-spoken."] —**bland·ly** *adv.* —**bland·ness** *n.*

blan·dish (blăn′dĭsh) *tr.v.* **-dished, -dishing, -dishes.** To coax by flattery or wheedling; cajole. [Middle English *blandishen,* from Old French *blandir* (present stem *blandiss-*), from Latin *blandīrī,* from *blandus,* flattering, BLAND.] —**blan·dish·er** *n.* —**blan·dish·ment** *n.*

blank (blăngk) *adj.* **blanker, blankest.** **1.** Bearing no writing, print, or marking of any kind. **2.** Not finished or filled in: *a blank questionnaire.* **3.** Having no finishing grooves or cuts: *a blank key.* **4. a.** Expressing nothing; vacant. **b.** Vacuous; having no inspiration: *my mind was blank.* **c.** Confused, uncomprehending: *a blank look.* **5.** Devoid of activity or character; empty. **6.** Barren; fruitless: *blank efforts.* **7.** Utter; complete: *a blank refusal.* **8.** Having no openings or ornamentation: *a blank wall.* —See Synonyms at **empty.**
~*n.* **1.** An empty space; void: *His memory was a complete blank.* **2. a.** An empty space on a document to be filled in. **b.** A document having one or more such spaces. **3.** An unfinished material, part, or article, such as a key form, that is prepared ready for eventual finishing. **4.** A gun cartridge with a charge of powder but no bullet. Also called "blank cartridge." **5.** A lottery ticket that wins no prize. **6.** A mark, usually a dash (—), indicating the omission of a word or letter. **7.** The center white circle of a target; the bull's eye. **8.** Something used to seal an opening. **9.** Any goal or target. —**draw a blank.** *Informal.* To fail utterly; achieve nothing.
~*tr.v.* **blanked, blanking, blanks.** **1.** To remove from view; obliterate: *The strong glare of the sun blanked it from view.* **2.** To omit; delete; invalidate. Often used with *out.* **3.** To prevent (an opponent in a game or sport) from scoring. **4.** To punch or stamp from flat stock, especially with a die. Often used with *out.* **5.** To seal or block (an opening or means of access). Often used with *off.* [Middle English *bla(u)nk,* white, not written on, from Old French *blanc.* See **blanch.**] —**blank·ly** *adv.* —**blank·ness** *n.*

blank check *n.* **1.** A check that has been signed, but which has not had the amount filled in. **2.** Unrestrained freedom of action or choice.

blank endorsement *n.* An endorsement on a check or negotiable note that names no payee, making it payable to the bearer. Also called "endorsement in blank."

blan·ket (blăng′kĭt) *n.* **1.** A large piece of wool or other thick cloth used as a covering for warmth, especially on a bed. **2.** A thick layer that covers or encloses: *a blanket of snow.*
~*adj.* Covering a wide range of conditions or requirements: *a blanket insurance policy.*
~*tr.v.* **blanketed, -keting, -kets.** **1.** To cover with or as if with a blanket. **2.** To conceal or suppress as if with a blanket. **3.** *Nautical.* To cut off (a sail boat) from the wind by passing close on the windward side. [Middle English, originally, a white woolen material, from Old French *blanquet, blanchet,* diminutive of *blanc,* white. See **blanch.**]

blanket stitch *n.* The buttonhole stitch, as used for edging around a blanket.

blank verse *n.* Verse consisting of unrhymed lines, usually of iambic pentameter.

blan·quette de veau (blän-kĕt′də-vō′) *n.* A stew or fricassee of veal in a white sauce. [French, white dish of veal. See **blanket.**]

Blan·qui (blän-kē′), **Louis Auguste** (1805–81). French revolutionary leader and political theorist. He fought for the deposition of Napoleon III and proclamation of the Paris Commune. His ideas, close to those of Karl Marx, were expressed in his treatise, *Critique Sociale,* published four years after his death.

Blan·tyre (blăn-tīr′). Also **Blan·tyre-Lim·be** (-lĭm′bā). The oldest and largest town in Malawi, in the Shire Highlands. It was founded as a mission of the Church of Scotland by David Livingstone (1876) and named after the village where he was born.

blare (blâr) *v.* **blared, blaring, blares.** —*intr.* To sound loudly and insistently. —*tr.* To utter or proclaim loudly.
~*n.* A loud, strident noise. [Middle English *bleren,* to bellow, from Middle Dutch.]

blar·ney (blär′nē) *n.* Smooth, flattering talk.
~*v.* **blarneyed, -neying, -neys.** —*tr.* To beguile with blarney. —*intr.* To flatter. [After the *Blarney Stone.*]

Blar·ney (blär′nē). A village in County Cork, Republic of Ireland. Blarney Castle (*c.* 1446) has on its southern wall the famous Blarney Stone, said to impart gifts of eloquence and flattery to those who kiss it.

Blas·co I·bá·ñez (blä′skō ē-bän′yäs), **Vicente** (1867–1928). Spanish politician and novelist. He founded the republican paper *El Pueblo* (1891), was elected to the Spanish parliament (1901), and spent more than 30 periods in prison for his antimonarchist views before settling in France (1923). His most famous novel is *The Four Horsemen of the Apocalypse* (1916).

bla·sé (blä-zā′, blä′zā) *adj.* **1.** Indifferent, unexcited, or lacking enthusiasm, especially as a result of habitual and excessive indulgence. **2.** Filled with ennui; weary. [French, past participle of *blaser,* to blunt, cloy, "to cause to be bloated with strong liquor," from Middle Dutch *blasen,* to blow up, cause to swell.]

blas·pheme (blăs-fēm′) *v.* **-phemed, -pheming, -phemes.** —*tr.* **1.** To speak of (God or something sacred) in an irreverent or impious manner. **2.** To revile; execrate: *"and every tongue/ Cursed and blasphemed him as he passed"* (P.B. Shelley). —*intr.* To utter blasphemy. [Middle English *blasfemen, blasphemen,* from Old French *blasfemer,* from Late Latin *blasphēmāre,* to reproach, blaspheme,

from Greek *blasphēmein,* from *blasphēmos,* evil-speaking, BLASPHE-MOUS.] —**blas·phem·er** *n.*

blas·phe·mous (blăs′fə-məs) *adj.* Impiously irreverent. —See Synonyms at **profane.** [Late Latin *blasphēmus,* from Greek *blasphēmos,* evil-speaking, impious.] —**blas·phe·mous·ly** *adv.* —**blas·phe·mous·ness** *n.*

blas·phe·my (blăs′fə-mē) *n., pl.* **-mies. 1. a.** Any contemptuous or profane act, utterance, or writing concerning God or something considered sacred. **b.** The act of claiming for oneself the attributes and rights of God. **2.** An irreverent or impious act, attitude, or utterance in regard to something considered inviolable or sacrosanct.

blast (blăst, bläst) *n.* **1. a.** A strong gust of wind. **b.** The battering effect of such a gust. **2.** A forcible stream of air or other gas from an opening, especially one in a blast furnace to aid combustion. **3. a.** The blowing of a whistle or wind instrument. **b.** The sound or noise produced by this. **4. a.** An explosion. **b.** A charge of explosive. **c.** The powerful, destructive rush of air resulting from an explosion. **5.** Any disease of plants that results in failure of flowers to open, or failure of fruit or seeds to mature. **6.** A violent verbal assault or outburst. **7.** A big or wild party. —See Synonyms at **wind.** —**(at) full blast.** At full speed, volume, or capacity.
~*v.* **blasted, blasting, blasts.** —*tr.* **1.** To tear to pieces by or as if by explosion; blow up. **2.** To cause to deteriorate; ruin; frustrate: *His dreams were all blasted by the news of his rejection.* **3.** To cause to shrivel, wither, or mature imperfectly by or as if by blast or blight. **4.** To make, dislodge, or open (something) by or as if by explosion: *blast a channel through the reefs.* **5.** *Slang.* To attack or criticize vigorously. **6.** *Slang.* To damn. Used euphemistically. —*intr.* **1.** To detonate explosives. **2.** To emit a sudden loud noise. **3.** To wither, shrivel, or mature imperfectly. **4.** *Slang.* To attack or criticize with vigor. **5.** *Slang.* To shoot. Sometimes used with *away.* **6.** *Electronics.* To distort sound recording or transmission by overloading a microphone or loud-speaker.
~*interj.* *Informal.* Used to express annoyance or frustration. [Middle English *blast,* Old English *blæst.*] —**blast·er** *n.*

-blast *suffix* Indicates a germ, sprout, or growth; for example, **erythroblast.** [Greek *blastos,* shoot, bud.]

blast·ed (blăs′tĭd, bläs′-) *adj.* **1.** Blighted; withered; shriveled. **2.** *Slang.* Damned.

blas·te·ma (blă-stē′mə) *n., pl.* **-mas** or **-mata** (-mə-tə). **1.** A segregated region of embryonic cells from which a specific organ develops. **2.** A mass of undifferentiated animal cells that develops into a new tissue or organ during regeneration of lost parts. [New Latin, from Greek *blastēma,* offspring, offshoot, from *blastos,* sprout, bud.] —**blas·te·mal** (blă-stē′məl), **blas·te·mat·ic** (blăs′tə-măt′ĭk), **blas·te·mic** (blă-stē′mĭk) *adj.*

blast furnace *n.* Any furnace in which combustion is intensified by a blast of air, especially a furnace for smelting iron by blowing air through a hot mixture of ore, coke, and flux.

-blastic *suffix.* Indicates buds, sprouts, or growth; for example, **diploblastic.**

blasting gelatin *n.* A **dynamite** *(see)* containing nitrocellulose in addition to nitroglycerin.

blasto- *prefix.* Indicates growth, budding, or germination; for example, **blastoderm.** [Greek *blastos.* See **-blast.**]

blas·to·coel, blas·to·coele (blăs′tə-sēl′) *n. Embryology.* The cavity of a **blastula** *(see).* Also called "segmentation cavity." [BLASTO- + -coel, variant of -CELE.] —**blas·to·coel·ic** *adj.*

blas·to·cyst (blăs′tə-sĭst) *n. Embryology.* **1.** The **blastula** *(see)* of mammals. **2.** The **germinal vesicle** *(see).* —**blas·to·cys·tic** *adj.*

blas·to·derm (blăs′tə-dûrm′) *n.* **1.** The layer of cells surrounding the blastocoel. It gives rise to the **germinal disc** *(see)* from which the embryo develops in most placental vertebrates. **2.** The embryonic structure resulting from cleavage in heavily yolked eggs, such as those of birds. [BLASTO- + -DERM.] —**blas·to·der·mat·ic, blas·to·derm·ic** *adj.*

blas·to·disc, blas·to·disk (blăs′tə-dĭsk′) *n. Embryology.* The **germinal disc** *(see).*

blast off *intr.v.* To commence flight; take off. Used of rockets or space vehicles.

blast·off, blast-off (blăst′ôf′, bläst′-) *n.* The launching of a rocket or space vehicle.

blas·to·gen·e·sis (blăs′tə-jĕn′ĭ-sĭs) *n. Biology.* **1.** The theory that inherited characteristics are transmitted from parent to offspring by germ plasm. **2.** Reproduction by budding or other asexual means. —**blas·to·ge·net·ic** (blăs′tə-jə-nĕt′ĭk), **blas·to·gen·ic** *adj.*

blas·to·mere (blăs′tə-mîr′) *n.* A cell formed during the cleavage of a fertilized ovum. [BLASTO- + -MERE.] —**blas·to·mer·ic** (blăs′tə-mĕr′ĭk) *adj.*

blas·to·pore (blăs′tə-pôr′, -pōr′) *n.* The mouthlike opening into the primitive intestinal cavity of the gastrula. [BLASTO- + PORE (orifice).] —**blas·to·po·ral** *adj.*

blas·tu·la (blăs′chōō-lə) *n., pl.* **-las** or **-lae** (-lē′). An early embryonic form, resulting from cleavage and consisting essentially of a hollow cellular sphere. Also called "blastosphere." [New Latin, from Greek *blastos,* bud, germ.] —**blas·tu·lar** (blăs′chōō-lər) *adj.* —**blas·tu·la·tion** (blăs′chōō-lā′shən) *n.*

bla·tant (blā′tənt) *adj.* **1.** Offensively conspicuous; obtrusive; obvious: *a blatant lie.* **2.** Unpleasantly loud and noisy. [First used by Spenser ("the blattant beast," a symbol of calumny), probably from Latin *blatīre,* to blab, gossip.] —**bla·tan·cy** *n.* —**bla·tant·ly** *adv.*

Usage: *Blatant* and *flagrant* are often confused. In the sense that causes the confusion, *blatant* has the meaning of "outrageous" or "egregious." *Flagrant* emphasizes wrong or evil that is glaring or notorious. Therefore, one who blunders may be guilty of a *blatant* (but not *flagrant*) error; one who intentionally violates a pledge commits a *flagrant* act.

blath·er (blăth′ər) *v.* **-ered, -ering, -ers.** Also **bleth·er** (blĕth′ər). —*intr.* To talk nonsense; babble. —*tr.* To speak foolishly or nonsensically.
∼*n.* Also **bleth·er.** Absurd or foolish talk; nonsense. [Middle English *blether,* from Old Norse *bladhra,* to prattle, akin to *bladhra,* bladder.] —**blath·er·er** *n.*

blath·er·skite (blăth′ər-skīt′) *n.* **1.** A babbling, foolish person. **2.** Absurd and foolish talk. [Earlier *bletherskate* : BLATHER + SKATE (fish).]

Bla·vat·sky (blə-văt′skē), **Helena Petrovna,** born Helena Petrovna Hahn (1831–91). Russian theosophist. She began the theosophist movement in Russia in the late 1850's and founded the Theosophical Society in New York. Her demonstrations of supernatural phenomena were declared fraudulent by the London Society for Psychical Research (1885).

blaze¹ (blāz) *n.* **1.** A brilliant burst of fire; a flame. **2. a.** Any bright, hot, steady light or glare. **b.** Any bright, conspicuous display: *a blaze of color; a blaze of publicity.* **3.** A destructive fire, especially one that spreads rapidly. **4.** A sudden outburst, as of emotion or activity. **5. blazes.** *Slang.* Hell. Used euphemistically especially in the phrase *go to blazes* and as an intensive: *gallop like blazes; What he blazes is going on here?*
∼*v.* **blazed, blazing, blazes.** —*intr.* **1.** To burn with a bright flame. **2.** To shine brightly. **3.** To be deeply excited, as by emotion. **4.** To shoot rapidly and continuously. Used with *away.* —*tr.* To shine or be resplendent with: *Her eyes blazed fire.* [Middle English *blase,* Old English *blæse,* torch, bright fire.] —**blaz·ing·ly** *adv.*
Synonyms: *flame, flare, flash, glare, glow, incandescence.*

blaze² *n.* **1.** A white or light-colored spot or stripe on the face of a horse or other animal. **2.** A mark cut on a tree to indicate a trail.
∼*tr.v.* **blazed, blazing, blazes. 1.** To mark (a tree) by cutting the bark. **2.** To indicate (a trail) by marking trees in this manner. **3.** To make (a trail) into new, unexplained areas of knowledge or research. Used in the phrase *blaze the trail.* [Probably from Middle Low German *bles.*]

blaz·er (blā′zər) *n.* **1.** One that blazes. **2.** A lightweight, informal sports jacket, often striped or brightly colored.

blaz·ing (blā′zĭng) *adj.* Very hot.
∼*adv.* Used as an intensive: *blazing hot.*

blazing star *n.* **1.** A North American plant, *Chamaelirium luteum,* having a long cluster of small white flowers. Also called "devil's bit." **2.** Any of various North American plants of the genus *Liatris,* having clusters of tuftlike purple or pinkish flowers. Also called "button snakeroot." **3.** A plant, *Mentzelia laevicaulis,* of western North America, having large, pale-yellow flowers.

bla·zon (blā′zən) *tr.v.* **-zoned, -zoning, -zons. 1.** To describe (a coat of arms) in proper heraldic terms. **2.** To paint or depict (a coat of arms) with accurate heraldic detail. **3.** To adorn or embellish with or as if with blazons. **4.** To announce publicly; proclaim loudly and widely. Often used with *abroad.*
∼*n.* **1.** A heraldic charge or coat of arms. **2. a.** The heraldic description or representation of a heraldic charge or coat of arms. **b.** The heraldic terms used to describe coats of arms. **3.** An ostentatious or showy display. [Middle English *blasoun,* shield, coat of arms, from Old French *blason*†.] —**bla·zon·er** *n.* —**bla·zon·ment** *n.*

bla·zon·ry (blā′zən-rē) *n., pl.* **-ries. 1.** The art of properly and accurately describing or representing heraldic bearings. **2.** Coats of arms and heraldic bearings collectively. **3.** Any showy or brilliant display.

bld. boldface.

bldg. building.

bleach (blēch) *v.* **bleached, bleaching, bleaches.** —*tr.* **1.** To remove the color from, as by means of sunlight or chemical agents. **2.** To make white or colorless. —*intr.* To become white or colorless.
∼*n.* **1.** Any chemical agent used for bleaching, by either oxidation or reduction. **2.** The degree of bleaching obtained. **3.** The act of bleaching. [Middle English *blechen,* Old English *blǣcan.*]

bleach·er (blē′chər) *n.* **1.** One that bleaches. **2.** *Usually* **bleachers.** An unroofed outdoor grandstand for seating spectators. [Sense 2, from the bleaching effect of exposure to sun.]

bleaching powder *n.* Any powder, such as chlorinated lime or calcium hypochlorite, used in solution as a bleach.

bleak¹ (blēk) *adj.* **bleaker, bleakest. 1.** Exposed to the elements; unsheltered; barren. **2.** Cold and cutting; harsh. **3.** Offering no hope or encouragement: *bleak prospects.* **4.** Gloomy and somber; depressing; dreary. [Middle English *bleike,* pale, from Old Norse *bleikr,* shining, white.] —**bleak·ly** *adv.* —**bleak·ness** *n.*

bleak² *n.* A European freshwater fish of the genus *Alburnus,* related to the carp, having silvery scales used in the manufacture of artificial pearls. [Middle English *bleke,* probably from Old Norse *bleikja,* "white color."]

blear (blîr) *tr.v.* **bleared, blearing, blears. 1.** To blur (the eyes) with or as if with tears. **2.** To blur; dim.
∼*adj.* Bleary. [Middle English *bleren,* probably of Low German origin, akin to Low German *blerr-*† (in *blerr-oged,* bleary-eyed).]

blear·y (blîr′ē) *adj.* **-ier, -iest. 1.** Blurred or dimmed as by tears or lack of sleep. Said of the eyes. **2.** Vague or indistinct; blurred. **3.** Exhausted; worn-out. —**blear·i·ly** *adv.* —**blear·i·ness** *n.*

blear·y-eyed (blîr′ē-īd′) *adj.* Also **blear-eyed** (blîr′īd′). **1.** With eyes blurred by or as if by tears or lack of sleep. **2.** Dull of mind or perception.

bleat (blēt) *v.* **bleated, bleating, bleats.** —*intr.* **1.** To utter the cry of a goat, sheep, or calf. **2.** To utter any similar sound, especially a whine. —*tr.* To utter in a whining voice.
∼*n.* **1.** The characteristic cry of a goat, sheep, or calf. **2.** Any similar sound, such as a whining cry. [Middle English *bleten,* Old English *blǣtan.*] —**bleat·er** *n.*

bleb (blĕb) *n.* **1.** A small blister or pustule. Compare **bulla. 2.** An air bubble. [Variant of BLOB.] —**bleb·by** *adj.*

bleed (blēd) *v.* **bled** (blĕd), **bleeding, bleeds.** —*intr.* **1.** To lose or emit blood. **2.** To suffer injury or death, as in battle. **3.** To feel sympathetic grief or anguish: *My heart bleeds for you.* **4.** To exude sap or a similar fluid, as a bruised plant does. **5.** *Slang.* To pay out money, especially an exorbitant amount. **6.** To become mixed or run, as dyes in wet cloth or paper. **7.** To show through a layer of paint, as a stain or resin in wood. **8.** *Printing.* To be printed so as to go over the edge or edges of a page, either purposely or by trimming the margins too closely. Often used with *off.* —*tr.* **1. a.** To take blood from, either surgically or with leeches. **b.** To extract sap or juice from. **2.** To exude (blood or sap, for example). **3. a.** To draw liquid or gaseous contents from; especially, to remove air from a hydraulic brake system or from a radiator in a central-heating system. **b.** To draw off (liquid or gaseous matter) from a container. **4.** *Slang.* To obtain large amounts of money from, especially by improper means. **5.** *Printing.* **a.** To print (an illustration, for example) so that it will go over the edge or edges of a page. **b.** To trim (a page or sheet, for example) too closely so as to mutilate the printed or illustrative matter. **6.** To feed (continuous small amounts of fluid) into a system.
∼*n. Printing.* **1.** Illustrative matter that purposely bleeds. **2.** A page trimmed so as to bleed. Also called "bleed page." **3.** The part thus trimmed off. [Bleed, bled, bled; Middle English *bleden, bledde, bledde,* Old English *blēdan, blēdde, blēdd,* from Common Germanic *blōthjan* (unattested), from *blōtham* (unattested), BLOOD.]

bleed·er (blē′dər) *n.* **1.** A **hemophiliac** *(see).* **2.** A bloodletter.

bleed·ing-heart (blē′dĭng-härt′) *n.* **1.** Any of several plants of the genus *Dicentra,* having nodding, pink flowers; especially, the widely cultivated species *D. spectabilis,* native to Japan. **2.** A person who is considered excessively sympathetic toward those who claim to be underprivileged or exploited.

bleeding-heart *A pink flower similar in appearance to the fuchsia; it is native to Japan and Siberia.*

bleep (blēp) *n.* A high-pitched noise of short duration produced electronically.
∼*intr.v.* **bleeped, bleeping, bleeps.** To blip. [Imitative.]

blem·ish (blĕm′ĭsh) *tr.v.* **-ished, -ishing, -ishes.** To impair or spoil by a flaw; mar.
∼*n.* A flaw or defect; a stain; a disfigurement. [Middle English *blemisshen,* from Old French *blemir, blesmir* (present stem *blemiss-*), to make pale, from Germanic.] —**blem·ish·er** *n.*
Synonyms: *defect, fault, flaw, imperfection.*

blench¹ (blĕnch) *intr.v.* **blenched, blenching, blenches.** To draw back or shy away, as in fear; quail; flinch. —See Synonyms at **recoil.** [Middle English *blenchen,* to deceive, start aside, evade, Old English *blencan,* to deceive.] —**blench·er** *n.*

blench². Variant of **blanch.**

blend (blĕnd) *v.* **blended** or **blent** (blĕnt), **blending, blends.** —*tr.* **1.** To combine or mix so as to render the constituent parts indistinguishable from one another. **2.** To mix (different varieties or grades of coffee or tea, for example) so as to obtain a new mixture of some particular quality or consistency. —*intr.* **1.** To form a uniform mixture; intermingle. **2.** To become merged into one; unite. **3.** To pass imperceptibly into one another: *"standing motionless beside that door, as though trying to make myself blend with the dark wood"* (William Faulkner). —See Synonyms at **mix.**
∼*n.* **1.** That which is blended; a mixture. **2.** The act of blending. **3.** *Linguistics.* A word produced by combining parts of other words, such as *smog,* from *smoke* and *fog;* a portmanteau word. **4.** To go together; harmonize: *The new carpet blends well with the curtains.* [Middle English *blenden,* from Old Norse *blanda* (stem *blend-*).]

blende (blĕnd) *n.* **1.** Any of various shiny minerals composed chiefly of metallic sulfides. **2.** A mineral, **sphalerite** *(see).* [German *Blende,* short for *blendendes Erz,* "deceptive ore" (often mistaken, on account of its metallic gleam, for a lead ore), from *blenden,* to blind, deceive, from Old High German *blenten.*]

blended whiskey *n.* Whiskey that is a blend of two or more straight whiskeys, or a blend of whiskey and neutral spirits.

blend·er (blĕn′dər) *n.* **1.** One that combines or blends. **2.** A mechanical device with rotating blades used for chopping, mixing, or liquefying foods.

Blen·heim Palace (blĕn′əm). The country seat of the dukes of Marlborough, outside Woodstock in Oxfordshire. The palace, designed by Sir John Vanbrugh, is considered to be one of the finest examples of the baroque in English architecture.

blen·ny (blĕn′ē) *n., pl.* **-nies.** Any of numerous small, elongated marine fishes of the families Blenniidae and Clinidae, especially a fish of the genus *Blennius,* which has a long dorsal fin and long, rayed pelvic fins. [Latin *blennius, blendius,* from Greek *blennos,* "slime" (from the slimy coating on its scales).]

blent. Alternate past tense and past participle of **blend.**

blesbok *Great herds of blesbok used to roam the grasslands of southern Africa. Hunting has now made the antelope rare in the wild, but it is preserved on private farms and in game reserves.*

bleph·a·ri·tis (blĕf'ə-rī'tĭs) *n.* Inflammation of the eyelid. [New Latin : Greek *blepharon*†, eyelid + -ITIS.]

bleph·a·ro·spasm (blĕf'ə-rō-spăz'əm) *n.* Uncontrollable winking, caused by involuntary contraction of an eyelid muscle. [New Latin *blepharospasmus* : BLEPHAR(ITIS) + SPASM.]

Blé·riot (blā-ryō', blĕr'ē-ō), **Louis** (1872–1936). French inventor and aviator. On July 25, 1909, he flew his 25-horsepower airplane over the English Channel from Calais to Dover, the first time that an airplane had flown across open sea.

bles·bok (blĕs'bŏk') *n., pl.* **-boks** or collectively **blesbok.** Also **bles·buck** (-bŭk'), *pl.* **-bucks** or collectively **blesbuck.** An African antelope, *Damaliscus albifrons,* having a reddish-brown coat and a face marked with white. [Afrikaans : *bles,* white mark on animal's face + *bok,* buck.]

bless (blĕs) *tr.v.* **blessed** (blĕst) or **blest, blessing, blesses. 1.** To make holy by religious rite; sanctify. **2.** To make the sign of the cross over, so as to sanctify. **3.** To invoke divine favor upon. **4.** To preserve from evil. Used as an exclamation: *Bless my soul!* **5.** To honor as holy; glorify: *Bless the Lord.* **6.** To confer well-being or prosperity upon. **7.** To endow or favor. Usually used in the passive: *blessed with good health.* **—bless you.** Used conventionally as an interjection after a person has sneezed. [Middle English *blessen,* Old English *blētsian, blœdsian,* from Common Germanic *blōthisōjan* (unattested), "to hallow with blood," from *blōtham* (unattested), BLOOD.] **—bless·er** *n.*

bless·ed (blĕs'ĭd) *adj.* Also **blest** (blĕst). **1.** Made sacred by a religious rite; consecrated. **2.** Worthy of profound respect or worship. **3.** *Roman Catholic Church.* Enjoying the eternal happiness of heaven. Used as a title for those who have been beatified. **4.** Enjoying happiness; fortunate. **5.** Bringing happiness or bliss. **6.** Damned. Used euphemistically or as an intensive. **—bless·ed·ly** *adv.* **—bless·ed·ness** *n.*

Bles·sed Sacrament (blĕs'ĭd) *n. Roman Catholic Church.* The consecrated Host.

Bles·sed Virgin (blĕs'ĭd) *n. Abbr.* **B.V.** The Virgin Mary.

bless·ing (blĕs'ĭng) *n.* **1. a.** The act of one who blesses. **b.** The prescribed words or ceremony for such an act. **2.** An expression or utterance of good wishes. **3.** A special favor granted by God. **4.** Anything promoting or contributing to happiness, well-being, or prosperity; a boon: *a blessing in disguise.* **5.** Approval: *This plan has my blessing.* **6.** A short prayer before or after a meal.

blest. 1. Alternate past tense and past participle of **bless. 2.** Variant of **blessed.**

blet (blĕt) *n.* Internal softening or incipient decay of certain fruits. The medlar is edible only when it has reached this state. [French *blettir,* become overripe, from *blet(te),* overripe, from Old French, from Germanic.]

blether. Variant of **blather.**

bleu cheese (blœ) *n.* Blue cheese.

blew. Past tense of **blow.**

blew·its (blo͞o'əts) *n. Used with a singular verb.* An edible mushroom, *Tricholoma saevum,* having a bluish stalk and a pale brown cap. [Probably from BLUE.]

Bligh (blī), **William** (1754–1817). British admiral, known chiefly from the mutiny of his ship the *Bounty* (1789). He accompanied James Cook on the explorer's last expedition (1776–79) as sailing master and served as governor of New South Wales (1805–08).

blight (blīt) *n.* **1.** Any of several plant diseases that result in sudden dying of leaves, growing tips, or an entire plant. **2.** An environmental condition, such as air pollution, that injures or kills plants or animals. **3.** Something that withers hopes or ambitions, impairs growth, or halts prosperity. **4.** The state or result of being blighted; dilapidation; decay: *urban blight.*

~v. **blighted, blighting, blights.** *—tr.* **1.** To cause to decline or decay. **2.** To ruin; destroy. **3.** To frustrate: *a mishap that blighted his hopes.* *—intr.* To suffer blight. [17th century : origin obscure.]

blight·er (blī'tər) *n. Chiefly British Slang.* **1.** An annoying or contemptible person. **2.** A person. Used affectionately: *You lucky blighter!*

blight·y (blī'tē) *n. Often* **Blighty.** *British Slang.* England; home. Used especially by soldiers serving abroad. [Hindi *bilāyatī, wilāyatī,* "foreign," "English," from Arabic *wilāyat,* district, realm, from *waliya,* he rules.]

bli·mey (blī'mē) *interj. British Slang.* Used to express surprise, irritation, or the like. [From *(God) blind me!*]

blimp¹ (blĭmp) *n.* A nonrigid, buoyant aircraft, such as a barrage balloon. [Probably (type) B + LIMP.]

blimp² *n. Chiefly British.* One whose views exhibit a blend of ultraconservative jingoism and misinformation. [After Colonel *Blimp,* a cartoon character invented by David Low.] **—blimp·ish** *adj.*

blind (blīnd) *adj.* **blinder, blindest. 1.** Without the sense of sight. **2.** Of or for sightless persons. **3.** Performed without the use of sight, relying wholly on instruments: *blind flying.* **4.** Performed without preparation, forethought, or knowledge: *a blind attempt.* **5.** Unable or unwilling to perceive or understand: *blind to all her faults.* **6.** Not based on reason or evidence: *blind faith.* **7.** *Informal.* Drunk. **8.** Acting without human control: *blind fate.* **9. a.** Difficult to comprehend or see; illegible: *blind writings.* **b.** Illegibly or incompletely addressed: *blind mail.* **10.** Hidden from sight: *a blind seam.* **11.** Affording poor visibility to an oncoming driver: *a blind corner.* **12.** Closed at one end: *a blind alley.* **13.** Having no opening: *a blind wall.* **14.** *Botany.* Failing to flower. Said of cultivated plants. **15.** *Informal.* Used as an intensive: *didn't take a blind bit of notice.*

~n. **1. a.** Something that hinders vision or shuts out light: *a Venetian blind.* **b.** A piece of fabric, usually mounted on rollers, used to cover a window. Also "window shade." **2.** A shelter for concealing hunters, especially duck hunters. **3.** Any subterfuge or front; a decoy. **4.** *British Slang.* A drinking bout. **5.** In poker, a bet made before seeing one's cards.

~adv. **1.** Without being able to see; blindly: *fly blind.* **2.** *Informal.* Into a stupor: *They drank themselves blind.* Also used as an intensive, chiefly in the phrase *blind drunk.* **3.** Without a filling, or with a temporary filling of dried peas, beans, or the like inserted merely to retain shape during cooking: *bake a pastry shell blind.*

~tr.v. **blinded, blinding, blinds. 1.** To deprive of sight. **2.** To dazzle. **3.** To deprive (a person) of the powers of perception or judgment. **4.** To eclipse. **5.** To deprive of light; darken. [Middle English *blind,* Old English *blind,* blind, obscure.] **—blind·ly** *adv.* **—blind·ness** *n.*

blind alley *n.* **1.** A passageway open only at one end; a dead end. **2.** *Informal.* Any project or situation that offers no prospect of progress or development.

blind date *n. Informal.* **1.** A social engagement between two people, usually a man and a woman, who have not previously met. **2.** Either of the persons keeping such an engagement.

blind·er (blīn'dər) *n.* **1.** One that causes blinding. **2. blinders.** A pair of leather flaps attached to a horse's bridle to curtail side vision. Also called "blinkers." **3.** *Western U.S.* A cloth used to cover a horse's eyes during saddling or shoeing. **4.** *British Slang.* A bout of drinking. Used chiefly in the phrase *go on a blinder.*

blind·fish (blīnd'fĭsh') *n., pl.* **-fishes** or collectively **blindfish.** Any of various fishes having rudimentary, nonfunctioning eyes; especially, the **cavefish** *(see).*

blind·fold (blīnd'fōld') *tr.v.* **-folded, -folding, -folds. 1.** To cover the eyes with or as if with a bandage. **2.** To hamper the sight or comprehension of; mislead; delude.

~n. A bandage over the eyes.

~adj. **1.** With eyes covered. **2.** Reckless. [Middle English *blindfolde, blindfelde,* past participle of *blindfellen,* to strike blind, from Old English *geblindfellian,* "to strike blind" : *ge-,* Y- + BLIND + *fellan,* to strike down, FELL.]

blind gut *n.* **1.** A digestive cavity having only one opening. **2.** *Anatomy.* The **cecum** *(see).*

blind hinge *n.* A hinge so constructed that it allows the hinged piece to swing shut by its own weight unless held open.

blind·ing (blīn'dĭng) *adj.* **1.** Tending to make sightless. **2.** Dazzling; overpowering. **—blind·ing·ly** *adv.*

blind·man's buff (blīnd'mănz') *n.* A game in which one person, blindfolded, tries to catch and identify one of the other players. [*Buff,* short for BUFFET (a blow).]

blind side *n.* The side away from which one is directing one's attention.

blind spot *n.* **1.** *Anatomy.* The small, optically insensitive region where the optic nerve enters the retina of the eye. **2.** Any part of an area that cannot be directly observed, especially that part of a motor-vehicle driver's surroundings that is not reflected in the vehicle's mirrors and cannot be seen without sharply turning the head. **3.** An area where radio reception is weak. **4.** A subject about which one is markedly ignorant or prejudiced.

blind staggers *n. Used with a singular verb.* A disease of horses, **staggers** *(see).*

blind·sto·ry (blīnd'stôr'ē, -stōr'ē) *n., pl.* **-ries.** *Architecture.* A story having no windows.

blind·worm (blīnd'wûrm') *n.* A lizard, the **slowworm** *(see).* [Perhaps so called because its eyes close after death.]

bli·ni (blē'nē, blĭn'ē) *pl.n.* Small buckwheat pancakes served with caviar or sour cream. [Russian, plural of *blin,* pancake, from Old Russian *blinŭ, mlinŭ.*]

blink (blĭngk) *v.* **blinked, blinking, blinks.** *—intr.* **1.** To close and open one or both eyes rapidly. **2.** To look through half-closed eyes, as in a bright glare; squint. **3.** To shine with intermittent gleams; flash on and off. **4.** To pretend not to be aware of something, especially something unpleasant. Used with *at.* **5.** To become startled or dismayed. Usually used with *at.* *—tr.* **1.** To close and open (the eyes or an eye) rapidly. **2.** To ignore or refuse to acknowledge. —See Usage note below.

~n. **1.** The act or an instance of blinking; a brief closing of the eyes. **2.** A quick look or glimpse; a glance. **3.** The time it takes to blink. **4.** A flash of light; a gleam; a twinkle; a glimmer. **5.** An **iceblink** *(see).* **—on the blink.** *Slang.* Not in proper working condition; out of order. [Middle English *blinken,* partly a variant of *blenchen,* BLENCH (flinch), and perhaps partly from Middle Dutch *blinken,* to glitter.]

Usage: The verb *blink* used transitively and without a preposition expresses evasion in the sense of deliberate refusal to face or recognize: *blink* (not *blink at*) *ugly facts.* In an intransitive sense, *blink at* (or more frequently, *wink at*) expresses evasion by condoning or tolerating: *blink at dishonest practices.* The first construction pertains basically to shirking and the second to complicity.

blink·er (blĭng'kər) *n.* **1.** A light that blinks in order to convey a message or warning, as, for example, on a control panel. **2.** *Slang.* An eye. **3. blinkers.** Goggles. **4. blinkers. Blinders** *(see).*

blink·ered (blĭng'kərd) *adj.* **1.** Wearing blinders. Said of a horse. **2.** Showing unwillingness or inability to understand; obtuse.

blintz (blĭnts) *n.* Also **blin·tze** (blĭn'tsə). A thin, folded pancake filled with cream cheese or cottage cheese, fruit, or seasoned mashed potatoes, and often served with sour cream. [Yiddish *blintse*, from Russian *blinyets*, diminutive of *blin*, BLINI.]

blip (blĭp) *n.* **1.** A spot of light on a radar screen. **2.** A regularly repeated sound. **3.** A brief interruption of the sound received in a television program as a result of blipping.
~*intr. v.* **blipped, blipping, blips. 1.** To produce a blip. **2.** To interrupt recorded sounds, as on a videotape: *blipped the expletive from the TV show.* [Imitative.]

bliss (blĭs) *n.* **1.** Serene happiness. **2.** The ecstasy of salvation; spiritual joy. —See Synonyms at **ecstasy.** [Middle English *blis(se)*, Old English *bliss, blīths*, from Common Germanic *blīthsjo* (unattested), from *blīthiz* (unattested), BLITHE.] **—bliss·ful** *adj.* **—bliss·ful·ly** *adv.* **—bliss·ful·ness** *n.*

blis·ter (blĭs'tər) *n.* **1.** A thin, rounded swelling of the skin, containing watery serum, caused by burning or friction. **2.** A similar swelling on a plant. **3.** An air bubble on a painted surface or in a casting. **4.** A rounded, often transparent protuberance on certain aircraft, used for observation or as a gun position.
~*v.* **blistered, -tering, -ters.** —*tr.* **1.** To cause a blister or blisters to form upon. **2.** To reprove harshly. —*intr.* To break out in blisters. [Middle English *blester, blister*, possibly from Old French *blestre*, from Middle Dutch *bluyster*, "swelling."] **—blis·ter·y** *adj.*

blister beetle *n.* Any of various beetles of the family Meloidae that secrete a substance capable of blistering the skin. Some species cause damage to crops. See **Spanish fly.**

blister copper *n.* An almost pure form of copper produced in an intermediate stage of copper refining. [From its blistered surface caused by release of gas in the refining process.]

blis·ter·ing (blĭs'tər-ĭng) *adj.* **1.** Intensely hot. **2.** Harshly condemnatory; scathing: *a blistering attack on government policy.* **3.** Very rapid: *a blistering pace.*

blister pack *n.* A type of package for pills or tablets with plastic bubbles that are pushed in to eject the pill or tablet through the backing foil.

blister rust *n.* Any of several diseases of pine trees, caused by various fungi of the genus *Cronartium,* and resulting in cankers and blisters on the bark.

B.Lit. or **B.Litt.** Bachelor of Letters. [Latin *Baccalaureus Litterarum.*]

blithe (blīth, blīth) *adj.* **1.** Filled with gaiety; cheerful. **2.** Frivolous; casual; carefree: *blithe optimism.* —See Synonyms at **jolly.** [Middle English *blithe*, Old English *blīthe*, from Common Germanic *blīthiz*† (unattested), gentle, mild.] **—blithe·ly** *adv.* **—blithe·ness** *n.*

blith·er (blĭth'ər) *intr.v.* **-ered, -ering, -ers.** To blather. [Alteration of BLATHER.]

blith·er·ing (blĭth'ər-ĭng) *adj.* **1.** Talking senselessly; jabbering. **2.** *British Informal.* Stupid; silly.

blithe·some (blīth'səm, blīth'-) *adj.* Cheerful; merry. **—blithe·some·ly** *adv.* **—blithe·some·ness** *n.*

blitz (blĭts) *n.* **1.** A blitzkrieg. **2.** An intensive air raid or series of air raids. **3.** Any intense campaign or effort: *I'm ready for a blitz on the spare room.* **—the Blitz.** The period in 1940–41 during which British cities and towns were subjected to continual nighttime bombing by the German Luftwaffe.
~*tr.v.* **blitzed, blitzing, blitzes.** To subject to a blitz. [Short for BLITZKRIEG.]

blitz·krieg (blĭts'krēg') *n.* **1.** A swift, sudden military offensive, usually by combined air and land forces. **2.** Any swift, concerted effort. [German *Blitzkrieg,* "lightning war."]

bliz·zard (blĭz'ərd) *n.* **1.** A violent windstorm accompanied by intense cold and driving, powdery snow or ice crystals. **2.** A very heavy snowstorm with high winds. [19th century : originally American, perhaps imitative.]

blk. 1. black. **2.** block. **3.** bulk.

bloat (blōt) *v.* **bloated, bloating, bloats.** —*tr.* **1.** To cause to swell up or inflate, as with liquid or gas. **2. a.** To puff up, as with vanity. **b.** To puff up (the face or body), as from overeating. **3.** To cure (herring or other fish) by soaking in brine and half-drying in smoke. —*intr.* To become swollen or inflated.
~*n. Veterinary Medicine.* A swelling of the rumen or intestinal tract of a domestic animal, caused by the gases of fermentation of green forage. [From *bloat,* swollen, earlier *blowt,* soft, flabby, from Middle English *blout,* probably from Old Norse *blautr,* soft, wet, soaked.]

bloat·er (blō'tər) *n.* A herring lightly smoked and salted.

blob (blŏb) *n.* **1.** A soft, amorphous mass. **2.** A shapeless splotch or daub of color.
~*tr.v.* **blobbed, blobbing, blobs.** To splash or mark with blobs; splotch. [Middle English, bubble (imitative).]

bloc (blŏk) *n.* A group of persons, parties, or nations united for common action or by a common interest. [French, BLOCK.]

Bloch (blŏk), **Ernest** (1880–1959). Swiss-born U.S. composer. He is famous for his chamber music, such as the Piano Quintet (1923) and his five string quartets, and also for works with Jewish themes, including the *Israel Symphony* (1916).

block (blŏk) *n. Abbr.* **blk. 1.** A large, solid piece of wood, stone, or other hard substance having one or more flat sides. **2. a.** Such a piece used in construction work. **b.** A child's toy model of such a piece: *a set of building blocks.* **3.** A large solid piece of wood, especially: **a.** One on which chopping or cutting is done: *a butcher's block.* **b.** One on which people were formerly beheaded. Usually preceded by *the.* **c.** One from which a horse may be mounted. **4.** A piece of wood, stone, or metal engraved for use in printing. **5. a.** A pulley or a system of pulleys set in a casing. **b.** The casing holding the pulleys. See **block and tackle. 6.** The casting containing the cylinders of an internal-combustion engine. **7.** A group acting or regarded as a unit; a bloc. **8.** A set or quantity of like items sold, handled, or regarded as a unit, such as theater tickets, shares, or postage stamps. **9.** A large building divided into separate units, such as apartments or offices. **10. a.** A rectangular section of a city or town bounded on each side by consecutive streets. **b.** A segment of a street bounded by successive cross streets, including its buildings and inhabitants. **c.** The distance between these streets: *The theater is three blocks away.* **11.** A length of railway track controlled by signals. See **block system. 12.** Something that hinders; an obstacle. **13.** An act of obstructing or hindering. **14.** *Sports.* An act of bodily obstruction; specifically, in football, legal interference with an opposing player to clear the path of the ballcarrier. **15.** In athletics, a **starting block** *(see).* **16.** *Medicine.* Interruption, especially obstruction, of a neural, digestive, or other physiological process. See **heart block, nerve block. 17.** *Psychology.* Sudden cessation of a thought or creative process without an immediate observable cause, sometimes considered to be a consequence of repression. **18.** *Slang.* A person's head. Used chiefly in the phrase *knock someone's block off.* **19.** *Computer Science.* A group of words or numbers treated as a unit in a storage device. **—off one's block.** Mad; crazy. **—on the block.** Up for auction. —See Synonyms at **obstacle.**
~*v.* **blocked, blocking, blocks.** —*tr.* **1.** To shape into a block or blocks. **2.** To support, strengthen, or retain in place by means of a block or blocks. **3.** To shape, mold, or form with or on a block: *block a hat.* **4.** To stop or impede the passage of or movement through; hinder or obstruct: *block traffic; block a piece of legislation.* **5.** *Sports.* To impede the movement of (one's opponent or the ball) by means of physical interference. **6.** *Medicine.* To interrupt the proper functioning of (a physiological process). **7.** To stamp or emboss a design or lettering on (the cover of a book), especially using gold or other foil. **8.** *Finance.* To restrict or prevent the use or conversion of (currency or assets). **9.** *Psychology.* To repress or fail to recognize (an area or subject that causes pain or anxiety). Often used with *out.* —*intr. Sports.* To obstruct the movement of an opponent. —See Synonyms at **hinder. —block out. 1.** To plan or project broadly without details; sketch out. **2.** To obscure from view. **—block up. 1.** To raise on a block or blocks, as a house or boat. **2.** To fill with solid material: *block up the windows of an old house.* [Middle English *blok(ke),* from Old French *bloc,* from Middle Dutch *blok,* trunk of a tree, from Germanic.] **—block** *adj.* **—block·er** *n.*

Block (blŏk), **Herbert Lawrence,** known as "Herblock" (1909–). U.S. editorial cartoonist. His works have appeared in *The Washington Post* and 200 other newspapers nationwide. In 1942 and 1954 he was awarded a Pulitzer Prize.

block·ade (blŏ-kād') *n.* **1.** The closing off of a country, city, harbor, or other area to traffic and communication by hostile ships or forces. **2.** The forces employed to close such an area. **—run a blockade.** To succeed in getting through a blockade.
~*tr.v.* **blockaded, -ading, -ades.** To set up a blockade against. [From BLOCK (after AMBUSCADE).] **—block·ad·er** *n.*

block·ade-run·ner (blŏ-kād'rŭn'ər) *n.* A ship or person that goes through or past a blockade. **—block·ade-ru·ning** *n.*

block·age (blŏk'ĭj) *n.* **1.** The act of blocking or obstructing. **2.** An obstruction.

block and tackle *n.* An apparatus of pulley blocks and ropes or cables used for hauling and hoisting heavy objects.

block·bust·er (blŏk'bŭs'tər) *n. Informal.* **1.** A powerful bomb capable of destroying large areas. **2.** Anything of devastating effect. **3.** A film or play that attracts large audiences and earns large amounts of money.

block diagram *n.* **1.** A diagram of a system, such as a computer program or electrical circuit, in which the essential units are represented by rectangles or blocks that are connected by lines showing the relationship between the units. **2.** A diagram that gives a three-dimensional representation of a landform or section of country.

block-graze (blŏk'grāz') *tr.v.* **-grazed, -grazing, -grazes.** *Chiefly Australian.* To graze (livestock) on an area of land until it is bare before moving them to the next area.

block·head (blŏk'hĕd') *n.* A stupid person; a dolt.

block·house (blŏk'hous') *n.* **1.** A military fortification constructed of concrete or other sturdy material, with loopholes for defensive firing or for observation. **2.** *Aerospace.* A heavily reinforced building used for protecting personnel and equipment during launch operations of missiles, rockets, or the like. **3.** A house made of squared timbers.

block·ish (blŏk'ĭsh) *adj.* **1.** Like or resembling a block. **2.** Dull; stupid. **—block·ish·ly** *adv.* **—block·ish·ness** *n.*

block lava *n.* Lava formed into sharp, angular blocks.

block letter *n.* **1.** A plain capital letter printed or written sans serif, often used when filling in forms. Also called "block capital." **2.** *Printing.* A sans-serif style of type. **—block-let·ter** *adj.*

block plane *n.* A small plane used by carpenters for cutting across the grain of wood.

block printing *n.* Printing from engraved or carved wooden or linoleum blocks.

block release *n. British.* A system whereby trainees and apprentices may leave work for a set period in order to study at a college. Compare **day release.**

block system *n.* A system for controlling and safeguarding the flow

blister beetle *One of the 2,000 species of the family* Meloidae *that secrete a substance containing cantharidin, an irritant chemical.*

PRONUNCIATION KEY

ă, pat; ā, pay; âr, care;
ä, father, are; b, bib;
ch, church; d, deed; ĕ, pet;
ē, be; f, fife; g, gag; h, hat;
hw, which; ĭ, pit; ī, pie;
îr, pier; j, judge; k, kick;
l, lid, needle; m, mum;
n, no, sudden; ng, thing;
ŏ, pot; ō, toe; ô, paw, for;
oi, noise; ou, out; o͝o, book;
o͞o, boot; p, pop; r, roar;
s, sauce; sh, ship, dish;
t, tight; th, thin, path;
th, this, bathe; ŭ, cut; ûr, fur;
v, valve; w, with; y, yes;
z, zebra, size; zh, vision;
ə, about, item, edible,
gallop, circus, peaceful

IN FOREIGN WORDS:

à, *Fr.* ami; œ, *Fr.* feu, *Ger.* schön; ü, *Fr.* tu, *Ger.* über;
KH, *Ger.* ich, *Scot.* loch;
N, *Fr.* bon; y', *Fr.* Compiègne

STRESS MARKS:

Primary stress: '
in·cite' (ĭn-sīt')
Secondary stress: '
in'sight' (ĭn'sīt')

of railway trains, in which the track is divided into sections or blocks, each controlled by automatic signals.

block tin *n.* An impure commercial form of tin cast in blocks.

block vote *n.* A single vote cast by the representative of a large group, as at a union conference, for example, that is held to represent the votes of all the members of that group.

block·y (blŏk′ē) *adj.* **-ier, -iest.** Resembling a block; stocky.

Bloem·fon·tein (blōōm′fŏn-tān′). City in South Africa, capital of the Orange Free State. Founded as a Boer fort (1846), it is unofficially called the judicial capital of South Africa because the appellate division of the Supreme Court sits here.

Blois (blwä). City in north-central France, lying on the Loire River. Its historical importance dates from the 6th century when it became the seat of the powerful counts of Blois, the ancestors of the royal Capetian line.

bloke (blōk) *n. Chiefly British Slang.* A fellow; a man.

blond (blŏnd) *adj.* **-er, -est. 1.** Having fair hair and skin and usually light eyes. **2.** Of a flaxen or golden color or of any light shade of auburn or pale yellowish brown: *blond hair.* **3.** Light-colored: *blond furniture.*
~*n.* A blond person. [Old French, probably from Germanic.] **—blond·ish** *adj.* **—blond·ness** *n.*
Usage: Blond as an adjective may be used of both sexes. *Blonde* and *brunette* as nouns are used only of females.

blonde (blŏnd) *adj.* **blonder, blondest.** Blond.
~*n.* A blonde woman or girl. [Old French, feminine of *blond.*]

Blon·din (blôn-dăn′), **Charles,** born Jean François Gravelet (1824–97). French acrobat and stunt performer whose speciality was tightrope walking. He walked across Niagara Falls several times, the first time in 1859, in a variety of ways—with a man on his back, on stilts, and blindfolded.

blood (blŭd) *n.* **1.** The fluid circulated by the heart through the vertebrate vascular system, carrying oxygen and nutrients throughout the body and waste materials to excretory channels. It consists of **blood plasma** (*see*) in which are suspended red blood cells (erythrocytes), white cells (leucocytes), and platelets. **2.** A functionally similar fluid in an invertebrate. **3.** A fluid resembling blood, such as the juice of certain plants. **4.** Loosely, life; lifeblood. **5.** Bloodshed; murder. **6.** Temperament; temper; disposition. **7.** Descent from a common ancestor; parental lineage. **8.** Family relationship; kinship. **9.** Descent from noble or royal lineage. Preceded by *the*: *a princess of the blood.* Said of animals. **10.** Recorded descent from purebred stock. **11.** Racial or national ancestry. **12.** Members or personnel, especially ones providing fresh or new impetus: *new blood in the organization.* **13.** A dashing young man; a rake; a dandy. **—blood is thicker than water.** Family ties and loyalties are stronger than any others. **—in cold blood.** Dispassionately; deliberately; coldly. **—in one's blood.** Fundamental or inherent in one's character. **—make one's blood boil.** To make extremely angry. **—make one's blood run cold.** To terrify.
~*tr.v.* **blooded, blooding, bloods. 1. a.** To give (a hound or hunting dog) its first taste of blood. **b.** To initiate a novice who has successfully followed hounds from find to death by marking the face with the blood of the fox. **2.** To initiate (a new member or recruit) into an organization. **3.** To subject (recruits) to the baptism of fire.
~*adj.* Purebred: *a blood mare.* [Middle English *blood,* Old English *blōd,* from Common Germanic *blōtham* (unattested).]

blood-and-thunder (blŭd′ən-thŭn′dər) *adj.* Designating or pertaining to a melodramatic, action-packed book or film.

blood bath *n.* A savage and indiscriminate killing; a massacre.

blood brother *n.* **1.** One's brother by birth. **2.** A boy or man who swears to treat another as his brother, often at a ceremony where the blood of the two is mingled.

blood count *n.* **1.** The number of red and white blood cells in a specific volume of blood. **2.** The determination of this number.

blood·cur·dling (blŭd′kûrd′lĭng) *adj.* Causing great horror; terrifying. **—blood·cur·dling·ly** *adv.*

blood donor *n.* A person who gives blood for transfusion.

blood·ed (blŭd′ĭd) *adj.* **1.** Having blood or a temperament of a specified kind. Used in combination: *a cold-blooded reptile; a hot-blooded person.* **2.** Thoroughbred.

blood feud *n.* A long-lasting dispute, usually between families or tribes, involving killing on both sides.

blood fluke *n.* A trematode worm, such as a **schistosome** (*see*), that lives in the blood vessels of its host.

blood group *n.* Any of several immunologically distinct, genetically determined classes of human blood, clinically identified by characteristic agglutination reactions based on the presence or absence of certain antigens. Also called "blood type."

blood·guilt (blŭd′gĭlt′) *n.* Guilt owing to murder or bloodshed.

blood heat *n.* The usual temperature (37°C; 98.6°F) of human blood.

blood·hound (blŭd′hound′) *n.* **1.** One of a breed of hounds with a smooth coat, drooping ears, sagging jowls, and a keen sense of smell. **2.** *Informal.* Any relentless pursuer.

blood·less (blŭd′lĭs) *adj.* **1.** Having no blood. **2.** Pale and anemic in color. **3.** Achieved without bloodshed. **4.** Lacking spirit or emotion. **—blood·less·ly** *adv.* **—blood·less·ness** *n.*

Bloodless Revolution *n.* The Glorious Revolution (*see*).

blood·let·ting (blŭd′lĕt′ĭng) *n.* **1.** The bleeding of a vein as a supposedly therapeutic measure; bleeding; venesection. **2.** A draining away, as of lifeblood. **3.** Bloodshed (*see*). **—blood·let·ter** *n.*

blood·line (blŭd′līn′) *n.* Direct line of descent; strain; pedigree.

blood money *n.* **1.** Money paid as compensation to the next of kin of a murder victim. **2.** Money paid to a hired killer. **3.** Money gained at the cost of another's life or livelihood.

blood plasma *n.* The pale-yellow or gray-yellow, protein-containing fluid portion of the blood in which the blood cells are normally suspended. Also called "plasma."

blood platelet *n.* A constituent of blood, a **platelet** (*see*).

blood poisoning *n.* Any condition in which the blood contains poisons or the bacteria that produce them; **septicemia** or **toxemia** (both of which see).

blood pressure *n.* Pressure of the blood against the walls of the arteries, primarily maintained by contraction of the left ventricle.

blood pudding *n.* A sausage prepared from cooked swine's blood and suet. Also *chiefly British* "black pudding."

---

blood

THE BODY'S INTERNAL TRANSPORT SYSTEM
The liquid that supports life in every cell of the body

Every cell of living tissue in the body is linked by the flow of blood. As it circulates, it acts as a transport system—carrying oxygen, vitamins, and nutrients to the body's tissues and waste products away from them. The blood has a defense mechanism that fights infection and a self-sealing power to repair wounds. It also carries hormones to the organs that need them, and it distributes body heat.

Human blood contains red cells, white cells, and platelets in a clear fluid called plasma. The red blood cells absorb oxygen in the lungs to provide energy for the body. The heart pumps oxygenated blood around the body and returns it, with waste products such as carbon dioxide, to the lungs. White blood cells defend the body against attacks by bacteria. Platelets enable the blood to clot after a cut.

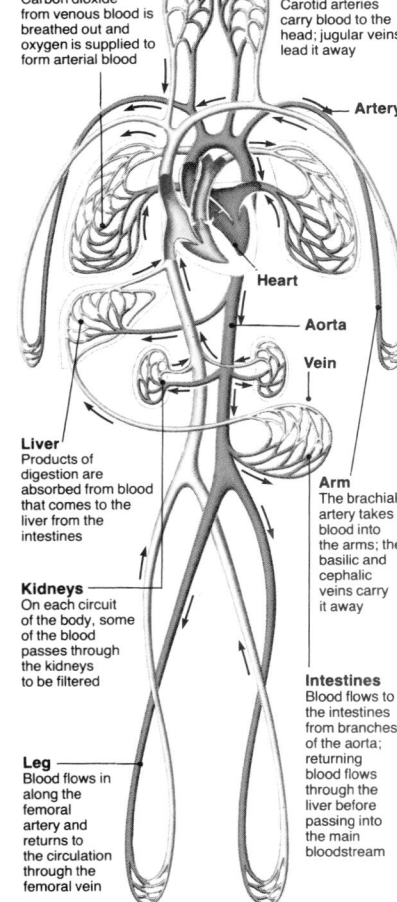

Lungs Carbon dioxide from venous blood is breathed out and oxygen is supplied to form arterial blood

Head Carotid arteries carry blood to the head; jugular veins lead it away

Artery

Heart

Aorta

Vein

Liver Products of digestion are absorbed from blood that comes to the liver from the intestines

Arm The brachial artery takes blood into the arms; the basilic and cephalic veins carry it away

Kidneys On each circuit of the body, some of the blood passes through the kidneys to be filtered

Leg Blood flows in along the femoral artery and returns to the circulation through the femoral vein

Intestines Blood flows to the intestines from branches of the aorta; returning blood flows through the liver before passing into the main bloodstream

CIRCULATION *The heart pumps blood through the lungs to absorb oxygen, then through the aorta, a large blood vessel, to the main arteries. These divide and subdivide before reaching the minute blood vessels called capillaries, which permeate the tissue and pass oxygen to it. Blood from the capillaries returns to the heart through the veins.*

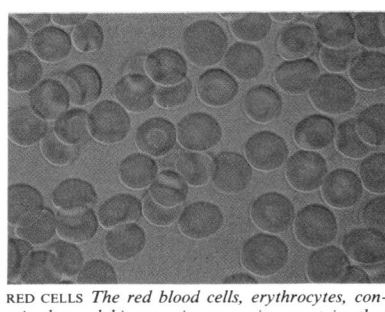

RED CELLS *The red blood cells, erythrocytes, contain hemoglobin, an iron-carrying protein that makes the blood red and transports oxygen around the body.*

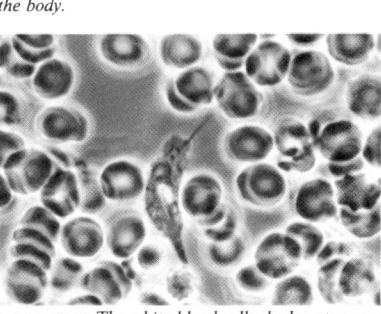

WHITE CELLS *The white blood cells, leukocytes, are part of the body's defense mechanism. They surround and "digest" any foreign bodies, such as bacteria in the blood.*

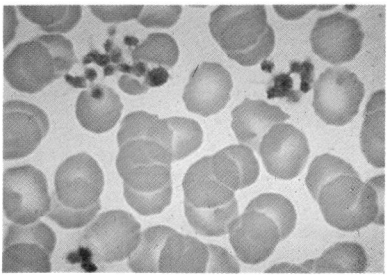

PLATELETS *Minute cells, called platelets (seen above as small, dark spots among red blood cells), cluster together and enable the blood to clot when a blood vessel is injured.*

blood rain *n.* Rain in which the raindrops are colored by fine, reddish dust particles brought from desert regions by the wind.
blood red *n.* Moderate to vivid red. —**blood-red** (blŭd′rĕd′) *adj.*
blood relation *n.* A person who is related by birth rather than by marriage. Also called "blood relative." —**blood relationship** *n.*
blood·root (blŭd′rōōt′, -rŏŏt′) *n.* See **sanguinaria.**
blood sausage *n.* **Blood pudding** (see).
blood serum *n.* Blood plasma with the fibrin removed.
blood·shed (blŭd′shĕd′) *n.* 1. The shedding of blood. 2. Carnage. Also called "bloodletting." —**blood·shed·der** *n.*
blood·shot (blŭd′shŏt′) *adj.* Red and inflamed: *bloodshot eyes.*
blood·stain (blŭd′stān′) *n.* A stain caused by blood. —**blood·stained** *adj.*
blood·stock (blŭd′stŏk′) *n.* Thoroughbred horses, especially racehorses.
blood·stone (blŭd′stōn′) *n.* A variety of deep-green chalcedony flecked with red jasper. Also called "heliotrope."
blood·stream (blŭd′strēm′) *n.* The stream of blood flowing through the circulatory system of a living body.
blood·suck·er (blŭd′sŭk′ər) *n.* 1. Any animal that sucks blood, as a leech. 2. One who clings to or preys upon another; a parasite. —**blood·suck·ing** *adj. & n.*
blood test *n.* Examination of a blood sample in order to determine the level of alcohol or drugs, the presence of bacteria, the blood group, or the like.
blood·thirst·y (blŭd′thûr′stē) *adj.* 1. **a.** Thirsting for bloodshed; murderous; cruel. **b.** Thirsting for violence. 2. Displaying or pandering to such feelings: *a bloodthirsty film.* —**blood·thirst·i·ly** *adv.* —**blood·thirst·i·ness** *n.*
blood type *n.* **Blood group** (see).
blood vessel *n.* Any elastic, tubular canal, such as an artery, vein, or capillary, through which blood circulates.
blood·worm (blŭd′wûrm′) *n.* Any of various segmented worms of the genera *Polycirrus* and *Enoplobranchus,* having bright-red bodies and often used for bait.
blood·wort (blŭd′wûrt′, -wôrt′) *n.* Any of various chiefly South American plants of the family Haemodoraceae, having roots that contain a red juice.
blood·y (blŭd′ē) *adj.* -ier, -iest. 1. Stained with blood. 2. Of, characteristic of, or containing blood. 3. Accompanied by or giving rise to bloodshed: *a bloody fight.* 4. Bloodthirsty; cruel. 5. Suggesting the color of blood; blood-red. 6. *British Slang.* Used as an intensive: *bloody fool.*
~*adv. British Slang.* Used as an intensive: *a bloody good film.*
~*tr.v.* **bloodied, -ying, -ies.** To stain, spot, or color with or as if with blood. —**blood·i·ly** *adv.* —**blood·i·ness** *n.*
bloody mary, Bloody Mary *n.* A drink made with vodka, tomato juice, and seasonings.
Bloody Mary. See **Mary I.**
bloom¹ (blōōm) *n.* 1. The flower or blossoms of a plant. 2. **a.** The condition or time of being in flower: *a rose in bloom.* **b.** A condition or time of vigor, freshness, and beauty; prime: *the bloom of girlhood.* 3. A fresh, rosy complexion. 4. *Botany.* A delicate, powdery coating, such as that found on some fruits, such as the plum, or on some leaves and stems. 5. A similar coating, as on newly minted coins. 6. A cloudy appearance on old paint or varnish.
~*v.* **bloomed, blooming, blooms.** —*intr.* 1. To bear flowers. 2. To shine with health and vigor; glow. 3. To grow or flourish. —*tr.* 1. To cause to flower. 2. To cause to flourish. 3. *British.* To coat the outer surface of (a lens) with a thin transparent layer so as to minimize reflection. [Middle English *blom, blome,* from Old Norse *blōm, blōmi.*] —**bloom·y** *adj.*
bloom² *n.* 1. A large bar of steel prepared for rolling. 2. A mass of wrought iron ready for further working. [Middle English *blome,* lump of metal, Old English *blōma.*]
bloom·er (blōō′mər) *n.* 1. **a.** A plant that blooms. **b.** One who attains full development of his or her abilities. 2. *Slang.* A blunder.
bloom·ers (blōō′mərz) *pl.n.* 1. A costume formerly worn by women and girls that was composed of loose trousers gathered about the ankles and sometimes worn under a short skirt. 2. Women's long and usually loose underpants. [After Amelia *Bloomer* (1818–94), U.S. reformer who advocated this type of undergarment.]
bloom·ing (blōō′mĭng) *adj.* 1. Flowering; blossoming. 2. Flourishing; growing. 3. *Slang.* Utter; thorough. Used as an intensive: *a blooming idiot.* [Sense 3, probably a euphemism for BLOODY.] —**bloom·ing·ly** *adv.* —**bloom·ing·ness** *n.*
bloop·er (blōō′pər) *n.* 1. *Baseball.* A short, weakly hit fly ball that carries just beyond the infield. 2. *Informal.* A clumsy mistake, especially one made in public; a faux pas. [From *bloop,* sound of such a hit (imitative).]
blos·som (blŏs′əm) *n.* 1. A flower or mass of flowers, especially on a plant that yields edible fruit. 2. The condition or time of flowering: *peach trees in blossom.*
~*intr.v.* **blossomed, -soming, -soms.** 1. To come into flower; bloom. 2. To develop; flourish: *She blossomed into a beauty.* [Middle English *blosme,* Old English *blōstm, blōstma.*] —**blos·som·y** *adj.*
blot¹ (blŏt) *n.* 1. A spot; a stain: *a blot of ink.* 2. A stain on one's reputation or character; a disgrace. 3. Something that detracts from beauty or excellence: *That factory is a blot on the landscape.*
~*v.* **blotted, blotting, blots.** —*tr.* 1. To spot or stain. 2. To bring moral disgrace to. [Sense 3, probably a euphemism for BLOODY.] Used with *out: "Whosoever hath sinned against me, him will I blot out of my book"* (Exodus 32:33). 4. To make obscure; darken; hide. Usually used with *out:*

clouds blotting out the moon. 5. To destroy utterly; annihilate. Used with *out.* 6. To dry or soak up with absorbent material. —*intr.* 1. To spill or spread in a blot or blots. 2. To become blotted; absorb or soak up: *a paper that blots easily.* —See Synonyms at **erase.** [Middle English *blot, blotte,* perhaps from Old French *blotte, blostre,* clod of earth, probably from Germanic.]
blot² *n.* 1. An exposed piece in backgammon. 2. *Archaic.* A weak point. [Probably from Dutch *bloot,* "naked," from Middle Dutch *bloot,* naked, poor.]
blotch (blŏch) *n.* 1. A spot or blot; a splotch. 2. A discoloration on the skin; a blemish. [Probably a blend of BLOT and BOTCH.] —**blotched** *adj.* —**blotch·i·ness** *n.* —**blotch·y** *adj.*
blot·ter (blŏt′ər) *n.* 1. A piece or pad of blotting paper, especially one with a firm backing. 2. A book containing daily records of occurrences or transactions: *a police blotter.*
blotting paper *n.* Absorbent paper used to soak up excess ink.
blot·to (blŏt′ō) *adj. Informal.* Very drunk. [Perhaps from BLOT.]
blouse (blouz, blous) *n.* 1. A woman's or child's loosely fitting shirtlike garment extending from the neck to the waist or slightly below the waist. 2. A loosely fitting garment resembling a long shirt, sometimes belted at the waist, often worn by European workmen. 3. A jacket or tunic worn as part of a uniform.
~*v.* **bloused, blousing, blouses.** —*intr.* To hang loosely. —*tr.* To make full and loose. [French *blouse*†.]
blou·son (blou′sŏn′, blōō′zŏn′) *n.* A short, loose jacket similar in style to a blouse and fitting tightly at the waist and often at the wrists. [French *blouson*†.]
blow¹ (blō) *v.* **blew** (blōō), **blown** (blōn), **blowing, blows.** —*intr.* 1. To be in a state of motion, as the wind. 2. **a.** To move along or be carried by or as if by the wind: *Her hat blew away.* **b.** To be brought into a specified state by the action of the wind: *The door blew open. The chimney blew down.* 3. To expel a current of air, as from the mouth or from a bellows. 4. To produce a sound by expelling a current of air, as in sounding a wind instrument. 5. To breathe hard; pant. 6. To storm: *It blew all night.* 7. To spout water and air. Used of a whale. 8. *Slang.* To boast. Used with *off.* 9. *Slang.* To go away; depart. 10. To break down as a result of excess current. Used of fuses or electronic components. —*tr.* 1. To cause to move by means of a current of air. 2. To bring into a specified state by means of a current of air: *The wind blew the door shut.* 3. To clear out or make free of obstruction by forcing air through: *to blow one's nose.* 4. **a.** To shape or form (glass, for example) by forcing air or gas through the material when molten. **b.** To shape or form by forcing air through the mouth: *blow a smoke ring.* 5. **a.** To cause (a wind instrument) to sound. **b.** To sound: *The bugle blew reveille.* 6. To cause (a horse) to be out of breath. 7. To cause to explode or bring into a specified state by means of an explosion. Used with *up, down, apart,* or other adverbs: *The bomb blew the windows out.* 8. To lay or deposit eggs in. Used of a fly. 9. To burn out or destroy (a fuse or other component) by excess current. 10. *Slang.* To spend (money) freely. 11. *Slang.* To handle ineptly; bungle: *blew his only chance.* 12. *Informal.* To curse; damn. Used euphemistically: *I'm blowed if I'll do it!* —**blow hot and cold.** To vacillate between favor and opposition. —**blow over.** 1. To subside; wane: *The storm blew over quickly.* 2. To be forgotten: *The scandal will soon blow over.* —**blow through.** *Australian & New Zealand Informal.* To leave.
~*n.* 1. **a.** A blast of air or wind. **b.** A storm. 2. The act of blowing. 3. A sound produced by blowing. [Blow, blew, blown; Middle English *blowen, blew, blowen,* Old English *blāwan, blēow, blāwen.*]
blow² *n.* 1. A sudden hard stroke or hit, as with the fist or an instrument. 2. A setback or unexpected shock. —**come to blows.** To begin to fight. [Middle English (northern dialect) *blaw,* perhaps from Germanic *bleuwan* (unattested), to strike.]
blow³ *n.* A mass of blossoms. Used chiefly in the phrase *in full blow.*
~*v.* **blew** (blōō), **blown** (blōn), **blowing, blows.** —*intr.* To bloom. —*tr.* 1. To cause to bloom. 2. To produce (blossoms). [Middle English *blowen,* to blossom, Old English *blōwan.*]
blow-by-blow (blō′bī-blō′) *adj.* Described exactly and in a detailed way: *a blow-by-blow account of the accident.*
blow-dry (blō′drī′) *n.* A method of styling the hair by drying it with a hand-held hair drier and shaping it with a brush at the same time. —**blow-dri·er** *n.* —**blow-dry** *v.*
blow·er (blō′ər) *n.* 1. One that blows, especially a mechanical device, such as a fan. 2. *Slang.* A braggart. 3. *British Informal.* A telephone.
blow·fish (blō′fĭsh′) *n., pl.* **-fishes** or collectively **blowfish.** The **puffer** (see).
blow·fly (blō′flī′) *n., pl.* **-flies.** Any of several flies of the family Calliphoridae that deposit their eggs in carcasses or carrion or in open sores and wounds. See **bluebottle.**
blow·hard (blō′härd′) *n.* A boaster; a braggart.
blow·hole (blō′hōl′) *n.* 1. A nostril at the highest point on the head of whales and other cetaceans. 2. A hole in ice through which whales, dolphins, seals, and other aquatic mammals come up for air. 3. A vent to permit the escape of air or other gas. 4. A virtually vertical vent that reaches from the roof of a sea cave to the cliff top.
blow in *intr.v. Informal.* To arrive casually or without warning.
blow-in (blō′ĭn′) *n. Australian Informal.* A stranger or newcomer, especially one who is unwelcome.
blow·lamp (blō′lămp′) *n.* A **blowtorch** (see).
blown (blōn) *adj.* Completely expanded or opened. Often used in combination: *a full-blown flower.*
blow off *tr.v.* To release or let off (steam from a boiler, for example).

bluebell *Common name for the wood hyacinth, a perennial plant with dark-blue or violet bell-shaped flowers. Bluebells flower in early summer in woodlands.*

blueberry *Grape-colored edible berries that grow well only in very acidic, well-drained, but moist soils.*

bluebottle *The large shiny-bodied relative of the common housefly makes a distinctive buzzing noise when it flies. The eggs it lays hatch into maggots that feed on carrion. Bluebottles may also lay eggs on household meat that has been left uncovered.*

—*intr.v.* **1.** To be released or let off. Used of gas or liquid under pressure. **2.** *Informal.* To give vent to pent-up emotions.

blow·off (blō'ôf', -ŏf') *n.* **1.** Something blown off, such as a gas. **2.** A device or channel for blowing off something.

blow out *intr.v.* **1.** To be extinguished by a current of air. Used of a candle or other flame. **2.** To burst suddenly. Used of a tire. **3.** To burn out or melt. Used of a fuse or other electrical device. **4.** To eject gas or oil in an uncontrolled flow. Used of a gas or oil well. —*tr. v.* To extinguish (a candle, for example) by blowing.

blow·out (blō'out') *n.* **1. a.** A sudden rupture or bursting, as of a car tire. **b.** The hole made in this way. **2.** A sudden escape of a confined gas. **3.** The burning out of a fuse. **4.** An uncontrolled flow from a gas or oil well. **5.** A basin-shaped or trough-shaped depression formed by wind eddying in a sand dune or sand deposit. **6.** *Slang.* A very large party or social affair.

blow·pipe (blō'pīp') *n.* **1.** A metal tube in which a flow of gas is mixed with a controlled flow of air to concentrate the heat of a flame. **2.** A long narrow pipe through which darts or pellets may be blown. **3.** A long narrow iron pipe used to gather, work, and blow molten glass.

blow·torch (blō'tôrch') *n.* **1.** A portable burner for mixing gas and oxygen to produce a very hot flame for welding, flame cutting, glass blowing, or the like. **2.** A portable hand burner fueled by paraffin or bottled gas and used by plumbers for soldering and by painters for removing old paint. Also called "blowlamp."

blow up *intr.v.* **1.** To come into being: *A storm blew up off the coast.* **2.** To explode. **3.** To lose one's temper. —*tr. v.* **1.** To cause to explode. **2.** To enlarge the size of (a photographic print). **3.** To increase the importance of. **4.** To fill with air.

blow·up (blō'ŭp') *n.* **1.** An explosion. **2.** A violent outburst of temper. **3.** A photographic enlargement.

blow·y (blō'ē) *adj.* **-ier, -iest.** Windy; breezy.

blow·zy, blow·sy (blou'zē) *adj.* **-zier, -ziest** or **-sier, -siest. 1.** Having a coarsely ruddy and bloated appearance. **2.** Disheveled; frowzy; unkempt: *blowzy hair.* —See Synonyms at **sloppy.** [From obsolete *blowse,* beggar wench, slattern, perhaps from *blowzy,* windy, from BLOW.]

blub (blŭb) *intr.v.* **blubbed, blubbing, blubs.** *British.* To blubber.

blub·ber¹ (blŭb'ər) *v.* **-bered, -bering, -bers.** —*intr.* To weep and sob in a noisy manner. —*tr.* To utter while crying and sobbing: *The child blubbered his name.* —See Synonyms at **cry.**
~*n.* A loud weeping and sobbing. [Middle English *bloberen, blubren,* to bubble, foam, from *blober, bluber,* foam, bubble (imitative).] **—blub·ber·er** *n.* **—blub·ber·ing·ly** *adv.*

blubber² *n.* **1.** The thick layer of fat between the skin and the muscle layers of whales and other marine mammals. **2.** Excessive body fat.
~*adj.* Swollen and protruding. [Middle English *blober, bluber,* foam, bubble, entrails, fish, or whale oil. See **blubber** (verb).] **—blub·ber·y** *adj.*

Blü·cher (blōō'kər), **Gebhard Leberecht von, Prince of Wahlstatt** (1742–1819). Prussian field marshal. His astute leadership of the Prussian army played a crucial part in the campaigns against Napoleon, culminating in 1815 when he arrived at Waterloo in time to secure Wellington's famous victory.

bludg·eon (blŭj'ən) *n.* A short, heavy club, usually of wood, that has one end loaded or thicker than the other.
~*tr.v.* **bludgeoned, -eoning, -eons. 1.** To hit with or as if with a bludgeon. **2.** To threaten or bully. [18th century : origin obscure.] **—bludg·eon·er, bludg·eon·eer** (blŭj'ə-nîr') *n.*

blue (blōō) *n.* **1.** *Abbr.* **bl.** Any of a group of colors that may vary in lightness and saturation, whose hue is that of a clear sky; the hue of that portion of the spectrum lying between green and violet; one of the additive or light primaries; one of the psychological primary hues, evoked in the normal observer by radiant energy of wavelength approximately 475 nanometers. **2. a.** Any pigment or dye imparting this color. **b. Bluing** *(see).* **3. a.** Any object of this color. **b.** Blue dress or clothing: *the girls in blue.* **4.** A person who wears a blue uniform. **5.** *Sometimes* **Blue. a.** A member of the Union Army in the Civil War. **b.** The Union Army itself. Compare **gray. 6. blues.** The blue uniform of the U.S. Navy. **7.** A small blue butterfly of the family Lycaenidae. **8.** A **bluestocking** *(see).* **9.** *British Informal.* A member of the Conservative Party or loosely, a politically conservative person. Used chiefly in the phrase *a true blue.* **—into the blue.** At a far distance or into the unknown. **—out of the blue. 1.** From an unexpected, unforeseen, or unknown source. **2.** At a completely unexpected time. **—the blue. 1.** The sea. **2.** The sky.
~*adj.* **bluer, bluest. 1.** *Abbr.* **bl.** Of the color blue. **2.** Bluish, or having parts that are blue or bluish. Used with plant and animal names: *blue spruce, blue whale.* **3.** Having a gray or purplish color, as from cold or contusion. **4.** Wearing blue. **5. a.** Gloomy; depressed. **b.** Dismal; dreary: *a blue day.* **c.** *Music.* Of or pertaining to the blues. **6.** *Physics.* Designating one of the three quark colors, the others being green and red. **7.** Puritanical; strict. **8.** Fiercely intellectual. Usually said of a woman. **9.** Aristocratic; patrician. **10. a.** Indecent; risqué: *a blue joke.* **b.** Pornographic: *blue films.* **—true blue.** *Informal.* **1.** Loyal and sincere. **2.** Genuine or real.
~*v.* **blued, bluing, blues.** —*tr.* **1.** To make blue. **2.** To use bluing on. **3.** *Slang.* To squander; waste. —*intr.* To become blue. [Middle English *bleu, blewe,* from Old French *bleu,* from Common Romance *blāvus* (unattested), from Germanic.] **—blue·ly** *adv.* **—blue·ness** *n.*

blue asbestos *n.* A variety of commercial asbestos, **crocidolite** *(see).*

blue baby *n.* An infant born with bluish skin caused by inadequate oxygenation of the blood, a symptom of a congenital malformation of the heart.

blue-back salmon (blōō'băk') *n.* The sockeye salmon *(see).*

blue·beard (blōō'bîrd') *n. Often* **Bluebeard.** Any man thought to be a wife-slayer or a killer of women. [French *Barbe-bleue,* character in fairy tale (by Charles PERRAULT) who murdered a number of wives in succession.]

blue·beat (blōō'bēt') *n.* A type of rhythmic West Indian popular music in 12/8 time with the accent on the third beat in every group of three beats.

blue·bell (blōō'bĕl') *n.* **1.** A European plant, *Endymion nonscriptus,* having a one-sided cluster of fragrant, blue-violet flowers. **2.** The **harebell** *(see),* which is the bluebell of Scotland. **3.** Any of various other plants with blue, bell-shaped flowers.

blue·ber·ry (blōō'bĕr'ē, -bər-ē) *n., pl.* **-ries. 1.** Any of several North American shrubs of the genus *Vaccinium,* having small, urn-shaped flowers and edible berries. **2.** The juicy, blue, purplish, or blackish berry of any of these shrubs.

blue·bird (blōō'bûrd') *n.* Any of several North American birds of the genus *Sialia,* having blue plumage and, in the male of most species, a rust-colored breast.

blue blood *n.* **1.** Noble or aristocratic descent. **2.** A member of the aristocracy or other high social group. [Translation of Spanish *sangre azul*; probably from the blue color of the veins of fair-complexioned aristocrats.] **—blue-blood·ed** *adj.*

blue·blos·som (blōō'blŏs'əm) *n.* A shrub, *Ceanothus thyrsiflorus,* of the west coast of the United States, having profuse clusters of small blue flowers.

blue·bon·net (blōō'bŏn'ĭt) *n.* **1.** A plant, *Lupinus subcarnosus,* of Texas and adjacent regions, having compound leaves and clusters of blue flowers. **2.** Any of several other plants having blue flowers. **3.** A broad, blue woolen cap worn in Scotland. **4.** A Scotsman wearing such a cap.

blue·book (blōō'bŏŏk') *n.* **1.** An official publication of the British government, so named from its blue covers. **2.** An official list of persons in the employ of the U.S. government. **3.** *Informal.* A book listing socially prominent people. **4.** A blank notebook with blue covers in which to write college examinations.

blue·bot·tle (blōō'bŏt'l) *n.* **1.** Any of several flies of the genus *Calliphora,* having a bright metallic-blue body and breeding in decaying organic matter. **2.** A plant, the **cornflower** *(see).*

blue cheese *n.* Any of various cheeses having a greenish-blue mold and a sharp flavor. Also called "bleu cheese."

blue chip *n.* **1.** *Finance.* A stock that sells at a high price because of public confidence in its long record of steady earnings. Also called "blue-chip stock." **2.** A valuable asset held in reserve. **3.** A blue-colored gambling chip of high value. **—blue-chip** *adj.*

blue cohosh *n.* A plant, *Caulophyllum thalictroides,* of eastern North America, having compound leaves and a cluster of greenish or purplish flowers.

blue-col·lar (blōō'kŏl'ər) *adj.* Of or pertaining to wage earners in jobs performed in clothing such as overalls and often involving manual labor, especially when such workers are regarded as a social class. Compare **white-collar.**

blue devils *pl.n.* **1.** *Slang.* Delirium tremens. **2.** *Informal.* A feeling of depression or despondency.

blue-eyed Mary (blōō'īd') *n.* A plant, *Collinsia verna,* of eastern North America, having two-lipped blue and white flowers.

Blue·fields (blōō'fēldz'). A port in southeast Nicaragua, the most important of the country's Caribbean ports. British and Dutch pirate ships used it as a harbor in the 16th and 17th centuries.

blue·fish (blōō'fĭsh') *n., pl.* **-fishes** or collectively **bluefish. 1.** A voracious bluish-colored food and game fish, *Pomatomus saltatrix,* of temperate and tropical waters of the Atlantic and Indian oceans. **2.** Broadly, any of various other fishes that are predominantly blue in color.

blue fox *n.* **1.** The **arctic fox** *(see)* during its summer color phase, when its pelt is bluish gray. **2.** The fur of such a fox.

blue·gill (blōō'gĭl') *n.* A common, edible sunfish, *Lepomis macrochirus,* of North American lakes and streams.

blue·grass (blōō'grăs', -gräs') *n.* **1.** Any of several grasses of the genus *Poa*; especially, *P. pratensis,* native to Eurasia but naturalized throughout North America. This species is also called "Kentucky bluegrass." **2.** A type of folk music that originated in the southern United States, characterized by rapid tempos, jazzlike improvisation, and emphasis on nonelectrified stringed instruments, such as banjos and guitars.

Blue·grass Country (blōō'grăs'). Also **Bluegrass Region** or **the Bluegrass.** Area in central Kentucky noted for its abundant bluegrass and also for the breeding of racehorses.

blue-green algae (blōō'grēn') *n.* Algae of the division Cyanophyta (or Myxophyceae), considered to be among the simplest forms of plants.

blue grouse *n.* A wildfowl, *Dendragapus obscurus,* of Western North America, having predominantly gray plumage.

blue·gum (blōō'gŭm') *n.* Also **blue gum.** A tall timber tree, *Eucalyptus globulus,* native to Australia, having aromatic leaves that yield a medicinal oil and outer bark that peels off in shreds.

blue·head (blōō'hĕd') *n.* A marine fish, *Thalassoma bifasciatum,* of tropical Atlantic waters, of which the male has a blue head and a green body.

blueing. Variant of **bluing.**

blueish. Variant of **bluish.**

blue-jack-et (blōō′jăk′ĭt) n. A sailor in the U.S. or British navy. [From the blue jacket of the Navy.]

blue jay n. A common North American bird, *Cyanocitta cristata,* having a crested head and predominantly blue plumage.

blue jeans pl.n. Heavy blue denim trousers. See **jean** (sense 2).

blue law n. 1. One of a body of laws in colonial New England designed to enforce certain moral standards. 2. A law designed to regulate Sunday activities.

blue mold n. Any of several fungi of the genus *Penicillium,* forming a bluish growth on food and other surfaces.

Blue Mountains. Uplifted, eroded part of the Columbia Plateau in northeastern Oregon and southeastern Washington. Lava flows cover much of the surface. The slopes are used for lumbering, and the surrounding lowlands for irrigated farming and dairying.

Blue Nile. *Arabic* **Bahr el Az-raq** (bä′hər ăl ăz′rŏk). A river rising in northwestern Ethiopia and flowing c. 1,610 kilometers (1,000 miles) southeast and then northwest to Sudan. At Khartoum it joins the White Nile to form the Nile.

blue-nose (blōō′nōz′) n. 1. A puritanical person. 2. Usually **Bluenose.** A person or ship from Nova Scotia.

blue note n. *Music.* A flatted note, especially the third or seventh note of a chord, in place of an expected major interval.

blue-pen-cil (blōō′pĕn′səl) tr.v. -ciled, -ciling, -cils. To edit, revise, or correct with or as if with a blue pencil; especially, to censor.

blue peter n. *Nautical.* A blue flag with a white square in the center, flown to signal that a ship is ready to sail. [Probably from the Christian name *Peter.*]

blue-print (blōō′prĭnt′) n. 1. A photographic reproduction, as of architectural plans or technical drawings, rendered as white lines on a blue background. Also called "cyanotype." 2. Any carefully designed plan or model.

~tr.v. **blueprinted, -printing, -prints.** 1. To make a blueprint of. 2. To lay a plan for.

blue ribbon n. 1. The first prize; highest award or honor. 2. The badge of various temperance societies. —**blue-rib-bon** adj.

Blue Ridge. Also **Blue Ridge Mountains.** A range of the Appalachian Mts. extending from southern Pennsylvania to northern Georgia. It is a major recreation area noted for its resorts and scenery.

blues (blōōz) n. *Sometimes used with a singular verb.* 1. A state of depression or melancholy. 2. A style of jazz evolved from black southern American secular songs and usually distinguished by slow tempo and flatted thirds and sevenths.

blue shift n. A shift of spectral lines toward shorter wavelengths, observed in the spectra of stars that are approaching the solar system. Compare **red shift.**

blue-sky law (blōō′skī′) n. A law designed to protect the public from buying fraudulent securities.

blue spruce n. An evergreen tree, *Picea pungens,* of the Rocky Mountain region, having bluish-green needles.

blue-stock-ing (blōō′stŏk′ĭng) n. A serious, intellectual, or scholarly woman. [After the *Blue Stocking Society,* name given derisively to a group of 18th-century intellectuals who met in the London houses of several prominent women. Some of the male members wore ordinary blue stockings instead of formal black silk.] —**blue-stock-ing** adj.

blue-stone (blōō′stōn′) n. 1. A bluish-gray sandstone used for paving and building. 2. Any similar stone.

blue tit n. A common European songbird, *Parus caeruleus,* with a blue crown and wings, a yellow breast, and a white face.

blu-ets (blōō′ĭts) n. *Used with a singular or plural verb.* A slender, low-growing plant, *Houstonia caerulea,* of eastern North America, having small, light-blue flowers with yellow centers. Also called "innocence," "Quaker-ladies." [French *bleuet, bluet,* diminutives of *bleu,* BLUE.]

blue vitriol n. *Chemistry.* The blue hydrated crystalline form of **copper sulfate** *(see).*

blue-weed (blōō′wēd′) n. A plant, viper's bugloss *(see).*

blue whale n. A very large whale, *Sibbaldus musculus,* having a bluish-gray back and longitudinal grooves along the throat and belly. Also called "sulphur-bottom," "Sibbald's rorqual."

bluff¹ (blŭf) v. **bluffed, bluffing, bluffs.** —tr. 1. To mislead, deceive, or hoodwink. 2. To impress, deter, or intimidate by a display of confidence greater than the facts support. 3. To try to mislead (opponents) in poker by heavy betting on a poor hand or by little or no betting on a good one. —intr. To feign strength when in a state of weakness, or, to feign weakness when strong.

~n. 1. The act or practice of bluffing. 2. One who bluffs. —**call someone's bluff.** To challenge or expose someone's bluff. [19th century (as poker term) : Dutch *bluffen,* to boast, from Middle Dutch, to swell up.] —**bluff-a-ble** adj. —**bluff-er** n.

bluff² n. A steep headland, promontory, river bank, or cliff.

~adj. **bluffer, bluffest.** 1. Presenting a broad, steep front. 2. Having a rough, blunt, but not unkind manner. —See Synonyms at **gruff.** [17th century (nautical use) : origin obscure.] —**bluff-ly** adv. —**bluff-ness** n.

blu-ing, blue-ing (blōō′ĭng) n. 1. Any of various coloring agents used to counteract the yellowing of laundered fabrics. Also called "blue." 2. A rinsing agent used to give a silver tint to graying hair.

blu-ish, blue-ish (blōō′ĭsh) adj. Somewhat or slightly blue. —**blu-ish-ness** n.

Blum (blōōm), **Léon** (1872-1950). French statesman, cofounder of the Socialist Party (1905), becoming its leader in 1920. He was premier in 1936-37 and again in 1938 and 1946-47.

Blun-den (blŭn′dən), **Edmund Charles** (1896-1974). British writer. He is best known for *Undertones of War* (1928), a collection of prose and poetry derived from his experiences in World War I.

blun-der (blŭn′dər) n. A stupid and serious mistake usually caused by ignorance, stupidity, or confusion. —See Synonyms at **error.** ~v. **blundered, -dering, -ders.** —intr. 1. To move awkwardly or clumsily, as if blind; stumble. 2. To make a stupid mistake because of ignorance or confusion. —tr. 1. To botch or bungle. 2. To say stupidly or thoughtlessly. [Middle English *blund(e)ren, blond(e)ren,* to proceed blindly, blunder, probably from Old Norse *blunda,* to shut the eyes.] —**blun-der-er** n. —**blun-der-ing-ly** adv.

blun-der-buss (blŭn′dər-bŭs′) n. 1. A short musket with a wide bore and flaring muzzle, formerly used to scatter shot at close range. 2. A stupid, clumsy person. [Alteration (influenced by BLUNDER) of Dutch *donderbus* : *donder,* thunder, + *bus,* gun, from Middle Dutch *busse,* box, tube, from Late Latin *buxis,* BOX.]

blunge (blŭnj) tr.v. **blunged, blunging, blunges.** To mix (clay, for example) with water for use in making ceramics, usually by means of a machine. [Blend of BLEND + PLUNGE.]

blung-er (blŭn′jər) n. A large vat in which water and clay or a similar substance are mixed. [From *blunge.*]

blunt (blŭnt) adj. **blunter, bluntest.** 1. Having a thick, dull edge or end; not sharp or pointed. 2. **a.** Having an abrupt and frank manner; brusque. **b.** Direct; straightforward: *a blunt refusal.* 3. Slow to understand or perceive; dull. —See Synonyms at **gruff.** ~v. **blunted, blunting, blunts.** —tr. 1. To make blunt. 2. To make less sensitive or alert: *senses blunted by too much drinking.* 3. To lessen the force or destructiveness of: *blunt the enemy's attack.* —intr. To become blunt. [Middle English *blont, blunt†,* dull, blunt, stupid.] —**blunt-ly** adv. —**blunt-ness** n.

blur (blûr) v. **blurred, blurring, blurs.** —tr. 1. To make indistinct and hazy in outline or appearance; obscure. 2. To smear or stain; smudge. 3. To lessen the perception of; dim. —intr. To become indistinct or smudged.

~n. 1. A blot or smudge. 2. A hazy and indistinct visual or mental image. [16th century : perhaps akin to BLEAR.] —**blur-ry** adj.

blurb (blûrb) n. A brief commendatory publicity notice, as on a book jacket. [Coined in the early 1900's by Gelett *Burgess* (1866-1951), American humorist and illustrator.]

blurt (blûrt) tr.v. **blurted, blurting, blurts.** To utter suddenly and impulsively. Often used with *out.* [Probably imitative.]

blush (blŭsh) v. **blushed, blushing, blushes.** —intr. 1. To become suddenly red in the face from modesty, embarrassment, or shame; flush: *"There's a blush for won't, and a blush for shan't / And a blush for having done it"* (Keats). 2. To become red or rosy. 3. To feel ashamed or regretful about something. Usually used with *at* or *for.* —tr. 1. To give a reddish hue to. 2. To reveal by blushing. ~n. 1. A sudden reddening of the face from modesty, embarrassment, or shame. 2. A red or rosy color. —**at** (or **on**) **first blush.** At first sight or glance.

~adj. Having the rosy color of a blush. [Middle English *blusshen, blisshen,* Old English *blyscan.*] —**blush-ful** adj. —**blush-ing-ly** adv.

blush-er (blŭsh′ər) n. 1. One that blushes. 2. A cosmetic used to give color to the cheeks.

blus-ter (blŭs′tər) v. -tered, -tering, -ters. —intr. 1. To blow in loud, violent gusts, as wind in a storm. 2. To speak noisily and boastfully. 3. To threaten ineffectually. —tr. To force or bully (one's way) with swaggering threats.

~n. 1. A violent, gusty wind. 2. Turbulence or noisy confusion. 3. Swaggering talk. [Middle English *blusteren,* probably akin to Low German *blüstern.*] —**blus-ter-er** n. —**blus-ter-y, blus-ter-ous** adj.

blvd. boulevard.

b.m. board measure.

B.M. 1. Bachelor of Medicine. 2. Bachelor of Music. 3. bench mark. 4. British Museum.

B.M.E. 1. Bachelor of Mechanical Engineering. 2. Bachelor of Mining Engineering.

BMR basal metabolic rate.

B.M.S. Bachelor of Marine Science.

B.Mus. Bachelor of Music.

bn., Bn. 1. baron. 2. battalion.

B.N.A. British North America.

B'nai B'rith (bnä′ brĭth′) n. A Jewish international fraternal society. [Hebrew *benē berîth,* "sons of the covenant."]

bo (bō) n., pl. **bos.** *Slang.* A fellow; a pal. Often used as a form of address. [Probably short for HOBO or BOZO.]

b.o. 1. box office. 2. branch office. 3. buyer's option.

B.O. n. *Informal.* Body odor; an unpleasant bodily smell.

bo-a (bō′ə) n. 1. Any of various large, nonvenomous, chiefly tropical snakes of the family Boidae, which includes the python, anaconda, boa constrictor, and other snakes that coil around and crush their prey. 2. A long, fluffy scarf made of fur, feathers, or other soft material. [New Latin *Boa* (genus), from Latin *boa†,* a large water snake.]

boa constrictor n. A large, nonvenomous snake, *Constrictor constrictor,* of tropical America, having brown markings, which kills its prey by constriction.

blue jay *North America's blue jay (above) is distinguished from the European jay by its coloring and by its mobile crest, shown here in the lowered position. But the birds have many similar habits. Both, for instance, bury acorns as a winter food reserve.*

blue tit *Insects and insect larvae are the chief food of the European blue tit, which often hunts upside down on the branches of trees.*

Boadicea. See **Boudicca.**

Bo·a·ner·ges¹ (bō′ə-nûr′jēz). The name given by Jesus to the Apostles John and James. Mark 3:17.

Boanerges² *n.* *Used with a singular verb.* A vociferous, loud-voiced preacher or orator. [Hebrew *bənē reghesh,* "sons of thunder."]

boar (bôr, bōr) *n.* **1.** An uncastrated male pig. **2.** A *wild boar* (see). [Middle English *bor,* Old English *bār,* from West Germanic *bairoz* (unattested).]

board (bôrd, bōrd) *n.* *Abbr.* **bd. 1.** A long, flat slab of sawed lumber; plank. **2.** A flat piece of wood or similarly rigid material, adapted for a special use: *a diving board; a notice board.* **3.** A flat, usually specially marked surface on which a game is played. **4.** The hard pasteboard cover of a book. **5. boards. a.** The stage of a theater. **b.** The acting profession. In both senses, preceded by *the.* **6. a.** A table, especially one set for serving food. **b.** Food or meals collectively: *board and lodging.* **7.** A table at which official meetings are held; a conference table. **8.** *Used with a singular or plural verb.* **a.** The directors of a company. Also used adjectivally: *a board meeting.* **b.** Any committee, body of administrators, or the like: *a board of trustees.* **9.** A panel, usually plastic, on which an electrical circuit is mounted, especially one serving as a base for a printed circuit: *printed circuit board.* **10.** *Nautical.* **a.** The side of a ship. **b.** A leeboard. **c.** A centerboard. **—across the board.** *Informal.* **1.** Designating a bet that a horse or dog will win, place, or show. **2.** Affecting all members or divisions equally. **—by the board.** Overboard. **—go by the board.** To be ruined, unnoticed, or ignored. **—on board.** Aboard. **—sweep the board.** To win every possible prize, event, or the like. **—tread the boards.** To perform on or as if on a theater stage.

~*v.* **boarded, boarding, boards.** —*tr.* **1.** To cover or close with boards. Used with *up*: *board up a door.* **2.** To furnish with meals in return for payment. **3.** To house where board is furnished. **4.** To enter or go aboard (a ship or public vehicle). **5.** To come alongside (a ship), especially in order to force one's way aboard. **6.** In ice hockey, to block (an opposing player) into the boards surrounding the rink. —*intr.* To receive meals, or meals and lodging, in return for payment. [Middle English *bord,* Old English *bord,* plank, table, border, ship's side.]

board·er (bôr′dər, bōr′-) *n.* **1.** One who pays a stipulated sum to stay in someone else's house and receive regular meals; lodger. **2.** A person who is detailed to go aboard an enemy ship.

board foot *n., pl.* **board feet.** *Abbr.* **bd. ft.** A unit of lumber measurement equal to the volume of a piece of wood one foot square by one inch thick.

boarding house, board·ing·house (bôr′dĭng-hous′, bōr′-) *n.* A private home that takes in paying guests and provides meals and lodging.

boarding school *n.* A school where pupils are provided with meals and lodging. Compare **day school.**

board measure *n.* *Abbr.* **b.m.** Measurement of lumber in board feet.

board of trade *n.* **1.** An association of bankers and businessmen formed to promote common commercial interests; a **chamber of commerce** (see). **2. Board of Trade.** A British government committee dealing with problems of trade and commerce.

board rule *n.* A measuring stick for determining a volume of lumber in board feet.

board·walk (bôrd′wôk′, bōrd′-) *n.* **1.** A path made of wooden planks. **2.** A promenade, especially of planks, along a beach or waterfront.

boar·fish (bôr′fĭsh′, bōr′-) *n., pl.* **-fishes** or collectively **boarfish.** Any of several marine fishes of the genus *Antigonia,* having a deep, flattened body, bright red coloring, and spiny fins.

boar·hound (bôr′hound′, bōr′-) *n.* A large dog, such as the Great Dane, used for hunting wild boars.

boar·ish (bôr′ĭsh, bōr′-) *adj.* Like a boar; coarse; lecherous; brutish. **—boar·ish·ly** *adv.* **—boar·ish·ness** *n.*

boart. Variant of **bort.**

Bo·as (bō′ăz′), **Franz** (1858–1942). German-born U.S. anthropologist. Boas laid special emphasis on the systematic analysis of language structures and culture and is considered one of the founders of American anthropology.

boast¹ (bōst) *v.* **boasted, boasting, boasts.** —*intr.* To speak with excessive pride about one's own accomplishments, talents, or possessions. Often used with *of* or *about.* —*tr.* **1.** To brag about with excessive pride. **2.** To take pride in, or be enhanced by the possession of: *The school boasts excellent sporting facilities.*

~*n.* **1.** An instance of excessive self-praise. **2.** Something that one is proud of. [Middle English *bosten,* from *bost,* bragging, threat, perhaps from Germanic, akin to German dialectal *bauste(r)n,* to swell.] **—boast·er** *n.* **—boast·ing·ly** *adv.*

Synonyms: brag, crow, vaunt.

boast² *tr.v.* **boasted, boasting, boasts.** To shape or form (stone) roughly with a broad chisel. [Origin obscure.]

boast·ful (bōst′fəl) *adj.* Tending to boast or brag. **—boast·ful·ly** *adv.* **—boast·ful·ness** *n.*

boat (bōt) *n.* **1.** A relatively small, usually open craft of a size that might be carried on a ship. **2.** A ship. Not in nautical usage. **3.** A dish shaped somewhat like a boat: *a gravy boat.* **—burn one's boats.** *Chiefly British.* To commit oneself irrevocably to a course of action; burn one's bridges. **—in the same boat.** In the same predicament. **—miss the boat.** *Informal.* To lose an opportunity by failing to act at the right moment. **—rock the boat.** To upset the

existing state of affairs; behave disruptively.

~*v.* **boated, boating, boats.** —*intr.* To travel by boat. —*tr.* To transport by boat. [Middle English *bo(o)t,* from Old English *bāt* and Old Norse *bātr.*]

boat·bill (bōt′bĭl′) *n.* A nocturnal tropical American wading bird, *Cochlearius cochlearius,* having a large bill shaped like an inverted boat. Also called "boat-billed heron."

boat·er (bō′tər) *n.* **1.** One who boats. **2.** A stiff straw hat with a flat crown.

boat hook *n.* A pole with a metal point and hook at one end, used to maneuver boats and other floating objects.

boat·house (bōt′hous′) *n.* A shed built at the water's edge or over the water, in which boats are kept.

boat·load (bōt′lōd′) *n.* The number of passengers or quantity of cargo that a boat carries or can safely carry.

boat·man (bōt′mən) *n., pl.* **-men** (-mĭn). One who works on, deals with, or operates boats. **—boat·man·ship** *n.*

boat people *pl.n.* Refugees, especially those from Vietnam or other parts of Southeast Asia, who have made their escape in small boats.

boat·swain, bo's'n, bo·sun (bō′sən) *n.* A warrant officer or petty officer in charge of a ship's deck crew, rigging, anchors, and cables, who has a whistle as his badge of office. [Middle English *botswein,* Old English *bātswān* : BOAT + SWAIN.]

boatswain's chair *n.* A short board secured by ropes and used as a seat by sailors when working aloft or over a ship's side.

boat train *n.* A train scheduled to take passengers to catch or meet a particular ship.

Bo·az (bō′ăz). The husband of Ruth. Ruth 2:4.

bob¹ (bŏb) *n.* **1. a.** A quick jerking movement of the head or body. **b.** A quick bow or curtsy. **2.** A short line at the end of a stanza of verse. **3. a.** Any small knoblike dangling object: *a plumb bob.* **b. bobs.** Small, unimportant objects: *bits and bobs.* **4.** A fishing float or cork. **5.** A small lock or curl of hair. **6.** A short haircut on a woman or child, in which the hair is cut to the same length all round the back and sides of the head. **7.** The docked tail of a horse. **8.** A polishing disk rotated by a spindle and impregnated with an abrasive. **9.** In bell-ringing, one of several types of change. **10.** A tap or a light blow.

~*v.* **bobbed, bobbing, bobs.** —*intr.* **1.** To move up and down: *The cork bobbed on the water.* **2.** To curtsy or bow. **3.** To grab at floating or hanging objects with the teeth. Usually used with *for*: *He bobbed for apples.* **4.** To fish with a bob. —*tr.* **1.** To move (especially the head) up and down. **2.** To cut short: *She bobbed her hair.* **3.** To hit lightly and quickly; tap. **—bob up.** To appear suddenly, as a cork emerging from under water. [As "a pendent object," Middle English *bobbe†,* cluster of flowers or fruit. As verb "to move up and down," Middle English *bobben* (probably imitative).] **—bob·ber** *n.*

bob² *n., pl.* **bob.** *British Slang.* A shilling (five pence). [19th century : origin obscure.]

bob·bin (bŏb′ĭn) *n.* **1.** A spool or reel that holds thread or yarn for spinning, weaving, knitting, sewing, or making lace. **2.** Narrow braid used as trimming. **3.** A spool wound with insulated wire that forms part of an electromagnetic device, such as an electric bell. [French *bobine* (expressive).]

bob·bi·net (bŏb′ə-nĕt′) *n.* A machine-woven net fabric with hexagonal meshes. [*bobbin* + *net.*]

bobbin lace *n.* An intricate handmade lace made by interlacing thread around small notched pins or bobbins stuck into a pillow according to a certain pattern. Also called "pillow lace."

bob·ble (bŏb′əl) *v.* **-bled, -bling, -bles.** —*intr.* To bob up and down. —*tr.* To fumble (a ball, for example). ~*n.* **1.** A fumble or a miss; a blunder. **2.** *Chiefly British.* An ornamental woolly ball, as on a knitted hat. [Frequentative of BOB (verb).]

bob·by (bŏb′ē) *n., pl.* **-bies.** *British Informal.* A policeman. [After Sir Robert PEEL, who was Home Secretary of England when the Metropolitan Police Force was created (1828).]

bob·by-daz·zler (bŏb′ē-dăz′lər) *n.* *British Informal.* A striking or exceptional person or thing.

bobby pin *n.* A small metal hair clip with the ends pressed tightly together. Also *British* "hairgrip." [From BOB (lock of hair).]

bobby socks, bobby sox *pl.n.* *Informal.* Ankle socks worn by girls or women. [From the name *Bobby,* pet form for the name *Robert* (influenced by BOBBY PIN).]

bob·by-sox·er (bŏb′ē-sŏk′sər) *n.* *Informal.* A teenage girl of the 1940's who followed current fads. [From the BOBBY SOCKS worn by the teenage girls.]

bob·cat (bŏb′kăt′) *n.* A wild cat, *Lynx rufus,* of North America, having reddish-brown fur with dark markings, tufted ears, and a short tail. Also called "bay lynx." [From its bobbed tail.]

bob·o·link (bŏb′ə-lĭngk′) *n.* An American migratory songbird, *Dolichonyx oryzivorus,* of which the male has black, white, and yellowish plumage in the breeding season. Also called "redbird." [Originally *bobolincon;* imitative of its call.]

bob skate *n.* A skate having two parallel bearing edges. [BOB(SLED) + SKATE.]

bob·sled (bŏb′slĕd′) *n.* **1.** A long racing sled with a steering mechanism controlling the front runners. **2. a.** A long sled made of two shorter sleds joined in tandem. **b.** Either of these two smaller sleds. ~*intr.v.* **bobsledded, -sledding, -sleds.** To ride or race in a bobsled. [From BOB (to cut short).]

bob·stay (bŏb′stā′) *n.* *Nautical.* A rope or chain used to steady the

bobcat *A North American wild cat that grows to about 75 centimeters (30 inches) long. It lives in forests, swamps, and deserts and is sometimes found even on the outskirts of towns. The bobcat's main prey are rabbits and hares.*

bowsprit. [From BOB (up-and-down motion).]

bob·tail (bŏb'tāl') n. 1. A short or shortened tail. 2. A horse or other animal having such a tail.
~adj. 1. Having the tail short or cut short: *a bobtail nag.* 2. Cut short; abbreviated; curtailed.
~tr.v. **bobtailed, -tailing, -tails.** 1. To cut the tail of (a horse or other animal); dock. 2. To cut short; abbreviate.

bob·white (bŏb-hwīt') n. A small North American quail, *Colinus virginianus,* having brown plumage with white markings. Sometimes called "partridge." [Imitative of its call.]

bo·cac·cio (bə-kä'chō, -chē-ō') n., pl. **-cios.** A rockfish, *Sebastodes paucispinus,* of American Pacific waters. [Mexican Spanish, probably from Spanish *bocacha,* big mouth.]

bo·cage (bō'kàzh') n. The representation of woodland scenes in ceramics. [French, from Old French, BOSCAGE.]

Boc·cac·cio (bō-kä'chē-ō, -chō), **Giovanni** (1313–75). French-born Italian poet and writer. His reputation rests chiefly on *Il Decameron* (1348–53), a collection of 100 tales exposing the nature of man, set against the melancholy background of the Black Death.

Boc·cher·i·ni (bō'kə-rē'nē), **(Ridolfo) Luigi** (1743–1805). Italian cellist and composer. He made his name as a composer, especially as a developer and prolific composer of chamber music.

boc·cie or **boc·ci** or **boc·ce** (bŏch'ē) n. A game of Italian origin similar to bowling that is played with wooden balls on a long narrow dirt or clay court. [Ital. *bocce,* pl. of *boccia,* ball.]

bock beer (bŏk) n. A strong dark beer, the first that is drawn from the vats in springtime. Also called "bock." [German *Bockbier,* short for *Eimbockbier* : *Eimbock, Einbeck* (town in Lower Saxony) + *Bier,* BEER.]

bod (bŏd) n. *Slang.* Body. [Shortened from BODY.]

BOD 1. biochemical oxygen demand. 2. biological oxygen demand.

bode¹ (bŏd) tr.v. **boded, boding, bodes.** 1. To be an omen of: *His ill will bodes no good.* 2. *Obsolete.* To predict; foretell. —*intr.* To be a sign or omen: *The fine weather bodes well for the game.* —See Synonyms at **foretell.** [Middle English *boden,* Old English *bodian,* to announce, proclaim, from *boda,* messenger.]

bode². Alternate past tense of **bide.**

bo·de·ga (bō-dā'gə) n. 1. A wineshop, sometimes combined with a grocery, especially in a Spanish-speaking country. 2. A warehouse for wine storage. [Spanish, from Latin *apothēca,* from Greek *apothēkē,* storehouse, from *apotithenai,* to put away : *apo-,* away + *tithenai,* to put, place.]

Bodensee. See **Constance, Lake.**

bodge (bŏj) tr.v. **bodged, bodging, bodges.** To spoil through clumsiness; make a mess of; botch.
~n. A carelessly done piece of work. [Variant of BOTCH.]

bod·ger (bŏj'ər) adj. Also **bod·gie** (bŏj'ē). *Australian Informal.* 1. Worthless; inferior. 2. False or assumed. Said especially of names.
~n. *British.* One who makes chairs out of beech wood. [From BODGE.]

bod·gie (bŏj'ē) n. *Australian.* 1. An unruly and unconventionally dressed young man, especially in the 1950's. 2. A worthless or uncouth person.
~adj. Variant of **bodger.**
~tr.v. **bodgied, -giing, -gies.** *Australian Informal.* To patch (something) up, especially temporarily. Used with *up.*

Bodh Gaya. See **Buddh Gaya.**

bo·dhi·satt·va (bō'dĭ-sŭt'və) n. *Buddhism.* One who, out of compassion, forgoes nirvana in order to save others. [Sanskrit, "one whose essence is enlightenment" : *bodhi,* enlightenment, from *bodhati,* he awakes + *sattva,* essence, from *sat, sant,* existing.]

bod·ice (bŏd'ĭs) n. 1. The fitted part of a dress that extends from the waist to the shoulder. 2. A woman's laced outer garment, worn like a vest over a blouse. 3. *Obsolete.* A corset. [Originally *bodies,* plural of BODY (originally referring to the two sides of a whalebone corset).]

bod·ied (bŏd'ēd) adj. 1. Having a body. 2. Having a specified kind of body: *strong-bodied; full-bodied wine.*

bod·i·less (bŏd'ē-lĭs, bŏd'ə-) adj. Having no body, form, or substance; incorporeal. —**bod·i·less·ness** n.

bod·i·ly (bŏd'ə-lē) adj. 1. Of, pertaining to, within, or exhibited by the body. 2. Physical as opposed to mental or spiritual.
~adv. 1. In the flesh; in person: *He was bodily but not mentally present.* 2. As a complete physical entity: *He carried her bodily from the room.*

bod·ing (bō'dĭng) n. An omen or foreboding, especially of evil.

bod·kin (bŏd'kĭn) n. 1. A small, sharply pointed instrument for making holes in fabric or leather. 2. A blunt needle for pulling tape or ribbon through a series of loops or a hem. 3. A long hairpin, usually with an ornamental head. 4. *Printing.* A pointed tool for extracting letters from set type when correcting. [Middle English *boidekyn†.*]

Bod·lei·an (bŏd'lē-ən, bŏd-lē'ən) n. The library of Oxford University. It is one of the five libraries that automatically receive a free copy of every book published in the United Kingdom, in accordance with the copyright laws. [After Sir Thomas *Bodley* (1545–1613), English diplomat who refounded it (1603).]

Bo·do·ni (bə-dō'nē) n. *Printing.* A style of typeface. [Designed by Giambattista *Bodoni* (1740–1813), Italian printer.]

bod·y (bŏd'ē) n., pl. **-ies. 1. a.** The entire material structure and substance of an organism, especially of a human being or an animal. **b.** A corpse or carcass. **2. a.** The trunk or torso of a human being or animal. **b.** The part of a garment covering the torso. **3.** *Informal.* A person. **4. a.** *Law.* A group of individuals regarded as an entity; a corporation. **b.** A number of persons, concepts, or things regarded collectively; a group: *We walked out in a body; a legislative body.* **5.** The main or central part of something, as: **a.** The nave of a church or the auditorium of a theater. **b.** The central content of a book or document as opposed to the prefatory matter, codicils, indexes, and the like. **c.** The passenger- and cargo-carrying part of an aircraft, ship, or vehicle. **d.** The sound box of a musical instrument. **e.** The majority: *The body of party opinion favored the reform.* **6. a.** Any bounded mass of matter: *a body of water.* **b.** Any perceptible three-dimensional piece of matter: *a foreign body in one's ear; heavenly bodies.* **7.** Consistency of substance, as in paint, textiles, wine, and the like: *a sauce with body.* **8.** *Printing.* The part of a block of type underlying the impression surface.
~tr.v. **bodied, -ying, -ies.** To give form or shape to. Usually followed by *forth:* "*Imagination bodies forth the form of things unknown*" (Shakespeare). [Middle English *body,* Old English *bodig,* from Germanic *bot-* (unattested), container.]

body blow n. 1. In boxing, a blow delivered to the front of the body above the waist. 2. A serious setback; a major disappointment.

body building n. The strengthening of the body by means of physical exercises, especially in a way that makes the muscles prominent. —**body builder** n.

body cavity n. The internal cavity of all multicellular animals except sponges, which contains the heart, digestive tract, and many other organs.

body-centered (bŏd'ē-sĕn'tərd) adj. Having a lattice point at the center of the body as well as at the corners. Said of a crystal. Compare **face-centered.**

body corporate n. *Law.* A corporation (see).

body count n. The total number of persons killed in a battle or war.

bod·y·guard (bŏd'ē-gärd') n. 1. A person or group of persons, usually armed, responsible for the physical safety of one or more specific persons. 2. An escort or retinue.

body image n. A person's concept of the identity, shape, and relative positions of the different parts of his body.

body language n. Unspoken communication through conscious and unconscious gestures and positioning of the body.

body louse n. A parasitic louse, *Pediculus humanus,* afflicting humans.

body paint n. Paint that is applied directly to the body for decoration.

body politic n. The people collectively of a politically organized nation or state.

body pop·ping n. A type of dancing characterized by convulsive body movements and mimed robotic gestures, popular in the 1980's. It is often combined with **breakdancing** (see). [20th century : origin obscure.]

bod·y·shoot (bŏd'ē-shōōt') tr.v. **-shot, -shooting, -shoots.** *Australian.* To surf (a wave) without a board.

body shop n. A shop or garage where the bodies of automotive vehicles are repaired.

body snatcher n. In former times, a person who stole corpses from graves for dissection.

body stocking n. A tight one-piece undergarment for the torso, sometimes also with sleeves and legs.

body suit n. A tight-fitting one-piece garment for the torso.

body surfing n. A form of surfing without a board in which one swims with a wave and allows it to carry one toward the shore. —**bod·y·surf** v.

body wall n. The part of an animal's body that encloses the body cavity, made up of ectoderm and mesoderm.

body work n. The act or process of repairing the bodies of automotive vehicles.

bod·y·work (bŏd'ē-wûrk') n. The usually metal external structure of a motor vehicle.

Boehme, Jakob. See **Böhme.**

boehm·ite (bā'mīt', bō'-) n. A natural, white, hydrated aluminum hydroxide, AlO(OH), that occurs as orthorhombic crystals in some bauxites. [German *Böhmit,* after J. *Böhm,* 20th-century German scientist.]

Boe·o·tia (bē-ō'shə). Region of ancient Greece, lying north of Attica and the Gulf of Corinth. In the 7th century B.C. the cities of the region formed the Boeotian League, although they never succeeded in escaping from the dominance of Thebes.

Boe·o·tian (bē-ō'shən) adj. 1. Of or pertaining to Boeotia or its inhabitants. 2. Stupid; boorish.
~n. 1. An inhabitant of Boeotia. 2. A stupid, boorish person.

Boer (bōr, bôr, bōōr) n. A Dutch colonist or a descendant of a Dutch colonist in South Africa. [Dutch, "peasant," "farmer," from Middle Dutch *gheboer.*] —**Boer** adj.

Boer War n. A war (1899–1902) in which Great Britain defeated the Boers of the Orange Free State and the Transvaal Republic in South Africa. Also called "Anglo-Boer War."

Bo·e·thi·us (bō-ē'thē-əs), **Anicius Manlius Severinus** (c. 480–c. 524). Roman philosopher. His famous work, *De Consolatione Philosophiae (On the Consolation of Philosophy),* written in prison in the weeks before his execution without trial by Theodoric the Ostrogoth, became one of the most influential accounts of classical thought.

boeuf bourguignon n. *French.* **Beef bourguignon** (see).

bof·fin (bŏf'ən) n. *British Informal.* A scientist or technical expert, originally one carrying out work for the Royal Air Force. [20th century : origin obscure.]

bof·fo (bŏf'ō) *adj.* Extremely successful; excellent; great. [Short for slang *boffola,* hit, success.]

Bo·fors gun (bō'fôrz') *n.* A double-barreled, automatic antiaircraft gun. [First made at the munitions works in *Bofors,* Sweden.]

bog (bŏg, bôg) *n.* **1.** Permanently water-logged ground, with a surface layer of decaying vegetation, particularly *Sphagnum* mosses, which forms highly acid peat. **2.** An area of such ground; a marsh; a swamp.
~*v.* **bogged, bogging, bogs.** —*tr.* To hinder; slow; impede. Usually used with *down.* —*intr.* To be hindered and slowed. Usually used with *down: bogged down in work.* [Scottish and Irish Gaelic *bogach,* from *bog,* soft.] —**bog·gish** *adj.* —**bog·gish·ness** *n.*

Bo·garde (bō'gärd'), **Dirk,** born Derek Niven van den Bogaerde (1921–). British actor and writer. Among his most famous films are *The Servant* (1963) and *Death in Venice* (1971).

Bo·gart (bō'gärt'), **Humphrey DeForest** (1899–1957). U.S. actor. In the 1930's, 1940's, and 1950's he appeared in numerous roles as a reticent, tough hero with a soft heart, in films such as *Casablanca* (1942), *The African Queen* (1951), and, with the actress Lauren Bacall (whom he married in 1945), *To Have and Have Not* (1944) and *The Big Sleep* (1946).

bog asphodel *n.* Either of two related bog plants, *Narthecium ossifragum,* of Europe, or *N. americanum,* of the southeastern United States, having a spike of yellow flowers and irislike leaves.

bog·bean (bŏg'bĕn', bôg'-) *n.* An aquatic or creeping plant, *Menyanthes trifoliata,* with pink or white flowers in spikes, and three-lobed leaves held conspicuously above the surface. Also called "buckbean."

bo·gey (bō'gē) *n., pl.* **-geys. 1.** In golf: **a.** An estimated standard score. **b.** One stroke over par on a hole. **2.** *Military Slang.* Any unidentified flying aircraft. **3.** *Slang.* A bit of mucus from the nose. **4.** Variant of **bogy.**

bo·gey·man (boog'ē-măn', bō'gē-, boo'gē-) *n.* Variant of **boogieman.**

bog·gle (bŏg'əl) *v.* **-gled, -gling, -gles.** —*intr.* **1.** To hesitate or evade as if in fear or doubt. Usually used with *at.* **2.** To shy away with fright or astonishment; be overcome. **3.** To botch; bungle. —*tr.* To cause to be overcome, as with fright or astonishment. ~*n.* The act of boggling. [Probably from *boggle,* Northern dialectal variant of BOGLE.] —**bog·gler** *n.*

bog·gy (bŏg'ē, bôg'ē) *adj.* **-gier, -giest. 1.** Like a bog; swampy. **2.** Full of bogs. —**bog·gi·ness** *n.*

bog hole *n.* A hole containing soft mud or quicksand.

bo·gie¹, bo·gy (bō'gē) *n., pl.* **bogies. 1.** A railway coach or locomotive undercarriage with two, four, or six wheels that swivel so that curves may be negotiated. Also called "bogie truck." **2.** One of several wheels or supporting and aligning rollers inside the tread of a tractor or tank. In this sense, also called "bogie wheel." **3.** A small railway truck used for transporting coal, ores, or the like. [19th century : Northern England dialect, origin obscure.]

bogie². Variant of **bogy** (hobgoblin).

bo·gle (bō'gəl) *n.* A hobgoblin, a **bogy** (see). [Scottish *bogill;* akin to Welsh *bwg,* ghost, *bwgwl,* menace, akin to Cornish *buccaboo,* the devil, BUGABOO.]

bog moss *n.* Peat moss *(see).*

bog myrtle *n.* The **sweet myrtle** *(see).*

Bog·nor Re·gis (bŏg'nər rē'jĭs). Resort town on the coast of West Sussex, in southern England. It gained the title "Regis" after George V convalesced here in 1929.

bo·gong (bō'gŏng) *n.* An edible nocturnal Australian moth. [From a native Australian language.]

bog orchid *n.* An orchid, *Malaxis* (or *Hammarkya*) *paludosa,* growing in bogs, with yellow-green flowers and oval leaves that usually have small bulbils on their edges.

Bo·go·tá (bō'gə-tä'). Former name of Santa Fe de Bogotá, largest city and capital of Colombia, on a high plateau in the Andes Mts., where several rivers meet to form the Bogotá River.

bog rosemary *n.* A low-growing evergreen shrub, *Andromeda polifolia,* growing in wet ground, and having small pink bell-like flowers. Also called "marsh andromeda," "moorwort."

bog rush *n.* A densely tufted plant, *Schoenus nigricans,* with narrow, wiry leaves and stems carrying black, pointed spikes.

bog·trot·ter (bŏg'trŏt'ər, bôg'-) *n. Slang.* An Irishman. Used derogatorily.

bo·gus (bō'gəs) *adj.* Counterfeit; fake. [19th century (U.S.) : perhaps of African origin; perhaps from Hausa *boko,* deceit, fraud.]

bog·wood (bŏg'wŏod', bôg'-) *n.* Wood that has been preserved in a peat bog. Also called "bog oak."

bo·gy¹, bo·gie, bo·gey (bō'gē) *n., pl.* **-gies. 1.** An evil or mischievous spirit; a hobgoblin. Also called "bogle." **2.** Something that causes annoyance or harassment. [Originally used as proper name; compare BOGLE, BUGBEAR.] —**bo·gy·ism** *n.*

bogy². Variant of **bogie** (railroad car undercarriage).

bogyman. Variant of **boogieman.**

Bo Hai or **Po Hai** (bō'hī'). Formerly **Gulf of Chih·li** (jē'lē'). Inlet of the Yellow Sea between Shandong and Liaoning provinces in northeast China, with important oil and natural-gas resources.

bo·hea (bō-hē') *n.* A black Chinese tea. The name originally referred to the choicest grade but later was applied to an inferior variety. [Chinese (Fujian dialect) *bu-i,* corresponding to Mandarin *wǔ-yí,* after *Wu-yi Shan,* a range of hills in northern Fujian Province, where the black tea is grown.]

bo·he·mi·a, Bo·he·mi·a (bō-hē'mē-ə) *n.* **1.** A community of persons with artistic or literary tastes whose manners and moral standards are unconventional. **2.** The district in which bohemians live.

Bo·he·mi·a (bō-hē'mē-ə). *Czech* **Če·chy** (chĕкн'ē). A historic region of present-day western Czechoslovakia and a former kingdom. The Czechs, a west Slav people, settled in the area between the 1st and 5th centuries A.D. They maintained the independence of Bohemia until the 15th century, when the crown passed to Hungary and then to the Habsburgs. Nationalist efforts by the Czechs in the 19th century failed to re-establish an independent Bohemia, and it became a province of the new republic of Czechoslovakia (1918), losing its provincial status in an administrative reorganization (1948).

Bo·he·mi·an (bō-hē'mē-ən) *n.* **1.** A native or inhabitant of Bohemia. **2.** A Gypsy. **3.** *Archaic.* The language of the Czechs. **4. bohemian.** A person with artistic or literary interests who disregards conventional standards of behavior. —**Bo·he·mi·an** *adj.* —**Bo·he·mi·an·ism** *n.*

Bohemian Brethren *pl.n.* A Protestant religious society organized in the 15th century by the Hussites.

Böhm (bōm), **Karl** (1894–1981). Austrian conductor. He was conductor of the Vienna State Opera (1943–45 and 1954–56) and throughout his career was closely associated with the Vienna Philharmonic.

Böh·me or **Boeh·me** (bē'mə), **Jakob** (1575–1624). German theosophist and mystic. His several books describe evil as a necessary antithesis to good.

Bohr (bōr), **Niels Henrik David** (1885–1962). Danish physicist. His pioneering theoretical work used quantum theory to explain and develop the nuclear model of the atom put forward by Ernest Rutherford. He was awarded the Nobel Prize in physics (1922). His son **Aage Niels Bohr** (1922–) also won a Nobel Prize for physics (1975).

Bohr-Som·mer·feld theory (bōr'zŏm'ər-fĕlt') *n.* A modification of the Bohr theory, allowing for elliptical as well as circular orbits. [After Arnold *Sommerfeld* (1868–1951), German physicist who produced the modification.]

Bohr theory *n.* A model of atomic structure, in which electrons travel around the nucleus in certain orbits representing specific energy states determined by quantum theory, a jump from one orbit to another being accompanied by the emission or absorption of a quantum of energy. The model explains the spectrum of the hydrogen atom. [After Niels BOHR.]

boil¹ (boil) *v.* **boiled, boiling, boils.** —*intr.* **1.** To vaporize a liquid by the application of heat. **2.** To reach the **boiling point** *(see).* **3.** To undergo the action of boiling; especially, to cook by boiling. **4.** To be in a state of agitation, as boiling water; seethe. **5.** To be greatly excited, as with rage or passion. —*tr.* **1.** To heat to the boiling point. **2.** To cook or clean by boiling. **3.** To separate by evaporation as a result of boiling. —**boil away.** To evaporate by boiling. —**boil down. 1.** To reduce in bulk or size by boiling. **2.** To condense or summarize. —**boil down to.** To be in essence; amount to. —**boil over. 1.** To overflow while boiling. **2.** To explode in rage or passion. —**boil up.** *Australian & New Zealand.* To make tea. ~*n.* The state, condition, or act of boiling. [Middle English *boillen,* from Old French *bo(u)illir,* from Latin *bullīre,* to bubble, boil.]

boil² *n.* A painful swelling of the skin and subcutaneous tissue with a hard pus-filled center, caused by bacterial infection, usually occurring at a hair follicle. Also called "furuncle." Compare **carbuncle.** [Middle English *bile, bule, boyl,* Old English *bȳl, bȳle.*]

Boi·leau-Des·pré·aux (bwä-lō'dā-prā-ō'), **Nicolas** (1636–1711). French poet and critic. His most celebrated work, *The Art of Poetry* (1674), a treatise in verse, was a comprehensive summation of classical rules and conventions in French literature.

boil·er (boi'lər) *n.* **1.** An enclosed vessel in which water is heated and circulated, either as hot water or as steam, for heating or power. **2.** A container for boiling liquids, such as a double boiler. **3.** A storage tank for hot water. **4.** A hen, usually old and tough, to be cooked by boiling. Also called "boiling fowl." **5.** *Australian Informal.* A nagging old woman; an old bag.

boil·er·mak·er (boi'lər-mā'kər) *n.* **1.** One who makes or repairs boilers. **2.** *Slang.* A drink of whiskey with beer as a chaser.

boil·er·plate (boi'lər-plāt') *n.* **1.** A steel plate used in making the shells of steam boilers. **2.** Journalistic material, such as syndicated material, available in plate or mat form.

boil·er·room (boi'lər-room', -room') *adj. Informal.* Of, relating to, or involving usually illegal, high-pressure telephone sales tactics, as used in selling stock, commodities, or land.

boiler suit *n. British.* Coveralls or overalls.

boil·ing (boi'lĭng) *adj. Informal.* Very hot.
~*adv.* Used as an intensive: *boiling hot.*

boiling point *n.* **1.** *Abbr.* **bp, b.p.** The temperature at which a liquid boils, especially under standard atmospheric conditions. **2.** *Informal.* The point at which a person loses his temper.

boil·ing-wa·ter reactor (boi'lĭng-wô'tər) *n. Abbr.* **BWR** A type of nuclear reactor in which boiling water is used as both moderator and coolant.

boil off *tr.v.* To remove (impurities) from a liquid mixture by boiling. —*intr.v.* To be removed by boiling. Used of impurities, fractions, and the like in liquid mixtures.

boil·off (boil'ôf', -ŏf') *n.* The vaporization of a liquid, such as a rocket fuel.

Bois de Bou·logne (bwä'də boo-lōn'). A large park in west Paris, situated between the suburbs of Neuilly and Boulogne-Billancourt. It includes within its boundaries the two famous racecourses of Auteuil and Longchamps.

bois de rose (bwä′də rōz′) *n.* Dusty deep pink. [French, "rosewood."]

Boi·se (boi′zē, -sē). Capital and largest city of Idaho in the southwestern part of the state on the Boise River. It is an important trade, transportation, and food-processing center for a largely agricultural region.

bois·ter·ous (boi′stər-əs, -strəs) *adj.* **1.** Rough and stormy; violent and turbulent. **2.** Loud, noisy, and unrestrained. [Middle English *boistres,* variant of *boist(e)ous†,* rude, fierce, stout.] **—bois·ter·ous·ly** *adv.* **—bois·ter·ous·ness** *n.*

bok choy (bŏk choi′) *n.* Variant of **pak choi.**

Bokhara. See **Bukhara.**

Bok·mål (bŏŏk′môl′, bŏk′-) *n.* One of the two officially recognized and mutually intelligible forms of Norwegian. It is the language in which newspapers and most literature are written. Also called "Dano-Norwegian," formerly "Riksmål." Compare **Nynorsk.** [Norwegian, "book language."]

bo·la (bō′lə) *n.* Also **bo·las** (-ləs). A rope with weights attached, used in South America to catch cattle or game by entangling the legs. [American Spanish *bolas,* plural of Spanish *bola,* ball, from Latin *bulla,* bubble, round object.]

bola tie. Variant of **bolo tie.**

bold (bōld) *adj.* **bold·er, bold·est. 1.** Fearless and daring; courageous. **2.** Requiring or exhibiting courage and bravery. **3.** Unduly forward and brazen in manner. **4.** Clear and distinct to the eye; standing out prominently: *bold handwriting.* **5.** Steep, as a cliff. **6.** *Printing.* Designating thick, heavy type; boldface. —See Synonyms at **brave, shameless. —make bold.** To take the liberty; dare. [Middle English *bold,* Old English *bald, beald.*] **—bold·ly** *adv.* **—bold·ness** *n.*

boldface (bōld′fās′) *n. Abbr.* **bf, bf., b.f., bld.** *Printing.* Type that has thick, heavy lines so as to give a conspicuous black impression. Compare **lightface.**

~*adj. Abbr.* **bf, bf., b.f., bld.** Printed in boldface.

~*tr.v.* **boldfaced, -facing, -faces. 1.** To mark (copy) for printing in boldface. **2.** To print or set in boldface.

bold-faced (bōld′fāst′) *adj.* **1.** Impudent; brazen. **2. a.** Printed or set in boldface. **b.** Marked for printing in boldface.

bole[1] (bōl) *n.* The trunk of a tree. [Middle English, from Old Norse *bolr.*]

bole[2] *n.* **1.** Any of various fine soft clays; especially, a reddish-brown variety used as a pigment. **2.** Moderate reddish brown. [Middle English, a red clay, from Medieval Latin *bōlus,* clod of earth, BOLUS.] **—bole** *adj.*

bo·lec·tion (bō-lĕk′shən) *n. Architecture.* A molding that projects from the surface of a panel. [18th century : origin obscure.]

bo·le·ro (bō-lâr′ō) *n., pl.* **-ros. 1.** A short jacket, usually with no front fastening, worn by both men and women. **2.** A Spanish dance in triple time. **3.** The music for this dance. [Spanish, apparently from *bola,* ball. See **bola.**]

bo·le·tus (bō-lē′təs) *n., pl.* **-tuses** or **-ti** (-tī′). Also **bo·lete** (bō′lēt). Any fungus of the genus *Boletus,* having an umbrella-shaped cap with spore-bearing tubules on the underside. Some species are poisonous and others edible. [New Latin *Boletus,* from Latin *bōlētus†,* fungus.]

Bo·leyn (bŏŏl′ĭn, bō-lĭn′), **Anne** (c. 1507-36). Second wife of Henry VIII and mother of Elizabeth I. In order to marry her, Henry VIII divorced his first wife, Catherine of Aragon, thus breaking with the Roman Catholic Church and providing the occasion for the official Reformation in England. Henry and Anne were secretly married (January 1533). She produced no male heir and was convicted of adultery and beheaded (1536).

bo·lide (bō′līd) *n.* A meteoric fireball. [French, from Greek *bolis†,* missile.]

bol·i·var (bŏl′ə-vər; bō-lē′vär) *n., pl.* **-vars** or **bolivares** (bō-lē-vä′rĕs). *Abbr.* **b., B. 1.** The basic monetary unit of Venezuela, equal to 100 centimos. **2.** A coin worth one bolivar. See feature at **currency.** [After Simón BOLÍVAR.]

Bo·lí·var (bō-lē′vär), **Simón** (1783-1830). Venezuelan revolutionary hero, known as "the Liberator." He defeated the Spanish forces at Boyacá (1819) and was made president of Greater Colombia (now Colombia, Venezuela, and Ecuador). He helped liberate (1823-34) Peru and present-day Bolivia (named after him) and became the most powerful man on the continent.

Bo·liv·i·a (bə-lĭv′ē-ə). A landlocked republic in west-central South America. The country was named after Simón Bolívar, who helped win its independence from Spain (1825). The western half of the country is dominated by the Andes Mts. and includes the populated plateau of the altiplano, 3,900 meters (13,000 feet) high, containing Lake Titicaca; the east is a lowland region of forests and plains. Most of the poulation is concentrated in the southern Andes plateau. Area, 1,098,581 square kilometers (424,165 square miles). Population, 7,300,000. Judicial capital, Sucre; administrative capital, La Paz. **—Bo·liv·i·an** *adj. & n.*

boll (bōl) *n.* The rounded seed pod of certain plants, such as flax or cotton. [Middle English *bolle,* from Middle Dutch.]

Böll (bœl), **Heinrich** (1917-85). German writer. His short stories include the collection *Traveller, If You Come to Spa* (1950); his novels include *Tomorrow and Yesterday* (1957), *The Clown* (1963), and *The Lost Honor of Katharina Blum* (1975). He was awarded the Nobel Prize for literature in 1972.

bol·lard (bŏl′ərd) *n.* **1.** A thick post on a ship or wharf, used for securing ropes and hawsers. **2.** *British.* **a.** A small marker post on a traffic island. **b.** A post placed on a pavement, path, or street to prevent traffic from driving or parking there. [Middle English : probably BOLE (tree trunk) + -ARD.]

bol·lix (bŏl′ĭks) *tr.v.* **-lixed, -lixing, -lixes.** Also **bol·lox** (-əks), **-loxed, -loxing, -loxes.** *Slang.* To throw into confusion; botch or bungle. Usually used with *up.* [From earlier *bollocks, ballocks,* testicles, Middle English *ballocks,* Old English *beallucas.*]

boll weevil *n.* A small, grayish, long-snouted beetle, *Anthonomus grandis,* of Mexico and the southern United States, having destructive larvae that hatch in and damage cotton bolls.

boll·worm (bōl′wûrm′) *n.* **1.** The larval stage of various moths, such as *Pectinophora gossypiella,* that feeds on and destroys cotton bolls. **2.** The **corn earworm** *(see).*

bo·log·na (bə-lō′nə, -nē, -nyə) *n.* Also *informal* **ba·lo·ney** (-nē), **bo·lo·ney.** A seasoned smoked sausage made of mixed meats. [After BOLOGNA, where it was originally made.]

Bo·lo·gna (bə-lō′nyə). An industrial town in the Emilia-Romagna region of north-central Italy. It has one of the world's oldest universities, founded as a law school (A.D. 425) and established as a university in the 11th century.

bo·lom·e·ter (bō-lŏm′ə-tər) *n.* An instrument that measures radiant heat by detecting the change in electrical resistance produced in prepared metal foil strips by the heating effect of the incident radiation. [Greek *bolē,* beam, ray + -METER.] **—bo·lo·met·ric** (bō′-lō-mĕt′rĭk) *adj.*

bolo tie, bola tie *n.* A necktie consisting of a piece of cord with an ornamental bar or clasp. [Alteration of BOLA + TIE.]

Bol·she·vik (bōl′shə-vĭk′, bŏl′-) *n., pl.* **-viks** or **-viki** (-vē′kē). **1. a.** A member of the Communist Party of the Soviet Union. **b.** A member of the left-wing majority group of the Russian Social Democratic Party adopting Lenin's theses on party organization (1903). Compare **Menshevik. 2.** *Often* **bolshevik.** Any extreme radical: *a literary bolshevik.* [Russian *Bol'shevik,* "one of the majority" : *bol'shii,* greater, from *bol'shoi,* large + noun suffix *-vik.*] **—Bol·she·vik** *adj.*

Bol·she·vism (bōl′shə-vĭz′əm, bŏl′-) *n.* Also **bolshevism. 1.** The strategy developed by the Bolsheviks between 1903 and 1917 with a view to seizing state power and establishing the dictatorship of the proletariat. **2.** Soviet Communism.

Bol·she·vist (bōl′shə-vĭst, bŏl′-) *n.* Also **bolshevist.** A Bolshevik. **—Bol·she·vist, Bol·she·vis·tic** *adj.*

bol·son (bōl′sən) *n. Southwestern U.S.* A flat arid valley surrounded by mountains and draining into a shallow central lake. [Spanish, "big pouch," augmentative of *bolsa-,* purse, from Late Latin *bursa.*]

bol·ster (bōl′stər) *n.* **1.** A long, narrow pillow or cushion, typically hard and stiff. **2.** A structural support, such as a horizontal bar across the top of a post or column.

~*tr.v.* **bolstered, -stering, -sters. 1.** To support or prop up, as with a pillow. **2.** To support or strengthen: *bolster one's confidence.* **3.** To apply padding to. [Middle English *bolster,* Old English *bolster,* cushion.] **—bol·ster·er** *n.*

bolt[1] (bōlt) *n.* **1.** A bar made of wood or metal that slides into a socket and is used to fasten doors and gates. **2.** A metal bar or rod in the mechanism of a lock, thrown or withdrawn by turning the key. **3.** A fastener consisting of an externally threaded cylindrical piece, formed from a pin, rod, or wire and having a head at one end. It is designed to be inserted through holes in assembled parts and secured by a mating nut that is tightened by application of torque.

boll *The boll of the cotton plant, shown here, produces the white strands that are spun into yarn.*

4. a. A sliding metal bar that positions the cartridge in breech-loading rifles, closes the breech, and ejects the spent cartridge. **b.** A similar device in any breech mechanism. **5.** A short, heavy arrow with a thick head, used especially with a crossbow. **6.** A flash of lightning or a thunderbolt. **7.** A sudden movement toward or away from something. **8.** A large roll of cloth of a definite length, especially as it comes from the loom. —**bolt from the blue.** A sudden, usually shocking, surprise. —**shoot one's bolt.** To do all that one can; exhaust one's resources.
~*v.* **bolted, bolting, bolts.** —*tr.* **1.** To secure or lock with or as if with a bolt or bolts. **2.** To arrange or roll (lengths of cloth, for example) on a bolt. **3.** To eat hurriedly and with little chewing; gulp. **4.** *Archaic.* To shoot or discharge (an arrow or other missile). **5.** To desert or withdraw support from (a political party). **6.** To utter impulsively; blurt out. —*intr.* **1.** To move or spring suddenly toward or from something. **2.** To break from the rider's control and run away. Used of a horse. **3.** To make off suddenly; run away. **4.** To break away from a political party or its policies. **5.** *Horticulture.* To flower or produce seeds prematurely.
~*adv.* Rigidly straight. Used in the phrase *bolt upright.* [Middle English *bolt,* Old English *bolt,* heavy arrow.]
bolt² *tr.v.* **bolted, bolting, bolts.** To pass through a sieve; sift. [Middle English *bulten, bolten,* from Old French *buleter,* from Middle Dutch *biutelen.*]
Bolt (bōlt), **Robert Oxton** (1924–). British playwright. His most popular successes have been *A Man for All Seasons* (1960) and *Vivat! Vivat Regina!* (1970). He has also written numerous screenplays and won Academy Awards for *Dr. Zhivago* (1965) and *A Man for All Seasons* (1966).
bolt·er¹ (bōl'tər) *n.* **1.** A horse given to bolting. **2.** One who gives up membership in or withdraws support from his political party.
bolt·er² *n.* **1.** A machine for bolting flour. **2.** One who operates a bolter.
Bol·ton (bōl'tən). Industrial town in the metropolitan county of Greater Manchester, in northwest England. It was the center of the woolen trade from the 14th to the 18th century, when its economy shifted to cotton spinning.
bol·to·ni·a (bŏl-tō'nē-ə) *n.* Any of several North American plants of the genus *Boltonia,* having daisylike flowers with white, violet, or pinkish rays. [New Latin, after James *Bolton,* 18th-century botanist.]
bolt·rope (bōlt'rōp') *n.* A rope sewn into the outer edge of a sail to prevent the sail from tearing.
Boltz·mann (bōlts'män), **Ludwig** (1844–1906). Austrian physicist, one of the founders of modern physics, whose chief contribution was the kinetic theory of gases. He developed the Stefan-Boltzmann law.
Boltzmann constant *n.* *Physics.* Symbol **k** The ratio of the universal gas constant to the Avogadro constant. It has the value $1.380\,622 \times 10^{-23}$ joule per kelvin. [After Ludwig BOLTZMANN.]
bo·lus (bō'ləs) *n., pl.* **-luses. 1.** A small round mass, particularly of chewed food. **2.** *Pharmacology.* A large pill or tablet. [Medieval Latin *bōlus,* from Greek *bōlos†,* lump, clod.]
bo·ma (bōm'ə, bō'mə) *n.* In Central and East Africa: **1.** A protective enclosure for domestic animals; a camp; a stockade. **2.** A military or police post. **3.** A magistrate's office. [Swahili.]
Bo·ma (bō'mə). A port and railway terminus on the Zaire River in southwest Zaire. It was an important slave market up to the 19th century and was the capital of the Congo Free State (the Belgian Congo after 1908) from 1886 to 1926.
bomb (bŏm) *n.* **1.** An explosive weapon detonated by impact, proximity to an object, a timing mechanism, or other predetermined means. **2.** Any of various weapons detonated to release smoke, gas, pellets, poisons, or other destructive materials. **3.** *Football.* A very long forward pass designed to achieve great yardage in a single play. **4.** A container for a radioactive substance used in radiotherapy: *a cobalt bomb.* **5. a.** A vessel for storing compressed gas. **b.** A portable, manually operated container that ejects a spray, foam, or gas under pressure. **6.** A spherical mass of molten rock ejected into the air during a volcanic eruption. **7.** *Chiefly British Slang.* A lot of money: *It cost a bomb.* **8.** *Chiefly British Slang.* An old car. **9.** *Slang.* A dismal failure or complete fiasco. —**the bomb.** Often **Bomb. 1.** The atom or hydrogen bomb. **2.** Nuclear weapons collectively.
~*v.* **bombed, bombing, bombs.** —*tr.* To attack, damage, or destroy with a bomb or bombs. —*intr.* **1.** To drop a bomb or bombs. **2.** *Slang.* To go, especially to drive, quickly. Often used with *along.* **3.** *Slang.* To fail miserably. Usually used with *out.* [French *bombe,* from Italian *bomba,* probably from Latin *bombus,* booming, humming, from Greek *bombos.*]
bom·bard (bŏm'bärd') *n.* An early form of cannon that fired stone balls.
~*tr.v.* (bŏm-bärd') **bombarded, -barding, -bards. 1.** To attack with bombs, explosive shells, or missiles. **2.** To attack persistently with arguments, criticism, or the like. **3.** *Physics.* To subject (an atom, nucleus, or the like) to a stream of high energy particles. **4.** *Archaic.* To attack with a bombard. —*See* Synonyms at **attack.** [Middle English *bombarde,* cannon, from Old French, from Medieval Latin *bombarda,* probably from Latin *bombus,* booming. See **bomb.**] —**bom·bard·er** *n.* —**bom·bard·ment** *n.*
bom·bar·dier (bŏm'bər-dîr') *n.* **1.** *Military.* The member of an aircraft crew who operates the bombing equipment. **2.** *British.* A corporal in the artillery. **3.** Formerly, a soldier who operated a

bombard. [French, from Old French *bombarde,* BOMBARD.]
bombardier beetle *n.* Any of various beetles of the genus *Brachinus* and related genera, that expel an acrid secretion from the posterior end of the abdomen.
bom·bar·don (bŏm-bärd'n, bŏm'bər-dən) *n.* **1.** A brass musical instrument resembling a tuba but with a lower pitch; a bass or contrabass tuba. **2.** A 16-foot reed stop on the organ. [French, from Italian *bombardone,* augmentative of *bombardo,* from *bombarda,* bombard, from Medieval Latin. See **bombard.**]
bom·bast (bŏm'băst) *n.* **1.** Grandiloquent and pompous speech or writing. **2.** Formerly, a soft material used for padding. [Earlier *bombace,* cotton padding, from Old French, from Late Latin *bombax,* cotton, silk, alteration of Latin *bombyx,* silkworm, silk, from Greek *bombux,* of Oriental origin, akin to Turkish *pambuk,* cotton.] —**bom·bast·er** *n.*
bom·bas·tic (bŏm-băs'tĭk) *adj.* Characterized by bombast; pompous; grandiloquent. —**bom·bas·ti·cal·ly** *adv.*
bom·bax (bŏm'băks) *n.* Any of various trees of the genus *Bombax,* especially the cotton tree. [New Latin, from Late Latin. See **bombast.**]
bombax cotton *n.* The silky, cottonlike fiber produced by various trees of the genus *Bombax.*
Bom·bay (bŏm-bā'). An industrial city and port on the northwest coast of India, built on the islands of Bombay and Salsette and connected to the mainland by a causeway. It is the capital of Maharashtra state and India's main seaport and commercial center.
Bombay duck *n.* **1.** A food fish, *Harpodon nehereus,* of India. **2.** The dried flesh of this fish or a dish prepared from it.
bom·ba·zine (bŏm'bə-zēn') *n.* A fine twilled fabric of silk and worsted or cotton, often dyed black and used for mourning clothes. [French *bombasin,* from Late Latin *bombacinum,* variant of *bombȳcīnum,* from Latin, neuter of *bombȳcīnus,* silken, from *bombyx,* silk. See **bombast.**]
bomb bay *n.* The compartment in the fuselage of a military aircraft from which bombs are dropped.
bomb calorimeter *n.* A device used to measure the calorific value of fuels, foods, and the like by burning them in oxygen at high pressure and noting the rise in temperature of the calorimeter and its contents.
bombe (bŏm; *French* bôNb) *n.* A dessert consisting of two or more layers of ice cream of different flavors or textures frozen in a round or melon-shaped mold. [French, "bomb" (from its shape).]
bombed (bŏmd) *adj. Slang.* Drunk or under the influence of drugs.
bomb·er (bŏm'ər) *n.* **1.** A military aircraft designed to carry and drop bombs. **2.** One who plants or drops bombs.
bom·bo·ra, bom·boo·ra (bŏm-bô'rə) *n. Australian.* A dangerous stretch of water above a submerged reef. [From a native Australian language.]
bomb·proof (bŏm'prōōf') *adj.* Designed and constructed to resist destruction by bombs.
bomb rack *n.* A framework or mechanical holder for bombs on a military aircraft.
bomb·shell (bŏm'shĕl') *n.* **1.** A bomb. **2.** A shocking surprise.
bomb shelter *n.* A shelter, often below ground, built to withstand attacks by bombs.
bomb·sight (bŏm'sīt') *n.* A device in aircraft for aiming bombs.
bomb·site (bŏm'sīt') *n.* Also **bomb site.** A derelict area, often an open space, where the buildings have been destroyed by bombing.
bom·by·cid (bŏm'bĭ-sĭd) *n.* A moth of the family Bombycidae, which includes the silkworm. [New Latin *Bombycidae,* from Latin *bombyx,* silkworm. See **bombast.**]
Bon (bŏn) *n.* A Japanese Buddhist festival held in July to honor ancestral spirits. Also called "Feast of Lanterns." [Japanese *bon,* basin, sacrificial vessel (later used as a festive lantern), from Chinese (Mandarin) *pén.*]
bo·na fi·de (bō'nə fīd', fī'dē, bŏn'ə) *adj.* **1.** Done or made in good faith; sincere: *a bona fide offer.* **2.** Authentic; genuine: *a bona fide Rembrandt.* [Latin, "in good faith."]
bona fi·des (fī'dēz) *n. Law.* Honest intention; good faith. [Latin, "good faith."]
Usage: Bona fides is a singular Latin noun that takes a singular verb: *His bona fides is not in question.* Use of a plural verb is incorrect, and arises from confusion with the adjectival form *bona fide,* as in *a bona fide traveler.*
bo·nan·za (bə-năn'zə) *n.* **1.** A rich mine, vein, or pocket of ore. **2.** Any source of great wealth or prosperity. [Spanish, fair weather, prosperity, from Vulgar Latin *bonacia* (unattested), from Latin *bonus,* good (after Latin *malacia,* calm at sea, taken as if from *malus,* bad).]
Bo·na·parte (bō'nə-pärt'), **Jérôme** (1784–1860). Napoleon's youngest brother, king of Westphalia (1807–13). He lost the Westphalian crown when Germany was liberated from Napoleon (1813). He then took part in the French army's campaigns and fought at Waterloo. He became marshal of France (1850) and president of the senate under Napoleon III.
Bonaparte, Joseph (1768–1844). Napoleon's eldest brother, king of Naples (1806–08) and of Spain (1808–13).
Bonaparte, Louis (1778–1846). Brother of Napoleon, king of Holland (1806–10). He served with Napoleon in the Italian campaign (1796–97) and was his aide-de-camp in Egypt (1798–99). He was the father of Napoleon III.
Bonaparte, Lucien (1775–1840). Brother of Napoleon. He played an important part in Napoleon's coup of 18 Brumaire (1799), but,

disillusioned with his brother's policies, he went to Italy. He was reconciled with Napoleon at Elba.

Bonaparte, Napoleon. See **Napoleon I.**

Bo·na·part·ist (bō′nə-pär′tĭst) n. A follower or supporter of Napoleon Bonaparte, his policies and dynastic claims, or of the Bonaparte family. —**Bo·na·part·ism** n.

bon ap·pe·tit (bôn′ ä-pā-tē′) interj. Used to wish someone a good appetite and a pleasant meal. [French.]

bo·na va·can·ti·a (bō′nə və-kăn′tē-yə) pl.n. Law. Unclaimed goods. [Latin, goods without an owner.]

bon·bon (bŏn′bŏn′) n. A candy having a center of fondant, fruit, or nuts, and coated with chocolate or fondant. [French, baby-talk reduplication of bon, good, from Latin bonus.]

bon·bon·niere (bŏn′bŏn-yâr′) n. 1. A small ornate box or dish for candy. 2. A confectioner's store.

bond (bŏnd) n. 1. Anything that binds, ties, or fastens together, as: **a.** A shackle; a fetter. **b.** A cord, rope, or band. 2. Often **bonds.** Archaic. Captivity; confinement. 3. Often **bonds.** A uniting force or tie; a link. 4. A binding agreement; a covenant. 5. The duty, promise, or obligation by which one is bound: "To trust a man on his oath or bond" (Shakespeare). 6. **a.** A substance or an agent that causes two or more objects or parts to cohere. **b.** Such a union or cohesion. 7. Chemistry. A **chemical bond** (see). 8. Law. **a.** Any written and sealed obligation, especially one requiring payment of a stipulated amount of money on or before a given day. **b.** A sum of money paid as bail or surety. **c.** One who acts as bail; bondsman. 9. Finance. **a.** A certificate of debt issued by a government or corporation, guaranteeing payment of the original investment plus interest by a specified future date. **b.** South African. A company loan or mortgage on a house or property. 10. Commerce. The state or condition of storing taxable goods in a warehouse until the taxes or duties due on them are paid. Used chiefly in the phrase in bond. 11. An insurance contract in which an agency guarantees payment to an employer in the event of unforeseen financial loss through the actions of an employee. 12. Any overlapping arrangement of bricks or other masonry components in a wall. 13. **Bond paper** (see). ~v. **bonded, bonding, bonds.** —tr. 1. To mortgage or place a guaranteed bond on. 2. To furnish a bond or surety for. 3. To place (an employee, for example) under bond or guarantee. 4. To join securely, as with glue or cement. 5. To lay (bricks or other building materials) in an overlapping pattern for solidity. —intr. To secure or hold something together with or as if with a bond. [Middle English bond, band, from Old Norse band.] —**bond·a·ble** adj. —**bond·er** n.

Bond (bŏnd), **Edward** (1934–). British playwright. His plays include Saved (1965), Lear (1972), and The Women (1978). He also wrote the libretto for the German composer Hans Werner Henze's opera We Come to the River (1976).

bond·age (bŏn′dĭj) n. 1. The condition of a slave or serf; serfdom; servitude. 2. A state of subjection to any force, power, or influence. 3. In early English law, **villeinage** (see). 4. The condition or practice of deriving sexual pleasure from being tied or chained up or tying or chaining up another. —See Synonyms at **servitude.** [Middle English, from Anglo-Latin bondāgium, from Middle English bonde, serf, peasant, Old English bōnda, householder, from Old Norse bōndi, būandi, "tiller of the soil," husbandman, from the present participle of būa, to live, dwell.]

bonded warehouse n. A warehouse certified by the U.S. Department of Internal Revenue in which dutiable goods are stored pending payment of duties or taxes.

bond·hold·er (bŏnd′hōl′dər) n. The owner of a bond or bonds.

bond·ing (bŏn′dĭng) n. Anthropology. The forming of close, specialized human relationships, such as those that link parent and child, husband and wife, or friend and friend.

bond·maid (bŏnd′mād′) n. A female bondservant.

bond paper n. A superior grade of strong white paper made wholly or in part from rag pulp. Also called "bond."

bond·ser·vant (bŏnd′sûr′vənt) n. 1. A person obligated to service without wages. 2. A slave or serf. Also called "bondslave." [Bond-, from Middle English bonde, serf. See **bondage.**]

bonds·man (bŏndz′mən) n., pl. -**men** (-mĭn). 1. A male bondservant. 2. A person who provides bond or surety for another.

bond·wom·an (bŏnd′woŏm′ən) n. A female bondservant.

bone (bōn) n. 1. **a.** The dense, semirigid, porous, calcified connective tissue of the skeleton of most vertebrates. **b.** Any of numerous anatomically distinct skeletal structures made of this material. **c.** A piece of this material. 2. **bones. a.** The skeleton. **b.** The body. 3. An animal structure or material, such as ivory, resembling bone. 4. Something made of bone or of material resembling bone, especially: **a.** A piece of whalebone or similar material used as a corset stay. **b. bones.** Informal. Dice. **c. bones.** Essentials; basic principles. Used chiefly in the phrase the bare bones. 6. **a. bones.** Flat clappers made of bone or wood used by the end man in a minstrel show. **b. Bones.** Used with a singular verb. The end man in a minstrel show. —**bone of contention.** The subject of a dispute. —**feel in one's bones.** To have an intuition of. —**have a bone to pick with.** To have grounds for a dispute with. —**make no bones about.** To be frank and candid about. ~adv. Used as an intensive: bone dry; bone idle. ~tr.v. **boned, boning, bones.** 1. To remove the bones from. 2. To stiffen (a corset or piece of clothing) with whalebone or similar material. 3. To fertilize with bone meal. —**bone up.** Informal. To study intensively, usually at the last minute. Often used with on.

[Middle English bon, ban, from Old English bān, from Germanic bainam (unattested).] See feature, next page.

bone ash n. The white, powdery calcium phosphate ash of burned bones, used as a fertilizer, in making ceramics, and in cleaning and polishing compounds.

bone·black (bōn′blăk′) n. Also **bone black.** A black pigment containing about 10 percent charcoal, made by roasting bones in an airtight container, and used in polishes, as a filtering medium, and in decolorizing sugar.

bone china n. Porcelain made of clay mixed with bone ash.

bone conduction n. The transmission of sound by bone, especially to the inner ear by the bones of the skull.

bone·fish (bōn′fĭsh′) n., pl. -**fishes** or collectively **bonefish.** A marine game fish, Albula vulpes, of warm, shallow waters, having silvery scales. [From its many small bones.]

bone·head (bōn′hĕd′) n. Slang. A stupid person; dunce. —**bone·head·ed** adj. —**bone·head·ed·ness** n.

bone marrow n. The tissue contained in the bone cavities that in early life forms the blood cells and platelets.

bone meal n. Bones crushed and ground to a coarse powder, used as plant fertilizer and animal feed.

bon·er (bō′nər) n. Slang. A blunder. [BON(E) + -ER.]

bone·set (bōn′sĕt′) n. Any of various plants of the genus Eupatorium; especially, E. perfoliatum, of eastern North America, having broad clusters of small white flowers. Also called "thoroughwort" and sometimes "agueweed" or "feverwort." [From its use as a folk medicine.]

bone·set·ter (bōn′sĕt′ər) n. A person with no medical qualifications who tends to broken bones or dislocated limbs.

bone·yard (bōn′yärd′) n. Informal. A cemetery.

bon·fire (bŏn′fīr′) n. A large outdoor fire. [Middle English banefyre, a fire in which bones were burned : BON(E) + FIRE.]

bong (bŏng, bông) n. A deep ringing sound, as of a bell. ~v. **bonged, bonging, bongs.** —tr. To announce or proclaim with or as if with a deep ringing sound: bong the hour. —intr. To ring. [Imitative.]

bon·go (bŏng′gō) n., pl. -**gos.** An antelope, Boocercus eurycerus, of central Africa, having a reddish-brown coat with narrow, vertical white stripes and spirally twisted horns. [Native African name.]

bongo drums pl.n. A pair of connected drums having parchment heads that can be tuned, played by beating with the hands. Also called "bongos," "bongoes." [American Spanish bongó (probably imitative).]

Bon·hoef·fer (bŏn′höf-ər), **Dietrich** (1906–45). German Protestant theologian and philosopher. In 1933 he denounced Hitler in a radio broadcast, and two years later he was forbidden to teach and banned from Berlin. He then worked for the anti-Nazi underground movement. In 1945 after spending two years in prison, during which time he wrote Letters and Papers from Prison, he was executed for alleged participation in a plot to assassinate Hitler. His most important philosophical work was his Ethics, compiled from his notes and published posthumously (1949).

bon·ho·mie (bŏn′ə-mē′) n. An outgoing affable disposition; good nature; geniality. [French, from bonhomme, good-natured man.]

bon·i·face (bŏn′ə-fĭs, -fās′) n. An innkeeper. [After Boniface, an innkeeper in The Beaux' Stratagem by George Farquhar (1678–1707), British dramatist.]

Bon·i·face (bŏn′ə-fās′), **Saint** (c. 675–754). English monk, known as "the Apostle of Germany." He was born in Devonshire, and his English name was Winfrid or Wynfrith. Pope Gregory II gave him the name of Boniface (718) and encouraged his missionary work in Germany, where he made many converts to Christianity and founded monasteries. He was killed by a mob in Friesland.

bo·ni·to (bə-nē′tō) n., pl. -**tos** or collectively **bonito.** 1. Any of several marine food and game fishes of the genus Sarda, related to and resembling the tuna. 2. Any of several similar fishes. [Spanish, "beautiful" (from its appearance), from Latin bonus, good.]

bon·kers (bŏng′kərz) adj. Slang. Mad; eccentric; crazy. [20th century : origin obscure.]

bon mot (bôn mō′) n., pl. **bons mots** (bôn′mōz′). A clever saying, usually a terse and apt witticism. [French, "good word."]

Bonn (bŏn). Capital of West Germany (1949–90), on the Rhine River in the western part of Germany. It was founded as a Roman garrison (1st century A.D.). Its baroque architectural character is due to its having been rebuilt in 1685 after being destroyed by Elector Frederick III of Brandenburg.

Bon·nard (bô-när′), **Pierre** (1867–1947). French painter and lithographer noted for his use of dazzling light and color.

bonne (bôn) n. A female servant; maid. [French, feminine of bon, good, from Latin bonus.]

bonne bouche (bôn′ boōsh′) n., pl. **bonnes bouches** (pronounced as singular). 1. Something small and tasty, often eaten at the end of a meal. 2. A short pleasing item, such as a musical encore. [French, "good mouth."]

bonne femme (bôn′ fĕm′) adj. Designating simple, home-style cooking. [French (à la) bonne femme, "(in the manner of) a good housewife."]

bon·net (bŏn′ĭt) n. 1. A hat that is held in place by ribbons tied under the chin, worn by women and girls. 2. Scottish. A brimless cap worn by men. 3. A feather headdress worn by some American Indians. 4. A removable metal plate over a valve or other machinery part. 5. Chiefly British. The hood of an automobile. 6. A wind screen for a chimney. 7. Nautical. A strip of canvas laced to a

bone

THE SCAFFOLDING OF THE HUMAN BODY
Bone is light, flexible, yet stronger than steel

The human body, like those of other animals, is built around a skeleton of bone. This internal scaffolding not only supports the flesh and decides the shape of the body, but is jointed to make movement possible. Bone is made of two-thirds calcium, phosphorus, and magnesium and one-third collagen, a protein giving elasticity. This combination gives strength greater than that of mild steel, with only one-third the weight.

Bone consists of alternate horizontal and vertical layers of minerals containing collagen fibers, compacted on the outside to form hard ivory bone, and spongy in the center, where cavities hold bone marrow, which makes red blood cells and contains much of the body's stored fat cells.

Bones are classified as long (a thigh bone), short (a finger bone), flat (a shoulder bone), or irregular (a heel bone). In the embryo they are modeled in soft cartilage (gristle) and membrane. Bone-forming (ossification) centers develop later, and at birth all major bones have ossification centers near the middle. In childhood, secondary ossification centers develop near the ends (epiphyses) of long bones, which is where growth mainly occurs.

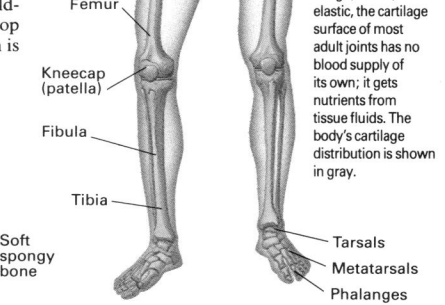

CORE OF MAN *More than 200 bones make up the human frame. All but the brain box are flexible and jointed. In reaction with contracted muscles, bones make possible all movement, such as breathing, walking, bending, and grasping.*

BONE STRUCTURE *Inside the hard ivory bone are layers (lamellae) containing Haversian canals, which carry blood and osteoblasts. These cells continually dissolve bone, replacing it with new minerals—the process that renews broken bones.*

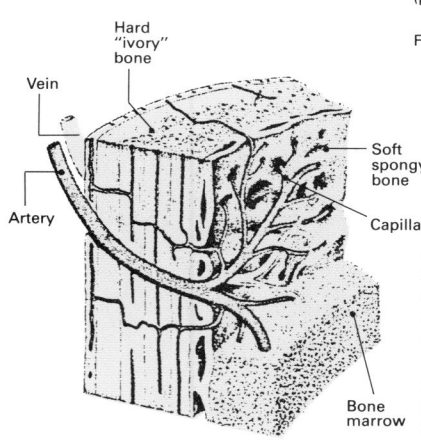

bonnet monkey *This southern Indian monkey's name comes from its distinctive cap of long hair. It lives in troops of about two dozen.*

fore-and-aft sail to increase sail area.
~*tr.v.* **bonneted, -neting, nets.** To put a bonnet on. [Middle English *bonet,* from Old French, from Medieval Latin *abonnis†,* cap.] —**bon·net·ed** *adj.*

bonnet monkey *n.* A macaque, *Macaca radiata,* having a thatch of hair on the head resembling a bonnet.

Bon·ne·ville Salt Flats (bŏn′ə-vĭl′). A very flat region of the Great Salt Lake Desert in northwest Utah. It forms part of the bed of the now-vanished ancient Lake Bonneville, named after a 19th-century French fur trader and explorer. The flats are regularly used in attempts to set land speed records.

Bon·ney (bŏn′ē), **William H.,** known as "Billy the Kid" (1859–81). U.S. outlaw. By the age of 21 he had murdered 21 men, two of them during an escape from jail after he had been sentenced to death. Sheriff Pat Garrett fulfilled a campaign promise by fatally shooting him, bringing to an end Bonney's murderous career.

Bonnie Prince Charlie. See **Stuart, Charles Edward.**

bonnock. Variant of **bannock.**

bon·ny (bŏn′ē) *adj.* **-nier, -niest.** Also **bon·nie.** *Chiefly Scottish.* **1.** Pleasing or attractive to the eye; pretty; fair. **2.** Healthy; robust. **3.** Cheerful; pleasant. [Perhaps from Old French *bon,* good, from Latin *bonus.*] —**bon·ni·ly** *adv.* —**bon·ni·ness** *n.*

bon·ny·clab·ber (bŏn′ē-klăb′ər) *n. British Regional.* Sour clotted milk. [Probably from Irish *bainne clabair,* "milk of the churn-dasher" : *bainne,* milk, from Middle Irish *banne,* milk, drop + *clabair,* genitive of *clabaire†,* dasher (part of a churn).]

bon·sai (bŏn-sī′) *n., pl.* **bonsai. 1.** The art of producing dwarfed trees or shrubs by growing them from normal seed in small, shallow pots and restricting root and shoot growth by pruning. **2.** A tree or

shrub grown by this method. [Japanese, "potted plant" : *bon,* basin, pot + *sai,* to plant.]

bon·spiel (bŏn′spēl′) *n.* Also **bon·spell** (-spəl). *Scottish.* A curling match. [Probably from Dutch *bon(d)spel* (unattested), "league game" : *bond,* league, from Middle Dutch *bont* + *spel,* game, from Middle Dutch, from Germanic *spillōn* (unattested), to play (see **spiel**).]

bon·te·bok (bŏn′tə-bŏk′) *n.* A rare South African antelope, *Damaliscus dorcas dorcas* (or *pygargus*), having a dark reddish coat, white underparts and rump, and a white mark on the face. [Afrikaans : *bont,* spotted, from Middle Dutch, probably from Latin *punctus,* spotted, pierced (see **point**) + *bok,* buck, from Middle Dutch *boc.*]

bon ton (bŏn′tŏn′) *n.* **1.** Sophisticated manners; style. **2.** Stylish or fashionable society. [French, "good tone."]

bo·nus (bō′nəs) *n., pl.* **-nuses. 1.** Something given or paid in addition to the usual or expected, especially an extra payment to employees at Christmas or for higher productivity. **2.** An extra dividend paid to shareholders from profits. **3.** Money paid to a state by a company in return for a corporate charter. **4.** A grant from the government to veterans of the armed forces. **5.** An incidental, extra, or unexpected benefit. **6.** A premium paid for a loan. [Latin *bonus,* good.]
   Synonyms: bounty, dividend, grant, gratuity, premium, reward, subsidy.

bonus issue *n.* A **scrip issue** *(see).*

bon vi·vant (bŏn vē-vän′) *n., pl.* **bons vivants** (pronounced as singular). *French.* A person who enjoys good food and drink and lives luxuriously.

bon voy·age (bŏn vwä-yäzh′) *interj.* Used to wish a departing traveler a pleasant journey. [French, "good journey."]

bon·y (bō′nē) *adj.* **-ier, -iest. 1.** Of, pertaining to, resembling, or made of bone. **2.** Having an internal skeleton of bones rather than cartilage. Said of fish. **3.** Having many bones. **4.** Having protruding or prominent bones; lean; gaunt. —**bon·i·ness** *n.*

bonze (bŏnz) *n.* A Mahayana Buddhist monk, especially of China, Japan, and adjacent countries. [French *bonze* or Portuguese *bonzo,* from Japanese *bonsō,* from Chinese *fàn sēng* : *fàn,* Buddhist, from Sanskrit *brahmanas* + *sēng* monk.]

bon·zer (bŏn′zər) *adj. Australian Slang.* Excellent; very good. Not in current usage. [Perhaps from BONANZA.]

boo¹ (bōō) *n., pl.* **boos.** A vocal sound uttered to show contempt, scorn, or disapproval.
~*interj.* Used to frighten or surprise, or to express disapproval or derision.
~*v.* **booed, booing, boos.** —*intr.* To utter "boo." —*tr.* To say "boo" to; jeer at. [Imitative.]

boo² *n. Slang.* Marijuana. [Origin unknown.]

boob (bōōb) *n. Slang.* A stupid or foolish person; a simpleton. [Short for BOOBY.]

boob·oi·sie (bōōb′wä-zē′) *n.* The class of the population composed of the stupid and gullible. [BOOB + (BOURGE)OISIE (coined by H.L. MENCKEN).]

boo-boo (bōō′bōō) *n., pl.* **-boos.** *Slang.* **1.** A stupid or thoughtless mistake; a blunder. **2.** A slight physical injury, especially on a child.

boob tube *n. Slang.* Television.

boo·by (bōō′bē) *n., pl.* **-bies. 1.** A stupid or childish person. **2.** *Slang.* A woman's breast. **3.** Any of several tropical sea birds of the genus *Sula,* typically with brightly colored bills and feet, resembling and related to the gannets. [Spanish *bobo,* from Latin *balbus,* stammering.]

booby hatch *n.* **1.** *Nautical.* A raised covering over a small hatchway. **2.** *Slang.* A mental hospital. [Sense 1, from BOOBY (bird), since these birds commonly light there at sea. Sense 2, from BOOBY (stupid person).]

booby prize *n.* An insignificant or comical prize given to the person who receives the lowest score in a game or contest.

booby trap *n.* **1.** A concealed or camouflaged device designed to be triggered by some unsuspecting action of the intended victim. **2.** Any device or situation that catches a person off guard.

boo·by-trap (bōō′bē-trăp′) *tr.v.* **-trapped, -trapping, -traps.** To fit with a booby trap.

boo·dle (bōōd′l) *n. Slang.* **1. a.** Money, especially counterfeit money. **b.** Money accepted as a bribe. **2.** Stolen goods; swag. **3.** A crowd or mob; caboodle.
~*v.* **boodled, -dling, -dles.** *Slang.* —*intr.* To accept a bribe. —*tr.* To bribe or swindle. [Dutch *boedel,* estate, effects, from Middle Dutch *bōdel,* riches, property.] —**boo·dler** *n.*

boo·gie (bōō′gē) *n.* Strongly rhythmic rock music.
~*intr.v.* **boogied, -gieing, -gies.** To dance to rock music. [Shortened from BOOGIE-WOOGIE.]

boog·ie·man (bōōg′ē-măn′, bōō′gē-) *n., pl.* **-men** (-mĕn′). Also **boog·y·man, boog·ey·man, bo·gy·man** (bō′gē-), **bo·gey·man.** A hobgoblin; a terrifying specter. [Boogie, alteration of *booger,* from dialectal *boggart,* specter, hobgoblin, akin to BOGLE.]

boog·ie-woog·ie (bōōg′ē-wōōg′ē) *n.* A style of jazz piano-playing characterized by a repeated rhythmic and melodic pattern in the bass. [20th century : probably of African origin; compare Hausa *buga,* to beat (drums), West African English (Sierra Leone) *bogi* (bogi), to dance.] —**boog·ie-woog·ie** *adj.*

boo·hoo (bōō′hōō′) *intr.v.* **-hooed, -hooing, -hoos.** To weep or pretend to weep noisily.
~*n., pl.* **boohoos.** Noisy or pretended weeping. [Imitative.]

book (bŏŏk) *n. Abbr.* **b., B., bk. 1.** A volume made up of written or printed pages fastened along one side, and having cardboard, leather, or paper protective covers. **2.** Any written or printed literary work. **3.** A bound volume of blank or ruled pages. **4. a.** Any of the volumes in which financial transactions are recorded. **b. books.** Such records collectively. **5.** A main division of a larger written or printed work: *a book of the Old Testament.* **6.** A libretto *(see).* **7.** The script of a play. **8. Book.** The Bible. Often preceded by *the.* **9. books.** *Informal.* Studies; lessons: *She's at her books.* **10.** Something regarded as a source of knowledge: *the book of life.* **11.** A number of similar items bound together between covers or in a small packet: *a book of matches.* **12.** A record of bets placed on a race. **13.** In card games, the number of tricks needed before any tricks can have scoring value, as the first six tricks taken by the declaring side in bridge. **14.** A bundle of tobacco leaves sliced lengthwise. **—bring to book. 1.** To compel to explain or account for. **2.** To reprimand. **—by the book.** Strictly according to established rules. **—close the books. 1.** In bookkeeping, to make no further entries in and to draw up statements from the records as they stand. **2.** To bring to an end. **—in one's book.** In one's opinion. **—in someone's good** (or **bad**) **books.** In favor (or disfavor) with someone. **—keep books.** To keep financial records. **—like a book.** Thoroughly; completely: *She knows him like a book.* **—make book.** *Slang.* To accept bets as a bookmaker, especially on a sporting event. **—one for the books.** *Informal.* Something noteworthy. **—on the books. 1.** Recorded or registered. **2.** Enlisted or enrolled. **—throw the book at.** *Slang.* **1.** To make all possible charges against (an offender or lawbreaker, for example). **2.** To reprimand or punish severely. ~*tr.v.* **booked, booking, books. 1.** To list or register in or as if in a book. **2.** To record charges against (a person) on a police blotter. **3.** To arrange for in advance; reserve (tickets, for example). **4.** To hire (entertainers, for example). [Middle English *bok,* Old English *bōc,* written document, composition.]

book·bind·er·y (bŏŏk′bīn′də-rē) *n., pl.* **-ies.** A business establishment where books are bound.

book·bind·ing (bŏŏk′bīn′dĭng) *n.* The art, trade, or profession of binding books. **—book·bind·er** *n.*

book·case (bŏŏk′kās′) *n.* A piece of furniture with shelves for holding books.

book club *n.* **1.** An organization that sells books, usually at a discount, to members who have agreed to buy a minimum number. **2.** A club for the reading and discussion of books.

book end *n.* A prop placed at the end of a row of books to keep them upright.

book·ie (bŏŏk′ē) *n. Slang.* A bookmaker *(see).*

book·ing (bŏŏk′ĭng) *n.* **1.** An engagement, as for a performance by an entertainer. **2.** A reservation, as of tickets or a hotel room. **3.** The recording of a person's name on a police blotter.

book·ish (bŏŏk′ĭsh) *adj.* **1.** Of, relating to, or resembling a book. **2.** Fond of books; studious. **3.** Relying on book learning rather than practical experience. **—book·ish·ly** *adv.* **—book·ish·ness** *n.*

book jacket *n.* A dust jacket *(see).*

book·keep·ing (bŏŏk′kē′pĭng) *n. Abbr.* **bkpg.** The art or practice of recording the accounts and transactions of a business. **—book·keep·er** *n.*

book learning *n.* Knowledge gained from books rather than from practical experience. Also called "booklore." **—book-learn·ed** *adj.*

book·let (bŏŏk′lĭt) *n.* A small bound book or pamphlet, usually with paper covers.

book·louse (bŏŏk′lous′) *n., pl.* **-lice** (-līs′). Any of various small, often wingless insects of the order Psocoptera (or Corrodentia), some species of which damage books.

book·mak·er (bŏŏk′mā′kər) *n.* **1.** One who edits, prints, publishes, or binds books. **2.** Someone who accepts bets, as on a horse race, and pays out winning bets. Also called "bookie."

book·man (bŏŏk′mən) *n., pl.* **-men** (-mĭn). **1.** One who is fond of books and reading. **2.** One who belongs to the literary world, such as a writer, critic, publisher, or bookseller.

book·mark (bŏŏk′märk′) *n.* A marker, such as a ribbon or a strip of leather, placed between the pages of a book.

book·mo·bile (bŏŏk′mō-bēl′) *n.* A small truck or trailer equipped to serve as a mobile lending library.

Book of Common Prayer *n.* The book of services and prayers used in the Church of England and, with certain modifications, in the other churches of the Anglican Communion.

Book of Kells. See **Kells.**

Book of Mormon *n.* The sacred text of the Mormon Church. See **Mormon.**

book·plate (bŏŏk′plāt′) *n.* A label usually pasted on the inside cover of a book that bears the owner's name or other identification.

book·rack (bŏŏk′răk′) *n.* **1.** A small rack or shelf for books. **2.** A frame or rack for supporting an open book. Also called "bookstand," "bookrest."

book review *n.* A critical analysis of a book.

book·sel·ler (bŏŏk′sĕl′ər) *n.* A person who sells books.

book·stall (bŏŏk′stôl′) *n.* A stall or stand where newspapers, magazines, or books are sold.

book·stand (bŏŏk′stănd′) *n.* **1.** A small counter where newspapers, magazines, or books are sold. **2.** A bookrack *(see).*

book·store (bŏŏk′stôr′, -stōr′) *n.* A store where books are sold. Also called "bookshop."

book value *n.* The value of a company's assets as set down in its financial records.

book·worm (bŏŏk′wûrm′) *n.* **1.** Any of various insects, especially booklice and silverfish, that infest books and feed on the paste in the bindings. **2.** One who spends much time reading or studying.

Boole (bŏŏl), **George** (1815–64). British mathematician and logician. He developed a calculus of symbolic logic, which was one of the first systems to show the use of symbolic mathematics as a tool in logical inference. It became one of the foundations of computer technology.

Bool·e·an algebra (bŏŏ′lē-ən) *n.* Any of various algebraic systems based on mathematical forms and relationships borrowed from the symbolic logic of George Boole.

boom¹ (bŏŏm) *v.* **boomed, booming, booms.** —*intr.* **1.** To make a deep, resonant, usually sustained sound: *His voice boomed down the corridor.* **2.** To flourish or progress usually with sudden rapid growth: *Business boomed.* —*tr.* To give forth or utter with a deep, resonant sound. Often used with *out.* ~*n.* **1.** A booming sound, as of an explosion. **2.** A time of general prosperity and economic growth. **3.** A sudden increase, as in growth, wealth, or popularity: *an investment boom; a baby boom.* ~*adj.* Of or resulting from a boom: *boom prices.* [Middle English *bomben, bummen* (imitative).]

boom² *n.* **1.** *Nautical.* A long spar extending from a mast to hold or extend the foot of a sail. **2.** A long pole extending upward at an angle from the mast of a derrick to support or guide objects lifted or suspended. **3. a.** A barrier composed of a chain of floating logs enclosing other free-floating logs. **b.** The area enclosed by such a barrier. **4.** A floating barrier serving to obstruct navigation or protect the entrance to a waterway. **5.** A long, movable arm used to maneuver an overhead microphone. ~*tr.v.* **boomed, booming, booms. 1.** *Nautical.* To extend (a sail) on a boom. Used with *out.* **2.** To obstruct (a river or the mouth of a harbor, for example) wih a floating barrier. [Dutch, tree, pole, from Middle Dutch.]

boom·er (bŏŏ′mər) *n.* **1.** A large male kangaroo. **2.** *Australian & New Zealand Informal.* Anything large, successful, or exciting.

boo·mer·ang (bŏŏ′mə-răng′) *n.* **1.** A flat, curved wooden missile, some types of which can be hurled so that they return to the thrower. It is used as a weapon by Australian aborigines. **2.** A statement or course of action that rebounds to the disadvantage of its originator. ~*intr.v.* **boomeranged, -anging, -angs.** To result in adverse effect upon the originator; backfire. [Native Australian word, variously recorded as *wo-mur-rāng, būmarin.*]

boom town *n.* A town which expands rapidly due to sudden prosperity, often through the discovery of local mineral resources.

boon¹ (bŏŏn) *n.* **1.** Something granted to benefit or please; a blessing: *Those phrase books are a boon to travellers.* **2.** A favor or request. [Middle English *bone,* prayer, thing prayed for, hence favor, from Old Norse *bōn,* prayer, request.]

boon² *adj.* Jolly; convivial. Used chiefly in the phrase *boon companion.* [Middle English *bone,* "good," from Old French *bon,* from Latin *bonus.*]

boon·docks (bŏŏn′dŏks′) *pl.n. Slang.* **1.** Wild and dense brush; jungle. Preceded by *the.* **2.** Back country; hinterland. Preceded by *the.* [Tagalog *bundok,* mountain.]

boon·dog·gle (bŏŏn′dôg′əl, -dŏg′əl) *intr.v.* **-gled, -gling, -gles.** *Informal.* To waste time on pointless and unnecessary work. ~*n.* Pointless, unnecessary, and time-wasting work. [20th century : origin obscure.] **—boon·dog·gler** *n.*

Boone (bŏŏn), **Daniel** (1734–1820). U.S. frontiersman and folk hero. He undertook the colonization of Kentucky, founding Boonesboro (or Boonesborough) on the Kentucky River (1775) after leading settlers across the Appalachian Mts.

boon·ies (bŏŏ′nēz) *pl.n. Slang.* See **Boondocks** (sense 2). [Shortening and alteration of BOONDOCKS.]

boor (bŏŏr) *n.* **1.** A peasant. **2.** A person with rude, clumsy manners and little respect for the feelings of others. [Dutch *boer,* farmer, peasant, from Middle Dutch *gheboer.*]

boor·ish (bŏŏr′ĭsh) *adj.* Like a boor; rude; ill-mannered. **—boor·ish·ly** *adv.* **—boor·ish·ness** *n.*

boost (bŏŏst) *v.* **boosted, boosting, boosts.** —*tr.* **1.** To raise or lift by or as if by pushing up from behind or below. **2.** To increase; raise: *boost production.* **3.** To encourage; help to improve: *boost someone's reputation; boost morale.* **4.** To promote or publicize; advocate actively. **5.** *Slang.* To steal, especially to shoplift. —*intr. Slang.* To steal. **—See Synonyms at lift.** ~*n.* **1.** A lift or help. **2.** An increase: *a boost in salary.* **3.** Anything that encourages or improves.

boost·er (bŏŏ′stər) *n.* **1.** Any device for increasing power or effectiveness. **2.** A person, thing, or event that is a source of encouragement or progress. **3.** *Electronics.* A radio-frequency amplifier. **4. a.** A rocket that assists the main propulsive system of an aircraft or spacecraft. **b.** A rocket used to launch a missile or space vehicle. In this sense, also called "booster rocket," "launch vehicle." **5.** A supplementary dose of a vaccine injected to maintain immunity. In this sense, also called "booster shot." **6.** A **supercharger** *(see).* **7.** *Slang.* One who shoplifts.

booster cable *n.* An electric cable used to connect a discharged automobile battery to a power source for charging. Also called "jumper cable," *chiefly British* "jump lead."

boot¹ (bŏŏt) *n.* **1.** A piece of footwear, usually of leather or rubber,

booby *There are six species of booby, a tropical relative of the gannet. Boobies catch fish by diving from high in the air. The conspicuously colored feet are used in displays to attract mates and warn off rivals.*

that covers the foot and part or all of the legs. **2.** A protective sheath for a horse's leg. **3.** An instrument of torture formerly used to crush the foot and leg. **4.** Any protective covering or sheath, especially a rubber sheath fitted over a coupling between two shafts. **5.** *British.* An automobile trunk. **6. a.** *Informal.* A kick. **b.** *Slang.* A swift, pleasurable feeling; thrill. **7.** A marine or navy recruit in basic training. **8.** *Slang.* A rude dismissal, as from work. Used with *the.*
~*tr.v.* **booted, booting, boots. 1.** To put boots on. **2.** *Informal.* To kick. **3.** *Informal.* To discharge; dismiss. Usually used with *out.* [Middle English *bote,* from Old French *bote†.*]

boot² *intr.v.* **booted, booting, boots.** *Archaic.* To be of help or advantage; avail.
~*n.* **1.** *Regional.* Something given in addition. **2.** *Archaic.* Advantage; avail. —**to boot.** In addition; besides. [Middle English *bote,* Old English *bōt,* advantage, addition, recompense.]

boot·black (boōt'blăk') *n.* A person who cleans and polishes shoes for a living.

boot camp *n.* A training camp for marine or navy recruits.

boot·ed (boō'tĭd) *adj.* **1.** Wearing boots. **2.** *Zoology.* In birds, having a horny sheath (in poultry, feathers) covering the lower part of the legs.

boo·tee (boō'tē) *n.* Also **boo·tie.** A soft, usually knitted, shoe for a baby. [Diminutive of BOOT (shoe).]

Bo·ö·tes (bō-ō'tēz) *n.* A constellation in the Northern Hemisphere near Virgo and Canes Venatici which contains the star Arcturus. [Latin *Boōtēs,* from Greek, "plowman," from *boōtein,* to plow, from *bous,* OX.]

booth (boōth) *n., pl.* **booths** (boōthz, boōths). **1.** A small enclosed compartment, usually accommodating only one person and providing privacy: *a telephone booth.* **2.** A seating area in a restaurant that has a table and seats whose backs serve as partitions. **3.** A small stall or stand for the display and sale of goods, as at a fairground. [Middle English *both, b(o)uth,* from Old Danish *bōth,* dwelling, stall.]

Booth (boōth). Family of actors, including **Junius Brutus** (1796–1852), a British-born Shakespearean actor who immigrated to the United States in 1821 and continued his highly acclaimed career. His two sons were born in America. **Edwin Thomas** (1833–93) began with supporting roles in his father's productions and later achieved accolades for a career highlighted by a 100-night appearance as Hamlet. The younger son, **John Wilkes** (1838–65), though also a talented actor, is infamous for the assassination of President Abraham Lincoln.

Booth, Charles (1840–1916). British social scientist. His 17-volume work, *Life and Labour of the People in London* (1891–1903), was one of the great early contributions to the modern study of social science.

Booth, William (1829–1912). British religious leader, the founder of the Salvation Army. He became a minister in the Methodist New Connection Church (1852). In 1861 he left the church to devote himself to independent evangelical work, establishing the East London Revival Society, later known as the Christian Mission (1865). In 1878 this organization became the Salvation Army, with Booth as its first general.

boot·jack (boōt'jăk') *n.* A forked device for holding a boot secure while the foot is being withdrawn.

boot·lace (boōt'lās') *n.* A strong lace for tying boots or shoes.

bootlace fungus *n.* The **honey fungus** (see).

bootlace worm *n.* A dark brown ribbon worm, *Lineus longissimus,* found in shallow waters. They grow up to 6 meters (20 feet) in length, and are the longest worms in existence.

boot·leg (boōt'lĕg') *v.* **-legged, -legging, -legs.** —*tr.* To make, sell, or transport (alcoholic liquor, for example) for sale illegally. —*intr.* To engage in bootlegging.
~*n.* Goods smuggled or illicitly produced or sold.
~*adj.* Produced, sold, or transported for sale illegally: *bootleg gin.* [From smugglers' practice of carrying liquor in the legs of tall boots.] —**boot·leg·ger** *n.*

boot·less (boōt'lĭs) *adj.* Having no advantage or benefit; useless; unavailing; fruitless: *a bootless effort.* —**boot·less·ly** *adv.* —**boot·less·ness** *n.*

boot·lick (boōt'lĭk') *v.* **-licked, -licking, -licks.** —*tr.* To be servile toward. —*intr.* To behave in a servile manner. —**boot·lick·er** *n.*

boots (boōts) *n., pl.* **boots.** *British.* A servant in a hotel who cleans and shines shoes.

boot·strap (boōt'străp') *n.* **1.** A leather or cloth loop sewn at each side or the top rear of a boot to help in pulling it on. **2.** *Computer Science.* A subroutine used to establish the full routine or another routine.
~*tr.v.* **-strapped, -strapping, -straps.** To establish (a program) with a bootstrap.
~*adj.* **1.** Undertaken or accomplished with minimal resources or help. **2.** Designating a technique or device for loading the first few programs into a computer so that the remaining programs can be introduced by way of an input device: *a bootstrap loader.* **3.** Denoting an electronic device, such as an amplifier, that uses the output voltage to bias the input. **4.** Denoting a self-consistent theory of nuclear interactions. —**by one's (own) bootstraps.** By one's own efforts.

boot tree *n.* A **shoetree** (see).

boo·ty (boō'tē) *n., pl.* **-ties. 1.** Plunder taken from an enemy in time of war. **2.** Any seized or stolen goods. **3.** Any valuable prize,

award, or gain. [Middle English *bottyne,* from Old French *butin,* from Middle Low German *būte,* exchange, from Common Germanic *būti-ōn* (unattested).]

booze (boōz) *Slang. n.* **1.** Alcoholic drink; especially, hard liquor. **2.** A drinking spree.
~*intr.v.* **boozed, boozing, boozes.** To drink alcoholic beverages excessively or chronically. [Middle English *bousen,* to carouse, from Middle Dutch *būsen†.*] —**booz·er** *n.* —**booz·y** *adj.*

bop¹ (bŏp) *tr.v.* **bopped, bopping, bops.** *Informal.* To hit or strike.
~*n.* A blow; a punch. [Imitative.]

bop² *n.* **1.** A style of jazz with a fast driving rhythm, very complex harmonies, and demanding virtuoso skills and techniques. Also called "bebop." **2.** *Informal.* A dance or a session of dancing to disco or pop music.
~*intr. v* **bopped, bopping, bops.** *Informal.* To dance to disco or pop music. [Short for BEBOP.]

Bo·phu·tha·tswa·na (bō'poō-tä-tswä'nə). One of the segregated areas known as Bantu homelands in South Africa. It consists of a number of widely separated districts located in Cape Province, the Orange Free State, and the Transvaal. It officially became a republic in 1977, but its independence has been recognized only by South Africa. Area, 40,430 square kilometers (15,610 square miles). Population, 1,200,000. Capital, Mmabatho.

bop·per (bŏp'ər) *n.* **1.** *Informal.* One who bops or plays bop. **2.** A **teenybopper** (see).

bor. borough.

bo·ra¹ (bôr'ə, bōr'ə) *n.* A violent cold wind from the northeast blowing on the Dalmatian coast of Yugoslavia in winter. [Italian (Venetian dialect), from Latin *Boreās,* BOREAS.]

bora² *n.* *Australian.* An Aboriginal initiation ceremony for boys going into manhood. [From a native Australian language.]

bo·rac·ic (bə-răs'ĭk, bô-) *adj.* Variant of **boric.** [Medieval Latin *borax* (stem *borac-*), BORAX + -IC.]

bo·rac·ite (bôr'ə-sīt', bōr'-) *n.* A white mineral consisting of borate and magnesium chloride, $Mg_6Cl_2B_{14}O_{26}$, found in some gypsum beds.

bor·age (bôr'ĭj, bŏr'-) *n.* A plant, *Borago officinalis,* native to southern Europe and northern Africa, having hairy leaves and star-shaped blue flowers. The young, cucumber-flavored leaves are sometimes used as seasoning. [Middle English, from Old French *bourrache,* from Medieval Latin *borrāgō,* probably from Arabic *abū 'āraq,* "father of sweat" (from its use medicinally as a sudorific).]

bo·rane (bôr'ān', bōr'-) *n.* Any of a series of boron-hydrogen compounds. [BOR(ON) + -ANE.]

bora ring *n.* *Australian.* A circle inside which an Aboriginal bora takes place.

bo·rate (bôr'āt', bōr'-) *n.* A salt or ester of boric acid.

bo·rax (bôr'ăks', -əks, bōr'-) *n.* **1.** A hydrated **sodium borate** (see). **2.** An anhydrous sodium borate used in the manufacture of glass and various ceramics. [Middle English *boras, borax,* from Old French *boras,* from Medieval Latin *borax,* from Arabic *būraq,* from Persian *būrah†.*]

borax bead *n.* A bead made of fused borax supported on a platinum wire, used in qualitative chemical analysis. When a substance of unknown composition is fused with the bead in a flame, the bead may change color depending on the presence of certain elements in the substance.

Bo·ra·zon (bôr'ə-zŏn', bōr'-) *n.* A trademark for an extremely hard boron nitride formed at very high pressures and temperatures. [BOR(ON) + AZ(O)- + -ON.]

bor·bo·ryg·mus (bôr'bə-rĭg'məs) *n.* Rumbling in the abdomen due to movement of fluid and gases in the intestines. [New Latin, from Greek (imitative).]

Bor·deaux¹ (bôr-dō'). A port in southwestern France, at the mouth of the Garonne River. Although it is an industrial town, its economy rests chiefly on the trade in Bordeaux wines.

Bor·deaux² (bôr-dō') *n., pl.* **Bordeaux** (bôr-dōz'). Any of the red or white wines produced in the regions around Bordeaux.

Bordeaux mixture *n.* A mixture of copper sulfate, lime, and water, used as a fungicide. [Translation of French *bouillie bordelaise.*]

bor·de·laise sauce (bôr-də-lĕz') *n.* A brown sauce made with Bordeaux wine and often with mushrooms. Also called "sauce bordelaise."

bor·del·lo (bôr-dĕl'ō) *n., pl* **-los.** A house of prostitution; a brothel. [Middle English, from Old French *bordel,* smallholding, small farm, diminutive of *borde,* from Frankish; akin to BOARD.]

Bor·den (bôrd'n), **Gail** (1801–74). U.S. surveyor and inventor. Concerned with the difficulty of transporting wholesome foods for long distances on the Western frontier, Borden developed a dried-beef biscuit (1851) and a method of condensing milk (patented 1856). His products were widely used during the Civil War.

Borden, Lizzie Andrew (1860–1927). Fall River, Massachusetts, woman who was accused of the ax murders of her father and step-mother on August 4, 1892. After a sensational trial, she was acquitted in June, 1893. The crime, still unsolved, has inspired many works of fiction, nonfiction, theater, and dance.

bor·der (bôr'dər) *n.* **1.** A margin, rim, or edge around or along something. **2.** A design or a decorative strip on the edge or rim of something, such as a plate. **3.** A strip of ground, around a lawn or along the side of a path for example, in which flowers or shrubs are planted. **4.** The line or frontier area separating political divisions or geographical regions; a boundary. —**the Borders.** The boundary

and adjacent areas between England and Scotland. —See Synonyms at **boundary**.
~adj. Of, pertaining to, forming, or located on a border.
~tr.v. bordered, -dering, -ders. 1. To put a border, rim, or edging on. **2.** To lie along or adjacent to the border of. —**border on** (or **upon**). **1.** To adjoin. **2.** To be almost like; approach in character: *an act that borders on heroism.* [Middle English *bordure*, from Old French, from *border*, to border, from *bord*, side of a vessel, border, from Frankish *bord* (unattested), board, plank.]
Synonyms: brim, brink, brow, edge, margin, rim, verge.

bor·der·er (bôr′dər-ər) *n.* A person who lives on or near a border, especially the border between Scotland and England.

bor·der·land (bôr′dər-lănd′) *n.* **1.** Land located on or near a border or frontier. **2.** An uncertain or indeterminate area, situation, or condition.

bor·der·line (bôr′dər-līn′) *n.* Also **border line. 1.** A line that establishes or marks a border; a demarcation. **2.** An indefinite or indeterminate division beween two qualities or conditions: *the borderline between genius and madness.*
~adj. 1. Verging on a given quality or condition; indeterminate; dubious: *a borderline case of paranoia.* **2.** Not quite or only just measuring up to an accepted standard, especially of behavior: *a borderline gesture.*

Borders Region. Since 1975 an administrative region of Scotland, in the southeast on the border with England. It includes the former counties of Roxburgh, Verwick, Peebles, and Selkirk. The administrative center is Newtown St. Boswells.

Border States. The former slave states of Delaware, Maryland, Kentucky, and Missouri, adjacent to the free states of the North and caught between opposing forces in the Civil War. None of the Border States seceded.

border terrier *n.* A small, hardy, rough-coated breed of terrier, bred to hunt foxes in the border country of Scotland and England.

Bor·det (bôr-dā′), **Jules** (1870–1961). Belgian serologist and immunologist. He helped develop the technique that led to the Wassermann test for syphilis. In 1906 he discovered the bacillus of whooping cough. He was awarded the Nobel Prize for medicine (1919).

bor·de·tel·la per·tus·sis (bôr′də-těl′ə pər-tŭs′ĭs) *n.* The coccobacillus that causes whooping cough. [NLat. : *Bordetella*, genus name (after Jules *Bordet*, 1870–1961) + *pertussis*, whooping cough.]

bor·dure (bôr′jər) *n. Heraldry.* A border around a shield. [Middle English, BORDER.]

bore¹ (bôr, bōr) *v.* **bored, boring, bores.** —*tr.* **1.** To make a hole in or through, as with a drill or lathe. **2.** To make (a tunnel or well, for example) by drilling, digging, or burrowing. **3.** To make (one's way) with difficulty. —*intr.* **1.** To make a hole in or through something by or as if by drilling. **2.** To advance steadily or laboriously.
~n. 1. A hole made by or as if by drilling, especially in order to find water or minerals; specifically, in Australia, an artesian well. Also called "borehole." **2. a.** The hollow part of a hole, tube, or cylinder. **b.** The interior diameter of this. **3.** The caliber of a firearm. Often used in combination: *12-bore.* **4.** A drilling tool. [Middle English *boren,* Old English *borian.*]

bore² *tr.v.* **bored, boring, bores.** To tire or weary with dullness, repetition, or tediousness.
~n. 1. A tiresome or tedious person or activity. **2.** A nuisance; a bother. [18th century : origin obscure.]

bore³ *n.* A high wave traveling upstream in the tidal reaches of certain rivers, caused by the surge of a flood tide upstream in a narrowing estuary or by colliding tidal currents. Also called "eagre." [Middle English *bare*, from Old Norse *bāra*, wave, billow.]

bore⁴. Past tense of **bear.**

bo·re·al (bôr′ē-əl, bōr′-) *adj.* **1.** Pertaining to the north; northern. **2.** Of or concerning the north wind. **3. Boreal.** Of or pertaining to the coniferous forest areas of the North Temperate Zone and Arctic region. **4. Boreal.** Of or designating a climatic zone with short summers and hard winters. **5. Boreal.** Of or designating a climatic period of cold winters and warm summers (7500 B.C. to 5500 B.C.). [Middle English *boriall*, from Late Latin *boreālis*, from BOREAS.]

Bo·re·as (bôr′ē-əs, bōr′-). **1.** The north wind. **2.** The god personifying the north wind in Greek mythology. [Middle English, from Latin *Boreās*, from Greek *Boreas*.]

bore·cole (bôr′kōl′, bōr′-) *n.* A vegetable, **kale** *(see).* [Dutch *boerenkool*, "peasants' cabbage" : *boer*, BOOR (peasant) + *kool*, cabbage, from Latin *caulis*, stalk (see **cole**).]

bore·dom (bôr′dəm, bōr′-) *n.* The condition of being bored.

bore·hole (bôr′hōl′, bōr′-) *n.* A bore, as for water or minerals; specifically, in South Africa, a narrow well drilled through to an underground source of water, which is usually pumped to the surface by means of a windmill.

bor·er (bôr′ər, bōr′-) *n.* **1.** A tool used for boring or drilling. **2.** One who works with such a tool. **3.** An insect or insect larva, such as the **corn borer** *(see),* that bores into plant material. **4.** Any of various mollusks that bore into soft rock or plant material.

Borg (bôrg), **Björn** (1956–). Swedish tennis player. He won his first major title at the Italian championships (1974) and from 1976 until 1980 won the Wimbledon men's singles championships five consecutive times, a record for the 20th century.

Bor·ges (bôr′hās), **Jorge Luis** (1899–1986). Argentinian writer. He was a poet, essayist, and literary critic, but he is best known for the metaphysical fantasy of his short stories, such as the collection *Ficciones* (1945).

Bor·gia (bôr′jä, -zhə), **Cesare** (c. 1475–1507). Italian soldier and politician, illegitimate son of Pope Alexander VI. The pope used his son to consolidate a papal empire, making him archbishop of Valenzia and then a cardinal. He was supposedly the model of the ruler in Machiavelli's *The Prince* (1532).

Borgia, Lucrezia (1480–1519). Italian noblewoman, daughter of Pope Alexander VI and sister of Cesare. Her three marriages helped increase the political power of the Borgia family. Later, her court at Ferrara became a cultural center of the Italian Renaissance.

Borgia, Rodrigo. See **Alexander VI.**

bo·ric (bôr′ĭk, bōr′-) *adj.* Also **bo·rac·ic** (bə-răs′ĭk). Of, pertaining to, derived from, or containing boron or boric acid.

boric acid *n.* A white or colorless crystalline compound, H_3BO_3, used as an antiseptic, preservative, and fireproofing agent. Also called "orthoboric acid."

boric oxide *n.* A white, colorless, transparent glass, B_2O_3, used in heat-resistant glassware, as a fire-resistant paint additive, and in the production of boron.

bo·ride (bôr′ĭd′, bōr′-) *n.* A binary compound of boron with a more electropositive element or radical. [BOR(ON) + -IDE.]

bor·ing¹ (bôr′ĭng, bōr′-) *n.* **1.** The making of a hole by or as if by drilling. **2.** A hole made in this way. **3. borings.** The material, chips, or dust produced by such drilling.

boring² *adj.* Uninteresting and tiresome; dull.
Synonyms: dreary, humdrum, irksome, monotonous, tedious, tiresome.

Bor·laug (bôr′lôg′), **Norman Ernest** (1914–). U.S. agronomist. For his contribution to progress in agriculture and attempts to overcome world hunger, he was awarded the Nobel Peace Prize (1970).

Bor·mann (bôr′män′), **Martin Ludwig.** (1900– c. 1945). German Nazi leader. He met Hitler in 1924 and became an important figure in the Nazi hierarchy. In 1942 he became Hitler's private secretary. He disappeared after Hitler's suicide in 1945 and was sentenced to death in his absence at the Nuremberg trials (1946). It is now thought that he committed suicide in May 1945.

born (bôrn). A past participle of **bear** (to give birth to). —See Usage note at **bear** (to carry).
~adj. 1. *Abbr.* **b., B.** Brought into life or being. **2.** Having or appearing with a specified innate quality or talent: *a born artist.*

Born (bôrn), **Max** (1882–1970). British theoretical physicist, born in Germany. He played an important part in the development of the new quantum and wave mechanics and was awarded the Nobel Prize for physics (1954).

born-a·gain (bôrn′ə-gĕn′) *adj.* **1.** Characteristic of or being a person who has undergone a personal, and usually very emotional conversion or reconversion, to Christianity, often through revelation or a similar experience; evangelical. **2.** Characterized by renewal, resurgence, or return: *born-again enthusiasm.*

borne¹ (bôrn, bōrn). A past participle of **bear** (to carry). —**borne in on** (or **upon**). Brought to the notice of; realized by: *The extent of our dilemma was gradually borne in on us.* —See Usage note at **bear** (to carry).

borne² *adj.* Carried or supported in a specified way. Often used in combination: *windborne; seaborne.*

Bor·ne·o (bôr′nē-ō). The largest island of the Malay Archipelago, lying north of Java and southwest of the Philippines. It is the third-largest island in the world. Kalimantan state, which occupies 70 percent of the island, belongs to Indonesia; the states of Sarawak in the west and Sabah in the north belong to Malaysia; and Brunei, in the northwest, is a British protectorate. The interior of the island consists of dense jungle and mountains, the coastal regions of mangrove swamp. The island is one of the most thinly populated parts of the nonpolar world.

bor·ne·ol (bôr′nē-ôl′, -ōl′) *n.* A solid terpene alchohol, $C_{10}H_{17}OH$, obtained from the tree *Dryobalanops camphora* and used in perfumery, the manufacture of celluloid, and as an antiseptic. [BORNEO + -OL.]

born·ite (bôr′nīt′) *n.* A brownish-bronze copper ore with composition Cu_5FeS_4. [After Ignaz von *Born* (1742–91), Austrian mineralogist.]

Bo·ro·bu·dur (bôr′ə-bə-dōōr′, bōr′-). One of the greatest of Buddhist shrines, in central Java in Indonesia. The monument was built in c. A.D. 800 and, although badly weathered, still stands.

Bo·ro·din (bôr′ə-dēn′) **Alexander Porfirevich.** (1834–87). Russian composer. His output was small, since he was primarily a chemist, but he is remembered for his opera, *Prince Igor* (unfinished at his death), and his two string quartets.

Bo·ro·di·no (bôr′ə-dē′nō). A village in central European U.S.S.R., west of Moscow. Nearby, Napoleon defeated the Russian forces defending Moscow on September 7, 1812. The battle, with heavy casualties on both sides, is described in Tolstoy's *War and Peace.*

bo·ron (bôr′ŏn′, bōr′-) *n. Symbol* **B** A nonmetallic element, extracted chiefly from kernite and borax, and used in flares, propellant mixtures, nuclear-reactor control elements, abrasives, and hard metallic alloys. It exists in two allotropic forms: a soft, brown, amorphous variety and a hard crystalline form. Atomic number 5, atomic weight 10.811, melting point 2300°C, sublimation 2,550°C, specific gravity (crystal) 2.34, valence 3. [BOR(AX) + (CARB)ON.]

boron carbide *n.* An extremely hard, black, crystalline compound, B_4C, used as an abrasive, in control rods for nuclear reactors, and as a reinforcing filament in composite structural materials.

boron chamber *n. Physics.* A type of particle detector that detects and counts slow neutrons by their effect on boron atoms.

boron nitride *n.* An inert white solid, BN, used as a lubricant, heat shield, and insulator at high temperatures. It has two crystalline forms: one similar to graphite and the other, **borazon** *(see),* similar to diamond.

bo·ro·sil·i·cate glass (bôr′ō-sĭl′ĭ-kĭt, bōr′ō-, -kāt′) *n.* A strong heat-resistant glass that contains a proportion of boron atoms in place of silicon atoms (up to five percent boric oxide).

bor·ough (bûr′ō, bûr′ə) *n. Abbr.* **bor.** **1.** A self-governing incorporated town in certain U.S. states. **2.** Any of the five administrative units of New York City. **3.** *British.* **a.** A town that was originally incorporated by royal charter and had a municipal corporation and certain rights, such as self-government. Compare **burgh.** **b.** A town that makes up the constituency of a member of Parliament. **c.** Any of the 32 divisions that make up Greater London. [Middle English *burgh, borugh,* Old English *burg, burh,* fortress, fortified town.]

bor·ough-Eng·lish (bûr′ō-ĭng′glĭsh) *n.* An old custom in certain boroughs of England whereby the right to inherit an estate went to the youngest son or, in default of issue, to the youngest brother. [Middle English, from Norman French *(tenure en) Burgh Engloys,* (tenure in) English borough.]

Bor·rel·i·a (bə-rĕl′ē-ə, -rē′lē-ə) *n.* A genus of locomotive helical bacteria of the family Spirochaetaceae, some of which cause relapsing fever in humans. [New Latin, after Amédée *Borrel* (1867–1936).]

Bor·ro·mi·ni (bôr′ō-mē′nē), **Francesco,** born Francesco Castelli (1599–1667). Baroque architect. He revolutionized architecture by conceiving a building as a collection of geometric shapes and by treating light and space as elements of the design.

bor·row (bôr′ō, bŏr′ō) *v.* **-rowed, -rowing, -rows.** —*tr.* **1.** To obtain or receive (something) on loan with the promise or understanding of returning it or its equivalent. **2.** To adopt or use as one's own: *They borrowed his ideas.* **3.** In subtraction, to increase a figure in the minuend by ten and make up for it by decreasing the next, larger denomination by one. **4.** *Nonstandard.* To lend. —*intr.* **1.** To take or receive a loan; obtain or receive something. **2.** *Golf.* To play a ball, especially when putting, so as to allow for the slope or wind. [Middle English *borwen,* Old English *borgian.*] —**bor·row·er** *n.*

bor·row·ing (bôr′ō-ĭng, bŏr′-) *n.* Something that is borrowed, especially a word borrowed from one language for use in another.

borscht, borsht (bôrsht) *n.* Also **borsch** (bôrsh). A Russian soup made from beets and sometimes cabbage, served hot or cold, often with sour cream. [Russian *borshch,* "cow parsnip" (the original base of the soup).]

borscht circuit *n. Slang.* The predominantly Jewish resort hotels of the Catskill Mountains that employ entertainers. [From the popularity of BORSCHT in their cuisine.]

bor·stal (bôr′stəl) *n. British.* A disciplinary institution for young offenders, aged 15 to 21. [After *Borstal* near Rochester, England, where the Borstal Institution for young offenders was established in 1901.]

bort, boart (bôrt) *n.* **1.** Poor-quality diamonds used for industrial cutting and abrasion. **2.** An impure diamond, a **carbonado** *(see).* [Perhaps from Dutch *boort,* perhaps from Old French *bourt,* bastard, from Latin *burdus,* hinny.] —**bort·y** *adj.*

bor·zoi (bôr′zoi) *n.* A rather large, slenderly built dog of a breed originating in Russia, having a narrow, pointed head and a silky, predominantly white coat. Also called "Russian wolfhound." [Russian *borzoi†,* "swift."]

bos·cage, bos·kage (bŏs′kĭj) *n.* A mass of trees or shrubs; a thicket. [Middle English *boskage,* from Old French *boscage,* from *bosc,* forest, from Germanic.]

Bosch (bŏs, bôs, bŏsh, bôsh), **Hieronymus** (c. 1450–1516). Flemish painter. He was strikingly original, producing surrealistically grotesque and allegorical canvases that have nothing in common with the prevailing Flemish style of the period.

Bosch (bŏsh, bôsh), **Karl** (1874–1940). German industrialist and chemist. He developed the Bosch process, but was more famous for his contribution to developing methods for the high-pressure synthesis of gases, especially ammonia. For this latter work he shared the Nobel Prize in chemistry with Friedrich Bergius (1884–1949).

Bosch process (bŏsh) *n.* A method of making hydrogen by the action of carbon monoxide on steam over a hot catalyst. [After K. BOSCH.]

Bose (bōs), **Sir Jagadis Chandra** (1858–1937). Indian physicist, plant physiologist, and founder of the Bose Research Institute in Calcutta. His most important work was in plant physiology. He was the inventor of an instrument used to measure the growth of plants.

Bose (bōs), **Satyenda Nath** (1894–1974). Indian physicist. In 1924 he was able to derive a radiation law for black bodies without using classical electrodynamics, as Max Planck had done. His work led to the **Bose-Einstein statistics.**

Bose-Ein·stein statistics (bōs′īn′shtīn, -stīn) *pl.n.* Quantum statistics concerning a system of identical bosons for which there can be any number of particles in the same quantum state simultaneously. [After S.N. BOSE and A. EINSTEIN.]

bosh (bŏsh) *n. Informal.* Meaningless talk or opinions; nonsense. [Turkish *boş,* empty, useless.]

bosk (bŏsk) *n.* A small wooded area or thicket. [Back-formation from BOSKY.]

bos·ky (bŏs′kē) *adj.* **1.** Covered with bushes, shrubs, or trees. **2.** Shaded by trees or bushes. [Middle English *bosky,* wooded, from *bosk, bush,* bush, from Old Norse *buskr.*] —**bos·ki·ness** *n.*

bo's'n. Variant of **boatswain.**

Bos·ni·a and Her·ce·go·vi·na (bŏz′nē-ə; hĕrt′sə-gō-vē′nə). Republic

in southern Europe. In 1946 the provinces of Bosnia and Hercegovina joined to form a constituent republic of Yugoslavia. The republic became independent in 1992. Area, 51,129 square kilometers (19,665 square miles). Population, 4,355,000. Capital, Sarajevo.

Bos·ni·an (bŏz′nē-ən) *adj.* Also **Bos·ni·ac** (-nē-ăk′). Of or pertaining to Bosnia.

—*n.* Also **Bos·ni·ac.1.** A native of Bosnia. **2.** The Serbo-Croatian language of this people.

bos·om (bo`oz′əm, boo′zəm) *n.* **1.** The chest of a human being; especially, the female breasts. **2.** The part of a garment covering the chest. **3.** The midst or heart: *"Deep in the bosom of the hills"* (George Eliot). **4.** A close enveloping relationship: *in the bosom of her family.* **5.** The chest considered as the source of feelings, hopes, and desires.

—*adj.* Beloved; intimate: *a bosom friend.* [Middle English *bosom,* Old English *bosm.*]

bos·om·y (boo′zə-mē, boo′zə-mē) *adj.* Having large breasts; busty.

bos·on (bō′sŏn) *n.* A particle, such as a photon, pion, or alpha particle, having zero or integral spin and obeying Bose-Einstein statistics. Compare **fermion.** [J.C. BOSE + -ON.]

Bos·po·rus (bŏs′pər-əs). The strait joining the Black Sea and the Sea of Marmara. Istanbul lies on its northern shore. Currents moving in opposite directions make the waters extremely turbulent.

boss¹ (bôs, bŏs) *n.* **1. a.** An employer or supervisor of workers; manager; foreman. **b.** A person who makes decisions or exercises authority. **2.** A professional politician who controls a party or political machine often by underhand or shady means.

—*v.* **bossed, bossing, bosses.** —*tr.* **1.** To supervise or control. **2.** To command in an arrogant or domineering manner. Often used with *around.* —*intr.* To be or act as a boss.

—*adj. Slang.* First-rate; topnotch. [Dutch *baas,* master, from Middle Dutch *baes,* from Germanic *basa-* (unattested).]

boss² *n.* **1.** A circular or knoblike protuberance, as on a shield. **2.** A raised area used as ornamentation. **3.** *Architecture.* A raised ornament, as at the intersection of the ribs in vaulted roofs. **4.** *Machinery.* **a.** An enlarged part of a shaft to which another shaft is coupled or to which a wheel or gear is keyed. **b.** A hub, especially of a propeller. **5.** A metal ornament used for protecting the corners or centers of books. **6.** *Geology.* An intrusive mound of igneous rock.

—*tr.v.* **bossed, bossing, bosses.** **1.** To decorate with bosses. **2.** To emboss. [Middle English *boce,* from Old French, from Vulgar Latin *bottia†* (unattested).]

boss³ (bôs, bŏs) *n.* A cow or calf. [Origin unknown.]

bossa nova (bŏs′ə nō′və) *n.* **1.** A rhythmic dance similar to the samba, originating in Brazil. **2. a.** A complex dance rhythm extending over two bars. **b.** A musical composition using this rhythm, as one written for the dance. [Portuguese, "new voice."]

bos·sism (bô′sĭz′əm, bŏs′ĭz′əm) *n.* The domination of a political organization by a political boss.

boss·y¹ (bô′sē, bŏs′ē) *adj.* **-ier, -iest.** Commanding, domineering, or overbearing. —**boss·i·ly** *adv.* —**boss·i·ness** *n.*

bossy² *adj.* Decorated with studs or similar raised ornaments.

bossy³ *n., pl.* **-sies.** *Informal.* A cow or calf. [From BOSS (cow).]

boss·y-boots (bô′sē-boots′, bŏs′ē-) *n. British Informal.* A bossy person.

Bos·ton¹ (bô′stən, bŏs′tən). Capital of Massachusetts, in the eastern part of the state on Boston Bay, an arm of the Atlantic Ocean. It played a prominent role in the developing opposition to colonial rule that led to the American Revolution. In the 19th century it was one of the centers of the movement to abolish slavery in the South. Today it is a major financial center and a leading port. Its industries include publishing, food processing, and the manufacture of machinery and electronic equipment. Tourism is also important to its economy.

Boston². Port in Lincolnshire in east-central England. Puritans sailed from Boston to Massachusetts Bay (1630) and gave the American settlement its name.

Boston bag *n.* A handbag or satchel for books and papers, with handles on both sides of the top opening.

Boston bull *n.* A dog, the **Boston terrier** *(see).*

Boston cream pie *n.* A cake with a custard filling.

Boston fern *n.* A fern, *Nephrolepis exaltata bostoniensis,* having arching or drooping fronds with opposite leaflets.

Boston ivy *n.* A widely cultivated climbing woody vine, *Parthenocissus tricuspidata,* native to Asia, that has three-lobed leaves and that frequently covers the outer walls of buildings. Also called "Japanese ivy."

Boston lettuce *n.* A type of cultivated lettuce forming a rounded head and having soft-textured, yellow-green leaves.

Boston rocker *n.* A 19th-century American wooden rocking chair with a curved seat, a high spindled back, and usually a headpiece with stenciled decorations.

Boston Tea Party *n.* A protest staged by American colonists in Boston (December 16, 1773) against the British tax on imported tea. The colonists, disguised as Indians, boarded British ships in Boston Harbor and threw chests of tea overboard.

Boston terrier *n.* A small dog of a breed that originated in New England as a cross between a bull terrier and a bulldog. Also called "Boston bull."

bosun. Variant of **boatswain.**

Bos·well (bŏz′wĕl′, -wəl) *n.* An assiduous and devoted admirer, student, and recorder of another's words and deeds. [After James BOSWELL.] —**Bos·wel·li·an** *adj.*

Boswell, James (1740–95). Scottish lawyer and author. He practiced law all his life, but his greatest interest was literature. His most famous work is the biography *The Life of Samuel Johnson* (1791).

Bos•worth Field (bŏz′wûrth′). Site of the final battle in the Wars of the Roses, near Leicester in central England, where Richard III, the last Plantagenet king, was defeated on August 22, 1485, by Henry Tudor.

bot, bott (bŏt) *n.* The parasitic larva of a botfly. [Middle English, probably of Low German origin; akin to Dutch *bot*†.]

bot. **1.** botanical; botanist; botany. **2.** bottle.

bo•tan•i•cal (bə-tăn′ĭ-kəl) *adj.* Also **bo•tan•ic** (bə-tăn′ĭk). *Abbr.* **bot.** Of or pertaining to plants, plant life, or the science of botany.
∼*n.* A drug, medicinal preparation, or similar substance obtained from a plant or plants. [French *botanique,* from Late Latin *botanicus,* from Greek *botanikos,* from *botanē*†, pasture, herb, plant.] **—bo•tan•i•cal•ly** *adv.*

botanical garden *n.* A place where plants are grown for scientific study and public exhibition, and at which herbaria and libraries are maintained.

botanical Latin *n.* An international language used by botanists to name and describe all new plant species.

bot•a•nist (bŏt′n-ĭst) *n. Abbr.* **bot.** One who specializes in the study of plants.

bot•a•nize (bŏt′n-īz′) *v.* **-nized, -nizing, -nizes.** *—intr.* **1.** To secure plants for botanical study. **2.** To examine plants scientifically. *—tr.* To investigate (an area) for botanical study. **—bot•a•niz•er** *n.*

bot•a•ny (bŏt′n-ē) *n., pl.* **-nies.** *Abbr.* **bot.** **1.** The study of plants, covering their classification, form, function, ecology, and economic importance. **2.** The plant life of a particular area or period. **3.** The characteristics of a plant group: *the botany of grasses.* **4.** A particular system of botany: *the botany of Linnaeus.* [From BOTANICAL.]

Bot•a•ny Bay (bŏt′n-ē). Inlet of the Tasman Sea, just south of Sydney in Australia. It was visited by Capt. James Cook (1770) and given its name by Sir Joseph Banks, the botanist in Cook's crew, for the variety of new flora he found on its shores.

Botany wool *n.* The wool of the merino sheep. [After BOTANY BAY.]

bo•tar•go (bə-târ′gō) *n.* A relish made from the roe of tuna or mullet. [From Italian *bottarga* (obsolete), from Egyptian Arabic *batārikh,* roe, from Coptic.]

botch (bŏch) *tr.v.* **botched, botching, botches.** **1.** To ruin through clumsiness. Often used with *up.* **2.** To make or perform clumsily; bungle. **3.** To repair or mend clumsily.
∼*n.* A ruined or defective piece of work: *"I have made a miserable botch of this description"* (Nathaniel Hawthorne). [Middle English *bocchen*†, to patch up, mend.] **—botch•er** *n.*

botch•y (bŏch′ē) *adj.* **-ier, -iest.** Carelessly or clumsily done or made; imperfect. **—botch•i•ly** *adv.*

bot•fly (bŏt′flī′) *n., pl.* **-flies.** Also **bot fly.** Any of various winged insects, chiefly of the families Gasterophilidae, Oestridae, and Cuterebridae, having larvae that are parasitic on man, livestock, rodents, and other animals. See **bots.**

both (bōth) *adj.* One and the other; two in conjunction: *Both boys arrived.*
∼*pron.* The one and the other: *Both are patriots.*
∼*conj.* Used with *and* to show that each of two coordinated words or things in coordinated phrases or clauses is included: *both Keats and Shelley.* [Middle English *bothe, bathe,* from Old Norse *bāthir.*]

Bo•tha (bō′tə), **Louis** (1862–1919). South African general in the Second Anglo-Boer War and first prime minister of the Union of South Africa after its establishment in 1910.

Botha, Pieter Willem (1916–). Prime minister of the Republic of South Africa from 1978 to 1989.

both•er (bŏth′ər) *v.* **-ered, -ering, -ers.** *—tr.* **1.** To irritate, particularly by small annoyances; pester; harass. **2. a.** To make agitated or nervous; fluster. **b.** To make confused or perplexed; bewilder; puzzle. **3.** To disturb, as by asking questions or by intrusion. **4.** To give trouble to: *a back condition that bothers him constantly.* *—intr.* To trouble or concern oneself. **—**See Synonyms at **annoy.**
∼*n.* **1.** A cause or state of disturbance or confusion. **2.** A person or thing that causes annoyance or disturbance. **3.** *British Slang.* Aggressive behavior or disturbance.
∼*interj. Chiefly British.* Used to express mild irritation. [18th century : Anglo-Irish, perhaps akin to POTHER.]

both•er•a•tion (bŏth′ə-rā′shən) *n.* Irritation; vexation; bother.
∼*interj.* Used to express irritation.

both•er•some (bŏth′ər-səm) *adj.* Causing vexation or irritation; troublesome.

Both•ni•a, Gulf of (bŏth′nē-ə). The northernmost arm of the Baltic Sea, lying between Sweden and Finland and separated from the Baltic by the Ahvenanmaa. The gulf is 725 kilometers (450 miles) long and is ice-covered for five months of the year.

Both•well (bŏth′wəl), **James Hepburn, 4th Earl of** (*c.* 1536–78). Scottish courtier, the third husband of Mary, Queen of Scots. He helped suppress the rebellion led by the Earl of Moray (1565) and became the adviser and confidant of the queen. In 1567 he was acquitted of the murder of her husband, Lord Darnley. He was forced to flee to Denmark soon after his own marriage to Mary.

both•y (bŏth′ē, bōth′-) *n., pl.* **bothies.** *Scottish.* A hut or other shelter, used by people, especially shepherds, working outdoors. [18th century : perhaps akin to BOOTH.]

bo tree (bō) *n.* An Asiatic tree, the **peepul** *(see).* According to Buddhist tradition, this is the tree under which the Buddha attained enlightenment. [Singhalese *bo,* from Pali *bodhi(taru),* "(tree of) wisdom," from Sanskrit *bodhi,* wisdom, enlightenment, from *bodhati,* he awakes.]

bot•ry•oi•dal (bŏt′rē-oid′l) *adj.* Also **bot•ry•oid** (bŏt′rē-oid′). Formed like a bunch of grapes. Said especially of minerals. [Greek *botruoeidēs* : *botrus*†, bunch of grapes + -OID.] **—bot•ry•oi•dal•ly** *adv.*

bots (bŏts) *n. Used with a singular or plural verb.* A disease of horses and cattle caused by infestation of the intestines with botfly larvae.

Bot•swa•na (bŏt-swä′nə). Formerly **Bech•u•a•na•land** (bĕch′wän′ə-lănd′, bĕch′ə-). Republic in southern Africa between Namibia in the west and Zimbabwe in the east, north of South Africa. It was named Botswana when it gained independence (1966). The country is a high tableland, mostly covered by arid desert sands. Cattle breeding is the chief economic activity, but important reserves of nickel, copper, diamonds, and coal were discovered in the 1960's. Area, 600,372 square kilometers (231,805 square miles). Population, 1,300,000. Capital, Gaborone. See map, next page.

bott. Variant of **bot.**

botte (bŏt) *n.* In fencing, a hit with the sword. [French, "hit."]

Bot•ti•cel•li (bŏt′ĭ-chĕl′ē), **Alessandro di Mariano di Vanni Filipepi,** known as "Sandro" (*c.* 1444–1510). Italian painter of the Florentine Renaissance. His flowing draftmanship is seen to advantage in his two best-known paintings, *Primavera* and the *Birth of Venus.*

bot•tle (bŏt′l) *n. Abbr.* **bot., btl.** **1.** A receptacle, usually glass, having a narrow neck and mouth that can be plugged, corked, or capped. **2.** The quantity a bottle contains. In the case of wine bottles, this is usually between 70 and 75 centiliters. **3. a.** A bottle filled with milk or other liquid and used to feed a baby. **b.** Intoxicating drink: *took to the bottle.* **4.** *Physics.* A configuration of magnetic fields used to confine a plasma in a fusion reactor.
∼*tr.v.* **bottled, -tling, -tles.** To place in a bottle. **—bottle up.** **1.** To hold in; restrain: *bottled up her emotions.* **2.** To seal up; block. **—hit the bottle.** *Slang.* To drink alcoholic liquor to excess. [Middle English *botel,* from Old French *botele, botaille,* from Medieval Latin *butticula,* diminutive of Late Latin *buttis,* cask, BUTT.] **—bot•tler** *n.*

bot•tle•brush (bŏt′l-brŭsh′) *n.* **1.** Any of various shrubs or trees of the genera *Callistemon* and *Melaleuca,* native to Australia. They have dense spikes of red flowers with protruding stamens that suggest a brush used to clean bottles. **2.** Any of various similar plants of the genus *Greyia,* native to southern Africa.

bottle club *n.* A private establishment where patrons may purchase bottles of liquor and keep them for consumption after legal closing hours.

bottled gas *n.* Gas, such as butane or propane, stored under pressure in portable tanks.

bottle-feed (bŏt′l-fēd′) *tr.v.* **-fed** (-fĕd), **-feeding, -feeds.** To feed (a baby) from a bottle rather than from the breast.

bottle gentian *n.* A plant, *Gentiana andrewsii,* of eastern and central North America, having deep-blue flowers that remain closed. Also called "closed gentian."

bottle gourd *n.* A vine, the **calabash** *(see),* or its fruit.

bottle green *n.* Dark bluish green. **—bot•tle-green** *adj.*

bot•tle•neck (bŏt′l-nĕk) *n.* **1.** The narrow part of a bottle near the top. **2. a.** A point on a road where traffic is held up because of an obstruction or narrow section. **b.** The hold-up so caused. **3. a.** Part of a process which is slower than other parts and delays the entire process. **b.** The delay caused. **4.** *Music.* A style of playing the guitar, especially in blues and country-and-western music, with a hollow metal cylinder which is held around the finger and slid along the strings.
∼*tr.v.* **bottlenecked, -necking, -necks.** To impede or slow down by creating a bottleneck.

bot•tle-nosed dolphin (bŏt′l-nōzd′) *n.* Any of several marine mammals of the genus *Tursiops,* having a short, protruding beak. Also called "bottlenose."

bottle tree *n.* Any of several trees of the genus *Brachychiton,* native to Australia, characterized by a bottlelike swelling of the trunk.

bot•tom (bŏt′əm) *n.* **1. a.** The lowest or deepest part of anything. **b.** The far end of something. **c.** The last place, as on a list. **d.** The worst or least favorable point: *started life at the bottom.* **2.** The underside. **3.** The supporting part of something; a foundation; base. **4.** The basic underlying cause or origin: *to find out what's at the bottom of the dispute.* **5.** The land below a body of water: *a river bottom.* **6.** *Often* **bottoms.** Low-lying alluvial land adjacent to a river; bottom land. **7. a.** *Nautical.* The part of a ship's hull below the water line. **b.** A ship: *"English merchants did much of their overseas trade in foreign bottoms"* (G.M. Trevelyan). **8. bottoms.** The trousers of pajamas. **9.** *Informal.* The buttocks. **10.** The seat of a chair. **11.** Staying power, as of a horse; stamina.
∼*adj.* Lowest; undermost; fundamental.
∼*v.* **bottomed, -toming, -toms.** *—tr.* **1.** To provide with an underside or foundation. **2.** To provide (a chair) with a bottom. **3.** To establish on a foundation or basis; ground; found. Used with *on* or *upon*: *The theory is bottomed on questionable assumptions.* **4.** To grasp the meaning of; fathom: *bottom a mystery.* *—intr.* To rest on or touch the bottom: *The submarine bottomed on the ocean floor.* **—at bottom.** Basically; actually. **—bottom out.** To descend to the lowest point possible, after which only a rise may occur: *Coffee bottomed out in the market.* **—bottoms up.** *Informal.* Drain your glass. [Middle English *botme,* Old English *botm,* from Germanic.] **—bot•tom•er** *n.*

botfly *A type of fly that bears some resemblance to a bee. The botfly often lays its eggs on horses' legs. When the horse licks the spot, the eggs are swallowed and later hatch into parasitic larvae inside the horse's stomach. The full-grown larvae, or maggots, eventually pass out in the animal's manure and undergo the transformation to adults in the soil.*

bottle-nosed dolphin *Dolphins—members of the air-breathing whale family—were once land mammals but readapted to life in the sea. Among the world's most intelligent animals, they communicate by using a vocabulary of grunts, squeaks, and whistles produced by forcing air past valves and flaps in their breathing holes.*

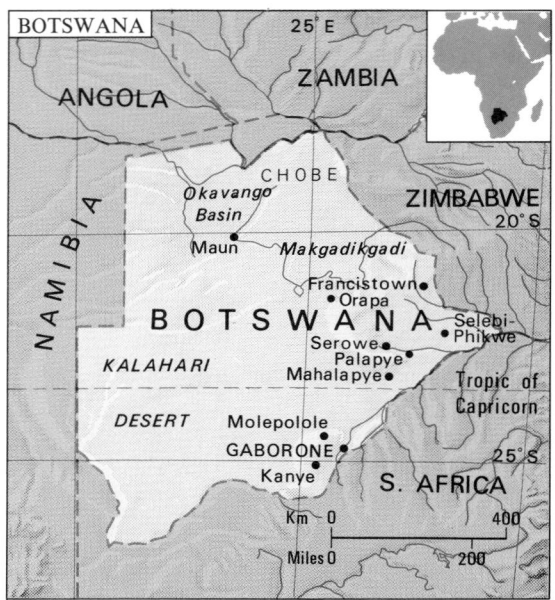

bottom break n. A branch arising from the stem base of a plant.
bottom drawer n. British. A **hope chest** (see).
bottom fauna n. Marine vegetation growing in the benthic region of the ocean depths.
bottom land n. Low land along a river.
bot·tom·less (bŏt′əm-lĭs) adj. **1.** Having no bottom. **2.** Too deep to be measured. **3.** Difficult or impossible to understand; unfathomable. **4.** Having no limit; limitless. —**bot·tom·less·ly** adv.
bottom line n. **1.** The lowest line in a financial statement, showing net income or loss. **2.** The results or basic implications of anything. **3.** The main or essential point.
bot·tom-line (bŏt′əm-lĭn′) adj. Concerned exclusively with costs and profits.
bot·tom·most (bŏt′əm-mōst′) adj. Deepest; most profound.
bottom round n. A cut of meat, as a steak or roast, taken from the outer section of a round of beef.
bot·tom·ry (bŏt′əm-rē) n. A contract by which a shipowner borrows money to finance a voyage, pledging the vessel as security. [BOTTOM (a ship) + -RY, by analogy with Dutch bodemerij.]
bot·u·lin (bŏch′ŏŏ-lĭn) n. Any of several nerve toxins produced by the bacterium Clostridium botulinum and found in improperly canned or improperly smoked foods. [New Latin botulinus, from Latin botulus, sausage.]
bot·u·li·num (bŏch′ə-lī′nəm) n. A bacterium, Clostridium botulinum, that secretes botulin. [New Latin, from Latin botulus, sausage.]
bot·u·lism (bŏch′ŏŏ-lĭz′əm) n. An often fatal food poisoning caused by botulin and characterized by vomiting, abdominal pain, coughing, muscular weakness, and visual disturbance. [German Botulismus, "sausage-poisoning," from Latin botulus, sausage.]
bou·chée (bŏŏ-shā′) n. A puff pastry case usually with a creamed filling. [French, "mouthful."]
Bou·cher (bŏŏ-shā′), **François** (1703-70). French painter. He was an outstanding representative of the rococo style of the 18th century, noted for his tapestries and fêtes galantes.
bou·clé (bŏŏ-klā′) n. **1.** A type of yarn, usually three-ply and having one thread looser than the others, which produces a rough-textured cloth. **2.** Fabric woven or knitted from this yarn. [French, "curled."]
Bou·dic·ca (bŏŏ-dĭk′ə). Also **Bo·a·di·ce·a** (bō-ăd′ə-sē′ə) (died A.D. 60). Queen of the Iceni people of eastern Britain. When her husband, King Prasutagus, died in 59 or 60, she led the **Iceni** in what is now Norfolk and Suffolk in a fierce and temporarily successful onslaught against the Romans who had seized her late husband's kingdom.
bou·doir (bŏŏ′dwär′, -dwòr′) n. A woman's private sitting room, dressing room, or bedroom. [French, "place for pouting," from Old French bouder, to pout, sulk (imitative).]
bouf·fant (bŏŏ-fänt′) adj. Puffed-out; full: a bouffant hair style. [French, present participle of bouffer, to swell, puff up (the cheeks), from Old French (imitative).]
bouffe (bŏŏf) n. Comic opera. See **opera buffa.**
Bou·gain·ville (bŏŏ′gən-vĭl′). Volcanic island in the South Pacific Ocean, the largest of the Solomon Islands. It forms part of Papua New Guinea.
Bougainville, Louis Antoine de (1729-1811). French navigator and explorer. In c. 1764 he established a short-lived French colony on the Falkland Islands and in 1766-69 made a voyage around the world with a crew that included astronomers and naturalists.
bou·gain·vil·le·a, bou·gain·vil·lae·a (bŏŏ′gən-vĭl′ē-ə, -vĭl′yə) n. Any of several woody tropical American vines of the genus Bougainvillea, having inconspicuous flowers surrounded by showy red,

purple, or orange bracts. [After Louis Antoine de BOUGAINVILLE.]
bough (bou) n. A large branch of a tree. [Middle English bow, bough, Old English bōg, bōh, from Germanic.]
bought. Past tense and past participle of **buy.**
bought·en. Regional. A past participle of **buy.**
bou·gie (bŏŏ′zhē, -jē) n. **1.** A wax candle. **2.** Medicine. **a.** A slender, pliable implement inserted into a bodily canal, such as the urethra or rectum, to dilate the passageway. **b.** A suppository. [French, from Old French, a fine wax imported from Bougie (Arabic Bujiya), town in Algeria.]
bouil·la·baisse (bŏŏ′yə-bās′) n. A highly seasoned fish stew made with several kinds of fish and shellfish. [French, earlier bouille-abaisse, from Provençal bouiabaisso, "boil (and) settle" (jocular command to the pot, because the fish is rapidly cooked).]
bouil·lon (bŏŏ′yŏn′, bŏŏl′yŏn′, -yən) n. The stock, often served as a broth, made from the liquid in which beef or chicken is simmered. [French, from Old French, from boulir, to boil, from Latin bullīre.]
bouillon cube n. A small cube of evaporated seasoned meat, poultry, or vegetable stock.
boul. boulevard.
Bou·lan·ger (bŏŏ-län-zhā′), **Georges Ernest Jean Marie** (1837-91). French general and politician. After the Franco-Prussian War he rallied the extreme right wing in France against Germany for the loss of Alsace-Lorraine. For a time he was the most popular French politician, but was dismissed from the government and the army (1887) by republicans who viewed him as a potential military dictator.
Boulanger, Nadia (1887-1979). French teacher of musical composition. She taught and influenced several generations of modern composers, including Milhaud, Copland, and Elliott Carter.
boul·der, bowl·der (bōl′dər) n. A large rounded mass of rock lying on the surface of the ground, or sometimes embedded in the soil, and generally different in composition from other rocks in the immediate vicinity. [Middle English bulder (ston), from Scandinavian, akin to dialectal Swedish bullersten, stone in a stream : buller-, "rounded object."]
boulder clay n. An unstratified clay deposited by glaciers and ice sheets. Also called "till."
Boulder Dam. See **Hoover Dam.**
bou·le[1] (bŏŏ′lē, bŏŏ-lā′) n. **1. a. Boule.** The senate of 400 members founded in ancient Athens by Solon. **b.** A legislative assembly in any of the states of ancient Greece. **2. Boule.** The lower house of the modern Greek legislature. [Greek boulē, "will," "council."]
boule[2] (bŏŏl) n. A pear-shaped synthetic sapphire, ruby, or other alumina-based gem, produced by fusing and tinting alumina. [French, "ball," from Latin bulla, bubble, ball.]
boule[3]. Variant of **buhl.**
boules (bŏŏl) n. Used with a singular verb. A version of bowling played in France with metal balls on a hard surface. [French, "bowls."]
boul·e·vard (bŏŏl′ə-värd′, bŏŏl′ə-) n. Abbr. **blvd., boul.** A broad city street, often tree-lined and landscaped. [French, from Old French boloart, belouart, rampart, promenade converted from an old rampart, from Middle Dutch bolwerc, from Middle High German, BULWARK.]
bou·le·var·dier (bŏŏ′lə-vär-dyā′, bŏŏl′ə-vär-dîr′) n. A man-about-town. [French, a man who frequents boulevards, from BOULEVARD.]
bou·le·ver·se·ment (bŏŏ′lə-věr′sə-mäN′) n. **1.** A reversal. **2.** A violent uproar; tumult. [French, from Old French bouleverser, to overturn : boule, ball + verser, to overturn, from Latin versare, to turn.]
Bou·lez (bŏŏ-lēz′), **Pierre** (1925-). French composer and conductor. He is a leading composer of the French avant garde, in particular as an adherent of 12-tone atonality. His best-known works are Le Marteau sans Maître (1955) and Pli selon Pli (1960).
boulle. Variant of **buhl.**
Bou·logne(-sur-Mer) (bŏŏ-lōn′sür-mâr′, -loin′-). Port and resort in Pas-de-Calais department in northwest France, on the English Channel. It has grown from its Celtic origins to be the leading fishing port in France.
Boult (bōlt), **Sir Adrian Cedric** (1889-1983). British orchestral conductor. In 1930 he became conductor of the new BBC Symphony Orchestra, with whom he stayed until 1950, when he became musical director of the London Philharmonic.
Bou·mé·di·enne (bŏŏ-mä-dē-ěn′), **Houari** (1928-78). Algerian independence leader and politician. He studied in Cairo in the early 1950's, then returned secretly to Algeria in 1955 to take part in guerrilla action against the French. He was head of the National Liberation Army operating from Tunisia (1960-67), and when Algeria gained its independence he served under Ahmed Ben Bella as minister of defense. He directed an army coup that overthrew Ben Bella (1965) and assumed the presidency of Algeria.
bounce (bouns) v. **bounced, bouncing, bounces.** —intr. **1. a.** To rebound elastically from an impact, as a rubber ball. **b.** To collide and rebound elastically several times in succession. **2.** To walk or move in a springy or excited way: The child bounced into the room. **3.** Informal. To be sent back by a bank as valueless: The check bounced. **4.** Informal. To recover after a setback. Used with back. —tr. **1.** To cause (a body, such as a ball) to collide and rebound. **2.** To cause to rebound repeatedly. **3.** Slang. To expel by force. **4.** Slang. To dismiss from employment.
~n. **1.** A bound or rebound. **2.** A sudden spring or leap. **3. a.** A loud or heavy blow or thump. **b.** Archaic. The sound of an explo-

sion: *"He speaks plain cannon fire, and smoke and bounce"* (Shakespeare). **4.** Capacity to bounce; spring: *A ball with bounce.* **5.** Spirit; liveliness. **6.** *Slang.* Expulsion; dismissal. **7.** *British.* An instance of impudent bluff: *"The whole story is a bounce of his own"* (Thomas De Quincey). [Middle English *bunsen, bonchen,* to beat, thrust, stamp (probably imitative).]

bounc·er (boun′sər) *n.* **1.** One that bounces. **2.** A person employed to expel disorderly people from a public place.

bounc·ing (boun′sĭng) *adj.* **1.** Vigorous; healthy: *a bouncing baby.* **2.** Spirited; lively.

bouncing Bet *n.* A plant, the **soapwort** *(see).* [*Bet,* pet form of *Elizabeth* (from its flower clusters, suggesting bouncing girls).]

bounc·y (boun′sē) *adj.* **-ier, -iest. 1. a.** Characterized by a capacity to bound or spring. **b.** Elastic; springy. **2.** Having vigor and buoyancy; lively. **—bounc·i·ly** *adv.*

bound[1] (bound) *intr.v.* **bounded, bounding, bounds. 1.** To leap forward or upward; spring. **2.** To progress quickly by bounds.
~*n.* **1.** A leap; jump. **2.** A bounce. [French *bondir,* to bounce, originally "to rebound," from Old French, to resound, from Vulgar Latin *bombitīre* (unattested), to hum, buzz, from Latin *bombīre,* to buzz, from *bombus,* a deep hollow sound, buzz, from Greek *bombos.*]

bound[2] *n.* **1.** *Usually* **bounds.** Boundary; limit: *His joy knew no bounds.* **2. bounds.** The territory on, within, or near limiting lines: *the bounds of the kingdom.* —See Synonyms at **boundary. —out of bounds. 1.** In an area outside official boundaries. **2.** Transgressing moral or conventional limits.
~*v.* **bounded, bounding, bounds.** —*tr.* **1.** To set a limit to. **2.** To constitute the boundary or limit of. **3.** To identify and set the boundaries of; demarcate. —*intr.* To border on another country, state, or place; adjoin. —See Synonyms at **limit.** [Middle English *bounde,* from Old French *bunde,* from Medieval Latin *bodina,* from Gaulish *bodina*† (unattested).]

bound[3]**.** Past tense and past participle of **bind.**
~*adj.* **1. a.** Confined by bonds; tied. **b.** Restricted; obstructed. Often used in combination: *snowbound.* **2.** Under legal or moral obligation; under contract: *bound by his promise.* **3.** Indentured: *a bound apprentice.* **4.** *Abbr.* **bd.** Encased in a cover or binding: *bound volumes.* **5.** Predetermined; certain: *We are bound to be late.* **6.** Constipated. **—bound up in.** Wholly dedicated to: *She is bound up in her career.*

bound[4] *adj.* **1.** Heading for; going toward: *bound for Sydney.* Often used after an expression of direction: *outward bound; homeward bound.* **2.** Intended for; on one's way to: *bound for a career in medicine.* [Middle English *boun,* prepared, ready to go, from Old Norse *būinn,* past participle of *būa,* to dwell, prepare.]

bound·a·ry (boun′drē, -də-rē) *n., pl.* **-ries. 1.** Something that indicates a border or limit. **2.** The border or limit so indicated. [From dialect *bounder,* from BOUND (limit).]
Synonyms: *border, bound, confine, end, frontier, limit.*

boundary layer *n. Physics.* The nearly motionless fluid layer found immediately adjacent to the surface of a solid, past which the fluid flows.

boundary rider *n. Australian.* A person employed to ride around the boundary of a sheep or cattle ranch and maintain the fences.

bound·en (boun′dən) *adj.* **1.** Obligatory: *his bounden duty.* **2.** *Archaic.* Under obligation; obliged. [From *bounden,* obsolete past participle of BIND.]

bound·er (boun′dər) *n.* **1.** One that bounds. **2.** *Chiefly British Informal.* A man who fails to behave like a gentleman.

bound form *n.* A linguistic element that always occurs as part of another word, as *-ly* in *lovely.* Compare **free form.**

bound·less (bound′lĭs) *adj.* Without limit; infinite. —See Synonyms at **infinite. —bound·less·ly** *adv.* **—bound·less·ness** *n.*

boun·te·ous (boun′tē-əs) *adj.* **1.** Giving generously and kindly. **2.** Copious; plentiful. [Middle English *bountevous, bounteuous,* from Old French *bontif, bontive,* benevolent, from *bonte,* BOUNTY.] **—boun·te·ous·ly** *adv.* **—boun·te·ous·ness** *n.*

boun·ti·ful (boun′tĭ-fəl) *adj.* **1.** Generous. **2.** Abundant; plentiful. **—boun·ti·ful·ly** *adv.* **—boun·ti·ful·ness** *n.*

boun·ty (boun′tē) *n., pl.* **-ties. 1.** Liberality in giving. **2.** Something that is given liberally. **3.** A reward, inducement, or payment, especially one given by a government for acts beneficial to the state, such as killing predatory animals or enlisting for military service. —See Synonyms at **bonus.** [Middle English *bounte,* from Old French *bonté,* from Latin *bonitās* (stem *bonitāt-*), goodness, from *bonus,* good.]

bounty hunter *n.* One who hunts predatory animals or criminals and outlaws for a bounty.

bou·quet (bō-kā′, bo͞o- *for sense 1;* bo͞o-kā′ *for sense 2*) *n.* **1.** A cluster of flowers; a nosegay. **2.** The fragrance typical of a wine or a liqueur. **3.** A compliment; praise. —See Synonyms at **smell.** [French, from Old North French *bosquet,* clump, diminutive of Old French *bosc,* forest, from Germanic.]

bou·quet gar·ni (bō-kā′ gär-nē′, bo͞o-) *n., pl.* **bouquets garnis** (bō-käz′gär-nē′, bo͞o-). A bunch of herbs tied together or wrapped in cheesecloth, immersed in a soup, stew, or the like as seasoning. [French, "garnished bouquet."]

bour·bon (bûr′bən) *n.* A whiskey distilled from a fermented mash containing not less than 51 percent corn. [After *Bourbon* County, Kentucky.]

Bour·bons (bo͝or′bənz). Members of the French royal line descending from Louis I, Duke of Bourbon (*c.* 1270–1342). They make up one of the most powerful ruling houses in modern European history. The first Bourbon king of France was Henry IV, and the line occupied the French throne until 1793 (when the French monarchy was abolished); it was briefly restored in 1814 and ruled again until the overthrow of Charles X in the July Revolution of 1830. The Bourbons have been kings of Spain since 1700, and another branch of the family ruled in Naples and Sicily from 1734 until 1860.

bour·don (bo͝or′dən) *n.* **1.** The monotonic drone bass of a bagpipe. **2.** An organ stop, commonly of the 16-foot pipes. [Middle English *burdoun,* from Old French *bourdon,* drone, from Vulgar Latin *burdō* (stem *burdon-*) (unattested), of imitative origin.]

Bourdon gauge *n.* A type of pressure gauge having a narrow spiral tube attached to a pointer and closed at one end, which tends to uncoil as the pressure in the tube increases. [After Eugène *Bourdon* (1808–84), French inventor.]

bourg (bo͝org; *French* bo͞or) *n.* **1.** A French medieval village, especially one situated near a castle. **2.** A French market town. [Middle English, fortified town, from Old French, from Late Latin *burgus.*]

bour·geois[1] (bo͝or-zhwä′, bo͝or′zhwä′) *n., pl.* **bourgeois. 1.** One belonging to the bourgeoisie. **2.** The middle classes; the bourgeoisie. **3.** One whose attitudes and behavior are marked by conformity to the standards and conventions of the middle class. **4.** In Marxist theory, a member of the property-owning class; a capitalist, as opposed to a member of the proletariat.
~*adj.* **1.** Of or typical of the middle class. Often used derogatorily to suggest such qualities as mediocrity or a preoccupation with respectability and material values. **2.** In Marxist theory, of, pertaining to, or dominated by the property-owning class. [French, from Old French *burgeis,* from *bourg,* fortified town, BOURG.]

bour·geois[2] (bər-jois′) *n. Printing.* A size of type, approximately 9-point. [French, middle class, perhaps from its middling size between long primer and brevier.]

bour·geoise (bo͝or-zhwäz′, bo͝or′zhwäz′) *n., pl.* **-geoises** (-zhwä′zĭz). A female member of the bourgeoisie. **—bour·geoise** *adj.*

bour·geoi·sie (bo͝or′zhwä-zē′) *n.* **1.** The middle classes. **2.** In Marxist theory, the social group opposed to the proletariat in the class struggle; the capitalist class. [French.]

bour·geoi·si·fy (bo͝or-zhwä′zə-fī) *tr. v.* **-fied, -fying, fies.** To turn (a member of the working class) into a member of the bourgeoisie; impart bourgeois values to. **—bour·geoi·si·fi·ca·tion** *n.*

bourgeon. Variant of **burgeon.**

Bourgogne. See **Burgundy** (region).

Bour·gui·ba (bo͝or-gē′bə), **Habib ben Ali** (1903–). Tunisian politician. His political career began in the 1930's, when he formed a nationalist party opposed to French rule. He took part in the pre-independence negotiations and was elected prime minister of independent Tunisia (1956). He became president (1957) and held that office until 1987, when he was removed by premier Zine el-Abidine Ben Ali.

Bourke-White (bûrk′hwīt′), **Margaret** (1906–71). U.S. photographer and author. Her many photographic books and essays explored such diverse subjects as the rural South, Soviet life, and the emancipation of concentration camp victims. She was an editor of *Life* magazine for 33 years.

bourn[1]**, bourne** (bôrn, bōrn, bo͝orn) *n.* A stream or small brook. [Middle English *burne,* variant of *burn,* BURN (brook).]

bourn[2]**, bourne** *n. Archaic.* **1.** The terminal point of a journey or course of action; a goal. **2.** A boundary, as between properties. [French *borne,* from Old French, BOUND (limit).]

Bourne·mouth (bôrn′məth, bōrn′-, bo͝orn′-). Resort town on England's southern coast, at the eastern border of Dorset. Until 1974 it was in Hampshire.

bour·rée (bo͞o-rā′, bo͞o-) *n.* **1.** An old French dance resembling the gavotte, and usually in quick duple time beginning with an upbeat. **2.** The music for this dance. [French, "faggot" (probably from its rude movements), from *bourrer,* to stuff, from Old French *bourre,* stuffing, fluff, from Late Latin *burra,* shaggy garment.]

Bourse (bo͝ors) *n.* The stock exchange of a city of continental Europe, especially Paris. [French, "purse," from Late Latin *bursa,* from Greek.]

bour·sin (bo͝or-săɴ′, bo͝or′săɴ) *n.* A soft, creamy French cheese, flavored with herbs and garlic or peppercorns.

bouse (bouz) *v.* **boused, bousing, bouses.** Also **bowse.** *Nautical.* —*tr.* To hoist or pull up with a tackle. —*intr.* To hoist. [16th century : origin obscure.]

bou·stro·phe·don (bo͞o′strə-fēd′n, -fē′dŏn′) *n.* An ancient method of writing in which the lines are inscribed alternately from right to left and from left to right. [Greek *boustrophēdon,* turning like an ox (while ploughing) : *bous,* ox + *strephein,* to turn.] **—bou·stroph·e·don·ic** (bo͞o-strŏf′ə-dŏn′ĭk) *adj.*

bout (bout) *n.* **1.** A contest between antagonists; a match: *a wrestling bout.* **2.** A period of time spent in a particular way or state; a spell: *bouts of depression and drinking.* [Earlier *bought,* a turn (as in ploughing), Middle English *bought,* bend, turn, from Middle Low German *bucht.*]

bou·tique (bo͞o-tēk′) *n.* A small retail shop that specializes in gifts, fashionable clothes, or accessories. [French, from Old Provençal *botica,* from Greek *apothēkē,* storeroom, from *apotithenai,* to put away : *apo-,* away + *tithenai,* to put, place.]

bou·ton (bo͞o-tôn′) *n.* A club-shaped enlargement at the end of a nerve fiber. [Fr., button.]

bou·ton·niere, bou·ton·nière (bo͞o′tə-nîr′, -tən-yâr′) *n.* A flower or

PRONUNCIATION KEY

ă, pat; ā, pay; âr, care;
ä, father, are; b, bib;
ch, church; d, deed; ĕ, pet;
ē, be; f, fife; g, gag; h, hat;
hw, which; ĭ, pit; ī, pie;
îr, pier; j, judge; k, kick;
l, lid, needle; m, mum;
n, no, sudden; ng, thing;
ŏ, pot; ō, toe; ô, paw, for;
oi, noise; ou, out; o͝o, book;
o͞o, boot; p, pop; r, roar;
s, sauce; sh, ship, dish;
t, tight; th, thin, path;
th, this, bathe; ŭ, cut; ûr, fur;
v, valve; w, with; y, yes;
z, zebra, size; zh, vision;
ə, about, item, edible,
gallop, circus, peaceful

IN FOREIGN WORDS:

à, *Fr.* ami; œ, *Fr.* feu, *Ger.* schön; ü, *Fr.* tu, *Ger.* über;
KH, *Ger.* ich, *Scot.* loch;
ɴ, *Fr.* bon; y′, *Fr.* Compiègne

STRESS MARKS:

Primary stress: ′
in·cite′ (ĭn-sīt′)
Secondary stress: ′
in′sight′ (ĭn′sīt′)

bowerbird *The bowerbird gets its name from the unusual courtship behavior of the male. It attracts a mate by building a bower and adorning it with brightly colored shells, flowers, and feathers.*

bowline knot *A bowline forms a loop that cannot close.*

small bunch of flowers worn in a buttonhole, usually on a lapel. [French.]

bou·var·di·a (bŏŏ-vär′dē-ə) *n.* Any of several tropical American shrubs of the genus *Bouvardia,* having clusters of white or red, often fragrant flowers. [New Latin *Bouvardia;* after Charles *Bouvard* (died 1658), French physician.]

Bou·vier des Flan·dres (bŏŏ-vyā′ də flän′dərz; *French* bŏŏ-vyā′ dä flän′dr′) *pl.* **Bouviers des Flandres** (*pronounced as singular*). A rough-coated dog of a breed originally used in Belgium for herding and guarding cattle. [French, "cowherd of Flanders."]

bou·zou·ki (bŏŏ-zŏŏ′kē, bə-) *n.* A Greek fretted string instrument resembling the mandolin. [Modern Greek *mpouzouki,* perhaps from Turkish *büyük,* large.]

Bo·vet (bō-vā′), **Daniel** (1907–92). Italian pharmacologist, born in Switzerland. For his discovery of gallamine and development of antihistamines, sulfa drugs, and other muscle relaxants used in surgery, he was awarded the Nobel Prize for medicine (1957).

bo·vid (bō′vĭd) *adj.* Of or belonging to the family Bovidae, which includes hoofed, hollow-horned ruminants such as cattle, sheep, goats, and buffaloes.
~*n.* A member of the Bovidae. [New Latin *Bovidae,* from Latin *bōs* (stem *bov-*), ox, cow.]

bo·vine (bō′vīn′, -vēn′) *adj.* 1. Of, pertaining to, or resembling an ox, cow, or other ruminant animal of the genus *Bos.* 2. Sluggish; dull; stolid.
~*n.* A bovine animal. [Late Latin *bovīnus,* from Latin *bōs* (stem *bov-*), ox, cow.]

bow¹ (bou) *n.* 1. The front section of a ship or boat. 2. The oar or oarsman closest to the bow of a boat.
~*adj.* Of or close to the bow. [Middle English, from Middle Low German *boog.*]

bow² (bou) *v.* **bowed, bowing, bows.** —*intr.* 1. To bend or curve downward; stoop. 2. To incline the body or head or bend the knee in greeting, consent, courtesy, acknowledgment, submission, or veneration. 3. To yield or comply; defer: *I bow to your superior knowledge.* —*tr.* 1. To bend (the head, knee, or body) in order to express greeting, consent, courtesy, submission, or veneration. 2. To convey (greeting or consent, for example) by bowing. 3. To escort deferentially and with bows: *He bowed us into the restaurant.* 4. To cause to acquiesce or submit. 5. To oppress; overburden. Often used with *down: Grief bowed him down.* —See Synonyms at **yield.** —**bow and scrape.** To behave in an obsequious manner. —**bow out.** To remove oneself from a situation or agreement.
~*n.* An inclination of the head or body, as in greeting, consent, courtesy, acknowledgment, submission, or veneration. —**make one's bow.** To enter or retire formally. —**take a bow.** To recognize and accept applause or an introduction. [Middle English *bowen,* Old English *būgan.*]

bow³ (bō) *n.* 1. Something that is bent, curved, or arched: *a bow in a road.* 2. A weapon consisting of a curved rod of a resilient material, especially wood, held tightly in an arch by a taut bowstring strung from end to end and used to propel arrows. 3. An archer, or archers collectively. 4. A rod having horsehair drawn tightly between its two raised ends, used in playing instruments such as the violin, cello, or viola. 5. a. A knot usually having two loops and two ends; a bowknot. b. This knot made with ribbon or braid and used to decorate the hair, clothing, or the like. 6. The loop forming the handle of a pair of scissors or large key. 7. a. A frame for the lenses of a pair of eye glasses. b. The part of such a frame passing over the ear. 8. A rainbow. 9. An ox-bow.
~*v.* **bowed, bowing, bows.** —*tr.* 1. To bend (something) into the shape of a bow. 2. To play (a stringed instrument) with a bow. —*intr.* 1. To bend into a curve or bow. 2. To play a stringed instrument with a bow. [Middle English *bowe,* Old English *boga,* bow, arch.]

bow compass (bō) *n.* A drawing compass with legs that are connected by an adjustable metal spring band. Also called "bow-spring compass."

Bowd·ler (boud′lər), **Thomas** (1754–1825). British editor, famous for his expurgated editions of classic literary works, especially his *Family Shakespeare* (1818).

bowd·ler·ize (bōd′lə-rīz′, boud′-) *tr.v.* **-ized, -izing, -izes.** To expurgate prudishly. [After Thomas BOWDLER.] —**bowd·ler·ism** *n.* —**bowd·ler·i·za·tion** *n.*

bow·el (bou′əl, boul) *n.* 1. An intestine, especially in humans. 2. *Often* **bowels.** The digestive tract below the stomach. 3. **bowels.** The inner depths of anything: *in the bowels of the ship.* 4. **bowels.** *Archaic.* The seat of pity or the gentler emotions.
~*tr.v.* **boweled, -eling, -els.** Also *Chiefly British* **-elled, -elling.** To remove the bowels or entrails from; disembowel. [Middle English *b(o)uel,* from Old French *bo(u)el, boiel,* from Latin *botellus,* diminutive of *botulus,* sausage.]

bowel movement *n.* 1. The discharge of waste matter from the body; defecation. 2. The matter discharged; feces.

Bow·en (bō′ən), **Elizabeth Dorothea Cole** (1899–1973). British novelist and short-story writer, born in Ireland. Her first collection of short stories, *Encounters,* appeared in 1923; her first novel, *The Hotel,* in 1927. Her most popular novels were *The House in Paris* (1935) and *The Heat of the Day* (1949).

bow·er¹ (bou′ər) *n.* 1. A shaded, leafy recess; an arbor. 2. *Poetic.* A private chamber; a boudoir. 3. *Poetic.* A rustic cottage; a country retreat.
~*tr.v.* **bowered, -ering, -ers.** *Poetic.* To enclose in or as if in a

bower; embower. [Middle English *bour,* dwelling, inner apartment, Old English *būr.*] —**bow·er·y** *adj.*

bower² *n.* In the game of euchre, either of the two highest cards, the jack of trumps (*right bower*) or the jack of the same color as the trump (*left bower*). [German *Bauer,* "farmer," "peasant," jack (in cards), from Middle High German *būre, gebūre,* from Old High German *gibūro.*]

bower³ *n.* The heaviest of a ship's anchors, carried at the bow. Also called "bower anchor."

bow·er·bird (bou′ər-bûrd′) *n.* 1. Any of various songbirds of the family Ptilonorhynchidae, of Australia and New Guinea. The males of many species build bowers of grasses, twigs, and colored materials to attract females. 2. *Australian Informal.* A person who collects trivia.

bow·er·y (bou′ər-ē, bou′rē) *n.* A farm or plantation owned by one of the early Dutch settlers of New York. [Dutch *bouwerij,* farm, estate, from *bouwen,* to cultivate, from Middle Dutch.]

Bow·er·y, the (bou′ər-ē, bou′rē). A street and section of lower Manhattan in New York City. The street was once a road to the farm, or *bouwerie,* owned by Peter Stuyvesant.

bow·fin (bō′fĭn′) *n.* A primitive, bony, freshwater fish, *Amia calva,* of central and eastern North America. Also called "dogfish," "mudfish."

bow-front (bō′frŭnt′) *adj.* Having an outward-curving front: *a bow-front bureau.*

bow·head (bō′hĕd′) *n.* A whale, *Balaena mysticetus,* of Arctic seas, having a large head. [From the curved top of its head.]

Bow·ie (bō′ē, bŏŏ′ē), **James** (1796–1836). Texas soldier. He was a colonel in the Texan forces during their struggle for independence from Mexico. He popularized the bowie knife, which was probably designed by his brother, Rezin P. Bowie. He died during the heroic defense of the Alamo.

bow·ie knife (bō′ē, bŏŏ′ē) *n.* A single-edged, steel hunting knife, about 38 centimeters (15 inches) in length, having a hilt and a crosspiece. [After Col. James BOWIE.]

bow·knot (bō′nŏt′) *n.* A knot with large, decorative loops.

bowl¹ (bōl) *n.* 1. a. A hemispherical container, wider than deep, for food or fluids. b. The contents of such a vessel. 2. A bowl-shaped part of something, such as a spoon or pipe. 3. a. A bowl-shaped building such as an amphitheater or a football stadium. b. Any of various football games played after the usual season between selected teams. 4. A bowl-shaped topographical depression. 5. *Archaic.* A drinking goblet. [Middle English *bolle,* Old English *bolla.*]

bowl² *n.* 1. A large, wooden ball weighted or slightly flattened so as to roll with a bias. 2. A roll or throw of the ball, as in bowling. 3. *Machinery.* A revolving cylinder or drum.
~*v.* **bowled, bowling, bowls.** —*intr.* 1. To participate in a game of bowling. 2. To throw or roll a ball in bowls or tenpin bowling. 3. To move smoothly and rapidly. Usually used with *along.* 4. *Cricket. Abbr.* **b** To deliver the ball from one end of the pitch toward the batsman at the other, keeping the arm straight throughout. —*tr.* 1. To throw or roll (a ball) in bowling. 2. To make or achieve by bowling. 3. *Cricket. Abbr.* **b** To retire (a batsman) with a bowled ball that knocks the bails off the wicket. Used with *out.* —**bowl over.** 1. To knock over (a person or thing); cause to fall. 2. *Informal.* To take by surprise; astound. [Middle English *boule, bowle,* originally "ball," from Old French *boule,* from Latin *bulla.*]

bowlder. Variant of **boulder.**

bow·leg (bō′lĕg′) *n.* A leg having an outward curvature in the region of the knee.

bow·leg·ged (bō′lĕg′ĭd, -lĕg′d) *adj.* Having bowlegs.

bowl·er¹ (bō′lər) *n.* One that bowls.

bowler² *n. Chiefly British.* A man's hat, a **derby** (see). [After John *Bowler,* 19th-century London hatmaker.]

bow·line (bō′lĭn, -līn′) *n.* 1. *Nautical.* A rope leading from the weather edge of a square sail to the bow to hold it forward when sailing close-hauled. 2. A knot forming a loop that does not slip. In this sense, also called "bowline knot." —**on a bowline.** *Nautical.* Close-hauled. [Middle English *bouline,* probably from Middle Low German *bōline : boog,* BOW (of a ship) + *līne,* line.]

bowl·ing (bō′lĭng) *n.* 1. A game played by rolling a ball down a wooden alley in order to knock down a triangular group of ten pins. Also called "tenpins." 2. Any of various similar games, such as skittles or ninepins. 3. Lawn bowling (see).

bowling alley *n.* 1. A smooth, level, wooden alley used in bowling. 2. A building or room containing such alleys.

bowling green *n.* A level grassy area for lawn bowling.

bow·man¹ (bō′mən) *n., pl.* **-men** (-mĭn). *Archaic.* An archer.

bow·man² (bou′mən) *n., pl.* **-men** (-mĭn). An oarsman stationed at the bow of a boat.

Bow·man's capsule (bō′mənz) *n. Anatomy.* In vertebrates, the cup-shaped end of a kidney tubule that surrounds a knot of blood capillaries and with them forms the Malpighian body. [After Sir William *Bowman* (1816–92), English surgeon.]

Bowman's glands *n.* The olfactory glands, which keep the olfactory surface moist.

bow·man's root (bō′mənz) *n.* A plant, *Gillenia trifoliata,* of eastern North America, having compound leaves and small white or pinkish flowers. Also called "Indian physic."

bow pen (bō) *n.* A bow compass with a pen at the end of one leg.

bow saw (bō) *n.* A type of saw with a narrow blade held in a large frame, used for cutting curves.

bowse. *Nautical.* Variant of **bouse.**

bow·shot (bō'shŏt') *n.* The distance an arrow can be shot.
bow-spring compass (bō'sprĭng') *n.* A **bow compass** (see).
bow·sprit (bou'sprĭt', bō'-) *n.* A spar extending forward from the stem of a ship. [Middle English *bouspret,* from Middle Low German *bōchsprēt, bugsprēt.*]
Bow Street runner (bō) *n.* A member of the first organized police force in London, set up in 1748 by Bow Street magistrate's court.
bow·string (bō'strĭng') *n.* The string of a bow.
bowstring hemp *n.* **1.** Any of various plants of the genus *Sansevieria,* having thick, erect leaves. **2.** The fiber from the leaves of these plants, used for cordage and in packing.
bow tie (bō) *n.* A man's small tie tied in the shape of a bow.
bow window (bō) *n.* A bay window built in a curve.
bow-wow (bou'wou'; bou'wou' *for sense 2*) *n.* **1.** An imitation or representation of the bark of a dog. **2.** A dog. Used by or to children. [Imitative.]
bow·yer (bō'yər) *n.* **1.** An archer. **2.** One who makes bows.
box¹ (bŏks) *n.* **1.** A rigid, usually rectangular container, typically having a lid or cover. **2.** The amount or quantity such a container can hold. **3.** A separate compartment in a public place, such as a theater, for the accommodation of a small group. **4. a.** A small structure serving as a shelter: *a sentry box.* **b.** Any of various containers used for a particular purpose, such as a *money box.* **5.** *British.* A small country house: *a shooting box.* **6.** A **box stall** (see). **7.** The raised seat for a driver of a coach or carriage. **8.** *Baseball.* **a.** An area marked out by chalk lines where the batter stands. **b.** Any of various designated areas for other team members, such as the pitcher, catcher, and coaches. **9.** Featured printed matter, enclosed by lines, a border, or white space and placed within or between text columns. **10.** A cut in the side of a tree through which sap is collected. **11.** An insulating, enclosing, or protective casing or part in a machine. **12.** An awkward or perplexing situation; predicament. *~tr.v.* **boxed, boxing, boxes. 1.** To pack or put in a box. **2.** To confine or as if in a box. Often used with *in* or *up.* **3.** *Nautical.* To boxhaul. **—box the compass. 1.** To name the points of the compass in proper order. **2.** To make a complete revolution or reversal. **—the box.** *Chiefly British Informal.* Television. [Middle English *box,* Old English *box,* from Late Latin *buxis,* variant of Latin *pyxis,* box (made of boxwood), from Greek *puxis,* from *puxos,* box tree.]
box² *n.* A blow or slap with the hand: *a box on the ear.*
~v. **boxed, boxing, boxes.** *—tr.* **1.** To hit with the hand or fist. **2.** To take part in a boxing match with. *—intr.* To fight with the fists; spar. [Middle English *box†.*]
box³ *n., pl.* **box** or **boxes. 1.** Any evergreen tree or shrub of the genus *Buxus;* especially, *B. sempervirens,* used for hedges, borders, and garden mazes. Also called "boxwood." **2.** The wood of this tree, **boxwood** (see). **3.** Any of several trees whose timber or foliage resembles that of box. [Middle English *box,* Old English *box,* from Latin *buxus,* from Greek *puxos.*]
Box and Cox *n. Sometimes* **box and cox. 1.** Two people who live in the same house but never see each other. **2.** Two people who take turns to perform the same role, function, or position. [After a stage farce by J. Maddison Morton (1811–91) in which two characters share a room in this way.] **—Box and Cox** *v.*
box calf *n.* Calfskin treated with chromium salts and having square markings on the grain. [After Joseph *Box,* 19th-century London bootmaker.]
box camera *n.* A camera shaped like a box with a simple lens and viewfinder.
box·car (bŏks'kär') *n.* An enclosed and covered railway car for the transportation of freight.
box coat *n.* **1.** A heavy overcoat formerly worn by coachmen. **2.** A coat designed to hang loose from the shoulders. [From BOX (seat for coach driver).]
box·el·der (bŏks'ĕl'dər) *n.* A widely cultivated maple tree, *Acer negundo,* of North America, having compound leaves with lobed leaflets. Also called "ash-leaved maple."
box·er¹ (bŏk'sər) *n.* One who boxes; specifically, a pugilist.
boxer² *n.* A short-haired dog of a breed developed in Germany, having a brownish coat and a short, square-jawed muzzle. [German *Boxer,* from English BOXER.]
Box·er (bŏk'sər) *n.* A member of a secret society in China that attempted in 1900 to drive foreigners from the country by violence and to force Chinese Christians to renounce their religion. [Rough translation of Mandarin Chinese *yì hé quán,* "righteous harmonious fists," altered from *yì hé tuán,* "Righteous Harmonious Brigade" (name of the society) : *yì,* righteousness + *hé,* harmony + *tuán,* brigade.]
boxer shorts *pl.n.* Men's full-cut undershorts.
box·fish (bŏks'fĭsh) *n., pl.* **-fishes** or collectively **boxfish.** A fish, the trunkfish (see).
box girder *n.* A hollow girder with a square or rectangular section.
box·haul (bŏks'hôl') *tr.v.* **-hauled, -hauling, -hauls.** To turn (a square-rigged ship) about on its heel by bracing the foresails against the wind and steering round.
box·ing¹ (bŏk'sĭng) *n.* Material used for boxes.
boxing² *n.* The sport or profession of fighting with the fists; especially, the modern sport of fighting with gloved hands, inside a raised ring.
Boxing Day *n. British.* The first weekday after Christmas, observed as a holiday in Britain and other Commonwealth countries, when Christmas boxes were traditionally given to household employees and other service workers.

boxing glove *n.* A heavily padded leather glove worn in boxing.
box jellyfish *n.* A highly venomous jellyfish, *Chironex fleckeri,* common in Australian waters.
box kite *n.* A tailless kite consisting of a rectangular, box-shaped frame, encircled with cloth or paper bands.
box lacrosse *n. Chiefly Canadian.* A form of lacrosse played in an enclosure by teams of seven players. Also informally called "boxla."
box lunch *n.* A lunch packed in a container, as a box, especially for traveling.
box office *n.* **1.** A ticket office, as of a theater or stadium. **2.** The drawing power of a theatrical entertainment or of a performer; popular appeal. **—box-of·fice** *adj.*
box pleat *n.* A double pleat formed by two facing folds.
box score *n.* A printed summary of a baseball or basketball game, in the form of a table listing each player and the statistics for his performance.
box seat *n.* A seat in a box at a theater, concert hall, or stadium.
box set *n.* A stage set with a ceiling and three walls.
box spanner *n.* A type of spanner with a socket that fits over the nut.
box spring *n.* A bedspring consisting of a frame enclosed with cloth and containing rows of coiled springs.
box stall *n.* An enclosed stall for a single animal.
box·thorn (bŏks'thôrn') *n.* A shrub, the **matrimony vine** (see).
box turtle *n.* Any of several North American turtles of the genus *Terrapene,* having a high-domed shell.
box·wood (bŏks'wŏod') *n.* **1.** The hard, light-yellow wood of the box tree, used to make musical instruments, rulers, inlays, and engraving blocks. **2.** A shrub or tree, **box** (see).
box·y (bŏk'sē) *adj.* **-ier, -iest.** Like a box.
boy (boi) *n.* **1.** A male child or youth. **2.** *Informal.* A grown man; fellow. Often used in the plural to imply a spirit of camaraderie among a group of men: *a night out with the boys.* **3.** A manservant. *~interj.* Used as a mild exclamation. [Middle English *boye, bay, bye,* originally "male servant," "knave," possibly from Norman French *abuié, embuié* (unattested), "fettered," from Old French *embuier,* to fetter, from Vulgar Latin *imboiāre* (unattested) : *in-,* in + *boiae,* collar for the neck, fetters, from Greek *boeiai (dorai),* ox(hides), hence thongs made from oxhide, from *bous,* ox.] **—boy·hood** *n.*
bo·yar (bō-yär') *n.* Also **bo·yard. 1.** A member of a former Russian aristocratic order abolished by Peter I. **2.** A member of a former aristocratic class of Romania. [Earlier *boiaren,* from Russian *boyarin,* from Old Russian, "of the highest rank," from Old Slavic *boljarinŭ,* from Old Turkic *boila,* a title.]
boy·cott (boi'kŏt') *tr.v.* **-cotted, -cotting, -cotts.** To abstain from using, buying, or dealing with, as a protest or means of coercion. *~n.* The act or an instance of boycotting. [After Charles C. *Boycott* (1832–97), land agent for the Earl of Erne, in County Mayo, Ireland, who was ostracized by the tenants for refusing to lower the rents.] **—boy·cott·er** *n.*
boy·friend (boi'frĕnd') *n.* Also **boy friend. 1.** A male friend. **2.** A favored male sexual or romantic partner; a sweetheart or lover.
boy·ish (boi'ĭsh) *adj.* Characteristic of or befitting a boy: *a boyish prank.* **—boy·ish·ly** *adv.* **—boy·ish·ness** *n.*
Boyle (boil), **Robert** (1627–91). Irish physicist and chemist, sometimes called "the father of chemistry" since his precision in defining chemical elements and chemical reactions was a major step in separating the science of chemistry from alchemy.
Boyle's law *n.* The principle that at a fixed temperature the pressure of a gas varies inversely with its volume. The law is obeyed only by a hypothetical ideal gas. Real gases approximately obey Boyle's law at high temperatures and low pressures. [After R. BOYLE.]
Boy Scout *n.* A member of a worldwide organization of young men and boys, founded in England in 1908, for character development and citizenship training.
boy·sen·ber·ry (boi'zən-bĕr'ē) *n., pl.* **-ries. 1.** A prickly bramble hybridized from the loganberry and various blackberries and raspberries. **2.** The large, wine-red, edible berry borne by this plant. [After Rudolph *Boysen,* 20th-century U.S. horticulturist.]
Boz (bŏz). Pen name of Charles Dickens (see).
bo·zo (bō'zō) *n., pl.* **-zos.** *Slang.* **1.** A fellow; guy. **2.** A dunce; fool. [Possibly from Spanish *bozot,* "down growing on the cheeks of youths."]
bp, b.pt. boiling point.
bp. bishop.
B.P. 1. Bachelor of Pharmacy. **2.** Bachelor of Philosophy. **3.** bills payable. **4.** British Pharmacopoeia.
B/P bills payable.
bpd, b.p.d. barrels per day.
B.Pd., B.Pe. Bachelor of Pedagogy.
B.P.E. Bachelor of Physical Education.
B.Ph., B.Phil. Bachelor of Philosophy.
bpi, b.p.i. bits per inch.
b.pl. birthplace.
B.P.O.E. Benevolent and Protective Order of Elks.
Br The symbol for the element bromine.
br. 1. branch. **2.** bridge. **3.** *Law.* brief. **4.** bronze. **5.** brother. **6.** brown.
Br. 1. Breton. **2.** Britain; British. **3.** Brother (religious).
B/R bills receivable.
bra (brä) *n.* A brassiere. **—bra·less** *adj.*

Bow Street Runner *One of the group of paid full-time "thief takers," who were the ancestors of modern policemen. The group was formed by the English novelist and playwright Henry Fielding after he became a magistrate at London's Bow Street Court in 1748. A runner's job was to detect and arrest criminals and to protect travelers from highwaymen and footpads.*

boxer *Often used as police and guide dogs, boxers are a hybrid breed descended from bulldogs and mastiffs.*

bracken *The largest and most common of British ferns, seen here on a hillside in Dorset, England.*

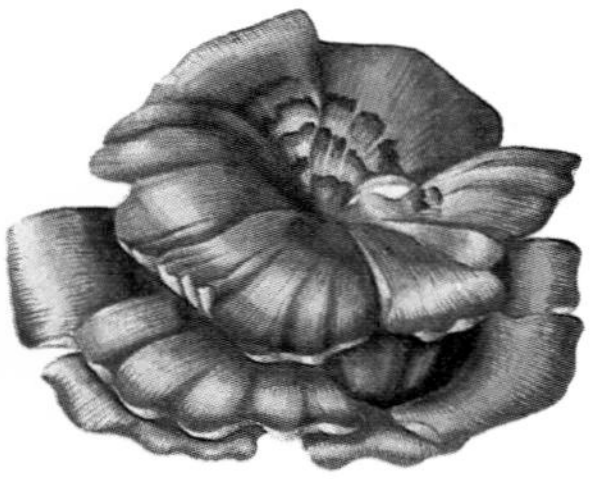

bracket fungus *A large, sometimes platelike, inedible fungus that grows on oak or beech trees in midwinter.*

PRONUNCIATION KEY

ă, pat; ā, pay; âr, care;
ä, father, are; b, bib;
ch, church; d, deed; ĕ, pet;
ē, be; f, fife; g, gag; h, hat;
hw, which; ĭ, pit; ī, pie;
îr, pier; j, judge; k, kick;
l, lid, needle; m, mum;
n, no, sudden; ng, thing;
ŏ, pot; ō, toe; ô, paw, for;
oi, noise; ou, out; o͝o, book;
o͞o, boot; p, pop; r, roar;
s, sauce; sh, ship, dish;
t, tight; th, thin, path;
th, this, bathe; ŭ, cut; ûr, fur;
v, valve; w, with; y, yes;
z, zebra, size; zh, vision;
ə, about, item, edible, gallop, circus, peaceful

IN FOREIGN WORDS:

à, *Fr.* ami; œ, *Fr.* feu, *Ger.* schön; ü, *Fr.* tu, *Ger.* über; KH, *Ger.* ich, *Scot.* loch; N, *Fr.* bon; y', *Fr.* Compiègne

STRESS MARKS:

Primary stress: ′
in·cite′ (ĭn-sīt′)
Secondary stress: ′
in′sight′ (ĭn′sīt′)

Bra·bant (brə-bănt′, -bänt′). A densely populated industrial and agricultural province of central Belgium, whose center is Brussels. It is the southern part of the old duchy of Brabant, which is now divided between Belgium and the Netherlands.

brab·ble (brăb′əl) *intr.v.* **-bled, -bling, -bles.** To quarrel noisily; to wrangle.
∼*n.* A petty dispute; a squabble. [Possibly from Middle Dutch *brabelen,* to jabber (imitative).] **—brab·bler** *n.*

brace (brās) *n., pl.* **braces** or **brace** (for sense 13 only). **1.** A device that holds or fastens two or more parts together or in place; a clamp. **2.** Any device that steadies or holds something erect, such as a supporting beam in a building. **3. braces.** *Chiefly British.* A pair of suspenders. **4.** *Medicine.* An appliance used to support a bodily part. **5.** *Often* **braces.** *Dentistry.* An arrangement of adjustable bands and wires fixed to the teeth to correct irregular alignment. **6.** *Nautical.* A rope by which a yard is controlled and secured on a square-rigged ship. **7.** *Archery.* A protective pad strapped to the bow arm. **8.** *Music.* A leather loop that slides to change the tension on the cords of a drum. **9.** *Music.* **a.** A symbol connecting two or more staves. **b.** A set of connected staves. **10.** A cranklike handle with an adjustable aperture at one end for securing and turning a bit. See **brace and bit. 11.** *Printing.* One of two symbols, { }, used to connect written or printed lines that should be considered together or are related in some way. **12.** *Mathematics.* Either of a pair of symbols, { }, used to indicate aggregation or to clarify the grouping of quantities when parentheses and square brackets have already been used. Also informally called "bracket." **13.** *pl.* **brace.** A pair of like things: *a brace of partridges.* —See Synonyms at **couple.**
∼*v.* **braced, bracing, braces.** —*tr.* **1.** To provide or strengthen with a brace or braces. **2.** To support or hold steady with or as if with a brace or braces. **3.** To prepare or position so as to be ready for an impact or danger. **4.** To invigorate; stimulate. **5.** *Nautical.* To turn (the yards of a ship) by the braces. —*intr.* **1.** To get ready; make preparations. **2.** *Military.* To assume a position of rigid attention. **—brace up.** To summon one's strength or endurance. [Middle English, arm guard, support, from Old French *brace,* the two arms, from Latin *bracchia,* plural of *bracchium,* arm, from Greek *brakhiōn.*]

brace and bit *n.* A hand tool for boring holes, consisting of a drilling bit rotated by a handle.

brace·let (brās′lĭt) *n.* **1.** An ornamental band or chain encircling the wrist. **2. bracelets.** *Slang.* Handcuffs. [Middle English, from Old French *bracelet,* diminutive of *bracel,* "little arm," armlet, from Latin *bracchiāle,* from *bracchium,* arm.]

brac·er[1] (brā′sər) *n.* **1.** Something or someone that braces. **2.** *Informal.* A stimulating drink, especially an alcoholic one; a tonic.

bracer[2] *n.* An arm or wrist guard worn by archers and fencers. [Middle English, arm guard, from Old French *brasseure,* from *bras,* arm, from Latin *bracchium.*]

bra·ce·ro (brə-sâr′ō) *n., pl.* **-ros.** A Mexican agricultural or industrial laborer permitted to enter the United States and work for a limited period of time. Compare **wetback.** [Spanish, manual laborer, from *brazo,* arm, from Latin *bracchium,* from Greek *brakhiōn.*]

bra·chi·a (brā′kē-ə, brăk′ē-ə) *n.* Plural of **brachium.**

bra·chi·al (brā′kē-əl, brăk′ē-) *adj.* Of, pertaining to, or resembling the arm or a similar or homologous part. [Latin *bracchialis,* from *bracchium,* arm, BRACHIUM.]

bra·chi·ate (brā′kē-ĭt, brăk′ē-, -āt′) *adj. Botany.* Having widely spreading branches arranged in pairs.
∼*intr.v.* (brā′kē-āt′, brăk′ē-) **brachiated, -ating, -ates.** To swing by the arms from branch to branch, as certain apes do. [Latin *bracchiātus,* from *bracchium,* arm, BRACHIUM.] **—bra·chi·a·tion** *n.*

brach·i·o·pod (brăk′ē-ə-pŏd′, brā′kē-) *n.* Any of various marine invertebrates of the phylum Brachiopoda, having bivalve dorsal and ventral shells and tentacled structures on either side of the mouth, used for feeding. Also called "lamp shell." [BRACHI(UM) + -POD.] **—brach·i·o·pod** *adj.*

bra·chi·o·saur·us (brăk′ē-ō-sôr′əs, brā′kē-) *n.* A dinosaur belonging to the genus *Brachiosaurus,* which grew up to 50 tons in weight and was the heaviest known dinosaur. [BRACHI(UM) + -SAURUS.]

bra·chis·to·chrone (brə-kĭs′tə-krōn′) *n. Mathematics.* A curve that is the path of an object falling freely between two points in the shortest possible time. [Greek *brakhistos,* shortest, superlative of *brakhus,* short + *khronos,* time.]

bra·chi·um (brā′kē-əm, brăk′ē-) *n., pl.* **brachia** (brā′kē-ə, brăk′ē-ə). An arm or a homologous anatomical structure, such as a flipper or wing. [Latin *bracchium,* arm, forearm, from Greek *brakhiōn.*]

brachy– *comb. form.* Indicates shortness; for example, **brachyuran.** [Greek *brakhus,* short.]

brach·y·ce·phal·ic (brăk′ē-sə-făl′ĭk) *adj.* Also **brach·y·ceph·a·lous** (-sĕf′ə-ləs). Having a short, almost round head, the width of which is at least 80 percent as great as the length. Compare **dolichocephalic, mesocephalic.** See **cephalic index.** [BRACHY- + -CEPHALIC.] **—brach·y·ceph·a·ly** (brăk′ē-sĕf′ə-lē), **brach·y·ceph·a·lism** (brăk′ē-sĕf-ə-lĭz′əm) *n.*

brach·y·dac·tyl·ic (brăk′ē-dăk-tĭl′ĭk) *adj.* Also **brach·y·dac·ty·lous** (-dăk′tə-ləs). Having abnormally short fingers or toes. [BRACHY- + -DACTYLIC.] **—brach·y·dac·tyl·i·a** (brăk′ē-dăk-tĭl′ē-ə), **brach·y·dac·ty·ly** (brăk′ē-dăk′tə-lē) *n.*

bra·chyl·o·gy (brə-kĭl′ə-jē) *n., pl.* **-gies. 1.** Brief, concise speech. **2.** A shortened or condensed phrase or expression. [Late Latin *brachylogia,* from Greek *brakhulogia* : BRACHY- + -LOGY.]

bra·chyp·ter·ous (brə-kĭp′tər-əs) *adj.* Having short wings. Said of certain insects. [Greek *brakhupteros* : BRACHY- + -PTEROUS.] **—bra·chyp·ter·ism** (brə-kĭp′tə-rĭz′əm) *n.*

brach·y·u·ran (brăk′ē-yo͝or′ən) *adj.* Also **brach·y·u·ral** (-əl), **brach·y·u·rous** (-əs). Of or belonging to the Brachyura, a group of crustaceans characterized by a short abdomen concealed under the cephalothorax, and including the true crabs.
∼*n.* A member of the Brachyura. [New Latin *Brachyura,* "short-tailed ones" : BRACHY- + *-ura,* plural of *-urus,* -UROUS.]

brac·ing (brā′sĭng) *adj.* Invigorating; strengthening.
∼*n.* **1.** A brace. **2.** Braces collectively; a system of braces. **—brac·ing·ly** *adv.* **—brac·ing·ness** *n.*

brack·en (brăk′ən) *n.* **1.** A fern, *Pteridium aquilinum,* having tough stems and branching, finely divided fronds. Also called "brake." **2.** An area overgrown with this fern. **3.** Any large, coarse fern. [Middle English (northern dialect) *braken,* from Old Norse *brakni* (unattested).]

brack·et (brăk′ĭt) *n.* **1.** A simple rigid structure in the shape of an L, one arm of which is fixed to a vertical surface, with the other projecting horizontally to support a shelf or other weight. **2.** Any of various functionally similar fixtures adapted to support loads. **3.** A small shelf or shelves supported by brackets. **4. a.** Either of a pair of symbols, [ ], used to enclose written or printed material or to indicate a mathematical expression considered in some sense a single quantity. Also called "square bracket." **b.** An **angle bracket** *(see).* **c.** *Informal.* A **brace** *(see).* **5.** A section or group within a classification, especially one of taxpayers according to income. **6.** *Military.* The space between two rounds of artillery, the first aimed beyond a target and the second aimed short of it, used to determine range.
∼*tr.v.* **bracketed, -eting, -ets. 1.** To support or hold with a bracket or brackets. **2. a.** To place (qualifying, explanatory, or unrelated material) within brackets. Often used with *off.* **b.** *Mathematics.* To put within brackets, especially angle brackets, to indicate a specified relationship. **c.** To enclose in a brace. Often used with *together.* **3.** To classify or group together. **4.** *Military.* To fire beyond and short of (a target) in order to determine range. [Earlier *bragget,* from Old French *braguette,* codpiece, diminutive of *brague,* mortise, breeches (in plural), from Old Provençal *braga,* from Latin *brāca.*]

bracket fungus *n.* Any of various fungi that form shelflike growths on tree trunks and wood structures.

brack·ish (brăk′ĭsh) *adj.* **1.** Containing some salt; briny. Usually said of water. **2.** Distasteful; unpalatable. [From obsolete *brack,* briny, brine, from Dutch *brak,* salty, from Middle Dutch *brac*†.] **—brack·ish·ness** *n.*

bract (brăkt) *n.* A leaflike plant part, usually small but sometimes showy and brightly colored, located below a flower or an inflorescence. [New Latin *bractea,* from Latin *bractea,* properly *brattea*†, metal plate or leaf.] **—brac·te·al** (brăk′tē-əl) *adj.*

brac·te·ate (brăk′tē-ĭt, -āt′) *adj. Botany.* Bearing bracts. [New Latin *bracteatus,* from *bractea,* BRACT.]

brac·te·o·late (brăk′tē-ə-lĭt, -lāt′) *adj. Botany.* Bearing small bracts, or bracteoles.

brac·te·ole (brăk′tē-ōl) *n.* Also **bract·let** (brăkt′lĭt). *Botany.* A small or secondary bract. [New Latin *bracteola,* from Latin, diminutive of *bractea,* metal plate or leaf. See **bract.**]

brad (brăd) *n.* A tapered nail with a small head or a slight side projection instead of a head. [Middle English *brad, brod,* from Old Norse *broddr,* spike.]

brad·awl (brăd′ôl′) *n.* A small awl with a chisel edge, used to make holes in wood for brads or screws.

Brad·bur·y (brăd′bĕr′ē), **Ray Douglas** (1920–). U.S. science fiction writer. Most of his works are a combination of social criticism and technological fantasy. His most successful novels have been *Fahrenheit 451* (1953), *Something Wicked This Way Comes* (1962), and *The Halloween Tree* (1972).

Brad·ford (brăd′fərd). Textile manufacturing town in the county of West Yorkshire in northern England, on the eastern slopes of the Pennines. It has been an important wool center since the 14th century and since the 18th century the most important worsted center in the country, both for its spinning mills and for its wool exchange.

Bradford, William (1590–1657). English Puritan colonist in America. A signer of the *Mayflower Compact* and an original settler of Plymouth Plantation, he was elected governor for 30 1-year terms and led the colony through its difficult early times.

Brad·laugh (brăd′lô), **Charles** (1833–91). British secularist and politician. In the 1860's and 1870's he campaigned for a number of unpopular causes, such as birth control, national education, and votes for women. In 1880 he was elected to the House of Commons for Northampton, but was refused permission to take his seat when he insisted on the right to affirm, rather than swear on the Bible. Eventually, after being re-elected by Northampton twice, he won the right for an atheist to sit in Parliament (1886).

Brad·ley (brăd′lē), **Omar Nelson** (1893–1981). U.S. general. He played a major part in the Allied victory in World War II. He was appointed chief of staff of the U.S. Army (1948) and was promoted to general (1950). He retired from the army in 1953.

brady– *prefix.* Indicates slowness; for example, **bradycardia.** [New Latin, from Greek *bradus*†, slow.]

Bra·dy (brā′dē), **Mathew B.** (*c.* 1823–96). U.S. photographer. He learned the daguerrotype process from Samuel Morse and opened his own studio in New York in 1844. He was famous for his por-

brachiation

HOW A GIBBON SWINGS THROUGH THE TREES
Acrobatic traveling by long-armed primates

The ability to brachiate (from the Latin *bracchiatus:* having arms) is a characteristic of all apes, although not all of them make frequent use of it. The undisputed masters of the art are the gibbons and siamangs, whose slight bodies, long arms, and hooked fingers are ideal for moving through trees. A gibbon traveling by this means (below) normally moves at human walking pace. But when excited, it can plunge through the tree-tops, or canopy, at astonishing speeds, covering 9 meters (30 feet) with each jump. Although gibbons have thumbs, they move so fast they do not have time to hook the thumbs around the branches.

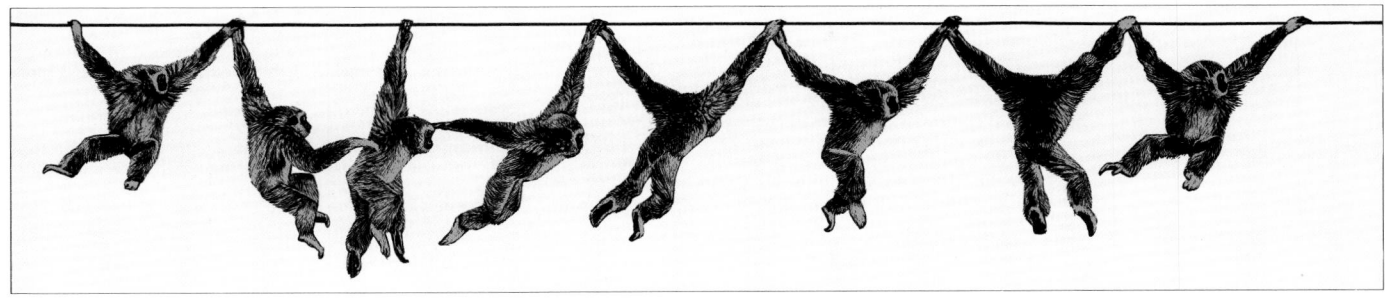

traits and was appointed official Union photographer of the Civil War (1861).

brad·y·car·di·a (brăd′ĭ-kär′dē-ə) *n.* Abnormally slow heartbeat, as less than 50 beats per minute. [New Latin : BRADY- + Greek *kardia,* heart (see **cardia**).] —**brad·y·car·dic** *adj.*

brad·y·kin·in (brăd′ĭ-kī′nən, brā′də-) *n.* A protein, $C_{50}H_{73}N_{15}O_{11}$, found in blood plasma that causes contraction of smooth muscle and dilates blood vessels. [BRADY- + Greek *kin(ēsis),* motion + -IN.]

brad·y·lex·i·a (brăd′ĭ-lĕk′sē-ə) *n.* A slowness of reading not attributable to lack of intelligence. [BRADY- + Greek *lexis,* speech, *legein,* to speak.]

brad·y·lo·gia (brăd′ə-lō′jə, -jē-ə) *n.* Abnormally slow speech. [New Latin : BRADY- + Greek *-logia,* -logy.]

brae (brā) *n. Scottish.* A hillside; slope. [Middle English (Scottish and northern dialects) *bra,* from Old Norse *brā,* eyelash.]

brag (brăg) *v.* **bragged, bragging, brags.** —*intr.* To talk boastfully about oneself, one's possessions, or the like. Often used with *about.* —*tr.* To assert boastfully: *He used to brag he'd become president.* —See Synonyms at **boast.** ~*n.* **1.** Arrogant or boastful speech or behavior. **2.** A braggart; boaster. **3.** A card game similar to poker. ~*adj.* **bragger, braggest.** Exceptionally fine; first-rate. [Middle English *braggen,* probably from *brag†,* "spirited," "mettlesome," hence boastful.] —**brag·ger** *n.*

Bra·ga (brä′gə). A city in northwestern Portugal, the capital of Braga district. It is said to have been founded by the Carthaginians and was an important settlement during Roman times. The city is now an agricultural trade center.

Bra·gan·ça (brə-gän′sə). Also **Bra·gan·za** (-zə). Town in northeast Portugal, capital of the province of the same name. It lies in the Sierra de la Culebra, almost on the border with Spain. Its 12th-century castle was the seat of the Bragança family who ruled Portugal from 1640 to 1910 and Brazil from 1822 to 1889.

Bragg (brăg), **Sir William Henry** (1862–1942). British physicist. He shared the Nobel Prize in physics (1915) with his son, **Sir William Lawrence Bragg** (1890–1971), for their analysis of x-ray spectra and the structure of crystals.

brag·ga·do·ci·o (brăg′ə-dō′shē-ō) *n., pl.* **-os. 1.** A braggart. **2. a.** Empty or pretentious bragging. **b.** Swaggering manner; cockiness. [After *Braggadocchio,* name coined by Spenser for his personification of boasting : *braggad-,* alteration of BRAGGART + *-occio,* Italian augmentative suffix.]

Bragg angle *n.* The angle between an incident x-ray beam and a set of crystal planes for which the reflected or transmitted radiation displays maximum intensity as a result of constructive interference. [After Sir William Lawrence BRAGG.]

brag·gart (brăg′ərt) *n.* One given to loud, empty boasting; a bragger. [French *bragard,* from *braguer,* to brag, obscurely related to Middle English *braggen,* BRAG.] —**brag·gart** *adj.*

Bragg's law *n.* The fundamental law of x-ray crystallography, $n\lambda = 2d\sin\theta$, where *n* is an integer, λ is the wavelength of a beam of x-rays incident on a crystal with lattice planes separated by distance *d,* and θ is the Bragg angle.

Bra·gi (brä′gē). Also **Bra·ge** (brä′gə). *Norse Mythology.* The son of Odin, husband of Ithunn, and god of poetry.

Bra·he (brä′ə), **Tycho** (1546–1601). Danish astronomer. His precise fixing of the planets and the stars, by far the most accurate positioning achieved until then, formed the foundation for **Johannes Kepler's** laws of planetary motion. He also made a detailed study of the supernova (first observed 1572) known as Tycho's star.

Brah·ma¹ (brä′mə) *n. Hinduism.* **1.** The personification of divine reality in its creative aspect as a member of the Hindu triad. See **Vishnu, Shiva. 2.** Variant of **Brahman.** [Sanskrit *bráhman,* prayer,

the universal soul, the Absolute, akin to *brahmán-,* priest. See **Brahman.**]

Brahma² (brä′mə, brä′-) *n. Sometimes* **brama.** A large domestic fowl of a breed originating in Asia, and having feathered legs. [Short for *Brahmaputra;* first brought from Lakhimpur, India, on the BRAHMAPUTRA river.]

Brah·man (brä′mən) *n., pl.* **-mans** (for senses 2, 3). Also **Brah·ma** (-mə), **Brah·min** (-mĭn). **1.** Also **Brah·ma.** *Hinduism.* The essential divine reality of the universe; the eternal spirit from which all being originates and to which all returns. **2.** Also **Brah·min.** *Hinduism.* A member of the highest caste, originally composed only of priests. **3.** Also **Brah·ma, Brah·min.** One of a breed of domestic cattle developed in the southern United States from stock originating in India, and having a hump between the shoulders and a pendulous dewlap. [Sanskrit *brāhmaṇas,* member of the Brahman caste, from *brahmán-,* priest.] —**Brah·man·ic** (brä-mǎn′ĭk), **Brah·man·i·cal** *adj.*

Brah·man·ism (brä′mən-ĭz′əm) *n.* Also **Brah·min·ism** (brä′mĭn-). **1.** The religious practices and beliefs of ancient India as reflected in the Vedas, the earliest religious texts. **2.** The social and religious system of the Brahmans and orthodox Hindus of India, characterized by a caste system and various forms of pantheism. —**Brah·man·ist** *n.*

Brah·ma·pu·tra (brä′mə-pōō′trə). A river rising in the Himalayas in southwestern Tibet and flowing 2,895 kilometers (1,800 miles) through northeastern India to join the Ganges River in Bangladesh. The river's lower course is sacred to Hindus.

Brah·min (brä′mĭn) *n.* **1.** Variant of **Brahman** (except for sense 1). **2.** A highly cultured and socially exclusive person, especially a member of one of the old New England families. —**Brah·min·ic** (brä-mĭn′ĭk), **Brah·min·i·cal** *adj.*

Brah·min·ism (brä′mĭn-ĭz′əm) *n.* **1.** Variant of **Brahmanism. 2.** The attitude or conduct typical of a social or cultural elite.

Brahms (brämz), **Johannes** (1833–97). German composer. His work was a blend of classical tradition with the new Romantic impulse. He wrote a relatively small number of large-scale works, including four symphonies (1876–85), the *German Requiem* (1868), two piano concertos (1881), a violin concerto (1878), and numerous chamber works.

braid (brād) *tr.v.* **braided, braiding, braids. 1.** To interweave three or more strands of; plait. **2.** To decorate or edge with an ornamental trim. **3.** To produce by interweaving: *braid a rug.* **4.** To fasten or entwine (hair) with a band or ribbon. ~*n.* **1.** A narrow length of fabric, hair, or other material that has been braided or plaited. **2.** A thin, flat, woven strip of cloth with a regular diagonal pattern, used for binding or decorating fabrics; an ornamental trim. **3.** A ribbon or band entwined in or used to fasten the hair. [Middle English *breyden,* to move quickly, pull, twist, braid, Old English *bregdan.*] —**braid·er** *n.*

braid·ing (brā′dĭng) *n.* **1.** A length of braid. **2.** Braided work.

brail (brāl) *n.* A line used to bring in a sail before furling it. ~*tr.v.* **brailed, brailing, brails.** To gather in (a sail) with brails. Usually used with *up.* [Middle English *brayle,* from Old French *brail, braiel,* belt, girdle, from Medieval Latin *brācāle,* from Latin *brāca,* breeches.]

Braille (brāl) *n.* Also **braille.** A system of writing and printing for the blind, in which varied arrangements of raised dots representing letters and numerals can be identified by touch. [After Louis BRAILLE.]

Braille (brāl), **Louis** (1809–52). French inventor of the Braille system. He was blinded himself at the age of three.

brain (brān) *n.* **1.** The portion of the central nervous system in the vertebrate cranium that is responsible for the interpretation of sensory impulses, the coordination and control of bodily activities, and the exercise of emotion, memory, and thought. **2.** A functionally similar portion of the invertebrate nervous system. **3. a.** Intellectual capacity or potential; mind: *She has a good brain.* **b.** *Often* **brains.** Intelligence; intellectual ability. **4.** *Informal.* A highly intelligent or intellectual person. **5.** *Often* **brains.** The planner or organizer of an enterprise or undertaking. **6. brains.** The brain of a calf, pig, or sheep used as food. **7.** An automatic device, as a computer, that is central to a computation or control process. —See Synonyms at **mind.** —**on the brain.** Obsessively in the mind or thoughts. —**pick someone's brains.** To elicit and use the ideas, knowledge, or thoughts of. —**rack one's brains.** To make a great mental effort. ~*tr.v.* **brained, braining, brains. 1.** To smash in the skull of. **2.** *Slang.* To hit on the head. [Middle English *brain,* Old English *brægen.*] See feature, previous page.

brain·child (brān'chīld') *n. Informal.* An original idea, plan, or the like, attributed to a specific person or group.

brain coral *n.* Any of several corals of the genus *Meandrina,* forming rounded colonies that resemble the surface of the human brain.

brain death *n.* Cessation of respiration and other vital reflexes due to irreversible brain damage, although the heart may continue beating with the aid of life-support systems. —**brain dead** *adj.*

brain drain *n.* The emigration of highly skilled or trained people, such as scientists or doctors, to another country, especially for higher salaries.

brain fever *n. Pathology.* Any of several diseases of the brain, such as **encephalitis** or **meningitis** *(both of which see).*

brain·less (brān'lĭs) *adj.* **1.** Devoid of intelligence; stupid. **2.** Lacking a brain. —**brain·less·ly** *adv.* —**brain·less·ness** *n.*

brain·pan (brān'păn') *n.* The part of the skull that contains the brain; the cranium.

brain·pick·ing (brān'pĭk'ĭng) *n.* The act of probing another's mind for information. —**brain·pick·er** *n.*

brain·pow·er (brān'pou'ər) *n.* **1.** Intellectual power or ability. **2.** People with well-developed mental ability.

brain scanner *n.* A **CAT scanner** *(see)* used to x-ray the brain.

brain·sick (brān'sĭk') *adj.* Of, pertaining to, or induced by insanity; mad. —**brain·sick·ly** *adv.* —**brain·sick·ness** *n.*

brain·stem (brān'stĕm') *n.* The part of the brain consisting of the medulla oblongata, pons, midbrain, and part of the forebrain, connecting the spinal cord to the forebrain and cerebrum.

brain·storm (brān'stôrm') *n.* **1.** A sudden and violent disturbance in the brain. **2. a.** A sudden clever idea. **b.** A foolish idea.

brain·storm·ing (brān'stôr'mĭng) *n.* A method of attacking problems or creating original ideas by intense discussion and spontaneous idea swapping within a group.

brain·teas·er (brān'tē-zər) *n. Informal.* A difficult or puzzling problem. Also called "brain-twister."

brain trust. Also *Chiefly British.* **brains trust.** A group of experts who serve as unofficial advisers and policy planners, especially in a government. —**brain truster** *n.*

brain·wash (brān'wŏsh', -wôsh') *tr.v.* **-washed, -washing, -washes.** To subject to brainwashing. [Back-formation from BRAINWASHING.]

brain·wash·ing (brān'wŏsh'ĭng, -wôsh'ĭng) *n.* Intensive indoctrination, usually political, aimed at changing a person's basic convictions and attitudes and replacing them with a fixed and

brain

THE MASTER CONTROLLER OF THE HUMAN BODY

A communications system that processes information from the senses

Wrinkled and grooved like an oversized walnut, the human brain consists of some 100 billion nerve cells and a complex system of interlinked pathways between them. This soft, gray mass of nerve tissue controls all the activities of the body, both conscious and unconscious, as well as being the seat of sensations, skills, emotions, intelligence, and memory.

All this potential is contained in a volume about the size of two clenched fists, weighing about 1.5 kilograms (3 pounds).

There are three main parts: the cerebrum, the largest and most developed part of the brain; the cerebellum; and the brainstem, which is an extension of the spinal cord.

The surface of the cerebrum has a layer of gray matter, known as the cortex, which is convoluted into folds to give it the maximum possible area for receiving and interpreting the stream of unsifted information that is relayed to it from the senses. The cortex surrounds a mass of nerve fibers, or white matter.

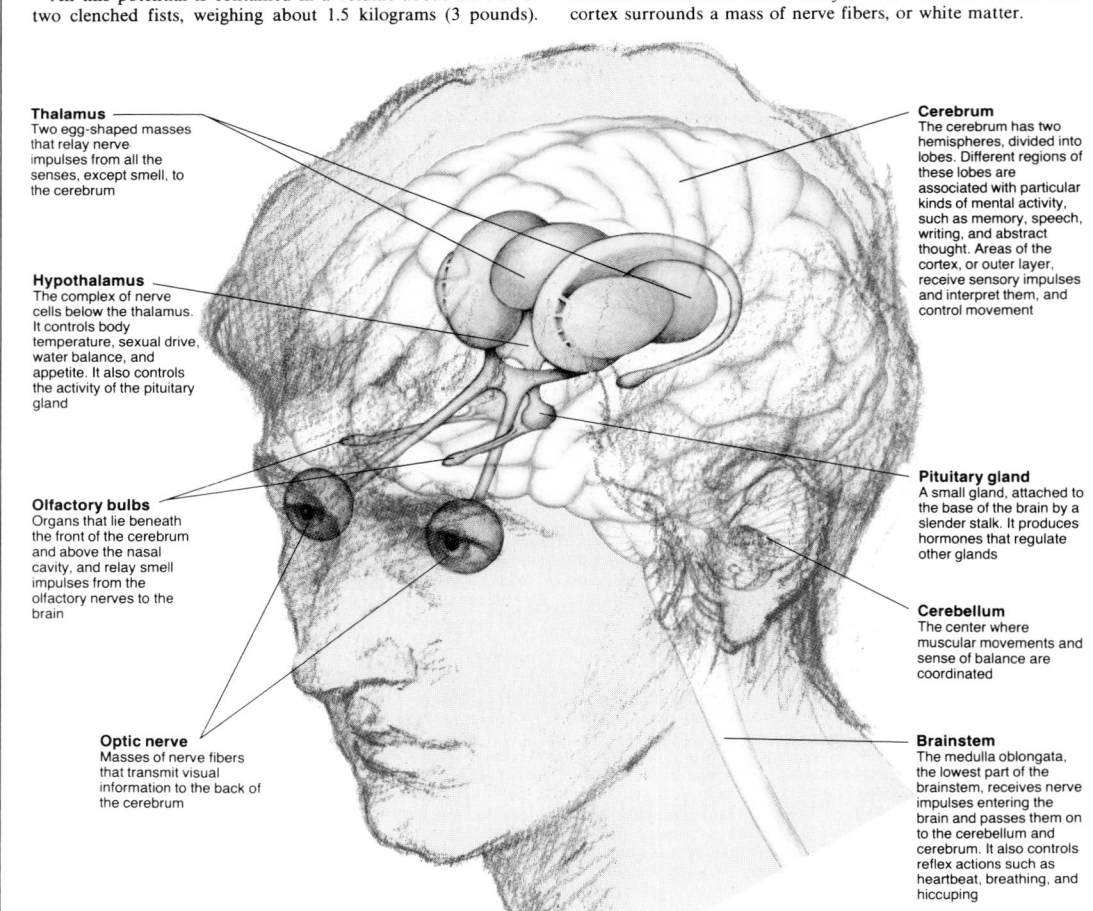

Thalamus
Two egg-shaped masses that relay nerve impulses from all the senses, except smell, to the cerebrum

Hypothalamus
The complex of nerve cells below the thalamus. It controls body temperature, sexual drive, water balance, and appetite. It also controls the activity of the pituitary gland

Olfactory bulbs
Organs that lie beneath the front of the cerebrum and above the nasal cavity, and relay smell impulses from the olfactory nerves to the brain

Optic nerve
Masses of nerve fibers that transmit visual information to the back of the cerebrum

Cerebrum
The cerebrum has two hemispheres, divided into lobes. Different regions of these lobes are associated with particular kinds of mental activity, such as memory, speech, writing, and abstract thought. Areas of the cortex, or outer layer, receive sensory impulses and interpret them, and control movement

Pituitary gland
A small gland, attached to the base of the brain by a slender stalk. It produces hormones that regulate other glands

Cerebellum
The center where muscular movements and sense of balance are coordinated

Brainstem
The medulla oblongata, the lowest part of the brainstem, receives nerve impulses entering the brain and passes them on to the cerebellum and cerebrum. It also controls reflex actions such as heartbeat, breathing, and hiccuping

unquestioned set of beliefs. [Translation of Mandarin Chinese *hsi³ nao³* : *hsi³*, to wash + *nao³*, brain.]

brain wave *n.* **1.** A fluctuation of electric potential between parts of the brain, as seen on an electroencephalogram. **2.** *Informal.* A sudden inspiration or brilliant idea.

brain·y (brā′nē) *adj.* **-ier, -iest.** *Informal.* Intelligent; learned; smart. —**brain·i·ly** *adv.* —**brain·i·ness** *n.*

braise (brāz) *tr.v.* **braised, braising, braises.** To cook (meat or vegetables) by browning in fat, then simmering in a small quantity of liquid in a covered container. [French *braiser*, from *braise,* hot charcoal, from Old French *brese,* from Germanic.]

brake¹ (brāk) *n.* **1.** A device for slowing or stopping motion, as of a vehicle or machine, especially by contact friction. **2.** *Often* **brakes.** Anything serving to slow or stop action or movement. **3.** A device for separating the fibers of flax or hemp by crushing or beating. **4.** A heavy harrow for breaking clods of earth. **5.** A handle on a pump or other machine. —*v.* **braked, braking, brakes.** —*tr.* **1.** To reduce the speed of with or as if with a brake. **2.** To crush (flax or hemp) in a brake. **3.** To break up (clods of earth) with a harrow. —*intr.* To operate or apply a brake or brakes. [Middle English *brake,* crushing instrument, pestle, flax brake, from Middle Dutch *braeke.*]

brake² *n.* Any of several ferns, especially **bracken** *(see).* [Middle English, variant of BRACKEN.]

brake³ *n.* An area overgrown with dense brushwood, briars, and undergrowth; a thicket. [Middle English *(ferne)* brake, Old English *(fearn)braca,* bed of fern : FERN + *bracu* (unattested), dense growth, thicket.]

brake⁴. Variant of **break** (carriage).

brake⁵. *Archaic.* Past tense of **break.**

brake·age (brā′kĭj) *n.* The action or capacity of a brake.

brake band *n.* A flexible belt that is tightened around a brake drum to arrest the motion of a wheel or shaft.

brake drum *n.* A metal cylinder to which pressure is applied in order to arrest rotation of a wheel or shaft attached to the cylinder.

brake fluid *n.* The liquid used in a hydraulic brake cylinder.

brake horsepower *n. Abbr.* **bhp., b.hp.** The useful horsepower of an engine, usually determined from the force exerted on a dynamometer connected to the engine's drive shaft.

brake light *n.* A red light on the back of a vehicle which lights up when the brakes are applied.

brake lining *n.* A renewable thin strip on the outside of a brake shoe to minimize wear.

brake·man (brāk′mən) *n., pl.* **-men** (-mĭn). A railroad employee who assists the conductor and checks on the operation of the train's brakes.

brake shoe *n.* A curved metal block that presses against and thereby arrests the rotation of a wheel or brake drum.

brak·ing rocket *n. Aerospace.* A retrorocket *(see).*

bram·ble (brăm′bəl) *n.* **1.** Any prickly plant or shrub of the genus *Rubus,* especially the blackberry. **2.** Any similar prickly shrub or bush such as the dog rose. [Middle English *brembel,* Old English *brǣmbel, brēmel.*] —**bram·bly** *adj.*

bram·bling (brăm′blĭng) *n.* A finch, *Fringilla montifringilla,* of northern Eurasia, having black, white, and rust-brown plumage. Also called "cock of the north." [BRAMB(LE) + -LING.]

Bram·ley (brăm′lē) *n.* A variety of cooking apple with firm juicy flesh. Also called "Bramley's seedling." [After Matthew *Bramley,* 19th-century English butcher, who may first have grown it.]

bran (brăn) *n.* **1.** The seed husk or outer coating of cereals such as wheat, rye, and oats, separated from the flour by sifting. **2.** Cereal by-products used as a food. [Middle English *bran, bren,* from Old French *bran,* perhaps from Gaulish *brenno-†* (unattested).]

branch (brănch, bränch) *n. Abbr.* **br. 1.** A secondary woody stem or limb growing from the trunk or main stem of a tree, bush, or shrub, or from another secondary limb. **2.** Any part resembling or suggestive of a branch. **3.** A limited part of a larger or more complex body, such as: **a.** An academic or vocational field of specialization. **b.** A local unit of a business, enterprise, bank, or the like. **c.** A division of a family, tribe, or other group believed to stem from a common ancestor. **4.** *Linguistics.* A subdivision of a family of languages. **5. a.** A tributary of a river. **b.** Any small stream, creek, or brook. **6.** *Geometry.* A part of a curve that is separated, as by discontinuities or extreme points. **7.** *Computer Science.* A change from a main program sequence into a subroutine. —*v.* **branched, branching, branches.** —*intr.* **1.** To put forth or spread out in branches. **2.** To separate into subdivisions; diverge. **3.** *Computer Science.* To depart from a sequence of instructions as a result of a branch. —*tr.* **1.** To separate (something) into or as if into branches. **2.** To embroider with a design of flowers or foliage. —**branch off. 1.** To divide into branches; fork. **2.** To separate from the main part or course; diverge. —**branch out.** To enlarge the scope of one's interest, business, or activities. [Middle English *braunche,* from Old French *branche,* from Late Latin *branca,* foot, paw.] —**branched** *adj.* —**branch·less** *adj.* —**branch·y** *adj.*

-branch *suffix. Zoology.* Indicates gills; for example, **elasmobranch.** [New Latin *-branchia,* from Latin *branchia,* BRANCHIA.]

branched chain *n. Chemistry.* A chain of atoms in a molecule with one or more side chains attached.

bran·chi·a (brăng′kē-ə) *n., pl.* **-chiae** (-kē-ē). *Zoology.* A gill or similar breathing organ. [Latin, from Greek *brankhia†,* gills.] —**bran·chi·al** *adj.*

bran·chi·ate (brăng′kē-ĭt, -āt′) *adj.* Having branchiae or gills.

bran·chi·o·pod (brăng′kē-ə-pŏd′) *n.* Any of various crustaceans of the subclass Branchiopoda, characteristically having a segmented body and flattened, limblike appendages. The group includes the water fleas. [New Latin *Branchiopoda* : BRANCHIA + -POD.]

branch line *n.* A minor railway line that branches off from a main line.

branch water *n.* Plain water, especially when mixed with liquor. [From *branch water,* water from a stream.]

Bran·cu·si (brän-kōō′zē, -sē), **Constantin** (1876-1957). Romanian sculptor, who settled in Paris in 1904. He broke sharply with the realist tradition in sculpture, making abstract sculptures of great geometric simplicity, chiefly in metal and stone.

brand (brănd) *n.* **1. a.** A trademark or distinctive name identifying a product or a manufacturer. **b.** The make of a product thus marked: *a popular brand of soap.* **2.** A particular type: *a strange brand of humor.* **3.** A mark indicating identity or ownership, burned on the hide of an animal with a hot iron. **4.** A mark formerly burned into the flesh of criminals or slaves. **5.** Any mark of disgrace or notoriety; a stigma. **6.** An iron that is heated and used for branding. **7.** A piece of burning or charred wood. **8.** *Archaic.* A sword: *"So flash'd and fell the brand Excalibur"* (Tennyson). **9.** A disease of plants caused by the rust fungus *Puccinia arenariae* in which brown spots appear on the leaves. —*tr.v.* **branded, branding, brands. 1.** To mark with or as if with a brand. **2.** To mark with disgrace or infamy; stigmatize. [Middle English *brand,* fire, torch, sword.]

Bran·deis (brăn′dīs), **Louis Dembitz** (1856-1941). Associate Justice U.S. Supreme Court (1916-39). As a young lawyer sensitive to the many social and economic problems of the day, he felt that law should be used to help the average citizen. Later, his liberalism and ardent defense of individual rights were the basis for many of his Supreme Court decisions.

Bran·den·burg¹ (brăn′dən-bûrg′). A former principality in Prussia, now lying in northeastern Germany, stretching at its greatest extent in the 18th century from west of the Elbe River beyond the Oder north to the Baltic Sea. Its center was Berlin. In 1701 Elector Frederick III took the title King of Prussia, and thereafter the history of Brandenburg is the history of Prussia.

Brandenburg². An industrial town in eastern Germany, on the Havel River. It was the headquarters of the ruling Hohenzollern family of Brandenburg (15th–early 18th century).

brand·ing iron *n.* A metal rod heated and used for branding.

bran·dish (brăn′dĭsh) *tr.v.* **-dished, -dishing, -dishes. 1.** To wave or flourish (a weapon, for example) menacingly. **2.** To display ostentatiously. —*n.* A menacing or defiant wave or flourish. [Middle English *braundisshen,* from Old French *brandir* (present stem *brandiss-*), from *brand,* sword, blade, from Germanic.] —**bran·dish·er** *n.*

brand·ling (brănd′lĭng) *n.* A common reddish-brown earthworm, *Eisenia foetida,* often used as bait by fishermen. [BRAND (because of its red markings) + -LING.]

brand name *n.* See **trade name** (sense 1).

brand-new (brănd′nōō′, -nyōō′) *adj.* In fresh and unused condition; completely new.

Bran·do (brăn′dō), **Marlon** (1924–). U.S. actor, chiefly famous for his appearance in films, most notably in *A Streetcar Named Desire* (1951). One of the outstanding representatives of method acting, he also won critical acclaim for *On the Waterfront* (1954).

Brandt (brănt, bränt), **Willy,** born Herbert Ernst Karl Frahm (1913–92). West German politician. He was elected to the Bundestag (1949) and became mayor of West Berlin (1957). He was chancellor (1969–74) until the revelation that one of his close aides was an East German spy. He was awarded the Nobel Peace Prize (1971) for his efforts to reduce tension between East and West.

bran·dy (brăn′dē) *n., pl.* **-dies.** A strong alcoholic drink distilled from wine or from fermented fruit juice. —*tr.v.* **brandied, -dying, -dies.** To mix, flavor, or preserve with brandy. [Earlier *brandy wine,* from Dutch *brandewijn, brantwijn* : *brant,* past participle of *branden,* to burn, distil + WINE.]

brandy bottle *n.* A plant, the **yellow water lily** *(see).*

Bran·dy·wine (brăn′dē-wīn′). A creek in southern Pennsylvania and northern Delaware. Here on September 11, 1777, that Gen. William Howe's British and Hessian troops defeated George Washington's army, largely made up of militiamen. Later that month Howe's forces entered Philadelphia.

branks (brăngks) *n. Used with a singular or plural verb.* A metal bridle with a bit to restrain the tongue, formerly used to punish scolds. [Perhaps an alteration of earlier *bernaks,* plural of Middle English *bernak,* bridle, from Norman French *bernac†.*]

bran·ni·gan (brăn′ĭ-gən) *n. Slang.* **1.** A noisy or confused quarrel. **2.** A spree; binge. [Probably from the proper name *Brannigan.*]

brant (brănt) *n., pl.* **brant** or **brants.** Also *British* **brent** (brĕnt). Any of several wild geese of the genus *Branta,* that breed in Arctic regions; especially, *B. bernicla,* having a black neck and head. [Probably from Scandinavian, akin to Swedish *brandgas,* "burnt goose" (from its black color) : *brand,* firebrand, from Old Norse *brandr* + *gas,* goose.]

Brant (brănt), **Joseph,** original name Thayendanegea (1742-1807). Indian leader. He supported Britain in the French and Indian War and remained loyal during the American Revolution, in which he led Mohawk warriors on devastating attacks on frontier settlements. After the war he settled in what is now Ontario, Canada.

Braque (bräk), **Georges** (1882-1963). French painter, a leading member of the School of Paris and cofounder of the cubist movement. His landscapes of 1908, painted after he had seen Picasso's *Demoiselles d'Avignon,* and described by Matisse as composed of little cubes, gave rise to the term "cubism." He later abandoned the cubist manner, painting still lifes with a flat perspective, large interior scenes, and in the 1950's the large black birds against a blue sky that dominate his last period.

brash¹ (brăsh) *adj.* **brasher, brashest. 1.** Hasty and unthinking; rash. **2.** Impudent; cocky. **3.** Brittle. Said of wood or timber. —See Synonyms at **shameless.** [Perhaps imitative, influenced by BREAK and RASH.] —**brash·ly** *adv.* —**brash·ness** *n.*

brash² *n.* A mass or pile of rubble or fragments. [Perhaps from French *brèche,* breach, from Old French, from Old High German

brehha, fracture, from *brehhan,* to break.]

Brasil. See **Brazil.**

Bra·sí·lia (brə-zĭl'yə). Capital of Brazil, a new town built in the central highlands of the country, 970 kilometers (603 miles) northwest of Rio de Janeiro. The city was laid out by the architect Lúcio Costa in the shape of an airplane; the civic buildings were almost all designed by Oscar Niemeyer.

brasilin. Variant of **brazilin.**

brass (brăs, bräs) *n.* **1.** An alloy of copper (more than 50 percent) and zinc with other metals in varying lesser amounts. **2.** Ornaments, objects, or utensils made of brass. **3.** *Often* **brasses.** *Music.* **a.** The family of wind instruments, such as the French horn and trombone, made of brass. **b.** *Sometimes used with a plural verb.* The section of an orchestra made up of these instruments. **4.** A memorial plaque made of brass, often inscribed with a representation of a dead person. See **brass rubbing. 5.** *Engineering.* A bushing sleeve or similar lining for a bearing, made from a copper alloy. **6.** *Informal.* Blatant self-assurance; effrontery; nerve. **7.** *Slang. Used with a plural verb.* High-ranking military officers or other high officials: *the top brass.* **8.** *Northern English Informal.* Money. [Middle English *bras,* Old English *bræs.†*] —**brass** *adj.*

bras·sard (brə-särd', brăs'ärd) *n.* Also **bras·sart** (brə-särt', brăs'ärt'). **1.** A cloth badge worn around the upper arm. **2.** A piece of armor for the arm. [French, from *bras,* arm, from Latin *brachium,* from Greek *brakhíōn.*]

brass·bound (brăs'bound', bräs'-) *adj.* **1.** Strengthened or ornamented with brass: *a brassbound wooden box.* **2.** Firmly and inflexibly established; rigid: *a brassbound tradition.*

brass·col·lar (brăs'kŏl'ər) *adj.* Voting the straight party ticket with no variation.

bras·se·rie (brăs'ə-rē', bräs-rē') *n.* **1.** A bar in which food may be served. **2.** A French-style restaurant. [French, "brewery."]

brass hat *n. Slang.* **1.** A high-ranking military officer. **2.** Any high-ranking official. [Because of the gold braid on his cap.]

bras·si·ca (brä'sĭ-kə) *n.* Any plant of the genus *Brassica,* indigenous to the Mediterranean region but widely cultivated as vegetables, such as cabbages, Brussels sprouts, and rutabagas. [Latin, "cabbage."]

brass·ie, brass·y (brăs'ē, bräs'ē) *n., pl.* **-ies.** A wooden golf club with a brass-plated sole, used for long low shots.

bras·siere, bras·sière (brə-zîr') *n.* A woman's undergarment worn to support and give contour to the breasts. Also called "bra." [French *brassière,* from Old French *braciere,* armor for the arm, arm guard, from *bras,* arm, from Latin *bracchium,* from Greek *brakhíōn.*]

brass knuckles *pl.n.* A weapon consisting of a metal strip or chain with holes or links into which the fingers fit.

brass rubbing *n.* **1.** The process of reproducing on paper the design on a memorial brass by rubbing with graphite or the like. **2.** The impression produced in this way.

brass tacks *pl.n. Informal.* Essential facts or details: *getting down to brass tacks.*

brass·y (brăs'ē, bräs'ē) *adj.* **-ier, -iest. 1.** Of or decorated with brass. **2.** Resembling brass in color. **3.** Resembling or characterized by the sound of brass instruments; strident. **4.** Cheap and showy; flashy. **5.** *Informal.* Brazen; insolent; impudent. —**brass·i·ly** *adv.* —**brass·i·ness** *n.*

brat (brăt) *n.* A child, especially an ill-mannered one. [Perhaps from dialectal *brat,* coarse garment, Middle English *brat,* Old English *bratt,* cloak, from Old Irish *bratt†.*] —**brat·tish, brat·ty** *adj.*

Bra·ti·sla·va (brät'ĭ-slä'və). Industrial city in southern Czechoslovakia, on the Danube River near the Austrian and Hungarian borders, the third-largest city in the country. From 1541 to 1784 it was the capital of Hungary.

brat·tice (brăt'ĭs) *n.* A partition, especially one erected in a mine for ventilation. ~*tr.v.* **bratticed, -ticing, -tices.** To equip with a brattice. [Middle English *bretais,* defensive structure, from Norman French *breteske,* variants of Old French *bretesque,* from Medieval Latin *(turris) brittisca,* perhaps "British (tower)," parapet (this type of fortification originated in Britain), probably from Latin *Britto,* BRITON.]

brat·tle (brăt'l) *n. Chiefly Scottish.* A rattling or clattering sound. ~*intr.v.* To make a brattle. [Imitative.]

brat·wurst (brăt'wûrst'; *German* brät'voorsht') *n.* A sausage made with finely chopped, seasoned fresh pork. [German *Bratwurst,* from Old High German *brātwurst : brāt(o),* meat + *wurst,* sausage, WURST.]

Braun), Eva (broun) (1912–45). German salesgirl, mistress and wife of Adolf Hitler. She went to live with him in 1936, but the liaison was kept secret and she was never seen in public with him. They married hours before committing suicide on April 30, 1945.

Braun, Wernher von (1912–77). U.S. aeronautical physicist, born in Germany. He worked on weapons and rocket research in Germany (1932–45), including the V-2 rockets that were used to bombard London (1944–45). After surrendering to Allied troops, he went to New Mexico to join the U.S. Army Ordnance Corps research and testing station at White Sands. He was the director of the army team that put the first American satellite, Explorer I, into space (January 1958). He retired in 1972.

Braunschweig. See **Brunswick.**

Braun·schwei·ger (broun'shwī'gər) *n.* A smoked liver sausage. [German *Braunschweig,* Brunswick, Germany.]

bra·va (brä'vä, brä-vä') *interj.* Used to express approval in applauding a woman.

THE POWERHOUSE OF MUSIC

Instruments that provide the strength of band and orchestra

Brass is the collective term for metal instruments that are blown directly through a cup-shaped or funnel-shaped mouthpiece. They include the trumpet, trombone, French horn, tuba, saxhorn, flugelhorn, cornet, and bugle. The saxophone is metal, but counts as woodwind because it has a reed mouthpiece.

Sound from a brass instrument is originated by air vibrated by the player's lips against the mouthpiece, which, together with the bell and

bore of the tube, also controls the quality of tone. A cupped mouthpiece, cylindrical bore, and narrow bell give a hard, bright tone as in the trumpet. A funnel-shaped mouthpiece, conical bore, and wide bell give the soft sound of the horn. Most brass instruments have valves that change the sounding length of the tube to give a wider range of notes. A trombone's tube length is varied by a telescopic slide operated by the player.

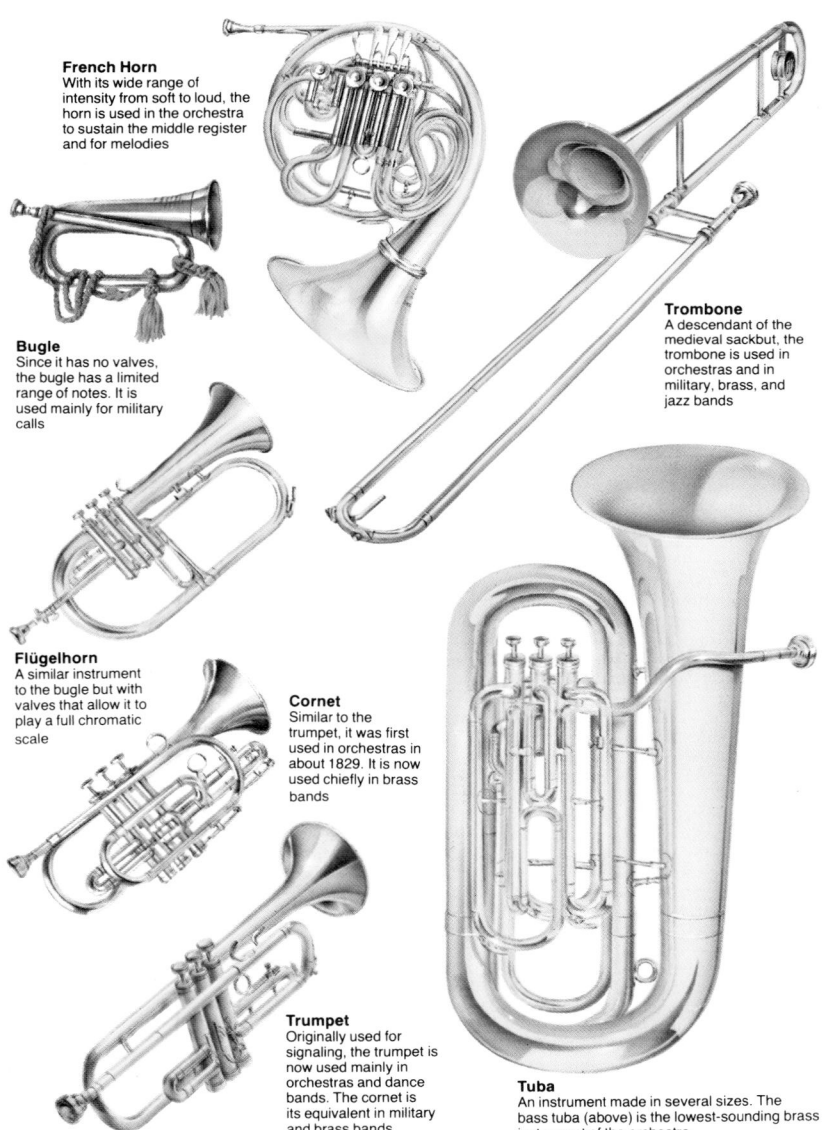

French Horn
With its wide range of intensity from soft to loud, the horn is used in the orchestra to sustain the middle register and for melodies

Bugle
Since it has no valves, the bugle has a limited range of notes. It is used mainly for military calls

Flügelhorn
A similar instrument to the bugle but with valves that allow it to play a full chromatic scale

Cornet
Similar to the trumpet, it was first used in orchestras in about 1829. It is now used chiefly in brass bands

Trumpet
Originally used for signaling, the trumpet is now used mainly in orchestras and dance bands. The cornet is its equivalent in military and brass bands

Trombone
A descendant of the medieval sackbut, the trombone is used in orchestras and in military, brass, and jazz bands

Tuba
An instrument made in several sizes. The bass tuba (above) is the lowest-sounding brass instrument of the orchestra

~*n.* A shout or cry of "brava." [Ital., fem. of *bravo,* bravo.]

bra·va·do (brə-vä′dō) *n., pl.* **-does** or **-dos. 1.** Defiant or swaggering show of courage; false bravery. **2.** *Rare.* An instance of such behavior. [Spanish *bravada, bravata,* from *bravo,* BRAVE.]

Bra·vais lattice (brä′vā, brä-vā′) *n. Physics.* A **space lattice** *(see).* [After Auguste *Bravais* (died 1863), French physicist.]

brave (brāv) *adj.* **braver, bravest. 1.** Possessing or displaying courage; valiant. **2.** Making a fine display; splendid. **3.** *Archaic.* Excellent.
~*n.* **1.** A North American Indian warrior. **2.** *Obsolete.* A boast or challenge. **3.** *Obsolete.* A bully.
~*tr. v.* **braved, braving, braves. 1.** To undergo or face courageously. **2.** To defy; challenge. [Old French *brave,* courageous, noble, from Italian and Spanish *bravo,* from Vulgar Latin *brabus* (unattested), wild, savage, altered from Latin *barbarus,* foreign, barbarous, from Greek *barbaros.*] **—brave·ly** *adv.* **—brave·ness** *n.*
Synonyms: *audacious, bold, courageous, daring, dauntless, doughty, fearless, gallant, game, gritty, intrepid, mettlesome, plucky, undaunted, valiant, valorous.*

brave new world *n.* A future that holds out a promise of social progress and human contentment. Often used ironically. [After the title of a novel (1932) by Aldous Huxley, which was itself taken from Shakespeare's *The Tempest* (*c.* 1611).]

brav·er·y (brā′və-rē, brāv′rē) *n., pl.* **-ies. 1.** The state or quality of being brave; courage. **2.** Splendor, as of attire; show. —See Synonyms at **courage.**

bra·vo[1] (brä′vō, brä-vō′) *interj.* Used to express approval.
~*n., pl.* **bravos.** A shout or cry of "bravo." [Italian, fine, BRAVE.]

bra·vo[2] (brä′vō) *n., pl.* **-voes** or **-vos.** A hired assassin; killer. [Italian, "brave."]

bra·vu·ra (brə-vyŏŏr′ə) *n.* **1.** *Music.* **a.** Brilliant technique or style in performance. **b.** A piece of music requiring this. **2.** A bold or showy manner. [Italian, "bravery," spirit, from *bravo,* BRAVE.] **—bra·vu·ra** *adj.*

braw (brô) *adj.* **brawer, brawest.** *Scottish.* Fine or splendid. [Earlier *brawf,* Scottish variant of BRAVE.]

brawl (brôl) *n.* A noisy quarrel or fight.
~*intr.v.* **brawled, brawling, brawls. 1.** To fight or quarrel noisily. **2.** To flow noisily: *a brawling stream.* [Middle English *brawlen, brallen,* probably related to Dutch and Low German *brallen* (imitative).] **—brawl·er** *n.* **—brawl·ing·ly** *adv.*

brawn (brôn) *n.* **1.** Solid and well-developed muscles. **2.** Muscular strength and power. **3.** *British.* A pickled or preserved preparation, made from meat of the head or feet of a pig. [Middle English, from Norman French *braun,* variant of Old French *braon,* flesh, muscle.]

brawn·y (brô′nē) *adj.* **-ier, -iest.** Strong and muscular. **—brawn·i·ly** *adv.* **—brawn·i·ness** *n.*

bray[1] (brā) *v.* **brayed, braying, brays.** —*intr.* **1.** To utter the loud, harsh cry of a donkey. **2.** To sound loudly and harshly. —*tr.* To utter loudly and harshly.
~*n.* **1.** A loud, harsh cry, as of a donkey. **2.** Any sound resembling this. [Middle English *brayen,* to make noise, roar, from Old French *braire,* probably from Celtic.] **—bray·er** *n.*

bray[2] *tr.v.* **brayed, braying, brays. 1.** To crush and pound in or as if in a mortar. **2.** To spread (printing ink) thinly over type. [Middle English *brayen,* from Old French *breier,* to break, from Germanic.]

bray·er (brā′ər) *n. Printing.* A small hand roller used to spread ink thinly and evenly over type.

Braz. Brazil; Brazilian.

braze[1] (brāz) *tr.v.* **brazed, brazing, brazes.** *Archaic.* To make hard like brass. [Middle English *brasen,* Old English *brasian,* from *bræs,* BRASS.]

braze[2] *tr.v.* **brazed, brazing, brazes.** To solder (two pieces of metal) together using a hard solder with a high melting point. [Probably from French *braser,* from Old French, to burn, from *brese,* burning coals, from Germanic.] **—braz·er** *n.*

bra·zen (brā′zən) *adj.* **1.** Made of brass. **2.** Resembling brass in color, quality, or hardness. **3.** Having a loud, resonant sound like that of a brass trumpet. **4.** Impudent; bold. —See Synonyms at **shameless.**
~*tr.v.* **brazened, -zening, -zens.** To face or undergo with bold or brash self-assurance. Usually used with *out.* [Middle English *brasen,* Old English *bræsen,* from *bræs,* BRASS.] **—bra·zen·ly** *adv.* **—bra·zen·ness** *n.*

bra·zen·faced (brā′zən-fāst′) *adj.* Impudent and shameless.

bra·zier[1] (brā′zhər) *n.* One who works in brass. [Middle English *brasier,* from *bras,* BRASS.]

brazier[2] *n.* A metal stand for holding burning coals or charcoal, usually used outdoors. [French *brasier,* from *braise,* burning coals, from Old French *brese,* from Germanic.]

Bra·zil (brə-zĭl′). *Abbr.* **Braz.** *Portuguese* **Bra·sil** (brä-). Republic in eastern South America and the largest Latin American country, occupying nearly half of the South American continent. The capital is Brasília. Northern and western Brazil consists of the densely forested lowlands of the Amazon basin and is sparsely inhabited by South American Indian tribes. The more temperate southern part of the country produces three quarters of the national agricultural and industrial output. Brazil contains huge deposits of iron ore, perhaps a quarter of the world's total. It produces a quarter of the world's coffee. The country was ruled by Portugal from 1500 until 1822. It became a republic (1889) when Emperor Pedro II was forced to abdicate. Area, 8,511,965 square kilometers (3,286,488 square miles). Population, 150,400,000. See map, next page. **—Bra·zil·i·an** *adj. & n.*

braz·i·lin, bras·i·lin (brăz′ə-lĭn, brə-zĭl′ən) *n.* A crystalline compound, $C_{16}H_{14}O_5$, obtained from brazilwood and used as a dye. [French *brésiline,* from *brésil,* brazilwood.]

Brazil nut *n.* **1.** A tree, *Bertholletia excelsa,* of tropical South America, bearing hard, round, woody pods that contain the nuts. **2.** The edible nut of this tree. Also called "brazil." [After BRAZIL.]

bra·zil·wood (brə-zĭl′wŏŏd′) *n.* The red wood of any of several tropical trees of the genus *Caesalpinia,* used especially for cabinetwork and as the source of a red or purple dye, brazilin. [Middle English *brasil,* from Old French *bresil,* "red-dye wood," probably from *brese,* burning coals, from Germanic.]

Braz·os (brăz′əs). A river of eastern New Mexico and central Texas. It flows 1,400 kilometers (870 miles) to the Gulf of Mexico at Freeport, southwest of Galveston.

Braz·za·ville (brăz′ə-vĭl′). Capital and largest city of the Congo. It is on the Zaire River and is an important port, receiving rubber, wood, and agricultural products and sending them on to the coast for export. The city was founded (1880) by the French explorer Savorgnan de Brazza (1852–1905) and was the capital of French Equatorial Africa (1910–58).

breach (brēch) *n.* **1.** A violation or infraction, as of a law, obligation, contract, or promise. **2.** A gap or rift, especially in a solid structure such as a dike or fortification. **3.** A breaking up or disruption of friendly relations; an estrangement. **4.** The leaping of a whale from the water. **5.** The breaking of waves or surf.
~*v.* **breached, breaching, breaches.** —*tr.* To make a hole or gap in; break through. —*intr.* To leap from the water. Used of a whale. [Middle English *breche, brek,* partly from Old French *breche,* from Old High German *brehha,* from *brehhan,* to break, and partly from Old English *brǣc, brēc,* from *brecan,* to break.]
Synonyms: *encroachment, infraction, infringement, transgression, trespass, violation.*

breach of promise *n. Law.* Formerly, the failure to fulfill a promise, especially a promise to marry someone.

breach of the peace *n. Law.* A disturbance of public order caused, for example, by fighting or rioting.

bread (brĕd) *n.* **1.** A staple food made from flour or meal mixed with a liquid, usually combined with a leavening agent, and kneaded, shaped into loaves, and baked. **2.** Food in general, regarded as necessary for sustaining life. **3. a.** The necessities of life; livelihood: *earn one's bread.* **b.** *Slang.* Money.
~*tr.v.* **breaded, breading, breads.** To coat with breadcrumbs, as before cooking. [Middle English *bread, bred,* Old English *brēad.*]

bread and butter *n. Informal.* **1.** A means of support; a livelihood. **2.** A staple, but not exclusive, source of income.

bread-and-but·ter (brĕd′n-bŭt′ər) *adj.* **1.** Providing a basic income: *a bread-and-butter job.* **2.** Of fundamental concern; basic: *an election campaign fought on bread-and-butter issues.* **3.** Expressing gratitude for hospitality: *a bread-and-butter note.*

bread·bas·ket (brĕd′băs′kĭt, -bäs′kĭt) *n.* **1.** An important cereal-producing region. **2.** *Slang.* The stomach.

bread·board (brĕd′bôrd′, -bōrd′) *n.* **1.** A board on which bread is sliced. **2.** An experimental model, especially of an electronic circuit; prototype.

bread·fruit (brĕd′frōōt′) *n., pl.* **-fruits** or collectively **breadfruit. 1.** A tree, *Artocarpus communis,* of Polynesia, having deeply lobed leaves and round, usually seedless fruit. **2.** The edible fruit of this tree, having a texture like that of bread when baked or roasted.

bread·line (brĕd′līn′) *n.* A line of persons waiting to be given free food, either from a relief agency or as charity. **—on the breadline.** Living at subsistence level; destitute.

bread mold *n.* A fungus, *Rhizopus nigricans,* that forms a dense, cottony growth on bread and other foods.

bread·nut (brĕd′nŭt′) *n.* **1.** A tree, *Brosimum alicastrum,* of Central America and the West Indies, bearing round, nutlike fruit. **2.** The fruit of this tree, ground to produce a substitute for wheat flour.

breadth (brĕdth) *n.* **1.** *Abbr.* **b., B.** The measure or dimension from side to side of something, as distinguished from length or thickness; width. **2.** An extent or piece of something, usually conforming to a standard width: *a breadth of canvas.* **3.** Wide extent or scope. **4.** Freedom from narrowness, as of views or interests. [Middle English *brede,* Old English *brǣdu,* from Germanic *braidjōn* (unattested), from *braithaz* (unattested), BROAD.]

breadth·wise (brĕdth′wīz′) *adv.* Also **breadth·ways** (-wāz′). In the direction of the breadth. **—breadth·wise** *adj.*

bread·win·ner (brĕd′wĭn′ər) *n.* One who supports a family or household by his or her earnings.

break (brāk) *v.* **broke** (brōk) or *archaic* **brake** (brāk), **broken** (brō′kən), **breaking, breaks.** —*tr.* **1.** To separate or reduce to pieces with sudden or violent force; smash. **2.** To crack without actually separating into pieces. **3.** To render unusable or inoperative. **4.** To part or pierce the surface of. **5.** To cause to burst. **6.** To fracture a bone of. **7.** To force or make a way through; penetrate: *break the sound barrier.* **8.** To force one's way out of; escape from. **9.** To put an end to by force or strong opposition: *break a strike.* **10.** To fail to conform to; act contrary to; violate. **11. a.** To bring abruptly to an end: *A scream broke the silence.* **b.** To discontinue temporarily; interrupt; suspend: *break a journey.* **12.** To cause to give up a habit. Used with *of.* **13.** To train to obey; tame; especially, to accustom (a horse) to the saddle. **14.** To disrupt or destroy the order or regularity of: *break ranks.* **15.** To destroy the completeness of: *break a set*

Brazil nuts *These edible nuts are harvested from a South American tree,* Bertholletia excelsa. *The nuts are contained in segmented shells that fit inside large spherical seedpods.*

breadfruit *In the 17th century this Pacific island fruit was introduced from Tahiti to the West Indies. It was during an expedition to collect the plant that the mutiny on H.M.S* Bounty *took place.*

PRONUNCIATION KEY

ă, pat; ā, pay; âr, care;
ä, father, are; b, bib;
ch, church; d, deed; ĕ, pet;
ē, be; f, fife; g, gag; h, hat;
hw, which; ĭ, pit; ī, pie;
îr, pier; j, judge; k, kick;
l, lid, needle; m, mum;
n, no, sudden; ng, thing;
ŏ, pot; ō, toe; ô, paw, for;
oi, noise; ou, out; ŏŏ, book;
ōō, boot; p, pop; r, roar;
s, sauce; sh, ship, dish;
t, tight; th, thin, path;
th, this, bathe; ŭ, cut; ûr, fur;
v, valve; w, with; y, yes;
z, zebra, size; zh, vision;
ə, about, item, edible, gallop, circus, peaceful

IN FOREIGN WORDS:

à, *Fr.* ami; œ, *Fr.* feu, *Ger.* schön; ü, *Fr.* tu, *Ger.* über; KH, *Ger.* ich, *Scot.* loch; N, *Fr.* bon; y′, *Fr.* Compiègne

STRESS MARKS:

Primary stress: ′
in·cite′ (ĭn-sīt′)
Secondary stress: ′
in′sight′ (ĭn′sīt′)

BRAZIL

of books. **16.** To lessen in force or effect: *break a fall.* **17.** To weaken or destroy, as in spirit or health: *"For a hero loves the world till it breaks him"* (W.B. Yeats). **18.** To overwhelm with grief or sorrow: *break one's heart.* **19.** To cause to be without money or to go into bankruptcy. **20.** *Military.* To reduce in rank; demote. **21.** To reduce to or exchange for smaller monetary units: *break a ten-dollar bill.* **22.** To surpass or outdo: *break a record.* **23.** To make known (news, for example). **24.** To find the solution or key to; decipher. **25.** *Law.* To invalidate (a will) by judicial action. **26.** *Tennis.* To win a game against (the service of an opponent). **27.** *Electricity.* To open: *break a circuit.* —*intr.* **1.** To become separated into pieces or fragments; come apart. **2.** To become unusable or inoperative. **3.** To give way; collapse. **4.** To diminish or discontinue abruptly: *His fever broke.* **5.** To rise to or emerge from the surface of the water. Used of fish. **6.** To move away or escape suddenly. **7.** To weaken in spirit, resolve, or self-control: *He broke under torture.* **8. a.** To come into being or public notice, especially suddenly: *The story broke at 12:00.* **b.** To dawn. **9.** To come to an end after a long time: *The cold spell finally broke.* **10.** To be overwhelmed with sorrow. Used of the heart. **11.** To begin abruptly to utter, express, or do something: *Her face broke into a smile. The horse broke into a gallop.* **12.** To interrupt or discontinue an activity. Often used with *up: The meeting broke up after noon.* **13.** *Linguistics.* To undergo breaking. Used of a vowel. **14.** To collapse or crash into surf or spray. Used of waves. **15. a.** To change from one tone quality to another, as from emotion. Used of the voice. **b.** To change from one musical register to another. **16.** In boxing and wrestling, to disengage from one's opponent after a clinch. —**break bread.** To eat or share a meal. —**break camp.** To pack up and leave a campsite. —**break even.** To operate economically, making neither a profit nor a loss. —**break (new) ground.** To discover or pioneer: *broke ground in cancer research.* —**break in on** (or **upon**). To interrupt or intrude on. —**break into.** **1.** To enter forcibly, suddenly, or illegally. **2.** To interrupt. **3.** To begin to draw on (a reserve): *break into one's savings.* **4.** To become employed or established in a profession or sphere of activity: *trying to break into publishing.* —**break off.** **1.** To stop suddenly, as in speaking. **2.** To discontinue (a relationship). —**break the ice.** To get started, as in an enterprise or conversation. —**break with.** **1.** To discontinue a relationship with. **2.** To depart from (a tradition or precedent, for example).

~*n.* Also **brake** (for sense 19). **1.** The act of breaking; a separating into parts. **2.** The result of breaking; a fracture or crack. **3. a.** A beginning; a coming into being: *the break of day.* **b.** An opening; a clearing. **4.** A dash, especially to escape: *made a break for it.* **5.** An interruption or disruption of continuity or regularity. **6.** A brief rest or holiday, as from work. **7.** A sudden or marked change. **8.** *Informal.* A chance occurrence; especially, an unexpected opportunity. **9.** A severing of ties. **10.** A sudden decline in prices, especially in the stock market. **11.** *Prosody.* A pause in a line; a caesura. **12.** *Tennis.* An instance of winning a game against an opponent's

breaker *There are three ways in which a wave breaks into foam against a reef or shoreline: plunging breakers (shown here) surge up from a steeply rising bottom and curl over to break with a sudden crash; spilling breakers break slowly over a long stretch of the seabed; surging breakers neither spill nor plunge—they break as they flow over the beach face.*

serve. **13.** *Electricity.* Interruption of a flow of current. **14.** *Music.* **a.** The point at which a register or a tonal quality changes to another register or tonal quality. **b.** The change itself. **c.** In jazz, an improvised solo cadenza played during the pause between the regular phrases or choruses of a melody. **15.** *Baseball & Cricket.* The swerving of a ball from a straight path of flight when thrown. **16.** *Billiards.* The opening shot. **17.** *Billiards & Croquet.* A run or unbroken series of successful shots. **18.** *Bowling.* Failure to score a strike or a spare in a given frame. **19.** A high, open, horse-drawn carriage with four wheels. [Break, broke, broken; Middle English *breken, brok* (or *brak*), *broken,* Old English *brecan, bræc* (plural *brǣcon*), *brocen,* from Germanic *brekan* (unattested).]

Synonyms: *burst, crack, crush, fracture, rupture, shatter, shiver, smash, splinter, split.*

break·a·ble (brā′kə-bəl) *adj.* Capable of being broken. —See Synonyms at **fragile.**

~*n.* **breakables.** Articles capable of being broken easily. —**break·a·ble·ness** *n.*

break·age (brā′kĭj) *n.* **1.** The act or result of breaking. **2.** A quantity or article broken. **3. a.** Loss or damage as a result of breaking. **b.** An allowance in compensation for such a loss or damage.

break away *intr.v.* **1.** To withdraw, especially from a main group. **2.** To depart from former ways or tradition.

break·a·way (brā′ə-wā′) *adj.* **1.** Withdrawing, or favoring withdrawal, from a main group: *a breakaway political faction.* **2.** Designed to break or fall apart easily: *breakaway stage scenery.* ~*n.* **1.** One that breaks away. **2.** *Australian.* A sudden mad rush, as of cattle, for example; a stampede.

break·bone fever (brāk′bōn′) *n.* A viral disease, **dengue** *(see).*

break·danc·ing (brāk′dăn′sĭng) *n.* A type of dance incorporating gymnastics such as handsprings, popular in the 1980's. It may accompany **body popping** *(see).* [20th century : origin obscure.]

break down *intr.v.* **1.** To fail to function; cease to be useful or operable. **2.** To have a physical or mental collapse. **3.** To become seriously distressed or upset. **4.** To end prematurely or inconclusively: *Peace talks have broken down.* **5.** To undergo chemical decomposition. —*tr.v.* **1.** To distress; upset. **2.** To overcome (opposition, for example). **3.** To consider in parts; analyze. **4.** To effect chemical decomposition in. **5.** To demolish; destroy.

break·down (brāk′doun′) *n.* **1. a.** The act or an instance of failing to function or ceasing to be effective. **b.** The condition resulting from this. **2.** *Electricity.* The failure of an insulator or insulating medium to prevent discharge or current flow. **3.** A collapse in physical or mental health. **4.** An analysis, outline, or summary consisting of itemized data or essentials. **5.** Disintegration or decomposition into parts or elements. **6.** An electrical discharge between electrodes that occurs at a certain voltage in a gas discharge tube.

break·er¹ (brā′kər) *n.* **1.** One that breaks. **2.** A machine or plant for breaking up some hard substance, such as rock or coal. **3.** *Electricity.* A **circuit breaker** *(see).* **4.** A wave that crests or breaks into foam, especially against a shoreline.

breaker² *n.* A small water cask for use on a ship's lifeboat. [Spanish *bareca, barrica,* BARREL.]

break-e·ven point (brāk′ē′vən) *n.* The stage at which a business, project, or speculator can operate economically without making a loss, but not yet making a profit.

break·fast (brĕk′fəst) *n.* The first meal of the day. [Middle English *brekfast, brekefast,* from *breken faste,* to break (one's) fasting.] —**break·fast** *v.* —**break·fast·er** *n.*

break·front (brāk′frŭnt′) *n.* A high, wide cabinet or bookcase having a central section projecting beyond the end sections.

break in *tr.v.* **1.** To train (a horse, for example) to obey; tame. **2.** To accustom to duties. **3.** To wear or use until comfortable or suited to one's requirements. —*intr.v.* **1.** To break into premises, usually to steal. **2.** To interrupt a speaker.

break-in (brāk′ĭn′) *n.* **1.** An act of forcible entry, as into a building, dwelling, or office, for an illegal purpose such as theft. **2.** A training or testing period of someone or something that is new.

break·ing (brā′kĭng) *n.* *Linguistics.* The change of a simple vowel to a diphthong, often caused by the influence of neighboring consonants. Also called "vowel fracture."

breaking and entering *n.* *Law.* The gaining of unauthorized access, as by forcing a lock, to another's premises for the purpose of committing a crime.

breaking point *n.* **1.** The point at which the stress on a material is sufficient to cause it to break. **2.** The stage at which a person is no longer able to bear psychological stress.

break·neck (brāk′nĕk′) *adj.* Dangerous: *breakneck speed.*

break out *intr.v.* **1.** To begin or arise suddenly. **2.** To escape, as from prison. **3.** To become affected with eruptions or with a rash. Used of the skin, or of a skin-disease sufferer.

break-out (brāk′out′) *n.* An escape, as from prison.

Breakspear, Nicholas. See **Adrian IV.**

break through *intr.v.* **1.** To penetrate an obstacle or defense. **2.** To overcome a difficulty and be able to make progress.

break·through (brāk′throo′) *n.* **1.** An act of breaking through an obstacle or restriction. **2.** A military offensive that penetrates an enemy's lines of defense. **3.** A major achievement or success that permits further progress, as in scientific research.

break up *tr.v.* **1.** To disband or disrupt. **2. a.** To take apart; separate. **b.** To fragment, as by cutting or digging. **3.** To put a stop to; discontinue. **4.** *Informal.* To convulse with laughter. —*intr.v.* **1. a.** To end. Used of a relationship. **b.** To part. Used of partners, especially in or as in a marriage. **2.** *British.* To begin the holiday period at the end of a school term. **3.** To melt in the spring thaw. Used of ice on a frozen river or lake. **4.** *Informal.* To be overcome by laughter or emotion.

break·up (brāk′ŭp′) *n.* **1.** The act of breaking up; a separation or dispersal. **2.** A collapse; dissolution.

break·wa·ter (brāk′wô′tər, -wŏt′ər) *n.* A structure that protects a harbor or shore from the full impact of waves.

bream (brēm) *n., pl.* **bream. 1.** Any of several European freshwater fishes of the genus *Abramis,* having a deep, flattened body and silvery scales. **2.** Any of several similar or related fishes. [Middle English *breme,* from Old French *breme, bresme,* from Germanic.]

breast (brĕst) *n.* **1. a.** Either of two fleshy milk-secreting organs on a woman's chest; the human mammary gland. **b.** A homologous organ in other mammals. **2.** A source of nourishment. **3. a.** The front of the body, extending from the neck to the abdomen. **b.** A homologous part in other animals. **4.** This part of the human body regarded as the seat of affection or emotion. **5.** The section of a garment that covers this part of the body. **6.** Anything likened to this part of the body: *the breast of a hill.* **7.** A coal face. **—make a clean breast of.** To make a full confession of.
∼*tr.v.* **breasted, breasting, breasts. 1.** To meet with the breast: *The runner breasted the tape just ahead of the others.* **2.** To encounter or face bravely. **3.** To come to the breast of: *The figure breasted the hill.* [Middle English *brest,* Old English *brēost.*]

breast·bone (brĕst′bōn′) *n. Anatomy.* The **sternum** *(see).*

breast·feed (brĕst′fēd′) *v.* **-fed** (-fĕd′), **-feeding, -feeds.** —*tr.* To feed (a baby) mother's milk from the breast; suckle. —*intr.* To feed a baby in this way.

breast·plate (brĕst′plāt′) *n.* **1.** A piece of armor that covers the breast. **2.** A square cloth set with 12 precious stones representing the 12 tribes of Israel, worn by a Jewish high priest. **3.** The plastron of a turtle's or tortoise's shell.

breast stroke *n.* A swimming stroke in which one lies face down in the water and extends the arms in front of the head, then sweeps them both back laterally under the surface of the water while performing a frog kick.

breast·work (brĕst′wûrk′) *n.* A temporary, quickly constructed fortification, usually breast-high. —See Synonyms at **bulwark.**

breath (brĕth) *n.* **1.** The air inhaled and exhaled in respiration. **2.** The act or process of breathing; respiration. **3.** The capacity to breathe, especially as evidence of life. **4.** A single respiration. **5.** Exhaled air, as evidenced by vapor, odor, or heat. **6.** A momentary pause or rest. **7. a.** A momentary stirring of air. **b.** A slight gust of fragrant air. **8.** A trace or suggestion: *a breath of scandal.* **9.** A soft-spoken sound; a whisper. **10.** *Phonetics.* Exhalation of air without vibrating the vocal cords, as in the articulation of *p* and *s.* Compare **voice. —catch one's breath. 1.** To pause until one's normal breathing is regained. **2.** To be left breathless for a moment, as in admiration. **—in the same breath.** At the same time. **—out of breath.** Breathless, as from exertion. **—save one's breath.** Not to waste time in pointless excuses, pleading, or the like. **—take someone's breath away.** To leave one as if breathless from awe or surprise. **—under** (or **below**) **one's breath.** In a whisper or muted voice. [Middle English *breth,* vapor, air from the lungs, Old English *brǣth,* odor, exhalation.]

breath·a·lyze (brĕth′ə-līz′) *tr.v.* **-lyzed, -lyzing, -lyzes.** To test (a driver) for excessive consumption of alcohol, using a Breathalyzer.

Breath·a·lyz·er (brĕth′ə-lī′zər) *n.* A trademark for a device used to test whether a driver has consumed an excessive amount of alcohol, consisting of crystals which react to the presence of alcohol in the driver's breath by changing color. [BREATH + (AN)ALYZE + -ER.]

breathe (brē*th*) *v.* **breathed, breathing, breathes.** —*intr.* **1.** To inhale and exhale. **2.** To be alive; live. **3.** To move or stir gently, as air does. **4.** To take in oxygen for combustion. Used of machinery. **5.** To come into contact with, or allow the passage of, air: *open the wine and let it breathe.* —*tr.* **1.** To inhale and exhale during respiration. **2.** To impart (a quality) as if by breathing; instill: *breathe life into a portrait.* **3.** To exhale; emit. **4.** To utter, especially quietly; whisper: *Don't breathe a word of this.* **5.** To express; evince; manifest. **6.** To allow (a person or animal) to rest or regain breath. **7.** *Phonetics.* To utter with a voiceless exhalation of air. [Middle English *brethen,* from *breth,* BREATH.] **—breath·a·ble** *adj.*

breath·er (brē′*th*ər) *n.* **1.** One who breathes in a specified manner. **2.** *Informal.* A short rest period. **3.** An opening for ventilation.

breath·ing (brē′*th*ĭng) *n.* **1.** The act or process of respiration. **2.** Either of two marks used in writing Greek, indicating aspiration of an initial sound (‛), called *rough breathing,* or the absence of such aspiration (’), called *smooth breathing.*

breathing room *n.* Breathing space.

breathing space *n.* **1.** Sufficient space to permit ease of breathing or movement. **2.** Time allowing an opportunity to rest or solve a problem. In this sense, also called "breathing spell."

breathing spell *n.* See **breathing space** (sense 2).

breath·less (brĕth′lĭs) *adj.* **1.** Out-of-breath. **2.** Holding the breath from excitement or suspense. **3.** Inspiring or marked by sudden excitement that takes the breath away: *a breathless flight.* **4.** Having no air or breeze; still. **5.** Without breath; not breathing; dead. **—breath·less·ly** *adv.* **—breath·less·ness** *n.*

breath·tak·ing (brĕth′tā′kĭng) *adj.* Inspiring awe; deeply impressive or exciting. **—breath·tak·ing·ly** *adv.*

breath test *n. British.* A test for intoxication, usually using a Breathalyzer.

breath·y (brĕth′ē) *adj.* **-ier, -iest.** Marked by audible or noisy breathing: *a breathy voice.*

brec·ci·a (brĕch′ē-ə, brĕsh′-) *n.* Rock composed of angular fragments cemented in a fine matrix. [Italian, from Old High German *brehha,* breaking, fragment, from *brehhan,* to break.] **—brec·ci·at·ed** (brĕch′ē-ā′tĭd, brĕsh′-) *adj.*

Brecht (brĕkt, brĕKHt), **Bertolt** (1898–1956). German playwright. His most popular work, *The Threepenny Opera,* with music by Kurt Weill, was produced in 1928. In 1933 he fled to Denmark to escape the Nazis, and in 1941 came to the United States, where he wrote *The Caucasian Chalk Circle.* He settled in East Berlin (1949) and was awarded the Stalin Peace Prize (1954). **—Brecht·i·an** *adj. & n.*

bred. Past tense and past participle of **breed.**

Bre·da (brā-dä′). Industrial town in the southern Netherlands, at the confluence of the Merk and Aa rivers. Charles II of England lived here during much of his exile and issued the Declaration of Breda (1660) announcing the conditions for his return to the English throne.

brede (brēd) *n. Archaic.* An ornamental embroidered edging. [Alteration of BRAID.]

breech (brēch) *n.* **1.** The lower rear portion of the human trunk; the buttocks. **2.** The lower part of a pulley. **3.** The part of a firearm to the rear of the barrel or, in a cannon, to the rear of the bore. [Middle English *breech,* Old English *brēc,* breeches, plural of *brōc,* leg covering.]

breech·block (brēch′blŏk′) *n.* The metal part that closes the breech end of the barrel of a breechloading gun and that is removed to insert a cartridge and replaced before firing.

breech·cloth (brēch′klôth′) *n.* Also **breech·clout** (-klout′). A loincloth.

breech delivery *n.* Delivery of a baby with the buttocks or feet appearing first. Also called "breech birth."

breech·es (brĭch′ĭz) *pl.n.* **1.** Trousers extending to or just below the knee. **2.** *Informal & Regional.* Any trousers. [Plural of BREECH.]

breeches buoy *n.* An apparatus used for rescues at sea, consisting of sturdy canvas breeches for the rescued person's legs, attached at the waist to a ring buoy that is suspended from a pulley running along a rope from ship to shore or from ship to ship.

breech·ing (brĭch′ĭng, brē′chĭng) *n.* **1.** The strap of a harness that passes behind a draft animal's haunches. **2.** The parts of a gun that make up the breech. **3.** Formerly, a rope securing the breech of a cannon to the side of a ship to control the recoil.

breech·load·er (brēch′lō′dər) *n.* Any gun or firearm loaded at the breech. **—breech·load·ing** *adj.*

breech presentation *n.* The position of a fetus during labor in which the buttocks or feet appear first in the cervix.

breed (brēd) *v.* **bred** (brĕd), **breeding, breeds.** —*tr.* **1.** To produce (offspring); give birth to or hatch. **2.** To bring about; engender. **3. a.** To cause to reproduce; raise. **b.** To develop new or improved strains in (animals or plants) by selection, hybridization, and similar methods. —*intr.* **1.** To produce offspring. **2.** To be engendered; arise: *Panic bred in this atmosphere.*
∼*n.* **1.** A genetic strain or type of organism, usually a domestic animal, having consistent and recognizable inherited characteristics; especially, such a strain developed and maintained by man. **2.** A kind or type: *a new breed of university student.* [Middle English *breden, bred,* Old English *brēdan, bredd* (unattested).]

breed·er (brē′dər) *n.* **1.** A person who breeds animals or plants. **2.** An animal kept to produce offspring. **3.** One that breeds; a cause; source. **4.** A breeder reactor.

breeder reactor *n.* A nuclear reactor that produces, as well as consumes, fissionable material; especially, one that produces more fissionable material than it consumes.

breed·ing (brē′dĭng) *n.* **1.** One's line of descent: *a woman of noble breeding.* **2.** Training in the proper forms of social and personal conduct. —See Usage note at **culture.**

breeding ground *n.* **1.** A place to which animals go to breed. **2.** A place or set of circumstances that encourages certain ideas or conditions.

breeks (brēks) *pl.n. Chiefly Scottish.* Breeches; trousers. [Middle English (northern dialect) *breke,* variant of *brech,* BREECH.]

breeze¹ (brēz) *n.* **1.** A light air current; a gentle wind. **2.** *Meteorology.* A wind of from 6.5 to 50 kilometers (4 to 31 miles) per hour. **3.** *Chiefly British Informal.* A commotion or disturbance; an argument. **4.** *Informal.* An easily accomplished task. —See Synonyms at **wind.**
∼*intr.v.* **breezed, breezing, breezes. 1.** To blow lightly. **2.** *Informal.* To move in a quick and usually nonchalant manner: *She breezed in an hour late* **3.** To progress swiftly and effortlessly: *breezed through the test.* **—breeze up.** *Nautical.* To blow more strongly. Used of wind. [Perhaps from Old Spanish *briza*†, northeast wind.]

breeze² *n. British.* The refuse left when coal, coke, or charcoal is burned, used in brickmaking and as a concrete filler. [French *braise,* burning coals, from Old French *brese,* from Germanic.]

breeze·way (brēz′wā′) *n.* A roofed, open-sided passageway connecting two structures, such as a house and a garage.

breez·y (brē′zē) *adj.* **-ier, -iest. 1.** Exposed to breezes; windy. **2.** Fresh and animated; lively; sprightly. **3.** Casual; nonchalant. **—breez·i·ly** *adv.* **—breez·i·ness** *n.*

breg·ma (brĕg′mə) *n., pl.* **-mata** (-mə-tə). *Anatomy.* The junction of the sagittal and coronal sutures at the top of the skull. **—breg·mat·ic** (brĕg-măt′ĭk) *adj.*

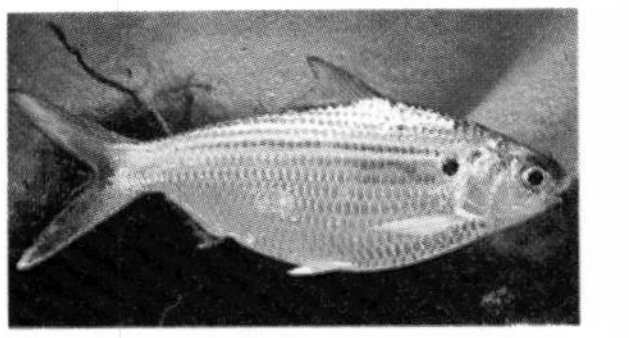

bream *A European freshwater fish that lives in lakes and slow-flowing rivers. Adult bream grow to between 300 and 500 millimeters (12–20 inches) long.*

PRONUNCIATION KEY

ă, pat; ā, pay; âr, care;
ä, father, are; b, bib;
ch, church; d, deed; ĕ, pet;
ē, be; f, fife; g, gag; h, hat;
hw, which; ĭ, pit; ī, pie;
îr, pier; j, judge; k, kick;
l, lid, needle; m, mum;
n, no, sudden; ng, thing;
ŏ, pot; ō, toe; ô, paw, for;
oi, noise; ou, out; ŏŏ, book;
ōō, boot; p, pop; r, roar;
s, sauce; sh, ship, dish;
t, tight; th, thin, path;
th, this, bathe; ŭ, cut; ûr, fur;
v, valve; w, with; y, yes;
z, zebra, size; zh, vision;
ə, about, item, edible, gallop, circus, peaceful

IN FOREIGN WORDS:

à, *Fr.* ami; œ, *Fr.* feu, *Ger.* schön; ü, *Fr.* tu, *Ger.* über; KH, *Ger.* ich, *Scot.* loch; N, *Fr.* bon; y′, *Fr.* Compiègne

STRESS MARKS:

Primary stress: ′
in·cite′ (ĭn-sīt′)
Secondary stress: ′
in′sight′ (ĭn′sīt′)

Bre·men (brĕm′ən, brā′mən). City in northern Germany, capital of the state of the same name, on the Weser River. It is Germany's second most important port after Hamburg and in the Middle Ages was a leading member of the Hanseatic League.

Bre·mer·ha·ven (brĕm′ər-hä′vən, -hä′-). Port in northern Germany, on the estuary of the Weser River. It has a deep natural harbor and is the largest fishing port in continental Europe.

brems·strah·lung (brĕms′shträ′lŏng) n. The electromagnetic radiation produced by an electrically charged subatomic particle, such as an electron, subjected to a change in velocity, as by deceleration in the electric field of an atomic nucleus. [German, "braking radiation" : *Bremse,* brake + *Strahlung,* radiation.]

Bren·dan (brĕn′dən), **Saint** (c. 484–c. 577). Irish abbot, also known variously as "Brenainn" (in Modern Irish), "Brandanus" (in Latin), and "Brandon." He is the legendary hero of a number of sea voyages, including one to America, and almost certainly visited the Scottish isles.

Bren·del (brĕn′dəl), **Alfred** (1931–). Austrian pianist. Although admired for his interpretation of the 19th-century masters generally, he has made his name as a performer of Schubert and Beethoven.

Bren gun (brĕn) n. A .303 caliber gas-operated, air-cooled light machine gun, adopted by the British Army in World War II. [Br(NO), Czechoslovakia, where it was first made + *En(field),* England, where it was later manufactured.]

Bren·ner Pass (brĕn′ər). One of the lowest Alpine passes, connecting Innsbruck, Austria, with Bolzano, Italy. It has been the major northern entrance to Italy since Roman times, but a road was not constructed through it until 1772. A railway through the pass, requiring 30 tunnels and 60 large bridges, was completed in 1867.

brent *British.* Variant of **brant.**

br'er (brûr, brĕr) n. *Southern U.S. Informal.* Brother.

Bre·scia (brĕsh′ə, brä′shə). Industrial city in northern Italy, at the junction of the Garza River and the Po plain. It is the capital of the province of the same name.

Brest¹ (brĕst). Port and naval station in northwest France, on the Brittany coast. Its large landlocked harbor was built by Cardinal Richelieu (1631) as a military base and arsenal, with a roadstead (24 kilometers; 14 miles long) leading to open water.

Brest². Formerly **Brest-Li·tovsk** (brĕst′lĭ-tôfsk′). Industrial city in Belarus, near the Polish border. It belonged to Lithuania, then Poland, before being ceded to Russia (1795). Germany and the U.S.S.R. signed the treaty of Brest-Litovsk ending World War I on the eastern front (March 1918).

Bretagne. See **Brittany.**

breth·ren (brĕth′rən). Plural of **brother.** Used chiefly in archaic, ceremonial, or ironic contexts.

Bret·on (brĕt′n) n. 1. A native or inhabitant of Brittany. 2. The Celtic language of Brittany. [French, from Old French, BRITON.] —**Bret·on** *adj.*

Bre·ton (brə-tôN′), **André** (1896–1966). French poet and literary theorist, founder of surrealism. He began to write after World War I, at first linking himself with dadaism, but breaking with that movement to write the first manifesto of surrealism (1924).

Breu·er (broi′ər) **Josef** (1842–1925). Austrian physician and psychologist. He collaborated with Freud in writing *Studies in Hysteria* (1895). He was the first man to relieve hysteria by cathartic methods, and it was his therapy that provided the basis of Freud's development of the theory of psychoanalysis.

Breughel. See **Bruegel.**

breve (brēv, brĕv) n. 1. A symbol (˘) placed over a vowel to show that it has a short sound. Compare **macron.** 2. *Prosody.* A similar symbol used to indicate that a syllable is short or unstressed. 3. *Music.* A single note equivalent to two whole notes. 4. *Archaic.* A letter of authority, especially one from a pope. [Middle English, variant of *bref,* BRIEF.]

bre·vet (brə-vĕt′; *British* brĕv′ĭt) n. *Abbr.* **brev., bvt.** A commission, often granted as an honor, promoting a military officer in rank without an increase in pay or authority.
~*tr.v.* **brevetted** or **-veted, -vetting** or **-veting, -vets.** To promote by brevet.
~*adj.* Held or awarded by brevet. [Middle English, from Old French *brevet,* diminutive of *bref,* letter, BRIEF.] —**bre·vet·cy** (brə-vĕt′sē) n.

bre·vi·ar·y (brē′vē-ĕr-ē, brĕv′ē-) n., *pl.* **-ies.** A book containing the hymns, offices, and prayers said or sung by Roman Catholic clergy at the canonical hours. [Latin *breviārium,* summary, abridgment, from *breviāre,* to abridge, from *brevis,* short, BRIEF.]

bre·vier (brə-vîr′) n. *Printing.* Formerly, a size of type, 8-point. [Dutch, "type size for breviaries," from Latin *breviārium,* BREVIARY.]

brev·i·ty (brĕv′ə-tē) n. 1. Briefness of duration. 2. Concise expression; terseness. [Latin *brevitās,* from *brevis,* BRIEF.]

brew (brōō) v. **brewed, brewing, brews.** —*tr.* 1. To make (ale or beer, for example) from malt and other ingredients by infusion, boiling, and fermentation. 2. To make (a beverage) by boiling, steeping, or mixing various ingredients. 3. To concoct; devise. —*intr.* 1. To brew ale or beer. 2. To be in the process of infusion. 3. To be imminent; impend. Used of storms. 4. To be in preparation. Used of plots, quarrels, or the like.
~*n.* 1. A beverage made by brewing. 2. The quality or quantity of beverage brewed at one time. 3. A concoction. [Middle English *brewen,* Old English *brēowan,* from Germanic.] —**brew·er** n.

brew·age (brōō′ĭj) n. 1. Something prepared by brewing. 2. The process of brewing.

brewer's yeast n. 1. A yeast, *Saccharomyces cerevisiae,* used in brewing and as a source of B complex vitamins. 2. The yeast obtained as a by-product of brewing.

brew·er·y (brōō′ər-ē) n., *pl.* **-ies.** An establishment for the manufacture of malt liquors.

brew·is (brōō′ĭs, brōōz) n. *Regional.* 1. A broth. 2. Bread soaked in broth, gravy, milk, or the like. [Middle English *browis, brewes,* from Old French *broez, bro(u)ez,* from *breu,* broth.]

Brey·ten·bach (brā′tən-bŭкн), **Breyten** (1939–). South African poet, a member of the so-called *Sestigers* (people of the sixties). After living in Paris for some years, he returned to South Africa in the 1970's and was imprisoned under the country's Terrorism Act.

Brezh·nev (brĕzh′nĕf), **Leonid Ilyich** (1906–82). Soviet politician and president. He joined the Komsomol (Communist Youth) in 1923 and the party in 1931. For the next 20 years he advanced his career as a protégé of Khrushchev in the Ukraine. In 1957 he was promoted to membership of the Presidium (now the Politburo) and became its chairman (1960). In 1964, when Khrushchev was dismissed, he replaced him as first secretary of the party. He became president in 1977. In 1968 when Soviet troops entered Czechoslovakia, he enunciated the "Brezhnev doctrine," which asserts that the U.S.S.R. has the right to enter any Warsaw Pact country in which the authority of the Communist government is threatened.

Bri·an Bo·ru (brī′ən bə-rōō′) (c. 926–1014). King of Ireland. Most of his life was spent fighting the Danes and their allies, the Norse of Ireland, Iceland, the Hebrides, and the Orkneys. In 1014 his forces routed the Danish coalition at Clontarf, ending Norse power in Ireland. He was killed at the end of the battle.

Bri·and (brē-äN′), **Aristide** (1862–1932). French politician and lawyer who became prime minister for the first of 11 times in 1909. His greatest achievements were as foreign minister (1925–32), when he was the chief architect of the Locarno Pact, guaranteeing the borders of Belgium, France, and Germany, and the Kellogg-Briand Pact (a declaration against war signed by 62 countries). He shared the Nobel Peace Prize (1926) with Gustav Stresemann.

bri·ar¹, bri·er (brī′ər) n. 1. A shrub or small tree, *Erica arborea,* of southern Europe, having a hard, woody root used to make tobacco pipes. Also called "tree heath." 2. A pipe made from briar-root or from a similar wood. [French *bruyère,* heath, from Gallo-Roman *brūcaria* (unattested), from Gaulish *brūko* (unattested).]

briar². Variant of **brier** (bush).

Bri·ar·e·us (brī-âr′ē-əs). *Greek Mythology.* A giant who aided Zeus and the Olympians against the Titans.

bri·ar-root (brī′ər-rōōt′, -rōōt′) n. The hard, woody root of the briar, *Erica arborea.*

bribe (brīb) n. 1. Anything, such as money, property, or a favor, offered or given to someone in a position of trust to induce him to act dishonestly. 2. Something offered or serving to influence or persuade.
~*v.* **bribed, bribing, bribes.** —*tr.* 1. To give, offer, or promise a bribe to. 2. To gain influence over or corrupt by bribery. —*intr.* To give, offer, or promise bribes. [Middle English *briben,* to purloin, steal, from Old French *briber, brimber†,* to beg.] —**brib·a·ble** *adj.* —**brib·er** n.

brib·er·y (brī′bə-rē) n., *pl.* **-ies.** The act of giving, offering, or taking a bribe.

bric-a-brac (brĭk′ə-brăk′) n. Miscellaneous, usually small, objects displayed in a room as ornaments and valued for their antiquity, rarity, or curiosity value. [French, from obsolete *à bric et à brac,* at random, perhaps based on *bric,* piece.]

brick (brĭk) n. 1. A molded, rectangular block of clay, baked by the sun or in a kiln until hard, and used as a building and paving material. 2. These blocks collectively. 3. Any object shaped like a brick. 4. *Informal.* A trustworthy or obliging person. 5. *Informal.* A tactless blunder. Used in the phrase *drop a brick.*
~*tr.v.* **bricked, bricking, bricks.** 1. To construct, line, or pave with brick. 2. To close or wall with brick. Usually used with *up* or *in: He bricked up the windows of the old house.* [Middle English *brike, breke,* probably from Middle Dutch *bricke,* akin to Middle Low German *brike†.*] —**brick** *adj.* —**brick·y** *adj.*

brick·bat (brĭk′băt′) n. 1. A piece of brick, especially one used as a weapon or missile. 2. A critical remark.

brick·lay·er (brĭk′lā′ər) n. A person who lays brick. —**brick·lay·ing** n.

brick red n. 1. Moderate reddish brown. 2. Moderate to strong brown. —**brick-red** *adj.*

brick·work (brĭk′wûrk′) n. 1. A structure made of bricks. 2. Construction with bricks.

brick·yard (brĭk′yärd′) n. A place where bricks are made.

bri·dal (brīd′l) n. A marriage ceremony; wedding.
~*adj.* Of or pertaining to a bride or a marriage ceremony; nuptial. [Middle English *bridale,* wedding feast, Old English *brȳdealu,* "bride ale" : BRIDE + ALE.]

bridal wreath n. Any of various shrubs of the genus *Spiraea,* cultivated for their profuse white flowers.

bride¹ (brīd) n. A woman who has recently been married or is about to be married. [Middle English *bride,* Old English *brȳd,* from Germanic *brūdhiz* (unattested).]

bride² (brīd) n. A loop, bar, or tie connecting pattern segments in lacework or needlework. [French, "bridle," from Middle High German *brīdel,* rein.]

Bride (brīd), **Saint** (c. 453–c. 523). Also **Bridg·et** (brīj′ĭt) or **Brig·id** (brĭj′ĭd, brē′ĭd). Irish holy woman, buried at Downpatrick with St. Patrick and St. Columba and, like them, a patron saint of Ireland. Her feast day is February 1.

bride·groom (brīd′grōōm′, -grōōm′) n. A man who has recently been married or is about to be married. [Alteration (influenced by GROOM) of Middle English bridegome, Old English brȳdguma : brȳd, BRIDE + guma, man.]

bride price n. In certain societies, money or goods given by a bridegroom's family to the bride's family. Also called "bride wealth."

brides·maid (brīdz′mād′) n. A woman, usually young and unmarried, who attends the bride at a wedding. Compare **maid of honor, matron of honor.**

bride·well (brīd′wĕl′, -wəl) n. A prison for petty offenders. [After St. Bride's Well, London, site of such a prison (16th century).]

bridge¹ (brĭj) n. Abb. **br.** 1. A structure spanning and providing passage over a road, waterway, railway, or other obstacle. 2. **a.** Anything resembling such a structure in form. **b.** Anything which forms a connection: a bridge between peoples. 3. The upper bony ridge of the human nose. 4. The part of a pair of eyeglasses that rests against this ridge. 5. Music. **a.** A thin, upright piece of wood in some stringed instruments that supports the strings above the soundboard. **b.** A transitional passage connecting two subjects or movements. 6. Dentistry. A fixed replacement for one or several, but not all, of the natural teeth, anchored at each end to a natural tooth. Also called "bridgework." 7. Nautical. A crosswise platform or area above the main deck of a ship from which the ship is controlled. 8. In games such as billiards, a notched piece of wood or a rest made with the hand on which to steady the cue. Also called "rest." 9. Electricity. Any of various circuits containing a branch that connects two points of equal potential and consequently carries no current when the circuit is suitably adjusted. 10. A platform above a theater stage. —**burn one's bridges.** To eliminate the possibility of retreat.
~tr.v. **bridged, bridging, bridges.** 1. To build a bridge over. 2. To cross by or as if by a bridge. 3. To form a link across (a period of time, for example). [Middle English brigge, Old English brycg, from Germanic.] —**bridge·a·ble** adj.

bridge² n. Any of several card games derived from whist, played with one pack of cards divided equally among four people. [19th century : origin obscure.]

bridge·board (brĭj′bôrd′, -bōrd′) n. A notched board at either side of a staircase, that supports the treads and risers.

bridge·build·er (brĭj′bĭl′dər) n. One who works for better relations between opposing groups; a conciliator. —**bridge·build·ing** n.

bridge·head (brĭj′hĕd′) n. 1. A military position established by advance troops on the enemy's side of a river or pass to afford protection for the main attacking force. 2. Any foothold established in hostile territory. [Translation of French tête de pont.]

Bridge of Sighs A stone bridge of the 16th century, in Venice, connecting the Doge's palace to the state prison, so named because prisoners were taken over the bridge from the hall in which they had been sentenced to the prison. The bridge over the Cam River, behind St. John's College, Cambridge, England, resembles the Venetian original and is often called by the same name.

Bridg·es (brĭj′ĭz), **Robert Seymour** (1844–1930). British poet, who became poet laureate in 1913. His poems are admired for their metrical invention and lyrical simplicity. His long poetic disquisition on the growth of the human soul, The Testament of Beauty (1929), is considered his finest achievement.

Bridget, Saint. See **St. Bride.**

Bridg·et of Sweden (brĭj′ĭt), **Saint** (1302–73). Swedish nun and patron saint of Sweden, who founded the Order of the Most Holy Savior (Bridgettines) for nuns and monks. She settled in Rome (1350), founded a house where she sheltered the poor, campaigned for Church reform, and worked, unsuccessfully, to bring the papacy back to Rome from Avignon. Her feast day is October 8.

Bridge·town (brĭj′toun′). Capital and largest city of Barbados, in the West Indies. It is the country's only seaport.

Bridge·wa·ter Canal (brĭj′wô′tər, -wŏt′ər). An inland canal in northwestern England, connecting Worsley to Liverpool. It was one of the great engineering feats of the early Industrial Revolution, completed in 1761 for the Duke of Bridgewater by James Brindley (1716–72). Brindley avoided the use of locks by designing the canal as an aqueduct on arches, allowing the water to flow by the natural force of gravity.

bridge·work (brĭj′wûrk′) n. Dentistry. 1. A bridge. 2. Prosthetics involving a bridge or bridges.

bridg·ing (brĭj′ĭng) n. Wooden braces between beams, as of a floor or roof, that provide reinforcement and distribution of stress.

bridging loan n. A short-term loan made by a bank to enable a house purchaser to buy a new house before the purchaser's previous house has been sold.

Bridg·man (brĭj′mən), **Percy Williams** (1882–1961). U.S. physicist who investigated the conduction of electricity in metals, the properties of crystals, and the behavior of matter when subjected to high pressure. For his contributions to the last of those fields he was awarded the Nobel Prize in physics (1946).

Bridg·wa·ter (brĭj′wô′tər, -wŏt′ər). Port and market town in Somerset, southwestern England, on an estuary of the Parrett River on the Bristol Channel. It was the site of medieval wool and wine fairs and now produces bricks and plastics.

bri·dle (brīd′l) n. 1. The harness fitted around a horse's head, nor-

mally consisting of a headstall, bit, and reins, used to restrain or guide the animal. 2. Any device or condition that controls or restrains free movement; a curb or check. 3. Nautical. A span of chain, wire, or rope that can be secured at both ends to an object and slung from its center point. 4. A bridling gesture.
~v. **bridled, -dling, -dles.** —tr. 1. To put a bridle on. 2. To control or restrain with or as if with a bridle. —intr. 1. To lift the head and draw in the chin as an expression of scorn or resentment. 2. To become scornful or angry; take offense. [Middle English bridel, Old English brīdel, from Germanic.] —**bri·dler** n.

bridle hand n. The left hand, in which the reins are usually held, as by a cavalry soldier.

bridle path n. A pathway suitable for horses.

bri·doon (brĭ-dōōn′) n. A part of certain military bridles that consists of a rein and a bit resembling a snaffle, which may be reined independently of the curb bit. [French bridon, from bride, a bridle. See bride (loop).]

Brie¹ (brē). Agricultural region of northern France, lying east of Paris between the Seine and Marne valleys. It is a region of wheat and sugar-beet cultivation, but is famous more for its rose nurseries and, above all, for Brie cheese.

Brie² n. A soft, white, mold-ripened, whole-milk cheese. [French, first made in BRIE.]

brief (brēf) adj. **briefer, briefest.** 1. Short in time or duration. 2. Short in length or extent. 3. Condensed in expression; succinct. 4. Curt; abrupt.
~n. 1. A short or condensed statement. 2. A condensation or abstract of a large document or series of documents. 3. Abbr. **br.** Law. A document containing all facts and points of law pertinent to a specific case, filed by an attorney before arguing the case in court. 4. Roman Catholic Church. A papal letter pertaining to matters of discipline. 5. A set of instructions; a briefing. 6. **briefs.** Short, tight-fitting underpants. 7. British Slang. A lawyer. —**in brief.** In short; in a few words.
~tr.v. **briefed, briefing, briefs.** 1. To give concise preparatory instructions or advice to. 2. To summarize. 3. British. To send a legal brief to (an attorney). 4. British. To authorize and retain (an attorney) as counsel. [As an adjective, Middle English bref, from Old French bref, from Latin brevis; as a noun, Middle English bref, letter of authority, from Old French brief, from Late Latin breve, summary, from Latin, neuter of brevis, short.] —**brief·ly** adv. —**brief·ness** n.

brief·case (brēf′kās′) n. A portable rectangular case of leather or similar material, used for holding books and papers. [From BRIEF (document).]

brief·ing (brē′fĭng) n. 1. The act or procedure of giving or receiving concise preparatory information, information, or advice. 2. The information conveyed during this procedure.

brief·less (brēf′lĭs) adj. Having no brief, thus no clients. Said of a lawyer.

bri·er¹ (brī′ər) n. Also **bri·ar.** Any of various thorny plants or bushes, especially a prickly-stemmed rosebush.

brier². Variant of **briar** (shrub).

brig¹ (brĭg) n. A two-masted sailing ship, developed from the brigantine and differing from it mainly by being square-rigged on both masts. [Short for BRIGANTINE.]

brig² 1. A ship's prison. 2. Military Slang. A guardhouse. [Probably from BRIG (ship).]

bri·gade (brĭ-gād′) n. 1. **a.** A military unit consisting of a variable number of combat battalions. **b.** A former unit of the U.S. Army composed of two or more regiments commanded by a brigadier general. 2. A group of persons organized for a specific purpose: a fire brigade.
~tr.v. **brigaded, -gading, -gades.** To form into a brigade. [French, from Old French, from Old Italian brigata, troop, company, from brigare, to form a troop, fight, from briga, strife, perhaps from Celtic.]

brig·a·dier (brĭg′ə-dîr′) n. A brigadier general. [French, from BRIGADE.]

brigadier general n., pl. **brigadier generals.** An officer ranking above a colonel and below a major general in the U.S. Army, Air Force, and Marine Corps. Also called "brigadier."

brig·and (brĭg′ənd) n. A robber, especially one of a gang of bandits. [Middle English brigaunt, foot soldier, bandit, from Old French brigand, from Italian brigante, from the past participle of brigare, to fight. See brigade.] —**brig·and·age** (brĭg′ənd-ĭj), **brig·and·ism** n.

brig·an·dine (brĭg′ən-dēn′) n. A protective jacket of canvas or leather lined with overlapping scales or plates, worn in medieval times.

brig·an·tine (brĭg′ən-tēn′) n. A two-masted sailing ship, square-rigged on the foremast and differing from a brig mainly by being fore-and-aft rigged with square topsails on the mainmast. [French, from Old French brigandin, from Italian brigantino, "pirate ship."]

bright (brīt) adj. **brighter, brightest.** 1. Emitting or reflecting light; shining. 2. **a.** Vivid or brilliant in color. **b.** Characterizing a dye that produces a highly saturated color. 3. Glorious; splendid. 4. Full of promise and hope; auspicious. 5. Happy; cheerful. 6. Clever; intelligent. —See Synonyms at **intelligent.**
~n. 1. A thin, flat paintbrush used for highlighting. 2. **brights.** High-beam headlights.
~adv. In a bright manner. [Middle English bright, Old English beorht, from Germanic.] —**bright·ly** adv.

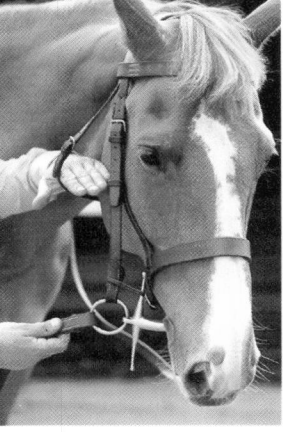

bridle The bit and reins by which a horse is controlled by its rider.

Synonyms: brilliant, incandescent, lambent, luminous, lustrous, radiant.

Bright (brīt), **John** (1811–89). British politician and one of the founders of the Anti-Corn Law League (1839). He was a leading campaigner in the movement that led to both the Second Reform Act (1867) and the Third (1884). From 1858 he represented Birmingham in Parliament, serving in Gladstone's administrations as president of the Board of Trade (1868–70) and Chancellor of the Duchy of Lancaster (1873–74 and 1880–82). He resigned from the cabinet in 1882 in protest against the bombardment of Alexandria, Egypt.

bright·en (brīt'n) v. **-ened, -ening, -ens.** —*tr.* To make bright or brighter. —*intr.* To become bright or brighter.

bright·ness (brīt'nĭs) n. **1.** The state or quality of being bright. **2. a.** The effect or sensation by means of which an observer is able to distinguish differences in luminance. **b.** *Physics.* **Luminance** *(see).* No longer in technical usage. **3.** The dimension of a color that represents its similarity to one of a series of achromatic colors ranging from very dim (dark) to very bright (dazzling).

Brigh·ton (brīt'n). Resort town on an old Saxon site on the East Sussex coast. Formerly known as Brighthelmstone, it became a fashionable resort after 1783, when the Prince of Wales, later George IV, began to frequent it. The famous pavilion, designed by John Nash in a combination of Chinese and Indian styles, was built for George IV.

Bright's disease n. Any of a group of kidney diseases marked by albumin in the urine and edema. [After Richard *Bright* (1789–1858), British physician who first described it.]

bright·work (brīt'wûrk') n. Metal parts or fixtures, especially on a ship, made bright by polishing.

Brigid, Saint. See St. Bride.

brill (brĭl) n., pl. **brills** or collectively **brill.** An edible flatfish, *Scophthalmus rhombus,* of European waters. [15th century : origin obscure.]

Bril·lat-Sa·va·rin (brē-yä'săv-ə-răN'), **Anthelme** (1755–1826). French politician and writer. He is best known for his *Physiologie de Goût* (1825), a witty dissertation on the art of dining.

bril·li·ance (brĭl'yəns) n. Also **bril·li·an·cy** (-yən-sē). **1.** Extreme brightness. **2.** Sharpness and clarity of musical tone. **3.** Splendor; magnificence. **4.** Exceptional clarity and agility of intellect or invention.

bril·liant (brĭl'yənt) adj. **1.** Full of light; shining. **2. a.** Brightly vivid in color. **b.** Designating a color that has a combination of high lightness and strong saturation. **2.** *Music.* Sharp and clear in tone. **4.** Glorious; splendid; magnificent. **5.** Superb; excellent; wonderful. Used also as a general term of approval. **6.** Marked by extraordinary powers of intellect or invention. —See Synonyms at **bright, intelligent.**
~n. **1.** A cut for precious gems, especially diamonds, having 58 facets and shaped like two cones joined at their bases with the top one cut off close to the base. **2.** A precious stone having this cut. [French *brillant,* present participle of *briller,* to shine, from Italian *brillare.*†] —**bril·liant·ly** adv. —**bril·liant·ness** n.

bril·lian·tine (brĭl'yən-tēn') n. **1.** An oily, perfumed preparation for the hair. **2.** A glossy fabric made from cotton and worsted or cotton and mohair. [French *brillantine,* from *brillant,* BRILLIANT.]

brim (brĭm) n. **1.** The rim or uppermost edge of a cup or other vessel. **2.** A projecting rim or edge: *the brim of a hat.* **3.** A border or edge, especially one surrounding a body of water.
~v. **brimmed, brimming, brims.** —*tr.* To fill to the brim. —*intr.* To be full to the brim; be filled. Used with *with.* —**brim over.** To overflow: *brim over with happiness.* [Middle English *brimme,* from Germanic; akin to Middle High German *brem.*]

brim·ful, brim·full (brĭm'fŏŏl') adj. Completely full.

brim·stone (brĭm'stōn') n. **1.** *Obsolete.* **Sulfur** *(see).* Now used chiefly in the phrase *fire and brimstone.* **2.** A bright yellow butterfly, *Gonepteryx rhamni,* common in northern temperate regions of Eurasia. **3.** A very common moth, *Opisthograptis luteolata,* of Europe and temperate Asia. [Middle English *brimston,* Late Old English *brynstān,* probably "burning stone," from *bryne,* burning.] —**brim·ston·y** adj.

brin (brĭn) n. Any of the ribs of a fan. [French *brin*†.]

Brin·di·si (brĭn'dĭ-zē). Ancient name **Brun·di·si·um** (brŭn-dĭz'ē-əm). Port in the Apulia region of southeastern Italy, on the Adriatic coast. In ancient times it was an important center of trade with the eastern Mediterranean, and it was also the point of departure for the Crusades of the Middle Ages.

brin·dle (brĭnd'l) adj. Brindled.
~n. **1.** A brindled color. **2.** A brindled animal.

brin·dled (brĭnd'əld) adj. Tawny or grayish with streaks or spots of a darker color. [Variant of earlier *brinded, brended,* from Middle English *brende,* perhaps from Scandinavian; akin to Old Norse *brandr,* piece of burning wood.]

brine (brīn) n. **1.** Water saturated with or containing large amounts of a salt, especially of sodium chloride. **2. a.** The water of a sea or ocean. **b.** A large body of salt water. **3.** Salt water used for preserving and pickling foods.
~tr.v. **brined, brining, brines.** To immerse or pickle in brine. [Middle English *brine,* Old English *brȳne*†, from Germanic.]

Bri·nell hardness (brĭ-nĕl') n. The relative hardness of metals and alloys, determined by forcing a steel ball into a test piece under standard conditions and measuring the surface area of the resulting indentation to calculate the relevant Brinell number. [After Johann

A. *Brinell* (1849–1925), Swedish engineer.]

Brinell number n. Abbr. **Bhn.** The numerical value assigned to the Brinell hardness of metals and alloys. It is calculated by dividing the load on the ball in kilograms by the area of the indentation in square millimeters.

brine shrimp n. Any of various small crustaceans of the genus *Artemia.* [So called because they have been observed living in highly saline water.]

bring (brĭng) tr.v. **brought** (brôt), **bringing, brings.** **1.** To take with oneself to a place; convey or carry along: *brought enough money with him.* **2.** To carry as an attribute or contribution: *brought years of experience to her new post.* **3.** To lead or cause to come to a specified state, situation, or location: *brought to ruin; brought tears to our eyes.* **4.** To succeed in persuading; induce: *His confession brought others to confess.* **5.** To cause to occur as a consequence or concomitant: *Floods brought death to the valley.* **6.** To cause to become apparent to the mind; recall: *bring back memories.* **7.** *Law.* To advance or set forth (charges or evidence, for example) in a court. **8.** To sell for; fetch. —**bring about.** To cause to happen. —**bring around** (or **round**). **1.** To cause to recover consciousness. **2.** To cause to adopt an opinion or course of action. —**bring down the house.** *Informal.* To cause wild or general applause. —**bring forth.** **1.** To give rise to; effect; produce. **2.** *Archaic.* To give birth to. —**bring forward.** **1.** To present; cite in argument: *bring forward an opinion.* **2.** *Accounting.* To carry (a sum) from one page or column to another. —**bring in.** **1.** To give or submit (a verdict). **2.** To produce or yield (profits or income). —**bring off.** To accomplish successfully. —**bring on.** **1.** To give rise to; cause. **2.** To cause to appear: *bring on the dessert.* —**bring out.** **1.** To reveal or expose. **2.** To produce or publish. **3.** To encourage; especially, to encourage (a shy person) to speak out or participate. —**bring over.** To win over. —**bring to.** **1.** To cause to recover consciousness. **2.** To cause (a ship) to turn into the wind and lose headway. —**bring up.** **1.** To take care of and educate (a child); rear. **2.** To introduce into discussion; mention. **3.** To vomit or cough up. [Bring, brought, brought; Middle English *bringen, broughte, brought,* Old English *bringan, brōhte, brōht,* from Germanic *brengen* (unattested).] —**bring·er** n.

bring down tr.v. **1.** To cause to fall, come down, or collapse. **2.** To reduce; lower. **3.** *Slang.* To cause to feel disappointed or depressed.

bring-down (brĭng'doun') n. Something that disturbs or disappoints.

bring·ing-up (brĭng'ĭng-ŭp') n. The care, training, and education of a child; upbringing.

brink (brĭngk) n. **1. a.** The upper edge of a steep or vertical declivity: *the brink of a cliff.* **b.** The margin of land bordering a body of water. **2.** The verge of something: *on the brink of discovery.* —See Synonyms at **border.** [Middle English *brinke, brenk,* akin to Middle Dutch *brink*†, slope.]

brink·man·ship (brĭngk'mən-shĭp') n. Also **brinks·man·ship** (brĭngks'-). The practice of seeking advantage by forcing a dangerous situation to crisis point in the hope that one's opponent will back down first. [BRINK + (GAMES)MANSHIP.]

brin·y (brī'nē) adj. **-ier, -iest.** Of, pertaining to, or resembling brine; salty.
~n. *Slang.* The sea. —**brin·i·ness** n.

bri·o (brē'ō) n. Vigor; vivacity. [Italian, "vivacity," from Gaulish *brigo-* (unattested), might, strength.]

bri·oche (brē-ōsh', -ŏsh') n. A soft, light-textured roll or bun made from eggs, butter, flour, and yeast. [French, from Old French, from *brier,* dialectal form of *broyer,* to knead, from Germanic.]

bri·o·lette (brē'ə-lĕt') n. A pear-shaped gem, especially a diamond, cut with long triangular facets. [French, *bri(ll)olette,* probably an irregular diminutive of *brillant,* BRILLIANT.]

bri·quette, bri·quet (brĭ-kĕt') n. A block of compressed coal dust or charcoal, used for fuel and kindling. [French *briquette,* from *brique,* BRICK.]

bri·sance (brĭ-zäns') n. The shattering effect of a sudden release of energy, as in an explosion. [French, from *brisant,* present participle of *briser,* to break, from Vulgar Latin *brisāre,* from Gaulish.] —**bri·sant** adj.

Bris·bane (brĭz'bən, -bān'). Capital of the state of Queensland, Australia, a port and transport hub on the Brisbane River near its mouth on Moreton Bay and the third-largest city in Australia. The city began as a penal colony (1824), was incorporated as a town (1834), and was named after Sir Thomas Brisbane, the governor of New South Wales (1821–25).

brisk (brĭsk) adj. **brisker, briskest. 1.** Moving or acting quickly; lively; energetic: *a brisk walk.* **2.** Sharp or abrupt in speech or manner: *a brisk greeting.* **3.** Stimulating and invigorating: *a brisk wind.* **4.** Pleasantly zestful: *a brisk tea.* —See Synonyms at **nimble.** [Probably a variant of BRUSQUE.] —**brisk·ly** adv. —**brisk·ness** n.

bris·ket (brĭs'kĭt) n. **1.** The chest of an animal. **2.** The ribs and meat from this part. [Middle English *brusket,* probably from a Scandinavian compound akin to Old Norse *brjōst,* breast + *ket*†, meat.]

bris·ling (brĭz'lĭng, brĭs'-) n. A fish, the **sprat** *(see),* which is usually preserved and canned. [From Norwegian and Danish.]

bris·tle (brĭs'əl) n. A short, coarse, stiff hair or hairlike part.
~v. **bristled, -tling, -tles.** —*intr.* **1.** To raise the bristles, as an angry, excited, or frightened animal does: *The dog bristled with fear.* **2.** To react with hostility or anger. **3.** To stand erect like bristles: *His hair bristled.* **4.** To be covered or thick with or as if with bristles: *The path bristled with thorns.* —*tr.* **1.** To furnish or supply with bristles; put bristles on. **2.** To make bristly; ruffle; disturb. [Mid-

brimstone The bright yellow brimstone butterfly of Europe and Asia takes its common English name from the color of brimstone, an early word for sulfur.

dle English *bristil, brustel,* from *brust,* bristle, Old English *byrst.*]
—bris·tly *adj.*

bris·tle·cone pine (brĭs′əl-kōn′) *n.* A small pine tree, *Pinus aristata,* native to the Rocky Mountains, that has the longest life span of any known conifer. Its annual rings are used in archaeological dating.

bris·tle·tail (brĭs′əl-tāl′) *n.* Any of various wingless insects of the order Thysanura, such as the silverfish, having bristlelike posterior appendages.

bristle worm *n.* A type of worm, the **polychaete** *(see).*

Bris·tol (brĭs′təl). City, port, and administrative center of Avon, in southwestern England, on the lower Avon River 11 kilometers (7 miles) from its mouth on the Bristol Channel. It has been a trading depot since the 12th century and is now a center of nuclear and aeronautical engineering works.

Bristol board *n.* A smooth, heavy pasteboard of fine quality. Also called "Bristol paper."

Bristol Channel. An inlet of the Atlantic Ocean, *c.* 137 kilometers (85 miles) long, broadening out from the mouth of the Severn River and separating Wales from southwestern England.

Bristol fashion *adj. British.* In good order; neat; tidy. Used especially in the phrase *all shipshape and Bristol fashion.* **—Bristol fashion** *adv.*

brit, britt (brĭt) *n.* **1.** The young of herring and similar fish. **2.** Minute marine organisms, such as crustaceans of the genus *Calanus,* that are a major source of food for many fish and whales. [Perhaps from Cornish *brȳthel,* mackerel.]

Brit (brĭt) *n. Informal.* A British person.

Brit. Britain; British.

Brit·ain (brĭt′n). *Abbr.* **Br., Brit.** See **Great Britain.**

bri·tan·ni·a (brĭ-tăn′yə, -tăn′ē-ə) *n.* Also **Britannia.** A white alloy of tin with copper, antimony, and sometimes bismuth and zinc. It is used in the manufacture of tableware and light bearings. Also called "britannia metal." [From BRITANNIA.]

Bri·tan·nia (brĭ-tăn′yə, -tăn′ē-ə) *n.* **1.** The ancient Roman province in Great Britain. **2.** *Poetic.* Great Britain. **3.** A female personification of Great Britain or the British Empire.

Bri·tan·nic (brĭ-tăn′ĭk) *adj.* British. Used chiefly in the phrase *His* (or *Her*) *Britannic Majesty.*

britch·es (brĭch′ĭz) *pl.n. Informal.* Breeches. **—too big for one's britches.** *Informal.* Overconfident; cocky; arrogant.

Brit·i·cism (brĭt′ə-sĭz′əm) *n.* Also **Brit·ish·ism** (brĭt′ĭsh-ĭz′əm). A word, phrase, or idiom characteristic of or peculiar to English as it is spoken in Great Britain.

Brit·ish (brĭt′ĭsh) *adj. Abbr.* **B., Br., Brit. 1.** Of, pertaining to, or characteristic of Great Britain, the United Kingdom, or the Commonwealth. **2.** Of, pertaining to, or characteristic of the ancient Britons.
—n. **1.** *Used with a plural verb.* The people of Great Britain. Preceded by *the.* **2. British English** *(see).* **3.** The language spoken by the ancient Britons.

British Antarctic Territory. Territory claimed by Britain. It lies in the extreme Southern Hemisphere, and is bounded by latitude 60°S and longitudes 20°W and 80°W. It includes the South Orkney Islands, Graham Land (on Antarctica), and the South Shetland Islands (parts of which are claimed by Argentina) and has been a colony administered from the Falkland Islands since 1962. Most of the small islands in the region are uninhabited except for a transient scientific population.

British Anti-Lew·is·ite (ăn′tē-lōō′ĭ-sīt′, -lyōō′-) *n.* A drug, BAL *(see).*

British Cameroons. See **Cameroon.**

British Co·lum·bi·a (kə-lŭm′bē-ə). *Abbr.* **B.C.** The westernmost province of Canada, bordering on the Pacific Ocean and stretching to the Yukon in the north. The capital is Victoria, on Vancouver Island, but the largest city is Vancouver. The province is almost entirely mountainous, with the Rocky Mts. in the east and the Coast Mts. in the west. Timber and pulp and paper manufacture are its leading industries, but mining of silver, copper, gold, iron ore, lead, and zinc is also important. The silver mine at Kimberley is the largest in the world, and Kimberley also has the world's largest reserves of lead and zinc. **—British Co·lum·bi·an** *n. & adj.*

British Commonwealth of Nations. See the **Commonwealth.**

British East Af·ri·ca (ăf′rĭ-kə). Collectively, the former British territories in eastern Africa, including Kenya, Uganda, Tanganyika, and Zanzibar.

British Empire. Collectively, all geographical and political units formerly under British control, including dominions, colonies, dependencies, trust territories, and protectorates.

British English *n.* The English language as spoken, pronounced, and written in Britain, as compared with the English spoken elsewhere.

Brit·ish·er (brĭt′ĭsh-ər) *n. Informal.* A native or inhabitant of Great Britain or a person of British origin.

British Guiana. See **Guyana.**

British Honduras. See **Belize.**

British In·di·a (ĭn′dē-ə). The part of the Indian subcontinent exclusive of the Indian states, under direct British administration until 1947. See **India.**

British In·di·an Ocean Territory (ĭn′dē-ən). British colony in the west Indian Ocean since 1965. The main islands include Diego Garcia, which has a U.S. base.

British Isles. A group of islands off the northwestern coast of Europe, comprising Great Britain, Ireland, and adjacent smaller islands.

British Movement *n.* A modern British fascist splinter group, noted for its virulent racism.

British North A·mer·i·ca (ə-mĕr′ə-kə). *Abbr.* **B.N.A.** Formerly, the British possessions in North America north of the United States; specifically, Canada.

British Somaliland. See **Somalialand.**

British thermal unit *n. Abbr.* **btu, B.th.u.** The quantity of heat required to raise the temperature of one pound of water by one degree Fahrenheit.

British Vir·gin Islands (vûr′jĭn). A British colony in the West Indies, in the eastern Caribbean. The colony, comprising *c.* 30 islands, lies east of Puerto Rico and the U.S. Virgin Islands. Its capital is Road Town, on Tortola Island.

British West Af·ri·ca (ăf′rĭ-kə). *Abbr.* **B.W.A.** The former British possessions in western Africa, including Nigeria, Gambia, Sierra Leone, and the Gold Coast and the trust territories of Togoland and Cameroons.

British West In·dies (ĭn′dēz). *Abbr.* **B.W.I.** The former name for the islands of the West Indies that were colonies or self-governing colonies of the United Kingdom.

Brit·on (brĭt′n) *n.* **1.** A native or inhabitant of Britain. **2.** One of a Celtic people who inhabited Britain before the Roman invasion.

britt. Variant of **brit.**

Brit·ta·ny (brĭt′n-ē). French **Bre·tagne** (brə-tän′yə). Region and former province of northwest France, between the English Channel and the Bay of Biscay. It has a deeply indented rocky coast with deep natural harbors at Brest and St. Malo.

Brit·ta·ny spaniel (brĭt′n-ē) *n.* A large spaniel of a breed originating in France. [After BRITTANY.]

Brit·ten (brĭt′n), **(Edward) Benjamin, Baron** (1913–76). British composer. His reputation rests chiefly on his vocal compositions, which fall into two main categories: song cycles such as *Les Illuminations* (1939) and the *Serenade* for tenor, horn, and string orchestra (1943); and the operas, including *Peter Grimes* (1945), *Albert Herring* (1947), and *Death in Venice* (1973).

brit·tle (brĭt′l) *adj.* **1.** Likely to break; fragile: *brittle porcelain.* **2. a.** Difficult to deal with; touchy; snappish: *a brittle disposition.* **b.** Lacking warmth or friendliness. **—See Synonyms at fragile.**
—n. A confection of caramelized sugar to which nuts are added: *peanut brittle.* [Middle English *brotel, britel,* Old English *brytel* (unattested), from Germanic.] **—brit·tle·ness** *n.*

brittle star *n.* Any of various marine organisms of the class Ophiuroidea, related to and resembling the starfish but having long, slender, whiplike arms.

Brix scale (brĭks) *n.* A density scale used in the sugar industry. A Brix hydrometer has a scale calibrated in units equivalent to the percentage of sugar in a pure sugar solution. [After A.F.W. Brix, 19th-century German inventor.]

Br·no (bûr′nō). German **Brünn** (brün). An industrial city in central Czechoslovakia. The Bren gun was developed there.

bro. brother.

broach[1] (brōch) *n.* **1.** A tapered and serrated tool used to shape or enlarge a hole. **2.** The handle made by such a tool. **3.** A spit for roasting meat. **4.** A narrow mason's chisel. **5.** A gimlet for tapping or broaching casks. **6.** Variant of **brooch.**
—tr.v. **broached, broaching, broaches. 1. a.** To begin to talk about: *broach a subject.* **b.** To announce: *"Ernest broached his plans for spending the next year or two"* (Samuel Butler). **2.** To pierce in order to draw off liquid: *broach a keg.* **3.** To draw off (a liquid) by piercing a hole in a cask, keg, or other container. **4.** To shape or enlarge (a hole) with a broach. **5.** To open and start using the contents of (a box, for example). **—See Synonyms at vent.** [Middle English *broche,* pointed rod or pin, from Old French, a spit, from Vulgar Latin *brocca* (unattested), a spike.] **—broach·er** *n.*

broach[2] *v.* **broached, broaching, broaches.** *Nautical.* **—***tr.* To cause to veer broadside to the wind and waves. **—***intr.* To veer broadside to the wind and waves. Used with *to.* [18th century : origin obscure.]

broad (brôd) *adj.* **broader, broadest. 1. a.** Extending a considerable distance from side to side. **b.** Of the specified extent from side to side; in breadth: *six feet broad.* **2.** Large in expanse; spacious: *a broad lawn.* **3.** Open to view; clear: *broad daylight.* **4.** Extensive in scope; generalized: *a broad rule.* **5.** Liberal; tolerant. **6.** Covering the essentials; comprehensive, but not detailed: *a broad outline of the problem.* **7.** Plain and clear; obvious: *a broad hint.* **8.** Outspoken; unrestrained. **9.** Vulgar; crude: *a broad joke.* **10.** Strongly marked by regional pronunciation: *a broad accent.* **11.** Phonetics. Designating a vowel that is pronounced with the tongue placed low and flat and with the oral cavity wide open, especially as when the *a* in *bath* is pronounced like the *a* in *bard.*
—n. **1.** The broad part of something. **2.** *Slang.* A woman or girl.
—adv. Fully; completely: *broad awake.* [Middle English *brood,* Old English *brād,* from Common Germanic *braithaz* (unattested). For noun sense 2, compare obsolete *broadwife* (*abroad* + *wife*), female slave separated from her husband, who was owned by a different master.] **—broad·ly** *adv.*

broad arrow *n.* **1.** An arrow with a wide, barbed head. **2.** A wide arrowhead mark identifying British government property and, formerly, prison clothing.

broad·ax, broad·axe (brôd′ăks′) *n., pl.* **-axes.** An ax with a wide, flat head and a short handle; battle-ax.

broad·band (brôd′bănd′) *adj.* Designating a wide band of electromagnetic frequencies: *broadband communications.* **—broad·band** *n.*

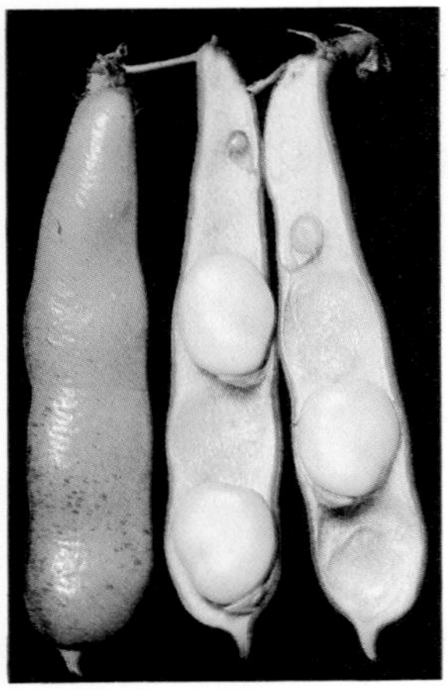

broad bean *The seeds of this plant, also known as fava bean, have been used as a vegetable for centuries. The plant, which is thought to have been introduced into northern Europe by the Romans, was an important crop in the Middle Ages.*

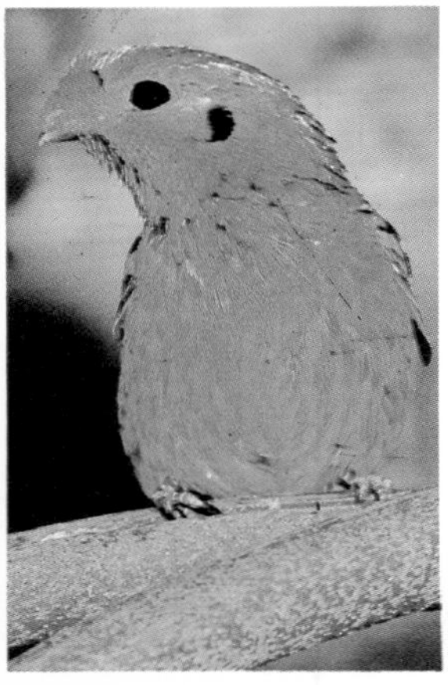

broadbill *The brightly colored broadbill is native to the tropical forests of Africa and Asia. Most of its 14 species live on insects, but the Malaysian green broadbill (above) feeds on fruit.*

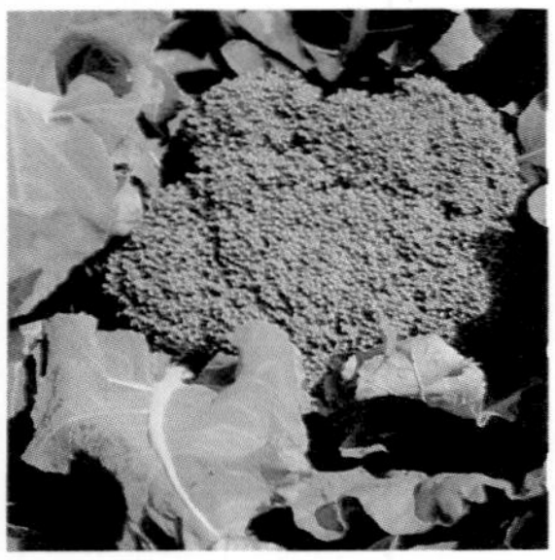

broccoli *The flower head of a green, or sometimes purple, edible plant of the same genus as the cabbage.*

broad bean *n.* **1.** A plant, *Vicia faba,* native to the Old World, cultivated for its edible pods and seeds. **2.** The somewhat flattened seed of this plant. Also called "fava bean," "horse bean."

broad·bill (brôd'bĭl') *n.* **1.** Any of various birds of the family Eurylaimidae, of Africa and tropical Asia, having a short, wide bill and brightly colored plumage. **2.** Any of several other broad-billed birds, such as the shoveler. **3.** The **swordfish** *(see).*

broad·brim (brôd'brĭm') *n.* **1.** A hat with a broad, flat brim, as those worn by Quakers. **2. Broadbrim.** *Informal.* A member of the Society of Friends; a Quaker.

broad·cast (brôd'kăst', -käst') *v.* **-cast** or **-casted, -casting, -casts.** *—tr.* **1.** To transmit (a program or signal) by radio or television. **2.** To make known over a wide area: *broadcast rumors.* **3.** To sow (seed) over a wide area, especially by hand. *—intr.* **1.** To transmit a radio or television program. **2.** To participate in a radio or television program.
~n. **1.** Transmission of a radio or television program or signal. **2.** A radio or television program, or the duration of such a program. **3.** The act of scattering seed.
~adj. Scattered over a wide area.
~adv. In a scattered manner; far and wide. [BROAD (adverb), "widely" + CAST (past participle).] **—broad·cast·er** *n.*

Broad Church *n.* Those members of the Anglican Communion favoring liberalism in matters of doctrine and ritual. Compare **High Church, Low Church. —Broad-Church** (brôd'chûrch') *adj.* **—Broad-Church·man** *n.*

broad·cloth (brôd'klôth', -klŏth') *n.* **1.** A densely textured woolen cloth with a plain or twill weave and a lustrous finish. **2.** A closely woven silk, cotton, or synthetic fabric with a narrow crosswise rib.

broad·en (brôd'n) *v.* **-ened, -ening, -ens.** *—tr.* To make broad or broader. *—intr.* To become broad or broader.

broad gauge *n.* A railway track with a width between the rails greater than the standard gauge of 56½ inches.

broad-gauge (brôd'găj') *adj.* **1.** Having a broad gauge. **2.** *Informal.* Having a wide scope; liberal.

broad jump *n.* A **long jump** *(see).*

broad·leaf (brôd'lēf') *n.* Any of various tobacco plants having broad leaves.

broad-leaved (brôd'lēvd') *adj.* Also **broad-leaf** (-lēf'), **broad-leafed** (-lēft'). Having relatively broad leaves, as evergreens such as the rhododendron and holly, rather than needles.

broad·loom (brôd'lo͞om') *adj.* Designating carpet woven on a wide loom and measuring from 1.3 meters (4½ feet) to 5.5 meters (18 feet) in width.
~n. A broadloom carpet.

broad-mind·ed (brôd'mīn'dĭd) *adj.* Having or arising from liberal or tolerant views. **—broad-mind·ed·ly** *adv.* **—broad-mind·ed·ness** *n.*

broad·ness (brôd'nĭs) *n.* The state, quality, or aspect of being broad. Compare **breadth.**

broad seal *n.* The official public seal of a state or nation.

Broads, the (brôdz). Region of inland waterways in East Anglia, chiefly in Norfolk but extending also into Suffolk. A great number of wide, shallow lakes are connected by the Yare and Bure rivers and their tributaries. The region is a wildlife sanctuary and recreational boating center.

broad·sheet (brôd'shēt') *n.* See **broadside** (sense 4).

broad·side (brôd'sīd') *n.* **1.** The side of a ship above the water line. **2. a.** All the guns on one side of a warship. **b.** Their simultaneous discharge. **3.** An explosive verbal attack or denunciation. **4. a.** A large sheet of paper printed on one side. **b.** Something, as an advertisement, printed on a broadside. **5.** Any broad, unbroken surface.
~adv. With the side turned to a given object.

broadside ballad *n.* A rhymed popular tale of romance, adventure, or crime, printed on a broadsheet and sold by hawkers from the 16th to the 19th century.

broad-spec·trum (brôd'spĕk'trəm) *adj.* Widely applicable or effective: *a broad-spectrum drug.*

broad·sword (brôd'sôrd', -sōrd') *n.* A cutting sword with a wide blade.

broad·tail (brôd'tāl') *n.* **1.** A breed of sheep, the **karakul** *(see).* **2.** The pelt of a newborn or prematurely born karakul lamb, having a flat surface with wavy markings. Compare **Persian lamb.**

Broad·way[1] (brôd'wā'). A thoroughfare in New York City and New York State. The longest street in the world, it begins at the southern tip of Manhattan Island and extends *c.* 242 kilometers (150 miles) north to Albany.

Broadway[2] *n.* **1.** The principal theater district of New York City, located on or near Broadway (thoroughfare). **2.** The American legitimate stage: *a career in television and on Broadway.* Compare **off-Broadway. —Broad·way** *adj.*

Brob·ding·nag·i·an (brôb'dĭng-năg'ē-ən, -dĭg-năg'-) *adj.* **1.** Gigantic; enormous. **2.** On a large scale; enlarged. [After *Brobdingnag,* the land of giants visited by Gulliver in *Gulliver's Travels* (1726), by Jonathan Swift.]

bro·cade (brō-kād') *n.* A heavy fabric interwoven with a rich, raised design.
~tr.v. **brocaded, -cading, -cades.** To weave with a raised design. [Earlier *brocado,* from Spanish or Portuguese, from Italian *broccato,* embossed fabric, from *brocco,* twisted thread, shoot, from Vulgar Latin *brocca* (unattested), a spike, from Latin *brocchus,* in *brocci dentes,* "projecting teeth."]

broc·a·tel, broc·a·telle (brŏk'ə-tĕl) *n.* A very heavy fabric resembling brocade, but with a more highly raised design. [French *brocatelle,* from Italian *broccatello,* diminutive of *broccato,* BROCADE.]

broc·co·li (brŏk'ə-lē) *n.* **1.** A plant, *Brassica oleracea italica,* closely related to the cabbage and the cauliflower, having a branched, greenish or purplish flower head. Also called "sprouting broccoli." **2.** The flower heads of this plant, eaten as a vegetable before the tightly clustered buds have opened. [Italian, plural of *broccolo,* cabbage sprout, diminutive of *brocco,* shoot. See **brocade.**]

broch (brŏk, brŭk, brŏch, brŭch) *n.* An ancient, round, dry-stone tower of a type found in northern Scotland, formerly used as a fortified dwelling. [From Old Norse *borg,* castle.]

bro·ché (brō-shā') *adj.* Woven with a raised pattern or design; brocaded. [French, past participle of *brocher,* to stitch, from *broche,* knitting needle, spit, from Old French, a spit, from Vulgar Latin *brocca* (unattested), a spike. See **brocade.**]

bro·chette (brō-shĕt') *n.* **1.** A small spit or skewer upon which meat, fish, or vegetables are roasted or grilled. **2.** A dish cooked on a brochette. [French, from Old French, diminutive of *broche,* spit. See **broché.**]

bro·chure (brō-sho͝or') *n.* A small pamphlet or booklet, especially one providing information about a service or product. [French, "a stitching" (from the former loose stitching of the pages), from *brocher,* to stitch.]

brock (brŏk) *n. British.* A badger. [Old English *broc,* from Celtic *brokko-* (unattested), badger.]

Brock·en (brŏk'ən). A large granite dome in central Germany, the highest peak (1,142 meters; 3,747 feet) in the Harz Mountains. The peak is the legendary site of the witches' sabbath, held on Walpurgis Night.

brock·et (brŏk'ĭt) *n.* **1.** A two-year-old stag with its first horns. **2.** Any of several small deer of the genus *Mazama,* of South America, having short, unbranched horns. [Middle English *broket,* from Old North French *brocard,* from *broque,* the horn of an animal, any pointed implement, variant of Old French *broche,* a spit.]

bro·de·rie an·glaise (brō'də-rē ŏn'glĕz, -glāz) *n.* Embroidery incorporating perforated patterns on fine white linen, cotton, or the like. [French, "English embroidery."]

bro·gan (brō'gən) *n.* A heavy, ankle-high work shoe. [Irish-Gaelic *brōgan,* diminutive of *brōg,* BROGUE (shoe).]

Bro·glie (brô-glē'), **Louis Victor, 7th Duc de** (1892–1987). French physicist. In 1927 he demonstrated by experiments that particles exhibit wavelike properties, thus establishing the field of wave mechanics. For this contribution to modern quantum theory he was awarded the Nobel Prize for physics (1929).

brogue[1] (brōg) *n.* A strong regional accent; especially, a strong Irish accent. [From BROGUE (shoe), with reference to the shoes of Irish and Scottish peasants.]

brogue[2] *n.* **1.** A heavy shoe of untanned leather, formerly worn in Scotland and Ireland. **2.** A strong oxford shoe, usually with ornamental perforations. [Irish and Scottish Gaelic *brōg,* from Old Irish *brōc,* shoe, apparently from Old Norse *brōk,* trousers.]

broi·der (broi'dər) *tr.v.* **-dered, -dering, -ders.** *Obsolete.* To ornament with needlework; embroider. **—broi·der·y** *n.*

broil[1] (broil) *v.* **broiled, broiling, broils.** *—tr.* **1.** To expose to great heat. **2.** To cook by direct radiant heat; grill. *—intr.* To become broiled.
~n. **1.** The act or condition of broiling. **2.** Something broiled. [Middle English *broillen, brulen,* from Old French *brul(l)er,* earlier *brusler,* to burn, from Vulgar Latin *brustulāre* (unattested), perhaps from Germanic.]

broil[2] *n.* A rowdy argument; a brawl.
~intr.v. **broiled, broiling, broils.** To engage in a brawl. [From obsolete *broil,* to confound, disturb, from Middle English *broilen,* from Old French *brouiller,* perhaps from *breu,* broth.]

broil·er (broi'lər) *n.* **1.** One who broils. **2. a.** A small electric oven used for broiling. **b.** The part of a stove used for broiling. **3.** A tender young chicken suitable for broiling.

broke (brōk). Past tense and *nonstandard* past participle of **break.**
~adj. Informal. Having no money.

bro·ken (brō'kən). Past participle of **break.**
~adj. **1.** Shattered or snapped into two or more pieces. **2.** Disregarded; not honored: *a broken promise.* **3.** Fragmentary; incomplete: *a broken set of books.* **4.** Disorganized; routed: *broken troops.* **5.** Intermittently stopping and starting; discontinuous. **6.** Varying abruptly, as in pitch: *broken sobs.* **7.** Spoken imperfectly: *broken English.* **8.** Topographically rough; uneven: *broken ground.* **9.** Subdued; humbled: *a broken spirit.* **10.** Tamed and trained: *a broken stallion.* **11.** Weakened; exhausted: *broken health.* **12. a.** Crushed by grief: *a broken heart.* **b.** Utterly demoralized: *a broken man.* **13.** Financially ruined; bankrupt. **14.** In which the marriage partners or parents are separated or divorced: *a broken home.* **15.** Not functioning. **—bro·ken·ly** *adv.*

bro·ken-down (brō'kən-doun') *adj.* **1.** Out of working order. **2.** Debilitated; infirm.

bro·ken-heart·ed (brō'kən-här'tĭd) *adj.* Extremely sad, as through the loss of a loved one.

Bro·ken Hill (brō'kən). Town in New South Wales, Australia, near the border with South Australia. It is named after a humped range of mountains, part of the Main Barrier Range. The town has one of the world's richest deposits of silver.

broken wind *n.* A disease of horses, the **heaves** *(see).*

bro·ker (brō'kər) *n.* **1.** One who acts as an agent for others in negotiating contracts, purchases, or sales in return for a fee or commission. **2.** A stockbroker. [Middle English, peddler, pawnbroker, go-between, from Norman French *brocour*†.]

bro·ker·age (brō′kər-ĭj) *n.* **1.** The business of a broker. **2.** A fee or commission paid to a broker.

brol·ly (brŏl′ē) *n., pl.* **-lies**. *British Informal.* An umbrella.

bro·mate (brō′māt′) *n.* A salt or ester of bromic acid. —*tr.v.* **bromated, -mating, -mates. 1.** To treat (a substance) chemically with a bromate. **2.** Loosely, to combine (a substance) chemically with bromine. [Probably German *Bromat* : BROM(O)- + -ATE.]

brome·grass (brōm′grăs′) *n.* Any grass of the genus *Bromus*, especially *B. mollis*, having spikelets in loose, often drooping clusters. Also called "brome." [New Latin *Bromus*, from Latin *bromos*, oats, from Greek *bromos*†.]

bro·me·li·ad (brō-mē′lē-ăd′) *n.* Any of various mostly epiphytic plants of the tropical American family Bromeliaceae, which includes the pineapple, Spanish moss, and many species grown as house plants. Typically, bromeliads have a rosette of fleshy, strap-shaped leaves and produce a long, central, often brightly colored spike of flowers. [From New Latin *Bromelia* (type genus), after Olaf *Bromelius* (1639–1705), Swedish botanist.]

bro·mic acid (brō′mĭk) *n.* A corrosive, colorless, unstable liquid, $HBrO_3$, used in making dyes and pharmaceuticals. [French *bromique* : BROM(O)- + -IC.]

bro·mide (brō′mīd′) *n.* **1.** Any chemical compound in which the element bromine has a valence of one, either as a negative ion or as an atom linked to another by a covalent bond. **2.** A sedative, **potassium bromide** (see). **3. a.** A commonplace remark or notion; a platitude. **b.** A tiresome person; bore. **4.** A photographic print on paper that has been treated with bromine and silver. **5.** A photographic print on bromide paper of a typeset page of a book, magazine, or the like, to which artwork is attached before filming and platemaking. —See Synonyms at **cliché**. [BROM(INE) + -IDE.] —**bro·mid·ic** (brō-mĭd′ĭk) *adj.*

bro·mi·nate (brō′mĭ-nāt′) *tr.v.* **-nated, -nating, -nates.** To combine (a substance) with bromine or a bromine compound. —**bro·mi·na·tion** *n.*

bro·mine (brō′mēn′) *n. Symbol* **Br** A heavy, volatile, corrosive, reddish-brown, nonmetallic liquid element, having a highly irritating vapor. It is used in producing gasoline antiknock mixtures, fumigants, dyes, and photographic chemicals. Atomic weight 79.909, atomic number 35, melting point –7.2°C, boiling point 58.78°C, specific gravity 3.119, valences 1, 3, 5, 7. [French *brome*, from Greek *bromos*†, stench + -INE.]

bro·mism (brō′mĭz′əm) *n.* Also **bro·min·ism** (brō′mə-nĭz′əm). Poisoning from overuse of bromides. Symptoms include skin eruptions, headache, sleepiness, apathy, and loss of strength. [Probably French *bromisme* : BROM(O)- + -ISM.]

bromo– *prefix.* Indicates bromine as the principal element in a chemical compound; for example, **bromoacetone.** [Probably from French *brome*, BROMINE.]

bro·mo·ac·e·tone (brō′mō-ăs′ə-tōn′) *n.* Also **brom·ac·e·tone** (brō-măs′ə-tōn′). A colorless liquid, $CH_2BrCOCH_3$, used as a constituent of tear gas. Also called "bromomethane." [BROMO- + -ACETONE.]

bro·mo·form (brō′mə-fôrm′, -fōrm′) *n.* A heavy, colorless liquid, $CHBr_3$, having a sweet taste and odor resembling chloroform, used in laboratory separations of minerals.

bron·chi. Plural of **bronchus.**

bron·chi·a (brŏng′kē-ə) *pl.n. Singular* **-chium** (-kē-əm). *Anatomy.* Bronchial tubes smaller than the bronchi and larger than bronchioles. [Late Latin, from Greek *bronkhia*, plural of *bronkhion*, diminutive of *bronkhos*, windpipe, BRONCHUS.]

bron·chi·al (brŏng′kē-əl) *adj. Anatomy.* Of or pertaining to the bronchi, the bronchia, or the bronchioles. —**bron·chi·al·ly** *adv.*

bronchial asthma *n.* A usually allergic asthma of the bronchi.

bronchial tube *n. Anatomy.* A bronchus or any of its branches.

bron·chi·ec·ta·sis (brŏng′kē-ĕk′tə-sĭs) *n. Pathology.* Chronic dilation of the bronchial tubes, with cough and formation of mucus and pus. [New Latin : BRONCH(O)- + *ectasis*, dilation, from Greek *ektasis*, stretching.]

bron·chi·ole (brŏng′kē-ōl′) *n. Anatomy.* Any of the fine, thin-walled, tubular extensions of a bronchus.

bron·chi·tis (brŏng-kī′tĭs) *n.* Chronic or acute inflammation of the mucous membrane of the bronchial tubes. Symptoms include coughing and breathing difficulties. [New Latin : BRONCH(O)- + -ITIS.] —**bron·chi·tic** (brŏng-kĭt′ĭk) *adj.*

broncho-, bronch– *prefix.* Indicates the bronchi or bronchial tubes; for example, **bronchoscope, bronchitis.** [Late Latin, from Greek *bronkh(o)-*, from *bronkhos*, windpipe, BRONCHUS.]

bron·cho·di·la·tor (brŏng′kō-dī′lā′tər) *n.* Any of various drugs that relax bronchial muscles and therefore widen the air passages, used to treat asthma, bronchitis, and other breathing difficulties.

bron·cho·pneu·mo·ni·a (brŏng′kō-nōō-mōn′yə, -nyōō-mōn′yə) *n.* Inflammation of the lungs spreading from and following infection of the bronchial tubes.

bron·cho·scope (brŏng′kə-skōp′) *n.* A slender tubular instrument with a small light on the end for inspection of the interior of the bronchial tubes. [BRONCHO- + -SCOPE.]

bron·chus (brŏng′kəs) *n., pl.* **-chi** (-kī′, -kē′). *Anatomy.* Either of two main branches of the trachea, having walls thickened with cartilage and branching into smaller air passages, leading directly to the lungs. [New Latin, from Greek *bronkhos*, trachea, windpipe, throat.]

bron·co (brŏng′kō) *n., pl.* **-cos.** A wild or semiwild horse of western North America. [Mexican Spanish, from Spanish, rough, wild.]

bron·co·bust·er (brŏng′kō-bŭs′tər) *n.* A cowboy who breaks wild horses to the saddle.

Bron·të (brŏn′tē), **Charlotte** (1816–55), **Emily** (1818–48), and **Anne** (1820–49). British novelists and poets, daughters of the Anglo-Irish clergyman and writer, Patrick Brunty, or Brontë, who was the curate at Haworth, Yorkshire, after 1820. In 1846 their first publication was issued, a volume of verse entitled *Poems by Currer, Ellis and Acton Bell.* In 1847 Charlotte published *Jane Eyre*, Emily *Wuthering Heights*, and Anne *Agnes Grey.* Anne's *The Tenant of Wildfell Hall* was published in 1848. Charlotte published *Shirley* in 1849 and *Villette* in 1853. Their brother, **(Patrick) Branwell** (1817–48), was an artist.

bron·to·sau·rus (brŏn′tə-sôr′əs) *n.* Also **bron·to·saur** (brŏn′tə-sôr′). A very large, plant-eating dinosaur of the genus *Apatosaurus* (or *Brontosaurus*), of the Late Jurassic period, having a long neck and tail and a small head. [New Latin *Brontosaurus* : Greek *brontē*, thunder + -SAUR.]

Bronx, the (brŏngks). Borough of New York City, the only one on the mainland. It is chiefly residential, except for the waterfront, which is crowded with warehouses and factories.

Bronx cheer *n. Slang.* An expression of derision or contempt, a **raspberry** (see).

bronze (brŏnz) *n.* **1. a.** Any of various alloys of copper and tin, sometimes with traces of other metals. **b.** Any of various alloys of copper, with or without tin, and antimony, phosphorus, or other components. **2.** A work of art made of bronze. **3.** A bronze medal. **4.** Metallic yellowish to olive brown. —*tr.v.* **bronzed, bronzing, bronzes. 1.** To give the appearance of bronze to. **2.** To give a suntanned appearance to. [French, from Italian *bronzo*, perhaps from Persian *birinj*, copper.] —**bronze** *adj.* —**bronz·y** *adj.*

Bronze Age *n.* A period of human culture between the Stone Age and the Iron Age, characterized by weapons and implements made of bronze. See feature, next page.

bronze diabetes *n.* Hemochromatosis *(see).*

Bronze Star *n.* A U.S. Army decoration awarded for heroism or meritorious achievement in ground combat.

brooch, broach (brōch, brōōch) *n.* An ornament worn on the clothing, attached by means of a pin and catch. [Middle English *broche*, brooch, BROACH (tool).]

brood (brōōd) *n.* **1.** The young of certain animals, such as birds or fish; especially, a group of young birds or fowl hatched at one time and cared for by the same mother. **2.** The children in one family. **3.** A group with a common origin or purpose: *a brood of troublemakers.* —*v.* **brooded, brooding, broods.** —*tr.* To sit on or hatch (eggs). —*intr.* **1.** To sit on or hatch eggs. **2.** To hover envelopingly: *"that gentle heat that brooded on the waters"* (Thomas Browne). **3.** To ponder moodily; sulk. —*adj.* Kept for breeding: *a brood mare.* [Middle English *brood*, Old English *brōd*, from Germanic *bro-* (unattested), heat.] —**brood·ing·ly** *adv.*

brood·er (brōō′dər) *n.* **1.** One that broods. **2.** A heated enclosure in which young chickens, other fowl, or young livestock are raised.

brood·y (brōō′dē) *adj.* **-ier, -iest. 1.** Moody; meditative. **2.** Inclined to sit on eggs to hatch them. Said of hens and other poultry.

brook¹ (brōōk) *n.* A small, natural freshwater stream. [Middle English *brook*, *broke*, Old English *brōc*.]

brook² *tr.v.* **brooked, brooking, brooks.** To put up with; bear; tolerate. Usually used in the negative: *I can't brook rudeness.* [Middle English *brouken*, *broken*, enjoy, to use (as food), to stomach, Old English *brūcan*.]

Brooke (brōōk), **Rupert Chawner** (1887–1915). British poet. His first volume of verse, *Poems*, was published in 1911. His *1914 and Other Poems* was published in 1915. The romantic patriotic lyricism of his war sonnets differs sharply in mood from the angry poems of the other leading war poets, Wilfred Owen and Siegfried Sassoon.

Brooke·bor·ough (brōōk′bûr-ō, -bə-rə), **Sir Basil Stanlake Brooke, 1st Viscount** (1888–1973). Northern Irish politician. After serving in the Special Constabulary in its struggle against the I.R.A., he was a member of the Northern Irish Assembly at Stormont (1929–68), serving as minister of agriculture (1933–41), minister of commerce (1941–45), and prime minister (1943–63). An outspoken opponent of Irish reunification and a fierce upholder of Protestant ascendancy in Northern Ireland, he was raised to the peerage (1952).

brook·ite (brōōk′īt′) *n.* A red-brown to black titanium dioxide mineral with characteristic orthorhombic crystals. [After Henry J. *Brooke* (1771–1857), English mineralogist.]

brook lamprey *n.* Any of several usually small lampreys that live mostly in brooks.

brook·let (brōōk′lĭt) *n.* A small brook.

brook·lime (brōōk′līm′) *n.* Either of two closely related trailing plants, *Veronica americana*, of North America, and *V. beccabunga*, native to Eurasia, growing in moist places and having small blue flowers resembling the speedwell. [Variant (influenced by LIME) of Middle English *brokelmke* : *broke*, BROOK + *lemke*, a kind of brooklime, Old English *hleomoce*.]

Brook·lyn (brōōk′lĭn). Borough of New York City, occupying the southwestern part of Long Island. It is both a residential and industrial borough, and in population it is the city's largest. It includes

bromeliad *The bromeliad family of plants is native to tropical America and the West Indies. The family contains more than 1,000 species, including the pineapple and the torch bromeliad shown here.*

brooch *A Victorian mosaic brooch. The earliest brooches were functional as well as decorative; they were used to fasten clothing.*

Bronze Age

THE METAL THAT BROUGHT THE STONE AGE TO AN END
Craftsmen who smelted copper with tin produced bronze for tools and weapons

It is thought that bronze was invented about 3000 B.C. in the city states of Mesopotamia. There, because the land was fertile through irrigation, there was no need for all the inhabitants to be occupied in food production. Craftsmen could be fed by the labors of their fellow men and had time to experiment; when they mixed tin and copper in their smelting furnaces, they produced bronze.

Bronze is much harder than copper. It was easily cast into hard tools and weapons that could be recast if they broke, straightened if they bent, and sharpened again and again. The new alloy eventually replaced stone for all agricultural tools and for weapons: the Stone Age had been succeeded by the Bronze Age.

The first bronze casts were made in flat molds carved out of stones or pressed into sand. Very early in the Bronze Age, casts were made in one-piece clay molds; these had to be broken for the cast to be taken out. Soon, molds were being prepared in two pieces, which were tied together with string or held by dowels during the casting and could be used more than once. Ax heads, daggers, sword blades, and shield mounts were made in either one-piece or two-piece molds.

For making finely modeled figures and small, intricate horse trappings a complex "lost wax" method was devised. It used less metal but required more skill. The object to be cast was modeled in clay and covered first with a layer of wax, then with a thick layer of clay in which two holes were made. Molten bronze was poured through one hole; it melted and forced out the wax through the other hole. A layer of bronze thus replaced the layer of wax and hardened to give a hollow cast.

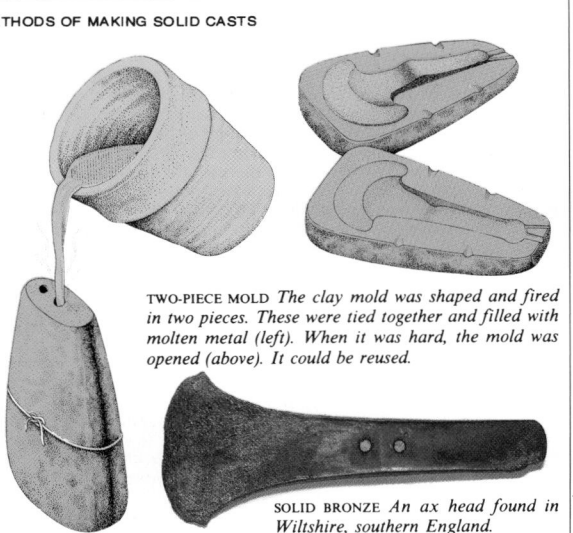

METHODS OF MAKING SOLID CASTS

ONE-PIECE MOLD *A beeswax model (top) of the object being cast, an ax head for example, was thickly encased in clay. This was fired to harden it (bottom). The beeswax melted and ran out. The mold was filled with molten bronze, and when the metal was hard, the mold was broken off.*

TWO-PIECE MOLD *The clay mold was shaped and fired in two pieces. These were tied together and filled with molten metal (left). When it was hard, the mold was opened (above). It could be reused.*

SOLID BRONZE *An ax head found in Wiltshire, southern England.*

HOLLOW BRONZE *This head of Sargon of Akkad, king of Mesopotamia 4,300 years ago, was made by the lost-wax process— the method still used for fine detail, as in the headdress and beard.*

broom *Common broom,* Sarothamnus scoparius, *is found throughout western Europe and temperate North America on sandy, acid soils. It grows up to 2 meters (6 feet) tall, bearing masses of golden flowers in early summer. Under its former name,* Planta genista, *broom was the badge of the English royal house of Plantagenet, who took their name from the plant.*

Coney Island, famous for its beach and amusement park.
Brooks (br $\overline{oo}$ ks), **Van Wyck** (1886–1963). U.S. literary historian, critic, and translator. He wrote many books on the literary history of America, including *The Flowering of New England* (1936), for which he won a Pulitzer Prize. His several volumes of memoirs were collected and published posthumously as *An Autobiography.*
brook trout *n.* A freshwater game fish, *Salvelinus fontinalis,* of eastern North America. Also called "speckled trout."
brook·weed (br $\overline{oo}$ k'wēd') *n.* Either of two related plants, *Samolus valerandi* of Europe and *S. floribundus* of North America, both having small white flowers and growing in moist areas. Also called "water pimpernel."
broom (br $\overline{oo}$ m, br $\overline{oo}$ m) *n.* **1.** A sweeping implement consisting traditionally of a bundle of twigs or straw bound to a stick, but now usually of synthetic bristles fastened to a long handle. **2.** Any shrub of the genus *Sarothamnus (Cytisus),* especially *S. scoparius,* native to Eurasia, having compound leaves and usually yellow flowers. **3.** Any of several similar or related shrubs, especially of the genus *Genista.*
~*tr.v.* **broomed, brooming, brooms.** To sweep with a broom. [Middle English *broom,* broom made of broom twigs, broom plant, Old English *brōm,* broom plant.] —**broom·y** *adj.*
broom·corn (br $\overline{oo}$ m'kôrn', br $\overline{oo}$ m'-) *n.* A grass, *Sorghum vulgare technicum,* having flower clusters with stiff, branching stalks that are used to make brooms and brushes.
broom moss *n.* Any moss of the genus *Dicranum,* especially *D. scoparium,* having leaves turned to one side along the stem.
broom·rape (br $\overline{oo}$ m'rāp', br $\overline{oo}$ m'-) *n.* Any of several leafless, parasitic plants of the genus *Orobanche,* having yellow, purple, or reddish-brown flowers and living on the roots of other plants. [Partial translation of New Latin *rapum genistae,* "tuber of Genista (a genus of broom)" (from the resemblance of one of the parasitic growths to a tuber on the roots of broom).]
broom·stick (br $\overline{oo}$ m'stĭk', br $\overline{oo}$ m'-) *n.* The long handle of a broom.
bros. brothers.
brose (brōz) *n.* A kind of oatmeal porridge eaten in Scotland. [Scottish form of BREWIS.]
broth (brôth, brŏth) *n., pl.* **broths** (brôths, brôthz, brŏths, brŏthz). **1.** The water in which meat, fish, or vegetables have been boiled; stock. **2.** A thin, clear soup based on stock, to which rice, barley, meat, or vegetables may be added. **3.** A nutrient medium for the culture of microorganisms and tissues. [Middle English, Old English, from Germanic.]
broth·el (brŏth'əl, brô'thəl) *n.* A house of prostitution. [Shortened from *brothel-house,* from Middle English *brothel,* worthless person, prostitute, from Old English *brēothan,* fall into ruin.]
broth·er (brŭth'ər) *n., pl.* **brothers** or *archaic* **brethren** (brĕth'rən). *Abbr.* **b., B., br., bro. 1.** A male having the same mother and father as another person *(full brother),* having one parent in common with another person *(half brother),* having one parent in common with another person, by marriage rather than by blood *(stepbrother),* or having the same father and mother after adoption *(foster brother).* **2.** One who shares a common ancestry, allegiance, character, or purpose with another or others, specifically: **a.** A kinsman. **b.** A fellow man. **c.** A fellow member, as of a trade union or profession. **d.** A close male friend; a comrade: *"Such a gallant set of fellows! Such a band of brothers!"* (Lord Nelson). **e.** *Informal.* Friend; fellow. Used as a term of address. **3.** *Ecclesiastical. Abbr.* **Br. a.** A member of a men's religious order who is not in holy orders, but engages in the work of the order. **b.** A lay member of a religious order of men. **c. Brother.** A form of address for such a person: *Brother Luke.* **4.** A black man or boy. Used as a term of address, especially by fellow blacks, to express solidarity. Compare **sister.**
~*interj.* Used to express annoyance, disgust, or the like. [Middle English, Old English *brōthor,* from Germanic.]
broth·er·hood (brŭth'ər-hood') *n.* **1.** The state or relationship of being a brother or brothers. **2.** The quality of being brotherly; fellowship. **3.** *Abbr.* **B.** An association of men united for common purposes; a union, society, or similar organization. **4.** All the members of a specific profession or trade.
broth·er-in-law (brŭth'ər-in-lô') *n., pl.* **brothers-in-law. 1.** The brother of one's husband or wife. **2.** The husband of one's sister. **3.** The husband of the sister of one's husband or wife.
Brother Jon·a·than (jŏn'ə-thən) *n. British Archaic.* **1.** A personification of the people or government of the United States. **2.** An American. Also called "Jonathan." [Originally applied by British soldiers to American patriots during the American War of Independence (probably from the frequent use of Old Testament first names in the New England colonies).]
broth·er·ly (brŭth'ər-lē) *adj.* **1.** Characteristic of or befitting brothers; fraternal. **2.** Kind; generous; affectionate: *brotherly love.* —**broth·er·li·ness** *n.* —**broth·er·ly** *adv.*

Brothers of the Christian Schools *pl.n.* The official name for the Christian Brothers *(see)*.

Brough (brŭf), **Althea Louise** (1923–). U.S. tennis player. Between 1948 and 1955 she won nine Wimbledon titles (four singles, three ladies' doubles, and two mixed doubles). With Margaret Osborne DuPont she formed the most successful doubles partnership in history. They were undefeated in the U.S. championships between 1942 and 1950.

brough·am (brŏŏm, brŏŏ'əm, brō'əm) *n.* **1.** A closed four-wheeled carriage with an open driver's seat in front. **2.** A car with an open driver's seat. **3.** An obsolete electrically powered car resembling a coupé. [After Henry Peter BROUGHAM.]

Brougham (brŏŏm, brōm), **Henry Peter, 1st Baron of Brougham and Vaux** (1778–1868). British politician and educational reformer, born in Scotland. A member of Parliament from 1810, he defended Queen Caroline in the divorce proceedings brought by George IV (1820) and, as Lord Chancellor (1830–34), played an important role in the passing of the 1832 Reform Act. He is remembered equally for his lifelong campaign against slavery, his great part in the extension of education, and his role as legal reformer.

brought. Past tense and past participle of **bring**.

brou·ha·ha (brŏŏ'hä-hä') *n.* An uproar; a hubbub. [French (imitative).]

Brou·wer (brou'wər), **Adriaen** (c. 1606–38). Flemish genre and landscape painter, the pupil of Hals. He is famous for his lively treatment of everyday peasant life and for his history of landscape.

brow (brou) *n.* **1.** *Anatomy.* **a.** The part of the face between the eyes and the hairline; the forehead. **b.** The eyebrow *(see).* **2.** A facial expression; countenance: *"Speak you this with a sad brow?"* (Shakespeare). **3.** The edge of a steep place; the top of a slope or hill. —See Synonyms at **border.** [Middle English *brow,* Old English *brū,* eyelash, eyelid, eyebrow, from Germanic.]

brow·beat (brou'bēt') *tr.v.* **-beat, -beaten** (-bēt'n), **-beating, -beats.** To intimidate or bully with an overbearing manner.

brown (broun) *n.* **1.** *Abbr.* **br.** Any of a group of colors between red and yellow in hue that are medium to low in lightness, and low to moderate in saturation. **2.** Any of various butterflies of the family Satyridae, such as the mountain ringlets and the heaths. In this sense, also called "satyr." —*adj.* **browner, brownest. 1.** *Abbr.* **br.** Of the color brown. **2.** Deeply sun-tanned. —*v.* **browned, browning, browns.** —*tr.* To make brown; specifically, to cook until brown. —*intr.* To become brown. [Middle English *broun, brown,* Old English *brūn.*] —**brown·ish** *adj.* —**brown·ness** *n.*

Brown (broun), **Sir Arthur Whitten** (1886–1948). British aviator. On July 14, 1919, with Sir John William Alcock, he made the first nonstop flight across the Atlantic Ocean.

Brown, Ford Madox (1821–93). British painter, born in France. He trained in Paris and Rome before settling in England (1845). He was closely associated with the pre-Raphaelites, but was never a member of the brotherhood. He painted chiefly historical subjects and scenes from contemporary life, of which the most famous is *Work* (1863).

Brown, John (1800–59). U.S. abolitionist commemorated in the song, "John Brown's Body Lies Amouldering in the Grave." A leading campaigner against slavery in the South, he enlisted men (1857) to give escaped slaves armed protection in a mountain stronghold. On October 16, 1859, they captured the U.S. arsenal at Harpers Ferry, Virginia. In the subsequent fighting his men were defeated, and Brown was hanged on December 2.

Brown, Lancelot (1716–83). British landscape gardener, known as "Capability Brown" from his habit of assuring his patrons of the great capabilities of their estates. He broke with the convention of geometrically laid-out gardens and planned parks and gardens in imitation of a natural landscape, as at Blenheim and Chatsworth. George III appointed him gardener at Hampton Court (1764).

Brown, Robert (1773–1858). British botanist. He discovered and named the nucleus of the cell, but he is most famous for his investigation of the sexual behavior of plants. It was the microscopic observation of pollination that brought about his discovery (1827) of the irregular movement of pollen grains. This observation led to the general physical concept known as Brownian motion.

brown algae *n.* Dark brown to olive green, chiefly marine algae of the division Phaeophyta, which includes the rockweeds and the kelps.

brown bagging *n.* **1.** The practice of taking one's own liquor into a restaurant or club, where setups are available. **2.** The practice of taking one's lunch to work, usually in a brown paper bag. —**brown bagger** *n.*

brown bear *n.* **1.** A very large bear, *Ursus arctos,* of Alaska and northern Eurasia, having brown to yellowish fur. Compare **grizzly bear, Kodiak bear. 2.** A brown variety of the American black bear.

brown Bet·ty (bĕt'ē) *n.* A baked pudding consisting of apples, raisins, and spices covered with bread crumbs, sugar, and butter.

brown bread *n.* **1.** A bread made of a dark flour, such as graham or whole-wheat. **2.** A steamed bread usually made of cornmeal, flour, and molasses.

brown coal *n.* A type of coal, **lignite** *(see).*

Browne (broun), **Charles Farrar,** known as "Artemus Ward" (1843–67). U.S. humorist and lecturer. His pieces, using backwoods characters and comic misspellings, chronicled the fictional adventures of an itinerant showman. In his writings on current events,

Browne often lampooned insincerity and sentimentality.

Browne, Hablot Knight (1815–82). British illustrator and caricaturist, who worked under the pseudonym "Phiz." Dickens invited him to illustrate *Pickwick Papers* (1836), and thereafter he illustrated a number of Dickens's novels.

Browne, Sir Thomas (1605–82). English writer. He was an eminent physician, but his most successful, enduring work was *Religio Medici* (1642), in which he attempted to reconcile the faith of a Christian with the growing body of scientific knowledge.

brown earth *n.* A type of soil, typically found where there is a mild climate and moderate rainfall, usually supporting deciduous forest.

brown fat *n.* Adipose tissue whose oxidation is a major source of heat in mammals.

Brown·i·an motion (brou'nē-ən) *n.* The random motion of microscopic particles suspended in a liquid or gas, caused by collision with molecules of the surrounding medium. Also called "Brownian movement." [After Robert BROWN, who described it.]

brown·ie (brou'nē) *n.* **1.** *Folklore.* A small sprite supposed to do helpful work at night, especially domestic chores. **2.** A small bar of rich, usually chocolate cake often with nuts. [Diminutive of BROWN. The sprite was thought of as a "wee brown man."]

Brownie *n.* A member of a junior branch of the Girl Scouts from 7 to 9 years of age. [From BROWNIE (sprite).]

Brownie point *n.* Credit considered as earned, especially by favorably impressing a superior. [From the practice of awarding points for achievement by Brownies in the Girl Scouts.]

Brown·ing (brou'nĭng), **Elizabeth Barrett** (1806–61). British poet. Her first volume of verse, *Poems* (1844), was read by Robert Browning; he subsequently married her and took her to live in Italy (1846), where she wrote *Sonnets from the Portuguese* (1850). Her verse novel *Aurora Leigh* was published in 1857.

Browning, Robert (1812–89). British poet. He published his first poem, *Pauline,* in 1833. After his initial visit to Italy, he wrote *Sordello* (1840) and *Pippa Passes* (1841). The collection *Bells and Pomegranates* was published in 1846, the year that he married Elizabeth Barrett in secret. For the next 15 years they lived together in Italy, where Browning wrote *Christmas Eve and Easter Day* (1850) and the collection *Men and Women* (1855). After Elizabeth's death (1861), he returned to England. *The Ring and the Book* (1868–69) is considered his masterpiece, but he is more widely known for his dramatic monologues, such as *My Last Duchess, Andrea del Sarto,* and *The Italian in England.*

Browning automatic rifle *n. Abbr.* **BAR** A .30 caliber air-cooled, automatic or semiautomatic, gas-operated, magazine-fed rifle used in World Wars I and II. [After John Moses *Browning* (1855–1926), U.S. firearms designer.]

Browning machine gun *n.* A .30 or .50 caliber automatic machine gun capable of firing ammunition at a rate of more than 500 rounds per minute.

brown·out (broun'out') *n.* A partial extinguishing or dimming of lights in a city, especially as a defensive measure against enemy bombardment or as a means of conserving electricity. [After BLACKOUT.]

brown rat *n.* A common and very destructive rodent pest, *Rattus norvegicus,* found in both town and country. Also called "common rat," "Norway rat."

brown rice *n.* Unpolished rice grains, retaining the germ and the yellowish outer layer containing the bran.

brown rot *n.* **1.** A disease of ripe fruits that is caused by fungi of the genus *Sclerotinia.* **2.** A disease of citrus trees that is caused by fungi of the genus *Phytophthora.*

Brown Shirts *pl.n.* A Nazi militia, **Sturmabteilung** *(see).*

brown·stone (broun'stōn') *n.* **1.** A brownish-red sandstone once widely used as a building material, especially for façades of houses. **2.** A house faced with such stone, especially in New York City. —**brown·stone** *adj.*

brown study *n.* A state of deep thought, melancholy, or reverie.

brown sugar *n.* **1. a.** Unrefined or partially refined sugar. **b.** Loosely, any sugar that is brown in color. **2.** *Slang.* A coarse, low-grade variety of heroin from Southeast Asia.

Brown Swiss *n.* One of a hardy breed of dairy cattle that originated in Switzerland.

brown thrasher *n.* A North American bird, *Toxostoma rufum,* having a reddish-brown back and a dark-streaked breast.

brown trout *n.* A freshwater fish, *Salmo trutta,* native to Europe, having yellow-brown sides with black and red spots, the latter circled by pale rings. Compare **sea trout.**

browse (brouz) *v.* **browsed, browsing, browses.** —*intr.* **1.** To look through or inspect something, such as a book or goods in a shop, in a leisurely and casual way. **2.** To feed on leaves, young shoots, and other vegetation. —*tr.* **1.** To nibble; crop. **2.** To graze on. —*n.* **1.** An instance of browsing. **2.** Young twigs, leaves, and tender shoots of plants or shrubs that animals eat. [From Old French *broust, brost,* shoot, twig, from Germanic.] —**brows·er** *n.*

Bru·beck (brŏŏ'bĕk), **Dave,** full name David Warren Brubeck (1920–). U.S. jazz pianist and composer. He was trained from the age of four as a classical pianist and studied composition under Milhaud and Schoenberg, but later turned entirely to jazz, forming an octet in 1946 and a successful quartet in 1951.

Bruce, Robert the. See Robert I.

bru·cel·lo·sis (brŏŏ'sə-lō'sĭs) *n.* A contagious disease of certain livestock caused by bacteria of the genus *Brucella* and transmissible to humans, for example through infected milk. Symptoms in humans

brown bear *Living throughout the Northern Hemisphere, brown bears eat almost anything, including roots, fruit, mice, and deer. They also hunt fish, flipping salmon from streams with their paws.*

include fever, headache, weakness, and painful joints and in animals, abortions. Also called "Malta fever," "Mediterranean fever," "undulant fever," and in animals "contagious abortion." [New Latin : *Brucella,* after Sir David *Bruce* (1855–1931), Australian bacteriologist and physician + -OSIS.]

bru·cine (broo'sēn', -sĭn) *n.* A poisonous white crystalline alkaloid, $C_{23}H_{26}O_4N_2 \cdot 2H_2O$, derived from nux vomica seeds. [After James *Bruce* (1730–94), Scottish explorer in Africa.]

Bruck·ner (brook'nər), **Anton** (1824–96). Austrian composer and organist. He did not write his first important work until he was in his forties, and it was not until his sixties that he became famous. His most important works are the nine symphonies and large choral works, especially the three masses and the *Te Deum.*

Brue·gel or **Breu·ghel** (broi'gəl), **Jan** (1568–1625). Flemish painter, second son of Pieter the Elder. He painted landscapes and often put figures or landscape backgrounds into other artists' paintings, including some of Rubens. His reputation now rests mainly on his paintings of still lifes, especially flowers.

Bruegel, Pieter the Elder (*c.* 1530–69). Foremost of a family of Flemish painters, he was one of the first painters to treat landscape as a worthy subject of itself. He is best known for his genre paintings, especially of peasant scenes, in which he combined minute observation of the Flemish tradition with the somewhat fantastical manner of Hieronymus Bosch.

Bruegel, Pieter the Younger (*c.* 1564–*c.* 1638). Flemish painter, son of Pieter the Elder. Many of his paintings are copies of his father's works. Owing to the scarcity of the latter's originals, Pieter the Younger is much better represented in museums and galleries.

Bruges (broozh). *Flemish* **Brug·ge** (broog'ə). Industrial city in northwestern Belgium, connected to the port of Zeebrugge on the North Sea by a canal. It was founded in the 9th century and in the 13th century was a leading member of the Hanseatic League. In the High Middle Ages, at the zenith of its prosperity, it was one of the most important wool-processing towns and commercial hubs of Europe.

bru·in (broo'ĭn) *n.* A name for bear, used especially in folktales and children's stories. [Dutch *bruin,* "brown."]

bruise (brooz) *v.* **bruised, bruising, bruises.** —*tr.* **1.** To damage the underlying tissue or bone of (part of the body) without breaking the skin. **2.** To damage or mar (fruit, for example). **3.** To pound into fragments; crush. **4.** To hurt psychologically; offend. —*intr.* To become discolored, as the skin does after a hard blow.
~*n.* An area of skin discoloration, caused by the escape of blood from ruptured capillaries following a blow; a contusion. [Middle English *brusen, brisen,* to crush, mangle, from Old English *brȳsan* and Old French *bruisier†,* to break, crush.]

bruis·er (broo'zər) *n. Slang.* A rough-looking, powerfully built man.

bruit (broot) *tr.v.* **bruited, bruiting, bruits.** To spread (a rumor, for example); report. Used with *about* or *abroad.*
~*n.* **1.** *Medicine.* An abnormal sound heard in the body during auscultation, especially a heart murmur. **2.** *Archaic.* A rumor. **3.** *Archaic.* A din; a clamor. [Middle English, noise, from Old French, from the past participle of *bruire,* to roar, from Vulgar Latin *brūgere* (unattested), variant of Latin *rugīre,* to roar.]

bru·mal (broo'məl) *adj. Archaic.* Of, pertaining to, or characteristic of winter; wintry. [Latin *brūmālis,* from *brūma,* winter solstice, "the shortest day," from *brevima* (unattested), the shortest, from *brevis,* short.]

brume (broom) *n.* Heavy fog or mist; dense vapor. [French, mist, winter, from Old French, from Old Provençal *bruma,* from Latin *brūma.* See brumal.] —**bru·mous** *adj.*

brum·ma·gem (brŭm'ə-jəm) *adj.* Cheap and showy; tawdry.
~*n.* Any cheap and gaudy imitation, especially of jewelry. [Dialect

---

Brueghel

THE PAINTER WHO "SPOKE" WITH HIS BRUSH
Brueghel's lively scenes are crowded with comment

The lively peasant scenes and crowded landscapes of Pieter Brueghel's canvases opened up a new door for the Flemish school of painters. Brueghel looked in on his subjects; there is satire and social comment in his compositions. Satire in the silly grin on the bride's face in *Peasant Wedding* (about 1567); social comment in the hungry looks of the musicians.

Little is known of Brueghel. It is not known where he was born, but it was between 1525 and 1530. By 1551 he was a master of the Painters' Guild at Antwerp. He visited Italy and on his return painted some impressive landscapes. He satirized sin and drunkenness in *The Fall of the Rebel Angels* (1562) and

Peasant Dance (1566), and produced two masterpieces on biblical themes, *Procession to Calvary* and *Massacre of the Innocents* (1566). A religious subject is embedded in the 16th-century detail in many of his works.

For a time after his death in Brussels in 1569, Brueghel's work seems to have been neglected, yet his observation of everyday life and his rapid, fluent style of brushwork were taken up by the Flemish painters who followed him. Among them were his sons, Pieter the Younger (*c.* 1564–1638), and Jan (1568–1625), known as Velvet Brueghel for his silky landscapes and detailed still-life paintings.

PEASANT WEDDING *Brueghel's observation of daily life shines through this vivid picture. All his characters say something about themselves: the bridegroom spooning his food thoughtfully, the friar and magistrate talking seriously, the little boy licking his plate.*

form of BIRMINGHAM, England (with reference to counterfeit coins made there in the 17th century).]

Brum·mell (brŭm′əl), **George Bryan,** known as "Beau Brummell" (1778–1840). British dandy and socialite. He became the close friend of the Prince of Wales and set the male fashion—dark, simply tailored clothes, trousers rather than breeches, and elaborate neckwear—of the prince's society at Brighton. He was a leader of society in London, but gambling forced him deeply into debt and he fled to France (1816) to escape his creditors. He never returned to England and died, after years of penniless squalor, in an insane asylum at Caen.

brunch (brŭnch) *n. Informal.* A meal eaten late in the morning as a combination of breakfast and lunch. [*br*eakfast + l*unch.*]

Brundisium. See **Brindisi.**

Bru·nei, State of (bro͞o′nī). Sultanate and former self-governing British protectorate on the northern coast of Borneo. It is split into two sections, each of which is an enclave within Malaysian territory. The only British dependency inhabited by Malays not to have entered the Federation of Malaysia (1963), it became fully independent at the end of 1983. The economy is largely dependent on the export of oil. Area, 5,800 square kilometers (2,226 square miles). Population, 266,000. Capital, Bandar Seri Begawan. See map at **Malaysia.**

Brunei Town. See **Bandar Seri Begawan.**

Bru·nel (bro͞o-nĕl′), **Isambard Kingdom** (1806–59). British civil engineer, son of Sir Marc. He was an engineer with the Great Western Railway and also helped build railways in Australia, Italy, and India. He worked with his father in the construction of the Thames Tunnel, but he is most famous for his design and construction of the three great ocean steamships, the *Great Western* (1838), which was the first transatlantic steamship, the *Great Britain* (1845), and the *Great Eastern* (1858).

Brunel, Sir Marc Isambard (1769–1849). British engineer and inventor, born in France. A royalist, he came to the United States in 1793 to escape the Reign of Terror and began his career as a civil engineer. By 1799 he had settled in England, where he patented a number of inventions, including a knitting machine. His greatest engineering achievement was the design and construction of the Thames Tunnel, which was completed in 1843.

Bru·nel·les·chi (bro͞o′nə-lĕs′kē), **Filippo** (1377–1446). Italian architect, the most celebrated of the 15th century Florentine Renaissance. He reintroduced Roman forms of perspective and methods of construction, but his greatest architectural feat, the dome of Florence cathedral (completed after his death), is in Gothic style. See feature, next page.

bru·net (bro͞o-nĕt′) *adj.* **1.** Of a dark complexion or coloring. **2.** Having dark brown or black hair or eyes.
~*n.* A person with brown hair. [French, from Old French, from *brun,* brown, from Germanic.]

bru·nette (bro͞o-nĕt′) *adj.* Having dark or brown hair.
~*n.* A girl or woman with dark or brown hair.

Brun·hild (bro͝on′hĭlt). *Norse Mythology.* A legendary queen of Iceland who is won as a bride by Gunther in the *Nibelungenlied.*

Brünn. See **Brno.**

Brun·ner (bro͝on′ər), **Emil** (1889–1966). Swiss Protestant theologian. With Karl Barth he was one of the foremost opponents of the rational, liberal school of modern theology and resolute in his insistence upon the importance of revelation in the relationship between God and humankind. Among his most influential writings were *The Divine Human Encounter* (1938) and *Christianity and Civilization* (1948–49).

Brünn·hil·de (bro͝on-hĭl′də). The heroine of Wagner's opera *Ring of the Nibelung,* a Valkyrie who is placed in a circle of fire by Wotan and is eventually released by Siegfried.

Bru·no (bro͞o′nō), **Giordano** (*c.* 1548–1600). Italian philosopher and cosmologist. He entered the Dominican order at the age of 15, but left it (1576) when he was charged with heresy and thereafter traveled throughout Europe. He was delivered to the Inquisition by the Venetian authorities (1592) and, after refusing to recant, was burned at the stake (1600) for immoral conduct, blasphemy, and heresy. His most important works were the series of dialogues in which he argued for the indivisibility of all matter and all forms and in which he extended Copernican thought to state that the universe is an infinite series of solar systems.

Bruno of Co·logne (kə-lōn′), **Saint** (*c.* 1030–1101). German monk, the founder of the Carthusian order. He was ordained a priest, but was deprived of his offices when he exposed the malpractices of an archbishop. In 1084 he retired with six fellow monks to the mountains of the Grande Chartreuse in southern France and founded a monastery.

Bruns·wick (brŭnz′wĭk). German **Braun·schweig** (broun′shvīk′). Former duchy and German state, mostly in present-day Lower Saxony and Saxony-Anhalt, Germany. The city of Brunswick, the former capital, is located on the Oker River.

brunt (brŭnt) *n.* **1.** The main impact or force, as of a blow or attack. Used especially in the phrase *bear the brunt of.* **2.** *Obsolete.* A violent attack. [Middle English *brunt*†.]

Brusa. See **Bursa.**

brush¹ (brŭsh) *n.* **1.** Any of various devices consisting of bristles, fibers, or other flexible material fastened into a handle, for such uses as scrubbing, polishing, applying paint, or grooming the hair. Often used in combination: *a toothbrush; a hairbrush.* **2.** An act of using such an implement. **3.** A light touch in passing; a graze. **4.** A brief, often unpleasant, contact or encounter: *had several brushes with the law.* **5.** The bushy tail of a fox, used especially as a hunting trophy. **6.** The art or profession of painting. Preceded by *the.* **7.** *Electricity.* A yielding or sliding connection completing a circuit between a fixed and a moving, especially rotating, conductor.
~*v.* **brushed, brushing, brushes.** —*tr.* **1.** To use a brush on, so as to clean, polish, paint, or groom. **2.** To apply with or as if with motions of a brush. **3.** To remove with or as if with motions of a brush. **4.** To dismiss or rebuff abruptly or curtly. Used with *aside* or *off*: *brushed the matter aside.* **5.** To touch lightly in passing; graze against. —*intr.* **1.** To use or apply a brush. **2.** To move past something so as to touch it lightly. **—brush up.** To refresh or improve one's knowledge of or skill at performing. [Middle English *brusshe,* from Old French *broisse, brosse,* perhaps from *broce,* BRUSH (brushwood).] **—brush·er** *n.* **—brush·y** *adj.*

brush² *n.* **1. a.** A dense growth of bushes or shrubs. **b.** Land covered by such a growth. **2.** Sparsely populated woodland. **3.** Cut or broken branches. [Middle English *brusch(e),* from Norman French *brousse,* from Old French *broce,* from Vulgar Latin *bruscia* (unattested).] **—brush·y** *adj.*

brush discharge *n.* A faintly visible, relatively slow, crackling discharge of electricity without sparking.

brushed (brŭsht) *adj.* Of or designating knitted or woven fabrics that have a nap produced by brushing during manufacture.

brush fire *n.* A fire in low-growing, scrubby trees and brush.

brush-off (brŭsh′ôf′, -ŏf′) *n.* An abrupt dismissal or snub; a rejection.

brush·wood (brŭsh′wo͝od′) *n.* **1.** Cut or broken-off branches. **2. a.** Dense undergrowth. **b.** An area covered by such growth.

brush·work (brŭsh′wûrk′) *n.* **1.** Work done with a brush. **2.** The manner in which a painter applies paint with the brush.

brusque, brusk (brŭsk) *adj.* Abrupt and curt in manner or speech; discourteously blunt. —See Synonyms at **gruff.** [French *brusque,* lively, fierce, harsh, from Italian *brusco,* sour, sharp, butcher's broom (as noun), from Vulgar Latin *bruscum*†.] **—brusque·ly** *adv.* **—brusque·ness** *n.*

brus·que·rie (brŭs′kə-rē′) *n.* Brusqueness; curtness.

Brus·sels (brŭs′əlz). *French* **Bru·xelles** (brü-sĕl′). Capital of Belgium, in Brabant province on the Senne River. Officially a bilingual (Flemish and French) city, it is the executive headquarters of the European Economic Community.

Brussels carpet *n.* A machine-made carpet consisting of small, colored woolen loops that form a heavy, patterned pile.

Brussels lace *n.* **1.** Fine needlepoint or bobbin lace worked in floral patterns. **2.** Net lace with an appliqué design, formerly made by hand but now usually made by machine.

Brussels sprout *n.* **1.** A variety of cabbage, *Brassica oleracea* or *B. gemmifera,* having a stout stem studded with budlike heads resembling miniature cabbages. **2. Brussels sprouts.** The small edible heads of this plant. Also called "sprouts."

brut (bro͞ot) *adj.* Very dry. Said of wines, especially champagne. Compare **sec.** [French, raw, rough, from Old French, from Latin *brūtus,* heavy.]

bru·tal (bro͞ot′l) *adj.* **1.** Characteristic of a brute; cruel; inhumane. **2.** Crude or unfeeling in manner or speech; insensitive. **3.** Harsh; unrelenting; merciless: *brutal criticism.* **—bru·tal·ly** *adv.*

bru·tal·ism *n.* A style of architecture that uses stark, geometric lines and large areas of unrelieved concrete to create an impression of monolithic strength. **—bru·tal·ist** *n.*

bru·tal·i·ty (bro͞o-tăl′ə-tē′) *n., pl.* **-ties. 1.** The state or quality of being brutal. **2.** A brutal act.

bru·tal·ize (bro͞ot′l-īz′) *tr.v.* **-ized, -izing, -izes. 1.** To make brutal. **2.** To treat brutally. **—bru·tal·i·za·tion** *n.*

brute (bro͞ot) *n.* **1.** Any animal other than a human being; a beast. **2. a.** *Informal.* A brutal person. **b.** *Informal.* A person who is much disliked.
~*adj.* **1.** Of or pertaining to beasts; animal: *"None of the brute creation requires more than food and shelter"* (Henry Thoreau). **2.** Characteristic of a brute: **a.** Entirely physical or instinctive: *brute force.* **b.** Lacking reason or intelligence. **3.** Savage; cruel. **4.** Gross; coarse. [Middle English, from Old French *brut,* rough. See **brut.**] **—brut·ism** *n.*

bru·ti·fy (bro͞o′tə-fī′) *v.* **-fied, -fying, -fies.** —*tr.* To brutalize. —*intr.* To become brutalized.

brut·ish (bro͞o′tĭsh) *adj.* **1.** Of or characteristic of a brute. **2.** Crude in feeling or manner. **3.** Sensual; carnal. **—brut·ish·ly** *adv.* **—brut·ish·ness** *n.*

Bru·tus (bro͞o′təs), **Marcus Junius** (*c.* 85–42 B.C.). Roman republican statesman and soldier. He joined Cassius in the successful plot to assassinate Caesar (44) and began to rally forces for the coming war against Mark Antony and Octavian. In Macedonia in 42 the opposing armies met; Brutus committed suicide after his defeat at the Battle of Philippi on October 23.

Bruxelles. See **Brussels.**

Bry·an (brī′ən), **William Jennings** (1860–1925). U.S. lawyer and Democratic politician. He was secretary of state in Woodrow Wilson's administration (1913–15). Many of the reforms of which he was a principal advocate—income tax, women's suffrage, prohibition—were later adopted.

Bry·ant (brī′ənt), **William Cullen** (1794–1878). U.S. poet and newspaper editor. After establishing himself as a fine nature poet in such works as "Thanatopsis," "Rizpah," and "Autumn Woods," he became the editor of the New York *Evening Post,* a position he held

PRONUNCIATION KEY

ă, pat; ā, pay; âr, care;
ä, father, are; b, bib;
ch, church; d, deed; ĕ, pet;
ē, be; f, fife; g, gag; h, hat;
hw, which; ĭ, pit; ī, pie;
îr, pier; j, judge; k, kick;
l, lid, needle; m, mum;
n, no, sudden; ng, thing;
ŏ, pot; ō, toe; ô, paw, for;
oi, noise; ou, out; o͝o, book;
o͞o, boot; p, pop; r, roar;
s, sauce; sh, ship, dish;
t, tight; th, thin, path;
th, this, bathe; ŭ, cut; ûr, fur;
v, valve; w, with; y, yes;
z, zebra, size; zh, vision;
ə, about, item, edible, gallop, circus, peaceful

IN FOREIGN WORDS:

à, *Fr.* ami; œ, *Fr.* feu, *Ger.* schön; ü, *Fr.* tu, *Ger.* über; KH, *Ger.* ich, *Scot.* loch; N, *Fr.* bon; y′, *Fr.* Compiègne

STRESS MARKS:

Primary stress: ′ **in·cite′** (ĭn-sīt′)
Secondary stress: ′ **in′sight′** (ĭn′sīt′)

Brunelleschi

THE FOUNDER OF RENAISSANCE ARCHITECTURE
Adapting classical architecture to produce a new style

The Renaissance style of architecture began in Florence, inspired by Filippo Brunelleschi (1377–1446), who lived at a time when Italians regarded the period of the Roman Empire as Italy's golden age. They believed that reviving their glorious past would bring about a new golden era. Brunelleschi did not copy the architecture of classical Rome, but adapted it to Gothic building techniques and produced a new style that influenced western architecture until the 20th century.

Brunelleschi worked as a sculptor in gold before turning to architecture and engineering. When the Florentines wished to complete their cathedral with a large dome, it was Brunelleschi who solved the problem of how to build it. Begun in 1420, the dome is second in size only to the Pantheon in Rome. It is unbuttressed, but supported by a chain of timber and iron at its base, and the drum it rests on is stabilized by

three semidomes below. The dome itself is strengthened by Gothic-arch ribs, and with them Brunelleschi combined two techniques of classical Rome—brickwork laced firmly together in a herringbone pattern and upper courses of tufa for lightness.

His other buildings—all in Florence—include the Foundling Hospital, which he began about 1419. The arcade was designed with mathematical precision as a row of square bays topped by a row of arches half the area of the squares.

Brunelleschi was an outstanding mathematician and geometrician who was as much interested in the construction of a building as in its aesthetic qualities. He worked out the mathematical rules governing perspective with a single vanishing point. These were eagerly adopted by Renaissance painters, who could now give a more realistic three-dimensional look to their work.

PAZZI CHAPEL *Built in the cloisters of Santa Croce, in the style of a Roman temple, the chapel (left and above) shows Brunelleschi's mathematical planning. Its square, domed nave is flanked by transepts half as wide as the nave. The choir and the porch at either end are a quarter the area of the nave; each is domed inside. The chapel was begun in about 1429 but was completed with a makeshift roof after Brunelleschi died.*

bryony *The white bryony and black bryony, both European plants, are entirely unrelated but are similar in appearance, and both bear poisonous red berries and yellow flowers. The white bryony (above) has paler flowers. The two types get their names from the color of their roots.*

for 49 years while continuing to write poetry.

Bryn·hild (brĭn′hĭld′). *Norse Mythology.* A Valkyrie in the *Volsunga Saga* who is revived from an enchanted sleep by Sigurd.

bryo– *prefix.* Indicates moss; for example, **bryophyte.** [New Latin, from Greek *bruon,* moss, akin to Greek *bruein,* to swell. See **embryo.**]

bry·ol·o·gy (brī-ŏl′ə-jē) *n.* The study of mosses and liverworts. [BRYO- + -LOGY.] —**bry·o·log·i·cal** *adj.*

bry·o·ny (brī′ə-nē) *n., pl.* -**nies.** Either of two European plants, the **black bryony** or the **white bryony** (both of which see). [Latin *bryōnia,* from Greek *bruōnia,* akin to Greek *bruein,* to swell. See **embryo.**]

bry·o·phyte (brī′ə-fīt′) *n.* Any plant of the major botanical division Bryophyta, which includes the mosses and liverworts. Bryophytes have stems and leaves but lack true roots and vascular tissue. [New Latin *Bryophyta* : BRYO- + -PHYTE.] —**bry·o·phyt·ic** *adj.*

bry·o·zo·an (brī′ə-zō′ən) *n.* Any of various small aquatic animals of the phylum Bryozoa that reproduce by budding and form moss-like or branching colonies. Also called "polyzoan." [New Latin *Bryozoa,* plural of *bryozoon* : BRYO- + -ZOON.] —**bry·o·zo·an** *adj.*

Bryth·on (brĭth′ən, -ŏn′) *n.* **1.** An ancient Celtic Briton of Cornwall, Wales, or Cumbria. **2.** One who speaks a Brythonic language.

Bry·thon·ic (brĭ-thŏn′ĭk) *adj.* Of, pertaining to, or characteristic of the Brythons or their language.
~*n.* The branch of the Celtic languages that includes Welsh, Breton, and Cornish.

B.S. 1. Bachelor of Science. **2.** balance sheet. **3.** bill of sale.

B.S.A. 1. Bachelor of Science in Agriculture. **2.** Boy Scouts of America.

B.S.Ed. Bachelor of Science in Education.

bsh. bushel.

bsk. basket.

Bt. baronet.

B.Th. Bachelor of Theology.

Btu British thermal unit.

bu bushel.

bu. 1. bureau. **2.** bushel.

bub (bŭb) *n. Informal.* Fellow. Used as a term of affectionate address. [From *bubby,* possibly a baby-talk variant of BROTHER.]

bub·ble (bŭb′əl) *n.* **1.** A thin transparent film of liquid, generally spherical, enclosing an accumulation of gas: *a soap bubble.* **2.** A small globule of gas trapped in a liquid or solid, as in a carbonated drink or in hardened glass. **3.** A sound made by or as if by the forming and bursting of bubbles. **4.** Anything insubstantial, groundless, or ephemeral, such as a scheme that comes to nothing. **5.** A glass or plastic dome, usually transparent.
~*v.* **bubbled, -bling, -bles.** —*intr.* **1.** To form or give off bubbles, as a boiling liquid does. **2.** To move or flow with a gurgling sound. **3.** To display irrepressible activity or animation. —*tr.* To cause to form bubbles. [Middle English *bobelen* (imitative).]

bubble and squeak *n. Chiefly British.* Leftover cabbage and mashed potatoes fried together, sometimes with meat added. [From the sounds it makes in cooking.]

bubble bath *n.* **1.** A perfumed liquid preparation added to bath water in order to make it foam. **2.** A bath to which such a preparation has been made.

bubble cap *n.* A perforated or slotted cap forming part of the plates of a distillation column that promotes the mixing of the condensate and the vapor.

bubble chamber *n. Physics.* An apparatus for detecting the paths of charged particles, or inferring the paths of electrically neutral particles, by examination of trails of bubbles that form on ions produced in a superheated liquid. Compare **cloud chamber.**

bubble gum *n.* Chewing gum that can be blown into bubbles.

bubble memory *n.* A computer memory in which information is stored in the form of binary digits represented by the presence or absence of magnetic bubbles.

bub·bler (bŭb′lər) *n.* A drinking fountain in which the water flows through a small vertical nozzle.

bub·bly (bŭb′lē) *adj.* -**blier, -bliest. 1.** Containing bubbles; effervescent. **2.** Lively; vivacious.
~*n. Informal.* Champagne.

Bu·ber (bōō′bər), **Martin** (1878–1965). Austrian-born philosopher and theologian. Much of his writing was devoted to interpreting the mysticism of the Chassidim, but he was also greatly influenced by the Christian existentialism of Kierkegaard. His highly personal interpretation of the direct dialogue between God and man, expressed in *I and Thou* (1923), was much drawn upon by contemporary Christian writers.

bu·bo (bōō′bō, byōō′-) *n., pl.* -**boes.** An inflamed swelling of a lymphatic gland, especially in the area of the armpit or groin. [Middle English, from Medieval Latin *bubo,* from Greek *boubōn,* groin, swollen gland.] —**bu·bon·ic** (bōō-bŏn′ĭk, byōō-) *adj.*

bubonic plague *n.* A contagious, often fatal epidemic disease caused by the bacterium *Pasteurella pestis,* transmitted by fleas from infected rats and characterized by chills, fever, vomiting, diarrhea, and buboes.

bu·bon·o·cele (bōō-bŏn′ə-sēl′, byōō-) *n.* An incomplete hernia of the groin; a partial inguinal hernia. [Greek *boubōn,* groin + -CELE.]

buc·cal (bŭk′əl) *adj.* Of or pertaining to the cheeks or mouth. [Latin *bucca,* cheek.]

buc·ca·neer (bŭk′ə-nîr′) *n.* A pirate, especially one of the freebooters who preyed upon Spanish shipping in the West Indies during the 17th century. [French *boucanier,* pirate, "one who cures meat on a barbecue frame" (as done by 17th-century French pirates), from *boucaner,* to cure meat, from *boucan,* barbecue frame, from Tupi *mukem.*]

buc·ca·neer·ing (bŭk′ə-nîr′ĭng) *adj.* Showing boldness and enterprise, often to the point of recklessness or unscrupulousness.

buc·ci·na·tor (bŭk′ə-nā′tər) *n.* A muscle of the cheek, important in chewing. [Latin, from *buccinare,* to blow a trumpet, from *buccina,* trumpet.]

Bu·ceph·a·lus (byōō-sĕf′ə-ləs). The war horse of Alexander the Great. [Latin *Būcephalus,* from Greek *Boukephalos,* "ox-headed" : *bous,* ox + -CEPHALOUS.]

Buch·an (bŭk′ən), **Sir John, 1st Baron Tweedsmuir** (1875–1940). British writer and politician. He was member of Parliament for the Scottish universities (1927–35), then was appointed governor general of Canada and raised to the peerage. He wrote a number of historical works, but his fame rests chiefly on his novels, especially *The Thirty-Nine Steps* (1915).

Bu·chan·an (byōō-kăn′ən, bə-), **James** (1791–1868). 15th president of the United States (1857–61). When he took office the tensions between the North and South were already rising. Although personally opposed to slavery, he sought to defend it under the Constitution. He attempted to quell the conflict between the states, but was unable to stop the secession of South Carolina on December 20, 1860.

Bu·cha·rest (bōō′kə-rĕst′, byōō′-). Romanian **Bu·cu·reş·ti** (bōō′-kōō-rĕsht′, -rĕsh′tē). Capital and largest city of Romania, in the southeastern region of Walachia, on the Dîmboviţa River. Founded in the 14th century the town was a fortress and a trading center on the trade route to Constantinople. It became the capital of Walachia in 1698 and, after the union of Walachia and Moldavia, the capital of Romania in 1861.

Bu·chen·wald (bōō′kən-wôld′). A village in central Germany, in the Buchenwald Forest near Weimar. It was the site of a Nazi concentration camp in World War II.

Buch·man (bo͝ok′mən, bŭk′-), **Frank Nathan Daniel** (1878–1961). U.S. evangelist, founder of the Moral Rearmament movement. A Lutheran minister, he preached "world-changing through life-changing" to Oxford undergraduates (1921). The movement emphasized the importance of purity, honesty, selflessness, and love, allied with reliance upon God.

Buch·man·ism (bo͝ok′mən-ĭz′əm, bŭk′-) *n.* The doctrine of **Moral Rearmament** *(see).* **—Buch·man·ite** *n.*

Buch·ner (bo͝oKH′nər), **Eduard** (1860–1917). German chemist, famous for his discovery (1896) that the alcoholic fermentation of sugars is caused not by the yeast cells themselves but by enzymes in the yeast. In 1903 he discovered zymase, the part of the enzyme system that produces fermentation. He was awarded the Nobel Prize for chemistry (1907).

Büch·ner (büKH′nər), **Georg** (1813–37). German playwright, one of the early founders of the school of social realism in the theater. He wrote only three plays, *Danton's Death* (1835), *Leonce and Lena* (1836), and the fragmentary *Woyzeck* (1836).

buck[1] (bŭk) *n., pl.* **bucks** or collectively **buck** (for senses 1, 2). **1.** The adult male of some animals, such as the deer or hare. Also used adjectivally: *a buck rabbit.* **2.** A male antelope. Often used in combination. **3.** *Informal.* **a.** A robust or high-spirited young man. **b.** A fop. [Middle English *bukke,* Old English *buc,* stag, and *bucca,* he-goat, from Old Norse.]

buck[2] *v.* **bucked, bucking, bucks.** *—intr.* **1.** To jump upward suddenly with a humped back. Used of a horse or mule. **2.** To be obstinately opposed. Often used with *at* or *against.* *—tr.* **1.** To throw (a rider or burden) by bucking. Often used with *off.* **2.** To oppose or resist stubbornly: *buck the system.* **—buck up.** *Informal.* To summon one's courage or spirits; pull oneself together.
~n. An act of bucking. [From BUCK (deer).] **—buck·er** *n.*

buck[3] *n.* **1.** A sawhorse. **2.** A leather-covered frame used for gymnastic vaulting. [Short for SAWBUCK.]

buck[4] *n. Slang.* A dollar. [Short for BUCKSKIN (a unit of trade with the American Indians).]

buck[5] *n.* A counter or marker formerly placed before a poker player to mark him as the next dealer. **—pass the buck.** To shift responsibility or blame to someone else. [Short for earlier *buckhorn knife,* from its use for this purpose.]

Buck (bŭk), **Pearl Sydenstricker** (1892–1973). U.S. novelist, whose fiction deals mainly with life in China, where she lived until 1924. She wrote more than 85 books, including *The Good Earth* (1931), which won a Pulitzer Prize. She won the Nobel Prize for literature (1938).

buck and wing *n.* A fast solo tap dance with much springing of the legs and clicking of the heels.

buck·a·roo, (bŭk′ə-ro͞o′) *n., pl.* **-roos.** A cowboy. [Variant of Spanish *vaquero,* VAQUERO, from *vaca,* a cow, from Latin *vacca.*]

buck·bean (bŭk′bēn′) *n.* A plant, the **bogbean** *(see).* [Translation of Dutch *boksboon.*]

buck·board (bŭk′bôrd′, -bōrd′) *n.* A four-wheeled open carriage with the seat attached to a flexible board extending from the front to the rear axle. [From obsolete *buck,* body of a wagon, "trunk of a body," belly, Old English *būc,* from Germanic.]

buck·et (bŭk′ĭt) *n.* **1.** A cylindrical vessel with a semicircular handle and an open top used for holding or carrying liquids or solids; a pail. **2.** Any of various machine compartments that receive and convey material, such as the scoop of a steam shovel. **3.** A bucketful. **4. buckets.** *Informal.* Large quantities: *She's got buckets of money.* **5.** *Computer Science.* A region on a direct-access storage device from which data can be read. **—kick the bucket.** *Informal.* To die. [Referring to the death throes of a slaughtered animal, from obsolete *bucket,* beam (from which freshly killed animals were suspended).]
~v. **bucketed, -eting, -ets.** *—tr.* **1.** To hold, carry, or put in a bucket. **2.** To ride (a horse) long and hard. *—intr.* **1.** To move or proceed rapidly and jerkily. **2.** To make haste; hustle. [Middle English *buket, boket,* from Norman French *buket,* bucket, tub, perhaps from Old English *būc,* belly, pitcher.]

buck·et·ful (bŭk′ĭt-fo͝ol′) *n., pl.* **-fuls** or **bucketsful.** The amount that a bucket will hold.

bucket seat *n.* A seat with a rounded or molded back, as in sports cars and airplanes.

bucket shop *n.* **1.** A fraudulent brokerage operation that accepts orders to buy or sell shares or commodities but delays executing the orders on the gamble that prices will change adversely to the interests of the customer, so that it can pocket what the customer thinks he has lost. **2.** *Chiefly British.* An unlicensed travel agency that buys airline tickets in bulk and sells them to the public at a discount. [Originally a place where small amounts of commodity gambling transactions took place and where the customer could buy alcoholic drink in buckets.]

buck·eye (bŭk′ī′) *n.* **1.** Any of several North American trees of the genus *Aesculus,* having compound leaves and erect clusters of white or reddish flowers. See **horse chestnut. 2.** The glossy brown nut of any of these trees. [BUCK (male deer) + EYE, referring to the appearance of the nut.]

buck fever *n. Informal.* Nervous excitement felt by a novice hunter at the first sight of game.

buck·horn (bŭk′hôrn′) *n.* The material of a buck's horn used for making handles for knives or other implements.

buck·hound (bŭk′hound′) *n.* A hound used for hunting deer.

Buck·ing·ham (bŭk′ĭng-əm, -hăm′), **George Villiers, 1st Duke of** (1592–1628). English courtier, statesman, and favorite of James I. He was murdered by John Felton, a discharged officer nursing a grievance.

Buckingham, George Villiers, 2nd Duke of (1628–87). English courtier and statesman, son of the 1st duke. A staunch Royalist during the Civil War, he fled to Holland (1648) and became a leading adviser to the exiled Charles II. On the restoration of Charles II (1660) he rose to prominence as a leading member of the royal administration, known as the Cabal. Financial malpractice and open philandering led to his dismissal from office (1674).

Buckingham Palace. The official London residence of the British sovereign, situated at the western end of St James's Park between Birdcage Walk and the Mall.

Buck·ing·ham·shire (bŭk′ĭng-əm-shîr, -shər). Also **Buck·ing·ham** (bŭk′ĭng-əm) or **Bucks** (bŭks). County in central England, almost entirely agricultural. It has extensive parklands and a great number of country estates, of which the most famous is Cliveden. The county town is Aylesbury.

buck·ish (bŭk′ĭsh) *adj. Archaic.* Foppish; dandified. **—buck·ish·ly** *adv.* **—buck·ish·ness** *n.*

buck·le[1] (bŭk′əl) *n.* **1.** A clasp, especially a metal frame with one or more movable tongues for fastening the two ends of a strap or belt. **2.** An ornament that resembles such a clasp.
~v. **buckled, -ling, -les.** *—tr.* To fasten or secure with a buckle. *—intr.* To become fastened or attached with a buckle. **—buckle down.** To apply oneself with determination. [Middle English *bocle,* from Old French *boucle,* metal ring, buckle, from Latin *buccula,* cheek strap of a helmet, diminutive of *bucca,* cheek.]

buckle[2] *v.* **-led, -ling, -les.** *—intr.* **1.** To bend, warp, or crumple under pressure or heat. **2.** To give way; collapse: *struts buckling under the stress.* *—tr.* To cause to bend, warp, or crumple. **—buckle under.** To surrender to another's authority; yield.
~n. A bend, bulge, or other distortion. [Middle English *boclen,* from Old French *boucler,* "to fasten with a buckle," from *boucle,* BUCKLE.]

buck·ler (bŭk′lər) *n.* **1.** A small round shield either carried or worn on the arm. **2.** A means of protection; a defense.
~tr.v. **bucklered, -lering, -lers.** To shield with or as if with a buckler; protect. [Middle English *boc(e)ler,* from Old French *bocler, boucler,* from *boucle,* boss on a shield, BUCKLE.]

buckler fern *n.* A shield fern *(see).*

Buck·ley (bŭk′lē), **William Frank, Jr.** (1925–). U.S. editor and author. In 1955 he founded and became editor of the *National Review.* Many of his works, including *Up From Liberalism* (1959), and his strong debating style have established him as an intellectual force in American conservatism. He also writes mystery novels such as *Saving the Queen* (1976) and *Marco Polo, If You Can* (1983).

buck·ling (bŭk′lĭng) *n. British.* A smoked herring. [German *Bückling,* bloater.]

buck·o (bŭk′ō) *n., pl.* **-oes. 1.** *Slang.* A swaggering bully. **2.** *Chiefly Irish.* A young man; a lad. Often used as a term of address. [From BUCK (young man).]

buck·ram (bŭk′rəm) *n.* **1.** A coarse cotton fabric heavily sized with glue, used for stiffening garments and in bookbinding. **2.** *Obsolete.* Stiffness; formality.
~adj. Made of buckram or resembling it in stiffness.
~tr.v. **buckramed, -raming, -rams.** To stiffen with buckram. [Middle English *bokram,* a fine linen, from Old French *boquerant,* obscurely from BOKHARA, from where the fine linen was once imported.]

Bucks. See **Buckinghamshire.**

buck·saw (bŭk′sô′) *n.* A wood-cutting saw, usually set in an H-shaped frame. [From BUCK (sawhorse).]

buck·shee (bŭk′shē) *n. British Slang.* **1.** A windfall or gratuity. **2.** An extra ration.
~adj. Free of charge; gratis. [Variant of BAKSHEESH.]

buck·shot (bŭk′shŏt′) *n.* A large lead shot for shotgun shells. [Originally the distance at which a buck could be shot.]

buck·skin (bŭk′skĭn′) *n.* **1.** The skin of a male deer. **2.** A strong, grayish-yellow leather once made from deerskins but now usually made from sheepskins. **3. buckskins.** A pair of breeches or shoes made from this leather.
~adj. Made of buckskin.

buck·thorn (bŭk′thôrn′) *n.* Any of various shrubs or trees of the genera *Rhamnus, Frangula,* or *Hippophaë;* especially, *R. catharticus,* native to Eurasia, with small greenish flowers, black berries, and often thorny branches. See **sea buckthorn.**

buck·tooth (bŭk′to͞oth′) *n., pl.* **-teeth** (-tēth′). A prominent, projecting upper front tooth. [From BUCK (deer).] **—buck·toothed** *adj.*

buck·wheat (bŭk′hwēt′) *n.* **1.** Any plant of the genus *Fagopyrum;* especially, *F. esculentum,* native to Asia, having fragrant white or pink flowers and small triangular seeds. **2.** The edible seeds of this plant, often ground into flour. [Partial translation of Middle Dutch *boecweite,* "beech wheat" (because its seeds resemble beech nuts) : *boek,* beech + *weite,* wheat.]

bu·col·ic (byo͞o-kŏl′ĭk) *adj.* **1.** Of or characteristic of shepherds and flocks; pastoral. **2.** Of or characteristic of the countryside or its people; rustic. —See Synonyms at **rural.**
~n. **bucolics.** A collection of pastoral poems. [Latin *būcolicus,* from Greek *boukolikos,* from *boukolos,* cowherd : *bous,* cow + *-kolos,* herd.] **—bu·col·i·cal·ly** *adv.*

București. See **Bucharest.**

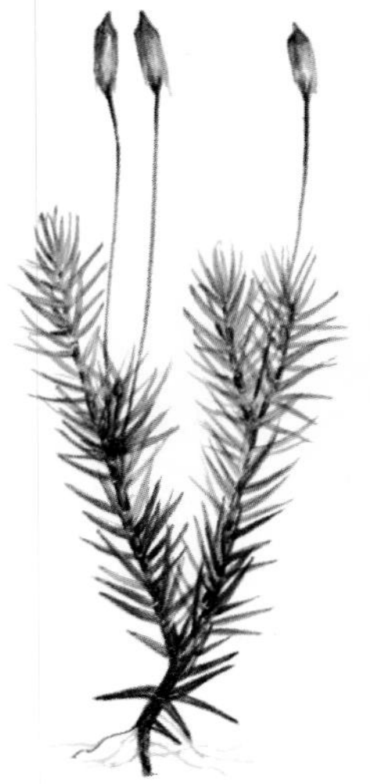

bryophyte *There are about 24,000 species of primitive green plants in the phylum* Bryophyta, *including mosses. This is* Polytrichum commune, *once used for stuffing mattresses and making brooms.*

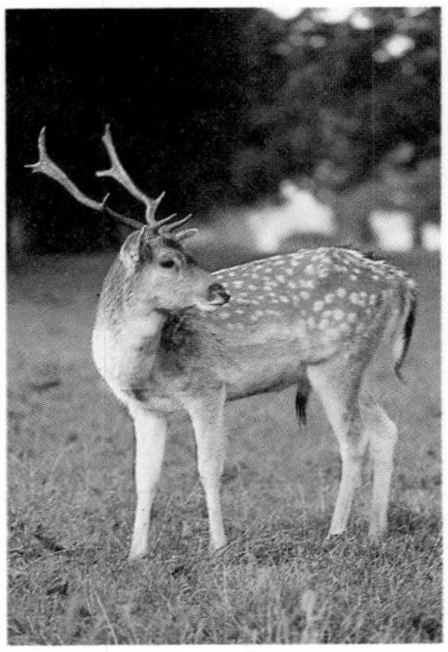

buck *Male deer are generally called bucks, although the male red deer is called a stag. This is a fallow buck in its summer coat.*

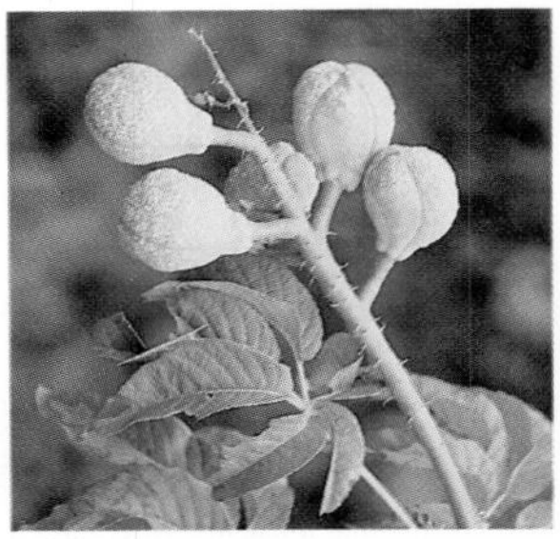

buckeye *A tree native to North America and related to the horse chestnut. It bears yellow, white, or reddish flowers and a smooth, rounded fruit.*

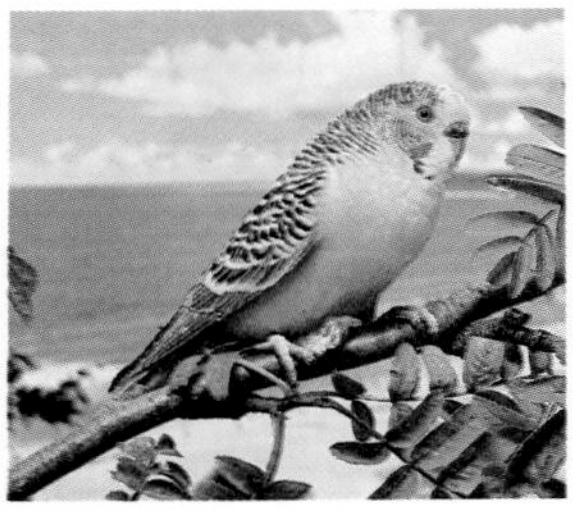

budgerigar *A small parakeet that lives in large flocks in the dry outback of Australia. Budgerigars are naturally green, but types with many other colors have been bred in captivity.*

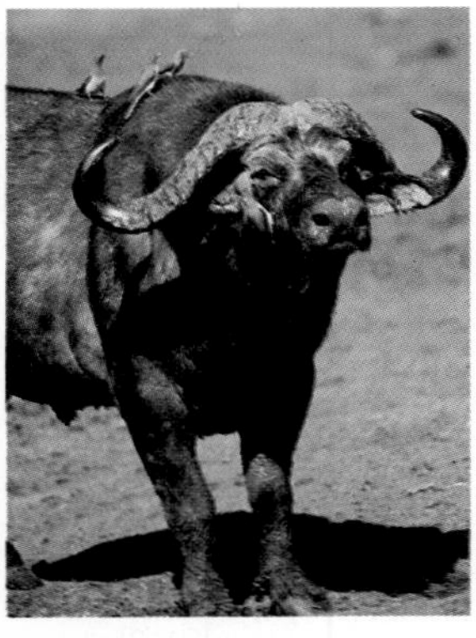

buffalo *The African buffalo, a grazing animal, weighs nearly a ton when fully grown. The birds on this buffalo's back are tick birds, also known as oxpeckers, which feed on the animal's insect parasites.*

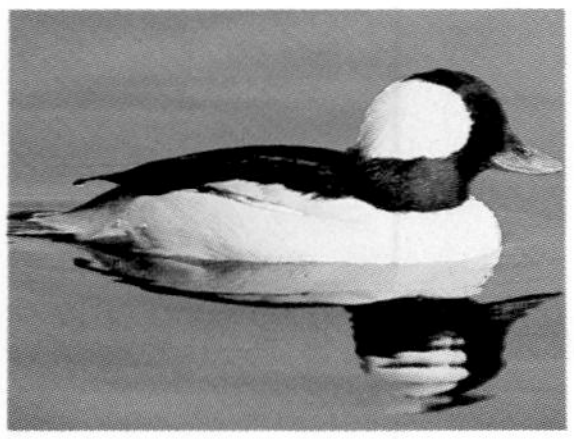

bufflehead *Old woodpecker holes are a favorite nesting place for the bufflehead. The duck, which is native to North America, lays up to a dozen eggs at a time.*

bud[1] (bŭd) *n.* **1.** *Botany.* **a.** An outgrowth on a stem or branch, often enclosed in protective scales, comprising a shortened stem and immature leaves or floral parts. **b.** The stage or condition of having buds. **c.** A partially opened flower. **2.** *Biology.* **a.** An asexually produced outgrowth, as on a polyp, that develops into a mature, complete organism. **b.** Any small, rounded organic part resembling a plant bud: *taste buds.* **—nip in the bud.** To stop (an idea, plan, or the like) in its initial stages.
~v. **budded, budding, buds.** *—intr.* **1.** To put forth or produce a bud or buds. **2.** To begin to develop or grow from or as if from a bud. *—tr.* **1.** To cause to put forth buds. **2.** To graft a bud onto (a plant). [Middle English *budde,* bud, perhaps from Low German *but,* perhaps from Old French *boter,* to push forth, from Germanic.] **—bud·der** *n.*

bud[2] *n.* Fellow; mister. Used as an informal term of address. [Short for BUDDY.]

Bu·da·pest (bo͞o′də-pĕst′). Capital and largest city of Hungary, on the Danube River in the northern part of the country. It was formed (1873) by the union of Buda and Óbuda on the right bank of the Danube with Pest on the left bank. Buda was the capital of Hungary from 1361 to 1541, when it was captured by the Ottoman Turks. In 1686 both Buda and Pest passed to the control of the Austro-Hungarian Empire. The city was the site of the counterrevolutionary uprising of 1956.

Bud·dha[1] (bo͞o′də, bo͝od′ə), born Gautama Siddhartha (*c.* 563–*c.* 483 B.C.). Indian mystic, the founder of Buddhism. He was the son of a prince of the Sakya clan in northern India and was brought up sheltered from the world, but at the age of about 29 he left the palace to wander about the world, deserting his wife and son. He studied yoga, then devoted himself to fasting and extreme asceticism. He is said to have gained perfect spiritual enlightenment at Buddh Gaya at the age of 35. Having thereby become the first Buddha, he lectured at Sarnath to five ascetic companions who became the first Buddhist disciples. He spent the rest of his life traveling through India preaching Buddhism to all listeners, regardless of caste. When he died, he was cremated and his ashes were distributed among eight Buddhist communities, who enshrined them in stupas.

Buddha[2] *n.* **1.** In Buddhism, one who has achieved a state of perfect spiritual enlightenment. **2.** A representation or likeness of Gautama Buddha. [Sanskrit, "awakened," past participle of *bōdhati,* he awakes, becomes aware.]

Buddh Ga·ya, Bodh Ga·ya (bo͝od′ gə-yä′). Village in Bihar state, east-central India. It was here, according to traditional belief, that Buddha gained enlightenment while sitting under a bo tree.

Bud·dhism (bo͞o′dĭz′əm, bo͝od′ĭz′əm) *n.* **1.** The doctrine, attributed to Gautama Buddha, that suffering is inseparable from existence but that inward extinction of the self and of worldly desire culminates in a state of spiritual enlightenment beyond both suffering and existence. **2.** The religion represented by the many groups, especially numerous in Asia, that profess varying forms of this doctrine and venerate Gautama Buddha. **—Bud·dhist** *n.* & *adj.* **—Bud·dhis·tic, Bud·dhis·ti·cal** *adj.*

bud·ding (bŭd′ĭng) *adj.* Beginning to develop; promising.

bud·dle (bŭd′l) *n.* An inclined trough on which ore is separated from waste by washing with running water.

bud·dlei·a (bŏd′lē-ə, bŭd-lē′ə) *n.* A shrub of the genus *Buddleia,* the **butterfly bush** *(see).* [After Adam *Buddle* (died 1715), British botanist.]

bud·dy (bŭd′ē) *n., pl.* **-dies.** *Informal.* A good friend. Often used as a term of address.
~adj. Informal. Of, pertaining to, or representing a close, warm relationship between two tough men: *a buddy movie.* [Probably from a baby-talk variant of BROTHER.]

bud·dy-bud·dy (bŭd′ē-bŭd′ē) *adj. Informal.* Showing great outward friendship.

buddy system *n.* An informal arrangement in which persons are paired, as for mutual safety or assistance.

budge[1] (bŭj) *v.* **budged, budging, budges.** *—intr.* **1.** To move or stir slightly. **2.** To alter a position or attitude. *—tr.* **1.** To cause or persuade to move slightly. **2.** To cause to alter a position or attitude. [Earlier *bouge,* from Old French *bouger, bougier,* from Vulgar Latin *bullicāre* (unattested), from Latin *bullīre,* to boil.]

budge[2] *n.* Fur, usually lambskin, treated to be worn with the wool outward.
~adj. Archaic. Extremely formal; solemn; pompous. [Middle English *bugee, bogey*†.]

Budge (bŭj), **(John) Donald** (1915–). U.S. tennis player, the first to win the Grand Slam (Wimbledon, French, U.S., and Australian titles) in one year (1938). He won all three titles (men's singles, men's doubles, and mixed doubles) at both Wimbledon and Forest Hills (1937, 1938).

budg·er·i·gar (bŭj′ə-rē-gär′) *n.* A parakeet, *Melopsittacus undulatus,* native to Australia, having green plumage in the wild. It is a popular cage bird and breeders have raised many different-colored varieties. Also *informal* "budgie." [Native Australian name : *budgeri,* good + *gar,* cockatoo.]

budg·et (bŭj′ĭt) *n.* **1.** An itemized summary of probable expenditures and income for a given period, usually embodying a systematic plan for meeting expenses. **2.** The total sum of money allocated for a particular purpose or time period.
~v. **budgeted, -eting, -ets.** *—tr.* **1.** To plan in advance the expenditure of (money or time, for example). **2.** To enter or plan for in a budget. [Middle English *bouget,* wallet, from Old French *bougette,* diminutive of *bouge,* leather bag, from Latin *bulga,* from Gaulish.] **—budg·et·ar·y** *adj.*

budg·ie (bŭj′ē) *n. Informal.* A budgerigar.

Bue·nos Ai·res (bwā′nəs âr′ēz, ĭr′ēz, bō′nəs). The capital, chief port, and largest city of Argentina, at the mouth of the Río de la Plata. Situated at the edge of the pampas, an intensely cultivated agricultural region, and connected by rivers to Brazil, Uruguay, and Paraguay, the city is one of the world's busiest ports. It is also one of the most heavily industrialized cities in South America. It was founded in 1536 by Spanish colonists and has been the capital since 1862.

buff[1] (bŭf) *n.* **1.** A soft, thick, undyed leather made chiefly from the skins of buffalo, elk, or oxen. **2.** The color of this leather; pale creamy yellow to light yellowish brown. **3.** *Informal.* The bare skin. Used chiefly in the phrase *in the buff.* **4.** A polishing implement covered with a soft material, such as velvet or leather.
~adj. **1.** Made of buff. **2.** Of the color of buff.
~tr.v. **buffed, buffing, buffs.** **1.** To polish or shine with a buff. **2.** To give (leather, for example) the velvety surface of buff, as with sandpaper. [Originally "buffalo," from Old French *buffle,* from Vulgar Latin *būfalus* (unattested), BUFFALO.]

buff[2] *tr.v.* **buffed, buffing, buffs.** To deaden the shock of.
~n. A buffet; a blow. [As verb, from obsolete *buff,* "to sound as a soft body when struck" (perhaps imitative); as noun, from Middle English *buffe,* from Old French, BUFFET.]

buff[3] *n. Informal.* One who is enthusiastic and knowledgeable about a specified subject: *an opera buff.* [Originally a New York volunteer fireman, hence an enthusiast, from the firemen's buff uniforms.]

buf·fa·lo (bŭf′ə-lō′) *n., pl.* **-loes** or **-los** or collectively **buffalo.** **1.** Any of several oxlike Old World mammals of the family Bovidae, having massive curved horns and humped backs, such as *Syncerus caffer* of Africa or the **water buffalo** *(see).* **2.** A related North American animal, the **bison** *(see).* [Portuguese *bufalo,* from Vulgar Latin *būfalus* (unattested), from Latin *būbalus,* from Greek *boubalos,* African antelope, buffalo, probably from *bous,* cow, ox.]

Buf·fa·lo (bŭf′ə-lō′). The second-largest city of New York State, in the west on Lake Erie and the Buffalo and Niagara rivers. Buffalo is an important Great Lakes port, especially for grain distribution, and has flour and steel mills, automobile factories, and other diversified manufactures.

buffalo berry *n.* **1.** Either of two North American shrubs, *Shepherdia argentea* of *S. canadensis,* having small yellowish flowers and red or yellowish berries. **2.** The berry of a buffalo berry.

Buffalo Bill. See William Frederick **Cody.**

buffalo bug *n.* Also **buffalo beetle.** The **carpet beetle** *(see).*

buffalo fish *n.* Any of several North American freshwater fishes of the genus *Ictiobus,* having a humped back.

buffalo gnat *n.* The **black fly** *(see).*

buffalo grass *n.* A short grass, *Buchloë dactyloides,* of the plains east of the Rocky Mountains.

buffalo robe *n.* The dressed skin of the North American bison, used as a lap robe, cape, or blanket.

buff·er[1] (bŭf′ər) *n.* An implement used to shine or polish, such as a soft cloth or a buffing wheel.

buffer[2] *n.* **1.** Something that lessens or absorbs the shock of an impact; especially, either of a pair of spring-loaded or hydraulically mounted steel pads attached to both ends of railway rolling stock and at the end of a railway line to reduce the shock of collision. **2.** One that protects by intercepting or moderating adverse pressures or influences. **3.** Something interposed between two rival powers, lessening the danger of conflict. Often used adjectivally: *a buffer zone.* **4.** *Chemistry.* An ionic solution capable of maintaining the relative concentrations of hydrogen and hydroxyl ions in a solution by neutralizing, within limits, added acids or bases. Also called "buffer solution." **5.** *Computer Science.* A memory device used for the temporary storage of data. **6.** *Electronics.* A circuit used to join two other circuits so as to minimize the reactance between them.
~tr.v. **buffered, -ering, -ers.** *Chemistry.* To treat (a solution) with a buffer.

buf·fet[1] (bə-fā′, bo͞o-) *n.* **1.** A large sideboard with drawers and cupboards. **2. a.** A counter or table from which meals or refreshments are served. **b.** A restaurant having such a counter. **3.** A meal at which guests serve themselves from various dishes displayed on a table or sideboard. Also used adjectivally: *a buffet lunch.* [French *buffet*†.]

buf·fet[2] (bŭf′ĭt) *n.* **1.** A blow or cuff with the hand. **2.** A blast of wind or the impact of a wave. **3.** A blow; a setback.
~v. **buffeted, -feting, -fets.** *—tr.* **1.** To strike against forcefully or repeatedly; batter. **2.** To contend with; struggle against. *—intr.* **1.** To struggle; contend. **2.** To force one's way by struggling. [Middle English, from Old French, diminutive of *buffe,* blow (imitative).] **—buf·fet·er** *n.*

Buf·fet (bo͞o-fā′), **Bernard** (1928–). French painter. His many works, including *The Horrors of War* and *The Angel of Destruction,* express disillusionment and misery.

buff·ing wheel *n.* A wheel covered with a soft material, such as velvet or leather, for shining and polishing metal.

buf·fle·head (bŭf′əl-hĕd′) *n.* A small North American duck, *Bucephala albeola,* having black and white plumage and a densely feathered, rounded head. Also called "butterball." [From obsolete *buffle,* a buffalo (from the duck's large head), from Old French. See **buff** (leather).]

Buddhism

THE EIGHTFOLD PATH TO ENLIGHTENMENT
Compassion and meditation in the quest for Nirvana

Buddhists try to emulate the life of Siddhartha Gautama—the Buddha—who founded the religion and philosophical system named after him in northeast India in the 6th century B.C.

According to tradition, Gautama was brought up in luxury and protected from all unpleasant sights during his early life. But one day he encountered in succession first an old man, then a sick man, and, finally, a corpse. These meetings made him aware of the sufferings of mankind and the impermanence of life, and he determined to leave his comforts and set out on a quest for spiritual truth.

Buddhism teaches Four Noble Truths: that the world is full of suffering; that suffering is caused by human desires; that suffering stops when desires are renounced; and that the Eightfold Path is the way to achieve this. The Eightfold Path consists of eight principles of behavior that make up the road to enlightenment: right understanding, right resolve, right speech, right action, right livelihood, right effort, right mindfulness, and right meditation.

Nirvana, the Buddhist's ultimate goal, is the ultimate state of blessedness, to which enlightenment gives entry. It is viewed in different ways by the two main Buddhist schools. The Hinayana school—the older, more conservative form of Buddhism—regards Nirvana as the means by which the individual is liberated from earthly existence. The Mahayana school, on the other hand, asserts that the disciple who gains enlightenment remains in the world, as a *Bodhisattva,* to help others along the path. The followers of Hinayana are chiefly found in Sri Lanka, Burma, Thailand, Laos, and Kampuchea; the Mahayana has most support in Tibet, Mongolia, China, Korea, and Japan. Today there are some 500 million Buddhists in the Far East, and a growing number in the West.

BUDDHIST SHRINE *The Swayambhunath Temple, near Katmandu in Nepal, is a typical example of Buddhist architecture.*

WHEEL OF BECOMING *The Bhavachakra, or Wheel of Becoming, is an image of the earthly existence from which the Buddhist seeks liberation; it is held by the demon of impermanence. The six segments represent the six possible states into which beings may be reborn: (clockwise from bottom) titans, hungry ghosts, humans, gods, demons, and animals.*

buf·fo (bōō′fō) *n., pl.* **-fi** (-fē). A male singer of comic opera roles. —*adj.* Characteristic of a buffo; comic. [Italian, "puff of wind," from *buffare,* to puff. See **buffoon.**]

Buf·fon (bōō-fôn′), **Georges-Louis Leclerc, Comte de** (1707–88). French biologist. In his 44-volume *Natural History* (1749) and *Epochs of Nature* (1778), he contributed greatly to the development of modern science by stressing a materialist, geological explanation of the world's origin and history. Buffon also wrote a *Discourse on Style* (1753), an analysis of literary expression that features the famous phrase, "the style is the man."

buf·foon (bə-fōōn′) *n.* **1.** A clown; a jester: *a court buffoon.* **2.** A witless person given to making coarse jokes. [French *bouffon,* from Italian *buffone,* from *buffare,* to puff (imitative).] —**buf·foon·er·y** *n.*

bug (bŭg) *n.* **1.** Any of various wingless or four-winged insects of the order Hemiptera, and especially the suborder Heteroptera, having mouthparts adapted for piercing and sucking. **2.** Broadly, any insect or similar organism. **3.** *Informal.* **a.** A disease-producing microorganism. **b.** A disease so caused, often spreading as a minor epidemic. **4.** A mechanical, electrical, or other systemic defect or difficulty, as in a computer system. **5.** *Slang.* An enthusiast or devotee; a buff; *a hi-fi bug.* **6.** *Informal.* A small hidden microphone or other device used for eavesdropping or surveillance. —*tr. v.* **bugged, bugging, bugs.** *Informal.* **1. a.** To annoy; pester. **b.** To worry; prey on: *That memory bugged me over the years.* **2.** To fit (a room, for example) with concealed electronic surveillance equipment. [17th century : origin obscure.]

Bug[1] (bōōg). Also **Western Bug.** A river rising in southwestern Ukraine. It flows northward 770 kilometers (480 miles) through Poland to the Vistula River near Warsaw.

Bug[2]. Also **Southern Bug.** A river rising in southwestern Ukraine. It flows 790 kilometers (490 miles) generally southeast to the Black Sea. It is navigable for *c.* 160 kilometers (100 miles) above its mouth.

bug·a·boo (bŭg′ə-bōō′) *n., pl.* **-boos. 1.** A bugbear. **2.** A steady source of concern. [Perhaps from Celtic; akin to Cornish *buccaboo,* the devil. Compare **bugbear** and **bogle.**]

Bu·gan·da (bōō-găn′də, byōō-). A former kingdom in East Africa, occupying the northern shores of Lake Victoria in present-day Uganda. It was ruled by the Ganda tribe until it became a British protectorate (1900). It was merged with Uganda when Uganda became an independent state (1962).

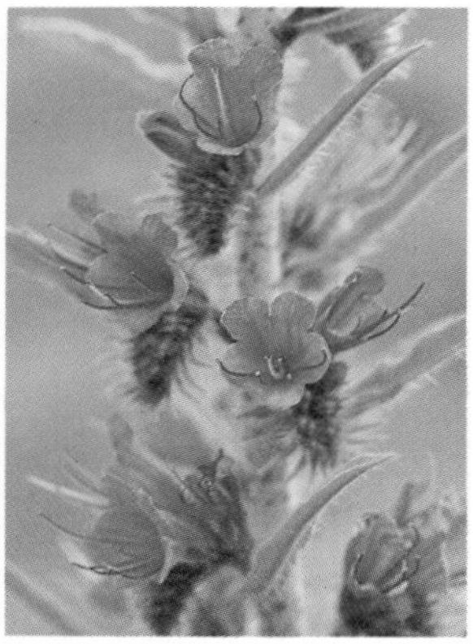

bugloss *The name of this wildflower is derived from two Greek words meaning "ox-tongued"—a reference to the shape and texture of its leaves. It grows on sandy soils throughout Europe and in the eastern United States.*

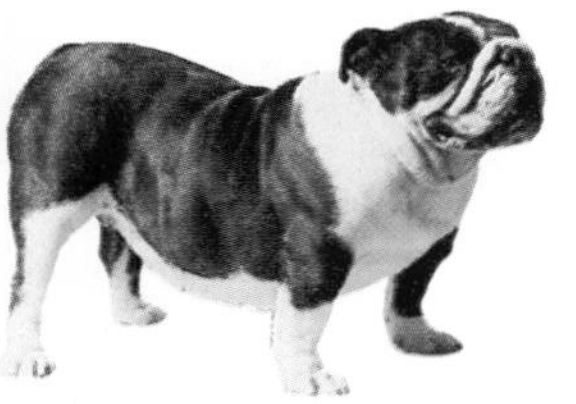

bulldog *This English breed of mastiff—noted for its tenacity—was once used to bait bulls.*

PRONUNCIATION KEY

ă, pat; ā, pay; âr, care;
ä, father, are; b, bib;
ch, church; d, deed; ĕ, pet;
ē, be; f, fife; g, gag; h, hat;
hw, which; ĭ, pit; ī, pie;
îr, pier; j, judge; k, kick;
l, lid, needle; m, mum;
n, no, sudden; ng, thing;
ŏ, pot; ō, toe; ô, paw, for;
oi, noise; ou, out; o͝o, book;
o͞o, boot; p, pop; r, roar;
s, sauce; sh, ship, dish;
t, tight; th, thin, path;
th, this, bathe; ŭ, cut; ûr, fur;
v, valve; w, with; y, yes;
z, zebra, size; zh, vision;
ə, about, item, edible,
gallop, circus, peaceful

IN FOREIGN WORDS:

à, *Fr.* ami; œ, *Fr.* feu, *Ger.* schön; ü, *Fr.* tu, *Ger.* über; KH, *Ger.* ich, *Scot.* loch; N, *Fr.* bon; y', *Fr.* Compiègne

STRESS MARKS:

Primary stress: ′
in·cite′ (ĭn-sīt′)
Secondary stress: ′
in′sight′ (ĭn′sīt′)

bug·bane (bŭg′bān′) *n.* Any of several plants of the genus *Cimicifuga;* especially, *C. americana* of eastern North America, having clusters of small white flowers supposed to repel insects.

bug·bear (bŭg′bâr′) *n.* **1.** An object of obsessive, but often groundless, dread. **2.** *Archaic.* A goblin reputed to eat naughty children. [Obsolete *bug,* from Middle English *bugge;* akin to Welsh *bwg(a),* ghost, and Cornish *buccaboo,* the devil.]

bug-eyed (bŭg′īd′) *adj. Slang.* Agog, as with amazement.

bug·ger[1] (bŭg′ər) *n.* **1.** *Slang.* A contemptible or disreputable person. **2.** A fellow; a chap.

bugger[2] *n. Informal.* A person who plants an electronic eavesdropping or surveillance device. [BUG + -ER[1].]

bug·gy[1] (bŭg′ē) *n., pl.* **-gies. 1.** A small, light, horse-drawn carriage. **2.** A baby carriage. [18th century : origin obscure.]

buggy[2] *adj.* **-gier, -giest. 1.** Infested with bugs. **2.** *Slang.* Crazy. **—bug·gi·ness** *n.*

bug·house (bŭg′hous′) *n. Slang.* An insane asylum. [From BUGGY (crazy).]

bu·gle[1] (byo͞o′gəl) *n.* **1.** A brass wind instrument somewhat shorter than a trumpet, and without keys or valves. **2.** A hunting horn. *~intr. v.* **bugled, -gling, -gles.** To play a bugle. [Middle English *bugle,* buffalo, horn, bugle, from Old French, from Latin *būculus,* diminutive of *bōs,* ox.] **—bu·gler** *n.*

bugle[2] *n.* A tubular glass or plastic bead used to trim clothing. Also called "bugle bead." [16th century : origin obscure.]

bugle[3] *n.* Any of several plants of the genus *Ajuga,* especially *A. reptans,* native to Eurasia, having spikes or dense clusters of small blue or white flowers. Also called "bugleweed." [Middle English, from Old French, from Late Latin *bugula,* perhaps from Latin *bugillō,* from Gaulish.]

bu·gle·weed (byo͞o′gəl-wēd′) *n.* **1.** A plant of the genus *Lycopus,* especially *L. virginicus,* having small, whitish flowers and an aromatic odor. **2.** A plant, the **bugle** *(see).* [Perhaps from its tubular flowers.]

bu·gloss (byo͞o′glŏs′, -glôs′) *n.* Any of several plants of the genera *Lycopsis, Echium,* and *Anchusa,* especially *L. arvensis,* having hairy stems and leaves and clusters of blue flowers. See **alkanet, viper's bugloss.** [Middle English *buglosse,* from Old French, from Latin *būglōssa,* from Greek *bouglōssos,* "ox-tongued" (from the broad, rough leaves) : *bous,* ox + *glōssa,* tongue.]

buhl, boule, boulle (bo͞ol) *n.* **1.** A style of furniture decoration in which elaborate designs are inlaid with tortoiseshell, ivory, and metals of various colors. **2.** A piece of furniture so decorated. [After André C. *Boulle* (1642–1732), French cabinetmaker.]

buhr·stone, burr·stone (bûr′stōn′) *n.* A tough limestone impregnated with silica, from which millstones were formerly made. [Variant of *bur(r)stone* : perhaps BUR + STONE.]

build (bĭld) *v.* **built** (bĭlt) or *archaic* **builded, building, builds.** *—tr.* **1.** To form by combining materials or parts; erect; construct. **2.** To develop and give form to according to a definite plan or process; fashion; mold; create. **3.** To establish and strengthen; create and add to: *build a savings account.* **4.** To establish a basis for; found or ground: *build an argument on fact.* **5.** *Card Games.* To accumulate combinations or sequences of (cards) according to suit or number. *—intr.* **1.** To construct something or have something constructed: *"Each of the three architects built in a different style"* (Dwight Macdonald). **2.** To be a builder. **3.** To develop an idea, argument, theory, or the like. Used with *on* or *upon.* **4.** *Card Games.* To accumulate combinations or sequences of cards. **5.** To progress toward a maximum, as of intensity, excitement, or the like. **—build in.** To construct as an integral or permanent part of.
~n. The physical make-up of a person or thing: *an athletic build.* [Middle English *bilden,* Old English *byldan,* from *bold,* a dwelling.]

build·er (bĭl′dər) *n.* **1.** One that builds; especially, a person who contracts for and supervises the construction of a building. **2.** An abrasive or filler used in a soap or a detergent.

build·ing (bĭl′dĭng) *n.* **1.** *Abbr.* **bldg.** Something that is built; a structure; an edifice. **2.** The act, process, or occupation of constructing.

build up *tr.v.* **1.** To renew the strength or health of. **2.** To construct or develop in stages or by degrees; create and add to: *build up a business.* **3.** To magnify (a person or thing) by extravagant praise or publicity. **4.** To fill up (an area) with buildings.

build-up, build·up (bĭld′ŭp′) *n.* **1.** The act of amassing or increasing. **2.** *Informal.* Extravagant praise; widely favorable publicity, especially by a systematic campaign. **3.** The result of building up: *the build-up of tension; the build-up of traffic.*

built. Past tense and past participle of **build.**
~adj. Having a physique or physical make-up of the specified type: *well built; heavily built.*

built-in (bĭlt′ĭn′) *adj.* **1.** Constructed as part of a larger unit; not detachable: *a built-in cabinet.* **2.** Forming a permanent or essential element or quality: *a built-in escape clause.*

built-up (bĭlt′ŭp′) *adj.* **1.** Occupied by or covered with many buildings. **2.** Made by fastening several layers or sections one on top of the other: *a built-up roof.*

Bu·jum·bu·ra (bo͞o′jəm-bo͝or′ə). Capital and largest city of Burundi, eastern Africa, situated on Lake Tanganyika.

Bu·kha·ra (bo͞o-kär′ə, -här′ə). Also **Bo·kha·ra** (bō-). A city in southern Uzbekistan, in the Zeravshan River valley. It is one of the oldest cultural and trading centers of Asia and was the capital of the khanate, or state, of Bukhara during its heyday from the 16th to the 19th century.

Bukhara rug *n.* Also **Bokhara rug.** A kind of rug, usually having a black and white pattern of large and small octagons on a red, brownish-red, or sometimes tan ground.

Bu·kha·rin (bo͞o-KHär′ĭn) **Nikolai Ivanovich** (1888–1938). Soviet politician, theoretician, and editor of *Pravda* (1915–29). In 1923 he became a full member of the Politburo and in the power struggle that followed Lenin's death (1924) supported Stalin. Later his advocacy of gradual agricultural collectivization and industrialization lost him major posts in the party (1929). He was executed for treason after the last of the Moscow "show trials" (1938).

Bu·la·wa·yo (bo͞o′lə-wä′yō, -wā′ō). Industrial city on the western border of Zimbabwe, on the Matsheumlope River. It is the second-largest city in Zimbabwe and was founded in 1893 when it was moved five kilometers (three miles) south of its old site, which was the seat of the last king of the Ndebele.

bulb (bŭlb) *n.* **1.** *Botany.* A modified underground stem, such as that of the onion or tulip, usually surrounded by scalelike modified leaves and containing stored food for the undeveloped shoots of the new plant enclosed within it. **2.** Loosely, an underground stem resembling this, such as a corm, rhizome, or tuber. **3.** Any plant that grows from a bulb. **4.** A rounded projection or part of something: *the bulb of a syringe.* **5.** An incandescent lamp or its glass housing. Also called "light bulb." **6.** *Anatomy.* Any of various rounded, enlarged, or bulb-shaped structures, especially the **medulla oblongata** *(see).* [Latin *bulbus,* bulb, onion, from Greek *bolbos†,* name of various bulbous plants.]

bul·bar (bŭl′bər, -bär′) *adj. Anatomy.* Of, pertaining to, or characteristic of a bulb, especially of the medulla oblongata: *bulbar poliomyelitis.*

bul·bil (bŭl′bĭl′) *n. Botany.* A small bulblike part growing above ground on a flower stalk or in a leaf axil. [French *bulbille,* diminutive of *bulbe,* BULB.]

bul·bous (bŭl′bəs) *adj.* **1.** Resembling a bulb in shape. **2.** *Botany.* Bearing bulbs or growing from a bulb.

bul·bul (bo͝ol′bo͝ol′) *n.* **1.** Any of various chiefly tropical Old World songbirds of the family Pycnonotidae, having grayish or brownish plumage. **2.** A songbird, thought to be a nightingale, often mentioned in Persian poetry. [Persian, from Arabic.]

Bulg. Bulgaria.

Bul·ga·nin (bo͝ol-gä′nĭn, -găn′ĭn), **Nikolai Alexandrovich** (1895–1975). Soviet politician. He rose to prominence during the Stalinist purges of the mid-1930s, later distinguishing himself as an administrator during World War II. After the war he was appointed a full member of the Politburo and deputy premier. In 1955 he replaced Malenkov as premier, but was dismissed by Khrushchev (1958) for his participation in the so-called anti-Party group.

Bul·gar·i·a (bŭl-gâr′ē-ə, bo͝ol-). *Abbr.* **Bulg.** Republic in the Balkan Peninsula of southeastern Europe, bordered on the west by Yugoslavia, on the north by Romania, on the east by the Black Sea, and on the south by Turkey and Greece. The center of the country is crossed from west to east by the Balkan Mts. Between these and the Danube, which forms most of the northern boundary, lies a broad, fertile plateau. Although the country has been considerably industrialized since 1945, agriculture remains the leading sector of the economy. Bulgaria is famous for its cultivation of damask roses, used to make attar of roses for perfumes. From the late 14th to the early 20th century, Bulgaria was ruled by Turkey. In 1946 it became a people's republic within the Soviet bloc. Area, 110,911 square kilometers (42,823 square miles). Population, 9,000,000. Capital, Sofia.

Bul·gar·i·an (bŭl-gâr′ē-ən, bo͝ol-) *adj.* Of, pertaining to, or characteristic of Bulgaria, its inhabitants, or their language.
~n. Also **Bul·gar** (bŭl′gər, bo͝ol′-) (for sense 1). **1.** A native or inhabitant of Bulgaria. **2.** The Slavonic language spoken by Bulgarians.

bulge (bŭlj) *n.* **1.** A protruding part; an outward curve or swelling. **2.** The rounded lower section of a ship's hull. **3.** *Slang.* An advantage.
~v. **bulged, bulging, bulges.** *—tr.* To cause to curve outward. *—intr.* **1.** To swell up or outward; grow larger or rounder. **2.** To be swollen because full: *a bulging wallet.* [Middle English, wallet, pouch, from Old French *bouge,* from Latin *bulga,* leather bag, probably from Gaulish.] **—bulg·i·ness** *n.* **—bulg·y** *adj.*

Bulge, Battle of the. The last major German counteroffensive of World War II, launched December 16, 1944, and repulsed by January 21, 1945. [So called because the line of combat formed a large bulge deep into Belgium.]

bul·gur, bul·ghur (bo͝ol′go͝or′, bŭl′gər) *n.* A cereal food prepared by boiling and drying coarsely ground wheat. [Turkish *burgul.*]

bu·lim·i·a (byo͞o-lĭm′ē-ə) *n.* Insatiable appetite. [New Latin, from Greek *boulimia* : *bous,* ox, cow + *limos,* hunger, famine.]

bulimia ner·vos·a (nûr-vō′sə) *n.* A psychological illness, often found in combination with **anorexia nervosa** *(see),* in which bouts of compulsive eating are followed by self-induced and ultimately involuntary vomiting. [New Latin, "nervous bulimia."]

bulk (bŭlk) *n.* **1.** Size, mass, or volume, especially when very large. **2. a.** A distinct mass or portion of matter, especially a large one. **b.** The body of a human being or animal, especially a large and corpulent body. **3.** The major portion or greater part of something: *"the great bulk of necessary work can never be anything but painful"* (Bertrand Russell). **4.** Thickness of paper or cardboard in relation to weight. **5.** *Abbr.* **blk.** A ship's hold or the cargo stowed there. **6.** Any substance that stimulates the action of the intestines; roughage. **—in bulk. 1.** Unpackaged; loose. **2.** In large numbers, amounts, or volume.

~v. bulked, bulking, bulks. —intr. 1. To appear to be, in terms of size, volume, or importance; loom: *"shopkeeping naturally bulks large among London occupations"* (G.D.H. Cole and Raymond Postgate). **2.** To grow or increase in size or importance. Usually used with *up*. **3.** To cohere or form a mass: *Certain paper pulps bulk well. —tr.* To gather together into a mass. [Middle English *bulke, bolke,* heap, mass, body, from Old Norse *bulki,* cargo.]

bulk buy *n.* A product bought in bulk. **—bulk-buy** *v.*

bulk density *n.* The mass of a substance divided by its volume when it is present in bulk. For example, the bulk density of coal is lower than its true density because of the air spaces between lumps.

bulk·head (bŭlk′hĕd′) *n.* **1.** Any of the upright partitions dividing a ship into compartments and serving to prevent the spread of leakage or fire. **2.** A wall or embankment constructed in a mine or tunnel to protect against earth slides, fire, water, or gas. **3.** A horizontal or sloping structure providing access to a cellar stairway or to an elevator shaft. [From BULK (ship's hold).]

bulk modulus *n.* A measure of the elasticity of a substance equal to the ratio of the stress applied to the resulting change in volume.

bulk·y (bŭl′kē) *adj.* **-i·er, -i·est. 1.** Extremely large; massive. **2.** Difficult to carry; unwieldy. **—bulk·i·ly** *adv.* **—bulk·i·ness** *n.*

bull¹ (bool) *n.* **1. a.** An adult male bovine mammal. **b.** The uncastrated adult male of domestic cattle. **2.** The male of certain other mammals, such as the elephant and whale. **3.** An exceptionally large, strong, and aggressive man. **4.** *Stock Market.* A person who buys stocks or shares in a market in anticipation of a rise in prices or who tries by speculative purchases to effect such a rise, in order to sell later at a profit. Compare **bear. 5. Bull.** The constellation and sign of the zodiac, **Taurus** *(see).* **6.** *Slang.* A policeman or detective. **7.** *Slang.* Empty, foolish, or boastful talk; nonsense. **—take the bull by the horns.** To deal with a problem directly and resolutely.

~v. bulled, bulling, bulls. —tr. 1. *Stock Market.* To engage in speculative buying so as to raise the price of (stocks) or prices in (a market). **2.** To push; force. **—intr. 1.** *Stock Market.* To rise in price. **2.** To push ahead or through forcefully.

~adj. 1. Male; masculine. **2.** Resembling a bull; large and strong. **3.** *Stock Market.* Characterized by rising prices: *a bull market.* Compare **bear.** [Middle English *bule, bole,* from Old English *bula,* from Old Norse *boli.* Stock Market senses, 18th century : term introduced to contrast with BEAR as descriptions of the two different types of speculators.]

bull² *n.* **1.** An official document issued by the pope and sealed with a bulla. **2.** The bulla itself. [Middle English *bulle,* from Old French *bulle,* from Medieval Latin *bulla,* seal, BULLA.]

Bull, John. See John Bull.

bul·la (bool′ə) *n., pl.* **bullae** (bool′ē). **1.** A round seal affixed to a papal bull. **2.** *Pathology.* A large blister or vesicle. Compare **bleb.** [Both senses, Medieval Latin, from Latin, bubble, seal.]

bul·lace (bool′ĭs) *n.* A plum, the **damson** *(see).* [Middle English *bolas,* from Old French *buloce, beloce,* sloe, probably from Medieval Latin *bolluca†.*]

bul·late (bool′āt′, bŭl′-) *adj.* Having a puckered or blistered appearance: *bullate leaves.* [New Latin *bulla,* bubble, from Latin.]

bull·bait·ing (bool′bā-tĭng) *n.* The setting of dogs upon bulls, once a popular sport in England.

bull·bat (bool′băt′) *n.* See **nighthawk** (sense 1). [From its roaring sound in flight.]

bull·dog (bool′dôg′, -dŏg′) *n.* **1.** A short-haired dog of a breed characterized by a large head, strong, square jaws with dewlaps, and a stocky body. **2.** A short-barreled revolver or pistol of a large caliber. **3.** *British.* A proctor's assistant at the universities of Oxford or Cambridge.

~adj. Resembling or having the qualities of a bulldog; stubborn; tenacious.

~tr.v. bulldogged, -dogging, -dogs. *Western U.S.* To throw (a steer) by seizing its horns and twisting its neck until it falls.

bulldog ant *n.* A large Australian ant of the genus *Myrmecia* measuring up to one inch long having powerful jaws and a painful sting. Also called "bull ant."

bull·doze (bool′dōz′) *tr.v.* **-dozed, -dozing, -dozes. 1.** To clear, dig up, or move with a bulldozer. **2.** *Slang.* To coerce by intimidation; bully. [Perhaps BULL + DOSE.]

bull·doz·er (bool′dō′zər) *n.* **1.** A tractor with a vertical metal scoop in front for moving earth and rocks, used especially to grade or clear land. **2.** An overbearing or bullying person.

bul·let (bool′ĭt) *n.* **1.** A spherical or pointed metallic projectile that is fired from a pistol, rifle, or other relatively small firearm. **2.** Such a projectile in a metal casing; a cartridge. **3.** Any object of similar shape, action, or effect. **4.** *Printing.* A heavy dot (●) used to call attention to a particular passage. **—bite the bullet.** *Informal.* To endure a painful or difficult situation bravely and stoically. [French *boulette,* diminutive of *boule,* ball, from Old French, from Latin *bulla,* bubble, ball.]

bul·le·tin (bool′ə-tən, -tĭn) *n.* **1.** A brief, authoritative statement on a matter of public interest, intended for immediate broadcast or publication. **2.** A brief, periodically broadcast summary of the news. **3.** A periodical published by an organization or society.

~tr.v. bulletined, -tining, -tins. To inform by bulletin. [French, probably from Old French *bullette,* from *bulle,* BULL (document).]

bulletin board *n.* A board mounted on a wall, on which notices are posted.

bul·let·proof (bool′ĭt-proof′) *adj.* Impenetrable by bullets. **~tr.v. bulletproofed, -proofing, -proofs.** To make impenetrable by bullets.

bull fiddle *n.* A double bass (see).

bull·fight (bool′fīt′) *n.* A public spectacle, especially in Spain and Latin America, in which a fighting bull is engaged in a series of traditional maneuvers culminating usually with the matador's ceremonial execution of the bull by sword. **—bull·fight·er** *n.* **—bull·fight·ing** *n.*

bull·finch (bool′fĭnch′) *n.* **1.** A European bird, *Pyrrhula pyrrhula,* having a short, thick bill and, in the male, a red breast, black head, wings, and tail and a gray and white back. **2.** Any of several other similar finches. [From its thick neck.]

bull·frog (bool′frôg′, -frŏg′) *n.* Any of several large frogs, chiefly of the genus *Rana;* especially, *R. catesbeiana,* of North America, having a characteristic deep, resonant croak.

bull·head (bool′hĕd′) *n.* **1.** Any of several North American freshwater catfishes of the genus *Ictalurus.* **2.** Any of several fishes of the family Cottidae, such as the **sculpin** and the **miller's thumb** (both of which see).

bull·head·ed (bool′hĕd′ĭd) *adj.* Very stubborn; obstinate; headstrong. **—bull·head·ed·ly** *adv.* **—bull·head·ed·ness** *n.*

bull·horn (bool′hôrn′) *n.* An electric megaphone that amplifies the volume of a voice or other sounds. Also *chiefly British* "loudhailer."

bul·lion (bool′yən) *n.* **1.** Gold or silver considered with respect to quantity rather than value. **2.** Gold or silver in the form of bars, ingots, or plates. **3.** A heavy lace trimming made of twisted gold or silver threads. [Middle English, from Norman French, "mint," perhaps variant of Old French *bouillon,* "a boiling," from *bouillir,* to BOIL.]

bull·ish (bool′ĭsh) *adj.* **1.** Like a bull; brawny or bull-headed. **2. a.** Causing, expecting, or characterized by rising stock-market prices. Compare **bearish. b.** Optimistic or confident. **—bull·ish·ly** *adv.* **—bull·ish·ness** *n.*

bull mastiff *n.* A heavy-set dog of a breed developed from the bulldog and the mastiff.

bull·necked (bool′nĕkt′) *adj.* Having a short, thick neck.

bul·lock (bool′ək) *n.* **1.** A castrated bull; a steer. **2.** A young bull. [Middle English *bullok,* Old English *bulluc,* diminutive of *bula,* BULL.]

bull·pen (bool′pĕn′) *n.* **1.** A pen for confining bulls. **2.** *Informal.* A place for the temporary detention of prisoners. **3.** *Baseball.* **a.** An area where relief pitchers warm up during a game. **b.** The relief pitchers of a team collectively.

bull·ring (bool′rĭng′) *n.* A circular arena for bullfights.

bull·roar·er (bool′rôr′ər, -rōr′ər) *n.* A small wooden slat attached to a string that makes a roaring noise when whirled.

Bull Run (bool′ rŭn) *n.* A small stream in northeastern Virginia, near Washington, D.C. It was the site of two Civil War battles (July 21, 1861, and August 29–30, 1862) in which the Confederates defeated Union troops. The battles are also known as the First and Second Battles of Manassas, after a small town nearby.

bull session *n. Informal.* An informal group discussion.

bull's-eye, bull's eye (boolz′ī′) *n.* **1. a.** The small central circle on a target. **b.** A shot that hits this circle. **2.** Anything that precisely achieves a desired goal. **3.** A thick, circular piece of glass set in a roof, pavement, ship's deck, or the like, to admit light. **4.** Any circular opening or window. **5. a.** A plano-convex lens used to concentrate light. **b.** A lantern or lamp having such a lens. **6.** *Nautical.* A small round or oval wooden pulley. **7.** A piece of round, hard candy.

bull snake *n.* Any of several nonvenomous North American snakes of the genus *Pituophis,* having yellow and brown or black markings. Some species are also called "gopher snake."

bull terrier *n.* A dog of a breed developed by crossing a bulldog and

bullfinch *Pyrrhula pyrrhula, the bullfinch, is native to Europe and lives on a diet of berries, buds, and seeds. It is sometimes considered a pest because of the damage it does to fruit trees. This is an adult male of the species; the female has broadly similar plumage but a brown instead of a pink chest.*

bullfrog *These large frogs are noted for their low, resonant mating call that can be heard up to 800 meters away (about half a mile). Their powerful hind legs, which enable them to jump 7.5 meters (25 feet) in a single leap, are eaten as a delicacy in some countries. Bullfrogs are found in North and South America, Africa, India, and Australia—this is an Australian species.*

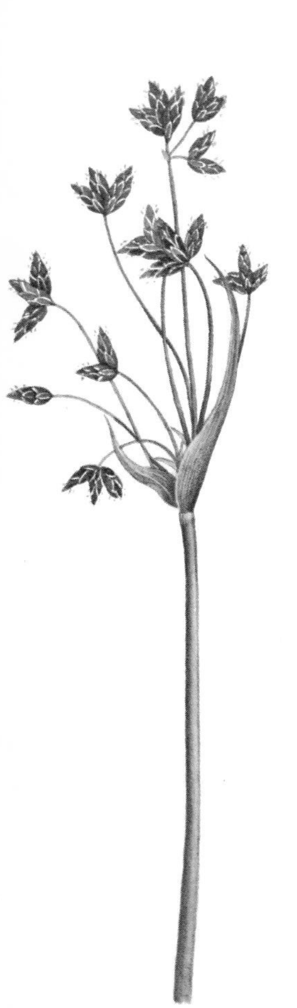

bulrush *In the Victorian painting,* Moses in the Bulrushes, *the artist showed the tall, cigar-shaped reed mace* (Typha latifolia); *but the true bulrush was the sedge grass* Scirpus lacustris, *shown here. Since then the name bulrush has gone into common usage for reed mace, and* Scirpus lacustris *no longer has a common name.*

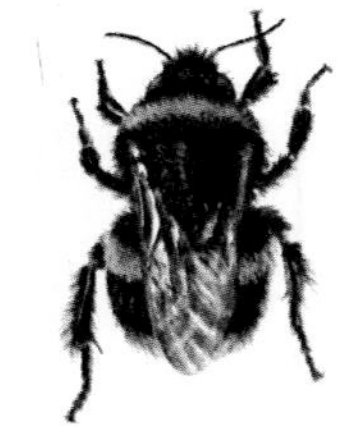

bumblebee *Distinguished by their furry, yellow-banded bodies, bumblebees live in colonies that last only one year. The queen bee, shown here, lays eggs that produce female workers who look after her and the nest. Male bees develop from eggs laid by the workers.*

the now extinct white English terrier, having a short, usually white coat and a tapering muzzle.

bull thistle *n.* A coarse weed, *Cirsium vulgare,* native to Eurasia, having spiny stems and leaves and purple flowers. [From its large head.]

bull tongue *n.* A heavy plow with a single shovel, used chiefly in cotton fields.

bull·whip (bo͝ol'hwĭp') *n.* A long, plaited rawhide whip with a knotted end.
~*tr.v.* **bullwhipped, -whipping, -whips.** To whip with a bullwhip.

bul·ly¹ (bo͝ol'ē) *n., pl.* **-lies. 1.** A person who is habitually cruel or overbearing toward smaller or weaker people. **2.** *Archaic.* A hired ruffian. **3.** *Obsolete.* A pimp. **4.** *Obsolete.* A fine fellow. **5.** *Obsolete.* A sweetheart.
~*v.* **bullied, -lying, -lies.** —*tr.* To intimidate with superior size or strength. —*intr.* To behave like a bully.
~*adj. Informal.* **1.** Excellent; splendid. **2.** Dashing; gallant.
~*interj.* Used to express admiration or approval: *bully for you.* [Originally "sweetheart," probably from Middle Dutch *boele,* lover, from Middle High German *buole,* perhaps of baby-talk origin.]

bully² *n.* Canned or pickled beef. [French *bouilli,* boiled (beef), from the past participle of *bouillir,* to BOIL.]

bully off *intr.v. British.* Formerly, to start or restart a game of hockey. Two players hit each other's sticks and then the ground three times before trying to hit the ball.

bul·ly-off (bo͝ol'ē-ôf', -ŏf') *n. British.* The former procedure for starting or restarting a game of hockey.

bul·ly·rag (bo͝ol'ē-răg') *tr.v.* **-ragged, -ragging, -rags.** Also **bal·ly·rag** (băl'-). To mistreat or intimidate by bullying or teasing.

bully tree *n.* A tropical American tree, the **balata** *(see).* [By folk etymology, variant of BALATA.]

Bü·low (byo͞o'lō), **Bernard Heinrich Martin, Prince von** (1849–1929). German politician, chancellor of the German Empire (1900–09). His chancellorship was marked by an aggressive foreign policy.

bul·rush (bo͝ol-rŭsh') *n.* **1.** Any of various grasslike sedges of the genus *Scirpus,* growing in wet places. **2.** A marsh plant, the **reed mace** *(see).* **3.** In the Old Testament, the **papyrus** *(see).* [Middle English *bulrish* : perhaps *bule,* BULL (in the sense "large") + *rish,* RUSH.]

bul·wark (bo͝ol'wərk, bŭl'-, -wôrk') *n.* **1.** A wall or wall-like structure raised as a defensive fortification; a rampart. **2.** Anything serving as a principal defense against attack or encroachment: *a bulwark against oppression.* **3.** A breakwater. **4.** *Usually* **bulwarks.** The part of a ship's side that is above the upper deck.
~*tr.v.* **bulwarked, -warking, -warks. 1.** To fortify with a bulwark. **2.** To provide defense or protection for. [Middle English *bulwerke,* from Middle High German *bolwerc* : *bole,* plank + *werc,* WORK.]
Synonyms: *barricade, bastion, breastwork, earthwork, parapet, rampart.*

Bulwer-Lytton, Edward. See **Lytton, 1st Baron.**

bum¹ (bŭm) *n.* **1.** A tramp; hobo. **2.** A person who avoids work and seeks to live off others. **3.** An incompetent or disagreeable person. **4.** One who is devoted to a specified activity: *ski bums.* **—on the bum.** *Slang.* **1.** Living as a tramp. **2.** Sponging or cadging.
~*v.* **bummed, bumming, bums.** *Informal.* —*intr.* **1.** To live by begging and scavenging from place to place. Often used with *around.* **2.** To loaf. —*tr.* To acquire by begging or sponging.
~*adj. Slang.* **1.** Of poor quality; worthless: *a bum deal.* **2.** Disabled; malfunctioning: *a bum shoulder.* [From earlier *bummer,* a loafer, probably from German *bummler,* from *bummeln*†, to loaf.]

bum² *intr.v.* **bummed, bumming, bums.** *Chiefly British.* To make a humming sound; drone.

bum³ *n. Chiefly British Slang.* The buttocks. [Middle English *bom*†.]

bum·bail·iff (bŭm-bā'lĭf) *n. British.* Formerly, a court officer who pursued debtors. Used derogatorily. [From BUM (buttocks), since he pursues and catches from behind.]

bum·ble¹ (bŭm'bəl) *v.* **-bled, -bling, -bles.** —*intr.* To speak or behave in a clumsy or faltering manner. —*tr.* To bungle; botch. [Variant of BUNGLE.] **—bum·bler** *n.* **—bum·bling·ly** *adv.*

bumble² *intr.v.* **-bled, -bling, -bles.** To make a humming or droning sound; buzz.
~*n.* A droning sound; a buzz. [Middle English *bomblen* (imitative).]

bum·ble·bee (bŭm'bəl-bē') *n.* Any of various large, hairy bees of the genus *Bombus.* [BUMBLE + BEE.]

bum·boat (bŭm'bōt') *n.* A small boat used to peddle provisions and small wares to ships anchored offshore. [Probably Dutch *bom*†, a kind of fishing boat + BOAT.]

Bu·mi·put·ra (bo͞o'mə-po͞o'trə) *n.* Any of the indigenous natives of Malaysia. **—Bu·mi·put·ra** *adj.*

bum·mer (bŭm'ər) *n. Slang.* **1. a.** A bad reaction to a hallucinogenic drug. **b.** A disagreeable person, event, or situation. **2.** A failure.

bump (bŭmp) *v.* **bumped, bumping, bumps.** —*tr.* **1.** To strike or collide with. **2.** To cause to knock against an obstacle. **3.** To knock to a new position; displace; dislodge. **4.** *Informal.* To displace by right of seniority or authority. —*intr.* **1.** To hit or knock with force. Often used with *against* or *into.* **2.** To proceed with jerks and jolts. Often used with *along.* **3.** To thrust the pelvis forward in a sensual way when dancing. Used chiefly in the phrase *bump and grind.* **—bump into.** To meet by chance. **—bump off.** *Slang.* To murder or kill.
~*n.* **1. a.** A light blow, collision, or jolt. **b.** The noise caused by this; a thud. **2.** A slight swelling or lump. **3.** A raised part on a generally even surface. **4.** One of the natural protuberances of the human skull. **5.** A sudden violent upward air current striking an airplane in flight. **6.** A sensual forward thrust of the pelvis when dancing.

bump·er¹ (bŭm'pər) *n.* **1.** One that bumps. **2.** Either of two metal or rubber structures, typically horizontal bars, attached to the front and rear of a motor vehicle to absorb the impact of a collision. **3.** A similar protective device on other objects.

bumper² *n.* **1.** A drinking vessel filled to the brim. **2.** Something unusually or extraordinarily large.
~*tr.v.* **bumpered, -ering, -ers. 1.** To fill to the brim. **2.** To propose a toast to.
~*adj.* Unusually good, large, or abundant: *a bumper crop.* [Perhaps from BUMP (lump, hence something large).]

bumper sticker *n.* A sticker bearing a printed message for display on a vehicle's bumper.

bum·per-to-bum·per (bŭm'pər-tə-bum'pər) *adj.* Traveling close together, with bumpers almost touching. Said of motor vehicles. **—bum·per-to-bum·per** *adv.*

bump·kin (bŭmp'kĭn, bŭm'-) *n.* Also **bum·kin** (bŭm'-) (for sense 2). **1.** An awkward, untutored rustic. **2.** A short spar projecting from the deck of a ship. Used to extend a sail or secure a block or stay. [Perhaps originally "Dutchman," probably from Dutch *boomken,* "little tree," squat person, diminutive of *boom,* tree, from Middle Dutch.]

bump·tious (bŭmp'shəs) *adj.* Crudely arrogant and self-assertive in behavior; pushy. [Perhaps a blend of BUMP and FRACTIOUS.] **—bump·tious·ly** *adv.* **—bump·tious·ness** *n.*

bump·y (bŭm'pē) *adj.* **-ier, -iest. 1.** Covered with bumps or protuberances: *a bumpy road.* **2.** Involving jerks and jolts: *a bumpy ride.* **—bump·i·ly** *adv.* **—bump·i·ness** *n.*

bum's rush *n. Slang.* Forcible ejection or dismissal. [From BUM (tramp).]

bun (bŭn) *n.* **1.** A small bread roll, often sweetened or spiced. **2.** A small round sweet bread roll, often made with dried fruit. **3.** A roll of hair worn at the back of a woman's head. [Middle English *bunne*†.]

Bu·na (bo͞o'nə, byo͞o'-) *n.* A trademark for a type of synthetic rubber made by polymerization of butadiene and sodium.

bunch (bŭnch) *n.* **1.** A group of like items growing, fastened, or placed together; a cluster or tuft. **2.** *Informal.* A small group of things or people. **3.** A lump or swelling.
~*v.* **bunched, bunching, bunches.** —*tr.* **1.** To gather or form into a cluster or tuft. **2.** To gather together in a group. **3.** To gather (fabric) into folds. —*intr.* **1.** To form a cluster or tuft. **2.** To gather together in a group; cluster. **3.** To be gathered up in folds. Used of fabric. [Middle English *bunche*†.] **—bunch·y** *adj.*

bunch·ber·ry (bŭnch'bĕr'ē) *n., pl.* **-ries.** A plant, the **dwarf cornel** *(see).*

Bunche (bŭnch), **Ralph Johnson** (1904–71). U.S. civil servant and political scientist. He was the first black to become a divisional head in the Department of State (1946). At the United Nations (1946–71) he carried out detailed research into colonial administration and race relations and was awarded the Nobel Peace Prize (1950) for his work as principal secretary of the UN Palestine Commission.

bunch·flow·er (bŭnch'flou'ər) *n.* A bog plant, *Melanthium virginicum,* of the eastern United States, having narrow leaves and a branching cluster of greenish flowers.

bun·co (bŭng'kō) *n., pl.* **-cos.** Also **bun·ko,** *pl.* **-kos.** *Informal.* A swindle; a confidence trick.
~*tr.v.* **buncoed, -coing, -cos.** Also **bunko, -koed, -koing, -kos.** *Informal.* To swindle; cheat. [Spanish *banca,* name of a card game, "bank" (in gambling), from Italian *banca,* BANK (financial establishment).]

bund¹ (bŭnd) *n.* **1.** In India and the Far East, an embankment or dyke. **2.** A street running along a harbor or waterway. [Hindi *band,* from Persian.]

bund² (bo͝ond, bŭnd) *n.* **1.** A confederation or league. **2. Bund.** A pro-Nazi German-American organization of the 1930's. [German *Bund,* "league."] **—bund·ist** *n.*

Bun·des·rat, Bun·des·rath (bo͝on'dəs-rät') *n.* **1.** The upper house of the federal legislative body of the republic of Germany, made up of ministers from each of the states. **2.** The federal council of certain countries, as of Switzerland and Austria. **3.** Formerly, a federal legislative council composed of representatives from the 26 states of the German Empire. [*Bundes,* genitive of BUND + *Rat,* council.]

Bun·des·tag (bo͝on'dəs-täg') *n.* The lower house of the federal legislative body of the republic of Germany, elected by universal suffrage. [German : *Bundes,* genitive of BUND + *-tag,* meeting.]

bun·dle (bŭnd'l) *n. Abbr.* **bdl. 1.** A number of objects bound, wrapped, or otherwise held together. **2.** Anything wrapped or tied up for carrying; a package. **3.** *Biology.* A cluster or strand of specialized cells. **4.** *Botany.* A **vascular bundle** *(see).* **5.** *Slang.* A large sum of money.
~*v.* **bundled, -dling, -dles.** —*tr.* **1.** To tie, wrap, fold, or otherwise secure together. **2.** To dispatch or cause to move quickly and unceremoniously; hustle. Usually used with *off* or *into.* **3.** To dress warmly. Used with *up.* —*intr.* To sleep in the same bed while fully clothed, a custom formerly practiced by engaged couples in early New England. [Middle English *bundel,* probably from Middle

Dutch, sheaf of papers, bundle.] —**bun·dler** *n.*

bung (bŭng) *n.* **1.** A stopper for a cask, flask, or the like. **2.** The hole itself; a bunghole. ~*tr.v.* **bunged, bunging, bungs. 1.** To close (a bunghole) with a cork or stopper. **2.** *Informal.* To beat up; bruise; maul. Often used with *up.* [Middle English *bunge,* from Middle Dutch *bonghe,* perhaps variant of *bonne,* perhaps from Late Latin *puncta,* hole, from the feminine past participle of Latin *pungere,* to prick.]

bun·ga·low (bŭng'gə-lō') *n.* A small cottage, usually of one story. [Earlier *bungale,* perhaps from Gujarati *bangalo,* from Hindi *banglā,* "of Bengal."]

bung·hole (bŭng'hōl') *n.* The hole in a cask, keg, or barrel through which liquid is poured in or drained out.

bun·gle (bŭng'gəl) *v.* **-gled, -gling, -gles.** —*intr.* To work or act ineptly or inefficiently. —*tr.* To manage (a task) badly; botch. ~*n.* A clumsy or inept job or performance. [Perhaps from Scandinavian, akin to Swedish (dialectal) *bangla,* to work ineffectually.] —**bun·gler** *n.*

bun·gling (bŭng'glĭng) *adj.* Performing clumsily or ineptly; incompetent. —See Synonyms at **awkward.** —**bun·gling·ly** *adv.*

Bu·nin (bōō'nĭn, -nyĭn), **Ivan Alexeyevich** (1870-1953). Russian writer. He gained international recognition with his novel *The Village* (1910), but he is best known for his short stories, especially *The Gentleman from San Francisco* (1915). He was awarded the Nobel Prize for literature (1933).

bun·ion (bŭn'yən) *n.* A painful, inflamed swelling at the bursa of the big toe. [Probably from earlier *bunny, bony,* swelling, from Old French *buignet†,* bump on the head.]

bunk[1] (bŭngk) *n.* **1.** A narrow berth attached like a shelf against a wall. **2.** Either of a pair of narrow beds stacked one on top of the other. Also called "bunk bed." **3.** *Informal.* Any place for sleeping. ~*intr.v.* **bunked, bunking, bunks. 1.** To sleep in a bunk. **2.** To go to bed. [Possibly short for BUNKER.]

bunk[2] *n. Slang.* Nonsense. [Short for BUNKUM.]

bun·ker (bŭng'kər) *n.* **1.** A bin or tank for fuel storage, as on a ship. **2.** A sand trap serving as an obstacle on a golf course. **3.** A fortified underground defensive position, with an overground projection for gun emplacements. ~*tr.v.* **bunkered, -kering, -kers. 1.** To store (fuel) in a bunker. **2.** To drive (a golf ball) into a bunker. [Earlier Scottish *bonker†.*]

Bun·ker Hill (bŭng'kər). Height in Charlestown, Boston, Massachusetts. The Battle of Bunker Hill (June 17, 1775), the first major engagement of the American Revolution, actually took place on nearby Breed's Hill. The British were victorious, but the American defense of the hill raised morale and stiffened colonial resistance.

bunk·house (bŭngk'hous') *n.* Sleeping quarters on a ranch or in a camp.

bunk·mate (bŭngk'māt') *n.* A person with whom one shares rough sleeping quarters.

bunko. Variant of **bunco.**

bun·kum, bun·combe (bŭng'kəm) *n.* Empty or meaningless talk, especially by a politician; claptrap. [After *Buncombe* County, North Carolina, from a remark made in about 1820 by its congressman, Felix Walker, who made a fatuous speech, calling it "a speech for Buncombe."]

bun·ny (bŭn'ē) *n., pl.* **-nies.** A rabbit. Used especially by and to children. [From dialectal *bun†,* squirrel.]

bunny hug *n.* A dance in ragtime rhythm popular in the United States during the early part of the 20th century.

bun·rak·u (bōōn-rä'kōō, bōōn'rä'-) *n.* **1.** The traditional Japanese puppet theater. **2.** One of the two schools of Japanese puppet theater. [Japanese : *bun,* literary composition + *raku,* easy.]

buns (bŭnz) *pl.n. Slang.* The buttocks. [From dialectal *bun,* hind part of a rabbit or squirrel, from Scottish Gaelic, stump, bottom.]

Bun·sen (bŭn'sən), **Robert Wilhelm** (1811-99). German chemist. He did important work in the analysis of gases and was a joint discoverer, with Gustav Kirchhoff (1824-87), of the elements caesium and rubidium. He also invented several pieces of laboratory equipment.

Bunsen burner *n.* A small laboratory burner consisting of a vertical metal tube connected to a gas source, and producing a hot flame from a mixture of gas and air let in through adjustable holes at the base. [After Robert Wilhelm BUNSEN, its inventor.]

bunt[1] (bŭnt) *v.* **bunted, bunting, bunts.** —*tr.* To butt (something) with or as if with the horns or head. **2.** *Baseball.* To bat (a pitched ball) with a half swing, and with the upper hand supporting the middle of the bat, so that the ball rolls slowly in front of the infielders. —*intr. Baseball.* To bunt a pitch. ~*n.* **1.** A butt with or as if with the horns or head. **2.** *Baseball.* **a.** The act of bunting. **b.** A bunted ball. [Probably from Celtic, akin to Breton *bounta,* to butt.]

bunt[2] *n.* **1.** *Nautical.* The middle section of a square sail. **2.** The sagging middle part of a fishnet. [Perhaps from Middle Low German *bunt,* bundle.]

bunt[3] *n.* A disease of wheat, rye, and other cereal grasses, caused by fungi of the genus *Tilletia* and resulting in sooty black spores in place of normal seeds. [18th century : origin obscure.]

bunt·ing[1] (bŭn'tĭng) *n.* **1.** A light cotton or woolen cloth used for making flags. **2.** Flags collectively. **3.** Long, variously colored strips of cloth or material used for festive decoration. [18th century : origin obscure.]

bunting[2] *n.* Any of various birds of the family Fringillidae, such as the **snow bunting** (see), having short, cone-shaped bills and brown-

ish or grayish plumage. [Middle English *buntynge†.*]

bunting[3] *n.* A snug-fitting, hooded sleeping bag for infants. [Origin unknown.]

bunt·line (bŭnt'lĭn, -līn') *n. Nautical.* A rope attached to a square sail when it is being hauled up for furling.

Bu·ñu·el (bōō-nyōō-ĕl'), **Luis** (1900-83). Spanish film director. In the 1920's he collaborated with Dali in making a number of surrealist films, notably *Un Chien Andalou* (1929), but he is most highly regarded for his studies of social manners and social conditions, such as *Belle de Jour* (1966) and *The Discreet Charm of the Bourgeoisie* (1972).

bun·ya (bŭn'yə) *n.* Also **bun·ya-bun·ya** (bŭn'yə-bŭn'yə). An evergreen tree, *Araucaria bidwilli,* native to Australia, having sharp-pointed, close-set leaves and large cones. [From a native Australian language.]

Bun·yan (bŭn'yən), **John** (1628-88). English writer and preacher. As a Puritan, he served in the Parliamentary army from 1644 to 1646 during the Civil War. He was imprisoned (1660-72) for unlicensed preaching. *The Pilgrim's Progress from This World to That Which Is to Come* was published in two parts in 1678 and 1684.

Bun·yan·esque (bŭn'yə-nĕsk') *adj.* **1.** Of, pertaining to, or suggestive of the allegorical writings of John Bunyan. **2. a.** Of, pertaining to, or suggestive of the stories about Paul Bunyan. **b.** Of astonishingly large size.

buoy (bōō'ē, boi) *n.* **1.** *Nautical.* A float moored in water as a warning of danger under the surface or as a marker for a channel. See **bell buoy. 2.** A device made of cork or other buoyant material for keeping a person afloat. In this sense, also called "lifebuoy." ~*tr.v.* **buoyed, buoying, buoys. 1.** *Nautical.* To mark with a buoy. **2.** To keep afloat. **3.** To uplift the spirits of; cheer; hearten. Used with *up.* [Middle English *boye,* probably from Old French *boie,* perhaps from Old High German *bouhhan.*]

buoy·ance (boi'əns, bōō'yəns) *n.* Buoyancy.

buoy·an·cy (boi'ən-sē, bōō'yən-) *n.* **1. a.** The tendency or capacity to remain afloat in a liquid or to rise in air or gas. **b.** The upward force of a fluid upon a floating or immersed object. **2.** The ability to recover quickly from setbacks. **3.** Lightness of spirit; cheerfulness.

buoy·ant (boi'ənt, bōō'yənt) *adj.* Having or marked by buoyancy. [Spanish *boyante,* present participle of *boyar,* to float, from *boya,* buoy, from Old French *boie,* BUOY.] —**buoy·ant·ly** *adv.*

bu·pres·tid (byōō-prĕs'tĭd) *n.* Any of various often brightly colored beetles of the family Buprestidae, many of which are destructive wood borers as larvae.

bur[1], **burr** (bûr) *n.* **1. a.** The rough, prickly, or spiny fruit husk, seed pod, or flower of various plants, such as the chestnut or the burdock. **b.** A plant producing burs. **2.** A person or thing that clings persistently. **3.** Any of various rotary cutting tools designed to be attached to a drill. [Middle English *burre,* probably from Scandinavian, akin to Old Swedish *borre.*]

bur[2]. **1.** Variant of **burr** (rough edge). **2.** Variant of **burr** (guttural trill). **3.** Variant of **burr** (washer).

Bur. 1. bureau. **2.** Burma.

bu·ran (bōō-rän') *n.* Also **bu·ra** (-rä'). A violent windstorm of the steppes of Russia, accompanied in summer by dust and in winter by snow. [Russian, *burya,* from Turkic; akin to Turkish and Kazan Tatar *buran.*]

Bur·bage (bûr'bĭj), **Richard** (c. 1567-1619). English actor, the foremost tragedian of his age. As the leading player in Shakespeare's company, the Chamberlain's Men, he was the first to play the title roles in *Hamlet, King Lear, Othello,* and *Richard III.*

Bur·bank (bûr'băngk). A city in southern California, in the Greater Los Angeles area. Aircraft manufacturing is the major industry. Several motion-picture and television studios are here.

Burbank, Luther (1849-1926). U.S. biologist and plant breeder. He applied Mendel's laws of heredity to create new varieties of plants. Besides the Burbank potato, he produced hundreds of new varieties of fruit and roses and a spineless cactus for use as cattle fodder.

bur·ble (bûr'bəl) *n.* **1.** A rushing or bubbling sound. **2.** A rapid, excited flow of speech. **3.** *Aviation.* A separation in the boundary layer of air about a moving streamlined body, causing a breakdown in the smooth airflow and resulting in turbulence. ~*intr.v.* **burbled, -bling, -bles. 1.** To bubble; gurgle. **2.** To speak quickly and excitedly. [Middle English *burblen,* to flow with a bubbling sound (imitative).]

bur·bot (bûr'bət) *n., pl.* **-bots** or collectively **burbot.** A freshwater fish, *Lota lota,* of the Northern Hemisphere, related to and resembling the cod. [Middle English *borbot,* from Old French *bourbotte, bourbete,* from *bourbeter,* to burrow in the mud, from *bourbe†,* mud.]

Burck·hardt (bōōrk'härt), **Jacob Christoph** (1818-97). Swiss historian, one of the founders of the modern school of history-writing. His great achievement was to direct historians away from an almost exclusive concentration on political and military events to a consideration of wider cultural history, as in his work *The Civilization of the Renaissance in Italy* (1860).

bur cucumber *n.* **1.** A climbing vine, *Sicyos angulatus,* of eastern North America, having lobed leaves, small greenish flowers, and bristly, egg-shaped fruit. **2.** The fruit of the bur cucumber.

bur·den[1] (bûr'dn) *n.* Also *archaic* **bur·then** (bûr'thən). **1. a.** Something that is carried. **b.** Something that is difficult to bear physically or emotionally. **2.** A responsibility or duty. **3. a.** The amount of cargo that a vessel can carry. **b.** The weight of the cargo carried by a vessel at one time. **4.** The carrying of heavy loads: *a beast of burden.*

~*tr.v.* **burdened, -dening, -dens.** Also *archaic* **burthen. 1.** To load or overload. **2.** To weigh down; oppress. [Middle English *burden,* *burthen,* Old English *byrthen.*]

burden² *n.* **1.** The chorus or refrain of a musical composition. **2.** A recurring idea or theme. **3.** The bass accompaniment to a song. **4.** The drone of a bagpipes. [Variant (influenced by BURDEN, load) of BOURDON, from the idea of the burden being carried along by the melody.]

burden of proof *n.* The responsibility of giving proof for a disputed charge or allegation. [Translation of Latin *onus probandi.*]

bur·den·some (bûrd′n-səm) *adj.* Heavy; hard to bear; onerous. —**bur·den·some·ly** *adv.* —**bur·den·some·ness** *n.*

    Synonyms: *arduous, demanding, exacting, harsh, onerous, oppressive, rigorous.*

bur·dock (bûr′dŏk′) *n.* Any of several coarse, weedy plants of the genus *Arctium,* native to Eurasia, having large, heart-shaped leaves, purplish flowers surrounded by hooked bristles, and prickly fruits. [BUR + DOCK (plant).]

bu·reau (byŏŏr′ō) *n., pl.* **-reaus** or **bureaux** (byŏŏr′ōz). **1.** A chest of drawers. **2.** *Chiefly British.* A writing desk or writing table with drawers. **3.** *Abbr.* **Bur, bu. a.** A government department or subdivision of a department. **b.** An office, usually of a large organization, that performs a specific duty: *a news bureau.* **c.** A business or office that offers information of a specified kind: *a travel bureau.* [French, bureau, woolen material used to cover writing desks, from Old French, *burel,* from *bure,* dark brown, from Latin *burrus,* bright red, from Greek *purros,* red.]

bu·reauc·ra·cy (byŏŏ-rŏk′rə-sē) *n., pl.* **-cies. 1. a.** Government administration through departments staffed by civil servants or similar officials. **b.** The officials in these departments. **2.** A form of administration in which authority is diffused among numerous offices and there is adherence to inflexible rules of operation. **3.** Any administration in which the need to follow complex procedures impedes effective action. [French *bureaucratie.*]

bu·reau·crat (byŏŏr′ə-krăt′) *n.* **1.** An official of a bureaucracy. **2.** Any official who insists on rigid adherence to rules, forms, and routines. —**bu·reau·crat·ic** *adj.* —**bu·reau·crat·i·cal·ly** *adv.*

bu·reau·crat·ese (byŏŏr′ə-krā-tēz′, -tēs′) *n.* A style of language used especially by bureaucrats that is characterized by jargon and euphemism.

bu·reau·cra·tize (byŏŏ-rŏk′rə-tīz′) *tr.v.* **tized, -tizing, -tizes.** To bring under bureaucratic influence or control. —**bu·reau·crat·iz·a·tion** *n.*

bu·rette, bu·ret (byŏŏ-rĕt′) *n.* A uniform-bore glass tube with fine graduations and a stopcock at the bottom, used especially in laboratory procedures for accurate dispensing and measurement of liquids. [French, originally "cruet," from Old French, cruet for sacramental wine, from *buire,* pitcher, variant of *buie,* from Frankish *būk* (unattested).]

burg (bûrg) *n.* **1.** A fortified town. **2.** *Informal.* A city or town. [Old English *burg, burh.*]

bur·gage (bûr′gĭj) *n.* A tenure in England and Scotland under which property of the king or a lord in a town was held in return for a yearly rent or other services. [Middle English, from Medieval Latin *burgāgium,* from *burgus,* fortified town, from Old English *burg,* BURG.]

bur·gee (bûr′jē, bər-jē′) *n.* A small distinguishing flag displayed by a ship or yacht. [Perhaps originally *burgee's flag,* from Channel Islands French *bourgeais,* shipowner, from Old French *burgeis,* owner, BURGESS.]

bur·geon (bûr′jən) *intr.v.* **-geoned, -geoning, -geons.** Also **bour·geon. 1.** To put forth new buds, leaves, or greenery; begin to sprout, grow, or blossom. **2.** To emerge and develop rapidly; flourish.

~*n.* Also **bour·geon.** A bud, sprout, or newly developing growth. [Middle English *burgenen,* from *burjon,* a bud, from Old French, from Vulgar Latin *burriō* (stem *burriōn-*) (unattested), from Late Latin *burra,* wool (probably from the down on some buds).]

    Usage: The verb *burgeon* and its past participle *burgeoning,* used as an adjective, are properly restricted to the actual or figurative sense of "to bud or sprout," or "to emerge and develop": *the burgeoning talent of the young Mozart.* They are not mere substitutes for the more general *expand, grow,* or *thrive.*

burg·er (bûr′gər) *n.* A hamburger (see).

bur·gess (bûr′jĭs) *n.* **1.** A freeman or citizen of an English borough. **2.** Formerly, a member of the English Parliament, representing a town, borough, or university. **3.** A member of the lower house of the colonial legislature of either Virginia or Maryland. [Middle English *burgeis,* from Old French, from Vulgar Latin *burgensis* (unattested), from Late Latin *burgus,* fortified place, from Germanic.]

Bur·gess (bûr′jĭs), **Anthony** (1917–). British novelist and essayist. His fame rests chiefly on his novels, in which he exhibits a flamboyant range and command of language. His most successful novels have been *A Clockwork Orange* (1962), *Nothing Like the Sun* (1964), and *End of the World News* (1982).

burgh (bûrg) *n.* A chartered town or borough in Scotland. Compare **borough.** [Scottish, variant of BOROUGH.] —**burgh·al** *adj.*

burgh·er (bûr′gər) *n.* **1. a.** A member of the mercantile class of a medieval city. **b.** A citizen of a medieval city. **2.** A solid citizen. [Either German *Bürger,* from Middle High German *burgære,* from Old High German *burgāri,* town-dweller, from *burg,* fortified place;

or Dutch *burger,* from Middle Dutch *burgher,* from Middle High German *burgære.*]

bur·glar (bûr′glər) *n.* One who commits burglary; a housebreaker. [Norman French *burgler,* from Medieval Latin *burgulator,* probably from Medieval Latin *burg-* (unattested), plunder.]

bur·glar·ize (bûr′glə-rīz′) *tr.v.* **-ized, -izing, -izes.** To commit burglary in. —See Synonyms at **rob.**

bur·gla·ry (bûr′glə-rē) *n., pl.* **-ries.** The crime or an act of breaking into and entering premises with intent to commit a felony.

bur·gle (bûr′gəl) *v.* **-gled, -gling, -gles.** *Informal.* —*tr.* To burglarize. —*intr.* To commit burglary. [Back-formation from BURGLAR.]

bur·go·mas·ter (bûr′gə-măs′tər, -mäs′tər) *n.* In the Netherlands, Flanders, Austria, and Germany, the principal magistrate of a city or town, comparable to a mayor. [Partial translation of Dutch *burgemeester* : *burg,* town + MASTER.]

bur·go·net (bûr′gə-nĭt, bûr′gə-nĕt′) *n.* A light steel helmet with a peak and hinged flaps covering the cheeks. [French *bourguignotte,* feminine of *bourguignot,* "of Burgundy," from *Bourgogne,* Burgundy.]

bur·goo (bûr′gŏŏ, bər-gŏŏ′) *n., pl.* **-goos. 1.** Thick oatmeal gruel, originally served to sailors. **2.** *Southern U.S.* **a.** A thick, spicy soup or stew of meat and vegetables. **b.** A picnic or gathering where this dish is served. [Perhaps from Arabic *burghul,* from Turkish *bulgur,* "bruised grain."]

Bur·gos (bŏŏr′gōs). A city in northern Spain, on a mountainous plateau near the Arlanzón River. It was founded in *c.* 884 and was the capital of the kingdom of Castile from 1035 to 1087. It was the headquarters of the Nationalists during the Spanish Civil War of 1936–39. Its limestone cathedral (13th to 16th centuries) is one of the finest examples of Gothic architecture in Europe.

Bur·goyne (bər-goin′), **John,** called "Gentleman Johnny" (1722–1792). British officer. A major general in the American Revolution, he captured Fort Ticonderoga on July 6, 1977. His army was defeated by an American force at the Battle of Saratoga on October 17, 1777. He also wrote several plays, including *The Heiress* (1786).

bur·grave (bûr′grāv′) *n.* **1.** In medieval Germany, the appointed governor of a town or military fortress. **2.** The hereditary lord of a German town and its surroundings. [Middle High German *burcgrāve* : *burc,* fortress, from Old High German *burg* + *grāve,* count.]

Bur·gun·dy¹ (bûr′gən-dē). *French* **Bour·gogne** (bŏŏr-gôn′y′). A historic region of eastern France. The region was first organized into a kingdom by the Burgundii tribe from Savoy in the late 5th century. The great age of Burgundian influence and power began (1364) when John II gave the duchy to his son Philip the Bold, who thus initiated the royal Valois-Bourgogne line. By the 15th century Burgundy had added most of present-day Belgium, Luxembourg, and the Netherlands to its territory and had become the most powerful duchy in France. Its historical importance and independence came to an end in the late 15th century, when Mary of Burgundy married the Emperor Maximilian I and so transferred Burgundy to the Hapsburgs. Today Burgundy is famous for its wines, produced in the Chablis district, the mountains of the Côte d'Or, and the Saône and Rhône river valleys.

Burgundy² *n., pl.* **-dies. 1. a.** Any of various red or white wines produced in Burgundy. **b.** Any of various similar full-bodied wines produced elsewhere. **2. burgundy.** A dark grayish or blackish purple to dark purplish red or reddish brown.

bur·i·al (bĕr′ē-əl) *n.* The interment of a dead body or an instance of this. [Middle English *biriel, buryel,* grave, singular of *buriels,* Old English *byrgels.*]

bu·rin (byŏŏr′ĭn, bûr′-) *n.* **1.** A pointed steel cutting tool used in engraving or in carving stone. **2.** The style or technique of an engraver's work. **3.** *Archaeology.* A primitive flint tool with a head like that of a chisel. [French, perhaps from Italian *burino.*]

burke (bûrk) *tr.v.* **burked, burking, burkes. 1.** To murder by suffocation so as to leave the body intact and suitable for dissection. **2.** To suppress quietly and unceremoniously. [After William *Burke* (1792–1829), Irish murderer executed in Edinburgh, for this crime.]

Burke (bûrk), **Edmund** (1729–97). British political writer and politician. As a member of Parliament from 1765, he played a major part until the French Revolution in developing liberal policy for the Whigs and in formulating the constitutional notion of party responsibility and a loyal opposition (1770). He pleaded on behalf of the American colonists' appeal for independence and in the 1780's led the campaign to reduce the influence of the Crown. The outbreak of the French Revolution caused him to abandon the Whigs and support Pitt.

Burke, Martha Jane, known as "Calamity Jane" (*c.* 1852–1903). U.S. frontierswoman who has became a legend of the Wild West. Often dressing in men's clothes, she is reputed to have been a crack shot and a skilled horsewoman.

Bur·ki·na Fa·so (bûr-kē′nə fä′sō). Also **Burkina.** Formerly **Upper Vol·ta** (vŏl′tə). Landlocked state in the Sahel region of West Africa. It is one of the world's poorest countries, depending on aid, mostly from France. Over 80 percent of its people are farmers, most at subsistence level. Some cattle and cotton are exported. A French colony since 1896, Burkina Faso became independent in 1960. Area, 274,200 square kilometers (105,869 square miles). Population, 9,000,000. Capital, Ouagadougou. See map at **West African States.**

burl (bûrl) *n.* **1.** A knot, lump, or slub in yarn or cloth. **2.** A large, rounded growth on the trunk or branch of a tree. **3.** The strongly marked wood from such a growth, especially walnut, usually cut into thin pieces and used as veneer.

~*tr.v.* **burled, burling, burls.** To dress or finish (fabric) by removing burls or loose threads. [Middle English *burle,* from Old French *bourle,* diminutive of *bourre,* coarse wool, from Late Latin *burra*†, wool.] **—burl·er** *n.*

bur·lap (bûr′lăp′) *n.* A coarsely woven cloth made of fibers of jute, flax, or hemp, used to make bags, to reinforce linoleum, and in interior decoration. [17th century : origin obscure.]

Burleigh, 1st Baron. See **Burghley.**

bur·lesque (bər-lĕsk′) *n.* **1.** A literary or dramatic work that makes a subject appear ridiculous by treating it in an incongruous style, as by presenting a lofty subject with vulgarity, or the inconsequential with mock dignity. **2.** Any ludicrous or mocking imitation; a travesty. **3.** A variety show characterized by broad, ribald comedy, dancing, and striptease.

~*v.* **burlesqued, -lesquing, -lesques.** —*tr.* To imitate mockingly: *"always bringing junk . . . home, as if he were burlesquing his role as provider"* (John Updike). —*intr.* To use the methods or techniques of burlesque.

~*adj.* **1.** Mockingly and ludicrously imitative. **2.** Of, pertaining to, or characteristic of theatrical burlesque, especially in its ribald aspects. [French, from Italian *burlesco,* from *burla,* joke, ridicule, from Vulgar Latin *burrula* (unattested), diminutive of Late Latin *burra,* trifle, bit of nonsense, perhaps from *burra,* wool, shaggy garment.] **—bur·lesque·ly** *adv.* **—bur·les·quer** *n.*

bur·ley, Bur·ley (bûr′lē) *n., pl.* **-leys.** A light-colored tobacco grown chiefly in Kentucky. [Probably from *Burley,* a proper name.]

bur·ly (bûr′lē) *adj.* **-lier, -liest.** Heavy, strong, and muscular; thickset. [Middle English *burli, borlich,* stately, probably from Old English *būrlic* (unattested), exalted.] **—bur·li·ly** *adv.* **—bur·li·ness** *n.*

Bur·ma (bûr′mə). *Abbr.* **Bur.** A republic in Southeast Asia. It is bordered on the west by the Indian Ocean, on the north by Bangladesh and India, and on the east by China, Laos, and Thailand. On both its northern and eastern borders it is cut off from its neighbors by large mountain ranges, between which lies the fertile Irrawaddy River valley, whose crops make Burma one of the world's largest producers of rice. Burma was made a province of British India (1886); it gained its independence in 1948, and in 1989 changed its name to the **Union of Myanmar.** Area, 676,552 square kilometers (261,218 square miles). Population, 41,700,000. Capital and largest city, Yangon (formerly Rangoon). See map, next page.

bur marigold *n.* Any of various plants of the genus *Bidens,* having yellow flowers and pointed seeds that cling to fur and clothing. Also called "beggar-ticks," "sticktight."

Bur·mese (bər-mēz′, -mēs′) *adj.* Also **Bur·man** (bûr′mən). Of, pertaining to, or characteristic of Burma, its people, their language, or their culture.

~*n., pl.* **Burmese.** Also **Bur·man** (for sense 1) *pl.* **-mans. 1.** A native or inhabitant of Burma. **2.** The Sino-Tibetan language spoken in Burma.

Burmese cat *n.* A cat of a breed resembling the Siamese but having a dark-brown or blue-gray coat.

burn[1] (bûrn) *v.* **burned** or **burnt** (bûrnt), **burning, burns.** —*tr.* **1. a.** To cause to undergo combustion. **b.** To destroy or consume with fire. **2.** To damage or injure the surface of by fire, heat, or a heat-producing agent: *He burned the toast.* **3.** *Slang.* To kill or execute. **4.** To produce by fire or heat: *burn a clearing in the brush.* **5.** To use as a fuel. **6.** To impart a sensation of intense heat to: *The chili burned his mouth.* **7.** To brand (an animal). **8.** To harden or impart a finish to by subjecting to intense heat; fire. **9.** To let (oneself or part of one's body) become sunburned. **10.** *Slang.* **a.** To defeat in a contest, especially by a narrow margin. **b.** To swindle or deceive; cheat. **11.** *Slang.* To execute in the electric chair; electrocute. —*intr.* **1.** To be on fire; undergo combustion; flame. **2.** To emit heat or light by or as if by means of fire. **3.** To be destroyed, injured, damaged, or changed by or as if by fire: *The house burned down.* **4.** To feel or look hot: *Her cheeks burned.* **5.** To be consumed with strong emotion. **6.** *Slang.* To be executed in the electric chair; be electrocuted. **—burn in.** To darken part of (a photographic print) by exposing unmasked areas. **—burn off.** To remove stubble from (land) by burning. **—burn up.** *Informal.* To make or become very annoyed; enrage.

~*n.* **1.** An injury produced by fire, heat, light, chemicals, electricity, or radiation. **2.** A burned place or area. **3.** The process or result of firing or burning, as in the manufacture of bricks. **4.** A sunburn. **5.** *Aerospace.* One firing of a rocket. [Middle English *bernen, burnen,* from Old English *beornan, byrnan* (intransitive) and *bærnan.*]

Usage: *burn, scorch, singe, sear, char, parch.* These verbs mean to injure or alter by heat. *Burn* can apply to the effect of exposure to any source of heat. *Scorch* usually refers to contact with flame or heated metal and involves superficial (surface) burning that discolors, damages texture, or makes brittle. *Singe* specifies superficial and momentary burning of edges through nearness to the heat source. *Sear* applies to surface burning of organic tissue, as by branding, cauterizing, or application of intense flames, as to meat. *Char* pertains to the reduction of a burning substance to carbon, or to any blackening or disintegration due to fire. *Parch* emphasizes surface drying and, often, fissuring by long exposure to sun.

burn[2] *n. Chiefly Scottish.* A small stream; a brook. Often used in Scottish place names: *Bannockburn.* [Middle English *burn, burne,* Old English *burn, burna,* spring, fountain; from Germanic.]

burn·back (bûrn′băk′) *n. Australian.* The deliberate burning off of strips of land in order to prevent bushfires.

burn·er (bûr′nər) *n.* **1.** One that burns something. **2.** The part of a stove, furnace, or lamp that is lit to produce a flame. **3.** A device in which something is burned: *an oil burner.*

bur·net (bər-nĕt′, bûr′nĭt) *n.* Any of several plants of the genus *Sanguisorba,* having cucumber-flavored leaves and clusters of small white, red, or greenish flowers. [Middle English, dark brown (from the brownish-red flowers), from Old French *burnete, brunette,* BRUNETTE.]

Bur·net (bər-nĕt′, bûr′nĭt), **Sir Frank Macfarlane** (1899–1985). Australian virologist. For his work in the development of immunity against influenza and his research with P.B. Medawar into the tolerance of the body to the introduction of foreign living tissues, he shared with Medawar the Nobel Prize for medicine (1960).

burnet rose *n.* A Eurasian wild rose, *Rosa pimpinellifolia,* having creamy white, rarely pink flowers and dark purple-black fruits.

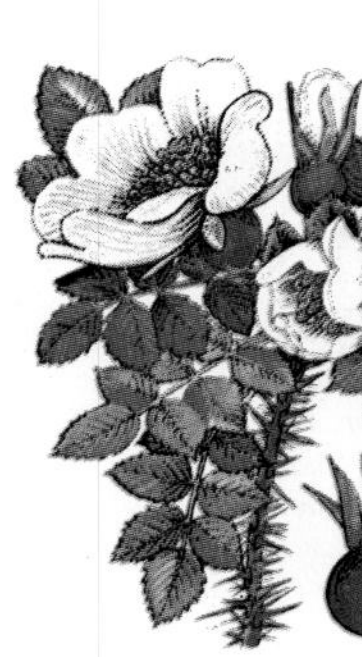

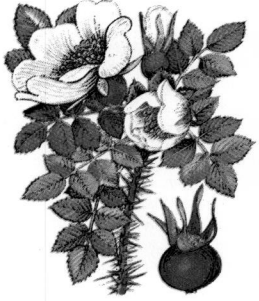

burnet rose *A European wild rose that grows on heaths and coastal sand dunes. Apart from its creamy white summer flowers, it can be identified by its spiny stem and by its berries, which are purplish-black instead of red, as in other wild roses.*

Bur·nett (bər-nĕt′), **Frances Eliza Hodgson** (1849–1924). U.S. writer, born in England. She lived in the United States after 1865 and became world-famous for her children's books, especially *Little Lord Fauntleroy* (1886) and *The Secret Garden* (1911).

Bur·ney (bûr′nē), **Fanny** (1752–1840). British diarist and novelist. Her diaries, begun in 1768 and continuing for more than 70 years, are a witty, sophisticated, and stylish record of the manners of the polished English society of her day.

burn·ing (bûr′nĭng) *adj.* **1.** Characterized by intense emotion; passionate. **2.** Of immediate import; urgent; pressing: *burning issues.* **—burn·ing·ly** *adv.*

burning bush *n.* **1.** Any of several plants or shrubs having foliage that turns bright red, such as the **summer cypress** *(see).* **2.** The **gas plant** *(see).* [So called from the burning bush in Exodus 3:2.]

burning glass *n.* A convex lens used to focus the sun's rays and produce heat, especially for ignition. Also called "sunglass."

bur·nish (bûr′nĭsh) *tr.v.* **-nished, -nishing, -nishes.** To polish or smooth by or as if by rubbing.

~*n.* A smooth, glossy finish or appearance; luster. [Middle English *burnischen,* from Old French *burnir* (present stem *burniss-*), variant of *brunir,* "to make brown," burnish, from *brun,* brown, shining, from Germanic.] **—bur·nish·er** *n.*

bur·noose, bur·nous (bər-no͞os′) *n.* A long hooded cloak worn by Arabs and Moors. [French, from Arabic *burnus,* from Greek *birros,* cloak.]

burn out *intr.v.* **1.** To stop burning or functioning from lack of fuel. Used of a fire, engine, or rocket. **2.** To wear out or become inoperative as a result of heat or friction. **3.** To become exhausted, especially as a result of long-term stress, overwork, or dissipation.

burn·out (bûrn′out′) *n.* **1.** A failure in a device attributable to burning, excessive heat, or friction. **2.** *Aerospace.* The termination of rocket or jet-engine operation because of fuel exhaustion or shutoff.

Burns (bûrnz), **Robert** (1759–96). Scottish poet. His first volume, *Poems, Chiefly in the Scottish Dialect* (1786) won him wide popularity through the humanity of its verse and the use of the Lallans dialect.

burn·sides (bûrn′sīdz′) *pl.n.* Mutton-chop whiskers and a moustache, worn with the chin clean-shaven. [After Ambrose E. *Burnside* (1824–81), U.S. general, who wore them.]

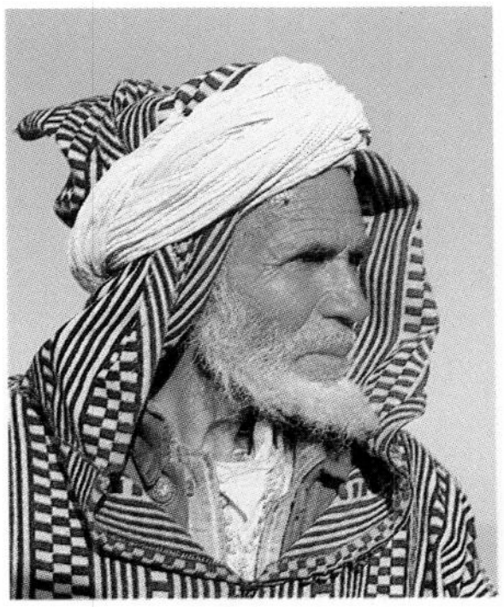

burnoose *Arabs, like this Berber tribesman from North Africa, wear hooded cloaks to keep out the sun, sand, and the chill of desert nights.*

burnt (bûrnt). Alternate past tense and past participle of **burn.**

~*adj.* **1.** Affected by or as if by burning; scorched. **2.** Treated by fire or calcined for a particular purpose. Said of bricks, certain pigments, or minerals, for example.

burnt offering *n.* An offering, such as a slaughtered animal, burnt on an altar as a religious sacrifice.

burnt orange *n.* A deep rust-colored orange. **—burnt-or·ange** *adj.*

burnt orchid *n.* An orchid, *Orchis ustulata,* having dark maroon flowers resembling those of the lady orchid.

burnt-out (bûrnt′out′) *adj.* Exhausted; spent; extinguished.

burnt sienna *n.* **1.** A reddish-brown pigment prepared by calcining raw sienna. **2.** Dark reddish orange. Also called "sienna."

burn-up (bûrn′ŭp′) *n. Chiefly British Informal.* A fast ride in a car or on a motorcycle.

bur oak *n.* A timber tree, *Quercus macrocarpa,* of eastern North America, having acorns enclosed within a deep, fringed cup.

bu·roo (bə-ro͞o′) *n., pl.* **-roos.** *Scottish & Irish Informal.* A social-security office. **—on the buroo.** Receiving unemployment benefits; on the dole. [From BUREAU.]

burp (bûrp) *n. Informal.* A belch.

~*v.* **burped, burping, burps.** *Informal.* —*intr.* To belch. —*tr.* To cause (a baby) to bring up wind after feeding. [Imitative.]

Bur·pee (bûr′pē). American family of horticulturalists and seedsmen, including **Washington Atlee** (1858–1915), founder of W. Atlee Burpee & Co., the world's largest mail-order seed company. His son **David** (1893–1980) headed the company after his father's death. The company's success was partially due to the family's constant experimentation, which produced many new strains of flowers and vegetables.

burp gun *n.* A portable, lightweight machine gun.

burr[1], bur (bûr) *n.* **1.** A rough edge or area remaining on metal or other material after it has been cast, cut, or drilled. **2.** Any rough protuberance; especially, a burl on a tree. **3.** A part in a surgical drill used for cutting into teeth or bone.

~*tr.v.* **burred, burring, burrs. 1.** To form a rough edge on. **2.** To remove a rough edge or edges from. [Middle English *burre,* rough edge, BUR.]

burr[2], bur *n.* **1.** A rough trilling of the letter *r,* as in Scottish pro-

nunciation. **2.** Any similar pronunciation or speech sound. **3.** A buzzing or whirring sound.
~*v.* **burred, burring, burrs.** —*tr.* To pronounce with a burr. —*intr.* **1.** To speak with a burr. **2.** To make a buzzing or whirring sound. [Imitative, associated with BUR, from its roughness.] —**bur·ry** *adj.*

burr³, bur *n.* **1.** A washer that fits around the smaller end of a rivet. **2.** A blank punched from a sheet of metal. [Variant of obsolete *burrow*†.]

burr⁴. Variant of **bur.**

Burr (bûr), **Aaron** (1756–1836). U.S. vice president (1801–05), soldier, and adventurer. In a duel on July 11, 1804, he mortally wounded his lifelong rival, Alexander Hamilton. Burr fled and began scheming to found an independent country in Mexico and several Western states. He was tried for treason but acquitted for lack of evidence.

bur reed *n.* Any of various marsh plants of the genus *Sparganium,* having narrow leaves and round, prickly fruit.

bur·ri·to (boo-rē′tō, bə-) *n.* A flour tortilla wrapped around a filling, as beef, beans, or cheese. [American Spanish, from Spanish, little donkey, diminutive of *burro,* burro.]

bur·ro (bûr′ō, boor′ō) *n., pl.* **-ros.** A small donkey, especially one used as a pack animal. [Spanish, from *borrico,* donkey, from Late Latin *burricus†,* small horse.]

Bur·roughs (bûr′ōz), **Edgar Rice** (1875–1950). U.S. novelist. He wrote many science-fiction and jungle tales, but is most famous for creating the character of Tarzan in *Tarzan of the Apes* (1914).

Burroughs, William (1914–). U.S. novelist. He became a cult figure of the beat generation after the publication of *The Naked Lunch* (1959), with its kaleidoscopic treatment of the brutality of contemporary life.

bur·row (bûr′ō) *n.* **1.** A hole or tunnel dug in the ground by a small animal, such as a rabbit or a mole, for habitation or refuge. **2.** Any similar narrow or snug place.
~*v.* **burrowed, -rowing, -rows.** —*intr.* **1.** To dig a burrow. **2.** To live or hide in a burrow. **3.** To move or progress through something as if by digging or tunneling. —*tr.* **1.** To make by or as if by tunneling or digging: *burrowed his way through the hedge; burrow a hole.* **2.** To dig a burrow in or through. **3.** To hide or seclude (oneself) in a burrow. [Middle English *borow,* probably a variant of BOROUGH.] —**bur·row·er** *n.*

burrowing owl *n.* A small, long-legged owl, *Speotyto cunicularia,* of American prairies, that nests in burrows dug by animals such as the prairie dog or rabbit.

burrstone. Variant of **buhrstone.**

bur·ry (bûr′ē) *adj.* **-rier, -riest. 1.** Like a bur; prickly. **2.** Full of or covered with burs.

bur·sa (bûr′sə) *n., pl.* **-sae** (-sē) or **-sas.** A saclike body cavity, especially one located between joints or at points of friction between moving structures. [New Latin, from Medieval Latin, bag, PURSE.]

Bur·sa (bûr′sə). Formerly **Bru·sa** (broo′sə). An industrial town and market center in northwest Turkey. It dates from the 3rd century B.C., when it was founded by Prusias I, king of Bithynia. Its baths have been famous since ancient times, and its importance as a silk-manufacturing center dates from the Middle Ages. It was the capital of the Ottoman Empire from 1326 to 1413.

bur·sal (bûr′səl) *adj.* **1.** *Anatomy.* Of or functioning as a bursa. **2.** *Archaic.* Pertaining to the public revenue; fiscal.

bur·sar (bûr′sər, -sär′) *n.* **1.** A treasurer or similar official in charge of funds and accounting, as at a school, college, or university. **2.** A scholarship student at a Scottish university. [Sense 1, Medieval Latin *bursārius,* from *bursa,* PURSE; sense 2, French *boursier,* from *bourse,* purse, from Medieval Latin *bursa.*]

bur·sa·ry (bûr′sə-rē′) *n., pl.* **-ries. 1.** A treasury, especially of a public institution or religious order. **2.** A scholarship, allowance, or award granted to a student at a school or university, especially at a Scottish university. [Medieval Latin *bursāria,* from *bursa,* purse.] —**bur·sar·i·al** *adj.*

burse (bûrs) *n.* **1.** *Ecclesiastical.* A flat cloth case for carrying the piece of linen, or corporal, that is used in celebrating the Eucharist. **2.** A foundation or fund for providing bursaries.

bur·seed (bûr′sēd′) *n.* A plant, the **stickseed** (see).

bur·si·form (bûr′sə-fôrm′) *adj. Anatomy.* Shaped like a pouch or sac. [Medieval Latin *bursa,* bag, purse + -FORM.]

bur·si·tis (bər-sī′tĭs) *n.* Inflammation of a bursa, especially of one of the shoulder, elbow, or knee joints. [New Latin : BURS(A) + -ITIS.]

burst (bûrst) *v.* **burst, bursting, bursts.** —*intr.* **1.** To come open or fly apart suddenly or violently, especially from internal pressure. **2.** To be full to the point of almost breaking open; swell: *a bag bursting with goodies.* **3.** To come forth, emerge, or arrive suddenly and in full force: *burst into the room; burst into flames.* **4.** To give sudden utterance or expression, especially to an emotion or feeling. Used with *into* or *out: burst into song; burst out laughing.* —*tr.* **1.** To cause or experience the rupture or bursting apart of: *burst a blood vessel.* **2.** To bring or force into a breached or opened state: *burst open the door.* **3.** *Computer Science.* To separate (a continuous roll of print-out) into individual sheets. —See Synonyms at **break.**
~*n.* **1.** A sudden breaking open or flying apart; an explosion. **2.** The result of bursting; a breach or rupture. **3.** A sudden, vehement outbreak or occurrence: *"blow with the strength of a hurricane in fitful bursts"* (Joseph Conrad). **4.** An abrupt, intense increase or spurt: *a burst of speed.* **5.** *Military.* **a.** The explosion of a projectile or bomb on impact or in the air. **b.** The number of bullets fired from an automatic weapon by one pull of the trigger. [Middle English *bersten,* Old English *berstan,* from Germanic.]

burst·er (bûr′stər) *n. Computer Science.* An offline device used to burst computer print-out.

burthen. *Archaic.* Variant of **burden.**

bur·ton (bûrt′n) *n. Nautical.* A light tackle having double or single blocks, used to hoist or tighten rigging. [Earlier *Breton (takles), Brytton (takles),* probably from BRETON.]

Bur·ton (bûrt′n), **Richard,** born Richard Jenkins (1925–84). Welsh-born actor. He was known as much for his tempetuous lifestyle, including his two marriages to actress Elizabeth Taylor, as for the variety of roles he played, ranging from Shakespeare to modern works such as *Who's Afraid of Virginia Woolf?* by Edward Albee.

Burton, Sir Richard Francis (1821–90). British explorer and orientalist. Disguised as a Pathan, he journeyed to the heart of Arabia. In 1858 he and John Hanning Speke (1827–64) became the first white men to explore the interior of Somaliland and to see Lake Tanganyika. His best-known work is his translation of *The Arabian Nights* (1885–1888).

Burton, Robert, pen name Democritus Junior (1577–1640). English clergyman and author. He was vicar of St. Thomas's at Oxford (1616–40). He is chiefly known for *The Anatomy of Melancholy,* a treatise on the causes, symptoms, and cure of melancholy that is a lively depiction of the everyday life of his time.

Bur·ton-up·on-Trent (bûrt′n-ə-pŏn-trĕnt′). Town in Staffordshire, west-central England, on the Trent River. It is a center for brewing, which was introduced by monks who founded a Benedictine abbey on the site in 1002.

Bu·run·di (boo-roon′dē). A republic in east-central Africa, between Rwanda and Tanzania on the northeastern extremity of Lake Tanganyika. The capital is Bujumbura, the only large town in the coun-

burying beetle *This beetle is also called the sexton beetle because it buries carrion, digging away the soil from beneath dead birds and small mammals in order to lay its eggs near the carcass. It is common throughout temperate latitudes.*

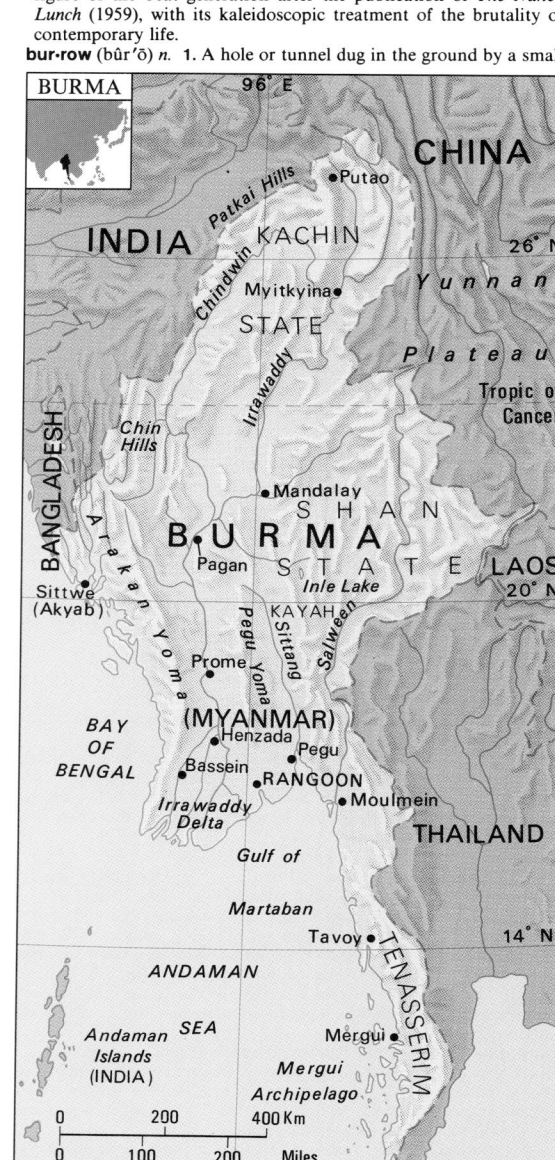

BURMA

CHINA
INDIA
KACHIN
STATE
Patkai Hills
•Putao
26° N
Myitkyina•
Yunnan
Chindwin
Irrawaddy
Plateau
Tropic of Cancer
BANGLADESH
Chin Hills
•Mandalay
S H A N
B U R M A   STATE
Pagan
Inle Lake
LAOS
20° N
Arakan Yoma
Sittwe (Akyab)
KAYAH
Salween
Sittang
Pegu Yoma
Prome•
(MYANMAR)
•Henzada
Pegu•
BAY OF BENGAL
•Bassein
•RANGOON
Irrawaddy Delta
•Moulmein
THAILAND
Gulf of Martaban
Tavoy•
14° N
TENASSERIM
ANDAMAN
Andaman Islands (INDIA)
SEA
Mergui•
Mergui Archipelago

0   200   400 Km
0   100   200   Miles

try. The western edge of the country is in the East African Rift Valley; the eastern parts are dominated by mountains. Burundi, one of the poorest nations in the world, exports coffee, but most of the people live by subsistence agriculture. It was part of Belgian-ruled Ruanda-Urundi until 1962, when it gained its independence (Ruanda becoming Rwanda and Urundi becoming Burundi). Following a military coup in 1966, Burundi became a republic. Area, 27,834 square kilometers (10,747 square miles). Population, 4,000,000. See map at **Tanzania.**

bur·weed (bûr′wēd) *n.* Any of various plants that bear burs, such as the burdock.

bur·y (bĕr′ē) *tr.v.* **-ied, -ying, -ies. 1.** To place in the ground; conceal by covering over with earth. **2.** To place (a dead body) in a grave, a tomb, or in the sea; inter. **3.** To cover from view; hide: *buried her head in her hands.* **4.** To embed; immerse or sink. **5.** To occupy (oneself) with deep concentration. **6.** To put an end to; forget; abandon. —See Synonyms at **hide.** [Middle English *berien, burien,* Old English *byrgan,* from Germanic.] **—bur·i·er** *n.*

Bur·y (bĕr′ē). A town in the metropolitan county of Greater Manchester, in northern England. It was the site of a Saxon settlement and, since the introduction of wool weaving by Flemish immigrants in the mid-14th century, has been a textile center.

Bur·yat Autonomous Soviet Socialist Republic (bŏŏr-yät′, bŏŏr′-ē-ăt). A constituent republic of the Soviet Union, lying north of Mongolia between Lake Baikal and the Yablonovy Mts. It is largely mountainous, with dense forests and many rivers and lakes rich in fish. Timber and mining are the main economic activities.

burying beetle *n.* Any of various black or black and orange beetles of the genus *Necrophorus,* that bury dead mice and other small animals, on which they feed and lay their eggs. Also called "sexton beetle."

bus (bŭs) *n., pl.* **buses** or **busses. 1.** A long motor vehicle, sometimes with two decks, used as a means of public transport, usually along a fixed route. Also called "omnibus." **2.** *Informal.* A large car or airplane. **3.** A four-wheeled cart for carrying dishes in a restaurant. **4.** *Electricity.* A **bus bar** *(see).* **—miss the bus.** To miss an opportunity; arrive too late.
~*v.* **bused** or **bussed, busing** or **bussing, buses** or **busses.** —*tr.* To transport in a bus, especially to schools in different areas in order to encourage racial integration. —*intr.* **1.** To travel in a bus. **2.** To work as a bus boy or bus girl. [Short for OMNIBUS.]
Usage: *Bus* is now well established as a transitive verb. It has the general meaning of "to transport (passengers)" and the specialized meaning of "to transport (schoolchildren) to achieve racial integration."

bus. business.

bus bar *n.* **1.** A conducting bar that carries heavy currents to supply several electric circuits. **2.** A conducting bar in a computer used to carry data from one part to another. Also called "bus."

bus boy *n.* A restaurant employee who clears away dirty dishes and serves as a waiter's assistant.

bus·by (bŭz′bē) *n., pl.* **-bies.** A tall, fur hat with a plume and a bag hanging at one side worn in certain regiments of the British Army, especially the hussars. [18th century : origin obscure.]

bus girl *n.* A girl or woman restaurant employee who clears away dirty dishes and serves as a waiter's assistant.

bush¹ (bŏŏsh) *n.* **1.** Any low, branching, woody plant, usually smaller than a tree; a shrub. **2.** A thick growth of shrubs; a thicket. **3. a.** Land covered with a dense growth of shrubs. **b.** Land remote from settled or cultivated areas, especially in Australia, New Zealand, Canada, or Africa. Usually preceded by *the.* **4.** A fox's tail. **5. a.** A clump of ivy formerly used as the sign of a tavern. **b.** *Obsolete.* A tavern. **—beat around** (or **about**) **the bush.** To delay in getting to the point.
~*v.* **bushed, bushing, bushes.** —*intr.* **1.** To grow or branch out like a shrub or bush. **2.** To extend in a bushy growth. —*tr.* To decorate, protect, or support with shrubs or bushes. [Middle English *busshe,* Old English *bysc* (unattested); akin to Old Norse *buski,* Old French *bosc,* all of Germanic origin.]

bush² *tr.v.* **bushed, bushing, bushes.** To furnish or line with a bush. [From Middle Dutch *busse,* bush of a wheel, wheel box, from Late Latin *buxis,* BOX.]

Bush (bŏŏsh), **George Herbert Walker** (1924–). 41st president of the United States. He was U.S. ambassador to the United Nations (1971–72) and China (1974–75), director of the Central Intelligence Agency (1976–77), and vice president under Ronald Reagan (1981–89). He served as president from 1989 to 1993.

bush baby *n.* Any of several small nocturnal primates of the genera *Galago* and *Euoticus,* having dense, woolly fur, large, round eyes, prominent ears, and a long tail. Also often called "galago."

bush Baptist *n. Australian Informal.* A person who has strong religious beliefs but who does not belong to any particular set.

bush bean *n.* A shrubby plant, *Phaseolus vulgaris humilis,* a variety of the string bean.

bush·buck (bŏŏsh′bŭk′) *n.* An African antelope, *Tragelaphus scriptus,* having a reddish-brown coat with white markings and twisted horns. Also called "harnessed antelope." [Translation of Afrikaans *bosbok.*]

bush clover *n.* Any of various plants or shrubs of the genus *Lespedeza,* having compound leaves with three leaflets and clusters of purple or yellowish flowers.

bush·craft (bŏŏsh′krăft′, -kräft′) *n. Australian.* Experience or knowledge of life or survival in the bush.

bush cricket *n.* A grasshopper of the family Tettigoniidae having long, threadlike antennae and tarsi feet divided into four segments.

bushed (bŏŏsht) *adj.* **1.** *Informal.* Extremely tired; exhausted. **2.** *Chiefly Australian & Canadian.* Lost or confused. [Probably from BUSH (wilderness).]

bush·el¹ (bŏŏsh′əl) *n. Abbr.* **bu, bu., bsh. 1. a.** A unit of volume or capacity in the U.S. Customary System, used in dry measure and equal to 4 pecks or 2,150.42 cubic inches. **b.** A unit of volume or capacity in the British Imperial System, used in dry and liquid measure, and equal to 2,219.36 cubic inches. **2.** A container with the capacity of this unit. **3.** *Informal.* A large amount; a great deal. [Middle English *busshel, boyschel,* from Old French *boissiel,* from *boisse,* one sixth of a bushel, from Gaulish *bostia*† (unattested), handful.]

bushel² *tr.v.* **-eled** or **-elled, -eling** or **-elling, -els.** To alter or mend (clothing). [German *bosseln,* to mend, do small jobs, probably from Middle High German *bōzeln,* to knock, tap repeatedly, from *bōzen,* to knock, shove, from Old High German *bōzan.*]

bush fly *n.* Any of the small and irritating flies that swarm about humans and animals in the bush.

bush hammer *n.* A hammer used for dressing stone, having a flat face with small pyramidal projections.

bush honeysuckle *n.* Any of several North American shrubs of the genus *Diervilla,* having yellow flowers that turn reddish.

bush-house (bŏŏsh′hous′) *n. Chiefly Australian.* **1.** A house or hut in the bush. **2.** A shed or hut in a garden.

Bu·shi·do, bu·shi·do (bōō′shē-dō′) *n.* The traditional code of the Japanese samurai, stressing self-discipline, bravery, and simple living. [Japanese *bushidō,* "the way of the warrior."]

bush·ie, bush·y (bŏŏsh′ē) *n., pl.* **-ies.** *Australian & New Zealand.* A person who lives in the bush, especially a person who is unsophisticated and ignorant of city life.

bush·ing (bŏŏsh′ĭng) *n.* **1.** A fixed or removable metal lining used to constrain, guide, or reduce friction. **2.** An insulating lining for an aperture through which a wire or other conductor passes. **3.** An adapter threaded to permit joining of pipes with different diameters. [From earlier *bush,* (metal lining).]

bush jacket *n.* A light, belted jacket with four patch pockets.

bush-law·yer (bŏŏsh′loi′ər) *n. Australian & New Zealand.* **1.** A layman who pretends or claims to have knowledge of the law. **2.** Loosely, an argumentative person.

bush league *n. Baseball Slang.* A minor league.

bush-league (bŏŏsh′lēg′) *adj. Slang.* **1.** *Baseball.* Of or belonging to a minor league **2.** Second-rate. **—bush-lea·guer** *n.*

Bush·man (bŏŏsh′mən) *n., pl.* **-men** (-mĭn). **1.** A member of a nomadic Negroid people of southwestern Africa, characteristically of short stature. **2.** Any of several Khoisan languages spoken by this people. **3. bushman.** *Chiefly Australian.* A person who lives in or knows the ways of life in the bush. [Translation of Afrikaans *boschjesman.*]

bush·mas·ter (bŏŏsh′măs′tər, -mäs′tər) *n.* A large, venomous snake, *Lachesis muta,* of tropical America, having brown and grayish markings.

Bush·nell (bŏŏsh′nəl), **David,** known as "father of the submarine" (1742–1824). U.S. inventor. In 1775 he designed a man-propelled submarine for use against British ships in the Revolution. A foot-operated valve in the keel let in water for submerging; two hand-operated pumps removed the water for ascending. The device proved ineffectual against the enemy and was ridiculed as "Bushnell's Turtle."

bush oyster *n. Australian Informal.* A testicle, usually of a sheep, that is cooked and eaten.

bush pig *n.* A wild pig, *Potamochoerus porcus,* of southern Africa, having long tufts of hair on the face and ears. [Translation of Afrikaans *bosvark.*]

bush pilot *n.* A pilot who flies a small airplane to and from areas inaccessible to larger aircraft or other means of transportation.

bush poppy *n.* The **tree poppy** *(see).*

bush·rang·er (bŏŏsh′rān′jər) *n.* **1.** A backwoodsman **2.** *Australian.* An outlaw living in the bush.

bush-sick (bŏŏsh′sĭk′) *adj. Chiefly Australian.* Of or designating livestock that are rapidly losing energy and weight due to mineral deficiencies in the soil. **—bush-sick·ness** *n.*

bush telegraph *n.* **1.** Word of mouth as a means by which rumors or gossip is rapidly spread. Also called "bush wire." **2.** Formerly, a means of disseminating information, especially amongst primitive tribes, as by beating drums.

bush·tit (bŏŏsh′tĭt′) *n.* Either of two small, long-tailed songbirds, *Psaltriparus minimus* or *P. melanotis,* of western North America, having predominantly gray plumage.

bush·veldt, bush·veld (bŏŏsh′fĕlt′, -vĕlt′) *n.* In South Africa, open country or veld whose flora consists predominantly of scrub or thorny bush.

bush week *n. Australian Informal.* **1.** A fictitious week during which bush dwellers come to town. **2.** A set of circumstances in which a person is easily duped: *What do you think this is—bush week?*

bush·whack (bŏŏsh′hwăk) *v.* **-whacked, -whacking, -whacks.** —*intr.* **1.** To make one's way through thick woods by cutting away bushes and branches. **2.** To travel through the woods, as in scouting. **3.** To fight as a guerrilla in the back country or bush. —*tr.* To attack suddenly from a place of concealment; ambush. [Back-formation from BUSHWHACKER.]

bush baby *Often called galagos, bush babies are small nocturnal primates of the African woodlands. They are tree-dwelling creatures and are able to make huge leaps from branch to branch.*

PRONUNCIATION KEY

ă, pat; ā, pay; âr, care;
ä, father, are; b, bib;
ch, church; d, deed; ĕ, pet;
ē, be; f, fife; g, gag; h, hat;
hw, which; ĭ, pit; ī, pie;
îr, pier; j, judge; k, kick;
l, lid, needle; m, mum;
n, no, sudden; ng, thing;
ŏ, pot; ō, toe; ô, paw, for;
oi, noise; ou, out; ŏŏ, book;
ōō, boot; p, pop; r, roar;
s, sauce; sh, ship, dish;
t, tight; th, thin, path;
th, this, bathe; ŭ, cut; ûr, fur;
v, valve; w, with; y, yes;
z, zebra, size; zh, vision;
ə, about, item, edible, gallop, circus, peaceful

IN FOREIGN WORDS:

à, *Fr.* ami; œ, *Fr.* feu, *Ger.* schön; ü, *Fr.* tu, *Ger.* über; KH, *Ger.* ich, *Scot.* loch; N, *Fr.* bon; y′, *Fr.* Compiègne

STRESS MARKS:

Primary stress: ′
in·cite′ (ĭn-sīt′)
Secondary stress: ′
in′sight′ (ĭn′sīt′)

bustard *The great bustard is the largest European land bird. It lives on open steppes and plains and can weigh as much as 14 kilograms (31 pounds), with a wingspan of up to 2.25 meters (7½ feet).*

bustle *Material used to push out a skirt from the back of the waist. Bustles, which first became fashionable in the 14th century, were fashioned from foxes' tails, kitchen dusters, down cushions, and wire cages. This one dates from the mid-19th century.*

bush·whacked (bo͝osh'hwăkt') *adj. Austrialian.* Bushed.

bush·whack·er (bo͝osh'hwăk'ər) *n.* **1.** One that bushwhacks. **2.** A woodsman. **3.** A guerrilla, especially a Confederate in the American Civil War. [BUSH + *whacker,* one who whacks, from WHACK.]

bush·y (bo͝osh'ē) *adj.* **-ier, -iest. 1.** Overgrown or thick with bushes. **2.** Shaggy and thick. **3.** Variant of **bushie. —bush·i·ly** *adv.* **—bush·i·ness** *n.*

bus·i·ly (bĭz'ə-lē) *adv.* In a busy manner.

busi·ness (bĭz'nĭs) *n. Abbr.* **bus. 1.** The occupation, work, or trade in which a person is engaged. **2.** Commercial, industrial, or professional dealings; the buying and selling of goods or services. **3.** Any commercial establishment, such as a store or factory. **4.** Volume or amount of commercial trade: *We're doing very good business.* **5.** Commercial policy or practice. **6.** One's rightful or proper concern or interest; responsibility: *Mind your own business.* **7.** Serious work or endeavor, especially pertaining to one's job: *went to Tokyo on business.* **8.** An affair or matter: *tired of this silly business.* **9.** Incidental actions performed by an actor on the stage to fill a pause between lines or to provide dramatic effect. Also called "stage business." **—get down to business.** To begin in earnest. **—mean business.** To be in dead earnest. [Middle English *bissinesse,* diligence, state of being busy, Old English *bisig,* BUSY.]

Usage: *business, industry, commerce, trade, traffic.* These nouns apply to forms of activity that have the objective of supplying commodities. *Business* pertains broadly to all gainful activity, though it usually excludes the professions and farming. *Industry* is the production and manufacture of goods and commodities, especially on a large scale, and *commerce* and *trade,* the exchange and distribution of commodities. Often *commerce* is applied to exchange of commodities for money, as within a country, while *trade* refers to exchange of commodities for commodities, as between countries. *Traffic* may suggest illegal trade, as in narcotics.

business administration *n.* A college or university course of studies that offers instruction in business principles and practices.

business card *n.* A small card that conveys information about a business or a business representative.

business end *n. Informal.* The end of something, such as a gun, knife, or the like, that actually performs the function for which the whole instrument has been designed.

business hours *pl.n.* The hours of the day during which a business, such as a store, bank, or the like, conducts business.

busi·ness·like (bĭz'nĭs-līk') *adj.* **1.** Methodical; systematic; efficient. **2.** Purposeful; earnest.

busi·ness·man (bĭz'nĭs-măn') *n., pl.* **-men** (-mĕn'). A man engaged in business, especially at an executive level.

business person *n.* A person engaged in business.

busi·ness·wom·an (bĭz'nĭs-wo͝om'ən) *n., pl.* **-women** (-wĭm'ĭn). A woman engaged in business, especially at an executive level.

bus·ing, bus·sing (bŭs'ĭng) *n.* The transportation of children by bus to schools outside their neighborhoods, especially as a means of achieving racial integration.

busk[1] (bŭsk) *n.* **1.** A thin, flexible strip of wood, whalebone, plastic, or metal sewn in a woman's undergarment as stiffening. **2.** *Regional.* A corset. [French *busc,* from Italian *busco,* splinter, from Germanic.]

busk[2] *intr.v.* **busked, busking, busks.** *British.* To entertain by singing, playing music, or dancing, especially in streets and public places, in return for money. [Perhaps from obsolete French *busquer,* to look for, seek.] **—busk·er** *n.*

busk[3] *tr.v.* **busked, busking, busks.** *Chiefly Scottish.* To make ready; prepare. [Middle English *busken,* from Old Norse *būask,* reflexive of *būa,* to prepare.]

bus·kin (bŭs'kĭn) *n.* **1.** A foot and leg covering reaching halfway to the knee, resembling a laced half-boot. **2.** A thick-soled laced half boot, worn by actors of tragedies in ancient Greece. Compare **sock. 3.** *Formal & Poetic.* Tragedy. Usually preceded by *the.* [Old French *bouzequin, brousequin,* akin to Spanish *borzeguí,* Italian *borzacchino*†.]

bus·man (bŭs'mən) *n., pl.* **-men** (-mĭn). One who operates a bus.

bus·man's holiday (bŭs'mənz) *n. Informal.* A holiday on which a person engages in recreation similar to his usual work. [A bus driver might go for a drive on a holiday.]

Bu·so·ni (bo͞o-zō'nē), **Gerruccio Benvenuto** (1866–1924). Italian composer, conductor, and pianist. He achieved great fame as a pianist in the flamboyant manner of Liszt and was a prolific composer, though few of his works are played today.

buss (bŭs) *v.* **bussed, bussing, busses.** *Regional. —tr.* To kiss with a loud smacking sound. *—intr.* To kiss loudly.
∼n. Regional. A smacking kiss. [From earlier *bass;* akin to French *baiser,* Latin *basiare.*]

bus·ses. 1. Alternate plural of **bus. 2.** Alternate third person singular of **bus.**

bus shelter *n.* A structure at a bus stop designed to protect waiting passengers from wind and rain.

bus·stop (bŭs'stŏp') *n.* A place on a bus route, usually marked, where passengers alight from or board buses.

bust[1] (bŭst) *n.* **1. a.** A woman's bosom. **b.** *Archaic.* The human chest. **2.** A piece of sculpture representing a person's head, shoulders, and upper chest. [French *buste,* from Italian *busto,* piece of sculpture, origin obscure.]

bust[2] *v.* **busted** or **bust, busting, busts.** *Informal. —tr.* **1.** To burst or break. **2.** To break up (a trust or monopoly). **3.** To break or tame (a horse) **4.** To cause to become bankrupt or short of money. **5.** To reduce the rank of; demote. **6.** To hit or punch. **7.** To place under arrest. *—intr.* **1.** To burst or break. **2.** To become bankrupt or short of money.
∼n. **1.** A failure; a flop. **2.** A state of bankruptcy. **3.** A time or period of widespread financial depression. Compare **boom. 4.** A punch or blow. **5.** A spree. **6.** An arrest. [Variant of BURST.]

Bus·ta·man·te (bo͞os'tə-măn'tē), **Sir William Alexander** (1884-1977). Jamaican politician, the first prime minister of independent Jamaica (1962–67). As a trade union leader he led the campaign for Jamaican independence and formed the Jamaica Labour Party (1943).

bus·tard (bŭs'tərd) *n.* Any of various large terrestrial Old World birds of the family Otididae, frequenting open, grassy regions. Bustards have long, strong legs, a stout body, and brown, mottled plumage. [Middle English *bustarde,* possibly from Norman French *bustarde* (unattested), blend of Old French *bistarde* and *oustarde,* both perhaps from Latin *avis tarda,* "slow bird" : *avis,* bird + *tarda,* feminine of *tardus,* slow (see **tardy**).]

bus·tee, bus·ti (bŭs'tē) *n.* A slum or shantytown in India.

bust·er (bŭs'tər) *n. Slang.* **1.** One who destroys or breaks up: *a crimebuster.* **2.** One who breaks horses; a broncobuster. **3.** Something especially large or remarkable. **4.** A spree. **5.** *Often* **Buster.** A man or boy. Used in direct address.

bus·tle[1] (bŭs'əl) *v.* **-tled, -tling, -tles.** *—intr.* To hurry energetically and busily. *—tr.* To cause to hurry.
∼n. Excited activity; commotion; stir. [Probably a variant of obsolete *buskle,* frequentative of dialectal *busk,* to prepare, from Middle English *busken,* from Old Norse *buāsk* : *būa,* to prepare + *-sk,* reflexive ending.]

bustle[2] *n.* **1.** A frame or pad worn, especially in the 19th and early 20th centuries, to support and extend the rear of a woman's skirt. **2.** A bow, peplum, or gathering of material at the back of a skirt below the waist. [Perhaps from German *Buschel*†, a bunch, pad.]

bust·y (bŭs'tē) *adj.* **-ier, -iest.** *Informal.* Full-bosomed.

bu·sul·fan (byo͞o-sŭl'fən) *n.* A drug, $C_6H_{14}O_6S_2$, that destroys cancer cells and is used mainly to treat certain forms of leukemia. [Blend of BUTANE and SULFONYL.]

bus·y (bĭz'ē) *adj.* **-ier, -iest. 1.** Actively engaged in some form of work; occupied. **2.** Crowded with activity: *a busy morning.* **3.** Meddlesome; prying. **4.** Temporarily in use. Said of a telephone line. **5.** Cluttered with minute and distracting detail: *a busy design.*
∼tr.v. **busied, -ying, -ies.** To make busy; occupy. Often used reflexively. [Middle English *bisy, busy,* Old English *bysig, bisig,* akin to Middle Low German *besicht*†.] **—bus·y·ness** *n.*

Usage: *busy, industrious, diligent, assiduous, sedulous.* All these words suggest active or sustained effort to accomplish something. *Busy* primarily applies to one engaged in present activity, without definite implication of kind, continuity, or duration of activity. *Industrious* implies continuing activity and a natural inclination to be so engaged. *Diligent* suggests intense activity in the accomplishment of a specific goal; often it implies keen interest in work of one's choosing. *Assiduous* emphasizes sustained devotion to work. *Sedulous* adds to assiduity the sense of earnest, persistent, painstaking labor.

bus·y·bod·y (bĭz'ē-bŏd'ē) *n., pl.* **-ies.** A person who meddles or pries into the affairs of others.

busy Liz·zie (lĭz'ē) *n.* A fast-growing hybrid plant of the genus *Impatiens,* having red, pink, white, or orange flowers, widely cultivated as a house plant.

busy signal *n.* A series of sharp buzzing tones heard over the telephone when the number dialed is in use.

bus·y·work (bĭz'ē-wûrk') *n.* Activity that takes up time but does not necessarily yield productive results.

but (bŭt, *unstressed* bət) *conj.* **1.** On the contrary. **2.** Contrary to expectation; however; yet. **3.** Except; save. **—**See Usage note below. **4.** With the exception that; except that. Used to introduce a dependent clause with *that* expressed: *They should have resisted but that they lacked courage.* **5.** Without the result that: *It never rains but it pours.* **6.** Other than: *I have no choice but to leave.* **7.** That. Often used after a negative: *There's no doubt but he'll win.* **8.** That . . . not. Used after a negative or question: *There never is a change made but someone complains.* **9.** Who . . . not; which . . . not: *None came to him but were treated well.* **10.** *Archaic.* Unless; if not: *"Beshrew me but I love her heartily"* (Shakespeare). **11.** *Archaic & Nonstandard.* Than: *"No sooner acquainted my brother, but he immediately wanted to propose it"* (Henry Fielding).
∼prep. With the exception of; barring; save: *none but the brave.* **—but for.** Were it not for: *But for luck, he would still be poor.*
∼adv. **1.** No more than; just: *but a month to live.* **2.** Only; simply: *If I had but known.* **3.** *Informal.* Really: *rich, but rich!* **—all but.** Nearly; almost: *His poem is all but finished.*
∼n. An objection, restriction, or exception: *no ifs, ands, or buts.* [Middle English *bute, but* (conjunction and adverb), Old English *būtan, būte* (conjunction and preposition).]

Usage: *But* is used to mean "except" in sentences like *No one but John can read it.* Some traditionalists have suggested that *but* is a conjunction in this use and so should be followed by nominative pronouns like *I* and *he* when the phrase in which it occurs is the subject of the sentence. But this use of *but* is perhaps better thought of as a preposition, since the verb always agrees with the subject preceding *but*; we say *no one but the boys has left* (not *have left*), and traditionalists themselves do not say *everyone but I am leaving,* which is clearly ungrammatical. Accordingly, this use of *but* should properly be accompanied by pronouns in the objective case, like *me* and *him*: *Everyone but me has received an answer.* *But* is redundant when used in combination with *however*, as in *But the army, however, went on with its own plans* (eliminate either *but* or *however*). *But* is often used in informal speech together with a negative in sentences like *It won't take but an hour.* The construction should be avoided in formal style; write *It won't take an hour.* *But what* is informal in sentences like *I don't know but what we'll get there before the boys do.* In writing, substitute *whether* or *that* for *but*. *But* is also informal when used in place of *than* in sentences like *It no sooner started but it stopped* (in writing, use *than*). *But* is usually not followed by a comma. Write *Kim wanted to go, but we didn't want to,* not *Kim wanted to go, but, we didn't want to,* which is incorrect. *But* can be used to begin a sentence, even in formal style. But it should not be followed by a comma here either. See also Usage notes at **doubt** and **than**.

but– *prefix.* Indicates a chemical compound containing four carbon atoms; for example, **butane**. [From BUTYRIC.]

bu·ta·di·ene (byōō′tə-dī′ēn′, -dī-ēn′) *n.* A colorless, highly flammable gaseous hydrocarbon, C_4H_6, obtained from petroleum and used in the manufacture of synthetic rubber. [BUTA(NE) + DI- + -ENE.]

bu·tane (byōō′tān′) *n.* Either of two isomers of a gaseous hydrocarbon, C_4H_{10}, produced synthetically from petroleum and used as a household fuel, refrigerant, and aerosol propellant, and in the manufacture of synthetic rubber.

bu·ta·no·ic acid (byōō′tə-nō′ĭk) *n.* **Butyric acid** (see).

bu·ta·nol (byōō′tə-nôl′, -nŏl′) *n.* **1.** An alcohol, C_4H_9OH, derived naturally from the bacterial fermentation of grain and used as a solvent for resins, plasticizers, hydraulic fluids, and as a dehydrating agent. **2.** An isomeric alcohol derived from the cracking of petroleum or natural gas and used as a solvent in varnishes, lacquers, and paint removers.

bu·ta·none (byōō′tə-nōn′) *n.* A colorless, flammable ketone, C_4H_8O, used in lacquers, paint removers, cements and adhesives, celluloid, and cleaning fluids. Also called "methyl ethyl ketone."

butch (bŏŏch) *n. Slang.* A woman who is masculine in appearance or manner; sometimes used of a lesbian assuming a pseudo-masculine role. —*adj. Informal.* **1.** Sturdily masculine in appearance. **2.** Assuming exaggeratedly masculine ways or appearance. Said of both male and female homosexuals. [From a boy's nickname, *Butch,* perhaps ultimately from BUTCHER.]

butch·er (bŏŏch′ər) *n.* **1.** One who slaughters and prepares animals for food or market. **2.** One who sells meat. **3.** One guilty of cruel or pointless killing. **4.** A vender of candy, magazines, and the like on a train. **5.** One who performs a task very unskillfully. —*tr.v.* **butchered, -ering, -ers. 1.** To slaughter or dress (animals) for market. **2.** To kill cruelly or pointlessly. **3.** To spoil by botching; bungle. [Middle English *bo(u)cher,* from Norman French, from Old French *bouchier,* from *boc,* he-goat.] —**butch·er·er** *n.*

butch·er·bird (bŏŏch′ər-bûrd′) *n.* Any of various birds that impale their prey on thorns; especially, a **shrike** (see).

butcher knife *n.* A heavy-duty knife about 8 inches long with a broad blade.

butch·ers¹ (bŏŏch′ərz) *n. British Slang.* A look; a glance. [Short for *butcher's hook,* rhyming slang for *look.*]

butchers² *adj.* Also **butcher's hook.** *Australian Informal.* Unwell; crook. —**go butcher's (or hook) at.** To become angry with.

butcher's broom *n.* A shrub, *Ruscus aculeatus,* native to Europe, having stiff, prickle-tipped, flattened stems resembling true leaves. [Formerly used as a broom by butchers.]

butch·er·y (bŏŏch′ə-rē) *n., pl.* **-ies. 1.** The trade of a butcher. **2.** A slaughterhouse. **3.** *South African.* A butcher's shop, where meat is sold. **4.** Wanton or cruel killing; carnage.

Bute (byōōt). Also **Bute·shire** (byōōt′shîr, -shər). Former county of Scotland, absorbed in 1975 into Strathclyde.

Bute, John Stuart, 3rd Earl of (1713–92). British politician. From 1751 he was tutor to the heir to the throne, later George III. In 1761 he was appointed secretary of state and helped bring about the defeat of the elder Pitt (1762). Bute succeeded Pitt as chief minister of the crown and worked to conclude peace with France (1763).

Bu·te·nandt (bōō′tə-nänt′), **Adolf Friedrich** (1903–). German chemist. Known especially for his work on sex hormones, he declined his share of the 1939 Nobel Prize for chemistry, following a Nazi edict prohibiting acceptance.

bu·te·o (byōō′tē-ō′) *n., pl.* **-os.** Any of various hawks of the genus *Buteo,* characterized by broad wings and broad, rounded tails. [New Latin, genus name, from Latin *buteo,* a kind of hawk or falcon.]

Bu·the·le·zi (bōō′tə-lā′zē) (Mangosuthu) Gatsha (1928–). Chief Minister of KwaZulu—one of the national states created as homelands for South Africa's blacks—and a prominent spokesman on South African racial and political affairs.

but·ler (bŭt′lər) *n.* A male head servant in a household, in charge of the table and the wine cellar. [Middle English *buteler,* servant in charge of the wine cellar, from Old French *bouteiller,* a bottle bearer, from *bouteille, botele,* BOTTLE.]

But·ler (bŭt′lər), **Nicholas Murray** (1862–1947). U.S. educator. Widely known for his theories on education and the training of teachers, he helped organize the School of Education at Columbia University. Butler worked widely for international peace and shared the Nobel Peace Prize (1931) with Jane Addams.

Butler, Samuel¹ (1612–80). English satirical poet. His reputation rests on one long poem, *Hudibras* (1663–78), a mock-heroic satire on the Puritans.

Butler, Samuel² (1835–1902). British novelist. He first gained literary notice with his novel, *Erewhon* (1872), a trenchant satire on English life and laws. Perhaps his greatest achievement was the semiautobiographical novel *The Way of All Flesh* (1903).

butler's pantry *n.* A serving and storage room between the kitchen and the dining room.

butt¹ (bŭt) *v.* **butted, butting, butts.** —*tr.* To hit or push against with the head or horns; ram. —*intr.* **1.** To hit or push something with the head or horns. **2.** To project forward or out. —**butt in.** *Informal.* To interfere or meddle; intrude. —*n.* A push or blow with the head or horns. [Middle English *butten,* from Norman French *buter, boter,* from Germanic.]

butt² *v.* **butted, butting, butts.** —*tr.* To attach the ends of; abut. —*intr.* To be joined at the ends. —*n.* **1. a.** The act of joining two objects end to end. **b.** A **butt joint** (see). **2.** A **butt hinge** (see). [From BUTT (end).]

butt³ *n.* **1.** A person or thing serving as an object of ridicule or contempt. **2.** A target. **3. butts.** A target range. **4.** A mound of earth, a wall, or another obstacle behind a target for stopping the shot. **5.** *Obsolete.* A limit; goal. [Middle English *butte,* target, from Old French *but*†.]

butt⁴ *n.* **1.** The larger or thicker end of something: *the butt of a rifle.* **2.** An unburned end, as of a cigarette. **3.** A short or broken remnant; a stub. **4.** *Slang.* A cigarette. **5.** *Informal.* The buttocks; the rear end. [Middle English *but, butte,* thicker end, from Germanic.]

butt⁵ *n.* **1.** A large cask. **2.** A unit of volume equal to 126 U.S. gallons. [Middle English, from Norman French *but,* variant of Old French *bot, bout,* from Late Latin *buttis.* See **bottle**.]

butte (byōōt) *n.* A hill rising abruptly above the surrounding area and having sloping sides and a flat top. [French, from Old French *but,* BUTT (mound behind targets).]

Butte (byōōt). A city in southwestern Montana. Butte was established as a gold-mining camp (1862), then became a silver center, and gained importance when copper was discovered (c. 1880). The city has a mining museum and offers tours of nearby mines.

but·ter¹ (bŭt′ər) *n.* **1.** A soft, yellowish or whitish emulsion of butterfat, water, air, and sometimes salt, churned from milk or cream and processed for use in cooking and as a food. **2.** Any of various similar substances, especially: **a.** A spread made from fruit, nuts, or other foods, as *apple butter.* **b.** A vegetable fat having a nearly solid consistency at ordinary temperatures, as **cocoa butter** (see). **3.** *Informal.* Flattery. —*tr.v.* **buttered, -tering, -ters. 1.** To put butter on or in. **2.** *Informal.* To flatter. Usually used with *up.* [Middle English *buter(e),* Old English *butere,* from West Germanic, from Latin *būtyrum,* from Greek *bouturon,* "cow cheese" : *bous,* cow + *turos,* cheese.]

but·ter² (bŭt′ər) *n.* One that butts with the head or horns.

but·ter-and-eggs (bŭt′ər-ən-ĕgz′) *n. Used with a singular or plural verb.* A North American plant, *Linaria vulgaris,* having numerous narrow leaves and a spike of spurred pale-yellow and orange flowers. Also called "toadflax."

but·ter·ball (bŭt′ər-bôl′) *n.* **1.** A ball of butter. **2.** *Informal.* A fat or chubby person. **3.** A duck, the **bufflehead** (see).

butter bean *n.* **1.** The **wax bean** (see). **2.** *Regional.* The **lima bean** (see). [From the yellow pods of the wax bean.]

but·ter·bur (bŭt′ər-bûr′) *n.* Any of several plants of the genus *Petasites,* having woolly leaves and fragrant whitish or purple flowers. [Its leaves are said to have been used to wrap butter.]

but·ter·cup (bŭt′ər-kŭp′) *n.* Any of various plants of the genus *Ranunculus,* characteristically having glossy yellow flowers, especially the meadow buttercup, *R. acris,* native to Europe, but widely introduced elsewhere.

but·ter·fat (bŭt′ər-făt′) *n.* The oily content of milk from which butter is made, consisting largely of the glycerides of oleic, stearic, and palmitic acids.

but·ter·fin·gers (bŭt′ər-fĭng′gərz) *n. Plural in form, used with a singular verb.* A clumsy or awkward person who drops things. —**but·ter·fin·gered** *adj.*

but·ter·fish (bŭt′ər-fĭsh′) *n., pl.* **-fishes** or collectively **butterfish. 1.** A marine food fish, *Poronotus triacanthus,* of the North American Atlantic coast, having a flattened body. **2.** Any of various similar or related fishes. [From their slippery mucous coating.]

but·ter·fly (bŭt′ər-flī′) *n., pl.* **-flies. 1.** Any of various diurnal insects of the order Lepidoptera, characteristically having slender bodies, knobbed antennae, and broad, usually colorful wings that are closed over the back at rest. **2.** A frivolous pleasure-seeker: *a social butterfly.* **3.** The **butterfly stroke** (see). **4. butterflies.** *Informal.* Nervous tremors in the stomach. [Middle English *butterflie,* from Old English *buttorflēoge* : *buter(e),* BUTTER + FLY, perhaps from the belief that butterflies steal butter.] See feature, next page.

butterfly bird *n.* A bird, the **wall creeper** (see).

butterfly bush *n.* Any of several shrubs of the genus *Buddleia,* cultivated for their clusters of purplish or white flowers. Also called "buddleia."

butterfly fish *n.* Any of various tropical marine fishes of the family Chaetodontidae, having brightly colored flattened bodies.

butterfly nut *n.* A **wing nut** (see).

butterfly pea *n.* A twining vine, *Clitoria mariana,* of the eastern United States, having compound leaves and pale-blue flowers.

butterfly stroke *n.* A swimming stroke, a variation of the breast stroke, in which both arms are drawn upward out of the water and

butterfly fish *These small tropical fish have deep, flattened bodies, a single dorsal fin, and a small mouth with brushlike teeth.*

butterfly

THE FLY-BY-DAYS

Scales of bright pigment make delicate wings of incomparable beauty

There are about 10,000 known species of butterflies in the world and, together with moths, they make up the order of insects known as Lepidoptera. This order gets its name from the Greek words *lepis* (scale) and *pteron* (wing). Butterflies fly during the day, while most species of moths fly at night.

A butterfly's wing is covered with thousands of minute scales, arranged in an overlapping pattern like slates on a roof. The dust that rubs so easily off a butterfly when it is handled is, in fact, composed of these scales. Seen under a microscope, each scale is a tiny flattened bag with a short stem that fits into a socket in the wing membrane. Some of the scales are filled with varied pigments and form the vivid patterns on the wings. Others contain no pigment but are grooved and polished on the outside so that they reflect light and color.

The beautiful coloring of butterflies' wings seems to serve as visual signaling. It may be that, as in some tropical fish and birds, the patterns help in finding or identifying a mate. In some species, however, the colors seem to be for defense, warning birds that the insect is distasteful or poisonous, or distracting predators toward less vulnerable parts of the body—by means of a bright tail spot, for example.

LARVA *The wanderer butterfly of Papua, New Guinea, emerges from the egg as a caterpillar, or larva.*

PUPA *The larva hangs from a twig and undergoes its final molt. The skin of the new pupa is still soft.*

CHRYSALIS *The skin hardens into a chrysalis—a protective case. Inside it, the larval structures re-form.*

TRANSFORMED *The pupa develops wings and legs while its turquoise chrysalis becomes clear and soft enough to split.*

EMERGENCE *The fully formed butterfly breaks free from its chrysalis and waits for its wings to expand and dry.*

ADULT *The new adult wanderer butterfly is poised to spread its wings in flight for the first time.*

BRIEF LIFE *A butterfly is a beautiful adult for only a few weeks—even days—in a year-long life cycle.*

forward with a simultaneous up-and-down kick of the feet.

butterfly table *n.* A small, drop-leaf table, the leaves of which have brackets shaped like a butterfly's wings.

butterfly valve *n.* **1.** A disk turning on a diametrical axis inside a pipe, used as a throttle valve or damper. **2.** A valve composed of two semicircular plates hinged on a common spindle, used to permit flow in one direction only. [Its action somewhat resembles that of a butterfly's wings.]

butterfly weed *n.* A North American plant, *Asclepias tuberosa,* having flat-topped clusters of bright-orange flowers. Also called "orange milkweed," "pleurisy root."

but·ter·milk (bŭt'ər-mĭlk') *n.* **1.** The sour liquid that remains after the butterfat has been removed from whole milk or cream by churning. **2.** Milk soured with certain microorganisms.

butter muslin *n.* A coarse loosely woven cotton gauze. [Formerly used for wrapping butter.]

but·ter·nut (bŭt'ər-nŭt') *n.* **1.** A tree, *Juglans cinerea,* of eastern North America, having compound leaves and egg-shaped nuts. Also called "white walnut." **2.** The edible, oily nut of this tree. **3.** The hard, grayish-brown wood of this tree. **4.** The bark of this tree, or an extract obtained from it, formerly used as a laxative. **5.** A brownish color or dye obtained from butternut bark **6.** butternuts. Clothing dyed with butternut extract. **7.** *Informal.* A Confederate soldier or partisan in the Civil War. **8.** The **souari nut** *(see).* [From the oiliness of the nut. Sense 7, from homemade uniforms dyed with butternut extract.]

butternut squash *n.* A small, yellowish, pear-shaped winter squash, with orange to yellow flesh.

but·ter·scotch (bŭt'ə-skŏch') *n.* **1.** A syrup, sauce, or flavoring made by melting butter, brown sugar, and sometimes artificial flavorings. **2.** A hard, sticky sweet made from these ingredients. [Perhaps originally made in Scotland.]

but·ter·weed (bŭt'ər-wēd') *n.* **1.** A plant, *Senecio glabellus,* of the southern and central United States, having yellow flowers. **2.** The **horseweed** *(see).* [From its yellow flowers.]

but·ter·wort (bŭt'ər-wûrt', -wôrt') *n.* Any plant of the genus *Pinguicula;* especially, *P. vulgaris,* of wet places, having violet-blue, spurred flowers and fleshy, greasy leaves. [From the oiliness of the leaves.]

but·ter·y[1] (bŭt'ə-rē) *adj.* **1.** Resembling, containing, or spread with butter. **2.** *Informal.* Effusively and insincerely flattering. **—but·ter·i·ness** *n.*

buttery[2] *n., pl.* **-ies.** *Chiefly British.* **1.** A pantry or wine cellar. **2.** A room or bar in colleges and universities where students can buy provisions. [Middle English *boteri, buttrie,* from Old French *boterie,* from *bot,* BUTT (cask).]

butt hinge *n.* A hinge composed of two plates attached to abutting surfaces of a door and door jamb and joined by a pin. Also called "butt." [From BUTT (abut).]

but·tin·sky, but·tin·ski (bŭ-tĭn'skē) *n., pl.* **-skies.** *Slang.* An interfering busybody. [One who *butts in* + *-sky,* surname suffix.]

butt joint *n.* A joint formed by two abutting surfaces placed squarely together. Also called "butt." [From BUTT (abut).]

but·tock (bŭt'ək) *n.* **1. a.** Either of the two rounded fleshy parts on the lower rear part of the human torso. **b.** The analogous part of the body of certain mammals. **2.** buttocks. These two parts together; the bottom. [Middle English, from Old English *buttuc,* end, ridge, strip of land.]

but·ton (bŭt'n) *n.* **1.** A fastener, usually disk-shaped, used to join two parts of a garment by fitting through a buttonhole or loop. **2.** Such an object used for decoration. **3.** Any of various objects of similar appearance, especially: **a.** A control switch, as on a bell or machine. **b.** In fencing, the tip of a foil. **c.** A fused metal or glass globule. **4.** Any of various knoblike organic structures, especially: **a.** The head of a young mushroom. **b.** The tip of a rattlesnake's tail. **5.** A round flat emblem bearing a design or printed information and pinned to the front of a garment. **6.** *Slang.* The end of the chin. *—v.* **buttoned, -toning, -tons.** *—tr.* **1.** To furnish with a button or buttons. **2.** To fasten with a button or buttons. Often used with *up.* *—intr.* **1.** To admit of being fastened with a button or buttons. Often used with *up.* **2.** *Informal.* To become uncommunicative. Used with *up.* [Middle English *boton,* from Old French *bouton,* bud, button, from *bouter,* to strike against, thrust, pierce, of Germanic origin.] **—but·ton·er** *n.* **—but·ton·y** *adj.*

But·ton (bŭt'n), **Richard Totten,** known as "Dick" (1929–). U.S. figure skater. In 1946 he became the youngest person ever to win the U.S. senior ice-skating championship. By 1948 he held all five major figure-skating titles in the world, including the Olympic gold medal. He won another Olympic championship in 1952. Button now organizes ice shows and is a television sports commentator.

but·ton·ball (bŭt'n-bôl') *n.* A North American tree, the **sycamore** *(see).* [From its button-shaped fruit.]

but·ton·bush (bŭt'n-bʊsh') *n.* A North American shrub, *Cephalanthus occidentalis,* having spherical clusters of small white flowers.

but·ton-down (bŭt'n-doun') *adj.* **1.** Having the ends of the collar fastened down by buttons: *a button-down shirt.* **2.** Also **but·toned-down** (bŭt'nd-). Conservative, conventional, or unimaginative: *buttoned-down diplomacy.*

but·ton·hole (bŭt'n-hōl') *n.* **1.** A slit in a garment or piece of fabric for fastening a button. **2.** *Chiefly British.* A flower worn in a buttonhole on the lapel of a coat or jacket.

—tr.v. **buttonholed, -holing, -holes. 1.** To make a buttonhole in.

2. To sew with a buttonhole stitch. **3.** To accost and detain in conversation. —**but·ton·hol·er** *n.*

buttonhole stitch *n.* A loop stitch that forms a reinforced edge, as around a buttonhole. Also called "close stitch."

but·ton·hook (bŭt′n-hŏŏk′) *n.* A small hook for buttoning shoes or gloves.

but·ton·mold (bŭt′n-mōld′) *n.* A piece of wood, plastic, or metal that is covered with fabric to form a button.

but·ton·quail (bŭt′n-kwāl′) *n.* Any of various small, quaillike birds of the family Turnicidae, occurring in warm grassland regions of the Old World.

but·tons (bŭt′nz) *n., pl.* **buttons.** *Informal.* A pageboy, especially in a pantomime. [From the buttons on his jacket.]

button snakeroot *n.* **1.** A plant, the **blazing star** *(see).* **2.** A plant, the **rattlesnake master** *(see).* [Probably from its button-like umbels.]

but·ton·wood (bŭt′n-wŏŏd′) *n.* A North American tree, the **sycamore** *(see).* [From the buttonlike fruit.]

butt plate *n.* A metal plate on the butt end of a gunstock.

but·tress (bŭt′rĭs) *n.* **1.** A structure, usually brick or stone, built against a wall for support or reinforcement. See **flying buttress.** **2.** Anything resembling a buttress, such as a projecting part of a hill. **3.** A horny growth on the heel of a horse's hoof. **4.** Anything that serves to support, prop, or reinforce. ~*tr.v.* **buttressed, -tressing, -tresses. 1.** To support or reinforce with a buttress. **2.** To sustain, prop, or bolster: *buttress an argument with evidence.* [Middle English *butres, boteras,* from Old French *bouterez,* shortened from *(ars) bouterez,* thrusting (arch), from *bouter,* to strike against.]

buttress root *n.* A root growing from and supporting the trunk of a tree, as in the mangrove.

butt shaft *n.* A blunt, unbarbed arrow.

butt weld *n.* A welded butt joint.

butt-weld (bŭt′wĕld′) *tr.v.* **-welded, -welding, -welds.** To join by a butt weld.

but·ty¹ (bŭt′ē) *n., pl.* **-ties.** *Chiefly Welsh.* A miner's mate. [Perhaps from BOOTY, as in the phrase *play booty,* to share takings.]

butty² *n., pl.* **-ties.** *Northern English.* A sandwich or a slice of buttered bread: *a jam butty.* [From BUTTER.]

bu·tut (bŏŏ′tŏŏt′) *n.* A coin equal to ¹⁄₁₀₀ of the dalasi of the Gambia. See feature at **currency.** [From a native Gambian language.]

bu·tyl (byōōt′l, byōō′tĭl) *n.* A hydrocarbon radical, C_4H_9, with the structure of butane and valence 1.

butyl alcohol *n.* Any of four isomeric alcohols widely used as solvents and in organic synthesis, each having the formula C_4H_9OH.

bu·ty·lene (byōōt′l-ēn′) *n.* Any of three gaseous isomeric ethylene hydrocarbons, C_4H_8, used principally in making synthetic rubbers.

butyl rubber *n.* A synthetic rubber produced by copolymerization of a butylene (98 percent) with isoprene or butadiene (2 percent), outstanding in gaseous impermeability and used in tires, insulation, and as a binder fuel in solid propellants for rockets.

bu·ty·ra·ceous (byōō′tə-rā′shəs) *adj.* Resembling butter in appearance, consistency, or chemical properties; buttery. [Latin *būtȳrum,* BUTTER + -ACEOUS.]

bu·tyr·al·de·hyde (byōō′tə-răl′də-hīd′) *n.* A transparent, extremely flammable liquid, $CH_3(CH_2)_2CHO$, used in synthesizing resins. [BUTYR(IC) + ALDEHYDE.]

bu·ty·rate (byōō′tə-rāt′) *n.* A salt or ester of butyric acid. [BUTYR(IC) + -ATE.]

bu·tyr·ic (byōō-tĭr′ĭk) *adj.* **1.** Of, pertaining to, containing, or derived from butter. **2.** Of, pertaining to, or derived from butyric acid.

butyric acid *n.* Either of two colorless isomeric acids, C_3H_7COOH, occurring in animal milk fats and used in disinfectants, emulsifying agents, and pharmaceuticals.

bu·ty·rin (byōō′tə-rĭn) *n.* Any one of three isomeric glyceryl esters of butyric acid, naturally present in butter. [Earlier *butirine,* from French : Latin *būtȳrum,* BUTTER + -INE.]

bux·om (bŭk′səm) *adj.* **1.** Full-bosomed and plump. Said of a woman. **2.** *Archaic.* Lively; blithe; vivacious. **3.** *Obsolete.* Obedient; yielding. [Earlier, flexible, gay, comely, Middle English *buhsum, buxum,* obedient, humble, bending, from Old English *gebūhsum* (unattested), easy to bend, pliable, from *būgan,* to bend.] —**bux·om·ly** *adv.* —**bux·om·ness** *n.*

Bux·te·hu·de (bŏŏks′tə-hŏŏ′də), **Dietrich** (1637–1707). Danish composer and organist. As church organist at Lübeck (1668–1707), he gained the admiration of Handel and Bach.

Bux·ton (bŭks′tən). Town in Derbyshire, central England, in the Peak District. It is *c.* 305 meters (1,000 feet) above sea level, overlooking the Wye River; the oldest section of the town is on a hill above the modern section. Buxton is a year-round resort, with mineral springs and baths.

buy (bī) *v.* **bought, bought** or *regional* **boughten, buying, buys.** —*tr.* **1.** To acquire in exchange for money or its equivalent; purchase. **2.** To be a means of obtaining or procuring: *Money buys power.* **3.** To acquire by sacrifice, exchange, or trade. **4.** To bribe. **5.** *Slang.* To accept the truth, merit, or feasibility of. —*intr.* To purchase goods; act as a purchaser: *to buy in bulk.* —**buy in** (or **into). 1.** To purchase (a supply of something) for future use. **2.** To purchase back for the original owner, as at an auction when the bidding is low. **3.** To purchase shares or an interest in (a company, for example). **4.** *Slang.* To pay money in exchange for joining (a social or business group). —**buy off.** To bribe in order to proceed without interference, or to be exempted from an obligation or from prosecution. —**buy out.** To purchase the controlling stock, business rights, or interests of. —**buy up.** To purchase all that is available of.

~*n.* Anything bought or capable of being bought; a purchase, especially something that is underpriced: *a good buy.* [Buy, bought (past tense), bought (past participle); Middle English *byen* (earlier *byggen*), *bo(g)hte, (i)bo(g)ht,* Old English *bycgan, bohte, geboht,* from Germanic *bugjan* (unattested).] —**buy·a·ble** *adj.*

Usage: **Buy,** as a noun denoting a purchase or bargain, is appropriate only to commercial usage. Its use in a more general context (as in *luxury gained at the expense of liberty is never a good buy*) is considered by many to be unacceptable in written usage.

buy·er (bī′ər) *n.* **1.** One who buys goods; a customer. **2.** A purchasing agent, especially one who buys for a company or store.

buyers' market *n. Economics.* A market condition characterized by low prices, occurring when the supply of commodities exceeds market demand. Compare **sellers' market.**

Buys Bal·lot's law (bīs′bə-lŏts′) *n. Meteorology.* The principle that in the northern hemisphere an observer standing with his back to the wind has a lower atmospheric pressure on his left. In the southern hemisphere the pressure is lower on his right. [After C.H.D. *Buys Ballot,* 19th-century Dutch meteorologist.]

buzz¹ (bŭz) *v.* **buzzed, buzzing, buzzes.** —*intr.* **1.** To make a low droning or vibrating sound like that of a bee. **2.** To talk excitedly in low tones. **3.** To move quickly and busily; bustle. —*tr.* **1.** To cause to buzz: *hornets buzzing their wings.* **2.** To spread (gossip). **3.** *Informal.* To fly low over: *The plane buzzed the control tower.* **4.** To signal (a person) with a buzzer. **5.** *Informal.* To telephone (a person). —**buzz off.** *Informal.* To go away. Usually used in the imperative.

~*n.* **1.** A rapidly vibrating, humming, or droning sound. **2.** A low murmur, as of many hushed voices speaking at once: *a buzz of talk.* **3.** *Informal.* A telephone call. **4.** *Slang.* A pleasant euphoric feeling, as induced by drugs; a high. [Middle English *bussen* (attested only in the verbal noun *bussyng*), to drone (imitative).]

buzz² *tr.v.* **buzzed, buzzing, buzzes.** *Chiefly British Regional.* To drink (a bottle or cup) to the last drop. [From BUZZ (sound).]

buz·zard (bŭz′ərd) *n.* **1.** Any of various North American vultures, such as the **turkey buzzard** *(see).* **2.** Any hawk of the genus *Buteo,* having broad wings and a broad tail. **3.** An avaricious or unpleasant person. [Middle English *busard,* from Old French, alteration of *buson,* from Latin *būteō* (stem *būteōn-*).]

Buz·zards Bay (bŭz′ərdz). Inlet of the Atlantic Ocean, *c.* 48 kilometers (30 miles) long and from 8 to 16 kilometers (5 to 10 miles) wide, in southeastern Massachusetts. It is connected with Cape Cod Bay by the Cape Cod Canal. Its shoreline is very irregular.

buzz bomb *n.* A robot bomb *(see)* of World War II. [From the buzzing noise made by its pulsejet engine.]

buzz·er (bŭz′ər) *n.* Any of various electric signaling devices that make a buzzing sound, such as a doorbell.

buzz saw *n.* A circular saw *(see).* [From the sound it makes.]

buzz session *n.* An informal group discussion, as in a workshop or classroom.

buzz word *n. Informal.* A catchword; a jargon word, often one used to convey an impression of specialized knowledge. [From the meaninglessness or frequency of the word in question.]

B.V. Blessed Virgin.

B.V.M. Blessed Virgin Mary.

bvt. brevet; brevetted.

B.W.A. British West Africa.

bwa·na (bwä′nə) *n. East African.* A boss or employer. Often used as a term of respectful address. [Swahili, from Arabic *abūna,* our father.]

B.W.I. British West Indies.

bx. box.

by¹ (bī) *prep.* **1.** Next to; close to: *the window by the door.* **2.** Passing along or through: *He came by the back road.* **3.** Up to and beyond; past: *He drove by the house.* **4.** In the period of; during: *sleeping by day.* **5.** Not later than: *by five o'clock.* **6.** Used to indicate: **a.** Rate or amount: *letters by the thousand.* **b.** Units: *paid by the hour.* **7.** To the extent of: *shorter by two inches.* **8. a.** According to: *by his own admission.* **b.** In accordance with: *play by the rules.* **9.** In the presence or name of. Used in oaths: *swear by the Bible.* **10.** Used to indicate: **a.** A means: *done by machine.* **b.** A creator or originator: *a novel by Dickens.* **c.** The doer of an action: *The window was broken by some children.* **11.** Used to indicate a cause or reason: *thrifty by necessity.* **12.** Used to indicate a sign or piece of evidence: *I knew by his face that he was lying.* **13.** Used to indicate a point of contact: *take by the hand.* **14.** As regards; in respect of: *a plumber by trade.* **15.** As far as it concerns: *It's all right by me.* **16.** In succession to; after: *day by day.* **17.** Used to link certain expressions to be taken together and indicating: **a.** Multiplication or division of quantities. **b.** Coordination of measurements: *a room 12 by 18 feet.* **c.** Alteration of a compass direction: *north by northeast.* —**by the way.** Incidentally.

~*adv.* **1.** On hand; nearby: *stand by.* **2.** Aside; away: *He put it by for later.* **3.** Up to, alongside, and past: *The car raced by.* **4.** Into the past: *as years go by.* —**by and by.** Soon enough; in good time. —**by and large.** Generally; on the whole. [Middle English *by,* Old English *bī, bi, be.*]

Usage: *by, through, with.* These prepositions indicate the agency or means by which something is accomplished. *By* usually intro-

Byzantium

A CHRISTIAN EMPIRE UNDER CONSTANT THREAT
Politically weak, it displayed enduring cultural strength

Christianity, whose adherents Rome persecuted, was the binding force that enabled Byzantium—the Byzantine Empire—to survive for more than 1,100 years, long after the Roman Empire that gave it birth had perished. Christianity also inspired the art and architecture of Byzantium.

Byzantium owed its wealth to its position astride both north-south and east-west trade routes. It owed its traditions of law and government to Rome and its learning to Greece. But at its heart lay the Christian city of Constantinople. The city, formerly Byzantium, was rebuilt and renamed in 330 by the Roman emperor Constantine, who made it his capital, judging it to be better placed to withstand the barbarian invasions that threatened Rome. The empire, which retained its ancient name, became an increasingly independent entity after 395.

Constantine was the first emperor to see Christianity as a unifying force and to encourage it—fortunately so, for without such a bond the empire would probably have fallen. In the subsequent 11 centuries, Byzantium rarely enjoyed a year's peace. Under a succession of weak emperors, internal conflicts made "Byzantine" a byword for intrigue. Though the empire always included at least parts of the Balkan Peninsula and Turkey, its borders shifted constantly. It was assailed in turn by Goths, Huns, Persians, Avars, Bulgars, Vikings, Slavs, Arabs, Berbers, Turks, Normans, and the Crusaders, who looted Constantinople in 1204. In 1453, the Turkish sultan Mohammed II captured the city—he called it a "monstrous head without a body"—and the empire fell to Islam.

Byzantium's legacy lives on, however. Its own version of Christianity, independent of Rome after 1054, formed the basis of today's Orthodox churches, which claim over 120 million members; it preserved classical literature, an inspiration during the Renaissance; and Justinian's legal code remains the foundation of much European civil law.

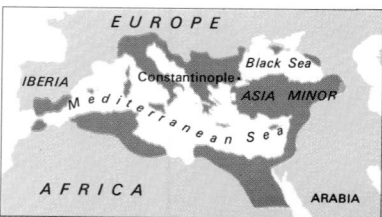

THE BYZANTINE EMPIRE *The blue area shows the extent of Byzantium in 550 after Justinian had retaken much of the former Roman Empire fringing the Mediterranean.*

EMPEROR JUSTINIAN *The greatest Byzantine emperor was Justinian (527–565). Backed by his formidable wife Theodora, he retook North Africa from the Vandals and Italy from the Ostrogoths. These gains were temporary, but his power enabled him to leave lasting monuments: gorgeous buildings, such as the Church of St. Sophia, and the codification of a millennium of Roman law. This massive work, the* Corpus Juris Civilis, *has influenced the intellectual, social, and political life of Europe ever since. It is a comprehensive guide to Roman law and the basic document of civil law throughout Europe today.*

GREEK FIRE *During the 7th century, when Arabs swept to conquest in the Middle East, they besieged Constantinople for five years (673–678). The city was saved by a new flame-throwing weapon. It emitted "Greek fire," an explosive mixture that probably contained sulfur, naphtha, and quicklime. The results were devastating, as this 14th-century painting shows.*

---

duces directly the agent (person) or agency (power): *named by him; struck by lightning. Through,* the least direct, is often followed by a person, in the sense of intermediary (*apply through a friend*), or by a word naming a condition as cause or means (*fail through indecision*). *With* is usually followed by an inanimate object denoting physical instrument (*fight with a sword*) or instrumentality (*soothe with kind words*).

by². Variant of **bye.**

by–, bye– *prefix.* Indicates: **1.** Close at hand or near; for example, **bystander. 2.** Out of the way or aside; for example, **byroad, by-election. 3.** Secondary or incidental; for example, **by-product.** [Middle English *by-, bi-,* from BY.]

by and by *adv.* At a later time; before long. [Middle English, side by side, again and again, one by one, from BY.]

by-and-by (bī′ən-bī′) *n.* **1.** Some future time or occasion. **2.** The hereafter.

by-bid·der (bī-bĭd′ər) *n.* A person who bids at an auction to raise prices for the owner.

Byb·los (bĭb′lŏs). An ancient Phoenician port and the chief city of Phoenicia during the 2nd millennium B.C. It stood northeast of present-day Beirut on the site of modern Jubayl (the biblical Gebal). It was famous for its papyrus.

by-blow (bī′blō′) *n. Archaic.* **1.** An indirect or chance blow. **2.** An illegitimate child; a bastard. [Sense 2 from the idea of a child begotten incidentally or by chance.]

Byd·goszcz (bĭd′gôshch). City, capital of Bydgoszcz province, in north-central Poland on the Brda River, a tributary of the Vistula. One of Poland's major inland ports, it is on the Bydgoszcz Canal (built 1773–74), a part of the Vistula-Oder waterway. Chartered in 1346, the city developed during the Middle Ages around the site of a prehistoric fort. In World War II it was occupied by German forces from 1939 to 1945 and suffered heavy damages.

bye, by (bī) *n.* **1.** A secondary matter; a side issue. **2.** *Sports.* The position of one who draws no opponent for a round in a tournament and so advances to the next round. **3.** *Golf.* One or more holes remaining unplayed at the end of a match. **4.** *Cricket.* A run made off a ball not touched by the batsman. Compare **leg bye. —by the bye** (or **by**). Incidentally; by the way. [From BY (aside, hence, "secondary").]

bye–. Variant of **by–.**

bye-bye (bī′bī′) *interj. Informal.* Goodbye. [Baby-talk form.]

bye-byes (bī′bīz′) *n. Informal.* Sleep; bed. Used especially to children. [From BYE-BYE.]

by-e·lec·tion, bye-e·lec·tion (bī′ĭ-lĕk′shən) *n.* A special election held between regular elections to fill a vacancy in a legislature; especially, in the United Kingdom and other Commonwealth countries, an election to Parliament occurring between general elections.

Byelorussia. See **Belorussia.**

Byelorussian. Variant of **Belorussian.**

by·gone (bī′gôn′, -gŏn′) *adj.* Past; gone by; former. ~ *n.* A past occurrence. **—let bygones be bygones.** To let past differences be forgotten; be reconciled.

by-lane (bī′lān′) *n.* A side road; a byway.

by-law (bī′lô′) *n.* **1.** A regulation made by a local authority, corporation, or the like, having legal effect only in the area governed by that authority. **2.** A law or rule governing the internal affairs of an organization. [Middle English *bilawe, bylawe,* "village law," probably from Old Norse *bȳr,* village + *lög,* law.]

by-line (bī′līn′) *n.* A line at the head or foot of a newspaper or magazine article with the author's name. ~ *tr.v.* **by-lined, -lining, -lines.** To write (an article) under a by-line. **—by-lin·er** *n.*

by-name (bī′nām′) *n.* **1.** A surname. **2.** A nickname.

Byng (bĭng), **George, Viscount Torrington** (1663–1733). English admiral. He persuaded the navy to support William of Orange against James II in 1688 and later repelled the attempted Jacobite invasions of 1708 and 1715. His greatest victory was the defeat of the Spanish fleet in the Strait of Messina (1718).

Byng, John (1704–57). English admiral, son of George Viscount Torrington. After his failure to relieve Menorca from a French siege and his subsequent withdrawal from the island, he was court-martialed and executed for neglect of duty.

BYOB, b.y.o.b. Bring your own bottle.

by-pass, by·pass (bī′păs′, -päs′) *n.* **1.** A road, especially a main road, that passes around or to one side of an obstructed or congested area; a detour. **2.** A pipe or channel to conduct gas or liquid around another pipe or a fixture. **3.** Any means of circumvention. **4.** *Electronics.* A shunt (*see*). **5.** *Medicine.* **a.** An apparatus used to keep the blood circulating and oxygenated while surgery is performed on the heart. **b.** A surgical operation to pass around an obstructed passage, as in an artery or intestine. Also used adjectivally: *by-pass surgery.* **c.** An alternative passage created in such an operation. **d.** A horseshoe-shaped length of tubing worn on the arm by a patient requiring regular treatment on a kidney machine. ~ *tr.v.* **by-passed, -passing, -passes.** Also **by·pass. 1.** To go around instead of through; avoid (an obstacle). **2.** To proceed heedless of; ignore or circumvent: *by-passing office procedures.* **3.** To cause (a fluid or electricity, for example) to follow a by-pass.

by-pass engine *n.* A jet engine in which some of the air intake by-passes the combustion zone, flowing directly into or around the main exhaust gas flow to provide additional thrust.

by-past (bī′păst′) *adj.* Past; bygone.

by-path (bī'păth', -päth') *n., pl.* **-paths** (-păthz, -päthz). An indirect or little-used path.

by-play (bī'plā') *n.* Secondary action or speech taking place while the main action proceeds, especially in a play.

by-prod-uct (bī'prŏd'əkt) *n.* **1.** Something, especially something useful, that is produced in the making of something else. **2.** A secondary result; a side effect.

Byrd (bûrd), **Richard Evelyn** (1888–1957). U.S. aviator and polar explorer. In 1926 he made the first flight over the North Pole. Between 1929 and 1956 he led five scientific and exploratory air expeditions to the South Pole, voyages that established the basis of American claims to territory in Antarctica.

Byrd, William (c. 1543–1623). English composer, one of the foremost of early English musicians. The best known of his works today are his settings of the Anglican service and his three Masses.

byre (bīr) *n.* A cowshed or barn. [Middle English *byre*, Old English *bȳre*, stall, hut, perhaps variant of BOWER.]

byr-nie (bûr'nē) *n. Archaic.* A breastplate or a coat or shirt of mail. [Middle English *brinie*, from Old Norse *brynja*.]

by-road (bī'rōd') *n.* A side road; a minor road.

By-ron (bī'rən), **George Gordon, 6th Baron** (1788–1824). British poet, one of the leading figures of the English romantic movement. The first two cantos of *Childe Harold's Pilgrimage*, which appeared in 1812, made him the darling of London society. *Manfred* (1817), in which the full "Byronic hero"—lonely, rebellious, secretive—appeared. His last work, *Don Juan* (1819–24), is considered by many to be the finest satirical and comic poem in the English language. In 1824 he sailed to Greece to help in the nationalist revolt against Turkish rule. He caught a fever and died.

By-ron-ic (bī-rŏn'ĭk) *adj.* Of or characteristic of Byron or his works; especially, adventurous and wildly romantic. **—By-ron-i-cal-ly** *adv.*

bys-sin-o-sis (bĭs'ə-nō'sĭs) *n.* A lung disease affecting textile workers, caused by prolonged exposure to cotton dust and characterized by wheezing. [New Latin, from Greek *bussinos,* of BYSSUS + -OSIS.]

bys-sus (bĭs'əs) *n., pl.* **-suses** or **byssi** (bĭs'ī'). **1.** *Zoology.* A mass of filaments by means of which certain bivalve mollusks, such as mussels, attach themselves to fixed surfaces. **2.** A fine-textured linen of ancient times, used by the Egyptians as wrapping for mummies. [Latin, from Greek *bussos,* flax, linen.]

by-stand-er (bī'stăn'dər) *n.* A person who is present at some event without participating in it.

by-street (bī'strēt') *n.* A small side street; an alley.

by-talk (bī'tôk') *n.* Unimportant talk; small talk.

byte (bīt) *n. Computer Science.* **1.** A group of bits of information, typically six or eight, treated as a unit in a computer process.

2. The space occupied by a single character in a computer store. [Probably from BIT + BITE.]

By-tom (bī'tôm). City of southwestern Poland, in the Katowice mining region. It is an important industrial center, with factories producing metal products and furniture. The city was chartered in 1254 and held by the Hapsburgs from 1526 until 1742, when it passed to Prussia. It was incorporated into Poland in 1945.

by-way (bī'wā') *n.* **1. a.** A small country road or lane. **b.** An unimportant or partially hidden side road. **2.** A secondary or unexplored field of study.

by-word (bī'wûrd') *n.* **1.** A well-known saying; a proverb. **2.** One that proverbially represents a type, class, or quality. **3.** An object of contempt or notoriety. **4.** A nickname or epithet. [Middle English *biword,* Old English *bīword* (translation of Latin *prōverbium,* PROVERB) : BY + WORD.]

by-work (bī'wûrk') *n.* Work done during one's spare time.

by-your-leave (bī'yər-lēv') *n.* A request for permission. Used chiefly in the phrase *without so much as a by-your-leave.*

byzant. Variant of **bezant.**

By-zan-tine (bĭz'ən-tēn', -tīn', bĭ-zăn'tīn) *adj.* **1.** Of, pertaining to, or characteristic of Byzantium, its inhabitants, or their culture. **2.** Of or designating the style of architecture developed from the 5th century A.D. in Byzantium, characterized by round arches, massive domes, intricate spires and minarets, and extensive use of mosaic. **3.** Of or designating the style of painting and design developed in Byzantium, characterized by formality of design, stylized presentation of figures, rich use of color, especially gold, and generally religious subject matter. **4.** Of the Eastern Orthodox Church or the rites performed in it. **5.** *Sometimes* **byzantine.** Complicated; labyrinthine; devious. **6.** *Sometimes* **byzantine.** Rigid; inflexible. *~n.* A native or inhabitant of Byzantium.

Byzantine Empire. *Arabic* **Rum** (rōom). The successor to the Roman Empire, dating from A.D. 330, when Constantine I rebuilt Byzantium, named it Constantinople, and made it the capital of the Roman Empire. It was also called the Eastern Empire, especially after 395, when Honorius became emperor in the east and Arcadius emperor in the west, thus making permanent the split in the Roman Empire. Although its extent varied through the centuries, the core of the empire was always the Balkan Peninsula and Asia Minor. The last Byzantine emperor was Constantine XI Palaeologus, who reigned from 1449–1453. Constantinople fell to the Ottoman Turks in 1453, a defeat that marked the end of the empire.

By-zan-ti-um (bĭ-zăn'shē-əm, -tē-əm). **1.** A Greek city on the site of which Constantine built the city of **Constantinople** *(see)* in A.D. 330. **2.** The Byzantine Empire and its culture.

C

cabbage *Green cabbage is known to have been eaten in the Bronze Age. It is cultivated in most countries of the world.*

c, C (sē) *n., pl.* **c's** or **C's. 1.** The third letter of the modern English alphabet. See feature at **alphabet. 2.** Any of the speech sounds represented by this letter. **3. C** The third best or highest in quality, class, or rank; especially, the third highest mark awarded for academic work. **4.** *Music.* **a.** The first tone in the scale of C major, or the third tone in the relative minor scale. **b.** The key or a scale in which C is the tonic. **c.** A written or printed note representing this tone. **d.** A string, key, or pipe tuned to the pitch of this tone. **5.** Something shaped like the letter **C**.

c, C, c., C. *Note:* As an abbreviation or symbol, *c* may be a small or a capital letter, with or without a period. Established forms or those generally preferred precede the definition. When no form is given, all four forms are in general use in that sense. **1. c** *Physics.* candle. **2. C** *Electricity.* capacitance. **3. c., C.** capacity. **4. c., C.** cape. **5. c** carat. **6. C** The symbol for the element carbon. **7. c., C.** carton. **8. c., C.** case. **9. C.** Catholic. **10. c., C.** *Baseball.* catcher. **11. C** Celsius. **12. C.** Celtic. **13. c., C.** cent. **14. c** centi-. **15. C** centigrade. **16. c., C.** centime. **17. c., C.** century. **18. C.** chancellor. **19. c., C.** chapter. **20. C** *Physics.* charge conjugation. **21. C.** chief. **22. c., C.** church. **23. c.** circa (usually italic *c.*). **24. C.** city. **25. c.** cloudy. **26. C.** companion. **27. c., C.** congius. **28. C.** Congress. **29. C.** Conservative. **30. c, C** *Mathematics.* constant. **31. c., C.** consul. **32. c., C.** copy. **33. c., C.** copyright. **34. c., C.** corps. **35. C** coulomb. **36. C.** court. **37. c** cubic. **38. c.** cup. **39. C** The Roman numeral for 100 [Latin *centum.*] **40.** The third in a series.

Ca The symbol for the element calcium.

CA 1. California (used with Zip Code). **2.** chronological age.

C.A. 1. Central America. **2.** chartered accountant. **3.** chronological age.

C.A.A. Civil Aeronautics Authority.

Caaba. See **Kaaba.**

cab¹ (kăb) *n.* **1.** A taxi (*see*). **2.** The covered compartment of a heavy vehicle or machine, such as a truck or locomotive, in which the operator or driver sits. **3.** Formerly, a one-horse vehicle for public hire. [Short for CABRIOLET.]

cab², kab *n.* A Hebrew measure equal to about two quarts. [Hebrew *qabh,* "hollow vessel."]

ca·bal (kə-băl′) *n.* **1.** A conspiratorial group of plotters or intriguers. **2.** A secret scheme or plot. —See Synonyms at **conspiracy.**
~*intr.v.* **caballed, -balling, -bals.** To form a cabal; plot; conspire. [French *cabale,* from Medieval Latin *cabala,* CABALA. The term was popularized during the reign of Charles II, when it was applied to the ministry of Clifford, Arlington, Buckingham, Ashley, and Lauderdale.]

cab·a·la, cab·ba·la, kab·a·la, kab·ba·la (kăb′ə-lə, kə-bä′lə) *n.* **1.** *Often* **Cabala.** An occult mystical philosophy of rabbinical origin, widely transmitted in medieval Europe, based on an esoteric interpretation of the Hebrew Scriptures. **2.** Any secret doctrine. [Medieval Latin, from Hebrew *qabbālāh,* received doctrine, tradition, from *qābal,* to receive.] —**cab·a·lism** *n.* —**cab·a·list** *n.*

cab·a·lis·tic (kăb′ə-lĭs′tĭk) *adj.* **1.** Of or pertaining to the Cabala. **2.** Having secret or hidden meaning; occult; mysterious.

cab·al·le·ro (kăb′ə-lâr′ō; *Spanish* kăb′əl-yâr′ō) *n., pl.* **-ros.** In Spanish-speaking countries, a gentleman; a cavalier. [Spanish, from Late Latin *caballārius,* a horse groom, from Latin *caballus,* a horse. See **cavalier.**]

ca·ban·a (kə-băn′ə, -băn′yə) *n.* Also **ca·ba·ña** (kə-bä′nyə). A shelter on a beach used as a bathhouse. [Spanish *cabaña,* from Late Latin *capanna,* hut. CABIN.]

cab·a·ret (kăb′ə-rā′) *n.* **1.** Live entertainment in a restaurant or nightclub, with performances by singers, comedians, dancers, and the like. **2.** A restaurant or nightclub that provides such entertainment. [French, tavern, from Old French, probably of dialect (Walloon) origin.]

cab·bage (kăb′ĭj) *n.* **1.** An edible plant, *Brassica oleracea capitata,* many varieties of which are grown in temperate climates throughout the world, having a short, thick stalk and a large head formed by tightly overlapping green or reddish leaves. **2.** The head of a cabbage. **3.** An edible leaf bud of the **cabbage palm** (*see*). **4.** *Slang.*

cabriole *The cabriole leg on chairs, cabinets, and tables was used by the ancient Chinese and by the Greeks. It became fashionable in Europe in the late 17th century.*

Money, especially in the form of bills.
~*intr.v.* **cabbaged, -baging, -bages.** To form or grow in a head, as cabbage does. [Middle English *caboche,* from Old North French, variant of Old French *caboce†,* "head."] —**cab·ba·gy** *adj.*

cabbage butterfly *n.* Any of several white butterflies of the genus *Pieris,* having larvae that feed on cabbages and other brassicas.

cabbage moth *n.* A brown-gray moth, *Mamestra brassicae,* whose caterpillars are a horticultural pest.

cabbage palm *n.* A tropical American palm tree, *Roystonea oleracea,* having leaf buds that are edible when young.

cabbage palmetto *n.* See **palmetto.**

cabbage rose *n.* A prickly shrub, *Rosa centifolia,* native to the Caucasus, having large, fragrant, many-petaled pink flowers. It is cultivated in gardens in many varieties.

cab·bage·worm (kăb′ĭj-wûrm′) *n.* Any of several caterpillars that feed on cabbage; especially, the bright green larva of the **cabbage butterfly** (*see*).

cabbage yellow *n.* A disease of cabbage marked by the yellowing of leaves and caused by the fungus *Fusarium conglutinans.*

cab·by, cab·bie (kăb′ē) *n., pl.* **-bies.** *Informal.* A taxi driver.

Cab·ell (kăb′əl), **James Branch** (1879–1958). U.S. essayist and novelist. He wrote many stories and novels that satirized life in Virginia, his home state. *Jurgen* (1919) was his best-known book. He was among the prestigious writers who edited the satirical magazine *American Spectator* (1932–35).

ca·ber (kā′bər, kä′-) *n.* A heavy wooden pole, usually the trunk of a young pine tree, thrown in the air as a trial of strength in Scottish Highland games: *tossing the caber.* [Gaelic *cabar.*]

ca·ber·net sau·vi·gnon (kăb′ər-nā′ sō-vēn-yōN′) *n.* A variety of black grape grown in France and many other countries. It is the main variety used in claret. [French.]

Ca·be·za de Va·ca (kə-bā′zə də vä′kə), **Alvar Núñez** (c. 1490–c. 1577). Spanish explorer and colonial administrator. After exploring parts of present-day Florida, Texas, and Mexico, he recounted vivid stories of riches and opportunity in the region, thus arousing Spain's interest in southern and southwestern North America.

cab·in (kăb′ĭn) *n.* **1.** A small, roughly or simply built house, cottage, or hut. **2. a.** In a ship, a room used as living quarters by an officer or passenger. **b.** In a boat, an enclosed compartment serving as a shelter or as living quarters. **c.** In an aircraft, the enclosed space for the crew, passengers, or cargo.
~*tr.v.* **cabined, -ining, -ins.** To confine, as in a cabin. [Middle English *cabane,* from Old French, from Old Provençal, from Late Latin *capanna†,* hut, cabin.]

cabin boy *n.* A boy servant aboard a ship.

cabin class *n.* A class of accommodation on some passenger ships, lower than first class and higher than tourist class. —**cab·in-class** *adj. & adv.*

cabin cruiser *n.* See **cruiser** (sense 3).

cab·i·net (kăb′ə-nĭt) *n.* **1.** An upright cupboard or case with shelves, drawers, or compartments for the display or display of a collection of objects or materials. **2.** A container for a record-player, television set, or the like. **3.** A small or private room set aside for some specific activity. **4.** *Often* **Cabinet.** A powerful advisory and policy-making body appointed by a head of state or prime minister, and comprising those ministers who head the most important government departments.
~*adj.* **1.** Of suitable value, beauty, or size to be kept or displayed in a cabinet: *a cabinet edition.* **2.** Belonging or pertaining to a political cabinet: *a cabinet minister.* **3.** Used for cabinetwork: *teak and other heavy cabinet woods.* [CABIN + -ET, after French *cabinet,* from *cabinet†,* a gambling house.]

cab·i·net·mak·er (kăb′ə-nĭt-mā′kər) *n.* A craftsman specializing in making fine wooden furniture. —**cab·i·net·mak·ing** *n.*

cab·i·net·work (kăb′ə-nĭt-wûrk′) *n.* Finished woodwork made by a cabinetmaker.

ca·ble (kā′bəl) *n.* **1.** A strong, large-diameter, heavy steel or fiber rope. **2.** *Electricity.* A bound or sheathed group of mutually insulated conductors. **3. a.** *Nautical.* A heavy rope or chain for mooring

or anchoring a ship. **b.** A unit of nautical length equal to about 720 feet in the United States and 608 feet in England. Also called "cable's length." **4.** A cablegram. **5.** A **cable stitch** *(see).*
~v. **cabled, -bling, -bles.** *—tr.* **1. a.** To send a cablegram to. **b.** To transmit (a message) by telegraph. **2.** To supply or fasten with a cable or cables. *—intr.* To send a cablegram. [Middle English, from Norman French, from Late Latin *capulum,* rope for fastening cattle, from Latin *capere,* to take.]
cable car *n.* A passenger car used on a cableway or cable railway.
ca·ble·cast (kā′bəl-kăst′) *n.* A telecast by cable television. **—ca′ble′cast′** *v.* **—ca′ble·cast′er** *n.*
ca·ble·gram (kā′bəl-grăm′) *n.* An overseas telegram sent by submarine cable.
ca·ble-laid (kā′bəl-lād′) *adj.* Made of three ropes of three strands each, twisted together counterclockwise.
cable railway *n.* A railway on which the cars are suspended on and moved by an endless cable driven by a stationary engine.
cable release *n.* A short length of flexible cable used to operate the shutter of a camera without moving or shaking the camera.
cable stitch *n.* A knitting technique or stitch that produces a twisted rope design. Also called "cable." **—ca·ble-stitch** *adj.*
ca·blet (kā′blĭt) *n.* A cable-laid rope with a circumference of less than 10 inches; a small cable. [Diminutive of CABLE.]
cable television *n.* A television system in which signals are delivered to subscribers' receivers by cable. Also called "cablevision."
ca·ble·vi·sion (kā′bəl-vĭzh′ən) *n.* **Cable television** *(see).*
ca·ble·way (kā′bəl-wā′) *n.* An overhead cable and apparatus for carrying materials, goods, and passengers, normally secured between terminal towers.
cab·man (kăb′mən) *n., pl.* **-men** (-mĭn). The driver of a cab.
cab·o·chon (kăb′ə-shŏn′) *n.* **1.** A highly polished, convex-cut, unfaceted gem. **2.** This style of cutting. [Old French, diminutive of Old North French *caboche, caboce,* head. See **cabbage.**]
ca·boo·dle (kə-bo͞od′l) *n. Informal.* The lot, group, or bunch. Used chiefly in the phrase *the whole kit and caboodle.* [19th century (U.S.) : perhaps contraction of phrase *kit and boodle.*]
ca·boose (kə-bo͞os′) *n.* **1.** The last car on a freight train, having kitchen and sleeping facilities for the train crew. **2.** *Obsolete.* **a.** A ship's galley. **b.** Any of various cast-iron cooking ranges used in such galleys during the early 19th century. **c.** An outdoor oven or fireplace. [Probably from Dutch *kabuis,* ship's supply room or galley, from Middle Low German *kabūse*†.]
Cab·ot (kăb′ət), **John** (*c.* 1425–98). *Italian* **Giovanni Ca·bo·to** (kä-bō′tə). Italian explorer from Genoa who settled in Bristol and led the first English expedition to America. In 1497, under letters patent from Henry VII, he set sail and discovered Newfoundland and Nova Scotia, thinking them to be part of Asia.
cab·o·tage (kăb′ə-täzh′) *n.* **1.** Trade or navigation in coastal waters. **2.** The exclusive right of a country to operate the air traffic within its territory. [French, from *caboter,* to coast, probably from Spanish *cabo,* cape, headland, from Latin *caput,* head.]
Ca·bri·ni (kə-brē′nē), **Saint Frances Xavier,** born Maria Francesca Cabrini, known as "Mother Cabrini" (1850–1917). Italian-born founder of the Missionary Sisters of the Sacred Heart and the first citizen of the United States to be canonized (1946).
cab·ri·ole (kăb′rē-ōl′) *n.* A form of furniture leg, characteristic of Queen Anne and Chippendale furniture, that curves outward and then narrows downward into an ornamental foot. [French, "caper" (from its resemblance to the foreleg of a capering animal). See **capriole.**]
cab·ri·o·let (kăb′rē-ə-lā′) *n.* **1.** A two-wheeled, one-horse vehicle with two seats and a folding top. **2.** A car with a folding roof; a convertible coupé. [French, diminutive of *cabriole,* caper (in allusion to its bounding motion). See **capriole.**]
cab·stand (kăb′stănd′) *n.* A place designated for taxicabs waiting for hire.
ca·ca·o (kə-kä′ō, -kā′ō) *n., pl.* **-os. 1.** An evergreen tropical American tree, *Theobroma cacao,* having yellowish flowers and reddish-brown seed pods. **2.** The seed of this tree, used in making chocolate, cocoa, and cocoa butter. In this sense, also called "cacao bean," "cocoa bean." [Spanish, from Nahuatl *cacahuatl,* cacao tree.]
cacao butter *n.* **Cocoa butter** *(see).*
cach·a·lot (kăsh′ə-lŏt′, kăsh′ə-lō′) *n.* The **sperm whale** *(see).* [French, from Spanish and Portuguese *cachalote*†.]
cache (kăsh) *n.* **1.** A hole or similar hiding place for the concealment and storage of provisions, weapons, or valuables. **2.** A store of goods or articles hidden in a cache.
~tr.v. **cached, caching, caches.** To store in a hiding place for future use. —See Synonyms at **hide.** [French, from *cacher,* to hide, from Vulgar Latin *cōacticāre* (unattested), to compress, from Latin *cōactāre,* to constrain, from *cōgere* (past participle *cōactus*), to drive together : *com-,* together + *agere,* to drive.]
ca·chet (kă-shā′) *n.* **1.** A seal on a letter or document. **2.** Distinction; prestige: *social cachet.* **3. a.** A commemorative design stamped on an envelope to mark some postal or philatelic event. **b.** A motto forming part of a postal cancellation. **4.** A kind of wafer capsule formerly used by pharmacists for presenting an unpleasant-tasting drug. [Old French, from *cacher,* to hide, press together. See **cache.**]
ca·chex·i·a (kă-kĕk′sē-ə) *n.* A general wasting of the body or weakening of the brain during any debilitating chronic disease. [Late Latin, from Greek *kakhexia,* bad condition of the body : CAC(O)- + *hexis,* condition, from *ekhein,* to hold, be in a condition.] **—ca·chec·tic** *adj.*
cach·in·nate (kăk′ə-nāt′) *intr.v.* **-nated, -nating, -nates.** To laugh loud, hard, or convulsively; guffaw. [Latin *cachinnāre*†.] **—cach·in·na·tion** *n.*
ca·chou (kă-sho͞o′, kăsh′o͞o) *n.* **1.** An astringent, **catechu** *(see).* **2.** A pastille used to sweeten the breath. [French, from Portuguese *cachu,* from Malayalam *cāccu.*]
ca·chu·cha (kä-cho͞o′chä) *n.* A Spanish solo dance in 3/4 time. [Spanish, origin obscure.]
ca·cique (kə-sĕk′) *n.* Also **ca·zique** (-zēk′). **1.** An Indian chief, especially in the Spanish West Indies and other parts of Latin America during colonial and postcolonial times. **2.** A powerful local politician in Latin America or Spain. **3.** Any of various tropical American orioles. [Spanish, of Arawakan origin; akin to Arawak *kassequa,* chief, Taino *cacique.*]
cack·le (kăk′əl) *v.* **-led, -ling, -les.** *—intr.* **1.** To make the shrill, broken cry characteristic of a hen after laying an egg. **2.** To laugh or talk in a similar manner. *—tr.* To utter in cackles.
~n. **1.** The act or sound of cackling. **2.** Shrill, brittle laughter. **3.** Foolish chatter. [Middle English *cakelen,* probably from Middle Low German *kakeln* (imitative).] **—cack·ler** *n.*
caco– *prefix.* Indicates bad, incorrect, or unpleasant; for example, **cacography.** [Greek *kako-,* from *kakos,* bad.]
cac·o·dyl (kăk′ə-dĭl′) *n.* **1.** The arsenic group $As(CH_3)_2$. **2.** A poisonous oil, $As_2(CH_3)_4$, with an obnoxious garlicky odor. [Greek *kakōdēs,* bad-smelling : CACO- + *-ōdēs,* from *ozein,* to smell + -YL.] **—cac·o·dyl·ic** *adj.*
cac·o·ë·thes (kăk′ō-ē′thēz) *n.* A mania or irresistible compulsion; a pernicious habit. [Latin, from Greek *kakoethes,* from the neuter of *kakoēthēs,* ill-disposed, abominable, malignant: CACO- + *ēthos,* custom, disposition.]
cac·o·gen·ics (kăk′ə-jĕn′ĭks) *n.* **Dysgenics** *(see).* [CACO- + -GENIC(S).] **—cac·o·gen·ic** *adj.*
ca·cog·ra·phy (kă-kŏg′rə-fē) *n.* **1.** Bad handwriting. Compare **calligraphy. 2.** Incorrect spelling. Compare **orthography.** [CACO- + -GRAPHY.]
cac·o·mis·tle (kăk′ə-mĭs′əl) *n.* Also **cac·o·mix·le** (-mĭx′səl) Either of two small, carnivorous mammals, *Bassariscus astutus,* of the southwest United States, or *Jentinkia sumichrasti,* of Central America, related to the raccoons and having grayish or brownish fur and a black-banded tail. Also called "ringtail," "ring-tailed cat." [Mexican Spanish, from Nahuatl *tlacomiztli* : *tlaco,* half + *miztli,* puma.]
ca·coph·o·nous (kə-kŏf′ə-nəs) *adj.* Having a harsh, unpleasant sound; discordant. [Greek *kakophōnos* : CACO- + *phōnē,* sound.] **—ca·coph′o·nous·ly** *adv.*
ca·coph·o·ny (kă-kŏf′ə-nē) *n., pl.* **-nies. 1.** Jarring, discordant sound; dissonance. **2.** The use of harsh-sounding or unharmonious language. Compare **euphony.** [French *cacophonie,* from Greek *kakophōnia,* from *kakophōnos* : CACO- + *phōnē,* sound.]
cac·tus (kăk′təs) *n., pl.* **-tuses** or **-ti** (-tī′). Any of a large group of plants of the family Cactaceae, mostly native to arid regions of the New World. They are characterized by thick, fleshy, often prickly stems that function as leaves and in some species have showy flowers and edible fruit. [New Latin, from Latin, the cardoon, from Greek *kaktos*†.]
Usage: The regular plural of this word, *cactuses,* is increasingly being used in formal contexts in place of *cacti.* In strictly technical usage, *cacti* remains the preferred form.
ca·cu·mi·nal (kă-kyo͞o′mə-nəl) *adj. Phonetics.* Pronounced with the tip of the tongue turned back and up toward the roof of the mouth; retroflex.
~n. Phonetics. A cacuminal consonant. [Latin *cacūmen* (stem *cacūmin-*), summit, treetop, point.]
cad (kăd) *n.* An ungentlemanly man. Now usually used humorously. [Short for CADDIE.] **—cad·dish** *adj.* **—cad·dish·ly** *adv.* **—cad·dish·ness** *n.*
ca·das·ter (kə-dăs′tər) *n.* Also **ca·das·tre.** A public record, survey, or map of the value, extent, and ownership of land as a basis of taxation. [French *cadastre,* from Italian *catastro,* variant of Old Italian *catastico,* from Late Greek *katastikhon,* list, from *kata stikhon,* "line by line."] **—ca·das·tral** *adj.*
ca·dav·er (kə-dăv′ər) *n.* A dead body, especially one considered for medical purposes or intended for dissection. [Latin, from *cadere,* to fall, "die."] **—ca·dav·er·ic** *adj.*
ca·dav·er·ine (kə-dăv′ə-rēn′) *n.* A syrupy, colorless fuming ptomaine, $NH_2(CH_2)_5NH_2$, formed from decaying animal flesh.
ca·dav·er·ous (kə-dăv′ər-əs) *adj.* **1. a.** Corpselike. **b.** Sickly pale. **2.** Gaunt and haggard; emaciated: *a cadaverous face.* **—ca·dav·er·ous·ly** *adv.* **—ca·dav·er·ous·ness** *n.*
cad·die, cad·dy (kăd′ē) *n., pl.* **-dies.** A golfer's hired attendant, who carries his clubs.
~intr.v. **caddied, -dying, -dies.** To serve as a caddie. [French *cadet,* CADET.]
cad·dis, cad·dice (kăd′ĭs) *n.* A coarse woolen fabric, yarn, or ribbon binding. [Middle English *cadas,* from Old French *cadaz,* from Provençal *cadarz*†.]
caddis fly *n.* Also **caddice fly.** Any of various four-winged insects of the order Trichoptera, found near lakes and streams. [17th century: origin obscure.]
caddis worm *n.* Also **caddice worm.** The aquatic, wormlike larva of the caddis fly, commonly enclosed in a cylindrical case covered with grains of sand, fragments of shell, or the like.

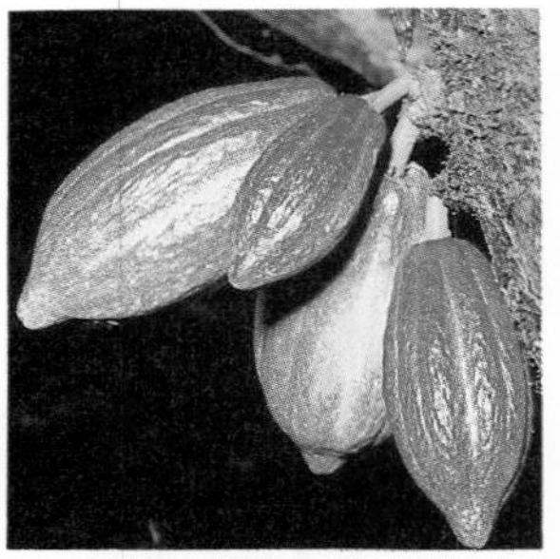
cacao *The reddish seedpods of* Theobroma cacao, *a tropical American tree, produce the beans from which chocolate is made.*

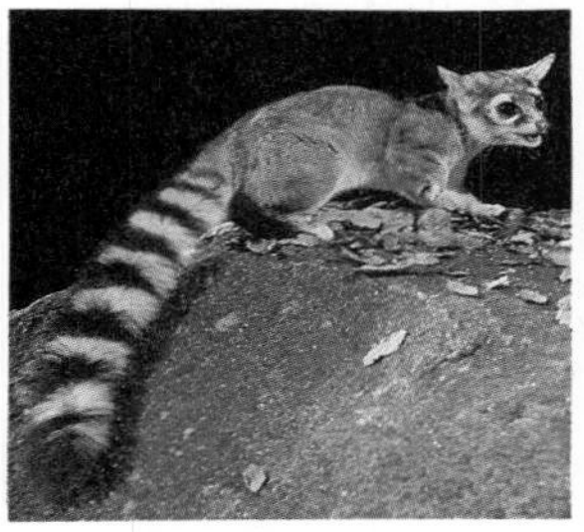
cacomistle *A native of the southwestern United States and Mexico, the cacomistle is a tree-dwelling relative of the raccoon and feeds at night on small animals, fruit, and vegetables.*

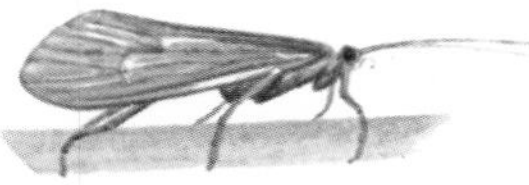
caddis fly *Adult caddis flies, like the one shown here, are nocturnal insects that resemble brownish moths. Some species are used as bait by anglers.*

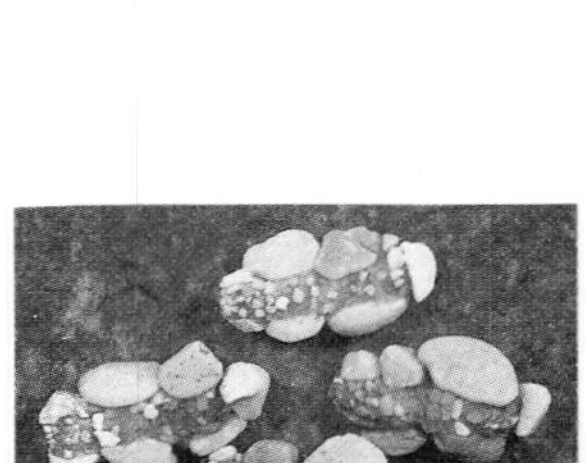
caddis worm *The larvae of many of the 5,000 species of the caddis fly construct portable cases of silk, covered with sand, leaves, and shells. They live in these cases with only their armored heads protruding until they are ready to become adults.*

cad·dy¹ (kăd′ē) *n., pl.* **-dies.** A small box or other container, especially for holding tea. [Originally "a container of one caddy of tea," from Malay *kātī* (weight of 605 grams; 1⅓ pounds).]

caddy². Variant of **caddie.**

cade¹ (kād) *adj.* Left by its mother and raised by hand: *a cade calf.* [Middle English *cad*†.]

cade² *n.* A juniper shrub, *Juniperus oxycedrus,* of the Mediterranean region, the wood of which yields an oily brown liquid *(oil of cade)* used to treat skin ailments. [French, from Old Provençal, from Medieval Latin *catanus,* probably from Gaulish *catănos* (unattested).]

Cade (kād), **Jack** (died 1450). English rebel who led an unsuccessful rebellion against Henry VI (1450) and called for the return of Richard Plantagenet, the Duke of York, from Ireland.

-cade *suffix.* Indicates procession or parade; for example, **motorcade.** [From CAVALCADE.]

ca·delle (kə-dĕl′) *n.* A small blackish beetle, *Tenebroides mauritanicus,* both the larval and adult forms of which damage stored grain and packaged foods. [French, from Provençal *cadello,* from Latin *catella,* feminine of *catellus, catulus,* offspring.]

ca·dence (kād′ns) *n.* **1.** Balanced, rhythmic flow, as of poetry or oratory. **2.** The measure or beat of movement, as in dancing or marching. **3. a.** A falling inflection of the voice, as at the end of a sentence. **b.** The general modulation of the voice; intonation. **4.** *Music.* A progression of chords moving to a harmonic close or point of rest. —See Synonyms at **rhythm.** [Middle English, from Old French, from Old Italian *cadenza,* from *cadere,* to fall, from Latin.] —**ca·denced** *adj.*

ca·dent (kād′nt) *adj.* **1.** Having cadence or rhythm. **2.** *Archaic.* Falling. [Latin *cadēns* (stem *cadent-*), present participle of *cadere,* to fall.]

ca·den·za (kə-dĕn′zə) *n. Music.* **1.** An elaborate ornamental flourish interpolated into an aria or other vocal piece. **2.** An extended, virtuoso section for the soloist near the end of a movement of a concerto. [Italian, CADENCE.]

ca·det (kə-dĕt′) *n.* **1.** A student training for service in the armed forces or police force, usually at a college. **2.** A younger son or brother.
—*adj.* Pertaining to or descended from a younger son: *the cadet branch of the family.* [French, from Gascon dialect *capdet,* captain, chief, from Late Latin *capitellum,* "small head," from Latin *caput,* head.] —**ca·det·ship** *n.*

cadge (kăj) *v.* **cadged, cadging, cadges.** *Informal.* —*tr.* To get by begging or pretending to borrow. —*intr.* To beg or borrow something without intent to repay. [Back-formation from *cadger,* carrier, Middle English *cadgear,* from *caggen*†, to carry wares.] —**cadg·er** *n.*

Cá·diz (kə-dīz′, kā′dīz). Capital of Cádiz province in Spain. Situated at the entrance to the Bay of Cádiz, it is an important seaport, founded by the Phoenicians in *c.* 1100 B.C. After the conquest of the Americas, it was used as a base for the Spanish treasure fleets.

Cad·me·an (kăd-mē′ən) *adj.* Pertaining to, associated with, or resembling Cadmus.

cad·mi·um (kăd′mē-əm) *n. Symbol* **Cd** A soft, bluish-white metallic element, occurring primarily in zinc, copper, and lead ores. It is easily cut with a knife and is used in low-friction, fatigue-resistant alloys, solders, dental amalgams, nickel-cadmium accumulators, neutron-absorbing control rods in nuclear reactors, and in rustproof electroplating. Atomic number 48, atomic weight 112.40, melting point 320.9°C, boiling point 765°C, specific gravity 8.65, valence 2. [New Latin, from Latin *cadmia,* zinc ore, CALAMINE (because cadmium is found together with calamine in the ore).] —**cadmic** *adj.*

cadmium cell *n.* A photocell of a type having a cadmium electrode that is sensitive to ultraviolet radiation.

cadmium sulfate *n.* A colorless crystalline solid, $CdSO_4$, used as an antiseptic.

cadmium sulfide *n.* An orange or yellow insoluble solid, CdS, used as a pigment in paints *(cadmium yellow).*

Cad·mus (kăd′məs). *Greek Mythology.* A Phoenician prince who killed a dragon and sowed its teeth, from which sprang up an army of men who fought one another until only five survived; with these Cadmus founded the city of Thebes.

cad·re (kăd′rē) *n.* **1.** A nucleus of trained personnel, especially in a military or political organization, around which a larger organization can be built and trained. **2.** A member of such a nucleus. [French, from Italian *quadro,* from Latin *quādrum,* a square, from *quādrus.*]

ca·du·ce·us (kə-dōo′sē-əs, kə-dyōo′-) *n., pl.* **-cei** (-sē-ī′). **1. a.** An ancient herald's wand or staff. **b.** *Greek Mythology.* A winged staff with two serpents twined around it, carried by the messenger-god Hermes. **2.** A similar staff used as the symbol of the medical profession. [Latin *cādūceus,* from Greek (Doric) *karukeion,* from *karux,* herald.] —**ca·du·ce·an** *adj.*

ca·du·ci·corn (kə-dōo′sĭ-kôrn, -dyōo′-) *adj.* Having horns that are shed annually, as certain deer. [Latin *cadūcus,* falling (from *cadere,* to fall) + *cornu,* horn.]

ca·du·ci·ty (kə-dōo′sə-tē, kə-dyōo′-) *n.* **1.** The frailty of old age; senility. **2.** Perishability; impermanence. [French *caducité,* from *caduc,* frail, falling, from Latin *cadūcus,* CADUCOUS.]

ca·du·cous (kə-dōo′kəs, kə-dyōo′-) *adj.* **1.** *Biology.* Dropping off or shedding at an early stage of development. Said of the gills of amphibians or the leaves of certain plants. **2.** Not long-lasting; imper-

manent; transitory. [Latin *cadūcus,* falling, frail, from *cadere,* to fall.]

cae·cil·i·an (sĭ-sĭl′yən, -sĭl′ē-ən, sĭ-sēl′-) *n.* Any of various legless, burrowing, wormlike amphibians of the order Gymnophiona (formerly Apoda), of tropical regions. [New Latin *Caecilia,* type genus, from Latin *caecilia,* lizard, from *caecus,* blind (in allusion to a lizard's small eyes).]

caecum Variant of **cecum.**

Caed·mon (kăd′mən) (died *c.* A.D. 680). The earliest known English poet, who, according to Bede, was a cowherd at the monastery of Whitby and who, as an old man, was told in a vision to sing "the beginning of all created things." He became a monk and spent the remainder of his days writing songs and poems based on the Scriptures.

Cae·li·an (sē′lē-ən). One of the seven hills of Rome.

Caen (kän). Port and administrative center of the department of Calvados, northwest France, on the Orne River. It first came to prominence under William the Conqueror, who founded the Abbaye aux Hommes where he is buried. His wife Matilda founded the Abbaye aux Dames. Caen was a Huguenot stronghold in the 16th and 17th centuries and saw heavy fighting in World War II. Its industries include machinery, textiles, and cement.

Caer·nar·von or **Caer·nar·fon** (kär-när′vən). County town and port on the south shore of Menai Strait, in Gwynedd, northern Wales. In 1284 Edward I built a castle, reputedly the birthplace of Edward II, the first Prince of Wales. Prince Charles, the 21st Prince of Wales, was invested here (1969).

Caer·nar·von·shire (kär-när′vən-shîr, -shər). Formerly, a county in north Wales, now a part of Gwynedd.

Caer·phil·ly¹ (kär-fĭl′ē). Market and industrial center in Mid Glamorgan, southern Wales, and the home of Caerphilly cheese. Caerphilly Castle, built between the 13th and 14th centuries, is the largest in Wales.

Caerphilly² *n.* A mild, crumbly white cheese originally from Wales. [After CAERPHILLY.]

Cae·sar (sē′zər) *n.* **1.** A surname of the early Roman emperors that after Hadrian became the title of the junior imperial colleague of the **Augustus** *(see).* **2.** A dictator or autocrat.

Caesar, Gaius Julius (*c.* 100–44 B.C.). Roman general, statesman, and writer. During his Gaul campaign, he invaded Britain (55) and returned to Rome a popular hero. He had, however, many political enemies, including Pompey, who persuaded the senate to order Caesar to resign his army command. Instead, Caesar took his legions across the Rubicon River (49) and crushed Pompey at Pharsalus (48). In 47 he pursued his enemies to Egypt where he installed Cleopatra as queen. It is widely believed that Cleopatra later gave birth to his son, Caesarion. Returning to Rome (45), he was given a mandate by the people to rule, as dictator, for life. He introduced many reforms, including the Julian calendar and public libraries. On March 15, 44 B.C. (the ides of March), Caesar was murdered in the senate by a group of republicans, led by Cassius and Brutus, who feared that he was about to establish a monarchy with himself as king.

Cae·sar·e·an, Cae·sar·i·an (sĭ-zâr′ē-ən) *adj.* Pertaining to Julius Caesar or the Caesars.
—*n.* A Caesarean section *(see).*

Caesarean section *n. Sometimes* **caesarian section.** A surgical incision through the abdominal wall and uterus, performed to deliver a baby. Also called "Caesarean." [From an unhistorical tradition that the eponymous ancestor of the Roman family *Caesar* (or Julius *Caesar* himself) was born by this operation, and named *ā caesō mātris ūterē,* "from the *incised* womb of his mother," from *caesus,* past participle of *caedere,* to cut.]

Cae·sa·re·a Pal·es·ti·nae (sē′zə-rē′ə păl′ə-stī′nē, sĕs′ə-, sēz′ə-). Ancient city in Israel, lying south of Haifa. It was founded by Herod the Great in 13 B.C. as a port on the Mediterranean coast. An early center of Christianity, often referred to in the New Testament, Caesarea became the capital of Roman Judaea. The port declined after Muslim occupation (A.D. 638) and, though revived by the Crusaders, was destroyed by the Muslims (1265).

Cae·sar·ism (sē′zə-rĭz′əm) *n.* Military dictatorship. —**Cae·sar·ist** *n.* —**Cae·sar·is·tic** *adj.*

caesar salad *n.* A salad made with lettuce, cheese, croutons, and dressed with raw egg, oil, and lemon juice.

caesium Variant of **cesium.**

caespitose Variant of **cespitose.**

cae·su·ra, ce·su·ra (sĭ-zhōor′ə, -zyōor′ə, -zōor′ə) *n., pl.* **-ras** or **-surae** (-zhōor′ē, -zyōor′ē, -zōor′ē). **1.** A pause in a line of verse dictated by sense or natural speech rhythm rather than by meter. It is conventionally indicated by an oblique stroke: *"Drink deep, / or taste not the Pierian Spring"* (Alexander Pope). **2.** In Latin and Greek verse, a break in a line caused by the ending of a word within a foot, especially when this coincides with a sense division: *"Arma virumque cano / Troiae qui primus ab oris"* (Virgil). **3.** *Music.* A pause or breathing at a point of rhythmic division in a melody. [Latin, "a cutting off," from *caedere,* to cut off.] —**cae·su·ral, cae·su·ric** *adj.*

ca·fé, ca·fe (kă-fā′, kə-) *n.* A coffee house, restaurant, or bar. [French, COFFEE.]

ca·fé au lait (kă-fā′ ō lā′) *n., pl.* **cafés au lait. 1.** Coffee served with hot milk. **2.** A light coffee color. [French, "coffee with milk."]

caf·e·te·ri·a (kăf′ə-tîr′ē-ə) *n.* A restaurant in which the customers are served at a counter and carry their meals to tables. [American

Caesar *Julius Caesar's likeness appears on the denarius, the principal Roman silver coin. Caesar laid the foundations of the Roman Empire, replacing the Republic that preceded it and profoundly influencing European history. The Russian and German imperial titles of Czar and Kaiser are forms of his name.*

Spanish, coffee shop, from Spanish *cafetero,* coffee maker or seller, from *café,* COFFEE.]

caf·feine, caf·fein (kă-fēn′, kăf′ē-ĭn) *n.* A bitter white alkaloid, $C_8H_{10}N_4O_2 \cdot H_2O$, derived from coffee, tea, and cocoa, and used as a stimulant and diuretic. [German *Kaffein,* from *Kaffee,* COFFEE.]

caf·tan, kaf·tan (kăf′tən, kăf-tăn′) *n.* **1.** In the Near East, a full-length tunic with long sleeves and a sash at the waist, worn under a coat. **2.** A westernized version of this consisting of a loose and often brightly colored waist-length or ankle-length tunic. [Russian *kaftan,* from Turkish *kaftān.*]

cage (kāj) *n.* **1.** A structure for confining birds or animals, enclosed on at least one side by a grating of wires or bars in order to let in air and light. **2. a.** Any enclosure that serves as a means of confining prisoners. **b.** Anything that confines, physically or psychologically. **3.** Any framework having a cagelike appearance or construction. **4.** A rudimentary elevator car, especially one used in a mine. **5.** *Baseball.* **a.** A backstop used for batting practices. **b.** A catcher's mask. **6.** *Basketball.* The basket. **7.** *Hockey.* The goal, made of a network frame.
~*tr.v.* **caged, caging, cages.** To put in a cage; lock up or confine. [Middle English, from Old French, from Latin *cavea,* a hollow, enclosure, from *cavus,* hollow.]

Cage (kāj), **John** (1912–92). Avant-garde U.S. composer, whose works include *Sonatas and Interludes,* for a prepared piano with its strings damped by wood and metal (1946–48), *Imaginary Landscape No. 4,* for 12 randomly tuned radios (1951), and *4 minutes 33 seconds,* silence in three movements for any instrument or instruments (1954).

cage bird *n.* A bird of a type that is often kept in a cage.

cage·ling (kāj′lĭng) *n.* A caged bird.

cag·ey, cag·y (kā′jē) *adj.* **-ier, -iest.** *Informal.* Wary; careful; unwilling to disclose information. [20th century (U.S.) : origin obscure.] —**cag·i·ly** *adv.* —**cag·i·ness** *n.*

Ca·glia·ri (kăl′yə-rē) Administrative and industrial center of Sardinia, Italy. Also a seaport, it lies at the mouth of the Mannu River on the south side of the island. Founded by the Carthaginians, the city has a Roman amphitheater, a basilica (5th century), a massive Pisan tower (1304), and a university (1606).

Ca·glio·stro (kăl-yô′strō), **Alessandro, Conte di,** born Giuseppe Balsamo (1743–95). Italian adventurer who became famous throughout Europe as an alchemist and magician. He died in Italy, following his incarceration for promoting freemasonry.

Cag·ney (kăg′nē), **James** (1899–1986). U.S. actor famous for his portrayals of gangsters, hard characters injected with elements of humanity. His films include *Public Enemy* (1931), *Angels with Dirty Faces* (1938), *The Roaring Twenties* (1939), and *Yankee Doodle Dandy* (1942), for which he won an Academy Award.

ca·hoots (kə-hōōts′) *pl.n. Informal.* Collaboration of a questionable nature. Used in the phrase *in cahoots.* [19th century : origin obscure.]

Cai·a·phas (kā′ə-fəs, kī′-), **Joseph.** Jewish high priest (A.D. *c.* 18–36); president of the council condemning Jesus. Matthew 26.

Caicos. See Turks and Caicos Islands.

cai·man, cay·man (kā′mən, kā-măn′, kī-măn′) *n., pl.* **-mans.** Any of various tropical American crocodilians of the genus *Caiman* and related genera, resembling and closely related to the alligators. [Spanish *caimán,* from Carib *cayman,* perhaps of African origin.]

cain Variant of **kain.**

Cain[1] (kān). The eldest son of Adam and Eve, who killed his brother Abel out of jealousy. Genesis 4. [Latin, from Greek *Kain,* from Hebrew *Qayin,* "creature."]

Cain[2] *n.* A murderer. —**raise Cain.** *Informal.* To create a great disturbance or uproar; make trouble. [From CAIN.]

-caine *suffix.* Indicates a synthetic alkaloid in anesthetic drugs; for example, **eucaine.** [From (CO)CAINE.]

cai·no·to·pho·bi·a (kā-nō′tə-fō′bē-ə) *n.* An abnormal fear of newness. [Greek *kainotēs,* newness + PHOBIA.]

ca·ique (kä-ēk′) *n.* **1.** A long, narrow rowing boat used in the Middle East. **2.** A small sailing vessel used in the eastern Mediterranean. [French, from Italian *caicco,* from Turkish *kayik.*]

caird (kârd) *n. Scottish.* A traveling tinker or handyman. [Scottish Gaelic *ceard,* artist, craftsman, from Old Irish *cerd,* art, artist.]

cairn (kârn) *n.* A mound of stones erected as a landmark or memorial. [Middle English *carne,* from Celtic *kar-n-, kr-ag-* (both unattested).] —**cairned** *adj.*

cairn·gorm (kârn′gôrm′) *n.* A smoky-brown or yellow variety of quartz, used as a semiprecious gem. Also called "smoky quartz." [After CAIRNGORM MOUNTAINS, where it is found.]

Cairn·gorm Mountains (kârn′gôrm′). Mountain range in northeast Scotland, forming part of the Grampians in Highland Region. A favorite winter sports resort, it includes Ben Macdhui, at 1,309 meters (4,295 feet) the second-highest peak in Scotland. The area was declared a nature reserve for arctic flora and fauna (1954).

Cairns (kârnz). Seaport on Trinity Bay in Queensland, Australia. It serves as an agricultural, timber, and mining region and is a tourist center for the Great Barrier Reef.

Cairn terrier *n.* A small dog of a breed developed in Scotland, having a broad head and a rough, shaggy coat. [So called because it hunts among cairns.]

Cai·ro (kī′rō). *Arabic* **Al Qa·hi·ra** (äl kä′hĭ-rō). Also **Al Fus·tat** (äl fōō-stät′). Capital of Egypt, lying on the east bank of the Nile River. It is the largest city in Africa and the Middle East and is one of the most important cultural, commercial, and political centers of

the Arab world. The pyramids at Giza, 13 kilometers (8 miles) southwest of Cairo, and Egypt's many other monuments and treasures, ensure a busy tourist industry. Other industries include textiles, food processing, plastics, and motor-vehicle assembly. Al Fustat, now Old Cairo, was established by Arab conquerors as a military camp (A.D. 642). Al Qahira was founded by the Fatimids as their capital (968). Saladin built the citadel (*c.* 1176), and extended the city's walls against Crusader attack. Cairo prospered under the Mamelukes, but fell to the Ottoman Turks (1517). Following Napoleon's occupation (1798–1801), it became the capital (1805–49) of a virtually independent kingdom under the pasha Mehemet Ali. The Al Azhar University (970) is reputedly the world's leading center for Koranic studies, and the city is also the headquarters of the Coptic Church in Egypt.

cais·son (kā′sŏn′, -sən) *n.* **1.** A watertight structure within which construction work is carried on. **2.** A watertight float, a **camel** (*see*). **3.** A floating structure used to close off the entrance to a dock or canal lock. **4.** A large box open at the top and one side, designed to fit against the side of a ship and used to repair damaged hulls under water. **5.** *Military.* **a.** A large box used to hold ammunition. **b.** A horse-drawn vehicle, usually two-wheeled, once used to carry ammunition. [French, from Old French *casson,* from Italian *cassa,* chest, box, from Latin *capsa.*]

caisson disease *n.* A disorder in divers and caisson and tunnel workers caused by a too rapid return from high pressure to atmospheric pressure, characterized by pains in the joints, cramps, paralysis, and eventual death unless treated by gradual decompression. Also called "aeroembolism," "the bends," "decompression sickness," "tunnel disease."

Caith·ness (kāth′nĕs′). Former county in northeast Scotland, part of Highland Region since 1975. Mainly infertile moorland and mountains, it sustains sheepherding, fishing, and farming.

cai·tiff (kā′tĭf) *n.* A base coward; a wretch.
~*adj.* Base and cowardly. [Middle English *caitif,* prisoner, captive, wretch, from Old French, from Latin *captivus,* CAPTIVE.]

caj·e·put, caj·u·put (kăj′ə-pət, -pōōt′) *n.* **1.** A tree, *Melaleuca leucadendron,* native to Australia, having whitish flowers and leaves that yield an aromatic medicinal oil. **2.** The oil obtained from this tree. [Malay *kayu puteh : kayu,* tree + *puteh,* white.]

ca·jole (kə-jōl′) *tr.v.* **-joled, -joling, -joles.** To persuade by means of flattery; coax; wheedle. [French *cajoler* †.] —**ca·jol·er** *n.* —**ca·jol·er·y** *n.* —**ca·jol·ing·ly** *adv.*

Ca·jun, Ca·jan (kā′jən) *n.* **1.** A native of Louisiana believed to be descended from the French exiles from Acadia. **2.** The dialect of these people. **3.** Cajun music. [Alteration of ACADIAN.]

Cajun music *n.* A type of folk music originating among the Cajuns, typically using accordions and fiddles.

cake (kāk) *n.* **1.** A sweetened baked mixture of flour, liquid, eggs, and other ingredients, usually in loaf or rounded layer form. **2.** A flat, thin mass of dough or batter, baked or fried, such as a pancake or oatcake. **3.** A patty of fried food, such as a fishcake. **4.** A shaped or molded piece, as of soap. **5.** An aggregate of benefits, especially financial benefits, that are to be divided up or to be distributed: *workers want a larger slice of the cake.* —**go** (or **sell**) **like hot cakes.** To be in great demand; sell in large quantities. —**take the cake.** *Informal.* To win the prize; be outstanding.
~*v.* **caked, caking, cakes.** —*tr.* To cause to dry out and harden around something; encrust. —*intr.* To form a hard, dried-out mass. [Middle English *cake, kake,* from Old Norse *kaka.*]

cakes and ale *pl.n.* Enjoyment of the good things in life.

cake·walk (kāk′wôk′) *n.* **1.** Formerly, a promenade or walk in which those performing the most complex and unusual steps won cakes as prizes. **2. a.** A strutting dance based on this promenade. **b.** The music for this dance. **3.** *Informal.* Something easily done.
~*intr.v.* **cakewalked, -walking, -walks.** To perform a cakewalk.

cal calorie (small).

Cal calorie (large).

cal. **1.** calendar. **2.** caliber.

Cal·a·bar bean (kăl′ə-bär′) *n.* The dark-brown poisonous seed of a woody vine, *Physostigma venenosum,* of tropical Africa. It is the source of the drug **physostigmine** (*see*). Also called "ordeal bean." [After *Calabar,* city in Nigeria.]

cal·a·bash (kăl′ə-băsh′) *n.* **1.** A vine, *Lagenaria siceraria,* native to the Old World, bearing large, hard-shelled gourds. Also called "bottle gourd." **2.** A tropical American tree, *Crescentia cujete,* bearing large, rounded fruit. Also called "bottle gourd." **3.** The hard-shelled fruit of a calabash vine or tree. **4.** A utensil, such as a dish, ladle, or tobacco pipe, made from the fruit of a calabash. [Obsolete French *calabasse,* from Spanish *calabaza*†.]

cal·a·boose (kăl′ə-bōōs′) *n. Slang.* A jail. [Louisiana French *calabouse,* from Spanish *calabozo*†, a dungeon.]

cal·a·bre·se (kăl′ə-brā′zē, -sē) *n.* **1.** An Italian variety of broccoli, *Brassica oleracea italica,* having a branched, greenish flower head. **2.** The flower head of this plant eaten as a vegetable before the green, tightly clustered buds have opened. [Italian, "Calabrian."]

Ca·la·bri·a (kə-lā′brē-ə, -lā′-). Region in Italy comprising the provinces of Cosenza, Cantanzaro, and Reggio di Calabria, forming the "toe of Italy" between the Ionian and Tyrrhenian seas. It is mainly mountainous, with extensive forests. Crotone is an industrial center, but the area is economically underdeveloped. The main sources of income are the cultivation of vines, citrus fruit, and olives, sheep and goat herding, and granite quarrying. Cantanzaro is the capital.
—**Ca·la·bri·an** *n. & adj.*

ca·la·di·um (kə-lā'dē-əm) *n.* Any of various tropical plants of the genus *Caladium,* widely cultivated as potted plants for their showy, variegated foliage. [New Latin *Caladium,* from Malay *kĕladi,* araceous plant.]

Ca·lais (kă-lā', kăl'ā). Industrial town and seaport in Pas-de-Calais department, France. It is 35 kilometers (22 miles) east-southeast of Dover, on the shortest crossing between England and France. Calais was conquered by Edward III (1347) after a siege in which six burghers offered their lives for the town, but intervention by Edward's queen, Philippa, saved them. Calais remained in English possession until 1558. It was almost destroyed in World War II during the Dunkirk withdrawal. Industries include fishing, boatbuilding, textiles, and clothing.

cal·a·man·co (kăl'ə-măng'kō) *n., pl.* **-cos** or **-coes.** A glossy woolen fabric with a check pattern on only one side. [16th century : origin obscure.]

cal·a·man·der (kăl'ə-măn'dər) *n.* The hard, black-and-brown-striped wood of certain tropical Asiatic trees of the genus *Diospyros,* used in furniture. [Probably from Dutch *kalamander(hout),* calamander (wood), perhaps metathetic variant of COROMANDEL COAST.]

cal·a·mine (kăl'ə-mīn', -mĭn) *n.* **1.** A white or sometimes iron- or copper-stained mineral, essentially $Zn_4Si_2O_7(OH)_2 \cdot H_2O$. Also called "hemimorphite." **2.** *Pharmacology.* A pink, odorless, tasteless powder of zinc oxide with a small amount of ferric oxide, dissolved in mineral oils and used in skin lotions. [French, from Medieval Latin *calamīna,* alteration of Latin *cadmia,* from Greek *kadmeia,* "Cadmean (earth)" (first found near Thebes, city founded by Cadmus), from *kadmeios,* of CADMUS.]

cal·a·mint (kăl'ə-mĭnt') *n.* Any of several aromatic plants of the genus *Calamintha;* especially, *S. calamintha,* native to Eurasia, having clusters of purplish or pink flowers. [Middle English *calament,* from Old French, from Medieval Latin *calamentum,* variant of Late Latin *calaminthē,* from Greek *kalaminthē†.]

cal·a·mite (kăl'ə-mīt) *n.* Any of various extinct treelike Carboniferous plants of the genus *Calamites,* resembling the horsetails, but much larger, and known only as fossils. [New Latin *Calamites,* from Late Greek *kalamitēs,* reedlike, from Greek, of a reed, from *kalamos,* reed.]

ca·lam·i·tous (kə-lăm'ə-təs) *adj.* Causing or involving a disaster. —**ca·lam·i·tous·ly** *adv.* —**ca·lam·i·tous·ness** *n.*

ca·lam·i·ty (kə-lăm'ə-tē) *n., pl.* **-ties.** **1.** A disaster, especially one that leads to personal loss and suffering. **2.** Dire distress. —See Synonyms at **disaster.** [Middle English *calamite,* from Old French, from Latin *calamitās* (stem *calamitāt-*).]

Calamity Jane. See Martha Jane **Burke.**

cal·a·mus (kăl'ə-məs) *n., pl.* **-mi** (-mī'). **1.** A plant, the **sweet flag** *(see),* or its aromatic root. **2.** Any of various tropical Asiatic palms of the genus *Calamus,* from some of which rattan is obtained. **3.** A part of a feather, a **quill** *(see).* [Latin, reed, cane, from Greek *kalamos.*]

ca·lan·do (kä-län'dō) *adj. Music.* Gradually diminishing in tempo and volume.
~*adv. Music.* In a calando manner. [Italian, from Latin *calandum,* a slackening, from *calāre, chalāre,* to let fall, slacken, from Greek *khalan.*]

cal·an·dri·a (kə-lăn'drē-ə) *n.* A heat exchanger, as in the core of a nuclear reactor, consisting of a vessel with vertical tubes passing through it.

ca·lash (kə-lăsh') *n.* Also **ca·lèche** (kə-lĕsh'). **1.** A carriage with low wheels and a collapsible top. **2.** The top of such a carriage. **3.** A woman's folding bonnet, fashionable in the late 18th century. [French *calèche,* from German *Kalesche,* from Czech *kolesa,* plural of *koleso,* wheel, from *kolo* (stem *koles-*), wheel, from Old Church Slavonic.]

cal·a·thus (kăl'ə-thəs) *n., pl.* **-thi** (-thī'). A vase-shaped basket represented in ancient Greek painting and sculpture. [Latin, from Greek *kalathos†.*]

cal·a·ver·ite (kăl'ə-vâr'īt') *n.* A rare ore of gold, essentially gold telluride, $AuTe_2$, often containing silver. [After *Calaveras,* county in California, where it was discovered.]

cal·ca·ne·o·cu·boid ligament (kăl-kā'nē-ō-kyōō'boid') *n.* The ligament that connects the calcaneus and the cuboid bones.

cal·ca·ne·us (kăl-kā'nē-əs) *n., pl.* **-nei** (-nē-ī'). Also **cal·ca·ne·um** (-nē-əm) *pl.* **-nea** (-nē-ə). The quadrangular bone at the back of the tarsus, forming the projection of the heel. Also called "heel bone." [Latin, "heel," from *calx* (stem *calc-*), heel.] —**cal·ca·ne·al** *adj.*

cal·car (kăl'kär') *n., pl.* **calcaria** (kăl-kâr'ē). *Biology.* An anatomical spur or spurlike projection. [Latin, spur, from *calx* (stem *calc-*), heel.]

cal·car·e·ous (kăl-kâr'ē-əs) *adj.* Composed of, containing, or characteristic of calcium carbonate, calcium, or limestone; chalky. [Latin *calcārius,* from *calx* (stem *calc-*), lime.]

cal·ca·rine fissure (kăl'kə-rīn') *n.* A calcarine sulcus.

calcarine sul·cus (sŭl'kəs) *n.* A sulcus on the occipital lobe of the brain. [CALCAR + -INE.]

cal·ce·i·form (kăl'sē-ə-fôrm') *adj. Botany.* Slipper-shaped; calceolate. [Latin *calceus,* shoe (see **calceolate**) + -FORM.]

cal·ce·o·lar·i·a (kăl'sē-ə-lâr'ē-ə) *n.* Any of various plants of the genus *Calceolaria,* native to tropical America and widely cultivated for their yellow, speckled, slipper-shaped flowers. Also called "slipperwort." [New Latin, from Latin *calceolārius,* shoemaker, from *calceolus,* small shoe. See **calceolate.**]

cal·ce·o·late (kăl'sē-ə-lāt') *adj. Botany.* Shaped like a slipper, as the blossoms of some orchids. [Latin *calceolus,* diminutive of *calceus†,* shoe.]

cal·ces. Alternate plural of **calx.**

calci-, calc- *prefix.* Indicates lime or calcium; for example, **calciferous, calcite.** [Latin *calx* (stem *calc-*), lime, limestone.]

cal·cic (kăl'sĭk) *adj.* Composed of, containing, derived from, or pertaining to calcium or lime.

cal·ci·cole (kăl'sĭ-kōl') *n. Botany.* A plant that thrives in soil rich in lime. [French : CALCI- + -cole, dweller, from Latin -cola (see **-colous**).] —**cal·cic·o·lous** *adj.*

cal·ci·co·sis (kăl'sĭ-kō'sĭs) *n.* A pneumoconiosis resulting from the inhalation of calcium carbonate dust. [CALCI- + -cosis (as in silicosis).]

cal·cif·er·ol (kăl-sĭf'ə-rôl', -rōl') *n.* One of the forms in which **vitamin D** *(see)* occurs. [Calciferous + ergosterol.]

cal·cif·er·ous (kăl-sĭf'ər-əs) *adj.* Of, forming, or containing calcium or calcium carbonate. [CALCI- + -FEROUS.]

cal·cif·ic (kăl-sĭf'ĭk) *adj.* Producing salts of lime, as in the formation of eggshells in birds.

cal·ci·fi·ca·tion (kăl'sə-fĭ-kā'shən) *n.* **1.** Impregnation with calcium or calcium salts, as with calcium carbonate. **2.** Hardening, as of tissue, by such impregnation. **3.** A substance, such as petrified wood, or a part so impregnated.

cal·ci·fuge (kăl'sə-fyōōj') *n.* A plant that does not thrive in lime-rich soil, preferring acid soil. —**cal·cif·u·gal, cal·cif·u·gous** *adj.*

cal·ci·fy (kăl'sə-fī') *v.* **-fied, -fying, -fies.** —*tr.* To make stony or chalky by deposition of calcium salts. —*intr.* To become stony or chalky by deposition of calcium salts. [CALCI- + -FY.]

cal·ci·mine (kăl'sə-mīn') *n.* Also **kal·so·mine.** A white or tinted liquid containing zinc oxide, water, glue, and coloring matter, used as a wash for walls and ceilings. Also *British* "distemper."
~*tr.v.* **calcimined, -mining, -mines.** To cover or wash with calcimine. [Alteration of trademark *Kalsomine.*]

cal·cine (kăl'sīn', kăl-sīn') *v.* **-cined, -cining, -cines.** —*tr.* To heat (a substance) to a high temperature but below the melting or fusing point, causing loss of moisture, reduction, or oxidation. —*intr.* To undergo oxidation as a result of heating. [Middle English *calcinen,* from Old French *calciner,* from Medieval Latin *calcīnāre,* from Latin *calx,* lime. See **calcium.**] —**cal·ci·na·tion** *n.*

cal·cite (kăl'sīt') *n.* A common crystalline form of natural calcium carbonate, the basic constituent of limestone, marble, and chalk. Also called "calcspar." —**cal·cit·ic** *adj.*

cal·ci·ton·in (kăl'sĭ-tō'nĭn) *n.* A hormone secreted by the thyroid that lowers the amount of calcium in the blood to within normal limits. Also called "thyrocalcitonin." [CALCI- + TON(IC) + -IN.]

cal·ci·um (kăl'sē-əm) *n. Symbol* Ca A silvery, moderately hard metallic element, constituting approximately three percent of the earth's crust, a basic component of bone, shells, and teeth. It occurs naturally in limestone, gypsum, and fluorite, and its compounds are used to make plaster, quicklime, Portland cement, and metallurgic and electronic materials. Atomic number 20, atomic weight 40.08, melting point 842 to 848°C, boiling point 1,487°C, specific gravity 1.55, valence 2. [New Latin, from Latin *calx* (stem *calc-*), lime, limestone, from Greek *khalix†,* pebble.]

calcium carbide *n.* A grayish-black crystalline compound, CaC_2, obtained by heating pulverized limestone or quicklime with carbon and used to generate acetylene, as a dehydrating agent, and in the manufacture of graphite and hydrogen.

calcium carbonate *n.* A colorless or white crystalline compound, $CaCO_3$, occurring naturally as chalk, limestone, marble, and other forms and used in a wide variety of manufactured products including commercial chalk, medicines, and toothpastes.

calcium chloride *n.* A white deliquescent compound, $CaCl_2$, used chiefly as a drying agent, refrigerant, and preservative.

calcium cyanamide *n.* A gray-black compound, $Ca(CN)_2$, used as a fertilizer and weedkiller. Also called "cyanamide."

calcium fluoride *n.* A white powder, CaF_2, used in emery wheels, carbon electrodes, and cements.

calcium hydroxide *n.* A soft white powder, $Ca(OH)_2$, used in making mortar, cements, calcium salts, paints, hard rubber products, and petrochemicals. Also called "lime," "slaked lime."

calcium hypochlorite *n.* A white crystalline solid, $Ca(OCl)_2$, used as a bactericide, fungicide, and bleaching agent.

calcium light *n.* An intense white light produced by incandescent lime, **limelight** *(see).*

calcium oxalate *n.* A white crystalline powder, CaC_2O_4, used to make oxalic acid and found in many plant cells.

calcium oxide *n.* A white caustic lumpy powder, CaO, used as a refractory, as a flux, in manufacturing steel, glassmaking, waste treatment, insecticides, and as an industrial alkali. Also called "lime," "quicklime," "unslaked lime," "calx."

calcium phosphate *n.* Any of several phosphate compounds, especially: **1.** A white crystalline powder, $CaHPO_4$ or $CaHPO_4 \cdot 2H_2O$, used as a food, as a plastic stabilizer, and in glass; dibasic calcium phosphate. **2.** A colorless deliquescent powder, $CaH_4(PO_4)_2 \cdot H_2O$, used in baking powders, as a plant food, plastic stabilizer, and in glass; monobasic calcium phosphate. **3.** A white amorphous powder, $Ca_3(PO_4)_2$, used in ceramics, rubber, fertilizers, plastic stabilizers, and as a food supplement; tribasic calcium phosphate.

calc-sin·ter *n.* Natural calcium carbonate, chiefly in the form of stalagmites or stalactites. See **travertine.** [German *Kalksinter* : *Kalk,* lime + *Sinter,* slag, SINTER.]

calc·spar (kălk′spär′) *n.* **Calcite** *(see).* [Partial translation of Swedish *kalkspar* : *kalk,* lime (see **calcium**) + SPAR (mineral).]

calc·tu·fa (kălk′to͞o′fə, -tyo͞o′fə) *n.* Also **calc-tuff** (-tŭf′). A porous or spongy deposit of calcium carbonate found in calcareous mineral springs. [*Cal*careous + *tufa.*]

cal·cu·la·ble (kăl′kyə-lə-bəl) *adj.* **1.** Capable of being calculated or estimated. **2.** That may be counted or depended on. **—cal·cu·la·bil·i·ty** *n.*

cal·cu·late (kăl′kyə-lāt′) *v.* **-lated, -lating, -lates.** *—tr.* **1.** To ascertain by computation; reckon. **2.** To make an estimate of; evaluate. **3.** To fit or plan for a purpose; design. Usually used in the passive: *His speech was cleverly calculated to stir up ill feeling against the government.* **4.** *Regional.* **a.** To purpose, intend. **b.** To think; suppose. *—intr.* **1.** To execute a mathematical process. **2.** To suppose; think; guess. [Latin *calculāre,* from *calculus,* small stone (used in reckoning), diminutive of *calx* (stem *calc-*), lime, limestone, from Greek *khalix,* pebble.]

Synonyms: *compute, estimate, reckon.*

cal·cu·lat·ed (kăl′kyə-lā′tĭd) *adj.* **1.** Estimated with forethought: *a calculated risk.* **2.** Deliberately planned to achieve a particular purpose. **3.** Determined by mathematical calculation. **—cal·cu·lat·ed·ly** *adv.* **—cal·cu·lat·ed·ness** *n.*

cal·cu·lat·ing (kăl′kyə-lā′tĭng) *adj.* **1.** Performing calculations: *a calculating machine.* **2. a.** Shrewd; crafty. **b.** Coldly scheming or conniving.

cal·cu·la·tion (kăl′kyə-lā′shən) *n.* **1.** The act, process, or result of calculating. **2.** An estimate based upon probabilities. **3.** *Often* **calculations. a.** Deliberation; foresight. **b.** Shrewd scheming. **—cal·cu·la·tive** *adj.*

cal·cu·la·tor (kăl′kyə-lā′tər) *n.* **1.** A mechanical or electronic device for the automatic performance of arithmetical operations. **2.** A person who performs calculations. **3.** A set of mathematical tables used as an aid in calculating.

cal·cu·lous (kăl′kyə-ləs) *adj. Medicine.* Pertaining to, caused by, or having a calculus or calculi.

cal·cu·lus (kăl′kyə-ləs) *n., pl.* **-li** (-lī′) or **-luses. 1.** *Pathology.* An abnormal concretion in the body, usually formed of mineral salts; a stone, as in the gall bladder, kidney, or urinary bladder. **2.** *Mathematics.* **a.** A method of analysis or calculation using a special symbolic notation. **b.** The combined mathematics of **differential calculus** and **integral calculus** *(both of which see).* [Latin, small stone (used in reckoning), reckoning. See **calculate.**]

calculus of variations *n.* The mathematical analysis of the maxima and minima of definite integrals, the integrands of which are functions of independent variables, dependent variables, and the derivatives of one or more dependent variables.

Cal·cut·ta (kăl-kŭt′ə). Capital city of West Bengal state, India. Built on the Hooghly River, it is India's largest city and one of the world's most densely populated. It was founded as a British East India Company trading post (*c.* 1690). Captured by Siraj-ud-Dawlah, the nawab of Bengal (1756), it was retaken by Robert Clive (1757). During the campaign, the nawab confined 146 prisoners overnight in a small guardhouse (see **Black Hole of Calcutta**). Calcutta is the chief port and industrial center of eastern India.

Cal·der (kôl′dər), **Alexander** (1898–1976). U.S. sculptor who created the mobile in Paris in the early 1930's.

cal·de·ra (kăl-dâr′ə, -dĭr′ə) *n.* A large crater formed by the collapse of a volcanic cone, or by a volcanic explosion that removes the top of the original cone. [Spanish, "kettle," "boiler," from Late Latin *caldāria,* CAULDRON.]

Cal·der·ón de la Bar·ca (kăl′də-rôn′ dā lə bär′kə) **Pedro** (1600–81). Spanish author. He was one of the greatest dramatists of Spain's Golden Age (17th century). Among his better known works are *The Surgeon and His Honor* (1635), *Life is a Dream* (1635), and *The Daughter of the Air* (1653).

cal·dron, caul·dron (kôl′drən) *n.* A large kettle or vat for boiling. [Middle English *caud(e)ron, caldron,* from Old North French *caud(e)ron,* from Late Latin *caldāria,* from Latin, warm bath, from *caldārius,* suitable for warming, from *cal(i)dus,* warm.]

Cald·well (kôl′dwĕl′, -dwəl), **Erskine Preston** (1903–87). U.S. author. His graphic novels about poverty and degeneration established him as a controversial and highly popular author. *Tobacco Road* (1932), *God's Little Acre* (1933), and *Trouble in July* (1940) are among his most critically successful novels. He also collaborated with his second wife, photographer Margaret Bourke-White, on *You Have Seen Their Faces* (1937) and other titles.

Ca·leb (kā′ləb). A Hebrew leader. He and Joshua were the only two allowed to enter the Promised Land. Numbers 14:24.

calèche. Variant of **calash.**

Cal·e·do·ni·a (kăl′ə-dō′nē-ə, -dōn′yə). The Roman name for Scotland. It was first used by Lucan, the Roman poet (1st century A.D.), to describe Britain north of the Antonine Wall, which reached from the Firth of Forth to the Firth of Clyde. Today Caledonia is chiefly used in the names of many Scottish institutions and in poetry.

Cal·e·do·ni·an (kăl′ə-dō′nē-ən, -yən) *adj.* **1.** *Poetic.* Of or pertaining to Scotland. **2.** *Geology.* Of or pertaining to the mountain-building episode that occurred in the late Silurian and Devonian periods. *~n. Poetic.* A native of Scotland.

cal·en·dar (kăl′ən-dər) *n. Abbr.* **cal. 1.** Any of various systems of reckoning time in which the beginning, length, and divisions of a year are arbitrarily defined or otherwise established. **2.** A table showing the months, weeks, and days in at least one specific year. **3.** A list or schedule, especially one arranged in chronological order, as of court cases awaiting trial, sporting events, or the like: *the next big event in the racing calendar.* **4.** *Library Science.* A chronological list of documents or manuscripts, usually annotated. **5.** *Obsolete.* A guide; an example.
~tr.v. **calendared, -daring, -dars.** To enter on a calendar; list; schedule. [Middle English *calender,* from Norman French, from Medieval Latin *kalendārium,* from Latin, a moneylender's account book (because the monthly interest was due on the calends), from *kalendae,* the CALENDS.] See feature, next page.

calendar month *n.* See **month** (sense 1).

cal·en·der (kăl′ən-dər) *n.* A machine in which paper or cloth is made smooth and glossy by being pressed through rollers.
~tr.v. **calendered, -dering, -ders.** To press in a calender. [French *calendre,* from Medieval Latin *calendra, celendra,* from Latin *cylindrus,* cylinder, roller, from Greek *kulindros,* from *kulindein,* to roll.] **—cal·en·der·er** *n.*

ca·len·dri·cal (kə-lĕn′drĭ-kəl) *adj.* Of, pertaining to, or used in a calendar.

cal·ends (kăl′əndz) *n., pl.* **calends.** Also **kal·ends.** *Used with a singular or plural verb.* In the ancient Roman calendar, the day of the new moon and the first day of the month. [Middle English *kalendes,* from Latin *kalendae.*] **—ca·len·dal** *adj.*

ca·len·du·la (kə-lĕn′jo͞o-lə) *n.* Any plant of the genus *Calendula,* having orange-yellow rayed flowers; especially, the **pot marigold** *(see).* [New Latin *Calendula,* from Medieval Latin *calendula,* marigold, from Latin *kalendae,* CALENDS (perhaps because it was thought to be a cure for menstrual disorders).]

cal·en·ture (kăl′ən-cho͝or′) *n.* A mild, brief, or sometimes persistent tropical fever. [Spanish *calentura,* from *calentar,* to heat, from Latin *calēns* (stem *calent-*), present participle of *calēre,* to be warm.]

calf[1] (kăf, käf) *n., pl.* **calves** (kăvz, kävz). **1.** A young cow or bull. **2.** The young of certain other mammals, such as the elephant or whale. **3.** Calfskin. **4.** A large, floating chunk of ice split from a glacier, iceberg, or floe. **5.** An awkward, callow youth. **—kill the fatted calf.** To prepare a feast of welcome; celebrate in grand style. [Middle English *calf, kelf,* Old English *cealf,* from West Germanic *kalbam* (unattested).]

calf[2] *n., pl.* **calves.** The fleshy, muscular back part of the human leg, between the knee and ankle. [Middle English, from Old Norse *kalfi*†.]

calf's-foot jelly, calves'-foot jelly (kăvz′fo͝ot′, kăvz′-) *n.* A gelatinous food made by boiling calves' feet.

calf·skin (kăf′skĭn′, käf′-) *n.* **1.** The hide of a calf. **2.** *Abbr.* **cf.** Fine leather made from the hide of a calf. In this sense, also called "calf."

Cal·ga·ry (kăl′gə-rē). City of southern Alberta, Canada. Situated at the confluence of the Bow and Elbow rivers, it is the market center for south Alberta and the heart of Canada's petroleum industry. It has a famous annual rodeo, the Calgary Stampede.

Cal·houn (kăl-ho͞on′), **John Caldwell** (1782–1850). U.S. vice president (1824–32) and political philosopher. As a South Carolina senator devoted to protecting the interests of the South, he argued that the citizens of individual states had the right to nullify any federal legislation that they deemed unconstitutional (1832–33). He wrote several theses elucidating his political views.

Cal·i·ban (kăl′ə-băn′) *n.* A man of savage and brutish character. [After a character in Shakespeare's *The Tempest,* perhaps alteration of CARIBAN.]

cal·i·ber (kăl′ə-bər) *n.* Also *chiefly British* **cal·i·bre. 1.** *Abbr.* **cal. a.** The diameter of the inside of a tube. **b.** The diameter of the bore of a gun. **c.** The diameter of a bullet or shell. **2.** Degree of excellence, worth, or distinction. [Old French *calibre,* from Old Italian *calibro,* from Arabic *qālib,* shoemaker's last, probably from Greek *kalapous,* "wooden foot" : *kalon,* wood, firewood, from *kaiein,* to burn + *pous,* foot.]

cal·i·brate (kăl′ə-brāt′) *tr.v.* **-brated, -brating, -brates. 1.** To check, adjust, or standardize systematically the graduations of a quantitative measuring instrument. **2.** To determine the caliber of (a tube). **—cal·i·bra·tion** *n.* **—cal·i·bra·tor** *n.*

ca·li·ces. Plural of **calix.**

ca·li·che (kə-lē′chē; *Spanish* kä-lē′chā) *n.* **1. a.** A crude sodium nitrate occurring naturally in Chile, Peru, and the southwestern United States, used as fertilizer. **b. Sodium nitrate** *(see).* **2.** A hard soil layer cemented by calcium carbonate and found in deserts and other arid or semiarid regions. [American Spanish, from Spanish, chip of limestone, from *cal,* lime(stone), from Latin *calx,* from Greek *khalix,* pebble.]

cal·i·co (kăl′ĭ-kō) *n., pl.* **-coes** or **-cos. 1.** A coarse cloth, usually printed with bright designs. **2.** *British.* A plain white cotton cloth.
~adj. **1.** Made of calico. **2.** Resembling printed calico; spotted; mottled: *a calico cat.* [Earlier *calicut,* after CALICUT.]

cal·i·co·back (kăl′ĭ-kō-băk) *n.* The **harlequin bug** *(see).*

calico bush *n.* A shrub, the **mountain laurel** *(see).*

Cal·i·cut (kăl′ə-kət). Also **Ko·zhi·kode** (kō′zhə-kōd′). City on the southwest coast of India. Vasco da Gama made his first landfall in India on the site, where the Portuguese, British, French, and Danes later established trading posts. Finally ceded to Britain (1792), Calicut became the chief port of southern India. It gave its name to calico, its main export in the 17th century.

calif. Variant of **caliph.**

Cal·i·for·nia (kăl′ə-fôrn′yə, -fôr′nē-ə). Pacific state of the United States. The third-largest state and the most populous, it is known as the "Golden State" because of its sunny climate and the discovery of gold in pioneering days. Its forested coastal ranges are noted for

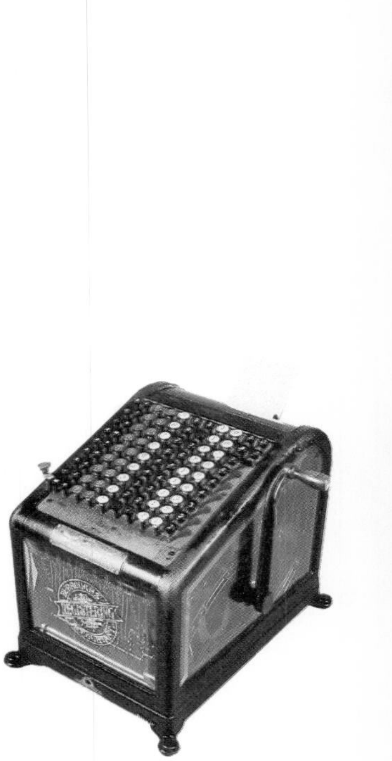

calculator *This Burroughs adding machine, one of the first mechanical calculators, was used by a British bank between 1897 and 1913. Digits were added by pressing the keys and the sum total was given by operating the handle. The machine is now in the Science Museum, London.*

calendar

MEASURING THE PASSAGE OF TIME
How cycles of the sun and moon are used to predict events

Almost every society has had to devise a system of measuring time in order to fix dates for annual events such as seasonal or religious festivals. Primitive societies calculated time by so many suns and moons, and the complex calendars of more sophisticated societies are also based on cycles of the sun and moon.

But the lunar and solar cycles are not compatible. The lunar month (the interval between two new moons) averages 29.5 days, 12 lunar months equaling

354 days. The solar year (the time the earth takes to orbit from one vernal equinox to the next) is 365 days 5 hours 48 minutes and 46 seconds (365.24 days), equaling 12.37 lunar months. So calendars based on a lunar year do not keep in step with the seasons.

The Roman Julian calendar of the 1st century B.C. was based on the solar cycle, having an average year of 365.25 days—the fractions of a day were taken up in a 366-day leap year every four years. But by 1582 it was

more than 10 days behind the seasons because the time difference between 365.24 and 365.25 days (11 minutes 14 seconds) amounts to 7-8 days over 1,000 years. Pope Gregory XIII therefore deleted 10 days in 1582, and to reduce future error he decreed that centennial years should be leap years only if divisible by 400 (so 1900, for example, was not a leap year but 2000 will be). The Gregorian calendar was adopted in Britain and the American colonies in 1752.

GREGORIAN A widely used calendar matching the seasons with a 365¼-day year.		HEBREW The year 5743 coincided with September 18, 1982–August 10, 1983.		MUSLIM In the Muslim year 1396, Muharram corresponded with January 1976.		CHINESE The ancient Chinese agricultural calendar has 24 seasonal segments each of about a fortnight. The Gregorian dates given are approximate.	
Month	days	Month	days	Month	days	Fortnight	Gregorian dates
January	31	Tishri (September–October)	30	Muharram	30	Li Chun (Spring Begins) ... February 5–19 Yu Shui (Rain Water) ... February 19–March 5	
February (Leap year 29)	28	Heshvan (October–November) (in some years ... 30)	29	Safar	29	Jing Zhe (Excited Insects) ... March 5–20 Chun Fen (Vernal Equinox) ... March 20–April 4/5	
March	31	Kislev (November–December) (in some years ... 30)	29	Rabī' I	30	Qing Ming (Clear and Bright) ... April 4/5–20 Gu Yu (Grain Rains) ... April 20–May 5	
April	30	Tevet (December–January)	29	Rabī' II	29	Li Xia (Summer Begins) ... May 5–21 Xiao Man (Grain Fills) ... May 21–June 5	
May	31	Shevat (January–February)	30	Jumādā I	30	Mang Zhong (Grain in Ear) ... June 5–21 Xia Zhi (Summer Solstice) ... June 21–July 7	
June	30	Adar (February–March) (in leap year ... 30)	29	Jumādā II	29	Xiao Shu (Slight Heat) ... July 7–23 Da Shu (Great Heat) ... July 23–August 7	
July	31	Nisan (March–April)	30	Rajab	30	Li Qiu (Autumn Begins) ... August 7–23 Chu Shu (Limit of Heat) ... August 23–September 7	
August	31	Iyar (April–May)	29	Sha'ban	29	Bai Lu (White Dew) ... September 7–23 Qui Fen (Autumn Equinox) ... September 23–October 8	
September	30	Sivan (May–June)	30	Ramadān	30	Han Lu (Cold Dew) ... October 8–23 Shuang Jiang (Frost Descends) ... October 23–November 7	
October	31	Tammuz (June–July)	29	Shawwāl	29	Li Dong (Winter Begins) ... November 7–22 Xiao Xue (Little Snow) ... November 22–December 7	
November	30	Av (July–August)	30	Dhū al-Qa'dah	30	Da Xue (Heavy Snow) ... December 7–22 Dong Zhi (Winter Solstice) ... December 22–January 6	
December	31	Elul (August–September)	29	Dhū al-Hijjah	29 or 30	Xiao Han (Little Cold) ... January 6–21 Da Han (Severe Cold) ... January 21–February 5	

FOUR CALENDARS IN USE TODAY *The Hebrew and Muslim calendars are based on the lunar year, the Gregorian on the solar year, and the Chinese on lunar and solar cycles. The Hebrew calendar periodically includes an extra month (First Adar), and the Chinese does so occasionally. In the Muslim calendar, an extra day is added to the last month in some years to ensure that the first day of the month coincides with the new moon. The Chinese calendar is banned in China but is still used in parts of Asia.*

their giant redwood trees. The state's products include fruit, wine, natural gas, gold, silver, and copper, while its manufacturing includes aerospace and defense-linked industries. California was colonized by the Spaniards and ceded to the United States in 1848. Sacramento is the capital. —**Cal·i·for·nian** *n. & adj.*

California laurel *n.* An aromatic evergreen tree, *Umbellularia californica*, of the North American Pacific Coast, having yellowish-green fleshy fruit and attractively grained wood. Also called "bay tree," "Oregon myrtle."

California lilac *n.* A shrub, the **blueblossom** (see).

California nutmeg *n.* An evergreen tree, *Torreya californica*, having spiny, pointed leaves and purple-streaked, greenish fruit.

California poppy *n.* A plant, *Eschscholtzia californica*, native to the Pacific Coast of North America but widely cultivated, having finely divided bluish-green leaves and orange-yellow flowers.

cal·i·for·ni·um (kăl′ə-fôr′nē-əm) *n. Symbol* Cf A synthetic element produced in trace quantities, originally by helium isotope bombardment of curium. All isotopes are radioactive, chiefly by emission of alpha particles. Atomic number 98, mass numbers 244–254, half-

lives varying from 25 minutes to 800 years. [New Latin; discovered at the University of *California* (Berkeley).]

ca·lig·i·nous (kə-lĭj′ə-nəs) *adj.* Dark; gloomy; shadowy. [Old French *caligineux,* from Latin *cālīginōsus,* dark, from *cālīgō†,* darkness.]

Ca·lig·u·la (kə-lĭg′yə-lə), born Gaius Caesar Augustus Germanicus (A.D. 12–41). Roman emperor (37–41). The son of Germanicus Caesar and Agrippina the Elder, he was adopted (A.D. 32) by Tiberius, on whose death he succeeded. He ennobled his favorite horse, claimed to be a manifestation of all the gods, and provoked a riot in Jerusalem by ordering a statue of himself to be erected in the temple. He was assassinated after alienating the army and threatening to execute the members of the senate. As a child, he wore military boots and was dubbed Caligula (little boot) by his father's soldiers.

cal·i·pash (kăl′ə-păsh′, kăl′ə-păsh′) *n.* An edible, gelatinous, greenish substance lying beneath a turtle's upper shell. [Probably alteration of Spanish *carapacho,* CARAPACE.]

cal·i·pee (kăl′ə-pē′, kăl′ə-pē′) *n.* An edible, gelatinous, yellowish substance lying above a turtle's lower shell. [Probably alteration of CALIPASH.]

cal·i·per, cal·li·per (kăl'ə-pər) **1.** *Usually* **calipers.** An instrument consisting essentially of two curved hinged legs, used to measure internal and external dimensions. **2.** A **vernier caliper** *(see).* **3.** *Medical.* Either of a pair of metal rods with straps and attachments for providing support to or exerting tension on a leg.
~*v.* **calipered, -pering, -pers.** —*tr.* To measure with calipers. —*intr.* To determine dimensions by using calipers. [Probably a variant of CALIBRE.]

ca·liph, ca·lif, ka·lif, kha·lif (kā'lĭf, kăl'ĭf) *n.* The secular and religious head of a Muslim state. [Middle English *caliphe, califfe,* from Old French *calife,* from Arabic *khalīfa,* "successor" (of Muhammad), from *khalafa,* to succeed.]

ca·liph·ate (kā'lĭf-āt', kăl'ĭf-, -ĭt) *n.* The office, jurisdiction, or reign of a caliph.

cal·i·sa·ya (kăl'ə-sā'ə) *n.* The bark of any tree of the genus *Cinchona,* from which quinine is obtained. Also called "calisaya bark," "yellowbark." [Spanish, probably after *Calisaya,* 17th-century Bolivian Indian who taught the Spanish the use of quinine contained in the bark.]

cal·is·then·ics, cal·lis·then·ics (kăl'əs-thĕn'ĭks) *pl.n.* **1.** Simple gymnastic exercises designed to develop muscular tone and to promote physical well-being **2.** *Used with a singular verb.* The practice of such exercises. [CAL(L)I- + Greek *sthenos,* strength (see **sthenia**).] —**cal'is·then'ic** *adj.*

calk¹ (kôk) *n.* A pointed extension on the toe or heels of a horseshoe designed to prevent slipping.
~*tr.v.* **calked, calking, calks. 1.** To supply with calks. **2.** To cut or injure with a calk. [Short for earlier *calkin,* Middle English *kakun,* from Middle Dutch *calcoen,* hoof of a horse, from Old French *calcain,* heel, from Latin *calcāneum, calcāneus,* from *calx*† (stem *calc-*).]

calk². Variant of **caulk.**

call (kôl) *v.* **called, calling, calls.** —*tr.* **1.** To cry out in a loud voice so as to attract attention. **2.** To summon. **3.** To convoke or convene (a meeting). **4.** To summon to a specified vocation or pursuit. **5.** To awaken. **6.** To telephone (someone). **7.** To name. **8.** To estimate as being; consider: *I call that fair.* **9.** To describe as; label: *Nobody calls me a liar.* **10.** *Law.* To bring to action or under consideration: *call a case to court.* **11.** To demand payment of (a loan or bond issue). **12.** *Baseball.* **a.** To stop (a game) because of bad weather or darkness. **b.** To indicate a decision in regard to (a pitch, ball, strike, or player) **13.** *Billiards.* **a.** To predict (the outcome of a shot) before playing **b.** To ask (another player) to do so. **14.** To forecast or predict accurately. **15.** *Poker.* To demand to see the hand of (an opponent) by equaling his bet. **16.** To read aloud (a register or list) to ascertain any absences. **17.** To shout (directions) in rhythm for square dances. —*intr.* **1.** To telephone. **2.** To pay a short visit. **3.** To attract attention by shouting. **4.** To urge one to go: *duty calls.* **5.** *Bridge.* To make a bid. **6.** To guess the result of the toss of a coin or spin of a racket. **7.** To make a characteristic cry. Used chiefly of birds. —**call back. 1.** To telephone in return. **2.** To retract or disavow. —**call down. 1.** To invoke, as from heaven. **2.** *Informal.* To find fault with or berate. —**call for. 1.** To go and get, or stop for. **2.** To be appropriate for; warrant: *This calls for a celebration.* —**call forth.** To evoke. —**call in. 1.** To collect or request payment of. **2.** To take out of circulation: *calling in silver dollars.* **3.** To summon for assistance or consultation: *call in a specialist.* —**call into being.** To create or cause to exist. —**call into question.** To raise doubt about. —**call off. 1.** To cancel or postpone. **2.** To restrain or recall. **3.** To read aloud, as from a list of names. —**call on** or **upon. 1.** To pay a short visit to. **2.** To request or order (someone) to do something. —**call out. 1.** To shout. **2.** To cause to assemble; summon: *call out the guard.*
~*n.* **1.** An act of calling. **2.** A shout or loud cry. **3. a.** The characteristic cry of an animal, especially a bird. **b.** An instrument or sound made to imitate such a cry, used as a lure. **4. a.** Need or occasion: *There was no call for that remark.* **b.** Demand: *There isn't much call for tiepins today.* **5. a.** A claim on a person's time or life: *the call of duty.* **b.** Attraction or appeal: *the call of the wild.* **6.** A short visit; especially, one made as a formality or for business or professional purposes. **7.** A summons or invitation. **8.** A signal, as made by a hunting horn, bugle, or bell. **9.** A vocation, as to the priesthood. **10.** An act of telephoning or instance of being telephoned. **11. a.** A notice summoning actors to rehearsal. **b.** A spoken message telling an actor to be ready to appear on stage. **12.** *Sports.* The decision of an umpire or linesman. **13. a.** *Poker.* A demand to see an opponent's hand. **b.** *Bridge.* A bid or turn to bid. **14.** A demand or request for the payment of a debt. **15.** *Finance.* **a.** A **call option** *(see).* **b.** An unpaid part of the price of a share. **c.** A demand for this outstanding amount. **d.** A demand for the presentation of redeemable bonds or shares. —**on call. 1.** Payable on demand. **2.** Available whenever summoned. —**within call.** Easily summoned; accessible. [Middle English *callen,* Old English *ceallian,* to call, shout, from Old Norse *kalla.*]

cal·la (kăl'ə) *n.* **1.** Any of several tropical or semitropical plants of the genus *Zantedeschia*; especially, *Z. aethiopica,* widely cultivated for its large, showy white spathe that encloses a yellow spadix. Also called "arum lily." **2.** A marsh plant, *Calla palustris,* of the North Temperate Zone, having small, densely clustered greenish flowers partly enclosed in a spreading white spathe. [New Latin *Calla,* probably from Greek *kallaia,* wattle of a cock, from *kallos,* beauty.]

Cal·la·ghan (kăl'ə-hən, -hăn') **(Leonard) James** (1912–). British Labour prime minister (1976–79). A former clerk who served in the Royal Navy during World War II, he entered Parliament in 1945 and was chancellor of the exchequer from 1964 until his resignation in protest against Wilson's devaluation of the pound (1967). He was home secretary (1967–70) and foreign secretary (1974–76).

Cal·lao (kä-you', -yä'ō). The major port of Peru, on the Pacific Ocean and now part of Greater Lima. Founded in 1537, it was frequently raided by pirates and adventurers.

Cal·las (kăl'əs, kä'ləs), **Maria,** born Maria Anna Kalogeropoulos (1923–77). U.S.-born Greek coloratura soprano. She made her debut in Athens at the age of 14 in the opera *Cavalleria Rusticana.* She became the prima donna at Milan's La Scala (1950) and made her American debut in Chicago (1954) as Bellini's *Norma.*

call·boy (kôl'boi') *n.* One who tells actors when it is time for them to go on stage.

call·er¹ (kô'lər) *n.* **1.** Someone or something that calls or cries out. **2.** A person paying a short visit. **3.** A person making a telephone call. **4.** A person who calls numbers at bingo. **5.** In square dancing, a person who calls out the changing sequence of movements.

cal·ler² (kăl'ər) *adj. Scottish.* **1.** Fresh. Said of food, especially fish. **2.** Cool and refreshing. Said of a breeze. [Middle English *calour,* earlier *calvur*†.]

call girl *n. Informal.* A prostitute who takes appointments by telephone.

calli– *prefix.* Indicates beauty; for example, **calliopsis.** [Latin, from Greek *kalli-,* from *kallos,* beauty.]

cal·lig·ra·phy (kə-lĭg'rə-fē) *n.* **1.** The art of fine handwriting. **2.** Penmanship; handwriting. Compare **cacography.** [French *calligraphie,* from Greek *kalligraphia* : CALLI- + -GRAPHY.] —**cal·lig·ra·pher, cal·lig·ra·phist** *n.* —**cal·li·graph·ic** (kăl'ə-grăf'ĭk) *adj.*

Cal·lim·a·chus (kə-lĭm'ə-kəs) (*c.* 305–240 B.C.). A poet and scholar of ancient Greece. The fragments of his work that survive include the catalogue of the library of Alexandria and 64 epigrams.

call·ing (kô'lĭng) *n.* **1.** An inner urge; a strong impulse. **2.** An occupation, profession, or career.

calling card *n.* A card bearing one's name and often one's address and telephone number, used for social or business purposes.

cal·li·o·pe (kăl'ē-ōp', kə-lī'ə-pē') A musical instrument fitted with steam whistles, played from a keyboard. It is usually heard at carnivals and circuses.

Cal·li·o·pe (kə-lī'ə-pē'). *Greek Mythology.* The Muse of epic poetry. [Latin, from Greek *Kalliopē,* "beautiful-voiced" : CALLI- + *ops,* voice.]

cal·li·op·sis (kăl'ē-ŏp'sĭs) *n.* A plant, the **coreopsis** *(see).* [New Latin, "having a beautiful appearance" : Greek *kallos,* beauty + -OPSIS.]

calliper. Variant of **caliper.**

cal·li·pyg·i·an (kăl'ə-pĭj'ē-ən) *adj.* Also **cal·li·pyg·ous** (-pī'gəs). Having beautifully proportioned buttocks. [Greek *kallipugos* : CALLI- + *pugē,* buttocks.]

callisthenics. Variant of **calisthenics.**

Cal·lis·to (kə-lĭs'tō) *n.* One of the satellites of Jupiter, shown by Voyager 2 to have an extremely smooth, icy surface. [After *Callisto,* in Greek mythology a nymph loved by Zeus.]

call letters *pl.n.* The identifying code letters or numbers of a radio or television transmitting station.

call loan *n.* A loan repayable on demand at any time.

call market *n.* The market for call money.

call money *n.* Money lent by banks, usually to stockbrokers, subject to repayment on demand at any time.

call number *n.* A number used in libraries to classify a book and indicate its place on the shelves.

call option *n.* An agreement in which a trader may, for a commission, buy a quantity of a stock or commodity for a specific price within a limited period of time. Also called "call."

cal·lose (kăl'ōs') *n.* A complex branched carbohydrate component of plant cell walls. [Latin *callosus,* callous.]

cal·los·i·ty (kă-lŏs'ə-tē, kə-) *n., pl.* **-ties. 1. a.** A calloused area. **b.** The condition of being calloused. **2.** Hard-heartedness; insensitivity. [Middle English *callosite,* from Old French, from Latin *callōsitās* (stem *callōsitāt-*), from *callōsus,* hardened, CALLOUS.]

cal·lous (kăl'əs) *adj.* **1.** Emotionally hardened; insensitive; unfeeling. **2.** Having calluses; toughened. [Middle English, from Old French *calleuse,* from Latin *callōsus,* from *callum, callus,* hard skin, CALLUS.] —**cal·loused** *adj.* —**cal·lous·ly** *adv.* —**cal·lous·ness** *n.*

cal·low (kăl'ō) *adj.* **1.** Immature; inexperienced. **2.** Not yet having feathers; unfledged. Said of birds. [Originally, "bald," hence unfledged, Middle English *calwe,* bald, Old English *calu,* probably from Latin *calvus,* bald.] —**cal·low·ly** *adv.* —**cal·low·ness** *n.*

call rate *n.* The rate of interest charged on call loans.

call sign *n.* A signal, often using code words or letters, used by a radio station to identify itself.

call up *tr.v.* **1.** To summon for military service. **2.** To telephone (someone). **3.** To cause to remember; evoke: *calling up old times.*

call-up (kôl'ŭp') *n.* **1.** A summons for military service. **2.** Those summoned for military service.

cal·lus (kăl'əs) *n., pl.* **-luses. 1. a.** A localized thickening and enlargement of the horny layer of the skin, resulting from continual pressure or friction; callosity. **b.** The hard bony tissue that develops around the ends of a fractured bone during healing. **2.** *Botany.* The hardened tissue that develops over a wound or cut in a woody stem.
~*intr.v.* **callused, -lusing, -luses.** To form or develop a callus. [Latin *callus, callum*†.]

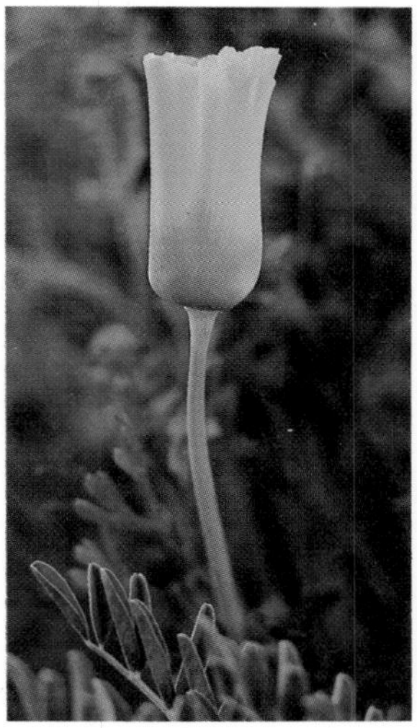

California poppy *A native of the western United States, the California poppy survives even in desert regions. The plant is cultivated as a hardy annual and bears a poppylike flower that closes in dull or cold weather.*

PRONUNCIATION KEY

ă, pat; ā, pay; âr, care;
ä, father, are; b, bib;
ch, church; d, deed; ĕ, pet;
ē, be; f, fife; g, gag; h, hat;
hw, which; ĭ, pit; ī, pie;
îr, pier; j, judge; k, kick;
l, lid, needle; m, mum;
n, no, sudden; ng, thing;
ŏ, pot; ō, toe; ô, paw, for;
oi, noise; ou, out; ŏŏ, book;
ōō, boot; p, pop; r, roar;
s, sauce; sh, ship, dish;
t, tight; th, thin, path;
th, this, bathe; ŭ, cut; ûr, fur;
v, valve; w, with; y, yes;
z, zebra, size; zh, vision;
ə, about, item, edible, gallop, circus, peaceful

IN FOREIGN WORDS:

à, *Fr.* ami; œ, *Fr.* feu, *Ger.* schön; ü, *Fr.* tu, *Ger.* über; KH, *Ger.* ich, *Scot.* loch; N, *Fr.* bon; y', *Fr.* Compiègne

STRESS MARKS:

Primary stress: '
in·cite' (ĭn-sīt')
Secondary stress: '
in'sight' (ĭn'sīt')

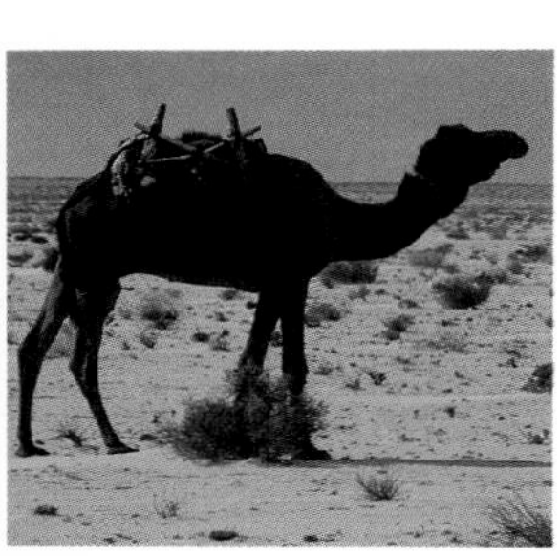

camel *Although camels can survive long periods without water, they have a correspondingly gargantuan thirst. A full-grown camel can drink up to 120 liters (27 gallons) at a time. The two-humped Bactrian camel, found in central Asia, is used for carrying loads in cold mountainous regions, while the single-humped dromedary (above) is better adapted to riding and load carrying in hot deserts. The humps of both types contain deposits of fat, which act as a food reserve.*

calm (käm) *adj.* **calmer, calmest. 1.** Undisturbed by wind. **2.** Free from excitement or agitation. **3.** Not affected by anxiety or qualms.
~n. **1.** An absence of disturbance or agitation; peacefulness. **2.** *Meteorology.* A condition of no wind or a wind with a velocity of less than 1 knot; force 0 on the Beaufort scale. **3.** Freedom from anxiety or qualms.
~v. **calmed, calming, calms.** *—tr.* To make calm; quiet. Often used with *down.* *—intr.* To become calm or quiet. Often used with *down.* [Middle English *calme,* from Old French, from Late Latin *cauma,* heat of the day, hence, a rest or resting place in the heat of the day, from Greek *kauma,* burning heat, from *kaiein,* to burn.] **—calm·ly** *adv.* **—calm·ness** *n.*
Synonyms: *peaceful, placid, quiet, serene, still, tranquil.*

calm·a·tive (kä′mə-tĭv, kăl′mə-) *adj.* Having relaxing or pacifying properties; sedative.
~n. A sedative or tranquilizer. [From CALM (after SEDATIVE).]

cal·o·mel (kăl′ə-məl′, -məl) *n.* A white, tasteless compound, Hg_2Cl_2, used as a purgative. [French, from New Latin *calomelas,* "beautiful black" (calomel, though white, was originally developed from a black powder) : Greek *kalos,* beautiful + *melas,* black.]

cal·o·re·cep·tor (kăl′ə-rĭ-sĕp′tər) *n.* A sensory receptor that detects warmth. [Latin *calor,* heat + RECEPTOR.]

ca·lor·ic (kə-lôr′ĭk, -lŏr′ĭk) *adj.* Of or pertaining to heat or calories.
~n. A hypothetically indestructible, uncreatable, highly elastic, self-repellent, all-pervading fluid, formerly thought responsible for the production, possession, and transfer of heat.

cal·o·rie (kăl′ər-ē) *n.* **1.** *Abbr.* **cal** Any of several approximately equal units of heat, each measured as the quantity of heat required to raise the temperature of 1 gram of water by 1°C from a standard initial temperature, especially from 3.98°C, 14.5°C, or 19.5°C, at 1 atmosphere pressure. Also called "gram calorie," "small calorie." **2.** *Abbr.* **cal** The unit of heat equal to $^1/_{100}$ the quantity of heat required to raise the temperature of 1 gram of water from 0 to 100°C at 1 atmosphere pressure. Also called "mean calorie." **3.** *Abbr.* **Cal** The unit of heat equal to the amount of heat required to raise the temperature of 1 kilogram of water by 1°C at 1 atmosphere pressure. Also called "kilocalorie," "kilogram calorie," "large calorie." **4.** The unit of heat equal to 4.184 joules. Also called "thermochemical calorie." The calorie has been replaced by the joule for all scientific purposes and some nonscientific uses. The calories used to express the energy value of foods are kilocalories (sense 3): 1 kilocalorie is equal to 4,184 joules. [French, from Latin *calor,* heat.]

cal·o·rif·ic (kăl′ə-rĭf′ĭk) *adj.* Pertaining to or generating heat or calories. [French *calorifique,* from Latin *calorificus* : *calor,* heat + -FIC.]

calorific value *n.* The quantity of heat, usually expressed in joules per kilogram, that will be produced by the complete combustion of a given mass of a fuel.

cal·o·rim·e·ter (kăl′ə-rĭm′ə-tər) *n.* **1.** An apparatus for measuring heat. **2.** The part of such an apparatus, usually a sample container, in which the heat measured causes a change of state. [Latin *calor,* heat + -METER.]

cal·o·rim·e·try (kăl′ə-rĭm′ə-trē) *n.* The measurement of the quantity of heat evolved or absorbed by a chemical reaction, change of state, or formation of a solution. **—cal·o·ri·met·ri·cal** (kăl′ə-rĭ-mĕt′rĭ-kəl) *adj.*

ca·lotte (kə-lŏt′) *n.* A skullcap, especially one worn by Roman Catholic clergymen. [French, diminutive of Old French *cale,* cap, from Germanic.]

ca·loy·er (kə-loi′ər, kăl′ə-yər) *n.* A monk of the Eastern Orthodox Church. [French, from obsolete Italian *caloiero,* from Medieval Greek *kalogēros,* venerable, "handsome old man" : Greek *kalos,* beautiful + *gēras,* old age.]

cal·pac, cal·pack, kal·pak (kăl′păk′, kăl-păk′) *n.* A large black cap, usually of sheepskin or felt, worn in Turkey, Armenia, and other Near Eastern regions. [Turkish *kalpāk.*]

calque (kălk) *n. Linguistics.* **1.** A form of semantic borrowing in which a word is given a special extended meaning by analogy with that of a word having the same basic meaning in another language. **2.** A **loan translation** *(see).*
~tr.v. **calqued, calquing, calques.** To model (the meaning of a word) upon that of an analogous word in another language. [French, tracing, imitation, close copy, from *calquer,* to trace, copy, from Italian *calcar,* to press, from Latin *calcāre,* to trample, stamp, from *calx,* a heel.]

cal·trop, cal·trap (kăl′trəp) *n.* **1.** *Military.* An iron ball with four projecting spikes so arranged that when three of the spikes were on the ground, the fourth pointed upward. It was formerly used to delay the advance of mounted and unmounted troops. Also called "crowfoot." **2.** Any of several plants having spiny burs or bracts, as members of the genus *Tribulus.* See **water chestnut.** [Middle English *cal(ke)trap(pe),* from Old French *chauchetrap,* iron ball with spikes, and Old English *calcatrippe,* spiny plant, brambles, both from Medieval Latin *calcatrappa, calcatrippa,* "foot trap" : Latin *calcāre,* to tread, from *calx,* heel + Medieval Latin *trappa,* trap, from Germanic.]

cal·u·met (kăl′yə-mĕt′, -mət, kăl′yə-mĕt′) *n.* A long-stemmed, ornamented pipe used by North American Indians for ceremonial purposes. Also called "peace pipe." [Canadian French, from French (Normandy dialect), variant of French *chalumeau,* a straw, from Late Latin *calamellus,* little reed, from *calamus,* a reed, from Greek *kalamos.*]

ca·lum·ni·ate (kə-lŭm′nē-āt′) *tr.v.* **-ated, -ating, -ates.** To make false and damaging statements about; slander. —See Synonyms at **malign.** [Latin *calumniārī,* from *calumnia,* CALUMNY.] **—ca·lum·ni·a·tion** *n.* **—ca·lum·ni·a·tor** *n.*

ca·lum·ni·ous (kə-lŭm′nē-əs) *adj.* Also **ca·lum·ni·a·to·ry** (-ə-tôr′ē, -tōr′ē). Containing or implying calumny; slanderous; defamatory. **—ca·lum·ni·ous·ly** *adv.*

cal·um·ny (kăl′əm-nē) *n., pl.* **-nies. 1.** A false statement, maliciously or knowingly made to injure someone's reputation. **2.** The utterance of such statements; slander. [Middle English, from Old French *calomnie,* from Latin *calumnia,* "trickery," "deception," from *calvī,* to deceive, trick.]

cal·u·tron (kăl′yə-trŏn′) *n. Physics.* A device for separating isotopes by deflecting ions in electric and magnetic fields. It is similar in action to a large mass spectrometer.

cal·va·dos (kăl′və-dōs′) *n.* A French brandy made from apples. [French, after *Calvados,* department in Normandy where it was originally made.]

cal·var·i·um (kăl-vâr′ē-əm) *n., pl.* **-iums** or **-ia** (-ē-ə). *Anatomy.* The top, rounded part of the skull. Also called "skullcap." [Late Latin, skull. See **Calvary.**]

cal·va·ry (kăl′vər-ē) *n., pl.* **-ries. 1.** A sculptured depiction of the Crucifixion. **2.** A spiritual ordeal. [After CALVARY.]

Cal·va·ry (kăl′və-rē). The hill outside the ancient city of Jerusalem where Jesus was crucified. [Middle English *Calvarie,* Old English *Calvarie,* from Late Latin *Calvāria,* from Latin *calvāria,* skull (translation of Greek *kranion,* translation of Aramaic *gulgūtha,* GOLGOTHA), from *calva,* scalp, from *calvus,* bald.]

Calvary cross *n. Heraldry.* A Latin cross set on three steps.

calve (kăv, käv) *v.* **calved, calving, calves.** *—intr.* **1.** To give birth to a calf. **2.** To break up and lose a mass of ice. Used of a glacier or an iceberg. *—tr.* **1.** To give birth to (a calf). **2.** To set loose (a mass of ice). [Middle English *calven,* Old English *cealfian,* from *cealf,* CALF (young cow).]

calves. Plural of **calf.**

calves'-foot jelly. Variant of **calf's-foot jelly.**

Cal·vin (kăl′vĭn), **John** (1509–64). French Protestant reformer and theologian who, after breaking with the Roman Catholic Church (1533), settled in Geneva (1541). Although he was never ordained into the priesthood, his brand of theology, published in his book *Institutes* and known today as Presbyterianism, had a profound effect on the Christian world.

Cal·vin·ism (kăl′vĭn-ĭz′əm) *n.* **1.** The religious doctrines of John Calvin, which emphasize the supremacy of the Scriptures in the revelation of truth, the omnipotence of God, the sinfulness of man, the salvation of the elect by God's grace alone, and a rigid moral code. **2.** Agreement with or advocacy of such doctrines. **—Cal·vin·ist** *n.* **—Cal·vin·is·tic** *adj.*

calx (kălks) *n., pl.* **calxes** or **calces** (kăl′sēz′). **1.** The crumbly residue left after a mineral or metal has been calcined or roasted. **2.** Lime; chalk. **3. Calcium oxide** *(see).* [Latin, lime, limestone, from Greek *khalix,* pebble.]

ca·ly·cine (kā′lə-sīn′, kăl′ə-) *adj.* Of, pertaining to, or resembling a calyx.

ca·ly·cle (kā′lə-kəl, kăl′ə-) *n.* **1.** *Botany.* An **epicalyx** *(see).* **2.** *Biology.* A calyculus. [French *calicule,* from Latin *calyculus,* diminutive of *calyx,* bud, CALYX.] **—ca·lyc·u·late** (kə-lĭk′yə-lāt′, -lĭt) *adj.*

ca·lyc·u·lus (kə-lĭk′yə-ləs) *n., pl.* **-li** (-lī′). *Biology.* A small cup-shaped structure. Also called "calycle." [Latin, CALYCLE.] **—ca·lyc·u·lar** *adj.*

ca·lyp·so[1] (kə-lĭp′sō) *n., pl.* **-sos.** An orchid, *Calypso bulbosa,* of the North Temperate Zone, having a pinkish flower with a slipper-shaped lip. [After CALYPSO.]

calypso[2] *n., pl.* **-sos** or **-soes. 1.** A type of song originating in the West Indies, notably in Trinidad, characterized by improvised lyrics on topical or broadly humorous subjects and a syncopated rhythm. **2.** A dance to calypso music. [After CALYPSO.]

Ca·lyp·so (kə-lĭp′sō). *Greek Mythology.* A sea nymph who delayed Odysseus on her island, Ogygia, for seven years. [Latin, from Greek *Kalupsō,* "she who conceals," from *kaluptein,* to cover, conceal.]

ca·lyp·tra (kə-lĭp′trə) *n. Botany.* **1.** The protective cap covering the spore case of a moss or related plant. **2.** Any similar hoodlike or caplike structure. [New Latin, from Greek *kaluptra,* veil, covering, from *kaluptein,* to cover, conceal.] **—ca·lyp·trate** (kə-lĭp′trāt′) *adj.*

ca·lyp·tro·gen (kə-lĭp′trə-jən) *n. Botany.* A layer of actively dividing cells at the end of a root tip, from which the root cap is formed.

ca·lyx (kā′lĭks, kăl′ĭks) *n., pl.* **-lyxes** or **calyces** (kā′lə-sēz′, kăl′ə-). **1.** The outer protective covering of a flower, consisting of a series of leaflike, usually green segments called sepals. Compare **corolla. 2.** A cuplike or funnel-shaped animal structure, such as one of those forming part of the kidney. [Latin, from Greek *kalux.*]

cam (kăm) *n.* An eccentric or multiply curved wheel mounted on a rotating shaft and used to produce variable or reciprocating motion in another engaged or contacted part. [Perhaps from French *came,* from German *Kamm,* "comb," from Old High German *kamb.*]

ca·ma·ra·de·rie (kä′mə-rä′də-rē, kăm′ə-răd′ə-) *n.* Good will and lighthearted rapport between or among friends; comradeship. [French, from *camarade,* COMRADE.]

Ca·margue, La (lä kə-märg′, kä-). Island in the delta of the Rhône River, Bouches-du-Rhône department, southern France. Much of the once predominantly marshy land has been reclaimed and now supports livestock including cattle, bulls for the bullrings of Spain, Portugal, and France, and horses.

cam·a·ril·la (kăm′ə-rīl′ə, -rē′ə) *n.* A group of confidential advisers; a cabal. [Spanish, "small room," from *cámara*, room, from Late Latin *camera*, from Latin, arched roof, from Greek *kamara*, vault.]

cam·as, cam·ass (kăm′əs) *n.* Also **quam·ash** (kwŏm′ăsh′). 1. Any of several North American plants of the genus *Camassia*; especially, *C. quamash*, of western North America, having a showy cluster of blue or white flowers and an edible bulb. 2. The **death camas** (*see*). [Chinook jargon *kamass*.]

cam·ber (kăm′bər) *n.* 1. a. A slightly arched surface, as of a road, a ship's deck, or an airfoil. b. The condition of having an arched surface. 2. A setting of the front wheels of an automotive vehicle so that they are closer together at the bottom than at the top. ~*v.* **cambered, -bering, -bers.** —*tr.* To give a slight arch to. —*intr.* To arch slightly. [Middle English *ca(u)mber*, curved, from Old French *cambre*, from Latin *camur(us)†*, curved inward.]

Cam·ber·well beauty (kăm′bər-wĕl′, -wəl) *n.* A butterfly, the **mourning cloak** (*see*). [After *Camberwell*, a district of south London.]

cam·bist (kăm′bĭst) *n.* 1. A manual giving exchange rates of different currencies and equivalents of different weights and measures. 2. A dealer in or expert on international exchange. [French *cambiste*, from Italian *cambista*, from *cambio*, exchange, from *cambiare*, to exchange, from Late Latin *cambiāre.*] —**cam·bis·try** *n.*

cam·bi·um (kăm′bē-əm) *n.* A layer of cells in the stems and roots of vascular plants that gives rise to phloem and xylem and thus increases the girth of the plant. [New Latin, "that which changes into new layers," from Medieval Latin, exchange, from Latin *cambiāre*, to exchange.] —**cam·bi·al** *adj.*

Cambodia. See Kampuchea. —**Cam·bo·di·an** (kăm-bō′dē-ən) *n. & adj.*

cam·bo·gi·a (kăm-bō′jē-ə) *n.* A resin, **gamboge** (*see*). [New Latin, variant of GAMBOGE.]

Cam·brai (kăm-brā′). Industrial town in northeast France. Famous for the cambric cloth that originated here in the 16th century, it still has a large cloth-dyeing and bleaching industry.

Cam·bri·a (kăm′brē-ə). The Latin name for Wales. [Latin, from Welsh *Cymru*, from Old Welsh *kombroges* (unattested), Welshmen, "compatriots" : *kom-*, with + *bro*, border, region.]

Cam·bri·an¹ (kăm′brē-ən) *adj.* Of or pertaining to Wales; Welsh. ~*n.* A Welshman.

Cambrian² *adj.* Of, belonging to, or pertaining to the geologic time, system of rocks, and sedimentary deposits of the first period of the Paleozoic era, characterized by warm seas and desert land areas. ~*n. Geology.* The Cambrian period. Preceded by *the*. [After CAMBRIA (Wales), where rocks and fossils of this period were found.]

cam·bric (kăm′brĭk) *n.* A finely woven white linen or cotton fabric. [Earlier *cameryk*, from Flemish *Kameryk*, CAMBRAI, where it was first made.] —**cam·bric** *adj.*

cambric tea *n.* A drink, especially for children, that is made of hot water, milk, sugar, and usually a small amount of tea. [So called because it is thin and white like CAMBRIC.]

Cam·bridge¹ (kăm′brĭj). City on the Cam River in Cambridgeshire. An important market center for East Anglia and the administrative center of the county, the city is best known for its university, which dates back to 1284.

Cambridge². City on the Charles River, opposite Boston, in Massachusetts, the seat of America's oldest university, Harvard (established 1636), and the Massachusetts Institute of Technology.

Cam·bridge·shire (kăm′brĭj-shîr, -shər). County in East Anglia, England. Consisting mainly of low-lying fens, it is chiefly agricultural and includes the former county of Huntingdonshire, the Soke of Peterborough, parts of west Suffolk, and the Isle of Ely. The chief towns, Cambridge, Peterborough, and Wisbech, have industries that include brickmaking, cement, electronics, and printing.

came¹ (kām) *n.* A slender, grooved lead bar used to hold together the panes in stained-glass or latticework windows. [Perhaps Scottish *calm*, casting mold.]

came². Past tense of **come.**

cam·el (kăm′əl) *n.* 1. A humped, long-necked ruminant mammal of the genus *Camelus*, domesticated in Old World desert regions as a beast of burden and as a source of wool, milk, and meat. See **Bactrian camel, dromedary.** 2. A device used to raise a sunken or submerged vessel. In this sense, also called "caisson." 3. A light fawn or brownish yellow. [Middle English, from Old English, from Latin *camēlus*, from Greek *kamēlos*, from Semitic; akin to Hebrew and Phoenician *gāmāl*, Arabic *jamal*.]

cam·el·back (kăm′əl-băk′) *adj.* Having a shape characterized by a hump or upward curve.

cam·el·eer (kăm′ə-lîr′) *n.* A person who drives or rides a camel.

camel hair. Variant of **camel's hair.**

ca·mel·ia (kə-mēl′yə) *n.* 1. Any of several shrubs or trees of the genus *Camellia*, native to Asia; especially, *C. japonica*, having shiny evergreen leaves and showy, usually white, pink, or red flowers. 2. The flower of a camellia. Also called "japonica." [New Latin; first described by George Joseph *Kamel* (1661-1706), Moravian Jesuit missionary.]

ca·mel·o·pard (kə-mĕl′ə-pärd′) *n.* 1. *Archaic.* A giraffe. 2. *Heraldry.* A bearing resembling a giraffe, but represented with long curved horns. [Medieval Latin *camēlopardus*, from Latin *camēlopardalis*, from Greek *kamēlopardalis* : *kamēlos*, CAMEL + *pardalis*, variant of *pardos*, PARD (leopard), so called because the giraffe has a head like a camel's and the spots of a leopard.]

Ca·mel·o·par·da·lis (kə-mĕl′ə-pär′də-lĭs) *n.* A constellation in the Northern Hemisphere near Ursa Major and Cassiopeia. [New Latin, CAMELOPARD.]

Cam·e·lot (kăm′ə-lŏt) *n.* 1. The legendary place where King Arthur held court with his Knights of the Round Table. 2. A place, time, or circumstance marked by idealized beauty, peacefulness, and enlightenment.

camel's hair *n.* Also **camel hair.** 1. The soft, fine hair of a camel or a substitute for it. 2. A soft, heavy cloth, usually light tan, made chiefly of camel's hair. —**cam·el's-hair** (kăm′əlz-hâr′) *adj.*

Cam·em·bert¹ (kăm′əm-bâr′). Village in Normandy, northwest France, famous for the cheese of the same name, originally made here.

Camembert² *n.* A creamy, mold-ripened cheese that softens on the inside as it matures.

cam·e·o (kăm′ē-ō′) *n., pl.* **-os.** 1. a. A technique of engraving in relief on a gem, stone, or shell, especially one with layers of different hues, cut so the raised design is of one color and the background of another. Compare **intaglio.** b. A gem, stone, or shell so cut. 2. A medallion with a profile cut in raised relief. 3. A brief literary work or dramatic sketch. 4. A brief but dramatic appearance of a prominent actress or actor in a single scene in a television play or in a film. In this sense, also called "cameo role." ~*tr.v.* **cameoed, -oing, -os.** 1. To make into or like a cameo. 2. To portray in sharp, delicate relief, as in a literary composition. [Middle English *cameu*, from Italian *cam(m)eo* and Old French *camaïeu*, perhaps from Arabic *qamā′īl*, plural of *qum′ūl*, flower bud.]

cameo ware *n.* Pottery having raised figures on a background of contrasting color.

cam·er·a (kăm′ər-ə, kăm′rə) *n., pl.* **-eras** or **-erae** (-ə-rē) (for sense 4). 1. Any apparatus for taking photographs, generally consisting of a lightproof enclosure having an aperture with a shuttered lens through which the image of an object is focused and recorded on a photosensitive film or plate. 2. The part of a television transmitting apparatus that receives the primary image on a light-sensitive cathode tube and transforms it into electrical impulses. 3. A **camera obscura** (*see*). 4. A room or chamber; specifically, a judge's private office. —**in camera.** 1. In court with only the judge and litigants or their representatives present. 2. In private; privately. [Late Latin, room, from Latin, arched roof, from Greek *kamara*, vault.] See feature, next page.

cam·er·al (kăm′ər-əl) *adj.* 1. Pertaining to a judge's chamber and to the judicial affairs that take place there. 2. Pertaining to public finance and state business or to a council that manages such matters. [Medieval Latin *camerālis*, from *camera*, office, department of state, CAMERA.]

camera lu·ci·da (lōō′sĭ-də) *n.* An optical device that projects a virtual image of an object onto a plane surface, especially for tracing. [New Latin, "light chamber" : CAMERA + Latin *lūcīda*, feminine of *lūcīdus*, LUCID.]

cam·er·a·man (kăm′ər-mən′, kăm′rə-) *n., pl.* **-men** (-mĕn′). A man who operates a motion-picture or television camera.

camera ob·scu·ra (ŏb-skyŏŏr′ə, əb-) *n.* A darkened chamber in which the real image of an object is received through a small opening and focused in natural color onto a facing surface. Also called "camera." [New Latin, "dark chamber" : CAMERA + Latin *obscūra*, feminine of *obscūrus*, OBSCURE.]

cam·er·a·shy (kăm′ər-ə-shī′, kăm′rə-) *adj.* Reluctant or nervous about being photographed.

camera tube *n.* The part of a television camera that converts the optical image into electrical signals.

cam·er·a·wom·an (kăm′ər-ə-wŏŏm′ən, kăm′rə-) *n., pl.* **-women** (-wĭm′ĭn). A woman who operates a motion picture or television camera.

cam·er·lin·go (kăm′ər-lĭng′gō) *n., pl.* **-gos.** Also **cam·er·len·go** (-lĕng′gō). *Roman Catholic Church.* The cardinal who manages the pope's secular affairs. [Italian *camarlingo*, from Germanic *kamarling* (unattested), "chamber servant" : *kamar* (unattested), room, from Late Latin *camera*, CAMERA + -LING.]

Cam·er·on (kăm′ər-ən), **Julia Margaret** (1815-79). British photographer noted for her pioneering work in artistic portrait photography. Tennyson, Darwin, and the actress Ellen Terry were among her subjects.

Cam·e·roon (kăm′ə-rōōn′). Country in west-central Africa. Originally the German colony of Kamerun, the country was divided between Britain and France (1919). It became a United Nations trust territory after World War II. French Cameroons was granted independence (1960) as the Cameroon Republic and was joined by the southern part of the British Cameroons (when the remainder of the British territory joined Nigeria) to form the Federal Republic of Cameroon (1961). In 1974 it became the United Republic of Cameroon. Its population of more than 150 different ethnic groups is mainly occupied in agriculture, with coffee, cocoa, and timber the main exports. Offshore oil deposits and large reserves of bauxite are being exploited. The main city and port is Douala. Area, 475,442 square kilometers (183,521 square miles). Population, 11,800,000. Capital, Yaoundé. See map, page 261.

cam·i·knick·ers (kăm′ə-nĭk′ərz) *pl.n. British.* An undergarment worn by women that consists of a pair of underpants combined with a camisole top. [*camisole* + *knickers.*]

cam·i·on (kăm′ē-ən, kà-myôN′) *n.* 1. A low, sturdy wagon. 2. a. A truck. b. A bus. [French, from Old French *chamion†.*]

ca·mi·sa (kə-mē′sə) *n. Southwestern U.S.* A shirt or chemise. [Spanish, from Late Latin *camīsia*, shirt.]

camellia Camellia reticulata *is one of the ornamental flowering species belonging to the Theaceae family of evergreen shrubs and trees. Camellias are native to India, China, and Japan.*

camera

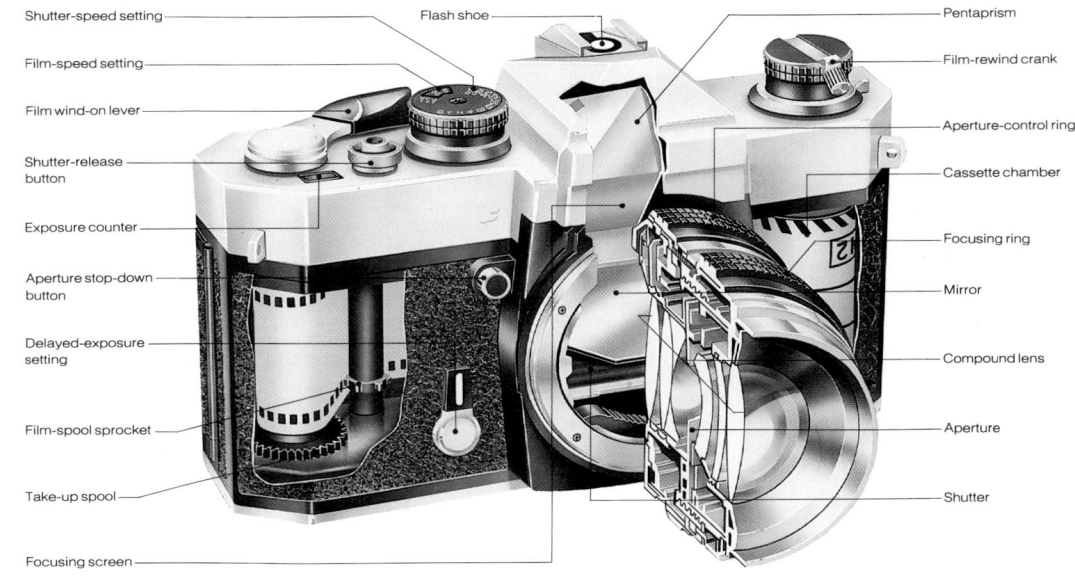

FOUR MAIN TYPES OF CAMERA
Different ways of seeing what the camera will record

In the VIEWFINDER CAMERA, the light image is focused on the film through the lens, but the eye of the photographer receives the image through the viewfinder, which is above the lens. The image received by the eye is slightly different from the image fixed on the film; some models of camera have a built-in adjustment to allow for this. The SINGLE-LENS REFLEX CAMERA (below) receives an image virtually identical to that fixed on the film, because a mirror and prism inside the camera reflect to the eye the image entering the lens. In the TWIN-LENS REFLEX CAMERA, the picture is taken through the lower lens, and the image is reflected by a mirror from the upper lens to a viewing screen on the top of the camera. Because the photographer looks into the camera from above, it need not be held at eye level. As in the viewfinder camera, there can be a slight difference between what the eye sees and the image fixed on the film through the lens. In the VIEW CAMERA, the eye receives the image directly through the lens.

Shutter-speed setting
Film-speed setting
Film wind-on lever
Shutter-release button
Exposure counter
Aperture stop-down button
Delayed-exposure setting
Film-spool sprocket
Take-up spool
Focusing screen
Flash shoe
Pentaprism
Film-rewind crank
Aperture-control ring
Cassette chamber
Focusing ring
Mirror
Compound lens
Aperture
Shutter

THE 35 MM SINGLE-LENS REFLEX CAMERA *The lens reverses the image of the scene before it. The mirror and pentaprism turn it the right way around and show it on the focusing screen for the photographer to view through the eyepiece (at the back of the camera) and adjust with the focusing ring. The aperture and shutter speeds are set to suit the lighting. When the shutter-release button is pressed, the mirror moves to block light from the eyepiece and the shutter opens to expose the film for the set time.*

camouflage *Like some other insects,* Gastropacha quercifolia *has a remarkable ability to merge with its surroundings. While it rests during the day, its folded wings look like a dead leaf.*

cam·i·sa·do (kăm'ə-sä'dō, -sā'dō) *n., pl.* **-dos.** *Archaic.* A surprise attack by night. [Probably from obsolete Spanish *camisada,* "shirted" (because attackers wore white shirts over armor for identification), from *camisa,* shirt, CAMISA.]

ca·mise (kə-mēz', -mēs') *n.* A loose shirt, shift, or tunic. [Arabic *qamīs,* from Late Latin *camīsia,* shirt.]

cam·i·sole (kăm'ə-sōl') *n.* **1.** A woman's sleeveless undergarment. **2.** A short negligee. [French, from Old Provençal *camisolla,* diminutive of *camisa,* shirt, from Late Latin *camīsia.*]

Cam·lan (kăm'lən) *n.* The legendary battlefield where King Arthur was mortally wounded.

cam·let (kăm'lĭt) *n.* **1.** A kind of rich cloth of Oriental origin, supposed to have been made formerly of camel's hair and silk, and later made of goat's hair and silk or other combinations. **2.** A garment made from this cloth. [Middle English *chamelet,* from Old French *c(h)amelot,* from Arabic *ḥamlat.*]

Ca·mões (kə-moinsh'), **Luis Vaz de.** Also **Cam·o·ëns** (kăm'ō-ĕnz) (1524–80). Portuguese poet and soldier noted for his book *Os Lusíadas* (1572), possibly the greatest of all Portuguese literary works.

camomile. Variant of **chamomile.**

Ca·mor·ra (kə-môr'ə, -mŏr'ə) *n.* **1.** A Neapolitan secret society organized about 1820 and notorious for practicing violence and blackmail. Compare **Mafia. 2. camorra.** An unscrupulous, clandestine group. [Italian, perhaps from *camorra†,* a kind of smock (said to have been worn by members of this society).] **—Ca·mor·rism** *n.* **—Ca·mor·rist** *n. & adj.*

cam·ou·flage (kăm'ə-fläzh', -fläj') *n.* **1. a.** The method or result of concealing personnel or material from an enemy by making them appear to be part of the natural surroundings: *Heavy nets were an effective camouflage for the planes.* **2. a.** The condition of an animal that is concealed from predators or prey by means of protective coloration or shape. **b.** The protective coloration or shape of an animal. **3. A** means of concealment or deception; dissimulation: *She used a sweet smile as camouflage for her anger.* **—v. camouflaged, -flaging, -flages.** *—tr.* To conceal by camouflage: *The decorator camouflaged the unattractive view with colorful curtains.* *—intr.* To use camouflage. [French, from *camoufler,* to disguise, from Italian *camuffare†,* to disguise, trick.]

camp¹ (kămp) *n.* **1. a.** A place where a body of people, such as soldiers, miners, or sportsmen, are temporarily lodged in tents, huts, or other makeshift shelters. **b.** The shelters in such a place. **c.** The persons using such shelters. **2.** A place where enemy aliens, political prisoners, and the like are detained. **3.** A place consisting of more or less permanent shelters, such as cabins or tents, used for vacationing or other recreational purposes. **4.** Military service; army life: *recruits getting used to the routine in camp.* **5.** A group of persons, parties, or states favorable to a common cause, doctrine, or political system: *the socialist camp.*
~*adj.* **1.** Pertaining to or used in a camp or camping. **2.** Being portable and usually collapsible: *a camp bed.*
~*intr.v.* **camped, camping, camps. 1.** To make or set up a camp. **2.** To live in or as if in a camp: *We camped in the apartment until the electricity was connected and the furniture arrived.* **—camp out.** To sleep in the open. [French, from Italian *campo,* from Latin *campus†,* open field.]

camp² *n.* **1. a.** An affectation or appreciation of manners and tastes commonly thought to be outlandish, vulgar, or banal. **b.** Behavior exhibiting such affectation or appreciation. **2.** Banality or artificiality when appreciated for its humor.
~*adj.* **1.** Theatrical, affected, or exaggerated in manner or style. **2.** Effeminately homosexual. Said of a man. **3.** In the style of an effeminate man; mannered.
~*intr.v.* **camped, camping, camps.** To act in a theatrical or effeminate manner. Used in the phrase *camp it up.* [20th century : origin obscure.] **—camp·i·ly** *adv.* **—camp·i·ness** *n.* **—camp·y** *adj.*

cam·paign (kăm-pān') *n.* **1.** A series of military operations undertaken to achieve a specific objective within a given area. **2.** An operation undertaken, as by means of propaganda, to attain some political, social, commercial, or personal goal: *We launched a campaign to raise funds for the hospital.*
~*intr.v.* **campaigned, -paigning, -paigns.** To engage or serve in a campaign: *Many of the city's businessmen campaigned for the mayor's re-election.* [French *campagne,* from Old French, battlefield, from Italian *campania,* from Late Latin *campānia,* countryside, from *campus,* field.] **—cam·paign·er** *n.*

Cam·pa·nia (kăm-pān′yə). Region in southern Italy spanning the provinces of Avellino, Benevento, Caserta, Napoli, and Salerno, with the islands of Capri, Ischia, Porcida, and the Pontine Islands. It joined Italy (1861) as part of the kingdom of Naples. The excavated Roman towns of Pompeii and Herculaneum and the region's many resorts give it a large tourist trade.

cam·pa·ni·le (kăm′pə-nē′lē) n., pl. **-les** (-lēz) or **-li** (-lē). A bell tower, especially one near but not attached to a church. [Italian, from *campana*, bell, from Late Latin *campāna*, bell (made of metal produced in Campania), from Latin *campānus*, of Campania.]

cam·pa·nol·o·gy (kăm′pə-nŏl′ə-jē) n. The art or study of bell ringing. [New Latin *campanologia* : Late Latin *campāna*, bell (see **campanile**) + -LOGY.] —**cam·pa·nol·o·gist** n.

cam·pan·u·la (kăm-păn′yə-lə) n. Any of various plants of the genus *Campanula*, which includes the bellflowers. [New Latin, diminutive of Late Latin *campāna*, bell. See **campanile**.]

cam·pan·u·late (kăm-păn′yə-lĭt, -lāt′). Also **cam·pan·i·form** (kăm-păn′ə-fôrm′). Bell-shaped: *campanulate flowers*. [New Latin *campanula*, small bell.]

Camp·bell (kăm′bəl), **Donald** (1921-67). Son of Sir Malcolm, he set the land speed record in a gas-turbine four-wheeled car on July 17, 1964, at Lake Eyre Salt Flats, Australia, reaching a top speed of 648.7 km/h (403.1 mph). Later that year he achieved the water speed record of 444.89 km/h (276.33 mph) at Dumbleyung Lake, Australia. Finally, during an attempt on the water speed record, his jet-powered boat *Bluebird* was wrecked and he was killed, having reached a speed of 527.8 km/h (328 mph), which is still the fastest time recorded.

Campbell, (Ignatius) Royston Dunnachie (1901-57). South African poet and satirist, who spent part of his working life in England, where he was associated with the Bloomsbury Group. He also translated several important French, Spanish, and Portuguese literary works into English.

Campbell, Sir Malcolm (1885-1948). British motor engineer who held the land speed record nine times between 1924 and 1935 and the water speed record three times between 1937 and 1939. His fastest time on land was 483 km/h (301 mph), and on water he reached a top speed of 227 km/h (141 mph).

Campbell, Mrs Patrick, born Beatrice Stella Tanner (1865-1940). Leading British actress, who played the original Eliza in *Pygmalion*, a part written especially for her by George Bernard Shaw. She also played roles in Shakespeare and Ibsen with great success.

Camp Da·vid (dā′vĭd). The official country retreat of the President of the United States, in the Appalachian Mountains, Maryland. It was here (1978) that President Jimmy Carter mediated at a meeting between Anwar el-Sadat, the Egyptian president, and Menachem Begin, the prime minister of Israel, to produce the framework for a peace treaty between their two countries. Signed by both parties (March 1979), the treaty was known as the Camp David Agreement. Technically, Camp David becomes the White House whenever the President is in residence.

camp·er (kăm′pər) n. **1.** A person who camps outdoors or who attends a camp for recreation. **2. a.** A compact vanlike vehicle resembling an automobile-and-trailer combination, designed to serve as a dwelling and used for camping or on long motor trips. **b.** A porta-

ble shelter resembling the top part of a trailer, made to be mounted on a pickup truck to form such a vehicle.

cam·pes·tral (kăm-pĕs′trəl) adj. Of, pertaining to, or growing in uncultivated land or open fields. [Latin *campester*, of the fields, from *campus*, field.]

camp·fire (kămp′fīr′) n. **1.** An outdoor fire in a camp, used for warmth or cooking. **2.** A meeting held around a campfire.

camp follower n. **1.** A civilian who follows a military unit from place to place to sell goods or services, especially sexual services. **2.** One who sympathizes with but does not belong to a main body or group.

cam·phene (kăm′fēn′) n. A colorless crystalline compound, $C_{10}H_{16}$, used in the manufacture of synthetic camphor and insecticides.

cam·phor (kăm′fər) n. A volatile crystalline compound, $C_{10}H_{16}O$, obtained from the wood of the camphor tree or synthesized and used as an insect repellent, in the manufacture of film, plastics, lacquers, and explosives, and medicinally as a stimulant, expectorant, and diaphoretic. [Middle English *ca(u)mfre*, from Old French *camphre*, from Medieval Latin *camphora*, from Arabic *kāfūr*, from Sanskrit *karpūram*.] —**cam·phor·ic** (kăm-fôr′ĭk, -fŏr′ĭk) adj.

cam·phor·ate (kăm′fə-rāt′) tr.v. **-ated, -ating, -ates**. To treat, fill, or saturate with camphor.

camphorated oil n. A liniment containing camphor and vegetable oil, used as a counterirritant.

camphor tree n. An evergreen tree, *Cinnamomum camphora*, native to eastern Asia, having aromatic wood that is a source of camphor.

cam·pi·on (kăm′pē-ən) n. Any of various plants of the genus *Lychnis*, or related genera, having red, pink, or white flowers. [Probably from *campion*, obsolete variant of CHAMPION; applied first to *lychnis coronaria*, "crowning lychnis" (whose leaves were formerly used to make crowns for athletic champions).]

Cam·pi·on (kăm′pē-ən), **Saint Edmund** (1540-81). English Jesuit martyr. Ordained an Anglican deacon, he was converted to Roman Catholicism (1571) in Douai. He was executed in England for circulating anti-Anglican literature (1581) and was canonized in 1970.

Campion, Thomas (1567-1620). English composer, poet, and physician. The *Poemata* and his *Masques* are among his best-known works.

camp meeting n. An evangelistic gathering held in a tent or outdoors and often lasting several days.

cam·po (kăm′pō, käm′-) n., pl. **-pos**. A large, grassy plain in South America with occasional bushes and small trees. [Portuguese, from Latin *campus*.]

camp·site (kămp′sīt′) n. An area suitable or used for camping or pitching tents.

camp·stool (kămp′stool′) n. A light folding stool.

cam·pus (kăm′pəs) n., pl. **-puses**. **1.** The grounds of a school, college, or university, especially when situated away from an urban center. **2.** A field in ancient Rome used for various events, such as games, military exercises, and public meetings. [Latin *campus*, field, plain (sense 1, first used at Princeton University).]

Cam·ranh Bay (kăm′răn′). Natural harbor in the South China Sea on the coast of southern Vietnam, 20 kilometers (12 miles) wide, and protected by two peninsulas. It was a naval, military, and air base during the Vietnam War.

cam·shaft (kăm′shăft′) n. An engine shaft fitted with a cam or cams, especially one used to operate the valves of an internal-combustion engine.

Ca·mus (kà-mü′), **Albert** (1913-60). French existentialist novelist. A member of the Algerian Communist Party (1934-35), he edited the French Resistance magazine *Combat* during the Nazi occupation of France. Among his best-known works are *The Stranger* (translated 1946) and *The Plague* (translated 1948). In 1957 he was awarded the Nobel Prize for literature.

cam·wood (kăm′wood′) n. **1.** An African tree, *Baphia nitida*, whose hard red-brown wood has been used as the source of a red dye. **2.** The wood of this tree.

can¹ (kăn; unstressed kən) v. Past tense **could** (kood), present tense **can** or archaic **canst** (kănst) (for second person singular). Used as an auxiliary, followed by an infinitive without *to*, or with the infinitive understood. It can indicate: **1. a.** Ability to do or perform: *I can meet you today.* **b.** With verbs of sense perception, ability plus achievement: *At last I can see the sun.* **2.** Possession of a specified power, right, or means: *Only the judge can save her from prison.* **3.** Possession of a specified capacity, faculty, or skill: *He can tune the harpsichord as well as play it.* **4.** Possibility or likelihood: *I wonder if she can be alive after all these years.* **5. a.** Right or sanction: *You can't drive without a license.* **b.** Permission granted according to one's conscience or feelings. Usually used in the negative: *I can't let you take such a risk.* **c.** A requesting or granting of permission: *Can I be excused? No, you cannot.* [Can, could; Middle English *can*, *coude* (also *couthe*), Old English *can* (also *con*), *cūthe*, first and third person present and past indicative of *cunnan*, to know how, from Germanic.]

Usage: In formal English, a clear distinction is maintained between *can* and *may*: the former refers to ability, the latter to permission or possibility (*I can sing. You may sing now. Tomorrow I may sing again*). In informal English, however, the use of *can* to refer to permission is becoming more frequent, and it is now heard even in relatively formal contexts. *May*, correspondingly, is becoming more restricted in its use, and usually implies a clear distinction in status between speaker and person referred to (*You may go. She may leave now*). In negative statements and questions, *mayn't* tends

campanile These bell towers are usually freestanding and generally near a church or town hall. Dating from 1329, this one in St. Mark's Square (Piazza San Marco) in Venice, Italy, was rebuilt in 1902.

CAMEROON 10° E

L. Chad

CHAD

Maroua

10° N

Garoua

N I G E R I A

N'Gaoundéré

CAMEROON   C.A.E.

Mt Cameroon
4070m Limbe
MALABO Douala
Bioko YAOUNDÉ

Sanaga

EQUATORIAL GUINEA

Principe Mbini

SÃO TOMÉ AND PRINCIPE

São Tomé

Annobón
(EQ. GUIN.)

GABON   CONGO

Equator

Km 0   400
Miles 0   200

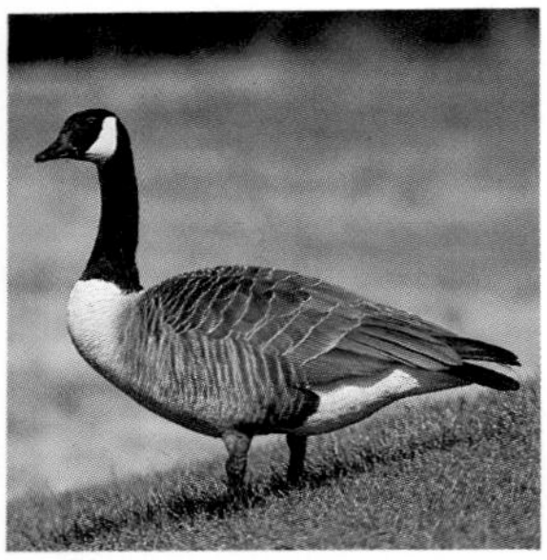

Canada goose *Though a native of Canada, this goose now lives wild throughout the Northern Hemisphere. It feeds mainly on grass but also on aquatic plants.*

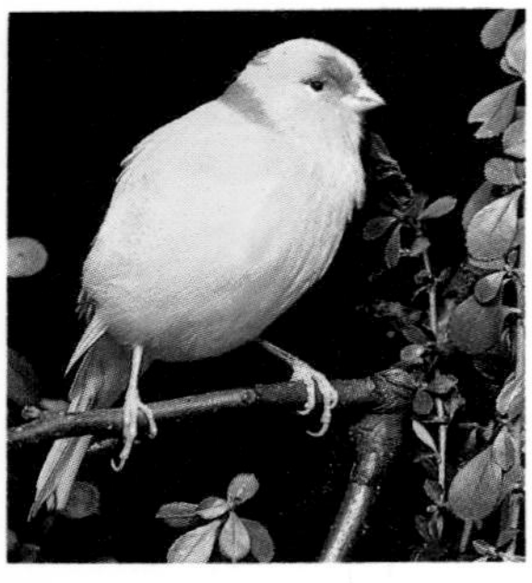

canary *Introduced into Europe in the 16th century as a cage bird, the canary takes its name from its native land—the Canary Islands. In its wild state it is mainly gray-green.*

to be avoided, on account of its awkwardness, but the uncontracted form *may not* is also quite cumbersome, especially in questions (*Why may I not buy that book?*). As a consequence, forms using *can* are increasingly replacing *may*: *Why can't I. . . ?*

can[2] (kăn) *n.* **1.** A metal container, open or with a lid, used for holding oil, gasoline, or the like. **2. a.** An airtight container in which foods are preserved. **b.** A cylindrical airtight metal container for cold drinks: *a beer can.* **c.** The contents of such a container. **3.** *Slang.* **a.** A jail or prison. **b.** A toilet or rest room. **c.** The buttocks. **—in the can.** Recorded and edited; completed. Said of film.
~*tr.v.* **canned, canning, cans. 1.** To seal (vegetables, meat, fruit, drinks, or jam) in a can or jar for future use. **2.** *Slang.* To make a recording of. **3.** *Slang.* **a.** To dismiss from employment or school. **b.** To stop or dispense with: *can the chatter.* [Middle English *canne,* Old English *canne,* from Common Germanic *kannōn-* (unattested).]

can. 1. canon. **2.** canto.

Can. Canada; Canadian.

Ca•na (kā'nə). Village in northern Palestine, 6.5 kilometers (4 miles) northeast of Nazareth, where Jesus performed his first miracle by changing water into wine. John 2:1, 11.

Ca•naan (kā'nən). The name given to ancient Palestine before it was occupied by the Jews. Covering an area approximately equal to that of Israel, western Jordan, and southern Syria, it was referred to in the Bible as the land promised by God to the Israelites.

Ca•naan•ite (kā'nən-īt') *n.* **1.** One of the Semitic inhabitants of the ancient land of Canaan before its conquest by the Israelites. **2.** The Semitic language of this people. **—Ca•naan•it•ic** (-ĭttĭk) *adj.*

Can•a•da (kăn'ə-də). *Abbr.* **Can.** A country occupying (with the exception of Alaska) the northern part of North America. The second-largest country in the world, it has six different time zones, ten provinces, two territories (the Northwest Territories and the Yukon), and two main languages (English and French). The population, concentrated in the southeast, includes Europeans (the main ethnic group), about 250,000 Indians, mostly living on reservations, and 17,000 Eskimos. The Canadian coast was reached by John Cabot who sailed from Bristol (1497), but it was Samuel de Champlain who founded the first permanent settlement at Port Royal (1605) and the settlement on the site of present-day Quebec (1608). Quebec, known as New France, became a royal province of the French crown (1663). With the British Hudson's Bay Company establishing fur-trading posts and strongholds in the Hudson Bay area, a seven-year war broke out between the British and the French (1756). In 1763 Canada was ceded to Britain. With the British North American Act (1867) the Dominion of Canada, a federation of the provinces of Lower Canada (Quebec), Upper Canada (Ontario), New Brunswick, and Nova Scotia, was formed. Between then and 1905, Rupert's Land (Northwest Territories) was acquired from the Hudson's Bay Company, and Manitoba, British Columbia, Prince Edward Island, Alberta, and Saskatchewan became part of the federation. The Statute of Westminster (1931) confirmed and defined Canada as an independent constitutional monarchy equal in status to Britain in the Commonwealth. Since Newfoundland joined the federation (1949), Canada has had ten provinces, in spite of the autonomist Parti Québecois in the largely French-speaking province of Quebec. Fishing is Canada's oldest industry, and modern and effective farming methods produce spring wheat, oats, barley, and hay. Manufacturing industries include paper, motor vehicles, iron, steel, and food processing. Canada is rich in mineral resources and exports natural gas, petroleum, iron ore, nickel, zinc, copper, gold, and uranium. With forests covering a third of the country, Canada supplies the world with wood pulp, newsprint, and timber. The traditional fur trade still flourishes. Area, 9,976,139 square kilometers (3,851,809 square miles). Population, 26,500,000. Capital, Ottawa. **—Ca•na•di•an** (kə-nā'dē-ən) *n. & adj.*

Canada balsam *n.* **1.** A viscous, yellowish, transparent resin obtained from the balsam fir and used as a mounting cement for microscopic specimens. **2.** A tree, the **balsam fir** *(see).*

Canada goose *n.* A common wild goose, *Branta canadensis,* originally of North America but introduced into Britain in the 17th century, having grayish plumage, a black neck and head, and a white face patch.

Canada thistle *n.* A plant, **creeping thistle** *(see).*

Canadian bacon *n.* Cured rolled bacon from the loin of a pig.

Canadian French *n.* The French language as spoken and written in Canada, chiefly in Quebec and the Maritime Provinces.

ca•naille (kə-nī', -nāl') *n.* The masses of common people; rabble or riffraff. [French, from Italian *canaglia,* "pack of dogs," from *cane,* dog, from Latin *canis.*]

ca•nal (kə-năl') *n.* **1.** A man-made waterway or artificially improved river used for irrigation, shipping, or travel. **2.** *Anatomy.* A tube or duct. **3.** *Astronomy.* One of the faint, hazy markings resembling straight lines on the surface of Mars.
~*tr.v.* **canalled** or **-naled, -nalling** or **-naling, -nals. 1.** To dig an artificial waterway through. **2.** To provide with a canal or canals. [Middle English, tube, from Latin *canālis,* channel, from *canna,* reed, from Greek *kanna.*]

Can•a•let•to (kăn'ə-lĕt'ō), **Antonio,** born Giovanni Antonio Canal or Canale (1697–1768). Venetian painter famous for his views of Venice and London. Canaletto was a master of light, flickering colors, and shadows, and his works influenced landscape artists for generations.

can•a•lic•u•lus (kăn'ə-lĭk'yə-ləs) *n., pl.* **-li** (-lī'). *Anatomy.* A small bodily channel, as a tear duct. [Latin, diminutive of *canālis,* CANAL.] **—can•a•lic•u•lar** *adj.*

can•a•li•za•tion (kăn'ə-lī-zā'shən) *n.* **1.** The act or an instance of canalizing. **2.** A system of canals.

can•a•lize (kăn'ə-līz') *tr.v.* **-lized, -lizing, -lizes. 1.** To furnish with, build, or convert into a canal or canals. **2.** To channel into a particular direction; provide an outlet for.

canal rays *pl.n.* Positively charged ions formed in a gas by electrical discharge and attracted to the cathode of the discharge tube. Not in current technical use. [Translation of German *Kanalstrahlen* (because the ions pass through fissures in the cathode).]

Canal Zone. Territory extending 8 kilometers (5 miles) on either side of the Panama Canal. It is administered by the United States under a 1977 treaty. The canal is scheduled to come under Panamanian control in 2000.

can•a•pé (kăn'ə-pā', -pē) *n.* A biscuit or small, thin piece of bread or toast spread with cheese, meat, or relish and served as an appetizer. [French, "couch" ("seat" for the relish), from Medieval Latin *canapeum.* See **canopy.**]

ca•nard (kə-närd') *n.* A false or unfounded and especially a deliberately misleading story or item of news. [French, "duck" (from the expression *vendre des canards à moitié,* "to half-sell ducks," swindle, deceive), from Old French *canart,* duck, from *caner,* to cackle (imitative).]

ca•nar•y (kə-nâr'ē) *n., pl.* **-ies. 1.** A songbird, *Serinus canaria,* native to the Canary Islands, that is greenish to yellow and has long been bred as a cage bird. **2.** *Slang.* A stool pigeon; informer. **3.** A sweet white wine, similar to Madeira, from the Canary Islands. **4.** A lively 16th-century French and English court dance. **5.** A light to moderate or vivid yellow. [French *canari* (bird), *canarie* (wine, dance), from Old Spanish *canario,* "of the Canary Islands," from *Islas Canarias,* CANARY ISLANDS, from Latin *Canaria,* from *Canis,* dog (one of the islands was famous among the Romans for its breed of large dogs).]

canary grass *n.* A grass, *Phalaris canariensis,* native to Europe, having straw-colored seeds used to feed birds.

Ca•nar•y Islands (kə-nâr'ē). Also **Ca•nar•ies** (-ēz). *Spanish* **Is•las Ca•nar•i•as** (ēz'läs kə-när'ē-äs). Group of volcanic islands in the North Atlantic Ocean, 96 kilometers (60 miles) off the northwest coast of Africa. It comprises two provinces of Spain, each named after their capitals: Las Palmas de Gran Canaria has the islands of Fuerteventura, Lanzarote, Gran Canaria, and six unhabited islands; Santa Cruz de Tenerife contains the islands of Tenerife, La Palma, Gomera, and Hierro. The islands were once possessions of Ferdinand and Isabella of Aragon-Castile (1476). After a treaty between Portugal and Aragon-Castile (1479), they became wholly subject to Spain. Having a mild climate, the islands are popular as a winter resort. With the help of irrigation, citrus fruits, bananas, tomatoes, peaches, onions, and potatoes are grown for export.

ca•nas•ta (kə-năs'tə) *n.* **1.** A card game for two to six players, related to rummy and requiring two packs of cards. **2.** A meld of seven cards in this game. [Spanish, "basket" (from the use of two packs, or a "basketful," of cards), from *canasto, canastro,* basket, from Latin *canistrum,* CANISTER.]

ca•nas•ter (kə-năs'tər) *n.* Tobacco made from dried leaves that have been roughly shredded. [Spanish *canastro,* basket (referring to the rush baskets in which the tobacco was shipped). See **canister.**]

Ca•nav•er•al, Cape (kə-năv'ər-əl). Known 1963–73 as **Cape Ken•ne•dy** (kĕn'ə-dē). Cape on the east coast of Florida. It is the site of NASA's Kennedy Manned Space Flight Center, the key launching site for all U.S. space missions.

Can•ber•ra (kăn'bĕr'ə, -bər-ə). Capital of Australia. Situated on the Molongo River in the Australian Capital Territory, it was founded in 1824, chosen as capital (1908), and planned by the U.S. architect Walter Burley Griffin (1876–1937). It is the site of the Australian National University.

can•can (kăn'kăn') *n.* An exuberant dance, popular especially in 19th-century France, performed by women and marked by high kicking. [French, earlier (16th century) "noise," "uproar," of obscure origin.]

can•cel (kăn'səl) *v.* **-celed, -celing, -cels.** Also *chiefly British* **-celled, -celling, -cels.** *—tr.* **1.** To call off (an event, appointment, or the like), usually without rescheduling: *They canceled the picnic because of rain.* **2.** To cross out with lines or other markings. **3. a.** To annul, revoke, or invalidate. **b.** To mark or perforate (a postage stamp or check, for example) to indicate that it may not be used again. **4.** To equalize or make up for; neutralize; offset. Usually followed by *out.* **5.** *Mathematics.* **a.** To remove (a common factor) from the numerator and denominator of a fractional expression. **b.** To remove (a common factor or term) from both members of an equation or inequality. **6.** *Printing.* To omit or delete. *—intr.* To balance or neutralize one another: *two forces that canceled out.* —See Synonyms at **erase, nullify.**
~*n.* **1. a.** The omission or deletion of typed or printed matter. **b.** The matter omitted or deleted or its replacement. **2.** A part of a book used as a substitute for an original part of the book. [Middle English *cancellen,* from Old French *canceller,* from Latin *cancellāre,* to make like a lattice, cross out, from *cancellī,* lattice, diminutive of *cancer, carcer,* jail.] **—can•cel•a•ble** *adj.* **—can•cel•er** *n.*

can•cel•late (kăn-sĕl'ĭt, kăn'sə-lāt') *adj.* Also **can•cel•lat•ed** (kăn'sə-lā'tĭd), **can•cel•lous** (kăn'sə-ləs, kăn-sĕl'əs). **1.** *Anatomy.* Having a coarse netlike or spongy structure. Said of bone. **2.** *Botany.* In the form of a network, as the vein pattern of a leaf. [Latin *cancellātus,*

CANADA

past participle of *cancellāre*, to make like a lattice. See **cancel**.]
can·cel·la·tion (kăn′sə-lā′shən) *n.* **1.** The act of canceling. **2.** Marks or perforations indicating canceling. **3.** Something that has been canceled. **4.** Something, such as a ticket or hotel room, that becomes available after a reservation has been canceled.
can·cer (kăn′sər) *n.* **1. a.** Any of various malignant neoplasms, caused by abnormal division of cells, that invade surrounding tissues and often spread to other parts of the body through the blood or lymph. **b.** The pathological condition characterized by such growths. **2.** A pernicious, spreading evil. [Latin *cancer*, crab, creeping ulcer (formed after Greek *karkinōma*, CARCINOMA).] —**can·cer·ous** *adj.*
Can·cer (kăn′sər) *n.* **1.** A constellation in the Northern Hemisphere near Leo and Gemini. **2. a.** The fourth sign of the **zodiac** *(see).* Also called the "Crab." **b.** One born under this sign. [Middle English, from Latin *cancer*, crab.]
can·croid (kăng′kroid′) *adj.* **1.** Similar to a cancer. **2.** Similar to a crab.
~*n.* A skin cancer. [Latin *cancer* (stem *cancr-*), crab, CANCER + -OID.]
can·del·a (kăn-děl′ə) *n. Abbr.* **cd** A unit of luminous intensity equal to 1/60 of the luminous intensity per square centimeter of a black-body radiating at the temperature of solidification of platinum (2,046°K). Also called "candle," "standard candle." [Latin *candēla,* CANDLE.]
can·de·la·bra (kăn′də-lä′brə, -lăb′rə, -lā′brə) *n., pl.* -**bras.** A candelabrum. —See Usage note at **candelabrum**.
can·de·la·brum (kăn′də-lä′brəm, -lăb′rəm, -lā′brəm) *n., pl.* -**bra** (-brə) *or* -**brums.** A large decorative candlestick having several arms or branches. [Latin *candēlābrum,* from *candēla,* CANDLE.]

   Usage: Two different usage trends have affected this word. First, its original Latin-based plural, *candelabra,* has been in conflict with a later English-based plural, *candelabrums,* considered to be incorrect in formal speech or writing. Secondly, *candelabra* has increasingly come to be used as a singular form, from which a new

English-based plural form has derived: *I bought a new candelabra today; The candelabras need cleaning.* This second development is widespread in all but the most formal and technical contexts.
can·dent (kăn′dənt) *adj.* Having a white-hot glow; incandescent. [Latin *candēns* (stem *candent-*), present participle of *candēre,* to shine, glow, be white.]
can·des·cence (kăn-děs′əns) *n.* The state of being white hot; incandescence. [Latin *candēscēns,* present participle of *candēscere,* inceptive of *candēre,* to shine, glow, be white.] —**can·des·cent** *adj.* —**can·des·cent·ly** *adv.*
Candia. See **Iráklion.**
can·did (kăn′dĭd) *adj.* **1.** Without pretense or reserve; straightforward and open. **2.** Without prejudice; impartial.. **3.** Not posed or rehearsed: *a candid snapshot.* —See Synonyms at **frank**.
~*n.* An unposed informal photograph. [French *candide,* from Latin *candidus,* glowing, white, pure, guileless, from *candēre,* to glow, be white.] —**can·did·ly** *adv.* —**can·did·ness** *n.*
can·di·da (kăn′dĭ-də) *n.* Any of the pathogenic yeastlike fungi of the genus *Candida.* [New Latin *Candida,* genus name, from Latin, feminine of *candidus,* white.]
can·di·date (kăn′də-dāt′, -dĭt) *n.* **1.** A person who seeks or is nominated for an office, prize, honor, or the like. **2.** A person who seems likely to gain a certain position or undergo a certain fate. **3.** Something that seems likely to be chosen: *The book is a candidate for the award.* [Latin *candidātus,* "(Roman candidate) clothed in a white toga," from *candidus,* white, CANDID.] —**can·di·da·cy** (kăn′-də-də-sē), **can·di·da·ture** (kăn′də-də-chōōr′, -chər) *n.*
candid camera *n.* Any small, easily operated camera with a fast lens for taking unposed or informal photographs.
can·di·di·a·sis (kăn′də-dī′ə-sĭs) *n.* Infection with a fungus of the genus *Candida,* usually affecting moist areas of the body. Also called "moniliasis." [New Latin *Candida* (genus name), from Latin *candidus,* white + -IASIS.]
can·died (kăn′dēd) *adj.* Permeated, covered, encrusted, or cooked with sugar: *candied fruit.*

Can·di·ot (kăn'dē-ŏt') adj. Also **Can·di·ote** (-ōt'). Of or pertaining to Candia (Iráklion) or Crete.
~n. A native or inhabitant of Crete.

can·dle (kăn'dəl) n. 1. A solid mass, usually a cylinder, of tallow, wax, or other fatty substance, containing a wick that is burned to provide light. 2. Something resembling a candle in use or shape. 3. a. Physics. An obsolete unit of luminous intensity, originally defined in terms of a wax candle with standard composition and equal to 1.02 candelas. Also called "international candle." b. A **candela** (see). —**burn the candle at both ends.** To exhaust oneself by leading too hectic a life. —**not hold a candle to.** To be not nearly as good as.
~tr.v. **candled, -dling, -dles.** To examine (an egg) for freshness in front of a light. [Middle English candel, Old English candel, from Latin candēla, from candēre, to shine.] —**can·dler** n.

can·dle·ber·ry (kăn'dəl-bĕr'ē) n., pl. **-ries.** A shrub or tree, the **wax myrtle** (see), or its fruit. [From the wax in the berry.]

can·dle·fish (kăn'dəl-fĭsh') n., pl. **candlefish** or **-fishes.** An oily, edible fish, Thaleichthys pacificus, of northern Pacific waters, formerly dried and used as a torch. Also called "eulachon."

can·dle·foot (kăn'dəl-foot') n. A **foot-candle** (see).

can·dle·hold·er (kăn'dəl-hōl'dər) n. A candlestick.

can·dle·light (kăn'dəl-līt') n. 1. Illumination from a candle or candles. 2. Dusk; twilight.

Can·dle·mas (kăn'dəl-məs) n. A church festival celebrated on February 2 as the feast of the purification of the Virgin Mary and the presentation of the infant Jesus in the temple. [Middle English candelmasse, Old English candelmæsse : CANDLE + -MAS (candles for church use were blessed at the feast).]

can·dle·nut (kăn'dəl-nŭt') n. 1. A tree, Aleurites moluccana, of tropical Asia and Polynesia, bearing nuts that yield an oil used in paints and varnishes. 2. The nut of this tree. [From the use of the oily nuts as candles.]

can·dle·pin (kăn'dəl-pĭn') n. 1. A slender bowling pin used in a variation of the game of tenpins. 2. **candlepins.** Used with a singular verb. A bowling game played with a ball smaller than that used in tenpins and a different scoring system.

can·dle·pow·er (kăn'dəl-pou'ər) n. Luminous intensity of a light source expressed in standard candles.

can·dle·stick (kăn'dəl-stĭk') n. A holder, often ornamental, with a cup or spike for a candle.

can·dle·wick (kăn'dəl-wĭk') n. 1. The wick of a candle. 2. a. Soft, heavy cotton thread similar to that used to make wicks for candles. b. Embroidery made of tufts of candlewick.

can·dle·wood (kăn'dəl-wood') n. 1. A tree, the **ocotillo** (see). 2. The resinous wood of this or similar trees. [After the use of the wood for torches and as a substitute for candles.]

can·dor (kăn'dər) n. Also chiefly British **can·dour.** 1. Frankness of expression; sincerity; straightforwardness. 2. Freedom from prejudice; impartiality. [Latin candor, whiteness, purity, frankness, from candēre, to glow, be white.]

can·dy (kăn'dē) n., pl. **-dies.** 1. A rich, sweet confection, as one made with sugar or corn syrup, often flavored and combined with fruits or nuts. 2. A single piece of such confection.
~v. **candied, -dying, -dies.** —tr. 1. To reduce to sugar crystals. 2. To cook, preserve, saturate, or coat with sugar or syrup. —intr. 1. To crystallize. Used of sugar. 2. To become coated with sugar or syrup. [Short for sugar candy, from French sucre candi, from Arabic sukkar qandī, from qand, sugar, from Persian, from Sanskrit khanda, sugar in lumps.]

Candy. See **Kandy.**

can·dy-striped (kăn'dē-strīpt') adj. Having stripes, usually of bright colors, against a plain background.

candy strip·er (strī'pər) n. A usually teenage volunteer nurse's aide in a hospital. [From the resemblance of the volunteer's red and white striped uniform to a candy cane.]

can·dy·tuft (kăn'dē-tŭft') n. Any of various plants of the genus Iberis, cultivated for their clusters of white, red, or purplish flowers. [Candy, obsolete variant of Candia, Crete + TUFT.]

cane (kān) n. 1. a. A slender, jointed stem, woody but usually flexible, as of bamboo, rattan, or certain palm trees. b. Any plant having such a stem. c. Such stems, or strips of such stems, used for wickerwork. 2. A grass, Arundinaria gigantea, of the southeastern United States, having long stiff stems and often forming canebrakes. 3. The long, woody stem of the raspberry, blackberry, certain roses, or similar plants. 4. **Sugar cane** (see). 5. A stick used as an aid in walking or carried as an accessory. 6. A rod used for flogging, especially in schools.
~tr.v. **caned, caning, canes.** 1. To make, supply, or repair with cane. 2. To hit or beat with a cane. [Middle English, from Old French, from Latin canna, from Greek kanna, reed.] —**can·er** n.

Ca·ne·a or **Ka·ne·a** (kə-nē'ə). Greek **Khan·iá** (KHän-yä'). Capital of the Greek island of Crete and of the Canea nome (province) in the northwest of the island. It prospered under the Venetians between the 13th and the 17th century until it was taken by the Turks in 1645. The Venetian fortifications and town walls can still be seen.

cane·brake (kān'brāk') n. A dense thicket of cane.

ca·nes·cent (kə-nĕs'ənt) adj. 1. Biology. Covered with whitish or grayish down; hoary. 2. Turning white or grayish. [Latin cānēscēns (stem cānescent-), present participle of cānescere, to grow white, turn gray, from cānēre, to be white or gray, from cānus, white, gray.] —**ca·nes·cence** n.

cane sugar n. A sugar yielded by sugar cane, **sucrose** (see).

cannabis Also known as hemp, Cannabis sativa is the plant from which hashish and marijuana are derived. It is a native of Asia and its possession in most Western countries is prohibited.

Ca·nes Ve·nat·i·ci (kā'nēz vĭ-năt'ə-sī') n. A constellation in the Northern Hemisphere near Ursa Major and Boötes, under the Big Dipper's handle. [Latin, "hunting dogs."]

cangue (kăng) n. An old Chinese device for punishing petty criminals, consisting of a heavy wooden yoke enclosing the neck and hands of the offender. [French, from Portuguese canga, a yoke, from Vietnamese gong.]

Ca·nic·u·la (kə-nĭk'yə-lə) n. A star, **Sirius** (see). [Latin, diminutive of canis, dog.]

ca·nic·u·lar (kə-nĭk'yə-lər) adj. 1. Of or pertaining to the Dog Star. 2. Of or pertaining to the dog days in July and August.

canikin. Variant of **cannikin.**

ca·nine (kā'nīn') adj. 1. Of or pertaining to dogs. 2. Of, pertaining to, or characteristic of the family Canidae, which includes the dogs, wolves, and foxes. 3. Of or designating one of the conical teeth located between the incisors and the first bicuspids.
~n. 1. A canine animal. 2. A canine tooth. Also called "eyetooth." [Latin canīnus, from canis, dog.]

Ca·nis Ma·jor (kā'nĭs mā'jər) n. A constellation in the Southern Hemisphere near Puppis and Lepus. It contains the star Sirius. [Latin, "the larger dog."]

Canis Mi·nor (mī'nər) n. A constellation in the equatorial region of the Southern Hemisphere near Hydra and Monoceros. It contains the star Procyon. [Latin, "the smaller dog."]

can·is·ter (kăn'ĭ-stər) n. 1. A container, usually of thin metal, for holding dry foods, chemicals, and the like. 2. Military. A metallic cylinder that when fired from a gun bursts and scatters the shot packed inside it. Also called "canister shot," "case shot." 3. The part of a gas mask containing a filter for removing poison gas from the air. [Latin canistrum, reed basket, from Greek kanastron, from kanna, reed.]

can·ker (kăng'kər) n. 1. An ulcerous sore of the mouth and lips. 2. An area of dead or decaying tissue in a plant surrounded by healthy wood or bark. 3. Any of several animal diseases characterized by chronic inflammation of affected parts and attacking especially the ears of dogs and cats. 4. Any source of spreading corruption or debilitation.
~v. **cankered, -kering, -kers.** —tr. 1. To attack or infect with canker. 2. To cause to decay or become corrupt. —intr. To become infected with or as if with canker. [Middle English, from Old English cancer and Old Northern French cancre, both from Latin cancer, CANCER.]

can·ker·ous (kăng'kər-əs) adj. 1. Of, pertaining to, or infected with a canker; ulcerous. 2. Causing canker; ulcerating.

canker sore n. A small, painful ulcer, usually of the mouth.

can·ker·worm (kăng'kər-wûrm') n. The larva of either of two moths, Paleacrita vernata or Alsophila Pometaria, that are destructive to fruit and shade trees.

can·na (kăn'ə) n. Any of various tropical plants of the genus Canna, having broad leaves and showy red or yellow flowers for which they are widely grown for ornament. [New Latin Canna, from Latin canna, reed, CANE.]

can·na·bi·di·ol (kăn'ə-bī-dī'ôl', -ōl') n. A chemical constituent of cannabis, $C_{21}H_{29}(OH)_2$.

can·na·bin (kăn'ə-bĭn) n. A resinous material extracted from cannabis. [CANNAB(IS) + -IN.]

can·na·bis (kăn'ə-bĭs) n. 1. A plant of the genus **Cannabis, hemp** (see). 2. A preparation made from the dried flowering tops of the hemp plant, and smoked, chewed, or drunk for its euphoric or relaxing effect. See **marijuana, hashish.** [New Latin, from Latin, hemp, from Greek kannabis.] —**can·na·bic** adj.

canned (kănd) adj. 1. Preserved and sealed in a can. 2. Informal. Recorded or taped: "So if television is to have canned laughter, how about canned tears?" (Jack Paar).

can·nel (kăn'əl) n. A type of bituminous coal that burns brightly with much smoke. Also called "cannel coal." [From cannel coal, dialectal form for candle coal (from its bright flame).]

can·nel·lo·ni (kăn'ə-lō'nē) n. An Italian pasta dish of large-sized macaroni stuffed with a meat or cheese mixture, baked, and served with tomato sauce or cream sauce. [Italian, plural of cannellone, from cannello, diminutive of canna, reed, CANE.]

can·ne·lure (kăn'ə-loor', -əl-yoor') n. A groove or fluting, especially that around the cylindrical part of a bullet. [French, from canneler, to make a groove, channel, from canne, CANE.]

can·ner (kăn'ər) n. Someone or something that cans.

can·ner·y (kăn'ə-rē) n., pl. **-ies.** An establishment where meat, vegetables, or other foods are canned.

Cannes (kăn). Resort and port in Alpes-Maritimes department, southern France. It has been a fashionable French Riviera resort since Lord Brougham (1778–1868) built a villa here. It has the oldest monastery in Western Europe (on the Île St. Honorat). Each spring Cannes hosts an international film festival.

can·ni·bal (kăn'ə-bəl) n. 1. A person who eats the flesh of human beings. 2. Any animal that feeds on others of its own kind. [Spanish Canibales (plural), variant (recorded by Columbus) of Caribes, the man-eating Caribs of Cuba and Haiti.] —**can·ni·bal·ism** n. —**can·ni·bal·is·tic** adj.

can·ni·bal·ize (kăn'ə-bə-līz') tr.v. **-ized, -izing, -izes.** 1. a. To remove serviceable parts from (damaged aircraft, cars, or other machinery) for use in the repair of other equipment. b. To extract material from (a book or magazine, for example) for use in another work. 2. To deprive (an organization) of personnel or equipment for use in another organization. [Originally, "to eat human flesh," from CANNIBAL.] **—can·ni·bal·i·za·tion** *n.*

can·ni·kin, can·i·kin (kăn′ĭ-kĭn) *n.* A little can or cup. [Dutch *kanneken,* diminutive of CAN.]

Can·ning (kăn′ĭng), **George** (1770–1827). British statesman, remembered for his achievements as foreign secretary (1807–09, 1822–27). After resigning (1809) over Viscount Castlereagh's handling of the Napoleonic Wars, he was wounded in the thigh by Castlereagh in a duel. During his second term as foreign secretary, he liberalized Tory politics, withdrew from Emperor Alexander I of Russia's Holy Alliance, and supported the rebellion of the Spanish-American colonies (1823) and the Greeks in their struggle for freedom from the Turks (1825–27). In 1827 he became prime minister, but half the cabinet and over 40 ministers refused to serve under him. He resigned, in failing health, after four months.

Can·niz·za·ro (kä′nē-zär′ō), **Stanislao** (1826–1910). Italian chemist whose ideas are the basis of much of modern chemistry. He expanded on Avogadro's work in distinguishing between molecular and atomic weights and employed Avogadro's hypothesis to solve the problem of representing compounds by formulas.

can·non (kăn′ən) *n., pl.* **cannon** or **-nons. 1.** A weapon used for firing projectiles that consists of a heavy metal tube mounted on a carriage. **2. a.** A heavy firearm larger than 0.60 caliber. See **gun, howitzer, mortar. b.** An automatic gun mounted on an aircraft. **3.** The loop at the top of a bell by which the bell is suspended. **4.** A round bit for a horse. **5. a.** The section of leg containing the cannon bone. **b.** The cannon bone. **6.** *Chiefly British.* A shot in billiards in which the cue ball strikes two other balls in succession.
∼*v.* **cannoned, -noning, -nons.** —*tr.* To bombard or batter with cannon. —*intr.* **1.** To fire cannon. **2.** *Chiefly British.* To make a cannon shot in billiards. **3.** *Chiefly British.* To crash into with violence; collide. Used with *into.* [Middle English *canon,* from Old French, from Italian *cannone,* "large tube, barrel," from *canna,* reed, tube, CANE.]

can·non·ade (kăn′ə-nād′) *v.* **-aded, -ading, -ades.** —*tr.* To assault or bombard with heavy artillery fire. —*intr.* To deliver heavy artillery fire.
∼*n.* An extended, usually heavy, discharge of artillery. [French *canonade,* discharge of artillery, from Italian *cannonata,* from *cannone,* CANNON.]

can·non·ball (kăn′ən-bôl′) *n.* **1.** A round projectile fired from a cannon. **2.** A jump into water made with the arms grasping the upraised knees. **3.** Something moving with great speed, as a fast train. **4.** A fast low serve in tennis.
∼*intr.v.* **cannonballed, -balling, -balls. 1.** To travel rapidly in the manner of a cannonball: *The truck cannonballed down the highway.* **2.** To make a cannonball jump into water.

cannon bone *n.* The bone located between the back of the knee and the fetlock of a horse or ruminant, made up of fused, elongated metatarsals or metacarpals. [So called from its shape.]

can·non·eer (kăn′ə-nîr′) *n.* A gunner or artilleryman. [Old French *canonier,* from *canon,* CANNON.] **—can·non·eer·ing** *n.*

cannon fodder *n.* Soldiers considered as expendable material of warfare. [Translation of German *Kanonenfutter.*]

can·non·ry (kăn′ən-rē) *n., pl.* **-ries. 1.** Artillery; cannons collectively. **2.** Artillery fire.

cannon shot *n.* **1.** Ammunition for a cannon. **2.** A shot or shots fired by cannon. **3.** The firing distance of a cannon.

can·not (kăn′ŏt′, kə-nŏt′, kă-) *v.* The negative form of **can.** —See Usage note at **can.**

can·nu·la, can·u·la (kăn′yə-lə) *n., pl.* **-las** or **-lae** (-lē′). A tube inserted into a bodily cavity to drain fluid or insert medication. [New Latin, from Latin, diminutive of *canna,* a reed, tube, CANE.]

can·nu·lar (kăn′yə-lər) *adj.* Cannulate.

can·nu·late (kăn′yə-lāt′) *tr.v.* **-lated, -lating, -lates.** To insert a cannula into.
∼*adj.* Tubular; hollow. **—can·nu·la·tion** *n.*

can·ny (kăn′ē) *adj.* **-nier, -niest. 1.** Shrewd and prudent, especially in looking after one's own interests. **2.** Cautious in spending money; thrifty. **3.** *Chiefly Scottish.* **a.** Pleasant; attractive. **b.** Gentle; mild. [From CAN (to know how, be able).] **—can·ni·ly** *adv.* **—can·ni·ness** *n.*

ca·noe (kə-no͞o′) *n.* A light, slender boat with pointed ends, propelled by paddles.
∼*v.* **canoed, -noeing, -noes.** —*tr.* To carry or send by canoe, especially as a sport or hobby. —*intr.* To travel in or propel a canoe. [Earlier *canoa,* from Spanish, from Arawakan (recorded by Columbus), from Cariban.] **—ca·noe·ist** *n.*

can of worms *n. Informal.* A complicated situation or problem that is likely to become more complicated with any attempt to resolve it.

can·on¹ (kăn′ən) *n. Abbr.* **can. 1.** An ecclesiastical law or code of laws established by a church council. **2.** A secular law, rule, or code of law. **3.** A basis for judgment; a standard; a criterion. **4.** The books of the Bible officially recognized as the Holy Scripture. **5.** *Often* **Cannon.** The part of the Mass beginning after the Sanctus and ending just before the Lord's Prayer. **6.** The calendar of saints accepted by the Roman Catholic Church. **7.** An authoritative list, as of the works of an author. **8.** *Music.* A composition or passage in which the same melody is repeated by one or more voices, overlapping in time in the same or a related key. See **fugue, round. 9.** *Printing.* A size of type, 48-point. [Middle English *cano(u)n,* from Old English and Old French *canon,* both from Late Latin *canōn,* from Latin, measuring line, rule, model, from Greek *kanōn,* rod, rule.]

canon² *n.* **1.** A member of a chapter of priests serving in a cathedral or collegiate church. **2.** A member of certain religious communities living under a common rule and bound by vows. [Middle English *cano(u)n,* from Norman French *canunie,* from Late Latin *canōnicus,* one living under a rule, from *canōn,* CANON (rule).]

cañon. Variant of **canyon.**

can·on·ess (kăn′ə-nĭs) *n.* A member of a religious community of women, living under a common rule but not bound by vows.

ca·non·i·cal (kə-nŏn′ĭ-kəl) *adj.* Also **ca·non·ic** (-ĭk). **1.** Of, pertaining to, required by, or abiding by canon law. **2.** Of or appearing in the Biblical canon. **3.** Authoritative; officially approved; orthodox. **4.** *Music.* Having the form of a canon. **5.** Of, pertaining to, or belonging to a cathedral chapter. **—ca·non·i·cal·ly** *adv.* **—can·on·ic·i·ty** (kăn′ə-nĭs′ə-tē) *n.*

canonical form *n.* **1.** *Mathematics.* A diagonal matrix (one in which all nondiagonal elements are zero), obtained by transformations on a given matrix. **2.** The simplest form of something.

canonical hours *pl.n.* **1.** *Ecclesiastical.* **a.** A special set of prayers, prescribed by canon law, normally to be recited at specific times of the day. They are matins (with lauds), prime, terce, sext, nones, vespers, and complin. **b.** The times of day set aside for these prayers. **2.** *British.* The hours between 8 A.M. and 6 P.M., during which marriages may legally take place in parish churches.

ca·non·i·cals (kə-nŏn′ĭ-kəlz) *pl.n.* The dress prescribed by canon law for officiating clergy.

ca·non·i·cate (kə-nŏn′ĭ-kāt′, -kĭt) *n.* The office or dignity of a canon; canonry. [Medieval Latin *canōnicātus,* from Late Latin *canōnicus,* a canon, from *canōn,* CANON (rule).]

can·on·ist (kăn′ə-nĭst) *n.* A person skilled in canon law. **—can·on·is·tic, can·on·is·ti·cal** *adj.*

can·on·ize (kăn′ə-nīz′) *tr.v.* **-ized, -izing, -izes. 1.** To declare (a deceased person) to be a saint and entitled to be fully honored as such. Compare **beatify. 2.** To include in the Biblical canon. **3.** To approve as being within canon law. **4.** To glorify; exalt. **—can·on·i·za·tion** *n.* **—can·on·iz·er** *n.*

canon law *n.* The body of officially established rules governing the faith and practice of the members of a Christian church.

can·on·ry (kăn′ən-rē) *n., pl.* **-ries. 1.** The position or benefice of one who is an ecclesiastical canon. **2.** Canons collectively.

Ca·no·pic (kə-nō′pĭk, -nŏp′ĭk) *adj.* Designating an ancient Egyptian vase, urn, or jar used to hold the viscera of the dead. [Latin *Canopicus,* from *Canopus,* ancient Egyptian port east of Alexandria.]

Ca·no·pus (kə-nō′pəs) *n.* A star in the constellation Carina, 650 light-years from Earth, the second-brightest star in the sky. [Latin, from Greek *Kanōpos*†.]

can·o·py (kăn′ə-pē) *n., pl.* **-pies. 1.** A cloth covering fastened or held horizontally above a person or an object for protection or ornamentation. **2.** *Architecture.* An ornamental, rooflike projection, as over an altar, pulpit, or the like. **3.** A high covering: *a vast canopy of foliage.* **4. a.** The transparent, movable enclosure over the cockpit of an aircraft. **b.** The hemispherical fabric surface of a parachute.
∼*tr.v.* **canopied, -pying, -pies.** To overhang with a canopy; form a canopy over: *Mist canopied the landscape.* [Middle English *canape, canope,* from Medieval Latin *canopeum,* (couch with a) mosquito net, from Greek *kōnōpeion,* from *kōnōps,* gnat.]

ca·no·rous (kə-nôr′əs, -nōr′əs, kăn′ər-əs) *adj.* Agreeable to the ears; melodious. [Latin *canōrus,* from *canor,* tune, melody, from *canere,* to sing.] **—ca·no·rous·ly** *adv.* **—ca·no·rous·ness** *n.*

Ca·nos·sa (kə-nŏs′ə). A village in north-central Italy, in the Apennines. In January 1077 the Holy Roman Emperor Henry IV did penance here to obtain a pardon from his excommunication by Pope Gregory VII.

Ca·no·va (kə-nō′və), **Antonio** (1757-1822). Italian neoclassical sculptor whose works include *The Tomb of Clement XIII* (1792) and *Pauline Borghese as Venus Victrix* (1807).

canst (kănst). *Archaic.* The second person singular present tense of **can.** Used with *thou.*

cant¹ (kănt) *n.* **1.** Angular deviation from a vertical or horizontal plane or surface; inclination; slant; slope. **2. a.** A thrust or motion that tilts something. **b.** The tilt caused by such a motion. **3.** An outer corner, as of a building. **4.** A slanted edge or surface.
∼*v.* **canted, canting, cants.** —*tr.* **1.** To set at an oblique angle; cause to slant or tilt. **2.** To give a slanting edge to; bevel. **3.** To change the direction of suddenly. —*intr.* **1.** To tilt to one side; slant. **2.** To take an oblique direction or course; swing around. Used of a ship. [Middle English, side, edge, ultimately from Latin *cant(h)us,* iron tire, rim of a wheel, from Celtic.]

cant² *n.* **1.** Hypocritically pious language. **2.** Platitudes uttered mindlessly. **3.** The special vocabulary peculiar to the members of a group on the fringe of society, such as thieves, for example; argot. **4.** The special terminology understood among the members of a profession, discipline, or class, but obscure to the general population; jargon. **5.** Whining speech, as used by beggars.
∼*intr.v.* **canted, canting, cants. 1.** To speak in a whining, pleading tone. **2.** To speak tediously or sententiously; moralize. **3.** To use special jargon or argot. [Perhaps from Norman French *cant,* musical sound, singing, whining speech of beggars (sense perhaps derived from original application to the singing of religious mendicants), from *canter,* to sing, tell, from Latin *cantāre,* frequentative of *canere,* to sing.] **—cant·ing·ly** *adv.*

can't (kănt, känt). Contraction of *cannot.* —See Usage note at **can.**

can·ta·bi·le (kän-tä′bə-lā′) *adv. Music.* In a smooth, lyrical, flowing

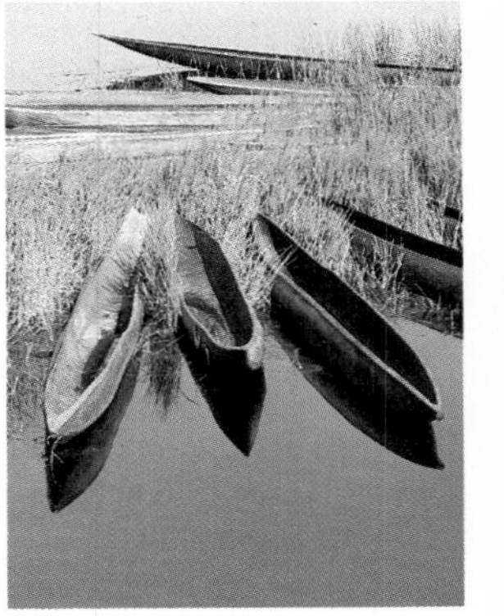

canoe *Primitive canoes—like these in New Guinea—are made by hollowing out the center of a log and are called dugouts.*

PRONUNCIATION KEY

ă, **pat**; ā, **pay**; âr, **care**;
ä, **father**, **are**; b, **bib**;
ch, **church**; d, **deed**; ĕ, **pet**;
ē, **be**; f, **fife**; g, **gag**; h, **hat**;
hw, **which**; ĭ, **pit**; ī, **pie**;
îr, **pier**; j, **judge**; k, **kick**;
l, **lid**, **needle**; m, **mum**;
n, **no**, **sudden**; ng, **thing**;
ŏ, **pot**; ō, **toe**; ô, **paw**, **for**;
oi, **noise**; ou, **out**; o͝o, **book**;
o͞o, **boot**; p, **pop**; r, **roar**;
s, **sauce**; sh, **ship**, **dish**;
t, **tight**; th, **thin**, **path**;
th, **this**, **bathe**; ŭ, **cut**; ûr, **fur**;
v, **valve**; w, **with**; y, **yes**;
z, **zebra**, **size**; zh, **vision**;
ə, **about**, **item**, **edible**,
gallop, **circus**, **peaceful**

IN FOREIGN WORDS:

à, *Fr.* **ami**; œ, *Fr.* **feu**, *Ger.* **schön**; ü, *Fr.* **tu**, *Ger.* **über**;
KH, *Ger.* **ich**, *Scot.* **loch**;
N, *Fr.* **bon**; y′, *Fr.* **Compiègne**

STRESS MARKS:

Primary stress: ′
in·cite′ (ĭn-sīt′)
Secondary stress: ′
in′sight′ (ĭn′sīt′)

style. Used as a direction to the performer.

~n. Music. A cantabile passage or movement. [Italian, from Late Latin *cantābilis*, singable, from Latin *cantāre*, frequentative of *canere*, to sing.] —**can·ta·bi·le** *adj.*

Can·ta·bri·an Mountains (kăn-tā′brē-ən). Mountain range in the north of Spain stretching *c.* 480 kilometers (300 miles) east to west along the Bay of Biscay. Its highest peak is Torre de Cerredo (2,642 meters; 8,668 feet).

Can·ta·brig·i·an (kăn′tə-brĭj′ē-ən) *adj.* 1. Of or pertaining to Cambridge in England or Cambridge in Massachusetts. 2. Of or pertaining to Cambridge University.
~n. 1. A native or resident of Cambridge. 2. A student or graduate of Cambridge University. [Medieval Latin *Cantabrigia*, CAMBRIDGE.]

can·ta·la (kăn-tä′lə) *n.* 1. A century plant, *Agave cantula*, native to tropical America, cultivated for its coarse, tough fiber. 2. The fiber of the cantala. [Origin unknown.]

can·ta·loupe, can·ta·loup (kăn′tə-lōp′) *n.* 1. A variety of melon, *Cucumis melo cantalupensis,* having fruit with a ribbed, rough rind and aromatic orange flesh. 2. Any of several similar melons. 3. The fruit of any of these plants. [French *cantaloup,* from Italian *cantalupo,* first grown at *Cantalupo,* a papal villa.]

can·tan·ker·ous (kăn-tăng′kər-əs) *adj.* Ill-tempered and quarrelsome. [Perhaps from Middle English *contekour,* rioter, brawler, from *contek,* quarrel, strife, from Norman French *contek†.*] —**can·tan·ker·ous·ly** *adv.* —**can·tan·ker·ous·ness** *n.*

can·ta·ta (kən-tä′tə) *n.* A vocal and instrumental composition comprising choruses, arias, and recitatives. [Italian *(aria) cantata,* "sung (aria)," from *cantare,* to sing, from Latin *cantāre.* See cant (jargon).]

can·teen (kăn-tēn′) *n.* 1. An institutional recreation hall or cafeteria. 2. A temporary or mobile eating place, especially one set up in an emergency. 3. **a.** A store for on-base military personnel. **b.** *Chiefly British.* A recreational club for soldiers. 4. **a.** A mess kit. **b.** A box divided into compartments containing a set of cooking gear. 5. A flask for drinking water of the kind carried by soldiers. [French *cantine,* from Italian *cantina,* a wine cellar, from *canto,* edge, from Latin *cant(h)us.* See cant (angle).]

can·ter (kăn′tər) *n.* 1. A horse's gait, slower than the gallop but faster than the trot, in which a three-beat rhythm commences on the inside leg. 2. A ride at this gait.
~v. **cantered, -tering, -ters.** —*intr.* To move or ride at a canter. —*tr.* To make (a horse) go at a canter. [18th century : short for *Canterbury gallop, trot,* or the like, supposedly the slow pace at which mounted pilgrims rode to Canterbury in the Middle Ages.]

Can·ter·bur·y (kăn′tər-bĕr′ē). City at the foot of the North Downs, on the Stour River, in east Kent, England. The 11th- to 16th-century cathedral, where Thomas Becket was martyred (1170), dominates the city and is the seat of the archbishop and primate of the Anglican Communion. The original cathedral, founded by St. Augustine (597), was destroyed by fire (1067). The shrine erected to commemorate the canonization of Becket was a focal point for pilgrims for three centuries and inspired Chaucer's *Canterbury Tales.*

Can·ter·bur·y bells (kăn′tər-bĕr′ē). *Used with a singular or plural verb.* A plant, *Campanula medium,* native to Europe, widely cultivated for its bell-shaped, violet-blue flowers. [The flowers resemble the bells on the horses of Canterbury pilgrims.]

can·thar·i·des (kăn-thăr′ə-dēz′) *pl.n. Singular* **can·tha·ris** (kăn′thər-ĭs). *Used with a singular or plural verb.* A toxic preparation of the crushed, dried bodies of the beetle *Lytta vesicatoria* (or *Cantharis vesicatoria*), formerly used as a counterirritant for skin blisters and as an aphrodisiac. Also called "Spanish fly." [Latin, plural of *cantharis,* from Greek *kantharis,* blister beetle, from *kantharos†,* dung beetle.]

can·thi·tis (kăn-thī′tĭs) *n.* Inflammation of the canthus.

cant hook *n.* A wooden pole with a hinged hook near the end, used for moving logs, similar to a **peavey** *(see)* but with a blunt end. [From CANT (angle).]

can·thus (kăn′thəs) *n., pl.* **-thi** (-thī′). The corner at either side of the eye, formed by the meeting of the upper and lower eyelids. [Late Latin, from Greek *kanthos†.*]

can·ti·cle (kăn′tĭ-kəl) *n.* A song or chant; specifically, a nonmetrical hymn with words taken directly from a Biblical text. [Middle English, from Latin *canticulum,* diminutive of *cantus,* song, from *canere,* to sing.]

Canticle of Canticles *n.* In the Douay Bible, the **Song of Solomon** *(see).*

can·ti·le·na (kăn′tə-lā′nə, -lē′nə) *n. Music.* A sustained, smooth-flowing melodic line. [Italian.]

can·ti·le·ver (kăn′tə-lē′vər, -lĕv′ər) *n.* 1. A projecting beam or other structure supported only at one end. 2. A beam or other part projecting beyond a fulcrum and supported by a balancing part or a downward force behind the fulcrum. 3. A bracket or block supporting a balcony or cornice.
~v. **cantilevered, -vering, -vers.** —*tr.* To build as a cantilever. —*intr.* To extend outward as or like a cantilever. [17th century : origin obscure.]

cantilever bridge *n.* A bridge formed by two projecting beams or trusses that are joined in the center by a connecting part and are supported on piers and anchored by counterbalancing parts.

can·til·late (kăn′tə-lāt′) *v.* **-lated, -lating, -lates.** —*tr.* To chant or recite in a musical monotone, as in Jewish or other rituals. —*intr.* To recite in a musical monotone. [Latin *cantillāre,* to sing in a low

voice, hum, from *cantāre,* frequentative of *canere,* to sing.] —**can·til·la·tion** *n.*

can·ti·na (kăn-tē′nə) *n. Southwestern U.S.* An establishment that serves liquor; a bar or saloon. [Spanish, CANTEEN.]

cant·ing (kăn′tĭng) *adj. Heraldry.* Of, pertaining to, or being a visual allusion to the owner's or bearer's name.

can·tle (kăn′təl) *n.* 1. The rear part of a saddle. 2. A corner or portion, especially when cut off from something, such as a piece of land or cheese; a slice. [Middle English *cantel,* from Norman French, diminutive of *cant,* corner, CANT.]

can·to (kăn′tō) *n., pl.* **-tos. Abbr. can.** Any of the principal divisions of a long poem. [Italian, from Latin *cantus,* song, from *canere,* to sing.]

can·ton (kăn′tən, -tŏn′) *n.* 1. **a.** A small territorial division of a country; especially, any of the constituent states of Switzerland. **b.** A subdivision of an arrondissement in France. 2. *Heraldry.* A small, square division of a shield, usually in the upper right corner. 3. A division of a flag, usually rectangular, occupying the upper corner next to the staff.
~*tr.v.* (kăn′tən, -tŏn′ *for sense 1;* kăn-tŏn′, -tōn′ *for sense 2)* **cantoned, -toning, -tons.** 1. To divide into parts, especially into cantons or territorial districts. 2. To assign quarters to (troops); billet. [French, corner, subdivision, from Old French, from Italian *cantone,* augmentative of *canto,* CANT (corner).] —**can·ton·al** (kăn′tə-nəl, kăn-tŏn′əl) *adj.*

Canton. See Guangzhou.

Can·ton crepe (kăn-tŏn′) *n.* A soft fabric of silk or similar material with a finely crinkled texture. It is similar to crêpe de Chine but heavier. [After CANTON, China, where it was originally made.]

Can·ton·ese (kăn′tə-nēz′, -nēs′) *n., pl.* **Cantonese.** 1. The dialect of Chinese spoken in Guangdong province in southern China. 2. A native or inhabitant of Guangdong province in southern China. —**Can·ton·ese** *adj.*

Canton flannel *n.* Flannelette. [After CANTON, China.]

can·ton·ment (kăn-tŏn′mənt, kăn-tŏn′-) *n.* 1. A group of more or less temporary buildings for housing troops. 2. The assignment of troops to temporary quarters.

Canton ware *n.* Ceramic ware, including blue-and-white enameled porcelain, exported from China, especially during the 18th and 19th centuries. [After CANTON, China.]

can·tor (kăn′tər) *n.* 1. The official soloist or chief singer of the liturgy in a synagogue. 2. The person who leads a church choir or congregation in singing; a precentor. [Latin, singer, from *canere,* to sing.] —**can·to·ri·al** (kăn-tôr′ē-əl, -tōr′ē-əl) *adj.*

Can·tor (kăn′tôr), **Georg** (1845–1918). Russian mathematician, noted for setting the concept of infinity on a mathematical foundation. Born in St. Petersburg, he moved to Germany with his family in 1856. His main achievements were in applying ideas of symbolic logic to sets of numbers and formulating his theory of sets. Attacked by many of his contemporaries, he had a breakdown (1884) and died in an asylum.

can·trip (kăn′trĭp) *n. Scottish.* 1. A magic spell; a witch's trick. 2. A mischievous trick; a prank. [18th century : origin obscure.]

can·tus fir·mus (kăn′təs fîr′məs, fûr′məs) *n.* A plainsong melody serving as the basis of a polyphonic composition by the addition of contrapuntal voices, as in 15th-century polyphony. [Medieval Latin, "fixed melody."]

canula. Variant of cannula.

Ca·nute or **Cnut** (kə-nōōt′, -nyōōt′) (*c.* 994–1035). Danish King of England (from 1016), Denmark (from 1019), and Norway (from 1028). He repelled Viking attacks on England and temporarily subjugated Malcolm II and the Scots (1028). To prove to flatterers that even his powers were limited, he is reputed to have taken his court to the seashore and commanded the incoming waves to recede.

can·vas (kăn′vəs) *n.* 1. A heavy, coarse, closely woven fabric of cotton, hemp, or flax, used for making tents and sails. 2. **a.** A piece of such material on which a painting, especially an oil painting, is executed. **b.** A painting of this kind. 3. Sailcloth. 4. **a.** A sail. **b.** Sails collectively. 5. **a.** A tent. **b.** Tents collectively. **c.** A circus tent. 6. A fabric of coarse open weave, used as a foundation for needlework. 7. The floor of a ring in which boxing or wrestling takes place. 8. A covering made of canvas to enclose the section at the front or back of a racing boat in order to keep out water. —**under canvas.** 1. In a tent or tents. 2. With sails spread. [Middle English *canevas,* from Norman French, from Vulgar Latin *cannabāceus* (unattested), "made of hemp," from Latin *cannabis,* hemp, from Greek *kannabis.*]

can·vas·back (kăn′vəs-băk′) *n.* A North American duck, *Aythya valisneria,* having a reddish-brown head and neck and a whitish back.

canvas duck *n.* A fabric made of lightweight cotton or linen.

can·vass (kăn′vəs) *v.* **-vassed, -vassing, -vasses.** —*tr.* 1. **a.** To go through (a region) or go to (persons) to solicit votes, orders, subscriptions, or the like. **b.** To conduct a survey of (public opinion) on a given subject; poll. 2. To examine carefully or discuss thoroughly; scrutinize. —*intr.* 1. To solicit political support, sales orders, or opinions. 2. To make a thorough examination or conduct a detailed discussion.
~n. 1. **a.** A solicitation of votes, sales orders, or opinions. **b.** A survey of public opinion. 2. An examination or discussion. [From CANVAS, probably from the idea of "tossing a person in a canvas sheet," hence to agitate, harangue.] —**can·vass·er** *n.*

can·yon (kăn′yən) *n.* Also **ca·ñon.** A narrow chasm with steep cliff walls, usually formed by running water; a gorge. [American Spanish *cañon*, from Spanish, pipe, tube, conduit, augmentative of *caña*, tube, cane, from Latin *canna*, a reed, from Greek *kanna*.]

Can·yon·lands National Park (kăn'yən-lăndz'). A national park covering 104,344 hectares (257,640 acres) in southeastern Utah. The park is in a desert region and has deep canyons, unusual rock pinnacles and arches, and high mesas.

can·zo·ne (kăn-zō′nĕ, känt-sô′nä) *n.*, *pl.* **-nes** (-nĕz, -näz) or **-ni** (-nē). **1.** A poetic form that was the dominant lyric genre of 13th-century Italy, consisting of a sequence of equal stanzas with various standard rhyme schemes developed as a synthesis of pre-existing Provençal forms by Dante and others. **2.** A polyphonic song form evolving from this and resembling the madrigal in style. [Italian, from Latin *cantiō* (stem *cantiōn-*), song, from *canere*, to sing.]

can·zo·net (kăn′zə-nĕt′) *n.* Also **can·zo·net·ta** (-nĕt′ə). A short, lighthearted song or air. [Italian *canzonetta*, diminutive of CANZONE.]

caou·tchouc (kou′chook′, -chook′) *n.* Natural **rubber** *(see).* [French, from obsolete Spanish *cauchuc*, from Quechua.]

cap (kăp) *n.* **1.** A covering for the head, usually soft and close-fitting and often having a visor. **2.** A special head covering worn to indicate rank, occupation, or membership in a particular group: *a cardinal's cap.* **3.** Any of numerous objects that cover, protect, or seal: *a bottle cap.* **4.** *Architecture.* The capital of a column. **5.** The top part, or pileus, of a fungus such as a mushroom or toadstool. **6. a.** A percussion cap *(see).* **b.** A small explosive charge enclosed in paper for use in a toy gun. **7.** An academic mortarboard. Used especially in the phrase *cap and gown.* **8.** *British.* **a.** *Sports.* A token award made to a player on each appearance for a special team, especially an international football or cricket team. **b.** A sportsman awarded a cap. **9.** Any of several sizes of writing paper. See foolscap. **10.** Something that limits or restrains: *put a cap on government spending.* **—set one's cap for.** To attempt to attract and win (a man) as a lover or husband.
~*tr.v.* **capped, capping, caps. 1.** To put a cap on: *Engineers capped the oil well to contain the fire.* **2.** To lie over or on top of; serve as a cap for; cover: *Snow capped the hills.* **3.** To apply the finishing touch to; complete: *cap a meal with dessert.* **4.** To surpass; outdo. **5.** *British.* To name (a sportsman) as a member of a special team. [Middle English *cappe*, Old English *cæppe*, from Late Latin *cappa*, hood, probably from Latin *caput*, head.]

cap. 1. capacity. **2.** capital (city). **3.** capital letter.

ca·pa·bil·i·ty (kā′pə-bĭl′ə-tē) *n.*, *pl.* **-ties. 1.** The quality of being capable; physical, mental, or moral capacity; ability. **2.** Potential ability: *live up to one's capabilities.* **3.** The capacity to be used, treated, or developed for a specific purpose.

ca·pa·ble (kā′pə-bəl) *adj.* **1.** Having capacity or ability; competent; efficient; able: *a capable administrator.* **2.** Having the required mental or physical capacity; qualified. Used with *of.* **3.** Open; susceptible. Used with *of*: *an error capable of remedy.* [French, from Old French, from Late Latin *capābilis*, "able to hold," from *capere*, to hold.] **—ca·pa·ble·ness** *n.* **—ca·pa·bly** *adv.*

ca·pa·cious (kə-pā′shəs) *adj.* Able to contain a large quantity; spacious; roomy. [Latin *capāx* (stem *capāc-*), able to hold, from *capere*, to hold, contain.] **—ca·pa·cious·ly** *adv.* **—ca·pa·cious·ness** *n.*

ca·pac·i·tance (kə-păs′ə-təns) *n. Symbol* **C 1.** The ratio of charge to potential on an electrically charged, isolated conductor. **2.** The ratio of the electric charge transferred from one to the other of a pair of conductors to the resulting potential difference between them. Formerly called "capacity." **3. a.** The property of a circuit element that permits it to store charge. **b.** The part of a circuit exhibiting capacitance. [CAPACIT(Y) + -ANCE.] **—ca·pac·i·tive** *adj.* **—ca·pac·i·tive·ly** *adv.*

ca·pac·i·tate (kə-păs′ə-tāt′) *tr.v.* **-tated, -tating, -tates.** To render fit; make qualified; enable. **—ca·pac·i·ta·tion** *n.*

ca·pac·i·tor (kə-păs′ə-tər) *n.* An electric circuit element used to store charge temporarily, consisting typically of two metallic plates separated by a dielectric. Formerly called "condenser."

ca·pac·i·ty (kə-păs′ə-tē) *n.*, *pl.* **-ties.** *Abbr.* **c., C., cap. 1.** The ability to receive, hold, or absorb. **2.** A measure of this ability; volume. **3.** The maximum amount that can be contained: *a trunk filled to capacity.* **4.** The maximum or optimum amount of production: *factories operating below capacity.* **5.** The ability to learn or retain knowledge. **6.** The ability to do something; faculty; aptitude. Used with *of, for,* or an infinitive: *a capacity for self-expression.* **7.** The quality of being suitable for or receptive to specified treatment: *the capacity of elastic to be stretched.* **8.** The position in which one functions; a role: *in her capacity as hostess.* **9.** Legal qualification or authority: *the capacity to make an arrest.* **10.** *Electricity.* **a.** *Obsolete.* Capacitance. **b.** A measure of the electric output of a generator. **—See Synonyms at ability.**
~*adj.* As large or numerous as possible: *a capacity crowd on opening night.* [Middle English *capacite*, from Old French, from Latin *capācitās* (stem *capācitāt-*), from *capāx*, CAPACIOUS.]

cap-a-pie, cap-à-pie (kăp′ə-pē′) *adv.* From head to foot. [Old French *(de) cap a pie*, from Old Provençal *de cap a pe* : *cap*, head, from Latin *caput* + *pe*, foot, from Latin *pēs*.]

ca·par·i·son (kə-păr′ə-sən) *n.* **1.** A cover, usually ornamental, placed over a horse's saddle or harness; trappings. **2.** Richly ornamented clothing; finery.
~*tr.v.* **caparisoned, -soning, -sons.** To equip with a caparison. [Old French *caparaçon*, from Spanish *caparazón*, saddle blanket, "mantle with hood," probably from *capa*, CAPE (garment).]

cape¹ (kāp) *n.* A sleeveless garment fastened at the throat and worn hanging over the shoulders. [French, from Old Provençal *cape* and Spanish *capa*, both from Late Latin *cappa*, hood, cloak, from Latin *caput*, head.]

cape² *n. Abbr.* **c., C.** A point or head of land projecting into a sea or other body of water; a promontory. Compare **peninsula.** [Middle English *cap*, from Old French, from Old Provençal, from Latin *caput*, head.]

Cape, Cape of. For names of actual capes, see the specific element of the name, as **Hatteras, Cape; Good Hope, Cape of; Cod, Cape.** Other names beginning with *Cape* are entered under **Cape,** as **Cape Province.**

Cape Bret·on Island (kāp brĕt′n). Island forming northern Nova Scotia, eastern Canada. A causeway links it to the mainland.

Cape Coast. Town on the Gulf of Guinea, Ghana. The capital of the British colony of the Gold Coast until 1877, it was formerly known as Cape Coast Castle after the castle built by the Swedes (1652). The Dutch followed the Swedes as the colonial power before handing it over to the British (1664). Cocoa is its chief export.

Cape Cod Canal (kŏd). A sea level canal, 28.2 kilometers (17.5 miles) long, at the base of Cape Cod in Massachusetts. It was built (1910–14) with private funds and purchased by the U.S. government in 1927. The canal can accommodate oceangoing vessels and cuts the distance between New York and Boston by 121 kilometers (75 miles).

Cape Cod National Seashore. A scenic area, *c.* 18,060 hectares (44,600 acres), on Cape Cod in southeastern Massachusetts. It includes beaches, sand dunes, heathlands, marshes, freshwater ponds, and historic sites.

Cape colored *n.* A South African of mixed racial descent who lives in or near the Cape Peninsula.

Cape cowslip *n.* Any of various bulbous South African plants of the genus *Lachenalia,* having clusters of drooping red, green, or yellow flowers and widely cultivated as a potted plant.

Cape gooseberry *n.* A plant, *Physalis peruviana,* native to tropical America, having yellow flowers and edible yellow berries.

Cape jasmine *n.* A species of **gardenia** *(see).*

cap·e·lin (kăp′ə-lĭn) *n.* Also **cap·lin** (kăp′lĭn). A small, edible marine fish, *Mallotus villosus,* of northern Atlantic and Pacific waters, related to and resembling the smelts. [French, from Provençal, "smelt," CHAPLAIN.]

Ca·pel·la (kə-pĕl′ə) *n.* A double star in Auriga, the brightest star in the constellation, approximately 46 light-years from Earth. [New Latin, from Latin, diminutive of *capra,* she-goat, from *caper,* goat.]

Cape Province. Officially, Province of the Cape of Good Hope. *Abbr.* **C.P.** Largest and most southerly province of South Africa. The first settlers (1652) were Dutch. Ceded to Britain (1814), it became Cape Colony (Crown Colony of the Cape of Good Hope) and joined the Union of South Africa as a province (1910). It produces diamonds, copper, asbestos, manganese, iron ore, fruit, and vegetables. Its capital is Cape Town.

ca·per¹ (kā′pər) *n.* **1.** A playful leap or hop; a skip. **2.** A wild escapade. **3.** A criminal plot or enterprise.
~*intr.v.* **capered, -pering, -pers.** To leap or frisk about; frolic; gambol. [Short for CAPRIOLE.] **—ca·per·er** *n.*

caper² *n.* **1.** A spiny, trailing shrub, *Capparis spinosa,* of the Mediterranean region. **2. a.** A pickled flower bud of this shrub, having a pungent taste and used as a condiment. **b.** Any similar pickled bud or pod. [From earlier *capres* (mistaken as plural), Middle English *caperis,* from Latin *capparis,* from Greek *kapparis†.*]

cap·er·cail·lie (kăp′ər-kāl′yē, -kā′lē) *n.* Also **cap·er·cail·zie** (-kāl′zē). A large grouse, *Tetrao urogallus,* of northern Europe, having dark plumage and, in the male, a fanlike tail. [Scottish Gaelic *capalcoille,* "horse of the wood" : *capall,* horse, probably from Latin *caballus* + *coille,* forest, probably from Old Irish *caill.*]

Ca·per·na·um (kə-pûr′nē-əm). Ancient town on the northern shore of the Sea of Galilee, Israel. Closely associated with Christ's teachings, it is the scene of many Biblical events.

cape·skin (kāp′skĭn′) *n.* Soft leather made from sheepskin. [After CAPE PROVINCE, where it was originally made.]

Ca·pet (kā′pĭt, kăp′ĭt, kä-pā′). Dynasty of French kings (987–1328) descended from **Robert the Strong** (died 866), including **Hugh Capet** (*c.* 940–99) who was elected king in 987, permanently removing the Carolingians from power, and ruled until his death. Their gradual expansion of territory and centralization of power initiated the movement toward a unified France.

Ca·pe·tian (kə-pē′shən) *adj.* Pertaining or belonging to the Capet dynasty. **—Ca·pe·tian** *n.*

Cape Town. Legislative capital of South Africa and the capital city of Cape Province. Founded by Jan van Riebeeck (1652) as a supply post on the Atlantic coast for the Dutch East India Company, it is the oldest white settlement in South Africa. The chief seaport and second-largest city in the country (after Johannesberg), it is an important commercial and industrial center producing chemicals, textiles, and motor vehicles.

Cape Verde (vûrd). *Portuguese* **Ca·bo Ver·de** (kä′boo vĕr′dĭ). Country occupying an archipelago in the North Atlantic Ocean. Settled by the Portuguese in the mid-15th century, the ten islands and five islets became a Portuguese colony in 1495, an overseas province in 1951, and independent in 1975. The islands, of volcanic origin, have a poor economy based on subsistence farming. Area, 4,033 square kilometers (1,557 square miles). Population, 370,000. Capital, Praia. See map at **Atlantic Ocean.**

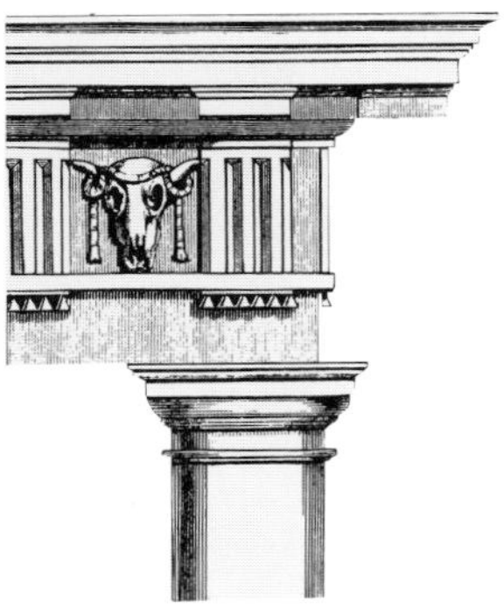

capital *A column was first designed with a capital for a practical purpose: to concentrate the load of the roof above onto the column. But the capital soon became a focus for decoration. Designs range from the simplicity of this Roman Doric capital to the elaborate Corinthian and Gothic capitals.*

Cape York Peninsula (yôrk). Northern part of Queensland, Australia, situated between the Gulf of Carpentaria and the Coral Sea. The low-lying peninsula, tipped by Cape York, the most northerly point of the Australian mainland, supplies bauxite to Australia's aluminium industries.

cap·ful (kăp′fo͝ol′) *n., pl.* **-fuls.** The amount a cap will hold.

cap gun *n.* A cap pistol.

caph. Variant of **kaph.**

Cap-Ha·ï·tien (kăp-hā′shən, kȧ-pȧ-ē-syăɴ′). Also **Le Cap** (lə kăp′). Seaport and resort on the north coast of Haiti. Under French rule, it was the capital of the colony until superseded by Port-au-Prince.

ca·pi·as (kā′pē-əs) *n. Law.* A writ authorizing an officer to arrest the person named in it. [Middle English, from Latin *capias,* "you are to arrest" (first word of the writ), from *capere,* to seize, take.]

cap·il·lar·i·ty (kăp′ə-lăr′ə-tē) *n., pl.* **-ties.** The interaction between contacting surfaces of a liquid and a solid that, as a result of surface tension, distorts the liquid surface from a planar shape.

cap·il·lar·o·scope (kăp′ə-lăr′ə-skōp′) *n.* A microscope used in capillaroscopy. [CAPILLAR(Y) + -SCOPE.]

cap·il·la·ros·co·py (kăp′ə-lə-rŏs′kə-pē) *n.* The diagnostic examination of the capillaries. [CAPILLAR(Y) + -SCOPY.]

cap·il·lar·y (kăp′ə-lĕr′ē) *adj.* **1.** Pertaining to or resembling a hair; fine and slender. **2.** Having a very small internal diameter. Said of tubes. **3.** *Anatomy.* In, of, or pertaining to the capillaries. **4.** *Physics.* Of or pertaining to capillarity.
~*n., pl.* **capillaries. 1.** *Anatomy.* Any of the minute blood vessels that connect the arteries and veins. **2.** A tube with a small internal diameter. [Latin *capillāris,* from *capillus*†, hair.]

capillary attraction *n.* The force that results in the raising of the surface molecules of a liquid in contact with a solid surface, when the attraction between the solid and the liquid molecules is greater than that between the liquid molecules themselves.

capillary repulsion *n.* The force that results in the lowering of the surface molecules of a liquid in contact with a solid surface, when the attraction between the solid and the liquid molecules is less than that between the liquid molecules themselves.

cap·i·tal[1] (kăp′ə-təl) *n.* **1.** *Abbr.* **cap.** A town or city that is the official seat of government in a state, nation, or other political entity. **2.** Wealth in the form of money or property, owned, used, or accumulated in business by an individual, partnership, or corporation. **3.** Any form of material wealth used or available for use in the production of more wealth. **4. a.** *Accounting.* The remaining assets of a business after all liabilities have been deducted; net worth. **b.** The funds contributed to a business by the owners or stockholders. **5.** Capitalists considered as a group or class. **6.** Any asset or advantage. **7.** A **capital letter** *(see).*
~*adj.* **1.** First and foremost; chief; principal. **2.** Of, pertaining to, or being a political capital. **3.** First-rate; excellent: *a capital fellow.* **4.** Extremely serious; fatal: *a capital blunder.* **5.** Involving death or calling for the death penalty: *a capital crime.* **6.** Of or pertaining to monetary capital. **7.** Designating an upper-case letter. [Middle English, from Old French, from Latin *capitālis,* "of the head," important, chief, from *caput,* head.]

capital[2] *n. Architecture.* The top part, or head, of a pillar or column. [Middle English *capitale,* from Norman French *capitel,* from Late Latin *capitellum,* "small head," from Latin *caput,* head.]

capital account *n.* **1.** An account stating the amount of funds and assets invested in a business by the owners or stockholders, including retained earnings; the owner's interest in the firm. **2.** *Accounting.* A statement of the net worth of a business enterprise at a given time.

capital assets *pl.n.* Long-term assets, as land, buildings, or shares belonging to an individual.

capital expenditure *n.* Funds spent for additions or improvements to plant or equipment.

capital gain *n.* Profit acquired by the sale of capital assets.

capital goods *pl.n.* Goods used in the production of commodities. Also called "producer goods." Compare **consumer goods.**

cap·i·tal·ism (kăp′ə-tə-lĭz′əm) *n.* **1.** An economic system characterized by a free competitive market with private and corporate ownership of production and distribution means, in which development is proportionate to the accumulation and reinvestment of profits. **2.** A political or social system regarded as being based on this. Compare **socialism.**

cap·i·tal·ist (kăp′ə-tə-lĭst) *n.* **1.** An investor of capital in business; especially, one having a major financial interest in an important enterprise. **2.** *Informal.* Any person of great wealth. **3.** A supporter of capitalism.
~*adj.* Capitalistic.

cap·i·tal·is·tic (kăp′ə-tə-lĭs′tĭk) *adj.* **1.** Of or pertaining to capitalism or capitalists. **2.** Favoring or practicing capitalism. **—cap·i·tal·is·ti·cal·ly** *adv.*

cap·i·tal·i·za·tion (kăp′ə-tə-lə-zā′shən) *n.* **1.** The act, practice, or result of capitalizing. **2. a.** The total value of shares in a business firm; the total investment of shareholders. **b.** The authorized or outstanding stock or bonds in a corporation. **3.** The process of converting anticipated future income into present value. **4.** The use of capital letters in printing or writing.

cap·i·tal·ize (kăp′ə-tə-līz′) *v.* **-ized, -izing, -izes.** *—tr.* **1.** To utilize as capital; convert into capital. **2.** To supply with capital or investment funds. **3.** To authorize the issue of a certain amount of capital stock of (a business). **4.** To convert (debt) into capital stock or shares. **5.** To estimate the present value of (a stock, annuity, or real estate, for example). **6.** *Accounting.* To include (expenditures) in business accounts as assets instead of expenses. **7. a.** To write or print in upper-case letters. **b.** To begin (a word) with an upper-case letter. *—intr.* To turn something to advantage; exploit an opportunity. Often used with *on*: *capitalize on an opponent's error.* **—cap·i·tal·iz·a·ble** *adj.* **—cap·i·tal·iz·er** *n.*

capital letter *n. Abbr.* **cap.** An upper-case letter; a letter written or printed in a size larger than and often in a form differing from its corresponding lower-case letter. Also called "capital."

capital levy *n.* A tax on capital assets or real property.

capital punishment *n.* The infliction of the death penalty for the commission of crimes.

capital ship *n.* A warship, such as a battleship or aircraft carrier, of the largest class.

capital stock *n.* **1.** The total amount of stock authorized for issue by a corporation. **2.** The total stated or par value of the permanently invested capital of a corporation.

cap·i·tate (kăp′ə-tāt′) *adj.* **1.** *Zoology.* Enlarged or globular at an end, as some tentacles and bones. **2.** *Botany.* Forming a headlike mass or dense cluster. Said of certain flowers. [Latin *capitātus,* having a head, from *caput* (stem *capit-*), head.]

cap·i·ta·tion (kăp′ə-tā′shən) *n.* **1.** A tax fixed at an equal sum per person; a per capita or poll tax. **2.** A payment or fee of a fixed amount per person. [Late Latin *capitātiō* (stem *capitātiōn-*), from *caput* (stem *capit-*), head, person.] **—cap·i·ta·tive** (kăp′ə-tā′tĭv) *adj.*

cap·i·tol (kăp′ə-təl) *n.* **1. Capitol.** The ancient temple of Jupiter on the Capitoline Hill in Rome. **2.** The building in which a state legislature assembles. **3. Capitol.** The building in Washington, D.C., occupied by the Congress of the United States. [Middle English *Capitol(ie),* Jupiter's temple in Rome, from Latin *Capitōlium,* probably "the chief (temple)," from *caput* (stem *capit-*), head.]

Cap·i·to·line (kəp′ə-tə-līn) *adj.* Of or pertaining to the Roman Capitol or to the Capitoline Hill.

Capitoline Hill. The highest of the seven hills of Rome.

Capitol Reef National Park. An area of 13,355 hectares (33,000 acres) in south-central Utah. The park contains cliff dwellings, petrified trees, and highly colored sandstone cliffs.

ca·pit·u·lar (kə-pĭch′ə-lər) *adj.* **1.** Pertaining or belonging to a chapter, especially an ecclesiastical chapter: *capitular clergy.* **2.** Of or pertaining to a capitulum. [Medieval Latin *capitulāris,* from *capitulum,* (ecclesiastical) chapter, from Late Latin, division (of a book), chapter. See **capitulate.**] **—ca·pit·u·lar·ly** *adv.*

ca·pit·u·lar·y (kə-pĭch′ə-lĕr′ē) *n., pl.* **capitularies. 1.** A member of an ecclesiastical or similar chapter. **2. capitularies.** Ordinances or a set of them; especially, those promulgated by Charlemagne and his successors.

ca·pit·u·late (kə-pĭch′ə-lāt′) *intr.v.* **-lated, -lating, -lates. 1.** To surrender under specified conditions; come to terms. **2.** To give up all resistance; acquiesce. —See Synonyms at **yield.** [Originally "to propose or make terms (of surrender)," from Medieval Latin *capitulāre,* to draw up under heads or chapters, from Late Latin *capitulum,* chapter, from Latin, heading, from *caput,* head.] **—ca·pit·u·lant** *n.* **—ca·pit·u·la·tor** *n.*

ca·pit·u·la·tion (kə-pĭch′ə-lā′shən) *n.* **1. a.** The act of capitulating; surrender. **b.** A document containing the terms of surrender. **2.** An enumeration of the main parts of a subject; a summary. —See Synonyms at **surrender. —ca·pit·u·la·to·ry** *adj.*

ca·pit·u·lum (kə-pĭch′ə-ləm) *n., pl.* **-la** (-lə). **1.** *Botany.* A dense, headlike cluster of stalkless flowers, seen in the daisy and related plants. **2.** *Anatomy.* A small knob or head-shaped part, such as the end of a bone or the knoblike tip of an insect's antenna. [New Latin, from Latin, diminutive of *caput,* head.]

caplin. Variant of **capelin.**

ca·po[1] (kā′pō) *n., pl.* **-pos.** A small movable bar placed across the fingerboard of a guitar or other similar instrument for altering the pitch of all the strings simultaneously. [Italian *capo (di tasto),* "cap (of the keys)," from Latin *caput,* head.]

ca·po[2] (kā′pō, kăp′ō) *n., pl.* **capos.** The head of an organized crime syndicate or one of its branches. [Italian, head, chief.]

ca·pon (kā′pŏn′, -pən) *n.* A rooster castrated when young to improve the quality of its flesh for food. Compare **poulard.** [Middle English *capon,* Old English *capūn* and Norman French *capon,* both from Latin *capō* (stem *cāpōn-*).]

Ca·pone (kə-pōn′) **Alphonse,** "Al" and also known as "Scarface." (1899–1947). Italian-born U.S. gangster. He ruled the Chicago underworld ruthlessly, as in the St. Valentine's Day Massacre (1929), when he had seven members of Bugs Moran's gang shot to death. Never successfully prosecuted for any of his gangland crimes, he was finally convicted of tax evasion and sent to Alcatraz prison (1931).

cap·o·ral (kăp′ər-əl, kăp′ə-răl′) *n.* A strong, dark cigarette and pipe tobacco. [French *(tabac de) caporal,* "corporal's tobacco" (superior to *tabac de soldat,* private soldier's tobacco), from Italian *caporale,* corporal, from *capo,* head, chief, from Latin *caput,* head.]

ca·pote (kə-pōt′) *n.* A long cloak or coat, usually hooded. [French, from Old French *cape,* CAPE (cloak).]

Ca·po·te (kə-pō′tē), **Truman** (1924–84). U.S. novelist and journalist best known for the book *In Cold Blood* (1966). *Breakfast at Tiffany's* (1958) enjoyed great success as a film.

Capp (kăp), **Al,** born Alfred Gerald Caplin (1909–79). U.S. cartoonist who created the Li'l Abner comic strip, first published in the New York *Mirror* (1934). His characters satirized events and personalities of the time.

Cap·pa·do·ci·a (kăp′ə-dō′shē-ə, -shə). An ancient region of eastern Asia Minor, now forming the central part of Turkey. —**Cap·pa·do·cian** adj. & n.

cap pistol n. A toy pistol with a hammer action that detonates a mildly explosive cap.

cap·puc·ci·no (kăp′ə-chē′nō, kä′pə-) n., pl. **-nos. 1.** Espresso coffee mixed or topped with steamed milk or cream. **2.** A cup of such coffee. [Italian, Capuchin (alluding to the monks' brown hoods).]

Cap·ra (kăp′rə), **Frank** (1897–1991). U.S. film director, born in Italy, whose comedies dealt with the individual's battles against corruption. His successful films included *Platinum Blonde* (1932), *It Happened One Night* (1934), *Mr. Smith Goes to Washington* (1939), and *It's a Wonderful Life* (1946).

cap·re·o·late (kăp′rē-ə-lāt′, kə-prē′-) adj. *Biology.* Having or like tendrils. [Latin *capreolus,* wild goat, wooden prop (suggesting horns) supporting tendrils of vines.]

Ca·pri (kə-prē′, kä′prē). Small island in the Bay of Naples, Italy. Warm and picturesque, it has been a tourist resort since Roman times. It has the remains of Emperor Tiberius's villas and the Blue Grotto, discovered in 1826.

cap·ric acid (kăp′rĭk) n. *Chemistry.* A white crystalline compound, $C_{10}H_{2}O_2$, derived from coconut oil by fractional distillation. It is chiefly used in the manufacture of esters for artificial fruit flavors and perfumes, and as a base for plasticizers and resins. Also called "decanoic acid." [Latin *caper,* goat (from the unpleasant odor of the acid).]

ca·pric·cio (kə-prē′chō, -chē-ō′) n., pl. **-cios.** *Music.* An instrumental work with an improvisatory style and a free form. [Italian, CA-PRICE.]

ca·pric·cio·so (kə-prē′chō′sō) adv. *Music.* Lively and free. Used as a direction. [Italian, from *capriccio,* CAPRICE.] —**ca·pric·cio·so** adj.

ca·price (kə-prēs′) n. **1.** An impulsive change of mind. **2.** An inclination to make such changes. **3.** *Music.* A capriccio. [French, from Italian *capriccio,* "head with hair standing on end," hence horror, whim (in sense influenced by *capra,* goat, from Latin *caper*) : *capo,* head, from Latin *caput* + *riccio,* hedgehog, from Latin *ēricius,* from *ēr,* hedgehog.]

   Synonyms: fancy, notion, vagary, whim.

ca·pri·cious (kə-prĭsh′əs, -prē′shəs) adj. Characterized by or subject to whim; impulsive and unpredictable; fickle. —**ca·pri·cious·ly** adv. —**ca·pri·cious·ness** n.

Cap·ri·corn (kăp′rĭ-kôrn′) n. **1. a.** The tenth sign of the **zodiac** *(see).* Also called the "Goat." **b.** One born under this sign. **2.** Variant of **Capricornus.**

Cap·ri·cor·nus (kăp′rĭ-kôr′nəs) n. Also **Cap·ri·corn** (kăp′rĭ-kôrn′). A constellation in the equatorial region of the Southern Hemisphere, near Aquarius and Sagittarius. [Latin (translation of Greek *aigokeros,* "goat-horned") : *caper,* goat + *cornū,* horn.]

cap·ri·fi·ca·tion (kăp′rə-fĭ-kā′shən) n. A method of assuring pollination of the edible fig by allowing certain wasps to carry pollen from the flowers of the caprifig to those of the edible variety. [Latin *caprificātio* (stem *caprificātiōn-*), from *caprificāre,* to ripen figs by caprification, from *caprificus,* CAPRIFIG.]

cap·ri·fig (kăp′rə-fĭg′) n. A wild variety of fig, *Ficus carica sylvestris,* of the eastern Mediterranean region, used in the caprification of the edible fig. [Middle English *caprifige, caprificus,* from Latin *caprificus,* "goat fig" : *caper,* goat + *ficus,* FIG.]

cap·rine (kăp′rīn′) adj. Of or like a goat. [Middle English, from Latin *caprīnus,* from *caper,* he-goat.]

cap·ri·ole (kăp′rē-ōl′) n. **1.** An upward leap in dressage made by a trained horse without going forward and with all feet off the ground. **2.** A leap or jump in ballet.

   intr.v. **caprioled, -oling, -oles.** To perform a capriole. [French, from Italian *capriola,* "leap of a goat," from *capriolo,* wild goat, roebuck, from Latin *capreolus,* diminutive of *caper,* goat.]

ca·pro·ic acid (kə-prō′ĭk, kă-) n. A liquid fatty acid, $C_6H_{12}O_2$, found in animal fats and oils and used in the manufacture of pharmaceuticals and flavors. [Latin *caper* (stem *capr-*), goat (referring to its smell).]

capsaicin. Variant of **capsicin.**

cap screw n. A screw with a head that has a shaped groove, usually six-sided, and is turned by a wrench that fits into this groove.

Cap·si·an (kăp′sē-ən) adj. Of or designating a Paleolithic culture of northern Africa and southern Europe. [French *capsien,* after *Capsa,* ancient name of *Gafsa,* Tunisia, near which remains of the culture were found.]

cap·si·cin (kăp′sə-sĭn) n. Also **cap·sa·i·cin** (kăp-sā′ə-sĭn). n. A peppery, reddish-brown liquid, $C_{18}H_{27}O_3N$, obtained from plants of the genus *Capsicum* and used in flavoring vinegar and pickles and medicinally as an irritant. [CAPSIC(UM) + -IN.]

cap·si·cum (kăp′sĭ-kəm) n. **1.** Any of various tropical plants of the genus *Capsicum.* See **pepper. 2.** The dried fruit of pungent varieties of *C. frutescens,* used medicinally as a gastric stimulant and counterirritant. [New Latin, probably from Latin *capsa,* box (from its podlike fruit). See **capsule.**]

cap·sid[1] (kăp′sĭd) n. Any bug of the family Miridae (formerly Capsidae), especially one that feeds on and damages crop plants. [New Latin *Capsus* (former genus name).]

capsid[2] n. The proteinaceous covering of a virus particle. [French *capside,* from Latin *capsa,* box.]

cap·size (kăp′sīz′, kăp-sīz′) v. **-sized, -sizing, -sizes.** —*intr.* To overturn. Used typically of a boat or ship. —*tr.* To cause to capsize. [18th century : origin obscure.]

cap·stan (kăp′stən, -stăn′) n. **1.** *Nautical.* An apparatus consisting of a vertical cylinder rotated manually by a lever (*capstan bar*) or by motor, used for hoisting weights by winding in a cable. **2.** *Electronics.* A small cylindrical pulley used to regulate the speed of magnetic tape in a tape recorder. [Middle English, from Old Provençal *cabestan, cabestran,* from *cabestre,* rope noose, from Latin *capistrum,* halter, from *capere,* to take, seize.]

capstan lathe n. A lathe fitted with a rotatable head capable of holding a number of different tools.

capstan screw n. A screw with a number of radial holes through the head, turned by a bar that fits through one of these holes.

cap·stone (kăp′stōn) n. Also **cope·stone** (kōp′-). **1.** The top stone of a structure or wall. Compare **coping. 2.** The crowning or final stroke; the culmination; the acme.

cap·su·lar (kăp′sə-lər, -syə-lər) adj. Of, pertaining to, or characteristic of a capsule.

cap·su·late (kăp′sə-lāt′, -lĭt, kăp′syə-) adj. Also **cap·su·lat·ed** (-lā′tĭd). In or formed into a capsule. —**cap·su·la·tion** n.

cap·sule (kăp′səl, -sōol) n. **1.** *Pharmacology.* A soluble container, usually of gelatin, enclosing a dose of an oral medicine. **2.** A seal or airtight cap, as for the mouth of a bottle. **3.** *Anatomy.* A fibrous, membranous, or fatty envelope enclosing an organ or part, such as the sac surrounding the kidney. **4.** *Microbiology.* A mucopolysaccharide layer enveloping certain bacteria. **5.** *Botany.* **a.** A dry fruit that contains two or more seeds that are released when it splits open. **b.** The spore case of a moss or other bryophyte. **6.** A pressurized modular compartment of an aircraft or spacecraft, especially one designed to accommodate a crew or to be ejected if required. ~*adj.* Condensed into a small or brief unit; concise; compact: *a capsule description.*

   ~*tr.v.* **capsuled, -suling, -sules. 1.** To enclose in or furnish with a capsule. **2.** To devise or present in a very brief form; condense or summarize. [French, from Latin *capsula,* diminutive of *capsa,* box, chest.]

cap·sul·ize (kăp′sə-līz′) *tr.v.* **-ized, -izing, -izes.** To capsule. —**cap·sul·i·za·tion** n.

Capt. captain.

cap·tain (kăp′tən) n. **1.** One who commands, leads, or guides others, specifically: **a.** The officer in command of a ship, aircraft, or spacecraft. **b.** A precinct chief in a police or fire department. **c.** The designated leader of a team or crew in sports. **2.** *Abbr.* **Capt. a.** A commissioned officer in the Army, Air Force, or Marine Corps who ranks below a major and above a first lieutenant. **b.** A commissioned officer in the Navy who ranks below a commodore or rear admiral and above a commander. **3.** A figure in the forefront; a leader: *a captain of industry.* **4.** A headwaiter.

   ~*tr.v.* **captained, -taining, -tains. 1.** To act as captain of (a team, for example). **2.** To command or direct. [Middle English *capitane, captein,* from Old French *capitain(e),* from Late Latin *capitāneus,* chief, from Latin *caput,* head.] —**cap·tain·cy** n. —**cap·tain·ship** n.

cap·tan (kăp′tən, -tăn′) n. An agricultural fungicide, $C_9H_8CI_3NO_25$. [Short for MERCAPTAN.]

cap·tion (kăp′shən) n. **1.** A title, short explanation, or description accompanying an illustration or photograph. **2.** A subtitle in a film. **3.** A title or heading, as of a document or chapter in a book. **4.** *Law.* The part of a legal document that states the time, place, and authority of its execution.

   ~*tr.v.* **captioned, -tioning, -tions.** To furnish a caption for. [Originally "arrest," hence record of execution of a commission, from Middle English *capcioun,* arrest, seizure, from Latin *captiō* (stem *captiōn-*), from *capere,* to take, seize.]

cap·tious (kăp′shəs) adj. **1.** Marked by a disposition to find fault and make petty criticisms; carping. **2.** Intended to entrap or confuse: *a captious question.* [Middle English *capcious,* from Old French *captieux,* from Latin *captiōsus,* "ensnaring," from *captiō,* seizure, CAPTION.] —**cap·tious·ly** adv. —**cap·tious·ness** n.

cap·ti·vate (kăp′tə-vāt′) *tr.v.* **-vated, -vating, -vates. 1.** To fascinate or hold the attention of by special charm, interest, or beauty. **2.** *Archaic.* To capture. [Late Latin *captīvāre,* to capture, from Latin *captīvus,* CAPTIVE.] —**cap·ti·va·tion** n. —**cap·ti·va·tor** n.

cap·tive (kăp′tĭv) n. **1.** One that is forcibly confined, restrained, or subjugated, such as a prisoner. **2.** One who is enslaved by a strong emotion or passion.

   ~*adj.* **1.** Held as prisoner. **2.** Under restraint or control. **3.** Captivated; enraptured. **4.** Obliged to be present: *a captive audience.* **5.** Forced to buy from a particular source: *a captive market.* [Middle English *captif,* from Latin *captīvus,* from *capere,* to seize.]

cap·tiv·i·ty (kăp-tĭv′ə-tē) n., pl. **-ties.** The state or a period of being captive.

cap·tor (kăp′tər, -tôr′) n. One who takes or keeps someone or something captive. [Late Latin, from Latin *capere,* to seize.]

cap·ture (kăp′chər) *tr.v.* **-tured, -turing, -tures. 1.** To take captive; seize or catch by force or craft. **2.** To win possession or control of, as in a contest. **3.** To succeed in preserving in a fixed form: *capture a likeness in a painting.*

   ~*n.* **1.** The act of capturing; seizure. **2.** One that is seized, caught, or won; a catch or prize. **3.** *Physics.* **a.** The phenomenon whereby an atomic nucleus absorbs a subatomic particle, especially an orbiting electron, often with the subsequent emission of radiation. **b.** The phenomenon whereby an atom, molecule, or positive ion takes up an extra electron. [French, from Old French, from Latin *captūra,* from *capere,* to seize.]

captured rotation n. *Astronomy.* An orbit of a satellite in which the satellite's orbital period is equal to its rotation period. This means that the satellite always points the same hemisphere to its primary, as in the case of the Moon in relation to Earth. Also called "synchronous rotation."

Cap·u·a (kăp′yo͞o-ə). Market town in Campania, southern Italy, near Naples. It rose to prominence under the Romans when it was linked to Rome by the Appian Way.

ca·puche (kə-po͞och′, -po͞osh′) *n.* A hood on a cloak; especially, the long, pointed cowl worn by a Capuchin monk. [Italian *cappuccio,* from *cappa,* hood, from Late Latin, hood, cloak, from Latin *caput,* head.]

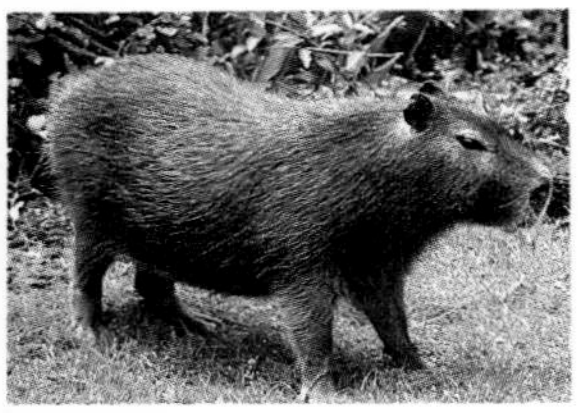

capybara *An aquatic rodent related to the guinea pig family and found in South America. It is the world's largest rodent, growing to a length of about 1.2 meters (4 feet) and weighing up to 50 kilograms (110 pounds).*

cap·u·chin (kăp′yə-chĭn, kə-pyo͞o′-, -shĭn) *n.* **1. Capuchin.** A monk belonging to the Order of Friars Minor Capuchins, an independent branch of the Franciscans, founded in 1525, and licensed in 1619. **2.** A hooded cloak worn by women. **3.** Any of several long-tailed monkeys of the genus *Cebus,* of Central and South America, many of which have hoodlike tufts of hair on the head. In this sense, also called "sapajou." [French, from Old French, from Italian *cappuccino,* "hooded one," from *cappuccio,* CAPUCHE.]

cap·y·ba·ra (kăp′ə-bä′rə, -băr′ə) *n.* A large, short-tailed, semiaquatic rodent, *Hydrochoerus hydrochaeris,* of tropical South America, often attaining a length of four feet. [Portuguese *capibara,* from Tupi.]

car (kär) *n.* **1.** An automobile; motor car. **2.** A conveyance, such as a streetcar, with wheels that run along tracks. **3.** *Archaic.* A chariot. **4.** A boxlike enclosure, such as an elevator car, for passengers on a conveyance. [Middle English *car(re),* cart, wagon, from Norman French, from Vulgar Latin *carra* (unattested), variant of Latin *carrus,* two-wheeled wagon.]

car. carat.

car·a·bao (kăr′ə-bou′, kä′rə-) *n., pl.* **-baos.** The **water buffalo** *(see).* [Visayan *karabáw,* akin to Malay *karbaw.*]

car·a·bid (kăr′ə-bĭd, kə-răb′ĭd) *n.* Any of various black carnivorous beetles of the family Carabidae.
~*adj.* Of or belonging to the Carabidae. [New Latin *Carabidae,* from Latin *cārabus,* from Greek *karabos*†, crayfish, horned beetle.]

carabin, carabine. Variants of **carbine.**

car·a·bi·neer, car·a·bi·nier (kăr′ə-bə-nîr′) *n.* Also **car·bi·neer** (kär′bə-). A soldier armed with a carbine.

ca·ra·bi·nie·re (kär′ə-bən-yâr′ā, kä′rə-) *n, pl.* **-nieri** (-yâr′ē). An Italian policeman under military command. [Italian.]

car·a·cal (kăr′ə-kăl′) *n.* A wild cat, *Lynx caracal,* of Africa and southern Asia, having short, fawn-colored fur and long, tufted ears. Also called "desert lynx." [French, from Turkish *kara kŭlāk,* "black ear" : *kara,* black + *kŭlāk,* ear.]

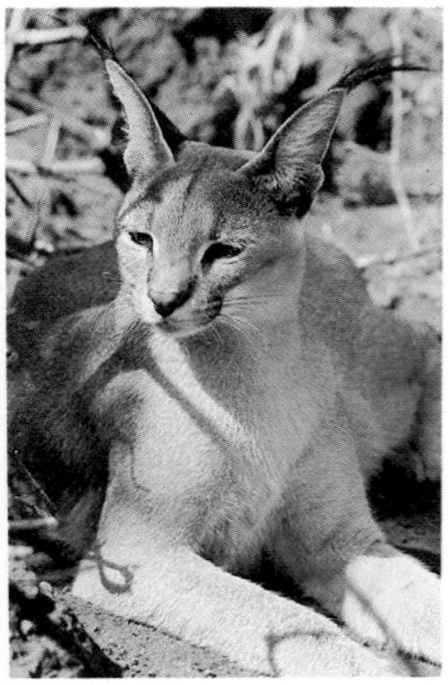

caracal *A wild cat native to the drier parts of Africa and Asia. Caracals normally live alone and hunt by night and are fast enough to knock a low-flying bird out of the air.*

Car·a·cal·la (kăr′ə-kăl′ə) (A.D. 188–217). Roman emperor from the age of 23. He was obsessed with and sought to imitate Alexander the Great. However his bloody, undisciplined rule of the empire left only a legacy of infamy. He was assassinated by the order of the commander of the imperial guard and next emperor, Macrinus (A.D. 164–218).

ca·ra·ca·ra (kä′rə-kä′rə, -kə-rä′) *n.* Any of several large, carrion-eating or predatory birds of the subfamily Caracarinae, of South and Central America and the southern United States, related to the hawks and falcons. [Spanish *caracara* and Portuguese *caracará,* from Tupi *caracara* (imitative).]

Ca·ra·cas (kə-rä′kəs, -răk′əs). Capital of Venezuela. In a basin at 1,000 meters (3,280 feet) above sea level, it is connected to its port and airport at La Guaira by a tunneled motorway 18 kilometers (11 miles) long. Caracas was founded by the Spanish in 1567. It now earns much of its wealth from oil.

carack. Variant of **carrack.**

car·a·cole (kăr′ə-kōl′) *n.* Also **car·a·col** (-kŏl′). A half turn to either side performed by a horse in dressage.
~*intr.v.* **caracoled, -coling, -coles.** To perform a caracole or caracoles. [French, from Spanish *caracol*†, snail, winding stair.]

car·a·cul (kăr′ə-kəl) *n.* **1.** The loosely curled fur of a karakul lamb. **2.** Variant of **karakul.**

ca·rafe (kə-răf′, -räf′) *n.* **1.** A glass bottle for serving water or wine at the table; a decanter. **2.** The amount a carafe will hold. [French, from Italian *caraffa,* from Spanish *garaffa,* from Arabic *gharrāfa,* from *gharafa,* to dip.]

car·a·mel (kăr′ə-məl, -mĕl′, kär′məl) *n.* **1.** A smooth, chewy candy made with sugar, butter, cream or milk, and flavoring. **2.** Burnt sugar, used for coloring and sweetening foods. [French, from Old Spanish, probably from Late Latin *calamellus,* diminutive of Latin *calamus,* reed, cane, from Greek *kalamos.*]

car·a·mel·ize (kăr′ə-mə-līz′, kär′mə-) *v.* **-ized, -izing, -izes.** —*tr.* To convert (sugar) into caramel. —*intr.* To change into caramel. **—car·a·mel·i·za·tion** *n.*

ca·ran·gid (kə-răn′jĭd, -răng′gĭd) *n.* Any of various fishes of the family Carangidae, which includes the jacks, pilot fish, and pompanos, having a compressed body and forked tail.
~*adj.* Of or belonging to the Carangidae. [New Latin *Carangidae* : *Caranx* (stem *Carang-*) (genus), from French *carangue,* mackerel, from Spanish *caranga*† + -IDAE.]

car·a·pace (kăr′ə-pās′) *n.* **1.** *Zoology.* A hard bony or chitinous outer covering, such as the fused dorsal plates of a turtle or the portion of the exoskeleton covering the head and thorax of a crustacean. **2.** A protective covering similar to a carapace. [French, from Spanish *carapacho.*]

car·at (kăr′ət) *n.* **1.** *Abbr.* **c, car.** A unit of weight for precious stones, equal to 200 milligrams. **2.** Variant of **karat.** [French, from Old French, from Medieval Latin *carratus,* from Arabic *qīrāṭ,* small weight, carat, from Greek *keration,* "little horn," carob fruit, carat, diminutive of *keras,* horn.]

Ca·ra·vag·gio (kăr′ə-vä′jō), born Michelangelo Merisi (*c.* 1565–1610). Italian baroque painter, born in Caravaggio, Lombardy. Refusing to conform to the tradition of earlier European art with its idealized religious figures, he chose instead to use peasants and street people as the models for many of his sacred subjects. The altarpiece *Death of the Virgin* and the painting *Supper at Emmaus* are examples of his work. His mastery of light and shade influenced Velázquez and Rembrandt. He fled from Rome in 1606 after killing a man in a dispute over a tennis match, and his final years were spent in exile in Naples, Malta, and Sicily.

car·a·van (kăr′ə-văn′) *n.* **1.** A company of travelers journeying together, especially across a desert. **2.** A single file of vehicles or pack animals. **3.** A large covered vehicle, as one used by gypsies; van. **4.** *Chiefly British.* An unmotorized furnished vehicle, often attached as a trailer to a car or truck and used as living quarters, a temporary office, or a vacation home. [French *caravane* or Italian *caravana, carovana,* from Persian *kārwān*†.]

car·a·van·sa·ry (kăr′ə-văn′sə-rē) *n., pl.* **-ries.** Also **car·a·van·se·rai** (-sə-rī′). **1.** In the Near or Far East, an inn built around a large court for accommodating caravans at night. **2.** Any large inn or hostelry. [Persian *kārwānsarāī* : *kārwān,* CARAVAN + *sarāī,* palace, inn.]

car·a·vel, car·a·velle (kăr′ə-vĕl′) *n.* Also **car·vel** (kär′vəl, -vĕl′). A small, light sailing ship of the kind used by the Spanish and Portuguese in the 15th and 16th centuries. [French *caravelle, carvelle,* from Portuguese *caravela,* diminutive of *cáravo,* ship, from Latin *cārabus,* from Greek *karabos*†, crayfish, light ship.]

car·a·way (kăr′ə-wā′) *n.* **1.** A plant, *Carum carvi,* native to Eurasia, having finely divided leaves and clusters of small, whitish flowers. **2.** The pungent, aromatic seeds of this plant, used in baking and cooking. [Middle English *car(a)way,* probably from Old Spanish *alcarahueya* and Medieval Latin *carvi,* both from Arabic *alkarāwiyā,* probably from Greek *karon*†, cumin.]

carb·an·i·on (kär-băn′ī′ən, -ī′ŏn′) *n.* A negatively charged organic ion, such as H_3C^-, having one more electron than the corresponding free radical. [CARBO- + AN- + ION.]

car·bide (kär′bīd′) *n.* **1.** A binary carbon compound consisting of carbon and a more electropositive element. **2. Calcium carbide** *(see).* [CARB(O)- + -IDE.]

car·bine (kär′bīn′, -bēn′) *n.* Also **car·a·bin** (kăr′ə-bĭn), **car·a·bine** (-bīn′, -bēn′). A light shoulder rifle with a short barrel, originally for cavalry use. [French *carabine,* carbine, carabineer, from Old French *carabin,* cavalryman, soldier armed with a musket, probably derisively from *escarrabin,* "one who lays out plague corpses," variant of *escarabilh, scarabée,* dung beetle, from Latin *scarabeus,* a beetle. See **scarab.**]

carbineer, carabinier. Variants of **carabineer.**

car·bi·nol (kär′bə-nôl′, -nōl′) *n.* **1.** Wood alcohol, **methanol** *(see).* **2.** An alcohol derived from methanol by substitution of one or more hydrogen atoms by other hydrocarbon groups. [German *Karbinol* : CARB(O)- + -IN + -OL.]

carbo–, carb– *prefix.* Indicates carbon; for example, **carbohydrate, carbolic acid.** [French, from *carbone,* CARBON.]

car·bo·hy·drate (kär′bō-hī′drāt′) *n.* Any of a group of chemical compounds, including sugars, starches, and cellulose, containing carbon, hydrogen, and oxygen only, with the ratio of hydrogen to oxygen atoms usually 2:1.

car·bo·lat·ed (kär′bə-lā′tĭd) *adj.* Containing or treated with carbolic acid.

car·bol·ic acid (kär-bŏl′ĭk) *n.* An organic compound, **phenol** *(see).* [CARB(O)- + -OL + -IC.]

car·bon (kär′bən) *n.* **1.** *Symbol* **C** A naturally abundant nonmetallic element that occurs in many inorganic and in all organic compounds, exists in amorphous, graphitic, and diamond forms, and is capable of chemical self-bonding to form an enormous number of chemically, biologically, and commercially important molecules. Atomic number 6; atomic weight 12.01115; sublimes above 3,500°C; boiling point 4,827°C; specific gravity of amorphous carbon 1.8 to 2.1, of diamond 3.15 to 3.53, of graphite 1.9 to 2.3; valences 2, 3, 4. **2. a.** A sheet of carbon paper. **b.** A copy made by using carbon paper. **3.** *Electricity.* **a.** Either of two rods through which current flows to form an arc in lighting or in welding. **b.** A carbonaceous electrode in an electric cell.
~*adj.* **1.** Of, pertaining to, or like carbon. **2.** Treated with carbon. [French *carbone,* from Latin *carbō* (stem *carbōn-*), charcoal.] **—car·bon·ous** *adj.*

carbon 14 *n.* A naturally radioactive carbon isotope with atomic mass 14 and half-life 5,700 years, used in dating ancient carbon-containing objects. Also called "radiocarbon."

car·bo·na·ceous (kär′bə-nā′shəs) *adj.* Consisting of, containing, pertaining to, or yielding carbon.

car·bo·nade, car·bon·nade (kär′bə-näd′) *n.* A rich stew of beef, onions, and beer, of Belgian origin. [French.]

car·bo·na·do[1] (kär′bə-nā′dō, -nä′dō) *n., pl.* **-does** or **-dos.** A piece of scored and broiled fish, poultry, or meat.
~*tr.v.* **carbonadoed, -doing, -dos. 1.** To score and broil (fish, poultry, or meat). **2.** *Archaic.* To slice; slash; chop. [Spanish *carbonada,* from *carbón,* charcoal, coal, from Latin *carbō,* CARBON.]

carbonado[2] *n., pl.* **-does.** A form of opaque or dark-colored diamond, chiefly Brazilian, used for drills. Also called "black diamond," "bort." [Portuguese, "carbonated," from *carbone*, carbon, from French, CARBON.]

carbon arc *n.* An electric arc produced by a carbon electrode, as in an arc lamp or welder.

Car·bo·na·ri (kär′bə-nä′rē) *pl.n. Singular* **Car·bo·na·ro** (-rō). The members of a secret society originally organized in Naples in the early 19th century to establish a liberal, unified Italian republic. [Italian, "charcoal burners," name adopted by members of the society apparently after disguising themselves as such after being driven into hiding in the forest of the Abruzzi.] —**Car·bo·na·rism** *n.* —**Car·bo·na·rist** *n. & adj.*

car·bon·ate (kär′bə-nāt′) *tr.v.* **-ated, -ating, -ates. 1.** To add carbon dioxide gas to (a cold drink, for example) to produce fizz. **2.** To burn to carbon; carbonize. **3.** To change into a carbonate. ~*n.* (-nāt′, -nĭt). A salt or ester of carbonic acid. —**car·bon·a·tion** *n.* —**car·bon·a·tor** *n.*

carbonated water *n.* Soda water *(see).*

carbon bisulfide *n.* Carbon disulfide *(see).*

carbon black *n.* Any of various finely divided forms of carbon derived from the incomplete combustion of natural gas or petroleum oil and used principally in rubber and ink.

carbon copy *n.* **1.** *Abbr.* **C.C., c.c.** A replica, as of a letter, made by using carbon paper. **2.** *Informal.* A close copy or reproduction; duplicate.

carbon cycle *n.* **1.** *Astrophysics.* The **carbon-nitrogen cycle** *(see).* **2.** *Biology.* The cycle of natural processes in which atmospheric carbon in the form of carbon dioxide is converted by photosynthesis in plants to carbohydrates that are eaten and metabolized by animals and ultimately returned to the atmosphere as carbon dioxide through respiration or decomposition.

carbon dating *n.* Determination of the approximate age of carbon-containing objects by the use of the radiation rate of carbon 14.

carbon dioxide *n.* A colorless, odorless, incombustible gas, CO_2, formed during respiration, combustion, and organic decomposition and used in food refrigeration, carbonated beverages, inert atmospheres, fire extinguishers, and aerosols.

carbon dioxide snow *n.* Solid carbon dioxide, used as a refrigerant.

carbon disulfide *n.* A clear flammable liquid, CS_2, used to manufacture viscose rayon and cellophane, as a solvent for fats, rubber, resins, waxes, and sulfur, and in matches, fumigants, and pesticides. Also called "carbon bisulfide."

carbon fiber *n.* A fine filament of almost pure crystalline carbon made by heating stretched textile threads and extensively used in composite plastic and metal materials, as for aircraft parts.

car·bon·ic acid (kär-bŏn′ĭk) *n.* A weak, unstable acid, H_2CO_3, present only in solutions of carbon dioxide in water.

carbonic acid gas *n.* Carbon dioxide.

Car·bon·if·er·ous (kär′bə-nĭf′ər-əs) *adj.* **1.** *Geology.* Of, belonging to, or designating a period of the Paleozoic era following the Devonian and preceding the Permian. It was characterized by swamp formation and deposition of plant remains that later hardened into coal. **2. carboniferous.** Producing or containing coal or carbon. ~*n. Geology.* The Carboniferous period. Preceded by *the.*

car·bo·ni·um (kär-bō′nē-əm) *n.* A positively charged organic ion, such as H_3C^+, having one electron fewer than a corresponding free radical and behaving chemically as if the positive charge were localized on the carbon atom.

car·bon·i·za·tion (kär′bə-nə-zā′shən) *n.* **1.** The process of carbonizing. **2.** The decomposition by destructive distillation of bituminous coal to obtain coke and other by-products.

car·bon·ize (kär′bə-nīz′) *tr.v.* **-ized, -izing, -izes. 1.** To reduce or convert to carbon, as by partial burning. **2.** To coat or combine with carbon. —**car·bon·iz·er** *n.*

carbon microphone *n.* A type of microphone in which an electric current passes through a diaphragm with carbon powder packed behind it. Sound waves vibrate the diaphragm, producing a varying pressure on the carbon and changing its electrical resistance.

carbon monoxide *n.* A colorless, odorless, highly poisonous gas, CO, formed by the incomplete combustion of carbon or any carbonaceous material.

car·bon·ni·tro·gen cycle (kär′bən-nī′trə-jən) *n.* A chain of thermonuclear reactions in which nitrogen isotopes are formed in intermediate stages and carbon acts essentially as a catalyst to convert four protons into one helium nucleus. The sequence is thought to generate significant amounts of energy in certain classes of stars. Also called "carbon cycle," "nitrogen cycle."

carbon paper *n.* A lightweight paper faced on one side with a dark waxy pigment that is transferred by the impact of typewriter keys or by writing pressure to any copying surface, such as paper.

carbon process *n.* A photographic printing process using permanent pigments, such as carbon, contained in a sensitized tissue or film of gelatin.

carbon steel *n.* A type of steel composed mainly of iron with added carbon. Compare **alloy steel.**

carbon tetrachloride *n.* A poisonous, nonflammable, colorless liquid, CCl_4, used as a solvent.

car·bon·yl (kär′bə-nĭl′, -nēl′) *n.* **1.** The bivalent radical CO. **2.** A metal compound containing the CO group bound directly to a metal atom or ion. —**car·bon·yl·ic** (kär′bə-nĭl′ĭk) *adj.*

carbonyl chloride *n.* A poisonous gas, **phosgene** *(see).*

Car·bo·run·dum (kär′bə-rŭn′dəm) *n.* A trademark for a silicon carbide abrasive.

car·box·yl (kär-bŏk′səl) *n.* A univalent radical, COOH, characteristic of all organic acids. [CARB(O)- + OX(Y)- + -YL.]

car·box·yl·ase (kär-bŏk′sə-lās′, -lāz′) *n.* An enzyme that produces an aldehyde and carbon dioxide from certain acids.

car·box·yl·ic acid (kär′bŏk-sĭl′ĭk) *n. Chemistry.* An organic acid with the general formula RCOOH, where R is an organic group. See **fatty acid.**

car·boy (kär′boi′) *n.* A large glass or plastic bottle, usually encased in a protective basket or crate and often used to hold corrosive liquids. [Persian *qarāba*, from Arabic *qarrābah.*]

car·bun·cle (kär′bŭng′kəl) *n.* **1.** An extensive skin eruption, resembling a boil but much larger and having multiple openings, usually caused by infection with *Staphylococcus aureus.* Compare **boil.** **2.** *Obsolete.* A deep-red precious stone, especially the garnet, unfaceted and convex. [Middle English, from Old French, from Latin *carbunculus*, small glowing ember, tumor, diminutive of *carbō* (stem *carbōn-*), charcoal, ember.] —**car·bun·cled** *adj.* —**car·bun·cu·lar** (kär-bŭng′kyə-lər) *adj.*

car·bu·ret (kär′bə-rāt′, kär′byə-, -rĕt′) *tr.v.* **-reted** or **-retted, -reting** or **-retting, -rets.** To combine or mix with carbon or hydrocarbons in order to increase available fuel energy. [From obsolete *carbure(t)*, carbide, from French *carbure*, from Latin *carbō*, CARBON.]

car·bu·re·tor (kär′bə-rā′tər, kär′byə-) *n.* Also *chiefly British* **car·bu·ret·tor, car·bu·ret·ter** (-rĕt′ər). A device used in internal-combustion engines to produce an efficient explosive vapor of fuel and air. [From CARBURET.]

car·bu·rize (kär′bə-rīz′, kär′byə-) *tr.v.* **-rized, -rizing, -rizes.** To treat (iron or steel, for example) with carbon. [CARBUR(ET) + -IZE.] —**car·bu·ri·za·tion** *n.*

car·byl·a·mine (kär-bĭl′ə-mēn′, kär′bĭl-ăm′ēn′) *n.* A type of chemical compound, an **isocyanide** *(see).*

car·ca·jou (kär′kə-jōō′, -zhōō′)) *n. Canadian.* An animal, the **wolverine** *(see).* [Canadian French, from Algonquian *karkajou.*]

car·cass (kär′kəs) *n.* Also *archaic* **car·case. 1.** The dead body of an animal or bird, especially one slaughtered and gutted. **2.** The body of a human being. Used humorously or derogatorily. **3.** Something from which the substance or character is gone: *the carcass of a once-glorious empire.* **4.** A framework or basic structure, as of a ruined building. [Middle English *carcasse*, from Old French *c(h)arcois†*.]

Car·cas·sonne (kär′kə-sôn′, -sŏn′). Capital of Aude department on the Canal du Midi and the Aude River in southwest France. It includes an old fortified medieval hill town (La Cité) and a modern town (Ville Basse).

Car·che·mish (kär′kə-mĭsh′). Ancient city on the Euphrates River, in southern Turkey. A Hittite stronghold until the empire's collapse in the 12th century B.C., it survived as an independent kingdom until taken by the Assyrians under Sargon (717 B.C.). It was the scene of the Egyptians' defeat at the hands of Nebuchadnezzar II and the Babylonians (605 B.C.).

car·cin·o·gen (kär-sĭn′ə-jən, kär′sə-nə-jĕn′) *n.* A cancer-causing substance. [Greek *karkinos*, cancer, crab + -GEN.] —**car·cin·o·gen·ic** (kär′sə-nə-jĕn′ĭk) *adj.*

car·ci·no·ma (kär′sə-nō′mə) *n., pl.* **-mas** or **-mata** (-mə-tə). A malignant tumor arising in epithelial tissue. [Latin *carcinōma*, cancerous ulcer, from Greek *karkinōma*, from *karkinos*, cancer, crab.] —**car·ci·no·ma·toid** (kär′sə-nō′mə-toid′, -nŏm′ə-toid′), **car·ci·nom·a·tous** (-nŏm′ə-təs, -nō′mə-təs) *adj.*

car·ci·no·ma·to·sis (kär′sə-nō′mə-tō′sĭs) *n.* The existence of carcinomas at many bodily sites. [New Latin : Latin *carcinōma* (stem *carcinōmat-*), CARCINOMA + -OSIS.]

card¹ (kärd) *n.* **1.** A small, flat piece of stiff paper, thin pasteboard, or plastic, usually rectangular, with numerous uses, as: **a.** Any of a set bearing significant numbers, symbols, and figures, used in numerous games and in fortunetelling. See **cards. b.** One used to send messages; especially, a postcard. **c.** One printed with a suitable illustration and greeting and sent in an envelope, as for Christmas. **d.** A card or membership card, bearing a person's name and other information and used for purposes of identification or classification. **e.** One used for cataloguing information in a file, such as a reference card. **f.** A credit card *(see).* **2.** A notice or advertisement printed on cardboard. **3.** *Sports.* A list of events or competitors, such as a **scorecard** *(see).* **4.** A compass card *(see).* **5.** *Computer Science.* A punch card *(see).* **6.** *Informal.* An amusing or eccentric person. —**have a card up one's sleeve.** To have a secret resource or plan held in reserve. ~*tr.v.* **carded, carding, cards. 1.** To furnish with or attach to a card. **2.** To list on a card; catalogue. **3.** *Informal.* To check the identification of, especially in order to verify legal age. [Middle English *carde*, from Old French *carte*, from Latin *charta*, leaf of papyrus, from Greek *khartēs*, probably from Egyptian.]

card² *n.* **1.** A wire-toothed brush or comblike machine used to disentangle fibers, as of wool, prior to spinning. **2.** A similar device used to raise the nap on a fabric. ~*tr.v.* **carded, carding, cards.** To comb out or brush with a card. [Middle English *carde*, from Old French, from *carder*, to card, from Old Provençal *cardar*, from Vulgar Latin *caritāre* (unattested), from Latin *cārere*, to card.] —**card·er** *n.*

Card. *Roman Catholic Church.* cardinal.

car·da·mom, car·da·mum (kär′də-məm) *n.* Also **car·da·mon** (-mən). **1. a.** A tropical Asiatic perennial plant, *Elettaria cardamomum*, having large, hairy leaves and capsular fruit. **b.** The fruit and seeds of this plant, used as a condiment and in medicine. **2. a.** An East Indian plant, *Amomum cardamomum.* **b.** The fruit and seeds

caracara *The caracara, a type of hawk, spends much of its life on the ground, where its long legs enable it to run swiftly. It feeds on carrion, small animals, and birds. This is the striated caracara.*

of this plant, used as an inferior substitute for true cardamom seed. [Latin *cardamōmum,* from Greek *kardamōmon* : *kardamon*†, cress + *amōmon*†, an Indian spice.]

card·board (kärd'bôrd', -bōrd') *n.* A thin, stiff pasteboard made of paper pulp, used for making cartons and boxes. ~*adj.* **1.** Made of cardboard. **2.** Superficial; two-dimensional: *cardboard characters.*

card-car·ry·ing (kärd'kăr'ē-ĭng) *adj.* **1.** Being an enrolled member, especially of a political organization: *a card-carrying Communist.* **2.** Being strongly identified with or devoted to a group, as of persons with shared ideals: *a card-carrying liberal.*

card catalog *n.* An alphabetical listing, especially of books in a library, made with a separate card for each item.

car·di·a (kär'dē-ə) *n.* The opening of the esophagus into the stomach. [New Latin, from Greek *kardia,* heart, cardiac orifice of the stomach.]

car·di·ac (kär'dē-ăk') *adj.* **1.** Of, near, or pertaining to the heart. **2.** Of or pertaining to the cardia. ~*n.* A person with a heart disorder. [Latin *cardiacus,* from Greek *kardiakos,* from *kardia,* heart.]

cardiac arrest *n.* The cessation of effective pumping of blood by the heart, resulting in loss of consciousness, absence of the pulse, and cessation of breathing.

cardiac massage *n.* A procedure to restore circulation in an individual by rhythmic manual compression either of the chest or of the heart through an opening in the chest wall.

cardiac muscle *n.* The striated muscle of the heart.

car·di·al·gi·a (kär'dē-ăl'jē-ə, -jə) *n.* **1.** Heartburn *(see).* **2.** Pain in or close to the heart. [New Latin, from Greek *kardialgia* : CARDI(O)- + -ALGIA.]

Car·diff (kär'dĭf). Capital of Wales, situated in South Glamorgan on the Taff River. Cardiff is the administrative center of South and Mid Glamorgan. With the expansion of the South Wales coal and iron mines in the 19th century, Cardiff grew from a small market town into one of the world's leading coal exporters. It was chosen as the capital of Wales only in 1955. After World War II the port declined, and Tiger Bay, the quayside area, is now a residential suburb. Industries include general shipping, ship repairs, steel, engineering, chemicals, and cement.

car·di·gan (kär'dĭ-gən) *n.* A sweater or knitted jacket worn by both sexes and opening down the front. [After the Earl of CARDIGAN.]

Car·di·gan (kär'dĭ-gən). Town on the Teifi River, Dyfed, south Wales, noted for its salmon and sea-trout angling. It was the county town of the former county of Cardiganshire.

Car·di·gan (kär'dĭ-gən), **James Thomas Brudenell, 7th Earl of** (1797–1868). British cavalry officer. He is remembered chiefly for leading the suicidal Charge of the Light Brigade at Balaclava (1854) in the Crimean War.

Car·di·gan·shire (kär'dĭ-gən-shĭr, -shər). Also **Car·di·gan** Former county in Wales, which became part of the county of Dyfed (1974).

Car·din (kär-dăn'), **Pierre** (1922–). French fashion designer who made his mark in the 1950's with his slim-line coats, large collars, and Eastern-influenced designs.

car·di·nal (kärd'n-əl, kärd'nəl) *adj.* **1.** Of foremost importance; pivotal. **2.** Of a dark to deep or vivid red color. ~*n.* **1.** *Abbr.* **Card.** *Roman Catholic Church.* A member of the Sacred College or College of Cardinals. Members are appointed by the pope and elect a new pope when the Holy See is vacated. **2.** A dark to deep or vivid red. **3.** A North American bird, *Richmondena cardinalis,* having a crested head, a short, thick bill, and bright red plumage in the male. **4.** A short, hooded cloak, originally of scarlet cloth, worn by women in the 18th century. **5.** A **cardinal number** *(see).* [Middle English, from Old French, from Late Latin *cardinālis,* from Latin, principal, of a hinge, from *cardō*† (stem *cardin-*), hinge.]

car·di·nal·ate (kärd'n-ə-lĭt, kärd'nə-, -lāt') *n.* Also **car·di·nal·ship** (-shĭp'). *Roman Catholic Church.* **1.** The College of Cardinals. **2.** The position, rank, dignity, or term of a cardinal.

cardinal beetle *n.* A bright red European beetle of the genus *Pyrodehroa,* especially *P. coccinea* and *P. serraticornis,* whose coloration and unpleasant taste help to protect it from predatory birds.

cardinal flower *n.* A plant, *Lobelia cardinalis,* of eastern North America, having a terminal cluster of brilliant scarlet flowers.

cardinal number *n.* A number, such as 3 or 11 or 412, used to indicate quantity but not order. Compare **ordinal number.** **2.** A symbol denoting the size of a transfinite set.

cardinal point *n.* Any of the four principal directions on a compass: north, south, east, or west.

cardinal sins *pl.n.* The **seven deadly sins** *(see).*

cardinal virtues *pl.n.* The four qualities of justice, prudence, fortitude, and temperance. Also called "natural virtues."

cardio-, cardi- *prefix.* Indicates the heart; for example, **cardiogram, cardioid.** [Greek *kardi(o)-,* from *kardia,* heart.]

car·di·o·ac·cel·er·a·tor (kär'dē-ō'ăk-sĕl'ə-rā'tər) *n.* An agent that increases the heart rate.

car·di·o·gen·ic (kär'dē-ō-jĕn'ĭk, -jē'nĭk) *adj.* Having origin in a cardiac condition.

car·di·o·gram (kär'dē-ə-grăm') *n.* **1.** The curve traced by a cardiograph, used in the diagnosis of heart defects. **2.** An electrocardiogram *(see).* [CARDIO- + -GRAM.]

car·di·o·graph (kär'dē-ə-grăf', -gräf') *n.* **1.** An instrument used to record the mechanical movements of the heart. **2.** An electrocardiograph *(see).* [French *cardiographe* : CARDIO- + -GRAPH.] —car-

di·og·ra·pher (kär'dē-ŏg'rə-fər) *n.* —**car·di·o·graph·ic** (kär'dē-ə-grăf'ĭk), **car·di·o·graph·i·cal** *adj.* —**car·di·o·graph·i·cal·ly** *adv.* —**car·di·og·ra·phy** (kär'dē-ŏg'rə-fē) *n.*

car·di·oid (kär'dē-oid') *n.* A heart-shaped plane curve, the locus of a fixed point on a circle that rolls on the circumference of another circle with the same radius. [CARDI(O)- + -OID.]

car·di·ol·o·gy (kär'dē-ŏl'ə-jē) *n.* The medical study and treatment of the diseases and functioning of the heart. [CARDIO- + -LOGY.] —**car·di·ol·o·gist** *n.*

car·di·o·meg·a·ly (kär'dē-ō-mĕg'ə-lē) *n. Pathology.* **Megalocardia** *(see).* [CARDIO- + *-megaly,* from MEGALO-.]

car·di·o·pul·mo·nar·y (kär'dē-ō-pōōl'mə-nĕr'ē) *adj.* Of or pertaining to the heart and the lungs.

car·di·o·res·pir·a·to·ry (kär'dē-ō-rĕs'pər-ə-tôr'ē, -rĭ-spīr'ə-tôr'ē, -tōr'ē) *adj.* Of or pertaining to the heart and the respiratory system.

car·di·o·vas·cu·lar (kär'dē-ō-văs'kyə-lər) *adj.* Pertaining to or involving the heart and the blood vessels.

car·di·tis (kär-dī'tĭs) *n.* Inflammation of the heart.

car·doon (kär-dōōn') *n.* A plant, *Cynara cardunculus,* of southern Europe, closely related to the artichoke and having spiny leaves, purple flowers, and an edible leafstalk. [French *cardon,* from Provençal, from Late Latin *cardō* (stem *cardōn-*), thistle, from Latin *carduus,* thistle, artichoke.]

Car·do·zo (kär-dō'zō), **Benjamin Nathan** (1870–1938). U.S. jurist, justice of the Supreme Court (1932–38), and author. Appointed to the Supreme Court by Herbert Hoover, he blended his confidence in the Constitution and concern for social inadequacies into a broader interpretation of the role of federal government.

card reader *n. Computer Science.* A device for reading data from punched cards into a computer or storage device.

cards (kärdz) *n. Usually used with a singular verb.* **1.** Any game played with cards, such as bridge, whist, or poker, usually in packs of 52 cards divided into four suits: spades, hearts, diamonds, and clubs. **2.** The playing of such games. —**in the cards.** Likely to occur; probable. —**play one's cards right.** To carry out one's plans in the cleverest possible manner. —**put** or **lay one's cards on the table.** To make an open and honest declaration of one's position.

card·sharp (kärd'shärp') *n.* Also **card·sharp·er** (-shär'pər). A person expert in cheating at cards. —**card·sharp·ing** *n.*

card vote *n.* A method of voting, used especially at European trade-union conferences, in which the vote of each delegate counts for a specific number of his constituents.

care (kâr) *n.* **1.** Mental distress and uncertainty; worry. **2.** Mental suffering; grief. **3.** An object or source of worry, attention, or solicitude: *The preparation of meals was my particular care.* **4.** Caution in avoiding harm or danger; heedfulness: *handle with care.* **5.** Protection; supervision; charge: *in the care of a nurse.* **6.** Attentiveness to detail; painstaking application: *The report should be prepared with great care.* —**(in) care of.** *Abbr.* **c/o, c.o.** At the address of. Used in addressing letters and other mail. —**take care.** To act cautiously or prudently. —**take care of.** To look after or deal with. ~*v.* **cared, caring, cares.** —*intr.* **1.** To have a strong feeling or opinion; be concerned or interested: *The senator cares about human rights.* **2.** To have a fondness, regard, liking, or attachment: *I care for her deeply. They don't care for classical music.* **3.** To have an objection; mind: *I won't care if you borrow my car.* **4.** To look after; provide care: *an agency that cares for the homeless.* ~*tr.* **1.** To be concerned to the degree of: *I don't care a damn.* **2.** To be inclined; wish: *We don't care to attend the party.* [Middle English *care,* Old English *caru, cearu.*]

ca·reen (kə-rēn') *v.* **-reened, -reening, -reens.** —*intr.* **1.** To lean to one side; sway or heel, in the manner of a ship sailing in the wind. **2.** *Nautical.* To turn a ship on its side for cleaning, caulking, or repairing. **3.** To move rapidly and erratically. —*tr. Nautical.* **1.** To cause to lean to one side; tilt. **2.** To lean (a ship) on one side for cleaning, caulking, or repairing. [French *(en) carène,* "(on) the keel," from Old French *carene,* keel, from Old Italian *carena,* from Latin *carīna,* keel of a ship, nutshell.] —**ca·reen·er** *n.*

Usage: Both *careen* and *career* may refer to rapid and uncontrolled movement, the similarity in their form having promoted their use as synonyms. Many people try to maintain a distinction in meaning between the words, restricting *career* to forward movement, and *careen* to leaning and tilting, as in nautical usage. *Careen* is generally accepted in informal contexts, however, in statements such as *The car careened across the icy pavement.*

ca·reen·age (kə-rē'nĭj) *n.* **1.** A place for careening ships. **2.** The careening of ships. **3.** The charge for careening.

ca·reer (kə-rîr') *n.* **1.** An occupation, especially one with the possibility of advancement; a profession that lasts most of one's working lifetime. **2.** A path, course, or progress through life or history; especially, the course of a working life. **3.** Rapid progress; swift movement; speed. Often used with *full:* "*My hasting days fly on with full career.*" (Milton). ~*adj.* Engaged in a specified occupation as a chosen career: *a career diplomat.* ~*intr.v.* **careered, -reering, -reers.** To move or run at full speed; go headlong; rush. —See Usage note at **careen.** [French *carrière,* racecourse, course, career, from Old French, from Old Provençal *carriera,* street, from Medieval Latin *(via) carrāria,* (road) for vehicles, from Latin *carrus,* a kind of vehicle.]

ca·reer·ism (kə-rîr'ĭz'əm) *n.* The practice of seeking one's professional advancement by all possible means. —**ca·reer·ist** *n. & adj.*

care·free (kâr′frē′) *adj.* Free of worries and responsibilities.
care·ful (kâr′fəl) *adj.* **1.** Cautious in thought, speech, or action; circumspect; prudent. **2.** Thorough; painstaking; conscientious: *careful investigation.* **3.** Solicitous; protective. Used with *of.* **4.** *Chiefly British Informal.* Frugal, often to the point of meanness. **—care·ful·ly** *adv.* **—care·ful·ness** *n.*
care·less (kâr′lĭs) *adj.* **1.** Inattentive; negligent. **2.** Marked by or resulting from lack of thought, thoroughness, or planning: *a careless mistake.* **3.** Inconsiderate: *a careless remark.* **4.** Unconcerned; unmindful: *careless about her health.* **5.** Unstudied; effortless: *careless grandeur.* **—care·less·ly** *adv.* **—care·less·ness** *n.*
Synonyms: *heedless, lax, negligent, thoughtless.*
ca·ress (kə-rĕs′) *n.* A gentle touch or gesture of fondness, tenderness, or love.
~tr.v. **caressed, -ressing, -resses. 1.** To touch or stroke in an affectionate or loving manner. **2.** To touch or stroke gently. [French *caresse,* from Italian *carezza,* endearment, from *caro,* dear, from Latin *cārus.*] **—ca·ress·er** *n.* **—ca·ress·ing·ly** *adv.*
car·et (kăr′ĭt) *n.* A proofreading symbol used to indicate where something is to be inserted in printed or written matter. [Latin, "there is lacking," from *carēre,* to cut off, be without.]
care·tak·er (kâr′tā′kər) *n.* **1.** A person employed to look after or take charge of goods, property, or a person; a custodian. **2.** One taking charge temporarily. Also used adjectivally: *a caretaker government.*
care·worn (kâr′wôrn′, -wōrn′) *adj.* Showing the effects of anxiety; weary from worry. —See Synonyms at **haggard.**
car·fare (kär′fâr′) *n.* Fare charged a passenger.
car·go (kär′gō) *n., pl.* **-goes** or **-gos.** The freight carried by a ship, airplane, or other vehicle. [Spanish *cargo, carga,* load, cargo, from *cargar,* to load, from Late Latin *carricāre,* from Latin *carrus,* a kind of vehicle.]
cargo cult *n.* A religious cult, existing mainly in the South Pacific islands of Melanesia, based on a belief that suitable actions will bring the future arrival from boats and airplanes of rich and desirable goods.
Car·ib (kăr′ĭb) *n., pl.* **-ibs** or collectively **Carib. 1.** A member of a group of American Indian peoples of northern South America and the Lesser Antilles. **2.** Any of the languages of these peoples. **—Car·ib** *adj.*
Car·ib·be·an (kăr′ə-bē′ən, kə-rĭb′ē-ən) *n.* A Carib Indian.
~adj. **1.** Of, pertaining to, or originating in the Caribbean Sea and its islands. **2.** Of or pertaining to the Carib or their language.
Caribbean Sea. Part of the western Atlantic Ocean, separated from the main section of the ocean by the West Indies. This tropical sea, covering 2,590,000 square kilometers (1,000,000 square miles), has been an important shipping route since the opening of the Panama Canal in 1914. It takes its name from the original inhabitants of the area, the Caribs.
car·i·bou (kăr′ə-bo͞o′) *n., pl.* **-bous** or collectively **caribou.** A deer, *Rangifer tarandus,* of arctic regions of the New World, having antlers in both sexes. It also occurs in northern Europe and Asia, where it is called a reindeer. [Canadian French, probably from Algonquian.]
car·i·ca·ture (kăr′ĭ-kə-cho͝or′) *n.* **1.** A representation, especially pictorial, in which the subject's distinctive features or peculiarities are deliberately exaggerated or distorted to produce a comic or grotesque effect. **2.** The process or art of creating such representations. **3.** An imitation or copy so inferior as to be absurd.
~tr.v. **caricatured, -turing, -tures.** To represent or imitate in or as if in a caricature; satirize. [French, from Italian *caricatura,* caricature, "exaggeration," from *caricare,* to load, from Late Latin *carricāre,* from Latin *carrus,* a kind of vehicle.] **—car·i·ca·tur·ist** *n.*
Synonyms: *lampoon, parody, satire, spoof, takeoff.*
car·ies (kâr′ēz) *n.* Decay of a bone or a tooth. [Latin *cariēs,* caries, decay.]
car·il·lon (kăr′ə-lŏn′, -lən) *n.* **1.** A set of chromatically tuned bells that are housed in a tower and are usually played from a keyboard. **2.** A stop on an organ that produces a bell-like sound. **3.** A composition written or arranged for or played on a carillon.
~intr.v. **carillonned, -lonning, -lons.** To play a carillon. [French, variant of Old French *carignon, quarregnon,* from Vulgar Latin *quadriniō* (stem *quadriniōn-*) (unattested), set of four bells, variant of Late Latin *quaterniō,* set of four, from *quaternī,* four each, from *quater,* four times.]
car·il·lon·neur (kăr′ə-lə-nûr′) *n.* A person who plays a carillon.
ca·ri·na (kə-rī′nə, -rē′nə) *n., pl.* **-nae** (-nē). *Biology.* A keel-shaped ridge, such as that on the breastbone of a bird or in the petals of certain flowers. [New Latin, from Latin *carīna,* keel.]
Ca·ri·na (kə-rī′nə, -rē′nə) *n.* A constellation in the Southern Hemisphere near Vela containing the star Canopus. [Latin, "the Keel."]
car·i·nate (kăr′ə-nāt′, -nĭt) *adj.* Also **car·i·nat·ed** (-nā′tĭd). *Biology.* Having or shaped like a keel; ridged.
Carinthia. See **Kärnten.**
car·i·o·ca (kăr′ē-ō′kə) *n.* **1.** A South American ballroom dance that originated in Rio de Janeiro. **2.** The music for this dance. **3. Carioca.** A native or resident of Rio de Janeiro. [Portuguese *Carioca,* from Tupi.]
car·i·o·gen·ic (kăr′ē-ō-jĕn′ĭk) *adj.* Producing caries, especially of the teeth. [CARIES + -GENIC.]
car·i·ole, car·ri·ole (kăr′ē-ōl′) *n.* **1.** A small, open, one-horse vehicle with two wheels. **2.** A light, covered cart. [French *carriole,* from Old Provençal *carriola,* diminutive of *carri,* chariot, from Vulgar Latin *carrium* (unattested), from Latin *carrus,* a kind of vehicle.]
car·i·ous (kâr′ē-əs) *adj.* Having caries; decayed. Said of teeth and bones. **—car·i·os·i·ty** (kăr′ē-ŏs′ə-tē) **car·i·ous·ness** *n.*
car·line[1] (kär′lən, -līn′) *n.* A thistlelike Eurasian plant, *Carlina vulgaris,* having spiny leaves and flower heads surrounded by slender, raylike, straw-colored bracts. [French, from Medieval Latin *carlina,* perhaps variant of *cardina* (through association with *Carolus* (*Magnus*), Charlemagne, from Latin *cardo,* thistle.]
car·line[2], car·lin (kär′lən) *n. Scottish.* **1.** A woman, especially an old woman. **2.** A witch. [See **carling.**]
car·ling (kär′lĭng, -lĭn) *n. Nautical.* Any of the short timbers running fore and aft that connect the transverse beams supporting the deck of a ship. [French *carlingue,* from Old French *cal(l)ingue,* probably from Old Norse *kerling,* "old woman," from *karl,* man.]
Car·lisle (kär-līl′, kär′līl′). City and administrative center of Cumbria, England, on the Eden River. Once a Roman fortress, it was destroyed by the Danes in 875 and rebuilt (1092) by William Rufus. Mary, Queen of Scots was imprisoned in its 11th-century castle.
Carl·ist (kär′lĭst) *n.* In Spain, a supporter of Don Carlos, the pretender to the throne, or his heirs. **—Carl·ism** *n.* **—Carl·ist** *adj.*
car·load (kär′lōd′) *n.* The amount a car carries or is able to carry.
Carlovingian. Variant of **Carolingian.**
Car·low (kär′lō). A largely agricultural county in Leinster, southeast Republic of Ireland. Carlow is the chief town.
Carls·bad Caverns National Park (kärlz′băd). Area of 18,935 hectares (46,753 acres) in southeastern New Mexico, in the Guadalupe Mts. These limestone caves, discovered *c.* 1900, began forming 60 million years ago when ground water began dissolving the rock. There are remarkable stalactite and stalagmite formations.
Carlsruhe. See **Karlsruhe.**
Car·lyle (kär-līl′), **Thomas** (1795-1881). Scottish historian and essayist, well known for a literary style characterized by complex syntax and rich vocabulary. His book *Sartor Resartus* (1833–34), a blend of fiction, autobiography, and philosophy, was followed by *The French Revolution* (1837). His other works include *Past and Present* (1843), an attack on England's social and political ills.
car·man (kär′mən) *n., pl.* **-men** (-mĭn). **1.** A man who drives a car or cart. **2.** A driver or conductor, as of a streetcar.
Car·mar·then (kər-mär′*th*ən, kär-). One of the oldest towns in Wales, on the Towey River in Dyfed, south Wales. It was once the site of a Roman fort.
Car·mar·then·shire (kər-mär′*th*ən-shîr, -shər, kär-). Former county in southwest Wales. It became part of Dyfed in 1974.
Car·mel (kär-mĕl′). Also **Car·mel-by-the-Sea** (-bī-thə-sē′). Village in western California, on Carmel Bay at the southern end of the Monterey peninsula. It is known as a writers' and artists' community and is popular with tourists.
Car·mel (kär′məl), **Mount.** A limestone ridge, 546 meters (1,791 feet) at its highest, in northwest Israel. It was the scene of Elijah's struggle with the priests of Baal. The religious order of the Carmelites was founded here in the 12th century.
Car·mel·ite (kär′mə-līt′) *n.* **1.** A monk or mendicant friar belonging to the order of Our Lady of Mt. Carmel, founded at Mt. Carmel in about 1155. Also called "White Friar." **2.** A member of a community of nuns of this order, founded in 1452. **—Car·mel·ite** *adj.*
Car·mi·chael (kär′mī-kəl), **Hoagland Howard,** known as "Hoagie" (1899–1981). U.S. songwriter. He wrote his first successful song, "Riverboat Shuffle," while in college. He moved to New York City in the 1920's and dedicated himself to music. He wrote many popular songs, such as "Stardust" (1929) and "Georgia on My Mind" (1931).
car·min·a·tive (kär-mĭn′ə-tĭv, kär′mə-nā′-) *adj.* Inducing expulsion of gas from the stomach and intestines.
~n. A carminative drug. [Middle English, from Medieval Latin *carminātīvus,* from *carmināre* (past participle *carminātus*), to card wool, comb out impurities, from Latin *carmen,* a card for wool, from *cārere,* to card.]
car·mine (kär′mĭn, -mīn′) *n.* **1.** A deep vivid red color with a purplish tinge. **2.** A crimson pigment derived from **cochineal** *(see).*
~adj. Vivid red or purplish red. [French *carmin,* from Medieval Latin *carminium* : Arabic *qirmiz,* KERMES + Latin *minium,* MINIUM.]
Car·nac (kär′năk). Small coastal village in Brittany, France, famous for its prehistoric standing stones extending in parallel rows for c. 5 kilometers (3 miles).
car·nage (kär′nĭj) *n.* **1.** Massive slaughter, as in war; massacre. **2.** *Obsolete.* Corpses, especially of men killed in battle: *a battlefield bloody with carnage.* [Old French, from Medieval Latin *carnāticum,* slaughter of animals, from Latin *carō* (stem *carn-*), flesh, meat.]
car·nal (kär′nəl) *adj.* **1.** Pertaining to the desires and appetites of the flesh or body; sensual. **2.** Worldly or earthly; temporal. [Middle English, from Medieval Latin *carnālis,* from Latin *carō* (stem *carn-*), flesh.] **—car·nal·i·ty** (kär-năl′ə-tē) *n.* **—car·nal·ly** *adv.*
carnal knowledge *n.* Sexual intercourse.
car·nall·ite (kär′nə-līt′) *n.* A white, brownish, or reddish mineral, $KMgCl_3 \cdot 6H_2O$, that is used in the manufacture of potassium salts. [German *Carnallit,* after Rudolf von Carnall (1804–74), German mining engineer.]
car·nas·si·al (kär-năs′ē-əl) *adj.* Adapted for tearing apart flesh. Said of teeth.
~n. A carnassial tooth, either the last upper premolar or the first lower molar in carnivorous mammals. [French *carnassier,* carnivorous, from Provençal, from *carnasso,* meat in abundance, from *carn,* flesh, from Latin *carō* (stem *carn-*), flesh.]

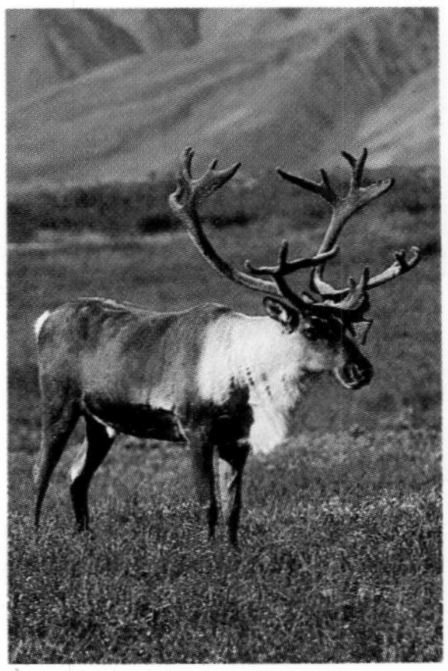

caribou *This North American deer is the same species as the reindeer of Europe and Asia. The thick hair and furry muzzle protect it against cold, and, unlike other deer, both sexes have antlers.*

car·na·tion (kär-nā'shən) n. **1. a.** A plant, *Dianthus caryophyllus,* native to Eurasia, widely cultivated for its fragrant, variously colored flowers with fringed petals. **b.** The flower of this plant. **2.** A flesh-colored tint once used in painting. [French, flesh-colored, carnation, from Italian *carnagione,* complexion, from *carne,* flesh, from Latin *carō* (stem *carn-*), flesh.]

car·nau·ba (kär-nô'bə, -nou'bə) n. **1.** A palm tree, *Copernica cerifera,* of tropical South America. **2.** A hard wax obtained from the leaves of this tree, used as a polish and in candles. In this sense, also called "carnauba wax." [Portuguese, probably of Tupi origin.]

Car·neg·ie (kär'nə-gē, kär-nĕg'ē) **Andrew** (1835–1919). Scottish-born U.S. industrialist and philanthropist. Arriving in the United States as a penniless young boy, he became one of the world's richest men and gave millions of dollars to charities in the United States and in the United Kingdom.

car·nel·ian (kär-nēl'yən) n. Also **cor·nel·ian** (kôr-). A reddish or reddish-brown variety of chalcedony, used in jewelry. [Middle English *corneline,* from Old French, probably "cherry-colored," from *cornelle,* CORNEL (cherry).]

car·net (kär-nā') n. A permit or customs license allowing a motor vehicle to be imported or driven across certain national frontiers. [French, "notebook."]

carney. Variant of **carny.**

car·ni·val (kär'nə-vəl) n. **1.** The season just before Lent, celebrated by processions, dancing, merrymaking, and feasting. See **Mardi gras. 2.** A time of revelry; a festival. **3.** A traveling amusement show. **4.** *Australian.* A large-scale sporting event: *a surfing carnival.* [Italian *carnevale,* from Old Italian *carnelevare,* "the putting away of flesh," Shrovetide, from Medieval Latin *carnelevāmen* : Latin *carō* (stem *carn-*), flesh + *levāre,* to raise, remove.]

car·ni·vore (kär'nə-vôr', -vōr') n. **1.** *Zoology.* Any animal belonging to the order Carnivora, which includes predominantly flesh-eating mammals such as dogs, cats, bears, and weasels. **2.** Any flesh-eating or predatory organism, such as a bird of prey or an insectivorous plant. [French, from Latin *carnivorus,* CARNIVOROUS.]

car·niv·o·rous (kär-nĭv'ər-əs) adj. **1.** Belonging or pertaining to the order Carnivora. **2.** Flesh-eating or predatory. **3.** *Botany.* Capable of trapping and absorbing insects or other small organisms; insectivorous. Said of plants such as the pitcher plant and the Venus's-flytrap. [Latin *carnivorus* : *carō* (stem *carn-*), flesh + -VOROUS.] —**car·niv·o·rous·ly** adv. —**car·niv·o·rous·ness** n.

Car·not (kär-nō'), **Nicolas Léonard Sadi** (1796–1832). French physicist, engineer, and soldier who founded the science of thermodynamics. His investigations on the motive power of heat established that heat and work are reversible conditions. The Carnot cycle and Carnot's principle are described in his study *Réflexions sur la Puissance Motrice du Feu* (1824).

Carnot, Lazare Nicolas Marguerite (1753–1823). Father of Sadi Carnot and statesman and military engineer whose book *De la Défense de Places Fortes* (1810) became a classic study on fortifications.

Carnot cycle n. *Physics.* The thermodynamic cycle of an ideal heat engine, consisting of an adiabatic compression, an isothermal expansion, an adiabatic expansion, and an isothermal compression, the sequence restoring the initial conditions of the system. [After N.L.S. CARNOT.]

car·no·tite (kär'nə-tīt') n. A yellow uranium ore with composition $K_2(UO_2)_2(VO_4)_2H_2O$. [French, after M.A. *Carnot* (died 1920), French inspector general of mines.]

Carnot's principle n. *Physics.* The principle that the efficiency of a perfect heat engine does not depend on the substance used. [After N.L.S. CARNOT.]

car·ny (kär'nē) n., pl. **-nies.** Also **car·ney** pl. **-neys.** *Slang.* **1.** A carnival. **2.** A person who works with a carnival.

car·ob (kär'əb) n. **1.** An evergreen tree, *Ceratonia siliqua,* of the Mediterranean region, having compound leaves and edible pods. Also called "algarroba," "locust." See **St. John's bread. 2.** The edible pod of the carob tree, used as animal fodder and to make a preparation resembling chocolate. [Obsolete French *caro(u)be,* from Medieval Latin *carrūbium,* from Arabic *kharrūbah.*]

ca·roche (kə-rōch', -rōsh') n. A stately carriage of the 16th and 17th centuries. [French *carroche,* from Old Italian *carroccio,* augmentative of *carro,* vehicle, from Latin *carrus.*]

car·ol (kär'əl) v. **-oled, -olings, -ols.** Also chiefly British **-olled, -olling.** —*tr.* **1.** To celebrate in song. **2.** To sing (something) joyously. —*intr.* **1.** To sing in a joyous manner; warble. **2.** To go from house to house singing Christmas carols.

~n. **1.** A song of praise or joy, especially one celebrating the birth of Christ. **2.** An old round dance often accompanied by singing. [Middle English *carolen,* from Old French *caroler,* of obscure origin.] —**car·ol·er** n.

Car·ol II (kär'əl) (1893–1953). King of Romania. Because of his love for a commoner, Magda Lupescu, he renounced his right to succession (1925) in favor of his son Michael, who became king in 1927. He returned to his country in 1930 and was proclaimed king, but his reign lasted only until 1940. After failure to prevent Nazi domination of the kingdom, he abdicated and settled in Mexico.

Car·o·le·an (kär'ə-lē'ən) adj. Caroline. [Medieval Latin *Carolus,* Charles.]

Car·o·li·na (kär'ə-lī'nə). An English colony in southern North America, first settled in 1653 and divided into what became North and South Carolina in 1729. The colonies and present-day states of North and South Carolina are called **the Carolinas.**

Car·o·line (kär'ə-līn', -lĭn) adj. **1.** Of or pertaining to the life and times of Charles I or Charles II of England. **2.** Of or pertaining to Charlemagne or his time. [New Latin *Carolinius,* from Medieval Latin *Carolus,* CHARLES.]

Car·o·line Islands (kär'ə-līn'). Also **Car·o·lines** (-līnz'). Archipelago in the western Pacific Ocean, comprising four main groups: Ponape, Truk, Yap, and Palau. Formerly part of the U.S. Trust Territory of the Pacific Islands (1947–80), all but Palau joined the Federated States of Micronesia. Palau was renamed Belau and became an independent republic (1981).

Car·o·lin·gi·an (kär'ə-lĭn'jē-ən, -jən) adj. Also **Car·lo·vin·gi·an** (kär'lə-vĭn'jē-ən, -jən). Related to, designating, or belonging to the Frankish dynasty that was founded by Pepin the Short in 751 and that lasted until 987 in France and 911 in Germany.

~n. Also **Car·lo·vin·gi·an.** A member of this dynasty. [French *Carolingien,* variant of *Carlovingien,* probably a blend of Medieval Latin *Carolus,* Charles, and *Mérovingien,* MEROVINGIAN.]

car·om (kär'əm) n. **1. a.** A shot in billiards in which the cue ball successively strikes two other balls. **b.** A similar shot in related games, such as pool. **2.** A collision followed by a rebound.

~v. **caromed, -oming, -oms.** —*intr.* **1.** To collide with and rebound: *The boat caromed off the dock.* **2.** To make a carom, as in billiards. —*tr.* To cause to carom. [Earlier *carambole,* from Spanish *carambola,* a kind of fruit, from Portuguese, from Marathi *karambal†.*]

Ca·ro's acid (kä'rōz) n. A strong acid, **peroxysulfuric acid** *(see).* [After Heinrich *Caro* (1834–1910), German chemist.]

car·o·tene (kär'ə-tēn') n. Also **car·o·tin** (-tĭn). An orange-yellow to red hydrocarbon, $C_{40}H_{56}$, existing in six isomeric forms, occurring in many plants as a pigment. Three of the isomers may be converted to vitamin A in the liver. [German *Karotin* : Latin *carōta,* CARROT + -ENE.]

ca·rot·e·noid, ca·rot·i·noid (kə-rŏt'n-oid') n. Any of a class of yellow to deep red pigments, such as the carotenes, occurring in many vegetable oils and some animal fats.

ca·rot·id (kə-rŏt'ĭd') n. Either of the two major arteries in the neck that carry blood to the head.

~adj. Of or pertaining to either of these arteries. [French *carotide,* from Greek *karōtides,* from *karoun,* to stupefy (it was once thought that pressure on the carotids causes stupor).]

ca·rous·al (kə-rou'zəl) n. A jovial, riotous drinking party; boisterous merrymaking; revelry.

ca·rouse (kə-rouz') n. A carousal.

~intr.v. **caroused, -rousing, -rouses.** To drink excessively; go on a drinking spree. [Old French *carrousse,* from *(boire) carous,* (to drink) all out, from German *garaus (trinken)* : *gar,* quite, entirely + *aus,* out.] —**ca·rous·er** n.

car·ou·sel, car·rou·sel (kär'ə-sĕl', -zĕl') n. **1.** A tournament in which knights or horsemen engaged in various exercises and races. **2.** A **merry-go-round** *(see).* **3.** A rotating conveyor system, as for delivering luggage in an airport. [French *carrousel,* probably from Italian dialectal *carosello†,* a kind of tournament.]

carp¹ (kärp) intr.v. **carped, carping, carps.** To find fault and complain constantly; harp on petty grievances; grumble. Often used with *at.* [Middle English *carpen,* from Old Norse *karpa,* to boast.] —**carp·er** n. —**carp·ing·ly** adv.

carp² n., pl. **carps** or collectively **carp. 1.** An edible freshwater fish, *Cyprinus carpio,* frequently bred in ponds and lakes. **2.** Any of various other fishes of the family Cyprinidae. [Middle English *carpe,* from Old French, from Late Latin *carpa†.*]

-carp suffix. *Botany.* Indicates fruit or similar reproductive structure; for example, *mesocarp.* [New Latin *-carpium,* from Greek *-karpion,* from *karpos,* fruit.]

Car·pac·cio (kär-pä'chō, -chē-o) **Vittore,** born Vittore Scarpazza (c. 1460–c. 1525). Venetian painter noted for his views of the city and his narrative cycles. Influenced by Gentile and Giovanni Bellini, his works include the cycle *Scenes from the Life of St. Ursula* and *The Miracle of the Cross.*

car·pal (kär'pəl) adj. *Anatomy.* Of, pertaining to, or near the carpus.

~n. Any bone of the carpus. [New Latin *carpalis,* from Greek *karpos,* wrist.]

car park n. *Chiefly British.* A parking lot.

Car·pa·thi·an Mountains (kär-pā'thē-ən). Also **Car·pa·thi·ans** (-ənz). Mountain range extending through central and eastern Europe in an arc 1,400 kilometers (900 miles) long. It forms part of the Czechoslovak-Polish border, crosses southwest Ukraine into Romania, and swings back to the Danube at the Iron Gate on the Romanian-Yugoslavian frontier. Sparsely inhabited, it is a resort area and rich in mineral deposits.

car·pe di·em (kär'pĕ dē'ĕm', -əm, dī'-) n. The admonition to seize the pleasures of the moment without thought for the future. [Latin, "seize the day."]

car·pel (kär'pəl) n. *Botany.* The central, ovule-bearing female organ of a flower, consisting of an ovary, style, and stigma. Carpels may be separate or fused to form a single pistil. [New Latin *carpellum,* from Greek *karpos,* fruit.] —**car·pel·lar·y** (kär'pə-lĕr'ē) adj.

car·pel·late (kär'pə-lāt', -lĭt) adj. *Botany.* Having carpels.

Car·pen·tar·ia (kär'pən-târ'ē-ə). **Gulf of.** A large inlet of the Arafura Sea between Arnhem Land and Cape York Peninsula in north Australia. It is approximately 480 kilometers (300 miles) west to east and 595 kilometers (370 miles) north to south.

car·pen·ter (kär'pən-tər) n. One whose occupation is constructing

carnation *A species of the genus Dianthus, a group of annual or perennial herbs and flowers that also includes sweet William.*

carnelian *Although this translucent semiprecious stone is found in many parts of the world, it is commercially exploited mainly in Brazil and Uruguay.*

and repairing wooden objects and structures, especially large solid ones, such as ships or houses.
~v. **carpentered, -tering, -ters.** —*tr.* To make, build, or repair (wooden objects or structures). —*intr.* To work as a carpenter. [Middle English, from Norman French, from Latin *carpentārius (artifex),* carriage(-maker), from adjective, from *carpentum,* two-wheeled vehicle, wagon, from Celtic.] —**car·pen·try** (kär′pən-trē) *n.*
carpenter moth *n.* Any of various moths of the family Cossidae, the larvae of which are harmful to the wood of various trees.
Car·pen·tier (kär-pôn-tyā′), **Georges** (1894-1975). French boxer who held the world light-heavyweight title (1920-22). His fight against Jack Dempsey (1921) was the first to realize a million dollars in takings.
car·pet (kär′pĭt) *n.* **1. a.** A thick, heavy covering for a floor, usually made of wool or synthetic fibers. **b.** The fabric used for this. **2.** A surface similar to a carpet in texture or appearance: *a carpet of leaves and pine needles.* —**on the carpet.** *Informal.* In the position of being reprimanded by one in authority.
~*tr.v.* **carpeted, -peting, -pets.** To cover with or as if with a carpet: *The pool was carpeted with green sponge"* (Rachel Carson). [Middle English *carpete,* from Old French *carpite,* from Old Italian *carpita,* from *carpire,* to pluck, tear, from Latin *carpere.*]
car·pet·bag (kär′pĭt-băg′) *n.* An old-fashioned kind of traveling bag made of carpet fabric.
car·pet·bag·ger (kär′pĭt-băg′ər) *n.* **1.** A politician who for political interest seeks to represent an area with which he has no personal connections. **2.** A Northerner who went to the South after the Civil War for political or financial advantage. Compare **scalawag.** —**car·pet·bag·ger·y, car·pet·bag·gism** *n.*
carpet beetle *n.* Any of various small beetles of the genera *Anthrenus* and *Attagenus,* having larvae injurious to fabrics, furs, and other plant and animal products. Also called "buffalo bug."
car·pet·ing (kär′pĭ-tĭng) *n.* **1.** Material or fabric used for making carpets. **2.** Carpets.
carpet shark *n.* Any of certain sharks of the family Orectolobidae, having a back patterned in brown and white and a fringe of fleshy growths around the sides of the head.
carpet snake *n.* A nonvenomous Australian snake, *Morelia variegata,* marked on its back with a pattern resembling that of a Persian carpet.
carpetsweeper *n.* A hand-operated household implement with a revolving brush, used for sweeping carpets.
car·pet·weed (kär′pĭt-wēd′) *n.* A low-growing weedy plant, *Mollugo verticillata,* forming dense mats and having whorled leaves and small greenish-white flowers.
carpo– *prefix.* Indicates fruit or similar reproductive structure; for example, *carpogonium, carpology.* [Greek *karpos,* fruit.]
car·po·go·ni·um (kär′pə-gō′nē-əm) *n., pl.* **-nia** (-nē-ə). *Botany.* The female reproductive structure of red algae, comprising a swollen base enclosing the ovum and a long neck along which the male gametes pass. [New Latin : CARPO- + -GONIUM.] —**car·po·go·ni·al** *adj.*
car·pol·o·gy (kär-pŏl′ə-jē) *n.* The area of botany concerned with fruits and seeds. [CARPO- + -LOGY.]
car·po·met·a·car·pus (kär′pō-mĕt′ə-kär′pəs) *n.* A bone in a bird's wing made up of the metacarpal bones and some of the carpal bones fused together. [CARPO- + META- + CARPUS.]
car·pool (kär′pōōl′) *n.* **1.** An arrangement whereby several commuters travel together in one car. **2.** A group, as of commuters, participating in a car-pool.
car·poph·a·gous (kär-pŏf′ə-gəs) *adj.* Feeding on fruit; fruit-eating. [Greek *karpophagos* : CARPO- + -PHAGOUS.]
car·po·phore (kär′pə-fôr′, -fōr′) *n. Botany.* **1.** The elongated part of the axis of certain flowers to which the carpels and stamens are attached. **2.** A fruiting body or the stalk of a fruiting body in certain fungi. [CARPO- + -PHORE.]
car·port (kär′pôrt′, -pōrt′) *n.* A roof projecting from the side of a building, used as a shelter for a motor vehicle.
car·po·spo·ran·gi·um (kär′pə-spə-răn′jē-əm) *n., pl.* **-gia** (-jē-ə). A specialized sporangium in red algae, in which carpospores are formed. [New Latin : CARPO- + SPORANGIUM.]
car·po·spore (kär′pə-spôr′, -spōr′) *n. Botany.* A nonmotile haploid or diploid spore formed within the carposporangium of red algae.
–carpous, –carpic *suffix.* Indicates a specified number or kind of fruit; for example, *polycarpous, monocarpic.* [New Latin *-carpus,* from Greek *karpos,* fruit.]
car·pus (kär′pəs) *n., pl.* **-pi** (-pī′). *Anatomy.* **1. a.** The wrist *(see).* **b.** The bones of the wrist. **2.** Any joint corresponding to the wrist in quadrupeds. [New Latin, from Greek *karpos,* wrist.]
car·rack, car·ack (kär′ək) *n.* A type of merchant ship used in the 14th, 15th, and 16th centuries; a galleon. [Middle English *caryk, carrake,* from Old French *caraque,* from Old Spanish *carraca,* from Arabic *qarāqīr,* plural of *qurqūr,* carrack.]
car·ra·geen, car·ra·gheen (kär′ə-gēn′) *n.* A seaweed, **Irish moss** *(see).* [After *Carragheen,* Ireland, where it flourishes.]
Car·ran·tuo·hill (kär′ən-tōō′əl). Mountain in Macgillicuddy's Reeks in County Kerry, Republic of Ireland. At 1,041 meters (3,414 feet), it is Ireland's highest peak.
Car·ran·za (kə-rän′zə, -rän′-), **Venustiano** (1859-1920). Mexican revolutionary statesman. He became the first president of the new Mexican Republic after the overthrow of dictator Porfirio Díaz (1911). After he tried to engineer the election of his chosen successor, an armed rebellion forced him to flee the capital. He was be-

trayed and murdered while hiding in the mountains.
Car·ra·ra (kə-rär′ə). City in north-central Italy, famous for the white marble quarried nearby that was favored by Michelangelo.
car·rel (kär′əl) *n.* Also **car·rell.** A small separate enclosure, especially in a library, used for private study. [Variant of CAROL (in obsolete sense "small enclosure").]
Car·rel (kə-rĕl′, kär′əl), **Alexis** (1873-1944). French surgeon and biologist, who worked in the United States (1905-39). For his development of a method of suturing blood vessels, he was awarded the Nobel Prize in physiology and medicine in 1912.
car·riage (kär′ĭj; kăr′ē-ĭj *for sense 6b*) *n.* **1.** A four-wheeled, horse-drawn passenger vehicle, often of an elegant design. **2.** *Chiefly British.* A railroad car for passengers. **3.** A baby carriage; perambulator. **4.** A wheeled support or frame for moving a heavy object, such as a cannon. **5.** A moving part of a machine for holding or shifting another part, as on a lathe. **6. a.** The act or process of transporting or carrying. **b.** The cost or charge for transporting. **7.** The manner of holding and moving one's head and body; posture or bearing. —See Synonyms at **bearing.** [Middle English *cariage,* from Old North French, from *carier,* to transport in a vehicle, CARRY.]
carriage dog *n.* The **Dalmatian** *(see).*
carriage trade *n.* Wealthy patrons, as of a restaurant.
car·rick bend (kär′ĭk) *n. Nautical.* A type of knot used to fasten two cables or hawsers together. [From obsolete *carrick,* carrack, from Middle English *caryk,* CARRACK.]
carrick bitt *n. Nautical.* Either of the two posts that support the windlass on a ship's deck. [See **carrick bend.**]
car·ri·er (kär′ē-ər) *n.* **1.** One that transports or conveys. **2.** An organization or individual that deals in transporting passengers or goods. **3.** A mechanism or device by which something is conveyed or conducted. **4.** *Medicine.* A person or animal that shows no symptoms of a disease but transmits it directly or indirectly to others or, in the case of a hereditary disease, to offspring. **5.** *Pathology.* A **vector** *(see).* **6.** *Electronics.* **a.** A **carrier wave** *(see).* **b.** A charge-carrying entity, especially an electron or a hole in a semiconductor. **7.** An **aircraft carrier** *(see).* **8. a.** *Chemistry.* A support, such as alumina or asbestos, for a solid catalyst. **b.** A molecule or ion that transports an atom or group between molecules. **c.** The solid that adsorbs a dyestuff in the formation of a lake. **d.** An inert substance containing a radioactive isotope, used to introduce the isotope into a system for tracer studies.
carrier bag *n. Chiefly British.* A large plastic or paper bag used especially for carrying shopping.
carrier pigeon *n.* A **homing pigeon** *(see),* especially one trained to carry messages.
carrier wave *n.* A radio wave or other electromagnetic wave that can be modulated in frequency, amplitude, phase, or otherwise to transmit speech, music, images, or other signals.
carriole. Variant of **cariole.**
car·ri·on (kär′ē-ən) *n.* Dead and decaying flesh.
~*adj.* **1.** Of or similar to carrion. **2.** Carrion-eating. [Middle English *carion, caroine,* from Norman French *caroine,* from Vulgar Latin *carōnia* (unattested), from Latin *carō* (stem *carn-*), flesh.]
carrion crow *n.* A common scavenging and predatory crow, *Corvus corone,* of Europe and Asia, resembling the rook but having a pure black bill.
carrion flower *n.* **1.** A climbing vine, *Smilax herbacea,* of eastern North America, having clusters of small, greenish flowers with an odor of decaying flesh. **2.** Any of several other plants having flowers with an unpleasant odor.
Car·roll (kär′əl), **Charles,** known as "Carroll of Carrollton" (1737-1832). U.S. Revolutionary leader. Barred from entering Maryland colonial politics because he was a Roman Catholic, he became active in the movement for independence from Great Britain. He signed the Declaration of Independence in July 1776.
Carroll, John (1735-1813). U.S. Jesuit clergyman and cousin of Charles Carroll. He was named the first Roman Catholic bishop in the United States (1789) and the first archbishop of Baltimore (1808). He actively promoted missions to the Indians and founded what is now Georgetown University (1791).
Carroll, Lewis. See Charles Lutwidge **Dodgson.**
car·rot (kär′ət) *n.* **1.** A widely cultivated plant, *Daucus carota sativa,* having finely divided leaves, flat clusters of small white flowers, and an edible, yellow-orange root. **2.** The long, tapering root of this plant, eaten as a vegetable. **3.** Something offered as a means of persuasion; an incentive. [Old French *carotte,* from Latin *carōta,* from Greek *karōton.*]
car·rot-and-stick (kär′ət-ən-stĭk′) *adj.* Combining a promised reward with a threat or punishment: *a carrot-and-stick approach to getting things done.*
car·rot·y (kär′ə-tē′) *adj.* **1.** Similar to a carrot, especially in color. **2.** Having orange-red hair.
carrousel. Variant of **carousel.**
car·ry (kär′ē) *v.* **-ried, -rying, -ries.** —*tr.* **1.** To bear or convey from one place to another; transport: *carry cargo.* **2.** To make known, take, bring, or communicate (a message, for example). **3.** To serve as a means for the conveyance or transmission of; transmit: *Flies carry disease.* **4.** To hold or bear while moving: *The plane carried us to safety.* **5. a.** To hold or be capable of holding: *The car carries four people.* **b.** To sustain the weight of; support. **6.** To support or sustain the responsibility of. **7.** To keep or have on one's person. **8.** To be pregnant with. **9. a.** To hold and move (the body or a part of it) in a specified way. **b.** To behave or conduct (oneself) in a specified

carrion crow *Native to Europe and Asia, the carrion crow feeds mainly on the ground and eats almost anything, including the eggs and young of other birds.*

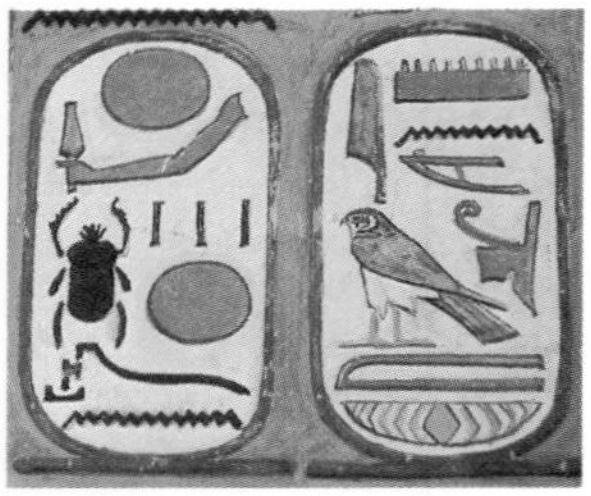

cartouche *In ancient Egypt these oblong or oval frames enclosed the name of the pharaoh, spelled out in pictorial hieroglyphics. They were often inscribed on Egyptian monuments, but smaller cartouches were also used as royal seals.*

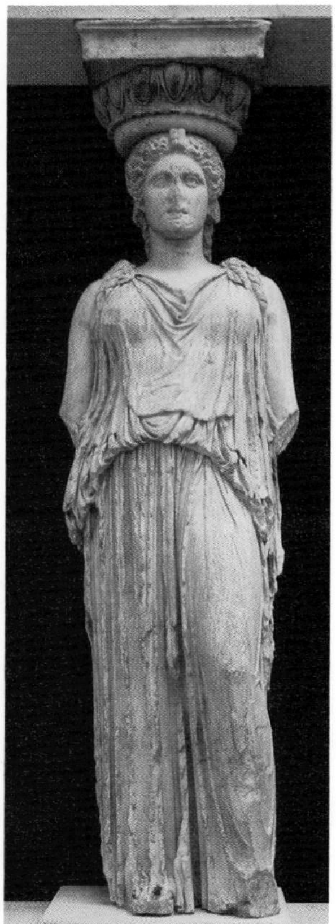

caryatid *A sculptured female figure used as a column. This example is from the Acropolis at Athens. It was carved in about 415* B.C.

manner. **10.** To extend or continue in a certain direction or to a given point or degree: *carry a joke too far.* **11.** To cause to move; drive; impel. **12.** To take or seize, especially by force; capture: *"The Turks carried the defenses of Jebel Subh"* (T.E. Lawrence). **13.** To gain victory, support, or acceptance for; especially, to secure the adoption of (a motion or bill). **14.** To be successful in; win. **15.** To include as part of a publication, broadcast, or the like. **16.** To sway; move; gain the interest of: *Her enthusiasm carried the audience.* **17.** To have as a customary, necessary, or characteristic attribute or accompaniment: *an appliance carrying a five-year guarantee; a critic whose views carry a lot of weight.* **18.** To involve necessarily as a condition, consequence, effect, or the like: *The crime carried a five-year sentence.* **19.** To keep in stock; offer for sale: *carry a large selection of china and glass.* **20.** *Mathematics.* To transfer (a number) from one column of digits for inclusion in the calculations of another. **21.** To include in another set of accounts: *carry a loss over to the following year.* **22.** To make up for the deficiencies of (a colleague, for example). **23.** To yield (a crop, for example). **24.** To support or sustain (livestock): *An acre can carry 60 sheep.* **25.** *Golf.* To cover (a distance) or advance beyond (a point or object) in one stroke. **26.** In hunting, to keep and follow (a scent). —*intr.* **1.** To act as a bearer: *She used to fetch and carry for her old aunt.* **2.** To reach; cover a distance or range: *a soprano voice that carries to the back of the hall; guns that carry for 500 feet.* **3.** To be accepted or approved: *The motion carried by a wide margin.* —See Synonyms at **convey.** —**carry away.** To move emotionally or excite greatly: *carried away by his beauty.* —**carry forward.** **1.** To progress with: *carried forward the program.* **2.** *Accounting.* To transfer (an entry) to the next column, page, book, or to another account. —**carry off.** **1.** To cause the death of: *carried off by a fever.* **2.** To handle or cope with (a situation, for example) successfully. **3.** To win (a prize or award, for example). —**carry through.** **1.** To accomplish; complete. **2.** To enable to endure; sustain: *Fortitude carried her through the ordeal.*

~*n., pl.* **carries.** **1.** The act or process of carrying. **2. a.** The range of a gun or projectile. **b.** The distance traveled by a ball, especially a golf ball. **3.** *Football.* The act or an instance of rushing with the ball. [Middle English *carien,* from Old North French *carier,* to transport in a vehicle, from *car(re),* vehicle, from Latin *carrus.*]

car·ry·all (kăr′ē-ôl′) *n.* **1. a.** A covered one-horse carriage with two seats. **b.** A closed automobile with two lengthwise seats facing each other. **2.** A large bag, basket, or pocketbook.

car·ry·cot (kăr′ē-kŏt′) *n. Chiefly British.* A portable bed for a baby, usually made from canvas stretched over a metal frame or occasionally from wickerwork.

carrying charge *n.* The interest charged on the balance owed when paying in installments.

car·ry·ings-on (kăr′ē-ĭngz-ŏn′, -ôn′) *pl.n.* **1.** Behavior that is regarded as improper or frivolous: *Grandmothers do not generally hold with the carryings-on of the young.* **2.** Noisy or excitable behavior.

carry on *tr.v.* To conduct; continue the process or activities of: *will carry on the business in my absence.* —*intr.v.* **1. a.** To persevere; continue: *carry on in the face of disaster.* **b.** To resume after stopping: *carry on where you left off.* **2.** *Informal.* To have a usually illicit sexual involvement: *Mrs. Brown is carrying on with the mailman.* **3.** To behave in an excited or foolish manner; act hysterically or childishly.

car·ry·on (kăr′ē-ŏn′, -ôn′) *n.* An item, such as luggage, that is small or compact enough to be carried aboard an airplane by a passenger. —**car·ry·on** *adj.*

carry out *tr.v.* **1.** To put into practice or effect; accomplish. **2.** To follow or obey: *carry out orders.*

car·ry·out (kăr′ē-out′) *n.* Food or drink intended to be consumed away from the premises where it is prepared or sold. —**car·ry·out** *adj.*

carry over *tr.v.* **1.** *Accounting.* To transfer (an entry) to another column, page, book, or account. **2.** To continue at another time; put off: *carry over a problem until the next meeting.*

car·ry·o·ver (kăr′ē-ō′vər) *n.* **1.** A part or quantity, as of goods or commodities, left over or held for future use. **2.** *Accounting.* A sum transferred to a new column, page, book, or account.

carse (kärs) *n. Scottish.* An alluvial plain beside a river or an estuary. [Middle English, of obscure origin.]

car·sick (kär′sĭk) *adj.* Suffering nausea from vehicular motion. —**car·sick·ness** *n.*

Car·son (kär′sən), **Christopher,** known as "Kit" (1808–68). U.S. trapper, guide, and Indian agent. An almost legendary figure among the Indian fighters and heroes of the West, he was a guide of John C. Frémont's three expeditions in the 1840's and became a national hero during the Mexican War.

Carson, Rachel Louise (1907–64). U.S. marine and genetic biologist and science writer. Her *The Sea Around Us* (1951) deals with the biology, chemistry, history, and geography of the sea. *Silent Spring* (1962) is a condemnation of the use of pesticides.

Carson City. The capital (since 1864) of Nevada, in the western part of the state. It became important (1859) after the discovery of gold and silver at the Comstock Lode.

cart (kärt) *n.* **1.** A two-wheeled vehicle usually drawn by a horse or other animal and used for transporting goods. **2.** A light, open two-wheeled vehicle pulled by a pony, horse, or dog. **3.** A small, light vehicle moved by hand, as a grocery cart.

~*tr.v.* **carted, carting, carts.** **1. a.** To convey in a cart. **b.** To convey laboriously, as in a cart; lug. **2.** To remove or transport (a person or thing) in an unceremonious manner or by force. Often used with *away* or *off*: *He was carted off to jail.* [Middle English *carte, cart,* partly from Old English *cræt,* partly from Old Norse *kartr.*] —**cart·a·ble** *adj.* —**cart·er** *n.*

cart·age (kär′tĭj) *n.* **1.** The act or process of transporting by cart. **2.** The cost of transporting by cart or other means.

Car·ta·ge·na[1] (kär′tə-gā′nə, -jē′-). Capital of the Bolívar department on Colombia's Caribbean coast. The Spanish built a fortified stronghold here (1533) to export precious metals.

Cartagena[2]. A fortified naval base and seaport on the Mediterranean Sea, in the Spanish province of Murcia. The Carthaginian leader Hasdrubal founded it *c.* 225 B.C.

Carte, Richard D'Oyly. See **D'Oyly Carte.**

carte blanche (kärt blänsh′) *n.* Unrestricted power to act at one's own discretion; unconditional authorization. [French, "blank card."]

car·tel (kär-tĕl′) *n.* **1.** A combination of independent business organizations formed to regulate production, pricing, and marketing of goods by the members. **2.** An official agreement between governments at war, especially one concerning the exchange of prisoners. **3.** In some European countries, a political group united in a common cause; a bloc. [German *Kartell,* from French *cartel,* from Italian *cartello,* diminutive of *carta,* CARD.]

Car·ter (kär′tər), **Howard** (1874–1939). British archaeologist who excavated ancient Egyptian tombs, including that of the pharaoh Tutankhamen (1922–32).

Carter, James Earl, Jr., known as "Jimmy" (1924–). 39th president of the United States (1977–81). A Democrat, he was twice elected senator for Georgia (1962, 1964) and governor of Georgia (1970–74). He was elected president in the wake of the Watergate scandal. After promising a more "open" style of government, he lost popularity because of the failure of his economic measures and the lack of confidence in his social reforms. He was also hurt politically by his handling of the hostage crisis in Iran (November 1979–January 1981). First he appeared to do nothing, then he ordered an abortive mission aimed at rescuing the hostages (April 1980). Eight servicemen were killed and five injured in the raid when a helicopter and cargo plane collided. His main achievements were to cut national energy consumption and to negotiate the Camp David Agreement between Egypt and Israel (1979).

Car·te·sian (kär-tē′zhən) *adj.* **1.** Of or pertaining to Descartes or to the philosophy or methods of Descartes. **2.** Of or forming a Cartesian coordinate.

~*n.* A person who follows the philosophy or methods of Descartes. —**Car·te·sian·ism** *n.*

Cartesian coordinate *n.* A coordinate in a Cartesian coordinate system.

Cartesian coordinate system *n. Mathematics.* **1.** A rectangular coordinate system, usually in two or three dimensions, in which the location of a point in rectangular space is identified by its distance from the mutually perpendicular axes. **2.** A three-dimensional coordinate system in which the coordinates of a point are its distances from each of three intersecting, often mutually perpendicular planes along lines parallel to the intersection of the other two.

Car·thage (kär′thĭj). Ancient city-state in North Africa on the Bay of Tunis, near modern Tunis. Founded by the Phoenicians (9th century B.C.), it became the center of Carthaginian power in the western Mediterranean from the 6th century B.C. Its trading empire included colonies in Senegal and Guinea, and it grew rich on the sale of slaves, ivory, and gold from the tropics of Africa. The three Punic Wars with Rome resulted in the complete destruction of Carthage (146 B.C.). In 44 B.C. Julius Caesar refounded the city, and it became the commercial, cultural, and administrative center of Roman Africa. The Vandals took it (A.D. 439) and made it their capital. Carthage was recaptured by the Byzantines (534), but virtually destroyed by Arabs (698). Only a few Punic and Roman ruins survive. —**Car·tha·gin·i·an** (kär′thə-jĭn′ē-ən) *adj. & n.*

cart·horse (kärt′hôrs′) *n.* A large, heavily built horse bred for pulling carts or similar vehicles.

Car·thu·sian (kär-tho͞o′zhən) *n. Roman Catholic Church.* A member of a contemplative order of monks founded in 1084 in Chartreuse, France, by St. Bruno. —**Car·thu·sian** *adj.*

Car·tier (kär-tyā′, kär′tē-ā′), **Jacques** (1491–1557). French explorer. King Francis I of France commissioned him to explore the northern lands of the New World. His explorations of the St. Lawrence River and the surrounding region gave rise to France's future claims to Canada.

Car·ti·er-Bres·son (kär-tyā′brĕ-sôN′), **Henri** (1908–). French photographer and pioneer of photojournalism. He took up photography in 1931 and worked with the film director Jean Renoir (1936–39). Imprisoned by the Nazis (1940–43), he escaped and set up underground photographic units. He is the author of many photographic books, including *The Decisive Moment* (1952).

car·ti·lage (kär′tə-lĭj) *n.* A tough fibrous connective tissue attached at the joints between bones. It is a major constituent of the young vertebrate skeleton that is largely converted to bone with maturation. Also called "gristle." [Latin *cartilāgo* (stem *cartilāgin-*).]

cartilage bone *n.* A bone developed from cartilage. Compare **membrane bone.**

car·ti·lag·i·nous (kär′tə-lăj′ə-nəs) *adj.* **1.** Of or pertaining to cartilage. **2.** Having a skeleton consisting mainly of cartilage.

cartilaginous fish *n.* Any fish of the class Chondrichthyes, which includes the sharks, skates, and rays, having a skeleton entirely or mainly made up of cartilage.

cart·load (kärt'lōd') n. The amount that is or that can be carried in a cart.

car·to·gram (kär'tə-grăm') n. A presentation of statistical data in geographical distribution using lines, dots, and other marks on a map. [French *cartogramme : carte*, map, CARD + -GRAM.]

car·tog·ra·phy (kär-tŏg'rə-fē)) n. The art or technique of making maps or charts. [French *cartographie : carte*, map, CARD + -GRAPHY.] —**car·tog·ra·pher** n. —**car·to·graph·ic** (kär'tə-grăf'ĭk), **car·to·graph·i·cal** adj.

car·to·man·cy (kär'tə-măn'sē) n. The telling of fortunes using playing cards, such as the tarot pack. [French *cartomancie : carte*, CARD + -mancie, -MANCY.]

car·ton (kärt'n) n. **1.** Abbr. **C., c., ctn.** A cardboard box or other container, especially: **a.** A box closed by flaps on the top or on one end, used for transporting goods. **b.** A container for liquids: *a milk carton.* **2.** The contents of a carton. [French, from Italian *cartone*, pasteboard, from *carta*, CARD.]

car·toon (kär-tōōn') n. **1.** A drawing in a newspaper, magazine, or the like, often accompanied by a caption that depicts a humorous situation or makes a satirical comment on a subject of current public interest. **2.** A preliminary sketch similar in size to the work, as a fresco, mosaic, or tapestry, that is to be copied from it. **3.** An **animated cartoon** (see). **4.** A **comic strip** (see). [Italian *cartone*, pasteboard, CARTON.] —**car·toon·ist** n.

car·touche, car·touch (kär-tōōsh') n. **1.** Architecture. A scroll-like tablet used either to provide space for an inscription or for ornamental purposes. **2.** In ancient Egyptian hieroglyphics, an oval or oblong figure that encloses characters expressing the names or epithets of royal or divine personages. **3.** A case containing the combustible materials in some varieties of fireworks. **4.** An elaborate or decorative frame, as a panel on a map for displaying the title and scale. **5.** Obsolete. A cartridge. [French, cartridge, from Italian *cartoccio*, from *carta*, paper, card. See **carton**.]

car·tridge (kär'trĭj) n. **1. a.** A tubular metal or cardboard-and-metal case containing the propellant powder and primer of small arms ammunition or shotgun shells. **b.** Such a case loaded with shotgun pellets. **c.** Such a case fitted with a projectile, such as a bullet, for use in rifles, small arms, machine guns, or the like. **2.** A small modular unit of equipment, especially: **a.** A removable case containing the stylus and electric conversion circuitry in a phonograph pickup. **b.** A cassette for use in tape recorders, video recorders, and the like. **c.** A case with photographic film that can be loaded directly into a camera. **d.** A disposable ink reservoir for a pen. [From earlier *cartage*, variant of French CARTOUCHE (cartridge).]

cartridge belt n. A belt for carrying ammunition, with loops or pockets for cartridges or clips of cartridges.

cartridge clip n. A metal container or frame for holding cartridges to be loaded into an automatic rifle or pistol.

car·tu·lar·y (kär'chə-lĕr'ē) n., pl. **-ies.** Also **char·tu·lar·y** (kär'-). A collection of deeds or charters; especially, a register of titles to all the property of an estate or monastery. [Medieval Latin *c(h)artulārium*, from Latin *chartula*, little paper, diminutive of *charta*, leaf of papyrus. See **card**.]

cart·wheel (kärt'hwēl') n. **1.** The wheel of a cart. **2.** A somersault or handspring in which the body turns over sideways with the arms and legs spread like the spokes of a wheel.

cart·wright (kärt'rīt') n. A person who makes carts.

car·un·cle (kär'ŭng'kəl, kə-rŭng'-) n. **1.** A fleshy, naked outgrowth, such as a fowl's wattles. **2.** Botany. An excrescence on a seed at or near the hilum. [Obsolete French *caruncule*, from Latin *caruncula*, diminutive of *carō* (stem *carn-*), flesh.] —**ca·run·cu·lar** (kə-rŭng'kyə-lər) adj. —**ca·run·cu·late** (kə-rŭng'kyə-lĭt, -lāt'), **ca·run·cu·lat·ed** (-lā'tĭd) adj.

Ca·ru·so (kə-rōō'sō), **Enrico** (1873–1921). Italian tenor opera singer who made his debut at the Teatro Nuovo, Naples (1894). His final performance was with the Metropolitan Opera, New York (1920), when he ruptured a blood vessel in his throat while singing. He died of related complications. His most popular roles included Canio in *Pagliacci;* Rodolpho in *La Bohème;* and the Duke in *Rigoletto.*

car·va·crol (kär'və-krôl', -krŏl') n. A liquid phenol, $C_{10}H_{14}O$, used in flavorings and fungicides. [From New Latin *carvi*, specific epithet of *Carum carvi*, caraway + Latin *acer, acr-*, sharp + -OL.]

carve (kärv) v. **carved, carving, carves.** —tr. **1. a.** To divide into pieces or slices by cutting: *carve a chicken.* **b.** To divide by parceling out: *carve up an estate.* **2.** To cut into a desired shape; fashion by cutting: *carve the wood into a figure.* **3.** To produce or form by or as if by cutting: *carve initials in the bark; carved out a career.* **4.** To decorate by carving. —intr. **1.** To engrave or cut figures as a hobby or trade. **2.** To disjoint, slice, and serve meat or poultry. ~n. An act or stroke of slicing or carving. [Middle English *kerven, carven*, Old English *ceorfan.*] —**carv·er** n.

carvel. Variant of **caravel.**

car·vel-built (kär'vəl-bĭlt', kär'vĕl'-) adj. Designating a boat or ship built with the hull planks lying flush or edge to edge, rather than overlapping. Compare **clinker-built.**

carvel joint (kär'vəl, -vĕl') n. A joining of wood planks so that they lie flush or edge to edge.

carv·en (kär'vən) adj. Produced, formed, or decorated by carving; carved.

Carver (kär'vər), **George Washington** (c. 1864–1943). U.S. bota-

---

Cartier-Bresson

---

nist, agricultural chemist, and educator. In his laboratory at Tuskegee Institute, Alabama, he produced hundreds of peanut products, including soap, wood stains, and even shaving cream. His research prompted southern farmers to raise peanuts, which became an important cash crop in the region.

carv·ing (kär'vĭng) n. **1.** The cutting of material such as wood or stone to form a figure or design. **2.** A figure or design formed by carving.

carving knife n. A knife with a long blade for slicing meat.

Car·y (kâr'ē), **(Arthur) Joyce Lunel** (1888–1957). British novelist. His major works, *The Horse's Mouth* (1944) and *Prisoner of Grace* (1952), deal with the classic themes of conflict between the generations, the individual and society, and the artist and the middle classes.

car·y·at·id (kăr'ē-ăt'ĭd) n., pl. **-ids** or **-ides** (-ĭ-dēz'). Architecture. A supporting column sculptured in the form of a woman in classical Greek dress. Compare **telamon.** [Latin *Caryātidēs* (plural), from Greek *Karuatidēs*, caryatids, priestesses of Artemis at *Karuai*, village in Laconia.]

caryo-. Variant of **karyo-.**

car·y·op·sis (kăr'ē-ŏp'sĭs) n., pl. **-ses** (-sēz) or **-sides** (-sĭ-dēz') Botany. A one-seeded dry fruit, such as a grain of barley or wheat, having its outer coat fused to the seed coat. [New Latin : CARY(O)- + -OPSIS.]

ca·sa·ba, cas·sa·ba (kə-sä'bə) n. A variety of **winter melon** (see) having a yellow rind and sweet, whitish flesh. [From *Kasaba*, former name of Turgutlu, Turkey.]

Ca·sa·blan·ca (kăs'ə-blăngk'ə, käz'-). Arabic **Dar-al-Bei·da** (där-ăl'bä'də). Seaport on the Atlantic coast of Morocco. It was founded by the Portuguese in the early 16th century. Taken by the French in 1907, it remained for many years a center of French influence in Africa. It is now Morocco's largest city.

Ca·sals (kə-sälz'), **Pablo** (1876–1973). Spanish cellist, conductor, and composer. He founded the Barcelona Orchestra (1919), but left Spain in 1939 after Franco came to power. He was acclaimed as one of the greatest interpreters of Bach's unaccompanied cello suites and the cello concertos of Dvořák, Elgar, and Schumann.

Ca•sa•no•va (kăz′ə-nō′və, kăs′-), **Giovanni Giacomo, Chevalier de Seingalt** (1725–98). Italian adventurer and legendary lover. After being expelled from a seminary for immoral conduct, he lived in many European cities and worked as a violinist, a spy, a writer, and a librarian. His adventures are chronicled in his memoirs.

Casanova *n.* An ostentatiously promiscuous man; libertine.

casava. Variant of **cassava.**

Cas•bah (kăz′bä′, käz′-) *n.* Also **Kas•bah. 1.** The citadel and palace of a sovereign in northern Africa. **2.** The native quarter in any of several cities in northern Africa. [French, from dialectal Arabic *qaṣbah,* from Arabic *qaṣabah,* fortress.]

cas•cade (kăs-kād′) *n.* **1. a.** A waterfall or a series of small waterfalls over steep rocks. **b.** Anything that falls loosely or freely: *a cascade of flowers.* **2.** *Physics.* An analogous structure or phenomenon, as: **a.** A cosmic-ray shower generated by the successive alternate production of electron–positron pairs by pair production and of photons by bremsstrahlung, continuing until the energy of each single particle is below the threshold for pair production. **b.** A process occurring in an electrical discharge in a gas by which at least one member of an ion pair is accelerated by the field to sufficiently high energy to produce another pair of ions in a collision. **c.** An **avalanche** *(see),* as in a Geiger counter. **3.** *Electricity.* A series of components or networks, the output of each of which serves as the input for the next. **4.** *Chemistry.* A series of compressed gases of successively lower boiling points, the expansion of which produces successively lower temperatures. This arrangement is used to liquefy gases.
~*intr.v.* **cascaded, -cading, -cades.** To fall from one level to another in a continuous series; fall loosely or freely. [French, from Italian *cascata,* from *cascare,* to fall, from Vulgar Latin *casicāre* (unattested), from Latin *cadere* (past participle *cāsus*).]

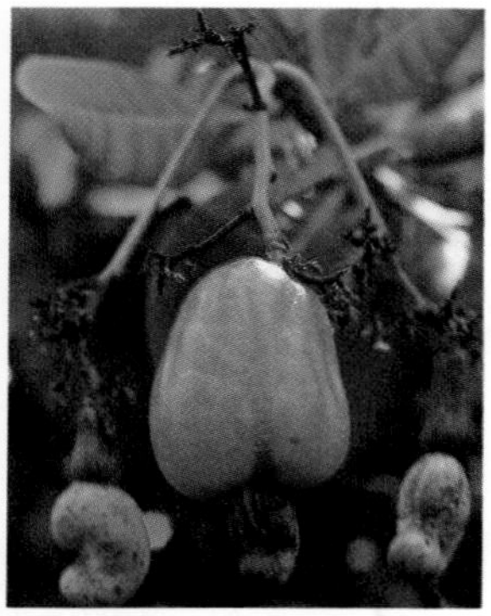

cashew *The edible kidney-shaped nuts grow beneath the reddish, fleshy fruit of the cashew tree, a small evergreen native to tropical America.*

Cascade Range. Mountain chain, *c.* 1,125 kilometers (700 miles) long, extending from southern British Columbia to northern California, where it joins the Sierra Nevada. Many of its highest peaks, including Mt. Ranier, are volcanic cones covered with snowfields and glaciers.

cas•car•a (kăs-kăr′ə) *n.* **1.** The cascara buckthorn. **2.** Cascara sagrada. [Spanish *cáscara,* bark, from *cascar,* to break, break off, from Vulgar Latin *quassicāre* (unattested), from Latin *quassāre,* from *quatere* (past participle *quassus*), to shake.]

cascara buckthorn *n.* A shrub or tree, *Rhamnus purshiana,* of northwestern North America, the bark of which is the source of cascara sagrada.

cascara sa•gra•da (sə-grä′də) *n.* The dried bark of the cascara buckthorn, used as a stimulant, cathartic, and laxative.

cas•ca•ril•la (kăs′kə-rĭl′ə) *n.* **1.** A shrub, *Croton eluteria,* of the West Indies, having bitter, aromatic bark. **2.** The bark of this shrub, used as a tonic. In this sense, also called "cascarilla bark." [Spanish, diminutive of *cáscara,* bark. See **cascara.**]

case[1] (kās) *n.* **1.** An instance or exemplification of the existence or occurrence of something. **2. a.** An occurrence of disease or disorder: *He had a bad case of pneumonia.* **b.** A client, as of a doctor, psychiatrist, lawyer, or social worker. **3. a.** A particular set of circumstances or state of affairs: *will make an exception in this case.* **b.** The actual situation; the truth: *It simply isn't the case.* **4.** A set of circumstances subject to or requiring investigation, especially for a formal or official body: *a detective's most famous case.* **5.** A set of reasons, arguments, or supporting facts offered in justification of a statement, action, situation, or thing: *the case for legalized abortion.* **6.** A question or problem; a matter: *a case of honor.* **7.** *Law.* **a.** An action or suit. **b.** Just grounds for legal action. **c.** The facts or evidence offered in support of a claim. **8.** *Informal.* A peculiar or eccentric person. **9.** *Linguistics.* **a.** The syntactic relationship of a noun, pronoun, or adjective to the other words of a sentence, indicated in inflected languages typically by endings and in noninflected languages by word order or prepositions. **b.** The form or position of a word that indicates this relationship. **c.** Such forms, positions, or relationships collectively. —See Synonyms at **example.** **—in any case.** Regardless of what occurred or will occur. **—in case. 1.** As a preventive measure: *I took along a sandwich just in case.* **2.** If. **—in case of.** In the event of; if there should happen: *In case of fire, sound the alarm.* [Middle English *cas,* an occurrence, from Old French, from Latin *cāsus,* fall, event, occurrence, from the past participle of *cadere,* to fall.]

case[2] *n.* **1. a.** A container or receptacle. **b.** A suitcase. **2. a.** A decorative or protective covering or cover. **b.** A glass box for exhibiting items of interest; showcase. **3.** *Abbr.* **C., c., cs.** A box with its contents, especially when of a standard quantity; for example, a case of wine usually contains 12 bottles. **4.** A set or pair, as of pistols. **5.** The frame or framework of a window, door, or stairway. **6.** *Printing.* A shallow, compartmented tray for storing type or type matrices. **7.** A cover of stiff boards ready to be attached to a book.
~*tr.v.* **cased, casing, cases. 1.** To put into, cover, or protect with or as if with a case. **2.** *Slang.* To examine carefully, as in planning a crime: *cased the bank before the robbery.* [Middle English, from Old North French *casse,* from Latin *capsa,* chest, case.]

ca•se•ate (kā′sē-āt′) *intr.v.* **-ated, -ating, -ates.** To undergo caseation. [Latin *cāseus,* CHEESE.]

ca•se•a•tion (kā′sē-ā′shən) *n.* **1.** The production of cheese from casein in the coagulation of milk. **2.** The degeneration of dead bodily tissue into a cheeselike substance. [From CASEATE.]

case•book (kās′bo͝ok′) *n.* **1.** A book containing a record of medical or legal cases. **2.** A book containing source materials in a specific area that is used as a reference and in teaching.

case ending *n.* A letter or letters added to the stem of a noun, pronoun, or adjective in inflected languages to indicate case.

case•hard•en (kās′härd′n) *tr.v.* **-ened, -ening, -ens. 1.** To harden the surface of (iron or steel) by high-temperature shallow infusion of carbon followed by quenching. **2.** To harden the spirit or emotions of; make callous. [From CASE (covering).]

case history *n.* An organized set of facts relevant to the development of an individual or group under study or treatment, especially in social work, psychiatry, or medicine.

ca•sein (kā′sēn′, -sē-ĭn) *n.* A white, tasteless, odorless protein, precipitated from milk by rennin. It is the basis of cheese and is used to make plastics, adhesives, paints, and foods. [Probably French *caséine* : Latin *cāseus,* CHEESE + -IN.]

case knife *n.* **1.** A knife kept in a sheath or case. **2.** A table knife.

case law *n.* Law based on judicial decision and precedent rather than statute.

case load *n.* The number of cases for which a social worker, doctor, or similar professional person is responsible at any one time.

case•mate (kās′māt′) *n. Military.* **1.** On a warship, a fortified enclosure for artillery. **2.** A recess in a rampart with openings, or embrasures, from which artillery can be fired. [Old French, from Italian *casamatta,* perhaps from Greek *khasmata,* plural of *khasma,* gap, CHASM.] **—case•mat•ed** *adj.*

case•ment (kās′mənt) *n.* **1. a.** A window frame that opens outward or inward by means of hinges along one side. **b.** A window with such frames. **2.** A case or covering. [Middle English *casement*†.] **—case•ment•ed** *adj.*

Case•ment (kās′mənt), **Sir Roger David** (1864–1916). British consular official and Irish nationalist. He retired to Ireland in 1912, and with the outbreak of World War I he attempted to obtain German help for the Irish nationalist cause. Caught returning to Ireland in a German submarine, he was convicted for treason and hanged.

ca•se•ous (kā′sē-əs) *adj.* Resembling cheese. [Latin *cāseus,* CHEESE.]

ca•sern, ca•serne (kə-zûrn′) *n.* A military barracks. [French *caserne,* from Old French, small room for the night watch, from Old Provençal *cazerna,* group of four persons, from Vulgar Latin *quaderna* (unattested), from Latin *quater,* four times.]

Ca•ser•ta (kə-zĕr′tə). A market town in southern Italy, and capital of Caserta province. In the 19th century it was the center of operations for Giuseppe Garibaldi's campaigns for the unification of Italy. The German forces in Italy in World War II surrendered to the Allied Command at Caserta (1945).

case shot *n.* **1.** A **canister** *(see).* **2.** The shot in a canister. **3.** A shrapnel shell.

case study *n.* A detailed analysis of an individual or group, especially as a model of medical, psychological, or social phenomena.

case•work (kās′wûrk′) *n.* The part of a social worker's duties dealing with the problems of a particular case. **—case•work•er** *n.*

case•worm (kās′wûrm′) *n.* An insect larva, such as a caddis worm, that constructs a protective case around its body.

cash[1] (kăsh) *n.* **1.** Ready money; currency or coins. **2.** Payment for goods or services in money or by check, as opposed to credit.
~*tr.v.* **cashed, cashing, cashes.** To exchange for or convert into ready money: *cash a check.* **—cash in. 1.** To withdraw from a venture by or as if by settling one's account. **2.** *Slang.* To die. **—cash in on.** To take advantage of. [Old French *casse,* money box, CASE (box).]

cash[2] *n., pl.* **cash.** Any of various Oriental coins of small denomination; especially, a copper and lead coin with a square hole in its center. [Portuguese *caixa,* from Tamil *kācu,* a small copper coin, from Sanskrit *karṣa*†, a certain weight.]

cash-and-car•ry (kăsh′ən-kăr′ē) *n.* The practice of selling for cash on the spot and usually removal by the purchaser.
~*adj.* Sold in accordance with the policy of cash-and-carry.

cash•book (kăsh′bo͝ok′) *n.* A book in which a record of cash receipts and expenditures is kept.

cash•box (kăsh′bŏks′) *n.* A receptacle, especially a compartmented metal box with a lid, in which to keep cash.

cash crop *n.* A crop grown especially for sale, often to another country, and usually constituting an important source of income.

cash discount *n. Abbr.* **c.d.** A reduction in the price of an item for sale allowed if payment is made within a stipulated period.

cash•ew (kăsh′o͞o, kə-sho͞o′) *n.* **1.** A widely cultivated tropical American evergreen tree, *Anacardium occidentale,* bearing kidney-shaped nuts that protrude from a fleshy receptacle. **2.** The nut of this tree, edible when roasted. In this sense, also called "cashew nut." [Portuguese *cajú, acajú,* from Tupi *acajú.*]

cash flow *n.* The movement of money into and out of a business. **—cash-flow** *adj.*

cash•ier[1] (kă-shîr′) *n.* **1.** The person in a bank or business concern in charge of paying and receiving money. **2.** An employee whose major function is to handle cash transactions for any of various business operations, such as a restaurant or supermarket. [Dutch *cassier,* from French *caissier,* from *caisse,* money box, from Old French *casse,* CASE (box).]

cashier[2] *tr.v.* **-shiered, -shiering, -shiers.** To dismiss from a position of command or responsibility, as in the armed forces, especially for disciplinary reasons. [Dutch *casseren,* from Old French *casser,* to discharge, annul, from Latin *quassāre,* to shake, break in pieces, from *quassus,* past participle of *quatere,* to shake.]

cashier's check *n.* A check drawn by a bank on its own funds and signed by the bank's cashier.

cash·mere (kăzh′mîr′, kăsh′-) *n.* **1.** Fine, downy wool growing beneath the outer hair of the Cashmere goat. **2.** A soft fabric made of wool from this goat or of similar fibers.

Cashmere. See **Kashmir.**

Cashmere goat *n.* Also **Kashmir goat.** A goat native to the Himalayan regions of India and Tibet and prized for its wool.

cash register *n.* A machine that tabulates the amount of sales transactions, displays the amount of each, has a tape for making a permanent and cumulative record of them, and has a drawer in which cash may be kept.

cas·ing (kā′sĭng) *n.* **1.** Something that encases; an outer cover. **2.** The cleaned intestines of cattle, sheep, or pigs used for encasing processed meat. **3.** The frame or framework for a window or door. **4.** A metal pipe or tube used as a lining for water, oil, or gas wells. **5.** The outer covering of a pneumatic tire.

ca·si·no (kə-sē′nō) *n., pl.* **-nos. 1.** A public room or building for entertainment, especially for gambling. **2.** Variant of **cassino. 3.** A summer or country house in Italy. [Italian, diminutive of *casa,* house, from Latin *casa*†, hut, cottage.]

cask (kăsk, käsk) *n. Abbr.* **ck. 1.** A barrel of any size. **2.** The quantity contained in a barrel. [Spanish *casco,* helmet, cask, perhaps from *cascar,* to crack, break, from Vulgar Latin *quassicāre* (unattested), to shake, break, from Latin *quassāre.*]

cas·ket (kăs′kĭt, kä′skĭt) *n.* **1.** A small case or chest for jewels or other valuables. **2.** A coffin.
~*tr.v.* **-keted, -keting, -kets.** To enclose in a casket. [Middle English, from Old French *cassette.* See **cassette.**]

Cas·par (kăs′pər). Also **Gas·par** (găs-pär′). One of the three Magi who traveled to see the infant Jesus.

Cas·par·i·an strip (kă-spăr′ē-ən, kă-spä′rē-ən) *n. Botany.* A band of thickening in the walls of certain cells in the plant stem surrounding the conducting tissues, forming a ring impervious to liquids and gases. Also called "Casparian band."

Cas·pi·an Sea (kăs′pē-ən). The world's largest inland sea. It lies between southeast Europe and Asia and covers 393,898 square kilometers (152,084 square miles). It is slowly shrinking due to dam construction on the Volga River, which feeds the lake. Its fisheries produce the world's finest caviar.

casque (kăsk) *n.* **1.** A helmet or other piece of armor for the head. **2.** *Zoology.* A helmetlike structure or protuberance. [French, from Spanish *casco,* CASK.] **—casqued** (kăskt) *adj.*

cassaba. Variant of **casaba.**

Cas·san·dra[1] (kə-săn′drə). *Greek Mythology.* A daughter of Priam, King of Troy, endowed with the gift of prophecy but fated by Apollo never to be believed.

Cassandra[2] *n.* A prophet of doom, especially one whose prophecies go unheeded. [After CASSANDRA.]

cas·sa·reep (kăs′ə-rēp′) *n.* The boiled juice of the cassava root, used as a condiment. [Earlier *casserepo,* of Cariban origin.]

cas·sa·tion (kă-sā′shən, kə-) *n.* Abrogation; annulment. [Middle English *cassacioun,* from Old French *cassation,* from *casser,* to annul. See **cashier** (dismiss).]

Cas·satt (kə-săt′), **Mary** (1845–1926). U.S. painter. She is noted for her studies of mothers and their children and was associated with the French impressionist movement.

cas·sa·va, ca·sa·va (kə-sä′və) *n.* **1.** Any of various tropical American plants of the genus *Manihot,* having a large starchy root. Also called "manioc." **2.** A starch derived from the root of the cassava, used to make tapioca and as a staple food in the tropics. [Spanish *cazabe,* cassava, from Taino *caçábi.*]

Cas·se·grain·i·an telescope (kăs′ə-grā′nē-ən) *n.* A reflecting telescope in which a concave primary mirror reflects incident light to a convex secondary mirror that in turn reflects the light back through a central hole in the primary mirror onto the focal plane. [After N. *Cassegrain,* 17th-century French physician, who invented it.]

Cassel. See **Kassel.**

cas·se·role (kăs′ə-rōl′) *n.* **1.** A dish, usually of earthenware, glass, or cast iron, in which food is both baked and served. **2.** Food prepared and served in such a dish. **3.** *Chemistry.* A small-handled, deep porcelain crucible used for heating and evaporating.
~*tr.v.* **casseroled, -roling, -roles.** To cook in a casserole. [French, saucepan, from Old French, from *casse,* ladle, dripping pan, from Old Provençal *cassa,* from Medieval Latin *cattia,* dipper, from Greek *kuathion,* small ladle, diminutive of *kuathos*†, ladle.]

cas·sette (kə-sĕt′, kă-) *n.* **1.** A case containing reeled magnetic tape, with a pickup reel, and guide and feed mechanisms that is used instead of separate reels in certain tape recorders, tape players, and video recorders. **2.** A lightproof camera cartridge, for daylight loading of photographic film. [French, small box, from Old French, diminutive of *casse,* CASE (box).]

cas·sia (kăsh′ə) *n.* **1.** Any of various chiefly tropical trees, shrubs, and plants of the genus *Cassia,* having compound leaves, usually yellow flowers, and long pods. See **senna. 2.** A tree, *Cinnamomum cassia,* of tropical Asia, having bark similar to cinnamon but of inferior quality. **3.** The bark of *Cinnamomum cassia,* used as a spice. In this sense, also called "cassia bark." [Middle English *cassia,* Old English *cassia,* from Latin *cas(s)ia,* a kind of plant, from Greek *kas(s)ia,* from Hebrew *kesi'ah,* bark resembling cinnamon.]

cassia oil *n.* An oil derived from the bark of the tree *Cinnamomum cassia* and used in medicine and as a flavor.

cas·si·mere (kăz′ə-mîr′, kăs′-) *n.* A twilled fabric, **kerseymere** *(see).* [From *Cassimere,* variant of KASHMIR.]

Cas·si·ni's division (kə-sē′nēz) *n.* A gap 2,500 miles across in the ring structure of Saturn. The Voyager missions have shown that it contains some ring particles that themselves are arranged in ring formations. [After Gian Domenico *Cassini* (1625–1712), Italian astronomer.]

cas·si·no, ca·si·no (kə-sē′nō) *n.* A card game for two to four players in which cards on the table are matched by cards in the hand. [From CASINO.]

Cas·si·no (kə-sē′nō). Town in Latium, central Italy. During World War II the town and the Benedictine monastery of Monte Cassino were destroyed (1944).

Cas·si·o·pe·ia (kăs′ē-ə-pē′ə) *n.* A W-shaped constellation in the Northern Hemisphere near Camelopardalis and Cepheus.

Cas·sir·er (kə-sîr′ər, kä-), **Ernst** (1874–1945). German philosopher. Primarily a Kantian, he was concerned with concept formation and the mind's functions as they pertain to cultural values. *The Philosophy of Symbolic Forms* (translated 1953–57) is his major work.

cas·sis (kə-sēs′, kă-) *n.* **1.** A European bush, *Ribes nigrum,* that bears black currants. **2.** A cordial made from the berries of the cassis. [French, black currant.]

cas·sit·er·ite (kə-sĭt′ə-rīt′) *n.* A red-brown or black mineral, SnO_2, that is the chief ore of tin. Also called "tinstone." [French *cassiterite,* from Greek *kassiteros,* tin, from Elamite *kassi-ti-ra,* "coming from the land of the Kassi," an Elamite people.]

Cas·sius Lon·gi·nus (kăsh′əs lŏn-jī′nəs), **Gaius** (died 42 B.C.). Roman general and politician. He was a leading member of the conspiracy to assassinate Julius Caesar. After the defeat of the Republican forces at Philippi, he committed suicide.

Cas·si·ve·lau·nus (kăs′ē-və-lô′nəs). King of the Catuvellauni, a people from north of the Thames River who temporarily resisted Julius Caesar's invasion of southeast Britain (54 B.C.) but finally agreed on peace terms with the Romans.

cas·sock (kăs′ək) *n.* A long garment, usually black, reaching to the feet and worn by members of the clergy, choristers, and others assisting in church services. [Old French *casaque,* from Persian *kazagand*†, padded jacket.]

cas·sou·let (kăs′ə-lā′) *n.* A stew originating in France made of beans, sausages, and goose, pork, or duck. [French, diminutive of dialectal *cassolo,* CASSEROLE (saucepan).]

cas·so·war·y (kăs′ə-wĕr′ē) *n., pl.* **-ies.** Any of several large, flightless birds of the genus *Casuarius,* of northern Australia, New Guinea, and adjacent islands, having a large, bony projection on the top of the head, coarse dark plumage, and a brightly colored head, neck, and wattles. [Malay *kĕsuari.*]

cast (kăst, käst) *v.* **cast, casting, casts.** —*tr.* **1.** To throw, especially with violence or force; hurl; toss; fling. **2.** To throw off or away. **3.** To shed; molt. **4.** To throw forth or drop (a fishing net or anchor, for example). **5. a.** To throw to the ground, as in wrestling. **b.** To overthrow; defeat. **6.** To put or place, especially with haste or violence. **7.** To throw aside; dismiss; discard: *cast one's doubts aside.* **8.** To deposit or register (a vote). **9.** To turn or direct (one's eyes). **10.** To cause (light, for example) to fall upon or over something or in a certain direction. **11.** *Archaic.* To bestow; confer. Used with *upon.* **12. a.** To draw (lots). **b.** To throw (dice). **13.** To express, utter, or give rise to (doubt or criticism, for example): *cast aspersions on his ability.* **14.** To cause (hounds) to scatter and circle in search of a lost scent. **15. a.** To choose actors for (a play or film). **b.** To assign a certain role to (an actor). **c.** To assign an actor to (a part). **16. a.** To form (liquid metal or plaster, for example) into a particular shape by pouring into a mold. **b.** To produce (an object) in this way. **17.** To arrange in some system. **18.** To contrive; formulate: *cast a spell.* **19.** To calculate or compute; add up (a column of figures). Often used with *up.* **20.** To calculate astrologically: *cast a horoscope.* **21.** To warp; twist. **22.** *Printing.* To stereotype or electroplate. **23.** *Nautical.* To turn (a ship); change to the opposite tack. —*intr.* **1.** To throw; especially, to throw out a lure or bait at the end of a fishing line. **2. a.** To add a column of figures; make calculations. **b.** To calculate horoscopes, tides, or the like. **3.** To receive form or shape in a mold. **4.** To spread out and search for a lost scent. Used of hunting hounds. **5.** *Nautical.* **a.** To veer to leeward from a former course; fall off. **b.** To put about; tack. **6.** To choose the actors for a play, film, or the like. **7.** To become warped. —See Synonyms at **throw. —cast about. 1.** To search or look for. **2.** To devise means; contrive; scheme. **—cast back.** To refer or direct to something past: *cast your mind back to last summer.* **—cast down.** To make dejected or disappointed. **—cast on.** To make the first row of stitches in knitting. **—cast out.** To drive out by force; expel.
~*n.* **1. a.** The act of casting or throwing. **b.** The distance thrown. **2. a.** The throwing of a fishing line or net into the water. **b.** The line or net thrown. **c.** *Chiefly British.* The leader with flies or baited hooks attached. **3. a.** A throw of dice. **b.** The number thrown. **c.** A stroke of fortune or fate; one's lot. **4. a.** A slight squint in the eye. **b.** A turning of the eye; a glance in a particular direction. **5.** A quantity or thing thrown off, out, or away, such as the mass of waste and earth excreted by an earthworm, the skin shed by an insect, or a mass of feathers, bones, and other matter ejected from the crop of an owl. **6. a.** The addition of a column of figures; a calculation. **b.** A conjecture or forecast. **7. a.** The act of casting or founding. **b.** The amount of molten material poured into a mold at a single operation. **c.** Something formed by this means. **8. a.** An

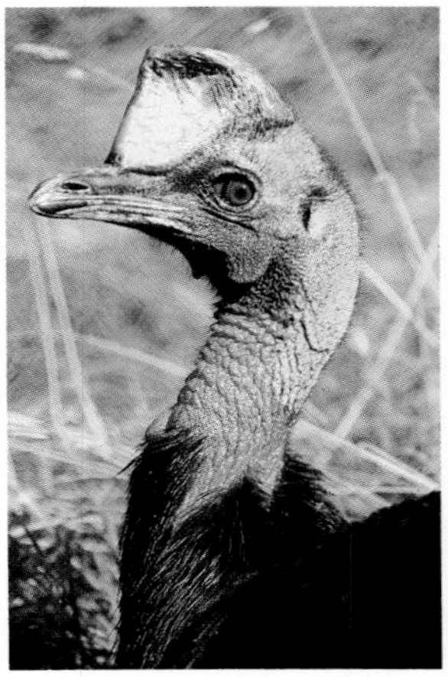

cassowary *A close relative of the emu, the cassowary—of which there are several species—is a flightless bird found in Australia and New Guinea. It can grow up to 150 centimeters (5 feet) tall and has long powerful legs with sharp claws. This is* Casuarius unappendiculatus.

PRONUNCIATION KEY

ă, pat; ā, pay; âr, care;
ä, father, are; b, bib;
ch, church; d, deed; ĕ, pet;
ē, be; f, fife; g, gag; h, hat;
hw, which; ĭ, pit; ī, pie;
îr, pier; j, judge; k, kick;
l, lid, needle; m, mum;
n, no, sudden; ng, thing;
ŏ, pot; ō, toe; ô, paw, for;
oi, noise; ou, out; ŏŏ, book;
ōō, boot; p, pop; r, roar;
s, sauce; sh, ship, dish;
t, tight; th, thin, path;
th, this, bathe; ŭ, cut; ûr, fur;
v, valve; w, with; y, yes;
z, zebra, size; zh, vision;
ə, about, item, edible, gallop, circus, peaceful

IN FOREIGN WORDS:

à, *Fr.* ami; œ, *Fr.* feu, *Ger.* schön; ü, *Fr.* tu, *Ger.* über; KH, *Ger.* ich, *Scot.* loch; N, *Fr.* bon; y′, *Fr.* Compiègne

STRESS MARKS:

Primary stress: ′
in·cite′ (ĭn-sīt′)
Secondary stress: ′
in′sight′ (ĭn′sīt′)

impression formed in a mold or matrix; a mold. **b.** *Geology.* A three-dimensional replica or solidified impression, as of ripple marks or footprints; especially, a fossil formed by a mineral substance that has filled a hole left by an object, such as a shell, that has been dissolved out of a rock or earth mass. **9.** The form in which something is made or constructed; an arrangement; a disposition. **10.** The actors in a play, film, or the like. **11.** A rigid dressing, usually made of gauze and plaster of Paris, for immobilizing a broken bone, an arthritic joint, or part or all of the spine. Also called "plaster cast." **12. a.** A slight trace of color. **b.** A tinge or shade of any quality. **13.** Outward form or aspect; appearance. **14.** A sort; a type. **15.** An inclination; a tendency. **16.** A distortion or twist. **17.** A pair of hawks released by a falconer at one time. **18.** The circling of hounds to pick up a scent. [Middle English *casten,* to throw, from Old Norse *kasta†.*]

cas·ta·nets (kăs′tə-nĕts′) *pl.n.* A pair of slightly concave shells of ivory or hardwood, held in the palm of the hand by a connecting cord over the thumb and clapped together with the fingers as a rhythmical accompaniment to dancing. [Spanish *castañeta,* from *castaña,* chestnut, from Latin *castanea,* CHESTNUT.]

cast away *tr.v.* **1.** To shipwreck; strand. Usually used in the passive. **2.** To throw away; squander.

cast·a·way (kăst′ə-wā′, kăst′-) *n.* **1.** One who has been shipwrecked. **2.** An outcast. —**cast·a·way** *adj.*

caste (kăst, käst) *n.* **1.** One of the four major hereditary classes into which Hindu society is divided. Each caste is distinctly separated from the others by restrictions placed upon occupation and marriage. See **Brahman, Kshatriya, Vaisya, Sudra.** **2.** Any social class separated from others by distinctions of hereditary rank, profession, or the like. **3.** A social system or principle of organization based on these distinctions. Also used adjectively: *a caste system.* **4.** The social position or status conferred by such a system: *lose caste.* **5.** *Zoology.* In social insects, any of the various kinds of specialized individuals, such as drones or workers. [Spanish and Portuguese *casta,* caste, race, breed, from the feminine of *casto,* pure, chaste, from Latin *castus.*]

Cas·tel Gan·dol·fo (käs-tĕl′ gän-dôl′fō). Village on the shore of Lake Albano, central Italy, where the pope has his summer residence.

cas·tel·lan (kăs′tə-lən) *n.* The governor or keeper of a castle. [Middle English *castelain,* from Norman French, from Latin *castellānus,* "of a castle," from *castellum,* CASTLE.]

cas·tel·lat·ed (kăs′tə-lā′tĭd) *adj.* Furnished with turrets and battlements in the style of a castle. [Medieval Latin *castellātus,* past participle of *castellāre,* to fortify as a castle, from Latin *castellum,* CASTLE.] —**cas·tel·la·tion** *n.*

cast·er (kăs′tər, kä′stər) *n.* Also **cas·tor** (for senses 2, 3). **1.** A person or thing that casts. **2. a.** A small container, as of silver or glass, having a perforated top and used for sprinkling sugar or spices. **b.** A stand, often rotating, for holding condiment containers such as casters and cruets. **3.** A small wheel on a swivel attached to the underside of a piece of furniture or other heavy object to make it easier to move.

caster sugar *n.* *Chiefly British.* A very finely granulated white sugar.

cas·ti·gate (kăs′tə-gāt′) *tr.v.* **-gated, -gating, -gates. 1.** To punish or chastise. **2.** To criticize severely. —See Synonyms at **punish.** [Latin *castīgāre,* to correct, punish : *castus,* pure + *agere,* to do, make.] —**cas·ti·ga·tion** *n.* —**cas·ti·ga·tor** *n.*

Cas·ti·gli·o·ne (kä′stē-lyō′nə), **Baldassare** (1478–1529). Italian courtier, writer, and humanist. He is best known for *Il Cortegiano* (1528), which describes the perfect courtier.

Cas·tile (kăs-tēl′). *Spanish* **Cas·til·la** (kä-stēl′yə). Region in the high plateau of central Spain. Stretching from the Bay of Biscay in the north to Sierra Morena in the south, it became an independent kingdom in 1035. In 1230 it joined the kingdom of León, and in 1479 after the marriage of Isabella of Castile and Ferdinand II of Aragon, the nucleus of modern Spain was established. The name Castile probably derives from the number of castles that were built here against the Moorish invasions.

Cas·tile soap (kăs-tēl′) *n.* Also **castile soap.** A fine, hard, white, odorless soap made with olive oil and sodium hydroxide.

Cas·til·ian (kăs-tĭl′yən) *n.* **1.** The dialect of Spanish spoken in Castile, now the standard and official form of the Spanish language in Spain. **2.** A native or inhabitant of Castile. —**Cas·til·ian** *adj.*

cast·ing (kăs′tĭng, kä′stĭng) *n.* **1.** The act or process of one that casts. **2.** That which is cast in a mold, as a metal piece. **3.** That which is cast off or out, as skin or earth excreted by worms; a cast.

casting vote *n.* The vote of a presiding officer in an assembly or committee, given to decide a question when the votes of the members are tied.

cast iron *n.* A hard, brittle nonmalleable iron-carbon alloy containing 2.0 to 4.5 percent carbon, 0.5 to 3 percent silicon, and lesser amounts of sulfur, manganese, and phosphorus.

cast-i·ron (kăst′ī′ərn, kăst′-) *adj.* **1.** Made of cast iron. **2.** Rigid; inflexible: *a cast-iron rule.* **3.** Tough; resilient: *a cast-iron stomach.* **4.** Unquestionable; indisputable: *a cast-iron alibi.*

cas·tle (kăs′əl, kä′səl) *n.* **1.** A fortified building or group of buildings designed to defend a town, route, or territory, especially in medieval Europe. **2.** A former stronghold of this kind converted to residential use; a mansion. **3.** A place that provides security or refuge; a stronghold. **4. a.** A small defensive tower on the deck of a medieval warship. Compare **forecastle. b.** A small tower carried on

the back of an elephant in war. **5.** *Chess.* The **rook** *(see).* —**castle in the air** or **in Spain.** An aspiration that is unlikely to be realized; daydream.

—*v.* **castled, -tling, -tles.** —*tr.* **1.** To place in or as if in a castle. **2.** *Chess.* To move (the king) from his own square two squares to one side and then, in the same move, bring the rook from that side to the square immediately past the king. —*intr. Chess.* To move the king and rook by castling. [Middle English *castel,* from Old English *castel,* from Late Latin *castellum,* village, from Latin *castellum,* castle, diminutive of *castrum,* fortified place.]

cas·tled (kăs′əld, kä′səld) *adj.* Castellated; fortified.

Cas·tle·reagh (kăs′əl-rā′), **Robert Stewart, Viscount,** also called "2nd Marquis of Londonderry" (1769–1822). British statesman. As the Irish chief secretary he was able to quell the 1798 rebellion and form a political union with Great Britain in 1800, thereby protecting Ireland from the threat of French invasion.

cast off *tr.v.* **1.** To discard or reject. **2.** To set loose; especially, to detach (a boat) from its moorings. **3.** To estimate the space (a manuscript) will occupy when set into type. **4.** To loop (a knitted stitch or stitches) over the next, thus leaving a short finished edge. —*intr.v.* **1.** To finish the last row in a strip of knitting by looping each stitch in turn over the next. **2.** To detach a boat from its moorings.

cast-off (kăst′ôf′, -ŏf′, kăst′-) *adj.* Discarded; rejected: *The little boy hated wearing his big brother's cast-off clothes.*

cast-off (kăst′ôf′, -ŏf′, kăst′-) *n.* **1.** Someone or something that has been discarded, especially an item of clothing. **2.** *Printing.* A calculation of the amount of space a manuscript will occupy when set into type.

cas·tor¹ (kăs′tər, kä′stər) *n.* **1.** An oily, brown, odorous substance obtained from glands in the groin of the beaver and used as a perfume fixative. **2.** A beaver hat. [Middle English, beaver, from Latin, from Greek *kastōr,* beaver.]

castor². Variant of **caster.**

Cas·tor (kăs′tər, kä′stər) *n.* A double star in the constellation Gemini, the brightest star in the group, approximately 46 light-years from Earth.

Castor and Pol·lux (pŏl′əks). *Greek Mythology.* The twin sons of Leda, one by Tyndareus, the other by Zeus. They were transformed by Zeus into the constellation Gemini so that they would not be separated. Also called "Dioscuri."

castor bean *n.* **1.** The castor-oil plant. **2.** The very poisonous seed of the castor bean.

castor oil *n.* A colorless or yellowish oil extracted from castor-oil plant seeds and used as a laxative and a fine lubricant. [Probably from a mistaken connection with the substance CASTOR.]

cas·tor-oil plant (kăs′tər-oil′, kä′stər-) *n.* A large evergreen plant, *Ricinus communis,* native to tropical Africa and Asia, with lobed, bronze- or purple-flushed leaves, grown for ornament and for the commercial extraction of castor oil from its poisonous seeds.

cas·trate (kăs′trāt′) *tr.v.* **-trated, -trating, -trates. 1.** To remove the testicles of; geld. **2.** To remove the ovaries of; spay. **3.** To deprive of strength or vigor. **4.** To bowdlerize. [Latin *castrāre.*] —**cas·tra·tion** *n.*

cas·tra·to (kă-strä′tō) *n., pl.* **-ti** (-tē) or **-tos.** A male singer castrated in boyhood so as to retain a soprano or alto voice. [Italian, "castrated (one)."]

Cas·tries (kă-strē, kăs′trēs′). Capital and the chief port of St. Lucia, in the Windward Islands, the West Indies.

Cas·tro (kăs′trō), **Fidel,** born Fidel Castro Ruz (1927–). Cuban statesman and prime minister. He overthrew the corrupt regime of the dictator Fulgencio Batista and became the head of the Cuban government in February 1959. He seized U.S. and other foreign-owned property and established a socialist state. Under Castro, Cuba has become one of the leading Third World countries. —**Cas·tro·ism** *n.* —**Cas·tro·ist** *n.*

cast steel *n.* Carbon steel that has been cast into shape rather than wrought.

cas·u·al (kăzh′ōō-əl) *adj.* **1.** Resulting from or occurring by chance; accidental. **2.** Occurring at irregular intervals; occasional. **3. a.** Without ceremony; informal or relaxed. **b.** Suitable for informal occasions: *casual clothes.* **4.** Showing little interest; nonchalant: *a casual manner.* **5.** Not serious or thorough; superficial: *a casual inspection.* **6.** Not close or intimate: *a casual acquaintance.* **7.** Pertaining to or associated with accidents. —See Synonyms at **chance.**

—*n.* **1.** A person who works at irregular intervals. **2.** A soldier temporarily attached to a unit while awaiting permanent assignment. **3.** Casual clothing or footwear. [Middle English *casuel,* from Old French, from Late Latin *cāsuālis,* from Latin *cāsus,* fall, chance, CASE.] —**cas·u·al·ly** *adv.* —**cas·u·al·ness** *n.*

cas·u·al·ty (kăzh′ōō-əl-tē) *n., pl.* **-ties. 1.** An unfortunate accident, especially one involving loss of life. **2.** One who is injured or killed in an accident. **3.** One injured, killed, captured, or missing in action against an enemy: *We suffered heavy casualties in the invasion.* **4.** A person or thing that has suffered injury, loss, or destruction as the result of a particular occurrence or circumstance: *one of the casualties of the recent cabinet reshuffle.* [Middle English *casuelte,* from *casuel,* CASUAL.]

cas·u·a·ri·na (kăzh′ōō-ə-rī′nə) *n.* Any of various tropical trees of the genus *Casuarina,* which includes the beefwoods. [New Latin, from Malay *kĕsuari,* CASSOWARY (from the resemblance of its twigs to the drooping feathers of the cassowary).]

castle

FORTRESS RESIDENCE OF THE MIDDLE AGES

A castle defended a route or territory as well as housing a lord and his family

The castle of medieval Europe was both a fortress and the private residence of the lord who owned it. Earlier, the Roman fortress, unlike the castle, was built for occupation by a garrison, and the defense works of Anglo-Saxon Britain, known as burhs, consisted of little more than ditches and timber stockades. It was the Normans, in the 10th century, who built private fortresses, which spread with the Norman conquests throughout the countries of western Europe.

The Norman motte-and-bailey castle was a two-story wooden tower on a steep-sided, flat-topped mound (the motte), round or oval at its base. The motte was surrounded by a ditch filled with water or sharpened stakes. At the foot of the motte was an enclosed courtyard called a bailey.

In the 12th century, stone walls replaced the stockades of the motte-and-bailey, and the keep, or donjon (a stone tower, three or more stories high), became the focal point of the castle. Concentrically planned castles, having a series of walls one within the other, were introduced in the 13th century. Castles as fortresses did not survive the introduction of firearms in the 15th and 16th centuries, and some (Windsor Castle, for example) became private or royal residences.

CONCENTRIC CASTLE *Defenders in the keep could shoot over the heads of the men on the lower outer walls. Walls, towers, and turrets were fortified with battlements—parapets indented with openings called crenels, or embrasures. Archers shot through these and sought protection behind the merlons between them. The gatehouse was protected by a tower—the barbican—and a portcullis, a grating of iron-plated oak. A drawbridge was raised or lowered from inside the gatehouse.*

cas·u·ist (kăzh′o͞o-ĭst) *n.* **1.** One who argues plausibly but falsely; a sophist. **2.** One who determines what is right and wrong in matters of conscience or conduct. [French *casuiste,* from Spanish *casuista,* from Latin *cāsus,* chance, CASE.]

cas·u·is·tic (kăzh′o͞o-ĭs′tĭk) *adj.* Also **cas·u·is·ti·cal** (-tĭ-kəl). Of or pertaining to casuists or casuistry. **—cas·u·is·ti·cal·ly** *adv.*

cas·u·ist·ry (kăzh′o͞o-ĭ-strē) *n.* **1.** Plausible but false reasoning; sophistry. **2.** The determination of right and wrong in questions of conduct or conscience by the application of general principles of ethics. [From CASUIST.]

ca·sus bel·li (kā′səs bĕl′ī′, kä′səs bĕl′ē′) *n.* An act or event that justifies or leads directly to a declaration of war. [Latin, "occasion of war."]

cat (kăt) *n.* **1. a.** A carnivorous mammal, *Felis catus* (or *F. domesticus*), domesticated since early times as a catcher of rats and mice and as a pet and existing in several distinctive breeds and varieties. **b.** Any of the other animals of the family Felidae, which includes the lion, tiger, lynx, and leopard. **c.** The fur of a domestic cat. **2.** A spiteful woman. **3.** A cat-o'-nine-tails. **4.** A catfish. **5.** *Nautical.* **a.** A cathead. **b.** A device for raising an anchor to the cathead. **c.** A catboat. **6.** *Slang.* A man. **—let the cat out of the bag.** To let a secret be known. **—play cat and mouse with.** To play with, tease, or keep in suspense in an unkind way. **—rain cats and dogs.** To rain heavily. See feature, next page.

~*tr.v.* **catted, catting, cats. 1.** To flog with a cat-o'-nine-tails. **2.** To hoist (an anchor) to the cathead. [Middle English *cat(te),* Old English *cat(t),* from Common Germanic *kattuz* (unattested).]

CAT (kăt) *n.* Computerized axial tomography.

cat. catalogue.

cata– *prefix.* Indicates: **1.** Reversing of a process; for example, **cataplasia. 2.** Lower in position or down from; for example, **cataphyll, catadromous.** [In borrowed Greek compounds *kata-* indicates: **1.** Down, as in **catabolism. 2.** Down from, as in **catalepsy. 3.** Off or away, as in **catalectic. 4.** Against, as in **category. 5.** Wrongly or overly, as in **catachresis. 6.** According to, as in **catechize. 7.** Completely or thoroughly, as in **catalogue.** Greek *kata-,* from *kata,* down, down from, according to.]

ca·tab·o·lism (kə-tăb′ə-lĭz′əm) *n.* The metabolic change of complex into simple molecules with the release of energy; destructive metabolism. Compare **anabolism.** [Greek *katabolē,* a throwing down, from *kataballein,* to throw down : *kata-,* down + *ballein,* to throw.] **—cat·a·bol·ic** (kăt′ə-bŏl′ĭk) *adj.* **—cat·a·bol·i·cal·ly** *adv.*

ca·tab·o·lite (kə-tăb′ə-līt′) *n.* A substance produced in the process of catabolism. [CATABOL(ISM) + -ITE.]

ca·tab·o·lize (kə-tăb′ə-līz′) *v.* **-lized, -lizing, -lizes. —tr.** To break down (complex molecules) by metabolic processes. **—intr.** To undergo catabolism.

cat·a·caus·tic (kăt′ə-kô′stĭk) *adj.* Designating a caustic curve or surface formed by reflected light rather than refracted light. **~**n.* A catacaustic curve or surface. Compare **diacaustic.**

cat·a·chre·sis (kăt′ə-krē′sĭs) *n., pl.* **-ses** (-sēz′). **1. a.** Strained use of a word or phrase, as for rhetorical effect. **b.** A deliberately paradoxical figure of speech. **2.** Incorrect use of a word. [Latin *catachrēsis,* from Greek *katakhrēsis,* excessive use, misuse, from *katakhrēsthai,* to misuse, use up : *kata-,* wrongly + *khrēsthai,* to use.] **—cat·a·chres·tic** (kăt′ə-krĕs′tĭk) *adj.*

cat·a·cla·sis (kăt′ə-klā′sĭs) *n., pl.* **-ses** (-sēz′). *Geology.* The process in which rocks are deformed by mechanical shearing, or in which selected rock minerals are granulated. [CATA- + -CLASIS.] **—cat·a·clas·tic** (kăt′ə-klăs′tĭk) *adj.*

cat·a·clysm (kăt′ə-klĭz′əm) *n.* **1.** A violent and sudden change in the earth's crust. **2.** Any violent or destructive upheaval, especially one that brings fundamental change. **3.** A devastating flood. **—See** Synonyms at **disaster.** [French *cataclysme,* from Latin *cataclysmos,* deluge, flood, from Greek *kataklusmos,* from *katakluzein,* to deluge, inundate : *kata-,* down + *kluzein,* to wash.] **—cat·a·clys·mic** (kăt′ə-klĭz′mĭk), **cat·a·clys·mal** (-məl) *adj.*

cat·a·comb (kăt′ə-kōm′) *n.* **1.** *Usually* **catacombs.** A series of underground chambers or tunnels with recesses for graves, especially those in Rome. **2.** An underground cemetery. [From Old French *catacombe,* a subterranean chamber, probably from Old Italian *catacomba,* from Late Latin *catacumba†.*]

cat·a·di·op·tric (kăt′ə-dī-ŏp′trĭk) *adj.* Pertaining to or designating an optical instrument, such as a telescope, that uses lenses and

cat

HUNTERS BY STEALTH

Success in catching prey has spread wildcats around the globe

From the domestic cat to the lion, all feline species catch their prey by stealth. They stalk it and pounce on it, or lie in wait to ambush it, rather than run it down over long distances as dogs do. Cats are strong, speedy, and agile, and their good vision, hearing, and sense of smell make them formidable hunters by night or day. Success in hunting means that wildcats are found on every continent except Australasia and the Antarctic.

Black leopard (panther)
Far East, especially Indonesia
Length 2.4 meters
(8 feet)

Ocelot
Central and
South America
Length 1.45
meters
(4 feet 10
inches)

Snow Leopard
Central Asia
Length 2.3 meters
(7 feet 8 inches)

Leopard
Africa and Asia
Length 2.4 meters (8 feet)

African wildcat
Africa
Length 75 centimeters
(2 feet 6 inches)

Bobcat
North America
Length 90 centimeters
(3 feet)

European wildcat
Europe and
West Asia
Length 80 centimeters
(2 feet 8 inches)

Lynx
Poland,
Scandinavia,
Siberia
Length 1.4 meters
(4 feet 8 inches)

Domestic cat
Worldwide
Length 65 centimeters
(2 feet 2 inches)

Golden cat
Africa and Southeast Asia
Length 1.25 meters
(4 feet 2 inches)

Puma
North and South America
Length 2.4 meters (8 feet)

Lion
Africa, rarely India
Length 3.75 meters
(12 feet 3 inches)

Tiger
Asia
Length 3.8 meters
(12 feet 6 inches)

All lengths represent an average, measuring from
the nose to the tip of the tail

mirrors in its operation. [CATA- + DIOPTRIC.]

ca·tad·ro·mous (kə-tăd′rə-məs) *adj.* Migrating down river to breed in marine waters, as some fishes do. Compare **anadromous**. [CATA- + -DROMOUS.]

cat·a·falque (kăt′ə-fălk′, -fôlk′) *n.* The raised structure upon which a coffin rests, as during a state funeral. [French, from Italian *catafalco†*.]

Cat·a·lan (kăt′l-ăn′, -ən) *adj.* Of or pertaining to Catalonia, its people, language, or culture. —*n.* **1.** A native or inhabitant of Catalonia. **2.** The Romance language of Catalonia.

cat·a·lase (kăt′l-ās′, -āz′) *n.* An enzyme that catalyzes the decomposition of hydrogen peroxide into water and oxygen. [CATAL(YSIS) + -ASE.]

cat·a·lec·tic (kăt′l-ĕk′tĭk) *adj.* Designating a verse that lacks part of the last foot. [Late Latin *catalēcticus*, from Greek *katalēktikos*, incomplete, from *katalēgein*, to leave off : *kata-*, off, away + *lēgein*, to leave off, stop.]

cat·a·lep·sy (kăt′l-ĕp′sē) *n.* A condition marked by muscular rigidity, lack of awareness of environment, and lack of response to external stimuli that is often associated with encephalitis, schizophrenia, and hysteria. [Learned respelling of earlier *catalency*, from Middle English *cathalempsia*, from Medieval Latin *catalepsia*, from Late Latin *catalēpsis*, from Greek *katalēpsis*, "a seizing," from *katalambanein*, to seize : *kata-*, down from + *lambanein*, to take.] —**cat·a·lep·tic** (kăt′l-ĕp′tĭk) *adj.*

Catalina Island. See **Santa Catalina.**

catalo. Variant of **cattalo.**

cat·a·logue, cat·a·log (kăt′l-ôg′, -ŏg′) *n. Abbr.* **cat. 1. a.** A systematized list, usually in alphabetical order, often with descriptions of the listed items. **b.** A publication, such as a book, containing such a list. **2.** A card catalog. **3.** A series of related or similar things: *a catalogue of disasters.* —*v.* **catalogued, -loguing, -logues** or **cataloged, -loging, -logs.** —*tr.* **1.** To list in a catalogue; make a catalogue of. **2.** To add (a new item) to an existing catalogue. —*intr.* To make a catalogue. [Middle English *cateloge*, from Old French *catalogue*, from Late Latin *catalogus*, an enumeration, from Greek *katalogos*, from *katalegein*, to recount, enumerate : *kata-*, thoroughly + *legein*, to gather, speak.] —**cat·a·logu·er** *n.*

Cat·a·lo·nia (kăt′l-ōn′yə, -ō′nē-ə). *Spanish* **Ca·ta·lu·ña** (kä′tə-lōō′nyə). A mountainous, industrialized region of northeast Spain, extending from the Pyrenees along the Mediterranean coast. It is an autonomous region comprising the provinces of Barcelona, Gerona, Lérida, and Tarragona.

ca·tal·pa (kə-tăl′pə, -tôl′pə) *n.* Any of several chiefly North American trees of the genus *Catalpa*, having large leaves, showy clusters of whitish flowers, and long, slender pods. Also called "Indian bean." [Creek *kutuhlpa*, "head with wings" (from the shape of its flowers).]

ca·tal·y·sis (kə-tăl′ə-sĭs) *n.* The action of a catalyst in modifying the rate of a chemical reaction. [Greek *katalusis*, dissolution, from *kataluein*, to dissolve : *kata-*, down + *luein*, to loosen, release.] —**cat·a·lyt·ic** (kăt′l-ĭt′ĭk) *adj.* —**cat·a·lyt·i·cal·ly** *adv.*

cat·a·lyst (kăt′l-ĭst) *n.* **1.** *Chemistry.* A substance that modifies, and especially increases, the rate of a chemical reaction without being consumed or chemically changed in the process. **2.** One that precipitates a process or event, especially without being involved in or changed by the consequences. [From CATALYSIS (by analogy with ANALYST and ANALYSIS).]

catalytic converter *n.* A reaction chamber, typically containing a finely divided platinum-iridium catalyst, into which exhaust gases from an automotive engine are passed together with excess air so that carbon monoxide and hydrocarbon pollutants are oxidized to carbon dioxide and water.

catalytic cracker *n.* An oil-refinery unit in which catalytic **cracking** *(see)* of petroleum is performed.

cat·a·lyze (kăt′l-īz′) *tr.v.* **-lyzed, -lyzing, -lyzes.** To modify the rate of (a chemical reaction) by catalysis. —**cat·a·lyz·er** *n.*

cat·a·ma·ran (kăt′ə-mə-răn′) *n.* **1.** A boat with two parallel hulls. **2.** A raft of logs or floats lashed together. [Tamil *kaṭṭumaram* : *kaṭṭu-*, to tie + *maram*, tree, timber.]

cat·a·me·ni·a (kăt′ə-mē′nē-ə) *n. Physiology.* Menstruation. [New Latin, from Greek *katamēnia*, neuter plural of *katamēnios*, monthly : *kata-*, according to + *mēn*, month.] —**cat·a·me·ni·al** *adj.*

cat·a·mite (kăt′ə-mīt′) *n.* A boy kept by a pederast. [Latin *catamītus*, from *Catamītus*, Ganymede, from Greek *Ganumēdēs*, GANYMEDE (cupbearer of the gods).]

cat·a·mount (kăt′ə-mount′) *n.* Also **cat·a·moun·tain** (kăt′ə-moun′tən). Any of various wild felines, as a mountain lion. [Short for *catamountain*, variant of earlier *cat of the mountain*.]

Ca·ta·nia (kə-tā′nyə). Capital city of Catania province in Sicily, situated at the foot of Mt. Etna.

cat·a·pho·re·sis (kăt′ə-fə-rē′sĭs) *n. Chemistry.* **Electrophoresis** *(see).* [New Latin : CATA- + -PHORESIS.] —**cat·a·pho·ret·ic** (kăt′ə-fə-rĕt′ĭk) *adj.* —**cat·a·pho·ret·i·cal·ly** *adv.*

cat·a·phyll (kăt′ə-fĭl′) *n. Botany.* A modified or rudimentary leaf, such as a bud scale. [CATA- + -PHYLL (translation of German *Niederblatt*, "lower leaf").]

cat·a·pla·sia (kăt′ə-plā′zhə, -zhē-ə) *n.* Degenerative reversion of cells or tissue to a less differentiated form. [New Latin : CATA- + -PLASIA.] —**cat·a·plas·tic** (kăt′ə-plăs′tĭk) *adj.*

cat·a·plasm (kăt′ə-plăz′əm) *n. Medicine.* A **poultice** *(see).* [Old

French *cataplasme,* from Late Latin *cataplasma,* from Greek *kataplasma,* from *kataplassein,* to plaster over : *kata-,* thoroughly + *plassein,* to mold.]

cat·a·plex·y (kăt'ə-plĕk'sē) *n.* A sudden temporary paralysis; especially, the hypnotic state assumed by animals when shamming death. [From Greek *kataplēxis* : *kata-,* CATA- + *plēxis,* from *plēssein,* to strike.] **—cat·a·plec·tic** (kăt'ə-plĕk'tĭk) *adj.*

cat·a·pult (kăt'ə-pŭlt', -po͝olt') *n.* **1.** An ancient military machine for hurling missiles, as stones. **2.** A mechanism for launching aircraft without a runway, as from the deck of a ship. **3.** A slingshot.
~*v.* **catapulted, -pulting, -pults.** —*tr.* **1. a.** To hurl or launch from or as if from a catapult. **b.** To shoot at with a catapult. **2.** To bring or move suddenly or abruptly: *catapulted to fame by the success of her first novel.* —*intr.* To become catapulted; spring up abruptly. [Old French *catapulte,* from Latin *catapulta,* from Greek *katapaltēs, katapeltēs* : *kata-,* down + *pallein,* to sway, brandish.]

cat·a·ract (kăt'ə-răkt') *n.* **1. a.** A very large waterfall, especially one with a sheer drop. **b.** A series of rapids on a stretch of river. **2.** A great downpour. **3.** *Pathology.* Opacity of the lens or capsule of the eye, causing partial or total blindness. [Middle English *cataracte,* floodgate, from Old French, portcullis, cataract (of the eye), from Latin *cataractēs,* waterfall, portcullis, from Greek *katar(rh)aktēs,* "a down-swooping," from *katarassein,* to dash down : *kata-,* down + *rassein,* to strike.]

ca·tarrh (kə-tär') *n.* Inflammation of mucous membranes, especially of the nose and throat, causing excessive secretion of phlegm or mucus. [Old French *catarrhe,* from Late Latin *catarrhus,* from Greek *katarrhous,* a flowing down, from *katarrhein,* to flow down : *kata-,* down + *rhein,* to flow.] **—ca·tarrh·al** *adj.*

cat·arrh·ine (kăt'ə-rīn') *adj.* Of or designating a group of primates that includes the Old World monkeys, higher apes, and man, characterized by close-set nostrils directed forward or downward.
~*n.* A catarrhine primate. [New Latin *Catarrhina,* from Greek *katarrhin,* hook-nosed : *kata-,* down + *rhis* (stem *rhin-*), nose.]

ca·tas·ta·sis (kə-tăs'tə-sĭs) *n., pl.* **-ses** (-sēz'). **1.** In classical tragedy, the intensified part of the action directly preceding the catastrophe. **2.** The climax of a play. [Greek *katastasis,* settlement, establishment, from *kathistanai,* to set in order, bring down : *kata-,* down + *histanai,* to set, place.]

ca·tas·tro·phe (kə-tăs'trə-fē) *n.* **1.** A great and sudden calamity causing extreme, often widespread ruin or destruction; a disaster. **2.** A sudden violent change in the earth's surface; a cataclysm. **3.** A complete failure; fiasco. **4.** The dénouement of a play, especially a classical tragedy. —See Synonyms at **disaster.** [Greek *katastrophē,* from *katastrephein,* to turn down, overturn : *kata-,* down + *strephein,* to turn.] **—cat·a·stroph·ic** (kăt'ə-strŏf'ĭk) *adj.* **—cat·a·stroph·i·cal·ly** *adv.*

catastrophe theory *n.* A mathematical theory applied to a wide range of phenomena that show different structures or sudden discontinuous changes, such as biological differentiation, mechanical failure, social conflict, and the like. It depends on representation of different states of the system by geometrical shapes, and on topological analysis of shape and changes of shape.

ca·tas·tro·phism (kə-tăs'trə-fĭz'əm) *n. Geology.* The theory that geological changes in the past were caused by sudden catastrophic disturbances. The theory is also used to account for extinction of plant and animal species. Compare **uniformitarianism.**

cat·a·to·ni·a (kăt'ə-tō'nē-ə) *n.* A condition associated with schizophrenia and certain organic brain disorders and characterized by catalepsy and negativism. [New Latin, from German *Katatonie* : CATA- + -TONIA.] **—cat·a·ton·ic** (kăt'ə-tŏn'ĭk) *adj. & n.*

cat·bird (kăt'bûrd') *n.* **1.** Any of various Australian bowerbirds of the generus *Ailuroedus.* **2.** A North American songbird, *Dumetella carolinensis,* having predominantly slate-gray plumage. [After one of its calls, resembling the mewing of a cat.]

catbird seat *n.* A position of power or prominence.

cat·boat (kăt'bōt') *n.* A broad-beamed sailing boat carrying a single sail on a mast stepped well forward. Also called "cat."

cat·bri·er (kăt'brī'ər) *n.* Any of several thorny vines of the genus *Smilax,* especially *S. rotundifolia,* having heart-shaped leaves, small green flowers, and blackish berries.

cat burglar *n.* A burglar who enters buildings by climbing to the upper stories.

cat·call (kăt'kôl') *n.* A harsh or shrill call expressing disapproval or derision. **—cat·call** *v.*

catch (kăch) *v.* **caught** (kôt), **catching, catches.** —*tr.* **1.** To capture or seize, especially after a chase. **2.** To take by trapping or snaring. **3.** To come upon suddenly, unexpectedly, or accidentally. **4. a.** To lay hold of forcibly or suddenly; grasp: *caught my arm.* **b.** To grab so as to stop the motion of: *tried to catch the ball.* **5. a.** To reach; especially, to reach and overtake. **b.** To reach in time to board, attend, or otherwise make use of: *catch a plane; caught the last mail.* **6. a.** To entangle; grip. **b.** To cause to become suddenly or accidentally hooked, entangled, or the like. **7.** To hit; strike: *a punch that caught him in the stomach.* **8.** To check (oneself) in some sort of action. **9.** To become subject to, as by exposure or contagion; contract: *caught a cold.* **10.** To become affected by: *caught the joyous mood of the festival.* **11.** To take or get suddenly, momentarily, or quickly: *caught a glimpse of the President.* **12. a.** To grasp mentally; comprehend. **b.** To grasp by the senses; apprehend: *I didn't quite catch his last remark.* **13.** To apprehend and reproduce accurately, especially by artistic means; capture: *a novel that catches the flavor of the period.* **14.** To attract and fix; arrest: *catch the waiter's attention.* **15.** *Informal.* To watch or listen to (a theatrical performance, for example). —*intr.* **1.** To become held, entangled, or fastened. **2.** To be communicable or infectious; spread. **3.** To take fire; kindle and burn. **4.** To act as catcher in baseball. **—catch at. 1.** To try to catch; snatch or grab at. **2.** To clutch at gratefully or eagerly. **—catch it.** *Informal.* To receive some form of punishment or scolding. **—catch on.** *Informal.* **1.** To understand or perceive. **2.** To become popular. **—catch one's breath. 1.** To rest so as to be able to go on. **2.** To cease breathing briefly. **—catch out.** To detect (someone) in a mistake. **—catch up. 1.** To lift up suddenly; grab; snatch. **2.** To entangle: *caught up in some barbed wire.* **3. a.** To come up from behind and draw level. **b.** To reach the same level or amount. Used with *with*: *When will the supply catch up with the demand?* **c.** To have an expected, usually undesirable effect, especially after a lapse of time. Used with *with*: *Years of riotous living finally caught up with him.* **4.** To cause to become involved, often unwillingly. Used in the passive: *caught up in the scandal.* **5. a.** To deal with an accumulation of work or the like. Used with *on* or *with*: *catch up on one's correspondence.* **b.** To become acquainted with the latest information. Used with *on* or *with*: *catch up on the gossip.* **6.** To absorb completely; engross. Used in the passive: *He is caught up in his work.*
~*n.* **1.** The act of catching; a taking and holding. **2.** Something that catches, especially a device for fastening or for checking motion. **3.** Something that is caught. **4.** The amount caught. **5.** A choking or stoppage of the breath or voice. **6.** *Informal.* One worth catching, especially as a partner in marriage. **7.** *Informal.* A tricky or unsuspected drawback or condition. **8.** A snatch or fragment. **9.** *Music.* A type of round for three or more voices, popular especially in the 17th and 18th centuries. **10. a.** The grabbing and holding of a thrown, kicked, or batted ball before it hits the ground. **b.** A game of throwing and catching a ball. [Catch, caught, caught; Middle English *cacchen, cauhte, cauht,* to chase, catch, from Old North French *cachier,* to hunt, from Vulgar Latin *captiāre* (unattested), from Latin *captāre,* to chase, strive to seize, from *capere* (past participle *captus*), to take, seize.]

catch·all (kăch'ôl') *n.* **1.** A receptacle for a variety of odds and ends. **2.** Something, such as a phrase or law, that covers a variety of situations. **—catch·all** *adj.*

catch-as-catch-can (kăch'əz-kăch-kăn') *n.* A style of wrestling in which a contestant is permitted to hold his opponent below the waist and to trip and tackle.
~*adj.* Using any available means or opportunity.

catch crop *n.* **1.** A crop grown between two staple crops in consecutive seasons. **2.** A crop grown between the rows of a staple crop.

catch·er (kăch'ər) *n.* One that catches, especially in baseball.

catch·fly (kăch'flī') *n., pl.* **-flies.** Any of several plants of the genus *Silene* and related genera, having white, pink, or red flowers with characteristically sticky stems and calyxes.

catch·ing (kăch'ĭng) *adj. Informal.* **1.** Infectious. **2.** Attractive; alluring.

catch·ment (kăch'mənt) *n.* **1.** A catching or collecting of water. **2. a.** A structure, such as a basin, for collecting or draining water. **b.** The amount of water collected. **3.** A **catchment area** *(see).*

catchment area *n.* The geographical area from which people are drawn to an institution, as a hospital.

catch·pen·ny (kăch'pĕn'ē) *adj.* Designed and made to sell without concern for quality; cheap. **—catch·pen·ny** *n.*

catch phrase *n.* A word or phrase that is often repeated in popular use; slogan.

catch·pole, catch·poll (kăch'pōl') *n.* A sheriff's officer, especially one who arrests debtors. [Middle English *cacchepol,* Old English *cæccepol,* from Old North French *cachepol,* "chicken chaser" : *cachier,* variant of Old French *chacier,* to hunt, CHASE + *poul, pol,* rooster, from Latin *pullus,* young animal, young fowl.]

Catch-22 (kăch'twĕn'tē-to͞o') *n.* A paradox or predicament in which seeming alternatives actually cancel each other out, leaving no means of escape from a dilemma. [After *Catch-22* (1961), a novel by Joseph Heller (born 1923).]

catchup. Variant of **ketchup.**

catch·weight (kăch'wāt') *adj. Sports.* Having no weight restriction. Used especially in wrestling.

catch·word (kăch'wûrd') *n.* **1.** A catch phrase, especially one associated with a political party. **2.** *Printing.* **a.** A word placed at the head of a column or page, as in a dictionary or encyclopedia, to indicate the first or last entry on the page. **b.** The first word of a page printed at the bottom of the preceding page.

catch·y (kăch'ē) *adj.* **-ier, -iest. 1.** Catching one's attention or interest; striking. **2.** Easily remembered and quickly popular.

cat·e·che·sis (kăt'ə-kē'sĭs) *n., pl.* **-ses** (-sēz'). Instruction of catechumens. [Late Latin *catēchēsis,* from Greek *katēkhēsis,* from *katēkhein,* to CATECHIZE.] **—cat·e·chet·ic** (kăt'ə-kĕt'ĭk), **cat·e·chet·i·cal** *adj.*

cat·e·chin (kăt'ə-kĭn') *n.* A soluble yellow solid substance, $C_{15}H_{14}O_6$, derived from catechu and used in tanning and dyeing. [CATECH(U) + -IN.]

cat·e·chism (kăt'ə-kĭz'əm) *n.* **1.** A short book giving, in question-and-answer form, a brief summary of the basic principles of a religion, especially Christianity. **2.** A book of similar form giving instruction in other subjects. **3.** A question-and-answer examination, as of a political candidate. [Late Latin *catēchismus,* from Late Greek *katēkhismos,* from *katēkhizein,* to CATECHIZE.] **—cat·e·chis·mal** (kăt'ə-kĭz'məl) *adj.*

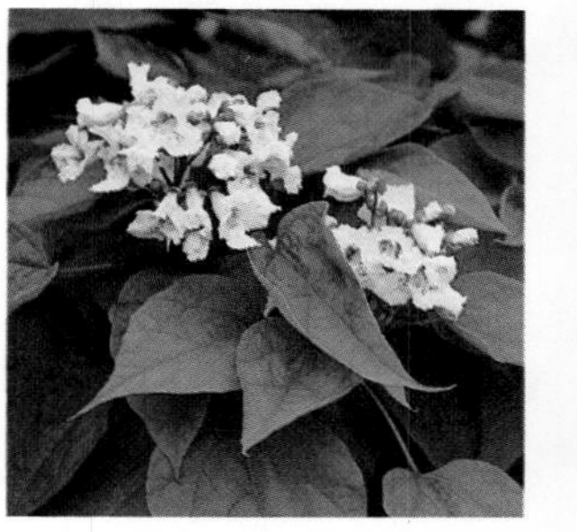

catalpa *Native to Asia and South America, but widely grown in North America as well, the catalpa tree flowers in summer. It is also called the Indian bean.*

PRONUNCIATION KEY

ă, pat; ā, pay; âr, care;
ä, father, are; b, **bib;**
ch, **church;** d, **deed;** ĕ, pet;
ē, be; f, **fife;** g, **gag;** h, **hat;**
hw, **which;** ĭ, pit; ī, pie;
îr, **pier;** j, **judge;** k, **kick;**
l, **lid,** needle; m, **mum;**
n, **no,** sudden; ng, **thing;**
ŏ, pot; ō, **toe;** ô, **paw,** for;
oi, **noise;** ou, **out;** o͝o, **book;**
o͞o, **boot;** p, **pop;** r, **roar;**
s, **sauce;** sh, **ship,** dish;
t, **tight;** th, **thin,** path;
th, **this,** bathe; ŭ, cut; ûr, **fur;**
v, valve; w, **with;** y, **yes;**
z, zebra, size; zh, vision;
ə, about, item, edible, gallop, circus, peaceful

IN FOREIGN WORDS:

à, *Fr.* ami; œ, *Fr.* feu, *Ger.* schön; ü, *Fr.* tu, *Ger.* über; KH, *Ger.* ich, *Scot.* loch; N, *Fr.* bon; y', *Fr.* Compiègne

STRESS MARKS:

Primary stress: '
in·cite' (ĭn-sīt')
Secondary stress: '
in'sight' (ĭn'sīt')

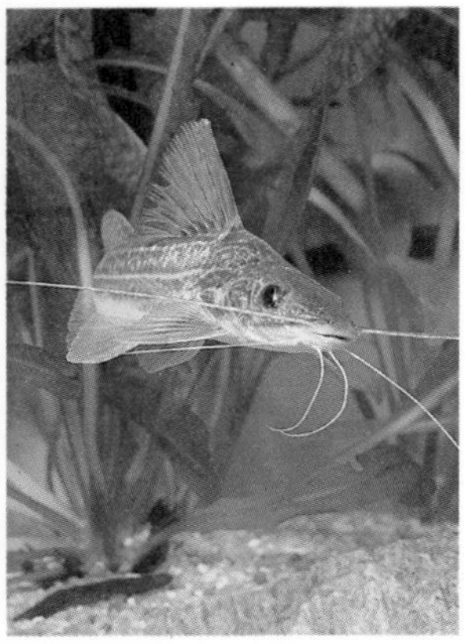

catfish *The catfish group contains a large number of species of freshwater fish identified by their catlike whiskers. The barbels beneath the chin help the fish to locate food on riverbeds.*

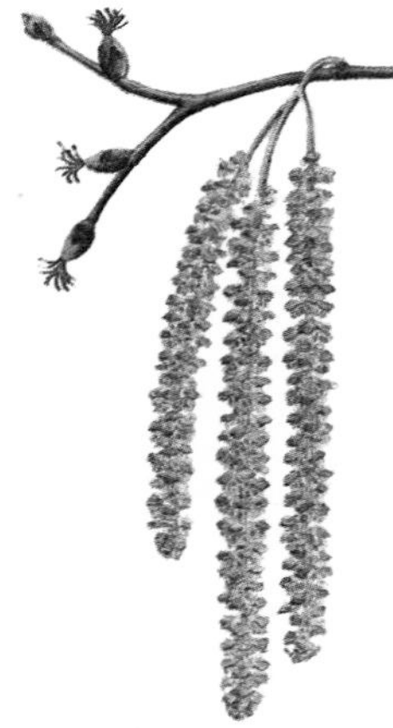

catkin *Many plants produce the long tassellike flower spikes known as catkins. The yellow catkins shown here are the male flowers of the alder tree. The small red blooms are the tree's female flowers.*

cat·e·chist (kăt'ə-kĭst) *n.* A person who catechizes, especially one who instructs catechumens in preparation for baptism. [Late Latin *catēchista,* from Late Greek *katēkhistēs,* from *katēkhizein,* to CATECHIZE.] **—cat·e·chis·tic** (kăt'ə-kĭs'tĭk), **cat·e·chis·ti·cal** *adj.*

cat·e·chize (kăt'ə-kīz') *tr.v.* **-chized, -chizing, -chizes. 1.** To instruct orally in the principles of a religious creed by means of questions and answers. **2.** To question searchingly or persistently. [Late Latin *catēchizāre,* from Late Greek *katēkhizein,* from Greek *katēkhein,* to teach by word of mouth : *kata-,* according to + *ēkhein,* to sound, from *ēkhē,* sound.] **—cat·e·chi·za·tion** *n.* **—cat·e·chiz·er** *n.*

cat·e·chol (kăt'ə-kôl', -kōl') *n.* A colorless crystalline derivative of phenol, $C_6H_4(OH)_2$, used as a photographic developer. [CATECH(U) + -OL.]

cat·e·cho·la·mine (kăt'ə-kō'lə-mēn', -kô'lə-mēn') *n.* Any of a group of amine derivatives of catechol that have important physiological effects on the central nervous system and include epinephrine, norepinephrine, and dopamine.

cat·e·chu (kăt'ə-cho͞o') *n.* Any of several water-soluble, resinous, astringent substances used in tanning and dyeing, as that obtained from a tree, *Acacia catechu,* of southern Asia, or from a woody vine, *Uncaria gambier,* of Malaya. Also called "cachou," "cutch." [Probably from Malay *kachu,* probably from Dravidian, akin to Malayalam *kāccu,* CACHOU.]

cat·e·chu·men (kăt'ə-kyo͞o'mən) *n.* One who is being taught the principles of Christianity; a neophyte. [Middle English *cathecumyn,* from Old French *cathecumene,* from Late Latin *catēchūmenus,* from Greek *katēkhoumenos,* present passive participle of *katēkhein,* to CATECHIZE.]

cat·e·gor·i·cal (kăt'ə-gôr'ĭ-kəl, -gŏr'ĭ-kəl) *adj.* Also **cat·e·gor·ic** (-ĭk). **1.** Without exception or qualification; absolute. **2.** Of, concerning, or included in a category. **—cat·e·gor·i·cal·ly** *adv.*

categorical imperative *n.* In Kant's ethical system, an absolute and universally binding moral law derived from pure reason. Compare **hypothetical imperative.**

cat·e·go·rize (kăt'ə-gə-rīz') *tr.v.* **-rized, -rizing, -rizes.** To put into a category; classify. **—cat·e·go·ri·za·tion** *n.*

cat·e·go·ry (kăt'ə-gôr'ē, -gōr'ē) *n., pl.* **-ries. 1.** A specifically defined division in a system of classification; a class. **2.** *Logic.* Any of the basic classifications into which all knowledge can be placed. [Late Latin *catēgoria,* accusation, predicament, category of predicables, from Greek *katēgoria,* from *katēgorein,* to accuse : *kata-,* against + *-agorein,* to speak publicly, from *agora,* assembly.]

ca·te·na (kə-tē'nə) *n., pl.* **-nae** (-nē') or **-nas.** A closely linked series, especially of commentaries on the Bible by church fathers. [Latin *catēna*†, chain.]

cat·e·nar·y (kăt'ə-nĕr'ē, kə-tē'nə-rē) *n., pl.* **-ies. 1.** The curve theoretically formed by a perfectly flexible, uniformly dense and thick, inextensible cable suspended from two points. **2.** Anything having the shape of this curve. **3.** The overhead wire system of an electric railway. [New Latin *catenaria,* from Latin *catēnāria,* feminine of *catēnārius,* of a chain, from *catēna*†, chain.] **—cat·e·nar·y** *adj.*

catenary bridge *n.* A suspension bridge hanging from chains or cables.

cat·e·nate (kăt'ə-nāt') *tr.v.* **-nated, -nating, -nates.** To connect in a series of ties or links; form into a chain. [Latin *catēnāre,* from *catēna*†, chain.] **—cat·e·na·tion** *n.*

cat·e·noid (kăt'ə-noid') *n.* A geometrical solid generated by rotating a catenary about its axis.

ca·ten·u·late (kə-tĕn'yə-lĭt, -lāt') *adj. Biology.* Consisting or formed of chainlike links. [From Latin *catēnula,* little chain, diminutive of Latin *catēna*†, chain.]

ca·ter (kā'tər) *v.* **-tered, -tering, -ters.** *—intr.* **1.** To provide food or entertainment, usually for large dinners, banquets, and receptions. **2.** To provide anything wished for or needed: *He read books that catered to his appetite for adventure.* **3.** To behave with special thoughtfulness: *catered to the unhappy invalid.* *—tr.* To provide food or entertainment for: *catering a banquet.* [From obsolete *cater,* a buyer of provisions, caterer, from Middle English *catour,* short for *acatour,* from Norman French, from *acater,* to buy, from Vulgar Latin *accaptāre* (unattested), to buy, procure, from Latin *acceptāre,* to ACCEPT.]

cat·er·an (kăt'ər-ən) *n.* A former robber of the Scottish highlands. [Middle English, probably from Scottish Gaelic *ceathairneach.*]

cat·er·cor·nered (kăt'ər-kôr'nərd, kăt'ē-) *adj.* Also **cat·ty-cor·nered** (kăt'ē-). Diagonal. [From obsolete *cater,* four at dice, from Middle English, from Old French *quatre,* four, from Latin *quattuor.*] **—cat·er·cor·nered** *adv.*

ca·ter·er (kā'tər-ər) *n.* One that caters; specifically, a person or company whose business is to supply and serve food and drinks for large social gatherings, banquets, and the like.

cat·er·pil·lar (kăt'ər-pĭl'ər, kăt'ə-) *n.* **1. a.** The wormlike, often brightly colored hairy or spiny larva of a butterfly or moth, having many legs and biting jaws. **b.** Any of various similar insect larvae. **2. Caterpillar.** A trademark for a tractor or bulldozer equipped with a pair of endless chain treads. [Middle English *catyrpel,* probably from Old French *catepelose,* "hairy cat" : *cate,* female cat, from Late Latin *catta,* CAT + *pelose, pelouse,* feminine of *pelous,* hairy, from Latin *pilōsus,* from *pilus,* hair.]

cat·er·waul (kăt'ər-wôl') *intr.v.* **-wauled, -wauling, -wauls. 1.** To cry or screech like a sexually aroused cat. **2.** To have a noisy argument. *~n.* **1.** The cry of a sexually aroused cat. **2.** Any similar cry. [Middle English *caterw(r)awen,* perhaps from Low German *katerwaulen* : *kater,* tomcat, from Common Germanic *kattuz* (unattested), CAT + *waulen,* to screech (perhaps imitative).]

cat·fish (kăt'fĭsh') *n., pl.* **-fishes** or collectively **catfish.** Any of numerous scaleless, chiefly freshwater fishes of the order Siluriformes, characteristically having whiskerlike barbels extending from the upper jaw.

cat·gut (kăt'gŭt') *n.* A tough, thin cord or thread made from the dried intestines of certain animals (usually sheep, but not cat), used for stringing musical instruments and tennis rackets and for surgical ligatures. [16th century : origin obscure.]

cath. cathedral.

Cath·ar (kăth'är') *n., pl.* **Cath·ars** or **Cath·a·ri** (kăth'ə-rī'). An adherent of Catharism.

Cath·a·rism (kăth'ə-rĭz'əm) *n.* The teachings of an ascetic sect of Gnostic heretics that existed in Europe between the 10th and 14th centuries, whose adherents regarded all matter as the creation of an evil deity opposed to God. **—Cath·a·rist** *adj. & n.*

ca·thar·sis (kə-thär'sĭs) *n., pl.* **-ses** (-sēz') **1.** *Medicine.* Purgation, especially for the digestive system. **2.** A purifying or figurative cleansing or release of the emotions, especially as experienced by the audience of a drama. **3.** *Psychoanalysis.* **a.** A technique used to relieve tension and anxiety by bringing repressed material to consciousness. **b.** The result of this process; abreaction. [New Latin, from Greek *katharsis,* from *kathairein,* to purge, purify, from *katharos*†, pure.]

ca·thar·tic (kə-thär'tĭk) *adj.* Inducing catharsis; purgative; cleansing.
~n. A cathartic agent, especially a laxative. [Late Latin *catharticus,* from Greek *kathartikos,* from *kathairein,* to purge, purify.]

Ca·thay (kă-thā'). *Archaic & Poetic.* China. [Medieval Latin *Catay, Kitai,* from Old Turkic *Qitar, Qitan,* name of a Turkic tribe that invaded the north of China in the 10th century and subsequently ruled China as the Liao Dynasty (A.D. 907–1101).]

cat·head (kăt'hĕd') *n.* A beam projecting outward from the bow of a ship and used as a support to lift the anchor. [CAT (nautical) + HEAD.]

ca·thec·tic (kə-thĕk'tĭk) *adj.* Of or pertaining to cathexis.

ca·the·dra (kə-thē'drə) *n., pl.* **-drae** (-drē). **1.** The official chair or throne of a bishop. **2.** The office or see of a bishop. See **ex cathedra. 3.** The official chair of an office or position, as of a professor. [Latin, chair, from Greek *kathedra,* seat : *kata-,* down + *hedra,* seat.]

ca·the·dral (kə-thē'drəl) *n. Abbr.* **cath.** The principal church of a bishop's see and one that contains his throne.
~adj. Of or pertaining to a cathedral. [Originally *cathedral church,* from Middle English *cathedral,* of a cathedra, from Old French, from Late Latin *cathedrālis,* from Latin *cathedra,* CATHEDRA.]

ca·thep·sin (kə-thĕp'sĭn) *n.* Any of a group of enzymes, found in animals, that digest proteins. [Greek *kathepsein,* "to boil down," soften.]

Cath·er (kă*th*'ər), **Willa Sibert** (1873–1947). U.S. author. Growing up in frontier Nebraska, she experienced the trials of pioneer and small-town life that became dominant themes in her works, including *O Pioneers!* (1913), *The Song of the Lark* (1915), and her Pulitzer Prize winner *One of Ours* (1922).

Cath·e·rine II (kăth'rĭn, -ər-ĭn), known as "Catherine the Great" (1729–96). German-born empress of Russia. When her husband, Peter III, succeeded to the throne (1762), Catherine deposed Peter, who was later murdered, and seized the crown. She had schools built, encouraged public health, extended education for women, and promoted religious tolerance. During her reign Russia's frontiers were extended to include most of Poland, the Crimea, and tracts of land bordering the Black Sea.

Catherine de Me·di·ci (də mĕd'ə-chē) (1519–89). Wife of Henry II of France. She ruled France as regent during the minority of her son, Charles IX (1560–63) and, unofficially, until Charles' death (1574). Her plotting was largely responsible for the massacre of Protestants on St. Bartholemew's Day, 1572.

Catherine of Ar·a·gon (ăr'ə-gŏn') (1485–1536). The first wife of Henry VIII of England and mother of Mary I. Henry's insistence on a divorce from her (1533) caused his break with Roman Catholicism and the beginning of the English Reformation.

Catherine of Bra·gan·za (brə-găn'zə) (1638–1705). Portuguese princess and wife of Charles II of England. She married Charles in 1662, but her staunch Roman Catholicism and her failure to produce an heir led to unpopularity with the English people.

cath·er·ine wheel (kăth'ər-ĭn, kăth'rĭn) *n.* **1.** A circular firework that rotates around a pin; pinwheel. **2.** A circular window with ribs radiating from its center. [After St. *Catherine* of Alexandria (died *c.* A.D. 307), who was condemned to be tortured on a wheel.]

cath·e·ter (kăth'ə-tər) *n. Medicine.* A slender, flexible tube of metal, rubber, or plastic inserted into a body channel, such as a vein, to introduce or remove fluid. [Late Latin *cathetēr,* from Greek *kathetēr,* something inserted, from *kathienai,* let fall, send down : *kata-,* down + *hienai,* to send.]

cath·e·ter·ize (kăth'ə-tə-rīz') *tr.v.* **-ized, -izing, -izes.** To introduce a catheter into (a bodily passage). **—cath·e·ter·i·za·tion** *n.*

cath·e·tom·e·ter (kăth'ə-tŏm'ə-tər) *n.* An instrument that measures vertical distances, especially small differences in the level of liquids in tubes. [*catheto-* (see **catheter**) + -METER.]

ca·thex·is (kə-thĕk'sĭs) *n., pl.* **-es** (-sēz'). The concentration of emotional energy upon some object or idea. [New Latin (adopted to translate German *Besetzung,* the term used by Freud), from Greek *kathexis,* a holding, retention, from *katekhein,* to hold fast : *kata-,* down + *ekhein,* to have, hold.]

cath·ode (kăth′ōd′) *n.* **1.** Any negatively charged electrode, as of an electrolytic cell, storage battery, or electron tube. **2.** The positively charged terminal of a primary cell or of a storage battery that is supplying current. [Greek *kathodos,* way down, descent : *kata-,* down + *hodos,* way.] **—ca·thod·ic** (kă-thŏd′ĭk) *adj.* **—ca·thod·i·cal·ly** *adv.*

cathode ray *n.* A stream of electrons emitted by the cathode in an electrical discharge tube.

cath·ode-ray tube (kăth′ōd-rā′) *n.* A vacuum tube, as one used in television sets, in which a hot cathode emits electrons that are accelerated as a beam through a relatively high voltage anode, further focused or deflected electrostatically or electromagnetically, and allowed to fall on a fluorescent screen to produce a visible spot of light.

cath·o·lic (kăth′ə-lĭk, kăth′lĭk) *adj.* **1.** Universal; general; all-inclusive. **2.** Broad and comprehensive in interests, sympathies, or the like; liberal. [Old French *catholique,* from Late Latin *catholicus,* from Greek *katholikos,* from *katholou,* in general : *kata-,* according to + *holou,* neuter genitive of *holos,* whole.] **—ca·thol·i·cal·ly** (kə-thŏl′ĭ-kə-lē, -ĭk-lē) *adv.*

Cath·o·lic (kăth′ə-lĭk, kăth′lĭk) *adj. Abbr.* **C. 1.** Of, pertaining to, or designating the universal Christian church. **2.** Of, pertaining to, or designating the ancient undivided Christian church. **3.** Of, pertaining to, or designating any of those churches that have claimed to be representatives of the ancient undivided church, especially the Roman Catholic Church. **4.** Of, pertaining to, or designating the Western Church as opposed to the Eastern Orthodox Church.

∼*n. Abbr.* **C.** A member of any Catholic church; specifically, a Roman Catholic.

Catholic Apostolic Church *n.* A religious sect founded in England in 1832 and based on the principles of the Rev. E. Irving, whose liturgies follow those of the Roman Catholic, Eastern Orthodox, and Anglican churches.

Catholic Church *n.* The **Roman Catholic Church** *(see).*

Ca·thol·i·cism (kə-thŏl′ə-sĭz′əm) *n.* The faith, doctrine, system, and practice of a Catholic church, especially the Roman Catholic Church. See **Roman Catholicism.**

cath·o·lic·i·ty (kăth′ə-lĭs′ə-tē) *n.* **1.** The condition or quality of being catholic; liberality; broad-mindedness. **2.** General prevalence or acceptance; universality. **3. Catholicity.** Roman Catholicism.

ca·thol·i·cize (kə-thŏl′ə-sīz′) *v.* **-cized, -cizing, -cizes.** *—tr.* **1.** To make catholic. **2.** To convert to Catholicism. *—intr.* To become catholic. **2.** To be converted to Catholicism.

ca·thol·i·con (kə-thŏl′ə-kŏn′) *n.* A universal remedy; a panacea. [French, from Medieval Latin, from Greek *katholikon,* neuter of *katholikos,* CATHOLIC.]

Cat·i·line (kăt′l-īn′) (*c.* 108–62 B.C.). Roman politician and conspirator. He led an unsuccessful revolt against the Roman Republic while Cicero was a consul. His movement died with him and most of his followers in a battle at Pistoria (Pistoia, Italy).

cat·i·on (kăt′ī′ən) *n.* An ion having a positive charge and, in electrolytes, characteristically moving toward a negative electrode. Compare **anion.** [Greek *kation,* neuter of *katiōn,* present participle of *katienai,* to go down : *kata-,* down + *ienai,* to go.] **—cat·i·on·ic** (kăt′ī-ŏn′ĭk) *adj.*

cation exchange *n.* A chemical process used in water softening in which cations of like charge are exchanged equally between a solid, as zeolite, and a solution, as water.

cat·kin (kăt′kĭn) *n. Botany.* A dense, often drooping flower cluster, such as that of a birch, consisting of small, scalelike flowers. Also called "ament." [Translation of obsolete Dutch *katteken,* "little cat" (the cluster resembles a kitten's tail).]

cat·like (kăt′līk′) *adj.* Like a cat; especially, stealthy and silent.

Cat·lin (kăt′lĭn), **George** (1796–1872). U.S. painter. In 1824, after seeing a convention of North American Indians in Philadelphia, he dedicated his life and talent to preserving and publicizing Indian culture with his artwork. His hundreds of paintings, sketches, and etchings are a reliable, detailed record of Indian life and customs.

cat nap *n.* A short nap; a light sleep.

cat·nip (kăt′nĭp′) *n.* A hairy, aromatic blue-flowered plant, *Nepeta cataria,* native to Eurasia, to which cats are attracted.

Ca·to the Elder (kā′tō), **Marcus Porcius** (234–149 B.C.). Roman statesman who wrote the first history of Rome. Opposing luxury and decadence, he attempted, as censor, to restore simplicity to Roman life. After a mission to Africa (153) he was convinced that Rome would always be threatened by Carthage and reportedly ended all his speeches in the Senate, whatever the subject, with *Delenda est Carthago* ("Carthage must be destroyed").

Cato the Younger, Marcus Porcius (95–46 B.C.). Roman politician and great-grandson of Cato the Elder. A conservative opponent of Julius Caesar's political ambitions, he supported Pompey against Caesar in the civil war (49–46 B.C.).

cat-o'-nine-tails (kăt′ə-nīn′tālz′) *n.* A whip consisting of nine knotted cords fastened to a handle, formerly used for flogging. [So called because it leaves marks like the scratches of a cat.]

ca·top·tric (kə-tŏp′trĭk) *adj.* Of or pertaining to mirrors and reflected images. [Greek *katoptrikos,* from *katoptron,* mirror : *kata-,* against + *optos,* visible.] **—ca·top·trics** *n.*

CAT scan *n.* A cross-sectional picture produced by a CAT scanner.

CAT scanner *n.* A device that makes cross-sectional x-rays of the body using computerized axial tomography.

CAT scanning *n.* The act or process of using a CAT scanner.

cat's cradle *n.* A child's game in which an intricately looped string is transferred from the hands of one player to the next, resulting in a succession of different loop patterns.

cat scratch disease *n.* Also **cat scratch fever.** A viral disease transmitted to humans following a skin injury, such as a cat scratch, and characterized by fever and glandular swelling.

cat's-ear (kăts′îr′) *n.* Any of various European plants of the genus *Hypochoeris,* having yellow dandelionlike flowers.

cat's-eye (kăts′ī′) *n.* **1.** Any of various semiprecious gems displaying a band of reflected light that shifts position as the gem is turned. **2.** A colored reflector attached to the back of a vehicle to indicate its presence on the road at night.

cat's-foot (kăts′fo͝ot′) *n.* A small European plant, *Antennaria dioica,* having woolly flowers that form a cluster resembling a cat's paw.

Cats·kill Mountains (kăt′skĭl). Mountain range in New York State, west of the Hudson River and at the north end of the Appalachians. The well-forested mountains, rising to 1,281 meters (4,203 feet) at Slide Mt., provide water and resort areas for New York.

cat's-paw, cats·paw (kăts′pô′) *n.* **1.** A person used by another as a dupe or tool. **2.** A light breeze that ruffles small areas of a water surface. **3.** *Nautical.* A hitch in the bight of a rope, on which a tackle is hooked. ["These he useth as the Monkey did the cat's paw to scrape the nuts out of the fire." M. Hawke, *Killing Is Murder* (1657).]

catsup. Variant of **ketchup.**

cat·tail (kăt′tāl′) *n.* Any of several marsh plants of the genus *Typha,* especially *T. latifolia,* having long straplike leaves and a dense cylindrical head of minute brown flowers. Also called "reed mace."

cat·ta·lo (kăt′l-ō′) *n., pl.* **-loes** or **-los.** Also **cat·a·lo.** A hardy, fertile hybrid breed resulting from a cross between the American buffalo and domestic cattle. [CAT(TLE) + (BUFF)ALO.]

Cattegat. See **Kattegat.**

cat·ter·y (kăt′ə-rē) *n, pl.* **-ies.** A place where cats are bred or boarded.

cat·tle (kăt′l) *pl.n.* **1.** Various animals of the genus *Bos,* especially those of the domesticated species *B. taurus,* raised in many breeds for meat and dairy products. **2.** Human beings, especially when viewed as a mob. [Middle English *catel,* personal property, livestock, from Old North French, from Medieval Latin *capitāle,* property, from Latin, neuter of *capitālis,* chief, primary, from *caput,* head.]

cattle cake *n. Chiefly British.* Concentrated cattle food made up into cake-shaped slabs.

cattle grid *n. Chiefly British.* A ditch covered by a grid of parallel bars that prevents livestock from crossing but allows the passage of vehicles and pedestrians.

cat·tle·man (kăt′l-mən, -măn′) *n., pl.* **-men** (-mĭn, -mĕn′). A man who tends or rears cattle.

cattle plague *n.* **Rinderpest** *(see).*

cattle prod *n.* An electric prod for driving cattle.

cat·tley·a (kăt′lē-ə) *n.* Any orchid of the genus *Cattleya,* having showy rose-purple or white flowers. [New Latin, after William *Cattley* (died 1832), British patron of botany.]

cat·ty¹, cat·tie (kăt′ē) *n., pl.* **-ties.** A unit of weight used in China and Southeast Asia generally equivalent to 1⅓ pounds avoirdupois. [Malay *kati.*]

catty² *adj.* **-tier, -tiest.** Subtly cruel or malicious; spiteful: *a catty remark.* **—cat·ti·ly** *adv.* **—cat·ti·ness** *n.*

catty-cornered. Variant of **cater-cornered.**

Ca·tul·lus (kə-tŭl′əs), **Gaius Valerius** (*c.* 84–54 B.C.). Roman lyric poet whose best-known poems tell of his love, from the beginning to the final disillusionment, for Lesbia, an aristocratic Roman woman whose real name was Clodia.

cat·walk (kăt′wôk′) *n.* A narrow platform or pathway, as along the sides of a bridge.

cat whisker *n.* **1.** A fine, pointed wire formerly used to make electrical contact in a crystal radio receiver. **2.** A wire used to make contact with a semiconductor.

Cau·ca·sian (kô-kā′zhən, -kăzh′ən) *n.* **1.** A member of the Caucasoid ethnic division; especially, a white person. **2.** A native or inhabitant of the Caucasus. **3.** The group of languages spoken in the area of the Caucasus that are neither Indo-European nor Altaic, including Circassian and Georgian.

∼*adj.* **1.** Of or pertaining to the Caucasus, its people, or their languages and culture. **2.** Caucasoid.

Cau·ca·soid (kô′kə-soid′) *adj. Anthropology.* **1.** Of, pertaining to, or designating a major ethnic division of the human species having certain distinctive physical characteristics such as skin color varying from very light to brown and fine hair ranging from straight to wavy or curly. This division is considered to include groups of peoples indigenous to or inhabiting Europe, northern Africa, southwestern Asia, and the Indian subcontinent, and persons of this ancestry in other parts of the world. **2.** Of, pertaining to, or characteristic of Caucasoids.

∼*n.* A member of the Caucasoid ethnic division.

Cau·ca·sus (kô′kə-səs). Also **Cau·ca·sia** (kō-kā′zhə, -shə). Historic region between the Black and Caspian seas. Its earliest inhabitants, before 2000 B.C., were Caucasoid peoples, and today, after many invasions, more than 40 languages are spoken, including Circassian, Armenian, Georgian, and Azerbaijani. It is divided in two by the **Caucasus Mts.,** whose highest peak is Mt. Elbrus (5,633 meters; 18,481 feet), the highest mountain in Europe.

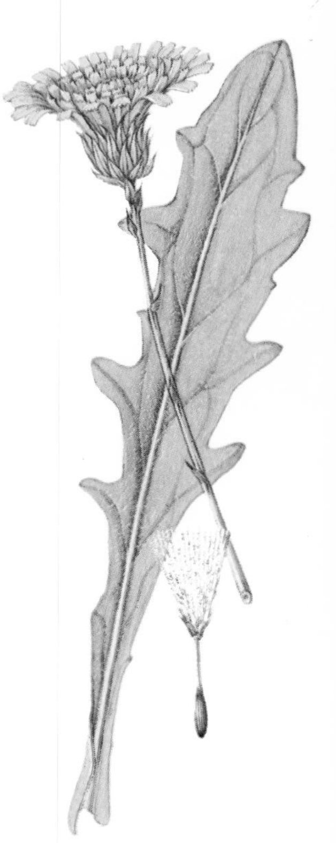

cat's-ear Hypochoeris radicata *is one of many wildflowers that belong to the daisy family. The flower heads, up to 4 centimeters (1½ inches) across, decorate the pastures and woodlands of Europe and North America, but the plants are regarded as weeds by gardeners.*

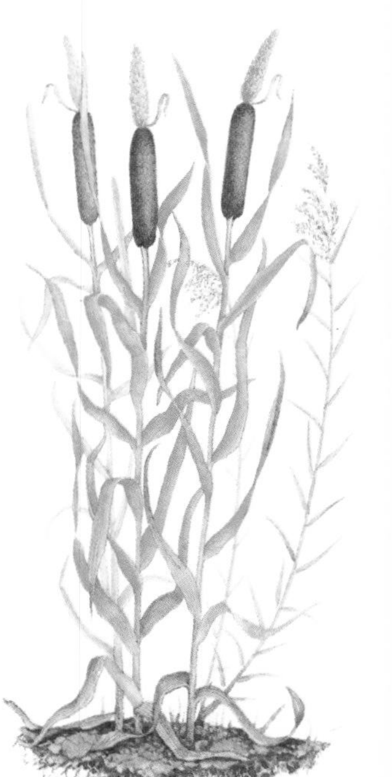

cattail *One of the common names for the reed mace, a waterside plant also known as the bulrush.*

cau·cus (kô'kəs) n., pl. **-cuses** or **-cusses**. 1. *Chiefly British.* A group of activists within a political party, sometimes considered as unrepresentative or undemocratic. 2. a. A closed meeting of the members of a political party within a legislative body to decide upon questions of policy and the selection of candidates for office. b. These members as a group. ~intr.v. **-cused** or **-cussed, -cusing** or **-cussing, -cuses** or **-cusses**. To assemble in or hold a caucus. [Perhaps from Algonquian *caucauasu,* counselor (a term recorded by Capt. John Smith).]

cau·dad (kô'dăd') adv. *Anatomy.* Toward the tail or posterior part of the body. Compare **cephalad**. [Latin *cauda†,* tail + -AD.]

cau·dal (kôd'l) adj. 1. *Anatomy.* Of, at, or near the tail or hind parts; posterior. 2. *Zoology.* Of, pertaining to, or resembling the tail. [New Latin *caudalis,* from Latin *cauda†,* tail.] —**cau·dal·ly** adv.

caudal fin n. The tail fin of a fish.

cau·date (kô'dāt') adj. Also **cau·dat·ed** (-dā'tĭd). Having a tail or a taillike part. [New Latin *caudatus,* from Latin *cauda†,* tail.]

caudate nucleus n. A large ganglion in the lateral ventricle of the brain that functions in motor control.

cau·dex (kô'dĕks') n., pl. **-dices** (-də-sēz') or **-dexes**. *Botany.* 1. The thickened base of the stem of some perennial plants. 2. A woody, trunklike stem, such as that of a tree fern. [Latin *caudex, cōdex†,* stem, tree trunk.]

cau·di·llo (kou-*th*ēl'yō, -*th*ē'yō) n., pl. **-llos**. In Spanish-speaking countries, a military leader who sets himself up as a dictator. [Spanish, chieftain, from Late Latin *capitellum,* small head, diminutive of *caput,* head.]

cau·dle (kôd'l) n. A warm beverage formerly given to invalids, consisting of wine or ale mixed with sugar, eggs, bread, and various spices. [Middle English *caudel,* from Old North French *caudel, chaudel,* from *chaud,* warm, from Latin *cal(i)dus.*]

caught. Past tense and past participle of **catch**.

caul (kôl) n. 1. A portion of the membrane that surrounds a fetus, which is sometimes found on the head at birth and considered a sign of good luck. 2. The large omentum covering the intestines. [Middle English *calle,* probably from Old French *cale,* cap, from Germanic.]

cauldron. Variant of **caldron**.

cau·les·cent (kô-lĕs'ənt) adj. *Botany.* Having a stem showing above the ground. [Latin *caulis,* stem.]

cau·li·cle (kô'lĭ-kəl) n. *Botany.* A small stem. [Latin *cauliculus,* diminutive of *caulis,* stem.]

cauliflower *A flowering vegetable, of which only the white head is normally eaten.*

cau·li·flow·er (kô'lĭ-flou'ər, kŏl'ĭ-) n. 1. A plant, *Brassica oleracea botrytis,* related to the cabbage and broccoli and having an enlarged, crowded flower head. 2. The compact, whitish flower head of this plant, eaten as a vegetable. [Earlier *colie-florie,* probably from Italian *caoli-fiori,* plural of *cavolo-fiore,* "flowered cabbage" : *cavolo,* cabbage, from Late Latin *caulus,* variant of Latin *caulis,* stem + *fiore,* flower, from Latin *flōs* (stem *flōr-*).]

cauliflower ear n. An ear swollen and deformed by repeated blows, as in boxing.

cau·line (kô'līn) adj. *Botany.* Of, having, or growing on a stem. [New Latin *caulinus,* from Latin *caulis,* stalk, stem.]

caulk, calk (kôk) tr.v. **caulked, caulking, caulks** or **calked, calking, calks**. 1. *Nautical.* To make (a boat) watertight by packing seams with oakum or tar. 2. To make (pipes, for example) watertight or airtight by filling in cracks. [Middle English *ca(u)lken,* from Old North French *cauquer,* to trample, tread, from Latin *calcāre,* from *calx* (stem *calc-*), a heel.] —**caulk·er** n.

cau·ri (kou'rē) n., pl. **-ris**. A monetary unit of Guinea, equal to ¹⁄₁₀₀ of a syli. See feature at **currency**.

caus·al (kô'zəl) adj. 1. Pertaining to, constituting, or involving a cause: *a number of causal factors.* 2. Expressing a cause or reason. ~n. A word or grammatical element that expresses a cause or reason. —**caus·al·ly** adv.

cau·sal·gia (kô-zăl'jə, -jē-ə) n. A burning pain felt in a limb along the course of a peripheral nerve that has been injured. It may be accompanied by changes in the appearance of the skin. [New Latin, from Greek *kausos,* fever, burning + -ALGIA.] —**cau·sal·gic** (kô-zăl'jĭk) adj.

cau·sal·i·ty (kô-zăl'ə-tē) n., pl. **-ties**. 1. The relationship between cause and effect. 2. A causal agency, force, or quality.

cau·sa·tion (kô-zā'shən) n. 1. The act or process of causing. 2. The relationship between cause and effect.

caus·a·tive (kô'zə-tĭv) adj. 1. Functioning as a cause; effective. 2. Designating a verb or verbal affix that expresses causation. In the phrase *to fell a tree, fell* is a causative verb. ~n. A word or form expressing causation. —**caus·a·tive·ly** adv.

cause (kôz) n. 1. That which produces an effect, result, or consequence; the person, event, or condition responsible for an action or result. 2. A basis for an action or decision; ground; reason; motive. 3. Good or sufficient reason or ground. 4. A goal, principle, or concern that is actively pursued: *the cause of mental health.* 5. The interests of a person or group engaged in a struggle: *"The cause of America is in great measure the cause of all mankind"* (Thomas Paine). 6. *Law.* a. A ground for legal action. b. A lawsuit. 7. A subject under debate or discussion. ~tr.v. **caused, causing, causes**. To be the cause of; make happen; bring about. [Middle English, from Old French, from Latin *causa†,* reason, purpose, motive, lawsuit.] —**caus·a·ble** adj. —**caus·er** n.

Usage: **cause, reason, occasion**. These nouns denote things or prior conditions that bring about, or are associated with, certain effects. A *cause,* singly or as one of a series, must exist for an effect logically to occur: *Deficiency in vitamin C is the cause of scurvy. Reason* refers to what explains the occurrence or nature of an effect in terms of human thought rather than objective or external factors: *There was no reason to leave.* An *occasion* is the situation or time that permits existing causes to come into play: *The occasion for the robbery was the absence of the regular night watchman.*

cause cé·lè·bre (kōz' să-lĕb'r') n., pl. **causes célèbres** (pronounced as singular). 1. A celebrated legal case. 2. A controversial issue arousing heated public debate and partisanship. [French, "celebrated case."]

cause list n. *Law.* A list of cases awaiting trial.

cau·se·rie (kōz-rē', kō'zə-rē') n. 1. An informal talk or chat. 2. A short, conversational piece of writing. [French, from *causer,* to talk.]

cause·way (kôz'wā') n. 1. A raised roadway, as across water or marshland. 2. A paved highway. [Middle English *caucewei* : *cauce,* from Old North French *cauciee,* from Vulgar Latin *calciāta* (unattested), paved (as with limestone), from Latin *calx* (stem *calc-*), limestone, small stone, from Greek *khalix,* small stone + *wei,* WAY.]

caus·tic (kô'stĭk) adj. 1. Able to burn, corrode, dissolve, or otherwise eat away by chemical action. 2. Marked by sharp and bitter wit; cutting: *"Her new clothes were the subject of caustic comment"* (Willa Cather). 3. *Optics.* Of or designating a curve or surface of revolution formed by rays of an initially parallel beam of light after they have been reflected or refracted by an optical system that does not bring the rays to a single focus. —See Usage note at **sarcastic**. ~n. 1. A caustic material or substance. 2. A caustic curve or surface. [Latin *causticus,* from Greek *kaustikos,* from *kaiein,* to burn.] —**caus·ti·cal·ly** adv. —**caus·tic·i·ty** (kô-stĭs'ə-tē) n.

caustic lime n. Calcium hydroxide (see).

caustic potash n. Potassium hydroxide (see).

caustic soda n. Sodium hydroxide (see).

cau·ter·ize (kô'tə-rīz') tr.v. **-ized, -izing, -izes**. To burn or sear with a cautery. [Old French *cauteriser,* from Late Latin.] —**cau·ter·i·za·tion** n.

cau·ter·y (kô'tə-rē) n., pl. **-ies**. 1. A caustic agent or a very hot or very cold instrument used, especially in the treatment of wounds, to destroy abnormal tissue. 2. The act or result of using a cautery; cauterization. [Latin *cautērium,* branding iron, from Greek *kautērion,* from *kaiein,* to burn.]

cau·tion (kô'shən) n. 1. a. Forethought to avoid danger or harm. b. An instinctive avoidance of risks and danger. 2. A warning; an admonishment. 3. *British Law.* An official warning, given to a person suspected of or arrested for a crime, that if he chooses to speak, anything he says may be set down and used in evidence. 4. *Informal.* Someone or something that is striking or amusing. ~tr.v. **cautioned, -tioning, -tions**. 1. To warn, especially against danger; put on guard. 2. *British Law.* To give a caution to (a person suspected of a crime). —See Synonyms at **warn**. [Middle English *caucion,* from Old French *caution,* from Latin *cautiō* (stem *cautiōn-*), a guarding, from *cavēre* (past participle *cautus*), to watch, take heed.]

cau·tion·ar·y (kô'shə-nĕr'ē) adj. 1. Of, pertaining to, or being a caution. 2. Giving or serving as a warning.

caution money n. *British.* Money deposited as a surety, as for example against possible debts or damage.

cau·tious (kô'shəs) adj. 1. Showing or practicing caution; wary; careful. 2. Showing prudence and deliberation; guarded; tentative: *cautious optimism.* —**cau·tious·ly** adv. —**cau·tious·ness** n.

cav. cavalry.

cav·al·cade (kăv'əl-kād', kăv'əl-kād') n. 1. A ceremonial procession, especially of horsemen or horse-drawn carriages. 2. A colorful procession or display. 3. A succession: *a cavalcade of stars.* [French, from Italian *cavalcata,* from *cavalcare,* to ride on horseback, from Vulgar Latin *caballicāre* (unattested), from Latin *caballus,* horse.]

Cav·al·can·ti (kăv'əl-kăn'tē), **Guido** (c. 1255–1300). Florentine poet whose major themes were love and emotional suffering. A friend of Dante, he died in exile, banished for his political meddlings.

cav·a·lier (kăv'ə-lîr') n. 1. A gentleman accomplished in arms and horsemanship. 2. A gallant courtly gentleman, especially one escorting a lady. 3. **Cavalier.** A supporter of Charles I of England in his struggles against the Parliamentarians; a Royalist. ~adj. 1. Showing arrogant self-assurance; offhand: *He dismissed my objection with a cavalier wave of his hand.* 2. Carefree and gay. 3. **Cavalier.** Of or pertaining to the Cavaliers. [French, from Italian *cavaliere,* from Late Latin *caballārius,* horseman, rider, from Latin *caballus,* horse.] —**cav·a·lier·ly** adv.

Cavalier poets pl.n. A group of English poets, including Lovelace and Suckling, associated with the court of Charles I.

ca·val·la (kə-văl'ə) n., pl. **-las** or **cavalla**. Also **ca·val·ly** (-văl'ē) pl. **-lies** or **cavally**. 1. Any of various tropical marine food fishes of the family Carangidae. 2. The **king mackerel** (see). [Spanish *caballa,* horse mackerel, from Late Latin, feminine of Latin *caballus,* horse.]

cav·al·ry (kăv'əl-rē) n., pl. **-ries**. *Abbr.* **cav.** 1. Troops mounted on horseback. 2. A highly mobile army unit using armored vehicles, helicopters, and the like. [French *cavallerie,* from Italian *cavalleria,* cavalry, chivalry, from *cavaliere,* CAVALIER.]

cav·al·ry·man (kăv'əl-rē-mən) n., pl. **-men** (-mĭn). A soldier in the cavalry.

Cav·an (kăv'ən). County in the Republic of Ireland, in Ulster. It is a predominantly hilly region, infertile and boggy with many lakes. The county town is also named Cavan.

cav·a·ti·na (kăv′ə-tē′nə, kä′və-) *n. Music.* 1. A short operatic solo in a simple style. 2. An instrumental piece or movement in a simple style. [Italian.]

cave (kāv) *n.* 1. A hollow beneath the earth's surface, often having an opening in the side of a hill or cliff. 2. *British.* A dissident group formally seceding from a political party.
~*v.* **caved, caving, caves.** —*tr.* To hollow out. —*intr.* To explore caves. [Middle English, from Old French, from Latin *cava,* from the neuter plural of *cavus,* hollow.]

ca·ve·at (kā′vē-ăt′, kăv′ē-, kä′vē-ăt′) *n.* 1. *Law.* A formal application filed by an interested party to a court or officer, requesting the postponement of proceedings until he is heard. 2. A warning or caution.
~*v.* **caveated, -ating, -ats.** —*intr. Law.* To enter a caveat. —*tr. Slang.* To do or say (something) with an accompanying warning or caution. [Latin, let him beware, from *cavēre,* to beware, take care.]

caveat emp·tor (ĕmp′tôr′) *n.* The principle in commerce that the buyer alone is responsible for assessing the quality of a purchase before buying it. [Latin, "let the buyer beware."]

cave·fish (kāv′fĭsh′) *n., pl.* **fishes** or collectively **cavefish.** Any of various freshwater fishes of the family Amblyopsidae, of subterranean waters, having rudimentary eyes. Also called "blindfish."

cave in *intr.v.* 1. To fall in; collapse, as from being undermined. 2. *Informal.* To cease resistance. —*tr.v.* To cause to collapse.

cave-in (kāv′ĭn′) *n.* 1. An act of caving in. 2. A place where a structure, such as a mineshaft, has caved in.

Cav·ell (kăv′əl), **Edith** (1865-1915). British nurse who remained in Brussels after the German occupation (1915) helping to smuggle Allied troops to the Dutch border. Caught by the Germans, she was executed by firing squad.

cave·man (kāv′măn′) *n., pl.* **-men** (-mĕn′). 1. A prehistoric man who lived in caves. 2. *Informal.* A man who is crude or brutal, especially toward women.

cav·en·dish (kăv′ən-dĭsh) *n. British.* Tobacco that has been sweetened and molded into plugs or cakes. [Perhaps from the name of the first manufacturer.]

Cav·en·dish (kăv′ən-dĭsh), **Henry** (1731-1810). English physicist and chemist who discovered (1766) the properties of hydrogen and later established that water was a compound of hydrogen and oxygen. Using the universal gravitational constant, he measured the density of the earth in 1798.

cave painting *n.* 1. A painting made by prehistoric man on a cave wall. 2. Prehistoric art found on cave walls.

cav·er (kā′vər) *n.* One who explores caves.

cav·ern (kăv′ərn) *n.* 1. A large cave. 2. Something resembling a cavern in depth, hollowness, or darkness.
~*tr.v.* **caverned, -erning, -erns.** 1. To enclose in or as if in a cavern. 2. To hollow. Used with *out.* [Middle English *caverne,* from Old French, from Latin *caverna,* from *cavus,* hollow.]

cav·er·nic·o·lous (kăv′ər-nĭk′ə-ləs) *adj.* Inhabiting caverns or caves.

cav·ern·ous (kăv′ər-nəs) *adj.* 1. Filled with caverns. 2. Like a cavern in depth, vastness, or darkness. 3. Filled with cavities; porous. —**cav·ern·ous·ly** *adv.*

cav·es·son (kăv′ĭ-sən) *n.* A strong noseband used when breaking in difficult horses. [French *caveçon,* from Italian *cavezzone,* augmentative of *cavezza,* halter, from Medieval Latin *capitium,* head covering, from Latin *caput* (stem *capit-*), head.]

ca·vet·to (kə-vĕt′ō) *n., pl.* **-vetti** (-vĕt′ē) or **-tos.** A concave molding for cornices, shaped like a circular quadrant. [Italian, from *cavo,* hollow, from Latin *cavus.*]

cav·i·ar, cav·i·are (kăv′ē-är′, kä′vē-) *n.* The roe of a large fish, especially a sturgeon, that is salted, seasoned, and eaten as a delicacy. [Earlier *caviari, cavialy,* probably from French *caviar,* from Italian *caviaro,* from Turkish *kāvyār.*]

cav·il (kăv′əl) *intr.v.* **-iled, -iling, -ils.** Also *chiefly British* **-illed, -illing.** To raise unnecessary or trivial objections; carp. Used with *at, about,* or *with.*
~*n.* A captious or trivial objection. [French *caviller,* from Latin *cavillārī,* to satirize, criticize, from *cavilla,* a jeering.] —**cav·il·er** *n.*

cav·ing (kā′vĭng) *n.* The exploration of caves as a sport or scientific pursuit.

cav·i·tar·y (kăv′ə-tĕr′ē) *adj.* Of, pertaining to, or marked by cavitation in the body.

cav·i·ta·tion (kăv′ə-tā′shən) *n.* 1. The sudden formation and collapse of low-pressure bubbles in liquids by means of mechanical forces, such as those resulting from rotation of a marine propeller. 2. The formation of cavities in tissue or an organ, especially as a result of disease. [From CAVITY.]

cav·i·ty (kăv′ə-tē) *n., pl.* **-ties.** 1. A hollow or hole. 2. A hollow area within the body: *a sinus cavity.* 3. A pitted area in a tooth caused by caries *(see).* —See Synonyms at **hole.** [French *cavité,* Old French *cavete,* from Late Latin *cavitās,* hollowness, from Latin *cavus,* hollow.]

cavity resonator *n. Electronics.* A microwave device containing an enclosed space in which an oscillating electromagnetic field can be maintained. The dimensions of the cavity determine the frequency of the oscillations. Also called "rhumbatron."

cavity wall *n.* A wall, usually of masonry, consisting of two layers separated by an air space for insulation.

ca·vort (kə-vôrt′) *intr.v.* **-vorted, -vorting, -vorts.** 1. To bound or prance about in a sprightly manner; caper. 2. To make merry; frolic. [Perhaps variant of CURVET.]

Ca·vour (kə-voor′), **Count Camillo Benso di** (1810-61). Italian liberal statesman who helped unify Italy. Prime minister of Sardinia-Piedmont (1852-59, 1860-61) he made various alliances to oust the Austrians from Italy and with Giuseppi Garibaldi, created the kingdom of Italy under the king of Sardinia-Piedmont, Victor Emmanuel II.

ca·vy (kā′vē) *n., pl.* **-vies.** Any of various short-tailed or apparently tailless South American rodents of the family Caviidae, which includes the guinea pig. [New Latin *Cavia,* probably from Galibi *cabiai.*]

caw (kô) *n.* The hoarse, raucous sound uttered by a crow or similar bird.
~*intr.v.* **cawed, cawing, caws.** To utter a caw. [Imitative.]

Cawnpore. See Kanpur.

Cax·ton (kăk′stən), **William** (c. 1422-91). The first English printer and publisher, formerly a cloth merchant. *Recuyell of the Historyes of Troye* (c. 1475) was the first book printed in English. He set up his own press (1476) at Westminster where he published and printed *Canterbury Tales* (1478) and the first illustrated English book, an encyclopedia, *Myrrour of the Worlde* (1481).

cay (kē, kā) *n.* A small, low islet composed largely of coral or sand; a key. [Spanish *cayo,* probably from Old French *quai, cay,* QUAY.]

Cay·enne (kī-ĕn′, kā-). The capital and chief seaport of French Guiana, situated on the coast of the Île de Cayenne. The French founded it in 1643, and it was a penal colony (1854-1938).

cay·enne pepper (kī-ĕn′, kā-) *n.* A condiment made from the very pungent fruit of a variety of the plant *Capsicum frutescens.* Also called "cayenne," "red pepper." [Earlier *kian, chian* (influenced by CAYENNE), from Tupi *kyinha.*]

cayman. Variant of **caiman.**

Cay·man Islands (kā-măn′, kā′mən). A group of three low-lying coral islands in the Caribbean Sea approximately 320 kilometers (200 miles) northwest of Jamaica. The largest, Grand Cayman, includes Georgetown, the capital. Little Cayman and Cayman Brac make up the rest of this British colony. Columbus discovered the islands in 1503.

Ca·yu·ga (kā-yōō′gə, kī-) *n., pl.* **-gas** or collectively **Cayuga.** 1. A member of an American Indian people formerly living around Cayuga and Seneca lakes in central New York. 2. The Iroquoian language spoken by this people. —**Ca·yu·ga** *adj.*

Cayuga Lake. The longest of the Finger Lakes in west-central New York. It is 61 kilometers (38 miles) long and 1.6 to 5.6 kilometers (1 to 3.5 miles) wide.

cay·use (kī-yōōs′, kī′yōōs′) *n. Western U.S.* A horse; especially, an Indian pony. [After the CAYUSE Indians.]

Cay·use (kī-yōōs′, kī′yōōs′) *n., pl.* **-uses** or collectively **Cayuse.** 1. A member of an American Indian people of Oregon. 2. The Sahaptin language of this tribe. —**Cay·use** *adj.*

cazique. Variant of **cacique.**

Cb The symbol for the element columbium.

CB (sē-bē′) *n., pl.* **CB's. Citizens band** *(see).*

CBC 1. Canadian Broadcasting Corporation. 2. complete blood count.

C.B.D. cash before delivery.

C.B.E. Commander of the (Order of the) British Empire.

CBS Columbia Broadcasting System.

cc cubic centimeter.

cc. chapters.

c.c., C.C. carbon copy.

C.C.A. Circuit Court of Appeals.

CCC 1. Civilian Conservation Corps. 2. Commodity Credit Corporation.

C clef *n. Music.* A clef sign used to form any of three clefs, soprano, alto, or tenor, by locating middle C on, respectively, the lowest line of the staff, the middle line, or the fourth (next to the highest) line.

cd *Physics.* candela.

Cd The symbol for the element cadmium.

c.d. cash discount.

C.D. 1. civil defense. 2. compact disc.

CDC Center for Disease Control.

Cdr. commander.

Ce The symbol for the element cerium.

C.E. 1. chemical engineer. 2. chief engineer. 3. civil engineer. 4. common era.

ce·a·no·thus (sē′ə-nō′thəs) *n.* A shrub of the North American genus *Ceanothus,* often grown for ornament. [New Latin, from Greek *keanōthos,* a type of thistle.]

cease (sēs) *v.* **ceased, ceasing, ceases.** —*tr.* To put an end to; discontinue. —*intr.* 1. To come to an end; stop. 2. To desist; discontinue. Often used with *from.*
~*n.* Pause or end. Used in the phrase *without cease.* [Middle English *ces(s)en,* from Old French *cesser,* from Latin *cessāre,* to delay, stop, frequentative of *cēdere* (past participle *cessus*), to CEDE.]

cease-fire (sēs′fīr′) *n.* 1. An order to cease firing. 2. A suspension of active hostilities; a truce.

cease·less (sēs′lĭs) *adj.* Without stop; endless. —See Synonyms at **continual.** —**cease·less·ly** *adv.*

Ceau·şes·cu (chou-shĕs′kōō), **Nicolae** (1918-89). Romanian Communist leader. As Romania's first president (1974-89) he maintained

cave painting *Some prehistoric paintings, such as this one discovered at Lascaux in France, are at once realistic and highly stylized. Painting in the caves at Lascaux began in about 15,000 B.C.*

close ties with the U.S.S.R., but restricted its interference in Romania's national affairs. He was tried and executed by the military.

Čechy. See **Bohemia.**

Cecil, William. See William Cecil, 1st Baron **Burghley.**

ce·cum, cae·cum (sē′kəm) *n., pl.* **-ca** (-kə). **1.** A cavity with only one opening. **2.** *Anatomy.* The large blind pouch forming the beginning of the large intestine. [New Latin, from Latin *(intestinum) caecum,* blind (intestine), from *caecus,* blind.]

ce·dar (sē′dər) *n.* **1.** Any of several coniferous evergreen trees of the genus *Cedrus,* native to the Old World and having spreading branches and barrel-shaped cones, as the **cedar of Lebanon** *(see).* **2.** Any of various similar evergreen trees, mostly of the genera *Thuja, Chamaecyparis,* and *Juniperus.* **3.** The durable, aromatic, often reddish wood of a cedar. [Middle English *cedre,* from Old French, from Latin *cedrus,* cedar, juniper, from Greek *kedros*†.]

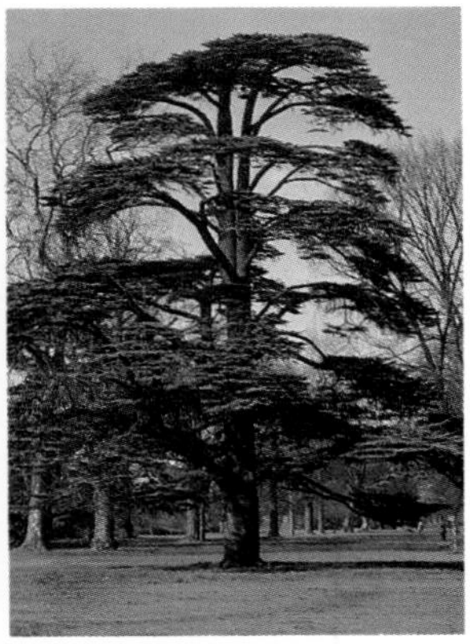

cedar of Lebanon *These trees, native to the mountains of Lebanon, Syria, and Asia Minor, yield a hard and durable timber. In biblical times, they became a symbol of longevity.*

cedar of Lebanon *n.* A tall evergreen tree, *Cedrus libani,* of Asia Minor, having level spreading branches, short dark needles, and fragrant hard wood. [Translation of Late Latin *cedrus libani* (translation of Hebrew *arzē Ləbānōn*).]

Cedar Rapids. A city of east-central Iowa, on the Cedar River. A thriving commercial and industrial city, Cedar Rapids is a distribution and rail center for an extensive agricultural area. Its museum has a collection of paintings by Grant Wood.

cedar waxwing *n.* A North American bird, *Bombycilla cedrorum,* having a crested head and predominantly brown plumage. [Probably so called because it eats the berries of the red cedar.]

cede (sēd) *tr.v.* **ceded, ceding, cedes. 1.** To surrender possession of officially or formally. **2.** To yield; grant. —See Synonyms at **relinquish.** [French *céder,* from Latin *cēdere,* to withdraw, yield.]

ce·di (sā′dē) *n., pl.* **cedi** or **-dis. 1.** The basic monetary unit of Ghana, equal to 100 pesewas. See feature at **currency. 2.** A note worth one cedi.

ce·dil·la (sĭ-dĭl′ə) *n.* A mark (̧) placed beneath the letter *c* in the spelling of French, Portuguese, and older Spanish to indicate that the letter is to be pronounced (s), as in the French word *garçon.* The cedilla is also used for various purposes in Turkish and Romanian spelling. [Obsolete Spanish *cedilla,* diminutive of *ceda,* the letter zee, from Late Latin *zēta,* ZETA (so called because a small *z* was formerly used to make a hard *c* sibilant).]

cei·ba (sā′bə) *n.* Any of various large tropical trees of the genus *Ceiba,* which includes the silk-cotton tree, the source of the fiber kapok. [New Latin, from Spanish, probably from Arawakan.]

ceil (sēl) *tr.v.* **ceiled, ceiling, ceils. 1.** To make a ceiling for. **2.** To provide (a ship) with interior planking. [Middle English *celen,* perhaps a back-formation from CEILING.]

cei·lidh (kā′lē) *n.* An Irish or Scottish social gathering with traditional music, dancing, and storytelling. [Gaelic.]

ceil·ing (sē′lĭng) *n.* **1.** The interior upper surface of a room. **2.** The planking applied to the interior framework of a ship. **3.** A maximum limit, especially on wages or prices. **4.** Any of various vertical boundaries, especially of atmospheric visibility, cloud-cover altitude, or operable aircraft altitude. [Middle English *celing*†.]

ceil·om·e·ter (sē-lŏm′ə-tər) *n.* A photoelectric instrument for ascertaining cloud heights. [CEIL(ING) + -METER.]

cel·a·don (sĕl′ə-dŏn′) *n.* **1.** A pale to very pale green. **2.** A kind of pottery with a pale grayish-green glaze that was originally produced in China. [French *céladon,* from *Céladon,* wan character in Honoré d'Urfé's *L'Astrée* (1607–19).] **—cel·a·don** *adj.*

cel·a·don·ite (sĕl′ə-də-nīt′) *n.* A soft mica having a green hue and a high iron content.

Ce·lae·no[1] (sĭ-lē′nō). *Greek Mythology.* One of the **Pleiades** *(see).*

Celaeno[2] *n.* One of the six stars in the Pleiades cluster visible to the naked eye. [After CELAENO.]

cel·an·dine (sĕl′ən-dīn′, -dēn′) *n.* **1.** A plant, *Chelidonium majus,* native to Eurasia, having deeply divided leaves, yellow flowers, and yellow-orange juice. Also called "swallowwort." **2.** The **lesser celandine** *(see).* [Middle English *celidoine,* from Old French, from Medieval Latin *celidonia,* from Latin *chelidonia, chelidonium,* from Greek *khelidonion,* from *khelidōn,* swallow (the ancients associated the plant with the habits of the swallow).]

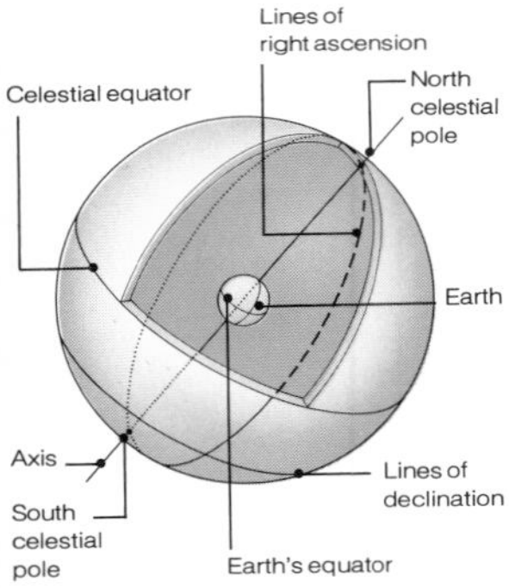

celestial sphere *The imaginary celestial sphere, with the observer at its center, is used to identify the position of a heavenly body.*

-cele[1] *suffix.* Indicates a tumor or hernia; for example, **cystocele.** [From Greek *kēlē*†, tumor.]

-cele[2], **-coel, -coele** *suffix.* Indicates a hollow chamber; for example, **hematocele, blastocoel, blastocoele.**

Celebes. See **Sulawesi.**

cel·e·brant (sĕl′ə-brənt) *n.* **1.** The priest officiating at the celebration of the Eucharist or other religious ceremony. **2.** A person who participates in a celebration.

cel·e·brate (sĕl′ə-brāt′) *v.* **-brated, -brating, -brates.** *—tr.* **1.** To mark or observe (a special day or event) with ceremonies of respect, festivity, or rejoicing. **2.** To perform (a religious ceremony). **3.** To extol; praise. *—intr.* **1.** To observe an occasion with appropriate ceremony, festivity, or merrymaking. **2.** To perform a religious ceremony. —See Synonyms at **observe.** [Latin *celebrāre,* to frequent, fill, celebrate, from *celeber,* numerous, much frequented.] **—cel·e·bra·tion** *n.* **—cel·e·bra·tor** *n.*

cel·e·brat·ed (sĕl′ə-brā′tĭd) *adj.* Famous.

ce·leb·ri·ty (sə-lĕb′rə-tē) *n., pl.* **-ties. 1.** A famous person. **2.** Notoriety or renown; fame. [Latin *celebritās* (stem *celebritāt-*), from *celeber,* numerous.]

ce·le·ri·ac (sə-lĭr′ē-ăk′, sə-lĕr′-) *n.* A variety of celery, *Apium graveolens rapaceum,* cultivated for its edible, turniplike root. [Unexplained derivative of CELERY.]

ce·ler·i·ty (sə-lĕr′ə-tē) *n.* Swiftness of action or motion; speed. [Middle English *celerite,* from Old French, from Latin *celeritās,* from *celer,* swift.]

cel·er·y (sĕl′ə-rē) *n., pl.* **-ies.** A plant, *Apium graveolens dulce,* native to Eurasia and widely cultivated for its edible stalks and its small seeds, used as seasoning. [French *céleri,* from Italian (Lombardy dialect) *seleri,* plural of *selero,* from Late Latin *selīnum,* from Greek *selinon*†, celery.]

ce·les·ta (sə-lĕs′tə) *n.* Also **ce·leste** (sə-lĕst′). A musical instrument having a keyboard and metal plates struck by hammers that produce bell-like tones. [French *célesta,* coined from *céleste,* celestial, from Latin *caelestis,* CELESTIAL.]

ce·les·tial (sə-lĕs′chəl) *adj.* **1.** Of or pertaining to the sky or the heavens. **2.** Of, from, or suggestive of heaven; divine or spiritual: *celestial beings.* **3.** Supreme in nature or kind; heavenly: *celestial happiness.* **4.** Of or pertaining to the Chinese people or to the former Chinese Empire. [Middle English, from Old French, from Latin *caelestis,* from *caelum*†, sky, heaven.]

celestial body *n.* Any object occurring naturally in space, especially a planet, star, or comet.

Celestial Empire *n.* The Chinese Empire. [Translation of Chinese *tiān cháo,* literally "celestial dynasty" (from the belief that the emperors were sons of Heaven).]

celestial equator *n.* A great circle on the celestial sphere in the same plane as the earth's equator. Also called "equinoctial," "equinoctial circle," "equinoctial line."

celestial globe *n.* A model of the celestial sphere showing the stars and other celestial bodies.

celestial guidance *n.* The guiding of missiles or spacecraft by reference to the positions of one or more celestial bodies.

celestial horizon *n.* See **horizon** (sense 2c).

celestial latitude *n.* The angular distance of a celestial body north (counted positive) or south (counted negative) of the ecliptic, measured on the great circle through the body and the poles of the ecliptic.

celestial longitude *n.* The angular distance of a celestial body from the vernal equinox, measured eastward along the ecliptic to its intersection with the great circle through the body and the poles of the ecliptic. Also called "longitude."

celestial mechanics *n. Used with a singular verb.* The science of the motion of celestial bodies under the influence of gravitational forces.

celestial navigation *n.* Ship or aircraft navigation based on the positions of celestial bodies. Also called "astronavigation."

celestial pole *n.* Either of two diametrically opposite points at which the extensions of the earth's axis intersect the celestial sphere.

celestial sphere *n.* An imaginary sphere of infinite extent with the earth at its center. The stars, planets, and other heavenly bodies appear to be located on its imaginary surface.

cel·es·tite (sĕl′ĭ-stīt′, sə-lĕs′tīt′) *n.* A white, red-brown, or light-blue strontium ore, essentially strontium sulfate, $SrSO_4$. [German *Zölestin,* from Latin *caelestis,* CELESTIAL (from its blue color).]

ce·li·ac, coe·li·ac (sē′lē-ăk′) *adj.* Of or relating to the abdomen. [Latin *coeliacus,* from Greek *koiliakos,* from *koilia,* abdomen, from *koilos,* hollow.]

celiac disease *n.* A chronic nutritional disturbance of infants and young children, caused by improper absorption of fats and resulting in malnutrition, distended abdomen, and diarrhea.

cel·i·ba·cy (sĕl′ə-bə-sē) *n.* The condition of being unmarried or sexually abstinent, especially by reason of religious vows. [Latin *caelibātus,* celibacy, from *caelebs*† (stem *caelib-*), unmarried.]

cel·i·bate (sĕl′ə-bĭt) *n.* One who remains unmarried, especially by religious vow, or abstains from sexual intercourse.
~adj. **1.** Unmarried. **2.** Not having sexual intercourse; chaste. [From Latin *caelebs*† (stem *caelib-*), unmarried.]

cell (sĕl) *n.* **1.** A small, narrow room, as in a prison or monastic institution. **2.** Any small and humble dwelling. **3.** A small religious house dependent on a larger one, such as a priory within an abbey. **4.** The primary organizational unit of a subversive or revolutionary political group, consisting of a few members usually living or working in the same place. **5.** A small group of Christian lay persons working for the propagation of the faith. **6.** *Biology.* The smallest structural unit of an organism that is capable of independent functioning, consisting of one or more nuclei, cytoplasm, various organelles, and inanimate matter, all surrounded by a semipermeable plasma membrane. Plant cells have cellulose outer cell walls. **7.** *Biology.* A small, enclosed cavity or space, such as a compartment in a honeycomb or within a plant ovary, or an area bordered by veins in an insect's wing. **8. a.** A single unit for electrolysis or for conversion of chemical into electric energy, usually consisting of a container with electrodes and an electrolyte. **b.** A single unit that converts radiant energy into electric energy: *a solar cell.* **9.** *Computer Science.* The smallest unit of data, capable of storing a single bit in part of a computer memory.
~v. **celled, celling, cells.** *—tr.* To store in a honeycomb. *—intr.* To live in a cell. [Middle English *celle,* from Old French, from Latin *cella,* cella, storeroom, chamber.]

cel·la (sĕl′ə) *n., pl.* **cellae** (sĕl′ē′). The inner room of an ancient Greek or Roman temple. [Latin *cella,* cella, CELL.]

cel·lar (sĕl′ər) *n.* **1.** A room used for storage, usually beneath the ground or under a building. **2. a.** A dark, cool room for storing wines. **b.** A stock of wines. **3.** *Informal.* The lowest level, especially in the standing of an athletic team.

~*tr.v.* **cellared, -laring, -lars.** To store in a cellar. [Middle English *celer*, from Norman French, from Late Latin *cellārium*, storehouse, larder, from Latin *cella*, storeroom, CELL.]

cel·lar·age (sĕl′ər-ĭj) *n.* **1.** A fee charged for storage in a cellar. **2.** The amount of storage space in a cellar. **3. a.** A cellar. **b.** Cellars collectively.

cel·lar·er (sĕl′ər-ər) *n.* The member of a monastic community responsible for the maintenance of adequate supplies of food and drink. [Middle English *celerer*, from Norman French, from Late Latin *cellāriārius*, from *cellārium*, CELLAR.]

cel·lar·et, cel·lar·ette (sĕl′ə-rĕt′) *n.* A cabinet used for storing bottles of wine. [Diminutive of CELLAR.]

cell division *n.* The process by which a cell divides and multiplies. See *amitosis, meiosis, mitosis.*

celled (sĕld) *adj.* Having cells of the specified type or number. Used in combination: *single-celled.*

Cel·li·ni (chə-lē′nē), **Benvenuto** (1500–71). Italian goldsmith and sculptor, famous also for his *Autobiography*, which described court life in Rome, Florence, and Paris and the siege of Rome (1527). *Perseus*, at the Loggia dei Lanzi, Florence, is considered his masterpiece as a sculptor.

cell membrane *n.* A **plasma membrane** (see).

cel·lo (chĕl′ō) *n., pl.* **-los.** A four-stringed instrument of the violin family, pitched lower than the viola but higher than the double bass and held upright between the knees. Also called "violoncello." [Short for VIOLONCELLO.] —**cel·list** (chĕl′ĭst) *n.*

cel·loi·din (sə-loid′n) *n.* A pure pyroxylin in which specimens being sectioned for microscopic examination are embedded. [CELL(U-LOSE) + -OID + -IN.]

cel·lo·phane (sĕl′ə-fān′) *n.* A thin, flexible, transparent cellulose material made from wood pulp and used as a moistureproof wrapping. [CELL(ULOSE) + -PHANE.]

cel·lu·lar (sĕl′yə-lər) *adj.* **1.** Of, pertaining to, or resembling a cell. **2.** Consisting of or containing a cell or cells. **3.** Containing a number of small compartments or cavities. Said of rock. —**cel·lu·lar·i·ty** (sĕl′yə-lăr′ə-tē) *n.*

cel·lu·lase (sĕl′yə-lās′, -lāz′) *n.* Any of several enzymes, found in fungi, bacteria, and lower animals, that hydrolyze cellulose. [CEL-LUL(OSE) + -ASE.]

cel·lule (sĕl′yōol) *n. Biology.* A small cell. [French, monk's cell, from Latin *cellula*, small apartment, diminutive of *cella*, CELL.]

cel·lu·lite (sĕl′yə-līt′) *n.* A fatty deposit, found particularly around the thighs and buttocks and the tops of the arms. [CELLUL(E) + -ITE.]

cel·lu·li·tis (sĕl′yə-lī′tĭs) *n.* Inflammation of subcutaneous tissue, causing pain and fever. [New Latin : Latin *cellula*, cell (see **cellule**) + -ITIS.]

cel·lu·loid (sĕl′yə-loid′) *n.* A colorless, flammable material made from nitrocellulose and camphor and used for toys, toilet articles, and photographic film. [Originally a trademark.]

cel·lu·lose (sĕl′yə-lōs′, -lōz′) *n.* A polysaccharide, ($C_6H_{10}O_5$)$_x$, of high tensile strength, the main constituent of plant cell walls and used in the manufacture of many fibrous products, including paper, textiles, and explosives. [French, from *cellule*, biological cell, CEL-LULE.] —**cel·lu·lo·sic** (sĕl′yə-lō′sĭk, -zĭk) *adj.*

cellulose acetate *n.* A cellulose resin used in lacquers, photographic film, transparent sheeting, and cigarette filters.

cellulose nitrate *n.* A tough thermoplastic, **nitrocellulose** (see).

cell wall *n.* The rigid outermost layer of a plant cell, consisting of cellulose and other polysaccharides.

celom. Variant of **coelom.**

Cel·si·us (sĕl′sē-əs, -shəs) *adj. Abbr.* **C** Of or pertaining to a temperature scale that registers the freezing point of water as 0°C and the boiling point as 100°C under normal atmospheric pressure. Also called "centigrade." The designation *Celsius* has been official since 1948, but *centigrade* remains in common use. [After Anders *Celsius* (1701–44), Swedish astronomer who devised the scale.]

celt (sĕlt) *n.* A prehistoric axlike tool. [Late Latin *celtis, celtes†*, chisel, a possible misreading of *certe*, surely, in a disputed text of the Vulgate (Job 19:24) (influenced in form by CELT).]

Celt (kĕlt, sĕlt) *n.* **1.** A member of an ancient people of western and central Europe, including the Britons, the Irish, and the Gauls. **2.** A speaker or a descendant of speakers of a Celtic language. [French *Celte*, singular of *Celtes*, from Latin *Celtae*, from Greek *Keltoi†*.]

Celt·ic (kĕl′tĭk, sĕl′-) *n. Abbr.* **C., Celt.** A subfamily of the Indo-European family of languages, subdivided into the Brythonic branch, consisting of Cornish, Welsh, and Breton, and the Goidelic branch, consisting of Irish Gaelic, Scottish Gaelic, and Manx. ~*adj.* Of or pertaining to the Celtic people and languages.

Celtic Church *n.* The Church as it existed throughout the British Isles until the late 6th century and as it remained, at variance with the Church of Rome, in Wales and Ireland for some time.

Celtic cross *n.* An upright cross superimposed on a circle.

Celt·i·cism (kĕl′tə-sĭz′əm, sĕl′-) *n.* A Celtic custom or idiom.

Celt·i·cist (kĕl′tə-sĭst, sĕl′-) *n.* A specialist in Celtic culture or Celtic languages.

Celtic Sea. A section of the Atlantic Ocean bounded by southern Ireland, Wales, Cornwall, Brittany, and southwest England.

cem·ba·lo (chĕm′bə-lō′) *n., pl.* **-los.** A harpsichord. [Italian, short for *clavicembalo*, from Medieval Latin *clāvicymbalum* : Latin *clāvis*, key + *cymbalum*, CYMBAL.] —**cem·ba·list** *n.*

ce·ment (sĭ-mĕnt′) *n.* **1.** Any of various construction adhesives, consisting essentially of powdered, calcined rock and clay materials,

cell division

THE BUILDING BLOCKS OF LIFE
Every living organism grows from a single cell

All growth is the result of cells splitting in two, a process triggered by the genetic instructions carried in the core, or nucleus, of each cell in the form of DNA (deoxyribonucleic acid). In single-celled animals such as amoebas, this division, or "mitosis," results in two separate but identical individuals. But in multicelled plants and animals, the process is more complex.

In humans, for example, the mother's ovum, which is a single cell just visible to the naked eye, begins to divide soon after conception. It becomes two, then four, then eight, then sixteen cells, and so on. The cells are identical at first. But as growth continues, the cluster of cells forms a hollow ball with two distinct layers—an

inner endoderm and an outer ectoderm. Later a third layer, the mesoderm, forms between the two.

Eventually, ectoderm cells give rise to skin or nerve tissue. Endoderm cells develop into glands, the digestive system, and the lungs. Mesoderm cells become blood, bone, and muscle. But every cell still carries within it the genetic blueprint for the entire individual. At birth a baby contains 20 trillion cells, and the number increases to about 50 trillion by adulthood. Then, apart from the replacement of blood cells and of tissue such as skin—which is renewed by cell division every few days—and the repair of wounds with scar tissue, all growth stops.

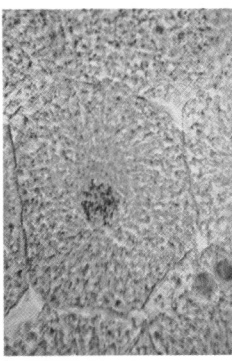
PROPHASE *Strands of chromosomes in the nucleus darken as they duplicate themselves before splitting.*

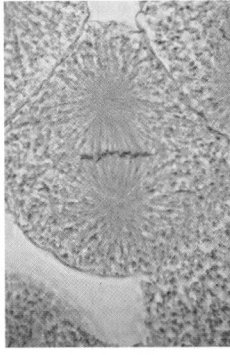
METAPHASE *Minute fibers draw the strands, which contain the cell's genetic instructions, into a line.*

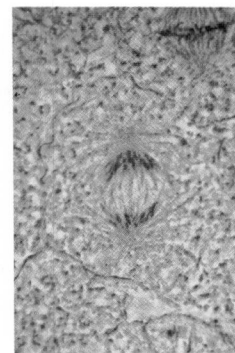
ANAPHASE *The fibers contract, pulling the strands apart into two identical sets of chromosomes.*

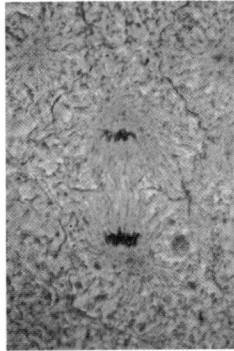
EARLY TELOPHASE *The separated sets—seen here more than 300 times lifesize—gather into clusters.*

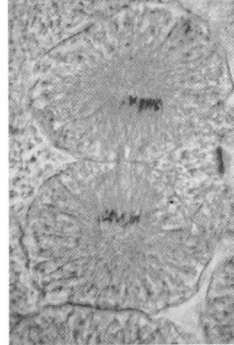
LATE TELOPHASE *Cell walls form around the two new nuclei to complete the hour-long process of division.*

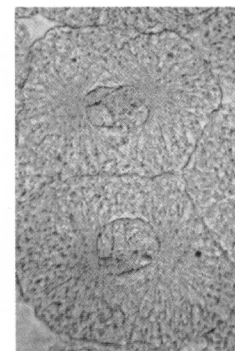
INTERPHASE *Chromosome strands spread through the nucleus until a new division begins 10–20 hours later.*

that form a paste with water and can be molded or poured to set as a solid mass, especially when mixed with sand and aggregate to form concrete. See **Portland cement, hydraulic cement. 2.** Any substance that hardens to act as an adhesive; glue. **3.** Any of various substances used in dentistry to form fillings or fix crowns in place. **4.** *Geology.* A chemically precipitated substance that binds particles of clastic rocks. **5. Cementum** (see). ~*v.* **cemented, -menting, -ments.** —*tr.* **1.** To bind with or as if with cement. **2.** To cover or coat with cement. **3.** To make firm and united; bind closely: *cement a friendship.* —*intr.* To become cemented. [Middle English *siment, cyment*, from Old French *ciment*, from Latin *caementum*, rough quarried stone, and its plural *caementa*, marble chips (used to make lime), from *caedere*, to cut, hew.] —**ce·ment·er** *n.*

ce·men·ta·tion (sē′mĕn-tā′shən) *n.* **1.** The process or result of cementing. **2.** A metallurgical coating process in which iron or steel is immersed in a powder of another metal, such as zinc, chromium, or aluminum, and heated to a temperature below the melting point of either. **3.** A similar process in which wrought iron is heated in a bed of charcoal to produce steel.

ce•ment•ite (sĭ-mĕn′tīt′) *n.* A hard, brittle iron carbide, Fe_3C, formed in steel with more than 0.85 percent carbon.

cement mixer *n.* A **concrete mixer** *(see).*

ce•ment•um (sĭ-mĕn′təm) *n.* A bony substance that covers the root of a tooth and anchors the tooth in the socket. [New Latin, from Latin *caementum,* rough stone, CEMENT.]

cem•e•ter•y (sĕm′ə-tĕr′ē) *n., pl.* **-ies.** A place for burying the dead; graveyard. [Middle English *cimitery,* from Late Latin *coemētērium,* from Greek *koimētērion,* sleeping room, burial place, from *koiman,* to put to sleep.]

cen. **1.** central. **2.** century.

cen–, ceno–. Variants of **coeno-.**

cen•a•cle (sĕn′ə-kəl) *n.* **1.** A small social group that meets to discuss shared interests; especially, a literary clique. **2.** A small dining room, usually on an upper floor. **3.** A retreat house. [Middle English, from Old French, from Late Latin *cēnāculum,* dining room, the Cenacle of the Last Supper, from Latin *cēna,* dinner.]

–cene *suffix.* Indicates a recent geological period; for example, **Miocene.** [From Greek *kainos,* new, fresh.]

cen•o•bite, coen•o•bite (sĕn′ə-bīt′, sē′nə-) *n.* A member of a monastic community. [Late Latin *coenobīta,* from *coenobium,* convent, from Greek *koinobion,* life in community : *koinos,* common + *bios,* life.] **—cen•o•bit•ic** (sĕn′ə-bĭt′ĭk, sē′nə-), **cen•o•bit•i•cal** (-ĭ-kəl) *adj.*

ce•no•gen•e•sis, coe•no•gen•e•sis (sē′nō-jĕn′ə-sĭs, sĕn′ō-) *n.* The environmentally determined development of characteristics or structures in an organism. [Greek *kainos,* new + GENESIS.] **—ce•no•ge•net•ic** (sē′nō-jə-nĕt′ĭk, sĕn′ō-) *adj.*

ce•no•spe•cies (sē′nə-spē′shēz, sĕn′ə-) *n., pl.* **cenospecies.** Any of a group of species that are capable of interbreeding: *Donkeys and horses are cenospecies.* [From Greek *koinos,* common + SPECIES.]

cen•o•taph (sĕn′ə-tăf′, -täf′) *n.* A monument erected in honor of a dead person or persons whose remains lie elsewhere. [French *cénotaphe,* from Latin *cenotaphium,* from Greek *kenotaphion,* empty tomb : *kenos,* empty + *taphos,* tomb.]

Ce•no•zo•ic (sē′nə-zō′ĭk, sĕn′ə-) *adj.* Of, belonging to, or designating the latest era of geological time, which includes the Tertiary and Quaternary periods and is characterized by the evolution of mammals, birds, plants, modern continents, and glaciation.
~n. Geology. The Cenozoic era. Preceded by *the.* [Greek *kainos,* new, fresh + -ZOIC.]

cense (sĕns) *tr.v.* **censed, censing, censes.** **1.** To perfume with incense. **2.** To offer incense to. [Middle English *censen,* short for *encensen,* to burn incense, from Old French *encenser,* from *encens,* INCENSE (noun).]

cen•ser (sĕn′sər) *n.* A vessel in which incense is burned, especially at religious ceremonies. Also called "thurible." [Middle English *censer,* from Old French *censier,* short for *encensier,* from *encens,* INCENSE (noun).]

cen•sor (sĕn′sər) *n.* **1.** An authorized examiner of literature, plays, films, or other material, who may prohibit what he considers morally, politically, or otherwise objectionable. **2.** An official, as in the armed forces or a prison, who examines personal mail and official dispatches to remove any information considered secret or improper. **3.** Any person who condemns or censures. **4.** In ancient Rome, either of two officials responsible for supervising the public census and public behavior and morals. **5.** *Psychoanalysis.* The agent responsible for censorship.
~tr.v. **censored, -soring, -sors.** To examine and expurgate. [Latin *cēnsor,* from *cēnsēre,* to assess, estimate, judge.] **—cen•so•ri•al** (sĕn-sôr′ē-əl, sĕn-sōr′-) *adj.*

cen•so•ri•ous (sĕn-sôr′ē-əs, sĕn-sōr′-) *adj.* **1.** Tending to reprimand or censure; highly critical. **2.** Expressing censure. [Latin *cēnsōrius,* of a censor, from *cēnsor,* CENSOR.] **—cen•so•ri•ous•ly** *adv.* **—cen•so•ri•ous•ness** *n.*

cen•sor•ship (sĕn′sər-shĭp′) *n.* **1.** The act or process of censoring. **2.** The office or authority of a Roman censor. **3.** A program or policy of censoring. **4.** *Psychoanalysis.* The inhibition, by either ego or superego, of conscious awareness of painful feelings or ideas.

cen•sur•a•ble (sĕn′shər-ə-bəl) *adj.* Deserving censure. **—cen•sur•a•ble•ness, cen•sur•a•bil•i•ty** *n.* **—cen•sur•a•bly** *adv.*

cen•sure (sĕn′shər) *n.* An expression of disapproval or severe criticism: *passed a vote of censure.*
~tr.v. **censured, -suring, -sures.** To criticize severely; express strong disapproval of; blame. —See Synonyms at **criticize.** [Latin *cēnsūra,* censorship, the office of a censor, from *cēnsor,* CENSOR.] **—cen•sur•er** *n.*

cen•sus (sĕn′səs) *n.* An official, periodic enumeration of population that usually also includes the collection of related demographic information. [Latin *cēnsus,* registration of citizens, from *cēnsēre,* to assess, tax.]

census taker *n.* One who gathers information for a census.

cent (sĕnt) *n. Abbr.* **c., C., ct.** **1. a.** *Symbol* **¢** A monetary unit equal to 1/100 of the U.S. dollar. **b.** A monetary unit equal to 1/100 of the dollar of various other countries, such as Australia, Canada, New Zealand, Hong Kong, and Zimbabwe. **c.** A monetary unit equal to 1/100 of various standard monetary units, such as the leone of Sierra Leone, the rand of South Africa, the rupee of Sri Lanka, and the yuan of China. **d.** A monetary unit equal to 1/100 of the shilling of Kenya, Tanzania, Uganda, and Somalia. See feature at **currency.** **2.** A coin or note worth one cent. [Old French, "hundred," from Latin *centum,* hundred.]

cent. **1.** centime. **2.** central. **3.** century.

cen•taur (sĕn′tôr′) *n.* **1.** *Greek Mythology.* One of a race of monsters, born of Ixion, having the head, arms, and trunk of a man and the body and legs of a horse. **2. Centaur.** Variant of **Centaurus.** [Middle English *Centaur,* from Latin *Centaurus,* from Greek *Kentauros*†, originally the name of a primitive Thessalian tribe.]

Cen•tau•rus (sĕn-tôr′əs) *n.* Also **Cen•taur** (sĕn′tôr′). A constellation in the Southern Hemisphere near Vela and Lupus. [Latin, CENTAUR.]

cen•tau•ry (sĕn′tôr′ē) *n., pl.* **-ries.** **1.** Any of several plants of the genus *Centaurium,* native to Eurasia; especially, *C. umbellatum,* having clusters of rose-purple flowers. **2.** A plant of the genus *Centaurea,* which includes the cornflower and knapweed. [Middle English *centaure,* from Old French *centauree,* from Late Latin *centaurea,* variant of Latin *centaureum,* from Greek *kentaureion,* centaury, from *Kentauros,* CENTAUR (its medicinal properties were supposedly discovered by the centaur Chiron, a physician).]

cen•ta•vo (sĕn-tä′vō) *n., pl.* **-vos.** **1. a.** A monetary unit equal to 1/100 of the Portuguese escudo. **b.** A monetary unit equal to 1/100 of the standard monetary unit of various countries in Central and South America, such as the cruzeiro of Brazil or the peso of Mexico. **c.** A monetary unit equal to 1/100 of the escudo of Cape Verde. See feature at **currency.** **2.** A coin worth one centavo. [Spanish, "a hundredth," from Latin *centum,* hundred.]

cen•te•nar•i•an (sĕn′tə-nâr′ē-ən) *n.* A person who is one hundred years old or older. [From Latin *centēnārius,* CENTENARY.] **—cen•te•nar•i•an** *adj.*

cen•ten•a•ry (sĕn-tĕn′ə-rē, sĕn′tə-nĕr′ē) *adj.* **1.** Of or pertaining to a 100-year period. **2.** Of or pertaining to a 100th anniversary.
~n., pl. **centenaries.** **1.** A 100-year period. **2.** A centennial. [Latin *centēnārius,* of a hundred, from *centēnī,* a hundred each, from *centum,* hundred.]

cen•ten•ni•al (sĕn-tĕn′ē-əl) *adj.* **1.** Of, pertaining to, or existing for a 100-year period. **2.** Occurring once every 100 years. **3.** Of or pertaining to a 100th anniversary.
~n. **1.** A 100th anniversary. **2.** A celebration of a centennial. [Latin *centum,* hundred + (BI)ENNIAL.] **—cen•ten•ni•al•ly** *adv.*

cen•ter (sĕn′tər) *n.* Also *chiefly British* **cen•tre.** *Abbr.* **ctr.** **1.** A point equidistant or at the average distance from all points on the sides or outer boundaries of anything. **2.** *Geometry.* **a.** A point equidistant from the vertexes of a regular polygon. **b.** A point equidistant from all points on the circumference of a circle or on the surface of a sphere. **3.** A point around which something revolves; an axis. **4.** A part of an object that is surrounded by the rest; a core: *a chocolate with a soft center.* **5.** An area that is roughly in the middle of a larger area: *the center of town.* **6. a.** The main area in which a particular activity is concentrated: *the center of the steel industry.* **b.** An area of special influence: *a center of power.* **c.** A place used for a specified purpose or activity: *an arts center.* **7.** A person or thing that is the chief object of attention, interest, activity, or emotion. **8.** A person, object, or group occupying a middle position. **9.** A political group or a set of policies representing a compromise between the right and the left. **10.** In some team sports, a player who holds a middle position on the field, court, or forward line. **11.** A collection of nerve cells in the central nervous system that controls a particular function: *the respiratory center.* **12.** A small conical hole made in a piece of work with a center punch in order to center a drill within it accurately. **13.** A bar with a conical point used to support work, as during turning in a lathe.
~v. **centered, -tering, -ters.** Also *chiefly British* **centre, -tred, -tring, -tres.** *—tr.* **1.** To place in or on a center. **2.** To concentrate at a center. **3.** To pass (a football) from the line to a back. *—intr.* To have a center; be concentrated: *The dispute centered on the issue of overtime rates.*
~adj. Also *chiefly British* **centre.** Being at the center; middle. [Middle English, from Old French, from Latin *centrum,* center, stationary point of a compass, from Greek *kentron,* sharp point, needle, from *kentein,* to prick.]

center bit *n.* A drill bit having a sharp center point, used in carpentry for boring holes.

cen•ter•board (sĕn′tər-bôrd′, -bōrd′) *n. Nautical.* A flat board or metal plate that can be lowered through the bottom of a sailing boat to prevent drifting and provide stability.

center field *n. Baseball.* **1.** The middle part of the outfield, behind second base. **2.** The position of center field. **—center fielder** *n.*

cen•ter•fold (sĕn′tər-fōld′) *n.* An illustration that fills the center spread of a magazine or newspaper.

center of gravity *n.* **1.** *Abbr.* **c.g.** The point in or near a body at which the gravitational potential energy of the body is equal to that of a single particle of the same mass located at that point and through which the resultant of the gravitational forces on the component particles of the body acts. **2.** The point of greatest importance, most concentrated activity, or the like; the focal point.

center of mass *n.* The point in a body or system of bodies through which all external forces may be considered to act and at which the entire mass is apparently concentrated. Also called "barycenter."

cen•ter•piece (sĕn′tər-pēs′) *n.* **1.** Something in a central position; especially a decorative object or arrangement placed at the center of a table. **2.** A part or item intended as the principal or most impressive feature: *the centerpiece of the party's manifesto.*

center punch *n.* A tool with a sharp point used in metalwork to mark centers or center lines on pieces to be drilled.

cen•tes•i•mal (sĕn-tĕs′ə-məl) *adj.* Of, pertaining to, or characterized

centaur *For the ancient Greeks the mythical centaurs—half men, half horses—represented lawlessness, animal passions, and barbarism. They were often pictured, as here, being ridden by Eros, the god of love—an allusion to their amorous nature.*

PRONUNCIATION KEY

ă, pat; ā, pay; âr, care;
ä, father, are; b, bib;
ch, church; d, deed; ĕ, pet;
ē, be; f, fife; g, gag; h, hat;
hw, which; ĭ, pit; ī, pie;
îr, pier; j, judge; k, kick;
l, lid, needle; m, mum;
n, no, sudden; ng, thing;
ŏ, pot; ō, toe; ô, paw, for;
oi, noise; ou, out; ŏŏ, book;
ōō, boot; p, pop; r, roar;
s, sauce; sh, ship, dish;
t, tight; th, thin, path;
th, this, bathe; ŭ, cut; ûr, fur;
v, valve; w, with; y, yes;
z, zebra, size; zh, vision;
ə, about, item, edible, gallop, circus, peaceful

IN FOREIGN WORDS:

à, *Fr.* ami; œ, *Fr.* feu, *Ger.* schön; ü, *Fr.* tu, *Ger.* über; KH, *Ger.* ich, *Scot.* loch; N, *Fr.* bon; y′, *Fr.* Compiègne

STRESS MARKS:

Primary stress: ′
in·cite′ (ĭn-sīt′)
Secondary stress: ′
in′sight′ (ĭn′sīt′)

by division into hundredths. [From Latin *centēsimus,* hundredth, from *centum,* hundred.] **—cen·tes·i·mal·ly** *adv.*

cen·tes·i·mo (sĕn-tĕs′ə-mō′; *Italian* chän-tā′zĕ-mō′) *n., pl.* **-mi** (-mē). A monetary unit equal to ¹/₁₀₀ of the lira of Italy and the shilling of Somalia. See feature at **currency.** [Italian, "hundredth," from Latin *centēsimus,* CENTESIMAL.]

cen·tés·i·mo (sĕn-tĕs′ə-mō′; *Spanish* sĕn-tĕ′sē-mō′) *n., pl.* **-mos.** A monetary unit equal to ¹/₁₀₀ of the balboa of Panama, the escudo of Chile, and the nuevo peso of Uruguay. See feature at **currency.** [Spanish, "hundredth," from Latin *centēsimus,* CENTESIMAL.]

cen·te·sis (sĕn-tē′sĭs) *n., pl.* **-ses** (-sēz′). The surgical puncture of a membrane or body cavity, usually for diagnostic purposes. [Greek *kentēsis,* act of pricking, from *kentein,* to prick.]

centi-, cent- *prefix. Abbr.* **c** Indicates a hundred or hundredth; for example, **centinewton, centiliter.** [French, from Latin *centum,* hundred.]

cen·ti·grade (sĕn′tĭ-grād′) *adj.* **1.** Consisting of or divided into 100 degrees. **2.** *Abbr.* **C** Designating the **Celsius** temperature scale. [French : CENTI- + GRADE.]

cen·ti·gram (sĕn′tĭ-grăm′) *n. Abbr.* **cg** One hundredth (10⁻²) of a gram.

cen·tile (sĕn′tīl, -tĭl′) *n.* **Percentile** (see).

cen·ti·li·ter (sĕn′tə-lē′tər) *n. Abbr.* **cl** One hundredth (10⁻²) of a liter. [French : CENTI- + LITER.]

cen·til·lion (sĕn-tĭl′yən) *n.* **1.** In British and German usage, the cardinal number represented by one followed by 600 zeros, usually written 10⁶⁰⁰. **2.** In U.S. and French usage, the cardinal number represented by one followed by 303 zeros, usually written 10³⁰³. [CENTI- + (MI)LLION.]

cen·time (sän′tēm′; *French* sän-tēm′) *n. Abbr.* **c., C., cent. 1. a.** A monetary unit equal to ¹/₁₀₀ of the French franc. **b.** A monetary unit equal to ¹/₁₀₀ of the franc of various other countries, such as Belgium, Luxembourg, and Switzerland. See feature at **currency. 2.** A coin worth one centime. [French, from *cent,* hundred. See **cent.**]

cen·ti·me·ter (sĕn′tə-mē′tər, sän′-) *n. Abbr.* **cm** A unit of length equal to one hundredth (10⁻²) of a meter or 0.3937 inch. [French *centimètre* : CENTI- + -METER.]

cen·ti·me·ter-gram-sec·ond system (sĕn′tə-mē′tər-grăm′sĕk′ənd) *n. Abbr.* **cgs, CGS** A coherent system of units for mechanics, electricity, and magnetism, in which the basic units of length, mass, and time are the centimeter, gram, and second.

cén·ti·mo (sĕn′tə-mō′) *n., pl.* **-mos. 1.** A monetary unit equal to ¹/₁₀₀ of various standard monetary units, such as the bolívar of Venezuela, the colón of Costa Rica, and the peseta of Spain. See feature at **currency. 2.** A coin worth one céntimo. [Spanish *céntimo,* from French *centime,* CENTIME.]

cen·ti·new·ton (sĕn′tə-nōō′tən, -nyōō′tən) *n. Abbr.* **cN** One hundredth (10⁻²) of a newton.

cen·ti·pede (sĕn′tə-pēd′) *n.* Any of various wormlike arthropods of the class Chilopoda, having numerous body segments, each with a pair of legs, the front pair modified into venomous biting organs. Compare **millipede.** [Latin *centipeda* : CENTI- + -PEDE.]

cen·ti·poise (sĕn′tə-poiz′) *n. Abbr.* **cP** One hundredth (10⁻²) of a poise.

cent·ner (sĕnt′nər) *n.* **1.** A unit of weight corresponding to the hundredweight, equal to 50 kilograms (110.23 pounds), used in several European countries. **2.** An assaying unit equal to one dram. [German *Zentner,* from Old High German *centenāri,* from Medieval Latin *centēnārius,* weighing a hundred pounds, from Latin, CENTENARY.]

cen·to (sĕn′tō) *n., pl.* **-tos.** A literary work pieced together from the works of several authors. [Latin *centō,* patchwork, cento.]

cen·tral (sĕn′trəl) *adj. Abbr.* **cen., cent. 1.** At, in, near, or being the center. **2.** Of, pertaining to, or constituting that from which other things proceed or upon which they depend: *central government.* **3.** Of great importance; essential: *the central theme of the book.* **4.** Easily reached from various points: *tried to find a central location for the new store.* **5.** Of or being a single source controlling all components of a mechanical system: *installed central air conditioning.* **6.** *Anatomy & Physiology.* **a.** Of or pertaining to the central nervous system. **b.** Of or pertaining to a centrum. **7.** *Phonetics.* Pronounced with the tongue in a neutral position, as *e* in *mister.* ~*n.* **1.** A telephone exchange. **2.** An operator at a telephone exchange. [Latin *centrālis,* from *centrum,* CENTER.] **—cen·tral·ly** *adv.*

Central African Republic. Formerly **U·ban·gi-Sha·ri** (ōō-bäng′gē-shär′ē, yōō-). A country in central Africa. Known from 1976 to 1979 as the Central African Empire, it was, from 1894 to 1960, Ubangi-Shari, one of the four territories of French Equatorial Africa. It was granted independence in 1960, and in 1966 a coup brought Jean Bédel Bokassa to power. In 1976 he had himself crowned Emperor Bokassa I. Following allegations of corruption and massacres, he fled, and the short-lived empire became once again the Central African Republic. The country, one of the world's poorest, is covered by savanna. More than 90 percent of its workers are subsistence farmers, but the republic does export diamonds, uranium, cotton, and coffee. Area, 622,984 square kilometers (240,472 square miles). Population, 3,000,000. Capital, Bangui. See map at **Chad.**

Central America. *Abbr.* **C.A.** See **Americas, the.**

Central A·mer·i·can States (ə-mĕr′ĭ-kən). The countries that comprise Central America, south of Mexico and north of Colombia.

central angle *n.* An angle having radii as sides and the center of a circle as its vertex.

central dogma *n.* The hypothesis of biochemical genetics that genetic information is carried only one way in the cell, from DNA to RNA to protein.

Central European Time *n. Abbr.* **CET, C.E.T.** The standard time adopted by some countries of Central Europe, Western Europe, and Africa. It is one hour ahead of Greenwich Mean Time. See map at **Time Zone.**

central heating *n.* A method of or apparatus for heating the rooms of a building, as a house or office, by means of water-filled radiators or hot-air vents connected to a central boiler or heat source.

Central Intelligence Agency *n. Abbr.* **CIA** The coordinating agency for the intelligence and espionage activities of the U.S. government.

cen·tral·ism (sĕn′trə-līz′əm) *n.* The act or policy of concentrating control, as of the making of decisions, in a central authority or organization. **—cen·tral·ist** *n.* **—cen·tral·is·tic** *adj.*

cen·tral·i·ty (sĕn-trăl′ə-tē) *n.* **1.** The state or quality of being central. **2.** The tendency to be or remain at the center.

cen·tral·ize (sĕn′trə-līz′) *v.* **-ized, -izing, -izes.** *—tr.* **1.** To draw into or toward a center; consolidate. **2.** To bring under a single, central authority. *—intr.* To come together at a center; concentrate. **—cen·tral·i·za·tion** *n.* **—cen·tral·iz·er** *n.*

central nervous system *n. Abbr.* **CNS** The portion of the vertebrate nervous system consisting of the brain and spinal cord. Compare **autonomic nervous system.**

Central Powers *pl.n.* The alliance comprising Germany, Austria-Hungary, Bulgaria, and Turkey in World War I.

central processing unit *n. Abbr.* **CPU** The central part of a computer, in which all the logical and arithmetical operations are performed.

Central Region. Since 1975 a Scottish local government region formed from Clackmannan, most of Stirlingshire, south Perthshire, and a small part of West Lothian. Extending from the Grampian Mts. to the Central Lowlands, it includes the Forth River valley. Stirling is the county town.

Central Standard Time *n. Abbr.* **CST, C.S.T.** The local civil time of the 90th meridian west of Greenwich, England, observed in the central United States, Canada, and Mexico and in some countries of Central America. It is six hours behind Greenwich Mean Time. See map at **Time Zone.** Also called "Central Time."

Central Sudanic *n.* A group of African languages of the Chari-Nile family, spoken in Chad, Central African Republic, Congo, Sudan, and Uganda.

centre. *Chiefly British.* Variant of **center.**

cen·tric (sĕn′trĭk) *adj.* Also **cen·tri·cal** (-trĭ-kəl). **1.** At, of, or having a center. **2.** *Physiology.* Of or originating at a nerve center. [Greek *kentrikos,* from *kentron,* CENTER.] **—cen·tri·cal·ly** *adv.* **—cen·tric·i·ty** (sĕn-trĭs′ə-tē) *n.*

-centric *suffix.* Indicates possession of a specified center; for example, **anthropocentric.**

cen·trif·u·gal (sĕn-trĭf′yə-gəl, -trĭf′ə-gəl) *adj.* **1.** Moving or directed away from a center or axis. Compare **centripetal. 2.** Operated by means of centrifugal force. **3.** *Physiology.* Transmitting impulses away from the central nervous system; efferent. **4.** *Botany.* Developing outward from a center or axis. Said of certain inflorescences. [New Latin *centrifugus* : Latin *centrum,* CENTER + *fugere,* to flee.] **—cen·trif·u·gal·ly** *adv.*

centrifugal force *n.* The component of apparent force on a body in curvilinear motion, as observed from that body, that is directed away from the center of curvature or axis of rotation; the equilibrant of centripetal force.

cen·tri·fuge (sĕn′trə-fyōōj′) *n.* Any apparatus consisting essentially of a compartment spun about a central axis, used to separate con-

centipede *Unlike the millipede, which has two pairs of legs on each body segment, the centipede has only a single pair of legs to each segment. It is also armed with venomous fangs for killing prey. Centipedes are found in most temperate and tropical countries and may grow up to 200 millimeters (8 inches) in length.*

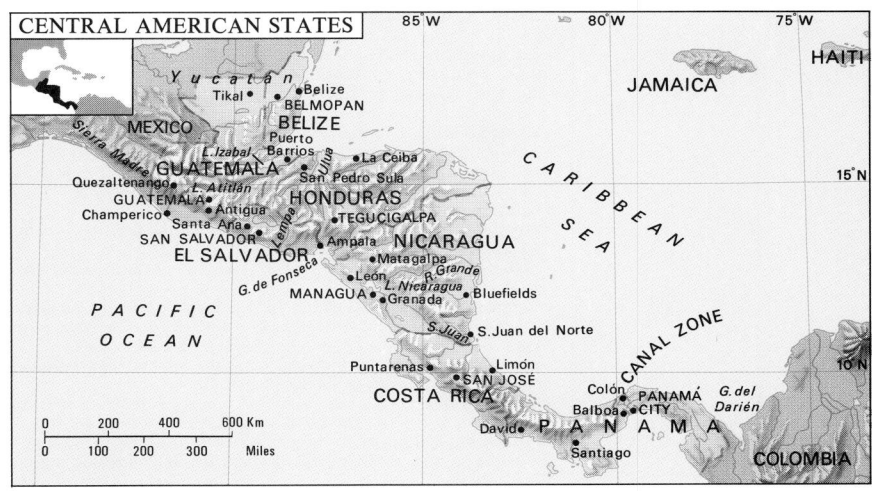

tained materials of different density or to simulate gravity with centrifugal force.

~*tr.v.* **centrifuged, -fuging, -fuges.** To separate, dehydrate, or test by means of a centrifuge. [French, from New Latin *centrifugus,* CENTRIFUGAL.] —**cen·tri·fu·ga·tion** (sĕn-trĭf′yə-gā′shən, -trĭf′ə-) *n.*

cen·tri·ole (sĕn′trē-ōl′) *n. Genetics.* Either of two tiny cylindrical organelles in most animal cells that form the poles of the spindle during mitosis. [Latin *centrum,* CENTER + -OLE.]

cen·trip·e·tal (sĕn-trĭp′ə-təl) *adj.* **1.** Directed or moving toward a center or axis. Compare **centrifugal. 2.** Operated by means of centripetal force. **3.** *Physiology.* Transmitting impulses toward the central nervous system; afferent. **4.** *Botany.* Developing inward toward the center or axis. Said of some forms of inflorescence. [New Latin *centripetus* : Latin *centrum,* CENTER + -PETAL.] —**cen·trip·e·tal·ly** *adv.*

centripetal force *n.* The component of force acting on a body in curvilinear motion that is directed toward the center of curvature or axis of rotation.

cen·trism (sĕn′trĭz′əm) *n.* A political philosophy of avoiding extremes by taking a position in the center.

cen·trist (sĕn′trĭst) *n.* One taking a position in the political center; a moderate. [CENTR(O)- + -IST.]

centro-, centr- *prefix.* Indicates center; for example, **centromere, centrist.** [Greek *kentron,* CENTER.]

cen·tro·bar·ic (sĕn′trə-bär′ĭk) *adj.* Of or relating to the center of gravity. [Late Greek *kentrobarikos,* from Greek *kentrobarikē,* the theory of the center of gravity : *kentron,* CENTER + *bareos,* genitive of *baros,* weight.]

cen·tro·cli·nal (sĕn′trə-klī′nəl) *n. Geology.* Designating a rock formation in which the strata slope down and inward toward a central point or area. [CENTRO- + -CLINE.]

cen·troid (sĕn′troid′) *n.* The center of mass of an object having constant density. [CENTR(O)- + -OID.]

cen·tro·mere (sĕn′trə-mîr′) *n. Genetics.* The region of a chromosome to which the spindle is attached during mitosis. [CENTRO- + -MERE.]

cen·tro·some (sĕn′trə-sōm′) *n. Genetics.* A small mass of differentiated cytoplasm containing the centriole. [CENTRO- + -SOME (body).] —**cen·tro·so·mic** (sĕn′trə-sō′mĭk, -sŏm′ĭk) *adj.*

cen·tro·sphere (sĕn′trə-sfîr′) *n. Genetics.* The mass of cytoplasm surrounding the centriole in a centrosome.

cen·trum (sĕn′trəm) *n., pl.* **-trums** or **-tra** (-trə). The major part of a vertebra, exclusive of the bases of the neural arch. [Latin, CENTER.]

cen·tum (kĕn′təm) *adj.* Of, pertaining to, or designating those Indo-European languages that retained the velar *k* and the labiovelar *kw* of primitive Indo-European. Compare **satem.** [From Latin *centum,* hundred (chosen as a typical word in which initial *c* represents initial Indo-European *k*).]

cen·tu·ple (sĕn′tə-pəl, sĕn-tōō′pəl, -tyōō′pəl) *adj.* Multiplied by a hundred; hundredfold.

~*tr.v.* **centupled, -pling, -ples.** To increase a hundredfold; multiply by a hundred. [French, from Late Latin *centuplus* : Latin *centum,* hundred + *-plus,* "-fold."]

cen·tu·pli·cate (sĕn-tōō′plĭ-kāt′, sĕn-tyōō′-) *tr.v.* **-cated, -cating, -cates.** To multiply by one hundred.

~*adj.* (-kĭt, -kāt′). Hundredfold. [Latin *centuplicāre,* from *centuplex,* hundredfold : *centum,* hundred + *-plex,* "-fold."] —**cen·tu·pli·ca·tion** (sĕn-tōō′plĭ-kā′shən, sĕn-tyōō′-) *n.*

cen·tu·ri·on (sĕn-tōōr′ē-ən, sĕn-tyōōr′-) *n.* An officer commanding a century in the Roman army. [Middle English *centurioun,* from Old French *centurion,* from Latin *centuriō* (stem *centuriōn-*), from *centuria,* CENTURY.]

cen·tu·ry (sĕn′chə-rē) *n., pl.* **-ries.** *Abbr.* **c., C., cen., cent. 1.** A period of 100 years. **2.** Each of the successive periods of 100 years before or since the advent of the Christian era. **3.** A unit of the Roman army, originally consisting of 100 men. **4.** One of the 193 groups into which the Roman people were divided for purposes of electing the consuls and other state officials. **5.** A group of 100 things. [Latin *centuria,* a group of a hundred, from *centum,* hundred.]

century plant *n.* Any of several fleshy plants of the genus *Agave,* some species of which bloom only once in 10 to 20 years and then die; especially, *A. americana,* having large grayish leaves and greenish flowers.

ce·orl (chä′ôrl′) *n.* In Anglo-Saxon England, a freeman of the lowest class. Also called "churl." [Old English *ceorl,* CHURL.]

cepe, cep (sĕp) *n.* An edible mushroom, *Boletus edulis,* having a brown shiny cap. [French *cèpe,* from dialect (Gascon) *cep,* from Latin *cippus,* stake.]

ceph·a·lad (sĕf′ə-lăd′) *adv. Anatomy.* Toward the head or anterior section. Compare **caudad.** [CEPHAL(O)- + -AD.]

ceph·al·al·gia (sĕf′ə-lăl′jə, -jē-ə) *n.* Pain in the head; headache. [CEPHAL(O)- + -ALGIA.]

ce·phal·ic (sə-făl′ĭk) *adj.* **1.** Of or relating to the head or skull. **2.** Located on, in, or near the head. [Old French *cephalique,* from Latin *cephalicus,* from Greek *kephalikos,* from *kephalē,* head.]

-cephalic *suffix.* Indicates head or skull; for example, **orthocephalic.** [From Greek *-kephalos,* -CEPHALOUS.]

cephalic index *n.* The ratio of the maximum width of the head to its maximum length, multiplied by 100. Compare **cranial index.**

ceph·a·lin (sĕf′ə-lĭn) *n.* A phosphatide derived from the brain and spinal cord, usually of cattle, and used as a homeostatic agent. [CEPHAL(O)- + -IN.]

ceph·a·li·za·tion (sĕf′ə-lə-zā′shən) *n. Zoology.* The gradually increasing concentration of nervous tissue and feeding and sensory organs at the head end during animal evolution. [CEPHAL(O)- + -IZ(E) + -ATION.]

cephalo-, cephal- *prefix.* Indicates head; for example, **cephalopod, cephalad.** [Latin, from Greek *kephalo-,* from *kephalē,* head.]

ceph·a·lo·chor·date (sĕf′ə-lə-kôr′dāt′) *adj.* Of or belonging to the subphylum Cephalochordata, which includes primitive forerunners of the vertebrates such as the lancelet.

~*n.* A cephalochordate animal. [New Latin *Cephalochordata* : CEPHALO- + CHORDATE.]

ceph·a·lo·pod (sĕf′ə-lə-pŏd′) *n.* Any of various mollusks of the class Cephalopoda, such as an octopus or nautilus, having a beaked head, an internal shell in some species, and prehensile tentacles. ~*adj.* Also **ceph·a·lop·o·dous** (sĕf′ə-lŏp′ə-dəs). Of, pertaining to, or belonging to the Cephalopoda. [New Latin *Cephalopoda* : CEPHALO- + -POD.] —**ceph·a·lop·o·dan** (sĕf′ə-lŏp′ə-dən) *n. & adj.*

ceph·a·lo·spo·rin (sĕf′ə-lə-spôr′ĭn, -spōr′ĭn) *n.* Any of a group of antibiotics, derived from the mold *Cephalosporium* and used to treat a wide variety of infections. [New Latin *Cephalosporium* : CEPHALO- + SPORE.]

ceph·a·lo·tho·rax (sĕf′ə-lə-thôr′ăks′, -thōr′ăks′) *n.* The anterior section of arachnids and many crustaceans, consisting of the fused head and thorax.

-cephalous *suffix.* Indicates a head; for example, **hydrocephalous.** [New Latin *-cephalus,* from Greek *-kephalos,* from *kephalē,* head.]

-cephalus *suffix.* Indicates an abnormality of the head; for example, **hydrocephalus.** [New Latin *-cephalus,* -CEPHALOUS.]

-cephaly *suffix.* Indicates a head; for example, **megalocephaly.** [From Greek *-kephalos,* -CEPHALOUS.]

Ce·phe·id variable (sē′fē-ĭd, sĕf′ē-) *n.* Either of two classes of intrinsically variable stars with exceptionally regular periods of light pulsation. Also called "Cepheid." [From CEPHEUS.]

Ce·pheus (sē′fyōōs′, sē′fē-əs, sĕf′ē-) *n.* A constellation in the Northern Hemisphere near Cassiopeia and Draco. [Latin *Cēpheus,* from Greek *Kēpheus,* a mythical king.]

ce·ra·ceous (sə-rā′shəs) *adj.* Waxy or waxlike. [Latin *cēra,* wax (see **cerate**) + -ACEOUS.]

ce·ram·al (sə-răm′əl) *n.* **Cermet** (*see*). [CERAM(IC) + AL(LOY).]

ce·ram·ic (sə-răm′ĭk) *n.* **1.** Any of various hard, brittle, heat-resistant and corrosion-resistant materials made by firing a nonmetallic mineral, as clay, at a high temperature. **2. a.** An object made of ceramic. **b. ceramics.** *Used with a singular verb.* The art or technique of making objects of ceramic, especially from fired clay or porcelain. [Probably French *céramique,* "of pottery," from Greek *keramikos,* from *keramos,* potter's clay, earthenware.] —**ce·ram·ic** *adj.* —**ce·ram·ist** *n.*

ce·rar·gy·rite (sə-rär′jə-rīt′) *n.* A gray to yellow mineral, AgCl, used as a source of silver. Also called "horn silver." [From Greek *keras,* horn + *arguros,* silver + -ITE.]

ce·ras·tes (sə-răs′tēz) *n., pl.* **cerastes.** Either of the two species of desert-dwelling, venomous snakes of the genus *Cerastes,* especially the **horned viper** (*see*). [Middle English, from Latin *cerastēs,* from Greek *kerastēs,* horned (serpent), from *keras,* horn.]

ce·rate (sîr′āt′) *n.* A hard, oily, fat- or wax-based solid, sometimes medicated, formerly applied to the skin directly or on dressings. [Latin *cērātum,* a wax plaster, wax salve, from *cēra,* wax, akin to Greek *kēros†,* wax.]

ce·rat·o·dus (sə-răt′ə-dəs) *n., pl.* **-duses.** Any of various extinct lungfishes of the genus *Ceratodus,* of the Triassic and Cretaceous periods. [New Latin *Ceratodus,* "horn-tooth" : Greek *keras* (stem *kerat-*), horn + *odous,* tooth.]

cer·a·toid (sĕr′ə-toid′) *adj.* Hornlike. [Greek *keratoeidēs* : *keras* (stem *kerat-*), horn + -OID.]

Cer·ber·us (sûr′bər-əs). *Greek & Roman Mythology.* A three-headed dog guarding the entrance of Hades. [Latin, from Greek *Kerberos†.*] —**Cer·be·re·an** (sûr′bə-rē′ən) *adj.*

cer·car·i·a (sər-kâr′ē-ə) *n., pl.* **-iae** (-ē-ē′) or **-as.** The parasitic larva of a trematode worm, having a tail that disappears in the adult stage. [New Latin, "the tailed one" : Greek *kerkos,* tail + *-aria,* from *-arius,* -ARY.] —**cer·car·i·al** *adj.*

cer·co·pi·the·coid (sûr′kə-pī-thē′koid′, -pĭth′ə-koid′) *adj.* Of or belonging to the family Cercopithecidae, which includes Old World monkeys such as the baboons, mandrills, macaques, and langurs. ~*n.* A member of the Cercopithecidae. [Latin *cercopithēcus,* long-tailed ape, from Greek *kerkopithēkos* : *kerkos,* tail + *pithēkos,* ape + -OID.]

cere¹ (sîr) *tr.v.* **cered, cering, ceres.** To wrap (a corpse, for example) in or as if in cerecloth. [Middle English *ceren,* to cover with wax, from Old French *cirer,* from Latin *cērāre,* from *cēra,* wax. See **cerate.**]

cere² *n.* A fleshy or waxlike swelling at the base of the upper part of the beak in certain birds, such as parrots and some birds of prey. [Middle English *sere,* from Old French *cire,* from Medieval Latin *cēra,* from Latin, wax. See **cerate.**] —**cered** (sîrd) *adj.*

ce·re·al (sîr′ē-əl) *n.* **1.** An edible grain, such as wheat, oats, or corn. **2.** A grass producing such a grain. **3.** A food prepared from such a grain, especially one eaten at breakfast. [Latin *cereālis,* of grain, "of Ceres," from *Cerēs,* CERES.] —**ce·re·al** *adj.*

cer·e·bel·lum (sĕr′ə-bĕl′əm) *n., pl.* **-lums** or **-bella** (-bĕl′ə). The structure of the brain responsible for regulation and coordination of

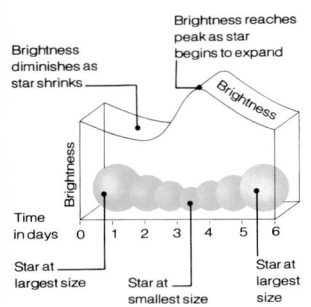

Cepheid variable *Delta Cephei, after which Cepheid variable stars are named, was discovered in 1784. It contracts and expands over a period of 5 days 9 hours. Such stars are used in the calculation of distances in the universe.*

complex voluntary movement, lying below the occipital lobes of the cerebral hemispheres. [Medieval Latin, from Latin, diminutive of *cerebrum,* brain.] —**cer·e·bel·lar** (sĕr′ə-bĕl′ər) *adj.*

cer·e·bral (sĕr′ə-brəl, sə-rē′-) *adj.* **1.** Of or pertaining to the brain or cerebrum. **2.** Appealing to or involving the workings of the intellect, rather than of the emotions. —**ce·re·bral·ly** *adv.*

cerebral cortex *n.* The extensive outer layer of gray matter of the cerebral hemispheres, largely responsible for higher nervous functions. Also called "mantle," "pallium."

cerebral hemisphere *n.* Either hemisphere of the cerebrum of the brain, divided by a deep groove running lengthwise.

cerebral palsy *n.* Impaired muscular power and coordination and weakness of the limbs resulting from brain damage usually occurring at or before birth.

cer·e·brate (sĕr′ə-brāt′) *intr.v.* **-brated, -brating, -brates.** To use the power of reason; think. [Back-formation from CEREBRATION.]

cer·e·bra·tion (sĕr′ə-brā′shən) *n.* The action of thinking; thought. [From Latin *cerebrum,* CEREBRUM.]

cerebro-, cerebr- *prefix.* Indicates the brain or cerebrum; for example, **cerebral, cerebration.**

cer·e·bro·side (sĕr′ə-brə-sīd′, sə-rē′-) *n.* Any of a group of lipids found in the brain and other nerve tissue, yielding on decomposition a fatty acid, an unsaturated amino alcohol, and a sugar. [CEREBR(UM) + -OS(E) + -IDE.]

cer·e·bro·spi·nal (sĕr′ə-brō-spī′nəl, sə-rē′brō-) *adj.* Of or pertaining to the brain and spinal cord. [CEREBR(UM) + SPINAL.]

cerebrospinal fluid *n.* The serumlike fluid that bathes the ventricles of the brain and the cavity of the spinal cord.

cerebrospinal meningitis *n.* An acute, infectious, epidemic meningitis that is caused by the bacterium *Neisseria meningitidis* and is often fatal. Also called "spinal meningitis," "cerebrospinal fever."

cer·e·bro·vas·cu·lar (sĕr′ə-brō-văs′kyə-lər, sə-rē′brō-) *adj.* Of or pertaining to the blood vessels supplying the brain or to the blood they carry.

cerebrovascular accident *n.* A sudden interruption of the supply of blood to the brain, caused by rupture (as in a cerebral hemorrhage) or blocking of a cerebral artery and resulting in a stroke.

cer·e·brum (sĕr′ə-brəm, sə-rē′-) *n., pl.* **-brums** or **-bra** (-brə). The large rounded structure of the brain occupying most of the cranial cavity, divided into two cerebral hemispheres and joined at the bottom by the corpus callosum. [Latin, brain.]

cere·cloth (sîr′klôth′, -klŏth′) *n.* Cloth coated with wax, formerly used for wrapping the dead. [Earlier *cered cloth,* waxed cloth. See **cerate.**]

cere·ment (sîr′mənt) *n. Often* **cerements.** Cerecloth. [French *cirement,* from *cirer,* to wax. See **cerate.**]

cer·e·mo·ni·al (sĕr′ə-mō′nē-əl) *adj.* Of, appropriate to, or characterized by ceremony; formal; ritual.
~*n.* **1.** The ceremonies to be observed on an official or religious occasion; a rite. **2.** The observance of these ceremonies. —**cer·e·mo·ni·al·ism** *n.* —**cer·e·mo·ni·al·ist** *n.* —**cer·e·mo·ni·al·ly** *adv.*

Usage: The similarity in form between *ceremonial* and *ceremonious* often leads to a confusion of senses, but a clear distinction is maintained in standard English. *Ceremonial* relates primarily to what involves or is involved in ceremony: *ceremonial occasions, ceremonial dress. Ceremonious* stresses formality and display, often in the unfavorable sense of pompousness: *He met me at the door and delivered a ceremonious greeting.*

cer·e·mo·ni·ous (sĕr′ə-mō′nē-əs) *adj.* Having, showing, or indicative of a fondness for ceremony; rigidly or elaborately formal. —See Usage note at **ceremonial.** —**cer·e·mo·ni·ous·ly** *adv.* —**cer·e·mo·ni·ous·ness** *n.*

cer·e·mo·ny (sĕr′ə-mō′nē) *n., pl.* **-nies. 1. a.** A formal act or set of acts performed as prescribed by ritual, custom, or etiquette. **b.** Such acts collectively; pomp. **2.** A conventional social gesture or act without intrinsic purpose. **3.** Strict observance of formalities or etiquette. —**stand on ceremony.** To insist on or behave with excessive formality. [Middle English *ceremonie,* from Old French, from Latin *caerimōnia†,* sacredness, religious rite.]

Če·ren·kov radiation (chə-rĕng′kôf′) *n. Physics.* The light emitted by a beam of high-energy particles passing through transparent, nonconducting material at a speed greater than the speed of light in that medium. [After Pavel A. *Čerenkov* (1904–), Russian physicist.]

Ce·res¹ (sîr′ēz). *Roman Mythology.* The goddess of agriculture; identified with the Greek goddess Demeter. [Latin *Cerēs.*]

Ceres² *n.* The first asteroid to be discovered (1801), having an orbit between Mars and Jupiter. [After CERES.]

ce·re·us (sîr′ē-əs) *n.* Any of several tall tropical American cacti of the genus *Cereus* or other genera, such as the **night-blooming cereus** (*see*). [New Latin, "candle" (from the shape), from Latin, taper, from *cēra,* wax. See **cerate.**]

ce·ric (sîr′ĭk, sĕr′-) *adj.* Of, pertaining to, or containing cerium, especially with valence 4.

ceric oxide *n.* A pale yellow-white powder, CeO_2, used in ceramics, to polish glass, and to sensitize photosensitive glass.

ce·rise (sə-rēs′, -rēz′) *n.* Purplish pink. [French, from Old French CHERRY.] —**cerise** *adj.*

ce·ri·um (sîr′ē-əm) *n. Symbol* **Ce** A lustrous, iron-gray, malleable metallic rare-earth element that occurs chiefly in the mineral monazite, exists in four allotropic states, is a constituent of lighter flint alloys, and is used in various metallurgical and nuclear applications. Atomic number 58, atomic weight 140.12, melting point

795°C, boiling point 3,468°C, specific gravity 6.67 to 8.23, valences 3, 4. [New Latin, after the asteroid CERES, discovered shortly before the element.]

cer·met (sûr′mĕt′) *n.* A material consisting of processed ceramic particles bonded with metal and used in high-strength and high-temperature applications. Also called "ceramal." [CER(AMIC) + MET(AL).]

CERN (sûrn) *n.* The research center of the European Organization for Nuclear Research in Geneva. [French *Conseil Européen Pour Recherches Nucléaires.*]

cer·nu·ous (sûr′nyŏŏ-əs) *adj. Botany.* Hanging downward; drooping; nodding. [Latin *cernuus†.*]

ce·ro·plas·tics (sîr′ō-plăs′tĭks, sĕr′ō-) *n. Used with a singular verb.* The art of modeling in wax. [Latin *cēra,* wax (see **cerate**) + PLASTICS.] —**ce·ro·plas·tic** *adj.*

ce·ro·tic acid (sə-rō′tĭk, -rŏt′ĭk) *n.* An acid, $C_{25}H_{51}COOH$, occurring in waxes, such as beeswax and carnauba wax. [From Latin *cērōtum,* wax plaster, from Greek *kērōton,* from *kēros,* wax. See **cerate.**]

ce·ro·type (sîr′ə-tīp′, sĕr′ə-) *n.* The process of preparing a printing surface for electrotyping by first engraving on a wax-coated metal plate. [Greek *kēros,* wax (see **cerate**) + -TYPE.]

ce·rous (sîr′əs) *adj.* Of, pertaining to, or containing cerium, especially with valence 3. [CER(IUM) + -OUS.]

cert. certificate; certification; certified.

cer·tain (sûrt′n) *adj.* **1.** Definitely known; determined beyond doubt. **2. a.** Sure; destined; bound: *certain to be a best seller.* **b.** Sure to happen; inevitable: *At such speeds, an accident would mean certain death.* **3.** Confident or convinced; having no doubt about something. **4.** Sound; dependable; unerring. **5.** Of a particular but unspecified character or identity: *has a certain rustic charm; a certain well-known politician.* **6.** Designating a person not known or previously mentioned: *a certain Mr. Harvey.* **7.** Some but not much; limited: *to a certain degree.* —See Synonyms at **sure.**
~*pron.* An indefinite but limited number; some. —**for certain.** Definitely; without doubt. [Middle English, from Old French, from Vulgar Latin *certānus* (unattested), from Latin *certus,* past participle of *cernere,* to decide, determine.]

Usage: Because *certain* implies an absolute lack of doubt, purists have criticized such constructions as *more certain, most certain, quite certain, fairly certain, very certain,* and so on. But such qualifications are widespread in all styles and dialects and would generally be considered to be standard.

cer·tain·ly (sûrt′n-lē) *adv.* **1.** Undoubtedly; indeed. **2.** By all means; of course. **3.** Admittedly.

cer·tain·ty (sûrt′n-tē) *n., pl.* **-ties. 1.** The fact, quality, or state of being certain. **2.** A clearly established fact. **3.** Something that is bound to happen.
Synonyms: assurance, certitude, conviction.

cer·tes (sûr′tēz, sûrts) *adv. Archaic.* Certainly; truly; verily. [Middle English, from Old French, from Vulgar Latin *certās* (unattested), from Latin *certus,* CERTAIN.]

cer·ti·fi·a·ble (sûr′tə-fī′ə-bəl) *adj.* **1.** Capable of being certified. **2.** Fit to be declared insane. —**cer·ti·fi·a·bly** *adv.*

cer·tif·i·cate (sər-tĭf′ĭ-kĭt) *n. Abbr.* **cert., ct. 1.** A document testifying to the truth of a given fact, such as a person's date of birth or ownership of shares. **2. a.** A document issued to a person completing a course of study. **b.** A document certifying that a person may officially practice in certain professions.
~*tr.v.* (-kāt′) **certificated, -cating, -cates.** To furnish with, testify to, or authorize by a certificate. [Middle English *certificat,* from Old French, from Medieval Latin *certificātum,* from the neuter past participle of Late Latin *certificāre,* to CERTIFY.]

certificate of deposit *n.* A certificate from a bank stating that the named person has a specified sum on deposit.

cer·ti·fi·ca·tion (sûr′tə-fĭ-kā′shən) *n. Abbr.* **cert. 1.** The act of certifying or certificating. **2.** The state of being certified. **3.** A certified statement.

cer·ti·fied (sûr′tə-fīd′) *adj. Abbr.* **cert. 1.** Guaranteed in writing; vouched for; endorsed. **2.** Holding a certificate. **3.** Declared legally insane.

certified check *n.* A check guaranteed by a bank to be covered by sufficient funds on deposit.

certified mail *n.* Uninsured first-class mail whose delivery is recorded by having the addressee sign for it.

certified public accountant *n. Abbr.* **C.P.A.** A public accountant who has received a certificate stating that he has met a state's legal requirements.

cer·ti·fy (sûr′tə-fī′) *v.* **-fied, -fying, -fies.** —*tr.* **1. a.** To confirm formally as true, accurate, or genuine, especially in writing. **b.** To guarantee as meeting a standard. **2.** To acknowledge in writing on the face of (a check) that the signature of the maker is genuine and that there are sufficient funds on deposit for its payment. **3.** To issue a license or certificate to. To declare legally insane. —*intr.* To testify: *certify to the facts.* —See Synonyms at **approve.** [Middle English *certifien,* from Old French *certifier,* from Late Latin *certificāre,* to make certain : Latin *certus,* CERTAIN + *facere,* to make.] —**cer·ti·fi·er** *n.*

cer·ti·o·rar·i (sûr′shē-ə-râr′ĭ, -râ′rē) *n. Law.* A writ from a higher court to a lower one requesting a transcript of the proceedings of a case for review. [Medieval Latin *certiorārī volumus,* "we wish to be informed" (words used in the writ), from *certiorāre,* to inform, certify, from *certior,* comparative of *certus,* CERTAIN.]

cer·ti·tude (sûr′tə-tōōd′, -tyōōd′) *n.* Complete assurance. —See Synonyms at **certainty.** [Middle English, from Late Latin *certitūdō,* from Latin *certus,* CERTAIN.]

ce·ru·le·an (sə-rōō′lē-ən) *adj.* Sky-blue; azure. [Latin *caeruleus,* dark-blue, azure, from *caelum,* sky. See **celestial.**]

ce·ru·men (sə-rōō′mən) *n.* A yellowish waxy secretion of the external ear; earwax. [New Latin, from Latin *cēra,* wax. See **cerate.**]

ce·ruse (sə-rōōs′, sĭr′ōōs′) *n.* **White lead** *(see).* [Middle English, from Old French, from Latin *cērussa,* perhaps from Greek *kēroessa* (unattested), white wax cosmetic, from *kēroun,* to wax, from *kēros,* wax. See **cerate.**]

ce·rus·site (sə-rŭs′īt′) *n.* Natural lead carbonate, PbCO₃, a lead ore. [German *Zerussit* : Latin *cērussa,* CERUSE + -ITE.]

Cer·van·tes Sa·a·ve·dra (sər-văn′tĕz sä′ə-vä′drə), **Miguel de** (1547-1616). Spanish writer. He is best known for *Don Quixote* (1605-15), the story of a middle-aged landowner who equips himself as a knight in armor and sets out into the world with his cunning squire, Sancho Panza, to right the wrongs of mankind.

cer·ve·lat (sûr′və-lăt′, -lät′) *n.* A kind of spiced smoked sausage made from pork or a mixture of beef and pork. [Obsolete French, from Italian *cervellata.*]

cer·vi·cal (sûr′vĭ-kəl) *adj. Anatomy.* Pertaining to the neck or the cervix. [New Latin *cervicalis,* from Latin *cervīx* (stem *cervic-*), CERVIX.]

cervical smear *n.* A specimen of material taken from the cervix of the uterus and examined for the presence of cancer.

cer·vi·ci·tis (sûr′vĭ-sī′tĭs) *n.* Inflammation of the cervix of the uterus. [New Latin : CERVIX + -ITIS.]

cer·vine (sûr′vīn′) *adj.* Pertaining to, resembling, or characteristic of a deer. [Latin *cervīnus,* from *cervus,* deer.]

cer·vix (sûr′vĭks) *n., pl.* **-vixes** *or* **-vices** (sûr′və-sēz′, sər-vī′sēz′). *Anatomy.* **1.** The neck. **2.** Any neck-shaped anatomical structure; especially, the narrow outer end of the uterus. [Latin *cervīx,* neck.]

Cesarean. Variant of **Caesarean.**

ce·si·um, cae·si·um (sē′zē-əm) *n. Symbol* **Cs** A soft, silvery-white ductile metal, liquid at room temperature, the most electropositive and alkaline of the elements, used in photoelectric cells and to catalyze hydrogenation of some organic compounds. Atomic number 55, atomic weight 132.905, melting point 28.5°C, boiling point 690°C, specific gravity 1.87, valence 1. [New Latin, from Latin *caesius,* bluish gray (from its blue spectral lines).]

cesium clock *n.* A form of atomic clock based on the frequency of the radiation absorbed in changing the state of cesium nuclei in a magnetic field. It is used in the definition of the second.

Československo. See **Czechoslovakia.**

ces·pi·tose, caes·pi·tose (sĕs′pĭ-tōs′) *adj.* Growing in dense tufts. or turflike clumps; matted. [New Latin *caespitosus,* from Latin *caespes,* turf.]

cess¹ (sĕs) *n.* Any of various taxes, especially one formerly levied in Britain, Ireland, and British India. [Variant of *sess,* from obsolete *assess* (noun). See **assess.**]

cess² *n. Irish.* Luck: *Bad cess to him!* [Perhaps from CESS (tax).]

ces·sa·tion (sĕ-sā′shən) *n.* A ceasing; a discontinuance. [Middle English *cessacioun,* from Latin *cessātiō* (stem *cessātiōn-*), from *cessāre,* to CEASE.]

ces·ser (sĕs′ər) *n. Law.* The end, as of a term or annuity; ceasing. [Norman French and Old French, from *cesser,* to CEASE.]

ces·sion (sĕsh′ən) *n.* The act or an instance of giving up or ceding something to which one has a claim; especially, a surrendering of territory to another country by treaty. [Middle English, from Old French, from Latin *cessiō* (stem *cessiōn-*), from *cēdere* (past participle *cessus*), to yield.]

ces·sion·ar·y (sĕsh′ə-nĕr′ē) *n., pl.* **-ies.** One to whom a cession is made; a transferee; an assignee.

cess·pool (sĕs′pōōl′) *n.* **1.** A covered hole or pit for receiving sediment or drained sewage. **2.** A filthy or disgusting place. Also called "cesspit." [Variant (influenced by POOL) of earlier *cesperalle,* drainpipe, from Middle English *suspiral,* from Old French *souspirail,* breathing hole, from *sou(s)pirer,* to breathe, SUSPIRE.]

ces·tode (sĕs′tōd′) *n.* Any flatworm of the class Cestoda, including tapeworms. [New Latin *Cestoda,* variant of *Cestoidea,* "ribbon-shaped ones" : Latin *cestus,* CESTUS (belt) + -OID.]

ces·tus¹ (sĕs′təs) *n., pl.* **-ti** (-tī′). A woman's belt or girdle, especially as formerly worn by a bride. [Latin *cestus,* girdle, belt, from Greek *kestos.*]

cestus² *n., pl.* **-tuses.** A covering for the hand, made of leather straps weighted with iron or lead, worn by ancient Roman boxers. [Latin *caestus, cestus,* boxing glove, from *caedere,* to strike.]

cesura. Variant of **caesura.**

CET, C.E.T. Central European Time.

ce·ta·cean (sĭ-tā′shən) *adj.* Of or belonging to the order Cetacea, which includes fishlike aquatic mammals such as the whale and porpoise.
~ *n.* Any mammal of the order Cetacea. [New Latin *Cetacea,* from the neuter plural of *cetaceus,* of whales : Latin *cētus,* whale, from Greek *kētos*† + -ACEAN.] —**ce·ta·ceous** (sĭ-tā′shəs) *adj.*

ce·tane (sē′tān′) *n.* A colorless liquid, C₁₆H₃₄, used as a solvent and in standardized hydrocarbons to determine the cetane number of diesel fuels. [Latin *cētus,* whale (so called because it belongs to a series of compounds found in sperm whale oil) + -ANE.]

cetane number *n.* The performance rating of a diesel fuel, expressed as the percentage of cetane that must be mixed with liquid methylnaphthalene to produce the same ignition performance as the diesel fuel being rated. Also called "cetane rating." Compare **octane number.**

cete (sēt) *n.* A company of badgers. [Probably from Latin *coetus, coitus,* meeting, reunion, assembly, COITUS.]

ce·ter·is par·i·bus (kā′tər-ĭs păr′ə-bəs, sĕt′ər-ĭs) *adv.* With all other factors or things being the same. [New Latin, with other things equal.]

ce·tol·o·gy (sĭ-tŏl′ə-jē) *n.* The zoology of whales and related aquatic mammals. [Latin *cētus,* whale (see cetacean) + -LOGY.] —**ce·to·log·i·cal** (sē′tə-lŏj′ĭ-kəl) *adj.* —**ce·tol·o·gist** *n.*

Ce·tus (sē′təs) *n.* A constellation in the equatorial region of the Southern Hemisphere near Aquarius and Eridanus. [Latin *cētus,* whale. See **cetacean.**]

ce·tyl alcohol (sēt′l) *n.* A waxy alcohol, C₁₆H₃₃OH, used in cosmetics and pharmaceutical products. Also called "hexadecanol."

Cé·vennes (sā-vĕn′). A mountain range at the extreme southeast of the Massif Central, France. Its highest peak is Mont Mézenc at 1,754 meters (5,753 feet). It is the source of many rivers, including the Allier, the Loire, the Lot, and the Tarn.

Ceylon. See **Sri Lanka.**

Cey·lon moss (sĭ-lŏn′) *n.* A red seaweed, *Gracilaria lichenoides,* of the East Indies, used for making agar.

Cé·zanne (sā-zăn′), **Paul** (1839-1906). French painter whose works led to the development of cubism and abstract art. His most famous paintings include a celebrated view of Mont Sainte-Victoire and *The Card Players.*

Cf The symbol for the element californium.

cf. 1. calfskin **2.** compare (Latin *confer.*)

c.f., C.F. cost and freight.

C/F *Accounting.* carried forward.

CFAFr. franc communauté financière africaine.

c.f.i., C.F.I. cost, freight, and insurance.

cg centigram.

c.g. 1. center of gravity. **2.** consul general.

C.G. 1. coast guard. **2.** commanding general. **3.** consul general.

cgs, CGS centimeter-gram-second (system of units).

ch chain (measurement).

ch. 1. chaplain. **2.** chapter. **3.** chief. **4.** church.

Ch. 1. chaplain. **2.** chief. **3.** China; Chinese. **4.** church.

c.h., C.H. 1. clearing-house. **2.** courthouse. **3.** customhouse.

Cha·blis (shă-blē′, shä-, shăb′lē) *n.* A very dry white Burgundy wine produced in the region of Chablis, in east-central France.

cha-cha (chä′chä) *n.* **1.** A rhythmic ballroom dance that originated in Latin America. **2.** The music for the cha-cha.
~ *intr.v.* **cha-chaed, -chaing, -chas.** To dance the cha-cha. [American Spanish *cha-cha-cha.*]

chac·ma (chăk′mə) *n.* A grayish-black baboon, *Chaeropithecus ursinus* (or *Papio ursinus*), of southern and eastern Africa. [Hottentot.]

cha·conne (shä-kôn′, -kŏn′, -kün′) *n.* **1.** A slow and stately dance of the 18th century. **2.** The music for this dance. **3.** A musical form consisting of variations based on a repeated harmonic pattern. Compare **passacaglia.** [French, from Spanish *chacona* (perhaps imitative of the castanets used for the music).]

chad (chăd) *n.* The small disks of paper, card, or the like removed by punching from paper tape or computer cards. [Perhaps alteration of CHAFF (rubbish).]

Chad (chăd). *French* **Tchad** (chäd). A landlocked country in north-central Africa, formerly a territory of French Equatorial Africa (1897-1960). The Sahara covers its northern half. Its population is predominately Muslim in the north with Bantu peoples in the south, a cultural rift reflected from 1965 in costly civil war. In 1980 fighting broke out between the factions of Hissené Habré and Col. Goukouni Oueddei, and Oueddei was aided by Libyan troops sent by Col. Muammar el-Qaddafi, who declared a union of the two countries (1981). The Libyans withdrew, and an Organization of African Unity peace-keeping force entered Chad (1982). When this failed, Habré's troops took the capital, and Oueddei fled into exile. Chad is one of the world's poorest countries and relies on foreign aid. Most of its people live as subsistence farmers, but some cotton is exported and oil has been discovered. Area, 1,284,000 square kilometers (495,624 square miles). Population, 5,700,000. Capital N'djamena. —**Chad·i·an** *n. & adj.*

Chad, Lake. A shallow lake in north-central Africa, partitioned between Chad, Cameroon, Nigeria, and Niger. It is watered by the Shari, and has no outlet. It reaches 20,700 square kilometers (7,990 square miles) in extent during the wet season between May and October, but shrinks to half that size by April. The lake was first sighted by Europeans in 1823.

cha·dor (chŭd′ər, chä′dôr′) *n.* A garment worn by women in Muslim and Hindu countries, especially Iran and India, made from a long, usually black cloth covering the upper body, head, and part of the face. [Hindi, from Persian *chaddar.*]

Chad·wick (chăd′wĭk′), **Sir James** (1891-1974). British physicist who discovered the neutron (1932), pointing the way to the fission process that, in turn, led to the atom bomb. He was awarded the Nobel Prize for physics (1935).

chae·ta (kē′tə) *n., pl.* **-tae** (-tē′). *Zoology.* A bristle, or seta, on the body of annelid worms, such as the earthworms, used in locomotion. [New Latin, from Greek *khaitē,* long hair.]

chae·tog·nath (kē′tŏg-năth′) *n.* Any of various marine worms of the phylum Chaetognatha, which includes the arrow worms. [New

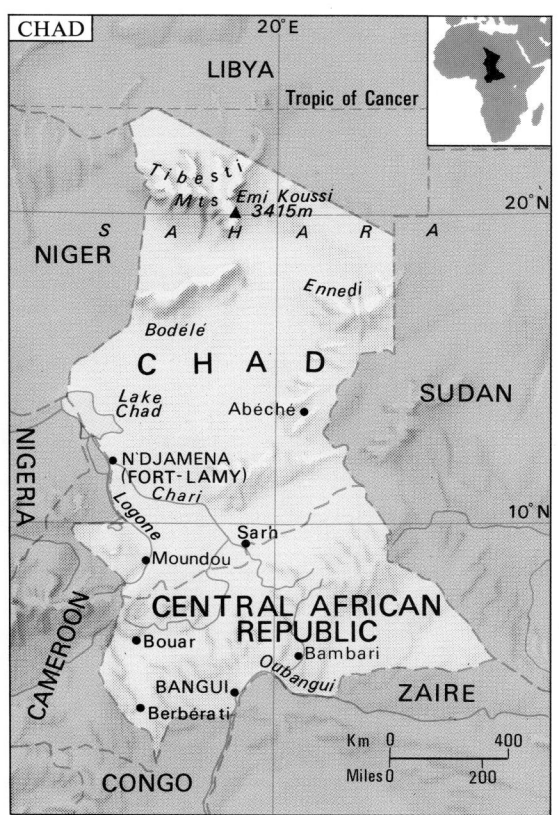

CHAD

LIBYA

Tropic of Cancer

20°E

NIGER

Tibesti Mts. ▲Emi Koussi 3415m

20°N

S A H A R A

Ennedi

Bodélé

C H A D

SUDAN

Lake Chad

Abéché ●

NIGERIA

●N'DJAMENA (FORT-LAMY)

Chari

10°N

Sarh ●

Moundou ●

CAMEROON

Logone

CENTRAL AFRICAN REPUBLIC

●Bouar

●Bambari

Oubangui

BANGUI ●

ZAIRE

●Berbérati

CONGO

Km 0   400
Miles 0   200

Latin *Chaetognatha,* "bristle-jaw" (so named from the spines at the jaws) : CHAETA + *gnathos,* jaw.]

chafe (chāf) *v.* **chafed, chafing, chafes.** —*tr.* **1.** To wear away or irritate by rubbing. **2.** To annoy; vex. **3.** To heat or warm by rubbing. —*intr.* **1.** To cause friction; rub. **2.** To become worn or sore from rubbing. **3.** To be or become irritated, impatient, or frustrated. ~*n.* **1.** Warmth, wear, or soreness produced by friction. **2.** Annoyance; irritation; vexation. [Middle English *chaufen,* from Old French *chauf(f)er,* to warm (by rubbing), from Vulgar Latin *calefāre* (unattested), variant of Latin *calefacere* : *calēre,* to be warm + *facere,* to make.]

cha·fer (chā′fər) *n.* Any of various beetles of the family Scarabaeidae, such as the cockchafer. [Middle English *cheaffer,* Old English *ceafor.*]

chaff[1] (chăf) *n.* **1.** The husks of grain after separation from the seed. **2.** Finely cut straw or hay used as fodder. **3.** Trivial or worthless matter. **4.** Strips of metal foil released in the atmosphere to inhibit radar. [Middle English *chaf(f),* Old English *ceaf.*]

chaff[2] *v.* **chaffed, chaffing, chaffs.** —*tr.* To make fun of good-naturedly; tease. —*intr.* To engage in good-natured teasing. ~*n.* Good-natured teasing; banter. [Probably a blend of CHAFF (trivia) and CHAFE (to irritate).] —**chaff′er** *n.*

chaf·fer (chăf′ər) *intr.v.* **-fered, -fering, -fers. 1.** To bargain or haggle. **2.** To bandy words; chatter. ~*n.* A bargaining or haggling. [Middle English *chaffare, cheapfare,* trade, merchandise, Old English *ceapfaru,* "bargain journey." See **cheap, fare.**] —**chaf·fer·er** *n.*

chaf·finch (chăf′inch) *n.* A small European songbird, *Fringilla coelebs,* having predominantly reddish-brown plumage and black and white wings. [Middle English *chaffynche,* Old English *ceaffinc* : CHAFF + FINCH.]

chafing dish *n.* A dish set above a heating device, used to cook or maintain the warmth of food at the table.

Cha·gall (shə-gäl′), **Marc** (1887-1985). Russian-born artist noted for his brilliant colors and dreamlike, fanciful imagery. Among his works is a huge painting, completed in 1964, for the ceiling of the Paris Opera House.

Cha·gas disease (shä′gəs) *n.* A South American form of trypanosomiasis caused by the protozoan *Trypanosoma cruzi,* which is carried by a bloodsucking insect. [First described by Carlos *Chagas* (1879-1934), Brazilian physician.]

cha·grin (shə-grĭn′) *n.* A feeling of embarrassment, annoyance, or humiliation caused by failure or disappointment. ~*tr.v.* **chagrined, -grining, -grins.** To cause to feel chagrin; discomfit. Usually used in the passive. [French, sadness, from *chagrin†,* sad.]

chain (chān) *n.* **1. a.** A connected, flexible series of links, usually of metal, used for binding, connecting, or other purposes. **b.** Such a set of links, often of precious metal and with pendants attached,

worn as an ornament or symbol of office. **2.** Anything that restrains or confines. **3. chains.** Bonds, fetters, or shackles. **4. chains.** Captivity or oppression; bondage. **5.** A number of events or processes that form a continuous or interconnected series: *a chain of coincidences.* **6.** A number of establishments, such as stores, restaurants, or theaters, under common ownership or management. **7.** A mountain range. **8.** *Chemistry.* A group of atoms bonded in a spatial configuration resembling a chain. **9. a.** A measuring instrument for surveying, consisting of 100 linked pieces of iron or steel. **b.** *Abbr.* **ch** The length of this instrument as a unit of length, equal to 100 links or 66 feet. Also called "Gunter's chain." **10. a.** A similar instrument used in engineering. **b.** *Abbr.* **ch** The length of this instrument used as a unit of length, equal to 100 feet. Also called "engineer's chain." —See Synonyms at **series.** ~*tr.v.* **chained, chaining, chains.** To bind or confine with or as if with a chain or chains: *The spectators of the football game were chained to their seats by excitement.* [Middle English *chayne, cheyne,* from Old French *chaine, chaeine,* from Latin *catēna,* CATENA.]

Chain (chān), **Sir Ernst Boris** (1906-79). British biochemist, born in Germany. He worked with Sir Howard Florey on antibiotic substances produced by various microorganisms and isolated and purified penicillin. With Sir Alexander Fleming, who discovered penicillin, Chain and Florey were jointly awarded the Nobel Prize for discovering the healing properties of the antibiotic (1945).

chain gang *n.* A group of convicts chained together and set to outdoor labor.

chain letter *n.* A letter instructing the recipient to send out multiple copies, so that its circulation increases in a geometrical progression as long as the instructions are followed.

chain mail *n.* Flexible armor of joined metal links or scales.

chain·man (chān′mən) *n., pl.* **-men** (-mĭn). In surveying, either of the two people who hold the measuring chain.

chain printer *n.* A printer used in computer systems in which the type is arranged in a continuous chain.

chain pump *n.* A pump that lifts water by means of containers, attached to an endless chain, that pass under water and up over a wheel.

chain·re·act (chān′rē-ăkt′) *intr.v.* **-acted, -acting, -acts.** To undergo a chain reaction.

chain reaction *n.* **1.** A series of events each of which induces or otherwise influences its successor. **2.** *Physics.* A self-sustaining series of nuclear reactions; especially, a fission reaction in which neutrons are released and cause other nuclei to split, leading to a succession of fissions and an increasing number of neutrons. **3.** *Chemistry.* A series of reactions in which one product of a reacting set is a reactant in the following set.

chain rule *n.* A mathematical theorem used in the differentiation of a function of a function. If *y* is a function of *x* and *u* is a function of *y,* then $du/dx = (du/dy) (dy/dx)$.

chain saw *n.* A power saw with teeth linked in an endless chain.

chain-smoke (chān′smōk′) *v.* **-smoked, -smoking, -smokes.** —*intr.* To smoke cigarettes or cigars in a continuous succession. —*tr.* To smoke (cigarettes or cigars) in a continuous succession. —**chain smoker** *n.*

chain stitch *n.* A decorative stitch in which loops are connected like the links of a chain. —**chain-stitch** (chān′stĭch′) *v.*

chain store *n.* Any of a group of retail shops under the same ownership.

chair (châr) *n.* **1. a.** A piece of furniture consisting of a seat, legs, back, and often arms, designed to accommodate one person. **b.** Any of various types of seats designed for a particular purpose. Used in combination: *a deck chair; a sedan chair.* **2. a.** A seat of office, authority, or dignity, such as that of a bishop. **b.** A professorship. **3.** The office or position of a person having authority. **4.** A person who holds such an office or position; especially, one who presides over a meeting. **5.** A metal block for supporting and holding railroad tracks in position. **6.** *Slang.* The electric chair. —**take the chair.** To preside as chairman at a meeting. ~*tr.v.* **chaired, chairing, chairs.** **1.** To preside over (a meeting). **2.** To install in a position of authority, especially as a presiding officer. **3.** *British.* To carry (a person) aloft in triumph, usually in a chair. [Middle English *chaiere, chare,* from Old French *chaiere,* bishop's chair, from Latin *cathedra,* chair, from Greek *kathedra,* seat : *kata-,* down + *hedra,* seat.]

chair car *n.* A parlor car.

chair lift *n.* A cable-suspended, power-driven chair assembly used to transport people up or down mountains. See **ski lift.**

chair·man (châr′mən) *n., pl.* **-men** (-mĭn). *Abbr.* **chm. 1.** A person who presides over an assembly, meeting, committee, or board. **2.** Formerly, one employed to carry a sedan chair. —See Usage note at **-person.** ~*tr.v.* **-manned, -manning, -mans.** To act as chairman of.

chair·man·ship (châr′mən-shĭp′) *n.* The office or term of a chairman.

chair·per·son (châr′pûr′sən) *n.* A person who presides over an assembly, meeting, committee, or board. —See Usage note at **-person.**

chair·wom·an (châr′wŏom′ən) *n., pl.* **-women** (-wĭm′ən). A woman who presides over an assembly, meeting, committee, or board. —See Usage note at **-person.**

chaise (shāz) *n.* **1.** Any of various light, open carriages, often with a collapsible hood; especially, a two-wheeled carriage drawn by one

chalice *The chalice has been used in the Christian church to celebrate the Eucharist since ancient times. At first it was usually made out of glass, semiprecious stone, or horn, but after Christianity was recognized by the Roman Empire in the fourth century, gold and silver became the usual materials, and chalices were often adorned with precious stones and carvings.*

chambered nautilus *A spiraling series of chambers fills the curves of a nautilus shell. The nautilus—a mollusk related to squids and octopuses—occupies the large outer chamber and fills the others with gas to control its buoyancy.*

horse. **2.** A **post chaise** *(see).* [French, chair, seat, from Old French, variant of *chaiere,* CHAIR.]

chaise longue (shāz lông′) *n., pl.* **chaise longues** or **chaises longues** (*pronounced as singular*). A reclining chair with a seat long enough to support the outstretched legs of the sitter. [French, "long chair."]

chak•ra (chŭk′rə) *n.* In yoga philosophy, one of the seven centers of spiritual energy in the human body. [Sanskrit, wheel.]

chalah. Variant of **challah.**

cha•la•za (kə-lā′zə, -lăz′ə) *n., pl.* **-zae** (-zē′) or **-zas. 1.** *Zoology.* Either of the two spiral bands of tissue in an egg, connecting the yolk to the lining membrane. **2.** *Botany.* The part of an ovule that is opposite the micropyle and that serves as a point of attachment for the integuments and the nucellus. [New Latin, from Greek *khalaza,* hailstone, small cyst.]

cha•la•zi•on (kə-lā′zē-ən, -ŏn′) *n., pl.* **-zi•a** (-zē-ə). A cyst in the eyelid formed by a blocked and swollen sebaceous gland. [New Latin, diminutive of Greek *khalaza,* small cyst, hailstone, CHALAZA.]

chal•can•thite (kăl-kăn′thīt′, kăl′kən-) *n.* A blue mineral, $CuSO_4 \cdot 5H_2O$, that occurs in some copper ores. [Latin *chalcanthum,* copper sulfate solution, from Greek *khalkanthon* : *khalkos,* CHALCO- + *anthos,* flower.]

chal•ced•o•ny (kăl-sĕd′n-ē) *n., pl.* **-nies.** A translucent to transparent milky or grayish quartz, SiO_2, with distinctive microscopic crystals arranged in slender fibers in parallel bands. [Middle English *calcedonie,* from Late Latin *chalcēdonius,* from Greek *khalkēdōn,* a mystical stone (Revelation 21:19), perhaps after *Khalkēdōn,* Chalcedon, town in Asia Minor.] **—chal•ce•don•ic** (kăl′sĭ-dŏn′ĭk) *adj.*

chal•cid (kăl′sĭd) *n.* Any of various minute wasps of the superfamily Chalcidoidea, of which the larvae of many species are parasitic on the larval stages of other insects. Also called "chalcid wasp." [New Latin *Chalcis* (genus), "copper (fly)" (from its metallic color and sheen), from Greek *khalkos,* copper.]

Chal•cid•i•ce (kăl-sĭd′ē-ə). *Greek* **Khal•ki•dhi•kí** (käl′kə-thī-kē′). Mountainous peninsula of northeast Greece. It terminates in the three parallel promontories of Kassandra, Sithonia, and Akte. The latter is the site of Mt. Athos, a monastic center of the Greek Orthodox Church.

Chal•cis (kăl′sĭs). *Greek* **Khal•kis** (käl′kĭs). The principal town on the island of Euboea in eastern Greece. A prosperous city-state from the 8th century B.C., its traders established settlements in Italy, Sicily, Syria, and mainland Greece.

chalco-, chalc- *prefix.* Indicates copper or bronze; for example, **Chalcolithic.** [Greek *khalkos,* copper.]

chal•co•cite (kăl′kə-sīt′) *n.* An important copper ore, essentially Cu_2S. [French *chalcos(ine)* : Greek *khalkos,* copper + -ITE.]

Chal•co•lith•ic (kăl′kə-lĭth′ĭk) *adj. Archaeology. Sometimes* **chalcolithic.** Of or relating to a period of man's development in which both stone and copper implements were in use.
∼*n.* The Chalcolithic period. Preceded by *the.* [CHALCO- + -LITH.]

chal•co•py•rite (kăl′kə-pī′rīt′) *n.* An important copper ore, essentially $CuFeS_2$. Also called "copper pyrites." [New Latin *chalcopyrites* : Greek *khalkos,* copper + PYRITES.]

chal•co•sis (kăl-kō′sĭs) *n.* Copper poisoning, sometimes with the formation of copper deposits in the tissues. [Greek *khalkos,* copper + -OSIS.]

Chal•de•a or **Chal•dae•a** (kăl-dē′ə). Area of southern Babylonia that produced the last Babylonian dynasty, the so-called Chaldean or neo-Babylonian dynasty. It achieved supremacy under Nabopolassar (626–605 B.C.) and reached its height under Nebuchadnezzar II, who extended the kingdom to include Syria and Palestine and rebuilt Babylon. The Persians destroyed the empire in 539 B.C.

Chal•de•an, Chal•dae•an (kăl-dē′ən) *n.* Also **Chal•dae•an, Chal•dee** (kăl′dē′). **1.** A member of an ancient Semitic people who ruled in Babylonia. **2.** The Semitic language of the Chaldeans. **3.** A person versed in occult learning; an astrologer, soothsayer, or sorcerer. **—Chal•da•ic** (kăl-dā′ĭk) *n. & adj.* **—Chal•de•an** *adj.*

Chal•dee (kăl′dē′) *n.* **1. Biblical Aramaic** *(see).* **2.** Variant of **Chaldean.**

chal•dron (chôl′drən) *n.* A unit of dry measure, as for coke, coal, or lime, equal to 32 to 36 bushels, formerly used in England. [Old French *chauderon,* augmentative of *chaudiere,* kettle, from Late Latin *caldāria,* CALDRON.]

cha•let (shă-lā′, shăl′ā) *n.* **1.** A house with a gently sloping overhanging roof, common in Switzerland and other Alpine regions. **2.** The hut of a herdsman in the Alps. **3.** A small, often wooden cottage, as one for vacationers, built in the style of a chalet. [French, from Swiss French, cabin, perhaps a diminutive of *cala* (unattested), stone shelter, from a Mediterranean root *cal-,* "stone."]

Cha•leur Bay (shə-lo͝or′). Inlet of the Gulf of St. Lawrence, *c.* 135 kilometers (85 miles) long and from 24 to 40 kilometers (15 to 25 miles) wide, between northern New Brunswick and the Gaspé Peninsula of eastern Quebec. It is a famous fishing ground for cod, herring, mackerel, and salmon.

Cha•lia•pin (shə-lyä′pĭn), **Feodor Ivanovich** (1873–1938). Russian opera singer. He is best known for his bass performances as Boris Godunov and Mephistopheles.

chal•ice (chăl′ĭs) *n.* **1.** A cup for the consecrated wine of the Eucharist. **2.** A cup or goblet. **3.** A cup-shaped blossom. [Middle English, from Norman French, from Latin *calix,* cup, goblet.]

chal•i•co•there (kăl′ĭ-kə-thîr′) *n.* Any of various extinct ungulate mammals of the Eocene to Pleistocene epochs, having distinctive three-clawed, three-toed feet. [New Latin *Chalicotherium* (genus), "fossil beast" : Greek *khalix,* stone, pebble (see **calcium**) + Greek *thērion,* diminutive of *thēr,* beast.]

chalk (chôk) *n.* **1.** A soft, compact calcium carbonate, $CaCO_3$, a type of limestone, with varying amounts of silica, quartz, feldspar, or other mineral impurities, generally gray-white or yellow-white and derived chiefly from the remains of small marine organisms. **2.** A piece of chalk or chalklike substance, often calcium sulfate, frequently colored, used for marking on a blackboard or other surface. **3.** A mark or picture made with chalk. **4.** A reckoning, as of credit given; tally. **—by a long chalk.** *British Informal.* By a wide margin: *This isn't the last you'll see of them by a long chalk.*
∼*tr.v.* **chalked, chalking, chalks. 1.** To mark, draw, or write with chalk. **2.** To smear or cover with chalk. **3.** To treat (soil, for example) with chalk. **—chalk up. 1.** To earn or score: *chalk up points.* **2.** To credit: *Chalk that up to experience.*
∼*adj.* Made with or consisting of chalk. [Middle English *chalk,* Old English *cealc,* from Latin *calx,* stone, pebble, from Greek *khalix.*] **—chalk•i•ness** *n.* **—chalk•y** *adj.*

chalk•board (chôk′bôrd′, -bōrd′) *n.* A panel, usually green or black, for writing on with chalk; blackboard.

chalk•stone (chôk′stōn′) *n. Medicine.* A **tophus** *(see).*

chalk stripe *n.* A striped fabric in two colors such that thin stripes of one color alternate with thick stripes of the other. Compare **pinstripe. —chalk-stripe** (chôk′strīp′) *adj.*

chal•lah, cha•lah, hal•lah (KHä′lə) *n.* A yeast-leavened white egg bread, usually in a braided loaf, traditionally eaten by Jews on the Sabbath, holidays, and ceremonial occasions. [Hebrew *ḥallāh.*]

chal•lenge (chăl′ənj) *n.* **1. a.** A call to engage in a contest or fight. **b.** Any act or statement likely to produce conflict or confrontation: *a challenge to the government's authority.* **2.** A demand for an explanation or justification. **3.** A sentry's call for identification. **4. a.** The quality of requiring full use of one's abilities, energy, or resources: *a career that offers plenty of challenge.* **b.** An undertaking having this quality. **5.** *Law.* A formal objection, especially to the qualifications of a juror or jury. **6. a.** A test of immunity following immunization treatment. **b.** A dose of the antigen or substance administered in such a test.
∼*v.* **challenged, -lenging, -lenges.** —*tr.* **1.** To call to engage in a contest or fight. **2.** To call into question; dispute: *a book that challenges established beliefs.* **3.** To order to halt and be identified. **4.** *Law.* To object formally to (a juror or jury, for example). **5.** To claim; call for: *events that challenge our attention.* **6.** To present a challenge to; stimulate: *a problem that challenges the imagination.* **7.** To test (a patient or laboratory animal) for immunity following immunization treatment. —*intr.* To make or give voice to a challenge. [Middle English *c(h)alenge,* accusation, challenge, from Old French *c(h)alenge,* from Latin *calumnia,* trickery, false accusation, from *calvī,* to deceive.] **—chal•lenge•a•ble** *adj.*

chal•leng•er (chăl′ən-jər) *n.* **1.** One that challenges. **2.** One who takes part in a sporting contest against the holder of a title or championship.

chal•leng•ing (chăl′ən-jĭng) *adj.* Calling for full use of one's abilities and resources; difficult but stimulating.

chal•lis (shăl′ē) *n.* A light fabric usually printed and made of wool, cotton, or rayon. [Perhaps from the surname *Challis.*]

chal•one (kăl′ōn′, kā′lōn′) *n.* Any of a group of internal secretions that inhibit a metabolic process. [Greek *khalōn,* present participle of *khalan,* to slacken, let down.]

cha•lyb•e•ate (kə-lĭb′ē-ĭt, -lē′bē-ĭt) *adj.* **1.** Impregnated with or containing salts of iron. **2.** Tasting like iron. Said of mineral water.
∼*n.* Water or medicine containing iron in solution. [New Latin *chalybeatus,* from Latin *chalybs,* steel, from Greek *khalups* (stem *khalub-*), from *Khalups*†, the Chalybes, ancient people in Asia Minor famous for their work in iron and steel.]

cham (kăm) *n. Archaic.* A Tatar or Mogul khan. [French, from Persian *khān,* from Turkish, KHAN.]

Cha•mae•leon, Cha•me•leon (kə-mēl′yən, -mē′lē-ən) *n.* A constellation in the southern polar region near Apus and Mensa. [Latin *chamaeleōn,* chameleon.]

cham•ae•phyte (kăm′ə-fīt′) *n.* A plant whose winter buds are situated close to the soil surface. [Greek *khamai,* on the ground + -PHYTE.]

cham•ber (chām′bər) *n.* **1.** A room where a person of authority, rank, or importance receives visitors. **2. a.** A hall for the meeting of an assembly, especially a legislative assembly. **b.** A legislative, judicial, or deliberative assembly. **3. a.** A room in a house, especially a bedroom. **b. chambers.** *Chiefly British.* A suite of rooms in an office building. **4.** *Usually* **chambers.** An office to which a judge withdraws, as for consultations with attorneys, and in which some legal matters can be dealt with. **5.** A place where state or municipal funds are received and held; a treasury. **6.** An enclosed space or compartment, as one in the body or in a piece of machinery; a cavity. **7. a.** An enclosed space in the bore of a gun that holds the charge. **b.** The part of a cylinder of a revolver that receives the cartridge.
∼*tr.v.* **chambered, -bering, -bers. 1.** To put in or as if in a chamber; enclose; confine. **2.** To furnish with a chamber. [Middle English *chambre,* from Old French, from Late Latin *camera, camara,* from Latin, vault, arched roof, from Greek *kamara.*]

chambered nautilus *n.* A cephalopod mollusk, *Nautilus pompilius,* of the Pacific and Indian oceans, having a partitioned shell lined with a pearly layer. Also called "pearly nautilus."

cham·ber·lain (chām′bər-lən) *n.* **1.** An official who manages the household of a sovereign or nobleman; a chief steward. **2.** An official who receives the rents and fees of a municipality; a treasurer. **3.** *Roman Catholic Church.* A papal attendant, usually honorary. [Middle English *chamberleyn,* from Old French *chamberlenc,* from Frankish *kamerling* (unattested), bedchamber servant : CHAMBER + -LING.]

Chamberlain (chām′bər-lĭn), **(Arthur) Neville** (1869–1940). As Conservative prime minister (1937–40), he advocated a policy of appeasement toward the fascist regimes of Europe. In the hope of preventing war, he visited Hitler three times in 1938 before reaching the Munich Agreement that recognized Hitler's annexation of the Sudetenland. Germany's subsequent invasion of Czechoslovakia forced Chamberlain to abandon his policy. In September 1939 he declared war on Germany after Hitler's invasion of Poland. He resigned as prime minister and joined Churchill's war cabinet (May 1940).

Chamberlain, Owen (1920–). U.S. physicist, who contributed to the development of the atom bomb. In 1955 he and Emilio Segrè discovered the antiproton by bombarding a copper target with high-energy protons. They were awarded the Nobel Prize in physics (1959).

Cham·ber·lin (chām′bər-lĭn), **Thomas Chrowder** (1843–1928). U.S. geologist, who with the astronomer Forest Ray Moulton (1872–1952) proposed the planetismal hypothesis (1906) of the formation of the planets in the solar system.

cham·ber·maid (chām′bər-mād′) *n.* A female servant who cleans and cares for bedrooms, now chiefly in hotels.

chamber music *n.* Music appropriate for performance in a private room or small concert hall and composed for a small group of instruments.

chamber of commerce *n. Abbr.* **C. of C.** An association of business persons and merchants for the promotion of business interests in its community. Also called "board of trade."

chamber orchestra *n.* A small orchestra, usually with only one instrument to a part, playing chamber music.

chamber pot *n.* A portable vessel used in a bedroom as a toilet.

Cham·bers (chām′bərz), **(Jay David) Whittaker** (1901–61). U.S. journalist. For some 15 years after 1924 Chambers was a member of the Communist Party, but in 1938 or 1939 he left the party. In 1948 he testified before the House Committee on Un-American Activities, implicating Alger Hiss as a fellow party worker. His autobiography, *Witness,* was published in 1952.

Cham·bé·ry (shäɴ-bā-rē′). Capital of Savoie department in the French Alps. It is popular with tourists.

cham·bray (shăm′brā′) *n.* A fine, lightweight fabric woven with white threads across a colored warp. [After CAMBRAI.]

cha·me·leon (kə-mēl′yən, -mē′lē-ən) *n.* **1.** Any of various tropical Old World lizards of the family Chamaeleontidae, characterized by their ability to change color. **2.** A lizard, the **anole** *(see).* **3.** A changeable or inconstant person. **4. Chameleon.** Variant of **Chamaeleon.** [Middle English *camelion,* from Latin *chamaeleōn,* from Greek *khamaileōn,* "ground lion" : *khamai,* on the ground + *leōn,* LION.] **—cha·me·le·on·ic** (kə-mē′lē-ŏn′ĭk) *adj.*

cham·fer (chăm′fər) *tr.v.* **-fered, -fering, -fers. 1.** To cut off the edge or corner of; bevel. **2.** To cut a groove in; flute.
~*n.* **1.** A flat surface made by cutting off the edge or corner of something, such as a block of wood. **2.** A furrow or groove, as in a piece of wood. [Perhaps a back-formation from *chamfering,* from French *chanfrein,* a bevel, from Old French *chanfrein(t),* past participle of *chanfraindre,* to break the edge off : *chant,* edge, rim, from Latin *canthus,* iron ring of a wheel, from Celtic + *fraindre,* to break, from Latin *frangere.*]

cham·ois (shăm′ē; shăm-wä′ *for sense 1 only*) *n., pl.* **chamois** (shăm′ēz; shăm-wä′ *for sense 1 only*). Also **cham·my, sham·my** (for sense 2) *pl.* **-mies. 1.** A hoofed mammal, *Rupricapra rupricapra,* of mountainous regions of Europe, having upright horns with backward-hooked tips. **2. a.** The soft leather made from the hide of this animal or others such as deer or sheep. **b.** A piece of such leather, used for polishing windows and the like. **3.** A moderate to grayish yellow. [Old French, probably from Late Latin *camox*†.]

cham·o·mile, cam·o·mile (kăm′ə-mīl′) *n.* **1.** Any of various plants of the genus *Anthemis;* especially, *A. nobilis,* an aromatic plant native to Eurasia, with finely dissected leaves and white flowers. **2.** Any of several similar plants of the genus *Matricaria;* especially *M. chamomilla,* native to Eurasia. [Middle English, from Old French *camomile,* from Late Latin *chamomilla,* from Greek *khamaimēlon,* "earth-apple" (referring to the apple scent of the flowers).]

Cha·mo·nix (shȧ-mô-nē′). Tourist resort in the Haute-Savoie department of the French Alps. It is close to Mont Blanc and is a winter sports center.

champ[1] (chămp) *v.* **champed, champing, champs.** Also **chomp** (chŏmp), **chomped, chomping, chomps.** *—tr.* To bite or chew upon noisily or impatiently. *—intr.* To work the jaws and teeth vigorously. **—champ at the bit.** To be impatient or frustrated at being held back. [Probably imitative.]

champ[2] *n. Informal.* A champion.

cham·pagne (shăm-pān′) *n.* **1. a.** A sparkling white wine produced in the Champagne region of France. **b.** A wine that is similar to champagne but is produced elsewhere. **2.** A pale orange yellow to grayish yellow.
~*adj.* Of, pertaining to, or being champagne.

Cham·pagne (shăm-pān′). Ancient province of northeast France, now chiefly in Marne department. The sparkling wine that takes its name from the province was first produced around 1700.

cham·paign (shăm-pān′) *n.* A stretch of level and open country; a plain.
~*adj.* Pertaining to or like a champaign; level and open. [Middle English *champayn,* from Old French *champagne,* from Late Latin *campānia,* from Latin *Campānia,* Campagna (province in central Italy), from *campus,* plain, field. See **camp, campaign.**]

cham·pak, cham·pac (chăm′păk′, chŭm′pŭk) *n.* A tree, *Michelia champaca,* of India and the East Indies, having yellow flowers and yielding a camphorlike substance and an oil used in perfumes. [Hindi *campak,* from Sanskrit *campaka,* of Dravidian origin.]

cham·pers (shăm′pərz) *n. British Slang.* Champagne. [CHAMP(AGNE) + -ERS (humorous suffix).]

cham·per·ty (chăm′pər-tē) *n., pl.* **-ties.** *Law.* An illegal sharing in the proceeds of a lawsuit by an outside party who has promoted it. [Middle English *champartie,* from Norman French, from Old French *champart,* division of farm produce : *champ,* field, from Latin *campus* (see **camp**) + *part,* PART.]

cham·pi·gnon (shăm-pĭn′yən) *n.* Any of various edible mushrooms, especially the common species *Agaricus campestris.* [French, from Old French *champigneul,* probably from Vulgar Latin *(fungus) campāniolus* (unattested), "(fungus) growing in the fields," from Late Latin *campānia,* countryside, CHAMPAIGN.]

cham·pi·on (chăm′pē-ən) *n.* **1.** One that holds first place or wins first prize in a contest, especially in sports. **2.** One who fights for, defends, or supports a cause or another person: *champion of the oppressed.* **3.** One who fights; a warrior.
~*tr.v.* **championed, -oning, -ons. 1.** To fight as champion of; defend; support: *"championed the government and defended the system of taxation"* (Samuel Chew). **2.** *Obsolete.* To defy or challenge. —See Synonyms at **support.**
~*adj.* Holding first place or prize; superior to all others: *She was the champion chess player in her class.* [Middle English *champi(o)un,* from Old French *champion,* from Medieval Latin *campiō* (stem *campiōn-*), warrior, from Latin *campus,* field. See **camp.**]

cham·pi·on·ship (chăm′pē-ən-shĭp′) *n.* **1.** The position or title of a champion. **2.** Defense or support; advocacy. **3.** *Often* **championships.** A competition or series of competitions to determine a winner.

Cham·plain, Lake (shăm-plān′). A lake, 201 kilometers (125 miles) long and from .8 to 22.5 kilometers (.5 to 14 miles) wide, forming part of the border between New York and Vermont. Lake Champlain is a link in the Hudson River–St. Lawrence waterway. There are many resorts in the scenic region.

Champlain, Samuel de (*c.* 1567–1635). French explorer. In 1605 he founded the colony of Port Royal, and three years later he founded Stadacona, on the site of present-day Quebec.

champ·le·vé (shäɴ-lə-vā′) *n.* A technique of decorating silver and other metals in which hollowed-out areas are filled with colored enamel. [From French *champ,* field, flat surface + *levé,* raised area.] **—champ·le·vé** *adj.*

Cham·pol·lion (shäɴ-pô-lyôɴ′), **Jean François** (1790–1832). French Egyptologist. In 1821, working from the Rosetta stone, he became the first person to decipher Egyptian hieroglyphics.

chance (chăns, chäns) *n.* **1. a.** The abstract nature or quality shared by unexpected, random, or unpredictable events; contingency. **b.** This quality regarded as a cause of such events; luck. **2. a.** A possibility: *There's just a chance that the letter has gone astray.* **b.** *Often* **chances.** Likelihood; probability: *What are the chances of our catching the plane?* **3. a.** An opportunity. **b.** A risk or gamble. **c.** A raffle or lottery ticket. **4. a.** An unexpected, random, or unpredicted event. **b.** A fortuitous event.
~*v.* **chanced, chancing, chances.** *—intr.* To happen by chance; occur by accident. *—tr.* To take the risk or hazard of. Often used in the phrase *chance it.* —See Synonyms at **happen. —chance on** (or **upon**). To find or meet accidentally; happen upon.
~*adj.* Occurring as or in consequence of chance. [Middle English, from Old French, from Vulgar Latin *cadentia* (unattested), "a fall," happening, from Latin *cadere,* to fall.]
Synonyms: *casual, desultory, haphazard, random.*

chan·cel (chăn′səl, chän′-) *n.* The space around the altar of a church for the clergy and choir, often enclosed by a lattice or railing. [Middle English *chauncel,* from Old French *chancel,* from Late Latin *cancellus,* altar, from Latin *cancellī,* grating, lattice, plural diminutive of *cancer,* lattice.]

chan·cel·ler·y, chan·cel·lor·y (chăn′sə-lə-rē, -slə-rē, chän′-) *n., pl.* **-ies. 1.** The rank or position of a chancellor. **2.** The office or department of a chancellor or the building in which it is located. **3.** The official place of business of an embassy, consulate, or legation. [Middle English *chancelerie,* from Old French, from *chancelier,* CHANCELLOR.]

chan·cel·lor (chăn′sə-lər, -slər, chän′-) *n. Abbr.* **C. 1.** Any of various officials of high rank; especially: **a.** A secretary to a king or nobleman. **b.** *Chiefly British.* The chief secretary of an embassy. **c.** The chief minister of state in some European countries, such as West Germany. **2. a.** *Chiefly British.* The honorary or titular head of a university. **b.** The president of certain American universities. **3.** An Episcopal bishop's administrative officer who is responsible especially for matters of canon law. [Middle English *cha(u)nceler,* from Norman French *chanceler,* from Old French *chancelier,* from Late

chameleon *A lizard that lives in trees and bushes in Africa and Asia. It is famous for its ability to change color to blend in with its surroundings. The skull is crested and the tongue is at least half as long as the animal itself—and in some species longer.*

chamois *Chamois are mountain antelopes native to Europe and the eastern Mediterranean. Their specially adapted rubbery hoof pads make them sure-footed even on slippery rocks. Adult males live apart from the herd for most of the year; but during the November breeding season they rejoin the herd, drive out the young males, and fight among themselves for possession of the females.*

Latin *cancellārius,* secretary, doorkeeper, from *cancellus,* grating, CHANCEL.] —**chan·cel·lor·ship** *n.*

Chancellor of the Exchequer *n.* The senior finance minister in the British Cabinet.

Chan·cel·lors·ville (chăn'səl-ərz-vĭl', -slərz-vĭl', chän'-). Village in northeastern Virginia, site of a major Civil War battle (May 2-4, 1863) in which the Confederate Army under Robert E. Lee defeated a Union force that was double its size. Gen. Stonewall Jackson was killed in the battle.

chance-med·ley (chăns'mĕd'lē, chăns'-) *n.* **1.** *Law.* An action, especially manslaughter, that is largely but not wholly accidental. **2.** A random or haphazard action. [Middle English, from Norman French *chance medlee,* "mixed chance" : Old French *chance,* CHANCE + *medlee,* past participle of *medler,* to MEDDLE.]

chanc·er (chăn'sər, chän'-) *n. British Informal.* One who risks doing something, especially something likely to incur disapproval, in the hope of avoiding loss or discovery.

chan·cer·y (chăn'sə-rē, chän'-) *n., pl.* **-ies. 1.** *Often* **Chancery.** One of the five divisions of the High Court of Justice in Great Britain, presided over by the Lord High Chancellor. **2. a.** A court of equity. Also called "court of chancery." **b.** The proceedings and practice of a court of equity. **3.** *British.* The political section of a diplomatic mission. **4.** *Ecclesiastical.* A diocesan office controlling archives and legal matters. **5.** An office of public record; an archive. **6.** A chancellery. —**in chancery. 1.** *Law.* In litigation or pending in a court of chancery. **2.** *Wrestling.* Having the head locked firmly in an opponent's arm and held against his chest. **3.** *Informal.* In an embarrassing or hopeless predicament. [Middle English *chancerie,* contraction of *chancelerie,* CHANCELLERY.]

chan·cre (shăng'kər) *n.* A dull-red, hard, insensitive lesion that is the first manifestation of syphilis. [French, from Latin *cancer,* ulcer, CANCER.] —**chan·crous** *adj.*

chan·croid (shăng'kroid') *n.* A soft, nonsyphilitic, usually venereal lesion of the genital region, caused by infection with the bacterium *Haemophilus ducreyi.* Also called "soft sore." [French *chancroide* : CHANCR(E) + -OID.]

chanc·y (chăn'sē, chän'-) *adj.* **-ier, -iest.** *Informal.* Uncertain or hazardous.

chan·de·lier (shăn'də-lîr') *n.* A branched fixture that holds a number of light bulbs or candles, and is usually suspended from a ceiling. [French, from Old French, from Vulgar Latin *candēlārum* (unattested), from Latin *candēlābrum,* CANDELABRUM.]

chan·delle (shăn-dĕl') *n.* A sudden, steep climbing turn of an aircraft, executed to alter flight direction and gain altitude simultaneously. [French, "candle," from Old French. See **chandler.**] —**chan·delle** *v.*

Chan·di·garh (chŭn'dē-gər). The joint capital of Punjab and Haryana states in northern India, situated below the foothills of the Himalayas. It was planned as the new Punjabi capital when Lahore became part of Pakistan (1947). The city, opened in 1953, was laid out in spacious rectangular blocks by a European team of architects under Le Corbusier.

chan·dler (chănd'lər, chänd'-) *n.* **1.** A person who makes or sells candles. **2.** A dealer in specified goods or equipment: *a ship's chandler.* [Middle English *chandeler,* from Old French *chandelier,* from *c(h)andelle,* candle, from Latin *candēla,* CANDLE.]

Chan·dler (chănd'lər), **Raymond** (1888-1959). U.S. novelist noted for creating the character Philip Marlowe, a cynical and incorruptible private eye. His works include *The Big Sleep* (1939), *Farewell My Lovely* (1940), and *The Long Goodbye* (1953).

Chandler wobble *n.* A small periodic variation in the location of the geographic poles on the Earth's surface. It has an interval of about 14 months. [After Seth Carlo *Chandler* (1846-1913), U.S. astronomer.]

chan·dler·y (chănd'lə-rē, chänd'-) *n., pl.* **-ies.** The stock or business of a chandler.

Chan·dra·se·khar (chŭn'drə-shā'kər), **Subrahmanyan** (1910-). Indian-born U.S. astronomer noted for his work on the evolution of stars, especially the small, low-mass white dwarf.

Cha·nel (shə-nĕl'), **Gabrielle,** known as "Coco" (1883-1971). French fashion designer, noted for her classic dresses and suits and later for her range of perfumes, particularly Chanel No. 5. She retired in 1939, but returned to work in 1954.

Cha·ney (chā'nē), **Lon** (1883-1930). U.S. actor. The son of deaf-mute parents, he developed his pantomime skill at an early age. With this skill and his mastery of make-up he brought eerily sensitive, human qualities to horribly ugly monsters in movies such as *The Hunchback of Notre Dame* (1923) and *The Phantom of the Opera* (1925).

Changan. See **Xi'an.**

Ch'ang Chiang. See **Chang Jiang.**

Ch'ang-chou or **Changchow.** See **Changzhou.**

Chang·chun or **Ch'ang-ch'un** (chăng'chōōn'). *Japanese* **Hsin·king** (shĭn'jĭng). Capital of Jilin province in northeast China. It grew in the early years of this century as a key station on the Chinese Eastern Railway, connecting the Trans-Siberian Railway with lines to Vladivostok and Port Arthur (now part of Lü-da).

Chang·de or **Ch'ang-te** (chăng'dŏō'). City of Hunan province, southeast China, on the Yüan River. The center of a "rice bowl," it was formerly a treaty port.

change (chānj) *v.* **changed, changing, changes.** —*tr.* **1. a.** To cause to be different; alter. **b.** To give a completely different form or appearance to; transform. **2.** To give and receive reciprocally; interchange. **3.** To exchange for or replace by another, usually of the same kind or category: *change one's name.* **4.** To lay aside or leave for another; switch: *change sides.* **5.** To transfer from (one vehicle) to another: *change planes.* **6.** To give or receive the equivalent of (money) in lower denominations or in foreign currency. **7.** To engage a higher or lower (gear) in a motor vehicle. **8.** To put fresh clothes or coverings on: *change a baby.* —*intr.* **1.** To become different or altered. **2.** To go from one phase to another. Used of the Moon. **3.** To pass from one state or position to another according to an established pattern: *Wait till the traffic lights change before you cross the street.* **4.** To transfer from one vehicle, as a train or airplane, to another. **5.** To put on other clothing: *She changed for dinner.* **6.** To become deeper in pitch. Used of the voice. —**change hands.** To pass from one owner to another. —**change off. 1.** To alternate with another person in performing a task. **2.** To perform two tasks at once by alternating or a single task by alternate means. ~*n.* Also '**change** (for sense 9). **1. a.** The process or condition of changing. **b.** An instance of changing; an alteration or modification: *make a few changes.* **c.** The replacing of one thing for another; substitution. **2.** A transition from one state, condition, or phase to another: *the change of seasons.* **3. a.** Something different; a substitution. **b.** Variety; novelty: *ate early for a change.* **4.** A different or fresh set of clothing, especially one kept in reserve. **5.** The money of smaller denomination given or received in exchange for money of higher denomination. **6.** The balance of money returned when an amount given is more than what is due. **7.** Any coins, especially when of low value. **8.** A pattern or order in which bells are rung. **9.** A market or exchange where business is transacted. —**ring the changes. 1.** To ring bells with every possible variation. **2.** To do or say something familiar or routine in a new and different way. [Middle English *changen,* from Old French *changier,* from Late Latin *cambiāre,* probably from Celtic.] —**chang·er** *n.* —**change·less** *adj.*
  Synonyms: alter, convert, modify, transform, transmute, vary.

change·a·ble (chān'jə-bəl) *adj.* **1.** Liable to change. **2.** Capable of being altered. **3.** Changing color or appearance when seen from different angles or in different lights: *changeable taffeta.* —**change·a·bil·i·ty, change·a·ble·ness** *n.* —**change·a·bly** *adv.*

change·ful (chānj'fəl) *adj.* Likely to change; variable.

change·ling (chānj'lĭng) *n.* **1.** A child believed to have been secretly exchanged for another, especially by fairies. **2.** *Archaic.* A changeable, fickle person.

change of life *n.* The **menopause** (see).

change over *intr.v.* To make a complete change; convert to a new system, position, or attitude: *The accounting department changed over to computers.*

change·o·ver (chānj'ō'vər) *n.* A conversion, as to a different method, attitude, or system.

change ringing *n.* The ringing of a set of chimes or bells with every possible unrepeated variation.

Chang Jiang or **Ch'ang Chiang** (chäng' jē-äng'). Also **Yang·tze Kiang** (yäng'tsĕ' jē-äng', kē-äng') or **Yang·tze.** Longest river of China. Rising in the Kunlun Shan in southwestern Qinghai province, it flows some 5,520 kilometers (3,430 miles) southeastward along the Tibet-Sichuan border and then mainly eastward to enter the East China Sea at Shanghai through a delta.

Chang·sha (chäng'shä'). Capital of Hunan province, south China, on the Xiang Jiang River. This historic trade center is set in rice-growing country and is famous for its handicrafts. Industries include engineering and chemicals and zinc and lead mining.

Ch'ang-te. See **Changde.**

Chang·zhou or **Ch'ang-chou** or **Chang·chow** (chäng'jō'). Formerly (until 1949) **Wu·tsin** (wōō'jĭn'). City in southern Jiangsu province, eastern China. It lies on the Grand Canal and is an agricultural and industrial center.

chan·nel[1] (chăn'əl) *n.* **1.** The bed of a stream or river. **2.** The deeper part of a river or harbor; especially, a deep navigable passage. **3.** A broad strait, especially one that connects two seas: *the English Channel.* **4.** A tubular passage for liquids. **5.** A course or passage through which something may be moved or directed: *a channel of thought.* **6.** *Often* **channels.** A means of communication or access, especially one that is officially recognized: *went through the proper channels.* **7.** *Electronics.* **a.** A specific frequency band for the transmission and reception of electromagnetic signals, as of television signals. **b.** Loosely, a television station: *What channel is it on?* **c.** A thin layer of semiconductor between the source and the drain of a field-effect transistor. **d.** Any path along which signals, data, or the like can travel. **8.** A trench, furrow, or groove. **9.** A rolled metal bar with a bracket-shaped section. Also called "channel bar," "channel iron." **10.** *Computer Science.* Any of the rows of punched holes in a punched-paper tape used to store information. ~*tr.v.* **channeled, channeling, channels.** Also *chiefly British* **channelled, -nelling. 1.** To make or cut channels in: *"No more shall trenching war channel her fields."* (Shakespeare). **2.** To form a channel or flute in. **3.** To direct or guide along some desired course. [Middle English *chanel,* from Old French, from Latin *canālis,* CANAL.]

channel[2] *n. Nautical.* A wood or steel ledge projecting from a sailing vessel's sides to spread the shrouds and keep them clear of the gunwales. [Earlier *chainwale* : CHAIN (fastening) + WALE (plank).]

Chan·nel Islands (chăn'əl). *Abbr.* **C.I.** An island group in the English Channel. They were settled by the Vikings and formed part of the duchy of Normandy, being united with the English crown in 1066. When England lost mainland Normandy in the 15th century, the islands remained possessions of the Crown. They have a measure of autonomy; British laws do not apply until approved by their own legislative bodies. The islands were occupied by the Germans in World War II. Jersey and Guernsey are famous for potato and tomato crops, woolen sweaters, and pedigreed cattle. Tourism is a major industry.

chan·nel·ize (chăn′ə-līz′) *tr.v.* **-ized, -izing, -izes.** To channel. **—chan·nel·i·za·tion** *n.*

chan·son de geste (shän-sôn′ də zhĕst′) *n., pl.* **chansons de geste** *(pronounced as singular).* A genre of Old French epic poem falling into cycles of poems celebrating the deeds of heroic or historical figures. [French, "song of heroic deeds."]

chant (chănt, chänt) *n.* Also *archaic* **chaunt** (chônt, chänt). **1.** A short, simple melody in which a number of syllables or words are sung on each note. **2.** A psalm or canticle sung in this manner. **3.** A repetitive rhythmic intonation of words or slogans, as by political demonstrators, striking workers, or spectators at a football game. **4.** A singsong way of speaking. **~v. chanted, chanting, chants.** *—tr.* To sing or intone as a chant. *—intr.* **1.** To sing; especially, to sing chants. **2.** To intone words or slogans in a repetitive, rhythmic manner. [Middle English *chanten,* to sing, from Old French *chanter,* from Latin *cantāre,* from *canere.*]

chant·er (chăn′tər, chän′-) *n.* **1.** A person who chants; especially, a chorister or precentor. **2.** The pipe on a set of bagpipes on which the melody is played.

chan·te·relle (shăn′tə-rĕl′, shän′-) *n.* An edible yellow mushroom, *Cantharellus cibarius,* having a pleasant fruity odor. [French, from New Latin *cantharella,* "little cup" (from its shape), diminutive of Latin *cantharus,* drinking vessel, from Greek *kantharos†.*]

chan·teuse (shän-tœz′) *n.* A woman singer, especially a nightclub singer. [French, feminine of *chanteur,* singer, from *chanter,* to sing, CHANT.]

chan·tey (shăn′tē, chăn′-) *n., pl.* **-teys.** Also **chan·ty,** *pl.* **-ties.** A song that is sung by sailors to the rhythm of their motions while working. [Probably from French *chantez,* imperative of *chanter,* to sing, CHANT.]

chan·ti·cleer (chăn′tə-klîr′, shăn′-) *n.* A cock or rooster. [Middle English *Chantecleer,* from Old French *Chantecler* (the cock in *Reynard the Fox*) : *chanter,* to CHANT + *cler,* CLEAR.]

Chan·til·ly (shăn-tĭl′ē). Town in the Oise department of northern France. It was famous in the 17th and 18th centuries for fine chantilly lace, no longer made there.

chan·try (chăn′trē, chän′-) *n., pl.* **-tries.** *Ecclesiastical.* **1.** In medieval times, an endowment to cover expenses for the saying of masses and prayers, usually for the soul of the founder of the endowment. **2.** An altar or chapel endowed for this purpose. [Middle English *chaunterie,* from Old French *chanterie,* from *chanter,* to CHANT.]

chanty. Variant of **chantey.**

Cha·nu·kah, Cha·nuk·kah, Ha·nu·kah, Ha·nuk·kah (кнä′nə-kə, hä′-) *n.* A Jewish festival beginning on the 25th day of the month of Kislev and lasting eight days. It commemorates the victory of the Maccabees over the Syrians in 165 B.C. and the rededication of the Temple at Jerusalem. Also called "Feast of Lights," "Feast of Dedication." [Hebrew *ḥanukkāh,* "dedication," from *ḥānakh,* he dedicated.]

Cha·nute (shə-nōōt′), Octave (1832–1910). U.S. engineer and aviation pioneer, born in France. After establishing himself as a civil engineer he studied aerodynamics; designed, improved, and flew many gliders; and encouraged the Wright brothers' experiments, greatly advancing man's quest for powered flight.

chao (dou) *n.* Also **hao** (hou). A monetary unit of Vietnam equal to 1/10 of a dong. See feature at **currency.** [Vietnamese.]

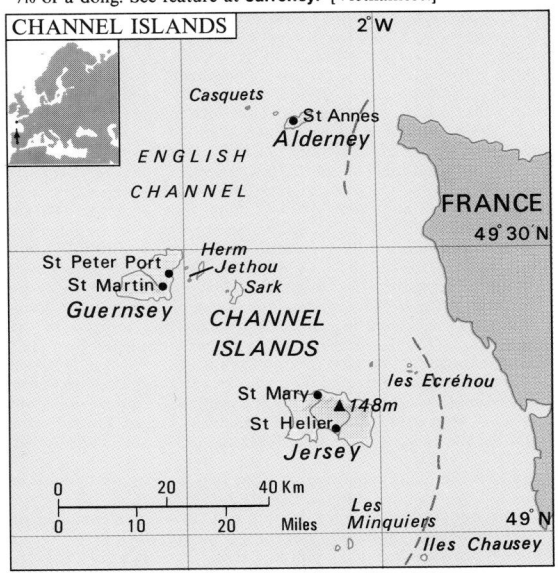

CHANNEL ISLANDS

Chao Phra·ya (chou prī′ə). River in north Thailand. It flows some 365 kilometers (225 miles) north to south, passing through Krung Thep (Bangkok) and emptying into the Gulf of Thailand.

cha·os (kā′ŏs′) *n.* **1.** A condition of total disorder or confusion. **2.** *Often* **Chaos.** The disordered state of unformed matter and infinite space supposed to have existed prior to the ordered universe according to some religious cosmological views. **3.** *Obsolete.* A vast abyss or chasm. [Latin, from Greek *khaos,* empty space, chaos.] **—cha·ot·ic** (kā-ŏt′ĭk) *adj.* **—cha·ot·i·cal·ly** *adv.*

chap¹ (chăp) *v.* **chapped, chapping, chaps.** *—tr.* To cause (the skin) to split or roughen, especially as a result of cold or exposure. *—intr.* To split or become rough and sore. **~n.** A sore roughening of the skin, caused especially by cold or exposure. [Middle English *chappen,* perhaps of Low German origin, akin to Middle Low German *kappen,* to chop off.]

chap² *n.* *Informal.* A man or boy; a fellow. [Short for CHAPMAN.]

chap. chapter.

cha·pa·re·jos, cha·pa·ra·jos (shăp′ə-rā′ōs) *pl.n.* Southwestern U.S. Heavy leather trousers worn by cowboys, **chaps** *(see).* [Probably from Mexican Spanish *chaparreras* (influenced by Spanish *aparejo,* equipment), from *chaparro,* CHAPARRAL.]

chap·ar·ral (shăp′ə-răl′) *n.* A dense thicket of shrubs and small trees, especially in the southwestern United States and Mexico, that is similar to the maquis of southern Europe. [Spanish, from *chaparro,* evergreen oak, probably from Basque *txapar,* diminutive of *saphar,* thicket.]

cha·pat·ti, cha·pa·ti (chə-pä′tē, -pät′ē) *n.* In the cookery of India, a thin flat cake of coarse unleavened bread. [Hindi.]

chap·book (chăp′bŏŏk′) *n.* A small book or pamphlet containing poems, ballads, stories, or religious tracts. [Originally, "a book sold by chapmen" : CHAP(MAN) + BOOK.]

chape (chāp, chăp) *n.* A metal tip or mounting on a scabbard or sheath. [Middle English, from Old French, *cape,* from Late Latin *cappa,* hood, "head covering," from Latin *caput,* head.]

cha·peau (shă-pō′) *n., pl.* **-peaux** (-pōz′) or **-peaus** (-pōz′). A hat. [French, from Old French *chapel,* from Vulgar Latin *cappellus* (unattested), diminutive of Late Latin *cappa,* head covering. See **chape.**]

chap·el (chăp′əl) *n.* **1.** A place of Christian worship that is smaller than and subordinate to a church. **2.** A place of worship in a college, hospital, or other institution. **3.** A recess or room in a church that has its own altar and is set apart for special or small services. **4. a.** In England and Wales, a place of worship for those not connected with or not members of the established church. **b.** In Scotland, a Roman Catholic church. **5.** The services held in a chapel. **6. a.** An association of workers in a print shop. **b.** *Obsolete.* A printing house or print shop. **~adj.** *Chiefly British.* Belonging to a Nonconformist church. Compare **church.** [Middle English, from Old French *chapele,* from Medieval Latin *cappella,* originally a shrine containing the cape of St. Martin of Tours, diminutive of Late Latin *cappa,* cape. See **chape.**]

chap·er·on, chap·er·one (shăp′ə-rōn′) *n.* A person, especially an older or married woman, who for propriety supervises a group of young unmarried people or accompanies a young unmarried woman in public. **~tr.v. chaperoned, -oning, -ons.** To act as chaperon to or for. **—See Synonyms at accompany.** [French, "hood," protection, protectress, from Old French, from *chape,* CHAPE.] **—chap·er·on·age** (shăp′ə-rō′nĭj) *n.*

chap·i·ter (chăp′ə-tər) *n.* *Architecture.* The capital of a column. [Middle English *chapitre,* from Latin *capitulum.* See **chapter.**]

chap·lain (chăp′lən) *n. Abbr.* **ch., Ch. 1.** A clergyman attached to a chapel. **2.** A clergyman attached to a hospital, prison, university, or other institution. **3.** A clergyman attached to a military unit or on board a ship. [Middle English *chapeleyn,* from Old French *chapelain,* from Medieval Latin *cappellānus,* from *cappella,* CHAPEL.] **—chap·lain·cy** (-sē), **chap·lain·ship** (-shĭp′) *n.*

chap·let (chăp′lĭt) *n.* **1.** A wreath or garland for the head. **2.** A string of beads; especially, a string of prayer beads having one third the number of a rosary's beads. **3.** *Architecture.* A small molding carved in a way resembling a string of beads. [Middle English *chapelet,* from Old French, diminutive of *chapel,* CHAPEAU.] **—chap·let·ed** *adj.*

Chap·lin (chăp′lĭn), **Sir Charles Spencer,** known as "Charlie" (1889–1977). British film star, director, producer, choreographer, and composer, knighted in 1975. His early films, in which he created a tramp in baggy trousers with a bowler hat and twirling cane, made him an immediate success. His productions included *The Kid* (1920), *The Gold Rush* (1924), *City Lights* (1931), *Modern Times* (1936), and *The Great Dictator* (1940). His later films include *Monsieur Verdoux* (1947), in which he played a murderer; and *Limelight* (1952), in which he portrayed an aging music-hall comic. A victim of the McCarthy anti-Communist witch-hunt of the early 1950's, he left the United States for Switzerland in 1952.

chap·man (chăp′mən) *n., pl.* **-men** (-mĭn). *Archaic.* A dealer or merchant, especially a peddler. [Middle English *chapman,* Old English *cēapman* : *cēap,* trade (see **cheap**) + MAN.]

Chapman (chăp′mən), **George** (*c.* 1560–1634). English poet, dramatist, and scholar noted for his translations of Homer's *Iliad* (1598–1611) and *Odyssey* (1616), which later prompted John Keats to compose his sonnet *On First Looking Into Chapman's Homer.*

Chapman, John, known as "Johnny Appleseed" (*c.* 1775–1845). U.S. pioneer and hero of many legends. Born in New England, he

chanterelle *An edible fungus with the color and smell of apricot. It is found in woodlands, particularly beech woods, from July to December.*

settled in the Ohio River valley after 1800, traveling widely over the countryside to plant apple seeds and prune the young trees.

chap·pal (chŭp′əl, chăp′-) *n.* A type of Indian sandal, usually made of leather. [Hindi.]

chap·pie (chăp′ē) *n. Chiefly British Informal.* A fellow; chap.

chaps (chăps, shăps) *pl.n.* Heavy leather trousers without a seat, worn over ordinary trousers by cowboys to protect their legs. Also called "chaparejos." [Short for Mexican Spanish *chaparreras,* CHAPAREJOS.]

chap·ter (chăp′tər) *n. Abbr.* **chap., ch., c., C. 1.** Any of the main divisions of a book or other piece of writing, usually numbered or titled. **2.** A distinct period or sequence of connected events, as in history or in a person's life. **3.** *British.* A numbered division of a session of Parliament relating to a specific Act of Parliament. **4.** *Ecclesiastical.* **a.** An assembly of the canons of a cathedral or collegiate church. **b.** The canons collectively. **5.** *Ecclesiastical.* An assembly of the members or representatives of a religious community or knightly order. **6.** A local branch of an organization, as a college fraternity or a club. [Middle English *chapitre,* from Old French, from Late Latin *capitulum,* from Latin, small head, chapiter, from *caput,* head.]

chapter and verse *n.* The exact source or authority for a statement or action. [Referring to citing the chapter and verses of books of the Bible.]

chapter house *n.* **1.** A building in which the chapter of a cathedral or monastery assembles. **2.** A house in which a chapter of a fraternity or sorority lives and holds its meetings.

char[1] (chär) *v.* **charred, charring, chars.** —*tr.* **1.** To burn the surface of; scorch. **2.** To reduce to charcoal by incomplete combustion. —*intr.* To become charred. **—See Usage note at burn.**
~*n.* A substance that has been charred; charcoal. [Back-formation from CHARCOAL.]

char[2] *n., pl.* **chars** or collectively **char.** Also **charr.** Any of several fishes of the genus *Salvelinus,* related to the trout; especially, the widely distributed *S. alpinus.* [17th century : origin obscure.]

char[3] *n.* **1.** A chore or odd job, especially a household task. **2.** A charwoman.
~*intr.v.* **charred, charring, chars. 1.** To do small jobs, tasks, or chores. **2.** To work as a charwoman. [Middle English *char(re),* piece of work, Old English *cerr,* piece of work, a turning, from *cierran,* to turn, from Germanic.]

char·a·banc (shăr′ə-băng′) *n., pl.* **-bancs.** *Chiefly British.* A large bus or coach, often used for sightseeing, group outings, or the like. [French *char à bancs,* "carriage with benches."]

char·a·cin (kăr′ə-sĭn) *n.* Also **char·a·cid** (-sĭd). Any of numerous chiefly tropical freshwater fishes of the family Characidae, related to the carp, many of which are popular aquarium fishes. [New Latin *Characinidae* (earlier family name) : *Charax* (genus), from Greek *kharax* (stem *kharak-*), a kind of fish, pointed stake + -IDAE.]

char·ac·ter (kăr′ək-tər) *n.* **1.** The combination of qualities or features that distinguishes one person, group, or thing from another. **2.** One such distinguishing feature or attribute; a characteristic. **3.** The moral or ethical nature of a person or group. **4.** Moral or ethical strength; integrity and fortitude. **5.** The quality of being distinctive or outstanding: *an old house of great character.* **6.** Status; capacity; role: *in his character as a father.* **7.** *Informal.* **a.** A person: *There's some character at the door asking to see you.* **b.** A person who is amusing or eccentric. **8.** A person portrayed in a drama, novel, or other artistic piece. **9.** A statement regarding an employee's competence and dependability; reference. **10.** A symbol or mark used in a writing system, as a letter of the alphabet. **11.** *Printing.* A letter, punctuation mark, numeral, or the like, cast in type and usually occupying a fixed amount of space. **12.** A style of printing or writing. **13.** *Computer Science.* **a.** One of a set of symbols, as letters or numbers, arranged to express information. **b.** The multi-bit code representing a character. **14.** *Genetics.* A structure, function, or attribute determined by a gene or group of genes. —See Synonyms at **disposition, quality, type. —in** (or **out of**) **character.** Consistent (or inconsistent) with the usual nature of a person.
~*adj.* **1.** Specializing in roles portraying odd, eccentric, or unusual personality types: *a character actor.* **2.** Calling for the abilities of such an actor: *a character part.*
~*tr.v.* **charactered, -tering, -ters.** *Archaic.* **1.** To portray, describe, or represent. **2.** To write, print, engrave, or inscribe. [Learned respelling of Middle English *caracter,* from Old French *caractere,* from Latin *charactēr,* character, mark, instrument for branding, from Greek *kharaktēr,* engraved mark, brand, from *kharassein,* to brand, sharpen, from *kharax* (stem *kharak-*), pointed stake.]

character assassination *n.* The malicious slandering of the reputation of a person, especially a public figure.

char·ac·ter·is·tic (kăr′ək-tə-rĭs′tĭk) *adj.* Pertaining to, indicating, or constituting a distinctive character, quality, or disposition; typical.
~*n.* **1.** A distinguishing feature or attribute. **2.** *Mathematics.* The integral part of a logarithm as distinguished from the mantissa: *6 is the characteristic of the logarithm 6.3214.* **—char·ac·ter·is·ti·cal·ly** *adv.*
Synonyms: *distinctive, individual, peculiar, typical.*

char·ac·ter·i·za·tion (kăr′ək-tər-ə-zā′shən) *n.* **1.** The act of characterizing; especially, a description of the qualities or peculiarities of a person or thing. **2.** The creation or delineation of a character or characters on the stage, in a film, or in writing, especially by imitating or describing actions, gestures, or speech.

char·ac·ter·ize (kăr′ək-tə-rīz′) *tr.v.* **-ized, -izing, -izes. 1.** To describe the qualities or peculiarities of: *characterized him as ruthless.* **2.** To be a distinguishing trait or mark of.

char·ac·ter·less (kăr′ək-tər-lĭs) *n.* Without any distinguishing or interesting features or qualities.

character sketch *n.* A brief portrayal or summary of a person's qualities, distinguishing features, idiosyncrasies, or the like.

char·ac·ter·y (kăr′ək-tə-rē, kə-răk′-) *n., pl.* **-ies. 1.** The use of characters or symbols to express or convey thought and meaning. **2.** Such characters or symbols collectively.

cha·rade (shə-rād′) *n.* **1. a. charades.** A game in which a word or phrase is acted out syllable by syllable until it is guessed by the other players or team. **b.** An episode or word in this game. **2.** A readily perceived pretense; travesty. [French, from Provençal *charrado,* chat, from *charra,* to chat (imitative).]

char·broil (chär′broil′) *tr.v.* **-broiled, -broiling, -broils.** To broil over charcoal: *charbroiled our steaks.* [CHAR[1] + BROIL.]

char·coal (chär′kōl′) *n.* **1.** A black, porous carbonaceous material produced by the destructive distillation of wood and used as a fuel, filter, and absorbent. **2.** A drawing pencil or crayon made from this substance. **3.** A drawing executed with such a pencil or crayon. **4.** A dark smoky gray to black.
~*tr.v.* **charcoaled, -coaling, -coals.** To draw, write, or blacken with charcoal. [Middle English *charcole* : perhaps Old French *charbon,* charcoal (see **carbon**) + COAL.]

charcoal rot *n.* A disease of plants that is caused by a fungus, *Macrophomina phaseoli,* and that results in black, decayed tissue.

Char·cot (shär-kō′), **Jean Martin** (1825–93). French physiologist noted for his research into the nervous system. Sigmund Freud was one of his students.

char·cu·te·rie (shär-ko͞o′tə-rē′) *n.* **1.** Cooked meats, as ham and sausages. **2.** A shop selling charcuterie. [French, from *charcutier,* seller of cooked meat, from Old French, from *chair cuite,* "cooked meat" : *chair,* from Latin *caro* (stem *carn-*), flesh + *cuite,* past participle of *cuire,* from Latin *coquere,* to cook.]

chard (chärd) *n.* A variety of beet, *Beta vulgaris cicla,* having large leaves used as a vegetable. Also called "Swiss chard," "leaf beet." [French *carde,* edible stalks of the cardoon, from Old French, cardoon, from Late Latin *cardō,* from Latin *carduus,* artichoke.]

Chardin, Pierre Teilhard de. See **Teilhard de Chardin.**

char·don·nay (shär′də-nā′) *n.* A variety of white grape used for making fine white Burgundy wine. [French.]

Cha·rente (shə-räɴt′). River in western France. It rises in the foothills of the Massif Central and flows 354 kilometers (220 miles) through Angoulême and Rochefort to the Bay of Biscay.

charge (chärj) *v.* **charged, charging, charges.** —*tr.* **1.** To place a burden on; entrust with a duty, responsibility, task, or obligation. **2.** To command, instruct, or urge with authority: *The judge charged the court to be silent.* **3.** To blame or accuse; impute something to. Often used with *with*: *charged with murder.* **4.** To set or ask (a given amount) as a price. **5.** To hold financially liable; demand payment from: *Customers will be charged for any breakage.* **6.** To postpone payment on (a service or purchase) by recording as a debt: *charge the dress to my account.* **7.** To attack by rushing violently toward: *The soldiers charged the fort.* **8.** To load (a gun or other firearm). **9.** To fill fully: *His mind was charged with ideas.* **10.** *Electricity.* **a.** To cause formation of a net electric charge on or in (a conductor, for example). **b.** To energize (a storage battery). Often used with *up*: *charge up the battery.* **11. a.** To cause to be saturated; impregnate: *The air was charged with perfume.* **b.** To fill so as to intensify: *The argument was charged with emotion.* **12.** *Heraldry.* To depict a heraldic charge on. —*intr.* To make an attack by rushing forward: *The cows charged toward the gate.* —See Synonyms at **command.**
~*n.* **1. a.** Care or custody: *children in the charge of their teacher.* **b.** Supervision; a position of responsibility or authority: *Who's in charge here?* **2.** An obligation or responsibility. **3.** A person or thing entrusted to one's care or management. **4.** An order, command, or injunction. **5.** An address, given by a judge to a jury at the end of a trial, of instruction about such matters as legal points and the weight of evidence. **6.** An accusation or indictment: *a charge of conspiracy to defraud.* **7.** *Abbr.* **chg.** The price set or demanded for an article or service: *bank charges.* **8.** Expense: *gave the banquet at his own charge.* **9.** *Abbr.* **chg.** A debt or an entry in an account recording a debt. **10.** A rushing, forceful attack. **11.** The maximum quantity of anything that an apparatus or container can hold at one time. **12.** The quantity of explosive with which a firearm is loaded for one shot. **13.** *Electricity.* **a.** The intrinsic property of matter responsible for all electric phenomena, in particular for the force of the electromagnetic interaction, occurring in two forms arbitrarily designated *negative* and *positive.* **b.** A measure of this property. **c.** The net measure of this property possessed by a body or contained in a bounded region of space. **14.** *Heraldry.* A device, figure, or emblem depicted on a shield. **15.** *Informal.* A feeling of pleasant excitement; thrill: *We got a real charge out of the movie.* —See Synonyms at **price.** [Middle English *chargen,* to load, from Old French *charger,* from Late Latin *carricāre,* from Latin *carrus,* CAR.]

charge·a·ble (chär′jə-bəl) *adj.* **1.** That may be or is suitable to be charged, as to an account. **2.** Liable to be accused.

charge account *n.* A credit arrangement in which a customer receives purchases or services prior to payment.

charge conjugation *n. Symbol* **C** *Physics.* **1.** A mathematical op-

PRONUNCIATION KEY

ă, pat; ā, pay; âr, care;
ä, father, are; b, bib;
ch, church; d, deed; ĕ, pet;
ē, be; f, fife; g, gag; h, hat;
hw, which; ĭ, pit; ī, pie;
îr, pier; j, judge; k, kick;
l, lid, needle; m, mum;
n, no, sudden; ng, thing;
ŏ, pot; ō, toe; ô, paw, for;
oi, noise; ou, out; o͝o, book;
o͞o, boot; p, pop; r, roar;
s, sauce; sh, ship, dish;
t, tight; th, thin, path;
th, this, bathe; ŭ, cut; ûr, fur;
v, valve; w, with; y, yes;
z, zebra, size; zh, vision;
ə, about, item, edible,
gallop, circus, peaceful

IN FOREIGN WORDS:

à, *Fr.* ami; œ, *Fr.* feu, *Ger.* schön; ü, *Fr.* tu, *Ger.* über; KH, *Ger.* ich, *Scot.* loch; N, *Fr.* bon; y′, *Fr.* Compiègne

STRESS MARKS:

Primary stress: ′
in·cite′ (ĭn-sīt′)
Secondary stress: ′
in′sight′ (ĭn′sīt′)

erator that changes the sign of the charge and of the magnetic moment of every particle in the system to which it is applied. **2.** Loosely, the theoretical conversion of matter to antimatter or of antimatter to matter.

char·gé d'af·faires (shär-zhā' də-fâr') n., pl. **chargés d'affaires** (-zhā', -zhāz'). **1.** A governmental official temporarily placed in charge of diplomatic affairs while the ambassador or minister is absent. **2.** A low-ranking diplomat representing his government in a country to which no higher-ranking diplomat has been appointed. [French, "(one) charged with affairs."]

charge density n. The electric charge per unit area or per unit volume of a body or of a region of space.

charge hand n. British. A workman, usually below the rank of foreman, who is in charge of a particular section or group of workers.

charge nurse n. A nurse in charge of a hospital ward.

charg·er[1] (chär'jər) n. **1.** One that charges. **2.** A powerful horse trained for battle; a cavalry horse. **3.** An instrument that charges or replenishes storage batteries.

charger[2] n. A large, shallow dish; a platter. [Middle English *chargeour*, from Norman French, probably from CHARGE, "to fill."]

charge sheet n. A document kept in a police station listing persons arrested and the charges made against them.

Char·ing Cross (chär'ĭng). District in the London borough of the City of Westminster, where Whitehall and the Strand once met. There, in about 1290, Edward I set up the last of a series of crosses in memory of his queen, Eleanor. The cross was destroyed during the English Civil War, but another was erected (1865) in front of Charing Cross Station, a major railway terminus.

Cha·ri-Nile (shä'rē-nīl') n. A family of languages spoken in eastern and central Africa, including the East and Central Sudanic languages.

char·i·ot (chăr'ē-ət) n. **1.** An ancient horse-drawn two-wheeled vehicle used in war, races, and processions. **2.** A light four-wheeled carriage used for ceremonial occasions or for pleasure.
~v. **charioted, -oting, -ots.** —tr. To convey or ride in a chariot. —intr. To ride in or drive a chariot. [Middle English, from Old French, augmentative of *char*, vehicle, from Latin *carrus*, CAR.]

char·i·o·teer (chăr'ē-ə-tîr') n. **1.** A person who drives a chariot. **2.** **Charioteer.** The constellation Auriga (*see*).

cha·ris·ma (kə-rĭz'mə) n., pl. **-mata** (-mə-tə). Also **char·ism** (kăr'ĭz'əm). **1.** An exceptional ability to attract and influence others; marked personal charm or magnetism. **2.** Theology. A divinely inspired gift or power, such as the ability to heal or to perform miracles. [Greek *kharisma*, favor, divine gift, from *kharizesthai*, to favor, from *kharis*, grace, favor.]

char·is·mat·ic (kăr'ĭz-măt'ĭk) adj. **1.** Of, pertaining to, or marked by charisma. **2.** Theology. Inspired or bestowed by the Holy Spirit. **3.** Of, pertaining to, or following a charismatic movement. ~n. A follower of a charismatic group or movement. —**char·is·mat·i·cal·ly** adv.

charismatic movement n. A movement among various Christian churches, seeking to reassert the influence of the Holy Spirit in the world and reviving certain practices of the early Church, such as the ministry of healing and speaking in tongues.

char·i·ta·ble (chăr'ə-tə-bəl) adj. **1.** Generous in giving money or other help to the needy. **2.** Mild or tolerant in judging others; lenient. **3.** Of, for, or concerned with charity: *a charitable organization.* —**char·i·ta·ble·ness** n. —**char·i·ta·bly** adv.

char·i·ty (chăr'ə-tē) n., pl. **-ties.** **1.** The provision of help or relief to the poor. **2.** An institution, organization, or fund established to help the needy or carry out other socially useful work. **3.** Something that is given to help the needy; alms. **4.** An act or feeling of benevolence, good will, or affection. **5.** Indulgence or forbearance in judging others; leniency: *The teacher showed charity toward the less gifted students.* **6.** Theology. **a.** The benevolence of God toward man. **b.** The love of man for his fellow men; brotherly love. [Middle English *charite*, Christian love, from Old French, from Latin *cāritās* (stem *cāritāt-*), love, regard, from *cārus*, dear.]

cha·ri·va·ri (shĭv'ə-rē', shĭv'ə-rē') n., pl. **-ris.** Also **chiv·a·ree, shiv·a·ree.** A noisy mock serenade to newlyweds. [French, from Late Latin *caribaria*, headache, from Greek *karēbaria*, "heavy head" : *karē, kara*, head + *barus*, heavy.]

char·kha, char·ka (chûr'kə-, chär'-) n. In India, a spinning wheel, especially one used for cotton. [Hindi *carkha*, from Persian *charkha*, wheel.]

char·la·dy (chär'lā'dē) n., pl. **-dies.** British. A charwoman (*see*).

char·la·tan (shär'lə-tən) n. A person who claims to possess knowledge or skill that he does not have; quack. [French, from Italian *ciarlatano*, from *ciarlare*, to chatter, babble (as when peddling quack remedies), probably imitative.] —**char·la·tan·ic** (shär'lə-tăn'ĭk) adj. —**char·la·tan·ism** n.

Char·le·magne (shär'lə-mān'), also called "Charles the Great" (c. 742–814). King of the Franks (768–814) and founder of the first empire in Western Europe after the fall of Rome. The elder son of King Pepin the Short, he built an empire that encompassed the entire heartland of Western Europe, stretching from the Danube River to the Pyrenees, from Rome to the North Sea. Pope Leo III crowned him emperor on Christmas Day, 800. Charlemagne's court at Aix-la-Chapelle became the center of a cultural rebirth in Europe, known as the Carolingian Renaissance.

Charles (chärlz), **Prince Philip Arthur George** (1948–). The eldest son of Elizabeth II and heir to the British throne. He was

invested as Prince of Wales (1969). He was educated at Gordonstoun and Cambridge and later served in the Royal Navy and RAF. He married Lady Diana Spencer (1981).

Charles, Ray (1930–). U.S. singer and pianist. Blind from the age of six, he became an outstanding blues singer.

Charles I (1600–49). King of England, Scotland, and Ireland (1625–49) and son of James I. His clashes with Parliament on constitutional issues led to the English Civil War. Conflict with three successive parliaments (1625, 1626, and 1628–9) on the issue of his right to raise taxes without parliamentary consent led to 11 years' rule without Parliament. His arbitrary rule, High Church leanings, and indulgence in the Roman Catholic faith of his wife, Henrietta Maria, culminated in an attempt to force Archbishop William Laud's Anglican prayer book on Presbyterian Scotland and led to the Bishops' Wars against Scotland (1639–40). Charles summoned a parliament that refused him financial support unless grievances were discussed. This so-called Short Parliament (April–May 1640) was dissolved, but a new one was summoned in November after a military defeat by the Scots. The Long Parliament vigorously opposed Charles, and, following the failure of his attempt to have five of its members arrested for treason (January 1642), the king raised his standard against Parliament on August 22. The Battle of Naseby (1645) was decisive, and Charles surrendered to the Scots at Newark in the following year. In January 1647 he was handed over to Parliament. In November he escaped to the Isle of Wight, where he secretly enlisted the Scots against Parliament, a move that failed. Charles was tried for treason and executed in January 1649.

Charles II (1630–85). King of England, Scotland, and Ireland (1660–85). Exiled during the Commonwealth, Charles was invited to return in 1660. Seeking to free the monarchy from financial dependence on Parliament, he negotiated the secret Treaty of Dover (1670) with Louis XIV, agreeing to help the French against the Dutch. Parliament responded with the Test Act (1673) excluding Dissenters and Roman Catholics from office. Fear of Roman Catholicism came to a head with the Popish Plot (1678), which fabricated a plan to place Charles's brother and heir, later James II, on the throne. Charles resisted parliamentary attempts to exclude James from the succession and from 1681 ruled without Parliament.

Charles V (1500–58). Holy Roman Emperor (1519–56). The son of Philip of Burgundy, he inherited Burgundy with its Dutch possessions on his father's death in 1506, succeeded to the throne of Spain in 1516, and was elected Holy Roman Emperor on the death of his grandfather, Maximilian I.

Charles XIV, King of Sweden and Norway, born Jean Baptiste Jules Bernadotte (1763–1844). French Revolutionary general and king of Sweden and Norway (1818–44). He served brilliantly under Napoleon Bonaparte in the Italian campaign (1796–97) and became minister of war (1799) and marshal of the empire (1804). Sweden was in need of an heir to the throne and approached Bernadotte. With Napoleon's support, he accepted, and was elected crown prince in 1810. In 1814 he marched into Denmark and forced the Danes to cede Norway to Sweden; both countries became united under the same crown. His reign was peaceful and marked by internal improvements, such as the building of the Göta Canal. He was the founder of the present Swedish royal dynasty.

Charles Mar·tel (mär-tĕl') (c. 689–741). Frankish ruler and illegitimate son of Pepin of Herstal, mayor of the palace of the eastern Frankish kingdom of Austrasia. He was the grandfather of Charlemagne.

Charles's law n. Physics. The law that the volume of a fixed mass of gas held at a constant pressure varies directly with the absolute temperature. Also called "Gay-Lussac's law." [After Jacques *Charles* (1746–1823), French physicist.]

Charles's Wain (wān) n. A constellation, the **Big Dipper** (*see*).

Charles·ton[1] (chärl'stən). City in South Carolina, on the southeastern coast, on a peninsula between the Ashley and Cooper rivers. It was founded in 1670 and is a major port and industrial center. On April 12, 1861, Confederates fired the first shots of the Civil War on Union-occupied Ft. Sumter in Charleston harbor.

Charleston[2]. The capital and largest city of West Virginia, in the west-central part of the state. It is an important transportation, manufacturing, and trading center.

Charleston[3] n. A fast dance $\frac{4}{4}$ time, characterized by kicks out to the side from the knees, and first popular during the 1920s. [After CHARLESTON, South Carolina.]

char·ley horse (chär'lē) n. Informal. A cramp or muscular stiffness caused by injury or excessive exertion. [Origin unknown.]

char·lock (chär'lək, -lŏk') n. A weedy plant, *Brassica kaber*, native to Eurasia, having hairy stems, foliage, and yellow flowers. Also called "wild mustard." [Middle English *cherlok, carlok*, Old English *cerlic*†.]

char·lotte (shär'lət) n. **1.** A cold dessert, **Charlotte russe** (*see*). **2.** A dessert, served either hot or cold, consisting of a mold of sponge cake or bread with a filling of fruits, whipped cream, custard, or the like. [French, from the name *Charlotte.*]

Char·lotte A·ma·lie (shär'lət ə-mäl'yə). Capital of the U.S. Virgin Islands, on St. Thomas Island.

Char·lot·ten·burg (shär-lŏt'ən-bûrg'). A residential area of Berlin in Germany. Once a city in its own right, it contains a 17th-century castle with museum and art gallery.

charlotte russe (rōos) n. A cold dessert of whipped cream or a custard mixture set in a mold lined with ladyfingers. Also called "charlotte." [French, "Russian charlotte."]

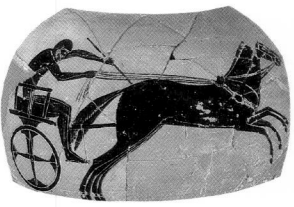

chariot *A detail of an Athenian black-figure vase, depicting a light racing chariot. The vase was made in about 550 B.C.*

Charolais *A heavy, milky white French-bred cow. Charolais cattle are extensively crossed with animals such as Holsteins to produce quick-maturing beef calves from dairy herds.*

chateau *Azay-le-Rideau, a 16th-century French moated castle. Some chateaux are more modest manor houses.*

Char·lottes·ville (shär′ləts-vĭl′). A city of central Virginia, in a piedmont area known for its apples. The University of Virginia is in Charlottesville. Monticello, Thomas Jefferson's home, is nearby.

Char·lotte·town (shär′lət-toun′). Capital city of Prince Edward Island province, Canada. It was the site of the conference (1864) that laid the foundations of the confederation of Canada in 1867.

charm[1] (chärm) *n.* **1.** The power or quality of pleasing, attracting, or fascinating. **2.** A particular quality or feature that fascinates or attracts: *The painting's charm is its simplicity.* **3.** A trinket or small ornament worn on a bracelet or other piece of jewelry. **4.** Anything that is worn for its supposed magical effect, as in warding off evil; an amulet. **5.** Any action or formula thought to have magical power. **6.** A chanting of a magic word or verse; an incantation. **7.** *Physics.* A quantum property of one of the quarks whose conservation explains the absence of certain strange-particle decay modes and that accounts for the longevity of the particle.
~*v.* **charmed, charming, charms.** —*tr.* **1.** To attract or delight greatly or irresistibly; fascinate. **2.** To act upon with or as if with magic; bewitch. —*intr.* **1.** To be alluring or pleasing. **2.** To act as an amulet or charm. **3.** To employ spells. [Middle English *charme,* chant, magic spell, from Old French, from Latin *carmen,* song, incantation.] **—charm·less** *adj.*

charm[2] *n.* **1.** *Archaic.* A confused sound of voices or bird calls. **2.** A company of finches. [Middle English *cherme* (influenced by *charme,* incantation, CHARM), Old English *cirm, cierm,* clamor, cry, of imitative origin.]

charmed (chärmd) *adj.* **1.** Affected or protected by or as if by a charm: *a charmed life.* **2.** *Physics.* Exhibiting the property of charm.

charmed circle *n.* A very exclusive group.

charm·er (chär′mər) *n.* **1.** One who charms or has the power to charm. **2.** A sorcerer.

charm·ing (chär′mĭng) *adj.* **1.** Having charm or a pleasant manner. **2.** Delightful; appealing.
~*interj.* Used ironically to express indignation or distaste. **—charm·ing·ly** *adv.*

char·mo·ni·um (chär-mō′nē-əm) *n. Physics.* Any of various elementary particles consisting of a charmed quark and the antiparticle of a quark. [CHARM + *-onium,* pseudoscientific suffix representing typical technical words (*ammonium, plutonium,* and so on).]

char·nel (chär′nəl) *n.* A charnel house.
~*adj.* Resembling or suggesting a charnel house; sepulchral; deathlike. [Middle English, from Old French, from Medieval Latin *carnāle,* from Late Latin *carnālis,* carnal, from Latin *carō* (stem *carn-*), flesh.]

charnel house *n.* A building, room, or vault in which the bones or bodies of the dead are placed.

Char·o·lais (shăr′ə-lā′) *n.* Any of a French breed of large white beef cattle.

Char·on (kâr′ən). *Greek Mythology.* The ferryman who conveyed the dead to Hades over the river Styx.

char·poy (chär′poi′) *n.* A light bedstead used especially in India. [Urdu *chārpāi.*]

char·qui (chär′kē) *n.* Cured or jerked meat, especially beef. Also called "jerky." [Spanish, from Quechua *ch'arki.*]

charr. Variant of **char** (fish).

chart (chärt) *n.* **1. a.** A map showing coastlines, water depths, or other information of use to navigators. **b.** A map of the sky showing the positions of the stars. **2.** An outline map on which special information, such as weather data, can be plotted. **3.** A sheet presenting information in the form of graphs, tables, or other figures. **4.** A **graph** *(see).* **5. charts.** A list, as of phonograph records, whose members are ranked in accordance with popularity or sales.
~*tr.v.* **charted, charting, charts. 1.** To make a chart of. **2.** To plan in detail. **3.** To record (progress, for example). [Old French *charte,* from Latin *charta,* papyrus leaf, paper, CARD.]

char·ta·ceous (kär-tā′shəs) *adj.* Resembling paper; papery. [Late Latin *chartāceus,* from Latin *charta,* papyrus leaf, paper. See **card.**]

char·ter (chär′tər) *n.* **1.** A document issued by a sovereign, legislative body, or other authority, creating a public or private corporation, such as a city, college, or bank, and defining its privileges and purposes. **2.** A written grant from the sovereign power of a country conferring certain rights and privileges upon a person, a corporation, or the people. **3.** *Often* **Charter.** A document outlining the principles, functions, and organization of a corporate body; constitution. **4.** A document claiming or asserting certain rights. **5.** A special privilege or immunity. **6.** A charter party. **7. a.** The hiring or leasing of an aircraft, vessel, or land vehicle. **b.** An agreement for such a hiring or leasing. **8.** A written instrument given as evidence of agreement, transfer, or contract; a deed.
~*tr.v.* **chartered, -tering, -ters. 1.** To grant a charter to; establish by charter. **2.** To hire or lease by charter. **3.** To hire (a vehicle). [Middle English *chartre,* from Old French, from Latin *chartula,* diminutive of *charta,* papyrus leaf, CARD.] **—char·ter·er** *n.*

char·ter·age (chär′tər-ĭj) *n.* **1.** The act or business of chartering, especially of ships. **2.** The fee charged by a ship broker.

charter colony *n.* A British colony in America, as Massachusetts, Connecticut, or Rhode Island, that was created by a royal charter exempting it from direct interference by the Crown.

chartered accountant *n. Abbr.* **C.A.** *Chiefly British.* A member of an institute of accountants granted a royal charter.

charter flight *n.* A flight by a specially chartered aircraft; especially, one providing cheap fares for members of the chartering group.

char·ter·house (chär′tər-hous′) *n.* A Carthusian monastery. [Middle English, altered (by assimilation to HOUSE) from Norman French *Chartrous,* (La Grande) Chartreuse. See **Carthusian.**]

charter member *n.* An original member or founder of an organization.

charter party *n.* A contract for the commercial leasing of a vessel or space on a vessel.

Chart·ism (chär′tĭz′əm) *n.* The principles and practices of a movement of social and political reformers, chiefly workingmen, active in England from 1838 to 1848. Their views were stated in the People's Charter, published in 1838. **—Chart·ist** *n.* & *adj.*

Chartres (shärt, shär′trə). Capital of the Eure-et-Loir department of northwest France, on the Eure River. Its 13th-century cathedral is one of the masterpieces of Gothic architecture and is famous for its magnificent statuary and stained glass.

char·treuse (shär-trōōz′, -trōōs′, -trœz′) *n.* **1.** Either of two liqueurs, green or yellow, made from herbs and spices by the Carthusian monks. **2.** Strong to brilliant greenish yellow to moderate or strong yellow green. [French, first made at *la Grande Chartreuse,* Carthusian monastery near Grenoble.] **—char·treuse** *adj.*

chartulary. Variant of **cartulary.**

char·wom·an (chär′wŏŏm′ən) *n., pl.* **-women** (-wĭm′ĭn). *Chiefly British.* A woman hired to do cleaning or similar work in an office or home. [CHAR (chore) + WOMAN.]

char·y (châr′ē) *adj.* **-ier, -iest. 1.** Careful; wary. **2.** Fastidious; finicky. **3.** Shy: *chary of meeting people.* **4.** Sparing: *chary of compliments.* [Middle English *charig, charry,* cherished, dear, Old English *cearig,* sorrowful, from Germanic *karō* (unattested), CARE.] **—char·i·ly** *adv.* **—char·i·ness** *n.*

Cha·ryb·dis (kə-rĭb′dĭs). *Greek Mythology.* A whirlpool off the Sicilian coast, opposite the cave of **Scylla** *(see).*

chase[1] (chās) *v.* **chased, chasing, chases.** —*tr.* **1.** To pursue in order to catch or overtake. **2.** To follow (game) in order to capture or kill; hunt. **3. a.** To try to obtain. **b.** *Informal.* To pursue and force one's attentions on (a woman, for example). **4.** To put to flight; drive. Often used with *away, out,* or *off.* —*intr.* **1.** To go or follow in pursuit. **2.** *Informal.* To go hurriedly; rush. Often used with *after* or *off.*
~*n.* **1.** The act of chasing; pursuit. **2.** The sport of hunting. Preceded by *the.* **3.** That which is hunted or pursued; a quarry. **4.** *Chiefly British.* **a.** A privately owned, unenclosed game preserve. **b.** The right to hunt or keep game on the land of others. **—give chase.** To pursue; chase. [Middle English *chacen, chasen,* from Old French *chasser, chacier,* from Vulgar Latin *captiāre* (unattested), from Latin *captāre,* to seize, frequentative of *capere,* to take.]

chase[2] *n. Printing.* A rectangular steel or iron frame into which type is locked for printing or plate making. [Probably from French *châsse,* a case, from Latin *capsa,* box, CASE.]

chase[3] *n.* **1. a.** A groove cut in any object; a slot. **b.** A trench or channel for drainpipes or wiring. **c.** A longitudinal groove for a tenon or tongue. **2.** The part of a gun that contains the bore.
~*tr.v.* **chased, chasing, chases. 1.** To decorate (metal) by engraving or embossing. **2. a.** To groove; indent. **b.** To cut or finish (the thread of a screw). [Old French *chas,* "enclosure," from Latin *capsus,* from *capsa,* box, CASE.]

chas·er[1] (chā′sər) *n.* **1.** One that chases or pursues. **2.** A gun on the bow or stern of a ship, used during pursuit or flight. Also called "chase gun." **3.** *Informal.* A drink, as of water or beer, taken after hard liquor.

chaser[2] *n.* **1.** One who decorates metal by engraving or embossing. **2.** A steel tool for cutting or finishing screw threads.

chasm (kăz′əm) *n.* **1.** A deep cleft or crack in the earth's surface; an abyss or narrow gorge. **2.** A sudden and considerable interruption of continuity; a gap; a hiatus. **3.** Any marked difference of opinion, interests, loyalty, or the like. [Latin *chasma,* from Greek *khasma,* akin to *khainein,* to gape.] **—chas·mal** (kăz′məl) *adj.*

chas·sé (shă-sā′) *n.* A dance movement consisting of one or more quick, gliding steps with the same foot always leading.
~*intr.v.* **chasséd, -séing, -sés.** To make or perform a chassé. [French, from the past participle of *chasser,* to CHASE.]

chasse·pot (shăs′pō′) *n.* A type of breech-loading rifle introduced into the French army in 1866. [French, after Antoine *Chassepot* (1833–1905), French gunsmith.]

chas·seur (shă-sûr′) *n.* **1.** A soldier; especially, one of certain light cavalry or infantry troops of the French army, trained for rapid maneuvers. **2.** A huntsman. **3.** A uniformed footman.
~*adj.* Served with a sauce of mushrooms and white wine: *chicken chasseur.* [French, "huntsman," from *chasser,* to CHASE.]

Chas·si·dim, Has·si·dim (KHä-sē′dĭm) *pl.n. Singular* **Chas·sid, Has·sid** (KHä′sĭd). A sect of Jewish mystics founded in Poland (about 1750) in opposition to the formalistic Judaism of the period and to ritual laxity. [Hebrew *ḥasīdhīm,* "pious ones," from *ḥāsīdh,* pious.] **—Chas·si·dic** (KHə-sĭd′ĭk, -sē′dĭk) *adj.* **—Chas·si·dism** *n.*

chas·sis (shăs′ē, chăs′ē) *n., pl.* **chassis** (-ēz). **1.** The rectangular steel frame, supported on springs and attached to the axles, that holds the body and engine of an automotive vehicle. **2.** The landing gear of an aircraft, including the wheels, floats, and other structures that support the aircraft on land or water. **3.** The frame on which a casement gun carriage moves forward and backward. **4.** The framework to which the functioning parts of a radio, television, record player, tape recorder, or other electronic equipment are attached. [French *châssis,* from Old French *chassis,* from Vulgar Latin *capsī-*

cium (unattested), from Latin *capsa,* box, CASE.]

chaste (chāst) *adj.* **chaster, chastest. 1.** Morally pure in thought and conduct; decent and modest. **2. a.** Not having experienced sexual intercourse; virginal. **b.** Abstaining from unlawful sexual intercourse. **c.** Abstaining from all sexual activity; celibate. **3.** Pure or simple in design or style; not ornate, extreme, or artificial. [Middle English, from Old French, from Latin *castus,* morally pure.] —**chaste·ly** *adv.* —**chaste·ness** *n.*

chas·ten (chā′sən) *tr.v.* **-tened, -tening, -tens. 1.** To punish, either physically or morally; chastise. **2.** To restrain; moderate. **3.** To refine; purify: *chasten one's style.* [From obsolete *chaste* (verb), from Middle English *chasten, chastien,* from Old French *chastier,* from Latin *castigāre,* to CASTIGATE.] —**chas·ten·er** *n.*

chaste tree *n.* A shrub, *Vitex agnus-castus,* of southern Europe, often cultivated for its spikes of lilac-blue flowers. [Translation of New Latin *agnus castus,* by folk etymology (influenced by Latin *agnus,* lamb) from Greek *agnos*† (confused with *hagnos,* holy, chaste).]

chas·tise (chăs-tīz′) *tr.v.* **-tised, -tising, -tises. 1.** To punish, usually by beating. **2.** To criticize severely. **3.** *Archaic.* To purify. —See Synonyms at **punish.** [Middle English *chastisen,* variant of *chastien,* to CHASTEN.] —**chas·tise·ment** (chăs-tīz′mənt, chăs′tĭz-) *n.* —**chas·tis·er** *n.*

chas·ti·ty (chăs′tə-tē) *n.* **1.** The state or quality of being chaste or pure. **2. a.** Celibacy. **b.** Virtuousness. **c.** Virginity. [Middle English *chastete,* from Old French, from Latin *castitās* (stem *castitāt-*), from *castus,* CHASTE.]

chastity belt *n.* Any of various devices worn by medieval women to prevent sexual intercourse.

chas·u·ble (chăz′ə-bəl, chăzh′ə-, chăs′ə-) *n.* A long, sleeveless vestment worn over the alb by the priest at Mass. [French, from Old French, from Late Latin *casubla,* hooded garment, irregularly from Latin *casula,* cloak (literally, little house, cottage), diminutive of *casa,* house.]

chat (chăt) *intr.v.* **chatted, chatting, chats.** To converse in an easy, informal, or familiar manner. —**chat up.** *British Informal.* To engage (a person) in friendly or flirtatious conversation, especially so as to win personal favor or strike up a sexual relationship. ~*n.* **1.** An informal or familiar conversation. **2.** Any of several birds known for their chattering call, such as: **a.** Any of several Old World birds of the genus *Saxicola.* See **stonechat, whinchat. b.** A North American bird, *Icteria virens,* having a yellow breast and a greenish back. This species is also called "yellow-breasted chat." **c.** Any of several Australian wrens of the genus *Ephthianura.* [Middle English *chatten,* short for *chatteren,* to CHATTER.]

cha·teau, châ·teau (shă-tō′) *n., pl.* **-teaux** (-tōz′). **1.** A French castle or manor house. **2.** A country house; especially, one resembling a French castle. [French *château,* from Old French *chastel,* from Latin *castellum,* CASTLE.]

cha·teau-bot·tled (shă-tō′bŏt′ld) *adj.* Designating a wine coming from the vineyards attached to a chateau and bottled within its domain.

Châ·teau·bri·and (shă-tō′brē-än′) *n. Sometimes* **châteaubriand. 1.** A double-thick tender center cut of beef tenderloin. **2.** A cut of Châteaubriand in which a pocket is cut and filled with various seasonings before grilling. [Probably invented by the chef of the Vicomte de CHATEAUBRIAND.]

Chateaubriand, François René, Vicomte de (1768–1848). French author and diplomat and a leading figure in the early romantic movement in France. His 12 volumes of memoirs, *Mémoires d'Outre-tombe,* were published after his death.

chat·e·lain (shăt′ə-lān′) *n.* The keeper of a castle; a castellan. [Middle English *chateleyn,* from Old French *chastelain,* from Latin *castellānus,* from *castellum,* CASTLE.]

chat·e·laine (shăt′ə-lān′) *n.* **1.** The lady or mistress of a castle, chateau, or large, fashionable household. **2.** A clasp or chain worn at the waist for holding keys, a purse, or a watch.

Chat·ham Islands (chăt′əm). Small Pacific island group forming part of New Zealand. They were discovered in 1791. Sheep farming is the main occupation. See map at **Pacific Ocean.**

cha·toy·an·cy (shə-toi′ən-sē) *n.* The quality or state of being chatoyant.

cha·toy·ant (shə-toi′ənt) *adj.* Having a changeable luster. ~*n.* A chatoyant stone or gemstone, such as the cat's-eye. [French, present participle of *chatoyer,* gleam like a cat's eyes, from *chat,* CAT.]

chat show *n. Chiefly British.* A talk show.

Chat·ta·noo·ga (chăt′ə-nōō′gə). City in southeast Tennessee on the Tennessee River. It is a major rail terminus, celebrated in the song "Chattanooga Choo Choo."

chat·tel (chăt′l) *n.* **1.** *Law.* An article of personal, movable property. **2.** A slave. [Middle English *chatel,* property, goods, from Old French. See **cattle.**]

chattel mortgage *n.* A mortgage on personal property as security for an obligation or debt.

chat·ter (chăt′ər) *intr.v.* **-tered, -tering, -ters. 1.** To utter a rapid series of short, inarticulate, speechlike sounds. Used of a bird or animal. **2.** To talk rapidly or incessantly, especially on a trivial subject; jabber. **3.** To click together quickly, as the teeth do from cold. **4.** To vibrate or rattle while in operation, as a power tool does. —See Synonyms at **speak.** ~*n.* **1.** Idle or trivial talk. **2.** The jabbering of an animal or bird. **3.** A rattling or clicking, as of the teeth. **4.** A rattling or vibration,

as of a power tool in operation. [Middle English *chat(t)eren* (imitative).] —**chat·ter·er** *n.*

chat·ter·box (chăt′ər-bŏks′) *n.* An extremely talkative person.

chatter mark, chat·ter·mark (chăt′ər-märk′) *n.* **1.** A riblike marking on wood or metal, caused by vibration of a cutting tool. **2.** *Geology.* Any of a series of short scars on a glaciated rock surface.

Chartres

CHARTRES CATHEDRAL: A SPLENDOR OF MEDIEVAL ART
Its windows preserve pictures showing local life of 700 years ago

Unsurpassed stained glass, superb sculpture, and fine high-Gothic architecture make the 13th-century Chartres Cathedral one of the outstanding medieval cathedrals of Europe. The light cast through its 173 stained glass windows, including the great western rose window, gives a twilight radiance dominated by red and deep, vivid blue—the unique "Chartres blue." Many of the windows were donated by medieval guilds, and pictures of the donors' trades and crafts are worked into the designs.

The cathedral replaced one that was destroyed by fire in 1194; the most sacred relic,

said to be the Virgin's tunic, survived the fire and inspired the rebuilding. The use of flying buttresses allowed the building of thinner walls and more windows than had been possible in previous cathedrals. The windows cover some 2,000 square meters (22,000 square feet). The Royal Portal (1145–55) at the west front, a remainder from the earlier building, has fine examples of the sculpture of its period.

The northern tower was given a new spire after the old one was destroyed by lightning in 1506. It does not compare with the southern tower, one of the most beautiful in Europe.

GOTHIC GRANDEUR *Few cathedrals have the unity of design of the great 13th-century high-Gothic cathedral of Notre Dame at Chartres, most of it built within 30 years (1194–1220). Only the ornamented north tower and eastern St. Piat Chapel are later exterior work.*

NORTH PORCH CARVINGS *The Old Testament figures in the central bay of the porch include Abraham about to sacrifice Isaac (second left) and King David carrying a spear (extreme right).*

STAINED GLASS *Pisces is one sign of the zodiac depicted on the left side of a south ambulatory window. On the right side there are scenes showing seasonal labors performed during that month.*

Chaucer *A portrait of the 14th-century poet taken from an illustration in an early manuscript of his best-known work,* The Canterbury Tales.

Chat·ter·ton (chăt′ər-tən), **Thomas** (1752–70). English poet. As a youth he fooled readers by ascribing his works to a 15th-century monk, Thomas Rowley. Although some of his works were published under his own name, he was unable to support himself with writing. Starving and dejected, he took his life at the age of 18. His work and example greatly influenced the romantic poets.

chat·ty (chăt′ē) *adj.* **-tier, -tiest. 1.** Given to informal conversation. **2.** Marked by a familiar, conversational style: *a chatty letter.* **—chat·ti·ly** *adv.* **—chat·ti·ness** *n.*

Chau·cer (chô′sər), **Geoffrey** (*c.* 1342–1400). English poet, considered the father of English poetry. He was also a diplomat and customs official, traveling widely in Europe under Richard II. *The Book of the Duchess* (1369), written in honor of the wife of John of Gaunt, was his first work, followed by others including the *Parliament of Fowls* and *Troilus and Criseyde.* His *Canterbury Tales,* a collection of stories supposedly told by a party of pilgrims traveling from London to Canterbury, is his most famous work.

Chau·ce·ri·an (chô-sîr′ē-ən) *adj.* Of, pertaining to, or characteristic of Chaucer or his writings.
~*n.* A scholar specializing in the study of Chaucer.

chaud·froid (shō-frwä′) *n.* **1.** A jellied white or brown sauce used as an aspic for cold meats or fish. **2.** Molded cold meat or fish dishes garnished with a chaudfroid sauce. [French, "hot-cold."]

chauf·feur (shō′fər, shō-fûr′) *n.* One employed to drive a private or official car.
~*v.* **chauffeured, -feuring, -feurs.** —*tr.* To serve as a driver for. —*intr.* To serve as a chauffeur. [French, stoker, from *chauffer,* to warm. See **chafe.**]

chaul·moo·gra (chôl-mo͞o′grə) *n.* Any of several trees of tropical Asia, especially *Taraktogenos kurzii* and those of the genus *Hydnocarpus,* having seeds that yield an oil formerly used in treating leprosy. [Bengali *cāulmugrā* : *cāul,* rice + *mugrā,* hemp.]

chaunt. *Archaic.* Variant of **chant.**

chausses (shōs) *pl.n.* Medieval armor of mail for the legs and feet. [Middle English *chauces,* from Old French, from Medieval Latin *calcia,* clothing for the leg, from Latin *calceus,* shoe. See **calceate.**]

chau·vin·ism (shō′və-nĭz′əm) *n.* **1.** Militant devotion to and glorification of one's country; fanatical patriotism. **2.** Prejudiced belief in the superiority of one's own group: *male chauvinism.* [French *chauvinisme,* after Nicolas *Chauvin,* veteran of the First Republic and Empire noted for his patriotic fervor, popularized as a character in the play *La Cocarde tricolore* (1831).] **—chau·vin·ist** *n.* **—chau·vin·is·tic** (shō′və-nĭs′tĭk) *adj.* **—chau·vin·is·ti·cal·ly** *adv.*

Chá·vez (chä′vĕz), **Cesar Estrada** (1927–). U.S. labor organizer. In 1962 he founded the National Farm Workers Association and organized the workers of California's prime agricultural areas. In 1968 he launched a two-year nationwide boycott of California grapes, which led to important concessions by the grape growers.

chaw (chô) *v.* **chawed, chawing, chaws.** *Regional.* —*intr.* To chew. —*tr.* To chew (something). **—chaw** *n.*

Cha·yef·sky (chī-ĕf′skē, chä-), **Paddy** (1923–81). U.S. playwright and screenwriter. Considered one of the most successful early television writers, he depicted the unglamorous drama of everyday life. Many of his television dramas were made into movies. He earned Academy Awards for *Marty* (1955) and *Hospital* (1971).

cha·yo·te (chä-yō′tā) *n.* **1.** A tropical American vine, *Sechium edule,* bearing edible squashlike fruit. **2.** The fruit of the chayote. [Spanish, from Nahuatl *chayotli.*]

cha·zan, chaz·zen, haz·zan (KHä′zən) *n.* A cantor in a synagogue. [Late Hebrew *ḥazzān,* officer, cantor.]

Ch.E. chemical engineer.

cheap (chēp) *adj.* **cheaper, cheapest. 1.** Relatively low in cost; inexpensive. **2.** Charging low prices: *a cheap restaurant.* **3.** Worth more than the price paid. **4.** Involving little effort or loss: *a cheap victory.* **5.** Of small value. **6.** Of poor quality; shoddy. **7.** Not worthy of respect; vulgar; despicable. **8.** Ashamed or abashed. **9.** *Economics.* **a.** Obtainable at a low rate of interest. **b.** Devalued, as in buying power.
~*adv.* Inexpensively. [Middle English *chep,* sale, bargain, purchase, Old English *cēap,* from West Germanic *kaupaz* (unattested), trader, from Latin *caupō,* innkeeper.] **—cheap·ly** *adv.* **—cheap·ness** *n.*

cheap·en (chē′pən) *v.* **-ened, -ening, -ens.** —*tr.* **1.** To make cheap or cheaper. **2.** To lower in estimation; degrade. —*intr.* To become cheap or cheaper. **—cheap·en·er** *n.*

cheap·ie (chē′pē) *n. Informal.* Something that is cheap and often of poor quality.

cheap-jack (chēp′jăk′) *adj.* **1.** Selling overpriced goods of poor quality. **2.** Of poor quality; worthless. [CHEAP + JACK (fellow), originally a hawker or dealer in shoddy goods.]

cheap·o (chē′pō) *adj. Informal.* Cheap.

cheap shot *n. Informal.* An unjust action or statement, especially one directed at a vulnerable target, as a public figure.

Cheap·side (chēp′sīd′). Street in the City of London. It was the central market area of medieval London. St. Mary le Bow, built here by Christopher Wren in 1680, is the church of Bow Bells.

cheap·skate (chēp′skāt′) *n. Informal.* A stingy person; a miser. [CHEAP + SKATE (chap).] **—cheap·skate** *adj.*

cheat (chēt) *v.* **cheated, cheating, cheats.** —*tr.* **1.** To deceive by trickery; swindle. **2.** To mislead; fool. **3.** To elude; escape: *cheat death.* —*intr.* **1.** To act dishonestly to gain some advantage: *cheat at cards.* **2.** To act fraudulently. **3.** *Informal.* To be unfaithful, especially to one's spouse: *cheating on his wife.*
~*n.* **1.** A fraud or swindle. **2.** One who cheats. **3.** *Law.* The fraudulent acquisition of another's property. [Middle English *cheten,* to revert, short for *acheten,* variant of *escheten,* from *eschete,* ESCHEAT.] **—cheat·er** *n.* **—cheat·ing·ly** *adv.*

check (chĕk) *n.* Also *chiefly British* **cheque** (for sense 10). **1.** An abrupt stopping or interruption of motion or progress; a halt or delay. **2.** Restraint or control. **3.** Someone or something that restrains or controls: *I tried to put a check on my emotions.* **4.** An inspection or examination, as to assess or verify accuracy, efficiency, attendance, or the like. **5.** A standard of comparison used in such an inspection; a test. **6. a.** A pattern of small squares, as on a chessboard. **b.** Any of the squares of such a pattern. **c.** A fabric patterned with such squares. **7.** A small crack or fault, especially in a piece of timber. **8.** *Chess.* **a.** A move that directly attacks an opponent's king but does not constitute a checkmate. **b.** The position or tactical condition of a king so attacked. **9.** A ticket or slip of identification: *a baggage check.* **10.** A written order to a bank to pay the amount specified from funds on deposit; draft. **11.** A bill in a restaurant or bar. **12.** A mark indicating verification or approval. **13.** A gambling chip or counter. **—in check.** Under restraint; in control.
~*interj.* **1.** *Chess.* A declaration made to an opponent that his king is in check. **2.** *Informal.* Used to express affirmation.
~*v.* **checked, checking, checks.** —*tr.* **1.** To arrest the motion or progress of abruptly; halt. **2.** To hold in restraint; curb. **3.** To slow the growth of; retard. **4.** To rebuke or rebuff. **5. a.** To test or examine, as for accuracy or efficiency. **b.** To ascertain or verify: *I'll just check that I've locked the door.* **6.** *Chess.* To move so as to put (an opponent's king) under direct attack. **7.** *Ice Hockey.* To impede (an opponent in control of the puck). **8.** To put a check mark on or next to. **9.** To deposit for temporary safekeeping, as in a cloakroom. —*intr.* **1.** To come to an abrupt halt; stop. **2.** To make an examination or investigation, as to verify something or to assess accuracy. Often used with *up, on,* or *upon.* **3.** To correspond accurately; agree. **4.** To pause to relocate a scent. Used of hunting dogs. **5.** *Chess.* To place an opponent's king in check. **—See Synonyms at restrain, delay.** [Middle English *chek,* attack, quarrel, check at chess, from Old French *eschec, eschac,* from Arabic *shāh,* king, check at chess, from Persian, king.] **—check·a·ble** *adj.*

check·book (chĕk′bo͝ok′) *n.* A book containing blank checks issued by a bank.

checked (chĕkt) *adj.* **1.** Having a pattern of squares. **2.** Held in check; restrained. **3.** Situated in a stopped or closed syllable: *a checked vowel.*

check·er (chĕk′ər) *n.* Also *chiefly British* **cheq·uer. 1.** One of the disks used in the game of checkers. **2. a.** A pattern of checks or squares. **b.** One of the squares in such a pattern. **3.** One who checks, examines, or supervises. **4.** A person who processes purchases at a check-out, as in a supermarket.
~*tr.v.* **checkered, -ering, -ers.** Also *chiefly British* **cheq·uer. 1.** To mark into a pattern of squares. **2.** To diversify, as in color or character; variegate. [Middle English, from *cheker,* chessboard, from Old French *eschequier,* from *eschec,* CHECK.]

check·er·ber·ry (chĕk′ər-bĕr′ē) *n., pl.* **-ries. 1.** A plant, the **wintergreen** *(see).* **2.** The red, edible, spicy berry of this plant. [CHECKER (a name for the fruit of the service tree) + BERRY.]

check·er·bloom (chĕk′ər-blo͞om′) *n.* A plant, *Sidalcea malvaeflora,* of California, with long clusters of rose-pink flowers. [CHECKER, the wild service tree + BLOOM.]

check·er·board (chĕk′ər-bôrd′, -bōrd′) *n.* A game board divided into 64 squares of two alternating colors on which chess and checkers are played.

check·ers (chĕk′ərz) *n.* Also *chiefly British* **cheq·uers.** *Used with a singular verb.* A game played on a checkerboard by two players each using 12 pieces.

check in *intr.v.* To register on one's arrival, as at work or an airport. —*tr.v.* To register (passengers or luggage, for example) on arrival.

check-in (chĕk′ĭn′) *n.* **1.** The act of checking in, as at an airport. **2.** The place or time at which one checks in.

checking account *n.* A bank account in which checks may be written against amounts on deposit.

check·list (chĕk′lĭst′) *n.* A list against which items can be compared, verified, or identified.

check·mate (chĕk′māt′) *tr.v.* **-mated, -mating, -mates. 1.** *Chess.* To attack (an opponent's king) in such manner that no escape or defense is possible, thus ending the game. **2.** To defeat completely.
~*n.* **1.** *Abbr.* **chm.** *Chess.* **a.** A move that constitutes an inescapable and indefensible attack on an opponent's king. **b.** The position of a king so attacked. **2.** Utter defeat.
~*interj. Chess.* A call declaring the checkmate of an opponent's king. [Middle English *chekmate,* from Old French *eschec mat,* from Persian *shāh māt,* the king is dead.]

check·off (chĕk′ôf′, -ŏf′) *n.* The collection of dues from members of a union by authorized deduction from their wages.

check out *intr.v.* **1.** To pay one's bill and depart, as from a hotel. **2.** To record one's departure, as from a workplace.
~*tr.v.* To process through a check-out, as in a supermarket.

check-out (chĕk′out′) *n.* **1.** The act, time, or place of checking out, as at a supermarket or hotel. **2.** A test, as of a machine, for proper functioning. **3.** An investigation or inspection.

check·point (chĕk′point′) *n.* A place where people or vehicles are stopped for inspection.

check·rein (chĕk′rān′) *n.* **1.** A short rein connected from a horse's

bit to the saddle to keep the horse from lowering its head. Also called "bearing rein." **2.** A rein joining the bit of one of a span of horses to the driving rein of the other horse.

check·room (chĕk'rōōm', -rŏŏm') *n.* A place where items, as clothing or packages, can be stored temporarily.

check·row (chĕk'rō') *n.* A row, as of corn, in which the distance between plants is the same as the distance between adjacent rows to permit cross cultivation.
~*tr.v.* **checkrowed, -rowing, -rows.** To plant in checkrows.

checks and balances *pl.n.* The system of maintaining a balance of power between various branches of a government.

check·up (chĕk'ŭp') *n.* **1.** A thorough examination, as for verification or accuracy. **2.** A physical examination.

Ched·dar[1] (chĕd'ər). Town in Somerset in southwest England, in the valley of the Axe River. Cheddar cheese was first produced here in the 17th century. Cheddar Gorge, cutting through the Mendip Hills to the east, has limestone caverns and rare flora.

Ched·dar[2] (chĕd'ər) *n. Sometimes* **cheddar.** Any of several types of smooth, hard cheese varying in flavor from mild to extra sharp. [After CHEDDAR, where it was originally made.]

cheek (chēk) *n.* **1.** The fleshy part of either side of the face below the eye and between the nose and ear. **2.** Something resembling this in shape or position, as either of two sides of something. **3.** *Informal.* A buttock. **4.** Sauciness; impudence. —See Synonyms at **temerity.** —**cheek by jowl.** Side by side; close. —**turn the other cheek.** To submit to unjust or unkind treatment without retaliating.
~*tr.v.* **cheeked, cheeking, cheeks.** *Informal.* To speak impudently to. [Middle English *che(e)ke,* Old English *cēce, cēace,* from Germanic *kækōn-* (unattested).]

cheek·bone (chēk'bōn') *n.* A bone in the upper cheek, the **zygomatic bone** *(see).*

cheek pouch *n.* A pouch inside the mouth of many rodents and certain other animals, used for holding food.

cheek·y (chē'kē) *adj.* **-ier, -iest.** Saucy; impudent; brazen. —**cheek·i·ly** *adv.* —**cheek·i·ness** *n.*

cheep (chēp) *n.* A faint, shrill sound like that of a young bird; a chirp.
~*v.* **cheeped, cheeping, cheeps.** —*tr.* To utter with a chirp. —*intr.* To chirp; peep. [Imitative.] —**cheep·er** *n.*

cheer (chîr) *n.* **1.** Gaiety; animation. **2.** A shout of approval, encouragement, or congratulation. **3.** Something that gives joy or comfort; encouragement. **4.** Food or drink; refreshment.
~*v.* **cheered, cheering, cheers.** —*tr.* **1. a.** To fill with joy. **b.** To comfort. Often used with *up.* **2.** To encourage with or as if with cheers; urge. Often used with *on.* **3.** To salute or acclaim with cheers; applaud. —*intr.* **1.** To shout cheers; applaud. **2.** To become cheerful. Often used with *up.* [Middle English *chere,* cheer, disposition, countenance, face, from Old French *ch(i)ere,* face, from Late Latin *cara,* from Greek *karē, kara,* head.] —**cheer·er** *n.* —**cheer·ing·ly** *adv.*

cheer·ful (chîr'fəl) *adj.* **1.** Being in good spirits; happy. **2.** Promoting cheer; pleasant. —See Synonyms at **glad.** —**cheer·ful·ly** *adv.* —**cheer·ful·ness** *n.*

cheer·i·o (chîr'ē-ō') *interj. Chiefly British Informal.* **1.** Used as a farewell or greeting. **2.** Used as a toast. [From CHEER.]

cheer·lead·er (chîr'lē'dər) *n.* One who leads group cheering, especially at sporting events.

cheer·less (chîr'lĭs) *adj.* **1.** Lacking cheer; gloomy. **2.** Pessimistic; in low spirits. —**cheer·less·ly** *adv.* —**cheer·less·ness** *n.*

cheers (chîrz) *interj.* Used as a toast.

cheer·y (chîr'ē) *adj.* **-ier, -iest.** In good spirits; cheerful. —**cheer·i·ly** *adv.* —**cheer·i·ness** *n.*

cheese[1] (chēz) *n.* **1. a.** A solid or semisolid food prepared from the pressed curd of milk. **b.** A molded mass of this substance. **2.** Something like cheese in shape, smell, or consistency. [Middle English *chese,* Old English *cēse,* from Germanic *kasjus* (unattested), from Latin *cāseus†.*] See feature, next page.

cheese[2] *tr.v.* **cheesed, cheesing, cheeses.** *Slang.* To stop. —**cheese it.** *Slang.* Look out; get away fast. [Origin unknown.]

cheese[3] *n. Slang.* An important person: *He thinks he's a big cheese.* [Perhaps from Urdu *chīz,* thing, from Persian.]

cheese·burg·er (chēz'bûr'gər) *n.* A hamburger topped with melted cheese.

cheese·cake (chēz'kāk') *n.* **1.** A cake made of sweetened cottage cheese or cream cheese, eggs, milk, sugar, and flavoring. **2.** *Slang.* Photographs, as in advertisements, of attractive women scantily clothed. Compare **beefcake.**

cheese·cloth (chēz'klôth', -klŏth') *n.* A coarse, loosely woven cotton gauze, originally used for wrapping cheese.

cheesed off (chēzd) *adj. British Slang.* Annoyed; fed up. [From CHEESE (to stop).]

cheese mite *n.* A white mite, *Tyrophagus longior,* sometimes found in moldy cheese, on which it feeds.

cheese·par·ing (chēz'pâr'ĭng) *n.* Stinginess; parsimony.
~*adj.* Miserly; stingy.

chees·y (chē'zē) *adj.* **-ier, -iest.** **1. a.** Resembling cheese. **b.** Containing cheese. **2.** *Slang.* Of poor quality; shoddy: *That was a cheesy movie.* —**chees·i·ly** *adv.* —**chees·i·ness** *n.*

chee·tah (chē'tə) *n.* A long-legged, swift-running feline mammal, *Acinonyx jubatus,* of Africa and southwestern Asia, having black-spotted, tawny fur and partially retractile claws. It is sometimes trained to pursue game. Also called "hunting leopard." [Hindi *cītā,* from Sanskrit *citrakāya,* tiger : *citra,* speckled + *kāya,* body.]

Chee·ver (chē'vər), **John** (1912–82). U.S. author. In many of his more than 100 short stories and five novels he humorously and compassionately depicted life in the American suburbs. He won America's most respected literary awards, including a Pulitzer Prize for *The Stories of John Cheever* (1978).

chef (shĕf) *n.* A cook; especially, the chief cook of a large kitchen staff. [French, CHIEF.]

chef-d'oeu·vre (shā-dœ'vr', -dûrv') *n., pl.* **chefs-d'oeuvre** *(pronounced as singular).* A masterpiece, especially in literature or art. [French, "chief work."]

chef's salad *n.* A green salad that usually includes raw vegetables, hard-boiled egg, and julienne strips of cheese and meat.

chei·lo·sis (kī-lō'sĭs) *n.* Inflammation and cracking of the lips, a symptom of riboflavin (Vitamin B_2) deficiency and other nutritional disorders. [New Latin, from Greek *kheilos,* lip + -OSIS.]

cheiro-. Variant of **chiro-.**

Che·ka (chā'kä, -kə, chĕk'ə) *n.* The Soviet security service organized in 1918 by Lenin. Reorganized many times, it acquired in 1954 the designation **KGB** *(see).* [Russian, short for *Chrezvychaynaya Komissiya,* "extraordinary commission."]

Che·khov (chĕk'ôf'), **Anton Pavlovich** (1860–1904). Russian playwright and short-story writer. Between 1898 and 1904 he had four plays produced at the Moscow Art Theatre: *The Seagull, Uncle Vanya, The Three Sisters,* and *The Cherry Orchard.* All are now acknowledged masterpieces.

Chekiang. See **Zhejiang.**

che·la (kē'lə) *n., pl.* **-lae** (-lē). A pincerlike claw of arthropods, as of a lobster, crab, or similar crustacean. [New Latin, from Latin *chēlē,* from Greek *khēlē,* claw.]

che·late (kē'lāt') *adj.* **1.** *Zoology.* Having or characteristic of a chela. **2.** *Chemistry.* Of or pertaining to a heterocyclic ring containing a metal ion attached by coordinate bonds to at least two nonmetal ions in the same molecule.
~*tr.v.* **chelated, -lating, -lates.** To form a ring compound by joining a chelating agent to (a metal ion). —**che·late** *n.* —**che·la·tion** (kē-lā'shən) *n.*

che·lic·er·a (kə-lĭs'ər-ə) *n., pl.* **-erae** (-ə-rē') Either of the first pair of appendages near the mouth of a spider or other arachnid, often modified for grasping food. [New Latin : CHELA + Greek *keras,* horn.] —**che·lic·er·ate** (kə-lĭs'ə-rāt') *adj.*

che·li·form (kē'lə-fôrm') *adj.* Shaped like a chela; pincerlike.

Chel·li·an, Chel·le·an (shĕl'ē-ən) *adj. Archaeology.* Abbevillian. [French *chelléen,* of *Chelles,* site near Paris where some archaeological specimens were found.]

Chelms·ford (chĕmz'fərd, chĕlmz'-). City in Essex in southeast England, the administrative center of the county. Marconi began the world's first broadcasting service here (1920).

cheloid. Variant of **keloid.**

che·lo·ni·an (kə-lō'nē-ən) *adj. Zoology.* Of or belonging to the Chelonia, an order of reptiles that includes the turtles and tortoises.
~*n.* A member of the Chelonia. [New Latin *Chelonia,* from Greek *khelōnē,* tortoise.]

Chel·sea (chĕl'sē). District in the west London royal borough of Kensington and Chelsea, on the north bank of the Thames, popular since the 18th century with writers and artists. It is now a fashionable residential and shopping area.

chem-, chemi-. Variants of **chemo-.**

chem. chemical; chemist; chemistry.

chem·i·cal (kĕm'ĭ-kəl) *adj. Abbr.* **chem. 1.** Of, used in, or pertaining to chemistry. **2.** Of, employing, or pertaining to the properties or actions of chemicals.
~*n.* A substance produced by or used in a chemical process. [Earlier *chimical,* from *chimic,* an alchemist, from New Latin *chimicus,* from Medieval Latin *alchimicus,* from *alchimia, alchymia,* ALCHEMY.] —**chem·i·cal·ly** *adv.*

chemical bond *n.* Any of several forces or mechanisms, especially the **ionic bond, covalent bond, coordinate bond,** and **metallic bond** *(all of which see),* by which atoms or ions are bound in a molecule or crystal.

chemical engineering *n.* The technology of large-scale chemical and chemical materials production. —**chemical engineer** *n.*

chemical equation *n.* A representation of a chemical reaction using the chemical symbols of the elements taking part. The amount of substance of the reactants and products is usually given in moles.

Chemical Mace *n.* A trademark for a mixture of organic chemicals used in aerosol form as a weapon to disable with intense burning eye pain, blepharospasm, acute bronchitis, and respiratory irritation. Also called "Mace."

chemical reaction *n.* An interaction between substances involving changes in the outer electron structure and energy content of their molecules, atoms, or ions.

chemical warfare *n.* Warfare using chemicals other than explosives, especially irritants, asphyxiants, contaminants, poisons, and incendiaries, as direct weapons.

chemical weathering *n.* The wearing away of rocks or soil; **leaching** or **corrosion** *(both of which see).*

chem·i·lu·mi·nes·cence (kĕm'ə-lōō'mə-nĕs'əns, kē'mə-) *n.* The emission of light as a result of a chemical reaction at environmental temperatures.

che·min de fer (shə-măN' də fâr') *n.* A gambling game that is a variation of baccarat. [French, "road of iron," railroad.]

che·mise (shə-mēz') *n.* **1.** A woman's loose, shirtlike undergarment. **2.** A dress, a **shift** *(see).* [Middle English, from Old French, shirt,

cheetah *The cheetah, which is native to Africa and southwest Asia, is the world's fastest mammal. It can sprint at up to 110 kilometers (70 miles) per hour in pursuit of prey such as antelope. Unlike other big cats, the cheetah cannot retract its claws; instead they remain extended, helping it to grip the ground as it runs.*

THE MAGIC OF CURDS AND WHEY

How curdled milk is turned into Camembert and Caerphilly

All cheese begins as milk—mostly cows' milk, although it can be the milk of ewes or goats—and it was being eaten about 3000 B.C. in the ancient civilization of Sumer, Mesopotamia. Cheese is made by adding rennet—a preparation derived from a calf's stomach—to milk to produce curds and whey. The curds are drained of whey (which is used as a protein-rich animal feed), heated, salted, and pressed into drum-shaped molds. The cheeses are then ripened—sometimes for years. Variations of this method, together with the amount of fermentation that takes place during ripening, determine the final flavor and texture. Blue cheeses, such as Stilton, Danish Blue, and Gorgonzola, get their distinctive veining from bacteria allowed to grow on and into the cheeses.

HARD AND MEDIUM CHEESES

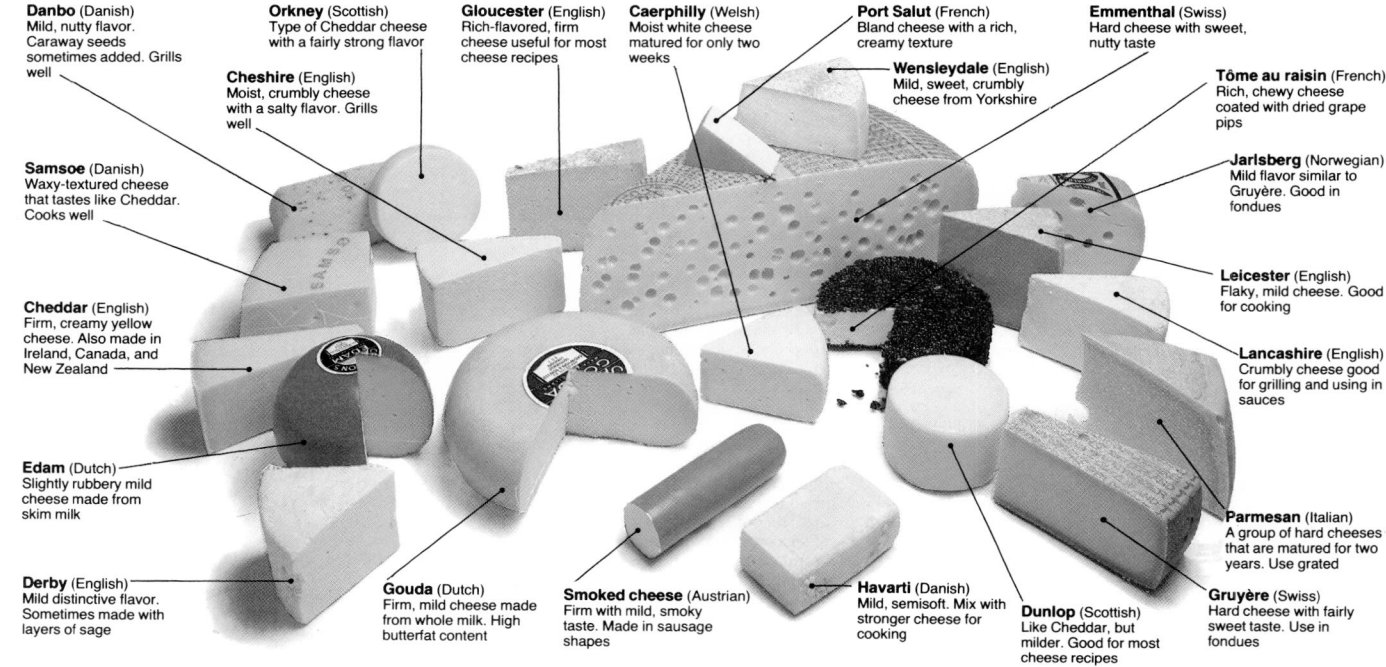

Danbo (Danish)
Mild, nutty flavor. Caraway seeds sometimes added. Grills well

Orkney (Scottish)
Type of Cheddar cheese with a fairly strong flavor

Gloucester (English)
Rich-flavored, firm cheese useful for most cheese recipes

Caerphilly (Welsh)
Moist white cheese matured for only two weeks

Port Salut (French)
Bland cheese with a rich, creamy texture

Emmenthal (Swiss)
Hard cheese with sweet, nutty taste

Cheshire (English)
Moist, crumbly cheese with a salty flavor. Grills well

Wensleydale (English)
Mild, sweet, crumbly cheese from Yorkshire

Tôme au raisin (French)
Rich, chewy cheese coated with dried grape pips

Samsoe (Danish)
Waxy-textured cheese that tastes like Cheddar. Cooks well

Jarlsberg (Norwegian)
Mild flavor similar to Gruyère. Good in fondues

Cheddar (English)
Firm, creamy yellow cheese. Also made in Ireland, Canada, and New Zealand

Leicester (English)
Flaky, mild cheese. Good for cooking

Lancashire (English)
Crumbly cheese good for grilling and using in sauces

Edam (Dutch)
Slightly rubbery mild cheese made from skim milk

Parmesan (Italian)
A group of hard cheeses that are matured for two years. Use grated

Derby (English)
Mild distinctive flavor. Sometimes made with layers of sage

Gouda (Dutch)
Firm, mild cheese made from whole milk. High butterfat content

Smoked cheese (Austrian)
Firm with mild, smoky taste. Made in sausage shapes

Havarti (Danish)
Mild, semisoft. Mix with stronger cheese for cooking

Dunlop (Scottish)
Like Cheddar, but milder. Good for most cheese recipes

Gruyère (Swiss)
Hard cheese with fairly sweet taste. Use in fondues

BLUE-VEINED AND CREAM CHEESES

Brie (French)
Delicately flavored, farm-produced cheese

Cottage cheese (English)
Acid taste. Made from sour skim milk

Gorgonzola (Italian)
Rich, strong blue cheese matured for up to a year

Boursin (French)
Triple-cream cheese flavored with garlic, herbs, or pepper

Mozzarella (Italian)
Firm, unpressed cheese with a sharp taste. Use on pizza

Stilton (English)
Blue cheese with rich, creamy flavor. Matured for six months

Danish blue
Crumbly with sharp, salty flavor. Very white cheese is underripe

Bel paese (Italian)
Mild and rich. Foil-packed cheese is softer than cheese sold loose. Use on pizza

Dolce latte (Italian)
Strong-flavored cheese similar to Gorgonzola. Creamy when ripe

Camembert (French)
Originally from Normandy, now widely imitated. Best when soft

Mycella (Danish)
Very soft with rich flavor. Should be soft enough to spread

Caboc (Scottish)
Mild, semisoft cheese rolled in toasted oatmeal

Demi-sel (French)
Bland taste like fresh cream. Use with fruit and in cold desserts

Roquefort (French)
Rich blue cheese with sharp, peppery taste and strong smell

Cream cheese (English)
Double-cream cheese is 45–50% fat; single is 25–30% fat

Petit suisse (French)
Cream cheese made from whole milk and cream. Serve with sugar

Bleu de Bresse (French)
Soft blue cheese with a buttery flavor. Can be salty

from Late Latin *camīsia,* linen shirt, nightgown.]

chem·i·sette (shĕm′ĭ-zĕt′) *n.* **1.** A short, sleeveless underbodice, formerly worn by women. **2.** A blouse front formerly worn by women to fill in the neckline of a dress. [French, diminutive of CHEMISE.]

chem·i·sorb (kĕm′ĭ-sôrb′) *tr.v.* **-sorbed, -sorbing, -sorbs.** Also **chem·o·sorb** (kĕm′ə-). To take up and chemically bind (a substance) on the surface of another substance. [CHEMI- + (AB)SORB.] **—chem·i·sorp·tion** (kĕm′ĭ-sôrp′shən) *n.*

chem·ist (kĕm′ĭst) *n. Abbr.* **chem. 1.** A scientist specializing in chemistry. **2.** *Chiefly British.* A pharmacist. **3.** *Obsolete.* An alchemist. [Earlier *chimist,* from New Latin *chimista,* short for Medieval Latin *alchymista,* ALCHEMIST.]

chem·is·try (kĕm′ĭ-strē) *n., pl.* **-tries.** *Abbr.* **chem. 1.** The science of the composition, structure, properties, and reactions of matter, especially of atomic and molecular systems. **2.** The composition, structure, properties, and reactions of a substance. **3.** Spontaneous interaction, as between two individuals: *the chemistry of love.* [Earlier *chimistrie,* from *chimist,* CHEMIST.]

chemo–, chemi–, chem– *prefix.* Indicates chemicals or chemical reactions; for example, **chemisorb, chemosmosis, chemotaxis.** [CHEM(ICAL) + -O-.]

chem·o·pro·phy·lax·is (kĕm′ō-prō′fə-lăk′sĭs, kē′mō-) *n.* The use of chemicals to prevent infectious disease. **—chem·o·pro·phy·lac·tic** *adj.*

chem·o·re·cep·tion (kĕm′ō-rĭ-sĕp′shən, kē′mō-) *n.* The reaction of a sense organ to a chemical stimulus. **—chem·o·re·cep·tive** *adj.* **—chem·o·re·cep·tiv·i·ty** *n.*

chem·o·re·cep·tor (kĕm′ō-rĭ-sĕp′tər, kē′mō-) *n.* A nerve ending or sense organ, such as a taste bud, sensitive to chemical stimuli.

chem·os·mo·sis (kĕm′ŏz-mō′sĭs, kĕm′ŏs-) *n.* The phenomenon of ionic or molecular transport across a membrane. **—chem·os·mot·ic** (kĕm′ŏz-mŏt′ĭk, kĕm′ŏs-) *adj.*

chem·o·sphere (kĕm′ə-sfîr′, kē′mə-) *n.* The region of the atmosphere between 20 and 120 miles altitude in which photochemical reactions initiated by solar radiation occur.

che·mo·sur·ger·y (kē′mō-sûr′jə-rē, kĕm′ō-) *n.* The combined use of surgery and chemotherapy to remove tumors of the skin.

chem·o·syn·the·sis (kĕm′ō-sĭn′thə-sĭs, kē′mō-) *n.* The synthesis of organic substances from carbon dioxide by certain bacteria using the energy of chemical reactions. **—chem·o·syn·thet·ic** (kĕm′ō-sĭn-thĕt′ĭk, kē′mō-) *adj.* **—chem·o·syn·thet·i·cal·ly** *adv.*

chem·o·tax·is (kĕm′ō-tăk′sĭs, kē′mō-) *n.* Characteristic orientation or motion of a freely moving living organism in response to a chemical substance. [New Latin : CHEMO- + -TAXIS.] **—chem·o·tac·tic** (kĕm′ō-tăk′tĭk, kē′mō-) *adj.* **—chem·o·tac·ti·cal·ly** *adv.*

chem·o·ther·a·py (kĕm′ō-thĕr′ə-pē, kē′mō-) *n.* The treatment of disease with chemicals; especially, the use of drugs rather than radiotherapy to treat cancer. **—chem·o·ther·a·peu·tic** (kĕm′ō-thĕr′ə-pyōō′tĭk, kē′mō-) *adj.* **—chem·o·ther·a·pist** *n.*

chem·ot·ro·pism (kĕm-ŏt′rə-pĭz′əm) *n.* Growth of an organism, especially a plant, in response to chemical stimuli. [German *Chemotropismus* : CHEMO- + -TROPISM.] **—chem·o·trop·ic** (kĕm′ō-trŏp′ĭk, -trō′pĭk, kē′mo-) *adj.*

chem·ur·gy (kĕm′ər-jē, kĕ-mûr′-) *n.* The development of new industrial chemical products from organic raw materials, especially from those of agricultural origin. [CHEM(O)- + -URGY.] **—chem·ur·gic** (kĕ-mûr′jĭk), **chem·ur·gi·cal** *adj.*

Cheng-chou, Chengchow. See **Zhengzhou.**

Cheng·du or **Cheng·tu** (chĕng′dōō′) or **Ch'eng-too.** Capital of Sichuan province in central China and one of the country's largest and oldest cities, founded before 770 B.C. It lies on the Min Jiang, an irrigation system more than 2,000 years old.

Ché·nier (shā-nyā′), **André Marie de** (1762–94). French poet. He is considered the greatest 18th-century French poet, although the vast majority of his work was not published until 25 years after his death by guillotine during the last days of the Reign of Terror.

che·nille (shə-nēl′) *n.* **1.** A soft, tufted cord of silk, cotton, or worsted used in embroidery or for fringing. **2.** Fabric made of this cord.
~*adj.* Of, made of, or resembling chenille: *a chenille bedspread.* [French, "caterpillar," from Latin *canīcula,* diminutive of *canis,* dog (from its hairy pile).]

Chen·nault (shə-nôlt′), **Claire Lee** (1890-1958). U.S. aviator and air-force officer. While commandant of the 19th Pursuit Group, Hawaii, he studied aerial combat strategies and the effectiveness of paratroops. He was named brigadier general in 1942 and led the U.S. Army Air Forces in China until his resignation in 1945.

che·no·pod (kē′nə-pŏd′, kĕn′ə-) *n.* Any plant of the goosefoot family, Chenopodiaceae, which includes spinach and beets as well as many common weeds. [New Latin *Chenopodiaceae,* from *Chenopodium* (genus) : Greek *khēn,* goose + -PODIUM.] **—che·no·po·di·a·ceous** (kē′nə-pō′dē-ā′shəs, kĕn′ə-) *adj.*

cheong·sam (chông′săm′) *n.* A light tight-fitting dress with a high collar and a slit skirt, typically worn by Chinese women. [Cantonese *cheung saam,* "long gown."]

Che·ops (kē′ŏps) (2590–2567 B.C.). Also **Khu·fu** (kōō′fōō′). Egyptian king. The second king of the fourth dynasty (*c.* 2613–*c.* 2494), he is renowned as the builder of the Great Pyramid at Giza, the largest single manmade structure at that time.

cheque. *Chiefly British.* Variant of **check** (sense 10).

cheque card *n. Chiefly British.* A **bankcard** *(see).*

chequer. *Chiefly British.* Variant of **checker.**

Cheq·uers (chĕk′ərz). The country residence of the prime minister of Great Britain, near Princes Risborough, Buckinghamshire. It was given to the nation by Lord Lee of Fareham (1917).

Cher·bourg (shâr′bōōrg′). Port in the Manche department of northwest France on the Cotentin Peninsula. It serves cross-Channel lines to Southampton.

cher·i·moy·a (chĕr′ə-moi′ə) *n.* **1.** A tropical American tree, *Annona cherimola,* having yellow flowers and edible fruit with white, soft, aromatic pulp. **2.** The fruit of this tree. [American Spanish *chirimoya,* from Quechua *chirimuya.*]

cher·ish (chĕr′ĭsh) *tr.v.* **-ished, -ishing, -ishes. 1.** To hold dear; treat with affection and tenderness. **2.** To keep fondly in mind; cling to: *We cherished the memory of our trip.* —See Synonyms at **appreciate.** [Middle English *cherissen, cherishen,* from Old French *cherir* (present stem *cheriss-*), from *cher,* dear, from Latin *cārus.*] **—cher·ish·er** *n.* **—cher·ish·ing·ly** *adv.*

cherished number plate *n. Chiefly British.* A **vanity plate** *(see).*

Cher·nen·ko (chûr-nyĕng′kō), **Konstantin Ustinovich** (1911–85). Soviet politician, president of the U.S.S.R. (1984–85).

cher·no·zem (chĕr′nə-zĕm′, -zhôm′) *n.* A black soil, rich in humus, ypical of cool to temperate semiarid regions, such as the grasslands of European Russia. Also called "black earth." [Russian, contraction of *chërnaya zemlya,* "black earth" : *chërnyĭ,* black + *zemlya,* earth.]

Cher·o·kee (chĕr′ə-kē′, chĕr′ə-kē′) *n., pl.* **-kees** or collectively **Cherokee. 1. a.** A tribe of North American Indians that formerly inhabited North Carolina and northern Georgia and are now settled in Oklahoma. **b.** A member of this tribe. **2.** The Iroquoian language of the Cherokee. **—Cher·o·kee** *adj.*

Cherokee rose *n.* A climbing rose, *Rosa laevigata,* of Chinese origin, having large, white, fragrant flowers.

che·root (shə-rōōt′, chə-) *n.* A cigar with square-cut ends. [Tamil *curuṭṭu, śurruṭṭu,* from *śuruḷ,* a curl.]

cher·ry (chĕr′ē) *n., pl.* **-ries. 1. a.** Any of several trees of the genus *Prunus,* having small, fleshy, globe-shaped or heart-shaped fruit with a small, hard stone; especially, *P. avium,* the common wild cherry, and *P. cerasus,* the sour cherry. **b.** The fruit or wood of any of these trees. **2.** A moderate or strong red to purplish red.
~*adj.* **1.** Of the color cherry: *She bought a cherry dress.* **2.** Made from the wood of a cherry tree: *a cherry highboy.* [Middle English *chery,* from Old Northern French *cherise,* variant of Old French *cerise,* from Vulgar Latin *ceresia* (unattested), from Latin *cerasus,* cherry tree, from Greek *kerasos*†.]

cherry Prunus "Kanzan," *an ornamental Japanese cherry tree, which is widely grown for its spectacular spring blossoms. The fruit on ornamental cherries are insignificant.*

cherry brandy *n.* A liqueur made from brandy and crushed cherry stones.

cherry laurel *n.* An evergreen European shrub, *Prunus laurocerasus,* having white flowers and blackish fruits.

cherry picker *n.* Any of various large, usually mobile cranes having a long, maneuverable obliquely vertical boom often supporting a work platform.

cherry pie *n. Chiefly British.* A widely cultivated garden heliotrope, *Heliotropium peruvianum.*

cherry plum *n.* A tree, the **myrobalan** *(see).*

cherry tomato *n.* A variety of the common tomato, *Lycospermum esculentum cerasiforme,* having small red or yellow fruit.

chert (chûrt) *n.* Any of various microscopically crystalline mineral varieties of silica, usually occurring in bands or layers of modules in sedimentary rocks. [17th century : origin obscure.]

cher·ub (chĕr′əb) *n., pl.* **-ubim** (-ə-bĭm′, -yə-bĭm′) for senses 1, 2) or **-ubs** (for senses 3, 4). **1.** A winged celestial being. Genesis 3:24. **2.** In medieval angelology, any of the second order of angels. See **angel. 3.** A representation of an angelic cherub, portrayed as a winged child with a chubby, rosy face. **4.** A delightful or innocent-looking child. [Hebrew *kərūbh.*] **—che·ru·bic** (chə-rōō′bĭk) *adj.* **—che·ru·bi·cal·ly** *adv.*

Che·ru·bi·ni (kĕr′ə-bē′nē, kā′rōō-), **(Maria) Luigi Carlo Zenobio Salvatore** (1760–1842). Italian composer. His 29 operas helped form the transition between classicism and romanticism. He did most of his composing in France, where he was appointed director of the Paris Conservatoire in 1822.

cher·vil (chûr′vəl) *n.* **1.** An aromatic plant, *Anthriscus cerefolium,* native to Eurasia, having leaves used in soups and salads. **2.** Any of several related plants, especially *Chaerophyllum bulbosum,* having an edible root. [Middle English *cherville,* Old English *cerfille,* from West Germanic *kervila* (unattested), from Latin *chaerephylla,* from Greek *khairephullon* : *khairein,* to delight in + *phullon,* leaf.]

Cheshire cat *A colored version of Tenniel's drawing that appeared in Lewis Carroll's* Alice's Adventures in Wonderland.

Ches. Cheshire.

Ches·a·peake Bay (chĕs′ə-pēk′). An inlet 320 kilometers (200 miles) long on the eastern seaboard of Virginia and Maryland. Baltimore is its main port.

Chesapeake Bay retriever *n.* A hunting dog of a breed developed in the United States, having a thick, short, brownish coat.

Chesh·ire (chĕs′ər, -îr). *Abbr.* **Ches.** County in western England, bounded by the Welsh border to the west and Merseyside to the north. It is noted for dairy produce, including Cheshire cheese. Extensive salt beds supply an important chemical industry. Chester is the administrative center.

Cheshire cat *n.* In *Alice's Adventures in Wonderland,* by Lewis Carroll, a cat that faded until only its grin remained visible.

Chesh·ire cheese (chĕsh′ər) *n.* A fairly hard, crumbly English cheese made from cow's milk. [From CHESHIRE.]

chess[1] (chĕs) *n.* A board game for two players, each possessing an initial force of a king, a queen, two bishops, two knights, two rooks, and eight pawns, all maneuvered following individual rules of movement with the objective of checkmating the opposing king. [Middle English *ches*, short for Old French *esches*, plural of *eschec*, CHECK (at chess).]

chess² *n.* One of the floorboards of a pontoon bridge. [Middle English *ches*, tier, from Old French *chasse*, frame, from Latin *capsa*, box.]

chess·board (chĕs′bôrd′, -bōrd′) *n.* A board used in playing chess, marked with 64 squares.

ches·sel (chĕs′əl) *n.* A mold used in the manufacture of cheese. [Probably CHEESE + WELL.]

chess·man (chĕs′măn′, -mən) *n., pl.* **-men** (-mĕn′, -mĭn). Any of the pieces used in playing the game of chess. Also called "chess piece."

chest (chĕst) *n.* **1.** The part of the body between the neck and the abdomen, enclosed by the ribs and the breastbone. **2. a.** A sturdy box with a lid and often a lock, used for storage and protection of articles. **b.** A chest of drawers; dresser. **c.** A small closet or cabinet with shelves. **3. a.** The treasury of a public institution. **b.** The funds kept there. **4. a.** A box for the shipping of certain goods, such as tea. **b.** The quantity packed in such a box. [Middle English *chest*, Old English *cest, cist*, box, from West Germanic *kistā* (unattested), from Latin *cista*, from Greek *kistē*.] **—chest·ed** *adj.*

Ches·ter (chĕs′tər). City and administrative center of Cheshire, on the Dee River. The Romans, who built a fort here to command the river crossing into Wales, called it Deva. It has an 11th-century cathedral.

ches·ter·field (chĕs′tər-fēld′) *n.* **1.** A single-breasted or double-breasted overcoat, usually with concealed buttons and a velvet collar. **2.** A large, overstuffed sofa with straight armrests of the same height as the back. [After an Earl of *Chesterfield* of the 19th century.]

Ches·ter·ton (chĕs′tər-tən), **Gilbert Keith** (1874–1936). British author, poet, and literary critic. His works include studies of *Robert Browning* (1903) and *Charles Dickens* (1906). His skills as a writer of mystery and fantasy were shown in *The Napoleon of Notting Hill Gate* (1904) and *The Man Who Was Thursday* (1908). In 1911 he published the first of his popular Father Brown stories, featuring a Roman Catholic priest as a detective.

Chester White *n.* A white hog of a breed that originated in Chester County, Pennsylvania.

chest·nut (chĕs′nŭt′, -nət) *n.* **1. a.** Any of several trees of the genus *Castanea*, of the Northern Hemisphere, bearing nuts enclosed in a prickly bur. **b.** The nut of any of these trees, edible when cooked. **c.** The hard wood of these trees, used in furniture and as a building material. **2.** The **horse chestnut** *(see)*. **3.** A grayish brown to rich reddish brown. **4.** A reddish-brown horse. **5.** A small, hard callus on the inner surface of a horse's foreleg. **6.** *Informal.* Anything lacking freshness or originality, as a joke, song, or story. ~*adj.* **1.** Of the color chestnut: *chestnut hair*. **2.** Of or pertaining to chestnut: *chestnut purée*. [Earlier *chesten nut* : Middle English *chesten, chasteine*, chestnut, from Old French *chastaigne*, from Latin *castanea*, from Greek *kastanea*† + NUT.]

chestnut blight *n.* A disease of the native American chestnut tree that is caused by a fungus, *Endothia parasitica*, and that results in cankers on the trunk and branches and eventual death.

chestnut soil *n.* A dark brown, friable type of chernozem found in arid areas of steppe that have little grass.

chest of drawers *n.* A piece of furniture consisting of a set of drawers that fit in a frame.

chest register *n.* The lowest register of the human voice. Also called "chest voice."

chest·y (chĕs′tē) *adj.* **-ier, -iest.** *Informal.* **1.** Having a large or well-developed chest. **2.** Arrogant; proud; conceited. **—chest·i·ness** *n.*

Chet·nik (chĕt′nĭk) *n., pl.* **-niks** or **Chetnici** (chĕt-nēt′sē). A Serbian guerrilla fighter, especially in World War II. [Serbian *četnik*, from *četa*†, troop.]

chet·rum (chĕ′trəm, chĕt′rəm) *n.* A monetary unit of Bhutan equal to ¹⁄₁₀₀ of a ngultrum. See feature at **currency**. [Native word in Bhutan.]

che·val-de-frise (shə-văl′də-frēz′) *n., pl.* **che·vaux-de-frise** (shə-vō′-). **1.** A defensive obstacle composed of barbed wire or spikes attached to a wooden frame. **2.** An obstacle in the form of jagged glass or spikes set in the masonry on the top of a wall. [French, "Frisian horse." It was first used in Friesland to compensate for a lack of cavalry.]

che·val glass (shə-văl′) *n.* A long mirror mounted on swivels in a frame. [French *cheval*, support, "horse."]

chev·a·lier (shĕv′ə-lîr′) *n.* **1.** A member of certain orders of knighthood or merit, such as the Legion of Honor in France. **2.** A knight. **3.** A chivalrous, gallant man. [Middle English *chevaler*, from Old French *chevalier*, from Late Latin *caballārius*, horseman, CAVALIER.]

Che·va·lier (shə-văl′yā), **Maurice** (1888–1972). French singer and film actor. His career began in cabaret, but he moved to Hollywood to take part in screen musicals in the 1930's. *Gigi* (1958) is his best-known film.

che·ve·lure (shəv-lür′) *n.* A head of hair. [Old French, from Latin *capillātūra*, the hair, from *capillus*, hair.]

che·vet (shə-vā′) *n.* The rounded east end of a church, usually with apses. [French, "pillow," from Latin *capitium*, from *caput*, head.]

Chev·i·ot (shĕv′ē-ət, chĕv′-) *n.* **1.** A sheep of a breed with short, thick wool, originally bred in the Cheviot Hills. **2. cheviot.** A woolen fabric with a coarse twill weave, used chiefly for suits and overcoats and originally made from the wool of the Cheviot sheep.

Cheviot Hills. Range of hills bordering England and Scotland. The

Cheviot (816 meters; 2,677 feet) is the highest peak.

chev·ron (shĕv′rən) *n.* **1.** A badge or insignia consisting of parallel stripes meeting at an angle, worn on the sleeve of a policeman or a noncommissioned officer in the armed forces and indicating rank, merit, or length of service. **2.** *Heraldry.* A device shaped like an inverted V. **3.** A V-shaped pattern, especially a kind of architectural molding. [Middle English, from Old French, beam, rafter, from Vulgar Latin *capriō* (unattested), from Latin *capra*, feminine of *caper*, goat.]

chev·ro·tain (shĕv′rə-tān′) *n.* Any of several small, hornless ruminants of the genera *Hyemoschus* and *Tragulus* of central Africa and southeastern Asia. The males have tusklike upper canine teeth. Also called "mouse deer." [French *chevrotin*, from Old French, diminutive of *chevrot*, kid, diminutive of *chevre*, goat, from Latin *capra*. See **chevron**.]

chevy. Variant of **chivvy**.

chew (chōō) *v.* **chewed, chewing, chews.** —*tr.* To bite and grind with the teeth; masticate. —*intr.* To make a crushing and grinding motion with the teeth. **—chew out.** *Slang.* To scold or reprimand. **—chew over.** To meditate upon; ponder. **—chew the fat** (or **rag**). To talk casually or idly; chat. **—chew up.** To grind, crush, or damage with or as if with the teeth: *heavy trucks that chew up the road.* ~*n.* **1.** The act of chewing. **2.** Something held in the mouth and chewed: *a chew of tobacco.* [Middle English *chewen*, Old English *cēowan*.] **—chew·er** *n.*

chewing gum *n.* A sweetened, flavored preparation with a rubbery texture for chewing, usually made of chicle.

chew·y (chōō′ē) *adj.* **-ier, -est.** Of a texture that requires chewing: *a chewy caramel.*

Chey·enne¹ (shī-ăn′, -ĕn′). Capital of Wyoming, in the southeast part of the state. It was founded (1867) as a station of the Union Pacific Railway and became a cattle center.

Cheyenne² *n., pl.* **-ennes** or collectively **Cheyenne. 1. a.** A tribe of North American Indians that formerly inhabited central Minnesota and North and South Dakota and are now settled in Montana and Oklahoma. **b.** A member of this tribe. **2.** The Algonquian language of the Cheyenne. [Canadian French, from Dakota *šahíyena*.] **—Chey·enne** *adj.*

Cheyne-Stokes respiration (chān′stōks′) *n.* An abnormal type of respiration, seen particularly in comatose patients, characterized by alternating shallow and deep breathing. [After John *Cheyne* (1777–1836), Scottish physician, and William *Stokes* (1804–78), Irish physician.]

chez (shā) *prep.* French. At the home or place of business of.

chg. charge.

chi, khi ((kī)) *n.* The 22nd letter in the Greek alphabet, written Χ, χ. Transliterated in English as *ch* or *kh*, and sometimes as *h*, especially for Modern Greek words. See feature at **alphabet**. [Greek *khi*.]

Chiang Ch'ing. See Jiang Qing.

Chiang-hsi. See Jiangxi.

Chiang Kai-shek. Jiang Jieshi.

Chiang-su. See Jiangsu.

Chi·an·ti (kē-än′tē, -än′tē) *n.* **1.** A fruity dry red wine produced in the Monte Chianti region of Tuscany in Italy. **2.** A wine similar to Chianti.

chiao (tyou) *n., pl.* **chiao.** A monetary unit equal to ¹⁄₁₀ of the yuan of the People's Republic of China. See feature at **currency**. [Chinese (Mandarin) *jiao³*.]

chi·a·ro·scu·ro (kē-är′ə-skoor′ō, -skyoor′ō) *n., pl.* **-ros. 1.** The technique of using light and shade in pictorial representation. **2.** The arrangement of light and dark elements in a pictorial work of art. **3.** The use of contrast in literary works. [Italian : *chiaro*, light, clear, from Latin *clārus*, clear + *oscuro*, dark, from Latin *obscūrus*.] **—chi·a·ro·scu·rist** *n.*

chi·as·ma (kī-ăz′mə) *n., pl.* **-mata** (-mə-tə) or **-mas.** Also **chi·asm** (kī′ăz′əm). **1.** *Anatomy.* A crossing or intersection of two tracts, such as that of the two optic nerves in the brain. **2.** *Genetics.* A point of contact between homologous chromosomes, considered the cytological manifestation of crossing over. [New Latin, from Greek *khiasma*, cross, from *khiazein*, to mark with the letter CHI.] **—chi·as·mal, chi·as·mic, chi·as·mat·ic** (kī′ăz-măt′ĭk) *adj.*

chi·as·mus (kī-ăz′məs) *n., pl.* **-mi** (-mī′). A rhetorical inversion of the second of two parallel structures, as *He went onward, but home went she.* [New Latin, from Greek *khiasmos*, from *khiazein*, to mark with the letter CHI.]

chi·as·to·lite (kī-ăs′tə-līt′) *n.* A mineral variety of andalusite with carbonaceous impurities symmetrically arranged along the longer axis of the crystal. In cross-section the crystals show a black cross, hence the name. Also called "macle." [German *Chiastolith* : Greek *khiastos*, crossed, past participle of *khiazein*, to mark with the letter CHI + -LITE.]

Chib·cha (chĭb′chə) *n., pl.* **-chas** or collectively **Chibcha. 1.** A member of an extinct Indian people once inhabiting Colombia. **2.** The extinct language of this people.

Chib·chan (chĭb′chən) *n.* **1.** A South American or Central American Indian ethnic stock including the Chibcha. **2.** The language spoken by these people. ~*adj.* Of or pertaining to this ethnic stock or language.

chi·bouk, chi·bouque (chĭ-book′, shĭ-) *n.* A Turkish tobacco pipe with a long stem and a red clay bowl. [French *chibouque*, from Turkish *çubuk, çibuk*, tube.]

chic (shēk) *adj.* **1.** Sophisticated; stylish. **2.** Dressed smartly and fashionably; elegant.

Cheviot *The fleece of this sheep, which was first bred in the Cheviot hills of northern England, is used for carpets, tweeds, and flannel. Both crossbred and purebred flocks are also reared for meat.*

~*n.* **1.** Sophistication in dress and manner; elegance. **2.** The quality of being fashionable; stylishness. [French, perhaps from German *Schick*, skill, Middle High German *schicken†*, to arrange, prepare.] —**chic·ly** *adv.*

Chi·ca·go (shə-kä′gō, -kô′-). Third-largest city in the United States and a major port on the Illinois shore of Lake Michigan. During the Prohibition years (1919–33), it became a notorious center of gangsterism and corruption. Chicago is a vital focus of industry, trade, finance, and communications.

chi·cane (shĭ-kān′, chĭ-) *v.* **-caned, -caning, -canes.** —*tr.* **1.** To trick; deceive. **2.** To quibble over; cavil. —*intr.* To use tricks or chicanery.
~*n.* **1.** Chicanery. **2.** In bridge or whist, a hand without trumps. **3.** In automobile racing, an obstacle on the track intended to slow the cars down. [French *chicaner,* from Old French *chicaner†,* to quibble.] —**chi·can·er** *n.*

chi·can·er·y (shĭ-kā′nə-rē, chĭ-) *n., pl.* **-ies. 1.** Deception by trickery or sophistry. **2.** A trick; a subterfuge.

Chi·ca·no (chĭ-kä′nō, shĭ-) *n., pl.* **-nos.** A Mexican-American. [American Spanish *Chicano,* variant of *Mejicano,* a Mexican, from *Méjico,* MEXICO.] —**Chi·ca·no** *adj.*

Chich·es·ter (chĭch′ĭ-stər). City in southern England, the administrative center of West Sussex. Laid out by the Romans, it prospered in the medieval wool trade. Parts of its ancient walls and gates survive.

Chichester, Sir Francis Charles (1901–77). British pilot and yachtsman. He made the first long-distance seaplane flight (1931) and won the first solo transatlantic yacht race (1960). He sailed around the world alone (1966–67).

chi·chi (shē′shē) *adj.* **1.** Elaborate; fussy; frilly. **2.** Pretentiously fashionable; precious. [French.]

chick (chĭk) *n.* **1. a.** A young chicken. **b.** The young of any bird. **2.** A child. **3.** *Slang.* A girl or young woman. [Middle English *chike,* short for CHICKEN.]

chick·a·dee (chĭk′ə-dē′) *n.* Any of several small, plump North American birds of the genus *Parus,* having predominantly gray plumage and a dark-crowned head. [Imitative of its cry.]

Chick·a·saw (chĭk′ə-sô′) *n., pl.* **-saws** or collectively **Chickasaw. 1.** A member of a North American Indian people, originally of Mississippi, later removed to Oklahoma. **2.** The Muskhogean language of this tribe. —**Chick·a·saw** *adj.*

chick·en (chĭk′ən) *n.* **1.** A young bird, especially of the common domestic fowl. **2.** The flesh of the common domestic fowl. **3.** Any of various birds similar or related to the common domestic fowl, such as the **prairie chicken** *(see).* —**count one's chickens before they are hatched.** To rely on an outcome that is still uncertain. ~*adj. Slang.* Cowardly; timid. ~*intr.v.* **chickened, -ening, -ens.** *Slang.* To act in a cowardly manner; lose one's nerve. Usually used with *out.* [Middle English *chiken,* Old English *cīcen,* from Germanic.]

chicken feed *n. Slang.* A trifling amount of money.

chicken hawk *n.* Any of various hawks that prey on or have the reputation of preying on chickens.

chick·en-heart·ed (chĭk′ən-här′tĭd) *adj.* Cowardly; timid.

chick·en-liv·ered (chĭk′ən-lĭv′ərd) *adj.* Cowardly; timid.

chicken louse *n.* A louse, *Menopon pallidum* (or *gallinae*), parasitic on domestic fowl.

chicken pox *n.* An acute contagious viral disease, usually of children, characterized by skin eruption, slight fever, and mild constitutional symptoms. Also called "varicella." [Perhaps alluding to the mildness of the disease.]

chicken wire *n.* A light-gauge galvanized wire fencing, usually made with hexagonal mesh.

chick·pea (chĭk′pē′) *n.* **1.** A bushy plant, *Cicer arietinum,* grown in the Mediterranean region and central Asia and bearing edible seeds. **2.** Any of the pealike seeds of this plant, widely used as food. Also called "garbanzo." [Earlier *chich-pease* : Middle English *chiche,* chickpea, from Old French, from Latin *cicer†* + *pease,* PEA.]

chick·weed (chĭk′wēd′) *n.* Any of various plants of the genera *Cerastium* and *Stellaria;* especially, *S. media,* a weedy plant with white flowers. [So called because it is eaten by chickens.]

chic·le (chĭk′əl) *n.* The coagulated juice of the sapodilla, used as the main ingredient of chewing gum. [Spanish, from Nahuatl *chictli.*]

chic·o·ry (chĭk′ə-rē) *n., pl.* **-ries. 1.** A widely cultivated plant, *Cichorium intybus,* having usually blue flowers, and leaves used in salads. **2.** The root of this plant, dried, roasted, and ground for mixing with coffee or as a coffee substitute. See endive. [Middle English *cicoree,* from Old French, from Latin *cichorium,* from Greek *kikhora†.*]

chide (chīd) *v.* **chided** or **chid** (chĭd), **chided** or **chid** or **chidden** (chĭd′n), **chiding, chides.** —*intr.* To scold; rebuke. —*tr.* To state one's disapproval of so as to correct or improve; scold: *chided the child for being sloppy.* [Middle English *chiden,* Old English *cīdan,* from *cīd†,* strife.] —**chid·er** *n.* —**chid·ing·ly** *adv.*

chief (chēf) *n. Abbr.* **C., ch., Ch. 1.** One who is highest in rank or authority; a leader: *a meeting of party chiefs.* **2.** The head man of a tribe or clan. **3.** *Slang.* A boss. **4.** *Heraldry.* The upper section of a shield. —**in chief. 1.** Having the highest or most important position: *the commander in chief.* **2.** Chiefly.
~*adj.* **1.** Highest in rank, authority, or office. **2.** Principal; most important.
~*adv. Archaic.* Chiefly. [Middle English *chief, chef,* from Old French, from Vulgar Latin *capum* (unattested), from Latin *caput,* head.]

Synonyms: *foremost, leading, main, primary, principal.*

chief constable *n.* In Britain, a high-ranking police officer in command of a regional police force.

chief·dom (chēf′dəm) *n.* The office or domain of a chief, especially of a tribal leader.

Chief Justice *n. Abbr.* **C.J.** The presiding judge of a court of several judges, especially the Supreme Court of the United States.

chief·ly (chēf′lē) *adv.* **1.** Above all; especially. **2.** Mostly; mainly.
~*adj.* Of, befitting, or similar to a chief.

chief of staff *n. Abbr.* **C.S. 1.** The senior staff officer of a major military formation. **2.** *Often* **Chief of Staff.** The commanding officer of the U.S. Army, Navy, or Air Force.

chief petty officer *n.* The highest rank of noncommissioned officer in the navy or coast guard.

Chief Rabbi *n.* The religious leader of the Jewish community within a country.

chief·tain (chēf′tən) *n.* The leader of a clan or tribe. [Middle English *chieftaine, cheftaine,* from Old French *chevetain,* from Late Latin *capitāneus,* from Latin *caput,* head.]

chiff-chaff (chĭf′chăf′) *n.* A small European warbler, *Phylloscopus collybita,* with brownish-gray plumage. [Imitative of its cry.]

chif·fon (shĭ-fŏn′, shĭf′ŏn′) *n.* **1.** A fabric of sheer silk or rayon. **2.** *Often* **chiffons.** Ribbons, laces, or other ornamental accessories for women's clothing.
~*adj.* **1.** Of or relating to chiffon. **2.** Having a light and fluffy consistency. Said of food. [French, "rag," from *chiffe,* old rag, variant of Old French *chipe,* from Middle English *chip,* CHIP.]

chif·fo·nier, chif·fon·nier (shĭf′ə-nîr′) *n.* A narrow, high chest of drawers, often with a mirror attached. [French *chiffonnier,* "bureau for rags," from CHIFFON.]

chig·ger (chĭg′ər) *n.* **1.** Any of various small six-legged larvae of mites of the family Trombidiidae, causing intensely irritating itching when lodged on the skin. Also called "chigoe," "jigger," "harvest bug," "harvest mite." **2.** A flea, the **chigoe** *(see).* [Variant of CHIGOE.]

chi·gnon (shēn-yŏn′, shēn′yŏn′) *n.* A roll or knot of hair worn at the back of the head or nape of the neck by women. [French, variant of Old French *chaignon,* chain, from Vulgar Latin *catēniō* (unattested), from Latin *catēna,* CATENA.]

chig·oe (chĭg′ō, chē′gō) *n.* **1.** A small tropical flea, *Tunga penetrans,* of which the fertile female burrows under the skin, causing intense irritation and sores that may become severely infected. Also called "chigger," "jigger," "sand flea." **2.** A flea, the **chigger** *(see).* [Cariban *chigo.*]

Chihli, Gulf of. See Bo Hai.

Chi·hua·hua¹ (chĭ-wä′wä, -wə). Capital of Chihuahua state in northern Mexico. It is situated in a valley of the Sierra Madre.

Chihuahua² *n.* A very small dog of a breed originating in Mexico, having pointed ears and a smooth coat. [After CHIHUAHUA, Mexico.]

chil·blain (chĭl′blān′) *n.* An inflammation followed by itchy irritation on the hands, feet, or ears, resulting from exposure to moist cold. [CHIL(L) + BLAIN.] —**chil·blained** *adj.*

child (chīld) *n., pl.* **children** (chĭl′drən). **1.** Any person between birth and puberty. **2. a.** An unborn infant; a fetus. **b.** An infant; a baby. **3.** One who is childish or immature. **4.** A son or daughter. **5. children.** In Biblical usage, members of a tribe; descendants. **6.** A person or thing considered as the product of a specified influence or phenomenon: *a child of nature.* —**with child.** Pregnant. [Child, children; Middle English *child(e), childre(ns),* Old English *cild, cildra,* from Common Germanic *kiltham* (unattested).] —**child·less** *adj.* —**child·less·ness** *n.*

child-bear·ing (chīld′bâr′ĭng) *n.* The process of pregnancy and childbirth. Also used adjectivally: *of childbearing age.*

child·bed (chīld′bĕd) *n.* The state of a woman in childbirth.

childbed fever *n.* Puerperal fever *(see).*

child·birth (chīld′bûrth′) *n.* The process of giving birth to a child; parturition.

child care *n.* Professional supervision, as by a local authority, of the welfare of children, especially in the absence or failure of parental supervision.

childe (chīld) *n. Archaic.* A young man of noble birth. [Middle English *child(e),* CHILD.]

Chil·ders (chĭl′dərz), **Robert Erskine** (1870–1922). Irish nationalist. He was active in the cause of Irish Home Rule and became a Sinn Fein deputy in the Irish Assembly (1921). He acted as publicity director for the I.R.A. during the Irish civil war. Arrested in 1922 for carrying arms, he was tried and shot. His son, **Erskine Hamilton Childers** (1905–74), became Irish president (1973–74).

child·hood (chīld′hŏŏd′) *n.* The time or state of being a child.

child·ish (chīld′ĭsh) *adj.* **1.** Of, similar to, or suitable for a child. **2.** Foolishly immature. —**child·ish·ly** *adv.* —**child·ish·ness** *n.*

Usage: *Childish* applied to adults is almost invariably a term of reproach but lacks such connotation when applied to children. *Childlike* is generally favorable on all age levels, suggesting endearing traits characteristic of children.

child·like (chīld′līk′) *adj.* Also *rare* **child·ly** (-lē). Like or befitting a child, as in innocence or guilelessness. —See Usage note at childish.

child·mind·er (chīld′mīn′dər) *n. Chiefly British.* A baby sitter *(see).*

child-proof (chīld′prŏŏf′) *adj.* Safe against tampering by children.

chil·dren. Plural of **child.**

chicory *This native of Europe is now grown worldwide. Its roots are dried, roasted, and ground, then added to coffee to strengthen its flavor.*

Children of Israel *pl.n.* The Jews.

child's play *n. Informal.* **1.** Anything that is very easy to do. **2.** A trivial matter.

Chil·e (chĭl′ē). A long, narrow country on the western seaboard of South America. The Spaniards colonized it from 1541, and the country declared its independence in 1818. After World War I cut off its markets and sources of manufactured goods, economic chaos and political unrest ensued. The military seized power in 1924 and ran the country for six months. A new constitution restoring presidential powers was promulgated in 1925 but was followed by several years of unrest. Constitutional normality returned in 1932. Salvador Allende's Marxist coalition was elected (1970) and instituted sweeping reforms and nationalization, but inefficiency and costly welfare schemes brought economic collapse and street violence. The armed forces staged a bloody coup in 1973, and under the repressive regime of President Augusto Pinochet Ugarte, the economy revived. Elections were held in 1980, and a Christian Democrat, Patricio Aylwin, became president in 1990. Chile has large energy resources: oil and gas in Patagonia, hydroelectric power in the Andes, and coal. The fertile central valley is its economic heartland, with industries concentrated around Concepción and Santiago. Exports include copper, iron ore, nitrates, wood products, fruit, and wine. Area, 756,945 square kilometers (292,181 square miles). Population, 13,200,000. Capital, Santiago. —**Chil·e·an** *adj. & n.*

chil·e con car·ne, chil·i con car·ne (chĭl′ē kŏn kär′nē) *n.* A highly spiced dish made of red peppers, meat, and usually beans. Also called "chili." [Spanish, "chili with meat."]

Chile saltpeter *n. Chemistry.* **Sodium nitrate** *(see).*

chil·i, chil·e, chil·li (chĭl′ē) *n., pl.* **-ies, -es, -lies. 1. a.** The very pungent red fruit of several varieties of a woody plant, *Capsicum frutescens.* **b.** A condiment made from the dried fruits of this plant. In both senses, also called "chili pepper." **2. Chile con carne** *(see).* [Spanish *chile, chilli,* from Nahuatl *chilli.*]

chil·i·ad (kĭl′ē-ăd′, -əd) *n.* **1.** A group containing 1,000 elements. **2.** One thousand years. [Late Latin *chīliās* (stem *chīliad-*), from Greek *khilias,* thousand, from *khilioi,* thousand.]

chil·i·asm (kĭl′ē-ăz′əm) *n.* **Millenarianism** *(see).* [New Latin *chiliasmus,* from Greek *khiliasmos,* from *khilias,* CHILIAD.] —**chil·i·ast** (kĭl′ē-ăst′) *n.* —**chil·i·as·tic** (kĭl′ē-ăs′tĭk) *adj.*

chili sauce *n.* A spiced sauce made with chilies and tomatoes.

chill (chĭl) *n.* **1.** A moderate but penetrating coldness. **2. a.** A sensation of coldness, marked by shivering. **b.** An illness characterized by this: *catch a chill.* **3.** A checking or dampening of enthusiasm, spirit, or joy. **4.** A sudden numbing fear or dread. ~*adj.* **1.** Chilly. **2.** Depressing; discouraging. ~*v.* **chilled, chilling, chills.** —*tr.* **1.** To affect with cold. **2.** To discourage; dispirit. **3.** To cool, as in a refrigerator: *Serve the wine chilled.* **4.** *Metallurgy.* To harden (a metallic surface) by rapid cooling. —*intr.* **1.** To be seized with cold. **2.** To become cold: *jelly that chills quickly.* **3.** *Metallurgy.* To become hard by rapid cooling. [Middle English *chile, chele,* frost, Old English *c(i)ele.*] —**chill·ing·ly** *adv.* —**chill·ness** *n.*

chill·er (chĭl′ər) *n.* One that chills or frightens; a thriller.

Chil·lon (shĭ-lŏn′, shĭl′ən). Castle in Switzerland, at the east end of Lake Geneva, near Montreux. Byron's poem *The Prisoner of Chillon* (1816) describes the fate of François de Bonnivard (1496–1570), a Genevan patriot imprisoned here (1530–36).

chill·y (chĭl′ē) *adj.* **-ier, -iest. 1.** Cool or cold enough to cause shivering. **2.** Seized with cold; shivering. **3.** Distant and cool; unfriendly. —**chill·i·ly** *adv.* —**chill·i·ness** *n.*

chi·lo·pod (kī′lə-pŏd) *n.* Any of various arthropods of the class Chilopoda, which includes the centipedes. [New Latin *Chilopoda,* "foot jaws" (the foremost pair of legs are jawlike appendages) : Greek *kheilos,* lip + -POD.]

Chiltern Hundreds *pl.n. British.* A now merely formal office applied for by Members of Parliament when they wish to resign from the House of Commons. [After a Crown manor in England's Chiltern Hills (the administration of which would require resignation from the House of Commons).]

chi·mae·ra (kī-mîr′ə, kī-) *n.* **1.** Any deep-sea cartilaginous fish of the order *Chimaeriformes* having a smooth-skinned tapering body and a whiplike tail. See **rabbitfish. 2.** Variant of **chimera.**

chime (chīm) *n.* **1.** An apparatus for striking a bell or bells to produce a musical sound. **2.** *Often* **chimes.** A set of bells tuned to a scale and used as an orchestral instrument or in a clock. **3.** A single bell. **4.** The musical sound produced by a bell or bells. **5.** Agreement; accord. ~*v.* **chimed, chiming, chimes.** —*intr.* **1.** To sound with a harmonious ring when struck. **2.** To make a musical sound by striking a chime. **3.** To agree; harmonize. Usually used with *with.* —*tr.* **1.** To produce (music) by striking bells. **2.** To strike (a bell) to produce music. **3.** To make known (the hour) by chiming. —**chime in. 1.** To break into a conversation, especially to express agreement. **2.** To accord harmoniously. [Middle English *chime, chimbe,* cymbal, chime, perhaps from Old French *chimbe,* from Latin *cymbalum,* CYMBAL.] —**chim·er** *n.*

chi·me·ra, chi·mae·ra (kī-mîr′ə, kī-) *n.* **1. Chimera.** *Greek Mythology.* A fire-breathing she-monster usually represented as a composite of a lion, a goat, and a serpent. **2.** A creation of the imagination; an impossible and foolish fancy. **3.** *Biology.* **a.** An organism, especially a cultivated plant, containing tissues from at least two distinct genetic types, often because of grafting. **b.** An animal or plant produced by genetic engineering, in which DNA from two distinct parent species is artificially combined to produce an individual with a double chromosome complement. [Latin *Chimaera,* from Greek *khimaira,* chimera, "she-goat."]

chi·mere (shə-mîr′, chə-) *n.* A long black or scarlet robe, often with lawn sleeves, worn over a rochet by Anglican bishops. [Middle English, perhaps from Medieval Latin *chimēra,* "sheepskin" (see **chimera**); akin to Spanish *zamarra,* sheepskin cloak.]

chi·mer·i·cal (kī-mĕr′ĭ-kəl, -mîr′ĭ-kəl, kī-) *adj.* Also **chi·mer·ic** (-mĕr′ĭk, -mîr′ĭk). **1.** Like a chimera; imaginary; unreal. **2.** Given to unrealistic fantasies. —**chi·mer·i·cal·ly** *adv.*

chim·ney (chĭm′nē) *n., pl.* **-neys. 1.** A passage through which smoke and gases escape from a fire or furnace; a flue. **2. a.** The usually vertical structure containing a flue. **b.** The part of such a structure that rises above a roof. **3.** A glass tube for enclosing the flame of a lamp. **4.** Anything resembling a chimney, such as a narrow cleft in a mountain by which a climber may ascend. **5.** The vent of a volcano. [Middle English *chimenee,* from Old French *cheminee,* from Late Latin *caminata,* from Latin *camīnus,* furnace, from Greek *kaminos†.*]

chimney breast *n.* The projection of a chimney from the walls surrounding it.

chili *Mature chilies on display in an African market. Fresh or dried, they are used in cooking.*

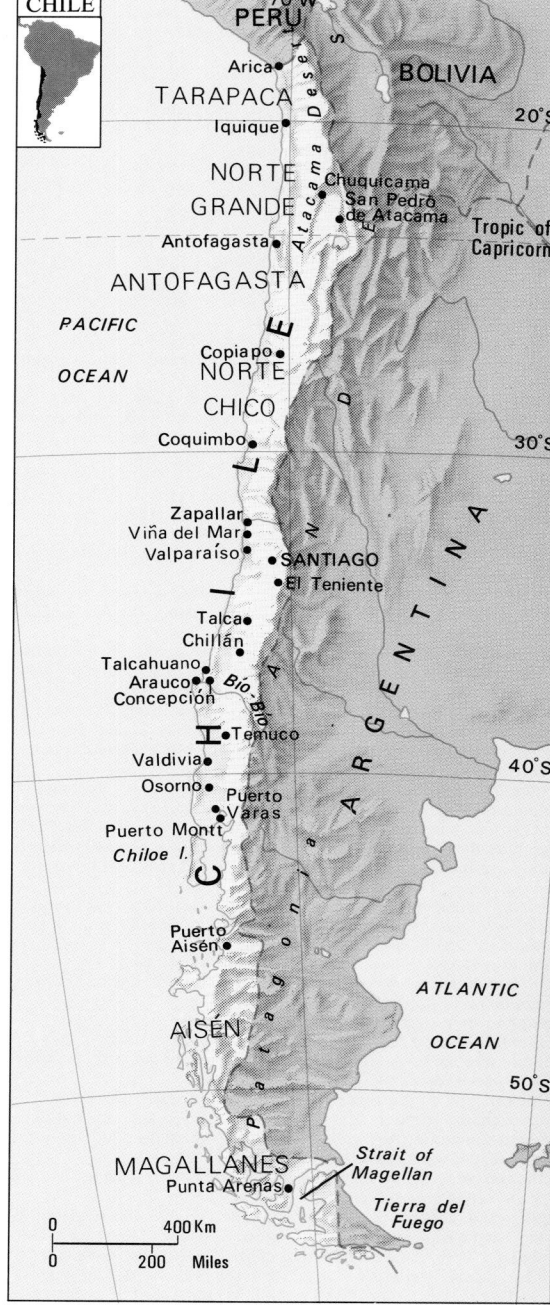

CHILE

PERU

BOLIVIA

Arica

TARAPACA

Iquique

20°S

NORTE GRANDE

Chuquicama
San Pedro
de Atacama

Antofagasta

Tropic of Capricorn

ANTOFAGASTA

PACIFIC OCEAN

Copiapo

NORTE CHICO

30°S

Coquimbo

Zapallar
Viña del Mar
Valparaíso

SANTIAGO

El Teniente

Talca
Chillán

Talcahuano
Arauco
Concepción

Bío-Bío

Temuco

ARGENTINA

Valdivia

40°S

Osorno
Puerto Varas

Puerto Montt

Chiloe I.

Puerto Aisén

ATLANTIC OCEAN

AISÉN

50°S

MAGALLANES
Punta Arenas

Strait of Magellan

Tierra del Fuego

0   400 Km

0   200 Miles

chimney corner *n.* A recessed seat inside or next to a large, old-fashioned fireplace.

chim·ney·piece (chĭm′nē-pēs′) *n.* **1.** The mantel of a fireplace. **2.** A decoration over a fireplace.

chimney pot *n.* A pipe placed on the top of a chimney to improve the draft.

chimney stack *n.* **1.** The part of a chimney rising above the roof of a building; stack. **2.** The masonry enclosing a number of flues.

chimney sweep *n.* Also **chimney sweeper.** A worker employed to clean soot from chimneys. Also called "sweep."

chimney swift *n.* A small, dark, swallowlike North American bird, *Chaetura pelagica,* that frequently nests in chimneys.

chimp (chĭmp) *n. Informal.* A chimpanzee.

chim·pan·zee (chĭm′păn-zē′, chĭm-păn′zē) *n.* An anthropoid ape, *Pan troglodytes,* of tropical Africa, having dark hair, gregarious, somewhat arboreal habits, and a high degree of intelligence. [French *chimpanzé,* from Kongo.]

chin (chĭn) *n.* The central forward portion of the lower jaw. **—take it on the chin.** To undergo misfortune or defeat.
~ *v.* **chinned, chinning, chins.** —*tr.* **1.** To pull (oneself) up with the arms while grasping an overhead horizontal bar until the chin is level with the bar. **2.** To place (a violin) under the chin. —*intr.* **1.** *Informal.* To chatter. **2.** To chin oneself. [Middle English *chin,* Old English *cin(n),* from Germanic.]

Chin. China; Chinese.

Ch'in or **Qin** (chĭn). A dynasty that ruled China from 221 to 206 B.C.

chi·na (chī′nə) *n.* **1.** High-quality porcelain or ceramic ware, originally made in China. **2.** Any porcelain ware. **3.** Tableware, as plates and cups, of porcelain or earthenware. **—chi·na** *adj.*

Chi·na (chī′nə). *Abbr.* **Ch., Chin.** Officially, People's Republic of China. The world's most populous and third-largest country, lying in East Asia. Its heartland is formed by three great river systems running west to east: the Huang He in the north, the Chang Jiang and the Xi Jiang in the south. The country also includes the barren plateau of Tibet and deserts in the north and west. China is the home of the oldest surviving civilization, traditionally dated from the first emperor (c. 2700 B.C.). The Shang dynasty emerged c. 1525 B.C. on the North China Plain. Bronzework had already evolved and a form of writing was in use. Under the Chou (Zhou) dynasty (c. 1027–221 B.C.), Confucian and Taoist thought spread. The Ch'in (Qin) dynasty (221–206 B.C.) founded the first unified empire and linked up the sections of the Great Wall against nomadic invasion. The Han dynasty (206 B.C.–A.D. 220) made great advances, and frontiers were extended, the "silk road" to Rome was opened up, and Buddhism introduced. The empire fell into decay, but was reunited by the Sui (581). Under the T'ang (618–960) a golden age in the arts and great expansion in trade occurred. The Song (960–1279) were removed by the Mongols, who set up the Yuan dynasty at Beijing (Peking), which Marco Polo visited. During the native Ming dynasty (1368–1644) the first European seafarers reached China. The Manchus, a northern people, set up the (Ch'ing) Qing dynasty (1644–1911), under which the 18th century was a period of stability, but in the later Ch'ing (Qing), isolation and stagnation led to backwardness. China was defeated in the Opium War (1839–42), by Japan (1895), was humiliated in the Boxer Rising (1900), and was forced to accept treaty ports for foreign trade. After a popular revolution, Sun Zhong-shan inaugurated a republic (1912), but civil war between the nationalist Guomindang and the Chinese Communist Party broke out. Japanese encroachments from 1931 led to war (1937), and an uneasy alliance against the invader. After a civil war (1946–49), the People's Republic was established under chairman Mao Ze-dong, and the nationalists fled to Taiwan. China made strides in modernization and social and economic development, but Soviet aid ceased (1960) after an ideological break between the two countries, and Mao launched the Cultural Revolution (1966). In 1971 China was admitted to the United Nations. Mao's failing health led to a period of confusion during which the Gang of Four, led by his wife, Jiang Qing, made a bid for power. Mao died in 1976 and was succeeded by Hua Guofeng. Under Hua and Deng Xiao-ping, modernization was resumed, and relations with the West and Japan greatly improved. In 1989 pro-democracy protests held by young people were ruthlessly suppressed. Chinese agriculture, the basis of the economy, is organized on a commune system and is traditionally dependent on rice. Cotton and tea are grown for export. Pigs are widely farmed. Coal, mined in most provinces, is the main mineral product. China is also a leading producer of oil, natural gas, iron ore, and antimony. Steel, machinery, and fertilizers are the major manufacturing industries, and fishing is important. Some 94 percent of China's vast population is Han Chinese, a Sinitic group of the Mongoloid race. There are over 20 cities with more than a million inhabitants, the largest by far being Shanghai, which is also the main port. Area, 9,596,991 square kilometers (3,704,427 square miles). Population, 1,139,100,000. Capital, Beijing.

China aster *n.* A plant, *Callistephus chinensis,* native to China, widely cultivated for its variously colored asterlike flowers.

chi·na·ber·ry (chī′nə-bĕr′ē) *n., pl.* **-ries. 1.** A spreading tree, *Melia azedarach,* native to Asia, widely grown for its white or purple flower clusters. Also called "China tree," "azedarach." **2.** A soapberry tree, *Sapindus marginatus* (or *S. saponaria),* of the West Indies, Mexico, and the southwestern United States. **3.** The fruit of either of these trees.

chi·na·graph pencil (chī′nə-grăf′) *n.* A type of colored pencil that can write on surfaces such as china or glass.

Chi·na·man (chī′nə-mən) *n., pl.* **-men** (-mĭn). A Chinese man. An offensive term.

Chi-nan. See Jinan.

chimpanzee *Thought to be the primates most closely related to man, chimpanzees are highly intelligent apes found in the forests of West Africa. They are one of the few tool-using animals and will use sticks to dig up ants for food.*

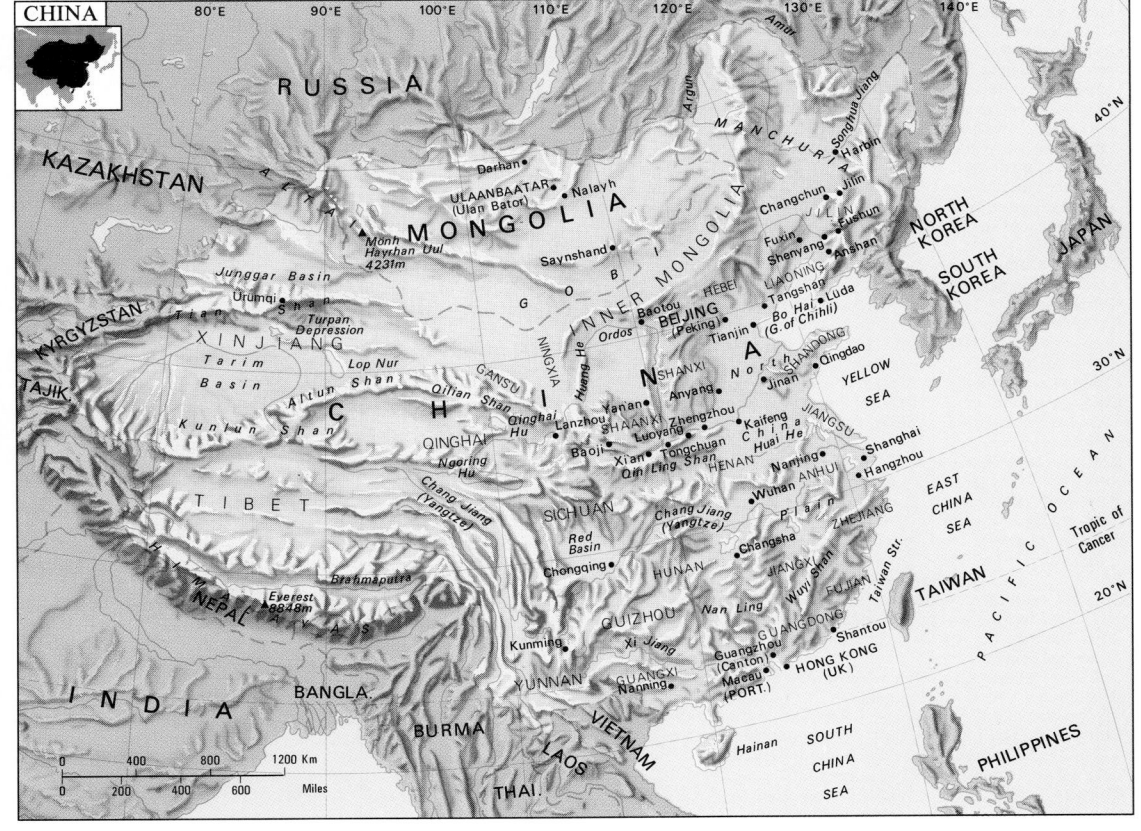

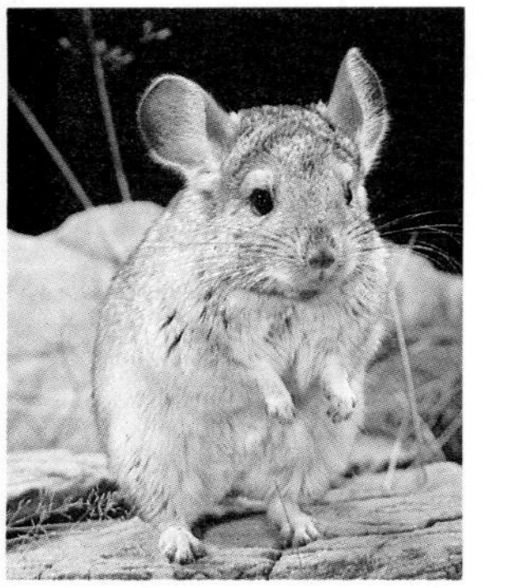

chinchilla *A rodent native to South America, the chinchilla is farmed worldwide for its blue-gray fur.*

China rose *n.* **1.** A shrub, *Rosa chinensis,* that has fragrant red or pink flowers and is the original ancestor of many cultivated hybrid roses. **2.** A dwarf, red-flowered rose, *Rosa semperflorens.*

Chi·na·town (chī'nə-toun') *n.* A district of a city inhabited mainly by Chinese people.

chi·na·ware (chī'nə-wâr') *n.* Porcelain or similar ware.

chinch (chĭnch) *n. Regional.* A bedbug. [Spanish *chinche,* from Latin *cīmex* (stem *cīmic-*), bug.]

chinch bug *n.* **1.** A small black and white European insect, *Ischnodemus sabuleti,* that is very destructive to grains and grasses. **2.** A similar American insect, *Blissus leucopterus.*

chin·che·rin·chee (chĭn'chə-rĭn-chē', chĭng'kə-) *n.* A bulbous plant, *Ornithogalum thyrsoides,* of southern Africa, having long clusters or spikes of white or yellow flowers. [Imitative of the squeaky sound made by its stalks.]

chin·chil·la (chĭn-chĭl'ə) *n.* **1. a.** A squirrellike rodent, *Chinchilla laniger,* native to the mountains of South America and widely bred in captivity for its soft pale gray fur. **b.** The fur of this animal. **2.** A thick, twilled cloth of wool and cotton, used for overcoats. **3.** *Often* **Chinchilla. a.** A breed of domesticated rabbit having a thick bluish-gray coat. **b.** A breed of long-haired cat having silvery-white fur. [Spanish, perhaps from Aymara.]

chin-chin (chĭn'chĭn') *interj. British.* Used as a toast or expression of farewell. [Pidgin English, from Chinese *qǐng qǐng,* "please please."]

Chin·co·teague pony (shĭng'kə-tēg', chĭng'-) *n.* A type of small, inbred North American horse that runs wild on certain islands off the Virginia coast. [From *Chincoteague* Island, Virginia, where the breed developed.]

chine[1] (chīn) *n.* **1.** The backbone; the spine. **2.** A cut of meat containing part of the backbone. **3.** A ridge or crest. **4.** The line of intersection between the side and bottom of a boat.
~*tr.v.* **chined, chining, chines.** To separate the backbone from the ribs of (a piece of meat). [Middle English *chyne,* from Old French *eschine,* probably from Germanic.]

chine[2] *n. British Regional.* A deep, narrow cleft in a cliff wall. [Old English *cinu,* cleft, chink, from Germanic.]

Chi·nese (chī-nēz', -nēs') *adj. Abbr.* **Ch., Chin.** Of or pertaining to China, its culture, people, or languages.
~*n., pl.* **Chinese. 1. a.** A native or inhabitant of China. **b.** A person of Chinese ancestry. **2.** A branch of the Sino-Tibetan language family that consists of the various dialects spoken in China. **3.** Any of the dialects spoken by the Chinese people.
Usage: This is the normal term for someone of Chinese origin, other forms being generally considered derogatory or nonstandard. Many people find *a Chinese* and other singular uses awkward and somewhat formal and prefer an adjectival construction—*a Chinese man came in.*

Chinese anise *n.* A tree, the **star anise** *(see),* or its fruit.

Chinese cabbage *n.* **1.** A Chinese plant, *Brassica pekinensis,* related to the common cabbage, having a cylindrical head of crisp, edible leaves. **2.** A plant similar to Chinese cabbage, **pak choi** *(see).*

Chinese calendar *n.* The lunar calendar of the Chinese people, supposed to have begun in 2397 B.C. Years are reckoned in cycles of 60, each year having a name that is a combination of two characters derived schematically from two series of signs, the celestial and the terrestrial. Months are reckoned also in cycles of 60 that are renewed every 5 years, and each month consists of 28 to 30 days. See feature at **calendar.**

Chinese checkers *n.* A game that is played on a board with a six-pointed star in which marbles or pegs are transferred, via holes or depressions in the board, from one point of the star to the point opposite it.

Chinese Chippendale *n.* Chippendale furniture characterized by certain Oriental influences.

Chinese date *n.* A tree, the **jujube** *(see),* or its fruit.

Chinese evergreen *n.* A plant, *Aglaonema simplex,* of tropical Asia, that has glossy, pointed leaves and is widely grown as a house plant. Also called "Japanese leaf."

Chinese gooseberry *n.* A plant, the **kiwi** *(see),* or its fruit.

Chinese houses *n. Used with a singular or plural verb.* A plant, *Collinsia bicolor,* of California, having showy white or rose-purple flowers.

Chinese lantern *n.* **1.** A decorative, collapsible lantern of thin, brightly colored paper. **2.** One of the papery, inflated seed cases of the **winter cherry** *(see).*

Chinese lantern plant *n.* The **winter cherry** *(see).*

Chinese puzzle *n.* **1.** A very intricate puzzle. **2.** Any very difficult problem.

Chinese red *n.* **Vermilion** *(see).*

Chinese restaurant syndrome *n.* A group of symptoms, including dizziness, facial pressure, sweating, and headache, that may occur after the ingestion of food containing large amounts of monosodium glutamate.

Chinese Revolution *n.* **1.** The revolution of 1911–12 in which the Republic of China was founded. **2.** The revolution culminating in the proclamation of the People's Republic of China (1949).

Chinese sacred lily *n.* A variety of the polyanthus narcissus, *Narcissus tazetta orientalis,* that has fragrant yellow and white flowers and is frequently grown as a house plant.

Chinese Turkestan. See **Xinjiang Uigur Zizhiqu.**

Chinese white *n.* A paint pigment, **zinc oxide** *(see).*

Chinese windlass *n. Machinery.* A **differential windlass** *(see).*

Chinese wood oil *n.* **Tung oil** *(see).*

Ch'ing or **Qing** (chĭng). A Manchu dynasty that in 1644 took Beijing from the Ming and became the last ruling dynasty of China.

Ch'ing-hai. See **Qinghai.**

Chingiz Khan. See **Genghis Khan.**

chink[1] (chĭngk) *n.* A crack or fissure; a narrow opening.
~*tr.v.* **chinked, chinking, chinks. 1.** To make chinks in. **2.** To fill chinks in. [Perhaps variant of earlier *chine,* from Middle English *chine,* crack, Old English *cinu, cine.*]

chink[2] *n.* A short, metallic sound.
~*v.* **chinked, chinking, chinks.** —*tr.* To strike (something) and make a chink. —*intr.* To make a chink. [Imitative.]

chin·less (chĭn'lĭs) *adj.* Having a small or receding chin.

chinless wonder *n. British Informal.* An upper-class man, especially a stupid or ineffectual one.

Chin-men. See **Jinmen.**

Chinnereth, Sea of. See **Galilee, Sea of.**

chi·no (chē'nō, shē'-) *n., pl.* **-nos. 1.** A coarse, twilled cotton fabric used for uniforms and sports clothes. **2. chinos.** Boys' and men's trousers of this material. [American Spanish *chino*†, "toasted" (from its original tan color).]

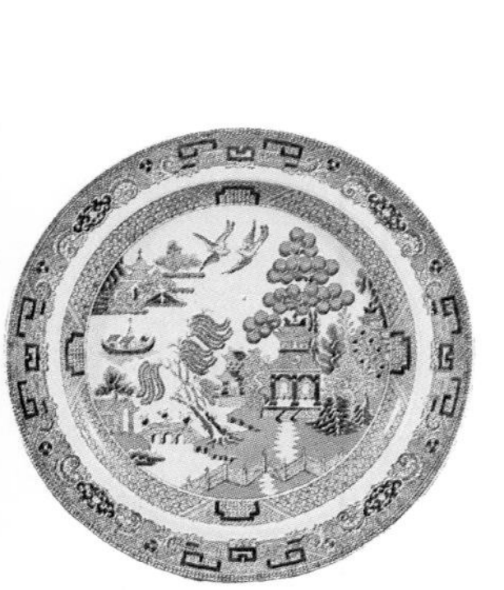

chinoiserie *A decorative style, seen here on a 19th-century willow pattern plate. In Britain, the Chinese-derived style had two vogues: after about 1775 it faded away, but it returned with the building of the Brighton Pavilion between 1815 and 1821.*

chi·noi·se·rie (shēn'wäz-rē') *n.* **1.** A style, especially of the 17th and 18th centuries, primarily in the decorative arts, in which Chinese motifs, such as the willow tree, are employed. **2.** An object in this style. [French.]

Chi·nook (shĭ-no͝ok', chĭ-) *n., pl.* **-nooks** or collectively **Chinook. 1.** A member of a North American Indian people formerly inhabiting the Columbia River basin in Oregon and speaking one of the Chinookan languages. **2.** The language of this people. **3. chinook.** A moist, warm wind blowing from the sea on the Oregon and Washington coasts. **4. chinook.** A warm, dry wind that descends from the eastern slopes of the Rocky Mountains, causing a rapid rise in temperature.

Chi·nook·an (shĭ-no͝ok'ən, chĭ-) *n.* A North American Indian language family of Washington and Oregon.

Chinook jargon *n.* A language combining simple English, French, Chinookan, and other North American Indian dialects, formerly used by Indians and fur traders of the Pacific Northwest.

Chinook salmon *n.* A salmon, *Oncorhynchus tshawytscha,* of northern Pacific waters, valued as a food fish.

chintz (chĭnts) *n.* A printed and glazed cotton fabric, usually of bright colors. [Variant of earlier *chints,* plural of *chint,* from Hindi *chīṇt,* from Sanskrit *chitra* many-colored, bright.]

chintz·y (chĭnt'sē) *adj.* **-ier, -iest. 1.** Of, pertaining to, or decorated with chintz. **2.** Characterized by a bright, fussy, flowery style that attempts to evoke an old-fashioned atmosphere. **3. a.** Gaudy; trashy. **b.** Cheap: *too chintzy to pay for my coffee.*

chin·wag (chĭn'wăg') *n. Slang.* A gossip or conversation.

chip (chĭp) *n.* **1.** A small piece broken or cut off. **2.** A crack or other mark caused by chipping. **3. a.** A small disk or counter used in gambling to represent money. **b.** *Slang.* Money: *They won the lottery and are in the chips now.* **4.** *Electronics.* A minute square of a thin semiconducting material, such as silicon or germanium, doped and otherwise processed to have specific electrical characteristics; especially, such a square before attachment of electrical leads and packaging as an electronic component or integrated circuit. **5. a.** A thin, brittle slice of a food, usually fried in deep fat: *a potato chip.* **b. chips.** *Chiefly British.* French-fried potatoes. **6.** A chip shot in golf. **7.** Wood, palm leaves, straw, or similar material cut and dried for weaving. **8.** A fragment of dried animal dung used as fuel. **—chip off the old block.** *Informal.* One who resembles a parent, especially in behavior. **—have a chip on one's shoulder.** To behave in an aggressive, challenging, truculent manner, especially owing to sensitivity about one's imagined social inferiority.
~*v.* **chipped, chipping, chips.** —*tr.* **1.** To break a small piece from: *fell and chipped a tooth.* **2.** To chop or cut with an implement, especially an ax. **3.** To shape or carve by cutting or chopping. **4.** To hit (a golf ball) with a short, lofted stroke. —*intr.* **1.** To become broken off. **2.** To play a chip shot in golf. **—chip in.** *Informal.* **1.** To contribute money, labor, or the like. **2.** To interject; interrupt. [Middle English *chip,* Old English *cipp*†, beam, piece cut off a beam.]

chip basket *n. Chiefly British.* **1.** A wire basket for holding food during deep-frying. **2.** A basket made of thin woven strips of split wood.

chip·board (chĭp'bôrd', -bōrd') *n.* A hard, flat material made from sawdust and wood chips compressed and bound with resin.

chip·munk (chĭp'mŭngk') *n.* A small rodent, *Tamias striatus,* of eastern North America, or any of several similar rodents of the genus *Eutamias,* of western North America and northern Asia, resembling a squirrel but smaller and having a striped back. [Variant of earlier *chitmunk,* from Algonquian.]

chip·o·la·ta (chĭp'ə-lä'tə) *n.* A small sausage with a spicy flavor. [French, from Italian *cipollata,* "onion-flavored (dish or mixture)," from *cipolla,* onion.]

Chip·pen·dale (chĭp'ən-dāl') *adj.* Of, pertaining to, or designating a type of furniture characterized by flowing lines and rococo ornamentation. [After Thomas CHIPPENDALE (1718–79).]

Chip·pen·dale (chĭp'ən-dāl'), **Thomas** (1718–79). British furniture maker whose name is associated with elegant mid-18th century taste. His son, **Thomas Chippendale** (*c.* 1749–1822), expanded the business to include fabrics and wallpaper.

chip·per (chĭp′ər) *adj. Informal.* Active; cheerful; brisk; pert. [Perhaps from northern English dialect *kipper,* active, cheerful.]

chip·py (chĭp′ē) *n., pl.* **-pies.** *Slang.* A prostitute. [From *chip,* chirp (imitative).]

chip shot *n.* A short, lofted golf stroke used in approaching the green.

Chi·rac (shîr′ăk, shē-räk′), **Jacques** (1932–). French politician and prime minister (1974–76). A Gaullist, he served as prime minister in the government of Giscard d'Estaing, but resigned (1976), reorganizing Gaullist forces in the Rassemblement des Français pour la République.

chi·ral (kī′rəl) *adj.* Of or pertaining to the handedness or chirality of an asymmetric molecule. [Greek *kheir,* hand.]

chi·ral·i·ty (kī-răl′ĭ-tē) *n. Chemistry.* The concept of left or right-handedness applied to stereoisometric molecules. A figure representing the configuration of a molecule is said to have chirality if its image in a plane mirror cannot be superimposed on it.

chi-rho (kī′rō′, kē′-) *n.* A monogram and symbol for Christ, consisting of the superimposed Greek letters chi (X) and rho (P). [CHI + RHO, first two letters of Greek *khristos,* CHRIST.]

chiro–, cheiro– *prefix.* Indicates of or with the hand; for example, **chiropractic.** [Latin, from Greek *kheir,* hand.]

Chi·ri·co (kîr′ĭ-kō′), **Giorgio de** (1888–1978). Italian painter, born in Greece. He produced distinctive canvases that feature enigmatically arranged statues and objects set against semideserted backgrounds of Italian architecture. He founded the Italian metaphysical school of painting (1917).

chi·rog·ra·phy (kī-rŏg′rə-fē) *n.* Penmanship. [French *chirographie* : CHIRO- + -GRAPHY.] **—chi·rog·ra·pher** *n.* **—chi·ro·graph·ic** (kī′rə-grăf′ĭk), **chi·ro·graph·i·cal** *adj.*

chi·ro·man·cy (kī′rə-măn′sē) *n.* The art or practice of foretelling a person's future by studying the palm of the hand; palmistry. [CHIRO- + -MANCY.] **—chi·ro·man·cer** *n.*

Chi·ron (kī′rŏn′). *Greek Mythology.* The wise centaur who tutored Achilles, Nestor, and Asclepius.

chi·rop·o·dy (kə-rŏp′ə-dē, shə-) *n. Medicine.* **Podiatry** *(see).* [CHIRO- + -PODY.] **—chi·rop·o·dist** *n.*

chi·ro·prac·tic (kī′rə-prăk′tĭk) *n.* A system of therapy in which disease is considered the result of neural malfunction and manipulation of the spinal column and other bodily structures is the preferred method of treatment. [CHIRO- + Greek *praktikos,* effective, PRACTICAL.] **—chi·ro·prac·tor** (kī′rə-prăk′tər) *n.*

chi·rop·ter·an (kī-rŏp′tər-ən) *n.* Also **chi·rop·ter** (kī′rŏp′tər). Any flying mammal of the order Chiroptera, which includes the bats. [New Latin *Chiroptera* : CHIRO- + -PTER + -AN.] **—chi·rop·ter·an** *adj.*

chirp (chûrp) *v.* **chirped, chirping, chirps.** *—intr.* **1.** To utter a short, high-pitched sound, like that of a small bird or grasshopper. **2.** To speak in a quick, sprightly manner. *—tr.* To utter with a short, high-pitched sound.
~*n.* A short, high-pitched sound; a tweet. [Middle English *chirpen* (attested only in gerund *chirpinge*), to chirp, twitter (imitative).] **—chirp·er** *n.*

chirp·y (chûr′pē) *adj.* **-ier, -iest.** *Informal.* Cheerful; bright; in a good or lively mood. **—chirp·i·ly** *adv.* **—chirp·i·ness** *n.*

chirr (chûr) *intr.v.* **chirred, chirring, chirrs.** To make a harsh, trilled sound, as a cricket does. [Imitative.] **—chirr** *n.*

chir·rup (chûr′əp, chĭr′-) *v.* **-ruped, -ruping, -rups.** *—intr.* To utter a series of chirps; make a light, tremulous sound. *—tr.* To sound with chirps. [Variant of CHIRP.] **—chir·rup** *n.*

chis·el (chĭz′əl) *n.* A metal tool with a sharp, beveled edge, used to cut and shape stone, wood, or metal.
~*v.* **chiseled, -eling, -els.** Also *chiefly British* **-elled, -elling.** *—tr.* **1.** To shape or cut with or as if with a chisel. **2.** *Slang.* To cheat or swindle. *—intr.* **1.** To use a chisel. **2.** *Slang.* To use unethical methods; cheat. [Middle English, from Old North French, from Vulgar Latin *cīsellus, caesellus* (both unattested), diminutive formation from *caedere* (past participle *caesus*), to cut.] **—chis·el·er** *n.*

Chis·holm (chĭz′əm), **Shirley Anita St. Hill** (1924–). U.S. politician. Concerned with education and social reform, she used her straightforward manner and genuine interest to earn the trust of her constituents. She served as New York State assemblywoman (1965–67) and as a U.S. congresswoman (1969–81). Her campaign slogan also served as the title of her book *Unbought and Unbossed* (1970).

chi-square test (kī′skwâr′) *n. Statistics.* A test used in relation to a hypothesis concerning the discrepancy between observed and expected results. The result of the test, the *chi-square distribution,* is calculated as the sum of the squares of observed values minus expected values divided by the expected values.

chit¹ (chĭt) *n.* **1.** A statement of an amount owed for food and drink; check. **2.** *Chiefly British.* A small slip of paper, as one carrying a memo. [Short for earlier *chitty,* from Hindi *ciṭṭhi,* note, pass, from Sanskrit *chitra,* mark.]

chit² *n.* A child, girl, or young woman, especially one thought to be impertinent. [Middle English *chittet*, young animal.]

chi·tal (chē′təl) *n.* The **axis deer** *(see).* [Hindi *cītal,* from Sanskrit *citrala,* spotted, from *chitra,* bright, variegated.]

chit·chat (chĭt′chăt′) *n.* **1.** Casual, light conversation. **2.** Gossip. [Dissimilated reduplication of CHAT.] **—chit·chat** *v.*

chi·tin (kīt′n, kī′tĭn) *n.* A semitransparent horny substance, primarily a mucopolysaccharide, forming the principal component of arthropod exoskeletons and the cell walls of certain fungi. [French *chitine,* from New Latin CHITON (mollusk).] **—chi·tin·ous** *adj.*

chi·ton (kīt′n, kī′tŏn′) *n.* **1.** A tunic worn by men and women in ancient Greece. **2.** Any of various marine mollusks of the class Amphineura, especially of the genus *Chiton,* living on rocks and having shells consisting of eight overlapping transverse plates. [New Latin, mollusk (with tuniclike shell), from Greek *khiton,* tunic, from Semitic, akin to Hebrew *kəthōnet.*]

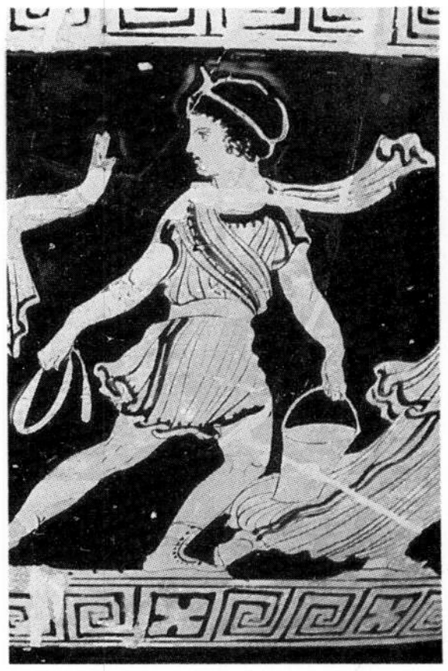

chiton *A tunic worn by the men and women of ancient Greece. The women's version was ankle length but the chiton normally worn by men, like the one shown here, barely reached the knees. Chitons worn by slaves were designed to leave the right arm bare and part of the chest exposed.*

Chit·ta·gong (chĭt′ə-gŏng′). Port and city in Bangladesh, near the mouth of the Karnaphuli River. It is the southern terminus of all the country's major land, river, and air routes, and Bangladesh's second-largest industrial center, processing cotton, jute, and tea.

chi·tar·ro·ne (kē′tə-rō′nā) *n., pl.* **-ni** (-nē). A large baroque lute. [Italian, augmentative of *chittara,* lute, GUITAR.]

chit·ter·lings (chĭt′lĭnz) *pl.n.* Also **chit·lins, chit·lings.** The small intestines of pigs, cooked and eaten as food. [Middle English *chiterling,* perhaps diminutive of Old English *cieter* (unattested), intestines.]

Chiu-lung. See **Jiulong.**

chiv·al·rous (shĭv′əl-rəs) *adj.* Also **chi·val·ric** (shĭ-văl′rĭk, shĭv′əl-). **1. a.** Having the qualities of gallantry and honor attributed to an ideal knight. **b.** Courteous, considerate, and protective, especially to women. Said of men. **2.** Of or pertaining to chivalry. **—chiv·al·rous·ly** *adv.* **—chiv·al·rous·ness** *n.*

chiv·al·ry (shĭv′əl-rē′) *n., pl.* **-ries.** **1. a.** The medieval institution of knighthood. **b.** The principles and customs of this institution. **2. a.** The qualities idealized by knighthood, as bravery, courtesy, honor, and readiness to help the weak. **b.** The manifestation of any of these qualities. **3.** A group of knights. [Middle English *chivalrie,* from Old French *chevalerie,* knightliness, from *chevalier,* knight, from Late Latin *caballārius,* horseman, CAVALIER.]

chivaree. Variant of **charivari.**

chive (chīv) *n.* **1.** A plant, *Allium schoenoprasum,* native to Eurasia, having rose-pink flowers and hollow, grasslike leaves. **2. chives.** The leaves of this plant, used as a seasoning. [Middle English *cyve, cheve,* from Old French *cive,* from Latin *cēpa,* onion, perhaps akin to Greek *kapiat*, onions.]

chiv·vy, chiv·y (chĭv′ē) *tr.v.* **-vied, -vying, -vies** or **-ied, -ying, -ies.** Also **chev·y** (chĕv′ē) **-ied, -ying, -ies.** *Chiefly British.* To cause to act or move more quickly; chase or harass. [English dialectal *chevy,* short for *chevy chase,* confusion, pursuit, from *Chevy Chase,* name of a Middle English ballad about the battle of Otterburn (1388), which arose from a hunt *(chase)* near the CHEVIOT HILLS.]

chla·myd·e·ous (klə-mĭd′ē-əs) *adj. Botany.* Having a floral envelope. [Latin *chlamys* (stem *chlamyd-*), mantle, CHLAMYS.]

chla·myd·o·spore (klə-mĭd′ə-spôr′, -spōr′) *n.* A thick-walled fungus spore derived from a hyphal cell; a resting spore. [Latin *chlamys* (stem *chlamyd-*), mantle, CHLAMYS + SPORE.]

chlam·ys (klā′mĭs, klăm′ĭs) *n., pl.* **-myses** or **chlamydes** (klăm′ə-dēz′). A short mantle fastened at the shoulder, worn by men in ancient Greece. [Latin *chlamys,* from Greek *khlamus*†.]

chlo·as·ma (klō-ăz′mə) *n., pl.* **-mata** (-mə-tə). A brown patch on the skin, usually on the face, that may occur during pregnancy and the menopause. [New Latin, from Late Greek *khloasma,* greenness, from *khloazein,* to be green, from *khloos,* green color.]

chlor·ac·ne (klôr-ăk′nē, klōr-) *n.* An acnelike skin disorder caused by prolonged exposure to chlorinated hydrocarbons.

chlo·ral (klôr′əl, klōr′-) *n.* A colorless, mobile, oily liquid, CCl_3CHO, a penetrating lung irritant, used to manufacture DDT and chloral hydrate. [French : CHLOR(O)- + AL(COHOL).]

chloral hydrate *n.* A colorless crystalline compound, $CCl_3CH(OH)_2$, used medicinally as a sedative and hypnotic.

chlor·am·bu·cil (klôr-ăm′byə-sĭl, klōr-) *n.* A drug, $C_{14}H_{19}Cl_2NO_2$, administered orally in the treatment of cancers.

chlo·ra·mine (klôr′ə-mēn′, klōr′-) *n.* Any of several compounds containing nitrogen and chlorine; especially, an unstable colorless liquid, NH_2Cl, used to make hydrazine. [CHLOR(O)- + AM(MONIA) + -INE.]

chlo·ram·phen·i·col (klôr′ăm-fĕn′ĭ-kôl′, -kōl′, klōr′-) *n.* An antibiotic, $C_{11}H_{12}O_2N_2Cl_2$, derived from the soil bacterium *Streptomyces venezuelae* or produced industrially by chemical synthesis. [CHLOR(O)- + AM(IDE) + PHE(NO)- + NI(TRO)- + (GLY)COL.]

chlo·rate (klôr′āt′, klōr′-) *n.* The inorganic group ClO_3 or a compound containing it. [CHLOR(O)- + -ATE.]

chlor·dane (klôr′dān′, klōr′-) *n.* Also **chlor·dan** (-dăn′). An amber-colored, odorless viscous liquid, $C_{10}H_6Cl_8$, used as an insecticide. [CHLOR(O)- + (IN)D(ENE) + -ANE.]

chlor·di·az·e·pox·ide (klôr′dī-ăz′ə-pŏk′sīd′, klōr′-) *n.* A drug used as a sedative and mild tranquilizer.

chlo·rel·la (klə-rĕl′ə) *n.* Any of various minute green algae of the genus *Chlorella,* widely used in studies of photosynthesis. [New Latin *Chlorella* : CHLOR(O)- + *-ella,* diminutive suffix.]

chlo·ren·chy·ma (klə-rĕng′kə-mə) *n.* Plant tissue containing chlorophyll. [CHLOR(OPHYLL) + -ENCHYMA.]

chlo·ric (klôr′ĭk, klōr′-) *adj.* Of, pertaining to, or containing chlorine, especially with a valence of 5. [CHLOR(O)- + -IC.]

chloric acid *n.* A strongly oxidizing unstable acid, $HClO_3 \cdot 7H_2O$.

chlo·ride (klôr′īd′, klōr′-) *n.* Any binary compound of chlorine. [CHLOR(O)- + -IDE.] **—chlo·rid·ic** (klə-rĭd′ĭk) *adj.*

chlo·rin·ate (klôr′ə-nāt′, klōr′-) *tr.v.* **-ated, -ating, -ates.** To treat or combine with chlorine or with a chlorine compound. **—chlo·ri·na·tion** *n.* **—chlo·ri·na·tor** *n.*

chlorinated lime *n.* A white powder of varying composition, as

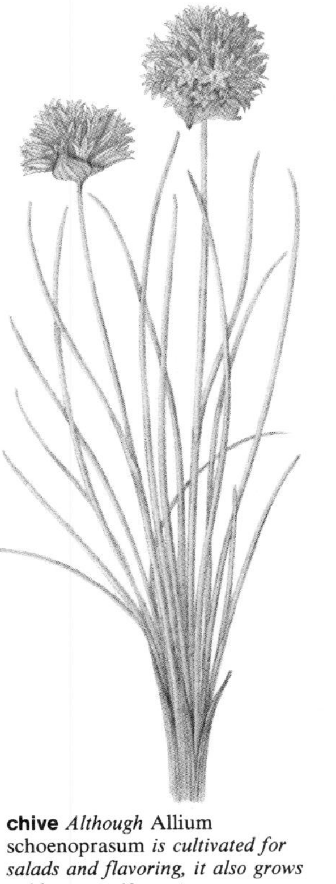

chive *Although* Allium schoenoprasum *is cultivated for salads and flavoring, it also grows wild—up to 40 centimeters (16 inches) tall.*

$CaCl (ClO) \cdot 4H_2O$, produced by chlorinating slaked lime and used as a bleach.

chlo·rine (klôr'ēn', klôr'-, -ĭn) n. Symbol **Cl** A highly irritating, greenish-yellow gaseous halogen, capable of combining with nearly all other elements, produced principally by electrolysis of sodium chloride and used widely to purify water, as a disinfectant, a bleaching agent, and in the manufacture of many important compounds including chloroform and carbon tetrachloride. Atomic number 17, atomic weight 35.45, freezing point $-100.98°C$, boiling point $-34.0°C$, specific gravity 1.56 ($-33.6°C$), valences 1, 3, 5, 7. [CHLOR(O)- + -INE.]

chlo·rite¹ (klôr'īt', klôr'-) n. A generally green or black secondary mineral, (Mg, Fe), Al (Al, Si₃)O₁₀ (OH)₉, often formed by metamorphic alteration of primary dark rock minerals. [Latin *chlorītis*, a green precious stone, from Greek *khlōritis*, from *khlōros*, greenish yellow.]

chlorite² n. The inorganic group ClO_2 or a compound containing it. [CHLOR(O)- + -ITE.]

chloro–, chlor– prefix. Indicates: 1. The color green; for example, **chlorosis**. 2. The presence of chlorine; for example, **chloroform**, **chlorate**. [Greek *khlōros*, greenish yellow.]

chlo·ro·a·ce·tic acid (klôr'ō-ə-sē'tĭk, -sĕt'ĭk, klôr'-) n. Also **chlor·a·ce·tic acid** (klôr'ə-sē'tĭk, -sĕt'ĭk, klôr'-) 1. A colorless crystalline solid, $CH_2ClCOOH$, prepared by chlorinating acetic acid and used as an intermediate. 2. A colorless liquid, $CHCl_2COOH$, used in the manufacture of dyes. 3. A deliquescent crystalline solid, **trichloroacetic acid** (see).

chlo·ro·ben·zene (klôr'ō-bĕn'zēn', -bĕn-zēn', klôr'-) n. A colorless, volatile flammable liquid, C_6H_5Cl, used to prepare phenol, DDT, aniline, and as a general solvent.

chlo·ro·eth·ene (klôr'ō-ĕth'ēn', klôr'-) n. **Vinyl chloride** (see).

chlo·ro·form (klôr'ə-fôrm', klôr'-) n. A clear, colorless, heavy liquid, $CHCl_3$, used in refrigerants, propellants, and resins and as an anesthetic. —tr.v. **chloroformed, -forming, -forms.** 1. To anesthetize or kill with chloroform. 2. To apply chloroform to. [CHLORO- + FORM(YL).]

chlo·ro·hy·drin (klôr'ō-hī'drĭn, klôr'-) n. An aliphatic organic chemical compound that is both an alkyl chloride and an alcohol, frequently containing a single chlorine atom and a single hydroxyl group on adjacent carbon atoms. [CHLORO- + HYDR(O)- + -IN.]

Chlo·ro·my·ce·tin (klôr'ō-mī-sēt'n, klôr'-) n. A trademark for **chloramphenicol** (see).

chlo·ro·phyll, chlo·ro·phyl (klôr'ə-fĭl', klôr'-) n. Any of a group of related green pigments found in plants that trap energy from sunlight for use in photosynthesis, especially: 1. *Chlorophyll a*, a waxy blue-black microcrystalline green-plant pigment, $C_{55}H_{72}MgN_4O_5$, with a characteristic blue-green alcohol solution. 2. *Chlorophyll b*, a similar green-plant pigment, $C_{55}H_{70}MgN_4O_6$, having a brilliant green alcohol solution. [French *chlorophylle* : CHLORO- + -PHYLL.]

chlo·ro·pic·rin (klôr'ə-pĭk'rĭn, klôr'-) n. An oily colorless liquid, CCl_3NO_2, used to make poison gas, in dyestuffs, disinfectants, insecticides, and fumigants. Also called "nitrochloroform," "vomiting gas." [CHLORO- + PICR(O)- + -IN.]

chlo·ro·plast (klôr'ə-plăst', klôr'-) n. Also **chlo·ro·plas·tid** (klôr'-ə-plăs'tĭd, klôr'-). Botany. A plastid containing chlorophyll in photosynthetic plants. [CHLORO- + -PLAST.]

chlo·ro·prene (klôr'ə-prēn', klôr'-) n. A colorless liquid, C_4H_5Cl, used as the monomer of neoprene rubber. [CHLORO- + (ISO)PRENE.]

chlor·o·quine (klôr'ə-kwīn', -kwĕn', klôr'-) n. A drug, $C_{18}H_{26}ClN_3$, used mainly in the treatment and prevention of malaria.

chlo·ro·sis (klə-rō'sĭs) n. 1. Botany. An abnormal condition of plants, characterized by absence of or deficiency in green pigment and caused by lack of light, mineral deficiency, or genetic disorders. 2. Pathology. An iron-deficiency anemia chiefly affecting girls at puberty and characterized by greenish skin color. Also called "greensickness." [CHLOR(O)- + -OSIS.]

chlo·rous (klôr'əs, klōr'-) adj. Of, pertaining to, or containing chlorine, especially with a valence of 3.

chlor·prom·a·zine (klôr-prŏm'ə-zēn', -prō'mə-zēn', klōr-) n. An oily liquid, $C_{17}H_{19}ClN_2S$, derived from phenothiazine and used as a sedative, tranquilizer, and antiemetic. [CHLOR(O)- + PRO(PYL) + METH(YL) + AZINE.]

chlor·tet·ra·cy·cline (klôr'tĕt-rə-sī'klēn', klôr'-) n. An antibiotic, $C_{22}H_{23}ClN_2O_8$, obtained from the soil bacterium *Streptomyces aureofaciens* and used for treating a variety of infections.

chm. 1. chairman. 2. Chess. checkmate.

cho·a·na (kō'ə-nə) n., pl. **-nae** (-nē'). Anatomy. A funnel-shaped opening; especially, either of the two internal openings of the nose into the pharynx. [Greek *khoanē*, funnel, from *khein*, to pour.]

cho·an·o·cyte (kō-ăn'ə-sīt') n. Biology. One of the flagellated cells that line the body cavity of a sponge. Also called "collar cell." [Greek *khoanē*, funnel, from *khein*, to pour + -CYTE.]

cho·cho (chō'chō) n. The cucumberlike fruit of the vine *Sechium edule*, eaten especially in the West Indies, Australia, and New Zealand. [Brazilian native name *chuchy*.]

chock (chŏk) n. 1. A block or wedge placed under something, such as a boat, barrel, or wheel, to keep it from moving. 2. Nautical. A heavy fitting of metal or wood with two jaws curving inward, through which a rope or cable may be run. —tr.v. **chocked, chocking, chocks.** To fit, secure, or wedge with a chock or chocks.

—adv. As completely or closely as possible. [17th century : origin obscure.]

chock-a-block (chŏk'ə-blŏk') adj. 1. Completely full; jammed: *chock-a-block with cars.* 2. Archaic. Drawn so close as to have the blocks touching. Said of a ship's hoisting tackle. —**chock-a-block** adv.

chock-full (chŏk'fŏŏl', chŭk'-) adj. Completely filled; stuffed. Used with of. [Middle English *chokkeful*, probably from CHOCK (to ram tight with chocks).]

choc·o (chŏk'ō, chŏ'kō) n., pl. **-os.** Australian Slang. During World War II, a military recruit. [Shortened from *chocolate soldier*.]

choc·o·late (chŏk'ə-lĭt, chôk'-, chŏk'ə-lĭt, chôk'-) n. 1. Husked, roasted, and ground cacao seeds, often combined with a sweetener or flavoring agent. 2. A candy or beverage made from chocolate. 3. A grayish to deep reddish brown. [Spanish, from Aztec *xococ*, bitter + *atl*, water.] —**choc·o·late** adj.

choc·o·late-box (chô'kə-lĭt-bŏks', chŏk'lĭt-, chŏk'ə-lĭt-, chôk'lĭt-) adj. Pretty in a sentimental way. Usually said of pictures.

choc·taw (chŏk'tô) n. In figure-skating, a turn from either edge of one skate to the opposite edge of the other. [After CHOCTAW.]

Choc·taw (chŏk'tô) n., pl. **-taws** or collectively **Choctaw.** 1. A member of a North American Indian people, formerly living in southern Mississippi and Alabama, now settled in Oklahoma. 2. The Muskhogean language of this tribe.

chog·yal (chŏg'yäl') n. The traditional title of the ruler of Sikkim.

choice (chois) n. 1. The act of choosing; selection; election. 2. The power, right, or liberty of choosing; option. 3. The person or thing chosen. 4. a. A sufficient number or variety from which to choose. b. A supply chosen with care. 5. The best part; the pick. 6. An alternative. —adj. **choicer, choicest.** 1. Of fine quality; select; excellent. 2. Selected with care. 3. Appealing to refined taste. [Middle English *chois*, from Old French, from *choisir*, to CHOOSE.]

   Synonyms: alternative, option, preference, selection.

choir (kwīr) n. 1. a. An organized company of singers, especially one performing church music or singing in a church. b. The part of a church used by such singers. 2. Architecture. The part of a cruciform church between the nave and the main altar. Compare **chancel.** 3. a. A musical group or band. b. A section of a musical group or band. —intr.v. **choired, choiring, choirs.** To sing in chorus. [Earlier *quier, quire*, Middle English *quere*, from Old French *cuer*, from Medieval Latin *chorus*, CHORUS.]

choir·boy (kwīr'boi') n. A boy member of a choir.

choir loft n. A gallery for a church choir.

choke (chōk) v. **choked, choking, chokes.** —tr. 1. To interfere with or terminate the normal breathing of (a person, for example), especially by constricting or breaking the windpipe or by polluting the air. 2. To stop by or as if by strangling; silence; suppress. Often used with off, down, or back: *choke back tears.* 3. To reduce the air intake of (a carburetor), thereby enriching the fuel mixture. 4. To check or slow down the movement, growth, or development of (plants, for example). 5. To block up or obstruct by filling or crowding; clog; congest. 6. To fill completely; jam; pack. Often used with up. 7. To cause to be temporarily overcome with strong emotion. Usually used in the passive. —intr. 1. To become suffocated; have difficulty in breathing, swallowing, or speaking. 2. To be blocked up or obstructed. —n. 1. The act or sound of choking. 2. That which constricts or chokes; a narrow part, such as the chokebore of a gun. 3. A device used in an internal-combustion engine to enrich the fuel mixture by reducing the flow of air to the carburetor. 4. Electronics. A coil of wire with a high impedance used to smooth the output of a rectifier or prevent the passage of high frequencies. 5. The inner part of a globe artichoke, composed of small inedible hairs. [Middle English *choken, cheken*, short for *achoken, acheken*, Old English *ācēocian*, from Germanic *kēkōn-* (unattested), CHEEK.]

choke-bore (chōk'bôr', -bōr') n. 1. A shotgun bore that narrows toward the muzzle to prevent wide scattering of the shot. 2. A gun with a chokebore.

choke-damp (chōk'dămp') n. A gaseous mixture, **blackdamp** (see). [So called because it causes suffocation in mines.]

chok·er (chō'kər) n. 1. One that chokes. 2. a. A necklace or band that fits closely round the throat. b. A high, tight collar.

cho·key (chō'kē) n., pl. **-keys.** British Slang. Prison. [Hindi *chaukī*, (police) station, shed.]

cho·lan·gi·og·ra·phy (kō-lăn'jē-ŏg'rə-fē) n. Examination by x-ray of the bile ducts in order to detect obstruction or the presence of stones. [CHOLE- + ANGIO- + -GRAPHY.] —**cho·lan·gi·o·graph·ic** (kō-lăn'jē-ə-grăf'ĭk) adj.

chole–, chol– prefix. Indicates gall or bile; for example, **cholecyst**, **choline**. [Greek *kholē*, bile, gall.]

cho·le·cal·cif·er·ol (kō'lĭ-kăl-sĭf'ə-rôl', -rōl') n. One of the forms in which **Vitamin D** (see) occurs.

cho·le·cyst (kō'lə-sĭst', kōl'ə-) n. The gallbladder. [New Latin *cholecystis* : CHOLE- + CYST.]

cho·le·cys·tec·to·my (kō'lə-sĭ-stĕk'tə-mē, kōl'ə-) n., pl. **-mies.** Surgical removal of the gallbladder.

chol·er (kŏl'ər, kō'lər) n. 1. Archaic. a. One of the four humors of the body thought in the Middle Ages to cause anger and bad temper when present in excess; yellow bile. b. Biliousness. 2. Anger; irritability. [Middle English *colre, coler(a)*, from Old French *colere*, from Latin *cholera*, bilious diarrhea, from Greek *kholera*, from *kholē*, bile, gall.]

chol·er·a (kŏl′ər-ə) *n.* An acute infectious epidemic disease caused by the bacterium *Vibrio comma*, characterized by watery diarrhea, vomiting, cramps, suppression of urine, and collapse. [Latin *cholera*, bilious diarrhea. See **choler**.] —**chol·er·a·ic** (kŏl′ə-rā′ĭk) *adj.* —**chol·er·oid** (kŏl′ə-roid′) *adj.*

chol·er·ic (kŏl′ər-ĭk, kə-lĕr′ĭk) *adj.* Bad-tempered; irascible. —**chol·er·i·cal·ly, chol·er·ic·ly** *adv.*

cho·les·ter·ol (kə-lĕs′tə-rôl′, -rōl′) *n.* A glistening white soapy crystalline substance, $C_{27}H_{45}OH$, the most common animal sterol, a precursor of a form of Vitamin D and a universal tissue constituent, occurring notably in bile, gallstones, the brain, blood cells, plasma, egg yolk, and seeds. Also called "cholesterin." [CHOLE- + Greek *stereos*, hard, solid + -OL (so called because it was first found in gallstones).]

cho·li (chō′lē) *n.* A short-sleeved woman's bodice worn mainly by women in India. [Hindi *coli*.]

cho·lic acid (kō′lĭk) *n.* An abundant crystalline bile acid, $C_{24}H_{40}O_5$. [Greek *kholikos*, bilious, from *kholē*, bile.]

cho·line (kō′lēn′) *n.* A natural amine, $C_5H_{15}NO_2$, sometimes classed in the vitamin B complex and a precursor of various phospholipids and acetylcholine. [CHOL(E)- + -INE (from its function in preventing fat accumulation in the liver).]

cho·lin·er·gic (kō′lə-nûr′jĭk) *adj.* **1.** Activated by or capable of liberating **acetylcholine** (*see*). Said of certain nerve fibers. **2.** Having physiological effects similar to acetylcholine. [(ACETYL)CHOLIN(E) + Greek *ergon*, work + -IC.]

cho·lin·es·ter·ase (kō′lə-nĕs′tə-rās′, -rāz′) *n.* An enzyme that hydrolyzes acetylcholine to form acetic acid and choline. Also called "acetylcholinesterase." [CHOLIN(E) + ESTERASE.]

chol·la (choi′ə) *n.* Any of several very spiny cacti of the genus *Opuntia*, characterized by cylindrical stem segments. See **prickly pear**. [Mexican Spanish, from Spanish *cholla*, head, possibly from Old French *cholle*, head, from Germanic.]

chomp. Variant of **champ** (bite).

Chom·sky (chŏm′skē), **Noam** (1928–). U.S. language theorist whose works revolutionized the study of linguistics. He argues that the structure of language is determined by the structure of the human mind, and that human language differs radically from the way animals communicate or machines may be programmed. —**Chom·sky·an** *adj. & n.*

chon (chŏn) *n., pl.* **chon.** A coin equal to $^1/_{100}$ of the won, the monetary unit of South Korea. See feature at **currency**. [Korean.]

chon·dri·fy (kŏn′drə-fī′) *v.* **-fied, -fying, -fies.** —*tr.* To change into cartilage. —*intr.* To become cartilage. [CHONDRI- + -FY.] —**chon·dri·fi·ca·tion** *n.*

chon·dri·o·some (kŏn′drē-ə-sōm′) *n. Biology.* A **mitochondrion** (*see*). [CHONDRI- + -SOME.]

chon·drite (kŏn′drīt′) *n.* A stone of meteoric origin characterized by chondrules. [CHONDR(O)- + -ITE.] —**chon·drit·ic** (kŏn-drĭt′ĭk) *adj.*

chondro–, chondr–, chondri– *prefix.* Indicates: **1.** Cartilage; for example, **chondroma, chondrify. 2.** Granule or chondrule; for example, **chondrite.** [Greek *khondros*, granule, cartilage.]

chon·dro·cra·ni·um (kŏn′drō-krā′nē-əm) *n., pl.* **-ums** or **-nia** (-nē-ə). The embryonic cartilaginous cranium, especially as distinguished from the **osteocranium** (*see*).

chon·dro·ma (kŏn-drō′mə) *n., pl.* **-mas** or **-mata** (-mə-tə). A benign cartilaginous tumor. [New Latin : CHONDR(O)- + -OMA.]

chon·drule (kŏn′drōōl′) *n. Geology.* A small round granule of mineral or glass embedded in some meteorites. [CHONDR(O)- + -ULE.]

Chong·qing, Ch'ung-ch'ing, or **Chung-king** (chōōng′chĭng′, -kĭng′). City and river port in Sichuan province of central China, on the Chang Jiang. It was made capital of China (1937–46) during the war with Japan. Coal and iron are mined nearby.

choose (chōōz) *v.* **chose** (chōz), **chosen** (chō′zən), **choosing, chooses.** —*tr.* **1.** To decide upon and pick out from a number of possible alternatives; select. **2.** To prefer to others. **3.** To want; desire: *choose to go.* —*intr.* To make a choice; select; decide. [Choose, Middle English *chosen*, Old English *cēosan* (later *cēosan*). Chose, chosen; Middle English *chosen* (past plural), *chosen*, both from the infinitive *chosen*. All from Germanic *kiusan* (unattested).] —**choos·er** *n.*

Synonyms: elect, pick, select.

choos·y, choos·ey (chōō′zē) *adj.* **-ier, -iest.** Unwilling to settle for less than the best; hard to please. —**choos·i·ness** *n.*

chop¹ (chŏp) *v.* **chopped, chopping, chops.** —*tr.* **1.** To cut by striking with a heavy, sharp tool, such as an ax. **2.** To make by chopping. **3.** To cut into bits; mince: *chop onions.* **4.** *Sports.* To hit or hit at with a short, swift downward stroke. **5.** To cut short: *chopped off the sentence midway.* —*intr.* **1.** To make heavy, cutting strokes. **2.** To move roughly or suddenly. ~*n.* **1.** The act of chopping. **2.** A swift, short cutting blow or stroke. **3.** A chopped-off piece; especially, a cut of meat, usually taken from the rib, shoulder, or loin and containing a bone. **4.** A short, irregular motion of waves. **5.** *Australian Slang.* A share, as of winnings. —**get the chop.** *British Slang.* To be dismissed from one's job. [Middle English *choppen*, variant of *chappen*, CHAP (to split).]

chop² *intr.v.* **chopped, chopping, chops.** To change direction suddenly, as a ship in the wind; swerve. [Originally, "to exchange," from Middle English *choppen*, variant of *chappen, chepen*, to barter,

trade, Old English *cēapian*, ultimately from Latin *caupō*, innkeeper; akin to CHEAP.]

chop³ *n.* **1.** An official stamp or permit in the Far East. **2.** Quality: *a painter of the first chop.* [Hindi *chhāp†*, seal.]

chop-chop (chŏp′chŏp′) *adv. Informal.* Quickly. [Pidgin English, from Cantonese *gap gap*, "quickly," reduplication of *gap*, corresponding to Mandarin *ji*, urgent.]

chop·house (chŏp′hous′) *n.* A restaurant that specializes in serving chops and steaks.

Chopin (shō′păn′), **Frédéric François** (1810–49). Polish pianist and composer, of French parentage. He became a celebrated figure in the romantic age and was known for his affair with the novelist George Sand, with whom he lived for nine years. His music, written chiefly for the piano, drew inspiration from the romance and melancholy of traditional Polish dance music.

chop·log·ic (chŏp′lŏj′ĭk) *n.* Cunning but fallacious argument. —**chop·log·ic** *adj.*

chop·per (chŏp′ər) *n.* **1.** One that chops. **2.** A butcher's cleaver. **3.** A device that interrupts an electric current or beam of radiation. **4.** A motorcycle, especially one that is customized. **5.** *Slang.* A helicopter. **6. choppers.** *Slang.* Teeth, especially false teeth.

chop·py (chŏp′ē) *adj.* **-pier, -piest. 1.** Abruptly shifting or breaking, as waves: *choppy seas.* **2.** Marked by abrupt transitions; jerky: *choppy prose.*

chops (chŏps) *pl.n.* The jaws, cheeks, or jowls of an animal or human being. [Origin unknown.]

chop·sticks (chŏp′stĭks′) *pl.n.* A pair of slender sticks made of wood, ivory, or plastic and used as eating utensils by the Chinese, Japanese, and some other Asian peoples. [Pidgin English chop, fast (see **chopchop**) + STICK(S), a loose translation of Cantonese *kuàizi*, "fast ones."]

chop su·ey (chŏp sōō′ē) *n.* A Chinese-style dish consisting of small pieces of meat or chicken cooked with bean sprouts and other vegetables and served with rice. [Cantonese *tsaap sui*, corresponding to *zá sui*, "mixed pieces."]

cho·ra·gus (kə-rā′gəs) *n., pl.* **-gi** (-jī′). **1.** In Greek drama: **a.** The leader of the chorus. **b.** An elected official supervising the production of dramatic performances in the festival of Dionysus at Athens. **2.** The leader of a choir. [Latin, from Greek *khoragos* : *khoros*, CHORUS + -*agos*, leader, from *agein*, to lead.] —**cho·rag·ic** *adj.*

cho·ral (kôr′əl, kōr′-) *adj.* **1.** Of or pertaining to a chorus or choir. **2.** Written for performance by a chorus. ~*n.* Variant of **chorale.** [Medieval Latin *chorālis*, from *chorus*, CHORUS.] —**cho·ral·ly** *adv.*

cho·rale, cho·ral (kə-răl′, -räl′) *n.* **1.** A Protestant hymn tune. **2.** A harmonized hymn, especially one for organ: *a Bach chorale.* **3.** A chorus or choir. [German *Choral(gesang)*, "choral (song)," from Medieval Latin *chorālis*, CHORAL.]

chorale prelude *n. Music.* A composition for the organ, chiefly in baroque style, characterized by an elaborate contrapuntal structure based on the melody of a hymn or chorale.

chord¹ (kôrd, kōrd) *n.* **1.** A combination of three or more usually concordant notes sounded simultaneously. **2.** An emotional feeling or response: *Her words struck a sympathetic chord.* [Alteration (influenced by Latin *chorda*, string, CORD) of Middle English *cord*, agreement, harmony, short for ACCORD.]

chord² *n.* **1.** *Geometry.* A line segment that joins two points on a curve. **2.** *Aviation.* An imaginary straight line connecting the leading and trailing edges of an airfoil. **3.** *Archaic.* The string of a musical instrument. **4.** *Engineering.* A part of a truss, especially a member lying along the top or the bottom. [16th century : respelling (influenced by Latin *chorda*, string) of CORD.]

chord³. Variant of **cord.**

chord·al (kôrd′l) *adj. Music.* **1.** Relating to or consisting of a harmonic chord. **2.** Giving prominence to harmonic rather than contrapuntal structure: *chordal music.*

chor·date (kôr′dāt′, -dĭt) *n. Zoology.* Any of numerous animals belonging to the phylum Chordata, which includes all vertebrates and certain marine animals having a notochord, such as the lancelets. ~*adj. Zoology.* Of or belonging to the Chordata. [New Latin *Chordata*, from *chorda*, notochord, from Latin, CORD.]

chor·do·phone (kôr′də-fōn′) *n.* Any musical instrument producing its sound through the vibration of strings.

chore (chôr, chōr) *n.* **1.** A routine or minor task. **2.** An unpleasant or burdensome task. —See Synonyms at **task.** [Variant of CHARE, CHAR.]

–chore *suffix.* Indicates a plant distributed by a specified agency; for example, **anemochore, zoochore.** [Greek *khōrein*, to move, spread abroad.]

cho·re·a (kô-rē′ə, kō-) *n.* Any of various nervous disorders marked by uncontrollable and irregular movements of the muscles of the arms, legs, and face, one of which is "St. Vitus' dance." Also informally "jerks." [Latin *chorea*, dance, from Greek *khoreia*, choral dance, from *khoros*, dance, CHORUS.]

chor·e·o·graph (kôr′ē-ə-grăf′, -gräf′, kōr′-) *v.* **-graphed, -graphing, -graphs.** —*tr.* To create the choreography of (a ballet or other stage work). —*intr.* To serve as a choreographer. [Back-formation from CHOREOGRAPH.]

chor·e·og·ra·pher (kôr′ē-ŏg′rə-fər, kōr′-) *n.* One who creates, arranges, or directs dances, especially ballets.

chor·e·og·ra·phy (kôr′ē-ŏg′rə-fē, kōr′-) *n.* **1.** The art of creating and arranging ballets or dances. **2.** The steps and movements of a dance or ballet. **3.** The art and technique of dance notation. **4.** The art of dancing. [French *chorégraphie* : Greek *khoreios*, of a dance, from *khoros*, dance, CHORUS + -GRAPHY.] —**chor·e·o·graph·ic** (kôr′-ē-ə-grăf′ĭk, kōr′-) *adj.* —**cho·re·o·graph·i·cal·ly** *adv.*

chor·i·amb (kôr′ē-ămb′, kōr′-) *n., pl.* -**ambs**. Also **cho·ri·am·bus** (kôr′ē-ăm′bəs, kōr′-) *pl.* -**bi** (-bī′) or -**buses**. In Greek and Latin verse, a metrical foot consisting of a trochee followed by an iamb, much employed in Aeolic poetry and in the choric odes of tragedy. [Late Latin *choriambus*, from Greek *khoriambos* : *khoreios*, of a chorus, hence trochee, from *khoros*, CHORUS + *iambos*, IAMBUS.] —**chor·i·am·bic** *adj.*

chor·ic (kôr′ĭk, kōr′-, kŏr′-) *adj.* Of, pertaining to, or in the style of a singing or speaking chorus. Used with reference to Greek poetry or drama: *choric dance.* [Late Latin *choricus*, from Greek *khorikos*, from *khoros*, CHORUS.]

cho·rine (kôr′ēn′, kōr′-) *n. Slang.* A chorus girl.

cho·ri·on (kôr′ē-ŏn′, kōr′-) *n.* The outer membrane enclosing the embryo in reptiles, birds, and mammals. Compare **amnion**. [Greek *khorion*, afterbirth.] —**cho·ri·on·ic** *adj.*

chor·is·ter (kôr′ĭs-tər, kōr′-, kŏr′-) *n.* A choir singer; especially, a choirboy. [Learned respelling of Middle English *queristre*, from Norman French *cueristre* (unattested), from Medieval Latin *chorista*, from *chorus*, CHORUS.]

cho·ri·zo (chə-rē′zō, -sō) *n.* A spicy pork sausage, traditionally made in Spain. [Spanish.]

cho·rog·ra·phy (kə-rŏg′rə-fē) *n.* **1.** The technique of mapping a region or district. **2.** *Archaic.* A description or map of a region. [Latin *chōrographia*, from Greek *khōrographia* : *khoros*, place, + -GRAPHY.] —**cho·rog·ra·pher** *n.* —**cho·ro·graph·ic** (kôr′ə-grăf′ĭk, kōr′-), **cho·ro·graph·i·cal** *adj.* —**cho·ro·graph·i·cal·ly** *adv.*

cho·roid (kôr′oid′, kōr′-) *n.* The dark brown vascular coat of the eye between the sclera and the retina.
~*adj.* Also **cho·ri·oid** (kôr′ē-oid′, kōr′-). *Anatomy.* **1.** Resembling the chorion. **2.** Resembling the corium. **3.** Of or pertaining to the choroid. [Greek *khoroeidēs*, scribal error for *khorioeidēs*, resembling an afterbirth : *khorion*, afterbirth, CHORION + -OID.]

choroid plexus *n.* A network of blood vessels in the ventricles of the brain that secretes cerebrospinal fluid.

cho·rol·o·gy (kə-rŏl′ə-jē) *n.* **1.** The study of the geographical distribution of plants and animals. **2.** The study of geographical features and their relationship within a particular region. [German *Chorologie* : Greek *khoros*, place + -*logie*, -LOGY.]

chor·tle (chôrt′l) *intr.v.* -**tled**, -**tling**, -**tles**. To chuckle throatily: "*He chortled in his joy*" (Lewis Carroll).
~*n.* A snorting, joyful chuckle. [Blend of CHUCKLE and SNORT, coined by Lewis Carroll.] —**chor·tler** *n.*

cho·rus (kôr′əs, kōr′-) *n., pl.* -**ruses**. **1.** *Music.* **a.** A composition in four or more parts written for a large number of singers. **b.** A song refrain in which the audience joins the soloist. **c.** A solo section in jazz based on the main melody and played by a member of the group. **d.** A body of singers who perform choral compositions. **e.** A body of singers or dancers who support the soloists and leading actors in an opera, musical, or revue. **2.** In drama or poetry recitation, a group of persons who speak or sing a given part or composition in unison. **b.** In Elizabethan drama, an actor who recites the prologue and epilogue to a play and sometimes comments on the action. **c.** The lines spoken by this actor. **3.** In Greek poetry and drama: **a.** A ceremonial dance performed to the singing of odes. **b.** The portion of a drama consisting of choric dance and ode. **c.** The body of actors whose choric performance comments upon and accompanies the action of the play. **4. a.** Any speech, song, or other utterance made in concert by many people. **b.** Any simultaneous utterance by a number of persons or animals: *the dawn bird chorus.* —**in chorus**. With simultaneous utterance; all together.
~*v.* **chorused**, -**rusing**, -**ruses**. —*tr.* To sing or utter in chorus. —*intr.* To speak or sing in chorus. [Latin *chorus*, from Greek *khoros*, dance, chorus.]

chorus girl *n.* A girl who dances in a theatrical chorus.

chose¹. Past tense of **choose**.

chose² (shōz) *n. Law.* An item of personal property; a chattel. [French, "thing," from Old French, from Latin *causa*, thing, CAUSE.]

cho·sen (chō′zən). Past participle of **choose**.
~*adj.* **1.** Selected from or preferred above others. **2.** *Theology.* Elect.
~*n., pl.* **chosen**. **1.** One of the elect. **2.** The elect collectively. Preceded by *the*.

Cho·sen (chō′sĕn′) **1.** A name traditionally designating Korea since the 2nd millennium B.C. **2.** See **Korea**.

chosen people *pl.n.* The Israelites regarded as the people chosen to receive God's revelation. Nehemiah 9:8.

Choson. See **Korea**.

cho·ta (chō′tə) *adj. Indian.* Small; lesser in size or importance. [Hindi.]

chott. Variant of **shott**.

Chou or **Zhou** (jō). A dynasty that ruled China from *c.* 1027 to 221 B.C., enlarging the empire and promoting philosophy.

Chou En-Lai. See **Zhou En-lai**.

chough (chŭf) *n.* A crowlike Old World bird of the genus *Pyrrhocorax*, especially *P. pyrrhocorax*, having black plumage and red legs. [Middle English *choge*, *chowe*, from Germanic, proably imitative; akin to Old English *cēo*, jackdaw, jay, Middle Dutch *cauwe*, chough (imitative).]

choux pastry (shoo) *n.* A light glossy pastry made with eggs, typi-

cally used for making eclairs. [Partial translation of French *pâte choux*, "cabbage dough" (from its round shape), plural of *chou*, cabbage.]

chow¹ (chou) *n.* Also **chow chow**. A heavy-set dog of a breed originating in China, having a long, dense, reddish-brown or black coat and a blackish tongue. [Pidgin English, perhaps from Cantonese *gao*, dog.]

chow² *n. Slang.* Food. [Pidgin English, probably from Cantonese *chaau*, to fry, cook.]

chow·chil·la (chou′chĭl′ə) *n.* The **auctioneer-bird** (see).

chow-chow (chou′chou′) *n.* A relish consisting of chopped vegetables pickled in mustard. [Pidgin English.]

chow·der (chou′dər) *n.* A thick soup or stew containing fish or shellfish, especially clams, and vegetables, often in a milk base. [French *chaudière*, stew pot, from Old French, from Late Latin *caldāria*, caldron, from Latin *caldārius*, suitable for heating, from *caldus*, *calidus*, hot.]

chow mein (chou′ mān′) *n.* A Chinese-style dish consisting of any of various combinations of stewed vegetables and meat, served over fried noodles. [Cantonese *chaau min* or Mandarin *chāo mian* : *chāo*, to shallow fry + *mian*, noodles.]

Chr. Christ; Christian.

chres·ard (krĕs′ərd) *n.* Water present in the soil and available for plant absorption. [Greek *khrēsis*, use, from *khrēsthai*, to use + *ardein†*, to water.]

chres·tom·a·thy (krĕs-tŏm′ə-thē) *n., pl.* -**thies**. A selection of literary passages used in studying literature or a language. [Greek *khrēstomatheia*, "useful learning" : *khrēstos*, useful, from *khrēsthai*, to use + -*matheia*, learning, from *manthanein*, to learn.] —**chres·to·math·ic** (krĕs′tə-măth′ĭk) *adj.*

Chré·tien de Troyes (krā-tyăN′ də trwä′) (*c.* 1135–*c.* 1183). French poet and author of the earliest surviving Arthurian romances, including *Lancelot, Knight of the Barrow.*

chrism (krĭz′əm) *n.* **1.** A mixture of oil and balsam consecrated by a bishop and used for anointing in various church sacraments, such as baptism and confirmation. **2.** A sacramental anointing, especially upon confirmation into the Eastern Orthodox Church. [Middle English *crisme*, Old English *crisma*, from Late Latin *chrisma*, from Greek *khrisma*, ointment, from *khriein*, to anoint.] —**chris·mal** (krĭz′məl) *adj.* —**chris·ma·tion** (krĭz-mā′shən) *n.*

chris·om (krĭz′əm) *n.* **1.** A white cloth or robe worn by an infant at baptism. **2.** *Archaic.* An infant wearing a baptismal robe; a baby. [Middle English *crisom*, variant of *chrism*, CHRISM.]

Christ (krīst) *n. Abbr.* **Chr. 1.** The Anointed; the Messiah, as foretold by the prophets of the Old Testament. **2.** See **Jesus**. **3.** *Christian Science.* "The divine manifestation of God, which comes to the flesh to destroy incarnate error" (Mary Baker Eddy).
~*interj. Slang.* Used as an oath to express surprise, irritation, or the like. [Middle English *Crist*, Old English *Crist*, from Latin *Christus*, from Greek *Khristos*, "the anointed (one)," from *khriein*, to anoint.] —**Christ·li·ness** *n.* —**Christ·ly** *adj.*

Chris·ta·del·phi·an (krĭs′tə-dĕl′fē-ən) *n.* A member of a Christian sect, founded in the United States by Dr. John Thomas (1805–71) in the mid-19th century, that believes in the **millennium** (see) and rejects the doctrine of the Trinity. [From CHRIST + Greek *adelphos*, brother.] —**Chris·ta·del·phi·an** *adj.*

Christ·church¹ (krīst′chûrch′). Capital of Canterbury province in New Zealand, situated on the Banks Peninsula in the eastern part of South Island.

Christchurch². Coastal resort in Dorset in southern England, at the mouths of the Stour and Avon rivers.

christ-cross (krĭs′krŏs′, -krôs′) *n. Archaic.* The cross, used as a signature by someone who cannot write. [From *Christ's cross.*]

chris·ten (krĭs′ən) *tr.v.* -**tened**, -**tening**, -**tens**. **1.** To baptize into a Christian church. **2.** To give a name to at baptism. **3.** To name and dedicate ceremonially: *christen a ship.* **4.** *Informal.* To use for the first time. [Middle English *cristen*, *cristnen*, Old English *cristnian*, from *Cristen*, CHRISTIAN.]

Chris·ten·dom (krĭs′ən-dəm) *n.* **1.** Christians collectively. **2.** The Christian world. **3.** *Obsolete.* Christianity. [Middle English *Cristendom*, Old English *Cristendōm* : *Cristen*, CHRISTIAN + -DOM.]

chris·ten·ing (krĭs′ə-nĭng) *n.* The Christian sacrament of baptism, including the bestowal of a name upon an infant.

Chris·tian (krĭs′chən) *adj.* **1.** Professing belief in Jesus as Christ or following the religion based on his teachings. **2.** Pertaining to or derived from Jesus or his teachings. **3.** Manifesting the qualities or spirit of Christ; Christlike. **4.** Pertaining to or characteristic of Christianity or its adherents. **5.** *Informal.* Neighborly, decent, or generous.
~*n.* **1.** *Abbr.* **Chr.** One who professes belief in Jesus as the Christ or follows the religion based on his teachings. **2.** One who lives according to the teachings of Jesus. **3.** *Informal.* A kind or generous human being. [Middle English *Cristen*, *Christen*, Old English *Crīsten*, from Latin *Christiānus*, believer in Christ, from Greek *Khristianos*, from *Khristos*, CHRIST.] —**Chris·tian·ly** *adj. & adv.*

Chris·tian X (krĭs′chən) (1870–1947). King of Denmark (1912–47), notable for his passive resistance to the German occupation of his country during World War II. He rejected Nazi demands for anti-Jewish legislation (1942) and was kept in confinement until 1945.

Christian Brothers *pl.n.* An order of Roman Catholic laymen concerned with education of the poor. Also officially called "Brothers of the Christian Schools."

Christian era *n.* The period beginning with the birth of Jesus (con-

Christianity

CHRISTIANITY, THE WORLDWIDE RELIGION
Almost a quarter of the world's people embrace the teachings of Christ

The traditional basis of the Christian faith is that in Jesus Christ, God himself—in the person of his eternal son—became man, lived and taught on earth, died on the cross, and rose from the dead, all for the salvation of mankind. Today more than 1.2 billion people are professedly Christian and are associated, however loosely, with a Christian denomination. The belief that forgiveness of sins and eternal life are found only in Christ remains at the heart of the Christian allegiance.

Christianity arose in Roman-occupied Palestine 2,000 years ago, when Jesus was proclaimed by his disciples after his death as the awaited Messiah, or Deliverer, of his people. This claim, and repudiation of the need to accept Jewish Law completely to gain salvation, led to the final breach between Christians and Jews. Although rooted in the Old Testament, Christianity developed in the Greco-Roman world, which largely determined its thought and culture.

THE CRUCIFIXION *The 15th-century Italian artist Stefano da Zevio painted this death of Christ (above). On the left are Mary, the mother of Jesus, Mary Magdalene, and Mary, the mother of James and John. On the right, Roman soldiers cast lots for Christ's robes.*

THE RESURRECTION *During the miracle of Christ's resurrection, four Roman soldiers sleep outside the tomb. Painted by Piero della Francesca around 1460, the fresco (right) can be seen in his hometown of Borgo San Sepolcro in central Italy.*

---

ventionally in A.D. 1). Dates in this era are marked A.D., and dates before it, B.C. Also called "common era."

chris·ti·a·ni·a (krĭs′tə-ă′nē-ə, krĭs′chē-ăn′ē-ə) *n.* A ski turn in which the body is swung around with the skis parallel, to change direction or to make a stop. Also called "christie," "christy." [Norwegian, after CHRISTIANIA.]

Christiania. See **Oslo.**

Chris·ti·an·i·ty (krĭs′chē-ăn′ə-tē) *n., pl.* **-ties. 1.** The Christian religion, founded on the teachings of Jesus. **2.** Christians as a group; Christendom. **3.** The state or fact of being a Christian.

Chris·tian·ize (krĭs′chə-nīz′) *v.* **-ized, -izing, -izes.** —*tr.* **1.** To convert to Christianity. **2.** To instill with Christian principles and qualities. —*intr. Rare.* To adopt Christianity. —**Chris·tian·i·za·tion** *n.* —**Chris·tian·iz·er** *n.*

Christian name *n.* A name other than a surname given to a person at birth or when christened.

Christian Science *n. Abbr.* **C.S.** The church and the religious system founded by Mary Baker Eddy, emphasizing healing through spiritual means as an important element of Christianity, and teaching pure divine goodness as underlying the scientific reality of existence. Also officially called "Church of Christ, Scientist." —**Christian Scientist** *n.*

chris·tie (krĭs′tē) *n.* A ski turn, the **christiania** *(see).*

Chris·tie (krĭs′tē), **Dame Agatha Mary Clarissa** (1890–1976). British author of detective fiction. Her play *The Mousetrap* (1952) set a world record for the longest continuous run in one theater.

Chris·ti·na (krĭs-tē′nə) (1626–89). Swedish queen (1632–54; crowned 1644). The sole heir of King Gustavus II, she was crowned at the age of 18. Highly intelligent and a great patron of the arts, she confused much of Europe when she abdicated the throne, converted to Roman Catholicism, and spent most of the rest of her life in Rome.

Christ Jesus. See **Jesus.**

Christ·like (krīst′līk′) *adj.* Having the spiritual qualities or attributes of Christ. —**Christ·like·ness** *n.*

Christ·mas (krĭs′məs) *n.* **1.** December 25, a holiday celebrated by Christians as the anniversary of the birth of Jesus. **2.** The Christian church festival extending from December 24 (Christmas Eve) to January 6 (Epiphany). In this sense, also called "Christmastide." [Middle English *Cristesmasse,* Old English *Crīstesmæsse* : *Crīstes,* genitive of *Crīst,* CHRIST + *mæsse,* -MAS.]

Christmas berry *n.* A shrub, the **toyon** *(see).*

Christmas box *n.* In Britain, a small gift, usually of money, given at Christmas to those who provide services, such as postmen.

Christmas cactus *n.* A spineless, epiphytic cactus, *Zygocactus truncatus,* of South America, cultivated as a house plant for its showy red flowers. Also called "crab cactus."

Christmas disease *n.* A type of hemophilia that is caused by a deficiency of the plasma thromboplastin component. [After Stephen *Christmas,* the first patient in whom the disease was diagnosed and studied.]

Christmas Eve *n.* The evening or the day before Christmas.

Christmas fern *n.* The dagger fern *(see).*

Christmas Island¹. A coral atoll just north of the equator in the central North Pacific Ocean. It is a territory of Kiribati.

Christmas Island². An island territory of Australia, in the Indian Ocean southwest of Java. Phosphates are mined here.

Christmas pudding *n.* A plum pudding *(see).*

Christmas rose *n.* An evergreen plant, *Helleborus niger,* native to Europe, having white or pinkish-green flowers that bloom in late autumn or winter. Also called "hellebore."

Christmas stocking *n.* A stocking hung up by children on Christmas Eve, to be filled with presents by Santa Claus.

Christ·mas·sy, Christ·mas·y (krĭs′mə-sē) *adj. Informal.* Characteristic of Christmas.

Christ·mas·tide (krĭs′məs-tīd′) *n.* See **Christmas** (sense 2).

Christmas tree *n.* An evergreen or artificial tree decorated with lights and ornaments during the Christmas season.

Chris·tol·o·gy (krĭs-tŏl′ə-jē) *n., pl.* **-gies. 1.** The study of Christ's person, qualities, and deeds. **2.** Any doctrine or theory based on Christ or his teachings. —**Chris·to·log·i·cal** (krĭs′tə-lŏj′ĭ-kəl) *adj.*

Chris·to·pher (krĭs′tə-fər), **Saint** (*fl. c.* 3rd century A.D.). Christian martyr. Often depicted as a giant who converted to Christianity and thereafter devoted himself to carrying travelers across a river, he is

Christmas rose *A clump of* Helleborus niger, *or Christmas rose—so named because its flowers, which resemble wild roses, bloom in winter.*

the patron saint of travelers and, with the advent of the automobile, motorists.

Christ's-thorn (krīsts'thôrn') *n.* Any of several plants of the Near East, such as the jujube or *Paliurus spina-christi*, having spiny thorns and popularly believed to have been used for Christ's crown of thorns.

chris·ty (krĭs'tē) *n., pl.* **-ties.** A ski turn, the **christiania** *(see).*

chro·ma (krō'mə) *n.* That aspect of color in the Munsell color system by which a sample appears to differ from a gray of the same lightness or brightness. Chroma corresponds to **saturation** *(see)* of the perceived color. [Greek *khrōma*, color.]

chro·mate (krō'māt') *n.* A salt or ester of chromic acid. [CHROM(O)- + -ATE.]

chro·mat·ic (krō-măt'ĭk) *adj.* **1. a.** Pertaining to colors or color. **b.** Pertaining to color perceived to have a saturation greater than zero. **2.** *Music.* **a.** Of, pertaining to, or based on the chromatic scale. **b.** Pertaining to chords or harmonies based on nonharmonic notes. [Greek *khrōmatikos*, from *khrōma*, color, modification of musical note.] —**chro·mat·i·cal·ly** *adv.* —**chro·mat·i·cism** (krō-măt'ə-sĭz'əm) *n.*

chromatic aberration *n.* Color distortion in an image produced by a lens because of the focusing of light of different wavelengths by the lens at different points.

chro·ma·tic·i·ty (krō'mə-tĭs'ə-tē) *n.* The aspect of color that includes consideration of its dominant wavelength and purity.

chro·mat·ic·ness (krō-măt'ĭk-nĭs) *n.* *Physics.* Hue and saturation considered together as an attribute of color.

chro·mat·ics (krō-măt'ĭks) *n. Used with a singular verb.* The scientific study of color. Also called "chromatology." —**chro·ma·tist** (krō'mə-tĭst) *n.*

chromatic scale *n.* *Music.* A scale consisting of 12 semitones.

chro·ma·tid (krō'mə-tĭd) *n.* *Genetics.* Either of two daughter strands of a duplicated chromosome while still joined by a single centromere. [CHROMAT(O)- + -ID.]

chro·ma·tin (krō'mə-tən) *n.* *Genetics.* A complex of nucleic acids and proteins in the nucleus of a cell, characterized by intense staining with basic dyes. [CHROMAT(O)- + -IN.]

chromato-, chromat– *prefix.* Indicates: **1.** Color, staining, or pigmentation; for example, **chromatophore, chromatid.** **2.** Chromatin; for example, **chromatolysis.** [Greek *khrōma* (stem *khrōmat-*), color.]

chro·mat·o·gram (krō-măt'ə-grăm') *n.* **1.** The absorbent column or strip of material containing the stratographically differentiated constituents separated from a solution or mixture by chromatography. **2.** A graph or graphlike diagram indicating quantitatively the substances present in a chromatographic analysis. [CHROMATO- + -GRAM.]

chro·ma·tog·ra·phy (krō'mə-tŏg'rə-fē) *n.* Any of several methods of separating chemical substances for analysis in which the substance is passed through a selectively absorbent medium such as treated filter paper (*paper chromatography*) or a column of powder (*column chromatography*). [CHROMATO- + -GRAPHY.] —**chro·ma·tog·ra·pher** *n.* —**chro·mat·o·graph·ic** (krō-măt'ə-grăf'ĭk) *adj.*

chro·ma·tol·o·gy (krō'mə-tŏl'ə-jē) *n.* Chromatics *(see).* —**chro·ma·to·log·i·cal** (krō'mə-tə-lŏj'ĭ-kəl), **chro·ma·to·log·ic** *adj.* —**chro·ma·tol·o·gist** (krō'mə-tŏl'ə-jĭst) *n.*

chro·ma·tol·y·sis (krō'mə-tŏl'ə-sĭs) *n.* *Biology.* The disintegration of chromatin within a cell. [CHROMATO- + -LYSIS.]

chro·mat·o·phore (krō-măt'ə-fôr', -fōr') *n.* *Biology.* A pigment-containing or pigment-producing cell; especially, a pigment-containing animal cell, as in certain lizards, that by expansion or contraction can change the overall color of the skin. Also called "pigment cell." [CHROMATO- + -PHORE.] —**chro·ma·to·phor·ic** (krō'mə-tə-fôr'ĭk, -fōr'ĭk) *adj.*

chrome (krōm) *n.* **1. a.** Chromium. **b.** Anything plated with a chromium alloy. **2.** A pigment containing chromium.
~*tr.v.* **chromed, chroming, chromes. 1.** To plate with chromium. **2.** To tan or dye with a chromium compound. [French, from Greek *khrōma*, color (from the brilliant colors of the chromium compounds).]

–chrome *suffix.* Indicates pigment, color, or colored; for example, **autochrome.** [Greek *khrōma*, color.]

chrome alum *n.* A violet-red crystalline compound, CrK(SO₄)₂. 12H₂O, used in tanning, as a mordant, and in photography.

chrome green *n.* **1.** Any of a class of green pigments consisting of chrome yellow and iron blue in various proportions. **2.** Very dark yellowish green to moderate or strong green.

chrome red *n.* A light orange to red pigment consisting of basic lead chromate with varying proportions of PbCrO₄ and PbO.

chrome steel *n.* Any of various hard, rustproof steels that contain chromium. Also called "chromium steel."

chrome yellow *n.* Lead chromate, PbCrO₄, a yellow pigment often combined with lead sulfate, PbSO₄, for lighter hues.

chro·mic (krō'mĭk) *adj.* Of, pertaining to, or containing chromium, especially with valence 3.

chromic acid *n.* **1.** A corrosive, oxidizing acid, H₂CrO₄, known only in solution. **2.** The anhydride of this acid, CrO₃, a purplish crystalline material that reacts explosively with reducing agents and is used in chromium plating and to color glass and rubber.

chromic oxide *n.* A bright green, crystalline powder, Cr₂O₃, used in metallurgy and as a paint pigment.

chro·mi·nance (krō'mə-nəns) *n.* The quality of light that creates the sensation of color and is determined by comparing it with a reference source of the same brightness and of known chromaticity. [CHROMO- + LUMINANCE.]

chro·mite (krō'mīt') *n.* **1.** A widely distributed black to brownish-black chromium ore, FeCr₂O₄. **2.** A salt of chromous acid. [CHROM(O)- + -ITE.]

chro·mi·um (krō'mē-əm) *n. Symbol* **Cr** A lustrous, hard, steel-gray metallic element, resistant to tarnish and corrosion, and found primarily in chromite. It is used as a catalyst, to harden steel alloys, to produce stainless steels, in corrosion-resistant decorative platings, and as pigment in glass. Atomic number 24, atomic weight 51.996, melting point 1,890°C, boiling point 2,482°C, specific gravity 7.18, valences 2, 3, 6. [New Latin, from French *chrome*, CHROME.]

chromium steel *n.* Chrome steel.

chromo-, chrom– *prefix.* Indicates: **1.** Color, colored, staining, or pigment; for example, **chromophore, chromosome. 2.** Chromium or chromic acid; for example, **chromate.** [Greek *khrōma*, color.]

chro·mo·dy·nam·ics (krō'mō-dī-năm'ĭks) *n. Used with a singular verb.* The physics of the relationship between quarks and the nature of the strong interaction, color, and the exchange of gluons. Also called "quantum chromodynamics."

chro·mo·gen (krō'mə-jən) *n.* **1.** *Chemistry.* A substance capable of chemical conversion into a pigment or dye. **2.** *Biology.* A strongly pigmented or pigment-generating organ, organelle, or microorganism. [CHROMO- + -GEN.] —**chro·mo·gen·ic** (krō'mə-jĕn'ĭk) *adj.*

chro·mo·lith·o·graph (krō'mō-lĭth'ə-grăf', -gräf') *n.* A colored print produced by chromolithography.

chro·mo·li·thog·ra·phy (krō'mō-lĭ-thŏg'rə-fē) *n.* The art or process of printing color pictures from a series of stone or zinc plates by lithography. —**chro·mo·li·thog·ra·pher** *n.* —**chro·mo·lith·o·graph·ic** (krō'mō-lĭth'ə-grăf'ĭk) *adj.*

chro·mo·mere (krō'mə-mîr') *n.* One of the serially aligned chromatin granules forming a chromosome. [CHROMO- + -MERE.]

chro·mo·ne·ma (krō'mə-nē'mə) *n., pl.* **-mata** (-mə-tə). The coiled threadlike core of a chromosome. [CHROMO- + Greek *nēma*, thread.] —**chro·mo·ne·mal** (krō'mə-nē'məl), **chro·mo·ne·mat·ic** (krō'mə-nī-măt'ĭk), **chro·mo·ne·mic** (krō'mə-nē'mĭk) *adj.*

chro·mo·phore (krō'mə-fôr', -fōr') *n.* A molecular group capable of selective light absorption resulting in coloration of aromatic compounds. [CHROMO- + -PHORE.] —**chro·mo·phor·ic** (krō'mə-fôr'ĭk, -fōr'ĭk) *adj.*

chro·mo·plast (krō'mə-plăst') *n.* *Botany.* A colored plastid containing a pigment other than or in addition to chlorophyll. [CHROMO- + -PLAST.]

chro·mo·pro·tein (krō'mō-prō'tēn', -prō'tē-ĭn) *n.* A substance consisting of a protein forming a complex with a pigmented group.

chro·mo·scope (krō'mə-skōp') *n.* *Electronics.* A device used in sonar systems that displays information about objects detected by the sonar beam on a screen, in colors whose shade and intensity vary according to the density of the object.

chro·mo·some (krō'mə-sōm') *n.* Any of a number of threadlike structures in the cell nuclei of plants and animals, consisting of DNA, RNA, and protein, that carry genetic information in the form of genes and are responsible for the determination and transmission of hereditary characteristics. [CHROMO- + -SOME (body).] —**chro·mo·so·mal** (krō'mə-sō'məl) *adj.* —**chro·mo·so·mal·ly** *adv.*

chro·mo·sphere (krō'mə-sfîr') *n.* **1.** An incandescent, transparent layer of gas, primarily hydrogen, several thousand miles in depth, that lies above and surrounds the photosphere of the sun but is distinctly separate from the corona. **2.** A similar gaseous layer around a star. [CHROMO- (from its rosy color) + SPHERE.] —**chro·mo·spher·ic** (krō'mə-sfîr'ĭk, -sfĕr'ĭk) *adj.*

chro·mous (krō'məs) *adj.* Of, pertaining to, or containing chromium, especially with valence 2.

chro·myl (krō'məl) *adj.* Of or designating a chemical compound that contains the divalent radical CrO₂. [CHROM(O)- + -YL.]

chro·nax·y, chro·nax·ie (krō'năk'sē) *n., pl.* **-ies.** Also **chro·nax·i·a** (krō-năk'sē-ə). The time interval necessary to stimulate a muscle or nerve fiber electrically, using twice the minimum current needed to elicit a threshold response. [French *chronaxie* : CHRON(O)- + Greek *axia*, value, from *axios*, worthy.]

chron·ic (krŏn'ĭk) *adj.* **1.** Of long duration; continuing; constant. **2.** Prolonged or developing slowly. Said of certain diseases. Compare **acute. 3.** Subject to a disease or habit for a long time; inveterate. [French *chronique*, from Latin *chronicus*, from Greek *khronikos*, pertaining to time, from *khronos†*, time.] —**chron·i·cal·ly** *adv.* —**chron·ic·i·ty** (krō-nĭs'ə-tē) *n.*

chron·i·cle (krŏn'ĭ-kəl) *n.* A chronological record of events.
~*tr.v.* **chronicled, -cling, -cles.** To record in, or in the form of, a chronicle. [Middle English *cronicle*, from Norman French, from Old French *cronique*, from Latin *chronica*, from Greek *(biblia) khronika*, "chronological (books)," from *khronikos*, chronological. See **chronic.**] —**chron·i·cler** (krŏn'ĭ-klər) *n.*

Chron·i·cles (krŏn'ĭ-kəlz) *pl.n. Abbr.* **Chron.** Either of two books in the Old Testament, I and II Chronicles.

chrono-, chron– *prefix.* Indicates time; for example, **chronaxy, chronometer.** [Greek *khronos*, time. See **chronic.**]

chron·o·bi·ol·o·gy (krŏn'ō-bī-ŏl'ə-jē) *n.* The branch of biology concerned with biorhythms.

chron·o·gram (krŏn'ə-grăm') *n.* **1.** The record produced by a chronograph. **2.** An inscribed phrase in which certain letters can be read as Roman numerals indicating a specific date. [CHRONO- + -GRAM.] —**chron·o·gram·mat·ic** (krŏn'ə-grə-măt'ĭk) *adj.* —**chron·o·gram·mat·i·cal·ly** *adv.*

chron·o·graph (krŏn′ə-grăf′, -gräf′) *n.* An instrument that registers or graphically records time intervals such as the duration of an event. [CHRONO- + -GRAPH.] **—chron·o·graph·ic** (krŏn′ə-grăf′ĭk) *adj.* **—chron·o·graph·i·cal·ly** *adv.*

chron·o·log·i·cal (krŏn′ə-lŏj′ĭ-kəl, krō′nə-) *adj.* Also **chron·o·log·ic** (-lŏj′ĭk). *Abbr.* **chron., chronol. 1.** Arranged in order of time of occurrence. **2.** In accordance with or relating to chronology. **—chron·o·log·i·cal·ly** *adv.*

chronological age *n. Abbr.* **CA, C.A.** The number of years a person has lived, used in psychometrics as a comparison standard for various performance measures. Compare **mental age.**

chro·nol·o·gy (krə-nŏl′ə-jē) *n., pl.* **-gies.** *Abbr.* **chron., chronol. 1.** The determination of dates and the sequence of events. **2.** The arrangement of events in time. **3.** A chronological list or table. [CHRONO- + -LOGY.] **—chro·nol·o·gist** *n.*

chro·nom·e·ter (krə-nŏm′ə-tər) *n.* An exceptionally precise clock, watch, or other timepiece. [CHRONO- + -METER.] **—chron·o·met·ric** (krŏn′ə-mĕt′rĭk, krō′nə-) **—chron·o·met·ri·cal** *adj.* **—chron·o·met·ri·cal·ly** *adv.*

chro·nom·e·try (krə-nŏm′ə-trē) *n.* The scientific measurement of time. [CHRONO- + -METRY.]

chro·non (krō′nŏn) *n.* A unit of time equal to about 10^{-24} second, the time taken for a photon to traverse an electron. [CHRONO- + -ON.]

chron·o·scope (krŏn′ə-skōp′, krō′nə-) *n.* An optical instrument for measuring minute time intervals. [CHRONO- + -SCOPE.] **—chron·o·scop·ic** (krŏn′ə-skŏp′ĭk, krō′nə-) *adj.*

-chroous *suffix.* Indicates colored; for example, **isochroous.** [Greek *khrōs,* flesh, complexion, color.]

chrys·a·lid (krĭs′ə-lĭd) *n. Entomology.* A chrysalis.
~*adj.* Also **chry·sal·i·dal** (krĭ-săl′ə-dəl) Pertaining to or resembling a chrysalis.

chrys·a·lis (krĭs′ə-lĭs) *n., pl.* **-lises** or **chrysalides** (krĭ-săl′ə-dēz′). **1.** *Entomology.* A pupa; especially, the pupa of a moth or butterfly, enclosed in a firm case or cocoon. **2.** A state of incomplete development; a transitional stage. [Latin *chrȳsallis,* from Greek *khrusallis,* the golden pupa of a butterfly, from *khrusos,* gold. See **chryso-**.]

chry·san·the·mum (krĭ-săn′thə-məm) *n.* **1.** Any of various plants of the genus *Chrysanthemum,* the cultivated forms of which have showy flowers of various sizes and colors, especially red, yellow, white, and brown. **2.** The flower of any of these plants. [Latin *chrȳsanthemum,* from Greek *khrusanthemon,* "gold flower" : CHRYS(O)- + *anthemon,* flower, from *anthos,* flower.]

chrys·a·ro·bin (krĭs′ə-rō′bən) *n.* A medicine obtained from a deposit found in the wood of the araroba tree and formerly used to treat certain chronic skin conditions. [CHRYS(O)- (from its golden color) + (AR)AROB(A) + -IN.]

chrys·el·e·phan·tine (krĭs′ĕl-ə-făn′tēn′, -tīn′) *adj.* Made of or overlaid with gold and ivory. Said especially of ancient Greek statues. [Greek *khruselephantinos* : CHRYS(O)- + *elephantinos,* of ivory, from *elephas,* ivory (see **elephant**).]

chryso-, chrys- *prefix.* Indicates gold or the color of gold; for example, **chrysotile, chrysarobin.** [Greek *khrusos,* gold, from Semitic; akin to Hebrew *ḥarūz,* gold.]

chrys·o·ber·yl (krĭs′ə-bĕr′əl) *n.* A green to yellow vitreous mineral, $BeAl_2O_4$, used as a gemstone. [Latin *chrȳsobēryllus* : CHRYSO- + BERYL.]

chrys·o·lite (krĭs′ə-līt′) *n.* A mineral, **olivine** *(see).* [Middle English *crisolite* : CHRYSO- + -LITE.]

chrys·o·prase (krĭs′ə-prāz′) *n.* An apple-green chalcedony used as a gemstone. [Middle English *crisopase,* from Old French *crisopace, crisopras,* from Latin *chrȳsoprasus,* from Greek *khrusoprasos,* "gold green" : CHRYSO- + *prason,* leek.]

Chrys·o·stom (krĭs′əs-təm), **Saint John** (*c.* 347–407). Greek Church Father, archbishop of Constantinople (398–404). He earned the name of *Chrysostom* (golden-mouthed) by preaching in Antioch.

chrys·o·ther·a·py (krĭs′ō-thĕr′ə-pē) *n.* The treatment of certain diseases, especially rheumatoid arthritis, with gold compounds.

chrys·o·tile (krĭs′ə-tĭl′) *n.* A fibrous mineral variety of serpentine used as a variety of commercial asbestos. Also called "white asbestos." [CHRYSO- + Greek *tilos,* something plucked, fine hair, from *tillein*†, to pluck.]

chthon·ic (thŏn′ĭk) *adj.* Also **chtho·ni·an** (thō′nē-ən). Pertaining to the gods and spirits of the underworld. [Greek *khthonios,* under the earth, from *khthōn,* earth.]

chub (chŭb) *n., pl.* **chubs** or collectively **chub. 1.** Any of various freshwater fishes of the family Cyprinidae, related to the carps and minnows, especially a Eurasian species, *Leuciscus cephalus.* **2.** Any of various North American fishes, such as a whitefish of the genus *Coregonus* or a marine fish of the genus *Kyphosus.* [15th century : origin obscure.]

chub·by (chŭb′ē) *adj.* **-bier, -biest.** Rounded and plump. —See Synonyms at **fat.** [Probably from CHUB, from the plumpness of the fish.] **—chub·bi·ness** *n.*

Chuchiang. See **Zhujiang.**

chuck[1] (chŭk) *tr.v.* **chucked, chucking, chucks. 1.** To pat or squeeze fondly or playfully, especially under the chin. **2.** *Informal.* To throw; toss. **3.** *Informal.* To throw out; discard. Often used with *out.* **4.** *Informal.* To expel forcibly; eject. Used with *out: chucking out the troublemakers.*
~*n.* **1.** An affectionate pat or squeeze under the chin. **2.** *Informal.* A throw, toss, or pitch. [Perhaps from Old French *choquer, chuquer,* to strike, SHOCK.]

chuck[2] *n.* **1.** A cut of beef extending from the neck to the ribs and including the shoulder blade. **2.** *Western U.S. Slang.* Food. **3.** A clamp with adjustable jaws that holds a tool, or the material being worked, in a machine such as a drill or a lathe. [Variant of CHOCK (wedge).]

chuck[3] *intr.v.* **chucked, chucking, chucks.** To make a clucking sound. [Imitative.] **—chuck** *n.*

chuck[4] *n. Informal.* A woodchuck.

chuck·le (chŭk′əl) *intr.v.* **-led, -ling, -les.** To laugh quietly or to oneself.
~*n.* A quiet laugh of mild amusement or satisfaction. [Probably frequentative of CHUCK (to make a clucking sound).] **—chuck·ler** *n.*

chuck·le·head (chŭk′əl-hĕd′) *n. Informal.* A stupid and gauche person; a blockhead. **—chuck·le·head·ed** *adj.*

chuck wagon *n.* A wagon equipped with food and utensils, as in lumber camp.

chuck·wal·la (chŭk′wŏl′ə) *n.* A lizard, *Sauromalus obesus,* of the southwestern United States and Mexico, related to the iguana. [Mexican Spanish *chacahuala,* from Shoshonean *tcaxxwal.*]

chuck-will's-wid·ow (chŭk′wĭlz-wĭd′ō) *n.* A bird, *Caprimulgus carolinensis,* of the southern and central United States, resembling but larger than the whippoorwill. [Imitative of its song.]

chu·fa (cho͞o′fə) *n.* A sedge, *Cyperus esculentus,* native to warm regions of the Old World, having edible, nutlike tubers. [Spanish, fluff, nonsense, from Old Spanish, from *chufar, chuflar,* to hiss at, laugh at, from Vulgar Latin *sufilāre* (unattested), variant of Latin *sībilāre,* to whistle at, hiss down.]

chuff (chŭf) *n.* A short, usually repeated, puffing sound.
~*intr.v.* **chuffed, chuffing, chuffs.** To make a regular puffing sound. Used especially of steam trains. [Imitative.]

chug (chŭg) *n.* A dull, low sound, usually short and repeated, made by or as if by a laboring engine.
~*intr.v.* **chugged, chugging, chugs. 1.** To make such sounds. **2.** To travel or move while making such sounds. Often used with *along.* [Imitative.]

chu·kar (chə-kär′) *n.* An Old World partridge, *Alectoris graeca,* having a black-striped brownish plumage and red legs and bill. [Hindi *chakor,* from Sanskrit *cakōra.*]

Chuk·chi (cho͝ok′chē) *n., pl.* **-chis** or collectively **Chukchi.** Also **Chuk·chee,** *pl.* **-chees** or collectively **Chukchee. 1.** A member of a Mongoloid people of northeastern Siberia. **2.** The language of this people, noted for being pronounced differently by men and women.

Chukiang. See **Zhujiang.**

chuk·ka (chŭk′ə) *n.* A short, ankle-length boot, usually made of suede, having two pairs of eyelets. Also called "chukka boot." [From CHUKKER (polo players wear a kind of chukka boot).]

chuk·ker, chuk·kar (chŭk′ər) *n.* One of the periods of play, lasting 7 to 7 1/2 minutes, in a polo match. [Hindi *cakkar,* circle, turn, from Sanskrit *cakra-,* wheel.]

chum[1] (chŭm) *n.* An intimate friend or companion.
~*v.* **chummed, chumming, chums.** —*intr.* To be or become an intimate friend of. Often used with *up* or *up with.* —*tr. Scottish.* To accompany; escort. [17th century : Oxford University slang, probably from *chamber fellow,* "roommate."]

chum[2] *n.* Bait usually consisting of oily fish ground up and scattered on the water.
~*intr.v.* **chummed, chumming, chums.** To fish with chum. [Origin unknown.]

chum·my (chŭm′ē) *adj.* **-mier, -miest.** *Informal.* Intimate; friendly; amicable. —See Synonyms at **familiar. —chum·mi·ly** *adv.* **—chum·mi·ness** *n.*

chump (chŭmp) *n.* **1.** *Informal.* A blockhead; a dolt. **2.** A blunt end of something, such as a piece of wood. [Probably a blend of CHUNK and LUMP or STUMP.]

chump chop *n. British.* A chop, especially of pork or lamb, cut from between the leg and loin.

Ch'ung-ch'ing, Chungking. See **Chongqing.**

chunk (chŭngk) *n.* **1.** A thick mass or piece of something: *a chunk of bread.* **2.** *Informal.* A fair or substantial amount. [Probably a nasalized variant of CHUCK (cut of beef).]

chunk·y (chung′kē) *adj.* **-ier, -iest. 1.** Short; thickset; stocky. **2.** In chunks. **3.** Being or knitted with thick wool: *a chunky sweater.* **—chunk·i·ness** *n.*

church (chûrch) *n. Abbr.* **Ch., C., ch., c. 1. Church.** The body of all Christians throughout the world. **2.** A building for public worship, especially Christian worship. **3.** A congregation. **4.** Public divine worship in a church; a religious service. **5.** *Usually* **Church.** A specified Christian denomination: *the Presbyterian Church.* **6.** Ecclesiastical power as distinguished from secular power. **7.** The clerical profession; the clergy. **8.** *Christian Science.* "The structure of Truth and Love" (Mary Baker Eddy). See feature, next page.
~*tr.v.* **churched, churching, churches.** To conduct church services for; especially, to perform a religious service for (a woman after childbirth).
~*adj.* **1.** Of or pertaining to the church; ecclesiastical. **2.** *Chiefly British.* Being a member of the Anglican church. Compare **chapel.** [Middle English *chirche,* Old English *cirice,* from West Germanic *kirika* (unattested), from Late Greek *kurikon,* variant of *(dōma) kuriakon,* the Lord's (house), from Greek *kuriakos,* of the Lord, from *kurios,* lord.]

church·go·er (chûrch′gō′ər) *n.* One who attends church regularly. **—church·go·ing** *adj. & n.*

Church·ill[1] (chûr′chĭl). River, 1,610 kilometers (1,000 miles) long,

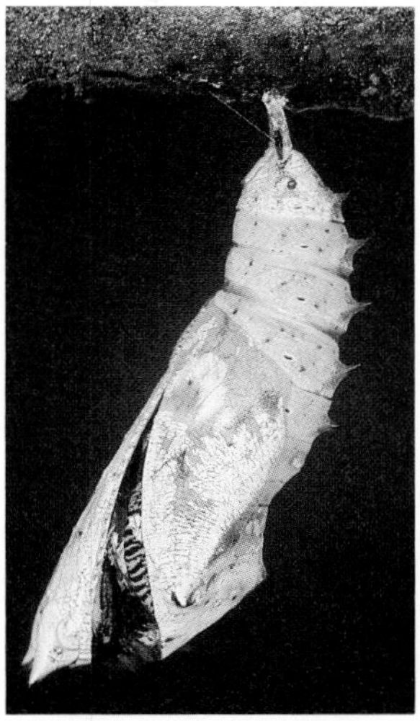

chrysalis *The intermediate stage between caterpillar and adult in the life cycle of butterflies and moths. The metamorphosis is usually completed within a protective case, or cocoon. When it has taken place, the adult may split the case and chew its way out or it may emerge after secreting a fluid that softens the covering.*

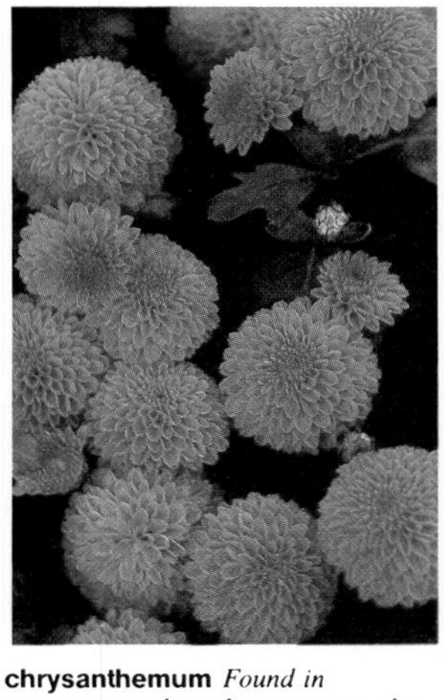

chrysanthemum *Found in temperate and northern regions, the chrysanthemum genus contains more than 200 species and a large number of garden varieties. The blooms vary in shape and formation, from a daisylike flower to a pompom of tightly packed petals such as the variety "Fairie" shown here.*

church

A CHRISTIAN HOUSE OF WORSHIP
Three main designs: basilica, Greek cross, and cruciform

The earliest churches were private homes where the first Christians, a small, often persecuted minority, met to worship. With the spread of Christianity such meetings became more common. Private homes were adapted into community houses for use as meeting places. Only after the Roman emperor Constantine officially recognized Christianity in A.D. 313 were the first churches specifically built as places for public Christian worship.

Naturally, early designs were modeled on existing public halls or Roman basilicas. The basilican plan consists of a nave flanked on each side by one or two aisles. Rows of columns separate the aisles from the nave. The aisles are lower in height than the nave, so the nave can be lit by rows of windows built into its upper walls (the clerestory, or clear story).

Crucifixion was a common form of execution for criminals in ancient Rome so the cross did not quickly become a Christian symbol—it would have seemed as gruesome a choice as a hangman's noose might today. The crucifix did eventually emerge from these shadows, and buildings were erected to reflect its powerful symbolism.

The eastern remnant of imperial Rome became the empire of Byzantium and the Greek cross plan of architecture originated there. Churches of this type have a square, domed central area from which four wings extend.

The Latin cross, or cruciform shape, that was adopted elsewhere has different proportions. The longest arm of the Latin cross is the nave, which usually points west. Shorter transepts to the north and south cross the top of the nave and the short eastern arm is extended as the chancel. The complete structure is truly cruciform.

There are round churches based on the original basilican plan and others based on the rectangular design of the mosque al-Aqsa in Jerusalem. When the Crusaders took Jerusalem in 1099, the mosque was believed to be the Temple of Solomon and replicas were constructed by the powerful Knights Templars all over Europe.

In the 20th century architects have not been constrained by any particular design but have used a variety of plans.

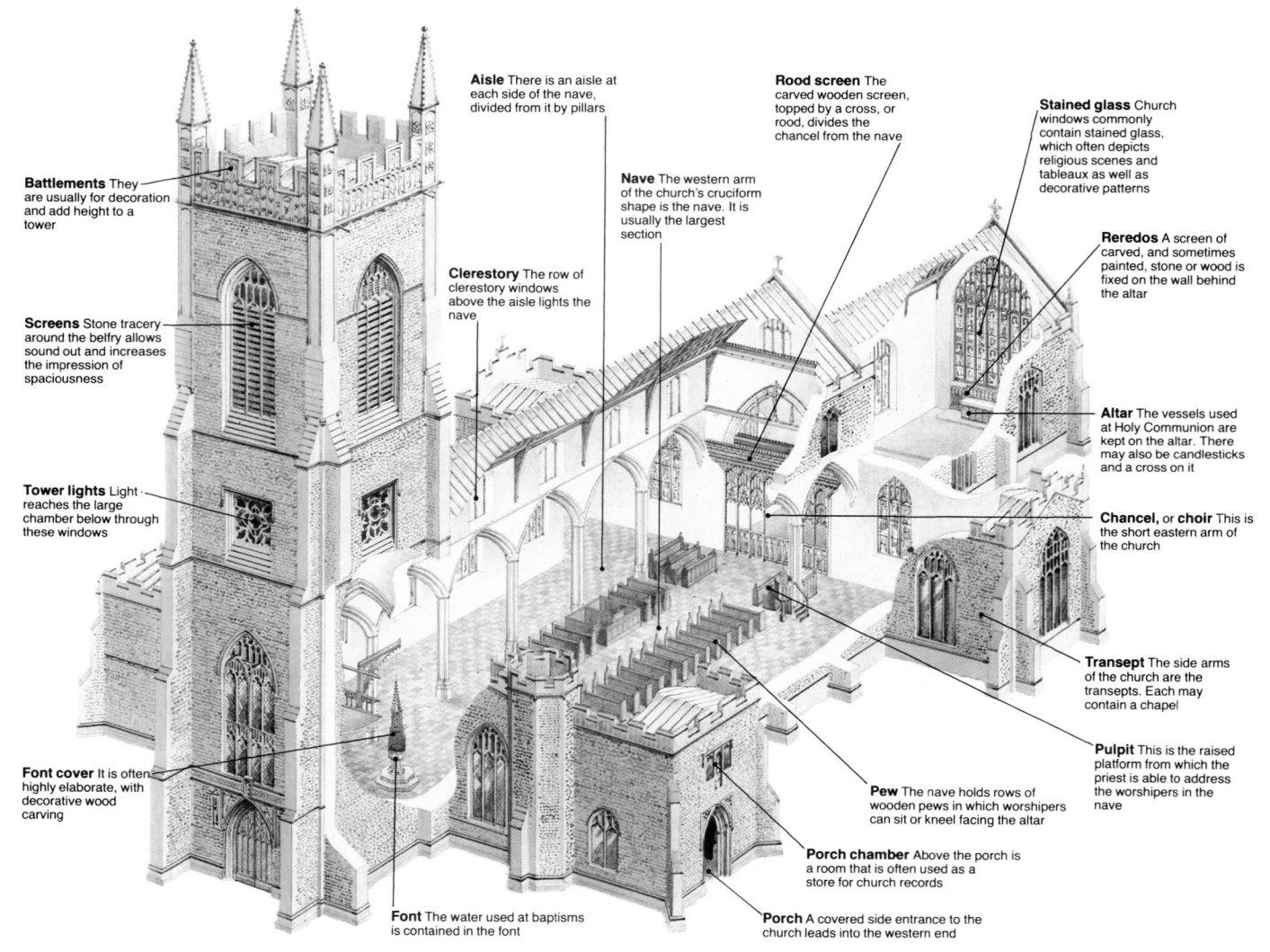

Battlements They are usually for decoration and add height to a tower

Screens Stone tracery around the belfry allows sound out and increases the impression of spaciousness

Tower lights Light reaches the large chamber below through these windows

Font cover It is often highly elaborate, with decorative wood carving

Aisle There is an aisle at each side of the nave, divided from it by pillars

Clerestory The row of clerestory windows above the aisle lights the nave

Nave The western arm of the church's cruciform shape is the nave. It is usually the largest section

Font The water used at baptisms is contained in the font

Rood screen The carved wooden screen, topped by a cross, or rood, divides the chancel from the nave

Pew The nave holds rows of wooden pews in which worshipers can sit or kneel facing the altar

Porch chamber Above the porch is a room that is often used as a store for church records

Porch A covered side entrance to the church leads into the western end

Stained glass Church windows commonly contain stained glass, which often depicts religious scenes and tableaux as well as decorative patterns

Reredos A screen of carved, and sometimes painted, stone or wood is fixed on the wall behind the altar

Altar The vessels used at Holy Communion are kept on the altar. There may also be candlesticks and a cross on it

Chancel, or **choir** This is the short eastern arm of the church

Transept The side arms of the church are the transepts. Each may contain a chapel

Pulpit This is the raised platform from which the priest is able to address the worshipers in the nave

in western Canada. It flows from Saskatchewan to Hudson Bay.
Churchill². River in eastern Canada. It flows some 970 kilometers (600 miles) through Labrador into the Atlantic Ocean.
Churchill, Lord Randolph Henry Spencer (1849–95). British statesman and father of Winston Churchill. He was leader of the so-called Fourth Party, a group of Conservative M.P.'s who pressed for social and constitutional reform.
Churchill, Sir Winston Leonard Spencer (1874–1965). British statesman and author. He became a Conservative M.P. (1900), but joined the Liberals over tariff reform (1904). He held office in several Liberal governments and Lloyd George's coalition government, but rejoined the Conservative Party (1924). As Chancellor of the Exchequer (1924–29) he forcefully opposed the General Strike

(1926). With the rise of Nazism in Germany he urged British rearmament and on the outbreak of war (1939) became first lord of the admiralty and succeeded Neville Chamberlain as prime minister, heading the coalition government (1940–45). He was returned as prime minister (1951) and knighted (1953). He published several volumes including *The Second World War* (1948–53) and was awarded the Nobel Prize for literature (1953). He resigned as prime minister in 1955, subsequently publishing his major study, *A History of the English Speaking Peoples* (1956–58).
church·ly (chûrch'lē) *adj.* Of, pertaining to, or fit for a church. **—church·li·ness** *n.*
church·man (chûrch'mən) *n., pl.* **-men** (-mĭn). **1.** A clergyman; a

priest. **2.** A male member of a church. **—church·man·ly** *adj.* **—church·man·ship** *n.*
Church militant *n.* The Church on earth viewed as fighting against evil. Compare **Church triumphant.**
Church of Christ, Scientist *n.* The official name of the Christian Science Church. See **Christian Science.**
Church of England *n. Abbr.* **C. of E.** The episcopal and liturgical national church of England, which withdrew its recognition of papal authority in the 16th century. See **Anglican Communion.**
Church of Jesus Christ of Latter-day Saints *n.* The official name of the Mormon Church. See **Mormon.**
Church of Rome *n.* The **Roman Catholic Church** *(see).*
Church of Scotland *n.* The established Presbyterian church in Scotland.
Church Slavonic *n.* The literary language of Slavonic manuscripts written after the early 11th century, still used as a liturgical language in the Eastern Orthodox Church.
church text *n. Printing.* **Black letter** *(see).*
Church triumphant *n.* That part of the Church that has overcome evil and reached heaven. Compare **Church militant.**
church·war·den (chûrch′wôrd′n) *n.* **1.** In the Anglican Church, a lay officer chosen annually by the vicar or the congregation to handle the secular and legal affairs of the parish. **2.** One of two elected chief lay officers of the vestry in the Episcopal Church. **3.** A clay pipe with a long stem.
church·wom·an (chûrch′wo͝om′ən) *n., pl.* **-women** (-wĭm′ĭn). A female member of a church.
church·yard (chûrch′yärd′) *n.* A yard adjacent to a church, often used as a graveyard.
chu·rin·ga (chə-rĭng′gə) *n., pl.* **-gas** or collectively **churinga.** An Australian aboriginal sacred amulet. [From a native Australian language.]
churl (chûrl) *n.* **1.** A rude, boorish person. **2.** A miser; a niggard. **3. a.** A **ceorl** *(see).* **b.** A medieval English peasant. [Middle English *churl, cherl,* man, husband, Old English *ceorl,* man, free man of the lowest rank, from West Germanic *kerl-* (unattested), man.]
churl·ish (chûr′lĭsh) *adj.* **1. a.** Rude; surly. **b.** Boorish. **2.** Difficult to work: *churlish soil.* **—churl·ish·ly** *adv.* **—churl·ish·ness** *n.*
churn (chûrn) *n.* **1.** A vessel or device in which cream or whole milk is agitated to separate the oily globules used to make butter. **2.** *British.* A large can used to carry milk.
~*v.* **churned, churning, churns.** *—tr.* **1.** To stir or agitate (milk or cream) in a churn in order to make butter. **2.** To make by the agitation of milk or cream: *churn butter.* **3.** To shake or agitate vigorously. *—intr.* **1.** To make butter by operating a churn. **2.** To move with great agitation: *My stomach churned at the prospect.* **—churn out.** To produce in large quantities, as if mechanically and usually at the expense of quality. [Middle English *chirne, cherine,* Old English *cyrin, cyrn,* from Germanic *kernjōn* (unattested).] **—churn·er** *n.*
churn·ing (chûr′nĭng) *n.* The amount of butter churned at one time.
churr (chûr) *n.* The sharp, whirring or trilling sound made by some insects and birds. [Imitative.] **—churr** *v.*
chute (sho͞ot) *n.* **1.** An inclined trough, passage, or channel down which things may pass. **2.** A waterfall or rapid. **3.** *Informal.* A parachute. [French, a fall, from Old French *cheoite,* feminine past participle of *cheoir,* to fall, from Vulgar Latin *cadēre* (unattested), from Latin *cadere.*]
chut·ney (chŭt′nē) *n.* A pungent relish made of fruit, vinegar, spices, and herbs. [Hindi *caṭnī*†.]
chutz·pah (ᴋʜo͝ots′pə) *n. Slang.* Brazenness; gall. [Yiddish.]
Chu·vash (cho͞o-väsh′) *n., pl.* **-vashes** or collective **Chuvash. 1.** A member of a Tatar people living chiefly in the Chuvash A.S.S.R. **2.** The Turkic language of this people. [Russian, from Chuvash *čăvaš,* akin to Turkish *yavaş,* gentle.]
Chuvash Autonomous Soviet Socialist Republic. A part of the Russian Soviet Federative Socialist Republic, in the west-central U.S.S.R. Its capital is Cheboksary.
chyle (kīl) *n.* A thick white or pale-yellow fluid, consisting of lymph and finely emulsified fat, that is taken up by the lacteals from the intestine in digestion. [Latin *chȳlus,* juice, from Greek *khulos,* from *khein,* to pour.] **—chy·la·ceous** (kī-lā′shəs), **chy·lous** (kī′ləs) *adj.*
chy·lo·mic·ron (kī′lō-mī′krŏn′) *n.* Any of the microscopic fat particles present in the blood after fat has been digested and absorbed from the small intestine. [From *chylo-,* CHYLE + Greek *mikron,* particle, from *mikros,* small.]
chyme (kīm) *n.* The thick semifluid mass of partly digested food in the stomach that passes into the duodenum. [Late Latin *chȳmus,* from Greek *khumos,* juice, from *khein,* to pour. See **chyle.**] **—chy·mous** (kī′məs) *adj.*
chy·mo·sin (kī′mə-sĭn) *n.* An enzyme, **rennin** *(see).* [CHYM(E) + -OS(E) + -IN.]
chy·mo·tryp·sin (kī′mə-trĭp′sĭn) *n.* A protein-digesting enzyme secreted by the pancreas in an inactive form, which is activated by trypsin. [CHYM(E) + TRYPSIN.]
Ci curie.
C.I. Channel Islands.
CIA Central Intelligence Agency.
Cia·no (chä′nō), **Conte Galeazzo** (1903–44). Italian fascist statesman. He became an influential figure after marrying Benito Mussolini's daughter Edda in 1930. Having urged Italy to join the Axis powers in World War II, he later favored a separate peace with the Allies and was among those who forced Mussolini's resignation. He was captured, tried for treason, and executed on Mussolini's order.
ciao (chou) *interj.* Used informally to express greeting or farewell. [Italian.]
Ciar·di (chär′dē), **John Anthony** (1916–86). U.S. poet and author. In his clear, simple poems and works of literary criticism, including *How Does a Poem Mean?* (1960), he was concerned with making poetry more accessible to adults and children. He also produced a much-heralded translation of Dante's *Divine Comedy* (1954–70).
ci·bo·ri·um (sĭ-bôr′ē-əm, sĭ-bōr′-) *n., pl.* **-boria** (-bôr′ē-ə, -bōr′ē-ə) A covered receptacle for holding the consecrated wafers of the Eucharist. [Medieval Latin *cibōrium,* from Latin, drinking vessel, from Greek *kibōrion,* the seed vessel of the Indian lotus, hence, a cup made from this, probably from Semitic.]
ci·ca·da (sĭ-kā′də, -kä′də) *n., pl.* **-das** or **-dae** (-dē′). Any of various insects of the family Cicadidae, having a broad head, membranous wings, and, in the male, a pair of resonating organs that produce a characteristic high-pitched, droning sound. [Latin *cicāda,* probably of Mediterranean origin.]
cic·a·trix (sĭk′ə-trĭks′, sĭ-kā′trĭks) *n., pl.* **cicatrices** (sĭk′ə-trī′sēz, sĭ-kā′trə-sēz′). Also **cic·a·trice** (sĭk′ə-trəs). **1.** Recently formed connective tissue on a healing wound; scar tissue. **2.** *Botany.* A scar left where a leaf or a branch has been detached. [Middle English *cicatrice,* from Latin *cicātrix*†.] **—cic·a·tri·cial** (sĭk′ə-trĭsh′əl), **ci·cat·ri·cose** (sĭ-kăt′rĭ-kōs′) *adj.*
ci·ca·trize (sĭk′ə-trīz′) *v.* **-trized, -trizing, -trizes.** *—tr.* To heal by the forming of a scar. *—intr.* To become healed or closed by the forming of a scar.
cic·e·ly (sĭs′ə-lē) *n., pl.* **-lies.** See **sweet cicely.** [Middle English *ciceli, seseli,* from Latin *seselis,* from Greek *seselis*†.]
cic·e·ro (sĭs′ə-rō′) *n., pl.* **-ros.** *Printing.* A unit of measurement for type, slightly larger than the pica, used in Europe. [After an edition (1458) of Cicero, in which it was first used.]
Cic·e·ro (sĭs′ə-rō′), **Marcus Tullius** (106–43 B.C.). Roman orator and statesman, a leading figure during the last years of the republic. **—Cic·e·ro·ni·an** (sĭs′ə-rō′nē-ən) *adj.*
cic·e·ro·ne (sĭs′ə-rō′nē) *n., pl.* **-nes** or **-ni** (-nē). A guide who conducts sightseers. [Italian *cicerone,* originally "a learned antiquarian," from *Cicerone,* CICERO.]
cich·lid (sĭk′lĭd) *n.* Any of various tropical freshwater fishes of the family Cichlidae, many of which are popular as aquarium fish. ~*adj.* Of or belonging to the Cichlidae. [New Latin *Cichlidae,* from *Cichla,* type genus, from Greek *kikhlē,* thrush, also, a sea fish.]
ci·cis·be·o (chē′chĭz-bā′ō) *n. pl.* **-bei** (-bā′-ē′). *Italian.* The male lover or companion of a married woman, especially in the 18th century. [Italian : origin obscure.]
Cid, The. See **El Cid.**
C.I.D. Criminal Investigation Department (Scotland Yard).
-cide *suffix.* Indicates: **1.** Killer of; for example, **insecticide. 2.** Murder or killing of; for example, **genocide, regicide.** [French, from Latin *-cīda,* killer, and *-cīdium,* killing, from *caedere,* to kill.]
ci·der (sī′dər) *n.* Also *chiefly British* **cy·der.** The juice pressed from apples or, formerly, from other fruit, and used to produce a beverage or vinegar. [Middle English *cidre, sidre,* from Old French *sidre, cisdre,* from Medieval Latin *sīcera,* from Greek (Septuagint) *sikera,* strong drink, from Hebrew *shēkār.*]
c.i.f. cost, insurance, freight.
cig (sĭg) *n. Informal.* A cigarette.
ci·gar (sĭ-gär′) *n.* A small, compact roll of tobacco leaves prepared for smoking. [Spanish *cigarro.*]
cig·a·rette (sĭg′ə-rĕt′) *n.* A small roll of finely cut tobacco for smoking, usually enclosed in a wrapper of thin paper. [French *cigarette,* diminutive of *cigare,* from Spanish *cigarro,* CIGAR.]
cigarette holder *n.* A thin tube with a mouthpiece for holding a cigarette while smoking it.
cigarette paper *n.* A thin piece of gummed paper in which tobacco is rolled to make a cigarette.
cig·a·ril·lo (sĭg′ə-rĭl′ō) *n., pl.* **-los.** A small, narrow cigar. [Spanish, diminutive of *cigarro,* CIGAR.]
ci·lan·tro (sĭ-lăn′trō) *n.* The parsleylike leaves of fresh coriander, used in Oriental cookery. [Spanish, coriander, from Late Latin *coliandrum,* from Latin *coriandrum,* CORIANDER.]
cil·i·a (sĭl′ē-ə) *pl.n. Singular* **-ium** (-ē-əm). **1.** Microscopic hairlike growths extending from the surface of a cell or organism. Their rhythmical beating causes movement of the cell or of the surrounding medium. **2.** The eyelashes. [New Latin, plural of *cilium,* eyelash, hairlike process, from Latin, the lower eyelid.]
cil·i·ar·y (sĭl′ē-ĕr′ē) *adj.* **1.** Of, pertaining to, or resembling cilia. **2.** Of or pertaining to the ciliary body.
ciliary body *n.* The thickened part of the vascular tunic of the eye that connects the choroid with the iris.
cil·i·ate (sĭl′ē-ĭt, -āt′) *adj.* Also **cil·i·at·ed** (sĭl′ē-ā′tĭd). **1.** Having cilia. **2.** Of or belonging to the protozoan class Ciliata.
~*n.* Any of various protozoans of the class Ciliata, having numerous cilia. [New Latin *Ciliata,* plural of *ciliatus,* having cilia, from CILIA.]
cil·ice (sĭl′ĭs) *n.* **1.** A coarse cloth; haircloth. **2.** A garment made from this cloth. [French, from Latin *cilicium,* from Greek *kilikion,* coarse cloth made of Cilician goats' hair, from *Kilikia,* Cilicia.]
Ci·li·cian Gates (sə-lĭsh′ən). *Turkish* **Kü·lek Bo·ğa·zi** (kyo͞o-lĕk′ bō-gä′zē). Mountain pass through the Taurus Mountains of southern Turkey.
cil·i·o·late (sĭl′ē-ə-lāt′) *adj.* Having minute cilia. [New Latin *ciliolum,* minute cilium, from *cilium,* singular of CILIA.]

churn *This type of butter churn, commonly called a tumbling churn because of its end-over-end motion, was developed in 1880. The slatted frame, called a diaphragm, was set loosely inside the barrel to increase the agitation of the cream.*

cicada *Male cicadas attract females by means of special drumlike organs at the base of their abdomens. Muscles vibrate the stretched membranes of these organs to produce a shrill noise. The sound is related to temperature—the hotter the weather, the louder the noise.*

cichlid *Because of their bright colors, cichlids are popular in aquariums. They are found mainly in slow-moving rivers and in lakes in Africa and South America. This is* Hemichromis bimaculatus *of Lake Tanganyika.*

Ci·ma·bu·e (chē'mä-bōō'ā), **Giovanni Cenni de Peppi** (*c.* 1240–*c.* 1302). Florentine artist, considered the originator of the Italian Renaissance in painting. He worked within the tradition of Byzantine art, but introduced a new expressiveness and sense of three-dimensional reality.
cim·ba·lom (sĭm'bə-ləm) *n.* A type of dulcimer, used especially in Hungary. [Hungarian, from Italian (see **cembalo**).]
ci·met·i·dine (sī-mĕt'ĭ-dēn', -dīn') *n.* A drug that reduces acid secretion in the stomach and is used to treat peptic ulcers and other digestive disorders.
ci·mex (sī'mĕks') *n., pl.* **cimices** (sĭm'ĭ-sēz'). Any insect of the genus *Cimex,* which includes the bedbugs. [New Latin *Cimex,* from Latin *cīmex*†, bedbug.]
Cim·me·ri·an (sĭ-mîr'ē-ən) *adj.* Gloomy; dark.
~*n.* One of a mythical people described by Homer as inhabiting a land of perpetual darkness.
C in C, C-in-C commander in chief.
cinch (sĭnch) *n.* **1.** A girth for a pack or saddle. **2.** A firm grip. **3.** *Slang.* **a.** Something easy to accomplish. **b.** A certainty.
~*v.* **cinched, cinching, cinches.** —*tr.* **1.** To put a saddle girth on. **2.** To get a tight grip on. **3.** To make certain of: *cinch a victory.* —*intr.* To tighten a saddle girth. Often used with *up.* [Spanish *cincha,* "girdle," from Latin *cingula,* from *cingere,* to gird.]
cin·cho·na (sĭng-kō'nə, sĭn-chō'nə) *n.* **1.** Any of various trees and shrubs of the genus *Cinchona,* native to South America, whose bark yields quinine and other medicinal alkaloids. **2.** The dried bark of any of these trees. In this sense, also called "Peruvian bark." **3.** Any drug derived from this bark. [New Latin, after Francisca Henriquez de Ribera, countess of *Chinchón* (1576–1639), who introduced it into Europe after recovering from a fever through the use of cinchona bark.] **—cin·chon·ic** (sĭng-kŏn'ĭk, sĭn-chŏn'ĭk) *adj.*
cin·cho·nine (sĭng'kə-nēn') *n.* An alkaloid, $C_{19}H_{22}N_2O$, derived from the bark of various cinchona trees and used as an antimalarial agent.
cin·cho·nism (sĭng'kə-nĭz'əm) *n.* A pathological condition resulting from an overdose of cinchona, marked by deafness, headache, giddiness, and dimming eyesight.
Cin·cin·nat·i (sĭn'sə-năt'ē, -năt'ə). A city of extreme southwestern Ohio, on the Ohio River. Founded in 1788, the city is a river port and an important industrial, commercial, and cultural center for an extensive area in southern Ohio and northern Kentucky.
Cin·cin·na·tus (sĭn'sə-năt'əs), **Lucius Quinctius** (*c.* 519–*c.* 438 B.C.). A peasant farmer, twice called to assume the dictatorship of Rome during crises. He was regarded as a model of simple virtue, especially because of his refusal to accept permanent dictatorship.
cinc·ture (sĭngk'chər) *n.* **1.** A belt; a girdle. **2.** Something that encompasses or surrounds.
~*tr.v.* **cinctured, -turing, -tures.** To gird or encompass. [Latin *cinctūra,* girdle, from *cingere* (past participle *cinctus*), to gird.]
cin·der (sĭn'dər) *n.* **1.** A burned or partly burned substance, such as coal or wood, that is not reduced to ashes, but is incapable of further combustion. **2.** A partly charred substance that can burn further, but without flame; an ember. **3. cinders.** Ashes. **4. cinders.** *Geology.* Volcanic **scoria** *(see).* **5.** *Metallurgy.* **Slag** *(see).*
~*tr.v.* **cindered, -dering, -ders.** To burn or reduce to cinders. [Middle English *cinder, sinder,* Old English *sinder,* (iron) slag, dross.] **—cin·der·y** *adj.*
Cin·der·el·la (sĭn'də-rĕl'ə) *n.* **1.** A person or thing that achieves recognition after a period of obscurity. **2.** A person or thing whose worth or beauty remains unrecognized. [After the fairy-tale character who, with the help of a fairy godmother, escaped from a life of drudgery and married a prince.]
cine- *prefix.* Indicates motion pictures or film-making; for example, **cinecamera.**
cin·e·aste (sĭn'ē-ăst) *n.* A person who is enthusiastic and knowledgable about motion pictures; a film buff. [French : CINE- + *enthousiaste,* enthusiast.]
cin·e·cam·e·ra (sĭn'ə-kăm'rə) *n.* A motion-picture camera.
cin·e·ma (sĭn'ə-mə) *n.* **1.** A motion picture. **2.** A motion-picture theater. **3. a.** Motion pictures collectively. **b.** The motion-picture industry. **4.** The art of making motion pictures. [French *cinéma,* shortened from *cinématographe,* CINEMATOGRAPH.]
Cin·e·ma·Scope (sĭn'ə-mə-skōp') *n.* A trademark for a process using an anamorphic lens to create films that can be projected onto a wide, curved screen.
cin·e·ma·theque (sĭn'ə-mə-tĕk') *n.* A small theater showing experimental, artistic, and less commercially successful films. [French, originally "film library" : CINEMA + *bibliothèque,* library.]
cin·e·mat·ic (sĭn'ə-măt'ĭk) *adj.* **1.** Of, in, or relating to motion pictures: *her stage and cinematic performances; cinematic art.* **2.** Peculiar to or characteristic of motion pictures: *a vivid, highly cinematic movie.* **—cin·e·mat·i·cal·ly** *adv.*
cin·e·mat·o·graph (sĭn'ə-măt'ə-grăf, -gräf) *n. British.* A camera or projector used in cinematography. [French *cinématographe* : Greek *kinēma* (stem *kinēmat-*), motion, from *kinein,* to move + -GRAPH.] **—cin·e·mat·o·graph·ic** (sĭn'ə-măt'ə-grăf'ĭk) *adj.* **—cin·e·mat·o·graph·i·cal·ly** *adv.*
cin·e·ma·tog·ra·phy (sĭn'ə-mə-tŏg'rə-fē) *n.* The practice or technique of making motion pictures. **—cin·e·ma·tog·ra·pher** *n.*
cin·é·ma vér·i·té (sē'nā-mä' vĕr'ē-tā') *n.* A style of film-making that tries to achieve an effect of realism and spontaneity by techniques such as the use of hand-held cameras and minimal editing of sound and image. [French, "cinema truth."]
cin·e·ol, cin·e·ole (sĭn'ē-ōl') *n.* **Eucalyptol** *(see).* [New Latin *cina*†, wormseed + Latin *oleum,* OIL.]
cin·e·ra·di·og·ra·phy (sĭn'ə-rā'dē-ŏg'rə-fē) *n.* Also **cin·e·mat·o·ra·di·og·ra·phy** (sĭn'ə-măt'ə-rā'dē-ŏg'rə-fē). A radiographic investigation of an organ or part in which a film is made from a series of successive x-rays to show the organ in motion.
cin·e·rar·i·a (sĭn'ə-râr'ē-ə) *n.* A plant, *Senecio cruentis,* native to the Canary Islands but widely cultivated as a house plant, having flat clusters of blue or purplish daisylike flowers. [New Latin, from the feminine of Latin *cinerārius,* of ashes (from the ash-colored down on its leaves). See **cinerarium.**]
cin·e·rar·i·um (sĭn'ə-râr'ē-əm) *n., pl.* **-ia** (-ē-ə) A place for keeping the ashes of a cremated body. [Latin, from *cinerārius,* of ashes, from *cinis* (stem *ciner-*), ashes.] **—cin·er·ar·y** (sĭn'ə-rĕr'ē) *adj.*
ci·ne·re·ous (sĭ-nîr'ē-əs) *adj.* **1.** Consisting of or like ashes. **2.** Of the color of ashes; gray tinged with black. [Latin *cinereus,* from *cinis,* ashes.]
cin·gu·lum (sĭng'gyə-ləm) *n., pl.* **-la** (-lə). *Biology.* A girdlelike structure or band. [New Latin, from Latin, girdle, from *cingere,* to gird.] **—cin·gu·late** (sĭng'gyə-lĭt) **cin·gu·la·ted** (-lā'tĭd) *adj.*
Cin·na (sĭn'ə), **Lucius Cornelius** (died 84 B.C.). Roman consul, expelled by Sulla (87). Joining forces with Marius, he captured Rome, forcing Sulla's exile. He restored order as consul (86–84), but was killed by his own troops.
cin·na·bar (sĭn'ə-bär') *n.* **1.** A heavy reddish mineral form of mercuric sulfide, HgS, that is the principal ore of mercury. **2.** Red mercuric sulfide used as a pigment; vermilion. **3.** Bright red; vermilion. [Middle English *cynoper, cynabare,* from Old French *cenobre,* from Latin *cinnābaris,* from Greek *kinnabari,* of Oriental origin.]
cin·nam·ic acid (sə-năm'ĭk) *n.* A white insoluble organic acid, $C_6H_5CH{:}CHCOOH$, existing in two isomeric forms and used in perfumes.
cin·na·mon (sĭn'ə-mən) *n.* **1.** Either of two trees, *Cinnamomum zeylanicum* or *C. loureirii,* of tropical Asia, having very aromatic bark. **2.** The yellowish-brown bark of either of these trees, dried and often ground, used as a spice. **3.** Any of several trees yielding a spice similar to this, such as cassia. **4.** A deep reddish brown. [Middle English *sinamome, cynamone,* from Old French *cinnamome,* from Latin *cinna(mo)mum, cinnamon,* from Greek *kinna(mō)mon,* from Hebrew *qinnāmown.*] **—cin·nam·ic** (sĭ-năm'ĭk), **cin·na·mon·ic** (sĭn'ə-mŏn'ĭk) *adj.*
cinnamon bear *n.* The American black bear during the phase when its color is reddish-brown.
cinnamon stone *n.* A mineral, **essonite** *(see).*
cinque (sĭngk, săngk) *n.* The number five, in cards or dice. [Middle English *cink,* from Old French *cinq,* from Latin *quīnque.*]
cin·que·cen·to (chĭng'kwĭ-chĕn'tō) *n.* The 16th century, especially in Italian art and architecture. [Italian, short for *(mil) cinquecento,* "(one thousand) five hundred."]
cinque·foil (sĭngk'foil', săngk'-) *n.* **1.** Any of various plants of the genus *Potentilla,* having compound leaves, often with five lobes. Also called "five-finger." **2.** *Architecture.* A design having five sides composed of converging arcs, usually used as a frame for glass or a panel. [Middle English *cincfoil,* from Old French *cincfoille,* from Latin·*quīnquefolium,* "five leaves" (translation of Greek *pentaphullon*) : *quīnque,* five + *folium,* a leaf.]

cinquefoil *So called because of its five-lobed leaves, this plant was used as a medicine by the ancient Greeks. In the Middle Ages in Britain, it was hung over doorways to ward off witches.*

Cinque Ports (sĭngk). An association of ports in southeast England, formed in the 11th century to defend the English Channel coast. There were five original members: Sandwich, Dover, Hythe, Romney, and Hastings. Winchelsea and Rye joined later.
Cintra. See **Sintra.**
CIO, C.I.O. Congress of Industrial Organizations.
ci·pher, cy·pher (sī'fər) *n.* **1.** The mathematical symbol (0) denoting absence of quantity; zero. **2.** Any Arabic numeral or figure; a number. **3.** The Arabic system of numerical notation. **4.** A person or thing without influence or value; a nonentity. **5. a.** Any system of secret writing in which units of text of regular length, usually letters, are arbitrarily transposed or substituted according to a predetermined key. Compare **code. b.** The key to such a system. **6.** A message in cipher. **7.** A design combining or interweaving letters or initials; a monogram. **8.** The continuous sounding of a pipe in an organ resulting from mechanical failure.
~*v.* **ciphered, -phering, -phers.** —*intr.* To solve problems in arithmetic; calculate. —*tr.* **1.** To put (a message) in secret writing; encipher. **2.** To solve (a problem) by means of arithmetic. [Middle English *cifre,* zero, from Old French, from Medieval Latin *cifra,* from Arabic *ṣifr.*]
cir., circ. 1. circular. **2.** circulation. **3.** circumference.
cir·ca (sûr'kə) *prep. Abbr.* **ca, c.** About. Used before approximate dates or figures. [Latin *circā,* from *circum,* round about, from *circus,* circle.]
cir·ca·di·an (sər-kā'dē-ən) *adj. Biology.* Exhibiting approximately 24-hour periodicity: *circadian rhythm.* See **biorhythm.** [Latin *circā,* about, CIRCA + *diēs,* day.]
Cir·cas·sia (sər-kăsh'ə, -kăsh'ē-ə). Region of southwestern Russia, northwest of the Caucasus Mts.
Cir·cas·sian (sər-kăsh'ən, -kăsh'ē-ən) *n.* Also **Cir·cas·sic** (-kăs'ĭk). **1.** An inhabitant of Circassia; especially, a member of a Caucasian people inhabiting Circassia, noted for thier striking physical beauty. **2.** The North Caucasian language of this people.
~*adj.* Of or pertaining to Circassia, its people or their language.
Circassian walnut *n.* The mottled or veined light-brown wood of the English walnut, used especially in decorative cabinetwork.

Cir·ce (sûr′sē). An enchantress described in Homer's *Odyssey* who detains Odysseus for a year and turns his men into swine.

Cir·ce·an (sûr′sē-ən, sər-sē′ən) *adj.* Dangerously and deceptively beautiful; bewitching. [From CIRCE.]

cir·ci·nate (sûr′sə-nāt′) *adj.* 1. Ring-shaped. 2. Rolled up from the tip, as a young fern frond or a butterfly's tongue. [Latin *circinātus*, from *circināre*, to make circular, from *circinus*, pair of compasses, from *circus*, CIRCLE.] —**cir·ci·nate·ly** *adv.*

Cir·ci·nus (sûr′sə-nəs) *n.* A constellation in the Southern Hemisphere near Musca and Triangulum Australe. [Latin *circinus*, a pair of compasses. See **circinate**.]

cir·cle (sûr′kəl) *n.* 1. A plane curve with the property that all points on the curve are equidistant from a given fixed point, the center. See **great circle, small circle.** 2. A planar region bounded by such a curve. 3. a. Anything shaped like a circle, such as a region or halo: *the Arctic Circle.* b. A group of things or people in a circle. 4. A circular course, circuit, or orbit. 5. An upper curved section or tier of seats in a theater: *dress circle.* 6. A series or process that finishes at its starting point or continuously repeats itself; a cycle. 7. *Sometimes* **circles.** A group of people sharing an interest, activity, achievement, or the like: *publishing circles; circle of friends.* 8. *Archaeology.* A ring of megalithic stones, such as Stonehenge, often thought to have some religious significance. 9. A sphere of influence or interest; a domain. 10. *Logic.* A fallacy in reasoning in which the premise is used to prove the conclusion, and the conclusion used to prove the premise. Also called "vicious circle." 11. In field hockey, a **striking circle** (see). —**come full circle.** To arrive back at a starting point. —**go** (or **run**) **around in circles.** To expend effort fruitlessly.
~*v.* **circled, -cling, -cles.** —*tr.* 1. To make or form a circle around; enclose. 2. To move in a circle around. —*intr.* To move in circles; revolve: *Crows circled overhead.* —See Synonyms at **turn.** [Middle English *cercle*, from Old French, from Latin *circulus*, diminutive of *circus*, ring.] —**cir·cler** (sûr′klər) *n.*
    Synonyms: clique, club, coterie, set, society.

cir·clet (sûr′klĭt) *n.* A small circle; especially, a circular ornament worn on the head. [Middle English *cerclett*, band, from Old French, diminutive of *cercle*, CIRCLE.]

cir·cuit (sûr′kĭt) *n.* 1. a. A closed, usually circular, curve. b. The area enclosed by such a curve. 2. a. Any path or route, the complete traversal of which without local change of direction requires returning to the starting point. b. The act of following such a path. c. A journey made on such a path or route. 3. *Electricity.* a. A closed path followed or capable of being followed by an electric current. b. Any configuration of electrically or electromagnetically connected components or devices. See **closed circuit, open circuit.** 4. a. A regular or accustomed course from place to place, such as that of a judge or salesman; a round. b. The area or district thus covered; especially, a territory under jurisdiction of a judge, in which he holds periodic court sessions. 5. An administrative unit of the Methodist Church. 6. An association of theaters, usually under a single management, in which plays, acts, or motion pictures move from one to another for presentation. 7. An association of teams or clubs, especially for the playing of a particular sport.
~*v.* **circuited, -cuiting, -cuits.** —*tr.* To make a circuit of. —*intr.* To move about in a circuit. [Middle English, from Old French, from Latin *circuitus*, from *circuīre, circumīre*, to go round : *circum-*, round + *īre*, to go.]

circuit breaker *n.* An automatic switch that stops the flow of electric current in a suddenly overloaded or otherwise abnormally stressed electric circuit.

circuit court *n.* In some states, the lowest court of record, in some instances holding sessions in different places.

circuit diagram *n.* A diagram representing the interconnections between elements of an electrical or electronic circuit.

circuit element *n.* A resistor, capacitor, inductor, transistor, or other device used in constructing electrical circuits.

circuit judge *n.* A judge who holds a circuit court.

cir·cu·i·tous (sər-kyōō′ə-təs) *adj.* Being or taking a roundabout, lengthy course. [Medieval Latin *circuitōsus*, from *circuitus*, CIRCUIT.] —**cir·cu·i·tous·ly** *adv.* —**cir·cu·i·tous·ness, cir·cu·i·ty** *n.*

circuit rider *n.* A minister who travels from church to church in a circuit, especially in a rural or frontier area.

cir·cuit·ry (sûr′kĭ-trē) *n.* 1. The design of or a detailed plan for an electric circuit. 2. Electric circuits collectively.

cir·cu·lar (sûr′kyə-lər) *adj. Abbr.* **cir., circ.** 1. Of or pertaining to a circle. 2. a. Having the shape of a circle. b. Having a shape approximately that of a circle; round. 3. Moving in or forming a circle. 4. Circuitous; indirect; roundabout. 5. a. Addressed or distributed to a large number of persons. b. Using the premise to prove the conclusion, which is used in turn to prove the premise: *a circular argument.* 6. *Mathematics.* a. Having a base in the shape of a circle: *a circular cone.* b. Designating a helix in which the distance from the curve to the axis is constant.
~*n.* A printed advertisement, directive, or notice intended for distribution. [Middle English, from Norman French, from Old French *circulier*, from Late Latin *circulāris*, from *circulus*, CIRCLE.] —**cir·cu·lar·i·ty** (sûr′kyə-lăr′ĭ-tē) *n.* —**cir·cu·lar·ly** *adv.*

circular file *n. Informal.* A wastepaper basket. Used humorously.

circular function *n. Mathematics.* A **trigonometric function** (see).

cir·cu·lar·ize (sûr′kyə-lə-rīz′) *tr.v.* **-ized, -izing, -izes.** 1. To make circular. 2. To distribute circulars to. —**cir·cu·lar·i·za·tion** (sûr′-kyə-lə-rī-zā′shən) *n.* —**cir·cu·lar·iz·er** *n.*

circular measure *n.* The measure of angles in **radians** (see).

circular mil *n. Abbr.* **c.m.** A unit of cross-sectional measurement, especially of wire, equal to the area of a circle with a diameter of one mil.

circular polarization *n. Physics.* A type of polarization of electromagnetic radiation in which the plane of polarization rotates at a uniform rate about the direction of propagation of the radiation.

circular saw *n.* A power-driven saw consisting of a toothed steel disk rotated at high speed. Also called "buzz saw."

cir·cu·late (sûr′kyə-lāt′) *v.* **-lated, -lating, -lates.** —*intr.* 1. To move in or flow through a circle or circuit. 2. To move around, as from person to person, or place to place. 3. To move about or flow freely; be diffused, as air. 4. To spread widely among persons or places; disseminate. —*tr.* To cause to move about or be distributed. [Latin *circulāre*, from *circulus*, CIRCLE.] —**cir·cu·la·tive** (sûr′-kyə-lə-tĭv, -lā′tĭv) —**cir·cu·la·tor** *n.* —**cir·cu·la·to·ry** (sûr′kyə-lə-tôr′ē, -tōr′ē) *adj.*

circulating decimal *n. Mathematics.* A **repeating decimal** (see).

circulating library *n.* A lending library.

circulating medium *n.* Currency or coin that can be exchanged for goods without endorsement.

cir·cu·la·tion (sûr′kyə-lā′shən) *n. Abbr.* **cir., circ.** 1. Movement in a circle or circuit. 2. The movement of blood around the body through the arteries and veins as a result of the heart's pumping action. 3. Any movement or passage through a system of vessels, as of water through pipes or sap through a plant. 4. Free movement or passage. 5. The passing of something, as money or news, from place to place or from person to person. 6. The condition of being passed about and widely known; distribution. 7. The distribution of printed material, especially copies of newspapers or magazines, among readers. 8. The number of copies sold or distributed of a given or an average issue of a publication.

circulatory system *n.* The system of vessels by which blood is circulated throughout the body by the heart.

circum– *prefix.* Indicates around or on all sides; for example, **circumlunar.** [Latin, from *circum*, around, from *circus*, circle.]

cir·cum·am·bi·ent (sûr′kəm-ăm′bē-ənt) *adj.* Surrounding; enclosing. [Latin *circumambiēns* (stem *circumambient-*) : CIRCUM- + AMBIENT.] —**cir·cum·am·bi·ence, cir·cum·am·bi·en·cy** *n.*

cir·cum·cen·ter (sûr′kəm-sĕn′tər) *n. Mathematics.* The center of a circumscribed circle.

cir·cum·cir·cle (sûr′kəm-sûr′kəl) *n. Mathematics.* A circumscribed circle.

cir·cum·cise (sûr′kəm-sīz′) *tr.v.* **-cised, -cising, -cises.** 1. a. To remove the foreskin of (a male). b. To remove the clitoris of (a female). c. To perform the religious rite of circumcision for. 2. To purify spiritually: *"Circumcise yourselves to the Lord"* (Jeremiah 4:4). [Middle English *circumcisen*, from Latin *circumcīdere* (past participle *circumcīsus*), "to cut round" (translation of Greek *peritemnein*) : CIRCUM- + *caedere*, to cut.] —**cir·cum·cis·er** *n.*

cir·cum·ci·sion (sûr′kəm-sĭzh′ən) *n.* 1. *Medicine.* The act of circumcising. 2. A religious ceremony in which someone is circumcised. 3. Spiritual purification.

cir·cum·fer·ence (sər-kŭm′fər-əns) *n. Abbr.* **cir., circ.** 1. a. The boundary line of a circle. b. The boundary line of any closed figure; a perimeter. 2. The length of such a boundary. [Middle English, from Old French, from Latin *circumferentia*, from *circumferēns*, present participle of *circumferre*, to carry around : CIRCUM- + *ferre*, to carry.] —**cir·cum·fer·en·tial** (sər-kŭm′fə-rĕn′shəl) *adj.*

cir·cum·flex (sûr′kəm-flĕks′) *n.* A mark (ˆ) used over a letter in certain languages, such as French, or in phonetic keys, to indicate quality of pronunciation, such as lengthening of a vowel.
~*adj.* Marked with a circumflex.
~*tr.v.* **circumflexed, -flexing, -flexes.** To mark with a circumflex. [Latin *circumflexus*, "a bending around," from *circumflectere*, to bend round : CIRCUM- + *flectere*, to bend, to FLEX.]

cir·cum·fuse (sûr′kəm-fyōōz′) *tr.v.* **-fused, -fusing, -fuses.** 1. To pour or diffuse around; spread. 2. To surround, as with liquid; suffuse. [Latin *circumfundere* (past participle *circumfūsus*), to pour around : CIRCUM- + *fundere*, to pour.] —**cir·cum·fu·sion** *n.*

cir·cum·lo·cu·tion (sûr′kəm-lō-kyōō′shən) *n.* 1. The use of prolix and indirect language. 2. Evasion in speech or writing. 3. A roundabout expression. [Middle English *circumlocucioun*, from Latin *circumlocūtiō* (stem *circumlocūtiōn-*), from *circumloquī*, "to speak in a roundabout way" : CIRCUM- + *loquī*, to speak.] —**cir·cum·loc·u·to·ry** (sûr′kəm-lŏk′yə-tôr′ē, -tōr′ē) *adj.*

cir·cum·lu·nar (sûr′kəm-lōō′nər) *adj.* Revolving around or surrounding the moon.

cir·cum·nav·i·gate (sûr′kəm-năv′ĭ-gāt′) *tr.v.* **-gated, -gating, -gates.** To sail or fly completely around. [Latin *circumnāvigāre* : CIRCUM- + *nāvigāre*, NAVIGATE.] —**cir·cum·nav·i·ga·tion** (sûr′kəm-năv′ĭ-gā′-shən) *n.* —**cir·cum·nav·i·ga·tor** *n.*

cir·cum·nu·tate (sûr′kəm-nōō′tāt′, -nyōō′tāt′) *intr.v.* **-tated, -tating, -tates.** *Botany.* To exhibit circumnutation. [CIRCUM- + Latin *nūtāre*, to nod, sway.]

cir·cum·nu·ta·tion (sûr′kəm-nōō-tā′shən, -nyōō-tā′shən) *n. Botany.* An elliptical or spiral direction of growth shown by certain plant parts, such as the apex of a growing tendril.

cir·cum·po·lar (sûr′kəm-pō′lər) *adj.* 1. Located or found in one of the polar regions. 2. *Astronomy.* Designating a star that from a given observer's latitude does not go below the horizon.

cir·cum·scis·sile (sûr′kəm-sĭs′əl) *adj. Botany.* Splitting or opening along a transverse circular line: *a circumscissile seed capsule.* [CIR-

cithara *A Greek statue of a woman playing the cithara, similar in construction to the lyre. The statue was carved in about 200* B.C.

CUM- + Latin *scissilis,* capable of being cut, from *scissus* (see **scission**).]

cir·cum·scribe (sûr′kəm-skrīb′) *tr.v.* **-scribed, -scribing, -scribes. 1.** To draw a line around; encircle. **2.** To confine within bounds; limit; restrict. **3.** To determine the limits of. **4.** *Geometry.* To enclose (a geometric figure) within another geometric figure, so that the enclosed object touches but does not intersect with the enclosing figure. —See Synonyms at **limit.** [Middle English *circumscriben,* from Latin *circumscrībere* : CIRCUM- + *scrībere,* to write.] **—cir·cum·scrib·a·ble** *adj.* **—cir·cum·scrib·er** *n.*

cir·cum·scrip·tion (sûr′kəm-skrĭp′shən) *n.* **1. a.** The act of circumscribing. **b.** The state of being circumscribed. **2.** Something that circumscribes. **3.** A circumscribed space; a limited area. **4.** A circular inscription, as on a coin or medallion. **—cir·cum·scrip·tive** *adj.* **—cir·cum·scrip·tive·ly** *adv.*

cir·cum·spect (sûr′kəm-spĕkt) *adj.* Taking into account all circumstances or consequences; prudent. [Middle English, from Latin *circumspectus,* past participle of *circumspicere,* to look round, take heed : CIRCUM- + *specere,* to look.] **—cir·cum·spec·tion** (sûr′kəm-spĕk′shən) *n.* **—cir·cum·spect·ly** *adv.*

cir·cum·stance (sûr′kəm-stăns′) *n.* **1.** One of the conditions or facts attending an event and having some bearing upon it; a determining or modifying factor. **2.** One of the conditions or facts that determine or that must be considered in the determining of a course of action. **3.** The sum of determining factors beyond willful control: *a victim of circumstance.* **4.** *Usually* **circumstances.** Financial status or means: *living in reduced circumstances.* **5.** Additional or accessory information; detail. **6.** Formal display; ceremony: *pomp and circumstance.* —See Synonyms at **occurrence. —under no circumstances.** In no case; never. **—under** (or **in**) **the circumstances.** Given these conditions; such being the case. [Middle English, from Old French, from Latin *circumstāntia,* accessory details, from *circumstāns,* present participle of *circumstāre,* to stand around, be accessory : CIRCUM- + *stāre,* to stand.]

cir·cum·stanced (sûr′kəm-stănst′) *adj.* Placed in specified circumstances, especially with regard to finance.

cir·cum·stan·tial (sûr′kəm-stăn′shəl) *adj.* **1.** Of, pertaining to, or dependent upon circumstances. **2.** Of no primary significance; incidental; inessential. **3.** Complete and particular; full of detail. **—cir·cum·stan·ti·al·i·ty** (sûr′kəm-stăn′shē-ăl′ə-tē) *n.* **—cir·cum·stan·tial·ly** *adv.*

circumstantial evidence *n. Law.* Evidence not bearing directly on the fact in dispute, but on various attendant circumstances from which the judge or jury might infer the occurrence of the fact in dispute.

cir·cum·stan·ti·ate (sûr′kəm-stăn′shē-āt′) *tr.v.* **-ated, -ating, -ates.** To support or verify with detailed evidence or proof. **—cir·cum·stan·ti·a·tion** *n.*

cir·cum·val·late (sûr′kəm-văl′āt′) *tr.v.* **-lated, -lating, -lates.** To surround with a rampart or other defensive barrier.
~*adj.* (sûr′kəm-văl′ăt′, -văl′ĭt). Surrounded by or as if by a rampart. [Latin *circumvallāre* : CIRCUM- + *vallāre,* to wall, from *vallum,* wall.] **—cir·cum·val·la·tion** *n.*

cir·cum·vent (sûr′kəm-vĕnt′) *tr.v.* **-vented, -venting, -vents. 1.** To surround and entrap (an enemy, for example). **2.** To overcome by artful maneuvering; outwit. **3.** To avoid by or as if by passing around. [Latin *circumvenīre* (past participle *circumventus*) : CIRCUM- + *venīre, to come.*] **—cir·cum·vent·er, cir·cum·ven·tor** *n.* **—cir·cum·ven·tion** *n.* **—cir·cum·ven·tive** *adj.*

cir·cum·vo·lu·tion (sər-kŭm′və-lo͞o′shən, sûr′kəm-vō-) **1.** An act or instance of turning, coiling, or folding about a center core or axis. **2.** A single turn, coil, or fold; convolution. [Middle English *circumvolucioun,* from Medieval Latin *circumvolūtiō* (stem *-volūtion-*), from Latin *circumvolvere* (past participle *circumvolūtus*), CIRCUMVOLVE.]

cir·cum·volve (sûr′kəm-vŏlv′) *v.* **-volved, -volving, -volves.** —*intr.* To revolve. —*tr.* To cause to revolve. [Latin *circumvolverse* : CIRCUM- + *volvere,* to roll.]

cir·cus (sûr′kəs) *n.* **1.** A public entertainment consisting typically of a variety of performances by acrobats, clowns, and trained animals. **2.** A traveling company that performs such entertainments. **3.** A circular arena, surrounded by tiers of seats and often covered by a tent, in which such entertainments are performed. **4.** A roofless, oval enclosure surrounded by tiers of seats and used in ancient times for public spectacles. **5.** *British.* An open circular place where several streets intersect. **6.** *Informal.* A place or activity given over to rowdy or noisy disorder. [Latin *circus,* ring, CIRCLE.]

cire per·due (sēr′ pĕr-dü′) *n.* A technique used in casting bronze, the **lost wax process** *(see).* [French, "lost wax."]

cirque (sûrk) *n.* A steep, bowl-shaped hollow, often containing a small lake, occurring at the upper end of some mountain valleys. Also called "corrie" in Scotland, "cwm" in Wales. [French, from Latin *circus,* ring, CIRCLE.]

cir·rate (sĭr′āt′) *adj.* Also **cir·rose** (sĭr′ōs′), **cir·rous** (sĭr′əs). Having or of the nature of a cirrus or cirri. [Latin *cirrātus,* curled, from *cirrus,* curl, CIRRUS.]

cir·rho·sis (sĭ-rō′sĭs) *n.* **1.** A chronic disorder of the liver, in which normal tissue is replaced by fibrous tissue similar to scar tissue, caused for example by alcoholism or hepatitis. **2.** Interstitial inflammation of any tissue or organ. [New Latin, "orange-colored disease" (from the color of the diseased liver) : Greek *kirrhos*†, orange tawny + -OSIS.] **—cir·rhot·ic** (sĭ-rŏt′ĭk) *adj.*

cir·ri·pede (sĭr′ə-pēd′) *n.* Also **cir·ri·ped** (sĭr′ə-pĕd′) Any of various crustaceans of the subclass Cirripedia, which includes the barnacles and similar organisms that attach themselves to objects or become parasitic in the adult stage. [New Latin *Cirripedia,* "the cirrus-footed ones" : CIRR(US) + *-ped.*] **—cir·ri·ped** *adj.*

cir·ro·cu·mu·lus (sĭr′ō-kyo͞om′yə-ləs) *n.* A high-altitude cloud composed of a series of small, regularly arranged cloudlets in the form of ripples or grains. [New Latin : CIRR(US) + CUMULUS.]

cir·ro·stra·tus (sĭr′ō-strā′təs, -străt′əs) *n.* A high-altitude, thin, hazy, veil-like cloud, usually covering the sky and often producing a halo effect around the sun. [New Latin : CIRR(US) + STRATUS.]

cir·rus (sĭr′əs) *n., pl.* **cirri** (sĭr′ī′). **1.** A high-altitude cloud composed of narrow bands or patches of thin, generally white, fleecy parts. **2.** *Botany.* A mass of coherent spores that are discharged through an ostiole. **3.** *Zoology.* A slender, flexible appendage, such as a tentacle. [New Latin, from Latin *cirrus*†, curl, filament, tuft.]

cis– *prefix.* **1.** Indicates location on this or the near side; for example, **cislunar. 2.** *Chemistry.* Indicates an isomer in which two atoms or groups in a molecule occupy positions on the same side of a line, usually a chemical bond, or a center. Compare **trans-.** [Latin, from *cis,* on this side of.]

Cis·al·pine Gaul (sĭs-ăl′pīn′ gôl). The part of ancient Gaul south of the Alps of northern Italy.

cis·at·lan·tic (sĭs′ət-lăn′tĭk) *adj.* On this (the speaker's) side of the Atlantic. [CIS- + ATLANTIC]

Cis·cau·ca·sia (sĭs′kô-kā′zhə, -shə). Also **North Cau·ca·sia** (kô-kā′zhə, -shə). A steppeland region in southwestern Russia.

cis·co (sĭs′kō) *n., pl.* **-coes** or **-cos** or collectively **cisco.** Any of several North American whitefish, especially the **lake herring** *(see)* of the Great Lakes. [Canadian French *ciscoette,* from Ojibwa *pemitewiskawet,* oily-skinned fish.]

cis·lu·nar (sĭs-lo͞o′nər) *adj.* Of or pertaining to the region between the earth and the moon. Compare **translunar.**

cis·mon·tane (sĭs-mŏn′tān′) *adj.* On this (the speaker's) side of the mountains. [French *cismontain,* from Latin *cismontānus* : CIS- + *montānus,* of the mountains, MONTANE.]

cis·soid (sĭs′oid′) *n. Mathematics.* A type of geometric curve with a cusp and two branches, both asymptotic to a straight line. Its equation is $x^3 = y^2(2a - x)$, with the cusp at the origin and the asymptote being the line $x = 2a$.
~*adj.* Lying between the concave sides of two curves. Compare **sistroid.** [Greek *kissoeidēs,* ivy-shaped, from *kissos,* ivy.]

cissy. *British.* Variant of **sissy.**

cist (kĭst, sĭst) *n.* Also **kist** (kĭst). A Neolithic stone coffin. [Welsh, "chest," from Latin *cista,* basket, wicker receptacle, from Greek *kistē.*]

Cis·ter·cian (sĭ-stûr′shən) *n.* A member of a contemplative monastic order founded by reformist Benedictines in France in 1098.
~*adj.* Of, pertaining to, or belonging to this order. [French *Cistertien,* from Medieval Latin *Cistercium,* Cîteaux, near Dijon, site of the original abbey.]

cis·tern (sĭs′tərn) *n.* **1.** A receptacle for holding water or other liquid, especially, a water tank in the roof of a house or connected to a toilet. **2.** *Anatomy.* A cisterna. [Middle English *cisterne,* from Old French, from Latin *cisterna,* water tank, from *cista,* box, from Greek *kistē,* basket.] **—cis·ter·nal** (sĭ-stûr′nəl) *adj.*

cis·ter·na (sĭ-stûr′nə) *n., pl.* **-nae** (-nē′). Any fluid-containing sac or space in the body of an organism. Also called "reservoir." [New Latin, from Latin, CISTERN.]

cis-trans isomerism (sĭs′trănz′) *n. Chemistry.* A type of isomerism in which two atoms or groups in a molecule can occupy positions on the same side (*cis*) or opposite sides (*trans*) of a line or center. It is found especially in organic compounds containing double bonds and in inorganic square and octahedral coordination complexes. Also called "geometrical isomerism." **—cis-trans isomer** *n.*

cis·tron (sĭs′trŏn′) *n.* A unit of genetic function: a section of DNA controlling the production of a single polypeptide chain of a protein molecule. [From *cis-trans* + -ON (molecular unit).]

cit. 1. citation. **2.** cited. **3.** citizen.

cit·a·del (sĭt′ə-dəl, -dĕl′) *n.* **1.** A fortress in a commanding position in or near a city. **2.** Any stronghold or fortified place; a bulwark. **3.** A Salvation Army meeting hall. [French *citadelle* or Italian *cittadella,* diminutive of obsolete *cittade,* city, from Latin *cīvitās,* citizenry, state, CITY.]

ci·ta·tion (sī-tā′shən) *n. Abbr.* **cit. 1.** The act of citing. **2.** A quoting of an authoritative source for substantiation. **3.** A source so cited; a quotation. **4.** *Law.* A reference to previous court decisions or authoritative writings. **5.** An official commendation for meritorious action, especially in military service. **6.** A summons, especially one calling for appearance in court. **—ci·ta·to·ry** (sī′tə-tôr′ē, -tōr′ē) *adj.*

cite (sīt) *tr.v.* **cited, citing, cites. 1.** To quote as an authority or example. **2.** To mention or bring forward as support, illustration, or proof. **3.** To commend (a unit or individual in the armed forces) in dispatches, for meritorious action. **4.** To summon before a court of law. **5.** *Archaic.* To call to action; rouse. [Middle English *citen,* to summon, from Old French *citer,* from Latin *citāre,* frequentative of *ciēre,* to set in motion, summon.]

cith·a·ra (sĭth′ə-rə, kĭth′-) *n.* An ancient musical instrument resembling the lyre. [Latin, from Greek *kithara*†.]

cith·er (sĭth′ər, sĭth′-) *n.* Also **cith·ern** (sĭth′ərn, sĭth′-). A musical instrument, a **cittern** *(see).* [French *cithare,* from Latin *cithara,* CITHARA.]

cit·i·fied (sĭt′ĭ-fīd′) *adj.* Having customs, manners, fashions, or other characteristics attributed to city people.

cit·i·fy (sĭt′ĭ-fī′) *tr.v.* **-fied, -fying, -fies. 1.** To cause to become like a city; make urban. **2.** To cause to acquire the styles or manners of city people. **—cit·i·fi·ca·tion** (sĭt′ĭ-fĭ-kā′shən) *n.*

cit·i·zen (sĭt′ə-zən) *n. Abbr.* **cit. 1.** A person owing loyalty to and entitled by birth or naturalization to the protection of a given nation. **2.** A resident of a city or town, especially one entitled to vote and enjoy other privileges there. [Middle English *citisein,* from Norman French *citesein,* variant of Old French *citeien,* from *cite,* CITY.] **—cit·i·zen·ly** *adj.*

cit·i·zen·ry (sĭt′ə-zən-rē) *n., pl.* **-ries.** Citizens collectively.

citizen's arrest *n.* An arrest made by an ordinary member of the public, in accordance with the right of any citizen to arrest someone who has committed an arrestable offense or a breach of the peace.

citizens band *n.* A range of radio frequencies officially allocated for radio communications between private individuals. Often used adjectivally: *citizens band radio.* Also called "CB."

cit·i·zen·ship (sĭt′ĭ-zən-shĭp′) *n.* The status of a citizen with its attendant duties, rights, and privileges.

Ci·tlal·té·petl (sē′tläl-tā′pĕt-l). An extinct volcanic peak in southern Mexico, situated between Mexico City and Veracruz. At 5,699 meters (18,697 feet) it is Mexico's highest peak.

cit·ral (sĭt′răl′) *n.* A free-flowing pale yellow liquid, $C_{10}H_{16}O$, derived from lemon-grass oil and used in perfumery and as a flavoring. It exists in two isomeric forms: the cis-isomer (**geranial**) and the trans-isomer (**neral**). [CITR(US) + -AL (aldehyde).]

cit·rate (sĭt′rāt′) *n.* A salt or ester of citric acid.

cit·ric (sĭt′rĭk) *adj.* Of or obtained from citrus fruits.

citric acid *n.* A colorless translucent crystalline acid, $C_6H_8O_7$, principally derived by fermentation of carbohydrates or from lemon, lime, and pineapple juices, and used to prepare citrates, in flavorings, and in metal polishes.

citric acid cycle *n.* The **Krebs cycle** *(see).*

cit·ri·cul·ture (sĭt′rĭ-kŭl′chər) *n.* The cultivation of citrus fruits. [*citrus* + *culture.*] **—cit·ri·cul·tur·ist** (sĭt′rĭ-kŭl′chə-rĭst) *n.*

cit·rine (sĭt′rĭn, -rēn′) *n.* **1.** A pale-yellow variety of quartz, resembling topaz. **2.** The greenish-yellow color of a lemon. [Middle English, from Old French *citrin,* from Medieval Latin *citrīnus,* from Latin *citrus,* citron tree, CITRUS.] **—cit·rine** *adj.*

cit·ron (sĭt′rən) *n.* **1.** A tree, *Citrus medica,* native to Asia, having lemonlike fruit with a thick, aromatic rind. **2.** The fruit of this tree. **3.** A variety of watermelon, *Citrullus vulgaris citroides,* having fruit generally considered inedible and a hard rind used as flavoring. In this sense, also called "citron melon." **4.** The preserved or candied rind of either of these fruits, used especially in baking. **5.** Grayish green yellow. [French, from Old French, from Latin *citrus*†, citron tree.] **—cit·ron** *adj.*

cit·ron·el·la (sĭt′rə-nĕl′ə) *n.* **1.** A tropical Eurasian grass, *Cymbopogon nardus,* having bluish-green, lemon-scented leaves. Also called "citronella grass." **2.** A light yellow, aromatic oil obtained from this grass and used in insect repellents and perfumery. Also called "citronella oil." [New Latin, from French *citronnelle,* lemon oil, diminutive of *citron,* CITRON.]

cit·ron·el·lal (sĭt′rə-nĕl′ăl′) *n.* A colorless mixture of isomeric liquids, $C_9H_{17}CHO$, the chief constituent of citronella oil. [CITRONELL(A) + -AL (aldehyde).]

cit·rus (sĭt′rəs) *adj.* Also **cit·rous. 1.** Of or pertaining to trees or shrubs of the genus *Citrus,* many of which bear edible fruit such as the orange, lemon, lime, and grapefruit. **2.** Of or characteristic of the fruits of these trees or shrubs.
~*n., pl.* **citruses** or collectively **citrus.** A citrus tree or shrub. [New Latin, from Latin *citrus*†, citron tree, citrus tree.]

Città del Vaticano. See **Vatican City.**

cit·tern (sĭt′ərn) *n.* A 16th-century guitar with a pear-shaped body. Also called "cither." [Variant (assimilated to GITTERN or CITHER).]

cit·y (sĭt′ē) *n., pl.* **-ies.** *Abbr.* **C. 1.** A town of significant size. **2.** In the United States, an incorporated municipality with definite boundaries and legal powers set forth in a charter granted by the state. **3.** In Canada, a municipality of high rank, usually determined by population but varying according to province. **4.** In Great Britain, a large incorporated town, usually the seat of a bishop, with its title conferred by the Crown. **5.** In various other countries, a large town, designated as a city according to population, the presence of a cathedral, or other factors. **6.** The inhabitants of a city as a group. **7.** An ancient Greek city-state. **—the City.** The commercial and financial district of London, in which the stock exchange and the Bank of England are situated.
~*adj.* Of, in, or belonging to a city. [Middle English *cite,* from Old French, from Latin *cīvitās* (stem *cīvitat-*), citizenry, state, (later) city, from *cīvis,* citizen.]

city editor *n.* **1.** A newspaper editor responsible for handling local news and reporters' assignments. **2.** In Great Britain, the editor who handles commercial and financial news.

city fathers *pl.n.* The members of the governing body of a city.

city hall *n.* **1.** The building housing the administrative offices of a municipal government. **2.** The officials of a municipal government.

city manager *n.* An administrator appointed by a city council to manage the affairs of the municipality.

city slicker *n. Informal.* A person with the sophisticated or smooth manners traditionally associated by rural people with city dwellers. Often used derogatorily.

cit·y-state (sĭt′ē-stāt′) *n.* A sovereign state consisting of an independent city and its surrounding territory, especially as in ancient Greece.

Ciu·dad Bo·lí·var (syo͞o-däd′ bō-lē′vär). Seaport on the Orinoco River in eastern Venezuela, renamed Bolívar in 1849.

Ciudad Re·al (rā-äl′). Town in New Castile province in south-central Spain, founded in the 13th century.

Ciudad Trujillo. See **Santo Domingo.**

civ. civil; civilian.

civ·et (sĭv′ĭt) *n.* **1.** Any of various catlike mammals of the family Viverridae, of Africa and Asia, having spotted or blotched fur and anal scent glands that secrete a fluid with a musky odor. Also called "civet cat." **2.** This fluid, used in the manufacture of perfumes. **3.** The fur of a civet. [French *civette,* from Old French, from Italian *zibetto,* from Arabic *zabād.*]

civ·ic (sĭv′ĭk) *adj.* Of, pertaining to, or belonging to a city, to a citizen, or to citizenship; municipal or civil. [Latin *cīvicus,* from *cīvis,* citizen.] **—civ·i·cal·ly** *adv.*

civic center *n.* A building or complex containing the municipal offices of a city, often with other facilities such as a hall.

civ·ics (sĭv′ĭks) *n. Used with a singular verb.* **1.** The study of the rights and duties of a citizen. **2.** The branch of political science that deals with civic affairs.

civies. Variant of **civvies.**

civ·il (sĭv′əl) *adj. Abbr.* **civ. 1.** Of, pertaining to, or befitting citizens or the citizen as an individual. **2.** Of or pertaining to citizens and their relations with one another or with the state. **3.** Of ordinary citizens or ordinary community life, as distinguished from the military or the ecclesiastical. **4.** Of or in accordance with organized society and government; civilized. **5.** Observing or befitting accepted social usages; proper; polite. **6.** Designating or according to legally recognized divisions of time: *a civil year.* **7.** *Law.* **a.** Of or in accordance with Roman civil law or with its medieval and modern derivatives. **b.** Pertaining to the rights of private individuals and to legal proceedings concerning these rights. Used to distinguish a court, proceeding, or rule that is not criminal, military, or international. —See Synonyms at **polite.** [Middle English, from Old French, from Latin *cīvīlis,* from *cīvis,* citizen.] **—civ·il·ly** *adv.*

civet *The scent glands of these catlike meat eaters are used in the manufacture of some perfumes. Civets, which also eat fruit and nuts, are native to the tropical forests of Southeast Asia, India, and Africa. They are related to the mongoose.*

civil day *n.* A **mean solar day** *(see).*

civil death *n. Law.* Formerly, the total deprivation of civil rights resulting from conviction for treason or other serious offenses.

civil defense *n. Abbr.* **C.D. 1.** The activities of an organized body of civilian volunteers to protect life and property in the case of a natural disaster or an attack by an enemy. **2.** These civilian volunteers.

civil disobedience *n.* The refusal to obey civil laws that are regarded as unjust, usually by employing methods of passive resistance to bring about political change.

civil engineer *n. Abbr.* **C.E.** An engineer trained in the design and construction of public works.

ci·vil·ian (sə-vĭl′yən) *n. Abbr.* **civ.** A person following the pursuits of civil life, as distinguished from one serving in the armed forces.
~*adj.* Of or pertaining to civilians or civil life; nonmilitary. [Middle English, practitioner of civil law, jurist, from *civile,* civil law, from Latin, from *(jūs) cīvīle,* from *cīvīlis,* CIVIL.]

ci·vil·i·ty (sə-vĭl′ə-tē) *n., pl.* **-ties. 1.** Politeness; courtesy. **2.** A courteous act or utterance.

civ·i·li·za·tion (sĭv′ə-lə-zā′shən) *n.* **1.** A condition of human society marked by an advanced stage of development in the arts and sciences and by corresponding social, political, and cultural complexity. **2.** Those nations or peoples regarded as having arrived at this stage. **3.** The type of culture and society developed by a particular group, nation, or region, or by any of these in some particular epoch. **4.** The act or process of civilizing or of reaching a civilized state. **5.** The state of being cultured or having good taste. **6.** Populated areas, especially urban areas, and the conveniences associated with them.

civ·i·lize (sĭv′ə-līz′) *tr.v.* **-lized, -lizing, -lizes. 1.** To bring out of a primitive or savage state into a more developed one. **2.** To educate or enlighten. **—civ·i·liz·a·ble** *adj.* **—civ·i·liz·er** *n.*

civ·i·lized (sĭv′ə-līzd′) *adj.* **1.** Having a highly developed society and culture. **2.** Of, pertaining to, or characteristic of a people or nation so developed. **3.** Polite or cultured; refined.

civil law *n.* **1.** The body of law dealing with the rights of private citizens in a particular state or nation, as distinguished from criminal law, military law, or international law. Compare **criminal law. 2.** The law of ancient Rome, especially that which applied to private citizens. **3.** Any system of law having its origin in Roman law, as distinguished from common law or canon law.

civil liberty *n.* A liberty legally guaranteeing to the individual a right, such as free speech, thought, or action, limited only insofar as its use must not interfere with the rights of others.

civil list *n.* In Great Britain, the yearly provision by Parliament of funds for the personal and household expenses of the monarch.

civil marriage *n.* A marriage ceremony performed by a civil official, such as a registrar.

civil rights *pl.n.* Rights belonging to a person by virtue of his or her status as a citizen or as a member of civil society. Also used adjectivally to designate efforts to win political, economic, and social equality for U.S. blacks: *the civil rights movement.*

civil servant *n.* A person employed in the civil service.

civil service *n. Abbr.* **C.S. 1.** All branches of government administration that are not legislative, judicial, military, or naval. **2.** Collectively, the persons employed by these branches of the government.

civil time *n.* **Mean solar time** *(see).*

civil war *n.* A war between factions or regions of one country.

Civil War *n.* **1.** In the United States, the war between the Union (the

PRONUNCIATION KEY

ă, pat; ā, pay; âr, care;
ä, father, are; b, **bib;**
ch, **church;** d, **deed;** ĕ, pet;
ē, be; f, **fife;** g, **gag;** h, **hat;**
hw, **which;** ĭ, pit; ī, **pie;**
îr, **pier;** j, **judge;** k, **kick;**
l, **lid,** needle; m, **mum;**
n, **no,** sudden; ng, **thing;**
ŏ, pot; ō, **toe;** ô, **paw,** for;
oi, **noise;** ou, **out;** o͝o, **book;**
o͞o, **boot;** p, **pop;** r, **roar;**
s, **sauce;** sh, **ship, dish;**
t, **tight;** th, **thin, path;**
th, **this, bathe;** ŭ, **cut;** ûr, **fur;**
v, **valve;** w, **with;** y, **yes;**
z, **zebra,** size; zh, vision;
ə, about, item, edible,
gallop, circus, peaceful

IN FOREIGN WORDS:

à, *Fr.* **ami;** œ, *Fr.* **feu,** *Ger.* **schön;** ü, *Fr.* **tu,** *Ger.* **über;**
KH, *Ger.* **ich,** *Scot.* **loch;**
N, *Fr.* **bon;** y′, *Fr.* **Compiègne**

STRESS MARKS:

Primary stress: ′
in·cite′ (ĭn-sīt′)
Secondary stress: ′
in′sight′ (ĭn′sīt′)

North) and the Confederacy (the South) from 1861 to 1865. Also called "War Between the States," "War of Secession." **2.** In Great Britain, the war between the Parliamentarians and the Royalists from 1642 to 1652. Also called the "Great Rebellion."

Ci·vi·ta·vec·chia (chē'vē-tä-vĕk'yə). Fishing port on the west coast of central Italy. The old town was founded by Trajan, and Roman baths survive. Michelangelo designed the citadel.

civ·vies, civ·ies (sĭv'ēz) *pl.n. Slang.* Civilian clothes, as distinguished from military dress. [Short for CIVILIAN.]

Civ·vy Street (sĭv'ē) *n. Slang.* Civilian life.

C.J. 1. chief justice. **2.** corpus juris.

ck. cask.

cl centiliter.

Cl The symbol for the element chlorine.

cl. 1. class; classification. **2.** clause. **3.** clearance. **4.** clergyman. **5.** closet. **6.** cloth.

c.l. 1. carload. **2.** *Sports.* center line. **3.** common law.

clab·ber (klăb'ər) *n.* Sour, curdled milk. —*v.* **clabbered, -bering, -bers.** —*tr.* To cause to curdle. —*intr.* To become curdled. [Short for earlier *bonnyclabber,* from Irish : *bainne,* milk, from Middle Irish *banne,* a drop + *clabair*†, thick sour milk.]

clach·an (klăKH'ən) *n. Scottish.* A village or hamlet. [Scottish Gaelic, from *clach,* stone.]

clack (klăk) *v.* **clacked, clacking, clacks.** —*intr.* **1.** To make an abrupt, dry sound, as by the collision of two wooden surfaces. **2.** To chatter thoughtlessly or at length. **3.** To cackle or cluck, as a hen does. —*tr.* To cause to make an abrupt, dry sound. —*n.* **1.** A clacking sound. **2.** Something that makes a clacking sound. **3.** Thoughtless, prolonged talk; chatter. [Middle English *clacken,* from Old Norse *klaka* (imitative).] —**clack·er** *n.*

Civil War

THE CONFLICT THAT SPLIT THE UNITED STATES

Deeply divided along many lines, the Union was restored at terrible cost

Well over a century after the last gunfire, the American Civil War (1861–65) is more likely to arouse dispute than bring consensus. Long before the Confederate shelling of Fort Sumter, South Carolina, opened the shooting war, sectional rivalries had already split families, friendships, churches, political parties—and the nation itself.

A divided nation played cruel tricks with allegiances. Mary Todd, the wife of President Abraham Lincoln (1809–65), had three brothers who fought and died for the South. Robert E. Lee (1807–70), more respected in the Confederacy than even its president, Jefferson Davis (1808–89), was offered command of the Union forces but became a Rebel because he would not fight against his native Virginia. Before the war, Lee had captured the abolitionist zealot John Brown (1800–59). Brown was hanged and the poem "John Brown's Body" and a Southern

melody combined to become a marching song of Union troops. With lyrics (1862) by Julia Ward Howe (1819–1910), it became "The Battle Hymn of the Republic."

Lincoln's Emancipation Proclamation made slaves free as of January 1, 1863, in states "in rebellion"—but not in loyal border states. His priority was to "save the Union," and alienating loyal states would not help that cause. Worn down by the North's industrial and manpower edge, the South began to fold in 1864. On April 9, 1865, Lee surrendered to Ulysses S. Grant (1822–85) at Appomattox Court House, Virginia. Five days later, screaming "the South is avenged!" John Wilkes Booth assassinated Lincoln. The last Confederate force gave up on May 26. Counting deaths from disease (about 315,000), some 530,000 perished in the war—more Americans than died in World Wars I and II combined.

NEAR THE END *Prisoners from the Front by Winslow Homer shows three captured Confederate soldiers, with and without uniforms, confronting a Union officer. On assignment for* Harper's Weekly, *Homer competed with photographers to bring images of the war to the Northern homefront.*

Clack·man·nan (klăk-măn'ən). Also **Clack·man·nan·shire** (-shîr, -shər). Former county in central Scotland, the smallest in the country. In 1975 it became Clackmannan district in Central Region.

clack valve *n.* A hinged or ball valve that permits fluids to flow in only one direction.

Clac·to·ni·an (klăk-tō'nē-ən) *adj. Archaeology.* Of or pertaining to a lower Paleolithic culture of northwestern Europe. [From *Clacton-on-Sea,* southeast England, site of the discovery of artifacts from which the culture was classified.]

clad¹ (klăd) *tr.v.* **clad, cladding, clads.** To sheathe or cover (a metal) with a metal, as for decoration or protection. [Middle English *cladden,* from *cladde,* past participle of *clathen, clothen,* CLOTHE.]

clad². Alternate past tense and past participle of **clothe.**

clad–, clado– *prefix.* Indicates a sprout or branch; for example, **cladistics.** [Greek *klados,* branch.]

clad·ding (klăd'ĭng) *n.* **1.** A metal coating bonded onto another metal. **2.** A protective or insulating layer fixed to the outside of a building or other structure.

clade (klăd) *n.* A group of organisms that share a common ancestor. [Greek *klados,* branch.]

cla·dist (klā'dĭst) *n.* One who practices cladistics.

cla·dis·tics (klə-dĭs'tĭks) *n. Used with a singular verb.* A method of scientific classification in which organisms are placed in the same taxonomic group when they share features thought to indicate recent common ancestry. [CLADE + -ISTICS.] —**cla·dis·tic** *adj.*

cla·doc·er·an (klə-dŏs'ər-ən) *n.* Any of various small aquatic crustaceans of the order Cladocera, which includes the water fleas. —*adj.* Of or belonging to the Cladocera. [New Latin *Cladocera* : Greek *klados,* branch, shoot + *keras,* horn.]

clad·ode (klăd'ōd') *n.* A leaflike plant stem, a **cladophyll** (see).

cla·do·gram (klăd'ə-grăm') *n.* A diagram used in cladistics to show the relationships between organisms, consisting of a series of branches that repeatedly divide into two, each point of branching representing divergence from a common ancestor. [CLADE + -GRAM.]

clad·o·phyll (klăd'ə-fĭl') *n.* A branch or portion of a stem that resembles a leaf. Also called "cladode," "phylloclade." [New Latin *cladophyllum* : Greek *klados,* twig + *phullon,* leaf, -PHYLL.]

clag (klăg) *v.* **clagged, clagging, clags.** —*tr.* **1.** To clog. **2.** To stick; adhere. —*intr.* **1.** To become clogged. **2.** To become stuck. —*n.* A clog or clot. [Middle English *claggen,* to daub with mud, from Scandinavian; akin to Danish *klagge,* mud.] —**clag·gy** *adj.*

claim (klām) *v.* **claimed, claiming, claims.** —*tr.* **1.** To demand as one's due; assert one's right to. **2.** To take by or as if by right: *He claimed the reward.* **3.** To state to be true; assert or maintain. **4.** To deserve or call for; require. **5.** To demand (money) under an insurance policy, as after an accident. —*intr.* To make a claim, especially an insurance claim.
—*n.* **1.** A demand for something as one's rightful due; affirmation of a right. **2.** A basis for demanding something; a title or right. **3.** Something claimed in a formal or legal manner; especially, a tract of land staked out by a miner or prospector. **4. a.** A sum of money demanded, as after an accident, in accordance with an insurance policy or other formal arrangement. **b.** A demand for such money. **5.** A statement of something as a fact; an assertion of truth. —**lay claim to.** To assert one's right to or ownership of. [Middle English *claimen,* from Old French *clamer* (present stem *claim-*), to cry, appeal, from Latin *clāmāre,* to call.] —**claim·a·ble** *adj.* —**claim·er** *n.*

claim·ant (klā'mənt) *n.* A person making a claim.

Clair (klâr), **René** (1898–1981). French film director. As an early exponent of sound productions, he directed the classics *Sous les Toits de Paris* (1929) and *Le Million* (1931).

clair·au·di·ence (klâr-ô'dē-əns) *n.* The supposed faculty of hearing things outside the normal range of perception. [French *clair,* CLEAR + AUDIENCE, by analogy with CLAIRVOYANCE.] —**clair·au·di·ent** *n. & adj.*

clair de lune (klâr' də lōōn') *n.* **1.** A pale, grayish-blue glaze applied to various kinds of Chinese porcelain. **2.** The color of this glaze. [French, "moonlight."] —**clair-de-lune** *adj.*

clair·schach, clar·sach (klär'shəKH) *n.* An ancient Irish harp. [Middle English *clareschaw,* from Scottish Gaelic *clārsach*†.]

Clair·vaux (klâr-vō'). Village in the Aube department of northeast France. Its abbey, founded by St. Bernard of Clairvaux in 1115, became the most influential center of the Cistercian order.

clair·voy·ance (klâr-voi'əns) *n.* **1.** The supposed power to see or know things that are out of the natural range of human perception. **2.** Acute intuitive insight or perceptiveness. [French *clairvoyant,* "clear-seeing" : *clair,* clear, from Latin *clārus* + *voyant,* present participle of *voir,* to see, from Latin *vidēre.*] —**clair·voy·ant** *n. & adj.*

clam¹ (klăm) *n.* **1.** Any of various usually burrowing marine and freshwater bivalve mollusks, including members of the genera *Venus, Mya,* and others, many of which are edible. See **quahog. 2.** The soft, tasty, edible flesh of such a mollusk. **3.** *Informal.* An uncommunicative person. —*intr.v.* **clammed, clamming, clams.** To hunt for clams. —**clam up.** To cease talking or remain silent. [Shortened from *clamshell,* "bivalve that shuts tight like a clamp," from CLAM (clamp).]

clam² *n.* A clamp or vise. [Middle English, Old English *clamm,* bond, fetter.]

cla·mant (klā'mənt) *adj.* **1.** Clamorous; loud. **2.** Urgent; compelling. [Latin *clāmāns* (stem *clāmant-*), present participle of *clāmāre,* to cry out.]

clam·a·to·ri·al (klăm′ə-tôr′ē-əl, -tōr′ē-əl) *adj. Ornithology.* Of or pertaining to the American flycatchers, a group of perching and singing birds. [New Latin *clamatores,* plural of Latin *clāmātor,* shouter, from *clāmāre,* to cry out.]

clam·bake (klăm′bāk′) *n.* **1.** A seashore picnic where clams, fish, and other foods are baked in layers on buried hot stones. **2.** *Informal.* A party, especially a noisy and lively one.

clam·ber (klăm′ər, klăm′bər) *intr.v.* **-bered, -bering, -bers.** To climb with difficulty, especially on all fours; scramble.
~*n.* The act of clambering. [Middle English *clambren,* from Old Norse *klembra,* originally, "to grip."] **—clam·ber·er** *n.*

clam chowder *n.* Any of various soups made from shelled clams, salt pork, potatoes, and onions.

clam·my (klăm′ē) *adj.* **-mier, -miest. 1.** Disagreeably moist and usually cold. **2.** Humid; damp. Said of weather. [Middle English, from *clammen,* to stick, smear, Old English *clǣman.*] **—clam·mi·ly** *adv.* **—clam·mi·ness** *n.*

clam·or (klăm′ər) *n.* Also *chiefly British* **clam·our. 1.** A loud outcry or shouting; hubbub. **2.** A vehement expression of discontent or protest; a public outcry. **3.** Any loud and sustained noise; din; blare. **—See Synonyms at noise.**
~*v.* **clamored, -oring, ors.** Also *chiefly British* **clam·our.** —*intr.* **1.** To make a clamor. **2.** To make vigorous demands or complaints. —*tr.* To exclaim insistently and noisily. [Middle English *clamor,* from Old French, from Latin *clāmor,* from *clāmāre,* to cry out.] **—clam·or·er** *n.*

clam·or·ous (klăm′ər-əs) *adj.* Making, full of, or characterized by clamor. **—clam·or·ous·ly** *adv.* **—clam·or·ous·ness** *n.*

clamp (klămp) *n.* Any of various devices used to join, grip, support, or compress mechanical or structural parts.
~*tr.v.* **clamped, clamping, clamps.** To fasten, grip, or support with or as if with a clamp. [Middle English, from Middle Dutch *clampe.*]

clamp down *intr.v.* To repress, restrict, or prohibit something not approved of. Used with *on.* **—clamp-down** (klămp′doun′) *n.*

clamp·er (klăm′pər) *n.* A spiked plate attached to the sole of a shoe to prevent slipping on ice.

clam·shell (klăm′shĕl′) *n.* **1.** The shell of a clam. **2.** A dredging bucket made of two hinged jaws. **3.** Either of a pair of doors in an airplane that open outward and away from each other.

clam·worm (klăm′wûrm′) *n.* Any of various segmented marine worms of the genus *Nereis;* especially, *N. cultrifera,* swimming by means of paired, paddlelike appendages. Also called "ragworm."

clan (klăn) *n.* **1.** A traditional social unit in Scotland, consisting of a number of families claiming a common ancestor and following the same hereditary chieftain. **2.** In some tribal societies, a division of a tribe tracing descent from a common ancestor. **3.** Any numerous group of relatives, friends, or associates. [Middle English, from Scottish Gaelic *clann,* children, family, from Latin *planta,* shoot, PLANT.]

clan·des·tine (klăn-dĕs′tən) *adj.* Concealed, usually for some secret or illicit purpose. **—See Synonyms at secret.** [French *clandestin,* from Old French, from Latin *clandestīnus,* in secret (after *intestīnus,* inward, INTESTINE).] **—clan·des·tine·ly** *adv.* **—clan·des·tine·ness, clan·des·ti·ni·ty** (klăn′dĕs-tĭn′ə-tē) *n.*

clang (klăng) *n.* **1.** A loud, metallic, resonant sound. **2.** The strident call of a crane or goose.
~*v.* **clanged, clanging, clangs.** —*intr.* To make a clang. —*tr.* To cause to clang. [Latin *clangere,* to resound (imitative).]

clang·er (klăng′ər) *n. Slang.* An embarrassing or tactless blunder. [Imitative, also influenced by Latin *clangor,* resounding noise.]

clan·gor (klăng′ər, klăng′gər) *n.* Also *chiefly British* **clan·gour.** A clang or repeated clanging; a loud ringing; a din. [Latin, from *clangere,* CLANG.] **—clangor** *v.* **—clan·gor·ous** *adj.* **—clan·gor·ous·ly** *adv.*

clank (klăngk) *n.* A metallic sound, sharp and hard but not as resonant as a clang.
~*v.* **clanked, clanking, clanks.** —*intr.* To make a clank. —*tr.* To cause to clank. [Imitative.]

clan·nish (klăn′ĭsh) *adj.* **1.** Of, pertaining to, or characteristic of a clan. **2.** Inclined to cling together in a group and exclude outsiders. **—clan·nish·ly** *adv.* **—clan·nish·ness** *n.*

clans·man (klănz′mən) *n., pl.* **-men** (-mĭn). A person belonging to a clan.

clans·wom·an (klănz′wŏŏm′ən) *n., pl.* **-women** (-wĭm′ĭn). A woman belonging to a clan.

clap¹ (klăp) *v.* **clapped, clapping, claps.** —*intr.* **1.** To strike the palms of the hands together with a sudden, explosive sound, as in applauding. **2.** To come together suddenly with a sharp noise. —*tr.* **1.** To strike (the hands, for example) together with a brisk movement and an abrupt, loud sound. **2.** To applaud (actors, for example) by clapping the hands. **3.** To strike lightly but firmly with the open hand, as in greeting: *clapped him on the shoulder.* **4.** To put or place quickly or firmly: *clapped him in jail.* **5.** To flap (the wings). **—clap eyes on.** *Informal.* To catch sight of. **—clap hold of.** *Informal.* To grip.
~*n.* **1. a.** The act or sound of clapping the hands. **b.** A loud, sharp, or explosive noise, especially that made by thunder. **2.** A sharp blow with the open hand; a slap. [Middle English *clappen,* from Old English *clappian,* to throb, beat, from Germanic *klap-* (unattested), imitative.]

clap² *n. Slang.* Gonorrhea. [Old French *clapoir,* venereal sore; akin

to *clapier,* brothel, and Old Provençal *clap†,* heap of stones.]

clap·board (klăb′ərd, klăp′bôrd′, -bōrd′) *n.* A long, narrow board with one edge thicker than the other, overlapped to cover the outer walls of frame houses. Also called "weatherboard."
~*tr.v.* **clapboarded, -boarding, boards.** To cover with clapboards. [Partial translation of Middle Dutch *clapholt* : *clappen,* to crack, split, akin to Old English *clappian,* to CLAP + *holt,* board, wood.]

cla·po·tis (klə-pō′tĭs) *n.* A type of wave formation in which standing waves that have no horizontal motion of crests are formed by the approach of waves to a sea wall, breakwater, or other barrier. [French, from *clapoter,* (of a liquid) agitate with waves.]

clap·per (klăp′ər) *n.* **1.** A person or thing that claps. **2.** The part of a bell that strikes the side. **3.** **clappers.** A rattle consisting of two pieces of wood that strike together to make a clapping sound. **4.** *Slang.* The tongue.

clap·per·board (klăp′ər-bôrd, -bōrd) *n.* A device used in filmmaking consisting of two hinged pieces of wood that are held before the camera bearing the scene number and clapped together to allow the synchronization of the soundtrack and the image.

clap·per·claw (klăp′ər-klô′) *tr.v.* **-clawed, -clawing, -claws.** *Archaic.* **1.** To claw or scratch. **2.** To berate or revile. [Probably CLAPPER + CLAW.]

clapper rail *n.* A North American marsh bird, *Rallus longirostris,* having brownish plumage, a long bill, and a clattering cry.

clap·trap (klăp′trăp′) *n. Informal.* Pretentious, insincere, or empty language. [CLAP + TRAP ("a trick to win applause").]

claque (klăk) *n.* **1.** A group of persons hired to applaud at a performance. **2.** Any group of adulating or fawning admirers. [French, from *claquer,* to clap (imitative).]

clar·a·bel·la (klăr′ə-bĕl′ə) *n.* An eight-foot organ stop producing soft, sweet tones. [Latin *clāra,* feminine of *clārus,* CLEAR + *bella,* feminine of *bellus,* pretty.]

Clare (klâr). A county in Munster province on the Atlantic coast of the Irish Republic. It is a farming district, with salmon fisheries in the Shannon estuary.

Clare, John (1793–1864). British poet, known for his lyrical evocations of the English countryside. His works, which include *The Shepherd's Calendar* (1827) and *The Rural Muse* (1835), sold poorly and he was destitute. After 1841 he spent his life in a mental hospital, where he produced some of his best poetry.

clar·ence (klăr′əns) *n.* A four-wheeled closed carriage with seats for four passengers. [After the Duke of *Clarence* (1765–1837), later William IV.]

clar·en·don (klăr′ən-dən) *n. Printing.* A variety of boldface roman type. [After the *Clarendon* Press, printing house of Oxford University.]

Clare of As·si·si (klâr; ə-sē′sē, -ze), **Saint** (1194–1253). Italian nun, who founded the first Franciscan order of nuns, the Poor Clares. She has become the patron saint of television because she is said to have once witnessed a mass celebrated far away.

clar·et (klăr′ət) *n.* **1. a.** The dry red table wine from the Bordeaux region of France. **b.** Any of various similar red wines made elsewhere. **2.** Dark or grayish purplish red. [Middle English, from Old French, from Medieval Latin *(vīnum) clārātum,* "clarified (wine)," from Latin *clārāre,* to make clear, purify, from *clārus,* CLEAR.] **—claret** *adj.*

claret cup *n.* A chilled mixed drink of red wine with spirits, fruit, and other ingredients.

clar·i·fy (klăr′ə-fī′) *v.* **-fied, -fying, -fies.** —*tr.* **1.** To make clear or easier to understand; elucidate. **2.** To make clear by removing impurities, often by heating gently: *clarify butter.* —*intr.* To become clear. [Middle English *clarifien,* from Old French *clarifier,* from Late Latin *clārificāre* : Latin *clārus,* CLEAR + *facere,* to make.] **—clar·i·fi·ca·tion** (klăr′ə-fĭ-kā′shən) *n.* **—clar·i·fi·er** *n.*

clar·i·net (klăr′ə-nĕt′) *n.* Also *rare* **clar·i·o·net** (klăr′ē-ə-nĕt′). **1.** A woodwind instrument having a straight, cylindrical tube with a flaring bell and a single-reed mouthpiece, played by means of finger holes and keys. **2.** An eight-foot organ stop producing a sound suggestive of a clarinet. [French *clarinette,* from Italian *clarinetto,* diminutive of *clarino,* trumpet, from Latin *clārus,* CLEAR.] **—clar·i·net·ist, clar·i·net·tist** *n.*

cla·ri·no (klə-rē′nō) *n., pl.* **-nos.** *Music.* **1.** The high register of the trumpet, especially in baroque music. **2.** A high, trumpetlike organ stop. [Italian, trumpet, probably from Spanish *clarin.*]

clar·i·on (klăr′ē-ən) *n.* **1.** A medieval trumpet with a shrill, clear tone. **2.** The sound made by this instrument or any sound resembling it. **3.** An organ stop with a high, shrill tone.
~*adj.* Shrill and clear: *a clarion call to resistance.* [Middle English *clarioun,* from Medieval Latin *clāriō* (stem *clārion-*), trumpet, from Latin *clārus,* CLEAR.]

clar·i·ty (klăr′ə-tē) *n.* **1.** Clearness. **2.** Plainness; lucidity: *clarity of style.* [Middle English *clarite,* from Latin *clāritās,* from *clārus,* CLEAR.]

Clark (klärk), **George Rogers** (1752–1818). U.S. military leader and frontiersman. During the American Revolution he led a band of less than 200 men on many successful raids against hostile Indians and British troops. His efforts contributed to England's concession of the Northwest Territory to the United States in 1783.

Clark, Kenneth Mackenzie, Baron (1903–83). British art critic and historian. *The Gothic Revival* (1929) was the first of his many influential books, and *The Nude* (1955) perhaps his most famous.

Clark, William (1770–1838). U.S. explorer and soldier. With Meriwether Lewis, he explored the American northwest in search of a land passage to the Pacific (1804–06). During the expedition he studied the flora and fauna and carefully mapped the region, helping to open the area to settlers. He was the brother of George Rogers Clark.

Clark cell *n. Physics.* A former standard voltaic cell with an emf of 1.4345 volts (15°C). It has a zinc cathode in zinc sulfate and a mercury anode in mercury sulfate. [After Josiah L. *Clark* (1822–98), English engineer.]

clark·i·a (klär′kē-ə) *n.* Any of several annual plants of the genus *Clarkia,* of western North America, especially *C. pulchella,* which is cultivated for its red, purple, and white flowers. [New Latin, after William CLARK, who discovered it.]

clarsach. Variant of **clairschach.**

clart (klärt) *n. Northern British.* A dirty or sticky smear. [Middle English, origin obscure.] —**clart·y** *adj.*

clar·y (klâr′ē) *n., pl.* **-ies.** Any of several European plants of the genus *Salvia,* especially *S. sclarea,* an aromatic herb with bluish-white flowers. Also called "clary sage." [Middle English *clarye, sclarey,* from Old French *sclaree,* from Medieval Latin *sclarea†.]*

–clase *suffix.* Indicates a mineral with a specified cleavage; for example, **plagioclase.** [French, from Greek *klasis,* a breaking, from *klan,* to break.]

clash (klăsh) *v.* **clashed, clashing, clashes.** —*intr.* **1.** To collide with a loud, harsh noise. **2.** To conflict, as in a fight, contest, or debate; be in opposition. **3.** To create an unpleasant visual impression when combined. Used of colors. **4.** To occur at the same time; coincide: *The date of the meeting clashes with my dental appointment.* —*tr.* To strike together with a harsh, metallic noise. —*n.* **1.** A loud, resounding, metallic noise, such as that made by two objects colliding. **2.** A conflict, opposition, or disagreement. **3.** An inharmonious grouping, for example of colors. —See Synonyms at **discord.** [Imitative.]

clasp (klăsp, kläsp) *n.* **1.** A fastening, such as a hook or buckle, used to hold two objects or parts together. **2. a.** An embrace; a hug. **b.** A grip or grasp of the hand. **3.** A small metal bar attached to a military decoration indicating the action for which it was awarded. —*tr.v.* **clasped, clasping, clasps. 1.** To fasten with or as if with a clasp. **2.** To hold in a tight grasp; embrace. **3.** To grip firmly in or with the hand. [Middle English *claspe,* from *claspen, clapsen,* to grip, grasp, perhaps from Old English *clyppan,* to embrace.] —**clasp·er** *n.*

clas·pers (klăs′pərz, kläs-) *pl.n.* A pair of appendages, found in male insects and certain fish, that are specialized for the introduction of sperm into the female reproductive tract.

clasp knife *n.* A pocketknife with a single blade.

class (klăs, kläs) *n. Abbr.* **cl. 1. a.** A set, collection, group, or configuration containing members having or thought to have at least one attribute in common; a kind; a sort. **b.** *Statistics.* Any interval in a **frequency distribution** *(see).* See **set** (in mathematics). **2.** Any division of people or objects by quality, rank, or grade. **3.** A social stratum whose members share similar economic, social, and cultural characteristics. **4. a.** The division of society into relative strata or ranks: *discrimination on grounds of class.* **b.** Social rank or caste, especially high rank. **5. a.** A group of pupils or students studying the same subject or following the same course. **b.** The period during which such a group meets. **c.** A group of students graduating in the same year. **6.** *Biology.* A taxonomic category ranking below a phylum (animals) or division (plants) and above an order. **7.** The quality of accommodation on a public vehicle: *travel in first class.* **8.** *Informal.* Good taste in manner or dress; stylishness: *a girl with class.* —*tr.v.* **classed, classing, classes.** To arrange, group, or rate according to qualities or characteristics; assign to a class; classify. [French *classe,* from Late Latin *classis,* from Latin, one of the six divisions of the Roman people, army, fleet.]

class. 1. classic; classical. **2.** classification; classified; classify.

class action *n.* A legal action undertaken on behalf of all unnamed persons having the same interest in the alleged wrong as the named plaintiffs.

class-con·scious (klăs′kŏn′shəs) *adj.* Aware of belonging to a particular socioeconomic class, often to the extent of being hostile to or envious of other classes. —**class-con·scious·ness** *n.*

clas·sic (klăs′ĭk) *adj.* **1.** Of the highest rank or class. **2.** Serving as an outstanding representative of its kind; model. **3.** Having lasting significance or recognized worth. **4.** *Abbr.* **class.** Pertaining to ancient Greek or Roman literature or art; classical. **5. a.** Of or in accordance with established principles and methods in the arts and sciences. **b.** Having a simple and harmonious design unaffected by passing fashions. **6.** Of lasting historical or literary significance. **7.** *Informal.* Of a well-known or traditional type; remarkably typical: *a classic mistake.* —*n.* **1.** An artist, author, or work generally considered to be of the highest rank or excellence. **2. classics.** The literature of ancient Greece and Rome. **3.** Something considered to be typical or traditional. **4.** A traditional, usually annual, sporting event: *The World Series is the fall classic of baseball.*

Usage: Classic and classical are sometimes interchangeable when used as adjectives, as in such phrases as *classic/classical design* or *look. Classical* is more common in senses pertaining to ancient Greek or Roman culture. *Classic* has a more general range of use, including the broad sense of "highest rank or excellence": *a classic story; Edward Lear's classic limericks.* In this sense it would be different from *a classical story,* in that there is not necessarily any

implication of historical origins. *Classic* has also undergone considerable semantic development in recent years, with its meaning of "typical," "appropriate," and its widespread ironic use in informal speech: *That's classic!* See also Usage note at **-ic, -ical.**

clas·si·cal (klăs′ĭ-kəl) *adj. Abbr.* **class. 1. a.** Of, pertaining to, or in accordance with the precedents of ancient Greek and Roman art, architecture, and literature. **b.** Learned in or studying Greek and Roman art, architecture, or literature. **2.** Of or concerning the most artistically developed stage of a civilization: *Chinese classical poetry.* **3.** *Music.* **a.** Pertaining to or designating the European music, such as that of Haydn and Mozart, of the latter half of the 18th century. **b.** Designating any music in the educated European tradition, as distinguished from popular or folk music. **4.** Conventional and authoritative rather than new or experimental. **5.** Showing artistic restraint and respect for principles of traditional design. **6.** Of or pertaining to nonrelativistic or nonquantum physics: *classical mechanics.* —See Usage note at **classic.** —**clas·si·cal·ism, clas·si·cal·ness** *n.* —**clas·si·cal·ly** *adv.*

Classical Greek *n.* The forms of Greek used in classical literature, chiefly Attic-Ionic, Doric, and Aeolic.

Classical Latin *n.* The form of Latin used in classical literature. Compare **Vulgar Latin.**

clas·si·cism (klăs′ə-sĭz′əm) *n.* **1.** Aesthetic attitudes and principles based on the culture, art, architecture, and literature of ancient Greece and Rome and characterized by emphasis on form, simplicity, proportion, and restraint. **2.** Classical scholarship. **3.** A Greek or Latin form or idiom.

clas·si·cist (klăs′ə-sĭst) *n.* A student of classics.

clas·si·fi·a·ble (klăs′ə-fī′ə-bəl) *adj.* Capable of being classified.

clas·si·fi·ca·tion (klăs′ə-fĭ-kā′shən) *n. Abbr.* **cl., class. 1.** The act or result of classifying. **2.** A category in which something may be classified. **3.** In South Africa, any of various racial groups as distinguished in law. **4.** *Biology.* The systematic grouping of organisms into categories based on shared characteristics or traits; taxonomy. **5.** The designation of information as officially secret. **6.** One of a series of degrees of availability for conscription assigned to men by a selective service system. —**clas·si·fi·ca·to·ry** (klăs′ə-fĭ-kə-tôr′ē, -kə-tōr′ē) *adj.*

class·i·fied (klăs′ə-fīd′) *adj.* **1.** Arranged in classes or categories. **2.** Designated as secret and available only to authorized persons.

classified advertisement *n.* An advertisement in a newspaper, usually brief and in small type. Also called "classified."

clas·si·fy (klăs′ə-fī′) *tr.v.* **-fied, -fying, -fies. 1.** To arrange or organize according to class or category. **2.** In South Africa, to assign to or register under any of the various racial groups. **3.** To designate (a document, for instance) as secret and available only to authorized persons: *The report was classified top secret.* [Latin *classis,* CLASS + -FY.] —**clas·si·fi·er** *n.*

clas·sis (klăs′ĭs) *n., pl.* **classes** (klăs′ēz′). *Ecclesiastical.* **1.** In certain Reformed churches, a governing body of pastors and elders having jurisdiction over local churches. **2.** The district or churches governed by such a body. [New Latin, from Latin, division, CLASS.]

class·less (klăs′lĭs) *adj.* **1.** Not divided economically or socially; lacking class distinctions. **2.** Not belonging to any particular social class.

class mark *n. Statistics.* The numerical value given for computational convenience to a statistical observation falling within a number of intervals. Also called "mark."

class·mate (klăs′māt′, kläs′-) *n.* A member of the same class at school.

class·room (klăs′rōōm′, -rŏŏm′, kläs′-) *n.* A room in which classes are conducted in a school.

class struggle *n.* Conflict between social classes; especially, in Marxist theory, the conflict for economic and political power between an exploiting class, as the capitalist bourgeoisie, and an exploited class, as the proletariat. Also called "class war."

class·y (klăs′ē, kläs′ē) *adj.* **-ier, -iest.** *Informal.* Stylish; elegant. —**class·i·ness** *n.*

clast (klăst) *n. Geology.* A fragment of rock. [Greek *klastos,* fragmented, from *klān,* to break.]

–clast *suffix.* Indicates one that breaks or destroys; for example, **osteoclast, iconoclast.** [Medieval Latin *-clastēs,* from Medieval Greek *-klastēs,* breaker, from *klān,* to break.]

clas·tic (klăs′tĭk) *adj.* **1.** Separable into parts or having removable sections: *a clastic anatomical model.* **2.** *Geology.* Made up of fragments; fragmental. **3.** *Biology.* Dividing into parts. [Greek *klastos,* broken, from *klān,* to break.]

clath·rate (klăth′rāt′, kläth′-) *adj. Biology.* Having a latticelike structure or appearance. —*n. Chemistry.* An inclusion complex in which atoms or molecules of one substance are trapped within the crystal structure of another. Also called "clathrate compound." [Latin *clāthrātus,* past participle of *clāthrāre,* to provide with a lattice, from *clāthrī, clātra,* lattice, from Greek *klēithra,* from *klēithron,* door bar, from *kleiein,* to close.]

clat·ter (klăt′ər) *n.* **1.** A loud rattling sound or sounds. **2.** A loud disturbance; a commotion. —*v.* **clattered, -tering, -ters.** —*intr.* **1.** To make a clatter; move with a clatter. —*tr.* To cause to clatter. [Middle English *clatren,* Old English *clatrian* (attested in gerund, *clatrung*) (imitative).] —**clat·ter·er** *n.*

Claude Lor·rain (klōd lô-răn′), born Claude Gellée (1600–82). French landscape painter, who settled in Rome. He produced luminous landscapes and coastal scenes suffused with golden light.

Clau·di·an (klô′dē-ən), born Claudius Claudianus (*c.* A.D. 370–404). Roman poet, considered the last in the classical tradition. He is best known for his epic *The Rape of Proserpine.*

clau·di·ca·tion (klô′dĭ-kā′shən) *n.* A halt in one's walk; a limp; lameness. [Middle English *claudicacioun,* from Latin *claudicātiō* (stem *claudicātiōn-*), from *claudicāre,* to limp, from *claudus†,* lame.]

Clau·di·us I (klô′dē-əs) (10 B.C.–A.D. 54). Roman emperor (A.D. 41–54) and historian. Physically disabled and considered weak in the head, he was excluded from public life until Caligula made him consul (37). When Caligula was murdered (41), Claudius became emperor and proved a sound, efficient ruler.

claus·al (klô′zəl) *adj.* 1. Of the nature of a clause. 2. Of or pertaining to clauses.

clause (klôz) *n. Abbr.* **cl.** 1. A group of words containing a subject and a predicate that forms part of a compound or complex sentence. See **subordinate clause, main clause.** 2. A section of a legal document, contract, or the like; a distinct article, stipulation, or provision in a document. [Middle English, from Old French, from Medieval Latin *clausa,* close of a rhetorical period, conclusion of a legal argument, hence section of a law, from *claudere* (past participle *clausus*), to close.]

Clau·se·witz (klou′zə-vĭts), **Karl von** (1780–1831). Prussian general and military theorist. In his *On War* he argued for the mobilization of the national effort in a concept of total warfare that dominated Prussian and German military strategy up to World War I.

Clau·si·us (klou′zē-ōōs), **Rudolph Julius Emanuel** (1822–88). German molecular physicist, who formulated the second law of thermodynamics (1850) that "heat cannot of itself pass from a colder to a hotter body." He developed the concept of entropy and a kinetic theory of gases.

claustral. Variant of **cloistral.**

claus·tro·pho·bi·a (klôs′trə-fō′bē-ə) *n.* A pathological fear of confined spaces. [New Latin : Latin *claustrum,* enclosed place, CLOISTER + -PHOBIA.]

claus·tro·pho·bic (klôs′trə-fō′bĭk) *adj.* 1. Suffering from claustrophobia; fearful of confined spaces. 2. Uncomfortably confined or crowded: *a claustrophobic little room.*

cla·vate (klā′vāt′) *adj.* Having one end thickened; club-shaped; claviform. [New Latin *clavatus,* from Latin *clāva,* club.] —**cla·vate·ly** *adv.*

clave. *Archaic.* 1. Past tense of **cleave** (to split). 2. Past tense of **cleave** (to cling).

cla·ver (klā′vər) *intr.v.* **-vered, -vering, -vers.** *Scottish.* To gossip or talk idly.
—*n. Scottish.* Gossip; idle talk. [Scottish Gaelic *clabaire†,* babbler.]

clav·i·chord (klăv′ĭ-kôrd) *n.* An early musical keyboard instrument with a soft sound produced by brass pins (tangents) striking horizontal strings. [Medieval Latin *clāvichordium* : Latin *clāvis,* key + *chorda,* CHORD.]

clav·i·cle (klăv′ĭ-kəl) *n.* 1. In human beings, either of the two bones connecting the upper part of the breastbone with the shoulder blades. Also called "collarbone." 2. The corresponding structure in the pectoral girdle of certain other vertebrates. [Medieval Latin *clāvicula,* diminutive of Latin *clāvis,* key (referring to the shape).] —**cla·vic·u·lar** (klă-vĭk′yə-lər) *adj.* —**cla·vic·u·late** (klă-vĭk′yə-lāt′) *adj.*

clav·i·corn (klăv′ĭ-kôrn′) *adj.* Belonging to or designating a group of beetles of the section Clavicornia, having club-shaped antennae, including the ladybugs and grain beetles. [New Latin *Clavicornia* (family name) : Latin *clāva,* club + Latin *cornū,* horn.]

cla·vier (klə-vîr′, klā′vē-ər, klăv′ē-ər) *n.* 1. A keyboard. 2. Any stringed keyboard instrument, such as a harpsichord or piano. [German *Klavier,* piano, from French *clavier,* keyboard, from Old French *clavier,* key-bearer, from Latin *clāvis,* key.]

clav·i·form (klăv′ə-fôrm′) *adj.* Club-shaped; clavate. [Latin *clāva,* club + -FORM.]

claw (klô) *n.* 1. **a.** A sharp, often curved, nail on the toe of a mammal, reptile, or bird. **b.** The foot of a mammal, reptile, or bird having such nails. 2. **a.** A chela or similar pincerlike structure on the limb of a crustacean or other arthropod. **b.** A limb terminating in such a structure. 3. Anything resembling a claw, such as the cleft end of a hammerhead. 4. *Botany.* The narrowed basal part of certain petals or sepals.
—*v.* **clawed, clawing, claws.** —*tr.* To scratch, tear, grab, or pull with or as if with claws. —*intr.* To make scratching or digging motions with or as if with claws. [Middle English *clawe,* Old English *clawu,* from Germanic.]

claw hammer *n.* A hammer having a head with one end forked for removing nails.

claw hatchet *n.* A hatchet having one end of the head forked.

clay (klā) *n.* 1. A fine-grained, firm, natural material, plastic when wet, that consists primarily of hydrated silicates of aluminum and is widely used in making bricks, tiles, and pottery. 2. Any earth that forms a paste with water and hardens when heated or dried. 3. Moist earth; mud. 4. The human body as distinct from the spirit. Used in literary or poetic contexts. [Middle English *cley, clay,* Old English *clæg,* from Germanic.] —**clay·ey** (klā′ē), **clay·ish** *adj.*

Clay, Cassius Marcellus. See Muhammad Ali.

Clay, Henry (1777–1852). U.S. statesman. A U.S. congressman and senator, his efforts to reconcile the free and slave states through the Missouri Compromise (1820), the compromise tariff of 1833, and the Compromise of 1850 earned him the nickname "the Great

Compromiser." He ran unsuccessfully for president in 1824, 1832, and 1844.

clay court *n.* A tennis court having a surface made of clay or a synthetic substance resembling clay.

clay mineral *n.* Any of a group of hydrated silicates, mainly of aluminum and magnesium, present in clays and responsible for their plastic properties.

clay·more (klā′môr′, -mōr′) *n.* A large, double-edged broadsword formerly used by Scottish Highlanders. [Gaelic *claidheamh mòr,* "great sword" : *claidheamh,* sword + *mòr,* great.]

clay·pan (klā′păn′) *n.* 1. *Geology.* A layer of compact clay beneath the surface soil, causing poor drainage and waterlogging. 2. In Australia, a hollow or slight depression in the ground that has a bottom of clay and holds water after rain.

clay pigeon *n.* A clay disk thrown or propelled into the air as a flying target to be shot at for sport. Also called "bird."

clay·to·ni·a (klā-tō′nē-ə) *n.* Any North American or eastern Siberian succulent plant of the genus *Claytonia,* many of which are cultivated as ornamentals. [After John *Clayton* (1693–1773), U.S. botanist.]

–cle *suffix.* Indicates small size; for example, **particle.** [Middle English, from Old French, from Latin *-culus.*]

clean (klēn) *adj.* **cleaner, cleanest.** 1. Free from dirt, stains, or impurities; unsoiled. 2. **a.** Free from foreign matter; unadulterated. **b.** Not infected: *a clean wound.* 3. Producing little radioactive fallout or contamination. 4. **a.** Without imperfections or blemishes; regular; perfect: *a clean line.* **b.** Well-formed or elegant; streamlined. 5. Free from clumsiness; deft; adroit: *a clean throw.* 6. Without restrictions or encumbrances: *a clean bill of health.* 7. Entire; thorough; complete: *a clean sweep.* 8. Having few alterations or corrections; legible. 9. Blank: *a clean page.* 10. Morally pure; unsullied; sinless. 11. Not ribald or obscene. 12. Honest; fair, as in sports: *a clean fighter.* 13. *Slang.* **a.** Possessing no hidden drugs, weapon, stolen goods, or the like. **b.** Innocent of a crime. 14. Having or showing no record or history of crimes, offenses, or misdeeds: *a clean past.* 15. In religious and biblical contexts: **a.** Free from defilement. **b.** Not prohibited by dietary law. 16. Fresh; pleasantly sharp: *a clean taste.* 17. *Informal.* Able to control urination and defecation.
—*adv.* 1. In a clean manner; cleanly. 2. *Informal.* Entirely; wholly; thoroughly. —**come clean.** *Slang.* To admit the truth; confess.
—*v.* **cleaned, cleaning, cleans.** —*tr.* 1. To rid of dirt or other impurities. 2. To remove (dirt or impurities) from something. 3. To prepare (fowl or other food) for cooking. —*intr.* To undergo or perform the act of ridding of dirt and impurities. —**clean out.** 1. To rid of dirt, rubbish, or impurities. 2. To rid or empty of contents or occupants. 3. To drive or force out. 4. *Informal.* To deprive completely of money or material wealth: *The robbery cleaned them out.* 5. *Informal.* To exhaust (a supply of goods or money).
—*n.* An act or instance of cleaning. [Middle English *clene,* Old English *clēne,* from West Germanic *klaini* (unattested).] —**clean·a·ble** *adj.* —**clean·ness** *n.*

clean-cut (klēn′kŭt′) *adj.* 1. Clearly and sharply defined or outlined. 2. Wholesome; neat and well-dressed.

clean·er (klē′nər) *n.* 1. A person who is employed to clean houses, offices, and the like. 2. A machine, device, or chemical agent that cleans.

clean·ers (klē′nərz) *n. Used with a singular or plural verb.* A commercial establishment providing a dry-cleaning service. —**take to the cleaners.** *Slang.* 1. To swindle or rob. 2. To take all the money or possessions of; ruin. 3. To subject to withering criticism.

clean·ly (klĕn′lē) *adj.* **-lier, -liest.** Habitually and carefully neat and clean.
—*adv.* (klēn′lē). 1. In a clean manner. 2. Smoothly; deftly or easily: *cut the wood cleanly.* —**clean·li·ness** *n.*

cleanse (klĕnz) *tr.v.* **cleansed, cleansing, cleanses.** 1. To free from dirt, defilement, or guilt; purge or clean. 2. To clean (a wound). 3. To use a cleanser on. [Middle English *clensen,* Old English *clēnsian.*]

cleans·er (klĕn′zər) *n.* 1. One that cleans. 2. A detergent, powder, or other chemical agent that removes dirt, grease, or stains. 3. A skin lotion or cream that is used to clean the face.

clean-shav·en (klēn-shā′vən) *adj.* 1. Having the beard or hair shaved off. 2. Having recently shaved.

clean up *intr.v.* 1. To rid a place of dirt or disorder. 2. To make oneself clean, neat, or presentable. 3. *Informal.* To finish; conclude. 4. *Informal.* To make a large profit. —*tr.v.* 1. To clean and make tidy (a room or oneself, for example); remove dirt or debris from. 2. *Informal.* To rid (a town, for example) of corruption.

clean·up (klēn′ŭp′) *n.* 1. A thorough cleaning or tidying. 2. *Informal.* The process of ridding a place of corruption or dishonesty. 3. *Informal.* The final often routine tasks that complete a project. 4. *Informal.* A large profit.

clear (klîr) *adj.* **clearer, clearest.** 1. Free from anything that dims, obscures, or darkens; unclouded. 2. Free from flaw, blemish, or impurity. 3. Free from impediment, obstruction, or hindrance; open. 4. Plain or evident. 5. Easily perceptible to the eye or ear; distinct. 6. Free of guilt; untroubled: *a clear conscience.* 7. **a.** Free from doubt or confusion; certain; sure. **b.** Logical and incisive: *a clear thinker.* 8. Free from qualification or limitation; absolute: *a clear winner.* 9. Resonant; ringing, as certain sounds. 10. Freed from contact or connection; disengaged. Used with *of:* *We are now clear of danger.* 11. Free from roughness or protrusions, as timber

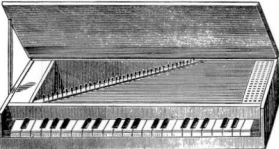

clavichord *The clavichord was originally designed for organists to practice on. The basic clavichord, illustrated here, consists of a single keyboard, but there are examples with two keyboards and a pedal board—reproducing on a small scale the effect of an organ with two manuals.*

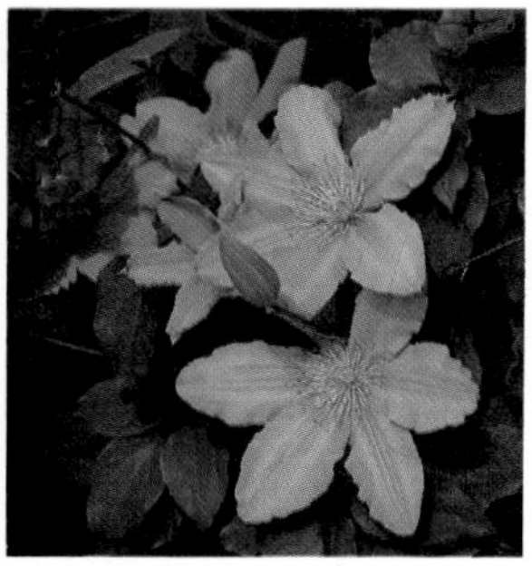

clematis *There are approximately 200 species of* Clematis *found in temperate regions. The climbing species (vines) are the most common, and this hybrid variety is known as "The President."*

12. Freed from burden or obligation. **13.** Without charges or deductions; net: *She earns a clear $15,000.* **14.** Transparent: *clear soup.* **15.** Not cloudy or raining. Said of weather. **16.** Empty: *a clear desk; a clear ship.* **17.** In show jumping, having incurred no penalties: *a clear round.* **—in the clear.** Free from burdens, dangers, difficulties, or suspicion.
~*adv.* **1.** Distinctly; clearly. **2.** *Informal.* All the way; completely; entirely: *He slept clear through the night.* **3.** Out of the way; completely away: *stand clear of the doors.*
~*v.* **cleared, clearing, clears.** —*tr.* **1.** To make clear, light, or bright. **2.** To rid of impurities, blemishes, muddiness, or foreign matter. **3.** To free from confusion, doubt, or ambiguity; make plain or intelligible. **4. a.** To rid of obstructions or entanglements: *clear the road of snow.* **b.** To make (a way, path, clearing, or the like) by removing obstacles or entanglements: *clear a space in the snow.* **c.** To remove or get rid of (obstacles or entanglements): *clear snow from the road.* **5.** To free from a legal charge or imputation of guilt; acquit. **6.** To pass by, under, or over without contact. **7.** To settle (a debt). **8.** To gain (a given amount) as net profit or earnings. **9. a.** To pass (a check or other bill of exchange) through a clearing-house. **b.** To pass (a check) through the banking system and debit and credit the relevant accounts. **10.** To free (a ship or cargo) from legal detention at a harbor by fulfilling the customs and harbor requirements. **11.** To free (the throat) of phlegm by coughing. **12.** To empty; remove objects from: *clear the cupboard.* **13.** To leave; evacuate: *If the fire alarm goes off, everyone must clear the building.* **14.** To declare (a person) fit to see secret or classified documents or to take part in confidential matters. **15.** To pass through by complying with or satisfying certain conditions: *clear customs.* **16.** *Sports.* To kick, hit, throw, or carry (a ball or puck) away from the defended goal. **17.** *Computer Science.* To remove (stored data) from a storage device. **18.** To make (a microscope specimen) transparent by immersing in a fluid such as xylene. —*intr.* **1.** To become clean, fair, or bright. **2.** To exchange checks and bills or settle accounts, through a clearing-house. **3.** To pass through the banking system and be debited and credited to the relevant accounts. Used of a check. **4.** To be enabled to pass through by satisfying certain conditions; especially, to comply with customs regulations. **5.** To become empty or unblocked. **6.** To stop raining or become less cloudy; brighten. **7.** To go away; disappear. Used of fog, mist, rain, or the like. **—clear off.** *Informal.* To go away; leave quickly. Often used in the imperative. **—clear up. 1.** To make clear. **2.** To become fair and sunny after having been cloudy. **3.** To rid of confusion or mystery; explain. [Middle English *clere,* from Old French *cler,* from Latin *clārus,* bright, clear.] **—clear·a·ble** *adj.* **—clear·er** *n.* **—clear·ly** *adv.* **—clear·ness** *n.*

clear-air turbulence (klîr′âr′) *n. Abbr.* **CAT** A type of turbulence encountered by aircraft at high altitudes, caused by waves formed at the interface between two unmixed air layers.

clear·ance (klîr′əns) *n.* **1.** The act of clearing. **2.** A space cleared; a clearing. **3.** *Abbr.* **cl.** The amount by which a moving object clears something. **4.** An intervening distance or space enabling free play, such as that between machine parts. **5.** Permission for an aircraft, ship, or other vehicle to proceed, as after an inspection of equipment or cargo or during certain traffic conditions. **6.** Official certification of blamelessness, trustworthiness, or suitability. **7.** A sale, generally at reduced prices, to dispose of old merchandise. **8.** *Abbr.* **cl.** The passage of checks and other bills of exchange through a clearing-house.

clear·cole (klîr′kōl′) *n.* A primer or size that contains whiting. **—clear·cole** *v.*

clear-cut (klîr′kŭt′) *adj.* **1.** Distinctly and sharply defined or outlined. **2.** Plain; evident.

clear-eyed (klîr′īd′) *adj.* **1. a.** Having sharp, bright eyes. **b.** Keen-sighted. **2.** Mentally acute or perceptive.

clear-head·ed (klîr′hĕd′ĭd) *adj.* Having a clear, orderly mind; sensible. **—clear-head·ed·ly** *adv.* **—clear-head·ed·ness** *n.*

clear·ing (klîr′ĭng) *n.* **1.** A tract of land within a wood or other overgrown area from which the trees and other obstructions have been removed. **2.** In banking, the exchange among banks of checks, drafts, and notes, and the settlement of differences arising from it.

clear·ing-house (klîr′ĭng-hous′) *n. Abbr.* **c.h., C.H.** An office where banks exchange checks and drafts and settle accounts.

clear out *tr.v.* To tidy or empty by removing rubbish or unwanted articles. —*intr.v. Informal.* To leave. **—clear·out** (klîr′out′) *n.*

clear-sight·ed (klîr′sī′tĭd) *adj.* **1.** Having sharp, clear vision. **2.** Discerning. **—clear-sight·ed·ly** *adv.* **—clear-sight·ed·ness** *n.*

clearstory. Variant of **clerestory.**

clear·wing (klîr′wĭng′) *n.* Any of various moths of the family Sesiidae (or Aegeriidae), having scaleless, transparent wings and resembling wasps.

cleat (klēt) *n.* **1.** A strip of wood or iron used to strengthen or support the surface to which it is attached. **2.** A piece of iron, rubber, or leather attached to the underside of a shoe to preserve the sole or prevent slipping. **3.** A piece of metal or wood having projecting arms or ends on which a rope can be wound or secured. **4.** A wedge-shaped piece of wood or other material fastened onto something such as a spar to act as a support or to prevent slipping. **5.** A spurlike device used in gripping a tree or pole in climbing. **6.** *Mining.* A joint or system of joints developed in a coal seam.
~*tr.v.* **cleated, cleating, cleats. 1.** To supply or support with a cleat or cleats. **2.** *Nautical.* To secure (a rope, for example) to or with a cleat. [Middle English *clete,* Old English *clēat* (unattested), lump, wedge.]

cleav·age (klē′vĭj) *n.* **1.** The act of splitting or cleaving. **2.** The state of being split or cleft; a fissure or division. **3.** *Mineralogy.* The splitting of a crystal, or the tendency to split, along definite crystalline planes *(cleavage planes),* yielding smooth surfaces. **4.** *Zoology.* The process of cell division that produces a blastula (hollow ball of cells) from a fertilized ovum. Also called "segmentation." **5.** *Informal.* The hollow or line between a woman's breasts, especially that exposed by a low neckline.

cleave[1] (klēv) *v.* **cleft** (klĕft) or **cleaved** or **clove** (klōv) or *archaic* **clave** (klāv), **cleft** or **cleaved** or **cloven** (klō′vən) or *archaic* **clove, cleaving, cleaves.** —*tr.* **1.** To split or separate, as with an ax. **2.** To make or accomplish as if by cutting: *cleave a path through the forest.* **3.** To pierce or penetrate. —*intr.* **1.** To split or separate, especially along a natural line of division. **2.** To make one's way; penetrate; pass. Used with *through.* —See Synonyms at **tear.** [Cleave, clove, cloven; Middle English *cleven, clave, cloven,* Old English *clēofan, clēaf* (past singular), *clofen.* The weak form *cleft,* Middle English *cleved, cleft,* from the infinitive *cleven.*]

cleave[2] *intr.v.* **cleaved** or *archaic* **clave** (klāv) or **clove** (klōv), **cleaved, cleaving, cleaves.** *Archaic.* **1.** To adhere, cling, or stick fast. Used with *to.* **2.** To be faithful. Used with *to: "Cleave to that which is good"* (Romans 12:9). [Middle English *clevien,* Old English *cleofian.*]

cleav·er (klē′vər) *n.* A heavy, axlike knife or hatchet used especially by butchers.

cleav·ers (klē′vərz) *n., pl.* **-ers.** Any of several plants of the genus *Galium;* especially, *G. aparine,* having small white flowers and prickly stems and fruits. This species is also called "goose grass." [Middle English *clivre* (probably influenced by *clivres,* claws), Old English *clīfe,* "the clinging plant," from *cleofian,* CLEAVE (cling.]

cleek (klēk) *n.* **1.** A number-one golf iron, having very little loft to the club face. **2.** *Scottish.* A large hook. [Middle English *cleche, cleike,* "grasping," from *clechen,* to grasp, seize, Old English *clǣcan* (unattested), probably akin to CLUTCH (verb).]

clef (klĕf) *n.* A symbol on a musical staff, indicating the pitch of the notes. See **alto clef, bass clef, treble clef.** [French, key, musical key, from Old French, from Latin *clāvis,* key.]

cleft (klĕft). A past tense and past participle of **cleave** (to split).
~*adj.* **1.** Divided; split; separated. **2.** *Botany.* Having deeply divided lobes or divisions: *a cleft leaf.*
~*n.* **1.** A crack; a crevice; a split. **2.** A split or indentation between two parts, as of the chin. **3.** A **rill** *(see)* on the moon's surface. [Middle English *clift,* rift, fissure, Old English *geclyft.*]

cleft palate *n.* A congenital fissure in the roof of the mouth, often associated with a cleft in the upper lip (a harelip).

cleg (klĕg) *n.* A horsefly. [Old Norse *kleggi.*]

clei·do·ic egg (klī-dō′ĭk) *n.* An egg with a tough shell that limits water loss but permits gas exchange, characteristic of reptiles, birds, and insects. [Greek *kleidoun,* to lock in, from *kleis* (stem *kleid-*), key.]

cleis·tog·a·mous (klī-stŏg′ə-məs) *adj.* Also **cleis·to·gam·ic** (klī′stə-găm′ĭk). *Botany.* Characterized by self-fertilization in an unopened, budlike state, as in the violet. [Greek *kleistos,* closed + -GAMOUS.] **—cleis·tog·a·mous·ly** *adv.* **—cleis·tog·a·my** (klī-stŏg′ə-mē) *n.*

cleis·to·the·ci·um (klī′stə-thē′sē-əm) *n. Botany.* In fungi, a type of ascocarp in which the ascospores are completely enclosed and released by decay of its wall. [Greek *kleistos,* closed + New Latin *-thecium,* case, from Greek *thēkē,* case.]

Cle·land (klē′lənd), **John** (1709–89). English author, best known for the racy novel *Fanny Hill* (1749).

clem·a·tis (klĕm′ə-tĭs) *n.* Any of various northern temperate plants or vines of the genus *Clematis,* many of which are cultivated as ornamentals, having white or variously colored flowers and plumelike seeds. See **traveler's-joy.** [New Latin *Clematis,* from Latin *clēmatis,* from Greek *klēmatis,* from *klēma,* twig.]

Cle·men·ceau (klĕm′ən-sō′), **Georges** (1841–1929). French statesman and prime minister (1906–09, 1917–20), whose polemical style earned him the nickname "the Tiger." He played a key role in negotiating the Treaty of Versailles (1919).

clem·en·cy (klĕm′ən-sē) *n., pl.* **-cies. 1.** Mildness of temper, especially toward an offender or enemy; leniency; mercy. **2.** Mildness, especially of weather. —See Synonyms at **mercy.**

Clem·ens (klĕm′ənz), **Samuel Langhorne,** pen name "Mark Twain" (1835–1910). U.S. author and humorist. Influenced by his early years on the Mississippi River, he brought his unmatched humor and sarcasm to southern life in such works as *The Adventures of Tom Sawyer* (1876), *Life on the Mississippi* (1883), and *The Adventures of Huckleberry Finn* (1884).

clem·ent (klĕm′ənt) *adj.* **1.** Lenient or merciful in disposition. **2.** Mild. Said of weather or climate. [Middle English, from Latin *clēmēns*† (stem *clēment-*), gentle.] **—clem·ent·ly** *adv.*

clem·en·tine (klĕm′ən-tēn, -tīn) *n.* A type of citrus fruit resembling a tangerine, possibly a hybrid between a tangerine and an orange. [French *clémentine,* probably from the feminine name.]

clench (klĕnch) *tr.v.* **clenched, clenching, clenches. 1.** To bring together (hands or teeth) tightly; close up: *clenched his fist in anger.* **2.** To grasp or grip tightly. **3.** To clinch (a nail or bolt, for example). **4.** *Nautical.* To fasten with a clinch.
~*n.* **1.** A tight grip or grasp. **2.** Anything that clenches or holds fast, such as a mechanical device. **3.** *Nautical.* A kind of knot, a

clinch *(see).* [Middle English *clenchen,* Old English *beclencan.*]

cle·o·me (klē-ō′mē) *n.* Any of various mostly tropical plants of the genus *Cleome;* especially, *C. spinosa,* cultivated for its clusters of white or purplish flowers with long, conspicuous stamens. Also called "spiderflower." [New Latin *Cleome*†.]

Cle·on (klē′ŏn′) (died 422 B.C.). Athenian statesman and orator, known for his vigorous opposition to Sparta and its allies in the Peloponnesian War.

Cle·o·pat·ra VII (klē′ə-păt′rə, -pä′trə) (69–30 B.C.). Queen of Egypt (51–49 B.C., 48–30 B.C.), noted for her beauty and charisma. Her lovers included Julius Caesar and Mark Antony.

clepe (klēp) *tr.v.* **cleped** (klēpt, klĕpt) or **clept, cleping, clepes.** Also *past participle* **ycleped** or **yclept** (i-klĕpt′, i-klēpt′). *Archaic.* To call by the name of; name. [Middle English *clepen,* to speak, call out, Old English *cleopian, clipian*†, to call out, call by name.]

clep·sy·dra (klĕp′sə-drə) *n., pl.* **-dras** or **-drae** (-drē′). An ancient device that measured time by marking the regulated flow of water through a small opening. Also called "water clock." [Latin, from Greek *klepsudra,* "water stealer" (from the "stealthy" flow of the water) : *kleps-,* stem of *kleptein,* to steal + *hudōr,* water.]

clere·sto·ry, clear·sto·ry (klîr′stôr′ē, -stōr′ē) *n., pl.* **-ries. 1.** The upper part of the nave, transepts, and choir of a church, containing windows. **2.** Any similar windowed wall or construction used for light and ventilation. [Middle English : *clere,* lighted, CLEAR + STORY (of a building).]

cler·gy (klûr′jē) *n., pl.* **-gies.** The body of women and men ordained for religious service. Compare **laity.** [Middle English *clergie,* from Old French (influenced by *clerge,* body of clerks), from *clerc,* ecclesiastic, CLERK.]

cler·gy·man (klûr′jē-mən) *n., pl.* **-men** (-mĭn). *Abbr.* **cl.** A male member of the clergy.

clergyman's throat *n.* Hoarseness after a long period of talking, especially as suffered by professional speechmakers.

cler·gy·wom·an (klûr′jē-wo͝om′ən) *n., pl.* **-women** (-wĭm′ĭn). A female member of the clergy.

cler·ic (klĕr′ĭk) *n.* A member of the clergy. [Medieval Latin *clēricus,* CLERK.]

cler·i·cal (klĕr′ĭ-kəl) *adj.* **1. a.** Of or pertaining to clerks or office workers. **b.** Of, pertaining to, or designating office work such as filing and correspondence. **2.** Of, pertaining to, or characteristic of the clergy or a member of the clergy. **3.** Advocating clericalism.
~*n.* **1.** A member of the clergy. **2. clericals.** The distinctive garb of a member of the clergy. **3.** A person or party advocating clericalism. **—cler·i·cal·ly** *adv.*

clerical collar *n.* A stiff white collar in the shape of a band fastening at the back of the neck, worn by clergymen.

cler·i·cal·ism (klĕr′ĭ-kəl-ĭz′əm) *n.* A policy of supporting the power or influence of the clergy in secular matters. **—cler·i·cal·ist** *n.*

cler·i·hew (klĕr′ə-hyo͞o′) *n.* A humorous rhyming quatrain about a person whose name generally serves as one of the rhymes. [After Edmund *Clerihew* BENTLEY, writer who invented it.]

cler·i·sy (klĕr′ə-sē) *n.* Educated people as a class; the literati. [German *Klerisei,* from Medieval Latin *clēricia,* the clergy, from Late Latin *clēricus,* CLERK.]

clerk (klûrk; *British* klärk) *n.* **1.** A person who works in an office performing such tasks as keeping records, attending to correspondence, or filing. **2.** A person who keeps the records and performs the regular business of a court or legislative body. **3.** A person who works at a service or sales counter; as in a store. **4.** *Anglican Church.* A lay minister who helps the parish clergyman to perform his duties. **5.** *Archaic.* A clergyman. **6.** *Archaic.* **a.** A literate person. **b.** A scholar.
~*intr.v.* **clerked, clerking, clerks.** To work or serve as a clerk. [Middle English, from Old English and Old French *clerc,* from Late Latin *clēricus,* a cleric, from Greek *klērikos,* belonging to inheritance, cleric (with reference to the Levites whose only inheritance was the Lord), from *klēros,* allotment, inheritance.] **—clerk·dom** *n.* **—clerk·ship** *n.*

clerk·ly (klûrk′lē) *adj.* **-lier, -liest. 1.** Of or pertaining to a clerk or clerks. **2.** *Archaic.* Scholarly. **—clerk·li·ness** *n.*

Cleve·land[1] (klēv′lənd). A small county in northeast England, formed in 1974 from parts of southern Durham and northern Yorkshire. Its center is the industrial region of Teeside.

Cleveland[2]. A city of northeastern Ohio, a port of entry on Lake Erie at the mouth of the Cuyahoga River. The city was laid out in 1796 and grew rapidly after the opening of the Ohio and Erie Canal in 1827 and the arrival of the railroad in 1851. It is a leading oil and steel center.

Cleveland, (Stephen) Grover (1837–1908). 22nd and 24th U.S. president (1885–89, 1893–97). Recognized as an honest, independent president, he lost his bid for re-election in 1888 primarily because he advocated a lower tariff. He was re-elected in in 1892 to a politically trying term highlighted by the repeal of the Sherman Silver Purchase Act (1893).

clev·er (klĕv′ər) *adj.* **cleverer, cleverest. 1.** Mentally quick and original; bright. **2.** Nimble with the hands; dexterous. **3.** Showing quick-wittedness; ingenious: *a clever story.* **4.** *Informal.* Superficial or contrived. **5.** *Regional.* Handy; suitable. —See Synonyms at **intelligent.** [Probably from Middle English *cliver,* dexterous, perhaps from Scandinavian; akin to Old Norse *kleyfr.*] **—clev·er·ly** *adv.* **—clev·er·ness** *n.*
Synonyms: *cunning, ingenious, shrewd.*

clev·is (klĕv′ĭs) *n.* A U-shaped metal piece with holes in each end through which a pin or bolt is run, used for attaching a drawbar to a plow, for example. [Probably plural of *clevi,* "cleft instrument," from Scandinavian, akin to Old Norse *klofi,* cleft, fissure.]

clew[1] (klo͞o) *n.* **1.** *Archaic.* A ball of yarn or thread. **2.** *Greek Mythology.* The ball of thread used by Theseus as a guide through the labyrinth of Minos on Crete. **3. clews.** The cords by which a hammock is suspended. **4.** *Nautical.* **a.** One of the two lower corners of a square sail. **b.** The lower aft corner of a fore-and-aft sail.
~*tr.v.* **clewed, clewing, clews. 1.** To roll or coil into a ball. **2.** *Nautical.* To raise the lower corners of (a square sail) by means of clew lines. Used with *up.* [Middle English *clewe(n),* Old English *cliewen, clewe(n).*]

clew[2]. Variant of **clue.**

clew line *n.* A rope for raising the clew of a sail up to the yard or mast.

cli·an·thus (klē-ăn′thəs) *n.* Any of several plants of the genus *Clianthus,* native to Indochina, Australia, and New Zealand, having showy clusters of elongated scarlet flowers.

cli·ché (klē-shā′) *n.* **1.** A trite or overused expression or idea. **2.** *Printing.* A stereotype or electrotype plate. [French, "stereotyped," from *clicher,* to stereotype (imitative of the sound made when the matrix is dropped into the molten metal to make a stereotype plate).]
Synonyms: *banality, bromide, commonplace, truism.*

cli·chéd (klē-shād′) *adj.* Hackneyed; trite.

click (klĭk) *n.* **1.** A brief, sharp, nonresonant sound: *the click of a door latch.* **2.** A mechanical device that snaps into position, such as a detent or pawl. **3.** *Phonetics.* An oral ingressive speech sound, common in some African languages, produced by drawing air into the mouth and clicking the tongue. Also called "suction stop."
~*v.* **clicked, clicking, clicks.** —*intr.* **1.** To produce one or a series of clicks. **2.** *Slang.* **a.** To become a success. **b.** To establish an immediate rapport. **c.** To become clear; fall into place. —*tr.* To cause to click. [Imitative.] **—click·er** *n.*

click beetle *n.* Any of various beetles of the family Elateridae, characterized by the ability to right itself from an overturned position by flipping into the air with a clicking sound. Also called "snapping beetle," "skipjack."

click languages *pl.n.* A set of African languages employing the phonetic click, including the **Khoisan** *(see)* family and the Nguni group.

cli·ent (klī′ənt) *n.* **1.** One for whom services, usually professional services, are rendered. **2.** A customer or patron. **3.** One dependent on the patronage of another. **4.** One receiving the attention and care of a social worker or doctor. [Middle English, from Old French, from Latin *cliēns* (stem *client-*), dependent, follower, earlier *cluēns,* from *cluere,* to follow, obey.] **—cli·en·tal** (klī-ĕn′təl) *adj.* **—cli·ent·ship** *n.*

cli·en·tele (klī′ən-tĕl′, klē-äɴ-tĕl′) *n.* Customers, patrons, or clients of a restaurant, professional person, or the like, considered collectively. [French *clientèle,* from Latin *clientēla,* from *cliēns,* CLIENT.]

client state *n.* A country that is economically or politically dependent on a larger or more powerful country.

cliff (klĭf) *n.* A high, steep, or overhanging face of rock. [Middle English *clif,* Old English *clif,* from Germanic *klibam* (unattested).] **—clif·fy** *adj.*

cliff dweller *n.* **1.** A member of certain prehistoric Indian tribes of the southwestern United States who lived in caves in the sides of cliffs. **2.** *Slang.* A person who lives in a large apartment house, especially in a city. **—cliff-dwel·ling** *adj.*

cliff·hang·er (klĭf′hăng′ər) *n.* **1.** A situation of great suspense occurring usually at the end of a chapter in a book, scene in a film, or episode in a serial. **2.** A serial in which each episode ends in suspense. **3.** A situation, as in a competition or election, in which the outcome is uncertain until the very end. **—cliff·hang·ing** *adj.*

cliff swallow *n.* A North American swallow, *Petrochelidon pyrrhonota,* that builds a bottle-shaped mud nest on the face of a cliff or bluff or under the eaves of a roof.

cli·mac·ter·ic (klī-măk′tər-ĭk, klī′măk-tĕr′ĭk) *n.* **1. a.** The **menopause** *(see).* **b.** A corresponding period in the male, marked by a reduction in sexual activity. **2.** *Archaic.* A critical period or year in a person's life when major changes in health or fortune take place. **3.** *Botany.* The increase in respiration rate associated with fruit ripening and senescence. **4.** Any critical period.
~*adj.* Also **cli·mac·ter·i·cal** (klī′măk-tĕr′ĭ-kəl) Pertaining to a critical stage, period, or year. [Latin *clīmactēricus,* from Greek *klimaktērikos,* from *klimaktēr,* rung of a ladder, crisis, from *klimax,* ladder. See **climax.**]

cli·mac·tic (klī-măk′tĭk) *adj.* Pertaining to or constituting a climax. **—cli·mac·ti·cal·ly** *adv.*

cli·ma·gram, cli·mo·gram (klī′mə-grăm′) *n.* A **climograph** *(see).*

climagraph. Variant of **climograph.**

cli·mate (klī′mĭt) *n.* **1.** The meteorological conditions, including temperature, rainfall, and wind, that characteristically prevail in a particular region. **2.** A region having particular meteorological conditions. **3.** A prevailing set of attitudes or opinions in human affairs: *the political climate.* [Middle English *climat,* from Old French, from Late Latin *clīma,* climate, zone of latitude, from Greek *klima,* sloping surface of the earth.] **—cli·mat·ic** (klī-măt′ĭk), **cli·ma·tal** (klī′mə-təl), **cli·mat·i·cal** *adj.* **—cli·mat·i·cal·ly** *adv.*

cli·mat·o·graph (klī-măt′ə-grăf′, -gräf′) *n. Meteorology.* A circular graph showing the yearly variations of average temperature (as dis-

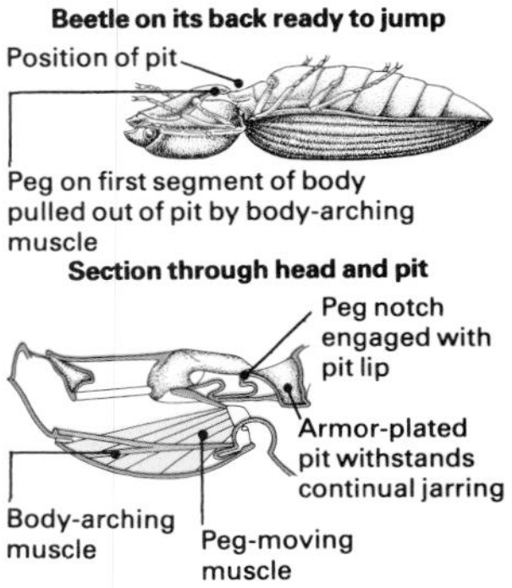
Beetle on its back ready to jump
Position of pit
Peg on first segment of body pulled out of pit by body-arching muscle
Section through head and pit
Peg notch engaged with pit lip
Armor-plated pit withstands continual jarring
Body-arching muscle
Peg-moving muscle

click beetle *When adult click beetles fall onto their backs, their special click mechanism (above), between their head and body, enables them to regain their feet and escape predators. When triggered, the mechanism can catapult them up to 300 millimeters (12 inches) into the air. The beetles' larvae, known as wireworms, are serious crop pests, living underground for up to five years and feeding on plant roots.*

PRONUNCIATION KEY

ă, pat; ā, pay; âr, care; ä, father, are; b, bib; ch, church; d, deed; ĕ, pet; ē, be; f, fife; g, gag; h, hat; hw, which; ĭ, pit; ī, pie; îr, pier; j, judge; k, kick; l, lid, needle; m, mum; n, no, sudden; ng, thing; ŏ, pot; ō, toe; ô, paw, for; oi, noise; ou, out; o͝o, book; o͞o, boot; p, pop; r, roar; s, sauce; sh, ship, dish; t, tight; th, thin, path; *th,* this, bathe; ŭ, cut; ûr, fur; v, valve; w, with; y, yes; z, zebra, size; zh, vision; ə, about, item, edible, gallop, circus, peaceful

IN FOREIGN WORDS:

à, *Fr.* ami; œ, *Fr.* feu, *Ger.* schön; ü, *Fr.* tu, *Ger.* über; кн, *Ger.* ich, *Scot.* loch; ɴ, *Fr.* bon; y′, *Fr.* Compiègne

STRESS MARKS:

Primary stress: ′ in·cite′ (ĭn-sīt′)
Secondary stress: ′ in′sight′ (ĭn′sīt′)

tance from center) against time of year (as angular position). [CLIMATE + -GRAPH.]

cli·ma·tol·o·gy (klī'mə-tŏl'ə-jē) *n.* The meteorological study of climate. [CLIMAT(E) + -LOGY.] —**cli·ma·to·log·ic** (klī'mə-tə-lŏj'ĭk), **cli·ma·to·log·i·cal** *adj.* —**cli·ma·tol·o·gist** (klī'mə-tŏl'ə-jĭst) *n.*

cli·max (klī'măks') *n.* **1. a.** The point of greatest intensity, excitement, or interest in any series or progression of events; the culmination. **b.** Such a point in a literary or dramatic work. **2.** An orgasm. **3.** *Rhetoric.* **a.** A series of statements or ideas in an ascending order of force or intensity. **b.** The final statement in such a series. **4.** The stage in ecological development or evolution in which the community of organisms becomes stable. —See Synonyms at **summit**.
~*v.* **climaxed, -maxing, -maxes.** —*intr.* To reach a climax. —*tr.* To bring to a climax. [Latin, rhetorical climax, from Greek *klimax*, ladder.]

climax community *n. Ecology.* The mature or stabilized stage in a successional series of communities, usually associated with maximum complexity, when dominant species are completely adapted to environmental conditions, as in tropical rain forests.

climb (klīm) *v.* **climbed** or *archaic* **clomb** (klōm), **climbing, climbs.** —*tr.* To move up or mount, especially by using the hands and feet; ascend. —*intr.* **1.** To rise to a higher position; move upward: *The sun climbed in the sky.* **2.** To rise slowly or with effort in rank, status, or fortune. **3.** To slant or slope upward. **4.** To grow in an upward direction, as some plants do, by twining about or clinging to another object for support. **5.** To move in a specified direction by or as if by clambering: *climbed out of the window.* —See Synonyms at **rise**.
~*n.* **1.** An act of climbing; an ascent. **2.** A place to be climbed. [Climb, clomb; Middle English *climben, clomb,* Old English *climban, clamb* (or *clomb*).] —**climb·a·ble** *adj.*

Usage: Both *up* and *down* are used with this verb in standard English. *Climb up* has been said to contain an unnecessary element, in that climbing implies ascent. By the same token, *climb down* is said to be self-contradictory, but both uses are well established.

climb down *intr.v.* **1.** To move downward by using the limbs. **2.** To retreat in an argument or dispute; back down.
~*tr.v.* To descend by using the limbs. —See Usage note at **climb**.

climb-down (klīm'doun') *n.* An act of yielding or backing down in an argument or dispute.

climb·er (klī'mər) *n.* **1.** Something or someone that climbs; especially, a person who climbs mountains. **2.** *Informal.* A person seeking to gain a higher social or professional position. Used derogatorily. **3.** A plant that grows upward by clinging to or twining about something.

climbing frame *n.* A structure, usually of metal tubing, for children to climb on.

climbing irons *pl.n.* Iron bars with spikes or spurs attached, which are strapped to a shoe or boot and used in climbing telegraph poles, trees, or ice slopes.

clime (klīm) *n. Poetic.* Climate or region. [Middle English, region of the earth, zone, from Late Latin *clīma,* CLIMATE.]

-clinal *suffix.* Indicates a slope or inclination; for example, **anticlinal, synclinal.** [-CLINE + -AL.]

cli·mo·graph, cli·ma·graph (klī'mə-grăf', -gräf') *n. Meteorology.* A graph in which one climatic feature at a location is plotted against another, for example temperature against humidity. Also called "climagram," "climogram." [CLIMATE + -GRAPH.]

clin-. Variant of *clino-.*

cli·nan·dri·um (klĭ-năn'drē-əm) *n., pl.* **-dria** (-drē-ə). *Botany.* A hollow containing the anther in the upper part of the column of an orchid. [New Latin, "stamen bed" : CLIN(O)- + -*andrium,* "stamen," from Greek *anēr* (stem *andr*-), man.]

clinch (klĭnch) *v.* **clinched, clinching, clinches.** —*tr.* **1.** To fix or secure (a nail or bolt, for example) by bending down or flattening the end that has been driven through something. **2.** To fasten together in this way. **3.** To settle definitely and conclusively; make final. **4.** *Nautical.* To fasten with a clinch. —*intr.* **1.** In boxing and wrestling, to hold the opponent's body with one or both arms to prevent or hinder his movements. **2.** *Informal.* To embrace.
~*n.* **1.** The act of clinching. **2.** Something that clinches, such as a clinched nail or clamp. **3.** The clinched part of a nail, bolt, rivet, or the like. **4.** In boxing and wrestling, the act or an instance of clinching. **5.** *Nautical.* A knot in a rope made by a half hitch with the end of the rope fastened back by seizing. Also called "clench." **6.** *Informal.* An amorous or romantic embrace. [Variant of CLENCH.]

clinch·er (klĭn'chər) *n.* **1.** One that clinches; specifically, a tool for clinching nails or bolts. **2.** *Informal.* A decisive point, fact, or remark, as in an argument.

clincher-built. Variant of **clinker-built.**

cline (klīn) *n.* **1.** *Ecology.* A continuous variation in form within members of a species or population, resulting from gradual changes or transitions in the environment over a wide range. **2.** Loosely, a continuum. [Greek *klinein,* to slope, lean.]

-cline *suffix.* Indicates slope; for example, **anticline, syncline.** [Greek *klinein,* to slope.]

cling (klĭng) *intr.v.* **clung** (klŭng), **clinging, clings. 1.** To hold fast or adhere to something, as by grasping, sticking, or entwining. **2. a.** To stay near; remain close. **b.** To resist separation. **3.** To hold on, often stubbornly; remain attached: *cling to old-fashioned ideas.* [Cling, clung (past tense), clung (past participle); Middle English *clingen, clong* (past singular), *clungen* (past plural), *clungen,* Old English *clingan, clang, clungon, clungen.*] —**cling·er** *n.*

cling·fish (klĭng'fĭsh) *n., pl.* **-fishes** or collectively **clingfish.** Any of various small marine fishes of the family Gobiesocidae, having an adhesive disk under the front part of the body, by which it fastens itself to rocks and seaweed.

clinging vine *n.* A person who shows excessive dependence on his or her spouse.

cling peach *n.* A clingstone peach.

cling·stone (klĭng'stōn') *n.* A fruit, especially a peach, having pulp that adheres partially to the stone. Compare **freestone.** —**clingstone** *adj.*

cling·y (klĭng'ē) *adj.* **-gier, -giest.** Tending to cling: *a clingy dress.*

clin·ic (klĭn'ĭk) *n.* **1.** An establishment, often a department of a hospital specializing in a particular branch of medicine, devoted to the treatment and care of outpatients. **2.** A medical establishment run by several specialists working cooperatively. **3.** A private hospital or nursing home. **4.** A group meeting or seminar devoted to the study of problems in a particular field, or offering to teach certain skills to those who attend: *a tennis clinic.* [French *clinique,* originally "a bedridden person," from Greek *klinikē,* medical treatment at sickbed, from *klinikos,* "of a bed," doctor who visits bedridden persons, from *klinē,* bed.]

-clinic *suffix.* Indicates: **1.** Inclination or slope; for example, **isoclinic. 2.** A specified number of oblique axial intersections; for example, **triclinic.** [-CLINE + -IC.]

clin·i·cal (klĭn'ĭ-kəl) *adj.* **1.** Pertaining to or connected with a clinic. **2.** Of or pertaining to direct observation and treatment of patients: *a clinical lecture.* **3.** Analytical; highly objective; rigorously scientific: *clinical details.* **4.** Suggestive of a hospital or clinic; austere; antiseptic: *a clinical style of decor.*
~*n.* A class in which medical students are instructed in the examination and treatment of patients at the bedside. —**clin·i·cal·ly** *adv.*

clinical thermometer *n.* A thermometer used to measure body temperature; especially, a small mercury-in-glass thermometer designed with a narrowing in the base so that the mercury column stays in position when the instrument is removed from the body.

cli·ni·cian (klĭ-nĭsh'ən) *n.* A doctor, psychologist, or psychiatrist specializing in clinical studies or practice. [French *clinicien,* from *clinique,* CLINIC.]

clink¹ (klĭngk) *n.* A soft, sharp, ringing sound.
~*v.* **clinked, clinking, clinks.** —*intr.* To make a clink. —*tr.* To cause to clink. [Middle English, from Middle Dutch *klinken.*]

clink² *n. Slang.* Prison. [16th century (as *the Clink,* name of former prison near London) : origin obscure.]

clink·er (klĭng'kər) *n.* **1.** The incombustible residue, fused into irregular lumps, that remains after the combustion of coal. **2.** A partially vitrified brick or a mass of bricks fused together. **3.** An extremely hard burned brick. **4.** Vitrified matter expelled by a volcano. **5.** *Slang.* A conspicuous mistake or failure.
~*intr.v.* **clinkered, -ering, -ers.** To form clinker while burning. [Earlier *clincart, klincard,* from obsolete Dutch *klinckaerd,* "one that clinks" (from its clinking sound when struck), from Middle Dutch *klinken, clinken,* CLINK.]

clink·er-built (klĭng'kər-bĭlt') *adj.* Also **clinch·er-built** (klĭn'chər-). Built with overlapping planks or boards. Said of ships or boats. Compare **carvel-built.** [From *clinker,* a fastening or clinching with nails, from Middle English *clinken,* probably variant of *clenchen,* CLENCH.]

clink·stone (klĭngk'stōn') *n. Mineralogy.* Phonolite *(see).*

clino-, clin- *prefix.* Indicates slope or slant; for example, **clinometer, clinandrium.** [New Latin, from Greek *klinein,* to slope, and *klinē,* bed.]

cli·nom·e·ter (klī-nŏm'ə-tər, klĭ-) *n.* An instrument for measuring the angle of an incline, as of an embankment. Also called "inclinometer." [CLINO- + -METER.] —**cli·no·met·ric** (klī'nə-mĕt'rĭk), **cli·no·met·ri·cal** *adj.* —**cli·nom·e·try** (klī-nŏm'ə-trē) *n.*

cli·no·stat (klī'nō-stăt') *n. Botany.* An apparatus used to study plant growth, consisting of a rotating disk to which the plant is attached. Rotation ensures that all parts of the plant receive identical stimulation, for example from light or gravity. [CLINO- + -STAT.]

clint (klĭnt) *n. Geology.* Any of a number of irregularly shaped blocks making up a type of flat, exposed limestone formation. [Middle English, perhaps from Scandinavian; akin to Danish and Swedish *klint,* Old Norse *klettr,* cliff.]

Clin·ton (klĭnt'ŭn), **William "Bill" Jefferson** (1946–). 42nd president of the United States. A lawyer, he was elected twice as governor of Arkansas (1977–81; 1983–93). In 1993, he was inaugurated as president.

clin·to·ni·a (klĭn-tō'nē-ə) *n.* Any plant of the genus *Clintonia,* having narrow leaves, white, greenish-yellow, or purplish flowers, and usually blue berries. [New Latin, after DeWitt *Clinton* (1769–1828), U.S. statesman.]

Cli·o (klī'ō). *Greek Mythology.* The Muse of history. [Latin *Clīō,* from Greek *Kleiō,* "teller," from *kleiein, klein,* to tell, praise.]

cli·o·met·rics (klī'ə-mĕt'rĭks) *n. Used with a singular verb.* The use of statistics in the study of history. —**cli·o·met·ric** *adj.*

clip¹ (klĭp) *tr.v.* **clipped, clipping, clips. 1.** To cut off or cut out with or as if with scissors or shears: *clip an article from a newspaper; clipped three seconds off the record.* **2.** To make shorter by cutting; trim. **3.** To cut off the edge of: *clip a coin.* **4. a.** To cut short (a word or words) by leaving out letters or syllables. **b.** To enunciate with clarity and precision: *clip one's speech.* **5.** *British.* To punch a hole in (a ticket). **6.** *Informal.* To hit with a sharp blow. **7.** *Slang.* To cheat or overcharge.

~*n.* **1.** The act of clipping. **2.** A short extract from a film or videotape. **3. a.** The wool shorn at one shearing. **b.** A season's shearing. **4.** *Informal.* A quick, sharp blow: *a clip on the ear.* **5.** *Informal.* A brisk pace. **6. clips.** A pair of shears or clippers. [Middle English *clippen,* from Old Norse *klippa*†, to cut short.]

clip[2] *n.* **1.** A device for holding things together; a clasp. **2.** A piece of jewelry fastened by a clip; a brooch. **3.** A **cartridge clip** *(see).* ~*tr.v.* **clipped, clipping, clips. 1.** To fasten with a clip. **2.** *Football.* To block (an opponent who is not carrying the ball) illegally from the rear. [Middle English *clipp,* from *clippen,* to embrace, fasten, Old English *clyppan.*]

clip·board (klĭp′bôrd, -bōrd′) *n.* A small writing board with a spring clip at the top for holding papers or a writing pad.

clip joint *n. Slang.* A restaurant or place of public entertainment where customers are overcharged or otherwise defrauded.

clip-on (klĭp′ŏn′) *adj.* Designating an article that is attached by means of a clip: *clip-on earrings; a clip-on bow tie.*

clip·per (klĭp′ər) *n.* **1.** One who cuts, clips, or shears. **2. clippers.** An instrument or tool for cutting, clipping, or shearing: *nail clippers.* **3.** A sharp-bowed sailing vessel of the mid-19th century, having tall masts and sharp lines and built for great speed. Also called "clipper ship." **4.** *Electronics.* A **limiter** *(see).*

clip·ping (klĭp′ĭng) *n.* **1.** Something that is cut off or out: *nail clippings.* **2.** An item cut out of a newspaper.

clique (klēk, klĭk) *n.* An exclusive group of friends or associates; coterie. —See Synonyms at **circle.** [French, from Old French, probably "a group of applauders," from *cliquer,* to click, clap, applaud (imitative).]

cli·quish (klē′kĭsh, klĭk′ĭsh) *adj.* Also **cli·quey, cli·quy** (klē′kē, klĭk′ē). Of, like, or characteristic of a clique; exclusive. **—cli·quish·ly** *adv.* **—cli·quish·ness** *n.*

cli·tel·lum (klī-tĕl′əm, klī-) *n., pl.* **-tella** (-tĕl′ə). A swollen, glandular, saddlelike region in the epidermis of certain annelid worms, such as the earthworm, serving to bind worms together during copulation. [New Latin, from Latin *clītellae,* packsaddle.]

clit·o·rid·ec·to·my *n.* The ritualistic mutilation of the clitoris, as performed on prepubertal girls in certain cultures. [New Latin *clitoris* (stem *clitorid-*), CLITORIS + -ECTOMY.]

clit·o·ris (klĭt′ə-rĭs, klī-tôr′əs) *n.* A part of the female genitalia lying above the vagina and urethra, consisting of a small, highly sensitive, erectile organ, which plays a major role in the female orgasm. [New Latin, from Greek *kleitoris,* "little hill," diminutive of *kleitor-* (unattested), hill, from *klinein,* to incline.] **—clit·o·ral** (klĭt′ə-rəl) *adj.*

Clive of Plas·sey (klīv; plăs′ē), **Robert, Baron,** also known as "Clive of India" (1725–74). British soldier and statesman, famous for securing British interests in India.

clo·a·ca (klō-ā′kə) *n., pl.* **-cae** (-sē′, -kē′). **1.** *Zoology.* The cavity into which the intestinal, genital, and urinary tracts open in vertebrates such as fish, reptiles, birds, and some primitive mammals. **2.** A sewer. [Latin *cloāca,* sewer, canal.] **—clo·a·cal** (klō-ā′kəl) *adj.*

cloak (klōk) *n.* **1.** A loose outer garment, usually sleeveless. **2.** Anything that covers or conceals. ~*tr.v.* **cloaked, cloaking, cloaks. 1.** To cover with a cloak. **2.** To cover up; hide; conceal. —See Synonyms at **hide.** [Middle English *cloke,* from Old French *cloque,* bell, "bell-shaped garment." See **clock.**]

cloak-and-dagger (klōk′ən-dăg′ər) *adj.* Concerned with or suggestive of melodramatic intrigue.

cloak·room (klōk′rōōm′, -rŏŏm′) *n.* **1.** A room where coats and other articles may be left temporarily, as in a school or theater. **2.** A private lounge for members of a legislative chamber.

clob·ber[1] (klŏb′ər) *tr.v.* **-bered, -bering, -bers.** *Slang.* **1.** To strike violently and repeatedly; batter or maul. **2.** To defeat completely. **3.** To criticize or condemn harshly. [20th century : origin obscure; perhaps akin to *club* (to beat).]

clobber[2] *n. British Slang.* **1.** Belongings; equipment. **2.** Clothes. [19th century : origin obscure.]

cloche (klōsh, klŏsh) *n.* **1.** A semicylindrical or bell-shaped cover, usually of glass, used to protect young plants. **2.** A close-fitting woman's hat with a bell-like shape. [French, bell, from Old French, bell, CLOCK.]

clock[1] (klŏk) *n.* **1.** An instrument for measuring or indicating time; especially, a mechanical device, larger than a watch, with a numbered dial and moving hands or pointers. **2.** Any of various scientific devices for the accurate measurement or standardization of time. **3.** *Informal.* Any of various instruments that indicate measurement by a dial and pointer or by a digital display, such as a speedometer or the meter on a taxi. **4.** An electronic circuit that produces regular pulses. See **clock pulse. 5.** A **time clock** *(see).* **6.** *Botany.* The downy flower head of a dandelion that has gone to seed. **—put the clock back. 1.** To revert to outmoded practices or ideas; regress. **2.** To revert to a former, preferable, and idealized state of affairs. See feature, next page. ~*v.* **clocked, clocking, clocks.** —*tr.* **1.** To record the time or speed of, as with a stopwatch. **2.** To register or record (a distance traveled, a speed attained, or the like). Used with *up.* **3.** *Electronics.* To regulate (a circuit) with clock pulses. —*intr.* **1.** To register the time of arrival at work. Used with *in*: *She clocked in early.* **2.** To register the time of departure from work. Used with *out.* [Middle English *clok,* from Middle Dutch *clocke,* bell, clock, from Old French *cloche, cloque,* bell, from Late Latin *clocca* (imitative).] **—clock·er** *n.*

clock[2] *n.* An embroidered or woven decoration on the side of a stocking or sock. [Perhaps originally "a bell-shaped ornament," from Middle Dutch *clocke,* bell, CLOCK.]

clock pulse *n.* One of a series of regular electrical pulses used to drive an electronic circuit such as a computer logic circuit.

clock radio *n.* An appliance that combines an alarm clock with a radio that can be set to start playing at a particular time.

clock-watch·er (klŏk′wŏch′ər) *n.* A person who continually checks the time while at work. **—clock-watch·ing** *n.*

clock·wise (klŏk′wīz′) *adv.* In the same direction as the rotating hands of a clock. **—clock·wise** *adj.*

clock·work (klŏk′wûrk′) *n.* A mechanism of gears driven by a wound spring, as in a mechanical clock, toy, or the like. **—like clockwork.** With machinelike regularity and precision; perfectly. **—clock·work** *adj.*

clod (klŏd) *n.* **1.** A lump of earth or clay. **2.** Earth or soil. **3.** A dull, ignorant, or stupid person; an oaf. **4.** A cut of the shoulder of beef. [Middle English *clodde,* Old English *clod-* (only in compounds), variant of *clott,* lump.] **—clod·dish** *adj.* **—clod·dish·ness** *n.*

clod·hop·per (klŏd′hŏp′ər) *n.* **1.** A clumsy, coarse person; a lout or bumpkin. **2. clodhoppers.** Big, heavy shoes. [Originally "farmer" : CLOD (earth) + HOPPER.] **—clod·hop·ping** *adj.*

clog (klŏg) *n.* **1.** A heavy wooden or wooden-soled shoe. **2.** A block or other weight attached to the leg of an animal to hinder movement. **3.** *Archaic.* An obstacle or hindrance. ~*v.* **clogged, clogging, clogs.** —*tr.* **1.** To block up; obstruct. **2.** To impede or encumber; hamper. —*intr.* **1.** To become obstructed or choked up. **2.** To thicken or stick together; coagulate. **3.** To do a clog dance. [Middle English *clog, clogge*†, block of wood.] **—clog·gy** *adj.*

clog dance *n.* A dance performed wearing clogs and characterized by heavy, stamping steps.

cloi·son·né (kloi′zə-nā′; *French* klwä-zô-nā′) *n.* **1.** A kind of enamelware in which the surface decoration is formed by different colors of enamel separated by thin strips of metal. **2.** The process or method of producing such enamelware. ~*adj.* Of or designating this ware or method. [French, past participle of *cloisonner,* to partition, from Old French *cloison,* partition, from Vulgar Latin *clausiō* (unattested), enclosure, from Latin *claudere,* to close.]

clois·ter (kloi′stər) *n.* **1.** Sometimes **cloisters.** A covered walk with an open colonnade on one side, running along the walls of buildings that face a quadrangle. **2.** A place devoted to religious seclusion; especially, a monastery or convent. **3.** Life in a monastery or convent. Preceded by *the.* ~*tr.v.* **cloistered, -tering, -ters. 1.** To shut away from the world in or as if in a cloister; seclude. **2.** To furnish (a building) with a cloister. [Middle English *cloistre,* from Old French, variant of *clostre* (influenced by *cloison,* partition, CLOISONNÉ), from Medieval Latin *claustrum,* from Latin, enclosed place, from *claudere,* to close.]

clois·tral (kloi′strəl) *adj.* Also **claus·tral** (klôs′trəl). Of, resembling, or suggesting a cloister; secluded. [Middle English *claustral,* from Medieval Latin *claustrālis,* from *claustrum,* CLOISTER.]

clomb. *Archaic.* Past tense and past participle of **climb.**

clomp (klŏmp) *intr.v.* **clomped, clomping, clomps.** To walk heavily; clump. [Variant of CLUM.]

clone (klōn) *n.* **1.** A group of genetically identical cells descended from a single common ancestor. **2.** One or more organisms descended asexually from a single ancestor. **3.** An exact copy of a person or thing; a duplicate. ~*v.* **cloned, cloning, clones.** —*intr.* To create a genetic duplicate of an individual organism through asexual reproduction, as by stimulating a single cell or taking cuttings of plants. —*tr.* **1.** To duplicate (an organism) asexually by cloning. **2.** To create (a new organism) in this way. **3.** To create a duplicate of. [Greek *klōn,* twig, shoot.] **—clon·al** (klō′nəl) *adj.* **—clon·al·ly** *adv.*

clonk (klŏngk) *n.* A dull, metallic sound. ~*v.* **clonked, clonking, clonks.** —*intr.* To make a clonk. —*tr.* **1.** To cause to clonk. **2.** *Informal.* To hit; punch.

clo·nus (klō′nəs) *n., pl.* **-nuses.** A convulsion characterized by rapidly alternating muscular contraction and relaxation. [New Latin, from Greek *klonos,* agitation, turmoil.] **—clo·nic** (klō′nĭk, klŏn′ĭk) *adj.* **—clo·nic·i·ty** (klō-nĭs′ə-tē, klō-), **clo·nism** (klō′nĭz′əm, klŏn′ĭz′əm) *n.*

clop (klŏp) *n.* The sound of a horse's hoof striking a paved surface. ~*intr.v.* **clopped, clopping, clops.** To make or move with this sound. [Imitative.]

close (klōs) *adj.* **closer, closest. 1.** Separated by only a small distance; not far off in space or time; near. **2.** Near in relationship: *close relatives.* **3.** Having all elements or parts near to each other; compact; dense: *a close weave.* **4.** Near the surface; short: *a close haircut.* **5.** Nearly even; decided by a narrow margin: *a close finish.* **6.** Fitting tightly. **7.** Not deviating substantially from an original or model: *a close resemblance.* **8.** Complete; thorough; rigorous: *a close examination.* **9.** Bound by mutual interests, loyalties, or affection: *close friends.* **10.** Enclosed or confined. **11.** Confined to specific persons or groups; restricted: *a close secret.* **12.** Heavily guarded; allowing no means of escape: *under close arrest.* **13.** Secretive in manner; reticent. **14.** Not generous; miserly. **15.** Airless; stuffy; oppressive. **16.** *Phonetics.* Spoken with the tongue near the palate. Said of vowels. —See Synonyms at **familiar, stingy.** ~*v.* (klōz) **closed, closing, closes.** —*tr.* **1.** To shut. **2.** To bar or obstruct: *The road is closed for repairs.* **3.** To bring together all the

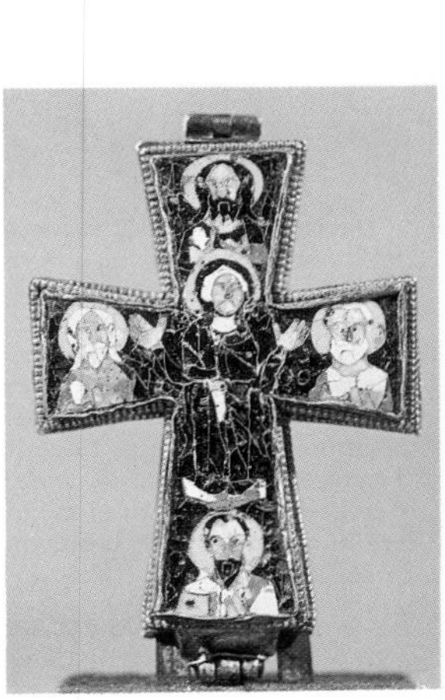

cloisonné *The Hope-Beresford Cross, a 9th-century Byzantine icon now in the Victoria and Albert Museum, London. Each section of the design is made of enamel, separated from the adjoining sections by thin strips of metal.*

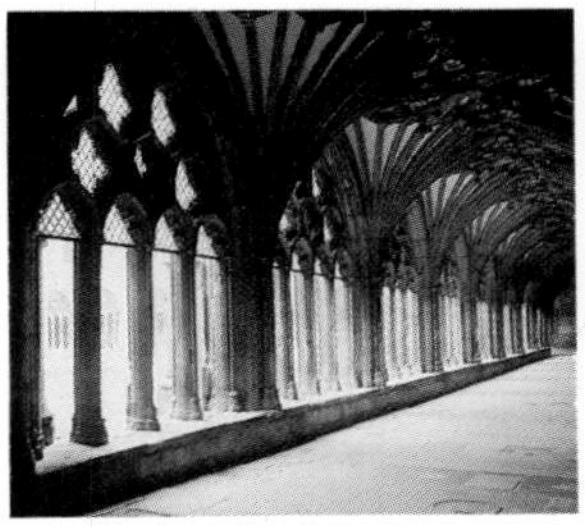

cloister *In medieval monasteries, cloisters were the places where the elders studied and younger monks were educated.*

PRONUNCIATION KEY

ă, pat; ā, pay; âr, care;
ä, father, are; b, bib;
ch, church; d, deed; ĕ, pet;
ē, be; f, fife; g, gag; h, hat;
hw, which; ĭ, pit; ī, pie;
îr, pier; j, judge; k, kick;
l, lid, needle; m, mum;
n, no, sudden; ng, thing;
ŏ, pot; ō, toe; ô, paw, for;
oi, noise; ou, out; ŏŏ, book;
ōō, boot; p, pop; r, roar;
s, sauce; sh, ship, dish;
t, tight; th, thin, path;
th, this, bathe; ŭ, cut; ûr, fur;
v, valve; w, with; y, yes;
z, zebra, size; zh, vision;
ə, about, item, edible,
gallop, circus, peaceful

IN FOREIGN WORDS:

à, *Fr.* ami; œ, *Fr.* feu, *Ger.* schön; ü, *Fr.* tu, *Ger.* über;
KH, *Ger.* ich, *Scot.* loch;
N, *Fr.* bon; y′, *Fr.* Compiègne

STRESS MARKS:

Primary stress: ′
in·cite′ (ĭn-sīt′)
Secondary stress: ′
in′sight′ (ĭn′sīt′)

SEVEN CENTURIES OF IMPROVING TIMEKEEPING

Precision that has increased with the advance of technology

The mechanical clock was invented in Europe in the 13th century. Its driving power was a falling weight on a cord, and the escapement—the method of converting the power into a regular beat or tick—was a swinging spindle, or verge. The clocks were used in churches and monasteries. They could be regulated by moving a weight on a bar known as the foliot bar, but the system was inaccurate. A keeper had to correct the clock by a sundial every few days. Nevertheless the verge escapement remained in use for 550 years.

In the early 15th century the energy stored in a wound-up spiral mainspring was first used as the driving force for clocks. It made possible light, portable clocks—and also pocket watches. The rate at which the spring turned the wheels was kept steady by a fusee and chain.

The first practical pendulum clock was designed by a Dutchman, Christian Huygens, about 1656. It was based on the observation that no matter how far a certain pendulum swings, each swing takes the same length of time. Such absolute regularity gave much greater accuracy to clocks. The pendulum replaced the foliot bar in large clocks. Huygens's pendulum mechanism was improved by the invention of the anchor escapement about 1670. It limited the swing to a narrow arc and led to grandfather clocks.

Later Huygens invented the spiral balance wheel. This replaced the swinging foliot bar in small clocks and watches and could make them accurate to within 2 minutes a day. Combined with the lever escapement invented about 1754, it became the regulating device of modern mechanical clocks and watches, still in use alongside electric and quartz-crystal timepieces.

VERGE ESCAPEMENT

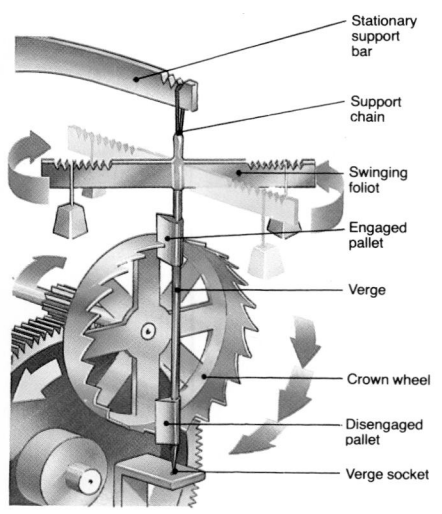

The turning crown wheel, powered by a falling weight, is checked as its teeth engage with one pallet after the other. As the teeth escape the pallets, the foliot swings to and fro, regulating the turning of the crown wheel.

FUSEE AND CORD OR CHAIN

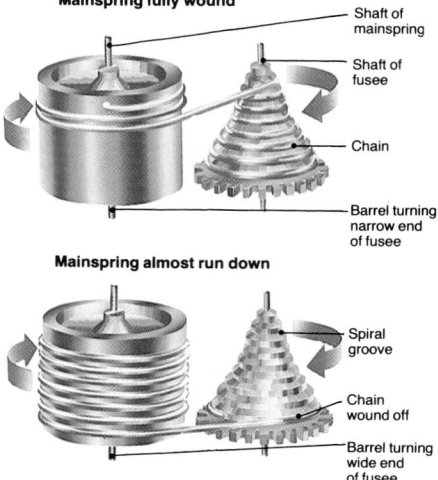

The fully wound mainspring inside the barrel makes it turn the fusee's narrow end. As the spring runs down it loses force, but compensates by turning the fusee's wider end, driving the mechanism at the same rate.

ANCHOR ESCAPEMENT

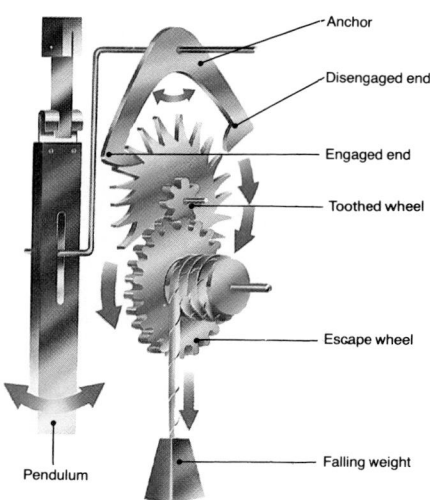

The anchor rocks with each pendulum swing; alternately its ends halt the toothed wheel and through it the escape wheel, which is turned by the weight. Each swing lets the mechanism move forward one tooth, or "tick."

LEVER ESCAPEMENT

Right motion

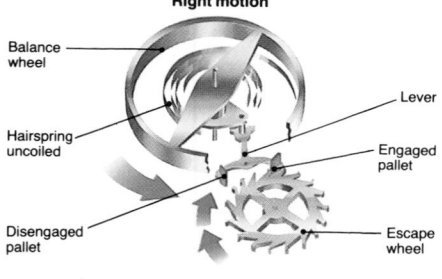

Left motion

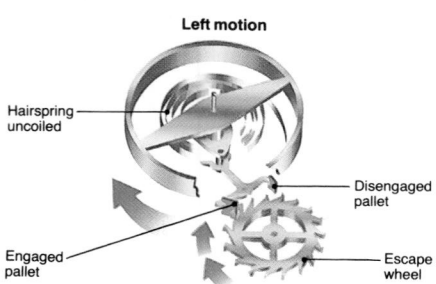

The balance wheel oscillates five times a second and keeps the hairspring coiling and uncoiling. This rocks the lever; the pallets, one after another, halt the escape wheel so that it turns one tooth, or "tick," at a time.

QUARTZ-CRYSTAL CLOCK

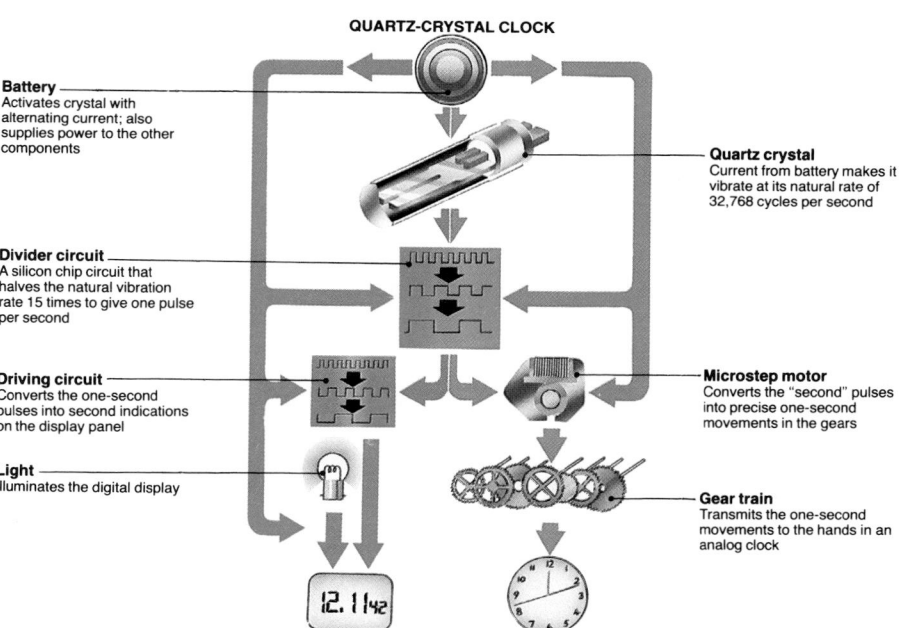

The battery makes the crystal oscillate at its natural rate of 32,768 cycles per second. The divider circuit converts the vibration rate to one per second. A driving circuit or a motor converts these vibrations into one-second "ticks," which are then transmitted to the digital display or the clock face.

elements of; end; finish. **4.** To bring to an end, temporarily or permanently, the operations of (a business establishment, factory, or the like). **5.** To settle (an account) finally, by withdrawing any money credited to it and settling outstanding debts. **6.** To join or unite; bring into contact: *close a circuit.* **7.** *Archaic.* To enclose on all sides. *—intr.* **1.** To become shut. **2.** To finish or conclude. **3.** To cease operations, temporarily or permanently. **4.** To engage at close quarters; begin to fight. Used with *with.* **5.** To reach an agreement; come to terms. Used with *with.* **6.** To have a specified value at the end of the day's trading: *Gold closed at 520 dollars an ounce.* **—See Synonyms at complete. —close in.** To surround and advance upon, so as to eliminate the possibility of escape. Often used with *on* or *upon.* **~n.** (klōz *for senses* 1,2,3; klōs *for senses* 4,5). **1.** A conclusion; a finish. **2.** The concluding part of a musical phrase or theme; a cadence. **3.** *Archaic.* A fight at close quarters. **4.** An enclosed place, especially land surrounding a cathedral. **5.** *Chiefly British.* **a.** A narrow passage or alley leading to the back of a house or to the common stairway of an apartment building. **b.** A cul-de-sac. **~adv.** (klōs). Closely. **—close on.** Approximately; practically. [Middle English *clos*, from Old French, from Latin *clausus*, past participle of *claudere*, to close.] **—close·ly** (klōs′lē) *adv.* **—close·ness** (klōs′nĭs) *n.* **—clos·er** (klō′zər) *n.*

close call (klōs) *n. Informal.* A narrow escape.
closed (klōzd) *adj.* **1.** Having complete boundaries; enclosed. **2.** Blocked or barred to passage or entry. **3.** Having explicitly limited membership; restricted; exclusive. **4.** *Phonetics.* Ending in a consonant. Said of a syllable. **5.** *Geometry.* **a.** Of or pertaining to a curve, such as a circle, having no end points. **b.** Of or pertaining to a surface having no boundary curves.
closed book *n. Informal.* A person or matter that is not known or understood.
closed-cap·tioned (klōzd′kăp′shənd) *adj.* Broadcast with captions that appear only on the screens of specially equipped receivers: *A closed-captioned television program for the hearing-impaired.*
closed chain *n.* A chemical ring *(see).* Compare **open chain.**
closed circuit *n.* **1.** A television transmission circuit with a limited number of reception stations and no broadcasting facilities. **2.** An electric circuit providing an uninterrupted, endless path for the flow of current. Compare **open circuit.**
close down (klōz) *intr.v.* **1.** To stop or cease operations entirely. **2.** To end transmission for the day. Used of a radio or television station. **—close-down** (klōz′doun′) *n.*
closed season (klōzd) *n.* The period in the year when the law prohibits the killing for sport of certain animals, birds, and fish. Compare **open season.**
closed shop *n.* A business or industrial establishment in which the employers have a contractual agreement with a particular trade union to employ only members of that union. Compare **open shop, union shop.**
close-fist·ed (klōs′fĭs′tĭd) *adj.* Miserly; tight-fisted.
close-grained (klōs′grānd′) *adj.* Dense or compact in structure or texture: *close-grained wood.*
close harmony (klōs) *n.* A singing arrangement in which the three upper parts lie close together, usually within an octave.
close-hauled (klōs′hôld′) *adv. Nautical.* With sails trimmed flat for sailing as close to the wind as possible. **—close-hauled** *adj.*
close-knit (klōs′nĭt′) *adj.* Bound together by social or cultural ties: *a close-knit village community.*
close-mouthed (klōs′mouthd′, -moutht′) *adj.* Not disposed to talk; reticent; taciturn.
close out (klōz) *tr.v.* To dispose of (goods), usually at greatly reduced prices.
close-out (klōz′out′) *n.* A sale in which all remaining goods are disposed of, usually at greatly reduced prices.
close packing (klōs) *n.* An arrangement of objects, such as spheres or atoms in a crystal, such that the total occupies the minimum possible volume. In the close packing of equal spheres each sphere has 12 near neighbors. **—close packed** *adj.*
close quarters (klōs) *pl.n.* Close range; close proximity. Used chiefly in the phrase *at close quarters.*
close shave (klōs) *n.* A narrow escape.
close stitch (klōs) *n.* The **buttonhole stitch** *(see).*
clos·et (klŏz′ĭt, klô′zĭt) *n. Abbr.* **cl. 1.** A small room, cabinet, or recess for storing linens or supplies, hanging clothes, or the like. **2.** *Archaic.* A small private chamber for studying, meditating, praying, or the like. **3.** A water closet; a toilet. **—come out of the closet.** To give up concealing proclivities, opinions, or affiliations considered undesirable by others. **~tr.v. closeted, -eting, -ets.** To enclose or shut up in a private room, as for discussion or meditation. Usually used reflexively. **~adj. 1.** Concealed; confidential: *a closet liberal.* **2.** Based upon theory and speculation rather than practice: *closet plans.* [Middle English, from Old French, diminutive of *clos*, enclosure, from Medieval Latin *clausum*, from Latin *clausus*, enclosed, CLOSE.]
close up (klōz) *tr.v.* **1.** To close entirely. **2.** To bring nearer together. *—intr.v.* To come nearer together.
close-up (klōs′ŭp′) *n.* **1.** A picture, such as a film or television shot, taken at close range. **2.** A close or intimate view or description.
clos·trid·i·um (klōs-trĭd′ē-əm) *n., pl.* **-tridia** (-trĭd′ē-ə). Any of various rod-shaped, spore-forming, chiefly anaerobic bacteria of the genus *Clostridium*, including some of the nitrogen-fixing bacteria found in soil and those causing botulism and tetanus. [New Latin,

"small spindle," from Greek *klōstēr*, spindle, from *klōthein*, to spin. See **Clotho.**]
clo·sure (klō′zhər) *n.* **1.** The act of closing or the condition of being closed. **2.** Something that closes or shuts. **3.** A finish; a conclusion. **4.** *Geology.* The vertical distance from the highest point of a structure and the lowest surrounding contour. **5.** *Mathematics.* The property of an algebraic structure, such as a group, by which combinations of elements produce other elements that belong to the set. **6.** Variant of **cloture.** **~tr.v. closured, -suring, -sures.** To end (a debate) by cloture. [Middle English, from Old French, from Latin *clausūra*, from *clausus*, enclosed, CLOSE.]
clot (klŏt) *n.* **1.** A thick, viscous, or coagulated mass or lump, as of blood. **2.** *British Slang.* A stupid person; blockhead. **~v. clotted, clotting, clots.** *—intr.* To form into clots. *—tr.* To cause to clot; fill or cover with clots. [Middle English *clot*, Old English *clott*, lump.]
cloth (klôth, klŏth) *n., pl.* **cloths** (klôths, klôthz, klŏths, klŏthz). **1.** *Abbr.* **cl.** Fabric or material formed by weaving, knitting, pressing, or felting natural or synthetic fibers. **2.** A piece of fabric or material used for a specific purpose. Often used in combination: *tablecloth; dishcloth.* **3.** *Nautical.* **a.** Canvas. **b.** A sail. **4.** Professional attire or mode of dress. **—the cloth.** The clergy. [Middle English *cloth*, Old English *clāth*, from Germanic.] **—cloth** *adj.*
cloth-bound (klôth′bound′, klŏth′-) *adj.* Designating a book bound in boards and covered with cloth.
cloth-cap (klôth′kăp′, klŏth′-) *adj. British.* Of or considered as characteristic of the working class: *a cloth-cap mentality.*
clothe (klōth) *tr.v.* **clothed** or **clad** (klăd), **clothing, clothes. 1.** To put clothes on; dress. **2.** To cover as if with clothes. [Middle English *clothen, clathen*, Old English *clāthian*, from *clāth*, CLOTH.]
clothes (klōz; klōthz) *pl.n.* **1.** Articles of dress; garments. **2. Bedclothes** *(see).* [Middle English, from Old English *clāthas*, plural of *clāth*, CLOTH.]
clothes·horse (klōz′hôrs′, klōthz′-) *n.* **1.** A frame on which clothes are hung to dry or air. **2.** A person considered to be excessively concerned with dress.
clothes·line (klōz′līn′, klōthz′-) *n.* A cord, rope, or wire on which clothes are hung to dry or air.
clothes moth *n.* Any of various moths of the family Tineidae, the larvae of which feed on wool, hair, fur, and feathers.
clothes·pin (klōz′pĭn′, klōthz′-) *n.* A clip of wood or plastic for fastening clothes to a clothesline. Also *British* "clothespeg."
clothes tree *n.* An upright pole or stand with hooks or pegs on which to hang garments.
cloth·ier (klōth′yər, klō′thē-ər) *n.* One who deals in clothing, especially men's clothing.
cloth·ing (klō′thĭng) *n.* **1.** Clothes collectively; attire. **2.** A covering.
Clo·tho (klō′thō). *Greek Mythology.* One of the three **Fates** *(see).* She spins the thread of life. [Greek *klōthō*, "spinner," from *klōthein*, to spin, akin to *kalathos*, CALATHUS.]
cloth of gold *n.* Silk or woolen cloth interwoven with gold threads.
clot·ted cream (klŏt′ĭd) *n.* Thick cream made by scalding milk.
clo·ture (klō′chər) *n.* Also **clo·sure** (klō′zhər). A parliamentary procedure by which debate is ended and an immediate vote is taken on the matter under discussion. **~tr.v. clotured, -turing, -tures.** To close (a parliamentary debate) by cloture. [French *clôture*, variant of Old French *closure*, CLOSURE.]
cloud (kloud) *n.* **1.** A visible body of very fine droplets of water or particles of ice dispersed in the atmosphere above the earth's surface at various altitudes ranging up to several miles. **2.** Any visible mass in the air, as of steam, smoke, or dust. **3.** A large mass of things moving in the air; a swarm. **4.** Anything that darkens, threatens, or fills with gloom. **5.** A dark region or blemish on a polished stone or gem. **6.** An appearance of dimness or milkiness, as in glass or a liquid. **—have one's head in the clouds.** To be impractical; live in a world of fantasy. **—under a cloud.** Under suspicion or out of favor. **~v. clouded, clouding, clouds.** *—tr.* **1.** To cover with or as if with clouds; darken; dim. **2.** To make gloomy, sullen, or troubled. *—intr.* To become cloudy or overcast. Often used with *over* or *up.* [Middle English *cloud*, hill, mass of earth, cloud, Old English *clūd*, rock, hill.] **—cloud·less** *adj.* See feature, next page.
cloud·ber·ry (kloud′běr′ē) *n., pl.* **-ries. 1.** A creeping plant, *Rubus chamaemorus*, of northern regions, having white flowers and edible fruit. **2.** The reddish-orange fruit of this plant.
cloud·burst (kloud′bûrst′) *n.* A sudden rainstorm; a downpour.
cloud chamber *n.* A device for detecting charged subatomic particles by the formation of small droplets of liquid along the paths of the particles as they pass through supersaturated vapor. The droplets condense on ions produced by the particles. Compare **bubble chamber.**
cloud-cuck·oo-land (kloud′kōō′kōō-lănd′) *n.* An ideal realm of imagination or fantasy. Often used derogatorily. [Translation of Greek *Nephelokokkugia* (*nephelē*, cloud + *kokkux*, cuckoo), a comic utopia in Aristophanes' comedy *The Birds* (414 B.C.).]
cloud nine *n. Informal.* A state of great happiness. Used in the phrase *on cloud nine.* [Originally *on cloud seven;* the phrase is perhaps related to *in the seventh heaven* (in some Jewish and Muslim literature the seventh and final heaven is the abode of God).]
cloud seeding *n.* A technique of stimulating rainfall, especially by distributing quantities of dry-ice crystals or silver iodide smoke

cloudberry *A wild relative of the blackberry and raspberry that grows in damp patches on exposed moors of northern regions. White flowers produce amber berries in late summer.*

TEN TYPES OF CLOUDS AND WHAT THEY MEAN

How tomorrow's rain and snow are stored in reservoirs in the sky

Moisture from the world's seas, rivers, plants, and soil is constantly evaporating. As a result, large quantities of water rise unseen from the earth into the atmosphere. When air rises it cools and its capacity to hold the invisible water vapor is reduced until the air becomes saturated. Further cooling then causes the formation of tiny water particles and—at low temperatures—of ice crystals, which develop into various types of clouds. A vast number of cloud particles must join together to form a drop of rain, hail, or snow large enough to fall to earth. Clouds are classified according to appearance and height.

CIRRUS *High-level ice-crystal clouds, often a sign of bad weather to come*

NIMBOSTRATUS *A solid mass of low clouds means that rain is imminent*

CIRROCUMULUS *High-level rippling clouds on the edge of unsettled weather*

STRATOCUMULUS *Low rolls, usually associated with dry, overcast weather*

CIRROSTRATUS *High milky clouds, often bringing rain within 12 hours*

STRATUS *Low, shapeless, foggy clouds that often bring drizzle*

ALTOCUMULUS *Midlevel banded masses, usually breaking up to give sunny periods*

CUMULUS *Fluffy cauliflowers of low cloud associated with sunny spells*

ALTOSTRATUS *Midlevel thin gray sheet that can develop into rain clouds*

CUMULONIMBUS *Tall, towering thunderheads appearing before a thunderstorm*

through clouds. Also informally called "rainmaking."

cloud·y (klou'dē) *adj.* **-ier, -iest. 1.** *Abbr.* **c.** Full of or covered with clouds; overcast. **2.** Of or like a cloud or clouds. **3.** Marked with indistinct masses or streaks: *cloudy marble.* **4.** Not transparent; milky. Said of liquids. **5.** Obscure; vague. **6.** Troubled; gloomy. **—cloud·i·ly** *adv.* **—cloud·i·ness** *n.*

clout (klout) *n.* **1.** A blow, especially with the fist. **2.** *Slang.* A long, powerful hit in baseball. **3.** *Informal.* Power, prestige, or influence; pull: *political clout.* **4.** An archery target. **5.** *Archaic & Regional.* A piece of cloth. **6.** A short nail with a wide flat head. Also called "clout nail."
~*tr.v.* **clouted, clouting, clouts. 1.** To hit with much force. **2.** *Archaic & Regional.* To patch. [Middle English *clout,* from Old English *clūt* (noun), lump, piece of material, patch, *clūtian,* to patch.]

clove[1] (klōv) *n.* **1.** An East Indian evergreen tree, *Eugenia aromatica,* of which the aromatic unopened flower buds are used, whole or ground, as a spice. **2.** The small dried flower bud of this tree. [Middle English *clowe (of gilofre),* "nail-shaped bud (of clove)," from Old French *clou (de girofle)* : *clou,* nail, from Latin *clāvus* + *girofle,* clove tree (see **gillyflower**).]

clove[2] *n.* Any of the small sections of a separable bulb, such as that of garlic. [Middle English *clove,* Old English *clufu.*]

clove[3]. **1.** Alternate past tense and *archaic* past participle of **cleave** (to split). **2.** *Archaic.* Past tense of **cleave** (to cling).

clove hitch *n.* A knot used to secure a line to a spar, post, or other object, consisting of two turns with the second held under the first. [*Clove,* from CLOVEN (split).]

clo·ven (klō'vən). Alternate past participle of **cleave** (to split). ~*adj.* Split; divided.

cloven foot *n.* A cloven hoof. **—clo·ven-foot·ed** *adj.*

cloven hoof *n.* **1.** A divided or cleft hoof, as in deer or cattle. **2.** The symbol of Satan, who is often depicted with such hooves. **—clo·ven-hoofed** (klō'vən-hŏŏft', -hōōft') *adj.*

clove pink *n.* A plant, *Dianthus caryophyllus,* having pink flowers from which the garden carnations have been bred.

clo·ver (klō'vər) *n.* **1.** Any plant of the genus *Trifolium,* having compound leaves with usually three leaflets and tight heads of small flowers. Many species provide valuable pasturage. **2.** Any of several related plants, such as the sweet clover, or **melilot** *(see).* **—in clover.** Living a carefree life of ease, comfort, or prosperity. [Middle English *clover, claver,* Old English *clǣfre,* clover, from Germanic *klaibrōn* (unattested).]

clo·ver·leaf (klō'vər-lēf') *n., pl.* **-leaves** (-lēvz') or **-leafs.** A highway interchange in the shape of a four-leafed clover at which two roads crossing each other on different levels are provided with curving access and exit ramps, enabling vehicles to go in any of four directions.

Clo·vis (klō'vĭs) (*c.* A.D. 466–511). King of the Franks (481–511), the greatest of the early Merovingian dynasty, who united Gaul as a single kingdom and set up his capital in Paris. His name, Gallicized as "Louis," was given to 18 later French monarchs.

clown (kloun) *n.* **1.** A buffoon or jester, often wearing outlandish clothes and make-up, who entertains by jokes, antics, and tricks, in a circus, play, or other presentation. **2.** A person who acts the fool or behaves in a comic way. **3.** An ignorant or boorish person. **4.** *Archaic.* A rustic or peasant. See feature, next page.
~*intr.v.* **clowned, clowning, clowns. 1.** To behave in a silly, clownlike fashion. Often used with *around.* **2.** To perform as a clown. [Probably from Scandinavian, akin to Icelandic *klunni,* clumsy person.] **—clown·ish** *adj.* **—clown·ish·ly** *adv.* **—clown·ish·ness** *n.*

cloy (kloi) *v.* **cloyed, cloying, cloys.** —*tr.* To supply with too much of something, especially with something too rich or sweet; surfeit. —*intr.* To cause a feeling of surfeit. [Short for obsolete *accloy,* to nail, hence, to clog, satiate, Middle English *acloien,* to obstruct, hamper, from Old French *encloer,* to nail, from Vulgar Latin *inclāvāre* (unattested) : Latin *in,* in + *clāvāre,* to nail, from *clāvus,* nail.] **—cloy·ing** *adj.* **—cloy·ing·ly** *adv.* **—cloy·ing·ness** *n.*

club[1] (klub) *n.* **1.** A stout, heavy stick, usually thicker at one end than at the other, suitable for use as a weapon; a cudgel. **2.** A bat or stick used in certain games to drive a ball; especially, a stick with a curved head used in golf. **3.** *Botany.* A club-shaped structure or organ. **4. a.** The black symbol appearing on one of the four suits of playing cards, in the shape of a trefoil or cloverleaf. **b.** A card bearing this symbol. See **clubs. 5.** *Nautical.* A spar.
~*tr.v.* **clubbed, clubbing, clubs. 1.** To strike or beat with or as with a club. **2.** To gather or combine (hair, for example) into a clublike mass; tangle: *clubbed roots.* [Middle English *clubbe,* from Old Norse *klubba,* billet, club.]

club[2] *n.* **1. a.** A group of people organized for a common purpose; especially, a group that meets regularly. **b.** An association of people formed for social purposes, having premises providing meals, accommodation, and other facilities. **c.** *Sports.* An association that organizes and provides teams, matches, facilities, and events, in a particular game or sport: *a tennis club; a golf club.* **2.** The room, building, or other facilities used by such a group or association. —See Synonyms at **circle.**
~*v.* **clubbed, clubbing, clubs.** —*tr.* To contribute for a joint or common purpose. —*intr.* To join or combine for a common purpose. Used with *together*: *They clubbed together to buy her a farewell present.* [Probably from CLUB (to gather into a mass).]

club·ba·ble (klŭb'ə-bəl) *adj. Informal.* Suited to membership in a social club; sociable.

club car *n.* A railroad passenger car equipped with lounge chairs, tables, a buffet or bar, and other extra comforts.

club chair *n.* An upholstered easy chair with arms and a low back.

club·foot (klŭb'fŏŏt') *n., pl.* **-feet** (-fēt). **1.** Congenital deformity of the foot, marked by a misshapen appearance often resembling a club. Also called "talipes." **2.** A foot so deformed. **—club·foot·ed** *adj.*

club·house (klŭb'hous') *n.* A building occupied by a club.

club·man (klŭb'mən, -măn') *n., pl.* **-men** (-mĭn, -mĕn'). A man who is an active member of a fashionable club or clubs.

club moss *n.* Any of various erect or creeping mosslike plants of the genus *Lycopodium,* having tiny, scalelike, overlapping leaves and reproducing by spores. Some species are also called "ground pine." Also called "lycopodium." [After the club-shaped strobiles on some species.]

club root *n.* A disease of cabbage and related plants, caused by a fungus of the genus *Plasmodiophora,* and resulting in large, distorted swellings on the roots.

clubs (klŭbz) *n. Used with a singular or plural verb.* One of the four suits of playing cards, distinguished by black trefoil figures printed on the face of each card.

club sandwich *n.* A sandwich, usually of three slices of toast, with a filling of various meats, tomato, lettuce, and dressing.

club soda *n.* An effervescent, unflavored water used in various alcoholic and nonalcoholic drinks.

club steak *n.* **Delmonico steak** *(see).*

cluck (klŭk) *v.* **clucked, clucking, clucks.** —*intr.* To utter a cluck or clucks. —*tr.* To express by clucking: *He clucked his disapproval.*
~*n.* **1. a.** The characteristic sound made by a hen when brooding or calling her chicks. **b.** Any sound resembling this. **2.** *Informal.* A stupid or foolish person: *a dumb cluck.* [Imitative.]

clue, clew (klōō) *n.* Anything that guides or directs in the solution of a problem or mystery. **—not have a clue.** *Informal.* To be ignorant or incapable.
~*tr.v.* **clued, clueing** or **cluing, clues.** Also **clew, clewed, clewing, clews.** To give (someone) guiding information. Used with *in.* [Variant of CLEW (ball of yarn).]

Clum·ber spaniel (klŭm'bər) *n.* A dog of a breed developed in England, having short legs and a silky, predominantly white coat. [After *Clumber,* a country estate in Nottinghamshire.]

clump (klŭmp) *n.* **1.** A clustered mass; a lump. **2.** A thick grouping, as of plants. **3.** A heavy dull sound; a thud, as of footsteps.
~*v.* **clumped, clumping, clumps.** —*intr.* **1.** To walk with a heavy dull sound. **2.** To form clumps. —*tr.* **1.** To gather into or form clumps of. **2.** To cause (blood cells or bacteria for example) to form clumps. [Low German *klump,* from Middle Low German *klumpe.*] **—clump·y** *adj.*

clum·sy (klŭm'zē) *adj.* **-sier, -siest. 1.** Lacking physical coordination, skill, or grace; awkward. **2.** Awkwardly made; unwieldy. **3.** Gauche; inept: *a clumsy excuse; a clumsy compliment.* —See Synonyms at **awkward.** [From obsolete *clumse,* to be numb with cold, Middle English *clumsen,* probably from Scandinavian, akin to Swedish dialectal *klumsen,* benumbed, from Germanic *klum-* (unattested).] **—clum·si·ly** *adv.* **—clum·si·ness** *n.*

clung. Past tense and past participle of **cling.**

clunk (klŭngk) *n.* **1.** A heavy blow. **2.** A dull, hollow sound; thump. [Imitative.]

clunk·er (klŭng'kər) *n.* **1.** An old, broken-down car or other machine. **2.** A failure; flop.

Clu·ny (klōō'nē). Town in Saône-et-Loire department of east-central France, on the Grosne River. The Cluniac order of Benedictine monks was established here in 910 at an abbey which survives to this day.

clu·pe·id (klōō'pē-ĭd)) *n.* Any of various fishes of the family Clupeidae, which includes herrings, sardines, and sprats. [New Latin *Clupeidae,* from Latin *clupea*†, a kind of small fish.] **—clu·pe·id** *adj.*

clus·ter (klŭs'tər) *n.* **1.** Any configuration of elements gathered or occurring closely together; a group; a bunch. **2.** Two or more successive consonants in a word; for example, *cl* and *st* in the word *cluster.* **3.** *Astronomy.* A group of stars or galaxies moving together.
~*v.* **clustered, -tering, -ters.** —*intr.* To gather or grow in clusters. —*tr.* To cause to grow or form into clusters. [Middle English *cluster,* Old English *clyster, cluster*†.]

cluster bomb *n.* A bomb consisting of a collection of **fragmentation bombs** *(see)* that are dispersed on impact.

cluster fly *n.* A fly of the family Calliphoridae that gathers with others of its kind in crevices or corners of buildings.

cluster pine *n.* A tree, the **pinaster** *(see).*

clutch[1] (klŭch) *v.* **clutched, clutching, clutches.** —*tr.* **1.** To grasp and hold tightly. **2.** To seize or snatch. —*intr.* To attempt to grasp or seize. Used with *at.*
~*n.* **1.** The hand, claw, talon, paw, or the like, used in the act of grasping. **2.** A tight grasp. **3.** *Usually* **clutches.** Control or power: *She had them in her clutches.* **4.** *Machinery.* **a.** Any of various devices for engaging and disengaging two working parts of a shaft or of a shaft and a driving mechanism, as in a car. **b.** The pedal, lever, or other apparatus that activates such a device. **—in the clutch.** *Informal.* In a crucial or critical situation. [Middle English *clicchen, clucchen,* Old English *clyccan,* from Germanic *klukjan* (unattested).]

clutch[2] *n.* **1.** The number of eggs produced or incubated by one bird or in one nest at one time. **2.** A brood of chickens. **3.** *Informal.* A group of people or things.

clove hitch *This is made of two adjustable loops that jam together, fastening the rope securely. It is often used for mooring boats.*

clover *An inconspicuous meadow plant that can absorb nitrogen from the air. Red clover (above) is often grown and plowed into the ground in order to enrich it with nitrogen, a vital plant food.*

Clumber spaniel *This English breed of sporting dog was developed at Clumber Park in Nottingham. It is one of the largest types of spaniel and, like other spaniels, was originally used to retrieve and flush out game animals such as pheasants, ducks, and rabbits.*

Clydesdale *A tall and powerful workhorse once widely used for plowing and for pulling heavy farm wagons and brewers' drays.*

~*tr.v.* **clutched, clutching, clutches.** To hatch (chicks). [18th century : variant of dialectal *cletch,* from Middle English *clecken,* to hatch, give birth, from Old Norse *klekja†.*]

clutch bag *n.* A small handbag without a strap or handles.

clut·ter (klŭt′ər) *n.* **1.** A confused or disordered state or collection; a jumble. **2.** *Archaic.* A confused noise; a clatter. **3.** *Electronics.* Noise, echoes, or other unwanted signals on a radar display. ~*tr.v.* **cluttered, -tering, -ters.** To litter or pile in a disordered state. Used with *up.* [Middle English *clotteren,* to clot, coagulate, heap, from *clot,* lump, CLOT.]

Clwyd (klōō′ĭd). County in northeast Wales, formed in 1974 from Flintshire and parts of Denbighshire and Merionethshire. It is bounded by England to the east. Upland pastures, rising to 690 meters (2,265 feet) at Foel Wen in the south are broken by the fertile valleys of the Clwyd and Dee rivers, where sheep and cattle are farmed. Its county town is Mold.

Clyde (klīd). River in western Scotland. It rises in the Southern Uplands and flows 170 kilometers (106 miles) northwest through Glasgow and Clydebank to the sea at the Firth of Clyde, an inlet of the Atlantic Ocean.

Clyde·bank (klīd′băngk′). Town in the Strathclyde Region, on the lower Clyde River. Many ocean liners were built in its shipyards, including the *Queen Mary* and *Queen Elizabeth.*

Clydes·dale (klīdz′dāl′) *n.* **1.** A large, powerful draft horse of a breed developed in the Clyde valley in Scotland. **2.** A type of small terrier.

clyp·e·ate (klĭp′ē-ĭt) *adj.* Also **clyp·e·i·form** (klĭp′ē-ə-fôrm). **1.** Shaped like a round shield. **2.** Having a clypeus.

clyp·e·us (klĭp′ē-əs) *n., pl.* **-ei** (-ē-ī′). *Biology.* A shieldlike structure, especially a plate on the front of the head of an insect. [New Latin, from Latin *clipeus, clupeus†,* round shield.] —**clyp′e·al** *adj.*

clys·ter (klĭs′tər) *n. Medicine. Rare.* An enema. [Middle English *clister,* from Old French *clistere,* from Latin *clystēr,* from Greek *klustēr,* "liquid for washing out," from *kluzein,* to wash out.]

Cly·tem·nes·tra (klī′təm-nĕs′trə). *Greek Mythology.* The wife of Agamemnon and mother of Orestes and Electra. With her lover Aegisthus she murdered Agamemnon and was killed by her son in revenge.

cm centimeter; centimeters.

Cm The symbol for the element curium.

c.m. **1.** circular mil. **2.** court-martial.

CMA certified medical assistant.

Cmdr. commander.

C.M.G. Companion (of the Order) of St. Michael and St. George.

cml. commercial.

cN centinewton.

C/N credit note.

CND Campaign for Nuclear Disarmament.

cni·dar·i·an (nī-dâr′ē-ən) *n.* Any of various aquatic invertebrates of the Cnidaria, a chiefly marine subphylum of the Coelenterata that includes the jellyfish, sea anemones, and corals. ~*adj.* Of or belonging to the Cnidaria. [New Latin *Cnidaria,* from Greek *knidē,* nettle.]

Cnossos. See **Knossos.**

CNS central nervous system.

Cnut. See **Canute.**

Co The symbol for the element cobalt.

CO Colorado (with Zip Code).

co– *prefix.* Indicates: **1.** Joint, jointly, together, or mutually; for example, **co-education, cooperate, copilot. 2.** Same, similar; for example, **coconscious. 3.** Complement of an angle; for example, **cosine, coaltitude.** [In borrowed Latin compounds, *co-* is the reduced form of *com-* (see **com-**), used before *h, gn,* and usually before vowels, as in COHERE, COGNATE, and COALESCE.]

co., Co. 1. company. **2.** county.

c.o. 1. care of. **2.** *Accounting.* carried over. **3.** cash order.

C.O. 1. commanding officer. **2.** conscientious objector.

c/o care of.

co·ac·er·vate (kō-ăs′ər-vāt′) *n. Chemistry.* A cluster of droplets separated out of a lyophilic colloid. [Latin *coacervātus,* past participle of *coacervāre,* to heap together : *co-,* together + *acervāre,* to heap, ACERVATE.]

---

clown

THE FOOL WHO IS SUFFERED GLADLY

A tradition of buffoonery that goes back to ancient Greece

Clowns are mostly found today in the circus, but the professional buffoon has a long tradition behind him. He was seen on the stages of ancient Greece and Rome, and as the Old Vice (attendant on the Devil) in medieval religious drama.

From Italian Renaissance comedy—the *commedia dell'arte* — came Punch and Pierrot and the comic character of 19th-century English pantomime. A character called Clown in pantomime was mainly the creation of the London actor Joseph Grimaldi (1779–1837), who played in pantomime from the age of four.

In Grimaldi's honor the present-day circus clown, who has inherited many of his characteristics, is known as "Joey." He has as his butt the "Auguste," according to some an 1870's invention of the French circus, but attributed by some others to Tom Belling in a Berlin circus in 1864. The Auguste is a shambling figure with a bulbous red nose and a fright wig, who interrupts and ruins all Clown's tricks and trips over anything in his way.

AUGUSTE *Coco, who performed with Bertram Mills's Circus in Britain for 30 years, was an Auguste, the clown who does everything wrong and often has buckets of water thrown over him.*

WHITE-FACED CLOWN *In the Cirque de Paris, a white-faced clown plays to the audience on a clarinet, before his performance is wrecked by the clumsy assistance of an Auguste.*

co·ac·er·va·tion (kō-ăs′ər-vā′shən) n. The process of becoming a coacervate.

coach (kōch) n. 1. A large, closed horse-drawn carriage with four wheels. 2. A railway carriage. 3. *Chiefly British.* A motor bus. 4. Economy-class seating on a train or airplane. 5. A person who trains athletes or sports teams. 6. A private tutor employed to prepare a student for an examination. ~v. **coached, coaching, coaches.** —*tr.* 1. To teach or train; tutor. 2. To transport by coach. —*intr.* 1. To act as a coach. 2. To ride in a coach. —See Synonyms at **teach.** [French *coche,* from German *Kutsche,* from Hungarian *kocsi,* after *Kocs,* a town in Hungary, where such carriages originated. Sense 6: 19th-century university slang use of *coach* (carriage).] —**coach·er** n.

coach-built (kōch′bĭlt′) adj. Designating a vehicle body built specially by craftsmen.

coach dog n. The **Dalmatian** (see). [Formerly trained as a fashionable pet to run behind a coach.]

coach·ing inn (kō′chĭng) n. An inn where the horses pulling a long-distance coach could be changed for a fresh team.

coach·man (kōch′mən) n., pl. **-men** (-mĭn). 1. A person who drives a horse-drawn coach. 2. A type of artificial fishing fly.

coach·wood (kōch′wŏŏd′) n. An Australian tree yielding closely grained wood suitable for making furniture.

coach·work (kōch′wûrk′) n. The bodywork of a motor vehicle.

co·ac·tion (kō-ăk′shən) n. 1. Joint action. 2. *Archaic.* Compulsion. [Middle English *coaccioun,* from Old French *coaction,* from Latin *coactiō,* from *cōgere* (past participle *cōactus*), to drive together, force. See **coagulum.**] —**co·ac·tive** adj. —**co·ac·tive·ly** adv.

co·ad·ju·tant (kō-ăj′ə-tənt) adj. Helping each other. ~n. A coworker; an assistant.

co·ad·ju·tor (kō′ə-jōō′tər, kō-ăj′ə-tər) n. *Abbr.* **coad.** 1. The assistant to a bishop. 2. Any coworker; an assistant. [Middle English *coadjutour,* from Old French *coadjuteur,* from Latin *coadjūtor* : *cō-,* together + *adjūtor,* assistant, from *adjūtāre,* to assist, AID.]

co·ad·u·nate (kō-ăj′ə-nĭt, -nāt′) adj. Closely joined by growing together; connate. [Late Latin *coadūnāre* : *cō-,* together + *adūnāre,* to unite to : Latin *ad-,* to + *ūnāre,* to unite, from *ūnus,* one.] —**co·ad·u·na·tion** (kō-ăj′ə-nā′shən) n. —**co·ad·u·na·tive** (kō-ăj′ə-nā′tĭv, -nə-tĭv) adj.

co·ag·u·lant (kō-ăg′yə-lənt) n. An agent that causes coagulation. —**co·ag·u·lant** adj.

co·ag·u·lase (kō-ăg′yə-lās′, -lāz′) n. An enzyme, such as thrombin, that causes blood clotting. [COAGUL(ATE) + -ASE.]

co·ag·u·late (kō-ăg′yə-lāt′) v. **-lated, -lating, -lates.** —*tr.* To cause transformation of (a liquid or solid, such as blood) into a soft, semisolid, or solid mass. —*intr.* To become such a mass. [Middle English *coagulaten,* from Latin *coāgulāre,* to curdle, from COAGULUM.] —**co·ag·u·la·ble** (kō-ăg′yə-lə-bəl) adj. —**co·ag·u·la·bil·i·ty** (kō-ăg′yə-lə-bĭl′ə-tē) n. —**co·ag·u·la·tion** (kō-ăg′yə-lā′shən) n. —**co·ag·u·la·tive** (kō-ăg′yə-lā′tĭv, -lə-tĭv) adj. —**co·ag·u·la·tor** n.

coagulation factor n. Any factor in the blood or plasma that contributes to the clotting of blood.

co·ag·u·lum (kō-ăg′yə-ləm) n., pl. **-la** (-lə). A coagulated mass; a clot; a curd. [Latin *coāgulum,* from *cōgere,* to drive together, condense : *cō-,* together + *agere,* to drive.]

coal (kōl) n. 1. A natural dark brown to black solid used as a fuel, formed from fossilized plants, and consisting of carbon with various organic and some inorganic compounds. 2. A piece of this substance. 3. A glowing or charred piece of coal, wood, or other solid fuel; an ember. —**haul** (or **drag**) **over the coals.** To reprimand; scold. —**take coals to Newcastle.** To take something to a place where it is already plentiful. ~v. **coaled, coaling, coals.** —*tr.* To provide (a ship, for example) with coal. —*intr.* To take on coal. [Middle English *cole,* Old English *col,* coal, live coal.]

coal bunker n. A place for storing coal outside a house or in a ship.

coal·er (kō′lər) n. A ship that transports coal.

co·a·lesce (kō′ə-lĕs′) intr.v. **-lesced, -lescing, -lesces.** 1. To grow together; fuse. 2. To come together so as to form one whole; unite. —See Synonyms at **mix.** [Latin *coalēscere,* to grow together : *cō-,* together + *alēscere,* to grow, inceptive of *alēre,* to nourish.] —**co·a·les·cence** (kō′ə-lĕs′əns) n. —**co·a·les·cent** (kō′ə-lĕs′ənt) adj.

coal·face (kōl′fās′) n. The exposed seam in a mine from which the coal is cut.

coal·field (kōl′fēld′) n. An area with large deposits of coal.

coal·fish (kōl′fĭsh′) n., pl. **-fishes** or collectively **coalfish.** An edible deep-water marine fish, *Gadus virens,* closely related to the cod, with a blackish back and chin barbel. Also called "coley," "saithe."

coal gas n. 1. A gaseous mixture produced by the destructive distillation of bituminous coal and formerly used as a commercial fuel. 2. The gaseous mixture released by burning coal.

coal·i·fy (kō′lə-fī′) v. **-fied, -fying, -fies.** —*tr.* To cause (plant material) to form coal. —*intr.* To form coal. Used of plant material. —**coal·i·fi·ca·tion** (kō′lə-fĭ-kā′shən) n.

co·a·li·tion (kō′ə-lĭsh′ən) n. 1. An alliance, especially a temporary one, of factions, parties, or nations. 2. A combination or fusion into one body. [French, from Medieval Latin *coalitiō* (stem *coalitiōn-*), from Latin *coalēscere,* COALESCE.] —**co·a·li·tion·ist** n.

coal measures pl.n. *Geology.* 1. **Coal Measures.** A stratigraphic unit equivalent to the uppermost division of the Pennsylvanian or Upper Carboniferous periods. 2. Strata of the Carboniferous period containing coal deposits.

coal oil n. 1. An oil formed during the distillation of coal. 2. **Kerosene** (see).

Coal·port (kōl′pôrt′, -pōrt′) n. An antique type of translucent bone china, decorated with brightly colored patterns on a white base. [After *Coalport,* Shrewsbury, England, where it was made.] —**Coalport** adj.

Coal·sack (kōl′săk′) n. 1. A dark nebula near the Southern Cross, appearing as a hole in the Milky Way. 2. A similar dark region of the sky, the Northern Coalsack, near the Northern Cross.

coal scuttle n. A metal container, usually with a handle, in which coal is kept by a hearth.

coal tar n. A viscous black liquid obtained by the destructive distillation of coal, used as a raw material for many dyes, drugs, medications, and organic chemicals and for waterproofing, paints, roofing, and insulation materials. —**coal-tar** (kōl′tär′) adj.

coal-tar pitch n. A heavy black pitch produced by the distillation of coal tar, used as a binder in smokeless fuels and in road surfacing.

coam·ing (kō′mĭng) n. A raised rim or curb around an opening in a ship's deck or the roof of a building, designed to keep out water. [17th century : origin obscure.]

co-an·chor (kō-ăng′kər) n. A newscaster who anchors a news broadcast with another or others. —**co-an·chor** v.

co·ap·ta·tion (kō-ăp-tā′shən) n. The adjustment of parts to each other; especially, the joining of broken bones or the edges of a wound. [Late Latin *coaptātiō* (stem *coaptātiōn-*), a careful fitting together, from Latin *co-,* together + *aptāre,* to fit.]

co·arc·tate (kō-ärk′tāt′) adj. *Entomology.* Describing an insect pupa in which the final larval cuticle remains to form a hardened shell around the body. [Latin *coarctātus,* past participle of *coarctāre, coartāre,* to press together : *cō-,* together + *artāre,* to press, from *artus,* narrow, tight.] —**co·arc·ta·tion** (kō′ärk-tā′shən) n.

coarse (kôrs, kōrs) adj. **coarser, coarsest.** 1. Of low, common, or inferior quality. 2. **a.** Lacking in delicacy or refinement. **b.** Obscene or improper. Said of language. 3. Consisting of large particles; not fine in texture. 4. Rough; harsh. [Middle English *co(a)rs,* ordinary, coarse, probably from *co(u)rs,* COURSE ("the usual practice").] —**coarse·ly** adv. —**coarse·ness** n.
  Synonyms: crass, gross, obscene, ribald, vulgar.

coarse fish n. *British.* Any freshwater fish that does not belong to the salmon or trout families. —**coarse fishing** n.

coarse-grained (kôrs′grānd′, kōrs′-) adj. 1. Having a rough or coarse texture. 2. Not refined; indelicate; crude.

coars·en (kôr′sən, kōr′sən) v. **-ened, -ening, -ens.** —*intr.* To become coarse. —*tr.* To make coarse.

coast (kōst) n. 1. The land next to the sea; the seashore. 2. *Obsolete.* The frontier or border of a country. 3. The act of sliding or coasting; a slide. 4. A hill or other slope down which one may coast, as on a toboggan. —**the Coast.** The Atlantic or Pacific coast of the United States. —**the coast is clear.** *Informal.* There are no dangers or hindrances. ~v. **coasted, coasting, coasts.** —*intr.* 1. **a.** To move along without power, as a freewheeling car does. **b.** To progress effortlessly, at an unhurried pace. 2. To slide down a slope, as on a sled. 3. To sail near or along a coast. —*tr.* To sail or move along the coast or border of. [Middle English *cost,* from Old French *coste,* from Latin *costa,* rib, side.] —**coast·al** (kōs′təl) adj.

coast·er (kōs′tər) n. 1. A ship engaged in coastal trade. 2. A disk placed under a bottle or glass to protect a table top. 3. A small tray or stand, often wheeled, for passing a wine decanter around a table, for example. 4. A sled or toboggan for coasting.

coaster brake n. A brake in the hub of the rear wheel of a bicycle, engaged by pedaling backward.

coast guard n. 1. *Abbr.* **C.G.** The military or naval coastal patrol of a nation, responsible for the protection of life and property at sea, coastal defense, and enforcement of customs, immigration, and navigation laws. 2. A member of a coast guard; coastguardsman.

coast-guards·man (kōst′gärdz′mən) n., pl. **-men** (-mĭn). A member of a coast guard.

coast·line (kōst′līn′) n. The shape or boundary of a coast.

Coast Mountains. Range of western British Columbia and southeastern Alaska, extending *c.* 1,610 kilometers (1,000 miles) northward from the Cascade Range. The mountains have been heavily eroded by glaciers and slope steeply to the Pacific Ocean, where the shoreline is deeply indented by fjords.

Coast Ranges. The mountain ranges along the Pacific coast of North America, extending from southeastern Alaska to Lower California. North of San Francisco the ranges are thickly forested; the southern parts are dry and covered with brush and grass.

coast·ward (kōst′wərd) adj. Directed toward a coast. ~adv. Also **coast·wards** (kōst′wərdz). Toward the coast.

coast·wise (kōst′wīz′) adj. Following the coast. ~adv. By way of or along the coast.

coat (kōt) n. 1. An outer garment covering the body from the shoulders to the waist or below, worn primarily for protection from cold or bad weather. 2. **a.** A woman's garment extending to just below the waist and usually forming the top part of a suit. **b.** The jacket of a man's suit. 3. A natural integument or outer covering, such as the fur of an animal. 4. A layer of some material covering something else; a coating: *a coat of dust; a coat of paint.* ~tr.v. **coated, coating, coats.** 1. To provide or cover with a coat. 2. To cover with a layer, as of paint or chocolate. [Middle English *cote,* from Old French, from Frankish *kotta* (unattested), from West Germanic *kotta* (unattested).]

cobra *The Indian cobra (above) has a larger hood than the African varieties. Some species can spit venom, at a distance and with great accuracy, into the eyes of an approaching aggressor.*

cobweb *Spider's cobweb spun in a dead tree. Cobwebs are made of silk exuded from the spider's body. But only the central trap is sticky; the supporting threads are dry.*

cockatoo *There are 16 species in this group of crested parrots, all native to Australia and nearby islands. They range in color from pink and black to white and yellow; this is the sulfur-crested cockatoo.*

coat·ed (kō'tĭd) *adj.* **1.** Having an outer layer, coat, or covering. **2.** Having a highly polished surface suitable for halftone printing: *coated paper.* **3.** *Optics.* Having a thin layer to minimize reflection; bloomed. Said of a lens.

co·a·ti (kō-ä'tē) *n.* Any of several omnivorous mammals of the genus *Nasua,* of South and Central America and the southwestern United States, related to and resembling the raccoon but having a longer snout and tail. Also called "coatimundi." [Portuguese *coatí,* from Tupi *coatí, coatim,* "belt-nosed" : *cua,* belt, band + *tim,* nose.]

co·a·ti·mun·di (kō-ä'tē-mŭn'dē) *n.* The **coati** *(see).*

coat·ing (kō'tĭng) *n.* **1.** A layer of any substance spread over a surface for protection or decoration. **2.** Cloth for making coats.

coat of arms *n.* **1.** A tabard or surcoat blazoned with heraldic bearings. **2.** The heraldic bearings of a family, city, or the like, usually represented on an escutcheon or shield and accompanied by a crest and motto.

coat of mail *n., pl.* **coats of mail.** An armored coat made of chain mail, interlinked rings, or overlapping metal plates.

coat·tails (kōt'tālz') *pl.n.* The long divided part at the back of a formal or dress coat. **—on (someone's) coattails.** Benefiting from someone else's advancement.

co-au·thor (kō-ô'thər) *n.* A collaborating or joint author.
~tr.v. **co-authored, -thoring, -thors.** To be a co-author of.

coax[1] (kōks) *v.* **coaxed, coaxing, coaxes.** *—tr.* **1.** To persuade or try to persuade by pleading or flattery; cajole; wheedle. **2.** To obtain by persistent persuasion. *—intr.* To use persuasion or inducement. —See Synonyms at **urge.** [Earlier *coaks, cokes,* to fool, from *cokes*†, fool.] **—coax·er** *n.* **—coax·ing·ly** *adv.*

co·ax[2] (kō'ăks') *n.* A **coaxial cable** *(see).*

co·ax·i·al (kō-ăk'sē-əl) *adj.* Having or mounted on a common axis.

coaxial cable *n.* A high-frequency cable used for telephone, telegraph, or television transmission, consisting of a conducting metal tube enclosing and insulated from a central conducting wire core.

cob[1] (kŏb) *n.* **1.** The central core of an ear of corn; corncob. **2.** A male swan. Compare **pen. 3.** A thick-set, stocky, short-legged horse. **4.** A tree, the **cobnut** *(see),* or its edible nut. [Middle English *cobbe*†, lump, round object.]

cob[2] *n.* A mixture of clay and straw formerly used as a building material. [17th century : origin obscure.]

co·balt (kō'bôlt') *n. Symbol* **Co** A hard, brittle metallic element, found associated with nickel, silver, lead, copper, and iron ores and resembling nickel and iron in appearance. It is used chiefly for magnetic alloys, high-temperature alloys, and in the form of its salts for blue glass and ceramic pigments. Atomic number 27, atomic weight 58.9332, melting point 1,495°C, boiling point 3,100°C, specific gravity 8.9, valences 1, 2, 3. [German *Kobalt, Kobold,* from Middle High German *kobolt,* an underground goblin (cobalt was thought to be injurious to silver ores).]

cobalt–60 *n.* A radioactive isotope of cobalt with mass number 60 and exceptionally intense gamma-ray activity, used in radiotherapy, metallurgy, and materials testing.

cobalt blue *n.* **1.** A blue to green pigment consisting of a variable mixture of cobalt and aluminum oxides. **2.** Vivid or strong greenish blue. **—co·balt-blue** *adj.*

cobalt bomb *n.* **1.** An apparatus for producing a beam of gamma rays from a cobalt-60 source, used in medical radiation treatment. **2.** A nuclear weapon designed to release large amounts of radioactive cobalt-60 into the atmosphere.

co·bal·tic (kō-bôl'tĭk) *adj.* Of or containing cobalt. Said especially of chemical compounds containing cobalt with valence 3.

co·bal·tite (kō'bôl-tīt') *n.* Also **co·balt·ine** (-tēn'). A silver-white to gray mineral, CoAsS, that is an important cobalt ore and is used in ceramics.

co·bal·tous (kō-bôl'təs) *adj.* Of or containing cobalt. Said especially of chemical compounds containing cobalt with valence 2.

cob·ber (kŏb'ər) *n. Australian.* Comrade; mate. [Origin unknown.]

Cob·bett (kŏb'ĭt), **William** (1763–1835). British radical author known for his *Weekly Political Register* (1802–35). His *Rural Rides* (1830) described horseback tours of England, charting the decline of traditional values and liberties with industrialization.

cob·ble[1] (kŏb'əl) *n.* **1.** A cobblestone. **2. cobbles.** Coal in lumps about the size of cobblestones.
~tr.v. **cobbled, -bling, -bles.** To pave with cobblestones. [Back-formation from COBBLESTONE.]

cobble[2] *tr.v.* **-bled, -bling, -bles. 1.** To make or mend (boots or shoes). **2.** To put together quickly and roughly: *She cobbled together a speech.* [Probably back-formation from COBBLER.]

cob·bler[1] (kŏb'lər) *n.* **1.** One who mends boots and shoes. **2.** *Archaic.* A clumsy worker; bungler. [Middle English *cobelere*†.]

cobbler[2] *n.* **1.** A deep-dish fruit pie with a thick upper crust. **2.** An iced drink made of wine or liqueur, sugar, and citrus fruit. [Perhaps from COBBLER (mender).]

cob·ble·stone (kŏb'əl-stōn') *n.* A naturally rounded stone, formerly used for paving streets and walls. Also called "cobble." [Middle English *cobelston* : *cobel-,* probably diminutive of *cobbe,* COB (lump) + STONE.]

Cob·den (kŏb'dən), **Richard** (1804–65). British economist and a leading spokesman for free trade. He was a supporter of the Anti-Corn-Law League (1838–46), which brought about the repeal of protectionist legislation.

co·bel·lig·er·ent (kō'bə-lĭj'ər-ənt) *n.* A nation associated with another or others in waging war.

co·bi·a (kō'bē-ə) *n.* A large game fish, *Rachycentron canadum,* of tropical and subtropical seas. [Origin obscure.]

co·ble (kō'bəl) *n. British.* A small, flat-bottomed fishing boat with a lugsail on a raking mast. [Old English *cobel,* from Celtic; akin to Old Breton *caubal.*]

Coblenz. See **Koblenz.**

cob·nut (kŏb'nŭt') *n.* **1.** A European hazel tree, *Corylus avellana grandis.* **2.** The large, edible nut of this tree. Also called "cob."

CO·BOL (kō'bôl') *n.* A computer language based on English words and phrases, used for various business applications. [*CO*mmon *B*usiness *O*riented *L*anguage.]

co·bra (kō'brə) *n.* Any of several venomous snakes of the genus *Naja* and related genera, of Asia and Africa, capable of expanding the skin of the neck to form a flattened hood. [Short for Portuguese *cobra (de capello),* "snake (with a hood)," from Latin *colubra,* feminine of *coluber*†, snake.]

cob·web (kŏb'wĕb') *n.* **1.** The web spun by a spider to catch its prey. **2.** A single thread of such a web. **3.** Something resembling a cobweb in fineness or flimsiness. **4. cobwebs. a.** Any musty accumulation, especially as a result of disuse or neglect. **b.** Confusion; disorder: *cobwebs in the brain.*
~tr.v. **cobwebbed, -webbing, -webs.** To cover with or as if with cobwebs. [Middle English *coppeweb* : *coppe,* spider, Old English *(āttor)coppe* + WEB.] **—cob·web·by** *adj.*

co·ca (kō'kə) *n.* **1.** A South American tree, *Erythroxylon coca,* having leaves that contain cocaine and related alkaloids. **2.** The dried leaves of this shrub or related plants, chewed by people of the Andes as a stimulant. [Spanish, from Quechua *kúka, cuca.*]

co·caine (kō'kān', kō-kān') *n.* A colorless or white crystalline narcotic alkaloid, $C_{17}H_{21}NO_4$, extracted from coca leaves and used as a stimulant or local anesthetic. [COCA + -INE.]

co·cain·ism (kō-kā'nĭz'əm) *n.* The habitual use of cocaine.

coc·cid (kŏk'sĭd) *n.* An insect of the family Coccidae, which includes the scale insects and mealybugs. [New Latin *Coccidae,* from *Coccus* (genus), from Greek *kokkos,* kermes berry, pit.]

coc·cid·i·o·sis (kŏk-sĭd'ē-ō'sĭs) *n.* A disease of many animals, including cattle, pigs, sheep, dogs, cats, and poultry, but rarely of humans, resulting from an infection of the digestive tract by parasitic protozoa of the order Coccidia. [New Latin : *Coccidia,* from COCCUS + -OSIS.]

coc·cus (kŏk'əs) *n., pl.* **cocci** (kŏk'sī', kŏk'ī'). **1.** A bacterium with a spherical or spheroidal shape. Compare **bacillus, spirillum. 2.** *Botany.* A division that contains a single seed and splits apart from a many-lobed fruit. [New Latin, from Greek *kokkos,* kermes berry, pit.] **—coc·coid** (kŏk'oid'), **coc·cal** (kŏk'əl) *adj.*

-coccus *suffix.* Indicates a microorganism that is spheroidal in shape; for example, **streptococcus.** [New Latin, from COCCUS.]

coc·cyx (kŏk'sĭks) *n., pl.* **coccyges** (kŏk-sī'jēz, kŏk'sə-jēz'). In humans and certain apes, a small bone at the base of the spinal column, consisting of several fused rudimentary vertebrae, which represents a vestigial tail. [New Latin, from Greek *kokkux,* cuckoo, coccyx (bone shaped like the cuckoo's beak) (imitative).] **—coc·cyg·e·al** (kŏk-sĭj'ē-əl) *adj.*

Co·chin[1] (kō'chĭn, kōch'ĭn). Port on the Malabar Coast of southwest India. It was the first European settlement in India, colonized by the Portuguese from 1502.

Cochin[2] *n.* A large domestic fowl of a breed developed in Asia, having thickly feathered legs. Also called "Cochin China." [After COCHIN CHINA.]

Cochin Chi·na (chī'nə). The European name for a historic region of central and southern Vietnam. French Cochin China (1862–67) was a territory surrounding Saigon and the Mekong delta. It was subsequently incorporated into the French Union of Indochina (1887–1945) and now forms part of Vietnam.

coch·i·neal (kŏch'ə-nēl', kŏch'ə-nēl') *n.* **1.** A tropical American scale insect, *Dactylopius coccus,* that feeds on certain species of cacti. Also called "cochineal insect." **2.** A brilliant red dye, used especially in cooking, made by drying and pulverizing the bodies of the females of this insect. **3.** Vivid red. [French *cochenille,* from Spanish *cochinilla,* from Latin *coccinus,* scarlet, from Greek *kokkinos,* from *kokkos,* kermes berry.] **—coch·i·neal** *adj.*

Co·chise (kō-chēs', -chēz') (*c.* 1812–74). U.S. Indian leader. An Apache chief, he was falsely imprisoned for kidnapping a white child. When he escaped, hostilities began between Indians and U.S. troops. He and his warriors took refuge in the Dragoon Mts. until 1872, when a treaty relegated the Apaches to an Arizona reservation.

coch·le·a (kŏk'lē-ə) *n., pl.* **-leae** (-lē-ē'). A spiral tube of the inner ear resembling a snail shell and containing nerve endings essential for hearing. [New Latin, from Latin, snail shell, from Greek *kokhlias,* from *kokhlos,* land snail.] **—coch·le·ar** (kŏk'lē-ər) *adj.*

cochlear nerve *n.* The nerve connecting the cochlea to the brain, responsible for the nerve impulses relating to hearing. It is a division of the **acoustic nerve** *(see).*

coch·le·ate (kŏk'lē-ĭt, -āt') *adj.* Also **coch·le·at·ed** (-ā'tĭd). Shaped like a snail shell; spirally twisted. [Latin *cochleātus,* from *cochlea,* snail. See **cochlea.**]

Coch·ran (kŏk'rən), **Jacqueline** (1910–80). U.S. aviator and businesswoman. In the 1930's she studied aviation and founded a cosmetics company. During World War II she trained women as auxiliary pilots for English and American armed forces. She was the first woman to break the sound barrier (1953).

cock[1] (kŏk) *n.* **1.** The adult male of the domestic fowl; rooster. **2. a.** The male of various other birds. **b.** The male of certain other

animals, such as the lobster and the salmon. **3.** A weathervane in the shape of a cock; a weathercock. **4.** A valve by which the flow of a liquid or gas can be regulated. **5. a.** The hammer in a firearm. **b.** Its position when ready for firing. **6.** A tilting or turning upward.
~v. **cocked, cocking, cocks.** *—tr.* **1.** To set the hammer of (a firearm) in a position ready for firing. **2.** To tilt or turn (the ears, for example) up or to one side, usually in a jaunty or alert manner. *—intr.* **1.** To cock the hammer of a firearm. **2.** To turn or stick up.
~adj. Male. Said of birds and, sometimes, other animals: *a cock lobster.* [Middle English, Old English *cocc,* probably from Medieval Latin *coccus* (imitative).]

cock² *n.* A cone-shaped pile of straw or hay.
~tr.v. **cocked, cocking, cocks.** To arrange (straw or hay) in such piles. [Middle English *cok,* Old English *cocc* (attested only in place names), perhaps from Scandinavian.]

cock·ade (kŏk-ăd′) *n.* A rosette or knot of ribbon worn especially on the hat as a badge. [Originally *cockard,* from French *cocarde,* jauntily tilted hat, from Old French *coquard,* strutting, vain, from *coq,* COCK.] **—cock·ad·ed** (kŏk-ā′dĭd) *adj.*

cock-a-doo·dle-doo (kŏk′ə-do͝od′l-do͞o′) *n.* A representation of the characteristic crow of a cock. [Imitative.]

cock-a-hoop (kŏk′ə-ho͞op′, -ho͝op′) *adj.* **1.** In a state of elation or exultation. **2.** Boastful. **3.** Askew. [From the expression *set cock a hoop,* perhaps "to set a cock on a hoop or measure of grain."] **—cock-a-hoop** *adv.*

Cock·aigne, Cock·ayne (kŏ-kān′) *n.* An imaginary land of easy and luxurious living. [Middle English *cockayne,* from Old French *(pais de) quoquaigne,* "(land of) delicacies," probably from Middle Low German *kōkenje,* small fancy sugar cake, diminutive of *kōke,* cake.]

cock-a-leek·ie, cock·ie·leek·ie (kŏk′ə-lē′kē) *n.* A cream soup of Scottish origin, made with leeks and chicken.

cock·a·lo·rum (kŏk′ə-lôr′əm, -lōr′əm) *n.* **1.** A little man with an unduly high opinion of himself. **2.** Boastful talk. **3.** A children's jumping game like leapfrog. [Pseudo-Latin : COCK ("strutting leader") + Latin *-orum,* genitive plural ending.]

cock-and-bull story (kŏk′ən-bo͝ol′) *n.* An absurd or highly improbable tale. [Originally a rambling animal fable about a cock changed into a bull.]

cock·a·tiel (kŏk′ə-tēl′) *n.* A crested parrot, *Nymphicus hollandicus,* of Australia, having gray and yellow plumage. Also called "quarrion." [Dutch *kaketielje,* probably from Portuguese *cacatilha,* diminutive of *cacatua,* COCKATOO.]

cock·a·too (kŏk′ə-to͞o′) *n., pl.* **-toos.** Any of various parrots of the genus *Cacatuinae* and related genera, of Australia and adjacent areas, characterized by a long, erectile crest. [Dutch *kaketoe,* from Malay *kakatua.*]

cock·a·trice (kŏk′ə-trĭs, -trīs′) *n.* A mythical serpent reputed to be hatched from a cock's egg and supposed to have the power of killing by its glance. Compare **basilisk.** [Middle English *cocatrice,* basilisk, crocodile, from Old French *cocatris,* from Medieval Latin *cocātrix,* variant of Late Latin *calcātrix,* "the tracker" (translation of Greek *ikhneumōn,* ICHNEUMON), from *calcāre,* to track, from *calx,* heel.]

cock·boat (kŏk′bōt′) *n.* A small rowing boat kept on a ship. [Middle English *cokbote* : *cok,* cockboat, from Old French *coque, coche,* probably from Late Latin *caudica,* canoe (made from the trunk of a tree), from Latin *caudex,* trunk of a tree + BOAT.]

cock·chaf·er (kŏk′chā′fər) *n.* Any of various Old World beetles of the Scarabaeidae family; especially, *Melolontha melolontha,* the larvae of which often destroy plant roots. Also called "May bug." [COCK (bird) + CHAFER (so called probably from its large size).]

Cock·croft (kŏk′krôft′, -krŏft′) **Sir John Douglas** (1897–1967). British pioneer of atomic physics. He invented, with E.T.S. Walton, the first machine to split the atom (1932). He contributed to the wartime development of the atomic bomb and was director of the Atomic Energy Research Establishment at Harwell (1946–59). He and Walton were awarded the 1951 Nobel Prize for physics.

Cockcroft-Walton accelerator *n.* An early linear particle accelerator consisting of an ion source and a series of cylindrical high-voltage electrodes to accelerate the ions on to a target. It was used in producing the first artificial disintegration of an atomic nucleus. Also called "Cockcroft-Walton generator." [After Sir John Douglas COCKCROFT and Ernest Thomas Sinton WALTON, the inventors.]

cock·crow (kŏk′krō′) *n.* The time of day when the cock crows; early morning; dawn.

cocked hat (kŏkt) *n.* A hat with the brim turned up in two or three places; especially, a three-cornered hat; a tricorn. **—knock into a cocked hat.** *Informal.* To defeat or nullify utterly.

cock·er¹ (kŏk′ər) *n.* **1.** A cocker spaniel. **2.** A person who keeps or trains fighting cocks.

cocker² *tr.v.* **-ered, -ering, -ers.** To pamper, spoil, or coddle. [Middle English *cokerenägger.*]

cock·er·el (kŏk′ər-əl) *n.* A young rooster. [Middle English *cokerelle,* diminutive of COCK.]

cocker spaniel *n.* A dog of a breed originally developed in England, having long, drooping ears and a variously colored silky coat. [Originally used for hunting woodcocks.]

cock-eyed (kŏk′īd′) *adj.* **1.** Cross-eyed. **2.** *Slang.* **a.** Crooked; askew. **b.** Foolish; ridiculous; absurd. **c.** Drunk.

cock·fight (kŏk′fīt′) *n.* A fight between gamecocks that are often fitted with metal spurs. **—cock·fight·ing** *adj. & n.*

cock·horse (kŏk′hôrs′) *n.* A rocking horse.

cockieleekie. Variant of **cock-a-leekie.**

cock·le¹ (kŏk′əl) *n.* **1.** Any of various bivalve mollusks of the family Cardiidae, especially *Cardium edule,* having rounded or heart-shaped shells with radiating ribs. **2.** The shell of any of these mollusks; a cockleshell. **3.** A wrinkle or pucker. **4.** A small and shallow boat. **—the cockles of one's heart.** One's innermost feelings.
~v. **cockled, -ling, -les.** *—tr.* To cause to wrinkle or pucker. *—intr.* To become wrinkled or puckered. [Middle English *cokille,* from Old French *coquille,* shell, from Vulgar Latin *conchīllia* (unattested), variant of Latin *conchȳllium,* from Greek *konkhullion,* diminutive of *konkhē,* mussel, conch.]

cockle² *n.* Any of several plants often growing as weeds in grain fields, especially the corn cockle. [Middle English *cok(k)el,* Old English *coccel,* from Medieval Latin *cocculus* (unattested), diminutive of Latin *coccus,* kermes berry.]

cock·le·bur (kŏk′əl-bûr′) *n.* **1.** Any of several coarse weeds of the genus *Xanthium,* especially *X. spinosum,* bearing prickly burs. **2.** The bur of any of these plants.

cock·le·shell (kŏk′əl-shĕl′) *n.* **1. a.** The shell of a cockle. **b.** A shell similar to that of a cockle. **2.** A small, light boat.

cock·loft (kŏk′lôft′, -lŏft′) *n.* A small loft. [16th century : perhaps COCK (fowl) + LOFT, from its use as a roosting place.]

cock·ney (kŏk′nē) *n., pl.* **-neys. 1.** *Often* **Cockney.** A native of the East End of London or adjacent areas. **2.** The dialect or accent of cockneys.
~adj. Of or like cockneys or their dialect. [Middle English *cokeney,* "cock's egg," pampered brat, effeminate youth, townsman (of London) : *cokene,* genitive plural of *cok,* COCK + *ey,* egg, Old English *ǣg.*]

cock of the north *n.* The **brambling** *(see).*

cock-of-the-rock (kŏk′əv-*thə*-rŏk′) *n., pl.* **cocks-of-the-rock.** Either of two South American birds, *Rupicola rupicola* or *R. peruviana,* having a distinctive crest and bright-orange or reddish plumage in the male. [From its habit of nesting on rocks.]

cock of the walk *n.* **1.** The leader or most important person in a group. **2.** An overbearing or domineering person.

cock·pit (kŏk′pĭt′) *n.* **1.** A pit or enclosed space for cockfights. **2.** A site of many battles. **3. a.** In old warships, a section used as quarters for junior officers and as a station for the wounded during a battle. **b.** In small decked vessels, an area from which the vessel is steered. **4. a.** The space for the pilot, and sometimes passengers, in the fuselage of a small aircraft. **b.** The space set apart for the pilot and crew in a large airliner; the flight deck. **5.** The place where the driver of a racing car sits.

cock·roach (kŏk′rōch′) *n.* Any of various oval, flat-bodied insects of the family Blattidae, several species of which are common household pests. [Earlier *cacarootch,* from Spanish *cucaracha*†.]

cocks·comb (kŏks′kōm′) *n.* Also **cox·comb** (for senses 2, 4). **1.** The comb of a rooster. **2.** The cap of a jester, decorated to resemble this. **3.** Any of several plants of the genus *Celosia*; especially, *C. argentea cristata,* having a showy crested or rolled flower cluster. **4.** A pretentious fop.

cocks·foot (kŏks′fo͝ot′) *n., pl.* **-foots.** A perennial grass, *Dactylis glomerata,* sown as a pasture grass in North America and South Africa. [From its appearance.]

cock·shy (kŏk′shī′) *n., pl.* **-shies.** *British.* **1.** A target aimed at in throwing contests. **2.** The throw itself. **3.** A target for abuse or ridicule. [In the earliest form of this game, the contestants shied or threw sticks at a cock.]

cock·spur (kŏk′spûr′) *n.* **1.** A small, thorny North American tree, *Crataegus crus-galli,* having white flowers and small red fruit. **2.** An annual grass, *Echinochloa crus-galli,* widely distributed in warm temperate and tropical areas. [From the resemblance of its thorn to a cock's spur.]

cock·sure (kŏk′sho͝or′) *adj.* Too sure of oneself or one's opinions; overconfident. [16th century : perhaps from *cock,* euphemistic for GOD + SURE.] **—cock·sure·ly** *adv.* **—cock·sure·ness** *n.*

cock·tail¹ (kŏk′tāl′) *n.* **1.** Any of various mixed alcoholic drinks, often served chilled, consisting usually of a spirit combined with fruit juices or other ingredients, such as bitters or vermouth. **2.** An appetizer typically consisting of seafood or mixed fruits: *a prawn cocktail.* **3.** A mixture of medicinal drugs in drinkable form.
~adj. **1.** Of, pertaining to, or served with cocktails: *cocktail sausages.* **2.** Suitable for wear on semiformal occasions: *a cocktail dress.* [19th-century : apparently from COCKTAIL (horse), but the connection is obscure.]

cocktail² *n.* A horse that has had its tail docked. [Earlier, "docked tail (of horse)," from COCK (fowl) + TAIL.]

cocktail party *n.* A party, usually in the early evening, at which cocktails are served.

cock·up (kŏk′ŭp′) *n.* **1.** *British Slang.* **a.** A blunder. **b.** Something that has been bungled; a mess. **2.** *Archaic.* A hat or cap with upturned front.

cock·y (kŏk′ē) *adj.* **-ier, -iest.** *Informal.* Cheerfully self-assertive or self-confident; conceited. Said especially of or about males. **—cock·i·ly** *adv.*

co·co (kō′kō) *n., pl.* **-cos. 1.** A tree, the **coconut palm** *(see).* **2.** Its fruit, the coconut.
~adj. Made of fibers from the coconut shell: *coco matting.* [Spanish, from Portuguese *coco,* goblin, grimace (referring to the base of the coconut shell, which resembles a face).]

co·coa (kō′kō) *n.* **1.** A powder made from cocoa beans after they have been roasted, ground, and freed of most of their fatty oil. **2.** A

cockchafer *Also known as the May bug, this large beetle can be up to 25 millimeters (1 inch) long.*

cockle *These edible shellfish live under the sand, completely buried except for the tips of the feeding tubes through which they siphon plankton. The tidal zones of some beaches may contain over 1,000 cockles per square meter. Their shells—some still hinged—become visible only when they are washed up on beaches after the animals die.*

cock-of-the-rock *In tropical rain forests, the brightly colored male cock-of-the-rock struts and postures on communal mating grounds known as leks. The females have plain brown plumage.*

beverage made by combining this powder with water or milk and sugar. **3.** Moderate brown to reddish brown. [Variant of CACAO, by confusion with COCO (nut).] —**co·coa** *adj.*

cocoa bean *n.* The seed of the cacao.

cocoa butter *n.* A yellowish-white, waxy solid obtained from cocoa beans and used in the manufacture of pharmaceuticals, confections, and soap. Also called "cacao butter."

coco de mer (kō′kō də mĕr′) *n.* **1.** A Seychelles palm tree, *Lodoicea maldivica,* bearing a large fruit that contains a two-lobed edible nut. **2.** The nut of this palm. [French, "sea coconut."]

co·con·scious (kō′kŏn′shəs) *adj.* Being aware or conscious of the same things.
~*n.* Also **co·con·scious·ness** (ko′kŏn′shəs-nĭs). *Psychiatry.* Mental processes outside the realm of conscious activity or awareness, as with schizophrenic individuals.

co·co·nut, co·coa·nut (kō′kə-nŭt′, -nət) *n.* The fruit of the coconut palm, a large seed with a thick, hard shell that encloses edible white meat and has a milky fluid, *coconut milk,* filling the hollow center.

coconut butter *n.* A solid form of coconut oil used for making soap, candles, and other products.

coconut crab *n.* The **robber crab** (see).

coconut matting *n.* A type of coarse matting made from the outer fibers of the coconut.

coconut oil *n.* The oil obtained from the white flesh of the coconut, used especially in the manufacture of soaps and cosmetics.

coconut palm *n.* A tall palm tree, *Cocos nucifera,* native to the East Indies, bearing coconuts as fruit. Also called "coco," "coco palm," "coconut tree."

coconut shy *n.* *British.* A sideshow at a fair in which balls are thrown at coconuts to knock them off their stands and win a prize.

co·coon (kə-kōōn′) *n.* **1.** A covering of silk or similar fibrous material spun by the larvae of moths and other insects as protection for their pupal stage. **2.** Any similar protective covering or structure, such as that of a spider or earthworm. **3.** A protective plastic coating placed over stored inactive military or naval equipment.
~*v.* **cocooned, -cooning, -coons.** —*tr.* To cover or envelop in, or as if in, a cocoon. —*intr.* To form a cocoon. [French *cocon,* from Provençal *cocoun,* from *coco,* eggshell, hence, cocoon, from Latin *coccum, coccus,* kermes berry, from Greek *kokkos.*]

co·co·pan (kō′kō-păn′) *n.* In South Africa, a small truck on a mine railway. [Possibly from Zulu *nqukumbana,* small cart.]

Co·cos Islands (kō′kəs). Also **Kee·ling Islands** (kē′lĭng). A group of coral island territories of Australia in the eastern Indian Ocean. They were discovered in 1609 and settled from 1826.

co·cotte (kô-kôt′) *n.* **1.** A prostitute or demimondaine. **2.** A small dish used for baking individual portions, especially of egg dishes. [French, originally a baby's word for hen, from *coq,* cock.]

co·co·yam (kō′kō-yăm′) *n.* A tropical plant, the **taro** (see).

Coc·teau (kôk-tō′), **Jean** (1889–1963). French artist, poet, and dramatist. His works, including *Orpheé* (1950) and *La Machine Infernale* (1934), show a fascination with dreams and myths.

Co·cy·tus (kō-kī′təs) *n.* *Greek Mythology.* One of the six rivers of Hades. [Latin, from Greek *Kōkutos,* "river of lamentation," from *kōkuein,* to wail, lament.]

cod¹ (kŏd) *n., pl.* **cods** or collectively **cod.** Any of various marine fishes of the family Gadidae; especially, *Gadus morhua* (or *G. callarias*), an important food fish of Northern Atlantic waters and a source of cod-liver oil. Also called "codfish." [Middle English, perhaps from COD (bag), from its shape.]

cod² *n. British Slang.* Nonsense. [Shortened from CODSWALLOP.]

cod³ *n.* **1.** *Regional.* A husk or pod. **2.** *Obsolete.* A bag. **3.** *Archaic.* The scrotum. [Middle English *cod,* Old English *codd,* bag, husk.]

Cod, Cape (kŏd). A low, sandy peninsula 105 kilometers (65 miles) long in Massachusetts Bay. It encloses Cape Cod Bay, where the Pilgrims first landed in America (1620). Cape Cod is a popular resort area.

COD, C.O.D. **1.** cash on delivery. **2.** collect on delivery.

Cod. codex.

co·da (kō′də) *n.* **1.** *Music.* A passage added on to the end of a movement or composition that brings it to a formal close. **2.** In ballet, the closing part of a pas de deux. [Italian, "tail," from Latin *cōda, cauda.*]

cod·dle (kŏd′l) *tr.v.* **-dled, -dling, -dles.** **1.** To cook in water just below boiling point. **2.** To treat indulgently; pamper. —See Synonyms at **pamper.** [Variant of CAUDLE.] —**cod·dler** *n.*

code (kŏd) *n.* **1. a.** A systematically arranged and comprehensive collection of laws. **b.** Any systematic collection of regulations and rules of procedure or conduct: *the military code.* **2.** A generally accepted set of principles: *a code of conduct.* **3.** A system of signals used to represent letters or numbers in transmitting messages. **4.** A system of symbols, letters, or words given certain arbitrary meanings, used for transmitting messages requiring secrecy or brevity. Compare **cipher. 5.** A system of symbols used to identify something for classification or selection. See **genetic code.**
~*v.* **coded, coding, codes.** —*tr.* **1.** To systematize and arrange (laws and regulations) into a code; codify. **2.** To encode. **3.** To carry the genetic information for (a specific amino acid, for example). —*intr.* To be or carry genetic information. Used with *for.* [Middle English, from Old French, from Latin *cōdex,* CODEX.] —**cod·er** *n.*

co·deine (kō′dēn′, kō′dē-ĭn) *n.* An alkaloid narcotic, $C_{18}H_{21}NO_3$, derived from opium or morphine, used for relieving coughing, as an analgesic, and as a hypnotic. [French *codéine* : Greek *kōdeia,* pop-

coconut palm *This tall Indonesian palm tree bears the hard-shelled seed used for oil, confectionery, and beauty preparations. One tree may produce 50 or more coconuts a year.*

pyhead, from *koos,* hollow place, cavity + -INE.]

Code Na·po·lé·on (kōd′ nä-pô-lā-ôn′) *n.* The code of French civil law, prepared under the direction of Napoleon Bonaparte between 1804 and 1807.

co·dex (kō′dĕks′) *n., pl.* **codices** (kō′də-sēz′, kŏd′ə-). *Abbr.* **Cod.** A manuscript volume, especially of the Scriptures or of a classic work. [Latin *cōdex, caudex,* tree trunk, board, writing tablet, book (of laws).]

Co·dex Ju·ris Ca·non·i·ci (kō′dĕks′ jŏŏr′ĭs kə-nŏn′ə-sī′) *n.* The code of law that has governed the Roman Catholic Church since 1918. [Latin, "book of canon laws."]

cod·fish (kŏd′fĭsh′) *n., pl.* **-fishes** or collectively **codfish.** The **cod** (see).

codg·er (kŏj′ər) *n.* *Informal.* An old man; especially, an eccentric one. Used in the phrase *old codger.* [Perhaps a variant of *cadget.* See **cadge.**]

cod·i·cil (kŏd′ə-sĭl) *n.* **1.** *Law.* A supplement or appendix to a will. **2.** Any supplement or appendix. [Middle English, from Old French *codicille,* from Latin *cōdicillus,* diminutive of *cōdex,* CODEX.] —**cod·i·cil·la·ry** (kŏd′ə-sĭl′ə-rē) *adj.*

cod·i·fy (kŏd′ə-fī′, kō′də-) *tr.v.* **-fied, -fying, -fies.** **1.** To reduce to a code: *codify laws.* **2.** To arrange or systematize. —**cod·i·fi·ca·tion** (kŏd′ə-fĭ-kā′shən) *n.* —**cod·i·fi·er** *n.*

cod·ling¹ (kŏd′lĭng) *n.* Also **cod·lin** (-lĭn). *British.* **1.** A long, tapering apple. **2.** An unripe apple. [Middle English *querdlyng,* from Norman French *quer de lion,* "lion's heart," from its elongated shape.]

codling² *n., pl.* **-lings** or collectively **codling.** A young cod.

codling moth *n.* Also **codlin moth.** A small grayish moth, *Laspreyresia pomonella,* the larvae of which are destructive to various fruits, especially apples.

cod·lins-and-cream (kŏd′lĭnz-ən-krēm′) *n.* A Eurasian plant, *Epilobium hirsutum,* having hairy stems and leaves and purple-red flowers in a stalked spike. [From CODLING (apple).]

cod-liv·er oil (kŏd′lĭv′ər) *n.* An oil obtained from the livers of cod and containing a rich supply of vitamins A and D.

co·do·main (kō′dō-mān′) *n.* *Mathematics.* The **range** (see) of a function.

co·don (kō′dŏn′) *n.* *Genetics.* A sequence of three adjacent nucleotides on a DNA molecule that specifies the insertion of an amino acid in a specific structural position during protein synthesis. [COD(E) + -ON.]

cod·piece (kŏd′pēs′) *n.* A pouch at the crotch of the tight-fitting breeches worn by men in the 15th and 16th centuries. [Middle English : COD (bag, scrotum) + PIECE.]

co-driv·er (kō′drī′vər) *n.* One who takes turns with another to drive a car, especially in a race or rally.

cods·wal·lop (kŏdz′wŏl′əp) *n.* *British Slang.* Nonsense, especially when put forward as a serious statement. [20th century : origin obscure.]

Co·dy (kō′dē), **William Frederick,** known as "Buffalo Bill." (1846–1917). U.S. frontiersman and showman, who from 1883 toured the United States and Europe with his Wild West Show.

co-ed, co·ed (kō′ĕd′) *n.* *Informal.* A woman student attending a co-educational school, college, or university.
~*adj. Informal.* Co-educational. [Short for *co-educational student.*]

co-ed·u·ca·tion (kō′ĕj-ōō-kā′shən) *n.* The system of education in which both male and female pupils or students attend the same institution or classes. —**co-ed·u·ca·tion·al** *adj.*

co-ef·fi·cient (kō′ə-fĭsh′ənt) *n.* **1.** *Mathematics.* **a.** A numerical factor of an elementary algebraic term, such as 4 in the term 4*x.* **b.** The product of all but one of the factors of an expression, the product being regarded as a distinct entity with respect to the excluded factor and to a designated operation. See **correlation coefficient. 2.** A numerical measure of a physical or chemical property that is constant for a system under specified conditions. [New Latin *coefficiens* : CO- (together) + EFFICIENT.]

coefficient of self-induction *n.* **Self-inductance** (see).

coel- *prefix.* Indicates a cavity within a body or bodily organ; for example, **coelenterate.** [New Latin, from Greek *koilos,* hollow.]

-coel, -coele. Variants of **-cele** (hollow chamber).

coe·la·canth (sē′lə-kănth′) *n.* Any of various fishes of the order Coelacanthiformes, known only in fossil form until a living species, *Latimeria chalumnae,* of African marine waters, was identified in 1938. [New Latin *coelacanthus,* "hollow-spined" : COEL- + Greek *akanthos,* spine, thorn, from *akantha,* thorny plant.] —**coe·la·can·thine** (sē′lə-kăn′thĭn′, -thĭn) *adj.* —**coe·la·can·thous** (sē′lə-kăn′thəs) *adj.*

coe·len·ter·ate (sĭ-lĕn′tə-rāt′, -rĭt) *n.* Any invertebrate animal of the phylum Coelenterata, characterized by a radially symmetrical body with a saclike internal cavity, and including the jellyfishes, hydras, sea anemones, and corals. See **cnidarian, ctenophore.**
~*adj.* Of or belonging to the Coelenterata. [New Latin *coelenterata,* "hollow-intestined ones" : COEL- + ENTER(ON) + -ATE.] —**coe·len·ter·ic** (sĭ-lĕn′tĕr′ĭk) *adj.*

coe·len·ter·on (sĭ-lĕn′tə-rŏn′, -rən) *n., pl.* **-tera** (-tər-ə). *Zoology.* The saclike body cavity of a coelenterate. [New Latin : COEL- + ENTERON.]

coeliac. Variant of **celiac.**

coe·lom, ce·lom (sē′ləm) *n., pl.* **-loms** or **-lomata** (sĭ-lō′mə-tə). The body cavity in all animals higher than the coelenterates and certain primitive worms, formed by the splitting of the mesoderm into two layers. [German *Koelom,* from Greek *koilōma,* cavity, from *koilos,* hollow.]

coe·lo·stat (sē′lə-stăt′) *n. Astronomy.* A movable mirror that rotates slowly so as to compensate for the earth's rotation, used to direct light from a fixed region of the sky into a telescope or other optical instrument. [COEL- + -STAT.]

coeno–, ceno– *prefix.* Also **coen–, cen–.** Indicates common; for example, **coenurus.** [New Latin, from Greek *koino-,* from *koinos,* common.]

coenobite. Variant of **cenobite.**

coen·o·bi·um (sē-nō′bē-əm) *n. Botany.* A colony of motile cells formed by certain green algae. [New Latin, from Greek *koinobion,* convent : *koinos,* common + *bios,* life.]

coe·no·cyte (sē′nə-sīt′) *n. Botany.* An organism consisting of a multinucleate protoplasmic mass resulting from nuclear division without the formation of a new cell wall or membrane, as in slime molds and certain fungi and algae. [COENO- + -CYTE.] —**coe·no·cyt·ic** (sē′nə-sīt′ĭk) *adj.*

coenogenesis. Variant of **cenogenesis.**

coe·no·sarc (sē′nə-särk) *n.* The system of tissues connecting the polyps of compound zoophytes such as corals. [COENO- + Greek *sarx* (stem *sark-*), flesh.]

coe·nu·rus (sĭ-nyŏŏr′əs) *n., pl.* **-nuri** (-nyŏŏr′ī′). The encysted larval stage of a tapeworm, *Taenia multiceps* (or *Multiceps multiceps*), that attacks the central nervous system of ruminant animals. [New Latin, "having a common tail" (because it has many heads and only one tail) : COEN(O)- + -UR(O)US.]

co·en·zyme (kō-ĕn′zīm′) *n.* A heat-stable organic molecule that must be loosely associated with certain enzymes for them to function.

co·e·qual (kō-ē′kwəl) *adj.* Equal with one another, as in rank or size. —*n.* An equal. —**co·e·qual·i·ty** (kō′ē-kwŏl′ə-tē) *n.* —**co·e·qual·ly** *adv.*

co·erce (kō-ûrs′) *tr.v.* **-erced, -ercing, -erces. 1.** To force to act or think in a given manner; compel: *The suspect was coerced into confessing.* **2.** To dominate, restrain, or control forcibly. **3.** To achieve by means of force; enforce: *coerce an agreement.* —See Synonyms at **force.** [Middle English *cohercen,* from Old French *cohercier,* from Latin *coercēre,* to constrain : *cō-,* together + *arcēre,* to restrain, confine.] —**co·erc·er** *n.* —**co·er·ci·ble** *adj.*

co·er·cion (kō-ûr′shən) *n.* **1.** The act or practice of coercing. **2.** A government or power that coerces. —**co·er·cion·ar·y** (kō-ûr′shə-nĕr′ē) *adj.*

co·er·cive (kō-ûr′sĭv) *adj.* Characterized by or inclined to coercion. —**co·er·cive·ly** *adv.* —**co·er·cive·ness** *n.*

coercive force *n. Physics.* The external magnetic field strength required to demagnetize a given sample.

co·er·civ·i·ty (kō′ər-sĭv′ə-tē) *n. Physics.* The external magnetic field strength required to demagnetize a given sample that has been magnetized to saturation.

co·es·sen·tial (kō′ĭ-sĕn′shəl) *adj. Theology.* Having the same nature or essence. —**co·es·sen·ti·al·i·ty** (kō′ĭ-sĕn′shē-ăl′ə-tē), **co·es·sen·tial·ness** *n.* —**co·es·sen·tial·ly** *adv.*

co·e·ta·ne·ous (kō′ĭ-tā′nē-əs) *adj.* Of equal age, duration, or period; contemporary. [Latin *coaetāneus* : *co-,* same + *aetās,* age.] —**co·e·ta·ne·ous·ly** *adv.* —**co·e·ta·ne·ous·ness** *n.*

co·e·ter·nal (kō′ĭ-tûr′nəl) *adj.* Equally eternal; eternally existing with one another. —**co·e·ter·nal·ly** *adv.* —**co·e·ter·ni·ty** (kō′ĭ-tûr′nĭ-tē) *n.*

Coeur de Lion. See **Richard I.**

co·e·val (kō-ē′vəl) *adj.* Originating or existing during the same period of time; lasting through the same era. [Latin *coaevus* : *cō-,* same + *aevum,* age.] —**co·e·val** *n.* —**co·e·val·ly** *adv.*

co·ex·ist (kō′ĭg-zĭst′) *intr.v.* **-isted, -isting, -ists. 1.** To exist together, at the same time or in the same place. **2.** To exist together in peace.

co·ex·is·tence (kō′ĭg-zĭs′təns) *n.* **1.** The condition of existing together: *"excitement in coexistence with an overbalance of pleasure"* (Wordsworth). **2.** The concurrent but separate existence of two or more nations of great ideological disparity. —**co·ex·is·tent** *adj.*

co·ex·ten·sive (kō′ĭk-stĕn′sĭv) *adj.* Extending over the same space or time; having the same scope. —**co·ex·ten·sive·ly** *adv.*

co·fac·tor (kō′făk′tər) *n.* **1.** *Mathematics.* A determinant associated with a given element of a matrix, formed by removing the row and column containing this element. **2.** *Biochemistry.* A nonprotein portion of certain enzymes, essential for their activity, such as a coenzyme or a metal ion, such as of sodium or potassium.

C. of C. chamber of commerce.

C. of E. Church of England.

cof·fee (kô′fē, kŏf′ē) *n.* **1.** Any of several trees of the genus *Coffea,* native to eastern Asia and Africa, bearing berries containing beans used in the preparation of a beverage; especially, *C. arabica,* the chief commercial source of these beans. **2. a.** The seeds or beans of the coffee tree. **b.** Such beans roasted and ground. **3. a.** An aromatic, mildly stimulating beverage prepared from ground coffee beans. **b.** A cup of coffee. **4.** Moderate to dark yellowish brown. —*adj.* **1.** Of, pertaining to, or accompanied by the drink coffee: *a coffee hour.* **2.** Having the color coffee. [Italian *caffè,* from Turkish *kahve,* from Arabic *qahwah.*]

coffee cake *n.* A sweet cake to be eaten with coffee, often containing nuts or raisins and topped with icing.

coffee cup *n.* A usually small cup from which coffee is drunk.

coffee house, cof·fee·house (kô′fē-hous′, kŏf′ē-) *n.* An establishment serving coffee and other refreshments, popular especially in the 17th and 18th centuries as a rendezvous for fashionable people.

coffee mill *n.* A device for grinding roasted coffee beans.

cof·fee·pot (kô′fē-pŏt′, kŏf′ē-) *n.* A pot for making or serving coffee.

coffee shop *n.* A small restaurant in which light meals are served.

coffee table *n.* A long, low table, often placed before a sofa.

coffee tree *n.* **1.** Any tree of the genus *Coffea,* producing coffee beans. **2.** The **Kentucky coffee tree** *(see).*

cof·fer (kô′fər, kŏf′ər) *n.* **1. a.** A chest. **b.** A strongbox. **2. coffers.** Funds; a treasury. **3.** A decorative sunken panel in a soffit, ceiling, dome, or vault. **4.** A cofferdam. —*tr.v.* **coffered, -fering, -fers. 1.** To supply with decorative sunken panels. **2.** To put in a coffer. [Middle English *cof(f)re,* box, chest, from Old French, from Latin *cophinus,* basket. See **coffin.**]

cof·fer·dam (kô′fər-dăm′, kŏf′ər-) *n. Engineering.* **1.** A temporary watertight enclosure built in the water and pumped dry to expose the bottom so that construction, as of piers, may be undertaken. **2.** A watertight chamber attached to a ship's side to facilitate repairs below the water line.

cof·fin (kô′fən, kŏf′ən) *n.* **1.** An oblong box in which a corpse is buried or cremated. **2.** A horse's hoof. **3.** A thick, usually lead, container for transporting radioactive materials. —*tr.v.* **coffined, -fining, -fins.** To place in or as if in a coffin. [Middle English, box, basket, from Old French *cofin,* from Latin *cophinus,* from Greek *kophinus†,* basket, measure of capacity.]

coffin bone *n.* The bone inside the hoof of a horse or similar animal.

cof·fle (kô′fəl, kŏf′əl) *n.* A file of animals, prisoners, or slaves, chained together in transit. [Arabic *qāfilah,* caravan.]

C. of S. chief of staff.

cog[1] (kŏg) *n.* **1.** Any of a series of teeth on the rim of a wheel which by engagement transmit motive force to a corresponding wheel or toothed rack. **2.** A cogwheel. **3.** A subordinate member within a given organization. —*tr.v.* **cogged, cogging, cogs.** To roll (steel ingots) to convert into blooms. [Middle English *cogge,* probably from Scandinavian, akin to Swedish *kugge.*]

cog[2] *v.* **cogged, cogging, cogs.** *Archaic Slang.* —*tr.* To load or manipulate (dice) fraudulently. —*intr.* To cheat, especially at dice. [16th century : origin obscure.]

cog[3] *n.* A tenon projecting from a wooden beam and fitting into an opening in another beam to form a joint. —*tr.v.* **cogged, cogging, cogs.** To join with such tenons. [19th century : origin obscure.]

cog. cognate.

co·gent (kō′jənt) *adj.* **1.** Forcibly convincing. **2.** Compelling; powerful. [Latin *cōgens* (stem *cogent-*), present participle of *cōgere,* to force, drive together : *cō-,* together + *agere,* to drive.] —**co·gen·cy** (kō′jən-sē) *n.* —**co·gent·ly** *adv.*

cog·i·tate (kŏj′ə-tāt′) *v.* **-tated, -tating, -tates.** —*intr.* To take long and careful thought; meditate; ponder. —*tr.* To think carefully about; consider intently. [Latin *cōgitāre* : *cō-* (intensive) + *agitāre,* to turn in mind, consider, AGITATE.] —**cog·i·ta·ble** (kŏj′ə-tə-bəl) *adj.* —**cog·i·ta·tor** *n.*

cog·i·ta·tion (kŏj′ə-tā′shən) *n.* **1.** Thoughtful consideration; meditation. **2.** A serious thought; a reflection.

cog·i·ta·tive (kŏj′ə-tā′tĭv) *adj.* Meditative. —**cog·i·ta·tive·ly** *adv.* —**cog·i·ta·tive·ness** *n.*

cog·i·to (kŏg′ĭ-tō) *n. Philosophy.* The principle that establishes a person's existence from the fact of his thinking and awareness. [Latin, "I think" (abstracted from Descartes' phrase, *cogito, ergo sum,* "I think, therefore I am").]

co·gnac (kōn′yăk′, kŏn′-, kŏn′-) *n.* A brandy produced in the vicinity of Cognac in western France.

Co·gnac (kōn′yăk′, kŏn′-). Town in the Charente department of western France, on the Charente River. Only brandy produced in a limited area around the town can be called cognac.

cog·nate (kŏg′nāt′) *adj. Abbr.* **cog. 1.** Related by blood; having a common ancestor, especially a maternal one. **2.** *Linguistics.* Akin. Said especially of languages or of words in different languages derived from the same root. **3.** Related or analogous in nature, character, or function. —*n. Abbr.* **cog.** A person or thing cognate with another. [Latin *cōgnātus* : *cō-,* same + *gnātus,* born, from *gnāscī, nāscī,* to be born.] —**cog·na·tion** (kŏg-nā′shən) *n.*

cog·ni·tion (kŏg-nĭsh′ən) *n.* **1.** The mental process or faculty by which knowledge is acquired. **2.** That which comes to be known, as through perception, reasoning, or intuition; knowledge. [Middle English *cognicioun,* from Latin *cognitiō* (stem *cognition-*), from *cognōscere,* to get to know, learn : *cō-* (intensive) + *gnōscere,* to know.] —**cog·ni·tion·al** *adj.*

cog·ni·tive (kŏg′nə-tĭv) *adj.* Of, pertaining to, or constituting cognition: *cognitive processes such as perception and comparison.*

cog·ni·za·ble (kŏg′nə-zə-bəl, kŏg-nī′-) *adj.* **1.** Knowable or perceptible. **2.** Within a court's jurisdiction. —**cog·ni·za·bly** *adv.*

cog·ni·zance (kŏg′nə-zəns) *n.* **1.** Conscious knowledge or awareness. **2.** The range of what one can know or understand. **3.** *Law.* **a.** The examination of a case by a court. **b.** The right or power of a court's jurisdiction. **4.** *Heraldry.* A crest or badge worn to distinguish the bearer. —**take cognizance of.** To take notice of; acknowledge. [Middle English *co(g)nisaunce,* from Old French *conoissance,* from *conoistre,* to know, from Latin *cognōscere,* to learn. See **cognition.**]

coffee *The coffee tree* Coffea arabica *yields the seeds (above) used to make coffee. A native of Asia and Africa, the tree was introduced into Brazil in 1727 and that country is now the world's leading coffee producer.*

cog·ni·zant (kŏg′nə-zənt) *adj.* **1.** Fully informed; conscious. Used with *of*. **2.** *Philosophy.* Having cognition. [From COGNIZANCE.]

cog·nize (kŏg-nīz′, kŏg′nīz′) —*tr.v.* **-nized, -nizing, -nizes.** *Philosophy.* To have cognition of. [Back-formation from COGNIZANCE, by analogy with *recognize,* and so on.]

cog·no·men (kŏg-nō′mən) *n., pl.* **-mens** or **-nomina** (-nŏm′ə-nə). **1.** A family name; a surname. **2.** The third and usually last name of a citizen of ancient Rome, such as *Caesar* in *Caius Julius Caesar.* Compare **nomen, praenomen. 3.** Any name, especially a descriptive nickname. [Latin *cōgnōmen,* "additional name" (formed after *cognōscere,* to learn) : *cō-,* together + *nōmen,* name.] —**cog·nom·i·nal** (kŏg-nŏm′ə-nəl) *adj.*

co·gno·scen·te (kŏn′yō-shĕn′tē) *n., pl.* **-ti** (-tē). A person of expert knowledge or superior taste; a connoisseur. [Obsolete Italian, "the knowing one," from Latin *cognōscēns* (stem *cognōscent-*), present participle of *cognōscere,* to get to know. See **cognition.**]

cog·no·vit (kŏg-nō′vĭt) *n. Law.* A written admission by a defendant of his liability, made to avoid the expense of a trial. [Latin, "he has acknowledged," from *cognōscere,* to get to know, recognize, acknowledge. See **cognition.**]

cog railway *n.* A railway designed to operate on steep slopes, having locomotives with a center cogwheel that engages with a cogged center rail to provide traction. Also called "rack railway."

cog·wheel (kŏg′hwēl′) *n.* Any of a set of cogged wheels within a given mechanism.

co·hab·it (kō-hăb′ĭt) *intr.v.* **-ited, -iting, -its.** To live together in a sexual relationship when not legally married. Used with *with.* [Late Latin *cohabitāre* : *cō-,* together + *habitāre,* to inhabit.] —**co·hab·it·ant, co·hab·it·ee** *n.* —**co·hab·i·ta·tion** *n.*

Co·han (kō′hăn′), **George Michael** (1878–1942). U.S. singer, songwriter, and playwright. Perhaps best remembered for his patriotic hits "Over There" (1917) and "You're a Grand Old Flag" (1906), he also wrote many successful musical comedies, including *The Yankee Prince* (1909), *Broadway Jones* (1912), and *American Born* (1925).

co·here (kō-hîr′) —*intr.v.* **-hered, -hering, -heres.** **1.** To stick or hold together. **2.** To be logically or contextually connected or consistent. [Latin *cohaerēre* : *cō-,* together + *haerēre,* to cling to.]

co·her·ence (kō-hîr′əns, -hĕr′-) *n.* Also **co·her·en·cy** (-ən-sē). The quality or state of logical or orderly relationship of parts; consistency; logical or contextual congruity.

Usage: Standard English makes a clear distinction between *coherence* and *cohesion. Coherence* refers to the logical or orderly relationship of parts, especially in speech or writing. *Cohesion* refers to the literal sticking together of objects or substances, or figuratively to a close connection established between people.

co·her·ent (kō-hîr′ənt, kō-hĕr′-) *adj.* **1.** Sticking together; cohering. **2.** Marked by an orderly or logical relation of parts that allows comprehension or recognition: *coherent speech.* **3.** *Physics.* Of or pertaining to waves with a continuous relationship among phases. **4.** Designating or pertaining to a system of units of measurement in which a small number of basic units are defined from which all others in the system are derived by multiplication or division only. —**co·her·ent·ly** *adv.*

co·he·sion (kō-hē′zhən) *n.* **1.** The process or condition of cohering; a becoming or remaining united, especially in a tangible or explicit way. **2.** *Physics.* The mutual attraction by which the elements of a body are held together. Compare **adhesion. 3.** *Botany.* The congenital joining of two parts, such as flower petals. —See Usage note at **coherence.** [Latin *cohaesus,* past participle of *cohaerēre,* COHERE.]

co·he·sive (kō-hē′sĭv, -zĭv) *adj.* Showing or producing cohesion or unity. —**co·he·sive·ly** *adv.* —**co·he·sive·ness** *n.*

co·hort (kō′hôrt′) *n.* **1.** Any of the ten divisions of a Roman legion, consisting of 300 to 600 men. **2.** A group or band united in some struggle. **3.** *Informal.* An associate. [Middle English, from Old French *cohorte,* from Latin *cohors* (stem *cohort-*), enclosed yard, company of soldiers, multitude.]

co·ho salmon (kō′hō) *n.* A food and game fish, *Oncorhyncus kisutch,* native to the North Pacific coasts and introduced in the Great Lakes. Also called "silver salmon." [*Coho,* probably from an American Indian language.]

co·hune (kō-hōōn′) *n.* A tropical American palm tree, *Attalea cohune,* having long featherlike leaves and oily nuts. Also called "cohune palm." [American Spanish, from Mosquito *ókhun.*]

coif (koif) *n.* **1.** A tight-fitting cap worn under a veil, as by nuns. **2. a.** A white skullcap formerly worn by English lawyers and sergeants at law. **b.** The office or rank of sergeant at law. —*tr.v.* (koif; *also* kwôf *for sense 2*) **coifed, coifing, coifs. 1.** To cover with or as if with a coif. **2.** To arrange or dress (the hair, especially of women). [Middle English *coyfe,* from Old French *coiffe, coife,* from Late Latin *cofia†.*]

coif·feur (kwä-fœr′) *n. Feminine* **coif·feuse** (kwä-fœz′). A hairdresser. [French, from COIF.]

coif·fure (kwä-fyōōr′) *n.* A way of arranging the hair; a woman's hairstyle. —*tr.v.* **coiffured, -furing, -fures.** To arrange or dress (women's hair). [French, from *coiffer,* to COIF.]

coign (koin) *n.* A projecting corner, a **quoin** *(see).* [Variant of COIN (quoin).]

coil (koil) *n.* **1.** A series of connected spirals or concentric rings formed by gathering or winding: *a coil of rope.* **2.** An individual spiral or ring within such a series. **3.** A spiral pipe or series of spiral pipes, as in a radiator. **4.** *Electricity.* **a.** A wound spiral of two or more turns of insulated wire, used to introduce inductance into a

circuit or to provide a magnetic field. **b.** Any device of which such a spiral is the major component. **5.** An **intrauterine device** *(see)* shaped like a coil. **6.** A transformer in a gasoline engine that supplies the high voltage to the spark plugs through the distributor. ~*v.* **coiled, coiling, coils.** —*tr.* **1.** To wind in loops, spirals, or concentric rings. **2.** To wind into a shape resembling a coil. —*intr.* **1.** To form coils. **2.** To move in a spiral course. **3.** To move in a sinuous way. [Middle English *coilen,* to collect, cull, from Old French *coillir,* from Latin *colligere* : *com-,* together + *legere,* to gather.] —**coil·er** *n.*

coil spring *n.* A spring formed from a helical coil of wire.

Co·im·bra (kō-ĭm′brə). City in central Portugal, situated on the Mondego River. It has the oldest university in the country and a fine Romanesque cathedral.

coin (koin) *n.* **1.** A small piece of metal, usually flat and circular, authorized by a government for use as money. **2.** Metal money collectively. **3.** *Architecture.* A corner or cornerstone. ~*tr.v.* **coined, coining, coins. 1. a.** To make (coins) from metal; mint; strike: *coin silver dollars.* **b.** To make coins from (metal): *coin gold.* **2.** To invent (a word or phrase). [Middle English *coyne,* wedge, design stamped on a coiner's die, coin, from Old French *coing, coin,* wedge, from Latin *cuneus†,* wedge.] —**coin·a·ble** *adj.* —**coin·er** *n.*

coin·age (koi′nĭj) *n.* **1.** The act or process of making coins. **2. a.** Metal currency. **b.** A system of metal currency. **3. a.** A coined word or phrase. **b.** The invention of new words.

co·in·cide (kō′ĭn-sīd′) *intr.v.* **-cided, -ciding, -cides. 1. a.** To occupy the same position simultaneously. **b.** To have identical dimensions. **2.** To happen at the same time or during the same period. **3.** To correspond exactly; be identical. **4.** To concur; agree. —See Synonyms at **agree.** [Medieval Latin *coincidere* : *cō-,* together + *incidere,* to happen.]

co·in·ci·dence (kō-ĭn′sə-dəns, -dĕns′) *n.* **1.** The state or fact of coinciding. **2.** An accidental sequence of events that appear to have a causal relationship. —**co·in·ci·dent** *adj.*

coincidence gate *n. Electronics.* A circuit or device that produces an output only when both its input terminals receive pulses within a specific short interval; a **gate** *(see).*

co·in·ci·den·tal (kō-ĭn′sə-dĕn′təl) *adj.* Occurring as or resulting from coincidence. —**co·in·ci·den·tal·ly** *adv.*

coin-op (koin′ŏp′) *n.* A self-service laundry in which the machines are operated by the insertion of coins. Also called "coin-op laundry."

co·in·sur·ance (kō′ĭn-shōōr′əns) *n.* **1.** Insurance held jointly with another or others. **2.** A form of insurance in which a person insures property for less than its full value and agrees to be responsible for the difference. —**co·in·sure** *v.* —**co·in·sur·er** *n.*

Coin·treau (kwän-trō′) *n.* A trademark for a colorless liqueur made from brandy and oranges.

coir (koir) *n.* The fiber obtained from the husk of a coconut, used in making rope and matting. [Malayalam *kāyar,* cord.]

co·i·tus (kō′ə-təs) *n.* Also **co·i·tion** (kō-ĭsh′ən). Sexual intercourse. [Latin *coitus,* "meeting," from *coīre,* to come together : *cō-,* together + *īre,* to go.] —**co·i·tal** *adj.*

coitus in·ter·rup·tus (kō′ə-təs ĭn′tə-rŭp′təs) *n.* Sexual intercourse deliberately interrupted by withdrawal of the penis prior to ejaculation. [Latin, "interrupted intercourse."]

coke[1] (kōk) *n.* **1.** The solid carbonaceous residue obtained from coal after removal of volatile material by destructive distillation, used as fuel. **2.** A similar material formed in different ways; especially, the layer of carbon formed within an engine as a result of incomplete combustion of the fuel. ~*v.* **coked, coking, cokes.** —*tr.* To convert or change into coke. —*intr.* To become coke. [Middle English *coke†.*]

coke[2] *n. Slang.* Cocaine.

Coke *n.* A trademark for Coca-Cola, a soft drink.

Coke (kōōk, kōk), **Sir Edward** (1552–1634). English jurist. As the chief justice of the court of common pleas (1606–16) he ruled that the common law was the supreme law, even when the Crown disagreed. His bill of liberties (1628), which became the Petition of Right, melded ancient English legal precedents into a charter that limited the royal prerogative.

col (kŏl) *n.* **1.** A pass between two peaks or a gap in a ridge. **2.** *Meteorology.* A region of intermediate pressure between two anticyclones and two depressions. [French, from Old French, neck, from Latin *collum.*]

col. **1.** collect; collected; collector. **2.** college; collegiate. **3.** colonial; colony. **4.** color. **5.** column.

Col. **1.** Colombia. **2.** colonel. **3.** Colossians (New Testament).

col–[1]. Variant of **com–.** Used before *l.*

col–[2]. Variant of **colo–.**

co·la[1], **ko·la** (kō′lə) *n.* **1.** Either of two African trees, *Cola nitida* or *C. acuminata,* cultivated in the tropics for their seeds. See **cola nut. 2.** A soft carbonated drink flavored with an extract from cola nuts. [Probably a variant of Mandingo *kolo,* nut.]

co·la[2]. Alternative plural of **colon.**

col·an·der (kŭl′ən-dər, kŏl′-) *n.* A bowl-shaped kitchen utensil with a perforated bottom for draining off liquids and rinsing food. [Middle English *colyndore, culatre,* from Old Provençal *colador* (unattested), from Vulgar Latin *cōlātor* (unattested), from Latin *cōlāre,* to strain, from *cōlum,* sieve, filter.]

cola nut, kola nut *n.* The seed of the cola tree, containing caffeine and theobromine and yielding an extract used in carbonated drinks and in pharmaceutical products.

co·lat·i·tude (kō′lăt′ĭ-tōōd′, -tyōōd′) *n.* *Astronomy.* The complement of the celestial latitude; (90°-β), where β is the celestial latitude.

Col·bert (kôl-bâr′, kōl′-), **Claudette,** born Lily Claudette Chauchoin (1905-). French film actress, later a U.S. citizen. She made her name with vivacious performances in comedies such as *It Happened One Night* (1934).

Colbert, Jean-Baptiste (1619-83). French statesman and leading adviser to Louis XIV. To encourage trade, he reformed taxes, centralized the administration, and improved road and canal networks. He also developed the French navy and codified laws.

col·can·non (kŏl-kăn′ən) *n.* An Irish dish of mashed potatoes and cabbage. [Irish Gaelic *cal ceannan,* "white-headed cabbage" : *cal,* cabbage, from Old Irish, from Latin *caulis* + *ceannan,* whiteheaded, from *ceann,* head.]

Col·ches·ter (kōl′chĭs-tər). Town in Essex in southeast England, on the Colne River. Parts of the old Roman town, called Camulodunum, have been excavated, and relics are displayed in a fine Norman castle.

col·chi·cine (kŏl′chə-sēn′, kŏl′kə-) *n.* A poisonous alkaloid, $C_{22}H_{25}NO_6$, used experimentally to induce chromosome doubling and medicinally to treat gout. [German *Kolchizin,* from New Latin *colchicum,* COLCHICUM.]

col·chi·cum (kŏl′chĭ-kəm, kŏl′kĭ-) *n.* **1.** Any of various bulbous plants of the genus *Colchicum,* such as the **autumn crocus** *(see).* **2.** The dried seeds or corms of the autumn crocus, a source of colchicine. [New Latin, from Latin, a poisonous root, from Greek *Kolkhikon,* from *Kolkhikos,* of Colchis, belonging to the witch Medea of Colchis, from *Kolkhis,* Colchis, ancient region on the Black Sea.]

col·co·thar (kŏl′kə-thər, -thär′) *n.* A brownish-red iron oxide obtained as a residue after heating ferrous sulfate, used in glass polishing and as a pigment. [French *colcotar,* from Spanish, from Arabic *qolqoṭār.*]

cold (kōld) *adj.* **colder, coldest. 1. a.** Having a low or lower than usual temperature. **b.** Lacking heat: *the cold light of the moon.* **2.** Feeling no warmth; uncomfortably chilled. **3.** Designating a color or tone that suggests little warmth, such as pale gray. **4.** Served without heating after being processed or cooked: *cold cereal; cold chicken.* **5.** *Informal.* **a.** Unconscious; insensible: *knocked cold.* **b.** Dead. **6.** Not affected by emotion; objective: *cold logic.* **7.** Without appeal to the senses or feelings; depressing: *cold decor.* **8.** Not affectionate or friendly: *a cold reception.* **9.** Without sexual desire; frigid. **10.** Unenthusiastic; apathetic: *The prospect left him cold.* **11.** Without freshness; faint; weak. Said of a scent in hunting. **12.** *Informal.* In guessing and searching games, far removed from the object sought. *~adv. Informal.* **1.** Completely; thoroughly: *turned our offer down cold.* **2.** Without preparation or rehearsal. *~n.* **1.** The relative lack of warmth. **2.** The sensation resulting from lack of warmth. **3.** A viral infection characterized by inflammation of the mucous membranes of the respiratory passages and accompanying fever, chills, coughing, and sneezing. **4.** A condition of low air temperature; cold weather. **—out in the cold.** Neglected; ignored. [Middle English *cold, cald,* Old English *ceald,* from Germanic.] **—cold′ly** *adv.* **—cold′ness** *n.*

cold-blood·ed (kōld′blŭd′ĭd) *adj.* **1.** Ruthless; unfeeling; heartless. **2.** *Zoology.* Having a body temperature that varies with the external environment; poikilothermic. **3.** *Informal.* Likely to feel the cold. **—cold′-blood′ed·ly** *adv.* **—cold′-blood′ed·ness** *n.*

cold cathode *n.* An electrode from which electrons are emitted at ambient temperatures as a result of a high surface potential gradient.

cold chisel *n.* A chisel made of hardened, tempered steel and used for cutting cold metal.

cold comfort *n.* Something that gives little consolation or cheer.

cold cream *n.* An emulsion for cleansing and softening the skin.

cold cuts *pl.n.* Slices of assorted cold meats.

cold desert *n.* **1.** A polar area with no vegetation. **2.** A tundra. **3.** A high plateau in a continental interior, cut off from moist maritime influences.

cold-drawn (kōld′drôn′) *adj.* Designating a metal wire, bar, or the like that has been pulled through a die without heating to reduce its thickness or change its toughness or appearance.

cold duck *n.* An alcoholic drink combining champagne and burgundy. [Translation of German *Kalte Ente,* a drink made from a mixture of wines.]

cold feet *n. Informal.* Failure of nerve.

cold frame *n.* A structure consisting of a frame with a glass top, used for protecting young plants from the cold.

cold front *n.* The leading portion of a cold atmospheric air mass moving into the base of and eventually replacing a warm air mass.

cold-heart·ed (kōld′här′tĭd) *adj.* Unkind; stern.

cold light *n.* **1.** Light producing little or no heat. **2.** Light emitted by a process other than incandescence.

cold pack *n.* **1.** *Medicine.* A therapeutic pack consisting of a cold, damp sheet, used to lower body temperature. **2.** A canning process in which uncooked food is packed in cans, then sterilized by heat.

cold rubber *n.* A durable, strong, synthetic rubber polymerized at low temperatures.

cold shoulder *n. Informal.* Deliberately unkind or unfriendly treatment; a snub. Preceded by *the.*

cold-shoul·der (kōld′shōl′dər) *tr.v.* **-dered, -dering, -ders.** *Informal.* To give (someone) the cold shoulder; slight; snub.

cold snap *n.* A sudden, brief spell of cold weather.

cold sore *n.* A small sore on the lips that often accompanies a fever or cold and is caused by a viral infection; a fever blister. Also called "fever blister," "herpes simplex."

cold storage *n.* **1.** The protective storage of foods, furs, or the like in a refrigerated place. **2.** *Informal.* A state of temporary suspension.

Cold·stream (kōld′strēm′). Town in Borders Region in southeast Scotland, on the Tweed River. The regiment of Coldstream Guards, for which it is famous, was first formed here in 1660.

cold sweat *n.* A reaction to extreme nervousness, characterized by a cold, moist skin.

cold turkey *n. Informal.* Immediate, complete withdrawal from something on which one has become dependent, such as an addictive drug. [Originally, a blunt statement, with reference to a plain ungarnished dish of cold meat; hence, a "blunt" withdrawal from drugs.]

cold type *n.* Typesetting, such as photocomposition, done without the casting of metal.

cold war *n.* **1.** A state of political tension and rivalry between nations, stopping short of actual full-scale war. **2. Cold War.** The state of such rivalry beginning between the Soviet and Western blocs following World War II and ending in 1990. **—cold warrior** *n.*

cold wave *n.* **1.** An abrupt onset of unusually cold weather brought by a cold air mass following a depression. **2.** A form of permanent wave in which the hair is set by chemicals rather than heat. See **perm.**

cold-weld (kōld′wĕld′) *tr.v.* **-welded, -welding, -welds.** To join (two metals) together without heat by forcing their surfaces together under pressure.

cold-work (kōld′wûrk′) *tr.v.* **-worked, -working, -works.** To shape or form (metal) in the absence of heat.

cole (kōl) *n. Rare.* Any of various plants of the genus *Brassica,* such as the cabbage or rape. Also called "colewort." [Middle English *col, coole,* Old English *cāl, cāul,* from Latin *caulis,* plant stalk, cabbage.]

Cole (kōl), **Nat "King"** (1919-65). U.S. singer and pianist. In 1937 he formed the King Cole Trio, which drew enthusiastic crowds on the jazz circuit. In 1943 he began recording a string of hits, including "Nature Boy, "The Christmas Song," and "Mona Lisa," making him one of the most popular recording artists of the 1940's and 1950's.

Cole, Thomas (1801-48). U.S. painter, born in England. The acknowledged leader of the Hudson River School, America's first native painting movement, he traveled the country capturing nature on canvas. Later he created religious and symbolic works, including *Course of Empire* (1835-36) and *The Voyage of Life* (1839).

co·lec·to·my (kə-lĕk′tə-mē) *n., pl.* **-mies.** Surgical removal of part or all of the colon. [COL(O)- + -ECTOMY.]

cole·man·ite (kōl′mə-nīt′) *n.* A natural white or colorless hydrated calcium borate, $Ca_2B_6O_{11} \cdot 5H_2O$, a principal source of borax. [After William T. *Coleman* (1824-93), U.S. pioneer, owner of the mine where it was discovered.]

co·le·op·ter·an (kō′lē-ŏp′tər-ən, kŏl′ē-) *n.* Also **co·le·op·ter·on** (-tə-rŏn′). Any insect of the order Coleoptera, characterized by forewings modified to form tough protective covers for the hind wings, and including the beetles. *~adj.* Also **co·le·op·ter·ous** (-tər-əs) Of or belonging to the Coleoptera. [New Latin *Coleoptera,* "sheath-winged ones," from Greek *koleopteros,* sheath-winged : *koleon,* sheath + -PTEROUS.] **—co·le·op·ter·ist** *n.*

co·le·op·tile (kō′lē-ŏp′tĭl, kŏl′ē) *n. Botany.* A leaflike structure in grasses and similar monocotyledons, forming a protective sheath around the plumule. [New Latin *coleoptilum,* "sheathed plume" : Greek *koleon,* sheath + *ptilon,* plume, down.]

co·le·o·rhi·za (kō′lē-ə-rī′zə, kŏl′ē-) *n., pl.* **-zae** (-zē). *Botany.* A protective sheath around the embryonic root of grasses and similar monocotyledons. [New Latin, "root sheath" : Greek *koleon,* sheath + *rhiza,* root.]

Cole·ridge (kōl′rĭj), **Samuel Taylor** (1772-1834). British poet and critic. With William Wordsworth he published *Lyrical Ballads* (1798), which contained *The Rime of the Ancient Mariner,* his best-known poem. Other works include the visionary poem "Kubla Khan" (published 1816) and the critical and philosophical *Biographia Literaria* (1817).

cole·slaw (kōl′slô′) *n.* Also **cole slaw.** A salad consisting mainly of finely shredded raw cabbage with a dressing. Also called "slaw." [Dutch *koolsla* : *kool,* cabbage, from Middle Dutch *cōle,* from Latin *caulis* + *sla,* short for *salade,* SALAD.]

Col·et (kŏl′ĭt), **John** (c. 1466-1519). English humanist theologian and champion of Renaissance scholarship within the Catholic Church. He founded St. Paul's School, London (1509), to promote classical as well as scriptural learning.

Co·lette (kô-lĕt′), born Sidonie Gabrielle Claudine Colette (1873-1954). French novelist, famous especially for her sensuous and idyllic evocations of childhood and nature. Her works include *Gigi* (1944) and the series of *Claudine* books.

co·le·us (kō′lē-əs) *n.* Any of various plants of the genus *Coleus,* of Eurasia and Africa, cultivated for their showy leaves, which are often marked with red, yellow, or white. [New Latin *Coleus,* from Greek *koleos, koleon,* sheath (from the way its filaments are joined).]

colchicum *A crocuslike flower whose blooms appear in autumn, the autumn crocus,* Colchicum autumnale, *is found in meadowland.*

cole·wort (kōl′wûrt′, -wôrt′) *n.* A plant, **cole** *(see)*.

co·ley (kō′lē) *n., pl.* **coleys** or collectively **coley.** Any of several edible fishes, especially the **coalfish** *(see)*. [Probably shortened from *coalfish*.]

col·ic (kŏl′ĭk) *n.* **1.** Acute, paroxysmal pain in the abdomen, caused by spasm, obstruction, or distension of the intestine. **2.** Severe abdominal pain in infants, usually resulting from accumulation of gas in the alimentary canal. [Middle English *colike,* from Old French *colique,* from Latin *cōlicus,* from Greek *kōlikos,* suffering in the colon, from *kōlon,* variant of *kolon,* COLON (intestine).] —**col·ick·y** (kŏl′ĭ-kē) *adj.*

col·i·cin (kŏl′ə-sən, kŏl′ə-) *n.* A protein produced by some strains of coliform bacteria such as *Escherichia coli* that is lethal to other strains of the same species. [New Latin, *coli* (specific name of the bacterium) + -*c*- (connective) + -IN.]

co·li·form bacteria (kŏl′ə-fôrm′, kōl′ə-) *pl.n.* A group of rod-shaped bacteria most commonly occurring in the intestines of man and other vertebrates, some of which can cause disease. [COL(ON) + -FORM.]

col·i·se·um, col·os·se·um (kŏl′ə-sē′əm) *n.* A large amphitheater for public entertainment or assemblies. [After the COLOSSEUM in Rome.]

Coliseum. See **Colosseum.**

co·lis·tin (kə-lĭs′tĭn, kō-) *n.* An antibiotic produced by the bacterium *Bacillus colistinus* that is used mainly in treating gastrointestinal infections. [New Latin *colistinus* (specific name of the bacterium).]

co·li·tis (kō-lī′tĭs) *n.* Inflammation of the mucous membrane of the colon. [New Latin : COL(O)- + -ITIS.]

coll. 1. collateral. **2.** collect; collection; collector. **3.** college; collegiate. **4.** colloquial; colloquialism.

coll–. Variant of **collo–.**

col·lab·o·rate (kə-lăb′ə-rāt′) *intr.v.* **-rated, -rating, -rates. 1.** To work together, especially in a joint intellectual or artistic effort. **2.** To cooperate treasonably, especially with an enemy occupying one's country. [Late Latin *collabōrāre* : Latin *com-,* together + *labōrāre,* to work, from *labor,* labor.] —**col·lab·o·ra·tion** *n.* —**col·lab·o·ra·tor** *n.*

col·lab·o·ra·tion·ist (kə-lăb′ə-rā′shən-ĭst) *n.* A person who collaborates with an occupying enemy. —**col·lab·o·ra·tion·ism** *n.*

col·lage (kō-läzh′) *n.* **1.** An artistic composition of materials and objects pasted over a surface. **2.** Such compositions as an art form. **3.** An assemblage of images or sounds on a theme. [French, from *coller,* to glue, paste, from *colle,* glue, from Vulgar Latin *colla* (unattested), from Greek *kolla.*]

col·la·gen (kŏl′ə-jən) *n.* A fibrous protein occurring in bone, cartilage, and connective tissue. [Greek *kolla,* glue + -GEN.] —**col·la·gen·ic** (kŏl′ə-jĕn′ĭk), **col·lag·e·nous** (kə-lăj′ə-nəs) *adj.*

col·lap·sar (kə-lăp′sär′) *n.* A star which has collapsed under its own gravitational force; a black hole.

col·lapse (kə-lăps′) *v.* **-lapsed, -lapsing, -lapses.** —*intr.* **1.** To fall down or inward suddenly; cave in. **2.** To break down suddenly in health or strength; lose consciousness or energy. **3.** To suffer a complete loss of power, effectiveness, or the like: *Opposition to the proposals has collapsed.* **4.** To fold compactly. —*tr.* To cause to collapse. —*n.* **1.** The act of falling down or inward, as from external pressure or loss of supports. **2.** An abrupt failure of function, strength, or health. [Back-formation from *collapsed,* from Latin *collāpsus,* past participle of *collābī,* to fall together, fall in ruin : *com-,* together + *lābī,* slide, fall.] —**col·laps·i·ble, col·laps·a·ble** *adj.* —**col·laps·i·bil·i·ty** *n.*

col·lar (kŏl′ər) *n.* **1.** The part of a garment that encircles the neck. **2.** A necklace, choker, or similar ornament for the neck. **3.** A restraining or identifying band of leather or metal put around the neck of an animal. **4.** The cushioned part of a harness that presses against the shoulders of a draft animal. **5.** *Biology.* An encircling structure or bandlike marking suggestive of a collar. **6.** Any of various ringlike devices or parts used to limit, guide, or secure a machine part. —**hot under the collar.** *Informal.* Angry; annoyed. —*tr.v.* **collared, -laring, -lars. 1.** To furnish with a collar. **2.** To seize by the collar. **3.** *Informal.* To seize or detain. [Middle English *coler,* from Norman French, from Latin *collāre,* necklace, collar, from *collum,* neck.]

collar beam *n.* A timber beam connecting the midpoints of the sloping rafters of a pitched roof.

col·lar·bone (kŏl′ər-bōn′) *n. Anatomy.* The **clavicle** *(see)*.

collar cell *n. Biology.* A **choanocyte** *(see)*.

col·lard (kŏl′ərd) *n.* **1.** A variety of kale, *Brassica oleracea acephala,* having a crown of edible leaves. **2. collards.** The leaves of this plant used as a vegetable. [Variant of COLEWORT.]

col·lared dove *n.* A common European dove, *Streptopelia decaocto,* having a pale, brownish-gray plumage with a black band around the back of the neck.

collat. collateral.

col·late (kə-lāt′, kŏl′āt′, kō′lāt′) *tr.v.* **-lated, -lating, -lates. 1.** To examine and compare carefully (texts) in order to note points of difference and agreement. **2.** In bookbinding, to examine (gathered signatures) in order to arrange them in proper sequence before binding. **3.** To verify the order and completeness of (the pages of a volume). **4.** To assemble in proper numerical or logical sequence. **5.** *Ecclesiastical.* To admit (a cleric) to a benefice. [Latin *collātus* (past participle of *conferre,* to bring together) : *com-,* together +

lātus, "carried."] —**col·la·tor** (kə-lā′tər, kŏl′ā-tər, kō′lā-) *n.*

col·lat·er·al (kə-lăt′ər-əl) *adj. Abbr.* **coll., collat. 1.** Situated or running side by side; parallel. **2.** Coinciding in tendency or effect; concomitant; accompanying. **3.** Serving to support or corroborate: *collateral evidence.* **4.** Of a secondary nature; subordinate. **5.** *Finance.* Of, designating, or guaranteed by a security pledged against the performance of an obligation: *a collateral loan.* **6.** Descended from the same ancestor, but through a different line: *a collateral branch of the family.* In this sense, compare **lineal.** —*n.* **1.** *Finance.* Property acceptable as security for a loan or other obligation. **2.** A collateral relative. [Middle English, from Medieval Latin *collaterālis* : *com-,* together + *laterālis,* of the side, LATERAL.] —**col·lat·er·al·ly** *adv.*

col·la·tion (kə-lā′shən, kŏ-, kō-) *n.* **1.** The act or process of collating. **2.** A description of the material aspects of a book. **3.** In the Roman Catholic Church, a light meal permitted on fast days. **4.** Any light meal. [Middle English, from Old French, from Latin *collātiō* (stem *collātiōn-*), a bringing together (see **collate**). Senses 3, 4 : from the custom in Benedictine monasteries of reading from Cassian's *Collationes Patrum (Lives of the Fathers)* before taking a light meal on fast days.]

col·league (kŏl′ēg′) *n.* A fellow member, typically of a profession, staff, or academic faculty; an associate. —See Synonyms at **partner.** [French *collègue,* from Old French, from Latin *collēga,* one chosen to serve with another : *com-,* together + *lēgāre,* to choose.] —**col·league·ship** *n.*

col·lect¹ (kə-lĕkt′) *v.* **-lected, -lecting, -lects.** —*tr.* **1.** To bring together in a group; assemble. **2.** To accumulate as a hobby or for study. **3.** To obtain payment of (rents or taxes, for example). **4.** To recover control of. **5.** To call for; go and fetch. **6.** *Informal.* To win or receive (money, for example). —*intr.* **1.** To gather together; congregate. **2.** To take in payments or donations. —See Synonyms at **gather.** —*adj.* With payment to be made by the receiver: *a collect phone call.* —*adv.* So that the receiver is charged: *phone collect.* [Middle English *collecten,* from Latin *colligere* (past participle *collectus*), to gather together : *com-,* together + *legere,* to gather.] —**col·lect·i·ble, col·lect·a·ble** *adj.*

col·lect² (kŏl′ĭkt, -ĕkt′) *n. Ecclesiastical.* A brief formal prayer used in various Western liturgies before the epistle at Mass or Holy Communion and varying with the day. [Middle English *collecte,* from Old French, from Medieval Latin *collēcta,* from *ōrātiō ad collēctam,* "prayer at the congregation," from Late Latin *collēcta,* assembly, from *collēctus,* collected. See **collect¹.**]

col·lec·ta·ne·a (kŏl′ĕk-tā′nē-ə) *pl.n.* A selection of passages from one or more authors; an anthology. [Latin, "things collected," from *collēctāneus,* collected, from *collēctus.* See **collect¹.**]

col·lect·ed (kə-lĕk′tĭd) *adj.* **1.** Self-possessed; composed. **2.** Brought or placed together from various sources: *the collected poems of W.H. Auden.* —See Synonyms at **cool.** —**col·lect·ed·ly** *adv.* —**col·lect·ed·ness** *n.*

col·lec·tion (kə-lĕk′shən) *n. Abbr.* **coll. 1.** The act or process of collecting. **2.** A group of things that have been brought together, especially: **a.** A set of like objects collected as a hobby or for exhibition: *a postcard collection.* **b.** A set of literary works assembled in a single volume: *a collection of short stories.* **c.** A range of clothes exhibited by a fashion designer. **3.** An accumulation; deposit. **4. a.** A collecting of money, as in church. **b.** The sum collected. **5.** A removal of letters for delivery from a mailbox.

col·lec·tive (kə-lĕk′tĭv) *adj.* **1.** Formed by collecting; assembled or accumulated into a whole. **2.** Of, pertaining to, characteristic of, or made by a number of individuals taken or acting as a group: *a collective decision.* —*n.* **1.** A collective enterprise, such as **workers' cooperative** *(see),* or the persons working in it. **2.** A group of people working together for mutual support or advancement: *a women's collective.* **3.** *Grammar.* A collective noun. —**col·lec·tive·ly** *adv.* —**col·lec·tive·ness** *n.*

collective bargaining *n.* Negotiation between trade-union representatives and employers to determine wages, hours, rules, and working conditions.

collective farm *n.* A farm or a group of farms organized as a unit, managed and worked cooperatively by a group of workers, typically under government supervision. See **kibbutz, kolkhoz.**

collective fruit *n. Botany.* A **multiple fruit** *(see)*.

collective noun *n. Grammar.* A noun, such as *family* or *committee,* that denotes a collection of persons or things regarded as a unit.

Usage: A collective noun takes a singular verb when it refers to the collection as a whole and a plural verb when it refers to the members of the collection as separate persons or things: *The orchestra was playing,* but *The orchestra have all gone home.* A collective noun should not be treated as both singular and plural in the same construction. Thus: *The family is determined to press its* (not *their*) *claim.*

col·lec·tiv·ism (kə-lĕk′tə-vĭz′əm) *n.* The principle or system of ownership and control of the means of production and distribution by the people collectively. —**col·lec·tiv·ist** *adj. & n.*

col·lec·tiv·i·ty (kŏl′ĕk-tĭv′ə-tē, kə-lĕk′-) *n.* **1.** The condition or quality of being collective. **2.** The people as a whole.

col·lec·tiv·ize (kə-lĕk′tə-vīz′) *tr.v.* **-ized, -izing, -izes.** To organize (an economy, industry, or enterprise) on the basis of collectivism. —**col·lec·tiv·i·za·tion** *n.*

col·lec·tor (kə-lĕk′tər) *n.* **1.** A person or thing that collects. **2.** *Abbr.*

col., coll. A person employed to collect taxes, duties, or other payments. **3.** A person who collects things as a hobby, such as stamps. **4.** Formerly, the chief administrative officer of a district in British India. **5. a.** *Electricity.* A conducting contact between moving and stationary parts of an electric circuit. **b.** *Electronics.* The output terminal of a three-terminal semiconducting device, especially of a transistor. **—col·lec·tor·ship** *n.*

col·leen (kŏl'ēn', kŏ-lēn') *n.* An Irish girl. [Irish *cailīn,* diminutive of *caile,* girl, from Old Irish *calé,* probably from Latin *pellex,* concubine, akin to Greek *pallakē,* Sanskrit *pallavaki,* of non-Indo-European origin.]

col·lege (kŏl'ĭj) *n. Abbr.* **col., coll. 1. a.** An institution offering courses in higher education that grants the bachelor's degree in liberal arts or science or both. **b.** Any of the undergraduate divisions or schools of a university offering courses or granting degrees in a particular field. **c.** A technical or professional school, often affiliated with a university, offering the bachelor's or master's degree: *a teachers' college.* **d.** The building or buildings occupied by any such school. **e.** *Chiefly British.* A self-governing body of scholars incorporated within a university. **f.** In France, an institution for secondary education not supported by the state. **2.** A company or assemblage; especially, a body of persons having a common purpose, common professional interests, or common duties: *a college of surgeons.* **3.** A body of clergymen living together on an endowment. [Middle English, from Old French, from Latin *collēgium,* corporate institution, partnership, from *collēga,* COLLEAGUE.]

College of Arms *n.* A royal corporation in Britain that deals with matters of heraldry. Also called "Heralds' College."

College of Cardinals *n. Roman Catholic Church.* A body comprising all the cardinals that elects the pope, assists him in governing the church, and administers the Holy See when vacant. Also called "Sacred College."

col·le·gi·al·i·ty (kə-lē'jē-ăl'ĭ-tē) *n.* **1.** Shared authority among colleagues. **2.** *Roman Catholic Church.* The principle that the bishops, together with the pope, share collectively the responsibility of ruling the Church.

col·le·gian (kə-lē'jən, -jē-ən) *n.* A student or recent graduate of a college.

col·le·giate (kə-lē'jĭt, -jē-ĭt) *adj.* Also **col·le·gi·al** (kə-lē'jē-əl, -jəl). *Abbr.* **col., coll. 1.** Of, pertaining to, or resembling a college. **2.** Of, for, or typical of college students. **3.** Of or pertaining to a collegiate church. [Medieval Latin *collēgiātus,* from Latin *collēgium,* COLLEGE.]

collegiate church *n.* **1.** A Roman Catholic or Anglican church other than a cathedral, having a chapter of canons and presided over by a dean or provost. **2. a.** A church in the United States associated with others under a common body of pastors. **b.** An association of such churches. **3.** In Scotland, a church served by two or more ministers at the same time.

col·le·gi·um (kə-lē'jē-əm) *n., pl.* **-gia** (-jē-ə) or **-giums.** An executive council or committee of equally empowered members; specifically, one supervising an industry, commissariat, or other organization in the U.S.S.R. [Russian *kollegya,* from Latin *collēgium,* COLLEGE.]

col·lem·bo·lan (kə-lĕm'bə-lən) *n.* Any small wingless insect of the order Collembola; a springtail. [New Latin *Collembola,* from Greek *kolla,* glue + *embolon,* wedge, peg (referring to a projecting pouch characteristic of all members of the order).] **—col·lem·bo·lan** *adj.*

col·len·chy·ma (kə-lĕng'-kə-mə) *n. Botany.* Supportive tissue of plants, consisting of elongated, approximately rectangular cells with cell walls thickened with cellulose and pectin. [New Latin, "glue tissue" : COLL(O)- + -ENCHYMA.] **—col·len·chym·a·tous** (kŏl'-ən-kĭm'ə-təs) *adj.*

Col·les' fracture (kŏl'ĭs) *n.* A fracture of the wrist, at the lower end of the radius, in which the hand is displaced backwards. [After Abraham *Colles* (died 1843), Irish surgeon.]

col·let (kŏl'ĭt) *n.* **1.** A cone-shaped sleeve used for holding circular or rodlike machine pieces. **2.** A metal collar used in watchmaking to join one end of a balance spring to the balance staff. **3.** A circular flange or rim, as in a ring, into which a gem is set.
~tr.v. **colleted, -leting, -lets.** To set in or supply with a collet. [French, diminutive of *col,* neck, collar, from Latin *collum,* neck.]

col·lide (kə-līd') *intr.v.* **-lided, -liding, -lides. 1.** To come together with violent, direct impact. **2.** To meet in opposition; clash; conflict. [Latin *collīdere* : *com-,* together + *laedere,* to strike, injure.]

col·lie (kŏl'ē) *n.* A large dog of a breed originating in Scotland and widely used as a sheep dog, having long hair and a long, narrow muzzle. [Scottish, possibly from *colly,* "black like coal" (its original color), from *coll,* variant of COAL.]

col·li·er (kŏl'yər) *n. British.* **1.** A coal miner. **2.** A coal ship. [Middle English *colier,* from *col, cole,* COAL.]

col·lier·y (kŏl'yər-ē) *n., pl.* **-ies.** *British.* A coal mine.

col·li·gate (kŏl'ĭ-gāt') *tr.v.* **-gated, -gating, -gates. 1.** To tie together. **2.** *Logic.* To bring (isolated observations) together by an explanation or hypothesis that applies to them all. [Latin *colligāre* : *com-,* together + *ligāre,* to tie.] **—col·li·ga·tion** *n.*

col·li·ga·tive (kŏl'ĭ-gā'tĭv) *adj.* Designating the physical properties of a substance that depend on the concentrations of molecules, atoms, or ions present rather than on their nature: *colligative properties.*

col·li·mate (kŏl'ə-māt') *tr.v.* **-mated, -mating, -mates. 1.** To make parallel; line up. **2.** To adjust the line of sight of (a transit, telescope, or other optical device). [New Latin *collimare,* to adjust, misreading of Latin *collīneāre,* to direct in a straight line : *com-* (intensive) + *līneāre,* to make straight, from *līnea,* LINE.] **—col·li·ma·tion** *n.*

col·li·ma·tor (kŏl'ə-mā'tər) *n.* **1.** Any device capable of collimating radiation, such as a long narrow tube in which strongly absorbing or reflecting walls permit only radiation travelling parallel to the tube axis to traverse the entire length. **2.** A small telescope attached to a larger one as an aid to adjusting its line of sight.

col·lin·e·ar (kō'lĭn'ē-ər, kə-) *adj.* **1.** Lying on the same line. **2.** Containing a common line; coaxial. [COM- + LINEAR.]

col·lins (kŏl'ənz) *n.* A tall iced drink made with gin, vodka, rum, or other spirits, and lemon or lime juice, soda water, and sugar. [20th century : origin obscure.]

Collins *n. Chiefly British Informal.* A letter written to thank a host for his hospitality. [After William *Collins,* a character in Jane Austen's *Pride and Prejudice* (1813).]

Col·lins (kŏl'ənz), **Michael** (1890–1922). Irish nationalist. He took part in the Easter Rising in Dublin (1916) and was elected a Sinn Fein member of the Dáil (1919). He helped to negotiate the establishment of the Irish Free State (1921) but was killed in an ambush by republican opponents.

Collins, (William) Wilkie (1824–89). British novelist, a pioneer of the mystery story, best remembered for *The Woman in White* (1860) and *The Moonstone* (1868).

col·lin·si·a (kə-lĭn'zē-ə) *n.* Any of various North American plants of the genus *Collinsia,* having blue-and-white or purplish flowers.

col·li·sion (kə-lĭzh'ən) *n.* **1.** A direct, violent striking together; crash. **2.** A clash of ideas or interests; a conflict. **3.** *Physics.* A dynamic event consisting of the interaction between two or more bodies, usually of very brief duration, resulting in a change of momentum of at least one participating body. [Middle English, from Latin *collīsiō* (stem *collīsion-*), from *collīdere,* COLLIDE.]

collision course *n.* A course, as of moving objects or ideas, that will end in collision or conflict if continued unchanged.

collo–, coll– *prefix.* Indicates: **1.** Glue; for example, **collenchyma. 2.** Colloid; for example, **collotype.** [New Latin, from Greek *kolla,* glue.]

collie *The initiative and intelligence of the collie—one of the oldest breeds of sheepdog—make it a popular working dog for farmers. This is a rough collie, named for its thick shaggy coat.*

col·lo·cate (kŏl'ō-kāt') *v.* **-cated, -cating, -cates.** *—tr.* To place together or in proper order; arrange. *—intr. Linguistics.* To occur habitually and naturally together; for example, *quick* collocates with *temper,* but *fast* does not. [Latin *collocāre* : *com-,* together + *locāre,* to place, LOCATE.]

col·lo·ca·tion (kŏl'ō-kā'shən) *n.* **1. a.** The act of collocating. **b.** The state of being collocated. **2.** An arrangement or juxtaposition; especially, a group of words habitually occurring together.

col·lo·di·on (kə-lō'dē-ən) *n.* Also **col·lo·di·um** (kə-lō'dē-əm). A highly flammable, colorless or yellowish syrupy solution of **pyroxylin** *(see)* in ether and alcohol, used to hold surgical dressings, as a coating for certain skin diseases, and for making photographic plates. [New Latin *collodium,* from Greek *kollōdēs,* gluelike, from *kolla,* glue.]

col·logue (kə-lōg') *intr.v.* **-logued, -loguinq, -logues.** *British Regional.* To confer secretly; conspire. [Probably from obsolete verb *colleague,* to be a colleague, ally, conspire (influenced by Latin *colloquī,* to converse), from Old French *colleguer,* from Latin *colligāre,* to tie together, COLLIGATE.]

col·loid (kŏl'oid', kō'loid') *n.* **1.** *Chemistry.* **a.** A suspension of finely divided particles in a continuous medium (a gaseous, liquid, or solid substance), such as an atmospheric fog, a paint, or foam rubber, containing suspended particles that are approximately 1 to 1,000 nanometers in size, do not settle out of the medium rapidly, and are not readily filtered. **b.** The particulate matter so suspended. See **sol, gel, emulsion, foam. 2.** *Physiology.* A clear gelatinous secretion of the thyroid gland. Also called "thyroid colloid." **3.** *Pathology.* Gelatinous material resulting from tissue degeneration.
~adj. Also **col·loi·dal** (kə-loid'l, kō-). Of, pertaining to, or having the nature of a colloid. [French *colloïde* : COLL(O)- + -OID.]

col·lop (kŏl'əp) *n.* **1.** A small portion or slice, especially of meat. **2.** A roll of flesh on the body. [Middle English *coloppe, colhoppe*†.]

col·lo·qui·al (kə-lō'kwē-əl) *adj. Abbr.* **coll., colloq. 1.** Characteristic of or appropriate to the spoken language or to writing that seeks its effect; informal in diction or style of expression. **2.** Pertaining to conversation; conversational. [From COLLOQUY.] **—col·lo·qui·al·ly** *adv.* **—col·lo·qui·al·ness** *n.*

col·lo·qui·al·ism (kə-lō'kwē-əl-ĭz'əm) *n. Abbr.* **coll., colloq. 1.** Colloquial style or quality. **2.** A colloquial expression.

col·lo·qui·um (kə-lō'kwē-əm) *n., pl.* **-ums** or **-quia** (-kwē-ə). An academic seminar on some broad field of study, usually led by a different lecturer at each meeting. [Latin *colloquium,* COLLOQUY.]

col·lo·quy (kŏl'ə-kwē) *n., pl.* **-quies. 1.** A conversation, especially one that is formal or mannered. **2.** A written dialogue. [Latin *colloquium,* conversation, from *colloquī,* to converse : *com-,* together + *loquī,* to speak.]

col·lo·type (kŏl'ə-tīp') *n.* **1.** A printing process utilizing a glass plate with a gelatin surface carrying the image to be reproduced. Also called "photogelatin process." **2.** A print made by this process. [COLLO- + -TYPE.]

col·lude (kə-lōōd') *intr.v.* **-luded, -luding, -ludes.** To be in collusion; act together secretly. [Latin *collūdere* : *com-,* together + *lūdere,* to play, deceive, from *lūdus,* game.] **—col·lud·er** *n.*

col·lu·sion (kə-lōō'zhən) *n.* **1.** Secret agreement between two or more persons for a deceitful or fraudulent purpose. **2.** A secret agreement between the parties in a lawsuit to obtain a specific verdict. —See Synonyms at **conspiracy.** [Middle English *collucioun,* from Old French *collusion,* from Latin *collūsiō* (stem *collūsiōn-),* from *collūdere,* COLLUDE.]

col·lu·sive (kə-lōō'sĭv, -zĭv) *adj.* Secretly arranged for fraudulent purposes. —**col·lu·sive·ly** *adv.* —**col·lu·sive·ness** *n.*

col·lu·vi·um (kə-lōō'vē-əm) *n., pl.* **-via** (-vē-ə) or **-ums.** A loose deposit of rock debris accumulated at the base of a cliff or slope. [Latin *colluvium, colluviō,* collection of filth, washings, from *colluere,* to wash thoroughly, wash out : *com-* (intensive) + *lavere,* to wash.] —**col·lu·vi·al** *adj.*

col·lyr·i·um (kə-lîr'ē-əm) *n., pl.* **-ums** or **-ia** (-ē-ə). A medicinal lotion applied to the eye; eyewash. [Latin, from Greek *kollurion,* poultice, diminutive of *kollura†,* roll of bread.]

col·ly·wob·bles (kŏl'ē-wŏb'əlz) *pl.n. Informal.* **1.** A pain in the stomach, especially due to nervousness. **2.** A state of nervous apprehension. [19th century : fanciful coinage, from COLIC + WOBBLE.]

colo-, col- *prefix.* Indicates the colon; for example, **colostomy, colitis.** [New Latin, from Latin *colon,* COLON (intestine).]

col·o·bo·ma (kŏl'ə-bō'mə) *n., pl.* **-ma·ta** (-mə-tə). A lesion or fissure of the eye or eyelid. [New Latin, from Greek *kolobōma,* a mutilation, from *koloboun,* to mutilate, from *kolobos,* cut, docked.]

col·o·bus (kŏl'ə-bəs) *n.* Any Old World monkey of the genus *Colobus* of West and Central Africa, having a long tail, long silky fur, and short thumbs. [New Latin, from Greek *kolobos,* cut short (referring to its reduced thumbs).]

col·o·cynth (kŏl'ə-sĭnth') *n.* **1.** A vine, *Citrullus colocynthis,* of the Mediterranean region, bearing a small, bitter fruit. **2.** The fruit of this plant, used as a cathartic. Also called "bitter apple." [Latin *colocynthis,* from Greek *kolokunthis,* from *kolokunthē†,* round gourd.]

co·log·a·rithm (kō-lŏg'ə-rĭth'əm) *n.* The logarithm of the reciprocal of a number, expressed with a positive mantissa.

co·logne (kə-lōn') *n.* A scented liquid made of alcohol and various fragrant oils. Also called "cologne water," "eau de cologne." [French *eau de cologne,* "water of COLOGNE."]

Cologne. See **Köln.**

Co·lom·bi·a (kə-lŭm'bē-ə). *Abbr.* **Col.** Country in northwest South America. It was settled by the Spaniards in 1510. In 1740 it became part of the viceroyalty of New Granada, which was liberated from Spain by Simón Bolívar (1819). By 1903 Colombia had its present boundaries and had suffered 27 civil wars. Land and other reforms were slow, and strife led to military intervention (1953). However, agreements in 1957 and 1974 left Colombia a fragile democracy. The country, formerly dependent on coffee, is diversifying, and coffee now accounts for about half its exports. With industrialization Colombia has become an importer instead of an exporter of oil. It also has large reserves of coal and emeralds. Area, 1,138,914 square kilometers (439,735 square miles). Population, 33,000,000. Capital, Santa Fe de Bogotá. —**Co·lom·bi·an** *adj. & n.*

Co·lom·bo (kə-lŭm'bō). Capital of Sri Lanka, a port on the west coast of the island near the mouth of the Kelani River. It is noted for gem cutting and ivory carving.

Colombo, Cristoforo. See Christopher **Columbus.**

co·lon¹ (kō'lən) *n., pl.* **-lons** or **-la** (-lä) (for sense 2). **1. a.** A punctuation mark (:) used after a word introducing a quotation, explanation, example, or series, and after the salutation of a formal letter. **b.** The sign (:) used between numbers or groups of numbers, as in

colobus *Unlike other primates, these African monkeys have almost no thumb. They spend most of their lives in trees, feeding on leaves, and descend to the ground only to lick salt from the earth.*

ratios (1:2), biblical references (Genesis 4:1-5), or expressions of time (8:45 A.M.). **2.** A section of a rhythmical period in Greek and Latin verse, consisting of two to six feet and having one principal accent. [Latin *colon,* unit of verses, from Greek *kōlon,* "limb."]

co·lon² (kō'lən) *n., pl.* **-lons** or **-la** (-lə). The section of the large intestine extending from the cecum to the rectum. [Middle English, from Latin, from Greek *kolon†,* large intestine.] —**co·lon·ic** (kə-lŏn'ĭk) *adj.*

co·lón (kə-lōn') *n., pl.* **-lóns** (-lōnz') or *Spanish* **colónes** (kə-lō'nās'). **1. a.** The basic monetary unit of Costa Rica, equal to 100 céntimos. **b.** The basic monetary unit of El Salvador, equal to 100 centavos. **2.** A coin or note worth one colón. See feature at **currency.** [Spanish *colón,* after *Cristóbal Colón,* Christopher Columbus.]

Colón, Archipiélago de. See **Galápagos Islands.**

Colón, Cristóbal. See Christopher **Columbus.**

colo·nel (kûr'nəl) *n. Abbr.* **Col. 1. a.** An officer in the U.S. Army, Air Force, or Marine Corps ranking immediately above a lieutenant colonel and below a brigadier general. **b.** An officer of similar rank in other military or paramilitary organizations. **2.** An honorary title awarded by some states of the United States. [French, from Italian *colonnello,* "commander of a column," diminutive of *colonna,* column (of soldiers), from Latin *columna.*] —**colo·nel·cy, colo·nel·ship** *n.*

Colonel Blimp (blĭmp) *n.* A pompous reactionary, especially an army officer or government official. [After *Colonel Blimp,* character in cartoons by Sir David Low (1891-1963).]

co·lo·ni·al (kə-lō'nē-əl) *adj. Abbr.* **col. 1.** Of, pertaining to, possessing, or inhabiting a colony or colonies. **2.** *Often* **Colonial. a.** Of or pertaining to the 13 British colonies that became the original United States of America. **b.** Of or pertaining to the colonial period in the United States. **3.** *Often* **Colonial.** Designating an architectural style prevalent in the American colonies in the 17th and 18th centuries. ∼*n.* An inhabitant of a colony, especially a settler or one descended from settlers. —**co·lo·ni·al·ly** *adv.*

co·lo·ni·al·ism (kə-lō'nē-ə-lĭz'əm) *n.* A policy by which a nation maintains or extends its control over foreign dependencies. —**co·lo·ni·al·ist** *n. & adj.*

colonic irrigation *n.* The washing out of the contents of the large intestine by injecting large quantities of fluid through the rectum.

col·o·nist (kŏl'ə-nĭst) *n.* **1.** An original settler or founder of a colony. **2.** An inhabitant of a colony.

col·o·ni·za·tion (kŏl'ə-nə-zā'shən) *n.* The act or process of establishing a colony or colonies.

col·o·nize (kŏl'ə-nīz') *v.* **-nized, -nizing, -nizes.** —*tr.* **1. a.** To establish a colony or colonies in. **b.** To migrate to and settle in; occupy as a colony. **c.** To establish in a colony. **2.** To register party supporters as votes in (a district) so as to influence an election there. —*intr.* **1.** To set up or form a colony. **2.** To settle in a colony or colonies. —**col·o·niz·er** *n.*

col·on·nade (kŏl'ə-nād') *n. Architecture.* A series of columns placed at regular intervals. [French, from Italian *colonnato,* from *colonna,* column, from Latin *columna.*] —**col·on·nad·ed** *adj.*

col·o·ny (kŏl'ə-nē) *n., pl.* **-nies. 1.** A group of emigrants or their descendants who settle in a distant land but remain subject to or intimately connected with the parent country. **2.** A territory thus settled. **3.** *Abbr.* **col.** Any region politically controlled by a distant country; a dependency. **4. Colony.** Any of the 13 British colonies that became the original United States of America. **5. a.** A group of people with the same interests or ethnic origin, concentrated in a particular area. **b.** The area or place occupied by such a group. **6.** An area or institution in which a specified group of people is kept apart from others: *a leper colony; a penal colony.* **7.** *Biology.* **a.** A group of the same kind of animals or plants living or growing together. **b.** A group of individuals structurally connected and functioning as a single unit, as in sponges and corals. **8.** *Microbiology.* A visible growth of microorganisms in a nutrient medium. [Middle English *colonie,* from Old French, from Latin *colōnia,* farm, settlement, from *colōnus,* farmer, settler, from *colere,* to cultivate, inhabit.]

col·o·phon (kŏl'ə-fŏn', -fən) *n.* **1.** An inscription placed at the end of a book, giving facts pertaining to its publication. **2.** A publisher's emblem or trademark placed usually on the title page of a book. [Latin *colophōn,* from Greek *kolophōn,* summit, finishing.]

co·loph·o·ny (kə-lŏf'ə-nē) *n.* **Rosin** *(see).* [Latin *Colophonia rēsina,* "resin of *Colophon*" (ancient city in Lydia).]

col·or (kŭl'ər) *n.* Also *chiefly British* **col·our.** *Abbr.* **col. 1.** That aspect of things that is caused by differing qualities of the light reflected or emitted by them. It may be defined in terms of the observer (sense a) or by the light (sense b): **a.** The appearance of objects or light sources described in terms of the individual's perception of them, involving hue, lightness, and saturation for objects, and hue, brightness, and saturation for light sources. **b.** The characteristics of light by which the individual is made aware of objects or light sources through the receptors of the eye, described in terms of dominant frequency, luminance, and purity. **2.** Any of the gradations of this aspect, conventionally divided into shades as, for example, red, green, or brown. See **primary color, secondary color. 3.** A dye, pigment, paint, or other substance that imparts color. **4. a.** A redness of complexion, considered as a sign of normal health. **b.** A reddening of the face, as from indignation or embarrassment. **5.** The skin pigmentation of a person not classed as a Caucasian, especially that of a Negro. **6. colors. a.** An identifying

COLOMBIA / 70° W / Caribbean Sea / Barranquilla / Cartagena / 10°N / PANAMA / VENEZUELA / Medellín / Cúcuta / Bucaramanga / PACIFIC OCEAN / Manizales / SANTA FE DE BOGOTÁ / C O L O M B I A / Cali / Meta / Equator / Caqueta / ECUADOR / PERU / BRAZIL / 400 Km / 200 Miles

flag or banner, as of a country, organization, or military unit. **b.** A ceremony of lowering or raising military colors. **7. colors. a.** Any distinguishing symbol, badge, ribbon, or mark: *the colors of a college.* **b.** *British.* Such a badge or ribbon awarded for representing one's school, for example at sport. **8.** Character or nature: *appear in one's true colors.* **9.** Outward, often deceptive, appearance. Used chiefly in the phrase *under color of.* **10.** Appearance of truth or authenticity; plausibility. **11. colors.** An opinion or position: *Stick to your colors.* **12.** Variety of effect or expression. **13.** Picturesque and authentic detail, as in a film or novel, for example. **14.** Vitality; exuberance: *She loved the color of Mediterranean life.* **15.** In art, the use or effect of color as distinct from form. **16.** *Music.* Tonal quality. **17.** *Printing.* The amount, shade, or tone of ink used. **18.** *Law.* An apparent or prima-facie right, pretext, or ground. **19.** A particle or bit of gold found in auriferous gravel or sand. **20.** *Physics.* A hypothetical property associated with quark theory. Each quark may exist in any of three states designated red, blue, and green. The combination of certain color and quark types produces the various baryons and mesons. **—with flying colors.** With great success.

∼v. **colored, -oring, -ors.** *—tr.* **1.** To impart color to or change the color of. **2.** To give a distinctive character or quality to; modify or influence. **3.** To misrepresent, especially by distortion or exaggeration. *—intr.* **1.** To take on color or become colored. **2.** To change color. **3.** To become red in the face, as from embarrassment or indignation. [Middle English, from Old French, from Latin *color.*] **—col·or** *adj.* **—col·or·er** *n.*

col·or·a·ble (kŭl′ər-ə-bəl) *adj.* **1.** Seemingly true or genuine. **2.** Feigned; pretended. **—col·or·a·bil·i·ty, col·or·a·ble·ness** *n.* **—col·or·a·bly** *adv.*

Col·o·ra·do[1] (kŏl′ə-rä′dō, -răd′ə). State in the west-central United States, where the Rocky Mts. meet the Great Plains. The Rockies contain reserves of molybdenum, uranium, and oil. Denver is the capital.

Colorado[2]. River in the southwestern United States. It rises in the Rocky Mts. of Colorado and flows 2,336 kilometers (1,450 miles) southwest through Utah and Arizona, reaching the sea in Mexico at the Gulf of California. It supplies the Hoover Dam.

Colorado beetle *n.* A small black-and-yellow striped beetle, *Leptinotarsa decemlineata,* native to Central America but now widespread in Europe, that is a major pest of potatoes. Also called "Colorado potato beetle," "potato beetle." [After COLORADO, where it first became a major pest of potatoes.]

Colorado Springs. A city of central Colorado, at the foot of Pikes Peak. It is a year-round vacation center and health resort and has thriving industries. The U.S. Air Force Academy is nearby.

col·or·ant (kŭl′ər-ənt) *n.* Anything that colors or modifies the color of something else, especially a dye, pigment, ink, or paint.

col·or·a·tion (kŭl′ə-rā′shən) *n.* Arrangement of colors.

col·or·a·tu·ra (kŭl′ər-ə-to͝or′ə, -tyo͝or′ə) *n.* **1.** Florid ornamental trills and runs in vocal music. **2.** Music characterized by such ornamentation. **3.** A singer, especially a soprano, specializing in this. [Obsolete Italian, "coloring," from Late Latin *colōrātūra,* from Latin *colōrāre,* to COLOR.]

col·or-blind (kŭl′ər-blīnd′) *adj.* **1.** Partially or totally unable to distinguish certain colors. See **deuteranopia, protanopia, tritanopia. 2. a.** Not subject to racial prejudices. **b.** Not recognizing racial distinctions. **—color blindness** *n.*

col·or·breed (kŭl′ər-brēd′) *tr.v.* **-bred** (-brĕd′), **breeding, -breeds.** To breed (plants or animals) selectively to produce new or desired colors. **—col·or·bred** *adj.*

color code *n.* A method of distinguishing items, such as parts, components, wires, or resistors, using distinctive colors for identification. **—col·or-cod·ed** (kŭl′ər-kō′dĭd) *adj.*

col·ored (kŭl′ərd) *adj.* **1.** Having color. **2.** Distorted or biased, as by irrelevant or incorrect information.

∼n. Often **Colored.** In South Africa, a person of racially mixed descent belonging to a population grouping that is distinct from Asians, blacks, and whites.

col·or·fast (kŭl′ər-făst′, -fäst′) *adj.* Having color that will not run or fade with washing or wear. Said of fabrics. **—col·or·fast·ness** *n.*

color filter *n.* A photographic filter used to increase contrast or in taking photographs through haze.

col·or·ful (kŭl′ər-fəl) *adj.* **1.** Full of color; abounding in colors. **2.** Characterized by rich variety; vivid; distinctive. **—col·or·ful·ly** *adj.* **—col·or·ful·ness** *n.*

color guard *n.* The ceremonial escort for the flag, as of a country or an organization.

col·or·if·ic (kŭl′ə-rĭf′ĭk) *adj.* **1.** Producing or imparting color. **2.** Of or pertaining to color.

col·or·im·e·ter (kŭl′ə-rĭm′ə-tər) *n.* **1.** Any of various instruments used to determine or specify colors, as by comparison with spectroscopic or visual standards. **2.** An instrument that measures the concentration of a known solution constituent by comparison with colors of standard solutions of that constituent. **—col·or·i·met·ric** (kŭl′ər-ə-mĕt′rĭk) *adj.* **—col·or·i·met·ri·cal·ly** *adv.* **—col·or·im·e·try** *n.*

color index *n.* **1.** *Astronomy.* The numerical difference between the apparent photographic magnitude and the apparent visual magnitude of a star, as an indication of its color and temperature. **2.** *Geology.* The percentage of dark and colored minerals in a rock, calculated on the basis of its total mineral content.

col·or·ing (kŭl′ər-ĭng) *n.* **1.** The art, manner, or process of applying color. **2.** Any substance used to color something. **3.** Appearance with regard to color. **4.** The arrangement of or patterns created by colors. **5.** A false or misleading appearance.

col·or·ist (kŭl′ər-ĭst) *n.* An artist skilled in achieving special effects with color. **—col·or·is·tic** *adj.*

col·or·less (kŭl′ər-lĭs) *adj.* **1.** Without color. **2.** Weak or dull in color; pallid. **3.** Lacking animation, variety, or distinction; uninteresting; dull. **4.** Without bias; neutral; objective. **—col·or·less·ly** *adv.* **—col·or·less·ness** *n.*

color phase *n.* **1.** A seasonal variation in the color of the fur or feathers of some animals, especially those living in arctic regions. **2.** Variation in the color of animals of the same species.

color scheme *n.* An arrangement of colors, especially one planned for a certain effect, as in interior decorating.

Co·los·sae (kə-lŏs′-ē). An ancient city in western Asia Minor, the seat of a congregation to which St. Paul addressed the Epistle to the Colossians. **—Co·los·sian** (kə-lŏsh′ən) *adj. & n.*

co·los·sal (kə-lŏs′əl) *adj.* **1.** Enormous in size or extent; gigantic. **2.** *Informal.* Great in degree; enormous: *a colossal waste of time.* —See Synonyms at **enormous.** [French, from Latin *colossus,* COLOSSUS.] **—co·los·sal·ly** *adv.*

colosseum. Variant of **coliseum.**

Col·os·se·um, Col·i·se·um (kŏl′ə-sē′əm). An amphitheater in Rome built by Vespasian and Titus (A.D. *c.* 75–80). [Latin, from *colossēus,* huge, from *colossus,* COLOSSUS.] See feature, next page.

Co·los·sians (kə-lŏsh′ənz, -lŏs′ē-ənz) *n. Used with a singular verb. Abbr.* **Col.** A book of the New Testament, an epistle of Saint Paul to the Christians of Colossae.

co·los·sus (kə-lŏs′əs) *n., pl.* **-lossi** (-lŏs′ī′) or **-suses. 1.** A huge statue. **2.** Any person or thing of outstanding size or importance. [Latin, from Greek *kolossos,* probably of Mediterranean origin.]

Colossus of Rhodes (rōdz). A huge statue of Apollo, about 36 meters (120 feet) high, built about 280 B.C. and later destroyed by an earthquake. It was set at the entrance to the harbor of Rhodes and was one of the Seven Wonders of the World.

co·los·to·my (kə-lŏs′tə-mē) *n., pl.* **-mies.** The surgical construction of an artificial excretory opening from the colon onto the surface of the abdomen. [COLO- + -STOMY.]

co·los·trum (kə-lŏs′trəm) *n.* The first secretion of the mammary glands immediately after childbirth, lasting for a few days and consisting of serum, white blood cells, and antibodies. Also called "foremilk." [Latin *colostrum, colostra*†.]

colour. *Chiefly British.* Variant of **color.**

-colous *suffix.* Indicates habitat in or among; for example, **arenicolous.** [Latin *-cola,* inhabitant.]

col·pi·tis (kŏl-pī′tĭs) *n.* **Vaginitis** *(see).* [New Latin : Greek *kolpos,* bosom, womb, vagina + -ITIS.]

col·por·tage (kŏl′pôr′tĭj, -pōr′tĭj) *n.* The work of a colporteur.

col·por·teur (kŏl′pôr′tər, -pōr′tər) *n.* A peddler of devotional literature. [French, from Old French *comporteur* (influenced by *col,* neck), from *comporter,* to peddle, COMPORT.]

col·po·scope (kŏl′pə-skōp′) *n.* A speculum that is used to examine the tissues of the vagina and the cervix of the uterus. [Greek *kolpos,* womb, vagina + -SCOPE.] **—col·pos·co·py** (kŏl-pŏs′kə-pē) *n.*

colt (kōlt) *n.* **1.** A young male horse. **2. a.** A youthful or inexperienced person; a novice or beginner. **b.** *Sports.* An inexperienced player; a player on a junior team. **3.** A rope whip formerly used for shipboard discipline. [Middle English *colt,* Old English *colt,* young ass or camel, perhaps from Scandinavian; akin to Swedish dialectal *kult, kulter*†, half-grown animal, boy.]

Colt *n.* A trademark for a type of revolver invented by Samuel Colt.

Colt (kōlt) **Samuel** (1814–62). U.S. firearms inventor and manufacturer. He developed the revolver, the first single-barrel, multishot pistol (1836). Colt used assembly-line techniques, interchangeable parts, and quality control to efficiently manufacture the guns, which played an important part in the settling of the West.

col·ter, coul·ter (kōl′tər) *n.* A blade or wheel on a plow for making vertical cuts in the sod. [Middle English *culter, colter,* from Old English *culter* and Old French *coltre,* both from Latin *culter,* knife, plowshare.]

colt·ish (kōl′tĭsh) *adj.* **1.** Of or like a colt. **2.** Lively and playful; frisky. **—colt·ish·ly** *adv.* **—colt·ish·ness** *n.*

Col·trane (kōl′trān′, kōl′-), **John William** (1912–67). U.S. musician and composer. He brought his mastery of the saxophone to several jazz bands. His controversial, occasionally violent style and his incorporation of the music of India into his work made him a respected and much-imitated musician.

colts·foot (kōlts′fo͝ot′) *n., pl.* **-foots.** A plant, *Tussilago farfara,* native to the Old World, having yellow, daisylike flowers that appear before the heart-shaped leaves. [From the shape of its leaves.]

col·u·brid (kŏl′ə-brĭd, kŏl′yə-) *n.* Any of numerous chiefly nonvenomous snakes of the family Colubridae, which includes the garter snake.

∼adj. Of or belonging to the Colubridae. [New Latin *Colubridae,* from Latin *coluber,* snake.]

col·u·brine (kŏl′ə-brīn′, kŏl′yə-) *adj.* **1.** Of or like a snake. **2.** Of or belonging to the Colubrinae, a subfamily of nonvenomous colubrid snakes. [Latin *colubrīnus,* from *coluber,* snake.]

co·lu·go (kə-lo͞o′gō) *n., pl.* **-gos.** A mammal, the **flying lemur** *(see).* [Malay.]

Co·lum·ba (kə-lŭm′bə) *n.* A constellation in the Southern Hemisphere near Caelum and Puppis. Also called the "Dove." [New Latin, from Latin *columba,* dove.]

Columba, Saint (521–97). Irish saint and missionary. He founded a

Colorado beetle *A devastating pest of potato crops, this insect spread eastward as the settlers moved west across the United States.*

colossus *Some 20 meters (70 feet) tall, these Colossi of Memnon are statues of the Egyptian pharaoh Amenhotep III.*

PRONUNCIATION KEY

ă, pat; ā, pay; âr, care; ä, father, are; b, bib; ch, church; d, deed; ĕ, pet; ē, be; f, fife; g, gag; h, hat; hw, which; ĭ, pit; ī, pie; îr, pier; j, judge; k, kick; l, lid, needle; m, mum; n, no, sudden; ng, thing; ŏ, pot; ō, toe; ô, paw, for; oi, noise; ou, out; o͝o, book; o͞o, boot; p, pop; r, roar; s, sauce; sh, ship, dish; t, tight; th, thin, path; *th,* this, bathe; ŭ, cut; ûr, fur; v, valve; w, with; y, yes; z, zebra, size; zh, vision; ə, about, item, edible, gallop, circus, peaceful

IN FOREIGN WORDS:

à, *Fr.* ami; œ, *Fr.* feu, *Ger.* schön; ü, *Fr.* tu, *Ger.* über; KH, *Ger.* ich, *Scot.* loch; N, *Fr.* bon; y', *Fr.* Compiègne

STRESS MARKS:

Primary stress: ′ **in·cite′** (ĭn-sīt′)
Secondary stress: ′ **in′sight′** (ĭn′sīt′)

Colosseum

THEATER OF DEATH WHERE 2,000 GLADIATORS MIGHT FIGHT ON A SINGLE ROMAN HOLIDAY

The Colosseum remains as a monument to the ingenuity of Roman engineering

The Colosseum is a four-storied complex of arches and arcades 48 meters (157 feet) high, with 80 arches around the exterior. It was constructed with a soundness that has endured for almost two millennia and is a striking monument to the skills of Roman engineers.

Overall the Colosseum is 189 meters (620 feet) long and 156 meters (513 feet) across, by far the largest of the Roman amphitheaters that, despite centuries of vandalism, still stand. Its present name was not used until the Middle Ages; it derives not from the amphitheater's dimensions but perhaps from those of the colossal statue of Nero that used to stand nearby.

Mortal combat between men, or men and beasts, was the dramatic form most often staged in the vast Roman amphitheaters. Gladiatorial combat was intro-

duced in 264 B.C., when the consul Decimus Junius Brutus held games for his father's funeral in the tradition of the ancient Etruscan funeral rites. These fights to the death provided blood to give strength to the deceased. Contests gradually became celebrations of imperial Roman victories but ostensibly remained tributes to the dead until Julius Caesar's games of 46 B.C.

Gladiators drawn from the ranks of slaves, criminals, and prisoners of war were trained in special schools and then made to fight lions, panthers, bears, bulls, and other beasts that had been goaded into savagery by fear and hunger.

The emperor Nero (A.D. 37–68) sent Christians into the arena to face wild beasts, but such persecution was

unusual until the 2nd century A.D., when it became commonplace.

Gladiatorial combats and the "hunting" of wild animals were first held in a closed-off part of the Forum, the public marketplace. From 80 B.C. stone buildings were constructed throughout the Roman world, from Caerleon in Wales to Aspendos in Turkey, to house the increasingly popular spectacles. By the late 1st century A.D., when the Colosseum was built in Rome, they were held once or twice a week as a diversion for the people. Five thousand wild animals were killed on the day in A.D. 80 when the Colosseum was inaugurated by the emperor Titus, son of its originator Vespasian. On a single public holiday 2,000 gladiators might be scheduled to fight.

STRUCTURE OF THE COLOSSEUM *A Roman amphitheater was usually built into the side of a hill, which gave structural support. The Colosseum is unusual in being freestanding and is a story higher than any other. The arena was open to the sky with only a giant canvas awning to shield it when necessary from the sun. Cells beneath the arena accommodated beasts and performers. The spectators entered through the ground-floor arches, the gladiators and the emperor through underground corridors. The imperial throne, set on a podium and surrounded by seats for officers of state, was just behind the wall, 4.5 meters (15 feet) high, that encircles the arena.*

church and monastery on the island of Iona (563). This became the center of evangelical activity in Scotland, from which the northern Picts were converted.

col·um·bar·i·um (kŏl′əm-bâr′ē-əm) *n., pl.* **-ia** (-ē-ə). **1. a.** A vault with niches for urns containing ashes of the dead. **b.** Any of the niches in such a vault. **2.** A dovecote. [Middle English *columba(i)re*, dovecote, from Latin *columbārium*, from *columba*, dove.]

Co·lum·bi·a¹ (kə-lŭm′bē-ə) *n. Poetic.* A feminine personification of the United States. [After Christopher COLUMBUS.]

Columbia². River in western Canada and the northwestern United States. It rises in British Columbia and flows 1,950 kilometers (1,210 miles) southwest to the Pacific in Oregon. For much of its length it forms the border between the states of Washington and Oregon.

Columbia³. The capital of South Carolina, in the central part of the state on the Congaree River. It is an important trade and commercial center in the heart of a rich farm region. Most of the original city was burned on February 17, 1865, by Gen. William T. Sherman's soldiers.

Columbia, District of. See **District of Columbia**.

col·um·bine (kŏl′əm-bīn′) *n.* Any of several plants of the genus *Aquilegia*, having variously colored flowers with five conspicuously spurred petals. [Middle English, from Medieval Latin (*herba*) *columbīna*, from Latin *columbīnus*, dovelike (from the resemblance of the inverted flower to a cluster of five doves), from *columba*, dove.]

Columbine *n.* In pantomime, the partner or sweetheart of Harlequin.

co·lum·bite (kə-lŭm′bīt′) *n.* A black mineral, essentially (Fe,

Mn)(Nb, Ta)₂O₆, used as a source of niobium and tantalum. [CO-LUMB(IUM) + -ITE.]

co·lum·bi·um (kə-lŭm′bē-əm) *n. Symbol* **Cb** The element **niobium** (*see*). [New Latin, after *Columbia* (name of a personification of the United States), because it was discovered in a mineral found in Connecticut.] **—co·lum·bic** *adj.*

Co·lum·bus (kə-lŭm′bəs). The capital of Ohio, in the central part of the state, on the Scioto River. It is a port of entry and a major industrial and trade center in a rich farm region. Its early growth was stimulated in the early 1800's by the Ohio and Erie Canal, the National Road, and the arrival of the railroad.

Columbus, Christopher (1451–1506). *Italian* **Cristoforo Co·lom·bo** (kō-lōm′bō). *Spanish* **Cristóbal Co·lón** (kō-lôn′). Italian explorer in the service of Spain, the first modern European to discover America. Believing that the earth was not flat, Columbus concluded that it must be possible to reach the east by sailing westward. He reached the Bahamas (1492) and discovered Puerto Rico, Jamaica, and other islands (1493–96). On a third voyage (1498–1500) he reached Trinidad and the mouth of the Orinoco in South America. Having set up colonies in the New World, he was charged with mismanaging them and returned to Spain in chains (1500). On a fourth voyage (1502–04), he landed at Honduras, Costa Rica, and Panama.

col·u·mel·la (kŏl′yə-mĕl′ə, kŏl′ə-) *n., pl.* **-mellae** (-mĕl′ē). Any of several small, columnlike structures in various plants and animals, such as the central part of the sporangium of certain fungi and mosses. [New Latin, from Latin, diminutive of *columna*, COLUMN.] **—col·u·mel·lar** *adj.*

col·umn (kŏl′əm) n. Abbr. **col.** **1.** A pillar consisting of a base, a cylindrical shaft, and a capital, used as a support or standing alone as a monument. **2.** Anything resembling a pillar in form or function: a column of smoke. **3.** Any of two or more vertical sections of printed lines lying side by side on a page and separated by a rule or blank space. **4.** A section of a newspaper or magazine that regularly contains an article by a particular writer or is devoted to a particular subject: the personal column. **5.** A vertical row of numbers on a page. **6.** A formation, as of troops, vehicles, ships, or aircraft, in which the elements follow one behind the other. **7.** Botany. An organ in an orchid flower formed by the fusion of stamens and style. [Middle English columpne, from Old French colomne, from Latin columna.] —**co·lum·nar** (kə-lŭm′nər), **col·umned** (kŏl′əmd) adj.
co·lum·ni·a·tion (kə-lŭm′nē-ā′shən) n. The use or arrangement of columns in a building.
column inch n. A unit used to measure advertising space in newspapers or magazines, one column wide and one inch deep.
col·um·nist (kŏl′əm-nĭst, -ə-mĭst) n. A writer of a regular column in a newspaper or periodical.
co·lure (kə-lyōor′, -lŏŏr′, kō′-) n. Astronomy. Either of two great circles passing through the celestial poles on the celestial sphere: one passing through the equinoxes (equinoctial colure) and the other through the solstices (solstitial colure). [Middle English, from Late Latin, from Greek kolouros, "dock-tailed," truncated (because the view of the lower part of the circles is cut short) : kolos, docked + oura, tail.]
col·za (kŏl′zə, kōl′-) n. A plant, **rape** (see). [French, from Dutch koolzaad, "cabbage seed."]
COM (kŏm) n. A process that enables computer output to be presented directly in the form of photographic film or fiche. [Computer Output on Microfilm.]
com- prefix. Indicates with, together, jointly; for example, **com·measure, commingle.** [In borrowed Latin compounds, com- indicates: 1. With, together, joint, jointly, mutually, collectively, as in **compose, compact.** 2. Altogether, comprehensively, inclusively, intensively, as in **comfort, combust.** 3. Same, similar, as in **concord, consubstantial.** 4. Together in mind, mentally, as in **compute, comprehend.** (The semantic function of com- is often so indistinct as to be indefinable, as in **concave.**) Before l and r, com- is assimilated to col- and cor-; before h, gn, and usually before vowels, it is reduced to co- (hence English **co-**); before all other consonants except b, p, and m, it becomes con-. Com- is the preverbal form of the Old Latin preposition com, which in classical Latin became cum, with.]
com. **1.** comedy; comic. **2.** commerce; commercial. **3.** committee.
Com. **1.** commander. **2.** commission; commissioner. **3.** committee. **4.** commodore. **5.** communist.
co·ma¹ (kō′mə) n., pl. **-mas.** A state of deep, prolonged unconsciousness, usually the result of injury, disease, or poison. [New Latin, from Greek kōma, deep sleep, lethargy.]
coma² n., pl. **-mae** (-mē). **1.** Astronomy. The nebulous luminescent cloud containing the nucleus and constituting the major portion of the head of a comet. **2.** Botany. A tuft of hairs, as on some seeds. **3.** Optics. The distorted image of a point source, appearing as a diffuse, pear-shaped spot. It is the result of errors in an optical system. [Latin, hair, from Greek komē†.] —**co·mal** adj.
Co·ma Ber·e·ni·ces (kō′mə bĕr′ə-nī′sēz) n. A constellation in the northern sky near Boötes and Leo. It contains the coma cluster of galaxies. Also called "Berenice's Hair."
Co·man·che (kə-măn′chē) n., pl. **-ches** or collectively **Comanche.** **1.** A member of a Uto-Aztecan-speaking North American Indian people, formerly ranging over the western plains from Wyoming to Texas, now living in Oklahoma. **2.** The language of this people. —**Co·man·che** adj.
Co·man·che·an (kə-măn′chē-ən) adj. Of, belonging to, or designating the geologic time, system of rocks, or sedimentary deposits of the Mesozoic era between the Jurassic and the Upper Cretaceous. ~n. The Comanchean period. [After Comanche, a county in Texas.]
Co·ma·neci (kŏm′ə-nēch), **Nadia** (1961–). Romanian gymnast. She became Olympic champion at the Montreal Olympic Games (1976).
co·mate (kō′māt′) adj. Also **co·mose** (-mōs′). Botany. Having or resembling a tuft of hairs. [Latin comātus, from coma, hair, from Greek komē.]
co·ma·tose (kō′mə-tōs′, kŏm′ə-) adj. Pathology. **1.** Of, pertaining to, or affected with coma; unconscious. **2.** Lethargic or torpid. —**co·ma·tose·ly** adv.
co·mat·u·lid (kə-măch′ŏŏ-lĭd) n. Also **co·mat·u·la** (-lə) pl. **-lae** (-lē). Any of several marine invertebrates of the order Crinoidea, including the feather stars, that are attached to a surface by a stalk when young but are free-swimming as adults. [New Latin Comatulidae (former designation), from Late Latin comātulus, with neatly curled hair, from Latin comātus, having hair, COMATE.]
comb (kōm) n. **1.** A thin, toothed strip of plastic, bone, rubber, or other material, used to smooth, arrange, or fasten the hair. **2.** Something resembling a comb in shape or use, such as: **a.** A card for dressing and cleansing wool or other fibers. **b.** A toothed part, as in a shearing device, guiding hair or fleece toward the blade. **3.** A currycomb (see). **4.** The fleshy crest or ridge that grows on the crown of the head of domestic fowl and other birds and is most prominent in the male. **5.** Something suggesting a fowl's comb in appearance or position. **6.** A honeycomb (see). ~v. combed, combing, combs. —tr. **1.** To dress or arrange with or as if with a comb. **2.** To card (wool or other fibers). **3.** To search thoroughly; look through. —intr. To roll and break. Used of waves. —**comb out.** To isolate and get rid of (something unwanted). [Middle English comb, Old English comb, camb.]
comb. **1.** combination. **2.** combining.
com·bat (kəm-băt′, kŏm′băt′) v. **-bated, -bating, -bats.** Also chiefly British **-batted, -batting.** —tr. **1.** To fight against; contend with; oppose in battle. **2.** To oppose vigorously; resist. —intr. To engage in fighting; contend; struggle. Used with with or against: combat against laziness. —See Synonyms at **oppose.** ~n. (kŏm′băt′). Fighting, especially armed battle; strife. Also used adjectively: combat troops. —See Synonyms at **conflict.** [Old French combattre, from Vulgar Latin combattere (unattested), to fight with : Latin com-, with + battuere, beat.]
com·bat·ant (kəm-băt′ənt, kŏm′bə-tənt) n. One taking part in armed combat. —**com·bat·ant** adj.
combat fatigue n. A nervous disorder, usually temporary but sometimes leading to a permanent neurosis, brought on by the exhaustion and stress of combat or similar situations, and characterized by deep anxiety, depression, irritability, and other related symptoms. Also called "battle fatigue." Compare **shell shock.**
com·bat·ive (kəm-băt′ĭv) adj. Eager or disposed to fight. —**com·bat·ive·ly** adv. —**com·bat·ive·ness, com·ba·tiv·i·ty** n.
comb·er (kō′mər) n. **1.** One that combs. **2.** A long, cresting wave of the sea; breaker.
com·bi·na·tion (kŏm′bə-nā′shən) n. Abbr. **comb. 1. a.** The act of combining. **b.** The state of being combined. **2.** Something resulting from combining; a compound; an aggregate: passed the exam through a combination of luck and hard work. **3.** An alliance or association of persons or parties for a common purpose. **4.** A sequence of numbers or letters used to open a combination lock. **5.** A one-piece undergarment consisting of an undershirt or chemise and drawers. **6.** Mathematics. One or more elements selected from a set without regard to order of selection. **7.** Chemistry. The union of two or more compounds, as a result of chemical reaction, to form another compound. —**com·bi·na·tion·al** adj.
combination lock n. A lock that will open only when its dial is turned through a predetermined sequence of positions identified on the dial face by numbers or letters.
com·bi·na·tive (kŏm′bə-nā′tĭv, kəm-bī′nə-tĭv) adj. **1.** Of, pertaining to, or resulting from combination. **2.** Tending, serving, or able to combine.
com·bi·na·to·ri·al (kŏm′bə-nə-tôr′ē-əl, -tōr′-, kəm-bī′nə-) adj. **1.** Pertaining to or involving combinations. **2.** Mathematics. Pertaining to the arrangement and manipulation of combinations and permutations and mathematical elements in sets: combinatorial analysis.
com·bi·na·tor·ics (kŏm′bə-nə-tôr′ĭks, -tōr′-, kəm-bī′nə-) n. Combinatorial mathematics.
com·bine (kəm-bīn′) v. **-bined, -bining, -bines.** —tr. **1.** To bring into a state of unity; join; merge; blend. **2.** To possess or exhibit in combination. —intr. **1.** To become united; coalesce. **2.** To join forces for a common purpose; enter into an alliance. **3.** Chemistry. To form a chemical compound. —See Synonyms at **join, mix.** ~n. (kŏm′bīn′). **1.** An association of persons or firms united for commercial interests, such as control of prices. **2.** A combine harvester. **3.** A combination. [Middle English combinen, from Old French combiner, from Late Latin combīnāre : Latin com-, together + bīnī, two at a time.] —**com·bin·er** n.
combine harvester (kŏm′bīn′) n. A harvesting machine that cuts, threshes, and cleans grain. Also called "combine."
comb·ings (kō′mĭngz) pl.n. Hairs, wool, or other material removed with a comb.
combining form n. Grammar. A word element that can form new words by combining with complete words, other combining forms, or sometimes with affixes; for example, **-logy,** as in **gynecology; macro-,** as in **macrochemistry; Sino-,** as in **Sino-Soviet.**
combining weight n. Equivalent weight (see).
comb jelly n. A marine organism, a ctenophore (see).
com·bo (kŏm′bō) n., pl. **-bos. 1.** Informal. A small group of musicians, usually jazz musicians. **2.** Slang. The result or product of combining; combination. [Short for COMBINATION.]
com·bust (kəm-bŭst′) adj. Astrology. Not visible because of proximity to the sun. Said of a star or planet. ~v. combusted, -busting, -busts. —tr. To cause to burn. —intr. To burn; undergo combustion. [Middle English, "burned," from Old French, from Latin combustus, past participle of comburere, to burn up (infixed b probably influenced by amburere, to burn up) : com- (intensive) + ūrere, to burn.] —**com·bus·tive** adj.
com·bus·ti·ble (kəm-bŭs′tə-bəl) adj. **1.** Capable of igniting and burning. **2.** Easily aroused or excited. ~n. A combustible substance. —**com·bus·ti·bil·i·ty** n. —**com·bus·ti·bly** adv.
com·bus·tion (kəm-bŭs′chən) n. **1.** The act or process of burning. **2.** Chemistry. A chemical change, especially oxidation, accompanied by the production of heat and light. [Middle English, from Old French, from Late Latin combustio (stem combustiōn-), from Latin combustus. See combust.]
combustion chamber n. An enclosure in which combustion, especially of a fuel or propellant, is initiated and controlled.
com·bus·tor (kəm-bŭs′tər) n. The combustion system of a jet engine or gas turbine, consisting of a combustion chamber together with its igniter and fuel injection system.

columbine This group of hardy border plants with funnel-shaped flowers is related to the buttercup. The Latin name for the group is Aquilegia.

comdg. commanding.

Comdr. commander.

Comdt. commandant.

come (kŭm) v. **came** (kām), **come, coming, comes.** —intr. **1. a.** To advance toward the speaker or toward a specified place; approach. **b.** To advance in a specified manner. **2.** To arrive as a result of moving or making progress. **3.** To reach a particular point in a series or as a result of orderly progression. **4.** To move into view; appear. **5.** To occur in time. **6. a.** To arrive at a particular result or end: *come to an understanding.* **b.** To arrive at or reach a particular state or condition: *came to like him; didn't come to any harm.* **c.** To move or be brought to a particular position: *The bus came to an abrupt halt.* **7.** To extend; reach: *hair coming to the waist.* **8.** To exist at a particular point or place: *The letter T comes before U.* **9. a.** To happen: *How did you come to know that?* **b.** To happen as a result: *This comes of your carelessness.* **10.** To be allotted or given: *On my death the jewels will come to you.* **11.** To occur in the mind: *An idea came to her.* **12. a.** To issue forth: *A loud scream came from the next room.* **b.** To descend; originate: *comes of an old Scottish family.* **c.** To be derived. **13.** To be a native or have been a resident of. **14.** To be moving toward a concluding or culminating stage; develop; evolve: *The project is coming along very well.* **15.** To become: *The knot came loose.* **16.** To be available or obtainable: *Houses here don't come cheap; It comes in two sizes.* **17.** To prove or turn out to be: *His wish came true.* **18.** To be achieved or mastered as specified: *Math comes easily to some people.* —**come about. 1.** To occur; take place; happen. **2.** *Nautical.* To change tack. —**come across. 1.** To encounter or find by chance. **2.** To leave an impression: *He comes across as a very pushy young man.* **3.** *Slang.* To do or give what is wanted. —**come again. 1.** To come or go back; return. **2.** *Informal.* To repeat what one has just said. Used in the imperative. —**come along. 1.** To improve; progress; advance. **2.** To appear; arrive: *Don't just take the first job that comes along.* —**come around** (or **round**). **1.** To recover; revive. **2.** To change one's opinion or position. —**come at. 1.** To attack; rush at. **2.** To obtain; get. —**come between.** To cause the separation or estrangement of. —**come by.** To acquire or get, especially by chance. —**come clean.** To confess all. —**come down on** (or **upon**). **1.** To descend upon; attack. **2.** *Informal.* To criticize; scold. —**come forward.** To volunteer one's services. —**come in. 1.** To turn out to be: *Some matches would come in handy.* **2.** To become popular or fashionable. **3.** To be received as income. **4.** To finish a race: *My horse came in last as usual.* **5.** To rise; flow. Used of the tide. —**come in for.** *Informal.* **1.** To be eligible for. **2.** To get; receive; acquire. —**come into.** To inherit. —**come off. 1.** To happen; occur. **2.** To acquit oneself. **3.** To have an intended effect; succeed. —**come off it.** *Informal.* To stop talking nonsense. Used in the imperative. —**come out. 1.** To be disclosed or made public. **2.** To declare oneself openly as to be something, especially a homosexual or lesbian. **3.** To make a formal social debut. **4.** To result; end up. **5.** *Chiefly British.* To go on strike. **6.** To become available; be published: *His new book is coming out next month.* **7.** To be developed successfully. Used of photographic film: *Our holiday photos didn't come out.* —**come out with. 1.** To disclose publicly; declare. **2.** To put into words; say. —**come over. 1.** To seize; possess: *Strange feelings came over me.* **2.** To change sides. **3.** *Informal.* To visit. —**come through. 1.** To recover; survive. **2.** *Informal.* To do as expected. **3.** To become manifest: *His love of nature comes through in his paintings.* —**come to. 1.** To recover consciousness. **2.** To amount to. **3.** To be a matter of; concern: *When it comes to fixing things, he's in a class of his own.* **4.** *Nautical.* **a.** To bring a ship's bow into the wind. **b.** To anchor. —**come to grips with.** To face squarely: *came to grips with the problem.* —**come up. 1.** To be regurgitated. **2.** To manifest itself; arise: *Something came up and we couldn't go.* —**come up against. 1.** To struggle or do battle with. **2.** To encounter (a problem, for example). —**come upon. 1.** To meet by accident. **2.** To attack. —**come up to. 1.** To reach or extend to; meet. **2.** To equal. —**come up with.** *Informal.* To propose; produce. —**how come.** *Informal.* Why. Used interrogatively. ~interj. Used to express anger, impatience, or remonstrance: *Come now, that's enough.* ~prep. As from; by: *Come next Friday, our financial problems will be solved.* [Come, came, come; Middle English *comen* or *cumen* (infinitive), *com* or *cam* (past singular), *comen* or *camen* (past plural), *comen* or *cumen* (past participle), Old English *cuman, cōm, c(w)ōmon, cumen,* from Germanic.]

come back intr.v. **1.** To return to popularity; become fashionable again. **2.** To return to memory. **3.** To retort. Usually used with *at.*

come·back (kŭm′băk′) n. **1.** A return to former prosperity or status. **2.** A retort; a piece of repartee. **3.** A recourse; a means of redress.

Com·e·con (kŏm′ē-kŏn, kŏm′ĭ-) n. A trade association of Communist states founded in 1949 and disbanded in 1991. Its members included the U.S.S.R. and its European allies, Cuba, Mongolia, and Vietnam. [Council for Mutual Economic Assistance.]

co·me·di·an (kə-mē′dē-ən) n. **1.** A professional entertainer who tells jokes, does impersonations, or performs various other comic acts. **2.** An actor in comedy. **3.** A comedy writer. **4.** An amusing person; clown.

co·me·dic (kə-mē′dĭk) adj. Of or relating to comedy.

co·me·di·enne (kə-mē′dē-ĕn′) n. A female professional entertainer who tells jokes, does impersonations, or performs various other comic acts. [French.]

com·e·do (kŏm′ə-dō′) n., pl. **-dos** or **-do·nes** (-dō′nēz). A **blackhead**

(see). Used in technical contexts. [New Latin, from Latin *comedo,* glutton, from *comedere,* to eat up : *com-* (intensive) + *edere,* to eat.]

come down intr.v. **1.** To lose status or wealth. **2.** To become ill. Used with *with: come down with measles.* **3.** To move to a lower position; drop. **4.** To reach a decision about a matter: *They came down on the side of the union.* **5.** To be transmitted through history; be passed down. Often used with *to.* **6.** To amount to. Used with *to*: *It comes down to this.* **7.** *Slang.* To come out of a drug-induced state.

come·down (kŭm′doun) n. **1.** A decline or drop to a lower status or level. **2.** *Informal.* A disappointment.

com·e·dy (kŏm′ĭ-dē) n., pl. **-dies.** Abbr. **com. 1.** A play, film, or other work that is humorous in its treatment of theme and character and usually has a happy ending. **2.** Any literary composition with humorous themes or characters. **3.** The branch of literature dealing with comedies. **4.** The art or technique of composing or acting in comedy. **5.** A comic element of literature or life. **6.** A comic occurrence. [Middle English *comedie,* from Old French, from Latin *cōmoedia,* from Greek *kōmōidia,* from *kōmōidos,* originally "a singer in the revels" : *kōmos†,* revel + *ōidos, aoidēs,* singer, from *aeidein,* to sing.]

comedy of manners n. A comedy satirizing fashionable society.

come-hith·er (kŭm′hĭth′ər) adj. Seductive; alluring.

come·ly (kŭm′lē) adj. **-lier, -liest. 1.** Having a pleasing appearance; attractive. —See Synonyms at **beautiful. 2.** Suitable; proper; seemly: *comely behavior.* [Middle English *comli, comeli(ch),* Old English *cȳmlic,* lovely, splendid, from *cȳme†,* beautiful.] —**come·li·ness** n.

Co·me·ni·us (kə-mē′nē-əs), **John Amos** (1592-1671). Czech **Jan Ko·men·ský** (kō′mən-skē). Czech theologian and educational reformer, who believed that science exalted divine majesty rather than threatened it. He held that learning should be by observation rather than through authoritarian dogma.

come on intr.v. **1.** To make progress; improve; develop. **2.** To enter or appear, as on a theater stage. **3.** To begin: *I feel a cold coming on.* **4.** *Informal.* To try to attract; allure. —tr.v. To find or encounter; happen on.

come-on (kŭm′ŏn′, -ôn′) n. Something offered to allure or attract; an inducement.

com·er (kŭm′ər) n. **1.** One that arrives or comes. Usually used in combination: *a latecomer; a newcomer.* **2.** *Informal.* One showing great promise.

co·mes·ti·ble (kə-mĕs′tə-bəl) adj. Edible. ~n. **comestibles.** Food. [Old French, from Medieval Latin *comestibilis,* from Latin *comedere* (past participle *comestus*), to eat up : *com-* (intensive) + *edere,* eat.]

com·et (kŏm′ĭt) n. Astronomy. A celestial body, observed only in that part of its orbit that is relatively close to the sun, having a head consisting of a solid nucleus surrounded by a nebulous coma, an elongated curved vapor tail arising from the coma when sufficiently close to the sun, and thought to consist chiefly of ammonia, methane, carbon dioxide, and water. [Middle English *comete,* Old English *comēta,* from Latin *comēta, comētēs,* from Greek *(astēr) komētēs,* "long-haired (star)," from *koman,* to wear long hair, from *komē†,* hair.] —**com·et·ar·y** (kŏm′ə-tĕr′ē), **co·met·ic** (kə-mĕt′ĭk) adj.

come·up·pance (kŭm′ŭp′əns) n. Informal. Punishment or retribution that one deserves; one's just deserts. [From phrase *come up,* sense development obscure.]

com·fit (kŭm′fĭt, kŏm′-) n. A sugar-coated sweet. [Middle English *confit,* from Old French, from Latin *confectum,* "preparation," from Latin *conficere,* to prepare : *com-* (intensive) + *facere,* to make.]

com·fort (kŭm′fərt) tr.v. **-forted, -forting, -forts. 1.** To soothe in time of grief or fear; console. **2.** To ease physically; relieve of pain or discomfort. —See Synonyms at **relieve.** ~n. **1.** A state of ease or well-being; freedom from pain or anxiety. **2.** Relief; consolation; solace. **3.** A source of consolation or support. **4.** A source of physical well-being: *home comforts.* **5.** Capacity to give physical ease and well-being: *enjoying the comfort of his favorite chair.* —See Synonyms at **rest.** [Middle English *comforten,* from Old French *conforter,* from Late Latin *confortāre,* to strengthen : Latin *com-* (intensive) + *fortis,* strong.] —**com·fort·ing·ly** adv.

com·fort·a·ble (kŭm′fər-tə-bəl, kŭmf′tər-bəl) adj. **1.** Providing or giving comfort. **2.** Being in a state of comfort; at ease. **3.** *Informal.* **a.** Providing adequately for one's material needs: *a comfortable income.* **b.** Having an adequate income. —**com·fort·a·ble·ness** n. —**com·fort·a·bly** adv.

Synonyms: cozy, restful, snug.

com·fort·er (kŭm′fər-tər) n. **1.** One that comforts. **2. Comforter.** The Holy Spirit. **3.** A quilted bedcover. **4.** *Chiefly British.* A woolen neck scarf.

comfort station n. A public toilet or rest room.

com·frey (kŭm′frē) n., pl. **-freys.** Any of several usually hairy or bristly plants of the genus *Symphytum,* native to the Old World, having clusters of blue, purplish, or white flowers. [Middle English *conferie,* from Old French *cumfirie, confire,* from Latin *conferva,* a water plant, "healer," from *confervēre,* to boil together, heal : *com-,* together + *fervēre,* to boil.]

com·fy (kŭm′fē) adj. **-fier, -fiest.** Informal. Comfortable.

com·ic (kŏm′ĭk) adj. Abbr. **com. 1.** Of, characteristic of, or pertaining to comedy. **2.** Of or pertaining to comic strips. **3.** Amusing; humorous.

~*n. Abbr.* **com. 1. a.** A comedian. **b.** A person who is comical. **2. a. comics.** Comic strips. **b.** A comic book. **c. comics.** The part of a newspaper devoted to comic strips. **3.** Something that provokes humor in art or life. [Latin *cōmicus,* from Greek *kōmikos,* from *kōmos,* revelry, merrymaking. See **comedy.**]

com·i·cal (kŏm′ĭ-kəl) *adj.* **1.** *Obsolete.* Of or pertaining to comedy. **2.** Provoking mirth; funny; amusing. —**com·i·cal·i·ty** (kŏm′ĭ-kăl′ə-tē), **com·i·cal·ness** *n.* —**com·i·cal·ly** *adv.*

comic book *n.* A magazine of comic strips.

comic opera *n.* An opera or operetta with a humorous plot, spoken dialogue, and, usually, a happy ending.

comic strip *n.* A narrative series of cartoons.

com·ing (kŭm′ĭng) *adj.* **1.** Approaching; next. **2.** *Informal.* Showing promise of fame or success; up-and-coming. ~*n.* Arrival; advent.

com·ing-out (kŭm′ĭng-out′) *n. Informal.* A social debut. Also used adjectivally: *a coming-out party.*

Com·in·tern (kŏm′ĭn-tûrn) *n.* The Third **International** *(see)* or, especially, its executive committee in Moscow. [*Communist International.*]

com·i·ti·a (kə-mĭsh′ē-ə, -mĭsh′ə) *n., pl.* **comitia.** A popular assembly in ancient Rome having legislative or electoral duties. [Latin, plural of *comitium,* meeting place : *com-,* together + *īre* (past participle *itus*), to go.] —**co·mi·tial** (kə-mĭsh′əl) *adj.*

com·i·ty (kŏm′ə-tē) *n., pl.* **-ties.** *Formal.* Civility; courtesy. [Latin *cōmitās,* from *cōmis,* courteous.]

comity of nations *n.* **1.** Courteous recognition accorded by one nation to the laws and institutions of another. **2.** The nations observing such courtesy.

comm. 1. commerce. **2.** commission; commissioner. **3.** commonwealth. **4.** communication.

com·ma (kŏm′ə) *n.* **1.** A punctuation mark (,) used to indicate a separation of ideas or of elements within the structure of a sentence, and, in some countries, to precede a decimal fraction. **2.** A pause or separation; caesura. **3.** Any of several butterflies of the genus *Polygonia,* having wings with brownish coloring and irregularly notched edges. [Latin, from Greek *komma,* a cut, section, clause, from *koptein,* to cut.]

comma bacillus *n.* A bacillus, *Vibrio comma,* that causes Asiatic cholera. [From its commalike shape.]

comma fault *n. Grammar.* Improper use of a comma between independent clauses not joined by a conjunction.

com·mand (kə-mănd′, -mänd′) *v.* **-manded, -manding, -mands.** —*tr.* **1.** To direct with authority; give orders to. **2.** To have control or authority over; rule. **3.** To have at one's disposal: *The country commands enormous mineral resources.* **4.** To deserve and receive as due; require: *His bravery commanded respect.* **5.** To dominate by position; overlook. —*intr.* **1.** To give commands. **2.** To exercise authority as a commander; be in control. ~*n.* **1.** The act of commanding or giving orders. **2.** An order so given. **3.** The authority to command. **4.** The possession and exercise of authority to command: *using all the skill at his command.* **5.** Ability to control; mastery: *an impressive command of the language.* **6.** Dominance by location; extent of view. **7. a.** The jurisdiction of a commander. **b.** *Military.* A unit, post, or region under the control of one officer. **c.** *U.S. Air Force.* A unit consisting of a specified number of wings, generally three or more, under the authority of an officer. **8.** *British.* An invitation from the reigning monarch. **9.** *Computer Science.* An instruction. Also used adjectivally: *a command file.* [Middle English *com(m)aunden,* from Norman French *comaunder,* from Old French *comander,* from Late Latin *commandāre,* to **COMMEND.**]

Synonyms: *bid, charge, direct, enjoin, instruct, order.*

com·man·dant (kŏm′ən-dănt′, -dänt′) *n. Abbr.* **Comdt. 1.** A commanding officer of a military organization. **2.** *South African.* A lieutenant-colonel.

com·man·deer (kŏm′ən-dîr′) *tr.v.* **-deered, -deering, -deers. 1.** To force into military service. **2.** To seize (property) for military use; confiscate. **3.** *Informal.* To take arbitrarily or by force. [Afrikaans *kommandeer,* from French *commander,* to **COMMAND.**]

com·mand·er (kə-măn′dər, kə-män′-) *n.* **1.** A person who commands; leader. **2. a.** *Abbr.* **Comdr., Cdr., Com., Cmdr.** An officer in the U.S. Navy who ranks next above a lieutenant commander and next below a captain. **b.** The chief commissioned officer of a military unit, regardless of his rank. **3.** A chief or an officer in certain knightly or fraternal orders.

commander in chief *n., pl.* **commanders in chief. 1.** *Often* **Commander in Chief.** *Abbr.* **CINC, C in C.** The supreme commander of all the armed forces of a nation. **2.** The officer commanding a major armed force.

com·mand·er·y (kə-măn′dər-ē, kə-män′-) *n., pl.* **-ies. 1.** The district or office of a commander, especially of an order of knights. **2.** A lodge or local branch of certain fraternal orders.

com·mand·ing (kə-măn′dĭng, kə-män′-) *adj.* **1.** *Abbr.* **comdg.** Having command; controlling. **2.** Impressive. **3.** Dominating, as by height or position. —**com·mand·ing·ly** *adv.*

commanding officer *n. Abbr.* **C.O.** An officer in charge of any military unit.

com·mand·ment (kə-mănd′mənt, kə-mänd′-) *n.* **1.** A command; edict. **2.** *Sometimes* **Commandment.** Any of the **Ten Commandments** *(see).*

command module *n.* The portion of a spacecraft in which the astronauts live and operate controls during a flight.

com·man·do (kə-măn′dō, kə-män′-) *n., pl.* **-dos** *or* **-does. 1. a.** A small fighting force specially trained for making quick, destructive raids against enemy-held areas. Also used adjectivally: *a commando unit.* **b.** A member of such a force. **2. a.** Originally, in South Africa, an organized force of Boer troops. **b.** A raid made by such a force. [Afrikaans *kommando,* from Dutch *commando,* unit of troops, from Spanish *comando,* from *comandar,* to command, from Vulgar Latin *commandāre* (unattested), **COMMAND.**]

command performance *n.* A theatrical performance, entertainment, or the like, given at the request of a head of state.

command post *n. Abbr.* **C.P.** The field headquarters used by the commander of a military unit.

com·meas·ure (kə-mĕzh′ər) *tr.v.* **-ured, -uring, -ures.** To coincide

---

comet

REGULAR VISITORS FROM SPACE

Long trails of gas and dust lit up by the sun

More than 1,600 comets have been recorded, but only a few are visible with the naked eye. A comet is a ball of gas and dust with a starlike nucleus; probably space debris, it spins around the sun in an elongated orbit and can be seen from earth for only a short part of its journey. As it nears the sun, the comet shines by reflected sunlight, the gas warms up and evaporates, and a streaming tail of gas and dust is formed—always pointing away from the sun.

Orbits may take a few years or thousands of years. Encke's comet has the shortest-known orbital period —just over three years. Halley's comet, a bright comet visible to the naked eye for a few months every 76 years, was the first for which an orbital period was calculated. It was used by Edmund Halley (1656–1742), the English astronomer, as proof of Newton's theory of gravitation. In 1687 Newton had published his theories and calculations on the laws of motion that govern all bodies, including comets. Halley had observed a comet in 1682. Using Newton's equations, he calculated that its orbital period was 76 years. He then found records of a great comet in 1607 and 1531, and predicted its return in 1758. It actually appeared in December 1758 and was named after him.

At once it became clear that many previous sightings had been made. In 1301, the Italian painter Giotto used the comet later to become known as Halley's as a model for the Star of Bethlehem. Its appearance in 1066 was recorded in the Bayeux Tapestry. Chinese astronomers noted it in 240 B.C. It returned in the winter of 1985–86 and could be seen at its best in early 1986. Gravitational pulls from other planets can slightly shorten or lengthen the orbital period.

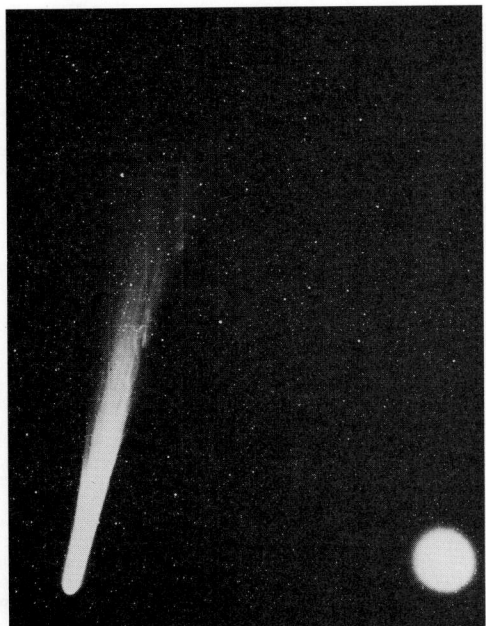

STREAKING THROUGH SPACE *The glowing tail, millions of miles long, streams behind Halley's comet as it is photographed passing Venus. On its appearance in 1986, the comet was more difficult to see than in 1910, but a space probe monitored it.*

with; be coextensive with. [COM- + MEASURE.] —**com·meas·ur·a·ble** *adj.*

com·me·dia dell'ar·te (kə-mā′dē-ə dĕl-är′tĕ) *n.* A type of comedy developed in Italy in the 16th century, characterized by improvisation from a plot outline and by the use of stock characters. [Italian, "comedy of art."]

comme il faut (kô mĕl fō′) *adj. French.* As one or it should be; proper.

com·mem·o·rate (kə-mĕm′ə-rāt′) *tr.v.* **-rated, -rating, -rates.** 1. To honor the memory of (a person or event) in speech or writing, or with a ceremony. 2. To serve as a memorial to. —See Synonyms at **observe.** [Latin *commemorāre,* to call to mind clearly : *com-* (intensive) + *memorāre,* to remind, speak of, from *memor,* mindful.] —**com·mem·o·ra·tor** *n.*

com·mem·o·ra·tion (kə-mĕm′ə-rā′shən) *n.* 1. The act of commemorating. 2. Something that commemorates. 3. A commemorative celebration.

com·mem·o·ra·tive (kə-mĕm′ər-ə-tĭv, -ə-rā′tĭv) *adj.* 1. Serving to commemorate. 2. Issued to commemorate a notable person or event. Said of coins, stamps, or the like. —*n.* Anything that commemorates.

com·mence (kə-mĕns′) *v.* **-menced, -mencing, -mences.** —*tr.* To begin; start. —*intr.* To come into existence; have a beginning. —See Synonyms at **begin.** [Middle English *commencen,* from Old French *comencer,* from Vulgar Latin *cominitiāre* (unattested) : Latin *com-* (intensive) + *initiāre,* to INITIATE.] —**com·menc·er** *n.*

com·mence·ment (kə-mĕns′mənt) *n.* 1. A beginning; start. 2. A ceremony at which academic degrees or diplomas are conferred.

com·mend (kə-mĕnd′) *tr.v.* **-mended, -mending, -mends.** 1. To represent as worthy, qualified, or desirable; recommend. 2. To express approval of; praise. 3. To commit to the care of another; entrust. —See Synonyms at **praise.** [Middle English *commenden,* from Latin *commendāre,* to commit to one's charge, commend, recommend : *com-* (intensive) + *mandāre,* to entrust.] —**com·mend·a·ble** *adj.* -**com·mend·a·bly** *adv.* —**com·mend·er** *n.*

com·men·da·tion (kŏm′ən-dā′shən) *n.* 1. The act of commending; recommendation; approval. 2. An award or honor: *a commendation for bravery.* —**com·men·da·to·ry** (kə-mĕn′də-tôr′ē, -tōr′ē) *adj.*

com·men·sal (kə-mĕn′səl) *adj.* 1. *Rare.* Eating at the same table. 2. *Biology.* Pertaining to or characterized by commensalism. —*n.* 1. *Rare.* A mealtime companion. 2. *Biology.* An organism participating in commensalism. [Middle English, from Medieval Latin *commensālis* : Latin *com-,* together + *mēnsa,* table.] —**com·men·sal·ly** *adv.*

com·men·sal·ism (kə-mĕn′səl-ĭz′əm) *n. Biology.* A relationship in which two or more organisms live in close association, and in which one may derive some benefit, but in which neither harms or is parasitic on the other. Compare **symbiosis.**

com·men·su·ra·ble (kə-mĕn′sər-ə-bəl, -shər-ə-bəl) *adj.* 1. Able to be measured by a common standard or in units having the same dimensions. 2. Properly proportioned; commensurate. 3. *Mathematics.* Exactly divisible by the same unit an integral number of times. Said of two quantities. [Late Latin *commēnsūrābilis* : *com-,* same + *mēnsūrābilis,* measurable, from *mēnsūrāre,* to measure, from Latin *mēnsūra,* MEASURE.] —**com·men·su·ra·bil·i·ty** *n.* —**com·men·su·ra·bly** *adv.*

com·men·su·rate (kə-mĕn′sə-rĭt, -shə-rĭt) *adj.* 1. Of the same size, extent, or duration; coextensive. 2. Corresponding in scale or measure; proportionate: *a salary commensurate with the job's responsibilities.* 3. Having a common measure or standard; commensurable. [Late Latin *commēnsūrātus* : *com-,* same + *mēnsūrātus,* past participle of *mēnsūrāre,* to MEASURE.] —**com·men·su·rate·ly** *adv.* —**com·men·su·ra·tion** *n.*

com·ment (kŏm′ĕnt′) *n.* 1. a. A remark, as in criticism or observation. b. A brief statement of fact or opinion, especially one that expresses a personal reaction or attitude. 2. *Usually* **comments.** A written note intended as an explanation, illustration, or criticism of a passage in a book or other writing; an annotation. 3. Talk; gossip: *caused a lot of comment.* 4. Something that exemplifies; an illustration: *The incident was a sad comment on our times.* —*intr.v.* **commented, -menting, -ments.** To make a comment; remark. Often used with *on.* [Middle English, from Latin *commentum,* contrivance, interpretation, from *commentus,* past participle of *comminīscī,* to contrive by thought.]

com·men·tar·y (kŏm′ən-tĕr′ē) *n., pl.* **-ies.** 1. A series of annotations, explanations, or interpretations of a literary text. 2. *Often* **commentaries.** An expository treatise or essay; exegesis. 3. A series of descriptive observations of an event, especially a sports event, as it happens in a radio or television broadcast. 4. An illustration; comment. 5. *Often* **commentaries.** A personal narrative; memoir. —**com·men·tar·i·al** (kŏm′ən-târ′ē-əl) *adj.*

com·men·tate (kŏm′ən-tāt′) *v.* **-tated, -tating, -tates.** —*tr.* To make a commentary on. —*intr.* To serve as commentator; make a commentary, especially for a film or a radio or television broadcast. Used with *on.*

com·men·ta·tor (kŏm′ən-tā′tər) *n.* 1. An author of commentaries, especially on current or political events. 2. A person who makes radio or television commentaries.

com·merce (kŏm′ərs) *n.* 1. *Abbr.* **com., comm.** The buying and selling of goods, especially on a large scale, as between cities or nations; business; trade. 2. Intellectual exchange or social intercourse. 3. Sexual intercourse. —See Usage note at **business.**

[Old French, from Latin *commercium* : *com-* (collective) + *merx* (stem *merc-*), merchandise.]

com·mer·cial (kə-mûr′shəl) *adj. Abbr.* **com., cml.** 1. a. Of, pertaining to, or engaged in commerce. b. Suitable for commerce; profitable: *valuable minerals in commercial quantities.* 2. Produced in large quantities for use by industry; unrefined. Said especially of chemicals. 3. a. Viewed purely in terms of financial returns: *The play was a commercial success.* b. Having profit, success, or immediate results as chief aim: *a commercial painter.* 4. Financed by advertising revenue: *commercial television.* —*n.* An advertisement on radio or television.

commercial bank *n.* A privately owned bank, usually with a large umber of branches, the principal functions of which are to operate deposit and checking accounts and to make short-term loans.

com·mer·cial·ism (kə-mûr′shə-lĭz′əm) *n.* 1. The practices, methods, aims, and spirit of commerce or business. 2. An attitude that emphasizes or overemphasizes tangible profit or success. —**com·mer·cial·ist** *n.* —**com·mer·cial·is·tic** *adj.*

com·mer·cial·ize (kə-mûr′shə-līz′) *tr.v.* **-ized, -izing, -izes.** 1. To make commercial; apply methods of business to. 2. a. To exploit, do, or make mainly for financial gain. b. To sacrifice the quality of for profit. —**com·mer·cial·i·za·tion** *n.*

commercial paper *n.* Any of various short-term negotiable papers originating in business transactions.

commercial traveler *n.* A traveling salesman *(see).*

commercial vehicle *n.* A vehicle used for transporting merchandise by road.

com·mi·na·tion (kŏm′ə-nā′shən) *n.* 1. A formal denunciation; a threatening. 2. In the Anglican liturgy, a recital of God's judgment and anger against sinners, read on Ash Wednesday. [Middle English *comminacioun,* from Old French *commination,* from Latin *comminātiō* (stem *comminātiōn-*), from *comminārī,* to threaten : *com-* (intensive) + *minārī,* threaten, from *minae,* threats.] —**com·min·a·to·ry** (kə-mĭn′ə-tôr′ē, -tōr′ē, kŏm′ĭ-nə-) *adj.*

com·min·gle (kə-mĭng′gəl) *v.* **-gled, -gling, -gles.** —*intr.* To blend together; mix. —*tr.* To mix together; combine.

com·mi·nute (kŏm′ə-nōōt′, -nyōōt′) *tr.v.* **-nuted, -nuting, -nutes.** To reduce to powder; pulverize; triturate. [Latin *comminuere* : *com-* (intensive) + *minuere,* to lessen.] —**com·mi·nu·tion** *n.*

com·mis·er·ate (kə-mĭz′ə-rāt′) *v.* **-ated, -ating, -ates.** —*tr.* To feel or express sorrow or pity for; sympathize with. —*intr.* To feel or express sympathy. [Latin *commiserārī* : *com-,* with + *miserārī,* to pity, from *miser,* wretched, pitiable.] —**com·mis·er·a·tive** *adj.* —**com·mis·er·a·tive·ly** *adv.* —**com·mis·er·a·tor** *n.*

com·mis·er·a·tion (kə-mĭz′ə-rā′shən) *n.* A feeling or expression of sorrow or sympathy for the distress of another; compassion. —See Synonyms at **pity.**

com·mis·sar (kŏm′ə-sär′) *n.* 1. An official of the Communist Party charged with the teaching of political principles and the enforcement of party loyalty. 2. Formerly, the head of a commissariat in the U.S.S.R. [Russian *kommissar,* from French *commissaire,* COMMISSARY.]

com·mis·sar·i·at (kŏm′ə-sâr′ē-ĭt) *n.* 1. a. A department of an army in charge of providing food and other supplies for the troops. b. The officers in charge of this. 2. A food supply. 3. Formerly, any major government department in the U.S.S.R. [Russian *kommissariat,* from French and Medieval Latin *commissariatus,* from *commissārius,* COMMISSARY.]

com·mis·sar·y (kŏm′ə-sĕr′ē, -sâr′ē) *n., pl.* **-ies.** 1. A person to whom a special duty is given by a higher authority; a representative; deputy. 2. a. A supermarket for the use of soldiers in a camp, employees, diplomatic personnel, or the like. b. A cafeteria on a film set or in a television studio. 3. Formerly, an army officer in charge of supplying provisions. [Middle English *commissarie,* from Medieval Latin *commissārius,* commissioner, agent, from *committere,* to entrust, commission, COMMIT.] —**com·mis·sar·y·ship** *n.*

com·mis·sion (kə-mĭsh′ən) *n.* 1. a. An act of committing or giving authority to carry out a particular task or duty, or granting certain powers; an entrusting. b. A document conferring such authority. 2. The authority, duty, or task conferred in this way. 3. The state of being authorized to perform certain functions. 4. *Abbr.* **Com., comm.** A group of people lawfully authorized to perform certain duties or functions, such as a government agency. 5. A committing or perpetrating: *commission of a crime.* 6. A fee or percentage allowed to a salesman or agent for his services. 7. *Abbr.* **Com., comm.** a. An official document issued by a government, conferring the rank of a commissioned officer in the armed forces. b. The rank and powers so conferred. —**in** (or **out of**) **commission.** 1. In (or out of) active service. Said of a ship. 2. In (or out of) working condition or use. —*tr.v.* **commissioned, -sioning, -sions.** 1. To grant a commission to. 2. To place an order for. 3. *Nautical.* To put (a ship) into active service. [Middle English *commissioun,* from Old French *commission,* from Latin *commissiō* (stem *commissiōn-*), from *committere* (past participle *commissus*), COMMIT.] —**com·mis·sion·al, com·mis·sion·ar·y** (kə-mĭsh′ə-nĕr′ē) *adj.*

com·mis·sion·aire (kə-mĭsh′ə-nâr′) *n. Chiefly British.* A uniformed doorman. [French *commissionnaire,* from Old French *commission,* COMMISSION.]

commissioned officer *n.* Any officer in the armed forces who holds a commission and ranks as a second lieutenant or above in the U.S. Army, Air Force, or Marine Corps, or as an ensign or above in the U.S. Navy or Coast Guard. Compare **noncommissioned officer, warrant officer.**

com·mis·sion·er (kə-mĭsh′ən-ər) n. Abbr. **Com., Comr., comm.** 1. A person authorized by a commission to perform certain duties. 2. A member of a commission. 3. An official in charge of a particular department: *commissioner of police.* 4. *Sports.* An official selected by an athletic association or league to exercise judicial or regulatory power: *a baseball commissioner.* —**com·mis·sion·er·ship** n.

commission merchant n. A person who buys and sells goods for others on a commission basis.

commission plan n. A type of municipal government in which legislative and administrative functions and powers are vested in an elected commission rather than in a mayor and city council.

com·mis·sure (kŏm′ə-shoor′) n. 1. A line or place at which two things are joined; seam; juncture. 2. *Anatomy.* **a.** A tract of nerve fibers passing from one side to the other of the spinal cord or brain. **b.** The angle or corner of such structures as the lips, eyelids, or cardiac valves. 3. *Botany.* A surface by which adhering carpels, leaf lobes, or other parts are joined. [Middle English, from Latin *commissūra,* from *committere,* COMMIT.] —**com·mis·su·ral** (kŏm′ə-shoor′əl, kə-mĭsh′ər-əl) adj.

com·mit (kə-mĭt′) tr.v. **-mitted, -mitting, -mits.** 1. To do, perform, or perpetrate (especially something bad or wrong): *commit a murder.* 2. To place in trust or charge; consign; entrust. 3. To place officially in confinement or custody; especially, to place in a mental institution. 4. To consign for future use or reference or for preservation: *commit a poem to memory.* 5. To put in some place to be kept safe or be disposed of: *commit old love letters to the flames.* 6. **a.** To pledge (oneself) to a position on some issue. **b.** To bind or obligate, as by a pledge. **c.** To assign for a particular purpose; pledge. 7. To refer (a bill, for example) to a committee. [Middle English *committen,* from Latin *committere,* to join, connect, entrust : *com-,* together + *mittere,* to send, put.] —**com·mit·ta·ble** adj.
Synonyms: assign, confide, consign, entrust.

com·mit·ment (kə-mĭt′mənt) n. Also **com·mit·tal** (kə-mĭt′l) (for senses 1, 2, 3, 8). 1. **a.** The act of committing; a giving in charge or entrusting. **b.** The state of being committed. 2. Official consignment, as to a prison or mental hospital. 3. *Law.* A court order authorizing consignment to a prison; a mittimus. 4. **a.** A pledge to do something. **b.** Something pledged. 5. An engagement by contract involving financial obligation. 6. The state of being bound emotionally or intellectually to some way of thinking or course of action: *a deep commitment to liberal policies.* 7. A perpetration, as of a crime. 8. The act of referring a legislative bill to a committee.

com·mit·tee (kə-mĭt′ē) n. Abbr. **com., Com.** 1. A group of people, usually appointed from a larger body, delegated to perform a function, such as investigating, considering, or acting on a matter. 2. *Law.* Formerly, a person to whom the care of an estate or incompetent person is committed; a trustee; guardian. —**in committee.** Under consideration by a committee. Said of a legislative measure. [Middle English *committe,* trustee, from *committen,* COMMIT.]

com·mit·tee·man (kə-mĭt′ē-mən, -măn′) n., pl. **-men** (-mĭn, -mĕn′). A committee member.

committee of the whole n. The whole membership of a legislative body sitting as a committee to consider the details of a proposal.

com·mit·tee·wom·an (kə-mĭt′ē-woom′ən) n., pl. **-women** (-wĭm′ĭn). A female committee member.

com·mix (kə-mĭks′, kŏ-) v. **-mixed, -mixing, -mixes.** *Rare.* —*tr.* To mix together. —*intr.* To mix; blend. [Middle English, back-formation from *commixt,* from Latin *commixtus,* past participle of *commiscēre,* to mix together : *com-,* together + *miscēre,* mix.]

com·mix·ture (kə-mĭks′chər, kŏ-) n. 1. The act or process of mixing together. 2. The result of this; a mixture.

com·mode (kə-mōd′) n. 1. A low cabinet or chest of drawers, often elaborately decorated and usually on legs or short feet. 2. Formerly: **a.** A movable stand or cupboard containing a washbowl. **b.** A chair containing a concealed chamber pot. 3. A toilet. 4. A woman's ornate lace headdress, fashionable around 1700. [French, "convenient," from Latin *commodus,* COMMODIOUS.]

com·mo·di·ous (kə-mō′dē-əs) adj. 1. Spacious; roomy. 2. *Archaic.* Convenient; suitable. [Middle English, from Old French *commodieux,* from Medieval Latin *commodiōsus,* from Latin *commodus,* convenient, "(conforming) with (due) measure" : *com-,* with + *modus,* measure.] —**com·mo·di·ous·ly** adv. —**com·mo·di·ous·ness** n.

com·mod·i·ty (kə-mŏd′ə-tē) n., pl. **-ties.** 1. Anything useful or that can be turned to commercial or other advantage. 2. *Economics.* **a.** An article of trade or commerce that can be transported, especially an agricultural or mining product. **b.** Any economic unit that can be exchanged, such as a service or a product. 3. *Obsolete.* **a.** Convenience; profit; expediency: *"kings break faith upon commodity"* (Shakespeare). **b.** A quantity of goods. [Middle English *commodite,* profit, income, property, from Old French *commodite,* from Latin *commoditās* (stem *commoditat-*), advantage, convenience, from *commodus,* convenient, COMMODIOUS.]

com·mo·dore (kŏm′ə-dôr′, -dōr′) n. Abbr. **Com., COMO, Como.** 1. *U.S. Navy.* Formerly, an officer ranking below rear admiral and above captain. This rank was abolished in 1899 but temporarily restored during World War II. 2. *British Navy.* An unofficial designation for a captain temporarily in command of a fleet division or squadron. 3. **a.** The senior captain of a naval squadron or merchant fleet. **b.** The presiding officer of a yacht club. [Dutch *komandeur,* commander, from French *commandeur,* commander.]

com·mon (kŏm′ən) adj. **-moner, -monest.** 1. Belonging equally to two or more; shared by all alike; joint: *common interests.* 2. Pertaining to the community as a whole; public: *the common good.* 3. Generally known: *common knowledge.* 4. Widespread; prevalent; general. 5. Of frequent or habitual occurrence; usual. 6. Most widely known or occurring most frequently; ordinary: *the common crow.* 7. Without special designation, status, or rank: *a common sailor.* 8. Not distinguished by superior or other characteristics; average: *the common spectator.* 9. Of no special quality; standard; plain: *common courtesy.* 10. Of mediocre or inferior quality; not costly or rare: *common cloth.* 11. Vulgar; unrefined; coarse. 12. Of variable length; either short or long. Said of a syllable in verse. 13. *Grammar.* **a.** Either masculine or feminine in gender. **b.** Representing one or all the members of a class; not designating a unique entity. 14. *Anatomy.* Having several branches: *common bile duct.* —See Usage note at **mutual.**
~n. 1. **commons.** The common people; commonalty. 2. **commons.** *Used with a singular or plural verb. British.* **a.** The political class comprising the commoners. **b.** The parliamentary representatives of this class. **c. Commons.** The House of Commons. 3. *Sometimes* **commons.** A tract of land belonging to or used by a community as a whole. 4. *Law.* The right of a person to use the lands or waters of another, as for fishing or grazing cattle. 5. *Sometimes* **Common.** A church service used for a particular class of festivals. 6. **commons.** *Used with a singular verb.* A building or hall for dining. —**in common.** Equally with or by all; jointly. [Middle English *commun(e),* from Old French, from Latin *commūnis.*] —**com·mon·ness** n.
Synonyms: familiar, ordinary, prevalent.

com·mon·age (kŏm′ə-nĭj) n. 1. The right to pasture animals on common land. 2. The use of this right. 3. The state of being held in common. 4. That which is held in common, especially land.

com·mon·al·i·ty (kŏm′ən-ăl′ə-tē) n. 1. The state of being held in common or shared by numerous people or things. 2. An object or attribute so shared. 3. A common occurrence. 4. The common people; commonalty.

com·mon·al·ty (kŏm′ən-əl-tē) n., pl. **-ties.** 1. The common people, as opposed to the upper classes. 2. A body corporate; corporation. 3. An entire group or body. [Middle English *communalte,* from Old French *comunalte,* from Medieval Latin *commūnālitās* (stem *commūnālitat-*), from *commūnālis,* COMMUNAL.]

common blue n. A blue butterfly, *Polyommatus icarus,* of the temperate Old World, the male of which is bright violet-blue and the female of which is dark brown.

common carrier n. A carrier by land, water, or air which is prepared to accept any passengers or goods that require transport. Compare **private carrier.**

common cold n. A respiratory viral infection, characterized by sneezing, nasal congestion, coughing, and inflammation of the nasal mucous membranes.

common denominator n. 1. A quantity into which all the denominators of a set of fractions may be evenly divided. 2. A quality or belief common to all the members of a particular group, and considered to characterize them as a group.

common divisor n. A quantity that is a factor of two or more quantities. Also called "common factor," "common measure."

com·mon·er (kŏm′ə-nər) n. 1. One of the common people. 2. One who is not a noble. 3. In certain British universities and public schools, a student who does not hold a scholarship or similar award.

common era n. Abbr. **C.E.** The Christian Era (see).

common fraction n. A simple fraction (see).

common gender n. Gender that may refer to either masculine or feminine categories; for example, *child, person.* Compare **natural gender, grammatical gender.**

common ground n. Points of agreement between the parties in a discussion providing a basis for argument or negotiation.

common law n. Abbr. **c.l.** 1. The system of laws originated and developed in England, based on court decisions, on the doctrines implicit in those decisions, and on customs and usages, rather than on codified written laws. Compare **statute law.** 2. The part of a system of laws of any state or nation that is of a general and universal application. —**com·mon-law** adj.

common-law marriage n. 1. In English law, a marriage contracted in circumstances not allowing an official ceremony. 2. A marriage existing by mutual agreement between a man and a woman without a civil or religious ceremony.

common logarithm n. A logarithm to the base 10. Compare **natural logarithm.**

com·mon·ly (kŏm′ən-lē) adv. 1. Generally; ordinarily. 2. In a common manner.

Common Market n. 1. The **European Economic Community** (see). 2. *Usually* **common market.** Any economic union between countries in which trade barriers are removed.

common measure n. 1. *Music.* **Common time** (see). 2. A **common divisor** (see).

common meter n. A form of stanza used in hymns and carols, consisting of four lines, alternately of eight and six syllables.

common multiple n. A quantity that is a multiple of each of two or more given quantities.

common noun n. *Grammar.* A noun that represents one or all of the members of a class; for example, *book, woman.* Compare **proper noun.**

Commonwealth

THE BAND OF NATIONS THAT GREW OUT OF THE BRITISH EMPIRE
A billion people of many languages, cultures, and political systems

The Commonwealth grew out of the old British Empire, as former colonies achieved their independence and joined together in a loose association for consultation and cooperation.

As the British Commonwealth, it developed gradually between 1919 and 1949, the Statute of Westminster (1931) referring to the self-governing dominions of Australia, Canada, New Zealand, and South Africa as "freely associated members." In April 1949, membership was broadened to include republics (notably India) prepared to acknowledge the British reigning monarch as head of the Commonwealth, and "British" was dropped from the title. The Republic of Ireland withdrew in 1949, South Africa in 1961 because of its apartheid policy, and Fiji withdrew in 1987. Pakistan left in 1972 and rejoined in 1989. In

1990, the admission of Namibia brought membership to 50 nations.

The Commonwealth has no formal constitution. Members accept the Singapore Declaration of Commonwealth Principles (1971) calling for individual liberty, international peace and cooperation, free and fair international trade for a more equitable international society, and opposition to all forms of racial oppression. A Commonwealth Secretariat was established in London in 1965. Heads of government meet every two years, with the emphasis on informal sessions and private discussion. Commonwealth Day is the second Monday in March, and the Commonwealth Games are held every four years; the 1990 venue was Auckland, New Zealand.

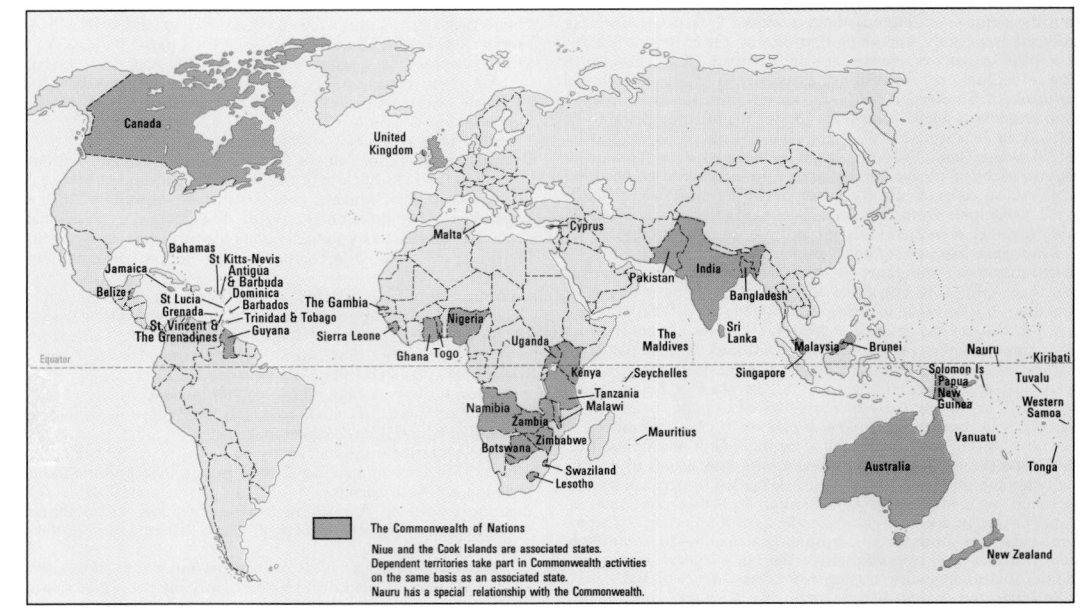

☐ The Commonwealth of Nations
Niue and the Cook Islands are associated states.
Dependent territories take part in Commonwealth activities on the same basis as an associated state.
Nauru has a special relationship with the Commonwealth.

---

com·mon·place (kŏm′ən-plās′) *adj.* Ordinary; uninteresting; common. —See Synonyms at **trite.**
~*n.* **1.** A trite or obvious remark; platitude. **2.** Something ordinary or common. **3.** A passage in a book marked for reference or entered in a commonplace book. —See Synonyms at **cliché.** [Translation of Latin *locus commūnis,* translation of Greek *koinos topos,* "common place," literary passage of universal application.] —**com·mon·place·ness** *n.*

commonplace book *n.* A personal journal in which quotable passages, literary excerpts, and comments are written.

common pleas *n.* A **Court of Common Pleas** *(see).*

Common Prayer *n.* **1.** The liturgy for public worship in the Church of England. **2.** The **Book of Common Prayer** *(see).*

common rat *n.* The **brown rat** *(see).*

common room *n.* A sitting room or lounge in an educational or similar institution.

common salt *n.* **1.** Salt *(see).* **2.** Sodium chloride *(see).* **3.** Table salt *(see).*

common sense *n.* **1.** Native good judgment. **2.** A set of general unexamined assumptions as distinguished from specially acquired concepts. [Translation of Latin *sensus commūnis* and Greek *koinē aisthēsis,* total perception of the five senses.] —**com·mon·sense, com·mon-sense** (kŏm′ən-sĕns′) *adj.*

common stock *n.* Ordinary capital shares of a corporation that have exclusive residual claim on the net assets and net income of the corporation after all prior claims have been paid.

common time *n. Music.* A meter having four quarter notes to the measure. It is written ⁴/₄. Also called "common measure."

com·mon·weal (kŏm′ən-wēl′) *n.* **1.** The public good. **2.** *Archaic.* A commonwealth.

com·mon·wealth (kŏm′ən-wĕlth′) *n.* **1.** The people of a nation or state; the body politic. **2.** *Abbr.* **comm.** A nation or state governed by the people; republic. **3. Commonwealth. a.** The official title of some U.S. states, including Kentucky, Virginia, Massachusetts, and Pennsylvania. **b.** The official title of Puerto Rico, indicating its special status as a self-governing, autonomous political unit voluntarily associated with the United States. **4.** *Obsolete.* The public welfare.

Also *archaic* "commonweal." —**the Commonwealth. 1.** The political community consisting of the United Kingdom, its dependencies, and certain former colonies. Also officially called the "Commonwealth of Nations," formerly the "British Commonwealth of Nations." **2. a.** The period of republican government in Britain between 1649 and 1660. **b.** The parts of this period that preceded (1649–53) and followed (1659–60) Oliver Cromwell's personal protectorship. **c.** The form or forms of government during these periods. Also called the "Commonwealth of England." **3. Australia** *(see).*

Commonwealth of Independent States *n. Abbr.* **CIS, C.I.S.** An alliance of 11 former Soviet republics formed in 1991 for the purpose of economic, political, and cultural cooperation. Its headquarters are at Minsk, Belarus.

com·mo·tion (kə-mō′shən) *n.* **1.** Violent or turbulent motion; agitation. **2.** Political disturbance; disorder. **3.** A confused noise, suggesting upheaval; tumult. [Middle English *commocioun,* from Old French *commotion,* from Latin *commōtiō* (stem *commōtiōn-*), from *commovēre* (past participle *commōtus*), to move violently : *com-* (intensive) + *movēre,* to move.] —**com·mo·tion·al** *adj.*

com·move (kə-mōōv′) *tr.v.* **-moved, -moving, -moves.** To agitate; disturb; excite. [Middle English *commeven, comm(o)even,* from Latin *commovēre.* See **commotion.**]

com·mu·nal (kə-myōōn′əl, kŏm′yə-nəl) *adj.* **1.** Of or pertaining to a commune or community. **2.** Of, pertaining to, or shared by the people of a community or members of a group; common: *communal washing facilities.* **3.** Of or concerning different and opposed communities, especially in India: *communal riots between Hindus and Muslims.* [French, from Old French *comunal,* from Medieval Latin *commūnālis,* from *commūna, commūnia,* **COMMUNE** (community).] —**com·mu·nal·i·ty** (kŏm′yə-năl′ə-tē) *n.* —**com·mu·nal·ly** *adv.*

com·mu·nal·ism (kə-myōōn′əl-īz′əm, kŏm′yə-nəl-) *n.* **1.** A theory or system of government in which local communities are loosely bound in a federation. **2.** Belief in or practice of communal ownership, as of goods and property. **3.** Strong devotion to the interests of one's own cultural or ethnic group rather than those of society as a whole. —**com·mu·nal·ist** *n.* —**com·mu·nal·is·tic** *adj.*

com·mu·nal·ize (kə-myōōn′əl-īz′, kŏm′yə-nəl-) *tr.v.* **-ized, -izing.**

-izes. To convert into municipal or community property.

Com·mu·nard (kŏm′yə-närd′) n. **1.** A member or supporter of the **Paris Commune** (see). **2. communard.** A member of a commune. [French, from commune, COMMUNE (division).]

com·mune¹ (kə-myōōn′) intr.v. **-muned, -muning, -munes. 1.** To have close or intimate rapport or communication. Often used with with. **2.** To receive Communion. ~n. (kŏm′yōōn′). Intimate conversation or communion. [Middle English communen, to distribute, share, communicate, from Old French comuner, from comun, commun, COMMON. Sense 2 of verb : back-formation from COMMUNION.]

com·mune² (kŏm′yōōn′) n. **1.** The smallest local political division of France, Belgium, Italy, and Switzerland, governed by a mayor and municipal council. **2. a.** A local community organized legally for promoting local interests. **b.** A municipal corporation in the Middle Ages. **3.** A small, often rural community whose members have common interests and in which property is often shared or owned jointly. **4.** The people of a commune. **—the Commune. 1.** The revolutionary committee that governed Paris from 1789 to 1795. **2.** The **Paris Commune** (see). [French, from Medieval Latin communia, community, from Latin communis, public, COMMON.]

com·mu·ni·ca·ble (kə-myōō′nĭ-kə-bəl) adj. **1.** Able to be communicated or transmitted. **2.** Talkative. **3.** Medicine. Liable to be readily passed on from one person to another; infectious. Said of a disease. **—com·mu·ni·ca·bil·i·ty, com·mu·ni·ca·ble·ness** n. **—com·mu·ni·ca·bly** adv.

com·mu·ni·cant (kə-myōō′nĭ-kənt) n. **1.** A person who receives, or is entitled to receive, Communion. **2.** One who communicates. ~adj. Communicating.

com·mu·ni·cate (kə-myōō′nə-kāt) v. **-cated, -cating, -cates. —tr. 1.** To make known; impart: communicate information. **2.** To transmit (a disease, for example). **—intr. 1.** To share or convey information. **2. a.** To have an interchange, as of ideas. **b.** To have mutual sympathy or good mutual understanding. **3.** To express oneself in such a way that one is readily and clearly understood. **4.** To receive Communion. **5.** To be connected or form a connecting passage. [Latin communicāre, "to make common," make known, from communis, COMMON.] **—com·mu·ni·ca·tor** n.

com·mu·ni·ca·tion (kə-myōō′nə-kā′shən) n. Abbr. **comm. 1.** The act of communicating; transmission. **2.** The exchange of thoughts, messages, or the like, as by speech, signals, or writing. **3.** Something communicated. **4. communications.** A means of communicating, especially: **a.** A system for sending and receiving messages, as by mail, telephone, or telegram. **b.** Any method by which human beings pass information to one another, including publishing, broadcasting, and telecommunications. **c.** Military. A network of routes for sending messages and transporting troops and supplies. **5.** Any connective passage or channel. **6. communications.** The art and technology of communicating in all its forms.

communications satellite n. A satellite used to aid communications, as by reflecting a radio signal. Also called "comsat."

com·mu·ni·ca·tive (kə-myōō′nə-kā′tĭv, -nĭ-kə-tĭv) adj. **1.** Inclined to communicate readily; talkative. **2.** Of communication.

com·mun·ion (kə-myōōn′yən) n. **1.** A possessing or sharing in common; participation. **2.** The act of communing; the sharing of thoughts or feelings; close rapport: in communion with nature. **3. a.** A religious or spiritual fellowship. **b.** A body of Christians with a common religious faith who practice the same rites; a denomination. **4. a. Communion.** The **Eucharist** (see). **b.** The consecrated elements of a Eucharist. **c.** The part of the Mass in which the sacrament of the Eucharist is received. [Middle English communioun, from Old French communion, from Late Latin communio (stem communion-), the Eucharist, from Latin, participation by all, from communis, COMMON.]

com·mu·ni·qué (kə-myōō′nə-kā′, kə-myōō′nə-kā′) n. An official announcement made to the press and public. [French, from communiquer, to inform, announce, from Latin communicāre, COMMUNICATE.]

com·mu·nism (kŏm′yə-nĭz′əm) n. **1.** A social system characterized by the absence of classes and by common ownership of the means of production and subsistence. **2. a.** A political, economic, and social doctrine aiming at the establishment of such a society. **b.** Often **Communism.** The Marxist-Leninist doctrine of revolutionary struggle toward this goal, the political movement representing it, or, loosely, socialism as practiced in countries ruled by communist parties. **c.** Communalism. **3.** Loosely, left-wing activity aiming at revolution. [French communisme, from commun, COMMON.]

Communism Peak. A mountain in Tajikistan, in west-central Asia, situated in the Pamir range. It rises to 7,495 meters (24,590 feet) above sea level.

com·mu·nist (kŏm′yə-nĭst) n. **1.** Often **Communist.** Abbr. **Com.** A member of a Marxist-Leninist party. **2.** A supporter of such a party or movement. **3.** A communalist. **4.** A Communard. **5.** Any radical viewed as a subversive or revolutionary. ~adj. Often **Communist.** Pertaining to, characteristic of, or resembling communism or communists.

com·mu·nis·tic (kŏm′yə-nĭs′tĭk) adj. Of, characteristic of, or inclined to communism. **—com·mu·nis·ti·cal·ly** adv.

Communist International n. The Third **International** (see).

Communist Manifesto n. A pamphlet, issued in 1848 by Karl Marx and Friedrich Engels, constituting the first statement of the principles of modern Communism.

Communist Party n. Abbr. **C.P.** A Marxist-Leninist party, usually

one originally belonging to the Third **International** (see).

com·mu·ni·tar·i·an (kə-myōō′nə-târ′ē-ən) n. A member or supporter of a communistic community.

com·mu·ni·ty (kə-myōō′nə-tē) n., pl. **-ties. 1. a.** A group of people living in the same locality or under the same local government. **b.** The district or locality in which they live. **2.** A social group or class having common characteristics. **3.** Any group having common interests: the scientific community. **4.** Joint participation or common ownership: community of property. **5.** Similarity or identity: a community of interests. **6.** Society as a whole; the public. Preceded by the. **7.** Ecology. **a.** A group of plants and animals living in a specific region under relatively similar conditions, and interacting with each other through food webs and other relationships. **b.** The region in which they live. [Middle English communite, from Old French comunete, from Latin communitās (stem communitat-), from communis, COMMON.]

community center n. A meeting place used by members of a community for social, cultural, or recreational purposes.

community chest n. A welfare fund financed by private contributions for aiding various charitable organizations.

com·mu·nize (kŏm′yə-nīz′) tr.v. **-nized, -nizing, -nizes. 1.** To make public all the property of a community. **2.** To convert to Communist principles or control. [From Latin communis, COMMON.] **—com·mu·ni·za·tion** n.

com·mut·a·ble (kə-myōō′tə-bəl) adj. **1.** Capable of being commuted; interchangeable. **2.** Law. Capable of being reduced in length or severity. Said of a sentence. **—com·mut·a·bil·i·ty** n.

com·mu·tate (kŏm′yə-tāt′) tr.v. **-tated, -tating, -tates. 1.** To reverse the direction of (an alternating electric current) each half-cycle. **2.** To convert (an alternating electric current) into a direct current. [Back-formation from COMMUTATION.]

com·mu·ta·tion (kŏm′yə-tā′shən) n. **1.** A substitution, exchange, or interchange. **2. a.** The substitution of one kind of payment for another. **b.** The payment substituted. **3.** The travel of a commuter. **4.** Electricity. **a.** The conversion of alternating to direct electric current. **b.** The reversing of current direction. **5.** Law. A reduction of a penalty to a less severe one. [Middle English, from Old French, from Latin commutātiō (stem commutātiōn-), from commutāre, COMMUTE.]

commutation ticket n. A ticket issued at a reduced rate by a railroad, bus, or other transportation company for passage over a given route for a specified number of trips.

com·mu·ta·tive (kŏm′yə-tā′tĭv, kə-myōō′tə-tĭv) adj. **1.** Pertaining to, involving, or characterized by substitution, interchange, or exchange. **2.** Mathematics & Logic. Independent of the order of terms. Said of a combining operation, such as multiplication.

commutative group n. Mathematics. An algebraic group in which the result of multiplying one member by another is independent of the order of the members. Also called "Abelian group."

commutative law n. Mathematics & Logic. The law that certain operations, such as addition, multiplication, and conjunction, are independent of the order of the terms to which they are applied.

com·mu·ta·tor (kŏm′yə-tā′tər) n. A cylindrical arrangement of insulated metal bars connected to the coils of an electric motor or generator to provide a unidirectional current from the generator or a reversal of current into the coils of the motor.

com·mute (kə-myōōt′) v. **-muted, -muting, -mutes. —tr. 1.** To substitute; exchange; interchange. **2.** To convert; change; transform. **3.** To change (a penalty, debt, or payment) to a less severe one. **—intr. 1. a.** To compensate. **b.** To serve as a substitute. **2.** To pay in gross, usually at a reduced rate, rather than in individual payments. **3.** To travel as a commuter. **4.** Mathematics & Logic. To satisfy or engage in a commutative operation. [Middle English commuten, from Latin commutāre, to exchange : com-, mutually + mutāre, to change.]

com·mut·er (kə-myōō′tər) n. A person who travels regularly from one place to another, especially between work and home.

Co·mo, Lake (kō′mō). Lake in Lombardy in north Italy, in the southern margin of the Alps. It is a popular tourist center.

Com·o·ros (kŏm′ə-rōz′). Country consisting of the Comoro archipelago (except Mayotte Island), in the Indian Ocean. Most people are of mixed African, Arab, and Malay descent. The islands became a French colony (1912) and a French overseas territory in 1947. In 1974 all the islands except Mayotte voted for independence, which was attained in 1975. The islands export vanilla, sisal, copra, coffee, and perfume oils. Area, 2,200 square kilometers (849 square miles). Population, 500,000. Capital, Moroni. See map at **Madagascar.**

comose. Variant of comate.

comp¹ (kŏmp) intr. v. **comped, comping, comps.** Music. To play a jazz accompaniment, as on a piano or guitar.

comp² n. Informal. Something, as a theater ticket, given free of charge. [Short for COMPLIMENTARY.]

comp. 1. comparative. **2.** complete. **3.** composer. **4.** composite; composition; compositor. **5.** compound. **6.** comprehensive. **7.** comprising.

com·pact¹ (kəm-păkt′, kŏm-, kŏm′păkt′) adj. **1.** Closely and firmly united or packed together; dense. **2.** Packed into or arranged within a relatively small space. **3.** Expressed briefly and concisely. **4.** Designating a car that is small and inexpensive to run. ~tr.v. (kəm-păkt′) **compacted, -pacting, -pacts. 1.** To press or join firmly together; condense; consolidate. **2.** To make or compose by pressing or joining together. ~n. (kŏm′păkt′). **1.** A small case containing a mirror, face powder, and a powder puff. **2.** A small economical car. [Middle English, from Latin *compactus,* past participle of *compingere,* to join together : *com-,* together + *pangere,* to fasten.] **—com·pact·er** *n.* **—com·pac·tion** *n.* **—com·pact·ly** *adv.* **—com·pact·ness** *n.*

com·pact[2] (kŏm′păkt′) *n.* An agreement or covenant. [Latin *compactum,* from *compactus,* past participle of *compacīscī,* to agree together : *com-,* together + *pacīscī,* to agree.]

compact disc *n. Abbr.* **C.D.** A compact laser disc for reproducing recorded sound when it is played on a specially designed record player.

com·pac·tor (kəm-păk′tər, kŏm′păk′-) *n.* An apparatus that compresses refuse into relatively small packs for handy disposal.

com·pa·dre (kəm-pä′drā) *n. Southwestern U.S.* A friend or close companion. [Spanish, godfather, from Medieval Latin *compater,* "joint father," godfather : Latin *com-,* with, + *pater,* father.]

com·pan·der, com·pan·dor (kəm-păn′dər, kŏm-) *n. Electronics.* A system for reducing the noise level of a channel by compressing the volume range of the signal at the transmitter or recorder and restoring it to its original value at the receiving or reproducing device. [*Com*pression + Ex*pander.*]

com·pan·ion[1] (kəm-păn′yən) *n.* **1. a.** A person who accompanies or associates with another; comrade. **b.** One who lives with another as an intimate, but without formal legal ties. **2.** A person employed to assist, live with, or travel with another. **3.** Any of two or more matching or complementary things; mate; match. Also used adjectivally: *a companion volume.* **4.** A guidebook or handbook. **5.** *Abbr.* **C.** A member of the lowest rank or grade in certain orders of knighthood. **6.** The fainter part of a double star.
~*tr.v.* **companioned, -ioning, -ions.** *Rare.* To be a companion to; associate with; accompany. [Middle English *compai(g)noun,* from Old French *compaignon,* from Vulgar Latin *compāniō* (stem *compāniōn-*), "one who eats bread with another" : Latin *com-,* together + *pānis,* bread.]

companion[2] *n.* **1.** A raised frame on the open deck of a ship, containing windows to light the cabins or closed deck below. **2.** A companionway. [Obsolete Dutch *kompanje,* quarterdeck, from Old French *compagne,* from Italian *(camera della) compagna,* ship's storeroom, perhaps related to COMPANION (comrade).]

com·pan·ion·a·ble (kəm-păn′yə-nə-bəl) *adj.* Suited to be a good companion; sociable; friendly. **—com·pan·ion·a·bly** *adv.*

com·pan·ion·ship (kəm-păn′yən-shĭp′) *n.* The relationship existing between companions; fellowship.

com·pan·ion·way (kəm-păn′yən-wā′) *n.* A stairway leading from a ship's deck to the cabins or deck below.

com·pa·ny (kŭm′pə-nē) *n., pl.* **-nies. 1.** A group of people; an assembly; gathering. **2.** People assembled for a social purpose. **3.** A guest or guests. **4. a.** Companionship; fellowship. **b.** A source of companionship: *She'll be company for you.* **c.** A person's companions: *bad company.* **5.** A social environment; society: *she's rather shy in company.* **6.** A business enterprise; firm. **7.** *Abbr.* **co., Co.** A partner or partners not specifically named in a firm's title: *John Rogers and Company.* **8.** A troupe of dancers or dramatic or musical performers: *a repertory company.* **9.** *Military.* A subdivision of a regiment or battalion, usually under the command of a captain. **10.** A ship's crew and officers. **11.** A medieval guild. **—keep company.** To associate, as in courtship. **—keep someone company.** To accompany. **—part company.** To end an association or friendship.
~*v.* **companied, -nying, -nies.** *Archaic.* —*tr.* To accompany or associate with. —*intr.* To keep company; associate. [Middle English *compaignie,* from Old French *compagnie,* from *compain,* COMPANION.]

compar. comparative.

com·pa·ra·ble (kŏm′pər-ə-bəl) *adj.* **1.** Able to be compared; similar or equivalent. **2.** Worthy of comparison. **—com·pa·ra·bil·i·ty, com·pa·ra·ble·ness** *n.* **—com·pa·ra·bly** *adv.*

com·par·a·tist (kəm-păr′ə-tĭst) *n.* A person who employs the comparative method, as in linguistics.

com·par·a·tive (kəm-păr′ə-tĭv) *adj. Abbr.* **comp., compar. 1.** Pertaining to, based on, or involving comparison: *comparative studies.* **2.** Estimated by comparison; relative: *a comparative failure.* **3.** *Grammar.* Expressing or involving the intermediate degree of comparison of adjectives and adverbs. Compare **positive** and **superlative.**
~*n. Grammar.* **1.** The comparative degree. **2.** An adjective or adverb expressing the comparative degree; for example, *brighter* is the comparative of *bright; more keenly* is the comparative of *keenly.* **—com·par·a·tive·ly** *adv.*

comparative linguistics *n.* The study of two languages or linguistic varieties which are usually synchronous, with the emphasis on common features or divergence from a common source. Compare **historical linguistics.**

com·pa·ra·tor (kŏm′pə-rā′tər, kəm-păr′ə-tər) *n.* **1.** Any of various devices for comparing an aspect of an object, such as shape, color, or brightness, with a standard. **2.** An electrical device containing a circuit for comparing two signals.

com·pare (kəm-pâr′) *v.* **-pared, -paring, -pares.** —*tr.* **1.** To represent as similar, equal, or analogous; liken. Used with *to.* **2.** *Abbr.* **cf., cp.** To examine in order to note similarities or differences. Used with *with* or *and.* **3.** *Grammar.* To form the positive, comparative, or superlative degrees of (an adjective or adverb). —*intr.* **1.** To be worthy of comparison; be considered as similar or equal. Used with *with: Nothing can compare with real silk.* **2.** To draw comparisons.
~*n.* Comparison: *a musician beyond compare.* [Middle English *comparen,* from Old French *comparer,* from Latin *comparāre,* to pair, match, from *compar,* like, equal : *com-,* mutually + *pār,* equal.] **—com·par·er** *n.*
Usage: In formal usage, *compare to* and *compare with* have different interpretations. In the sense "represent as similar," *compare to* is usual: *He compared the meeting to a battlefield.* In the sense "examine in order to note similarities and differences," *compare with* is usual: *He compared Shelley's poetry with Wordsworth's.*

com·par·i·son (kəm-păr′ə-sən) *n.* **1.** A comparing or being compared; a statement or estimate of similarities and differences. **2.** The quality of being capable or worthy of being compared; similarity; likeness. **3.** *Grammar.* The modification or inflection of an adjective or adverb to denote the three degrees (positive, comparative, and superlative). [Middle English *comparisoun,* from Old French *comparaison,* from Latin *comparātiō* (stem *comparātiōn-*), from *comparāre,* COMPARE.]

com·part (kəm-pärt′) *tr.v.* **-parted, -parting, -parts.** To divide into parts or compartments; partition. [Italian *compartire,* from Late Latin *compartīrī,* to divide, share with : *com-,* with + *partīrī,* to share, from *pars* (stem *part-*), a part.]

com·part·ment (kəm-pärt′mənt) *n.* **1.** Any of the parts or spaces into which an area is subdivided. **2.** Any separate room, section, or chamber: *a storage compartment.* **3.** Any separate part or division. **4.** A separate section of a railroad car. [French, *compartiment,* from Italian, *compartire,* from Late Latin *compartīrī,* to divide, share with : *com-,* with + *partīrī,* to share, from *pars* (stem *part-*), a part + -MENT.]

com·part·men·tal·ize (kŏm′pärt-mĕn′təl-īz′, kəm-pärt′-) *tr.v.* **-ized, -izing, -izes.** To divide or partition into compartments or categories. **—com·part·men·tal·i·za·tion** *n.*

compass *Seamen of the 12th century are the first known to have used a compass for navigation. It was simply a magnetized needle floating in a bowl of water. Decorative compass cards such as the one in this compass were common in the 18th and 19th centuries. A similar highly decorative device showing directions was usually included on a map or chart of the time, and is known as a compass rose.*

com·pass (kŭm′pəs, kŏm′-) *n.* **1. a.** A device used to determine geographical direction, usually consisting of a magnetic needle horizontally mounted or suspended and free to pivot until aligned with the magnetic field of the earth. **b.** Any other device for determining geographical direction, such as a **radio compass** or a **gyrocompass** *(both of which see).* **2.** *Sometimes* **compasses.** A V-shaped device for drawing circles or circular arcs, consisting of a pair of rigid, hinged arms, one of which is equipped with a pen or pencil and the other with a sharp point providing a central anchor or pivot about which the drawing arm is turned. Also called "pair of compasses." **3.** An enclosing line or boundary; circumference. **4.** An enclosed space or area. **5.** A range or scope; extent. **6.** *Music.* The range of a voice or instrument; register.
~*tr.v.* **compassed, -passing, -passes. 1.** To go around; circle. **2.** *Literary.* To surround; encircle. **3.** To understand; comprehend. **4.** To achieve; obtain; accomplish. **5.** To contrive, especially by scheming or plotting. —See Synonyms at **reach.** [Middle English *compas,* measure, circle, compasses, compass, from Old French, from *compasser,* to measure (with compasses), from Vulgar Latin *compassāre* (unattested), "to measure off by steps" : Latin *com-* (intensive) + *passus,* PACE.] **—com·pass·a·ble** *adj.*

compass card *n.* A freely pivoting circular disk carrying the magnetic needles of a compass and marked with the 32 points of the compass and the 360 degrees of the circle.

com·pas·sion (kəm-păsh′ən) *n.* A deep feeling of pity for the suffering of another, and an inclination to give aid or support, or to show mercy. —See Synonyms at **pity.** [Middle English *compassioun,* from Old French *compassion,* from Late Latin *compassiō* (stem *compassiōn-*), from *compatī* (past participle *compassus*), to sympathize with : *com-,* with + *patī,* to suffer.]

com·pas·sion·ate (kəm-păsh′ən-ĭt) *adj.* Feeling or showing pity or compassion; sympathetic. —See Synonyms at **kind. —com·pas·sion·ate·ly** *adv.* **—com·pas·sion·ate·ness** *n.*

compass plant *n.* **1.** A tall plant, *Silphium laciniatum,* of central North America, having yellow flowers and lower leaves that tend to align in a north-south plane. Also called "rosinweed." **2.** Any of several similar plants.

compass rose *n.* A circle resembling a compass card, often decorated, printed onto a chart or map to indicate the points of the compass relative to the land depicted in the map or chart.

compass saw *n.* A handsaw with a narrow blade for making curved cuts.

compass window *n.* A bay window that has a rounded rather than square projection.

com·pat·i·ble (kəm-păt′ə-bəl) *adj.* **1.** Capable of living or performing in harmonious, consistent, or congenial combination with another or others. **2.** Capable of efficient integration and operation with each other or with other elements in a system. Said of pieces of machinery, electronic equipment, or the like. **3.** Capable of forming a chemically or biochemically stable system. **4.** *Botany.* Capable of being successfully grafted. Said of plants. **5.** Of or pertaining to a television system in which color broadcasts can be received in black and white by sets incapable of color reception. [Middle English, from Old French, from Medieval Latin *compatibilis,* from Late Latin *compatī,* to sympathize with. See **compassion.**] **—com·pat·i·bil·i·ty, com·pat·i·ble·ness** *n.* **—com·pat·i·bly** *adv.*

com·pa·tri·ot (kəm-pā′trē-ət, -ŏt′) *n.* **1.** A fellow countryman or countrywoman. **2.** *Informal.* A colleague. [French *compatriote,* from Late Latin *compatriōta* : *com-,* together + *patriōta,* PATRIOT.] **—com·pa·tri·ot·ic** *adj.*

com·peer (kəm-pîr′, kŏm′pîr′) *n.* **1.** A person of equal status, ability, or rank; a peer or equal. **2.** A comrade, companion, or associate. [Middle English *comper,* from Old French, from Latin *compār* : *com-,* with + *pār,* an equal, PEER.]

com·pel (kəm-pĕl′) *tr.v.* **-pelled, -pelling, -pels. 1.** To force, drive, or constrain. **2.** To obtain or bring about by or as if by force; exact: *compel obedience; compel respect.* **3.** *Archaic.* To gather or unite by force; herd. —See Synonyms at **force.** [Middle English *compellen,* from Old French *compeller,* from Latin *compellere,* "to drive (cattle) together," force : *com-,* together + *pellere,* drive.] —**com·pel·la·ble** *adj.* —**com·pel·la·bly** *adv.* —**com·pel·ler** *n.*

com·pel·la·tion (kŏm′pə-lā′shən, kŏm′pĕl-ā′-) *n. Rare.* **1.** An addressing or designating by name or title. **2.** The name or title used; an appellation. [Latin *compellātiō* (stem *compellātiōn-*), from *compellāre,* to accost, address.]

com·pel·ling (kəm-pĕl′ĭng) *adj.* **1.** Forceful. **2.** Worthy of serious attention or interest; convincing. —**com·pel·ling·ly** *adv.*

com·pen·di·ous (kəm-pĕn′dē-əs) *adj.* Containing or stating briefly and concisely all the essentials of something; terse; succinct. —See Synonyms at **concise.** [Middle English, from Latin *compendiōsus,* from *compendium,* COMPENDIUM.] —**com·pen·di·ous·ly** *adv.* —**com·pen·di·ous·ness** *n.*

com·pen·di·um (kəm-pĕn′dē-əm) *n., pl.* **-ums** or **-dia** (-dē-ə). **1.** A short, complete summary; an abridgment. **2.** *British.* A collection of useful information. [Latin, "that which is weighed together," gain, saving, abridgment, from *compendere,* to weigh together : *com-,* together + *pendere,* to weigh.]

com·pen·sa·ble (kəm-pĕn′sə-bəl) *adj.* Entitled to compensation; capable of being compensated.

com·pen·sate (kŏm′pən-sāt′) *v.* **-sated, -sating, -sates.** —*tr.* **1.** To make up for or offset; counterbalance. **2.** To make equivalent or satisfactory reparation to; recompense or reimburse. **3.** To provide (a pendulum, for example) with a mechanism to offset the effects of variations such as expansion. —*intr.* **1.** To provide or serve as a substitute or counterbalance. **2.** *Biology & Psychology.* To make up for a failing, defect, or unwanted effect by cultivating some other characteristic: *compensated for his lack of height by an aggressive manner.* [Latin *compensāre,* to weigh one thing against another, counterbalance : *com-,* mutually, reciprocally + *pensāre,* frequentative of *pendere,* to weigh.] —**com·pen·sa·tive** (-sā′tĭv, kəm-pĕn′sə-tĭv), **com·pen·sa·to·ry** (kəm-pĕn′sə-tôr′ē, -tōr′ē) *adj.* —**com·pen·sa·tor** *n.*

com·pen·sa·tion (kŏm′pən-sā′shən) *n.* **1. a.** The act of compensating or making amends. **b.** The state of being compensated. **2.** Something given or received as an equivalent or as reparation for a loss, service, or debt; a recompense; an indemnity. **3.** *Biology.* The counterbalancing of any functional defect in one organ by the supplementary development or activation of another organ or another part of the defective structure. **4.** *Psychology.* Behavior designed to compensate for real or imagined defects. —**com·pen·sa·tion·al** *adj.*

com·pere (kŏm′pâr′) *n. British.* The master of ceremonies of a television program, variety show, cabaret, or the like. [Old French, "godfather" : *com-* (joint) + *père,* father.] —**com·pere** *v.*

com·pete (kəm-pēt′) *intr.v.* **-peted, -peting, -petes.** To strive or contend with another or others for profit, prize, position, or the necessities of life; vie. —See Synonyms at **rival.** [Latin *competere,* "to strive together" : *com-,* together + *petere,* to seek, strive.]

com·pe·tence (kŏm′pə-təns) *n.* Also **com·pe·ten·cy** (-tən-sē). **1.** The state or quality of being capable or competent; adequate skill or ability. **2.** Sufficient means for a comfortable existence. **3.** *Law.* The quality or condition of being legally qualified, eligible, or admissible; legal authority, qualification, or jurisdiction. **4.** *Linguistics.* The knowledge underlying an individual's ability to speak or understand a language. Compare **langue, performance. 5.** The ability possessed by embryonic cells at an early stage of development to differentiate into any of various types of cells. —See Synonyms at **ability.**

com·pe·tent (kŏm′pə-tənt) *adj.* **1.** Properly or well qualified; having adequate skill or ability; capable. **2.** *Law.* Legally qualified or fit; admissible. **3.** Rightly or properly belonging; permissible. Used with *to.* **4.** Adequate for the purpose; suitable. **5.** Able to differentiate in any of various ways. Said of embryonic cells at an early stage of development. [Middle English, from Old French, from Latin *competēns* (stem *competent-*), present participle of *competere,* to be competent, COMPETE.] —**com·pe·tent·ly** *adv.*

com·pe·ti·tion (kŏm′pə-tĭsh′ən) *n.* **1. a.** The action of competing with another or others for profit, prize, position, or the necessities of life; rivalry. **b.** The person or persons competing; one's competitors considered collectively. **2. a.** A contest, match, or other trial of skill or ability. **b.** A series of such contests. **3.** The rivalry between two or more businesses striving for the same customer or market: *Competition tends to keep prices down.* **4.** *Ecology.* The struggle between organisms in a community for scarce resources.

com·pet·i·tive (kəm-pĕt′ə-tĭv) *adj.* **1.** Of, involving, or determined by competition. **2.** Comparatively low in price. **3.** Having an urge to compete; inclined to rivalry. —**com·pet·i·tive·ly** *adv.* —**com·pet·i·tive·ness** *n.*

com·pet·i·tor (kəm-pĕt′ə-tər) *n.* Someone or something that competes; rival. —See Synonyms at **opponent.**

Com·piègne (kôN-pyĕn′y′). Town in the Oise department of northern France, on the Oise River. The Armistice that ended World War I (1918) was signed in a railroad car in Compiègne forest, and Hitler insisted that the same coach be used to conclude the agreement by which France fell to the Germans (1940).

com·pi·la·tion (kŏm′pə-lā′shən) *n.* **1.** The act of collecting or compiling. **2.** Something compiled, such as a set of data, a report, or an anthology.

com·pile (kəm-pīl′) *tr.v.* **-piled, -piling, -piles. 1.** To gather (facts, literature, or other material) into one book or corpus. **2.** To put together or compose (a book, outline, or other collection) from materials gathered from several sources. **3.** *Computer Science.* To convert to machine language. [Middle English *compilen,* from Old French *compiler,* from Latin *compīlāre,* "to heap together," plunder, plagiarize : *com-,* together + *pīlāre,* to plunder, "pile up (booty)," from *pīla,* "pile," PILLAR.]

com·pil·er (kəm-pī′lər) *n.* **1.** A person who compiles something. **2.** *Computer Science.* A computer program that converts from a high-level language into machine language. Each language needs its own compiler for each type of computer.

com·pla·cen·cy (kəm-plā′sən-sē) *n.* Also **com·pla·cence** (-səns). **1. a.** A feeling of contentment or satisfaction; gratification. **b.** Equanimity, sometimes excessive, in the face of real or potential problems. **2.** Self-satisfaction; smugness.

com·pla·cent (kəm-plā′sənt) *adj.* **1.** Having or showing complacency. **2.** Complaisant. [Originally "pleasing," from Latin *complacēns* (stem *complacent-*), present participle of *complacēre,* to please : *com-* (intensive) + *placēre,* to please.] —**com·pla·cent·ly** *adv.*

com·plain (kəm-plān′) *intr.v.* **-plained, -plaining, -plains. 1.** To express feelings of pain, dissatisfaction, or resentment. **2.** To describe one's pains, problems, or dissatisfactions. Used with *of.* **3.** To make a formal accusation or report a grievance officially: *complained to the police about the neighbor's dog.* —See Synonyms at **object.** [Middle English *compleinen,* from Old French *complaindre,* from Vulgar Latin *complangere* (unattested) : Latin *com-* (intensive) + *plangere,* to lament.] —**com·plain·er** *n.*

com·plain·ant (kəm-plā′nənt) *n. Law.* A person who makes a complaint or files a formal charge, as in a court of law; plaintiff.

com·plaint (kəm-plānt′) *n.* **1.** An expression of pain, dissatisfaction, resentment, discontent, or grief. **2.** A cause or reason for complaining; grievance. **3.** A cause of physical pain; malady; illness. **4.** A literary outpouring of grief, typically a poem lamenting lost love. **5.** *Law.* A formal allegation made by the plaintiff in a civil action. [Middle English *compleint(e),* from Old French *complainte,* from *complaint,* past participle of *complaindre,* COMPLAIN.]

com·plai·sance (kəm-plā′səns, -zəns) *n.* Willing compliance with the wishes of others; obligingness.

com·plai·sant (kəm-plā′sənt, -zənt, kŏm′plā-zănt′) *adj.* Showing a desire or willingness to please; cheerfully obliging. [French, pleasing, agreeable, from Old French, present participle of *complaire,* to please, from Latin *complacēre.* See **complacent.**] —**com·plai·sant·ly** *adv.*

com·pleat (kəm-plēt′) *adj. Archaic.* Complete: *"The Compleat Angler"* (Izaak Walton). Often used humorously.

com·plect (kəm-plĕkt′) *tr.v.* **-plected, -plecting, -plects.** To join by weaving or twining together; interweave. [Latin *complectī, complectere* : *com-,* together + *plectere,* to entwine.]

com·plect·ed (kəm-plĕk′tĭd) *adj. Regional.* Complexioned. Used only in combination: *dark-complected.* [Irregularly from COMPLEXION.]

com·ple·ment (kŏm′plə-mənt) *n.* **1.** Something that completes, makes up a whole, or perfects. **2.** The quantity or number needed to make up a whole. **3.** Either of two parts that complete the whole or mutually complete each other. **4.** The full quantity, allowance, or amount; a complete set. **5.** *Geometry.* An angle related to another so that the sum of their measures is 90 degrees. **6.** *Grammar.* A word or words used after a verb to complete a predicate construction; for example, *their best player* acts as the complement in the sentence *They considered her their best player.* **7.** An interval in music that completes an octave when added to a given interval. **8.** The full crew of officers and men required to man a ship. **9.** *Biochemistry.* The heat-sensitive substance found in normal blood serum that helps to destroy pathogenic bacteria and other materials. In this sense, also formerly called "alexin."
~*tr.v.* (kŏm′plə-mĕnt′) **complemented, -menting, -ments.** To add or serve as a complement to. [Middle English, from Latin *complēmentum,* from *complēre,* to COMPLETE.]

Usage: Complement and compliment are often confused because of their identical pronunciations, as are the adjectival pair *complementary* and *complimentary.* The former has the sense of completion, the latter the sense of praising.

com·ple·men·tal (kŏm′plə-mĕn′təl) *adj.* Complementary. —**com·ple·men·tal·ly** *adv.*

com·ple·men·ta·ry (kŏm′plə-mĕn′tə-rē, -mĕn′trē) *adj.* **1.** Forming or serving as a complement; completing. **2.** Complementing each other; supplying what is needed to make whole or complete. **3.** *Genetics.* Producing effects when in combination that are different from those produced separately. Said of genes. —**com·ple·men·ta·ri·ness** *n.*

complementary angles *pl.n.* Two angles whose sum is 90 degrees.

complementary color *n.* Either of a pair of colors, such as blue-green and red, that appear as white or gray when mixed in the correct proportions.

complement fixation *n. Biochemistry.* The joining of a complement to the antigen-antibody pair for which it is specific. It is used as a test for the presence of specific antigens and antibodies and hence used in the diagnosis of certain infections.

com·plete (kəm-plēt′) *adj. Abbr.* **comp. 1.** Having all necessary or

PRONUNCIATION KEY

ă, pat; ā, pay; âr, care; ä, father, are; b, bib; ch, church; d, deed; ĕ, pet; ē, be; f, fife; g, gag; h, hat; hw, which; ĭ, pit; ī, pie; îr, pier; j, judge; k, kick; l, lid, needle; m, mum; n, no, sudden; ng, thing; ŏ, pot; ō, toe; ô, paw, for; oi, noise; ou, out; ŏŏ, book; ōō, boot; p, pop; r, roar; s, sauce; sh, ship, dish; t, tight; th, thin, path; *th,* this, bathe; ŭ, cut; ûr, fur; v, valve; w, with; y, yes; z, zebra, size; zh, vision; ə, about, item, edible, gallop, circus, peaceful

IN FOREIGN WORDS:

à, *Fr.* ami; œ, *Fr.* feu, *Ger.* schön; ü, *Fr.* tu, *Ger.* über; KH, *Ger.* ich, *Scot.* loch; N, *Fr.* bon; y′, *Fr.* Compiègne

STRESS MARKS:

Primary stress: ′ **in·cite′** (ĭn-sīt′)
Secondary stress: ′ **in′sight′** (ĭn′sīt′)

normal parts; entire; whole. **2.** *Botany.* Having all characteristic floral parts, including sepals, petals, stamens, and a pistil. **3.** Brought to a satisfactory conclusion; ended: *Work on the new bridge is almost complete.* **4.** Thorough; exhaustive: *a complete report on the accident.* **5.** Total; absolute: *a complete stranger.* **6.** Fully supplied or equipped: *comes complete with its own instruction manual.* **7.** *Archaic.* Skilled; accomplished.
~tr.v. **completed, -pleting, -pletes. 1.** To make whole or complete. **2.** To fill in (a form). **3.** To conclude. [Middle English *complet(e),* from Old French, from Latin *complētus,* past participle of *complēre,* to fill up : *com-* (intensive) + *plēre,* to fill.] **—com·plete·ly** *adv.* **—com·plete·ness** *n.* **—com·ple·tive** *adj.*

Synonyms: *close, conclude, end, finish, terminate.*

Usage: In formal English, anything that is *complete* is absolutely so. It is therefore incorrect to use such qualifying words as *more, most, very, quite,* and so on, unless the implication is one of comprehensiveness of scope or thoroughness of treatment (where degrees of completeness are felt to exist), as in *Her report is a more complete account of the situation than is mine.*

com·ple·tion (kəm-plē′shən) *n.* **1.** The act of concluding, perfecting, or making entire. **2.** The state of being completed. **3.** Accomplishment; realization; fulfillment.

com·plex (kəm-plĕks′, kŏm′plĕks′) *adj.* **1.** Consisting of interconnected or interwoven parts; composite; compound. **2.** Involved or intricate, as in structure; complicated. **3.** *Grammar.* **a.** Pertaining to or designating a word consisting of at least one bound form, such as *slowly.* **b.** Pertaining to a **complex sentence** *(see).* **4.** *Mathematics.* Of, pertaining to, or designating a number or variable that has both a real and an imaginary part.
~n. (kŏm′plĕks′). **1.** A whole composed of intricate or interconnected parts. **2.** *Psychology.* A connected group of repressed ideas that compel characteristic or habitual patterns of thought, feeling, and action. **3.** *Informal.* An exaggerated or obsessive concern or fear. **4.** A group of buildings designed for a particular purpose or supplying a variety of related facilities: *an apartment complex; an industrial complex.* **5.** *Chemistry.* **a.** A complex ion. **b.** Any compound in which two molecules or groups are linked to each other by a coordinate bond. [Latin *complexus,* past participle of *complectī, complectere,* to entwine : *com-,* together + *plectere,* to twine, plait.] **—com·plex·ly** *adv.* **—com·plex·ness** *n.*

Synonyms: *complicated, intricate, involved, knotty.*

complex conjugate *n. Mathematics.* A complex number that differs from another complex number only by the reversal of the sign of the imaginary part. For example, $a + bi$ has as complex conjugate $a - bi$.

complex fraction *n.* A fraction in which the numerator or denominator or both contain fractions, such as $^{1}/_{5/6}$. Also called "compound fraction."

com·plex·i·fy (kəm′plĕks′ĭ-fī, kŏm′-) *v.* **-fied, -fying, -fies.** *—tr.* To make more complex. *—intr.* To become more complex. **—com·plex·i·fi·ca·tion** *n.*

complex ion *n. Chemistry.* An ion or radical in which several groups or ions are attached to a central atom by coordinate bonds. Also called "complex," "coordination compound."

com·plex·ion (kəm-plĕk′shən) *n.* **1.** The natural color, texture, and appearance of the skin, especially on the face. **2.** General character, aspect, or appearance. **3.** In medieval physiology, the combination of the four humors of cold, heat, moistness, and dryness in specific proportions, thought to control the temperament and the constitution of the body. [Middle English *complexioun,* physical constitution, temperament, from Old French *complexion,* from Medieval Latin *complexiō* (stem *complexiōn-*), "combination of corporeal humors," from Latin, connection, combination, from *complexus.* See **complex.**] **—com·plex·ion·al** *adj.*

com·plex·ioned (kəm-plĕk′shənd) *adj.* Of or having a specified complexion. Used in combination: *fair-complexioned.*

com·plex·i·ty (kəm-plĕk′sə-tē) *n., pl.* **-ties. 1.** The state or condition of being intricate or complex. **2.** Something intricate or complex.

complex number *n.* A number consisting of a real and imaginary part, usually expressed in the form $a + bi$ where a and b are real numbers and i is the imaginary unit such that $i^2 = -1$.

complex plane *n.* A plane that has complex numbers as its points.

complex salt *n.* A salt containing one or more complex ions.

complex sentence *n. Grammar.* A sentence containing one main clause and one or more subordinate clauses; for example, the sentence *When the rain stops, we'll leave* is a complex sentence. Compare **simple sentence.**

complex variable *n.* An expression of the form $x + iy$, where x and y are real variables and $i^2 = -1$.

com·pli·ance (kəm-plī′əns) *n.* Also **com·pli·an·cy** (-ən-sē). **1.** The act of yielding to a wish, request, or demand; acquiescence. **2.** A disposition or tendency to yield to others. **3. a.** *Mechanics.* The extension or displacement of a loaded structure per unit load. **b.** Flexibility. Not in technical usage.

com·pli·ant (kəm-plī′ənt) *adj.* Also *archaic* **com·pli·a·ble** (kəm-plī′ə-bəl). Yielding; submissive. —See Synonyms at **obedient.** [COM-PL(Y) + -ANT.] **—com·pli·ant·ly** *adv.*

com·pli·ca·cy (kəm-plĭk′ə-sē) *n., pl.* **-cies.** *Rare.* **1.** The state of being complicated. **2.** A complication.

com·pli·cate (kŏm′plĭ-kāt′) *tr.v.* **-cated, -cating, -cates. 1.** To make complex, intricate, or perplexing. **2.** To combine so as to produce a more complex result. **3.** *Pathology.* To aggravate (an existing disease).
~adj. (kŏm′plə-kĭt). **1.** *Biology.* Folded longitudinally one or several times, as certain leaves or the wings of some insects are. **2.** *Archaic.* Complex; intricate; involved. [Latin *complicāre,* to fold together : *com-,* together + *plicāre,* to fold.]

com·pli·cat·ed (kŏm′plə-kā′tĭd) *adj.* Containing intricately combined or involved parts; not easily understood or untangled. —See Synonyms at **complex. —com·pli·cat·ed·ly** *adv.* **—com·pli·cat·ed·ness** *n.*

com·pli·ca·tion (kŏm′plə-kā′shən) *n.* **1.** The act of complicating. **2.** A confused or intricate relationship of parts. **3.** Any factor, condition, or event that is complicated or that complicates. **4.** *Pathology.* A condition occurring during the course of or as a consequence of another disease and often aggravating it.

com·plice (kŏm′plĭs) *n. Obsolete.* An associate or accomplice. [Middle English, from Old French, from Latin *complex,* closely connected, hence a confederate : *com-,* together + *-plex,* -fold.]

com·plic·i·ty (kəm-plĭs′ə-tē) *n., pl.* **-ties. 1.** The state of being an accomplice in a wrongful act. **2.** *Rare.* Complexity.

com·pli·er (kəm-plī′ər) *n.* A person who complies or yields.

com·pli·ment (kŏm′plə-mənt) *n.* **1.** An expression of praise, admiration, or congratulation. **2.** A formal act of civility, courtesy, or respect. **3.** *Usually* **compliments.** A formal or ceremonious greeting or expression of regards: *Please give my compliments to your parents.* **4.** *Archaic.* A gift presented for services rendered; gratuity.
~tr.v. **complimented, -menting, -ments. 1.** To pay a compliment to. **2.** To show fondness, regard, or respect for (someone) by giving a gift or performing a favor. —See Usage note at **complement.** [French, from Spanish *cumplimiento,* from *cumplir,* to complete, behave properly, be courteous, from Latin *complēre,* to fill up : *com-* (intensive) + *plēre,* to fill.]

com·pli·men·ta·ry (kŏm′plə-mĕn′tər-ē, -trē) *adj.* **1.** Expressing, using, or resembling a compliment. **2.** Given free of charge to repay a favor, as an act of courtesy, or for publicity purposes. **—com·pli·men·ta·ri·ly** *adv.*

com·pline, com·plin (kŏm′plĭn) *n. Ecclesiastical.* **1.** The last of the seven **canonical hours** *(see).* **2.** The time of day set aside for this prayer, usually just before retiring to bed. [Middle English *compline,* from Old French *complie,* from Medieval Latin *(hōra) complēta,* "completed (hour)," from Latin *complētus,* past participle of *complēre,* COMPLETE.]

com·ply (kəm-plī′) *intr.v.* **-plied, -plying, -plies. 1.** To act in accordance with a command, request, rule, wish, or the like. Used with *with.* **2.** *Obsolete.* To be courteous or obedient. [Italian *complire,* from Spanish *cumplir,* to complete, do what is proper, be courteous, from Latin *complēre,* to fill up : *com-* (intensive) + *plēre,* to fill.]

com·po (kŏm′pō) *n., pl.* **-pos.** Any of various combined substances, such as mortar or plaster, formed by mixing ingredients. [Short for COMPOSITION.]

com·po·nent (kəm-pō′nənt) *n.* **1.** A constituent part of a complex whole, especially of a mechanical or electrical device. **2.** *Mathematics.* Any of a set of two or more vectors having a sum equal to a given vector. **3.** *Chemistry.* Any of the minimum number of substances required to specify completely the composition of all phases of a chemical system.
~adj. Being or functioning as a component; constituent. [Latin *compōnens* (stem *compōnent-*), present participle of *compōnere,* to place together : *com-,* together + *pōnere,* to put.]

com·po·ny (kəm-pō′nē, kŏm-) *adj. Heraldry.* Composed of a row of squares in alternating tinctures. [Old French *componé,* "made of pieces," from *compon, copon,* piece. See **coupon.**]

com·port (kəm-pôrt′) *v.* **-ported, -porting, -ports.** *—tr.* To conduct or behave (oneself) in a specified manner. *—intr.* To agree, correspond, or harmonize. Used with *with.* [Old French *comporter,* to support, conduct, from Latin *comportāre,* to bring together, later to support : *com-,* together + *portāre,* to carry, bear.] **—com·port·ment** *n.*

com·pose (kəm-pōz′) *v.* **-posed, -posing, -poses.** *—tr.* **1.** To make up or be the constituent parts of; constitute or form. —See Usage note at **comprise. 2.** To make or create by putting together parts or elements. **3.** To create or produce (a literary or musical piece). **4.** To make (oneself) calm or tranquil; quiet. **5.** To settle (arguments or differences); reconcile. **6. a.** To arrange aesthetically or artistically (the constituents of a painting, for example). **b.** To put in order; arrange (one's thoughts, for example). **7.** *Printing.* To arrange or set (type or matter to be printed). *—intr.* **1.** To create literary or musical pieces. **2.** *Printing.* To set type. [Middle English, from Old French *composer* : *com-,* together, from Latin + *poser,* to place, from Latin *pausāre,* to cease, repose, hence to place, from *pausa,* a pause, from Greek *pausis,* from *pauein,* to stop.]

com·posed (kəm-pōzd′) *adj.* Calm; serene; self-possessed. —See Synonyms at **cool. —com·pos·ed·ly** (kəm-pō′zĭd-lē) *adv.* **—com·pos·ed·ness** (kəm-pō′zĭd-nĭs) *n.*

com·pos·er (kəm-pō′zər) *n. Abbr.* **comp.** A person who composes, especially one who composes music.

composing stick *n. Printing.* Especially formerly, a small shallow tray, usually metal and with an adjustable end, in which a compositor sets type before it is placed in the galley.

com·pos·ite (kəm-pŏz′ĭt) *adj. Abbr.* **comp. 1.** Made up of distinct components; compound. **2.** *Mathematics.* Having factors; factorable. **3.** *Botany.* Of, belonging to, or characteristic of the Compositae, a large plant family characterized by flower heads consisting of both **ray flowers** and **disk flowers** *(both of which see),* as in the daisy, of disk flowers only, as in wormwood, or of ray flowers only, as in

PRONUNCIATION KEY

ă, pat; ā, pay; âr, care;
ä, father, are; b, bib;
ch, church; d, deed; ĕ, pet;
ē, be; f, fife; g, gag; h, hat;
hw, which; ĭ, pit; ī, pie;
îr, pier; j, judge; k, kick;
l, lid, needle; m, mum;
n, no, sudden; ng, thing;
ŏ, pot; ō, toe; ô, paw, for;
oi, noise; ou, out; o͝o, book;
o͞o, boot; p, pop; r, roar;
s, sauce; sh, ship, dish;
t, tight; th, thin, path;
th, this, bathe; ŭ, cut; ûr, fur;
v, valve; w, with; y, yes;
z, zebra, size; zh, vision;
ə, about, item, edible,
gallop, circus, peaceful

IN FOREIGN WORDS:

à, *Fr.* ami; œ, *Fr.* feu, *Ger.* schön; ü, *Fr.* tu, *Ger.* über; KH, *Ger.* ich, *Scot.* loch; N, *Fr.* bon; y′, *Fr.* Compiègne

STRESS MARKS:

Primary stress: ′
in·cite′ (ĭn-sīt′)
Secondary stress: ′
in′sight′ (ĭn′sīt′)

the dandelion. **4. Composite.** *Architecture.* Pertaining to or designating the Composite order.
~*n.* **1.** A composite structure or entity. **2.** A complex material, such as wood or fiberglass, in which two or more distinct, structurally complementary substances, especially metals, ceramics, glasses, and polymers, combine to produce some structural or functional properties not present in any individual component. **3.** A composite plant.
~*tr.v.* **composited, -iting, -ites.** To make composite or into something composite. [Latin *compositus,* past participle of *compōnere,* to put together : *com-,* together + *pōnere,* to put.] **—com·pos·ite·ly** *adv.* **—com·pos·ite·ness** *n.*

composite number *n.* An integer exactly divisible by at least one number other than itself or 1.

Composite order *n. Architecture.* A late Roman style of capital formed by superimposing Ionic volutes on a Corinthian capital.

com·po·si·tion (kŏm′pə-zĭsh′ən) *n. Abbr.* **comp. 1.** A putting together of parts or elements to form a whole; a combining. **2.** The manner in which such parts are combined or related; constitution; make-up. **3.** The result or product of composing; mixture; compound. **4.** The arrangement of artistic parts so as to form a unified whole. **5.** The art or act of composing a literary or musical work. **6.** Any work of art, literature, or music, or its structure and arrangement. **7. a.** An essay; especially, one written as a school exercise. **b.** An exercise or class in writing poetry or prose. **8.** *Linguistics.* The formation of compound words from separate words. **9.** *Printing.* Typesetting. **10.** *Law.* **a.** A settlement whereby the creditors of a debtor about to enter bankruptcy agree to accept partial payment in lieu of full payment for debts. **b.** The sum thus agreed upon. **11.** *Archaic.* Settlement by mutual agreement or compromise. [Middle English *composicioun,* from Old French *composition,* from Latin *compositiō* (stem *composition-*), from *compōnere,* to put together, arrange : *com-,* together + *pōnere,* to put.] **—com·po·si·tion·al** *adj.*

composition of forces *n.* The finding or determination of a vector that is the resultant of a given set of forces.

com·pos·i·tor (kəm-pŏz′ə-tər) *n. Abbr.* **comp.** *Printing.* A typesetter. **—com·pos·i·to·ri·al** (kəm-pŏz′-ə-tôr′ē-əl, -tōr′-) *adj.*

com·pos men·tis (kŏm′pəs mĕn′tĭs) *adj.* Of sound mind; sane. [Latin, having control of one's mind.]

com·post (kŏm′pōst) *n.* **1.** A mixture of decaying organic matter, such as leaves and manure, used as fertilizer. **2.** A composition; mixture.
~*tr.v.* **composted, -posting, -posts. 1.** To fertilize with compost. **2.** To change (vegetable matter) to compost. [Middle English, stew, compote, from Old French *composte,* stewed fruit, and *compost,* mixture, respectively from Latin *composita* and *compositum,* feminine and neuter of *compositus,* put together, COMPOSITE.]

com·po·sure (kəm-pō′zhər) *n.* Self-possession; calmness; tranquillity. —See Synonyms at **equanimity.** [From COMPOSE.]

com·pote (kŏm′pōt; *French* kôɴ-pôt′) *n.* **1.** Fruit stewed or cooked in syrup. **2.** A long-stemmed dish for holding fruit, nuts, or candy. [French, from Old French *composte,* stewed fruit, COMPOST.]

com·pound¹ (kŏm-pound′, kəm-) *v.* **-pounded, -pounding, -pounds.** —*tr.* **1.** To combine; mix. **2.** To produce or create by combining ingredients or parts. **3.** *Pharmacology.* To mix (drugs) according to prescription. **4.** To settle (a debt, for example) by agreeing on an amount less than the claim; adjust. **5.** To compute (compound interest). **6.** *Law.* To agree, for payment or other consideration, not to prosecute: *compound a felony.* **7.** To add to or intensify (a difficulty, an error, or the like). —*intr.* **1.** To come to terms; agree. **2.** To settle or compromise with a creditor. —See Synonyms at **mix.**
~*adj.* (kŏm′pound, kŏm-pound′). Consisting of two or more substances, ingredients, elements, or parts.
~*n.* (kŏm′pound). *Abbr.* **comp., cpd. 1.** A combination of two or more elements or parts. **2.** *Linguistics.* **a.** A word formed either from other words, for example *racehorse,* or by the addition or combination of affixes or combining forms, for example *geography* or *isometric.* **b.** An intonational pattern exhibiting a primary stress and a terminal juncture. **c.** A verb form, in any of various tenses, the passive mood, or the like, consisting of a main verb and at least one auxiliary verb; for example, *may have been eaten.* **d.** In transformational grammar, a sequence of words not connected by a functional element in surface structure but functioning as a grammatical unit in deep structure. **3.** *Chemistry.* A pure, macroscopically homogeneous substance consisting of atoms or ions of two or more different elements in definite proportions, and usually having properties unlike those of its constituent elements. [Middle English *compounen,* from Old French *compon(d)re,* from Latin *compōnere,* to put together : *com-,* together + *pōnere,* to put.] **—com·pound·a·ble** *adj.* **—com·pound·er** *n.*

com·pound² (kŏm′pound) *n.* **1.** In the Orient, an enclosure for a factory or group of European residences. **2.** In South Africa, living quarters, usually inside an enclosure, for black workers. **3.** A large enclosed area inside a prison, concentration camp, or the like. [Portuguese *campon* or Dutch *kampoeng,* from Malay *kampong,* village, cluster of buildings.]

com·pound-com·plex sentence (kŏm′pound-kŏm′plĕks) *n.* A sentence consisting of at least two coordinate main clauses and one or more subordinate clauses.

compound engine *n.* **1.** A steam engine in which the steam is expanded in two or more stages in different cylinders. **2.** A gas or diesel engine in which the exhaust gases are used to drive a turbine-powered supercharger.

compound eye *n.* The eye of most insects and some crustaceans, composed of many light-sensitive elements, each with its own refractive system and each forming a portion of an image.

compound flower *n.* A flower head of a composite plant, such as a daisy, consisting of numerous small flowers appearing as a single bloom.

compound fraction *n. Mathematics.* A **complex fraction** *(see).*

compound fracture *n.* A fracture in which broken bone lacerates soft tissue.

compound interest *n.* Interest computed on the accumulated unpaid interest as well as on the original principal. Compare **simple interest.**

compound leaf *n.* A leaf consisting of two or more separate leaflets borne on a single leafstalk.

compound microscope *n.* A microscope consisting of an objective and an eyepiece, that is, two lenses or lens systems, at opposite ends of an adjustable tube.

compound number *n.* A quantity, such as 10 pounds 5 ounces or 3 feet 4 inches, involving different units of measure.

compound pendulum *n.* See **pendulum.**

compound sentence *n.* A sentence of two or more coordinate main clauses, often joined by a conjunction or conjunctions, as *The problem was difficult, but I finally found the answer.*

compound tense *n. Grammar.* A tense in which the verb is expressed by means of at least one auxiliary; for example, the present perfect tense of "go," *I have gone,* as opposed to the simple past tense, *I went.* Compare **simple tense.**

compound time *n. Music.* Time in which each beat in a bar is divisible into thirds, sixths, and so on; for example, 6/8 time.

com·pra·dor, com·pra·dore (kŏm′prə-dôr′) *n.* Formerly, in China and certain other Asian countries, a native agent for a foreign business. [Portuguese, "buyer," from Late Latin *comparātor,* from Latin *comparāre,* provide, buy, prepare : *com-* (collectively) + *parāre,* to prepare.]

com·pre·hend (kŏm′prĭ-hĕnd′) *tr.v.* **-hended, -hending, -hends. 1.** To grasp mentally; understand or fathom. **2.** To take in; include; embrace. —See Synonyms at **apprehend, include.** [Middle English *comprehenden,* from Latin *comprehendere,* to grasp mentally : *com-,* together in mind, mentally + *prehendere,* to seize, grasp.]

com·pre·hen·si·ble (kŏm′prĭ-hĕn′sə-bəl) *adj.* Capable of being comprehended or understood; intelligible. **—com·pre·hen·si·bil·i·ty, com·pre·hen·si·ble·ness** *n.* **—com·pre·hen·si·bly** *adv.*

com·pre·hen·sion (kŏm′prĭ-hĕn′shən) *n.* **1.** The act of or capacity for comprehending or understanding. **2.** Comprehensiveness. **3.** *Logic.* The attributes making up a concept; intension. **4.** An exercise designed to test students' powers of comprehension.

com·pre·hen·sive (kŏm′prĭ-hĕn′sĭv) *adj.* **1.** Including or comprehending much; large in scope or content. **2.** Marked by or showing extensive understanding: *comprehensive knowledge.* **3.** Designating a type of motor-vehicle insurance that provides wide-ranging cover.
~*n.* **1.** Often **comprehensives.** *Informal.* Examinations covering the entire field of major study, given in the final undergraduate or graduate year of college. **2.** An advertising layout showing all the elements planned for an advertisement but not ready for actual reproduction. **—com·pre·hen·sive·ly** *adv.* **—com·pre·hen·sive·ness** *n.*

com·press (kəm-prĕs′) *tr.v.* **-pressed, -pressing, -presses.** To press together or force into a smaller space; condense; compact. —See Synonyms at **contract.**
~*n.* (kŏm′prĕs′). *Medicine.* **1.** A soft pad of gauze or other material, either hot or cold, dry or moistened with water or medication, applied to a part of the body to alleviate pain or reduce inflammation. **2.** A soft pad of gauze or other material applied with force to reduce bleeding. **3.** A machine for compressing, especially for baling cotton. [Middle English *compressen,* from Old French *compresser,* from Late Latin *compressāre,* frequentative of Latin *comprimere* (past participle *compressus*), to press together : *com-,* together + *premere,* to press.] **—com·press·i·bil·i·ty, com·press·i·ble·ness** *n.* **—com·press·i·ble** *adj.*

com·pressed (kəm-prĕst′) *adj.* **1.** Pressed together or into less space; made compact. **2.** *Biology.* Flattened laterally or lengthwise. Said of certain seed pods or the bodies of many fish.

compressed air *n.* Air under greater than atmospheric pressure, especially when used to power a mechanical device or provide a portable supply of oxygen.

compressed air illness *n.* **Decompression sickness** *(see).*

com·pres·sion (kəm-prĕsh′ən) *n.* **1. a.** The act or process of compressing. **b.** The state of being compressed. **2. a.** The process by which the working substance in a heat engine, such as the vapor mixture in the cylinder of an internal-combustion engine, is compressed. **b.** The engine cycle during which this process occurs.

com·pres·sion-ig·ni·tion engine (kəm-prĕsh′ən-ĭg-nĭsh′ən) *n.* A **diesel-engine** *(see).*

compression ratio *n.* The ratio of the volume of the combustion chamber of an internal-combustion engine with the piston at the bottom of its stroke to the volume when the piston has reached the top of its stroke.

compression wave or **compressional wave** *n.* A wave, as of sound, propagated by means of the compression of an elastic medium.

com·pres·sive (kəm-prĕs′ĭv) *adj.* Compressing or capable of compressing. **—com·pres·sive·ly** *adv.*

Composite order *A combination by the Romans of the scrolls (or volutes) of the Greeks' Ionic order and the acanthus leaves of the Corinthian order. The Composite style appeared in the first century* A.D.

compound eye *The horsefly (genus* Tabanus, *above), like other insects and crustaceans, has eyes made up of many separate elements that are effectively individual eyes. Each element transmits a single spot of light, so that the insect sees the world as a shifting mosaic of dots.*

com·pres·sor (kəm-prĕs′ər) n. 1. A device or machine for compressing a gas. 2. The part of a gas turbine that compresses the air before it enters the combustion chambers. 3. *Electronics*. A device for reducing the variation in signal amplitude in a communication channel. 4. *Anatomy*. Any muscle that acts to compress an organ or part. 5. *Medicine*. An instrument used for holding down a tissue or part of the body.

com·prise (kəm-prīz′) tr.v. **-prised, -prising, -prises.** 1. To consist of; be composed of. 2. To include; contain. 3. To constitute; make up. —See Synonyms at **include.** [Middle English *comprisen,* from Old French *comprendre* (past participle *compris*), to comprehend, include, from Latin *comprehendere,* to grasp mentally : *com-,* together, in mind, mentally + *prehendere,* to seize.] —**com·pris·a·ble** *adj.*

Usage: The traditional rule states that the whole *comprises* the parts; the parts *compose* the whole. In strict usage: *The Union comprises fifty states. Fifty states compose* (or *constitute* or *make up*) *the Union.* While this distinction is still maintained by many writers, *comprise* is increasingly used, especially in the passive, in place of *compose: The Union is comprised of fifty states.* This last example is considered unacceptable by many.

com·pro·mise (kŏm′prə-mīz′) n. 1. A settlement of differences in which each side makes concessions. 2. Anything resulting from such a settlement. 3. Something midway between different things or courses of action, combining certain of their qualities. Also used adjectivally: *a compromise proposal.* 4. Loosely, a concession, especially one involving one's principles or integrity: *She had to make a lot of compromises to keep this job.*

~v. **compromised, -mising, -mises.** —*tr.* 1. To settle by concessions. 2. To expose or make liable to scandal, suspicion, or disrepute. 3. To make concessions damaging to (one's interests, principles, or integrity). —*intr.* To make a compromise. [Middle English *compromis,* from Old French, from Latin *comprōmissum,* from *comprōmittere,* to promise mutually (to abide by an arbiter's decision) : *com-,* mutually + *prōmittere,* to PROMISE.] —**com·pro·mis·er** *n.*

Comp·tom·e·ter (kŏmp-tŏm′ə-tər) n. A trademark for a high-speed calculating and adding machine.

Comp·ton (kŏmp′tən), **Arthur Holly** (1892–1962). U.S. physicist, noted for his research into radiation. In 1923 he discovered the Compton effect, an important step toward the development of quantum mechanics. He was awarded the Nobel Prize for physics with C.T.R. Wilson (1927).

Comp·ton-Bur·nett (kŏmp′tən-bər-nĕt′), **Dame Ivy** (1892–1969). British novelist. She is best remembered for a series of popular novels about life in the wealthy households of England, at the turn of the century.

Compton effect n. The increase in wavelength of electromagnetic radiation, especially of an x-ray or gamma-ray photon, scattered by an electron. [After A.H. COMPTON, who discovered it.]

comptroller. Variant of **controller** (sense 2).

com·pul·sion (kəm-pŭl′shən) n. 1. The act of compelling or forcing; coercion; constraint. 2. The state of being compelled. 3. *Psychology.* **a.** An irresistible impulse to act in a certain way, regardless of the rationality of the motivation. **b.** An act or acts performed in response to such an impulse. [Middle English *compulsioun,* from Old French *compulsion,* from Late Latin *compulsiō* (stem *compulsiōn-*), from Latin *compellere* (past participle *compulsus*), COMPEL.]

com·pul·sive (kəm-pŭl′sĭv) adj. 1. Having the power to or tending to compel. 2. *Psychology.* Acting from or conditioned by compulsion or obsession: *a compulsive gambler.* —**com·pul·sive·ly** *adv.* —**com·pul·sive·ness** *n.*

com·pul·so·ry (kəm-pŭl′sə-rē) adj. 1. Obligatory; required; enforced. 2. Employing or exerting compulsion; coercive; compelling. [Medieval Latin *compulsōrius,* from Latin *compellere,* to COMPEL.] —**com·pul·so·ri·ly** *adv.* —**com·pul·so·ri·ness** *n.*

com·punc·tion (kəm-pŭngk′shən) n. 1. A strong uneasiness caused by a sense of guilt; remorse. 2. A slight uneasiness or feeling of regret. —See Synonyms at **qualm.** [Middle English, from Old French *componction,* from Late Latin *compunctiō* (stem *compunctiōn-*), "prick of conscience," from Latin, puncture, from *compungere,* to prick hard : *com-* (intensive) + *pungere,* to prick, sting.] —**com·punc·tious** *adj.* —**com·punc·tious·ly** *adv.*

com·pur·ga·tion (kŏm′pər-gā′shən) n. *Law.* The former practice, especially in the Middle Ages, of clearing an accused person of a charge by having a number of people swear to a belief in his innocence or good character. [Late Latin *compurgātiō* (stem *compurgātiōn-*), from Latin *compurgāre,* to purify completely : *com-* (intensive) + *purgāre,* to purify.] —**com·pur·ga·tor** *n.*

com·pu·ta·tion (kŏm′pyōō-tā′shən) n. 1. The act, process, or method of computing. 2. The result of computing.

com·pute (kəm-pyōōt′) v. **-puted, -puting, -putes.** —*tr.* To determine by mathematics, especially by numerical methods or with the aid of a computer. —*intr.* 1. To determine an amount or number. 2. To perform mathematical or logical calculations. Used of a computer. —See Synonyms at **calculate.**

~n. Computation; calculation. Used in the phrase *beyond compute.* [Latin *computāre,* to reckon together : *com-,* together in mind, mentally + *putāre,* to think, reckon.] —**com·put·a·bil·i·ty** *n.* —**com·put·a·ble** *adj.*

com·put·er (kəm-pyōō′tər) n. One that computes; specifically, an electronic machine that performs high-speed mathematical or logical calculations or that assembles, stores, correlates, or otherwise processes and prints information derived from coded data in accordance with a predetermined **program** *(see).* See **digital computer, analog computer.**

com·pu·ter·ese (kəm-pyōō′tə-rēz′, -rēs′) n. The technical language or jargon of the computer profession.

com·put·er·ize (kəm-pyōō′tə-rīz′) tr.v. **-ized, -izing, -izes.** 1. To perform (an operation) or process (information) with an electronic computer or system of computers. 2. To furnish with a computer or computer system. —**com·put·er·i·za·tion** *n.*

com·put·er·ized axial tomography (kəm-pyōō′tə-rīzd′) n. Abbr. **CAT** A radiological technique for examining the soft tissues of the body. X-ray slices are recorded by a **CAT scanner** *(see)* and integrated by computer to give a three-dimensional image of the tissue or organ.

computer language n. A code used to provide data and instructions to computers; a code for programming computers.

computer typesetting n. A method of setting type using the output of a computer to drive the typesetting machine.

Comr. commissioner.

com·rade (kŏm′răd, -rĭd, kŭm′-) n. 1. A friend, associate, or companion. 2. A person who shares one's interests, occupation, or activities. 3. *Often* **Comrade.** A fellow member; especially, a fellow member of a Communist or socialist party. [Earlier *camerade, cumrade,* from Old French *camarade,* roommate, soldier sharing the same room, from Spanish *camarada,* from *camara,* room, from Late Latin *camera,* from Latin, arched roof, from Greek *kamara,* vault.] —**com·rade·ship** *n.*

com·sat (kŏm′săt′) n. A **communications satellite** *(see).*

Comte (kônt), **(Isidore) Auguste (Marie François)** (1798–1857). French philosopher and the founder of modern sociology, a term he coined. He believed that intellectual life had developed through three stages: theological, metaphysical, and positivist. Sociology, he held, formed the apex of a hierarchy of sciences and would help to build a better future.

Com·tism (kŏm′tĭz-əm) n. The philosophy of Auguste Comte; positivism. —**Com·tist** (kŏm′tĭst) *adj. & n.*

Co·mus (kō′məs). In Roman mythology, a god or the spirit of revelry. [Latin, from Greek *Kōmos,* personification of *kōmos,* revel, festival procession. See **comedy.**]

con[1] (kŏn). *Informal.* One that votes or argues against. Used in the phrase *pros and cons.* [Middle English, short for *contra,* against, from Latin *contrā.*]

con[2] tr.v. **conned, conning, cons.** 1. To study, peruse, or examine carefully. 2. To learn or commit to memory. [Middle English *connen, cunnen,* to know how, be able, master, Old English *cunnan.*] —**con·ner** *n.*

con[3], **conn** tr.v. **conned, conning, cons.** *Nautical.* To direct the steering or course of (a ship).

~n. *Nautical.* 1. The station or post of the person who cons. 2. The act or process of conning. [Earlier *cond, cund,* from Middle English *conduen, condien,* to guide, from Old French *conduire,* to conduct, from Latin *condūcere,* "to bring together" : *com-,* together + *dūcere,* to lead.]

con[4] tr.v. **conned, conning, cons.** *Slang.* To swindle or defraud by first winning the confidence of; dupe.

~n. *Slang.* A swindle; trick. [Short for CONFIDENCE TRICK.]

con[5] n. *Slang.* A convict.

con. 1. concerto. 2. *Law.* conclusion. 3. connection. 4. consolidate; consolidated.

Con. 1. conformist. 2. Conservative. 3. consul.

Con·a·kry (kŏn′ə-krē). Capital and chief port of Guinea, situated on Tombo Island off the west coast of Africa. It is connected by a causeway to the mainland.

con a·mo·re (kŏn ä-mō′rā) adv. *Music.* Lovingly; tenderly. Used as a direction. [Italian, "with love."]

Conan Doyle, Sir Arthur. See Sir Arthur Conan **Doyle.**

Co·nant (kō′nənt), **James Bryant** (1893–1978). U.S. educator, diplomat, and author. In addition to his duties as president of Harvard (1933–53) and U.S. ambassador to West Germany (1955–57), he wrote many books on education, including *Education for a Classless Society* (1951), and *The American High School Today* (1959).

co·na·tion (kō-nā′shən) n. *Psychology.* The aspect of mental processes or behavior directed toward action or change and including impulse, desire, volition, and striving. [Latin *cōnātiō* (stem *cōnātiōn-*), endeavor, effort, from *cōnātus,* past participle of *cōnārī,* to endeavor.] —**co·na·tion·al** *adj.*

co·na·tive (kŏn′ə-tĭv, kō′nə-) adj. 1. *Psychology.* Of, pertaining to, or involving conation. 2. *Grammar.* Being or designating a verb, verb form, verbal aspect, or affix in certain inflected languages, such as Russian, that expresses an attempt to perform an action that is not necessarily achieved.

~n. A conative linguistic form.

co·na·tus (kō-nā′təs) n., pl. **conatus.** Any natural tendency, impulse, or directed effort. [Latin *cōnātus,* attempt, effort, from the past participle of *cōnārī,* to endeavor. See **conation.**]

con bri·o (kŏn brē′ō) adv. *Music.* With spirit and vigor. Used as a direction. [Italian, "with vigor."]

conc. concentrate; concentrated.

con·cat·e·nate (kŏn-kăt′ə-nāt′) tr.v. **-nated, -nating, -nates.** To connect or link in a series or chain.

~adj. (-nĭt, -nāt′). Connected or linked in a series. [Late Latin *concatēnāre* : *com-,* together + *catēnāre,* to link, chain, from Latin *catēna,* CATENA.] —**con·cat·e·na·tion** *n.*

computer

A DIGITAL COMPUTER SYSTEM
How the equipment stores, retrieves, and processes information

The chief components of the multipurpose, and most widely used, digital computer are a central processing unit (CPU), consisting of control and arithmetic/logic sections, that processes information (data); a main memory unit (the ROM in the illustration) in which information is held while being processed; and devices that respectively feed information into the CPU (input) and provide the user with the results of the computation (output). These components are termed hardware. Information such as details of employees' salaries is held on magnetic tape in the back-up memory store and can be obtained by the CPU when it is required.

Programs, sets of instructions to the computer, are called software. They are required to convert the information into the binary notation in which the computer operates, and computer languages, such as BASIC, FORTRAN, ALGOL, and COBOL, translate the programs into a form comprehensible to the computer.

The programs are stored in the main memory unit. The output required, the total salary bill, for example, can be displayed on a visual display unit (VDU) or printed out. An operator may communicate directly with the computer using the VDU and keyboard.

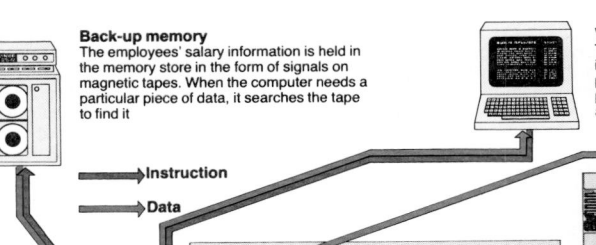

Back-up memory
The employees' salary information is held in the memory store in the form of signals on magnetic tapes. When the computer needs a particular piece of data, it searches the tape to find it

Visual display unit
The computer is told how to combine the information about hours worked and rates of pay by a sequence of instructions called the program. The program is "read" from a tape and can be modified through a keyboard

Printer
The calculated pay for all the company's employees can be displayed on the VDU or it can be printed out at rates of 200 characters a second or more. The results can be stored on tapes or disks

→ **Instruction**
→ **Data**

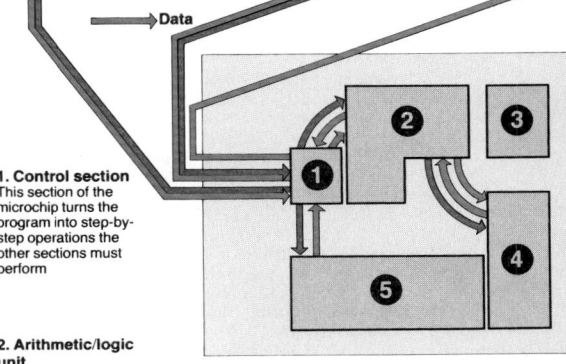

1. Control section
This section of the microchip turns the program into step-by-step operations the other sections must perform

2. Arithmetic/logic unit
Arithmetical calculations are carried out in this unit

3. Clock
The computer's actions are synchronized by a built-in clock. At each "tick" all the computer parts perform one step of their operations

4. Random-access memory
Results and information that might be needed again are entered in the random-access memory (RAM). They can be called quickly from any part of this memory at random. It is the computer's "notepad"

5. Read-only memory
Information that the computer will need when performing a program is stored in a special unit called the read-only memory (ROM), because it is not changed or added to in normal operation

Actual size of the microchip

MICROPROCESSOR *An entire computer can be etched onto a single silicon chip called a microprocessor. In this payroll computing system, the chip is housed in a visual display unit (VDU). The program is fed in from magnetic tapes, which also provide additional memory storage (back-up memory). Employees' wages can be displayed on the VDU and also printed out on paper by a printer linked to the microprocessor. The computer can list the employees' names in any given order.*

---

con·cave (kŏn-kāv′) *adj.* Curved like a section of the inner surface of a sphere: *a concave mirror.* Compare **convex.**
~*n.* A concave surface, structure, or line. [Middle English, from Old French, from Latin *concavus,* vaulted, hollow : *com-* (intensive) + *cavus,* hollow.] —**con·cave·ly** *adv.* —**con·cave·ness** *n.*
con·cav·i·ty (kŏn-kăv′ə-tē) *n., pl.* **-ties. 1.** The condition or state of being concave. **2.** A concave surface or structure.
con·ca·vo-con·cave (kŏn-kā′vō-kŏn-kāv′) *adj.* Concave on both surfaces, as certain lenses are.
con·ca·vo-con·vex (kŏn-kā′vō-kŏn-vĕks′) *adj.* **1.** Concave on one side and convex on the other; convexo-concave. **2.** Designating a lens with greater concave than convex curvature.
con·ceal (kən-sēl′) *tr.v.* **-cealed, -cealing, -ceals. 1.** To prevent from being noticed or discovered: *couldn't conceal her disgust.* **2.** To keep out of sight; hide: *a concealed entrance.* —See Synonyms at **hide.** [Middle English *concelen,* from Old French *conceler,* from Latin *concēlāre* : *com-* (intensive) + *cēlāre,* to hide.] —**con·ceal·a·ble** *adj.* —**con·ceal·er** *n.* —**con·ceal·ment** *n.*
con·cede (kən-sēd′) *v.* **-ceded, -ceding, -cedes.** —*tr.* **1.** To acknowledge as true, just, or proper; admit. **2.** To yield or grant (a privilege or right, for example). **3.** To allow an opponent to score (a goal, points, or the like). —*intr.* **1.** To make a concession. **2.** To admit defeat, as in an election. —See Synonyms at **acknowledge.** [French *concéder,* from Latin *concēdere,* to yield : *com-* (intensive) + *cēdere,* to go away, withdraw.] —**con·ced·ed·ly** *adv.* —**con·ced·er** *n.*
con·ceit (kən-sēt′) *n.* **1.** A high, often exaggerated, opinion of one's own abilities, worth, or personality; vanity. **2.** An ingenious, fanciful, or witty thought or expression. **3. a.** A far-fetched or exaggerated metaphor. **b.** The use of such metaphors. **c.** A poem or verse constructed entirely around an elaborate conceit. **4.** *Archaic.* A thought or idea; opinion.
~*tr.v.* **conceited, -ceiting, -ceits.** *Obsolete.* **1.** To imagine or consider. **2.** *Regional.* To take a fancy to. [Middle English *conceite,* concept, notion, from *conceiven,* to CONCEIVE (by analogy with DE-CEIVE, DECEIT).]
con·ceit·ed (kən-sē′tĭd) *adj.* **1.** Holding too high an opinion of oneself; vain. **2.** *Regional.* Inclined to be fanciful or whimsical. —**con·ceit·ed·ly** *adv.* —**con·ceit·ed·ness** *n.*
con·ceiv·a·ble (kən-sē′və-bəl) *adj.* Capable of being conceived or imagined; possible. —**con·ceiv·a·bil·ity, con·ceiv·a·ble·ness** *n.* —**con·ceiv·a·bly** *adv.*
con·ceive (kən-sēv′) *v.* **-ceived, -ceiving, -ceives.** —*tr.* **1. a.** To become pregnant with. **b.** To begin or induce the conception of: *a test-tube baby conceived outside the womb.* **2. a.** To form in the mind; become possessed by: *conceived an instant dislike for her.* **b.** To formulate; devise: *conceive a plan.* **3.** To apprehend mentally; imagine or understand. Often followed by a clause. **4.** To think or consider. Often followed by a clause. —*intr.* **1.** To form an idea. Used with *of.* **2.** To become pregnant. [Middle English *conceiven,* from Old French *conceivre,* from Latin *concipere,* to take to oneself, hence to be impregnated, to take into the mind : *com-,* comprehensively + *capere,* to take.] —**con·ceiv·er** *n.*
con·cel·e·brate (kən-sĕl′ə-brāt′) *intr.v.* **-brated, -brating, -brates.** To take part in a concelebration. [Latin *concelebrāre* : *com-,* together + *celebrāre,* to CELEBRATE.]
con·cel·e·bra·tion (kən-sĕl′ə-brā′shən) *n.* The celebration of the Eucharist by two or more clergymen.
con·cen·ter (kŏn-sĕn′tər) *v.* **-tered, -tering, -ters.** —*tr.* To direct toward a common center. —*intr.* To come together at a common

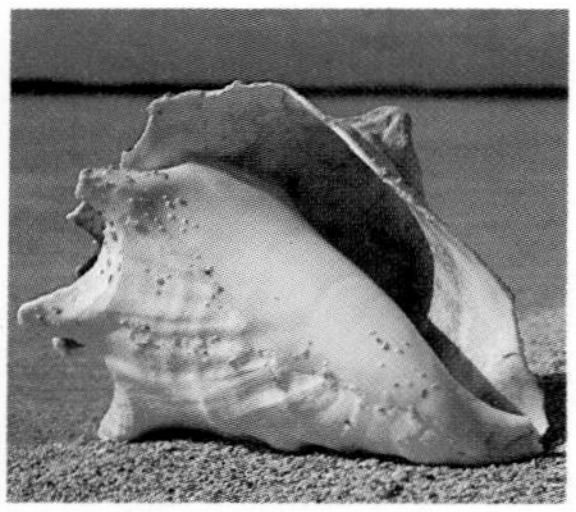

conch *In Greek mythology, the sea god Triton used the shell of the trumpet conch,* Charonia tritonis, *as his horn. Although conches are still sometimes used as musical instruments, they are now mainly valued as the material from which cameos are carved. Conches are large edible snails—sometimes weighing over 2 kilograms (4½ pounds) without their shells—and are found around the world in warm coastal waters. This shell is from a Caribbean species.*

center. [French *concentrer,* to CONCENTRATE.]

con·cen·trate (kŏn′sən-trāt′) *v.* **-trated, -trating, -trates.** —*tr.* **1.** To direct or draw toward a common center, purpose, or the like; focus: *tried to concentrate her mind on her work.* **2.** *Chemistry.* To increase the concentration of (a solution or mixture). —*intr.* **1.** To converge toward a center. **2. a.** To focus one's thoughts or attention. Often used with *on* or *upon.* **b.** To keep one's attention closely on a matter at hand.
~*n. Abbr.* **conc.** *Chemistry.* A product of concentration.
~*adj. Abbr.* **conc.** Concentrated. [French *concentrer* : *com-,* same + *center,* CENTER.] —**con·cen·tra·tor** *n.*

con·cen·tra·tion (kŏn′sən-trā′shən) *n.* **1.** The act or process of concentrating or the condition of being concentrated. **2.** A concentrated mass; an accumulation. **3.** Closely directed thoughts or attention. **4.** *Chemistry.* The amount of a given substance in a unit amount of another substance, usually expressed as the number of moles of solute in a liter or a cubic decimeter of solvent.

concentration camp *n.* An internment camp of a type first used by the British in the Boer War, where prisoners of war, enemy aliens, and political prisoners are confined and sometimes, as in those of Nazi Germany, subjected to brutal treatment. [Referring to the *concentration* of large numbers of such prisoners in one area.]

con·cen·tric (kən-sĕn′trĭk) *adj.* Having a common center. Compare **eccentric.** [Middle English *concentrik,* from Old French *concentrique,* from Medieval Latin *concentricus* : Latin *com-,* same + *centrum,* CENTER.] —**con·cen·tri·cal·ly** *adv.* —**con·cen·tric·i·ty** (kŏn′sĕn-trĭs′ĭ-tē) *n.*

con·cept (kŏn′sĕpt) *n.* **1.** A general idea or understanding, especially one derived from specific instances or occurrences. **2.** A thought or notion, especially one that is abstract or theoretical. **3. a.** A way of thinking about something. **b.** The structure or design of something, considered in the abstract. —See Synonyms at **idea.** [Late Latin *conceptus,* a thing conceived, thought, from past participle of *concipere,* to take to oneself, CONCEIVE.]

con·cep·ta·cle (kən-sĕp′tə-kəl) *n.* A cavity in certain algae and fungi that opens to the exterior and contains reproductive structures. [French, from Latin *conceptāculum,* from *concipere,* to receive, contain, CONCEIVE.]

con·cep·tion (kən-sĕp′shən) *n.* **1. a.** The fertilization of an egg cell by a sperm in the uterus to form an embryo capable of survival and maturation in normal conditions. **b.** The entity so formed; an embryo. **2.** A beginning. **3.** The ability to form mental concepts; invention. **4.** That which is mentally conceived; a concept, plan, design, idea, or thought. —See Synonyms at **idea.** [Middle English *concepcioun,* from Old French *conception,* from Latin *conceptiō* (stem *conceptiōn-*), from *concipere,* to take to oneself, CONCEIVE.] —**con·cep·tion·al** *adj.*

con·cep·tive (kən-sĕp′tĭv) *adj.* Able to conceive mentally.

con·cep·tu·al (kən-sĕp′cho͞o-əl) *adj.* Of or pertaining to concepts or mental conception. —**con·cep·tu·al·ly** *adv.*

conceptual art *n.* Art that is intended to convey an idea or concept to the perceiver and need not involve the creation or appreciation of a traditional art object such as a painting or sculpture.

con·cep·tu·al·ism (kən-sĕp′cho͞o-əl-ĭz′əm) *n. Philosophy.* The doctrine that universals, or abstract concepts, exist only within the mind and have no external or substantial reality. —**con·cep·tu·al·ist** *n.* —**con·cep·tu·al·is·tic** *adj.*

con·cep·tu·al·ize (kən-sĕp′cho͞o-əl-īz′) *v.* **-ized, -izing, -izes.** —*tr.* To form concepts or a concept of. —*intr.* To form concepts, theories, or ideas. —**con·cep·tu·al·i·za·tion** *n.*

con·cern (kən-sûrn′) *v.* **-cerned, -cerning, -cerns.** —*tr.* **1. a.** To pertain or relate to. **b.** To be of interest or importance to; affect. **2.** To engage or involve the mind or interests of. Used reflexively or in the passive: *concern oneself with trivia.* **3.** To cause anxiety or uneasiness in; trouble. —*intr. Obsolete.* To be of importance.
~*n.* **1. a.** A matter that relates to or affects one. **b.** Something of interest or importance. **2.** Regard for or interest in someone or something: *concern for her well-being.* **3.** A matter about which one is concerned. **4.** Anxiety; worry. **5.** A business establishment or enterprise; a company. —See Synonyms at **anxiety.** [Middle English *concernen,* from Old French *concerner,* from Medieval Latin *concernere,* to relate to, involve with, from Latin, to mix in a sieve (before sifting) : *com-,* together + *cernere,* to sift.]

con·cerned (kən-sûrnd′) *adj.* **1.** Interested or affected; involved. **2.** Anxious; troubled; disturbed.

con·cern·ing (kən-sûr′nĭng) *prep.* With reference to; regarding; about.

con·cern·ment (kən-sûrn′mənt) *n.* **1.** A matter that concerns one; an affair. **2.** Reference, relation, or importance. **3.** Anxiety; worry.

con·cert (kŏn′sûrt) *n.* **1.** A musical performance in which a number of singers or players participate. **2.** Agreement in purpose, feeling, or action. —**in concert. 1.** All together; in agreement. **2.** Playing or singing live, at a concert.
~*adj.* Pertaining to, playing in, or designed for concerts.
~*tr.v.* (kən-sûrt′) **concerted, -certing, -certs. 1.** To plan or arrange by mutual agreement. **2.** To contrive or devise. [French, from Italian *concerto,* from Old Italian *concertare*†, to bring into agreement, harmonize.]

con·cert·ed (kən-sûr′tĭd) *adj.* **1.** Planned or accomplished together; combined: *a concerted effort.* **2.** *Music.* Arranged in parts for voices or instruments. —**con·cert·ed·ly** *adv.*

concert grand *n.* The largest type of grand piano, being roughly 2.8 meters (9 feet) in length.

con·cer·ti·na (kŏn′sər-tē′nə) *n.* A small, hexagonal accordion with bellows, and buttons for keys. [CONCERT + Italian *-ina* (feminine diminutive suffix).]

con·cer·ti·no (kŏn′chĕr-tē′nō) *n., pl.* **-nos** or **-ni** (-nē). *Music.* **1.** A short concerto. **2.** The solo instrument group in a concerto grosso. [Italian, diminutive of *concerto,* concerto, CONCERT.]

con·cer·tize (kŏn′sər-tīz′) *intr.v.* **-tized, -tizing, -tizes.** To give, or perform in, concerts.

con·cert·mas·ter (kŏn′sərt-măs′tər, -mäs′tər) *n.* The first violinist and assistant conductor in a symphony orchestra.

con·cer·to (kən-chĕr′tō) *n., pl.* **-tos** or **-ti** (-tē). *Abbr.* **con.** A composition for an orchestra and one or more solo instruments, typically in three movements. [Italian, CONCERT.]

concerto gros·so (kən-chĕr′tō grō′sō) *n., pl.* **concerti grossi** (kən-chĕr′tē grō′sē). A composition for a small group of solo instruments and a full orchestra. [Italian, "great concerto."]

concert pitch *n.* **1.** *Music.* A pitch to which orchestral instruments are tuned with the A above middle C at 440 hertz. Also called "international pitch." **2.** *Informal.* The state of being ready and tensely alert.

con·ces·sion (kən-sĕsh′ən) *n.* **1.** The act of conceding, granting, or yielding. **2.** Any thing or point so conceded. **3.** Something granted by a government or controlling authority, such as a right to land or exploration, to be used for a specific purpose. **4. a.** The right to operate a subsidiary business within a larger establishment. **b.** The space allotted for such a business. [Middle English, from Old French, from Latin *concessiō* (stem *concessiōn-*), from *concēdere* (past participle *concessus*), to CONCEDE.]

con·ces·sion·aire (kən-sĕsh′ən-âr′) *n.* Also **con·ces·sion·er** (-sĕsh′-ən-ər). The operator or holder of a concession.

con·ces·sion·ar·y (kən-sĕsh′ən-ĕr′ē) *adj.* Of the nature of or granted by a concession.

con·ces·sive (kən-sĕs′ĭv) *adj.* **1.** Of the nature of or containing a concession; tending to concede. **2.** *Grammar.* Expressing concession, as the conjunction *although.* [Latin *concessīvus,* from *concessus,* past participle of *concēdere,* to CONCEDE.]

conch (kŏngk, kŏnch) *n., pl.* **conchs** (kŏngks) or **conches** (kŏn′-chĭz). **1.** Any of various tropical marine gastropod mollusks of the genus *Strombus* and other genera, having large, often brightly colored spiral shells and, in some species, edible flesh. **2.** The shell of any of these mollusks, used for ornament, in making cameos, or as a horn. **3.** A concha. [Middle English *conche, conk,* from Latin *concha,* from Greek *konkhē.*]

con·cha (kŏng′kə) *n., pl.* **-chae** (-kē). **1.** *Anatomy.* A shell-like structure, such as the external ear. **2.** *Architecture.* The half dome over an apse. [Latin, CONCH.]

con·chif·er·ous (kŏng-kĭf′ər-əs) *adj.* **1.** Having or forming a shell. **2.** Containing shells. Said of certain rocks. [CONCH(O)- + -FEROUS.]

con·chi·o·lin (kŏng-kī′ə-lĭn, kŏn-) *n.* A fibrous protein, $C_{32}H_{98}N_2O_{11}$, that is the principal constituent of mollusk shells. [From CONCH.]

concho-, conch-, conchi- *prefix.* Indicates shell; for example, **conchology.** [Greek *konkho-,* from *konkhē,* shell.]

con·choid (kŏng′koid′) *n.* In geometry, a curve having two branches with a common asymptote, so that a line from a fixed point that intersects both branches is of constant length between the asymptote and either branch. [CONCH + -OID (referring to the shape of the curve).]

con·choi·dal (kŏng-koid′l) *adj.* Of or designating rocks, such as flint or obsidian, having bivalve shell-like surfaces when fractured. [Greek *konkhoeidēs,* shell-like : CONCH(O)- + -OID.]

con·chol·o·gy (kŏng-kŏl′ə-jē) *n.* The study of mollusks and their shells. [CONCHO- + -LOGY.] —**con·cho·log·i·cal** (kŏng′kə-lŏj′ĭ-kəl) *adj.* —**con·chol·o·gist** (kŏng′kŏl′ə-jĭst) *n.*

con·ci·erge (kŏn′sē-ûrzh; *French* kôɴ-syârzh′) *n.* A person who attends the entrance of a building and acts as caretaker. [French, from Old French *cumcerges,* from Vulgar Latin *conservius* (unattested), variant of Latin *conservus,* a fellow slave : *com-,* together + *servus,* slave.]

con·cil·i·ar (kən-sĭl′ē-ər) *adj.* Of or pertaining to a council, especially an ecclesiastical council.

con·cil·i·ate (kən-sĭl′ē-āt′) *tr.v.* **-ated, -ating, -ates. 1.** To overcome the distrust or animosity of; win over; placate; soothe. **2.** To gain, win, or secure (favor, friendship, or goodwill, for example) by friendly overtures. **3.** To reconcile. —See Synonyms at **pacify.** [Latin *conciliāre,* to bring together, unite, from *concilium,* union, gathering, meeting.] —**con·cil·i·a·ble** (kən-sĭl′ē-ə-bəl) *adj.* —**con·cil·i·a·tor** *n.* —**con·cil·i·a·to·ry** (kən-sĭl′ē-ə-tôr′ē, -tōr′ē) *adj.*

con·cil·i·a·tion (kən-sĭl′ē-ā′shən) *n.* **1.** The act or process of conciliating; placation; propitiation. **2.** The process of settling differences between employers and employees through the good offices of a third party but without resort to arbitration. —See Synonyms at **mediation.**

con·cin·ni·ty (kən-sĭn′ə-tē) *n., pl.* **-ties. 1.** A skillful, harmonious arrangement of parts. **2.** Elegance of literary style. [Latin *concinnitās,* from *concinnus,* placed fitly together, from *concinnāre,* to place fitly together, arrange in good order : *com-,* together + *cinnus*†, a mixed drink.]

con·cise (kən-sīs′) *adj.* Expressing much in few words; short and to the point; succinct. [Latin *concīsus,* past participle of *concīdere,* to cut up : *com-* (intensive) + *caedere,* to cut.] —**con·cise·ly** *adv.* —**con·cise·ness** *n.*

Synonyms: *compendious, epigrammatic, laconic, pithy, succinct, summary, terse.*

con·ci·sion (kən-sĭzh'ən) *n.* **1.** The quality of being concise; terseness; brevity; succinctness. **2.** *Archaic.* A cutting apart or off. [Middle English *concisioun,* from Latin *concīsiō* (stem *concīsiōn-*), from *concīsus,* CONCISE.]

con·clave (kŏn'klāv, kŏng'-) *n.* **1.** A confidential or secret meeting. **2. a.** The private rooms in which the cardinals of the Roman Catholic Church meet to elect a pope. **b.** The meeting so held. [Middle English, from Old French, from Latin *conclāve,* "room locked with a key" : *com-,* together + *clāvis,* key.]

con·clude (kən-klōōd') *v.* **-cluded, -cluding, -cludes.** —*tr.* **1.** To bring to an end; wind up; finish. **2.** To arrive finally at (an agreement or settlement); settle: *conclude a peace treaty.* **3.** To infer or deduce. **4.** To determine; decide. —*intr.* **1.** To come to an end; close. **2.** To form a final judgment; come to a decision or an agreement. —See Synonyms at **complete, decide.** [Middle English *concluden,* from Latin *conclūdere,* to shut up closely : *com-* (intensive) + *claudere,* to shut.] —**con·clud·er** *n.*

con·clu·sion (kən-klōō'zhən) *n.* **1.** The close or termination of something; the end; the finish. **2.** The closing or last part, as of a speech, paper, or the like, often containing a summing up. **3.** A final outcome or result: *Their election victory was a foregone conclusion.* **4.** A judgment, inference, or decision reached after deliberation. **5.** A final arrangement or settlement, as of a treaty. **6.** *Law. Abbr.* **con. a.** The close of a plea or deed. **b.** An estoppel *(see).* **7.** *Logic.* **a.** In a syllogism, the proposition that must follow from the major and minor premises. **b.** The proposition concluded from one or more premises; a deduction. —**try conclusions with.** *Archaic.* To engage in a contest or argument. [Middle English *conclusioun,* from Old French *conclusion,* from Latin *conclūsiō* (stem *conclūsiōn-*), from *conclūdere,* to shut up closely, CONCLUDE.]

con·clu·sive (kən-klōō'sĭv) *adj.* Serving to put an end to doubt or question; decisive; final. —See Synonyms at **valid.** —**con·clu·sive·ly** *adv.* —**con·clu·sive·ness** *n.*

con·coct (kən-kŏkt') *tr.v.* **-cocted, -cocting, -cocts. 1.** To prepare by mixing ingredients, as in cookery. **2.** To invent or fabricate; contrive: *concoct a plausible story.* [Latin *concoquere* (past participle *concoctus*), to cook together : *com-,* together + *coquere,* to cook.] —**con·coct·er, con·coc·tor** *n.* —**con·coc·tion** *n.* —**con·coc·tive** *adj.*

con·com·i·tance (kən-kŏm'ə-təns) *n.* Also **con·com·i·tan·cy** (-tən-sē) *pl.* **-cies. 1.** Occurrence together or in connection with another; accompaniment. **2.** A concomitant. **3.** *Theology.* The coexistence of the body and blood of Christ in each element of the Eucharist.

con·com·i·tant (kən-kŏm'ə-tənt) *adj.* Existing or occurring concurrently as an attendant feature or circumstance; accompanying. —See Synonyms at **contemporary.** ~*n.* A concomitant state, circumstance, or thing. [Latin *concomitāns* (stem *concomitant-*), present participle of *concomitārī,* to accompany : *com-,* together + *comitārī,* to accompany, from *comes* (stem *comit-*), companion.]

con·cord (kŏn'kôrd, kŏng'-) *n.* **1.** Harmony or agreement of interests or feelings; concurrence; accord. **2.** A treaty establishing peaceful relations. **3.** *Grammar.* Agreement between words in person, number, gender, or case. **4.** A harmonious combination of simultaneously sounded notes; consonance. Compare **discord.** [Middle English, from Old French *concorde,* from Latin *concordia,* from *concors,* "of the same mind" : *com-,* same, mutually + *cors* (stem *cord-*), the heart, mind.]

Con·cord[1] (kŏng'kərd). A city of eastern Massachusetts, on the Concord River. It is the site of the Revolutionary War Battle of Concord (April 19, 1775). There are many fine old houses in the city.

Concord[2]. The capital of New Hampshire, in the south-central part of the state on the Merrimack River. The city is famous for its granite and also has varied industries.

con·cor·dance (kən-kôr'dəns) *n.* **1.** A state of agreement; harmony; concord. **2.** An index of all the words in a text or corpus of texts, showing every contextual occurrence of a word.

con·cor·dant (kən-kôr'dənt) *adj.* Harmonious; agreeing; corresponding. [Middle English *concordaunt,* from Old French *concordant,* from Latin *concordāns* (stem *concordant-*), present participle of *concordāre,* to agree, from *concors,* agreed. See **concord.**] —**con·cor·dant·ly** *adv.*

con·cor·dat (kən-kôr'dăt') *n.* A formal agreement; especially, an agreement between the pope and a government for the regulation of church affairs. [French, from Medieval Latin *concordātum,* from Latin *concordāre,* to agree. See **concordant.**]

Con·corde (kŏn'kôrd, kŏng'-) *n.* An Anglo-French supersonic airliner, capable of flying at speeds greater than Mach 2. [French, *concord,* unity, referring to Anglo-French cooperation in producing it.]

Concord grape *n.* A variety of grape having purple-black fruit with a bluish bloom. [Discovered (1846) at CONCORD, Massachusetts.]

con·course (kŏn'kôrs, -kōrs, kŏng'-) *n.* **1.** A great crowd; throng; multitude. **2.** A coming, moving, or flowing together. **3. a.** A large open space for the gathering or passage of crowds, as in a railroad station. **b.** A broad thoroughfare. [Middle English, from Old French *concours,* from Latin *concursus,* from the past participle of *concurrere,* to run together : *com-,* together + *currere,* to run.]

con·cres·cence (kən-krĕs'əns) *n.* The uniting, especially the growing together, of related parts, as of physical particles or anatomical structures. [Latin *concrēscentia,* from *concrēscēns* (stem *concrēscent-*), present participle of *concrēscere,* to grow together : *com-,* together + *crēscere,* to grow.]

con·crete (kŏn-krēt', kŏn'krēt) *adj.* **1.** Pertaining to an actual, specific thing or instance; not general; particular. **2.** Existing in reality or in real experience; perceptible by the senses; real. **3.** Designating a material object or thing as opposed to an abstraction or quality. **4.** Formed by the coalescence of separate particles or parts into one mass; solid. **5.** Made of concrete. —See Synonyms at **real.** ~*n.* (kŏn'krēt, kŏn-krēt'). **1.** A construction material consisting of sand, gravel, pebbles, broken stone, or the like in a mortar or cement matrix. **2.** A mass formed by the coalescence of particles. ~*v.* (kŏn'krēt, kŏn-krēt') **concreted, -creting, -cretes.** —*tr.* **1.** To form into a mass by coalescence or cohesion of particles. **2.** To build, treat, or cover with concrete. —*intr.* To coalesce; solidify. [Middle English *concret,* from Old French, from Latin *concrētus,* past participle of *concrēscere,* to grow together, harden : *com-,* together + *crēscere,* to grow.] —**con·crete·ly** *adv.* —**con·crete·ness** *n.*

concrete mixer *n.* A machine with a revolving drum in which cement, sand, gravel, and water are combined into concrete. Also called "cement mixer."

concrete noun *n.* A noun designating a material object as opposed to an abstract idea or quality. Compare **abstract noun.**

concrete poetry Poetry in which the physical representation or arrangement of the words conveys or adds meaning.

con·cre·tion (kən-krē'shən) *n.* **1.** The act or process of growing together or becoming united in one mass; coalescence. **2.** A solid or concrete mass. **3.** *Geology.* A rounded or irregular mass of mineral matter found in sedimentary rock. **4.** *Pathology.* A solid mass of inorganic material formed in a cavity or tissue of the body; a calculus. —**con·cre·tion·ar·y** (kən-krē'shə-nĕr'ē) *adj.*

con·cret·ism (kŏn-krē'tĭz'əm) *n.* The theory or practice of concrete poetry. —**con·cret·ist** *n.*

con·cre·tize (kŏn'krĭ-tīz') *tr.v.* **-tized, -tizing, -tizes.** To render concrete; make real or specific. —**con·cre·ti·za·tion** *n.*

con·cu·bi·nage (kŏn-kyōō'bə-nĭj) *n.* **1.** Cohabitation without legal marriage. **2.** The state of being a concubine.

con·cu·bine (kŏng'kyə-bīn', kŏn'-) *n.* **1.** A woman who cohabits with and is supported by a man without being married to him. **2.** In certain polygamous societies, a secondary wife, usually of inferior legal and social status. [Middle English, from Old French, from Latin *concubīna,* "one to sleep with" : *com-,* together + *cubāre,* to lie down.] —**con·cu·bi·nar·y** *adj.*

con·cu·pis·cence (kŏn-kyōō'pə-səns) *n.* **1.** Sexual desire; lust. **2.** Any abnormally strong desire. [Latin *concupīscēns,* present participle of *concupīscere,* inceptive of *concupere,* to have a strong desire for : *com-* (intensive) + *cupere,* to desire.] —**con·cu·pis·cent** *adj.*

con·cur (kən-kûr') *intr.v.* **-curred, -curring, -curs. 1.** To have the same opinion; agree. **2.** To act together; cooperate. **3.** To occur at the same time; coincide. —See Synonyms at **assent.** [Middle English *concurren,* from Latin *concurrere,* to run together : *com-,* together + *currere,* to run.]

Usage: *Concur in* is generally used to express approval or joint action: *concur in a plan. Concur with* expresses agreement: *concur with her view.*

con·cur·rence (kən-kûr'əns) *n.* **1.** Agreement in opinion; accord. **2.** Cooperation or combination, as of agents, causes, circumstances, or events. **3.** Simultaneous occurrence; coincidence. **4.** In geometry, the intersection of three or more lines. **5.** *Rare.* Competition; rivalry. **6.** *Law.* A power or claim held jointly.

con·cur·rent (kən-kûr'ənt) *adj.* **1. a.** Happening at the same time or place. **b.** Intended to run simultaneously. **2.** Operating in conjunction. **3.** Meeting at or tending to meet at the same point. **4.** In accordance or agreement; harmonious. **5.** Exercising equal authority or having the same jurisdiction. —See Synonyms at **contemporary.** [Middle English, from Old French, from Latin *concurrēns* (stem *concurrent-*), present participle of *concurrere,* to run together, CONCUR.] —**con·cur·rent·ly** *adv.*

concurrent resolution *n.* A resolution adopted by both houses of a bicameral legislature that does not have the force of law and does not require the signature of the chief executive. Compare **joint resolution.**

con·cuss (kən-kŭs') *tr.v.* **-cussed, -cussing, -cusses. 1.** To injure by concussion. **2.** *Rare.* To shake or agitate; disturb severely. [Late Latin *concutere* (past participle *concussus*), to shake violently : Latin *com-* (intensive) + *-cutere,* from *quatere,* to shake, dash.]

con·cus·sion (kən-kŭsh'ən) *n.* **1.** An injury of a soft structure, especially of the brain, resulting from a violent blow and usually causing loss of consciousness. **2.** Any violent jarring shock. —**con·cus·sive** (kən-kŭs'ĭv) *adj.*

Con·dé (kôn-dā'), Louis I (1530–69). French prince of a branch of the Bourbon dynasty. He was leader of the Huguenots during the French Wars of Religion.

Condé, Louis II, also known as "the Great Condé" (1621–86). Great-grandson of Louis Condé I. He was a brilliant general who won famous victories for France during the Thirty Years' War.

con·demn (kən-dĕm') *tr.v.* **-demned, -demning, -demns. 1.** To express disapproval of; censure; criticize. **2. a.** To pronounce judgment against; sentence. **b.** To force into an undesirable state; doom. **3.** To demonstrate the guilt of; convict. **4.** To judge or declare to be unfit for use or consumption, usually by official order:

condemn an old building. —See Synonyms at **criticize**. [Middle English *condem(p)nen,* from Old French *condem(p)ner,* from Latin *condemnāre* : *com-,* (intensive) + *damnāre,* to damage, condemn, from *damnum,* damage, fine.] —**con·dem·na·ble** *adj.* —**con·demn·er** *n.*

con·dem·na·tion (kŏn′dĕm-nā′shən) *n.* **1.** The act of condemning. **2.** The state of being condemned. **3.** Severe reproof; strong censure. **4.** A reason or occasion for condemning. —**con·dem·na·to·ry** (kən-dĕm′nə-tôr′ē, -tōr′ē) *adj.*

con·demned cell (kən-dĕmd′) *n.* The prison cell of a person who has been condemned to death.

con·den·sate (kən-dĕn′sāt′) *n.* A liquid formed by condensation. [Latin *condēnsātus,* past participle of *condēnsāre,* to CONDENSE.]

con·den·sa·tion (kŏn′dən-sā′shən) *n.* **1.** The act of condensing. **2.** The state of being condensed. **3.** A product of condensing, especially, abridgment. **4.** *Physics.* **a.** The physical process by which a liquid is removed from a vapor or vapor mixture. **b.** The liquid so removed; a condensate, especially water droplets forming on cold glass as air cools. **5.** *Chemistry.* A chemical reaction in which water or another simple substance is released by the combination of two or more molecules. **6.** *Psychoanalysis.* The process by which a single idea or word is invested with the emotional content of a group of ideas.

condensation trail *n.* A vapor trail *(see).*

con·dense (kən-dĕns′) *v.* **-densed, -densing, -denses.** —*tr.* **1.** To reduce the volume of; compress. **2.** To abridge (a literary work, for example). **3. a.** To form a condensate from (a vapor, for example). **b.** To subject (a vapor, for example) to condensation. —*intr.* **1.** To become more compact. **2.** To undergo condensation. —See Synonyms at **contract**. [Middle English *condensen,* from Old French *condenser,* from Latin *condēnsāre* : *com-* (intensive) + *dēnsāre,* to make dense, from *dēnsus,* dense.] —**con·dens·a·bil·i·ty** *n.* —**con·dens·a·ble** *adj.*

con·densed (kən-dĕnst′) *adj.* **1. a.** Made more compact. **b.** Abridged: *a condensed book.* **2.** *Printing.* Narrower than normal in proportion to its height. Said of type. Compare **expanded.** **3.** *Botany.* Having stalkless or nearly stalkless flowers tightly crowded together. Said of certain inflorescences.

condensed milk *n.* Cow's milk with sugar added, and reduced by evaporation to a thick consistency. Compare **evaporated milk.**

con·dens·er (kən-dĕn′sər) *n.* **1.** One that condenses. **2.** *Physics.* An apparatus used to condense vapor. **3.** *Electricity.* A capacitor *(see).* **4.** A mirror, lens, or combination of lenses used to gather light and direct it upon an object or projection lens.

con·de·scend (kŏn′dĭ-sĕnd′) *intr.v.* **-scended, -scending, -scends.** **1.** To come down voluntarily to the level of inferiors with whom one is dealing; deign. **2.** To behave in a patronizing manner. [Middle English *condescenden,* from Old French *condescendre,* from Medieval Latin *condēscendere,* to stoop to : Latin *com-* (intensive) + *dēscendere,* to descend : *dē-,* down + *scandere,* to climb.] —**con·de·scend·er** *n.*

con·de·scen·dence (kŏn′dĭ-sĕn′dəns) *n.* **1.** *Scottish Law.* A list of facts or grounds presented by the plaintiff. **2.** Condescension.

con·de·scend·ing (kŏn′dĭ-sĕn′dĭng) *adj.* Showing or assuming an air of superiority; patronizing. —**con·de·scend·ing·ly** *adv.*

con·de·scen·sion (kŏn′dĭ-sĕn′shən) *n.* **1. a.** The act of condescending. **b.** An instance of this. **2.** Patronizing behavior or manner.

con·dign (kən-dīn′) *adj.* Deserved; adequate; merited. Said of punishment or censure. [Middle English *condigne,* from Old French, from Latin *condignus,* wholly worthy : *com-* (intensive) + *dignus,* worthy.] —**con·dign·ly** *adv.*

Con·dil·lac (kôn′-dē-yäk′), **Étienne Bonnot de** (1715–80). French philosopher, a leading figure in the Enlightenment. He developed John Locke's view that all knowledge derives from the senses.

con·di·ment (kŏn′də-mənt) *n.* A seasoning for food, such as mustard, vinegar, or a spice. [Middle English, from Old French, from Latin *condīmentum,* from *condīre,* to season, preserve by pickling, perhaps variant of *condere,* to bring together, store up.] —**con·di·men·tal** *adj.*

con·di·tion (kən-dĭsh′ən) *n.* **1.** The particular mode or state of being of a person or thing, especially: **a.** State of health. **b.** State of readiness or preparation: *out of condition for the race.* **c.** State of repair or fitness for use. **d.** Rank or social position. **2.** A disease or ailment: *a heart condition.* **3.** Something indispensable to the appearance or occurrence of something else; a prerequisite: *The Moon's atmosphere lacks the essential conditions for supporting human life.* **4.** Something required as prerequisite to the fulfillment or performance of something else; stipulation. **5.** Something that restricts or modifies something else; qualification. **6.** *Usually* **conditions.** The existing or external circumstances: *poor driving conditions.* **7.** *Grammar.* The dependent clause of a conditional sentence. **8.** *Logic.* A proposition upon which another proposition depends; the antecedent of a conditional proposition. **9.** *Law.* A provision making the effect of a legal instrument contingent upon the occurrence of some uncertain future event. **b.** The event itself. —See Synonyms at **state.**
~*tr.v.* **conditioned, -tioning, -tions.** **1.** To make conditional; govern. Often used in the passive. **2.** To render fit; put into the desired condition. **3. a.** *Psychology.* To cause to respond in a specific manner to a specific stimulus. **b.** To accustom (a person) to adopt or conform to certain attitudes, modes of behavior, or the like. **4.** To treat with conditioner: *conditioned his hair.* [Middle English *condicioun,* from Old French *condicion,* from Latin *conditiō* (stem *condi-*

tiōn-), agreement, stipulation, probably (irregularly) from *condīcere,* to talk together, agree : *com-,* together + *dīcere,* to talk.]

con·di·tion·al (kən-dĭsh′ən-əl) *adj.* **1.** Imposing, depending on, or containing a condition or conditions. **2.** *Grammar.* Stating or implying a condition. **3.** *Psychology.* Brought about by conditioning. ~*n.* *Grammar.* A mood, tense, clause, or word expressing a condition. —**con·di·tion·al·i·ty** *n.* —**con·di·tion·al·ly** *adv.*

conditional probability *n.* The probability that an event will take place provided that some other event has occurred or will occur.

con·di·tioned (kən-dĭsh′ənd) *adj.* **1.** Subject to or dependent upon conditions or stipulations. **2. a.** Physically fit; in good physical condition. **b.** Prepared for a specific action or process. **3.** *Psychology.* Exhibiting or trained to exhibit a conditioned response.

conditioned response *n.* *Psychology.* A response, elicited by conditioning, to a stimulus that does not really cause it. Also called "conditioned reflex."

conditioned stimulus *n.* *Psychology.* A stimulus rendered capable of eliciting a response like that of a specific **unconditioned stimulus** *(see)* by conditioning.

con·di·tion·er (kən-dĭsh′ən-ər) *n.* **1.** A person or thing that conditions. **2.** An additive or application that improves the condition of something: *a soil conditioner; a hair conditioner.*

con·di·tion·ing (kən-dĭsh′ən-ĭng) *n.* *Psychology.* The process of altering behavior by modifying the stimuli associated with it. In *classical conditioning* the stimulus that normally causes the response is paired with a different stimulus until a conditioned response is elicited by the second stimulus alone. In *operant,* or *instrumental, conditioning* the response is modified by reinforcement (reward or punishment).

con·dole (kən-dōl′) *v.* **-doled, -doling, -doles.** —*intr.* To mourn or express sympathy with someone in pain, grief, or misfortune. Used with *with.* —*tr. Archaic.* To commiserate with or grieve over. [Late Latin *condolēre,* to feel another's pain : Latin *com-,* together + *dolēre,* to feel pain, grieve.] —**con·do·la·to·ry** (kən-dō′lə-tôr′ē, -tōr′ē) *adj.* —**con·dol·er** *n.*

con·do·lence (kən-dō′ləns) *n.* **1.** Sympathy with a person in pain, grief, or misfortune. **2.** **condolences.** A formal declaration of such sympathy. —See Synonyms at **pity.** —**con·do·lent** *adj.*

con·dom (kŏn′dəm) *n.* A sheath, usually made of thin rubber, designed to cover the penis during sexual intercourse, for contraception or as protection against venereal disease. [18th century : origin obscure.]

con·do·min·i·um (kŏn′də-mĭn′ē-əm) *n.* **1. a.** Joint sovereignty; especially, the joint rule of a territory by two or more states. **b.** The territory so governed. **2. a.** An apartment building in which the apartments are owned individually. **b.** An apartment in such a building. Also informally called "condo." [New Latin : CON- + DOMINIUM.]

con·do·na·tion (kŏn′dō-nā′shən) *n.* **1.** The condoning or overlooking of an offense. **2.** *Law.* A forgiving by a wife or husband of an offense by the other, especially adultery.

con·done (kən-dōn′) *tr.v.* **-doned, -doning, -dones.** To forgive, overlook, or disregard (an offense) without protest or censure. —See Synonyms at **forgive.** [Latin *condōnāre,* to give up, forgive : *com-* (intensive) + *dōnāre,* to give away, from *dōnum,* gift.] —**con·don·er** *n.*

con·dor (kŏn′dôr, -dər) *n.* **1.** Either of two very large, black and white New World vultures, *Vultur gryphus* of the Andes or *Gymnogyps californianus* of the mountains of California. **2.** Any of several gold coins of some South American countries bearing the figure of a condor. [Spanish *cóndor,* from Quechua *kúntur.*]

con·dot·tie·re (kŏn′dō-tyâr′ā) *n., pl.* **-tieri** (-tyâr′ē). **1.** A leader of mercenary soldiers in Europe between the 14th and 16th centuries. **2.** A mercenary soldier. [Italian, leader, from *condotto,* conduct, leadership, from Latin *conductum,* from *condūcere,* to lead together, CONDUCT.]

con·duce (kən-dōōs′, -dyōōs′) *intr.v.* **-duced, -ducing, -duces.** To contribute or lead to a particular end or result. Used with *to* or *toward.* [Middle English *conducen,* from Latin *condūcere,* to lead together, be useful, contribute : *com-,* together + *dūcere,* to lead.] —**con·duc·er** *n.*

con·du·cive (kən-dōō′sĭv, -dyōō′sĭv) *adj.* Conducing; promoting; contributive. Used with *to.* —See Synonyms at **favorable.** —**con·du·cive·ness** *n.*

con·duct (kən-dŭkt′) *v.* **-ducted, -ducting, -ducts.** —*tr.* **1.** To direct the course of; manage; carry out: *conduct an opinion poll.* **2.** To guide or escort: *conduct a tour.* **3.** To direct or guide (an orchestra or other musical group), with movements of the hands or a baton. **4.** To serve as a medium or channel for conveying; transmit (heat or electricity, for example). **5.** To behave. Used reflexively. —*intr.* **1.** To act as a conductor. **2.** To be capable of transmitting heat, electricity, or other forms of energy. —See Synonyms at **accompany.**
~*n.* (kŏn′dŭkt). **1.** The way a person acts; behavior. **2.** The act of directing or controlling; management; administration. **3.** *Obsolete.* A guide or escort. [Middle English *conducten,* from Medieval Latin *condūcere,* to escort, from Latin, to lead together : *com-,* together + *dūcere,* to lead.] —**con·duct·i·bil·i·ty** *n.* —**con·duct·i·ble** *adj.*
Synonyms: control, direct, manage, oversee, supervise.

con·duc·tance (kən-dŭk′təns) *n.* A measure of a material's ability to conduct electric charge, the real part of the complex representation of **admittance** *(see).*

con·duc·tim·e·try (kŏn′dŭk-tĭm′ĭ-trē) *n.* The study of chemical analyses that involve titrations based on changes in the electrical conductance of a solution.

con·duc·tion (kən-dŭk'shən) n. The transmission or conveying of something through a medium or passage, especially: **1.** The transmission of electric charge or heat through a conducting medium without perceptible motion of the medium itself. **2.** The transmission of a nerve impulse along a nerve fiber.

con·duc·tive (kən-dŭk'tĭv) adj. Exhibiting conductivity.

con·duc·tiv·i·ty (kŏn'dŭk-tĭv'ə-tē) n. Symbol σ **1.** A measure of the ability of a material to conduct an electric charge, the reciprocal of **resistivity** (see). See **thermal conductivity. 2.** The ability or power to conduct or transmit.

con·duc·tor (kən-dŭk'tər) n. **1.** A person who conducts or leads. **2.** The person in charge of a railroad train, bus, or streetcar. **3.** One who conducts an orchestra or other musical ensemble. **4.** Physics. A substance or medium that conducts heat, sound, or an electric current. **5.** A lightning rod. —**con·duc·tor·ship** n.

con·duc·tress (kən-dŭk'trəs) n. A woman who works as a bus or train conductor.

con·duit (kŏn'dĭt, -dōō-ĭt) n. **1.** A channel or pipe for conveying water or other fluids. **2.** A tube or duct for enclosing electric wires or cable. **3.** Archaic. A fountain. [Middle English, from Old French, conveyance, from Medieval Latin conductus, escort, transportation, from Latin, past participle of conducere, to lead together, CONDUCT.]

con·du·pli·cate (kŏn-dōō'plə-kĭt, kŏn-dyōō'-) adj. Botany. Folded in half lengthwise. Said especially of unopened leaves. [Latin conduplicatus, past participle of conduplicare, to double, fold together : com-, together + duplicare, to double, DUPLICATE.] —**con·du·pli·ca·tion** n.

con·dyle (kŏn'dīl) n. A rounded articulatory prominence at the end of a bone. [French, from Latin condylus, knuckle, from Greek kondulos†.] —**con·dy·lar** adj. —**con·dy·loid** adj.

con·dy·lo·ma (kŏn-də-lō'mə) n., pl. **-mas** or **-mata** (-mə-tə). A wartlike growth near the anus or external genitalia, usually a result of venereal infection. [New Latin, from Greek kondulōma : kondulos, knuckle, CONDYLE + -OMA.] —**con·dy·lom·a·tous** adj.

Con·dy's fluid (kŏn'dīz) n. A solution of potassium permanganate, used especially as a disinfectant or in the treatment of snakebites. [After Henry Bollman Condy, 19th-century British chemist.]

cone (kōn) n. **1.** Geometry. **a.** A surface generated by a straight line, the generator, passing through a fixed point, the vertex, and moving along the intersection with a fixed curve, the directrix. **b.** The surface generated by such a generator passing through a vertex lying on the perpendicular axis of a circular directrix. **2. a.** The figure formed by such a surface bound, or regarded as bound, by its vertex and a plane section taken anywhere above or below the vertex. **b.** Anything having the shape of this figure. **3. a.** A conical, spheroidal, or cylindrical structure borne by certain trees, such as the pines, firs, and hemlocks, consisting of clusters of stiff, overlapping, woody scales, between which are the naked ovules. **b.** Any similar structure, such as the fruit of the magnolia or hop or the reproductive structure of pteridophytes. Also called "strobilus." **4.** A photoreceptor in the retina of the eye that is sensitive to color and bright light. Compare **rod. 5.** Any of various gastropod mollusks of the family Conidae, of tropical seas, having a conical, often vividly marked shell. Also called "cone shell." **6.** A volcanic peak having a wide base. ~tr.v. **coned, coning, cones.** To shape like a cone or cone segment. [French cône, from Latin cōnus, from Greek kōnos.]

cone·flow·er (kōn'flou'ər) n. Any of various North American plants of the genera Rudbeckia, Ratibida, and Echinacea, having rayed flowers with a conelike center of tubular florets.

cone·nose (kōn'nōz') n. Any of several assassin bugs; especially, Triatoma sanguisuga, of the southern and western United States and Mexico, having sucking mouth-parts and capable of inflicting a painful, toxic bite. Also called "cone-nosed bug."

coney. Variant of cony.

Co·ney Island (kō'nē). A beach resort and amusement area of Brooklyn, New York, on the southwestern tip of Long Island.

conf. conference.

con·fab (kŏn'făb') n. Informal. A confabulation; chat. ~intr.v. (kən-făb', kŏn'făb') **confabbed, -fabbing, -fabs.** Informal. To talk informally; confabulate.

con·fab·u·late (kən-făb'yə-lāt') intr.v. **-lated, -lating, -lates. 1.** To talk informally; chat. **2.** Psychiatry. To replace fact with fantasy in memory. [Latin confābulārī : com-, together + fābulārī, to talk, from fābula, story, conversation, from fārī, to speak.] —**con·fab·u·la·tion** n. —**con·fab·u·la·tor** n. —**con·fab·u·la·to·ry** (kən-făb'yə-lə-tôr'ē, -tōr'ē) adj.

con·fect (kən-fĕkt') tr.v. **-fected, -fecting, -fects. 1.** To put together; make. **2.** To make into a confection or preserve. ~n. (kŏn'fĕkt'). A candy or other sweet confection. [Middle English confecten, from Latin conficere (past participle confectus), to prepare : com- (intensive) + facere, to make.]

con·fec·tion (kən-fĕk'shən) n. **1.** The act or a product of compounding, mixing, or preparing. **2.** A sweet preparation, such as candy or preserves. **3.** A sweetened medicinal compound. **4.** Especially formerly, a stylish article of women's clothing.

con·fec·tion·ar·y (kən-fĕk'shən-ĕr'ē) adj. Pertaining to or resembling confections or their preparation.

con·fec·tion·er (kən-fĕk'shən-ər) n. One who makes or sells confections, especially sweets.

confectioners' sugar n. Finely pulverized sugar with some cornstarch added.

con·fec·tion·er·y (kən-fĕk'shən-ĕr'ē) n., pl. **-ies.** Also **con·fec·tion·ar·y** (for sense 3). **1.** Candies and other confections collectively. **2.** The art or occupation of a confectioner. **3.** A confectioner's shop.

con·fed·er·a·cy (kən-fĕd'ər-ə-sē) n., pl. **-cies. 1.** A union of persons, parties, or states; alliance; league. **2.** A combination for unlawful practices; conspiracy. **3. Confederacy.** The Confederate States of America. [Middle English confederacie, from Norman French, from Latin confoederātiō, union, from confoederāre, to unite. See **confederate.**]

con·fed·er·ate (kən-fĕd'ər-ĭt) n. **1.** A member of a confederacy; an ally. **2.** One who assists in a plot; an accomplice. **3. Confederate.** Formerly, a supporter of the Confederate States of America. —See Synonyms at **partner.** ~adj. **1.** United in a confederacy; allied. **2. Confederate.** Of or pertaining to the Confederate States of America. ~v. (kən-fĕd'ə-rāt') **confederated, -ating, -ates.** —tr. To form into a confederacy. —intr. To unite into, or become part of, a confederacy. [Middle English confederat, from Latin confoederātus, from past participle of confoederāre, to unite in a league : com-, together + foederāre, to unite, from foedus, league.] —**con·fed·er·a·tive** adj.

Confederate rose n. The cotton rose (see).

Confederate States of America n. Abbr. **C.S.A.** The confederation of 11 Southern states that seceded from the United States (1860-65), comprising Alabama, Arkansas, Florida, Georgia, Louisiana, Mississippi, North Carolina, South Carolina, Tennessee, Texas, and Virginia. Also called the "Confederacy," "Southern Confederacy."

con·fed·er·a·tion (kən-fĕd'ə-rā'shən) n. Abbr. **confed. 1.** An act of confederating or a state of being confederated. **2.** A group of confederates, especially of states or nations, united for a common purpose; a league. Compare **federation.** —**con·fed·er·a·tion·ism** n. —**con·fed·er·a·tion·ist** n.

con·fer (kən-fûr') v. **-ferred, -ferring, -fers.** —tr. **1.** To bestow (an honor or degree, for example). Used with on or upon. **2.** Obsolete. To compare. —intr. To hold a conference; compare views; consult together. [Latin conferre, to bring together, contribute, bestow : com-, together + ferre, to bring, bear.] —**con·fer·ment, con·fer·ral** n. —**con·fer·ra·ble** adj. —**con·fer·rer** n.

con·fer·ee, con·fer·ree (kŏn'fə-rē') n. **1.** A participant in a conference. **2.** One upon whom something is conferred.

con·fer·ence (kŏn'fə-rəns, -frəns) n. Abbr. **conf. 1. a.** A meeting for consultation or discussion. **b.** An exchange of views. **c.** A meeting of committees to settle differences between two legislative bodies. **2.** A formal meeting, especially one held annually, at which delegates representing different states or organizations, or different branches of the same organization, discuss and debate matters of common interest. **3.** In the Methodist and some other Protestant churches, the annual assembly of clerical and lay members that constitutes the governing body of such churches. **4.** An association for mutual benefit. **5.** The act of conferring, as of a degree; bestowal or conferral. —**in conference.** Taking part in a meeting or discussion. [Old French, from Medieval Latin conferentia, from Latin conferēns (stem conferent-), present participle of conferre, to CONFER.] —**con·fer·en·tial** adj.

conference call n. A conference by telephone in which several persons participate by means of a central switching unit.

con·fer·va (kən-fûr'və) n., pl. **-vae** (-vē) or **-vas.** Any of various bright green, threadlike freshwater algae, especially any of the genus Tribonema. [New Latin, from Latin conferva, COMFREY.] —**con·fer·void** n. & adj.

con·fess (kən-fĕs') v. **-fessed, -fessing, -fesses.** —tr. **1.** To disclose or acknowledge (something damaging or inconvenient to oneself). **2.** To concede the truth or validity of; admit. **3.** To acknowledge belief or faith in. **4. a.** To make known (one's sins), especially to a priest for absolution. **b.** To confess thus the sins of (oneself). **c.** To hear the confession of. Used of a priest. —intr. **1.** To admit or acknowledge a crime or deed. Sometimes used with to. **2.** To tell one's sins to a priest. —See Synonyms at **acknowledge.** [Middle English confessen, from Old French confesser, from Late Latin confessāre, frequentative of confitērī (past participle confessus), to acknowledge : com- (intensive) + fatērī, to admit.]

con·fess·ed·ly (kən-fĕs'ĭd-lē) adv. By one's own admission; admittedly.

con·fes·sion (kən-fĕsh'ən) n. **1.** The act or an instance of confessing; acknowledgment; avowal; admission. **2.** A formal declaration of guilt. **3.** The disclosure of sins to a priest for absolution. **4.** An avowal of belief in the doctrines of a particular faith. Also called "confession of faith." **5.** A church or group of worshipers adhering to a particular creed.

con·fes·sion·al (kən-fĕsh'ən-əl) adj. Of, pertaining to, or resembling confession. ~n. **1.** A small enclosed stall in a church, in which a priest hears confessions. **2.** The act or practice of confessing to a priest.

con·fes·sor (kən-fĕs'ər) n. **1.** A priest who hears confession and gives absolution. **2.** One who confesses. **3.** One who confesses faith in Christianity in the face of persecution but does not suffer martyrdom: King Edward the Confessor.

con·fet·ti (kən-fĕt'ē) n. Used with a singular verb. Small pieces of colored paper thrown during festive celebrations, especially at the bride and groom after a wedding. [Italian, plural of confetto, con-

condor With a wingspan of up to about 2.75 meters (10 feet), the condors of the Andes and the California condor (above) are among the world's largest flying birds. Both are vultures of mountain regions; the California condor is one of the world's rarest birds.

fection, from Medieval Latin *confectum,* from Latin *confectus,* past participle of *conficere,* to put together, prepare, CONFECT.]

con·fi·dant (kŏn′fə-dănt′, -dänt′, kŏn′fə-dănt, -dänt) *n.* One to whom secrets or private matters are confided. [French *confident,* from Italian *confidente,* from Latin *confīdēns* (stem *confīdent-*), present participle of *confīdere,* to CONFIDE.]

con·fi·dante (kŏn′fə-dănt′, -dänt′, kŏn′fə-dănt, -dänt) *n.* A woman to whom secret or private matters are confided. [French *confidente,* feminine of *confident,* CONFIDANT.]

con·fide (kən-fīd′) *v.* **-fided, -fiding, -fides.** —*tr.* **1.** To tell (something) in confidence. **2.** To entrust (something) to another. —*intr.* To tell private matters to another in confidence. Used with *in.* —See Synonyms at **commit.** [Middle English *confiden,* from Old French *confider,* from Latin *confīdere* : *com-* (intensive) + *fīdere,* to trust.] —**con·fid·er** *n.*

con·fi·dence (kŏn′fə-dəns) *n.* **1.** Trust in a person or thing. **2.** A trusting relationship in which secrets may be imparted: *took us into her confidence.* **3.** Something confided, such as a secret. **4.** A feeling of assurance or certainty, especially in oneself and one's capabilities. —**in confidence.** As a secret. —See Synonyms at **trust.**

confidence game *n.* A swindle in which the victim is defrauded after his confidence has been won. Also *informal* "con game."

confidence interval *n.* A statistical range, bounded by confidence limits, with a stipulated probability that a given parameter lies within the range.

confidence limit *n.* One of the two values reasonably chosen to specify the limits of a confidence interval.

confidence man *n.* One who swindles by using a confidence game. Also *informal* "con man."

con·fi·dent (kŏn′fə-dənt) *adj.* **1.** Having or indicating assurance or certainty, as of success. **2.** Having confidence in oneself; self-assured. **3.** Very bold; presumptuous. **4.** *Obsolete.* Confiding; trustful. —See Synonyms at **sure.**
~*n.* A confidant. [Latin *confīdens* (stem *confīdent-*), present participle of *confīdere,* to CONFIDE.] —**con·fi·dent·ly** *adv.*

con·fi·den·tial (kŏn′fə-dĕn′shəl) *adj.* **1.** Done or communicated in confidence; told in secret. **2.** Entrusted with the confidence of another; intimate: *a confidential secretary.* **3.** Denoting trust or intimacy: *a confidential tone of voice.* —**con·fi·den·ti·al·i·ty** (kŏn′fə-dĕn′shē-ăl′ə-tē), **con·fi·den·tial·ness** *n.* —**con·fi·den·tial·ly** *adv.*

con·fid·ing (kən-fī′dĭng) *adj.* Trusting; unsuspicious. —**con·fid·ing·ly** *adv.* —**con·fid·ing·ness** *n.*

con·fig·u·ra·tion (kən-fĭg′yə-rā′shən) *n.* **1. a.** The arrangement of the parts or elements of something. **b.** The form of a figure as determined by the arrangement of its parts; outline; contour. **2.** *Psychology.* A **gestalt** *(see).* **3.** *Chemistry.* **Conformation** *(see).* [Late Latin *configūrātiō* (stem *configūrātiōn-*), from Latin *configūrāre,* "to form together," fashion after : *com-,* together + *figūrāre,* to form, from *figūra,* shape, FIGURE.] —**con·fig·u·ra·tive, con·fig·u·ra·tion·al** *adj.* —**con·fig·u·ra·tion·al·ly** *adv.*

con·fig·u·ra·tion·ism (kən-fĭg′yə-rā′shə-nĭz′əm) *n.* **Gestalt psychology** *(see).*

con·fine (kən-fīn′) *v.* **-fined, -fining, -fines.** —*tr.* **1.** To keep within bounds; restrict. **2.** To shut within an enclosure; imprison. **3.** To keep (a woman who is about to give birth) in bed. Used in the passive. —*intr. Archaic.* To border; be adjacent. —See Synonyms at **limit.**
~*n.* (kŏn′fīn′ *for senses 1, 3;* kən-fīn′ *for sense 2*). **1.** *Usually* **confines.** A border or limit; boundary. **2.** *Archaic.* Confinement. **3.** *Obsolete.* A place of confinement. —See Synonyms at **boundary.** [Old French *confiner,* from *confin,* boundary, limit, from Latin *confīne,* from *confīnis,* having the same border : *com-,* together + *fīnis,* border, end.] —**con·fin·a·ble, con·fine·a·ble** *adj.* —**con·fin·er** *n.*

con·fine·ment (kən-fīn′mənt) *n.* **1.** The act of confining or the state of being confined. **2.** The state of being confined prior to and during childbirth. **3.** *Physics.* The theory that the attractive force between two quarks increases as the quarks are pulled apart as a result of the exchange of gluons, used to explain why quarks cannot be found as free particles.

con·firm (kən-fûrm′) *tr.v.* **-firmed, -firming, -firms.** **1.** To assure the certainty or validity of; corroborate; verify. **2.** To make more firm; strengthen: *She confirmed my suspicions.* **3.** To make valid or binding by a formal or legal act; ratify. **4.** To administer the religious rite of confirmation to. [Middle English *confirmen,* from Old French *confirmer,* from Latin *confirmāre* : *com-* (intensive) + *firmāre,* to make firm, strengthen, from *firmus,* firm.] —**con·firm·a·ble** *adj.* —**con·firm·er** *n.*
Synonyms: *authenticate, corroborate, establish, prove, ratify, substantiate, validate, verify.*

con·fir·ma·tion (kŏn′fər-mā′shən) *n.* **1.** An act of confirming. **2.** That which confirms; corroboration or verification. **3.** A rite admitting a baptized person to full membership in a church. —**con·firm·a·to·ry** (kən-fûr′mə-tôr′ē, -tōr′ē), **con·firm·a·tive** (kən-fûr′mə-tĭv) *adj.*

con·firmed (kən-fûrmd′) *adj.* Firmly established in a given state or habit, and unlikely to change; inveterate: *a confirmed bachelor.* —**con·firm·ed·ly** (kən-fûr′mĭd-lē) *adv.*

con·fis·ca·ble (kən-fĭs′kə-bəl) *adj.* Subject to confiscation.

con·fis·cate (kŏn′fĭs-kāt′) *tr.v.* **-cated, -cating, -cates.** **1.** To seize (private property) for a public treasury, especially by way of penalty. **2.** To seize by or as by authority.
~*adj.* **1.** Confiscated; appropriated. **2.** Having lost property through confiscation. [Latin *confiscāre,* to lay up in a chest, confiscate : *com-* (collective) + *fiscus,* chest, the treasury.] —**con·fis·ca·tion** *n.* —**con·fis·ca·tor** *n.*

Con·fit·e·or (kən-fēt′ē-ôr) *n. Roman Catholic Church.* A prayer in which confession of sins is made. [Latin, "I confess" (first word of the prayer).]

con·fla·grant (kən-flā′grənt) *adj.* Burning intensely; blazing. [Latin *conflagrāns* (stem *conflagrant-*), present participle of *conflagrāre,* to burn up. See **conflagration.**]

con·fla·gra·tion (kŏn′flə-grā′shən) *n.* A large, blazing, and destructive fire. [Latin *conflagrātiō* (stem *conflagrātiōn-*), from *conflagrāre,* to burn up : *com-* (intensive) + *flagrāre,* to burn, blaze.]

con·flate (kən-flāt′) *tr.v.* **-flated, -flating, -flates.** To fuse or blend into a single unit (especially two versions of a text).

con·fla·tion (kən-flā′shən) *n.* **1.** A combining, as of two variant texts into one text. **2.** A product of this; especially, a text or reading arrived at by fusing material from different sources. [Middle English *conflacioun,* from Late Latin *conflātiō* (stem *conflātiōn-*), from Latin *conflāre,* "to blow together," combine two readings : *com-,* together + *flāre,* to blow.]

con·flict (kŏn′flĭkt) *n.* **1.** A prolonged battle; a struggle. **2.** The clash of opposing ideas or forces; disagreement; opposition. **3.** *Psychology.* Inner struggle resulting from the opposition of irreconcilable impulses, desires, or tendencies. **4.** A crashing together; collision. —See Synonyms at **discord.**
~*intr.v.* (kən-flĭkt′) **conflicted, -flicting, -flicts.** **1.** To come into opposition; collide; differ. **2.** To fight; do battle. [Middle English, from Latin *conflīctus,* from the past participle of *conflīgere,* to clash together, contend : *com-,* together + *flīgere,* to strike.] —**con·flic·tion** *n.* —**con·flic·tive** *adj.*
Synonyms: *affray, combat, contest, fight, melee, scuffle.*

con·flic·ting (kən-flĭk′tĭng) *adj.* Mutually incompatible or contradictory: *conflicting ideologies; conflicting reports.* —**con·flic·ting·ly** *adv.*

con·flu·ence (kŏn′flo͞o-əns) *n.* Also **con·flux** (-flŭks). **1.** A flowing together, as of two or more streams. **2.** The point of juncture of such streams. **3.** A gathering together; crowd.

con·flu·ent (kŏn′flo͞o-ənt) *adj.* **1.** Flowing together; blended into one. **2.** *Pathology.* Merging together so as to form a mass. Said of sores in a rash. **3.** *Anatomy.* Coalesced. Said for example of two originally separate bones.
~*n.* **1.** A confluent stream. **2.** A tributary. [Middle English, from Latin *confluēns* (stem *confluent-*), present participle of *confluere,* to flow together : *com-,* together + *fluere,* to flow.]

con·fo·cal (kŏn-fō′kəl) *adj.* Having the same focus or foci.

con·form (kən-fôrm′) *v.* **-formed, -forming, -forms.** —*intr.* **1.** To come to have the same form or character as another or each other. **2.** To act or be in accord or agreement; comply. Used with *to* or *with.* **3.** To act in accordance with current customs or modes. **4.** To comply with the usages of an established church, especially the Church of England. —*tr.* **1.** To make similar. **2.** To bring into agreement or correspondence. Often used reflexively. —See Synonyms at **agree.** [Middle English *conformen,* from Old French *conformer,* from Latin *conformāre,* "to have the same form" : *com-,* same, similar + *formāre,* to shape, from *forma,* form, shape.] —**con·form·er** *n.*

con·form·a·ble (kən-fôrm′ə-bəl) *adj.* **1.** In harmony or agreement; corresponding; similar. Often used with *to.* **2.** Quick to comply; submissive. **3.** *Geology.* Designating strata that are parallel to each other without interruption. —**con·form·a·bil·i·ty, con·form·a·ble·ness** *n.* —**con·form·a·bly** *adv.*

con·for·mal (kən-fôr′məl) *adj.* **1.** *Mathematics.* Designating a depiction of a surface or region upon another surface so that all angles between intersecting curves remain unchanged. **2.** Of, pertaining to, or designating a map projection in which angles around any point are true, and at any point the scale is the same in any direction, so that small areas are rendered with true shape. [Late Latin *confōrmālis,* having the same form : Latin *com-,* same, similar + *fōrmālis,* having a form, FORMAL.] —**con·for·mal·ly** *adv.*

con·for·mance (kən-fôr′məns) *n.* Conformity.

con·for·ma·tion (kŏn′fər-mā′shən) *n.* **1.** The structure or outline of something as determined by the arrangement of its parts. **2.** The act of conforming or state of being conformed; adjustment; adaptation. **3.** *Chemistry.* The shape of a molecule or an atom as determined by the three-dimensional arrangement of its constituents. Also called "configuration."

conformation theory *n. Chemistry.* The theory that the stability and reactivity of a molecule can be predicted from its three-dimensional structure, especially with respect to the conformation of organic molecules and their substituents.

con·form·ist (kən-fôr′mĭst) *n.* **1.** One who conforms to current standards or customs. **2.** *Abbr.* **Con.** One who complies with the usages of an established church, especially the Church of England. Compare **dissenter, nonconformist.** —**con·form·ism** *n.*

con·form·i·ty (kən-fôr′mə-tē) *n., pl.* **-ties.** Also **con·form·ance** (-fôr′məns). **1.** Similarity in form or character; correspondence; agreement. **2.** Action or behavior in correspondence with current customs, rules, or styles. **3.** Compliance with the usages of an established church, especially the Church of England.

con·found (kən-found′, kŏn-) *tr.v.* **-founded, -founding, -founds.** **1.** To cause to become confused or disordered; bewilder. **2.** To mix up (incompatible elements or ideas). **3.** To fail to distinguish; confuse; mix up. **4.** To cause to be ashamed; abash. **5.** To defeat;

PRONUNCIATION KEY

ă, pat; ā, pay; âr, care;
ä, father, are; b, bib;
ch, church; d, deed; ĕ, pet;
ē, be; f, fife; g, gag; h, hat;
hw, which; ĭ, pit; ī, pie;
îr, pier; j, judge; k, kick;
l, lid, needle; m, mum;
n, no, sudden; ng, thing;
ŏ, pot; ō, toe; ô, paw, for;
oi, noise; ou, out; o͝o, book;
o͞o, boot; p, pop; r, roar;
s, sauce; sh, ship, dish;
t, tight; th, thin, path;
th, this, bathe; ŭ, cut; ûr, fur;
v, valve; w, with; y, yes;
z, zebra, size; zh, vision;
ə, about, item, edible,
gallop, circus, peaceful

IN FOREIGN WORDS:

à, *Fr.* ami; œ, *Fr.* feu, *Ger.* schön; ü, *Fr.* tu, *Ger.* über; KH, *Ger.* ich, *Scot.* loch; N, *Fr.* bon; y′, *Fr.* Compiègne

STRESS MARKS:

Primary stress: ′
in·cite′ (ĭn-sīt′)
Secondary stress: ′
in′sight′ (ĭn′sīt′)

overthrow. **6.** To damn. Used in mild oaths: *Confound it!* —See Synonyms at **puzzle**. [Middle English *confounden*, from Old French *confondre*, from Latin *confundere*, to pour together, mix up : *com-*, together + *fundere*, to pour.] —**con·found·er** *n.*

con·found·ed (kən-foun′dĭd, kŏn-) *adj.* **1.** Confused; befuddled. **2.** Damned. Used as a mild oath: *a confounded fool.* —**con·found·ed·ly** *adv.* —**con·found·ed·ness** *n.*

con·fra·ter·ni·ty (kŏn′frə-tûr′nə-tē) *n., pl.* **-ties.** An association of men united by profession or in some common purpose, usually of a religious or charitable nature. [Middle English *confraternite*, from Old French, from Medieval Latin *confrāternitās* (stem *confrāternitāt-*), from *confrāter*, colleague, CONFRERE.]

con·frere (kŏn′frâr) *n.* A fellow member of a fraternity or profession; a colleague. [Middle English, from Old French, from Medieval Latin *confrāter*, colleague, fellow member : Latin *com-*, together + *frāter*, brother.]

con·front (kən-frŭnt′) *tr.v.* **-front·ed, -front·ing, -fronts.** **1.** To come face to face with; stand in front of. **2.** To face with hostility or defiance. **3.** To bring close together for comparison; compare. **4.** To cause to meet or face: *confronted them with the evidence of their guilt.* **5.** To come up against; encounter. [Old French *confronter*, from Medieval Latin *confrontāre*, to have a common border : Latin *com-*, together + *frōns* (stem *front-*), forehead, FRONT.] —**con·front·er** *n.*

con·fron·ta·tion (kŏn′frən-tā′shən) *n.* The act of confronting or state of being confronted; especially, a condition or stance of conflict and rivalry rather than of conciliation. —**con·fron·ta·tion·al** *adj.* —**con·fron·ta·tion·ist** *adj. & n.*

Con·fu·cian (kən-fyo͞o′shən) *adj.* Of, pertaining to, or characteristic of Confucius, his teachings, or his followers.
∼*n.* One who adheres to the teachings of Confucius.

Con·fu·cian·ism (kən-fyo͞o′shən-ĭz′əm) *n.* The ethical system based on the teachings of Confucius, emphasizing personal virtue, devotion to family (including the spirits of one's ancestors), and justice. —**Con·fu·cian·ist** *n.*

Con·fu·cius (kən-fyo͞o′shəs) (*c.* 551–479 B.C.). *Chinese* **Kong-zi** (ko͝ong′dzə), **Kong-fu-zi** (-fo͞o′dzə). Chinese philosopher, who was a statesman and adviser to various feudal lords. When none would implement his philosophy of perfecting one's own moral character, he became a teacher. Many books and sayings have been attributed to him, but few can be authenticated.

con·fuse (kən-fyo͞oz′) *tr.v.* **-fused, -fus·ing, -fus·es.** **1.** To disturb the thought process, perceptions, or purpose of; perplex. **2.** To assemble without order or sense; jumble. **3.** To make less distinct; blur: *confuse an important issue.* **4.** To fail to distinguish between; mix up: *confuse a word with a near synonym.* [Back-formation from Middle English *confused*, from Old French *confus*, from Latin *confūsus*, past participle of *confundere*, to mix up, CONFOUND.] —**con·fus·ed·ly** (kən-fyo͞o′zĭd-lē) *adv.* —**con·fus·ed·ness** *n.* —**con·fus·er** *n.* —**con·fus·ing·ly** *adv.*

con·fu·sion (kən-fyo͞o′zhən) *n.* **1.** The act of confusing or state of being confused. **2.** Disorder; jumble. **3.** Distraction; bewilderment. —**con·fu·sion·al** *adj.*

con·fu·ta·tion (kŏn′fyo͞o-tā′shən) *n.* **1.** An act of confuting. **2.** Something that confutes. —**con·fu·ta·tive** (kən-fyo͞o′tə-tĭv) *adj.*

con·fute (kən-fyo͞ot′) *tr.v.* **-fut·ed, -fut·ing, -futes.** To prove conclusively to be wrong or in error: *confute a theory.* [Latin *confūtāre*, to check, restrain.] —**con·fut·a·ble** *adj.* —**con·fut·er** *n.*

cong. *Pharmacology.* congius.

Cong. **1.** Congregational. **2.** Congress; Congressional.

con·ga (kŏng′gə) *n.* **1.** A dance of Latin-American origin in which the dancers form a long, winding line. **2.** Music for this dance.
∼*intr.v.* **con·gaed, -ga·ing, -gas.** To dance the conga. [American Spanish *(danza) Conga*, "the Congo (dance)," from CONGO.]

conga drum *n.* A tall, narrow bass drum beaten with the hands.

con game *n. Slang.* A **confidence game** *(see).*

con·gé (kôN-zhā′, kŏn′jā′) *n.* Also **con·gee** (kŏn′jē). **1.** Formal or authoritative permission to depart. **2.** An abrupt dismissal. **3. a.** *Archaic.* A formal bow. **b.** A leave-taking. **4.** *Architecture.* A kind of concave molding.
∼*intr.v.* **con·géed, -gé·ing, -gées.** *Archaic.* **1.** To take ceremonious leave. **2.** To make a formal bow. [French, from Old French *congie*, from Latin *commeātus*, "a going to and fro," from *commeāre*, to go to and fro : *com-*, mutually, back and forth + *meāre*, to go.]

con·geal (kən-jēl′) *v.* **-gealed, -geal·ing, -geals.** —*intr.* **1.** To solidify, as by freezing. **2.** To coagulate; jell. —*tr.* To cause to solidify or coagulate. [Middle English *congelen*, from Old French *congeler*, from Latin *congelāre*, to freeze solid : *com-*, together + *gelāre*, to freeze.] —**con·geal·a·ble** *adj.* —**con·geal·er** *n.* —**con·geal·ment** *n.* —**con·ge·la·tion** (kŏn′jə-lā′shən) *n.*

con·gee (kŏn′jē) *intr.v.* **-geed, -gee·ing, -gees.** *Archaic.* **1.** To take ceremonious leave. **2.** To make a formal bow.
∼*n.* Variant of **congé**. [Middle English *congeien*, from Old French *congier*, from *congie*, leave of absence, CONGÉ.]

con·ge·ner (kŏn′jə-nər, kən-jē′-) *n.* **1.** A member of the same kind, class, or group. **2.** An organism belonging to the same genus as another or others. [Latin, of the same race : *com-*, same + *genus* (stem *gener-*), race, kind.] —**con·ge·ner·ic** (kŏn′jə-nĕr′ĭk), **con·gen·er·ous** (kən-jĕn′ər-əs) *adj.*

con·gen·i·al (kən-jēn′yəl) *adj.* **1.** Having the same tastes, habits, or temperament; sympathetic. **2.** Agreeably suited to one's needs or tastes; pleasant. **3.** Of a pleasant disposition; friendly and sociable. [CON- (same) + GENIAL.] —**con·ge·ni·al·i·ty** (kən-jē′nē-ăl′ə-tē), **con·gen·ial·ness** *n.* —**con·gen·ial·ly** *adv.*

con·gen·i·tal (kən-jĕn′ə-təl) *adj.* **1.** Existing at birth but not hereditary: *a congenital defect.* **2.** Having a specified character as if by nature: *a congenital thief.* —See Synonyms at **innate**. [Latin *congenitus*, born together with : *com-*, together + *genitus*, born, past participle of *gignere*, to beget.] —**con·gen·i·tal·ly** *adv.*

con·ger eel (kŏng′gər) *n.* Any of various large marine eels of the family Congridae; especially, *Conger oceanicus*, of Atlantic waters. [Middle English *congre*, from Old French, from Latin *conger*, *congrus*, from Greek *gongros*, of Mediterranean origin.]

con·ge·ries (kən-jîr′ēz, kŏn′jə-rēz′) *n. Used with a singular verb.* A collection of things heaped together; an aggregation. [Latin *congeriēs*, heap, pile, from *congerere*, to bring together, CONGEST.]

con·gest (kən-jĕst′) *v.* **-gest·ed, -gest·ing, -gests.** —*tr.* **1.** To overfill or overcrowd; clog. **2.** *Pathology.* To cause excessive accumulation of blood in (a vessel or organ). **3.** To block (the nose). Used of mucus. —*intr.* To become congested. [Latin *congerere* (past participle *congestus*), to bring together, heap up : *com-*, together + *gerere*, to carry.] —**con·ges·tive** *adj.*

con·ges·tion (kən-jĕs′chən) *n.* **1. a.** An excessive accumulation of blood in a body part. **b.** An accumulation of mucus in the nose. **2.** An overcrowded condition, especially as caused by traffic.

con·gi·us (kŏn′jē-əs) *n., pl.* **-gii** (-jē-ī′). *Abbr.* **c., C., cong.** *Pharmacology.* A gallon. [Middle English, from Latin *congius*, perhaps from Greek *konkhos*, conch, shell.]

con·glo·bate (kŏn-glō′bāt′, kŏng′glō-) *v.* **-bat·ed, -bat·ing, -bates.** Also **con·globe** (kŏn-glōb′), **-globed, -glob·ing, -globes.** —*intr.* To become a globe or globule. —*tr.* To gather into a globe or ball.
∼*adj.* Shaped like or formed into a ball. [Latin *conglobāre* : *com-*, together + *globāre*, to make into a globe, from *globus*, globe.] —**con·glo·ba·tion** *n.*

con·glom·er·ate (kən-glŏm′ə-rāt′) *v.* **-at·ed, -at·ing, -ates.** —*tr.* To collect into a cohesive mass. —*intr.* To form into an adhering or rounded mass.
∼*n.* (kən-glŏm′ər-ĭt). **1.** A collected heterogeneous mass; a cluster. **2.** *Geology.* A rock consisting of pebbles and gravel embedded in a loosely cementing material. Also called "pudding stone." **3.** A business corporation made up of a number of different companies that operate in widely diversified fields.
∼*adj.* (kən-glŏm′ər-ĭt). **1.** Gathered into a cohesive mass; clustered. **2.** *Geology.* Made up of cemented heterogeneous material. [Latin *conglomerāre*, to roll together : *com-*, together + *glomerāre*, to roll into a ball, from *glomus*, ball.] —**con·glom·er·at·ic** (kən-glŏm′ə-răt′ĭk) *adj.*

con·glom·er·a·tion (kən-glŏm′ə-rā′shən) *n.* **1.** The process of conglomerating or state of being conglomerated. **2.** A collection or cohesive mass of miscellaneous things.

con·glu·ti·nant (kən-glo͞ot′ə-nənt) *adj. Medicine.* Promoting adhesion, as of the lips of a wound. [Latin *conglūtināns* (stem *conglūtinant-*), present participle of *conglūtināre*, to glue together, CONGLUTINATE.]

con·glu·ti·nate (kən-glo͞ot′ə-nāt′) *v.* **-nat·ed, -nat·ing, -nates.** —*intr.* **1.** To become stuck or glued together; adhere. **2.** *Medicine.* To become reunited. Used of bones or tissues. —*tr.* **1.** To stick or glue together. **2.** *Medicine.* To cause (bones or tissues) to reunite. [Middle English *conglutinaten*, from Latin *conglūtināre*, to glue together : *com-*, together + *glūtināre*, to glue, from *glūten*, glue.] —**con·glu·ti·na·tion** *n.* —**con·glu·ti·na·tive** (kən-glo͞ot′ə-nā′tĭv, -nə-tĭv) *adj.*

Con·go[1] (kŏng′gō). Country in west-central Africa. Oil from offshore fields and timber are the main exports. The Portuguese encountered the powerful Kongo kingdom in the 15th and 16th centuries. The area was claimed by France and in 1910 became the Middle Congo, a territory of French Equatorial Africa. In 1960 it was granted independence as the Republic of the Congo (Brazzaville). The country became Africa's first Marxist state in 1970. In 1977 the military junta assumed control. Area, 342,000 square kilometers (132,047 square miles). Population, 2,300,000. Capital, Brazzaville. See map, next page.

Congo[2]. See **Zaire**[1].

Congo, Democratic Republic of the. See **Zaire**[2].

congo eel *n.* An eellike amphibian, ***Amphiuma means***, of the southeastern United States, having two pairs of tiny, nonfunctioning legs.

Con·go·lese (kŏng′gə-lēz′) *adj.* Of or pertaining to the region of the Congo and the two Congo republics or their inhabitants.
∼*n., pl.* **Congolese.** An inhabitant of the region of the Congo or of either of the two Congo republics.

Congo peacock *n.* A variety of **peacock** *(see).*

Congo red *n.* A brownish-red powder, $C_{32}H_{22}N_6O_6S_2Na_2$, used as a diagnostic and chemical indicator, a dye, and a biological stain.

con·grat·u·late (kən-grăch′o͞o-lāt′) *tr.v.* **-lat·ed, -lat·ing, -lates.** **1.** To express pleasure at the success or good fortune of: *congratulated him on his promotion.* **2.** To take pride in (oneself) for an achievement. [Latin *congrātulārī*, to rejoice with someone : *com-*, with + *grātulārī*, to express one's joy, rejoice, from *grātus*, pleasing.] —**con·grat·u·la·tor** (kən-grăch′o͞o-lā′tər) *n.*

con·grat·u·la·tion (kən-grăch′o͞o-lā′shən) *n.* **1.** The act of congratulating. **2. congratulations.** Acknowledgment of the success or good fortune of another. Often used as an interjection.

con·grat·u·la·to·ry (kən-grăch′o͞o-lə-tôr′ē, -tōr′ē) *adj.* Conveying or expressing congratulations: *a congratulatory telegram.*

con·gre·gant (kŏng′grə-gənt) *n.* A member of a congregation.

con·gre·gate (kŏng′grə-gāt′) *v.* **-gat·ed, -gat·ing, -gates.** —*intr.* To come together in a crowd; assemble. —*tr.* To bring together in a

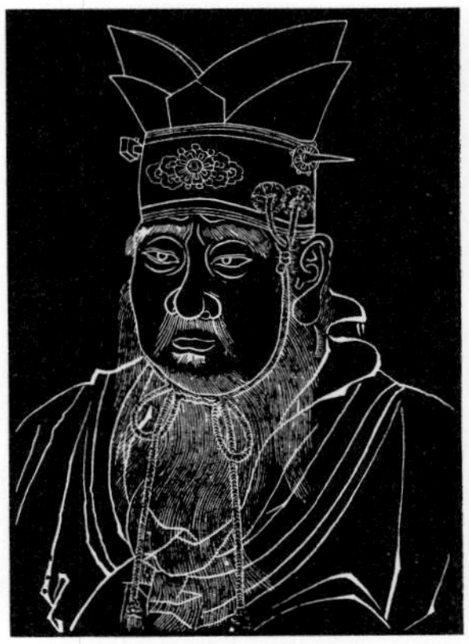

Confucius *The social and moral teachings of this Chinese philosopher, who was born in the sixth century B.C., became after his death the philosophical underpinning of classical Chinese civilization. The teachings emphasize a network of mutual duties binding families, friends, and nations.*

crowd or an assembly; collect. [Middle English *congregaten,* from Latin *congregāre,* to assemble : *com-,* together + *gregāre,* to flock together, from *grex* (stem *greg-*), herd, flock.] —**con·gre·ga·tive** *adj.* —**con·gre·ga·tor** *n.*

con·gre·ga·tion (kŏng′grə-gā′shən) *n.* **1.** An act of congregating. **2.** A body of assembled people or things; a gathering. **3. a.** A group of people gathered for religious worship. **b.** The members of a specific religious group who regularly worship at a particular church. **4.** *Roman Catholic Church.* **a.** A religious institute in which only simple vows, not solemn vows, are taken. **b.** Any of several committees of the **Curia** (see). **5.** *Chiefly British.* An assembly of the senior members of a university.

con·gre·ga·tion·al (kŏng′grə-gā′shən-əl) *adj.* **1.** Of or pertaining to a congregation. **2. Congregational.** *Abbr.* **Cong.** Of or pertaining to Congregationalism or Congregationalists.

Congregational Church. An evangelical Protestant denomination practicing Congregationalism and, since 1957, merged with the United Church of Christ.

con·gre·ga·tion·al·ism (kŏng′grə-gā′shən-əl-ĭz′əm) *n.* **1.** A type of church government in which each local congregation is self-governing. **2. Congregationalism.** The system of government and religious beliefs of the Congregational Church, in which each member church is self-governing. —**con·gre·ga·tion·al·ist, Con·gre·ga·tion·al·ist** *n. & adj.*

Congregation of the Holy Office *n.* The official name for the **Holy Office** (see).

con·gress (kŏng′grĭs) *n.* **1.** A formal assembly of representatives, as of various nations or of an association, to discuss problems and policy. **2.** The national legislative bodies of certain nations, especially of republics. **3. Congress.** *Abbr.* **Cong., C. a.** The national legislative body of the United States, consisting of the Senate and the House of Representatives. **b.** The two-year session of this legislature between elections of the House of Representatives. **4.** A coming together; a meeting. **5.** Sexual intercourse. [Middle English *congresse,* a coming together, from Latin *congressus,* from *congredī,* to come together : *com-,* together + *gradī,* to go.]

con·gres·sion·al (kən-grĕsh′ən-əl) *adj.* **1.** Of or pertaining to a congress. **2. Congressional.** *Abbr.* **Cong.** Of or pertaining to the Congress of the United States.

congressional district *n.* Any of the districts of each state of the United States, entitled to one representative in Congress.

Congressional Medal of Honor *n.* The Medal of Honor (see).

con·gress·man (kŏng′grĭs-mən) *n., pl.* **-men** (-mĭn). *Sometimes* **Congressman.** A member of the U.S. Congress, especially of the House of Representatives.

con·gress·wom·an (kŏng′grĭs-wŏom′ən) *n., pl.* **-women** (-wĭm′ĭn). *Sometimes* **Congresswoman.** A female member of the U.S. Congress, especially of the House of Representatives.

Con·greve (kŏn′grĕv, kŏng′-), **William** (1670–1729). English dramatist, brought up in Ireland. He is best known for his witty comedies, including *Love for Love* (1695) and *The Way of the World* (1700).

con·gru·ence (kŏng′grŏo-əns, kən-grŏo′əns) *n.* Also **con·gru·en·cy** (kŏng′grŏo′ən-sē). **1.** Agreement; conformity. **2.** *Mathematics.* **a.** The state of being congruent. **b.** A mathematical statement that two quantities are congruent.

con·gru·ent (kŏng′grŏo-ənt, kən-grŏo′ənt) *adj.* **1.** Corresponding; congruous. **2.** *Mathematics.* **a.** Coinciding exactly when superim-

posed: *congruent triangles.* **b.** Having a difference divisible by a modulus: *congruent numbers.* [Middle English, from Latin *congruēns* (stem *congruent-*), present participle of *congruere†,* to meet together, agree.] —**con·gru·ent·ly** *adv.*

con·gru·i·ty (kən-grŏo′ə-tē) *n., pl.* **-ties.** **1.** The quality or fact of being congruous. **2.** A point of agreement. **3.** *Geometry.* Exact coincidence when superimposed.

con·gru·ous (kŏng′grŏo-əs) *adj.* Corresponding in character or kind; appropriate; harmonious. [Latin *congruus,* from *congruere†,* to meet together, agree.]

con·ic (kŏn′ĭk) *adj.* Also **con·i·cal** (kŏn′ĭ-kəl). **1.** Shaped like a cone. **2.** Pertaining to a cone.
~ *n. Mathematics.* A conic section. [New Latin *conicus,* from Greek *kōnikos,* from *kōnos,* CONE.]

conic projection *n.* In cartography, a method of projecting pictures of parts of the earth's spherical surface onto a tangent cone, which is then flattened to a plane surface having concentric circles as parallels of latitude and radiating lines from the apex as meridians. Also called "conical projection."

conic section *n.* One of a group of plane curves, including the circle, ellipse, hyperbola, and parabola, generated by: **1.** An intersection of a right circular cone and a plane. **2.** The plane locus of a point that moves so that the ratio of its distance to a fixed point to its distance from a fixed line is a positive constant. **3.** A graph of the general quadratic equation in two variables.

co·nid·i·o·phore (kə-nĭd′ē-ə-fôr′, -fōr′) *n.* A specialized hyphal filament in certain fungi, bearing conidia. [CONIDI(UM) + -PHORE.]

co·nid·i·um (kə-nĭd′ē-əm) *n., pl.* **-ia** (-ē-ə). An asexual spore in certain fungi that is produced at the tip of a conidiophore. [New Latin (diminutive), from Greek *konis,* dust.] —**co·nid·i·al** *adj.*

con·i·fer (kŏn′ə-fər, kō′nə-) *n.* Any tree of the order Coniferales, typically evergreen and bearing cones, including the pine, spruce, and fir. [New Latin *Coniferae* (family name), from Latin *cōnifer,* cone-bearing : *cōnus,* CONE + -FER.] See feature, pages 372–373.

co·nif·er·ous (kō-nĭf′ər-əs) *adj.* **1.** Bearing cones. **2.** Of or composed of conifers.

co·ni·ine (kō′nē-ēn′) *n.* A poisonous, colorless liquid alkaloid, $C_8H_{17}N$, obtained from the poison hemlock and formerly used in the treatment of spasmodic disorders. Also called "Z-propylpiperidine." [German *Koniin* : CONIUM + -IN.]

co·ni·um (kō′nē-əm) *n.* Any of several poisonous plants of the genus *Conium,* including the **poison hemlock** (see). [New Latin *Conium,* from Late Latin *cōnium,* poison hemlock, from Greek *kōneion,* perhaps from *kōnos,* cone (from its indented, pinnatifid leaves suggesting pine cones).]

con·i·za·tion (kŏn′ə-zā′shən) *n.* Surgical removal of a cone of tissue, especially from the cervix of the uterus. [CON(E) + -IZ(E) + -ATION.]

conj. 1. conjugation. **2.** *Grammar.* conjunction; conjunctive. **3.** *Astronomy.* conjunction.

con·jec·tur·al (kən-jĕk′chər-əl) *adj.* **1.** Involving conjecture. **2.** Inclined to conjecture. —**con·jec·tur·al·ly** *adv.*

con·jec·ture (kən-jĕk′chər) *v.* **-tured, -turing, -tures.** —*tr.* To infer from inconclusive evidence; guess. —*intr.* To make a conjecture.
~ *n.* **1.** Inference based on inconclusive or incomplete evidence; guesswork. **2.** An opinion or conclusion based on incomplete evidence. [Middle English, from Old French, from Latin *conjectura,* conclusion, interpretation, from *conjicere,* "to throw together," put together mentally, conjecture, interpret : *com-,* together + *jacere,* to throw.] —**con·jec·tur·a·ble** *adj.* —**con·jec·tur·a·bly** *adv.* —**con·jec·tur·er** *n.*
Synonyms: *guess, infer, presume, speculate, surmise.*

con·join (kən-join′) *v.* **-joined, -joining, -joins.** —*tr.* To join together; connect; unite. —*intr.* To become joined or connected. [Middle English *conjoinen,* from Old French *conjoindre,* from Latin *conjungere* : *com-,* together + *jungere,* to join.] —**con·join·er** *n.*

con·joint (kən-joint′) *adj.* **1.** Joined together; connected; associated. **2.** Of, pertaining to, or involving two or more associated parties; joint. [Middle English, from Old French, past participle of *conjoindre,* from CONJOIN.] —**con·joint·ly** *adv.*

con·ju·gal (kŏn′jə-gəl) *adj.* Of or pertaining to marriage or the marital relationship. [Old French, from Latin *conjugālis,* from *conjux* (stem *conjug-*), a spouse, from *conjungere,* to join together (in marriage) : *com-,* together + *jungere,* to join.] —**con·ju·gal·i·ty** (kŏn′jə-găl′ə-tē) *n.* —**con·ju·gal·ly** *adv.*

conjugal rights *pl.n.* A right to sexual intercourse with one's husband or wife.

con·ju·gant (kŏn′jə-gənt) *n.* Either of a pair of organisms, cells, or gametes undergoing conjugation. [Latin *conjugāns* (stem *conjugant-*), present participle of *conjugāre,* to CONJUGATE.]

con·ju·gate (kŏn′jə-gāt′) *v.* **-gated, -gating, -gates.** —*tr. Grammar.* To give the inflectional forms of (a verb) in a fixed order according to person, number, tense, mood, and voice. —*intr.* **1.** *Biology.* To undergo conjugation. **2.** *Grammar.* To inflect or admit of inflection. Used of a verb.
~ *adj.* (kŏn′jə-gĭt). **1.** Joined together, especially in a pair or pairs; coupled. **2.** *Mathematics & Physics.* Inversely or oppositely related with respect to one of a group of otherwise identical properties; especially, designating either or both of a pair of complex numbers differing only in the sign of the imaginary term. **3.** *Geometry.* Designating two angles that together have a sum of 360°. **4.** Having the same derivation and usually a related meaning: *conjugate words.*
~ *n.* (kŏn′jə-gĭt). **1.** One of two or more conjugate words. **2.** *Mathe-*

matics & Physics. Either of a pair of conjugate quantities. [Middle English *conjugat,* joined, from Latin *conjugātus,* past participle of *conjugāre,* to yoke or join together : *com-,* together + *jugāre,* to yoke, from *jugum,* yoke.] **—con·ju·ga·tive** (kŏn′jə-gā′tĭv) *adj.* **—con·ju·ga·tor** (kŏn′jə-gā′tər) *n.*

con·ju·gat·ed (kŏn′jə-gā′tĭd) *adj. Chemistry.* **1.** Designating a double bond that is separated from another double bond in a molecule by one single bond. **2.** Designating a molecule or compound containing two or more double bonds that alternate with single bonds. **3.** Formed by the combination of two compounds.

conjugated protein *n.* A compound consisting of a protein attached to a nonprotein group, such as a lipid or a carbohydrate.

con·ju·ga·tion (kŏn′jə-gā′shən) *n. Abbr.* **conj. 1.** *Grammar.* **a.** The inflection of a particular verb. **b.** A presentation of the complete set of inflected forms of a verb. **c.** A class of verbs having the same type of inflected forms. Compare **declension. 2.** *Biology.* **a.** A process of sexual reproduction in ciliate protozoans, certain algae, and some bacteria, in which two individuals of the same species temporarily couple and exchange genetic material. **b.** Chromosome pairing in the first meiotic division. **c.** The fusion of gamete nuclei; karyogamy. **d.** The union of sex cells; syngamy. **—con·ju·ga·tion·al** *adj.* **—con·ju·ga·tion·al·ly** *adv.*

conjugation tube *n.* A slender protoplasmic tube formed between two algae undergoing conjugation, through which exchange of gametes between the individuals occurs.

con·junct (kən-jŭngkt′, kŏn′jŭngkt) *adj.* **1.** Joined together; united. **2.** Associated with another; joint. **3.** *Music.* Pertaining to progression by intervals no larger than a major second. Compare **disjunct.** [Middle English, from Latin *conjunctus,* past participle of *conjungere,* to join together : *com-,* together + *jungere,* to join.] **—con·junct·ly** (kən-jŭngkt′lē) *adv.*

con·junc·tion (kən-jŭngk′shən) *n.* **1.** The act of joining or state of being joined; combination. **2.** Simultaneous occurrence; coincidence. **3.** *Abbr.* **conj.** *Grammar.* A part of speech consisting of words that connect other words, phrases, clauses, or sentences. Some English conjunctions are *and, but, because.* See **coordinate conjunction, copulative conjunction, correlative conjunction, subordinate conjunction. 4.** *Abbr.* **conj.** *Astronomy.* The position of two celestial bodies on the celestial sphere when they have the same celestial longitude. **5.** *Logic.* **a.** A compound proposition in which the components are joined by the word *and,* which is true only if both or all the components are true. **b.** The relationship between the components of such a proposition. **—con·junc·tion·al** *adj.* **—con·junc·tion·al·ly** *adv.*

con·junc·ti·va (kŏn′jŭngk-tī′və) *n., pl.* **-vas** or **-vae** (-vē). The mucous membrane that lines the inner surface of the eyelid and covers the exposed surface of the eyeball. [Middle English, from Medieval Latin *(membrāna) conjunctīva,* "the connective (membrane)," from Late Latin *conjunctīvus,* CONJUNCTIVE.] **—con·junc·ti·val** *adj.*

con·junc·tive (kən-jŭngk′tĭv) *adj.* **1.** Joining; connective. **2.** Joined together; combined. **3.** *Abbr.* **conj.** *Grammar.* **a.** Designating or used as a conjunction. **b.** Serving to connect elements of meaning and construction in a sentence, as *and* and *but.*
∼*n. Abbr.* **conj.** *Grammar.* A connective word, especially a conjunction. [Late Latin *conjunctīvus,* from Latin *conjunctus,* CONJUNCT.] **—con·junc·tive·ly** *adv.*

con·junc·ti·vi·tis (kən-jŭngk′tə-vī′tĭs) *n. Pathology.* Inflammation of the conjunctiva. [New Latin : CONJUNCTIV(A) + -ITIS.]

con·junc·ture (kən-jŭngk′chər) *n.* **1.** A combination of circumstances or events. **2.** A critical set of circumstances; a crisis.

con·ju·ra·tion (kŏn′jŏŏ-rā′shən) *n.* **1.** Threat of conjuring. **2.** A solemn invocation. **3.** A magic spell or incantation. **4.** Magic; legerdemain.

con·jure (kŏn′jər; *in tr. sense 1* kən-jŏŏr′) *v.* **-jured, -juring, -jures.** —*tr.* **1.** To call upon or entreat solemnly, especially by an oath. **2.** To summon (a devil or spirit) by incantation or magic spell. **3.** To cause or effect by or as by magic. —*intr.* **1.** To practice magic; especially, to perform tricks using sleight of hand. **2.** To summon a devil by incantation or magic spell. **—conjure up. 1.** To bring into existence as if by magic. **2.** To bring to the mind's eye; evoke. [Middle English *conjuren,* from Old French *conjurer,* from Medieval Latin *conjūrāre,* to invoke with oaths or incantations, from Latin, to swear together, conspire : *com-,* together + *jūrāre,* to swear.]

con·jur·er, con·ju·ror (kŏn′jər-ər) *n.* One who practices magic tricks or sleight of hand, especially as an entertainer.

conk[1] (kŏngk) *n. Slang.* **1.** The head. **2.** A blow on the head.
∼*tr.v.* **conked, conking, conks.** *Slang.* To hit on the head. **—conk out. 1.** To fail suddenly: *The motor conked out.* **2.** To tire or fall asleep. **3.** To faint. [Probably alteration of CONCH.]

conk[2] *n.* The hard, shelflike fruiting body of a tree fungus. [Probably alteration of CONCH.]

conk[3] *tr.v.* **conked, conking, conks.** To straighten (kinky hair), usually by a chemical method. [Perhaps alteration of *congolene,* a substance for straightening hair.] **—conk** *n.*

con·ker (kŏng′kər) *n. British.* **1.** The brown shiny nut of the horse chestnut *(see).* **2. conkers.** A children's game in which each player swings a horse chestnut on a string and tries to break one held by the opponent. [From dialect *conker,* snail shell (later replaced by horse chestnuts in the game), perhaps (through influence of CONQUER) an alteration of CONCH.]

con man *n. Slang.* A **confidence man** *(see).*

con moto (kŏn mō′tō) *adv. Music.* With movement; in a spirited manner. Used as a direction. [Italian.]

conn. Variant of **con** (to steer).

Conn. Connecticut.

Con·nacht (kŏn′əKHt, -ət). Formerly **Con·naught** (-ôt). Province in the northwest of the Republic of Ireland. It consists of counties Galway, Leitrim, Mayo, Roscommon, and Sligo.

con·nate (kŏn′āt′) *adj.* **1.** Part of or existing in someone or something from birth; inborn; innate. **2.** Coexisting since birth or origin; cognate; related. **3.** *Biology.* Congenitally or firmly united. Said of similar parts or organs. [Late Latin *connātus,* past participle of *connascī,* to be born together : *com-,* together + Latin *nascī,* to be born.] **—con·nate·ly** *adv.* **—con·nate·ness** *n.*

con·nat·u·ral (kə-năch′ər-əl) *adj.* **1.** Innate; congenital; natural. **2.** Related or similar in nature; cognate. [Medieval Latin *connātūrālis* : *com-,* together + Latin *nātūrālis,* NATURAL.] **—con·nat·u·ral·ly** *adv.* **—con·nat·u·ral·ness** *n.*

con·nect (kə-nĕkt′) *v.* **-nected, -necting, -nects.** —*tr.* **1.** To join or fasten together; link; unite. **2.** To associate or consider as related. **3.** To establish communication between, especially by telephone. **4.** To join to a communications circuit. —*intr.* **1.** To be or become joined or united. **2.** To operate so that passengers can easily transfer from one route to another: *The trains connect at Chicago.* **3.** *Sports.* To make a successful hit, kick, or shot; make contact. **4.** *Informal.* To be successful; have the desired effect. —See Synonyms at **join.** [Middle English *connecten,* from Latin *connectere* : *com-,* together + *nectere,* to bind, tie.] **—con·nect·ed·ly** *adv.* **—con·nect·a·ble, con·nect·i·ble** *adj.* **—con·nec·tor** (kə-nĕk′tər), **con·nect·er** *n.*

Con·nect·i·cut (kə-nĕt′ə-kət). *Abbr.* **Conn.** State in the northeastern United States, in New England. Connecticut was one of the original 13 states. Its capital is Hartford.

con·nect·ing rod (kə-nĕk′tĭng) *n.* **1.** A rod linking rotating parts of a machine in reciprocating motion. **2.** Such a rod connecting the crankshaft of an internal-combustion engine to a piston. Also called "piston rod."

con·nec·tion (kə-nĕk′shən) *n.* Also *British* **con·nex·ion.** *Abbr.* **con. 1.** The act of joining or state of being joined; union. **2.** Anything that joins, relates, or connects; a bond; a link. **3. a.** The fact of being related or associated: *wanted in connection with a series of robberies.* **b.** A point of relationship or association: *What was her connection with the deceased?* **4.** The logical ordering of words or ideas; coherence. **5.** The relation of a word or idea to the surrounding text; context. **6.** A person with whom one is associated, especially by professional or family ties: *has some useful connections in New York.* **7. a.** The meeting of various means of transportation for the transfer of passengers. **b.** A connecting train, plane, or the like: *missed my connection.* **8.** A line of communication between two points in a telephone system. **9.** A point of contact in an electrical circuit: *a loose connection.* **10.** A religious organization or denomination. **11.** *Slang.* **a.** A dealer in illegal drugs. **b.** A major supply route for illegal drugs. **—in this connection.** Relating to the matter at hand. **—con·nec·tion·al** *adj.*

con·nec·tive (kə-nĕk′tĭv) *adj.* Serving or tending to connect.
∼*n.* **1.** Anything that connects. **2.** *Grammar.* A word, such as a conjunction, that connects words, phrases, clauses, and sentences. **3.** *Botany.* The tissue of a stamen that forms the division between the two lobes of an anther. **—con·nec·tive·ly** *adv.* **—con·nec·tiv·i·ty** (kŏn′ĕk-tĭv′ə-tē) *n.*

connective tissue *n.* Tissue arising chiefly from the embryonic mesoderm, consisting typically of a jellylike matrix in which are embedded collagen and elastic fibers, fat cells, fibroblasts, and mast cells. It forms the supporting and connecting structures of the body and occurs in tendons, ligaments, cartilage, and bone.

Con·ne·ma·ra (kŏn′ə-mär′ə). Region of County Galway in the west of the Republic of Ireland, between the Atlantic Ocean and Mask and Corrib loughs.

con·ning tower (kŏn′ĭng) *n.* **1.** A raised, enclosed observation post in a submarine, also usually used as a means of entrance and exit. **2.** The armored pilothouse of a warship. [From CON (to steer).]

con·nip·tion (kə-nĭp′shən) *n. Informal.* A fit of anger or hysteria. [19th century : origin obscure.]

con·niv·ance (kə-nī′vəns) *n.* **1.** The act of conniving. **2.** *Law.* Knowledge of, and tacit consent to, the commission of an illegal act by another.

con·nive (kə-nīv′) *intr.v.* **-nived, -niving, -nives. 1.** To feign ignorance of a wrong, thus implying tacit encouragement or consent. Usually used with *at.* **2.** To cooperate secretly or conspire. Used with *with.* [French *conniver,* from Latin *connivēre, cōnivēre,* to close the eyes, be indulgent.] **—con·niv·er** *n.*

con·ni·vent (kə-nī′vənt) *adj. Biology.* Converging and touching, but not fused together. Said especially of stamens or an insect's wings. [Latin *connivēns* (stem *connivent-*), present participle of *connivēre,* "to bend together," close the eyes, CONNIVE.]

con·nois·seur (kŏn′ə-sûr′) *n.* A person with informed and astute discrimination, especially concerning the arts or matters of taste. [Obsolete French, from Old French *connoisseor,* from *connoistre,* to know, from Latin *cognōscere,* to get acquainted with, know thoroughly : *co-,* together + *gnōscere, nōscere,* to know.] **—con·nois·seur·ship** *n.*

Con·nors (kŏn′ərz), **James Scott,** known as "Jimmy" (1952–). U.S. tennis player. He twice won both the U.S. and the Wimbledon men's singles titles (1974, 1982) and also won the U.S. title in 1976, 1978, and 1983.

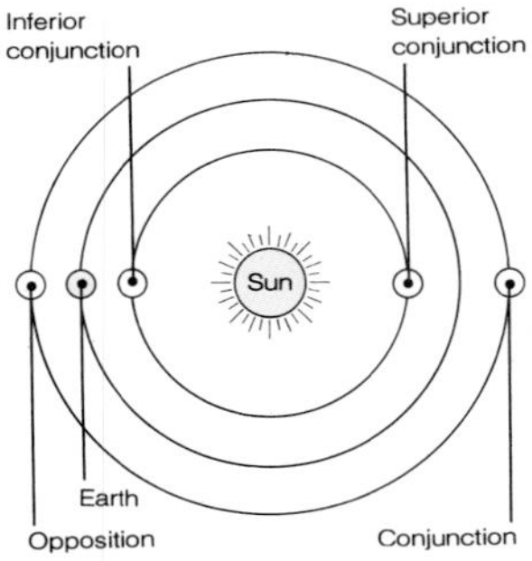

conjunction *Two heavenly bodies are said to be in conjunction when they align with the sun. The diagram shows the two conjunctions of the planet Mercury with Earth. When Mercury lies on the opposite side of the sun from Earth, it is known as a superior conjunction. When it lies between the sun and Earth, it is called an inferior conjunction.*

TREES THAT FLOURISHED IN THE WORLD'S ANCIENT FORESTS

Conifers thrive in extreme conditions and at high altitudes

Conifers, or cone-bearing trees, flourished in the prehistoric forests in which dinosaurs lived, and their descendants are found over one third of the earth's land surface. They grow in subtropical and temperate areas; on dry, hot mountainsides; and in the moister, colder zones up to and beyond the Arctic Circle.

Unlike broad-leaved trees, which have flowers pollinated by wind or insects, the narrow-leaved conifers reproduce when some of the wind-borne pollen grains from male cones—carrying the male cells—alight on the female cones and fertilize them. The rest of the pollen grains may be blown miles away, sometimes in

Hybrid larch
Larix x eurolepsis
Scotland
Up to 32 meters (105 feet)

European larch
Larix decidua
Central Europe, Britain
Up to 38 meters (125 feet)

Japanese larch
Larix kaempferi
Japan, Europe
Up to 35 meters (115 feet)

Cedar of Lebanon
Cedrus libani
Lebanon, Europe, North America
Up to 35 meters (115 feet)

Giant fir
Abies grandis
North America, western Europe
Up to 55 meters (180 feet)

Norway spruce
Picea abies
Northern Europe, Russia, North America
Up to 40 meters (131 feet)

Sitka spruce
Picea sitchensis
Northwest America, Europe
Up to 46 meters (150 feet)

Scots pine
Pinus sylvestris
Europe, Siberia, North America
Up to 36 meters (118 feet)

Shore pine
Pinus contorta
Northwest America, Europe
Up to 24 meters (79 feet)

Austrian pine
Pinus nigra
North America, Europe
Up to 35 meters (115 feet)

Common juniper
Juniperus communis
Britain, North America, Scandinavia
Up to 6 meters (20 feet)

con·no·ta·tion (kŏn'ə-tā'shən) *n.* **1.** An act or instance of connoting. **2. a.** The configuration of suggestive or associative implications constituting the general sense of an abstract expression beyond its literal, explicit sense. **b.** A secondary meaning suggested by a word in addition to its literal meaning. **3.** *Logic.* The total of the attributes constituting the meaning of a term; intension. **—con·no·ta·tive** (kŏn'ə-tā'tĭv, kə-nō'tə-tĭv) *adj.* **—con·no·ta·tive·ly** *adv.*

con·note (kə-nōt') *tr.v.* **-noted, -noting, -notes. 1.** To suggest or imply in addition to literal meaning: *The word "safari" connotes adventure.* **2.** To involve as a condition or consequence. **—See Usage note at denote.** [Medieval Latin *connotāre,* "to mark in addition" : Latin *com-,* together with + *notāre,* to mark, note, from *nota,* a mark, note.]

con·nu·bi·al (kə-nōō'bē-əl, -nyōō'-) *adj.* Of marriage or the married state; conjugal. [Latin *connūbiālis,* from *connūbium,* marriage : *com-,* together + *nūbere,* to marry.] **—con·nu·bi·al·i·ty** (kə-nōō'bē-ăl'ə-tē, -nyōō'-) *n.* **—con·nu·bi·al·ly** *adv.*

co·no·dont (kō'nə-dŏnt') *n.* Any of various small, toothlike Paleozoic fossils of unknown origin. [Greek *kōnos,* cone + -ODONT.]

co·noid (kō'noid') *adj.* Also **co·noid·al** (kō-noid'l). Shaped like a cone.

  ~*n.* **conoid. 1.** Something that is shaped like a cone. **2.** A geometric surface obtained when a parabola, ellipse, or hyperbola is rotated about one axis. [CON(E) + OID.]

con·quer (kŏng'kər) *v.* **-quered, -quering, -quers. —***tr.* **1.** To defeat or subdue by force, especially by force of arms. **2.** To gain or secure control of by or as if by force of arms. **3.** To overcome or surmount by physical, mental, or moral force: *conquer one's fear of flying.* **4.** To climb (a mountain) successfully. **—***intr.* To be victorious; win. **—See Synonyms at defeat.** [Middle English *conqueren,* from Old French *conquerre,* from Vulgar Latin *conquaerere* (unattested), variant of Latin *conquīrere,* to search for, procure, win : *con-* (intensive) + *quaerere,* to seek.] **—con·quer·a·ble** *adj.*

billowing, yellow clouds. There are more than 500 species of conifers, including pines, junipers, yews, cedars, monkey puzzles, spruces, firs, and the different kinds of larch, one of the few cone-bearing trees to shed its leaves each year.

Conifers vary in size from small shrubs to the spectacular coast redwoods and giant sequoias of the United States. Some of these are more than 3,000 years old and include the world's most massive living object—the giant sequoia "General Sherman," which is 85.4 meters (280 feet) tall and weighs about 2,020 tons. It has enough timber to make 5 billion matches. The world's tallest tree—at 111.6 meters (366 feet 2 inches) is a coast redwood.

Although most conifers are spread throughout the Northern Hemisphere, a few coniferous trees are found in the Southern Hemisphere. They include the ornamental bunya pine that grows in eastern Australia, and the totara yellowwood, kauri, and red pine of New Zealand.

The conifer's soft wood is used to make posts, poles, crates, boxes, and cabinets; and the trees are a valuable source of resins, oils, tars, and turpentines. The wood pulp provides paper for newsprint.

Noble fir
Abies procera
North America, western Europe
Up to 46 meters (150 feet)

Douglas fir
Pseudotsuga menziesii
North America, Europe, Australasia
Up to 100 meters (330 feet)

Coast redwood
Sequoia sempervirens
Northwest America
Up to 111.6 meters (366 feet)

Monkey puzzle
Araucaria araucana
South America, Europe
Up to 24 meters (79 feet)

Common yew
Taxus baccata
Europe, North America, Asia
Up to 20 meters (60 feet)

Leyland cypress
x Cupressocyparis leylandii
Europe, North America
Up to 30 meters (98 feet)

Totara pine
Podocarpus totara
New Zealand
Up to 38 meters (125 feet)

Kauri pine
Agathis australis
New Zealand
Up to 46 meters (150 feet)

Rimu, or Red pine
Dacrydium cupressinum
New Zealand
Up to 24 meters (79 feet)

Bunya-bunya pine
Araucaria bidwillii
Australia
Up to 43 meters (141 feet)

con·quer·or (kŏng′kər-ər) *n.* Someone who conquers. **—the Conqueror. William I** of England *(see).*

con·quest (kŏn′kwĕst, kŏng′-) *n.* **1.** The act or process of conquering. **2.** Something acquired by conquering, especially territory. **3.** A successful amorous exploit: *boasting about his latest conquest.* **4.** Someone whose love or favor has been captured. **—the Conquest.** The **Norman Conquest** *(see).* [Middle English *conquest(e),* from Old French, from Vulgar Latin *conquaesītus* (unattested), past participle of *conquaerere* (unattested), to CONQUER.]

con·qui·an (kŏng′kē-ən) *n.* A card game resembling rummy, for two players. Also called "cooncan." [(Mexican) Spanish *con quién,* with whom?]

con·quis·ta·dor (kŏn-kēs′tə-dôr′, -kwĭs′-) *n., pl.* **conquistadores** (kŏn-kēs′tə-dôr′ās, -dôr′ĕz, -kwĭs′-) or **-dors.** A conqueror; specifically, any of the Spanish conquerors of Central and South America, especially Mexico and Peru, in the 16th century. [Spanish, from *conquistar,* to conquer, from Medieval Latin *conquestāre,* frequentative of Vulgar Latin *conquaerere* (unattested). See **conquer.**]

Con·rad (kŏn′răd), **Joseph,** born Teodor Jósef Konrad Korzeniowski (1857–1924). Polish-born novelist who became a major English literary figure. His masterpieces include *Lord Jim* (1900), *The Heart of Darkness* (1902), and *Under Western Eyes* (1911).

cons. 1. consigned; consignment. **2.** consonant. **3.** constable. **4.** constitution; constitutional. **5.** construction.

Cons. 1. Constable. **2.** Consul.

con·san·guin·e·ous (kŏn′săng-gwĭn′ē-əs) *adj.* Also **con·san·guine** (kŏn-săng′gwĭn). Of the same lineage or origin; especially, related by blood. [Latin *consanguineus* : *com-,* joint + *sanguineus,* of blood, SANGUINE.] **—con·san·guin·e·ous·ly** *adv.*

con·san·guin·i·ty (kŏn′săng-gwĭn′ə-tē) *n.* **1.** Blood relationship. **2.** Any close connection or affinity.

con·science (kŏn′shəns) *n.* **1.** The faculty of recognizing the distinction between right and wrong in regard to one's own conduct, together with the feeling that one ought not to do wrong: *the voice* *of conscience.* **2.** A feeling or consciousness of conformity to one's own sense of right conduct: *a clear conscience.* **3.** *Archaic.* Consciousness. **—in (all) conscience. 1.** In fairness; reasonably. **2.** To be sure; certainly. **—on one's conscience.** Causing remorse. [Middle English, from Old French, from Latin *conscientia,* from *consciēns* (stem *conscient-*), present participle of *conscīre,* to be conscious, know well : *com-* (intensive) + *scīre,* to know.] **—con·science·less** *adj.*

conscience clause *n.* A clause in a law that recognizes or exempts persons whose moral scruples forbid compliance.

conscience money *n.* Money paid to atone for some concealed dishonest or morally wrong act.

con·science-strick·en (kŏn'shəns-strĭk'ən) *adj.* Feeling guilty or remorseful about something one has done or failed to do.

con·sci·en·tious (kŏn'shē-ĕn'shəs) *adj.* **1.** Governed by or accomplished according to conscience; scrupulous. **2.** Thorough and painstaking; careful and diligent. **—See Synonyms at meticulous.** [French *conscientieux,* from Medieval Latin *conscientiōsus,* from Latin *conscientia,* CONSCIENCE.] **—con·sci·en·tious·ly** *adv.* **—con·sci·en·tious·ness** *n.*

conscientious objector *n. Abbr.* **CO, C.O.** One who on the basis of religious or moral principles refuses to bear arms or participate in military service.

con·scion·a·ble (kŏn'shən-ə-bəl) *adj. Obsolete.* Conscientious. [From *conscions,* obsolete variant of CONSCIENCE + -ABLE.]

con·scious (kŏn'shəs) *adj.* **1. a.** Having an awareness of one's own existence, sensations, and thoughts and of one's environment. **b.** Having a particular preception; aware: *conscious of having offended her.* **2.** Not asleep or stuporous; awake: *conscious after surgery.* **3.** Subjectively known and felt: *She spoke with conscious pride.* **4.** Intentionally conceived or done; deliberate: *a conscious insult.* **5.** Having or showing self-consciousness: *conscious of her limp.* **6.** Concerned about or interested in something. Often used in combination: *fashion-conscious.*
~*n.* The component of waking awareness perceptible by an individual at any given instant. Preceded by *the.* [Latin *conscius,* knowing with others, participating in knowledge, aware of : *com-,* with + *scīre,* to know.] **—con·scious·ly** *adv.*
Usage: Conscious, *subconscious, preconscious,* and *unconscious.* These are psychological terms referring to aspects of the workings of the mind. *Conscious* refers to mental processes, such as thoughts or emotional reactions, of which a person is aware. *Subconscious* pertains to thoughts or feelings outside the immediate awareness either wholly or partly. *Preconscious* refers to mental processes that are outside the consciousness, but are easily brought into the conscious mind. *Unconscious* alludes to all mental processes that a person is not aware of, including thoughts or feelings that have been forgotten or repressed, and also images, instincts, desires, and the like. It is often used interchangeably with *subconscious.*

con·scious·ness (kŏn'shəs-nĭs) *n.* **1.** The state or condition of being conscious. **2.** The essence or totality of attitudes, opinions, and sensitivities held or thought to be held by an individual or group: *national consciousness.* **3.** The conscious. **4.** A critical awareness of one's own indentity and situation.

con·scious·ness-rais·ing (kŏn'shəs-nĭs-rā'zĭng) *n.* A process whereby one achieves greater personal or social awareness.

con·script (kŏn'skrĭpt) *n.* One who is compulsorily enrolled for service in the armed forces; a draftee.
~*adj.* (kŏn'skrĭpt). Enrolled compulsorily; drafted.
~*tr.v.* (kən-skrĭpt') **conscripted, -scripting, -scripts. 1.** To enroll compulsorily for military service; draft. **2.** To force into service. [Old French, enlisted, from Latin *conscriptus,* past participle of *conscrībere,* to write together, enter in a list, enrol : *com-,* together + *scrībere,* to write.]

con·scrip·tion (kən-skrĭp'shən) *n.* Compulsory enrollment for military service.

con·se·crate (kŏn'sə-krāt') *tr.v.* **-crated, -crating, -crates. 1.** To make, declare, or set apart as sacred: *consecrate a church.* **2. a.** To change (the bread and wine of the Eucharist) into the body and blood of Christ, according to the doctrines of the Roman Catholic Church. **b.** To sanctify (bread and wine) to be taken as a memorial of Christ, according to the beliefs of the Reformed churches. **3.** To initiate (a priest) into the order of bishops. **4.** To dedicate to some service or goal: *consecrated her life to helping the poor.* **5.** To make venerable: *a tradition consecrated by time.* **—See Synonyms at devote.**
~*adj.* Dedicated to a sacred purpose; sanctified. [Middle English *consecraten,* from Latin *consecrāre* : *com-* (intensive) + *sacrāre,* to make sacred, from *sacer,* sacred.] **—con·se·cra·tive** (kŏn'sə-krā'tĭv) *adj.* **—con·se·cra·tor** (kŏn'sə-krā'tər) *n.* **—con·se·cra·to·ry** (kŏn'sə-krə-tôr'ē, -tōr'ē) *adj.*

con·se·cra·tion (kŏn'sə-krā'shən) *n.* **1.** The act, process, or ceremony of consecrating. **2.** The state of being consecrated.

con·se·cu·tion (kŏn'sə-kyōō'shən) *n.* **1.** A sequence or succession. **2.** The relation of consequent to antecedent; deduction; inference. [Latin *consecūtiō* (stem *consecūtiōn-*), sequence, from *consequī,* to follow up. See **consequent.**]

con·sec·u·tive (kən-sĕk'yə-tĭv) *adj.* **1.** Following successively without interruption. **2.** Marked by logical sequence. **3.** *Music.* Designating harmonic intervals of a similar kind. **4.** *Grammar.* Expressing a consequence. [French *consécutif,* Medieval Latin *consecūtīvus,* from *consequī,* to follow up. See **consequent.**] **—con·sec·u·tive·ly** *adv.* **—con·sec·u·tive·ness** *n.*

con·sen·su·al (kən-sĕn'shōō-əl) *adj.* **1.** Based on or involving mutual consent or consensus. **2.** *Physiology.* Responding to reflex stimulation. Said especially of certain reflex actions by parts of the body that respond to stimulation of another part. [From CONSENSUS (after SENSUAL).] **—con·sen·su·al·ly** *adv.*

con·sen·sus (kən-sĕn'səs) *n.* Collective opinion or concord; general agreement or accord; a majority view. Also used adjectively: *consensus politics.* [Latin, from *consentīre,* to agree, CONSENT.]
Usage: The phrase *consensus of opinion* is widely used in informal speech and writing, and is sometimes used in formal speech. But people aware of the definition of *consensus* (which already contains the notion of "opinion") avoid the phrase, on the grounds that it contains a redundant element.

con·sent (kən-sĕnt') *intr.v.* **-sented, -senting, -sents. 1.** To give assent or permission; accede; agree. **2.** *Archaic.* To agree in opinion; to be of the same mind. **—See Synonyms at assent.**
~*n.* **1.** Voluntary acceptance or allowance of what is planned or done by another; permission. **2.** Agreement as to opinion or a course of action: *by common consent.* [Middle English *consenten,* from Old French *consentir,* from Latin *consentīre,* to feel together, agree : *com-,* together + *sentīre,* to feel.] **—con·sent·er** *n.*

con·sen·ta·ne·ous (kŏn'sĕn-tā'nē-əs) *adj.* **1.** Manifesting agreement; accordant. **2.** Done by common consent; unanimous. [Latin *consentāneus,* from *consentīre,* to feel together, CONSENT.] **—con·sen·ta·ne·i·ty** (kən-sĕn'tə-nē'ə-tē), **con·sen·ta·ne·ous·ness** *n.* **—con·sen·ta·ne·ous·ly** *adv.*

con·sen·tient (kən-sĕn'shənt) *adj.* United in agreement; of the same opinion.

con·se·quence (kŏn'sə-kwĕns', -kwəns) *n.* **1.** That which rationally or naturally follows from an action or condition; an effect; a result: *He must face the consequences of his thoughtlessness.* **2.** A logical result or inference. **3.** Importance in rank: *someone of consequence.* **4.** Significance: *a matter of little consequence.* **—in consequence** As a result; hence. **—See Synonyms at effect, importance.**

con·se·quent (kŏn'sə-kwĕnt', -kwənt) *adj.* **1. a.** Following as a natural effect, result, or conclusion: *a reduction in taxes with a consequent loss of revenue; a water shortage consequent to the drought.* **b.** Following as a logical conclusion. **2.** Logically correct or consistent. **3.** *Geology.* Having a position or direction relating to or resulting from the original slope of the earth's surface: *consequent rivers.* *In this sense, compare* **obsequent, subsequent.**
~*n.* **1.** Anything that follows something else, usually with causal relation. **2.** An outcome or result. **3.** *Logic.* The second part of a conditional proposition, whose truth is dependent on the truth of the antecedent. **4.** *Mathematics.* The second term of a ratio. [Middle English, from Old French, from Latin *consequēns* (stem *consequent-*), present participle of *consequī,* to follow up, accompany : *com-,* together + *sequī,* to follow.]
Usage: The usual prepositions following the adjectival sense of this word are *on* or *upon.* *To* is also common, but this usage increases the likelihood of confusion with *subsequent to. Consequent* usually implies a causal or logical relationship with what has gone before; *subsequent* has no such meaning, being equivalent to "after."

con·se·quen·tial (kŏn'sə-kwĕn'shəl) *adj.* **1.** Following as an effect, result, or conclusion; resultant; consequent. **2.** Having important consequences; significant. **3.** Self-important; pompous. **—con·se·quen·ti·al·i·ty** (kŏn'sə-kwĕn'shē-ăl'ə-tē), **con·se·quen·tial·ness** *n.* **—con·se·quen·tial·ly** *adv.*

con·se·quent·ly (kŏn'sə-kwĕnt'lē, -kwənt-) *adv.* As a result; therefore.

con·ser·van·cy (kən-sûr'vən-sē) *n., pl.* **-cies. 1.** Conservation, especially of natural resources. **2.** *British.* A commission supervising fisheries and navigation.

con·ser·va·tion (kŏn'sər-vā'shən) *n.* **1.** The act of conserving; preservation from loss, depletion, waste, or harm. **2.** The systematic preservation of the environment, especially of natural resources such as topsoil, forests, and waterways. **—con·ser·va·tion·al** *adj.*

con·ser·va·tion·ist (kŏn'sər-vā'shən-ĭst) *n.* One who practices or advocates the preservation of natural resources and the protection of wildlife and the environment.

conservation law *n.* **1.** *Physics.* A law stating that a given quantity, such as mass, energy, or charge, cannot be created or destroyed regardless of changes of distribution of that quantity within a system. **2.** A law by which a government seeks to prohibit certain actions in order to preserve a natural amenity or resource.

conservation of energy *n. Physics.* An exact conservation law stating that the total energy of an isolated system remains constant regardless of changes within the system.

conservation of mass *n. Physics.* The classical principle that the total mass of an isolated system is unchanged by interaction of its parts.

conservation of momentum *n. Physics.* An exact conservation law stating that the total linear or angular momentum of an isolated system remains constant regardless of changes within the system.

con·ser·va·tism (kən-sûr'və-tĭz'əm) *n.* **1.** The disposition in politics or culture to maintain the existing order and to resist or oppose change or innovation. **2.** The principles and practices of persons or groups so disposed. **3. Conservatism.** The principles and practices of the Conservative Party.

con·ser·va·tive (kən-sûr'və-tĭv) *adj.* **1.** Tending to favor the preservation of the existing order; averse to and distrustful of change. **2. Conservative.** *Abbr.* **Con.** Belonging to, supporting, or character-

istic of the Conservative Party of the United Kingdom. **3. Conservative.** Adhering to or characteristic of Conservative Judaism. **4.** Marked by moderation; prudent; cautious: *a conservative estimate.* **5.** Traditional in manner or style; not showy. **6.** Tending to conserve; conserving; preservative.
~*n.* **1.** A conservative person; especially, one who supports or belongs to a conservative political party. **2. Conservative.** *Abbr.* **C.** A member or supporter of the Conservative Party. —**con·ser·va·tive·ly** *adv.* —**con·ser·va·tive·ness** *n.*

Conservative Judaism *n.* A branch of Judaism that holds a modified view of the sanctity of the Torah and is flexible in its submission to the authority of the Rabbinical Law, accepting some liturgical and ritual changes in the light of the needs of modern life. Compare **Orthodox Judaism, Reform Judaism.**

Conservative Party *n.* The major right-wing political party of the United Kingdom, which supports private enterprise and privatization and opposes state control and nationalization.

con·ser·va·tor (kən-sûr′və-tər) *n.* **1.** Someone who preserves from injury or violation; a protector. **2.** A custodian of an art gallery or museum. **3.** *Law.* A guardian; a keeper.

con·ser·va·to·ry (kən-sûr′və-tôr′ē, -tōr′ē) *n., pl.* **-ries. 1.** A glass-enclosed room or greenhouse, usually forming part of a dwelling, in which plants are grown and displayed. **2.** A school of music or dramatic art.

con·serve (kən-sûrv′) *tr.v.* **-served, -serving, -serves. 1.** To protect from loss or wasteful depletion; preserve. **2.** To preserve (fruits) with sugar.
~*n.* (kŏn′sûrv). *Often* **conserves.** A jam containing whole fruit or whole pieces of fruit, especially one made of a mixture of fruits. [Middle English *conserven,* from Old French *conserver,* from Latin *conservāre : com-* (intensive) + *servāre,* to keep, preserve.] —**con·serv·a·ble** *adj.* —**con·serv·er** *n.*

con·sid·er (kən-sĭd′ər) *v.* **-ered, -ering, -ers.** —*tr.* **1.** To deliberate upon; examine; study. **2.** To regard as; think or deem to be: *considered him a fool.* **3.** To believe, especially after deliberation; judge: *considers waste criminal.* **4.** To take into account; make allowance for: *Consider that he's just a beginner.* **5.** To have regard for; pay attention to: *Consider her feelings.* **6.** To regard highly; esteem. **7.** To think about as possible or acceptable: *refused to consider the other possibilities.* —*intr.* To think carefully; reflect. [Middle English *consideren,* from Old French *considerer,* from Latin *consīderāre,* to observe (originally a term of augury meaning "to observe the stars carefully").] —**con·sid·er·er** *n.*
  Synonyms: *account, deem, reckon, regard.*

con·sid·er·a·ble (kən-sĭd′ər-ə-bəl) *adj.* **1.** Fairly large in amount, extent, or degree: *a man of considerable influence.* **2.** Worthy of consideration; important; significant: *a considerable poet.*
~*n. Informal.* A considerable amount, extent, or degree. —**con·sid·er·a·bly** *adv.*

con·sid·er·ate (kən-sĭd′ər-ĭt) *adj.* **1.** Having regard for the needs or feelings of others. **2.** Characterized by careful thought; deliberate. —See Synonyms at **thoughtful.** [Latin *consīderātus,* past participle of *consīderāre,* to be considerate, CONSIDER.] —**con·sid·er·ate·ly** *adv.* —**con·sid·er·ate·ness** *n.*

con·sid·er·a·tion (kən-sĭd′ə-rā′shən) *n.* **1.** Careful thought; deliberation. **2.** A factor to be considered in forming a judgment or decision: *Health is the major consideration.* **3.** Thoughtful concern for others; solicitude. **4.** Payment given in exchange for a service rendered. **5.** A thought produced by considering; a thoughtful opinion. **6.** *Law.* Something promised, given, or done that has the effect of making an agreement a legally enforceable contract. **7.** High regard. —**in consideration of. 1.** In view of; on account of. **2.** In return for.

con·sid·ered (kən-sĭd′ərd) *adj.* **1.** Reached after deliberation or careful thought. **2.** Regarded; esteemed.

con·sid·er·ing (kən-sĭd′ər-ĭng) *prep.* In view of; taking into consideration.
~*adv. Informal.* With all things considered: *He does well, considering.*
~*conj. Informal.* In view of the fact that; inasmuch as: *Considering he's only six, he reads very well.*

con·sign (kən-sīn′) *tr.v.* **-signed, -signing, -signs. 1.** To give over to the care of another; entrust. **2.** To turn over permanently; commit irrevocably. **3.** To ship (goods) to an agent for sale, custody, or use. —See Synonyms at **commit.** [Middle English *consignen,* to certify by a seal, from Old French *consigner,* from Latin *consignāre : com-* (intensive) + *signāre,* to seal, from *signum,* seal, mark.] —**con·sign·a·ble** *adj.* —**con·sig·na·tion** (kŏn′sĭg-nā′shən) *n.* —**con·sig·nor** (kŏn′sī-nôr′, kən-sī′nər), **con·sign·er** *n.*

con·sign·ee (kŏn′sī-nē′, kən-sī′nē) *n.* A person to whom goods are consigned.

con·sign·ment (kən-sīn′mənt) *n. Abbr.* **cons. 1.** The consigning of goods or cargo, especially to an agent for sale or custody. **2.** That which is consigned; a shipment of goods. —**on consignment.** Sent to a dealer who pays only for what is sold.

con·sist (kən-sĭst′) *intr.v.* **-sisted, -sisting, -sists. 1.** To be made up or composed. Used with *of.* **2.** To have a basis; lie; rest. Used with *in.* **3.** To be compatible; accord. [Old French *consister,* from Latin *consistere,* to stand still, exist : *com-* (intensive) + *sistere,* to cause to stand, place.]

con·sis·ten·cy (kən-sĭs′tən-sē) *n., pl.* **-cies.** Also **con·sis·tence** (-təns). **1.** Agreement or logical coherence among things or parts. **2.** Compatibility or agreement among successive acts, ideas, or

events. **3.** Degree or texture of firmness, density, or viscosity.

con·sis·tent (kən-sĭs′tənt) *adj.* **1.** In agreement; compatible; not contradictory. Often used with *with.* **2.** Constantly conforming to the same principles, course of action, or standards. [Latin *consistens* (stem *consistent-*), present participle of *consistere,* to stand firmly, CONSIST.] —**con·sis·tent·ly** *adv.*

con·sis·to·ry (kən-sĭs′tər-ē) *n., pl.* **-ries. 1.** *Roman Catholic Church.* A gathering, either of cardinals alone *(secret consistory),* or with others present *(public consistory),* presided over by the pope for the solemn promulgation of papal acts, such as the appointment of cardinals or bishops or the canonization of a saint. **2.** In certain Reformed churches, a governing body of a local congregation, composed of the ministers and elders. **3.** In Lutheran churches, a court appointed to regulate ecclesiastical affairs. **4.** In the Anglican Church, a diocesan court presided over by the bishop's chancellor or commissary. **5.** The meeting place, or the meeting itself, of any such body. **6.** A council or tribunal. [Middle English *consistorie,* from Old French, from Medieval Latin *consistōrium,* from Late Latin, place of assembly, from Latin *consistere,* to take one's place (at a meeting), stand, CONSIST.] —**con·sis·to·ri·al** (kŏn′sĭs-tôr′ē-əl, -tōr′-), **con·sis·to·ri·an** *adj.*

con·so·ci·ate (kən-sō′shē-āt′) *v.* **-ated, -ating, -ates.** —*tr.* To bring into friendly association. —*intr.* To come into friendly association.
~*adj.* (kən-sō′shē-ĭt). Associated; united.
~*n.* (kən-sō′shē-ĭt). An associate; a companion; a partner. [Middle English *consociat,* associate, from Latin *consociātus,* past participle of *consociāre,* to associate, join : *com-,* together + *sociāre,* to join, from *socius,* ally, companion.]

con·so·ci·a·tion (kən-sō′sē-ā′shən, -shē-) *n.* **1.** The act of consociating. **2.** A subdivision of an ecological association having one dominant species of plant.

con·so·la·tion (kŏn′sə-lā′shən) *n.* **1. a.** The act or an instance of consoling. **b.** The state of being consoled. **2.** Someone or something that consoles; a comfort. —**con·sol·a·to·ry** (kən-sŏl′ə-tôr′ē, -tōr′ē, -sōl′ə-) *adj.*

consolation prize *n.* A prize given to a competitor who loses.

con·sole¹ (kən-sōl′) *tr.v.* **-soled, -soling, -soles.** To comfort in time of grief, disappointment, or trouble; solace. [French *consoler,* from Old French, from Latin *consōlārī : com-* (intensive) + *sōlārī,* to comfort.] —**con·sol·a·ble** *adj.* —**con·sol·er** *n.* —**con·sol·ing·ly** *adv.*

con·sole² (kŏn′sōl) *n.* **1.** A decorative bracket for supporting a cornice, shelf, bust, or other object. **2.** A console table. **3.** The desklike part of an organ that contains the keyboard, stops, and pedals. **4.** A cabinet for a radio, television set, or record player, designed to stand on the floor. **5.** A panel housing the controls for electrical, electronic, or mechanical equipment; especially, the control panel of a computer. [French, short for *consolateur,* a carved human figure used to support cornices, from Latin *consōlātor,* one that consoles, hence a support, from *consōlārī,* to CONSOLE.]

console table *n.* **1.** A table supported by decorative consoles fixed to a wall. **2.** A small table, often with curved legs resembling consoles, designed to be set against a wall.

con·sol·i·date (kən-sŏl′ə-dāt′) *v.* **-dated, -dating, -dates.** —*tr.* **1.** To make firm or coherent; form into a compact mass; solidify. **2.** To make strong or secure; strengthen: *consolidated their empire.* **3.** To unite into one system or body; combine; merge. —*intr.* To become solidified or united. —See Synonyms at **join.** [Latin *consolidāre : com-* (intensive) + *solidāre,* to make solid or firm, from *solidus,* solid.] —**con·sol·i·da·tor** (kən-sŏl′ə-dā′tər) *n.*

consolidated school *n.* A public school, usually rural, for pupils from several adjacent districts.

con·sol·i·da·tion (kən-sŏl′ə-dā′shən) *n.* **1.** The act of consolidating or the state of being consolidated. **2.** The process of combining or uniting, as of separate corporations into a single new corporation. **3.** *Geology.* The process by which a loose deposit is compressed and cemented into solid rock.

con·sols (kŏn′sōlz, kən-sōlz′) *pl.n.* The perpetual governmental securities of Great Britain. Also called "bank annuities." [Short for *consolidated annuities.*]

con·so·lute (kŏn′sə-lōōt′) *adj.* Designating two or more liquids that are mutually soluble in all proportions. [Latin *consolūtus : con-,* together + *solūtus,* past participle of *solvere,* to dissolve.]

con·som·mé (kŏn′sə-mā′) *n.* A clear soup made of meat, fish, or vegetable stock or a combination of these. [French, "concentrate," from Old French *consommer,* to consume, from Latin *consummāre : com-* (intensive) + *summa,* SUM.]

con·so·nance (kŏn′sə-nəns) *n.* **1.** Agreement; harmony; accord. **2. a.** Correspondence or recurrence of sounds. **b.** In poetry, a similarity or recurrence of terminal consonants but not of vowels in two or more syllables, words, or lines, as in *rain* and *tone.* Compare **assonance. 3.** *Music.* A simultaneous combination of sounds conventionally regarded as pleasing and final in effect. Compare **dissonance.**

con·so·nant (kŏn′sə-nənt) *adj.* **1.** In agreement or accord: *remarks consonant with his beliefs.* **2.** Corresponding in sound. **3.** Harmonious in sound. **4.** Consonantal.
~*n. Abbr.* **cons. 1.** *Phonetics.* A speech sound produced by a partial or complete obstruction of the air stream by any of various constrictions of the speech organs. **2.** A letter or character representing such a sound, such as *p, t, g, k;* a letter that is not a vowel. [Middle English from Old French, from Latin *(littera) consonāns* (stem *consonant-*), "(letter) sounded with (a vowel)," from the pres-

ent participle of *consonāre,* to sound at the same time, harmonize, agree : *com-,* together + *sonāre,* to sound.] **—con·so·nant·ly** *adv.*

con·so·nan·tal (kŏn'sə-năn'təl) *adj.* **1.** Of, relating to, or having the nature of a consonant. **2.** Containing a consonant or consonants. **—con·so·nan·tal·ly** *adv.*

con sor·di·no (kŏn sôr-dē'nō) *adv. Music.* Using the mute. Used as a direction. [Italian.]

con·sort (kŏn'sôrt) *n.* **1.** A husband or wife; especially, the spouse of a monarch. **2.** A companion or partner. **3.** A ship accompanying another. **4. a.** *Archaic.* A harmonious combination of voices or musical instruments. **b.** A group of singers or instrumentalists. ~*v.* (kən-sôrt') **consorted, -sorting, -sorts.** —*intr.* **1.** To keep company; associate, especially with undesirable characters. **2.** To be in accord or agreement. —*tr.* To bring together. [Middle English, from Old French, from Latin *consors* (stem *consort-*), "one who shares the same fate," companion, partner : *com-,* together + *sors,* fate, share.]

con·sor·ti·um (kən-sôr'tē-əm, -shē-əm, -shəm) *n., pl.* **-tia** (-tē-ə, -shē-ə, -shə). **1.** An association of business organizations or financial institutions for carrying out a project requiring extensive financial resources, especially in international finance. **2.** Any association or partnership. **3.** *Law.* A married person's right to the company, help, and affection of his or her spouse. [Latin, fellowship, participation, from *consors,* partner, companion, CONSORT.]

con·spe·cif·ic (kŏn'spĭ-sĭf'ĭk) *adj. Biology.* Of the same species.

con·spec·tus (kən-spĕk'təs) *n.* **1.** A general survey of a subject. **2.** An outline or synopsis. [Latin, "view," "survey," from the past participle of *conspicere,* to observe (see **conspicuous**).]

con·spic·u·ous (kən-spĭk'yōō-əs) *adj.* **1.** Easy to notice; obvious. **2.** Attracting attention by being unusual or remarkable. [Latin *conspicuus,* from *conspicere,* to look at closely, observe : *com-* (intensive) + *specere,* to look.] **—con·spic·u·ous·ly** *adv.* **—con·spic·u·ous·ness** *n.*

conspicuous consumption *n.* Showy extravagance pursued in order to enhance one's prestige in society.

con·spir·a·cy (kən-spĭr'ə-sē) *n., pl.* **-cies. 1.** An agreement to perform together an illegal, treacherous, or evil act. **2.** A combining or acting together, as if by evil design: *a conspiracy of natural forces.*

3. *Law.* An agreement between two or more persons to commit a crime or to accomplish a legal purpose through illegal action. [Middle English *conspiracie,* from Norman French, variant of Old French *conspiration,* from Latin *conspīrātiō,* from *conspīrāre,* to CONSPIRE.]
    Synonyms: cabal, collusion, intrigue, plot.

conspiracy of silence *n.* A secret agreement that nothing should be said on a particular matter, usually in order to promote or protect the interests of the conspirators.

con·spir·a·tor (kən-spĭr'ə-tər) *n.* A person engaged in a conspiracy; a plotter.

con·spir·a·to·ri·al (kən-spĭr'ə-tôr'ē-əl, -tōr'-) *adj.* Pertaining to or suggestive of conspirators or a conspiracy: *gave me a conspiratorial wink.* **—con·spir·a·to·ri·al·ly** *adv.*

con·spire (kən-spĭr') *v.* **-spired, -spiring, -spires.** —*intr.* **1.** To plan together with another or others secretly, especially to commit an illegal or evil act. **2.** To combine or act together, especially to do harm: *factors that conspired against his re-election.* —*tr.* To plan or plot secretly. [Middle English *conspiren,* from Old French *conspirer,* from Latin *conspīrāre,* "to breathe together," agree, unite, plot : *com-,* together + *spīrāre,* to breathe, blow.] **—con·spir·er** *n.* **—con·spir·ing·ly** *adv.*

con spi·ri·to (kŏn spĭr'ĭ-tō') *adv. Music.* With spirit and vigor. Used as a direction.

const. 1. constable. **2.** constant. **3.** constitution. **4.** construction.

Const. 1. constable. **2.** constitution.

con·sta·ble (kŏn'stə-bəl, kŭn'-) *n. Abbr.* **cons., Cons., const., Const. 1.** A peace officer with less authority and smaller jurisdiction than a sheriff, empowered to serve writs and warrants and to make arrests. **2.** In medieval monarchies, an officer of high rank, usually serving as military commander in the ruler's absence. **3.** The governor of a royal castle. **4.** *British.* A policeman. [Middle English, from Old French, from Late Latin *comes stabulī,* "count of the stable" : Latin *comes,* companion, count + *stabuli,* genitive of *stabulum,* STABLE.] **—con·sta·ble·ship** *n.*

Con·sta·ble (kŭn'stə-bəl, kŏn'-), **John** (1776–1837). British landscape painter. His direct observations of nature and free use of broken color were original and influential. *The Hay Wain* (1821) is his best-known work.

con·stab·u·lar·y (kən-stăb'yə-lĕr'ē) *n., pl.* **-ies. 1.** The body of constables of a district or city. **2.** The district under the jurisdiction of a constable. **3.** An armed police force organized like a military unit. ~*adj.* Also **con·stab·u·lar** (-lər). Of or pertaining to constables or to constabularies.

Constance. See **Konstanz.**

Con·stance, Lake (kŏn'stəns). *German* **Bo·den·see** (bō'dən-zā'). Alpine lake on the border between West Germany, Austria, and Switzerland.

con·stan·cy (kŏn'stən-sē) *n.* **1.** Steadfastness in purpose or loyalty; faithfulness. **2.** An unchanging quality or state.

con·stant (kŏn'stənt) *adj.* **1. a.** Continuous; unremitting: *constant noise.* **b.** Continually recurring; persistent: *a constant worry.* **2.** Unchanging in nature, value, or extent; invariable. **3.** Steadfast in purpose, loyalty, or affection; faithful. —See Synonyms at **continual, faithful, steady.** ~*n.* **1.** A thing that is unchanging or invariable. **2.** *Abbr.* **const.** *Symbol* **c, C. a.** A quantity taken to have a fixed value in a specific mathematical context. **b.** An experimental or theoretical condition, factor, or quantity that occurs or is regarded as invariant in specific circumstances. [Middle English, from Old French, from Latin *constāns* (stem *constant-*), present participle of *constāre,* to stand together, remain steadfast : *com-,* together + *stāre,* to stand.] **—con·stant·ly** *adv.*

Con·stant (kôN-stôN'), **Benjamin** (1767–1830). French writer and political figure who wrote pamphlets defending the French Revolution, but opposed Napoleon and went into exile (1803). He had a long affair with Madame de Staël that he used as the basis for his novel *Adolphe* (1816).

con·stant·an (kŏn'stən-tăn') *n.* An alloy of copper nickel, used chiefly in electrical instruments because of its constant resistance. [Coined from CONSTANT.]

Con·stan·tine II (kŏn'stən-tēn). (1940–). King of Greece (1964–67). He went into exile after a right-wing coup by army officers (1967). Greece became a republic (1973).

Constantine the Great (c. A.D. 285–337). Roman emperor who ruled the Western Roman Empire (312–24) and became sole emperor (324–37). He adopted the Christian faith (312) and suspended the persecution of Christians. He rebuilt Constantinople (modern Istanbul) as the new Rome (330).

Con·stan·ti·no·ple (kŏn'stăn-tə-nō'pəl). Formerly **By·zan·ti·um** (bĭ-zăn'shē-əm, -tē-əm). Capital of the Byzantine Empire (330–1453) and of Turkey (1453–1923). The city was founded by Greeks in 667 B.C., captured by Roman forces in A.D. 196, and rebuilt by Constantine (330), who changed its name to Constantinople. The city enjoyed a golden age under Justinian the Great (532–62), when the church of Hagia Sophia was built. Constantinople finally fell to the Ottoman Turks (1453) and, as their capital, expanded across the Bosporus. Hagia Sophia became a mosque. In 1923 the Turkish capital was moved to Ankara and Constantinople was renamed Istanbul (1930).

Constanz. See **Konstanz.**

con·sta·ta·tion (kŏn'stə-tā'shən) *n.* **1.** The act of ascertaining or verifying. **2.** A statement or fact that has been ascertained.

Constable

RURAL SCENES FROM BOYHOOD MADE CONSTABLE A PAINTER

The artist who tried to capture nature's serenity

So influenced was John Constable (1776–1837) by his native Suffolk that the rural vistas of his boyhood became the theme of his paintings. "These scenes made me a painter, and I am grateful," he once declared. He became the greatest exponent of the English Picturesque style of painting.

Constable painted landscapes at a time when the function of artists was to represent man. He hoped to elevate the genre by replacing its conventions with what he himself called the "light-dews-breezes-bloom-and-freshness" of nature. He saw himself as a "natural" artist, but he is counted among the Romantics. His paintings exemplify the Romantic preference for color to express nature's changing moods, rather than the neoclassical ideal of purity of form and elegance of composition.

The somber moods that lowering storm clouds imposed on the landscape depressed him, and he preferred to paint nature in its more serene moments.

WEYMOUTH BAY *In this landscape painted about 1817, and in many others, Constable sought to capture in pigment scudding clouds and their shadows, and the transient reflections of light on water. His work anticipated Impressionism by more than 50 years.*

[French, from *constater,* to verify, from Latin *constat,* it is certain.]

con·stel·late (kŏn′stə-lāt′) *v.* **-lated, -lating, -lates.** —*tr.* To cause to form a group or cluster. —*intr.* To form a group or cluster. [Back-formation from CONSTELLATION.]

con·stel·la·tion (kŏn′stə-lā′shən) *n.* **1.** *Astronomy.* **a.** Any of 88 scientifically arbitrary groupings of stars as seen from Earth, considered to resemble and named after various mythological characters, inanimate objects, and animals. **b.** An area of the celestial sphere occupied by such a group. **2.** *Astrology.* The position of the stars at the time of one's birth, regarded as determining one's character or fate. **3.** A brilliant gathering or assemblage. **4.** A set or configuration of objects, properties, or individuals, especially a structurally or systematically related grouping. [Middle English *constellacioun,* from Old French *constellation,* from Late Latin *constellātiō* (stem *constellātiōn-*), group of stars : Latin *com-,* together + *stellātus,* starred, from *stella,* star.] **—con·stel·la·to·ry** (kən-stĕl′ə-tôr′ē, -tōr′ē) *adj.*

con·ster·nate (kŏn′stər-nāt′) *tr.v.* **-nated, -nating, -nates.** To fill with consternation. Usually used in the passive. [Latin *consternāre,* to stretch out, overcome, perplex : *com-* (intensive) + *sternere,* to spread out.]

con·ster·na·tion (kŏn′stər-nā′shən) *n.* Sudden confusion, amazement, or frustration.

con·sti·pate (kŏn′stə-pāt′) *tr.v.* **-pated, -pating, -pates. 1.** To cause constipation in. **2.** To repress; restrain. [Latin *constīpāre,* to press or crowd together (in Medieval Latin, "to confine the bowels") : *com-,* together + *stīpāre,* to press, cram.]

con·sti·pa·tion (kŏn′stə-pā′shən) *n.* Difficult, incomplete, or infrequent evacuation of the bowels.

con·stit·u·en·cy (kən-stĭch′o͞o-ən-sē) *n., pl.* **-cies. 1. a.** The body of voters represented by an elected legislator or executive. **b.** The district represented. **2.** Any group of supporters or people whose wishes must be considered.

con·stit·u·ent (kən-stĭch′o͞o-ənt) *adj.* **1.** Serving as part of a whole; component. **2.** Authorized to make or amend a constitution. **3.** Empowered to elect representatives.
~*n.* **1.** Someone represented by an elected official. **2.** Someone represented by another; a client. **3.** A constituent part; a component. **4.** *Grammar.* Any of the functional elements into which a construction or compound may be divided by analysis, being either immediate, as *He/ works on the railroad,* or ultimate, as *He/work/s/ on/the/rail/road.* [Latin *constituēns* (stem *constituent-*), present participle of *constituere,* to CONSTITUTE.] **—con·stit·u·ent·ly** *adv.*

con·sti·tute (kŏn′stə-to͞ot′, -tyo͞ot′) *tr.v.* **-tuted, -tuting, -tutes. 1. a.** To be the elements or parts of; make up; compose: *Ten members constitute a quorum.* **b.** To be equivalent or tantamount to: *Does this constitute a precedent?* **2.** To give legal form to (an assembly, court, or the like). **3.** To establish formally; found (an institution, for example). **4.** To set up; enact (a law, for example). **5.** To appoint to an office or task; designate. [Middle English *constituten,* from Latin *constituere,* to cause to stand, set, fix : *com-* (intensive) + *statuere,* to set up.] **—con·sti·tut·er, con·sti·tu·tor** *n.*

con·sti·tu·tion (kŏn′stə-to͞o′shən, -tyo͞o′-) *n. Abbr.* **cons., const., Const. 1.** The act or process of constituting or establishing. **2.** The composition of something made of a number of parts; make-up. **3.** A person's physical make-up as it relates to his or her characteristic state of health: *a strong constitution.* **4. a.** The system of fundamental laws and principles that prescribes the nature, functions, and limits of a government or other institution. **b.** The document in which this system is recorded. **5.** In former times, a decree or enactment. **—the Constitution.** The Constitution of the United States, adopted in 1787 and put into effect in 1789.

con·sti·tu·tion·al (kŏn′stə-to͞o′shən-əl, -tyo͞o′-) *adj. Abbr.* **cons. 1.** Of or proceeding from the basic structure or nature of a person or thing; essential. **2.** Contained in or consistent with a constitution. **3.** Regulated by or operating under a constitution. **4.** For the sake of one's general health.
~*n.* A walk taken for the sake of one's health. **—con·sti·tu·tion·al·i·ty** *n.* **—con·sti·tu·tion·al·ly** *adv.*

con·sti·tu·tion·al·ism (kŏn′stə-to͞o′shən-əl-ĭz′əm, -tyo͞o′-) *n.* **1.** Government in which power is distributed and limited by a system of laws that must be obeyed by the rulers. **2.** Advocacy of such government. **—con·sti·tu·tion·al·ist** *n.*

constitutional monarchy *n.* A monarchy in which the powers of the ruler are restricted to those granted under the constitution and laws of the nation.

con·sti·tu·tive (kŏn′stə-to͞o′tĭv, -tyo͞o′-) *adj.* **1.** Making a thing what it is; essential. **2.** Having power to institute, establish, or enact. **—con·sti·tu·tive·ly** *adv.*

constitutive enzyme *n.* An enzyme that is always present in a cell, being synthesized at a constant rate regardless of substrate.

constr. construction.

con·strain (kən-strān′) *tr.v.* **-strained, -straining, -strains. 1. a.** To compel by physical, moral, or circumstantial force; oblige. **b.** To bring about by compulsion; enforce. **2.** To keep within close bounds; confine. **3.** To check the freedom or mobility of; restrain. —See Synonyms at **force.** [Middle English *constreinen,* from Old French *constraindre,* from Latin *constringere,* to draw or bind tightly together : *com-,* together + *stringere,* to draw tight.] **—con·strain·a·ble** *adj.* **—con·strain·er** *n.*

con·strained (kən-strānd′) *adj.* **1.** Resulting from constraint; restrained. **2.** Forced; unnatural: *a constrained smile.* **—con·strain·ed·ly** (kən-strā′nĭd-lē) *adv.*

con·straint (kən-strānt′) *n.* **1.** The threat or use of force to prevent, restrict, or dictate the action or thought of others. **2.** The state or sense of being restricted to a given course of action or inaction. **3.** Something that restricts, limits, or regulates. **4.** A lack of ease; embarrassed reserve or reticence. [Middle English *constreint(e),* from Old French *constrainte,* from *constraindre,* to CONSTRAIN.]

con·strict (kən-strĭkt′) *tr.v.* **-stricted, -stricting, -stricts. 1.** To make smaller or narrower, as by shrinking or contracting. **2.** To squeeze or compress by or as if by narrowing or tightening. **3.** To limit; inhibit. —See Synonyms at **contract.** [Latin *constringere* (past participle *constrictus*), to draw or bind tightly together, CONSTRAIN.] **—con·stric·tive** *adj.* **—con·stric·tive·ly** *adv.*

con·stric·tion (kən-strĭk′shən) *n.* **1. a.** The act or process of constricting. **b.** The condition of being constricted. **2.** A feeling of pressure or tightness. **3.** A constricted or narrow part.

con·stric·tor (kən-strĭk′tər) *n.* **1.** Something that constricts. **2.** *Anatomy.* A muscle that compresses an organ or causes narrowing of a duct or passage. **3.** Any of various snakes, such as a python or boa, that coil around and crush their prey.

con·stringe (kən-strĭnj′) *tr.v.* **-stringed, -stringing, -stringes.** To cause to shrink or contract. [Latin *constringere,* to CONSTRAIN.] **—con·strin·gen·cy** *n.* **—con·strin·gent** *adj.*

con·struct (kən-strŭkt′) *tr.v.* **-structed, -structing, -structs. 1.** To form by assembling parts; build; erect. **2.** To create (an argument or sentence, for example) by systematically arranging ideas or expressions; devise with the mind. **3.** *Mathematics.* To draw (a geometric figure) according to specific requirements, usually with instruments limited to a ruler and compass.
~*n.* (kŏn′strŭkt). Something synthesized or constructed from simple elements, especially a concept. [Latin *construere* (past participle *constructus*), to pile up together, build : *com-,* together + *struere,* to pile up.] **—con·struc·tor** (kən-strŭk′tər), **con·struct·er** *n.* **—con·struct·i·ble** *adj.*

con·struc·tion (kən-strŭk′shən) *n. Abbr.* **cons., const., constr. 1. a.** The act or process of constructing. **b.** The business or work of building. Also used adjectivally: *the construction industry.* **2.** That which is constructed; a structure or building. **3.** The way in which a thing is put together; structure. **4.** The interpretation or explanation given to an action or statement. **5.** *Grammar.* The particular arrangement of words in a phrase, clause, or sentence. **—con·struc·tion·al** *adj.* **—con·struc·tion·al·ly** *adv.*

con·struc·tive (kən-strŭk′tĭv) *adj.* **1.** Serving to advance a good purpose; helpful. **2.** Of or pertaining to construction; structural. **3.** *Law.* Based on an interpretation; inferred but not directly expressed. **—con·struc·tive·ly** *adv.* **—con·struc·tive·ness** *n.*

con·struc·tiv·ism (kən-strŭk′tĭv-ĭz′əm) *n.* Also **Constructivism.** A movement in modern art that developed in Russia around 1920, in which glass, sheet metal, and other industrial materials are used to create nonrepresentational, often geometric objects. **—con·struc·tiv·ist** *adj.* & *n.*

con·strue (kən-stro͞o′) *v.* **-strued, -struing, -strues.** —*tr.* **1.** *Grammar.* **a.** To analyze the structure of (a clause or sentence). Compare **parse. b.** To use syntactically: *The noun "fish" can be construed as singular or plural.* **2.** To deduce and explain the meaning of; especially, to put a particular construction or interpretation upon: *construed his remark as offensive.* **3.** To translate, especially aloud. —*intr.* **1.** To analyze grammatical structure. **2.** To be capable of grammatical analysis. Used of a phrase or sentence.
~*n.* (kŏn′stro͞o). An interpretation or translation. [Middle English *construen,* from Late Latin *construere,* from Latin, to CONSTRUCT.]

con·sub·stan·tial (kŏn′səb-stăn′shəl) *adj.* Having the same substance, nature, or essence. [Middle English *consubstancial,* from Late Latin *consubstantiālis* : Latin *com-,* same + *substantiālis,* SUBSTANTIAL.]

con·sub·stan·ti·ate (kŏn′səb-stăn′shē-āt′) *v.* **-ated, -ating, -ates.** —*tr.* To unite in one common substance, nature, or essence. —*intr.* To become united in one common substance. [New Latin *consubstantiare* : *com-,* together + SUBSTANTIATE.]

con·sub·stan·ti·a·tion (kŏn′səb-stăn′shē-ā′shən) *n. Theology.* The Lutheran doctrine that the body and blood of Christ coexist with the elements of bread and wine during the Eucharist. Compare **transubstantiation.**

con·sue·tude (kŏn′swĭ-to͞od′, -tyo͞od′) *n. Chiefly Law.* Custom; usage; habit. [Middle English, from Latin *consuētūdo,* from *consuēscere,* to accustom : *com-* (intensive) + *suēscere,* to become accustomed.] **—con·sue·tu·di·nar·y** (kŏn′swĭ-to͞o′də-nĕr′ē, -tyo͞o′-) *adj.*

con·sul (kŏn′səl) *n. Abbr.* **c., C., Con., Cons. 1.** An official appointed by a government to reside in a foreign city and represent its commercial interests and give assistance to its citizens there. **2.** Either of the two chief magistrates of the Roman Republic, elected for a term of one year. **3.** Any of the three chief magistrates of the French Republic from 1799 to 1804. [Middle English, Roman magistrate, from Old French, from Latin *consul,* akin to *consulere,* to CONSULT.] **—con·su·lar** (kŏn′sə-lər) *adj.* **—con·sul·ship** *n.*

con·su·late (kŏn′sə-lĭt) *n.* **1.** The official premises occupied by a consul. **2.** The office or term of office of a consul. **3.** Government by, or the period of government by, consuls. [Middle English *consulat,* from Old French, from Latin *consulātus,* from *consul,* CONSUL.]

consul general *n., pl.* **consuls general.** *Abbr.* **c.g., C.G.** A consular officer of the highest rank.

con·sult (kən-sŭlt′) *v.* **-sulted, -sulting, -sults.** —*tr.* **1. a.** To seek the advice or opinion of: *consult an attorney.* **b.** To refer to: *consult*

PRONUNCIATION KEY

ă, pat; ā, pay; âr, care; ä, father, are; b, bib; ch, church; d, deed; ĕ, pet; ē, be; f, fife; g, gag; h, hat; hw, which; ĭ, pit; ī, pie; îr, pier; j, judge; k, kick; l, lid, needle; m, mum; n, no, sudden; ng, thing; ŏ, pot; ō, toe; ô, paw, for; oi, noise; ou, out; o͝o, book; o͞o, boot; p, pop; r, roar; s, sauce; sh, ship, dish; t, tight; th, thin, path; *th,* this, bathe; ŭ, cut; ûr, fur; v, valve; w, with; y, yes; z, zebra, size; zh, vision; ə, about, item, edible, gallop, circus, peaceful

IN FOREIGN WORDS:

à, *Fr.* ami; œ, *Fr.* feu, *Ger.* schön; ü, *Fr.* tu, *Ger.* über; KH, *Ger.* ich, *Scot.* loch; N, *Fr.* bon; y′, *Fr.* Compiègne

STRESS MARKS:

Primary stress: ′ **in·cite′** (ĭn-sīt′)
Secondary stress: ′ **in′sight′** (ĭn′sīt′)

a directory. **2.** To have an eye to; consider: *consult a checkbook balance before buying.* —*intr.* **1.** To exchange views; confer. Often used with *with.* **2.** To give expert advice as a professional. [Old French *consulter,* from Latin *consultāre,* frequentative of *consulere*†, to take counsel.]

con·sul·tan·cy (kən-sŭl′tən-sē) *n., pl.* **-cies.** The business or position of a consultant.

con·sul·tant (kən-sŭl′tənt) *n.* **1.** A person who gives expert or professional advice. **2.** A person who consults another. **3.** A specialist physician who is asked to confirm a diagnosis.

con·sul·ta·tion (kŏn′səl-tā′shən) *n.* **1.** The act or procedure of consulting. **2.** A conference at which advice is given or views are exchanged.

con·sul·ta·tive (kən-sŭl′tə-tĭv) *adj.* Of or pertaining to consultation; advisory.

con·sult·ing (kən-sŭl′tĭng) *adj.* Acting in an advisory capacity in a specialized field: *a consulting engineer.*

consulting room *n.* A room in which a doctor sees patients.

con·sume (kən-so͞om′) *v.* **-sumed, -suming, -sumes.** —*tr.* **1.** To eat or drink up; ingest. **2.** To use up; expend: *consume fuel.* **3.** To waste; squander. **4.** To destroy totally, especially by fire. **5.** To absorb completely; engross: *consumed with curiosity.* —*intr.* To be destroyed or expended; waste away. [Middle English *consumen,* from Old French *consumer,* from Latin *consūmere,* to take completely, consume : *com-* (intensive) + *sūmere,* to take up.] —**con·sum·a·ble** *adj.* & *n.*

con·sum·ed·ly (kən-so͞o′mĭd-lē) *adv.* Excessively.

con·sum·er (kən-so͞o′mər) *n.* **1.** One that consumes. **2.** *Economics.* One who acquires goods or services; a buyer. **3.** *Ecology.* An organism, such as an animal or insectivorous plant, that feeds on other organisms. Compare **producer.**

consumer credit *n. Economics.* Credit granted to a consumer, permitting the individual to own or use goods while making payments on them.

consumer goods *pl.n. Economics.* Goods, such as food, clothing, or household appliances, that directly satisfy human wants, as distinguished from those used in the production of other goods. Compare **capital goods.**

con·sum·er·ism (kən-so͞o′mə-rĭz′əm) *n.* **1.** Protection of the interests of the consumer, as through fair advertising, improved safety standards, and honest packaging. **2.** *Economics.* The theory that a progressively greater consumption of goods is economically desirable. —**con·sum·er·ist** *n.* & *adj.*

consumer price index *n.* An index of prices used to measure the change in the cost of basic goods and services in comparison with a fixed base period. Also called "cost-of-living index."

consumer research *n.* Investigation into what purchasers of goods and services buy and what they require.

con·sum·mate (kŏn′sə-māt′) *tr.v.* **-mated, -mating, -mates.** **1.** To bring to completion, perfection, or fulfillment; conclude: *consummate a business transaction.* **2.** To fulfill (a marriage) with the first act of sexual intercourse after the ceremony.
~*adj.* (kən-sŭm′ĭt, kŏn′sə-mĭt). **1.** Supremely accomplished or skilled: *a consummate artist.* **2.** Completely perfect: *consummate happiness.* **3.** Total, utter: *a consummate bore.* [Middle English *consummaten,* from Latin *consummāre,* to bring together, sum up : *com-,* together + *summa,* a SUM.] —**con·sum·mate·ly** *adv.* —**con·sum·ma·tive** (kŏn′sə-mā′tĭv, kən-sŭm′ə-tĭv), *adj.* —**con·sum·ma·tor** (kŏn′sə-mā′tər) *n.*

con·sum·ma·tion (kŏn′sə-mā′shən) *n.* **1.** The act of consummating, especially the consummating of a marriage. **2.** An ultimate end or goal.

con·sump·tion (kən-sŭmp′shən) *n.* **1. a.** The act or process of consuming. **b.** The state of being consumed. **2.** The amount consumed. **3.** *Economics.* The using up of consumer goods and services. **4.** A wasting away of the body, especially as caused by tuberculosis of the lungs. [Middle English *consumpcioun,* from Old French *consumption,* from Latin *consūmptiō,* from *consūmere,* to CONSUME.]

con·sump·tive (kən-sŭmp′tĭv) *adj.* **1.** Tending to consume; wasteful; destructive. **2.** Pertaining to or afflicted with consumption, especially tuberculosis of the lungs.
~*n.* A person afflicted with tuberculosis of the lungs.

cont. **1.** containing. **2.** contents. **3.** continent; continental. **4.** continue; continued. **5.** contract. **6.** contraction.

con·tact (kŏn′tăkt) *n.* **1. a.** The coming together of objects or surfaces so that there is no space between them. **b.** The fact or relation of not being separated by space or another object. **2.** The state of being in communication: *in contact with the doctor.* **3.** An acquaintance who might be of use; a connection. **4.** *Electricity.* **a.** A connection between two conductors that permits a flow of current. **b.** A part or device that makes or breaks such a connection. **5.** *Medicine.* A person exposed to a contagious disease and potentially able to transmit it. **6.** A contact lens.
~*v.* (kŏn′tăkt, kən-tăkt′) **contacted, -tacting, -tacts.** —*tr.* **1.** To bring into contact. **2.** To communicate with: *Contact your lawyer.* —*intr.* To be in or come into contact.
~*adj.* (kŏn′tăkt). **1.** Of, sustaining, or making contact. **2. a.** Caused or transmitted by contact: *a contact skin rash.* **b.** Activated or operating by means of contact: *a contact insecticide.* [Latin *contāctus,* from the past participle of *contingere,* to touch, border upon, attain to : *com-,* together + *tangere,* to touch.] —**con·tac·tu·al** (kən-tăk′cho͞o-əl) *adj.* —**con·tac·tu·al·ly** *adv.*

contact dermatitis *n.* Inflammation of the skin caused by direct contact with an irritating substance, especially a chemical.

contact flight *n.* Aircraft navigation by visual reference to the horizon or to landmarks. Also called "contact flying."

contact lens *n.* A thin corrective lens fitted over the cornea.

contact print *n.* A photographic print made by exposing a photosensitive surface that is in direct contact with the negative.

con·ta·gion (kən-tā′jən) *n.* **1.** Disease transmission by direct or indirect contact. **2.** A disease that is or may be so transmitted. **3.** A contagium. **4.** A harmful or corrupting influence. **5.** The tendency to spread, as of an idea or emotional state: *the contagion of laughter.* [Middle English *contagioun,* from Old French *contagion,* from Latin *contāgiō* (stem *contāgiōn-*), from *contingere,* to touch, touch with pollution, CONTACT.]

con·ta·gious (kən-tā′jəs) *adj.* **1.** Transmissible by direct or indirect contact; communicable. Said of certain diseases. **2.** Carrying or capable of carrying disease. **3.** Spreading or tending to spread from one to another; catching. Compare **infectious.** —**con·ta·gious·ly** *adv.* —**con·ta·gious·ness** *n.*

contagious abortion *n.* **Brucellosis** *(see)* of cattle.

con·ta·gi·um (kən-tā′jē-əm) *n., pl.* **-gia** (-jē-ə). The direct cause, such as a virus, of a communicable disease. [Latin, from *contāgiō,* CONTAGION.]

con·tain (kən-tān′) *tr.v.* **-tained, -taining, -tains.** **1.** To have within; enclose. **2.** To have as component parts; comprise; include. **3.** To be able to hold; have capacity for. **4.** *Mathematics.* To be exactly divisible by. **5.** To hold or keep within limits; restrain; confine: *contain one's emotions.* **6.** To prevent the expansion of (a country or power bloc, for example), as by encircling it with hostile alliances. [Middle English *conteinen,* from Old French *contenir,* from Latin *continēre,* to hold together, enclose, contain : *com-,* together + *tenēre,* to hold.] —**con·tain·a·ble** *adj.*
Synonyms: *accommodate, hold.*

con·tain·er (kən-tā′nər) *n.* **1.** One that contains; especially, something used for holding or carrying, such as a box. **2.** A large, usually rectangular, receptacle used for transporting cargo.

con·tain·er·ize (kən-tā′nər-īz′) *tr.v* **-ized, -izing, -izes.** To package (cargo) in large, standardized containers to facilitate shipping and handling. —**con·tain·er·i·za·tion** *n.*

container ship *n.* A ship specially designed for transporting containerized cargo.

con·tain·ment (kən-tān′mənt) *n.* The act of containing; especially, the act or policy of keeping a hostile power or bloc within existing limits of influence.

con·tam·i·nant (kən-tăm′ə-nənt) *n.* Something that contaminates.

con·tam·i·nate (kən-tăm′ə-nāt′) *tr.v.* **-nated, -nating, -nates.** **1.** To make impure or corrupt by contact or mixture. **2.** To expose to radioactivity. [Middle English *contaminaten,* from Latin *contāmināre.*] —**con·tam·i·na·tive** *adj.* —**con·tam·i·na·tor** (kən-tăm′ə-nā′tər) *n.*

con·tam·i·na·tion (kən-tăm′ə-nā′shən) *n.* **1. a.** The act or process of contaminating. **b.** The state of being contaminated. **2.** One that contaminates; an impurity. **3.** The alteration of a word form through association with a related form. For example, *miniscule* is a contamination of *minuscule* through association with *miniature.*

con·tan·go (kən-tăng′gō) *n., pl.* **-gos.** **1.** On the London Stock Exchange, an arrangement whereby the settlement for the delivery of stock is carried forward from one account to the next. **2.** The fee paid for this postponement. [19th century : arbitrary coinage apparently based on *continuation.*]

contd. continued.

conte (kônt) *n., pl.* **contes** (kônt). A short story; especially, a tale of adventure. [French, from Old French *conter, compter,* COUNT (to relate).]

con·temn (kən-tĕm′) *tr.v.* **-temned, -temning, -temns.** To view with contempt; despise. [Middle English *contempnen,* from Old French *contem(p)ner,* from Latin *contemnere* : *com-* (intensive) + *temnere*†, to despise.] —**con·temn·er** (kən-tĕm′ər, -tĕm′nər) *n.*

con·tem·plate (kŏn′təm-plāt′) *v.* **-plated, -plating, -plates.** —*tr.* **1.** To look at pensively: *contemplate the stars.* **2.** To ponder or consider thoughtfully. **3.** To have in mind as a purpose; intend: *contemplate marriage.* **4.** To regard as possible; take seriously. —*intr.* To engage in serious thought, especially about spiritual matters; meditate. —See Synonyms at **see.** [Latin *contemplārī,* to observe carefully (originally a term of augury) : *com-* (intensive) + *templum,* open space marked out by augurs for observation.] —**con·tem·pla·tor** *n.* —**con·tem·pla·tion** *n.*

con·tem·pla·tive (kən-tĕm′plə-tĭv, kŏn′təm-plā′-) *adj.* **1.** Disposed to or characterized by contemplation. **2.** Devoted to religious contemplation. —See Usage note at **pensive.**
~*n.* **1.** A person given to contemplation. **2.** A member of a religious order dedicated to meditation. —**con·tem·pla·tive·ly** *adv.* —**con·tem·pla·tive·ness** *n.*

con·tem·po·ra·ne·ous (kən-tĕm′pə-rā′nē-əs) *adj.* Originating, existing, or happening during the same period of time: *The reign of Philip II was contemporaneous with that of Elizabeth I.* —See Synonyms at **contemporary.** [Latin *contemporāneus* : *com-,* same + *tempus* (stem *tempor-*), time.] —**con·tem·po·ra·ne·i·ty** (kən-tĕm′pə-rə-nē′ə-tē, -nā′ə-tē), **con·tem·po·ra·ne·ous·ness** *n.* —**con·tem·po·ra·ne·ous·ly** *adv.*

con·tem·po·rar·y (kən-tĕm′pə-rĕr′ē) *adj.* **1.** Belonging to the same period of time: *a fact documented by two contemporary sources.* **2.** Of about the same age. **3. a.** Belonging to the present time; current. **b.** Very modern; up-to-date.

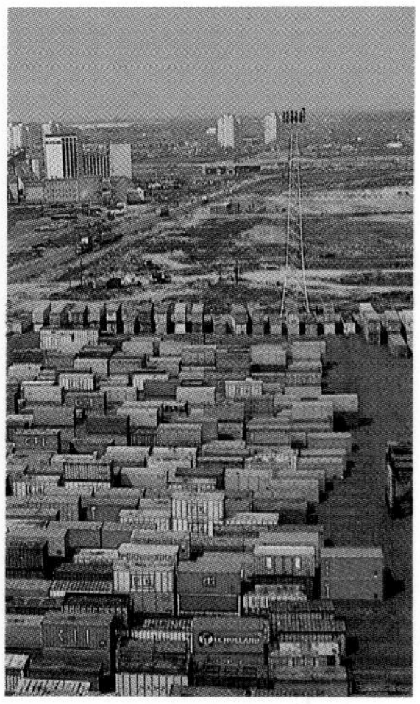

container *Rows of containers fill a dockyard in London. Containers were introduced in the 1960's to speed the movement of freight and make it easier to transfer goods between ships, trains, airplanes, and trucks.*

~*n., pl.* **-ies. 1.** One belonging to the same period of time as another. **2.** A person of about the same age as another. **3.** A modern. [Medieval Latin *contemporārius* : Latin *com-*, together + *tempus* (stem *tempor-*), time (see **temporal**).]

Synonyms: *coincident, concomitant, concurrent, contemporaneous, simultaneous, synchronous.*

Usage: When *contemporary* is used in reference to something in the past, its meaning is not always clear. *Contemporary critics of Shakespeare* may mean critics in his time or critics in our time. When the context does not make the meaning clear, misunderstanding may be avoided by using such phrases as "critics in Shakespeare's time" or "modern critics."

con·tem·po·rize (kən-tĕm'pə-rīz') *tr.v.* **-rized, -rizing, -rizes.** To relate in time; synchronize. [From CONTEMPORARY (after TEMPORIZE).]

con·tempt (kən-tĕmpt') *n.* **1.** Reproachful disdain, as for something vile or dishonorable; bitter scorn. **2.** The state of being scorned, despised, or dishonored: *hold someone in contempt.* **3.** Open disrespect or willful disobedience of the authority of a court of law or a legislative body. Also called "contempt of court." [Middle English, from Latin *contemptus,* from the past participle of *contemnere,* to CONTEMN.]

con·tempt·i·ble (kən-tĕmp'tə-bəl) *adj.* Deserving contempt; despicable. **—con·tempt·i·bil·i·ty, con·tempt·i·ble·ness** *n.* **—con·tempt·i·bly** *adv.*

con·temp·tu·ous (kən-tĕmp'chŏo-əs) *adj.* Manifesting or feeling contempt; scornful; disdainful: *contemptuous of her wealth.* **—con·temp·tu·ous·ly** *adv.* **—con·temp·tu·ous·ness** *n.*

con·tend (kən-tĕnd') *v.* **-tended, -tending, -tends.** *—intr.* **1.** To strive, as in battle; fight. **2.** To compete, as in a contest; vie. **3.** To strive in controversy or debate; dispute. *—tr.* To maintain or assert. **—See Synonyms at discuss.** [Middle English *contenden,* from Old French *contendre,* from Latin *contendere,* to strain, strive with : *com-*, with + *tendere,* to stretch, strain, strive.]

con·tend·er (kən-tĕn'dər) *n.* One who takes part in a contest, as for a championship or political office.

con·tent¹ (kŏn'tĕnt) *n.* **1.** *Abbr.* **cont.** *Usually* **contents.** That which is contained in a receptacle: *the content of a drawer.* **2. a.** *Sometimes* **contents.** The subject matter, as of a book or speech. **b. contents.** The chapter or other division headings of a book or document: *table of contents.* **3.** The meaning or significance of a literary or artistic work, as distinguished from its form. **4.** Ability to receive and hold; capacity. **5.** The amount held; volume. **6.** The proportion of a specified substance: *a high fat content.* [Middle English, from Medieval Latin *contentum,* from Latin *contentus,* past participle of *continēre,* to CONTAIN.]

con·tent² (kən-tĕnt') *adj.* **1.** Not desiring more than what one has; satisfied. **2.** Resigned to circumstances. *~tr.v.* **contented, -tenting, -tents.** To make content or satisfied. **—content oneself with.** To limit oneself to: *He contented himself with one slice of cake.* *~n.* **1.** Contentment; satisfaction. **2.** *British.* An affirmative vote or voter in the House of Lords. [Middle English, from Old French, from Latin *contentus,* restrained, satisfied, past participle of *continēre,* to restrain, CONTAIN.]

con·tent·ed (kən-tĕn'tĭd) *adj.* Satisfied with things as they are; content. **—con·tent·ed·ly** *adv.* **—con·tent·ed·ness** *n.*

con·ten·tion (kən-tĕn'shən) *n.* **1.** A verbal struggling; dispute; controversy. **2.** A striving to win in competition; a state of rivalry. **3.** An assertion put forward in argument. **—See Synonyms at discord.** [Middle English *contencioun,* from Old French *contention,* from Latin *contentiō* (stem *contentiōn-*), from *contendere,* CONTEND.]

con·ten·tious (kən-tĕn'shəs) *adj.* **1.** Given to contention; quarrelsome. **2.** Involving or likely to cause contention; controversial. **—See Synonyms at belligerent. —con·ten·tious·ly** *adv.* **—con·ten·tious·ness** *n.*

con·tent·ment (kən-tĕnt'mənt) *n.* The state of being contented; satisfaction.

con·ter·mi·nous (kən-tûr'mə-nəs) *adj.* Also **co·ter·mi·nous** (kō-). **1.** Having a boundary in common; contiguous. **2.** Contained in the same boundaries; coextensive. [Latin *conterminus* : *com-*, together + *terminus,* boundary, limit.] **—con·ter·mi·nous·ly** *adv.*

con·tes·sa (kən-tĕs'ə) *n.* An Italian countess. [Italian.]

con·test (kŏn'tĕst) *n.* **1.** A struggle for superiority or victory between rivals. **2.** A dispute; a debate. **3.** Any competition; especially, one in which entrants perform separately and are rated by judges. **—See Synonyms at conflict.** *~v.* (kən-tĕst', kŏn'tĕst) **contested, -testing, -tests.** *—tr.* **1.** To compete or strive for: *Six candidates contested the seat at the last election.* **2.** To attempt to disprove or invalidate; dispute; challenge: *contest a will.* *—intr.* To struggle or compete; contend. **—See Synonyms at oppose.** [Old French *conteste,* from *contester,* from Latin *contestārī,* bring in (a lawsuit) by calling witnesses (from both parties) : *com-*, together + *testārī,* to bear witness, from *testis,* a witness.] **—con·test·a·ble** *adj.* **—con·test·er** *n.*

con·test·ant (kən-tĕs'tənt) *n.* **1.** One who takes part in a contest; a competitor. **2.** One who contests something, such as an election or a will.

con·tes·ta·tion (kŏn'tĕs-tā'shən) *n.* Controversy; disputation.

con·text (kŏn'tĕkst) *n.* **1.** The part of a written or spoken statement that surrounds a particular word or passage and can clarify its meaning. **2.** The circumstances in which something occurs or exists; background or setting. [Middle English, from Latin *contextus,*

coherence, sequence of words, from the past participle of *contexere,* to join together, weave : *com-*, together + *texere,* to join, weave, plait.]

con·tex·tu·al (kən-tĕks'chŏo-əl) *adj.* Of, pertaining to, or depending upon the context. **—con·tex·tu·al·ly** *adv.*

con·tex·tu·al·ize (kən-tĕks'chŏo-əl-īz') *—tr.v.* **-ized, -izing, -izes.** To place (a word, an idea, or an activity, for example) in an appropriate context. **—con·tex·tu·al·i·za·tion** *n.*

con·tex·ture (kən-tĕks'chər) *n.* **1.** The act of weaving or assembling parts. **2.** An arrangement of interconnected parts; a structure. **—con·tex·tur·al, con·tex·tured** *adj.*

con·ti·gu·i·ty (kŏn'tĭ-gyŏo'ə-tē) *n., pl.* **-ties. 1.** The state of being contiguous. **2.** A continuous mass or series.

con·tig·u·ous (kən-tĭg'yŏo-əs) *adj.* **1.** Sharing an edge or boundary; touching. **2.** Nearby; neighboring; adjacent. **3.** Adjacent in time; immediately preceding or following. [Latin *contiguus,* from *contingere,* to touch on all sides, CONTACT.] **—con·tig·u·ous·ly** *adv.* **—con·tig·u·ous·ness** *n.*

con·ti·nence (kŏn'tə-nəns) *n.* **1.** Self-restraint; moderation. **2.** Control of the bodily functions of urination and defecation. **3.** Partial or complete abstention from sexual activity. **—See Synonyms at abstinence.**

con·ti·nent¹ (kŏn'tə-nənt) *n.* **1.** *Abbr.* **cont.** One of the principal land masses of the earth, usually regarded as including Africa, Antarctica, Asia, Australia, Europe, North America, and South America. **2.** *Archaic.* A thing that holds or retains. **—the Continent.** The mainland of Europe. [Latin *(terra) continēns* (stem *continent-*), "continuous (land)," from the present participle of *continēre,* to hold together, continue. See **continent** (adjective).]

continent² *adj.* **1.** Self-restrained; moderate. **2.** Able to control the bodily functions of urination and defecation. **3.** Partially or completely abstaining from sexual activity. [Middle English, from Old French, from Latin *continēns* (stem *continent-*), present participle of *continēre,* to hold together, CONTAIN.] **—con·ti·nent·ly** *adv.*

con·ti·nen·tal (kŏn'tə-nĕn'təl) *adj.* **1.** Of, pertaining to, or characteristic of a continent. **2.** *Usually* **Continental.** Of or relating to the mainland of Europe; European. **3. Continental.** Of or pertaining to the American colonies during and immediately after the Revolutionary War. *~n. Usually* **Continental. 1.** An inhabitant of the mainland of Europe; a European. **2. Continental.** A soldier in the Continental Army during the Revolutionary War. **3.** A piece of paper money issued by the Continental Congress during the Revolutionary War. **—con·ti·nen·tal·ly** *adv.*

continental breakfast *n.* A light meal consisting of rolls, usually with butter and jam, and coffee.

Continental Congress *n.* Either of two American legislative assemblies that governed the United States during the Revolutionary era. The first convened in 1774 to voice grievances against Great Britain. The second, convening in 1775, established the Continental Army and served as both the legislative and the executive arm of the government until the Constitution took effect in 1789.

continental divide *n.* **1.** An extensive stretch of high ground from each side of which the river systems of a continent flow in opposite directions. **2. Continental Divide.** In North America, such a stretch formed by the crests of the Rocky Mountains. In this sense, also called "Great Divide."

continental drift *n.* The theory that the earth's continents are not fixed in position but move slowly over the surface of the earth, their present positions resulting from the break-up of a single landmass about 200 million years ago. See **plate tectonics.**

continental shelf *n.* A generally shallow, flat submerged portion of a continent, extending to a point of steep descent to the ocean floor.

con·tin·gence (kən-tĭn'jəns) *n.* **1.** A joining or touching. **2.** The condition of contingency.

con·tin·gen·cy (kən-tĭn'jən-sē) *n., pl.* **-cies. 1. a.** An event that may occur but that is not certain or intended; a possibility. **b.** A possibility that must be prepared against; a future emergency. Sometimes used adjectivally: *a contingency fund.* **2.** The condition of being dependent upon chance; uncertainty; fortuitousness. **3.** Something incidental to something else. **4.** *Statistics.* The degree of association between theoretical and observed frequencies of certain types of variable.

con·tin·gent (kən-tĭn'jənt) *adj.* **1.** Likely but not certain to occur; possible. **2.** Dependent upon conditions or events not yet established; conditional. Often used with *on* or *upon.* **3.** Happening by chance or accident; fortuitous. **4.** *Philosophy.* Neither necessarily true nor necessarily false. Said of a proposition. *~n.* **1.** A contingency. **2.** A share or quota, as of troops, contributed to a general effort. **3.** A representative group forming part of a larger group. [Middle English, from Old French, from Latin *contingēns* (stem *contingent-*), present participle of *contingere,* to touch on all sides, happen, CONTACT.] **—con·tin·gent·ly** *adv.*

con·tin·u·al (kən-tĭn'yŏo-əl) *adj.* **1.** Repeated regularly and frequently; recurring often: *continual interruptions.* **2.** Continuing indefinitely; unending; incessant: *a source of continual worry.* **—con·tin·u·al·ly** *adv.*

Synonyms: *ceaseless, constant, continuous, eternal, incessant, interminable, perennial, perpetual.*

con·tin·u·ance (kən-tĭn'yŏo-əns) *n.* **1.** The act or fact of continuing. **2.** The time during which something exists or lasts; duration. **3.** A continuation; a sequel. **4.** *Law.* Adjournment to a future date.

Usage: *Continuance,* except in its legal sense, and *continuation* are sometimes interchangeable; but usually the former emphasizes the duration of a condition (*a machine's continuance in working order*), whereas the latter stresses prolongation or resumption of action (*the continuation of the story*).

con·tin·u·ant (kən-tĭn′yo͞o-ənt) *n. Phonetics.* A consonant, such as *s*, *z*, or *f*, that may be prolonged as long as the breath lasts without a change in quality. Compare **stop.** [French, from Latin *continuāns* (stem *continuant-*), present participle of *continuāre*, to CONTINUE.]

con·tin·u·a·tion (kən-tĭn′yo͞o-ā′shən) *n.* **1. a.** The act or fact of continuing. **b.** The state of being continued. —See Usage note at **continuance. 2.** A part by which something is carried on or extended; a supplement or sequel.

con·tin·u·a·tive (kən-tĭn′yo͞o-ā′tĭv) *adj.* **1.** Serving to continue or cause continuation. **2.** *Grammar.* Expressing continuation. Said of a word or clause.
~*n.* Something that expresses or causes continuation. —**con·tin·u·a·tive·ly** *adv.*

con·tin·u·a·tor (kən-tĭn′yo͞o-ā′tər) *n.* One that continues; especially, a person who resumes the work of another.

con·tin·ue (kən-tĭn′yo͞o) *v.* **-ued, -uing, -ues.** —*intr.* **1.** To exist over a prolonged period; last; persist. **2.** To exist over an extended space; extend. **3.** To remain in the same state, capacity, or place. **4.** To go on after an interruption; resume. —*tr.* **1.** To carry forward; keep up; persist in. **2.** To carry further in time, space, or development; extend. **3.** To carry on after an interruption; resume. **4.** *Law.* To postpone (a trial or other legal proceeding). [Middle English *continuen*, from Old French *continuer*, from Latin *continuāre*, from *continuus*, continuous, from *continēre*, to hold together, be continuous, CONTAIN.] —**con·tin·u·a·ble** *adj.* —**con·tin·u·er** *n.*

continuing education *n.* **1.** An educational program that brings participants up to date in a particular field. **2.** A course of study designed for part-time adult students.

con·ti·nu·i·ty (kŏn′tə-no͞o′ə-tē, -nyo͞o′-) *n., pl.* **-ties. 1.** The state or quality of being continuous. **2.** An uninterrupted succession; an unbroken course. **3. a.** A detailed script or scenario consulted to avoid errors and prevent discrepancies from shot to shot in a film. **b.** Spoken matter serving to link parts of a radio or television program so that no break occurs.

con·tin·u·o (kən-tĭn′yo͞o-ō) *n., pl.* **-os.** A bass part, typically played on a stringed or keyboard instrument, in which numerals indicate the successive chords, the actual notes played being left to the performer. Also called "basso continuo," "figured bass." [Italian, "continuous."]

con·tin·u·ous (kən-tĭn′yo͞o-əs) *adj.* **1.** Extending or prolonged without interruption or cessation; unceasing. **2.** *Mathematics.* Designating a function in which no sudden changes in value occur as the variable increases or decreases gradually. **3.** *Grammar.* **Progressive** (*see*). —See Synonyms at **continual.** [Latin *continuus*, from *continēre*, to hold together, CONTINUE.] —**con·tin·u·ous·ly** *adv.* —**con·tin·u·ous·ness** *n.*

continuous assessment *n.* Assessment of a student's work throughout a course, as opposed, for example, to assessment based solely on a final examination.

continuous creation *n.* The hypothesis that the universe did not start at a particular instant but has been continuously created throughout time. This hypothesis is a part of the **steady-state theory** (*see*).

continuous spectrum *n. Physics.* A spectrum having no breaks, especially a spectrum of radiation distributed over an uninterrupted range of wavelengths.

con·tin·u·ous-wave (kən-tĭn′yo͞o-əs-wāv′) *adj. Abbr.* **cw, CW** Emitting or capable of emitting continuously; not pulsed. Said especially of lasers.

con·tin·u·um (kən-tĭn′yo͞o-əm) *n., pl.* **-tinua** (-tĭn′yo͞o-ə) or **-tinuums. 1.** A continuous extent, succession, or whole, no part of which can be distinguished from neighboring parts except by arbitrary division. **2.** *Mathematics.* A set having the same number of points as all the real numbers in an interval. [Latin, neuter of *continuus*, CONTINUOUS.]

con·tort (kən-tôrt′) *v.* **-torted, -torting, -torts.** —*tr.* To twist or bend severely out of shape. —*intr.* To become twisted into a strained shape or expression: *His face contorted with pain.* —See Usage note at **distort.** [Latin *contorquēre* (past participle *contortus*), to twist together : *com-*, together + *torquēre*, to twist.] —**con·tor·tion** *n.* —**con·tor·tive** *adj.*

con·tort·ed (kən-tôr′tĭd) *adj.* **1.** Twisted or strained out of shape. **2.** *Botany.* Twisted or bent upon itself. —**con·tort·ed·ly** *adv.* —**con·tort·ed·ness** *n.*

con·tor·tion·ist (kən-tôr′shən-ĭst) *n.* An acrobat who can twist his body into extraordinary positions. —**con·tor·tion·is·tic** *adj.*

con·tour (kŏn′to͞or) *n.* **1.** The outline of a figure, body, or mass; shape. **2.** A line that represents such an outline. **3.** Often **contours.** A surface, especially a curving form. **4.** A **contour line** (*see*). —See Synonyms at **form.**
~*tr.v.* **contoured, -touring, -tours. 1.** To make or shape the outline of; represent in contour. **2.** To build (a road, for example) to follow the contour of the land.
~*adj.* **1.** Following the contour lines of uneven terrain to limit erosion of topsoil: *contour plowing.* **2.** Shaped to fit the outline or form of something. [French, from Italian *contorno*, from *contornare*, to go around, draw in outline : *con-* (intensive), from Latin *con-*, *com-* + *tornare*, to turn in a lathe, from Latin *tornāre*, from *tornus*, lathe, from Greek *tornos*.]

contour feather *n.* Any of the outermost feathers of a bird, forming the visible body contour and plumage.

contour line *n.* An imaginary line, or its representation on a contour map, joining points of equal elevation.

contour map *n.* A map showing elevations and surface configuration by means of contour lines.

contr. 1. contract. **2.** contraction. **3.** contralto.

con·tra (kŏn′trə) *prep.* **1.** Against. Used chiefly in the phrase *pro and contra.* **2.** Contrary to the view or evidence of: *They believe, contra recent opinion polls, that they can win the election.* [Latin.]

contra– *prefix.* Indicates: **1.** Against, opposing, or contrary; for example, **contradistinction, contraindicate. 2.** Pitched next below a specified musical instrument; for example, **contrabassoon.** [Middle English, from Latin *contrā-*, from *contrā*, against.]

con·tra·band (kŏn′trə-bănd′) *n.* **1.** Goods prohibited by law or treaty from being imported or exported. **2. a.** Illegal traffic in such goods; smuggling. **b.** Smuggled goods. **3.** *International Law.* Goods that may be confiscated by a belligerent if supplied to another belligerent by a neutral. Also called "contraband of war." **4.** During the Civil War, an escaped slave who fled to or was taken behind Union lines. [French *contrebande*, from Italian *contrabbando* : *contra-*, against, from Latin *contrā-* + *bando*, proclamation, from Late Latin *bannus, bannum*.] —**con·tra·band** *adj.* —**con·tra·band·ist** *n.*

con·tra·bass (kŏn′trə-bās′) *n. Music.* A **double bass** (*see*).
~*adj. Music.* Pitched an octave below the normal bass range. [Obsolete Italian *contrabasso* : *contra-*, pitched below, from Latin *contrā-*, against + *basso*, low, bass, from Late Latin *bassus*.] —**con·tra·bass·ist** *n.*

con·tra·bas·soon (kŏn′trə-bə-so͞on′) *n.* The largest and lowest-pitched of the double-reed wind musical instruments, sounding an octave below the bassoon. Also called "double bassoon."

con·tra·cep·tion (kŏn′trə-sĕp′shən) *n.* Prevention of conception; birth control. [CONTRA- + (CON)CEPTION.]

con·tra·cep·tive (kŏn′trə-sĕp′tĭv) *adj.* Capable of preventing conception.
~*n.* A contraceptive agent or device, such as a condom.

con·tract (kŏn′trăkt′) *n. Abbr.* **contr., cont. 1.** An agreement between two or more parties, especially one that is written and enforceable by law. **2.** The writing or document containing such an agreement. **3.** The branch of law dealing with contracts. **4.** An agreement by which property is transferred; a conveyance. **5.** Marriage as a formal agreement; betrothal. **6.** In the game of bridge: **a.** The last and highest bid of one hand. **b.** The number of tricks thus bid. **7.** *Slang.* An arrangement to kill someone for a fee.
~*v.* (kən-trăkt′, kŏn′trăkt′) **contracted, -tracting, -tracts.** —*tr.* **1.** To enter into by contract; establish or settle by formal agreement. **2. a.** To acquire or incur (a debt, for example). **b.** To catch (a disease). **3.** To reduce in size by drawing together; shrink. **4.** To pull together; wrinkle. **5.** To shorten (a word or words) by omitting or combining some of the letters or sounds: *to contract "I am" to "I'm."* —*intr.* **1.** To enter into or make a contract. **2.** To become reduced in size by or as if by being drawn together. —**contract out.** To arrange to purchase (services, for example) by contract. [Middle English, from Old French, from Latin *contractus*, from the past participle of *contrahere*, to draw together, bring about, enter into an agreement : *com-*, together + *trahere*, to draw.] —**con·tract·i·bil·i·ty** *n.* —**con·tract·i·ble** *adj.*

Synonyms: *compress, condense, constrict, contract, shrink.*

contract bridge *n.* A form of auction bridge in which tricks in excess of the contract may not count toward game. Compare **auction bridge.**

con·trac·tile (kən-trăk′təl) *adj.* Capable of contracting or causing contraction. —**con·trac·til·i·ty** (kŏn′trăk-tĭl′ə-tē) *n.*

contractile root *n.* A specialized root formed by certain bulbs and corms that pulls the bulb or corm down to the appropriate depth in the soil.

contractile vacuole *n.* A vesicle found in many protozoa that expels water to the exterior and so regulates osmosis.

con·trac·tion (kən-trăk′shən) *n. Abbr.* **cont., contr. 1.** The act of contracting or the state of being contracted. **2.** *Grammar.* **a.** A shortened word or words formed by omitting or combining some of the letters or sounds; for example, *isn't* for *is not.* **b.** The formation of such a word. **3.** *Physiology.* The shortening and thickening of functioning muscle, especially that which occurs in childbirth. **4.** *Medicine.* Any abnormal, often irreversible, shrinking or shortening of a body or part. **5.** *Physics.* A decrease in size caused by a reduction in temperature.

con·trac·tor (kŏn′trăk′tər, kən-trăk′tər) *n.* **1.** One who agrees to furnish materials or perform services at a specific price, especially in the building trade. **2.** Something that contracts, especially a muscle.

con·trac·tu·al (kən-trăk′cho͞o-əl) *adj.* Of, connected with, or having the nature of a contract.

con·trac·ture (kən-trăk′chər) *n.* A drawing together, as of muscle or scar tissue, resulting in distortion or deformity.

contradance. Variant of **contredanse.**

con·tra·dict (kŏn′trə-dĭkt′) *v.* **-dicted, -dicting, -dicts.** —*tr.* **1.** To assert or express the opposite of (a statement). **2.** To deny the statement or assertions of. **3.** To be contrary to; be inconsistent with: *His actions contradict his beliefs.* —*intr.* To utter a contradictory statement. —See Synonyms at **deny.** [Latin *contrādīcere*, to speak against : *contrā-*, against + *dīcere*, to speak.] —**con·tra·dict·a·ble** *adj.* —**con·tra·dict·er, con·tra·dic·tor** *n.*

con·tra·dic·tion (kŏn′trə-dĭk′shən) *n.* **1. a.** The act of contradicting.

b. The state of being in disagreement or opposition. **2.** A statement that contradicts; a denial. **3.** Inconsistency or discrepancy. **4.** Something that contains contradictory elements: *a contradiction in terms.*

con·tra·dic·tious (kŏn′trə-dĭk′shəs) *adj.* Tending to contradict; argumentative.

con·tra·dic·to·ry (kŏn′trə-dĭk′tə-rē) *adj.* **1.** Involving or having the nature of a contradiction; mutually inconsistent. **2.** Given to contradicting. —See Synonyms at **opposite.**
∼*n., pl.* **contradictories.** *Logic.* Either of two propositions related in such a way that it is impossible for both to be true or both to be false. Compare **contrary.** —**con·tra·dic·to·ri·ly** *adv.* —**con·tra·dic·to·ri·ness** *n.*

con·tra·dis·tinc·tion (kŏn′trə-dĭ-stĭngk′shən) *n.* Distinction by contrast or opposing qualities. —**con·tra·dis·tinc·tive** *adj.* —**con·tra·dis·tinc·tive·ly** *adv.*

con·tra·dis·tin·guish (kŏn′trə-dĭ-stĭng′gwĭsh) *tr.v.* **-guished, -guishing, -guishes.** To distinguish by contrasting qualities.

con·trail (kŏn′trāl′) *n.* A visible trail of water droplets or ice crystals sometimes forming in the wake of an aircraft or rocket. Also called "vapor trail." [CON(DENSATION) + TRAIL.]

con·tra·in·di·cate (kŏn′trə-ĭn′də-kāt′) *tr.v.* **-cated, -cating, -cates.** To indicate the inadvisability of: *An allergic reaction contraindicates the use of penicillin.* —**con·tra·in·di·cant** (kŏn′trə-ĭn′də-kənt) *n.* —**con·tra·in·di·ca·tion** *n.*

con·tral·to (kən-trăl′tō) *n., pl.* **-tos** or **-ti** (-tē). *Abbr.* **contr.** *Music.* **1.** The lowest female voice or voice part, intermediate in range between soprano and tenor. **2.** A woman having such a voice. [Italian : *contra-,* pitched below, from Latin *contrā-,* against + ALTO.]

con·tra·po·si·tion (kŏn′trə-pə-zĭsh′ən) *n.* An opposite position; opposition; antithesis.

con·trap·tion (kən-trăp′shən) *n.* A mechanical contrivance; a device or gadget. [Humorous blend of CONTRIVE and TRAP + -TION.]

con·tra·pun·tal (kŏn′trə-pŭnt′l) *adj. Music.* Of, pertaining to, or incorporating counterpoint. [From Italian *contrapunto* : *contra-,* against + *punto,* POINT.] —**con·tra·pun·tal·ly** *adv.*

con·tra·pun·tist (kŏn′trə-pŭn′tĭst) *n.* A specialist in contrapuntal music.

con·tra·ri·e·ty (kŏn′trə-rī′ə-tē) *n., pl.* **-ties.** **1.** The quality or condition of being contrary. **2.** Something contrary; a discrepancy or inconsistency. [Middle English, from Old French *contrarieté,* from Late Latin *contrārietās* (stem *contrārietāt-*), from *contrārius,* CONTRARY.]

con·trar·i·ous (kən-trâr′ē-əs) *adj. Archaic.* Perverse; contrary; adverse. [Middle English, from Medieval Latin *contrāriōsus,* from *contrārius,* CONTRARY.] —**con·trar·i·ous·ly** *adv.*

con·trar·i·wise (kŏn′trĕr′ē-wīz′, kən-trâr′ē-) *adv.* **1.** From a contrasting point of view. **2.** In the opposite way or reverse order. **3.** Contrarily; perversely.

con·tra·ry (kŏn′trĕr′ē; *in sense 4 also* kən-trâr′ē) *adj.* **1.** Opposed, as in character or purpose; completely different: *contrary beliefs.* **2.** Opposite in direction or position. **3.** Adverse; unfavorable: *contrary winds.* **4.** Given to acting or speaking in opposition to others; obstinate; willful. —**contrary to.** In opposition to; despite: *contrary to my request, she left early.* —See Synonyms at **opposite.**
∼*n., pl.* **contraries.** **1.** That which is contrary; the opposite. **2.** Either of two contrary, opposing, or incompatible things or conditions. **3.** *Logic.* A proposition related to another in such a way that if the latter is true, the former must be false, but if the latter is false, the former is not necessarily true. In this sense, compare **contradictory.** —**by contraries.** In opposition to what is expected. —**on the contrary.** Quite the opposite; in complete disagreement; conversely. —**to the contrary.** To a contrasting or opposite effect: *in the absence of any evidence to the contrary.*
∼*adv.* In opposition; contrariwise. [Middle English *contrarie,* from Old French *contraire,* from Latin *contrārius,* from *contrā,* against.] —**con·tra·ri·ly** *adv.* —**con·tra·ri·ness** *n.*

Synonyms: *adverse, obstinate, perverse, stubborn, wayward, willful.*

con·trast (kən-trăst′) *v.* **-trasted, -trasting, -trasts.** —*tr.* To set in opposition or compare in order to show differences: *contrast one style of writing with another.* —*intr.* To show differences or differing qualities when compared.
∼*n.* (kŏn′trăst′). **1.** The act of contrasting or the state of being contrasted. Often used in the phrases *by contrast, in contrast with,* and *in contrast to.* **2.** A striking dissimilarity between things compared. **3.** Something that shows a striking dissimilarity when compared to something else. **4.** In a work of art, the use of opposing elements, such as colors, forms, or lines, in proximity to produce an effect. **5.** The extent of difference between the light and dark areas of a photographic image or television picture. [French *contrester, contraster,* to contrast, resist, from Italian *contrastare,* from Medieval Latin *contrāstāre* : Latin *contrā-,* against + *stāre,* to stand.] —**con·trast·a·ble** *adj.* —**con·trast·ing·ly** *adv.*

Usage: As a verb, *contrast* is usually followed by *with.* As a noun the usual preposition is *between* (*the contrast between X and Y*), but *with* and *to* are also used (*the contrast with last year; as a contrast to his father.*). The phrase *in contrast* is usually followed by *with,* but *to* is also used, especially when the notion of opposition is being stressed.

con·tras·tive (kən-trăs′tĭv) *adj.* Tending to or resulting in contrast. —**con·tras·tive·ly** *adv.*

con·trast·y (kŏn′trăs′tē) *adj. Photography.* Having or producing sharp contrasts between light and dark.

con·tra·sug·gest·ible (kŏn′trə-səg-jĕs′tə-bəl) *adj. Psychology.* Tending to do or believe the opposite in response to a suggestion.

con·tra·vene (kŏn′trə-vēn′) *tr.v.* **-vened, -vening, -venes.** **1.** To act or be counter to (especially laws or regulations); violate; infringe. **2.** To oppose in argument. [Old French *contravenir,* from Late Latin *contrāvenīre,* to come against, oppose : Latin *contrā-,* against + *venīre,* to come.] —**con·tra·ven·er** *n.*

con·tra·ven·tion (kŏn′trə-vĕn′shən) *n.* An act of contravening; a violation; an infringement.

con·tre·danse, con·tra·dance (kŏn′trə-dăns′, -däns′; *French* kôN-trə-däNs′) *n.* **1.** A folk dance performed in two lines with the partners facing each other. **2.** The music for such a dance. [French, from English COUNTRY DANCE (influenced by French *contre,* against, opposite, because the partners face each other).]

con·tre·temps (kŏn′trə-täN′; *French* kôN-trə-täN′) *n., pl.* **contretemps** (-täNz′; *French* -täN′). **1.** An inopportune or embarrassing occurrence; a mishap. **2.** An argument or confrontation. [French : *contre-,* against, from Latin *contrā-* + *temps,* time, from Latin *tempus.*]

con·trib·ute (kən-trĭb′yo͞ot) *v.* **-uted, -uting, -utes.** —*tr.* **1.** To give or supply in common with others; give to a common fund or for a common purpose. **2.** To submit (an article, for example) for inclusion in a publication. —*intr.* **1.** To make a contribution. **2.** To act as a significant factor; play an important part. Used with *to*: *We have all contributed to his failure.* **3.** To submit material for publication. [Latin *contribuere,* to bring together, unite, collect : *com-,* together + *tribuere,* to allot, grant (see **tribute**).] —**con·trib·ut·a·ble** *adj.* —**con·trib·u·tive** *adj.* —**con·trib·u·tive·ly** *adv.* —**con·trib·u·tive·ness** *n.*

con·tri·bu·tion (kŏn′trə-byo͞o′shən) *n.* **1.** The act of contributing. **2.** Something contributed, as a piece of writing submitted to a publication or money donated to a cause. **3.** An impost or levy for a special, especially military, purpose.

con·trib·u·tor (kən-trĭb′yə-tər) *n.* One who contributes; especially, one who contributes articles or features to a newspaper or magazine.

con·trib·u·to·ry (kən-trĭb′yə-tôr′ē, -tōr′ē) *adj.* **1.** Pertaining to or involving a contribution. **2.** Contributing toward a result. **3.** Designating an employees' pension fund to which both employer and employee make contributions. **4.** Subject to an impost or levy.
∼*n., pl.* **contributories.** One that contributes.

contributory negligence *n. Law.* Carelessness on the part of the injured party as a factor in causing the injury suffered.

con·trite (kən-trīt′, kŏn′trīt′) *adj.* **1.** Humbled by guilt and repentant for one's sins; penitent; remorseful. **2.** Arising from contrition: *contrite resolutions.* [Middle English *contrit,* from Old French, from Medieval Latin *contrītus,* "broken in spirit," repentant, from Latin, past participle of *conterere,* to bruise, grind : *com-* (intensive) + *terere,* to rub, grind.] —**con·trite·ly** *adv.* —**con·trite·ness** *n.*

con·tri·tion (kən-trĭsh′ən) *n.* **1.** Sincere remorse for wrongdoing. **2.** *Theology.* Repentance for sin, as *perfect contrition,* repentance with a sincere desire to amend, arising from pure love of God, or *imperfect contrition,* repentance arising from a motive less than the pure love of God. Compare **attrition.**

con·tri·vance (kən-trī′vəns) *n.* **1. a.** The act or manner of contriving. **b.** The ability to contrive; inventiveness. **2.** Something contrived, such as a mechanical device or a clever plan.

con·trive (kən-trīv′) *v.* **-trived, -triving, -trives.** —*tr.* **1.** To plan or devise with cleverness or ingenuity. **2.** To plot with evil intent; scheme: *contrived his murder.* **3.** To invent or fabricate, especially by improvisation: *had to contrive excuses on the spur of the moment.* **4.** To manage or succeed in, as by scheming. —*intr.* To plot or scheme. [Middle English *contreven, controven,* from Old French *controver,* from Late Latin *contropāre,* to represent figuratively, compare : Latin *com-,* together + *tropus,* figure of speech, trope, from Greek *tropos,* turn, manner, style.] —**con·triv·a·ble** *adj.* —**con·triv·er** *n.*

con·trived (kən-trīvd′) *adj.* Achieved by artifice; artificial; unnatural. —**con·triv·ed·ly** (kən-trī′vĭd-lē) *adv.*

con·trol (kən-trōl′) *tr.v.* **-trolled, -trolling, -trols.** **1. a.** To exercise authority or a dominating influence over; direct: *control an empire.* **b.** To regulate; operate: *This button controls the lights.* **2.** To hold in restraint; check: *could not control her anger.* **3.** To reduce the severity or spread of: *control an outbreak of measles.* **4.** To verify or regulate (a scientific experiment) by conducting a parallel experiment in which the variable to be tested is absent or held constant, or by comparing with some other standard. —See Synonyms at **conduct.**
∼*n.* **1.** Authority or ability to regulate, direct, restrain, or dominate: *under the control of the local authority; lost control of her temper; remained in control of the project.* **2.** An act or means of regulating or verifying; a check or curb: *go through passport control; price controls.* **3. a.** A standard of comparison for checking or verifying the results of an experiment. **b.** An individual or group used as a standard of comparison in a control experiment. Also used adjectivally: *a control group.* **4.** Any of a set of instruments used to operate, regulate, or guide a machine or vehicle. Also used adjectivally: *control panel.* **5.** The organization, personnel, and equipment used in directing a space flight: *control mission.* **6.** In spiritualism, a spirit presumed to act through a medium. [Middle English *controllen,* from Old French *cont(r)eroller,* from Medieval Latin *contrārotulāre,* to check by a counter roll or duplicate register, from

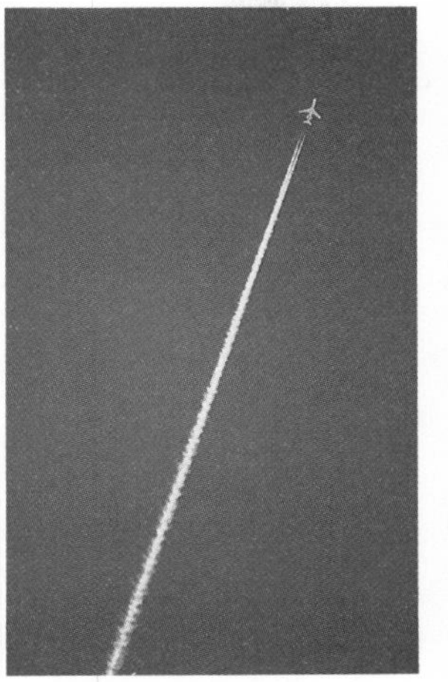

contrail *Water vapor from the exhaust of a Boeing 727 condenses in the chill of high-altitude air to form a white contrail of water droplets and ice crystals behind the jet. The same condensation principle is at work in the creation of clouds.*

contrārotulus, counter roll, duplicate register : Latin *contrā-,* against, opposite + *rotulus,* roll, "little wheel," from *rota,* wheel.] —**con·trol·la·bil·i·ty** *n.* —**con·trol·la·ble** *adj.*

control chart *n. Statistics.* A graph of a quantitative characteristic of a manufacturing process, usually determined from small, periodically repeated samples and evaluated with respect to control limits rendered as parallel horizontal lines above and below a line representing the expected or average value of the characteristic.

control experiment *n.* An experiment designed to check or verify a parallel experiment or as part of a set of experiments testing the effects of a variable or variables, in which the variable factors are controlled so that the effects of changing one at a time can be observed.

con·trolled response (kən-trōld′) *n.* A response to a military attack by limited military means in an effort to avoid nuclear war.

con·trol·ler (kən-trō′lər) *n.* Also **comp·trol·ler** (kən-trō′lər) (for sense 2). **1.** One who controls. **2.** An officer who audits accounts and supervises the financial affairs of a corporation or government body. **3.** A regulating mechanism, as in a vehicle or electrical device.

control rod *n. Physics.* One of a number of rods that can be moved into or out of the core of a nuclear reactor, used to control the rate of the reaction. They are made of a material that absorbs neutrons, such as boron.

control stick *n.* A lever used in small aircraft to control the angle of the elevators and ailerons; a joystick.

control surface *n.* A movable airfoil, especially a rudder, aileron, or elevator, used to control or guide an aircraft, guided missile, or rocket.

control tower *n.* A usually glass-enclosed tower at an airport from which air traffic is controlled by radio.

con·tro·ver·sial (kŏn′trə-vûr′shəl) *adj.* **1.** Subject to, surrounded by, or likely to produce controversy. **2.** Fond of controversy; disputatious. —**con·tro·ver·sial·ist** *n.* —**con·tro·ver·sial·ly** *adv.*

con·tro·ver·sy (kŏn′trə-vûr′sē) *n., pl.* **-sies. 1.** A dispute or debate, especially a lengthy and public one, between sides holding opposing views. **2.** Disputation; contention: *an affair surrounded by controversy.* —See Synonyms at **argument.** [Middle English *controversie,* from Latin *contrōversia,* from *contrōversus,* turned against, disputed : *contrō-,* variant of *contrā-,* against + *versus,* past participle of *vertere,* to turn.]

con·tro·vert (kŏn′trə-vûrt′) *tr.v.* **-verted, -verting, -verts. 1.** To raise arguments against; voice opposition to; deny. **2.** To argue or dispute about; debate. [From CONTROVERSY (by analogy with CONVERT, REVERT).] —**con·tro·vert·i·ble** *adj.*

con·tu·ma·cious (kŏn′tōō-mā′shəs, -tyōō-) *adj.* Obstinately disobedient or rebellious; insubordinate. —**con·tu·ma·cious·ly** *adv.* —**con·tu·ma·cious·ness** *n.*

con·tu·ma·cy (kŏn′tōō-mə-sē, -tyōō-) *n., pl.* **-cies. 1.** Obstinate or contemptuous resistance to authority. **2.** Willful disobedience to a court order. [Middle English *contumacie,* from Latin *contumācia,* from *contumāx,* stubborn, disobedient.]

con·tu·me·ly (kŏn′tōō-mə-lē, -tyōō-, kən-tōō′mə-lē, -tyōō′-) *n., pl.* **-lies. 1.** Rudeness or contempt in behavior or speech; insolence. **2.** An insulting remark or act. [Middle English *contumelie,* from Old French, from Latin *contumēlia,* insult, reproach.] —**con·tu·me·li·ous** (kŏn′tōō-mē′lē-əs, -tyōō-) *adj.* —**con·tu·me·li·ous·ly** *adv.*

con·tuse (kən-tōōz′, -tyōōz′) *tr.v.* **-tused, -tusing, -tuses.** To injure without breaking the skin; bruise. [Middle English *contusen,* from Old French *contuser,* from Latin *contundere* (past participle *contūsus*), to beat, pound : *com-* (intensive) + *tundere,* to beat.]

con·tu·sion (kən-tōō′zhən, -tyōō′-) *n.* An injury in which the skin is not broken; a bruise.

co·nun·drum (kə-nŭn′drəm) *n.* **1.** A riddle in which a fanciful question is answered by a pun. **2.** A puzzling problem or question admitting of no satisfactory solution. [16th century : perhaps originally a mock-Latin university slang word.]

con·ur·ba·tion (kŏn′ər-bā′shən) *n.* A large urban sprawl including smaller towns that have spread and joined together. [CON- + Latin *urbs,* city (see **urban**) + -ATION.]

con·va·lesce (kŏn′və-lĕs′) *intr.v.* **-lesced, -lescing, -lesces.** To return to health after illness, particularly by resting; recuperate. [Latin *convalēscere* : *com-* (intensive) + *valēscere,* to grow strong, from *valēre,* to be strong or well.]

con·va·les·cence (kŏn′və-lĕs′əns) *n.* **1.** Gradual return to health and strength after illness, particularly by resting. **2.** The period needed for this.

con·va·les·cent (kŏn′və-lĕs′ənt) *n.* One who is regaining health and strength after illness. —**con·va·les·cent** *adj.*

con·vect (kən-vĕkt′) *v.* **-vected, -vecting, -vects.** —*tr.* To transfer (heat) by convection. —*intr.* To undergo convection.

con·vec·tion (kən-vĕk′shən) *n.* **1.** The act or process of transmitting or conveying. **2.** *Physics.* **a.** Heat transfer by fluid motion between regions of unequal density that result from nonuniform heating. Also called "natural convection." **b.** Fluid motion caused by an external force such as a fan. Also called "forced convection." **3.** *Meteorology.* The transfer of heat or other atmospheric properties by massive motion within the atmosphere, especially by such motion directed upward. [Late Latin *convectiō* (stem *convectiōn-*), from *convehere,* to carry together, bring along : *com-,* together + *vehere,* to carry.] —**con·vec·tion·al** *adj.* —**con·vec·tive** *adj.* —**con·vec·tive·ly** *adv.*

con·vec·tor (kən-vĕk′tər) *n.* A heating unit typically having an enclosed electrically heated element from which warm air circulates by natural convection.

con·vene (kən-vēn′) *v.* **-vened, -vening, -venes.** —*intr.* To assemble, usually for an official or public purpose; meet formally. —*tr.* **1.** To cause to come together or assemble; convoke. **2.** To summon to appear, as before a court of law. [Middle English *convenen,* from Old French *convenir,* to come together, meet, hence agree, be suitable, from Latin *convenīre* : *com-,* together + *venīre,* to come.] —**con·ven·a·ble** *adj.*

con·ven·er, con·ve·nor (kən-vē′nər) *n.* A person, usually elected, who convenes or is the chairperson of a meeting, committee, or the like.

con·ven·ience (kən-vēn′yəns) *n.* **1.** The quality of being convenient; suitability or handiness. **2.** Personal comfort or advantage: *for the passenger's convenience.* **3.** A suitable time: *Call at your convenience.* **4.** Something that increases comfort or makes work less difficult, as an appliance or service. **5.** *Chiefly British.* A lavatory.

convenience food *n.* Packaged food requiring minimal preparation.

con·ven·ien·cy (kən-vēn′yən-sē) *n., pl.* **-cies.** *Archaic.* Convenience.

con·ven·ient (kən-vēn′yənt) *adj.* **1.** Suited or favorable to one's comfort, purpose, or needs. **2.** Easy to reach; accessible. **3.** *Obsolete.* Fitting and proper; appropriate. [Middle English, from Latin *conveniēns* (stem *convenient-*), present participle of *convenīre,* to be suitable. See **convene.**] —**con·ven·ient·ly** *adv.*

con·vent (kŏn′vənt, -vĕnt′) *n.* **1.** A community, especially of nuns, bound by vows to a religious life under a superior. **2.** The building or buildings occupied by such a community; especially, a nunnery. **3.** A convent school. [Middle English *covent,* from Old French, from Medieval Latin *conventus,* from Latin, a coming together, assembly, from *convenīre,* to come together, CONVENE.]

convent school *n.* A school in which the teaching staff are nuns.

con·ven·ti·cle (kən-vĕn′tĭ-kəl) *n.* **1.** A religious meeting, especially a secret or illegal one, such as those held by dissenters in England and Scotland in the 16th and 17th centuries. **2.** A building used for such a meeting. [Middle English, from Latin *conventiculum,* a place of meeting, diminutive of *conventus,* assembly, CONVENT.] —**con·ven·ti·cler** *n.*

con·ven·tion (kən-vĕn′shən) *n.* **1.** A formal assembly or meeting of members, representatives, or delegates of a group, such as a political party or trade union. **2.** The body of persons attending such an assembly. **3.** An agreement or compact; especially, an international agreement, less formal than a treaty, dealing with a specific subject, as the treatment of war prisoners. **4.** General agreement on or acceptance of certain practices or attitudes. **5.** A practice or procedure widely established in a group, especially in social matters; a custom. **6.** A widely used and accepted device or technique, as in drama, literature, or painting. **7.** In card games, a prearranged method of bidding or play that conveys information to partners. [Middle English *convencioun,* from Old French *convention,* from Latin *conventiō* (stem *conventiōn-*), assembly, agreement, from *convenīre,* to come together, CONVENE.]

con·ven·tion·al (kən-vĕn′shən-əl) *adj.* **1.** Developed, established, or approved by general usage; customary. **2.** Conforming to or rigidly following established practice or accepted standards; not adventurous or spontaneous. **3.** Marked by or dependent upon convention to the point of artificiality; stereotyped; trite. **4.** *Art.* Represented in simplified or abstract form. **5.** *Law.* Based upon mutual consent or agreement; contractual. **6.** Of or having to do with an assembly. **7.** Using means other than nuclear power: *conventional warfare.* —**con·ven·tion·al·ly** *adv.*

conventional current *n.* An electric current that flows from a positive point to a negative, as distinguished from the actual current, which is a flow of electrons in the opposite direction.

con·ven·tion·al·ism (kən-vĕn′shən-əl-ĭz′əm) *n.* **1.** Advocacy of or adherence to existing conventions. **2.** *Philosophy.* The view that principles and laws, especially in science, are formulated and adopted according to convention and conventional ways of interpreting evidence rather than purely by reason. —**con·ven·tion·al·ist** *n.*

con·ven·tion·al·i·ty (kən-vĕn′shən-ăl′ə-tē) *n., pl.* **-ties. 1.** The state, quality, or character of being conventional. **2.** A conventional act, principle, or practice. **3.** Adherence to convention.

con·ven·tion·al·ize (kən-vĕn′shən-əl-īz′) *tr.v.* **-ized, -izing, -izes.** To make conventional. —**con·ven·tion·al·i·za·tion** *n.*

conventional wisdom *n.* A body of established, received ideas accepted uncritically.

con·ven·tion·eer, con·ven·tion·er (kən-vĕn′shə-nîr′) *n.* One who attends a convention.

con·ven·tu·al (kən-vĕn′chōō-əl) *n.* **1.** A member of a convent. **2. Conventual.** A member of a branch of the Franciscan order that permits the accumulation and possession of common property. —**con·ven·tu·al** *adj.*

con·verge (kən-vûrj′) *v.* **-verged, -verging, -verges.** —*intr.* **1.** To approach the same point from different directions; tend toward a meeting or intersection. **2.** To tend or move toward union or toward a common conclusion or result. **3.** *Mathematics.* To approach a limit. Compare **diverge.** —*tr.* To cause to converge. [Late Latin *convergere,* to incline together : Latin *com-,* together + *vergere,* to bend, turn, incline.]

con·ver·gence (kən-vûr′jəns) *n.* Also **con·ver·gen·cy** (-jən-sē), *pl.* **-cies. 1.** The act, condition, quality, or fact of converging. **2.** *Mathematics.* The property or manner of approaching a limit such as a point, line, surface, or value. **3.** The point or degree of converging. **4.** *Physiology.* The coordinated turning of the eyes inward to focus on a nearby point. **5.** *Biology.* The adaptive evolution of superficially similar structures, such as the wings of birds and insects, in unrelated species subjected to similar environments. Also called "convergent evolution." **6.** *Meteorology.* A condition characterized by a horizontal net inflow of air over a region, which may be compensated by an upward air current giving rise to clouds and rain. **—con·ver·gent** *adj.*

convergent thinking *n. Psychology.* A type of thinking characterized by the use of logical reasoning to arrive at a single correct solution to a problem. Compare **divergent thinking.**

con·vers·a·ble (kən-vûr'sə-bəl) *adj.* Easy to talk to; affable. **—con·vers·a·ble·ness** *n.*

con·ver·sant (kən-vûr'sənt, kŏn'vər-) *adj.* Familiar, as by study or experience: *conversant with Roman history.* [Middle English *conversaunt,* from Old French *conversant,* from Latin *conversāns* (stem *conversant-*), present participle of *conversārī,* to associate with, CONVERSE.] **—con·ver·sance, con·ver·san·cy** *n.* **—con·ver·sant·ly** *adv.*

con·ver·sa·tion (kŏn'vər-sā'shən) *n.* **1.** An informal spoken exchange of thoughts and feelings; a talk. **2.** *Archaic.* Close acquaintance or association. **3.** *Archaic.* Manner of life; behavior. **4.** *Archaic.* Sexual intercourse. **—make conversation.** To talk for the sake of politeness.

con·ver·sa·tion·al (kŏn'vər-sā'shən-əl) *adj.* **1.** Of, pertaining to, or in the style of conversation; informal. **2.** Adept at or given to conversation. **—con·ver·sa·tion·al·ly** *adv.*

con·ver·sa·tion·al·ist (kŏn'vər-sā'shən-əl-ĭst) *n.* Also **con·ver·sa·tion·ist** (-shən-ĭst). One given to or skilled at conversation.

conversation piece *n.* **1.** A type of painting, especially popular in the 18th century, depicting a group of fashionable people. **2.** An unusual object that arouses comment or interest.

con·ver·sa·zi·o·ne (kŏn'vər-sät'sē-ō'nē) *n., pl.* **-nes** or **-ni** (-nē). A meeting for conversation or for discussion, especially of the arts. [Italian, "conversation."]

con·verse[1] (kən-vûrs') *intr.v.* **-versed, -versing, -verses.** **1.** To engage in spoken exchange of thoughts and feelings; talk. **2.** *Archaic.* To consort; associate. —See Synonyms at **speak.**

~*n.* (kŏn'vûrs'). Spoken interchange of thoughts and feelings; conversation. [Middle English *conversen,* to dwell, associate with, from Old French *converser,* from Latin *conversārī,* to associate with : *com-,* with + *versārī,* to live, occupy oneself, from *versāre,* frequentative of *vertere,* to turn.]

con·verse[2] (kən-vûrs', kŏn'vûrs') *adj.* Reversed, as in position, order, or action; contrary.

~*n.* (kŏn'vûrs'). **1.** Something that is contrary; the opposite. **2.** *Logic.* A proposition obtained by conversion. [Latin *conversus,* past participle of *convertere,* to turn around. See **convert.**] **—con·verse·ly** (kən-vûrs'lē) *adv.*

con·ver·sion (kən-vûr'zhən, -shən) *n.* **1.** The act of converting or the state of being converted. **2.** Something that has been changed from one use or form to another. **3.** A change in which one adopts a new religion. **4.** A change from one belief, opinion, or practice to another. **5.** *Law.* **a.** The unlawful appropriation of another's property. **b.** The changing of real property to personal property or vice versa. **6.** *Finance.* The exchange of one type of security or currency for another. **7.** *Logic.* The interchange of the subject and predicate of a proposition. **8.** *Football.* A successful attempt for an extra score after making a touchdown. **9.** *Psychiatry.* The symbolic manifestation of repressed ideas or impulses in motor or sensory abnormalities such as paralysis. Also called "conversion hysteria." **10.** *Physics.* The process in which an atomic nucleus in an excited state of energy changes to a lower state, the energy being taken up by an orbiting electron that is ejected from the atom. Also called "internal conversion." **11.** The act or result of converting a quantity in one system of units into another system of units, as meters into feet and inches. [Middle English *conversioun,* from Old French *conversion,* from Latin *conversiō* (stem *conversiōn-*), from *convertere,* to turn about, CONVERT.] **—con·ver·sion·al, con·ver·sion·ar·y** *adj.*

conversion factor *n.* A numerical factor used to multiply or divide a quantity in order to convert it from one system of units into another.

con·vert (kən-vûrt') *v.* **-verted, -verting, -verts.** —*tr.* **1.** To change into another form, substance, state, or product; transform; transmute: *convert water into ice.* **2.** To persuade or induce to adopt a particular religion, belief, or practice. **3. a.** To change from one use to another; adapt to a new or different purpose: *converted the bedroom into a study.* **b.** To make structural alterations to (a building). **4.** To exchange for something of equal value. **5.** *Finance.* To exchange (a security or bond, for example) by substituting an equivalent in another form. **6.** To express (a quantity) in alternative units. **7.** *Logic.* To transform (a proposition) by conversion. **8.** *Law.* **a.** To appropriate without right (another's property) to one's own use. **b.** To change (property) from real to personal, from joint to separate, or vice versa. —*intr.* **1.** To be converted or convertible; undergo a change: *a sofa that converts into a bed.* **2.** *Football.* To make a conversion. —See Synonyms at **change.**

~*n.* (kŏn'vûrt'). One who has been converted, especially from one religion or belief to another. [Middle English *converten,* from Old French *convertir,* from Medieval Latin *convertere,* to convert religiously, from Latin, to turn around, transform : *com-* (intensive) + *vertere,* to turn.]

con·vert·er, con·ver·tor (kən-vûr'tər) *n.* **1.** One that converts. **2.** A furnace in which pig iron is converted into steel by the Bessemer process. **3. a.** A device that changes electric current from one kind to another, especially one that converts direct current into alternating current. **b.** A radio device that changes one frequency to another. **c.** A device that transforms information from one code to another. **4.** A converter reactor.

converter reactor *n.* A nuclear reactor designed to change one type of nuclear fuel into another. Also called "converter." Compare **breeder reactor.**

con·vert·i·ble (kən-vûr'tə-bəl) *adj.* **1.** Capable of being converted. **2.** Having a top that may be folded back or removed: *a convertible automobile.* **3.** *Finance.* Capable of being lawfully exchanged for gold or another currency: *dollars convertible into pounds.*

~*n.* **1.** A convertible automobile. **2.** Something that can be converted. **—con·vert·i·bil·i·ty, con·vert·i·ble·ness** *n.* **—con·vert·i·bly** *adv.*

con·vert·i·plane, con·vert·a·plane (kən-vûr'tə-plān') *n.* An airplane that is designed to fly vertically as well as forward. [CONVERTI(BLE) + (AIR)PLANE.]

con·vex (kŏn'vĕks', kən-vĕks') *adj.* **1.** Having a surface or boundary that curves or bulges outward, as the exterior of a sphere. Compare **concave.** **2. a.** Thicker at the center than at the edges. Said of a lens. **b.** Having a convex reflecting surface. Said of a mirror. **3.** *Mathematics.* Designating a set in which the line segment between any two points is also contained in the set. [Latin *convexus,* arched, convex.] **—con·vex·ly** *adv.*

con·vex·i·ty (kən-vĕk'sə-tē) *n., pl.* **-ties.** **1.** The state of being convex. **2.** A convex surface, body, part, or line.

con·vex·o-con·cave (kən-vĕk'sō-kən-kāv') *adj.* **1. Concavo-convex** *(see).* **2.** *Optics.* Having greater convex than concave curvature. Said of a lens.

con·vex·o-con·vex (kən-vĕk'sō-kən-vĕks') *adj.* Convex on both sides; doubly convex; biconvex.

con·vey (kən-vā') *tr.v.* **-veyed, -veying, -veys.** **1.** To take or carry from one place to another; transport. **2.** To serve as a medium of transmission for; conduct; transmit. **3.** To communicate or make known: *"a look intended to convey sympathetic comprehension"* (Saki). **4.** *Law.* To transfer ownership of or title to. **5.** *Obsolete.* To steal. [Middle English *conveien,* from Old French *conveier,* from Medieval Latin *conviāre,* to go with, escort : Latin *com-,* with + *via,* way.] **—con·vey·a·ble** *adj.*

Synonyms: *bear, carry, convey, transfer, transmit, transport.*

con·vey·ance (kən-vā'əns) *n.* **1.** The act of transporting, transmitting, or communicating. **2.** A means of conveying; especially, a vehicle such as a bus. **3.** *Law.* **a.** The transfer of title to property from one person to another. **b.** The document by which this transfer is effected.

con·vey·anc·ing (kən-vā'ən-sĭng) *n.* **1.** The branch of legal practice dealing with the conveyance of property. **2.** An act or instance of conveying property. **—con·vey·anc·er** *n.*

con·vey·or, con·vey·er (kən-vā'ər) *n.* **1.** One that conveys. **2.** Any mechanical contrivance, especially a conveyor belt, that transports materials.

conveyor belt *n.* A continuous moving belt, usually driven by rollers, that transports objects or packages from one place to another, as on an assembly line in a factory. Also called "belt."

con·vict (kən-vĭkt') *tr.v.* **-victed, -victing, -victs.** **1.** To find or prove (someone) guilty of an offense, especially by the verdict of a court. **2.** To convince (someone) of his own guilt or sinfulness.

~*n.* (kŏn'vĭkt'). **1.** A person found or declared guilty of an offense or crime. **2.** A person serving a sentence of imprisonment. [Middle English *convicten,* from Latin *convincere* (past participle *convictus*), to prove guilty, CONVINCE.]

con·vic·tion (kən-vĭk'shən) *n.* **1.** The act or process of finding or proving guilty of an offense. **2.** The state or an instance of being convicted: *a string of previous convictions.* **3.** The act or process of convincing. **4.** The state of being convinced or persuaded. **5.** A fixed or strong belief. **6.** The quality of being convincing; plausibility: *His defense of government policy doesn't carry much conviction.* —See Synonyms at **certainty, opinion.** **—con·vic·tion·al** *adj.*

con·vince (kən-vĭns') *tr.v.* **-vinced, -vincing, -vinces.** To bring by argument and evidence to belief; cause to believe something; persuade: *convinced him to tell the truth; I am convinced that he is evil; convince them of our sincerity.* —See Synonyms at **persuade.** [Latin *convincere,* to overcome, refute, prove guilty : *com-* (intensive) + *vincere,* to conquer, overcome.] **—con·vince·ment** *n.* **—con·vinc·er** *n.* **—con·vin·ci·ble** *adj.*

con·vinc·ing (kən-vĭn'sĭng) *adj.* **1.** Persuading or satisfying by evidence or argument. **2.** Believable; plausible: *a convincing story.* —See Synonyms at **valid.** **—con·vinc·ing·ly** *adv.* **—con·vinc·ing·ness** *n.*

con·viv·i·al (kən-vĭv'ē-əl) *adj.* **1.** Fond of feasting, drinking, and good company; sociable; jovial. **2.** Appropriate to or of the nature of a festive occasion; warm and friendly: *a convivial atmosphere at the office party.* —See Synonyms at **jolly.** [Late Latin *convīviālis,* from Latin *convīvium,* "a living together," banquet : *com-,* together + *vīvere,* to live.] **—con·viv·i·al·i·ty** (kən-vĭv'ē-ăl'ə-tē) *n.* **—con·viv·i·al·ly** *adv.*

con·vo·ca·tion (kŏn'vō-kā'shən) *n.* **1.** The act of convoking or calling together. **2.** A group of people assembled by summons. **3.** *Anglican Church.* A clerical assembly similar to a synod, but assembling only when called. **4.** *Episcopal Church.* **a.** An assembly of the clergy and representative laity of a section of a diocese.

PRONUNCIATION KEY

ă, pat; ā, pay; âr, care;
ä, father, are; b, bib;
ch, church; d, deed; ĕ, pet;
ē, be; f, fife; g, gag; h, hat;
hw, which; ĭ, pit; ī, pie;
îr, pier; j, judge; k, kick;
l, lid, needle; m, mum;
n, no, sudden; ng, thing;
ŏ, pot; ō, toe; ô, paw, for;
oi, noise; ou, out; o͝o, book;
o͞o, boot; p, pop; r, roar;
s, sauce; sh, ship, dish;
t, tight; th, thin, path;
th, this, bathe; ŭ, cut; ûr, fur;
v, valve; w, with; y, yes;
z, zebra, size; zh, vision;
ə, about, item, edible, gallop, circus, peaceful

IN FOREIGN WORDS:

à, *Fr.* ami; œ, *Fr.* feu, *Ger.* schön; ü, *Fr.* tu, *Ger.* über; KH, *Ger.* ich, *Scot.* loch; N, *Fr.* bon; y', *Fr.* Compiègne

STRESS MARKS:

Primary stress: '
in·cite' (ĭn-sīt')
Secondary stress: '
in'sight' (ĭn'sīt')

b. The district represented at such an assembly. **5.** In certain British universities, a deliberative or legislative assembly, typically composed of graduates of the university. Compare **senate, congregation.** —**con·vo·ca·tion·al** adj.

con·voke (kən-vōk′) tr.v. **-voked, -voking, -vokes.** To cause to assemble; convene. [Old French convoquer, from Latin convocāre, to call together, summon : com-, together + vocāre, to call.] —**con·vok·er** n.

con·vo·lute (kŏn′və-lōōt′) adj. Rolled or folded together with one part over another; twisted; coiled.
~v. **convoluted, -luting, -lutes.** —tr. To coil or wind around. —intr. To coil up. [Latin convolūtus, past participle of convolvere, to CONVOLVE.] —**con·vo·lute·ly** adv.

con·vo·lut·ed (kŏn′və-lōō′tĭd) adj. **1.** Exhibiting convolutions; coiled; twisted. **2. a.** Intricate; complicated. **b.** Difficult to understand because lengthy, roundabout, or tortuous: a convoluted explanation.

con·vo·lu·tion (kŏn′və-lōō′shən) n. **1. a.** A coiling or twisting together. **b.** An entangling or interlacing, so as to make intricate. **2.** Any of the convex folds of the surface of the brain. See **gyrus. 3.** Mathematics. A function that measures how the shape of one function affects another, defined by the integral of the product $g(t)f(x-t)$ with respect to the variable t.

con·volve (kən-vŏlv′) v. **-volved, -volving, -volves.** —tr. To roll together; coil up. —intr. To form convolutions. [Latin convolvere, to roll together, enwrap : com-, together + volvere, to roll.]

con·vol·vu·lus (kən-vŏl′vyə-ləs) n., pl. **-luses** or **-li** (-lī′). Any of several trailing or twining plants of the genus Convolvulus, which includes the bindweeds. [New Latin Convolvulus, from Latin convolvulus, bindweed, from convolvere, to interweave, CONVOLVE.]

con·voy (kŏn′voi′, kən-voi′) tr.v. **-voyed, -voying, -voys.** To accompany on the way for protection, either by sea or land; escort.
~n. (kŏn′voi′). **1.** An accompanying and protecting force; a convoying vessel, fleet, or troop. **2.** That which is convoyed, such as ships or troops. **3.** The act of convoying. **4.** A group, as of vehicles, traveling together. [Middle English convoyen, conveien, from Old French convoier, conveier, to CONVEY.]

con·vul·sant (kən-vŭl′sənt) n. A drug or other agent that produces convulsions. —**con·vul·sant** adj.

con·vulse (kən-vŭls′) tr.v. **-vulsed, -vulsing, -vulses. 1.** To shake or agitate violently. **2.** To cause to shake with laughter. **3.** To affect with irregular and involuntary muscular contractions; throw into convulsions. [From Latin convellere (past participle convulsus), to pull violently, wrest : com- (intensive) + vellere, to pull.]

con·vul·sion (kən-vŭl′shən) n. **1.** A violent involuntary contraction or series of contractions of the muscles. **2.** An uncontrolled fit of laughter. **3.** A violent turmoil.

con·vul·sion·ar·y (kən-vŭl′shən-ĕr′ē) adj. Of, pertaining to, affected with, or of the nature of convulsions.
~n., pl. **convulsionaries.** A person affected with convulsions, especially as a result of religious fervor.

con·vul·sive (kən-vŭl′sĭv) adj. **1.** Marked by or of the nature of convulsions. **2.** Having or producing convulsions. —**con·vul·sive·ly** adv. —**con·vul·sive·ness** n.

Con·wy (kŏn′wē). Formerly **Con·way** (-wā). Town in Gwynedd, near the mouth of the Conwy River in northwest Wales.

co·ny (kō′nē, kŭn′ē) n., pl. **-nies.** Also **co·ney** pl. **-neys. 1.** A rabbit, especially the Old World species Oryctolagus cuniculus. **2.** The fur of a rabbit. **3.** A mammal, the **pika** (see). **4.** In the Old Testament, a mammal, the **hyrax** (see). Deuteronomy 14:7. [Middle English coni(n)g, cunin, from Old French conin, conil, from Latin cunīculus, rabbit.]

coo (kōō) v. **cooed, cooing, coos.** —intr. **1.** To utter the characteristic murmuring sound of a dove or pigeon, or a sound resembling this. **2.** To talk amorously or fondly in murmurs. Usually used in the phrase bill and coo. —tr. To utter gently or amorously, as with a murmuring sound.
~n., pl. **coos.** The murmuring sound made by a dove or pigeon, or a sound resembling this.
~interj. Chiefly British. Used to express surprise, admiration, or amazement. [Imitative.]

coo·ee (kōō′ē) n., pl. **-ees.** Also **coo·ey** pl. **-eys.** A prolonged shrill cry used as a signal by the Australian aborigines and later adopted by the settlers.

cook (kōōk) v. **cooked, cooking, cooks.** —tr. **1.** To prepare for eating by applying heat, as by boiling, frying, or baking. **2.** To subject to heat. **3.** Informal. To falsify (accounts, records, or statistics). Used chiefly in the phrase cook the books. —intr. **1.** To prepare food for eating by applying heat. **2.** To undergo cooking. **3.** Slang. To happen, develop, or take place: What's cooking in town? —**cook up.** Informal. To fabricate; concoct: cook up an excuse.
~n. A person who prepares food for eating. [Middle English coken, from cok(e), a cook, Old English cōc, from Vulgar Latin cōcus (unattested), from Latin cocus, coquus, from coquere, to cook.]

Cook (kōōk), **James,** known as "Captain Cook" (1728–79). British explorer and navigator. From 1768–71 in his ship Endeavour, Cook charted the coasts of New Zealand, reached eastern Australia, landed at Botany Bay, and skirted the Great Barrier Reef. On the voyage he conquered scurvy by providing fresh vegetables for his crew. His second voyage (1772–75) reached as far south as the Antarctic Circle, charting Easter Island and most of the major island groups in the South Pacific. On his third voyage (1776–79) he dis-

covered the Sandwich (now Hawaiian) Islands and charted the Bering Strait.

Cook, Mount. Maori **A·o·rang·i** (ä-ō-räng′gē). The highest mountain in New Zealand, on the west of South Island in the Southern Alps. It is 3,763 meters (12,346 feet) high.

cook·book (kōōk′bōōk′) n. A book containing recipes and other information about the preparation of food.

cook·er (kōōk′ər) n. **1.** An appliance or utensil used for cooking: a pressure cooker. **2.** A person employed to operate a cooking apparatus in the commercial preparation of food and drink. **3.** British. A stove.

cook·er·y (kōōk′ər-ē) n. **1.** The art or practice of preparing food. **2.** A place for cooking.

cookery book n. British. A cookbook.

cook·house (kōōk′hous′) n. A place or building where the cooking is done, as on a ranch.

cook·ie, cook·y (kōōk′ē) n., pl. **-ies. 1.** A small, usually flat cake made from sweet dough. **2.** Scottish. A bun. [Dutch koekje, diminutive of koek, cake, from Middle Dutch koeke.]

cook·ing (kōōk′ĭng) adj. **1.** Used in or for cooking: cooking utensils. **2.** Suitable primarily for use in cooking: cooking sherry; cooking apples.

Cook Islands. An associated state of New Zealand, in the southwest Pacific Ocean. Discovered by Captain Cook (1773), the group comprises 15 islands, including Rarotonga, with Avarua the administrative center.

cook·out (kōōk′out′) n. An outing or gathering at which a meal is cooked and served outdoors.

Cook Strait. Sea channel between North Island and South Island, New Zealand, 26 to 145 kilometers (16 to 90 miles) wide.

cook·ware (kōōk′wâr′) n. Utensils used in cooking.

cool (kōōl) adj. **cooler, coolest. 1.** Moderately cold; neither warm nor very cold. **2.** Reducing discomfort in hot weather; allowing a feeling of coolness: a cool blouse. **3.** Not excited; calm; controlled: a cool head in a crisis. **4.** Showing dislike, disdain, or indifference; unenthusiastic; not cordial: a cool greeting. **5.** Calmly audacious; impudent: gave him a cool look and walked away. **6.** Designating or characteristic of colors, such as blue and green, that produce the impression of coolness. **7.** Marked by a quietly self-possessed, unruffled attitude. **8.** Slang. **a.** Excellent; first-rate. **b.** Acceptable; O.K.: Tonight, if that's cool with you. **9.** Informal. Without exaggeration; entire; full: He lost a cool million.
~v. **cooled, cooling, cools.** —tr. **1.** To make less warm. Often used with down or off. **2.** To make less ardent, intense, or zealous; calm. —intr. **1.** To become less warm. Often used with down or off: We cooled off with a swim. **2.** To become less ardent, intense, or zealous; become calm. Often used with down or off. —**cool it.** Slang. Calm down; relax. —**cool one's heels.** To be kept waiting.
~n. **1.** A cool atmosphere: the cool of early morning. **2.** The state or quality of being cool. **3.** Slang. Composure: lose one's cool. [Middle English col, Old English cōl, from Germanic.] —**cool·ly** adv. —**cool·ness** n.
   Synonyms: collected, composed, detached, imperturbable, nonchalant, unruffled.

coo·la·bah, coo·li·bah (kōō′lə-bä′) n. An Australian eucalyptus tree, Eucalyptus microtheca, found near rivers. [From a native Australian language.]

cool·ant (kōō′lənt) n. An agent that produces cooling; especially, a fluid that draws off heat by circulating through a machine or by bathing a mechanical part. [COOL + -ant, by analogy with lubricant.]

cool·er (kōō′lər) n. **1.** A device or container that cools something or keeps it cool. **2.** Anything that cools, such as an iced drink. **3.** Slang. Jail.

Cool·ey's anemia (kōō′lēz) n. **Thalassemia** (see). [After Thomas B. Cooley (1871–1945), U.S. pediatrician.]

cool·head·ed (kōōl′hĕd′ĭd) adj. Not easily excited or flustered.

Coo·lidge (kōō′lĭj), **(John) Calvin** (1872–1933). U.S. Republican statesman and 30th president (1923–29). He succeeded Warren Harding (1923) and helped to restore public trust after the scandals of his predecessor's administration.

coo·lie, coo·ly (kōō′lē) n., pl. **-lies.** In India and the Far East, an unskilled laborer. [Hindi kulī, qulī, perhaps from Kulī, Kolī, an aboriginal tribe of Gujarat, India.]

cool·ing-off period (kōō′lĭng-ôf′, -ŏf′) n. A break during negotiations to allow time for the parties in a dispute to calm down and take stock of their positions.

Coomassie. See **Kumasi.**

coomb (kōōm) n. British. A short valley, especially in coastal areas. [Old English cumb, probably from Celtic.]

coon (kōōn) n. Informal. A raccoon. [Short for RACCOON.]

coon·can (kōōn′kăn′) n. A card game, **conquian** (see).

coon·hound (kōōn′hound′) n. A smooth-coated black and tan hound of a breed developed in the southeastern United States to hunt raccoons.

coon's age n. Slang. A long time.

coon·skin (kōōn′skĭn′) n. **1.** The pelt of the raccoon. **2.** An article made of coonskin, such as a hat. —**coon·skin** adj.

coon·tie (kōōn′tē) n. An evergreen plant, Zamia floridana, of southern Florida, having underground stems that yield a starch resembling arrowroot. [Mikasuki (Seminole) kuntie, flour.]

coop (kōōp) n. **1.** An enclosure or cage, as for poultry or small

animals. **2.** *Slang.* Any place of confinement. **—fly the coop.** *Slang.* To escape.
~tr.v. **cooped, cooping, coops.** To confine in a limited space. Usually used with *up.* [Middle English *c(o)upe,* wicker basket, chicken coop, probably from Middle Low German *kūpe,* basket, cask, tub, barrel.]

co-op (kō′ŏp′, kō-ŏp′) *n.* A cooperative.

coop·er (ko͞o′pər) *n.* One who makes or repairs wooden tubs and casks.
~v. **coopered, -ering, -ers.** *—tr.* To make or repair (wooden tubs and casks). *—intr.* To work as a cooper. [Middle English *couper,* probably from Middle Low German *kūper,* from *kūpe,* cask, COOP.]

Coop·er (ko͞o′pər), **Gary,** born Frank James Cooper (1901–61). U.S. film actor, who specialized in "strong, silent" hero roles in Hollywood westerns, such as the classic *High Noon* (1952).

Cooper, James Fenimore (1789–1851). U.S. novelist. He is best remembered for his novels of frontier life, such as *The Last of the Mohicans* (1826).

coop·er·age (ko͞o′pər-ĭj) *n.* A cooper's work, shop, or products.

co·op·er·ate (kō-ŏp′ə-rāt′) *intr.v.* **-ated, -ating, -ates. 1.** To work or act together toward a common end or purpose. **2.** To adopt a helpful and willing attitude. **3.** To practice economic cooperation. [Latin *cooperārī* : *co-,* together + *operārī,* to work, from *opus,* work.] **—co·op·er·a·tor** (kō-ŏp′ə-rā′tər) *n.*

co·op·er·a·tion (kō-ŏp′ə-rā′shən) *n.* **1.** The act of cooperating. **2.** Help or a helpful attitude: *We need your cooperation.* **3.** An association of persons for mutual benefit. **—co·op·er·a·tion·ist** *n.*

co·op·er·a·tive (kō-ŏp′ər-ə-tĭv, -ŏp′rə-, -ə-rā′tĭv) *adj.* **1.** Done in cooperation with others: *a cooperative effort.* **2.** Marked by willingness to cooperate: *a cooperative patient.* **3.** Of, pertaining to, or functioning as a cooperative: *a cooperative farm.*
~n. An enterprise, such as a farm, factory, shop, or set of houses or dwellings, that is collectively owned and operated for mutual benefit. Also called "co-op." **—co·op·er·a·tive·ly** *adv.* **—co·op·er·a·tive·ness** *n.*

Cooper pair *n. Physics.* A pair of interacting electrons responsible for carrying the electric current in a superconductor. [After Leon N. *Cooper* (born 1930), U.S. physicist.]

Coo·pers Creek (ko͞o′pərz). Intermittent watercourse in eastern Australia. It flows 1,420 kilometers (880 miles) southwest from the Great Dividing Range into Lake Eyre.

co-opt (kō-ŏpt′, kō′ŏpt′) *tr.v.* **-opted, -opting, -opts. 1.** To elect as a fellow member of a group. **2.** To appoint summarily. **3.** To preempt; appropriate. **4.** To absorb or take over, especially by assimilation into an established group or culture. [Latin *cooptāre* : *cō-,* together + *optāre,* to choose, elect.] **—co-op·ta·tion** (kō′ŏp-tā′shən), **co-op·tion** *n.* **—co-op·ta·tive** (kō-ŏp′tə-tĭv), **co-op·tive** *adj.*

co·or·di·nate (kō-ôr′də-nĭt, -nāt′) *n.* **1.** One that is equal in importance, rank, or degree. **2.** *Mathematics.* **a.** Any of a set of numbers that determines the location of a point in a space of a given dimension. **b.** Any of a set of two or more magnitudes used to determine the position of a point, line, curve, or plane. **3. coordinates.** Items of clothing or accessories designed to match and be worn together.
~adj. (kō-ôr′də-nĭt, -nāt′). **1.** Of equal importance, rank, or degree; not subordinate. **2.** Of or involving coordination. **3.** Of or based on coordinates.
~v. (kō-ôr′də-nāt′) **coordinated, -nating, -nates.** *—tr.* **1.** To place in the same order, class, or rank. **2.** To arrange in the proper relative position. **3.** To bring together in a common and harmonious action or effort. **4.** *Chemistry.* To cause (an atom, ion, or the like) to form a coordinate bond. *—intr.* **1.** To work together harmoniously. **2.** *Chemistry.* To form a coordinate bond. [Back-formation from COORDINATION.] **—co·or·di·nate·ly** *adv.* **—co·or·di·nate·ness** *n.* **—co·or·di·na·tive** *adj.* **—co·or·di·na·tor** (kō-ôr′də-nā′tər) *n.*

coordinate bond *n.* A covalent chemical bond in which both electrons forming the bond are supplied by one atom. Also called "semipolar bond," "dative bond."

coordinate conjunction *n.* Also **coordinating conjunction.** *Grammar.* A conjunction that connects parallel grammatical elements; for example, *or* in *She doesn't know whether she's coming or going.* Compare **subordinate conjunction.**

coordinate geometry *n.* A branch of geometry, **analytical geometry** *(see).*

coordinate system *n. Mathematics.* A method of specifying the positions of points in space by reference to fixed points, lines, or planes. See **Cartesian coordinates, cylindrical coordinates, polar coordinates.**

co·or·di·na·tion (kō-ôr′də-nā′shən) *n.* **1.** The act of coordinating. **2.** The state of being coordinated; harmonious adjustment or interaction. **3.** *Physiology.* The coordinated functioning of muscles or groups of muscles in the execution of a complex task. [French, from Late Latin *coōrdinātiō* (stem *coōrdinātiōn-*), arrangement in the same order : Latin *cō-,* same + *ōrdinātiō,* arrangement, from *ōrdināre,* to arrange in order, from *ōrdō,* order.]

coordination compound *n.* A chemical compound or complex ion formed by joining independent molecules or ions to a central metallic atom. Also called "coordination complex."

coot (ko͞ot) *n.* **1.** Any of several dark-gray aquatic birds of the genus *Fulica;* especially *F. americana* of the New World, and *F. atra* of the Old World. **2.** A duck, the **scoter** *(see).* **3.** *Informal.* A foolish old man. [Middle English *cote,* probably from Middle Dutch *coet, cuut*†.]

coo·tie (ko͞o′tē) *n. Slang.* A body louse. [Perhaps from Malay *kutu.*]

cop[1] (kŏp) *n.* **1.** A cone-shaped or cylindrical roll of yarn or thread wound on a spindle. **2.** *Archaic.* A summit or crest. [Middle English *cop, coppe,* summit, top, tip, Old English *copp,* from Late Latin *cuppa,* from Latin *cūpa,* tub.]

cop[2] *n. Informal.* A policeman.
~tr.v. **copped, copping, cops.** *Slang.* **1.** To seize; catch. **2.** To steal. **— cop a plea.** *Slang.* To plead guilty to a lesser charge so as to avoid having to stand trial on a more serious one. [Probably from obsolete *cap,* to arrest, from Old French *caper,* to seize.]

cop. copyright.

co·pa·cet·ic, co·pa·set·ic (kō′pə-sĕt′ĭk) *adj. Slang.* Excellent; first-rate. [20th century : origin obscure.]

co·pai·ba (kō-pī′bə, -pā′-) *n.* A transparent, yellowish, viscous resin from South American trees of the genus *Copaifera,* used in varnishes and tracing papers. [Spanish, from Portuguese *copaíba,* from Tupi *copaiba.*]

co·pal (kō′pəl) *n.* A brittle, aromatic, yellow to red resin of recent or fossil origin, obtained from various tropical trees and used in varnishes. [Spanish, from Nahuatl *copalli,* resin.]

Co·pán (kō-pän′). A ruined city of the ancient Maya on the Copán River in western Honduras, discovered by the Spanish in the early 16th century. Copán, second largest of the great Maya cities, flourished from *c.* 300 B.C.–A.D. 900.

co·par·ce·nar·y (kō-pär′sə-nĕr′ē) *n., pl.* **-ies. 1.** *Law.* Joint ownership of inherited property. Also called "parcenary." **2.** Any joint ownership. **—co·par·ce·nar·y** *adj.*

co·par·ce·ner (kō-pär′sə-nər) *n. Law.* Any of two or more persons sharing an undivided inheritance. Also called "parcener."

co·part·ner, co-part·ner (kō-pärt′nər) *n.* A partner, as in a business enterprise; an associate. **—co·part·ner·ship** *n.*

cope[1] (kōp) *intr.v.* **coped, coping, copes. 1.** To contend or struggle successfully. Used with *with: coping with career and family.* **2.** To contend with difficulties and attempt to overcome them. Often used with *with.* [Middle English *co(u)pen,* to contend with, join in battle with, from Old French *couper,* to strike, from *coup,* a blow, from Late Latin *colpus,* from Latin *colaphus,* from Greek *kolaphos.*]

cope[2] *n.* **1.** A long cloaklike ecclesiastical vestment worn over the alb or surplice. **2.** Any covering resembling a cloak or mantle.
~tr.v. **coped, coping, copes.** To provide (a wall, for example) with coping. [Middle English *cope,* Old English *(cantel)cāp,* from Late Latin *cāpa, cappa,* cloak, hood, from Latin *caput,* head.]

copeck. Variant of **kopeck.**

Co·pen·ha·gen (kō′pən-hā′gən, -hä′-). *Danish* **Kø·ben·havn** (kœ′bən-houn′). The capital of Denmark, on the Baltic coast of Sjaelland opposite the coast of southern Sweden.

co·pe·pod (kō′pə-pŏd′) *n.* Any of numerous small marine and freshwater crustaceans of the subclass *Copepoda.* [New Latin *Copepoda,* "oar-footed ones" : Greek *kōpē,* oar handle, oar + POD.]

cop·er (kō′pər) *n. British.* A horse dealer. [From obsolete *cope,* to buy, exchange, from Low German; akin to Dutch *koopen,* German *kaufen,* to buy.]

Co·per·ni·can system (kō-pûr′nə-kən) *n.* The description of the solar system published by Copernicus in 1543, with the sun at the center and the planets moving around it in, as originally formulated, circular orbits and epicycles. Compare **Ptolemaic system.**

Co·per·ni·cus (kō-pûr′nə-kəs, kə-), **Nicolaus** (1473–1543). *Polish* **Mikolaj Ko·per·nik** (kô-pĕr′nĭk). Polish astronomer. The difficulties he encountered in trying to calculate the position of the planets within the framework of the well-established Ptolemaic system led him to reject Ptolemy's belief that the heavenly bodies moved around the earth and to place the sun at the center of the universe. **—Co·per·ni·can** *adj.*

cope·stone (kōp′stōn′) *n.* **1.** A **capstone** *(see).* **2.** A coping stone.

cop·i·er (kŏp′ē-ər) *n.* **1.** Any of various office machines that make copies. **2.** A copyist or transcriber. **3.** An imitator.

co·pi·lot, co-pi·lot (kō′pī′lət) *n.* The second or relief pilot of an aircraft.

cop·ing (kō′pĭng) *n.* The top part of a wall or roof, usually slanted. [From COPE (vestment).]

coping saw *n.* A narrow, short-bladed saw with a thin blade in a U-shaped frame, used for cutting designs in wood.

coping stone *n.* A stone used in or as a coping.

co·pi·ous (kō′pē-əs) *adj.* **1.** Yielding or containing plenty; affording ample supply. **2.** Large in quantity; abundant. **3.** Abounding in matter, thoughts, or words; wordy. [Middle English, from Old French *copieux,* from Latin *cōpiōsus,* from *cōpia,* abundance.] **—co·pi·ous·ly** *adv.* **—co·pi·ous·ness** *n.*

co·pla·nar (kō-plā′nər) *adj.* Lying or occurring in the same plane.

Cop·land (kōp′lənd), **Aaron** (1900–90). U.S. pianist and composer. His works include the ballets *Rodeo* (1942) and *Appalachian Spring* (1944) and his highly acclaimed *Third Symphony* (1946).

Cop·ley (kŏp′lē), **John Singleton** (1738–1815). U.S. painter. A member of a Loyalist Boston family, he earned a reputation as a fine portraitist, painting such colonial dignitaries as Paul Revere and John Hancock. When the Revolution seemed imminent he went overseas (1774) and settled in England, where he continued to paint until his death.

co·pol·y·mer (kō-pŏl′ə-mər) *n.* A polymer of two or more different monomers. **—co·pol·y·mer·ic** (kō-pŏl′ə-mĕr′ĭk) *adj.*

co·pol·y·mer·ize (kō-pŏl′ə-mə-rīz′) *v.* **-ized, -izing, -izes.** *—tr.* To polymerize (different monomers) together. *—intr.* To react to form a copolymer. **—co·pol·y·mer·i·za·tion** *n.*

cop out *intr.v. Slang.* **1.** To evade a difficult question, situation, or

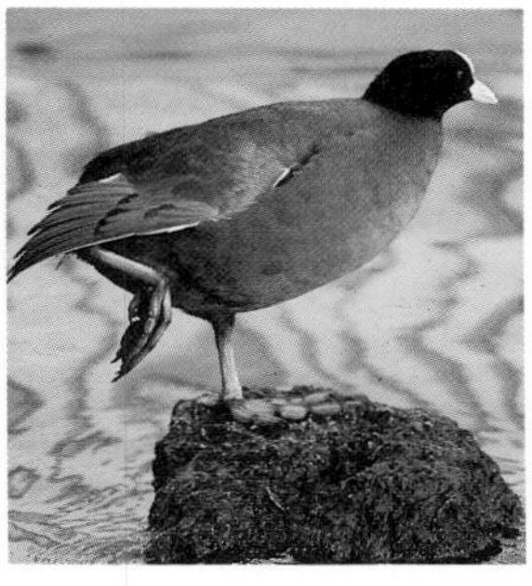

coot *A bird of lakes and ponds, found on all continents except Australia and Antarctica. It has lobed, not webbed, feet and swims and dives to feed on water plants.*

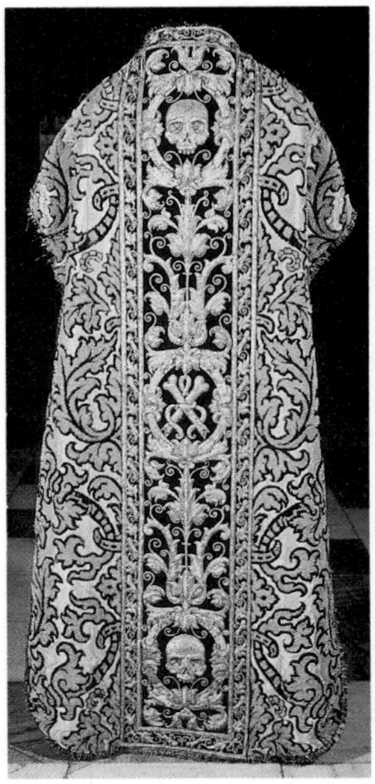

cope *A full-length and often richly embroidered church vestment.*

commitment. **2.** To back down, as on a promise. **3.** To compromise one's principles. [From COP (to seize).]
cop-out (kŏp′out′) *n. Slang.* An act of copping out; a failure to commit oneself or abide by one's principles.
cop·per¹ (kŏp′ər) *n.* **1.** *Symbol* **Cu** A ductile, malleable, reddish-brown metallic element that is an excellent conductor of heat and electricity and is widely used for electrical wiring, water piping, and corrosion-resistant parts either pure or in alloys such as brass and bronze. Atomic number 29, atomic weight 63.54, melting point 1,083°C, boiling point 2,595°C, specific gravity 8.96, valences 1, 2. **2.** A coin of low value made of copper or a copper alloy. **3.** *Chiefly British.* A large boiler made of copper or often of iron, especially one used for laundry. **4.** Any of various small butterflies of the subfamily Lycaeninae, having predominantly copper-colored wings.
~*tr.v.* **coppered, -pering, -pers.** To coat or finish with a layer of copper. [Middle English, Old English *coper, copor,* from Common Germanic *kupar* (unattested), from Late Latin *cuprum,* from Latin *Cyprium (aes),* "(copper) of Cyprus" (Cyprus was known in ancient times as the source of the best copper).] **—cop·per·y** *adj.*
copper² *n. Slang.* A policeman. [From COP (to seize).]
cop·per·as (kŏp′ər-əs) *n.* A greenish, crystalline, hydrated ferrous sulfate, $FeSO_4 \cdot 7H_2O$, used in the manufacture of fertilizers and inks and in water purification. [Middle English *coperose,* from Old French *co(u)perose,* from Medieval Latin *cup(e)rosa,* probably short for *aqua cup(e)rosa,* "copper water."]
copper beech *n.* A variety of the European beech, *Fagus sylvatica,* having copper-colored or purple leaves.
Cop·per·belt (kŏp′ər-bĕlt′). A region of central Africa, extending in an arc from southeastern Zaire into northern Zambia. It has the largest copper deposits in Africa.
cop·per·head (kŏp′ər-hĕd′) *n.* **1.** A venomous snake, *Agkistrodon contortrix* (or *Ancistron contortrix*), of the eastern United States, having reddish-brown markings. **2. Cooperhead.** A Northerner who sympathized with the South during the Civil War.
Cop·per·mine (kŏp′ər-mīn′). River, 845 kilometers (525 miles) long, in central Mackenzie district, Northwest Territories, Canada. It flows northwest to the Arctic Ocean. Its many falls give it great hydroelectric power potential.
copper nickel *n.* A nickel ore, **niccolite** *(see).*
cop·per·plate (kŏp′ər-plāt′) *n.* **1.** A copper printing plate, engraved or etched to form a recessed pattern of the matter to be printed. **2.** A print or engraving made by using such a plate. **3.** An ornate, cursive handwriting style based on copperplate engraved models and characterized by a slant to the right, regular loops, and vertical strokes thicker than horizontal strokes.
copper pyrites *n.* A copper ore, **chalcopyrite** *(see).*
cop·per·smith (kŏp′ər-smĭth′) *n.* **1.** A worker or manufacturer of objects in copper. **2.** A brightly colored bird, *Megalaima haemacephala,* of southeastern Asia, having a ringing, metallic call.
copper sulfate *n.* A poisonous crystalline copper salt, $CuSO_4$, used in agriculture, textile dyeing, leather treatment, electroplating, and the manufacture of germicides. It is white when anhydrous; the hydrate, $CuSO_4 \cdot 5H_2O$, is blue and is also called "blue vitriol."
cop·pice (kŏp′ĭs) *n. Chiefly British.* A thicket or copse. [From Old French *copeïz,* from Vulgar Latin *colpaticium* (unattested), from *colpare* (unattested), to cut, from Medieval Latin *colpus,* blow. See **cope** (to contend).]
cop·ra (kŏp′rə) *n.* Dried coconut meat from which coconut oil is extracted. [Portuguese, from Malayalam *koppara.*]
copro– *prefix.* Indicates dung or excrement; for example, **coprolite.** [From Greek *kopros,* dung.]
cop·ro·lite (kŏp′rə-līt′) *n.* Fossilized excrement. [COPRO- + -LITE.] **—cop·ro·lit·ic** (kŏp′rə-lĭt′ĭk) *adj.*
cop·rol·o·gy (kŏp-rŏl′ə-jē) *n.* Scatology. [COPRO- + -LOGY.]
cop·roph·a·gous (kŏp-rŏf′ə-gəs) *adj.* Feeding on excrement: *coprophagous insects.* [New Latin *coprophagus,* from Greek *koprophagos* : COPRO-´ + -PHAGOUS.] **—cop·roph·a·gy** (kŏp-rŏf′ə-jē) *n.*
cop·ro·phil·i·a (kŏp′rə-fĭl′ē-ə) *n.* An abnormal attraction to fecal matter. [New Latin : COPRO- + -PHILIA.]
copse (kŏps) *n.* A thicket of small trees or shrubs, especially one grown for periodic cutting. [Short for COPPICE.]
Copt (kŏpt) *n.* **1.** A native of Egypt descended from ancient Egyptian stock. **2.** A member of the Coptic Church. [French *Copte,* from New Latin *Coptus,* from Arabic *quft, qubt,* the Copts, from Coptic *gyptios,* from Greek *Aiguptios,* from *Aiguptos,* EGYPT.]
cop·ter (kŏp′tər) *n. Informal.* A helicopter.
Cop·tic (kŏp′tĭk) *n.* The Afro-Asiatic language of the Copts, used today only in the liturgy of the Coptic Church. **—Cop·tic** *adj.*
Coptic Church *n.* The Christian church of Egypt, adhering to the Monophysite doctrine.
cop·u·la (kŏp′yə-lə) *n., pl.* **-las** or **-lae** (-lē). **1.** A verb, such as *feel, become, seem,* or any form of *be,* that identifies the predicate of a sentence with the subject. In the sentence *The child seems unhappy,* the copula is *seems.* **2.** *Logic.* The word or set of words that serves as a link between the subject and predicate of a proposition. [Latin *cōpula,* link, bond.] **—cop·u·lar** (kŏp′yə-lər) *adj.*
cop·u·late (kŏp′yə-lāt′) *intr.v.* **-lated, -lating, -lates.** To engage in sexual intercourse. [Latin *cōpulāre,* to fasten together, link, from *cōpula,* link, bond.] **—cop·u·la·tion** *n.*
cop·u·la·tive (kŏp′yə-lā′tĭv, -lə-tĭv) *adj.* **1.** Joining or uniting. **2.** *Grammar.* **a.** Serving to connect coordinate words or clauses: *a copulative conjunction.* **b.** Serving as a copula: *a copulative verb.* **3.** Of or pertaining to copulation.
~*n. Grammar.* A copulative word or group of words. **—cop·u·la·tive·ly** *adv.*
copulative conjunction *n.* Any of various conjunctions that serve to connect words or word groups in a coordinate relationship; for example, the conjunction *and.*
co·punc·tal (kō-pŭngk′təl) *adj. Mathematics.* Having a point in common. Said of three or more intersecting planes or surfaces.
cop·y (kŏp′ē) *n., pl.* **-ies. 1.** An imitation or reproduction of something original; a duplicate. **2.** One specimen or example of a printed text or picture: *an autographed copy of a novel.* **3.** *Abbr.* **c., C. a.** Manuscript or other material to be printed. **b.** Text, especially advertising material, as distinct from graphic material. **4.** Suitable source material, as for a newspaper story: *Celebrities make good copy.*
~*v.* **copied, -ying, -ies.** —*tr.* **1.** To make a copy or copies of; transcribe or reproduce. **2.** To follow as a model or pattern; imitate. —*intr.* **1.** To make one or more copies or reproductions. **2.** To cheat, as in an examination, by copying another's work. **3.** To admit of being reproduced. —See Synonyms at **imitate.** [Middle English *copie,* from Old French, from Medieval Latin *cōpia,* transcript, right of reproduction, from Latin, abundance, power.]
cop·y·book (kŏp′ē-bo͝ok′) *n.* **1.** A book of models, especially of penmanship, for imitation. **2.** A book for copies, as of documents.
~*adj.* Unoriginal; trite: *a copybook phrase.*
copy boy *n.* An employee in a newspaper office who carries copy and runs errands.
cop·y·cat (kŏp′ē-kăt′) *n. Informal.* One who imitates, especially in a slavish way. **—cop·y·cat** *adj.*
copy desk *n.* The desk in a newspaper office where copy is edited and prepared for printing.
cop·y·ed·it (kŏp′ē-ĕd′ĭt) *tr.v.* **-ited, -iting, -its.** To correct and prepare (a manuscript or other material) for printing. **—copy editor** *n.*
cop·y·graph (kŏp′ē-grăf′, -gräf′) *n.* A **hectograph** *(see).*
cop·y·hold (kŏp′ē-hōld′) *n.* **1.** Formerly in England, tenure based on the customs of the local manor. **2.** Land held in this way.
cop·y·hold·er (kŏp′ē-hōl′dər) *n.* **1.** An assistant who reads manuscript aloud to a proofreader. **2.** A device that holds copy in place for the typesetter. **3.** Formerly, one holding land by copyhold.
cop·y·ist (kŏp′ē-ĭst) *n.* One who makes written copies.
cop·y·read·er (kŏp′ē-rē′dər) *n.* One who edits and corrects newspaper copy for publication.
cop·y·right (kŏp′ē-rīt′) *n. Abbr.* **c., C., cop.** The right granted by law to an author, composer, playwright, publisher, or distributor, to exclusive publication, production, sale, or distribution of a literary, musical, dramatic, or artistic work. In the United States, this right extends for a period of 28 years, with the privilege of renewal for an additional 28 years.
~*adj.* Also **cop·y·right·ed.** Protected by copyright.
~*tr.v.* **copyrighted, -righting, -rights.** To secure a copyright for. **—cop·y·right·a·ble** *adj.* **—cop·y·right·er** *n.*
copy typist *n.* One who types out written rather than dictated material. Compare **audiotypist.**
cop·y·writ·er (kŏp′ē-rī′tər) *n.* One who writes advertising or publicity copy. **—cop·y·writ·ing** *n.*
coq au vin (kōk′ ō văN′) *n.* Chicken cooked in red wine, with mushrooms, onions, and garlic. [French, "cock in wine."]
co·quet (kō-kĕt′) *intr.v.* **-quetted, -quetting, -quets. 1.** To play the coquette; flirt. **2.** To trifle; dally. [French *coqueter,* to flirt, from *coquet,* flirtatious man. See **coquette.**]
co·quet·ry (kō′kĭ-trē, kō-kĕt′rē) *n., pl.* **-ries.** Dalliance; flirtation. [French *coquetterie,* from COQUETTE.]
co·quette (kō-kĕt′) *n.* A woman who flirts with men. [French, feminine of *coquet,* flirtatious man, diminutive of *coq,* cock, from Old French *coc,* from Late Latin *coccus,* from Latin *coco,* cackle. See **cock.**] **—co·quet·tish** *adj.* **—co·quet·tish·ly** *adv.* **—co·quet·tish·ness** *n.*
co·quil·la nut (kō-kēl′yə, -kē′yə) *n.* The nut of a South American palm tree, *Attalea funifera,* having a hard oval shell used for decorative carving or turning. [Portuguese *coquilho,* diminutive of *côco,* COCO.]
co·quille (kō-kēl′) *n.* A scallop-shaped dish or a scallop shell in which various seafood dishes are browned and served. [French, variant (influenced by *coque,* shell) of Latin *conchylia,* plural of *conchylium,* mussel, from Greek *konkhulion,* mussel, cockle, diminutive of *konkhē,* CONCH.]
co·qui·na (kō-kē′nə) *n.* **1.** Any of various small bivalve mollusks of warm marine waters, having variously colored, often striped or banded shells. **2.** A soft porous limestone, essentially of shell and coral fragments, used as construction material. [Spanish, shellfish, cockel, irregular diminutive of concha, shell, mussel, from Latin, CONCH.]
co·qui·to (kō-kē′tō) *n., pl.* **-tos.** A Chilean palm tree, *Jubaea spectabilis,* whose sap gives a sweet edible syrup. [Spanish, diminutive of *coco,* coco palm, from Portuguese *côco,* COCO.]
cor. **1.** corner. **2.** cornet. **3.** coroner. **4.** corpus. **5.** correction. **6.** correspondence; correspondent; corresponding.
Cor. Corinthians (New Testament).
cor·a·ci·i·form (kôr′ə-sī′ə-fôrm′) *adj.* Of, belonging to, or pertaining to the Coraciiformes, an order of birds that includes the kingfishers, hornbills, hoopoes, and bee-eaters. [From New Latin *Coracias* (genus), from Greek *korakias,* chough.]
cor·a·cle (kôr′ə-kəl, kŏr′-) *n.* A small, rounded boat made of waterproof material stretched over a wicker or wooden frame. Also *Scot-*

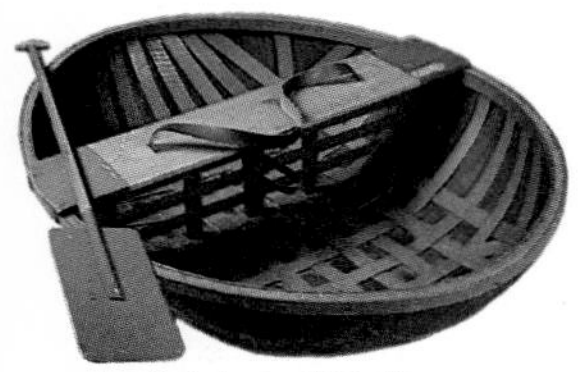

coracle *A light and highly maneuverable fishing boat still found in parts of Britain and Ireland. Coracles are made from a wicker or wood frame covered in leather or tarred cloth. The design dates back to prehistoric times.*

PRONUNCIATION KEY

ă, pat; ā, pay; âr, care;
ä, father, are; b, bib;
ch, church; d, deed; ĕ, pet;
ē, be; f, fife; g, gag; h, hat;
hw, which; ĭ, pit; ī, pie;
îr, pier; j, judge; k, kick;
l, lid, needle; m, mum;
n, no, sudden; ng, thing;
ŏ, pot; ō, toe; ô, paw, for;
oi, noise; ou, out; o͝o, book;
o͞o, boot; p, pop; r, roar;
s, sauce; sh, ship, dish;
t, tight; th, thin, path;
th, this, bathe; ŭ, cut; ûr, fur;
v, valve; w, with; y, yes;
z, zebra, size; zh, vision;
ə, about, item, edible,
gallop, circus, peaceful

IN FOREIGN WORDS:

à, *Fr.* ami; œ, *Fr.* feu, *Ger.* schön; ü, *Fr.* tu, *Ger.* über; KH, *Ger.* ich, *Scot.* loch; N, *Fr.* bon; y′, *Fr.* Compiègne

STRESS MARKS:

Primary stress: ′
in·cite′ (ĭn-sīt′)
Secondary stress: ′
in′sight′ (ĭn′sīt′)

tish & Irish "currach." [Earlier *corougle,* from Welsh *corwgl, cwrwgl.* See **currach.**]

cor·a·coid (kôr′ə-koid′, kŏr′-) *n.* A paired cartilage bone projecting from the scapula toward the sternum in teleost fish and quadrupeds. In mammals it is reduced to a peg, the *coracoid process.* [New Latin *coracoides,* "(bone) shaped like a crow's beak," from Greek *korakoeidēs,* like a raven : *korax,* raven + -OID.] **—cor·a·coid** *adj.*

cor·al (kôr′əl, kŏr′-) *n.* **1.** Any of numerous chiefly colonial marine coelenterates of the class Anthozoa, characterized by calcareous skeletons massed in a wide variety of shapes, and often forming reefs or islands. **2.** The often hard, rocklike structure formed by such organisms. **3.** The material forming such a structure; especially, the red-orange, pinkish, or white stony substance secreted by corals of the genus *Corallium,* used to make jewelry and ornaments. **4.** An object made of coral. **5.** Deep or strong pink to moderate red or reddish orange. [Middle English, from Old French, from Latin *corallium,* from Greek *korallion,* probably of Semitic origin, akin to Hebrew *gōrāl,* a pebble.] **—cor·al** *adj.*

cor·al·bells (kôr′əl-bĕlz′, kŏr′-) *n. Used with a singular or plural verb.* A plant, *Heuchera sanguinea,* of the western United States, widely cultivated for its clusters of small, bell-shaped red flowers.

cor·al·ber·ry (kôr′əl-bĕr′ē, kŏr′-) *n.* **1.** A North American shrub, *Symphoricarpos orbiculatus,* having red or purplish fruit. **2.** The fruit of this shrub.

cor·al·line (kôr′ə-lĭn, -līn′, kŏr′-) *adj.* **1.** Of, consisting of, or producing coral. **2.** Resembling coral; especially, coral-colored.
~n. **1.** A corallike animal, such as certain polyzoans or hydrozoans. **2.** Any of various red algae, especially of the genus *Corallina,* covered with a calcareous substance and forming stony deposits.

cor·al·loid (kôr′ə-loid′, kŏr′-) *adj.* Resembling coral.

coral reef *n.* A marine ridge or mound consisting chiefly of compacted coral together with algal material and biochemically deposited magnesium and calcium carbonates.

cor·al·root (kôr′əl-ro͞ot′, -ro͝ot′, kŏr′-) *n.* Any of several saprophytic orchids of the genus *Corallorhiza,* having small yellow-green or purplish flowers and branched roots that resemble coral.

Cor·al Sea (kôr′əl, kŏr′-). A region of the South Pacific Ocean, between northeast Australia and the New Britain–New Caledonia island chain. It contains the Great Barrier Reef, the largest coral reef in the world.

coral snake *n.* Any of various venomous snakes of the genus *Micrurus,* of tropical America and the southern United States, characteristically having brilliant red, black, and yellow banded markings.

cor an·glais (kôr än-glā′) *n., pl.* **cors anglais** (kôrz). A musical instrument, the **English horn** *(see).* [French, "English horn."]

cor·beil (kôr′bəl, kôr-bā′) *n.* Also **cor·beille** (kôr-bā′). A sculptured basket of flowers or fruit used as an architectural ornament. [French *corbeille,* from Late Latin *corbicula,* diminutive of Latin *corbis,* basket.]

cor·bel (kôr′bəl) *n.* A bracket of stone, wood, brick, or other building material, projecting from the face of a wall and generally used to support a cornice or an arch.
~tr.v. **corbeled** or **-belled, -beling** or **-belling,** or **-bels.** To provide with or support by a corbel or corbels. [Middle English, from Old French, diminutive of *corp,* raven (early corbels were wedge-shaped, like ravens' beaks), from Latin *corvus.*]

cor·bel·ing (kôr′bə-lĭng) *n.* An overlapping arrangement of bricks or stones in which each course extends farther out from the vertical of the wall than the course below.

cor·bie (kôr′bē) *n. Scottish.* A raven, crow, or rook. [Middle English, diminutive of Old French *corb,* from Latin *corvus,* crow.]

corbie gable *n.* A gable roof with corbie-steps.

cor·bie-step (kôr′bē-stĕp′) *n.* Also **corbel step.** Any of a series of steps or steplike projections on the top of a gable wall. [From Middle English *corbie,* raven (the steps being accessible only to birds), from Old French *corbin,* from Latin *corvīnus,* ravenlike.]

cor·bi·na (kôr-bē′nə) *n.* Also **cor·vi·na** (-vē′nə). A game fish, *Menticirrhus undulatus,* of North American Pacific coastal waters. [Spanish *corvina,* from *corvino,* ravenlike (from its color), from Latin *corvīnus,* from *corvus,* raven.]

Corbusier, Le. See **Le Corbusier.**

Corcyra. See **Corfu.**

cord (kôrd) *n.* Also **chord** (for sense 5 only). **1.** A string or small rope of twisted strands or fibers. **2.** An insulated, flexible electric wire fitted with a plug or plugs. **3.** An influence, feeling, or force that binds or restrains. **4.** The hangman's rope. **5.** An anatomical structure resembling a cord: *spinal cord; umbilical cord.* **6.** A raised rib on the surface of cloth, as on corduroy. **7.** A fabric with such ribs. **8. cords.** Trousers made of corduroy. **9.** A unit of quantity for cut fuel wood, equal to 128 cubic feet in a stack measuring 4 by 4 by 8 feet.
~tr.v. **corded, cording, cords.** **1.** To fasten or bind with a cord or cords. **2.** To pile (wood) in cords. [Middle English, from Old French *corde,* from Latin *chorda,* catgut, cord, from Greek *khordē.*] **—cord·er** *n.*

cord·age (kôr′dĭj) *n.* **1.** The ropes in the rigging of a ship. **2.** The amount of wood in an area, as measured in cords.

cor·date (kôr′dāt′) *adj. Biology.* Having a heart-shaped outline: *a cordate leaf.* [New Latin *cordatus,* from Latin *cor* (stem *cord-*), heart.] **—cor·date·ly** *adv.*

Cor·day (kôr-dā′), **Charlotte,** born Marie Anne Charlotte Corday d'Armont (1768–93). French noblewoman who assassinated Jean Paul Marat (1793). Of an impoverished Norman aristocratic family, she sympathized with the Girondins in the French Revolution. She was guillotined in 1793.

cord·ed (kôr′dĭd) *adj.* **1.** Furnished with or made of cords. **2.** Bound with cords. **3.** Ribbed or twilled, as corduroy. **4.** Stacked in cords, as firewood. **5.** Standing out like tightened cords. Said of muscles.

cor·dial (kôr′jəl) *adj.* **1.** Warm and sincere; hearty. **2.** Serving to invigorate; stimulating; reviving.
~n. **1.** A stimulant. **2.** A **liqueur** *(see).* [Middle English, of the heart, from Medieval Latin *cordiālis,* from Latin *cor* (stem *cord-*), heart.] **—cor·di·al·i·ty** (kôr′jē-ăl′ə-tē, -jăl′-), **cor·dial·ness** *n.* **—cor·dial·ly** *adv.*

cor·di·er·ite (kôr′dē-ə-rīt′) *n.* A dichroic violet-blue to gray mineral silicate of magnesium, aluminum, and sometimes iron. Also called "dichroite," "iolite." [French, after Pierre L.A. *Cordier* (1777–1861), French geologist who first described it.]

cor·di·form (kôr′də-fôrm′) *adj.* Heart-shaped. [French *cordiforme* : Latin *cor* (stem *cord-*), heart + -FORM.]

cor·dil·le·ra (kôr′dĭl-yâr′ə, kôr-dĭl′ər-ə) *n.* A series of broadly parallel mountain ranges; especially, the principal mountain system of a large land mass. [Spanish, from *cordilla,* diminutive of *cuerda,* cord, chain, from Latin *chorda,* CORD.] **—cor·dil·le·ran** *adj.*

Cor·dil·ler·as (kôr′dĭl-yâr′əz). The entire chain of mountain ranges of western North, Central, and South America. The Cordilleras extend from northern Alaska to Cape Horn and include the Rocky Mts., the Sierra Nevada, and the Andes.

cord·ite (kôr′dīt′) *n.* A smokeless explosive powder consisting of nitrocellulose, nitroglycerin, and petrolatum dissolved in acetone, dried, and extruded in cords. [From CORD.]

cord·less (kôrd′lĭs) *adj.* Operated by battery.

cór·do·ba (kôr′də-bə) *n.* The basic monetary unit of Nicaragua, equal to 100 centavos. [After Francisco de *Córdoba* (*c.* 1475–1526), Spanish explorer.]

Cór·do·ba[1] (kôr′də-bə). Capital of Córdoba province, southern Spain, on the Guadalquivir River. As a Moorish capital (756–1031) it was a brilliant cultural center.

Córdoba[2]. Capital of Córdoba province in central Argentina. It lies on the Primero River, and was founded in 1573.

cor·don (kôr′dən) *n.* **1.** A line of troops, military posts, ships, or the like, stationed around an area to enclose or guard it. **2.** A cord or braid worn as a fastening or an ornament. **3.** A ribbon, worn usually diagonally across the chest as a badge of honor or a decoration. **4.** *Architecture.* An ornamental band of stone or masonry, a **stringcourse** *(see).* **5.** *Horticulture.* A fruit tree trained and pruned to grow along wires or other supports.
~tr.v. **cordoned, -doning, -dons.** To form a cordon around (an area) so as to prevent movement in or out. Often used with *off.* [French, from Old French, diminutive of *corde,* CORD.]

cor·don bleu (kôr-dôN′ blœ′) *n., pl.* **cordons bleus** *(pronounced as singular).* **1.** The blue ribbon worn as a decoration by members of the Order of the Holy Ghost, the highest order of French chivalry under the Bourbon monarchy. **2.** A person highly distinguished in his field; especially, a master chef.
~adj. Of the highest standard of cooking. [French, "blue ribbon."]

cor·don sa·ni·taire (kôr-dôN′ sä-nē-târ′) *n., pl.* **cordons sanitaires** *(pronounced as singular).* **1.** A chain of buffer states organized around a nation considered ideologically dangerous or potentially hostile. **2.** Any physical or figurative barrier devised so as to keep off some potential danger. [French, "quarantine line."]

cor·do·van (kôr′də-vən) *n.* A fine leather made originally at Córdoba, Spain, first of goatskin but now more frequently of split horsehide. Also called "cordovan leather."
~adj. Made of this leather. [Spanish *cordobán,* from CÓRDOBA, Spain.]

Cor·do·van (kôr′də-vən) *n.* An inhabitant or native of Córdoba. [Spanish *Cordován,* from *Córdova,* CÓRDOBA, Spain.] **—Cor·do·van** *adj.*

cor·du·roy (kôr′də-roi′, kôr′də-roi′) *n.* **1.** A durable cut-pile fabric, usually made of cotton, with vertical ribs or wales. **2. corduroys.** Corduroy trousers; cords.
~adj. **1.** Made of or resembling corduroy. **2.** Made of logs laid together transversely: *a corduroy road.*
~tr.v. **corduroyed, -roying, -roys.** To build (a road) of logs laid together transversely. [Probably from CORD (ribbed cloth) + obsolete *duroy, deroy*†, a coarse woolen fabric.]

cord·wood (kôrd′wo͝od′) *n.* Wood piled or sold in cords.

core (kôr, kōr) *n.* **1.** The hard or fibrous central part of certain fruits, such as the apple or pear, containing the seeds. **2. a.** The innermost or most important part of anything; the heart; the center; the essence. **b.** A group or body forming the essential basis of something, as of an organization. **3.** *Electricity.* A soft iron rod in the coil of an electromagnet or transformer that intensifies and provides a path for the magnetic field produced by the windings. **4.** A mass of dry sand placed within a mold to provide openings or shape to a casting. **5.** The base, usually of soft or inferior wood, to which veneer woods are glued. **6.** *Computer Science.* **a.** Any of the tiny magnetic rings used to store a bit of information in a computer memory. Also called "magnetic core." **b.** A computer memory made up of such magnetic rings. **7.** The central part of the earth lying below the mantle. **8. a.** The central part of any planet that is differentiated into layers. **b.** The central part of a star, in which the energy is produced. **9.** *Physics.* The part of a nuclear reactor in

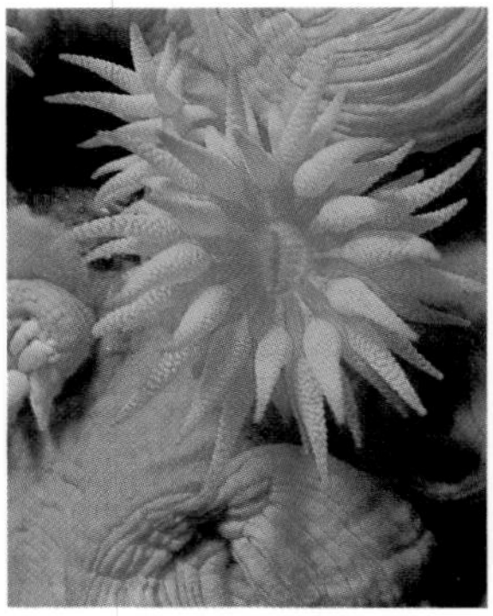

coral *The coral polyp is a soft-bodied animal that builds itself a protective, chalky skeleton into which it can withdraw. Its flowerlike tentacles usually emerge only at night to feed on tiny fish and plankton. When corals live together in large colonies, their skeletons accumulate to form reefs. Australia's Great Barrier Reef, which is some 1,930 kilometers (1,200 miles) long, is composed of the skeletons of billions of polyps, each only a few millimeters across.*

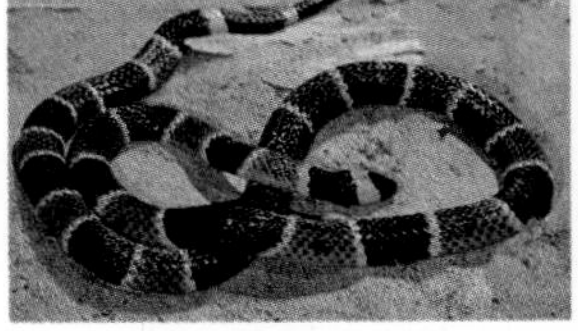

coral snake *Although this relative of the cobra is highly venomous, it seldom attacks man. Coral snakes, which are native to the tropical regions of the Americas and to the southern United States, live mostly under cover or in a burrow, emerging to feed on small animals.*

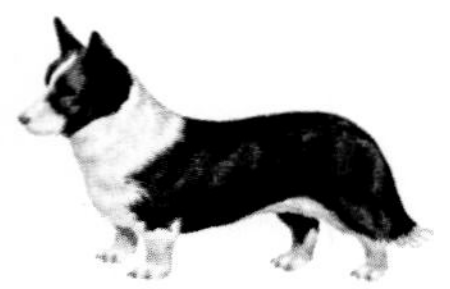

corgi *The Welsh corgi was originally a farm dog, bred to herd cattle by nipping at their heels. This is a Cardigan corgi, which has a long tail.*

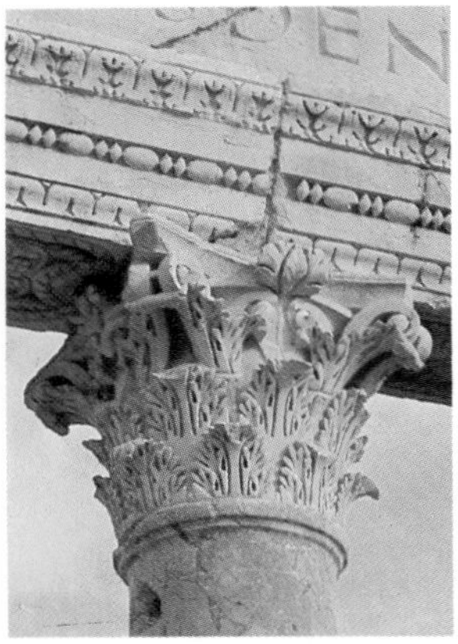

Corinthian order *This is the most richly ornamented style of pillar capital in ancient Greek architecture—an inverted, bell-shaped cluster of acanthus leaves.*

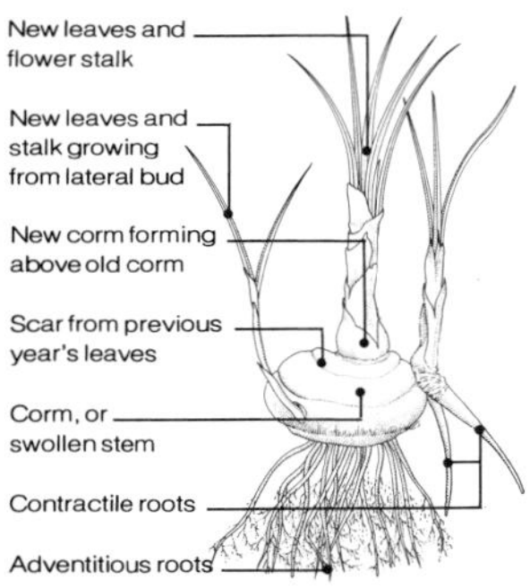
New leaves and flower stalk
New leaves and stalk growing from lateral bud
New corm forming above old corm
Scar from previous year's leaves
Corm, or swollen stem
Contractile roots
Adventitious roots

corm *A swollen underground stem, such as that of the gladiolus, which stores food from one season to the next.*

which the reaction occurs, containing the fuel and control rods. **10.** *Geology.* A cylindrical sample of the earth's crust obtained by a hollow drill or piston.
∼*tr.v.* **cored, coring, cores.** To remove the core of: *core apples.* [Middle English *core, coor*†.] —**cor·er** *n.*

core dump *n.* A listing in the form of a print-out or a display on a screen of the data stored in a computer core.

core-dump (kôr′dŭmp′, kōr′-) *tr.v.* **-dumped, -dumping, -dumps.** To print out or display (the data in a computer core).

corelate. *Chiefly British.* Variant of **correlate.**

co·re·lig·ion·ist (kō′rĭ-lĭj′ə-nĭst) *n.* One having the same religion as another.

Co·rel·li (kə-rĕl′ē), **Arcangelo** (1653–1713). Italian composer and violinist and an important innovator of violin technique in the baroque era. As a composer he is best remembered for his 12 *concerti grossi,* which shaped the development of the concerto.

co·re·op·sis (kôr′ē-ŏp′sĭs) *n.* Any of several plants of the genus *Coreopsis,* having daisylike yellow or variegated flowers. Also called "tickseed" and sometimes "calliopsis." [New Latin, "resembling a bedbug" (from the shape of the seed) : Greek *koris,* bedbug + -OPSIS.]

co·re·spon·dent (kō′rĭ-spŏn′dənt) *n. Law.* A person cited as having committed adultery with the defendant (respondent) in a divorce suit. —**co·re·spon·den·cy** *n.*

corf (kôrf) *n., pl.* **corves** (kôrvz). *British.* A wagon, tub, or basket used in a mine. [Middle English, basket, from Middle Dutch *corf* or Middle Low German *korf,* probably from Latin *corbis*†.]

Cor·fam (kôr′făm′) *n.* A trademark for a synthetic leather, used especially for shoes.

Cor·fu (kôr′fo͞o, -fyo͞o). *Ancient* **Cor·cy·ra** (kôr-sī′rə). *Greek* **Kér·ky·ra** (kər-kîr′ə). Island in the Ionian Sea off northwest Greece. It is probably the Scheria of Homer. The island passed through the hands of Rome, Byzantium, Sicily, and Venice and was under British protection from 1815 to 1864, when it was ceded to Greece. Corfu's beaches attract many tourists.

cor·gi (kôr′gē) *n.* A dog belonging to either of two long-bodied, short-legged breeds, the *Cardigan corgi* or the *Pembroke corgi.* Also called "Welsh corgi." [Welsh : *cor,* dwarf + *ci,* dog.]

co·ri·a·ceous (kôr′ē-ā′shəs) *adj.* Of or like leather, especially in texture; tough. [Late Latin *coriāceus,* from Latin *corium,* leather, hide.]

co·ri·an·der (kôr′ē-ăn′dər, kōr′-) *n.* **1.** A herb, *Coriandrum sativum,* widely cultivated for its aromatic seeds. **2.** The dried ripe seeds of this plant, used especially to flavor food. [Middle English *coriandre,* from Old French, from Latin *coriandrum,* from Greek *koriandron, koriannon,* perhaps of Mediterranean origin.]

Cor·inth (kôr′ĭnth, kŏr′-). *Greek* **Kó·rin·thos** (kôr′ĭn-thôs′). Port in southern Greece, on the Isthmus of Corinth. It became rich and influential in the 7th and 6th centuries B.C. as the region's leading pottery producer and maritime power, but it was later overshadowed by Athens. Medieval exports included currants, which get their name from the city.

Corinth, Isthmus of. A neck of land, *c.* 32 kilometers (20 miles) long and 6.5 to 13 kilometers (4 to 8 miles) wide, connecting the Peloponnese to the rest of Greece. It is between the Gulf of Corinth, an inlet of the Ionian Sea, and the Saronic Gulf.

Co·rin·thi·an (kə-rĭn′thē-ən) *adj.* **1.** Of or pertaining to ancient Corinth. **2.** Given to luxury; licentious; profligate. **3.** Elegantly or elaborately ornate. **4.** Pertaining to the Corinthian order.
∼*n.* **1.** A native or inhabitant of Corinth. **2.** A wealthy amateur sportsman, especially a yachtsman. **3.** A man-about-town. **4. Corinthians.** *Abbr.* **Cor.** Either of two epistles addressed by Saint Paul to the Christian community at Corinth, each forming a book of the New Testament. In this sense, also called "Epistle to the Corinthians."

Corinthian order *n.* The most ornate of the three classical orders of architecture, characterized by a slender fluted column having an ornate bell-shaped capital decorated with acanthus leaves. Compare **Doric order, Ionic order.**

Cor·i·o·la·nus (kôr′ē-ō-lā′nəs), **Gaius Marcius** (5th century B.C.). Roman general, commemorated in Shakespeare's play *Coriolanus.* Of noble birth, he is alleged to have won his name at the siege of Corioli in the war against the Volsci (493 B.C.).

Cor·i·o·lis force (kôr′ē-ō′lĭs) *n. Physics.* A fictitious force used mathematically to describe motion relative to a noninertial, uniformly rotating frame of reference. It is used, for example, to describe the motion of air relative to the rotating earth. [After Gaspard G. de *Coriolis* (1792–1843), French mathematician.]

co·ri·um (kôr′ē-əm, kōr′-) *n., pl.* **coria** (-ə). The **dermis** *(see).* [New Latin, from Latin, skin, hide.]

cork (kôrk) *n.* **1.** The light, porous, elastic outer bark of the cork oak, used widely in industry and the arts. **2.** Something made of cork, especially a bottle stopper. **3.** A bottle stopper made of other material, such as plastic or rubber. **4.** A small float used on a fishing line or net to buoy up the line or to indicate when a fish bites. **5.** *Botany.* Cork cambium.
∼*tr.v.* **corked, corking, corks. 1.** To stop or seal with or as if with a cork. **2.** To hold back; restrain or check. Usually used with *up.* **3.** To blacken with burnt cork. [Middle English, from Dutch *kurk* or Low German *korck,* from Spanish *alcorque,* cork sole or shoe, probably from Spanish Arabic *al-qūrq.*]

Cork[1] (kôrk). A county in Munster in the southwest of the Republic of Ireland. Its hills are scattered with fortified castles, including the 15th-century Blarney Castle, famous for the Blarney Stone.

Cork[2]**.** The administrative center of County Cork at the mouth of the Lee River in the southwest of the Republic of Ireland. It is Ireland's second-largest city.

cork·age (kôr′kĭj) *n.* A charge exacted at a restaurant for opening and serving bottles of wine or other alcoholic beverages not bought on the premises.

cork·board (kôrk′bôrd′, -bōrd′) *n.* A construction and insulating sheet material made of compressed and baked granules of cork.

cork cambium *n. Botany.* A layer of continually dividing cells situated near the surface of woody plant stems and roots, which forms cork to the outside and secondary cortical cells to the inside. Also called "cork," "phellem."

corked (kôrkt) *adj.* **1.** Sealed with a cork. **2.** Designating wine that has been impaired in taste by a poor or decaying cork. **3.** Blackened by burnt cork. **4.** *British Slang.* Drunk.

cork·er (kôr′kər) *n.* **1.** One that inserts corks, as in bottles. **2.** *Slang.* Someone or something that is remarkable or astounding. **3.** *Slang.* An unanswerable fact or argument.

cork·ing (kôr′kĭng) *adj. Informal.* Excellent; splendid; fine. [From CORK (verb), probably influenced in meaning by CORKER.] —**cork·ing** *adv.*

cork oak *n.* An evergreen oak tree, *Quercus suber,* of the Mediterranean region, having a porous outer bark that is the source of cork. Also called "cork tree."

cork·screw (kôrk′skro͞o′) *n.* A device for drawing corks from bottles, consisting typically of a pointed metal spiral attached to a handle.
∼*adj.* Resembling a corkscrew in shape; spiral; helical.
∼*v.* **corkscrewed, -screwing, -screws.** —*tr.* To cause to move in a spiral or winding course. —*intr.* To move spirally.

cork·wood (kôrk′wo͝od′) *n.* **1.** A small tree or shrub, *Leitneria floridana,* of the southeastern United States, having a very light wood that is used for fishing-net floats. **2.** Any of several other trees having light, porous wood. **3.** The wood of these.

cork·y (kôr′kē) *adj.* **-ier, -iest. 1.** Of or like cork. **2.** *Informal.* Lively; buoyant. **3.** Tasting of cork; corked. —**cork·i·ness** *n.*

corm (kôrm) *n. Botany.* An underground stem, such as that of the gladiolus, similar to a bulb but having papery, rather than fleshy, scale leaves. [New Latin *cormus,* from Greek *kormos,* a trimmed tree trunk, from *keirein,* to shear.]

cor·mel (kôr′məl) *n. Botany.* A young corm that arises at the base of a fully developed corm.

cor·mo·phyte (kôr′mə-fīt′) *n.* Any of a former botanical division, Cormophyta, consisting of plants having roots, stems, and foliage. [New Latin *Cormophyta* : Greek *kormos,* tree trunk (see **corm**) + -PHYTE.] —**cor·mo·phyt·ic** (kôr′mə-fĭt′ĭk) *adj.*

cor·mo·rant (kôr′mər-ənt) *n.* **1.** Any of several widely distributed aquatic birds of the genus *Phalacrocorax,* especially *P. carbo,* having dark plumage, webbed feet, a hooked bill, and a distensible pouch. **2.** A greedy or rapacious person. [Middle English *cormeraunt,* from Old French *cormoran, cormaran, cormareng* : *corp,* raven, from Latin *corvus* + *marenc,* of the sea, from Latin *marīnus,* MARINE.]

corn[1] (kôrn) *n.* **1. a.** Any of several varieties of a tall, widely cultivated cereal plant, *Zea Mays,* bearing seeds or kernels on large ears. **b.** The seeds or kernels of this plant, used for food or fodder, and yielding an edible oil. **c.** The ears of this plant. Also called "Indian corn," "maize." **2.** *British.* **a.** Any of several cereal plants producing edible seed, especially when the main crop of a region, such as wheat in England and oats in Scotland. **b.** The seeds of such a plant or crop; grain. **3. a.** A single seed of a cereal plant; a grain. **b.** A seed or fruit of various other plants. **4.** *Informal.* Corn whiskey. **5.** *Slang.* Anything considered trite, dated, or unduly sentimental.
∼*tr.v.* **corned, corning, corns. 1. a.** To preserve and season with granulated salt. **b.** To preserve in brine. **2.** To feed (animals) with corn or grain. [Middle English *corn,* Old English *corn.*]

corn[2] *n.* A horny painful thickening of the skin, usually on or near a toe, resulting from pressure or friction. [Middle English *corne,* from Old French *corne,* corn on the foot, horn, from Latin *cornū,* horn.]

Corn. Cornwall.

corn·ball (kôrn′bôl′) *n. Slang.* An unsophisticated or overly sentimental person. —**corn·ball** *adj.*

Corn Belt. A region of the midwestern United States, stretching across Ohio, Indiana, Illinois, Iowa, Minnesota, South Dakota, Missouri, Kansas, and Nebraska, where the chief products are corn and corn-fed livestock.

corn borer *n.* **1.** The larva of a moth, *Pyrausta nubilalis,* native to the Old World, that feeds on and destroys corn and other plants. **2.** Any of various similar insect larvae that infest corn.

corn bread, corn·bread (kôrn′brĕd′) *n.* A bread made of cornmeal.

corn·cake, corn cake (kôrn′kāk′) *n.* A bread made with white cornmeal cooked either as small cakes on a griddle or oven-baked in a pan. Also called "johnnycake."

corn·cob (kôrn′kŏb′) *n.* **1.** The hard core of an ear of corn to which the kernels are attached. **2.** A corncob pipe.

corncob pipe *n.* A pipe with a bowl made of a dried corncob.

corn cockle *n.* A plant, *Agrostemma githago,* native to Europe, having red flowers and growing in grain fields and by roadsides.

corn·crake (kôrn′krāk′) *n.* A common Old World bird, *Crex crex,* having brownish plumage and frequenting cornfields and meadows.

corn·dodg·er (kôrn′dŏj′ər) *n.* A corncake either baked, pan-fried, or broiled. [CORN + DODGER.]

cor·ne·a (kôr′nē-ə) *n.* The transparent anterior portion of the outer fibrous coat of the vertebrate eye, a uniformly thick, nearly circular, convex structure that refracts light onto the lens. [Medieval Latin *cornea (tēla),* "horny (tissue)," from Latin, feminine of *corneus,* horny, from *cornū,* horn.] **—cor·ne·al** *adj.*

corn earworm *n.* The large, destructive larva of a moth, *Heliothis armigera,* that feeds on corn and many other plants. Also called "bollworm."

corned beef *n.* A type of beef preserved with salt and spices.

Cor·neille (kôr-nā′), **Pierre** (1606–84). French playwright, the pioneer of French classical drama. His plays, including *Le Cid* (*c.* 1637) and *Horace* (1640), dramatize grand moral themes within measured and elegant verse.

cor·nel (kôr′nəl) *n.* Any of various plants of the genus *Cornus,* which includes the dogwoods. [German *Kornel(beere), Kornel(baum),* cornel (berry), cornel (tree), from Old High German *kornul-,* from Medieval Latin *corna* (unattested), from Latin *cornus*†, cornel tree.]

cornelian. Variant of **carnelian.**

cor·nel·ian cherry (kôr-nēl′yən) *n.* A shrub or small tree, *Cornus mas,* native to Eurasia, having very small yellow flowers and bright-red edible fruit. [From CORNEL.]

Cor·nell (kôr-nĕl′), **Katharine** (1893–1974). U.S. actress and producer. She made her Broadway debut in 1921 and that same year won acclaim for her starring role in *A Bill of Divorcement.* One of her most popular roles was Elizabeth Barrett Browning in *The Barretts of Wimpole Street,* which first opened in 1931.

cor·ne·ous (kôr′nē-əs) *adj.* Made of horn or a hornlike substance; horny. [Latin *corneus,* from *cornū,* horn.]

cor·ner (kôr′nər) *n. Abbr.* **cor. 1.** The position at which two lines or surfaces meet. **2.** The immediate interior or exterior region of the angle formed at this position, bounded by the two lines or surfaces. **3.** The point or place where the sides of roads, streets, or walls join, meet, or intersect. **4.** A threatening or embarrassing position, especially one from which escape is difficult or impossible: *backed into a corner.* **5.** Any part, quarter, or region: *from every corner of the globe.* **6.** A remote, secluded, or secret place, area, or part. **7.** A guard or decoration fitted on various kinds of corners, as of a bookbinding. **8.** A speculative monopoly of a stock or commodity created by purchasing all or most of the available supply in order to raise its price. **9.** In boxing and wrestling, either of two diagonally opposite corners of the ring in which opponents rest between rounds. **—cut corners. 1.** To take the shortest route around obstacles, often dangerously or illegally. **2.** To reduce expenses; economize. **—turn the corner.** To get over or come through the worst part of an illness, financial difficulty, or the like; pass the critical point.

~v. **cornered, -nering, -ners.** *—tr.* **1.** To furnish with corners. **2.** To place or drive into a corner. **3.** To get a corner in (a stock or commodity). *—intr.* **1.** To get a corner in a stock or commodity. **2.** To turn, as at a corner.

~adj. **1.** On or at a corner. **2.** Designed for or used in a corner. [Middle English, from Old French *cornere, corniere,* from Vulgar Latin *cornārium* (unattested), from Latin *cornū,* horn, extremity.]

cor·ner·stone (kôr′nər-stōn′) *n.* **1.** A stone at the corner of a building uniting two intersecting walls; a quoin. **2.** Such a stone ceremonially laid and often inscribed with the date of construction. **3.** The indispensable and fundamental basis of something: *Free speech is the cornerstone of a democracy.*

cor·net (kôr-nĕt′ *for sense 1*; kôr′nĭt *for senses 2–6*) *n.* **1.** *Abbr.* **cor.** A musical wind instrument of the trumpet class, having three valves operated by pistons. **2.** A piece of paper twisted into a cone and used to hold small wares such as candy and nuts. **3.** *British.* A wafer, usually cone-shaped, topped with ice cream. **4.** A large white headdress worn by certain nuns. **5.** A headdress, often cone-shaped, worn by women in the late Middle Ages. **6. a.** Formerly, the fifth commissioned officer in a British cavalry troop. **b.** The standard carried by such an officer. [Middle English, from Old French, diminutive of *corn,* horn, from Latin *cornū.*]

cor·net·cy (kôr′nĭt-sē) *n., pl.* **-cies.** Formerly, the rank or commission of a cornet cavalry officer.

cor·net·ist, cor·net·tist (kôr-nĕt′ĭst) *n.* One who plays a cornet.

corn-fed (kôrn′fĕd′) *adj.* **1.** Fed on corn. **2.** Well-fed and healthy, but provincial and unsophisticated.

corn·field (kôrn′fēld′) *n.* A field planted with corn.

corn·flakes (kôrn′flāks′) *pl.n.* A crisp, flaky, commercially prepared cold cereal made from coarse cornmeal.

corn·flour (kôrn′flou′ər) *n. British.* Cornstarch.

corn·flow·er (kôrn′flou′ər) *n.* A garden plant, *Centaurea cyanus,* native to Eurasia, having blue, purple, pink, or white flowers. Also called "bachelor's-button," "bluebottle." [So called because it is found in cornfields.]

corn·husk (kôrn′hŭsk′) *n.* The leafy husk surrounding an ear of corn. Also called "corn shuck."

cor·nice (kôr′nĭs) *n.* **1.** *Architecture.* **a.** A horizontal molded projection that crowns or completes a building or wall. **b.** The uppermost part of an entablature. **2.** A molding at the top of the walls of a room, between the walls and ceiling. **3.** An ornamental horizontal molding or frame used to conceal curtain rods, picture hooks, or other devices. **4.** An overhanging mass of snow at a precipice.

~tr.v. **corniced, -nicing, -nices.** To supply, decorate, or finish with, or as with, a cornice. [French *corniche,* from Italian *cornice,* perhaps from Latin *cornix* (stem *cornic-*), crow, also influenced by Greek *korōnis,* curved line, coping stone, from *korōnē,* anything curved, from *korōnos,* curved.]

cor·niche (kôr-nēsh′) *n.* A coast road, often along the side of a cliff. [French. See **cornice.**]

cor·nic·u·late (kôr-nĭk′yə-lāt′, -lĭt) *adj.* Having horns or hornlike projections. [Latin *corniculātus,* from *corniculum,* little horn, diminutive of *cornū,* horn.]

Cor·ning (kôr′nĭng). City in southern New York State, on the Chemung River in a dairy and vineyard region. It is famous for its glassworks dating from 1868 and its glass museum.

Cor·nish (kôr′nĭsh) *adj.* Of or pertaining to Cornwall in southwest England, its inhabitants, or their language.

~n. The Brythonic Celtic language of Cornwall, extinct since the late 18th century. **—Cor·nish·man** *n.*

Cornish hen *n.* See **Rock Cornish hen.**

Corn Laws *pl.n.* A series of British laws in force before 1846 regulating the grain trade and restricting imports of grain.

corn lily *n.* Any of several bulbous plants of the genus *Ixia,* native to southern Africa, having variously colored lilylike flowers.

corn marigold *n.* A Eurasian plant, *Chrysanthemum segetum,* having yellow or white daisylike flowers.

corn·meal, corn meal (kôrn′mēl′) *n.* Meal ground from corn.

corn pone (pōn) *n. Southern U.S.* Corn bread made without milk or eggs. Also called "pone."

corn poppy *n.* An Old World plant, *Papaver rhoeas,* having bright-red flowers, frequently a weed in cultivated fields. Also called "Flanders poppy."

corn rose *n. British.* Any of several red-flowered plants growing in grain fields, such as the corn poppy or the corn cockle.

corn·row (kôrn′rō′) *tr.v.* To style (hair) by dividing into sections and braiding in parallel rows close to the scalp. **—corn·row** *n.*

corn rule *n. Chemistry.* A rule for indicating the optical activity of amino acids with the formula $RCH(NH_2)(COOH)$. If the molecule were observed along the H–C direction, the COOH, R, and NH_2 groups would be arranged clockwise in dextrorotatory acids and counterclockwise in levorotatory acids. [From *CO*OH *R* NH_2.]

corn salad *n.* Any of several plants of the genus *Valerianella;* especially, *V. locusta* (or *V. olitoria*), native to Europe, having small bluish flowers and leaves that are used in salad. Also called "lamb's-lettuce." [So called because it is found in cornfields.]

corn shuck *n.* A **cornhusk** *(see).*

corn silk *n.* The silky styles that appear as a tuft or tassel at the tip of an ear of corn.

corn·stalk (kôrn′stôk′) *n.* A stalk or stem of corn.

corn·starch (kôrn′stärch′) *n.* A starch made from corn and used as a thickener in cooking.

corn sugar *n.* **Dextrose** *(see).*

corn syrup *n.* A syrup prepared from corn, containing glucose combined with dextrin and maltose.

cor·nu (kôr′nyōō, -nōō) *n., pl.* **-nua** (-nyōō-ə, -nōō-ə). *Anatomy.* A structure resembling a horn. [Latin *cornū,* horn.] **—cor·nu·al** *adj.*

cor·nu·co·pi·a (kôr′nə-kō′pē-ə) *n.* **1.** A goat's horn overflowing with fruit, flowers, and corn, signifying prosperity; a horn of plenty. **2.** An overflowing store; an abundance. **3.** Any cone-shaped receptacle or ornament. [Late Latin *cornūcōpia,* horn of plenty, from Latin *cornū cōpiae* : *cornū,* horn + *cōpiae,* genitive of *cōpia,* plenty.] **—cor·nu·co·pi·an** *adj.*

cor·nute (kôr-nōōt′, -nyōōt′) *adj.* Also **cor·nut·ed** (kôr-nōō′tĭd, -nyōō′tĭd). **1.** Horn-shaped. **2.** Having horns or horn-shaped anatomical processes. [Latin *cornūtus,* horned, from *cornū,* horn.]

Corn·wall (kôrn′wôl′). *Abbr.* **Corn.** County in the extreme southwest of England. At its extremity is Land's End, the westernmost point of the English mainland. Tin was mined in Cornwall in ancient times and is still mined in a number of places. Following the Roman and Saxon invasions of Britain, Cornwall became a bastion of Celtic culture and its language, of Celtic origin, has never entirely disappeared. Truro is the administrative center, and Penzance the largest town.

Corn·wal·lis (kôrn-wŏl′ĭs), **Charles, 1st Marquess** (1738–1805). British soldier and statesman who commanded British forces in South Carolina during the American Revolution. His surrender at Yorktown on October 19, 1781, marked the final British defeat. As governor general of India (1786–93) he introduced a series of land reforms to secure administrative control of India for the East India Company.

corn whiskey *n.* Whiskey distilled from corn.

corn·y (kôr′nē) *adj.* **-ier, -iest.** *Informal.* **1.** Trite or mawkishly sentimental: *a corny love story.* **2.** Lacking subtlety; unsophisticated: *corny jokes.* [From CORN (from the supposedly unsophisticated humor of farmers).]

co·rol·la (kə-rŏl′ə) *n. Botany.* The inner envelope of a flower, consisting of fused or separate petals. Compare **calyx.** [New Latin, from Latin, diminutive of *corōna,* garland, CORONA.]

cor·ol·lar·y (kôr′ə-lĕr′ē, kŏr′-) *n., pl.* **-ies. 1.** A proposition that follows with little or no additional proof from one already proved. **2.** A deduction or inference. **3.** A natural consequence or effect; a result.

~adj. Consequent or resultant. [Middle English *corolarie,* from Latin *corollārium,* money paid for a garland, gratuity, from *corolla,* small garland, diminutive of *corōna,* garland, CORONA.]

Cor·o·man·del Coast (kôr′ə-măn′dĕl). The southern reaches of India's eastern seaboard, from Point Calimere to the mouth of the Krishna River. It is lashed by rough seas and monsoons.

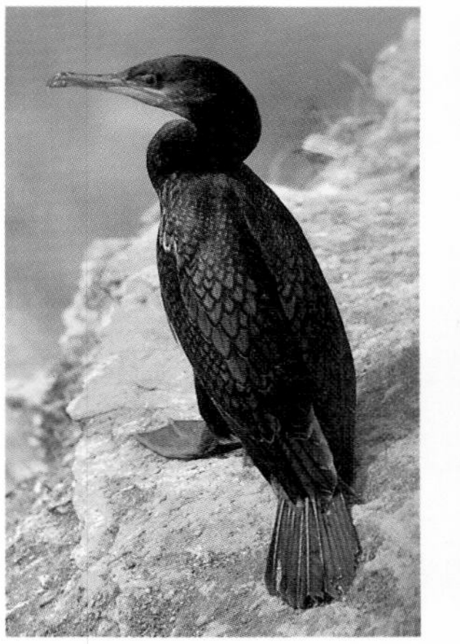

cormorant *In Japan, these diving birds—which are found in coastal waters in most parts of the world—have been used by fishermen for centuries. The birds are trained to dive for fish from boats and to return with their catch; tight leather collars prevent them from swallowing the fish. The cormorant's plumage is not oiled to resist water, and between hunting expeditions the bird often perches with its wings spread out to dry.*

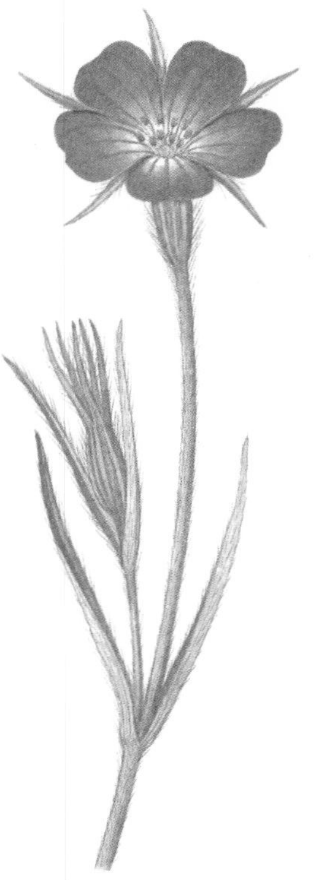

corn cockle Agrostemma githago *was once a common weed in northern European cornfields. But, since it grew among the corn, it lowered the quality of the flour; with improved methods of agriculture, this wildflower is becoming less common.*

co·ro·na (kə-rō′nə) *n., pl.* **-nas** or **-nae** (-nē). **1.** *Astronomy.* **a.** A faintly colored luminous ring around a celestial body visible through a haze or thin cloud, especially such a ring around the moon or sun, caused by diffraction of light from small suspended ice crystals in the upper atmosphere. **b.** The luminous irregular envelope of highly ionized gas outside the chromosphere of the sun. **2.** *Architecture.* The top projecting part of a cornice. **3.** A cigar having a long tapering body and blunt ends. **4.** A circular chandelier hanging from the ceiling of a church. **5.** *Anatomy.* A crownlike or upper part or structure, such as the top of the head. **6.** *Botany.* A crownlike part of a flower, usually between the petals and stamens, but sometimes an appendage of the corolla, as in daffodils. Also called "crown." **7.** *Electricity.* A faint glow enveloping the high-field electrode in a **corona discharge** *(see),* often accompanied by streamers directed toward the low-field electrode. [Latin *corōna,* garland, crown, from Greek *korōnē,* something curved, kind of crown, from *korōnos,* curved.]

Corona Aus·tra·lis (ô-strā′lĭs) *n.* A constellation in the Southern Hemisphere near Telescopium and Sagittarius. Also called the "Southern Crown."

Corona Bo·re·al·is (bôr′ē-ăl′ĭs, -ä′lĭs, bōr′ē-) *n.* A constellation containing the Corona Borealis cluster of galaxies, in the Northern Hemisphere near Hercules and Boötes. Also called the "Northern Crown."

co·ro·nach (kôr′ə-nəкн, kŏr′-) *n.* In Ireland or the Highlands of Scotland, a Gaelic funeral dirge. [Irish *coranach* and (Scottish) Gaelic *corranach* : *comh-,* together + *rānach,* a crying.]

Co·ro·na·do (kôr′ə-nä′dō, kŏr′-), **Francisco Vásquez de** (1510-54). Spanish explorer and colonial administrator. The governor of a Mexican province, he was intrigued by stories of immeasurable wealth to the north. He led an expedition through present-day southwest America in search of gold (1540), but was considered a failure when he returned to Mexico with only stories of the Grand Canyon and other natural wonders discovered on the journey.

corona discharge *n.* An electrical discharge characterized by a corona and occurring when one of two electrodes in a gas has a shape such that the electric field strength close to its surface is significantly greater than that between the electrodes.

co·ro·na·graph, co·ro·no·graph (kə-rō′nə-grăf′, -gräf′) *n. Astronomy.* A type of refracting telescope designed for study of the sun's corona, having a central disk to block light from the sun's surface. **—co·ro·na·graph·ic** *adj.*

cor·o·nal (kôr′ə-nəl, kŏr′-) *n.* **1.** A garland, wreath, or circlet. **2.** *Anatomy.* The coronal suture. **3.** *Phonetics.* A coronal speech sound.
~adj. **co·ro·nal** (kə-rō′nəl, kôr′ə-nəl, kŏr′-) **1.** Of or pertaining to a coronal. **2.** *Anatomy.* Of, designating, or having the direction of the coronal suture. **3.** *Phonetics.* Articulated with the blade of the tongue raised. [Middle English, from Old French *coronal,* from Latin *corōnālis,* of a crown, from CORONA.]

coronal suture *n.* The line of union of the two parietal bones with the frontal bone of the skull. Also called "coronal."

cor·o·nar·y (kôr′ə-něr′ē, kŏr′-) *adj.* **1.** Encircling. Said of arteries, ligaments, nerves, and the like that encircle a structure. **2.** Of or pertaining to the coronary arteries. **3.** Loosely, of or pertaining to the heart.
~n., pl. **coronaries.** A coronary thrombosis. [Latin *corōnārius,* of a wreath or garland, from *corōna,* garland, crown, CORONA.]

coronary artery *n.* Either of the two arteries that originate in the aorta and supply blood to the heart.

coronary occlusion *n.* The partial or complete obstruction of blood flow in a coronary artery, as by a blood clot or spasm.

coronary thrombosis *n.* The obstructing of a coronary artery by a blood clot, often leading to destruction of heart muscle and causing severe pain in the chest.

cor·o·na·tion (kôr′ə-nā′shən, kŏr′-) *n.* The act or ceremony of crowning a sovereign or a sovereign's consort. [Middle English *coronacioun,* from Old French *coronation,* from Medieval Latin *corōnātiō* (stem *corōnātiōn-*), from Latin *corōnāre* (past participle *corōnātus*), to crown, from CORONA.]

cor·o·ner (kôr′ə-nər, kŏr′-) *n. Abbr.* **cor.** A public officer, normally a physician, whose primary function is to investigate by inquest any death that may not have been from natural causes. [Middle English, officer charged with maintaining the record of the Crown's pleas, from Norman French *corouner,* from *coro(u)ne,* CROWN.] **—cor·o·ner·ship** *n.*

coroner's jury *n.* A group of people summoned to a coroner's inquest to determine the cause of the death under investigation.

cor·o·net (kôr′ə-nět′, kŏr′-) *n.* **1.** A small crown worn by princes and other nobles below the rank of sovereign. **2.** A chaplet or headband decorated with gold or jewels. **3.** The upper margin of a horse's hoof. [Middle English *coronette,* from Old French, diminutive of *coro(u)ne,* CROWN.]

Co·rot (kô-rō′), **Jean Baptiste Camille** (1796-1875). French landscape painter. His early informal sketches of the Italian countryside are today among his most highly regarded works, though they were never exhibited in his lifetime. His larger compositions are somewhat more mannered, characterized by soft contours and muted, silvery tones.

corp. corporation.

cor·po·ra. Plural of **corpus.**

cor·po·ral¹ (kôr′pər-əl) *adj.* Of the body; bodily. [Middle English *corporal, corporel,* from Old French, from Latin *corporālis,* from

corpus (stem *corpor-*), body.] **—cor·po·ral·i·ty** (kôr′pə-răl′ə-tē) *n.* **—cor·po·ral·ly** *adv.*
Usage: The similarity in form between *corporal* and *corporeal* sometimes leads to confusion. *Corporal* means simply "of the body" and is used in many phrases where the physical form of the body is involved (*corporal punishment, corporal needs*). *Corporeal* adds the implication of "bodily as opposed to spiritual or intangible" (*corporeal substance*). For *body* in the sense of "group of people united for some common end," the related adjective is *corporate.*

corporal² *n. Abbr.* **Cpl.** A noncommissioned officer of the lowest rank in the U.S. Army, Air Force, or Marine Corps. [Obsolete French, variant (probably influenced by *corporal,* bodily, as if meaning "leader of a body of troops") of CAPORAL.]

corporal³ *n.* **cor·po·ra·le** (kôr′pə-rä′lē) *Ecclesiastical.* A white linen cloth on which the consecrated elements are placed during the celebration of the Eucharist. [Middle English *corporale,* from Old French *corporal,* from Medieval Latin *corporāle,* from the neuter of Latin *corporālis,* of the body, CORPORAL.]

corporal punishment *n.* Physical punishment, such as beating.

cor·po·rate (kôr′pər-ĭt) *adj.* **1.** Formed into a corporation; incorporated. **2.** Of a corporation. **3.** United or combined into one body; collective. **4.** Considered as, pertaining to, or shared by a united body. **—See Usage note at corporal. 5.** Variant of **corporative.** [Latin *corporātus,* past participle of *corporāre,* to make into a body, from *corpus* (stem *corpor-*), CORPUS.] **—cor·po·rate·ly** *adv.*

cor·po·ra·tion (kôr′pə-rā′shən) *n. Abbr.* **corp. 1.** A body of persons granted a charter legally recognizing them as a separate entity having its own rights, privileges, and liabilities distinct from those of its members. Also called "body corporate." **2.** Such a body created for purposes of government, especially that of a city. **3.** Any group of people acting as one body. **4.** *Informal.* A potbelly.

cor·po·ra·tive (kôr′pə-rā′tĭv, -pər-ə-tĭv) *adj.* Also **cor·po·rate** (kôr′pər-ĭt). **1.** Of, pertaining to, or associated with a corporation. **2.** Of or designating a government or political system in which the principal economic functions, such as banking, industry, labor, and government, are organized as corporate entities with some official status. **—cor·po·rat·ism** *n.*

cor·po·re·al (kôr-pôr′ē-əl, -pōr′-) *adj.* **1.** Of, pertaining to, or characteristic of the body. **2.** Of a material rather than spiritual nature; tangible. **—See Usage note at corporal.** [From Latin *corporeus,* of the body, from *corpus* (stem *corpor-*), CORPUS.] **—cor·po·re·al·ly** *adv.* **—cor·po·re·al·ness** *n.*

cor·po·re·i·ty (kôr′pə-rē′ə-tē) *n.* Also **cor·po·re·al·i·ty** (kôr′pə-rē-ăl′ə-tē). The state of being material or corporeal; physical existence.

cor·po·sant (kôr′pə-zănt′, -sănt′) *n.* A luminous electrical phenomenon, **St. Elmo's fire** *(see).* [Portuguese *corpo-santo,* "holy body."]

corps (kôr, kōr) *n., pl.* **corps** (kôrz, kōrz). **1.** *Abbr.* **c., C.** *Military.* **a.** A separate branch or department of the armed forces having a specialized function. **b.** A tactical unit of ground combat forces, composed of two or more divisions and auxiliary service troops. **2.** A body of persons acting together or associated in a common calling or purpose. [French, from Latin *corpus,* body, CORPUS.]

corps de bal·let (kôr′ də bă-lā′) *n.* The dancers in a ballet troupe who perform as a group and have no solo parts. [French, "ballet troupe."]

corpse (kôrps) *n.* A dead body, especially of a human being. [Middle English *corps, cors,* from Old French, from Latin *corpus,* body.]

cor·pu·lence (kôr′pyə-ləns) *n.* Fatness; obesity. [Middle English, from Latin *corpulentia,* from *corpulentus,* from *corpus,* body, CORPUS.]

cor·pu·lent (kôr′pyə-lənt) *adj.* Large in body; obese. **—See Synonyms at fat. —cor·pu·lent·ly** *adv.*

cor·pus (kôr′pəs) *n., pl.* **-pora** (-pər-ə). *Abbr.* **cor. 1.** A large collection of writings or other artistic compositions of a specific kind or having a specific theme; especially, the complete body of work of an author. **2.** *Anatomy.* **a.** A structure constituting the main part of an organ. **b.** Any distinct mass or body. **3.** The principal or capital, as distinguished from the interest or income, of a fund, estate, investment, or the like. **4.** A human or animal body, especially when dead. [Middle English, from Latin, body, substance.]

corpus cal·lo·sum (kə-lō′səm) *n., pl.* **corpora callosa** (-sə). *Anatomy.* A wide arched band of white matter connecting the cerebral hemispheres of the brain at the base of the longitudinal fissure. [New Latin, "callous body."]

Cor·pus Chris·ti (kôr′pəs krĭs′tē). A city of southern Texas, on Corpus Christi Bay, an inlet of the Gulf of Mexico. The city is a petroleum and natural gas center, with much heavy industry and a large shrimp fleet.

Corpus Christi *n. Roman Catholic Church.* A festival celebrated in honor of the Eucharist on the first Thursday after Trinity Sunday. [Middle English, from Medieval Latin, "body of Christ."]

cor·pus·cle (kôr′pə-səl, -pŭs′əl) *n.* **1.** *Biology.* A cell, such as an erythrocyte or leucocyte, that is capable of free movement in a fluid or matrix, as distinguished from a cell fixed in tissue. **2.** *Anatomy.* The encapsulated ending of a secondary nerve. **3.** A discrete particle such as a photon or electron. **4.** Any minute globular particle. [Latin *corpusculum,* diminutive of CORPUS.] **—cor·pus·cu·lar** (kôr-pŭs′kyə-lər) *adj.*

corpuscular theory *n. Physics.* The theory that light consists of streams of small particles. Compare **wave theory.** See **light.**

corpus de·lic·ti (dĭ-lĭk′tī) *n.* **1.** *Law.* **a.** The material substance upon which a crime has been committed. **b.** The material evidence of the fact that a crime has been committed, such as the discovered corpse of a murder victim. **2.** Loosely, the victim's corpse in a murder case. [New Latin, "body of the crime."]

cor·pus ju·ris (jŏŏr′ĭs) *n. Abbr.* **C.J.** The collective or comprehensive body of all the laws of a nation or state. [Late Latin, "body of law."]

Corpus Juris Ca·non·i·ci (kə-nŏn′ə-sī′) *n. Roman Catholic Church.* The body of decrees and canons constituting the standard of ecclesiastical law until replaced in 1918 by Codex Juris Canonici. [Late Latin, "body of canon law."]

Corpus Juris Ci·vil·is (sĭ-vĭl′ĭs) *n.* The body of civil or Roman law comprising the Digest, the Institutes, the Code, and the Novels, assembled and issued (529–535) during Justinian's reign and forming the basis of most continental European law. [Latin, "body of civil law."]

corpus lu·te·um (lōō′tē-əm) *n., pl.* **corpora lutea** (-ə). A yellow mass of endocrine cells in a ruptured mature Graafian follicle of the ovary, formed after the release of an ovum. It secretes the hormone progesterone, which maintains pregnancy. [New Latin, "yellowish body."]

corpus stri·a·tum (strī-ā′təm) *n., pl.* **corpora striata** (-tə). Either of two gray-and-white, striated ganglionic masses of the brain stem in the lower lateral wall of each cerebral hemisphere. [New Latin, "striated body."]

corr. 1. correction. **2.** correspondence; correspondent.

cor·rade (kə-rād′) *v.* **-raded, -rading, -rades.** —*tr.* To wear away by friction of objects such as sand and gravel moving by gravity or carried in waves, running water, wind, or ice. —*intr.* To be worn away in this way. [Latin *corrādere,* to scrape together : *com-,* together + *rādere,* to scrape.] —**cor·ra·sion** (kə-rā′zhən) *n.* —**cor·ra·sive** (kə-rā′sĭv, -zĭv) *adj.*

cor·ral (kə-răl′) *n.* **1.** An enclosure for confining livestock. **2.** An enclosure formed by a circle of wagons for defense against attack while encamped.
~*tr.v.* **corralled, -ralling, -rals. 1.** To drive into and hold in a corral. **2.** To arrange (wagons) in a corral. **3.** *Informal.* To seize; capture. [Spanish and Portuguese, possibly of Hottentot origin. See also **kraal.**]

cor·rect (kə-rĕkt′) *tr.v.* **-rected, -recting, -rects. 1.** To remove the errors or mistakes from. **2.** To indicate or mark the errors of. **3.** To admonish or punish for the purpose of improving. **4.** To remove, remedy, or counteract (a malfunction, for example). **5.** To adjust so as to meet a standard or other required condition.
~*adj.* **1.** Free from error or fault; true or accurate. **2.** Conforming to accepted standards; proper: *correct behavior.* [Middle English *correcten,* from Latin *corrigere* (past participle *correctus*), to make straight, correct : *com-* (intensifier) + *regere,* to lead straight, rule.] —**cor·rect·a·ble, cor·rect·i·ble** *adj.* —**cor·rect·ly** *adv.* —**cor·rect·ness** *n.* —**cor·rec·tor** *n.*
Synonyms: amend, rectify, redress, reform, remedy, revise.

cor·rec·tion (kə-rĕk′shən) *n. Abbr.* **cor., corr. 1.** The act or process of correcting. **2.** That which is offered or substituted for a mistake, fault, or abnormality; an improvement. **3.** Punishment intended to rehabilitate or improve. **4.** An amount or quantity that is added or subtracted by way of correcting. **5.** A decline in stock market prices or activity following a rise. —**cor·rec·tion·al** *adj.*

cor·rec·ti·tude (kə-rĕk′tə-tōōd′, -tyōōd′) *n.* The state or quality of being correct, especially in manners and behavior; propriety.

cor·rec·tive (kə-rĕk′tĭv) *adj.* Tending or intended to correct.
~*n.* Something that corrects. —**cor·rec·tive·ly** *adv.*

Cor·reg·gio (kə-rĕj′ō, -rĕj′ē-ō), born Antonio Allegri da Correggio (c. 1494–1534). Italian painter, a master of the High Renaissance, whose name derived from his home town in northern Italy. He produced devotional pictures that include *Holy Night* and frescoes, such as those in the convent of San Paolo, Parma (1518).

Cor·reg·i·dor (kə-rĕg′ə-dôr′). An island at the entrance to Manila Bay, in the Philippines. It was the site of a World War II battle (April 9–May 6, 1942), after which the Philippines were surrendered to the Japanese. The island was recaptured in March 1945 and is now a national shrine.

correl. correlative.

cor·re·late (kôr′ə-lāt′, kŏr′-) *v.* **-lated, -lating, -lates.** Also *chiefly British* **co·re·late.** —*tr.* **1.** To put or bring into causal, complementary, parallel, or reciprocal relation: *correlate data from several sources.* **2.** To establish or demonstrate as having a correlation: *correlated drug abuse and crime.* —*intr.* To be related by a correlation.
~*adj.* (kôr′ə-lĭt, -lāt′, kŏr′-) Related by a correlation; especially, having corresponding characteristics.
~*n.* (kôr′ə-lĭt, -lāt′, kŏr′-) Either of two entities related by a correlation; a correlative. [Back-formation from CORRELATION.]

cor·re·la·tion (kôr′ə-lā′shən, kŏr′-) *n.* **1.** A causal, complementary, parallel, or reciprocal relationship; especially, a structural, functional, or qualitative correspondence between two comparable entities: *a correlation between recession and unemployment.* **2.** *Statistics.* **a.** The simultaneous increase or decrease in value of two numerically valued random variables. Also called "positive correlation." **b.** The simultaneous increase in the value of one and decrease in the value of the other of two numerically valued random variables. Also called "negative correlation." **3.** The act of correlating or the condition of being correlated. [Medieval Latin *correlātiō* (stem *correlātiōn-*): *com-,* together + *relātiō,* relation, from *relātus,* "carried back" (see **relate**).] —**cor·re·la·tion·al** *adj.*

correlation coefficient *n. Statistics.* A measure of the interdependence of two random variables that ranges in value from -1 to $+1$,

indicating perfect negative correlation at -1, absence of correlation at 0, and perfect positive correlation at $+1$.

cor·rel·a·tive (kə-rĕl′ə-tĭv) *adj. Abbr.* **correl. 1.** Related; corresponding. **2.** Reciprocally related.
~*n. Abbr.* **correl. 1.** Either of two related entities; a correlate. **2.** *Grammar.* A correlative word or expression. —**cor·rel·a·tive·ly** *adv.* —**cor·rel·a·tive·ness, cor·rel·a·tiv·i·ty** *n.*

correlative conjunction *n. Grammar.* Either of a pair of conjunctions indicating a reciprocal or complementary grammatical relation. *Neither* and *nor* are correlative conjunctions.

cor·re·spond (kôr′ĭ-spŏnd′, kŏr′-) *intr.v.* **-sponded, -sponding, -sponds. 1.** To be in agreement, harmony, or conformity; be consistent or compatible: *Our goals correspond.* **2.** To be similar or equivalent in some way, such as character, meaning, or function. Used with *to* or *with: English "good-by" corresponds to French "adieu."* **3.** To communicate by letter, usually over a period of time. —See Synonyms at **agree.** [Old French *correspondre,* from Medieval Latin *correspondēre* : *com-,* together, mutually + *respondēre,* RESPOND.]

cor·re·spon·dence (kôr′ə-spŏn′dəns, kŏr′-) *n. Abbr.* **cor., corr., cor-resp. 1.** The act, fact, or state of agreeing or conforming. **2.** Similarity or analogy. **3. a.** Communication by the exchange of letters. **b.** The letters written or received.

correspondence principle *n. Physics.* The principle that predictions of quantum theory approach those of classical physics in the limit of large quantum numbers.

correspondence school *n.* A school that offers instruction by mail, sending lessons and examinations to students at home.

cor·re·spon·dent (kôr′ə-spŏn′dənt, kŏr′) *n. Abbr.* **cor., corr. 1.** One who communicates by means of letters. **2.** Someone employed by a newspaper, magazine, or broadcasting company to supply news or articles from a distant place or on a specific subject: *a foreign correspondent.* **3.** A person who writes letters to a newspaper or magazine. **4.** A person or firm having regular business relations with another, especially at a distance. **5.** A thing that corresponds to something else.
~*adj.* Corresponding; consistent. —**cor·re·spon·dent·ly** *adv.*

cor·re·spond·ing (kôr′ə-spŏn′dĭng, kŏr′-) *adj. Abbr.* **cor. 1.** Agreeing or conforming; consistent. **2.** Analogous or equivalent. —**cor·re·spond·ing·ly** *adv.*

corresponding angle *n. Mathematics.* Either of a pair of angles formed when two lines are cut by a third (the transversal). The pairs of corresponding angles are angles that lie on the same side of each line and the same side of the transversal. If the two lines are parallel, the corresponding angles are equal.

cor·re·spon·sive (kôr′ə-spŏn′sĭv, kŏr′-) *adj.* Corresponding. —**cor·re·spon·sive·ly** *adv.*

cor·ri·da (kô-rē′də) *n.* A bullfight. [Spanish, "a running," from the feminine past participle of *correr,* to run, from Latin *currere.*]

cor·ri·dor (kôr′ĭ-dər, -dôr′, kŏr′-) *n.* **1.** A narrow hallway, passageway, or gallery, generally with rooms or apartments opening onto it. **2.** A similar passageway alongside the compartments of a train. **3.** A tract of land forming a passageway, such as that which allows an inland country access to the sea through another country. **4.** A lane for the passage of aircraft. [French, from Italian *corridore,* "a run," from *correre,* to run, from Latin *currere.*]

cor·rie (kôr′ē, kŏr′ē) *n. Scottish.* A **cirque** *(see).* [Scottish Gaelic *coire,* cauldron, hollow, whirlpool.]

cor·ri·gen·dum (kôr′ə-jĕn′dəm, kŏr′-) *n., pl.* **-da** (-də). **1.** An error to be corrected, especially a printer's error. **2. corrigenda.** A list of errors shown with their corrections in a book or other publication. [Latin, gerundive of *corrigere,* to CORRECT.]

cor·ri·gi·ble (kôr′ĭ-jə-bəl, kŏr′-) *adj.* Capable of being corrected, reformed, or improved. [Middle English, from Old French, from Medieval Latin *corrigibilis,* from Latin *corrigere,* to CORRECT.] —**cor·ri·gi·bil·i·ty** *n.* —**cor·ri·gi·bly** *adv.*

cor·ri·val (kə-rī′vəl, kō-) *n.* A rival or opponent.
~*adj.* Rival or opposing. [Old French *corrival,* from Latin *corrīvālis,* joint rival : *com-,* together + *rīvālis,* RIVAL.] —**cor·ri·val·ry** *n.*

cor·rob·o·rant (kə-rŏb′ər-ənt) *adj. Archaic.* **1.** Corroborating. **2.** Strengthening.
~*n. Archaic.* Something that corroborates.

cor·rob·o·rate (kə-rŏb′ə-rāt′) *tr.v.* **-rated, -rating, -rates.** To strengthen or support (other evidence); attest the truth or accuracy of. —See Synonyms at **confirm.** [Latin *corrōborāre* : *com-* (intensive) + *rōborāre,* to strengthen, from *rōbur,* hard kind of oak, strength.] —**cor·rob·o·ra·tion** *n.* —**cor·rob·o·ra·tor** *n.*

cor·rob·o·ra·tive (kə-rŏb′ə-rā′tĭv, -ər-ə-tĭv) *adj.* Also **cor·rob·o·ra·to·ry** (kə-rŏb′ər-ə-tôr′ē, -tōr′ē) Confirming or tending to confirm. —**cor·rob·o·ra·tive·ly** *adv.*

cor·rob·o·ree (kə-rŏb′ə-rē) *n. Australian.* **1.** An aboriginal dance festival held at night to celebrate tribal victories or other events. **2.** Any large or noisy celebration. [Native Australian *korobra.*]

cor·rode (kə-rōd′) *v.* **-roded, -roding, -rodes.** —*tr.* **1.** To eat away or wear away gradually, especially by chemical action. **2.** To impair steadily; slowly destroy. —*intr.* To be eaten or worn away; become corroded. [Middle English *corroden,* from Latin *corrōdere,* to gnaw to pieces : *com-* (intensive) + *rōdere,* to gnaw.] —**cor·rod·i·ble, cor·ro·si·ble** (kə-rō′sə-bəl) *adj.* —**cor·rod·ent** *n.*

cor·ro·sion (kə-rō′zhən) *n.* **1.** The act or process of corroding; especially, the wearing away of metals. **2.** A substance, such as rust, resulting from such a process. **3.** The condition produced by such a process. **4.** *Geology.* The wearing down of rocks by chemical means such as solution or oxidation. Also called "chemical weathering." **5.** Slow destruction, as of a relationship. [Middle English *corosioun,* from Old French *corrosion,* from Late Latin *corrōsiō* (stem *corrōsiōn-*), from Latin *corrōsus,* past participle of *corrōdere,* to CORRODE.]

cor·ro·sive (kə-rō′sĭv) *adj.* **1. a.** Capable of corroding. **b.** Inclined to produce corrosion. **2.** Spiteful, malicious, or malevolent. **3.** Insidiously destructive.
~*n.* A corrosive substance. **—cor·ro·sive·ly** *adv.* **—cor·ro·sive·ness** *n.*

corrosive sublimate *n. Chemistry.* An inorganic compound, **mercuric chloride** *(see).*

cor·ru·gate (kôr′ə-gāt′, kŏr′-) *v.* **-gated, -gating, -gates.** *—tr.* To shape into folds or parallel and alternating ridges and grooves. *—intr.* To become corrugated. [Latin *corrūgāre,* to make full of wrinkles : *com-,* together + *rūgāre,* to wrinkle, from *rūga,* wrinkle.] **—cor·ru·gat·ed** *adj.* **—cor·ru·ga·tion** *n.*

corrugated iron *n.* A structural sheet steel, usually galvanized, shaped in parallel grooves and ridges for rigidity.

cor·rupt (kə-rŭpt′) *adj.* **1.** Morally debased and perverted; depraved. **2.** Marked by or guilty of venality and dishonesty, especially bribery: *a corrupt mayor.* **3.** Decaying; putrid. **4.** Infected; contaminated; unclean. **5.** Containing errors or alterations, as a text: *a corrupt translation.*
~*v.* **corrupted, -rupting, -rupts.** *—tr.* **1.** To destroy or subvert the honesty or integrity of, especially by bribery. **2.** To ruin morally; pervert. **3.** To taint; contaminate; infect. **4.** To cause to become rotten; spoil. **5.** To change the original form of (a text, language, or the like). **6.** *Computer Science.* To change (stored data) so that it cannot be used. *—intr.* To become corrupt. [Middle English, from Old French, from Latin *corruptus,* past participle of *corrumpere,* break to pieces, destroy, ruin : *com-,* completely + *rumpere,* to break.] **—cor·rupt·er, cor·rup·tor** (kə-rŭp′tər) *n.* **—cor·rup·tive** *adj.* **—cor·rupt·ly** *adv.* **—cor·rupt·ness** *n.*

cor·rupt·i·ble (kə-rŭp′tə-bəl) *adj.* Capable of being corrupted, as by bribery or depravity. **—cor·rupt·i·bil·i·ty, cor·rupt·i·ble·ness** *n.* **—cor·rupt·i·bly** *adv.*

cor·rup·tion (kə-rŭp′shən) *n.* **1.** The act or result of corrupting. **2.** The state of being corrupt. **3.** An altered or debased form of a word or text. **4.** *Archaic.* Anything that corrupts; a corrupting influence.

cor·rup·tion·ist (kə-rŭp′shən-ĭst) *n.* One who defends or practices corruption.

cor·sage (kôr-säzh′) *n.* **1.** A small bouquet of flowers worn by a woman at the shoulder or waist or on the wrist. **2.** The bodice or waist of a dress. [Middle English, from Old French, torso, bust, from *cors, corps,* body, from Latin *corpus,* CORPUS.]

cor·sair (kôr′sâr′) *n.* **1.** A privateer, especially along the Barbary Coast of North Africa. **2.** A swift pirate ship. **3.** A pirate. [Old French *corsaire,* pirate, from Old Provençal *corsari,* from Old Italian *corsaro,* from Medieval Latin *cursārius,* from *cursus,* plunder, from Latin, "a run," from the past participle of *currere,* to run.]

corse (kôrs) *n. Archaic.* A corpse. [Middle English *cors,* CORPSE.]

corse·let (kôrs′lĭt *for sense 1*; kôr′sə-lĕt′ *for sense 2*) *n.* Also **cors·let** (for sense 1 only). **1.** Body armor; especially, a breastplate. **2.** A one-piece undergarment consisting of a light corset and a brassiere. [Old French *corselet,* diminutive of *cors,* body. See **corpse.**]

cor·set (kôr′sĭt) *n.* **1.** A close-fitting undergarment, often reinforced by elastic or stays, worn especially by women to support and shape the waistline, hips, and abdomen. **2.** A medieval outer garment, especially a laced jacket or bodice.
~*tr.v.* **corseted, -seting, -sets.** To enclose in or as if in a corset; fit a corset on. [Middle English, from Old French, diminutive of *cors,* body. See **corpse.**]

cor·se·tière (kôr′sə-tyâr′) *n. Masculine* **corsetier** (kôr′sə-tyā′). A maker, fitter, or seller of corsets. [French, from CORSET.]

Cor·si·ca (kôr′sĭ-kə). A rugged Mediterranean island forming two departments of France. Napoleon Bonaparte was born here. The landscape and poor communications have contributed to a tradition of banditry. Sheep and goats are raised, and vines, olives, lemons, and tobacco are grown. Ajaccio is the capital and Bastia the largest city. **—Cor·si·can** *adj. & n.*

cor·tege, cor·tège (kôr-tĕzh′, -tāzh′) *n.* **1. a.** A ceremonial procession. **b.** A funeral procession. **2.** A train of attendants; a retinue, as of a distinguished person. [French *cortège,* from Italian *corteggio,* from *corteggiare,* to pay honor, court, from *corte,* court, from Latin *cohors* (stem *cohort-*), enclosure, court.]

Cor·tes (kôr′tĕs) *n.* The legislative assembly of Spain. [Spanish, plural of *corte,* COURT.]

Cor·tés or **Cor·tez** (kôr-tĕz′), **Hernán** or **Hernando** (1485–1547). Spanish soldier and explorer who won Aztec Mexico for Spain. With an army of native Tlaxcalans he reached the Aztec capital, Tenochtitlán, in 1519 and took their ruler, Montezuma, hostage. In his absence the Aztecs rebelled and drove the Spaniards out. Cortés besieged the city (1521) and razed it to the ground. Appointed governor of New Spain, he reorganized land tenure and launched expeditions to Central America (1524–26).

cor·tex (kôr′tĕks′) *n., pl.* **-tices** (-tə-sēz′) or **-texes. 1.** *Anatomy.* The outer layer of an organ or part, as of the kidney, adrenal gland, cerebrum, or cerebellum. **2.** *Botany.* **a.** A layer of tissue in roots and stems lying between the epidermis and the vascular tissue. **b.** An external layer such as bark or rind. [Latin, bark, shell, rind.]

cor·ti·cal (kôr′tĭ-kəl) *adj.* **1.** Of, pertaining to, or consisting of cortex. **2.** Of, pertaining to, associated with, or depending on the cerebral cortex. [New Latin *corticalis,* from Latin *cortex* (stem *cortic-*), bark, shell, CORTEX.] **—cor·ti·cal·ly** *adv.*

cor·ti·cate (kôr′tĭ-kĭt, -kāt′) *adj.* Also **cor·ti·cat·ed** (-kā′tĭd). Having a bark, rind, or similar specialized outer layer. [Latin *corticātus,* covered with bark, from *cortex* (stem *cortic-*), bark, CORTEX.]

cortico–, cortic– *prefix.* Indicates cortex; for example, **corticosteroid.** [Latin *cortex* (stem *cortic-*), CORTEX.]

cor·tic·o·lous (kôr-tĭk′ə-ləs) *adj. Biology.* Growing or living on tree bark. [French *corticicole* : CORTI(CO)- + -COLOUS.]

cor·ti·co·ster·oid (kôr′tĭ-kō-stĕr′oid′, -stîr′-) *n.* Also **cor·ti·coid** (kôr′tĭ-koid′). Any of the steroid hormones of the adrenal cortex.

cor·ti·co·ster·one (kôr′tĭ-kŏs′tə-rōn′, kôr′tĭ-kō-stĕr′ōn′, -stîr′ōn′) *n.* A corticosteroid, $C_{21}H_{30}O_4$, that induces hyperglycemia and deposition of glycogen in the liver. [CORTICO- + STER(OL) + -ONE.]

cor·ti·co·tro·pin (kôr′tĭ-kō-trō′pĭn) *n.* Also **cor·ti·co·tro·phin** (-trō′fĭn). An anterior pituitary hormone, **ACTH** *(see).* [CORTICO- + -TROP(IC) + -IN.]

cor·ti·sol (kôr′tə-sôl′, -sōl′) *n.* A corticosteroid, **hydrocortisone** *(see).* [CORTIS(ONE) + -OL.]

cor·ti·sone (kôr′tə-sōn′, -zōn′) *n.* A corticosteroid, $C_{21}H_{28}O_5$, active in carbohydrate metabolism and used to treat rheumatoid arthritis, adrenal insufficiency, certain allergies, diseases of connective tissue, and gout. [Short for CORTICOSTERONE.]

co·run·dum (kə-rŭn′dəm) *n.* An extremely hard mineral, aluminum oxide, sometimes containing iron, magnesia, or silica, occurring in gem varieties such as ruby and sapphire and in a common gray, brown, or blue form used chiefly in abrasives. [Tamil *kuruntam,* probably ultimately from Sanskrit *kuruvinda*†, ruby.]

cor·us·cate (kôr′əs-kāt′, kŏr′-) *intr.v.* **-cated, -cating, -cates. 1.** To give forth flashes of light; sparkle; glitter; scintillate. **2.** To make a brilliant display, as of wit. [Latin *coruscāre,* to thrust, vibrate, glitter.] **—co·rus·cant** (kə-rŭs′kənt) *adj.* **—cor·us·ca·tion** *n.*

cor·vée (kôr-vā′) *n.* A day of unpaid labor, as on roads, required of a vassal by his feudal lord. **2.** Labor exacted by a local authority for little or no pay or instead of taxes, used especially in the maintenance of roads. [Middle English *corve,* from Old French, from Late Latin *(opera) corrogāta,* "(works) collected," feminine past participle of Latin *corrogāre,* to summon together, collect : *com-,* together + *rogāre,* to ask.]

corves. Plural of **corf.**

cor·vette (kôr-vĕt′) *n.* **1.** A fast, lightly armed warship, smaller than a destroyer. **2.** Formerly, a warship, smaller than a frigate, usually armed with one tier of guns. [French, from Old French, probably from Middle Dutch *corf,* basket, kind of small ship, CORF.]

corvina. Variant of **corbina.**

cor·vine (kôr′vīn′, -vĭn) *adj.* Of, resembling, or characteristic of crows, ravens, or related birds. [Latin *corvīnus,* from *corvus,* raven.]

Cor·vus (kôr′vəs) *n.* A constellation in the Southern Hemisphere near Crater and Virgo. [New Latin, from Latin, raven.]

Cor·y·bant (kôr′ə-bănt′, kŏr′-) *pl.* **-bants** or **Corybantes** (kôr′ə-băn′tēz, kŏr′-). *Greek Mythology.* A priest of the ancient Phrygian goddess Cybele whose rites were celebrated with music and ecstatic dances. [Latin *Corybas* (stem *Corybant-*), from Greek *Korubas,* probably of Phrygian origin.] **—Cor·y·ban·tian, Cor·y·ban·tic** *adj.*

co·ryd·a·lis (kə-rĭd′ə-lĭs) *n.* Any of various plants of the genus *Corydalis,* having finely lobed leaves and spurred two-lipped yellow, cream, or pinkish flowers. [New Latin, from Greek *korudallis,* crested lark (the shape of the flowers resembles the bird's spur), variant of *korudos.*]

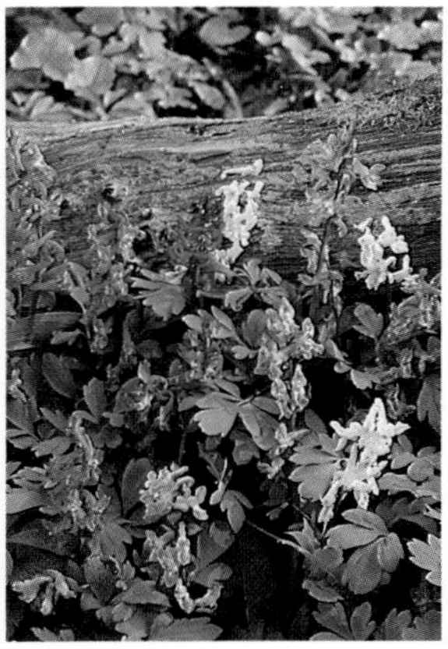

corydalis *There are about 20 species in the* Corydalis *genus. This is* Corydalis cava, *a European species that grows to about 150 millimeters (6 inches) high and flowers between February and May.*

Cor·y·don (kôr′ə-dən, -dŏn′, kŏr′-). A conventional name for a shepherd in many pastoral poems. [Latin, from Greek *Korudōn*†, proper name.]

cor·ymb (kôr′ĭmb, -ĭm, kŏr′-) *n. Botany.* A flat-topped flower cluster in which the individual stalks grow upward from various points of the main stem to approximately the same height. [French *corymbe,* from Latin *corymbus,* cluster, from Greek *korumbos,* uppermost point, cluster of fruits or flowers.] **—co·rym·bose** (kə-rĭm′bōs′, kôr′ĭm-bōs′, kŏr′-), **co·rym·bous** (kə-rĭm′bəs) *adj.* **—co·rym·bose·ly** *adv.*

cor·y·phae·us (kôr′ə-fē′əs, kŏr′-) *n., pl.* **-phaei** (-fē′ī′). **1.** The leader of the chorus in ancient Greek drama. **2.** Any leader or spokesman. [Latin *coryphaeus,* leader, chief, from Greek *koruphaios,* leader, leader of the chorus, from *koruphē,* head, top.]

cor·y·phée (kôr′ə-fā′) *n.* A ballet dancer ranking above the ordinary members of the corps de ballet but below the principal soloists. [French, from Latin *coryphaeus,* leader, CORYPHAEUS.]

co·ry·za (kə-rī′zə) *n.* An acute inflammation of the nasal mucous membrane marked by discharge of mucus, sneezing, and watering of the eyes; a head cold. [Late Latin *coryza,* from Greek *koruza*†, catarrh.]

cos[1] (kôs, kŏs) *n.* A lettuce, **romaine** *(see).* [After Cos, Aegean island where it originated.]

cos[2] cosine.

Cos (kŏs, kôs). *Greek* **Kos.** Greek island in the Dodecanese group. It joined the Delian League in the 5th century B.C. and was a seat of learning.

COS, C.O.S. cash on shipment.

Co·sa Nos·tra (kō′zə nōs′trə, kō′sə) *n.* A crime syndicate active throughout the United States, hierarchic in structure and comprising locally independent units known as families. It is believed to have an important relationship with the Sicilian Mafia. [Italian, "our thing," "our enterprise."]

PRONUNCIATION KEY

ă, pat; ā, pay; âr, care;
ä, father, are; b, bib;
ch, church; d, deed; ĕ, pet;
ē, be; f, fife; g, gag; h, hat;
hw, which; ĭ, pit; ī, pie;
îr, pier; j, judge; k, kick;
l, lid, needle; m, mum;
n, no, sudden; ng, thing;
ŏ, pot; ō, toe; ô, paw, for;
oi, noise; ou, out; o͝o, book;
o͞o, boot; p, pop; r, roar;
s, sauce; sh, ship, dish;
t, tight; th, thin, path;
th, this, bathe; ŭ, cut; ûr, fur;
v, valve; w, with; y, yes;
z, zebra, size; zh, vision;
ə, about, item, edible,
gallop, circus, peaceful

IN FOREIGN WORDS:

à, *Fr.* ami; œ, *Fr.* feu, *Ger.* schön; ü, *Fr.* tu, *Ger.* über;
KH, *Ger.* ich, *Scot.* loch;
N, *Fr.* bon; y′, *Fr.* Compiègne

STRESS MARKS:

Primary stress: ′
in·cite′ (ĭn-sīt′)
Secondary stress: ′
in′sight′ (ĭn′sīt′)

co·se·cant (kō-sē′kănt′, -kənt) n. Abbr. **cosec, csc** Trigonometry. The **secant** (see) of the complement of a directed angle or arc.

cosech hyperbolic cosecant.

co·seis·mal (kō-sīz′məl, -sīs′-) adj. Also **co·seis·mic** (-mĭk). Pertaining to or designating a line connecting the points on a map that indicate the places simultaneously affected by an earthquake shock. ~n. A coseismal line. [CO- (together) + SEISM(O)- + -AL.]

co·set (kō′sĕt′) n. Mathematics. A set associated with a subgroup of a group and formed by the products of elements of the group and elements of the subgroup.

Cos·grave (kŏs′grāv′), **William Thomas** (1880–1965). Irish statesman. A Sinn Fein supporter, he fought in the Easter Rising (1916) and was imprisoned. Released the next year, he was elected to the Dáil and served in the illegal Republican ministry (1918–21). He was the first president of the Irish Free State (1922–32).

cosh[1] (kŏsh) n. British. **1.** A heavy stick, such as a truncheon or bludgeon, used as a weapon. **2.** An attack with such a weapon. ~tr.v. **coshed, coshing, coshes.** British. To bludgeon. [19th century : origin obscure.]

cosh[2] hyperbolic cosine.

cosh·er (kŏsh′ər) tr.v. **-ered, -ering, -ers.** To coddle; pamper. [19th century : origin obscure.]

co·sign (kō-sīn′, kō′sīn′) tr.v. **-signed, -signing, -signs. 1.** To sign (a document) jointly with another or others. **2.** To endorse (a signature), as for a loan or mortgage. —**co·sign·er** n.

co·sig·na·to·ry (kō-sĭg′nə-tôr′ē, -tōr′ē) adj. Signed jointly with another or others. ~n., pl. **cosignatories.** One who signs a document jointly with another or others; a cosigner.

co·sine (kō′sīn′) n. Abbr. **cos 1.** In a right-angled triangle, the function of an acute angle that is the ratio of the adjacent side to the hypotenuse. **2.** A trigonometric function of an angle, given by the X-coordinate of the end of a line of unit length drawn from the origin at the stated angle to the positive X-axis. [CO- + SINE.]

cosine rule n. Mathematics. The rule that in any triangle $a^2 = b^2 + c^2 - 2bc \cos A$, where a, b, and c are the lengths of the sides and A is the angle opposite side a.

cos lettuce (kŏs, kŏz) n. Romaine (see).

cos·met·ic (kŏz-mĕt′ĭk) n. A preparation, such as a skin cream or lipstick, designed to beautify the body, especially the face, by direct application. ~adj. **1.** Serving to beautify the body, especially the face. **2.** Serving to improve or modify the appearance of the body, especially the face: cosmetic surgery. **3.** Decorative or superficial only; not having any significant effect or function: Fenders on cars are now essentially cosmetic. [French cosmétique, from adjective, "of adornment," from Greek kosmētikos, skilled in arranging, from kosmētos, well ordered, from kosmein, to arrange, from kosmos, order, COSMOS.] —**cos·met·i·cal·ly** adv.

cos·me·ti·cian (kŏz′mə-tĭsh′ən) n. A person whose occupation is manufacturing, selling, or applying cosmetics.

cos·me·tol·o·gy (kŏz′mə-tŏl′ə-jē) n. The study or art of cosmetics and their use. [French cosmétologie : cosmétique, COSMET(IC) + -LOGY.] —**cos·me·tol·o·gist** n.

cos·mic (kŏz′mĭk) adj. Also **cos·mi·cal** (kŏz′mĭ-kəl). **1. a.** Of or pertaining to the universe as distinct from the earth and its atmosphere or, sometimes, from the solar system. **b.** Of or pertaining to the universe as distinct from the earth and its atmosphere. **2.** Infinitely or inconceivably extended, as in space or time; vast: an issue of cosmic dimensions. **3.** Rare. Harmonious; orderly. [Greek kosmikos, of the universe, from kosmos, COSMOS.] —**cos·mi·cal·ly** adv.

cosmic background n. The **microwave background** (see).

cosmic censorship n. Astronomy. The principle that, in a black hole, the point at which the density could become infinite (the singularity) can never be observed because of a surrounding spherical boundary (the event horizon) that prevents the passage of information.

cosmic dust n. Fine solid particles of matter in interstellar space.

cosmic radiation n. Streams of ionizing radiation; cosmic rays.

cosmic ray n. Any of a number of high-energy ionizing particles or photons that can be observed moving through the earth's atmosphere or reaching the surface of the earth. Cosmic rays originate as primary radiation from space (mainly protons and atomic nuclei with some electrons) which interacts with atoms in the atmosphere to produce secondary radiation (pions, muons, electrons, and gamma rays).

cosmic year n. The time required for the sun to make one complete revolution about the center of the galaxy (about 220 million years). Also called "galactic year."

cosmo-, cosm- prefix. Indicates world or universe; for example, cosmology. [Greek kosmos, COSMOS.]

cos·mo·chem·is·try (kŏz′mō-kĕm′ĭs-trē) n. The branch of astronomy concerned with the chemical composition of the universe. —**cos·mo·chem·i·cal** adj.

cos·mo·drome (kŏz′mə-drōm′) n. A Soviet spacecraft-launching center. [COSMO- + -DROME.]

cos·mo·gen·ic (kŏz′mə-jĕn′ĭk) adj. Of or produced by cosmic rays. [COSMO- + -GENIC.]

cos·mog·o·ny (kŏz-mŏg′ə-nē) n., pl. **-nies. 1.** The astrophysical study of the evolution of the universe. **2.** A specific theory or model of this evolution. [Greek kosmogonia, the creation of the world : COSMO- + gonos, creation.] —**cos·mo·gon·ic** (kŏz′mə-gŏn′ĭk), **cos·mo·gon·i·cal** adj. —**cos·mog·o·nist** (kŏz-mŏg′ə-nĭst) n.

cos·mog·ra·phy (kŏz-mŏg′rə-fē) n., pl. **-phies. 1.** The study of the constitution of nature. **2.** A description of the world or universe. [Greek kosmographia, description of the world : COSMO- + -GRAPHY.] —**cos·mog·ra·pher** n. —**cos·mo·graph·ic** (kŏz′-mə-grăf′ĭk), **cos·mo·graph·i·cal** adj.

cos·mol·o·gy (kŏz-mŏl′ə-jē) n. **1.** A branch of philosophy dealing with the origin, processes, and structure of the universe. **2. a.** The astrophysical study of the structure and constituent dynamics of the universe. **b.** A specific theory or model of such structure and dynamics. See **big-bang theory, steady-state theory.** [New Latin cosmologia : COSMO- + -LOGY.] —**cos·mo·log·ic** (kŏz′mə-lŏj′ĭk), **cos·mo·log·i·cal** adj. —**cos·mo·log·i·cal·ly** adv. —**cos·mol·o·gist** (kŏz-mŏl′ə-jĭst) n.

cos·mo·naut (kŏz′mə-nôt′) n. An astronaut, especially a Soviet astronaut. [Russian kosmonavt : COSMO- + Greek nautēs, sailor.]

cos·mo·pol·i·tan (kŏz′mə-pŏl′ə-tən) adj. **1. a.** At home in or familiar with many parts of the world or many spheres of interest. **b.** Sophisticated and broadminded. **2.** Inhabited by or composed of many races of people with differing cultural backgrounds. **3.** Common to the whole world. **4.** Biology. Growing or occurring in all or most parts of the world; widely distributed. ~n. A person who has lived or traveled in many parts of the world and is free from provincial or national prejudices. [French cosmopolitain, from Old French, from Greek kosmopolitēs, COSMOPOLITE.] —**cos·mo·pol·i·tan·ism** n.

cos·mop·o·lite (kŏz-mŏp′ə-līt′) n. **1.** A cosmopolitan. **2.** Biology. A cosmopolitan organism. [Greek kosmopolitēs, citizen of the world : COSMO- + politēs, citizen, from polis, city.] —**cos·mop·o·lit·ism** n.

cos·mo·ra·ma (kŏz′mə-rä′mə, -răm′ə) n. A series of scenes and pictures from all over the world viewed through an eyehole using mirrors, lenses, or the like. [COSM(O)- + (PAN)ORAMA.] —**cos·mo·ram·ic** (kŏz′mə-răm′ĭk) adj.

cos·mos (kŏz′məs, -mōs′, -mŏs′) n. **1.** The universe regarded as an orderly, harmonious whole. **2.** Any system regarded as ordered, harmonious, and whole. **3.** Harmony and order as distinct from chaos. **4.** Any of various tropical American plants of the genus Cosmos, having variously colored rayed flowers; especially, C. bipinnatus, widely cultivated as a garden plant. [Greek kosmos, order, the universe, the world.]

cos·mo·tron (kŏz′mə-trŏn′) n. Physics. A large synchrotron designed to produce high-energy protons. [COSMO- + -TRON.]

Cos·sack (kŏs′ăk) n. A member of a people of southern European Russia and adjacent parts of Asia, who were noted as cavalrymen, especially under the czars. —**Cos·sack** adj.

cos·set (kŏs′ĭt) tr.v. **-seted, -seting, -sets.** To pamper; spoil. ~n. A pet; especially, a pet lamb. [Noun ("pet lamb"), from Norman French cozet, coscet, from Old English cotsæta, cottager.]

cost (kôst) n. **1.** An amount paid or required in payment for a purchase or for the production or upkeep of something, often measured in terms of effort and time expended. **2.** A loss or sacrifice. **3. costs.** Law. The charges fixed for litigation, usually payable by the losing party. —See Synonyms at **price.** ~v. **cost, costing, costs.** —intr. To require a specified payment, expenditure, effort, or loss. —tr. **1.** To estimate or determine the cost of. **2.** Informal. To be costly to. [Middle English, from Old French, from coster, to cost, from Latin constāre, to stand with, stand at a particular price : com-, with + stāre, to stand.]

cos·ta (kŏs′tə) n., pl. **-tae** (-tē). Biology. A rib or a riblike part, such as the midrib of a leaf or a thickened anterior vein or margin of an insect's wing. [Latin, rib.] —**cos·tal** adj.

Cos·ta Bra·va (kŏs′tə brä′və). The Mediterranean coastline in eastern Spain, stretching from Barcelona to the French border. It is a popular tourist area.

cost accountant n. An accountant who keeps records of all the costs of production and distribution of an enterprise. —**cost accounting** n.

co·star, co-star (kō′stär′) n. A starring actor or actress given equal status with another or others in a play or film. ~v. (kō′stär′) **costarred, -starring, -stars.** —intr. To act as a costar. —tr. To present or feature as a costar.

cos·tard (kŏs′tərd, kôs′-) n. **1.** An English variety of apple tree or the fruit of this tree. **2.** Archaic Slang. The head. [Middle English, from Norman French, "ribbed one" (from its appearance), from coste, rib, from Latin costa.]

Cos·ta Ri·ca (kŏs′tə rē′kə). Country in Central America. Its heartland is a broad, upland plateau amid volcanic ranges. The country was claimed by Christopher Columbus (1502) as a territory of Spain. Its native Indian population almost disappeared under colonial rule, and the people are now of Spanish or mixed descent. Costa Rica became independent in 1821. In 1948 it abolished its army to make military coups impossible. Attempts are being made to stimulate industrial growth and tourism, but the economy is chiefly agricultural, and coffee and bananas are still the leading exports. Area, 50,700 square kilometers (19,575 square miles). Population, 3,000,000. Capital, San José. See map at **Central American States.**

cost benefit analysis n. An analysis that takes into account the losses or benefits in economic and social welfare that will be incurred if a particular project is undertaken.

cost-effective (kôst′ĭ-fĕk′tĭv) adj. Of or resulting in a profit or return that justifies the initial outlay.

cos·ter·mon·ger (kŏs′tər-mŭng′gər, -mŏng′gər, kôs′-) n. British. One who sells fruit, vegetables, fish, or other goods from a cart, barrow, or stall in the streets, especially in London. Also called "coster." [Originally *costardmonger,* "apple seller" : COSTARD + MONGER.]

cos·tive (kŏs′tĭv) *adj.* **1. a.** Constipated. **b.** Causing constipation. **2.** Slow; sluggish. **3.** Stingy. [Middle English *costif,* from Old French *costive,* past participle of *costiver,* to bind, constipate, from Latin *constīpāre,* to CONSTIPATE.]

cost·ly (kôst′lē) *adj.* **-lier, -liest. 1.** Of high price or value; expensive. **2.** Entailing loss or sacrifice. **—cost·li·ness** *n.*

    Synonyms: *dear, expensive, invaluable, precious, priceless, valuable.*

cost·mar·y (kôst′mâr-ē, kôst′-) *n.* A herb, *Chrysanthemum balsamita,* native to Asia, having aromatic foliage sometimes used as seasoning. [Middle English *costmarie* : *cost,* costmary, Old English *cost,* from Latin *costum,* from Greek *kostos,* from Arabic *kust* + *Mary* (so named because regarded as sacred to the Virgin Mary).]

cost of living *n.* The average cost of those goods and services considered necessary to provide a person with a basic or average standard of living.

cost-of-living adjustment (kôst′əv-lĭv′ĭng) *n.* An adjustment made in wages that corresponds with a change in the cost of living.

cost-of-living index *n.* The **consumer price index** (see).

cost-plus (kôst′plŭs′, kôst′-) *adj.* Of or designating a method of calculating prices based on the cost of production plus a fixed rate of profit.

cost price *n.* The price at which a merchant or retailer buys goods.

cost-push (kôst′poosh′) *adj.* Designating a type of inflation in which increased production costs, as from higher wages, tend to drive up prices. Compare **demand-pull.**

cos·trel (kŏs′trəl) *n. Archaic.* A flat, pear-shaped drinking vessel with loops for attachment to the belt of the user. [Middle English, from Old French *costerel,* perhaps from *costier,* "that which is at the side," from *coste,* side, rib, from Latin *costa.*]

cos·tume (kŏs′toom, -tyoom, kŏs-toom′, -tyoom′) *n.* **1.** A complete style of dress including clothes, accessories, and often hairstyle, characteristic of a particular country, period, or people. **2.** A set of clothes worn for a play, film, fancy-dress ball, or the like, designed to give the wearer the appearance of the role that he or she is playing. **3.** A woman's suit. **4.** A set of clothes appropriate for a usually specified occasion or season, such as a swimming costume. *~tr.v.* **costumed, -tuming, -tumes. 1.** To put a costume on; dress. **2.** To furnish a costume or costumes for (a play or film, for example). [French, from Italian, custom, dress, from Latin *consuētūdō* (stem *consuētūdin-),* CUSTOM.]

costume drama *n.* A stage or television play, or a film, set in a specific era, in which the actors wear the appropriate dress of the period.

costume jewelry *n.* Inexpensive jewelry made from cheap materials such as glass, diamante, or the like.

cos·tum·er (kŏs-too′mər, -tyoo′mər) *n.* Also **cos·tum·i·er** (kŏs-too′mər, -tyoo′myər; French kôs-tü-myā′). A person or company that makes or supplies costumes.

cosy. Variant of **cozy.**

cot¹ (kŏt) *n.* A narrow bed, especially a camp bed. [Anglo-Indian, from Hindi *khāṭ,* bedstead, couch, from Sanskrit *khátvā,* from Dravidian, akin to Tamil *kaṭṭil.*]

cot² *n.* **1.** A shelter or protective covering, especially a cote. **2.** A small house; a cottage. [Middle English *cot(e),* Old English *cot.*]

co·tan·gent (kō-tăn′jənt) *n. Abbr.* **ctn** Trigonometry. The tangent of the complement of a directed angle or arc. **—co·tan·gen·tial** *adj.*

cot death *n. Chiefly British.* **Crib death** (see).

cote¹ (kōt) *n.* **1.** A small shed or shelter for sheep or birds. **2.** *Regional.* A cottage; a hut. [Middle English *cote,* Old English *cote.*]

cote² *tr.v.* **coted, coting, cotes.** *Archaic.* To go round by the side of; pass. [Origin obscure.]

Côte d'A·zur (kōt′də-zoor′). The Mediterranean coast of France, especially its eastern end. It is part of the Riviera.

co·ten·ant (kō-tĕn′ənt) *n.* One of two or more tenants sharing common property. [CO- + TENANT.] **—co·ten·an·cy** *n.*

co·te·rie (kō′tə-rē) *n.* A small, usually select, group of persons who associate frequently, especially because of shared artistic interests. Sometimes used derogatorily. —See Synonyms at **circle.** [French, from Old French, an association of peasant tenants, probably from *cotier,* cottager, from *cote* (unattested), cottage, perhaps from Middle English *cot,* COT (cottage).]

coterminous. Variant of **conterminous.**

coth hyperbolic cotangent.

co·thur·nus (kō-thûr′nəs) *n., pl.* **-ni** (-nī′). Also **co·thurn** (kō′thûrn, kō-thûrn′). A buskin or thick-soled boot worn by actors of classical tragedy. [Latin, from Greek *kothornos,* perhaps from Lydian.]

co·ti·dal (kō-tīd′l) *adj.* **1.** Of or pertaining to a coincidence of the tides. **2.** Designating lines on a map that join places at which high or low tides occur simultaneously.

co·til·lion, co·til·lon (kō-tĭl′yən, kə-) *n.* **1.** A lively dance originating in France in the 18th century, with varied, intricate patterns and steps. **2.** A quadrille. **3.** A formal ball. [French *cotillon,* peasant dress, country dance, from Old French, petticoat, diminutive of *cote,* COAT.]

co·to·ne·as·ter (kə-tō′nē-ăs′tər) *n.* Any of various Old World shrubs of the genus *Cotoneaster,* having small white or pinkish flowers and frequently cultivated for their showy red fruit. [New Latin *Cotoneaster,* from Latin *cotōneum,* QUINCE.]

Co·to·pax·i (kō′tō-păk′sē). One of the highest active volcanoes in the world, in the Andes Mts. of northern Ecuador. It has erupted periodically since the first recorded outburst in 1532 and rises to 5,896 meters (19,457 feet).

cot·quean (kŏt′kwēn′) *n. Archaic.* **1.** A vulgar woman; a hussy. **2.** A man who does domestic work considered more suitable for women. [COT (cottage) + QUEAN.]

Cots·wold (kŏts′wōld, -wəld) *n.* A sheep of a breed known for its long wool and originally developed in the Cotswolds.

Cots·wolds (kŏts′wōldz, -wəldz). Also **Cotswold Hills.** Range of limestone hills in southwest England, chiefly in Gloucestershire.

cot·ta (kŏt′ə) *n., pl.* **cottae** (kŏt′ē) or **-tas.** A short ecclesiastical surplice, often sleeveless or short-sleeved. [Medieval Latin, from West Germanic *kotta* (unattested), COAT.]

cot·tage (kŏt′ĭj) *n.* **1.** A small house, typically in the suburbs or the country. **2.** A small summer house used during vacations. [Middle English *cotage,* from *cot(e),* COT (cottage).] **—cot·tag·ey** *adj.*

cottage cheese *n.* A soft, white cheese made of strained and seasoned curds of skimmed milk.

cottage industry *n.* An industry, such as weaving or sewing, carried out in the home by individual workers rather than in a factory.

cottage loaf *n. British.* A loaf of bread made of two round masses, with the smaller on top of the larger.

cottage piano *n.* An upright, usually small, piano of the 19th century.

cottage pie *n.* **Shepherd's pie** (see).

cottage pudding *n.* Plain cake covered with a sweet sauce.

cot·tag·er (kŏt′ĭj-ər) *n.* A person, especially a farm laborer, who lives in a cottage.

cottage tulip *n.* A type of tall-stemmed garden tulip, usually having pointed petals.

cot·ter (kŏt′ər) *n.* **1.** A bolt, wedge, key, or pin inserted through a slot in order to hold parts together. **2.** A cotter pin. [17th century : shortened from dialectal *cotterel†.*]

cotter pin *n.* A split cotter inserted through holes in two or more pieces and bent at the ends to fasten and prevent excessive sliding and rotation.

Cot·ti·an Alps (kŏt′ē-ən). A section of the western Alps between northwestern Italy and southeastern France. Its highest elevation is Mt. Viso (3,844 meters; 12,602 feet).

cot·ti·er (kŏt′ē-ər) *n.* **1.** In Ireland in former times, a peasant renting and cultivating a small piece of land directly from its owner, the rate having been fixed by public competition. **2.** A cottager. [Middle English, from Old French *cotier,* cottager, from *cote* (unattested), cottage, perhaps from Middle English *cot,* COT (cottage).]

cot·ton (kŏt′n) *n.* **1.** Any of various plants or shrubs of the genus *Gossypium,* cultivated in warm climates for the fiber surrounding their seeds. **2.** The soft, white, downy fiber attached to the seeds of the cotton plant, used in making textiles and other products. **3.** Cotton plants collectively. **4.** The crop of these plants. **5.** Thread or cloth manufactured from cotton fiber. **6.** Any of various soft, downy substances found in other plants. *~adj.* Of, pertaining to, or made from cotton. *~intr.v.* **cottoned, -toning, -tons.** *Informal.* To take a liking; become friendly. Used with *to.* **—cotton up to.** *Informal.* To flatter; make overtures to. [Middle English *cotoun,* from Old French, from Arabic (dialectal) *qoṭon,* variant of Arabic *quṭn.*]

cotton batting *n.* See **batting** (sense 2).

cotton candy *n.* **Spun sugar** (see).

cotton flannel *n.* A soft, warm, napped fabric woven of cotton.

cotton gin *n.* A machine that separates the seeds, seed hulls, and other small objects from the fibers of cotton. Also called "gin."

cotton grass *n.* Any of various grasslike bog plants of the genus *Eriophorum* that grow in colder north temperate zones, having densely tufted, cottony flower heads.

cotton leafworm *n.* The larva of a New World moth, *Alabama argillacea,* that feeds on and destroys cotton leaves.

cot·ton·mouth (kŏt′n-mouth′) *n.* A snake, the **water moccasin** (see). [Its mouth is lined with a white cottony substance.]

cotton rose *n.* **1.** A Chinese shrub, *Hibiscus mutabilis,* cultivated in warm regions for its white or pink flowers that turn deep red. Also called "Confederate rose." **2.** The **cudweed** (see).

cotton rust *n.* A disease of the cotton plant caused by the fungus *Puccinia stakmani* that produces yellowish discolorations on the leaves.

cot·ton·seed (kŏt′n-sēd′) *n., pl.* **-seeds** or collectively **cottonseed.** The seed of cotton, used as a source of oil and meal.

cottonseed meal *n.* Meal made from the residue of cottonseed after the oil has been removed, used as animal feed and fertilizer.

cottonseed oil *n.* A yellowish to dark red oil obtained by crushing cottonseed and used in cooking and as salad oil and in the manufacture of paints, soaps, and other products.

cotton stainer *n.* Any of various small, flat, red insects of the genus *Dysdercus,* that pierce cotton bolls and stain the fibers.

cot·ton·tail (kŏt′n-tāl′) *n.* Any of several New World rabbits of the genus *Sylvilagus,* having grayish or brownish fur and a tail with a white underside.

cotton tree *n.* A spiny tropical tree, *Bombox Malabaricum,* having seeds surrounded by a cottonlike fiber.

cot·ton·weed (kŏt′n-wēd′) *n.* Any of various plants covered with cottony down or having cottonlike tufts.

cot·ton·wood (kŏt′n-wood′) *n.* Any of several softwood trees of the genus *Populus,* having seeds with cottonlike tufts; especially, *P. deltoides,* of eastern and central North America.

cotton *Mexican Indians used the plant's natural fiber to weave clothes as early as 2400 B.C.*

cotton wool *n.* **1.** Cotton in its natural or raw state. **2. Absorbent cotton** *(see).*

cot·ton·y (kŏt'n-ē) *adj.* **1.** Of or resembling cotton; downy; fluffy. **2.** Covered with fibers resembling cotton; nappy.

cot·ton·y-cush·ion scale (kŏt'n-ē-ko͝osh'ən) *n.* A scale insect, *Icerya purchasi,* that attacks citrus trees.

cot·y·le·don (kŏt'ə-lēd'n) *n.* **1.** *Botany.* A simple leaf of a plant embryo, being in some species the first or one of the first to appear from the sprouting seed and that acts to store food in many seeds. Also called "seed leaf." See **dicotyledon, monocotyledon. 2.** *Anatomy.* A lobule of the placenta, especially of ruminants. [Latin *cotylēdon,* navelwort, from Greek *kotulēdōn,* cup-shaped hollow, navelwort, from *kotulē*†, anything hollow, cup.] **—cot·y·le·don·al, cot·y·le·do·nous** *adj.*

cot·y·loid (kŏt'ə-loid') *adj.* Also **cot·y·loi·dal** (kŏt'ə-loi'dəl) *Anatomy.* **1.** Shaped like a cup. **2.** Of or relating to the acetabulum. [Greek *kotuloeidēs,* cup-shaped : *kotulē,* anything hollow, cup (see **cotyledon**) + -OID.]

couch (kouch) *n.* **1. a.** A long piece of upholstered furniture with a back and arms that more than one person may sit on; a sofa. **b.** A bed, especially one with a headrest and low back, used by a psychoanalyst's patients, for example. **2. a.** The frame or floor on which grain, usually barley, is spread in malting. **b.** A layer of grain, usually barley, spread to germinate. **3.** Couch grass. **4.** In papermaking, a board or felt blanket on which sheets of paper are laid to dry. **5.** *Archaic.* The lair of a wild beast.
~*v.* **couched, couching, couches.** —*tr.* **1.** *Archaic.* To cause to lie down. Usually used passively. **2.** To express in a certain context or style. **3.** To embroider by laying thread flat on a surface and fastening by stitches at regular intervals. **4.** To spread (grain) on a frame or floor to germinate, as in malting. **5.** To lower (a spear, lance, or the like) to the position of attack. **6.** *Medicine.* To remove (a cataract) by downward and backward displacement of the lens. —*intr.* **1.** To lie in ambush or concealment; lurk. **2.** *Archaic.* **a.** To lie down; recline. **b.** To crouch. **3.** To be in a heap or pile. Used especially of leaves for decomposition or fermentation. [Middle English *couche,* from Old French, from *coucher,* to lay down, from Latin *collocāre,* to place together, put : *com-,* together + *locāre,* to place, LOCATE.] **—couch·er** *n.*

couch·ant (kou'chənt) *adj.* *Heraldry.* Lying down with the head raised. Used after the noun: *a lion couchant.* [Middle English, from Old French, present participle of *coucher,* to lay down, COUCH.]

cou·chette (ko͞o-shĕt') *n.* *British.* A folding bunk in a railroad sleeping car. [French, diminutive of *couche,* bed, COUCH.]

couch grass *n.* A grass, *Agropyron repens,* having whitish-yellow rootstocks by means of which it multiplies rapidly, becoming a troublesome weed. Also called "couch," "quack grass," "twitch grass." [Originally *quitch grass,* Middle English *quicche* (unattested), Old English *cwice;* perhaps akin to *cwicu,* alive, QUICK.]

couch·ing (kou'chĭng) *n.* Embroidery work in which heavy thread is attached at intervals to a material with minute stitches. [Middle English, from *couchen,* to embroider, COUCH.]

cou·dé (ko͞o-dā') *adj.* *Astronomy.* Of or pertaining to a system of deflecting light from the primary mirror of a reflecting telescope into the eyepiece. [French, "bent like an elbow," past participle of *couder,* to bend at right angles, from *coude,* elbow, from Latin *cubitum,* elbow, CUBIT.]

cou·gar (ko͞o'gər) *n.* The **mountain lion** *(see).* [French *couguar,* from Portuguese *cuguardo,* from Tupi *suasuarana,* "like a deer" (from its color) : *suasú,* deer + *ran, rā,* similar to.]

cough (kôf, kŏf) *v.* **coughed, coughing, coughs.** —*intr.* **1.** To expel air from the lungs suddenly and noisily. **2.** To make a noise like coughing. —*tr.* To expel or utter with a cough. Usually used with *up* or *out.* **—cough up.** *Slang.* To hand over (money, information, or the like) reluctantly.
~*n.* **1.** A sudden and noisy effort to expel the air from the lungs. **2.** An illness marked by coughing. [Middle English *coughen,* Old English *cohhian* (unattested), from an imitative root *kokh-.*]

cough drop *n.* A small, often medicated and sweetened lozenge taken to ease coughing or soothe a sore throat.

cough syrup *n.* A sweetened, medicated liquid taken to relieve coughing.

could. Past tense of **can,** but often used as an auxiliary verb for various shades of associated meanings indicating: **1.** Possibility: *This could be a world record.* **2.** Advice: *You could always take a taxi if you're in a hurry.* **3.** A polite appeal or request: *Could I ask you a favor?* **4.** Condition: *If you could just be more tolerant, people would like you better.*

could·n't (ko͝od'ənt). Contraction of *could not.*

couldst. *Archaic.* The second person singular past tense of *can.* Used with *thou.*

cou·lee, cou·lée (ko͞o'lē) *n.* **1.** A sheet of solidified lava. **2.** A stream of molten lava. **3.** In the western United States and Canada: **a.** A deep gulch or ravine formed by rainstorms or melting snow, often dry in summer. **b.** A stream in such a gulch. [Canadian French *coulée,* from French, a flow, a flow of lava, from the past participle of *couler,* to flow, from Latin *cōlāre,* to strain, filter, from *cōlum,* a sieve.]

cou·lisse (ko͞o-lēs') *n.* **1.** A grooved piece of timber in which a frame or panel slides. **2.** *Theater.* **a.** Any of the side scenes in the wings of a stage; a stage flat. **b.** The space between two side scenes. **3.** A body of unofficial dealers on a stock exchange, especially the Paris Stock Exchange. [French, groove, corridor (see **portcullis**); sense 3, after the dealers' corridors in the Paris Bourse.]

cou·loir (ko͞ol-wär') *n.* A deep mountainside gorge or gully, especially in the Alps. [French, colander, passageway, ravine, from *couler,* to slide, flow. See **coulee.**]

cou·lomb (ko͞o'lŏm', -lōm') *n.* *Abbr.* **C** A meter-kilogram-second unit of electrical charge equal to the quantity of charge transferred in one second by a steady current of one ampere. [After Charles A. de COULOMB.]

Cou·lomb (ko͞o-lôɴ'), **Charles Augustin de** (1736–1806). French physicist who pioneered research into magnetism and electricity and formulated Coulomb's law.

Coulomb field *n.* An electric field equivalent to one that would be produced by a point charge, substituted for a charged body so that the force due to the body at every point is described by Coulomb's law.

Coulomb force *n.* An attractive or repulsive electrostatic force described by Coulomb's law.

cou·lomb·me·ter, cou·lom·e·ter (ko͞o-lŏm'ə-tər) *n.* A **voltameter** *(see).*

cou·lomb·met·ric, cou·lo·met·ric (ko͞o'lə-mĕt'rĭk) *adj.* *Chemistry.* Of or pertaining to measurement of electric current. Said of techniques involving electrolysis, as in a voltameter, or electrolyte conduction, as in certain types of titration. **—cou·lomb·met·ri·cal·ly** *adv.*

Coulomb potential *n.* The potential at any point in a Coulomb field.

Coulomb scattering *n.* The scattering of a charged particle from another charged particle, especially from an atomic nucleus, principally or exclusively as a result of Coulomb forces.

Coulomb's law *n.* The principle that the force between two charged particles is directly proportional to the product of their charges and inversely proportional to the square of the distance between them.

cou·lom·e·try (ko͞o-lŏm'ĭ-trē) *n.* An analytical method for determining the amount of a substance released during electrolysis in which the number of coulombs used is measured. [COULO(MB) + -METRY.]

coulter. Variant of **colter.**

cou·ma·rin (ko͞o'mə-rĭn) *n.* A toxic fragrant organic compound, $C_9H_6O_2$, present in many plants including sweet clover and tonka beans. It is usually produced synthetically and used in perfumery. [French *coumarine,* from *coumarou,* tonka bean tree, from Spanish *coumarú,* from Tupi *cumaru, comaru.*] **—cou·ma·ric** *adj.*

coun·cil (koun'səl) *n.* **1.** An assembly of persons called together for consultation, deliberation, or discussion. **2. a.** A body of people elected or appointed to serve in an administrative, legislative, or advisory capacity. **b.** Such a body elected to serve as a local government authority. **3.** The discussion or deliberation that takes place in a council. **4.** An assembly of church officials and theologians convened for regulating matters of doctrine and discipline. **5.** The **Sanhedrin** *(see).* [Middle English *co(u)nceil,* from Norman French *concilie, cuncile,* assembly, from Latin *concilium,* meeting, assembly.]

Usage: Identity of pronunciation and relatedness of meaning between *council* and *counsel, councilor* and *counselor,* lead to regular spelling confusions. *Council* refers to a deliberative assembly; *councilor* to its member. *Counsel* may be either noun or verb, referring to advice and guidance in general; *counselor* or, in law, *counsel,* refers to the person who provides it.

coun·cil·man (koun'səl-mən) *n., pl.* **-men** (-mĭn). A councilor.

coun·cil·or, coun·cil·lor (koun'sə-lər) *n.* A member of a council, especially the local governing body of a city or town. —See Usage note at **council.**

coun·sel (koun'səl) *n., pl.* **-sels** or **counsel** (for sense 5). **1.** The exchanging of opinions and ideas; consultation; discussion. **2.** Advice or guidance, especially as given by a knowledgeable or qualified person. **3.** A deliberate resolution; a plan; a scheme. **4.** A private purpose or opinion: *keep one's own counsel.* **5.** A lawyer, group of lawyers, or others giving legal advice; especially, an attorney engaged to conduct a case in court. —See Usage notes at **council, lawyer.**
~*v.* **counseled** or **-selled, -seling** or **-selling, -sels.** —*tr.* **1.** To give counsel to; advise. **2.** To give professional help to on social or psychological problems. **3.** To urge the adoption of; recommend. —*intr.* To give or take counsel or advice. —See Usage note at **council.** [Middle English *counseil, conseil,* from Old French *conseil,* from Latin *consilium,* deliberation, consultation, akin to *consulere,* to CONSULT.]

coun·sel·or, coun·sel·lor (koun'sə-lər) *n.* **1. a.** A person who gives counsel; an adviser. **b.** Such a person employed to advise on personal or other problems as a social service. **2.** A lawyer, especially one appearing in court. Also called "counselor-at-law." **3.** A high-ranking diplomat. **4.** A person supervising children at a summer camp. —See Usage notes at **council, lawyer. —coun·se·lor·ship** *n.*

count¹ (kount) *v.* **counted, counting, counts.** —*tr.* **1.** To find out the total number of units by listing the individual units. **2.** To recite numerals in ascending order up to and including: *count three before firing.* **3.** To include in a reckoning; take account of: *ten dogs, counting the puppies.* **4.** To believe or consider to be; deem: *He counts himself lucky.* —*intr.* **1.** To recite or list numbers in order or enumerate items by units or groups: *count by tens; count to three.* **2.** To have importance, especially when a judgment is being made: *His ill-health counted against him.* **3.** To have a specified value or importance; amount. Usually used with *for: His opinions count for*

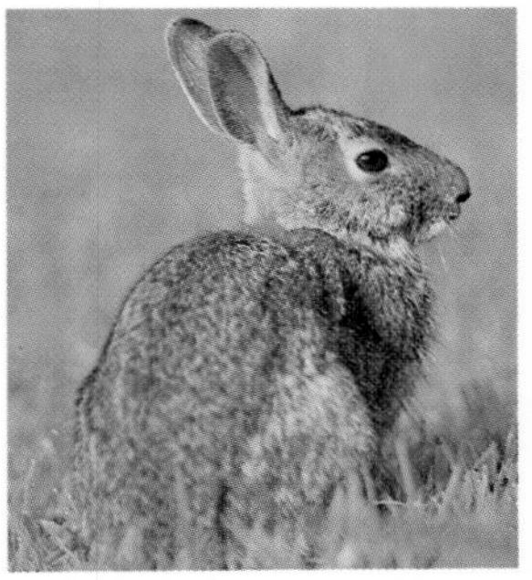

cottontail *The North American cottontail often relies on its ability to "freeze" in order to escape danger. Unlike the European rabbit, it does not dig itself an underground burrow. Its name is derived from the white fur on the underside of its tail.*

PRONUNCIATION KEY

ă, pat; ā, pay; âr, care; ä, father, are; b, bib; ch, church; d, deed; ĕ, pet; ē, be; f, fife; g, gag; h, hat; hw, which; ĭ, pit; ī, pie; îr, pier; j, judge; k, kick; l, lid, needle; m, mum; n, no, sudden; ng, thing; ŏ, pot; ō, toe; ô, paw, for; oi, noise; ou, out; o͝o, book; o͞o, boot; p, pop; r, roar; s, sauce; sh, ship, dish; t, tight; th, thin, path; *th,* this, bathe; ŭ, cut; ûr, fur; v, valve; w, with; y, yes; z, zebra, size; zh, vision; ə, about, item, edible, gallop, circus, peaceful

IN FOREIGN WORDS:

à, *Fr.* ami; œ, *Fr.* feu, *Ger.* schön; ü, *Fr.* tu, *Ger.* über; KH, *Ger.* ich, *Scot.* loch; N, *Fr.* bon; y', *Fr.* Compiègne

STRESS MARKS:

Primary stress: ' in·cite' (ĭn-sīt')
Secondary stress: ' in'sight' (ĭn'sīt')

little. **4.** *Music.* To keep time by counting beats. **5.** *Informal.* To rely. Used with *on.* —See Synonyms at **rely.** —**count in.** To include. —**count off.** To separate into groups by or as if by counting. —**count out. 1.** To exclude or discount. **2.** To count to ten and thereupon declare beaten (a boxer who has fallen to the floor). ∼*n.* **1.** The act of counting or calculating. **2.** A number reached by counting. **3.** A reckoning; an accounting. **4.** *Law.* Any of the separate and distinct charges in an indictment. **5.** A counting from one to ten seconds, during which time a boxer who is down must rise or be declared the loser. [Middle English *counten,* from Old French *conter, compter,* from Latin *computāre;* see **compute.**]

count² *n. Abbr.* **Ct.** In some European countries, a nobleman whose rank corresponds to that of an earl in Britain. [Middle English *counte,* from Old French *conte, comte,* from Late Latin *comes* (stem *comit-*), occupant of any state office, from Latin, companion.]

count·a·ble (kount′ə-bəl) *adj.* **1.** Capable of being counted. **2.** *Mathematics.* Capable of being put in a one-to-one correspondence with the positive integers. **3.** *Grammar.* Designating nouns that can be preceded by the indefinite article or a cardinal number and take a plural; for example, *cat* and *bag* are countable. Compare **noncountable.** —**count·a·bly** *adv.*

count·down (kount′doun′) *n.* **1.** The act or process of counting backward aloud to indicate the time elapsing before an imminent deadline that will initiate an event or operation. **2.** *Aerospace.* The act or process of making a timed scheduled series of successive checks during the preparation of a missile or space vehicle for launching. **3.** The time leading up to an important event.

coun·te·nance (koun′tə-nəns) *n.* **1.** Aspect; appearance; especially, the expression of the face. **2.** The face or facial features. **3.** Support or approval in general. **4.** Composure; bearing; self-control. —**out of countenance.** Visibly disconcerted or embarrassed. ∼*tr.v.* **countenanced, -nancing, -nances.** To give approval to; condone. [Middle English *contenaunce,* behavior, demeanor, from Old French *contenance,* from *contenir,* to behave, CONTAIN.] —**coun·te·nanc·er** *n.*

count·er¹ (koun′tər) *adj.* Contrary; opposing. ∼*n.* **1.** One that is counter; an opposite; a contrary. **2.** *Boxing.* A blow given while receiving or parrying another. **3.** *Fencing.* A parry in which one foil follows the other in a circular fashion. **4.** A stiff piece of leather around the heel of a shoe. **5.** The portion of a ship's stern extending from the water line to the end of the curved part. **6.** The part of a horse's chest between the shoulders and under the neck. **7.** The depression between the raised lines of a typeface. ∼*v.* **countered, -ering, -ers.** —*tr.* **1.** To meet or return (a blow) by another blow. **2.** To oppose; act counter to. **3.** To respond to by retaliating in kind. —*intr.* **1.** To give a return blow while receiving or parrying one, as in boxing. **2.** To retaliate. ∼*adv.* In a contrary manner or direction. [Middle English *countre,* from Old French *contre,* from Latin *contrā,* contrary to, against.]

counter² *n.* **1.** A table or similar flat surface on which money is counted, business is transacted, or food is served. **2.** A piece, as of wood or ivory, used for keeping a count or a place in games. **3.** An imitation coin; a token. —**under the counter.** In an underhand way. [Middle English *contour,* from Old French *comptouer, conteoir,* from Medieval Latin *computātōrium,* place of accounts, from Latin *computāre,* to COUNT.]

counter³ *n.* **1.** A person who counts. **2.** Any electronic or mechanical device that automatically counts occurrences or repetitions of phenomena or events. **3.** *Physics.* An apparatus that detects individual particles or photons.

counter– *prefix.* Indicates: **1.** Opposition, as in direction or purpose; for example, **countermarch, counteract. 2.** Reciprocation; for example, **countersign.** *Note:* Many compounds other than those entered here may be formed with *counter-.* In forming compounds, *counter-* is normally joined to the following element without a space or hyphen: *counterrevolution.* The adjective *counter* is written as a separate word, as in *Counter Reformation* or *counter word,* but except for these examples it is hardly ever used in an attributive position. Rather, the preference is for forming a compound with *counter-,* as evidenced by the entries that follow. [Middle English *countre-,* from Norman French, from Old French *contre-,* from Latin *contrā,* opposite to, COUNTER.]

coun·ter·act (koun′tər-ăkt′) *tr.v.* **-acted, -acting, -acts.** To oppose and mitigate the effects of by contrary action; check. —See Synonyms at **neutralize.** —**coun·ter·ac·tion** *n.* —**coun·ter·ac·tive** *adj.* —**coun·ter·ac·tive·ly** *adv.*

coun·ter·at·tack (koun′tər-ə-tăk′) *n.* A return attack. ∼*v.* **counterattacked, -tacking, -tacks.** —*intr.* To deliver a counterattack. —*tr.* To make a counterattack against.

coun·ter·at·trac·tion (koun′tər-ə-trăk′shən) *n.* A rival or alternative attraction.

coun·ter·bal·ance (koun′tər-băl′əns, koun′tər-băl′əns) *n.* **1.** Any force or influence equally counteracting another. **2.** A weight that acts to balance another; a counterpoise. ∼*tr.v.* (koun′tər-băl′əns, koun′tər-băl′əns) **counterbalanced, -ancing, -ances. 1.** To act as a counterbalance to; counterpoise. **2.** To oppose with an equal force; offset.

coun·ter·change (koun′tər-chănj′) *tr.v.* **-changed, -changing, -changes. 1.** To exchange; transpose. **2. a.** To make checkered. **b.** *Heraldry.* To reverse (colors and metals) on a field so that color comes next to metal and metal next to color.

coun·ter·charge (koun′tər-chärj′) *n.* A charge in opposition to a charge made by another.

∼*v.* (koun′tər-chärj) **countercharged, -charging, -charges.** —*tr.* To bring a charge against (one's accuser). —*intr.* To make a countercharge.

coun·ter·check (koun′tər-chĕk′) *n.* **1.** Something that serves to check or verify something else. **2.** Something that confirms or denies the correctness of a previous check. **3. a.** A restraint that reinforces another check. **b.** A restraint that counteracts another check. ∼*tr.v.* (koun′tər-chĕk′) **counterchecked, -checking, -checks. 1.** To oppose or check by a counteraction. **2.** To check again.

coun·ter·claim (koun′tər-klām′) *n.* A claim made in opposition to a claim made by another. ∼*v.* (koun′tər-klām′) **counterclaimed, -claiming, -claims.** —*tr.* To make a counterclaim against. —*intr.* To plead a counterclaim. —**coun·ter·claim·ant** *n.*

coun·ter·clock·wise (koun′tər-klŏk′wīz′) *adv.* Also **con·tra·clock·wise** (kŏn′trə-) In a direction opposite to that of the movement of the hands of a clock. Also *chiefly British* "anticlockwise." —**coun·ter·clock·wise** *adj.*

coun·ter·con·di·tion·ing (koun′tər-kən-dĭsh′ən-ĭng) *n. Psychology.* Conditioning intended to replace a negative response to a stimulus with a positive response.

coun·ter·coup (koun′tər-kōo′) *n.* A coup staged to reverse the effects of a previous coup.

coun·ter·cul·ture (koun′tər-kŭl′chər) *n.* A culture created by or for the alienated young in opposition to traditional lifestyles, values, and assumptions. —**coun·ter·cul·tur·al** *adj.*

coun·ter·cur·rent (koun′tər-kûr′ənt, -kŭr′-) *n.* An opposing current or flow. ∼*adj. Chemistry.* Involving or pertaining to an opposing flow. Said of certain analytical or industrial separation techniques.

coun·ter·dem·on·stra·tion (koun′tər-dĕm′ən-strā′shən) *n.* A demonstration held in opposition to another demonstration. —**coun·ter·dem·on·stra·tor** *n.*

coun·ter·es·pi·o·nage (koun′tər-ĕs′pē-ə-näzh′, -nĭj) *n.* Espionage undertaken to detect and counteract enemy espionage.

coun·ter·ex·am·ple (koun′tər-ĕg-zăm′pəl, -zăm′pəl, -ĭg-) *n.* An example that contradicts or disproves a previous one.

coun·ter·feit (koun′tər-fĭt) *v.* **-feited, -feiting, -feits.** —*tr.* **1.** To make a copy of, usually with the intent to defraud; forge. **2.** To imitate. **3.** To make a presence of; feign. —*intr.* **1.** To carry on a deception; feign; dissemble. **2.** To make imitations or forgeries. ∼*adj.* **1.** Made in imitation of what is genuine with the intent to defraud. **2.** Simulated; feigned. —See Synonyms at **artificial.** ∼*n.* **1.** A fraudulent imitation or facsimile. **2.** *Obsolete.* A portrait; an image. [Middle English *countrefeten,* from Old French *contrefaire* (past participle *contrefait*), from Medieval Latin *contrāfacere,* to make in contrast to, hence to make in imitation : Latin *contrā-,* opposite to + *facere,* to make.] —**coun·ter·feit·er** *n.*

coun·ter·flow (koun′tər-flō′) *n.* Fluid flow in opposite directions, as in adjacent parts of an apparatus, such as a heat exchanger, or in biological systems, such as the gills of a fish.

coun·ter·foil (koun′tər-foil′) *n.* The part of a check or other commercial paper retained by the issuer as a record of a transaction.

coun·ter·glow (koun′tər-glō′) *n.* **Gegenschein** *(see).*

coun·ter·in·sur·gen·cy (koun′tər-ĭn-sûr′jən-sē) *n.* Measures taken by a state against the activities of terrorists or other rebels.

coun·ter·in·tel·li·gence (koun′tər-ĭn-tĕl′ə-jəns) *n.* The branch of an intelligence service charged with keeping valuable information from enemy spies, preventing subversion and sabotage, and gathering political and military information.

coun·ter·in·tu·i·tive (koun′tər-ĭn-tōo′ə-tĭv, -tyōo′-) *adj.* Contrary to what is perceived intuitively.

coun·ter·ir·ri·tant (koun′tər-îr′ə-tənt) *n. Medicine.* An agent that induces local irritation to counteract general or deep irritation. —**coun·ter·ir·ri·ta·tion** *n.*

coun·ter·man (koun′tər-măn′, -mən) *n., pl.* **-men** (-mĕn′, -mĭn). One who serves at a counter, as in a cafeteria.

coun·ter·mand (koun′tər-mănd′, -mänd′) *tr.v.* **-manded, -manding, -mands. 1.** To cancel or reverse (a command or order). **2.** To recall by a contrary order. ∼*n.* An order or command reversing an earlier one. [Middle English *countremaunden,* from Old French *contremander* : COUNTER- + *mander,* to command, from Latin *mandāre.*]

coun·ter·march (koun′tər-märch′) *n.* **1.** A march back or in a reverse direction. **2.** A complete reversal of method or conduct. ∼*v.* (koun′tər-märch′) **countermarched, -marching, -marches.** —*tr.* To conduct in a countermarch. —*intr.* To execute a countermarch.

coun·ter·meas·ure (koun′tər-mĕzh′ər) *n.* A measure or action taken to oppose or compensate for another.

coun·ter·mine (koun′tər-mīn′) *n.* **1. a.** A mine or tunnel dug by the defenders of a fortress to intercept and destroy a tunnel made by the besiegers. **b.** A mine or charge of explosive placed so as to explode an enemy's mines. **2.** A counterplot. ∼*v.* (koun′tər-mīn′) **countermined, -mining, -mines.** —*tr.* **1.** To make or use a countermine against. **2.** To defeat or frustrate by secret measures. —*intr.* To make or lay down countermines.

coun·ter·move (koun′tər-mōov′) *n.* A move countering another move.

coun·ter·move·ment (koun′tər-mōov′mənt) *n.* A movement in an opposing direction.

coun·ter·of·fen·sive (koun′tər-ə-fĕn′sĭv) *n.* A large-scale attack by an army, designed to stop the offensive of an enemy force.

coun·ter·of·fer (koun′tər-ô′fər, -ŏf′ər) *n.* An offer made in return by one who rejects an unsatisfactory offer.

coun·ter·pane (koun′tər-pān′) *n.* A coverlet for a bed; a bedspread. [Earlier *counterpoint,* from Middle English, from Old French *contrepointe, coultepointe,* from Medieval Latin *culcita puncta,* "stitched quilt" : Latin *culcita,* QUILT + *puncta,* stabbed; see **point.**]

coun·ter·part (koun′tər-pärt′) *n.* 1. One that closely or exactly resembles another, as in function or relation. 2. a. One of two parts that fit and complete each other, such as a seal and its impression. b. One that is a natural complement to another.

coun·ter·plot (koun′tər-plŏt′) *n.* A plot intended to frustrate another plot. ~*v.* (koun′tər-plŏt′) **counterplotted, -plotting, -plots.** —*tr.* To oppose and frustrate by another plot. —*intr.* To devise a counterplot.

coun·ter·point (koun′tər-point′) *n.* 1. a. Melodic material that is added above or below an existing melody. b. The musical technique of combining two or more melodic lines in such a way that they establish a harmonic relationship while retaining their linear individuality. c. Music incorporating or consisting of composition in counterpoint. 2. A contrasting but parallel element, item, or theme. ~*tr.v.* **counterpointed, -pointing, -points.** 2. To compose in counterpoint. 2. To emphasize by means of contrasting detail.

coun·ter·poise (koun′tər-poiz′) *n.* 1. A counterbalancing weight. 2. Any force or influence that balances or equally counteracts another. 3. The state of being balanced or in equilibrium. ~*tr.v.* (koun′tər-poiz′) **counterpoised, -poising, -poises.** 1. To oppose with an equal weight; counterbalance. 2. To act against with an equal force or power; offset.

coun·ter·pro·duc·tive (koun′tər-prə-dŭk′tĭv) *adj.* Tending to hinder rather than serve one's purpose; harmful.

coun·ter·pro·pos·al (koun′tər-prə-pō′zəl) *n.* A proposal offered to nullify or substitute for a previous one.

coun·ter·ref·or·ma·tion (koun′tər-rĕf′ər-mā′shən) *n.* A reformation in opposition to previous reformation.

Counter Reformation *n.* A reform movement within the Roman Catholic Church during the 16th century and the first half of the 17th century organized in reaction to the Protestant Reformation.

coun·ter·rev·o·lu·tion (koun′tər-rĕv′ə-lōō′shən) *n.* A movement arising in opposition to a revolution and aiming to restore the prerevolutionary state of affairs. —**coun·ter·rev·o·lu·tion·ar·y** *adj. & n.* —**coun·ter·rev·o·lu·tion·ist** *n.*

coun·ter·scarp (koun′tər-skärp′) *n.* The outer wall of a ditch in a fortification.

coun·ter·shaft (koun′tər-shăft′) *n.* An intermediate shaft between the powered and driven shafts in a belt drive or gear train.

coun·ter·sign (koun′tər-sīn′) *tr.v.* **-signed, -signing, -signs.** To sign (a previously signed document), as for authentication. ~*n.* 1. A second or confirming signature, as on a previously signed document; a countersignature. 2. *Military.* A secret sign or signal to be given to a sentry in order to obtain passage; a password. 3. A secret sign or signal given in answer to another.

coun·ter·sig·na·ture (koun′tər-sĭg′nə-chər) *n.* A signature made in countersigning.

coun·ter·sink (koun′tər-sĭngk′) *tr.v.* **-sunk** (-sŭngk′), **-sinking, -sinks.** 1. To enlarge the top part of (a hole) so that a screw or bolthead will lie flush with or below the surface. 2. To fit (a screw or bolt) in this way. ~*n. Abbr.* **csk.** 1. A tool for making a countersunk hole. 2. A countersunk hole.

coun·ter·spy (koun′tər-spī′) *n.* A spy working in opposition to enemy espionage.

coun·ter·stain (koun′tər-stān′) *n.* A dye used to treat microscope specimens that have already been treated with another dye. The stain and the counterstain color different parts of the specimen. ~*tr.v.* **counterstained, -staining, -stains.** To treat with a counterstain.

coun·ter·ten·or (koun′tər-tĕn′ər) *n.* 1. An adult male voice with a range above that of tenor. 2. A part written for such a voice. 3. A singer with such a voice.

coun·ter·vail (koun′tər-vāl′, koun′tər-vāl′) *v.* **-vailed, -vailing, -vails.** —*tr.* 1. To act against with equal force. 2. To compensate for; offset. —*intr.* To avail. Used with *against.* [Middle English *countrevaillen,* to be equal in value, from Old French *contrevaloir,* COUNTER- + *valoir,* to be worth, from Latin *valēre,* to be strong, be worth.]

coun·ter·weigh (koun′tər-wā′) *v.* **-weighed, -weighing, -weighs.** —*tr.* To cause to counterbalance; counterpoise. —*intr.* To counterbalance.

coun·ter·weight (koun′tər-wāt′) *n.* A counterbalance. —**coun·ter·weight·ed** *adj.*

counter word *n.* A word commonly used without regard to its precise meaning, as *nice* or *awful.*

count·ess (koun′tĭs) *n.* 1. a. In various European countries, the wife or widow of a count. b. In Britain, the wife or widow of an earl. 2. A woman holding the title of count or earl in her own right. [Middle English *countes(se),* from Old French *contesse,* feminine of *conte,* COUNT.]

counting house *n.* An office in which a business firm carries on operations such as accounting and correspondence. Also called "counting room."

counting number *n.* Any of the numbers 0, 1, 2, 3, . . . used in counting objects.

count·less (kount′lĭs) *adj.* Too many to be counted; innumerable; very many. —See Synonyms at **infinite.**

count noun *n.* A countable (sense 3) noun. Compare **mass noun.**

count palatine *n., pl.* **counts palatine.** A noble originally exercising certain royal powers within his domain, a **palatine** (see).

coun·tri·fied, coun·try·fied (kŭn′trĭ-fīd′) *adj.* Resembling or having the characteristics of country life; rural; rustic.

coun·try (kŭn′trē) *n., pl.* **-tries.** 1. A large tract of land distinguishable by features of topography, biology, or culture. 2. A district outside cities and towns; a rural area. 3. The territory of a nation or state; land. 4. The people of a nation or state. 5. The land of a person's birth or citizenship or to which a person owes allegiance. 6. *Music.* Country music (see). —See Usage note at **nation.** —**go to the country.** *British.* To dissolve Parliament and hold a general election. ~*adj.* 1. Of or pertaining to rural areas. 2. Unsophisticated; rustic. [Middle English *cuntree, contre,* from Old French *contree,* from Medieval Latin *(terra) contrāta,* "(land) lying opposite or before one," from *contrātus,* lying opposite, from Latin *contrā,* against, opposite.]

country and western *n.* Country music (see).

country bumpkin *n.* A simple country dweller; a yokel; a bumpkin.

country club *n.* A club in the country or suburbs with facilities for outdoor sports and social activities.

country cousin *n.* One whose lack of familiarity with the ways of urban life is regarded as laughable by city dwellers.

country-dance *n.* A folk dance, typically one in which two lines of dancers face each other. —**country-dancing** *n.*

country gentleman *n.* 1. The proprietor of a country estate. 2. *Often* **Country Gentleman.** A variety of corn having small, sweet white kernels.

country house *n.* A mansion or other grand dwelling on a country estate.

coun·try·man (kŭn′trē-mən) *n., pl.* **-men** (-mĭn). 1. A man from one's own country. 2. A man from a particular region. 3. One who lives in the country and knows the countryside well.

country music *n.* A style of popular music based on folk music of the rural United States, especially of the southern or southwestern United States. Also called "country," "country and western."

country rock *n. Geology.* An existing rock within which a new rock, such as an igneous intrusion, is formed.

country seat *n.* 1. An estate in the country. 2. A mansion on such an estate.

coun·try·side (kŭn′trē-sīd) *n.* 1. The rural areas of a country. 2. The inhabitants of a rural area.

coun·try·wom·an (kŭn′trē-wŏom′ən) *n., pl.* **-women** (-wĭm′ən). 1. A woman from one's own country. 2. A woman from a particular region. 3. A woman who lives in the country and knows it well.

coun·ty (koun′tē) *n., pl.* **-ties.** *Abbr.* **co.** 1. In the United States, an administrative subdivision of a state. In Louisiana, also called "parish." 2. In Great Britain and Ireland a territorial division exercising administrative, judicial, and political functions. 3. The people living in a country. 4. *Obsolete.* a. The territory under the jurisdiction of a count or earl. b. A count or earl. ~*adj.* 1. Of or pertaining to a county. 2. *Chiefly British.* Belonging to or characteristic of the landed gentry in its interest in outdoor pursuits such as hunting and riding. [Middle English *co(u)nte,* from Norman French *counté,* from Medieval Latin *comitātus,* territory of a count, from Late Latin, retinue of a count, from *comes* (stem *comit-*), COUNT.]

county palatine *n.* The domain of a count palatine.

county seat *n.* A city or town that is the center of government in its county.

county town *n.* In Great Britain, a county seat. Also called "shire town."

coup (kōō) *n., pl.* **coups** (kōōz; *French* kōō). 1. A brilliantly executed stratagem; a masterstroke. 2. A coup d'état. [French, from Old French, from Late Latin *colpus,* from Latin *colaphus,* blow, from Greek *kolaphos,* a blow.]

coup de grâce (kōō′ də gräs′) *n., pl.* **coups de grâce** (*pronounced as singular*). 1. The mortal or finishing stroke, as delivered to someone mortally wounded. 2. Any finishing or decisive stroke. [Literally, "stroke of mercy."]

coup de main (kōō′ də măn′) *n., pl.* **coups de main** (*pronounced as singular*). *French.* A sudden action undertaken to surprise an enemy. [Literally, "stroke of hand."]

coup d'é·tat (kōō′ dā-tä′) *n., pl.* **coups d'état** (*pronounced as singular*). A sudden overthrowing of government and seizure of power by others. —See Synonyms at **rebellion.** [Literally, "stroke of state."]

coup de thé·â·tre (kōō′ də tā-ät′r′) *n., pl.* **coups de théâtre** (*pronounced as singular*). *French.* An unexpected and dramatic event that overturns some given situation. [Literally, "stroke of theater."]

coup d'oeil (kōō′ dœ′y′) *n., pl.* **coups d'oeil** (*pronounced as singular*). *French.* A glance; a quick survey. [Literally, "stroke of eye."]

coupe¹ (kōōp) *n.* 1. A dessert of ice cream or fruit-flavored ice, variously garnished with nuts, fruit, whipped cream, and the like, served in a special dessert glass. 2. a. The stemmed glass in which such a dessert is served. b. A shallow, bowl-shaped dessert dish. [French, "cup," from Late Latin *cuppa,* CUP.]

coupe² *n.* Variant of **coupé** (a two-door car).

cou·pé (kōō-pā′) *n.* Also **coupe** (kōōp) (for sense 1). 1. A closed streamlined two-door car. 2. A closed four-wheel carriage with two seats inside and one outside. [French, short for *(carrosse) coupé,* "cut-off (carriage)," from the past participle of *couper,* to cut off, from Old French *coup,* COUP.]

Cou·pe·rin (ko͞o-prăɴ′, ko͞o-pə-), **François** (1668–1733). The most famous of a family of French musicians. He was a court organist at Versailles under Louis XIV and wrote songs, chamber music, choral works, and organ pieces.

cou·ple (kŭp′əl) *n.* **1.** Two items of the same kind; a pair. **2.** Something that joins two things together; a connection; a link. **3.** Two people, especially a man and a woman, joined in a stable relationship such as marriage or cohabitation. **4.** Two people engaged in some joint activity, such as dancing. **5.** *Informal.* A few; several: *a couple of days.* **6.** *Physics.* A pair of forces of equal magnitude acting in parallel but opposite directions, capable of causing rotation but not translation. **7.** *Physics.* **a.** A pair of metals or semiconductors in direct contact developing an electromotive force across their junction, as in a thermocouple. **b.** A pair of metals in an electrolyte forming a galvanic cell. Also called "galvanic couple." **8. a.** A pair of hunting dogs. **b.** A double leash joining them.
~*v.* **coupled, -ling, -les.** —*tr.* **1.** To link together; attach; join. **2.** To form into pairs. **3.** To join as man and wife; marry. **4.** To combine. **5.** *Electricity.* To link (two circuits or currents) as by magnetic induction. —*intr.* **1.** To form pairs. **2.** To copulate. **3.** *Physics.* To interact as by electromagnetic interaction. Used of electrons or other elementary particles. [Middle English, pair, bond, from Old French *co(u)ple,* from Latin *cōpula,* bond, link.]
Synonyms: *brace, duo, pair, yoke.*
Usage: In informal usage, the meaning of *couple* has extended so that it is no longer restricted to two, but has the general sense of "a few." As the earlier meaning of "two" is still very much alive, however, the word is often ambiguous. *I've got a couple of dollars in my wallet* does not necessarily mean only two (though it might). On the other hand, *Lend me a couple of dollars* is likely to be interpreted in a precise way.

cou·pler (kŭp′lər) *n.* **1.** A device for coupling. **2.** A device connecting two organ keyboards so that they may be played together. **3.** A device for linking two electronic circuits.

cou·plet (kŭp′lĭt) *n.* **1.** A unit of verse consisting of two successive lines, usually rhyming and having the same meter. **2.** Two similar things; a pair. [Old French *couplet,* diminutive of *co(u)ple,* COUPLE.]

cou·pling (kŭp′lĭng) *n.* **1.** The act of forming couples. **2.** A device for connecting railway carriages or wagons. **3.** The part of the body connecting the hindquarters and forequarters of a four-footed animal. **4.** *Physics.* Interaction between elementary particles, especially between their magnetic moments.

cou·pon (ko͞o′pŏn′, kyo͞o′-) *n.* **1.** Any of a number of small, negotiable certificates attached to a bond that represent sums of interest due at stated maturities. **2.** A certificate or detachable part of an advertisement entitling the bearer to certain stated benefits, such as a cash discount or a gift, or for use as an order blank or inquiry form. **3.** Any of a number of detachable slips used when making installment payments. [French, from Old French *colpon,* "a piece cut off," from *colper, couper,* to cut off, from *coup,* a blow. See **coup.**]

cour·age (kûr′ĭj) *n.* **1.** The state or quality of mind or spirit that enables one to face danger and overcome fear. **2.** *Obsolete.* Heart; mind; disposition. [Middle English *corage,* heart as the seat of feeling, courage, from Old French, from Vulgar Latin *corāticum* (unattested), from Latin *cor,* heart.]
Synonyms: *backbone, bravery, fortitude, heroism, mettle, resolution, tenacity, valor.*

cou·ra·geous (kə-rā′jəs) *adj.* Having or characterized by courage; valiant. —See Synonyms at **brave.** —**cou·ra·geous·ly** *adv.* —**cou·ra·geous·ness** *n.*

cou·rante (ko͞o-ränt′) *n.* **1.** A French dance of the 17th century, characterized by running and gliding steps to an accompaniment in triple time. **2.** The second movement of the classical suite, typically following the allemande. [French, "running (dance)," from *courir,* to run, from Old French *courre,* from Latin *currere.*]

Cour·bet (ko͝or-bā′), **(Jean Désiré) Gustave** (1819–77). French painter who headed the realist school. He developed an earthy and uncompromising style, as in *Burial at Ornans* (1850), *Bonjour M. Courbet* (1854), and *The Artist's Studio* (1855).

cour·gette (ko͝or-zhĕt′) *n. Chiefly British.* A zucchini. [French, diminutive of *courge,* marrow, gourd.]

cour·i·er (ko͝or′ē-ər, kûr′-) *n.* **1.** A messenger employed on urgent business; especially, one working for a parcel delivery service. **2.** An official diplomatic messenger. **3.** A person who carries information back and forth between members of a secret service. **4.** A person employed to make arrangements for and attend to the requirements of travelers. [Middle English, from Old French *courrier,* from Italian *corriere,* "runner," from *correre,* from Latin *currere,* to run.]

cour·lan (ko͝or′lən) *n.* A bird, the **limpkin** *(see).* [French, variant of *courliri,* from Galibi *kurliri.*]

course (kôrs′, kōrs, ko͝ors) *n.* **1.** Onward movement in a particular direction; progress; advance. **2.** The direction of continuing movement. **3.** The route or path taken by something that moves, such as a stream. **4. a.** A designated area of land or water on which a race is held or a sport played. **b.** A **golf course** *(see).* **5.** Movement in time; duration: *in the course of a year.* **6.** A mode of action or behavior. **7.** A typical or natural manner of proceeding; customary passage from stage to stage; regular development: *The fad ran its course.* **8.** A systematic or orderly succession regarded as a unit: *a course of treatment.* **9.** *Architecture.* A continuous layer of building material, such as brick or tile, on a wall or roof of a building. **10.** *Education.* **a.** A prescribed body of studies to be followed by students. **b.** The subject matter studied. **11.** A part of a meal served as a unit at one time. **12.** The lowest sail on any mast of a square-rigged ship. **13.** A point on the compass; especially, the one toward which a ship is sailing. **14.** A hunt by hounds pursuing the quarry by sight rather than scent. —See Synonyms at **way.** —**in due course.** In proper order; at the right time. —**lay a course.** *Nautical.* **1.** To go in a particular course or direction without tacking. **2.** To plan some action or project. —**of course. 1.** In the natural order of things; naturally. **2.** Without any doubt; certainly.
~*v.* **coursed, coursing, courses.** —*tr.* **1.** To move swiftly through or over; traverse. **2.** To pursue or hunt, especially with hounds chasing the quarry by sight rather than scent. **3.** To set (hounds) to chase game; send into pursuit. —*intr.* **1.** To proceed on a course; follow a direction. **2. a.** To move swiftly; race. **b.** To run; flow: *"big tears now coursed down her face"* (Iris Murdoch). **3.** To hunt game with hounds. [Middle English *cours, course,* from Old French, from Latin *cursus,* from the past participle of *currere,* to run.]

cours·er[1] (kôr′sər, kōr′-, ko͝or′-) *n.* **1.** A dog trained for coursing. **2.** A person who courses hounds.

courser[2] *n. Poetic.* A swift horse.

courser[3] *n.* Any of various ploverlike birds of the family Glareolidae, found mainly in warm regions of Africa and Asia and characterized by the ability to run fast. [From New Latin *Cursorius* (genus), from Late Latin, "adapted for running," from Latin *cursus,* COURSE (forward movement).]

cours·ing (kôr′sĭng, kōr′-, ko͝or′-) *n.* The sport of hunting with dogs trained to chase game by sight instead of scent.

court (kôrt, kōrt) *n. Abbr.* **C., ct. 1.** An extent of open ground partially or completely enclosed by walls or buildings; a courtyard. **2.** A short street; especially, an alley walled by buildings on three sides. **3.** A large, open section of a building, often with a glass roof or skylight. **4.** Formerly, a mansion or other large building standing in a courtyard. Now used only in proper names. **5.** A level area, marked with appropriate lines, upon which tennis, squash, basketball, or some other game is played. **6.** The place of residence of a sovereign or dignitary; a royal mansion or palace. **7.** The retinue of a sovereign, including the royal family and his personal servants, advisers, ministers, and the like. **8.** A sovereign's governing body, including the council of ministers and state advisers. **9.** A formal meeting called for and presided over by a sovereign. **10. a.** A person or body of persons appointed to hear and submit a decision on legal cases. **b.** The building, hall, or room in which cases are heard and determined. **c.** The regular session of a judicial assembly. **11.** Any similar authorized tribunal having military or ecclesiastical jurisdiction. **12.** The body of directors of a corporation, company, or other organization. —**out of court. 1.** Without a trial. **2.** Being regarded as too trivial, rash, or ridiculous for discussion or consideration. —**pay court to. 1.** To flatter with solicitous overtures in an attempt to obtain something. **2.** To woo.
~*v.* **courted, courting, courts.** —*tr.* **1.** To attempt to gain the favor of by flattery or attention. **2.** To attempt to gain the affections or love of; woo. **3.** To attempt to gain; seek. **4.** To invite, often unwittingly or foolishly: *court disaster.* —*intr.* To be involved in regular social activities with a view to eventual marriage.
~*adj.* Of, pertaining to, or appropriate to a court. [Middle English, from Old French *cort,* from Latin *cohors* (stem *cohort-*), enclosure, court, cohort.]

court bouillon *n.* A light stock made from vegetables, herbs, and white wine, used for poaching fish. [French, "short bouillon."]

court card *n.* A **face card** *(see).* [Folk-etymological alteration of earlier *coat card.*]

cour·te·ous (kûr′tē-əs) *adj.* Characterized by graciousness and good manners; considerate toward others. —See Synonyms at **polite.** [Middle English *curteis, corteis,* having manners befitting a courtly gentleman, from Old French, from *cort,* COURT.] —**cour·te·ous·ly** *adv.* —**cour·te·ous·ness** *n.*

cour·te·san, cour·te·zan (kôr′tə-zən, kōr′-) *n.* A prostitute or kept woman, especially one associating with men of rank or wealth. [Old French *courtisane,* from Old Italian *cortigiana,* "female courtier," from *cortigiano,* courtier, from *corte,* court, from Latin *cohors* (stem *cohort-*), COURT.]

cour·te·sy (kûr′tə-sē) *n., pl.* **-sies. 1.** Polite behavior; gracious manner or manners. **2.** A polite gesture or remark. **3.** Consent or favor; indulgence: *called "doctor" by courtesy.* —**courtesy of. 1.** With the permission of. **2.** Paid for by. [Middle English *curteisie,* from Old French, from *curteis,* COURTEOUS.]

courtesy light *n.* An inside light in a car that is switched on automatically by the opening of a door.

courtesy title *n. British.* A title of nobility having no legal status; for example, the eldest son of the Duke of Bedford is called Marquis of Tavistock during his father's lifetime but is not a peer.

court hand *n.* A style of handwriting formerly used in English legal papers.

court·house (kôrt′hous′, kōrt′-) *n. Abbr.* **c.h., C.H.** A building housing judicial courts.

court·i·er (kôr′tē-ər, kōr′-, -tyər) *n.* **1.** An attendant at the court of a sovereign. **2.** One who seeks favor, especially by flattery or obsequious behavior. [Middle English *courteour,* from Norman French, from Old French *corteier,* to be at court, to court, from *cort, court,* COURT.] —**cour·ti·er·ly** *adv.*

court-leet (kôrt′lēt′, kōrt′-) *n.* A former court in Britain, a **leet** *(see).*

court·ly (kôrt′lē, kōrt′-) *adj.* **-lier, -liest. 1.** Suitable for a royal court; stately; dignified. **2.** Elegant in manners; polite; refined. **3.** Flattering; obsequious. **—court·li·ness** *n.*

courtly love *n.* A code of chivalrous devotion to an idealized beloved, usually a married lady, that became a regular theme of medieval and Renaissance literature.

court-mar·tial (kôrt′mär′shəl, kōrt′-) *n., pl.* **courts-martial.** *Abbr.* **c.m. 1.** A military or naval court of officers appointed by a commander to try persons for offenses under military law. See **general court-martial, special court-martial, summary court-martial. 2.** A trial by court-martial.
~tr.v. **court-martialed** or **-tialled, -tialing** or **-tialling, -tials.** To try by court-martial.

court of appeals *n.* A superior court to which appeals are made on points of law resulting from the judgment of a trial court.

court of chancery *n.* A court with jurisdiction in equity, a **chancery** *(see).*

Court of Claims *n.* A U.S. Federal court that determines claims of a specified sort by individuals against the United States.

Court of Common Pleas *n.* **1.** In some states of the United States, a court having general jurisdiction. **2.** Formerly, a court in Britain to hear civil cases between commoners.

Court of Exchequer *n.* Formerly, a court in Britain with jurisdiction in equity and common law, dealing originally with matters of revenue and later all kinds of cases, now merged with the High Court.

Court of Queen's Bench *n.* A superior court of common law in Britain, now merged with the High Court as the Queen's Bench Division. Called during the reign of a king "Court of King's Bench."

Court of St. James's *n.* The British royal court to which ambassadors are formally accredited.

court plaster *n.* An adhesive plaster formerly used to cover cuts or scratches on the skin. [Originally, referring to the black silk plaster used by ladies at court to make beauty spots.]

Courtrai. See **Kortrijk.**

court·room (kôrt′ro͞om′, kōrt′-, -ro͝om′) *n.* A room in which court proceedings are carried on.

court·ship (kôrt′shĭp′, kōrt′-) *n.* **1.** The act or period of courting before marriage. **2.** Mating rituals between animals.

court tennis *n.* A form of tennis played in a large indoor court having a specially marked-out floor and high cement walls off which the ball may be played.

court·yard (kôrt′yärd′, kōrt′-) *n.* An open space surrounded by walls or buildings, adjoining or within a large building.

cous·cous (ko͞os′ko͞os′) *n.* A North African dish of crushed semolina steamed and served with various meats, spices, and vegetables. [French, from Arabic *kouskous.*]

cous·in (kŭz′ən) *n.* **1.** A child of one's aunt or uncle. Also called "cousin-german," "first cousin," "full cousin." **2.** A relative descended from a common ancestor, such as a grandfather, by two or more steps in a diverging line; for example, one's first cousin's child is one's *first cousin once removed,* and the child of one's parent's first cousin is one's *second cousin.* **3.** *Obsolete.* A person related by descent from a common ancestor, but not a brother or sister. **4.** Loosely, any relative by blood or marriage. **5.** A member of a kindred group or country: *our Canadian cousins.* **6.** A title of address used by a sovereign to a nobleman or to another sovereign. [Middle English *cosin(e),* from Old French *cosin, cousin,* from Latin *consōbrīnus,* maternal first cousin : *com-,* together + *sōbrīnus,* maternal cousin.] **—cous·in·ly** *adj.*

cous·in-ger·man (kŭz′ən-jûr′mən) *n., pl.* **cousins-german.** A first cousin. See **cousin.**

Cou·steau (ko͞o-stō′), **Jacques Yves** (1910–). French pioneer of underwater exploration. He helped invent the Aqua Lung (1943) and later developed underwater laboratories.

cou·ter (ko͞o′tər) *n.* A piece of armor protecting the elbow. [Middle English, from Old French *coute* (modern French *coude*), elbow, from Latin *cubitum;* see **cubit.**]

couth (ko͞oth) *adj.* **1.** Refined; suave; cultured. Used humorously as a back-formation from "uncouth." **2.** *Obsolete.* Friendly; familiar. [Middle English *couth,* familiar, known, Old English *cūth.*]

couth·y, couth·ie (ko͞o′thē) *adj. Scottish.* Characterized by homeliness or affability. [Middle English. See **couth, uncouth.**]

cou·ture (ko͞o-to͝or′; *French* ko͞o-tür′) *n.* The business of a couturier, the designing and making of fashionable clothes for women. [French, tailoring, sewing, from Old French *cousture,* from Vulgar Latin *consūtūra* (unattested), from the feminine past participle of Latin *consuere,* to sew together : *com-,* together + *suere,* to sew.]

cou·tu·rier (ko͞o-to͞o-ryā′; *French* ko͞o-tü-ryā′) *n. Feminine* **cou·tu·rière** (ko͞o-to͞o-ryâr′; *French* ko͞o-tü-ryâr′) **1.** One who designs, makes, and sells fashionable, usually custom-made, women's clothing. **2.** An establishment engaged in this business. [French, from COUTURE.]

cou·vade (ko͞o-väd′) *n.* A practice among certain peoples in which the husband of a woman in labor takes to his bed as if he were bearing the child. [French, "a hatching," from *couver,* to hatch, sit on (eggs), from Latin *cubāre,* to lie down (on).]

cou·vert (ko͞o-vâr′, ko͞o-) *n.* **1.** A table setting at a restaurant table. **2.** A **cover charge** *(see).* [French, "cover."]

co·va·lence (kō-vā′ləns) *n.* Also **co·va·len·cy** (-lən-sē). *Chemistry.* The number of electron pairs an atom can share with other atoms in such bonds. **—co·va·lent** *adj.*

covalent bond *n.* A chemical bond formed by the sharing of one or more electrons, especially pairs of electrons, between atoms.

covalent crystal *n. Chemistry.* A crystal in which all the atoms are linked together by covalent bonds.

co·var·i·ance (kō-vâr′ē-əns) *n.* **1.** *Physics.* The principle that the laws of physics have the same form regardless of the system of coordinates in which they are expressed. **2.** *Statistics.* The expected value of the product of the deviations of corresponding values of two variables from their respective means.

co·var·i·ant (kō-vâr′ē-ənt) *adj.* **1.** *Physics.* Expressing, exhibiting, or pertaining to covariance. **2.** *Mathematics.* Varying with another variable quantity in a manner that leaves a specified relationship unchanged.

cove (kōv) *n.* **1.** A small, sheltered bay in the shoreline of a sea, river, or lake. **2. a.** A steep-walled mountain hollow. **b.** A steep-walled semicircular recess, especially one forming the head of a valley. **c.** A cave or cavern. **3.** A concave molding.
~tr.v. **coved, coving, coves.** To cause to arch over or curve inwards. [Middle English *cove,* closet, chamber, cave, Old English *cofa.*]

co·vel·lite (kō-vĕl′īt′, kō′və-līt′) *n.* An indigo-blue mineral form of copper sulfide, CuS; an important source of copper. [After Nicholas *Covelli* (1790–1829), Italian chemist who discovered it.]

cov·en (kŭv′ən, kō′vən) *n.* **1.** An assembly of witches. **2.** A group of 13 witches. [Perhaps from Middle English *covent,* a gathering, CONVENT.]

cov·e·nant (kŭv′ə-nənt) *n.* **1.** A binding agreement made by two or more parties; a compact; a contract. **2.** A solemn agreement or vow made by members of a church to defend and support its faith and doctrine. **3.** *Theology.* God's promises to man, as recorded in the Old and New Testaments. **4.** *Law.* **a.** A formal sealed agreement or contract, especially one to pay regular sums, as to a charity or relative. **b.** A particular clause of such a contract.
~v. **covenanted, -nanting, -nants.** *—tr.* To promise by a covenant. *—intr.* To enter into a covenant; contract. [Middle English, from Old French, from the present participle of *co(n)venir,* to agree, CONVENE.] **—cov·e·nant·al** *adj.* **—cov·e·nant·al·ly** *adv.*

cov·e·nant·ee (kŭv′ə-nən-tē′) *n.* The participant in a covenant to whom the promise is made.

cov·e·nant·er (kŭv′ə-nən-tər; *also* kŭv′ə-năn′tər *for sense 2*) *n.* **1.** One who makes a covenant. **2. Covenanter.** A Scottish Presbyterian who supported either of the agreements (National Covenant, 1638, or Solemn League and Covenant, 1643) intended to defend and extend Presbyterianism.

cov·e·nan·tor (kŭv′ə-nən-tər) *n.* The party to a covenant by whom the obligation expressed in it is to be performed.

Cov·en·try (kŭv′ən-trē). Industrial city in West Midlands, central England. A new cathedral was opened in 1962 and incorporates the ruins of the old, which was bombed in 1942. **—send to Coventry.** To refuse to associate with; ostracize. [*Send to Coventry,* from the sending of Royalist prisoners to Coventry during the English Civil War.]

cov·er (kŭv′ər) *v.* **-ered, -ering, -ers.** *—tr.* **1.** To place something upon, over, or in front of, so as to protect, shut in, or conceal; overlay or spread with something. **2.** To put a covering on; clothe. **3.** To put a cap, hat, or the like on (one's head). **4.** To bring upon (oneself or one's reputation). Used reflexively: *He covered himself in glory.* **5.** To serve as a covering for; occupy the surface of: *Dust covered the table.* **6.** To extend over; occupy: *a farm covering more than 100 acres.* **7.** To copulate with (a female). Used of animals, especially horses. **8.** To sit on (eggs); incubate; brood. **9.** To screen from view or detection; conceal. **10.** To protect or shield from harm, injury, or danger; shelter. **11.** To protect by insurance; insure against a specified risk or loss. **12.** To include; comprise: *a broad category that covers a variety of species.* **13.** To be sufficient to defray (a charge or expense); meet or offset (a liability). **14.** To make provision for; allow for: *This law does not cover such cases.* **15.** To deal with; treat of. **16.** To travel or pass over; traverse. **17.** To have as one's territory or sphere of work: *A single doctor has to cover the whole region.* **18.** To overwhelm; fill. Used in the passive: *covered in confusion.* **19.** *Military.* **a.** To overlook and dominate from a strategic position; have within range. **b.** To protect (a soldier, unit, or position, for example) by occupying a position from which enemy troops can be fired upon. **20.** *Journalism.* To be responsible for securing and reporting the details of (an event or situation): *cover a ball game.* **21.** *Sports.* To be responsible for marking (an opponent) or for defending (an area or position): *cover left field.* **22.** To match (an opponent's stake) in a wager. **23.** *Card Games.* To play a higher-ranking card than (the one previously played). **24.** *Obsolete.* To pardon or remit: *"Thou hast covered all their sins"* (Psalms 85:2). *—intr. Informal.* To act as a substitute or replacement during someone's absence. Often used with *for.*
~n. **1.** Something that covers or is laid, placed, or spread over or upon something else, especially: **a.** A blanket or sheet on a bed. **b.** The lid or top of a container. **c.** The binding at the front or back of a book. **d.** The front outer page of a magazine, or its outer front and back pages. **2.** *Military.* Natural or artificial shelter or protection by other armed units: *under a cover of mortar fire.* **3. a.** Vegetation covering an area, often serving to provide shade or prevent erosion. **b.** Undergrowth or other vegetation serving as protective concealment for wild animals. **4. a.** Something that screens or

PRONUNCIATION KEY

ă, pat; ā, pay; âr, care;
ä, father, are; b, bib;
ch, church; d, deed; ĕ, pet;
ē, be; f, fife; g, gag; h, hat;
hw, which; ĭ, pit; ī, pie;
îr, pier; j, judge; k, kick;
l, lid, needle; m, mum;
n, no, sudden; ng, thing;
ŏ, pot; ō, toe; ô, paw, for;
oi, noise; ou, out; o͝o, book;
o͞o, boot; p, pop; r, roar;
s, sauce; sh, ship, dish;
t, tight; th, thin, path;
th, this, bathe; ŭ, cut; ûr, fur;
v, valve; w, with; y, yes;
z, zebra, size; zh, vision;
ə, about, item, edible, gallop, circus, peaceful

IN FOREIGN WORDS:

à, *Fr.* ami; œ, *Fr.* feu, *Ger.* schön; ü, *Fr.* tu, *Ger.* über; KH, *Ger.* ich, *Scot.* loch; N, *Fr.* bon; y′, *Fr.* Compiègne

STRESS MARKS:

Primary stress: ′
in·cite′ (ĭn-sīt′)
Secondary stress: ′
in′sight′ (ĭn′sīt′)

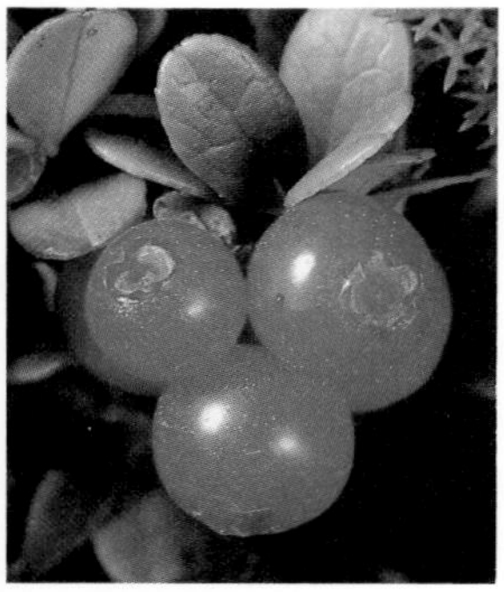

cowberry *This relative of the cranberry is found on boggy wetlands and in the acid woodlands of northern temperate regions. Its dark red bitter fruit ripens in August.*

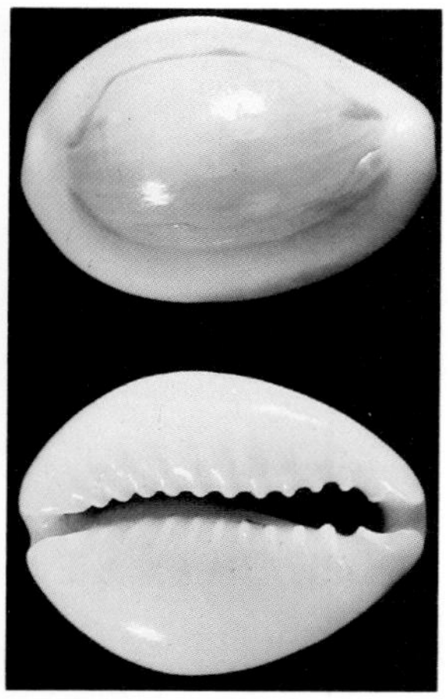

cowry *A marine snail found mainly in the coastal waters of the Indian and Pacific oceans. Unlike most shells, the cowry is glossy outside as well as inside. This is because its mantle—the sheet of tissue that produces the smooth, shiny lining of any mollusk's shell—can be extruded by the cowry to cover the outer surface as well. Cowries are still used as currency in parts of the Pacific, Asia, and West Africa.*

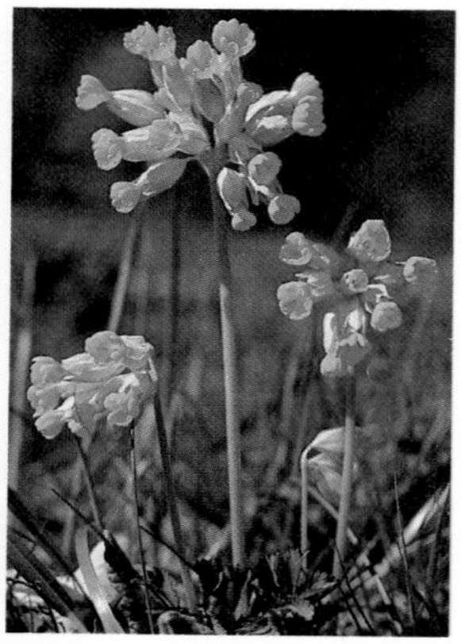

cowslip *Its fragrant yellow flowers were once common in pastures and meadowlands but are now becoming much rarer as old meadows are plowed.*

hides: *a heavy cloud cover.* **b.** Something that conceals or keeps secret, such as a pretext or disguise: *The secret agent's job in the bank is just a cover.* **5.** A table setting for one person. **6.** A **cover charge** *(see).* **7.** *Philately.* **a.** An envelope or wrapper for mail. **b.** An envelope, postcard, or the like bearing a stamp and postal markings of special interest to stamp collectors. **8.** *Finance.* **a.** Funds sufficient to meet an obligation or secure against loss. **b.** See **coverage** (sense 2). **9.** *Mathematics.* A collection of sets associated with a given set such that every point in the given set belongs to at least one other set in the collection. —See Synonyms at **shelter.** —**break cover.** To come out of hiding. —**take cover.** To seek concealment or protection, as from enemy fire. —**under cover. 1.** Operating secretly or under a guise; covert. **2.** Hidden; protected. [Middle English *coveren,* from Old French *covrir,* from Latin *cooperīre,* to cover completely : *co-,* completely + *operīre,* to cover.] —**cov·er·er** *n.*

cov·er·age (kŭv′ər-ĭj) *n.* **1.** The reporting and analysis of a news item. **2.** The extent of protection afforded by an insurance policy. **3.** The amount of funds reserved to meet liabilities. **4.** The way in which a subject is treated. **5.** The range achieved by a transmitter or communication medium.

cov·er·alls (kŭv′ər-ôlz′) *pl.n.* A loose-fitting one-piece garment worn by workmen to protect their clothes.

cover charge *n.* A fixed service charge added to the bill, at a night club, for entertainment or services. Also called "cover," "couvert."

cover crop *n.* A temporary crop planted to protect the soil from erosion in winter and provide humus or nitrogen when plowed under in the spring.

Cov·er·dale (kŭv′ər-dāl′), **Miles** (1488–1568). English Protestant theologian and translator of the Bible (1535).

covered bridge *n.* A bridge protected by a roof.

covered wagon *n.* A large wagon covered with an arched canvas top, used by American pioneers for prairie travel.

cover girl *n.* An attractive female model whose picture appears on magazine colors.

cover glass *n.* A **cover slip** *(see).*

cov·er·ing (kŭv′ər-ĭng) *n.* Something that covers for protection, concealment, or warmth.

covering board *n. Nautical.* A **plank-sheer** *(see).*

covering letter *n.* An explanatory letter enclosed with goods or other documents.

cov·er·let (kŭv′ər-lĭt) *n.* An ornamental cloth covering for a bed; a bedspread.

cover note *n. British.* A temporary document providing the holder with motor insurance until an official policy is issued.

covers versed cosine.

co·ver·sine (kō′vûr′sīn′) *n. Trigonometry.* A **versed cosine** *(see).*

cover slip *n.* A small, usually square, thin piece of glass used to cover a specimen on a microscope slide.

cov·ert (kŭv′ərt, kō′vərt) *adj.* **1.** Concealed; hidden; secret. **2.** *Rare.* Covered or covered over; sheltered. See **feme covert.** —See Synonyms at **secret.**
∼*n.* **1.** A covering or cover. **2.** A covered place or shelter; a hiding place. **3.** Thick undergrowth or woodland affording cover for game; cover. **4.** Covert cloth. **5.** *Zoology.* Any of the feathers covering the bases of the longer main feathers of a bird's wings or tail. [Middle English, from Old French, from the past participle of *covrir,* to COVER.] —**cov·ert·ly** *adv.* —**cov·ert·ness** *n.*

covert cloth *n.* A twilled cloth made of woolen or worsted yarn with cotton, silk, or rayon. It has a speckled appearance and is used for clothing. Also called "covert."

cov·er·ture (kŭv′ər-chər) *n.* **1.** A covering; shelter; concealment; disguise. **2.** *Law.* The legal status of a married woman.

cover up *tr.v.* **1.** To put a cover over. **2.** To conceal or attempt to conceal (a crime, for example). —*intr.v.* To conceal or attempt to conceal a crime, scandal, or the like.

cov·er-up (kŭv′ər-ŭp′) *n.* An effort or strategy designed to conceal something, such as a crime or scandal, that could be harmful or embarrassing if known. —**cov·er-up** *adj.*

cov·et (kŭv′ĭt) *tr.v.* **-eted, -eting, -ets. 1.** To desire (that which is another's). **2.** To wish for excessively and culpably; crave. [Middle English *coveiten,* from Old French *coveitier,* from Vulgar Latin *cupiditāre* (unattested), to desire, from Latin *cupiditās,* desire, CUPIDITY.] —**cov·et·a·ble** *adj.* —**cov·et·er** *n.*

cov·et·ous (kŭv′ə-təs) *adj.* **1.** Excessively desirous, especially of someone else's possessions; avaricious; greedy. **2.** Very desirous; eager for acquisition: *covetous of learning.* —**cov·et·ous·ly** *adv.* —**cov·et·ous·ness** *n.*

cov·ey (kŭv′ē) *n., pl.* **-eys. 1.** A family or small flock of partridges. **2.** A small group of people or things. [Middle English *covei(e),* from Old French *covee,* a brood, from *cover, couver,* to hatch, sit on (eggs), from Latin *cubāre,* to lie down (on).]

cov·in (kŭv′ĭn) *n. Law.* A secret arrangement to defraud or injure another person. [Middle English, from Old French *covin(e),* from Medieval Latin *convenium,* "a coming together," agreement, collusion, from Latin *convenīre,* to CONVENE.]

cov·ing (kō′vĭng) *n. Architecture.* **1.** A concave molding, often ready-made, used to form a junction between a ceiling and a wall. **2.** A curved part of a wall where it joins a ceiling.

cow[1] (kou) *n., pl.* **cows** or *archaic* **kine** (kīn). **1.** The mature female of cattle of the genus *Bos.* **2.** The mature female of other animals, such as whales, elephants, or moose. **3.** Broadly, any domesticated bovine. **4.** *Slang.* **a.** A fat or unpleasant woman. **b.** A woman. Used derogatorily. [Cow, kine; Middle English *cou, kin,* Old English *cū, cȳ(e).*]

cow[2] *tr.v.* **cowed, cowing, cows.** To frighten with threats or a show of force; intimidate. [Originally dialectal (as Scottish *kow*), perhaps ultimately from Old Norse *kūga,* to oppress.]

cow·ard (kou′ərd) *n.* One who lacks courage in the face of danger, pain, or an unpleasant situation; an ignobly frightened or timid person. [Middle English *couherde, coward,* from Old French *couard,* coward, perhaps "one with his tail between his legs," from *coue,* tail, from Latin *cauda,* tail.]

Cow·ard (kou′ərd), **Sir Noël** (1899–1973). British dramatist, composer, and entertainer. He began as an actor and won fame as a playwright, becoming especially noted for his witty and worldly comedies, including *Hay Fever* (1925) and *Private Lives* (1930).

cow·ard·ice (kou′ər-dĭs) *n.* Lack of courage in the face of danger, pain, difficulty, or opposition.

cow·ard·ly (kou′ərd-lē) *adj.* **1.** Lacking courage; ignobly fearful. **2.** Showing cowardice; befitting a coward.
∼*adv.* In the manner of a coward; basely; meanly. —**cow·ard·li·ness** *n.*

cow·bane (kou′bān) *n.* **1.** A plant, *Oxypolis rigidior,* of the southeastern and central United States, having poisonous roots and foliage, and clusters of small white flowers. **2.** Any of several related plants, such as the **water hemlock** *(see).*

cow·bell (kou′bĕl′) *n.* A bell hung from a collar around a cow's neck to aid in locating her.

cow·ber·ry (kou′bĕr′ē) *n., pl.* **-ries. 1.** A creeping evergreen shrub, *Vaccinium vitis-idaea,* having pink or reddish flowers and edible, slightly acid red berries. **2.** A berry of this plant. Also called "mountain cranberry," "lingonberry."

cow·bird (kou′bûrd′) *n.* Any of various blackbirds of the genus *Molothrus* and related genera, that lay their eggs in the nests of other birds; especially the common North American species, *M. ater.* [The birds feed on cattle vermin.]

cow·boy (kou′boi′) *n.* **1.** A hired man, especially in the western United States, who tends cattle, as on a ranch, and performs many of his duties on horseback. **2.** In the United States, a performer who demonstrates feats of horsemanship, as at a rodeo. **3.** A figure from the era of the Wild West, conventionally represented as fighting Indians. **4.** *Slang.* A speedy or reckless driver of a motor vehicle. **5.** One of a band of loyalist guerillas that operated between the British and American lines, mostly in Westchester County, New York, during the American Revolution.

cow·catch·er (kou′kăch′ər) *n.* An iron grille or frame that projects from the front of a locomotive and serves to clear the track of obstructions.

cow college *n. Informal.* **1.** An agricultural college. **2.** A college or university considered to be provincial and unsophisticated.

cow·er (kou′ər) *intr.v.* **-ered, -ering, -ers.** To cringe or shrink away, as from cold or in fear. —See Synonyms at **recoil.** [Middle English *couren,* from Middle Low German *kūren*†, lie in wait.]

Cowes (kouz). A town on the Medina River in the north of the Isle of Wight, off southern England. A yachting club was founded here in 1812, and the town stages an international regatta each August.

cow·fish (kou′fĭsh′) *n., pl.* **-fishes** or collectively **cowfish. 1.** Any of various small whales, porpoises, or similar aquatic mammals; especially, a whale of the genus *Mesopledon,* having a pointed snout. **2.** A fish, *Lactophrys quadricornis,* of warm Atlantic waters, having the body encased in a bony covering and hornlike spines over each eye.

cow·girl (kou′gûrl′) *n.* A hired woman, especially in the western United States, who tends cattle and performs many of her duties on horseback.

cow·hand (kou′hănd) *n.* A cowboy.

cow·herd (kou′hûrd′) *n.* A person who herds or tends cattle.

cow·hide (kou′hīd′) *n.* **1. a.** The hide of a cow. **b.** The leather made from this hide. **2.** A strong, heavy, flexible whip, usually made of braided leather.

cowl (koul) *n.* **1. a.** A hood worn by monks. **b.** The hooded robe of a monk or a similar garment. **c.** A loose collar that can be worn as a hood. **2.** A hood-shaped covering used to increase the draught of a chimney. **3.** A cowling.
∼*tr.v.* **cowled, cowling, cowls.** To put a cowl on or cover with a cowl. [Middle English *coule,* Old English *cugele, cūle,* from Late Latin *cuculla,* from Latin *cucullus*†, hood.]

cowled (kould) *adj.* **1.** Wearing or supplied with a cowl; hooded. **2.** Having the shape of a cowl.

Cow·ley (kou′lē), **Abraham** (1618–67). English poet and essayist. He published his first volume of poetry, *Poetical Blossoms,* at the age of 15. His best-known work is *Davideis,* an epic poem in four books recounting the Biblical history of King David.

cow·lick (kou′lĭk′) *n.* A projecting tuft of hair on the head that will not lie flat. [It appears to have been licked by a cow.]

cowl·ing (kou′lĭng) *n.* A removable metal covering for the engine of an aircraft or motor vehicle. Also called "cowl."

cow·man (kou′mən) *n., pl.* **-men** (-mĭn). **1.** *British.* A man who tends cows. **2.** The owner of a cattle ranch.

co·work·er (kō′wûrk′ər) *n.* A fellow worker.

cow parsnip *n.* Any of several tall, coarse plants of the genus *Heracleum,* such as *H. Lanatum,* of North America. Also called "masterwart."

cow pat *n.* A mass of cow dung.

cow·pea (kou′pē′) *n.* **1.** A tropical vine, *Vigna sinensis,* bearing long, hanging pods and grown in the southern United States for soil improvement and as animal feed. **2.** The edible, pealike seed of this plant. In this sense, also called "black-eyed pea."

Cow·per (ko͞o′pər, kou′-), **William** (1731–1800). British poet. His best-known works include *Table Talk* (1782) and *On the Loss of the Royal George* (published posthumously).

Cow·per's glands (kou′pərz, ko͞o′pərz) *pl.n.* A pair of small glands lying near the prostate gland that secrete mucus into the male urethra, thus contributing to the semen. [After William *Cowper* (1666–1709), English anatomist who discovered them.]

cow·poke (kou′pōk′) *n. Informal.* A cowboy, as on a ranch.

cow pony *n.* A small, agile horse used in roundups.

cow·pox (kou′pŏks′) *n.* A contagious viral disease of cattle characterized by vesicles on the skin, especially the udder. Inoculation of humans with cowpox virus confers temporary immunity to smallpox. Also called "vaccinia."

cow·punch·er (kou′pŭn′chər) *n. Informal.* A cowboy, as on a ranch.

cow·ry, cow·rie (kou′rē) *n., pl.* **-ries. 1.** Any of various tropical marine mollusks of the family Cypraeidae, having glossy, often brightly marked shells, some of which are used as money in the South Pacific and parts of Africa. **2.** The shell of any of these mollusks. [Hindi *kauṛī,* from Sanskrit *kaparda,* from Dravidian; akin to Tamil *kōṭu,* shell.]

cow shark *n.* Any of several sharks of the family Hexanchidae, of warm and temperate seas.

cow shed *n.* A shed for housing cows.

cow·skin (kou′skĭn′) *n.* **1.** The hide of a cow. **2.** Leather made from this hide.

cow·slip (kou′slĭp′) *n.* An Old World primrose, *Primula veris,* having yellow flowers borne in a cluster. [Middle English *cowslyppe,* Old English *cūslyppe,* "cow dung" (probably because some varieties are found in cow pastures) : *cū,* cow + *slyppe, slypa,* slime, paste.]

cow town *n.* A small town in a cattle-raising area.

cox (kŏks) *n. Informal.* A coxswain.
~*v.* **coxed, coxing, coxes.** *Informal.* —*tr.* To serve as coxswain for (a boat). —*intr.* To act as coxswain.

cox·a (kŏk′sə) *n., pl.* **coxae** (kŏk′sē′) **1.** *Anatomy.* The hip or hip joint. **2.** *Zoology.* The first segment of the leg of an insect or other arthropod, adjoining and attached to the body. [Latin *coxa,* the hip.]

cox·al·gi·a (kŏk-săl′jē-ə) *n.* Pain in or disease of the hip. [New Latin : COX(A) + -ALGIA.] —**cox·al·gic** *adj.*

coxcomb. Variant of **cockscomb** (senses 2, 4).

cox·comb·ry (kŏks′kōm′rē) *n., pl.* **-ries.** Arrogance and pretension in manner or behavior; foolishness; foppery.

cox·i·tis (kŏk-sī′tĭs) *n.* Inflammation of the hip joint. [COX(A) + -ITIS.]

Cox·sack·ie virus (ko͝ok-săk′ē) *n.* Any of a group of enteroviruses, some of which produce a disease resembling poliomyelitis without paralysis. [After *Coxsackie,* a town in New York state; the virus was first identified in a resident of the town.]

Cox's orange pippin (kŏk′sĭs) *n.* A variety of eating apple, having crisp flesh and a red-tinged green skin. Also called "Cox," "Cox's." [19th century : after R. *Cox,* Englishman who propagated it.]

cox·swain (kŏk′sən, kŏk′swān′) *n.* A person who steers a boat or racing shell or has charge of its crew. Also informally called "cox." [Middle English *cok swain* : *cok,* COCKBOAT + *swain,* servant, SWAIN.]

coy (koi) *adj.* **coyer, coyest. 1.** Shy and demure; retiring. **2.** Pretending shyness or modesty; coquettishly shy. **3.** Annoyingly unwilling to commit oneself; affectedly reticent. —See Synonyms at **shy.** [Middle English, from Old French *coi,* shy, quiet, from Vulgar Latin *quētus* (unattested), variant of Latin *quiētus,* QUIET.] —**coy·ly** *adv.* —**coy·ness** *n.*

coy·o·te (kī-ō′tē, kī′ōt) *n.* **1.** A wolflike carnivorous animal, *Canis latrans,* common in desert and prairie regions of western North America. **2.** *Slang.* A contemptible sneak. [Mexican Spanish, from Nahuatl *coyotl.*]

coy·pu (koi′po͞o) *n., pl.* **-pus. 1.** A large, beaverlike South American rodent, *Myocaster coypu,* valued for its fur. **2.** The fur of this animal. Also called "nutria." [American Spanish *coipú,* from Araucanian *kóypu.*]

coz (kŭz) *n. Archaic Informal.* Cousin.

coz·en (kŭz′ən) *v.* **-ened, -ening, -ens.** —*tr.* To deceive, by means of a petty trick or fraud. —*intr.* To act with intent to deceive. [16th century cant : perhaps akin to COUSIN.] —**coz·en·er** *n.*

coz·en·age (kŭz′ən-ĭj) *n.* **1.** The art or practice of cozening; cheating. **2.** A deception; a fraud.

co·zy (kō′zē) *adj.* **-zier, -ziest.** Also **co·sy, -sier, -siest. 1.** Snug and comfortable; warm. **2.** Marked by friendly intimacy. **3.** *Informal.* Marked by close association for devious purposes: *a cozy agreement.* —See Synonyms at **comfortable.**
~*n., pl.* **cozies.** Also **co·sy** *pl.* **-sies.** A padded or knitted covering placed over a teapot, for example, to keep the contents hot. [18th century (Scottish) : origin obscure.] —**coz·i·ly** *adv.* —**coz·i·ness** *n.*

cP centipoise.

cp. compare.

c.p. 1. candle power. **2.** chemically pure.

C.P. 1. Cape Province. **2.** command post. **3.** Communist Party.

CPA, C.P.A. certified public accountant.

cpd. compound.

Cpl. corporal.

C.P.O. chief petty officer.

cps cycles per second.

CPU central processing unit.

CQ (sē′kyo͞o′) *n.* Code letters used at the beginning of radio messages intended for all receivers. [C(all to) Q(uarters).]

Cr The symbol for the element chromium.

cr. 1. credit, creditor. **2.** creek. **3.** crescendo. **4.** crown.

craal. Variant of **kraal.**

crab[1] (krăb) *n.* **1. a.** Any of various predominantly marine crustaceans of the section Brachyura within the order Decapoda, characterized by a broad, flattened cephalothorax covered by a hard shell with the small abdomen concealed beneath it, and five pairs of legs, of which the front pair are large and pincerlike. **b.** The flesh of any edible variety of crab. **2.** Any of various similar related crustaceans, such as the **hermit crab** *(see).* **3.** The **horseshoe crab** *(see).* **4.** The crab louse. **5. Crab.** The constellation and sign of the zodiac, **Cancer** *(see).* **6.** The maneuvering of an aircraft partially into a crosswind in order to compensate for drift. **7.** Any of various machines for handling or hoisting heavy weights. **8. crabs.** *Informal.* The lowest throw, usually a two or three, of a pair of dice. **—catch a crab.** In rowing, to strike the water with an oar in recovering a stroke or to miss it in making one.
~*v.* **crabbed, crabbing, crabs.** —*intr.* **1.** To hunt or catch crabs. **2.** *Nautical.* To drift diagonally or sideways. **3.** To move sideways. —*tr. Aviation.* To direct (an aircraft) partly into a crosswind to eliminate drift. [Middle English *crab(be),* Old English *crabba,* from Germanic.]

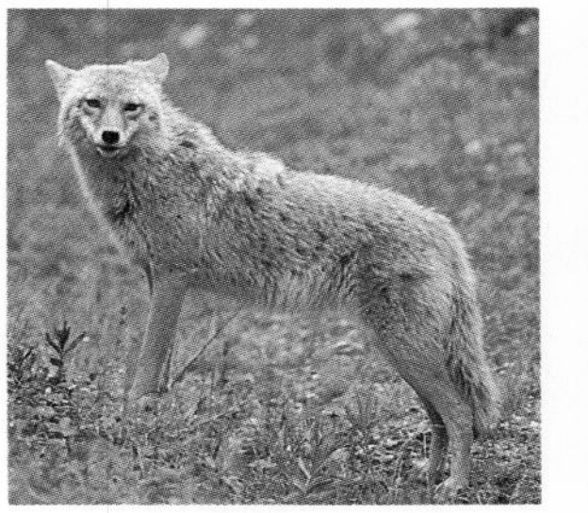

coyote A wild dog of western North America, with a distinctive, drawn-out howling call.

crab[2] (krăb) *n.* **1.** The crab apple or its fruit. **2.** A quarrelsome, ill-tempered person.
~*v.* **crabbed** (krăbd), **crabbing, crabs.** *Informal.* —*intr.* To criticize; find fault. —*tr.* **1.** To interfere with and ruin. **2.** To find fault with. [16th century : originally, (of hawks) to claw, fight, from Middle Low German *krabben;* akin to CRAB (crustacean).]

crab apple *n.* **1.** Any of several trees of the genus *Pyrus,* having white, pink, or red flowers and small, sour applelike fruit. **2.** The tart fruit of any of these trees, used for making jelly. [Middle English, perhaps alteration (through influence of CRAB) of earlier *scrab,* probably from Scandinavian.]

Crabbe (krăb), **George** (1754–1832). British poet. His first major poem was *The Village* (1783), in which he portrayed the ugliness of rural life, a theme taken up in subsequent works, including *The Parish Register* (1807) and *The Borough* (1810).

crab·bed (krăb′ĭd) *adj.* **1.** Irritable and perverse in disposition; ill-tempered. **2.** Difficult to understand; complicated. Said of a writer or his style. **3.** Difficult to read. Said of handwriting. [Middle English, partly from *crabbe,* CRAB, referring to the perversity of its gait, and partly from *crabbe,* CRAB (apple), referring to its sourness.] —**crab·bed·ly** *adv.* —**crab·bed·ness** *n.*

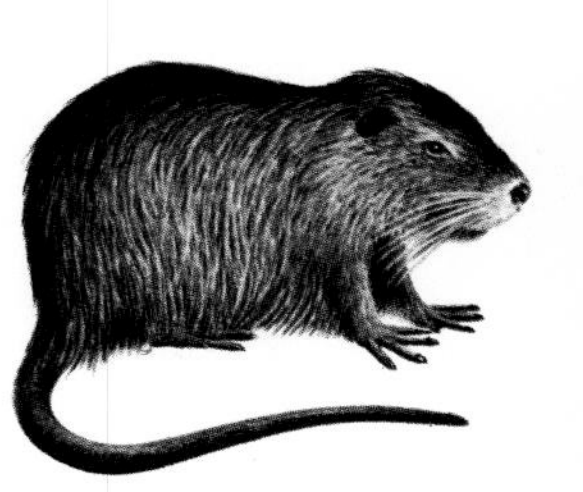

coypu A South American rodent found in marshes and rivers.

crab·ber (krăb′ər) *n.* **1.** A person whose occupation is fishing for crabs. **2.** The boat used in fishing for crabs.

crab·by (krăb′ē) *adj.* **-bier, -biest.** Irritable; bad-tempered.

crab cactus *n.* A **Christmas cactus** *(see).*

crab·grass (krăb′grăs′, -gräs′) *n.* Any of various coarse grasses of the genus *Digitaria,* that tend to spread and displace other grasses in lawns.

crab louse *n.* A body louse, *Phthirus pubis,* that generally infests the pubic region and causes severe itching.

Crab Nebula *n.* An expanding nebula of dust and gas about 5,000 light-years away in the constellation Taurus. It contains a pulsar and is the remnant of a supernova recorded in 1504. [So called from its shape.]

crabs (krăbz) *n. Informal.* Infestation by crab lice.

crab·stick (krăb′stĭk′) *n.* **1.** A stick made of crab-apple wood. **2.** A bad-tempered person.

crack (krăk) *v.* **cracked, cracking, cracks.** —*intr.* **1.** To break with a sharp, snapping sound. **2.** To make such a sound; snap. **3.** To break without dividing into parts; split slightly. **4.** To change sharply in pitch or timbre, as from hoarseness or emotion. Used of the voice. **5. a.** To break down; fail; give out. **b.** To give in to pressure. **6.** *Chemistry.* To decompose into simpler compounds. Used especially of large-molecule hydrocarbons from petroleum, which are broken by heat or catalysis to smaller molecules suitable for use as fuel. —*tr.* **1.** To cause to make a sharp, snapping sound; snap: *crack the whip.* **2.** To cause to break or split slightly or completely. **3.** To break with a sharp, snapping sound: *crack an egg.* **4.** To strike with a sudden, sharp sound. **5.** To break open or into. **6.** To discover the solution to, especially after considerable effort: *crack a problem.* **7.** To cause (the voice) to crack. **8.** *Informal.* To tell (a joke). **9.** To impair or diminish (a reputation, for example). **10.** *Chemistry.* To reduce (petroleum, for example) to simpler compounds by cracking. **11.** *Informal.* To open and drink (a bottle of wine, can of beer, or the like). —See Synonyms at **break.** **—cracked up to be.** *Informal.* Praised or lauded as; believed to be. **—get cracking.** *Informal.* To set about something promptly.
~*n.* **1.** A sharp, snapping sound, such as the report of a firearm. **2.** A partial split or break; a flaw; a fissure. **3.** A slight, narrow space: *The window was open a crack.* **4.** A sharp, resounding blow. **5.** A mental or physical impairment; a defect. **6.** A cracking vocal tone or sound, as in hoarseness. **7.** *Informal.* An attempt; a chance: *gave him a crack at the job.* **8.** *Informal.* **a.** A flippant or sarcastic remark. **b.** A humorous remark; a joke. **9.** A moment; an instant: *at the crack of dawn.* —See Synonyms at **joke.**
~*adj.* Excelling in skill or achievement; superior; first-rate: *a crack*

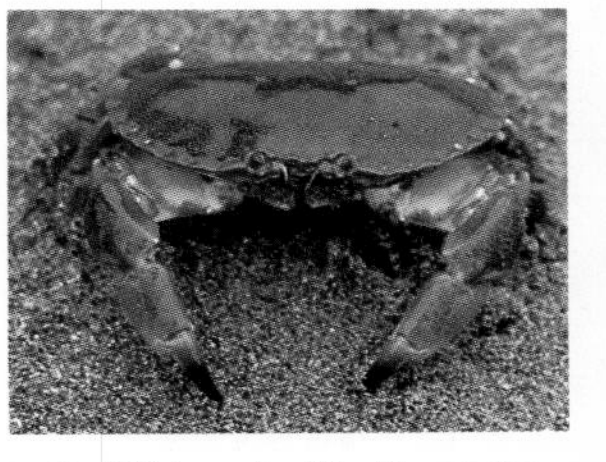

crab Edible crabs, like the species shown here, can grow to about 250 millimeters (10 inches) across. As a crab grows, it molts, shedding its old shell and forming a new one.

marksman. [Middle English *craken*, Old English *cracian*, to resound, from Germanic.]

crack·brain (krăk′brān′) *n.* A foolish or insane person. —**crack·brained** *adj.*

crack down *intr.v.* To become more demanding, severe, or strict. Often used with *on*: *crack down on student absences.*

crack-down (krăk′doun′) *n.* Sudden punitive action.

cracked (krăkt) *adj.* **1.** Having a crack or cracks. **2.** *Informal.* Crazy; foolish.

cracked stem *n.* A disease of the celery plant caused by a deficiency of boron and characterized by cracking of the stalks.

cracked wheat *n.* A cereal, **bulgur** (*see*).

crack·er (krăk′ər) *n.* **1.** A thin, crisp wafer or biscuit, usually made of unleavened, unsweetened dough. **2.** A firecracker. **3.** A small cardboard cylinder covered with decorative paper and containing a joke, a small toy, or the like and a weak explosive that makes a sharp popping noise when a paper strip is pulled at one or both ends and torn. **4.** *Chemistry.* A piece of apparatus in an oil refinery for cracking petroleum. **5.** A poor white person of the rural southeastern United States. Used disparagingly. **6.** One that cracks.

crack·er-bar·rel (krăk′ər-băr′əl) *adj.* Resembling or characteristic of the extended informal discussions carried on by persons habitually assembled at a general store; homespun and unsophisticated: *cracker-barrel theories.* [Cracker barrels were common fixtures in country stores.]

crack·er·jack (krăk′ər-jăk′) *adj. Slang.* Of excellent quality or ability; fine.
~*n. Slang.* Someone or something with excellent skills or abilities. [From CRACK (proficient) + JACK (man.)]

crack·ers (krăk′ərz) *adj. Chiefly British Slang.* Insane; crazy.

crack·ing (krăk′ĭng) *n. Chemistry.* Thermal decomposition, sometimes with catalysis, of a complex substance; especially, such decomposition of petroleum to extract low-boiling fractions, such as gasoline.
~*adj. British Informal.* Very good: *had a cracking time.* —**crack·ing** *adv.*

crack·le (krăk′əl) *v.* **-led, -ling, -les.** —*intr.* To make a succession of slight sharp, snapping noises, as a small fire may. —*tr.* **1.** To crush (paper, for example) with such sounds. **2.** To cause (china, for example) to become covered with a network of fine cracks.
~*n.* **1.** The act or sound of crackling. **2.** A network of fine cracks on the surface of glazed pottery, china, or glassware. **3.** Ware bearing this network of cracks. Also called "crackleware." [Frequentative of CRACK.]

crack·le·ware (krăk′əl-wâr′) *n.* Ceramic ware made with a surface network of cracks.

crack·ling (krăk′lĭng) *n.* **1.** A succession of slight sharp, snapping noises. **2.** The crisp browned rind of roasted pork. **3. cracklings.** The crisp bits that remain of pork fat after rendering.

crack·ly (krăk′lē) *adj.* Likely to crackle; crisp.

crack·nel (krăk′nəl) *n.* **1.** A hard, crisp biscuit. **2. cracknels.** Crisp bits of fried pork fat. [Middle English *crak(e)nel*, probably from Old French *craquelin*, from Middle Dutch *krākelinc*, from *krāken*, to crack.]

crack·pot (krăk′pŏt′) *n. Informal.* An eccentric person, especially one espousing bizarre ideas. —**crack·pot** *adj.*

crack up *intr.v. Informal.* **1.** To have a mental or physical breakdown. **2.** To laugh boisterously. **3.** To crash; collide.

crack-up (krăk′ŭp′) *n. Informal.* **1.** A mental or physical breakdown. **2.** A collision.

Cracow. See **Kraków.**

-cracy *suffix.* Indicates government or rule; for example, **aristocracy, mobocracy.** [Old French *-cratie*, from Late Latin *-cratia*, from Greek *-kratia*, from *kratos*, strength, power.]

cra·dle (krād′l) *n.* **1.** A small, low bed for an infant, often furnished with rockers. **2.** A place of origin; a birthplace. **3.** A framework of wood or metal used to support something, such as a ship undergoing construction or repair. **4.** A framework used to protect an injured limb. **5.** The part of a telephone upon which the handset rests. **6. a.** A frame projecting above a scythe, used to catch grain as it is cut so that it can be laid flat. **b.** A scythe equipped with such a frame. **7.** A low, flat framework that rolls on casters, for use by a mechanic working beneath a motor vehicle. **8.** A movable platform suspended by cables down the side of a building or ship, used by painters, window-cleaners, and the like. **9.** A boxlike device fitted with rockers, used for washing gem- or gold-bearing dirt. **10.** A metal frame inserted under bedclothes to keep them from touching an injured part of the body.
~*v.* **cradled, -dling, -dles.** —*tr.* **1.** To place into, rock, or hold in or as if in a cradle. **2.** To care for or nurture in infancy. **3.** To reap (grain) with a cradle. **4.** To place or support (a ship) in a cradle. **5.** *Mining.* To wash (gem- or gold-bearing dirt) in a cradle. —*intr. Rare.* **1.** To lie in or as if in a cradle. **2.** To reap grain with a cradle. [Middle English *cradel;* probably akin to Old High German *kratto*, basket.] —**cra·dler** *n.*

cradle cap *n.* Crusting of the scalp occurring in young babies. It is a type of seborrhoea.

cra·dle-snatch *v.* **-snatched, -snatching, -snatches.** —*tr.* To take (a much younger person) as a lover or spouse. —*intr.* To practice cradlesnatching. —**cra·dle·snatch·er** *n.*

cra·dle·song (krād′l-sông′, -sŏng′) *n.* A lullaby.

craft (krăft, kräft) *n., pl.* **crafts** or **craft** (for sense 5). **1.** Skill or ability in something, especially in handiwork or the arts; profi-

ciency; expertness. **2.** Skill in evasion or deception; cunning; guile. **3.** An occupation, art, or trade, especially one requiring manual dexterity. **4.** The membership of such an occupation or trade; a guild. **5.** A boat, ship, aircraft, or spacecraft.
~*tr.v.* **crafted, crafting, crafts. 1.** To make by hand. **2.** To make, produce, or create with painstaking skill and attention to detail. [Middle English *craft*, strength, skill, device, Old English *cræft*, from West Germanic *kraftaz, krab-taz* (both unattested), strength.]

-craft *suffix.* Indicates work, art, or practice of; for example, **woodcraft, stagecraft.** [From CRAFT.]

crafts·man (krăfts′mən, kräfts′-) *n., pl.* **-men** (-mĭn). **1.** A skilled worker who practices a craft by occupation. **2.** An artist considered with regard to technical skill. —**crafts·man·ly** *adj.* —**crafts·man·ship** *n.*

craft union *n.* A trade union limited in membership to workers engaged in the same type of work. Compare **industrial union.**

craft·y (krăf′tē, kräf′-) *adj.* **-ier, -iest. 1.** Skilled in underhandedness and deception; shrewd; cunning. **2.** *Archaic.* Skillful; ingenious; dexterous. —See Synonyms at **sly.** —**craft·i·ly** *adv.* —**craft·i·ness** *n.*

crag[1] (krăg) *n.* A steeply projecting mass of rock forming part of a rugged cliff or headland. [Middle English, from Celtic *kar-n-, krag-* (both unattested). See **cairn.**]

crag[2] *n. Geology.* **1.** A shelly deposit of sandstone, found especially in East Anglia. **2.** Strata containing this deposit. [18th century : perhaps specialized use of CRAG[1].]

crag·gy (krăg′ē) *adj.* **-gier, -giest.** Also **crag·ged** (krăg′ĭd). **1.** Having crags; steep and rugged. **2.** Uneven; rugged: *craggy features.* —**crag·gi·ly** *adv.* —**crag·gi·ness** *n.*

crake (krāk) *n.* Any of several birds of the family Rallidae, such as the corncrake, or a marsh bird of the genus *Porzana.* [Middle English *crak, crake*, crow, raven, from Old Norse *krāka* (imitative).]

cram (krăm) *v.* **crammed, cramming, crams.** —*tr.* **1.** To force, press, or squeeze into an insufficient space; stuff. **2.** To fill too tightly. **3.** To gorge with food. **4.** *Informal.* To prepare (a person) hastily or revise and study (a subject) intensively for an examination. —*intr.* **1.** To gorge oneself with food. **2.** *Informal.* To make a concentrated last-minute review of a given academic subject, as in studying for an examination.
~*n.* **1.** The act of, or condition resulting from, cramming. **2.** *Informal.* The knowledge acquired by cramming. [Middle English *crammen*, Old English *crammian* from Germanic.]

cram·bo (krăm′bō) *n., pl.* **-boes. 1.** A word game in which a player or team must find and express a rhyme for a word or line presented by the opposing player or team. **2.** Doggerel. [Obsolete *crambe*, "stale cabbage," tedious repetition, from Latin *crambē (repetīta)*, "cabbage (served up again)" (expression used by Juvenal), from Greek *krambē*.]

cram-full (krăm′fŏŏl′) *adj.* Filled to the maximum; stuffed.

cramp[1] (krămp) *n.* **1.** A sudden involuntary muscular contraction causing severe pain, often occurring in the calf or foot as the result of overexertion, chill, or salt loss. **2.** A temporary partial paralysis of habitually or excessively used muscles: *writer's cramp.* **3.** Sharp, persistent pains in the abdomen.
~*tr.v.* **cramped, cramping, cramps.** To affect or cause to be affected with or as if with a cramp. [Middle English *crampe*, from Old French, probably from Old High German *krampho*.]

cramp[2] *n.* **1.** A bar, usually of steel, with right-angle bends at both ends, used for permanently holding together stones, timber, and other building materials. Also called "cramp iron." **2.** A frame with an adjustable part to hold pieces together; a clamp. **3.** Anything that compresses or restrains. **4.** A confined position or part.
~*tr.v.* **cramped, cramping, cramps. 1.** To hold together with a cramp. **2.** To confine; restrict; hamper. [Middle English, from Middle Dutch *crampe*, hook, from Germanic; akin to CRAMP[1].]

cramped (krămpt) *adj.* **1.** Restricted; contracted; narrowed. **2.** Difficult to read or decipher: *cramped handwriting.*

cramp·fish (krămp′fĭsh′) *n., pl.* **-fish** or collectively **crampfish.** The **electric ray** (*see*). [From CRAMP, pain, from its ability to give electric shocks.]

cram·pon (krăm′pən) *n.* Also **cram·poon** (krăm-pŏŏn′) **1.** Either of a hinged pair of curved metal bars for raising heavy objects, such as stones or timber. **2.** An iron spike or spiked frame attached to the sole of a boot to prevent slipping when climbing or walking on ice. [Old French *crampon*, perhaps from Frankish *kramp* (unattested), hook; akin to CRAMP[2].]

cran (krăn) *n.* A British unit of capacity for fresh herring, equal to 37.5 imperial gallons in volume. [18th century : from Gaelic *crann†*.]

Cra·nach (krăn′ək), **Lucas,** also known as "Cranach the Elder," (1472–1553). German painter and engraver. His works include a famous *Adam and Eve*, as well as portraits of Elector John Frederick, Martin Luther, and others. His work was carried on by his son, **Lucas Cranach the Younger** (1515–86).

cran·age (krā′nĭj) *n.* **1.** The hire, loan, or use of a crane. **2.** The amount of money charged or paid for such use.

cran·ber·ry (krăn′bĕr′ē, -bər-ē) *n., pl.* **-ries. 1.** A slender, trailing North American shrub, *Vaccinium macrocarpon*, growing in damp ground and bearing tart red berries. **2.** The edible berry of this plant, often made into a sauce or jelly. **3.** Any of various similar or related plants, especially the European species *V. oxycoccous.* [Partial translation of (American colonial) Low German *kraanbere*, "crane-berry" (from the stamens which resemble a beak).]

cranberry *The berries of this marsh plant are made into a piquant sauce served with turkey or venison. This is the fruit of the North American high-bush cranberry.*

cranberry bush *n.* The **high-bush cranberry** *(see).*
crane (krān) *n.* **1.** Any of various large wading birds of the family Gruidae, having a long neck, long legs, and a long bill. **2.** Loosely, a similar bird, such as a heron. **3.** A machine for hoisting and moving heavy objects by means of cables attached to a movable boom. **4.** A movable arm on which a film or television camera is mounted.
~*v.* **craned, craning, cranes.** —*tr.* **1.** To hoist or move with or as if with a crane. **2.** To strain and stretch (the neck). —*intr.* **1.** To stretch one's neck for a better view. **2. a.** To balk and lean forward, as a horse does before jumping. **b.** To hesitate. [Middle English *crane,* Old English *cran,* from Germanic; akin to Latin *grus.*]
Crane (krān), **Hart,** born Harold Hart Crane (1899–1932). U.S. poet. His mature work is characterized by a passionate spiritual affirmation of America's democratic potential.
Crane, Stephen (1871–1900). U.S. novelist. He won fame with *The Red Badge of Courage* (1895), set in the Civil War.
crane fly *n.* Any of various flies of the family Tipulidae, having a slender body, long delicate wings, and long legs. Also *chiefly British* "daddy longlegs."
cranes·bill (krānz'bĭl') *n.* Any of various plants of the genus *Geranium* with fruits ending in a long, straight, pointed beak. See **wild geranium.**
cra·ni·al (krā'nē-əl) *adj.* Of or pertaining to the skull. [From CRANIUM.]
cranial index *n.* The ratio of the maximum width to the maximum length of the cranium, multiplied by 100. Compare **cephalic index.**
cranial nerve *n.* Any of several nerves that arise in pairs from the brainstem and reach the periphery through openings in the skull.
cra·ni·ate (krā'nē-ĭt, -nē-āt) *adj.* Having a skull.
~*n.* Any animal having a skull; a vertebrate. [CRANI(O)- + -ATE.]
cra·ni·ec·to·my (krā'nē-ĕk'tə-mē) *n., pl.* **-mies.** The surgical removal of a portion of the cranium.
cranio–, crani– *prefix.* Indicates cranium or cranial; for example, **craniology, craniate.** [From CRANIUM.]
cra·ni·o·ce·re·bral (krā'nē-ō-sə-rē'brəl, -sĕr'ə-brəl) *adj.* Of or pertaining to the cranium and the brain.
cra·ni·ol·o·gy (krā'nē-ŏl'ə-jē) *n.* The scientific study of the characteristics of the skull, such as size and shape, especially in humans. [CRANIO- + -LOGY.] **—cra·ni·o·log·i·cal** (krā'nē-ə-lŏj'ĭ-kəl) *adj.* **—cra·ni·o·log·i·cal·ly** *adv.* **—cra·ni·ol·o·gist** *n.*
cra·ni·om·e·ter (krā'nē-ŏm'ə-tər) *n.* An instrument for measuring skulls. [CRANIO- + -METER.] **—cra·ni·o·met·ric, cra·ni·o·met·ri·cal** *adj.* **—cra·ni·om·e·try** *n.*
cra·ni·o·sa·cral system (krā'nē-ō-săk'rəl, -sā'krəl) *n.* The **parasympathetic nervous system** *(see).*
cra·ni·ot·o·my (krā'nē-ŏt'ə-mē) *n., pl.* **-mies.** *Surgery.* **1.** The cutting or removal of part of the skull to relieve pressure or to expose the brain for examination. **2.** The cutting or breaking of the skull of a dead fetus to reduce its size for removal when normal delivery is not possible. [CRANIO- + -TOMY.]
cra·ni·um (krā'nē-əm) *n., pl.* **-ums** or **-nia** (-nē-ə). **1.** The skull of a vertebrate. **2.** The portion of the skull enclosing the brain comprising eight bones connected by immovable joints. [Medieval Latin *crānium,* from Greek *kranion.*]
crank[1] (krăngk) *n.* **1.** A device for transmitting rotary motion, consisting of a handle or arm attached at right angles to a shaft. **2.** A turn of speech; a verbal conceit. **3.** A peculiar or eccentric idea or action. **4.** *Informal.* **a.** A bad-tempered person. **b.** An eccentric.
~*v.* **cranked, cranking, cranks.** —*tr.* **1.** To start or operate (an engine, for example) by turning a crank. **2.** To make into the shape of a crank; twist; bend. **3.** To provide with a crank. —*intr.* **1.** To turn a crank. **2.** To twist; wind. **—crank out.** To produce, especially mechanically and rapidly: *cranks out memo after memo.* **—crank up.** To cause to start or to get started as if by turning a crank: *cranking up a massive publicity campaign.* [Middle English *crank,* Old English *cranc* (only in *crancstæf,* a weaving instrument), perhaps from *crincan,* to curl, twist, variant of *cringan,* to fall in a battle.]
crank[2] *adj. Nautical.* Liable to capsize; unstable. [Short for earlier *crank-sided*†, lopsided.]
crank[3] *adj. Regional.* Lively, cheerful; spirited. [Middle English *cranket.*]
crank·case (krăngk'kās') *n.* The metal case enclosing the crankshaft and associated parts in a reciprocating engine.
crank·pin (krăngk'pĭn') *n.* A bar or cylinder in the arm of a crank to which a reciprocating member or connecting rod is attached.
crank·shaft (krăngk'shăft', -shäft') *n.* A shaft that turns or is turned by a crank.
crank·y[1] (krăng'kē) *adj.* **-ier, -iest. 1.** *Informal.* Odd; eccentric. **2.** *Informal.* Ill-tempered; peevish. **3.** Full of bends and turns; crooked. **4.** Unreliable; mechanically faulty. [Perhaps from obsolete cant *crank,* a rogue pretending sickness; akin to Dutch *krank,* ill, weak.] **—crank·i·ly** *adv.* **—crank·i·ness** *n.*
crank·y[2] (krăng'kē) *adj.* **-ier, -iest. 1.** *Nautical.* Liable to capsize. **2.** Rickety; loose; shaky.
Cran·mer (krăn'mər), **Thomas** (1489–1556). English churchman, Archbishop of Canterbury (1533–53). A leading reformer, he worked on the English Prayer Books (1549 and 1552). He was burned at the stake during the Catholic reaction under Mary I.
cran·ny (krăn'ē) *n., pl.* **-nies.** A small opening, as in a wall or rock face; a crevice; a fissure. [Middle English *crani,* from Old French *cran, cren,* notch, perhaps from Late Latin *crēna.*] **—cran·nied** *adj.*
crape. Variant of **crepe.**
crape·hang·er (krāp'hăng'gər) *n.* A morose, gloomy, or pessimistic person.
crape jasmine (krāp) *n.* A fragrant shrub, *Tabernaemontana coronaria,* of India, cultivated in warm regions for its white flowers. [From the crinkled lobes of the corolla.]
crape myrtle *n.* An Oriental shrub, *Lagerstroemia indica,* widely cultivated in warm climates for its showy flowers.
crap·pie (krăp'ē) *n., pl.* **-pies.** Either of two edible North American freshwater fishes, *Pomoxis nigromaculatus* (the black crappie), or *P. annularis,* (the white crappie), related to the sunfishes. [Canadian French *crapet*†.]
craps (krăps) *n. Usually used with a singular verb.* A gambling game played with two dice in which a first throw of 7 or 11 wins, a first throw of 2, 3, or 12 loses the bet, and a first throw of any other number (a point) must be repeated to win before a 7 is thrown, which loses both the bet and the dice. [Louisiana French, from French *crabs, craps,* from obsolete English slang *crabs,* the lowest throw at hazard, plural of CRAB.]
crap·shoot·er (krăp'sho͞o'tər) *n.* One who plays craps.
crap·u·lence (krăp'yo͞o-ləns) *n.* **1.** Sickness caused by excessive eating or drinking. **2.** Excessive indulgence; intemperance. [Late Latin *crāpulentus,* drunk, from Latin *crāpula,* intoxication, from Greek *kraipalē,* intoxication, hangover.] **—crap·u·lent, crap·u·lous** *adj.*
cra·que·lure (krā-klo͝or') *n.* A pattern of tiny cracks on an old or deteriorated painting or its varnish. [French, from *craqueler,* to crackle, from *craquer,* to crack (imitative).]
crash[1] (krăsh) *v.* **crashed, crashing, crashes.** —*intr.* **1.** To fall or break noisily; smash. **2. a.** To collide. **b.** To undergo sudden damage or destruction on impact. **3.** To make a sudden loud noise. **4.** To move noisily or so as to cause damage. **5.** To fail suddenly, as a business or an economy might. **6.** *Computer Science.* To break down as a result of a malfunction of hardware or software. Used of computers and storage disks. **7.** *Slang.* To lodge temporarily; stay over: *Can I crash at your place tonight?* —*tr.* **1.** To cause to crash. **2.** To dash to pieces; smash. **3.** *Informal.* To join or enter without invitation; gate-crash. **—crash out.** *Slang.* To fall asleep; collapse with tiredness.
~*n.* **1.** A sudden loud noise, as of something breaking. **2.** A sudden accidental wrecking, smashing, or collision, especially of a car, train, or aircraft. **3.** A sudden business failure. **4.** *Computer Science.* An instance of crashing.
~*adj.* **1.** *Informal.* Of or characterized by an intensive effort to produce or accomplish something: *a crash program.* **2.** Abrupt or violent: *a crash tackle.* [Middle English *crashen* (imitative).] **—crash·er** *n.*
crash[2] *n.* **1.** A coarse, light, unevenly woven fabric of cotton or linen, used for towels and curtains. **2.** Starched reinforced fabric used to strengthen a book binding or the spine of a bound book. [Russian *krashenina,* a kind of colored linen, from *krashenie,* coloring, from *krasit',* to color, from *krasa,* beauty.]
crash barrier *n.* A barrier set up between traffic lanes, around racetracks, and the like, to limit the damage in the event of an accident.
crash cymbal *n.* A cymbal that produces an especially loud crashing sound when struck.
crash dive *n.* **1.** A rapid submerging of a submarine, especially in an emergency. **2.** A steep, uncontrolled fall to earth by an aircraft. **—crash-dive** *v.*
crash helmet *n.* A padded helmet, as worn by motorcyclists and pilots, to protect the head.
crash·ing (krăsh'ĭng) *adj. Informal.* **1.** Complete; utter; absolute: *a crashing bore.* **2.** Out of the ordinary; exceptional; unusual: *a crashing celebration.*
crash-land (krăsh'lănd') *v.* **-landed, -landing, -lands.** —*tr.* To land (an aircraft) in emergency conditions so as to minimize damage. —*intr.* To crash-land an aircraft. **—crash landing** *n.*
crash pad *n.* **1.** A padded area inside cars or other vehicles for protecting occupants in the event of an accident, sudden stop, or the like. **2.** *Slang.* A temporary lodging.
crash truck *n.* A truck specially designed and equipped to rescue victims of an airplane crash. Also called "crash wagon."
crash·wor·thy (krăsh'wûr'thē) *adj.* Capable of withstanding the effects of a crash: *new models of crashworthy cars.* **—crash·wor·thi·ness** *n.*
cra·sis (krā'sĭs) *n., pl.* **-ses** (-sēz'). Vowel contraction at the beginning and end of two adjacent words. [New Latin, from Greek *krasis,* "a mixture."]
crass (krăs) *adj.* **crasser, crassest. 1.** Grossly ignorant; unfeeling; stupid. **2.** *Rare.* Thick; coarse. —See Synonyms at **coarse, stupid.** [Latin *crassus*†, fat, gross, dense.] **—crass·ly** *adv.* **—crass·ness** *n.*
Cras·sus (krăs'əs), **Marcus Licinius** (*c.* 115–53 B.C.). Roman politician and general. A wealthy and politically powerful man, he joined Julius Caesar and Pompey in the first triumvirate to challenge the senate's power (60). Hungry for military glory, he invaded Parthia and was killed in battle.
-crat *suffix.* Indicates a participant in or supporter of a class or form of government; for example, **democrat, technocrat.** [French *-crate,* from Greek *-kratēs,* from *-kratia,* -CRACY.]
cratch (krăch) *n.* **1.** A frame for holding fodder, used for feeding farm animals out of doors. **2.** *Archaic.* A manger. [Middle English, from Old French *creche,* crib, CRÈCHE.]
crate (krāt) *n.* **1.** A container for storing or transporting objects,

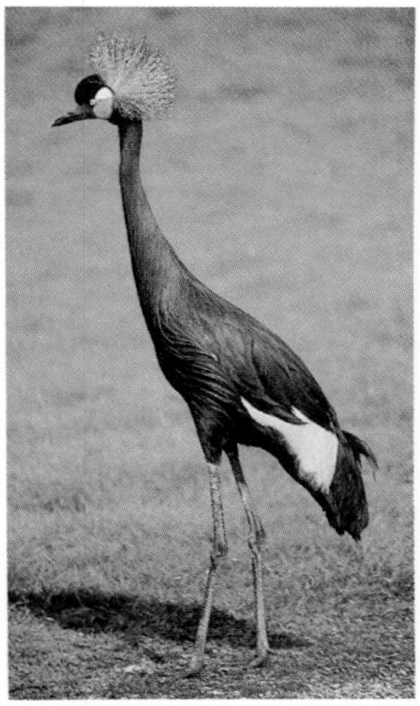

crane *Many of the 14 species of crane are marsh waders, but some—like this African crowned crane—also live on dry plains.*

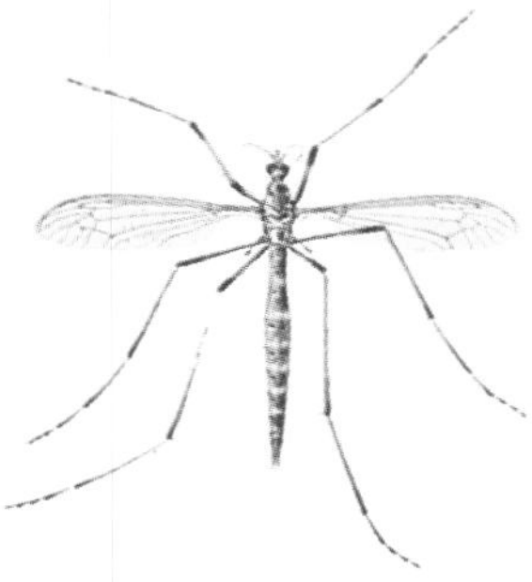

crane fly *Crane flies are found all over the world and can have a wingspan of up to 60 millimeters (2½ inches).*

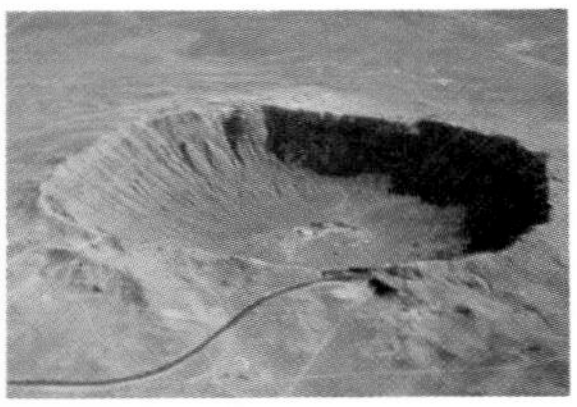

crater *Most natural craters are volcanic, but some have been created by the impact of meteorites. The one shown here is Meteor Crater, near Winslow in the Arizona desert. Made between 5,000 and 50,000 years ago, it is about 1,200 meters (4,000 feet) across and some 180 meters (600 feet) deep.*

usually consisting of a slatted wooden case or box or a wicker basket. **2.** *Slang.* An old, rickety vehicle, especially a car or aircraft.
~*tr.v.* **crated, crating, crates. 1.** To pack into a crate. Often used with *up.* **2.** To transport (goods) in a crate. [Latin *crātis,* wickerwork, hurdle.] **—crat·er** *n.*

cra·ter (krā′tər) *n.* **1.** A bowl-shaped depression at the mouth of a volcano or geyser. **2.** Any of numerous round, bowl-shaped depressions with raised rims covering the surface of the moon and various planets. **3.** Any bowl-shaped pit, especially when formed by an exploded projectile or by the impact of a meteor. **4.** A wide, two-handled bowl used in ancient Greece and Rome for mixing wine and water.
~*tr.v.* **cratered, -tering, -ters.** To cause craters to form on (the moon or a planet, for example). [Latin *crātēr,* bowl, crater, from Greek *kratēr,* mixing vessel.]

Cra·ter (krā′tər) *n.* A constellation in the Southern Hemisphere near Hydra and Corvus.

Crater Lake National Park. An area of *c.* 64,918 hectares (160,290 acres) in southwestern Oregon, in the Cascade Range. Crater Lake, 52 square kilometers (20 square miles), is the second-deepest lake in North America. It was created when the top of a prehistoric volcano was blown off by a violent eruption. The lake was discovered in 1853 by prospectors, who called it Deep Blue Lake because of the intense blue color of the water.

cra·ton, kra·ton (krā′tŏn′) *n.* A large part of the Earth's crust which has not been significantly deformed for many millions of years. Also called "shield."

cra·vat (krə-văt′) *n.* **1.** A small, light scarf, often of silk, worn round the neck and knotted at the front, usually by men. **2.** A necktie. [French *cravate,* originally a neckband worn by Croatian mercenaries in the service of France, from *Cravate,* a Croatian, from Flemish *Krawaat,* from Serbo-Croatian *Hrvat,* a CROAT.]

crave (krāv) *v.* **craved, craving, craves.** *—tr.* **1.** To have an intense desire for. **2.** To need urgently; require. **3.** To beg earnestly for; implore. *—intr.* To have an eager or intense desire. **—**See Synonyms at **beg.** [Middle English *craven,* Old English *crafian,* to beg, demand, from West Germanic *krabjan* (unattested), to demand, from the stem of *krab-taz* (unattested), strength.] **—crav·er** *n.* **—crav·ing·ly** *adv.*

cra·ven (krā′vən) *adj.* Characterized by abject fear; cowardly.
~*n.* A coward. [Middle English *cravant,* perhaps from Old French *crevant,* dying, from *crever,* to burst, die, from Latin *crepāre,* to crack, burst.] **—cra·ven·ly** *adv.* **—cra·ven·ness** *n.*

crav·ing (krā′vĭng) *n.* A consuming desire; a longing; a yearning.

craw (krô) *n.* **1.** The crop of a bird. **2.** The stomach of an animal. **—stick in one's craw.** To be unacceptable or offensive. [Middle English *crawe,* Old English *craga* (unattested). from Germanic.]

craw·fish (krô′fĭsh′) *intr.v.* **-fished, -fishing, -fishes.** *Informal.* To withdraw from an undertaking.
~*n.* Variant of **crayfish.**

Craw·ford (krô′fərd), **Joan,** born Lucille Le Sueur (1908–77). U.S. film actress. She specialized in portraying tough-minded and ambitious women in films such as *The Women* (1939) and *Mildred Pierce* (1945), for which she won an Academy Award.

crawl[1] (krôl) *intr.v.* **crawled, crawling, crawls. 1.** To move slowly on the hands and knees or by dragging the body along the ground; creep. **2.** To advance slowly, feebly, or laboriously: *Time crawls.* **3.** To proceed or act servilely. **4.** To be or feel as if covered with crawling things: *her flesh crawled in horror. The place was crawling with journalists.* **5.** To swim the crawl.
~*n.* **1.** The action of crawling. **2.** A rapid swimming stroke consisting of alternating overarm strokes and a flutter kick. See **Australian crawl.** [Middle English *craulen,* from Old Norse *krafla,* to crawl, creep.] **—crawl·ing·ly** *adv.*

crawl[2] *n.* A pen in shallow water, as for confining fish or turtles. [Dutch *kraal,* KRAAL.]

crawl·er (krô′lər) *n.* **1.** One that crawls, especially an insect. **2.** *Chiefly British Slang.* A toady; a fawning flatterer. **—**See Synonyms at **sycophant. 3.** A tractor with caterpillar tracks instead of wheels. **4. crawlers.** A one-piece garment worn by a baby. Compare **creeper** (sense 8).

crawl·space (krôl′spās′) *n.* A low or narrow space, as in the walls of a building, that gives workers access to plumbing or wiring equipment.

crawl·y (krô′lē) *adj.* **-ier, -iest.** *Informal.* **1.** Creepy. **2.** Feeling as if insects are crawling over one's skin.

cray·fish (krā′fĭsh′) *n., pl.* **-fishes** or collectively **crayfish.** Also **craw·fish** (krô′-). **1.** Any of various mostly freshwater crustaceans of the genera *Cambarus* and *Astacus,* resembling a lobster but considerably smaller. **2.** Broadly, a similar crustacean, such as the **spiny lobster** *(see).* [Alteration (influenced by FISH) of earlier *crevis, cravis,* Middle English *crevise,* from Old French, from Frankish *krabītja* (unattested), CRAB.]

cray·on (krā′ən, -ŏn′) *n.* **1.** A stick or pencil of colored wax, charcoal, or chalk, used for drawing. **2.** A drawing made with crayons.
~*tr.v.* **crayoned, -oning, -ons.** To draw, color, or decorate with crayons. [French, crayon, pencil, from *craie,* chalk, from Latin *crēta*†.] **—cray·on·ist** *n.*

craze (krāz) *v.* **crazed, crazing, crazes.** *—tr.* **1.** To cause to become mentally deranged or obsessed; make insane. **2.** To produce a network of fine cracks in (a ceramic, metal, or painted surface). *—intr.* **1.** To become mentally deranged or obsessed; go insane. **2.** To become covered with fine cracks.
~*n.* **1.** A short-lived popular fashion; a rage; a fad. **2.** A pattern of fine cracks. [Middle English *crasen,* to shatter, render insane, from Old Norse *krasa* (unattested), to shatter (probably imitative).]

cra·zy (krā′zē) *adj.* **-zier, -ziest. 1.** *Informal.* Affected with or suggestive of madness; insane. **2.** *Informal.* Departing from proportion or moderation, especially: **a.** Possessed by enthusiasm or excitement. **b.** Immoderately fond; infatuated. **c.** Not sensible; impractical. **3.** Rickety or dilapidated.
~*n., pl.* **-zies.** *Slang.* A mad or eccentric person. [From CRAZE.] **—cra·zi·ly** *adv.* **—cra·zi·ness** *n.*

crazy bone *n. Informal.* The **funny bone** *(see).*

Crazy Horse (*c.* 1849–1877). Sioux Indian chief. Resisting U.S. settlement in Dakota, he joined Sitting Bull at Little Bighorn and led the force that defeated Gen. George A. Custer's cavalry (1876). He surrendered (1877), but was killed while in custody.

crazy quilt *n.* **1.** A patchwork quilt of pieces of cloth of various shapes, colors, and sizes, arranged in no definite pattern. **2.** A disorderly mixture; a hodgepodge.

C-re·ac·tive protein (sē′rē-ăk′tĭv) *n.* A globulin that occurs in the blood in certain acute illnesses, such as rheumatic fever. [C(ARBOHYDRATE POLYSACCHARIDE) + REACTIVE.]

creak (krēk) *v.* **creaked, creaking, creaks.** *—intr.* **1.** To make a grating or squeaking sound. **2.** To move with such a sound or sounds. *—tr.* To cause to make a creaking sound.
~*n.* A grating or squeaking sound. [Middle English *creken* (imitative).] **—creak·ing·ly** *adv.*

creak·y (krē′kē) *adj.* **-ier, -iest. 1.** Tending or liable to creak. **2.** Dilapidated; decrepit. **3.** Suspect; unreliable: *a creaky argument.* **—creak·i·ly** *adv.* **—creak·i·ness** *n.*

cream (krēm) *n.* **1.** The yellowish fatty component of unhomogenized milk that tends to accumulate at the surface. **2.** The color of cream; pale yellow to yellowish white. **3.** Any of various substances resembling cream, such as certain cosmetics. **4.** The choicest part: *the cream of the crop.* **5.** A soup, dessert, or other dish containing cream or resembling cream in consistency.
~*v.* **creamed, creaming, creams.** *—intr.* **1.** To form cream. **2.** To form foam or scum at the top. *—tr.* **1.** To allow the cream to separate from (milk). **2.** To remove the cream from; skim. **3. a.** To select or remove the best part from. **b.** To select or remove (the best part) of something. Used with *off.* **4.** To beat (butter and sugar, for example) into a creamy consistency. **5.** To prepare or cook (a vegetable, for example) in or with a cream sauce. **6.** To add or apply cream or a similar substance to. **7.** *Slang.* To defeat overwhelmingly. [Middle English *creme, creime,* from Old French *cresme, craime,* blends of Late Latin *chrisma,* ointment, CHRISM, and Late Latin *crāmum*†, cream.] **—cream** *adj.*

cream cheese *n.* A soft white cheese made of cream and milk.

cream·cups (krēm′kŭps′) *n. Used with a singular or plural verb.* A plant, *Platystemon californicus,* of the southwestern United States, having long-stemmed, cream-colored or light-yellow flowers.

cream·er (krē′mər) *n.* **1.** A machine or device for separating cream from milk. **2.** A small jug or pitcher for cream. **3.** A refrigerator in which milk is placed to form cream.

cream·er·y (krē′mə-rē) *n., pl.* **-ies.** An establishment where dairy products are prepared or sold.

cream of tartar *n.* A chemical compound used in cookery, **potassium bitartrate** *(see).*

cream puff *n.* **1.** A shell of light pastry filled with whipped cream, custard, or ice cream. **2.** *Slang.* A sissy; an effeminate man.

cream sauce *n.* A white sauce made by heating a mixture of flour and butter and adding milk or cream.

cream soda *n.* A sweet soft drink flavored with vanilla.

cream·y (krē′mē) *adj.* **-ier, -iest.** Rich in cream or resembling cream. **—cream·i·ly** *adv.* **—cream·i·ness** *n.*

crease (krēs) *n.* **1.** A line made by pressing, folding, or wrinkling. **2.** *Cricket.* Any of the lines marking off the positions of the bowler and batsman or the space bounded by these lines. **3.** *Hockey.* The rectangular area marked off in front of each goal cage. **4.** *Lacrosse.* The circular area around each goal.
~*v.* **creased, creasing, creases.** *—tr.* **1.** To make a fold or wrinkle in. **2.** To graze with a bullet; wound superficially. *—intr.* To become wrinkled or creased. [Earlier *creast,* from Middle English *crest,* ridge, CREST.] **—creas·er** *n.* **—creas·y** *adj.*

cre·ate (krē-āt′) *v.* **-ated, -ating, -ates.** *—tr.* **1. a.** To cause to exist; bring into being; originate. **b.** To make or produce (something, especially an artistic work). **2.** To give rise to; bring about; produce: *Her remark created a stir.* **3.** To invest with office or title; appoint. **4.** To be first to portray and give character to (a role or part).
~*adj. Poetic.* Created. [Middle English *createn* from Latin *creāre.*]

cre·a·tine (krē′ə-tēn, -tĭn) *n.* Also **cre·a·tin** (-tĭn). A nitrogenous organic acid, $C_4H_9N_3O_2$, found, combined with phosphoric acid, mainly in the muscle tissue of many vertebrates and acting in muscular contraction. [Greek *kreas* (stem *kreat-*), flesh + -INE.]

creatine phosphate *n.* An organic compound, **phosphocreatine** *(see).*

cre·at·i·nine (krē-ăt′ə-nēn) *n.* The creatine anhydride $C_4H_7N_3O$, a normal metabolic waste. [CREATIN(E) + -INE.]

cre·a·tion (krē-ā′shən) *n.* **1. a.** The act of creating. **b.** The fact or process of being created. **2. Creation.** God's primal act of bringing the world into existence. Usually preceded by *the.* **3. a.** The world or universe and all things in it. **b.** All creatures or a class of creatures: *all creation.* **4.** An original product of human invention or imagination; a work. **5.** A specially designed garment or other article of fashion. **—cre·a·tion·al** *adj.*

cre·a·tion·ism (krē-ā′shən-ĭz′əm) *n.* **1.** The doctrine ascribing the origin of all matter and living forms as they now exist to distinct acts of creation by God. Compare **evolutionism. 2.** The doctrine that each human soul is a distinct and new creation by God. Compare **infusionism, traducianism. —cre·a·tion·ist** *n.*

cre·a·tive (krē-ā′tĭv) *adj.* **1.** Having the ability or power to create things. **2.** Creating; productive. Often used with *of.* **3.** Characterized by originality and expressiveness; imaginative. **4.** Stimulating to the imagination: *creative tension.* **5.** Extending its scope beyond normal limits, often for questionable purposes: *creative accounting.* **—cre·a·tive·ly** *adv.* **—cre·a·tiv·i·ty, cre·a·tive·ness** *n.*

cre·a·tor (krē-ā′tər) *n.* **1.** One that creates. **2. Creator.** God.

crea·ture (krē′chər) *n.* **1.** Anything created. **2.** A living being, especially an animal. **3.** A human being. Often used with a suggestion of pity or contempt. **4.** One dependent upon or subservient to another; a tool. **—crea·tur·al, crea·ture·ly** *adj.*

creature comforts *pl.n.* Material possessions that help ensure bodily comfort.

crèche (krĕsh) *n.* **1.** A representation of the Nativity scene. **2.** A foundling hospital. **3.** *Chiefly British.* A day nursery for very young children, in a place of work or study. [French, from Old French, from Vulgar Latin *creppja* (unattested), from Germanic *krippja* (unattested), manager, CRIB.]

Cré·cy, Battle of (krā-sē′) *n.* The first major land battle of the Hundred Years' War, fought near Crécy-en-Ponthieu in Somme department, northern France (August 26, 1346). English longbowmen outdistanced French crossbowmen and inflicted a crushing defeat on the French.

cre·dence (krē′dəns) *n.* **1.** Acceptance as true or valid; belief. **2.** Claim to acceptance; trustworthiness. **3.** Recommendation; credential: *a letter of credence.* **4.** *Ecclesiastical.* A small shelf or table to hold the bread and wine used in the Eucharist. In this sense, also called "credence table." [Middle English, from Old French, from Medieval Latin *crēdēntia,* belief, trust, hence a table holding food for tasting in order to detect poison, from Latin *crēdere,* to believe.]

cre·den·dum (krĭ-dĕn′dəm) *n., pl.* **-da** (-də). *Ecclesiastical.* An article or matter of faith. [Latin *crēdundum,* from the neuter gerundive of *crēdere,* to believe.]

cre·den·tial (krĭ-dĕn′shəl) *n.* **1.** That which entitles one to confidence, credit, or authority. **2. credentials. a.** A letter attesting one's right to credit, confidence, or authority. **b.** Written evidence of qualifications. [From Medieval Latin *crēdentiālis,* giving authority, from *crēdentia,* trust, CREDENCE.]

cre·den·za (krĭ-dĕn′zə) *n.* A cupboard or sideboard, especially one without legs, sometimes used as a credence table. [Italian, from Medieval Latin *crēdentia,* CREDENCE (table).]

cred·i·bil·i·ty (krĕd′ə-bĭl′ə-tē) *n.* Worthiness of belief.

credibility gap *n.* **1.** An inability to carry conviction because of previous failure to live up to promises; especially, the improbability of official claims and pronouncements when viewed against the apparent facts. **2.** Public scepticism about official claims.

cred·i·ble (krĕd′ə-bəl) *adj.* **1.** Capable of being believed; believable; plausible. **2.** Worthy of confidence; reliable. [Middle English, from Latin *crēdibilis,* from *crēdere,* to believe, entrust.] **—cred·i·ble·ness** *n.* **—cred·i·bly** *adv.*

Usage: *Credible, credulous,* and *creditable* are sometimes confused. *Credible* means "believable": *a credible story. Credulous* is used to refer to someone who is disposed to believe too readily: *a credulous person. Creditable* has nothing to do with the notion of belief; it means "deserving commendation": *a creditable result.*

cred·it (krĕd′ĭt) *n. Abbr.* **cr. 1.** Belief or confidence in the truth of something; trust. **2.** The quality or state of being trustworthy or credible. **3.** A reputation for sound character or quality; standing; repute. **4.** A source of honor or distinction: *He is a credit to his family.* **5.** Approval for some act, ability, or quality; praise. **6.** Influence based on the good opinion or confidence of others. **7. credits. a.** An acknowledgment of sources or contributors as in the production of a film, play, or book. **b.** A list appearing at the beginning or end of a film or broadcast, naming all those who have taken part. **8.** *Education.* **a.** Official certification that a student has successfully completed a course of study. **b.** A unit of study so certified. **c.** A distinction awarded for a high mark in a course of study. **9.** Reputation for solvency and integrity, entitling a person to be trusted in buying or borrowing. **10. a.** Confidence in a buyer's ability and intention to fulfill financial obligations at some future time. **b.** The commercial practice which allows such future payments. **c.** The time allowed for payment for anything sold on trust. **11.** *Accounting.* **a.** The acknowledgment of payment by a debtor by entry of the sum in an account. **b.** The right-hand side of an account on which such amounts are entered. **c.** An entry on this side. **d.** The sum of such entries. Compare **debit. 12.** The positive balance or amount remaining in a person's account. **13.** An amount placed by a bank, store, or the like, at the disposal of a client, against which he may draw. **—on credit.** With payment to be made at some time in the future.
~*tr.v.* **credited, -iting, -its. 1.** To believe; trust: *"she refused steadfastly to credit the reports of his death"* (Agatha Christie). **2.** *Archaic.* To bring honor or distinction to. **3. a.** To give credit to (a person) for something. Used with *with: credit him with the invention.* **b.** To ascribe (something) to a person; attribute. Used with *to: credit the invention to him.* **4.** *Accounting.* **a.** To give credit for (a sum paid). **b.** To give credit to (a payer). **c.** To make an entry in the right-hand side of (an account). Compare **debit. 5.** *Education.* To give or award credits to (a student). —See Synonyms at **attribute.** [French, from Italian *credito,* from Latin *crēditum,* "something entrusted," loan, from the past participle of *crēdere,* to believe, entrust.]

cred·it·a·ble (krĕd′ĭ-tə-bəl) *adj.* **1.** Deserving commendation. **2.** Capable of being credited or assigned. —See Usage note at **credible. —cred·it·a·bil·i·ty, cred·it·a·ble·ness** *n.* **—cred·it·a·bly** *adv.*

credit bureau *n.* An organization to which business firms apply for credit information on prospective customers. Also called "credit agency."

credit card *n.* A card issued by banks and business concerns authorizing the holder to buy goods or services on credit.

credit limit *n.* The maximum amount of credit to be extended to a customer. Also called "credit line," "line of credit."

credit line *n.* **1.** A line of copy acknowledging the source or origin of a news report, published article, film, or other work. **2.** A credit limit.

cred·i·tor (krĕd′ə-tər) *n.* A person or firm to whom money or its equivalent is owed. Compare **debtor.**

credit rating *n.* An estimate of the amount of credit that can be extended to a company or individual without undue risk.

credit squeeze *n.* **1.** The restriction by government of the availability of credit facilities by means of regulations limiting bank loans, overdrafts, and the like. **2.** A period of such restriction.

credit union *n.* A cooperative organization that makes loans to its members at low interest rates.

credit·wor·thy (krĕd′ĭt-wûr′*th*ē) *adj.* Designating a person or company to whom credit may be safely extended. **—cred·it·wor·thi·ness** *n.*

cre·do (krē′dō, krā′-) *n., pl.* **-dos. 1.** A statement of belief; a creed. **2.** *Often* **Credo. a.** The **Apostles' Creed** or the **Nicene Creed** *(both of which see).* **b.** A musical setting for either of these. [Latin *crēdo,* "I believe," the first word of the Apostles' Creed, from *crēdere,* to believe.]

cre·du·li·ty (krĭ-do͞o′lə-tē, -dyo͞o′lə-tē) *n.* A disposition to believe too readily; gullibility. [Middle English *credulite,* from Old French, from Latin *crēdulitās* (stem *crēdulitāt-*), from *crēdulus,* CREDULOUS.]

cred·u·lous (krĕj′o͞o-ləs, krĕd′yo͞o-) *adj.* **1.** Disposed to believe too readily; gullible. **2.** Arising from or characterized by credulity. —See Usage note at **credible.** [Latin *crēdulus,* from *crēdere,* to believe.] **—cred·u·lous·ly** *adv.* **—cred·u·lous·ness** *n.*

Cree (krē) *n., pl.* **Crees** or collectively **Cree. 1.** A member of a North American Indian people formerly living in Ontario, Manitoba, and Saskatchewan. **2.** The Algonquian language of this people. [Shortened from Canadian French *Christianaux,* by folk etymology from Ojibwa *Kenistenoag,* earlier *Kilistino* (unattested), tribal name.]

creed (krēd) *n.* **1.** A formal statement of religious belief; a confession of faith. **2.** An authoritative statement of certain articles of Christian faith that are considered essential; for example, the Apostles' Creed or the Nicene Creed. **3.** Any statement or system of belief, principles, or opinions. [Middle English *crede,* Old English *crēda,* from Latin *crēdo,* "I believe."] **—creed·al** *adj.*

creek (krēk, krĭk) *n.* **1.** A small stream, often a shallow or intermittent tributary to a river; a brook. **2.** *British.* A small tidal inlet in a shoreline. **—up the creek.** *Slang.* In a difficult or unfortunate position. [Middle English *creke, crike,* possibly from Old Norse *kriki,* a bend, nook.]

Creek (krēk) *n., pl.* **Creeks** or collectively **Creek. 1.** A member of any of several confederated American Indian peoples, formerly inhabiting parts of Georgia, Alabama, and northern Florida. **2.** Any of the languages of these peoples, of the Muskhogean family of languages.

creel (krēl) *n.* **1.** A wicker basket, especially one used by anglers for carrying fish. **2.** A wickerwork trap for fish or lobsters. **3.** A frame for holding bobbins or spools in a spinning machine. [Middle English (Scottish) *crel, crelle*†.]

Cree·ley (krē′lē), **Robert** (1926–). U.S. poet and author. The editor of the *Black Mountain Review* (1954–57), he has also written prose fiction, including the novel *The Island* (1963).

creep (krēp) *intr.v.* **crept** (krĕpt), **creeping, creeps. 1.** To move with the body close to the ground, as a reptile does. **2.** To move stealthily, cautiously, or very slowly. **3.** To behave obsequiously; fawn. **4.** *Botany.* To grow along a surface, rooting at intervals or clinging by means of suckers or tendrils. **5.** To slip out of place from pressure or wear; shift gradually. **6.** *Metallurgy.* To undergo slow deformation as a result of applied stress or high temperature. **7.** To have a tingling sensation: *made my flesh creep.*
~*n.* **1.** The action of creeping; a creeping motion or progress. **2.** *Slang.* An obnoxious or insignificant person. **3.** *Metallurgy.* A slow flow of metal when under high temperature or great stress. **4.** *Geology.* The slow movement of rock debris and soil, lubricated by rainwater, down a slope. **5.** Any slow deformation of an object, or slow distortion of the relative positions of two or more objects. **—the creeps.** *Informal.* A sensation of fear or repugnance, as if things were crawling on one's skin. [Creep: Middle English *crepen,* Old English *crēopan.* Crept: Middle English *creped, crept,* analogous formation from the infinitive *crepen.*]

creep·er (krē′pər) *n.* **1.** One that creeps. **2. creepers.** *Slang.* Shoes with thick soft soles. **3.** *Botany.* A plant having stems that grow along a surface, either rooting at intervals or clinging for support. **4. a.** Any of various birds that creep about in bushes looking for

PRONUNCIATION KEY

ă, **pat**; ā, **pay**; âr, **care**;
ä, **father, are**; b, **bib**;
ch, **church**; d, **deed**; ĕ, **pet**;
ē, **be**; f, **fife**; g, **gag**; h, **hat**;
hw, **which**; ĭ, **pit**; ī, **pie**;
îr, **pier**; j, **judge**; k, **kick**;
l, **lid, needle**; m, **mum**;
n, **no, sudden**; ng, **thing**;
ŏ, **pot**; ō, **toe**; ô, **paw, for**;
oi, **noise**; ou, **out**; o͝o, **book**;
o͞o, **boot**; p, **pop**; r, **roar**;
s, **sauce**; sh, **ship, dish**;
t, **tight**; th, **thin, path**;
th, **this, bathe**; ŭ, **cut**; ûr, **fur**;
v, **valve**; w, **with**; y, **yes**;
z, **zebra, size**; zh, **vision**;
ə, **about, item, edible, gallop, circus, peaceful**

IN FOREIGN WORDS:

à, *Fr.* **ami**; œ, *Fr.* **feu**, *Ger.* **schön**; ü, *Fr.* **tu**, *Ger.* **über**;
KH, *Ger.* **ich**, *Scot.* **loch**;
N, *Fr.* **bon**; y', *Fr.* **Compiègne**

STRESS MARKS:

Primary stress: ′
in·cite′ (ĭn-sīt′)
Secondary stress: ′
in′sight′ (ĭn′sīt′)

food. **b.** A treecreeper *(see)*. **5.** A grappling device for dragging lakes and rivers. **6.** A small platform on wheels for working underneath a car; a cradle. **7.** *Usually* **creepers.** A metal frame with spikes, attached to a shoe or boot to prevent slipping. **8. creepers.** A one-piece suit for a baby.

creeping bent grass *n.* A perennial grass, *Agrostis stolonifera,* of temperate regions.

creeping eruption *n.* An intensely irritating skin disease caused by larvae burrowing beneath the skin and characterized by spreading eruptions in the form of reddish lines.

creeping Jen·ny, creeping Jen·nie (jĕn′ē) *n.* Any of several creeping or trailing plants, such as **moneywort** *(see).*

creeping thistle *n.* A perennial plant, *Cirsium arrense,* having brushlike lilac flowers with purple bracts, found in waste places. Also called "Canada thistle."

creep·y (krē′pē) *adj.* **-ier, -iest. 1.** Creeping; slow-moving. **2.** *Informal.* Inducing or having a sensation of repugnance or fear, as of insects crawling on one's skin. **—creep·i·ness** *n.*

creese. Variant of **kris.**

cre·mains (krĕ-mānz′) *pl.n.* The ashes that remain after cremation of a corpse. [Blend of CREMATED and REMAINS.]

cre·mate (krē′māt, krĭ-māt′) *tr.v.* **-mated, -mating, -mates.** To burn (a corpse) to ashes. [Latin *cremāre,* to burn, consume by fire.] **—cre·ma·tion** *n.*

cre·ma·tor (krē′mā′tər, krĭ-mā′tər) *n.* **1.** One that cremates. **2.** *Chiefly British.* A furnace used for cremating.

cre·ma·to·ri·um (krē′mə-tôr′ē-əm, -tōr′ē-əm) *n., pl.* **-ums** or **-toria** (-tôr′ē-ə, -tōr′ē-ə). A crematory.

crem·a·to·ry (krē′mə-tôr′ē, -tōr′ē, krĕm′ə-) *adj.* Of or pertaining to cremation.
~*n., pl.* **crematories.** A furnace, building, or place for the cremation of corpses. [New Latin *crematorium,* from Latin *cremāre,* CREMATE.]

crème brû·lée (krĕm broo'lā) *n.* A rich, soft cream or custard dessert coated with a layer of hard caramelized sugar. [French, "burnt cream."]

crème caramel (krĕm) *n.* A solid but soft baked custard with a caramel sauce. [French "cream caramel."]

crème de ca·ca·o (krĕm′ də kə-kā′ō, kə-kä′ō) *n.* A sweet liqueur with a chocolate flavor. [French, "cream of cacao."]

crème de la crème (krĕm də lä krĕm′) *n.* **1.** The essence of excellence. **2.** The very best of a given kind. [French, "cream of the cream."]

crème de menthe (krĕm də mänt′) *n.* A sweet green or white liqueur, well flavored with mint. [French, "cream of mint."]

Cre·mo·na¹ (krĭ-mō′nə) A city on the Po River in Lombardy in northern Italy, famous for the making of fine stringed instruments.

Cremona² *n.* Any of the fine violins or other stringed instruments made in Cremona, from the 16th to the 18th century, especially by the Amati family, Antonio Stradivari, or Giuseppe Guarneri.

cre·nate (krē′nāt′) *adj.* Also **cre·nat·ed** (-nā′tĭd). *Biology.* Having a margin with rounded or scalloped projections: *a crenate leaf.* [New Latin *crenatus,* probably from Late Latin *crēnat,* notch.] **—cre·nate·ly** *adv.*

cre·na·tion (krĭ-nā′shən) *n.* **1.** A rounded projection; a crenature. **2.** The condition or fact of being crenate.

cren·a·ture (krĕn′ə-choŏr, krĕn′-) *n.* **1.** A crenation. **2.** A notch between crenations, as on a leaf.

cren·e·lat·ed (krĕn′ə-lā′tĭd) *adj.* Also *chiefly British* **cren·el·lat·ed 1.** Having battlements. **2.** Having square indentations: *a crenelated molding.* [French *crenel,* a crenelation, from Old French, perhaps from Vulgar Latin *crenellus* (unattested), diminutive of Late Latin *crēna,* notch.] **—cren·e·la·tion** *n.*

cren·u·late (krĕn′yə-lĭt, -lāt) *adj.* Also **cren·u·lat·ed** (-lā′tĭd). Having minutely notched or scalloped projections: *a crenulate shell.* [New Latin *crenulatus,* from *crenula,* perhaps diminutive of Late Latin *crēna,* notch.] **—cren·u·la·tion** *n.*

cre·o·dont (krē′ə-dŏnt′) *n.* Any of various extinct carnivorous mammals of the suborder Creodonta, of the Paleocene to Pliocene epochs. [New Latin *Creodonta,* "flesh-toothed ones" : Greek *kreas,* flesh + -ODONT.]

Cre·ole (krē′ōl′) *n.* **1.** Any person of European descent born in the West Indies or Spanish America. **2.** A person descended from or culturally related to the original French settlers of the southern United States, especially Louisiana. **3.** The French patois spoken by these people. **4.** A person descended from or culturally related to the Spanish and Portuguese settlers of the Gulf States. **5.** A person of Negro descent born in the West Indies or Spanish America, as distinguished from a Negro brought from Africa. Also called "Creole Negro." **6.** Any person of mixed European and Negro ancestry who speaks a Creole dialect. **7.** *Often* **creole.** A creolized language.
~*adj.* **1.** Of, relating to, or characteristic of creole or the Creoles. **2. creole.** Cooked with a spicy sauce containing tomatoes, onions, and peppers. [French *créole,* from Spanish *criollo,* from Portuguese *crioulo,* slave born in his master's house, from *criar,* to bring up, from Latin *creāre,* to create, beget.]

cre·o·lize (krē′ə-līz′) *tr.v.* **-lized, -lizing, -lizes.** To establish as a creolized language. **—cre·o·li·za·tion** *n.*

creolized language *n.* Any of several mixed languages of a kind that develops through contact between two language communities, incorporating the basic vocabulary of the dominant or colonial language with the grammar and an admixture of words from the subordinate or indigenous language. It then becomes the native tongue of the indigenous people. Compare **pidgin.**

Cre·on (krē′ŏn). In Greek legend, King of Thebes, successor to his nephew Oedipus and uncle of Antigone.

cre·o·sol (krē′ə-sōl′) *n.* A colorless to yellow aromatic liquid, $C_8H_{10}O_2$, that is a constituent of creosote and is obtained from beechwood tar. [CREOS(OTE) + -OL.]

cre·o·sote (krē′ə-sōt′) *n.* **1.** A colorless to yellowish oily liquid, obtained by the distillation of wood tar, especially from beechwood, and formerly used to treat chronic bronchitis. **2.** A yellowish to greenish-brown oily liquid obtained from coal tar and used as a wood preservative and disinfectant.
~*tr.v.* **creosoted, -soting, -sotes.** To treat or paint (wood or other material) with creosote. [German *Kreosot,* "flesh preserver" (from its antiseptic qualities) : Greek *kreas,* flesh + *sōtēr,* preserver, from *sōzein,* to preserve, save, from *saos,* safe.]

creosote bush *n.* A resinous shrub, *Larrea tridentata,* of the western United States and Mexico, exuding an odor like that of creosote. Also called "greasewood."

crepe, crêpe (krāp) *n.* Also **crape** (for senses 1-4). **1.** A light, soft, thin fabric of silk, cotton, wool, or other fiber, with a crinkled surface. **2.** A black band of this fabric, originally displayed or worn on the sleeve or hat as a sign of mourning. **3.** Crepe paper. **4.** Crepe rubber. **5.** A very thin pancake.
~*tr.v.* **creped, creping, crepes.** Also **crêpe, crape.** To cover or drape with crepe. [French *crêpe,* from Old French *crespe,* crisp, curly, from Latin *crispus.*] **—crep·y, crep·ey** *adj.*

crêpe de Chine (krāp′ də shĕn′, krĕp′) *n.* A silk crepe used for women's dresses and blouses. [French, "crepe of China."]

crepe hair *n.* False hair used in theatrical make-up for making artificial beards, sideburns, and the like.

crepe myrtle. Variant of **crape myrtle.**

crepe paper *n.* Crinkled tissue paper, resembling crepe, used for decorations. Also called "crepe."

crepe rubber *n.* A white or yellowish natural or synthetic rubber with a crinkled texture, used for shoe soles. Also called "crepe."

crêpe su·zette (krāp soo-zĕt′; *French* krĕp sü-zĕt′) *n., pl.* **crêpe suzettes.** A thin pancake usually rolled with hot orange or tangerine sauce and served with a flaming brandy or curaçao sauce. [French : CREPE (pancake) + *Suzette,* pet form of the name *Suzanne.*]

crep·i·tate (krĕp′ə-tāt′) *intr.v.* **-tated, -tating, -tates.** To make a creaking or rattling sound; crackle. [Latin *crepitāre,* to crackle, frequentative of *crepāre* (past participle *crepitus*), to crack, creak.] **—crep·i·ta·tion** *n.*

cre·pi·tus (krĕp′ə-təs) *n.* **1.** A rattling sound heard in the chest of someone suffering from a lung disease such as pneumonia. **2.** A grating sound produced by the rubbing together of the two edges of a broken bone. [Latin, from *crepāre,* to creak.]

crept. Past tense and past participle of **creep.**

cre·pus·cu·lar (krĭ-pŭs′kyə-lər) *adj.* **1.** Of or like twilight; hazy; dim. **2.** *Zoology.* Becoming active at twilight or before sunrise. Said of certain insects and birds. [From Latin *crepusculum,* twilight, from *creper,* dusky, dark.]

cres·cen·do (krĭ-shĕn′dō, -sĕn′dō) *n., pl.* **-dos** or **-di** (-dē). *Abbr.* **cr., cresc., cres. 1.** A gradual increase in the volume or intensity of sound. **2.** The direction or symbol indicating this in music. The sign < is displayed above the notes. **3.** A musical passage played in a crescendo. Compare **decrescendo.**
~*adj. Abbr.* **cresc., cres.** Gradually increasing in volume or intensity.
~*adv. Abbr.* **cresc., cres.** With a crescendo. Often used as a direction.
~*intr.v.* **crescendoed, -doing, -dos.** To increase gradually in volume. [Italian, "increasing," from *crescere,* to increase, from Latin *crēscere,* to grow.]

cres·cent (krĕs′ənt) *n.* **1.** The figure of the moon as it appears in its first or last quarters, with concave and convex edges terminating in points. **2.** Something shaped like this. **3.** *Often* **Crescent. a.** The Turkish emblem. **b.** Turkish or Muslim power. Often preceded by *the.* **4.** *British. Abbr.* **Cres.** A crescent-shaped street, often lined with Georgian houses. **5.** *Heraldry.* A crescent moon, especially with horns pointing upward, indicating a second son.
~*adj.* **1.** Crescent-shaped. **2.** Increasing; waxing, as does the moon. [Middle English *cressaunt,* from Old French *creissant,* waxing, increasing, from Latin *crēscēns* (stem *crēscent-*), present participle of *crēscere,* to increase, grow.] **—cres·cen·tic** *adj.*

cre·sol (krē′sōl′) *n.* Any of three isomeric phenols, $CH_3C_6H_4OH,$ found in coal tar and used in resins and as a disinfectant. [Variant of CREOSOL.]

cress (krĕs) *n.* Any of various plants of the cabbage family, such as those of the genera *Cardamine* and *Arabis,* having pungent leaves often used in salads and as a garnish. See **watercress, garden cress.** [Middle English *cresse,* Old English *cresse, cærse.*]

cres·set (krĕs′ĭt) *n.* A metal cup, often suspended on a pole, containing burning oil or pitch and used as a torch. [Middle English, from Old French *cresset, craisset,* from *craisse,* oil, grease, from Vulgar Latin *crassia* (unattested), animal fat, from Latin *crassus,* fat, thick.]

Cres·si·da (krĕs′ĭ-də). In medieval romances and in Shakespeare, a Greek lady who first returns the love of the Trojan Troilus but later forsakes him for the Greek Diomedes.

crest (krĕst) *n.* **1.** A tuft, ridge, or similar projection on the head of

creeping Jenny *Also known as moneywort and creeping Charlie. The plant is native to Europe but is grown in North America as well.*

a bird or other animal. **2. a.** A plume used as decoration on top of a helmet. **b.** A helmet. **c.** The ridge or raised part on a helmet. **3.** *Heraldry.* An emblem placed above the shield on a coat of arms and also used by itself on seals, stationery, and the like. **4. a.** The top of something, as a mountain or wave; a peak; a summit. **b.** A ridge. **5.** The ridge of an animal's neck or the mane growing on it. **6.** The ridge of a bone. **7.** *Architecture.* Cresting. ∼*v.* **crested, cresting, crests.** —*tr.* **1.** To serve as or decorate or furnish with a crest. **2.** To reach the crest of (a hill, for example). —*intr.* To form into a crest, as a wave might. [Middle English *creste,* from Old French, from Latin *crista,* crest, plume.] —**crest-ed** *adj.* —**crest-less** *adj.*

crest-fall-en (krĕst'fô'lən) *adj.* Dejected; dispirited; depressed. —**crest-fall-en-ly** *adv.*

crest-ing (krĕs'tĭng) *n. Architecture.* An ornamental ridge, as on top of a wall or roof.

cre-syl-ic (krĭ-sĭl'ĭk) *adj. Chemistry.* Of or pertaining to creosote or cresol. [CRES(OL) + -YL + -IC.]

Cre-ta-ceous (krĭ-tā'shəs) *adj.* **1.** Of, belonging to, or designating the geological time, system of rocks, and sedimentary deposits of the third and last period of the Mesozoic era, characterized by the deposition of chalk, the development of flowering plants, and the disappearance of dinosaurs. **2. cretaceous.** Of, containing, or resembling chalk. ∼*n. Geology.* The Cretaceous period. Preceded by *the.* [Latin *crētāceus : crētat,* chalk, clay (see also **crayon**) + -ACEOUS.]

Cretain mullein *n.* A plant, *Celsia cretica,* native to the Mediterranean region, having hairy foliage and yellow flowers splotched with purple.

Crete (krēt). *Greek* **Krí-ti** (krē'tē). The largest of the Greek islands, lying southeast of the mainland between the Mediterranean and Aegean seas. The Minoan civilization flourished in the mountainous island *c.* 3500–1400 B.C. and was celebrated in Greek mythology through the legends of King Minos, the Labyrinth, and the Minotaur. Modern excavations at Knossos have shown it to have been an advanced Bronze Age culture and a sea power. The civilization perished in the 15th century B.C., partly, it is thought, because of a catastrophic eruption. Crete was subsequently occupied by Romans, Byzantines, Muslims, Venetians, and Turks. It was ceded to Greece (1913) following unrest between its Christian and Muslim populations. In the World War II Battle of Crete (1941) Germany won the island through the world's first major airborne landing, using paratroops and troop-carrying gliders to defeat an Allied force that had been evacuated there from Greece. Crete was liberated in 1945. Sheep and goats are raised, and grapes, olives, and citrus fruits grown. Canea (Khaniá) is the capital; Iráklion, the chief port and center of the tourist industry. —**Cre-tan** *n. & adj.*

cre-tic (krē'tĭk) *n. Prosody.* A metrical foot consisting of one long syllable followed by a short and long syllable. [From Latin *crēticus,* from Greek *krētikos,* "Cretan (foot)," from *Krētē,* Crete.]

cre-tin (krē'tĭn, krĕt'n) *n.* **1.** One afflicted with cretinism. **2.** A fool; an idiot. [French *crétin,* idiot, from Swiss French *crestin,* CHRISTIAN, hence human being (an idiot being nonetheless human).] —**cre-tin-oid** *adj.* —**cre-tin-ous** *adj.*

cre-tin-ism (krē'tĭn-ĭz'əm) *n.* A condition caused by congenital deficiency of thyroid hormone and characterized by dwarfism and mental retardation.

cre-tonne (krĭ-tŏn', krē'tŏn') *n.* A heavy unglazed cotton, linen, or rayon fabric, colorfully printed and used for curtains and chair covers. [French, first made in *Creton,* village in Normandy.]

cre-vasse (krə-văs') *n.* **1.** A deep fissure, as in a glacier; a chasm. **2.** A crack in a dike or embankment. ∼*tr.v.* **crevassed, -vassing, -vasses.** To make crevasses in; fissure. [French, from Old French *crevace,* CREVICE.]

Crève-coeur (krĕv-kœr'), **Michel Guillaume Jean de** (1735–1813). French agriculturalist, author, and diplomat. A naturalized U.S. citizen, he farmed with his family in New York State until the American Revolution began. Returning to Europe, he published, among other works, *Letters from an American Farmer* (1782), a book of 12 essays that provided insight into American life.

crev-ice (krĕv'ĭs) *n.* A narrow crack or opening; a cleft. [Middle English *crevice, crevace,* from Old French *crevace,* from *crever,* to split, from Latin *crepāre,* to rattle, crack.] —**crev-iced** *adj.*

crew[1] (krōō) *n.* **1.** *Nautical.* **a.** All personnel manning a ship. **b.** All of a ship's personnel except the officers. **2.** All personnel manning an aircraft in flight. **3.** Any group of people working together; a team. **4.** A company; a crowd. Often used derogatorily. **5.** A team of oarsmen. ∼*v.* **crewed, crewing, crews.** —*tr.* To be a member of the crew on (a ship, aircraft, or boat in rowing). —*intr.* To work as a member of a crew. [Middle English *creue,* military reinforcement, from Old French *creue,* an increase, from the feminine past participle of *creistre,* to grow, from Latin *crēscere.*]

crew[2]. A past tense of **crow** (sense 1).

crew cut *n.* A close-cropped man's haircut. [Oarsmen formerly had this kind of haircut.] —**crew-cut** *adj.*

crew-el (krōō'əl) *n.* A loosely twisted worsted yarn used for embroidery, crochet, and the like. [Middle English *crulet.*]

crew neck *n.* A round, slightly raised neckline on a sweater. [After the style of sweaters worn by boat crews.]

crew sock *n.* A warm usually ribbed sock. [From its use by oarsmen.]

crib (krĭb) *n.* **1. a.** A child's bed; a cradle. **b.** A cot. **2.** A small building, bin, or box for storing grain. **3.** A rack or trough for fodder; a manger. **4.** A cattle stall. **5.** A small, crude cottage or room. **6.** A framework to support or strengthen a mine or shaft. **7.** A representation of the Nativity scene. **8.** *Informal.* **a.** A petty theft. **b.** Plagiarism. **9.** *Chiefly British Informal.* A translation or summary of a text, used by students, usually illicitly, as an aid in understanding the text or in answering examination questions. Also called "pony." **10.** *Cribbage.* A set of cards made up from discards by each player, used by the dealer. ∼*v.* **cribbed, cribbing, cribs.** —*tr.* **1.** To confine in or as in a crib. **2.** To furnish with a crib. **3.** *Informal.* To steal (something, especially an idea); plagiarize. **4.** To reinforce a mine or shaft with a wooden framework. —*intr. Informal.* To use a crib or copy from a neighbor in lessons or examinations; cheat. [Middle English *crib,* manger, stall, basket, Old English *cribb,* manger.] —**crib-ber** *n.*

crib-bage (krĭb'ĭj) *n.* A card game for from two to four players, in which the object is to score a given number of points with certain combinations of cards. [Perhaps from CRIB (noun), "basket," hence discard pile.]

crib-bing (krĭb'ĭng) *n.* **1.** A supporting framework, as of timber lining a shaft; a crib. **2.** Crib-biting.

crib-bit-ing (krĭb'bī'tĭng) *n.* A harmful habit of horses of biting at the edge of a feed trough or other object and swallowing air at the same time. —**crib-bite** *v.* —**crib-bit-er** *n.*

crib death *n.* The sudden and unexplained death of a baby during sleep. Also called "sudden infant death syndrome," and *chiefly British* "cot death."

cri-bel-lum (krĭ-bĕl'əm) *n. pl.* **-la** (-lə). An additional, sievelike, silk-spinning organ possessed by certain spiders, located between the spinnerets. [New Latin, diminutive of Latin *crībrum,* sieve.]

crib-ri-form (krĭb'rə-fôrm') *adj. Anatomy.* Perforated like a sieve. [Latin *crībrum,* sieve + -FORM.]

crib-work (krĭb'wûrk') *n.* A structural framework made of logs stacked one above the other, with the logs in each layer at right angles to those in the layer below, used in constructing mines, foundations, and the like.

cri-ce-tid (krĭ-sē'tĭd, -sĕt'ĭd) *n.* Any of various small rodents of the family Cricetidae, which includes muskrats and gerbils. [New Latin *Cricetidae,* family name, from *Cricetus,* hamster genus, of Slavic origin.] —**cri-ce-tid** *adj.*

Crich-ton (krī'tən), **James** (1560–82). Scottish prodigy whose accomplishments as a scholar, poet, linguist, and athlete earned him the nickname "the Admirable Crichton." In Italy after 1579, he was in the service of the Duke of Mantua until he was killed during a nocturnal brawl by the duke's son.

crick[1] (krĭk) *n.* A painful cramp or muscle spasm, as in the back or neck. ∼*tr.v.* **cricked, cricking, cricks.** To cause a crick in by turning or wrenching. [Middle English *crike, crykke†.*]

crick[2] (krĭk) *n. Regional.* A creek.

Crick (krĭk), **Francis Harry Compton** (1916–). British biophysicist who, with the U.S. geneticist James D. Watson, pioneered the study of DNA, proposing a spiral model for the molecular structure of DNA (1953). Crick subsequently investigated protein synthesis in the DNA molecule. He was awarded the Nobel Prize for medicine with Watson and Maurice Wilkins (1962).

crick-et[1] (krĭk'ĭt) *n.* **1.** Any of various insects of the family Gryllidae, having long antennae and legs adapted for leaping. The males of many species produce a shrill, chirping sound by rubbing their front wings together. **2.** Any of various similar insects, such as the bush cricket, or the mole cricket. [Middle English *criket,* from Old French *criquet,* from *criquer,* to click, creak (imitative).]

cricket[2] *n.* A field game, popular in Britain and many of its former colonies, played with bats and a ball on a large field with a 22-yard pitch between the wickets. The object is to score more runs than the opposing team. A full game consists of two innings by each team and can last up to five days. —**not cricket.** *Informal.* Unfair; unsporting. ∼*intr.v.* **cricketed, -eting, -ets.** To play cricket. [16th century : origin obscure.] —**crick-et-er** *n.*

cricket[3] *n.* A small, low wooden stool. [Origin obscure.]

cri-coid (krī'koid) *n. Anatomy.* A ring-shaped cartilage of the lower larynx. [Greek *krikoeidēs,* ring-shaped : *krikos,* ring + -OID.] —**cri-coid** *adj.*

cri de coeur (krē də kœr') *n., pl.* **cris de coeur.** A cry from the heart; a heartfelt appeal or utterance. [French, "cry from the heart."]

cri-er (krī'ər) *n.* **1.** One that cries. **2.** A person who shouts out public announcements; especially, a **town crier** (see). **3.** A hawker who advertises his wares by shouting.

crime (krīm) *n.* **1.** An act committed or omitted in violation of a law forbidding or commanding it, and for which punishment is imposed upon conviction. **2.** Unlawful activity in general. **3.** Any serious wrongdoing or offense. **4.** *Informal.* An unjust or senseless act or condition. [Middle English, from Old French, from Latin *crīmen,* verdict, judgment, crime.]

Cri-me-a (krī-mē'ə). A peninsula and region of Ukraine, extending into the Black Sea. In 1475 the Crimea was conquered by the Ottoman Turks and was governed as a tributary Tatar khanate until annexed by Russia in 1783. At the outset of the Crimean War (1853) much of the Tatar population was deported. After 1944 the remaining Tatars were exiled by the U.S.S.R., accused of collaborating with occupying German troops (1941–43) during

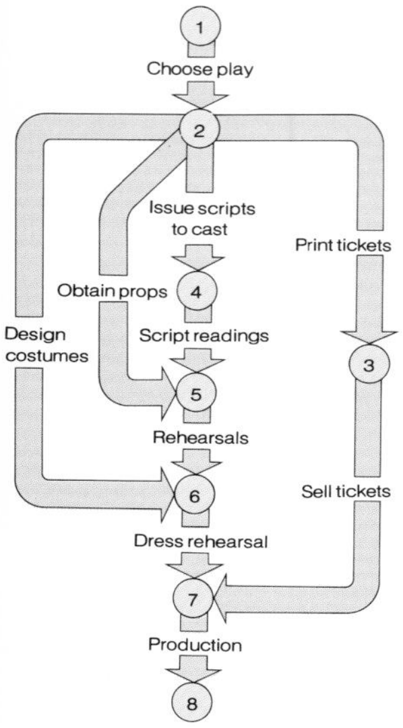

critical-path analysis *Critical-path network showing the preparation of a theatrical production. Delays matter only when they are on, or when they reach, the critical path down the center.*

World War II. Simferopol is the capital; Sevastopol the major port. —**Cri·me·an** *adj.*

Crimean War *n.* A war (1853–56) conducted mainly in the Crimea, in which Britain, France, Turkey, and Piedmont defeated Russia.

crime pas·si·o·nel (krĕm′ päs′ē-ə-nĕl′) *n., pl.* **crimes passionels** *(pronounced as singular).* A crime prompted by the heat of passion, usually unpremeditated and often connected with sexual jealousy. Also called "crime of passion." [French, "passionate crime."]

crim·i·nal (krĭm′ə-nəl) *adj. Abbr.* **crim.** **1.** Of, involving, or having the nature of crime. **2.** Pertaining to the administration of penal law as distinguished from civil law. **3.** Guilty of crime. **4.** *Informal.* Regrettable; senseless: *a criminal waste of space.*
~*n.* **1.** A person who has committed or been legally convicted of a crime. **2.** A person who habitually commits crime, usually theft. [Middle English, from Old French *criminel,* from Late Latin *crīminālis,* from Latin *crīmen* (stem *crīmin-*), CRIME.] —**crim·i·nal·ly** *adv.*

criminal conversation *n. Law.* Adultery.

crim·i·nal·i·ty (krĭm′ə-năl′ə-tē) *n., pl.* **-ties.** **1.** The state, quality, or fact of being criminal. **2.** A criminal action or practice.

criminal law *n.* Law involving crime and its punishment. Compare **civil law.**

crim·i·nate (krĭm′ə-nāt′) *tr.v.* **-nated, -nating, -nates.** **1.** To implicate in a crime; incriminate. **2.** To charge with a crime; accuse. **3.** To condemn as criminal; censure. [Latin *crīminārī,* to accuse, from *crīmen,* accusation, CRIME.] —**crim·i·na·tion** *n.* —**crim·i·na·tive, crim·i·na·to·ry** *adj.* —**crim·i·na·tor** *n.*

crim·i·nol·o·gy (krĭm′ə-nŏl′ə-jē) *n.* The study of crime, criminals, and criminal behavior. See **penology.** [Italian *criminologia* : CRIME + -LOGY.] —**crim·i·no·log·i·cal** *adj.* —**crim·i·no·log·i·cal·ly** *adv.* —**crim·i·nol·o·gist** *n.*

crimp[1] (krĭmp) *tr.v.* **crimped, crimping, crimps.** **1.** To press into small, regular folds or ridges; pleat; corrugate. **2.** To bend or mold (leather) into shape. **3.** To gash (the flesh of a raw fish, for example) to make it crisper and firmer when cooked. **4.** To form (hair) into tight curls or waves. **5.** To bend the edges of (metal) before joining. **6.** To hamper; obstruct.
~*n.* **1. a.** The act of crimping. **b.** Something that has been crimped. **2.** *Usually* **crimps.** Tightly curled or waved hair. **3.** The natural curliness of wool fibers. **4.** A fold or bend in sheet metal to provide stiffness or form a joint. —**put a crimp in.** *Informal.* To obstruct; hamper. [Middle English *crimpen,* to wrinkle, shrivel, Old English *gecrympan,* to curl.] —**crimp·er** *n.* —**crimp·y** *adj.*

crimp[2] *n.* Formerly, a person who procured men to serve as sailors or soldiers by tricking or coercing them.
~*tr.v.* **crimped, crimping, crimps.** To procure (sailors or soldiers) by trickery or coercion. [17th century : origin obscure.]

crimp·y (krĭm′pē) *adj.* **-ier, -est.** Full of crimps; wavy.

crim·son (krĭm′zən) *n.* A deep to vivid purplish red to vivid red.
~*v.* **crimsoned, -soning, -sons.** —*intr.* **1.** To become crimson. **2.** To blush. —*tr.* To make crimson. [Middle English *cremesin,* from Old Spanish, from Arabic *qirmizī,* from *qirmiz,* kermes insect (from which red dye was obtained).] —**crim·son** *adj.*

cringe (krĭnj) *intr.v.* **cringed, cringing, cringes.** **1.** To shrink back, as with fear, revulsion, or distaste. **2.** To behave in a servile manner; fawn. —See Synonyms at **recoil.**
~*n.* An act or instance of cringing. [Middle English *crengen,* probably ultimately from Old English *cringan,* to fall dead.]

crin·gle (krĭng′gəl) *n. Nautical.* A small ring or eyelet of rope or metal fastened to the edge of a sail. [Low German *kringel,* diminutive of *kring,* ring, circle, from Middle Low German *krink, kring.*]

cri·nite (krī′nīt′, krī′-) *adj. Biology.* Covered with delicate hairs or hairlike tufts. [Latin *crīnītus,* past participle of *crīnīre,* to provide with hair, from *crīnis,* hair.]

crin·kle (krĭng′kəl) *v.* **-kled, -kling, -kles.** —*intr.* **1.** To form into wrinkles or ripples. **2.** To make a soft, crackling sound; rustle. —*tr.* To cause to wrinkle or rustle.
~*n.* **1.** A wrinkle or ripple; a fold. **2.** A rustling sound. [Middle English *crinkelen,* akin to Middle Dutch *crinkelen.*] —**crin·kly** *adj.*

crin·kle·root (krĭng′kəl-ro͞ot′, -ro͝ot′) *n.* A woodland plant, *Dentaria diphylla,* of eastern north America, having fleshy rootstocks and clusters of white or pinkish flowers. Also called "pepperroot," "toothwort."

cri·noid (krī′noid′) *n.* Any of various marine invertebrates of the class Crinoidea, which includes the sea lilies and feather stars, characterized by feathery, radiating arms and a stalk by which they are attached to a surface.
~*adj.* **1.** Of or belonging to the Crinoidea. **2.** Resembling a lily in shape. [New Latin *Crinoidea* : Greek *krinon,* lily + -OID.]

crin·o·line (krĭn′ə-lĭn) *n.* **1.** A coarse, stiff cotton fabric, formerly made of horsehair and linen, used to line and stiffen garments. **2.** A petticoat made of this fabric. **3.** A **hoop skirt** *(see).* [French, from Italian *crinolino* : *crino,* horsehair, from Latin *crīnis,* hair + *lino,* flax, from Latin *līnum.*] —**crin·o·line** *adj.*

cri·num (krī′nəm) *n., pl.* **-nums.** Any of several mostly tropical plants of the genus *Crinum,* having long, strap-shaped leaves and clusters of lilylike flowers. Also called "crinum lily." [New Latin *Crinum,* from Greek *krinon*†, lily.]

cri·ol·lo (krē-ō′lō) *n., pl.* **-los.** **1.** A native of Latin America of Spanish descent. Compare **Creole.** **2.** Any of various domestic animals belonging to South American breeds. **3.** A high-grade type of cocoa. [Spanish, "native, local." See **Creole.**] —**cri·ol·lo** *adj.*

cri·o·sphinx (krī′ə-sfĭngks′) *n., pl.* **-sphinxes** or **sphinges** (-sfĭn′jēz). A sphinx with the head of a ram. [Greek, *krios,* ram + SPHINX.]

cripes (krīps) *interj.* Used to express surprise or dismay. [Euphemistic for *Christ!*]

crip·ple (krĭp′əl) *n.* **1.** One who is partly disabled or lame. **2.** One who is deficient in a specified way: *an emotional cripple.*
~*tr.v.* **crippled, -pling, -ples.** **1.** To make into a cripple. **2.** To disable or damage. [Middle English *crepel,* Old English *crypel,* from Germanic; akin to CREEP.] —**crip·pler** *n.*

Crip·ple Creek (krĭp′əl). A city of central Colorado, in the Rocky Mts. near Pikes Peak. After 1891 it was the center of a thriving gold-producing area, but declined as the deposits were exhausted. New veins were found in the 1930's.

Cripps (krĭps), **Sir (Richard) Stafford** (1889–1952). British statesman. As a Labour M.P. he helped form the Socialist League and was an advocate of the Popular Front alliance with the Communists. In World War II he was ambassador to Moscow (1940–42).

cri·sis (krī′sĭs) *n., pl.* **-ses** (-sēz′). **1. a.** A crucial point or situation in the course of anything; a turning point. **b.** An unstable condition in political, international, or economic affairs in which an abrupt or decisive change is impending. **2.** *Medicine.* A sudden change in the course of an acute disease, either toward improvement or deterioration. **3.** The point in a story or drama at which hostile forces are at their most tense state of opposition. [Latin, from Greek *krisis,* turning point, from *krinein,* to separate, decide.]

crisis center *n.* **1.** A place used as headquarters during an emergency for organizing relief work. **2.** A place providing advice or psychological support, as, for example, to victims of rape or assault.

crisp (krĭsp) *adj.* **crisper, crispest.** **1.** Firm but easily broken or crumbled; brittle. **2.** Firm and fresh: *crisp celery.* **3.** Brisk; invigorating; bracing. **4.** Animated; stimulating. **5.** Terse; pithy; sharp. **6.** Well defined; neat. **7.** Having small curls, waves, or ripples. —See Synonyms at **incisive.**
~*v.* **crisped, crisping, crisps.** —*tr.* To make crisp. —*intr.* To become crisp.
~*n. Chiefly British.* A potato chip. [Middle English, curly, from Old English, from Latin *crispus,* crisped, curly.] —**crisp·ly** *adv.* —**crisp·ness** *n.*

cris·pate (krĭs′pāt′) *adj.* Also **cris·pat·ed** (-pā′tĭd). Crimped, curled, or tightly waved. [Latin *crispātus,* from *crispāre,* to curl, from *crispus,* curly, CRISP.]

cris·pa·tion (krĭs-pā′shən) *n.* **1. a.** The act of crisping or curling. **b.** The state of being crisped or curled. **2.** A slight involuntary contraction or constriction, as of the skin. **3.** A minute undulation on the surface of a liquid, produced by vibration.

crisp·er (krĭs′pər) *n.* One that crisps; especially, a compartment in a refrigerator, used for storing vegetables to keep them fresh.

crisp·y (krĭs′pē) *adj.* **-ier, -iest.** Crisp. —**crisp·i·ly** *adv.* —**crisp·i·ness** *n.*

cris·sa. Plural of **crissum.**

criss·cross (krĭs′krôs′, -krŏs′) *v.* **-crossed, -crossing, -crosses.** —*tr.* **1.** To mark with crossing lines. **2.** To move crosswise through or over. —*intr.* To move crosswise or in a crossing direction.
~*n.* **1.** A mark or pattern made of crossing lines. **2.** A game, **ticktacktoe** *(see).*
~*adj.* Crossing one another or marked by crossings.
~*adv.* In a crisscross manner; in crossing directions. [Variant of CHRISTCROSS.]

cris·sum (krĭs′əm) *n., pl.* **crissa** (krĭs′ə). *Zoology.* The feathers or area surrounding a bird's cloacal opening. [New Latin, from Latin *crissāre, crisāre,* to move the haunches.] —**cris·sal** *adj.*

cris·ta (krĭs′tə) *n., pl.* **-tae** (-tē). *Biology.* A crest or ridge; especially, any of the infoldings of the inner membrane of a mitochondrion, or a sensory structure in the semicircular canal of the ear. [Latin, CREST.]

cris·tate (krĭs′tāt′) *adj.* Also **cris·tat·ed** (-tā′tĭd). Having or forming a crest. [Latin *cristātus,* from *crista,* tuft, crest.]

cris·to·bal·ite (krĭs-tō′bə-līt′) *n.* A white mineral form of silica, SiO_2, found in volcanic rocks. [From German, after Cerro San *Cristóbal,* Mexico, where it was discovered.]

crit. critic; critical; criticism.

cri·te·ri·on (krī-tîr′ē-ən) *n., pl.* **-teria** (-tîr′ē-ə) or **-rions.** A standard, rule, or test on which a judgment or decision can be based. [Greek *kritērion,* a means for judging, standard, from *kritēs,* a judge, umpire, from *krinein,* to separate, choose.]
Usage: *Criteria* is a plural form only. It should not be substituted for the singular *criterion.*

crit·ic (krĭt′ĭk) *n.* **1.** One who forms and expresses judgments of the merits and faults of anything. **2.** *Abbr.* **crit.** A professional specialist in the explication and judgment of literary or artistic works. **3.** A person who finds fault; a severe judge. **4.** *Obsolete.* A critique; a criticism. [Latin *criticus,* from adjective, "decisive," from Greek *kritikos,* able to discern, critical, from *kritos,* separated, chosen, from *krinein,* to separate, choose.]

crit·i·cal (krĭt′ĭ-kəl) *adj. Abbr.* **crit.** **1.** Inclined to judge severely; given to censuring. **2.** Characterized by careful and exact evaluation and judgment. **3.** Of, pertaining to, or characteristic of critics or criticism: *critical acclaim.* **4.** Forming or of the nature of a crisis; crucial. **5.** Fraught with danger or risk; perilous. **6.** Designating materials and products essential to some condition or project but in short supply. **7.** *Medicine.* Of or pertaining to a crisis. **8.** *Mathematics.* Of or pertaining to a point at which a curve has a maximum, minimum, or point of inflection. **9.** *Chemistry & Physics.* Of or pertaining to a condition causing an abrupt change in a quality, property, or phenomenon. —**go critical.** To produce a self-sustaining nuclear reaction, as when becoming operational. Used especially of a nuclear power station. **—crit·i·cal·i·ty** *n.* **—crit·i·cal·ly** *adv.*

Synonyms: *acute, crucial, serious.*

critical angle *n.* **1.** *Optics.* The smallest angle of incidence at which a light ray passing from one medium to another less refractive medium can be totally reflected from the boundary between the two. **2.** *Aviation.* The **stalling angle** *(see).*

critical apparatus *n.* An **apparatus criticus** *(see).*

critical constants *pl.n. Physics.* Constants, such as critical temperature, pressure, and volume, that characterize the critical point of a given substance.

critical mass *n.* The smallest mass of a fissionable material that will sustain a nuclear chain reaction.

crit·i·cal-path analysis (krĭt′ĭ-kəl-păth′, -päth′) *n.* A technique for finding the best way of completing a complex process in the minimum time by analyzing alternative combinations of stages.

critical point *n.* **1.** *Physics.* The condition in which the liquid and vapor phases of a pure stable substance have the same density. Also called "critical state." **2.** *Mathematics.* **a.** A maximum, minimum, or point of inflection. **b.** A point at which the derivative of a function is zero or infinite.

critical pressure *n.* The least applied pressure required at the critical temperature to liquefy a gas.

critical speed *n. Physics.* The speed above which fluid flow changes from smooth laminar flow to turbulent flows.

critical state *n. Physics.* See **critical point** (sense 1).

critical temperature *n.* The temperature above which a gas cannot be liquefied, regardless of the pressure applied.

critical volume *n.* The volume of one mole of a substance at its critical point.

crit·ic·as·ter (krĭt′ĭ-kăs′tər) *n.* A petty or inferior critic.

crit·i·cism (krĭt′ə-sĭz′əm) *n. Abbr.* **crit.** **1.** The act of making judgments or criticizing. **2. a.** The passing of unfavorable judgment; censure; disapproval. **b.** An instance of this; a critical comment or observation. **3.** The art, skill, or profession of making discriminating judgments and evaluations, especially of literary or other artistic works. **4.** A review or other article expressing such judgment and evaluation; a critique. **5.** The detailed investigation of the origin and history of literary documents, especially in order to produce the most authentic possible text. Also called "textual criticism."

crit·i·cize (krĭt′ə-sīz′) *v.* **-cized, -cizing, -cizes.** *—tr.* **1.** To judge the merits and faults of; analyze and evaluate. **2.** To judge with severity; find fault with; censure. *—intr.* **1.** To find fault. **2.** To act as a critic. **—crit·i·ciz·a·ble** *adj.* **—crit·i·ciz·er** *n.*

Synonyms: *blame, censure, condemn, denounce, reprehend.*

cri·tique (krĭ-tēk′) *n.* **1.** A critical review or commentary, especially one dealing with a literary or other artistic work. **2.** A critical discussion of some specified topic. **3.** The art of criticism.

~*tr.v.* **critiqued, -tiquing, -tiques.** To write a critique of; review. [French, from Greek *kritikē,* the art of criticism, from *kritikos,* critical. See **critic.**]

crit·ter (krĭt′ər) *n. Regional.* **1.** A creature, especially a domestic animal. **2.** A person. [Variant of CREATURE.]

croak (krōk) *v.* **croaked, croaking, croaks.** *—intr.* **1.** To utter the low, hoarse sound characteristic of frogs and crows. **2.** To speak with a low, hoarse voice. **3.** To talk discontentedly or dolefully. **4.** *Slang.* To die. *—tr.* **1.** To utter by croaking. **2.** *Slang.* To kill.

~*n.* A croaking sound. [Middle English *croken* (imitative).] **—croak·i·ly** *adv.* **—croak·y** *adj.*

croak·er (krō′kər) *n.* **1. a.** A croaking animal. **b.** A person who grumbles or habitually predicts evil. **2.** Any of various chiefly marine fishes of the family Sciaenidae, that make croaking sounds.

Croat (krōt, krō′ăt) *n.* **1.** A Slavonic native or inhabitant of Croatia. **2.** The language of the Croats; Croatian.

Cro·a·tia (krō-ā′shə). Republic in southern Europe. The Croats, a Slav people, occupied the area in the 7th century. Croatia was associated with the Hungarian crown from 1102 and then the Austro-Hungarian empire until 1918, when the Kingdom of Serbs, Croats, and Slovenes (later Yugoslavia) was formed. It became independent in 1992. Area, 56,538 square kilometers (21,745 square miles). Population, 4,601,000. Capital, Zagreb.

Cro·a·tian (krō-ā′shən) *adj.* Of or pertaining to Croatia, the Croats, their language, or their culture.

~*n.* **1.** A Croat. **2.** A form of the Serbo-Croatian language written using the Latin alphabet.

Cro·ce (krō′chā), **Benedetto** (1866–1952). Italian philosopher and political figure. He was minister of education (1920–21), and under Fascist rule he used his review *La Critica* (founded 1903) for veiled attacks on Mussolini's regime. He became a leader of the regrouped Liberal Party (1943) and its president (1947).

cro·ce·in (krō′sē-ĭn) *n.* Any of various red or orange acid azo dyes. [Latin *croceus,* saffron-colored, from *crocus,* saffron, CROCUS + -IN.]

cro·chet (krō-shā′) *v.* **-cheted** (-shād′), **-cheting** (-shā′ĭng), **-chets** (-shāz′). *—intr.* To make a piece of needlework by looping thread with a hooked needle. *—tr.* To make or decorate (a fabric) by looping thread with a hooked needle.

~*n.* A kind of needlework made by crocheting. [French, a hook, from Old French, diminutive of *croc(he),* a hook, from Frankish *krōk* (unattested).]

cro·cid·o·lite (krō-sĭd′ə-līt′) *n.* A fibrous, lavender-blue or greenish mineral, a sodium iron silicate that is used as a commercial form of asbestos. Also called "blue asbestos." [German *Krokydolith,* "fibrous stone" : Greek *krokus* (stem *krokud-*), nap of cloth + -LITE.]

crock[1] (krŏk) *n.* **1.** An earthenware vessel. **2.** A piece of broken earthenware; a potsherd. [Middle English *crokke,* Old English *crocc(a).*]

crock[2] *n. British Regional.* **1.** Soot. **2.** Coloring matter that rubs off from poorly dyed cloth.

~*v.* **crocked, crocking, crocks.** *British Regional. —tr.* To stain with or as with crock. *—intr.* To give off soot or color. [Possibly from CROCK (pot, hence "soot on a cooking pot").]

crock[3] *n. Chiefly British Informal.* One that is worn-out, decrepit, or impaired, especially a car.

~*v.* **crocked, crocking, crocks.** *Chiefly British Informal. —intr.* To get sick; become weak or disabled. Often used with *up. —tr.* To cause to collapse; disable. Sometimes used with *up.* [Middle English *crok,* perhaps from Scandinavian.]

crocked (krŏkt) *adj. Slang.* Drunk. [Perhaps from CROCK (to become disabled).]

crock·er·y (krŏk′ə-rē) *n.* Plates, cups, and the like collectively; china or earthenware.

crock·et (krŏk′ĭt) *n. Architecture.* An ornamental device, usually in the form of a cusp or curling leaf, placed along outer angles of pinnacles and gables, especially in the Gothic style. [Middle English *croket,* from Old North French *croquet,* variant of Old French *crochet,* hook. See **crochet.**]

Crock·ett (krŏk′ĭt), **David,** known as "Davy" (1786–1836). U.S. frontiersman and political figure who cultivated the image of a shrewd, homespun backwoodsman. He became a congressman (1827–31, 1833–35) and later joined the Texas revolutionaries fighting against Mexico. He died at the siege of the Alamo.

croc·o·dile (krŏk′ə-dīl′) *n.* **1.** Any of various large aquatic reptiles of the genus *Crocodylus* and related genera, of tropical regions, having thick, armorlike skin and long, tapering jaws. **2.** Broadly, any crocodilian reptile, such as an alligator, cayman, or gavial. **3.** Leather made from crocodile skin. [Middle English *cocodril,* from Old French, from Medieval Latin *cocodrillus,* from Latin *crocodīlus,* from Greek *krokodilos,* "worm of the pebbles" (from its habit of basking in the sun) : *krokē*†, pebbles + *drilos*†, worm.]

crocodile clip *n.* A small spring clip with long-toothed jaws, used to make temporary electrical connections.

crocodile tears *pl.n.* False tears; an insincere display of grief. [From the belief that crocodiles weep after eating their victims.]

croc·o·dil·i·an (krŏk′ə-dĭl′ē-ən, -dĭl′yən) *n.* Any of various reptiles of the order Crocodilia, which includes the alligators, crocodiles, caymans, and gavials. [New Latin *Crocodylia,* from Latin *crocodīlus,* CROCODILE.] **—croc·o·dil·ian** *adj.*

croc·oi·site (krŏk′wə-zīt′) *n.* Crocoite. [German *Krokoisit,* from French *crocoise,* from Greek *krokoeis,* saffron-colored, from *krokos,* saffron.]

croc·o·ite (krŏk′ō-īt′, krō′kō-) *n.* A rare orange to reddish mineral of lead chromate, $PbCrO_4$, found in oxidized lead deposits. [German *Krokoit,* alteration of *Krokoisit,* crocoisite.]

cro·cus (krō′kəs) *n., pl.* **-cuses** or **-ci** (-sī). **1.** Any plant of the genus *Crocus,* widely cultivated in gardens, and having showy, variously colored flowers and grasslike leaves. **2.** Grayish to light reddish purple. **3.** A red variety of iron oxide, Fe_2O_3, used in the form of an abrasive powder for polishing. [New Latin *Crocus,* from Latin *crocus,* saffron, from Greek *krokos,* from Semitic, akin to Hebrew *karkōm.*]

Croe·sus (krē′səs) (died *c.* 546 B.C.). Last king of Lydia (*c.* 560–546). He allied himself with Babylonia and Egypt and extended his kingdom, building a legendary prosperity on commerce.

croft (krôft, krŏft) *n. British.* **1.** A small enclosed field or pasture. **2.** An agricultural smallholding, especially in the Highlands and islands of Scotland. [Middle English *croft,* Old English *croft.*]

croft·er (krôf′tər, krŏf′-) *n. British & Scottish.* A person who rents or owns a croft, especially in Scotland.

crois·sant (krwä-sän′) *n.* A rich, crescent-shaped roll of leavened dough or puff pastry. [French, from Old French *croissant, creissant,* CRESCENT.]

Croix de Guerre (krwä′ də gâr′) *n.* A French military decoration for bravery in battle. [French, "cross of war."]

Cro-Mag·non (krō-măg′nən, -măn′yən) *adj.* Of, relating to, or designating an early form of modern man, *Homo sapiens sapiens,* inhabiting Europe in the late Palaeolithic era, characterized by a tall stature and known from skeletal parts found in the Cro-Magnon cave in southern France. **—Cro-Magnon** *n.*

crom·lech (krŏm′lĕk′) *n.* **1.** A prehistoric monument consisting of monoliths encircling a mound. **2.** A **dolmen** *(see).* [Welsh : *crom,* feminine of *crwn,* arched + *llech,* flat stone.]

Cromp·ton (krŏmp′tən) **Samuel** (1753–1827). British inventor of the spinning mule (1779), which combined the principles of Hargreaves's spinning jenny and Arkwright's water frame.

Crom·well (krŏm′wĕl′, -wəl, krŭm′-), **Oliver** (1599–1658). English soldier and statesman, lord protector of England (1653–58). A Puritan and critic of Charles I, he founded the New Model Army (1644). Originally working for reconciliation between army, Crown, and Parliament, he eventually sided with the army. During the second Civil War (1648) he came to support demands for Charles's execution (1649). As lord lieutenant of Ireland (1649–50), he ruthlessly suppressed rebellion and defeated the royalist rising of Scots at Worcester (1651). In 1653 he dismissed the governing Rump Parliament, and after the failure of the Barebones Parliament he

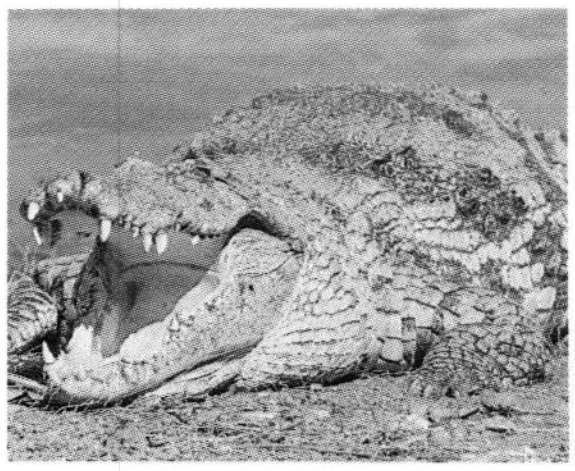

crocodile *The largest and among the oldest living reptiles, crocodiles have existed since the time of the dinosaurs, 150 million years ago. Some species can grow to more than 6.5 meters (20 feet) long.*

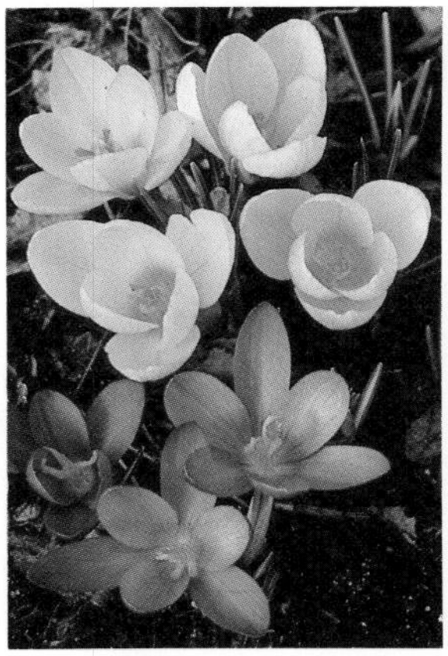

crocus *These low-growing plants—of which there are more than 70 species and numerous varieties—flower in the Northern Hemisphere between August and April.*

PRONUNCIATION KEY

ă, pat; ā, pay; âr, care; ä, father, are; b, bib; ch, church; d, deed; ĕ, pet; ē, be; f, fife; g, gag; h, hat; hw, which; ĭ, pit; ī, pie; îr, pier; j, judge; k, kick; l, lid, needle; m, mum; n, no, sudden; ng, thing; ŏ, pot; ō, toe; ô, paw, for; oi, noise; ou, out; o͝o, book; o͞o, boot; p, pop; r, roar; s, sauce; sh, ship, dish; t, tight; th, thin, path; *th*, this, bathe; ŭ, cut; ûr, fur; v, valve; w, with; y, yes; z, zebra, size; zh, vision; ə, about, item, edible, gallop, circus, peaceful

IN FOREIGN WORDS:

à, *Fr.* ami; œ, *Fr.* feu, *Ger.* schön; ü, *Fr.* tu, *Ger.* über; KH, *Ger.* ich, *Scot.* loch; N, *Fr.* bon; y′, *Fr.* Compiègne

STRESS MARKS:

Primary stress: ′ **in·cite′** (ĭn-sīt′)
Secondary stress: ′ **in′sight′** (ĭn′sīt′)

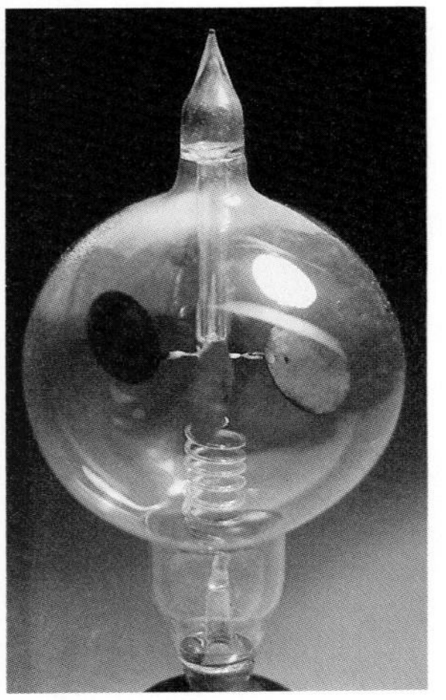

Crookes radiometer *The British physicist Sir William Crookes believed that electromagnetic radiation, such as light, caused the vanes in the bulb shown here to turn, but it is now known that the force of the radiation alone is too feeble. In fact, the dark sides of the vanes are warmed by absorbing more energy than the white sides; and the air molecules in the bulb gather on these warmer sides, causing a relative "breeze."*

PRONUNCIATION KEY

ă, pat; ā, pay; âr, care;
ä, father, are; b, **bib**;
ch, **church**; d, **deed**; ĕ, pet;
ē, be; f, **fife**; g, **gag**; h, **hat**;
hw, **which**; ĭ, pit; ī, pie;
îr, pier; j, **judge**; k, **kick**;
l, **lid**, need**le**; m, **mum**;
n, **no**, sudden; ng, **thing**;
ŏ, pot; ō, toe; ô, paw, for;
oi, noise; ou, **out**; o͝o, **book**;
o͞o, **boot**; p, **pop**; r, **roar**;
s, **sauce**; sh, **ship**, **dish**;
t, **tight**; th, **thin**, **path**;
th, **this**, **bathe**; ŭ, cut; ûr, **fur**;
v, **valve**; w, **with**; y, **yes**;
z, **zebra**, si**z**e; zh, vi**s**ion;
ə, **a**bout, it**e**m, ed**i**ble,
gall**o**p, circ**u**s, peacef**u**l

IN FOREIGN WORDS:

à, *Fr.* **ami**; œ, *Fr.* **feu**, *Ger.* **schön**; ü, *Fr.* **tu**, *Ger.* **über**;
KH, *Ger.* **ich**, *Scot.* **loch**;
N, *Fr.* **bon**; y', *Fr.* **Compiègne**

STRESS MARKS:

Primary stress: ′
in·cite′ (ĭn-sīt′)
Secondary stress: ′
in′sight′ (ĭn′sīt′)

accepted leadership of a kingless protectorate. As lord protector he pursued a vigorous foreign policy against Spain and conquered Jamaica (1655). At home he tried to restrain the excess of Puritan zeal but was beset by constitutional difficulties.

Cromwell, Richard (1626–1712). Son of Oliver, he succeeded him briefly as lord protector (1658–59) before the restoration of the monarchy under Charles II.

Cromwell, Thomas, Earl of Essex (*c.* 1485–1540). English lawyer and statesman who devised the legislation that made the English church independent of Rome, culminating in the Act of Supremacy (1534). From 1536 he supervised the dissolution of the monasteries. He lost favor, was accused of treason, and was executed.

Cromwell current *n.* A Pacific Ocean current at the equator, flowing eastward from the Hawaiian to the Galapagos islands. [After Townsend *Cromwell* (1922–1958), American oceanographer.]

Crom·wel·li·an (krŏm-wĕl′ē-ən, krŭm-) *adj.* Of, pertaining to, or characteristic of Oliver Cromwell or his time; especially, austere or puritanical.

crone (krōn) *n.* A withered old woman. [Middle English, from Middle Dutch *caroonje, croonje,* old ewe, dead body, from Old North French *carogne,* CARRION.]

Cro·nin (krō′nĭn), **Archibald Joseph** (1896–1981). British novelist, born in Scotland. A former physician, he published his first novel *Hatter's Castle* in 1931. Later titles include *The Keys of the Kingdom* (1941) and *The Minstrel Boy* (1975).

Cron·je (krôn-yä), **Piet Arnoldus** (*c.* 1840–1911). South African Boer general. He commanded the siege of Potchefstroom (1881) and headed the force that captured the Jameson Raiders (1896). In 1899 he was appointed general in command of the Boers' western forces, fighting off a major British assault at Magersfontein. He surrendered at Paardeburg (1900) and remained in captivity on St. Helena until the end of the war.

Cron·os, Kron·os (krō′nəs). *Greek Mythology.* A Titan who ruled the universe until dethroned by his son Zeus; identified with the Roman god Saturn.

cro·ny (krō′nē) *n., pl.* **-nies. 1.** A close friend or companion. **2.** An associate in some dishonest or questionable activity. [Earlier *chrony* (Cambridge University slang), "old companion," from Greek *khronios,* long-lasting, from *khronos,* time.]

cro·ny·ism (krō′nē-ĭz′əm) *n.* Favoritism shown to cronies, without regard for their qualifications, as in political appointments to office.

crook (kro͝ok) *n.* **1.** Something that is bent or curved; a hook or hooked part. **2.** An implement or tool that has a bent or curved part, such as a bishop's crosier or a shepherd's staff. **3.** A curve or bend; a turn. **4.** *Informal.* A person who makes a living by dishonest methods; a thief.
—*v.* **crooked, crooking, crooks.** —*tr.* To give a crook to or make a crook in; curve; bend. —*intr.* To become crooked. [Middle English *crok,* from Old Norse *krōkr,* a hook.]

crook·back (kro͝ok′băk′) *n. Archaic.* A hunchback. —**crook·backed** *adj.*

crook·ed (kro͝ok′ĭd) *adj.* **1.** Having bends, curves, or angles; not straight. **2.** *Informal.* Dishonest or unscrupulous; fraudulent. **3.** Misshapen; deformed. —**crook·ed·ly** *adv.* —**crook·ed·ness** *n.*

Crookes (kro͝oks), **Sir William** (1832–1919). British chemist and physicist. He discovered the element thallium (1861) and invented the radiometer. He pioneered research into cathode rays and produced a shield to protect the eyes of glassworkers.

Crookes dark space *n.* A small dark region near the cathode in a luminous gas discharge. [After Sir William CROOKES.]

Crookes glass *n.* A type of glass containing cerium, which cuts down the transmission of ultraviolet radiation. It is used in sunglasses and protective goggles. [After Sir William CROOKES.]

Crookes radiometer *n.* A device consisting of a small, evacuated glass bulb containing a set of four light, vertical metal vanes, each blackened on one side and mounted on a vertical, rotating spindle. When light or other radiation falls on the tube, the vanes rotate. The rate of rotation depends on the intensity of the radiation. [After Sir William CROOKES.]

Crookes tube *n.* A low-pressure discharge tube used to study the properties of cathode rays. [After Sir William CROOKES.]

crook·neck (kro͝ok′nĕk′) *n.* A type of squash having a long, curved neck and yellow flesh.

croon (kro͞on) *v.* **crooned, crooning, croons.** —*intr.* **1.** To sing or hum softly; murmur. **2.** To sing popular songs in a soft, sentimental manner. **3.** *British Regional.* **a.** To wail or cry softly, as when lamenting. **b.** To utter a deep, loud sound; roar. —*tr.* To sing by crooning.
—*n.* A soft singing, humming, or murmuring. [Middle English *croynen,* to boom, sing, from Middle Dutch *krōnen,* to groan, lament (imitative).] —**croon·er** *n.*

crop (krŏp) *n.* **1.** Cultivated plants or agricultural produce, such as grain, vegetables, or fruit. **2.** The quantity or quality of such produce of a particular season, place, or kind. **3.** A group, quantity, or supply appearing at one time: *this year's crop of students.* **4.** A short haircut. **5.** An animal hide, tanned and complete. **6. a.** A short whip used in horseback riding, with a loop serving as a lash. **b.** The stock of a whip. **7.** *Zoology.* **a.** A pouchlike enlargement of a bird's esophagus, in which food is stored or partially digested. **b.** A similar organ in earthworms, insects, and other invertebrates. **8.** The mark produced by cropping the ears of a domestic animal.
—*v.* **cropped, cropping, crops.** —*tr.* **1.** To cut or bite off the stems or top of (a plant). **2.** To cut (hair, for example) very short. **3.** To clip (an animal's ears or a photograph, for example). **4.** To reap; harvest. **5.** To cause to grow or yield a crop or crops. —*intr.* To plant, grow, or yield a crop or crops. —**crop out.** To project above the ground. Used of rock formations. —**crop up.** To appear or develop unexpectedly. [Middle English *crop,* Old English *cropp,* cluster, bunch, ear of corn, from Germanic.]

crop-dust·ing (krŏp′dŭs′tĭng) *n.* The spraying of crops with an insecticidal or fungicidal dust, usually from a light aircraft. —**crop-dust** *v.* —**crop-dust·er** *n.*

crop-eared (krŏp′îrd′) *adj.* **1.** Having the ears cropped. **2.** With the hair cut so short that the ears show.

crop·per¹ (krŏp′ər) *n.* **1.** A person, animal, or machine that crops. **2.** A person who works land in return for a share of the yield; a sharecropper. **3.** *Informal.* A plant that yields a crop of the specified type: *a generous cropper; a late cropper.*

cropper² *n.* **1.** A heavy fall; a tumble. **2.** A disastrous failure; a fiasco. —**come a cropper. 1.** To fall heavily. **2.** To fail miserably; come to grief. [From the phrase *neck and crop,* "completely," perhaps from CROP (to cut off).]

crop rotation *n.* A method of maintaining and renewing soil fertility by the successive planting of different crops on the same land.

cro·quet (krō-kā′) *n.* **1.** An outdoor game in which the players drive wooden balls through a series of loops using long-handled mallets. **2.** The act of driving away an opponent's croquet ball by hitting one's own ball when the two are in contact.
—*v.* **croqueted** (-kād′), **-queting** (-kā′ĭng), **-quets** (-kāz′). —*tr.* To drive away (an opponent's ball) with a croquet. —*intr.* To croquet an opponent's ball. [Perhaps dialect form of French *crochet,* a hook. See **crochet.**]

cro·quette (krō-kĕt′) *n.* A small cake of savory minced or molded food, coated with bread crumbs and deep-fried. [French, from *croquer,* to crunch, crack (imitative).]

cro·qui·gnole (krō′kĭn-yōl′) *n.* A kind of permanent wave in which the hair is wound around metal rods. [French, a biscuit, perhaps from *croquer,* to crunch. See **croquette.**]

Cros·by (krôz′bē, krŏz′-), **Bing,** born Harry Lillis Crosby (1904–77). U.S. singer, actor, and entertainer. He popularized a new, softer, and more relaxed style of singing and starred with Bob Hope in the *Road* series of comedy films.

cro·sier, cro·zier (krō′zhər) *n.* **1.** A staff with a crook at the end, carried by or before an abbot, bishop, or archbishop as a symbol of office. Also called "pastoral staff." **2.** *Botany.* A coiled tip of a plant stalk, as of a young fern frond. [Middle English *crocer,* from Old French *crossier,* staff-bearer, from *crosse,* bishop's staff, from Germanic.]

cross (krôs, krŏs) *n.* **1.** A structure, mark, or pattern formed typically by the intersection of two lines of equal length or two lines at right angles. **2.** An upright post with a transverse piece near the top, upon which condemned persons were executed in ancient times. **3.** Any of several representations of the cross upon which Jesus was crucified. **4.** A sign made by tracing the outline of a cross with the right hand upon the forehead and chest as a devotional act. **5.** A crucifix. **6. a.** Any of various symbolic or ornamental figures or structures in the form of a cross or modified cross, such as a medal or emblem. **b.** A monument in the form of a cross, often at a central place in a town or village. **7.** A source of trouble or sorrow; an affliction: *She too has her cross to bear.* **8.** A mark (X) used as a signature or to indicate an error, point of intersection, and the like. **9.** A pipe fitting with four branches in the form of a cross, used as a junction for intersecting pipes. **10.** *Biology.* **a.** A plant or animal produced by crossbreeding; a hybrid. **b.** The process of crossbreeding; hybridization. **11.** A combination of the qualities of two things or people. **12.** *Slang.* A swindle or fraud; especially, a contest whose outcome has been dishonestly prearranged. **13.** *Sports.* **a.** In boxing, a punch launched from the side, usually the right. **b.** In soccer, a shot that sends the ball across the pitch: *a long cross to the center.* —**the Cross. 1.** The cross upon which Jesus was crucified. **2.** Christianity; the Christian religion.
—*v.* **crossed, crossing, crosses.** —*tr.* **1.** To go across; pass from one side of to the other. **2.** To carry or convey across. **3.** To extend or pass across, through, or over; intersect. **4.** To make or put a line across. **5.** To lay across or over; place crosswise: *cross one's legs.* **6.** To make the sign of the cross upon (oneself) or over (another) as a sign of devotion. **7.** To encounter in passing: *His path crossed mine.* **8.** To thwart or obstruct; interfere with: *Do not cross me.* **9.** *Biology.* To crossbreed or cross-fertilize (plants or animals). —*intr.* **1.** To lie or pass across each other; intersect. **2.** To move or extend from one side to another. **3.** To encounter each other in passing: *Our paths crossed.* **4.** *Biology.* To crossbreed or cross-fertilize. **5.** To be in the mail simultaneously. Used of two letters addressed to each other's senders. —**cross off** or **out.** To cancel or eliminate by or as if by drawing a line or lines through.
—*adj.* **1.** Lying or passing crosswise; intersecting. **2.** Contrary or counter; opposing. **3.** Showing ill humor; annoyed. **4.** Crossbred; hybrid. [Middle English *cros,* Old English *cros,* from Old Irish *cross,* from Latin *crux* (stem *cruc-*), perhaps from Phoenician.] —**cross·er** *n.* —**cross·ly** *adv.* —**cross·ness** *n.*

cross·bar (krôs′bär′, krŏs′-) *n.* A horizontal beam or bar, as on a hurdle, on a bicycle, or on goalposts.

cross·beam (krôs′bēm′, krŏs′-) *n.* A beam that links or rests on two supports.

cross bedding *n. Geology.* The formation of laminations within a stratum at a different angle to that of the main bed. Also called "current bedding," "false bedding."

cross·bench (krôs′bĕnch′, krŏs′-) *n. British.* A bench in Parliament occupied by members who belong to neither government nor opposition. **—cross·bench·er** *n.*

cross·bill (krôs′bĭl′, krŏs′-) *n.* Any of several birds of the genus *Loxia,* having bills whose upper and lower parts curve and cross at their narrow tips.

cross·bones (krôs′bōnz′, krŏs′-) *n.* See **skull and crossbones.**

cross·bow (krôs′bō′, krŏs′-) *n.* A medieval weapon consisting of a bow fixed crosswise on a wooden stock, with grooves on the stock to direct the arrow or other projectile. **—cross·bow·man** *n.*

cross·breed (krôs′brēd′, krŏs′-) *v.* **-bred** (-brĕd), **-breeding, -breeds.** *—tr.* **1.** To mate individuals of different varieties or breeds; hybridize. **2.** To produce (a hybrid) by crossbreeding. *—intr.* To mate so as to produce a hybrid; interbreed.
~*n.* A hybrid produced by crossbreeding. Also called "intercross."

cross·check (krôs′chĕk′, krŏs′-) *tr.v.* **-checked, -checking, -checks.** To verify by comparing with supplementary data.
~*n.* (krôs′chĕk′, krŏs′-). An act of crosschecking.

cross-coun·try (krôs′kŭn′trē, krŏs′-) *adj.* **1.** Moving or directed across open country, rather than following roads. **2.** From one side of a country to the opposite side.
~*n.* A long running race over open country. **—cross-coun·try** *adv.*

cross-cul·tur·al (krôs′kŭl′chər-əl, krŏs′-) *adj.* Dealing with or involving two or more different cultures: *a cross-cultural study of marriage customs.*

cross·cur·rent (krôs′kûr′ənt, krŏs′-) *n.* **1.** A current flowing across another current. **2.** A conflicting movement, tendency, or inclination.

cross·cut (krôs′kŭt′, krŏs′-) *v.* **-cut, -cutting, -cuts.** *—tr.* **1.** To cut across transversely. **2.** In film-making, to intercut. *—intr.* To cut or run crosswise.
~*adj.* **1.** Used or constructed for cutting crosswise: *a crosscut saw.* **2.** Cut on the bias or across the grain.
~*n.* **1.** A course or cut going crosswise. **2.** A path more direct than the main path; a short cut. **3.** *Mining.* A level driven so that it intersects a vein of ore.

cross-dres·ser (krôs′drĕs′ər, krŏs′-) *n.* A **transvestite** *(see).* **—cross-dres·sing** *n.*

crosse (krôs, krŏs) *n.* A lacrosse stick. [French, from Old French *crosse,* staff. See **crosier.**]

crossed line *n.* A telephone connection between two callers in which another call can be heard.

cross-ex·am·ine (krôs′ĭg-zăm′ĭn, krŏs′-) *v.* **-ined, -ining, -ines.** *—tr.* **1.** To question (someone) closely, especially in order to check the resulting answers against answers previously made. **2.** *Law.* To question (a witness already examined by the opposing side). *—intr.* To question a person closely. **—cross-ex·am·i·na·tion** *n.* **—cross-ex·am·in·er** *n.*

cross-eye (krôs′ī′, krŏs′ī′) *n.* An eye defect in which one or both eyes turn toward the nose. See **strabismus. —cross-eyed** *adj.*

cross-fer·ti·li·za·tion (krôs′fûrt′l-ə-zā′shən, krŏs′-) *n.* **1.** *Biology.* The union of gametes from different individuals, usually of the same species. Cross-fertilization in plants is also called "allogamy." **2.** An interchange, as of ideas or methods, between different groups. **—cross-fer·tile** *adj.*

cross-fer·ti·lize (krôs′fûrt′l-īz′, krŏs′-) *v.* **-lized, -lizing, -lizes.** *—tr.* To fertilize by means of cross-fertilization. *—intr.* To be fertilized by means of cross-fertilization.

cross-file (krôs′fīl′, krŏs′-) *intr.v.* **-filed, -filing, -files.** To register as a candidate in the primaries of more than one political party. **—cross-fil·er** *n.*

cross·fire (krôs′fīr′, krŏs′-) *n.* **1.** *Military.* Lines of fire from two or more positions crossing one another at or near a single objective. **2.** Any situation in which things originating from different sources meet in conflict. **3.** A heated exchange of conflicting ideas.

cross-grained (krôs′grānd′, krŏs′-) *adj.* **1.** Having an irregular, transverse, or diagonal grain. **2.** Stubborn; contrary.

cross hair *n.* Either of two fine strands of wire crossed in the focus of an eyepiece of an optical instrument and used as a calibration or sighting reference.

cross·hatch (krôs′hăch′, krŏs′-) *tr.v.* **-hatched, -hatching, -hatches.** In drawing, to shade with two or more sets of intersecting parallel lines. **—cross·hatch·ing** *n.*

cross·head (krôs′hĕd, krŏs′-) *n.* **1.** *Engineering.* A beam that connects the piston rod to the connecting rod of a reciprocating engine. **2.** *Printing.* A subheading.
~*adj.* **1.** Designating a screw that has a cross-shaped notch in its head. **2.** Designating a screwdriver designed to fit such a screw.

cross-in·dex (krôs′ĭn′dĕks, krŏs′-) *v.* **-dexed, -dexing, -dexes.** *—tr.* To furnish (an index) with cross-references. *—intr.* To furnish cross-references.

cross·ing (krôs′ĭng, krŏs′-) *n.* **1.** A place at which roads, lines, or tracks intersect; an intersection. **2.** A place at which something, such as a river or road, may be crossed. **3.** An act or instance of crossing, especially in a ship: *a rough crossing from Bar Harbor to Yarmouth.* **4.** The intersection of the nave and transept in a cruciform church. **5.** The act of crossbreeding.

crossing over *n.* The exchange of genetic material between homologous chromosomes during the formation of gametes. Also called "crossover."

cross·jack (krôs′jăk′, krŏs′-) *n.* The square sail below the lowest mizzenmast spar on a ship. [CROSS + JACK (flag).]

cross-leg·ged (krôs′lĕg′ĭd, krŏs′-) *adj.* With one leg crossed over the other. **—cross-leg·ged** *adv.*

cross·let (krôs′lət, krŏs′-) *n. Heraldry.* A cross with a smaller cross at each of the four tips. [16th century *croslet,* diminutive of CROSS.]

cross-link (krôs′lĭngk′, krŏs′-) *n. Chemistry.* A short chain of atoms joined across two long chains in certain types of polymer.
~*v.* **cross-linked, -linking, -links.** *Chemistry. —tr.* To cause the formation of cross-links in (a polymer). *—intr.* To polymerize with cross-links.

cross matching *n.* The process by which blood compatibility between donor and recipient is tested before transfusion.

cros·sop·te·ryg·i·an (krŏ-sŏp′tə-rĭj′ē-ən) *n.* A member of the Crossopterygii, a group of mostly extinct bony fishes including the coelacanths, believed to have been the possible ancestors of terrestrial vertebrates. [New Latin *Crossopterygii,* "the fringed-winged ones" : Greek *krossoi*†, fringe + Greek *pterux,* wing, from *pteron,* feather, wing.] **—cros·sop·te·ryg·i·an** *adj.*

cross·o·ver (krôs′ō′vər, krŏs′-) *n.* **1.** A place at which or the means by which a crossing is made. **2.** A short connecting track by which a train can be transferred from one line to another. **3.** *Genetics.* **a.** A **crossing over** *(see).* **b.** A character combination resulting from crossing over.

cross·patch (krôs′păch′, krŏs′-) *n. Informal.* A peevish, irascible person. [CROSS (angry) + obsolete *patch,* jester, probably from Italian *pazzo*†.]

cross·piece (krôs′pēs′, krŏs′-) *n.* A transverse piece, such as a beam in a building.

cross-ply (krôs′plī′, krŏs′-) *adj.* Designating car tires that have fabric cords lying crosswise to stiffen the sidewalls.
~*n.* A cross-ply tire.

cross-pol·li·na·tion (krôs′pŏl-ə-nā′shən, krŏs′-) *n.* The transfer of pollen from the stamens of a flower of one plant to the stigma of a flower of another plant, either naturally by insects or wind, or artificially by hand. **—cross-pol·li·nate** *v.* **—cross-pol·li·na·tor** *n.*

cross product *n. Mathematics.* A **vector product** *(see).*

cross-pur·pose (krôs-pûr′pəs, krŏs-) *n.* A conflicting or contrary purpose; mutual misunderstanding. **—be at cross-purposes.** To have or act under a misunderstanding of each other's purposes.

cross-ques·tion (krôs′kwĕs′chən, krŏs′-) *tr.v.* **-tioned, -tioning, -tions.** To cross-examine; question closely.
~*n.* A question asked in the process of cross-examination.

cross-re·fer (krôs′rĭ-fûr′, krŏs′-) *v.* **-ferred, -ferring, -fers.** *—tr.* **1.** To refer (the reader) from one part or passage to another. **2.** To refer (one item or section in a text) to another. *—intr.* To make a cross-reference.

cross-ref·er·ence (krôs′rĕf′ər-əns, -rĕf′rəns, krŏs′-) *n.* A reference from one part of a book, index, catalogue, or file to another part containing related information.
~*tr.v.* **cross-referenced, -encing, -ences.** To supply (a text) with cross-references.

cross·road (krôs′rōd′, krŏs′-) *n.* **1.** A road that intersects another road. **2. crossroads. a.** A place where two or more roads meet. **b.** A place where different cultures meet. **c.** A crucial point or place.

cross·ruff (krôs′rŭf′, -rŭf′, krŏs′-) *n.* A series of plays in card games such as bridge and whist where partnership hands alternately trump the other's lead.
~*v.* **crossruffed, -ruffing, -ruffs.** *—intr.* To perform a crossruff or a series of crossruffs. *—tr.* To trump (one's partner's lead or a lead from the dummy) in alternating plays.

cross section *n.* **1.** A section formed by a plane cutting through an object, usually at right angles to an axis. **2.** A piece so cut or a graphic representation of such a piece. **3.** *Physics.* A measure of the probability of occurrence of a particular atomic or nuclear reaction. **4.** A representative sample meant to be typical of the whole. **—cross-sec·tion·al** *adj.*

cross-slide (krôs′slīd′, krŏs′-) *n.* The part of a lathe that moves the tool post at right angles to the bed of the lathe.

cross-stitch (krôs′stĭch′, krŏs′-) *n.* **1.** In sewing and embroidery, a double stitch forming an X. **2.** Needlework made with this stitch.
~*v.* **cross-stitched, -stitching, -stitches.** *—tr.* To make or embroider with cross-stitches. *—intr.* To work in cross-stitch.

cross-sub·si·dize *v.* **-dized, -dizing, -dizes.** *—tr.* To give financial support to (an unprofitable section of a firm or similar operation) from the profits of another. *—intr.* To cross-subsidize a financial operation. **—cross-sub·si·dy** *n.*

cross·talk (krôs′tôk′, krŏs′-) *n.* **1.** Noise or garbled sounds heard on a telephone or other electronic receiver, caused by interference from another channel. **2.** *British.* Exchange of repartee; witty conversation.

cross·tie (krôs′tī′, krŏs′-) *n.* **1.** A transverse beam or rod serving as a support or connection. **2.** A wood, concrete, or metal beam that connects and supports the rails of a railroad.

cross-town (krôs′toun′, krŏs′-) *adj.* Running across a city or town; specifically, running across the principal direction of traffic flow: *a cross-town bus.* **—cross-town** *adv.*

cross·tree (krôs′trē, krŏs′-) *n. Nautical.* Either of the two horizontal crosspieces at the upper ends of the lower masts in fore-and-aft-rigged vessels, serving to spread the shrouds.

cross-vine (krôs′vīn′, krŏs′-) *n.* A woody vine, *Bignonia capreolata,* of the southeastern United States, having large, trumpet-shaped, reddish flowers. Also called "bignonia." [So called because a cross

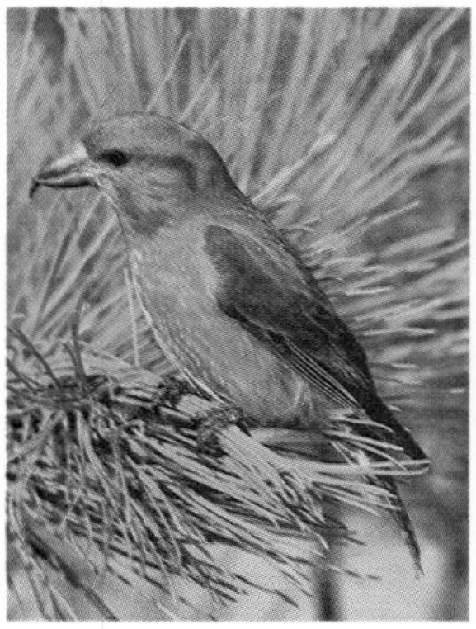

crossbill *The crossed tips of this bird's beak enable it to extract the seeds from pinecones. This is a male European crossbill,* Loxia curvirostra.

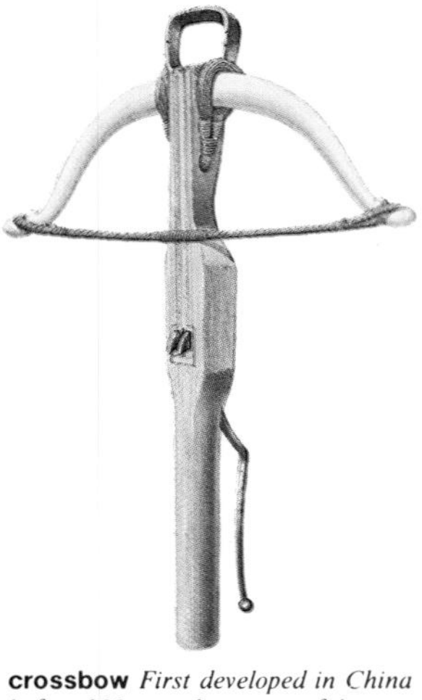

crossbow *First developed in China before 200 B.C., these powerful weapons were introduced to Europe in the 10th century A.D. Their wooden or iron bolts could pierce chain mail at a range of more than 350 meters (400 yards), but they could not be reloaded as quickly as a longbow.*

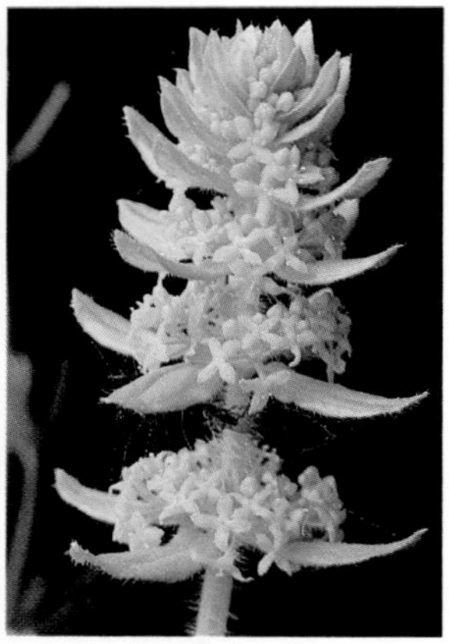

crosswort Galium cruciata, *the crosswort, is found in open woodland and hedgerows in Europe. Its honey-scented flowers grow in the angle between leaves and stem.*

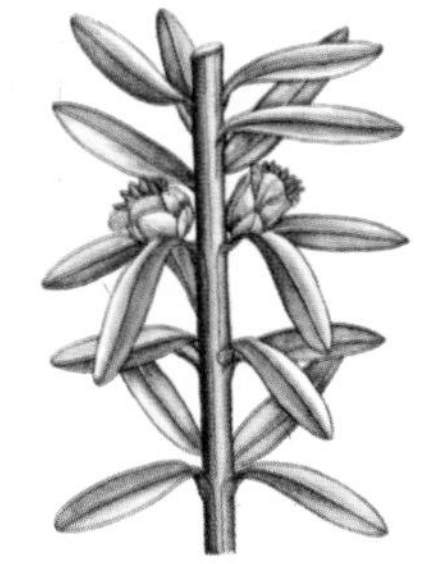

crowberry Empetrum nigrum, *the crowberry, grows throughout the Northern Hemisphere's cooler regions on boggy grasslands and mountain slopes. Its name may be derived from its edible black berries—the color of crows.*

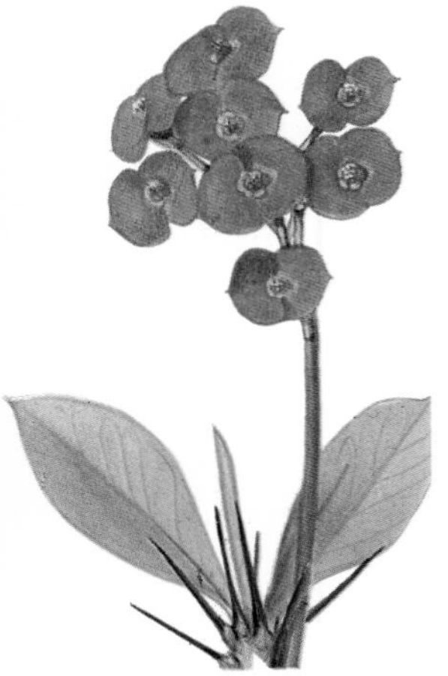

crown-of-thorns *The family Euphorbiaceae is one of the largest families of flowering plants. It includes both the tree from which rubber is harvested,* Hevea brasiliensis, *and this Madagascan plant, the crown-of-thorns* (Euphorbia splendens).

is found in a cross section of the stem.]
cross·way (krôs′wā′, krŏs′-) *n.* A crossroad.
crossways. Variant of **crosswise.**
cross·wind (krôs′wĭnd′, krŏs′-) *n.* A wind blowing more or less at right angles to a given direction, as to an aircraft's line of flight.
crosswise (krôs′wīz′, krŏs′-) *adv.* Also **cross·ways** (-wāz′). Transversely; across; diagonally.
cross·word puzzle (krôs′wûrd′, krŏs′-) *n.* A puzzle in which an arrangement of numbered squares has to be filled with words running across and down in answer to correspondingly numbered clues.
cross·wort (krôs′wôrt′, krŏs′-) *n.* A herbaceous perennial plant, *Galium cruciata,* having small yellow flowers borne at the leaf bases.
crotch (krŏch) *n.* **1.** The angle, or region of the angle, formed by the junction of parts or members, as by two branches, limbs, steps, or legs. **2.** The fork of a pole or other support. [Perhaps a variant of Middle English and Old French *croche,* hook. See **crochet.**] **—crotched** *adj.*
crotch·et (krŏch′ĭt) *n.* **1.** A small hook or hooklike structure. **2.** An odd, whimsical, or stubborn notion. **3.** *Music.* A **quarter note** *(see).* [Middle English *crochet,* small hook, from Old French. See **crochet.**]
crotch·et·y (krŏch′ĭ-tē) *adj.* **1.** Irritable; snappish. **2.** Capriciously stubborn or eccentric; perverse. **—crotch·et·i·ness** *n.*
cro·ton (krōt′n) *n.* **1.** Any of various chiefly tropical plants, shrubs, or trees of the genus *Croton.* See **croton oil.** **2.** Any of various tropical plants of the genus *Codiaeum;* especially, *C. variegatum pictum,* frequently grown as a house plant for its showy, varicolored foliage. [New Latin *Croton,* from Greek *krotōn*†.]
croton oil *n.* A yellowish-brown, violently cathartic oil obtained from the seeds of a tree, *Croton tiglium,* of southeastern Asia.
crouch (krouch) *v.* **crouched, crouching, crouches.** *—intr.* **1.** To bend low with the limbs pulled close to the body. **2.** To bend servilely or timidly; cringe. *—tr.* To cause to bend low, as in fear or humility.
∼n. The act or posture of crouching. [Middle English *cro(u)chen,* from Old French *crochir,* to be bent, from *croc(he),* a hook. See **crochet.**] **—crouch·ing·ly** *adv.*
croup¹ (kro͞op) *n.* A disorder affecting the throat in children, characterized by difficulty in breathing and a harsh cough and associated with inflammation and obstruction of the larynx. [Probably imitative of coughing.] **—croup·ous, croup·y** *adj.*
croup², croupe (kro͞op) *n.* The rump of certain animals, especially the horse. [Middle English *croupe,* from Old French, from Frankish *kruppa* (unattested).]
crou·pi·er (kro͞o′pē-ər, -pē-ā′) *n.* An attendant at a gaming table who deals the cards and collects and pays bets. [French, originally "rider on the rump (behind a rider)," from *croupe,* rump, CROUP.]
crou·ton (kro͞o′tŏn′, kro͞o-tŏn′) *n.* A small crisp cube of toasted or fried bread, often served in soup. [French *croûton,* from *croûte,* crust, from Old French *crouste,* from Latin *crusta,* CRUST.]
crow¹ (krō) *n.* **1.** Any of several large, glossy, black birds of the genus *Corvus,* having a characteristic raucous call; especially, *C. brachyrhynchos,* of North America. **2.** Loosely, any similar bird. **3.** A crowbar. **—as the crow flies.** In a straight line. **—eat crow.** *Informal.* To be forced into a humiliating situation, as from having been in error. [Middle English *croue,* Old English *crāwe,* akin to *crāwan,* to CROW.]
crow² (krō) *intr.v.* **crowed** or **crew** (kro͞o) (for sense 1), **crowing, crows. 1.** To utter the shrill cry characteristic of a cock. **2. a.** To boast, especially over the misfortune of another. **b.** To exult. **3.** To make a sound expressive of pleasure or well-being, like that of a baby. —See Synonyms at **boast.**
∼n. **1.** The shrill cry of a cock. **2.** An inarticulate sound expressive of pleasure or delight. [Middle English *crouen,* Old English *crāwan* (imitative).]
Crow (krō) *n., pl.* **Crows. 1.** A member of a North American Indian people, formerly inhabiting the region between the Platte and Yellowstone rivers and now settled in southeastern Montana. **2.** The Siouan language of the Crow.
crow·bar (krō′bär′) *n.* A straight bar of iron or steel, with the working end shaped like a forked chisel, used as a lever. Also called "crow." [From the resemblance of the forked end to a crow's foot.]
crow·ber·ry (krō′bĕr′ē) *n., pl.* **-ries. 1.** A low-growing evergreen shrub, *Empetrum nigrum,* of cool regions of the Northern Hemisphere, having small, purplish flowers and black, berrylike fruit. **2.** Any of several similar or related plants, such as the **bearberry** *(see).* **3.** The fruit of any of these plants.
crow blackbird *n.* The **grackle** *(see).*
crowd¹ (kroud) *n.* **1. a.** A large number of people gathered together; a throng. **b.** The mass of spectators, as at a football match. **2.** Ordinary people; people in general. Used with *the.* **3.** A specified social group; a clique: *the usual crowd; the arty crowd.* **4.** A large number of things grouped or considered together.
∼v. **crowded, crowding, crowds.** *—intr.* **1.** To throng; congregate closely. **2.** To advance by shoving. *—tr.* **1.** To press, cram, or force tightly together; compress. **2.** To fill or occupy to overflowing. **3.** *Informal.* To put pressure on; harass. **—crowd (on) sail.** *Nautical.* To spread a large amount of (sail) to increase speed. [Middle English *crouden, crowden,* to crowd, press, Old English *crūdan,* to hasten.] **—crowd·ed·ness** *n.* **—crowd·er** *n.*
crowd² (kroud, kro͝od) *n.* An ancient Celtic musical instrument, stringed and played with a bow. [Middle English *croud, crouth,* from Welsh *crwth.*]
crowd puller *n. Informal.* A very popular person, event, or the like, that is assured of a large audience.
crow·foot (krō′fo͝ot′) *n., pl.* **-foots** (for senses 1, 2) or **-feet** (-fēt) (for sense 3). **1.** Any of various plants of the genus *Ranunculus,* related to the buttercups, such as *R. aquatilis* and *R. sceleratus,* having small, inconspicuous yellow flowers and divided leaves. **2.** Loosely, any of various other plants having leaves or other parts resembling a bird's foot. **3.** *Military.* A defensive device, **caltrop** *(see).* **4.** *Nautical.* **a.** A block used in supporting the middle section of an awning. **b.** A set of small lines passed through holes of a batten or fitting to help support the backbone of an awning.
crown (kroun) *n.* **1.** An ornamental circlet or head covering, often made of precious metal set with jewels, and worn as a symbol of sovereignty. **2.** The power, position, or empire of a monarch. **3. a.** A decorative garland or wreath worn on the head as a symbol of victory, honor, or distinction. **b.** A championship title in a sport: *Borg's fifth Wimbledon crown.* **4.** Distinction or reward for achievement: *the crown of martyrdom.* **5.** Anything resembling a crown in shape, such as a badge, emblem, or heraldic bearing. **6.** A coin stamped with a crown or crowned head on the reverse side. **7. a.** A former British coin worth 5 shillings (25 pence). **b.** Any of several European coins with a name that means crown, such as the koruna, krona, and krone. **8. a.** The top or highest part of the head. **b.** The head itself. **9.** The top or upper part of a hat. **10.** The highest point of anything, especially: **a.** The summit of a hill or mountain. **b.** The highest point of a curved structure or surface, such as an arch or a cambered road. **11.** The highest or most outstanding state or point; the culmination: *the crown of her athletic career.* **12.** The most outstanding attribute or exemplar; the chief ornament. **13.** *Dentistry.* **a.** The part of a tooth that is covered by enamel and projects beyond the gum line. **b.** A gold, porcelain, or plastic substitute for the natural crown of a tooth. **14.** The lowest part of the shank of an anchor, where the arms are joined to it. **15. a.** The upper part of a tree, including the leaves and living branches. **b.** The part of a plant, usually at ground level, between the root and the stem. **c.** A flower part, the **corona** *(see).* **16.** The crest of an animal, especially of a bird. **17.** The portion of a cut gem above the girdle. **—the Crown. 1.** The monarch as the head of state or sovereign governing power. **2.** The power, position, or empire of a monarch.
∼tr.v. **crowned, crowning, crowns. 1.** To put a crown or garland upon the head of. **2.** To invest with regal power; make a monarch of; enthrone. **3.** To confer honor, dignity, or reward on. **4. a.** To cover or occupy the top of. **b.** To surmount or be the highest part of. **5.** To form the crown, top, or chief ornament of. **6.** To bring to completion or successful conclusion; complete; consummate. **7.** To put a crown on (a tooth). **8.** In checkers, to make (a piece that has reached the last row) into a king by placing another piece upon it. **9.** *Informal.* To hit on the head. [Middle English *crowne, coroune,* from Old French *corone,* from Latin *corōna,* garland, from Greek *korōnē,* anything curved, from *korōnos,* curved.] **—crown** *adj.*
crown canopy *n.* The canopy or cover formed by the upper branches of trees in a forest. Also called "crown cover."
crown cap *n.* An airtight bottle top for beer and soft drink bottles, consisting of a lined metal disk with its edge crimped over the mouth of the bottle.
crown colony *n.* A British colony in which the sovereign has control of legislation, usually administered by an appointed governor.
Crown Derby *n.* A fine porcelain, marked with a crown, made in Derby, England, in the late 18th and early 19th centuries.
crown gall *n.* A disease of plants caused by a bacterium, *Agrobacterium tumefaciens,* and characterized by warty, usually woody growths on roots and stems, especially near the soil line.
crown glass *n.* **1.** A clear soda-lime-silica optical glass with low refraction. Compare **flint glass. 2.** A form of window glass made by whirling a glass bubble to make a flat circular disk with a lump in the center formed by the craftsman's rod. **—crown-glass** *adj.*
crown graft *n.* A horticultural graft in which the scion is grafted onto the crown of the stock.
crown imperial *n.* A garden plant, *Fritillaria imperialis,* with a terminal cluster of orange bell-shaped flowers.
crown jewels *pl.n.* The jewels belonging to the regalia of a sovereign or royal family, used on state occasions.
crown lens *n.* The crown-glass element in an achromatic lens.
crown-of-thorns (kroun′əv-thôrnz′) *n.* **1.** A spiny, vinelike desert plant, *Euphorbia splendens* (or *E.milii*), often grown as a potted plant for its flowers, which have scarlet bracts. **2.** A starfish, *Acanthaster planci,* that is covered with spines and feeds on living coral.
crown prince *n.* The male heir apparent to a throne.
crown princess *n.* **1.** The wife of a crown prince. **2.** A female heir apparent to a throne.
crown roast *n.* Two or more rib sections of veal, pork, or especially lamb, secured together at the ends to form a circle and roasted.
crown saw *n.* A cylindrical saw with teeth on the bottom edge of the cylinder.
crow's-foot (krōz′fo͝ot′) *n., pl.* **-feet** (-fēt′). **1. crow's-feet.** The wrinkles at the outer corner of the eye, common in many adults. **2.** A three-pointed embroidery stitch used as finishing, as at the end of a seam. **3.** The set of ropes or strands of a rope attached to a single rope, used in sailing, ballooning, and the like.
crow's-nest (krōz′nĕst′) *n.* **1.** A small lookout platform with a high

protective railing and wind screen, located near the top of a ship's mast. **2.** Any similar lookout platform located ashore.

Croy·don (kroid'n). Borough of Greater London since 1965; it was formerly an important market town in Surrey.

croze (krōz) *n.* **1.** The groove at the ends of the staves of a barrel or cask into which the head is set. **2.** A cooper's tool, such as a plane, for making this groove. [French *creux,* from Old French *crues,* socket, groove, perhaps from Gallo-Roman *crosus†* (unattested).]

crozier. Variant of **crosier.**

CRT cathode-ray tube.

cru (krōō) *n.* A wine produced by certain superior French vineyards. [French, growth, from *crû,* past participle of *croître,* to grow.]

cru·ces. Alternate plural of **crux.**

cru·cial (krōō'shəl) *adj.* **1.** Of supreme importance in determining an outcome; critical; decisive: *a crucial election.* **2.** *Informal.* Very important or significant. **3.** Having the form of a cross; cross-shaped. —See Synonyms at **critical.** [French, from Latin *crux* (stem *cruc-*), CROSS.] —**cru·cial·ly** *adv.*

cru·ci·ate (krōō'shē-āt') *adj.* **1.** Cross-shaped. **2.** Overlapping or crossing, as the wings of some insects when at rest. [New Latin *cruciatus,* from Latin *crux,* CROSS.]

cru·ci·ble (krōō'sə-bəl) *n.* **1.** A vessel made of a refractory substance, such as graphite or porcelain, used for melting and calcining materials at high temperatures. **2.** The bottom of an ore furnace, in which the molten metal collects. **3.** A severe test or trial. [Middle English *crusible,* from Medieval Latin *crucibulum,* perhaps originally a lamp kept burning in front of a crucifix, from Latin *crux,* CROSS.]

crucible steel *n.* A high-grade steel made by fusing low-carbon steel with charcoal or cast iron in a graphite crucible and used in tools and dies.

cru·ci·fer (krōō'sə-fər) *n.* **1.** One who bears a cross in a religious procession. **2.** *Botany.* Any plant of the family Cruciferae, such as a mustard or cress, having four-petaled flowers suggestive of a cross. [Late Latin : Latin *crux,* CROSS + -FER.] —**cru·cif·er·ous** *adj.*

cru·ci·fix (krōō'sə-fĭks') *n.* A cross with an image of Christ on it. [Middle English, from Old French, from Late Latin *crucifixus,* from the past participle of *crucifīgere,* CRUCIFY.]

cru·ci·fix·ion (krōō'sə-fĭk'shən) *n.* **1.** The action of putting to death on a cross. **2.** A representation, as in painting or carving, of Christ on the Cross. —**the Crucifixion.** The crucifying of Christ on Calvary.

cru·ci·form (krōō'sə-fôrm') *adj.* Cross-shaped.
~*n.* A cross-shaped geometric curve having four branches forming similar asymptotes with two mutually perpendicular pairs of lines. [Latin *crux* (stem *cruc-*), CROSS + -FORM.]

cru·ci·fy (krōō'sə-fī') *tr.v.* **-fied, -fying, -fies. 1.** To put to death by nailing or binding to a cross. **2.** To mortify or subdue (the passions, for example). **3.** To torment; torture, especially mentally. **4. a.** *Slang.* To defeat overwhelmingly, as in a sporting contest. **b.** *Informal.* To criticize or ridicule mercilessly. [Middle English *crucifien,* from Old French *crucifier,* from Late Latin *crucifīgere* : Latin *crux* (stem *cruc-*), CROSS + *fīgere,* to fasten.] —**cru·ci·fi·er** *n.*

cruck (krŭk) *n. Architecture.* Either of a pair of sloping timbers, often curved, that help support a roof. [19th century : variant of CROOK (noun).]

crud (krŭd) *n. Slang.* **1.** A coating or incrustation of filth or refuse. **2.** A contemptible or disgusting person or thing. **3.** Nonsense; rubbish. **4.** Any disease, imaginary or real, especially one affecting the skin. [Middle English *crudde,* CURD.] —**crud·dy** *adj.*

crude (krōōd) *adj.* **cruder, crudest. 1.** In an unrefined or natural state; raw. **2.** *Archaic.* Unripe; immature. **3.** Lacking finish, tact, or polish. **4.** Not carefully, skillfully, or completely made; rough. **5.** *Statistics.* Not corrected, analyzed, or tabulated. Said of data. **6.** Undisguised or unadorned; blunt. **7.** Offensive and tasteless; vulgar.
~*n.* Crude oil (*see*). [Middle English, from Latin *crūdus,* bloody, raw.] —**crude·ly** *adv.* —**crude·ness, cru·di·ty** *n.*

crude oil *n.* Petroleum (*see*) in its unrefined state.

cru·el (krōō'əl) *adj.* **-eler** or **-eller, -elest** or **-ellest. 1.** Disposed to inflict pain or suffering. **2.** Causing suffering; painful: *a cruel hoax.* [Middle English, from Old French, from Latin *crūdēlis,* morally unfeeling, cruel; akin to *crūdus,* bloody, CRUDE.] —**cru·el·ly** *adv.*
   Synonyms: barbarous, ferocious, inhuman, pitiless, ruthless, sadistic, vicious.

cru·el·ty (krōō'əl-tē) *n., pl.* **-ties. 1.** The quality or condition of being cruel. **2.** Something that causes pain or suffering, such as a cruel action or remark. **3.** *Law.* Behavior that damages or endangers the physical or mental health of a spouse and constitutes grounds for divorce.

cru·et (krōō'ĭt) *n.* **1. a.** A small glass bottle for holding vinegar or oil. **b.** A small container for other condiments, such as a saltcellar, a pepperbox, or a mustard bowl. **2.** A pair or set of cruets, often on a tray or rack. **3.** Either of two small vessels used for wine and water at the Eucharist. [Middle English, from Norman French *cruet,* diminutive of Old French *crue,* flask, from Germanic.]

Cruik·shank (krŏok'shangk), **George** (1792–1878). British caricaturist and illustrator, best remembered for his illustrations of Dickens and other novelists. His own collections include his *Comic Almanack* (1835–53).

cruise (krōōz) *v.* **cruised, cruising, cruises.** —*intr.* **1.** To sail or travel about, as for pleasure or reconnaissance. **2.** To travel at a speed (*cruising speed*) that provides maximum operating efficiency for a sustained period. **3.** *Informal.* To wander about the street, frequent bars, and so on, in search of a sexual partner. —*tr.* **1.** To cruise or journey over. **2.** *Slang.* To appraise sexually.
~*n.* A sea voyage for pleasure, usually in a liner stopping at numerous ports. [Perhaps from Dutch *kruisen,* to sail to and fro, from Middle Dutch *crucen,* to cross, from *crūce,* a cross, from Latin *crux,* CROSS.]

cruise missile *n.* A subsonic, long-range guided missile armed with a nuclear warhead, which can fly low toward its target to avoid radar detection and which uses inbuilt computerized navigation equipment.

cruis·er (krōō'zər) *n.* **1.** One that cruises. **2.** Any of a class of fast warships of medium tonnage with a long cruising radius and less armor and firepower than a battleship. **3.** A large motorboat whose cabin is equipped with living facilities. Also called "cabin cruiser," "cruising yacht." **4.** *Informal.* A police **squad car** (*see*).

cruising radius *n.* The longest distance a ship or aircraft can go

cruck *A wooden frame used in medieval house building. The crucks form a supporting triangle from the roof ridge to the outer walls.*

---

crow

THE WORLDWIDE SUCCESS OF CROWS
One family with 100 thriving branches

Crows are found throughout the world in a wide range of habitats. They are large birds, up to 660 millimeters (26 inches) long, with rounded bills and usually black, glossy plumage. Often they are recognized by their harsh call, or caw. They are omnivorous. The crow family, Corvidae, has about 100 species. Of these 30 belong to the genus *Corvus,* the most common being the carrion crow of Eurasia and the American crow. The common name of 18 other *Corvus* species includes the word crow, but the rook, jackdaw, and raven also belong to the genus *Corvus.* The magpie and jay are close relatives from other branches of the vast Corvidae family.

JACKDAW
Corvus monedula
Gray nape
Dark gray underparts

Distinguished by its white iris and gray nape, the jackdaw is small, only 330 millimeters (13 inches) long, and a skilled aerobat. Its reputation as a thief is exaggerated: it is less likely than other crows to rob the nests of other birds.

RAVEN
Corvus corax
Stout bill
Shaggy throat feathers
Glossy black plumage

Wordsworth's "blithe croakers of death" were so long persecuted for pecking at corpses on the gibbet that ravens have retreated to the wilds. These—the largest of the world's perching birds, 660 millimeters (26 inches) long—feed on carrion but also hunt and forage.

CARRION CROW
Corvus corone corone
Heavy rounded bill
Glossy black plumage

Migrating from woodlands, carrion crows make their homes in cities and suburbs, scavenging on refuse and nesting on posts and pylons as well as in trees. They feed on grain and root crops and on the eggs and young of other birds. Length: 470 millimeters (18 inches).

ROOK
Corvus frugilegus
Bare face patch
Plumage black with purple gloss
Thigh feathers

Unlike crows, which nest alone, rooks live gregariously in rookeries consisting of anything from a few to several thousand nests, built usually in clusters of trees. A native of farmland, the rook is 460 millimeters (18 inches) long and distinguished by a bare face patch.

and return at cruising speed without refueling.

crul·ler (krŭl′ər) *n.* A small cake of sweet dough fried in deep fat, usually ring-shaped or twisted. [Dutch *krulle,* from *krullen,* to curl, from *krul,* curly, from Middle Dutch *crulle.*]

crumb (krŭm) *n.* **1.** A small piece broken or fallen from cake, bread, or other baked goods. **2.** Any small fragment or scrap. **3.** The soft inner portion of bread. Compare **crust. 4.** *Slang.* A contemptible, untrustworthy, or loathsome person.
~*v.* **crumbed, crumbing, crumbs.** —*tr.* **1.** To break into small pieces or crumbs; crumble. **2.** In cookery, to cover or prepare with breadcrumbs; bread. —*intr.* To break apart in crumbs. [Middle English *crome,* Old English *cruma.*]

crum·ble (krŭm′bəl) *v.* **-bled, -bling, -bles.** —*tr.* To break or cause to break into small parts or crumbs. —*intr.* To fall into tiny pieces; disintegrate. —See Synonyms at **decay.**
~*n. British.* A baked dessert of stewed fruit topped with a sweet, crumblike mixture of flour, fat, and sugar. [Earlier *crimble,* from Middle English *cremelen,* perhaps from Old English *gecrymian,* from *cruma,* CRUMB.]

crum·bly (krŭm′blē) *adj.* **-blier, -bliest.** Easily crumbled.

crum·horn, krumm·horn (krŭm′hôrn′) *n.* A medieval musical instrument, with a deep pitch, curving tube, and double reed. [From German *Krummhorn,* "carved horn."]

crum·mie (krŭm′ē) *n. Scottish.* A cow with crooked horns. [From Scottish *crum(b),* crooked, Middle English *croumb,* Old English *crumb.*]

crum·my (krŭm′ē) *adj.* **-mier, -miest.** Also **crumb·y, -ier, -iest.** *Slang.* Inferior, worthless, or unpleasant. [From CRUMB.]

crump (krŭmp) *v.* **crumped, crumping, crumps.** —*tr.* **1.** To crush or crunch with the teeth. **2.** To bombard or strike heavily with a crunching or thudding sound. —*intr.* To make a crunching sound.
~*n.* **1.** A crunching sound. **2.** The sound of a bomb or shell exploding. [Imitative.]

crum·pet (krŭm′pĭt) *n. Chiefly British.* **1.** A light, round teacake with holes in the top, made from a yeast batter, which is poured into special rings *(crumpet rings)* and cooked on one side on a heated baking sheet or a griddle and often toasted. **2.** *Slang.* Women collectively when considered sexually attractive. [Probably from Middle English *crompid (cake),* "curled cake," from *crampen,* *crumpen,* to curl, from *crump, crumb,* Old English *crump.*]

crum·ple (krŭm′pəl) *v.* **-pled, -pling, -ples.** —*tr.* To crush together or press into wrinkles; rumple. —*intr.* **1.** To become wrinkled; shrivel. Often used with *up.* **2.** To collapse; break down.
~*n.* An irregular fold, crease, or wrinkle. [Frequentative of obsolete *crump,* to curl up, from Middle English *crampen.* See **crumpet.**]

crunch (krŭnch) *v.* **crunched, crunching, crunches.** —*tr.* **1.** To chew with a noisy crackling sound. **2.** To crush, grind, or walk on noisily. —*intr.* **1.** To chew noisily with a crackling sound. **2.** To move with a crushing sound. **3.** To produce a crushing sound.
~*n.* **1.** The act or sound of crunching. **2. a.** A decisive confrontation. **b.** A critical situation.
~*adj.* Decisively important; crucial: *a crunch issue.* [Earlier *craunch* (imitative), assimilated to *munch.*]

crup·per (krŭp′ər) *n.* **1.** A leather strap looped under a horse's tail and attached to a harness or saddle to keep it from slipping forward. **2.** The rump of a horse. [Middle English *cropper, cropier,* from Old French *cropiere,* from *croupe,* rump, CROUP.]

cru·ral (krŏŏr′əl) *adj.* Of or pertaining to the leg, shank, or thigh. [Latin *crūrālis,* from *crūs* (stem *crūr-),* leg, CRUS.]

crus (krŏŏs, krŭs) *n., pl.* **crura** (krŏŏr′ə). **1.** The section of the leg or hind limb between the knee and foot; the shank. **2.** A leglike part. [Latin *crūs†,* leg.]

cru·sade (krŏŏ-sād′) *n.* **1.** *Often* **Crusade. a.** Any of the military expeditions undertaken by European Christians in the 11th, 12th, and 13th centuries to recover the Holy Land from the Muslims. **b.** Any holy war undertaken with papal sanction: *the Albigensian Crusade.* **2.** Any vigorous concerted movement for a cause or against an abuse.
~*intr.v.* **crusaded, -sading, -sades.** To engage in a crusade. [Earlier forms: (a) *croisade,* from Old French, variant of *croisée,* from the past participle of *croiser,* to bear the cross, from *crois,* cross, from Latin *crux;* (b) *crusado,* from Spanish *cruzada,* from *cruzar,* to bear the cross, from *cruz,* cross, from Latin *crux,* CROSS.] —**cru·sad·er** *n.*

cruse (krŏŏz, krŏŏs) *n.* A small jar or pot for holding water, wine, or oil. [Middle English *crouse,* perhaps from Middle Dutch *cruyse,* pot.]

crush (krŭsh) *v.* **crushed, crushing, crushes.** —*tr.* **1.** To press between opposing bodies so as to break, injure, or damage. **2. a.** To obtain juice from (a fruit). **b.** To obtain (juice) by crushing fruit thus. **3.** To crumple or rumple. **4.** To break, pound, or grind into small fragments or powder. **5.** To press upon, shove, or crowd. **6.** To put down; subdue. **7.** To overwhelm or humiliate, as in an argument or contest. **8.** To oppress severely: *Debt was crushing them.* —*intr.* **1.** To be or become crushed. **2.** To proceed or move by crowding or pressing. —See Synonyms at **break.**
~*n.* **1.** The act of crushing; extreme pressure. **2.** The state of being crushed. **3.** A great crowd or throng. **4.** A drink prepared from crushed fruit, or one made to taste like this. **5.** *Informal.* **a.** An infatuation. Usually used with *on.* **b.** The person who is the object of such an infatuation. [Middle English *crushen,* from Old French *croissir,* probably from Vulgar Latin *cruscīre†* (unattested).] —**crush·a·ble** *adj.* —**crush·er** *n.*

crush barrier *n. Chiefly British.* A safety barrier, often temporary, used to hold back a crowd.

Crusoe, Robinson. See **Robinson Crusoe.**

crust (krŭst) *n.* **1.** The hard outer portion or surface area of bread. Compare **crumb. 2.** A piece of bread consisting mostly of this part. **3.** A pastry shell, as of a pie or tart. **4.** Any hard, crisp covering or surface. **5.** A hard deposit produced by maturing wine on the interior of bottles. **6. a.** *Geology.* The solid exterior portion of the earth that lies above the Mohorovičić discontinuity. **b.** The outermost solid layer of a planet or moon. **7.** The hard outer covering or integument of certain plants and animals, such as lichens and crustaceans. **8.** *Pathology.* A coating or dry outer layer, as of pus or blood; a scab. **9.** *Informal.* Insolence; audacity; gall.
~*v.* **crusted, crusting, crusts.** —*tr.* **1.** To cover with a crust; encrust. **2.** To form (dough) into a crust. —*intr.* **1.** To become covered with a crust. **2.** To harden into a crust. [Middle English *cruste,* from Old French *crouste,* from Latin *crusta†,* shell.]

crus·ta·cean (krŭ-stā′shən) *n.* Any of various predominantly aquatic arthropods of the class Crustacea, including lobsters, crabs, shrimps, and wood lice, characteristically having a segmented body, a chitinous exoskeleton, and paired, jointed limbs. [From New Latin *crustacea,* "the shelled ones," from *crustaceus,* CRUSTACEOUS.] —**crus·ta·cean** *adj.*

crus·ta·ceous (krŭ-stā′shəs) *adj.* **1.** Having, resembling, or constituting a hard crust or shell. **2.** Crustacean. [New Latin *crustaceus* : Latin *crusta,* shell, CRUST + -ACEOUS.]

crus·tal (krŭs′təl) *adj.* Of or pertaining to a crust, especially that of the earth or the moon.

crust·y (krŭs′tē) *adj.* **-ier, -iest. 1.** Like or having a crust. **2.** Surly or short-tempered. —See Synonyms at **gruff.** —**crust·i·ness** *n.*

crutch (krŭch) *n.* **1.** A staff or support used by the lame or infirm as an aid in walking, usually having a crosspiece to fit under the armpit and often used in pairs. **2.** Any device similar to this in form or function. **3.** A forked support for the boom of a sailing vessel when the sails are furled. **4.** Anything or anyone depended upon for support; a prop. **5.** The human crotch.
~*tr.v.* **crutched, crutching, crutches.** To support on or as on crutches. [Middle English *crucche,* Old English *crycc,* from Germanic.]

crux (krŭks, krŏŏks) *n., pl.* **cruxes** or **cruces** (krŏŏ′sēz). **1.** A crucial or vital moment; a critical point. **2.** The basic or essential feature: *the crux of our argument.* **3.** A puzzling problem. [Latin, CROSS.]

Crux (krŭks) *n.* A constellation in the Southern Hemisphere near Centaurus and Musca. Also called "Southern Cross."

crux an·sa·ta (ăn-sā′tə) *n.* An **ansate cross** *(see).*

cru·zei·ro (krŏŏ-zā′rō, -rŏŏ) *n., pl.* **-ros. 1.** The basic monetary unit of Brazil, equal to 100 centavos. **2.** A coin worth one cruzeiro. [Portuguese, "(coin) bearing the figure of a cross," from *cruz,* cross, from Latin *crux,* CROSS.]

cry (krī) *v.* **cried, crying, cries.** —*intr.* **1.** To make inarticulate sobbing sounds expressing grief, sorrow, or pain. **2.** To produce moisture from the eyes; shed tears; weep. **3.** To call aloud; shout. Often used with *out.* **4.** To utter a characteristic sound or call. Used of an animal. **5.** To withdraw from an undertaking or back out of an agreement or promise. Used with *off.* —*tr.* **1.** To utter loudly. **2.** To proclaim or announce (especially goods for sale) in public. **3.** To beg for; beseech; implore: *cry forgiveness.* **4. a.** To bring into a specified condition by weeping: *cry oneself to sleep.* **b.** To weep or shed (tears). **5.** To belittle or disparage. Used with *down.* **6.** To break or withdraw from a promise, agreement, or undertaking. Used with *off.* **7.** To praise highly; extol. Used with *up.* —**cry out for.** To be in urgent need of; demand.
~*n., pl.* **cries. 1.** A loud utterance of some emotion, such as fear or anger. **2.** Any loud exclamation or utterance; a shout; a call. **3.** A fit of weeping. **4.** An urgent entreaty or appeal. **5.** A public or general demand or complaint; a clamor; an outcry. **6.** An advertising of wares by calling out. **7.** A rallying call or signal as in a battle or election campaign. **8.** A political slogan. **9.** The characteristic call or utterance of an animal or bird. **9.** A pack of hounds. —**a far cry. 1.** A very different state of affairs. **2.** A long way. —**in full cry.** In hot pursuit, as hounds hunting. [Middle English *crien,* from Old French *crier,* from Latin *quirītāre,* to cry out, to implore the aid of the citizens, from *Quirītēs,* plural of *Quirīs†,* a Roman citizen.]
   Synonyms: blubber, moan, sob, wail, weep, whimper.

cry·ba·by (krī′bā′bē) *n., pl.* **-bies.** A person who cries or complains frequently with little cause.

cry·ing (krī′ĭng) *adj.* Demanding or requiring immediate action or remedy: *a crying shame; a crying need.*

crymotherapy. Variant of **cryotherapy.**

cryo– *prefix.* Indicates cold, freezing, or frost; for example, **cryometer.** [From Greek *kruos†,* icy cold, frost.]

cry·o·bi·ol·o·gy (krī′ō-bī-ŏl′ə-jē) *n.* The study of the effects of very low temperatures on living organisms.

cry·o·gen (krī′ə-jən) *n.* A refrigerant used to obtain very low temperatures. [CRYO- + -GEN.]

cry·o·gen·ics (krī′ō-jĕn′ĭks) *n.* The science of low-temperature phenomena. [From CRYO- + -GENIC.] —**cry·o·gen·ic** *adj.*

cry·o·lite (krī′ə-līt′) *n.* A white, vitreous natural fluoride of aluminum and sodium, Na_3AlF_6, used chiefly as an electrolyte in aluminum refining and in the production of glass, enamel, and ceramics. Also called "Greenland spar." [CRYO- + -LITE.]

cry·om·e·ter (krī-ŏm′ə-tər) *n.* A thermometer capable of measuring very low temperatures. [CRYO- + -METER.]

cry·on·ics (krī-ŏn′ĭks) *n.* *Used with a singular verb.* The process of freezing and storing a dead human body to prevent tissue decomposition so that at some time in the future the individual might be brought back to life when new medical cures have been developed. [CRY(O)- + -*onics,* as in *bionics.*] —**cry·on′ic** *adj.*

cry·o·plank·ton (krī′ō-plangk′tən) *n.* *Biology.* Minute organisms living in snow, ice, or perpetually icy waters.

cry·o·scope (krī′ə-skōp′) *n.* An instrument used to measure the freezing point of a substance. [Back-formation from CRYOSCOPY.]

cry·os·co·py (krī-ŏs′kə-pē) *n.* The study of the freezing points of solutions. [CRYO- + -SCOPY.] —**cry·o·scop·ic** (krī′ə-skŏp′ĭk) *adj.*

cry·o·stat (krī′ə-stăt′) *n.* An apparatus used to maintain constant low temperature. [CRYO- + -STAT.]

cry·o·sur·ger·y (krī′ō-sûr′jə-rē) *n.* Surgery performed by local or general application of extreme cold to destroy unwanted tissue.

cry·o·ther·a·py (krī′ō-thĕr′ə-pē) *n.* Also **cry·mo·ther·a·py** (krī′mō-). The use of low temperatures in medical therapy.

cry·o·tron *n.* A small electronic switch that is based on the phenomenon of superconductivity. It works at the temperature of liquid helium, switching the conducting wire from a superconducting state to a nonsuperconducting state. [CRYO- + -TRON.]

crypt (krĭpt) *n.* **1.** An underground vault or chamber, especially one beneath a church that is used as a burial place. **2.** *Anatomy.* Any of various small pits, recesses, glandular cavities, or follicles in the body. [Latin *crypta,* from Greek *kruptē,* from *kruptos,* hidden, from *kruptein,* to hide.]

cryp·ta·nal·y·sis (krĭp′tə-năl′ə-sĭs) *n., pl.* **-ses** (-sēz). The analysis and deciphering of cryptograms, ciphers, codes, or other secret writings. [CRYPT(OGRAM) + ANALYSIS.] —**cryp·tan·a·lyst** *n.* —**cryp·tan·a·lyt·ic** *adj.*

cryp·tes·the·sia (krĭp′təs-thē′zhə, -zhē-ə) *n.* *Psychology.* A term describing the various modes of supposed paranormal perception, such as clairvoyance. [New Latin : CRYPT- + -ESTHESIA.]

cryp·tic (krĭp′tĭk) *adj.* Also **cryp·ti·cal** (-tĭ-kəl). **1.** Hidden; concealed. **2. a.** Mysterious; enigmatic. **b.** Intentionally obscure. **3.** Having esoteric or hidden meaning; mystifying. **4.** *Biology.* Tending to conceal or camouflage: *cryptic coloring.* [Late Latin *crypticus,* from Greek *kruptikos,* from *kruptos,* hidden. See **crypt.**]

crypto-, crypt- *prefix.* Indicates hidden or secret; for example, **cryptoclastic.** [New Latin, from Greek *kruptos,* hidden, from *kruptein,* to hide.]

cryp·to·clas·tic (krĭp′tō-klăs′tĭk) *adj.* Composed of microscopic fragments. Said of rocks.

cryp·to·crys·tal·line (krĭp′tō-krĭs′tə-lĭn) *adj.* Having a microscopic crystalline structure. Said of rocks and minerals.

cryp·to·gam (krĭp′tə-găm′) *n.* *Botany.* In former classification systems, any of the flowerless and seedless plants that reproduce by spores, such as fungi, algae, mosses, and ferns. Compare **phanerogam.** [French *cryptogame,* from New Latin *cryptogamia* : CRYPTO- + -GAMY.] —**cryp·to·gam·ic, cryp·tog·a·mous** *adj.*

cryp·to·gen·ic (krĭp′tə-jĕn′ĭk) *adj.* Also **cryp·tog·e·nous** (krĭp-tŏj′ə-nəs). Of obscure or unknown origin. Said of diseases.

cryp·to·gram (krĭp′tə-grăm′) *n.* **1.** Something written in code or cipher; a cryptograph. **2.** A figure having a secret or occult significance. [French *cryptogramme* : CRYPTO- + -GRAM (written).] —**cryp·to·gram·mic** *adj.*

cryp·to·graph (krĭp′tə-grăf′, -gräf′) *n.* **1.** A cryptogram. **2.** A system of secret or cipher writing; a cipher. **3. a.** A device for translating plain text into cipher. **b.** A device for deciphering codes and ciphers. [Back-formation from CRYPTOGRAPHY.]

cryp·tog·ra·phy (krĭp-tŏg′rə-fē) *n.* **1.** The art or process of writing in or deciphering secret code. **2.** Any secret or cipher code. [New Latin *cryptographia* : CRYPTO- + -GRAPHY.] —**cryp·tog·ra·pher, cryp·tog·ra·phist** *n.* —**cryp·to·graph·ic** *adj.* —**cryp·to·graph·i·cal·ly** *adv.*

cryp·tol·o·gy (krĭp-tŏl′ə-jē) *n.* **1.** The study of the use of secret codes or ciphers; cryptography. **2.** Cryptanalysis. [CRYPTO- + -LOGY.]

cryp·to·me·ri·a (krĭp′tə-mîr′ē-ə) *n.* An evergreen tree, *Cryptomeria japonica,* native to Japan, having short, inward-curving needles and soft, durable, fragrant wood. Also called "Japanese cedar." [New Latin : CRYPTO- + Greek *meros,* part, -MERE.]

cryp·to·nym (krĭp′tə-nĭm′) *n.* A secret name. [French *cryptonyme* : CRYPT(O)- + -ONYM.] —**cryp·ton·y·mous** (krĭp-tŏn′ə-məs) *adj.*

crypt·or·chism (krĭp-tôr′kĭz′əm) *n.* Also **crypt·or·chi·dism** (-kĭ-dĭz′əm). The condition of the testes failing to descend into the scrotum at puberty. [CRYPTO- + Greek *orkhis* (stem *orkhid*-), testicle + -ISM.]

cryp·to·zo·ite (krĭp′tə-zō′īt′) *n.* A sporozoite such as a malarial parasite as it exists in its host's tissues prior to invasion of the red blood cells. [CRYPTO- + (SPORO)ZOITE.]

cryst. **1.** crystalline. **2.** crystallography.

crys·tal (krĭs′təl) *n.* **1. a.** A three-dimensional atomic, ionic, or molecular structure consisting of periodically repeated, identically constituted, congruent unit cells. **b.** The unit cell of such a structure. **2.** A body, such as a piece of quartz, having such a structure, often characterized by external planar faces visible without magnification. **3.** An oscillator, detector, or other electronic device based on crystalline piezoelectricity, magnetism, semiconductivity, or other electric properties. **4. a.** A high-quality clear, colorless glass. **b.** An object, especially a vessel or ornament, made of such glass. **c.** Such objects collectively. **5.** A clear glass or plastic protective cover for the face of a watch or clock.

~*adj.* **1.** Of, pertaining to, made of, or based on crystal. **2.** Desig-

nating an electronic device operated by a crystal. **3.** Clear; transparent. [Middle English *cristal,* from Old French, from Latin *crystallum,* rock crystal, crystal, from Greek *krustallos†.*]

crystal ball *n.* A glass globe used in crystal gazing.

crystal counter *n.* A high-energy radiation detector in which particles strike a crystal, causing a brief increase in conductivity.

crystal detector *n.* A rectifying detector used especially in early radio receivers and consisting of a semiconducting crystal in point contact with a fine metal wire.

crystal gazing *n.* A foretelling or attempt to foretell the future by or as if by seeing future events in a crystal ball. —**crystal gazer** *n.*

crystall. crystallography.

crystall-. Variant of **crystallo-.**

crystal lattice *n.* A regular network of fixed points about which the ions, atoms, or molecules forming a crystal vibrate.

crys·tal·lif·er·ous (krĭs′tə-lĭf′ər-əs) *adj.* Also **crys·tal·lig·er·ous** (-lĭj′ər-əs). Producing or containing crystals.

crys·tal·line (krĭs′tə-lĭn) *adj.* **1.** *Abbr.* **cryst.** Pertaining to or made of crystal or crystals. **2.** Pertaining to crystals or their structure. **3.** Resembling crystal; transparent. [Middle English *cristallin,* from Old French, from Latin *crystallinus,* from Greek *krustallinos,* from *krustallos,* CRYSTAL.] —**crys·tal·lin·i·ty** *n.*

crystalline lens *n.* The lens (*see*) of the vertebrate eye.

crys·tal·lite (krĭs′tə-līt′) *n.* Any of numerous minute rudimentary, crystalline bodies found in glassy igneous rocks. [German *Kristallit* : CRYSTALL(O)- + -ITE.] —**crys·tal·lit·ic** (krĭs′tə-lĭt′ĭk) *adj.*

crys·tal·lize (krĭs′tə-līz′) *v.* **-lized, -lizing, -lizes.** —*tr.* **1.** To cause to form crystals or to assume a crystalline structure. **2.** To give a definite and permanent form to. **3.** To coat with sugar. —*intr.* **1.** To assume a crystalline form. **2.** To take on a definite and permanent form. [CRYSTALL(O)- + -IZE.] —**crys·tal·liz·a·bil·i·ty** *n.* —**crys·tal·liz·a·ble** *adj.* —**crys·tal·li·za·tion** *n.* —**crys·tal·liz·er** *n.*

crystallo-, crystall- *prefix.* Indicates crystal; for example, **crystallography, crystalloid.** [Greek *krustallos,* CRYSTAL.]

crys·tal·log·ra·phy (krĭs′tə-lŏg′rə-fē) *n.* *Abbr.* **cryst., crystall.** The science of the structure, form, and properties of crystals. [French *crystallographie,* from New Latin *crystallographia* : CRYSTALLO- + -GRAPHY.] —**crys·tal·log·ra·pher** *n.* —**crys·tal·lo·graph·ic, crys·tal·lo·graph·i·cal** *adj.* —**crys·tal·lo·graph·i·cal·ly** *adv.*

crys·tal·loid (krĭs′tə-loid′) *n.* **1.** *Chemistry.* A water-soluble crystalline substance capable of diffusion through a semipermeable membrane. **2.** *Botany.* Any of various minute crystalline protein particles, found in certain plant cells, especially oily seeds. —*adj.* Also **crys·tal·loi·dal** (krĭs′tə-loid′l). Resembling or having the properties of a crystal or crystalloid. [CRYSTALL(O)- + -OID.]

crystal pickup *n.* A record-player pickup that uses a piezoelectric crystal to convert stylus vibrations into electric impulses. Compare **magnetic pickup.**

crystal set *n.* An early radio receiver using a crystal detector.

crystal system *n.* Any of seven classifications into which crystals fall, depending on their symmetry: cubic, tetragonal, hexagonal, trigonal (sometimes regarded as a subsystem of hexagonal), orthorhombic, monoclinic, and triclinic.

crystal violet *n.* **Gentian violet** (*see*).

Cs The symbol for the element cesium.

cs. case.

c/s cycles per second.

C.S. **1.** chief of staff. **2.** Christian Science; Christian Scientist. **3.** civil service.

C.S.A. Confederate States of America.

csc cosecant.

CSC, C.S.C. Civil Service Commission.

csch hyperbolic cosecant.

CS gas *n.* A tear gas, *ortho*-chlorobenzylidine malonitrile C_6H_4ClCH: $C(CN)_2$, used in the control of civil disturbances. It causes tears, salivation, and breathing difficulties. [*CS,* after Ben Carson and Roger Staughton, its U.S. inventors.]

csk. **1.** cask. **2.** countersink.

CST, C.S.T. Central Standard Time.

CT Connecticut (with a Zip Code).

ct. **1.** carat. **2.** cent. **3.** certificate. **4.** court.

Ct. count (title).

C.T. Central Time.

cte·nid·i·um (tĭ-nĭd′ē-əm) *n., pl.* **-ia** (-ē-ə). *Zoology.* A comblike structure, such as the respiratory apparatus of a mollusk or a row of spines in some insects. [New Latin : Greek *kteis* (stem *kten*-), a comb.]

cten·oid (tĕn′oid′, tē′noid′) *adj.* *Biology.* Having narrow segments or spines resembling the teeth of a comb: *fishes with ctenoid scales.* [Greek *ktenoeidēs,* like a comb : *kteis* (stem *kten*-), comb + -OID.]

cten·o·phore (tĕn′ə-fôr′, -fōr′) *n.* Any of various marine coelenterate animals of the subphylum Ctenophora, having transparent, gelatinous bodies bearing eight rows of comblike cilia used for locomotion. Also called "comb jelly." [New Latin *Ctenophora* : Greek *kteis* (stem *kten*-), a comb + -PHORE.] —**cte·noph·o·ran** *adj.*

ctn cotangent.

ctn. carton.

ctr. center.

Cu The symbol for the element copper [Latin *cuprum*].

cu. cubic.

cub (kŭb) *n.* **1.** The young of certain carnivorous animals, such as the bear, wolf, or lion. **2.** An inexperienced, awkward, or ill-mannered youth. **3.** A novice or learner, particularly in journalism.

crystal *This naturally formed piece of rock crystal is a variety of quartz.*

Also used adjectivally: *a cub reporter.* **4. Cub.** A Cub Scout *(see).* [16th century : origin obscure.]

Cu·ba (kyōo′bə). Country in the Caribbean Sea and the largest island in the West Indies. Cuba was reached by Christopher Columbus (1492) and was a Spanish colony until 1898. Then it became nominally independent under the United States, which reserved the right to intervene in its affairs until 1934. From 1935 the dictator Fulgencio Batista dominated Cuba until he was overthrown by Fidel Castro (1959). Cuba began to import Soviet arms, and a U.S.-backed attempt to topple the regime resulted in disaster at the Bay of Pigs (1961). The Soviet installation of rocket bases caused a U.S. naval blockade and acute international tension until the missiles were withdrawn. In the 1970's and 1980's Cuba supplied troops and assistance to political movements in Africa and Latin America. Sugar is the mainstay of the economy, while nickel and tobacco are also exported. Area, 114,524 square kilometers (44,206 square miles). Population, 10,600,000. Capital, Havana. —**Cu·ban** *adj.* & *n.*

cub·age (kyōo′bij) *n.* Cubic content or volume.

Cuba li·bre, cuba li·bre (lē′brə) *n.* An iced drink of rum, a cola beverage, and lemon or lime juice. [American Spanish, "free Cuba."]

Cuban heel *n.* A moderately high heel, tapering only very slightly, for a boot or shoe.

cu·ba·ture (kyōo′bə-chŏor′) *n.* Also **cub·age** (kyōo′bij). **1.** The determination of the cubic contents of a solid. **2.** Cubic contents. [CUB(E) + (QUADR)ATURE.]

cub·by (kŭb′ē) *n., pl.* **-bies.** A small room; a cubbyhole. [From obsolete English *cub,* a stall, perhaps from Dutch *kub, kubbe,* trap, basket, from Middle Dutch *cubbe.*]

cub·by·hole (kŭb′ē-hōl′) *n.* **1.** A snug or cramped space or room. **2.** A small compartment. **3.** A small cupboard.

cube (kyōob) *n.* **1.** *Geometry.* A regular solid having six congruent square faces. **2.** Anything having such a shape. **3.** *Mathematics.* The third power of a number or quantity; the result of multiplying something by itself twice: *27 is the cube of 3.* ~*tr.v.* **cubed, cubing, cubes. 1.** To raise (a quantity or number) to the third power. **2.** To determine the cubic contents of. **3.** To form or cut into cubes or the shape of a cube; dice. **4.** To tenderize (meat) by breaking the fibers with superficial cuts in a pattern of squares. [French, from Latin *cubus,* a dice, cube, from Greek *kubos.*]

cu·bé, cu·be (kyōo′bā′, kyōo-bā′) *n.* **1.** Any of various tropical American shrubs or plants, especially of the genus *Lonchocarpus,* whose roots yield the chemical compound rotenone. **2.** An extract from the roots of these plants, used as a fish poison and insecticide. [American Spanish *cubé†.*]

cu·beb (kyōo′běb′) *n.* **1.** A treelike woody vine, *Piper cubeba,* of southeastern Asia, bearing brownish berries. **2.** Its dried, unripe, spicy fruit, used medicinally as a stimulant and diuretic and sometimes smoked in cigarettes. [Middle English *cubibe,* from Old French *cubebe,* from Medieval Latin *cubēba,* from Arabic *kabābah.*]

cube root *n.* The number that when cubed produces a given number: *3 is the cube root of 27.*

cube steak *n.* A thin round or square slice of beef made tender by cubing, usually pan-broiled.

cu·bic (kyōo′bĭk) *adj.* **1. a.** Having the shape of a cube. **b.** Having a shape similar to or approximating that of a cube. **2.** *Abbr.* **c, cu. a.** Having three dimensions. **b.** Having a volume equal to a cube whose edge is of a stated length: *a cubic foot.* **3.** *Mathematics.* Of the third power, order, or degree. **4.** *Crystallography.* Isometric. ~*n. Mathematics.* A cubic expression, curve, or equation.

cu·bi·cal (kyōo′bĭ-kəl) *adj.* **1.** Cubic. **2.** Of or pertaining to volume.

cubism *The cubist movement, with its emphasis on geometrical shapes and structure rather than the ordinary appearance of objects, broke away from the largely representational tradition of art and opened the way for modern abstract art. This oil on canvas,* Still Life with Bottles and Knife, *was painted in 1912 by the Spanish artist Juan Gris (1887–1927), who spent most of his adult life in Paris and was a neighbor and friend of Picasso.*

—**cu·bi·cal·ly** *adv.* —**cu·bi·cal·ness** *n.*

cu·bi·cle (kyōo′bĭ-kəl) *n.* **1.** A small sleeping compartment, especially one partitioned off from a larger room. **2.** Any small compartment or partitioned-off part: *a shower cubicle.* [Latin *cubiculum,* sleeping chamber, from *cubāre,* to lie down, sleep.]

cubic measure *n.* A unit, such as a cubic meter or a cubic foot, or a system of units used to measure volume or capacity.

cu·bi·form (kyōo′bə-fôrm′) *adj.* Having the shape of a cube.

cub·ism (kyōo′bĭz′əm) *n.* Often **Cubism.** A movement in painting and sculpture, initiated in Paris in the early 20th century by Picasso and Braque, that emphasized the structure of objects by combining lines, planes, and geometrical shapes to represent several viewpoints of an object simultaneously. [French, from CUBE (from a remark by Henri Matisse concerning the "small cubes" that predominated in a painting by Georges Braque).] —**cub·ist** *adj. & n.* —**cu·bis·tic** *adj.* —**cu·bis·ti·cal·ly** *adv.*

cu·bit (kyōo′bĭt) *n.* An ancient unit of linear measure, originally equal to the length of the forearm from the tip of the middle finger to the elbow, or from 17 to 22 inches. [Middle English *cubite,* from Latin *cubitum,* cubit, elbow.]

cu·bi·tal (kyōo′bĭ-təl) *adj.* **1.** Of, pertaining to, or situated near the forearm or elbow. **2.** Of or pertaining to measurement by cubits.

cu·boid (kyōo′boid) *adj.* Also **cu·boi·dal** (kōo-boid′l). **1.** Having the shape or approximate shape of a cube. **2.** *Anatomy.* Designating the bone on the side of the tarsus between the calcaneus and the fourth and fifth metatarsal bones of the foot. ~*n.* **1.** *Anatomy.* The cuboid bone. **2.** *Geometry.* A rectangular parallelepiped.

Cub Scout *n.* A member of the junior division of the Boy Scouts.

cu·chi·fri·to (kōo′chē-frē′tō) *n., pl.* **-tos.** A small deep-fried cube of pork. [American Spanish : *cuchi,* pig (from Spanish *cochino*) + Spanish *frito,* past participle of *freir,* to fry (from Latin *frigere*).]

Cu·chul·ain, Cu·chul·ainn (kōo-kŭl′ĭn). *Celtic Mythology.* A tribal hero of Ulster who single-handedly defended it against the rest of Ireland.

cuck·ing stool (kŭk′ĭng) *n.* A former instrument of punishment for prostitutes or dishonest tradesmen, consisting of a chair in which the offender was tied and exposed to public derision or ducked in water. Compare **ducking stool.** [Middle English *cucking stol,* "excreting stool" : *cucking,* present participle of *cukken,* to defecate, from Old Norse *kūka* (unattested) + *stol,* STOOL.]

cuck·old (kŭk′əld) *n.* A man whose wife has committed adultery. ~*tr.v.* **cuckolded, -olding, -olds.** To make a cuckold of. [Middle English *cukeweld, cokewold,* from Norman French *cucuald* (unattested), variant of Old French *cucualt,* pejorative form of *cucu,* cuckoo (perhaps because cuckoos leave their eggs in the nests of other birds).] —**cuck·old·ry** *n.*

cuck·oo (kōo′kōo, kŏŏk′ōō) *n., pl.* **-oos. 1. a.** A European bird, *Cuculus canorus,* having grayish plumage and a characteristic two-note call. It lays its eggs in the nests of other birds. **b.** Any of various related birds of the family Cuculidae. **2.** The call or cry of a cuckoo. **3.** A foolish person; a simpleton. ~*v.* **cuckooed, -ooing, -oos.** —*tr.* To repeat again and again. —*intr.* To utter or imitate a cuckoo's call. ~*adj. Informal.* Crazy; foolish. [Middle English *cuccu* (imitative).]

cuck·oo·bud (kōo′kōo-bŭd′, kŏŏk′ōo-) *n. Archaic.* A yellow-flowered plant, probably the buttercup: *"cuckoo-buds of yellow hue/ Do paint the meadows with delight"* (Shakespeare).

cuckoo clock *n.* A wall clock having a mechanical cuckoo announcing intervals of time.

cuck·oo·flow·er (kōo′kōo-flou′ər, kŏŏk′ōo-) *n.* **1.** A plant, *Cardamine pratensis,* of the North Temperate Zone, having white or rose-pink flowers. Also called "lady's-smock." **2.** A plant, the **ragged robin** (see).

cuck·oo·pint (kōo′kōo-pĭnt′, kŏŏk′ōo-) *n.* A European plant, *Arum maculatum,* having arrow-shaped leaves and a spadix enclosed in a purple-spotted spathe. Also called "lords-and-ladies." [Short for obsolete *cuckoo-pintle,* from Middle English *cokkupyntel* : *cokku, cuccu,* CUCKOO + *pintel,* penis, PINTLE (from the shape of the spadix).]

cuckoo shrike *n.* Any songbird of the family Campephagidae, of the Old World tropics, having long pointed wings and mainly gray plumage.

cuckoo spit *n.* A frothy mass of liquid secreted on plant stems as a protective covering by nymphs of the froghopper. Also called "frog spit," "toad spit."

cu·cu·li·form (kyōo′kə-lə-fôrm′) *adj.* Of or belonging to the order Cuculiformes, which includes the cuckoos and related birds. [New Latin Cuculiformes : Latin *cuculus,* cuckoo (imitative) + -FORM.]

cu·cul·late (kyōo′kə-lāt′, kyōo-kŭl′āt′) *adj.* Having the shape of a cowl or hood: *cucullate sepals.* [Medieval Latin *cucullātus,* from Latin *cucullus,* cap, hood. See cowl.] —**cu·cul·late·ly** *adv.*

cu·cum·ber (kyōo′kŭm′bər) *n.* **1.** A vine, *Cucumis sativus,* cultivated for its edible fruit. **2.** The usually cylindrical fruit of this vine, having a hard green rind and firm, white, succulent flesh. [Middle English *cucumer, cocumber,* from Old French *cocombre,* from Latin *cucumis,* of Mediterranean origin.]

cucumber mosaic *n.* A viral disease of the cucumber plant that produces a variegated spotting of the leaves and fruit.

cucumber tree *n.* **1.** A tree, *Magnolia acuminata,* of eastern and central North America, having cup-shaped greenish-yellow flowers and brown or scarlet cucumber-shaped fruit. **2.** A tree, *Averrhoa bilimbi,* of eastern Asia, having reddish-purple flowers and edible

CUBA

U.S.A.

GULF OF MEXICO

80° W — Freeport • Grand Bahama • Great Abaco

ATLANTIC OCEAN

Berry Is. • New Providence • Eleuthera — 25° N

NASSAU

75° W

BAHAMAS

Cat I.

Great Bahama Bank — Andros — Exuma Is.

San Salvador

Rum Cay

Cay Sal Bank

HAVANA (HABANA) • Matanzas — Arch. de Sabana — Long I. — Tropic of Cancer — Samana Cay

Marianao • Santa Clara — Crooked I.

Sierra de los Órganos • Pinar del Rio

Cienfuegos ▲1156m. — Arch. de Camagüey — Acklins I. — Mayaguana

Isle of Pines — Arch. de los Canarreos

C U B A

Camagüey • Holguín — Great Inagua — Little Inagua

Jardines de la Reina

Sierra Maestra • Santiago de Cuba • Guantánamo — 20° N

0 100 200 300 Km
0 50 100 150 Miles

CARIBBEAN SEA

Windward Passage

Cayman Is (UK)

fruit that resemble small cucumbers.

cu·cu·mi·form (kyo͞o-kyo͞o′mə-fôrm′) *adj.* Having the shape of a cucumber. [Latin *cucumis,* CUCUMBER + -FORM.]

cu·cur·bit (kyo͞o-kûr′bĭt) *n.* **1.** A gourd-shaped flask forming the body of an alembic, formerly used in distillation. **2.** Any of various vines of the family Cucurbitaceae, which includes the squash, pumpkin, and cucumber. [Middle English *cucurbite,* from Old French, from Latin *cucurbita,* GOURD.]

Cú·cu·ta (ko͞o′ko͞o-tä′). City of northeastern Colombia, near the border with Venezuela. Founded in 1733, Cúcuta is an industrial city and the center of a region producing coffee, oil, and minerals. The city was rebuilt after an earthquake in 1875.

cud (kŭd) *n.* Food regurgitated from the first stomach to the mouth of a ruminant and chewed again. **—chew the cud.** *Informal.* To ponder. [Middle English *cud(de),* Old English *cwudu, cudu,* from Germanic; akin to Old High German *kuti,* glue.]

cud·bear (kŭd′bâr′) *n.* A purplish-red coloring substance derived from certain lichens, especially of the genera *Rocella* and *Lecanora.* [From the name of Dr. *Cuthbert* Gordon, 18th-century Scottish chemist who patented the substance.]

cud·dle (kŭd′l) *v.* **-dled, -dling, -dles.** *—tr.* To fondle in the arms; hug tenderly. *—intr.* To nestle; snuggle. Often followed by *up.* *∼n.* The act of cuddling; a hug or embrace. [16th century : origin obscure.] **—cud·dle·some** *adj.* **—cud·dly** *adj.*

cud·dy¹ (kŭd′ē) *n., pl.* **-dies.** **1.** A small cabin or the cook's galley on a ship. **2.** A small room or cupboard. [Origin obscure.]

cuddy² *n., pl.* **-dies.** *Scottish.* **1.** A donkey. **2.** A fool; dolt. [Perhaps from *Cuddy,* nickname for *Cuthbert.*]

cudg·el (kŭj′əl) *n.* A short, heavy club. **—take up the cudgels.** To join in a dispute, especially in defense of a participant.
∼tr.v. **cudgeled, -eling, -els.** Also *chiefly British* **-elled, -elling.** To beat or strike with a cudgel. **—cudgel one's brains.** To think hard. [Middle English *cuggel,* Old English *cycgel.*] **—cudg·el·er** *n.*

cudg·el·play (kŭj′əl-plā′) *n.* **1.** A sporting contest with cudgels. **2.** The art of fighting with cudgels.

cud·weed (kŭd′wēd′) *n.* **1.** Any of various woolly plants of the genus *Gnaphalium,* having clusters of whitish or yellow buttonlike flowers. **2.** Any of several similar or related plants, especially a European plant, *Filago germanica.*

cue¹ (kyo͞o) *n.* **1.** In billiards and pool, the long, tapered rod used to propel the ball. **2.** A queue of hair; a long braid.
∼v. **cued, cuing, cues.** **1.** To strike (a ball) with a cue. **2.** To braid or twist (hair) into a cue. *—intr.* To strike a ball with a cue. [French *queue,* "tail" (from the shape of the cue), from Old French *coue,* from Latin *cauda,* tail.]

cue² *n.* **1. a.** A word or bit of stage action signaling the beginning of another action or speech. **b.** Any guide to a performer, such as a musician or singer, that serves as a signal for subsequent action. **2.** A hint or reminder; a prompting. **3.** *Psychology.* A perceived signal for action, especially one that produces an operant response. **—on cue.** Precisely at the right moment. **—take one's cue from.** To imitate the style of behavior of.
∼tr.v. **cued, cuing, cues.** To give (an actor or other performer) a cue. [16th century : origin obscure.]

cue³ *n.* The letter *q.*

cue ball *n. Billiards.* The ball that is hit directly with the cue.

Cuen·ca (kwĕng′kä). City of south-central Ecuador, at an altitude of *c.* 2,440 meters (8,000 feet). Founded in 1557, Cuena is the commercial center of a rich agricultural basin. It is known as "the Marble City" because of its many fine buildings.

Cuer·na·va·ca (kwâr′nə-vä′kə). City of southern Mexico, the capital of Morelos state. The city has flour mills and beverage, textile, and cement industries. It is also a popular tourist and health resort, with beautiful churches, monasteries, a formal garden, and a palace built by Hernán Cortés.

cues·ta (kwĕs′tə) *n.* A land elevation with a gentle slope on one side and a much steeper one on the other. [Spanish, sloping side, from Latin *costa,* side.]

cuff¹ (kŭf) *n.* **1. a.** The bottom of a sleeve. **b.** A fold or band used as trimming at the bottom of a sleeve. **2.** The turned-up fold at the bottom of a trouser leg. **3.** A band of linen, lace, or other fabric attached about the wrist, either under or over a sleeve. **4.** The part of a gauntlet that extends over the wrist. **5.** *Informal.* A **handcuff** *(see).* **—off the cuff.** *Informal.* Extemporaneously. **—on the cuff.** *Informal.* **1.** Without immediate payment; on credit. **2.** Without payment; gratis. [Middle English *cuffe*†, glove, mitten.]

cuff² *tr.v.* **cuffed, cuffing, cuffs.** To strike with the open hand; slap. *∼n.* A blow or slap with the open hand. [16th century : perhaps imitative.]

cuff links *pl.n.* A pair of linked buttons, used to fasten the cuffs of a shirt.

Cufic. Variant of **Kufic.**

cui·rass (kwĭ-răs′) *n.* **1.** A piece of armor for protecting the breast and back. **2.** The breastplate alone. **3.** *Zoology.* A protective covering of bony plates, scales, or shell.
∼tr.v. **cuirassed, -rassing, -rasses.** To protect with a cuirass. [Middle English *curace,* cuirass (especially one of leather), from Old French *cuirasse,* from Vulgar Latin *coriāca* (unattested), "leather buckler," from Latin *coriāceus,* of leather, from *corium,* hide, skin.]

cui·ras·sier (kwîr′ə-sîr′) *n.* Formerly, a horse soldier in European armies whose equipment included the cuirass.

cuir bouil·li (kwîr′ bo͞ol′yē) *n.* Leather soaked and left to harden, used as an early form of armor. [French, "boiled leather."]

Cui·se·naire (kwē′zə-nâr′) *n.* A trademark for a set of colored rods used to teach arithmetic.

cui·sine (kwĭ-zēn′) *n.* **1.** A characteristic manner or style of preparing food. **2.** Food prepared by a hotel, restaurant, or the like. [French, from Late Latin *coquīna,* a kitchen, cookery, from *coquere,* to cook.]

cuisine min·ceur (mäɴ-sœr′) *n.* A style of French cooking that seeks to minimize the use of rich ingredients such as flour, butter, and cream. [French, "slenderness cuisine."]

cuisse (kwĭs) *n.* Also **cuish** (kwĭsh). A piece of plate armor worn to protect the thigh. [Back-formation from Middle English *cussues, cushies,* from Old French *cuissaux,* plural of *cuissel,* from *cuisse,* thigh, from Latin *coxa,* thigh, hip.]

Cu·kor (kyo͞o′kər, -kôr, ko͞o′-), **George Dewey** (1899–1983). U.S. filmmaker. In his 50-year career, he used his skillful rapport with actresses and actors and his attention to detail to direct some of Hollywood's finest films, including *Little Women* (1933), *The Philadelphia Story* (1940), and *Adam's Rib* (1949). In 1964 he earned an Academy Award for his direction of *My Fair Lady.*

Cul·bert·son (kŭl′bərt-sən), **Ely** (1891–1955). U.S. contract bridge authority. He helped popularize contract bridge through his widely reported dominance of international matches and several books on the subject, including *The Contract Bridge Blue Book* (1930). He was also active in peace movements.

culch, cultch (kŭlch) *n.* **1.** A natural bed for oysters, consisting of gravel or crushed shells to which oyster spawn may adhere. **2.** The spawn of the oyster. **3.** Rubbish or refuse. [Perhaps from Old French *culche, couche,* bed, COUCH.]

cul-de-sac (kŭl′dĭ-săk′, ko͝ol′-) *n., pl.* **cul-de-sacs.** **1.** A dead-end street; a road closed at one end. **2.** *Anatomy.* A saclike cavity or tube open only at one end. [French, "bottom of the sack," blind alley.]

-cule *suffix.* Indicates smallness; for example, **molecule.** [French, from New Latin *-cula,* diminutive suffix from Latin *-culus, -cula, -culum.* See also **-cle.**]

Culebra Cut. See **Gaillard Cut.**

cu·let (kyo͞o′lĭt) *n.* **1.** The flat face of a gem cut as a brilliant. **2.** One of the plates of medieval armor covering the lower back. [French, diminutive of *cul,* the rump, from Latin *cūlus.*]

cu·lex (kyo͞o′lĕks) *n., pl.* **-lices** (-lə-sēz′). Any of various mosquitoes of the genus *Culex,* which includes the house mosquito, *C. pipiens.* [New Latin, from Latin *culex*†, gnat.]

Cu·lia·cán (kyo͞o′lyä-kän′). City of western Mexico, capital of Sinaloa state. Founded in 1531, it is located on a hot coastal plain that produces tropical fruits, sugar cane, cotton, beans, and corn; cattle raising is also important. In the Spanish colonial period the city was a point of departure for northern expeditions, including that of Francisco Coronado (1540).

cu·li·cide (kyo͞o′lə-sīd′) *n.* A chemical used to destroy mosquitoes or gnats. [Latin *culex* (stem *culic-*), gnat + -CIDE.]

cu·li·nar·y (kyo͞o′lə-nĕr′ē, kŭl′ə-) *adj.* Of or pertaining to a kitchen or to cookery. [Latin *culīnārius,* from *culīna,* kitchen, deformed variant of *coquīna,* cook.] **—cu·li·nar·i·ly** *adv.*

cull (kŭl) *tr.v.* **culled, culling, culls.** **1.** To pick out from others; select. **2.** To gather; collect. **3. a.** To remove and kill (weak or surplus animals in a herd or flock). **b.** To search through (a herd or flock) in order to remove and kill weak or surplus animals.
∼n. **1.** The act of culling. **2.** The amount culled. **3.** Something picked out from others; especially, something rejected because of inferior quality. [Middle English *coilen,* from Old French *cuillir,* from Latin *colligere,* to COLLECT.] **—cull·er** *n.*

Cul·len (kŭl′ən), **Countée** (1903–46). U.S. poet. Cullen established his reputation as a lyric poet with his first book, *Color* (1925). He also published a novel, *One Way to Heaven* (1932), several more books of verse, and an anthology of black poetry, *Caroling Dusk* (1927).

cullender. Variant of **colander.**

cul·let (kŭl′ĭt) *n.* Scraps of broken or waste glass gathered for remelting. [Perhaps variant of earlier *collet,* from French *collet,* "little neck" (the neck of glass broken off a newly blown vessel), diminutive of *col,* neck, from Old French, from Latin *collum.*]

cul·lis (kŭl′ĭs) *n., pl.* **-lises.** A gutter or groove in a roof. [Middle English *colis,* from Old French *coleïs,* channel, from *coler,* to pour, strain, from Latin *cōlāre,* to filter, strain, from *cōlum,* a sieve.]

Cul·lod·en Moor (kə-lŏd′n, -lō′dən). Moorland near Inverness in northeastern Scotland. It was the site of a battle in which the Jacobite forces of Charles Edward Stuart were defeated by an army commanded by the Duke of Cumberland (1746). The battle marked the final defeat of the Jacobite cause and was followed by savage repression in the Highlands.

culm¹ (kŭlm) *n.* The jointed stem of a grass or sedge. [Latin *culmus,* stalk.]

culm² *n.* **1.** Waste from anthracite coal mines, consisting of fine coal, coal dust, and dirt. **2. a.** *Often* **Culm.** *Geology.* A Lower Carboniferous formation consisting of shale and sandstone. Also called "culm measures." **b.** Inferior anthracite coal. [Middle English *colme,* coal dust, perhaps akin to *col,* COAL.]

cul·mi·nant (kŭl′mə-nənt) *adj.* Culminating; highest.

cul·mi·nate (kŭl′mə-nāt′) *intr.v.* **-nated, -nating, -nates.** **1.** To reach the highest point or degree; come to full effect; climax. Usually used with *in.* **2.** *Astronomy.* To cross the meridian of the observer; reach the highest point above an observer's horizon. Used of stars and other celestial bodies. [Late Latin *culmināre,* from Latin *cul-*

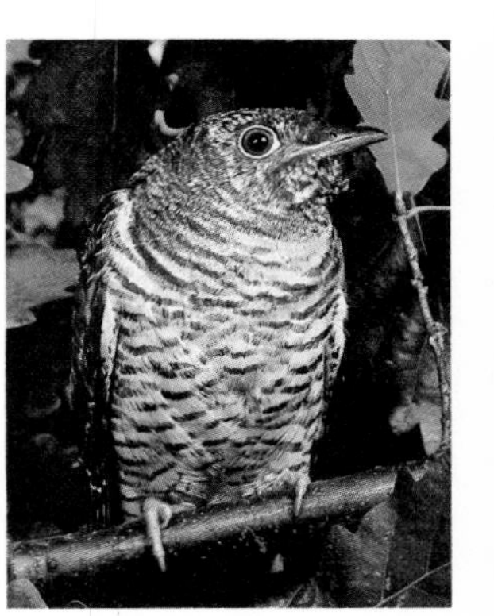

cuckoo *There are about 130 species of the cuckoo family distributed worldwide. Most are parasitic, laying their eggs in the nests of other birds. The young European cuckoo, seen here, is often reared in a reed warbler's nest.*

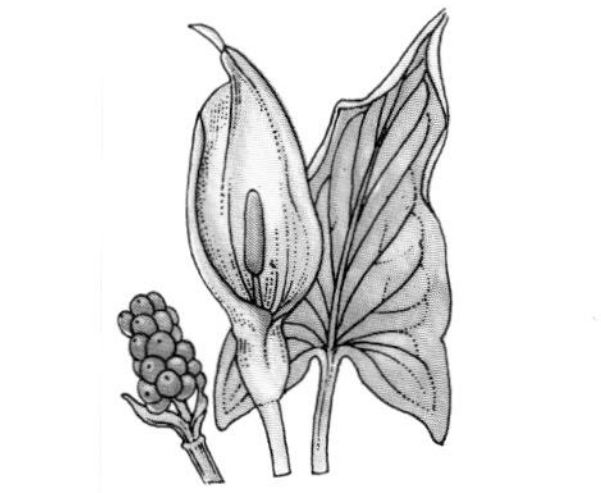

cuckoopint *In springtime, cuckoopint (*Arum maculatum*) is a common sight in the hedgerows of the Northern Hemisphere. The poisonous red berries that appear later can be fatal to humans if eaten. Cuckoopint is just one of many local names for this flower. An alternate name is lords-and-ladies.*

men (stem *culmin-*), top, summit.] —**cul·mi·na·tion** *n.*

cu·lottes (kōō-lŏts', kyōō-) *pl.n.* A woman's full trousers, usually knee-length, cut to resemble a skirt. [French, breeches, diminutive of *cul*, backside, from Latin *cūlus.*] —**cu·lotte** *adj.*

cul·pa (kŭl'pə, kōōl'-) *n. Law.* Fault; misconduct. [Latin.]

cul·pa·ble (kŭl'pə-bəl) *adj.* Responsible for wrong or error; deserving censure. [Middle English *coupable,* from Old French, from Latin *culpābilis,* from *culpāre,* to blame, from *culpa,* CULPA.] —**cul·pa·bil·i·ty** *n.* —**cul·pa·ble·ness** *n.* —**cul·pa·bly** *adv.*

Cul·pep·er (kŭl'pĕp'ər), **Nicholas** (1616–54). English herbalist and physician. He set up as an apothecary in 1640 and in 1649 angered the London College of Physicians by producing a popular translation from Latin of their official *Pharmocopoeia.* He is best remembered for *Culpeper's Herbal,* describing properties of herbs.

cul·prit (kŭl'prĭt) *n.* **1.** A person guilty of a fault or crime. **2.** A person charged with an offense or crime. [From the 17th-century legal phrase "*Culprit,* how will you be tried?", perhaps a mistake for Norman French "*Culpable. Prit d'averrer . . . ,*" "Guilty. (I am) ready to prove . . . ," the prosecutor's response to a plea of not guilty, which might have been abbreviated as "*Cul. prit, etc.*" : CUL-PABLE + *prit, prist,* ready, from Latin *praestus* (see presto).]

cult (kŭlt) *n.* **1.** A system or community of religious worship and ritual, especially one focusing upon a single deity or spirit. **2. a.** Obsessive devotion or veneration for a person, principle, or ideal. **b.** The object of such devotion. **3. a.** An exclusive group of persons sharing an esoteric interest. **b.** The object of such an interest. **4.** Any fashion or fad. Often used derogatorily.
~*adj.* Pertaining to or characteristic of a cult: *a cult figure.* [French *culte,* from Latin *cultus,* cultivation, a laboring, worship, from the past participle of *colere,* to CULTIVATE.] —**cul·tic** *adj.* —**cult·ism** *n.* —**cult·ist** *n. & adj.*

cultch. Variant of culch.

cul·ti. Alternate plural of cultus.

cul·ti·gen (kŭl'tə-jən) *n.* An organism, especially a cultivated plant such as maize, of a kind not known to have a wild or uncultivated counterpart. [CULTI(VATED) + -GEN.]

cul·ti·va·bie (kŭl'tə-və-bəl) *adj.* Also **cul·ti·vat·a·ble** (-vā'tə-bəl). Capable of being cultivated. —**cul·ti·va·bil·i·ty** *n.*

cul·ti·var (kŭl'tə-vär', -vâr') *n.* A horticulturally or agriculturally derived variety of a plant, as distinguished from a natural variety. [*Culti*vated + *vari*ety.]

cul·ti·vate (kŭl'tə-vāt') *tr.v.* **-vated, -vating, -vates. 1. a.** To improve and prepare (land), as by plowing or fertilizing, for raising crops; till. **b.** To loosen or dig (soil) around growing plants. **2.** To grow or tend (a plant or crop). **3.** To promote the growth of (a biological culture, for example). **4.** To nurture; foster. **5.** To form and refine, as by education. **6.** To seek the acquaintance or goodwill of. [Medieval Latin *cultīvāre,* from *(terra) cultīva,* tilled (land), from *cultīvus,* tilled, from Latin *cultus,* past participle of *colere,* to till, cultivate.]

cul·ti·vat·ed (kŭl'tə-vā'tĭd) *adj.* **1.** Cultured; refined. **2.** Specially nurtured or improved by cultivation. Said of plants.

cul·ti·va·tion (kŭl'tə-vā'shən) *n.* **1. a.** The act of cultivating. **b.** The state of being cultivated. **2.** Refinement; social polish. —See Usage Note at culture.

cul·ti·va·tor (kŭl'tə-vā'tər) *n.* **1.** One who cultivates. **2.** An implement or machine for loosening the earth and destroying weeds around growing plants.

cul·trate (kŭl'trāt') *adj.* Also **cul·trat·ed** (-trā'tĭd). Sharp-edged and pointed; knifelike: *a cultrate beak.* [Latin *cultrātus,* knifelike, from *culter* (stem *cultr-*), knife.]

cul·tur·al (kŭl'chər-əl) *adj.* **1.** Of or relating to culture, especially social, intellectual, or artistic pursuits. **2.** Obtained by specialized breeding, as cultured plant varieties are.

cultural anthropology *n.* The scientific study of human culture based on archaeological, ethnologic, ethnographic, linguistic, social, and psychological data and methods of analysis. Compare **physical anthropology.**

Cultural Revolution *n.* A political movement in China (1966–68), thought to have been launched by Mao Ze-dong, aimed at overthrowing entrenched bureaucracy and rekindling revolutionary fervor and ideals.

cul·ture (kŭl'chər) *n.* **1.** Social and intellectual formation. **2.** The totality of socially transmitted behavior patterns, arts, beliefs, institutions, and all other products of human work and thought characteristic of a community or population. **3.** A style of social and artistic expression peculiar to a society or class. **4. a.** Intellectual and artistic activity. **b.** Intellectual and social refinement resulting from such activity. **5.** The cultivation of the soil; tillage. **6.** The breeding of animals or growing of plants, especially to produce improved stock. **7.** *Biology.* **a.** The growing of microorganisms in a nutrient medium for scientific research or medical use. **b.** Such a growth or colony, as of bacteria.
~*tr.v.* **cultured, -turing, -tures. 1.** To cultivate. **2.** To develop (microorganisms or tissues, for example) in a culture medium. [Middle English, cultivation, tillage, from Old French, from Latin *cultūra,* from *cultus,* cultivation. See cultivate.]

Usage: **culture, cultivation, breeding, refinement, gentility, taste.** These nouns are applied to personal achievement in the development of intellect, manners, and aesthetic appreciation. *Culture,* which overlaps the others, implies enlightenment attained through close association with and appreciation of the highest level of civilization. *Cultivation* usually refers to the self-improvement or self-development by which a person acquires culture. *Breeding* is the development of good character and behavior, and is especially revealed in manners, poise, and sensitivity to the feelings of others. *Refinement,* the highest product of breeding, stresses aversion to coarseness; sometimes it may imply a delicacy of feeling associated with fastidiousness. *Gentility* is sometimes still synonymous with refinement or good birth; in modern usage it may suggest extreme elegance in behavior or manners. *Taste* is the capacity for recognizing and appreciating what is aesthetically superior.

cul·tured (kŭl'chərd) *adj.* **1.** Cultivated; refined. **2.** Produced under artificial and controlled conditions.

cultured pearl *n.* A pearl made to grow in the shell of an oyster or clam by inserting a small bead of mother-of-pearl, around which layers of nacre are deposited.

culture medium *n.* A substance, such as agar or blood, on which colonies of microorganisms, such as bacteria, are grown.

culture shock *n.* Severe and often distressing feelings of disorientation and isolation felt by a person on coming into contact with a completely alien society or foreign way of life.

culture vulture *n.* A person whose interest in art, literature, and the like is considered excessive or overzealous.

cul·tus (kŭl'təs) *n., pl.* **-tuses** or **-ti** (-tī). A religious cult. [New Latin, from Latin *cultus,* worship, CULT.]

cul·ver (kŭl'vər) *n. Poetic.* A dove; a pigeon. [Middle English *culver,* Old English *culufre,* from Vulgar Latin *columbra* (unattested), from Latin *columbula,* diminutive of *columba,* dove.]

Cul·ver City (kŭl'vər). City of southern California, a residential suburb of Los Angeles. It is a center of the motion-picture industry, which began in the city around 1915. The city's chief commercial products are electronic and aerospace equipment.

cul·ver·in (kŭl'vər-ĭn) *n.* **1.** A type of early musket. **2.** A heavy cannon used in the 16th and 17th centuries. [Middle English, from Old French *coulevrine,* "serpentine," from *couleuvre,* snake, from Vulgar Latin *colobra* (unattested), from Latin *colubra,* feminine of *coluber,* snake.] —**cul·ver·i·neer** *n.*

Cul·ver's root (kŭl'vərz) *n.* **1.** A North American plant, *Veronicastrum virginicum,* having spikes of small white or purplish flowers. **2.** The root of this plant, formerly used as a cathartic and emetic. [After a Dr. *Culver,* 18th-century U.S. physician.]

cul·vert (kŭl'vərt) *n.* **1.** A sewer or drain crossing under a road or embankment. **2.** A pipe or channel for an electric cable. [18th century : origin obscure.]

cum (kōōm, kŭm) *prep.* Together with; plus. Used in combination to indicate a dual nature or function: *her attic-cum-studio.* [Latin, with.]

Cu·mae (kyōō'mē). An ancient city of south-central Italy, near modern-day Naples. It was the earliest-known Greek colony in Italy, founded *c.* 750 B.C. At one time Cumae was a great power, with a number of colonies. It fell to the Samnites (late 5th century B.C.), later adopted Roman culture and civilization, and finally declined as neighboring cities rose to power.

Cu·ma·ná (kōō'mä-nä'). City of northeastern Venezuela, on the Manzanares River near its mouth on the Gulf of Cariaco, an inlet of the Caribbean Sea. Founded in 1521 to exploit nearby pearl fisheries, the city was frequently raided by the Dutch and British in the 16th and 17th centuries.

cum·ber (kŭm'bər) *tr.v.* **-bered, -bering, -bers. 1.** To weigh down; burden. **2.** To hamper; obstruct.
~*n.* A hindrance; an encumbrance. [Middle English *combren,* perhaps from Old French *combrer,* from *combre†,* hindrance.]

Cum·ber·land¹ (kŭm'bər-lənd). Former county of northwest England. Since 1974 it has been a part of the new county of Cumbria.

Cumberland². A river rising in southeastern Kentucky and flowing 1,105 kilometers (687 miles) through Kentucky and Tennessee to the Ohio River in western Kentucky.

Cumberland, William Augustus, Duke of (1721–65). British general, the third son of George II. Made commander in chief of the British army (1745), he crushed the Jacobite Rebellion at the Battle of Culloden (1746).

Cumberland Gap. A natural passage through the Cumberland Mts., at the junction of the borders of Kentucky, Virginia, and Tennessee. Daniel Boone's Wilderness Road traversed the Gap. It was a strategic point during the Civil War, held alternately by Union and Confederate forces.

cum·ber·some (kŭm'bər-səm) *adj.* **1.** Clumsy; unwieldy. **2.** Burdensome; onerous. —See Synonyms at heavy. —**cum·ber·some·ly** *adv.* —**cum·ber·some·ness** *n.*

cum·brance (kŭm'brəns) *n.* **1.** An encumbrance. **2.** Trouble. [Middle English *cumbraunce,* from *cumbren,* to CUMBER.]

Cum·bri·a (kŭm'brē-ə). County in northwest England, formed (1974) from Cumberland and Westmorland with parts of Yorkshire and Lancashire. It encompasses the Lake District and the Cumbrian Mts., which rise to 977 meters (3,205 feet) at Scafell Pikes, the highest point in England. Carlisle is the administrative center. —**Cum·bri·an** *adj. & n.*

cum·brous (kŭm'brəs) *adj.* Cumbersome. [Middle English, from *cumbren,* to CUMBER.]

cum gra·no sa·lis (kōōm grä'nō sä'lĭs, kŭm grā'no sā'lĭs) *adv. Latin.* With a grain of salt; with skepticism.

cum·in, cum·min (kŭm'ĭn) *n.* **1.** An Old World plant, *Cuminum cyminum,* having finely divided leaves and small white or pinkish flowers. **2.** The aromatic seeds of this plant, used as a condiment. [Middle English *comin,* from Old French *cumin,* from Latin *cumī-*

num, from Greek *kuminon,* from Semitic, akin to Hebrew *kammōn,* Akkadian *kamūnu.*]

cum lau·de (ko͝om lou′də, lou′dē, kŭm lô′dē) *adv.* With praise. Used on university and college diplomas to designate the third-highest degree of academic distinction. Compare **magna cum laude, summa cum laude.** [New Latin.]

cum·mer·bund (kŭm′ər-bŭnd′) *n.* A broad, pleated sash worn round the waist in men's formal dress. [Hindi *kamarband,* from Persian, loinband, waistband : *kamar,* loins, waist + *band,* band.]

Cum·mings (kŭm′ĭngz), **Edward Estlin,** known as "e e cummings" (1894–1962). U.S. poet, noted for his lyricism and unconventional use of punctuation and typography. He won fame through the bizarre format of his poetry, in which the visual impact of eccentric typography underlines the content.

cumquat. Variant of **kumquat.**

cum·shaw (kŭm′shô) *n.* A tip; a gratuity; a present. [Pidgin English, from Chinese dialect (Amoy) *kam sia,* to thank.]

cumul–. Variant of **cumulo–.**

cu·mu·late (kyo͞om′yə-lāt′) *v.* **-lated, -lating, -lates.** —*tr.* **1.** To accumulate. **2.** To combine into one unit; merge. **3.** To expand by an increment in new material. —*intr.* To become massed. [Latin *cumulāre,* from *cumulus,* heap.] **—cu·mu·la·tion** *n.*

cu·mu·la·tive (kyo͞om′yə-lā′tĭv, -yə-lə-tĭv) *adj.* **1.** Increasing or enlarging by successive addition. **2.** Acquired by or resulting from accumulation. **3.** *Finance.* **a.** Of or pertaining to interest or a dividend that increases if not paid when due. **b.** Designating shares that entitle holders to be paid arrears of dividend before any other payment is made to ordinary shareholders. **4.** *Law.* Designating additional or supporting evidence. **5.** *Statistics.* **a.** Of, pertaining to, or designating the sum of the frequencies of experimentally determined values of a random variable that are less than or equal to a given value. **b.** Of, pertaining to, or designating experimental error that increases in magnitude with each successive measurement. **—cu·mu·la·tive·ly** *adv.* **—cu·mu·la·tive·ness** *n.*

cumulative voting *n.* A system of voting, used, for example, by shareholders, in which each voter has as many votes as there are representatives to be elected and may give them all to one candidate or distribute them among several candidates.

cu·mu·li (kyo͞om′yə-lī′). Plural of **cumulus.**

cumuli–. Variant of **cumulo–.**

cu·mu·li·form (kyo͞om′yə-lə-fôrm′) *adj.* *Meteorology.* Having the shape of a cumulus cloud. [CUMUL(US) + -FORM.]

cumulo–, cumuli–, cumul– *prefix.* Indicates cumulus; for example, **cumulonimbus.** [From CUMULUS.]

cu·mu·lo·nim·bus (kyo͞om′yə-lō-nĭm′bəs) *n., pl.* **-buses** or **-bi** (-bī′). *Meteorology.* An extremely dense cumulus cloud developed vertically to a great height, usually producing heavy rains, thunderstorms, or hailstorms. [New Latin : CUMUL(US) + NIMBUS.]

cu·mu·lus (kyo͞om′yə-ləs) *n., pl.* **-li** (-lī). **1.** *Meteorology.* A dense, white, flat-based cloud with a multiple rounded top and a well-defined outline, occurring at heights of 2,000 to 3,000 feet, and usually formed by the ascent of thermally unstable air masses. Also called "cumulus cloud." **2.** A pile, mound, or heap. [New Latin, from Latin, heap, mass.] **—cu·mu·lous** *adj.*

cunc·ta·tion (kŭngk′tā′shən) *n.* Delay; procrastination. [Latin *cūnctātiō* (stem *cunctātion-*), from *cūnctātus,* past participle of *cūnctārī,* to delay.] **—cunc·ta·tive** *adj.* **—cunc·ta·tory** *adj.* **—cunc·ta·tor** *n.*

cu·ne·al (kyo͞o′nē-əl) *adj.* Wedge-shaped. [New Latin *cunealis,* from Latin *cuneus,* wedge. See **coin.**]

cu·ne·ate (kyo͞o′nē-ĭt, -āt′) *adj.* Wedge-shaped. Said especially of leaves that are narrow and triangular, and taper toward the base. [Latin *cuneātus,* from *cuneus,* wedge. See **coin.**] **—cu·ne·ate·ly** *adv.*

cu·ne·i·form (kyo͞o′nē-ə-fôrm′, kyo͞o-nē′-) *adj.* **1.** Wedge-shaped. **2.** Designating: **a.** The wedge-shaped characters used in ancient Sumerian, Akkadian, Assyrian, Babylonian, and Persian writing. **b.** Documents, stone tablets, or inscriptions written or engraved in such characters. **3.** *Anatomy.* Designating any of the three wedge-shaped bones in the tarsus of the foot.
~*n.* **1.** Cuneiform writing. **2.** A cuneiform bone. [French *cunéiforme* : Latin *cuneus,* wedge (see **coin**) + -FORM.]

Cu·ne·ne or **Ku·ne·ne** (ko͞o′nā-nə). River of southern Africa. It rises in central Angola and flows some 1,200 kilometers (about 750 miles) to the Atlantic, its lower course forming much of the Angola-Namibia border.

cun·ner (kŭn′ər) *n.* A marine fish, *Tautogolabrus adspersus,* of North American Atlantic waters. [Origin unknown.]

cun·ning (kŭn′ĭng) *adj.* **1.** Shrewd; crafty; artful. **2.** Executed with or exhibiting ingenuity. —See Synonyms at **clever, sly.**
~*n.* **1.** Skill in deception; craftiness; guile. **2.** Skill or adeptness in performance; adroitness; dexterity. [Middle English *conning,* perhaps from the present participle of *connen,* to know, Old English *cunnan.*] **—cun·ning·ly** *adv.* **—cun·ning·ness** *n.*

Cun·ning·ham (kŭn′ĭng-hăm′, -əm) **Merce** (1919–). U.S. choreographer, a pioneer of experimental ballet. He danced with Martha Graham's company (1939–45) and from 1942 often worked with the avant-garde composer John Cage.

Cu·no·be·li·nus (kyo͞o′nō-bə-lī′nəs) (died *c.* A.D. 42). *English* **Cym·be·line** (sĭm′bə-lēn). Ancient British ruler, chief of a tribe who ruled a territory corresponding to modern Hertfordshire.

cup (kŭp) *n.* **1.** A small, rounded, open container, typically with a flat bottom and a handle, used for drinking. **2. a.** Such a container and its contents. **b.** The contents alone. **3.** *Abbr.* **c. a.** A measure equal to 1/2 pint, 8 fluid ounces, or 16 tablespoons. **4.** The bowl of a drinking vessel. **5.** The chalice or the wine used in the celebration of the Eucharist. **6.** An ornamental cup-shaped vessel, usually two-handed, given to commemorate an event or as a prize or trophy. **7.** A sporting contest, often an elimination competition lasting several rounds, played for a cup as the prize. Also used adjectivally: *cup final; cup winner.* **8.** Either of the two rounded, hollow parts of a brassiere that contain or support the breasts. **9.** *Golf.* A hole or the metal container inside a hole. **10.** Any of various beverages, usually combining wine, fruit, and spices. **11.** Anything resembling a cup. **12.** *Biology.* A cuplike structure or organ. **13.** A lot or portion to be suffered or enjoyed. **—in one's cups.** Drunk. **—not one's cup of tea.** *Informal.* Not to one's taste; not agreeable.
~*tr.v.* **cupped, cupping, cups. 1.** To place in or as if in a cup. **2.** To shape like a cup: *cup one's hand.* **3.** *Medicine.* To practice cupping on. [Middle English *cuppe,* Old English *cuppe,* from Late Latin *cuppa*†, drinking vessel.]

cup·bear·er (kŭp′bâr′ər) *n.* One who serves wine, as in a royal household.

cup·board (kŭb′ərd) *n.* A cabinet or recessed portion of a room enclosed by a door, usually with shelves for storing food, crockery, and the like.

cupboard love *n.* *British.* Love shown or simulated in order to gain material goods or advantages.

cup·cake (kŭp′kāk′) *n.* A small cake baked in a cup-shaped container.

cu·pel (kyo͞o′pəl, kyo͞o-pĕl′) *n.* **1.** A shallow, porous vessel used in assaying to separate precious metals from less valuable elements. **2.** The bottom or receptacle in a silver-refining furnace.
~*tr.v.* **cupeled** or **cupelled, -peling** or **-pelling, -pels.** To separate from base metals in a cupel. [French *coupelle,* diminutive of *coupe,* cup, from Late Latin *cuppa,* CUP.] **—cu·pel·er** *n.*

cu·pel·la·tion (kyo͞o′pə-lā′shən) *n.* A refining process for nonoxidizing metals, such as silver and gold, in which the components of a metallic mixture oxidized at high temperatures are separated by absorption into the walls of a cupel.

cup·ful (kŭp′fo͝ol′) *n., pl.* **-fuls** or **cupsful. 1.** The amount a cup will hold. **2.** *Cooking.* A measure of capacity equal to 1/2 pint, 8 ounces, or 16 tablespoons.

cu·pid (kyo͞o′pĭd) *n.* A representation of the god Cupid as a winged boy holding a bow and arrow.

Cu·pid (kyo͞o′pĭd). The Roman god of love, identified with the Greek Eros. [Latin *Cupīdō,* personification of *cupīdō,* desire, from *cupere,* to desire.]

cu·pid·i·ty (kyo͞o-pĭd′ə-tē) *n.* Avarice; greed; strong desire for gain. [Middle English *cupidite,* from Old French, from Latin *cupiditās* (stem *cupiditāt-*), from *cupidus,* desiring, from *cupere,* to desire.]

cu·po·la (kyo͞o′pə-lə) *n.* **1. a.** A domed roof or ceiling. **b.** A small, usually domed structure surmounting a roof. **2.** A cylindrical vertical type of blast furnace used for remelting metals, usually iron, before casting. Also called "cupola furnace." **3.** A protective revolving dome on the guns of a warship. **4.** *Geology.* A small dome-shaped igneous intrusion. [Italian *cupola,* from Late Latin *cūpula,* diminutive of Latin *cūpa,* tub, vat.]

cup·ping (kŭp′ĭng) *n.* A therapeutic process, rarely used in modern medicine, in which glass cups (*cupping glasses*), partially evacuated by heating, are locally applied to the skin in order to draw blood toward or through the surface.

cup plant *n.* A coarse North American plant, *Silphium perfoliatum,* having yellow-rayed flowers. Also called "rosinweed." [From the cup formed around its stem by its leaves.]

cu·pre·ous (kyo͞o′prē-əs) *adj.* Of, resembling, or containing copper; coppery. [Late Latin *cupreus,* from *cuprum,* COPPER.]

cu·pric (kyo͞o′prĭk) *adj.* Of or containing divalent copper. [Late Latin *cuprum,* COPPER.]

cu·prif·er·ous (kyo͞o-prĭf′ər-əs) *adj.* Yielding copper. [Late Latin *cuprum,* COPPER + -FEROUS.]

cu·prite (kyo͞o′prīt′) *n.* A natural red copper ore, essentially Cu_2O. [German *Kuprit* : Late Latin *cuprum,* COPPER + -ITE.]

cupro-, cupri-, cupr- *prefix.* Indicates copper; for example, **cupronickel, cupriferous.** [Late Latin *cuprum,* copper.]

cu·pro·nick·el (ko͞o′prō-nĭk′əl, kyo͞o′-) *n.* An alloy of copper with up to 40 percent of nickel, highly resistant to corrosion.

cu·prous (kyo͞o′prəs) *adj.* Of, pertaining to, or containing univalent copper. [Late Latin *cuprum,* COPPER.]

cu·pu·la (kyo͞o′pyə-lə) *n., pl.* **-lae** (-lē). *Anatomy.* A cup-shaped or domed structure, such as the apex of the cochlea. [New Latin, CUPULE.]

cu·pu·late (kyo͞o′pyə-lāt′, -lĭt) *adj.* Also **cu·pu·lar** (-lər). **1.** Resembling a small cup; cup-shaped. **2.** Having or bearing a cupule.

cu·pule (kyo͞o′pyo͞ol′) *n.* *Biology.* A cup-shaped part, structure, or indentation; especially, the cuplike base of an acorn. [New Latin *cupula,* from Late Latin *cūpula,* little cask or tub, diminutive of Latin *cūpa,* a tub, vat.]

cur (kûr) *n.* **1.** A dog considered to be inferior, vicious, or undesirable; a mongrel. **2.** A base or cowardly person. [Middle English *curre,* short for *kur(dogge),* "growling dog," perhaps from Old Norse *kurra,* to growl.]

cur. 1. currency. **2.** current.

cur·a·ble (kyo͝or′ə-bəl) *adj.* Capable of being healed or cured. **—cur·a·bil·i·ty, cur·a·ble·ness** *n.* **—cur·a·bly** *adv.*

cu·ra·çao (kyo͝or′ə-sō′, -sou′, ko͝or′-) *n.* A liqueur flavored with the peel of the sour Curaçao orange. [From CURAÇAO.]

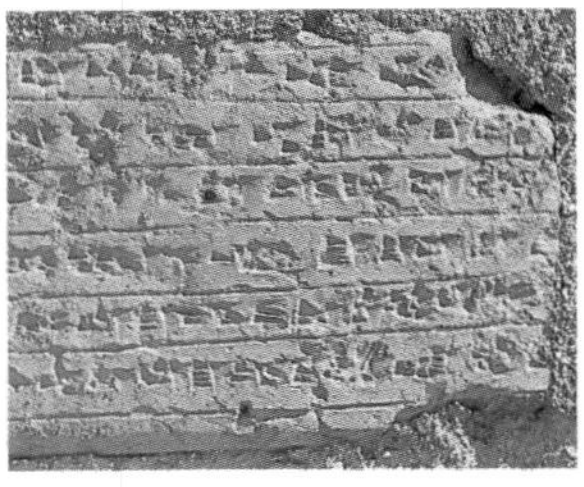

cuneiform *One of the earliest forms of writing. Its wedge-shaped characters have been found, baked into tablets of clay, in Mesopotamia. This tablet dates from about 1250* B.C.

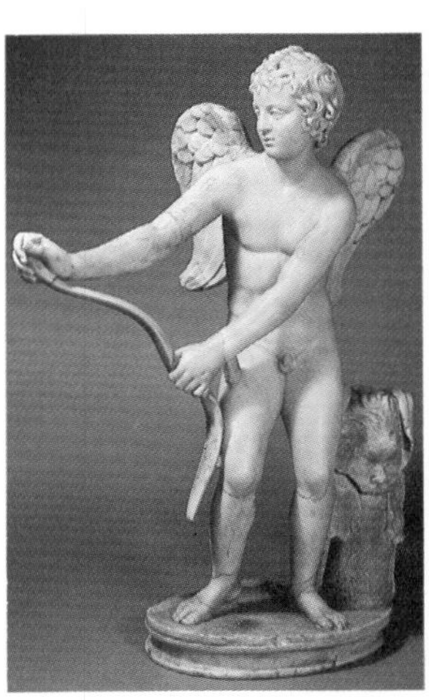

Cupid *The Roman winged god of love. Legend says he fires his arrows of love while blindfolded. This Roman statue of him dates from the second century* A.D.

Cu·ra·çao (kyōōr′ə-sō′, kōō′rä-sä′ō). The largest island in the Netherlands Antilles group, in the south Caribbean Sea. It was discovered and settled by Spain (1499) and occupied by the Dutch in the 17th century. It received autonomy under the Dutch Crown (1954). Willemstad is the administrative center.

cu·ra·cy (kyōōr′ə-sē) n., pl. **-cies.** The office, duties, or term of office of a curate.

curagh, curragh. Variants of **currach.**

cu·ra·re, cu·ra·ri (kōō-rär′ē, kyōō-) n. 1. A resinous substance obtained from several species of South American trees. It is used medicinally as a muscle relaxant and by some South American Indians as an arrow poison. 2. Any of the trees from which this substance is obtained. [Portuguese and Spanish, from Carib kurari.]

cu·ra·rine (kyōō-rär′ĭn, -ēn′) n. A poisonous alkaloid, $C_{19}H_{26}N_2O$, obtained from curare. [CURAR(E) + -INE.]

cu·ra·rize (kyōō-rär′īz) tr.v. **-rized, -rizing, -rizes.** 1. To poison with curare. 2. To treat with curare so as to paralyze the motor nerves. **—cu·ra·ri·za·tion** n.

cu·ras·sow (kyōōr′ə-sō′) n. Any of several long-tailed, crested tropical American birds of the family Cracidae, related to the pheasants and domestic fowl. [Variant of CURAÇAO (island).]

cu·rate (kyōōr′ĭt) n. 1. A clergyman who assists or deputizes for a rector or vicar. 2. A clergyman who has charge of a parish. [Middle English curat, from Medieval Latin cūrātus, "one having a (spiritual) cure or charge," from cūra, CURE.]

cur·a·tive (kyōōr′ə-tĭv) adj. 1. Serving or tending to cure. 2. Of or relating to the cure of disease.
~n. Something that cures; a remedy. **—cur·a·tive·ly** adv. **—cur·a·tive·ness** n.

cu·ra·tor (kyōō-rā′tər, kyōōr′ə-tər) n. The administrative director of a museum, library, zoo, or other similar institution. [Middle English curatour, from Old French curateur, from Latin cūrātōr, overseer, manager, from cūrāre, to take care of, from cūra, care, CURE.] **—cu·ra·to·ri·al** adj. **—cu·ra·tor·ship** n.

curb (kûrb) n. Also British **kerb** (sense 2). 1. Anything that checks or restrains. 2. A concrete border or row of joined stones forming part of a gutter along the edge of a street. 3. A chain or strap serving, with the bit, to restrain a horse. 4. A **curb exchange** (see).
~tr.v. **curbed, curbing, curbs.** 1. To check, restrain, or control. 2. To place a curb on (a horse). 3. To lead (a dog) off the sidewalk into the gutter so that it can eliminate waste. —See Synonyms at **restrain.** [Middle English, from Old French courber, from Latin curvāre, bend, CURVE.] **—curb·er** n.

curb broker n. A broker on a curb exchange.

curb exchange n. A market dealing in securities not listed on the regular stock exchange. Also called "curb."

curb·ing (kûr′bĭng) n. 1. The material used to construct a curb. 2. A row of curbstones; a curb.

curb roof n. A roof having two slopes on each side, the lower slope being the steeper.

curb·stone (kûrb′stōn′) n. Also British **kerb·stone.** A stone or row of stones that constitutes a curb.

cur·cu·li·o (kər-kyōō′lē-ō′) n., pl. **-os.** Any of several American weevils of the family Curculionidae, many of which are destructive to fruit and other plants. [New Latin, from Latin curculiō†, weevil.]

cur·cu·ma (kûr′kyə-mə) n. Any of various Old World tropical plants of the genus Curcuma, having aromatic rootstocks. C. longa provides turmeric (see). [New Latin, from Arabic kurkum, saffron.]

curd (kûrd) n. 1. Often **curds.** The coagulated part of milk, formed by the action of rennet or acid and used especially to make cheese. 2. Any coagulation resembling this. 3. The edible whitish flower head of the cauliflower.
~v. **curded, curding, curds.** —tr. To form into curd; cause to thicken; curdle. —intr. To become curd; curdle; coagulate. [Middle English curd, crudde†.] **—curd·y** adj.

curd cheese n. A soft, mild cheese made from skimmed milk curds.

cur·dle (kûrd′l) v. **-dled, -dling, -dles.** —intr. 1. To congeal; become curd; coagulate. 2. To go sour. —tr. 1. To cause to congeal or change into curd. 2. To make sour. [Frequentative of CURD.]

cure (kyōōr) n. 1. Restoration of health; recovery from disease. 2. A method or course of medical treatment used to restore health. 3. a. An agent, such as a drug, that restores health; a remedy. b. A remedy for a harmful or troublesome condition: a cure for unemployment. 4. Ecclesiastical. Spiritual charge or care of souls, as of a priest for his congregation. Also called "cure of souls." 5. The office or duties of a curate. 6. The act or process of preserving a product such as fish, meat, or tobacco.
~v. **cured, curing, cures.** —tr. 1. To restore to health; heal. 2. To get rid of; remedy: cure an evil. 3. To preserve (meat, fish, or the like), as by salting or smoking. 4. To prepare, preserve, or finish (a substance) by a chemical or physical process. 5. To vulcanize (rubber). —intr. 1. To effect a cure or recovery. 2. To be prepared, preserved, or finished by a chemical or physical process. [Middle English, care, spiritual charge, cure, from Old French, from Latin cūra, care, charge, healing.] **—cure·less** adj. **—cur·er** n.

cu·ré (kyōō-rā′, kyōōr′ā′) n. French. A parish priest.

cure-all (kyōōr′ôl) n. That which cures all diseases or evils; a panacea.

cu·ret·tage (kyōōr′ə-täzh′, kyōō-rĕt′ĭj) n. Surgical scraping of a bodily cavity, as of the uterus, with a curette. Also called "curettement." See **D & C.** [French, from CURETTE.]

cu·rette, cu·ret (kyōō-rĕt′) n. A surgical instrument shaped like a scoop or spoon, used to remove dead tissue or growths from a

curassow The turkeylike curassow lives in flocks in the forests of tropical America. The birds are sometimes kept as pets by villagers.

bodily cavity. [French, from curer, to clean, from Old French, from Latin cūrāre, from cūra, CURE.]

cu·rette·ment (kyōō-rĕt′mənt) n. Curettage (see).

cur·few (kûr′fyōō) n. 1. An order or regulation enjoining most people or specific members of the population to retire from the streets or from public premises at a prescribed hour. 2. A similar medieval regulation requiring fires to be extinguished. 3. a. The period during which any such regulation is in effect. b. The signal, such as a bell, announcing a curfew. c. The hour at which a curfew comes into effect. [Middle English curfeu, coeverfu, from Old French cuevrefeu, "a covering of the fire" : co(u)vrir, to COVER + feu, fire, from Latin focus, hearth (see **fuel**).]

cu·ri·a (kyōōr′ē-ə) n., pl. **curiae** (kyōōr′ē-ē′). 1. a. The Senate or any of the various buildings in which it met in republican Rome. b. The place of assembly of high councils in various Italian cities under Roman administration. 2. The ensemble of central administrative and governmental services in imperial Rome. 3. Often **Curia.** The central administration governing the Roman Catholic Church. 4. In medieval Europe: a. A feudal assembly or council. b. A royal court of justice. [Latin cūria, curia, council.] **—cu·ri·al** adj.

cu·rie (kyōōr′ē, kyōō-rē′) n. Abbr. **Ci** A unit of radioactivity, the amount of any nuclide that undergoes exactly 3.7×10^{10} radioactive disintegrations per second. [After Marie CURIE.]

Cu·rie (kyōōr′ē), **Marie,** born Maria Sklodowska (1867-1934). Polish chemist, famous for her discovery of radium (1898). She studied science in Paris and in 1895 married **Pierre Curie** (1859-1906), a French professor of physics. From 1896 the Curies investigated radioactivity and laid the foundations of nuclear physics. They were awarded the Nobel Prize for physics jointly with Henri Becquerel (1903). After her husband's death, Marie Curie continued her work and was awarded a second Nobel Prize, this time in chemistry for her discovery of radium and polonium and their properties (1911).

Curie law n. The law that magnetic susceptibility varies inversely with thermodynamic temperature in a paramagnetic substance. Also called "Curie's law." [After Pierre CURIE.]

Curie point n. A transition temperature marking a change in the magnetic properties of a substance, especially the change from ferromagnetism to paramagnetism. Also called "Curie temperature." [After Pierre CURIE.]

Cu·rie-Weiss law (kyōōr′ē-wīs′, -vīs′, kyōō-rē′-) n. The law that the magnetic susceptibility of a paramagnetic substance above the Curie point varies inversely with the excess of temperature above that point. [After Pierre CURIE and Pierre Weiss (1865-1940), French physicist.]

cu·ri·o (kyōōr′ē-ō′) n., pl. **-os.** A curious or unusual object of art or bric-a-brac. [Short for CURIOSITY.]

cu·ri·o·sa (kyōōr′ē-ō′sə, -zə) pl.n. Books, writings, or objects dealing with unusual, especially pornographic, topics; erotica. [New Latin, from Latin cūriōsa, neuter plural of cūriōsus, CURIOUS.]

cu·ri·os·i·ty (kyōōr′ē-ŏs′ə-tē) n., pl. **-ties.** 1. a. A desire to know or learn, especially about something new or strange. b. Excessive interest or eagerness to know; inquisitiveness. 2. That which arouses interest, as by being novel or extraordinary. 3. Strangeness; novelty. Also used adjectivally: curiosity value.

cu·ri·ous (kyōōr′ē-əs) adj. 1. Eager to acquire information or knowledge. 2. Unduly inquisitive; prying; nosy. 3. Interesting because of novelty or rarity; singular; odd. 4. Obsolete. Accomplished with skill or ingenuity. [Middle English, from Old French curios, from Latin cūriōsus, careful, diligent, inquisitive, from cūra, care, CURE.] **—cu·ri·ous·ly** adv. **—cu·ri·ous·ness** n.

Usage: curious, inquisitive, snoopy, nosy, intrusive. These adjectives apply to persons who show a marked desire for information or knowledge. Curious more often implies a legitimate desire to enlarge one's knowledge, but can suggest a less commendable urge to concern oneself in others' affairs. Inquisitive frequently suggests excessive curiosity and the asking of many questions. Snoopy implies an unworthy motive and underhandedness in implementing it. Nosy suggests excessive curiosity and impertinence in an adult; applied to a child, it may refer less unfavorably to habitual curiosity. Intrusive stresses unwarranted and unwelcome concern with another's affairs.

Cu·ri·ti·ba (kōō-rē-tē′bä). Capital of Paraná state, in southeastern Brazil. It is a commercial and processing center for an expansive agricultural and ranching area. The city was founded in 1654 and grew rapidly in the late 19th and early 20th centuries when German, Italian, and Slavic immigrants began to develop the surrounding hinterland.

cu·ri·um (kyōōr′ē-əm) n. Symbol **Cm** A silvery, metallic, synthetic, radioactive, transuranic element having 13 isotopes with mass numbers from 238 to 250 and half-lives from 64 minutes to 16.4 million years. Atomic number 96. [New Latin, after Marie and Pierre CURIE.]

curl (kûrl) v. **curled, curling, curls.** —tr. 1. To twist (the hair, for example) into ringlets or coils. 2. To form into the spiral or curved shape of a ringlet or coil. —intr. 1. To form ringlets or coils. 2. To assume a spiral or curved shape. Often used with up. 3. To move in a curve or spiral. 4. To play the game of curling. **—curl up.** 1. To assume a position with the legs drawn up. 2. To make oneself comfortable.
~n. 1. Something with a spiral or coiled shape. 2. A coil or ringlet of hair. 3. a. The act of curling. b. The state of being curled. 4. Mathematics. The vector product of the del operator and a vector function. Compare **divergence.** [Middle English curlen, crullen,

from *crulle,* curly, from Middle Dutch.]

curl·er (kûr′lər) *n.* **1.** One that curls. **2.** A pin, roller, or the like on which hair is wound for curling. **3.** A player of the game of curling.

cur·lew (kûrl′yo͞o, kûr′lo͞o′) *n.* Any of several brownish, long-legged shore birds of the genus *Numenius,* having long, slender, downward-curving bills. [Middle English *curleu,* from Old French *courlieu* (imitative).]

Cur·ley (kûr′lē), **James Michael** (1874–1958). U.S. political leader. He was mayor of Boston (1914–18, 1922–26, 1930–34, 1946–50) and governor of Massachusetts (1935–37); he also served in the U.S. House of Representatives (1911–14, 1943–47). Widely known for his flamboyant control of Boston's political machine, he was the inspiration for Edwin O'Connor's novel *The Last Hurrah* (1956).

curl·i·cue, curl·y·cue (kûr′lĭ-kyo͞o′) *n.* A fancy twist or curl, such as a flourish made with a pen. [CURLY + CUE (rod).] **—curl·i·cued, curl·y·cued** *adj.*

curl·ing (kûr′lĭng) *n.* A game originating in Scotland and played on ice, in which two four-man teams slide heavy, flat, round stones *(curling stones)* toward a fixed mark in the center of a circle.

curling iron *n.* Also **curling irons.** A scissorlike metal device, usually rod-shaped, that is heated and used to curl individual locks of hair.

curl paper *n.* A piece of soft paper on which a lock of hair is rolled up in order to make it curl.

curl·y (kûr′lē) *adj.* **-ier, -iest. 1.** Having curls. **2.** Having the tendency to curl. **3.** Having a wavy grain. Said of wood: *curly maple.* **—curl·i·ly** *adv.* **—curl·i·ness** *n.*

curly top *n.* A disease of plants caused by a virus, *Ruga verrucosans,* and resulting in severe stunting of plants.

cur·mudg·eon (kər-mŭj′ən) *n.* **1.** A surly person. **2.** A miser. [16th century : origin obscure.] **—cur·mudg·eon·ly** *adj.*

cur·rach, cur·agh, cur·ragh (kûr′əKH, kûr′ə) *n. Scottish & Irish.* A kind of boat, a **coracle** *(see).* [Middle English *currok,* from Scottish Gaelic *curach* and Irish Gaelic *currach*; akin to Welsh *corwgl, cwrwgl*†.]

cur·rant (kûr′ənt) *n.* **1.** A small, dried seedless grape of the Mediterranean region, used in cooking. **2.** Any of various shrubs of the genus *Ribes,* bearing clusters of red, black, or greenish fruit. See **black currant, red currant. 3.** The small, sour fruit of any of these plants, used chiefly for making jam and jelly. [Middle English *raysons of coraunce,* from Norman French *raisins de corauntz,* grapes of CORINTH (from where they were originally exported).]

cur·ra·wong (kûr′ə-wông, -wŏng) *n.* Any Australian bird of the genus *Strepera,* usually having a black plumage with white markings. Also called "bell magpie." [From a native Australian name.]

cur·ren·cy (kûr′ən-sē) *n., pl.* **-cies. 1.** *Abbr.* **cur.** Any form of money in actual use as a medium of exchange. **2.** A passing from hand to hand; circulation. **3.** Common acceptance; prevalence. [Medieval Latin *currentia,* "a flowing," from Latin *currēns* (stem *current-*), present participle of *currere,* to run. See **current.**] See feature, next page.

cur·rent (kûr′ənt) *adj.* **1. a.** Belonging to the time now passing; now in progress. **b.** Most recent: *the current issue.* **2.** Passing from one to another; circulating, as money does. **3.** Commonly accepted; prevalent. —See Synonyms at **prevailing.**

∼*n.* **1.** A steady and smooth onward movement, as of water. **2.** The part of any body of liquid or gas that has a continuous movement in a specific direction: *a river current.* **3.** A general tendency, movement, or course. **4.** *Symbol* **i, I** *Electricity.* **a.** A flow of electric charge. **b.** The amount of electric charge flowing past a specific circuit point per unit time. In this sense, also called "electric current." —See Synonyms at **tendency.** [Middle English *curraunt,* from Old French *corant,* present participle of *courre,* to run, from Latin *currere.*] **—cur·rent·ly** *adv.* **—cur·rent·ness** *n.*

current assets *pl.n.* Cash or other assets convertible into cash at short notice.

current bedding *n.* **Cross bedding** *(see).*

current density *n. Symbol* **J 1.** *Electricity.* The ratio of the magnitude of current flowing in a conductor to the cross-sectional area perpendicular to the current flow. **2.** *Physics.* The number of subatomic particles per unit time crossing a unit area in a designated plane perpendicular to the direction of motion of the particles.

current events *pl.n.* **1.** Topical news, usually of serious issues such as politics or international affairs. **2.** Discussion of such news, as on television. Also used adjectivally: *current events programs.* Also called "current affairs."

current ratio *n.* The arithmetic ratio of current assets to liabilities.

cur·ri·cle (kûr′ĭ-kəl) *n.* A light, open two-wheeled vehicle, drawn by two horses abreast. [Latin *curriculum,* a running, racecourse, racing chariot. See **curriculum.**]

cur·ric·u·lum (kə-rĭk′yə-ləm) *n., pl.* **-la** (-lə) or **-lums. 1.** All the courses of study offered by an educational institution. **2.** A particular course of study, often in a special field. [New Latin, from Latin, a running, course, from *currere,* to run.] **—cur·ric·u·lar** *adj.*

cur·ric·u·lum vi·tae (kə-rĭk′yə-ləm vī′tē, ko͞o-rĭk′o͝o-lo͝om wē′tī′) *n., pl.* **curricula vitae.** *Abbr.* **c.v.** A short résumé of one's educational background and career, as for a prospective employer. [Latin, the course of one's life.]

currie. Variant of **curry.**

cur·ri·er (kûr′ē-ər) *n.* One who curries something, especially leather. [Middle English *curr(e)iour,* from Old French, from Latin *coriārius,* a tanner, from *corium,* leather.]

Cur·ri·er (kŭr′ē-ər, kŭr′-), **Nathaniel** (1813–88). U.S. lithographer. With his business partner James Merritt Ives, he produced more than 7,000 prints depicting American life and tradition. The prints, each signed "Currier & Ives," are now valued collector's items.

cur·ri·er·y (kûr′ē-ə-rē) *n., pl.* **-ies.** The trade, work, or shop of a leather currier.

cur·rish (kûr′ĭsh) *adj.* Of or like a cur; snarling; bad-tempered. **—cur·rish·ly** *adv.*

cur·ry¹ (kûr′ē) *tr.v.* **-ried, -rying, -ries. 1.** To groom (a horse) with a currycomb. **2.** To prepare (tanned hides) for use by soaking, coloring, or other processes. **—curry favor.** To seek or gain favor by fawning or flattery. [Middle English *curreien,* from Old French *co(n)reer,* to prepare, equip, from Vulgar Latin *conrēdāre* (unattested) : *com-* (intensive), with + *rēdāre* (unattested), to prepare, from Germanic. Sense 2 is partly a back-formation from CURRIER.]

curry² *n., pl.* **-ries.** Also **cur·rie. 1.** A dish that originated in India, consisting of meat, fish, or vegetables prepared and cooked in a sauce made of various spices that give it a hot or piquant flavor. **2.** Curry powder or curry paste. **3.** A dish seasoned with curry powder or curry paste.

∼*tr.v.* **curried, -rying, -ries. 1.** To make a curry of. **2.** To season with curry. [Tamil *kari,* sauce.]

Cur·ry (kûr′ē), **John Anthony** (1949–). British ice skater, who brought the expressiveness of ballet to his art. He won the Olympic, European, and World figure-skating championships in a single season (1976). Curry has since toured extensively with his ice-dancing companies.

Curry, John Steuart (1897–1946). U.S. painter. He is noted for his vigorous depictions of the rural American scene, especially for his murals and oil paintings of Kansas, including *Baptism in Kansas* and *Tornado over Kansas.*

cur·ry·comb (kûr′ē-kōm′) *n.* A comb with metal teeth, used for grooming horses.

∼*tr.v.* **currycombed, -combing, -combs.** To groom with a currycomb.

curry paste *n.* A condiment prepared from pungent spices, as in curry powder, blended with oil, tomatoes, onions, and the like.

curry powder *n.* A blended condiment prepared from turmeric and other pungent spices such as cumin, coriander, and chili.

curse (kûrs) *n.* **1.** An appeal to a supernatural power for evil or injury to befall someone or something. **2.** The evil or injury thus invoked. **3.** Someone or something accursed. **4.** That which brings or causes evil; a scourge. **5.** Any profane oath or obscenity. **6.** *Ecclesiastical.* A censure, ban, or anathema. **7.** *Informal.* Menstruation. Preceded by *the.*

∼*v.* **cursed** or **curst, cursing, curses.** —*tr.* **1.** To invoke evil, calamity, or injury upon; damn. **2.** To swear at; abuse profanely. **3.** To bring harm upon; afflict. **4.** *Ecclesiastical.* To put under ban or anathema; excommunicate. —*intr.* To utter curses; swear. [Middle English *curs(e),* Old English *curs*†.] **—curs·er** *n.*

curs·ed (kûr′sĭd, kûrst) *adj.* Also **curst** (kûrst). **1.** Deserving to be cursed; wicked; detestable. **2.** Damned; under a curse. **—curs·ed·ly** *adv.* **—curs·ed·ness** *n.*

cur·sive (kûr′sĭv) *adj.* Designating writing or printing in which the letters are joined together; flowing.

∼*n.* **1.** A cursive character or letter. **2.** A manuscript written in cursive characters. **3.** *Printing.* A kind of type that imitates handwriting. [Medieval Latin *(scripta) cursīva,* "flowing (script)," from Latin *cursus,* past participle of *currere,* to run.]

cur·sor (kûr′sər) *n.* **1.** The point of a measuring or calculating instrument that slides; especially, the movable window on a slide rule. **2.** A visual indicator, such as a movable point of light, that is used to indicate a specific position on a visual display unit, such as where a deletion or insertion is to be made. [Latin, "runner," from *currere* (past participle stem *curs-*), to run.]

cur·so·ri·al (kûr-sôr′ē-əl, -sōr′ē-əl) *adj. Zoology.* Adapted to or specialized for running: *cursorial birds; cursorial legs.* [Late Latin *cursōrius,* of running. See **cursory.**]

cur·so·ry (kûr′sə-rē) *adj.* Hasty and superficial; not thorough. See Synonyms at **superficial.** [Late Latin *cursōrius,* of running, from Latin *cursor,* a runner, from *cursus.* See **cursive.**] **—cur·so·ri·ly** *adv.* **—cur·so·ri·ness** *n.*

curst. 1. Variant of **cursed. 2.** Alternate past tense and past participle of **curse.**

curt (kûrt) *adj.* **1.** Rudely brief or abrupt, as in speech or manner. **2.** Terse; concise. **3.** Shortened. —See Synonyms at **gruff.** [Latin *curtus,* cut short.] **—curt·ly** *adv.* **—curt·ness** *adj.*

cur·tail (kər-tāl′) *tr.v.* **-tailed, -tailing, -tails.** To reduce by or as if by cutting short. [Variant of obsolete *curtal,* to dock the tail of a horse, from CURTAL.] **—cur·tail·er** *n.* **—cur·tail·ment** *n.*

curtail step *n.* The widened step or steps at the foot of a flight of stairs. [Origin obscure.]

cur·tain (kûrt′n) *n.* **1.** A piece of cloth or similar material hanging in a window or other opening as a decoration, shade, or screen. **2.** *Theater.* **a.** A hanging barrier that rises at the beginning of a scene and falls at the end of a scene. **b.** A line, speech, or situation in a play that occurs at the very end or just before the curtain falls. **3.** The part of a rampart or parapet connecting two bastions or gates. **4.** Any barrier to visibility: *a curtain of fog.* **5.** Any barrier, such as a restriction on communication. **6. curtains.** *Informal.* The end; ruin.

∼*tr.v.* **curtained, -taining, -tains. 1.** To shut off with or as if with a curtain. Often used with *off.* **2.** To provide with curtains. [Middle English *curtin(e),* from Old French, from Late Latin *cortīna,* enclo-

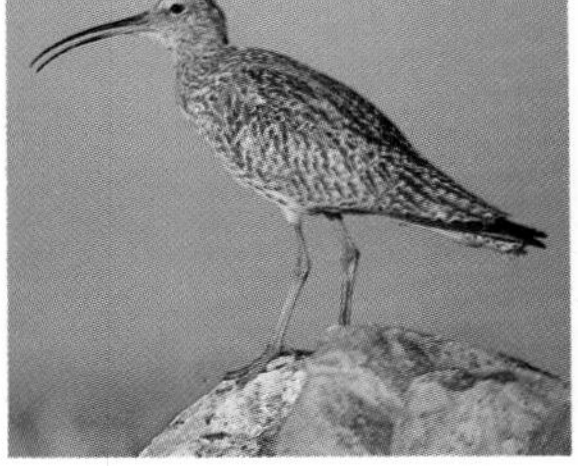

curlew *A common wader found worldwide on marshes and coastal mud flats. It feeds chiefly on mollusks and small crabs.*

currency

COUNTRY	BASIC UNIT	SUBDIVISION	ABBREV.
Afghanistan	afghani	100 puls	Af.
Albania	lek	100 quintars	Lk.
Algeria	dinar	100 centimes	D.A.
Angola	new kwanza	100 lwei	Kz.
Antigua and Barbuda	E. Caribbean dollar	100 cents	E.C. $
Argentina	peso	100 centavos	Arg. $
Armenia	tram	100 luma	
Australia	dollar	100 cents	A. $
Austria	schilling	100 groschen	S.
Azerbaijan	CIS* rouble	100 kopecks	Rbl.
Bahamas	dollar	100 cents	Ba. $
Bahrain	dinar	1,000 fils	B.D.
Bangladesh	taka	100 poisha	Tk.
Barbados	dollar	100 cents	Bds. $
Belarus	CIS* rouble	100 kopecks	Rbl.
Belgium	franc	100 centimes	B. Fr.
Belize	dollar	100 cents	Bz. $
Benin	CFAF**	100 centimes	CFAF
Bermuda	dollar	100 cents	Ber. $
Bhutan	ngultrum	100 tikchungs or N. chetrum	Nu.
Bolivia	boliviano	100 centavos	Bs.
Bosnia and Hercegovina	Yugoslav dinar	100 para	Din.
Botswana	pula	100 thebe	P.
Brazil	cruziero	100 centavos	Cr.
Brunei	dollar	100 cents	Br. $
Bulgaria	lev	100 stotinki	Lv.
Burkina Faso	CFAF**	100 centimes	CFAF.
Burundi	franc	100 centimes	Bu. Fr.
Cameroon	CFAF**	—	CFAF.
Canada	dollar	100 cents	Can. $
Cape Verde	escudo	100 centavos	C.V. Esc.
Cayman Islands	dollar	100 cents	C.I. $.
Central African Republic	CFAF**	100 centimes	CFAF.
Chad	CFAF**	—	CFAF.
Chile	peso	100 centavos	Ch. $
China	yuan	10 jiao or 100 fen	Y.
Colombia	peso	100 centavos	Col. $
Comoros	franc	100 centimes	C F.
Congo	CFAF**	—	CFAF.
Costa Rica	colón	100 céntimos	C.R. ₡
Croatia	dinar		
Cuba	peso	100 centavos	Cub. $
Cyprus	pound	100 cents	C. £
Czechoslovakia	koruna	100 haleru	Kčs.
Denmark	krone	100 øre	D. Kr.
Djibouti	franc	100 centimes	Dj. Fr.
Dominica	E. Caribbean dollar	100 cents	E.C. $
Dominican Republic	peso	100 centavos	R.D. $
Ecuador	sucre	100 centavos	Su.
Egypt	pound	100 piasters	£.E.
El Salvador	colón	100 centavos	E.S. ₡
Equatorial Guinea	franc	100 centimes	CFAF
Estonia	kroon	100 senti	
Ethiopia	birr	100 cents	Br.
Fiji	dollar	100 cents	$ F.
Finland	markka	100 penniä	F. Mk.
France	franc	100 centimes	Fr.
Gabon	CFAF**	—	CFAF.
Gambia	dalasi	100 bututs	Di.
Georgia	CIS* rouble	100 kopecks	Rbl.
Germany	deutsche mark	100 pfennig	DM
Ghana	cedi	100 pesewas	₡
Greece	drachma	100 lepta	Dr.
Grenada	E. Caribbean dollar	100 cents	E.C. $
Guatemala	quetzal	100 centavos	Q.
Guinea	franc	100 cauris	F.G.
Guinea-Bissau	peso	100 centavos	P.G.
Guyana	dollar	100 cents	G. $

COUNTRY	BASIC UNIT	SUBDIVISION	ABBREV.
Haiti	gourde	100 centimes	Gde.
Honduras	lempira	100 centavos	L.
Hong Kong	dollar	100 cents	H.K. $
Hungary	forint	100 fillér	Ft.
Iceland	króna	100 aurar	IS. Kr.
India	rupee	100 paise	I.R.
Indonesia	rupiah	100 sen	Rp.
Iran	rial	100 dinars	Rl.
Iraq	dinar	1,000 fils	I.D.
Ireland, Republic of	pound or punt Eirennach	100 pence or pighne	£ Ir.
Israel	new shekel	100 new agorot	NIS.
Italy	lira	100 centesimi	L IT.
Ivory Coast	CFAF**	100 centimes	CFAF.
Jamaica	dollar	100 cents	J. $
Japan	yen	100 sen	¥
Jordan	dinar	1,000 fils	J.D.
Kampuchea	riel	100 sen	K. RL.
Kazakhstan	CIS* rouble	100 kopecks	Rbl.
Kenya	shilling	100 cents	K. Sh.
Kuwait	dinar	1,000 fils	K.D.
Kyrgystan	CIS* rouble	100 kopecks	Rbl.
Laos	kip	100 at(s)	Kp.
Latvia	CIS* rouble	100 kopecks	Rbl.
Lebanon	pound	100 piasters	L.£.
Lesotho	loti (plural, maloti)	100 lisente	Lo. or Mo.
Liberia	dollar	100 cents	Lib.$
Libya	dinar	1,000 dirhams	L.D.
Lithuania	CIS* rouble	100 kopecks	Rbl.
Luxembourg	franc	100 centimes	L. Fr.
Madagascar	franc	—	Mg. Fr.
Malawi	kwacha	100 tambala	M. K.
Malaysia	ringgit	100 sen	Ma. $
Maldives	rufiyaa	100 laaris	Mv. R.
Mali	CFAF**	100 centimes	M. Fr.
Malta	Maltese pound	100 cents	L.M.
Mauritania	ouguiya	5 khoums	U.
Mauritius	rupee	100 cents	M.R.
Mexico	peso	100 centavos	Mex. $
Moldova	CIS* rouble	100 kopecks	Rbl.
Mongolia	tugrik	100 möngö	Tug.
Morocco	dirham	100 centimes	Dh.
Mozambique	metical	100 centavos	Mt.
Myanmar	kyat	100 pyas	
Namibia	rand	100 cents	R.
Nepal	rupee	100 paisa	N.R.
Netherlands	guilder or florin	100 cents	F.
Netherlands Antilles	guilder or florin	100 cents	N.A. f.
New Zealand	dollar	100 cents	N.Z. $
Nicaragua	córdoba oro	100 centavos	C. $
Niger	CFAF**	100 centimes	CFAF.
Nigeria	naira	100 kobo	₦.
North Korea	won	100 jun	N.K.W.
Norway	krone	100 øre	N. Kr.
Oman	rial Omani	1,000 baiza	O.R.
Pakistan	rupee	100 paisa	P.R.
Panama	balboa	100 centésimos	B.
Papua New Guinea	kina	100 toea	Ka.
Paraguay	guaraní	100 céntimos	₲.
Peru	nuevo sol	100 centavos	N.S.
Philippines	peso	100 centavos	P.P.
Poland	zloty	100 groszy	Zl.
Portugal	escudo	100 centavos	Esc.
Qatar	Qatar riyal	100 dirhams	Q.R.
Romania	leu (plural, lei)	100 bani	L.
Russia	CIS* rouble	100 kopecks	Rbl.
Rwanda	franc	100 centimes	R.F.

COUNTRY	BASIC UNIT	SUBDIVISION	ABBREV.
St. Lucia	E. Carib. dollar	100 cents	E.C. $
St. Vincent and the Grenadines	E. Caribbean dollar	—	E.C. $
São Tomé and Principe	dobra	100 centavos	Db.
Saudi Arabia	riyal or rial	100 halalahs	SRl.
Senegal	CFAF**	100 centimes	CFAF.
Seychelles	rupee	100 cents	S.R.
Sierra Leone	leone	100 cents	Le.
Singapore	dollar	100 cents	S. $
Slovenia	tolar		
Solomon Islands	dollar	100 cents	S.I. $
Somalia	shilling	100 cents	So. Sh.
South Africa	rand	100 cents	R.
South Korea	won	100 chon	S.K. W.
Spain	peseta	100 céntimos	Pta.
Sri Lanka	rupee	100 cents	S.L. R.
Sudan	dinar	10 pounds	Sd. D.
Surinam	guilder	100 cents	Sf.
Swaziland	lilangeni	100 cents	E.
Sweden	krona	100 öre	S. Kr.
Switzerland	franc	100 centimes or rappen	S. Fr.
Syria	pound	100 piasters	£.S.
Taiwan	New Taiwan dollar	100 cents	N.T. $
Tajikistan	CIS* rouble	100 kopecks	Rbl.
Tanzania	shilling	100 cents	T. Sh.
Thailand	baht	100 satang	Bt.
Togo	CFAF**	100 centimes	CFAF.
Tonga	pa'anga	100 seniti	T$
Trinidad and Tobago	dollar	100 cents	T.T. $
Tunisia	dinar	1,000 millièmes	T.D.
Turkey	lira	100 kurus or piasters	L.T.
Turkmenistan	CIS* rouble	100 kopecks	Rbl.
Uganda	shilling	100 cents	U. Sh.
Ukraine	CIS* rouble	100 kopecks	Rbl.
United Arab Emirates	dirham	100 fils	U.A.E.D.
United Kingdom	pound	100 pence	£
United States	dollar	100 cents	$
Uruguay	nuevo peso	100 centésimos	N.Ur. $
Uzbekistan	CIS* rouble	100 kopecks	Rbl.
Vanuatu	vatu	100 cents	VT.
Venezuela	bolívar	100 céntimos	Bs.
Vietnam	dong	10 hao or 100 xu	D.
Western Samoa	talà or dollar	100 sene or cents	W.S. $
Yemen	riyal	100 fils	Y.R.
Yugoslavia	dinar	100 para	Din.
Zaire	zaire	100 makuta	Z.
Zambia	kwacha	100 ngwee	K.
Zimbabwe	dollar	100 cents	Z. $.

* Commonwealth of Independent States

** Communauté Financière Africaine Franc (African Financial Community Franc)

USING FOREIGN CURRENCY AT HOME *Some smaller countries use other currencies besides their own. For instance, the Solomon Islands in the southwest Pacific use as legal tender the Australian dollar as well as their own. A few sovereign states use only foreign money—in San Marino and Vatican City, for example, the currency in use is the Italian lira.*

sure, curtain, translation of Greek *aulaia,* from *aulē,* court.]

curtain call *n.* The appearance of a performer or performers at the end of a performance in response to applause.

curtain lecture *n.* A private reprimand given to a husband by his wife, so called from the curtained beds in which such scoldings once took place.

curtain raiser *n.* **1.** A short entertainment presented before the principal dramatic production. **2.** Any preliminary event.

curtain speech *n.* **1.** A talk given in front of the curtain at the conclusion of a theatrical performance. **2.** The final speech of a play or of an act of a play.

cur·tal (kûr′təl) *n. Obsolete.* **1.** An animal with a docked tail. **2.** Anything cut short or docked.
~adj. Obsolete. **1.** Cut short or docked, as an animal's tail may be. **2.** Wearing a short frock: *a curtal friar.* [Old French *courtault,* horse with a cropped tail or mane, from *court,* short, from Latin *curtus,* shortened.]

curtal ax *n. Archaic.* A cutlass. [Variant (influenced by CURTAL and AX) of earlier *curtelace, coutelace,* CUTLASS.]

cur·tate (kûr′tāt′) *adj.* Shortened; abbreviated. [Latin *curtātus,* past participle of *curtāre,* to shorten, from *curtus,* short, CURT.]

cur·te·sy (kûr′tə-sē) *n., pl.* **-sies.** The life tenure which by common law is held by a man over the property of his deceased wife if children with rights of inheritance were born during the marriage. [Middle English *courteisie,* curtesy, COURTESY.]

cur·ti·lage (kûr′tə-lĭj) *n. Law.* The enclosed land surrounding a house or dwelling. [Middle English, from Old French *courtillage,* from *courtil,* little court, diminutive of *cort,* COURT.]

Cur·tiss (kûr′tĭs), **Glenn Hammond** (1878–1930). U.S. aviation pioneer. He developed and refined the first plane to complete a one-kilometer flight (1908), the first seaplane (1911), and the aileron (1911). He founded the Curtiss Aeroplane & Motor Company that produced thousands of biplanes for army and navy flight schools.

curt·sy (kûrt′sē) *n., pl.* **-sies.** Also **curt·sey,** *pl.* **-seys.** A gesture of respect or reverence made by women by bending the knees with one foot forward and lowering the body.
~intr.v. **curtsied, -sying, -sies.** Also **curt·sey, -seyed, -seying, -seys.** To make a curtsy. [Variant of COURTESY.]

cu·rule (kyŏŏr′ōōl) *adj.* Privileged to sit in a curule chair; of superior rank. [Latin *curūlis,* "of a chariot," of a curule chair (originally a throne mounted on a chariot), from *currus,* a chariot, from *currere,* to run.]

curule chair *n.* A seat with heavy, curved legs and no back, reserved for the use of the highest officials in ancient Rome. Also called "curule seat."

cur·va·ceous (kûr-vā′shəs) *adj.* **1.** Curving. **2.** *Informal.* Of, pertaining to, or designating a woman having a full or voluptuous figure; shapely. [CURV(E) + -ACEOUS.] **—cur·va·ceous·ly** *adv.*

cur·va·ture (kûr′və-chŏŏr) *n.* **1. a.** An act of curving. **b.** The state of being curved. **2.** *Mathematics.* **a.** The ratio of the change in tangent inclination over a given arc to the length of the arc. Also called "average curvature." **b.** The limit of this ratio as the length of the arc approaches zero. **3.** *Medicine.* A curving or bending, especially an abnormal one: *curvature of the spine.* [Latin *curvātūra,* from *curvātus,* past participle of *curvāre,* to bend, from *curvus,* curved.]

curve (kûrv) *n.* **1. a.** A line that deviates from straightness in a smooth, continuous fashion. **b.** A surface that deviates from a flat plane in a smooth, continuous fashion. **2.** A curved part, object, or region, such as a part of the human body. **3. a.** A line representing data on a graph. **b.** A trend derived from or as if from such a graph. **4.** *Mathematics.* **a.** The graph of a function on a coordinate plane. **b.** The intersection of two surfaces in three dimensions.
~v. **curved, curving, curves.** *—intr.* To move in or take the shape of a curve. *—tr.* To cause to curve. [From earlier *curve (line),* "curved (line)," from Middle English *curve,* curved, from Latin *curvus.*] **—curv·ed·ly** *adv.* **—curv·ed·ness** *n.* **—curv·y** *adj.*

curve ball *n.* **1.** *Baseball.* A pitched ball that veers or breaks to the left when thrown with the right hand and to the right when thrown with the left hand. **2.** *Slang.* A trick or deception.

cur·vet (kûr′vĭt) *n. Dressage.* A light leap by a horse, in which both hind legs leave the ground just before the forelegs are set down.
~v. **curvetted** or **-veted, -vetting** or **-veting, -vets.** *—intr.* **1.** To leap in a curvet. **2.** To prance; frolic. *—tr.* To cause to leap in a curvet. [Italian *corvetta,* "curving leap," from Old Italian, diminutive of *corva,* a curve, from Latin *curva,* feminine of *curvus,* curved, bent.]

cur·vi·lin·e·ar (kûr′və-lĭn′ē-ər) *adj.* Also **cur·vi·lin·e·al** (-əl). Formed, bounded, or characterized by curved lines. [Latin *curvus,* curved (see **curve**) + LINEAR.] **—cur·vi·lin·e·ar·ly** *adv.*

Cur·wen (kûr′wən), **John** (1816–80). British educator. He devised a method of teaching music by using the tonic sol-fa system of notation invented (*c.* 1812) by another music teacher, Sarah Ann Glover (1785–1867).

cus·cus (kŭs′kəs) *n.* Any of several marsupials of the genus *Phalanger,* of New Guinea and adjacent areas, having protruding eyes, a yellow nose, and a long, prehensile tail. [New Latin, probably from the native New Guinean name.]

cu·sec (kyōō′sĕk) *n.* A unit of volumetric flow of liquids, equal to one cubic foot per second. [CU(BIC) + SEC(OND).]

Cush[1] (kŭsh, kŏŏsh). The eldest son of Ham. Genesis 10:6.

Cush[2], **Kush** (kŭsh, kŏŏsh). **1.** A legendary ancient region of northeastern Africa where the Biblical descendants of Cush settled, often identified with Ethiopia. **2.** An ancient kingdom of Nubia in northern Sudan. It flourished from the 11th century B.C. until the 4th century A.D. when its capital, Merowe, fell to the Ethiopians.

cu·shaw (kə-shô′) *n.* A squash, *Cucurbita moschata,* having variably shaped, often crook-necked fruit. [Earlier *coscushaw,* from some Algonquian language of North Carolina or Virginia.]

Cush·ing (kŏŏsh′ĭng), **Caleb** (1800–79). U.S. politician, lawyer, and diplomat. As special envoy to China (1843–45), he negotiated a treaty that opened five ports to U.S. trade and established the principle of extraterritoriality for U.S. citizens in China. He later served as U.S. attorney general (1853–57) and minister to Spain (1874–77).

Cush·ing's disease (kŏŏsh′ĭngz) *n.* A disease resulting from excess corticosteroid hormones in the body, characterized by obesity, high blood pressure, and loss of minerals from the bones. Also called "Cushing's syndrome." [After Harvey *Cushing* (1869–1939), U.S. neurologist.]

cush·ion (kŏŏsh′ən) *n.* **1.** A pad or pillow with a soft filling, used for resting or reclining against or on. **2.** Anything resilient used as a rest, support, or shock absorber. **3.** Something that provides protection against harmful or distressing effects: *Her savings were a cushion against inflation.* **4.** The rim bordering the playing area on a billiard table. **5.** A pillow used in lacemaking. **6.** An **air cushion** *(see).*
~tr.v. **cushioned, -ioning, -ions.** **1.** To provide with a cushion. **2.** To place or seat on a cushion. **3.** To cover or hide with or as if with a cushion. **4.** To protect against or absorb the shock or adverse effects of something. [Middle English *cuisshen,* from Old French *coissin,* from Vulgar Latin *coxīnus* (unattested), "hip rest," cushion, from Latin *coxa,* hip.] **—cush·ion·y** *adj.*

Cush·it·ic, Kush·it·ic (kŏŏ-shĭt′ĭk) *n.* A group of Hamitic languages, including Somali and other languages spoken in Somalia and Ethiopia.
~adj. Of or pertaining to this group of languages.

Cush·man (kŏŏsh′mən), **Charlotte Saunders** (1816–76). U.S. actress. She made her debut in Boston in 1835, then appeared in New York and Philadelphia (1837–44) before traveling to London, where she disciplined and polished her talents as an actress who had the ability to move audiences passionately. She lived in Europe until 1870, but returned frequently to tour America, where she was acclaimed as the leading actress of her day.

cush·y (kŏŏsh′ē) *adj.* **-ier, -iest.** *Slang.* Comfortable; undemanding: *a cushy job.* [Anglo-Indian, from Hindi *khūsh,* from Persian *khōsh*†, pleasant.]

cusk (kŭsk) *n., pl.* **cusk** or **cusks.** A food fish, *Brosme brosme,* of North Atlantic coastal waters. [Probably variant of earlier *tusk,* from Norn.]

cusk eel *n.* Any of various eellike, chiefly marine fishes of the family Ophidiidae.

cusp (kŭsp) *n.* **1.** A point or pointed end. **2.** *Anatomy.* **a.** A prominence or projection on the chewing surface of a tooth. **b.** A fold or flap of a heart valve. **3.** *Geometry.* A point at which a curve crosses itself and at which the two tangents to the curve coincide. In this sense, also called "spinode." **4.** *Architecture.* The pointed figure formed by two intersecting arcs or foils. **5.** *Astronomy.* Either point of: **a.** A crescent moon. **b.** A satellite or inferior planet in a similar phase. **6.** *Astrology.* The transitional first or last part of a house or sign. [Latin *cuspis*†, a point, spear.]

cus·pate (kŭs′pāt) *adj.* Also **cus·pat·ed** (-pāt′ĭd), **cusped** (kŭspt). **1.** Having a cusp or cusps. **2.** Shaped like a cusp.

cus·pid (kŭs′pĭd) *n.* A tooth having one point; a canine tooth. [Back-formation from BICUSPID.]

cus·pi·date (kŭs′pə-dāt) *adj.* Also **cus·pi·dat·ed** (-dā′tĭd), **cus·pi·dal** (-dəl). **1.** Having a cusp or cusps. **2.** *Biology.* Terminating in or tipped with a sharp point: *a cuspidate leaf.* [Latin *cuspidātus,* from the past participle of *cuspidāre,* to make pointed, from *cuspis* (stem *cuspid-*), point, CUSP.]

cus·pi·da·tion (kŭs′pə-dā′shən) *n. Architecture.* Decoration with cusps.

cus·pi·dor (kŭs′pə-dôr′) *n.* A **spittoon** *(see).* [Portuguese, from *cuspir,* to spit, from Latin *conspuere,* to spit upon : *com-* (intensive), with + *spuere,* to spit.]

cuss (kŭs) *v.* **cussed, cussing, cusses.** *Informal.* *—intr.* To curse. *—tr.* To shout curses at.
~n. Informal. **1.** A curse. **2.** An odd or perverse creature. [Variant of CURSE.]

cuss·ed (kŭs′ĭd) *adj. Informal.* **1.** Cursed. **2.** Perverse; obstinate. **3.** Irritating; vexatious. **—cuss·ed·ly** *adv.* **—cuss·ed·ness** *n.*

cus·tard (kŭs′tərd) *n.* **1. a.** A thick, sweet, yellow sauce for desserts and puddings, made of sweetened milk and eggs, heated together and sometimes thickened with cornflour. **b.** A similar preparation made with sweetened milk and custard powder. **2.** A dessert of milk, sugar, sometimes cream, eggs, and usually flavoring, baked until set. [Middle English *crustade,* a kind of pie, from Norman French *crustade* (unattested), from *crute,* CRUST.]

custard apple *n.* **1.** A tropical American tree, *Annona reticulata,* bearing large, heart-shaped fruit. **2.** The fruit of this tree, having edible, fleshy pulp. **3.** Any of several related trees or fruit; especially, the **papaw** *(see).* [So called because its pulp resembles custard.]

Cus·ter (kŭs′tər), **George Armstrong** (1839–76). U.S. cavalry officer, made a brigadier general at the age of 23. Facing Sioux opposition under Sitting Bull and Crazy Horse, he rashly divided his force and led a party of 264 men to annihilation by an over-

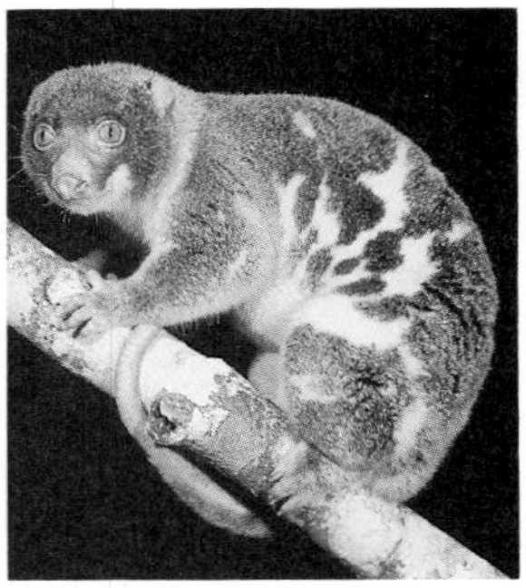

cuscus *Up to 60 centimeters (2 feet) long, these monkeylike marsupials live in the forests of New Guinea, northern Australia, and the Indonesian island of Sulawesi (Celebes).*

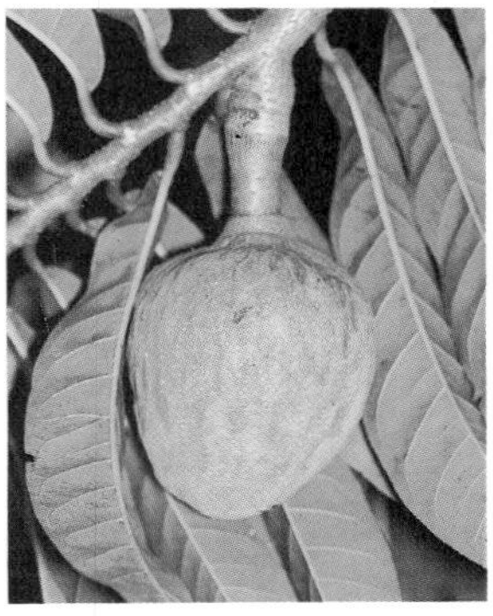

custard apple *The fruit of a group of trees native to the American tropics. The yellow pulp looks and tastes like custard.*

PRONUNCIATION KEY

ă, pat; ā, pay; âr, care;
ä, father, are; b, bib;
ch, church; d, deed; ĕ, pet;
ē, be; f, fife; g, gag; h, hat;
hw, which; ĭ, pit; ī, pie;
îr, pier; j, judge; k, kick;
l, lid, needle; m, mum;
n, no, sudden; ng, thing;
ŏ, pot; ō, toe; ô, paw, for;
oi, noise; ou, out; ŏŏ, book;
ōō, boot; p, pop; r, roar;
s, sauce; sh, ship, dish;
t, tight; th, thin, path;
th, this, bathe; ŭ, cut; ûr, fur;
v, valve; w, with; y, yes;
z, zebra, size; zh, vision;
ə, about, item, edible,
gallop, circus, peaceful

IN FOREIGN WORDS:

à, *Fr.* ami; œ, *Fr.* feu, *Ger.* schön; ü, *Fr.* tu, *Ger.* über;
KH, *Ger.* ich, *Scot.* loch;
N, *Fr.* bon; y′, *Fr.* Compiègne

STRESS MARKS:

Primary stress: ′
in·cite′ (ĭn-sīt′)
Secondary stress: ′
in′sight′ (ĭn′sīt′)

whelmingly larger Indian force at Little Bighorn (1876). The site of his defeat is marked by the Custer Battlefield National Monument, a national cemetery.

cus·to·di·al (kŭs-tō′dē-əl) *adj.* **1.** Of or pertaining to guarding or guardianship. **2.** Involving or necessitating imprisonment.

cus·to·di·an (kûs-tō′dē-ən) *n.* **1.** One who has charge of something; a warder or caretaker. **2.** A keeper, especially of a public building, art collection, or the like. **—cus·to·di·an·ship** *n.*

cus·to·dy (kûs′tə-dē) *n., pl.* **-dies. 1.** The act or right of guarding, especially such a right granted by a court to a guardian of a minor. **2.** The state of being kept or guarded. **3.** The state of being detained or held under guard, especially by the police. [Middle English *custodie,* from Latin *custōdia,* from CUSTOS.]

cus·tom (kûs′təm) *n.* **1.** A practice followed as a matter of course among a people or society; a conventional mode or form of action. **2.** A habitual practice of an individual. **3.** *Law.* A common tradition or usage so long established that it has the force or validity of law. **4. a.** Habitual patronage, as of a store or business. **b.** Collectively, those who patronize a store or business; customers. **5.** Tribute, service, or rent paid by a feudal tenant to his lord. —See Synonyms at **habit.**

~adj. Made to the specifications of an individual purchaser: *a custom car.* [Middle English *custume,* from Old French *costume,* from Latin *consuētūdō,* a being accustomed, from *consuēscere,* to accustom : *com-* (intensive), with + *suēscere,* to become accustomed.]

cus·tom·a·ble (kûs′təm-ə-bəl) *adj.* Subject to tariffs.

cus·tom·ar·y (kûs′tə-mĕr′ē) *adj.* **1.** Commonly practiced or used as a matter of course; usual. **2.** Based on custom or tradition rather than written law or contract. —See Synonyms at **usual.**

~n., pl. **customaries.** A written record of the customary laws of a community. **—cus·tom·ar·i·ly** *adv.* **—cus·tom·ar·i·ness** *n.*

cus·tom-built (kŭs′təm-bĭlt′) *adj.* Built according to the specifications of the buyer.

cus·tom·er (kŭs′təm-ər) *n.* **1.** A person or organization that buys goods or services. **2.** *Informal.* A person with whom one must deal: *a tough customer.*

custom·house (kŭs′təm-hous′) *n., pl.* **-houses** (-hou′zĭz). *Abbr.* **c.h., C.H.** A government building or office where customs are collected and ships are cleared for entering or leaving the country.

cus·tom·ize (kŭs′tə-mīz′) *tr.v.* **-ized, -izing, -izes.** To alter (a standard car model, for example) to the tastes of the buyer.

cus·tom-made (kŭs′təm-mād′) *adj.* Made according to the specifications of an individual purchaser.

cus·toms (kŭs′təmz) *n. Used with a singular or plural verb.* **1.** A duty or tax imposed on imported and, less commonly, exported goods. Also called "customs duty." **2.** The government department authorized to collect such duties. **3. a.** The procedure for inspecting goods and baggage entering a country. **b.** The place, as at an airport or frontier, where this inspection takes place.

customs union *n.* An international association organized to eliminate customs restrictions on goods exchanged between member nations and to establish a uniform tariff policy toward nonmember nations.

cus·tos (kŭs′tōs) *n., pl.* **custodes** (kŭs-tō′dēz). **1.** A guardian or keeper; a custodian. **2.** A superior in certain monastic orders. [Middle English, from Latin *custōs*†, guard, protector.]

cus·tu·mal (kŭs′cho͞o-məl, -tyo͞o-məl) *n.* A written record of the customs of a monastery or community. [Medieval Latin *custumāle,* from the neuter of *custumālis,* customary, from Old French *custume,* from *custome,* CUSTOM.]

cut (kŭt) *v.* **cut, cutting, cuts.** *—tr.* **1.** To penetrate with a sharp edge; strike a narrow opening in. **2.** To separate into parts with or as if with a sharp-edged instrument; sever: *cut cloth with scissors.* **3.** To sever the edges or outer extensions of; shorten; trim. **4.** To reap; harvest. **5.** To fell by sawing; hew. Often used with *down.* **6.** To have (a new tooth) grow through the gums. **7.** To form or shape by severing or incising: *a doll cut from paper.* **8.** To form by penetrating, probing, or digging. **9.** To separate or dissociate from a main body; detach: *cut off a chicken drumstick.* **10.** To pass through or across; cross. **11.** *Card Games.* To divide (a pack of cards) in two, as before dealing. **12. a.** To curtail the size, extent, or duration of; abridge. **b.** To reduce; diminish: *cut expenditure.* **13.** To lessen the strength of; dilute: *cut whiskey with water.* **14.** To dissolve by breaking down the fat of: *Soap cuts grease.* **15.** To injure the feelings of; hurt keenly. **16.** *Informal.* To deliberately fail to attend: *cut a class.* **17.** *Informal.* To cease; stop. **18. a.** *Sports.* To strike (a ball) with a slicing stroke so that it spins irregularly or is deflected. **b.** *Cricket.* To hit (a ball), usually with the bat held horizontally, on the off side in a direction between third man and cover. **19.** To perform: *cut a caper.* **20.** To terminate (a scene in a film). **21.** To record a performance on (a phonograph record). **22.** To edit (film or audio tape). **23.** *Informal.* To switch off (a car engine, for example). **24.** *Geometry.* To meet across (a line or curve). **25.** To castrate. *—intr.* **1.** To make an incision or separation. **2.** To allow incision or severing: *Butter cuts easily.* **3.** To use a sharp-edged instrument. **4.** To grow through the gums. Used of new teeth. **5.** To penetrate so as to cause injury. **6. a.** To change direction abruptly: *cut to the left.* **b.** *Cricket.* To turn abruptly on pitching. Used of a bowled ball. **7.** To go directly and often hastily: *cut across the field.* **8.** To divide a pack of cards into two parts in order, for example, to make a decision on the basis of the card or cards displayed. **9.** *Geometry.* To intersect. Used of lines. **10.** To stop filming or recording. Often used in the imperative. **—cut back. 1.** To shorten by cutting; prune. **2.** To reduce or decrease: *cut back production.* **—cut corners.** To do something quickly or cheaply to the detriment of quality; skimp. **—cut down to size.** To deflate the self-importance of. **—cut loose.** To become independent; break free. **—cut no ice with.** To fail to have an effect on; make no impression on. **—cut one's teeth on.** To gain early experience from. **—cut short.** To stop before the end; abbreviate.

~n. **1.** The act of incising, severing, or separating. **2.** The result of cutting; an incision; especially, a smallish wound or gash. **3.** A part that has been severed from a main body: *a cut of beef.* **4.** A passage or channel resulting from excavating or probing. **5. a.** An elimination or excision of a part: *a cut in a speech.* **b.** The eliminated part. **6. a.** A reduction: *a salary cut.* **b.** *Often* **cuts.** Reduction in government expenditure. **7.** The style in which hair or a garment is cut. **8.** *Informal.* A share of profits or earnings. **9.** *Informal.* **a.** A wounding remark; an insult. **b.** A snub. **10.** *Chemistry.* A fraction obtained by distilling. **11.** *Printing.* **a.** An engraved block or plate. **b.** A print made from such a block. **12.** *Sports.* A stroke played by cutting. **13.** *Card Games.* The act of dividing a pack of cards into two parts, as before dealing. **14.** A sharp transition between shots or scenes in a film. **15.** A **power cut** *(see).* **—a cut above.** A little better than. [Middle English *cutten, kitten,* probably from late Old English *cyttan* (unattested), akin to Icelandic *kuta,* to cut with a knife, of North Germanic origin.]

cut-and-dried (kŭt′ən-drīd′) *adj.* **1.** Prepared and arranged in advance; settled. **2.** Ordinary; routine; lacking spontaneity.

cu·ta·ne·ous (kyo͞o-tā′nē-əs) *adj.* Of, pertaining to, or affecting the skin. [New Latin *cutaneus,* from Latin *cutis,* skin.] **—cu·ta·ne·ous·ly** *adv.*

cutaneous anaphylaxis *n.* Anaphylaxis characterized by a violent skin reaction upon contact with the sensitizing substance.

cut·a·way (kŭt′ə-wā′) *n.* **1.** A diagram, as of a building or machine, that shows the interior by omitting the outer shell. **2.** A man's formal daytime coat, with front edges sloping diagonally from the waist and forming tails at the back. Also called "cutaway coat."

cut back *tr.v.* **1.** To prune severely; shorten (the stem of a plant, for example). **2.** To reduce; curtail. *—intr.v.* To make reductions; economize. Used with *on.*

cut·back (kŭt′băk′) *n.* **1.** A decrease; a curtailment: *a cutback in production.* **2.** A **flashback** *(see).* **3.** A sharp reversal of direction, as of a ballcarrier in football.

cutch (kŭch) *n.* A resinous substance, **catechu** *(see).* [Malay *kachu,* CATECHU.]

cut down *intr.v.* To reduce consumption, expenditure, or the like. Used with *on.* *—tr.v.* To kill, especially suddenly.

cut-down (kŭt′doun′) *n.* **1.** An act of cutting down; a reduction. **2.** Something reduced in size or extent.

~adj. Shortened; abridged.

cute (kyo͞ot) *adj.* **cuter, cutest. 1.** Delightfully pretty or dainty. **2.** Obviously contrived to charm; affected. **3.** Shrewd; clever. [Short for ACUTE.] **—cute·ly** *adv.* **—cute·ness** *n.*

cut glass *n.* Glassware shaped or decorated by cutting instruments or abrasive wheels. **—cut-glass** *adj.*

cut-grass (kŭt′grăs′, -gräs′) *n.* Any of several swamp and marsh grasses of the genus *Leersia,* having leaves with very rough margins.

Cuth·bert (kŭth′bərt), **Saint** (*c.* A.D. 635–687). English saint and missionary, who converted the Northumbrians to Christianity. His allegedly uncorrupted body was moved from the island of Farne for burial in Durham Cathedral in the 10th century.

cu·ti·cle (kyo͞o′tĭ-kəl) *n.* **1.** The strip of hardened skin at the base of a fingernail or toenail. **2.** The epidermis. **3.** *Zoology.* The noncellular, often horny protective outer covering in many invertebrates. **4.** *Botany.* The protective layer of cutin covering the epidermis of plants. [Latin *cutīcula,* diminutive of *cutis,* skin.] **—cu·tic·u·lar** *adj.*

cut·ie, cut·ey (kyo͞o′tē) *n., pl.* **-ies.** *Slang.* An attractive or charming person.

cut in *intr.v.* **1.** To move in front of another car too sharply, thus endangering or inconveniencing another motorist. **2.** To interrupt. **3.** To interrupt a dancing couple in order to dance with one of them. **4.** To take another player's place in a card game. *—tr.v.* *Informal.* To share with; give a share to: *cut him in.*

cut-in (kŭt′ĭn′) *n.* An inserted shot, often a still close-up, interrupting the continuity of the main action of a motion picture.

cu·tin (kyo͞o′tĭn) *n.* *Botany.* A waxlike, water-repellent material present in the walls of some plant cells, and forming the cuticle that covers the epidermis. [Latin *cut(is),* skin + -IN.]

cu·tin·ize (kyo͞o′tə-nīz′) *v.* **-ized, -izing, -izes.** *Botany.* *—tr.* To coat or impregnate with cutin. *—intr.* To become coated or impregnated with cutin. **—cu·tin·i·za·tion** *n.*

cu·tis (kyo͞o′tĭs) *n.* *Anatomy.* The **dermis** *(see).* [Latin *cutis,* skin.]

cut·lass, cut·las (kŭt′ləs) *n.* A short, heavy sword with a curved single-edged blade, once used as a weapon by sailors. [Variant of earlier *coutelace,* from Old French *coutelas,* from *coutel,* knife, from Latin *cultellus,* diminutive of *culter,* knife.]

cutlass fish *n.* Any of several marine fishes of the genus *Trichiurus,* having a long, narrow body and a pointed tail.

cut·ler (kŭt′lər) *n.* A person who makes, repairs, or sells knives, cutlery, or other cutting instruments. [Middle English, from Old French *coutelier,* from *coutel,* knife. See **cutlass.**]

cut·ler·y (kŭt′lĕr-ē) *n.* **1.** Cutting instruments and tools. **2.** Implements used as tableware. **3.** The occupation of a cutler.

cut·let (kŭt′lĭt) *n.* **1.** A thin slice of meat, usually veal or lamb, cut

PRONUNCIATION KEY

ă, pat; ā, pay; âr, care;
ä, father, are; b, bib;
ch, church; d, deed; ĕ, pet;
ē, be; f, fife; g, gag; h, hat;
hw, which; ĭ, pit; ī, pie;
îr, pier; j, judge; k, kick;
l, lid, needle; m, mum;
n, no, sudden; ng, thing;
ŏ, pot; ō, toe; ô, paw, for;
oi, noise; ou, out; o͝o, book;
o͞o, boot; p, pop; r, roar;
s, sauce; sh, ship, dish;
t, tight; th, thin, path;
th, this, bathe; ŭ, cut; ûr, fur;
v, valve; w, with; y, yes;
z, zebra, size; zh, vision;
ə, about, item, edible,
gallop, circus, peaceful

IN FOREIGN WORDS:

à, *Fr.* ami; œ, *Fr.* feu, *Ger.* schön; ü, *Fr.* tu, *Ger.* über; KH, *Ger.* ich, *Scot.* loch; N, *Fr.* bon; y′, *Fr.* Compiègne

STRESS MARKS:

Primary stress: ′
in·cite′ (ĭn-sīt′)
Secondary stress: ′
in′sight′ (ĭn′sīt′)

from the leg or ribs of an animal. **2.** A piece of fish cut across or widthwise, from between the head and middle part of the body of a large fish such as cod or halibut. **3.** A flat, cutlet-shaped croquette of chopped meat or fish. [French *côtelette,* from Old French *costelette,* diminutive of *coste,* rib, from Latin *costa,* rib.]

cut off *tr.v.* **1.** To detach by severing. **2.** To discontinue; stop. **3.** To interrupt or intercept. **4.** To separate; isolate. **5.** To disinherit. **6.** To disconnect (a power supply, for example).

cut-off (kŭt′ôf′, -ŏf′) *n.* **1.** A designated limit or point of termination. **2.** A new channel cut by a river across the neck of an oxbow lake. **3. a.** A checking or cutting off of a flow of steam, water, or other fluid. **b.** The device that cuts off.
~*adj.* Of or pertaining to a cut-off: *a cut-off point.*

cut-offs, cut·offs (kŭt′ôfs′, -ŏfs′) *pl.n.* Pants, as blue jeans, made into shorts by cutting off part of the legs.

cut out *tr.v.* **1.** To shape or fashion by cutting. **2.** To remove the background from behind a figure (as in a photograph or painting). **3.** *Informal.* To be temperamentally suited or fitted: *cut out for city life.* **4.** *Informal.* To cease or give up: *cut out cigarettes.* **5.** To outdo or take the place of (a rival). —*intr.v.* **1.** To cease functioning; switch off. **2.** To leave or be excluded from a card game.

cut-out (kŭt′out′) *n.* **1.** Something cut out or intended to be cut out. **2.** *Electricity.* A device that interrupts, bypasses, or disconnects a circuit or circuit element, especially as a safety measure.

cut·o·ver (kŭt′ō′vər) *adj.* Cleared of trees.

cut·purse (kŭt′pûrs′) *n. Archaic.* A pickpocket. [Originally one who cut off purses that were attached to a girdle.]

cut-rate (kŭt′rāt′) *adj.* Sold or on sale at a reduced price.

cut·ter (kŭt′ər) *n.* **1.** One who cuts, especially in tailoring or hairdressing. **2.** A device or machine that cuts. **3.** *Nautical.* **a.** A single-masted fore-and-aft-rigged sailing vessel with a running bowsprit, a mainsail, and two or more headsails. Compare **sloop. b.** A ship's boat, powered by a motor or oars, and used for transporting stores or passengers. **c.** A small, lightly armed motorboat used by the Coast Guard. **4.** A small sleigh, usually seating one person and drawn by a single horse.

cut·throat (kŭt′thrōt′) *n.* **1.** One who cuts throats; a murderer. **2.** *Chiefly British.* A razor having a long blade that folds into the handle. Also called "cutthroat razor."
~*adj.* **1.** Cruel; murderous. **2.** Relentless or merciless in competition. **3.** *Games & Sports.* Of or designating a form of game in which each of three players acts and scores for himself.

cut time *n. Music.* A kind of measure, **alla breve** *(see).*

cut·ting (kŭt′ĭng) *adj.* **1.** Capable of or designed for incising, shearing, or severing. **2.** Sharply penetrating; piercing and cold. **3.** Bitterly sarcastic or insulting. —See Synonyms at **incisive.**
~*n.* **1.** A part cut off from a main body. **2.** An excavation made through high ground in the construction of a road, railway, or the like. **3.** *Chiefly British.* An article, story, or other item cut out from a newspaper or magazine. **4.** The editing of film or audio tape. **5.** *Horticulture.* **a.** A twig, leaf, or plant part removed in order to form roots and propagate a new plant. **b.** Propagation by means of cuttings.

cut·tle (kŭt′l) *n. Rare.* A cuttlefish. [Middle English *codel,* Old English *cudele.* See **ku-** in Appendix.*]

cut·tle·bone (kŭt′l-bōn′) *n.* The calcareous internal shell of a cuttlefish, used as a dietary supplement for cage birds or ground into powder for use as a polishing agent.

cut·tle·fish (kŭt′l-fĭsh′) *n., pl.* **-fishes** or collectively **cuttlefish.** Any of various squidlike cephalopod marine mollusks of the genus *Sepia,* having ten arms and a calcareous internal shell, and secreting a dark, inky fluid. Also called "cuttle." [Middle English *codel,* Old English *cudele;* akin to *cod,* bag (see **codpiece**), referring to its ink sac.]

cut up *tr.v.* **1.** To divide into pieces. **2.** To inflict lacerations upon. **3.** *Informal.* To criticize severely. —*intr.v. Informal.* To behave mischievously.

cut·up (kŭt′ŭp′) *n. Informal.* A mischievous person; prankster.

cut·wa·ter (kŭt′wô′tər) *n.* **1.** The forward part of a ship's prow. **2.** The wedge-shaped end of a bridge pier, designed to divide the current and break up ice floes.

cut·work (kŭt′wûrk′) *n.* Openwork embroidery in which the ground fabric is cut away from the design.

cut·worm (kŭt′wûrm′) *n.* The larva of any of various moths of the family Noctuidae, feeding on a wide variety of plants. [So called because many species eat through stems of plants.]

Cu·vier (ko͞o′vē-ā′, kyo͞o′-), **Georges, Baron** (1769-1832). French naturalist, chiefly remembered for his pioneer work in comparing fossil remains with the anatomy of existing species. His main work was *The Animal Kingdom* (1817).

Cuy·a·ho·ga (kī′ə-hō′gə). River, c. 130 kilometers (80 miles), of northeastern Ohio. It flows southwest through the city of Cuyahoga Falls, a suburb of Akron, then north of Lake Erie, forming part of Cleveland harbor.

Cuz·co (ko͞os′kō). City in southern Peru, in the Andes. The capital of the Inca empire before the Spanish conquests, it contains the ruins of many impressive Inca temples.

c.v. curriculum vitae.

CVA cerebrovascular accident.

cvt. *Finance.* convertible.

cw, CW continuous wave.

cwm (ko͞om) *n. Welsh.* **1.** A valley. **2.** A steep hollow, a **cirque** *(see).*

CWO chief warrant officer.

c.w.o. cash with order.

CWS Chemical Warfare Service.

cwt. hundredweight.

-cy *suffix.* Indicates: **1.** A quality or condition; for example, **bankruptcy, infancy. 2.** Office or rank; for example, **baronetcy, magistracy.** [Middle English *-cie,* from Old French, from Latin *-cia, -tia,* and Greek *-kiā, -tiā,* both abstract noun suffixes.]

cy·an (sī′ăn) *n.* Greenish blue; one of the subtractive primary colors; a complement of red. [Greek *kuanos,* CYANO-.]

cy·an·a·mide (sī-ăn′ə-mīd) *n.* Also **cy·an·a·mid. 1.** An irritating caustic acidic crystalline compound, $NCNH_2$, prepared by continuous carbonation of calcium cyanamide in water. **2.** A compound, **calcium cyanamide** *(see).* **3.** A salt or ester of cyanamide. [French : CYAN(O)- + AMIDE.]

cy·a·nate (sī′ə-nāt′, -nət) *n.* A salt or ester of cyanic acid. [CYAN(O)- + -ATE.]

cy·an·ic (sī-ăn′ĭk) *adj.* **1.** Pertaining to or containing cyanogen. **2.** Blue or bluish. [CYAN(O)- + -IC.]

cyanic acid *n.* A poisonous, unstable, highly volatile organic acid, HOCN, used to prepare certain cyanates.

cy·a·nide (sī′ə-nīd′) *n.* Also **cy·an·id** (-nĭd). Any of various salts or esters of hydrogen cyanide containing a CN group; especially, the extremely poisonous compounds **potassium cyanide** and **sodium cyanide** *(both of which see).*
~*tr.v.* **cyanided, -niding, -nides. 1.** To treat (a metal surface) with cyanide to produce a hard surface. **2.** To treat (an ore) with cyanide to extract gold or silver. [CYAN(O)- + -IDE.]

cyanide process *n.* A process of extracting gold or silver from ores treated with a solution of sodium or calcium cyanide.

cy·a·nine (sī′ə-nīn) *n.* Any of various blue dyes, used to extend the range of color sensitivity of photographic emulsions. [CYAN(O)- + -INE.]

cyanite. Variant of **kyanite.**

cyano-, cyan- *prefix.* Indicates: **1.** A blue or dark-blue coloring; for example, **cyanine, cyanic. 2.** *Chemistry.* Cyanide or cyanogen; for example, **cyanate, cyanotype.** [German *zyan-,* from Greek *kuanos,* dark-blue enamel, the color blue, from an unknown language of Asia Minor.]

cy·a·no·ac·ry·late (sī′ə-nō-ăk′rə-lāt′, sī-ăn′ō-) *n.* An industrial and medical adhesive with an acrylic base.

cy·a·no·co·bal·a·min (sī′ə-nō′kō-bô′lə-mĭn) *n.* **Vitamin B_{12}** *(see).* [CYANO- + COBAL(T) + (VIT)AMIN.]

cy·an·o·gen (sī-ăn′ə-jən) *n. Chemistry.* A colorless, flammable, highly poisonous gas, C_2N_2, used as a rocket propellant, fumigant, military weapon, and in welding. [French *cyanogène* : CYANO- + -GEN.]

cyano group *n.* The univalent radical CN, found in simple and complex cyanide compounds.

cy·a·no·hy·drin (sī′ə-nō-hī′drĭn, sī-ăn′ō-) *n. Chemistry.* Any of a class of organic compounds containing both CN and OH groups attached to the same carbon atom. [CYANO- + HYDRO- + -IN.]

cy·a·nosed (sī′ə-nōzd′) *adj. Pathology.* Afflicted with cyanosis. [From CYANOSIS.]

cy·a·no·sis (sī′ə-nō′sĭs) *n. Pathology.* A bluish discoloration of the skin, resulting from inadequate oxygenation of the blood. [New Latin, from Greek *kuanōsis,* dark blue : CYAN(O)- + -OSIS.] —**cy·a·not·ic** (sī′ə-nŏt′ĭk) *adj.*

cy·an·o·type (sī-ăn′ə-tīp′) *n.* A **blueprint** *(see).*

cy·a·nu·ric acid (sī′ə-no͝or′ĭk, -nyo͝or′ĭk) *n.* A white crystalline acid, $C_3N_3(OH)_3$, that decomposes with heating to form cyanic acid. [CYAN(O)- + URIC ACID.]

Cyb·e·le (sĭb′ə-lē, kĭb′ə-lā). The Phrygian goddess of nature and mother of all living things.

cy·ber·nate (sī′bər-nāt′) *v.* **-nated, -nating, -nates.** —*tr.* To control (an industrial process) automatically by computer. —*intr.* To become so controlled. [From CYBERNET(ICS) + -ATE.] —**cy·ber·na·tion** *n.*

cy·ber·net·ics (sī′bər-nĕt′ĭks) *n. Used with a singular verb.* The theoretical study of control processes in electronic, mechanical, and biological systems; especially, the mathematical analysis of the flow of information in such systems. [Coined by Norbert Wiener from Greek *kubernētēs,* pilot, governor, from *kubernan,* to steer, guide, GOVERN.] —**cy·ber·net·ic** *adj.* —**cy·ber·net·i·cist** *n.*

cy·borg (sī′bôrg′) *n.* A human individual who has some of his vital bodily processes controlled by cybernetically operated devices. [CYB(ERNETIC) + ORG(ANISM).]

cy·cad (sī′kăd) *n.* Any seed-bearing gymnosperm plant of the family Cycadaceae, resembling a palm tree but surmounted by fernlike leaves. [New Latin *Cycas* (stem *Cycad-*), genus name, from Greek *kukas,* manuscript error for *koïkas,* accusative plural of *koïx,* doom palm, perhaps from Egyptian.] —**cy·cad·a·ceous** *adj.*

cycl-. Variant of **cyclo-.**

Cyc·la·des (sĭk′lə-dēz). *Greek* **Ki·klá·dhes** (kē-klä′*th*ēz). A group of more than 200 Greek islands, in the Aegean Sea southeast of the mainland. They include Naxos, the largest, Paros, and Delos. Hermoupolis, on Syros, is the capital.

cyc·la·mate (sī′klə-māt′, sĭk′lə-) *n.* A salt of cyclamic acid; especially, either of two very sweet crystalline compounds, **sodium cyclamate** *(see)* and calcium cyclamate, $C_{12}H_{24}N_2O_6S_2Ca$.

cyc·la·men (sī′klə-mən, sĭk′lə-, -mĕn′) *n.* Any of several plants of the genus *Cyclamen,* widely cultivated for their showy white, pink, or red flowers with reflexed petals. [New Latin, from Greek *kuklaminos,* probably from *kuklos,* a circle (from the bulbous roots).]

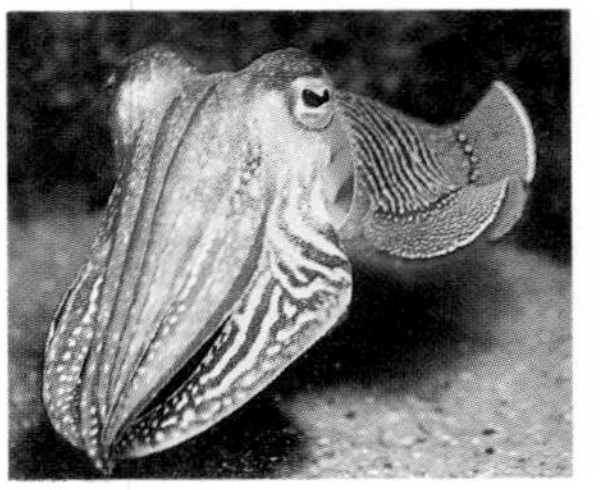

cuttlefish *Fossil evidence shows that this ancient genus of shellfish has existed in its present form for more than 20 million years, characterized by its cuttlebone, a type of internal, calcified shell, containing a network of hollow chambers. By regulating the amount of gas or water in these chambers, the cuttlefish controls its buoyancy, so that it can rise close to the surface to feed or sink to the seabed where it lives.* Sepia *is both its genus name and the word used for the brownish pigment that is obtained from its dried ink sac.*

$$CH_3CN + 2H_2 \rightarrow CH_3.CH_2.NH_2$$

methyl cyanide | hydrogen | ethylamine

cyanide *All cyanide compounds are highly poisonous, but some are useful too. Organic cyanides, for instance, such as methyl cyanide, are combined with hydrogen to form ethylamine—used in the manufacture of detergents.*

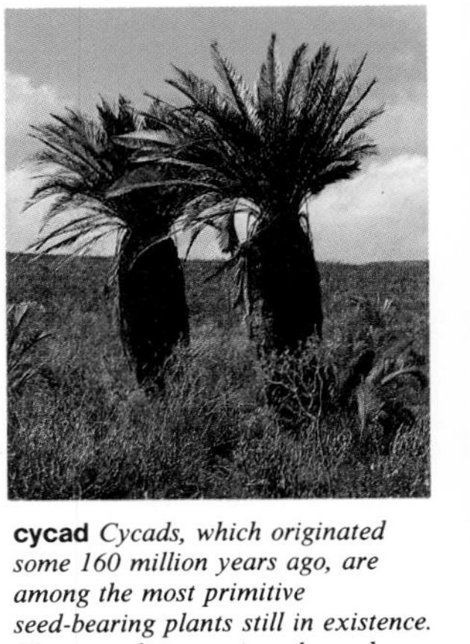

cycad *Cycads, which originated some 160 million years ago, are among the most primitive seed-bearing plants still in existence. They are slow-growing plants that resemble palm trees. But, unlike palms, they have no flowers. Instead they bear their seeds in cones that, in some species, can be 1 meter (3.3 feet) long and weigh more than 35 kilograms (77 pounds).*

cyc·la·mic acid (sĭk′lə-mĭk′, sī′klə-) n. A sour-sweet crystalline acid, $C_6H_{13}NO_3S$.

cy·clase (sī′klās, -klāz′) n. An enzyme that acts as a catalyst in the cyclization of a compound.

cy·cle (sī′kəl) n. 1. A time interval in which a characteristic, especially regularly repeated, event or sequence of events occurs. 2. a. A single complete execution of a periodically repeated phenomenon. b. A periodically repeated sequence of events. c. The time taken for the phenomenon or sequence to be completed. 3. The orbit of a celestial body. 4. A long period of time; an age; an eon. 5. a. The aggregate of traditional legends, stories, or tales concerning a central theme or hero: *the Arthurian cycle.* b. A series of poems or songs on the same theme. 6. A bicycle, tricycle, or the like. 7. *Botany.* A circular arrangement of flower parts such as petals or sepals. ~*intr.v.* **cycled, -cling, -cles.** 1. To occur in or pass through a cycle. 2. To move in or as if in a circle. 3. To ride a bicycle, tricycle, or similar vehicle. [French, from Late Latin *cyclus,* from Greek *kuklos,* circle.]

cy·cle·ry (sī′kəl-rē) n. A shop for the sale and service of bicycles.

cy·clic (sī′klĭk, sĭk′lĭk) adj. Also **cy·cli·cal** (sī′klĭ-kəl, sĭk′lĭ-). 1. a. Of, relating to, or characterized by cycles. b. Recurring or moving in cycles. 2. *Chemistry.* Of or pertaining to compounds having atoms arranged in a ring or closed-chain structure. 3. *Botany.* a. Having parts arranged in a whorl. b. Forming a whorl. 4. *Geometry.* Designating a polygon whose vertices lie on the circumference of a circumscribing circle: *a cyclic quadrilateral.* —**cy·cli·cal·ly** adv.

cyclic AMP n. *Biochemistry.* A cyclic form of adenosine monophosphate that has an important role in regulating metabolic processes, including the action of many hormones, in animals and humans.

cyclic GMP n. A cyclic nucleotide of guanosine believed to act as an antagonist to cyclic AMP in cellular processes.

cyclic pitch lever n. A helicopter control lever that alters the angle of attack of individual rotor blades, causing the aircraft to move forward, backward, or sideways.

cy·clist (sī′klĭst) n. Also **cy·cler** (-klər). One who rides a bicycle, motorcycle, or similar vehicle.

cy·cli·za·tion (sī′klə-zā′shən) n. The formation of rings in a hydrocarbon.

cyclo-, cycl- prefix. Indicates: 1. Circle; for example, **cyclometer, cyclorama.** 2. A cyclic compound; for example, **cyclohexane.** [Greek *kuklos,* circle, CYCLE.]

cy·clo·al·kane (sī′klō-ăl′kān′) n. **Cycloparaffin** (*see*).

cy·clo·hex·ane (sī′klō-hĕk′sān′) n. An extremely flammable, colorless, mobile liquid, C_6H_{12}, obtained from petroleum and benzene and used as a solvent, paint and varnish remover, and in the manufacture of nylon.

cy·clo·hex·i·mide (sī′klō-hĕk′sə-mīd, -mĭd) n. *Chemistry.* A compound, $C_{15}H_{23}NO_4$, that is used as an agricultural fungicide.

cy·cloid (sī′kloid′) adj. 1. Resembling a circle. 2. *Zoology.* Thin, rounded, and smooth-edged; disklike. Said of fish scales, such as those of the salmon. 3. *Psychiatry.* Designating a person suffering from **cyclothymia** (*see*). ~n. *Geometry.* The curve traced by a point on the circumference of a circle that rolls on a straight line. [French *cycloïde,* from Greek *kukloeidēs* : CYCL(O)- + -OID.] —**cy·cloi·dal** adj.

cy·clom·e·ter (sī-klŏm′ə-tər) n. 1. An instrument that records the revolutions of a wheel in order to indicate distance traveled. 2. An instrument that measures circular arcs. [CYCLO- + -METER.] —**cy·clo·met·ric** adj. —**cy·clom·e·try** n.

cy·clone (sī′klōn′) n. 1. *Meteorology.* a. A type of tropical atmospheric disturbance characterized by masses of air rapidly circulating clockwise in the southern and counterclockwise in the northern hemisphere, about a low-pressure center, usually accompanied by stormy, often destructive, weather. b. Formerly, a **depression** (sense 4). 2. Loosely, any violent, rotating windstorm, such as a **tornado** (*see*). [Probably from Greek *kuklōma,* coil, wheel, from *kuklos,* circle, CYCLE.] —**cy·clon·ic** (sī-klŏn′ĭk), **cy·clon·i·cal** adj.

cyclone′cellar n. An underground shelter in or adjacent to a house, used for protection from cyclones, tornadoes, or the like. Also called "storm cellar."

cy·clo·par·af·fin (sī′klō-păr′ə-fĭn) n. Any of a class of hydrocarbons, including cyclopropane, cyclopentane, and cyclohexane, in which at least three carbon atoms per molecule are joined in a ring structure and each such carbon in the ring is bonded to two hydrogen atoms or alkyl groups. Also called "cycloalkane."

cy·clo·pe·an (sī′klə-pē′ən, sī-klō′pē-ən) adj. 1. *Often* **Cyclopean.** Pertaining to or suggestive of the Cyclopes. 2. Pertaining to or designating a primitive style of masonry characterized by the use of massive stones of irregular shape and size.

cy·clo·pe·di·a, cy·clo·pae·di·a (sī′klə-pē′dē-ə) n. An encyclopedia. —**cy·clo·pe·dic** adj. —**cy·clo·pe·dist** n.

cy·clo·pen·tane (sī′klə-pĕn′tān, sĭk′lə-) n. A colorless flammable liquid, C_5H_{10}, derived from petroleum and used as a solvent and motor fuel.

cy·clo·ple·gi·a (sī′klə-plē′jē-ə) n. Loss of ability to focus vision because of paralysis of the ciliary muscles of the eye. [New Latin : CYCLO- + -PLEGIA.]

cy·clo·pro·pane (sī′klə-prō′pān′) n. A highly flammable, explosive, colorless gas, C_3H_6, used as an anesthetic.

Cy·clops (sī′klŏps). pl. **Cyclopes** (sī-klō′pēz), **Cyclopses, Cyclops.** *Greek Mythology.* 1. Any of the three one-eyed Titans who forged thunderbolts for Zeus. 2. Any of a race of one-eyed giants, reputedly descended from these Titans, inhabiting the island of Sicily.

cy·clo·ram·a (sī′klə-răm′ə, -rä′mə) n. 1. A large composite picture placed on the interior walls of a cylindrical room so as to appear in natural perspective to a spectator standing in the center. 2. A large curtain or wall, usually concave, placed or hung at the rear of a stage. [CYCL(O)- + (PAN)ORAMA.] —**cy·clo·ram·ic** adj.

cy·clo·ser·ine (sī′klō-sĕr′ēn′) n. An antibiotic active against a wide range of bacteria, used chiefly in the treatment of tuberculosis and infections of the urinary tract.

cy·clo·sis (sī-klō′sĭs) n., pl. **-ses** (-sēz′). The circulatory motion of protoplasm or organelles within certain cells and one-celled animals. [New Latin, from Greek *kuklōsis,* a surrounding, from *kukloun,* to surround, from *kuklos,* a circle, CYCLE.]

cy·clo·stome (sī′klə-stōm′) n. Any of various primitive eellike vertebrates of the class Agnatha, such as the lamprey, lacking jaws and true teeth and having a circular, sucking mouth. [New Latin *Cyclostomi,* "round-mouths" and *Cyclostomata,* "round-mouthed" : CYCLO- + -STOME.] —**cy·clos·to·mate, cy·clo·stom·a·tous** adj.

cy·clo·style (sī′klō-stīl′) n. A device consisting of a pen with a small toothed wheel producing a stencil from which copies can be made. ~*tr.v.* **cyclostyled, -styling, -styles.** To produce (copies) using a cyclostyle. [CYCLO- + Latin *stylus,* writing implement.]

cy·clo·thyme (sī′klə-thīm′) n. *Psychiatry.* A person afflicted with cyclothymia.

cy·clo·thy·mi·a (sī′klə-thī′mē-ə) n. *Psychiatry.* A form of depressive psychosis characterized by alternating periods of activity and excitement and periods of inactivity and depression. [New Latin, from German *Zyklothymie* : CYCLO- + -THYMIA.]

cy·clo·thy·mic (sī′klə-thī′mĭk) adj. Of or characterized by cyclothymia. ~n. A cyclothyme.

cy·clo·tron (sī′klə-trŏn′) n. *Physics.* A circular particle accelerator capable of generating particle energies between a few million and several tens of millions of electron volts, in which charged particles generated at a central source are accelerated spirally outward in a plane at right angles to a fixed magnetic field by an alternating electric field. [CYCLO- + -TRON.]

cyder. *Chiefly British.* Variant of **cider.**

cy·e·sis (sī-ē′sĭs) n., pl. **-ses** (-sēz′). Pregnancy; gestation. [New Latin, from Greek *kuēsis,* from *kuein,* to be pregnant, to swell.]

cyg·net (sĭg′nĭt) n. A young swan. [Middle English *sygnett,* diminutive of Old French *cygne,* swan, from Latin *cycnus, cygnus,* from Greek *kuknos.*]

Cyg·nus (sĭg′nəs) n. A constellation in the Northern Hemisphere near Lacerta and Lyra in the Milky Way. Also called "Northern Cross," "Swan." [Latin *cygnus,* swan. See **cygnet.**]

cyl·in·der (sĭl′ən-dər) n. *Abbr.* **cyl.** 1. *Geometry.* a. A surface generated by a straight line moving parallel to a fixed straight line and intersecting a plane curve. b. The portion of such a surface bounded by two parallel planes and the regions of the planes bounded by the surface. c. A solid consisting of two parallel planes bounded by two identical closed curves, usually circles. 2. Any cylindrical container or object. 3. a. The chamber in which the piston of a reciprocating engine moves. b. The chamber of a pump from which fluid is expelled by a piston. 4. The rotating chamber of a revolver that holds the cartridges. 5. Any of the rotating cylinders in a printing press that carry the paper or the curved printing plate, or receive the ink or impression. 6. *Archaeology.* A cylindrical stone or clay object with an engraved design or inscription. ~*tr.v.* **cylindered, -dering, -ders.** To press or furnish with a cylinder. [Old French *cylindre,* from Latin *cylindrus,* from Greek *kulindros,* roller, cylinder, from *kulindein,* to revolve, roll.]

cylinder block n. The casting containing the cylinders and cooling channels of an internal-combustion engine.

cylinder head n. The closed, often detachable, end of a cylinder or cylinders in an internal-combustion engine.

cy·lin·dri·cal (sə-lĭn′drĭ-kəl) adj. Also **cy·lin·dric** (-drĭk). *Abbr.* **cyl.** 1. Having the shape of a cylinder, especially a circular cylinder. 2. Of or pertaining to a cylinder. 3. Of or pertaining to the coordinate system, or to any of three coordinates in it, formed by two polar coordinates in a plane and a rectangular coordinate measured perpendicularly from the plane. —**cy·lin·dri·cal·i·ty** n. —**cy·lin·dri·cal·ly** adv.

cylindrical projection n. A map projection in which points on the globe are projected onto a cylinder placed at a tangent to or intersecting its surface, which is then opened and laid flat.

cyl·in·droid (sĭl′ĭn-droid′) n. A cylindrical surface or solid that is elliptical in cross section. ~adj. Resembling a cylinder.

cylix. Variant of **kylix.**

cy·ma (sī′mə) n., pl. **-mae** (-mē′) or **-mas.** 1. *Architecture.* A molding for a cornice, having a partly concave and partly convex curve in profile. A *cyma recta* has the concave curve uppermost, a *cyma reversa* the convex. 2. *Botany.* A cyme. [Greek *kuma,* anything swollen, waved molding, from *kuein,* to swell, be pregnant.]

cy·ma·ti·um (sī-mā′shē-əm, -tē-) n. **-tia** (-shē-ə). 1. A cyma. 2. The topmost molding of a classical cornice. [Latin *cymatium,* from Greek *kumation,* diminutive of *kuma,* moulding, CYMA.]

cym·bal (sĭm′bəl) n. 1. One of a pair of concave brass plates that are struck together as percussion instruments. 2. A single brass plate, sounded by hitting with a drumstick and often part of a set of drums. [Middle English, from Old French *symbale,* from Latin *cymbalum,* from Greek *kumbalon,* from *kumbē,* hollow of a vessel, a cup.] —**cym·bal·ist** n.

Cymbeline. See **Cunobelinus.**

cym·bid·i·um (sĭm-bĭd′ē-əm) *n.* Any orchid of the genus *Cymbidium,* cultivated as ornamentals for their sprays of long-lasting flowers. [New Latin, from Greek *kumbē,* cup.]

cyme (sīm) *n. Botany.* An often flat-topped flower cluster that blooms from the center toward the edges, and whose main axis always terminates in a flower. Also called "cyma." [New Latin *cyma,* from Latin *cyma,* young cabbage sprout, from Greek *kuma,* anything swollen, CYMA.] —**cy·mif·er·ous** *adj.*

cy·mene (sī′mēn′) *n. Chemistry.* Any of three colorless isomeric liquid hydrocarbons, $C_{10}H_{14}$, obtained chiefly from the essential oils of various plants and used in the manufacture of synthetic resins. [French *cymène,* from Greek *kuminon,* CUMIN.]

cym·ling (sĭm′lĭng) *n.* Also **cym·lin** (-lĭn), **sim·lin.** A greenish-white, flat, round squash with a scalloped edge. Also called "pattypan squash." [Probably variant of SIMNEL.]

cy·mo·gene (sī′mə-jēn′) *n.* A flammable gaseous fraction of petroleum, chiefly butane. [CYM(ENE) + -GENE.]

cy·moid (sī′moid′) *adj.* Resembling a cyma or cyme. [CYM(E) or CYM(A) + -OID.]

cy·mo·phane (sī′mə-fān′) *n.* A variety of chrysoberyl having an undulating luster. [French : Greek *kuma,* undulation, CYMA + -PHANE.]

cy·mose (sī′mōs′, sī-mōs′) *adj. Botany.* **1.** Pertaining to or resembling a cyme. **2.** Bearing a cyme or cymes. [CYM(E) + -OSE.] —**cy·mose·ly** *adv.*

Cym·ric, Kym·ric (kĭm′rĭk, sĭm′rĭk) *adj.* Of or pertaining to the Cymry or their languages, especially Welsh.
~*n.* **1.** The Welsh language. **2.** The Brythonic branch of the Celtic languages, including Welsh, Breton, and Cornish.

Cymru. See **Wales.**

Cym·ry, Cym·ri, Kym·ry (kĭm′rē, sĭm′rē) *n.* **1.** The Welsh. **2.** The branch of the Celtic people to which the Welsh, the Cornish, and the Bretons belong.

Cyn·e·wulf (kĭn′ə-wŏŏlf′) (*c.* A.D. 800). Anglo-Saxon poet, probably Northumbrian. He was the author of four poems that survive in 10th-century manuscripts: *Juliana, Elene, The Ascension,* and *The Fates of the Apostles.*

cyn·ic (sĭn′ĭk) *n.* **1. a.** One who believes that people are insincere and motivated by selfishness and who consequently expects the worst of human behavior. **b.** A scornful or mocking person. **2. Cynic.** A member of a sect, founded by Antisthenes of Athens, of ancient Greek philosophers who believed virtue to be the only good and self-control to be the only means of achieving virtue.
~*adj.* **1.** *Rare.* Cynical. **2. Cynic.** Of or pertaining to the Cynics or their doctrines. [Latin *cynicus,* from Greek *kunikos,* "doglike," currish (perhaps mistaken by the Greeks from the first part of *kunosarge,* the gymnasium where Antisthenes taught), from *kuōn* (stem *kun*-), dog.]

cyn·i·cal (sĭn′ĭ-kəl) *adj.* **1. a.** Scornful or skeptical of the motives or virtue of others. **b.** Bitterly mocking; sneering. **2.** Showing contempt for accepted morality or values: *a cynical cover-up by the authorities.* **3. Cynic.** Of or pertaining to the Cynics or their doctrines. —**cyn·i·cal·ly** *adv.* —**cyn·i·cal·ness** *n.*

cyn·i·cism (sĭn′ə-sĭz′əm) *n.* **1.** A cynical attitude or character. **2.** A cynical comment or act. **3. Cynic.** The beliefs and doctrines of the Cynics.

cy·no·sure (sī′nə-shŏŏr′, sĭn′ə-) *n.* **1.** An object or person that serves as a focal point of attention and admiration. **2.** Anything that serves to guide. [French, Ursa Minor, "the guiding star," from Latin *cynosūra,* from Greek *kunosoura,* "the dog's tail," Ursa Minor : *kunos,* genitive of *kuōn,* dog + *-ura,* plural of *-urus,* -UROUS.] —**cy·no·sur·al** *adj.*

Cyn·thi·a¹ (sĭn′thē-ə). *Greek Mythology.* Artemis, goddess of the moon. [Artemis was born on Mount *Cynthus,* on the island of Delos, Greece.]

Cynthia² *n. Poetic.* The moon or its personification.

CYO Catholic Youth Organization.

cypher. Variant of **cipher.**

cy·press (sī′prəs) *n.* **1.** Any evergreen coniferous tree of the genus *Cupressus,* having small, scalelike leaves and rounded cones. **2.** Any similar and related tree of the genus *Chamaecyparis,* such as *C. lawsoniana,* (Lawson's cypress). Also called "false cypress." **3.** Any of various other trees, such as the **swamp cypress** (*see*). **4.** The wood of any of these trees. **5.** Cypress branches used as a symbol of mourning. [Middle English *cipres,* from Old French, from Late Latin *cypressus,* from Greek *kuparissos,* of Mediterranean origin.]

cypress spurge *n.* A plant, *Euphorbia cyparissias,* native to Eurasia, having densely crowded, narrow leaves, and clusters of yellow-green flowers. [Probably because its narrow leaves suggest the needles of the cypress.]

cypress vine *n.* A tropical American vine, *Quamoclit pennata,* having finely divided compound leaves and scarlet flowers.

Cyp·ri·an (sĭp′rē-ən) *adj.* **1.** Of or pertaining to Cyprus, its people, their customs, or their language. **2.** Characteristic of or resembling the ancient worship of Aphrodite on Cyprus; licentious; wanton.
~*n.* **1.** A Cypriot (*see*). **2.** Often **cyprian.** *Obsolete.* A wanton person, especially a prostitute.

cy·pri·nid (sĭp′rə-nĭd) *n.* Any of numerous freshwater fishes of the family Cyprinidae, which includes the minnows, carps, and tench. [New Latin *Cyprinidae* : *Cyprinus* (genus name), from Latin *cyprīnus,* a carp, from Greek *kuprinos,* from *kupros,* "the henna plant,"

from Semitic, akin to Hebrew *kōpher* + -ID.] —**cy·pri·nid** *adj.*

cy·prin·o·dont (sĭ-prĭn′ə-dŏnt′, sī-prī′nə-) *n.* Any of various soft-finned fishes of the family Cyprinodontidae, which includes the killifishes, and many species popular in home aquariums. [New Latin *Cyprinodon* : Latin *cyprinus,* carp (see **cyprinid**) + -ODONT.]

cyp·ri·noid (sĭp′rə-noid′, sī-prī′-) *adj.* Of, pertaining to, or resembling a carp or related fish. [New Latin *Cyprinoidea* : *Cyprinus,* genus (see **cyprinid**) + -OID.] —**cyp·ri·noid** *n.*

Cyp·ri·ot, Cyp·ri·ote (sĭp′rē-ōt) *n.* **1.** A native or inhabitant of Cyprus. Also called "Cyprian." **2. a.** The ancient Greek dialect of Cyprus, belonging to the Arcado-Cyprian branch. **b.** The dialect of Modern Greek spoken in Cyprus. —**Cyp·ri·ot** *adj.*

cyp·ri·pe·di·um (sĭp′rə-pē′dē-əm) *n.* Any orchid of the genus *Cypripedium,* which includes the lady's-slippers. [New Latin, probably "Venus' slipper" : Late Latin *Cypris,* Venus, from Greek *Kupris,* Aphrodite, from *Kupros,* CYPRUS (supposedly her birthplace) + New Latin *-pedium,* probably a variant of Greek *pedilon,* sandal.]

cy·prot·er·one (sī-prŏt′ə-rōn′) *n.* A hormone that inhibits the secretion of androgen. [Probably Latin *Cypris,* Venus (from Greek *Kupris,* from *Kupros,* Cyprus) + (TESTOS)TERONE.]

Cy·prus (sī′prəs). Turkish **Ki·bris** (kē′brīs). Greek **Ky·ros** (kē′prôs). Island state in the east Mediterranean Sea. Dominated in turn by ancient Egypt, Assyria, Greece, Persia, the Romans, and Byzantium, it fell to the Ottoman Empire (1571) and passed to Britain (1878). Some Greek Cypriots sought *enosis* ("union") with Greece, and violence erupted in 1931 and again in 1955 under the EOKA movement. The island became an independent member of the British Commonwealth (1960), but violence between Turks (making up 18 percent of the population) and Greeks continued. President Makarios was overthrown (1974), and Turkey invaded the north. The island was partitioned, the northern part becoming known as the Turkish Federated State of Cyprus. In 1983 it was proclaimed the **Turkish Republic of Northern Cyprus.** Economic recovery in the south led to resumed exports of clothing, copper, vegetables, fruit, and wine, and a renewed tourist industry. Area, 9,251 square kilometers (3,572 square miles). Population, 700,000. Capital, Nicosia. See map at **Turkey.**

cyp·se·la (sĭp′sə-lə) *n., pl.* **-lae** (-lē′). *Botany.* A small dry fruit that resembles an achene but does not separate from its calyx, characteristic of composite plants. [New Latin, from Greek *kupselē,* hollow vessel, chest.]

Cy·ra·no de Ber·ge·rac (sîr′ə-nō də bûr′zhə-răk′), **Savinien de** (1619–55). French dramatist and novelist, whose spirited dramas *Le Pédant Joué* (*c.* 1654) and *La Mort d'Agrippine* (1653) ran counter to the classical taste of his day. He was the subject of Edmond Rostand's play *Cyrano de Bergerac* (1897), which depicted him as a chivalric duelist with a comically long nose.

Cyr·e·na·ic (sîr′ə-nā′ĭk, sĭr′-) *adj.* **1.** Of or pertaining to Cyrenaica or its major city, Cyrene. **2.** Of or pertaining to the hedonistic school of philosophy founded in Cyrene by Aristippus, who believed that pleasure was the only good in life.
~*n.* **1.** A native or inhabitant of Cyrenaica or Cyrene. **2.** A disciple of the Cyrenaic school of philosophy.

Cy·re·na·i·ca (sîr′ə-nā′ĭ-kə, sĭr′-). Region of eastern Libya, extending from the Mediterranean coast into the desert.

Cy·re·ne (sī-rē′nē). Ancient city in northeast Libya. Founded by Greeks (*c.* 630 B.C.), it became the chief city of Cyrenaica.

Cyr·il (sîr′əl), **Saint** (827–69). Macedonian missionary to the Slavs, the alleged inventor of the Cyrillic alphabet. From 863 he and his brother St. Methodius (825–84) worked among the Khazars of Moravia, translating the scriptures into the local language through an adaptation of the Greek alphabet.

Cy·ril·lic (sə-rĭl′ĭk) *adj.* **1.** Of or pertaining to St. Cyril, the 9th-century missionary to the Moravians. **2.** Of or designating the Cyrillic alphabet.
~*n.* The Cyrillic alphabet.

Cyrillic alphabet *n.* An old alphabet ascribed to St. Cyril, presently used in modified form for Russian, Bulgarian, Serbo-Croat, Macedonian, and certain languages of the former U.S.S.R., such as Ukranian. Also called "Cyrillic."

Cy·rus II (sī′rəs), called "the Great" (died 529 B.C.). King of Persia (550–529 B.C.) and founder of the Achaemenid empire. Having seized the empire of the Medes, he went on to conquer Lydia, the Ionian cities, and Babylon with its subject states in Syria. He was tolerant in religious matters, permitting the worship of native gods and allowing the Jews to return to Jerusalem (537).

cyst (sĭst) *n.* **1.** *Pathology.* An abnormal membranous sac containing a liquid or semisolid substance. **2.** *Anatomy.* Any sac or vesicle in the body. **3.** *Biology.* A capsulelike membrane enclosing certain organisms in a resting stage. [New Latin *cystis,* from Greek *kustis,* bladder, pouch.]

cyst-. Variant of **cysto-.**

cys·tec·to·my (sĭ-stĕk′tə-mē) *n., pl.* **-mies. 1.** Surgical excision of the gallbladder or of a portion of the urinary bladder. **2.** Surgical removal of a cyst.

cys·te·ine (sĭs′tē-ēn′, -tē-ĭn) *n.* An amino acid, $C_3H_7NO_2S$, found in most proteins, especially in keratin. [From CYSTINE.]

cys·tic (sĭs′tĭk) *adj.* **1.** Of, pertaining to, or like a cyst. **2.** Having or containing a cyst or cysts. **3.** Enclosed in a cyst. **4.** *Anatomy.* Pertaining to the gallbladder or urinary bladder.

cys·ti·cer·coid (sĭs′tə-sûr′koid) *n.* The larval stage of certain tapeworms, like a cysticercus but having the scolex completely filling the enclosing sac. [CYSTICERC(US) + -OID.]

cypress *The bald cypress (above), which is so called because it is deciduous, is native to the swamplands of the southern United States. Woody humps around the tree's base carry oxygen down to its waterlogged roots.*

CZECHOSLOVAKIA

cys·ti·cer·co·sis (sĭs′tə-sər-kō′sĭs) *n.* The condition of being infested with cysticerci. [CYSTICERC(US) + -OSIS.]

cys·ti·cer·cus (sĭs′tə-sûr′kəs) *n., pl.* **-ci** (-sī′). The larval stage of many tapeworms, consisting of a scolex, or head, enclosed in a fluid-filled sac. [New Latin, "bladder tail" : CYST(O)- + Greek *kerkos*, tail.]

cystic fibrosis *n.* A congenital disease of mucous and sweat glands throughout the body, usually developing during childhood and causing pancreatic insufficiency and pulmonary disorders.

cys·tine (sĭs′tēn) *n.* A white crystalline compound, $C_6H_{12}N_2O_4S_2$, the principal sulfur-containing amino acid of protein. [CYST(O)- + -INE.]

cys·ti·tis (sĭs-tī′tĭs) *n.* Inflammation of the urinary bladder. [New Latin : CYST(O)- + -ITIS.]

cysto-, cyst– *prefix.* Indicates a bladder or cyst; for example, **cystocele, cystoid.** [Greek *kustis,* bladder.]

cys·to·carp (sĭs′tə-kärp′) *n. Botany.* A structure consisting of fertile filaments and carpospores, developed after fertilization of the carpogonium in red algae. [CYSTO- + -CARP.]

cys·to·cele (sĭs′tə-sēl) *n.* A hernia of the bladder. [CYSTO- + -CELE (hernia).]

cys·toid (sĭs′toid′) *n.* A structure resembling a cyst but lacking an enclosing membrane. [CYST(O)- + -OID.] —**cys·toid** *adj.*

cys·to·lith (sĭs′tə-lĭth) *n.* **1.** *Botany.* A mineral concretion, usually calcium carbonate, formed in the cellulose wall of certain plant cells. **2.** *Pathology.* A urinary calculus. [CYSTO- + -LITH.]

cys·to·scope (sĭs′tə-skōp′) *n.* A tubular instrument fitted with a light and used to examine the urinary bladder and ureter. [CYSTO- + -SCOPE.] —**cys·to·scop·ic** (sĭs′tə-skōp′ĭk) *adj.*

cys·tos·co·py (sĭs-tŏs′kə-pē) *n.* Examination of the urinary bladder using a cystoscope in order to detect and remove polyp, take tissue specimens, or the like. [CYSTO- + -SCOPY.]

cys·tot·o·my *n.* Surgical cutting of the urinary bladder, usually through the abdominal wall. [CYSTO- + -TOMY.]

–cyte *suffix.* Indicates a cell; for example, **leucocyte.** [New Latin *-cyta,* from Greek *kutos,* hollow vessel.]

Cy·the·ra (sə-thîr′ə). Greek island, southernmost of the Ionian Islands, in the Mediterranean off the southern Peloponnese. In ancient times it was the chief center of the cult of Aphrodite.

Cytherea. See **Aphrodite.**

cyto-, cyt– *prefix.* Indicates cell; for example, **cytokinesis, cytology.** [Greek *kutos,* hollow vessel.]

cy·to·chem·is·try (sī′tō-kĕm′ĭs-trē) *n.* The chemistry of plant and animal cells. —**cy·to·chem·i·cal** *adj.*

cy·to·chrome (sī′tō-krōm′) *n.* Any of a class of compounds containing iron and protein, important for oxidation-reduction reactions in cells. [CYTO- + -CHROME.]

cytochrome oxidase *n.* An oxidizing enzyme that functions in cell respiration by reacting with oxygen in the reduced state.

cy·to·gen·e·sis (sī′tō-jĕn′ə-sĭs) *n.* Also **cy·tog·e·ny** (sī-tŏj′ə-nē). The formation and development of cells. [CYTO- + -GENESIS.] —**cy·to·ge·net·ic** (sī′tō-jə-nĕt′ĭk) *adj.*

cy·to·ge·net·ics (sī′tō-jə-nĕt′ĭks) *n. Used with a singular verb.* The study of heredity by cytological and genetic methods, particularly involving the study of chromosomes. —**cy·to·ge·net·i·cal** *adj.* —**cy·to·ge·net·i·cal·ly** *adv.* —**cy·to·ge·net·i·cist** *n.*

cy·to·ki·ne·sis (sī′tō-kī-nē′sĭs, -kĭ-nē′sĭs) *n.* The cleavage of cytoplasm during cell division. [New Latin : CYTO- + -KINESIS.]

cy·to·ki·nin (sī′tə-kī′nĭn) *n.* Any of various growth regulators that promote cell division in plants.

cy·tol·o·gy (sī-tŏl′ə-jē) *n. Abbr.* **cytol.** The branch of biology dealing with the study of the formation, structure, and function of cells. [CYTO- + -LOGY.] —**cy·to·log·i·cal** *adj.* —**cy·to·log·i·cal·ly** *adv.* —**cy·tol·o·gist** *n.*

cy·tol·y·sin (sī-tŏl′ə-sĭn) *n.* A substance capable of destroying an animal cell partially or completely. [CYTOLYS(IS) + -IN.]

cy·tol·y·sis (sī-tŏl′ə-sĭs) *n.* The dissolution of a cell. [New Latin : CYTO- + -LYSIS.] —**cy·to·lyt·ic** *adj.*

cy·to·me·gal·ic (sī′tō-mə-găl′ĭk) *adj.* Pertaining to or characterized by greatly enlarged cells.

cy·to·meg·a·lo·vi·rus (sī′tə-mĕg′ə-lō-vī′rəs) *n.* Any of a group of viruses that cause cellular enlargement and also cause a disease of infants characterized by circulatory dysfunction and microcephaly.

cy·to·path·ic (sī′tə-păth′ĭk) *adj.* Of or pertaining to pathologic changes in cells.

cy·toph·a·gy (sī-tŏf′ə-jē) *n.* The devouring of other cells by the phagocytes. [CYTO- + -PHAGY.] —**cy·to·phag·ic, cy·toph·a·gous** *adj.*

cy·to·pho·tom·e·try (sī′tə-fō-tŏm′ə-trē) *n.* The photometric study of a cell. —**cy·to·pho·to·met·ric** (sī′tə-fō-tə-mĕt′rĭk) *adj.*

cy·to·plasm (sī′tə-plăz′əm) *n.* The protoplasm outside a cell nucleus. [CYTO- + -PLASM.] —**cy·to·plas·mic** *adj.* —**cy·to·plas·mi·cal·ly** *adv.*

cy·to·plast (sī′tə-plăst′) *n.* The cytoplasm within a single cell. [CYTO- + -PLAST.] —**cy·to·plas·tic** *adj.*

cy·to·sine (sī′tō-sēn′, -zēn′, -sən) *n.* A pyrimidine base, $C_4H_5N_3O$, that is an essential constituent of both RNA and DNA. [CYT(O)- + -OS(E) + -INE.]

cy·to·tax·on·o·my (sī′tō-tăk-sŏn′ə-mē) *n.* The classification of organisms based on cellular structure, especially on the comparative morphology of chromosomes. —**cy·to·tax·o·nom·ic** *adj.* —**cy·to·tax·on·o·mist** *n.*

cy·to·tech·nol·o·gist (sī′tə-tĕk-nŏl′ə-jĭst) *n.* A technician who is trained in the medical examination and identification of cellular abnormalities.

cy·to·tox·ic *adj.* Destructive to cells. Said particularly of drugs that destroy cancer cells and are used in chemotherapy. [CYTO- + TOXIC.] —**cy·to·tox·ic·i·ty** *n.*

czar (zär) *n.* Also **tsar, tzar. 1.** A king or emperor, especially one of the former emperors of Russia. **2.** A tyrant; autocrat. **3.** *Informal.* One in authority; leader: *a czar in finance.* [Polish, from Russian *tsar',* from old Russian *tsĭsarĭ,* from Gothic *kaisar,* from Latin *Caesar,* emperor, CAESAR.] —**czar′dom** *n.*

Usage: Czar is the most common form in American usage and virtually the only one employed in the extended senses *(any tyrant* or, informally, *one in authority).* But *tsar* is preferred by most scholars of Slavic studies as a more accurate transliteration of the Russian, and is often found in scholarly writing with reference to one of the Russian emperors.

czar·das, csar·das (chär′dăsh) *n.* **1.** An intricate Hungarian dance characterized by variations in tempo. **2.** Music for this dance. [Hungarian *csárdás.*]

czar·e·vitch (zär′ə-vĭch) *n.* The eldest son of a czar. [Polish, from Russian *tsarevich : tsar',* CZAR + *-evich,* masculine patronymic suffix.]

cza·rev·na (zä-rĕv′nə) *n.* **1.** The daughter of a czar. **2.** The wife of a czarevitch. [Polish, from Russian *tsarevna : tsar',* CZAR + *-evna,* feminine patronymic suffix.]

cza·ri·na (zä-rē′nə) *n.* Also **cza·rit·za** (zä-rĭt′sə). The wife of a czar; an empress of Russia. [Polish, from Russian *tsarina : tsar',* CZAR + *-ina,* feminine suffix.]

czar·ism (zär′ĭz′əm) *n.* The system of government in Russia under the czars; absolute monarchy; autocracy. —**czar′ist** *adj.*

Czech (chĕk) *n.* **1.** A native or inhabitant of Czechoslovakia; especially, a Bohemian or Moravian. **2.** The West Slavonic language of these people. Formerly called "Bohemian." —**Czech** *adj.*

Czech·o·slo·vak·i·a (chĕk′ə-slō-vä′kē-ə, -väk′ē-ə). *Abbr.* **Czech.** *Czech* **Čes·ko·slo·ven·sko** (chĕs′kô-slô′vĕn-skô). Country in central Europe. Czechoslovakia was created (1918) out of the former Austrian territories of Bohemia and Moravia, with parts of Silesia. Ruthenia was added in 1920. The nation's name derives from the two main language groups: Czech in the west and Slovak in the east. Czechoslovakia developed in the interwar years under the democratic leadership of Tomáš Masaryk and Eduard Beneš. Tensions grew among its component nationalities, especially the German-speakers in the areas known as the Sudetenland, and the region was ceded to Germany by the Munich Agreement (1938). Hitler occupied the rest of the country (1939). After World War II the country fell within the Soviet orbit. Ruthenia was ceded to the U.S.S.R., and by 1948 the Communist Party was in control. In 1968 a liberal program, introduced by the new secretary of the Communist Party, Alexander Dubček, ended when Warsaw Pact tanks invaded and Dubček was ousted. The country returned to rigid pro-Soviet orthodoxy until 1989, when widespread demonstrations led to political reforms. Free elections were held in 1990. In 1993, Czechoslovakia divided into two nations: Czech Republic and Slovak Republic. Czechoslovakia is a highly industrialized country. Cereals, sugar beets, and potatoes are the chief crops, and timber is an important product. Area, 127,868 square kilometers (49,370 square miles). Population, 15,700,000. Capital, Prague. —**Czech·o·slo·vak, Czech·o·slo·va·ki·an** *adj. & n.*

Czer·ny (chĕr′nē), **Karl** (1791–1857). Austrian pianist and composer. A disciple of Ludwig van Beethoven and the teacher of Franz Liszt, he is most remembered and respected for his piano studies, including the *School of Velocity* and the *School of the Left Hand,* which have been toiled over by generations of beginning pianists.

PRONUNCIATION KEY

ă, pat; ā, pay; âr, care; ä, father, are; b, bib; ch, church; d, deed; ĕ, pet; ē, be; f, fife; g, gag; h, hat; hw, which; ĭ, pit; ī, pie; îr, pier; j, judge; k, kick; l, lid, needle; m, mum; n, no, sudden; ng, thing; ŏ, pot; ō, toe; ô, paw, for; oi, noise; ou, out; ŏŏ, book; ōō, boot; p, pop; r, roar; s, sauce; sh, ship, dish; t, tight; th, thin, path; *th,* this, bathe; ŭ, cut; ûr, fur; v, valve; w, with; y, yes; z, zebra, size; zh, vision; ə, about, item, edible, gallop, circus, peaceful

IN FOREIGN WORDS:

à, *Fr.* ami; œ, *Fr.* feu, *Ger.* schön; ü, *Fr.* tu, *Ger.* über; KH, *Ger.* ich, *Scot.* loch; N, *Fr.* bon; y′, *Fr.* Compiègne

STRESS MARKS:

Primary stress: ′
in·**cite**′ (ĭn-sīt′)
Secondary stress: ′
in′**sight** (ĭn′sīt′)

d, D (dē) *n., pl.* **d's** or **D's. 1.** The fourth letter of the modern English alphabet. See feature at **alphabet. 2.** Any of the speech sounds represented by this letter. **3. D** The lowest passing grade given to a student in a school or college. **4. D** *Music.* **a.** The second tone in the scale of C major, or the fourth tone of the relative minor scale. **b.** The key or a scale in which D is the tonic. **c.** A written or printed note representing this tone. **d.** A string, key, or pipe tuned to the pitch of this tone.

d, D, d., D. *Note:* As an abbreviation or symbol, *d* may be a small or a capital letter, with or without a period. Established forms or those generally preferred precede the definition. When no form is given, all four forms are in general use in that sense. **1. d.** dam (mother). **2. d.** date. **3. d.** daughter. **4. d** day. **5. D.** December. **6. d** deci-. **7. D, D.** Democrat; Democratic. **8. D.** department. **9. d., D.** deputy. **10. D.** Deus. **11. D** The symbol for deuterium. **12. d** *Physics.* deuteron. **13. d** dextro-. **14. d.** died. **15. D.** *Optics.* diopter. **16. D.** doctor (in academic degrees). **17. D.** Dominus. **18. D.** Don (title). **19. d., D.** dose. **20. d., D.** drachma. **21. D.** duchess. **22. D.** duke. **23. D.** Dutch. **24. D** The Roman numeral for 500. **25. d.** *British.* penny (Latin *denarius*). **26.** The fourth in a series.

d– *prefix. Chemistry.* Indicates a dextrorotatory compound. Usually written in italics; for example, "*d*-glucose." Compare **l–**.

D– *prefix. Chemistry.* Indicates an optically active compound with a molecular structure derived from or related to the structure of dextrorotatory glyceraldehyde; for example, "D-alanine." Compare **L–**. An isomer designated D- may itself be dextrorotatory (*d*-) but is not necessarily so.

–'d *suffix.* Indicates: **1.** Contraction of *had, should, would,* or *did,* as in *Who'd you see?* **2.** Contraction of *-ed,* as in *martyr'd.*

da¹ (dä) *n. Informal.* Father. [Of baby-talk origin.]

da² deca–.

Da. Danish.

D.A. district attorney.

dab¹ (dăb) *v.* **dabbed, dabbing, dabs.** *—tr.* **1.** To apply with short, poking strokes. **2.** To cover or press on lightly with or as if with something moist. **3.** To strike or hit lightly, as with a quick pat of the hand. *—intr.* **1.** To touch or poke gingerly at something. **2.** To tap gently; pat. **~** *n.* **1. a.** A small amount. **b.** A small mass or lump of a moist substance: *a dab of jam.* **2.** A quick, light pat, as with the hand. **3.** *Chiefly British Slang.* A fingerprint. [Middle English *dabben,* probably from Middle Dutch *dabben,* to tap (imitative).]

dab² *n.* Any of various small flatfishes, chiefly of the genera *Limanda* and *Hippoglossoides,* related to and resembling the flounders. [15th century : origin obscure.]

dab³ *n. British Informal.* An expert. [17th century : origin obscure.]

dab·ber (dăb'ər) *n.* **1.** One that dabs. **2.** *Printing.* A cushioned pad used with a brayer by printers and engravers to apply ink.

dab·ble (dăb'əl) *v.* **-bled, -bling, -bles.** *—tr.* **1.** To splash or spatter, as with a liquid. **2.** To move (a part of the body) in water. *—intr.* **1.** To splash liquid gently and playfully. **2.** To undertake something superficially or without serious intent: *dabble in antiques.* **3.** To bob forward and under in shoal water so as to feed off the bottom. [Probably from Dutch *dabbelen,* frequentative of *dabben,* to strike, tap, from Middle Dutch, to tap.]

dab·bler (dăb'lər) *n.* **1.** One who dabbles; dilettante. **2.** A duck of the genus *Anas* that feeds near the surface of the water or on land, including the mallard, teal, and widgeon. Compare **diving duck.**

dab·chick (dăb'chĭk') *n.* Any of various small grebes of the genus *Podiceps.* [Earlier *dapchick, dopchick : dop-,* probably from Middle English *doppe,* diving bird, Old English *doppa* + CHICK.]

dab hand *n. British Informal.* An expert; a skillful person: *a dab hand at sewing.*

da ca·po (dä kä'pō, də) *adv. Abbr.* **D.C.** *Music.* From the beginning. Used as a direction to repeat a passage: *da capo al fine.* [Italian.]

Dac·ca or **Dha·ka** (dăk'ə). Capital of Bangladesh, on a branch of the Dhaleswari River in the south of the country. Formerly the capital of Mogul Bengal (1608–1704), it came under British rule and was the capital of the province of East Bengal and Assam

(1905–12). After Indian independence (1947), Dacca was made the capital of East Pakistan (1956), which became Bangladesh in 1971.

dace (dās) *n., pl.* **daces** or collectively **dace.** Any of various small freshwater fishes of the family Cyprinidae, related to and resembling the minnows. [Middle English *dars, dase,* from Old French *dars,* probably from *dart,* DART (from its swift motion).]

da·cha (dä'chə) *n.* A Russian country house; a villa. [Russian *dacha,* gift, portion, land (granted by a prince), country or holiday house.]

Da·chau (dä'kou'). Town in southern Germany, near Munich in Bavaria. A Nazi concentration camp was built here in 1935, and an estimated 70,000 inmates died.

dachs·hund (däks'hōōnt', däks'hōōnd') *n.* A small dog of a breed developed in Germany for hunting badgers, having a long body with a usually short-haired brown or black and brown coat, drooping ears, and very short legs. [German *Dachshund : Dachs,* badger + *Hund,* dog.]

Da·cia (dä'shə). An ancient name for the area roughly corresponding to modern Romania. **—Da·cian** *adj. & n.*

da·coit, da·koit (də-koit') *n.* A member of any of the robber bands of India and Burma who live in the hills and attack in armed gangs, usually on horseback. [Hindi *ḍakait,* from *ḍākā,* "gang-robbery," from Sanskrit *daṣṭaka†,* crowded.]

da·coit·y (də-koi'tē) *n., pl.* **-ties.** Gang robbery in India or Burma. [Hindi *dakaiti.* See dacoit.]

Da·cron (dā'krŏn', dăk'rŏn') *n.* A trademark for a synthetic polyester textile fiber resistant to stretching and wrinkling.

dac·tyl (dăk'təl) *n.* Also **dac·ty·lus** (-tə-ləs), *pl.* **-li** (-lī') (for sense 2). **1.** *Prosody.* **a.** In accentual verse, a metrical foot consisting of one accented syllable followed by two unaccented. **b.** In quantitative verse, one long syllable followed by two short. **2.** *Zoology.* A finger, toe, or similar part or structure; digit. [Middle English *dactil,* from Latin *dactylus,* from Greek *daktulos†,* finger, hence dactyl (the three syllables of which correspond to the three joints of a finger).] **—dac·tyl·ic** (dăk-tĭl'ĭk) *adj. & n.* **—dac·tyl·i·cal·ly** *adv.*

dactylo–, dactyl– *prefix.* Indicates finger or toe; for example, **dactylogram.** [Greek *daktulos,* finger, DACTYL.]

dac·tyl·o·gram (dăk-tĭl'ə-grăm') *n.* A fingerprint. [DACTYLO- + -GRAM.]

dac·ty·log·ra·phy (dăk'tə-lŏg'rə-fē) *n.* The study of fingerprints as a method of identification. [DACTYLO- + -GRAPHY.] **—dac·ty·log·ra·pher** *n.* **—dac·ty·lo·graph·ic** (dăk'tə-lō-grăf'ĭk) *adj.*

dac·ty·lol·o·gy (dăk'tə-lŏl'ə-jē) *n.* The use of the fingers and hands to communicate, as in the manual alphabet. [DACTYLO- + -LOGY.]

dad (dăd) *n.* **1.** *Informal.* A father. **2.** *Slang.* A term of address used to an older male person other than one's father. [Of baby-talk origin.]

Da·da, da·da (dä'dä) *n.* Also **Da·da·ism** (-ĭz'əm). A western European artistic and literary movement (1916–24) that reacted against traditional cultural aesthetic values by emphasizing irrationality. [French *dada,* hobbyhorse, from baby talk (a name arbitrarily adopted first as the title of a Dadaist review of 1916).] **—Da·da·ist** *n.* **—Da·da·is·tic** *adj.* See feature, next page.

Dadd (dăd), **Richard** (1817–86). British painter. Of unstable temperament, he murdered his father and produced much of his best work in a lunatic asylum. He is known for his extraordinarily dense and intricate fantasy scenes of fairies, goblins, and sprites.

dad·dy (dăd'ē) *n., pl.* **-dies.** *Informal.* Father; dad. Used familiarly, especially by children. [Diminutive of DAD.]

daddy long·legs (lông'lĕgz', lŏng'-) *n., pl.* **daddy longlegs. 1.** Any of various arachnids of the order Phalangida, having a small, rounded body and long, slender legs. Also called "harvestman." **2.** *Chiefly British.* An insect, the **crane fly** (see).

da·do (dā'dō) *n., pl.* **-does. 1.** *Architecture.* The section of a pedestal between the base and crown. **2.** The lower portion of the wall of a room, decorated differently from the upper section, as with panels. **~** *tr.v.* **dadoed, -doing, -does.** To provide with a dado. [Italian, a die, cube, probably from Latin *datum,* gift, pawn (chessman), from the past participle of *dare,* to give.]

dabchick *The smallest of the grebe family, the dabchick is common on densely vegetated lakes in Europe, Asia, and Africa. The male (above left) has a red neck only during the breeding season in summer; at other times of the year, its plumage is brown, buff, and white. The female has similar but duller markings.*

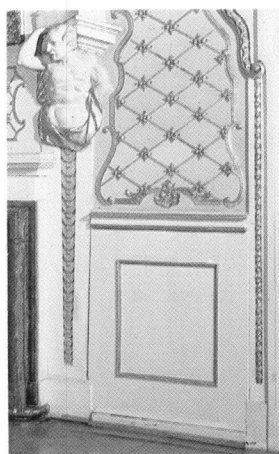

dado *The crisscross-painted plaster decoration on this wall extends down to a paneled dado.*

Dada

ART CREATED FROM CHANCE

Dada—French for "hobbyhorse"—was a name picked at random

Dada was born in Zurich in 1916 when a nightclub, the Cabaret Voltaire, was opened to operate as an agency for progressive and émigré artists. The movement's purpose was not to create a new style but to escape from artistic conventions and to explore materials and modes of communication not previously deemed suitable for the arts. An artist could use materials found by chance or arranged at random. The very name Dada, French for "hobbyhorse," was picked at random from a dictionary.

Leading figures in this "anti-art" movement were Jean Arp, Richard Hülsenbeck, and Tristan Tzara. The movement became international through artists such as Marcel Duchamps, Man Ray, and Francis Picabia in New York, André Breton and a literary cell in Paris, and Kurt Schwitters and Max Ernst in Germany. In the Berlin group, John Heartfield was perfecting the new form of photomontage that he later used for vivid anti-Nazi propaganda.

In 1924 Dada merged with surrealism.

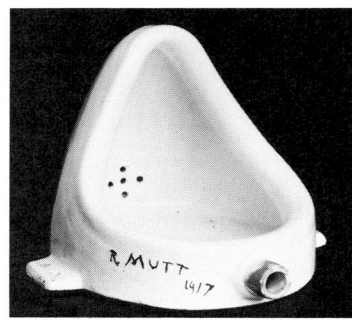

EXHIBIT REJECTED *Marcel Duchamp tried, and failed, to exhibit this urinal in New York in 1917. He called it* Fountain *and said it was a "ready-made" work of art.*

PAPER COLLAGE Hair Navel Picture *was done by the German Kurt Schwitters, who said an artist could mold paper into pictures "provided he is capable of molding a picture." In the subtlety of their colors, his works are widely seen as transcending Dada.*

dae·dal (dēd′l) *adj.* **1.** Ingenious and complex in design or function; intricate. **2.** Finely or skillfully made or employed; artistic. [Latin *daedalus*, from Greek *daidalos*, skillful.]

Daed·a·lus (dĕd′l-əs; *British* dēd′l-əs). *Greek Mythology.* A sculptor and inventor, father of Icarus and builder of the Labyrinth. —**Dae·da·li·an, Dae·da·le·an** (dĭ-dā′lē-ən, -dāl′yən) *adj.*

daemon. Variant of **demon.**

daf·fa·dil·ly, daf·fo·dil·ly (dăf′ə-dĭl′ē) *n., pl.* **-lies.** *Regional.* A daffo-

dil. Also called "daffadowndilly," "daffydowndilly."

daf·fo·dil (dăf′ə-dĭl) *n.* **1.** A bulbous plant, *Narcissus pseudonarcissus,* having usually yellow flowers with a trumpet-shaped central crown. **2.** Its flower. **3.** Brilliant to vivid yellow. [Probably from Dutch *de affodil,* the asphodel : *de,* the + *affodil,* from Medieval Latin *affodilus,* from Latin *asphodelus,* ASPHODEL.]

daf·fy (dăf′ē) *adj.* **-fier, -fiest.** *Informal.* Silly; foolish; zany. [Obsolete English *daff,* fool, Middle English *daffe,* probably related to *dafte,* gentle, foolish, DAFT.]

daft (dăft, däft) *adj.* **1.** Mad; crazy. **2.** Foolish; stupid. [Middle English *dafte,* gentle, modest, foolish, Old English *gedæfte,* mild, meek.] —**daft·ly** *adv.* —**daft·ness** *n.*

Da·fydd ap Gruff·ydd (dä′wĭth ăp grĭf′ĭth, dä′-) (died 1283). The last native Prince of Wales (1282–83), he fought his brother Llywelyn ap Gruffydd for the title, claiming it when his brother died (1282). He was captured by the English under Edward I and executed.

Dafydd ap Gwil·ym (gwĭl′əm) (c. 1320–c. 1380). Welsh poet. He was influenced by the troubadours of Europe and wrote in a tone more personal than the conventions of his day. He also popularized a new metrical form adopted by later bardic writers.

dag (dăg) *n.* **1.** A lock of matted or dung-coated wool. **2.** A loosely hanging end or shred. [Middle English *dagge†,* shred, tag.]

dag decagram.

Da·gan (dä′gän). The Babylonian god of the earth, considered by some to be identified with Baal.

Da·ge·stan (dăg′ə-stăn′, däg′ə-stän′). A part of Russia, bordered on the east by the Caspian Sea. It was annexed by Russia in 1813. Though comprising over 30 different nationalities, the population is chiefly Muslim. Its capital is the Caspian port of Makhachkala.

dag·ga (dăg′ə) *n. South African.* Indian hemp used as a narcotic; cannabis. [Afrikaans, from Hottentot *dachab.*]

dag·ger (dăg′ər) *n.* **1.** A short pointed weapon with sharp edges, used for stabbing. **2.** Something that agonizes, torments, or wounds. **3.** *Printing.* **a.** An **obelisk** *(see).* **b.** A double dagger *(see).* —**at daggers drawn.** Hostile; ready for confrontation. —**look daggers.** To glare angrily or hatefully.

~*tr.v.* **daggered, -gering, -gers.** **1.** To stab with a dagger. **2.** To mark with a dagger. [Middle English *daggere,* from obsolete *dag,* to pierce, influenced by Old French *dague,* from Old Provençal or Old Italian *daga,* perhaps from Vulgar Latin *daca* (unattested), "Dacian knife," feminine of Latin *Dācus,* Dacian, from DACIA.]

dagger fern *n.* An evergreen North American fern, *Polystichum acrostichoides,* having dense clusters of lance-shaped fronds. Also called "Christmas fern."

dag·lock (dăg′lŏk′) *n.* A lock of wool; a dag.

Da·gon (dā′gŏn′). The chief god of the ancient Philistines and later the Phoenicians, represented as half man and half fish. [Middle English, from Latin, from Greek *Dagōn,* from Hebrew *Dāgōn,* "small fish," diminutive of *dāg,* fish.]

Da·guerre (də-gâr′), **Louis Jacques Mandé** (1787–1851). French inventor of a photographic method in which sunlight formed a permanent image on a copper plate treated with silver iodide.

da·guerre·o·type (də-gâr′ə-tīp′) *n.* **1.** An early photographic process with the impression made on a light-sensitive silver-coated metallic plate and developed by mercury vapor. **2.** A photograph made by this process.

~*tr.v.* **daguerreotyped, -typing, -types.** To photograph by this process. [After Louis DAGUERRE.] —**da·guerre·o·typ·er** *n.* —**da·guerre·o·typ·y** *n.*

dah (dä) *n.* A dash in Morse code. Compare **dit.**

da·ha·be·ah, da·ha·bee·yah, da·ha·bi·ah (dä′hə-bē′ə) *n.* A houseboat used on the Nile, having sails and sometimes an engine. [Arabic *dahabīya,* "the golden" (that is, gilded barge), originally with reference to those used by Egyptian rulers.]

Dahl (däl), **Roald** (1916–90). British author, born in Wales of Norwegian parents. He wrote suspense stories and children's books, such as *Charlie and the Chocolate Factory* (1964).

dahl·i·a (dăl′yə, däl′-, dāl′-) *n.* **1.** Any of several plants of the genus *Dahlia,* native to Mexico and Central America, having tuberous roots and showy, variously colored flowers; especially, any of the horticultural forms derived from *D. pinnata* and *D. juarezii.* **2.** The flower of any of these plants. [New Latin *Dahlia;* named in honor of Anders *Dahl,* 18th-century Swedish botanist.]

Dahomey. See **Benin.**

da·hoon (də-hoon′) *n.* An evergreen shrub or small tree, *Ilex cassine,* of the southeastern United States, having red fruit. [Origin unknown.]

Dail Ei·reann (dô′əl â′rən). The lower legislative house of the Irish parliament. Also called "Dáil." See **Oireachtas.** [Irish : *dáil,* assembly, from Old Irish *dāl* + *Éireann,* genitive of *Éire,* Ireland, from Old Irish *Ériu,* "land."]

dai·ly (dā′lē) *adj.* Of, pertaining to, occurring, or published every day or every weekday.

~*n., pl.* **dailies.** **1.** A daily publication, especially a newspaper. **2.** *British.* A servant, especially a cleaning woman, who lives off the premises.

~*adv.* Each day; day after day. [Middle English *daili,* Old English *dæglīc,* from *dæg,* DAY.]

daily double *n. Horse Racing.* A bet won by choosing both winners of two specified races on one day.

dai·mio, dai·myo (dī′myō) *n., pl.* **daimio, daimyo, -mios,** or **-myos.**

A hereditary nobleman in feudal Japan. [Japanese *daimyō,* "great name."]

daimon. Variant of **demon.**

dain·ty (dān′tē) *adj.* **-tier, -tiest. 1.** Delicately beautiful or charming; exquisite: *"No dainty rhymes or sentimental love verses for you, terrible year"* (Walt Whitman). **2.** Delicious; choice. **3.** Of refined taste or manners. **4.** Too fastidious; fussy.
∼*n., pl.* **dainties.** Something delicious; a delicacy. [Middle English *deinte,* delicious, pleasant, from *deinte,* pleasure, delicacy, from Old French *deintie,* from Latin *dīgnitās* (stem *dīgnitāt-*), dignity, worth, from *dīgnus,* worthy.] **—dain·ti·ly** *adv.* **—dain·ti·ness** *n.*

dai·qui·ri (dī′kə-rē, dăk′ə-rē) *n., pl.* **-ris.** An iced cocktail of rum, lime or lemon juice, and sugar. [After *Daiquirí,* Cuba, source of the rum originally used in this drink.]

Dairen. See **Lü-da.**

dair·y (dâr′ē) *n., pl.* **-dairies. 1.** A commercial establishment that processes or sells milk and milk products. **2.** A place where milk and cream are stored and processed, such as a specially equipped building on a farm. **3. a.** A dairy farm. **b.** The herd of cattle on a dairy farm. **4.** The dairy business; dairying. **5.** Dairy products, as distinguished from meat, with reference to Jewish religious dietary laws. [Middle English *daierie,* from *daie,* dairymaid, Old English *dæge,* dough-kneader.] **—dair·y** *adj.*

dairy cattle *pl.n.* Cows bred and raised for milk rather than meat.

dairy farm *n.* A farm for producing milk and milk products.

dair·y·ing (dâr′ē-ĭng) *n.* **1.** The business of a dairy. **2.** Dairy farming. **—dair·y·ing** *adj.*

dair·y·maid (dâr′ē-mād′) *n.* A woman or girl who works in a dairy.

dair·y·man (dâr′ē-mən) *n., pl.* **-men** (-mĭn). **1.** A man who works in a dairy. **2.** A dairy manager or owner.

da·is (dā′ĭs, dās) *n., pl.* **-ises** (-ĭ-sĭz). A raised platform, as in a lecture hall or dining hall, used by speakers, dignitaries, or the like. [Middle English *deis,* from Old French, table, platform, from Latin *discus,* dish, quoit, DISK.]

dai·sy (dā′zē) *n., pl.* **-sies. 1.** Any of several related plants having rayed flowers; especially, in North America, a widely naturalized Eurasian plant, *Chrysanthemum leucanthemum,* having flowers with a yellow center and white rays. This species is also called "oxeye daisy," "white daisy." **2.** A low-growing European plant, *Bellis perennis,* having flowers with pink or white rays. This species is the daisy of literary tradition. Also called "English daisy," "bachelor's-button." **3.** The flower of any of these plants. **4.** *Slang.* Something excellent or notable. [Middle English *daisie, dayeseye,* Old English *dægesēage,* "day's eye" (the flower of some species opens to reveal a yellow disk in the morning and closes again in the evening) : *dæges,* genitive of *dæg,* DAY + *ēage,* eye.]

daisy fleabane *n.* Any of several plants of the genus *Erigeron,* especially *E. annuus,* a weedy North American plant having numerous small flowers with white or pinkish rays.

daisy wheel *n.* A printing device, used especially in the printing machines attached to computers and word processors, consisting of printing characters fixed at the end of spokes on a wheel.

dak (däk) *n.* In India, the post or mail. [Hindi and Marathi.]

Da·kar (də-kär′). Capital of Senegal, a port on Cape Verde Peninsula. A fort was built here by the French in 1857, and the city was the capital of French West Africa (1904–59).

dak bungalow *n.* In India, a place providing lodging for travelers.

Da·kin's solution (dā′kənz) *n.* A dilute solution of sodium hypochlorite in water, used as a surgical disinfectant. [Developed by Henry Drysdale *Dakin* (1880–1952), British biochemist.]

dakoit. Variant of **dacoit.**

Da·ko·ta[1] (də-kō′tə) *n., pl.* **-tas** or collectively **Dakota. 1.** A member of any of a large group of Siouan-speaking people of North American Plains Indians, commonly called Sioux, now living on reservations in North and South Dakota, Minnesota, and Montana. **2.** The Siouan language of these Indians. **—Da·ko·tan** *adj.* & *n.*

Dakota[2]. See **James** (river of North Dakota).

Dakota[3]. A U.S. territory (established 1861) comprising present-day North and South Dakota and much of Wyoming and Montana. It was reduced in size by the creation of the Montana Territory (1864) and Wyoming Territory (1868). The area was further divided (1889) into two new states, North and South Dakota. The two states are known as **the Dakotas.**

dal. Variant of **dhal.**

Da·la·dier (də-lä′dē-ā′), **Edouard** (1884–1970). French statesman and prime minister (1933, 1934, 1938–40). Daladier signed the Munich Agreement (1938) for France. He was arrested after France fell to the Germans in 1940 and remained in captivity until 1945.

Da·lai La·ma (dä-lī′ lä′mə) *n.* The traditional ruler and highest priest of the Buddhist religion in Tibet and Mongolia. The position is not hereditary or elective, but said to be held by the same individual in successive incarnations. Also called "Grand Lama." [Tibetan : Mongolian *dalai,* ocean, great + Tibetan *bla-ma,* superior one, a Buddhist monk, LAMA.]

dal·a·pon (dăl′ə-pŏn) *n.* A selective weedkiller used on unwanted grasses. [Probably *di-* + *alpha* + *propionic* acid.]

da·la·si (də-lä′sē) *n.* The basic monetary unit of Gambia, equivalent to 100 bututs. See feature at **currency.** [Native name in Gambia.]

dale (dāl) *n.* A valley. [Middle English *dale,* Old English *dæl.*]

d'A·lem·bert (dă-lăN-bâr′), **Jean le Rond** (1717–83). French mathematician and philosopher, who defined the laws of dynamics governing equilibrium and centrifugal force, known as d'Alembert's principle. A friend of Voltaire and Diderot, he contributed to the *Encyclopédie.*

dales·man (dālz′mən) *n., pl.* **-men** (-mĭn). A person who lives in a dale, especially in northern Yorkshire, England.

da·leth (dä′ləth) *n.* The fourth letter of the Hebrew alphabet. See feature at **alphabet.** [Hebrew *dāleth,* from *dālt,* door, daleth.]

Da·li (dä′lē), **Salvador** (1904–89). Spanish painter. He went to Paris in 1929 and joined the surrealist movement. Influenced by Freud's psychoanalytic theories of the unconscious, he painted disturbing images whose quasi-photographic finish heightens their disquieting effect, as in *Persistence of Memory* (1931).

Dal·las (dăl′əs). City on the Trinity River in northeast Texas. It grew on the site of Peter's Colony (founded 1841), becoming Dallas in 1845. The town prospered as a cotton center and expanded after 1915 with the discovery of oil nearby, becoming the largest city in Texas.

dal·li·ance (dăl′ē-əns) *n.* **1.** Frivolous spending of time; dawdling. **2.** Amorous play; flirtation.

Dal·lis grass (dăl′əs, -ĭs) *n.* A South American grass, *Paspalum dilatatum,* grown for pasturage in the southern United States. [*Dallis,* probably alteration of DALLAS.]

dal·ly (dăl′ē) *v.* **-lied, -lying, -lies.** —*intr.* **1.** To play amorously; flirt: *"Sylvester dallied about Lena until he began to make mistakes in his work"* (Willa Cather). **2.** To trifle; toy. **3.** To waste time; dawdle. —*tr.* To waste (time). Used with *away.* [Middle English *dalien,* from Old French *dalier*†, to chat.] **—dal·li·er** *n.* **—dal·ly·ing·ly** *adv.*

Dal·ma·tia (dăl-mā′shə). The southern part of Yugoslavia's coastline. The region is mountainous and the population mostly Croatian. It was dominated by Venice from the 15th to 18th century, then fell to Austria. Italy claimed Dalmatia in World War I, but it joined the Kingdom of Serbs, Croats, and Slovenes (1918), which became Yugoslavia (1929). During World War II much of it was held by Italy but was subsequently restored to Yugoslavia. Dalmatia's scenic coastline attracts many tourists, and the region produces wines and liqueurs. Split is the chief town.

Dal·ma·tian (dăl-mā′shən) *n.* **1.** A dog of a breed believed to have originated in Dalmatia, having a short, smooth, white coat covered with black or dark brown spots. Also called "coach dog," "carriage dog." **2.** A native or inhabitant of Dalmatia.
∼*adj.* Of or pertaining to Dalmatia or its inhabitants.

dal·mat·ic (dăl-măt′ĭk) *n.* **1.** *Roman Catholic Church.* A wide-sleeved garment formerly worn over the alb by the deacon at the celebration of High Mass and now worn by bishops and other prelates. **2.** A similar garment worn by an English monarch as a coronation robe. [Middle English *dalmatik,* from Old French *dalmatique,* from Late Latin *dalmatica (vestis),* "Dalmatian (garment)" (originally of Dalmatian wool), from *dalmaticus,* of DALMATIA.]

dal se·gno (däl sān′yo) *adv. Abbr.* **d.s., D.S.** *Music.* From the sign. Used as a direction to repeat from the place marked by the sign (§) to a designated point. [Italian.]

Dal·ton (dôlt′n), **John** (1766–1844). British chemist, whose pioneer work on the properties of gases led to his discovery in 1803 that the atoms of chemical elements differed in weight and to his formulation of the atomic theory.

dal·to·ni·an (dôl-tō′nē-ən) *adj.* Also **Dal·to·ni·an** (especially for sense 1). **1.** Of or pertaining to John Dalton or his atomic theory. **2.** Of or pertaining to daltonism.

dal·ton·ism (dôlt′n-ĭz′əm) *n.* Also **Dal·ton·ism. 1.** Red-green colorblindness. **2.** Any form of colorblindness. [After John DALTON, who was colorblind.] **—dal·ton·ic** (dôl-tŏn′ĭk) *adj.*

Dalton plan *n.* An educational system in which pupils learn by completing long-term study projects. [After *Dalton,* Massachusetts, where the plan was introduced.]

Dalton's law *n. Chemistry.* The principle that the pressure of a mixture of gases is the sum of the partial pressures of the components of the mixture. Also called "Dalton's law of partial pressures." [After John DALTON.]

dam[1] (dăm) *n.* **1.** A barrier constructed across a waterway to control the flow or raise the level of water. **2.** A natural barrier, such as an ice dam, across a watercourse. **3.** A body of water controlled by such a barrier. **4.** Any obstruction or hindrance.
∼*tr.v.* **dammed, damming, dams. 1.** To construct a dam across; hold back by means of a dam. **2.** To obstruct or restrain; confine. Usually used with *up.* —See Synonyms at **hinder.** [Middle English, probably from Middle Low German *dam,* from Germanic *dammjan* (unattested), to impede, dam.]

dam[2] *n.* **1.** *Abbr.* **d.** A female parent of a quadruped, such as a sheep or horse. **2.** *Archaic.* A mother. [Middle English, variant of DAME.]

dam decameter.

dam·age (dăm′ĭj) *n.* **1.** Harm done to a person or thing, usually reducing usefulness, value, soundness, or standing. **2. damages.** *Law.* Money paid or ordered to be paid as compensation for injury or loss. **3.** *Informal.* Cost; price: *What's the damage?*
∼*v.* **damaged, -aging, -ages.** —*tr.* To cause injury to; impair; harm. —*intr.* To suffer or be susceptible to damage. —See Synonyms at **injure, ruin.** [Middle English, from Old French, from *dam(me),* loss, damage, from Latin *damnum,* loss, harm, fine.] **—dam·age·a·ble** *adj.* **—dam·ag·ing·ly** *adv.*

da·man (dăm′ən) *n. Rare.* The hyrax, a small mammal of Africa and Asia Minor. [Arabic *damān (Isrā'īl),* "sheep of Israel."]

Da·man (də-män′). *Portuguese* **Da·mão** (dä-mouN′). Region of northwest India, on the eastern shore of the Gulf of Khambar

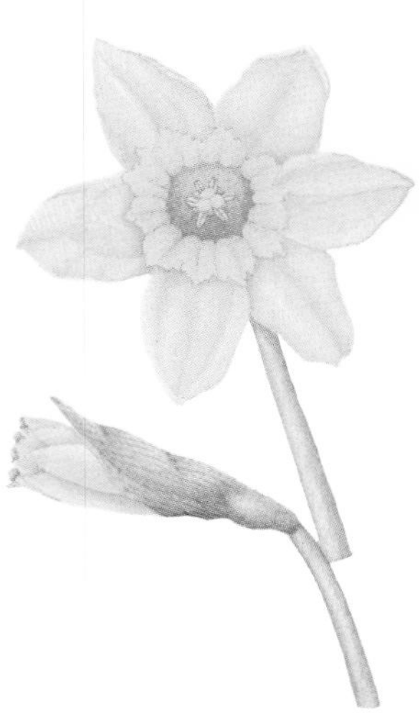

daffodil *The wild daffodil (above) gets its name from the plant that grew in the meadows of the nether world in Greek mythology. The Greeks called the plant* asphodelos, *which later became affadyl and then daffodil.*

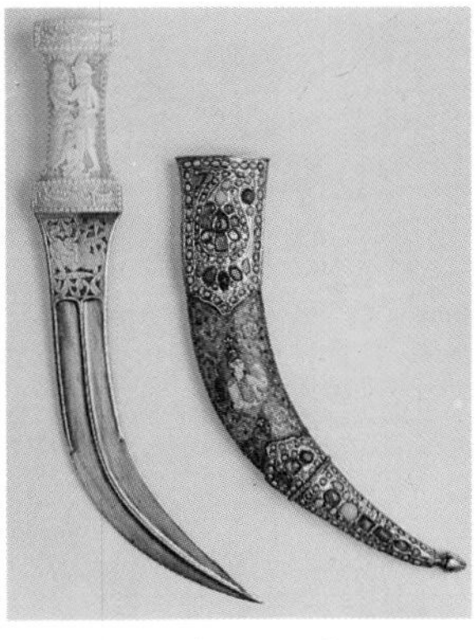

dagger *A 19th-century Persian dagger, with ivory handle and jeweled scabbard, now in the Victoria and Albert Museum, London.*

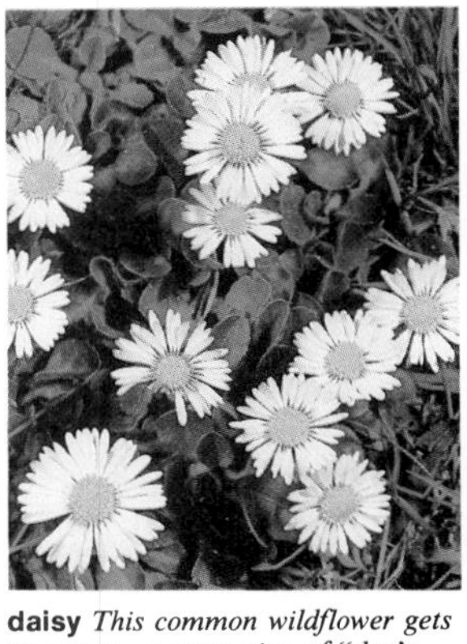

daisy *This common wildflower gets its name—a corruption of "day's eye"—from its habit of opening and closing with the sun.*

damascene *Detail from an iron damascened plaque, made in Milan in the mid-16th century. The wavy-patterned style gets its name from its resemblance to the ornamentation used by medieval Arab weavers and metalworkers in the Syrian capital, Damascus.*

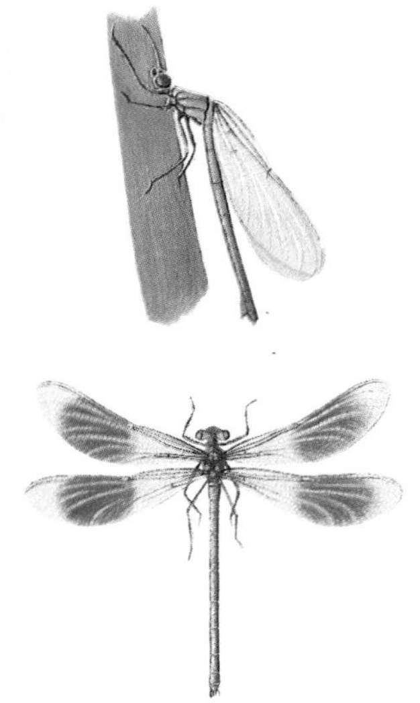

damselfly *These fragile relatives of the dragonflies live near streams and prey on tiny insects. In this species, the banded agrion, the males have dark blue bands on their wings; the females (top) do not.*

PRONUNCIATION KEY

ă, pat; ā, pay; âr, care;
ä, father, are; b, bib;
ch, church; d, deed; ĕ, pet;
ē, be; f, fife; g, gag; h, hat;
hw, which; ĭ, pit; ī, pie;
îr, pier; j, judge; k, kick;
l, lid, needle; m, mum;
n, no, sudden; ng, thing;
ŏ, pot; ō, toe; ô, paw, for;
oi, noise; ou, out; o͝o, book;
o͞o, boot; p, pop; r, roar;
s, sauce; sh, ship, dish;
t, tight; th, thin, path;
th, this, bathe; ŭ, cut; ûr, fur;
v, valve; w, with; y, yes;
z, zebra, size; zh, vision;
ə, about, item, edible,
gallop, circus, peaceful

IN FOREIGN WORDS:

à, *Fr.* ami; œ, *Fr.* feu, *Ger.* schön; ü, *Fr.* tu, *Ger.* über;
KH, *Ger.* ich, *Scot.* loch;
N, *Fr.* bon; y', *Fr.* Compiègne

STRESS MARKS:

Primary stress: ′
in·cite′ (ĭn-sīt′)
Secondary stress: ′
in′sight′ (ĭn′sīt′)

(Cambay). It was a Portuguese territory from the 16th century and was occupied by India in 1961. It now forms part of the territory of Goa, Daman, and Diu.

damar. Variant of **dammar.**

dam·as·cene (dăm′ə-sēn′, dăm′ə-sēn′) *tr.v.* **-cened, -cening, -cenes.** To decorate (metal) with wavy patterns of inlay, usually of gold or silver, or etching.
~n. Work decorated by damascening.
~adj. Of or pertaining to damascening or damask. [Middle English, from Old French *damasquiner,* "to decorate in the manner of Damascus blades or steel," from *damasquin,* of Damascus, from Italian *damaschino,* from Latin *Damascēnus,* from Greek *Damaskēnos,* from *Damaskos,* DAMASCUS.] **—dam·a·scen·er** *n.*

Dam·a·scene (dăm′ə-sēn′) *n.* A native or inhabitant of Damascus.
~adj. Of or pertaining to Damascus or its inhabitants.

Da·mas·cus (də-măs′kəs). *French* **Da·mas** (də-mä′). *Arabic* **Ash Sham** (ăsh shăm′) or **Di·mash** (dĭ-măsh′). Capital of Syria, on the Barada River in the southwest of the country. A city of great antiquity, it is mentioned in the Bible. Damascus fell to the Arabs (635) and was the capital of the Islamic empire under the Umayyad caliphs (661–750). A Saracen stronghold in the Crusades, the city was in Ottoman hands (1516–1918) and then occupied by the French before becoming the capital of independent Syria (1941). The city was once famous for its blades and armor and still produces fine metalware, textiles, glass, and leather goods.

Damascus steel *n.* An early form of steel having wavy markings, developed in Near Eastern countries, especially Persia, and used chiefly in sword blades. Also called "damask steel."

dam·ask (dăm′əsk) *n.* **1.** A rich patterned fabric of cotton, linen, silk, or wool. **2.** A fine, twilled table linen. **3.** Damascus steel. **4.** The wavy pattern on Damascus steel.
~tr.v. **damasked, -asking, -asks. 1.** To damascene. **2.** To decorate or weave with rich patterns.
~adj. **1.** Of or from Damascus. **2.** Made from damask or Damascus steel. [Middle English *damask (cloth),* from Medieval Latin *(pannus de) damasco,* "(cloth of) Damascus."]

damask rose *n.* A rose, *Rosa damascena,* native to Asia, having fragrant red or pink flowers that are used as a source of attar. [Medieval Latin *rosa Damascēna,* from Latin *Damascēnus,* of DAMASCUS, its supposed place of origin.]

dame (dām) *n.* **1.** A title formerly given to a woman in authority or to the mistress of a household. Now only used in expressions such as *Dame Fortune.* **2.** A married woman; matron. **3.** Slang. A woman; female. **4.** *British.* **a.** *Archaic.* The legal title of the wife or widow of a knight or baronet. **b.** A title of a woman, equivalent to that of a knight. **5.** *Obsolete.* A schoolmistress. [Middle English, from Old French, from Latin *domina,* feminine of *dominus,* master, lord.]

dame school *n.* Formerly, a small local school run by an elderly woman, usually for children of primary school age.

dame's rocket *n.* A plant, *Hesperis matronalis,* native to Europe, having clusters of fragrant purple or white flowers. Also called "dame's violet," "damewort." [Translation of its Latin name.]

Da·mien (dā′mē-ən), **Father,** born Joseph de Veuster Damien (1840–89). Belgian Roman Catholic missionary who volunteered in 1873 to supervise Hawaii's leper colony on Molokai Island. He died there of leprosy.

dam·mar, da·mar, dam·mer (dăm′ər) *n.* Any of various hard resins obtained from Indo-Malayan trees of the genera *Agathis* and *Shorea,* used in varnishes and lacquers. [Malay *damar,* resin.]

damn (dăm) *v.* **damned, damning, damns.** *—tr.* **1.** To pronounce an adverse judgment upon; criticize adversely. **2.** To bring about the failure of; ruin. **3.** To condemn as harmful, illegal, or immoral: *damn gambling and strong drink.* **4.** *Theology.* To condemn to everlasting punishment or a similar fate. **5.** To swear at by using the word "damn"; curse. *—intr.* To swear; curse.
~interj. Used to express anger, irritation, or disappointment.
~n. **1.** The saying of "damn"; a curse. **2.** *Informal.* The least valuable bit; a jot: *don't give a damn; not worth a damn.*
~adj. Damned.
~adv. *Informal.* Damned. Used as an intensive. [Middle English *dam(p)nen,* from Old French *dam(p)ner,* from Latin *damnāre,* to inflict loss upon, condemn, from *damnum,* loss, damage.]

dam·na·ble (dăm′nə-bəl) *adj.* **1.** Deserving condemnation; odious; hateful. **2.** Disagreeable; unpleasant: *damnable weather.* **—dam·na·ble·ness** *n.* **—dam·na·bly** *adv.*

dam·na·tion (dăm-nā′shən) *n.* **1.** The act of damning or condition of being damned. **2.** *Theology.* **a.** Condemnation to everlasting punishment; doom. **b.** Everlasting punishment. **3.** Failure or ruination incurred by adverse criticism.
~interj. Used to express anger or annoyance.

dam·na·to·ry (dăm′nə-tôr′ē, -tōr′ē) *adj.* Threatening with damnation; condemning; damning.

damned (dămd) *adj.* **1.** Condemned, especially to eternal punishment; doomed. **2.** *Informal.* **a.** Deserving condemnation; detestable. Used as an expression of irritation or disappointment: *This damned weather!* **b.** Absolute; utter. Used as an intensive: *a damned fool.* **3.** *Informal.* Used as an expression of surprise or refusal: *I'm damned if I'll lend him my car!*
~adv. Informal. Very; extremely: *a damned poor excuse.*
~n. Theology. Souls doomed to eternal punishment.

damned·est (dăm′dĭst) *adj. Informal.* Most extraordinary: *the damnedest thing I've ever heard.* **—do one's damnedest.** To do all one possibly can.

dam·ni·fy (dăm′nə-fī′) *tr.v.* **-fied, -fying, -fies.** *Law.* To cause loss or damage to. [Old French *damnifier,* from Late Latin *damnificāre,* from Latin *damnificus,* causing loss, harmful : *damnum,* loss, harm + *-ficus,* -FIC.] **—dam·ni·fi·ca·tion** *n.*

damn·ing (dăm′ĭng) *adj.* **1.** That condemns or criticizes: *a damning review.* **2.** That incriminates or gives proof of guilt: *damning evidence.* **—damn·ing·ly** *adv.*

Dam·o·cles (dăm′ə-klēz′). A member of the court of Dionysius the Elder, tyrant of Syracuse, who was forced by Dionysius to sit at a banquet under a sword suspended by a single hair to demonstrate the precariousness of a king's fortunes. **—Dam·o·cle·an** *adj.*

Da·mon and Pyth·i·as (dā′mən; pĭth′ē-əs). *Roman Mythology.* Two friends so devoted that Damon pledged his life as a hostage for the condemned Pythias.

dam·o·sel, dam·o·zel (dăm′ə-zĕl′) *n.* Also **dam·oi·selle** (dăm′ə-zĕl′). *Archaic.* A damsel. [Variant of DAMSEL.]

damp (dămp) *adj.* **damper, dampest. 1.** Slightly wet; moist; humid. **2.** *Archaic.* Dejected. —See Synonyms at **wet.**
~n. **1. a.** Moisture; humidity; mist. **b.** Moisture on the inside walls of a building caused by condensation, by rain entering through an outside wall, or by water seeping up from the ground *(rising damp).* **2.** Foul or poisonous gas that sometimes pollutes the air in mines. See **afterdamp, blackdamp, firedamp. 3.** *Archaic.* Lowness of spirits; depression. **4.** A restraint or check; discouragement.
~tr.v. **damped, damping, damps. 1.** To make damp or moist; moisten. **2.** To cut off the flow of air to (a fire) to reduce combustion. Often used with *down.* **3.** To restrain or check; discourage. Often used with *down.* **4.** To provide (the strings of a keyboard instrument) with dampers as a means of deadening the sound. **5.** *Physics.* To decrease the amplitude of (an oscillation or wave). **—damp off.** *Botany.* To be affected by **damping off** *(see).* [Middle English, poison gas, chokedamp, from Middle Low German and Middle Dutch, smoke, vapor, from Germanic *damp-* (unattested).] **—damp·ish** *adj.* **—damp·ly** *adv.* **—damp·ness** *n.*

damp course *n.* A strip of plastic or layer of other waterproof material placed between two courses of bricks close to the ground in a wall in order to prevent rising damp. Also called "dampproof course."

damp·en (dăm′pən) *v.* **-ened, -ening, -ens.** *—tr.* **1.** To moisten; make damp. **2.** To deaden; depress: *dampen one's spirits.* *—intr.* To become wet or moist. **—damp·en·er** *n.*

damp·er (dăm′pər) *n.* **1.** One that damps, restrains, or depresses. **2.** An adjustable plate in the flue of a furnace or stove for controlling the draft. **3.** *Music.* **a.** A device in various keyboard instruments for deadening the vibrations of the strings. **b.** A mute for various brass instruments. **4.** Any device that eliminates or progressively diminishes oscillations. **5.** *Australian.* An unleavened bread made from flour and water and cooked in an open fire. **—put a damper on.** *Informal.* To suppress; discourage.

Dam·pi·er (dăm′pē-ər), **William** (1652–1715). British pirate who later became an explorer and circumnavigated the globe, which he described in his *Voyage Round the World* (1697). In 1699 he was sent to the South Seas and discovered the Dampier Archipelago off northwest Australia.

damping off *n.* A disease of planted seeds or very young seedlings caused by fungi, particularly those of the genus *Pythium,* and resulting in death of the newly sprouted plants due to softening and collapse of the stem base.

dampproof (dămp′pro͞of′) *adj.* Resistant to damp.
~tr.v. **dampproofed, -proofing, -proofs.** To make dampproof, especially by providing a damp course.

dam·sel (dăm′zəl) *n.* A young woman or girl; maiden. [Middle English *damisele,* from Old French *dameisele,* from Vulgar Latin *dominicella* (unattested), diminutive of Latin *domina,* lady, DAME.]

dam·sel·fish (dăm′zəl-fĭsh′) *n., pl.* **-fishes** or collectively **damselfish.** Any of various small tropical marine fishes of the family Pomacentridae, having laterally compressed, usually brightly colored bodies. Also called "demoiselle."

dam·sel·fly (dăm′zəl-flī′) *n., pl.* **-flies.** Any of various slender-bodied, often brightly colored insects of the order Odonata, related to the dragonflies but differing in having wings that are folded together over the back when at rest. Also *rarely* "demoiselle."

dam·son (dăm′zən, -sən) *n.* **1.** A plum tree, *Prunus institia* (or *P. domestica institia*), native to Eurasia, cultivated since ancient times for its edible fruit. Also called "bullace." **2.** The oval, bluish-black, juicy plum borne by this tree. Also called "damson plum." [Middle English *damascene, damson,* from Latin *(prūnum) Damascēnum,* "(plum) of Damascus."]

dan (dăn, dän) *n.* *Sometimes* **Dan. 1.** In the oriental martial arts such as judo, any of twelve levels of proficiency at the grade of **black belt** *(see).* **2.** One who has achieved such a level. [Japanese.]

Dan[1] (dăn) *n.* **1.** The fifth son of Jacob. Genesis 30:6. **2.** One of the 12 tribes of Israel, descended from Dan.

Dan[2] *n. Obsolete.* A title of honor equivalent to *master* or *sir:* *"Dan Chaucer, well of English undefiled"* (Spenser). [Middle English *Dan, Daunz,* "master," "mister," originally a title of respect for a monk or priest, from Old French *Dan, Danz,* from Medieval Latin *Domnus,* contracted from Latin *dominus,* master, lord.]

Dan. 1. Daniel (Old Testament). **2.** Danish.

Da·na (dā′nə), **Richard Henry** (1815–82). U.S. lawyer and author. He wrote *Two Years Before the Mast* (1840), a popular description of his experience as a sailor voyaging from Boston to California. As a lawyer he specialized in maritime law and persuaded the Supreme Court to sanction the Union blockade of Southern ports (1861).

Dan·a·e, Dan·a·ë (dăn′ə-ē′). *Greek Mythology.* The mother of Perseus by Zeus, who visited her in the form of a shower of gold during her imprisonment by her father.

Dan·a·id, Dan·a·ïd (dăn′ē-ĭd) *n.* Any of the Danaides.

Da·na·i·des, Da·na·ï·des (də-nā′ə-dēz′) *pl.n. Greek Mythology.* The fifty daughters of Danaus who, with one exception, murdered their bridegrooms on their wedding night and were condemned in Hades to fill sieves with water. [Greek, from *Danaos,* DANAUS.] **—Dan·a·id·e·an** (dăn′ē-ĭd′ē-ən) *adj.*

Da Nang (də năng′). Formerly **Tou·rane** (to͞o-rän′). City and port on the South China Sea coast of Vietnam. A U.S. airforce base was sited here during the Vietnam War. The chief product is textiles.

Dan·a·us, Dan·a·üs (dăn′ē-əs). *Greek Mythology.* A king of Argos, father of the Danaides.

dance (dăns, däns) *v.* **danced, dancing, dances.** *—intr.* **1.** To move rhythmically, usually to music, using prescribed or improvised steps and gestures. **2. a.** To leap or skip about excitedly; caper; frolic. **b.** To move lightly or nimbly. **3.** To bob up and down. **4.** To be a dancer by profession. *—tr.* **1.** To engage in or perform (a dance). **2.** To cause to dance. **3.** To bring to a specified state or condition by dancing: *She danced him off his feet.* **—dance attendance.** To wait upon another attentively; lavish attentions on someone.
∼n. **1.** A series of rhythmical motions and steps, usually to music. **2.** A particular set of such prescribed movements. **3.** The art of dancing. Often preceded by *the.* **4.** A party or gathering of people for dancing. **5.** One round or turn of dancing. **6.** An act of dancing; a dance performance. **7.** A musical or rhythmical accompaniment composed or played for dancing. [Middle English *dansen, dauncen,* from Old French *danser,* from Vulgar Latin *dansāre*†.] **—danc·er** *n.* **—danc·ing·ly** *adv.*

dance·a·ble (dăns′ə-bəl, däns′-) *adj.* Suitable for dancing. Said of music.

Dance of Death *n.* In the art, music, and literature of medieval Europe, the concept of death as all-powerful, represented by a dance in which the living are led off to their graves in order of rank. Also called "danse macabre."

D and C *n.* **Dilation and curettage** *(see).*

dan·de·li·on (dăn′də-lī′ən) *n.* **1.** A plant, *Taraxacum officinale,* native to Eurasia and widely naturalized as a weed having many-rayed yellow flowers and deeply notched basal leaves that are sometimes used in salads. **2.** Any of several similar, related plants. [Middle English *dent-de-lion,* from Old French, translation of Medieval Latin *dēns leōnis,* "lion's tooth" (from its sharply indented leaves) : Latin *dēns* (stem *dent-*), tooth + *leōnis,* genitive of *leō,* LION.] **—dan·de·li·on** *adj.*

dan·der¹ (dăn′dər) *n. Informal.* Temper. **—get one's dander up.** *Informal.* To become angry or roused to vigorous action. [19th century : origin obscure.]

dander² *n.* Scurf from the coat of various animals, such as dogs, cats, or horses, often of an allergenic nature. [Short for DANDRUFF.]

dander³ *n. Scottish.* A saunter; a stroll.
∼intr.v. **dandered, -dering, -ders.** *Scottish.* To go for a stroll. [19th century : origin obscure.]

Dan·die Din·mont (dăn′dē dĭn′mŏnt′) *n.* A small terrier of a breed having a rough grayish or brownish coat and short legs. [After *Dandie Dinmont,* owner of two such dogs in *Guy Mannering* (1815), a novel by Sir Walter Scott.]

dan·di·fy (dăn′də-fī′) *tr.v.* **-fied, -fying, -fies.** To dress up or make resemble a dandy or fop. **—dan·di·fi·ca·tion** *n.*

dan·di·prat (dăn′dē-prăt′) *n.* **1.** *Archaic.* A little, insignificant, or contemptible fellow. **2.** A small 16th-century English coin. [16th century : origin obscure.]

dan·dle (dănd′l) *tr.v.* **-dled, -dling, -dles.** To move (a small child) up and down, usually on the knees or in the arms. [16th century : perhaps related to Italian *dandolare,* to dandle, swing (expressive formation).] **—dan·dler** *n.*

dan·druff (dăn′drəf) *n.* A scaly, whitish scurf formed on and shed from the scalp, often caused by seborrhea. [16th century : unexplained first element + *-ruff,* perhaps from Middle English *roufe,* scab, from Old Norse *hrufa.*]

dan·dy¹ (dăn′dē) *n., pl.* **-dies.** **1.** A man who affects extreme elegance in his clothes and manners. **2.** *Informal.* Something very good or agreeable. **3.** *Nautical.* A **yawl** *(see).*
∼adj. **dandier, -diest.** **1.** Like or dressed like a dandy; foppish. **2.** *Informal.* Fine; good. [Perhaps short for *jack-a-dandy,* pert person, fop : JACK (person) + A- (of) + *dandy,* probably from *Dandy,* Scottish nickname for the name *Andrew.*] **—dan·dy·ism** *n.*

dandy² *n. Pathology.* **Dengue** *(see).* Also called "dandy fever." [West Indian, variant of DENGUE.]

dandy-brush (dăn′dē-brŭsh) *n.* A stiff brush used for grooming horses.

dandy roll *n.* Also **dandy roller.** *Printing.* A cylinder of wire gauze pressed on drained but moist paper pulp before it starts through the rollers. It produces watermarks in the paper. [From DANDY (fine, neat).]

Dane (dān) *n.* A native or inhabitant of Denmark or a person of Danish ancestry. [Middle English *Dan* (replacing *Dene,* from Old English *Dene,* the Danes), from Old Norse *Danr.*]

Dane·geld (dān′gĕld′) *n.* Also **Dane·gelt** (-gĕlt′). A tax levied in England from the 10th to the 12th century, initially to finance protection against Danish invasion. It was later continued as a land tax. [Middle English (modeled upon some Scandinavian compound such as Old Danish *Danegjeld*) : *Dane,* genitive plural of *Dan,* DANE + *geld,* tribute, payment, Old English *gield.*]

Dane·law, Dane·lagh (dān′lô′) *n.* **1.** The body of law established by the Danish invaders and settlers in northeastern England in the 9th and 10th centuries. **2.** The area of northern and eastern England under jurisdiction of this law, roughly encompassing present-day Yorkshire, the east Midlands, and East Anglia. [Middle English *Dene laue,* Old English *Dena lagu,* "Danes' law" : *Dena,* genitive of *Dene,* the Danes + *lagu,* law.]

dane·wort (dān′wûrt′, -wôrt′) *n.* A Eurasian shrub, *Sambucus ebulus,* similar and related to the elder.

dan·ger (dān′jər) *n.* **1.** Exposure or vulnerability to harm or evil; risk; peril. **2.** A source or instance of risk or peril. **3.** *Obsolete.* Power, especially power to harm. **—on (or off) the danger list.** In (or out of) serious danger of death. [Middle English *daunger,* power, dominion, peril, damage, from Old French *dangier, dongier,* from Vulgar Latin *dom(i)niārium* (unattested), authority, from Latin *dominium,* sovereignty, from *dominus,* lord, master.]
Synonyms: *hazard, jeopardy, peril, risk.*

danger money *n. Chiefly British.* A payment made, in addition to basic wages, for work involving risk or danger.

dan·ger·ous (dān′jər-əs) *adj.* **1.** Involving or fraught with danger; perilous. **2.** Able or apt to do harm. **—dan·ger·ous·ly** *adv.* **—dan·ger·ous·ness** *n.*

dan·gle (dăng′gəl) *v.* **-gled, -gling, -glings.** *—intr.* **1.** To hang loosely and swing or sway to and fro. **2.** To hover around someone; follow; be a hanger-on. Usually used with *after.* *—tr.* **1.** To cause to dangle. **2.** To offer (something enticing) as an inducement or temptation.
∼n. **1.** The act of dangling. **2.** Something that is dangled. [Perhaps from Danish *dangle* or Swedish *dangla,* from Germanic *dang-* (unattested).] **—dan·gler** *n.* **—dan·gly** *adj.*

dan·gle·ber·ry (dăng′gəl-bĕr′ē) *n., pl.* **-ries.** **1.** A shrub, *Gaylussacia frondosa,* of eastern North America, having small, greenish-purple flowers and bluish-black fruit. **2.** The sweet, edible fruit of this shrub. Also called "tangleberry."

dangling participle *n. Grammar.* A participle that lacks clear connection with the word it modifies. In the sentence *Working at my desk, the sudden noise startled me, Working at my desk* is a dangling participle. The connection between the participle and the word it modifies may be clarified by revision: *Working at my desk, I was startled by the sudden noise.*

Dan·iel¹ (dăn′yəl). An Old Testament prophet during the Babylonian captivity whose faith protected him from death in a lions' den.

Daniel² *n. Abbr.* **Dan.** The book in the Old Testament containing the story and prophecies of Daniel.

Dan·iell (dăn′yəl), **John Frederic** (1790–1845). British chemist. In 1836 he invented the Daniell cell and the dewpoint hygrometer, which measures atmospheric humidity.

Daniell cell *n.* An electric cell in which the anode is a zinc rod in sulfuric acid and the cathode is a copper rod in copper sulfate solution, the two electrodes being separated by a porous partition. It has an emf of about 1.1 volts. [After J. F. DANIELL.]

da·ni·o (dā′nē-ō′) *n., pl.* **-os.** Any of various small, often brightly colored freshwater fishes of the genera *Danio* and *Brachydanio,* native to Asia and popular as aquarium fish. [New Latin *Danio*†.]

Dan·ish (dā′nĭsh) *adj. Abbr.* **Dan., Da.** Of or pertaining to Denmark, the Danes, their language, or their culture.
∼n. **1.** *Abbr.* **Dan., Da.** The North Germanic language of the Danes. **2.** *Informal.* A Danish pastry. [Middle English *Danish,* Old English *Denisc,* from *Dene,* the Danes.]

Danish blue *n.* A pungent, soft, blue-veined white cheese.

Danish pastry *n.* A sweet, buttery pastry made with raised dough, often filled with fruit and topped with icing, nuts, or other decoration. Also *informally* "Danish."

Dan·ite (dăn′īt′) *n.* A descendant of Dan. Judges 13:2.
∼adj. Of or pertaining to the Hebrew tribe descended from Dan.

dank (dăngk) *adj.* **danker, dankest.** Unpleasantly damp; chilly and wet: *a dank cellar.* —See Synonyms at **wet.** [Middle English *dank*†.] **—dank·ly** *adv.* **—dank·ness** *n.*

Danmark. See **Denmark.**

D'An·nun·zio (dä-no͞on′tsyō), **Gabriele** (1863–1938). Italian writer and nationalist. His first novel, *The Child of Pleasure,* appeared in 1898. In the same year his play, *City of Death,* written for Sarah Bernhardt, was first performed. He became a leading nationalist. In 1919 he headed an unofficial Italian expedition to seize the Dalmatian port of Fiume (now Rijeka) and held the city for 15 months in defiance of his government. He encouraged Mussolini's movement, helping to set up a Fascist seamen's union.

Da·no-Nor·we·gian (dā′nō-nôr-wē′jən) *n.* A form of the Norwegian language, **Bokmål** *(see).*

danse ma·ca·bre (däɴs mȧ-kȧ′br′) *n.* The **dance of death** *(see).*

dan·seur (däɴ-sœr′) *n., pl.* **-seurs** (-sœr′). A male ballet dancer. [French, from Old French, from *danser,* to DANCE.]

dan·seuse (däɴ-sœz′) *n. pl.* **-seuses** (-sœz′). A female ballet dancer. [French, see **danseur.**]

Dan·te A·li·ghie·ri (dăn′tā äl′ə-gyâ′rē) (1265–1321). Italian poet. Son of a noble burgher family in Florence, he remained in exile from the city after political rivals took over in 1302. He wrote *La Vita Nuova* (1292), the story of his boyhood love for a girl named

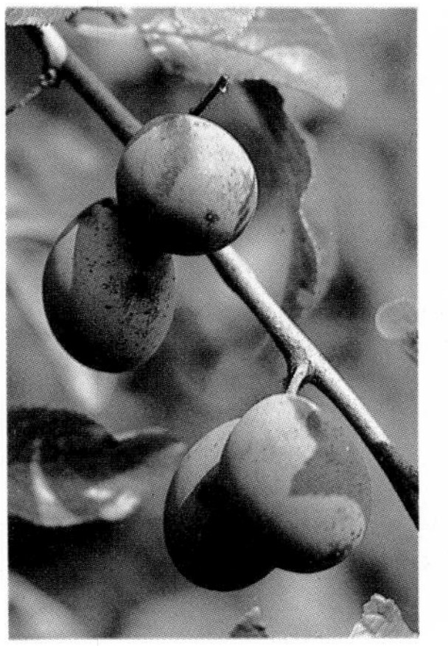

damson *A small blue plum. It gets its name from Damascus in Syria, where it was first cultivated.*

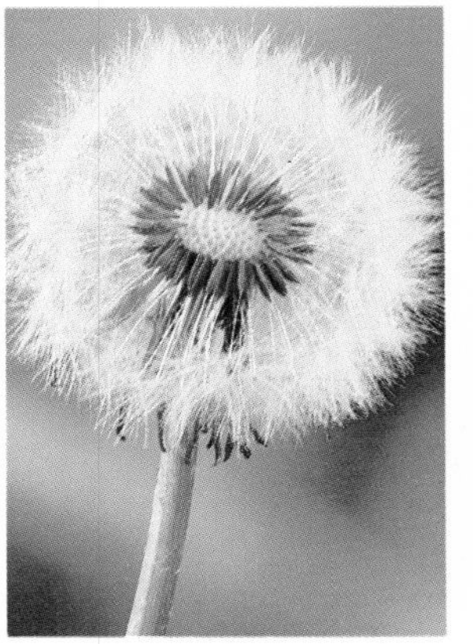

dandelion *The fluffy seed head of this plant is a favorite in the folklore of children everywhere, serving to tell the time or predict the number of one's future children by counting the seeds left after one or more puffs.*

Beatrice. *La Divina Commedia (The Divine Comedy)* he dates from a vision in 1300. It describes his progress through Hell and Purgatory (guided by Virgil) and Heaven (guided by Beatrice).

Dan·te·an (dăn′tē-ən, dăn-tē′ən) *adj.* **1.** Of or pertaining to Dante or his writings: *Dantean scholarship.* **2.** Dantesque.
~*n.* A scholar specializing in the life and writings of Dante.

Dan·tesque (dăn-tĕsk′) *adj.* Resembling or having the visionary literary style of Dante.

dan·tho·ni·a (dăn-thŏ′nē-ə) *n.* Any grass of the genus *Danthonia*, of the Southern Hemisphere. See **wallaby grass.** [New Latin, after E. *Danthoine*, 19th-century French botanist.]

Dan·ton (dăn-tôn′), **Georges Jacques** (1759–94). French lawyer and revolutionary leader. He took part in the storming of the Bastille in 1789, became minister of justice in 1792, and a member of the Committee for Public Safety. Danton supported the execution of Louis XVI in 1793, but the next year he joined the Jacobin moderates, opposing the Reign of Terror. Robespierre brought him before the revolutionary tribunal in 1794, and he was guillotined.

Da·nu (thä′nōō). *Irish Mythology.* The goddess of death and mother of the gods. [Irish, akin to Welsh *Don*†.]

Dan·ube (dăn′yōōb). *German* **Do·nau** (dō′nou). *Czech* **Du·naj** (dōō′nī). *Serbo-Croatian* **Du·nav** (dōō′năv). *Romanian* **Du·nă·rea** (dōō′nə-ryä). *Hungarian* **Du·na** (dōō′nô). The largest river in Europe, exceeding the Volga in volume though not in length. It rises in the Black Forest of southwestern Germany and flows 2,850 kilometers (1,770 miles) through central and southeastern Europe into the Black Sea in Romania. During the Middle Ages it was the chief route from Central Europe to Constantinople (Istanbul), and it remains a major trade artery. It passes through three European capitals—Vienna, Budapest, and Belgrade—and is connected to the Rhine, Main, Oder, and Tisza rivers by canals. —**Dan·u·bi·an** (dăn-yōōb′ē-ən) *adj.*

Danzig. See **Gdańsk.**

Dao. Variant of **Tao.**

Daoism. Variant of **Taoism.**

dap (dăp) *intr.v.* **dapped, dapping, daps. 1.** To fish by letting a baited hook fall gently on the water. **2.** To dip lightly or quickly into water, as a bird does. **3.** To skip or bounce, especially on the surface of water. [Probably alteration of DAB (to strike lightly), influenced by DIP.]

daph·ne (dăf′nē) *n.* Any of several shrubs of the genus *Daphne*, native to Eurasia, cultivated for their glossy evergreen foliage and clusters of bell-shaped flowers. See also **spurge laurel.** [New Latin *Daphne*, from Latin *daphnē*, laurel, from Greek. See **Daphne.**]

Daph·ne (dăf′nē). *Greek Mythology.* A nymph who chose to be turned into a laurel in order to escape from Apollo. [Latin *Daphnē*, from Greek, from *daphnē*, laurel, probably related to Latin *laurus*, LAUREL.]

daph·ni·a (dăf′nē-ə) *n., pl.* **daphnia.** Any of various small freshwater crustaceans of the genus *Daphnia*, some species of which are commonly used as food for aquarium fish. See also **water flea.** [New Latin *Daphnia*, perhaps from Latin *Daphnē*, DAPHNE.]

Da Pon·te (də pŏn′tā), **Lorenzo** (1749–1838). Italian author. He wrote the librettos for Mozart's operas *The Marriage of Figaro* (1786), *Don Giovanni* (1787), and *Cosi fan Tutti* (1790).

dap·per (dăp′ər) *adj.* **1.** Neatly dressed; trim. **2.** Small, compact, and active. [Middle English *dapyr*, elegant, probably from Middle Low German or Middle Dutch *dapper*, quick, nimble.] —**dap·per·ly** *adv.* —**dap·per·ness** *n.*

dap·ple (dăp′əl) *n.* **1. a.** Mottled or spotted marking, as on a horse's coat. **b.** An individual spot. **2.** An animal, especially a horse, with a mottled or spotted coat.
~*tr.v.* **dappled, -pling, -ples.** To mark or mottle with spots: *Sunlight dappled the lawn.*
~*adj.* Also **dap·pled** (-əld). Spotted or mottled. [Probably from DAPPLE-GRAY.]

dap·ple-gray (dăp′əl-grā′) *adj.* Gray with a mottled pattern of darker gray markings.
~*n.* A dapple-gray horse. [Middle English *dappel-grey*, perhaps alteration (influenced by Old Norse *depill*, a spot) of *appel-grey* (unattested), "apple-gray," probably from Old Norse *apalgrār* : *apall*, *epli*, apple + *grār*, gray.]

Dapsang. See **Godwin-Austin, Mt.**

dap·sone (dăp′sōn′, -zōn′) *n.* An antimicrobial agent, C₁₂H₁₂N₂OS, used against leprosy. [Contraction of *diaminodiphenyl sulfone*, a drug used to treat leprosy.]

DAR, D.A.R. Daughters of the American Revolution.

darb (därb) *n. Canadian Slang.* Something considered especially excellent or outstanding. [Perhaps variant of DAB (expert).]

dar·by¹ (där′bē) *n., pl.* **-bies.** A tool for smoothing a plaster surface. [After DERBY, England.]

darby² *n. British Slang.* A handcuff. [Originally *darbies* (plural), alluding to the phrase *Father Darby's bands*, a harsh binding agreement between a moneylender and a debtor.]

Dar·by and Joan (där′bē; jōn) *n.* An elderly married couple who live a placid, harmonious life together and are seldom seen apart. [After the elderly couple in a popular 18th-century English ballad.]

Dard (därd) *n., pl.* **Dards** or collectively **Dard.** A member of any of various Indo-European peoples speaking a Dardic language.

Dar·dan (där′dn) *n.* Also **Dar·da·ni·an** (där-dā′nē-ən). A Trojan. [After DARDANUS.] —**Dar·dan** *adj.*

Dar·da·nelles (där′dn-ĕlz′). Ancient name **Hel·les·pont** (hĕl′ĭs-pŏnt′). A strait linking the Aegean Sea with the Sea of Marmara

and separating Europe from Asia Minor. It was the site of the Dardanelles campaign (1915–16) of World War I. Allied landings were made at Gallipoli and Suvla Bay to try to secure the straits and open a route to Russia, forcing Turkey from the war. The attempt failed with the loss of many lives.

Dar·da·nus (därd′n-əs). *Greek Mythology.* The son of Zeus and Electra and founder of Troy.

Dar·dic (där′dĭk) *n.* The group of Indic languages of the upper Indus Valley.

dare (dâr) *v.* **dared** or *archaic* **durst** (dûrst), **daring, dare** or **dares.** —*tr.* **1.** To have the courage or boldness required for. Often used with an infinitive, with or without *to*: *No one dared oppose the dictator's wishes.* **2.** To challenge (a person) to do something requiring boldness: *I dare you to climb that tree.* —*intr.* To be courageous or bold enough to do or try something. —**dare say.** Also **dare·say.** To consider very likely or almost certain. Used only in the first person.
~*n.* A challenge, especially to give proof of bravery; an act of taunting or defying. [*Dare, durst*; Middle English *dar, dorste* (also *durste*), Old English *dear, dorste* (also *durste*), first and third person present and past indicative of *durran*, to venture, dare.] —**dar·er** *n.*

Dare (dâr), **Virginia** (1587–*c.* 87). First child born to English parents in America. She disappeared with the other members of the second colony on Roanoke Island, called the "Lost Colony."

dare·dev·il (dâr′dĕv′əl) *n.* One who is recklessly bold.
~*adj.* Recklessly bold. —**dare·dev·il·ry, dare·dev·il·try** *n.*

Dar-el-Beida. See **Casablanca.**

Dar es Sa·laam (där′ ĕs sə-läm′). City of Tanzania, an Indian Ocean port. It was founded by the sultan of Zanzibar (1862), and its name means "haven of peace." The German East Africa Company made it capital of German East Africa (1891–1916). It was later capital of Tanganyika, then of Tanzania.

darg (därg) *n. Chiefly British Regional.* **1.** A full day's work. **2.** An amount of work to be completed. [Middle English, syncopated form of *daywerk*, day-work.]

dar·ic (dăr′ĭk) *n.* A gold coin of ancient Persia. [Greek *Dar(e)ikos*, probably after *Dāreios*, DARIUS I.]

Da·ri·én (dâr′ē-ĕn′). Spanish colony founded by Vasco Núñez de Balboa (1510) in what is now Panama, on the west coast of the Gulf of Darién.

Darién, Gulf of. A wide bay of the Caribbean Sea between eastern Panama and northwestern Colombia.

Darién, Isthmus of. See **Panama, Isthmus of.**

dar·ing (dâr′ĭng) *adj.* Willing to take risks; fearless; bold; adventurous. —See Synonyms at **brave, reckless.**
~*n.* Active bravery; boldness; intrepidity. —**dar·ing·ly** *adv.* —**dar·ing·ness** *n.*

dar·i·ole (dâr′ē-ōl′) *n.* **1.** A small cream tart made with puff pastry in a circular mold. **2.** The mold itself. [French, from Old French, perhaps a diminutive formation from *dorer*, to gild, from Latin *dēaurāre* : *dē-* (intensive) + *aurāre*, to gild, from *aurum*, gold.]

Da·ri·us I (də-rī′əs), called "the Great" (*c.* 558–486 B.C.). King of Persia (521–486). He seized the throne after murdering a usurper, then divided the Persian Empire into provinces known as satrapies. Following unrest among subject Greek states, he invaded mainland Greece. A long war ended in defeat of the Persians at Marathon (490).

Dar·jee·ling¹ (där-jē′lĭng). Town in West Bengal, India, in the lower Himalayas. It is a tourist center 2,290 meters (7,500 feet) above sea level, with fine views of mounts Everest and Kangchenjunga. The surrounding district is famous for its tea.

Darjeeling² *n.* A fine variety of black tea from Darjeeling in India. Also called **"Darjeeling tea."**

dark (därk) *adj.* **darker, darkest.** *Abbr.* **dk. 1.** With very little or no light. **2.** Reflecting only a small fraction of the incident light. **3.** Lacking light or brightness; shaded; obscure: *a dark day.* **4.** Of a shade tending toward black or brown by comparison with *light, pale,* or *white*: *dark hair; dark green.* **5.** Characterized by or producing gloom; dreary; dismal. **6.** Sullen; threatening: *a dark scowl.* **7.** Hard to understand; obscure. **8.** Concealed; secret; mysterious. **9.** Unenlightened; uncivilized: *a dark era in history.* **10.** Evil or wicked; sinister: *a dark purpose.*
~*n.* **1.** Absence of light. **2.** A place having little light. **3.** Night; nightfall. **4.** A dark hue or color. —**in the dark. 1.** In secret: *things done in the dark.* **2.** In a state of ignorance; uninformed. —**whistle in the dark.** To put on a brave show to hide one's fears. [Middle English *derk*, Old English *deorc*; probably from Germanic.] —**dark·ish** *adj.*

Usage: *dark, dim, murky, dusky, obscure, opaque, shady, shadowy.* These adjectives indicate the absence of light or clarity. *Dark,* the most widely applicable, can refer to insufficiency of illumination for seeing, to deepness of shade of a color, as *dark brown,* or figuratively to absence of cheer or rectitude: *dark day; dark mood; dark comedy; dark deeds. Dim* suggests lack of clarity of outline of physical things or mental ones, such as memories or recollections, and can also apply to the source of light to indicate insufficiency. *Murky* usually implies darkness such as that produced by smoke or fog; less often it refers to extreme darkness or, figuratively, to unclear, sullen thoughts. *Dusky* applies principally to the dimness characteristic of twilight or to deepness of shade of a color. *Obscure* usually means unclear to the mind or senses but can refer to physical darkness. *Opaque* means incapable of being penetrated by light; figuratively it applies to what is incapable of perceiving reason and to what is unintelligible. *Shady* refers to what is sheltered from light, especially sunlight, or, figuratively, to what is covertly dishonest. *Shadowy* also implies obstructed light but suggests shifting illumination and indistinct vision.

dark adaptation *n.* The physical and chemical adjustments of the eye, including dilation of the pupil, that make vision possible in relative darkness. **—dark-a·dapt·ed** (därk′ə-dăp′tĭd) *adj.*

Dark Ages *n.* **1.** The early part of the Middle Ages from the fall of the Roman Empire in A.D. 476 until the coronation of Charlemagne in A.D. 800. **2.** The entire period from the end of classical civilization to the revival of learning in the West in about A.D. 1000, formerly regarded as a period lacking in cultural development.

Dark Continent *n.* Africa. [So called because its hinterland was largely unknown until the late 19th century.]

dark·en (där′kən) *v.* **-ened, -ening, -ens.** *—tr.* **1.** To shut out the light of; make dark or darker. **2.** To impart a darker hue to; render less white or clear. **3.** To fill with sadness; make gloomy. **4.** To obscure or cloud the meaning of; render vague. **5.** To strike with blindness. *—intr.* **1.** To become dark or darker. **2.** To become dark in color. **3.** To become obscure, vague, or uncertain. **4.** To grow clouded, gloomy, or sullen. **5.** To become blind. **—dark·en·er** *n.*

dark-field microscope (därk′fēld′) *n.* An **ultramicroscope** *(see).*

dark glasses *pl.n.* Glasses with tinted lenses worn to protect the eyes from glare.

dark horse *n.* **1.** A little-known entrant in a horse race, contest, or the like. **2.** One who receives unexpected support as a candidate for the nomination in a political convention. **3.** *Chiefly British.* A secretive person, especially one whose capabilities or talents are not yet revealed.

dark lantern *n.* A lantern whose light can be blocked by a sliding panel or other device.

dar·kle (där′kəl) *intr.v.* **-kled, -kling, -kles.** *Poetic.* **1.** To appear dark or indistinct. **2.** To grow dark. [Back-formation from DARKLING.]

dark·ling (därk′lĭng) *adv. Poetic.* In the dark.
~*adj. Poetic.* **1.** Being or happening in the dark or the night. **2.** Dim; obscure. [Middle English *derkeling* : DARK + -LING (condition).]

darkling beetle *n.* Any of various nocturnal, black or dark-brown beetles of the widely distributed family Tenebrionidae.

dark·ly (därk′lē) *adv.* **1.** So as to appear dark; in a dark manner. **2. a.** Mysteriously. **b.** In a sinister manner. **3.** Dimly; obscurely; faintly: *"For now we see through a glass, darkly."* (I Corinthians 13:12).

dark·ness (därk′nĭs) *n.* **1.** Total or almost total absence of light. **2.** The quality of being dark in color. **3.** Blindness. **4.** Lack of enlightenment; ignorance. **5.** Evil; wickedness. **6.** Secrecy; concealment. **7.** Lack of clearness; obscurity.

dark·room (därk′rōōm′, -rōōm′) *n.* A room in which photographic materials are processed, either in complete darkness or illuminated by sources of light to which the materials are not sensitive.

dark·some (därk′səm) *adj. Poetic.* Dark; darkish; somber.

dark star *n.* A star that is normally obscured or too faint for direct visual observation; especially, the component of an eclipsing binary detectable by spectral analysis or in the eclipse of the bright component.

dar·ling (där′lĭng) *n.* **1.** One who is very dear; a much-loved person. Often used as a term of address. **2.** One that is greatly liked or preferred; a favorite. **3.** A charming or attractive person or thing.
~*adj.* **1.** Regarded with great affection and tenderness; very dear; beloved. **2.** Regarded with special favor; favorite: *"Metaphysics and poetry . . . are my darling studies."* (S. T. Coleridge). **3.** *Informal.* Charming; amusing; pleasing: *a darling hat.* [Middle English *dereling,* Old English *dēorling* : DEAR + -LING (diminutive).]

Darling. River in New South Wales, in southeast Australia. It flows 2,739 kilometers (1,702 miles) from the Great Dividing Range to join the Murray River.

Darm·stadt (därm′stăt′). City in the state of Hesse in western Germany. In the 16th to 19th centuries it was the seat of the Hesse-Darmstadt royal house.

darn[1] (därn) *v.* **darned, darning, darns.** *—tr.* To mend by weaving thread or wool across a gap or hole. *—intr.* To mend or repair a hole or garment by darning.
~*n.* **1.** A hole repaired by darning. **2.** The act of darning. [Perhaps from obsolete *dern,* to hide, Old English *derne, dierne,* concealed, from Germanic.] **—darn·er** *n.*

darn[2] *interj.* Damn. Used euphemistically. **—darn** *adj. & adv.*

darned (därnd) *adj. Informal.* Damned. Used euphemistically and as an intensive: *a darned good player.* **—darned** *adv.*

dar·nel (där′nəl) *n.* Any of several grasses of the genus *Lolium,* native to Europe and Asia; especially, *L. tementulum* or *L. perenne.* [Middle English, akin to French dialect *darnelle*†, cockle.]

darning egg *n.* An egg-shaped object used to hold the shape of material being darned.

darning needle *n.* **1.** A long, large-eyed needle used in darning. **2.** *Informal.* A **dragonfly** *(see).*

Darn·ley (därn′lē), **Henry Stuart, Lord** (1545–67). Scottish earl, who was, by lineage, a possible successor to Elizabeth I of England. He married Mary, Queen of Scots, in 1565, chiefly to cement their joint claims to the throne. He became jealous of his wife's Italian secretary, Rizzio, and connived at his murder in 1566. Darnley himself was found murdered the following year, probably by Mary's lover, the Earl of Bothwell. His son by Mary became James VI of Scotland and the first Stuart king of England.

da·ro·gha (də-rō′gə) *n.* In India, an overseer, manager, or governor. [Urdu.]

Dar·row (dăr′ō), **Clarence Seward** (1857–1938). U.S. lawyer. A renowned defense lawyer, he used meticulous pretrial investigations and remarkable summations to juries to successfully defend Eugene V. Debs (1895), William D. Haywood (1906), and Leopold and Leob (1924), among many others. He opposed William Jennings Bryan in the landmark case of John T. Scopes, called the "Monkey Trial" (1925).

dar·shan (där′shən) *n. Hinduism.* A spiritual feeling experienced in the presence of a holy or revered person. [Hindi, from Sanskrit *darśana,* view.]

dart[1] (därt) *n.* **1.** A slender, pointed missile, often having tail fins, to be thrown by hand or shot, as from a blowgun. **2.** Anything like a dart in shape, use, or effect. **3.** *Zoology.* Any of various slender, pointed structures, such as an insect's sting. **4.** A rapid, sudden movement. **5.** In sewing, a tapered tuck to adjust the fit of a garment.
~*v.* **darted, darting, darts.** *—intr.* To move suddenly and swiftly. *—tr.* To throw or thrust suddenly or swiftly; shoot. [Middle English, from Old French, from Germanic *darōdhaz* (unattested), spear.]

dart[2] *n. Australian Informal.* A plan or scheme.

dart·board (därt′bôrd, -bōrd) *n.* A circular board divided into numbered segments with a small circle (bull's-eye) at the center, used as the target in the game of darts.

dar·ter (där′tər) *n.* **1.** One that moves suddenly and swiftly. **2.** Any of several long-necked, long-billed birds of the genus *Anhinga,* such as the **water turkey** *(see),* occurring in tropical and subtropical inland waters. **3.** Any of various small, often brightly colored freshwater fishes of the family Percidae, of eastern North America.

dar·tle (därt′l) *tr.v.* **-tled, -tling, -tles.** To thrust or shoot out repeatedly. [Frequentative of *dart,* to pierce with a dart, from Middle English *darten,* from DART.]

Dart·moor (därt′mōōr′). An expanse of high moorland in southwest Devon, England. Its many tors include High Willhays (621 meters; 2,038 feet), and there are ancient megalithic sites. The prison at Princetown was built (1806–09) for French prisoners of war and later housed American prisoners from the War of 1812. Since 1850 it has held long-term civilian prisoners.

Dartmoor pony *n.* A pony of a breed originating in the Dartmoor region of England.

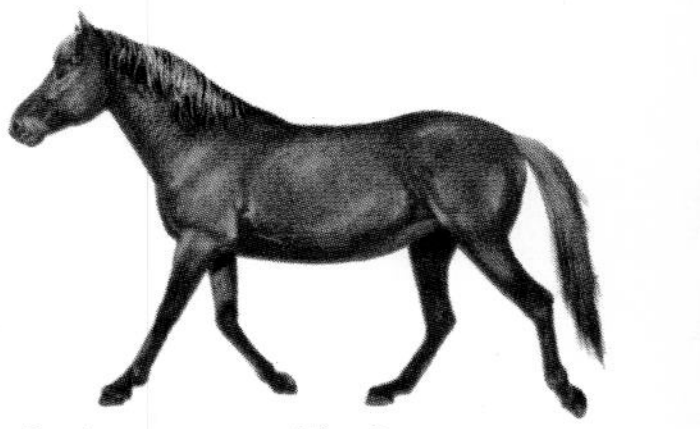

Dartmoor pony *The Dartmoor pony originated in southwest England and was once popular as a packhorse. It is muscular and hardy, standing 12 to 13 hands high at the shoulder (a hand equals 10 centimeters, or 4 inches).*

Dart·mouth (därt′məth). Seaport on the Dart estuary in Devon, southwest England. Richard I's crusaders embarked from here in 1190. In 1905 the Royal Naval College was opened.

darts (därts) *n. Used with a singular verb.* An indoor game in which darts are thrown at a target (a dartboard).

Dar·win (dâr′wĭn). Capital and seaport of Northern Territory, Australia. Founded as Palmerston (1869), it was renamed Port Darwin (1911). The modern city is an important stopover point on international air routes.

Darwin, Charles Robert (1809–82). British naturalist who revolutionized biological theory by putting forward his theory of evolution based on natural selection. His views, formed after his comprehensive observations of fossils and the diverse plant and animal life during his voyage (1831–36) around South America and the Pacific as naturalist on H.M.S. *Beagle,* were published in *On the Origin of Species.* His conclusions conflicted with traditional Christian opinion on the creation of the world and caused much controversy, especially where, as in his *The Descent of Man* (1871), evolutionary theories were applied to human origins.

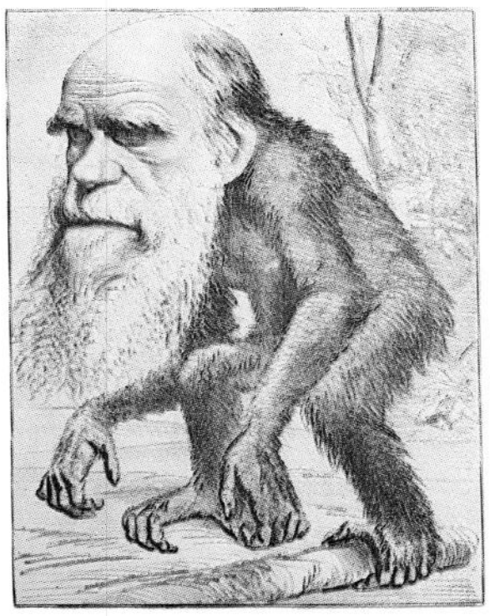

Darwin *A caricature of Charles Darwin from* The Hornet *magazine (1871). Some of Darwin's critics ridiculed the theory of evolution and its claim that man was descended from the apes, preferring to believe instead that all men were descended from Adam and Eve.*

Dar·win·ism (där′wə-nĭz′əm) *n.* A theory of biological evolution developed by Charles Darwin and others. It states that species of plants and animals develop through **natural selection** *(see)* of variations that increase the organism's ability to survive and reproduce. **—Dar·win·ist** *n.* **—Dar·win·is·tic** *adj.*

Darwin's finches *pl.n.* The finches of the subfamily Geospizinae, found only on the Galápagos Islands. Variations in their bill structure and feeding habits provided Charles Darwin with evidence to support his theory of evolution.

dash[1] (dăsh) *v.* **dashed, dashing, dashes.** *—tr.* **1.** To break or smash by striking violently. **2.** To hurl, knock, or thrust with sudden violence: *He was dashed to the ground.* **3.** To splash; bespatter. **4.** To write or execute hastily. Used with *off* or *down.* **5.** To destroy; frustrate: *His dreams were dashed.* **6.** To confound; abash: *She was dashed by the criticism.* **7.** To add an enlivening or altering element to; mix; adulterate: *"Some truth there was, but dash'd and brew'd with lies"* (John Dryden). *—intr.* **1.** To strike violently or with great force; smash. **2.** To move with haste; rush; race.
~*n.* **1.** A swift, violent blow or stroke. **2.** A splash. **3.** A small amount of an added ingredient: *a dash of salt.* **4.** A quick stroke, as with a pencil or brush. **5.** A sudden movement; a rush. **6.** A foot race run at top speed from the outset, usually less than a quarter-mile long. **7.** Spirited action or style; vigor; verve. **8.** A punctuation mark (—) used in writing and printing. —See Usage note below. **9.** In Morse code and similar codes, the long sound or signal used in combination with the dot, a shorter sound, and silent intervals to represent letters or numbers. [Middle English *daschen, dashen,* perhaps from Scandinavian, akin to Danish *daske,* to beat.]

Usage: The dash as a mark of punctuation has the following uses: 1. To set off a parenthetical clause: *Her face—or so it seemed to me—was never more radiant.* 2. To indicate a break in thought: *Then he ran—the fool.* 3. To mark an omission: *She doesn't give a*

d——. **4.** To mark a summing up: *Study and practice—this is the only solution.* **5.** To do the work of a colon: *Ten were chosen—five girls and five boys.* In modern writing, the dash is not used in combination with the colon or comma, though it can be followed immediately by a period at the end of a sentence. Indiscriminate use of the dash often leads to choppiness and confusion of expression.

dash² *Interj.* Damn. Used euphemistically.

dash³ *n. West African.* A tip or gratuity. —*tr.v.* **dashed, dashing, dashes.** *West African.* To give a tip or gratuity to. [Probably from Fanti.]

dash·board (dăsh'bôrd', -bōrd') *n.* A panel under the windshield of a car, aircraft, or the like, containing indicator displays, compartments, and control instruments.

da·sheen (dă-shēn') *n.* A plant, taro *(see).* [Perhaps alteration of French *de Chine,* of China.]

dash·er (dăsh'ər) *n.* **1.** One that dashes. **2.** The plunger of a churn or ice-cream freezer. **3.** *Informal.* A spirited person.

da·shi·ki (dä-shē'kē, də-) *n.* A loose, often brightly colored African tunic, usually worn by men. [Yoruba *danshiki.*]

dash·ing (dăsh'ĭng) *adj.* **1.** Audacious and gallant; bold; spirited. **2.** Marked by showy elegance; splendid: *a dashing new coat.* —**dash·ing·ly** *adv.*

dash·pot (dăsh'pŏt') *n.* A mechanical device for damping vibration in a machine, consisting of a piston moving in a cylinder of liquid.

dash·y (dăsh'ē) *adj.* **-ier, -iest.** Stylishly showy; dashing.

das·sie (dăs'ē) *n.* A mammal, the hyrax *(see).* [Afrikaans, diminutive of *das,* badger, hyrax, from Middle Dutch.]

das·tard (dăs'tərd) *n.* A base, sneaking coward. [Middle English, perhaps from obsolete *dasart,* dull person, influenced by *dotard.*]

das·tard·ly (dăs'tərd-lē) *adj.* Cowardly and mean-spirited; base. —**das·tard·li·ness** *n.*

Usage: *Dastardly* is employed most precisely when it refers to acts involving cowardice. It is loosely used when it applies to any reprehensible or risky act.

das·y·ure (dăs'ē-yŏor') *n.* Any of various marsupial mammals of the family Dasyuridae, of Australia and adjacent regions, ranging in size and appearance from that of a mouse to that of a dog. See **Tasmanian devil.** [New Latin *Dasyurus* (genus), "hairy-tailed" : Greek *dasus,* hairy, shaggy + -UROUS.]

dat. dative.

da·ta (dā'tə, dăt'ə, dä'tə) *pl.n. Singular* **da·tum** (dā'təm, dăt'əm, dä'təm). **1.** Information; especially, information organized for analysis or used as the basis for a decision. **2.** Numerical information in a form suitable for processing by computer. [Latin, plural of DATUM.]

Usage: Originally, data was used solely as the plural of *datum,* but it has increasingly come to be used as a singular, in such constructions as *the data is, this data, much data, two items of data.*

da·ta·bank, data bank (dā'tə-băngk', dăt'ə-) *n.* **1.** A database. **2.** An organization chiefly concerned with building, maintaining, and utilizing a databank.

da·ta·base, data base (dā'tə-bās', dăt'ə-, dä'tə-) *n.* A store of information; especially, a large store from which information can be selected by computer. Also called "databank."

data capture *n.* The process of converting data into a form in which it can be stored in or processed by a computer, as by keyboarding or optical character recognition (OCR).

data carrier *n.* The medium, as magnetic tape, selected to transport or communicate data.

data processing *n.* **1.** The preparation of information for processing by computers. **2.** The storing or processing of raw data by a computer. —**data processor** *n.*

da·ta·ry (dā'tə-rē) *n., pl.* **-ries.** *Roman Catholic Church.* **1.** The duty, formerly an official office of the curia, of investigating the fitness of candidates for papal benefices. **2.** A cardinal assuming the duty of datary. [Medieval Latin *datārius,* official who dated all papal letters, from Late Latin *data,* DATE (time).]

data set *n.* **1.** An electronic device that provides an interface in the transmission of data to a remote station. **2.** A collection of related computer records. **3.** A modem.

date¹ (dāt) *n. Abbr.* **d. 1.** A particular point or period of time at which something happened or existed or is to happen. **2.** The time during which something lasts; duration. **3.** The time or historical period to which something belongs: *artifacts of a later date.* **4. dates.** The years of a person's birth and death. **5.** The day of the month. **6.** An inscription or statement, as on a coin or letter, indicating when it was made or written. **7.** *Informal.* **a.** An appointment to meet socially at a particular time; especially, one with a member of the opposite sex. **b.** A person so met. —**to date.** Up to the present time; as yet.

—*v.* **dated, dating, dates.** —*tr.* **1.** To mark or supply (a letter, for example) with a date. **2.** To assign a date to; determine the date, occurrence, or origin of. **3.** To betray the age of. **4.** *Informal.* **a.** To go out on a date with. **b.** To go on dates regularly with. —*intr.* **1.** To have origin in a particular time in the past. Usually used with *back to* or *from: dates from 500 B.C.* **2.** To become old-fashioned. **3.** *Informal.* To have social engagements with persons of the opposite sex. [Middle English, from Old French, from Medieval Latin *data,* "given," "issued" (used for Latin *datum* in the letter-dating formula, e.g. *datum Romae,* issued at Rome) from Latin *datus,* past participle of *dare,* to give.] —**dat·able, date·able** *adj.* —**dat·er** *n.*

date² *n.* **1.** The sweet, oblong, edible fruit of the **date palm** *(see)* containing a narrow, hard seed. **2.** The date palm. [Middle English, from Old French, from Old Provençal *datil,* from Latin *dactylus,*

from Greek *daktulos,* "finger" (from the shape of the fruit). See **dactyl.**]

dat·ed (dā'tĭd) *adj.* **1.** Marked with or displaying a date. **2.** Old-fashioned; antiquated; outmoded. —**dat·ed·ness** *n.*

date·less (dāt'lĭs) *adj.* **1.** Having no date. **2.** Without limits; endless. **3.** Too old to be dated. **4.** Timeless or eternal.

date line *n. Sometimes* **Date Line.** An imaginary line through the Pacific Ocean roughly corresponding to 180 degrees longitude, to the east of which, by international agreement, the calendar date is one day earlier than to the west. Called in full "International Date Line."

date·line (dāt'līn') *n.* A phrase at the beginning of a newspaper or magazine article that gives the date and place of its origin.

date palm *n.* A palm tree, *Phoenix dactylifera,* of tropical and subtropical areas, having featherlike leaves and bearing clusters of dates.

date stamp *n.* A device with adjustable numerals and letters for marking a date on documents, goods, and other objects.

date-stamp (dāt'stămp') *tr.v.* **-stamped, -stamping, -stamps.** To mark a date on with a date stamp.

dating bar *n.* A singles bar *(see).*

da·tive (dā'tĭv) *n. Abbr.* **dat. 1.** The grammatical case in certain Indo-European languages, such as Greek, Latin, or Russian, that denotes the indirect object of a verb and the object of any of certain verbs and prepositions. **2.** A form or construction in this case. —*adj.* Also **da·ti·val** (dā-tī'vəl). *Abbr.* **dat.** Designating, pertaining to, or inflected in the dative case. [Middle English *datif,* from Latin (*cāsus*) *datīvus,* "(case) of giving" (translation of Greek *ptōsis dotikē*), from *dare,* to give.] —**da·tive·ly** *adv.*

dative bond *n. Chemistry.* A **coordinate bond** *(see).*

da·to, dat·to (dä'tō) *n., pl.* **-tos. 1.** The chief of a Muslim Moro tribe in the Philippines. **2.** The head man of a barrio or Malay tribe. [Spanish *dato,* from Tagalog *datò,* from Malay *dato',* "grandfather."]

da·tum (dā'təm, dăt'əm, dä'təm) *n., pl.* **-ta** (-tə) or **-tums** (for sense 3). **1.** An assumed, given, measured, or otherwise determined single fact or proposition used to draw a conclusion or make a decision; a single piece of information. —See Usage note at **data. 2.** The real or assumed point from which any reckoning or scale begins. **3.** A point, line, or level used as a reference, as in surveying or geology. [Latin, "something given," from the neuter past participle of *dare,* to give.]

da·tu·ra (də-tŏor'ə, -tyŏor'ə) *n.* Any of several plants of the genus *Datura,* including the **thorn apple** *(see),* having large trumpet-shaped flowers. [New Latin *Datura,* from Hindi *dhatūrā,* from Sanskrit *dhattūrā†.*]

daub (dôb) *v.* **daubed, daubing, daubs.** —*tr.* **1.** To cover, coat, or smear with an adhesive substance, such as plaster, mud, or grease. **2.** To apply paint to with hasty or crude strokes. —*intr.* To apply paint or coloring with crude, unskillful strokes.

—*n.* **1.** The act or a stroke of daubing. **2.** Any soft adhesive coating material that is daubed on, such as plaster or mud. See **wattle and daub. 3.** A crude or amateurishly inferior painting. [Middle English *dauben,* from Old French *dauber,* from Latin *dēalbāre,* to whitewash : *dē-,* completely + *albāre,* to whiten, from *albus,* white.] —**daub·er** *n.* —**daub·er·y** *n.* —**daub·ing·ly** *adv.* —**daub·y** *adj.*

daube (dōb) *n.* **1.** A method of cooking in which meat, usually beef, is braised in red wine. **2.** A stew so prepared. [French, from Spanish *doba* (unattested), from *dobar†,* to stew.]

Dau·bi·gny (dō-bē-nyē'), **Charles François** (1817-78). French landscape painter whose delight in the fleeting effects of light in the 1850's strongly influenced the young impressionists.

Dau·det (dō-dĕ'), **Alphonse** (1840-97). French novelist. He wrote *Lettres de mon moulin,* a collection of scenes from Provençal life in 1868. His novels include *Le Petit Chose* (1868) and *Tartarin de Tarascon* (1872).

daugh·ter (dô'tər) *n. Abbr.* **d. 1.** A female child considered in relation to her parents. **2.** A female descendant. **3.** A girl or woman attached to a country, organization, or the like as a child is to a parent: *a daughter of the nation.* **4.** Anything personified or regarded as a female descendant: *regarded Japan as a daughter of Chinese civilization.* Also used adjectivally: *a daughter cell.* **5.** A term of address used to a girl or woman by an older man other than her father, especially a priest. **6.** *Physics & Chemistry.* A particle, nucleus, ion, or the like produced by the decay or breakdown of another entity (the parent). Also used adjectivally: *a daughter nucleus.* [Middle English *doughter,* Old English *dohtor.*] —**daugh·ter·ly** *adj.*

daugh·ter-in-law (dô'tər-ĭn-lô') *n., pl.* **daughters-in-law.** The wife of one's son.

Daughters of the American Revolution *n. Abbr.* **DAR, D.A.R.** A society of women descended from American patriots of the Revolutionary War, organized in 1890.

Dau·mier (dō-myā'), **Honoré** (1808-79). French caricaturist and painter whose satirical lithographs in *La Caricature* and *Le Charivari* exposed the foibles of contemporary French government and society.

daunt (dônt, dänt) *tr.v.* **daunted, daunting, daunts. 1.** To intimidate. **2.** To discourage; dishearten. [Middle English *daunten,* from Old French *danter, donter,* from Latin *domitāre,* frequentative of *domāre,* to tame, subdue.] —**daunt·er** *n.* —**daunt·ing·ly** *adv.*

daunt·less (dônt'lĭs, dänt'-) *adj.* Incapable of being intimidated or discouraged; fearless; bold. —See Synonyms at **brave.** —**daunt·less·ly** *adv.* —**daunt·less·ness** *n.*

dau·phin (dô′fĭn; *French* dō-fäN′) *n.* The eldest son of the king of France. Used as a title from 1349 to 1830. [French, from Old French *dalphin, dalfin,* DOLPHIN. This title (originally borne by the lords of Viennois, whose coat of arms bore three dolphins) was adopted by the French crown princes as a condition when the Viennois province of Dauphiné was ceded to the crown.]

dau·phine (dô-fēn′; *French* dō-fēn′) *n.* Also **dau·phin·ess** (dô′fĭ-nĭs). The wife of the dauphin.

Dau·phi·né (dō-fē-nā′). Region in southeast France, comprising the present departments of Drôme, Hautes-Alpes, and Isère. Before 1343 it was ruled by a count known as a dauphin. It was then sold to Charles of Valois, the future Charles V of France. The king gave the province to his eldest son, and thereafter all eldest sons of the French kings inherited it with the title of dauphin.

DAV, D.A.V. Disabled American Veterans.

Da·vao (dä′vou). City of southeastern Mindanao, Phillippines, at the mouth of the Davao River on Davao Gulf. It is the chief commercial center and major port of the island of Mindanao.

dav·en·port (dăv′ən-pôrt′, -pōrt′) *n.* **1.** A large sofa, often convertible into a bed. **2.** *British.* A small writing desk with drawers and a hinged shelf to write on. [Perhaps from *Davenport,* name of the original manufacturer of the desk.]

Dav·en·port (dăv′ən-pôrt′, -pōrt′). City of east-central Iowa, on the Mississippi River. It is an important rail, commercial, and industrial center. Built on the site of an early trading post, the city prospered after the arrival (1856) of the first railroad to bridge the Mississippi.

Da·vid (dā′vĭd) (died 962 B.C.). King of Judah and Israel, who founded the Jewish royal dynasty at Jerusalem. He was born in Bethlehem and was acclaimed for his legendary boyhood feat of killing the Philistine giant, Goliath. Later outlawed by Saul, he seized the southern kingdom (Judah) on the king's death and gradually subdued the north (Israel), uniting the Israelites. He was succeeded by his son Solomon.

Da·vid (də-vēd), **Jacques Louis** (1748–1825). French painter and leading figure in the neoclassical movement. David welcomed the French Revolution in 1789 and painted pictures including *The Oath of the Horatii* (1785) and *Death of Marat* (1793) to promote republican feeling. He was elected to the national convention in 1792. He survived the downfall of his friend Robespierre to become court painter to Napoleon in 1804. His style became more richly decorative in such paintings as *Napoleon Crowning Josephine* (1805–07). With the fall of Napoleon, David was exiled and died in Brussels.

Da·vid (dā′vĭd), **Saint** (*c.* 520–600). Patron saint of Wales. The primate of the Celtic church in south Wales, set up his seat of government at Mynyw (now St. David's). His feast day is March 1.

David, Star of. A symbol of Judaism, the **Star of David** *(see).*

Da·vid·son (dā′vĭd-sən), **Jo,** born Joseph (1883–1952). U.S. sculptor. He is noted particularly for his portrait busts of contemporary Americans and French leaders, including Woodrow Wilson, Robert M. La Follette, Will Rogers, Marshal Foch, and Clemenceau.

da Vinci, Leonardo. See **Leonardo da Vinci.**

Da·vis (dā′vis), **Bette,** born Ruth Elizabeth Davis (1908–89). U.S. film actress. She made her screen debut in *The Man Who Played God* (1932) and twice won Academy Awards for her roles in *Dangerous* (1935) and *Jezebel* (1938). She was acclaimed for her role as an old and embittered former child star in *Whatever Happened to Baby Jane?* (1962).

Davis, Sir Colin (1927–). British conductor. He is noted for his interpretations of Mozart and his promotion of the music of Berlioz. He was knighted in 1980.

Davis, Jefferson (1808–89). President of the Confederate States during the Civil War (1861–65). An 1828 graduate of the U.S. Military Academy, he served as an officer till 1835 and in the Mexican War. He was also a Mississippi planter, a U.S. congressman and senator, and secretary of war. Davis supported slavery and states' rights against federal interference. After the election of Abraham Lincoln (1860), he withdrew his state from the Union (1861). As president of the Confederacy, Davis ordered the offensive that resulted in disaster at Gettysburg (1863). He was captured at Irwinville, Georgia (May 10, 1865), and was imprisoned for two years on a charge of treason.

Davis, Miles (1926–91). U.S. jazz trumpeter and composer. After playing with Charlie Parker in the 1940's he became one of the most influential musicians in jazz. Important recordings include *Birth of the Cool* (1949–50) and *Bitches Brew* (1970).

Davis, Richard Harding (1864–1916). U.S. journalist, editor, and novelist. As a war correspondent, he covered the Spanish-American War, the Boer War, and the Russo-Japanese War, among others, and became known as the leading reporter of his time. He also wrote vivid short stories, novels, and plays.

Davis, Sammy, Jr. (1925–90). U.S. entertainer. An exuberant, talented performer, he was successful in the recording studio, Broadway productions such as *Mr. Wonderful* (1956), movies, including *Porgy and Bess* (1959), and television specials.

Davis Cup *n.* **1.** A trophy awarded to the nation whose team is the winner of the annual International Lawn Tennis Championship for men. **2.** The competition held for this cup. [After Dwight F. *Davis* (1879–1945), American civic leader and government official who donated the trophy in 1900.]

dav·it (dăv′ĭt, dā′-) *n.* Any of various small cranes, usually one of a pair and made of shaped steel tubing, used on ships to hoist lifeboats, anchors, and cargo. [Middle English *daviot,* from Old French *daviot, daviet,* diminutive of the name *David,* also the name given to a carpenter's tool.]

Da·vos (dä-vôs′). An Alpine town in the Graubünden canton in east Switzerland. It is a tourist center, especially for winter sports.

Da·vy (dā′vē), **Sir Humphry** (1778–1829). British chemist and inventor of the Davy miner's safety lamp. He joined the Royal Institution in London and became a pioneer of electrochemistry. Davy was appointed president of the Royal Society (1820) and gave much encouragement to Michael Faraday.

Davy Jones *n.* The spirit of the sea. [Perhaps *Davy,* nickname for David + *Jones,* alteration of *Jonas, Jonah* (the prophet, with allusion to the whale in Jonah 1:17).]

Davy Jones's locker *n.* The bottom of the sea, especially as the grave of all who perish at sea.

Davy lamp *n.* An early safety oil lamp having a gauze surrounding the flame to prevent ignition of gas, used by coal miners. Also called "davy." [Invented by Sir Humphry DAVY.]

daw (dô) *n.* A bird, the **jackdaw** *(see).* [Middle English *dawe,* probably from Old English *dāwe* (unattested), from West Germanic *dǣgw-* (unattested).]

daw·dle (dôd′l) *v.* **-dled, -dling, -dles.** —*intr.* **1.** To move slowly; loiter; lag behind. **2.** To waste time by trifling; linger. —*tr.* To waste (time) in this manner. Usually used with *away: dawdling away the hours.* [17th century : probably of dialectal origin.] **—daw·dler** *n.* **—daw·dling·ly** *adv.*

Dawes (dôz), **Charles Gates** (1865–1951). U.S. financier and statesman. His report, known as the Dawes Plan (1924), provided a system for Germany to pay reparations for World War I damage. The plan helped the reconstruction of the German economy, and Dawes received the Nobel Peace Prize (1925). He became Republican vice president under Calvin Coolidge (1925–29).

dawn (dôn) *n.* **1.** The time each morning when daylight first appears. **2.** A first appearance; a beginning: *the dawn of history.* ~*intr.v.* **dawned, dawning, dawns. 1.** To begin to become light in the morning. **2.** To begin to appear or develop; emerge. **3.** To begin to be perceived or understood. Used with *on* or *upon*: *"the suspicion dawning on him that he was not a welcome visitor"* (Somerset Maugham). [Middle English *daunen,* probably back-formation from *dauninge,* daybreak, alteration of *dauinge,* Old English *dagung,* from *dagian,* to dawn.]

dawn chorus *n.* The singing of birds when they awaken at first light. Preceded by *the.*

dawn redwood *n.* A Chinese deciduous coniferous tree, *Metasequoia glyptostroboides,* discovered as an extant species after having long been considered extinct. It is often grown for ornament.

Daw·son (dô′sən). A town in Yukon Territory, northwest Canada. It was founded (1896) during the Klondike gold rush and was the territory's capital (1898–1951).

day (dā) *n. Abbr.* **d 1. a.** The period of light between dawn and nightfall; the interval from sunrise to sunset. **b.** The light of day; daylight. **2.** The 24-hour period during which the earth completes one rotation on its axis. See **mean solar day, sidereal day. 3.** The portion of a day devoted to work: *the eight-hour day.* **4.** A day reserved for a certain activity: *a day of rest.* **5.** *Usually* **Day.** A particular day connected with a special event or observance: *Mother's Day.* **6. a.** *Often* **days.** One's lifetime. **b.** The period of activity or prominence in one's lifetime: *a writer who has had his day.* **c.** A period of opportunity: *Every dog has his day.* **7.** *Often* **days.** A period of time; an age; an era: *in Napoleon's day; in days of old.* **8.** A unit of distance traveled in an ordinary day's journey. **9.** The contest or issue at hand: *carry the day.* **10.** *Astronomy.* The period during which a heavenly body completes one turn on its axis. **—call it a day.** *Informal.* **1.** To stop one's work or activity for the day. **2.** To terminate after any period of time. **—day after day.** Continuously; for many days. **—day in, day out.** Every day without fail; continuously. **—late in the day.** At a regrettably late stage. [Middle English *dai, day,* Old English *dæg,* from Germanic.]

Day (dā), **Clarence Shepard, Jr.** (1874–1935). U.S. author. He is best known for his autobiographical works, *God and My Father* (1932) and *Life with Father* (1935; dramatized in a highly successful version by Howard Lindsay and Russel Crouse in 1939), and his posthumous works *Life with Mother* (1937) and *Father and I* (1940).

Dayak. Variant of **Dyak.**

Da·yan (dī-än′), **Moshe** (1915–81). Israeli general and politician. He was chief of the general staff (1953–58) and minister of defense (1967, 1969–74). He became a national hero for directing Israel's victory in the Six-Day War (1967). In 1977 he was made foreign minister, resigning two years later.

day bed *n.* A couch or sofa that can be used as a bed, especially during the day.

day blindness *n. Pathology.* **Hemeralopia** *(see).*

day·book (dā′bo͝ok′) *n.* **1.** *Abbr.* **D.B.** *Bookkeeping.* A book in which daily transactions are recorded. **2.** A diary.

day·boy (dā′boi′) *n. Chiefly British.* A schoolboy who attends a boarding school but lives at home. Compare **boarder.**

day·break (dā′brāk′) *n.* The time each morning when light first appears; dawn.

day care *n.* The providing of daytime supervision, training, medical services, and the like, for children of preschool age or for the elderly or disabled.

day-care (dā′kâr′) *adj.* Of, relating to, or providing day care: *a day-care center.*

day coach *n.* An ordinary passenger car of a railroad train, as

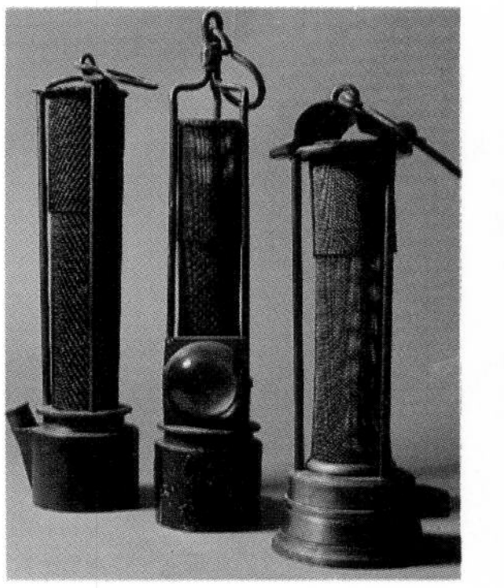

Davy lamp *The miners' safety lamp invented about 1815 has its oil flame surrounded by metal gauze. The metal allows light and air to pass through but conducts heat away so that it does not cause an explosion. The flame changes color in the presence of explosive gas.*

distinguished from other cars with special accommodations.

day·dream (dā'drēm') n. A dreamlike musing or fantasy while awake; idle reverie, especially of the fulfillment of wishes or hopes. ~intr.v. **daydreamed** or **-dreamt** (-drěmt'), **-dreaming, -dreams.** To have daydreams. —**day·dream·er** n.

day·flow·er (dā'flou'ər) n. Any of various plants of the genus *Commelina,* having blue or purplish flowers that wilt quickly.

day·fly (dā'flī') n., pl. **-flies.** An insect, the **mayfly** (see).

day·girl (dā'gûrl') n. Chiefly British. A schoolgirl who attends a boarding school but lives at home. Compare **boarder.**

Day-Glo (dā'glō') n. A trademark for a type of fluorescent paint that glows brightly in daylight.

day hospital n. A hospital as for the elderly or mentally ill, in which patients receive medical supervision but do not stay overnight.

day labor n. Labor hired and paid by the day. —**day laborer** n.

day letter n. A telegram sent during the day, usually less expensive but slower than a regular telegram.

day·light (dā'līt') n. 1. The light of day; direct light of the sun. 2. **a.** Daybreak. **b.** Daytime. 3. Exposure to public notice. 4. **daylights.** Slang. Sense; wits: *scared the living daylights out of him.* —**see daylight.** 1. To approach the end of a difficult endeavor. 2. To begin to understand what was formerly obscure.

daylight robbery n. Chiefly British Informal. Blatant swindling or overcharging.

day·light-sav·ing time (dā'līt'sā'vǐng) n. Abbr. **DST, D.S.T.** Time during which clocks are set one hour or more ahead of standard time to provide more daylight at the end of the working day during late spring, summer, and early autumn.

day lily n. 1. Any of various plants of the genus *Hemerocallis,* native to Eurasia, having sword-shaped leaves and yellow to red funnel-shaped flowers. Also called "hemerocallis." 2. The **plantain lily** (see).

day·long (dā'lông', -lǒng') adj. Lasting the whole day. ~adv. Through the whole day.

day-neutral (dā'nōō'trəl, -nyōō'-) adj. Of or designating plants whose ability to flower is not affected by the length of the day.

day nursery n. A nursery providing daytime care for children of preschool age.

Day of Atonement n. **Yom Kippur** (see).

Day of Judgment n. The **Judgment Day** (see).

day release n. British. A system whereby a worker is given regular, paid time off to attend an educational course. Compare **block release.**

day return n. British. A ticket, usually at a reduced fare, used when traveling to a place and back again on the same day.

day room n. A communal sitting room used for recreation, especially in institutions such as schools, hospitals, and prisons.

days (dāz) adv. Regularly or habitually in the daytime: *She prefers working days.*

day sailer n. A small sailboat for day trips.

day school n. 1. A private or state school for pupils living at home. Compare **boarding school.** 2. A school that holds classes during the day, as opposed to the evening, or on weekdays, as opposed to Sunday.

day·side (dā'sīd') n. The side of a planet facing the sun.

days·man (dāz'mən) n., pl. **-men** (-mǐn). Rare. An arbiter or mediator. [Middle English *dayesman : dayes,* genitive of DAY (appointed for settlement of dispute) + MAN.]

days of grace pl. n. Extra days, usually three, allowed for payment of a note or bill after it has fallen due. [Translation of Latin *diēs grātiae.*]

day·spring (dā'sprǐng') n. Poetic. The early dawn; daybreak.

day-star (dā'stär') n. 1. The morning star. 2. Poetic. The sun.

day·time (dā'tīm') n. The time between dawn and dark; day. ~adj. During the day.

day-to-day (dā'tə-dā') adj. 1. Occurring daily or on successive days. 2. Routine or regular; mundane.

Day·ton (dāt'n). A city on the Miami River in southwestern Ohio. It was the home of the aircraft pioneers Orville and Wilbur Wright.

Day·to·na Beach (dā-tō'nə). An Atlantic coastal city in northeast Florida. It is a beach resort, and its hard sands have been the venue for speed trials since 1903. The city is also the site of the Daytona International Speedway.

day-trip (dā'trǐp') n. An excursion to a place and back again completed in one day. —**day-trip-per** n.

daze (dāz) tr.v. **dazed, dazing, dazes.** 1. To stun, as with a heavy blow or shock; stupefy. 2. To dazzle, as with strong light. ~n. A stunned or bewildered condition: *wandering about in a daze.* [Middle English *dasen,* from Old Norse *dasa* (attested in the reflexive form *dasask,* to become weary).] —**daz·ed·ly** (dā'zəd-lē) adv.

daz·zle (dăz'əl) v. **-zled, -zling, -zles.** —tr. 1. To dim the vision of; blind temporarily with intense light. 2. To bewilder, amaze, impress or overwhelm with some spectacular display. —intr. 1. To inspire admiration or wonder: *dazzling wit and repartee.* 2. To become blinded: *"thy sight is young,/ And thou shalt read when mine begin to dazzle"* (Shakespeare). ~n. The act or quality of dazzling: *"the dazzle of league after league of featureless sand"* (T.E. Lawrence). [Frequentative of DAZE.] —**daz·zler** n. —**daz·zling·ly** adv.

dB, db decibel.

D.B. daybook.

d.b.a. doing business as.

D.B.A. Doctor of Business Administration.

D.B.E. Dame Commander of the Order of the British Empire.

d.b.h. Forestry. diameter at breast height.

D.Bib. Douay Bible.

dbl. double.

dc, DC direct current.

D.C. 1. Music. da capo. 2. District of Columbia. 3. district commissioner. 4. direct current.

D.C.L. Doctor of Civil Law.

D.C.M. Distinguished Conduct Medal.

D.D. 1. demand draft. 2. dishonorable discharge. 3. Doctor of Divinity (Latin *Divinitatis Doctor*).

D-day (dē'dā') n. The unnamed day on which a military offensive or other operation is to be launched; specifically, June 6, 1944, the day on which the Allied forces invaded France during World War II. [D (abbreviation for DAY) + DAY.]

D.D.S. Doctor of Dental Science; Doctor of Dental Surgery.

DDT n. A colorless contact insecticide, $(ClC_6H_4)_2CHCCl_3$, toxic to man and animals when swallowed or absorbed through the skin. [From *d(ichloro)d(iphenyl)t(richloroethane):* DI- + CHLORO- + DI- + PHENYL + TRI- + CHLORO- + ETHANE.]

de, De (də) prep. French. Of; from. Used in personal names, originally to show place of origin: *Guy de Maupassant.* [French, from Latin *dē,* from.]

DE Delaware (used with a Zip Code).

de- prefix. Indicates: 1. Reversal or undoing; for example, **decode, denationalize.** 2. Removal; for example, **deaminate, delouse.** 3. Degradation, reduction; for example, **declass.** 4. Disparagement; for example, **demean.** Note: Many compounds other than those entered here may be formed with *de-.* In forming compounds, *de-* is normally joined with the following element without space or hyphen: *decarbonize.* However, if the second element begins with *e,* it is separated with a hyphen: *de-escalate.* It is also preferable to use the hyphen if the compound brings together three or more vowels: *de-aerate.* In the rare case that the second element begins with a capital letter, it is separated with a hyphen: *de-Americanize.* [In borrowed Latin and French compounds, Latin *dē-* (French *dé-,* Old French *des-*) indicates: 1. Down, downward, as in **declivity, deject.** 2. Away, away from, off, as in **decide, deprecate.** 3. Reversal, undoing, as in **decrease, destroy.** 4. Removal, riddance, as in **defoliate, decapitate.** 5. Completely, carefully, intensively, as in **denominate, declare.** 6. Pejorative sense, as in **deride, deceive.** Latin *dē-,* from *dē,* from.]

de·ac·ces·sion (dē-ăk-sěsh'ən) v. **-sioned, -sioning, -sions.** —tr. To remove (an article) from the collection in a museum or gallery and sell it off in order to raise funds. —intr. To remove an article or articles in this way.

de·a·cid·i·fy (dē'ə-sǐd'ə-fī) tr.v. **-fied, -fying, -fies.** To remove the acid from or reduce the acid content of. —**de·a·cid·i·fi·ca·tion** n.

dea·con (dē'kən) n. 1. In the Anglican, Greek Orthodox, and Roman Catholic churches, a clergyman ranking just below a priest. 2. In various other Christian churches, a layman who assists the minister in various functions. ~tr.v. **deaconed, -coning, -cons.** Informal. 1. To read aloud lines or verses of (a hymn) to help the congregation in singing. 2. To arrange (fruit and vegetables) for sale so that inferior items are concealed. 3. To adulterate. [Middle English *dek(e)n,* Old English *dīacon,* from Late Latin *diāconus,* from Greek *diakonos,* "servant."] —**dea·con·ship** n.

dea·con·ess (dē'kə-nǐs) n. A woman appointed or elected to serve as an assistant in a church.

dea·con·ry (dē'kən-rē) n., pl. **-ries.** 1. The office or position of a deacon. 2. Deacons collectively.

de·ac·ti·vate (dē-ăk'tə-vāt') tr.v. **-vated, -vating, -vates.** 1. To render inactive; especially, to make (a bomb or radioactive sample, for example) harmless or ineffective. 2. Military. To remove from active status. —**de·ac·ti·va·tion** n.

dead (děd) adj. Sometimes **deader, deadest.** 1. No longer alive; lifeless. Compare **brain dead.** 2. Not having the capacity to live; inanimate: *as dead as a stone.* 3. **a.** Lacking feeling; numb: *My leg's gone dead.* **b.** Lacking sensitivity; unresponsive: *dead to all our entreaties.* 4. No longer in existence, use, force, or operation: *a dead language.* 5. Devoid of animation, interest, or excitement. 6. Not productive; idle: *dead capital.* 7. Informal. Weary and worn-out; exhausted. 8. Without brightness or luster. Said of colors. 9. Without resonance. Said of sounds. 10. Extinguished: *a dead match.* 11. Lacking elasticity or resilience. 12. Suggestive of the finality or absoluteness of death, especially: **a.** Abrupt: *dead stop.* **b.** Complete; utter: *dead silence.* **c.** Exact; unerring: *the dead center.* 13. Sports. Out of play. Said of a ball. 14. **a.** Lacking connection to a source of electric current or voltage. **b.** Drained of electric charge; discharged. Said of a battery. 15. Printing. No longer needed for use. Said of type. ~n. 1. A person who has died, or those who have died, collectively. Preceded by the. 2. The period of greatest intensity, as of cold or darkness: *the dead of winter.* ~adv. 1. Absolutely; altogether. 2. Directly; exactly: *dead ahead.* [Middle English *ded,* Old English *dēad,* from Germanic.] —**dead·ness** n.

Usage: *dead, deceased, departed, extinct, lifeless, inanimate.* These adjectives all mean without life. *Dead,* which has the widest use, applies in general to whatever once had physical life, function, or usefulness but no longer does. *Deceased* refers only to nonliving human beings, as does *departed,* a euphemistic term. *Extinct* can

D-Day

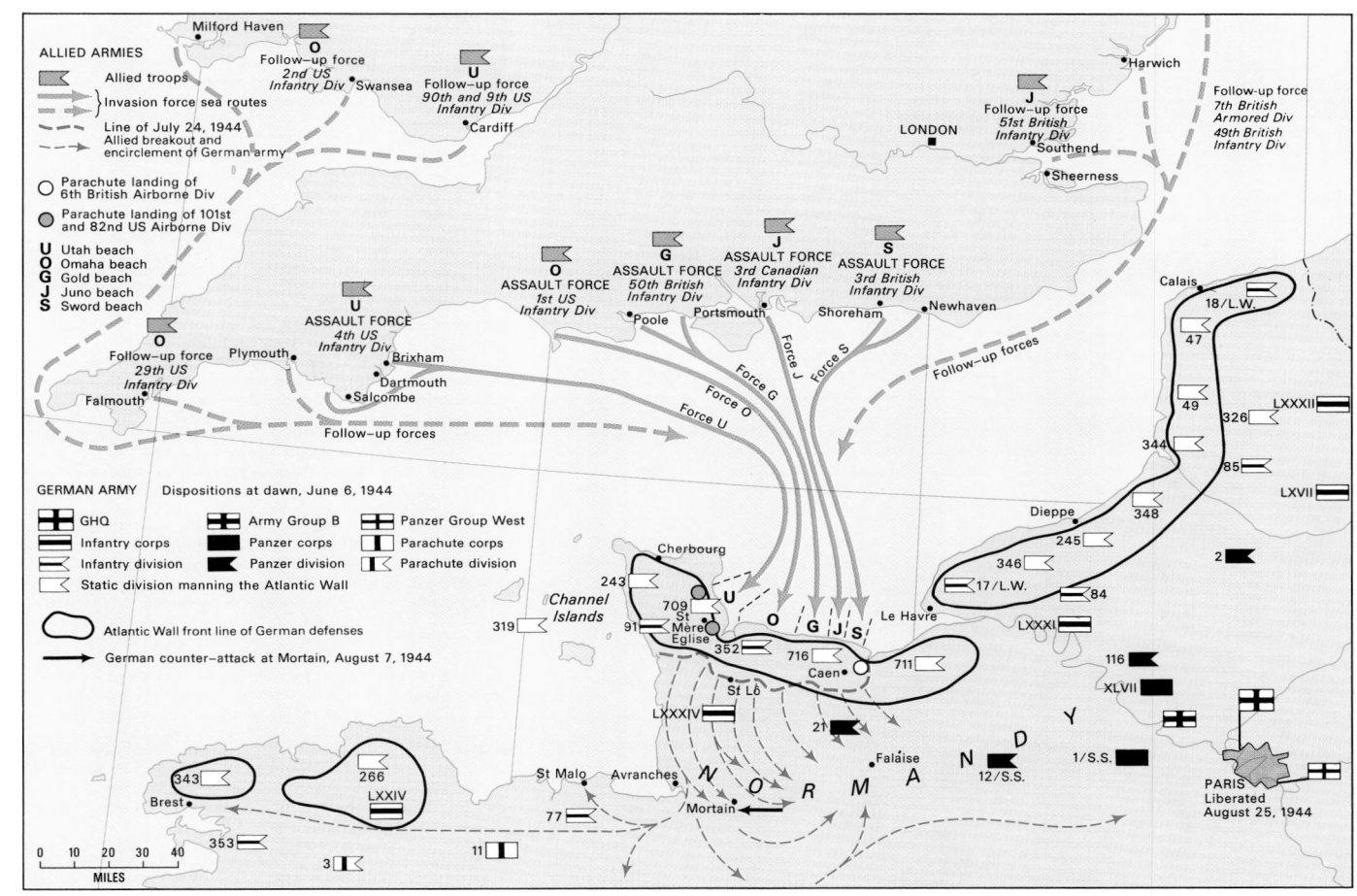

NORMANDY LANDINGS: THE INVASION OF OCCUPIED EUROPE
The Allied offensive that started the reconquest of occupied Europe

The turning point of World War II came in 1944. German forces had finally been forced on the defensive on the Russian front, and the growing demand for a second front to take the offensive against the enemy in western Europe was answered by Operation Overlord—the invasion of Normandy. On June 6, 1944, 156,000 men landed on five beaches between Caen and Cherbourg. This part of the French coast was chosen for its favorable tides and comparatively weak defenses. By feeding the Germans false intelligence reports, the Allies led them to believe that the main assault would be made around Calais. RAF bombers and two American airborne divisions prepared the way by attacking strategic targets. By June 11, the beachheads were completely in Allied hands. Specially designed artificial harbors enabled armored vehicles and heavy guns and artillery to land on the beaches and sustain the invasion.

refer to what has no living successors, such as an animal species, or to what is extinguished or inactive, such as a volcano. *Lifeless* applies to what no longer has physical life and to persons or things that lack animation or spirit. *Inanimate* is limited to what has never had physical life.

dead-air space (dĕd′âr′) *n.* An unventilated space.

dead ball line *n.* In Rugby football, a line behind the goal line, beyond which the ball is out of play (dead).

dead·beat¹ (dĕd′bēt′) *n.* **1.** *Informal.* Someone with no money; a destitute person. **2.** A lazy or lethargic person; a loafer. **3.** A person who does not pay his debts.
~*adj. Informal.* Completely exhausted. [Probably DEAD (completely) + BEAT (exhausted).]

deadbeat² *adj.* **1.** *Physics.* Lacking recoil, as the mechanism of a clock. **2.** Stopping without oscillation. [DEAD + BEAT (oscillation).]

dead center *n.* Either of two points in the path of a moving crank and connecting rod at the ends of a stroke when the two lie in a straight line. Also called "dead point."

dead duck *n. Slang.* A failure or a person or thing doomed to failure.

dead·en (dĕd′n) *v.* **-ened, -ening, -ens.** —*tr.* **1.** To render less sensitive, intense, or vigorous: *pills to deaden the pain.* **2.** To make soundproof. **3.** To make less colorful. —*intr.* To become dead or as if dead. —**dead·en·er** *n.*

dead end *n.* **1.** An end of a passage, such as a street or pipe, that affords no outlet or exit. **2.** Any point beyond which no movement or progress can be made; an impasse.

dead-end (dĕd′ĕnd′) *adj.* **1.** Not having an exit: *a dead-end street.* **2.** Without opportunity for advancement: *a dead-end job.* **3.** Infor-mal. Of or characteristic of the slums or life in the slums: *a dead-end gang.*

dead·en·ing (dĕd′n-ĭng) *n.* Material used for soundproofing.

dead-eye (dĕd′ī′) *n.* **1.** *Nautical.* A flat hardwood disk with a grooved perimeter, pierced by three holes through which the lanyards are passed, used to fasten the shrouds. **2.** *Slang.* An expert marksman. [Perhaps because the holes on the disk resemble the empty sockets in a human skull.]

dead-fall (dĕd′fôl′) *n.* **1.** A trap for large animals, in which a heavy weight is arranged to fall on and kill or disable the prey. **2.** A mass of fallen timber and tangled brush.

dead hand *n. Law. Mortmain (see).* [Middle English *dede hond,* translation of Old French *mortemain,* MORTMAIN.]

dead-head¹ (dĕd′hĕd′) *n.* **1.** A vehicle, such as a railway car or airplane, carrying no passengers or freight. **2.** A dull-witted or sluggish person. **3.** *Informal.* A person who uses a free ticket for admittance, accommodation, or entertainment.
~*tr.v.* **deadheaded, -heading, -heads.** *Informal.* To drive (a train, bus, or truck) carrying no passengers or freight.
~*adv. Informal.* Without passengers or freight; empty.

deadhead², dead-head *v. Chiefly British.* **-headed, -heading, -heads.** —*tr.* To remove the dead flowers from (a plant) to tidy it or prevent seeding. —*intr.* To remove the dead flowers from a plant. —**dead·head·ing** *n.*

dead heart *n. Australian.* The arid interior of Australia.

dead heat *n.* A race in which two or more contestants finish at the same time; a tie.

dead letter *n.* **1.** An unclaimed or undelivered letter that after a period of time is destroyed or returned to the sender by the post office. **2.** A law or directive still formally in effect but no longer valid or enforced.

dead·light (dĕd'līt') *n.* **1.** *Nautical.* **a.** A strong shutter or plate fastened over a ship's porthole or cabin window in stormy weather. **b.** A thick window set in a ship's side or deck. **2.** A skylight made so that it cannot be opened.

dead·line (dĕd'līn') *n.* **1.** A time limit, as for payment of a debt or completion of an assignment. **2.** The time after which copy for a newspaper, periodical, or the like will not be accepted. **3.** A boundary line in a prison that prisoners can cross only at the risk of being shot.

dead load *n.* *Engineering.* The fixed weight of a structure or piece of equipment, such as a bridge on its supports. Also called "dead weight." Compare **live load.**

dead·lock (dĕd'lŏk') *n.* **1.** A stoppage or standstill resulting from the opposition of two unrelenting forces. **2.** A door lock that combines the features of a **Yale lock** and a **mortise lock** (*both of which see*).

~*v.* **deadlocked, -locking, -locks.** —*tr.* To bring to a deadlock. —*intr.* To come to a deadlock.

dead·ly (dĕd'lē) *adj.* **-lier, -liest. 1.** Causing or tending to cause death; lethal. **2.** Suggestive of death; deathly: *deadly white.* **3.** Implacable; mortal: *deadly enemies.* **4.** Destructive in effect. **5.** Absolute; unqualified: *deadly accuracy.* **5.** *Informal.* Extremely dull and boring: *How deadly!* —See Synonyms at **fatal.**

~*adv.* **1.** So as to suggest death. **2.** To an extreme: *deadly earnest.* —**dead·li·ness** *n.*

Usage: *Deadly* (adjective) and *deathly* (adjective) overlap in meaning. But in modern usage *deadly* is largely confined to what causes death or extreme distress (such as disease or boredom) and *deathly* to what resembles or suggests death (such as silence or pallor).

deadly nightshade *n.* **1.** A poisonous plant, *Solanum nigrum,* having small white flowers and black fruit. Also called "black nightshade." **2.** A Eurasian plant, the **belladonna** (*see*).

deadly sins *pl.n.* See **seven deadly sins.**

dead-man's fingers (dĕd'mənz) *n. Used with a singular verb.* **1.** A soft coral, *Alcyonium digitatum,* consisting of a colony of flesh-pink, fingerlike polyps. **2.** A fungus, **devil's fingers** (*see*).

dead-man's handle *n.* A safety feature fitted to a train or other vehicle. It is kept depressed to control speed and, when not depressed and contact is broken, it will bring the vehicle to a stop.

dead march *n.* A slow, solemn march played for a funeral.

dead nettle *n.* Any of several weedy plants of the genus *Lamium,* native to the Old World, having nettlelike leaves and clusters of small purplish, white, or yellow flowers. [Because it does not sting.]

dead·pan (dĕd'păn') *adj.* Characterized by a blank or expressionless face or manner. —**dead·pan** *adv.*

dead point *n.* *Machinery.* **Dead center** (*see*).

dead reckoning *n.* **1.** *Navigation.* A method of determining the position of an aircraft or ship without external aids, such as astronomical observations or radio, by calculating from the direction and speed of travel from a known point. **2.** Calculation based on inference or guesswork. [From DEAD (probably "complete," "exact," because it is the closest estimate possible).]

Dead Sea (dĕd). *Arabic* **Bah·ret Lut** (bäh'rĕt loŏt'). Lake at the outlet of the Jordan River, partitioned between Israel and Jordan to the east. It is the lowest point on the earth's surface, being 396 meters (1,299 feet) below sea level. The surface waters have a salt content nearly nine times the average salinity of the ocean, allowing humans to float like corks. The sea contains no living things and has no outflow, its inflow being lost through evaporation.

Dead Sea Scrolls *pl.n.* A number of parchment scrolls, dated from about 250 B.C. to about A.D. 70, containing Hebrew and Aramaic Scriptural texts and the liturgical writings of an ascetic community. The first scrolls were found in 1947 in caves near the Dead Sea.

dead-set (dĕd'sĕt') *adj.* Determined; resolved: *dead-set on winning.*

dead weight *n.* **1.** The unrelieved weight of a heavy, motionless mass. **2.** An oppressive burden or difficulty affording no advantage whatever. **3.** *Engineering.* A dead load (*see*).

dead·wood (dĕd'woŏd') *n.* **1.** Dead branches or wood on a tree or shrub. **2.** Anything burdensome or superfluous, as useless phrases in writing or unnecessary personnel. **3.** *Nautical.* The vertical planking between the keel of a vessel and the sternpost, serving merely as a reinforcement.

deaf (dĕf) *adj.* **deafer, deafest. 1.** Partially or completely incapable of hearing. **2.** Unwilling or refusing to listen; heedless. [Middle English *de(a)f,* Old English *dēaf,* from Germanic.] —**deaf·ly** *adv.* —**deaf·ness** *n.*

deaf-aid (dĕf'ăd') *n. British.* A **hearing aid** (*see*).

deaf·en (dĕf'ən) *tr.v.* **-ened, -ening, -ens. 1.** To make deaf, especially momentarily by a loud noise. **2.** To make soundproof.

deaf·en·ing (dĕf'ən-ĭng) *adj.* Stunning to the ears; resoundingly loud. —**deaf·en·ing·ly** *adv.*

deaf-mute (dĕf'myoŏt') *n.* Also **deaf mute.** A person who can neither speak nor hear.

~*adj.* (dĕf-myoŏt'). Unable to speak or hear.

deal¹ (dēl) *v.* **dealt** (dĕlt), **dealing, deals.** —*tr.* **1.** To give to someone as a share; apportion. **2.** To distribute or pass out among several people. **3.** To administer; deliver (a blow, for example). **4.** *Card Games.* **a.** To distribute (playing cards) among players. **b.** To give (a specific card) to a player while so distributing. —*intr.* **1.** To be occupied or concerned; treat. Used with *in* or *with: a book dealing with the Middle Ages.* **2.** To behave in a specified way toward another or others; have transactions. Used with *with: deal honestly with competitors.* **3.** To take action. Used with *with: The committee will deal with this complaint.* **4.** To do business; trade: *dealing in diamonds.* **5.** *Card Games.* To distribute playing cards. —See Usage note at **distribute.**

~*n.* **1.** The act or a round of apportioning or distributing. **2.** *Card Games.* **a.** The distribution of the playing cards. **b.** The cards so distributed; a hand. **c.** The right or turn of a player to distribute the cards. **d.** The playing of one hand. **3.** An indefinite quantity, extent, or degree: *a great deal of experience.* **4.** An agreement arranged secretly, as in business or politics. **5.** *Informal.* Any agreement or business transaction. **6.** *Informal.* An exchange or bargain. **7.** *Informal.* Treatment received, especially as the result of an agreement: *a raw deal.* **8.** *Slang.* An important issue: *make a big deal out of nothing.* **9.** A program, such as a political platform, that offers

---

Dead Sea Scrolls

THE LIBRARY OF A JEWISH COMMUNITY
Religious texts that survived the ravages of 2,000 years

Early in 1947, a young Bedouin herdsman, searching for a stray lamb on the parched slopes west of the Dead Sea near Qumran, stumbled on some old clay jars in a cave. To his disappointment, they held only ancient scrolls.

However, as scholars deciphered the writings on the scrolls and on thousands of other parchment, papyrus, and copper fragments found in caves nearby, a fascinating story emerged—the story of a Jewish religious community with beliefs similar to those of the early Christians.

The scrolls were the sacred texts of an ancient Jewish sect—probably the Essenes—who were based at Qumran from the 2nd century B.C. to the 1st century A.D. They are thought to have been kept hidden in the caves after about A.D. 68 when the Romans threatened the community during a Jewish revolt.

From the scrolls, scholars have reconstructed the history of Palestine from the 4th century B.C. to A.D. 135 and dated the standardized Old Testament to about A.D. 70.

SACRED SCROLL *The discovery of these fragments from the Book of Exodus helped to confirm the authenticity of the Old Testament tradition. The scrolls are also valuable examples of contemporary Aramaic and Hebrew scripts.*

some specified treatment for those participating; especially, President Franklin Roosevelt's **New Deal** *(see).* [Middle English *delen,* Old English *dǣlan,* to divide, distribute, from Germanic.]

deal[2] *n.* **1.** A board of fir, pine, or similar wood cut to standard dimensions. **2.** Such boards or planks collectively. **3.** Fir, pine, or similar wood. [Middle English *dele,* from Middle Low German or Middle Dutch *dele.*]

Deal (dēl). Channel port in Kent, southeast England. In the 11th century it became one of the Cinque Ports, and its castle was built by Henry VIII (1539).

deal·er (dē′lər) *n.* **1.** A person or group engaged in buying and selling: *a used-car dealer.* **2.** *Card Games.* The person who distributes the cards. **3.** *Informal.* One who deals in illegal drugs.

deal·fish (dēl′fĭsh′) *n., pl.* **-fishes** or collectively **dealfish.** A marine fish, *Trachipterus arcticus,* of Atlantic waters, resembling the ribbonfishes. [DEAL (plank), from its long, thin body + FISH.]

deal·ing (dē′lĭng) *n.* **1.** *Usually* **dealings.** Transactions or relations with others, usually in business. **2.** Method or manner of conduct in relation to others; treatment: *honest dealing.*

de·am·i·nate (dē-ăm′ə-nāt′) *tr.v.* **-nated, -nating, -nates.** Also **de·am·i·nize** (-nīz′), **-nized, -nizing, -nizes.** To remove an amino group from (an organic compound, especially an amino acid). **—de·am·i·na·tion, de·am·i·ni·za·tion** *n.*

dean[1] (dēn) *n.* **1. a.** An administrative officer in charge of a college, faculty, or division in a university. **b.** In some universities and colleges, a member of the staff who counsels students and supervises the enforcement of rules. **2.** *Ecclesiastical.* The head of the chapter of canons governing a cathedral or collegiate church. **3.** *Chiefly British.* A priest appointed to oversee a group of parishes within a diocese. Also called "rural dean." **4.** *Roman Catholic Church.* **a.** A high-ranking official, usually a cardinal, who runs a department in the Vatican. **b.** The head of the College of Cardinals. **5.** The senior member of any body. [Middle English *deen, den,* from Norman French, from Late Latin *decānus,* "(one) set over ten," from Greek *dekanos,* from *deka,* ten.] **—dean·ship** *n.*

dean[2], dene. *British.* A valley.

Dean, Forest of (dēn). Woodland region of Gloucestershire in the west of England. Formerly an ancient royal hunting preserve, it became the first of Britain's National Forest Parks (1938).

Dean, James (1931–55). U.S. film actor. He was a youth hero of the rock 'n' roll era, whose screen image was one of moody rebellion. His films include *East of Eden* (1954) and *Rebel Without a Cause* (1955). He was killed in a car crash.

Dean, Jerome Herman, born Jay Hanna Dean, known as "Dizzy" (1911–74). U.S. baseball player. A right-handed pitcher, he played for the St. Louis Cardinals from 1930 to 1937. After his retirement in 1941, Dean became a sportscaster and was noted for his picturesque descriptions of baseball games.

dean·er·y (dē′nə-rē) *n., pl.* **-ies. 1.** The office, jurisdiction, or authority of a dean. **2.** A dean's official residence.

dear[1] (dîr) *adj.* **dearer, dearest. 1.** Beloved; loved; precious. **2.** Highly esteemed or regarded. Used as a conventional form of address at the beginning of a letter: *Dear Sir.* **3. a.** Expensive; costly. **b.** Charging high prices. **4.** Earnest; ardent: *fulfilled his dearest wishes.* **5.** Sweet; lovely: *a dear little kitten.* **6.** *Obsolete.* Noble; worthy. —See Synonyms at **costly.**
∼*n.* A greatly loved person; darling. Often used as a term of affectionate address: *my dear.*
∼*adv.* **1.** Fondly or affectionately. **2.** At a high cost: *Her mistake will cost her dear.*
∼*interj.* Used as a polite exclamation, as of dismay: *Oh dear. Dear me.* [Middle English *dere,* Old English *dēore,* from Germanic *deurjaz* (unattested), worthy, costly, dear.] **—dear·ness** *n.*

dear[2], dere *adj. Obsolete.* Severe; grievous; dire. [Middle English, *dere,* Old English *dēor*†.]

Dear·born (dîr′bôrn′, -bərn). A city of southeastern Michigan, on the Rouge River adjoining Detroit. It is a manufacturing, warehousing, and distribution center. Greenfield Village, Henry Ford's birthplace, is here.

Dear John letter *n. Informal.* A letter from a woman to her fiancé or lover informing him that their relationship is ended.

dear·ly (dîr′lē) *adv.* **1.** With deep affection; fondly. **2.** At great cost or price. **3.** Earnestly; ardently.

dearth (dûrth) *n.* **1.** Scarcity; lack; paucity. **2.** Shortage of food; famine. [Middle English *dearth(e),* costliness, scarcity, from *dere,* DEAR (expensive).]

dear·y, dear·ie (dîr′ē) *n., pl.* **-ies.** *Informal.* Darling; dear. Used as a term of address.

death (dĕth) *n.* **1. a.** The act of dying; termination of life. Compare **brain death. b.** An instance of dying or killing: *a number of deaths on the road.* **2.** The state of being dead. **3.** *Often* **Death.** A personification of the destroyer of life, usually represented as a skeleton holding a scythe. **4.** Termination; extinction: *the death of imperialism.* **5.** The cause of dying. **6.** A manner of dying: *a hero's death.* **7.** Loss or absence of spiritual life. **8.** *Law.* **Civil death** *(see).* **9.** *Christian Science.* The product of human belief of life in matter. **—be the death of someone.** To irritate or distress someone to an intolerable degree. **—catch one's death (of cold).** *Informal.* To catch a bad cold. **—do (or put) to death.** To kill or execute. **—like death warmed over.** Very ill or looking very ill. **—to death.** To an intolerable degree: *worried to death.* [Middle English *de(e)th,* Old English *dēath,* from Germanic.]

death adder *n.* A venomous Australian snake, *Acanthophis antarcticus,* resembling an adder.

death·bed (dĕth′bĕd′) *n.* **1.** The bed on which a person dies. **2.** The last hours before death. Also used adjectivally: *a deathbed plea.*

death bell *n.* A bell tolled to announce a death. Also called "passing bell."

death·blow (dĕth′blō′) *n.* **1.** A blow or stroke that causes death. **2.** Any fatal event or occurrence.

death camas. Also **death camass.** Any of several plants of the genus *Zygadenus,* of western North America, having grasslike leaves and clusters of greenish-white flowers. [So called because they are poisonous to livestock.]

death camp *n.* An **extermination camp** *(see).*

death cell *n.* A prison cell in which one who is condemned to death awaits execution.

death certificate *n.* An official document, signed by a doctor, giving details of the date, place, and cause of a person's death.

death cup *n.* A deadly poisonous, usually white mushroom, *Amanita phalloides,* having white gills and a prominent bulbous base. Also called "death angel."

death duty *n. British.* A tax on inherited property.

death·ful (dĕth′fəl) *adj.* **1.** Fatal; deadly. **2.** Deathly.

death house *n.* A cell block or other part of a prison in which prisoners condemned to death await execution.

death knell *n.* **1.** A bell tolled to announce a death. **2.** Anything that signals imminent death, as of a person or of hopes or plans.

death·less (dĕth′lĭs) *adj.* Not subject to death; immortal. **—death·less·ly** *adv.* **—death·less·ness** *n.*

death·ly (dĕth′lē) *adj.* **1.** Resembling or characteristic of death. **2.** Causing death; fatal; deadly. **3.** *Poetic.* Of death. —See Usage note at **deadly.**
∼*adv.* **1.** In the manner of death. **2.** Extremely; very: *deathly quiet.* **—death·li·ness** *n.*

death mask *n.* A cast of a person's face taken after death.

death penalty *n.* **1.** A sentence of death. **2.** Capital punishment.

death point *n.* An environmental limit, as of temperature, moisture, or radiation, beyond which a specified life form cannot survive.

death rate *n.* **1.** The ratio of total deaths to total population, usually expressed as deaths per 1,000, 10,000, or 100,000 population, in a specified community. Also called "mortality rate." **2.** The number of deaths per 100 persons having the same disease. In this sense, also called "fatality rate."

death rattle *n.* A rare respiratory gurgling or rattling in the throat of a dying person, caused by loss of the cough reflex and by the passage of breath through accumulating mucus in the throat.

death row *n.* A cell block or other part of a prison containing death cells. Also called "death house." **—on death row.** Under sentence of death.

death's-head (dĕths′hĕd′) *n.* The human skull or a representation of it, symbolizing mortality or death.

death's-head moth *n.* A large Eurasian hawk moth, *Acherontia atropos,* having a skull-like marking on the upper part of the thorax.

death squad *n.* Any of several unofficial groups of vigilantes, especially in Latin America, whose members kill criminals, political agitators, or others considered hostile to society.

death tax *n.* An **inheritance tax** *(see).*

death·trap (dĕth′trăp′) *n.* **1. a.** An unsafe building or structure, especially one susceptible to fire. **b.** An unsafe train, motor vehicle, or the like. **2.** Any perilous circumstance or situation.

Death Valley. An arid desert basin in eastern California. It acquired its name after a party crossing the valley in the 1849 gold rush died there. The valley is *c.* 225 kilometers (140 miles) long and is the hottest and deepest spot on the North American continent, 85 meters (282 feet) below sea level. The valley was made a national monument in 1933.

death warrant *n.* **1.** *Law.* An official order authorizing a person's execution. **2.** Anything that destroys hope, joy, or expectation.

death·watch (dĕth′wŏch′) *n.* **1.** A vigil kept beside a dying or dead person. **2. a.** Any of several beetles of the family Anobiidae, especially *Xestobium rufovillosum,* that strike their heads with a hollow, clicking sound against the wood into which they burrow. Also called "deathwatch beetle." **b.** A booklouse that makes a similar sound.

death wish *n. Psychology.* A conscious or unconscious wish for one's own or someone else's death.

Deau·ville (dō′vĭl, dō-vēl′). Coastal resort in the Calvados department of Normandy, northwest France. It has a casino, yachting harbor, and racecourse.

deave (dēv) *tr.v.* **deaved, deaving, deaves.** *British Regional.* To deafen or confuse with noise. [Middle English *deven,* Old English *ādēafian,* from *dēaf,* DEAF.]

deb (dĕb) *n. Informal.* A debutante.

deb. debenture.

de·ba·cle (dĭ-bä′kəl, -băk′əl) *n.* **1.** A sudden, disastrous overthrow or collapse; rout. **2.** The breaking up of ice in a river. **3.** A violent flood. —See Synonyms at **disaster.** [French *débâcle,* from *débâcler,* to unbar, from Old French *desbacler* : *des-,* from Latin *dē-* (removal) + *bacler,* to bar, from Old Provençal *baclar,* from Vulgar Latin *bacclāre* (unattested), from Latin *baculum,* rod, stick.]

de·bag (dē-băg′) *tr.v.* **-bagged, -bagging, -bags.** *British Slang.* To remove the trousers of (someone) as a joke or humiliation.

de·bar (dē-bär′) *tr.v.* **-barred, -barring, -bars. 1.** To exclude or bar; shut out. **2.** To forbid, hinder, or prevent. [Middle English *debar-*

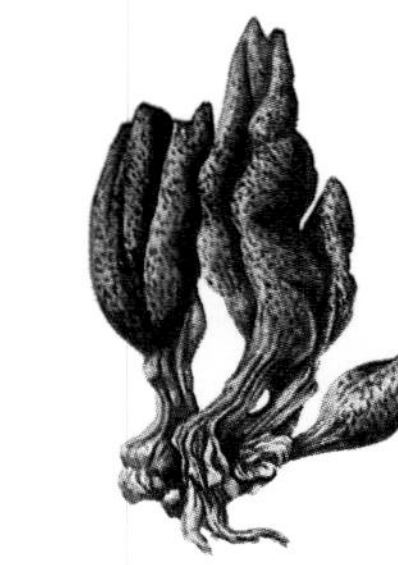

dead-man's fingers *An inedible hard-skinned, black fungus that grows on old tree stumps at all times of the year, sprouting in clusters up to 5 centimeters (2 inches) high.*

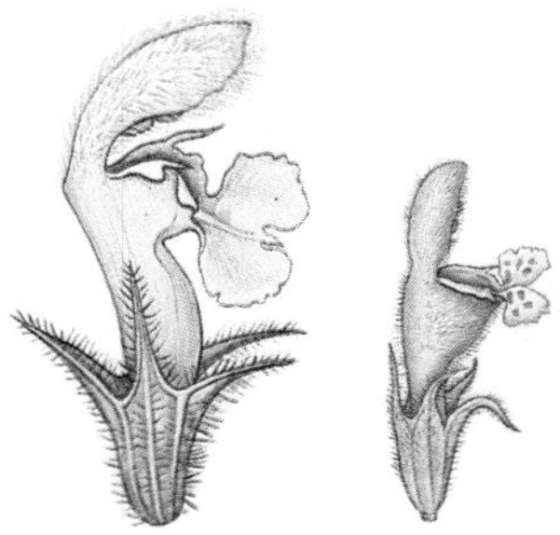

dead nettle *The flower heads of the white dead nettle,* Lamium album *(left), and the red dead nettle,* Lamium purpureum *(right). Both species are common wildflowers in the temperate zones of Europe and Asia. The plants are called "dead nettles" because, though they resemble nettles, they do not sting.*

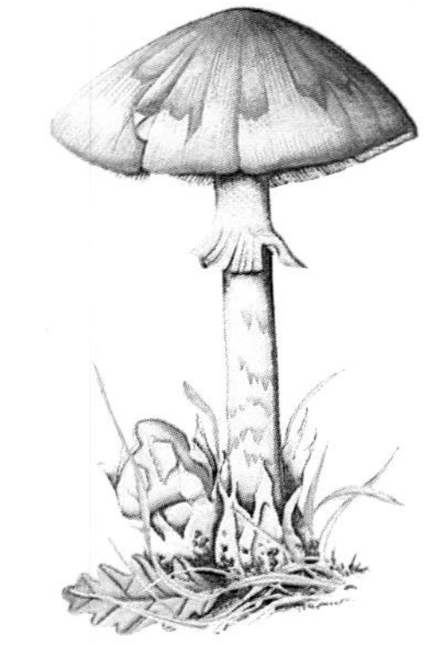

death cup *An aptly named fungus—it is deadly poisonous and there is no known antidote. It is particularly dangerous because it closely resembles the common field mushroom, which is edible; but, when old, the death cup can be recognized by its sickly smell.*

ren, from Old French *desbarrer,* to unbar : *des-,* from Latin *dē-* (removal) + *barrer,* to BAR.] **—de·bar·ment** *n.*

de·bark (dĭ-bärk′) *v.* **-barked, -barking, -barks.** *—tr.* To unload, as from a ship. *—intr.* To disembark. [French *débarquer,* from Old French *debarquer : de-,* from Latin *dē-* (removal) + *barque,* ship, BARK.] **—de·bar·ka·tion** *n.*

de·base (dĭ-bās′) *tr.v.* **-based, -basing, -bases. 1.** To reduce the value of (a coin) by adulterating with base metal. **2.** To lower in character, quality, or value; degrade; adulterate. [DE- (down) + BASE (low).] **—de·base·ment** *n.* **—de·bas·er** *n.*

de·bat·a·ble (dĭ-bā′tə-bəl) *adj.* **1.** Capable of being argued or discussed. **2.** In dispute; questionable. *—See Synonyms at* **doubtful. —de·bat·a·bly** *adv.*

de·bate (dĭ-bāt′) *v.* **-bated, -bating, -bates.** *—intr.* **1.** To deliberate; consider. **2.** To engage in argument; discuss opposing points. **3.** To engage in a formal discussion or argument. **4.** *Obsolete.* To fight; quarrel. *—tr.* **1.** To dispute or argue about. **2.** To discuss or argue (a question, for example) formally, as in a legislative assembly. **3.** To deliberate upon; consider. **4.** *Obsolete.* To fight or argue for or over. *—See Synonyms at* **discuss.**
~n. **1. a.** A discussion involving opposing points as in a legislative assembly. **b.** An argument; dispute. **2.** Deliberation; consideration. **3.** A formal argument in which two opposing teams defend and attack a given proposition. **4.** *Obsolete.* Conflict; strife; contention. [Middle English *debaten,* from Old French *debattre : de-, des-,* from Latin *dis-,* apart, against each other + *battre,* to fight, beat, from Latin *battere, battuere.*] **—de·bat·er** *n.*

de·bauch (dĭ-bôch′) *v.* **-bauched, -bauching, -bauches.** *—tr.* **1.** To corrupt morally; seduce; pervert: *"riches debauched one class with idleness of mind and body"* (Edward Bellamy). **2.** *Obsolete.* To cause to forsake allegiance. *—intr.* To indulge in dissipation.
~n. An act or period of dissipation. [French *débaucher,* Old French *desbaucher*†.] **—de·bauch·ed·ly** *adv.* **—de·bauch·er** *n.*

deb·au·chee (dĕb′ô-chē′, -shē′, dĭ-bô′chē) *n.* A person who habitually indulges in debauchery; libertine.

de·bauch·er·y (dĭ-bô′chə-rē) *n., pl.* **-ies. 1.** Extreme indulgence in sensual pleasures; intemperance; dissipation. **2.** *Archaic.* Seduction from morality, allegiance, or duty.

de·ben·ture (dĭ-bĕn′chər) *n. Abbr.* **deb., deben. 1.** A certificate or voucher acknowledging a debt. **2.** An unsecured bond, issued by a civil or governmental corporation or agency and backed only by the credit standing of the issuer. Also called "debenture bond." **3.** A customs certificate providing for the payment of a drawback. [Middle English *debentur,* from Latin *dēbentur,* "they are due," from *dēbēre,* to owe.]

de·bil·i·tate (dĭ-bĭl′ə-tāt′) *tr.v.* **-tated, -tating, -tates.** To make feeble; enervate. [Latin *dēbilitāre,* from *dēbilis,* weak.] **—de·bil·i·ta·tion** *n.* **—de·bil·i·ta·tive** *adj.*

de·bil·i·tat·ed (dĭ-bĭl′ə-tā′tĭd) *adj.* Tired; worn-out. *—See Synonyms at* **weak.**

de·bil·i·ty (dĭ-bĭl′ə-tē) *n.* A state of abnormal bodily weakness; feebleness. [Middle English *debilite,* from Old French, from Latin *dēbilitās,* from *dēbilis,* weak.]

deb·it (dĕb′ĭt) *n. Abbr.* **dr.** *Accounting.* **1.** An item of debt as recorded in an account. **2. a.** An entry of a sum in the left-hand side of an account, recording money paid out or goods supplied. **b.** The sum of such entries. Compare **credit. 3.** The left-hand side of an account or ledger where bookkeeping entries are made.
~tr.v. **debited, -iting, -its. 1.** To enter (a sum) on the left-hand side of an account or ledger. **2.** To charge with a debt. Compare **credit.** [Middle English *debite,* from Old French, from Latin *dēbitum,* DEBT.]

deb·o·nair, deb·o·naire, deb·on·naire (dĕb′ə-nâr′) *adj.* **1.** Suave; nonchalant; urbane. **2.** Affable; genial. **3.** Carefree; jaunty. [Middle English *debonaire,* from Old French, from *de bon aire,* "of good disposition."] **—deb·o·nair·ly** *adv.* **—deb·o·nair·ness** *n.*

Deb·o·rah (dĕb′ər-ə, dĕb′rə). A prophetess and judge of Israel who helped the Israelites free themselves from the Canaanites. Judges 4:4.

de·bouch (dĭ-bōōsh′) *v.* **-bouched, -bouching, -bouches.** *—intr.* **1.** *Military.* To march from a narrow or confined area into the open. **2.** To emerge or issue, especially into a less restricted space, as a river might. *—tr.* To cause to emerge or issue.
~n. A débouché. [French *déboucher : dé-,* out of + *bouche,* mouth, opening, from Old French, from Latin *bucca,* puffed-out cheek, mouth.]

dé·bou·ché (dā′bōō-shā′) *n.* **1.** An opening in military works for the passage of troops. **2.** An outlet, as for goods. [French, from *déboucher,* DEBOUCH.]

de·bouch·ment (dĭ-bōōsh′mənt) *n.* **1.** The act or an instance of emerging or debouching. **2.** A debouchure.

de·bou·chure (dā′bōō-shōōr′) *n.* A mouth or opening, especially of a river or channel.

De·brett (də-brĕt′), **John** (1752-1822). British publisher and founder of *Debrett's Peerage and Baronetage.* He took over a directory of the nobility in 1802 and made it into an authoritative guide to the British nobility and royalty.

dé·bride·ment (dā-brēd-män′, dĭ-brēd′mənt) *n.* The surgical excision of dead and devitalized tissue and the removal of all foreign matter from a wound. [French, from *débrider,* "to unbridle," from Old French *desbrider : des-,* from Latin *dē-* (removal) + *bride,* bridle, from Middle High German *brīdel.*]

de·brief (dē′brēf′) *v.* **-briefed, -briefing, -briefs.** *—tr.* **1.** To question

or interrogate (a diplomat, spy, or astronaut, for example) to obtain knowledge or intelligence gathered on a mission. **2.** To instruct (a government agent or similar employee) not to reveal secret information after his employment has ceased. *—intr.* To answer questions and provide information after returning from a mission.

de·brief·ing (dē-brē′fĭng) *n.* **1.** The act or process of being debriefed. **2.** The information conveyed during this procedure.

de·bris (də-brē′, dā′brē) *n.* Also **dé·bris** (dā′brē). **1.** The scattered remains of something broken or destroyed; ruins; fragments. **2.** *Geology.* An accumulation of loose material produced by disintegration of rocks. It includes rock fragments, sands, and clays. [French *débris,* from Old French *de(s)brisier,* to break to pieces : *des-,* from Latin *dē-* (intensive) + *brisier,* to break, from (unattested) Vulgar Latin *brīsāre.*]

de Bro·glie (də brō′glē), **Louis Victor, Prince** (1892–1987). French physicist. In 1923 he put forward the hypothesis of wave-particle duality. He was awarded the Nobel Prize (1929).

de Broglie wave *n. Physics.* A wave associated with a particle that represents its wavelike behavior under certain conditions, such as electron diffraction by crystals. The wavelength is given by $h/mv,$ where h is the Planck constant, m is the particle's mass, and v its velocity, interpreted in quantum mechanics as a wave of probability, in which the probability of finding the particle at a given point depends on the square of the wave function. [After Louis Victor DE BROGLIE.]

Debs (dĕbz), **Eugene Victor** (1855-1926). U.S. labor organizer and socialist leader. As president of the American Railway Union (1893) he was instrumental in strikes against the Northern Railroad and the Pullman Company (1894). He was nominated for president by the Socialist Party and ran unsuccessfully for that office five times.

debt (dĕt) *n.* **1.** Something owed, such as money, goods, or services. **2.** An obligation or liability to pay or render something to someone else. **3.** The condition of having such an obligation in debt. **4.** *Archaic.* An offense requiring forgiveness or reparation; sin; trespass. [Middle English *det(te),* from Old French *dette,* from Vulgar Latin *dēbita* (unattested), feminine of Latin *dēbitum,* debt, from *dēbitus,* past participle of *dēbēre,* to owe.]

debt of honor *n.* A debt that is morally binding but not legally recoverable, such as a gambling debt.

debt·or (dĕt′ər) *n. Abbr.* **dr.** A person who owes something to another. Compare **creditor.** [Middle English *det(t)our,* from Old French *det(t)or,* from Latin *dēbitor,* from *dēbēre,* to owe.]

de·bug (dē′bŭg′) *tr.v.* **-bugged, -bugging, -bugs. 1.** To remove insects from. **2.** To search for and eliminate malfunctioning elements in. **3.** To search for and eliminate sources of error in (a computer program, for example). **4.** To search for and remove concealed microphones from (a room, for example).

de·bunk (dĭ-bŭngk′) *tr.v.* **-bunked, -bunking, -bunks.** *Informal.* To expose or ridicule the falseness, sham, or exaggerated claims of. [DE- + BUNK (nonsense).] **—de·bunk·er** *n.*

De·bus·sy (də-byōō′sē), **Claude Achille** (1862–1918). French composer. He was the first exponent of musical impressionism, using unusual tone patterns to communicate mood and emotion. His works include *L'Après-midi d'un Faune* (1894) and the opera *Pelléas et Mélisande* (1892-1902).

de·but, dé·but (dĭ-byōō′, dā-, dā′byōō′) *n.* **1.** A first public appearance, as of an actor on the stage. **2.** The formal presentation of a girl to society. **3.** The beginning of a career or course of action. [French *début,* from *débuter,* to make one's debut, "give the first stroke in a game" : *dé-,* from Latin *dē-,* away + *but,* BUTT (target).]

deb·u·tant (dĕb′yōō-tänt′, dĕb′yōō-tänt′, dā′byōō-). A man making a debut, such as a sportsman playing on a team for the first time.

deb·u·tante, dé·bu·tante (dĕb′yōō-tänt′, dĕb′yōō-tänt′, dā′byōō-tänt′). A young lady making a debut into society. Also informally called "deb." [French *débutante,* from *débuter,* to make one's DEBUT.]

dec. 1. deceased. **2.** declaration. **3.** declension. **4.** declination. **5.** decrease.

Dec. December.

deca-, dec–, deka-, dek- *prefix. Abbr.* **da** Indicates ten; for example, **decahedron, decane.** [Greek *deka-,* from *deka,* ten.]

dec·ade (dĕk′ād′, dē-kād′) *n.* **1.** A period of ten years. **2.** A group or series of ten. [Middle English, from Old French, from Late Latin *decas* (stem *decad-*), from Greek *dekas,* ten.]

de·ca·dence (dĭ-kā′dəns, dĕk′ə-dəns) *n.* Also **de·ca·den·cy** (-dən-sē) *pl.* **-cies. 1.** A process, condition, or period of deterioration or decline, as in morals or art; decay. **2.** *Usually* **Decadence.** The period during which the Decadents flourished. [Old French, from Medieval Latin *dēcadentia,* from Vulgar Latin *dēcadere* (unattested), to DECAY.]

de·ca·dent (dĭ-kā′dənt, dĕk′ə-dənt) *adj.* **1.** In a state or condition of decline or decay. **2.** Of or pertaining to the Decadents.
~n. **1.** A person in a condition or process of mental or moral decay. **2.** *Usually* **Decadent.** A member of a group of French and English writers of the 19th century who often sought inspiration in the morbid, neurotic, or macabre and tended toward overrefinement of style. [From DECADENCE.] **—de·ca·dent·ly** *adv.*

de·caf·fein·ate (dē-kăf′ə-nāt) *tr.v.* **-ated, -ating, ates.** To remove most of the caffeine from (coffee).

dec·a·gon (dĕk′ə-gŏn′) *n.* A polygon with ten angles and ten sides. [New Latin *decagonum,* from Greek *dekagōnon,* "(one) having ten angles" : DECA- + -GON.] **—de·cag·o·nal** (dĭ-kăg′ə-nəl) *adj.* **—de·cag·o·nal·ly** *adv.*

dec·a·gram, dek·a·gram (děk'ə-grăm') n. Abbr. **dag** Ten grams. [French *décagramme* : DECA- + GRAM.]

dec·a·he·dron (děk'ə-hē'drən) n., pl. **-drons** or **-dra** (-drə). A polyhedron with ten faces. [New Latin : DECA- + -HEDRON.] —**dec·a·he·dral** adj.

de·cal (dē'kăl') n. A picture or design transferred by the process of **decalcomania** (see).

de·cal·ci·fy (dē-kăl'sə-fī') tr.v. **-fied, -fying, -fies.** To remove calcium or calcareous matter from (bones or teeth, for example). —**de·cal·ci·fi·ca·tion** n. —**de·cal·ci·fi·er** n.

de·cal·co·ma·ni·a (dē'kăl-kə-mā'nē-ə) n. **1.** The process of transferring pictures or designs printed on specially prepared paper to glass, metal, or other material. **2.** A picture so transferred; a decal. [French *décalcomanie* : *décalquer*, to transfer by tracing : *dé-*, from, from Latin *dē-* + *calquer*, to trace, from Italian *calcare*, to trace, trample, from Latin, to tread, from *calx* (stem *calc-*), heel (see **calk**) + *manie*, madness, from Late Latin *mania*, MANIA (from its mid-19th-century popularity).]

de·ca·les·cence (dē'kə-lĕs'əns) n. In a metal being heated, a sudden slowing in the rate of temperature increase as a result of an endothermic change in crystal structure. [DE- + Latin *calescere*, to become warm, from *calēre*, to be warm.] —**de·ca·les·cent** adj.

dec·a·li·ter, dek·a·li·ter (děk'ə-lē'tər) n. Ten liters.

Dec·a·logue (děk'ə-lôg', -lŏg') n. Also **Dec·a·log, dec·a·logue, dec·a·log.** The **Ten Commandments** (see). [Middle English *decalog*, from Old French *decalogue*, from Late Latin *decalogus*, from Greek *dekalogos* : DECA- + *logos*, speech, word.]

dec·a·me·ter, dek·a·me·ter (děk'ə-mē'tər) n. Abbr. **dam** Ten meters. [DECA- + METER.]

de·camp (dĭ-kămp') intr.v. **-camped, -camping, -camps. 1.** To depart from a camping ground; break camp. **2.** To depart secretly or suddenly; run away. [French *décamper*, from Old French *descamper* : *des-*, from Latin *dē-* (reversal) + *camper*, to camp, from *camp*, CAMP.] —**de·camp·ment** n.

dec·a·nal (děk'ə-nəl, dĭ-kā'nəl) adj. **1.** Of or pertaining to a dean or deanery. **2.** On the south side of a cathedral choir. [Late Latin *decānus*, DEAN.] —**dec·a·nal·ly** adv.

dec·ane (děk'ān') n. **1.** A straight-chain liquid hydrocarbon, $C_{10}H_{22}$, of the alkane series. Also called "normal decane." **2.** Any of various isomeric liquid alkanes with the formula $C_{10}H_{22}$. [DEC(A)- + -ANE.]

dec·ane·di·o·ic acid (děk'ān-dī-ō'ĭk) n. Chemistry. **Sebacic acid** (see). [DECANE + DI- + -OIC.]

dec·a·no·ic acid (děk'ə-nō'ĭk) n. Chemistry. **Capric acid** (see). [DECAN(E) + -OIC.]

de·cant (dĭ-kănt') tr.v. **-canted, -canting, -cants. 1.** To pour off (wine, for example) without disturbing the sediment. **2.** To pour (a liquid) from one container into another. **3.** Informal. To transfer (offices, for example) from one location to another. [Medieval Latin *decanthāre* : Latin *dē-*, from + *canthus*, rim of a vessel, from Latin, rim of a wheel, tire.] —**de·can·ta·tion** n.

de·cant·er (dĭ-kăn'tər) n. **1.** A decorative bottle used for serving wine or other drinks. **2.** A vessel used for decanting.

de·cap·i·tate (dĭ-kăp'ə-tāt') tr.v. **-tated, -tating, -tates.** To cut off the head of; behead. [Late Latin *decapitāre* : Latin *dē-* (removal) + *caput*, head.] —**de·cap·i·ta·tion** n. —**de·cap·i·ta·tor** n.

dec·a·pod (děk'ə-pŏd') n. **1.** Any crustacean of the order Decapoda, such as a crab, lobster, or shrimp, characteristically having five pairs of walking legs, each pair joined to a segment of the thorax. **2.** A cephalopod mollusk, such as a squid or cuttlefish, having ten armlike tentacles.
~adj. Of or pertaining to the Decapoda or a decapod. [New Latin *Decapoda*, "the ten-footed ones" : DECA- + -POD.] —**de·cap·o·dal** (dĭ-kăp'ə-dəl), **de·cap·o·dan, de·cap·o·dous** adj.

De·cap·o·lis (dĭ-kăp'ə-lĭs). A confederacy of 10 originally Greek cities, including Damascus, in the northeastern part of ancient Palestine, established in 63 or 62 B.C. and governed by Rome. [Greek *Dekapolis* : DECA- + *polis*, city.]

de·car·bon·ate (dē-kär'bə-nāt') tr.v. **-ated, -ating, -ates.** To remove carbon dioxide or carbonic acid from —**de·car·bon·a·tion** n.

de·car·bon·ize (dē-kär'bə-nīz') tr.v. **-ized, -izing, -izes.** To remove carbon from. —**de·car·bon·i·za·tion** n. —**de·car·bon·iz·er** n.

de·car·box·y·late (dē-kär-bŏk'sə-lāt') v. **-ated, -ating, -ates.** Chemistry. —tr. To remove a carboxyl group (−COOH) from (a chemical compound), usually with replacement by hydrogen. —intr. To lose a carboxyl group. —**de·car·box·y·la·tion** n.

dec·are, dek·are (děk'âr', -är') n. A metric unit of area equal to 10 ares, or 0.2471 acre. [French *décare* : DECA- + ARE.]

dec·a·stere, dek·a·stere (děk'ə-stîr') n. Ten steres.

dec·a·syl·la·ble (děk'ə-sĭl'ə-bəl) n. A word or line of verse having ten syllables. —**dec·a·syl·lab·ic** (děk'ə-sə-lăb'ĭk) adj.

de·cath·lon (dĭ-kăth'lŏn, -lən) n. An athletic contest in which contestants participate in ten different events. [French *décathlon* : DECA- + Greek *athlon*, contest (see **athlete**).] —**de·cath·lete** n.

De·ca·tur (dĭ-kā'tər), **Stephen** (1779–1820). U.S. naval officer. He led daring naval missions in the Tripolitan War (1801–05), in the War of 1812 (1812–15), and against the Barbary pirates (1815), and is remembered for his toast, " . . . our country, right or wrong" (1816). He was killed in a duel.

de·cay (dĭ-kā') v. **-cayed, -caying, -cays.** —intr. **1.** Biology. To decompose; rot. **2.** Physics. To disintegrate or diminish in magnitude. Used of such effects as radioactivity, phosphorescence, and magnetism. **3.** Aerospace. To decrease in orbit. Used of an artificial satellite. **4.** To become a ruin; fall into ruin. **5.** Pathology. To decline in health or vigor; waste away. **6.** To decline from a state of normality, excellence, or prosperity. —tr. To cause to decay.
~n. **1. a.** The destruction or decomposition of organic matter as a result of bacterial or fungal action; rot. **b.** Decaying matter. **2.** Physics. **a.** A reduction in or falling away of an effect such as radioactivity. **b.** A process in which an atomic nucleus disintegrates or emits a particle or gamma ray and transforms into a different nucleus. **c.** A process in which an elementary particle transforms spontaneously into one or more other particles. Also called "radioactive decay." **3.** The decrease in orbital altitude of an artificial satellite owing to conditions such as atmospheric drag. **4. a.** A gradual deterioration to an inferior state, as of health or mental capability. **b.** The state reached in this process. [Middle English *decayen*, from North French *decair*, from Vulgar Latin *decadere* (unattested), to fall down, decay : Latin *dē-*, down + *cadere*, to fall.]
Synonyms: crumble, decompose, disintegrate, putrefy, rot, spoil.

decay chain n. **Radioactive series** (see).

Dec·can¹ or **Dek·kan** (děk'ən). India south of the Narmada River. Its population is mostly Dravidian.

Deccan², the. The central plateau of southern India, bounded by the Eastern and Western Ghats. It is an ancient rock shield, and its fertile volcanic soils produce cotton and tea.

decd. deceased.

de·cease (dĭ-sēs') intr.v. **-ceased, -ceasing, -ceases.** To die.
~n. Death. [Middle English *decesen*, to die, from *deces*, death, from Old French, from Latin *dēcessus*, departure, death, from the past participle of *dēcēdere*, to depart : *dē-*, away + *cēdere*, to go.]

de·ceased (dĭ-sēst') adj. Abbr. **dec., decd.** No longer living; dead. —See Usage note at **dead**.
~n. A dead person or persons. Preceded by *the*.

de·ce·dent (dĭ-sē'dənt) n. Law. A deceased person. [Latin *dēcēdēns* (stem *dēcēdent-*), present participle of *dēcēdere*, to die, DECEASE.]

de·ceit (dĭ-sēt') n. **1.** An act of deceiving; misrepresentation; deception. **2.** A stratagem; a trick; a wile. **3.** A tendency to deceive or habit of deceiving; falseness; deceitfulness. [Middle English *deceit(e)*, from Old French, from Latin *dēcepta*, feminine of *dēceptus*, past participle of *dēcipere*, DECEIVE.]

de·ceit·ful (dĭ-sēt'fəl) adj. **1.** Given to cheating or deceiving. **2.** Misleading; deceptive. —See Synonyms at **dishonest**. —**de·ceit·ful·ly** adv. —**de·ceit·ful·ness** n.

de·ceive (dĭ-sēv') v. **-ceived, -ceiving, -ceives.** —tr. **1.** To trick into believing something false; delude; mislead. **2.** Archaic. To catch by guile; ensnare. —intr. To practice deceit. [Middle English *deceiven*, from Old French *deceivre, decevoir*, from Latin *dēcipere*, to take in, deceive : *dē-* (pejorative) + *capere*, to take, seize.] —**de·ceiv·a·bil·i·ty** n. —**de·ceiv·a·ble** adj. —**de·ceiv·a·bly** adv. —**de·ceiv·er** n. —**de·ceiv·ing·ly** adv.
Synonyms: bamboozle, beguile, betray, delude, double-cross, dupe, fool, hoodwink, mislead, outwit.

de·cel·er·ate (dē-sĕl'ə-rāt') v. **-ated, -ating, -ates.** —tr. **1.** To decrease the velocity of. **2.** To cause (a process, such as a chemical reaction) to slow down. —intr. **1.** To decrease in velocity. **2.** To be slowed down. [DE- + (AC)CELERATE.] —**de·cel·er·a·tor** n.

de·cel·er·a·tion (dē-sĕl'ə-rā'shən) n. Decrease in velocity.

de·cel·er·om·e·ter (dē-sĕl'ə-rŏm'ə-tər) n. Any instrument used to measure decrease in velocity. [DECELER(ATE) + -METER.]

de·cel·er·on (dē-sĕl'ə-rŏn') n. An aileron speed brake used primarily on jet aircraft. [*deceler*ation + *ailer*on.]

De·cem·ber (dĭ-sĕm'bər) n. Abbr. **Dec., D.** The 12th and last month of the year according to the Gregorian calendar. December has 31 days. See feature at **calendar**. [Middle English *decembre*, from Old French, from Latin *December*, "the tenth month," from *decem*, ten.]

De·cem·brist (dĭ-sĕm'brĭst) n. Any of the conspirators or participants in the attempted overthrow of Czar Nicholas I of Russia in December, 1825.

de·cem·vir (dĭ-sĕm'vər) n., pl. **-virs** or **-viri** (-və-rī'). A member of a body of ten Roman magistrates; especially, a member of either of two such bodies appointed in 451 and 450 B.C. to draw up a code of laws. **2.** A member of any commission or governing body that has ten members. [Middle English, from Latin, singular of *decemvirī*, from *decem virī*, ten men : *decem*, ten + *virī*, plural of *vir*, man.] —**de·cem·vi·ral** adj. —**de·cem·vi·rate** n.

de·cen·a·ry, de·cen·na·ry (dĭ-sĕn'ə-rē) adj. Of or pertaining to a tithing.
~n., pl. **decenaries.** Also **de·cen·na·ry.** A tithing. [Middle English *decennare*, tithing man, from Medieval Latin *decennārius*, from *decenna*, tithing, from Latin *decem*, ten.]

de·cen·cy (dē'sən-sē) n., pl. **-cies. 1.** The state or condition of being decent; propriety. **2.** Conformity to prevailing standards of propriety or modesty. **3. decencies.** The things considered necessary for leading a decent life. **4. decencies.** The proprieties.

de·cen·na·ry¹ (dĭ-sĕn'ə-rē) adj. Pertaining to a ten-year period.
~n., pl. **decennaries.** A decennium; a decade. [Latin *decennis*, of ten years. See **decennium**.]

decennary². Variant of **decenary**.

de·cen·ni·al (dĭ-sĕn'ē-əl) adj. **1.** Pertaining to or lasting for ten years. **2.** Occurring every ten years.
~n. **1.** An anniversary celebrated every ten years. **2.** The celebration of such an anniversary. [Latin *decennium*, DECENNIUM.] —**de·cen·ni·al·ly** adv.

de·cen·ni·um (dĭ-sĕn'ē-əm) n., pl. **-niums** or **-cennia** (-sĕn'ē-ə). A period of ten years; a decade. [Latin, from *decennis*, of ten years : *decem*, ten + *annus*, year.]

de·cent (dē′sənt) *adj.* **1.** Honest and respectable; conforming to recognized standards of morality and propriety. **2.** Proper; fitting. **3.** Free from indelicacy; modest. **4.** Adequate; passable: *a decent salary.* **5.** Kind; obliging; generous. **6.** *Informal.* Properly or modestly dressed. [Latin *decēns* (stem *decent-*), present participle of *decēre,* to be fitting, suit.] **—de·cent·ly** *adv.* **—de·cent·ness** *n.*

de·cen·tral·ize (dē-sĕn′trə-līz′) *v.* **-ized, -izing, -izes.** *—tr.* **1.** To distribute the administrative functions or powers of (a central authority) among regional authorities. **2.** To cause to withdraw from an area of concentration: *decentralize an industry.* *—intr.* To disperse across a greater area or range of authorities. **—de·cen·tral·i·za·tion** *n.*

de·cep·tion (dĭ-sĕp′shən) *n.* **1.** An act of deceiving; the use of deceit. **2.** The fact or state of being deceived. **3.** An act intended to deceive; a trick; a ruse. [Middle English *decepcioun,* from Old French *deception,* from Late Latin *dēceptiō* (stem *dēceptiōn-*), from Latin *dēcipere* (past participle *dēceptus*), DECEIVE.]

de·cep·tive (dĭ-sĕp′tĭv) *adj.* **1.** Intended or tending to deceive. **2.** Likely to confuse; misleading. **—de·cep·tive·ly** *adv.* **—de·cep·tive·ness** *n.*

de·cer·e·brate (dē-sĕr′ə-brāt′) *tr.v.* **-brated, -brating, -brates.** To eliminate the cerebral functions of (an experimental animal) by removing a large part of the brain or cutting across the brain below the cerebrum. [DE- + CEREBR- + -ATE.] **—de·cer·e·bra·tion** *n.*

deci- *prefix. Symbol* **d** Indicates one-tenth; for example, **decimeter.** [French *déci-,* from Latin *decimus,* tenth, from *decem,* ten.]

dec·i·are (dĕs′ē-âr′, -är′) *n.* One-tenth (10^{-1}) of an are.

de·ci·bel (dĕs′ĭ-bəl) *n. Abbr.* **dB, db** A unit used to express relative difference in power, usually between acoustic or electric signals, equal to ten times the common logarithm of the ratio of the two levels. [DECI- + BEL.]

de·cide (dĭ-sīd′) *v.* **-cided, -ciding, -cides.** *—tr.* **1.** To conclude or settle: *He decided which course to follow.* **2.** To influence or determine the conclusion of: *Sheer firepower decided the battle.* **3.** To cause to make a decision: *Your nagging decided me to buy it.* *—intr.* **1.** To pronounce a judgment; announce a verdict. Often used with *for* or *against.* **2.** To make up one's mind. [Middle English *deciden,* from Old French *decider,* from Latin *dēcīdere,* to cut off, determine : *dē-,* off + *cædere,* to cut.] **—de·cid·a·ble** *adj.* **—de·cid·er** *n.*

Synonyms: *conclude, determine, resolve, rule, settle.*

de·cid·ed (dĭ-sī′dĭd) *adj.* **1.** Unquestionable; definite. **2.** Resolute; unhesitating. **—de·cid·ed·ly** *adv.* **—de·cid·ed·ness** *n.*

Usage: *Decided* and *decisive* both have the sense "unquestionable" or "resolute." But *decided* usually means simply "definite," whereas *decisive* emphasizes the notion of decision-making or settling an issue beyond doubt. If one has *a decided advantage,* one is in a very strong position; but if one has a *decisive advantage,* then one is in the strongest possible position and cannot lose.

de·cid·er (dĭ-sī′dər) *n.* In a contest, a round that determines the winner.

de·cid·ing (dĭ-sī′dĭng) *adj.* Settling or able to settle a matter in dispute or doubt; decisive; conclusive: *the deciding vote.*

de·cid·u·a (dĭ-sĭj′o͞o-ə, -sĭd′yo͞o-ə) *n.* A mucous membrane that lines the uterus, modified during pregnancy and cast off during menstruation or at parturition. [New Latin *(membrana) decidua,* "(membrane) that falls off," from Latin *dēcidua,* feminine of *dēciduus,* DECIDUOUS.] **—de·cid·u·al** *adj.*

de·cid·u·ate (dĭ-sĭj′o͞o-ĭt, -sĭd′yo͞o-ĭt) *adj.* **1.** Characterized by or having a decidua. **2.** Characterized by shedding.

de·cid·u·ous (dĭ-sĭj′o͞o-əs, -sĭd′yo͞o-əs) *adj.* **1.** Falling off or shed at a specific season or stage of growth: *deciduous antlers; deciduous leaves.* **2.** Shedding or losing foliage at the end of the growing season: *deciduous trees.* Compare **evergreen. 3.** Not lasting; temporary. [Latin *dēciduus,* from *dēcidere,* to fall off : *dē-,* off + *cadere,* to fall.] **—de·cid·u·ous·ly** *adv.* **—de·cid·u·ous·ness** *n.*

dec·i·gram (dĕs′ĭ-grăm′) *n. Abbr.* **dg** One-tenth (10^{-1}) of a gram.

dec·i·li·ter (dĕs′ə-lē′tər) *n. Abbr.* **dl** One-tenth (10^{-1}) of a liter.

de·cil·lion (dĭ-sĭl′yən) *n.* **1.** The cardinal number represented by 1 followed by 33 zeros, usually written 10^{33}. **2.** *British.* The cardinal number represented by 1 followed by 60 zeros, usually written 10^{60}. [Latin *decem,* ten + (M)ILLION.] **—de·cil·lion** *adj.*

de·cil·lionth (dĭ-sĭl′yənth) *n.* **1.** The ordinal number decillion in a series. **2.** Any of a decillion equal parts. **—de·cil·lionth** *adj. & adv.*

dec·i·mal (dĕs′ə-məl) *n.* **1.** A linear array of integers that represents a fraction, every **decimal place** *(see)* indicating a multiple of a positive or negative power of 10; for example, the decimal .1 = $1/10$, .003 = $3/1000$. Also called "decimal fraction." **2.** Any number written using base 10. In this sense, also called "decimal number."
~*adj.* **1.** Expressed or expressible as a decimal. **2. a.** Based on ten. **b.** Numbered or ordered by tens. **3.** Loosely, not integral; fractional. [Medieval Latin *decimālis,* of tithes, from Latin *decimus,* tenth, from *decem,* ten.] **—dec·i·mal·ly** *adv.*

decimal currency *n.* A system of currency in which the monetary units are divided into or multiplied by further units of 10 or 100.

dec·i·mal·ize (dĕs′ə-mə-līz′) *tr.v.* **-ized, -izing, -izes.** To change to a decimal system. **—dec·i·mal·i·za·tion** *n.*

decimal place *n.* The position of a digit to the right of a decimal point, usually identified by successive ascending ordinal numbers with the digit immediately to the right of the decimal point being first. For example, in the decimal number 1.021, 2 is in the second decimal place.

decimal point *n.* A period, centered dot, or, in some countries, a comma, placed to the left of a decimal fraction. Also called "radix point."

decimal system *n.* **1.** A number system using the base 10. **2.** A measurement system in which all derived units are multiples of ten of basic units. **3.** A classification system using decimals.

dec·i·mate (dĕs′ĭ-māt′) *tr.v.* **-mated, -mating, -mates. 1.** To destroy or kill a large part of. **2. a.** To destroy or kill a tenth of. **b.** Especially in the ancient Roman army, to select by lot and kill one in every ten of, as a punishment for mutiny or cowardice: *decimate a cohort.* [Latin *decimāre,* from *decimus,* tenth, from *decem,* ten.] **—dec·i·ma·tion** *n.* **—dec·i·ma·tor** *n.*

Usage: The earlier meaning of *decimate* is, literally, "to kill one tenth of," but the word is now generally used to mean "to kill many of." This change in usage is still criticized by purists.

dec·i·me·ter (dĕs′ə-mē′tər) *n. Abbr.* **dm** One-tenth (10^{-1}) of a meter. [French *décimètre* : DECI- + METER.]

de·ci·pher (dĭ-sī′fər) *tr.v.* **-phered, -phering, -phers. 1.** To read or interpret (something ambiguous, obscure, or illegible). **2.** To convert from a code or cipher to plain text; decode. [DE- (reversal) + CIPHER (after Old French *deschiffrer*).] **—de·ci·pher·a·ble** *adj.* **—de·ci·pher·er** *n.* **—de·ci·pher·ment** *n.*

de·ci·sion (dĭ-sĭzh′ən) *n.* **1.** The passing of judgment on an issue under consideration. **2.** The act of reaching a conclusion or making up one's mind. **3.** A conclusion or judgment reached or pronounced; a verdict. **4.** Firmness of character or action; determination. **5.** *Boxing.* A victory won on points when no knockout has occurred. [Middle English *decisioun,* from Old French *decision,* from Latin *dēcīsiō* (stem *dēcīsiōn-*), from *dēcīdere,* DECIDE.]

de·ci·sion-mak·er (dĭ-sĭzh′ən-mā′kər) *n.* One who has the responsibility for making decisions; especially, an important administrator in business or government. **—de·ci·sion-mak·ing** *n. & adj.*

de·ci·sive (dĭ-sī′sĭv) *adj.* **1.** Able to settle a matter in dispute or doubt; conclusive. **2.** Characterized by firm decision; resolute; determined. **3.** Beyond doubt; unquestionable. —See Usage note at **decided. —de·ci·sive·ly** *adv.* **—de·ci·sive·ness** *n.*

deck[1] (dĕk) *n. Abbr.* **dk. 1.** *Nautical.* **a.** A platform extending horizontally from one side of a ship to the other. **b.** The space between two such platforms. **2.** Any similar platform or surface, as on a bus. **3.** The roadway on a bridge. **4.** A **tape deck** *(see).* **5.** *Informal.* The floor or ground. **6. a.** A pack of playing cards. **b.** *Computer Science.* A pile of punched computer cards. **7.** A packet of narcotic drugs. **—clear the deck.** To prepare for action. **—hit the deck.** *Slang.* **1.** To fall or drop to the floor or ground. **2.** To get out of bed. **3.** To prepare for action. **—on deck.** *Slang.* **1.** On hand; present. **2.** Waiting to take one's turn.
~*tr.v.* **decked, decking, decks.** To furnish with a deck. [Middle English *dekke,* from Middle Dutch *dec, decke,* roof, covering.]

deck[2] *tr.v.* **decked, decking, decks.** To clothe with finery; decorate; adorn. Often used with *out: decked out for a party.* [Middle Dutch *dekken,* to cover.]

deck chair *n.* A folding chair, usually with arms and a leg rest, found on the decks of passenger ships and now used generally for sitting outdoors.

deck hand *n.* A member of a ship's crew who works on deck.

deck·house (dĕk′hous′) *n.* A superstructure on the upper deck of a ship.

deck·le, deck·el (dĕk′əl) *n.* **1.** A frame used in making paper by hand to form paper pulp into sheets of a desired size. **2.** A deckle edge. **3.** A device for trimming mechanically made paper to the desired width. [German *Deckel,* diminutive of *Decke,* "a cover," from Old High German *decchī,* from *decchen,* to cover.]

deckle edge *n.* **1.** The rough, crimped edge of handmade paper formed in a deckle. Also called "featheredge." **2.** A similar edge produced by a machine. **—deck·le-edged** (dĕk′əl-ĕjd′) *adj.*

deck tennis *n.* A game in which a small ring or quoit is tossed back and forth over a net.

decl. declension.

de·claim (dĭ-klām′) *v.* **-claimed, -claiming, -claims.** *—intr.* **1.** To deliver an elocutionary recitation. **2.** To speak loudly and vehemently; inveigh. Used with *against.* *—tr.* To utter or recite with rhetorical effect. [Middle English *declamen,* from Latin *dēclāmāre* : *dē-* (intensive) + *clāmāre,* to cry out.] **—de·claim·er** *n.*

dec·la·ma·tion (dĕk′lə-mā′shən) *n.* **1.** An elocutionary recitation. **2. a.** Vehement oratory. **b.** A harangue; a tirade. **3. a.** Correct and expressive delivery of words to a musical accompaniment. **b.** The art or action of reading or reciting a literary text with the proper intonation and expression. [Middle English *declamacioun,* from Latin *dēclāmātiō* (stem *dēclāmātiōn-*), from *dēclāmāre,* DECLAIM.]

de·clam·a·to·ry (dĭ-klăm′ə-tôr′ē, -tōr′ē) *adj.* **1.** Having the quality of a declamation; loudly demanding attention. **2.** Pretentiously rhetorical; meaninglessly bombastic. **—de·clam·a·to·ri·ly** *adv.*

de·clar·a·ble (dĭ-klâr′ə-bəl) *adj.* Such as can or should be declared, as for payment of customs duty.

de·clar·ant (dĭ-klâr′ənt) *n.* **1.** *Law.* One making a declaration. **2.** One who has signed a declaration of intention of becoming a U.S. citizen.

dec·la·ra·tion (dĕk′lə-rā′shən) *n. Abbr.* **dec. 1.** An explicit or formal statement or announcement. **2.** Such a statement in written form. **3.** The act or process of declaring. **4.** A statement of taxable goods or of properties subject to duty. Used especially in the phrase *a customs declaration.* **5.** *Law.* **a.** Formerly, a formal statement by a plaintiff specifying the facts and circumstances constituting the cause of action. **b.** An unsworn statement of facts that may be

PRONUNCIATION KEY

ă, pat; ā, pay; âr, care;
ä, father, are; b, bib;
ch, church; d, deed; ĕ, pet;
ē, be; f, fife; g, gag; h, hat;
hw, which; ĭ, pit; ī, pie;
îr, pier; j, judge; k, kick;
l, lid, needle; m, mum;
n, no, sudden; ng, thing;
ŏ, pot; ō, toe; ô, paw, for;
oi, noise; ou, out; o͝o, book;
o͞o, boot; p, pop; r, roar;
s, sauce; sh, ship, dish;
t, tight; th, thin, path;
th, this, bathe; ŭ, cut; ûr, fur;
v, valve; w, with; y, yes;
z, zebra, size; zh, vision;
ə, about, item, edible, gallop, circus, peaceful

IN FOREIGN WORDS:

à, *Fr.* ami; œ, *Fr.* feu, *Ger.* schön; ü, *Fr.* tu, *Ger.* über; KH, *Ger.* ich, *Scot.* loch; N, *Fr.* bon; y′, *Fr.* Compiègne

STRESS MARKS:

Primary stress: ′
in·cite′ (ĭn-sīt′)
Secondary stress: ′
in′sight′ (ĭn′sīt′)

admissible as evidence. **6.** *Card Games.* **a.** A bid, especially the final bid of a hand. **b.** An announcement by a player of points made. **7.** *Cricket.* A decision by the captain of the batting side to end an innings before all the batsmen are out.

Declaration of Independence *n.* **1.** A proclamation by the Second Continental Congress declaring the 13 American colonies politically independent from Great Britain, formally adopted on July 4, 1776. **2.** The document in which this proclamation is recorded.

de·clar·a·tive (dĭ-klâr′ə-tĭv) *adj.* Serving to declare or state. **—de·clar·a·tive·ly** *adv.*

de·clar·a·to·ry (dĭ-klâr′ə-tôr′ē, -tōr′ē) *adj.* **1.** Declarative. **2.** *Law.* Explaining a point of law or setting out the rights of the parties.

de·clare (dĭ-klâr′) *v.* **-clared, -claring, -clares.** *—tr.* **1.** To bring into being by announcing officially or formally; decree: *declare war; declare an amnesty.* **2.** To admit to: *declare an interest.* **3.** To pronounce as being in a specified condition: *I declared him fit and well.* **4.** To state with emphasis or authority; affirm: *declare one's loyalty.* **5.** To reveal or manifest; prove: *His face declares his guilt.* **6.** To make a full statement of (dutiable goods, for example). **7.** To announce (a dividend) as payable. **8.** *Bridge.* To designate (a trump suit or no-trump) with the final bid of a hand. **9.** In various card games: **a.** To reveal (cards). **b.** To announce (points scored by such cards). *—intr.* **1.** To make a declaration. **2.** To proclaim one's choice, opinion, or resolution; act. Used with *for* or *against.* **3.** *Cricket.* To decide to end an innings before all one's batsmen are out. —See Synonyms at **assert.** [Middle English *declaren,* from Old French *declarer,* from Latin *dēclārāre,* to make clear : *dē-* (intensive) + *clārāre,* to make clear, from *clārus,* clear.] **—de·clar·ed·ly** *adv.* **—de·clar·er** *n.*

de·class (dē-klăs′, -kläs′) *tr.v.* **-classed, -classing, -classes.** To lower in class or standing; degrade; debase.

dé·clas·sé (dā-klă-sā′) *adj.* Also **de·classed** (dē-klăst′, -kläst′). Lowered in social standing. [French, from *déclasser,* to lower in class : *dé-,* from Latin *dē-,* down + *classe,* CLASS.]

de·clas·si·fy (dē-klăs′ə-fī′) *tr.v.* **-fied, -fying, -fies.** To remove official security classification from (information, documents, and the like); make (information) no longer secret. **—de·clas·si·fi·a·ble** *adj.* **—de·clas·si·fi·ca·tion** *n.*

de·clen·sion (dĭ-klĕn′shən) *n.* **1.** *Abbr.* **dec., decl.** *Linguistics.* **a.** In certain languages, the inflection of nouns, pronouns, and adjectives in such categories as case, number, and gender. **b.** A class of nouns, pronouns, and adjectives with the same or a similar system of inflections, such as the first declension in Latin. Compare **conjugation.** **2.** A descending slope; a descent. **3.** A decline or decrease; deterioration: *empires in their declension.* **4.** A deviation, as from a standard or practice. [Learned respelling of Middle English *declinson,* from Old French *declinaison,* from Late Latin *dēclīnātiō* (stem *dēclīnātiōn-*), grammatical declension, from Latin, DECLINATION.] **—de·clen·sion·al** *adj.*

dec·li·na·tion (dĕk′lə-nā′shən) *n. Abbr.* **dec** **1.** A sloping or bending downward. **2.** A falling off, especially from prosperity or vigor; a decline. **3.** A deviation, as from a specific direction or standard. **4.** A refusal to accept. **5. Magnetic declination** *(see).* **6.** *Astronomy. Symbol* δ The angular distance to a point on the celestial sphere, measured north or south from the celestial equator along the **hour circle** *(see).* [Middle English *declinacioun,* from Old French *declination,* from Latin *dēclīnātiō* (stem *dēclīnātiōn-*), from *dēclīnāre,* DECLINE.] **—dec·li·na·tion·al** *adj.*

de·cli·na·to·ry (dĭ-klī′nə-tôr′ē, -tōr′ē) *adj.* Involving or conveying declination; expressing refusal.

de·cline (dĭ-klīn′) *v.* **-clined, -clining, -clines.** *—intr.* **1.** To refuse to do or accept something. **2.** To slope downward. **3.** To deteriorate gradually; fail. **4.** To draw to a gradual close; wane. **5.** *Linguistics.* To have inflected forms. Used of nouns, pronouns, and adjectives in certain languages. *—tr.* **1.** To refuse (an offer or request, for example). **2.** To cause to slope downward. **3.** *Linguistics.* In certain languages, to give the inflected forms of (a noun, pronoun, or adjective). Compare **conjugate.** —See Synonyms at **refuse.**

~n. **1.** The process or result of declining; especially, gradual deterioration. **2.** A downward movement. **3.** The period when something is tending toward an end. **4.** A downward slope. **5.** Any disease, such as tuberculosis, that gradually weakens or wastes the body or a bodily part. [Middle English *declinen,* from Old French *decliner,* from Latin *dēclīnāre,* to turn aside, go down, inflect grammatically : *dē-,* away, aside + *clīnāre,* to bend.] **—de·clin·a·ble** *adj.* **—de·clin·er** *n.*

dec·li·nom·e·ter (dĕk′lə-nŏm′ə-tər) *n.* An instrument for measuring magnetic declination. [DECLIN(ATION) + -METER.]

de·cliv·i·tous (dĭ-klĭv′ə-təs) *adj.* Rather steep.

de·cliv·i·ty (dĭ-klĭv′ə-tē) *n., pl.* **-ties.** A descending slope, as of a hill. Compare **acclivity.** [Latin *dēclīvitās,* from *dēclīvis,* sloping down : *dē-,* down + *clīvus,* a slope.]

de·clutch (dē′klŭch′, dĭ-klŭch′) *intr.v.* **-clutched, -clutching, -clutches.** To disengage the clutch of an engine.

de·coct (dĭ-kŏkt′) *tr.v.* **-cocted, -cocting, -cocts.** **1. a.** To extract the flavor, essence, or other desired substance of by boiling. **b.** To steep in hot water. **2.** To concentrate by boiling; boil down. [Middle English *decocten,* from Latin *dēcoquere* (past participle *dēcoctus*), to boil to the dregs : *dē-* (intensive) + *coquere,* to cook.] **—de·coc·tion** *n.*

de·code (dē-kōd′) *tr.v.* **-coded, -coding, -codes.** To convert from code into plain, understandable language; decipher. **—de·cod·er** *n.*

de·coke (dē′kōk′, dĭ-kōk′) *tr.v. British.* To decarbonize (an engine). *~n.* An act of decarbonizing.

de·col·late[1] (dĭ-kŏl′āt′) *tr.v.* **-lated, -lating, -lates.** To behead. [Latin *decollāre, decollāt-* : *de-,* off + *collum,* neck.]

de·col·late[2] (dĕk′ə-lāt′, dē-kō′lāt′) *tr.v.* **-lated, -lating, -lates.** To separate out into individual copies. Used of documents produced in multiple copies. [DE- + COLLATE.]

dé·colle·tage (dā′kôl-tăzh′) *n.* **1.** A low neckline on a garment. **2.** A décolleté garment. [French, from *décolleter.* See **décolleté.**]

dé·colle·té (dā′kôl-tā′) *adj.* **1.** Having a low neckline: *a décolleté dress.* **2.** Wearing a garment with a low neckline. [French, past participle of *décolleter,* to uncover the neck, cut a low neckline : *dé-* (removal) + *collet,* collar, diminutive of *col,* neck, collar, from Old French, from Latin *collum,* neck.]

de·col·o·nize (dē-kŏl′ə-nīz′) *tr.v.* **-nized, -nizing, -nizes.** To give independence to (a former colony). **—de·col·o·ni·za·tion** *n.*

de·col·or (dē-kŭl′ər) *tr.v.* **-ored, -oring, -ors.** To deprive of color; bleach. **—de·col·or·a·tion** *n.*

de·col·or·ant (dē-kŭl′ər-ənt) *adj.* Able to remove color or to bleach. *~n.* A bleaching agent.

de·col·or·ize (dē-kŭl′ər-īz′) *tr.v.* **-ized, -izing, -izes.** To decolor. **—de·col·or·i·za·tion** *n.* **—de·col·or·iz·er** *n.*

de·com·pose (dē′kəm-pōz′) *v.* **-posed, -posing, -poses.** *—tr.* **1.** To separate into component parts or basic elements. **2.** To cause to rot. *—intr.* **1.** To break down into component parts; disintegrate. **2.** To break down into constituent parts by the action of bacteria or decay; putrefy. Used of organic matter. —See Synonyms at **decay.** [French *décomposer* : *dé-* (reversal) + *composer,* to COMPOSE, from Old French.] **—de·com·pos·a·ble** *adj.*

de·com·pos·er (dē′kəm-pōz′ər) *n.* Something that decomposes or causes decomposition; especially, an organism in an ecological community, such as a bacterium or fungus, that breaks down dead organic matter.

de·com·po·si·tion (dē-kŏm′pə-zĭsh′ən) *n.* The act or result of decomposing; especially: **1.** *Chemistry.* Separation into constituents by chemical reaction. **2.** *Biology.* Organic decay. **3.** *Geology.* Chemical breakdown of rock minerals with the resultant disintegration of the rocks themselves.

de·com·pound[1] (dē′kəm-pound′) *tr.v.* **-pounded, -pounding, -pounds.** **1.** To create (compounded things) by combining various elements.

~adj. **1.** Compounded or consisting of things or parts already compound. **2.** Having or consisting of subdivided or compound leaflets: *a decompound leaf.* [DE- (from) + COMPOUND (noun).]

decompound[2] *tr.v.* **-pounded, -pounding, -pounds.** To decompose. [DE- (reversal) + COMPOUND (verb).]

de·com·press (dē′kəm-prĕs′) *tr.v.* **-pressed, -pressing, -presses.** **1.** To relieve of pressure. **2.** To bring (a person working in a high pressure environment) back to normal air pressure by means of an air lock or a decompression chamber.

de·com·pres·sion (dē′kəm-prĕsh′ən) *n.* **1.** The act or process of decompressing. **2.** Any surgical procedure used to relieve pressure on an organ or part.

decompression chamber *n.* An apparatus in which the air pressure can be artificially varied for the use of divers and others while they gradually readjust from the high pressure of their working environment to normal pressure.

decompression sickness *n. Pathology.* **Caisson disease** *(see).*

de·con·gest·ant (dē′kən-jĕs′tənt) *adj.* Able to relieve congestion, especially in the nasal passages.

~n. A decongestant drug. [DE- + CONGEST + -ANT.]

de·con·se·crate (dē-kŏn′sə-krāt′) *tr.v.* **-crated, -crating, -crates.** To transfer (a church, for example) legally from religious to lay use or ownership. **—de·con·se·cra·tion** *n.*

de·con·tam·i·nate (dē′kən-tăm′ə-nāt′) *tr.v.* **-nated, -nating, -nates.** **1.** To eliminate contamination in. **2.** To make safe by eliminating poisonous or otherwise harmful substances, such as noxious chemicals or radioactive material. **—de·con·tam·i·nant** *n.* **—de·con·tam·i·na·tion** *n.* **—de·con·tam·i·na·tor** *n.*

de·con·trol (dē′kən-trōl′) *tr.v.* **-trolled, -trolling, -trols.** To free from control, especially from government control.

dé·cor, de·cor (dā′kôr′, dā-kôr′) *n.* **1. a.** A decorative style or scheme, as of a room, home, stage setting, or the like. **b.** The decorations and furnishings of a place. **2.** A stage setting; scenery. [French, from *décorer,* to DECORATE, from Latin *decorāre.*]

dec·o·rate (dĕk′ə-rāt′) *tr.v.* **-rated, -rating, -rates.** **1.** To furnish or adorn with fashionable or beautiful things; embellish; ornament. **2.** To confer a medal or other honor upon; present with a decoration. [Latin *decorāre,* from *decus* (stem *decor-*), ornament.]

dec·o·rat·ed (dĕk′ə-rā′tĭd) *adj. Architecture. Often* **Decorated.** Designating a style of English Gothic architecture of the 13th and 14th centuries, characterized by the use of the **ogee** *(see)* and elaborate tracery and carving.

dec·o·ra·tion (dĕk′ə-rā′shən) *n.* **1.** The act, process, technique, or art of decorating. **2.** An object or group of objects used to decorate; an ornament; an embellishment. **3.** A medal, badge, or other emblem of honor.

Decoration Day *n.* **Memorial Day** *(see).*

dec·o·ra·tive (dĕk′ər-ə-tĭv) *adj.* Serving to decorate; ornamental. **—dec·o·ra·tive·ly** *adv.* **—dec·o·ra·tive·ness** *n.*

decorative arts *pl.n.* The arts or crafts, such as pottery or cabinetmaking, that produce objects used as decoration or furnishings.

dec·o·ra·tor (dĕk′ə-rā′tər) *n.* An **interior decorator** *(see).*

dec·o·rous (dĕk′ər-əs, dĭ-kôr′əs) *adj.* Characterized by or exhibiting decorum; proper. [Latin *decōrus,* from *decor,* seemliness, elegance, beauty.] **—dec·o·rous·ly** *adv.* **—dec·o·rous·ness** *n.*

de·cor·ti·cate (dĭ-kôr′tĭ-kāt′) *tr.v.* **-cated, -cating, -cates. 1.** To remove the cortex from (an organ or structure), especially in surgery. **2.** To remove the bark, husk, or outer layer from; strip; peel. [Latin *dēcorticāre* : *dē-* (removal) + *cortex* (stem *cortic-*), bark.] **—de·cor·ti·ca·tion** *n.* **—de·cor·ti·ca·tor** *n.*

de·co·rum (dĭ-kôr′əm, -kōr′-) *n.* Respect for social convention and good manners; propriety. —See Synonyms at **etiquette.** [Latin *decōrum,* from *decōrus,* DECOROUS.]

de·cou·page, dé·cou·page (dā′ko͞o-päzh′) *n.* **1.** The technique of decorating a surface with paper cutouts. **2.** Something produced by decoupage. [French, from Old French *decouper,* to cut out : *de-,* from Latin *dē-,* away + *couper,* to cut, strike, from *coup,* stroke, COUP.]

de·cou·ple (dē-kŭp′əl) *tr.v.* **-pled, -pling, -ples. 1.** *Electronics.* To reduce or eliminate the coupling of circuits or mechanical parts. **2.** *Physics.* To decrease the seismic effects of (an explosion) by having it take place in an underground cavity. **—de·cou·pler** *n.*

de·coy (dē′koi′, dĭ-koi′) *n.* **1.** An enclosed place, such as a pond or a large trap, into which wildfowl are lured for capture. **2.** A living or artificial bird or other animal used to entice game into a trap or within shooting range. **3.** Someone who leads another into danger, deception, or a trap. **4.** Any means used to mislead or lead into danger.
~*v.* (dĭ-koi′) **decoyed, -coying, -coys.** —*tr.* To lure into danger or a trap; entrap by or as if by a decoy. —*intr.* To be lured by or as if by a decoy; fall into a trap. —See Synonyms at **lure.** [Perhaps from Dutch *de kooi,* "the cage" : *de,* the + *kooi,* cage, from Middle Dutch *cōie,* from Latin *cavea,* from *cavus,* hollow.] **—de·coy·er** *n.*

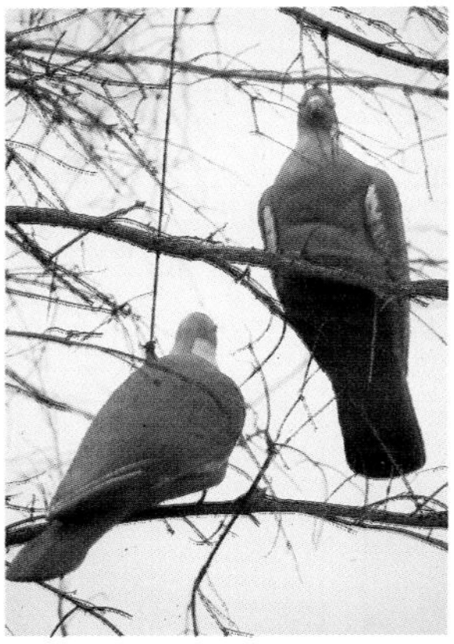

decoy *Two model pigeons hang from wires in a tree. The decoys, which appear to be perching on the branches, fool other birds into thinking that the tree is safe to approach—and lure them within range of the hunter's gun.*

de·crease (dĭ-krēs′) *v.* **-creased, -creasing, -creases.** —*intr.* To grow or become gradually less or smaller; diminish gradually; dwindle. —*tr.* To cause to grow or become less or smaller; make less; reduce.
~*n.* (dē′krēs′) *Abbr.* **dec. 1.** The act or process of decreasing, or the resulting condition. **2.** The amount by which something has been reduced. [Middle English *decresen,* from Old French *de(s)creistre* (present stem *decreiss-*), from Vulgar Latin *discrēscere* (unattested), variant of Latin *dēcrēscere* : *dē-* (reversal) + *crēscere,* to grow, increase.] **—de·creas·ing·ly** *adv.*
Synonyms: *abate, diminish, dwindle, lessen, reduce, shrink, subside.*

de·cree (dĭ-krē′) *n.* **1.** An authoritative order having the force of law. **2.** The judgment of a court of equity, admiralty, probate, or divorce. **3.** *Roman Catholic Church.* **a.** A doctrinal or disciplinary act of an ecumenical council. **b.** An administrative act applying or interpreting articles of canon law.
~*v.* **decreed, -creeing, -crees.** —*tr.* To ordain, establish, or decide by decree. —*intr.* To issue a decree. [Middle English *decre(t),* from Old French, from Latin *dēcrētum,* from *dēcrētus,* past participle of *dēcernere,* to decide : *dē-* (removal) + *cernere,* to sift.] **—de·cree·a·ble** *adj.* **—de·cre·er** *n.*

de·cree-law (dĭ-krē′lô′) *n.* A decree that has the force of a law enacted by a legislature, but usually issued on the sole authority of an absolute ruler or the executive branch of a government.

dec·re·ment (dĕk′rə-mənt) *n.* **1.** The act or process of decreasing or becoming gradually less. **2.** The amount lost by gradual diminution or waste. **3.** *Mathematics.* The amount by which a variable is decreased; a negative increment. **4.** *Physics.* The ratio of the amplitude of an oscillation to the amplitude after one period, used as a measure of damping. [Latin *dēcrēmentum,* from *dēcrēscere,* to DECREASE.]

de·crep·it (dĭ-krĕp′ĭt) *adj.* Weakened by old age, illness, or hard use; broken-down. —See Synonyms at **weak.** [Middle English, from Old French, from Latin *dēcrepitus,* probably "cracked" : *dē-* (intensive) + *crepitus,* past participle of *crepāre,* to crack, creak.] **—de·crep·it·ly** *adv.*

de·crep·i·tate (dĭ-krĕp′ĭ-tāt′) *v.* **-tated, -tating, -tates.** —*tr.* To roast or calcine (crystals or salts) until they emit a crackling sound or until this sound stops. —*intr.* To crackle when roasted. [Medieval Latin *dēcrepitāre* : Latin *dē-* (intensive) + *crepitāre,* frequentative of *crepāre,* to creak, crack.] **—de·crep·i·ta·tion** *n.*

de·crep·i·tude (dĭ-krĕp′ĭ-to͞od′, -tyo͞od′) *n.* The state of being decrepit; weakness; infirmity.

de·cre·scen·do (dē′krə-shĕn′dō) *n., pl.* **-dos.** *Abbr.* **decresc. 1.** A gradual decrease in force or loudness. **2.** A musical passage marked or performed in a decrescendo. Also called "diminuendo."
~*adj. Abbr.* **decresc.** Gradually diminishing in force or loudness; diminuendo.
~*adv. Abbr.* **decresc.** With a decrescendo; diminuendo. [Italian, from Latin *dēcrescendum,* gerund of *dēcrēscere,* to DECREASE.]

de·cres·cent (dĭ-krĕs′ənt) *adj.* Decreasing; waning. Said of the moon. Compare **increscent.** [Latin *dēcrescēns* (stem *dēcrescent-*), present participle *dēcrescere,* to DECREASE.]

de·cre·tal (dĭ-krēt′l) *n. Roman Catholic Church.* **1.** A decree; especially, a letter from the pope giving a decision on some point of canon law. **2. Decretals.** The body of papal laws and decrees forming a part of canon law. [Middle English, from Old French, from Medieval Latin *(epistola) dēcrētālis,* (letter) of decree, from Latin *dēcrētum,* DECREE.] **—de·cre·tal** *adj.*

de·cre·tive (dĭ-krē′tĭv) *adj.* Having the force of a decree.

dec·re·to·ry (dĕk′rə-tôr′ē, -tōr′ē) *adj.* Of or resulting from a decree.

de·crim·i·nal·ize (dē-krĭm′ə-nə-līz′) *tr.v.* **-ized, -izing, -izes.** To cause to be no longer illegal; regulate rather than prohibit: *decriminalize the use of marijuana.* **—de·crim·i·nal·i·za·tion** *n.*

de·cry (dĭ-krī′) *tr.v.* **-cried, -crying, -cries. 1.** To belittle or disparage openly; censure. **2.** To depreciate or devalue (currency, for example) by official proclamation or by rumor. [French *décrier,* from Old French *descrier,* "to cry down" : *des-,* from Latin *dē-,* down + *crier,* to CRY.] **—de·cri·er** *n.*
Synonyms: *belittle, depreciate, disparage.*

de·crypt (dē-krĭpt′) *tr.v.* **-crypted, -crypting, -crypts.** To decode a cipher, especially without knowledge of the key. [DE- + CRYPT(O-GRAM).] **—de·cryp·tion** *n.*

de·cu·bi·tus ulcer (dĭ-kyo͞o′bə-təs) *n. Medicine.* A **bedsore** *(see).* [Latin *dēcubitus,* past participle of *dēcumbere,* to lie down. See **decumbent.**]

de·cum·bent (dĭ-kŭm′bənt) *adj.* **1.** Reclining; lying down or lying flat; prostrate. **2.** *Botany.* Lying or growing along the ground but turning upward at or near the apex: *decumbent stems.* [Latin *dēcumbēns* (stem *dēcumbent-*), present participle of *dēcumbere,* to lie down : *dē-,* down + *cumbere,* to lie.] **—de·cum·bence, de·cum·ben·cy** *n.*

dec·u·ple (dĕk′yə-pəl) *adj.* Ten times as great; tenfold.
~*n.* A tenfold amount.
~*tr. v.* **decupled, -cupling, -cuples.** To multiply by ten or increase tenfold. [Middle English, from Old French, from Late Latin *decuplus* : Latin *decem,* ten + *-plus,* -fold.]

dec·u·plet (dĕk′yə-plət) *n.* A set of ten items of the same type. [From DECUPLE, by analogy with *triplet.*]

de·cu·ri·on (dĭ-kyo͝or′ē-ən) *n.* **1.** A commander in the Roman army in charge of ten men, especially in the cavalry. **2.** A member of the senate of a Roman colony or town. **3.** A member of a council in certain Italian towns. [Latin *decuriō* (stem *decuriōn-*), from *decuria,* company of ten, from *decem,* ten.]

de·cur·rent (dĭ-kûr′ənt) *adj. Botany.* Extending downward from the base along a stem: *decurrent leaves.* [Latin *dēcurrēns* (stem *dēcurrent-*), present participle of *dēcurrere,* to run down : *dē-,* down + *currere,* to run.] **—de·cur·rent·ly** *adv.*

dec·u·ry (dĕk′yə-rē) *n., pl.* **-ries. 1.** A division of the Roman army consisting of ten men. **2.** In ancient times, any group of ten men. [Latin *decuria.* See **decurion.**]

de·cus·sate (dĭ-kŭs′āt′) *v.* **-sated, -sating, -sates.** —*tr.* To intersect so as to form an X. —*intr.* To cross each other; intersect.
~*adj.* **1.** Intersected or crossed in the form of an X. **2.** *Botany.* Arranged on a stem in opposite pairs at right angles to those above or below. [Latin *decussāre* (past participle *decussātus*), from *decussis,* number ten, symbol X, coin worth ten asses : *decem,* ten + *ās,* AS (coin).] **—de·cus·sate·ly** *adv.*

de·cus·sa·tion (dē′kə-sā′shən) *n.* **1.** A crossing in the shape of an X. **2.** *Anatomy.* An X-shaped crossing of nerve fibers connecting corresponding parts on the two sides of the spinal cord or brain.

de·dans (dē′dəns) *n., pl.* **dedans. 1.** A screened gallery for spectators at the service end of a court-tennis court. **2.** The spectators at a court-tennis match. [French, "inside," "interior," from Old French, "from within" : *de,* from + *dans,* in, within, from Late Latin *deintus* : Latin *dē,* from + *intus,* within.]

ded·i·cate (dĕd′ə-kāt′) *tr.v.* **-cated, -cating, -cates. 1.** To set apart for a deity or for religious purposes; consecrate. **2.** To set apart for some special use; appropriate; devote. **3.** To address or inscribe (a literary work or artistic performance, for example) to someone as a mark of respect or affection. **4.** To commit (oneself) to a particular course of thought or action. **5.** To open (a building, for example) for public use or unveil (a monument), especially with a ceremony. —See Synonyms at **devote.**
~*adj.* Devoted; dedicated. [Middle English *dedicaten,* from Latin *dēdicāre,* to give out tidings, proclaim : *dē-,* away from oneself + *dicāre,* to say, proclaim.] **—ded·i·cat·ed·ly** *adv.* **—ded·i·ca·tee** (dĕd′ə-kə-tē′) *n.* **—ded·i·ca·tor** *n.*

ded·i·cat·ed (dĕd′ə-kā′tĭd) *adj.* **1.** Devoted to a particular vocation, aim, or cause. **2.** *Computer Science.* Designed to perform one particular function: *a dedicated word processor.*

ded·i·ca·tion (dĕd′ə-kā′shən) *n.* **1. a.** The act of dedicating. **b.** The state of being dedicated. **2.** A note prefixed to a literary, artistic, or musical work dedicating it to someone as a token of affection or esteem. **3.** A rite or ceremony of dedicating. **—ded·i·ca·tive** (dĕd′ə-kā′tĭv), **ded·i·ca·to·ry** (dĕd′ə-kə-tôr′ē, -tōr′ē) *adj.*

de·dif·fer·en·ti·a·tion (dē′dĭf-ə-rĕn′shē-ā′shən) *n. Biology.* The loss of specialized cellular form, especially prior to redifferentiation.

de·duce (dĭ-do͞os′, -dyo͞os′) *tr.v.* **-duced, -ducing, -duces. 1.** To reach (a conclusion) by reasoning. **2.** To infer from a general principle; reason deductively. **3.** To trace the origin or derivation of. [Middle English *deducen,* from Latin *dēdūcere,* to lead away, deduce : *dē-,* away + *dūcere,* to lead.] **—de·duc·i·ble** *adj.*

de·duct (dĭ-dŭkt′) *v.* **-ducted, -ducting, -ducts.** —*tr.* **1.** To take away (a quantity from another); subtract. **2.** To derive by deduction; deduce. —*intr.* To detract; diminish. Usually used with *from: Bad plumbing deducts from the value of the house.* [Latin *dēdūcere* (past participle *dēductus*), to lead or take away, DEDUCE.]

de·duct·i·ble (dĭ-dŭk′tə-bəl) *adj.* **1.** Capable of being deducted. **2.** Allowable as a tax deduction.

de·duc·tion (dĭ-dŭk′shən) *n.* **1.** The act of deducting; subtraction. **2.** That which is or may be deducted: *These expenses are legitimate tax deductions.* **3. a.** The act of deducing; the drawing of a conclusion by reasoning. **b.** *Logic.* The process of reasoning in which a conclusion follows necessarily from the stated premises; inference by reasoning from the general to the specific. **c.** *Logic.* A conclusion reached by this process. In this sense, compare **induction.**

de·duc·tive (dĭ-dŭk′tĭv) *adj.* **1.** Of or based on deduction. **2.** Involving deduction in reasoning. —**de·duc·tive·ly** *adv.*

Dee (dē). River in Grampian Region, northeast Scotland. It flows 140 kilometers (87 miles) from the Grampian Mts. into the North Sea at Aberdeen. *Dee* is an ancient British word for river: there is another one in southern Scotland, one in North Wales, and a fourth in County Limerick in the Republic of Ireland.

Dee, John (1527–1608). English mathematician, astronomer, astrologer, and magician. He wrote a preface to the first English translation of Euclid encouraging the practice of applied geometry. Elizabeth I consulted him as an astrologer.

deed (dēd) *n.* **1.** An act. **2.** A feat; an exploit. **3.** Action or performance in general, especially as distinguished from words: *They were found to be bold in deed as well as in speech.* **4.** *Law.* A document sealed as an instrument of bond, contract, or conveyance, especially one pertaining to property. ~*tr.v.* **deeded, deeding, deeds.** To transfer by means of a deed. [Middle English *dede,* Old English *dǣd.*]

deed poll *n., pl.* **deeds poll.** A deed made by one party, especially by a person changing his name.

dee·jay (dē′jā′) *n. Informal.* A *disc jockey (see).* [From the initials *d* and *j.*]

deem (dēm) *v.* **deemed, deeming, deems.** —*tr.* To judge; consider; think: *We deem it advisable to wait.* —*intr.* To have an opinion; suppose. —See Synonyms at **consider.** [Middle English *demen,* Old English *dēman.*]

de·em·pha·size (dē-ĕm′fə-sīz′) *tr.v.* **-sized, -sizing, -sizes. 1.** To remove emphasis from. **2.** To reduce the emphasis on.

deep (dēp) *adj.* **deeper, deepest. 1.** Extending to or located at: **a.** An unspecified, usually considerable, distance below a surface. **b.** A specified distance below a surface. **2.** Extending from front to rear, or inward from the outside, for: **a.** An unspecified distance. **b.** A specified distance. **3.** Arising from or penetrating to a depth. **4.** Far distant. **5. a.** Difficult to fathom or understand; obscure. **b.** Learned; understanding; wise. **c.** Cunning; crafty; sly. **6. a.** Profound; intense; extreme. **b.** Profoundly absorbed or immersed. **7.** Dark rather than pale in shade. **8.** Low in pitch; resonant. —**deep down.** *Informal.* In fact rather than in appearance; truthfully. —**go off the deep end.** *Informal.* To act recklessly or hysterically. —**in deep water.** In trouble. ~*n.* **1.** *Sometimes* **Deep.** Any deep place on land or in a body of water, especially in the ocean and over 3,000 fathoms in depth: *the Mindanao Deep.* **2.** The most intense or extreme part. **3.** *Nautical.* A distance estimated in fathoms between successive marks on a sounding line: *by the deep, 11.* —**the deep.** *Poetic.* The ocean. ~*adv.* **1.** Deeply; profoundly. **2.** Well on in time: *worked deep into the night.* —**in deep.** *Informal.* Completely committed. [Middle English *dep,* Old English *dēop,* from Germanic.] —**deep·ly** *adv.* —**deep·ness** *n.*

deep-drawn (dēp′drôn′) *adj.* Shaped by forcing through a die while cold. Said of metals.

deep-dyed (dēp′dīd′) *adj.* Unmitigated; absolute.

deep·en (dē′pən) *v.* **-ened, -ening, -ens.** —*tr.* To make deep or deeper. —*intr.* **1.** To become deep or deeper. **2.** To become more intensive: *a deepening depression.* —**deep·en·er** *n.*

Deep·freeze (dēp′frēz′) *n.* **1.** A trademark for a refrigerator designed to freeze and store food for long periods; a freezer. **2. deep-freeze.** *Informal.* Storage or preservation in, or as if in, a deepfreeze. **3. deepfreeze.** A state of suspended activity. —**deep-freeze** *v.*

deep-fry (dēp′frī′) *tr.v.* **-fried, -frying, -fries.** To fry by immersing in a deep pan of fat or oil.

deep-laid (dēp′lād′) *adj.* Elaborately worked out and kept secret. Said of a plan or scheme.

deep-root·ed (dēp′rōō′tĭd, -rŏŏ′tĭd) *adj.* Firmly implanted; ingrained.

deep-sea (dēp′sē′) *adj.* **1.** Abyssal. **2.** Of or pertaining to distant waters: *deep-sea fishing.*

deep-seat·ed (dēp′sē′tĭd) *adj.* Deeply rooted; ingrained.

deep-six (dēp′sĭks′) *tr.v.* **-sixed, -sixing, -sixes.** *Slang.* **1.** To toss overboard. **2.** To toss out; get rid of: *deep-sixed the incriminating papers.*

Deep South *n.* The southeasternmost part of the United States, especially the states of Alabama, Georgia, Louisiana, Mississippi, and South Carolina.

deep space *n.* The regions beyond the moon, encompassing interplanetary, interstellar, and intergalactic space.

deep structure *n. Linguistics.* In the standard theory of transformational grammar, an explicit representation of the parts of a sentence and their relations in a form that allows the sentence's meaning to be understood. For example, the deep structure of the sentence *Children want to play* may be displayed as *Children want (children play).* See **surface structure.**

deep therapy *n.* A type of radiotherapy using penetrating, high-frequency x-rays.

deer (dĭr) *n., pl.* **deer. 1.** Any of various hoofed ruminant mammals of the family Cervidae, characteristically having deciduous antlers usually borne only by the males. **2.** Any of various smaller deerlike mammals, such as the mouse deer. [Middle English *der,* animal, beast, deer, Old English *dēor.*]

deer fly *n.* Any of various blood-sucking flies of the genus *Chrysops,*

having dark bars or spots on the wings.

deer·hound (dĭr′hound′) *n.* A dog of a breed developed in Scotland, resembling a greyhound but larger and having a wiry coat. Also called "Scottish deerhound."

deer ked *n.* A wingless fly, the ked *(see).*

deer lick *n.* A salty spring or patch of ground, to which deer come to lick the salt and other minerals.

deer mouse *n.* Any of various New World mice of the genus *Peromyscus,* having large ears, white feet and underparts, and a long tail. Also called "white-footed mouse." [From its deerlike agility.]

deer·skin (dĭr′skĭn′) *n.* **1.** Leather made from the hide of a deer. **2.** A garment made from such leather.

deer·stalk·er (dĭr′stô′kər) *n.* **1.** A person who stalks deer, usually with the intention of killing them. **2.** A soft cloth hat, with peaks at the front and back and with earflaps that can be tied on its top.

deer's-tongue (dĭrz′tŭng′) *n.* A tall plant, *Frasera speciosa* of western North America, having whorls of greenish flowers.

deer·weed (dĭr′wēd′) *n.* Any of several bushlike, yellow-flowered plants of the genus *Lotus,* of southwestern North America, sometimes used as forage in arid regions.

de·es·ca·late (dē-ĕs′kə-lāt′) *tr.v.* **-lated, -lating, -lates.** To decrease the scope or intensity of: *de-escalated the war.* —**de·es·ca·la·tion** *n.*

deet (dēt) *n.* A colorless oily liquid, $C_{12}H_{17}NO$, that has a mild odor and is used as an insect repellent. [Pronunciation of *d.t.,* the abbreviation of DIETHYL TOLUAMIDE.]

def. 1. defective. **2.** defendant. **3.** defense. **4.** deferred. **5.** definite. **6.** definition.

de·face (dĭ-fās′) *tr.v.* **-faced, -facing, -faces. 1.** To spoil or mar the surface or appearance of; disfigure. **2.** To impair the usefulness, value, or influence of. **3.** To efface or obliterate. [Middle English *defacen,* from Old French *desfacier : des-,* from Latin *dē-* (undoing, ruin) + *face,* FACE.] —**de·face·a·ble** *adj.* —**de·face·ment** *n.* —**de·fac·er** *n.*

de fac·to (dē făk′tō) *adv.* In reality or fact; actually. ~*adj.* **1.** Actual. **2.** Actually exercising power. Compare **de jure.** ~*n. Australian & New Zealand.* A lover with whom one lives. [Latin, "from the fact."]

de·fal·cate (dĭ-făl′kāt′, -fôl′-, dĕf′əl-) *intr.v.* **-cated, -cating, -cates.** *Law.* To misuse funds; embezzle. [Medieval Latin *dēfalcāre,* to cut off : Latin *dē-,* off + *falx* (stem *falc-*), sickle.] —**de·fal·ca·tion** *n.* —**de·fal·ca·tor** *n.*

def·a·ma·tion (dĕf′ə-mā′shən) *n.* Slander or libel; calumny. —**de·fam·a·to·ry** (dĭ-făm′ə-tôr′ē, -tōr′ē) *adj.*

de·fame (dĭ-fām′) *tr.v.* **-famed, -faming, -fames.** To attack the good name of by slander or libel. —See Synonyms at **malign.** [Middle English *diffamen,* from Old French *diffamer, defamer,* from Latin *diffāmāre : dis-* (undoing, ruin) + *fāma,* report, fame.] —**de·fam·er** *n.*

de·fault (dĭ-fôlt′) *n.* **1.** A failure to perform a task or fulfill an obligation; especially, failure to meet a financial obligation. **2.** Failure to make a required appearance in court. **3.** The failure of one or more competitors or teams to participate in a contest: *win by default.* **4.** Lack or need. —**go by default.** To be ignored because absent or inconspicuous. —**in default of.** Through the failure, absence, or lack of. ~*v.* **defaulted, -faulting, -faults.** —*intr.* **1.** To fail to do that which is required. **2.** To fail to pay money when it is due. Often used with *on* or *in.* **3.** *Law.* To fail to appear in court when summoned. **b.** To lose a case by not appearing. **4.** *Sports.* To fail to compete in or complete a scheduled contest. —*tr.* **1.** To fail to perform or pay. **2. a.** To fail to take part in or complete (a contest, for example). **b.** To forfeit (a match, for example) through such failure. **3.** *Law.* **a.** To lose (a case) by failing to take part in it. **b.** To give judgment against (a defendant) because of failure to participate in the case. [Middle English *defaut,* from Old French *defaute,* from Vulgar Latin *dēfallita* (unattested), from *dēfallīre* (unattested), to fail : *dē-* (intensive) + *fallīre* (unattested), variant of Latin *fallere,* to FAIL.] —**de·fault·er** *n.*

de·fea·sance (dĭ-fē′zəns) *n.* **1.** An annulment or rendering void. **2.** *Law.* The voiding of a contract or deed. **3.** *Law.* A clause within a contract or deed providing for annulment. [Middle English *defesaunce,* from Old French *de(s)fesance,* from *de(s)fesant,* present participle of *de(s)faire,* to destroy, DEFEAT.]

de·fea·si·ble (dĭ-fē′zə-bəl) *adj. Law.* Capable of being annulled or forfeited. —**de·fea·si·bil·i·ty, de·fea·si·ble·ness** *n.*

de·feat (dĭ-fēt′) *tr.v.* **-feated, -feating, -feats. 1.** To win a victory over; vanquish. **2.** To prevent the success of; thwart. **3.** *Law.* To annul or make void. ~*n.* **1.** The act of defeating or state of being defeated. **2.** Failure to win; overthrow. **3.** A coming to naught; frustration. **4.** *Law.* A making null and void. [Middle English *defeten,* from Old French *de(s)faire* (past participle *desfait*), from Medieval Latin *disfacere,* to undo, destroy : Latin *dis-* (reversal) + *facere,* to do, make.] —**de·feat·er** *n.*

Synonyms: *beat, conquer, overcome, rout, subdue, subjugate, vanquish.*

de·feat·ism (dĭ-fē′tĭz′əm) *n.* Acceptance of or resignation to the prospect of defeat. —**de·feat·ist** *n.*

def·e·cate (dĕf′ə-kāt′) *v.* **-cated, cating, -cates.** —*intr.* To discharge feces from the bowels. —*tr.* To clarify (a chemical solution). [Latin *dēfaecāre : dē-* (removal) + *faex,* dregs, FECES.] —**def·e·ca·tion** *n.* —**def·e·ca·tor** *n.*

de·fect (dē′fĕkt′, dĭ-fĕkt′) *n.* **1.** The lack of something necessary or

desirable; a deficiency. **2.** An imperfection; a failing; a fault. **3.** *Physics.* An irregularity in a crystal lattice, such as a vacancy or line of missing atoms. —See Synonyms at **blemish**.
~*intr.v.* (dĭ-fĕkt′) **defected, -fecting, -fects. 1.** To desert one's proclaimed allegiance, political party, or the like. **2.** To leave one's country after disowning allegiance to it and take residence in another. [Middle English, from Old French, from Latin *dēfectus,* deficiency, lack, from the past participle of *dēficere,* to remove from, desert, fail, be wanting : *dē-,* away from + *facere,* to do, set.] **—de·fec·tion** *n.* **—de·fec·tor** *n.*

de·fec·tive (dĭ-fĕk′tĭv) *adj. Abbr.* **def. 1.** Lacking perfection; having a defect; faulty. —See Usage note below. **2.** Below average or below an acceptable standard, especially in mental powers. Said of a person. **3.** *Grammar.* Lacking one or more of the inflected forms normal for a particular category of word. In English, *may* is a defective verb.
~*n.* **1.** Something imperfect or damaged. **2.** Someone mentally incapacitated. **—de·fec·tive·ly** *adv.* **—de·fec·tive·ness** *n.*
Usage: The similarity in form and meaning between *defective* and *deficient* sometimes leads to a confusion in usage. *Defective* applies especially to what has a discernible fault and is therefore primarily concerned with quality: *a defective electric light; defective intelligence. Deficient* refers to insufficiency or incompleteness and is basically a quantitative term associated with deficit: *a deficient account; deficient in intelligence.*

defence. *Chiefly British.* Variant of **defense.**

de·fend (dĭ-fĕnd′) *v.* **-fended, -fending, -fends.** —*tr.* **1.** To protect from danger, attack, or harm; shield; guard. **2.** To support or maintain, as by argument or action; justify. **3.** *Law.* **a.** To represent (the defendant) in a civil or criminal case. **b.** To contest (a legal action or claim). **4.** *Sports.* **a.** To protect (oneself or one's goal) against the opposition's attacks. **b.** To compete in order to retain (a title or championship) against a challenger. —*intr.* To make a defense. [Middle English *defenden,* from Old French *defendre,* from Latin *dēfendere,* to ward off.] **—de·fend·a·ble** *adj.* **—de·fend·er** *n.*
Synonyms: *guard, preserve, protect, safeguard, shield.*

de·fen·dant (dĭ-fĕn′dənt) *n. Abbr.* **def.** *Law.* A person against whom an action is brought. Compare **plaintiff.**

Defender of the Faith *n.* A title of English sovereigns, originally conferred upon Henry VIII by Pope Leo X (1521).

de·fen·es·tra·tion (dē-fĕn′ə-strā′shən) *n.* An act of throwing something or someone out of a window. [DE- + FENESTRA + -TION.]

de·fense (dĭ-fĕns′) *n.* Also *chiefly British* **de·fence.** *Abbr.* **def. 1.** The act or policy of defending against attack, danger, or injury; protection. **2.** Anyone or anything that defends or protects. **3.** Military resources and activities designed to discourage or defend against enemy attack: *increased spending on defense.* **4. a.** An argument or set of arguments in support or justification of something. **b.** The speech, document, or the like, in which such arguments are contained. **5.** *Law.* **a.** The defendant's opposition to the complaints or allegations against him. **b.** The defendant and his legal counsel. **6.** *Psychology.* An unconsciously acquired and involuntary mental process such as regression, repression, or projection, that protects one from shame or anxiety. **7.** *Sports.* **a.** The action or policy of defending oneself or one's goal against the opposition's attacks. **b.** The team or those of its players attempting to do this. **c.** The participation in a contest or match against a challenger in order to retain one's title or championship.
~*tr.v.* **defensed, -fensing, -fenses.** *Football.* To act as defense: *defense a play.* **—de·fense·less** *adj.* **—de·fense·less·ly** *adv.* **—de·fense·less·ness** *n.*

defense mechanism *n.* **1.** *Biology.* Any reaction of an organism used in defending itself, as against germs. **2.** *Psychology.* A defense or the psychic structure or mechanism underlying a defense.

de·fen·si·ble (dĭ-fĕn′sə-bəl) *adj.* Capable of being defended, protected, or justified. **—de·fen·si·bil·i·ty, de·fen·si·ble·ness** *n.* **—de·fen·si·bly** *adv.*
Usage: *Defensible* and *defensive* come from the same root but have distinct meanings. *Defensible* means "capable of being defended": *a defensible position. Defensive* means "intended for or providing a defense" and is frequently used with pejorative connotations: *You're very defensive.*

de·fen·sive (dĭ-fĕn′sĭv) *adj.* **1.** Intended or appropriate for defense. **2.** Done for defense; defending. **3.** Of or pertaining to defense. —See Usage note at **defensible.**
~*n.* **1.** A means of defense. **2.** An attitude of defense. **—on the defensive.** Ready to defend or justify oneself. **—de·fen·sive·ly** *adv.* **—de·fen·sive·ness** *n.*

de·fer¹ (dĭ-fûr′) *v.* **-ferred, -ferring, -fers.** —*tr.* **1.** To put off until a future time; postpone. **2.** To postpone the induction of (one eligible for the military draft). —*intr.* To procrastinate; delay. [Middle English *differen,* from Old French *differer,* from Latin *differre* : *dis-,* away + *ferre,* to carry.] **—de·fer·rer** *n.*

defer² *intr.v.* **-ferred, -ferring, -fers.** To comply with or submit to the opinion or decision of another; be deferential. Used with *to.* —See Synonyms at **yield.** [Middle English *deferren,* from Old French *def(f)erer,* from Latin *dēferre,* to carry away, bring to, submit : *dē-,* away + *ferre,* to carry.] **—de·fer·rer** *n.*

def·er·ence (dĕf′ər-əns) *n.* **1.** Submission or courteous yielding to the opinion, wishes, or judgment of another. **2.** Courteous respect. —See Synonyms at **honor.**

def·er·ent¹ (dĕf′ər-ənt) *adj.* Showing deference; deferential.

deferent² *adj.* **1.** Carrying down or away. Said of nerves, blood vessels, and similar channels conveying impulses, fluids, or the like. **2.** Adapted to carry or transport.
~*n. Astronomy.* A circle with the earth at its center, marking the path of the center of a planet's epicycle in the Ptolemaic model of the universe. [Latin *dēferēns* (stem *dēferent-*), present participle of *dēferre,* to bring to, DEFER (to comply).]

def·er·en·tial (dĕf′ə-rĕn′shəl) *adj.* Marked by courteous respect: *"Mr. Bulstrode had also a deferential, bending attitude in listening"* (George Eliot). **—def·er·en·tial·ly** *adv.*

de·fer·ment (dĭ-fûr′mənt) *n.* Also **de·fer·ral** (-fûr′əl). The act or an instance of delaying or putting off; postponement.

de·fer·ra·ble (dĭ-fûr′ə-bəl) *adj.* **1.** Suitable for being postponed: *deferrable plans.* **2.** Eligible for deferment, especially from military service.

de·ferred (dĭ-fûrd′) *adj. Abbr.* **def. 1.** Postponed; delayed. **2.** With benefits or payments withheld until a future date.

de·fer·ves·cence (dē′fûr-vĕs′əns) *n.* The abatement of a fever. [DE- + Latin *fervescere,* inceptive of *fervēre,* to boil, be hot + -ENCE.]

de·fi·ance (dĭ-fī′əns) *n.* **1.** The disposition to defy or resist an opposing force or authority; resolute resistance. **2.** Intentionally provocative behavior or attitude; a challenge. [Middle English *defiaunce,* from Old French *desfiance,* from *desfier,* DEFY.]

de·fi·ant (dĭ-fī′ənt) *adj.* Marked by defiance. **—de·fi·ant·ly** *adv.*

de·fib·ril·la·tion (dē-fĭb′rə-lā′shən) *n. Medicine.* The administration of an electric shock to restore normal heart rhythm in cases of fibrillation. Electrodes from the apparatus used, a *defibrillator,* are placed over the chest wall or directly on the heart.

de·fi·cien·cy (dĭ-fĭsh′ən-sē) *n., pl.* **-cies.** Also *rare* **de·fi·cience** (-fĭsh′əns). **1.** The quality or condition of being deficient. **2.** A lack; a shortage; an insufficiency. **3.** *Genetics.* A **deletion** *(see).*

deficiency disease *n.* A disease caused by the lack of essential substances, especially vitamins, in the diet.

de·fi·cient (dĭ-fĭsh′ənt) *adj.* **1.** Lacking an essential quality or element; incomplete; defective. **2.** Inadequate in amount or degree; insufficient. —See Usage note at **defective.** [Latin *dēficiēns* (stem *dēficient-*), present participle of *dēficere,* to remove from, desert, fail, lack : *dē-,* away + *facere,* to make, do.] **—de·fi·cient·ly** *adv.*

def·i·cit (dĕf′ə-sĭt) *n.* **1.** The amount by which a sum of money falls short of the required or expected amount; a shortage. **2.** *Finance.* An excess of liabilities over assets, or expenditures over income. [French *déficit,* from Latin *dēficit,* it is lacking, from *dēficere,* to lack. See **deficient.**]

deficit spending *n.* Government spending of money obtained by borrowing, resulting in a deficit in the budget.

de fi·de (dā fē′dā′) *adj. Roman Catholic Church.* Designating a doctrine that is an essential part of the faith, especially when so ruled by the pope. [Latin, "of faith."]

def·i·lade (dĕf′ə-lād′) *tr.v.* **-laded, -lading, -lades.** *Military.* To arrange (fortifications) so as to give protection from enfilading and other fire.
~*n.* The act or procedure of defilading or the protection so provided. [DE- + (EN)FILADE.]

de·file¹ (dĭ-fīl′) *tr.v.* **-filed, -filing, -files. 1.** To make filthy or dirty. **2.** To tarnish the luster of; render impure; corrupt. **3.** To profane or sully (a good name or reputation, for example). **4.** To make unclean or unfit for ceremonial use; desecrate. **5.** To violate the chastity of. [Middle English *defilen,* probably alteration (influenced by *filen,* to sully) of *defoulen,* to trample down, injure, from Old French *defouler* : *de-,* from Latin *dē-,* down + *fouler,* to trample, FULL (verb).] **—de·file·ment** *n.* **—de·fil·er** *n.* **—de·fil·ing·ly** *adv.*

defile² *intr.v.* **-filed, -filing, -files. 1.** To march in single file. **2.** To march in files or columns.
~*n.* **1.** A narrow gorge, valley, or other feature of terrain that restricts lateral movement, as of troops. **2.** A marching in line, as of a single column of soldiers or travelers. [French *défiler* : *dé-,* from Latin *dē-,* off, away + *filer,* to march by files, from Old French, to spin, from Late Latin *fīlāre,* from Latin *fīlum,* thread.]

de·fine (dĭ-fīn′) *v.* **-fined, -fining, -fines.** —*tr.* **1.** To state the precise meaning of (a word or sense of a word, for example). **2.** To describe the nature or basic qualities of; explain: *define the properties of a new drug.* **3.** To delineate the outline or form of; make clear: *a shape defined by a line.* **4.** To specify distinctly; fix definitely: *define the weapons to be used in limited warfare.* **5.** To serve to distinguish; characterize. —*intr.* To make a definition. [Middle English *diffinen,* from Old French *definer,* from Vulgar Latin *dēfīnāre* (unattested), variant of Latin *dēfīnīre,* to set bounds to : *dē,* off + *fīnis,* end, boundary.] **—de·fin·a·bil·i·ty** *n.* **—de·fin·a·ble** *adj.* **—de·fin·a·bly** *adv.* **—de·fine·ment** *n.* **—de·fin·er** *n.*

de·fin·i·en·dum (dĭ-fĭn′ē-ĕn′dəm) *n., pl.* **-da** (-də). That which is defined by a definiens. [Latin, neuter of *dēfīniendus,* gerundive of *dēfīnīre,* to set bounds to, DEFINE.]

de·fin·i·ens (dĭ-fĭn′ē-ĕnz′) *n., pl.* **definientia** (dĭ-fĭn′ē-ĕn′shē-ə, -shə). The word or words serving to define another word or expression, as in a dictionary entry. [Latin *dēfīniēns,* present participle of *dēfīnīre,* DEFINE.]

def·i·nite (dĕf′ə-nĭt) *adj.* **1.** Having distinct limits: *definite restrictions on wine and liquor sales.* **2.** Known positively; for certain; sure: *a definite victory.* **3.** Clearly defined; precise; explicit: *a definite statement of the terms of the will.* **4.** *Abbr.* **def.** *Grammar.* Limiting or particularizing. **5.** *Botany.* **a.** Of a specified number not exceeding 20. Said of floral organs, especially stamens. **b.** Determinate. [Middle English *diffinite,* from Latin *dēfīnītus,* past participle of *dēfīnīre,* to determine, DEFINE.] **—def·i·nite·ness** *n.*

PRONUNCIATION KEY

ă, pat; ā, pay; âr, care;
ä, father, are; b, bib;
ch, church; d, deed; ĕ, pet;
ē, be; f, fife; g, gag; h, hat;
hw, which; ĭ, pit; ī, pie;
îr, pier; j, judge; k, kick;
l, lid, needle; m, mum;
n, no, sudden; ng, thing;
ŏ, pot; ō, toe; ô, paw, for;
oi, noise; ou, out; o͝o, book;
o͞o, boot; p, pop; r, roar;
s, sauce; sh, ship, dish;
t, tight; th, thin, path;
th, this, bathe; ŭ, cut; ûr, fur;
v, valve; w, with; y, yes;
z, zebra, size; zh, vision;
ə, about, item, edible,
gallop, circus, peaceful

IN FOREIGN WORDS:

à, *Fr.* ami; œ, *Fr.* feu, *Ger.* schön; ü, *Fr.* tu, *Ger.* über; KH, *Ger.* ich, *Scot.* loch; N, *Fr.* bon; y′, *Fr.* Compiègne

STRESS MARKS:

Primary stress: ′
in·cite′ (ĭn-sīt′)
Secondary stress: ′
in′sight′ (ĭn′sīt′)

Usage: *Definite* and *definitive* both apply to what is precisely defined or explicity set forth. But *definitive* more often refers, in addition, to what is unalterably final, and is not therefore usually interchangeable with *definite.* A *definite decision* is firm and clear-cut, and might come at any time and be provided by anyone. A *definitive decision,* by contrast, usually implies the conclusion of a process of decision-making ("less definite" decisions having previously been made) and suggests that the issues are complex or important and have received the attention of an authority.

definite article *n. Grammar.* The article that restricts or particularizes the noun or noun phrase following it; in English, the article *the.* Compare **indefinite article.**

definite integral *n.* An integral that is calculated between two specified limits, usually expressed in the form $\int_a^b f(x)dx$. The result of performing the integral is a number that represents the area under the curve of function $f(x)$ between the limits and the x-axis. Compare **indefinite integral.**

def·i·nite·ly (dĕf'ə-nĭt-lē, dĕf'nĭt-lē) *adv.* **1.** In a definite way. **2.** Certainly; undoubtedly.
∼*interj.* Used to express emphatic confirmation.

def·i·ni·tion (dĕf'ə-nĭsh'ən) *n. Abbr.* **def. 1.** The act of stating a precise meaning or significance, as of a word, phrase, or term. **2.** The statement of the meaning of a word, phrase, or term. **3.** The act or an instance of making clear and distinct: *a definition of one's intentions.* **4.** The state of being closely outlined or determined. **5.** A determining of outline, extent, or limits: *the definition of my authority.* **6.** *Telecommunications.* The degree of clarity with which a televised image is received or a radio receives a given station. **7.** *Optics.* The clarity of detail in an optically produced image, as in a photograph, produced by a combination of resolution and contrast. [Middle English *diffinicioun,* from Old French *definition,* from Latin *dēfīnītiō* (stem *dēfīnītiōn-*), from *dēfīnīre,* DEFINE.] **—def·i·ni·tion·al** *adj.* **—def·i·ni·tion·al·ly** *adv.*

de·fin·i·tive (dĭ-fĭn'ə-tĭv) *adj.* **1.** Precisely defining or outlining; explicit. **2.** Determining finally; conclusive; decisive. **3.** Designating a statement or work that can stand as the most complete and authoritative on its subject: *a definitive biography.* **4.** *Zoology.* In a complete, fully developed form. Said especially of parasites. **5.** Issued for permanent rather than commemorative or other use. Said of a postage stamp. **—**See Usage note at **definite.**
∼*n.* **1.** *Grammar.* A word that defines or limits, such as the definite article or a demonstrative pronoun. **2.** A definitive postage stamp. **—de·fin·i·tive·ly** *adv.* **—de·fin·i·tive·ness** *n.*

de·fin·i·tude (dĭ-fĭn'ə-to͞od', -tyo͞od') *n.* The quality of being definite or exact; precision.

def·la·grate (dĕf'lə-grāt') *v.* **-grated, -grating, -grates.** *—tr.* To cause to burn with great heat and intense light. *—intr.* To burn with great heat and intense light. [Latin *dēflagrāre* : *dē-* (intensive) + *flagrāre,* to burn.] **—def·la·gra·tion** *n.*

de·flate (dĭ-flāt') *v.* **-flated, -flating, -flates.** *—tr.* **1. a.** To release contained air or gas from. **b.** To collapse by releasing contained air or gas. **2.** To reduce or lessen the confidence, pride, self-esteem, or certainty of. **3.** *Economics.* **a.** To reduce the amount or availability of (currency or credit), effecting a decline in prices. **b.** To produce deflation in (an economy). In these senses, compare **reflate.** *—intr.* To be or become deflated. [DE- (reversal) + (IN)FLATE.] **—de·fla·tor** *n.*

de·fla·tion (dĭ-flā'shən) *n.* **1. a.** The act of deflating. **b.** The state of being deflated. **2.** *Economics.* A reduction in the general price level, brought on by a decrease in the amount of money in circulation or in the total volume of spending. Compare **inflation. 3.** *Geology.* The blowing away of loose rock particles by the wind. **—de·fla·tion·ar·y** *adj.* **—de·fla·tion·ist** *n.*

de·flect (dĭ-flĕkt') *v.* **-flected, -flecting, -flects.** *—tr.* To cause to swerve or turn aside. *—intr.* To swerve or turn aside. [Latin *dēflectere* : *dē-,* away + *flectere,* to bend, FLEX.] **—de·flect·a·ble** *adj.* **—de·flec·tive** *adj.* **—de·flec·tor** *n.*

de·flec·tion (dĭ-flĕk'shən) *n.* Also *British* **de·flex·ion. 1. a.** The act of deflecting. **b.** The condition of being deflected. **2.** Deviation or the amount of deviation. **3.** The deviation from zero shown by the indicator of a measuring instrument. **4.** The movement of a structure or structural part as a result of stress.

de·flexed (dĭ-flĕkst', dē'flĕkst') *adj. Botany.* Bent or turned downward at a sharp angle: *deflexed petals.* [Latin *dēflexus,* past participle of *dēflectere,* DEFLECT.]

deflexion. *British.* Variant of **deflection.**

de·floc·cu·late (dē-flŏk'yə-lāt') *v.* **-lated, -lating, -lates.** *—tr.* **1.** To disperse (an aggregate, such as clay or soil) into very fine particles. **2.** To prevent or hinder (a suspension or colloid) from forming an aggregate. *—intr.* To be dispersed into very fine particles. **—de·floc·cu·la·tion** *n.*

def·lo·ra·tion (dĕf'lə-rā'shən) *n.* The act of deflowering.

de·flow·er (dē-flou'ər) *tr.v.* **-ered, -ering, -ers. 1.** To strip of flowers. **2.** To rupture the hymen of (a virgin) by sexual intercourse. **3.** To spoil the appearance or nature of; mar. **4.** To destroy the innocence of; violate. [Middle English *deflouren,* from Old French *deflorer,* from Late Latin *dēflōrāre* : Latin *dē-* (removal) + *flōs* (stem *flōr-*), flower.] **—de·flow·er·er** *n.*

De·foe (dĭ-fō'), **Daniel** (1660–1731). English author. He took part in Monmouth's rebellion (1685) and later became a journalist. *Robinson Crusoe,* the most famous of his many novels, was published in 1719. Three major works appeared in 1722 alone: the novels *Moll Flanders* and *The History of Colonel Jack* and the pseudo-documentary *Journal of the Plague Year.*

de·fog (dē-fôg', -fŏg') *tr.v.* **-fogged, -fogging, -fogs.** To remove fog from. **—de·fog·ger** *n.*

de·fo·li·ant (dē-fō'lē-ənt) *n.* A chemical sprayed or dusted on plants to cause the leaves to fall off.

de·fo·li·ate (dē-fō'lē-āt') *v.* **-ated, -ating, -ates.** *—tr.* **1.** To deprive (a tree or other plant) of leaves. **2.** To cause the leaves of (a tree or other plant) to fall off, especially by the use of a chemical spray or dust. *—intr.* To lose foliage. [Late Latin *dēfoliāre* : Latin *dē,* removal + *folium,* leaf.] **—de·fo·li·ate** (dē-fō'lē-ĭt) *adj.* **—de·fo·li·a·tion** *n.* **—de·fo·li·a·tor** *n.*

de·force *tr.v.* **-forced, -forcing, -forces. 1. a.** In English feudal property law, to withhold by force from the rightful owner. **b.** *Law.* To deprive (a rightful owner) of property by force. **2.** In Scots law, to resist an officer of the law in the performance of his duty. [Middle English *deforcen,* from Norman French *deforcer,* variant of Old French *de(s)forcier* : *des-* (reversal) + *forcier,* to force, from Vulgar Latin *fortiāre* (unattested), from Latin *fortis,* strong.] **—de·force·ment** *n.*

de·for·ciant (dē-fôr'shənt, -fōr'-) *n. Law.* One who deforces a rightful owner.

de·for·est (dē-fôr'ĭst, -fŏr'-) *tr.v.* **-ested, -esting, -ests.** To cut down and clear away the trees or forests from. **—de·for·es·ta·tion** *n.* **—de·for·est·er** *n.*

De For·est (dĭ fôr'ĭst, fŏr'-), **Lee** (1873–1961). U.S. electrical engineer and inventor. Often called "the Father of Radio," he patented the triode electron tube (1907), which made possible the radio receiver. He received more than 300 patents and greatly contributed to the development of television and radar.

de·form (dĭ-fôrm') *v.* **-formed, -forming, -forms.** *—tr.* **1.** To spoil the natural form of; misshape. **2.** To deface; disfigure. **3.** To spoil the nature of; pervert. **4.** *Physics.* To alter the shape of by pressure or stress. *—intr.* To become deformed. **—**See Usage note at **distort.** [Middle English *deformen,* from Old French *deformer,* from Latin *dēformāre* : *dē-* (reversal) + *formāre,* to form, from *forma,* FORM.] **—de·form·a·bil·i·ty** *n.* **—de·form·a·ble** *adj.* **—de·for·ma·tion** (dē'fôr-mā'shən, dĕf'ər-) *n.*

de·formed (dĭ-fôrmd') *adj.* Misshapen; disfigured.

de·form·i·ty (dĭ-fôr'mĭ-tē) *n., pl.* **-ties. 1.** The state or condition of being deformed. **2.** A bodily malformation, such as a clubfoot or hunchback. **3.** A deformed person or thing. **4.** Gross ugliness or distortion, especially in art or morals.

de·fraud (dĭ-frôd') *tr.v.* **-frauded, -frauding, -frauds.** To take from or deprive (a person) of property by fraud; swindle. [Middle English *defrauden,* from Old French *defrauder,* from Latin *dēfraudāre* : *dē-* (intensive) + *fraudāre,* to cheat, from *fraus* (stem *fraud-*), FRAUD.] **—de·fraud·a·tion** *n.* **—de·fraud·er** *n.*

de·fray (dĭ-frā') *tr.v.* **-frayed, -fraying, -frays.** To meet or satisfy (costs or expenses) by payment; pay: *defray the cost of a trip.* [French *défrayer,* from Old French *deffrayer, desfrayer* : *des-* (removal) + *frai* (attested only in the plural *frais*), expense, cost, "damage," from Latin *fractum,* from *fractus,* past participle of *frangere,* to break.] **—de·fray·a·ble** *adj.* **—de·fray·al** *n.*

de·frock (dē-frŏk') *tr.v.* **-frocked, -frocking, -frocks.** To unfrock.

de·frost (dē-frôst', -frŏst') *v.* **-frosted, -frosting, -frosts.** *—tr.* **1.** To remove ice or frost from (a refrigerator, for example). **2.** To cause to thaw. *—intr.* **1.** To become free of ice or frost. **2.** To become unfrozen; thaw.

de·frost·er (dē-frôs'tər, -frŏs'-) *n.* A heating device designed to remove ice or frost or prevent its formation.

deft (dĕft) *adj.* Skillful; adroit. **—**See Synonyms at **dexterous.** [Middle English *defte,* originally "gentle," "meek," variant of *dafte,* DAFT.] **—deft·ly** *adv.* **—deft·ness** *n.*

de·funct (dĭ-fŭngkt') *adj.* **1.** Having ceased to live or exist; extinct; dead. **2.** No longer operative, effective, or respected. [Latin *dēfunctus,* past participle of *dēfungī,* to discharge, finish, die : *dē-* (intensive) + *fungī,* to discharge.] **—de·funct·ive** *adj.* **—de·funct·ness** *n.*

de·fuse (dē-fyo͞oz') *tr.v.* **-fused, -fusing, -fuses. 1.** To remove the fuse from (an explosive device). **2.** To make less dangerous, tense, or hostile: *defuse an international crisis.*

de·fy (dĭ-fī') *tr.v.* **-fied, -fying, -fies. 1.** To confront or stand up to; challenge: *defying convention.* **2.** To resist (an attempt, for example) successfully; withstand, especially in a puzzling way: *"so the plague defied all medicines"* (Daniel Defoe). **3.** To challenge or dare (a person) to perform something considered impossible. [Middle English *defien, diffien,* from Old French *desfier,* from Vulgar Latin *disfīdāre* (unattested), to renounce one's faith : *dis-* (reversal) + *fīdāre* (unattested), variant of Latin *fīdere,* to trust.] **—de·fi·er** *n.*

deg, deg. degree (thermometric).

dé·ga·gé (dā-gä-zhā') *adj.* Free and relaxed in manner; casual. [French, past participle of *dégager,* to disengage, release, from Old French *desgagier,* "to redeem a pledge" : *des-* (reversal) + *gage,* a pledge, gage, from Frankish (unattested) *wadi.*]

de·ga·me (də-gä'mə) *n.* Also **de·ga·mi** (-mē). **1.** A tree, *Calycophyllum candidissimum,* of tropical America, having hard, close-grained, yellowish wood. **2.** The wood of this tree. Also called "lemonwood." [American Spanish *dagame,* a native name.]

de·gas (dē-găs') *tr.v.* **-gassed, -gassing, -gasses** or **-gases. 1.** To remove poisonous gases from (a place or person). **2.** To evacuate gas from (a substance or device). **—de·gas·ser** *n.*

De·gas (də-gä'), **(Hilaire Germain) Edgar** (1834–1917). French

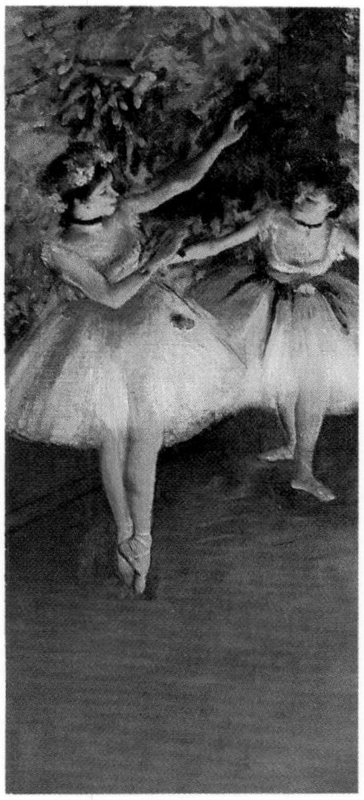

Degas painting *Detail from* Two Dancers on the Stage, *painted in 1874 by the French Impressionist artist Edgar Degas.*

painter and sculptor. He was noted for his portrayal of movement, as in his paintings of ballet dancers.

De Gaulle (də gōl′, gôl′), **Charles André Joseph Marie** (1890–1970). French soldier and statesman, president of France (1959–69). Based in London during World War II, he was made head of the Free French forces in exile and became the acknowledged leader of the Resistance movement in France. He led the provisional government briefly after the liberation (1944–46). With the Algerian crisis (1958), De Gaulle's supporters brought him out of retirement. He was made prime minister, empowered to redraw the constitution, and became president of the new Fifth Republic (1959). Despite violent hostility, he supervised Algeria's path to independence in 1962. He defended the French nuclear deterrent and reduced France's participation in NATO (1966). His leadership was severely tested by strikes and student riots in 1968, and he resigned the following year after proposed constitutional reforms were rejected in a referendum.

de·gauss (dē-gous′) *tr.v.* **-gaussed, -gaussing, -gausses.** To remove or neutralize the magnetic field of (a ship, piece of electronic apparatus, or the like). [DE- + GAUSS.]

de·gen·er·a·cy (dĭ-jĕn′ər-ə-sē) *n., pl.* **-cies. 1.** The state or condition of being degenerate. **2.** The process of degenerating. **3.** *Physics.* The number of quantum states with the same energy. **4.** Degenerate behavior, especially sexual perversion.

de·gen·er·ate (dĭ-jĕn′ə-rāt′) *intr.v.* **-ated, -ating, -ates. 1.** To become degenerate; deteriorate. **2.** *Biology.* To undergo degeneration.
~*adj.* (dĭ-jĕn′ər-ĭt). **1.** Characterized by deterioration; having declined in condition or quality. **2.** Having become debased or depraved; having declined morally. **3.** *Physics.* **a.** Having the same energy. Said of quantum states that are distinct but of equal energy: *degenerate orbitals.* **b.** Designating or pertaining to a semiconductor in which the number of conduction electrons approaches that in a metallic conductor. **c.** Having modes with equal frequencies. Said of a resonance device. **d.** Composed of nuclei and electrons; fully ionized. Said of matter in neutron stars.
~*n.* (dĭ-jĕn′ər-ĭt). **1.** A morally degraded person. **2. a.** A person lacking or having progressively lost normative biological or psychological characteristics. **b.** A person exhibiting antisocial, especially sexually deviant, behavior. [Latin *dēgenerāre,* to fall from one's ancestral quality : *dē-,* away from + *genus* (stem *gener-*), race.] **—de·gen·er·ate·ly** *adv.* **—de·gen·er·ate·ness** *n.* **—de·gen·er·a·tive** (dĭ-jĕn′ər-ə-tĭv) *adj.*

de·gen·er·a·tion (dĭ-jĕn′ə-rā′shən) *n.* **1.** The process of degenerating. **2.** The state or condition of being degenerate. **3.** *Biology.* **a.** The usually irreversible deterioration of specific cells or organs with corresponding functional impairment, caused by injury or disease and often resulting in necrosis or death. **b.** The loss of function of a part or organ over a period of time, as in the evolutionary development of vestigial organs. **4.** *Electronics.* Negative feedback of output power to an input signal in an amplifying circuit.

de·glu·ti·nate (dĭ-glo͞ot′n-āt′) *tr.v.* **-nated, -nating, -nates.** To extract the gluten from (wheat flour, for example). [Latin *dēglūtināre* : *dē* (removal) + *glūtināre,* to glue, from *glūten,* glue.] **—de·glu·ti·na·tion** *n.*

de·glu·ti·tion (dē′glo͞o-tĭsh′ən) *n.* The process or act of swallowing. [French, from Latin *dēglūtīre,* to swallow down : *dē-,* down + *glūtīre,* to swallow.] **—de·glu·ti·to·ry** (dĭ-glo͞o′tə-tôr′ē, -tōr′ē) *adj.*

deg·ra·da·tion (dĕg′rə-dā′shən) *n.* **1.** The act or process of degrading; specifically: **a.** A deposition, removal, or dismissal from rank or office. **b.** A reduction in worth or standing. **2.** A process of transition from a higher to a lower quality or level. **3.** The state or condition of being degraded; deterioration; degeneration. **4.** *Geology.* **a.** A general lowering of the earth's surface by erosion and removal of the eroded material. **b. Denudation** *(see).* **c.** The downward cutting action of a stream as it carves its bed. **5.** The changes in the nature of a soil as its chemicals are washed away. **6.** *Chemistry.* Decomposition of a compound into simpler compounds; especially, decomposition by stages exhibiting well-defined intermediate products. —See Synonyms at **disgrace.**

de·grade (dĭ-grād′) *tr.v.* **-graded, -grading, -grades. 1.** To reduce in grade, rank, or status; especially, to deprive of an office or dignity. **2.** To lower in moral or intellectual character; debase; corrupt. **3.** To reduce, divert, or pervert. **4.** To expose to contempt, dishonor, or disgrace. **5.** To impair or reduce in quality. **6.** *Geology.* To lower or wear down by erosion. Compare **aggrade. 7.** *Chemistry.* To cause (a compound) to undergo degradation. [Middle English *degraden,* from Old French *degrader,* from Late Latin *dēgradāre* : Latin *dē-,* down + *gradus,* rank, step.] **—de·grad·er** *n.* **—de·grad·a·ble** *adj.*
Synonyms: *abase, demean, discredit, humble, humiliate, mortify.*

de·grad·ed (dĭ-grā′dĭd) *adj.* **1.** Reduced in rank, honor, or position. **2.** Reduced in quality or value; distorted; vulgarized: *a degraded level of art.* **3.** Having declined in moral qualities; depraved; degenerate. **4.** Considered as below normal standards of civilization. **—de·grad·ed·ly** *adv.* **—de·grad·ed·ness** *n.*

de·grad·ing (dĭ-grā′dĭng) *adj.* **1.** Giving rise to embarrassment or humiliation; debasing. **2.** *Geology.* Eroding to a lower level; wearing down. **—de·grad·ing·ly** *adv.*

de·grease (dē-grēs′, -grēz′) *tr.v.* **-greased, -greasing, -greases.** To remove the grease from.

de·gree (dĭ-grē) *n.* **1.** One of a series of steps or stages in a process, course of action, progression, or retrogression. **2.** The relative distance, or a step, in a direct hereditary line of descent or ascent. **3.** Relative social or official rank, dignity, or position. **4.** Relative intensity or amount of a quality, attribute, or the like. **5.** Relative condition or extent; capacity; manner. **6.** The extent or measure of a state of being, action, or the like. **7.** *Abbr.* **deg, deg.** *Symbol* ° **a.** A unit division of a temperature scale. **b.** A unit division of various other scales of measurement, such as scales of hardness or relative density. **8.** *Symbol* ° A unit of angular measure equal in magnitude to the central angle subtended by 1/360 of the circumference of a circle. **9.** *Geography.* A unit of latitude or longitude, 1/360 of a great circle. **10.** *Algebra.* **a.** The greatest sum of the exponents of the variables in a term of a polynomial or polynomial equation. **b.** The exponent of the derivative of highest order in a differential equation in standard form; for example, the polynomial $ax^2 + bx + c$ is of the second degree. Compare **order. 11. a.** An academic title given by a college or university to a student who has completed a course of study. **b.** A similar title conferred as an honorary distinction. **12.** *Law.* **a.** A division or classification of a specific crime according to its seriousness. **b.** In Britain, either of the two classifications formerly applied to a felony. **13.** *Grammar.* One of the three forms used in the comparison of adjectives and adverbs. See **positive, comparative, superlative. 14.** *Music.* **a.** One of the seven notes of a diatonic scale. **b.** A space or line of the staff. **15.** Any of the three former classifications of a burn according to seriousness. **—by degrees.** Little by little; gradually. **—to a degree. 1.** To a great extent. **2.** Somewhat. [Middle English *degre,* from Old French, from Vulgar Latin *dēgradus* (unattested), "a step down" : Latin *dē-,* down + *gradus,* a step.]

de·gree-day (dĭ-grē′dā′) *n.* **1.** An indication of the extent of departure of the mean daily temperature from a standard. **2.** A unit used in estimating quantities of fuel and power consumption, based on a daily ratio of consumption and the mean temperature below 65°F (18°C).

degree of freedom *n.* **1.** *Statistics.* Any of the unrestricted, independent random variables that constitute a statistic. **2.** *Mechanics.* Any of the minimum number of coordinates required to specify completely the motion of a mechanical system. **3.** *Thermodynamics.* Any of the independent variables, such as pressure, temperature, or composition, required to specify a system with a given number of phases and components. See **phase rule.**

de·gres·sion (dĭ-grĕsh′ən, dē′-) *n.* **1.** A going down by stages or steps; a descent. **2.** The progressive reduction of the rate of tax on sums below a certain limit. [Middle English *digressioun,* from Medieval Latin *dēgressiō* (stem *dēgressiōn-*), from Latin *dēgredī* (past participle *dēgressus*), to step down : *dē-,* down + *gradī,* to go, step.] **—de·gres·sive** *adj.*

de·gum (dē-gŭm′) *tr.v.* **-gummed, -gumming, -gums.** To free from gum.

de·gust (dĭ-gŭst′, dē′-) *tr.v.* **-gusted, -gusting, -gusts.** To taste with relish or care; savor. [Latin *dēgustāre* : *dē-* (intensive) + *gustāre,* to taste.] **—de·gus·ta·tion** (dē′gŭs-tā′shən) *n.*

de Hav·il·land (də hăv′ə-lənd), **Sir Geoffrey** (1882–1965). British aircraft designer. He taught himself to fly in a plane of his own design (1910). His company produced the Moth biplane (1925), the Mosquito of World War II, and the Comet (1949), which in 1952 became the world's first commercial jet airliner.

de·hisce (dĭ-hĭs′) *intr.v.* **-hisced, -hiscing, -hisces.** To burst or split open along a line or slit, as do the ripe capsules or pods of some plants. [Latin *dēhiscere* : *dē-,* off + *hiscere,* to open, split, inceptive of *hiāre,* to be open, gape.]

de·his·cent (dĭ-hĭs′ənt) *adj.* Opening at pores or by splitting to release seeds within a fruit or pollen from an anther. Compare **indehiscent. —de·his·cence** *n.*

de·horn (dē-hôrn′) *tr.v.* **-horned, -horning, -horns. 1.** To remove the horns from. **2.** To prevent growth in the horns of (cattle, for example), as by cauterization.

Deh·ra Dun (dâr′ə do͞on′). City in Uttar Pradesh, north India. It was founded by a 17th-century Sikh community whose temple (1669) survives. The Indian Military Academy and Forestry Department have their headquarters here.

de·hu·man·ize (dē-hyo͞o′mə-nīz′) *tr.v.* **-ized, -izing, -izes. 1.** To deprive of human qualities or attributes. **2.** To offend human dignity or personality: *dehumanizing conditions.* **3.** To render mechanical and routine. **—de·hu·man·i·za·tion** *n.*

de·hu·mid·i·fy (dē′hyo͞o-mĭd′ə-fī′) *tr.v.* **-fied, -fying, -fies.** To remove atmospheric moisture from; decrease the humidity of. **—de·hu·mid·i·fi·ca·tion** *n.* **—de·hu·mid·i·fi·er** *n.*

de·hy·drate (dē-hī′drāt′) *v.* **-drated, -drating, -drates.** —*tr.* **1.** *Chemistry.* To eliminate water from or make anhydrous. **2.** To remove water from (vegetables, for example) for preservation. **3.** To cause to lose body fluids. —*intr.* **1.** To lose moisture; become dry. **2.** To become dehydrated. **—de·hy·dra·tor** *n.*

de·hy·dra·tion (dē′hī-drā′shən) *n.* **1.** The process of removing water from a substance or compound. **2.** *Pathology.* Excessive loss of water from the body or from an organ or bodily part.

de·hy·dro·gen·ase (dē′hī-drŏj′ə-nās′) *n.* An enzyme that removes hydrogen from a substrate in oxidation-reduction reactions.

de·hy·dro·ge·nate (dē′hī-drŏj′ə-nāt′) *tr.v.* **-nated, -nating, -nates.** *Chemistry.* To remove hydrogen from; dehydrogenize. **—de·hy·dro·ge·na·tion** *n.*

de·hy·dro·ge·nize (dē′hī-drŏj′ə-nīz′) *tr.v.* **-nized, -nizing, -nizes.** To dehydrogenate. **—de·hy·dro·ge·ni·za·tion** *n.*

de·hyp·no·tize (dē-hĭp′nə-tīz′) *tr.v.* **-tized, -tizing, -tizes.** To arouse from a hypnotic state.

PRONUNCIATION KEY

ă, pat; ā, pay; âr, care;
ä, father, are; b, bib;
ch, church; d, deed; ĕ, pet;
ē, be; f, fife; g, gag; h, hat;
hw, which; ĭ, pit; ī, pie;
îr, pier; j, judge; k, kick;
l, lid, needle; m, mum;
n, no, sudden; ng, thing;
ŏ, pot; ō, toe; ô, paw, for;
oi, noise; ou, out; o͝o, book;
o͞o, boot; p, pop; r, roar;
s, sauce; sh, ship, dish;
t, tight; th, thin, path;
th, this, bathe; ŭ, cut; ûr, fur;
v, valve; w, with; y, yes;
z, zebra, size; zh, vision;
ə, about, item, edible,
gallop, circus, peaceful

IN FOREIGN WORDS:

à, *Fr.* ami; œ, *Fr.* feu, *Ger.* schön; ü, *Fr.* tu, *Ger.* über; KH, *Ger.* ich, *Scot.* loch; N, *Fr.* bon; y′, *Fr.* Compiègne

STRESS MARKS:

Primary stress: ′
in·cite′ (ĭn-sīt′)
Secondary stress: ′
in′sight′ (ĭn′sīt′)

de·ice (dē-īs′) *tr.v.* **-iced, -icing, -ices.** To keep free of ice; remove ice from.

de·ic·er (dē-ī′sər) *n.* **1.** Any device, such as an electric heater, used to keep surfaces free from ice or remove ice after it has formed. **2.** Any compound used to prevent the formation of ice on windows, windshields, and the like.

de·i·cide (dē′ə-sīd′) *n.* **1.** The killing of a god. **2.** One who kills a god. [New Latin *deicida* : Latin *deus,* god, DEITY + -CIDE.]

deic·tic (dīk′tĭk) *adj.* **1.** *Logic.* Directly proving by argument. Compare **elenctic. 2.** *Grammar.* Designating a word, such as *this* or *you,* that specifies the object, person, or time referred to; demonstrative. [Greek *deiktikos,* from *deiktos,* able to show directly, from *deiknunai,* to show.] —**deic·ti·cal·ly** *adv.*

de·if·ic (dē-ĭf′ĭk) *adj.* **1.** Making or tending to make divine. **2.** Divine; godlike. [Old French *deifique,* from Late Latin *deificus* : Latin *deus,* god, DEITY + -FIC.]

de·i·fi·ca·tion (dē′ə-fĭ-kā′shən) *n.* **1.** The act or process of deifying. **2.** The condition of having been deified.

de·i·form (dē′ə-fôrm) *adj.* Embodying the qualities of a god; godlike. [Medieval Latin *deiformis* : *dei-,* genitive of *deus,* god + *-formis,* -FORM.]

de·i·fy (dē′ə-fī′) *tr.v.* **-fied, -fying, -fies. 1.** To raise to divine rank. **2.** To worship, revere, or personify as a god. **3.** To idealize; exalt. [Middle English *deifien,* from Old French *deifier,* from Late Latin *deificāre,* from *deificus,* DEIFIC.] —**de·i·fi·er** *n.*

deign (dān) *v.* **deigned, deigning, deigns.** —*intr.* **1.** To think it appropriate or suitable to one's dignity to do something. **2.** To agree in a condescending way to do something. —*tr.* To condescend to give or grant. [Middle English *deinen,* from Old French *deignier,* to regard as worthy, from Latin *dignārī,* from *dignus,* worthy.]

deil (dēl) *n. Scottish.* **1.** A devil. **2.** A mischievous person; imp.

de·in·sti·tu·tion·al·ize (dē-ĭn′stĭ-tōō′shə-nə-līz′, -tyōō′-) *tr.v.* **-ized, -izing, -izes. 1.** To remove the status of an institution from. **2.** To enable (one who is developmentally disabled or mentally ill, for example) to live away from an institution. —**de·in·sti·tu·tion·al·i·za·tion** *n.*

deip·nos·o·phist (dīp-nŏs′ə-fĭst) *n.* A person who is skilled in dinner-table conversation. [Greek *Deipnosophistai* (plural), title of work by Athenaeus (3rd century) describing learned conversations at banquets: *deipnon,* meal + *sophistai,* wise men (see **sophist**).]

Deir·dre (dîr′drə, -drē). *Irish Mythology.* A princess of Ulster who killed herself after her husband, Naoise, was murdered by King Conchobar, whom she had originally been meant to marry.

de·ism (dē′ĭz′əm) *n.* The belief that the truth of the existence of God can be discovered only by the individual through the evidence of reason and nature without resort to any particular church or to revelation. Compare **pantheism, theism.** [French *déisme,* from Latin *deus,* god.] —**de·ist** *n.* —**de·is·tic** *adj.* —**de·is·ti·cal·ly** *adv.*

de·i·ty (dē′ə-tē) *n., pl.* **-ties. 1.** A god or goddess. **2.** Divinity. —**the Deity.** God. [Middle English *deite,* from Old French, from Late Latin *deitās* (stem *deitāt-*), from Latin *deus,* god.]

dei·xis (dīk′sĭs) *n. Grammar.* The use of a deictic word.

dé·jà vu (dā-zhä vü′) *n.* The illusion or feeling of having already experienced something actually being experienced for the first time. [French, "already seen."]

de·ject (dĭ-jĕkt′) *tr.v.* **-jected, -jecting, -jects.** To dishearten; dispirit. [Middle English *dejecten,* from Latin *dējicere* (past participle *dējectus*), to cast down : *dē-,* down + *jacere,* to throw.]

de·jec·ta (dĭ-jĕk′tə) *pl.n.* Excremental matter; feces. [New Latin, from Latin, neuter plural of *dējectus,* past participle of *dējicere,* to cast down, DEJECT.]

de·ject·ed (dĭ-jĕk′tĭd) *adj.* Depressed; disheartened. —See Synonyms at **sad.** —**de·ject·ed·ly** *adv.* —**de·ject·ed·ness** *n.*

de·jec·tion (dĭ-jĕk′shən) *n.* **1.** A state of depression; melancholy. **2. a.** Evacuation of the bowels. **b.** Excrement. —See Synonyms at **despair.**

de ju·re (dē jōor′ē, dā yōo′rā) *adj.* By legal or constitutional right. Compare **de facto.** [Latin, "according to law."]

dek-, deka-. Variants of **deca-.**

dekagram. Variant of **decagram.**

dekaliter. Variant of **decaliter.**

dekameter. Variant of **decameter.**

Dek·ker (dĕk′ər), **Thomas** (*c.* 1572–1632). British dramatist and author. He wrote more than 40 plays, *The Shoemaker's Holiday* (1600) being the best known today.

dek·ko (dĕk′ō) *n., pl.* **-kos.** *British Slang.* A look; a glance. [Hindi *dekho,* imperative of *dekhnā,* to look.]

De Klerk (də-klûrk′), **Frederik W.** (1936–   ). Leader of South Africa's ruling National Party since 1989. He replaced P. W. Botha, who resigned due to poor health.

De Koo·ning (də kōō′nĭng, kōō′-), **Willem** (1904–   ). Dutch-born U.S. painter. He emigrated to the United States in 1926 and became connected with action painters. After 1950 he produced a series of female figures with distorted bodies and grimacing faces.

del (dĕl) *n. Symbol* ∇ *Mathematics.* The vector differential operator, having as components in three-dimensional Cartesian coordinates the first partial derivative operators with respect to each coordinate direction. Also called "nabla." [Short for DELTA (because it appears like an inverted delta).]

De·la·croix (dĕl′ə-kwrä′), **(Ferdinand Victor) Eugène** (1798–1863). French painter and leading figure in the romantic movement in art. Delacroix's *Massacre at Chios* caused a sensation when ex-

hibited at the Salon of 1824. Its rich tones and drama were in marked contrast to the sedate canvases of the classicists. Delacroix exalted color and tumult, as in the voluptuous *Death of Sardanapalus* (1827) and *Liberty Leading the People,* celebrating the Revolution of 1830.

de·laine (də-lān′) *n.* A light fabric of wool or cotton and wool. [French *(mousseline) de laine,* "(muslin) of wool," from Latin *lāna,* wool.]

de la Mare (də lə mâr′), **Walter John** (1873–1956). British poet and novelist. He published his first collection of poetry, *Songs of Childhood* (1902), under a pseudonym. *Memoirs of a Midget* (1921) is his best-known novel.

de·lam·i·nate (dē-lăm′ə-nāt′) *intr.v.* **-nated, -nating, -nates.** To split into thin layers.

de·lam·i·na·tion (dē-lăm′ə-nā′shən) *n.* **1.** A splitting or separating into layers. **2.** *Embryology.* The splitting of the blastoderm into two layers of cells.

de·late (dĭ-lāt′) *tr.v.* **-lated, -lating, -lates.** *Archaic.* **1.** To report (an offense). **2.** To inform against (a person). [Latin *dēlātus,* past participle of *dēferre,* to bring down, report, indict : *dē-,* down + *ferre,* to bear.] —**de·la·tion** *n.* —**de·la·tor** *n.*

De Lau·ren·tis (dē lô-rĕn′təs), **Dino** (1919–   ). Italian filmmaker. After a brief acting career, he turned to movie production and collaborated on many critically acclaimed films, including *Bitter Rice* (1949), *Europa '51* (1952), and *War and Peace* (1956).

Del·a·ware[1] (dĕl′ə-wâr′) *n., pl.* **-wares** or collectively **Delaware. 1.** A group of Algonquian-speaking North American Indian tribes, formerly inhabiting the Delaware River valley. **2.** A member of any of these tribes. **3.** Their language. Also called "Lenape," "Leni-Lenape," "Lenni-Lenape." —**Del·a·war·e·an** *n. & adj.*

Delaware[2] *n.* A variety of grape having sweet light-red fruit. [After the state of DELAWARE.]

Delaware[3]. *Abbr.* **Del.** The second-smallest of the United States, on the Atlantic seaboard. It covers 5,328 square kilometers (2,057 square miles) on the Delaware River. In 1776 it was one of the 13 founder states of the United States and fought on the Union side in the Civil War (1861–65). Wilmington is the industrial center. Dover is the capital.

Delaware[4]. River, *c.* 450 kilometers (280 miles) long, rising in the Catskill Mts. of southeastern New York and flowing generally south, forming the New York–Pennsylvania, Pennsylvania–New Jersey, and New Jersey–Delaware borders along its course. Its outlet is Delaware Bay, an inlet of the Atlantic Ocean extending 84 kilometers (52 miles) between Delaware and New Jersey. The lower Delaware River south of Trenton, New Jersey (the head of navigation), flows through a highly industrialized area.

De La Warr (dĕl′ə wâr′), **Baron Thomas West** (1577–1618). U.S. colonial administrator, born in England. He organized, fortified, and for two years directly governed the once-troubled Virginia Company colony. The state of Delaware and the Delaware River were named in his honor.

de·lay (dĭ-lā′) *v.* **-layed, -laying, -lays.** —*tr.* **1.** To postpone until a later time; defer. **2.** To cause to be late or detained; hinder. —*intr.* To be unduly slow in doing something; linger.
~*n.* **1.** The act of delaying; postponement. **2.** The condition of being delayed; detainment. **3.** The period of time during which one is delayed. **4.** The time interval between any two events. [Middle English *delaien,* from Old French *delaier, deslaier* : *des-,* from Latin *dē-,* off + *laier,* variant of *laissier,* to leave, let, from Latin *laxāre,* to slacken, undo, from *laxus,* slack, loose.] —**de·lay·er** *n.*
   Synonyms: *check, detain, retard, slow.*

de·layed-ac·tion (dĭ-lād′ăk′shən) *adj.* Also **de·lay-ac·tion** (dĭ-lā′-). **1.** Acting only after a predetermined time interval elapses. **2.** Detonating after impact.

delayed drop *n.* A parachute jump in which the parachutist delays opening the parachute for a certain period of time.

delayed neutron *n.* A neutron emitted by a product of nuclear fission several seconds or minutes after the fission occurs. Compare **prompt neutron.**

delay line *n. Electronics.* Any of various devices used to cause a controlled delay in the passage or action of a signal.

de·le (dē′lē) *n.* A sign indicating that something is to be removed from typeset matter.
~*tr.v.* **deled, -leing, -les. 1.** To take out or delete. **2.** To mark with a dele. Compare **stet.** [Latin *dēle,* imperative singular of *dēlēre,* DELETE.]

de·lec·ta·ble (dĭ-lĕk′tə-bəl) *adj.* Greatly pleasing, especially to the sense of taste; enjoyable. [Middle English, from Old French, from Latin *dēlectabilis,* from *dēlectāre,* to please, DELIGHT.] —**de·lec·ta·bil·i·ty, de·lec·ta·ble·ness** *n.* —**de·lec·ta·bly** *adv.*

de·lec·ta·tion (dē′lĕk-tā′shən) *n.* Pleasure; delight.

del·e·ga·cy (dĕl′ə-gə-sē) *n., pl.* **-cies. 1.** The authority, office, or position of a delegate. **2.** The act of delegating or being delegated. **3.** A body of delegates; a delegation.

del·e·gate (dĕl′ə-gāt′, -gĭt) *n. Abbr.* **del. 1.** A person authorized to act as representative for another or others, especially one elected or appointed to be a representative at a conference. **2. a.** An elected or appointed representative of a U.S. territory in the House of Representatives who is entitled to speak but not vote. **b.** A member of the House of Delegates, the lower house of the Maryland, Virginia, and West Virginia legislatures.
~*v.* (dĕl′ə-gāt′) **delegated, -gating, -gates.** —*tr.* **1.** To authorize or send (a person) as one's representative. **2.** To commit to one's agent

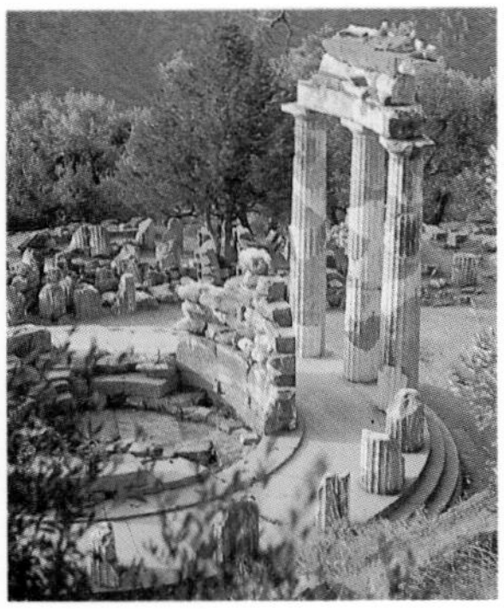

Delphi *The ancient Greeks considered the shrine at Delphi to be the "navel" of the world. This circle of ruined columns is all that remains of the shrine of the Delphic Oracle, dedicated to the god Apollo and built in the fourth century* B.C. *The oracle, the most important center for divination in ancient Greece, was consulted on political and military questions as well as private matters.*

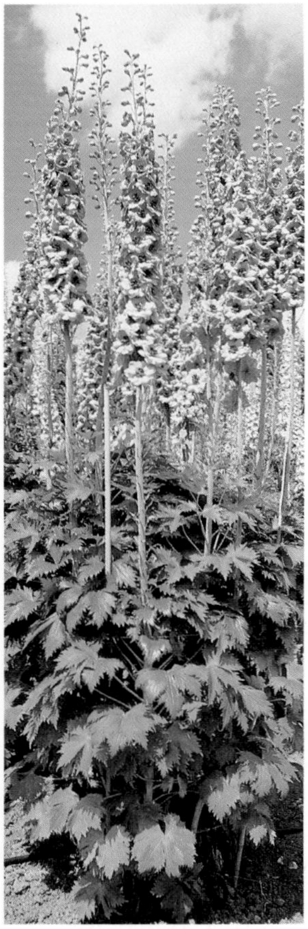

delphinium *"Loch Maree" (above) is a purple-blue perennial variety of this hardy annual, biennial, and perennial garden plant.*

or representative. **3.** To assign (work or duties) to employees or others over whom one has authority. **4.** *Law.* To appoint (one's debtor) as a debtor to one's creditor to replace oneself in satisfying a claim. —*intr.* To assign work or duties to employees or others over whom one has authority: *A manager must know how to delegate effectively.* [Middle English *delegat,* from Medieval Latin *dēlēgātus,* from Latin, past participle of *dēlēgāre,* to send away, dispatch : *dē-,* away + *lēgāre,* to send.]

del•e•ga•tion (dĕl′ə-gā′shən) *n.* **1. a.** The act of delegating. **b.** The condition of being delegated; appointment; deputation. **2.** *Abbr.* **del.** A person or group of persons officially elected or appointed to represent another or others.

de Lesseps, Ferdinand Marie, Vicomte. See **Lesseps.**

de•lete (dĭ-lēt′) *tr.v.* **-leted, -leting, -letes.** *Abbr.* **del.** To strike out or cancel; omit. —See Synonyms at **erase.** [Latin *dēlēre*†, to wipe out, efface.]

del•e•te•ri•ous (dĕl′ə-tîr′ē-əs) *adj.* Having a harmful effect; injurious. [Medieval Latin *dēlētērius,* from Greek *dēlētērios,* from *dēleisthai*†, to harm, injure.] —**del•e•te•ri•ous•ly** *adv.* —**del•e•te•ri•ous•ness** *n.*

de•le•tion (dĭ-lē′shən) *n.* **1.** An act of deleting; an omission or erasing. **2.** A word, passage, or the like that has been deleted from written, printed, or recorded matter. **3.** *Genetics.* A type of mutation in which part of a chromosome is missing. In this sense, also called "deficiency."

delft (dĕlft) *n.* Also **delf** (dĕlf). **1.** A style of glazed earthenware, usually blue and white, originally made in Delft. Also called "delftware." **2.** A piece of pottery in this style. **3.** Any pottery made in imitation of this style.

Delft (dĕlft). Town in South Holland province, southern Netherlands. A fine pottery† has been produced here since the late 16th century. The artist Vermeer lived and worked in Delft.

Del•hi (dĕl′ē). Capital of India, on the right bank of the Jumna River, a tributary of the Ganges. Delhi was an ancient capital of Hindu legend. Under its 17th-century Muslim ruler, Shah Jahan, Old Delhi was laid out within defensive walls 9 kilometers (5.5 miles) long. Chief among his monuments are the huge Red Fort (1638–48) and Great Mosque (1644–58). New Delhi was founded under the British in 1912 to replace Calcutta as the capital.

del•i (dĕl′ē) *n., pl.* **-is.** *Informal.* A delicatessen.

De•li•an (dē′lē-ən) *adj.* Of or pertaining to Delos or its inhabitants. ~*n.* A native or inhabitant of Delos.

de•lib•er•ate (dĭ-lĭb′ə-rāt′) *v.* **-ated, -ating, -ates.** —*intr.* **1.** To take careful thought; reflect. **2.** To consult with another or others as a process in reaching a decision. —*tr.* To consider (a matter) by carefully weighing alternatives or the like.
~*adj.* (dĭ-lĭb′ər-ĭt) **1.** Premeditated; intentional. **2. a.** Careful and slow in deciding or determining. **b.** Not rashly or hastily determined: *a deliberate choice.* **3.** Leisurely or slow in motion or manner; not hurried or impulsive. —See Synonyms at **voluntary.** [Latin *dēlīberāre,* to weigh well, ponder : *dē-,* completely + *lībrāre,* to weigh, from *lībra,* a scale, pound.] —**de•lib•er•ate•ly** *adv.* —**de•lib•er•ate•ness** *n.* —**de•lib•er•a•tor** *n.*

de•lib•er•a•tion (dĭ-lĭb′ə-rā′shən) *n.* **1.** The process of deliberating; thoughtful and lengthy consideration. **2.** *Often* **deliberations.** Formal discussion and debate of all sides of an issue. **3.** Thoughtfulness or care in decision or action.

de•lib•er•a•tive (dĭ-lĭb′ə-rā′tĭv, -ər-ə-tĭv) *adj.* **1.** Assembled or organized for deliberation or debate: *a deliberative legislature.* **2.** Characterized by or being the result of deliberation or debate. **3.** *Grammar.* Expressing doubt or deliberation. —**de•lib•er•a•tive•ly** *adv.* —**de•lib•er•a•tive•ness** *n.*

De•libes (də-lēb′), **(Clément Philibert) Léo** (1836–91). French composer. His compositions include the ballet *Coppélia* (1870) and the opera *Lakmé* (1883).

del•i•ca•cy (dĕl′ĭ-kə-sē) *n., pl.* **-cies.** **1.** The quality of being delicate. **2.** Frailty of bodily constitution or health. **3.** Sensitivity of perception, feeling, appreciation, or the like; refinement. **4. a.** Consideration of the feelings of others. **b.** Aversion to what is considered morally distasteful or injurious. **5.** A need of taste and tact in treating or handling: *a topic of some delicacy.* **6.** Softness or fineness of touch. **7.** Fineness or keenness of response or reaction. **8.** Something pleasing and appealing, especially a choice food. [Middle English *delicacie,* from *delicat,* DELICATE.]

del•i•cate (dĕl′ĭ-kĭt) *adj.* **1. a.** Exquisitely or pleasingly fine. **b.** Beautiful in a graceful or tender way. **c.** Characterized by precise skill, as in execution or workmanship. **2.** Frail in constitution or health. **3.** Easily broken or damaged. **4.** Requiring tasteful and tactful treatment. **5.** Keen in sense discrimination or perception. **6.** Manifesting extreme sensitivity and distaste toward anything immodest, impolite, or morally reprehensible; squeamish. **7.** Mindful of the feelings of others. **8.** Keenly accurate in response or reaction. **9.** Soft or gentle in touch or skill. **10.** Very subtle in difference or distinction. —See Synonyms at **fragile.** [Middle English *delicat,* from Latin *dēlicātus*†, alluring, charming, dainty.] —**del•i•cate•ly** *adv.* —**del•i•cate•ness** *n.*

del•i•ca•tes•sen (dĕl′ĭ-kə-tĕs′ən) *n.* A shop that sells cooked or prepared foods ready for serving, especially foreign or unusual foods. [German *Delikatessen,* plural of *Delikatesse,* delicacy, from French *délicatesse,* from Italian *delicatezza,* from *delicato,* delicate, dainty, from Latin *dēlicātus,* DELICATE.]

de•li•cious (dĭ-lĭsh′əs) *adj.* **1.** Highly pleasing or agreeable to the senses of taste or smell. **2.** Very pleasant; enjoyable; delightful. [Middle English, from Old French, from Late Latin *dēliciōsus,* pleasing, delightful, from Latin *dēlicia,* pleasure, from *dēlicere,* to entice away, DELIGHT.] —**de•li•cious•ly** *adv.* —**de•li•cious•ness** *n.*

De•li•cious (dĭ-lĭsh′əs) *n.* A variety of red or yellow apple having sweet fruit.

de•lict (dĭ-lĭkt′) *n.* **1.** In civil law, a misdemeanor; tort; an offense. **2.** In Scots and South African law, the branch of law corresponding to the English law of tort. **3.** In Roman law, the obligation to pay or make compensation for any wrong committed. [Latin *dēlictum,* from *dēlictus,* past participle of *dēlinquere,* to fail in duty, offend. See **delinquent.**]

de•light (dĭ-līt′) *n.* **1.** Great pleasure; gratification; joy. **2.** Something that gives great pleasure. —See Synonyms at **ecstasy.**
~*v.* **delighted, -lighting, -lights.** —*intr.* **1.** To take great pleasure or joy. **2.** To give great pleasure or joy. —*tr.* To please greatly. [Middle English *deliten,* from Old French *deleitier,* from Latin *dēlectāre,* frequentative of *dēlicere,* to allure, entice away : *dē-,* away + *lacere*†, to allure.]

de•light•ed (dĭ-lī′tĭd) *adj.* **1.** Filled with delight. **2.** *Obsolete.* Delightful. —**de•light•ed•ly** *adv.* —**de•light•ed•ness** *n.*

de•light•ful (dĭ-līt′fəl) *adj.* Affording keen satisfaction; greatly pleasing. —**de•light•ful•ly** *adv.* —**de•light•ful•ness** *n.*

de•light•some (dĭ-līt′səm) *adj.* Delightful. —**de•light•some•ly** *adv.* —**de•light•some•ness** *n.*

De•li•lah¹ (dĭ-lī′lə). A Philistine woman who betrayed Samson, her lover, to the Philistines by having his hair shorn as he slept, thus depriving him of his strength. Judges 16.

Delilah² *n.* A seductive, treacherous woman. [After DELILAH.]

de•lim•it (dĭ-lĭm′ĭt) *tr.v.* **-ited, -iting, -its.** Also **de•lim•i•tate** (dĭ-lĭm′ə-tāt′) **-tated, -tating, -tates.** **1.** To establish the limit or boundaries of; demarcate. **2.** To define: *Their authority is delimited in the constitution.* [French *délimiter,* from Latin *dēlīmitāre* : *dē-,* completely + *līmitāre,* to limit, from *līmes* (stem *līmit-*), LIMIT.] —**de•lim•i•ta•tion** *n.* —**de•lim•i•ta•tive** *adj.*

de•lim•it•er (dĭ-lĭm′ə-tər) *n.* *Computer Science.* A character marking the beginning or end of a unit of data.

de•lin•e•ate (dĭ-lĭn′ē-āt′) *tr.v.* **-ated, -ating, -ates.** **1.** To draw or trace the outline of; sketch out. **2.** To represent pictorially; depict. **3.** To depict in words or gestures; portray. [Latin *dēlīneāre* : *dē-,* completely + *līnea,* thread, LINE.] —**de•lin•e•a•tion** *n.* —**de•lin•e•a•tive** *adj.*

de•lin•e•a•tor (dĭ-lĭn′ē-ā′tər) *n.* **1.** One that delineates. **2.** An adjustable pattern used by tailors for cutting garments of various sizes.

de•lin•quen•cy (dĭ-lĭng′kwən-sē) *n., pl.* **-cies.** **1.** Negligence or failure in doing what is required. **2.** An offense or minor crime; a misdeed. **3.** A tendency to indulge in antisocial behavior, especially petty crime. See **juvenile delinquency.**

de•lin•quent (dĭ-lĭng′kwənt) *adj.* **1.** Engaging in delinquency. **2.** Failing to do what is required by law or obligation. **3.** Overdue in payment: *a delinquent account.*
~*n.* **1.** A delinquent person, especially a **juvenile delinquent** *(see).* **2.** A person who neglects or fails to do what law or obligation requires. [Latin *dēlinquēns* (stem *dēlinquent-*), present participle of *dēlinquere,* to fail in duty, offend, "leave undone" : *dē-* (intensive) + *linquere,* to leave.] —**de•lin•quent•ly** *adv.*

del•i•quesce (dĕl′ə-kwĕs′) *intr.v.* **-quesced, -quescing, -quesces.** **1.** *Chemistry.* To dissolve and become liquid by absorbing moisture from the air. **2.** *Botany.* **a.** To divide into numerous subdivisions that lack a main axis. **b.** To become fluid or soft on maturing, as do certain fungi. **3.** To melt away or disappear as if by melting. —See Synonyms at **melt.** [Latin *dēliquēscere* : *dē-,* completely + *liquēscere,* to melt, from *liquēre,* to be liquid.]

del•i•ques•cence (dĕl′ə-kwĕs′əns) *n.* **1.** The act or process of deliquescing. **2.** The liquid resulting from the process of deliquescing. —**del•i•ques•cent** *adj.*

de•lir•i•ous (dĭ-lîr′ē-əs) *adj.* **1.** Affected by delirium. **2.** Characteristic of or pertaining to delirium: *delirious speech.* —**de•lir•i•ous•ly** *adv.* —**de•lir•i•ous•ness** *n.*

de•lir•i•um (dĭ-lîr′ē-əm) *n., pl.* **-ums** or **-ia** (-ē-ə). **1.** A state of temporary mental confusion and clouded consciousness resulting from high fever, intoxication, or shock, and characterized by anxiety, tremors, hallucinations, delusions, and incoherence. **2.** A state of uncontrolled excitement or emotion. [Latin *dēlīrium,* from *dēlīrāre,* to deviate from a straight line, be deranged : *dē-,* away from + *līrā,* a furrow.] —**de•lir•i•ant** *adj.*

delirium tre•mens (trē′mənz) *n.* A severe psychotic delirium caused by the withdrawal of alcohol from an alcoholic or similar symptoms occurring when there is severe organic or functional brain disorder. Also informally called "D.T.'s." [New Latin, "trembling delirium."]

del•i•tes•cence (dĕl′ə-tĕs′əns) *n.* **1.** The unexpected disappearance or subsidence of disease symptoms. **2.** An incubation period of an infectious disease. [From Latin *dēlitēscens,* present participle of *dēlitēscere,* to hide away, lurk : *dē-,* away + *latēscere,* inceptive of *latēre,* to be concealed.] —**del•i•tes•cent** *adj.*

De•li•us (dē′lē-əs), **Frederick** (1862–1934). British composer, of German parentage. He emigrated to Florida as an orange planter and was influenced by Negro songs. He moved to France, there composing operas, concertos, orchestral music, songs, and chamber music. His works include *On Hearing the First Cuckoo in Spring* (1912).

de•liv•er (dĭ-lĭv′ər) *v.* **-ered, -ering, -ers.** —*tr.* **1.** To release or rescue from bondage, danger, or evil of any kind; set free. —See Synonyms at **save.** **2. a.** To assist (a female) in giving birth: *The doctor delivered her of twins.* **b.** To assist or aid in the birth of: *The midwife delivered the twins.* **3.** To put into another's possession or power; hand over. **4.** To take to the intended recipient: *deliver groceries.* **5.** To send forth (a blow, for example) by releasing, discharging, or throwing. **6.** To utter or pronounce. **7.** To produce or perform (something promised): *delivered the contract on time.* **—deliver oneself of.** To pronounce; utter. **—deliver the goods.** *Slang.* To perform as desired or promised. *—intr.* **1.** To take goods to the intended recipient: *Our grocer delivers.* **2.** *Informal.* To produce results as promised or expected. [Middle English *deliv(e)ren,* from Old French *delivrer,* from Late Latin *dēlīberāre* : Latin *dē-,* completely + *līberāre,* to set free, from *līber,* free.] **—de·liv·er·a·bil·i·ty** *n.* **—de·liv·er·a·ble** *adj.* **—de·liv·er·er** *n.*

de·liv·er·ance (dĭ-lĭv′ər-əns) *n.* **1.** The act of delivering; especially, rescue from bondage or danger. **2.** The state of being so delivered. **3.** A publicly expressed opinion, such as the verdict of a jury.

de·liv·er·y (dĭ-lĭv′ə-rē) *n., pl.* **-ies. 1.** The act of delivering or conveying. **2.** That which is delivered. **3.** The act of releasing or rescuing. **4.** The act of giving birth; parturition. **5.** *Law.* The act of transferring possession of an article from one person to another. **6.** A giving up; a surrender. **7. a.** Utterance. **b.** A manner of speaking or singing. **8.** The act or manner of throwing or discharging.

delivery room *n.* A room in a hospital equipped for delivering babies.

dell (dĕl) *n.* A small, secluded wooded valley. [Middle English *del,* Old English *dell,* from Germanic.]

del·la Rob·bi·a (dĕl′ə rō′bē-ə), **Luca** (*c.* 1400–82). Italian sculptor of the early Renaissance. One of his best-known works is a marble relief, *Cantoria,* in the Duomo, Florence. Much of his work was done with enameled terra cotta for which he developed a glazing.

Del·mon·i·co steak (dĕl-mŏn′ĭ-kō′) *n.* A small, often boned, steak from the front section of the short loin of beef. Also called "club steak." [After the *Delmonico* Restaurant, New York City, founded by Lorenzo Delmonico (1813–1881).]

de·lo·cal·ize (dē-lō′kə-līz′) *tr.v.* **-ized, -izing, -izes. 1.** To remove (something) from its native or usual locality. **2.** To broaden the range or scope of. **3.** *Physics & Chemistry.* To remove (electrons) from a particular position. **—de·lo·cal·i·za·tion** *n.*

De·lorme or **de l'Orme** (də-lôrm′), **Philibert** (*c.* 1510–1570). French architect. He was in charge of work at Fontainebleau, and later commissions included extending the palace of the Tuileries in 1565.

De·los (dē′lŏs). *Greek* **Dhí·los** (*thē*′lôs′). Greek island, virtually uninhabited, in the Aegean. It is the smallest of the Cyclades group, covering an area of barely 3 square kilometers (1 square mile). In Greek myth it was the birthplace of Apollo, and temples dedicated to the god have been excavated on the island.

de·louse (dē-lous′) *tr.v.* **-loused, -lousing, -louses.** To rid (a person or animal) of lice by physical or chemical means.

Del·phi (dĕl′fī′). Ancient site in central Greece, 10 kilometers (6 miles) inland from the Gulf of Corinth. It was the most important sanctuary of Apollo, lying in a secluded glade overlooked by Mt. Parnassus. The site, discovered in 1890, included Apollo's temple, where his oracle was consulted, a theater, and treasuries. The oracle fell into disuse with the rise of Christianity.

Del·phic (dĕl′fĭk) *adj.* Also **Del·phi·an** (-fē-ən). **1.** Of or pertaining to Delphi or to the oracle of Apollo at Delphi. **2.** *Sometimes* **delphic.** Obscure in meaning; ambiguous; oracular.

del·phin·i·um (dĕl-fĭn′ē-əm) *n.* Any plant of the genus *Delphinium*; especially, any of several tall cultivated varieties having spikes of variously colored, especially blue, spurred flowers, such as the larkspur. [New Latin *Delphinium* (genus), from Greek *delphinion,* larkspur, diminutive of *delphis* (stem *delphin-*), DOLPHIN (from the shape of the nectary).]

Del·phi·nus (dĕl-fī′nəs) *n.* A constellation in the Northern Hemisphere near Pegasus and Aquila. [New Latin, from Latin *delphīnus,* DOLPHIN.]

del·ta (dĕl′tə) *n.* **1.** The fourth letter in the Greek alphabet, written Δ, δ, transliterated in English as *d, D.* See feature at **alphabet. 2. a.** A usually triangular alluvial area at the mouth of a river. **b.** A similar deposit at the mouth of a tidal inlet, caused by tidal currents. **3.** Anything resembling the shape of a triangle. **4.** *Mathematics.* A finite increment in a variable. [Middle English, from Greek, from Semitic; akin to Hebrew *dāleth.*] **—del·ta·ic** (dĕl-tā′ĭk), **del·tic** (dĕl′tĭk) *adj.*

delta ray *n.* An electron ejected from matter by ionizing radiation.

delta wave or **delta rhythm** *n.* A low-frequency brain wave that emanates from the forward portion of the brain during deep sleep in normal adults.

delta wing *n.* An aircraft with sweptback wings that give it the appearance of an isoceles triangle.

del·toid (dĕl′toid′) *n.* A thick, triangular muscle covering the shoulder joint, used to raise the arm from the side.
~*adj.* **1.** Triangular. **2.** Pertaining to the deltoid. [New Latin *deltoides,* from Greek *deltoeidēs,* triangular : DELTA + -OID.]

de·lude (dĭ-lo͞od′) *tr.v.* **-luded, -luding, -ludes. 1.** To deceive the mind or judgment of; mislead. **2.** *Obsolete.* To elude or evade. **3.** *Obsolete.* To frustrate the hopes or plans of. —See Synonyms at **deceive.** [Middle English *deluden,* from Latin *dēlūdere,* to play false, deceive : *dē-* (pejorative) + *lūdere,* to play, from *lūdus,* game.] **—de·lud·a·ble** *adj.* **—de·lud·er** *n.* **—de·lud·ing·ly** *adv.*

del·uge (dĕl′yo͞oj) *tr.v.* **-uged, -uging, -uges. 1.** To overrun with water; flood. **2.** To inundate in overwhelming numbers: *deluged with inquiries.*
~*n.* **1.** A great flood; a heavy downpour. **2.** Anything that overwhelms as if by a great flood. **—the Deluge.** The great flood that occurred in the time of Noah. Genesis 7–10. [Middle English, from Old French, from Latin *dīluvium,* flood, from *dīluere,* to wash away : *dis-,* apart + *-luere,* from *lavere,* to wash.]

de·lu·sion (dĭ-lo͞o′zhən, -shən) *n.* **1. a.** The act or process of deluding; deception. **b.** The state of being deluded. **2. a.** A mistaken belief or idea. **b.** *Psychiatry.* A false belief, strongly held in spite of invalidating evidence. [Middle English *delusioun,* from Latin *dēlūsio* (stem *dēlūsiōn-*), from *dēlūdere* (past participle *dēlūsus*), DELUDE.] **—de·lu·sion·al** *adj.*

Usage: *Delusion* and *illusion* are seldom interchangeable, though closely related. *Delusion* refers to false belief held without reservation as a result of self-deception, the imposition of another, or mental disorder. It is the stronger term, often associated with harm. *Illusion* is applicable to a false impression, frequently based on fancy or on wishful thinking, or to a false perception (such as an optical illusion) that one eventually recognizes as false.

de·lu·sive (dĭ-lo͞o′sĭv) *adj.* Also **de·lu·so·ry** (-lo͞o′sə-rē). **1.** Tending to deceive or mislead; deceptive. **2.** Having the nature of a delusion; false. **—de·lu·sive·ly** *adv.* **—de·lu·sive·ness** *n.*

de luxe, de·luxe (dĭ-lo͝oks′, dĭ-lŭks′) *adj.* Of special elegance or luxury; superior: *a de luxe model.*
~*adv.* In an elegant manner; sumptuously. [French, "of luxury."]

delve (dĕlv) *v.* **delved, delving, delves.** *—intr.* **1.** To search deeply and painstakingly. **2.** *Archaic.* To dig the ground, as with a spade. *—tr. Archaic.* To dig (ground) with a spade. [Middle English *delven,* to dig, Old English *delfan.*] **—delv·er** *n.*

Dem. Democrat; Democratic.

de·mag·net·ize (dē-măg′nə-tīz′) *tr.v.* **-ized, -izing, -izes.** To remove magnetic properties from. **—de·mag·net·i·za·tion** *n.* **—de·mag·net·iz·er** *n.*

dem·a·gog·ic (dĕm′ə-gŏj′ĭk) *adj.* Also **dem·a·gog·i·cal** (-ĭ-kəl). Relating to, of the nature of, or characteristic of a demagogue. **—dem·a·gog·i·cal·ly** *adv.*

dem·a·gogue, dem·a·gog (dĕm′ə-gôg′, -gŏg′) *n.* **1.** A leader who obtains power by means of impassioned appeals to the emotions and prejudices of the populace. **2.** A leader of the common people in ancient times. [Greek *dēmagōgos,* popular leader : *dēmos,* common people + *agōgos,* leading, from *agein,* to lead.]

dem·a·gogu·er·y (dĕm′ə-gô′gə-rē, -gŏg′ə-rē) *n.* The practices or rhetoric of a demagogue. Also called "demagogism."

dem·a·go·gy (dĕm′ə-gō′jē, -gô′jē, -gŏj′ē) *n.* **1.** The quality or character of demagogues. **2.** Rule by a demagogue. **3.** Demagogues collectively.

de·mand (dĭ-mănd′, -mänd′) *v.* **-manded, -manding, -mands.** *—tr.* **1.** To ask for urgently or firmly, leaving no chance for refusal or denial. **2.** To claim as a right or due. **3.** To ask to be informed of: *demand the cause of his action.* **4.** To need or require as useful, just, proper, or necessary. **5.** *Law.* **a.** To summon to court. **b.** To claim formally; lay legal claim to. *—intr.* To make a demand.
~*n.* **1.** The act of demanding. **2.** Something that is demanded. **3. a.** The state of being sought after. **b.** An urgent requirement, need, or claim: *an ever-growing demand for investment.* **4.** *Archaic.* An emphatic question or enquiry. **5.** *Law.* A formal claim. **6.** *Economics.* **a.** The desire to possess something combined with the ability to purchase it. **b.** The amount of any commodity that people are ready and able to buy at a given time for a given price. Compare **supply. —in demand.** Much sought after. **—on demand.** Immediately obtainable on presentation or request. [Middle English *demaunden,* from Old French *demander,* to ask, charge with doing, from Latin *dēmandāre,* to give in charge, entrust : *dē-* (intensive) + *mandāre,* to entrust.] **—de·mand·a·ble** *adj.* **—de·mand·er** *n.*

Usage: *Demand* (verb) is commonly followed by a direct object in the form of a word (*demand payment*) or clause (*demand that he go*), or by an infinitive (*demand to know why*). The object is often followed by of or from: demand much of (or from) him. In a parallel construction, demand (noun) is followed by on: make a demand on him.

demand deposit *n.* A bank deposit that can be withdrawn by the depositor immediately and without advance notice.

de·mand·ing (dĭ-măn′dĭng, dĭ-män′-) *adj.* **1.** Making rigorous or excessive demands. **2.** Requiring careful attention or constant effort. —See Synonyms at **burdensome. —de·mand·ing·ly** *adv.*

demand note *n.* A bill or draft payable in lawful money on presentation or demand.

de·mand-pull (dĭ-mănd′po͝ol′, dĭ-mänd′-) *adj.* Designating a type of inflation in which increased demand for a limited amount of goods and services tends to drive up prices. Compare **cost-push.**

de·man·toid (dĭ-măn′toid′) *n.* A transparent, green variety of garnet, used as a gem. [German *Demantoid* : *Demant* (obsolete), diamond, from Middle High German *diemant,* from Old French *diamant,* DIAMOND + -OID.]

de·mar·cate (dĭ-mär′kāt′, dē′mär-kāt′) *tr.v.* **-cated, -cating, -cates. 1.** To set the boundaries of; delimit. **2.** To separate clearly as if by boundaries; discriminate. [Back-formation from DEMARCATION.] **—de·mar·ca·tor** *n.*

de·mar·ca·tion (dē′mär-kā′shən) *n.* **1.** The setting or marking of boundaries or limits. **2.** A separation; a distinction: *a line of demarcation.* **3.** *Chiefly British.* **a.** The practice of strictly differentiating the type of work carried out by members of individual trade unions.

PRONUNCIATION KEY

ă, pat; ā, pay; âr, care; ä, father, are; b, bib; ch, church; d, deed; ĕ, pet; ē, be; f, fife; g, gag; h, hat; hw, which; ĭ, pit; ī, pie; îr, pier; j, judge; k, kick; l, lid, needle; m, mum; n, no, sudden; ng, thing; ŏ, pot; ō, toe; ô, paw, for; oi, noise; ou, out; o͝o, book; o͞o, boot; p, pop; r, roar; s, sauce; sh, ship, dish; t, tight; th, thin, path; *th*, this, bathe; ŭ, cut; ûr, fur; v, valve; w, with; y, yes; z, zebra, size; zh, vision; ə, about, item, edible, gallop, circus, peaceful

IN FOREIGN WORDS:

à, *Fr.* ami; œ, *Fr.* feu, *Ger.* schön; ü, *Fr.* tu, *Ger.* über; KH, *Ger.* ich, *Scot.* loch; N, *Fr.* bon; y′, *Fr.* Compiègne

STRESS MARKS:

Primary stress: ′ **in·cite′** (ĭn-sīt′)
Secondary stress: ′ **in′sight′** (ĭn′sīt′)

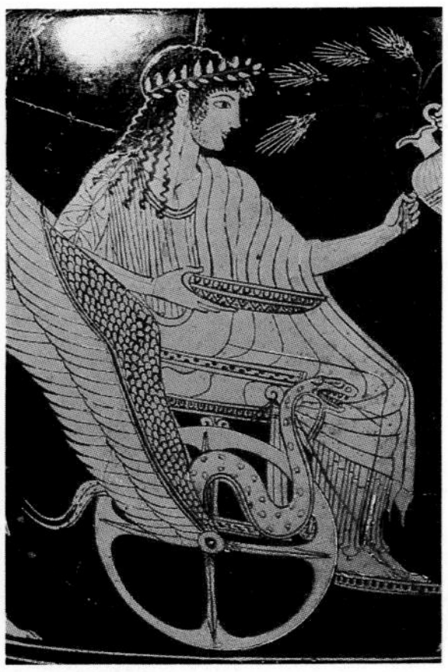

Demeter *The goddess of agriculture sending the gift of corn to mankind—a scene on a Greek vase from about 480* B.C. *When Demeter's daughter Persephone was carried off by Hades, god of the netherworld, Demeter in her grief allowed the earth to become barren. Her brother Zeus decided that Persephone should spend six months above ground and six below—the origin, according to Greek mythology, of the seasons.*

PRONUNCIATION KEY

ă, pat; ā, pay; âr, care;
ä, father, are; b, bib;
ch, church; d, deed; ĕ, pet;
ē, be; f, fife; g, gag; h, hat;
hw, which; ĭ, pit; ī, pie;
îr, pier; j, judge; k, kick;
l, lid, needle; m, mum;
n, no, sudden; ng, thing;
ŏ, pot; ō, toe; ô, paw, for;
oi, noise; ou, out; o͝o, book;
o͞o, boot; p, pop; r, roar;
s, sauce; sh, ship, dish;
t, tight; th, thin, path;
th, this, bathe; ŭ, cut; ûr, fur;
v, valve; w, with; y, yes;
z, zebra, size; zh, vision;
ə, about, item, edible, gallop, circus, peaceful

IN FOREIGN WORDS:

à, *Fr.* ami; œ, *Fr.* feu, *Ger.* schön; ü, *Fr.* tu, *Ger.* über; KH, *Ger.* ich, *Scot.* loch; N, *Fr.* bon; y', *Fr.* Compiègne

STRESS MARKS:

Primary stress: ′
in·cite′ (ĭn-sīt′)
Secondary stress: ′
in′sight′ (ĭn′sīt′)

b. An instance of this practice. [Spanish *demarcación,* from *demarcar,* to mark out the boundary : *de-,* completely + *marcar,* to mark, from Italian *marcare,* from Old Italian, from Germanic.]

dé·marche (dā-märsh′) *n.* **1.** An initiative or maneuver; a step. **2.** A diplomatic representation or protest. **3.** A statement or protest addressed to public authorities. [French, from Old French *demarche,* gait, from *demarchier,* to march : *de-,* from + *marchier,* to march, probably of Germanic origin.]

de·ma·te·ri·al·ize (dē′mə-tîr′ē-ə-līz′) *v.* **-ized, -izing, -izes.** —*tr.* To divest of material qualities or characteristics. —*intr.* To lose material character or form; disappear. **—de·ma·te·ri·al·i·za·tion** *n.*

deme (dēm) *n.* **1.** Any of the townships of ancient Attica. **2.** *Ecology.* A local, usually stable population of organisms of the same kind or species. [Greek *dēmos,* common people, deme.]

de·mean¹ (dĭ-mēn′) *tr.v.* **-meaned, -meaning, -means.** To conduct or behave (oneself) in a particular manner.
~*n. Archaic.* Behavior; demeanor. [Middle English *demeinen,* from Old French *demener* : *de-,* completely + *mener,* to lead, conduct, from Latin *mināre,* to drive (herds), from *minārī,* to threaten, from *minae,* threats.]

demean² *tr.v.* **-meaned, -meaning, -means.** **1.** To debase in dignity or stature. **2.** To humble (oneself). —See Synonyms at **degrade.** [DE- (pejorative) + MEAN (base).]

de·mean·or (dĭ-mē′nər) *n.* Also *British* **de·mean·our.** The way in which a person behaves or conducts himself; deportment; manner. —See Synonyms at **bearing.**

de·ment (dĭ-mĕnt′) *tr.v.* **-mented, -menting, -ments.** To make demented. [Late Latin *dēmentāre,* from Latin *dēmēns* (stem *dēment-*), mad : *dē-* (undoing) + *mēns,* mind.]

de·ment·ed (dĭ-mĕn′tĭd) *adj.* **1.** Insane. **2.** Suffering from dementia. **3.** Crazed, as through grief or worry. **—de·ment·ed·ly** *adv.* **—de·ment·ed·ness** *n.*

dé·men·ti (dā′mŏN-tē′) *n., pl.* **démentis** (-tēz, -tē). *French.* An official denial, as of a rumor or news story. Used in diplomacy.

de·men·tia (dĭ-mĕn′shə, -shē-ə) *n.* Deterioration of mental faculties combined with emotional disturbances, resulting from organic brain disorder. See **presenile dementia.** —See Synonyms at **insanity.** [Latin *dēmentia,* madness, from *dēmēns,* mad. See **dement.**]

dementia prae·cox (prē′kŏks′) *n.* **Schizophrenia** *(see).* [New Latin, "premature dementia."]

dem·e·rar·a (dĕm′ə-râr′ə, -rä′rə) *n.* **1.** A type of brown crystallized cane sugar. **2.** A type of blended rum. [After *Demerara,* Guyana, the main source of the sugar.]

Dem·e·ra·ra (dĕm′ə-râr′ə). River in Guyana. It flows 290 kilometers (180 miles) north from the Guiana Highlands to the Atlantic Ocean at Georgetown.

de·mer·it (dĭ-mĕr′ĭt) *n.* **1. a.** A quality or characteristic that deserves blame or censure; a fault. **b.** Absence of merit. **2.** A mark made on one's record by a superior, implying some loss of status or privileges for bad conduct or failure. [Middle English *demerite,* offense, guilt, originally "merit," "desert," from Old French, probably from Latin *dēmerēre,* to deserve : *dē-* (intensive) + *merēre, merērī,* to deserve, MERIT.] **—de·mer·i·tor·i·ous** *adj.* **—de·mer·i·tor·i·ous·ly** *adv.*

de·mer·sal (dĭ-mûr′səl) *adj.* Designating animal life in deep water, as at the bottom of the sea or a lake. [Latin *dēmergere* (past participle *dēmersus*), to plunge: *dē-,* down + *mergere,* to dip.]

de·mesne (dĭ-mān′, -mēn′) *n.* **1.** *Law.* Possession and use of one's own land. **2.** Lands retained by a feudal lord for his own use. **3.** The grounds belonging to a mansion or country house. **4.** An extensive piece of landed property; an estate. **5.** Any district; a territory. **6.** A realm; a domain. [Middle English *demesne, demeine,* from Old French *demaine,* DOMAIN.]

De·me·ter (dĭ-mē′tər). *Greek Mythology.* The goddess of agriculture, fertility, and marriage, identified with the Roman goddess Ceres.

demi– *prefix.* Indicates: **1.** Half; for example, **demisemiquaver. 2.** Less than full status; for example, **demigod.** [French, from *demi,* half, from Medieval Latin *dīmedius,* from Latin *dīmidius,* half, divided in half : *dis-,* apart + *medius,* half.]

dem·i·god (dĕm′ē-gŏd′) *n.* **1. a.** A mythological semidivine being, such as the offspring of a god and a mortal. **b.** An inferior deity; a minor god. **2.** A man with godlike attributes.

dem·i·god·dess (dĕm′ē-gŏd′ĭs) *n.* A woman regarded as a demigod.

dem·i·john (dĕm′ē-jŏn′) *n.* A large, narrow-necked bottle made of glass or earthenware, often encased in wickerwork. [Probably a variant of French *dame-Jeanne,* "Lady Jane," assimilated to DEMI- + the name *John.*]

de·mil·i·ta·rize (dē-mĭl′ə-tə-rīz′) *tr.v.* **-rized, -rizing, -rizes. 1.** To eliminate the military character of. **2.** To prohibit military forces or installations in. **3.** To replace military control of with civilian control. **—de·mil·i·ta·ri·za·tion** *n.*

demilitarized zone *n. Abbr.* **DMZ** A region, defined by diplomatic or political agreement, wherein military forces and installations may not be established.

De Mille (də mĭl′), **Agnes George** (1905–). U.S. choreographer. Among the premier American choreographers of the 1940's and 1950's, she introduduced innovative dance to much of the American public with her choreography of several successful Broadway shows and movies, including *Oklahoma!* (1943) and *Carousel* (1945).

De Mille, Cecil Blount (1881–1959). U.S. film producer and director, known for spectacular epics. He popularized religious and Biblical stories through the cinema with *The Ten Commandments* (1923) and *Samson and Delilah* (1949). His other films include *The Plainsman* (1936), *Union Pacific* (1939), and *The Greatest Show on Earth,* (1952), which won an Academy Award.

dem·i·lune (dĕm′ē-lo͞on′) *n.* **1.** A crescent or half-moon. **2.** *Military.* A crescent-shaped outwork to defend the entrance of a fort. **3.** A crescent-shaped mass of protoplasm found in salivary glands. [French *demi-lune* : DEMI- + *lune,* moon, from Latin *lūna.*]

dem·i·mon·daine (dĕm′ē-mŏn-dān′) *n.* A woman belonging to the demimonde. Also called "demirep."

dem·i·monde (dĕm′ē-mŏnd, dĕm′ē-mŏnd′) *n.* **1.** The social class of those women kept by wealthy lovers or protectors, especially as it existed in the 19th century. **2.** Any group existing on the margin of success or respectability: *the literary demimonde.* Also called "demiworld." [French *demi-monde,* "half-world," coined (1855) by Alexandre Dumas fils to designate "the class of the déclassé."]

de·min·er·al·ize (dē-mĭn′ər-ə-līz′) *tr.v.* **-ized, -izing, -izes.** To remove salts from (a liquid). **—de·min·er·al·i·za·tion** *n.*

de·mi-pen·sion (də-mē′päN-syôN′) *n.* Accommodation in a hotel comprising bed, breakfast, and one main meal. Also *British* "half board." [French, "half-board."]

dem·i·pique (dĕm′ē-pēk′) *n.* A military saddle used during the 18th century, having a pommel about half the height of those on earlier saddles. [Earlier *demipeak* : DEMI- + PEAK.]

dem·i·re·lief (dĕm′ē-rĭ-lēf′) *n. Sculpture.* **Mezzo-relievo** *(see).*

dem·i·rep (dĕm′ē-rĕp′) *n.* A demimondaine.

de·mise (dĭ-mīz′) *n.* **1.** Death. **2.** An ending or failure. **3.** The transfer of an estate by lease or will. **4.** The transfer of a ruler's authority by death or abdication: *demise of the crown.*
~*v.* **demised, -mising, -mises.** —*tr.* **1.** To transfer (an estate) by will or lease. **2.** To transfer (sovereignty) by abdication or will. —*intr.* **1.** To be transferred by will or descent. **2.** To die. [Middle English *dimise, demise,* transfer of property, from Old French, from feminine past participle of *demettre,* DEMIT.] **—de·mis·a·ble** *adj.*

dem·i·sem·i·qua·ver (dĕm′ē-sĕm′ē-kwā′vər) *n. Chiefly British.* A **thirty-second note** *(see).* [DEMI- + SEMI- + QUAVER (eighth note).]

de·mis·sion (dĭ-mĭsh′ən) *n.* The relinquishment of an office or function. [Middle English *dimissioun,* from Latin *dīmissiō* (stem *dīmissiōn-*), dismissal, from *dīmittere* (past participle *dīmissus*), to send away, DEMIT.]

de·mist (dē′mĭst′) *v.* **-misted, -misting, -mists.** *Chiefly British.* —*tr.* To clear condensation from (a surface, especially a car windshield). —*intr.* To become clear of condensation.

de·mist·er (dē′mĭs′tər) *n. Chiefly British.* A heating device designed to clean condensation from a car windshield or similar surface.

de·mit (dĭ-mĭt′) *v.* **-mitted, -mitting, -mits.** —*tr.* **1.** To relinquish (an office or function). **2.** *Obsolete.* To dismiss. —*intr.* To resign. [Middle English *dimitten,* to release, deliver, Old French *demettre,* from Latin *dīmittere,* to dismiss, renounce, send away : *dis-,* away + *mittere,* to send.]

dem·i·tasse (dĕm′ē-tăs′, -täs′) *n.* **1.** A small coffee cup. **2.** The strong black coffee drunk from such a cup. [French : DEMI- + *tasse,* cup, from Old French, from Arabic *tašt,* basin, from Persian *tašt* †.]

dem·i·urge (dĕm′ē-ûrj′) *n.* **1.** *Often* **Demiurge.** The name used by Plato to designate the deity who fashions the material world. **2.** *Often* **Demiurge.** In Gnostic philosophy, the creator of the material world. **3.** A public magistrate in some ancient Greek states. [Late Latin *dēmiūrgus,* from Greek *dēmiourgos,* "public craftsman" : *dēmios,* public, from *dēmos,* people + *ergon,* work.] **—dem·i·ur·geous, dem·i·ur·gic, dem·i·ur·gi·cal** *adj.* **—dem·i·ur·gi·cal·ly** *adv.*

dem·i·vierge (dĕm′ē-vyĕrzh′) *n.* A woman who engages in sexual activities but who retains her physiological virginity. [French, "half virgin."]

dem·i·volt, dem·i·volte (dĕm′ē-vōlt′) *n. Dressage.* A half-turn performed by a horse on its hind legs.

dem·i·world (dĕm′ē-wûrld′) *n.* **Demimonde** *(see).*

dem·o (dĕm′ō) *n., pl.* **-os.** *Informal.* **1. a.** A demonstration, as of a product or service. **b.** A record or tape recording presented to an agent, concert promoter, or the like to advertise a song or group. **2.** A product, such as an automobile, used for a demonstration and often sold later at a discount.

de·mob (dē-mŏb′) *tr.v.* **-mobbed, -mobbing, -mobs.** *British Informal.* To demobilize.
~*n. British Informal.* Demobilization.

de·mo·bil·ize (dē-mō′bə-līz′) *v.* **-ized, -izing, -izes.** —*tr.* To discharge from military service or use; disband or dismiss (troops, for example). —*intr.* To be demobilized. **—de·mo·bil·i·za·tion** *n.*

de·moc·ra·cy (dĭ-mŏk′rə-sē) *n., pl.* **-cies. 1.** Government by the people, exercised either directly or through elected representatives. **2.** A political or social unit based upon this form of rule. **3.** A social condition of equality and respect for the individual within the community. **4.** The people considered as a source of political authority. [Old French *democratie,* from Late Latin *dēmocratia,* from Greek *dēmokratia* : *dēmos,* common people + -CRACY.]

dem·o·crat (dĕm′ə-krăt′) *n.* **1.** An advocate of democracy. **2. Democrat.** *Abbr.* **D, D., Dem.** A member or supporter of the Democratic Party. [French *démocrate,* back-formation from *democratie,* DEMOCRACY.]

dem·o·crat·ic (dĕm′ə-krăt′ĭk) *adj.* **1.** Of, characterized by, or advocating democracy. **2.** Pertaining to, encompassing, or promoting the interests of the people. **3.** In favor of or practicing social equality; not snobbish. **4. Democratic.** *Abbr.* **D, D., Dem.** Pertaining to or characteristic of the Democratic Party. **—dem·o·crat·i·cal·ly** *adv.*

Democratic Party *n.* One of the two major political parties in the

United States. It owes its origin to a split in the Democratic-Republican Party under Andrew Jackson in 1828.

Dem·o·crat·ic-Re·pub·li·can Party (dĕm′ə-krăt′ĭk-rĭ-pŭb′lĭ-kən) n. A U.S. political party opposed to the Federalist Party, founded by Thomas Jefferson in 1792 and dissolved in 1828.

de·moc·ra·tize (dĭ-mŏk′rə-tīz′) v. **-tized, -tizing, -tizes.** —tr. To make democratic. —intr. To become democratic. —**de·moc·ra·ti·za·tion** n.

De·moc·ri·tus (dĭ-mŏk′rə-təs) (c. 460–370 B.C.). Greek philosopher and scientist. He developed an atomist theory of the universe, holding that it was made up of minute particles, or atoms, multifariously arranged to account for the differing properties of matter.

dé·mo·dé (dā′mō-dā′) adj. French. Outmoded.

de·mod·u·late (dē-mŏd′jōō-lāt′) tr.v. **-lated, -lating, -lates.** Electronics. To extract (information) from a modulated carrier wave. —**de·mod·u·la·tion** n.

de·mod·u·la·tor (dē-mŏd′jōō-lā′tər) n. A device used in demodulating radio signals. Also called "detector."

dem·o·graph·ics (dĕm′ə-grăf′ĭks, dē′mə-) n. Used with a plural verb. Demographic data that is used especially to identify consumer markets.

de·mog·ra·phy (dĭ-mŏg′rə-fē) n. The study of the characteristics of human populations, such as size, growth, density, distribution, and vital statistics. [French démographie : Greek dēmos, people + -GRAPHY.] —**de·mog·ra·pher** n. —**dem·o·graph·ic** (dĕm′ə-grăf′ĭk), **dem·o·graph·i·cal** adj. —**dem·o·graph·i·cal·ly** adv.

dem·oi·selle (dĕm′wə-zĕl′) n. **1.** A young lady or damsel. **2.** A small Old World crane, Anthropoides virgo, having gray and black plumage, long black breast feathers, and white plumes at the sides of the head. Also called "demoiselle crane." **3.** Rare. A damselfly (see). **4.** A damselfish (see). [French, from Old French dameisele, DAMSEL.]

de·mol·ish (dĭ-mŏl′ĭsh) tr.v. **-ished, -ishing, -ishes. 1.** To tear down completely; wreck; level. **2.** To do away with completely; put an end to. **3.** To destroy or defeat utterly: demolish the prosecution's case. **4.** Informal. To eat up completely. —See Synonyms at ruin. [Old French demolir (present stem demoliss-), from Latin dēmōlīrī, to throw down, demolish : dē- (reversal) + mōlīrī, to endeavor, strive, build, from mōlēs, mass.]

dem·o·li·tion (dĕm′ə-lĭsh′ən) n. **1.** The act or process of wrecking or destroying; specifically, the destruction, as of a building, by explosives. **2.** Military. **a.** Destruction by explosives. **b. demolitions.** Explosives used to demolish. [Old French, from Latin dēmōlītiō (stem dēmōlītiōn-), from dēmōlīrī, DEMOLISH.] —**dem·o·li·tion·ist** n.

de·mon (dē′mən) n. Also **dae·mon, dai·mon** (dī′mŏn′) (for senses 3, 4). **1.** A devil or evil being; especially, in the New Testament, an unclean spirit that possesses and afflicts a person. **2.** A persistently tormenting person, force, or passion. **3.** Greek Mythology. An inferior divinity, such as a deified hero. **4.** An attendant spirit; a genius. **5.** One who is extremely zealous, skillful, or engrossed in a given activity. **6.** Australian Slang. A policeman or detective. [Middle English, from Late Latin daemōn, evil spirit, from Latin, spirit, from Greek daimōn, divine power, fate, god.]

demon. Grammar. demonstrative.

de·mon·e·tize (dī-mŏn′ə-tīz′, -mŭn′-) tr.v. **-tized, -tizing, -tizes. 1.** To divest (a coin, for example) of monetary value. **2.** To stop using (a metal) as a monetary standard. [French démonétiser : dé-, away from + monēta, coin, MONEY.] —**de·mon·e·ti·za·tion** n.

de·mo·ni·ac (dĭ-mō′nē-ăk′) adj. Also **de·mo·ni·a·cal** (dē′mə-nī′ə-kəl). **1.** Arising or seeming to arise from possession by a demon. **2.** Befitting or suggestive of a devil; fiendish; frenzied.
~n. One who is or seems to be possessed by a demon. [Middle English demoniak, from Late Latin daemoniācus, from Greek daimoniakos, from daimonios, of a spirit, from daimōn, DEMON.] —**de·mo·ni·a·cal·ly** adv.

de·mon·ic (dĭ-mŏn′ĭk) adj. **1.** Befitting a demon; fiendish. **2.** Motivated by a spiritual force or genius; inspired. **3.** Showing a frenetic enthusiasm.

de·mon·ism (dē′mə-nĭz′əm) n. **1.** Belief in demons. **2.** The worship of demons. **3.** Demonology. —**de·mon·ist** n.

de·mon·ize (dē′mə-nīz′) tr.v. **-ized, -izing, -izes. 1.** To turn into or as if into a demon. **2.** To possess. Used of a demon.

de·mon·ol·o·gy (dē′mə-nŏl′ə-jē) n. **1.** The study of demons. Also called "demonism." **2.** A treatise on demons or demon worship. —**de·mon·ol·o·gist** n.

de·mon·stra·ble (dĭ-mŏn′strə-bəl) adj. Capable of being shown or proved. —**de·mon·stra·bil·i·ty, de·mon·stra·ble·ness** n. —**de·mon·stra·bly** adv.

de·mon·strant (dĭ-mon′strənt) n. One who participates in a demonstration.

dem·on·strate (dĕm′ən-strāt′) v. **-strated, -strating, -strates.** —tr. **1.** To prove or make manifest by reasoning or adducing evidence. **2.** To describe or illustrate by experiment or practical application. **3.** To manifest or reveal. **4.** To display the advantages of (a product, for example) to a prospective buyer, as by operation or explanation. —intr. To protest or participate in a demonstration, especially a public rally for a particular cause. [Latin dēmonstrāre, to point out : dē-, completely + monstrāre, to show, from monstrum, divine portent, from monēre, to warn.]

dem·on·stra·tion (dĕm′ən-strā′shən) n. **1.** The act of making evident or proving. **2.** Conclusive evidence; proof. **3.** An illustration or explanation, as of a theory or product, by exemplification or practical application. **4.** A manifestation, as of one's feelings. **5.** A

public display of group opinion, as by a rally or march. **6.** A show of military strength.

de·mon·stra·tive (dĭ-mŏn′strə-tĭv) adj. **1.** Serving to manifest or prove. **2.** Involving or characterized by demonstration. **3.** Given to or marked by the open expression of emotion, especially affection. **4.** Abbr. **demon.** Grammar. Designating a word, such as these or then, that specifies or singles out the person, thing, or time referred to. Compare **interrogative, relative.**
~n. Abbr. **demon.** Grammar. A demonstrative pronoun or adjective. —**de·mon·stra·tive·ly** adv. —**de·mon·stra·tive·ness** n.

dem·on·stra·tor (dĕm′ən-strā′tər) n. **1.** One who demonstrates something. **2.** A vehicle, domestic appliance, or the like used to demonstrate a product to a potential customer. **3.** Chiefly British. A person who demonstrates experiments and other practical work to students in a laboratory. **4.** One who takes part in a public demonstration.

dem·o·pho·bi·a (dĕm′ə-fō′bē-ə) n. Abnormal fear of crowds. [Greek dēmos, people, DEMOS + -PHOBIA.] —**dem·o·pho·bic** adj.

de·mor·al·ize (dĭ-môr′əl-īz′, -mŏr′-) tr.v. **-ized, -izing, -izes. 1.** To debase the morals of; corrupt. **2.** To undermine the confidence or morale of; dishearten. **3.** To put into disorder. —**de·mor·al·i·za·tion** n. —**de·mor·al·iz·er** n.

de·mos (dē′mŏs) n. **1.** The people of an ancient Greek state, considered as a social class or as a political entity. **2.** The common people; the populace. [Greek dēmos, district, people.]

De·mos·the·nes (dĭ-mŏs′thə-nēz′) (c. 384–322 B.C.). Athenian orator and statesman. He is famous for the Philippics, a series of orations attacking the political ambitions of Philip of Macedon.

de·mote (dĭ-mōt′) tr.v. **-moted, -moting, -motes.** To lower in rank or grade. [DE- (reversal) + (PRO)MOTE.] —**de·mo·tion** n.

de·mot·ic (dĭ-mŏt′ĭk) adj. **1. a.** Of or pertaining to the common people; in common use; popular. Said especially of language. **b.** Of the masses; unsophisticated or unrefined: demotic tastes in food. **2.** Of, pertaining to, or written in the simplified form of ancient Egyptian hieratic writing. **3. Demotic.** Of or pertaining to **Dhimotiki** (see).
~n. **1.** Demotic language. **2. Demotic.** The popular form of modern Greek, **Dhimotiki** (see). [Greek dēmotikos, from dēmotēs, commoner, from dēmos, common people, DEMOS.] —**de·mot·ist** n.

de·mount (dē-mount′) tr.v. **-mounted, -mounting, -mounts.** To remove (a gun or motor, for example) from a position on a mounting or other support. —**de·mount·a·ble** adj.

Demp·sey (dĕmp′sē), **Jack,** born William Harrison Dempsey (1895–1983). U.S. heavyweight boxer; world champion (1919–26).

demp·ster. Variant of **deemster.**

de·mul·cent (dĭ-mŭl′sənt) adj. Soothing.
~n. A soothing, usually mucilaginous or oily substance, used especially to relieve pain in inflamed or irritated mucous surfaces. [Latin dēmulcēns (stem dēmulcent-), present participle of dēmulcēre, to stroke down, caress, soothe : dē-, down + mulcēre†, to stroke.]

de·mur (dĭ-mûr′) intr.v. **-murred, -murring, -murs. 1.** To take exception; raise objections; object. **2.** Law. To enter or interpose a demurrer. **3.** To delay. —See Synonyms at **object.**
~n. Also **de·mur·ral** (dĭ-mûr′əl). **1.** The act of demurring. **2.** An objection. **3.** A delay. [Middle English demeoren, demuren, to delay, from French demorer, demurer, from Latin dēmorārī : dē- (intensive) + morārī, to delay, from mora, delay.] —**de·mur·ra·ble** adj.

de·mure (dĭ-myōōr′) adj. **-murer, -murest. 1.** Sedate or self-possessed in manner or behavior; reserved. Said especially of women and children. **2.** Feigning modesty or shyness. —See Synonyms at **shy.** [Middle English, from Old French demore, quiet, sedate, "settled," past participle of demorer, to stay, delay, DEMUR.] —**de·mure·ly** adv. —**de·mure·ness** n.

de·mur·rage (dĭ-mûr′ĭj) n. **1.** The detention of a ship or other cargo conveyance during loading or unloading beyond the scheduled time of departure. **2.** The compensation paid for this detention.

de·mur·rer (dĭ-mûr′ər) n. **1.** A person who demurs; an objector. **2.** Law. A plea to dismiss a lawsuit on the grounds that although the opposition's statements may be true, they are insufficient to sustain the claim. Compare **plea. 3.** An objection.

de·my (dĭ-mī′) n., pl. **-mies.** Any of several standard sizes of paper, especially: **1.** In Britain, paper measuring 15½ by 20 inches or 17½ by 22½ inches. **2.** In the United States, paper measuring 16 by 21 inches. [From DEMI-.]

de·mys·ti·fy (dē-mĭs′tə-fī′) tr.v. **-fied, -fying, -fies.** To make less complex or less ambiguous; make less difficult to understand. —**de·mys·ti·fi·ca·tion** n.

de·my·thol·o·gize (dē′mĭ-thŏl′ə-jīz′) tr.v. **-gized, -gizing, -gizes. 1.** To remove the mythical elements from (a piece of writing) so that the essential meaning may be made clear. **2.** To reinterpret mythical elements in (a piece of writing), especially in a way held to be more rational. **3.** To do away with the spurious reverence surrounding (a figure or institution).

den (dĕn) n. **1.** The shelter or retreat of a wild animal; a lair. **2.** A cave considered as a refuge or hiding place. **3.** A residence or abode, especially if hidden or squalid: a den of thieves. **4.** A small secluded room for study or relaxation. **5.** A unit of about eight to ten Cub Scouts.
~intr.v. **denned, denning, dens.** To inhabit or hide in a den. [Middle English den(ne), Old English denn, from Germanic.]

Den. Denmark.

de·nar·i·us (dĭ-nâr′ē-əs) n., pl. **-narii** (-nâr′ē-ī′). **1.** An ancient Ro-

denarius A Roman denarius minted during the reign of the emperor Augustus (63 B.C.–A.D. 14). The silver coin kept its value and its silver content under Augustus. But later emperors debased the coinage until, by the third century A.D., the denarius was almost worthless.

man silver coin, originally equivalent to four sesterces, or ten bronze asses. **2.** An ancient Roman gold coin valued at 25 silver denarii. [Middle English, from Latin *dēnārius*, from adjective, "consisting of ten," from *dēnī*, by tens.]

den·a·ry (dĕn′ə-rē) *adj.* **1.** Tenfold. **2.** Divided or counted by tens; decimal. [Latin *dēnārius*. See **denarius.**]

de·na·tion·al·ize (dē-năsh′ən-ə-līz′) *tr.v.* **-ized, -izing, -izes. 1.** To return (a nationalized industry or service) to private ownership. **2.** To deprive of national rights, status, or characteristics. —**de·na·tion·al·i·za·tion** *n.*

de·nat·u·ral·ize (dē-năch′ər-ə-līz′) *tr.v.* **-ized, -izing, -izes. 1.** To make unnatural. **2.** To deprive of the rights of naturalization or citizenship. —**de·nat·u·ral·i·za·tion** *n.*

de·na·tur·ant (dē-nā′chər-ənt) *n.* An evil-tasting chemical substance or vivid coloring that is added to a product to make it unfit for human consumption. [DENATURE + -ANT.]

de·na·ture (dē-nā′chər) *tr.v.* **-tured, -turing, -tures.** Also **de·na·tur·ize** (-chər-īz′), **-ized, -izing, -izes. 1.** To change the nature or natural qualities of. **2.** To render unfit to eat or drink; especially, to add methanol to ethyl alcohol for this purpose. **3.** *Physics.* To add nonfissionable matter to (fissionable material) to prevent use in an atomic weapon. **4.** *Biochemistry.* To cause (a protein) to unfold by subjecting it to a change of temperature, acidity, or the like. —**de·na·tur·a·tion** *n.*

denatured alcohol *n.* Ethyl alcohol made unfit for drinking by the addition of a substance, such as methanol.

de·na·zi·fy (dē-năt′sə-fī′, -nät′-) *tr.v.* **-fied, -fying, -fies.** To make or declare free of Nazi influence. —**de·na·zi·fi·ca·tion** *n.*

Den·bigh (dĕn′bē). Formerly county town of Denbighshire, Wales, now in Clwyd. Its castle was built in 1282 for Edward I.

Den·bigh·shire (dĕn′bē-shîr, -shər). Former county in north Wales. In 1974 it was divided between Clwyd (to the east) and Gwynedd (to the west).

den·dri·form (dĕn′drə-fôrm′) *adj.* Having the characteristic form or structure of a tree. [DENDRI- + -FORM.]

den·drite (dĕn′drīt′) *n.* **1. a.** A mineral crystallization in a branching or treelike form. **b.** A rock or mineral bearing such a crystal formation. **2.** In a nerve cell, a fine branch of a dendron. [DENDR(O)- + -ITE.]

den·drit·ic (dĕn-drĭt′ĭk) *adj.* Also **den·drit·i·cal** (-ĭ-kəl). **1.** Of, pertaining to, or resembling a dendrite. **2.** Tree-shaped; dendriform. [DENDRIT(E) + -IC.] —**den·drit·i·cal·ly** *adv.*

dendro–, dendri–, dendr– *prefix.* Indicates tree; for example, **dendrology, dendriform, dendrite.** [New Latin, from Greek, from *dendron,* tree.]

den·dro·chro·nol·o·gy (dĕn′drō-krə-nŏl′ə-jē) *n.* The study of the growth rings in trees as an aid in determining and dating past events. —**den·dro·chron·o·log·i·cal** (dĕn′drō-krŏn′ə-lŏj′ĭ-kəl) *adj.*

den·dro·cli·ma·tol·o·gy (dĕn′drō-clī′mə-tŏl′ə-jē) *n.* The determination of past climates and climatic conditions from a study of tree rings.

den·droid (dĕn′droid′) *adj.* Also **den·droi·dal** (dĕn-droid′l). Shaped like a tree. [Greek *dendroeidēs* : DENDR(O)- + -OID.]

den·drol·o·gy (dĕn-drŏl′ə-jē) *n.* The botanical study of trees. [DENDRO- + -LOGY.] —**den·dro·log·ic** (dĕn′drə-lŏj′ĭk), **den·dro·log·i·cal** *adj.* —**den·drol·o·gist** *n.*

den·dron (dĕn′drən) *n.* A protoplasmic process of a nerve cell that conducts impulses toward the cell body. [Greek, tree.]

dene¹ (dēn) *n. British Regional.* A sandy tract of land or low hill near the sea. [Probably akin to low German *düne.* See **dune.**]

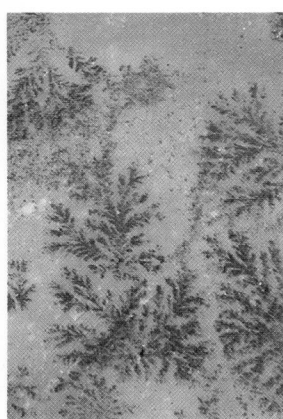
dendrite *These fernlike patterns are formed by impurities in minerals. Here, the dark impurity is manganese oxide; the surrounding stone is flint.*

dene². Variant of **dean** (valley).

De·neb (dĕn′ĕb) *n.* The brightest star in the constellation Cygnus, approximately 1,630 light years from Earth. [Arabic *dhanab,* tail.]

De·neb·o·la (dī-nĕb′ə-lə) *n.* The second-brightest star in the constellation Leo. [Arabic *dhanab al- (asad),* "tail of the (lion)."]

den·e·ga·tion (dĕn′ə-gā′shən) *n.* A denial. [Middle English *denegacioun,* from Old French *denegation,* from Latin *dēnegātiō* (stem *dēnegātiōn-*), from *dēnegātus,* past participle of *dēnegāre,* to DENY.]

dene hole *n. Archaeology.* A type of excavation found in chalk soils in Britain and France, consisting of a vertical shaft that widens out into several chambers. [Perhaps from DANE + HOLE.]

den·gue (dĕng′gē, dĕn′gā) *n.* An infectious, virulent, tropical and subtropical viral disease transmitted by mosquitoes and characterized by fever, rash, and severe pains in the joints. Also called "breakbone fever," "dandy." [Spanish, of African origin, akin to Swahili *kidinga.*]

Deng Xiao·ping or **Teng Hsiao-p'ing** (dŭng′ shou′pĭng′) (1904–). Vice premier of the state council of the People's Republic of China (1975–76, 1977–80), vice chairman of the Chinese Communist Party (1977–82), and chairman of the central military commission (1981–89). Dismissed during the Cultural Revolution as a "capitalist roader," he was rehabilitated in 1973 and became acting chairman in 1974. Disgraced again in 1976, he was rehabilitated a year later.

de·ni·a·ble (dī-nī′ə-bəl) *adj.* Capable of being denied; questionable. —**de·ni·a·bly** *adv.*

de·ni·al (dī-nī′əl) *n.* **1.** A negative reply, as to a request; a refusal to comply or satisfy. **2. a.** Refusal to grant the truth of a statement or allegation; contradiction. **b.** An assertion that a statement or allegation is untrue. **3.** A rejection, as of a doctrine or belief. **4.** A disowning or disavowal; repudiation. **5.** Abstinence; self-denial. [From DENY.]

de·nic·o·tin·ize (dē-nĭk′ə-tə-nīz′) *tr.v.* **-ized, -izing, -izes.** To remove nicotine from (tobacco, for example).

den·i·er¹ (də-nyâ′) *n.* **1.** (*also* dĕn′yər). A unit of fineness for rayon, nylon, and silk yarns, based on a standard of 50 milligrams per 450 meters of yarn. **2.** (*also* də-nîr′). A small coin of very low value current in France and western Europe from the 8th century until the French Revolution. [Middle English *denere,* a small coin, from Old French *denier,* from Latin *dēnārius,* DENARIUS.]

de·ni·er² (dī-nī′ər) *n.* One who denies.

den·i·grate (dĕn′ĭ-grāt′) *tr.v.* **-grated, -grating, -grates. 1. a.** To defame; calumniate. **b.** To belittle; undervalue. **2.** *Rare.* To blacken. [Latin *dēnigrāre* (past participle *dēnigrātus*), to blacken : *dē-,* completely + *nigrāre,* blacken, from *niger,* black.] —**den·i·gra·tion** *n.* —**den·i·gra·tor** *n.*

den·im (dĕn′əm) *n.* **1. a.** A coarse twilled cloth used for jeans, overalls, and work uniforms. **b. denims.** Garments, especially trousers, made of coarse denim. **2.** A finer grade of denim material used in draperies and upholstery. [French (*serge*) *de Nîmes,* serge of Nîmes.]

Den·is or **Den·ys** (dĕn′ĭs, də-nē′), **Saint** (died A.D. 270). Patron saint of France. He was sent to preach the Gospel to the Gauls and became the first bishop of Paris. He was martyred during the reign of Valerian.

de·ni·tri·fy (dē-nī′trə-fī′) *tr.v.* **-fied, -fying, -fies.** To remove nitrogen from (a material or chemical compound), as by bacterial action on soil. —**de·ni·tri·fi·ca·tion** *n.*

de·ni·tri·fy·ing bacteria (dē-nī′trə-fī′ĭng) *pl.n.* The soil bacteria that reduce nitrate to ammonia, including species of *Thiobacillus* and *Escherichia.*

den·i·zen (dĕn′ə-zən) *n.* **1.** An inhabitant; a resident. **2.** *British.* A foreigner permitted certain rights and privileges of citizenship. **3.** *Ecology.* An animal or plant naturalized in a region to which it is not indigenous.
~*tr.v.* **denizened, -zening, -zens.** *British.* To make a denizen of; naturalize. [Middle English *denisein,* from Old French *denzein,* from *deinz,* within, from Late Latin *deintus,* from within : Latin *dē-,* from + *intus,* within.] —**den·i·zen·a·tion** *n.*

Den·mark (dĕn′märk′). *Abbr.* **Den.** Danish **Dan·mark** (dän′märk′). A low-lying kingdom on the Jutland peninsula and islands, in northern Europe. It also has sovereignty over Greenland and the Faeroe Islands. In the 10th century Denmark was unified under the Viking king, Harold Bluetooth (died *c.* 985), who converted the people to Christianity. His expansionist policy was continued by his successors, who also brought England temporarily into the Danish fold (1013) under King Canute. Norway and Sweden came under the Danish crown in a union cemented at Kalmar in 1397. Sweden broke away (1523), and Denmark later lost Norway to Sweden (1814). It joined the European Economic Community in 1973. The country is intensively farmed and is noted for its beer, bacon, and butter. Its other exports include livestock, fish products, transport equipment, and fine ceramics and glassware. Area, 43,069 square kilometers (16,625 square miles). Population, 5,100,000. Capital, Copenhagen.

den mother *n.* A woman who supervises a den of Cub Scouts.

denom. denomination (religious sect).

de·nom·i·nal (dī-nŏm′ə-nəl) *adj.* Formed from a noun or adjective; denominative.

de·nom·i·nate (dī-nŏm′ə-nāt′) *tr.v.* **-nated, -nating, -nates.** To give a name to; designate. [Latin *dēnōmināre* : *dē-,* completely + *nōmināre,* to name, from *nōmen,* name.] —**de·nom·i·na·ble** (dī-nŏm′ə-nə-bəl) *adj.*

de·nom·i·nate number (dī-nŏm′ə-nĭt) *n.* A number that designates

DENMARK

Map shows: Skagerrak, Skagen, Frederikshavn, SWEDEN, Kattegat, Lim Fjord, Ålborg, Nykøbing, Randers, Viborg, JYLLAND (JUTLAND), Århus, DENMARK, Helsingør, Øresund, 56° N, Yding Skovhøj 173m, Horsens, COPENHAGEN, Esbjerg, Store Bælt, Odense, Sjælland (Zealand), Bornholm, Fyn (Funen), Rønne, den mother, Langeland, Lolland, Nyköbing, Møn, Falster, BALTIC SEA, Km 0 50 100 150, Miles 0 50, GERMANY, 12° E, 16° E

a quantity as a multiple of a unit. In the expression *12 feet, 12* is a denominate number.

de·nom·i·na·tion (dĭ-nŏm′ə-nā′shən) *n.* **1.** The act of naming. **2.** A name; a designation. **3.** The name of a class or group; a classification. **4.** A class of units having specific values, as in a system of currency or weights. **5.** *Abbr.* **denom.** A religious grouping with a common organization and name. —See Synonyms at **name.** —**de·nom·i·na·tion·al** *adj.* —**de·nom·i·na·tion·al·ly** *adv.*

de·nom·i·na·tion·al·ism (dĭ-nŏm′ə-nā′shən-ə-lĭz′əm) *n.* **1.** The tendency to separate into religious sects or denominations. **2.** Advocacy of such separation. **3.** Strict adherence to a denomination; sectarianism. —**de·nom·i·na·tion·al·ist** *n.*

de·nom·i·na·tive (dĭ-nŏm′ə-nā′tĭv, -nə-tĭv) *adj.* **1.** Giving or constituting a name; naming; appellative. **2.** *Grammar.* Formed from a noun or adjective.

~*n.* A word, especially a verb, that is derived from a noun or adjective, such as the verb *to bus* from the noun *bus.*

de·nom·i·na·tor (dĭ-nŏm′ə-nā′tər) *n.* The quantity below the line indicating division in a fraction; the quantity that divides the numerator; the divisor. Compare **numerator.**

de nos jours (də nō zhŏŏr′) *adj. French.* Of or pertaining to the present time; contemporary. [Literally, "of our days."]

de·no·ta·tion (dē′nō-tā′shən) *n.* **1.** The act of denoting; indication. **2.** A sign, symbol, or reference that denotes; an indicator. **3.** Something signified or referred to; a particular meaning of a symbol. **4.** The explicit meaning of a word, as opposed to its connotation.

de·no·ta·tive (dĭ-nō′tə-tĭv, dē′nō-tā′-) *adj.* **1.** Able to denote; designative. **2.** Explicit. —**de·no·ta·tive·ly** *adv.*

de·note (dĭ-nōt′) *tr.v.* **-noted, -noting, -notes. 1.** To reveal or indicate; mark. **2.** To serve as a symbol or name for; signify. **3.** To refer to specifically; mean explicitly. —See Synonyms at **mean** (convey sense). [French *dénoter,* from Latin *dēnotāre* : *dē-,* completely + *notāre,* mark, from *nota,* NOTE.] —**de·not·a·ble** *adj.* —**de·no·tive** *adj.*

Usage: Denote means "to mark" or "to signify directly." *Connote* means "to suggest or convey to the mind what is not explicit." Thus: *Frost denotes the coming of winter. For us winter connoted the beauty of frost on the windows and the coming of Christmas.* In speaking of words, *denote* is used to indicate the thing a word names, and *connote* to indicate our associations with that thing: *The word* bachelor *denotes an unmarried man and connotes a life of parties and carefree amusement.*

dé·noue·ment, de·noue·ment (dā-nōō-mäN′) *n.* **1.** The solution, clarification, or unraveling of the plot of a play or novel. **2.** Any outcome or final solution. [French, "an untying," from Old French *desnoue(u)r,* undo : *des-, de-,* reversing + *no(u)er,* to tie, from Latin *nōdāre,* from *nōdus,* knot.]

de·nounce (dĭ-nouns′) *tr.v.* **-nounced, -nouncing, -nounces. 1.** To condemn openly; censure, especially as evil. **2.** To accuse formally; inform against. **3.** To give formal announcement of the ending of (a treaty). —See Synonyms at **criticize.** [Middle English *denouncen,* from Old French *denoncier,* announce, from Latin *dēnūntiāre,* make an official announcement of : *dē-,* completely + *nūntiāre,* announce, from *nūntius,* messenger.] —**de·nounce·ment** *n.* —**de·nounc·er** *n.*

de nou·veau (də nōō-vō′) *adv. French.* Starting afresh; all over again; anew.

de no·vo (dē nō′vō, dā) *adv. Latin.* Afresh; anew.

dense (dĕns) *adj.* **denser, densest. 1. a.** Having relatively high density. **b.** Crowded closely together; compact. **2.** Thick; impenetrable. **3.** Thickheaded; dull. **4.** Comprehensible only through intellectual effort: *a dense argument.* **5.** *Photography.* Opaque, with good contrast between light and dark areas. Said of a developed negative. —See Synonyms at **stupid.** [Latin *dēnsus.*] —**dense·ly** *adv.* —**dense·ness** *n.*

den·sim·e·ter (dĕn-sĭm′ə-tər) *n.* An instrument used to determine density. [DENSE + -METER.] —**den·si·met·ric** (dĕn′sə-mĕt′rĭk) *adj.*

den·si·tom·e·ter (dĕn′sə-tŏm′ə-tər) *n.* An apparatus for measuring the optical density of a material, such as a photographic negative. [DENSITY + METER.]

den·si·ty (dĕn′sĭ-tē) *n., pl.* **-ties. 1. a.** The degree or a measure of the degree to which anything is filled or occupied. **b.** The condition or quality of being dense. **2.** *Physics.* **a.** The mass per unit volume of a substance under stipulated or standard conditions of pressure and temperature. **b.** The amount of something per unit measure, especially per unit length, area, or volume. See **charge density, current density, energy density. 3.** *Computer Science.* The number of units of useful information contained within a linear dimension. **4.** The number of inhabitants per unit geographical region. Also called "population density." **5.** The degree of optical opacity of a medium or material, as of a photographic negative. **6.** *Statistics.* **A probability density function** *(see).* Also called "density function." **7.** Thickness of consistency; impenetrability. **8.** Stupidity; dullness.

dent¹ (dĕnt) *n.* **1.** A depression in a surface made by pressure or a blow. **2.** A lessening or weakening effect: *a dent in his confidence.* ~*v.* **dented, denting, dents.** —*tr.* To make a dent in. —*intr.* To become dented. [Middle English *dent,* variant of *dint,* strike, blow, Old English *dynt,* from Germanic *dunti-* (unattested).]

dent² *n.* **1.** A toothlike protuberance, such as that on a gearwheel. **2.** The space between two wires on a loom through which a warp thread is drawn. [French, tooth.]

dent. dental; dentist; dentistry.

den·tal (dĕnt′l) *adj.* **1.** *Abbr.* **dent.** Of, pertaining to, or for the teeth.

2. *Abbr.* **dent.** Of, pertaining to, or for dentistry. **3.** *Phonetics.* Produced with the tip of the tongue near or against the upper front teeth.

~*n. Phonetics.* A dental consonant. [New Latin *dentalis,* from Latin *dēns* (stem *dent-*), tooth.]

dental appliance *n. Dentistry.* A **brace** *(see).*

dental caries *n.* Tooth decay.

dental floss *n.* A strong, usually waxed thread used to clean areas between the teeth. Also called "floss."

dental hygiene *n.* The maintenance of healthy teeth and gums, especially by regular brushing. Also called "oral hygiene."

dental hygienist *n.* A person trained in dental hygiene, who cleans and scales the teeth of dental patients and gives advice on general care. Also called "hygienist."

den·ta·li·um (dĕn-tā′lē-əm) *n., pl.* **-lia** (lē-ə) or **-liums.** Any tooth shell of the genus *Dentalium.* [New Latin, from Late Latin *dentālis,* of a tooth, DENTAL.]

dental plaque *n.* A film containing bacteria and other substances that forms on the surface of a tooth. Also called "plaque."

dental plate *n.* **1.** A plate fixed to the palate with a fitting used to correct the position of the teeth. **2.** A denture *(see).*

dental surgeon *n.* A dentist *(see).*

dental technician *n.* A person who repairs dentures and makes plaster casts of teeth.

den·tate (dĕn′tāt′) *adj.* Edged with toothlike projections; toothed. [Latin *dentātus,* from *dēns* (stem *dent-*), tooth.] —**den·tate·ly** *adv.*

den·ta·tion (dĕn-tā′shən) *n.* **1.** The condition of being dentate. **2.** A toothlike part or projection.

dent corn *n.* A tall-growing variety of corn, *Zea mays indentata,* having yellow or white kernels that are indented at the tip. Also *chiefly British* "dent maize."

denti-, dent- *prefix.* Indicates tooth; for example, **dentiform, dentoid.** [Latin *dēns* (stem *dent-*), tooth.]

den·ti·cle (dĕn′tĭ-kəl) *n.* A small tooth or toothlike projection. [Middle English, from Latin *denticulus,* diminutive of *dēns* (stem *dent-*), tooth.]

den·tic·u·late (dĕn-tĭk′yə-lāt′) *adj.* Also **den·tic·u·lat·ed** (-lā′tĭd). **1.** Finely toothed; minutely dentate. **2.** *Architecture.* Having dentils. [Latin *denticulātus,* from *denticulus,* DENTICLE.] —**den·tic·u·late·ly** *adv.* —**den·tic·u·la·tion** *n.*

den·ti·form (dĕn′tə-fôrm′) *adj.* Shaped like a tooth. [DENTI- + -FORM.]

den·ti·frice (dĕn′tə-frĭs) *n.* A substance, such as a powder or paste, for cleaning the teeth; toothpaste or tooth powder. [French, from Latin *dentifricium* : DENTI- + *fricāre,* to rub.]

den·til (dĕn′tĭl) *n. Architecture.* Any of a series of small rectangular blocks forming a molding or projecting beneath a cornice. [Obsolete French *dentille,* from Old French, diminutive of *dent,* tooth, from Latin *dēns* (stem *dent-*), tooth.]

den·ti·la·bi·al (dĕn′tĭ-lā′bē-əl) *adj. Phonetics.* Labiodental. —**den·ti·la·bi·al** *n.*

den·ti·lin·gual (dĕn′tĭ-lĭng′gwəl) *adj. Phonetics.* Interdental. —**den·ti·lin·gual** *n.*

den·tine (dĕn′tēn′) *n.* Also **den·tin** (-tĭn). The calcareous part of a tooth, beneath the enamel, containing the pulp chamber and root canals. [DENT(I)- + -INE.] —**den·ti·nal** *adj.*

den·tist (dĕn′tĭst) *n. Abbr.* **dent.** A person whose profession is dentistry. [French *dentiste,* from *dent,* tooth.]

den·tist·ry (dĕn′tĭ-strē) *n. Abbr.* **dent.** The diagnosis, prevention, and treatment of diseases of the teeth and related structures, including the repair or replacement of defective teeth.

den·ti·tion (dĕn-tĭsh′ən) *n.* **1.** *Biology.* The type, number, and arrangement of teeth, especially in humans and other animals. **2.** The process of cutting new teeth; a teething. [Latin *dentītiō* (stem *dentītiōn-*), from *dentītus,* past participle of *dentīre,* to teethe, from *dēns* (stem *dent-*), tooth.]

dent maize *n. Chiefly British.* Dent corn *(see).*

den·toid (dĕn′toid′) *adj.* Toothlike. [DENT(I)- + -OID.]

den·tu·lous (dĕn′chə-ləs) *adj.* Possessing teeth; toothed.

den·ture (dĕn′chər) *n.* **1.** A set of artificial teeth for a single jaw or part of it. Also called **dental plate.** **2. dentures.** A set of removable artificial teeth for both jaws. [French, from Old French, from *dent,* tooth.]

de·nu·cle·ar·ize (dē-nōō′klē-ə-rīz′, -nyōō′-) *tr.v.* **-ized, izing, -izes.** To remove nuclear installations from (a country or area).

de·nu·da·tion (dē′nōō-dā′shən, -nyōō-) *n.* **1.** *Geology.* The combined processes of erosion, weathering, and transporting away of the material removed. Also called "degradation." **2.** The act or process of denuding.

de·nude (dĭ-nōōd′, -nyōōd′) *tr.v.* **-nuded, -nuding, -nudes. 1. a.** To strip of covering; make bare. **b.** To divest; deprive completely. **2.** To cause to undergo denudation. —See Synonyms at **strip.** [Latin *dēnūdāre* : *dē-,* thoroughly + *nūdāre,* to make bare, from *nūdus,* NUDE.]

de·nu·mer·a·ble (dĭ-nōō′mər-ə-bəl, dĭ-nyōō′-) *adj.* Capable of being put into one-to-one correspondence with the positive integers; countable. —**de·nu·mer·a·bly** *adv.*

de·nun·ci·ate (dĭ-nŭn′sē-āt′, -shē-āt′) *tr.v.* **-ated, -ating, -ates.** *Rare.* To denounce. [Latin *dēnūntiāre,* to DENOUNCE.]

de·nun·ci·a·tion (dĭ-nŭn′sē-ā′shən, -shē-ā′shən) *n.* **1.** The act or an instance of denouncing; open condemnation or censure. **2.** The act of accusing another of a crime before a public prosecutor. **3.** A formal declaration of the termination of a treaty.

Den·ver (dĕn′vər). Capital of Colorado, in the north-central part of the state. It lies where the Rocky Mts. meet the Great Plains, a natural stopping point for early 19th-century settlers. The population boomed in 1859 during a gold rush. It is a railroad junction and industrial, tourist, and marketing center.

de·ny (dĭ-nī′) *tr.v.* **-nied, -nying, -nies. 1.** To declare untrue; assert the contrary of; contradict. **2.** To refuse to believe; reject. **3.** To refuse to recognize or acknowledge; disavow; disown. **4.** To refuse to grant; withhold. **—deny oneself.** To abstain from indulging oneself in. [Middle English *denien,* from Old French *denier,* from Latin *dēnegāre* : *dē-,* completely + *negāre,* to say no.]
Synonyms: contradict, gainsay, refute.

Denys. See **St. Denis.**

deoch an dor·is (dŏKH′ ən dŏr′ĭs) *n. Scottish & Irish.* A drink, usually of whisky, which is taken before departure. [Gaelic *deoch an doruis,* drink at the door.]

de·o·dand (dē′ə-dănd′) *n.* Formerly in English law, an object that caused the death of a person, either accidentally or intentionally, and that was then confiscated by the Crown to be used for charitable purposes. [Norman French *deodande,* from Latin *Deō dandum,* something to be given to God : *Deus,* God + *dare,* to give.]

deodar *In its home in the Himalayan foothills, this species of cedar is known as the Tree of God. Indians regard it as a symbol of fruitfulness and durability. Commercially, its timber is used to make railroad ties and bridges.*

de·o·dar (dē′ə-där′) *n.* A tall cedar, *Cedrus deodara,* native to the Himalayas, having drooping branches and wood valued as timber. [Hindi *dē′ odār,* from Sanskrit *devadāru* : *devás,* divine + *dāru,* tree.]

de·o·dor·ant (dē-ō′dər-ənt) *n.* **1.** A substance applied to counteract body odors. **2.** A chemical exposed to or sprayed into the air to counteract staleness. [DE- (removal) + Latin *odor,* odor + -ANT.] **—de·o·dor·ant** *adj.*

de·o·dor·ize (dē-ō′də-rīz′) *tr.v.* **-ized, -izing, -izes.** To disguise or absorb the odor of. **—de·o·dor·i·za·tion** *n.* **—de·o·dor·iz·er** *n.*

De·o gra·ti·as (dē′ō grā′shē-ăs, dā′ō grät′ē-äs′). *Latin.* Thanks be to God.

de·on·tic (dē-ŏn′tĭk) *adj.* **1.** *Logic & Philosophy.* Of or pertaining to such ethical concepts as obligation or commitment. **2.** *Linguistics.* Of or pertaining to the representation in language of obligation and permission, especially through various uses of the modal auxiliaries, for example, *must* and *may.* [Greek *deont-,* participial stem of *dei* (impersonal), it behooves, it is right.]

de·on·tol·o·gy (dē′ŏn-tŏl′ə-jē) *n. Philosophy.* The theory or study of moral obligation or commitment. [Greek *deon* (stem *deont-*), that which is binding or needful (influenced in meaning by *dein,* to bind), from *dei,* it is right + -LOGY.] **—de·on·to·log·i·cal** (dē-ŏn′tə lŏj′ĭ-kəl) *adj.* **—de·on·tol·o·gist** *n.*

De·o vo·len·te (dē′ō vō-lĕn′tē, dā′ō vō-lĕn′tā) *adv. Abbr.* **D.V.** *Latin.* God willing.

de·ox·i·dize (dē-ŏk′sə-dīz′) *tr.v.* **-dized, -dizing, -dizes.** To remove oxygen, especially chemically combined oxygen, from. **—de·ox·i·di·za·tion** *n.* **—de·ox·i·diz·er** *n.*

deoxy-, desoxy- *prefix.* Indicates that a molecule contains less oxygen than another to which it is related; for example, **deoxyribonucleic acid.**

de·ox·y·cor·ti·co·ster·one (dē-ŏk′sē-kôr′tĭ-kŏs′tə-rōn′) *n.* A steroid hormone, $C_{21}H_{30}O_3$, derived from the adrenal cortex, that regulates water and salt balance and is used to treat adrenal insufficiency.

de·ox·y·gen·ate (dē-ŏk′sə-jə-nāt′) *tr.v.* **-ated, -ating, -ates.** To remove oxygen from. **—de·ox·y·gen·a·tion** *n.*

de·ox·y·ri·bo·nu·cle·ic acid (dē-ŏk′sē-rī-bō-no͞o-klē′ĭk, -nyo͞o-) *n.* Also **des·ox·y·ri·bo·nu·cle·ic acid** (dĕs-). **DNA** *(see).*

de·ox·y·ri·bo·nu·cle·o·tide (dē-ŏk′sē-rī′bō-no͞o′klē-ə-tīd′, -nyo͞o′-) *n.* A nucleotide that contains deoxyribose and is a constituent of DNA. [DEOXYRIBO(SE) + NUCLEOTIDE.]

de·ox·y·ri·bose (dē-ŏk′sē-rī′bōs) *n.* Also **des·ox·y·ri·bose** (dĕs-). A sugar, $C_5H_{10}O_4$, that is a constituent of DNA.

dep. 1. depart; departure. **2.** department. **3.** deponent. **4.** deposit. **5.** depot. **6.** deputy.

Dep. dependency (territorial).

de·part (dĭ-pärt′) *v.* **-parted, -parting, -parts.** *—intr.* **1.** *Abbr.* **dep.** To go away; set forth; leave. **2.** To diverge, as from an established course; deviate: *depart from custom.* *—tr.* To leave. Used especially in the phrase *depart this life.* [Middle English *departen,* divide, from Old French *departir* : *de-,* away + *partir,* to go, divide, from Latin *partīre,* from *pars* (stem *part-*), PART.]

de·part·ed (dĭ-pär′tĭd) *adj.* **1.** Bygone; past. **2.** Dead. **—**See Usage note at **dead.**

de·part·ment (dĭ-pärt′mənt) *n. Abbr.* **D., dep., dept., dpt. 1.** A distinct division of a large organization, such as a company or shop, having a specialized function and personnel and often housed separately. **2.** *Usually* **Department.** Any of the principal administrative divisions of the government: *the Department of Energy.* **3.** An administrative district in the government of France. **4.** A division of a school, college, or university dealing with a particular field of study. **5.** *Informal.* An area of special knowledge or activity; sphere. [French *département,* from Old French, departure, from *departir,* divide, DEPART.]

de·part·men·tal (dē′pärt-mĕn′təl) *adj.* Pertaining to a department or departments. **—de·part·men·tal·ism** *n.* **—de·part·men·tal·ly** *adv.*

de·part·men·tal·ize (dē′pärt-mĕn′tə-līz′) *tr.v.* **-ized, -izing, -izes.** To organize into departments. **—de·part·men·tal·i·za·tion** *n.*

department store *n.* A large retail establishment offering a wide variety of merchandise and services, and organized into departments according to the kinds of goods sold.

de·par·ture (dĭ-pär′chər) *n. Abbr.* **dep. 1.** The act of leaving; a going away. **2.** A starting out, as on a trip or a new course of action. **3.** A deviation or divergence, as from an established rule, plan, or procedure. **4.** *Nautical.* **a.** The distance sailed due east or west by a ship on its course. **b.** A ship's bearing at the start of a voyage, used as a basis for dead reckoning.

de·pas·ture (dē-păs′chər, -päs′-) *v.* **-tured, -turing, -tures.** *Chiefly British.* *—tr.* **1.** To put out (cattle, for example) to graze. **2.** To empty or denude (a field, for example) by grazing. *—intr.* To graze in a pasture.

de·pend (dĭ-pĕnd′) *intr.v.* **-pended, -pending, -pends. 1.** To rely, as for support or aid. Used with *on* or *upon.* **2.** To be assured; place trust. Used with *on* or *upon.* **3.** To be determined, conditioned, or dependent. Usually used with *on* or *upon*: *It depends upon your taste.* **4.** To hang down. Used with *from.* **5.** *Informal.* To be pending or undecided. **—**See Synonyms at **rely.** [Middle English *dependen,* from Old French *dependre,* to hang down, from Latin *dēpendēre* : *dē-,* down + *pendēre,* to hang.]
Usage: Depend, indicating condition or contingency, is always followed by *on* or *upon: It depends (up)on who is in charge.* Omission of the preposition is typical of casual speech.

de·pend·a·ble (dĭ-pĕn′də-bəl) *adj.* Capable of being depended upon; trustworthy. **—**See Synonyms at **faithful. —de·pend·a·bil·i·ty, de·pend·a·ble·ness** *n.* **—de·pend·a·bly** *adv.*

de·pend·ence, de·pend·ance (dĭ-pĕn′dəns) *n.* **1.** The state or fact of being dependent; especially, subjection to, control by, or reliance upon someone or something else: *drug dependence.* **2.** Trust; reliance. **—**See Synonyms at **trust.**

de·pend·en·cy, de·pend·an·cy (dĭ-pĕn′dən-sē) *n., pl.* **-cies. 1.** Dependence. **2.** Anything dependent or subordinate. **3.** *Abbr.* **Dep.** A territory under the jurisdiction of another country from which it is separated geographically.

de·pend·ent, de·pend·ant (dĭ-pĕn′dənt) *adj.* **1.** Contingent upon something or someone else. **2.** Subordinate. **3.** Unable to exist or function satisfactorily without the aid or use of someone or something. **4.** Hanging down.
~n. One who relies on another for support, especially for financial support. **—de·pend·ent·ly** *adv.*

dependent clause *n. Grammar.* A clause that cannot stand alone as a full sentence and that functions as a noun, adjective, or adverb within a sentence. Also called "subordinate clause."

dependent variable *n. Mathematics.* A variable restricted to one or more of a set of values for every value assumed by an independent variable.

de·per·son·al·ize (dē-pûr′sə-nə-līz′) *tr.v.* **-ized, -izing, -izes. 1.** To deprive of personal or individual character. **2.** To render impersonal. **—de·per·son·al·i·za·tion** *n.*

de·phleg·ma·tor (dē-flĕg′mā′tər) *n.* A device used in distillation to condense the higher boiling constituents of a mixed vapor. [DE- + PHLEGM + -ATOR.]

de·pict (dĭ-pĭkt′) *tr.v.* **-picted, -picting, -picts. 1.** To represent in a picture or sculpture. **2.** To represent in words; describe. [Latin *dēpingere* (past participle *dēpictus*) : *dē-,* completely + *pingere,* to picture.] **—de·pic·tion** *n.*

dep·i·late (dĕp′ə-lāt′) *tr.v.* **-lated, -lating, -lates.** To remove hair from (the body). [Latin *dēpilāre* (past participle *dēpilātus*) : *dē-,* completely + *pilāre,* to deprive of hair, from *pilus,* hair.] **—dep·i·la·tion** *n.* **—dep·i·la·tor** *n.*

de·pil·a·to·ry (dĭ-pĭl′ə-tôr′ē, -tōr′ē) *adj.* Capable of removing hair.
~n., pl. **depilatories.** A liquid or cream used to remove unwanted hair from the body.

de·plane (dē-plān′) *intr.v.* **-planed, -planing, -planes.** To disembark from an airplane.

de·plete (dĭ-plēt′) *tr.v.* **-pleted, -pleting, -pletes. 1.** To reduce or lessen in quantity, value, or effectiveness; exhaust. **2.** To empty. [Latin *dēplēre* (past participle *dēplētus*), to empty : *de-* (reversal) + *plēre,* to fill.] **—de·plet·a·ble** *adj.* **—de·ple·tion** *n.*
Usage: deplete, drain, enervate, exhaust, impoverish. These verbs all signify depletion of strength or resources to the point of functional impairment. *Deplete* refers to using up gradually, and only hints at harmful consequences. *Drain* suggests reduction by gradually drawing off, and is stronger in implying harm. *Enervate* refers to weakening of vitality or moral strength. *Exhaust* stresses reduction to a point of no further usefulness in a given activity. *Impoverish* refers to severe reduction of resources or qualities essential to adequate functioning.

de·plor·a·ble (dĭ-plôr′ə-bəl, -plōr′-) *adj.* **1.** Worthy of severe reproach. **2.** Lamentable; grievous. **3.** Wretched; bad. **—de·plor·a·ble·ness, de·plor·a·bil·i·ty** *n.* **—de·plor·a·bly** *adv.*

de·plore (dĭ-plôr′, -plōr′) *tr.v.* **-plored, -ploring, -plores. 1.** To feel or express deep sorrow over; lament. **2.** To feel or express strong disapproval of; censure. [French *déplorer,* from Latin *dēplōrāre* : *dē-,* completely + *plōrāre*†, to wail.]

de·ploy (dĭ-ploi′) *v.* **-ployed, -ploying, -ploys.** *—tr.* **1.** To station (persons or forces) systematically over an area. **2.** *Military.* **a.** To spread out (troops) to form an extended front. **b.** To bring (forces or weapons) into action. **3.** To use or arrange for a particular effect. *—intr.* To be or become deployed. [French *déployer,* from Latin *displicāre,* to scatter : *dis-* (reversal) + *plicāre,* to fold.] **—de·ploy·ment** *n.*

de·plume (dē-plo͞om′) *tr.v.* **-plumed, -pluming, -plumes. 1.** To pluck the feathers from. **2.** To deprive of honor or pride. [Middle English *deplumen,* from Old French *deplumer,* from Medieval Latin *deplumāre* : Latin *de-,* removal + *plūma,* feather.] **—de·plu·ma·tion** *n.*

de·po·lar·i·za·tion (dē-pō′lə-rə-zā′shən) *n.* **1.** An instance or the

PRONUNCIATION KEY

ă, pat; ā, pay; âr, care; ä, father, are; b, bib; ch, church; d, deed; ĕ, pet; ē, be; f, fife; g, gag; h, hat; hw, which; ĭ, pit; ī, pie; îr, pier; j, judge; k, kick; l, lid, needle; m, mum; n, no, sudden; ng, thing; ŏ, pot; ō, toe; ô, paw, for; oi, noise; ou, out; o͝o, book; o͞o, boot; p, pop; r, roar; s, sauce; sh, ship, dish; t, tight; th, thin, path; *th,* this, bathe; ŭ, cut; ûr, fur; v, valve; w, with; y, yes; z, zebra, size; zh, vision; ə, about, item, edible, gallop, circus, peaceful

IN FOREIGN WORDS:

à, *Fr.* ami; œ, *Fr.* feu, *Ger.* schön; ü, *Fr.* tu, *Ger.* über; KH, *Ger.* ich, *Scot.* loch; N, *Fr.* bon; y′, *Fr.* Compiègne

STRESS MARKS:

Primary stress: ′ **in·cite′** (ĭn-sīt′)
Secondary stress: ′ **in′sight′** (ĭn′sīt′)

process of depolarizing. **2.** The sudden diffusion of ions across the membrane of a nerve cell that accompanies the passage of a nerve impulse and produces an action potential.

de·po·lar·ize (dē-pō′lə-rīz′) *tr.v.* **-ized, -izing, -izes.** To eliminate or counteract the polarization of.

de·pone (dĭ-pōn′) *v.* **-poned, -poning, -pones.** *Archaic.* —*tr.* To testify or declare under oath. —*intr.* To give testimony. [Medieval Latin *dēpōnere,* from Latin, to put down : *dē-,* down + *pōnere,* put.]

de·po·nent (dĭ-pō′nənt) *adj. Abbr.* **dep., dpt.** *Grammar.* Designating a verb of active meaning but passive form, such as certain Latin and Greek verbs.
∼*n. Abbr.* **dep., dpt. 1.** *Grammar.* A deponent verb. **2.** *Law.* A person who testifies under oath, especially in writing. [Late Latin *dēpōnēns* (stem *dēpōnent-*), "laying aside" (in grammar, referring to the idea that the verb has "laid aside" its active form, from Latin, present participle of *dēpōnere,* to put down, lay aside. See **depone.**]

de·pop·u·late (dē-pŏp′yə-lāt′) *v.* **-lated, -lating, -lates.** —*tr.* To reduce the population of. —*intr.* To be reduced in population. [Latin *dēpopulāre,* ravage : *dē-,* completely + *populāre,* to ravage, from *populus,* people.] —**de·pop·u·la·tion** *n.* —**de·pop·u·la·tor** *n.*

de·port (dĭ-pôrt′, -pōrt′) *tr.v.* **-ported, -porting, -ports. 1.** To expel from a country. **2.** To behave or conduct (oneself). —See Synonyms at **banish.** [(Sense 1, from French *déporter*), Old French *deporter,* behave, from Latin *dēportāre,* to carry off, carry away : *dē-,* away, off + *portāre,* to carry.]

de·por·ta·tion (dē′pôr-tā′shən, -pōr-) *n.* Banishment from a country; especially, the expulsion of an undesirable alien.

de·por·tee (dē′pôr-tē′, -pōr-) *n.* A deported person.

de·port·ment (dĭ-pôrt′mənt, -pōrt′-) *n.* **1.** Conduct; demeanor. —See Synonyms at **bearing. 2.** Posture; carriage.

de·pos·al (dĭ-pō′zəl) *n.* The act of deposing from office.

de·pose (dĭ-pōz′) *v.* **-posed, -posing, -poses.** —*tr.* **1.** To remove from office or a position of power. **2.** *Law.* To declare under oath, especially in writing. —*intr. Law.* To testify, especially in writing. [Middle English *deposen,* from Old French *deposer* : *de-,* away + *poser,* to put, POSE.] —**de·pos·a·ble** *adj.*

de·pos·it (dĭ-pŏz′ĭt) *v.* **-ited, -iting, -its.** —*tr.* **1.** To place carefully or safely in the proper repository. **2.** To lay down or cause to settle, especially in a layer or layers, by a natural process. **3.** To give (money) as partial payment or security. **4.** To entrust (money) to a bank or other institution. —*intr.* To become deposited; precipitate; settle.
∼*n. Abbr.* **dep. 1.** Something entrusted for safekeeping, such as a sum of money in a bank. **2.** The condition of being entrusted for safekeeping. Used chiefly in the phrase *on deposit.* **3.** A partial or initial payment of a cost or debt. **4.** A sum of money given as security for an item acquired for temporary use. **5.** A depository. **6.** Something deposited, especially by a natural process, as: **a.** *Geology.* Material that results from the process of deposition. **b.** *Physiology.* A sediment in a bodily fluid or a localized bodily accretion, as of calcium. **c.** A sediment or precipitate that has settled out of a solution. **7.** A coating or layer formed on a metal surface by electrolysis or by some other process, such as hot dipping. [Latin *dēpōnere* (past participle *dēpositus*), to put aside : *dē-,* aside + *pōnere,* put.] —**de·pos·i·tor** *n.*

deposit account *n. Chiefly British.* A bank account in which the money deposited earns interest and notice of withdrawal is sometimes required.

de·pos·i·tar·y (dĭ-pŏz′ə-tĕr′ē) *n., pl.* **-ies. 1.** A person or group entrusted with the preservation or safekeeping of something. **2.** A repository; a depository.

dep·o·si·tion (dĕp′ə-zĭsh′ən) *n.* **1.** The act of deposing, as from high office. **2.** The act of depositing. **3.** Something deposited; a deposit. **4.** *Law.* Testimony under oath; especially, a written statement by a witness for use in court in his absence. **5.** *Geology.* The laying down of material by natural processes, such as matter transported by wind or water or that resulting from the decay of living matter or organisms. **6. Deposition. a.** The taking down of Christ from the cross. **b.** A work of art depicting this scene.

de·pos·i·to·ry (dĭ-pŏz′ə-tôr′ē, -tōr′ē) *n., pl.* **-ries. 1.** A place where something is deposited for safekeeping; a repository. **2.** A trustee; a depositary.

de·pot (dē′pō, dĕp′ō) *n. Abbr.* **dep. 1.** A railroad or bus station. **2.** A warehouse or storehouse. **3.** *Military.* **a.** A centrally located installation for the storage, repair, or distribution of military equipment and materials. **b.** A station for receiving, classifying, and assembling personnel. [French *dépôt,* from Old French *depost,* from Latin *dēpositum,* deposit, from the neuter past participle of *dēpōnere,* to DEPOSIT.]

de·prave (dĭ-prāv′) *tr.v.* **-praved, -praving, -praves.** To deprive of rectitude; debase morally; corrupt. [Middle English *depraven,* from Old French *depraver,* to pervert, from Latin *dēprāvāre* : *dē-,* completely + *prāvus*†, distorted, crooked.] —**dep·ra·va·tion** (dĕp′rə-vā′shən) *n.* —**de·prav·er** *n.*

de·praved (dĭ-prāvd′) *adj.* Morally corrupt; debased; perverted. —**de·prav·ed·ly** (dĭ-prā′vĭd-lē) *adv.*

de·prav·i·ty (dĭ-prăv′ə-tē) *n., pl.* **-ties. 1. a.** Moral corruption. **b.** *Theology.* The innate corruption of human nature due to original sin. **2.** A wicked or perverse act.

dep·re·cate (dĕp′rə-kāt′) *tr.v.* **-cated, -cating, -cates. 1.** To express disapproval of; protest or plead against. **2.** To depreciate; belittle. —See Usage note below. [Latin *dēprecārī,* to ward off by prayer : *dē-,* away + *precārī,* pray.] —**dep·re·ca·tion** *n.* —**dep·re·ca·tor** *n.*

Usage: Similarity in form and meaning between *deprecate* and *depreciate* has led to a semantic development that is already well established. *Deprecate* means "express disapproval of": *He deprecated the use of force. Depreciate* means "belittle" or "mildly disparage": *depreciated my achievements.* However, examples such as *He deprecated my achievements* and associated forms such as *deprecation, self-deprecatory* are increasingly found and accepted.

dep·re·ca·to·ry (dĭp′rə-kə-tôr′ē, -tōr′ē) *adj.* Also **dep·re·ca·tive** (-kā′tĭv). **1.** Expressing deprecation; disapproving. **2.** Expressing apology, or regret; apologetic.

de·pre·ci·a·ble (dĭ-prē′shē-ə-bəl) *adj.* Liable to depreciation in value.

de·pre·ci·ate (dĭ-prē′shē-āt′) *v.* **-ated, -ating, -ates.** —*tr.* **1.** To lessen the price or value of. **2.** To make to seem less in value or importance; belittle. —*intr.* To diminish in value or price. —See Synonyms at **decry** and Usage note at **deprecate.** [Medieval Latin *dēpreciāre,* manuscript error for Late Latin *dēpretiāre* : *dē-,* down from + *pretium,* price.] —**de·pre·ci·a·tor** *n.*

de·pre·ci·a·tion (dĭ-prē′shē-ā′shən) *n.* **1.** A decrease or loss in value because of wear, age, or other cause. **2.** *Accounting.* An allowance made for this loss. **3.** A reduction in the purchasing value of money. **4.** A disparaging; a belittling.

de·pre·ci·a·to·ry (dĭ-prē′shē-ə-tôr′ē, -tōr′ē) *adj.* Also **de·pre·ci·a·tive** (-ā′tĭv). **1.** Diminishing in value. **2.** Disparaging.

dep·re·date (dĕp′rə-dāt′) *v.* **-dated, -dating, -dates.** —*tr.* To prey upon; plunder. —*intr.* To commit plunder. [Late Latin *dēpraedārī* : Latin *dē-,* completely + *praedārī,* to plunder, to make booty, from *praeda,* booty. —**dep·re·da·tion** *n.* —**dep·re·da·tor** *n.* —**dep·re·da·to·ry** (dĕp′rə-dā′tə-rē) *adj.*

de·press (dĭ-prĕs′) *tr.v.* **-pressed, -pressing, -presses. 1.** To dispirit; sadden. **2.** To press down; lower: *depress a pedal.* **3.** To lower prices in (a stock market). [Middle English *depressen,* from Old French *depresser,* from Latin *deprimere* (past participle *depressus*) : *de-,* down + *premere,* to press.]

de·pres·sant (dĭ-prĕs′ənt) *adj.* **1.** *Medicine.* Serving to lower the rate of vital activities. **2.** Causing dejection; depressing.
∼*n.* **1.** *Medicine.* A depressant drug. **2.** One that causes dejection or gloom.

de·pressed (dĭ-prĕst′) *adj.* **1.** Lacking energy and enthusiasm; melancholy; gloomy. **2.** *Botany.* Flattened downward, as if pressed from above. **3.** *Zoology.* Flattened along the dorsal and ventral surfaces. **4.** Sunk below the surrounding region: *the depressed center of a crater.* **5.** Economically and socially disadvantaged; marked by widespread poverty and unemployment: *The resort is a depressed area in the winter.* —See Synonyms at **sad.**

de·pres·sion (dĭ-prĕsh′ən) *n.* **1. a.** The act of depressing. **b.** The condition of being depressed. **2. a.** *Pathology.* An abnormal lowering of the rate of any physiological function or activity, such as heart beat. **b.** *Psychology.* A state of gloom and melancholy often accompanied by feelings of inadequacy and usually by a lack of energy. **3.** An area that is below or has sunk below its surroundings; a hollow. **4.** *Meteorology.* A region of low barometric pressure in high or mid latitudes. Also called "low," "disturbance," and formerly a "cyclone." **5.** *Surveying.* The angular distance below the horizontal plane through the point of observation. **6.** *Astronomy.* The angular distance of a celestial body below the horizon. **7.** *Economics.* **a.** A period of drastic decline in an economy, characterized by decreasing business activity, falling prices, and unemployment. **b. Depression.** The period during the 1930's when such a decline occurred in most industrialized countries. Preceded by *the.* —See Synonyms at **despair.**

Depression glass *n.* Glassware of many colors and patterns produced in large quantities during the 1920's and 1930's. [After the great *Depression,* a period of severe economic hardship during the 1930's.]

de·pres·sive (dĭ-prĕs′ĭv) *adj.* **1.** Causing depression. **2.** *Psychology.* Of or characterized by depression.
∼*n.* *Psychology.* A person suffering from depression. —**de·pres·sive·ly** *adv.* —**de·pres·sive·ness** *n.*

de·pres·so·mo·tor (dĭ-prĕs′ō-mō′tər) *adj.* Retarding or lessening physiological motor activity: *depressomotor nerves.*
∼*n.* A drug that causes such a retardation.

de·pres·sor (dĭ-prĕs′ər) *n.* **1.** Something that depresses or is used to depress. **2.** A **depressor nerve** *(see).* **3.** Any of several muscles that cause depression or contraction of a part. **4.** Any instrument, such as a tongue depressor, used to depress a part. **5.** *Phonetics.* A consonant that has the effect of lowering the tone of a following vowel.

depressor nerve *n.* A nerve that lowers arterial blood pressure. Also called "depressor."

de·pres·sur·ize (dē-prĕsh′ə-rīz′) *tr.v.* **-ized, -izing, -izes.** To reduce the pressure of air or gas within (a sealed container, room, or vehicle). —**de·pres·sur·i·za·tion** *n.*

dep·ri·va·tion (dĕp′rə-vā′shən) *n.* Also **de·priv·al** (dĭ-prī′vəl). **1. a.** The act of depriving. **b.** The condition of being deprived. **2.** Privation. **3.** A taking away of rank or office.

de·prive (dĭ-prīv′) *tr.v.* **-prived, -priving, -prives. 1.** To take something away from; dispossess; divest. **2.** To keep from the possession or enjoyment of something; deny. **3.** To take a position from; depose from office. [Middle English *depriven,* from Old French *depriver,* from Medieval Latin *dēprīvāre* : Latin *dē-,* completely + *prīvāre,* to deprive, from *prīvus,* individual, private.] —**de·priv·a·ble** *adj.*

de·prived (dĭ-prīvd′) *adj.* **1.** Lacking the financial means, education, family environment, or social ties considered necessary to achieve a fulfilling life: *a deprived childhood.* **2.** Lacking adequate housing, educational facilities, industry, and the like.

de·pro·fun·dis (dā′ prə-foŏn′dēs, prō-) *adv. Latin.* Out of the depths of misery or grief.

de·pro·gram (dē-prō′grăm′, -grəm) *tr.v.* **-grammed** or **-gramed, -gramming** or **-graming, -grams.** To counteract the effects of previous programming or indoctrination. —**de·pro·gram·mer** *n.*

dept. 1. department. **2.** deputy.

depth (dĕpth) *n.* **1.** The condition or quality of being deep; deepness. **2.** The extent, measurement, or dimension downward, backward, or inward. **3.** *Often* **depths.** A deep part of or place in something. **4.** *Often* **depths.** The middle, inner, or most remote or inaccessible part. **5.** *Often* **depths.** The most profound or intense part or stage: *the depths of despair.* **6.** *Often* **depths.** The severest or worst part: *in the depths of winter.* **7.** Intellectual penetration; profundity. **8.** The range of one's understanding or competence: *out of one's depth.* **9. depths.** An immoral condition; disgrace: *sink to such depths.* **10.** Richness; intensity; darkness: *depth of color.* **11.** Lowness in pitch, as of a voice or musical instrument. —**in depth.** Marked by thorough coverage or treatment: *a study in depth.* [Middle English *depthe,* from DEEP.]

depth charge *n.* Any explosive charge designed for detonation under water, especially such a charge dropped or catapulted from a ship's deck and used against submarines. Also called "depth bomb."

depth of field *n.* The distance in front of and behind an object focused by a camera, microscope, or the like, within which other objects would appear in focus. Compare **depth of focus.**

depth of focus *n.* The amount by which the distance between a camera lens and the film or plate can be varied without altering the sharpness of the image. Compare **depth of field.**

depth perception *n.* Perception of spatial relationships, especially of distances between objects, in three dimensions.

depth psychology *n.* **1.** Any psychology of the unconscious, especially as distinguished from the psychology of conscious behavior. **2.** Loosely, psychoanalysis.

dep·u·rate (dĕp′yə-rāt′) *v.* **-rated, -rating, -rates.** —*tr.* To cleanse or purify. —*intr.* To become cleansed or purified. [Medieval Latin *dēpūrāre* : Latin *dē-,* removal + *pūrāre,* to purify, from *pūrus,* pure.] —**dep·u·ra·tion** *n.* —**dep·u·ra·tive** *n. & adj.* —**dep·u·ra·tor** *n.*

dep·u·ta·tion (dĕp′yə-tā′shən) *n.* **1.** A person or group appointed to represent another or others; a delegation. **2. a.** The act of deputing. **b.** The state of being deputed.

de·pute (dĭ-pyoōt′) *tr.v.* **-puted, -puting, -putes. 1.** To appoint or authorize as an agent or representative. **2.** To appoint to carry out a particular job. **3.** To assign (authority or duties) to another or others; delegate. [Middle English *deputen,* from Old French *deputer,* from Late Latin *dēputāre,* to allot, from Latin, "to cut off," consider : *dē-,* off + *putāre,* to prune, cut, esteem.]

dep·u·tize (dĕp′yə-tīz′) *v.* **-tized, -tizing, -tizes.** —*tr.* To appoint as a deputy. —*intr.* To serve as a deputy.

dep·u·ty (dĕp′yə-tē) *n., pl.* **-ties.** *Abbr.* **d., D., dep., dept. 1.** A person named or empowered to act for another. **2.** An assistant exercising full authority in the absence of his superior and equal authority in emergencies. **3.** A representative in a legislative body in certain countries, such as France. **4.** A mining official who is responsible for safety precautions.
—*adj.* Acting as deputy. [Middle English *depute,* from Old French, from the past participle of *deputer,* to DEPUTE.]

De Quin·cey (dĭ kwĭn′sē), **Thomas** (1785–1859). British writer and critic. At Oxford he took opium, ostensibly to cure a toothache, and became addicted to the drug for the rest of his life. He is best known for his *Confessions of an English Opium Eater* (1821).

der. derivation; derivative.

de·rac·i·nate (dĭ-răs′ə-nāt′) *tr.v.* **-nated, -nating, -nates. 1.** To pull out by the roots; uproot. **2.** To displace from a natural environment; dislocate. [French *déraciner,* from Old French *desraciner* : *des-, de-* (undoing) + *racine,* root, from Late Latin *radīcīna,* from Latin *rādix* (stem *rādīc-*).] —**de·rac·i·na·tion** *n.*

dé·rac·i·né (dā′rä-sə-nā′) *adj.* Uprooted or rootless; having no ties with one's home or origins. [French.] —**dé·rac·i·né** *n.*

de·rail (dē-rāl′) *v.* **-railed, -railing, -rails.** —*tr.* To cause (a train) to run off the rails. —*intr.* To run off the rails. [French *dérailler* : *dé-,* off + *rail,* RAIL.] —**de·rail·ment** *n.*

de·rail·leur (dĭ-rā′lər) *n.* A device for changing gear on bicycles. [French, switch (for gears, rails), from *dérailler,* to go off rails, DE-RAIL.]

De·rain (də-răN′), **André** (1880–1954). French painter, illustrator, and theatrical designer. He was one of the original fauvists, but eventually adopted a more traditional style.

de·range (dĭ-rānj′) *tr.v.* **-ranged, -ranging, -ranges. 1.** To disturb the order or arrangement of; disorder; disarrange. **2.** To disturb the normal condition or functioning of; upset. **3.** To disturb the mental stability of; make insane. [French *déranger,* from Old French *desrengier* : *de-* (sense of undoing) + *reng, renc,* line, RANK.]

de·range·ment (dĭ-rānj′mənt) *n.* **1.** Severe mental disorder; insanity. **2.** The act or an instance of deranging. **3.** Disarrangement; confusion; disorder.

der·by (dûr′bē) *n., pl.* **-bies.** A stiff felt hat with a round crown and narrow, curved brim. Also called "bowler." [After DERBY (race).]

Der·by¹ (där′bē *for sense 1;* dûr′bē *for senses 2, 3*) *n.* **1.** A horse race for three-year-olds, held annually at Epsom Downs in Surrey, Eng-

land. Preceded by *the.* **2.** Any of various other horse races, especially the Kentucky Derby. **3. derby.** Any formal race with a more or less open field of contestants: *a soapbox derby.* [After Edward Smith Stanley (1752–1834), 12th Earl of *Derby,* founder of the English Derby.]

Der·by² (där′bē) *n.* A mild cheese originally made in Derby, England, often flavored with sage.

Der·by³ (där′bē). City at the foot of the Pennines in Derbyshire, central England. The country's first silk mill was founded here in 1719. The making of the porcelain known as Derbyware or Crown Derby was begun by William Duesbury (1725–86) and is still a major concern.

Der·by·shire (där′bē-shîr, -shər). A county in north-central England. The Peak District in the north is largely a national park supporting sheep farming and tourism. Coal is mined around Derby, its administrative center.

dere. Variant of **dear** (dire).

de·reg·u·late (dē-rĕg′yə-lāt′) *tr.v.* **1.** To remove rules or restrictions from, especially from governmental restrictions; decontrol: *deregulate the media.* **2.** To remove price controls from: *deregulate air fares.* —**de·reg·u·la·tion** *n.*

der·e·lict (dĕr′ə-lĭkt′) *adj.* **1.** Neglectful of duty or obligation; remiss; delinquent. **2.** Deserted by an owner or guardian; abandoned; forsaken. **3.** Dilapidated; falling into ruins; neglected.
—*n.* **1.** An item of abandoned property; especially, a ship abandoned at sea. **2.** A social outcast; a vagrant. **3.** *Law.* Land left dry by a permanent recession of the water line. **4.** One neglectful of duty or obligation. [Latin *dērelictus,* past participle of *dērelinquere,* to abandon : *dē-,* completely + *relinquere,* to leave behind : *re-,* behind + *linquere,* to leave.]

der·e·lic·tion (dĕr′ə-lĭk′shən) *n.* **1.** Willful neglect, as of duty. **2.** Abandonment. **3.** *Law.* **a.** A gaining of land by the permanent recession of the water line. **b.** The land so gained.

de·re·strict (dē′rĭ-strĭkt′) *tr.v.* To free from restriction; especially, to free (a road or area) from speed limits. —**de·re·stric·tion** *n.*

Dergue (dûrg) *n.* The ruling council established in Ethiopia after the overthrow of Haile Selassie in 1974.

de·ride (dĭ-rīd′) *tr.v.* **-rided, -riding, -rides.** To speak of or treat with contemptuous mirth; scoff at. —See Synonyms at **ridicule.** [Latin *dērīdēre* : *dē-* (pejorative) + *rīdēre,* to laugh at.] —**de·rid·er** *n.* —**de·rid·ing·ly** *adv.*

de ri·gueur (də rē-gœr′) *adj.* Required by the current fashion or custom; socially obligatory; proper. [French.]

de·ri·sion (dĭ-rĭzh′ən) *n.* **1. a.** Scoffing; ridicule. **b.** A state of being derided. **2.** An object of ridicule; a laughingstock. [Middle English *derisioun,* from Old French *derision,* from Late Latin *dērīsiō* (stem *dērīsiōn-*), from Latin *dērīsus,* past participle of *dērīdēre,* to DERIDE.] —**de·ris·i·ble** *adj.*

de·ri·sive (dĭ-rī′sĭv) *adj.* **1.** Mocking; scoffing. **2.** Liable to derision; absurd. —**de·ri·sive·ly** *adv.* —**de·ri·sive·ness** *n.*

de·ri·so·ry (dĭ-rī′sə-rē, -zə-rē) *adj.* **1.** Derisive. **2.** So small or inadequate as to be ridiculous: *a derisory pay offer.*

der·i·va·tion (dĕr′ə-vā′shən) *n. Abbr.* **der. 1.** The act or process of deriving. **2.** The condition or fact of being derived. **3.** Something derived; a derivative. **4.** The form or source from which something is derived; the origin; the descent. **5.** The historical origin and development of a word; an etymology. **6.** *Linguistics.* The morphological process by which new words are formed from existing words, chiefly by the addition of affixes to roots, stems, or words. **7.** *Mathematics.* A logical or mathematical process indicating through a sequence of statements that a result, such as a theorem or a formula, necessarily follows from the initial assumptions. —**der·i·va·tion·al** *adj.*

de·riv·a·tive (dĭ-rĭv′ə-tĭv) *adj.* Also **der·i·vate** (dĕr′ə-vāt′). *Abbr.* **der. 1.** Resulting from derivation; derived. **2.** Copied or adapted from others; lacking originality.
—*n.* **1.** Something derived. **2.** *Linguistics.* A word formed from another by derivation. Compare **primitive. 3.** *Mathematics.* The limit, as the increment in the argument of a function approaches zero, of the ratio of the increment in its value to the corresponding increment in the argument; loosely, the instantaneous rate of change of a function with respect to a variable. Also called "differential coefficient." **4.** *Chemistry.* Any compound derived or obtained from known or hypothetical substances and containing essential elements of the parent substance. —**de·riv·a·tive·ly** *adv.*

de·rive (dĭ-rīv′) *v.* **-rived, -riving, -rives.** —*tr.* **1.** To obtain or receive from a source. **2.** To arrive at by reasoning; deduce; infer : *derive a conclusion from facts.* **3.** To trace the origin or development of (a word, for example). **4.** *Chemistry.* To produce or obtain (a compound) from another substance by chemical reaction. —*intr.* To issue from a source; originate. [Middle English *deriven,* to conduct water from a source, spring from, from Old French *deriver,* from Latin *dērīvāre,* to draw off, derive : *dē-,* away, off + *rīvus,* stream.] —**de·riv·a·ble** *adj.* —**de·riv·er** *n.*

derived unit *n.* A unit of measurement obtained by multiplying or dividing two or more base units of a system of units without the introduction of numerical factors.

-derm *suffix. Biology.* Indicates skin; for example, **endoderm, echinoderm.** [French *-derme,* from Greek *derma,* skin.]

der·ma¹ (dûr′mə) *n.* Also **derm** (dûrm). *Anatomy.* A layer of skin, the **dermis** (*see*). [New Latin *derma, dermis,* from Greek *derma,* skin.]

derma² *n.* Beef or poultry casing stuffed with a seasoned mixture of matzo meal or flour, onion, and suet, that is boiled and then roasted. Also called "stuffed derma," "kishke." [Yiddish *derme*, plural of *darm*, intestine, from Middle High German, from Old High German.]

–derma *suffix*. Indicates skin or skin disease; for example, **scleroderma**. [New Latin, from Greek *derma*, skin.]

der·ma·bra·sion (dûr′mə-brā′zhən) *n*. A surgical procedure designed to remove skin imperfections, such as scars or wrinkles, through the abrasion of the frozen epidermis.

der·mal (dûr′məl) *adj*. Also **der·mic** (dûr′mĭk). Of or pertaining to the skin. [DERM(ATO)- + -AL.]

der·ma·ti·tis (dûr′mə-tī′tĭs) *n*. *Medicine*. Inflammation of the skin. [New Latin : DERMAT(O)- + -ITIS.]

dermato–, derm–, derma–, dermat– *prefix*. Indicates skin; for example, **dermatology, dermal, dermatome, dermatoid**. [Greek, from *derma*, skin.]

der·mat·o·gen (dûr-măt′ə-jən) *n*. *Botany*. The outer layer of **meristem** *(see)*, from which the epidermis is formed.

der·ma·toid (dûr′mə-toid′) *n*. Also **der·moid** (dûr′moid′). Resembling skin; skinlike. [DERMAT(O)- + -OID.]

der·ma·tol·o·gy (dûr′mə-tŏl′ə-jē) *n*. The branch of medicine concerned with the physiology and pathology of the skin and treatment of skin diseases. [DERMATO- + -LOGY.] **—der·ma·to·log·i·cal** (dûr′mə-tə-lŏj′ĭ-kəl) *adj*. **—der·ma·tol·o·gist** *n*.

der·ma·tome (dûr′mə-tōm′) *n*. 1. An area of skin with sensory fibers from a single spinal nerve. 2. An instrument used in cutting thin slices of the skin, as in skin grafting. 3. *Embryology*. The part of a somite that develops into the dermis. [DERMA(TO)- + -TOME.]

der·ma·to·phyte (dûr-măt′ə-fīt′, dûr′măt-ə-fīt′) *n*. Any of various fungi that cause skin disease. [DERMATO- + -PHYTE.] **—der·mat·o·phyt·ic** (dûr-măt′ə-fĭt′ĭk) *adj*.

der·ma·to·phy·to·sis (dûr′mə-tō′fī-tō′sĭs) *n*. Any fungal infection of the skin, especially of the feet, such as athlete's foot. [DERMATO-PHYT(E) + -OSIS.]

der·ma·to·plas·ty (dûr′mə-tō-plăs′tē) *n*. The use of skin grafts in plastic surgery to correct defects or replace skin loss. [DERMATO- + -PLASTY.]

der·ma·to·sis (dûr′mə-tō′sĭs) *n*., *pl*. **-ses** (-sēz′). A skin disease. [DERMAT(O)- + -OSIS.]

–dermatous *suffix*. Having a specified kind of skin; for example, **sclerodermatous**. [From Greek *derma, dermat-*, skin.]

dermic. Variant of **dermal**.

der·mis (dûr′mĭs) *n*. The living part of the skin that forms a thick layer below the epidermis and is made up of connective tissue containing blood and lymph vessels, nerve endings, sweat and sebaceous glands, and smooth muscle. Also called "corium," "derma," "derm." [New Latin, abstracted from EPIDERMIS.]

dermoid. Variant of **dermatoid**.

der·nier cri (dĕr′nyä krē′) *French*. The latest thing; the newest fashion. [Literally, "last cry."]

de·ro, der·ro (dĕr′ō) *n*., *pl*. **-ros**. *Australian Slang*. A vagabond; a tramp. [From DERELICT.]

der·o·gate (dĕr′ə-gāt′) *v*. **-gated, -gating, -gates**. —*intr*. 1. To detract; take away. Used with *from*. 2. To deviate from a standard or expectation; go astray. Used with *from*. —*tr*. To disparage; belittle. [Latin *dērogāre*, repeal, restrict, disparage : *dē-*, away + *rogāre*, ask.] **—der·o·ga·tion** (dĕr′ə-gā′shən) *n*. **—de·rog·a·tive** (dĭ-rŏg′ə-tĭv) *adj*.

de·rog·a·to·ry (dĭ-rŏg′ə-tôr′ē, -tōr′ē) *adj*. Deliberately offensive; detracting or disparaging. **—de·rog·a·to·ri·ly** *adv*. **—de·rog·a·to·ri·ness** *n*.

der·rick (dĕr′ĭk) *n*. 1. A large crane for hoisting and moving heavy objects, consisting of a movable boom equipped with cables and pulleys and connected to the base of an upright stationary beam. 2. A tall framework over the opening of an oil well or other drilled hole, used to support boring equipment or to hoist and lower pipe lengths. [Originally, a gallows, after *Derick*, noted hangman at Tyburn, England c. 1600.]

der·ri·ère (dĕr′ē-âr′; *French* dĕ-ryâr′) *n*. *Informal*. The buttocks; the rear. [French, "the rear."]

der·ring-do (dĕr′ĭng-dōō′) *n*. Daring spirit and action; valor. [Middle English *during don*, daring to do (mistaken for a noun phrase by Edmund Spenser and later by Sir Walter Scott) : *during*, present participle of *durren*, Old English *durran* to DARE + *don*, to DO.]

der·rin·ger (dĕr′ĭn-jər) *n*. A short-barreled pistol with a large bore. [After Henry *Deringer*, 19th-century U.S. gunsmith who invented it.]

der·ris (dĕr′ĭs) *n*. 1. Any of various woody vines of the genus *Derris*, of tropical Asia, whose roots yield rotenone. 2. The extract from the roots of such plants, which is a powerful insecticide. [New Latin, from Greek, covering, skin.]

derro. Variant of **dero**.

der·ry[1] (dĕr′ē) *n*., *pl*. **-ries**. A meaningless word used as a refrain or chorus in old songs.

derry[2] *n*. *Australian Informal*. A grudge; an aversion: *have a derry on a rival*. [Probably shortened from *derry down*, common refrain in folk songs, with allusion to the phrase *have a down on*.]

Derry. See **Londonderry**.

der·vish (dûr′vĭsh) *n*. A member of any of various Muslim orders of ascetics, some of which practice the achievement of collective ecstasy through whirling dances and the chanting of religious formulas. [Turkish *derviş*, mendicant, from Persian *darvēsh*†.]

Der·went (dûr′wənt). The name of several rivers in England, from a Celtic word meaning "clear water." The longest is in Derbyshire, flowing 96 kilometers (60 miles) into the Trent River.

DES (dē′ē-ĕs′) *n*. **Diethylstilbestrol** *(see)*.

De·sai (də-sī′), **Shri Morarji Ranchhodji** (1896–). Indian statesman. A disciple of Mahatma Gandhi, he later came to lead the Congress Party against Indira Gandhi, who as prime minister imprisoned him during a state of emergency. He defeated her in the 1977 elections and as prime minister led the newly formed Janata Party, but resigned in 1979.

de·sal·i·nate (dē-săl′ə-nāt′) *tr.v*. **-nated, -nating, -nates**. To desalinize. **—de·sal·i·na·tion** *n*.

de·sal·in·ize (dē-săl′ə-nīz′) *tr.v*. **-ized, -izing, -izes**. To remove (salts and other chemicals) from sea water or saline water. **—de·sal·i·ni·za·tion** *n*.

de·salt (dē-sôlt′) *tr.v*. **-salted, -salting, -salts**. To desalinize.

des·cant (dĕs′kănt) *n*. Also **dis·cant** (dĭs′-). 1. *Music*. **a**. An ornamental melody or counterpoint sung or played above a musical theme. **b**. The highest part sung in part music. 2. A discussion or discourse on a theme. ~*intr.v*. (dĕs-kănt′) **descanted, -canting, -cants**. Also **dis·cant** (dĭs-kănt′) (for sense 2). 1. To comment at length; discourse. Used with *on* or *upon*. 2. **a**. To sing or play a descant. **b**. To sing melodiously. [Middle English *discant*, from Old North French *descant*, from Medieval Latin *discantus*, refrain : *dis-*, apart + *cantus*, song, from the past participle of *canere*, to sing.] **—des·cant·er** *n*.

descant recorder *n*. *Music*. A recorder having the highest pitch of those in common use.

Des·cartes (dā-kärt′), **René** (1596–1650). French philosopher. Having rejected all his previously held beliefs, he built his philosophy on the one premise he held to be indisputable, the existence of himself as a thinking subject: "Cogito ergo sum" ("I think, therefore I am"), which he argued in his *Discourse on Method* (1637) and his *Meditations* (1641). As a mathematician, he introduced coordinates and the method of undetermined coefficients.

de·scend (dĭ-sĕnd′) *v*. **-scended, -scending, -scends**. —*intr*. 1. To move from a higher to a lower place, rank, pitch, or the like; come or go down. 2. To slope, extend, or incline downward: *"a rough path descended like a steep stair into the plain"* (J.R.R. Tolkien). 3. To come or be derived from ancestors. 4. To have hereditary derivation. 5. To lower oneself in behavior; stoop. 6. To arrive in an overwhelming manner. Used with *on* or *upon*. 7. To move down toward the horizon. Used of the sun and moon. —*tr*. To move from a higher to a lower part of; go down. [Middle English *descenden*, from Old French *descendre*, from Latin *dēscendere* : *dē-*, down + *scandere*, to climb.] **—de·scend·i·ble, de·scend·a·ble** *adj*.

de·scen·dant (dĭ-sĕn′dənt) *n*. 1. A person, animal, or plant descended from an individual, race, species, or earlier form; an immediate or remote offspring. 2. Anything descended from an earlier form. ~*adj*. Variant of **descendent**.

de·scen·dent, de·scen·dant (dĭ-sĕn′dənt) *adj*. 1. Moving downward; descending. 2. Proceeding by descent from an ancestor. Often used with *from*.

de·scend·er (dĭ-sĕn′dər) *n*. 1. One that descends. 2. *Printing*. **a**. The part of certain letters, such as *g, p*, or *y*, that extends below the bottom of most lower-case letters. **b**. Any such letter.

de·scent (dĭ-sĕnt′) *n*. 1. The act or an instance of descending; coming or going down. 2. A way down; downward incline or passage. 3. Hereditary derivation; ancestral extraction; lineage. 4. A generation of a specific lineage. 5. A lowering or decline, as in status or level. 6. A sudden attack; onslaught. 7. *Law*. Transference of property by inheritance. [Middle English *descent*, from Old French, from *descendre*, to DESCEND.]

de·scribe (dĭ-skrīb′) *tr.v*. **-scribed, -scribing, -scribes**. 1. To give a verbal account of; tell about in detail. 2. To transmit a mental image or impression of with words; picture verbally. 3. To trace or draw the figure of; outline: *describe a circle with a compass*. [Latin *dēscrībere*, to copy off, write down : *dē-*, down + *scrībere*, to write.] **—de·scrib·a·ble** *adj*. **—de·scrib·er** *n*.

de·scrip·tion (dĭ-skrĭp′shən) *n*. 1. The act, process, or technique of describing. 2. A statement or account describing someone or something. 3. The act of drawing or tracing a figure. 4. A kind; a sort: *costumes of every description*. [Middle English *descripcioun*, from Old French *description*, from Latin *dēscriptiō* (stem *dēscriptiōn-*), from *dēscriptus*, past participle of *dēscrībere*, to DESCRIBE.]

de·scrip·tive (dĭ-skrĭp′tĭv) *adj*. 1. Involving or characterized by description; serving to describe. 2. Concerned with description or classification rather than explanation: *descriptive science*. 3. *Grammar*. Expressing an attribute of the modified noun; for example, *green* in *green grass*. Said of an adjective or adjectival clause. 4. *Linguistics*. Of or pertaining to descriptive linguistics. **—de·scrip·tive·ly** *adv*. **—de·scrip·tive·ness** *n*.

descriptive geometry *n*. *Mathematics*. The collection of mathematical techniques used to describe geometric relationships among three-dimensional structures on a plane surface.

descriptive linguistics *n*. The study of a language or languages at a specific stage of development, with emphasis on constructing a complete grammatical analysis rather than on setting standards of usage, examining historical development, or making comparisons among languages.

de·scrip·ti·vism (dĭ-skrĭp′tĭv-ĭz′əm) *n*. 1. *Philosophy*. The doctrine that ethical propositions describe something about the real world and are true or false. Compare **emotivism, prescriptivism**. 2. *Lin-*

derringer *The American gunsmith Henry Deringer (1786–1868) gave his misspelled name to this short and easily concealed pistol—the weapon used to assassinate Abraham Lincoln. Deringer's original design was for a single-shot gun, but it was later modified into a two-shot model: the Remington double derringer shown here.*

desert

DRY AND DESOLATE WASTES
A third of the world's land surface consists of deserts

Deserts are uncultivated, mainly barren regions in which the annual rainfall is less than 250 millimeters (10 inches). There are two main types of desert: hot, arid deserts such as the Sahara and cold deserts such as polar regions.

Hot, arid deserts are the result of high atmospheric pressure combined with slowly descending dry air. They are the world's sunniest regions, where evaporation greatly exceeds rainfall. The cold, polar wastes—which form almost half the world's deserts—are marked by much frozen soil and ice and a lack of tall plants.

Some water-storing plants exist in parts of the hot deserts. Fennel, for instance, grows in cooler crevices in the Sahara, and cacti and agaves grow throughout the deserts of North and Central America.

DESERT DUNES *Ridges or dunes of loose sand, piled by the wind among the prevailing rocks or pebbles, are a feature of hot deserts.*

DESERT FLOWERS *The Atacama Desert of Chile has had droughts lasting for several years. Usually it has a little rain each year. Afterward plants may grow in surface cracks.*

guistics. The practice or advocacy of the methods of descriptive linguistics. Compare **prescriptivism**.

de·scry (dĭ-skrī′) *tr.v.* **-scried, -scrying, -scries.** **1.** To discern (something difficult to catch sight of): *through the mists they could descry the long arm of the mountains* (J.R.R. Tolkien). **2.** To discover by careful observation or investigation. —See Synonyms at **see**. [Middle English *descrien*, to cry out, proclaim, catch sight of, from Old French *descrier*, to decry : *des-*, used in pejorative sense, DIS- + *crier*, to CRY.] —**de·scri·er** *n.*

des·e·crate (dĕs′ə-krāt′) *tr.v.* **-crated, -crating, -crates.** To abuse the sacredness of; subject to sacrilege; profane. [DE- + (CON)SECRATE.] —**des·e·crat·er, des·e·cra·tor** *n.* —**des·e·cra·tion** *n.*

de·seg·re·gate (dē-sĕg′rə-gāt′) *v.* **-gated, -gating, -gates.** —*tr.* To abolish racial segregation in (a school, for example). —*intr.* To become desegregated. —**de·seg·re·ga·tion** *n.* —**de·seg·re·ga·tion·ist** *adj. & n.*

de·sen·si·tize (dē-sĕn′sə-tīz′) *tr.v.* **-tized, -tizing, -tizes.** To render

insensitive or less sensitive, as to light or pain. —**de·sen·si·ti·za·tion** *n.* —**de·sen·si·tiz·er** *n.*

Des·e·ret (dĕz′ə-rĕt′). A state proposed by the Mormons in 1849 as an independent state or, failing that, a state of the Union. Deseret would have included much of the southwestern United States, with a capital in Salt Lake City.

des·ert¹ (dĕz′ərt) *n.* **1.** A region rendered barren or partially barren by low precipitation (typically less than 250 millimeters or 10 inches a year), or by its exceptionally permeable surface. **2.** A place which lacks aesthetic or cultural appeal: *an architectural desert.* ~*adj.* Of, pertaining to, or characteristic of a desert; barren and uninhabited; desolate: *a desert island.* [Middle English, from Old French, from Late Latin *dēsertum*, from Latin, neuter past participle of *dēserere*, to abandon, DESERT.] See feature, next page.

de·sert² (dĭ-zûrt′) *n.* **1.** *Usually* **deserts.** That which is deserved or merited, especially a punishment: *received his just deserts.* **2.** The state or fact of deserving reward or punishment. **3.** *Obsolete.* A good deed. [Middle English *deserte*, from Old French, from *desert*, from *deservir*, to DESERVE.]

de·sert³ (dĭ-zûrt′) *v.* **-serted, -serting, -serts.** —*tr.* **1.** To forsake or leave; abandon: *"his set smile did not once desert him"* (Willa Cather). **2.** To leave (one's post, for example) in violation of orders or oath. —*intr.* To forsake one's duty or post; especially, to be absent without leave from the armed forces with no intention of returning. [French *déserter*, from Late Latin *dēsertāre*, from Latin *dēsertus*, past participle of *dēserere*, to abandon : *dē-*, reversal + *serere*, to join.] —**de·sert·er** *n.*

de·ser·tion (dĭ-zûr′shən) *n.* **1. a.** The act of deserting. **b.** The state of being deserted. **2.** *Law.* Willful abandonment of one's spouse or children, or both, without their consent and with the intention of forsaking all legal obligation.

desert lynx *n.* A wild cat, the **caracal** *(see).*

desert rat *n.* **1.** A **jerboa** *(see).* **2.** *British Informal.* A soldier who served in North Africa during World War II.

de·serve (dĭ-zûrv′) *v.* **-served, -serving, -serves.** —*tr.* To be worthy of; have a right to; merit: *"An American girl of college age . . . deserved instant inspection"* (Kingsley Amis). —*intr.* To be worthy. [Middle English *deserven*, to be entitled to in return for services, deserve, from Old French *deservir*, from Latin *dēservīre*, serve well : *dē-*, completely + *servīre*, to SERVE.]

de·served (dĭ-zûrvd′) *adj.* Merited or earned. Often used in combination: *a well-deserved holiday.* —**de·serv·ed·ly** (dĭ-zûr′vĭd-lē) *adv.* —**de·serv·ed·ness** *n.*

de·serv·ing (dĭ-zûr′vĭng) *adj.* Worthy of reward or praise; meritorious. ~*n.* Merit or demerit. —**de·serv·ing·ly** *adv.* —**de·serv·ing·ness** *n.*

de·sex (dē-sĕks′) *tr.v.* **-sexed, -sexing, -sexes.** To remove part or all of the reproductive organs of; spay or castrate.

de·sex·u·al·ize (dē-sĕk′shōō-ə-līz′) *tr.v.* **-ized, -izing, -izes.** **1.** To desex. **2.** To take away the sexual quality of. —**de·sex·u·al·i·za·tion** *n.*

deshabille. Variant of **dishabille**.

De Si·ca (də sē′kə), **Vittorio** (1901–74). Italian film director and actor. Among his best films are *Shoeshine* (1946), *Bicycle Thieves* (1948), and *Umberto D* (1952).

des·ic·cant (dĕs′ĭ-kənt) *n.* A substance, such as calcium oxide or sulfuric acid, that has a high affinity for water and is used as a drying agent to absorb moisture. [Latin *dēsiccāns* (stem *dēsiccant-*), present participle of *dēsiccāre*, to DESICCATE.] —**des·ic·cant** *adj.*

des·ic·cate (dĕs′ĭ-kāt′) *v.* **-cated, -cating, -cates.** —*tr.* **1.** To make thoroughly dry; dry out. **2.** To preserve (foods) by removing the moisture. **3.** To divest of spirit, spontaneity, or animation; make dry or uninteresting. —*intr.* To become dry. ~*adj.* Also **des·ic·cat·ed** (-kā′tĭd). Lacking spirit, spontaneity, or animation; arid. [Latin *dēsiccāre* : *dē-*, completely + *siccāre*, to dry up, from *siccus*, dry.] —**des·ic·ca·tion** (dĕs′ĭ-kā′shən) *n.* —**des·ic·ca·tive** (dĕs′ĭ-kā′tĭv) *adj.*

des·ic·ca·tor (dĕs′ə-kā′tər) *n.* **1.** A jar or box, especially one used in laboratories, that contains a desiccant and protects substances from atmospheric moisture. **2.** An apparatus for drying milk, fruit, or other natural products.

de·sid·er·ate (dĭ-sĭd′ə-rāt′) *tr.v.* **-ated, -ating, -ates.** To long for. [Latin *dēsīderāre*, to DESIRE.]

de·sid·er·a·tive (dĭ-sĭd′ə-rā′tĭv) *adj.* **1.** Of or pertaining to desire. **2. a.** Designating a category of verbs in some Indo-European languages, such as Latin, expressing a wish to perform the action denoted by the given verb. **b.** Being a verb, verb form, or affix in this category. ~*n.* A desiderative verb.

de·sid·er·a·tum (dĭ-sĭd′ə-rā′təm) *n., pl.* **-ta** (-tə). Something needed and desired. [Latin *dēsīderātum*, neuter past participle of *dēsīderāre*, to DESIRE.]

de·sign (dĭ-zīn′) *v.* **-signed, -signing, -signs.** —*tr.* **1.** To conceive; invent; contrive. **2.** To form a plan for. **3.** To draw a sketch of. **4.** To have as a goal or purpose; intend. —*intr.* **1.** To make or execute plans. **2.** To create designs. ~*n.* **1.** The invention and disposition of the forms, parts, or details of something according to a plan. **2.** A drawing or sketch. **3.** A decorative or artistic work. **4.** A visual composition; pattern. **5.** The art of creating designs. **6.** A plan; project; undertaking. **7.** A reasoned purpose; intention. **8.** *Often* **designs.** A sinister or hostile scheme; crafty plot. Used with *on, upon,* or *against.* [Old French *designer*, from Latin *dēsignāre*, to DESIGNATE.] —**de·sign·a·ble** *adj.*

des·ig·nate (dĕz′ĭg-nāt′) *tr.v.* **-nated, -nating, -nates.** **1.** To indicate or specify; point out. **2.** To give a name or title to; characterize. **3.** To select for a particular duty, office, or purpose; appoint. ~*adj.* (dĕz′ĭg-nĭt). Appointed but not yet installed in office. Used after the noun: *the chairwoman designate.* [Latin *dēsignāre*, designate, mark out : *dē-*, out + *signāre*, mark, from *signum*, sign.] —**des·ig·na·tive, des·ig·na·to·ry** (dĕz′ĭg-nə-tôr′ē, -tōr′ē) *adj.* —**des·ig·na·tor** *n.*

designated hitter *n. Baseball.* A player designated at the start of a game to bat instead of the pitcher in the lineup.

des·ig·na·tion (dĕz′ĭg-nā′shən) *n.* **1.** The act of designating; marking or pointing out. **2.** Nomination or appointment. **3.** A distinguishing name or mark; title.

de·sign·ed·ly (dĭ-zī′nĭd-lē) *adv.* On purpose; intentionally.

des·ig·nee (dĕz′ĭg-nē′) *n.* A person who has been designated.

de·sign·er (dĭ-zī′nər) *n.* **1.** A person who creates designs, usually commercial designs, as of clothing, fabrics, furniture, or machinery. **2.** A person who has designs; schemer; plotter. ~*adj.* Designed by a well-known fashion designer: *a designer dress.*

de·sign·ing (dĭ-zī′nĭng) *adj.* **1.** Conniving; artful; crafty. **2.** Showing or exercising forethought. —**de·sign·ing·ly** *adv.*

des·i·nence (dĕs′ə-nəns) *n.* **1.** A termination; finishing. **2.** *Grammar.* An inflectional ending. [Old French, from Medieval Latin *dēsinentia*, from Latin *dēsinēns*, present participle of *dēsinere*, to cease, leave off : *dē-*, off + *sinere*, to leave.]

de·sir·a·ble (dĭ-zīr′ə-bəl) *adj.* **1.** Worth seeking or deserving preference; pleasing; fine. **2.** Arousing desire, especially sexual desire. **3.** Worth wanting or doing; beneficial; advisable: *a desirable reform.* ~*n.* A desirable person or thing. —**de·sir·a·bil·i·ty,** (dĭ-zīr′ə-bĭl′ə-tē), **de·sir·a·ble·ness** *n.* —**de·sir·a·bly** *adv.*

de·sire (dĭ-zīr′) *tr.v.* **-sired, -siring, -sires. 1.** To wish or long for; want; crave. **2.** To express a wish for. ~*n.* **1.** A wish, longing, or craving. **2.** A request as expressed; petition. **3.** Something or someone longed for: *my heart's desire.* **4.** Sexual appetite; lust. [Middle English *desiren*, from Old French *desirer*, from Latin *dēsīderāre*.] —**de·sir·er** *n.*

de·sir·ous (dĭ-zīr′əs) *adj.* Having, expressing, or characterized by desire; desiring. Often used with *of: desirous of quick promotion.* —**de·sir·ous·ly** *adv.* —**de·sir·ous·ness** *n.*

de·sist (dĭ-zĭst′) *intr.v.* **-sisted, -sisting, -sists.** To cease doing something; forbear; abstain. Often used with *from.* [Old French *desister*, from Latin *dēsistere*, cease, stand off : *dē-*, from + *sistere*, to stop, stand.]

desk (dĕsk) *n.* **1.** A piece of furniture typically having a flat or sloping top for writing, and often drawers or other compartments. **2.** A table, counter, or booth at which specified services or functions are performed: *an information desk.* **3.** A department of a large organization, such as a government agency or newspaper, in charge of a specified operation: *city desk.* **4. a.** A music stand in an orchestra. **b.** Two string players using the same music stand in an orchestra. **5.** A bookrest for the service book in a church. [Middle English *deske*, from Medieval Latin *desca*, variant of Italian *desco*, table, from Latin *discus*, quoit, DISK.]

de·skill (dē-skĭl′) *tr.v.* **-skilled, -skilling, -skills.** To remove the need for skilled labor in (an industry), especially by introducing machines and computers: *Printing has been deskilled.*

des·man (dĕs′mən) *n., pl.* **-mans.** Either of two aquatic, insectivorous, molelike mammals, *Desmana moschata* of eastern Europe and western Asia, or *Galemys pyrenaicus* of southwestern Europe, having dense, brownish fur, a long snout, and a flattened, scaly tail. [Short for Swedish *desman(srätta),* musk(rat), from Middle Low German *desem*, musk, from West Germanic *dessem* (unattested), from Medieval Latin *bisamum*, from Semitic, akin to Hebrew *bśem*, mild odor.]

des·mid (dĕs′mĭd) *n.* Any of various green, unicellular freshwater algae of the family Desmidiaceae, often forming chainlike colonies. [New Latin *Desmidiaceae*, from *Desmidium* (genus) : Greek *desmos*, bond, from *dein*, to bind.]

Des Moines (də-moin′). Capital of Iowa, in the south-central part of the state. It is the center of the Corn Belt, a corn-growing and stock-raising region.

des·mo·some (dĕs′mə-sōm) *n. Zoology.* A strengthened area of contact between an epithelial cell and a smooth-muscle cell at which the cell membranes become thickened and fibrils extend into the cytoplasm. [Greek *desmos*, bond, from *dein*, to bind + -SOME (body).]

des·o·late (dĕs′ə-lĭt) *adj.* **1.** Devoid of inhabitants; deserted: *"streets which were usually so thronged now grown desolate"* (Daniel Defoe). **2.** Rendered unfit for habitation; laid waste; devastated. **3.** Dreary; dismal; gloomy. **4.** Without friends or hope; forlorn; lonely. —See Synonyms at **sad.** ~*tr.v.* (dĕs′ə-lāt′) **desolated, -lating, -lates. 1.** To rid or deprive of inhabitants. **2.** To devastate. **3.** To forsake; abandon. **4.** To make lonely, forlorn, or wretched. [Middle English *desolat*, from Latin *dēsōlātus*, past participle of *dēsōlāre*, abandon : *dē-*, completely + *sōlus*, alone.] —**des·o·late·ly** *adv.* —**des·o·late·ness** *n.* —**des·o·later, des·o·la·tor** *n.*

des·o·la·tion (dĕs′ə-lā′shən) *n.* **1.** The act of rendering desolate. **2.** The state of being desolate; ruin. **3.** A wasteland. **4.** Loneliness or misery; wretchedness.

de·sorb (dē-sôrb′, -zôrb′) *v.* **-sorbed, -sorbing, -sorbs.** *Chemistry.* —*intr.* To change from an adsorbed or absorbed state to a liquid or gaseous state. —*tr.* To change (a substance) from an adsorbed or absorbed state to a liquid or gaseous state. [DE- + (AD)SORB.] —**de·sorp·tion** *n.*

de Soto (dĭ sō′tō), **Hernando** (*c.* 1496-1542). Spanish explorer. After serving under Pizarro in Peru (1531-36), he was appointed governor of Cuba and given royal permission to conquer lands to the north. In 1539 he set out in search of riches with 600 men, landed in present-day Tampa Bay, and explored much of southern North America for two years. He died during the expedition and was laid to rest in his most important discovery, the Mississippi River.

desoxy- Variant of **deoxy-.**

desoxyribonucleic acid. Variant of **deoxyribonucleic acid.**

desoxyribose. Variant of **deoxyribose.**

de·spair (dĭ-spâr′) *intr.v.* **-spaired, -spairing, -spairs. 1.** To lose all hope; be overcome by a sense of futility or defeat. **2.** To lack trust or confidence, as in a favorable outcome or a person's abilities. Used with *of.* ~*n.* **1.** Utter lack of hope. **2.** That which destroys all hope. [Middle English *despeiren*, from Old French *desperer*, from Latin *dēspērāre* : *dē-* (reversal) + *spērāre*, to hope.] —**de·spair·ing·ly** *adv.*
   Synonyms: *dejection, depression, desperation, despondency, discouragement.*

despatch. Variant of **dispatch.**

des·per·a·do (dĕs′pə-rä′dō, -rā′dō) *n.* **-does** or **-dos.** A desperate, dangerous criminal, especially of the western U.S. frontier. [Pseudo-Spanish variant of DESPERATE.]

des·per·ate (dĕs′pər-ĭt) *adj.* **1.** Reckless or violent through despair; driven to take any risk. **2.** Undertaken as a last resort. **3.** Nearly hopeless; critical; grave: *a desperate illness.* **4.** Marked by, arising from, or showing despair; despairing: *the desperate look of hunger.* **5.** In an unbearable situation because of need or anxiety: *an artist desperate for recognition.* **6.** Extreme because of fear, danger, or suffering; very great: *in desperate need.* [Latin *dēspērātus*, past participle of *dēspērāre*, to DESPAIR.] —**des·per·ate·ly** *adv.* —**des·per·ate·ness** *n.*

des·per·a·tion (dĕs′pə-rā′shən) *n.* **1.** The condition of being desperate. **2.** Recklessness arising from despair. —See Synonyms at **despair.**

des·pi·ca·ble (dĕs′pĭ-kə-bəl, dĭ-spĭk′-) *adj.* Deserving of contempt or disdain; mean; vile. [Late Latin *dēspicābilis*, from Latin *dēspicārī*, to despise.] —**des·pi·ca·bil·i·ty, des·pi·ca·ble·ness** *n.* —**des·pi·ca·bly** *adv.*

de·spise (dĭ-spīz′) *tr.v.* **-spised, -spising, -spises.** To regard with contempt or disdain. [Middle English *despisen*, from Old French *despire* (present stem *despis-*), from Latin *dēspicere*, to look down on : *dē-*, down + *specere*, to look.] —**de·spis·er** *n.*

de·spite (dĭ-spīt′) *prep.* In spite of: *won despite overwhelming odds.* ~*n.* **1.** Contemptuous defiance. **2.** An act of such defiance; insult; offense. —**in despite of.** In spite of. [Preposition, short for *in despite of*, from Middle English *despit*, spite, from Old French, from Latin *dēspectus*, past participle of *dēspicere*, to DESPISE.]

de·spite·ful (dĭ-spīt′fəl) *adj. Archaic.* Full of malice; spiteful. —**de·spite·ful·ly** *adv.* —**de·spite·ful·ness** *n.*

de·spoil (dĭ-spoil′) *tr.v.* **-spoiled, -spoiling, -spoils.** To deprive of possessions or contents by force; plunder; ravage. [Middle English *despoilen*, from Old French *despoiller*, from Latin *dēspoliāre* : *dē-*, sense of undoing + *spoliāre*, to plunder, from *spolium*, booty, spoil.] —**de·spoil·er** *n.* —**de·spoil·ment** *n.*

de·spo·li·a·tion (dĭ-spō′lē-ā′shən) *n.* The act of despoiling or the condition of being despoiled. [Late Latin *dēspoliātiō* (stem *dēspoliātiōn-*), from Latin *dēspoliātus*, past participle of *dēspoliāre*, to DESPOIL.]

de·spond (dĭ-spŏnd′) *intr.v.* **-sponded, -sponding, -sponds.** To become disheartened. ~*n. Archaic.* Despondency. [Latin *dēspondēre*, to despond, promise to give, give up : *dē-*, away + *spondēre*, to promise.] —**de·spond·ing·ly** *adv.*

de·spon·den·cy (dĭ-spŏn′dən-sē) *n., pl.* **-cies.** Also **de·spon·dence** (-dəns). Lowness of spirits from loss of hope, confidence, or courage; dejection. —See Synonyms at **despair.**

de·spon·dent (dĭ-spŏn′dənt) *adj.* Feeling or expressing despondency; disheartened; dejected. [Latin *dēspondēns* (stem *dēspondent-*), present participle of *dēspondēre*, to DESPOND.] —**de·spon·dent·ly** *adv.*

des·pot (dĕs′pət) *n.* **1.** An autocratic ruler; a tyrant. **2.** Any autocratic or domineering person. **3.** A Greek title borne by Byzantine emperors and princes, by Christian rulers in the Balkans under the Turks, and by Eastern Orthodox bishops. [French, from Medieval Latin *despota*, from Greek *despotēs*, lord.] —**des·pot·ic** (dĭ-spŏt′ĭk) *adj.* —**des·pot·i·cal·ly** *adv.*

des·pot·ism (dĕs′pə-tĭz′əm) *n.* **1.** Rule by or as if by a despot; absolute power or authority. **2.** The actions of a despot; tyranny. **3. a.** A government or political system in which the ruler exercises absolute power. **b.** A state so ruled.

des·qua·mate (dĕs′kwə-māt′) *intr.v.* **-mated, -mating, -mates.** *Pathology.* To shed, peel, or come off in scales. Used of skin. [Latin *dēsquāmāre* : *dē-*, removal + *squāma*, scale.] —**des·qua·ma·tion** *n.*

Des·sa·lines (dā-sə-lēn′), **Jean Jacques** (1758-1806). Emperor of Haiti. A former slave, he rose in the slave revolt led by Toussaint L'Ouverture against the French and took over the leadership on Toussaint's capture in 1802. In 1803, with British help, he defeated the French and later declared himself emperor. His tyrannical rule provoked dissent, and he was assassinated.

des·sert (dĭ-zûrt′) *n.* **1.** The last course of a lunch or dinner, consist-

destroying angel *A highly poisonous fungus distinguishable from the edible common field mushroom by its white underside. Many species of this poisonous mushroom flourish in the United States.*

ing of a serving of a sweet food, such as fruit, ice cream, or pastry. **2.** *Chiefly British.* Especially formerly, fresh fruit, nuts, or sweetmeats served after the sweet course of a dinner. [French, from *desservir,* clear the table : *des-, de-,* reversal + *servir,* to SERVE.]

des·sert·spoon (dĭ-zûrt′spo͞on′) *n.* A spoon intermediate in size between a tablespoon and a teaspoon, used for eating dessert. **—des·sert·spoon·ful** *n.*

dessert wine *n.* A wine intended to be drunk with dessert.

de·sta·bil·ize (dē-stā′bə-līz) *tr.v.* **-ized, -izing, -izes.** To undermine and reduce the effective functioning of (a government or other political authority). **—de·sta·bil·i·za·tion** *n.*

de Stijl (də stīl′, stāl′) *n.* A school of art originating in the Netherlands in 1917 and characterized by the use of rectangular shapes and primary colors. [Dutch, "the style."]

des·ti·na·tion (dĕs′tə-nā′shən) *n.* **1.** The place or point to which someone or something is going or directed. **2.** The ultimate goal or purpose for which anything is created or intended.

des·tine (dĕs′tĭn) *tr.v.* **-tined, -tining, -tines. 1.** To determine beforehand; preordain to or as if to an inevitable outcome. Usually used with the infinitive: *destined to rule.* **2.** To assign or intend for a specific end, use, or purpose. **3.** To direct toward a given destination. [Middle English *destinen,* from Old French *destiner,* from Latin *dēstināre,* to determine, destine.]

des·tined (dĕs′tĭnd) *adj.* **1.** Preordained; assured through destiny. **2.** Intended for. **3.** Bound for a particular destination.

des·ti·ny (dĕs′tə-nē) *n., pl.* **-nies. 1.** The inevitable or necessary fate to which a particular person or thing is destined; one's lot. **2.** The preordained or inevitable course of events considered as something beyond human power or control. **3.** The power or agency thought to predetermine events; fate. **4. Destiny.** This power personified or regarded as a goddess. [Middle English *destine,* from Old French *destinee,* from the feminine past participle of *destiner,* to DESTINE.]

des·ti·tute (dĕs′tə-to͞ot′, -tyo͞ot′) *adj.* **1.** Utterly impoverished. **2.** Altogether lacking; devoid. Used with *of*: *destitute of experience.* **3.** *Obsolete.* Abandoned; deserted. —See Synonyms at **poor.** [Middle English *destitut,* from Latin *dēstitūtus,* past participle of *dēstituere,* to set down, desert : *dē-,* down, away from + *statuere,* to place.]

des·ti·tu·tion (dĕs′tə-to͞o′shən, -tyo͞o′shən) *n.* **1.** Extreme want of resources or the means of subsistence; complete poverty. **2.** Any deprivation or lack; deficiency.

des·tri·er (dĕs′trē-ər, -trîr) *n. Archaic.* A war-horse; a charger. [Middle English, from Old French, from Vulgar Latin *dextrārius* (unattested), from Latin *dexter,* right (the squire managed his own horse with his left hand and led his knight's horse with his right).]

de·stroy (dĭ-stroi′) *v.* **-stroyed, -stroying, -stroys.** *—tr.* **1.** To ruin completely; spoil so that restoration is impossible; consume: *The fire destroyed the ancient manuscripts.* **2.** To tear down or break up; raze; demolish. **3.** To do away with; get rid of; put an end to: *a speech that destroyed any chance of a settlement.* **4.** To kill. **5.** To render useless or ineffective. **6.** To subdue or defeat completely; crush. *—intr.* To be destructive or harmful: *"Too much money destroys as surely as too little"* (John Simon). —See Synonyms at **ruin.** [Middle English *destruyen,* from Old French *destruire,* from Vulgar Latin *dēstrūgere* (unattested), from Latin *dēstruere* (past participle *dēstructus*) : *dē-* (reversal) + *struere,* to build, pile up.]

de·stroy·er (dĭ-stroi′ər) *n.* **1.** One that destroys. **2.** A medium-sized, fast warship armed with guns, torpedoes, and depth charges, and noted for its high maneuverability.

destroyer escort *n.* A warship, usually smaller than a destroyer, used to convoy merchant vessels.

destroying angel *n.* Any of several poisonous mushrooms of the genus *Amanita,* especially *A. verna.*

de·struct (dĭ-strŭkt′) *n.* The intentional destruction of a space vehicle, rocket, or missile after launching.
~v. **destructed, -structing, -structs.** *—tr.* To destroy (a defective missile or space vehicle) after launching. *—intr.* To be destroyed deliberately, as a safety measure; self-destruct. Used of a missile or space vehicle. [Back-formation from DESTRUCTION.]

de·struc·ti·ble (dĭ-strŭk′tə-bəl) *adj.* Subject to destruction; capable of being destroyed: *destructible machine parts.* **—de·struc·ti·bil·i·ty, de·struc·ti·ble·ness** *n.*

de·struc·tion (dĭ-strŭk′shən) *n.* **1.** The act of destroying. **2.** The condition or fact of being destroyed. **3.** A cause or means of destroying. [Middle English *destruccioun,* from Old French *destruction,* from Latin *dēstructiō* (stem *dēstructiōn-*), from *dēstructus,* past participle of *dēstruere,* to DESTROY.]

de·struc·tion·ist (dĭ-strŭk′shən-ĭst) *n.* A person who favors destruction, especially of existing social institutions.

de·struc·tive (dĭ-strŭk′tĭv) *adj.* **1.** Tending to destroy; causing or wreaking destruction; ruinous. Often used with *of* or *to*: *destructive to national safety.* **2.** Designed or tending to disprove or discredit; negative; not constructive: *destructive criticism.* **—de·struc·tive·ly** *adv.* **—de·struc·tive·ness** *n.*

destructive distillation *n. Chemistry.* The simultaneous decomposition by heat and distillation of substances such as wood, coal, and oil shale to produce useful by-products such as coke, charcoal, oils, and gases. Also called "dry distillation."

de·struc·tor (dĭ-strŭk′tər) *n.* **1.** A furnace for disposing of rubbish, especially one that generates power from the heat so produced. **2.** A device which causes defective rockets and other space vehicles to explode.

des·ue·tude (dĕs′wə-to͞od′, -tyo͞od′) *n.* The state or condition of disuse: *words fallen into desuetude.* [French *désuétude,* from Latin *dēsuētūdō,* from *dēsuēscere,* to put out of use, become unaccustomed : *dē-* (reversal) + *suēscere,* to become accustomed.]

de·sul·fur·ize (dē-sŭl′fə-rīz′) *tr.v.* **-ized, -izing, -izes.** To eliminate sulfur from. **—de·sul·fu·ri·za·tion** *n.*

des·ul·to·ry (dĕs′əl-tôr′ē, -tōr′ē) *adj.* **1.** Moving or jumping from one thing to another; disconnected; rambling. **2.** Occurring haphazardly; random. —See Synonyms at **chance.** [Latin *dēsultōrius,* of a leaper, from *dēsultor,* a leaper, from *dēsultus,* past participle of *dēsilīre,* to leap down : *dē-,* down + *salīre,* to jump.] **—des·ul·to·ri·ly** *adv.* **—des·ul·to·ri·ness** *n.*

det. **1.** *Military.* detachment. **2.** detail.

de·tach (dĭ-tăch′) *tr.v.* **-tached, -taching, -taches. 1.** To separate, usually without violence or damage; disconnect. **2.** *Military.* To send (troops or ships, for example) on a special mission. [French *détacher,* from Old French *destachier* : *des-, de-,* apart + *atachier,* variant of *estachier,* to ATTACH.] **—de·tach·a·bil·i·ty** *n.* **—de·tach·a·ble** *adj.* **—de·tach·a·bly** *adv.*

de·tached (dĭ-tăcht′) *adj.* **1.** Standing apart from others; disconnected; separate: *a detached house.* **2.** Free from emotional, intellectual, social, or other involvement; without bias; disinterested. —See Synonyms at **cool, indifferent.**

de·tach·ment (dĭ-tăch′mənt) *n.* **1.** The act or process of disconnecting or detaching; separation. **2.** The state or condition of being separate or apart. **3.** Dissociation from or lack of involvement in worldly affairs or one's environment; aloofness. **4.** Absence of prejudice or bias; disinterest. **5.** *Military.* **a.** The dispatch of troops or ships selected from a larger unit for a special duty or mission. **b.** *Abbr.* **det.** The unit of troops or ships so dispatched. **c.** *Abbr.* **det.** A permanent unit, usually smaller than a platoon, organized for special duties.

de·tail (dĭ-tāl′, dē′tāl) *n. Abbr.* **det. 1.** An individually considered part, portion, or item; particular. **2.** Such an item considered as trivial or not worth attending to. **3.** Particulars considered separately and in relation to a whole: *careful attention to detail.* **4.** A small or secondary part of a painting, statue, building, or other work of art, especially when considered or represented in isolation. **5.** *Military.* **a.** The selection of one or more troops for a particular duty, usually a fatigue duty. **b.** The personnel so selected. **c.** The duty assigned. **—go into detail.** To discuss the finer points; cover most of the particulars. **—in detail.** With particulars; item by item.
~tr.v. **detailed, -tailing, -tails. 1.** To report or relate minutely or in detail. **2.** *Military.* To select and dispatch for a particular duty. [French *détail,* from Old French *detail,* piece cut off, from *detailler,* to cut up : *de-,* thoroughly + *tailler,* to cut, from Vulgar Latin *tāliāre* (unattested), to cut off.]

de·tailed (dĭ-tāld′, dē′tāld′) *adj.* Characterized by abundant use of detail or by thoroughness of treatment.

detail man *n.* A representative of a manufacturer of drugs or medical supplies who calls on doctors, pharmacists, and other professional users to promote new drugs and supplies.

de·tain (dĭ-tān′) *tr.v.* **-tained, -taining, -tains. 1.** To keep from proceeding; delay or retard. **2.** To keep in custody; confine. **3.** *Obsolete.* To retain or withhold. —See Synonyms at **delay.** [Middle English *deteynen,* from Old French *detenir,* from Latin *dētinēre,* to keep back : *dē-,* away + *tenēre,* to hold.] **—de·tain·ment** *n.*

de·tain·ee (dē′tā-nē′, dĭ-tā′-) *n.* A person held in custody: *a political detainee.*

de·tain·er (dĭ-tā′nər) *n. Law.* **1. a.** The unlawful withholding of the property of another. **b.** The detention of a person, especially in custody or confinement. **2.** A writ authorizing the further detention of a person in custody pending action.

de·tect (dĭ-tĕkt′) *tr.v.* **-tected, -tecting, -tects. 1.** To discover or discern the existence, presence, or fact of. **2.** To find out the true nature of. **3.** *Electronics.* To demodulate. [Middle English *detecten,* from Latin *dētegere* (past participle *dētectus*), to uncover : *dē-* (reversal) + *tegere,* to cover.] **—de·tect·a·ble, de·tect·i·ble** *adj.* **—de·tect·er** *n.*

de·tec·tion (dĭ-tĕk′shən) *n.* **1.** The act of finding out or the fact of being found out; discovery, as of something hidden or obscure. **2.** *Electronics.* Demodulation.

de·tec·tive (dĭ-tĕk′tĭv) *n.* A person, usually a police officer, whose work is investigating crimes and obtaining evidence.
~adj. **1.** Of or pertaining to detectives or their work. **2.** Suited for or used in detection.

de·tec·tor (dĭ-tĕk′tər) *n.* **1.** Any apparatus that detects; especially, a mechanical, electrical, or chemical device that automatically identifies and records or registers a stimulus such as an environmental change in pressure or temperature, an electric signal, or radiation from a radioactive material. **2.** A **demodulator** *(see).*

de·tent (dĭ-tĕnt′) *n. Engineering.* A **pawl** *(see).* [French *détente,* a loosening, a trigger, from Old French *destente,* from *destendre,* to release : *des-, de-,* apart + *tendre,* to stretch, from Latin *tendere.*]

dé·tente (dā-täNt′) *n.* A relaxing or easing, as of tension between nations. [French. See **detent.**]

de·ten·tion (dĭ-tĕn′shən) *n.* **1. a.** The act of detaining. **b.** The state of being detained. **2.** A form of punishment in schools, by which a pupil is made to remain in class after hours. **3.** A keeping in custody or confinement; especially, a period of temporary custody while awaiting trial. [French, from Late Latin *dētentiō* (stem *dētentiōn-*), from Latin *dētentus,* past participle of *dētinēre,* to DETAIN.]

de·ter (dĭ-tûr′) *tr.v.* **-terred, -terring, -ters.** To prevent or discourage (someone) from acting because of fear, doubt, or the like. [Latin *dēterrēre*, to frighten from : *dē-*, away from + *terrēre*, to frighten.] —**de·ter·ment** *n.*

de·terge (dĭ-tûrj′) *tr.v.* **-terged, -terging, -terges.** To wash or wipe off; cleanse. [French *déterger*, to cleanse, from Latin *dētergēre*, to wipe off : *dē-*, off, away + *tergēre†*, to wipe.]

de·ter·gen·cy (dĭ-tûr′jən-sē) *n.* Also **de·ter·gence** (-jəns) Cleansing power or quality.

de·ter·gent (dĭ-tûr′jənt) *n.* A cleansing substance, especially one that acts as a wetting agent and emulsifier and is made from a chemical compound such as an alkyl sulfonate, rather than from fats and lye. Compare **soap.** ~*adj.* Having cleansing power. [Latin *dētergēns* (stem *dētergent-*), present participle of *dētergēre.*]

de·te·ri·o·rate (dĭ-tîr′ē-ə-rāt′) *v.* **-rated, -rating, -rates.** —*intr.* To decline or grow worse in quality, condition, or value. —*tr.* To lower in quality, condition, or value. [Late Latin *dēteriōrāre*, from Latin *dēterior*, worse, comparative of *dēter* (unattested).] —**de·te·ri·o·ra·tive** *adj.*

de·te·ri·o·ra·tion (dĭ-tîr′ē-ə-rā′shən) *n.* **1.** The act or an instance of deteriorating. **2.** The state or condition of being deteriorated.

de·ter·mi·na·ble (dĭ-tûr′mə-nə-bəl) *adj.* **1.** Capable of being settled, fixed, or determined. **2.** *Law.* Liable to be terminated.

de·ter·mi·nant (dĭ-tûr′mə-nənt) *adj.* Tending or serving to determine; determinative. ~*n.* **1.** An influencing or determining factor. **2.** *Mathematics.* A square array of quantities, or elements, having a value determined by a rule of combination for the elements and used especially in solving certain classes of simultaneous equations.

de·ter·mi·nate (dĭ-tûr′mə-nĭt) *adj.* **1.** Precisely limited or defined. **2.** Settled; final. **3.** Firm in purpose; resolute. **4.** *Botany.* **a.** Terminating in a flower, and blooming in a sequence beginning with the uppermost or central flower: *a determinate inflorescence.* **b.** Not continuing indefinitely at the tip of an axis: *determinate growth.* [Middle English *determinat*, from Latin *dēterminātus*, past participle of *dētermināre*, to DETERMINE.]

de·ter·mi·na·tion (dĭ-tûr′mə-nā′shən) *n.* **1. a.** The act of making or arriving at a decision. **b.** The decision arrived at; a strong resolve. **2.** The quality of being resolute or firm in purpose; resoluteness. **3. a.** The act of settling a dispute, suit, or other question by an authoritative decision or pronouncement. **b.** The decision or pronouncement made. **4. a.** The ascertaining or establishing of the extent, quality, position, or character of anything. **b.** The result of such ascertaining. **5.** A fixed movement or tendency toward some object or end. **6.** *Logic.* **a.** The rendering of a concept or proposition more definite by further qualification. **b.** The factor or factors that so qualify. **c.** The defining of a concept through its constituent elements.

de·ter·mi·na·tive (dĭ-tûr′mə-nā′tĭv, -nə-tĭv) *adj.* Tending, able, or serving to determine or settle; limiting; deciding. ~*n.* **1.** Something that determines. **2.** *Grammar.* A determiner. —**de·ter·mi·na·tive·ness** *n.*

de·ter·mine (dĭ-tûr′mĭn) *v.* **-mined, -mining, -mines.** —*tr.* **1. a.** To decide or settle (a dispute, for example) conclusively and authoritatively. **b.** To end or decide by judicial or other final action. **2.** To establish or ascertain definitely, as after consideration, investigation, or calculation. **3.** To cause (someone) to come to a conclusion or resolution. **4.** To influence decisively; be the cause of; regulate. **5.** To give direction to; decide the course of. **6.** To limit in scope or extent; fix the bounds of. **7.** *Mathematics.* In geometry, to fix or define the position, form, or configuration of. **8.** *Logic.* To explain or limit (a concept or notion) by adding or requiring certain features or characteristics. **9.** *Law.* To put an end to; terminate. —*intr.* **1.** To reach a decision; resolve. **2.** *Law.* To come to an end. —See Synonyms at **decide.** [Middle English *determinen*, from Old French *determiner*, from Latin *dētermināre*, to limit : *dē-*, off + *termināre*, to limit, from *terminus*, boundary line.]

de·ter·mined (dĭ-tûr′mĭnd) *adj.* Marked by or showing determination or fixed purpose; resolute; unwavering; firm. —**de·ter·mined·ly** *adv.* —**de·ter·mined·ness** *n.*

de·ter·min·er (dĭ-tûr′mə-nər) *n.* **1.** One that determines. **2.** *Grammar.* A word, such as an article or a possessive adjective, that limits the meaning of a noun or noun phrase and precedes other adjectives that accompany it; for example, in the phrases *the new house, her young daughters*, and *both girls*, the words *the, her*, and *both* are determiners.

de·ter·min·ism (dĭ-tûr′mə-nĭz′əm) *n.* The philosophical doctrine that every event, act, and decision is the inevitable consequence of antecedents, such as physical, psychological, or environmental conditions, that are independent of the individual human will. Compare **free will.** —**de·ter·min·ist** *n. & adj.* —**de·ter·min·is·tic** *adj.*

de·ter·rence (dĭ-tûr′əns) *n.* **1.** The action or a means of deterring. **2.** A defensive policy or strategy involving the deployment of weapons at a level believed likely to deter potential aggressors.

de·ter·rent (dĭ-tûr′ənt) *n.* **1.** Something that deters: *a deterrent to theft.* **2.** Power of retaliation, especially in the form of weapons, considered as a means of discouraging enemy attack: *a nuclear deterrent.* —**de·ter·rent** *adj.*

de·test (dĭ-tĕst′) *tr.v.* **-tested, -testing, -tests.** To dislike intensely; abhor; loathe. [Latin *dētestārī*, to curse, execrate : *dē-* (pejorative) + *testārī*, to invoke, call to witness, from *testis*, a witness.] —**de·test·er** *n.*

de·test·a·ble (dĭ-tĕs′tə-bəl) *adj.* Deserving abhorrence or execration; odious; abominable. —See Synonyms at **hateful.** —**de·test·a·**

bil·i·ty, de·test·a·ble·ness *n.* —**de·test·a·bly** *adv.*

de·tes·ta·tion (dē′tĕ-stā′shən) *n.* **1.** Strong dislike; hatred or abhorrence. **2.** Someone or something that is detested.

de·throne (dē-thrōn′) *tr.v.* **-throned, -throning, -thrones.** To remove from a throne or high position; depose. —**de·throne·ment** *n.*

det·i·nue (dĕt′ĭ-nyōō′) *n. Law.* **1. a.** An action to recover possession or the value of property wrongfully detained. **b.** The writ authorizing such action. **2.** *Obsolete.* The act of unlawfully detaining personal property. [Middle English *detenewe*, from Old French *detenue*, detention, from the past participle of *detenir*, to DETAIN.]

det·o·na·ble (dĕt′n-ə-bəl) *adj.* Also **det·o·nat·a·ble** (dĕt′n-ā′tə-bəl). Capable of being detonated.

det·o·nate (dĕt′n-āt′) *v.* **-nated, -nating, -nates.** —*intr.* To explode suddenly and violently. Said of a bomb, explosive charge, or the like. —*tr.* To cause to explode. [Latin *dētonāre*, to thunder down : *dē-*, down + *tonāre*, to thunder.] —**det·o·na·tive** (dĕt′ə-nā′tĭv, dĕ′tə-) *adj.*

det·o·na·tion (dĕt′n-ā′shən) *n.* **1.** The act of detonating or exploding. **2.** A violent explosion.

det·o·na·tor (dĕt′n-ā′tər) *n.* **1.** A device, such as an electric generator, fuse, or percussion cap, used to set off explosives. **2.** An explosive.

de·tour (dē′tŏŏr′, dĭ-tŏŏr′) *n.* **1.** A roundabout way or course; especially, a byroad used temporarily instead of a main route. **2.** Deviation from the direct or shortest road, route, or course of action. ~*v.* **detoured, -touring, -tours.** —*intr.* To go by a roundabout way. —*tr.* To cause to go by a roundabout way or detour. [French *détour*, from Old French *destor*, from *destorner*, to turn away : *des-, de-*, away + *torner*, to TURN.]

de·tox (dē-tŏks′) *tr.v. Informal.* **-toxed, -toxing, -toxes.** To subject to detoxification. ~*n.* (dē′tŏks′). A section of a hospital in which patients are detoxified.

de·tox·i·fy (dē-tŏk′sə-fī′) *tr.v.* **-fied, -fying, -fies.** Also **de·tox·i·cate** (-kāt′) **-cated, -cating, -cates. 1.** To counteract or destroy the toxic properties of. **2.** To remove the effects of poison from. [DE- (reversal) + TOXI(C) + -FY.] —**de·tox·i·fi·ca·tion, de·tox·i·ca·tion** *n.*

de·tract (dĭ-trăkt′) *v.* **-tracted, -tracting, -tracts.** —*intr.* To take away a desirable or valuable quality; diminish. Used with *from.* —*tr.* To distract. [Middle English *detracten*, from Latin *dētrahere* (past participle *dētractus*), to pull down, draw away : *dē-*, away + *trahere*, to pull.]

de·trac·tion (dĭ-trăk′shən) *n.* **1.** A person or thing that detracts. **2.** The act of detracting or taking away; disparagement; depreciation. —**de·trac·tive** *adj.* —**de·trac·tor** *n.*

de·train (dē-trān′) *v.* **-trained, -training, -trains.** —*tr.* To cause to leave a railroad train. —*intr.* To leave a railroad train. —**de·train·ment** *n.*

de·trib·al·ize (dē-trī′bə-līz′) *tr.v.* **-ized, -izing, -izes.** To cause to lose tribal customs or habits, or tribal organization. —**de·trib·al·i·za·tion** *n.*

det·ri·ment (dĕt′rə-mənt) *n.* **1.** Damage, harm, or loss. **2.** Something that causes damage, harm, or loss. [Middle English, from Old French, from Latin *dētrīmentum*, to wear away : *dē-*, away + *terere*, to rub.]

det·ri·men·tal (dĕt′rə-mĕnt′l) *adj.* Causing damage or harm; injurious. Often used with *to.* —**det·ri·men·tal·ly** *adv.*

de·trit·ed (dĭ-trī′tĭd) *adj.* **1.** Worn down. **2.** *Geology.* Formed as detritus. [Latin *dētrītus*, past participle of *dēterere*, to wear down. See **detriment.**]

de·tri·tion (dĭ-trĭsh′ən) *n.* The act of wearing away by friction or rubbing. [Medieval Latin *dētrītiō* (stem *dētrītiōn-*), from Latin *dētrītus*, past participle of *dēterere*, to rub away. See **detriment.**]

de·tri·tus (dĭ-trī′təs) *n.* **1.** Loose fragments, particles, or grains that have been formed by the disintegration of rocks. **2.** Any disintegrated matter; debris. [French *détritus*, from Latin *dētrītus*, past participle of *dēterere*, to wear away. See **detriment.**]

De·troit (dĭ-troit′). City in southeastern Michigan, on the Canadian border. It was founded by French settlers in 1701. In the 20th century it became the center of the U.S. automobile industry. It is also a rail and shipping center serving the Great Lakes.

de trop (də trō′) *adj. French.* **1.** Too much; too many; excessive. **2.** Not wanted; superfluous: *I felt distinctly de trop with the honeymoon couple.*

de·trude (dĭ-trōōd′) *tr.v.* **-truded, -truding, -trudes.** To thrust down or away. [Latin *dētrūdere*, to thrust down : *dē-*, down, away + *trūdere*, to thrust.]

de·tu·mes·cence (dē′tŏŏ-mĕs′əns, -tyōō-mĕs′əns) *n.* Contraction following expansion, especially restoration of a swollen organ or part to normal size. [Latin *dētumescere*, to cease swelling : *dē-* (reversal) + *tumescere*, to swell up, from *tumēre*, to be swollen.] —**de·tu·mes·cent** *adj.*

Deu·ca·li·on (dōō-kā′lē-ən, dyōō-). *Greek Mythology.* A son of Prometheus who, with his wife Pyrrha, survived a deluge sent by Zeus and became the ancestor of the renewed human race.

deuce¹ (dōōs, dyōōs) *n.* **1. a.** A playing card or side of a die bearing two marks, symbols, or spots. **b.** A cast of the dice totaling two. **2.** *Tennis.* A score in which each player or side has 40 points (or 5 or more games each) and either player or side must win 2 successive points (or games) to win the game (or set). [Old French *deus*, two, from Latin *duōs*, accusative of *duo.*]

deuce² *n. Informal.* Bad luck; the devil. ~*interj.* Used to express annoyance, impatience, or surprise. Often preceded by *the* or *what the.* [Probably from Low German *duus,* deuce, two at dice (from the exclamation of the player making the lowest throw), ultimately from Latin *duōs,* two.]

deu·ced (dōō'sĭd, dyōō'sĭd) *adj. Informal.* Darned; confounded; extreme. Not in current usage. [From DEUCE (devil).] **—deu·ced, deu·ced·ly** *adv.*

deuces wild *n.* A variation of certain card games, such as poker, in which each deuce may represent any card the holder chooses.

De·us (dē'əs, dā'ŏŏs) *n. Abbr.* **D.** *Latin.* God.

de·us ex mach·i·na (dā'ŏŏs ĕks mä'kĕ-nä', dē'əs ĕks măk'ə-nə) *n.* **1.** A deity in ancient Greek and Roman drama who was brought in by stage machinery to intervene in a difficult situation. **2.** Any unexpected, artificial, or improbable character, device, or event suddenly intervening to resolve a situation or untangle a plot. [New Latin, "god from a machine" (translation of Greek *theos ek mēkhanēs*).]

Deut. Deuteronomy (Old Testament).

deu·ter·a·no·pi·a (dōō'tər-ə-nō'pē-ə, dyōō'-) *n.* A form of color-blindness characterized by confusion of green, bluish red, and neutral. [New Latin : DEUTER(O)- + AN- (lack of) + -OPIA (so called from the blindness to green, which is considered the second of the primary colors).] **—deu·ter·a·nope** *n.*

deu·ter·ide (dōō'tə-rīd, dyōō'-) *n.* A compound of deuterium and another element, analogous to a hydride.

deu·te·ri·um (dōō-tîr'ē-əm) *n. Symbol* **D** An isotope of hydrogen having an atomic weight of 2.0141. Also called "heavy hydrogen." [New Latin : DEUTER(O)- (because it is the second in the series of possible hydrogen isotopes) + -IUM.]

deuterium oxide *n.* An isotopic form of water with composition D_2O, present in natural water as approximately 1 part in 6,500 and isolated for use as a moderator in certain nuclear reactors. Also called "heavy water."

deutero-, deuter-, deuto- *prefix.* **1.** Indicates second or secondary; for example, **deuterocanonical, deuteranopia, deutoplasm. 2.** *Chemistry.* Indicates the presence of deuterium. [Greek *deuteros,* second.]

deu·ter·o·ca·non·i·cal (dōō'tə-rō-kə-nŏn'ĭ-kəl, dyōō'-) *adj.* **1.** Pertaining to or designating books or sections of books in the New Testament whose authority was once contested but later accepted. **2.** Pertaining to or designating books or sections of books in the Old Testament, considered canonical by Eastern Orthodox Christians and Roman Catholics, and apocryphal by many Protestants. See **Apocrypha.** [DEUTERO- + CANONICAL.]

deu·ter·og·a·my (dōō'tə-rŏg'ə-mē, dyōō'-) *n.* A second legal marriage, after the death or divorce of a first spouse.

Deu·ter·o·I·sa·iah (dōō'tə-rō-ī-zā'ə, dyōō'-). The name given to the author of chapters 40–66 of Isaiah, who was a Hebrew writer during the Babylonian captivity (597–538 B.C.).

deu·ter·on (dōō'tə-rŏn, dyōō'-) *n. Symbol* **d** The nucleus of a deuterium atom, a composite of a proton and a neutron, regarded as a subatomic particle with unit positive charge. [DEUTER(IUM) + -ON.]

Deu·ter·on·o·my (dōō'tə-rŏn'ə-mē, dyōō'-) *n. Abbr.* **Deut.** The fifth book of the Old Testament, in which the law of Moses is stated completely for the second time. [Middle English, from Late Latin *deuteronomium,* from Greek *deuteronomion,* from the Septuagint mistranslation (Deuteronomy 16:18) of Hebrew *mishnēh hattōrah hazzō'th,* "a copy of this law," as *deuteronomion (touto),* "(this) second law" : DEUTERO- + *nomos,* law.]

deu·to·plasm (dōō'tə-plăz'əm, dyōō'-) *n.* Also **deu·ter·o·plasm** (-tə-rō-). Food substance or yolk in the cytoplasm of an ovum or other cell. [DEUT(ERO)- + -PLASM.]

Deut·sche Mark, deut·sche-mark (doi'chə märk') *n.* Also **deutsch·mark** (doich'märk'). *Abbr.* **DM 1.** The basic monetary unit of Germany and formerly of West Germany, equal to 100 pfennigs. See feature at **currency. 2.** A coin worth one Deutsche Mark. See **mark**[2]. [German, "German Mark."]

Deutschland. See **Germany.**

deut·zi·a (dōōt'sē-ə, dyōōt'-) *n.* Any of various shrubs of the genus *Deutzia,* cultivated for their clusters of white or pinkish flowers. [New Latin *Deutzia,* after Jean *Deutz* (died c. 1784), Dutch patron of botany.]

de·va (dā'və) *n. Sometimes* **Deva.** In Buddhism and Hinduism, any of various gods or divinities. [Sanskrit, god.]

De Va·le·ra (dĕv'ə-lâr'ə, -lûr'ə), **Eamon** (1882–1975). Irish statesman. He was a battalion commander in the 1916 Easter Rising and was imprisoned by the British. He served as president of Sinn Fein (1917–26), prime minister of the Irish Free State (1932–48, 1951–54, 1957–59), and president of the Republic (1959–73).

de·val·u·ate (dē-văl'yōō-āt') *v.* -ated, -ating, -ates. Also **de·val·ue** (-văl'yōō). —*tr.* **1.** To lessen or annul the importance or value of. **2.** To lower the exchange value of (currency) against gold or other currencies by government action. Compare **revaluate.** —*intr.* To institute an official reduction in the value of a currency. **—de·val·u·a·tion** *n.*

De·va·na·ga·ri (dā'və-nä'gə-rē) *n.* The alphabet in which Sanskrit and many modern Indian languages are written. [Sanskrit *devanā-garī,* "the divine script of the city" : *deváḥ,* god + *nāgarī,* (script) of the city, from *nāgaram,* town, city, probably from Dravidian.]

dev·as·tate (dĕv'ə-stāt) *tr.v.* -tated, -tating, -tates. **1.** To reduce to a state of desolation; ravage; lay waste. **2.** *Informal.* To defeat, overwhelm, or confound. —See Synonyms at **ruin.** [Latin *dēvāstāre* : *dē-* (intensive) + *vāstāre,* to lay waste, from *vāstus,* waste.] **—dev·as·tat·ing·ly** *adv.* **—dev·as·ta·tion** *n.* **—dev·as·ta·tor** *n.*

de·vel·op (dĭ-vĕl'əp) *v.* -oped, -oping, -ops. —*tr.* **1.** To expand or realize the potentialities of; bring gradually to a fuller, greater, or better state. **2.** To elaborate or enlarge. **3.** *Music.* To unfold (a theme) with rhythmic and harmonic variations. **4.** To disclose (a plot, for example) gradually. **5.** To bring into being; make active; generate. **6.** To make more available; put to use. **7.** To convert (a tract of land) to a new function, and to increase its value, as by building extensively. **8.** To come to have gradually; acquire. **9.** To become affected with (a disease); contract. **10.** *Photography.* To process (a photosensitive material), especially with chemicals, in order to render a recorded image visible. **11.** *Chess.* To bring (a piece) into play from its starting position. **12.** *Mathematics.* To expand (a function) into a series. —*intr.* **1.** To grow; expand; progress to a more advanced state. **2.** To come gradually into existence or activity. **3.** To be disclosed. **4.** *Biology.* **a.** To progress from earlier to later stages of individual maturation. **b.** To progress from earlier to later or from simpler to more complex stages of evolution. [French *développer,* from Old French *desveloper* : *des-* (reversal) + *voloper,* to wrap up, perhaps from Celtic *vol-* (unattested), to roll.] **—de·vel·op·a·ble** *adj.*

de·vel·op·er (dĭ-vĕl'ə-pər) *n.* **1.** One that develops; especially, a person who develops property. **2.** *Photography.* A chemical used to render visible the image recorded on a photosensitive surface.

de·vel·op·ing (dĭ-vĕl'əp-ĭng) *adj.* In the process of improving living standards and attaining an economically viable level of industrial production: *developing countries.*

de·vel·op·ment (dĭ-vĕl'əp-mənt) *n.* **1.** The act, process, or result of developing. **2.** A developed state, condition, or form. **3.** Something, such as an event, factor, or piece of information, that has come into existence or been disclosed: *the latest developments in the police corruption scandal.* **4.** A group of dwellings built by the same contractor or in the same scheme. **5.** *Music.* The section of a composition in which a theme is elaborated with rhythmic and harmonic variations. **6.** *Chess.* The moving of pieces from their starting positions, or the state of play resulting from this. **—de·vel·op·men·tal** *adj.* **—de·vel·op·men·tal·ly** *adv.*

de·verb·a·tive (dĭ-vûr'bə-tĭv) *adj.* Also **de·verb·al** (dē-vûr'bəl). *Grammar.* **1.** Designating a word or word form derived from a verb; for example, *variable* is a deverbative adjective derived from the verb *vary.* **2.** Designating an element added to a verb form to produce a derivative; for example, the suffix -er in *worker* is a deverbative suffix. *—n.* Also **deverbal.** *Grammar.* A deverbative word or element.

de·vest (dĭ-vĕst') *tr.v.* -vested, -vesting, -vests. *Law.* To take (a title, estate, or right, for example) away from. [Old French *desvestir,* to undress, from Vulgar Latin *disvestire* (unattested) : Latin *dis-* (reversal) + *vestīre,* to dress, from *vestis,* garment.]

De·vi (dā'vē) *n. Hinduism.* The most powerful of the Hindu goddesses, mother and consort of Siva. She combines benevolence with ferocity.

de·vi·ant (dē'vē-ənt) *adj.* Differing from a norm or from the accepted standards of society; deviating. *—n.* A person whose attitude or behavior differs from the norm or from accepted social or moral standards. [Middle English *deviaunt,* from Late Latin *dēviāns* (stem *dēviant-*), present participle of *dēviāre,* to DEVIATE.] **—de·vi·ance** *n.*

de·vi·ate (dē'vē-āt') *v.* -ated, -ating, -ates. —*intr.* To turn or move increasingly away from a designated norm, as from a specific course or prescribed mode of behavior. —*tr.* To cause to turn aside or differ. *—n.* (dē'vē-ĭt). A deviant. [Late Latin *dēviāre* : Latin *dē-,* away from + *via,* road, way.] **—de·vi·a·tor** *n.*

de·vi·a·tion (dē'vē-ā'shən) *n.* **1.** The act or result of deviating or turning aside. **2.** An abnormality; departure: *That outburst was a deviation from her usual serenity.* **3.** *Statistics.* **a.** The difference, especially the absolute difference, between one of a set of numbers and their mean. **b.** Any variation from a trend. **4.** Divergence from an accepted or dominant policy or ideology. **5.** The deflection of a compass needle due to local magnetic disturbances. **—de·vi·a·tion·ism** *n.* **—de·vi·a·tion·ist** *n.*

de·vice (dĭ-vīs') *n.* **1.** Something devised or constructed for a particular purpose; especially, a machine used to perform one or more relatively simple tasks. **2.** An artistic contrivance in a literary or dramatic work used to achieve a particular effect. **3.** A plan or scheme, especially a malign one. **4.** A decorative design or pattern, such as one used in embroidery. **5.** A graphic symbol, emblem, or design, especially in heraldry. **6.** *Archaic.* The act, state, or power of devising. **—leave to one's own devices.** To allow to do as one pleases. [Middle English *devis, devise,* from Old French *devis,* division, contrivance, invention, and *devise,* difference, design, plan, both from *deviser,* to divide, DEVISE.]

dev·il (dĕv'əl) *n.* **1.** *Often* **Devil.** *Theology.* The major spirit of evil, ruler of Hell, and foe of God, often depicted as a man with horns, a tail, and cloven hoofs; Satan. **2.** A subordinate evil spirit. **3.** A wicked, malevolent, or ill-tempered person or animal. **4.** An unfortunate person or animal; a wretch: *poor devil.* **5.** A person who is energetic, mischievous, daring, or clever. **6.** The personification of something evil or undesirable. **7.** A printer's devil *(see).* **8.** Any of various mechanical devices with sharp teeth or spikes, as for tearing up rags. **9.** *Informal.* Anything difficult or hard to manage: *a devil of a job.* **10.** *Christian Science.* The opposite of Truth; error; a lie. **—(caught) between the devil and the deep blue sea.** Having to make a choice between two equally unsatisfactory options. **—give**

the devil his due. To acknowledge the ability or success of an evil or disliked person. **—go to the devil. 1.** To become thoroughly dissipated. **2.** Used as an exclamation of anger or irritation to a person who has annoyed one. **—(let the) devil take the hindmost.** To look after one's own interests and leave others to manage as best they can. **—the devil.** *Informal.* **1.** An exclamation or expletive used to express surprise, anger, disgust, vexation, or the like. **2.** Used as an intensive: *Where the devil is the waiter?* **—talk** (or **speak**) **of the devil.** Used when an absent person who has been the subject of conversation suddenly appears. **—the devil to pay.** Trouble to be faced as a result of some action.

~*v.* **deviled, -viling, -vils** or *chiefly British* **devilled, -villing.** *—tr.* **1.** To prepare (food) with pungent seasoning or condiments, such as mustard or cayenne pepper. **2.** To tear up (cloth or rags) in a toothed machine. **3.** To annoy, torment, or harass. *—intr.* To serve as a printer's devil. [Middle English *devel,* Old English *dēofol,* from Late Latin *diabolus,* from Late Greek *diabolos,* from Greek, slanderer, from *diaballein,* to slander, "throw across" : *dia-,* across + *ballein,* to throw.]

dev·il·fish (dĕv′əl-fĭsh′) *n., pl.* **-fishes** or collectively **devilfish. 1.** The **manta** *(see).* **2.** An **octopus** *(see),* or a similar cephalopod.

dev·il·ish (dĕv′ə-lĭsh) *adj.* **1.** Of, resembling, or characteristic of a devil; fiendish: *devilish cruelty.* **2.** *Informal.* Excessive; extreme: *devilish heat.*

~*adv. Informal.* Extremely; very. Not in current usage. **—dev·il·ish·ly** *adv.* **—dev·il·ish·ness** *n.*

dev·il-may-care (dĕv′əl-mā-kâr′) *adj.* Careless; reckless.

dev·il·ment (dĕv′əl-mənt) *n.* Devilish mischief.

devil's advocate *n.* **1.** *Roman Catholic Church.* An official appointed to present arguments against a proposed canonization or beatification. Also officially called "Promoter of the Faith." **2.** A person who opposes an argument with which he does not necessarily disagree, to determine its validity or be provocative. **3.** An adverse critic, especially of a good cause.

devil's bit *n.* A plant, the **blazing star** *(see).* [So called from the ragged bitten-off appearance of the roots.]

devil's darning needle *n. Informal.* A **dragonfly** *(see).*

devil's fingers *n. Usually used with a singular verb.* An ascomycete fungus, *Xylaria polymorpha,* that grows in blackish, club-shaped tufts on the stumps of deciduous trees. Also called "dead-man's fingers."

dev·il's-food cake (dĕv′əlz-fo͞od′) *n.* A rich, dark, dense-textured chocolate cake. [From the contrast with the white color of ANGEL FOOD CAKE.]

Dev·il's Island (dĕv′əlz). *French* **Île du Dia·ble** (ēl dü dyä′blə). Small island in the south Caribbean Sea, off French Guiana. A French penal colony for political prisoners from the late 19th century, it held Alfred Dreyfus (1894–99) and Henri Charrière ("Papillon"), who claimed to have made the first successful escape from it (1941). It was finally closed in 1945.

devil's paintbrush *n.* A plant, the **orange hawkweed** *(see).*

devil's walking stick *n.* A shrub, **Hercules'-club** *(see).*

dev·il·try (dĕv′əl-trē) *n., pl.* **-tries.** Also **dev·il·ry** (-əl-rē). **1.** Wanton or reckless mischief. **2.** Wickedness. **3.** Evil magic.

dev·il·wood (dĕv′əl-wo͝od′) *n.* A tree, *Osmanthus americanus,* of the southeastern United States, having fragrant greenish flowers and hard wood. [Because it is extremely difficult to cut.]

De Vin·ne (də vĭn′ē), **Theodore Low** (1828–1914). U.S. typographer. He was the best-known U.S. printer of his time and did much to advance the cause of good printing through his fine examples of workmanship and his influential writings, including *The Invention of Printing* (1876), *Historic Printing Types* (1886), and *The Practice of Typography* (1900–04).

de·vi·ous (dē′vē-əs) *adj.* **1.** Straying or deviating from the usual, straight, or direct course or way; circuitous; roundabout. **2.** Straying or departing from the correct or proper way; erring. **3.** Done, planned, used, or acting in an underhand manner; not straightforward; shifty: *a devious plot.* [Latin *dēvius,* off the main road : *dē-,* away from + *via,* way.] **—de·vi·ous·ly** *adv.* **—de·vi·ous·ness** *n.*

de·vis·a·ble (dĭ-vī′zə-bəl) *adj.* **1.** *Law.* Capable of being transmitted by will. Said of real property. **2.** Capable of being invented or contrived.

de·vi·sal (dĭ-vī′zəl) *n.* The act of devising.

de·vise (dĭ-vīz′) *tr.v.* **-vised, -vising, -vises. 1.** To form or arrange in the mind; plan; invent; contrive. **2.** *Law.* To transmit or give (real property) by will. **3.** *Obsolete.* To imagine; conceive.

~*n. Law.* **1.** The act of transmitting or giving real property by will. **2.** The property or lands so transmitted. **3.** A will or clause in a will devising real property. [Middle English *devisen,* to divide, distinguish, examine, design, from Old French *deviser,* from Vulgar Latin *dīvīsāre* (unattested), frequentative of Latin *dīvīdere* (past participle *dīvīsus*), to divide.] **—de·vis·er** *n.*

de·vi·see (dĭ-vī-zē′) *n. Law.* One to whom property is devised.

de·vi·sor (dĭ-vī′zər) *n. Law.* One who devises property.

de·vi·tal·ize (dē-vīt′l-īz′) *tr.v.* **-ized, -izing, -izes.** To reduce or destroy the vitality of.

de·vit·ri·fy (dē-vĭt′rə-fī′) *tr.v.* **-fied, -fying, -fies. 1.** To deprive of or destroy the glassy quality of. **2.** To treat (material such as glass) so as to cause crystallization, brittleness, and loss of transparency. [French *dévitrifier* : *dé-,* from Latin *dē-* (reversal) + *vitrifier,* VITRIFY.] **—de·vit·ri·fi·ca·tion** *n.*

de·vo·cal·ize (dē-vō′kə-līz′) *tr.v.* **-ized, -izing, -izes.** *Phonetics.* To unvoice (a speech sound). **—de·vo·cal·i·za·tion** *n.*

de·voice (dē-vois′) *tr.v.* **-voiced, -voicing, -voices.** *Phonetics.* To unvoice (a speech sound).

de·void (dĭ-void′) *adj.* Completely lacking; destitute; empty; without. Used with *of.* [Middle English *devoide,* from *devoiden,* to get rid of, from Old French *desvuidier* : *des-,* from Latin *dē-,* completely + *vuidier,* to empty, from Vulgar Latin *vocitāre* (unattested), from *vocitus* (unattested), empty, from Latin *vacāre,* to be empty.]

de·voir (də-vwär′, dĕv′wär′) *n.* **1.** *Usually* **devoirs.** Courteous attentions; compliments; respects: *pay one's devoirs to the host.* **2.** *Archaic.* Duty. [Middle English *dever, devoir,* duty, from Old French *devoir,* "that which is due," from *devoir,* to owe, from Latin *dēbēre.*]

de·vol·a·til·ize (dē-vŏl′ə-tl-īz′) *tr.v.* **-ized, -izing, -izes.** To remove volatile material from. **—de·vol·a·til·i·za·tion** *n.*

dev·o·lu·tion (dĕv′ə-lo͞o′shən) *n.* **1.** A passing down through successive stages. **2.** The passing to a successor of anything, such as properties, rights, or qualities. **3. a.** A delegating of authority or duties to a subordinate or substitute. **b.** The transfer of a certain amount of legislative or executive power from a central to a regional authority. **4.** Biological degeneration, as distinguished from evolution. [Medieval Latin *dēvolūtiō* (stem *dēvolūtiōn-*), from Latin *dēvolvere* (past participle *dēvolūtus*), to roll down, DEVOLVE.] **—dev·o·lu·tion·ar·y** *adj.*

de·volve (dĭ-vŏlv′) *v.* **-volved, -volving, -volves.** *—tr.* To pass on, delegate, or transfer (duty or authority, for example) to a successor or substitute. *—intr.* To fall or be passed on to a substitute or successor; be conferred. Used with *on, to,* or *upon:* "*With this high honor devolves upon you also a corresponding responsibility*" (Lincoln). [Middle English *devolven,* from Latin *dēvolvere,* to roll down : *dē-,* down + *volvere,* to roll.] **—de·volve·ment** *n.*

Dev·on[1] (dĕv′ən). Also **Dev·on·shire** (-shîr, -shər). County in southwest England, spanning the western peninsula between the Bristol Channel and English Channel. The land is hilly, rising to Dartmoor in the south and Exmoor to the northeast. The county is agricultural and famous for its cattle, clotted cream, and cider. The main towns are Exeter, the administrative center, and Plymouth.

Devon[2] *n.* Any of a breed of reddish cattle developed in Devon and raised primarily for beef.

Devon *Devon cattle, which are reared primarily for their beef, get their name from the southwestern English counties of Devon and Somerset, where they were originally bred. They are rarely found elsewhere.*

De·vo·ni·an (dĭ-vō′nē-ən) *adj.* **1.** Of or pertaining to Devon. **2.** *Geology.* Of, belonging to, or designating the geological time or system of rocks of the fourth period of the Paleozoic era, preceded by the Silurian and followed by the Mississippian or Carboniferous period, and characterized by the appearance of forests and amphibians.

~*n.* **1.** A native or inhabitant of Devon. **2.** *Geology.* The Devonian period or system of rocks. Preceded by *the.*

Devonshire cream *n.* A rich yellow clotted cream.

de·vote (dĭ-vōt′) *tr.v.* **-voted, -voting, -votes. 1.** To give or apply (one's time, attention, or self) entirely to a particular activity, pursuit, cause, or person. **2. a.** To dedicate by a vow or solemn act; consecrate. **b.** To set apart; give over to a particular purpose: *a broadcast devoted to Ireland.* **3.** *Rare.* To doom to destruction; curse. [Latin *dēvovēre* (past participle *dēvōtus*), to vow, devote : *dē-,* completely + *vovēre,* to vow.] **—de·vote·ment** *n.*

Synonyms: consecrate, dedicate, pledge.

de·vot·ed (dĭ-vō′tĭd) *adj.* **1.** Feeling or displaying strong affection or attachment: *devoted friends.* **2.** Consecrated; dedicated. —See Synonyms at **faithful. —de·vot·ed·ly** *adv.* **—de·vot·ed·ness** *n.*

dev·o·tee (dĕv′ə-tē′, -tā′) *n.* **1.** One ardently devoted or attached to anything; an enthusiast: *a devotee of sports.* **2.** One ardently or fanatically devoted to a religion.

de·vo·tion (dĭ-vō′shən) *n.* **1.** Ardent attachment or affection, as to a person or cause; faithfulness; loyalty. **2.** Religious ardor or zeal; piety. **3.** *Usually* **devotions.** An act of religious observance or prayer, especially when private. **4.** The act of devoting or the state of being devoted. —See Synonyms at **love, fidelity.**

de·vo·tion·al (dĭ-vō′shən-əl) *adj.* **1.** Of or pertaining to devotion. **2.** Used in worship.

~*n.* A short service of worship. **—de·vo·tion·al·ly** *adv.*

de·vour (dĭ-vour′) *tr.v.* **-voured, -vouring, -vours. 1.** To swallow or eat up greedily. **2.** To destroy, consume, or waste. **3.** To take in greedily with the senses or mind: *devour a novel.* **4.** To swallow up; engulf; absorb. [Middle English *devouren,* from Old French *devourer,* from Latin *dēvorāre* : *dē-,* completely + *vorāre,* to swallow, devour.] **—de·vour·er** *n.* **—de·vour·ing·ly** *adv.*

de·vout (dĭ-vout′) *adj.* **1.** Deeply religious; pious. **2.** Expressing reverence or piety. **3.** Sincere; earnest; devoted. [Middle English *devo(u)t,* from Old French *devot,* from Late Latin *dēvōtus,* from Latin, past participle of *dēvovēre,* to vow, DEVOTE.] **—de·vout·ly** *adv.* **—de·vout·ness** *n.*

De Vries (də vrēs′), **Peter** (1910–). U.S. author. With a comic, punning style, he has irreverently described American life in numerous novels such as *No But I Saw the Movie* (1952), *Reuben, Reuben* (1964), and *Slouching Towards Kalamazoo* (1983).

dew (do͞o, dyo͞o) *n.* **1.** Water droplets condensed from the air, usually at night, forming on cool surfaces, such as grass. **2.** Anything resembling or suggestive of dew; something moist, refreshing, or pure. **3.** Any moisture appearing in small drops, as tears.

~*tr.v.* **dewed, dewing, dews.** To wet with or as with dew; moisten; bedew. [Middle English *deu, de(a)w,* Old English *dēaw,* from Germanic.]

DEW distant early warning. See **DEW line.**

de·wan, di·wan (dĭ-wän′, -wôn′) *n.* Any of certain government officials in India, especially a finance minister, or the prime minister of

a state. [Hindi *dīwān,* from Persian *dīvān†,* register, account book, hence office of accounts, council of state. See also **divan.**]

Dew·ar flask (dōō'ər, dyōō'-) *n.* An insulated container used especially to store liquefied gases, having a double wall with evacuated space between the walls and silvered surfaces. [After Sir James *Dewar* (1842–1923), Scottish physicist who invented it.]

dew·ber·ry (dōō'bĕr'ē, dyōō'-) *n., pl.* **-ries. 1.** Any of several trailing forms of the blackberry, such as *Rubus hispidus,* of North America, and *R. caesius,* of Europe. **2.** The fruit of any of these plants.

dew·claw (dōō'klô', dyōō'-) *n.* A vestigial digit, claw, or hoof on the foot of certain mammals. [Because it reaches only the dewy surface of the ground.]

dew·drop (dōō'drŏp', dyōō'-) *n.* **1.** A drop of dew, or anything that resembles one. **2.** A North American plant, *Dalibarda repens,* having rounded leaves and white flowers.

Dew·ey (dōō'ē, dyōō'ē), **John** (1859–1952). U.S. philosopher and educator, one of the main exponents of philosophical pragmatism. He held that education should be as much concerned with physical and moral welfare as with intellectual development. His writings include *Democracy and Education* (1916), *Reconstruction in Philosophy* (1920), and *Experience and Nature* (1925).

Dewey decimal system *n. Library Science.* A system of classification of books and other publications into ten major categories, each category being further subdivided by number. Also called "Dewey classification." Compare **Library of Congress classification.** [After Melvil *Dewey* (1851–1931), U.S. librarian who devised it in 1876.]

dew·fall (dōō'fôl', dyōō'-) *n.* **1.** The formation of dew. **2.** The time of evening when dew begins to form. [From the erroneous assumption that dew falls like rain.]

dew·lap (dōō'lăp', dyōō'-) *n.* **1.** A fold of loose skin hanging from the neck region of certain animals, especially cattle. **2.** A similar pendulous part, such as the wattle of a bird. [Middle English *dewlappe* : DEW + *lappe,* LAP (loose flap).]

DEW line (dōō, dyōō) *n.* A line of radar stations at about the 70th parallel across the North American continent, designed to give advance warning of approaching aircraft and missiles. See **DEW.**

dew point *n.* The temperature at which air becomes saturated and produces dew.

dew pond *n. Chiefly British.* A manmade hollow, usually lined with clay or cement, found on chalk downs. Most of the water in it comes from condensation and rainfall.

dew·worm (dōō'wûrm', dyōō'-) *n.* Any earthworm found on or near the surface of the ground and used as fishing bait.

dew·y (dōō'ē, dyōō'ē) *adj.* **-ier, -iest. 1.** Wet or moist with or as if with dew. **2.** Pertaining to, resembling, or forming dew. **3.** *Poetic.* Suggestive of dew. **—dew·i·ly** *adv.* **—dew·i·ness** *n.*

dew·y-eyed (dōō'ē-īd', dyōō'-) *adj.* Characterized by childlike innocence and faith; naive.

dex (dĕks) *n. Slang.* Dextroamphetamine.

dex·ter (dĕk'stər) *adj.* **1.** Of or located on the right side. **2.** *Heraldry.* Located on the wearer's right and the observer's left. Compare **sinister. 3.** *Obsolete.* Auspicious; favorable. [Latin, on the right side.]

Dexter *n.* Any of a breed of small, hardy cattle originating in Ireland. [Perhaps from the surname of the breeder.]

dex·ter·i·ty (dĕk-stĕr'ə-tē) *n.* **1.** Skill in the use of the hands or body; adroitness. **2.** Mental skill or adroitness; cleverness: "*He admired the dexterity with which their host directed the conversation*" (Joyce). **3.** *Rare.* Right-handedness. [French *dextérité,* from Latin *dexteritās* (stem *dexteritāt-*), from *dexter,* skillful, DEXTER.]

dex·ter·ous, dex·trous (dĕk'strəs) *adj.* **1.** Adroit or skillful in the use of the hands, body, or mind; artful; clever. **2.** Done with dexterity. [Latin *dexter,* skillful, DEXTER.] **—dex·ter·ous·ly** *adv.* **—dex·ter·ous·ness** *n.*

   Synonyms: adroit, deft, handy, nimble.

dex·tral (dĕk'strəl) *adj.* **1.** Of, pertaining to, or located on the right side; right. **2.** Right-handed. Compare **sinistral. 3.** *Zoology.* Designating or pertaining to a gastropod shell that has its aperture to the right when facing the observer with the apex upward. [Medieval Latin *dextrālis,* from Latin *dexter,* DEXTER.] **—dex·tral·i·ty** (dĕk-străl'ə-tē) *n.* **—dex·tral·ly** *adv.*

dex·tran (dĕk'strən) *n.* Any of various heavy long-chain polymers of glucose that are used, depending on molecular weight, as a blood-plasma substitute, in confections, lacquers, and food additives. [DEXTR(O)- + -AN (chemistry).]

dex·trin (dĕk'strĭn) *n.* Also **dex·trine** (dĕk'strĭn, -strēn'). A white or yellow powder formed by the hydrolysis of starch, having colloidal properties, and used mainly as an adhesive and thickening agent. [DEXTR(O)- + -IN.]

dex·tro (dĕk'strō) *adj. Chemistry.* Dextrorotatory.

dextro-, dextr- *prefix. Abbr.* **d** Indicates on or toward the right-hand side; for example, **dextrorotatory, dextran.** [Latin, from *dexter,* on the right side.]

dex·tro·am·phet·a·mine (dĕk'strō-ăm-fĕt'ə-mēn', -mĭn) *n.* A drug, (C₉H₁₃N), that is the dextrorotatory form of amphetamine, acting as a stimulant on the central nervous system. It is commonly used as a sulfate or phosphate salt.

dex·tro·glu·cose (dĕk'strə-glōō'kōs', -kōz') *n.* **Dextrose** (see).

dex·tro·gy·rate (dĕk'strə-jī'rāt) *adj.* Dextrorotatory.

dex·tro·ro·ta·tion (dĕk'strə-rō-tā'shən) *n. Optics.* A turning to the right. Said especially of the plane of polarization of light.

dex·tro·ro·ta·to·ry (dĕk'strə-rō'tə-tôr'ē, -tōr'ē) *adj.* Also **dex·tro·ro·ta·ry** (-rō'tə-rē). **1.** *Optics.* Turning or rotating the plane of polariza-

Dexter *The smallest of British cattle, Dexters were bred in the mountains of western Ireland. Rarely found now, the breed is kept both for milk and beef.*

tion of light to the right or clockwise: *dextrorotatory crystals.* **2.** *Chemistry.* Of, pertaining to, or designating a solution that rotates the plane of polarized light to the right or clockwise; dextrogyrate. Compare **levorotatory.**

dex·trorse (dĕk'strôrs') *adj.* Growing upward in a spiral that turns from left to right: *a dextrorse vine.* Compare **sinistrorse.** [New Latin *dextrorsus,* from Latin, turned toward the right side : DEXTRO- + *versus,* past participle of *vertere,* to turn.] **—dex·trorse·ly** *adv.*

dex·trose (dĕk'strōs', -strōz') *n.* A dextrorotatory sugar, C₆H₁₂O₆·H₂O, found in animal and plant tissue and derived synthetically from starch. Also called "corn sugar," "dextroglucose," "grape sugar." [DEXTR(O)- + -OSE.]

dey (dā) *n.* **1.** The title of the governor of Algiers before the French conquest in 1830. **2.** Formerly, a title held by a ruler of Tunis or Tripoli. [French, from Turkish *dayı,* maternal uncle.]

DF direction finder.

DFC, D.F.C. Distinguished Flying Cross.

DFM, D.F.M. Distinguished Flying Medal.

dg decigram.

D.G. director-general.

DH designated hitter.

D.H. Doctor of Humanities.

dhak (däk, dôk) *n.* A tree, *Butea frondosa,* of tropical Asia that yields a red resin used as an astringent. [Hindi *ḍhāk†.*]

Dhaka. See **Dacca.**

dhal, dal (däl) *n.* **1.** A tropical shrub of the genus *Cajanus,* cultivated for its pealike seeds. Also called "pigeon pea." **2.** The edible seed of this shrub. **3.** An Indian dish made from dhal or other pulses, onions, and various spices. [Hindi *dāl,* (split) pulse, from Sanskrit *dal,* to split.]

dhar·ma (där'mə, dûr'-) *n. Hinduism & Buddhism.* **1.** The ultimate law of all things. **2.** Individual right conduct in conformity to this law. [Sanskrit, law.]

Dhílos. See **Delos.**

Dhi·mo·ti·ki (thē-mō'tē-kē) *n.* The colloquial form of Modern Greek. Also called "Demotic." Compare **Katharevusa.** [Greek, "demotic."]

D.H.L. Doctor of Hebrew Letters; Doctor of Hebrew Literature.

dho·bi (dō'bē) *n.* In India, a man who washes clothes. [Hindi, from *dhōb,* washing.]

dho·bi's itch (dō'bēz) *n.* Also **dhobi itch.** A fungal skin disease, *Tinea cruris.* [The disease being common in the tropics, and supposedly contracted from other people's dirty clothes.]

Dhodhekánisos. See **Dodecanese.**

dhole (dōl) *n.* A doglike, carnivorous mammal, *Cuon alpinus,* of Asia, having brownish fur, and often hunting in packs. [Of Anglo-Indian origin, akin to Kanarese *tōla,* wolf.]

dho·ti (dō'tē) *n., pl.* **-tis.** A long cloth worn round the waist and lower half of the body by Hindu men in India. [Hindi *dhōtī†.*]

dhow (dou) *n.* A lateen-rigged Arabian vessel. [Arabic *dāw†.*]

Dhul-Hij·ja, Dul-heg·gia (dūl'hĭj'ä). The 12th month of the Muslim year. Dhul-Hijja has 29 days. See feature at **calendar.** [Arabic *dhū'l-ḥijja,* "the one of the pilgrimage."]

Dhul-Qa·dah, Dul-kaa·da (dūl'käd'ä) *n.* The 11th month of the Muslim year. Dhul-Qadah has 30 days. See feature at **calendar.** [Arabic *dhū'l-ga'dah,* "the one of the sitting."]

di– *prefix.* Indicates: **1.** Twice, double, or two; for example, **dicotyledon. 2.** *Chemistry.* Having two atoms, molecules, or radicals; for example, **diacetylmorphine.** [Greek *di-,* two, twice.]

Di The symbol for didymium.

dia. diameter.

dia–, di– *prefix.* Indicates: **1.** Through or throughout; for example, **diachronic. 2.** Across or by transmission; for example, **diapophysis, diactinic. 3.** *Botany.* Over, across, or at right angles; for example, **diatropism. 4.** In opposite or different directions; for example, **diamagnetic.** [In borrowed Greek compounds, *dia-* indicates: 1. Through, throughout, as in **diapason.** 2. Across, as in **diagonal.** 3. Between, as in **diapause.** 4. Apart, as in **dialysis.** 5. From one to another, mutually, as in **dialogue.** 6. In different directions, as in **diathesis.** 7. Completely, as in **diaphragm.** 8. Made of, as in **diatessaron.** Greek *dia-* is the preverbal form of the preposition *dia†,* through.]

di·a·base (dī'ə-bās') *n.* **1.** Dark-gray to black, fine-textured igneous rock, composed mainly of feldspar and pyroxene, and used for monuments and as crushed stone. **2.** *Chiefly British.* Dolerite in which the pyroxene has been altered to amphibole. [French, from Greek *diabasis,* a crossing over, from *diabainein,* to cross over : *dia-,* across + *bainein,* to go.]

di·a·be·tes (dī'ə-bē'tĭs, -tēz) *n.* Any of several metabolic disorders marked by excessive discharge of urine and persistent thirst, especially diabetes mellitus. [Middle English *diabete,* from Medieval Latin *diabētēs,* from Greek *diabētēs,* "a crossing over or passing through" (from the symptomatic excessive urination), from *diabainein,* to cross over : *dia-,* across + *bainein,* to go.]

diabetes in·sip·i·dus (ĭn-sĭp'ə-dəs) *n.* A disease characterized by intense thirst and excessive urination, caused by a deficiency of the pituitary hormone vasopressin. [New Latin, "insipid diabetes."]

diabetes mel·li·tus (mə-lī'təs) *n.* A chronic disease of pancreatic origin, characterized by insulin deficiency, subsequent inability to utilize carbohydrates, excess sugar in the blood and urine, excessive thirst, hunger, and urination, weakness, emaciation, imperfect combustion of fats resulting in acidosis, and, without injection of insulin, eventual coma and death. [New Latin, "honey-sweet diabetes."]

di·a·bet·ic (dī′ə-bĕt′ĭk) *adj.* **1.** Of, pertaining to, or having diabetes. **2.** For the use of diabetics.
∼*n.* One afflicted with diabetes mellitus.

di·a·ble·rie (dē-ä′blə-rē; *French* dyä-blə-rē′) *n.* **1.** Dealings with demons or the devil; sorcery; witchcraft. **2. a.** The representation of devils or demons, as in paintings or fiction. **b.** Devil lore; demonology. **3.** Devilish conduct; deviltry. [French, from *diable,* devil, from Late Latin *diabolus,* DEVIL.]

di·a·bol·ic (dī′ə-bŏl′ĭk) *adj.* Also **di·a·bol·i·cal** (-ĭ-kəl). **1.** Of, concerning, or characteristic of the devil; satanic; hellish. **2.** Appropriate to a devil; extremely wicked; fiendishly cruel. [Middle English *deabolik,* from Old French *diabolique,* from Late Latin *diabolicus,* from *diabolus,* DEVIL.] **—di·a·bol·i·cal·ly** *adv.* **—di·a·bol·i·cal·ness** *n.*

di·ab·o·lism (dī-ăb′ə-lĭz′əm) *n.* **1.** Dealings with or worship of the devil or demons; sorcery; witchcraft. **2.** Devilish conduct or character. **—di·ab·o·list** *n.*

di·ab·o·lize (dī-ăb′ə-līz′) *tr.v.* **-lized, -lizing, -lizes. 1.** To cause to be diabolic or devilish. **2.** To bring under the influence of the devil. **3.** To represent as diabolic.

di·ab·o·lo (dē-ăb′ə-lō) *n., pl.* **-los. 1.** A game in which an hourglass-shaped top is spun and caught on a string held at each end by a stick. **2.** The top used in this game. [Italian, devil (the name of the top).]

di·a·caus·tic (dī′ə-kôs′tĭk) *n. Optics.* A caustic curve or surface formed by refracted rather than reflected light. Compare **catacaustic. —di·a·caus·tic** *adj.*

di·ac·e·tyl·mor·phine (dī-ăs′ə-təl-môr′fēn′) *n.* A drug, **heroin** *(see).*

di·a·chron·ic (dī′ə-krŏn′ĭk) *adj.* **1.** Considering phenomena as they occur or develop through time. **2.** *Linguistics.* Pertaining to or designating an approach to the study of language and linguistic phenomena from a historical perspective. Compare **synchronic.** [DIA- (through) + Greek *khronos,* time.]

di·ac·id (dī-ăs′ĭd) *adj.* Possessing two hydrogen atoms replaceable by metal atoms. Said of a salt.
∼*n.* An acid possessing two readily replaceable hydrogen atoms.

di·a·cid·ic (dī-ə-sĭd′ĭk) *adj.* Designating a base, such as calcium hydroxide, that is able to neutralize two protons. See **dibasic.**

di·ac·o·nal (dī-ăk′ə-nəl) *adj.* Of or concerning a deacon or the diaconate. [Late Latin *diācōnālis,* from *diāconus,* DEACON.]

di·ac·o·nate (dī-ăk′ə-nĭt) *n.* **1.** The rank or office of a deacon. **2.** A body of deacons. [Late Latin *diācōnātus,* from *diāconus,* DEACON.]

di·a·crit·ic (dī′ə-krĭt′ĭk) *adj.* **1.** Diacritical. **2.** *Medicine.* Diagnostic or distinctive.
∼*n.* A diacritical mark.

di·a·crit·i·cal (dī′ə-krĭt′ĭ-kəl) *adj.* Marking a distinction; distinguishing. [Greek *diakritikos,* distinguishing, from *diakrinein,* to distinguish : *dia-,* apart + *krinein,* to separate.] **—di·a·crit·i·cal·ly** *adv.*

diacritical mark *n.* A mark added to a letter to indicate a special phonetic value; for example, in French *façade,* the cedilla indicates that the *c* does not have its regular prevocalic value (k), but a sibilant value (s).

di·ac·tin·ic (dī′ăk-tĭn′ĭk) *adj.* Capable of transmitting chemically active, or actinic, radiation. Said of a lens filter, for example. [DI(A)- (across) + ACTINIC.] **—di·ac·tin·ism** (dī-ăk′tə-nĭz′əm) *n.*

di·a·del·phous (dī′ə-dĕl′fəs) *adj. Botany.* Having stamens in two bundles owing to the fusion of filaments. Compare **monadelphous.** [DI- (two) + -ADELPHOUS.]

di·a·dem (dī′ə-dĕm′) *n.* **1.** A crown or cloth headband, worn as a sign of royalty. **2.** Royal power or dignity. [Middle English *diademe,* from Old French, from Latin *diadēma,* from Greek *diadēma,* from *diadein,* to bind on either side : *dia-,* across + *dein,* to bind.] **—di·a·demed** *adj.*

diaeresis. Variant of **dieresis.**

diag. 1. diagonal. **2.** diagram.

di·a·gen·e·sis (dī′ə-jĕn′ĭ-sĭs) *n.* The changes that occur in sediments by which they become consolidated into rock, excluding weathering and metamorphism. **—di·a·ge·net·ic** (dī′ə-jə-nĕt′ĭk) *adj.* [DIA- (through) + -GENESIS.]

di·a·ge·ot·ro·pism (dī′ə-jē-ŏt′rə-pĭz′əm) *n. Botany.* The tendency of certain parts, such as rhizomes, to become oriented at right angles to the direction of gravitational force. [DIA- (over across) + GEOTROPISM.] **—di·a·ge·o·trop·ic** (dī′ə-jē′ə-trŏp′ĭk, -trō′pĭk) *adj.*

Di·agh·i·lev (dē-äg′ə-lĕf′), **Sergei Pavlovich** (1872–1929). Russian director and ballet impresario. He started his own company, Les Ballets Russes, in 1909 and influenced the evolution of the ballet as an art form. Among his collaborators were the artists Bakst, Picasso, and Cocteau and the musicians Stravinsky, Satie, and Milhaud.

di·ag·nose (dī′əg-nōs′, -nōz′) *v.* **-nosed, -nosing, -noses.** —*tr.* To distinguish or identify (a disease, for example) by diagnosis. —*intr.* To make a diagnosis. [Back-formation from DIAGNOSIS.] **—di·ag·nos·a·ble** *adj.*

di·ag·no·sis (dī′əg-nō′sĭs) *n., pl.* **-ses** (-sēz). **1.** *Medicine.* **a.** The act or process of identifying or determining the nature of a disease or injury through examination. **b.** The opinion derived from such an examination. **2. a.** The process of investigating and determining the nature of a condition or problem; especially, the identification and analysis of faults in a machine: *a computer diagnosis of faults in a car's electrical system.* **b.** The conclusion reached by such an investigation. **3.** *Biology.* A precise and detailed description of the characteristics of an organism for taxonomic classification. [New Latin, from Greek *diagnōsis,* discernment, from *diagignōskein,* to distinguish, discern : *dia-,* apart + *gignōskein,* to perceive.]

di·ag·nos·tic (dī′əg-nŏs′tĭk) *adj.* **1.** Of, pertaining to, or used in a diagnosis. **2.** Serving to identify a particular disease; characteristic.
∼*n.* **1.** *Often* **diagnostics.** The art or practice of medical diagnosis. **2.** A symptom serving as supporting evidence in a diagnosis. [Greek *diagnōstikos,* from *diagnōstos,* to be distinguished, from *diagignōskein,* to distinguish. See **diagnosis.**] **—di·ag·nos·ti·cal·ly** *adv.*

di·ag·nos·ti·cian (dī′əg-nŏ-stĭsh′ən) *n.* A person who diagnoses; especially, a medical practitioner specializing in medical diagnoses.

di·ag·nos·tics (dī′əg-nŏs′tĭks) *n. Used with a singular verb.* The science or practice of making medical diagnoses.

di·ag·o·nal (dī-ăg′ə-nəl) *adj. Abbr.* **diag. 1.** *Geometry.* **a.** Joining two nonadjacent vertices of a polygon. **b.** Joining two vertices of a polyhedron not in the same face. **2.** Having a slanted or oblique direction. **3.** Having oblique lines or markings.
∼*n. Abbr.* **diag. 1.** A diagonal line or plane. **2. a.** Anything arranged obliquely, such as a row, course, pattern, or part. **b.** A diagonal direction. **3.** A fabric woven with diagonal lines. [Latin *diagōnālis,* from Greek *diagōnios,* from angle to angle : *dia-,* across + *gōnia,* angle.] **—di·ag·o·nal·ly** *adv.*

di·ag·o·nal·ize (dī-ăg′ə-nə-līz′) *tr.v.* **-ized, -izing, -izes.** To order a matrix so that all the nonzero elements occur on the diagonal from upper left to lower right. **—di·ag·o·nal·iz·a·ble** *adj.* **—di·ag·o·nal·i·za·tion** *n.*

diagonal matrix *n.* A matrix that has been diagonalized.

di·a·gram (dī′ə-grăm′) *n. Abbr.* **diag. 1.** A plan, sketch, drawing, or outline, not necessarily representational, designed to demonstrate, describe, or explain something or clarify the relationship existing between the parts of a whole. **2.** A graphic representation of an algebraic or geometric relationship. **3.** A chart or graph.
∼*tr.v.* **diagrammed** or **diagramed, -gramming** or **-graming, -grams.** To indicate or represent by or as if by a diagram. [Latin *diagramma,* from Greek, from *diagraphein,* to mark out : *dia-,* apart + *graphein,* to write.] **—di·a·gram·ma·ble** *adj.* **—di·a·gram·mat·ic, di·a·gram·mat·i·cal** *adj.* **—di·a·gram·mat·i·cal·ly** *adv.*

di·a·graph (dī′ə-grăf′) *n.* **1.** An instrument used to draw copies of other drawings, such as maps, according to a desired scale. **2.** A protractor and scale combined. [French *diagraphe,* from Greek *diagraphein,* to mark out (in lines). See **diagram.**]

di·a·ki·ne·sis (dī′ə-kə-nē′sĭs) *n., pl.* **-ses** (-sēz). *Genetics.* The final stage of the prophase in meiosis, characterized by the separation of homologous chromosomes after chiasmata formation and the disappearance of the nucleoli and nuclear membrane. [DIA- (across) + -KINESIS (division).] **—di·a·ki·ne·tic** *adj.*

di·al (dī′əl, dīl) *n.* **1.** Any graduated, usually circular face or disk on which some measurement, as of speed, pressure, or temperature, is indicated by a moving needle or pointer. **2. a.** The face of a clock. **b.** A **sundial** *(see).* **3. a.** The panel or face on a radio or television receiver on which the frequencies or channels are indicated. **b.** The control on a radio or television receiver used to change the frequency or channel. **4.** A rotatable disk on a telephone with numbers and sometimes letters used to make connections. **5.** A miner's compass with sights, a spirit level, and a vernier, used for underground surveying.
∼*v.* **dialed** or **-alled, -aling** or **alling, -als.** —*tr.* **1.** To measure or survey with or as with a dial. **2.** To point to, indicate, or register by means of a dial. **3.** To telephone (the number of another telephone) by means of a dial. **4.** To select (a station or program) on a radio or television receiver by means of a dial. —*intr.* To use a dial, as on a telephone. [Middle English *diall,* sundial, from Medieval Latin *diāle,* clock dial, from *diālis,* daily, from Latin *diēs,* day.] **—di·al·er, di·al·ler** *n.*

dial. dialect; dialectal.

di·a·lect (dī′ə-lĕkt′) *n. Abbr.* **dial. 1.** A regional variety of a language, distinguished from other varieties by pronunciation, grammar, or vocabulary, especially: **a.** A variety of speech differing from the standard literary language or speech pattern of the culture in which it exists. Also used adjectivally: *a dialect word.* **b.** A variety of language that, with other varieties, constitutes a single language of which no single variety is standard: *the dialects of Ancient Greek.* **2.** The spoken language peculiar to the members of an occupational or professional group, an immigrant or minority group, or a particular social class. **3.** A manner or style of expressing oneself; idiom. **4.** A language considered as part of a larger family of languages or a linguistic branch: *Spanish and French are Romance dialects.* [Old French *dialecte,* from Latin *dialectus,* from Greek *dialektos,* speech, language, dialect, from *dialegesthai,* to converse : *dia-,* one with another + *legesthai,* middle voice of *legein,* to tell.]

di·a·lec·tal (dī′ə-lĕk′təl) *adj. Abbr.* **dial.** Pertaining to, characteristic of, or of the nature of a dialect. **—di·a·lec·tal·ly** *adv.*

di·a·lec·tic (dī′ə-lĕk′tĭk) *n.* **1.** The art of arriving at the truth by exposing the contradictions in an opponent's argument or beliefs and overcoming them; especially, the Socratic method of question and answer to elicit the truth. **2. a.** The process, formulated by Hegel, of reaching the truth or the absolute through change, whereby a proposition or idea (thesis) is transformed into its opposite (antithesis) and preserved and fulfilled by it, the combination of the two being resolved in a higher form of truth (synthesis), the ultimate synthesis being for Hegel the mind or thought. **b.** Hegel's critical method for the investigation of this process. **3.** The contradiction between two conflicting forces viewed as the determining factor in their continuing interaction. [Middle English *dialetik,* from Old French *dialetique,* from Latin *dialectica,* from Greek *dia-*

PRONUNCIATION KEY

ă, pat; ā, pay; âr, care;
ä, father, are; b, bib;
ch, church; d, deed; ĕ, pet;
ē, be; f, fife; g, gag; h, hat;
hw, which; ĭ, pit; ī, pie;
îr, pier; j, judge; k, kick;
l, lid, needle; m, mum;
n, no, sudden; ng, thing;
ŏ, pot; ō, toe; ô, paw, for;
oi, noise; ou, out; ŏŏ, book;
ōō, boot; p, pop; r, roar;
s, sauce; sh, ship, dish;
t, tight; th, thin, path;
th, this, bathe; ŭ, cut; ûr, fur;
v, valve; w, with; y, yes;
z, zebra, size; zh, vision;
ə, about, item, edible,
gallop, circus, peaceful

IN FOREIGN WORDS:

à, *Fr.* ami; œ, *Fr.* feu, *Ger.* schön; ü, *Fr.* tu, *Ger.* über; KH, *Ger.* ich, *Scot.* loch; N, *Fr.* bon; y′, *Fr.* Compiègne

STRESS MARKS:

Primary stress: ′
in·cite′ (ĭn-sīt′)
Secondary stress: ′
in′sight′ (ĭn′sīt′)

diamond *The many facets cut in this gemstone give it its brilliance. Because of their hardness, diamonds are also used as cutting tools in industry and science.*

diamondback *A coiled diamondback, one of the largest and most dangerous rattlesnakes, disturbed and getting ready to strike. The snake can grow to 2.5 meters (8 feet) long.*

lektikē (tekhnē), "(the art) of debate," from *dialektikos,* of conversation or discussion, from *dialektos,* discussion, debate, DIALECT.] **—di·a·lec·tic, di·a·lec·ti·cal** *adj.* **—di·a·lec·ti·cian** (dī'ə-lĕk-tĭsh'ən) *n.*

dialectical materialism *n.* The Marxist interpretation of reality, viewing matter as the primary subject of change and all change as the product of a constant conflict between opposites arising from the internal contradictions inherent in all things, these contradictions being resolved at higher levels and fresh contradictions arising. This theory has been applied to various areas of thought and scholarship, and especially to history. See **historical materialism.**

di·a·lec·tics (dī'ə-lĕk'tĭks) *n. Used with a singular verb.* **1.** Any method of argument or exposition that systematically weighs contradictory facts or ideas with a view to the resolution of their real or apparent contradictions. **2.** *Sometimes* **dialectic. a.** The Marxist doctrine, adopted from Hegel, of the process of change through the conflict of opposing forces, but asserting that matter, not mind, is the primary reality. **b.** The Marxist critique of this process. **3.** *Sometimes* **dialectic.** Logic, especially as used to expose invalid reasoning.

di·a·lec·tol·o·gy (dī'ə-lĕk-tŏl'ə-jē) *n.* The study of dialects. **—di·a·lec·to·log·i·cal** (dī'ə-lĕk'tə-lŏj'ĭ-kəl) *adj.* **—di·a·lec·tol·o·gist** *n.*

dial gauge *n.* A measuring instrument, the **indicator** *(see).*

di·a·log·ic (dī'ə-lŏj'ĭk) *adj.* Of, pertaining to, or written in dialogue. **—di·a·log·i·cal·ly** *adv.*

di·al·o·gism (dī-ăl'ə-jĭz'əm) *n.* **1.** *Obsolete.* A dialogue, especially an imaginary one contrived as a means of presenting divergent viewpoints. **2.** *Logic.* A form of argument having a single premise and resulting in a disjunctive conclusion.

di·al·o·gist (dī-ăl'ə-jĭst) *n.* **1.** One who writes dialogue. **2.** One who speaks in a dialogue. **—di·a·lo·gis·tic** (dī'ə-lō-jĭs'tĭk), **di·a·lo·gis·ti·cal** *adj.*

di·a·logue, di·a·log (dī'ə-lôg', -lŏg') *n.* **1.** A conversation between two or more people. **2.** A conversational passage in a play or narrative. **3.** The lines spoken by the characters in a play or narrative. **4.** A literary or philosophical work written in the form of a conversation: *the dialogues of Galileo.* **5.** An exchange of ideas or opinions. **6.** Diplomatic contact, negotiation, or discussion, especially between opposing nations or groups.
~v. **dialogued, -loguing, -logues.** Also **dialogged, -log·ging, -logs.** *—tr.* To express as or as in a dialogue. *—intr.* To converse in a dialogue. [Middle English *dialog(ue),* from Old French *dialogue,* from Latin *dialogus,* from Greek *dialogos,* from *dialegesthai,* to converse : *dia-,* one with another + *legesthai,* middle voice of *legein,* to tell, talk.] **—di·a·log·uer** *n.*

dial tone *n.* A low, steady tone in a telephone receiver indicating that a number may be dialed.

di·al·y·sis (dī-ăl'ə-sĭs) *n., pl.* **-ses** (-sēz'). The separation of smaller molecules from larger molecules, or of crystalloid particles from colloidal particles, in a solution by selective diffusion through a semipermeable membrane. **2. Renal dialysis** *(see).* [New Latin, from Greek *dialusis,* from *dialuein,* to tear apart : *dia-,* apart + *luein,* to loosen.] **—di·a·lyt·ic** (dī'ə-lĭt'ĭk) *adj.* **—di·a·lyt·i·cal·ly** *adv.*

di·a·lyze (dī'ə-līz') *v.* **-lyzed, -lyzing, -lyzes.** *—tr.* To subject to dialysis; separate by dialysis. *—intr.* To undergo dialysis. [Back-formation from DIALYSIS.]

di·a·lyz·er (dī'ə-līz'ər) *n.* An apparatus for performing dialysis, especially a kidney machine.

diam diameter.

di·a·mag·net (dī'ə-măg'nət) *n.* A diamagnetic substance.

di·a·mag·net·ic (dī'ə-măg-nĕt'ĭk) *adj.* Pertaining to or designating substances exhibiting diamagnetism.

di·a·mag·net·ism (dī'ə-măg'nə-tĭz'əm) *n.* The type of magnetism occurring in substances with a small negative magnetic susceptibility and a relative permeability of less than unity. It is caused by changes in the orbital motion of the electrons in the atoms of the substance and sometimes masked by the much stronger paramagnetism and ferromagnetism.

di·a·man·té (dē'ə-män'tā') *adj.* Decorated with or made from powdered glass or crystal, artificial jewels, or the like, in order to give the glittering effect of diamonds.
~n. **1.** Jewelry made from diamanté paste. **2.** Fabric having diamanté decoration. [French, past participle of *diamanter,* to stud with diamonds, from *diamant,* DIAMOND.]

di·a·man·tine (dī'ə-măn'tīn) *adj.* Of, pertaining to, or resembling diamonds. [French, from *diamant,* DIAMOND.]

di·am·e·ter (dī-ăm'ə-tər) *n. Abbr.* **dia., diam 1.** *Mathematics.* **a.** A straight line passing through the center of a figure, especially of a circle or sphere, and terminating at the periphery. **b.** The length of such a line. **2.** Loosely, the thickness or width of anything. [Middle English *diametre,* from Old French, from Latin *diametros,* from Greek *diametros (grammē),* "(line) which measures through" : *dia-,* through + *metron,* measure.] **—di·am·e·tral** *adj.*

di·a·met·ri·cal (dī'ə-mĕt'rĭ-kəl) *adj.* Also **di·a·met·ric** (-rĭk) (for sense 2). **1.** Of, pertaining to, or along a diameter. **2.** Exactly opposite; contrary.

di·a·met·ri·cal·ly (dī'ə-mĕt'rĭk-lē) *adv.* **1.** Along a diameter; straight across a circle or other figure. **2.** Absolutely; irreconcilably: *diametrically opposed ideologies.*

di·am·ine (dī-ăm'ēn, -ĭn, dī'ə-mēn', -mĭn) *n.* Any of various chemical compounds containing two amino groups, especially **hydrazine** *(see).* [DI- (two) + -AMINE.]

dia·mond (dī'mənd, dī'ə-) *n.* **1.** A highly refractive, colorless crystalline allotrope of carbon, used as a gemstone and in rock drills, abrasives, and cutting tools. It is the hardest naturally occurring substance and may be colored yellow, orange, blue, brown, or black by impurities. **2.** A figure with four equal sides forming two inner obtuse angles and two inner acute angles; a rhombus or lozenge. **3. a.** The red symbol appearing on one of the four suits of playing cards, in the shape of a diamond. **b.** A card bearing this symbol. See **diamonds. 4.** *Baseball.* **a.** The infield. **b.** The whole playing field. **5.** *Printing.* A small type size, 4½-point.
~adj. **1.** Of, resembling, or made with diamonds. **2.** Designating a 60th, or sometimes a 75th, anniversary: *diamond jubilee.*
~tr.v. **diamonded, -monding, -monds.** To adorn with or as with diamonds. [Middle English *diamaunt,* from Old French *diamant,* from Late Latin *diamas* (stem *diamant-*), variant of Vulgar Latin *adimas* (unattested), variant of Latin *adamas,* from Greek. See **adamant.**]

dia·mond·back (dī'mənd-băk', dī'ə-) *n.* **1.** Any of several large, venomous rattlesnakes of the genus *Crotalus,* of the southern and western United States and Mexico, having diamond-shaped markings. Also called "diamondback rattlesnake." **2.** Any of several turtles of the genus *Malaclémys,* of the southern Atlantic and Gulf coasts of the United States, having edible flesh and a carapace with roughly diamond-shaped, ridged or knobbed markings. Also called "diamondback terrapin." **3.** A moth, *Plutella maculipennis,* that is highly destructive to vegetables.

diamond bird *n.* Any bird of the species *Pardalotus,* found in Australia and Tasmania. Also called "pardalote." [From the diamond-shaped pattern of its plumage.]

Diamond Head. A promontory, 232 meters (761 feet) high, on the southeastern coast of Oahu Island in Hawaii. It is a famous symbol of the Hawaiian Islands and is now a national landmark to protect it from commercial development along Waikiki Beach.

dia·mond·if·er·ous (dī'mən-dĭf'ər-əs, dī'ə-) *adj.* Bearing or yielding diamonds.

diamond point *n.* A diamond-tipped stylus used for engraving.

dia·monds (dī'məndz, dī'ə-) *n. Used with a singular or plural verb.* One of the four suits of playing cards, distinguished by red diamond-shaped figures printed on the face of each card.

Di·an·a[1] (dī-ăn'ə). Princess of Wales, formerly Lady Diana Spencer (1961–). She married Charles, Prince of Wales and heir to the British throne, in a highly publicized wedding (1981). She is the mother of Prince William (1982–), second heir to the throne, and Prince Henry (1984–).

Diana[2]. *Roman Mythology.* The goddess of chastity, hunting, and the moon; identified with the Greek goddess Artemis.

Diana[3] *n. Poetic.* The moon. [From DIANA (moon goddess).]

di·an·drous (dī-ăn'drəs) *adj. Botany.* Having two stamens. [DI- (two) + -ANDROUS.]

Di·a·net·ics (dī'ə-nĕt'ĭks). A trademark used by the Church of Scientology and its affiliated organizations to designate the spiritual healing, technology, and related products and services offered by the Church and affiliated organizations and based on the writings of L. Ron Hubbard. See **Scientology.**

di·a·no·et·ic (dī'ə-nō-ĕt'ĭk) *adj.* Of or pertaining to reasoning; intellectual. [Greek *dianoētikos,* from *dianoia,* thought, process of thinking : *dia-,* through + *nous,* mind.]

di·an·thus (dī-ăn'thəs) *n.* Any plant of the genus *Dianthus,* which includes carnations and pinks. [New Latin *Dianthus* : DI- (two) + Greek *anthos,* flower.]

di·a·pa·son (dī'ə-pā'sən, -zən) *n. Music.* **1.** Either of the two principal stops on a pipe organ, the *open diapason* and the *stopped diapason,* which form the tonal basis for the entire scale of the instrument. **2. a.** The full range of notes; the compass of a voice or instrument. **b.** Range; breadth; scope. **3.** A former standard indication of pitch fixed in 1859 by the French Commission at the note A. Also called "diapason normal." See **concert pitch. 4.** A swelling burst of harmonious sound. [Middle English *dyapason,* from Latin *diapāsōn,* from Greek *(hē) dia pasōn (khordōn sumphonia),* (concord) through all (the notes) : *dia-,* through + *pasōn,* feminine genitive plural of *pas,* all.]

di·a·pause (dī'ə-pôz') *n. Biology.* A period during which growth or development is suspended, as in certain insects. [Greek *diapausis,* pause, from *diapauein,* to rest between times, pause : *dia-,* between + *pauein,* to stop, cease.]

di·a·pe·de·sis (dī'ə-pə-dē'sĭs) *n.* The passing of blood or any constituents, especially erythrocytes, through intact blood-vessel walls. [New Latin, from Greek *diapēdēsis,* "a leaping through," from *diapēdan,* to leap through, ooze : *dia-,* through + *pēdan,* to leap.] **—di·a·pe·det·ic** (dī'ə-pə-dĕt'ĭk) *adj.*

di·a·per (dī'ə-pər, dī'pər) *n.* **1.** A folded piece of cloth or other absorbent material placed between a baby's legs and pinned at the waist. Also *chiefly British* "nappy." **2.** A white cotton or linen fabric patterned with small diamond-shaped figures. **3.** A piece of such cloth, or such a pattern.
~tr.v. **diapered, -pering, -pers. 1.** To put a diaper on (a baby). **2.** To weave or decorate in a diamond-shaped pattern. [Middle English, from Old French *dia(s)pre,* from Medieval Latin *diasprum,* from Greek *diaspros,* ecclesiastical : DIA- (intensive) + *aspros,* white.]

di·aph·a·nous (dī-ăf'ə-nəs) *adj.* **1.** Allowing light to show through; transparent or translucent. **2.** Characterized by lightness or delicacy of form. [Medieval Latin *diaphanus,* from Greek *diaphanēs,* from *diaphanein,* to show through : *dia-,* through + *phainein,* to show.] **—di·aph·a·nous·ly** adv. **—di·aph·a·nous·ness** n.

di·aph·o·ny (dī-ăf'ə-nē) n., pl. **-nies.** Music. A simple form of polyphony; organum. [Medieval Latin diaphonia, from Greek diaphōnia, discord, dissonance, from diaphōnos, dissonant : dia-, apart + phōnē, sound.] **—di·a·phon·ic** (dī'ə-fŏn'ĭk) adj.

di·a·pho·re·sis (dī'ə-fə-rē'sĭs) n. Perspiration, especially when copious and medically induced. [Late Latin diaphorēsis, from Greek, from diaphorein, to disperse abroad (by perspiration) : dia-, in different directions + phorein, frequentative of pherein, to carry.]

di·a·pho·ret·ic (dī'ə-fə-rĕt'ĭk) adj. Producing perspiration. ~n. A diaphoretic medicine or agent.

di·a·phragm (dī'ə-frăm') n. 1. Anatomy. A muscular membranous partition separating the abdominal and thoracic cavities and functioning in respiration. 2. Any similar membranous part that divides or separates, such as a semipermeable membrane separating two solutions. 3. A thin disk, especially in a microphone or telephone receiver, the vibrations of which convert electric to acoustic signals or acoustic to electric signals. 4. A contraceptive consisting of a flexible cap that covers the uterine cervix. Also called "Dutch cap." 5. A disk having a fixed or variable opening used to restrict the amount of light traversing a lens or optical system. [Middle English diafragma, from Late Latin diaphragma, from Greek, from diaphrassein, to barricade : dia-, completely + phrassein, to enclose.] **—di·a·phrag·mat·ic** (dī'ə-frăg-măt'ĭk) adj. **—di·a·phrag·mat·i·cal·ly** adv.

di·aph·y·sis (dī-ăf'ə-sĭs) n., pl. **-ses** (-sēz'). The shaft of a long bone. [New Latin, from Greek diaphusis, spinous process of the tibia, from diaphuesthai, to grow between : dia-, between + phuesthai, middle voice of phuein, to bring forth, beget.] **—di·a·phys·i·al** (dī'ə-fĭz'ē-əl) adj.

di·a·poph·y·sis (dī'ə-pŏf'ĭ-sĭs) n., pl. **-ses** (-sēz). The superior or articular surface of a transverse vertebral process. **—di·ap·o·phys·i·al** (dī-ăp'ə-fĭz'ē-əl) adj.

di·ap·sid (dī-ăp'sĭd) n. In some classifications, a reptile of the subclass Diapsidia, having the upper and lower temporal regions of the skull distinct. [New Latin : DI- + Greek hapsis (stem hapsid-), arch.] **—di·ap·sid** adj.

di·ar·chy, dy·ar·chy (dī'är'kē) n., pl. **-chies.** Government by two joint rulers or ruling bodies. [DI- (two) + -ARCHY.] **—di·ar·chic** (dī'är'kĭk) adj.

di·a·rist (dī'ə-rĭst) n. A person who keeps a diary recording personal experiences and observations.

di·ar·rhe·a, di·ar·rhoe·a (dī'ə-rē'ə) n. 1. Excessive and frequent evacuation of watery feces. 2. Such feces themselves. 3. Any uncontrolled, excessive outpouring: verbal diarrhea. [Middle English diaria, from Late Latin diarrhœa, from Greek diarrhoia, "a flowing through," from diarrhein, to flow through : dia-, through + rhein, to flow.] **—di·ar·rhe·al, di·ar·rhe·ic, di·ar·rhet·ic** adj.

di·ar·thro·sis (dī'är-thrō'sĭs) n., pl. **-ses** (-sēz'). Any of several types of bone articulation permitting free motion in a joint. [New Latin, from Greek diarthrōsis, from diarthroun, to fasten by a joint, articulate : dia-, between + arthroun, to fasten, from arthron, joint.] **—di·ar·thro·di·al** adj.

di·a·ry (dī'ə-rē) n., pl. **-ries.** 1. A daily record, especially a personal record of events, experiences, and observations, or of engagements and appointments. 2. A book for keeping such a record; a journal. [Latin diārium, daily allowance, journal, from diēs, day.]

Di·as (dē'əs), Bartolomeu (c. 1450–1500). Portuguese navigator. In 1487 he set sail for Africa, but was blown off course by gales and rounded the Cape of Good Hope without sighting it. On his return from the Indian Ocean (1488) he finally sighted the Cape, the first European to do so, and named it the Cape of Storms.

di·a·scope (dī'ə-skōp) n. 1. A projector used to throw an optical image of a transparency onto a screen. Compare epidiascope. 2. Pathology. A flat glass plate that is pressed against the skin in order to examine superficial lesions. [DIA- + -SCOPE.]

Di·as·po·ra (dī-ăs'pər-ə) n. 1. a. The dispersion of the Jews after the Babylonian captivity. Also called the "Dispersion." b. The body of Jews living dispersed among the Gentiles after the Babylonian captivity. 2. The aggregate of Jews living outside Israel. 3. In the New Testament, the body of Christians living outside Palestine. 4. Often diaspora. A dispersion, as of any originally homogeneous people. [Greek, "dispersion" (Deuteronomy 28:25), from diaspeirein, to disperse : dia-, apart + speirein, to scatter.]

di·a·spore (dī'ə-spôr', -spōr') n. A white, pearly hydrous aluminum oxide, Al₂O₃·H₂O, found with corundum and emery and in bauxite. It is used as a refractory and abrasive. [Greek diaspora, scattering, DIASPORA (from the strong decrepitation of the mineral before the blowpipe).]

di·a·stase (dī'ə-stās') n. An amylase or a mixture of amylases that converts starch to maltose, found in certain germinating grains such as malt. [French, from Greek diastasis, separation, DIASTASIS.] **—di·a·sta·sic, di·a·stat·ic** (dī'ə-stăt'ĭk) adj.

di·a·sta·sis (dī-ăs'tə-sĭs) n., pl. **-ses** (-sēz). 1. Pathology. Separation of certain muscles during pregnancy, or of normally adjacent, unjoined bones without fracture. 2. Physiology. The last stage of diastole in the heart, occurring prior to contraction and during which little blood enters the filled ventricle. [New Latin, from Greek, separation, from diistanai, to set apart : dia-, apart + histanai, to cause to stand, set.] **—di·a·stat·ic** (dī'ə-stăt'ĭk) adj.

di·a·ste·ma (dī'ə-stē'mə) n., pl. **-mata** (-mə-tə). 1. Any bodily fissure or cleft, especially if congenital. 2. An abnormally large space between teeth. [New Latin, from Late Latin diastēma, from Greek,

interval, aperture, from diistanai, to set apart. See diastasis.]

di·as·ter (dī'ăs-tər) n. Biology. Anaphase (see). Not in current technical usage. [DI- (two) + Greek astēr, star.] **—di·as·tral** adj.

di·as·to·le (dī-ăs'tə-lē) n. Physiology. The normal rhythmically occurring relaxation and dilatation of the heart cavities, during which the cavities are filled with blood. [Greek diastolē, dilatation, separation, from diastellein, to expand, separate : dia-, apart + stellein, to put.] **—di·a·stol·ic** (dī'ə-stŏl'ĭk) adj.

di·as·tro·phism (dī-ăs'trə-fĭz'əm) n. The process or series of processes by which the major features of the earth's crust, including continents, mountains, and ocean basins, are formed. [Greek diastrophē, twisting, distortion, from diastrephein, to twist different ways, distort : dia-, in different directions + strephein, to turn, twist.] **—di·a·stroph·ic** (dī'ə-strŏf'ĭk) adj.

di·a·style (dī'ə-stīl') adj. Architecture. Having intervals of three to four diameters between the columns. ~n. Architecture. A diastyle building or arrangement of columns. [Latin, from Greek diastūlos, having spaced pillars : dia-, apart, through + stūlos, column, STYLE.]

di·a·tes·sa·ron (dī'ə-tĕs'ər-ən) n. 1. In Greek and medieval music, the interval of a fourth. 2. A single narrative made by combining the four Gospels. [Middle English, from Late Latin, from Greek dia tessarōn, consisting of four : dia, made out of + tessarōn, genitive of tessares, four.]

di·a·ther·mic (dī'ə-thûr'mĭk) adj. 1. Capable of transmitting heat or infrared radiation. 2. Of or pertaining to diathermy.

di·a·ther·my (dī'ə-thûr'mē) n. The therapeutic generation of local heat in body tissues by high-frequency electromagnetic waves. [DIA-, across, by transmission + Greek thermē, heat (see therm).]

di·ath·e·sis (dī-ăth'ə-sĭs) n., pl. **-ses** (-sēz'). A familial predisposition of the body to a disease, group of diseases, or structural or metabolic abnormality. [New Latin, from Greek, disposition, bodily state, from diatithenai, to dispose : dia-, in different directions + tithenai, to put, set.] **—di·a·thet·ic** (dī'ə-thĕt'ĭk) adj.

di·a·tom (dī'ə-tŏm', -təm) n. Any of various minute, unicellular or colonial algae of the class Bacillariophyceae, having siliceous cell walls consisting of two overlapping, symmetrical parts. [New Latin diatoma, from Greek diatomē, feminine of diatomos, cut in half, from diatemnein, to cut through, cut in half : dia-, through + temnein, to cut.]

di·a·to·ma·ceous (dī'ə-tə-mā'shəs) adj. Consisting of diatoms or their siliceous skeletons.

diatomaceous earth n. Diatomite.

di·a·tom·ic (dī'ə-tŏm'ĭk) adj. 1. Made up of two atoms. Said of a molecule. 2. Having two replaceable atoms or radicals.

di·at·o·mite (dī-ăt'ə-mīt') n. A fine, powdered siliceous earth, composed of the skeletons of diatoms, used in industry as a filler, filtering agent, absorbent, clarifier, and insulator. Also called "diatomaceous earth," "kieselguhr."

diatom ooze n. A siliceous sediment composed largely of the skeletons of diatoms, found on the deep (abyssal) ocean floor and on lake beds.

di·a·ton·ic (dī'ə-tŏn'ĭk) adj. Music. Of or using only the eight notes of a standard major or minor scale without chromatic variations. [French diatonique, from Late Latin diatonicus, from Greek diatonikos, from diatonos, "at the interval of a tone" : dia-, throughout, at the interval of + tonos, TONE.] **—di·a·ton·i·cal·ly** adv. **—di·a·ton·i·cism** (dī'ə-tŏn'ə-sĭz'əm) n.

di·a·tribe (dī'ə-trīb') n. A bitter and abusive criticism or denunciation; invective. [Latin diatriba, learned discourse, from Greek diatribē, "a wearing away," from diatribein, to rub hard, rub away, consume (time) : dia-, completely + tribein, to rub, wear out.]

di·at·ro·pism (dī-ăt'rə-pĭz'əm) n. The tendency of certain organisms or their parts to arrange themselves at right angles to the direction of a stimulus. [DIA- across, at right angles) + -TROPISM.] **—di·a·trop·ic** (dī'ə-trŏp'ĭk) adj.

Dí·az (dē'äs), Porfirio (1830–1915). Mexican soldier and politician. He became president of Mexico in 1876 following a coup and remained in office until 1880. He served a second term as president (1884–1911) but was forced to flee and died in exile.

di·az·e·pam (dī-ăz'ə-păm') n. A tranquilizer, Valium (see).

di·a·zine (dī'ə-zēn', -zĭn, dī-ăz'ĭn) n. A compound containing a benzene ring in which two of the carbon atoms have been replaced by nitrogen atoms; especially, any of three compounds so structured and having the composition C₄H₄N₂. [DIAZ(O) + -INE.]

di·az·o (dī-ăz'ō) Of, pertaining to, or consisting of a pair of nitrogen atoms bonded to each other and to an organic radical. [DI- (two) + A- (not) + Greek zoē, life.]

di·a·zole (dī-ăz'ōl, -ăz'ōl) n. An organic chemical in which the molecules contain a five-membered ring consisting of three carbon atoms and two nitrogen atoms.

di·az·o·me·thane (dī-ă'zō-mĕth'ān, -ăz'ō-) n. A yellow explosive gas, CH₂:N:N, used as a methylating agent.

di·a·zo·ni·um (dī'ə-zō'nē-əm) adj. Of, pertaining to, or containing the univalent cation RN² +, where R is an aromatic hydrocarbon radical. [DIAZ(O) + (AMM)ONIUM.]

diazonium salt n. An organic compound with the general formula RN² + X–, where R is an aromatic hydrocarbon and X– is an anion, such as the chloride ion, Cl–.

di·az·o·tize (dī-ăz'ə-tīz') tr.v. **-tized, -tizing, -tizes.** To cause (an aromatic hydrocarbon) to react with nitrous acid to produce a diazonium salt. **—di·az·o·ti·za·tion** (dī-ăz'ə-tə-zā'shən) n.

di·ba·sic (dī-bā'sĭk) adj. Chemistry. 1. Containing two replaceable

Dickens

THE MASTER STORYTELLER OF VICTORIAN ENGLAND

A gallery of immortal characters sprang to life from his pen

Charles Dickens was born in 1812 near Portsmouth—and his childhood was miserable. He had little regular schooling and, at the age of 12, after his father was jailed in London for debt, he was put to work in a shoe polish factory. The experience left him with an enduring sense of the intense harshness of industrial life in Victorian England and this provided the theme for such somber novels as *Bleak House* and *Hard Times*. He died suddenly of a stroke in June 1870, leaving unfinished his novel *The Mystery of Edwin Drood.*

AUTHOR'S DREAM *In this portrait Dickens dozes in his study, dreaming of the characters that crowd his books. Among them are Mr. Pickwick and Sam Weller, the comic heroes of his first literary success,* The Pickwick Papers *(published as a series of monthly chapters in 1836–37); Mr. Micaw-* *ber, the character based on Dickens's own father in the largely autobiographical novel* David Copperfield *(also published monthly in 1849–50); Fagin of Oliver Twist (published monthly in 1836–37); and the miser Scrooge in* A Christmas Carol *(1843).*

hydrogen atoms. **2.** Designating salts, or acids forming salts, with two atoms of a univalent metal. See **diacidic.** [DI- + BASIC.]

dib·ble¹ (dĭb′əl) *n.* Also **dib·ber** (dĭb′ər). A pointed gardening implement used to make holes in soil, especially for planting bulbs or seedlings.
~*tr.v.* **dibbled, -bling, -bles. 1.** To make holes in (soil) with a dibble. **2.** To plant by means of a dibble. [Middle English *debylle†.*]

dib·ble² *intr.v.* **-bled, -bling, -bles.** Also **dib** (dĭb), **dibbed, dibbing, dibs.** *British Regional.* In angling, to dip bait gently up and down in the water. [Probably variant of obsolete *dib,* to tap, dip, variant of DAB.]

di·bran·chi·ate (dī-brăng′kē-ĭt) *n.* Any of various two-gilled cephalopod mollusc of the former order Dibranchiata, which includes the octopuses, cuttlefish, and squids.
~*adj.* Of or belonging to the Dibranchiata. [New Latin *Dibranchiata* : DI- + BRANCHIATE.]

di·bro·mide (dī-brō′mīd′, -mĭd) *n.* A binary chemical compound containing two bromine atoms per molecule.

dibs (dĭbz) *pl.n. Slang.* Money, especially in small amounts. —**dibs on something.** *Slang.* A claim on (something); rights. [Short for *dibstones,* a children's game played with knucklebones, hence knucklebones, counters used in a game, money, probably from *dib,* to tap, dip, variant of DAB.]

di·car·box·yl·ic (dī-kär′bŏk-sĭl′ĭk) *adj.* Designating an acid that contains two carboxyl groups per molecule.

di·cast (dī′kăst′, dĭk′əst) *n.* In ancient Athens, one of the 6,000 citizens chosen each year to sit in the law courts, with functions resembling those of a judge and juror. [Greek *dikastēs,* judge, from *dikazein,* to judge, from *dikē,* custom, right, lawsuit.] —**di·cas·tic** *adj.*

dice (dīs) *n., pl.* **dice.** Also *singular* **die** (dī) (for sense 1). **1.** A small cube, as of ivory, bone, or plastic, marked on each side with a pattern of small dots, numbering from one to six, and used, usually in pairs, in games of chance. **2.** Any game of chance using dice. **3.** Any small cube. —**no dice.** *Slang.* **1.** Used to express a refusal. **2.** No luck or success.
~*v.* **diced, dicing, dices.** —*intr.* **1.** To play or gamble with dice.

2. To take risks: *dice with death.* —*tr.* **1.** To win or lose (money) by gambling with dice. **2.** To cut (food) into small cubes. **3.** To decorate with a pattern of squares. [Plural of DIE (cube).] —**dic·er** *n.*

di·cen·tra (dī-sĕn′trə) *n.* Any plant of the genus *Dicentra,* which includes the **bleeding-heart** and **Dutchman's-breeches** (both of which see). [New Latin *Dicentra,* "two-spurred" (from its dissected leaves) : *di-* (two) + Greek *kentron,* spur, point, center, from *kentein,* to prick.]

di·cey (dī′sē) *adj.* **-cier, -ciest.** Risky; unreliable. [From DICE (hence, risky).]

di·cha·si·um (dī-kā′zhē-əm) *n., pl.* **-sia** (-zhē-ə). *Botany.* A cyme in which two lateral branches occur at approximately the same level. Compare **monochasium.** [New Latin, from Greek *dikhasis,* division, from *dikhazein,* to divide in two, from *dikha,* in two.] —**di·cha·si·al** *adj.* —**di·cha·si·al·ly** *adv.*

di·chlo·ride (dī-klôr′īd, -ĭd, dī-klôr′-) *n.* A binary chemical compound containing two chloride atoms per molecule. Also called "bichloride."

di·chlo·ro·di·fluo·ro·me·thane (dī-klôr′ō-dī-flôr′ō-mĕth′ān, -flôr′ō-, dī-klôr′-) *n.* A colorless nonflammable gas, CCl₂F₂, used as an aerosol propellant, fire extinguisher, and refrigerant. See **Freon.**

di·chlor·o·di·phen·yl·tri·chlor·o·eth·ane (dī-klôr′ō-dī-fĕn′əl-trī-klôr′ō-ĕth′ān′, -klôr′ō-ĕth′ān′, dī-klôr′-) *n.* An organic compound, **DDT** (see).

dicho– *prefix.* Indicates two parts or a division into two parts; for example, **dichotomy, dichogamous.** [Late Latin, from Greek *dikho-,* from *dikha,* in two.]

di·chog·a·mous (dī-kŏg′ə-məs) *adj.* Having pistils and stamens that mature at different times, thus ensuring cross-fertilization rather than self-pollination. [DICHO- + -GAMOUS.] —**di·chog·a·my** *n.*

di·chot·o·mize (dī-kŏt′ə-mīz′) *v.* **-mized, -mizing, -mizes.** —*tr.* To separate into two parts or classifications. —*intr.* To be or become divided into parts or branches; fork. —**di·chot·o·mist** *n.* —**di·chot·o·mi·za·tion** *n.*

di·chot·o·mous (dī-kŏt′ə-məs) *adj.* Also **di·cho·tom·ic** (dī′kə-tŏm′ĭk). **1.** Divided or dividing into two parts or classifications. **2.** Characterized by dichotomy. —**di·chot·o·mous·ly** *adv.*

di·chot·o·my (dī-kŏt′ə-mē) *n., pl.* **-mies. 1. a.** Division into two usually contradictory parts or opinions; schism. **b.** Loosely, a lack of agreement or correspondence; discrepancy: *a dichotomy between their election promises and their performance.* **2.** *Logic.* The division or subdivision of a class into two mutually exclusive groups: *the dichotomy of truth and falsehood.* **3.** *Astronomy.* The phase of the moon, Mercury, or Venus when half of the disk is illuminated. **4.** *Botany.* Branching characterized by successive forking into two approximately equal divisions. [Greek *dikhotomia,* from *dikhotomos,* divided : DICHO- + *temnein,* to cut.]

di·chro·ic (dī-krō′ĭk) *adj.* Also **di·chro·it·ic** (dī′krō-ĭt′ĭk). **1.** Manifesting dichroism. **2.** Dichromatic. [Greek *dikhroos,* two-colored : DI- (two) + -CHROOUS.]

di·chro·ism (dī′krō-ĭz′əm) *n.* **1.** *Chemistry.* The property of showing different colors depending on the thickness of the medium or the relative concentration of coloring matter in it. **2.** The property possessed by some crystals of exhibiting different colors, especially two different colors, when viewed along different axes. Compare **pleochroism.** [Greek *dikhroos,* two-colored, DICHROIC.]

di·chro·ite (dī-krō′īt′) *n.* A mineral, **cordierite** (see). [DICHRO(IC) + -ITE.]

di·chro·mate (dī-krō′māt′) *n.* Any chemical compound which is a salt of the hypothetical acid, dichromic acid. A dichromate usually has a characteristic red-orange color. Also called "bichromate."

di·chro·mat·ic (dī′krō-măt′ĭk) *adj.* **1.** Possessing or exhibiting two colors. **2.** *Zoology.* Having two distinct color phases in the adult. Said of certain species of birds. **3.** *Pathology.* Capable of distinguishing only two colors. Also "dichroic," "dichromic."

di·chro·ma·tism (dī-krō′mə-tĭz′əm) *n.* The quality or condition of being dichromatic.

di·chro·mic (dī-krō′mĭk) *adj.* **1.** Dichromatic. **2.** *Chemistry.* Containing two chromium atoms per molecule.

dichromic acid *n.* An acid, H₂Cr₂O₇, known only in solution.

dick¹ *n. Slang.* A detective. [Shortened from DETECTIVE.]

dick² (dĭk) *n. British Slang.* A fellow. [From *Dick,* nickname for *Richard.*]

Dick (dĭk), **George Frederick** (1881–1967) and **Gladys Henry** (1881–1963). U.S. medical researchers. As a husband and wife team, they isolated the germ that causes scarlet fever and developed preventive medicine for the disease (1923). The next year they developed the Dick test, which determines a person's susceptibility to the disease.

dick·cis·sel (dĭk-sĭs′əl) *n.* A sparrowlike bird, *Spiza americana,* of central North America, of which the male has a yellow breast marked with black. [Imitative of its note.]

dick·ens (dĭk′ənz) *n.* Deuce; devil: *"I cannot tell what the dickens his name is"* (Shakespeare). [16th century : perhaps euphemistic for *(Old) Nick.*]

Dick·ens (dĭk′ənz), **Charles** (1812–70). British novelist. The son of an admiralty clerk who was imprisoned for debt, he was sent to work in a blacking factory at the age of 12. This, together with his school experiences, provided much of the material for his largely autobiographical *David Copperfield* (1849–50). After working in a solicitor's office, he became a journalist, going on to write sketches under the pen name "Boz" for the *Monthly Magazine. The Pickwick*

Papers, published from 1836 to 1837, established his popularity. His novels became an influential protest against the squalor and vices of Victorian society. Among his best-known books are *Oliver Twist, A Christmas Carol, Bleak House, A Tale of Two Cities, The Old Curiosity Shop, Nicholas Nickleby,* and *Great Expectations.*

Dick·en·si·an (dĭ-kĕn′zē-ən) *adj.* Of or characteristic of Charles Dickens, his novels, settings, and characters, or his literary style; especially, reminiscent of: **a.** The grim conditions of urban squalor and deprivation described in some of Dickens's novels: *the factory's Dickensian working conditions.* **b.** The cozy Victorian jollity of Dickens's sentimental family scenes.

dick·er (dĭk′ər) *v.* **-ered, -ering, -ers.** —*intr.* **1.** To bargain; barter; haggle. **2.** In politics, to make or attempt to make a deal by bargaining and barter. —*tr.* To trade or exchange.
~*n.* Barter or bargaining. [Probably from obsolete *dicker,* ten, ten hides (used as a unit of trade), Middle English *dyke,* Old English *dicor* (unattested), from West Germanic *dicura* (unattested), from Latin *dicuria,* set of ten, from *decem,* ten.]

dick·ey (dĭk′ē) *n., pl.* **-eys.** Also **dick·ie, dick·y** *pl.* **-ies. 1.** A woman's blouse front worn under a suit jacket or low-necked garment. **2.** A detachable shirt front. **3.** A collar for a shirt. **4.** A child's bib. **5.** *Informal.* Any small bird. Also called "dickybird." **7.** Either of two seats on a carriage, the forward outside driver's seat or a rear seat for servants. [From *Dick,* nickname for *Richard.*]

Dick·ey (dĭk′ē), **James** (1923–). U.S. poet. His volumes of energetic and technically versatile poetry include *Drowning with Others* (1962), *Helmets* (1964), and *Buckdancer's Choice* (1965). He is probably best known for his novel, *Deliverance* (1969), which was made into a highly successful motion picture.

Dick·in·son (dĭk′ən-sən), **Emily Elizabeth** (1830–86). U.S. poet. She wrote over 1,700 poems, although only 7 were published in her lifetime. The first volume of her work appeared in 1890.

Dick test *n.* A skin test for susceptibility to scarlet fever. [After Gladys and George Dick.]

di·cli·nous (dī-klī′nəs) *adj. Botany.* **1.** Having stamens and pistils in separate flowers: *a diclinous plant.* **2.** Having pistils but not stamens, or stamens but not pistils: *diclinous flowers.* [DI- (two) + Greek *klinē,* bed.] —**di·cli·ny** (dī′klī-nē) *n.*

di·cot·y·le·don (dī′kŏt′l-ēd′n) *n.* Also **di·cot** (dī′kŏt). Any plant of the Dicotyledoneae, one of the two major divisions of angiosperms, characterized by a pair of embryonic seed leaves that appear at germination, and including many trees, shrubs, and other flowering plants. Compare **monocotyledon.** —**di·cot·y·le·don·ous** *adj.*

di·cro·tism (dī′krə-tĭz′əm) *n.* A pathological doubling of the pulse with each beat of the heart. [From Greek *dikrotos,* double-beating : DI- (two) + *krotein,* to strike.] —**di·crot·ic** (dī-krŏt′ĭk) *adj.*

dict. 1. dictation. **2.** dictionary.

dic·ta. Plural of **dictum.**

Dic·ta·phone (dĭk′tə-fōn′) *n.* A trademark for a recording apparatus used for office dictation.

dic·tate (dĭk′tāt, dĭk-tāt′) *v.* **-tated, -tating, -tates.** —*tr.* **1.** To say or read aloud (something to be recorded or written by another). **2.** To prescribe expressly and with authority: *dictate a command.* **3.** To influence decisively; determine: *The choice of computer was dictated by the company's special needs.* —*intr.* **1.** To say or read aloud material to be transcribed by another. **2. a.** To issue orders or commands. **b.** To adopt an authoritarian attitude.
~*n.* (dĭk′tāt′). A directive or command: *the dictates of common sense.* [Latin *dictāre,* frequentative of *dīcere,* to say, tell.]

dic·ta·tion (dĭk-tā′shən) *n. Abbr.* **dict. 1.** The process of dictating material to another for transcription. **2.** The material dictated. **3.** *Formal.* Authoritative command or prescription; dictate.

dic·ta·tor (dĭk′tā-tər) *n.* **1.** A ruler having absolute authority and supreme jurisdiction over the government of a state; especially, one who is considered tyrannical or oppressive. **2.** One who has absolute authority or control in a particular sphere. **3.** One who dictates. **4.** In ancient Rome, a government official temporarily invested with absolute authority to deal with an immediate crisis or emergency.

dic·ta·to·ri·al (dĭk′tə-tôr′ē-əl, -tōr′ē-əl) *adj.* **1.** Tending to dictate; overbearing; domineering. **2.** Characteristic of or pertaining to a dictator; autocratic. —**dic·ta·to·ri·al·ly** *adv.* —**dic·ta·to·ri·al·ness** *n.*
Synonyms: *arbitrary, doctrinaire, dogmatic, imperious, overbearing.*

dic·ta·tor·ship (dĭk-tā′tər-shĭp′, dĭk′tā-) *n.* **1.** The office or tenure of office of a dictator. **2.** A state or government under dictatorial rule. **3.** Government by a dictator. **4.** Absolute or despotic control or power.

dic·tion (dĭk′shən) *n.* **1.** Choice and use of words in speech or writing; manner of expression. **2.** The degree of distinctness of speech; the manner of enunciation. [Latin *dictiō* (stem *dictiōn-*), from *dictus,* past participle of *dīcere,* to say.]
Synonyms: *articulation, enunciation.*

dic·tion·ar·y (dĭk′shə-nĕr′ē; *chiefly British* dĭk′shən-ə-rē) *n., pl.* **-ies.** *Abbr.* **dict. 1.** A reference book containing an explanatory alphabetical list of words, as: **a.** A book listing a comprehensive or restricted selection of the words of a language, identifying usually the pronunciation, grammatical function, and meanings of each word, often with other information on its origin and use. **b.** Such a book listing the words or other units of a particular category within a language: *a slang dictionary.* **2.** A book listing the words of a language with translations into another language. **3.** A book listing words or other linguistic items from particular fields, with special-

ized information about them: *a medical dictionary.* **4.** A reference book dealing with a particular subject: *a dictionary of modern history.* [Medieval Latin *dictiōnārium,* from Latin *dictiō,* DICTION.]

Dic·to·graph (dĭk′tə-grăf′, -gräf′) *n.* A trademark for a telephonic instrument that reproduces or records sounds from a transmitter by means of a small microphone.

dic·tum (dĭk′təm) *n., pl.* **dicta** (dĭk′tə) or **-tums. 1.** A dogmatic and authoritative pronouncement. **2.** *Law.* An **obiter dictum** (*see*). **3.** A popular saying; maxim. [Latin, from *dictus,* past participle of *dīcere,* to say.]

did. Past tense of **do.**

Did·a·che (dĭd′ə-kē) *n.* **1.** An anonymous church treatise of the 2nd century A.D. or possibly the 1st century A.D., known as the "Teaching of the Twelve Apostles." **2.** *didache. Theology.* The didactic element in early Christian teaching. Compare **kerygma.** [Greek *didakhē,* "a teaching," from *didaskein,* to teach.]

di·dact (dī′dăkt′) *n.* A person who is didactic. [Back-formation from DIDACTIC.]

di·dac·tic (dī-dăk′tĭk) *adj.* **1.** Intended to instruct; expository. **2.** Inclined to teach or moralize; pedantic. **3.** Intended to provide moral instruction, sometimes without regard for interest or style. Said especially of works of literature. [Greek *didaktikos,* skillful in teaching, from *didaktos,* taught, from *didaskein,* to teach.] —**di·dac·ti·cal** *adj.* —**di·dac·ti·cal·ly** *adv.* —**di·dac·ti·cism** (dī-dăk′tə-sĭz′əm) *n.*

di·dac·tics (dī-dăk′tĭks) *n.* *Used with a singular verb.* The art or science of teaching or instruction; pedagogy.

di·dap·per (dī′dăp′ər) *n.* A small grebe, such as the dabchick. [Middle English *didopper,* variant of *divedap, dovedop,* Old English *dūfedoppa,* pelican : *dūfan,* DIVE + *-doppa,* dapper.]

did·dle¹ (dĭd′l) *v.* **-dled, -dling, -dles.** Also *regional* **dad·dle** (dăd′l). —*tr. Informal.* To cheat; swindle. —*intr.* To waste time; dawdle. ~*n. Informal.* A swindle. [Probably back-formation from Jeremy Diddler, a dawdling, swindling character in *Raising the Wind* (1803), a farce by James Kenney, perhaps ultimately related to Old English *dydrian,* to delude, deceive.] —**did·dler** *n.*

did·dle² *v.* **-dled, -dling, -dles.** *Scottish.* —*tr.* To jerk back and forth. —*intr.* To move jerkily from side to side; shake. [Perhaps variant of dialectal *didder,* to quiver, Middle English *dideren,* probably variant of *doderen,* perhaps from Middle Low German.]

Di·de·rot (dē′də-rō′), **Denis** (1713–84). French philosopher and writer who helped to create the philosophical movement known as the Enlightenment through the *Encyclopédie* that he edited. This project ran to 28 volumes from 1751 to 1765.

did·ger·i·doo (dĭj′ə-rē-dōō′, dĭj′-ə-rē-dōō′) *n.* An Australian Aboriginal wind instrument, made from a long hollow wooden tube and blown to produce a droning sound. [Imitative.]

didn't (dĭd′ənt). Contraction of *did not.*

di·do (dī′dō) *n., pl.* **-dos** or **-does.** *Informal.* A mischievous prank or antic; caper. [19th century : origin obscure.]

Di·do (dī′dō). In Virgil's *Aeneid,* a Tyrian princess, founder and queen of Carthage, and lover of Aeneas.

Did·rik·son (dĭd′rĭk-sən), **Mildred Ella,** known as "Babe" (1914–56). U.S. athlete. One of the most talented and versatile athletes ever, she was an all-American basketball player (1930), won two Olympic track and field gold medals (1932), and then became a leading golfer, at one point winning 17 consecutive titles.

didst (dĭdst). *Archaic.* Second person singular, past tense, of **do.** Used with *thou.*

di·dy (dī′dē) *n., pl.* **-dies.** *Informal.* A baby's diaper. Typically said by or to children. [Variant of DIAPER.]

di·dym·i·um (dī-dĭm′ē-əm) *n. Symbol* **Di 1.** A metallic mixture, once considered an element, composed of neodymium and praseodymium. **2.** A mixture of rare-earth elements and oxides used chiefly in manufacturing and coloring various forms of glass. [New Latin, from Greek *didumos,* twin (so named from its association with lanthanum). See **didymous.**]

did·y·mous (dĭd′ə-məs) *adj. Botany.* Arranged or occurring in pairs; twin. [Greek *didumos,* twin.]

di·dyn·a·mous (dī-dĭn′ə-məs) *adj. Botany.* Having four stamens arranged in pairs that differ from one another, especially in length. [New Latin *Didynamia,* a former class of didynamous plants, "having two stamens stronger than the others" : DI- (two) + Greek *dunamis,* power (see **dynamic**).]

die¹ (dī) *v.* **died, dying, dies.** —*intr.* **1.** To cease living; become dead; expire. **2.** To cease existing, especially by degrees; fade or pass away: *The sunlight died in the west.* **3.** To lose vitality, activity, or force; become faint or weak. Often used with *away, out,* or *down: The storm died down.* **4.** To cease existing completely; become extinct. Often used with *off* or *out.* **5.** To cease functioning suddenly: *The engine died.* **6.** To experience the agony or suffering associated with death. **7.** To lose all attachment: *She died to the world.* **8.** *Informal.* To be completely overcome. Often used with *of: We died laughing. They were dying of thirst.* **9.** *Informal.* To desire something greatly or longingly: *dying for a drink; dying to go to the party.* **10.** *Theology.* To experience spiritual death. **11.** *Slang.* To get a very poor reception from an audience. —*tr.* To experience (a specified kind of death): *They died a peaceful death.* [Middle English *d(e)ien, deighen,* from late Old English *diegan,* from Old Norse *deyja.*]

Usage: *Die,* in its primary sense, it usually followed by *of* when expressing cause: *She died of a heart attack. From* is quite often used in informal speech.

Diesel engine

THE COMPRESSION-IGNITION ENGINE

The economy engine that is fired by hot air

Although the compression-ignition engine was invented in Britain in 1890, it was improved in Germany two years later by Rudolf Diesel. In this engine the fuel is not detonated by a spark as in the conventional internal-combustion engine but by the heat produced when air is compressed in a cylinder. It has several advantages over the gasoline engine. It needs no spark plugs or electric ignition system. Its fuel—diesel oil—is a heavier derivative of crude oil than gasoline and is cheaper.

At first Diesel's design was used as a stationary engine to generate electricity, and as a marine power unit in submarines and ships. Diesel engines are now used also in locomotives, trucks, taxis, buses, and many automobiles.

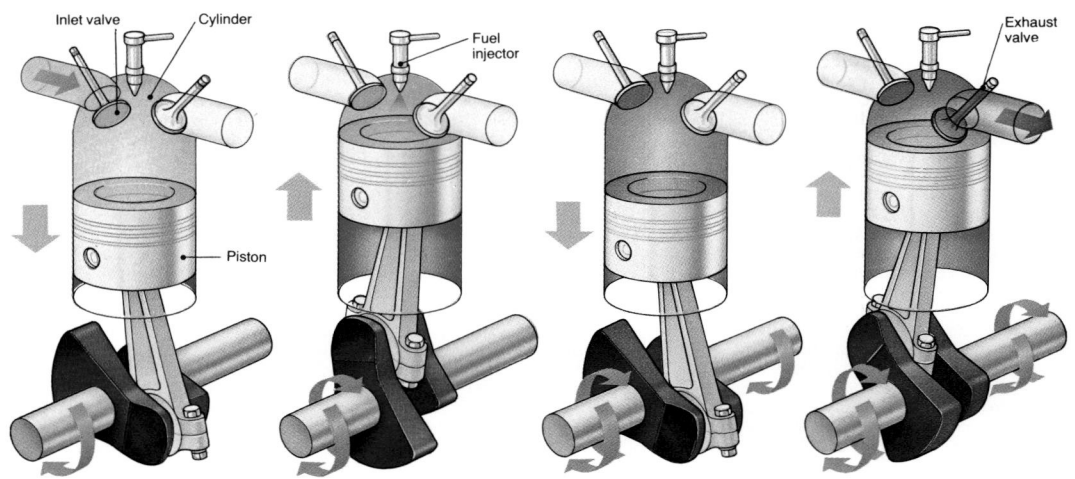

1. *Descending piston sucks air into cylinder through open inlet valve.*

2. *Inlet valve closes; ascending piston compresses and so heats air; fuel is injected.*

3. *Fuel, ignited by the heat, explodes and drives piston down.*

4. *Exhaust valve opens; ascending piston pushes burned gases out of cylinder.*

COMPRESSED POWER *In the diesel engine, the fuel is ignited by the heat developed when air is compressed in the cylinder. On the induction stroke the engine draws in a charge of air, and on the compression stroke subjects it to compression. This heats the air to a very high temperature. Fuel is injected and the temperature of the heated air is sufficient to ignite it.*

---

die² *n.*, *pl.* **dies** (for senses 1, 2) or **dice** (dīs) (for sense 3). **1.** Any of various devices used for cutting out, forming, or stamping material, especially: **a.** An engraved metal piece used for impressing a design upon a softer metal, as in minting coins. **b.** Any of several component pieces that are fitted into a diestock to cut threads on screws or bolts. Compare **tap. c.** A part on a machine that punches shaped holes in, cuts, or forms sheet metal, cardboard, or other material. **d.** A metal block containing small conical holes through which plastic, metal, or other ductile material is extruded or drawn. **2.** *Architecture.* The dado of a pedestal, especially when cube-shaped. **3.** One of a pair of **dice** (*see*). **—the die is cast.** The decision has been made and is irrevocable.
~*tr.v.* **died, dieing, dies.** To cut, form, or stamp with or as with a die. [Middle English *dee,* from Old French *de,* from Vulgar Latin *datum* (unattested), "playing piece," from Latin, neuter past participle of *dare,* to give, "play"; idiom, translation of Latin *alea jacta est,* supposedly said by Julius Caesar upon crossing the Rubicon.]

die back *intr.v.* To be affected by dieback.

die-back (dī′băk′) *n.* A condition leading to the gradual dying of plant shoots, starting at the tips, as a result of various diseases or climatic conditions.

die-cast (dī′kăst′) *tr.v.* **-cast, -casting, -casts.** To form by pressing molten metal into a die under pressure. **—die-cast·er** *n.*

diecious. Variant of **dioecious.**

dief·fen·bach·i·a (dēf′ən-băk′ē-ə) *n.* Also **dif·fen·bach·i·a** (dĭf′ən-). Any of various erect evergreen plants of the genus *Dieffenbachia,* native to tropical America, often kept as house plants for their attractive spotted foliage. Also called "dumb cane." [New Latin, after J.F. *Dieffenbach* (1794–1847), German botanist.]

die-hard, die·hard (dī′härd′) *n.* One who stubbornly refuses to abandon a position or resists apparently inevitable change. **—die-hard** *adj.* **—die-hard·ism** *n.*

diel·drin (dēl′drən) *n.* A contact insecticide based on a chlorinated naphthalene derivative, $C_{12}H_8OCl_6$, that is widely used for such purposes as mothproofing furnishings. [From *Diels-Alder reaction + -IN.*]

di·e·lec·tric (dī′ə-lĕk′trĭk) *n.* A nonconductor of electricity; especially, a substance with electrical conductivity of less than a millionth (10^{-6}) of a siemens. [DI(A)- (through) + ELECTRIC.] **—di·e·lec·tric** *adj.* **—di·e·lec·tri·cal·ly** *adv.*

dielectric constant *n.* Relative permittivity. See **permittivity.**

dielectric heating *n.* The heating of electrically nonconducting materials by a rapidly varying electrostatic field, widely used in the manufacture of furniture, plastics, foam rubber, and other products.

Diels (dēlz, dēls), **Otto Paul Herman** (1876–1954). German chemist whose work with Kurt Alder (1902–58) on converting linear organic molecules into cyclic molecules earned them the 1950 Nobel Prize.

Diels-Al·der reaction (dēls′ôl′dər, -ōl′dər) *n.* A chemical reaction in which an aromatic compound is formed from a diene and a compound containing a single double bond. [After Otto DIELS and Kurt *Alder* (1902–58), German chemists.]

Di·em (dē-ĕm′, dyĕm), **Ngo Dinh** (1901–63). Vietnamese political leader. After refusing to join the Communist Party, he fled Vietnam until 1954, when he returned to head the South Vietnamese government. A Catholic, he favored members of his religion in a predominantly Buddhist country. He was assassinated by his generals during a coup d'état.

Dien Bien (dyĕn′ byĕn′). Formerly **Dien Bien Phu** (foō′). A village in northeast Vietnam, where in 1954 a French fortress fell to Vietminh troops after almost three months of almost continuous fighting. The defeat led to the French withdrawal from Vietnam.

di·en·ceph·a·lon (dī′ĕn-sĕf′ə-lŏn′) *n.* The posterior part of the forebrain that connects the midbrain with the cerebral hemispheres and contains the thalamus, hypothalamus, and pituitary gland. Also called "interbrain," "thalamencephalon." [New Latin : DI(A)- (between) + ENCEPHALON.]

di·ene (dī′ēn′) *n.* An unsaturated hydrocarbon containing two double bonds. [DI- + -ENE.]

–diene *suffix. Chemistry.* Indicates a compound containing two double bonds; for example, **butadiene.** [DI- (two) + -ENE.]

Di·eppe (dē-ĕp′). Channel port and resort in Seine-Maritime department, northern France.

di·er·e·sis, di·aer·e·sis (dī-ĕr′ĭ-sĭs) *n.*, *pl.* **-ses** (-sēz′). **1.** A mark (¨) placed over the second of two adjacent vowels, and occasionally over a vowel following a consonant, to indicate: **a.** That two separate sounds are to be pronounced; for example, Noël. **b.** That a vowel which might otherwise have been interpreted as mute is to be pronounced; for example, **Brontë.** See **umlaut. 2.** The separation of two adjacent vowels into separate syllables. **3.** In poetry, a slight pause at the end of a line that occurs when the end of a word and the end of a metric foot coincide. Compare **syneresis.** [Late Latin, from Greek *diairesis,* division, separation; from *diairein,* to separate : *dia-,* apart + *hairein,* to take.]

die·sel (dē′zəl, -səl) *n.* **1.** A diesel engine. **2.** A vehicle, especially a locomotive, using a diesel engine. **3.** Diesel fuel. [After Rudolf *Diesel* (1858–1913), German engineer.] **—die·sel** *adj.*

diesel cycle *n.* A four-stroke engine cycle in which combustion takes place at constant pressure and heat is rejected at constant volume. Compare **Otto cycle.**

die·sel·e·lec·tric (dē'zəl-ĭ-lĕk'trĭk, dē'səl-) *adj.* Designating a locomotive in which a diesel engine drives an electric generator, the current from which is used to drive electric motors. —*n.* A diesel-electric locomotive.

diesel engine *n. Sometimes* **Diesel.** An internal-combustion engine that uses heat caused by high compression, rather than a spark plug, to ignite the fuel mixture. Also called "diesel motor," "diesel," "compression-ignition engine." [See **diesel.**]

diesel fuel *n.* A petroleum-based fuel used for diesel engines. Also called "diesel."

die·sel·ize (dē'zə-līz', -sə-līz') *tr.v.* **-ized, -izing, -izes.** To equip with a diesel engine or machinery using diesel engines.

Di·es I·rae (dī'ēz ī'rē; *Latin* dē'ās ē'rī) *n.* A medieval Latin hymn describing the Day of Judgment, used in some Masses for the dead. [Latin, "day of wrath."]

di·e·sis (dī'ə-sĭs) *n., pl.* **-ses** (-sēz') The **double dagger** *(see).* [Middle English, semitone, interval of a semitone (often indicated by a double dagger), from Latin, quarter tone, from Greek, "a letting through," from *diienai,* send through, discharge : *dia-,* through + *hienai,* to send.]

di·es non (dī'ēz nŏn') *n. Law.* A day on which courts may not convene nor any legal business be transacted. Also called "dies non juridicus." Compare **juridical days.** [Latin, short for *dies non juridicus,* "day without courts."]

die·stock (dī'stŏk') *n.* An apparatus for holding dies that cut threads on screws, bolts, pipes, or rods.

di·et¹ (dī'ət) *n.* **1.** The usual food and drink of a person or animal. **2.** A regulated selection of foods, especially as prescribed for gaining or losing weight or for other medical reasons: *a high-protein diet.* **3.** Anything taken or provided regularly: *her usual diet of thrillers.* —*v.* **dieted, -eting, -ets.** —*tr.* To regulate or prescribe food and drink for. —*intr.* **1.** To eat and drink according to a regulated system, especially in order to lose weight. **2.** *Archaic.* To eat or feed. [Middle English *diete,* from Old French, from Latin *diaeta,* from Greek *diaita,* mode of life, regimen, diet, from *diaitan,* to lead one's life.] —**di·et·er** *n.*

diet² *n.* **1.** *Sometimes* **Diet.** A legislative assembly in certain countries, such as Japan. **2.** *Scottish.* **a.** A single daily session of a court or local legislature. **b.** A day upon which a court convenes. **3.** **Diet.** The semiannual general assembly of the estates of the former Holy Roman Empire. [Middle English *diete, dyet,* day's journey, day for meeting, from Medieval Latin *diēta,* from Latin *diēs,* day.]

diet. dietetics.

di·e·tar·y (dī'ə-tĕr'ē) *adj.* Of or pertaining to diet. —*n., pl.* **dietaries. 1.** A system or regimen of dieting. **2.** A regulated daily food allowance.

dietary fiber *n.* **Roughage** *(see).*

dietary laws *pl.n.* In certain religions such as Judaism or Islam, a body of regulations prescribing the kinds and combinations of food that may be eaten by the orthodox.

di·e·tet·ic (dī'ə-tĕt'ĭk) *adj.* **1.** Of or pertaining to diet or its regulation. **2.** Specially prepared or processed for restrictive diets. [Late Latin *diaetēticus,* from Greek *diaitētikos,* from *diaita,* DIET.] —**di·e·tet·i·cal·ly** *adv.*

di·e·tet·ics (dī'ə-tĕt'ĭks) *n. Used with a singular verb. Abbr.* **diet.** The study of diet and dieting as it relates to health and hygiene.

di·eth·y·lene glycol (dī-ĕth'ə-lēn') *n.* A clear, colorless, extremely hygroscopic, syrupy liquid, $CH_2OHCH_2OCH_2CH_2OH$, widely used as an antifreeze, solvent, softening agent, and herbicide.

di·eth·yl ether (dī'ĕth'əl) *n.* **Ether** *(see).*

di·eth·yl·stil·bes·trol (dī-ĕth'əl-stĭl-bĕs'trôl') *n. Abbr.* **DES** A synthetic estrogen, $C_{18}H_{20}O_2$, used as an estrogen substitute, especially in the treatment of menstrual disorders. Also called "stilbestrol."

diethyl tol·u·am·ide (tŏl'yōō-ăm'īd') *n.* **Deet** *(see).* [DIETHYL TOLU(ENE) + AMIDE.]

di·e·ti·tian, di·e·ti·cian (dī'ə-tĭsh'ən) *n.* A person specializing in dietetics.

Die·trich (dē'trĭk), **Marlene,** born Maria Magdalena von Losch *(c.* 1901–92). German-American actress, singer, and screen star. Her international reputation was made in 1930 with Josef von Sternberg's German film *The Blue Angel.* Her Hollywood films include *Morocco* (1930), *Shanghai Express* (1932), and *Destry Rides Again* (1939).

dif., diff. difference; different.

diffenbachia. Variant of **dieffenbachia.**

dif·fer (dĭf'ər) *intr.v.* **-fered, -fering, -fers. 1.** To be unlike or dissimilar in nature, quality, amount, or form. Often used with *from.* **2.** To be of a different opinion; disagree; dissent. Often used with *with.* **3.** To quarrel. [Middle English *differen,* from Old French *differer,* from Latin *differre,* to carry in different directions, be different : *dis-,* apart + *ferre,* to carry.]

dif·fer·ence (dĭf'ər-əns, dĭf'rəns) *n. Abbr.* **dif., diff. 1.** The condition or degree of being unlike, dissimilar, or diverse; disparity; variation. **2.** A specific point of disparity or unlikeness; an instance of variation. **3.** *Archaic.* A distinct mark or peculiarity. **4.** A disagreement; quarrel. **5.** A distinction or discrimination. **6. a.** A substantial change: *Do you see a difference in her these days?* **b.** A critical factor in determining an outcome: *A good pension can be the difference between hardship and comfort in old age.* **7.** *Mathematics.* **a.** The amount by which one quantity is greater or less than another. **b.** The amount that remains after one quantity is subtracted from another. Also called "remainder." **8.** *Logic.* A differentia.

9. *Heraldry.* A distinguishing mark on a coat of arms to differentiate branches of the same family. —**make a difference.** To alter matters significantly. —*tr.v.* **differenced, -encing, -ences. 1.** To make or cause to make a difference between or in; distinguish. **2.** *Heraldry.* To add a distinguishing mark to (a coat of arms).

Usage: difference, discrepancy, dissimilarity, distinction, divergence, unlikeness, variation. These nouns refer to lack of correspondence, agreement, or equality, as revealed by comparison. *Difference,* the most general, applies to any such condition. *Discrepancy* stresses the idea of difference, such as conflict or contradiction, that should not exist, as discrepancies in two accounts of an incident or between financial statements. *Dissimilarity* points up difference between things otherwise alike or capable of close comparison. *Distinction* usually means a slight difference in detail between like or related things, determined only by close inspection. The difference is also subjectively determined rather than palpable or factual. *Divergence* implies a gradually developing difference between things originally similar or alike. *Unlikeness* usually implies greater and more obvious difference. *Variation* is difference between things of the same class or species; often it refers to modification of something original, prescribed, or typical.

dif·fer·ent (dĭf'ə-rənt, dĭf'rənt) *adj. Abbr.* **dif., diff. 1.** Characterized by a difference; unlike. **2.** Distinct; separate. **3.** Differing from the ordinary; special or unusual. —*adv. Nonstandard.* Differently. [Middle English, from Old French, from Latin *differēns* (stem *different-*), present participle of *differre,* to DIFFER.] —**dif·fer·ent·ly** *adv.* —**dif·fer·ent·ness** *n.*

Usage: A long-standing usage dispute focuses on the correct choice of word to use following *different* and *differently,* in such sentences as *This book is different . . . that, She behaves differently . . . Joan. Different from* is the traditional standard form, particularly when it is followed by a single noun or pronoun or by a short phrase or clause: *This illustration is different from that. This was different from what we expected.* But *different than* has wider acceptance, as an aid to conciseness, when the passage that follows is a clause (frequently a shortened or elliptical clause): *How different things seem now than yesterday,* rather than *How different things seem now from what they were yesterday.* Here the use of *different from* becomes ponderous; consequently the alternative to *different than* is to rephrase completely. *Different to,* a third form, is principally British. In an unrelated but common construction, *different* is superfluous: *Three different doctors examined him.*

dif·fer·en·ti·a (dĭf'ər-ĕn'shē-ə) *n., pl.* **-tiae** (-shē-ē', -shē-ī'). *Logic.* An attribute that characterizes and distinguishes a species from others of the same genus. [Latin, difference.]

dif·fer·en·ti·a·ble (dĭf'ə-rĕn'shē-ə-bəl) *adj.* **1.** Capable of being differentiated. **2.** *Mathematics.* Possessing a derivative. —**dif·fer·en·ti·a·bil·i·ty** *n.*

dif·fer·en·tial (dĭf'ə-rĕn'shəl) *adj.* **1.** Pertaining to or showing a difference or differences. **2.** Constituting or making a difference; distinctive. **3.** Dependent on or making use of a difference or distinction. **4.** *Mathematics.* Of or pertaining to differentiation. **5.** Involving differences in speed or direction of motion: *a differential pulley.* —*n.* **1.** A factor that constitutes or makes a difference. **2.** *Mathematics.* **a.** An infinitesimal increment in a variable. **b.** The product of the derivative of a function of one variable multiplied by the independent variable increment. **3.** A differential gear. **4.** A difference in costs, charges, or rates; especially, a difference in rates of pay, as between different types of work in the same industry or profession, or similar work done in different places or circumstances. —**dif·fer·en·tial·ly** *adv.*

differential analyzer *n.* A mechanical or electronic analog computer used to solve especially complicated differential equations.

differential calculus *n.* The mathematics of the variation of a function with respect to changes in independent variables; loosely, the study of slopes of curves, accelerations, maxima, and minima by means of derivatives and differentials.

differential coefficient *n. Mathematics.* A derivative *(see).*

differential diagnosis *n. Medicine.* The process or an instance of distinguishing between different diseases with similar signs or symptoms.

differential equation *n.* An equation containing derivatives or differentials of an unknown function.

differential gear *n.* An arrangement of gears in an epicyclic train permitting the rotation of two shafts at different speeds, used on the drive axle of motor vehicles to allow different rates of wheel rotation on curves.

differential operator *n. Symbol* ∇ A mathematical operator used in vector analysis.

differential windlass *n.* A hoisting device that has two drums of different sizes on the same axis. A line wound on the larger and unwound from the smaller provides extra lifting power. Also called "Chinese windlass."

dif·fer·en·ti·ate (dĭf'ə-rĕn'shē-āt') *v.* **-ated, -ating, -ates.** —*tr.* **1.** To constitute the difference in or between; serve to make a distinction between: *subspecies differentiated by the markings on their wings.* **2.** To perceive or show the difference in or between; discriminate; distinguish. **3.** To cause differences to develop in (something) by alteration or modification. Usually used in the passive. **4.** *Mathematics.* To calculate the derivative or differential of. —*intr.* **1.** To become distinct or specialized; acquire a different character. **2.** To make distinctions; discriminate. **3.** *Biology.* To develop into more specialized organs. Used especially of embryonic cells or tissues. —**dif·fer·en·ti·a·tion** *n.*

dif·fi·cult (dĭf′ĭ-kŭlt′, -kəlt) *adj.* **1.** Requiring effort or skill to do or achieve: *a difficult task.* **2.** Requiring mental effort to comprehend or solve: *a difficult puzzle.* **3.** Not easy to persuade, control, or manage ; stubborn; obstinate: *a difficult child.* —See Synonyms at **hard.** [Middle English, back-formation from DIFFICULTY.] —**dif·fi·cult·ly** *adv.*

dif·fi·cul·ty (dĭf′ĭ-kŭl′tē, -kəl-tē) *n., pl.* **-ties. 1.** The condition, fact, or quality of being difficult. **2.** Something not easily done, accomplished, comprehended, or solved. **3. a.** A problem; trouble: *I had difficulty catching her accent.* **b.** *Usually* **difficulties.** A troublesome or embarrassing state of affairs, especially one resulting from a shortage of money. **4.** A lack of normal ease: *Asthma can cause breathing difficulties.* **5.** A disagreement; dispute. **6.** An objection or impediment: *to make difficulties for someone.* [Middle English *difficulte,* from Latin *difficultās* (stem *difficultāt-*), from *difficilis* (earlier *difficul*), difficult : *dis-,* not + *facilis,* easy.]

dif·fi·dent (dĭf′ə-dənt, -dĕnt′) *adj.* **1.** Lacking self-confidence; timid. **2.** Not self-assertive. —See Synonyms at **shy.** [Middle English, from Latin *diffīdens* (stem *diffīdent-*), present participle of *diffīdere,* to mistrust : *dis-,* not + *fīdere, to trust.*] —**dif·fi·dence** *n.* —**dif·fi·dent·ly** *adv.*

dif·fract (dĭ-frăkt′) *tr.v.* **-fracted, -fracting, -fracts.** To cause to undergo diffraction. [Back-formation from DIFFRACTION.] —**dif·frac·tive** *adj.* —**dif·frac·tive·ly** *adv.* —**dif·frac·tive·ness** *n.*

dif·frac·tion (dĭ-frăk′shən) *n.* **1.** Modification of the intensity distribution of wave phenomena that are incident upon an object or aperture whose size is similar to that of the wavelength, resulting in dispersion and interference patterns. **2.** Any phenomenon resulting from such modification. [New Latin *diffractiō* (stem *diffractiōn-*), "a breaking up," from Latin *diffractus,* past participle of *diffringere,* to break to pieces : *dis-,* apart + *frangere,* to break.]

diffraction grating *n.* A usually glass or polished metal surface having a large number of very fine parallel grooves or slits cut in the surface and used to produce optical spectra by diffraction of transmitted or reflected light. Also called "grating."

dif·fuse (dĭ-fyōōz′) *v.* **-fused, -fusing, -fuses.** —*tr.* **1.** To pour out and cause (a gas or liquid, for example) to spread or disperse. **2.** To spread about or scatter; disseminate. **3.** To make less brilliant; soften. —*intr.* **1.** To spread out; become widely dispersed. **2.** *Physics.* To undergo diffusion.

~*adj.* (dĭ-fyōōs′). **1.** Characterized by excessive wordiness and poor organization; lacking conciseness. Said of speech or writing. **2.** Widely spread or scattered; dispersed. [Middle English, dispersed, from Old French *diffus,* from Latin *diffūsus,* past participle of *diffundere,* to pour out, spread : *dis-,* apart + *fundere,* to pour.] —**dif·fuse·ly** (dĭ-fyōōs′lē) *adv.* —**dif·fuse·ness** (dĭ-fyōōs′nĭs) *n.* —**dif·fus·i·ble** *adj.* —**dif·fus·i·bly** *adv.*

dif·fused junction (dĭ-fyōōzd′) *n.* A semiconductor junction formed by the diffusion of impurity atoms into semiconducting material to create p-type or n-type regions.

dif·fus·er, dif·fu·sor (dĭ-fyōō′zər) *n.* **1.** One that diffuses. **2.** A lighting fixture, such as a frosted globe or optically rough reflector, that diffuses light. **3.** A flow passage in a wind tunnel that decelerates a stream of gas or liquid from a high to a low velocity. **4.** A device, such as a cone or baffle, placed in front of a loudspeaker diaphragm to diffuse the sound waves. **5.** A medium that scatters light, used in photography to soften shadows.

dif·fu·sion (dĭ-fyōō′zhən) *n.* **1.** The process of diffusing or the condition of being diffused. **2.** *Physics.* The angular redistribution of radiation by a scattering, reflecting, or refracting system, ideally producing an isotropic distribution of intensity. **3.** *Physics.* The gradual mixing of the molecules of two or more substances, as a result of random thermal motion. **4. a.** Excessive wordiness; verbosity. **b.** Poor organization of material, as in a literary work, for example. **5.** *Anthropology.* The spreading of customs, skills, or the like from one group to another.

diffusion coefficient *n.* See **diffusivity** (sense 1).

dif·fu·sive (dĭ-fyōō′sĭv, -zĭv) *adj.* Characterized by diffusion; tending to diffuse. —**dif·fu·sive·ly** *adv.* —**dif·fu·sive·ness** *n.*

dif·fu·siv·i·ty (dĭ-fyōō′sĭv′ə-tē, -zĭv′-) *n.* *Physics.* **1.** The rate at which a substance diffuses between the opposite sides of a unit cube when there is unit concentration difference between them. Also called "diffusion coefficient." **2.** The ratio of the thermal conductivity of a substance to the product of its specific heat capacity and its density. **3.** The ability of a substance to undergo diffusion.

dig (dĭg) *v.* **dug** (dŭg) *or archaic* **digged** (dĭgd), **digging, digs.** —*tr.* **1.** To break up, turn over, or remove (earth or sand, for example) with a spade, the hands, or other tools; excavate. **2.** To make (a hole) by or as if by digging: *dig a grave.* **3.** To obtain by digging: *dig coal.* **4.** To mix with the earth when digging. Used with *in.* **5.** To learn or discover by careful research or investigation; unearth. Often used with *up* or *out.* **6. a.** To force or thrust into or against. Used with *into.* **b.** To prod or poke: *dug me in the ribs.* **7.** *Slang.* To comprehend, appreciate, or enjoy. —*intr.* **1.** To loosen or turn over the earth. **2.** To make one's way by or as if by digging. Used with *through, into,* or *under.* **3.** *Informal.* To study or work hard and diligently. —**dig in. 1.** *Military.* To dig holes or trenches. **2.** To entrench (oneself). **3.** *Informal.* To eat heartily.

~*n.* **1.** A poke; a thrust: *a dig in the ribs.* **2.** A sarcastic, taunting remark; a gibe. **3.** An archaeological excavation. **4. digs.** *Chiefly*

British *Informal.* Lodgings: *student digs.* [Middle English *diggen,* from Old French *diguer,* "to make a dike or ditch," from *digue,* ditch, from Germanic.]

dig. digest (compilation).

di·gam·ma (dī-găm′ə) *n.* A letter, written *F,* occurring in certain early forms of Greek and transliterated in English as *w.* [Latin, from Greek : DI- (two) + GAMMA (from its resemblance to two capital gammas placed one above the other).]

dig·a·my (dĭg′ə-mē) *n.* Remarriage after the death or divorce of one's first wife or husband. Also called "deuterogamy." [Late Latin *digamia,* from Late Greek : DI- (two) + -GAMY.] —**dig·a·mous** *adj.*

di·gas·tric (dī-găs′trĭk) *adj.* Having two fleshy ends connected by a thinner tendinous portion. Said of certain muscles.

~*n.* A lower jaw muscle that assists in lowering the jaw. [New Latin *digastricus,* "having two bellies" : DI- (two) + GASTRIC.]

di·gen·e·sis (dī-jĕn′ə-sĭs) *n.* **Alternation of generations** (see).

di·gest (dī-jĕst′, dĭ-) *v.* **-gested, -gesting, -gests.** —*tr.* **1.** To transform (food) into an assimilable condition, as by chemical and muscular action in the alimentary canal. **2.** To absorb or assimilate mentally. **3.** To organize into a systematic arrangement, usually by summarizing or classifying. **4.** *Archaic.* To endure or bear patiently. **5.** *Chemistry.* To soften or disintegrate by means of chemical action, heat, or moisture. —*intr.* **1.** To become assimilated into the body. **2.** To assimilate food substances. **3.** *Chemistry.* To undergo exposure to heat, liquids, or chemical agents.

~*n.* (dī′jĕst). **1.** *Abbr.* **dig.** A systematic organization or arrangement of summarized literary, scientific, or statistical materials or data; synopsis. **2.** A periodical containing literary abridgments, brief accounts of current affairs, and the like. **3.** *Law.* A systematic arrangement of statutes or court decisions. —**the Digest.** *Roman Law.* The **Pandects** *(see).* [Middle English *digesten,* from Latin *dīgerere* (past participle *dīgestus*), to divide, distribute, digest : *dī-,* apart + *gerere,* to bear, carry.]

di·gest·ant (dī-jĕst′ənt, dĭ-) *n.* A substance taken to aid digestion.

di·gest·er (dī-jĕst′ər, dĭ-) *n.* **1.** A person who makes a digest. **2.** *Chemistry.* An apparatus in which substances are softened or decomposed, usually for further processing.

di·gest·i·ble (dī-jĕst′ə-bəl, dĭ-) *adj.* Capable of being digested. —**di·gest·i·bil·i·ty, di·gest·i·ble·ness** *n.* —**di·gest·i·bly** *adv.*

di·gest·if (dī-zhĕs-tēf′) *n.* A drink, especially a brandy or liqueur, taken after a meal to aid digestion.

di·ges·tion (dī-jĕs′chən, dĭ-) *n.* **1.** *Physiology.* **a.** The primarily enzymatic bodily process by which foods are decomposed into simple, assimilable substances. **b.** The ability to digest food. **2.** The process of decomposing organic matter in sewage by bacteria. **3.** The assimilation of ideas or information; understanding.

di·ges·tive (dī-jĕs′tĭv, dĭ-) *adj.* **1.** Pertaining to or aiding digestion. **2.** Functioning to digest food.

~*n.* Any substance that aids digestion. —**di·ges·tive·ly** *adv.*

digestive gland *n.* Any of various endocrine and exocrine glands that secrete enzymes necessary for digestion.

digestive system *n.* The alimentary canal together with accessory glands including the salivary glands, liver, and pancreas, regarded as an integrated system responsible for digestion.

dig·ger (dĭg′ər) *n.* **1.** A person who digs, especially one who digs for gold. **2.** A motorized machine with an attachment for excavating earth. **3. Digger.** A member of a radical English Puritan group of the mid-17th century, advocating the communal ownership of land. **4.** *Informal.* A person, especially a soldier, from New Zealand or Australia. (Sense 4, with allusion to Australian gold miners.)

digger wasp *n.* Any of various wasps of the family Sphecidae, that burrow into the ground to build their nests.

dig·gings (dĭg′ĭngz) *pl.n.* **1.** An excavation site. **2.** Materials dug out. **3.** *Chiefly British.* Lodgings; digs. No longer in current usage.

dight (dīt) *tr.v.* **dight** *or* **dighted, dighting, dights.** *Archaic.* To dress; adorn. [Middle English *dighten,* Old English *dihtan,* to arrange, compose, from Latin *dictāre,* to DICTATE.]

dig·it (dĭj′ĭt) *n.* **1. a.** A finger or toe. **b.** Any of the corresponding parts of other vertebrates, the number of which may be reduced. In the horse, for example, there is a single digit on each leg. **2.** The breadth of a finger, used as a unit of measure, equal to about two centimeters (3/4 inch). **3.** Any one of the ten Arabic number symbols, 0 to 9. [Middle English, from Latin *digitus,* finger.]

dig·i·tal (dĭj′ə-təl) *adj.* **1.** Of, pertaining to, or resembling a digit, especially a finger. **2.** Done with the fingers. **3.** Having digits. **4.** Displaying measurements by means of changing numbers rather than by hands on a dial: *a digital clock.* **5.** *Computer Science.* Using digits to represent quantities. Compare **analog. 6.** Of or pertaining to digital recording.

~*n.* Any key played or operated with the finger, as on a piano. —**dig·i·tal·ly** *adv.*

digital computer *n.* A computer that performs operations with quantities represented electronically as digits, usually in the binary system. Compare **analog computer.**

dig·i·tal·in (dĭj′ə-tăl′ĭn) *n.* A poisonous white powder, $C_{36}H_{56}O_{14}$, used in the treatment of heart disease. [DIGITAL(IS) + -IN.]

dig·i·tal·is (dĭj′ə-tăl′ĭs) *n.* **1.** Any plant of the genus *Digitalis,* which includes the foxgloves. **2.** A drug prepared from the seeds and dried leaves of this plant, used as a cardiac stimulant. [New Latin, from Latin *digitālis,* digital (from the finger-shaped corollas of foxglove), from *digitus,* DIGIT.]

dig·i·tal·ize (dĭj′ə-tə-līz′) *tr.v.* **-ized, -izing, -izes. 1.** To treat medically with digitalis. **2.** To digitize. —**dig·i·tal·i·za·tion** *n.*

diffraction *A ray of light diffracts and breaks into the colors of the rainbow as it bounces off the finely ridged surface of a diffraction grating.*

dig·i·tate (dĭj′ə-tāt′) *adj.* Also **dig·i·tat·ed** (-tā′tĭd) **1.** Having digits or fingerlike parts. **2.** *Botany.* Having radiating fingerlike lobes or leaflets. **—dig·i·tate·ly** *adv.*

dig·i·ta·tion (dĭj′ə-tā′shən) *n.* **1.** Division into fingerlike parts; the condition of being digitate. **2.** A fingerlike part or anatomical projection.

dig·i·ti·grade (dĭj′ə-tə-grād′) *adj.* Walking so that only the digits touch the ground, as do horses, cats, and dogs.
∼*n.* A digitigrade animal. Compare **plantigrade.** [Latin *digitus,* finger, toe, DIGIT + -GRADE.]

dig·it·ize (dĭj′ə-tīz′) *tr.v.* **-ized, -izing, -izes.** To convert (continuous data) into digital form for computer processing. **—dig·it·i·za·tion** *n.*

dig·i·tox·in (dĭj′ə-tŏk′sĭn) *n.* A highly active glycoside, $C_{41}H_{64}O_{13}$, derived from digitalis. [DIGI(TALIS) + TOXIN.]

dig·i·tron (dĭj′ə-trŏn′) *n.* An electronic display tube consisting of an anode and a series of cathodes, each shaped as a number or letter, that can be separately lit by a glow discharge. Also called "Nixie tube." [DIGI(T) + -TRON.]

dig·ni·fied (dĭg′nə-fīd′) *adj.* Having or expressing dignity. **—dig·ni·fied·ly** (dĭg′nə-fīd′lē, -fī′ĭd-lē) *adv.*

dig·ni·fy (dĭg′nə-fī′) *tr.v.* **-fied, -fying, -fies. 1.** To confer dignity or honor upon. **2.** To impart a sense of dignity to. **3.** To elevate with the semblance of dignity. [Middle English *dignifien,* from Old French *dignifier,* from Late Latin *dignificāre* : Latin *dignus,* worthy + *facere,* to make, do.]

dig·ni·tar·y (dĭg′nə-tĕr′ē) *n., pl.* **-ies.** A person of high rank. [From DIGNITY.]

dig·ni·ty (dĭg′nə-tē) *n., pl.* **-ties. 1. a.** The presence of poise, self-control, and seriousness in one's deportment to a degree that inspires respect. **b.** Inherent nobility and worth: *the dignity of labor.* **c.** An imposing, formal quality; grandeur; stateliness. **2.** The respect and honor associated with an important position. **3. a.** A high office or rank. **b.** Standing or rank in relation to others. **4.** Self-esteem. **5. dignities.** The ceremonial symbols and observances attached to high office: *the dignities of office.* [Middle English *dignite,* from Old French, from Latin *dignitās* (stem *dignitāt-*), from *dignus,* worthy.]

di·graph (dī′grăf) *n.* **1.** A pair of letters that represents a single speech sound, such as the *ph* in *pheasant* or the *ea* in *beat.* **2.** Two letters run together to represent a special sound, such as Old English *æ.* [DI- + -GRAPH.] **—di·graph·ic** *adj.*

di·gress (dī-grĕs′, dĭ-) *intr.v.* **-gressed, -gressing, -gresses. 1.** To stray from the main subject in writing or speaking. **2.** To turn aside. [Latin *dīgredī* (past participle *dīgressus*), to go aside : *dis-,* apart, aside + *gradī,* to go.]

di·gres·sion (dī-grĕsh′ən, dĭ-) *n.* **1.** The act of digressing. **2.** An instance of digressing; especially, a written or spoken passage not bearing directly on the main subject. **—di·gres·sion·al** *adj.*

di·gres·sive (dī-grĕs′ĭv, dĭ-) *adj.* Characterized by digression; rambling. **—di·gres·sive·ly** *adv.* **—di·gres·sive·ness** *n.*

di·he·dral (dī-hē′drəl) *adj.* **1.** Formed by or having two plane faces; two-sided. **2.** Pertaining to, having, or forming a dihedral angle.
∼*n.* **1.** A dihedral angle. **2.** The upward or downward inclination of an aircraft wing from true horizontal. [DI- + -HEDRAL.]

dihedral angle *n.* **1.** *Geometry.* The angle formed by two intersecting planes. **2.** The acute angle between an aircraft wing and true horizontal. Also called "dihedral."

di·hy·brid (dī-hī′brĭd) *n. Genetics.* **1.** A cross whose parents differ in two distinct characters. **2.** An organism that is heterozygous for two pairs of alleles.

di·hy·dric (dī-hī′drĭk) *adj.* Containing two hydroxyl radicals.

Di·jon (dē-zhôN′). City in east-central France, capital of Côte-d'Or department, and once the capital of Burgundy. It is a railroad junction and gastronomic and industrial center, its best-known products being mustard and cassis, a black-currant liqueur.

dik-dik (dĭk′dĭk′) *n.* Any of several very small African antelopes of the genus *Madoqua.* [Native name in East Africa, imitative of its cry.]

dike, dyke (dīk) *n.* **1.** An embankment of earth and rock, especially: **a.** A levee built to prevent floods. **b.** *British.* A low wall, often of sod, dividing or enclosing lands. **c.** A barrier blocking a passage, especially for protection. **d.** A causeway. **2.** A ditch or channel. **3.** *Geology.* A long mass of igneous rock that cuts across the structure of adjacent rock.
∼*tr.v.* **diked, diking, dikes** or **dyked, dyking, dykes. 1.** To protect, enclose, or provide with a dike. **2.** To drain with dikes or ditches. [Middle English *dike,* Old English *dīc,* moat, ditch (possibly influenced in sense by Middle Low German *dīk,* ditch).] **—dik·er** *n.*

dik·kop (dĭk′ŏp) *n. South African.* A bird, the **stone curlew** *(see).* [Afrikaans : *dik,* thick + *kop,* head.]

dik·tat (dĭk-tät′) *n.* **1.** A unilaterally imposed settlement that deals harshly with a defeated party. **2.** An authoritative or dogmatic statement; command. [German, "dictation," "command," from Latin *dictātum,* neuter past participle of *dictāre,* to DICTATE.]

Di·lan·tin (dī-lăn′tĭn) *n.* A trademark for diphenylhydantoin sodium, used to treat epilepsy.

di·lap·i·date (dĭ-lăp′ə-dāt′) *v.* **-dated, -dating, -dates.** —*tr.* To bring into a state of ruin, decay, or disrepair. —*intr.* To fall into partial ruin or decay. [Latin *dīlapidāre,* to throw away, destroy : *dis-,* apart + *lapidāre,* to throw stones, from *lapis,* stone.] **—di·lap·i·da·tion** *n.*

di·lap·i·dat·ed (dĭ-lăp′ə-dā′tĭd) *adj.* Fallen into a state of disrepair; shabby; broken-down.

di·la·tan·cy (dī′lāt′n-sē, dĭ-) *n.* **1.** The increase in volume of a fixed amount of certain materials, such as wet sand, when it is subjected to a deformation that increases the interparticle distances of its constituents. **2.** Any of various related phenomena, such as increase in viscosity or solidification, resulting from such deformation.

di·la·tant (dī-lāt′ənt, dĭ-) *adj.* **1.** Tending to dilate; dilating. **2.** Exhibiting dilatancy.
∼*n.* A dilator.

dil·a·ta·tion (dĭl′ə-tā′shən, dī′lə-) *n.* **1.** The act or process of dilating; expansion; dilation. **2.** The state or condition of being dilated or stretched. **3.** *Medicine.* The condition of being abnormally enlarged or dilated. **4.** Lengthy explanation or elaboration of a subject in writing or speech. **—dil·a·ta·tion·al** *adj.*

di·late (dī-lāt′, dī′lāt′, dĭ-lāt′) *v.* **-lated, -lating, -lates.** —*tr.* To make wider or larger; cause to expand. —*intr.* **1.** To become wider or larger; expand. **2.** To write or speak at length on a subject; elaborate. Used with *on* or *upon.* [Middle English *dilaten,* from Old French *dilater,* from Latin *dīlātāre,* to enlarge, extend : *dis-,* apart + *lātus,* wide.] **—di·lat·a·bil·i·ty** *n.* **—di·lat·a·ble** *adj.* **—di·la·tion** *n.* **—di·la·tive** *adj.*

di·lat·ed (dī-lā′tĭd, dī′lā′tĭd, dĭ-lā′tĭd) *adj.* **1.** Widened; expanded. **2.** Distended.

dilation and curettage *n.* A surgical operation in which the cervix is opened using a dilator and the lining of the uterus is removed with a curette, performed after an incomplete miscarriage, for example. Also called "D and C."

dil·a·tom·e·ter (dĭl′ə-tŏm′ə-tər, dī′lə-) *n.* An instrument used to measure thermal expansion in solids, liquids, and gases. [DILATE + -METER.] **—dil·a·to·met·ric** (dĭl′ə-tə-mĕt′rĭk, dī′lə-) *adj.* **—dil·a·tom·e·try** *n.*

di·la·tor, di·lat·er (dī-lā′tər, dī′lā′tər, dĭ-lā′tər) *n.* Something that dilates an object, organ, or part; especially, a drug, surgical instrument, or muscle that induces dilation.

dil·a·to·ry (dĭl′ə-tôr′ē, -tōr′ē) *adj.* **1.** Intended to cause delay. **2.** Characterized by a tendency to postpone or delay. —See Synonyms at **tardy.** [Middle English *dilatorie,* from Latin *dīlātōrius,* from *dīlātor,* delayer, from *dīlātus* (past participle of *differre,* to postpone, DEFER) : *dis-,* apart + *-lātus,* "carried."] **—dil·a·to·ri·ly** *adv.* **—dil·a·to·ri·ness** *n.*

dil·do (dĭl′dō) *n., pl.* **-dos** or **-does.** An object shaped like an erect penis, usually used for sexual penetration. [17th century : origin obscure.]

di·lem·ma (dĭ-lĕm′ə) *n.* **1.** A situation that requires one to choose between two equally balanced and often equally unpleasant alternatives. **2.** A predicament that seemingly defies a satisfactory solution. **3.** *Logic.* An argument in which a choice of two or more alternatives, each being conclusive and fatal, is presented to an antagonist. —See Synonyms at **predicament.** [Latin, from Greek *dilēmma,* ambiguous proposition : DI- (double) + *lēmma,* proposition, LEMMA.] **—dil·em·mat·ic** (dĭl′ə-măt′ĭk) *adj.*

dil·et·tante (dĭl′ə-tänt′, -tän′tē, -tănt′, -tăn′tē, dĭl′ə-tänt′) *n., pl.* **-tantes** or **-tanti** (-tän′tē, -tăn′tē). **1.** One whose interest in a subject is not serious or professional; a dabbler, especially in the arts. **2.** A lover of the fine arts; connoisseur.
∼*adj.* Superficial or amateurish. [Italian *dilettante,* "amateur," from *dilettarsi,* to take pleasure in, from Latin *dēlectāre,* to DELIGHT.] **—dil·et·tan·tish** *adj.* **—dil·et·tan·tism** *n.*

dil·i·gence[1] (dĭl′ə-jəns) *n.* **1.** Earnest and persistent application to a matter in hand; steady effort; assiduity. **2.** Attentive care; heedfulness.

dil·i·gence[2] (dĭl′ə-jəns, dē′lē-zhäns′) *n.* In former times, a large public stagecoach. [French, from *diligence,* "speed," from *diligent,* DILIGENT.]

dil·i·gent (dĭl′ə-jənt) *adj.* **1.** Industrious; hard-working. **2.** Characterized by persevering, painstaking effort. —See Usage Note at **busy.** [Middle English, from Old French, from Latin *dīligēns* (stem *diligent-*), "loving," attentive, careful, from *dīligere,* to "single out," "choose," esteem highly, love : *dis-,* apart + *legere,* to choose, gather.] **—dil·i·gent·ly** *adv.*

dill (dĭl) *n.* **1.** An aromatic herb, *Anethum graveolens,* native to the Old World, having finely dissected leaves and small yellow flowers. **2.** The leaves or seedlike fruits of this plant, used as seasoning. Also called "dill weed." [Middle English *dile,* from Old English *dile,* from West Germanic *dilja* (unattested).]

Dil·lin·ger (dĭl′ĭn-jər), **John** (1902–34). U.S. outlaw. Named "public enemy number one" by the FBI (1933), he led a gang on a series of bank robberies, was captured and escaped from jail twice, and was involved in the deaths of three men. He was shot to death by FBI agents outside the Biograph Theater in Chicago.

dill pickle *n.* A cucumber pickled and flavored with dill.

dil·ly (dĭl′ē) *n., pl.* **-lies.** *Informal.* An excellent person or thing. [Obsolete *dilly,* delightful, from DELIGHTFUL.]

dilly bag *n. Australian.* A bag or basket, especially one made of woven rushes or bark. [From *dilli,* a native word in Queensland.]

dil·ly-dal·ly (dĭl′ē-dăl′ē) *intr.v.* **-lied, -lying, -lies.** *Informal.* **1.** To dawdle. **2.** To vacillate. [Reduplication of DALLY.]

dil·u·ent (dĭl′yo͞o-ənt) *adj.* Capable of diluting or serving to dilute.
∼*n.* A substance used to dilute. [Latin *dīluēns* (stem *dīluent-*), present participle of *dīluere,* to DILUTE.]

di·lute (dī-lo͞ot′, dĭ-) *tr.v.* **-luted, -luting, -lutes. 1.** To thin or reduce the strength or concentration of by adding water or a similar fluid. **2.** To lessen the force, strength, purity, or brilliance of, especially by admixture.
∼*adj.* **1.** Weakened; diluted. **2.** Designating a solution of a sub-

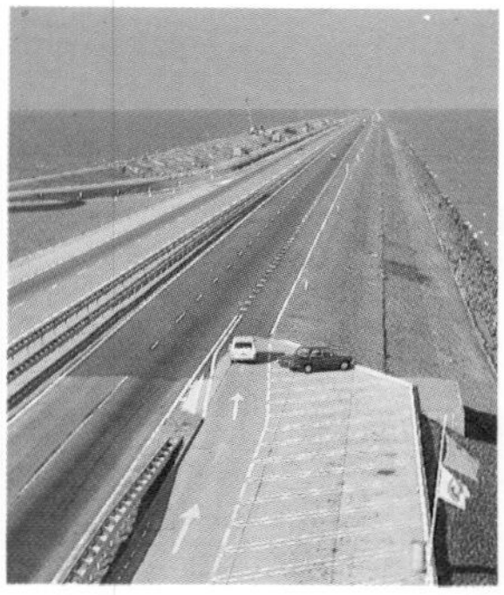

dike *This sea dike runs for 30 kilometers (19 miles) along the coast of Friesland, Holland.*

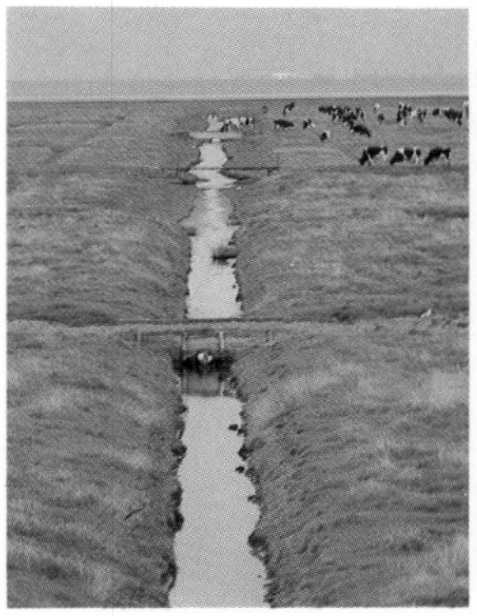

dike *An inland drainage dike in marshland near Greetsiel in northern Holland. The term is related to the Old English word* dīc, *meaning "ditch."*

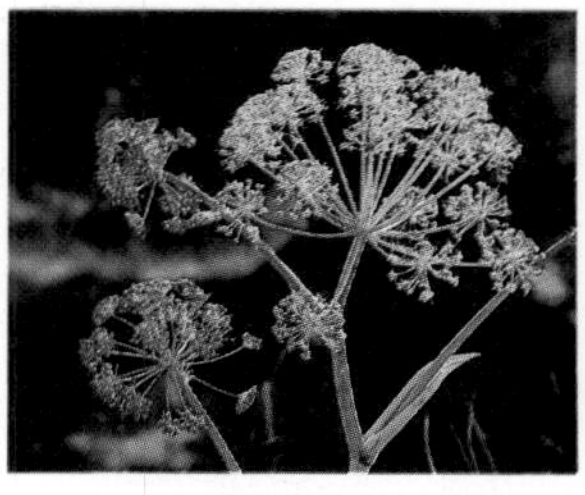

dill *An herb of the parsley family. The leaves and pungent seeds are used in cooking. The seeds are the source of dill oil, an extract used in some medicines.*

stance in which the substance is present in a low concentration. [Latin *dīluere* (past participle *dīlūtus*), to wash away, dilute : *dis-*, apart + *-luere*, from *lavere*, to wash.] **—di·lut·er** *n.*

di·lu·tion (dī-lo͞o′shən, dĭ-) *n.* **1. a.** The process of diluting or being diluted. **b.** A dilute or weakened condition. **2.** A diluted substance.

di·lu·vi·al (dĭ-lo͞o′vē-əl) *adj.* Also **di·lu·vi·an** (-ən). Of or produced by a flood, especially the Biblical Flood. [Late Latin *dīluviālis*, from Latin *dīluvium*, flood, from *dīluere*, to wash away, DILUTE.]

dim (dĭm) *adj.* **dimmer, dimmest. 1.** Faintly lit. **2.** Shedding a small amount of light; faint. **3.** Lacking brightness or luster; subdued; dull. **4.** Faintly outlined; indistinct; obscure. **5.** Lacking keenness of the senses, especially sight. **6.** *Informal.* Mentally slow; stupid. **7.** *Informal.* Negative, unfavorable, or disapproving: *She took a dim view of the plan.* —See Usage note at **dark.**
~*v.* **dimmed, dimming, dims.** —*tr.* **1.** To make dim. **2.** To put (headlights) on low beam. —*intr.* To become dim.
~*n.* **dims.** The parking lights on an automobile. [Middle English *dim(me)*, Old English *dimm*, from Germanic *dim-* (unattested).] **—dim·ly** *adv.* **—dim·ness** *n.*

dim. 1. dimension. **2.** diminished. **3.** *Music.* diminuendo. **4.** diminutive.

Di Mag·gi·o (də mä′zhē-ō), **Joseph Paul** (1914–). U.S. baseball player. Called "Jolting Joe" and the "Yankee Clipper" by his fans, he was a consistently excellent all-around player for the New York Yankees for 13 seasons. He amassed a career batting average of .325 and set a major league record by hitting safely in 56 consecutive games.

Dimash. See **Damascus.**

dime (dīm) *n.* **1.** A U.S. coin worth ten cents or $^1/_{10}$ of a dollar. **2.** A similar coin in Canadian currency. See feature at **currency.** [Middle English, a tenth part, tithe, from Old French *dime, disme*, from Latin *decima (pars)*, tenth (part), tithe, from *decimus*, tenth, from *decem*, ten.]

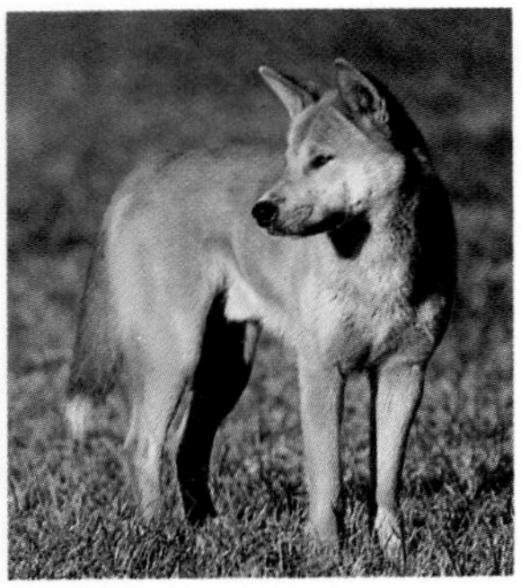

dingo *The warragal, or dingo, a type of dog, is one of the few Australian mammals that are not marsupial, or pouched. It is nocturnal and chiefly solitary and is thought to have been introduced by the aborigines from Asia about 8,000 years ago.*

di·men·hy·dri·nate (dī′mĕn-hī′drə-nāt′) *n.* An antihistamine, $C_{24}H_{28}ClN_5O_3$, used to treat travel sickness and allergic disorders.

dime novel *n.* A usually paperback romance or adventure novel.

di·men·sion (dĭ-mĕn′shən) *n. Abbr.* **dim. 1.** A measure of spatial extent, especially width, height, or length. **2.** *Often* **dimensions.** Extent; magnitude; size; scope. **3.** *Mathematics.* **a.** Any of the least number of independent coordinates required to specify a point in space uniquely. **b.** The range of any of these coordinates. **4.** *Physics.* A physical property, often mass, length, time, or some combination thereof, regarded as a fundamental measure, or as one of a set of fundamental measures, of a physical quantity: *Velocity has the dimensions of length divided by time.* **5.** An aspect of or way of regarding a whole: *This adds a whole new dimension to the problem.*
~*tr.v.* **dimensioned, -sioning, -sions.** To cut or shape to specific dimensions. [Middle English *dimensio(u)n*, from Old French *dimension*, from Latin *dīmēnsiō* (stem *dīmēnsiōn-*), "a measuring," from *dīmētīrī* (past participle *dīmēnsus*), to measure carefully : *dis-* (intensive) + *mētīrī*, to measure.] **—di·men·sion·al** *adj.* **—di·men·sion·al·i·ty** *n.* **—di·men·sion·al·ly** *adv.*

di·mer (dī′mər) *n. Chemistry.* **1.** A molecule consisting of two identical simpler molecules. **2.** A chemical compound consisting of such molecules. [DI- + Greek *meros*, part.]

di·mer·cap·rol (dī′mĕr-kăp′rôl′, -rōl′) *n.* See **BAL** (liquid).

di·mer·ic (dī-mĕr′ĭk) *adj.* **1.** *Biology.* Composed of two parts or divisions. **2.** *Chemistry.* Composed of dimers.

dim·er·ous (dĭm′ər-əs) *adj.* **1.** Consisting of two parts or segments, as does the tarsus in certain insects. **2.** *Botany.* Having flower parts, such as petals, sepals, and stamens, in sets of two. Also written *2-merous.* [New Latin *dimerus* : DI- + -MEROUS.] **—dim·er·ism** *n.*

dime store *n.* A **five-and-ten** *(see).*

dim·e·ter (dĭm′ə-tər) *n.* A verse consisting of two metrical feet or of two groups of two feet. [Late Latin, (verse) of two measures or meters, from Greek *dimetros*, having two meters : DI- + *metron*, METER.]

di·meth·yl·sulf·ox·ide (dī-mĕth′əl-sŭl-fŏk′sīd′) *n. Abbr.* **DMSO** A colorless hygroscopic liquid, $(CH_3)_2SO$, obtained from lignin, used as a solvent and in medicine as a skin penetrant to convey medications into the tissues.

dimin. 1. *Music.* diminuendo. **2.** diminutive.

di·min·ish (dĭ-mĭn′ĭsh) *v.* **-ished, -ishing, -ishes.** —*tr.* **1. a.** To reduce the size of; make smaller or less. **b.** To detract from the authority, rank, or prestige of. **2.** *Architecture.* To cause to taper. **3.** *Music.* To reduce (a perfect or minor interval) by a semitone. Compare **augment.** —*intr.* **1.** To become smaller or less. **2.** To become narrower; taper. —See Synonyms at **decrease.** [Middle English *deminishen*, blend of (a) *diminuen*, to reduce, lessen, from Old French *diminuer*, from Latin *dīminuere*, variant of *dēminuere* : *dē-*, from + *minuere*, to lessen; and (b) *minishen, minuisen*, to make smaller, from Old French *menuiser*, from Vulgar Latin *minūtiāre* (unattested), from Latin *minūtia*, smallness, from *minūtus*, small, from the past participle of *minuere*, to lessen.] **—di·min·ish·a·ble** *adj.* **—di·min·ish·ment** *n.*

diminishing returns *pl.n.* **1.** *Economics.* The principle that, after a certain point, further increases in a particular factor of production lead to progressively smaller increases in output. **2.** The idea that, after a certain point, more effort or investment in a project brings less reward or profit.

di·min·u·en·do (dĭ-mĭn′yo͞o-ĕn′dō) *n., pl.* **-dos** or **-does.** *Abbr.* **dim., dimin.** *Music.* A **decrescendo** *(see).* [Italian, "diminishing," from Latin *dīminuendum*, gerund of *dīminuere*, to DIMINISH.] **—di·min·u·en·do** *adj. & adv.*

dim·i·nu·tion (dĭm′ə-no͞o′shən, -nyo͞o′shən) *n.* **1. a.** The act or process of diminishing. **b.** The resulting reduction; decrease. **2.** *Music.* The repetition of a theme in notes of shorter duration than those of the original. Compare **augmentation.** [Middle English *diminucioun*, from Old French *diminution*, from Latin *dīminūtiō* (stem *dīminūtiōn-*), *dēminūtiō*, from *dēminuere*, to DIMINISH.]

di·min·u·tive (dĭ-mĭn′yə-tĭv) *adj. Abbr.* **dim., dimin. 1.** Of extremely small size; tiny. **2.** Designating certain affixes that denote smallness, youth, familiarity, affection, or contempt, such as *-let* in *booklet* or *-kin* in *lambkin.* Compare **augmentative.** —See Synonyms at **small.**
~*n. Abbr.* **dim., dimin. 1.** A diminutive word or affix. **2.** *Heraldry.* A smaller form of an ordinary when repeated on a shield. [Middle English *diminutif*, from Old French, from Latin *dīminūtīvus*, *dēminūtīvus*, from *dēminūtus*, past participle of *dēminuere*, to DIMINISH.] **—di·min·u·tive·ly** *adv.* **—di·min·u·tive·ness** *n.*

dim·is·so·ry (dĭm′ə-sôr′ē, -sōr′ē) *adj.* **1.** Formerly, designating a letter from a bishop granting a clergyman permission to depart for another diocese. **2.** Designating a bishop's letter certifying the eligibility of the bearer for ordination. [Late Latin *dīmissōrius* (used in *dīmissōriae litterae*, "letter of dismissal," letter granting leave), from Latin *dīmittere* (past participle *dīmissus*), to send away, DISMISS.]

dim·i·ty (dĭm′ĭ-tē) *n., pl.* **-ties.** A sheer, crisp cotton fabric with raised woven stripes or checks, used chiefly for curtains and dresses. [Middle English *demyt*, from Medieval Latin *dimitum*, from Medieval Greek *dimitos*, double-threaded : DI- + *mitos*, thread.]

dim·mer (dĭm′ər) *n.* **1.** A rheostat or other device used to vary the electric current to a light bulb, thereby altering the intensity of illumination. **2.** Parking lights on an automobile.

di·morph (dī′môrf′) *n.* Either of two forms exhibiting dimorphism.

di·mor·phic (dī-môr′fĭk) *adj.* Also **di·mor·phous** (-fəs). Exhibiting dimorphism.

di·mor·phism (dī-môr′fĭz′əm) *n.* **1.** *Botany.* The occurrence of two distinct forms of the same parts, such as leaves, flowers, or stamens, in a single plant or in plants of the same kind. **2.** *Chemistry & Physics.* Crystallization in two distinct forms. **3.** *Zoology.* The state of having two distinct forms in the same species, especially when these forms serve to distinguish two sexes. [Greek *dimorphos*, having two forms : DI- + -MORPHOUS.]

dim-out (dĭm′out′) *n.* **1.** The restricted use or exposure of lights in wartime or as a stage effect. **2.** The semidarkness resulting from this. Compare **blackout.**

dim·ple (dĭm′pəl) *n.* **1.** A small natural indentation in the flesh on a part of the human body, especially on the chin or cheek. **2.** Any slight depression or indentation in a surface.
~*v.* **dimpled, -pling, -ples.** —*tr.* To produce dimples in. —*intr.* To form dimples, as by smiling. [Middle English *dimple*, Old English *dympel* (unattested), pool, dimple.] **—dim·ply** *adj.*

dim sum (dĭm′so͝om′, sŭm′) *pl.n.* Light Chinese refreshments that include small steamed or fried dumplings and a variety of other delicacies. [Cantonese.]

dim·wit (dĭm′wĭt′) *n. Informal.* A stupid person. **—dim·wit·ted** *adj.* **—dim·wit·ted·ly** *adv.* **—dim·wit·ted·ness** *n.*

din (dĭn) *n.* A medley of resounding and discordant sounds; a continuing and unpleasant loud noise. —See Synonyms at **noise.**
~*v.* **dinned, dinning, dins.** —*tr.* **1.** To stun or assail with deafening noise. **2.** To teach or instill by wearying repetition. Usually used with *into*: *din an idea into someone's head.* —*intr.* To make a din. [Middle English *dine, dune*, Old English *dyne.*]

DIN (dĭn) *n.* A logarithmic scale used to express the speed of a photographic emulsion, film, or the like. The speed is equal to $-10 \log_{10}E$, where E is the exposure of a point 0.1 density units above the fog level. [German *Deutsche Industrie-Norm*, German Industry Standard.]

din. dinar.

di·nar (dĭ-när′, dē′när′) *n. Abbr.* **din. 1. a.** The basic monetary unit of Bahrain, Iraq, Jordan, and Kuwait, equal to 1,000 fils. **b.** The basic monetary unit of Algeria, equal to 100 centimes. **c.** The basic monetary unit of Libya, equal to 1,000 dirhams. **d.** The basic monetary unit of Tunisia, equal to 1,000 millimes. **e.** The basic monetary unit of Yugoslavia, equal to 100 para. **f.** The basic monetary unit of Yemen, equal to 100 fils. See feature at **currency. 2.** A monetary unit equal to $^1/_{100}$ of the rial of Iran. See feature at **currency. 3.** A coin or note worth one dinar. **4.** Any of several units of gold and silver currency used in the Middle East from the 8th to the 19th century. [Arabic *dīnār*, from Late Greek *dēnarion*, DENARIUS.]

Di·nar·ic Alps (dĭ-năr′ĭk ălps). *Serbo-Croatian* **Di·na·ra Pla·ni·na** (dē′nə-rä plä′nĭ-nä′). Mountain range stretching 700 kilometers (435 miles) from the Julian Alps of Slovenia southeastward along the Adriatic coast to the Balkan Mts. of Albania.

dine (dīn) *v.* **dined, dining, dines.** —*intr.* **1.** To eat dinner. **2.** To eat something for dinner: *"They dined upon mince and slices of quince"* (Edward Lear). —*tr.* To entertain at dinner; give dinner to: *wined and dined the boss.* **—dine out.** To dine away from home. [Middle English *dinen*, from Old French *di(s)ner*, to dine, breakfast, from Vulgar Latin *disjējūnāre* (unattested), to break one's fast : Latin *dis-* (reversal) + Latin *jējūnus*†, fasting, hungry.]

din·er (dī′nər) *n.* **1.** A person taking dinner. **2.** A railroad dining car. **3.** A restaurant with a long counter and booths, originally shaped like a railroad car.

PRONUNCIATION KEY

ă, pat; ā, pay; âr, care;
ä, father, are; b, bib;
ch, church; d, deed; ĕ, pet;
ē, be; f, fife; g, gag; h, hat;
hw, which; ĭ, pit; ī, pie;
îr, pier; j, judge; k, kick;
l, lid, needle; m, mum;
n, no, sudden; ng, thing;
ŏ, pot; ō, toe; ô, paw, for;
oi, noise; ou, out; o͝o, book;
o͞o, boot; p, pop; r, roar;
s, sauce; sh, ship, dish;
t, tight; th, thin, path;
th, this, bathe; ŭ, cut; ûr, fur;
v, valve; w, with; y, yes;
z, zebra, size; zh, vision;
ə, about, item, edible, gallop, circus, peaceful

IN FOREIGN WORDS:

à, *Fr.* ami; œ, *Fr.* feu, *Ger.* schön; ü, *Fr.* tu, *Ger.* über; KH, *Ger.* ich, *Scot.* loch; N, *Fr.* bon; y′, *Fr.* Compiègne

STRESS MARKS:

Primary stress: ′
in·cite′ (ĭn-sīt′)
Secondary stress: ′
in′sight′ (ĭn′sīt′)

Din·e·sen (dĭn′ə-sən), **Isak,** pen name of Karen Dinesen, Baroness Blixen-Finecke (1885–1962). Danish author who lived in Kenya, East Africa, from 1914 to 1933. Among her books are *Winter's Tales* (1943), *Last Tales* (1957), *Anecdotes of Destiny* (1958), and two collections of her memoirs, *Out of Africa* (1950) and *Shadows on the Grass* (1961).

di·nette (dī-nĕt′) *n.* **1.** A nook or alcove for informal meals. **2.** The table and chairs used in a dinette. [From DINE.]

ding (dĭng) *v.* **dinged, dinging, dings.** —*intr.* **1.** To ring; clang. **2.** *Informal.* To speak persistently and repetitiously. —*tr.* **1.** To cause to clang, as by striking. **2.** *Informal.* To hammer into or at with repetitious talk.
~*n.* A ringing sound. [Probably imitative, but influenced by *ding,* to strike. See **dingbat.**]

ding-a-ling (dĭng′ə-lĭng) *n. Informal.* A silly or eccentric person.

ding·bat (dĭng′băt′) *n.* **1.** Any unspecified gadget or other article; a thingamabob. **2.** *Printing.* A typographical symbol or ornament. **3.** *Informal.* A silly or eccentric person. [Probably obsolete *ding,* to strike, Middle English *dingen,* probably from Old Norse *dengja,* to cudgel, from Germanic *ding-* (unattested) + BAT (cudgel).]

ding-dong (dĭng′dông′, -dŏng′) *n.* **1.** The peal of a bell. **2.** Any similar repeating sound.
~*intr.v.* **ding-donged, -donging, -dongs.** To ring; peal.
~*adj.* Characterized by a vigorous exchange, as of blows or insults. [Imitative.]

din·ghy (dĭng′ē) *n., pl.* **-ghies.** Also **din·gey,** *pl.* **-eys.** Any small open boat. [Hindi *ḍiṅgī, ḍeṅgī,* diminutive of *ḍeṅgā*†, boat.]

din·gle (dĭng′gəl) *n.* A small, wooded valley; dell. [Middle English *dingle*†.]

din·go (dĭng′gō) *n., pl.* **-goes. 1.** A wild dog, *Canis dingo,* of Australia, having a yellowish-brown coat. **2.** *Australian Slang.* A cowardly or treacherous person. [From a native Australian name.]

ding·us (dĭng′əs) *n. Informal.* A gadget or other article whose name eludes one or is not known. [Dutch *dinges,* probably from German *Dinges,* genitive of *Ding,* thing, from Old High German *ding.*]

din·gy (dĭn′jē) *adj.* **-gier, -giest. 1.** Dark and dull, as from smoke, grime, or lack of daylight; dim, dirty, or discolored. **2.** Shabby; worn. [Possibly from Middle English *dinge,* rare variant of *dung, dong,* DUNG.] **—din·gi·ly** *adv.* **—din·gi·ness** *n.*

dining car *n.* A railroad car in which meals are served.

dining room *n.* A room in which meals are eaten.

di·ni·tro·ben·zene (dī-nī′trō-bĕn′zēn′, -bĕn-zēn′) *n.* Any of three isomeric compounds, $C_6H_4(NO_2)_2$, made from a mixture of nitric acid, sulfuric acid, and benzene and used in celluloid manufacture, in dyes, and in organic syntheses.

di·ni·tro·gen tetroxide (dī′nī′trə-jən, -nī′trō-) *n.* **Nitrogen tetroxide** *(see).*

Din·ka (dĭng′kä) *n., pl.***-kas** or collectively **Dinka. 1.** A member of a group of Nilotic tribes of the southern Sudan. **2.** The East Sudanic language of this people. [Dinka *jieng,* "people."]

dink·ey (dĭng′kē) *n., pl.* **-eys.** Also **dink·y,** *pl.* **-ies.** *Informal.* A small locomotive used in a railroad yard. [From DINKY.]

din·kum (dĭng′kəm) *adj. Australian & New Zealand. Informal.* True; genuine; real. Often used interjectionally in the phrase *fair dinkum.*
~*adv. Australian & New Zealand. Informal.* Truly; honestly. [19th century : origin obscure.]

dink·y (dĭng′kē) *adj.* **-ier, -iest. 1.** *Informal.* Of small size or consequence; insignificant. **2.** *British Informal.* Small and neat; dainty. [Probably from Scottish *dink*†, trim, neat.]

din·ner (dĭn′ər) *n.* **1.** The chief meal of the day, eaten at midday or in the evening. **2.** A banquet or formal meal, especially one in honor of some person or commemorating an occasion. **3.** The food prepared for a dinner. [Middle English *diner,* from Old French *di(s)ner,* from *di(s)ner,* to DINE.]

dinner jacket *n.* See **tuxedo** (sense 1).

dinner theater *n.* A restaurant that presents a play during or after dinner.

din·ner·ware (dĭn′ər-wâr′) *n.* **1.** The tableware other than utensils used in serving a meal. **2.** A set of dishes.

di·no·flag·el·late (dī′nō-flăj′ə-lĭt, -lāt′, -flə-jĕl′ĭt) *n.* Any of numerous minute, chiefly marine organisms, characteristically having two flagella and a cellulose outer envelope, and forming one of the chief constituents of plankton. They can be classified as protozoans (group Dinoflagellata) or algae (group Dinophyceae). [New Latin *Dinoflagellata,* "ones having whirling flagella" : Greek *dinos,* whirlpool, eddy, from *dinein*†, to whirl + FLAGELLUM.]

di·no·saur (dī′nə-sôr′) *n.* **1.** Any of various extinct, often gigantic reptiles of the orders Saurischia and Ornithischia, that existed during the Mesozoic era. **2.** An outmoded person or thing. [New Latin : Greek *deinos,* fearful, monstrous + -SAUR.] **—di·no·saur·i·an** *adj. & n.* **—di·no·sau·ric** *adj.* See feature, next page.

Dinosaur National Monument. An area of 772 square kilometers (298 square miles) in northwestern Colorado and northeastern Utah, set aside to preserve extensive remains of well-preserved animal fossils.

di·no·there (dī′nə-thîr′) *n.* Any of various extinct elephantlike mammals of the genus *Dinotherium,* that existed during the Miocene, Pliocene, and Pleistocene epochs. [New Latin *dinotherium* : Greek *deinos,* fearful, monstrous + -THERE.]

dint (dĭnt) *n.* **1.** Force or effort; power; exertion. Used in the phrase *by dint of.* **2.** A dent.
~*tr.v.* **dinted, dinting, dints.** To put a dent or dents in. [Middle English *dint, dunt,* Old English *dynt.* See **dent.**]

di·nu·cle·o·tide (dī-no͞o′klē-ə-tīd′, -nyo͞o′-) *n.* A compound consisting of two linked nucleotides, such as the coenzyme NAD.

Di·o Cas·si·us (dī′ō kăs′ē-əs) (*c.* A.D. 155–235). Roman historian. His 80 books, written in Greek, traced the history of Rome from the legendary arrival of Aeneas in Italy up to A.D. 229.

di·oc·e·san (dī-ŏs′ə-sən) *adj.* Of or pertaining to a diocese.
~*n.* **1.** A bishop of a diocese. **2.** A member of a diocese.

di·o·cese (dī′ə-sĭs, -sēs′, -sēz′) *n. Abbr.* **dioc.** The district or churches under the jurisdiction of a bishop; a bishopric. [Middle English *diocise,* from Old French, from Late Latin *diocēsis,* from Latin *dioecēsis,* jurisdiction, district, from Greek *dioikēsis,* "housekeeping," administration, from *dioikein,* to keep house, administer : *dia-,* completely + *oikein,* to inhabit, from *oikos,* house.]

Di·o·cle·tian (dī′ə-klē′shən), born Gaius Aurelius Valerius Diocletianus (A.D. 254–313). Roman emperor (284–305). In 286 he appointed Galerius (died A.D. 311) as his coemperor and divided the empire into east and west in order to govern more effectively. In 303, in a bid to revive the old religion, he instituted the last major persecution of the Christians. Two years later he and Galerius abdicated and retired to his grand palace at Salona (now Split, Yugoslavia).

di·ode (dī′ōd′) *n.* **1.** An electronic component having one semiconductor junction, used chiefly as a rectifier. **2.** A simple thermionic valve having two electrodes: a cathode and an anode. [DI- + -ODE.]

di·oe·cious, di·e·cious (dī-ē′shəs) *adj. Botany.* Having male and female flowers borne on separate plants. Compare **monoecious.** [New Latin *Dioecia* : DI- + Greek *oikia,* dwelling, from *oikos,* house.] **—di·oe·cious·ly** *adv.*

di·e·strus (dī-ĕs′trəs) *n. Biology.* A stage in the estrous cycle when the follicles and the uterus are small in size, and the epithelium layer surrounding the vagina is thin.

Di·og·e·nes (dī-ŏj′ə-nēz′), known as "the Cynic" (412–322 B.C.). Greek philosopher. Exiled with his father from Cinope in Asia Minor, he settled in Athens and founded the Cynic school of philosophy, promoting self-control, acceptance of suffering, the avoidance of physical pleasure, and a return to nature.

di·oi·cous (dī-oi′kəs) *adj. Botany.* Having antheridia and archegonia on separate plants; unisexual. Said of mosses and related plants. [New Latin *dioecus,* "having two houses" : DI- (two) + Greek *oikos,* house.]

di·ol (dī′ōl′, -ôl′) *n. Chemistry.* An alcohol that has two hydroxyl groups in its molecules; a dihydric alcohol. Also called "glycol."

Di·o·me·des (dī′ə-mē′dēz). Also **Di·o·med** (dī′ə-mĕd′), **Di·o·mede** (-mĕd). *Greek Mythology.* A king of Argos and, in the Homeric poems, one of the chief heroes at Troy.

Di·o·nys·i·a (dī′ə-nĭsh′ē-ə, -nĭzh′ē-ə, -nĭs′ē-ə) *pl.n.* Any of various festivals of ancient Attica, held in honor of the god Dionysus, especially: **1.** The lesser festival, held in the autumn, in which the tragedy as a dramatic and literary form is thought to have had its origin. **2.** The great spring festival in Athens, at which competing plays were presented from the time of Pisistratus.

Di·o·nys·i·ac (dī′ə-nĭs′ē-ăk′) *adj.* **1.** Of or pertaining to Dionysus or the Dionysia. **2.** *Sometimes* **dionysiac.** Dionysian, as opposed to Apollonian. **—Di·o·ny·si·a·cal·ly** (dī′ə-nĭ-sī′ĭk-lē) *adv.*

Di·o·nys·i·an (dī′ə-nĭsh′ən, -nĭzh′ən, -nĭs′ē-ən) *adj.* **1.** Of or pertaining to any of several historical persons named Dionysius. **2.** Of or pertaining to Dionysus or the Dionysia. **3.** *Often* **dionysian. a.** Of an ecstatic, orgiastic, or irrational character. **b.** Filled with tremendous creative energy. **4.** *Sometimes* **dionysian.** In the philosophy of Nietzsche, characteristic of the spontaneous, irrational, creative, passionate qualities of human nature. Compare **Apollonian.**

Di·o·nys·i·us the Ar·e·op·a·gite (dī′ə-nĭsh′ē-əs, -nĭsh′əs, -nī′sē-əs; ăr′ē-ŏp′ə-jīt′, -gīt′), **Saint** (1st century A.D.). Greek martyr. A judge of the Areopagus, he was converted to Christianity by St. Paul and became the first bishop of Athens.

Di·o·ny·sus, Di·o·ny·sos (dī′ə-nī′səs). *Greek Mythology.* The god of wine and ecstasy, idol of an orgiastic religion celebrating the power and fertility of nature. Also called "Bacchus."

Di·o·phan·tine equation (dī′ə-făn′tīn, -tēn, -tən) *n. Mathematics.* An equation of two or more variables with integral coefficients, for which sets of possible integer solutions are required. [After DIOPHANTUS of Alexandria.]

Di·o·phan·tus of Alexandria (dī′ō-făn′təs) (3rd or 4th century A.D.). Greek mathematician, credited with inventing algebra. His work, preserved by Arabic mathematicians, was translated into Latin in the 16th century.

di·op·side (dī-ŏp′sīd′) *n.* A monoclinic pyroxene mineral, $CaMgSi_2O_6$, used as a gemstone and as a refractory. [French : DI- (two) + Greek *opsis* (stem *opsid-*), appearance, sight.]

di·op·ter (dī-ŏp′tər) *n. Abbr.* **D.** *Optics.* A unit, equal to a reciprocal meter, of curvature and of the power of lenses, refracting surfaces, and other optical systems. [French, from Latin, from Greek *dioptra,* an optical instrument : *dia-,* through + *opsesthai,* to see.] **—di·op·tral** *adj.*

di·op·tom·e·ter (dī′ŏp-tŏm′ə-tər) *n.* An instrument for measuring ocular refraction. [DI- + Greek *optos,* visible (see **optic**) + -METER.] **—di·op·tom·e·try** *n.*

di·op·tric (dī-ŏp′trĭk) *adj.* Also **di·op·tri·cal** (-trĭ-kəl). *Optics.* **1.** Of or pertaining to dioptrics. **2.** Pertaining to optical refraction; refractive.

di·op·trics (dī-ŏp′trĭks) *n. Used with a singular verb. Optics.* The study of the refraction of light, especially within the eye. [Greek

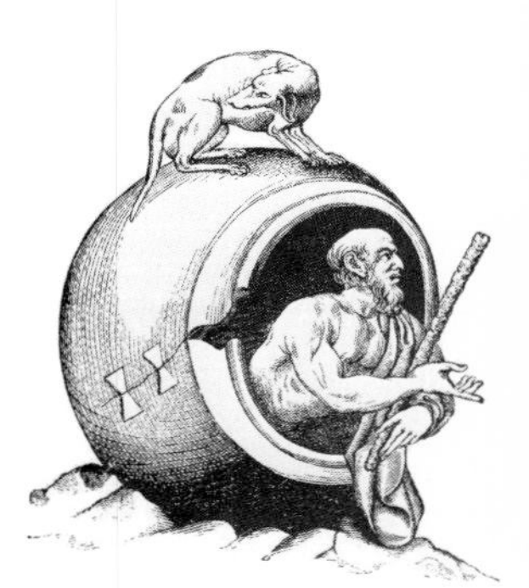

Diogenes *The Greek philosopher Diogenes rejected all luxury and is supposed to have made his home in a large earthenware barrel. His way of life earned him the name* kuon, *the Greek word for "dog"—a gibe from which is derived the word for followers of his ideas: Cynics.*

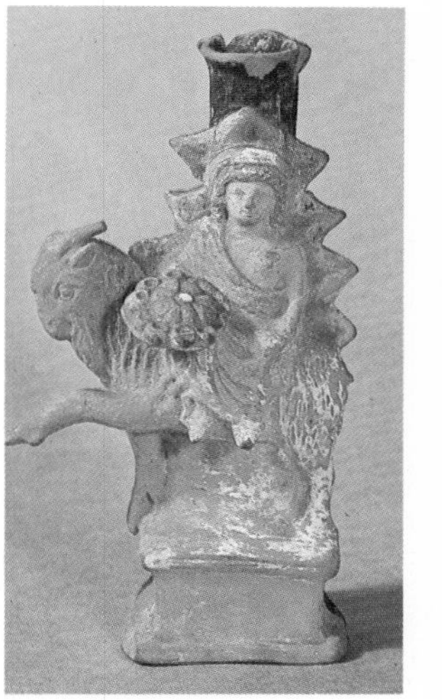

Dionysus *The Greek god of wine and revelry, here seen riding a goat on an Attic vase that was made in about 350* B.C.

dinosaur

THE RULING REPTILES OF PREHISTORY

The variety of creatures to be found among the dinosaurs—the "monstrous lizards"

Of the reptiles that dominated life on land during the Mesozoic era, about 250 to 66 million years ago, the dinosaurs (whose Greek-derived name means "monstrous lizards") were the most successful.

There were two dinosaur orders, distinguished by differences in pelvic structure. Some of the "lizard-hipped" Saurischia, the first order to evolve, number among the most gigantic creatures ever to exist. A reconstructed skeleton of the longest, *Diplodocus,* is 26.7 meters (87 feet) long including a tail 15 meters (50 feet) long; yet it weighed relatively little. Its hollow bone structure combined strength with lightness. The heaviest dinosaur was *Brachiosaurus,* which may have weighed some 50 tons.

Many dinosaurs were bipedal—they walked on two legs. The birdlike *Coelophysis* had a modified pelvic girdle, enabling it to walk more efficiently, and well-developed arms and hands to catch prey.

Most saurischians had a full set of pointed teeth. *Tyrannosaurus,* one of the last to appear and the largest terrestrial carnivore ever known, must have used its teeth to attack its prey since its tiny forelimbs were of little use.

The "bird-hipped" Ornithischia were not as large. Most of them lacked front teeth and browsed on plants; *Camptosaurus* was typical of these. But *Hadrosaurus,* called the "duck-billed" dinosaur from the shape of its jaw, had up to 2,000 side teeth for grinding conifer needles and twigs. It was a powerful swimmer and is thought to have taken to water whenever it was

startled. *Ankylosaurus,* a quadruped, was armored with a mosaic of bony plates fringed with spikes, and a tail that could be used as a club.

Stegosaurus had triangular bony plates along its neck and back, and a spiked tail. In common with many giant dinosaurs, *Stegosaurus* had an extra "brain," an enlarged area of the spinal cord located at the hip, which may have played a part in controlling the dinosaur's limbs and tail.

Climatic changes and consequent alterations in vegetation (possibly combined with a cataclysmic fire some 65 million years ago) may have been responsible for the disappearance of the dinosaurs. Yet they are aptly named Archosauria, or "ruling lizards," for they reigned for more than 100 million years.

Coelophysis
Triassic — Cretaceous
(250 – 66 million years ago)
2.4 meters (8 feet) long
23 kilograms (51 pounds)
Carnivorous

Brachiosaurus ("arm lizard")
Jurassic
(205 – 135 million years ago)
22.8 meters (75 feet) long
50 tons
Herbivorous

Diplodocus
Jurassic
(205 – 135 million years ago)
27 meters (87½ feet) long
10 tons
Herbivorous

Camptosaurus
Jurassic
(205 – 135 million years ago)
1.2 – 4.5 meters (4 – 15 feet) long
10 tons
Herbivorous

Ankylosaurus ("crooked lizard")
Early Cretaceous
(135 – 100 million years ago)
7.6 meters (25 feet) long
3 tons
Herbivorous

Hadrosaurus ("big lizard")
Cretaceous (135 – 66 million years ago)
9 meters (30 feet) long
3 tons
Herbivorous

Stegosaurus
Jurassic (205 – 135 million years ago)
6 meters (20 feet) long
1.8 tons
Herbivorous

Tyrannosaurus ("tyrant lizard")
Late Cretaceous (100 – 66 million years ago)
14 meters (46 feet) long
7 tons Carnivorous

dioptrikos, from *dioptra,* optical instrument : *dia-,* through + *optos,* visible.]

Di·or (dē-ôr'), **Christian** (1905-57). French fashion designer noted for his "new look" for women's fashions in 1947. His styling featured fitted bodices and long, full skirts.

di·o·ram·a (dī'ə-răm'ə, -rä'mə) *n.* **1.** A three-dimensional miniature scene with painted model or wax figures or stuffed animals against a background. Dioramas are often used for museum exhibits. **2.** A scene reproduced on cloth transparencies with various lights shining through the cloths to produce changes in effect, and viewed through a small aperture. [French : DI(A)- (through) + (PAN)O-RAMA.] **—di·o·ram·ic** *adj.*

di·o·rite (dī'ə-rīt') *n.* Any of various coarse-textured, crystalline igneous rocks rich in plagioclase and having little quartz, being intermediate between acid and basic rock. [French, from Greek *diorizein,* to distinguish : *dia-,* apart + *horizein,* to divide, from

horos, boundary.] **—di·o·rit·ic** (dī'ə-rĭt'ĭk) *adj.*

Di·o·scor·i·des Pe·dan·i·us (dī'ə-skôr'ĭ-dēz' pə-dăn'ē-əs) (c. A.D. 40-90). Greek physician. His *De Materia Medica* catalogued and described more than 600 plants and plant principles.

Di·os·cu·ri (dī-ŏs'kyə-rī', dī'ə-skyŏor'ī'). *Greek Mythology.* **Castor and Pollux** *(see).* [Greek *Dioskouroi,* "sons of Zeus" : *Dios,* genitive of ZEUS + *kouroi,* plural of *kouros,* boy, son.]

di·ox·ane (dī-ŏk'sān') *n.* A flammable, potentially explosive, colorless liquid, $C_4H_8O_2$, used as a solvent for fats, greases, and resins and in various products including paints, lacquers, and fumigants.

di·ox·ide (dī-ŏk'sīd') *n.* An oxide with two oxygen atoms per molecule.

di·ox·in (dī-ŏk'sĭn) *n.* An extremely toxic substance that causes chloracne and genetic mutation, formed as a by-product in the manufacture of the herbicide 2,4,5–T. Also called "TCDD."

dip (dĭp) *v.* **dipped, dipping, dips.** *—tr.* **1.** To plunge briefly in or into a liquid, usually in order to wet, coat, or saturate. **2.** To color or dye in this manner. **3.** To immerse (livestock) in a disinfectant solution. **4.** To make (a candle) by repeatedly immersing a wick in melted wax or tallow. **5.** To galvanize or plate (metal) by immersion. **6.** To scoop up by plunging the hand or a container into and out of a liquid; bail; ladle. **7.** To lower and raise (a flag) in salute. **8.** *Chiefly British.* To put (vehicle headlights) on low beam. *—intr.* **1.** To plunge into water or other liquid and come out quickly. **2.** To plunge the hand or a container into a liquid or another container, especially for the purpose of taking something up or out: *dipped into her pocket.* **3.** To drop or sink suddenly. **4.** To appear to sink. **5.** To slope downwards; decline. **6.** *Geology.* To lie at an angle to the horizontal plane, as a rock stratum may. **7.** To read here and there in a book or magazine; browse. Used with *into.* **8.** To investigate a subject superficially; dabble. **9.** To use up money, especially one's savings. Used with *into.*

∼n. **1.** A brief plunge or immersion; especially, a brief swim. **2.** A liquid into which something is dipped; especially, a **sheep dip** *(see).* **3.** A smooth creamed preparation into which crackers or other foods may be dipped. **4.** An amount taken up by dipping. **5.** A container for dipping. **6.** A candle made by repeated dipping in tallow or wax. **7.** A downward slope; a decline. **8.** *Geology.* The downward inclination of a rock stratum in reference to the plane of the horizontal. **9.** *Surveying.* The angular difference between eye level and the lower level of the horizon. **10. Magnetic dip** *(see).* **11.** A hollow; a depression. **12.** In gymnastics, an exercise on the parallel bars in which the body is lowered by bending the elbows until the chin reaches the level of the bars and then is raised by straightening the arms. **13.** A lowering or loss of altitude, as of an aircraft. **14.** *Slang.* A pickpocket. **15.** *Slang.* A foolish or gullible person. [Middle English *dippen,* Old English *dyppan,* from Germanic.]

di·pep·tide (dī-pĕp′tīd′) *n.* Any compound consisting of two amino acids linked by a peptide bond.

di·pet·al·ous (dī-pĕt′l-əs) *adj. Botany.* Having two petals.

di·phase (dī′fāz′) *adj.* Also **di·pha·sic** (dī-fā′zĭk). *Physics.* Having two phases.

di·phen·hy·dra·mine (dī′fĕn-hī′drə-mēn′) *n.* An antihistamine drug used to treat hay fever and other allergic conditions.

di·phen·yl (dī-fĕn′əl, -fē′nəl) *n. Chemistry.* **Biphenyl** *(see).*

di·phen·yl·a·mine (dī-fĕn-əl-ə-mēn′, -ăm′ĭn, dī-fē′nəl-) *n.* A colorless crystalline compound, $(C_6H_5)_2NH$, used as a stabilizer for plastics and in the manufacture of dyes, explosives, pesticides, and pharmaceuticals.

di·phen·yl·hy·dan·to·in sodium (dī-fĕn′əl-hī-dăn′tō-ĭn, dī-fē′nəl-) *n.* A white powder, $C_{15}H_{11}N_2O_2Na$, used as an anticonvulsant.

di·phe·nyl·ke·tone (dī-fĕn′əl-kē′tōn′, -fē′nəl-) *n.* **Benzophenone** *(see).*

di·phos·gene (dī-fŏz′jēn′) *n.* A colorless mobile liquid, $ClCOOCCl_3$, with a vapor used as a military poison gas, especially in World War I.

diph·the·ri·a (dĭf-thîr′ē-ə, dĭp-) *n.* An acute contagious disease caused by infection with the bacillus *Corynebacterium diphtheriae,* and characterized by the formation of a false membrane in the throat, causing difficulty in breathing, high fever, and weakness. [New Latin, from French *diphthérie,* from Greek *diphthera,* piece of leather (from the rough false membrane).] **—diph·the·rit·ic** (dĭf-thə-rĭt′ĭk, dĭp-), **diph·ther·ic** (dĭf-thĕr′ĭk, dĭp-), **diph·the·ri·al.** *adj.*

diph·thong (dĭf′thông′, -thŏng′, dĭp′-) *n. Phonetics.* **1.** A complex speech sound beginning with one vowel sound and moving to another vowel or semivowel position within the same syllable. For example, *oy* in the word *boy* is a diphthong. **2.** Either of the two ligatures *æ* or *œ,* originally pronounced as diphthongs in Classical Latin but in modern English rendered as single vowels. [Middle English *diptonge,* from Old French *diptongue,* from Late Latin *dipthongus,* from Greek *diphthongos* : DI- (two) + *phthongos*†, voice, sound. See also **monophthong, apothegm.**] **—diph·thon·gal** *adj.*

diph·thong·ize (dĭf′thông-īz′, dĭf′thŏng′-, dĭp′-) *v.* **-ized, -izing, -izes.** *—tr.* To pronounce as a diphthong. *—intr.* To become a diphthong. **—diph·thong·i·za·tion** *n.*

di·phy·cer·cal (dĭf′ĭ-sûr′kəl) *adj. Zoology.* Designating or having a tail fin in which the vertebral column extends to the tip, with symmetrical upper and lower parts. [Greek *diphuēs,* double, twofold + *kerkos,* tail.]

di·phy·let·ic (dī′fī-lĕt′ĭk) *adj.* Descended from two ancestral lines.

di·phyl·lous (dī-fĭl′əs) *adj. Botany.* Having two leaves. [New Latin *diphyllus* : DI- + -PHYLLOUS.]

di·phy·o·dont (dī-fī′ə-dŏnt′) *adj. Zoology.* Having two successive sets of teeth, as do humans and most other mammals. [Greek *diphuēs,* double, twofold : DI- (two) + *phuein,* to bring forth, grow + -ODONT.]

dipl. diplomat; diplomatic.

dip·la·cu·sis (dĭp′lə-ko͞o′sĭs, -kyo͞o′-) *n.* The hearing of a single sound as two sounds, due to a defect in the inner ear. [New Latin : DIPL(O)- + Greek *akousis,* hearing, from *akouein,* to hear.]

di·ple·gia (dī-plē′jə, -jē-ə) *n.* Paralysis of corresponding parts on both sides of the body. [DI- + -PLEGIA.]

di·plex (dī′plĕks′) *adj.* Capable of simultaneous transmission or reception of two messages in the same radio channel. [DI- + (DU)PLEX.]

diplo–, dipl– *prefix.* Indicates double; for example, **diploid.** [Greek, from *diploos,* double : DI- (two) + *-ploos,* "-fold."]

dip·lo·blas·tic (dĭp′lō-blăs′tĭk) *adj.* Having two distinct cellular layers. Said of lower invertebrate animals such as sponges and coelenterates. Compare **triploblastic.** [DIPLO- + -BLASTIC.]

dip·lo·car·di·ac (dĭp′lō-kär′dē-ăk′) *adj.* Having or characterizing a heart in which the two sides are distinctly separated, as in birds and mammals. [DIPLO- + Greek *kardia,* heart.]

dip·lo·coc·cus (dĭp′lō-kŏk′əs) *n., pl.* **-cocci** (-kŏk′sī′, -kŏk′ī′). Any of various paired spherical bacteria, including those of the genus *Diplococcus,* some of which are pathogenic. [New Latin : DIPLO- + -COCCUS.] **—dip·lo·coc·cal** (dĭp′lō-kŏk′əl), **dip·lo·coc·cic** (dĭp′-lō-kŏk′sĭk, -kŏk′ĭk) *adj.*

di·plod·o·cus (dĭ-plŏd′ə-kəs, dī-) *n.* A very large, extinct, long-necked, herbivorous dinosaur of the genus *Diplodocus,* that existed during the Jurassic period. [New Latin : DIPLO- + Greek *dokos,* beam.]

dip·lo·ë (dĭp′lō-ē′) *n.* The spongy, bony tissue between the outer and inner bone layers of the cranium. [New Latin, from Greek *diploē,* "doubling," "fold," from *diploos,* double. See **diplo-.**]

dip·loid (dĭp′loid′) *adj.* **1.** Double or twofold. **2.** *Genetics.* Having a homologous pair of chromosomes for each characteristic except sex, the total number of chromosomes being twice that of a gamete. Compare **haploid.**

∼n. Genetics. **1.** A diploid cell. **2.** An individual characterized by a diploid chromosome number. [DIPL(O)- + -OID.]

di·plo·ma (dĭ-plō′mə) *n.* **1.** A document or certificate issued by a university, college, school, or other educational institution indicating that a certain level of proficiency has been reached, examinations passed, or a particular course of study successfully completed. **2.** A certificate conferring a privilege or honor. **3.** An official document or charter. [Latin, from Greek *diplōma,* something doubled, folded paper, document, from *diploos,* double. See **diplo-.**]

di·plo·ma·cy (dĭ-plō′mə-sē) *n., pl.* **-cies.** **1.** The art or practice of conducting international relations, as in negotiating alliances, treaties, and agreements. **2.** Tact or skill in dealing with people. —See Synonyms at **tact.**

dip·lo·mat (dĭp′lə-măt′) *n.* **1.** *Abbr.* **dipl.** A person appointed to represent one government in its relations with others, such as an ambassador. **2.** One who possesses skill or tact in dealing with others. [French *diplomate,* back-formation from *diplomatique,* DIPLOMATIC.]

dip·lo·mate (dĭp′lə-māt′) *n.* One who has received a diploma; especially, a physician certified as a specialist by a board of examiners.

dip·lo·mat·ic (dĭp′lə-măt′ĭk) *adj.* **1.** *Abbr.* **dipl.** Of, pertaining to, or involving diplomacy or diplomats. **2.** Characterized by tact and sensitivity in dealing with people; discreet; politic. **3. a.** Of or pertaining to diplomatics. **b.** Being an exact copy of an original: *a diplomatic edition.* —See Synonyms at **suave.** [French *diplomatique,* connected with the documents that regulate international relations, from New Latin *diplomaticus,* connected with documents or diplomatics, from Latin *diplōma,* document. See **diploma.**] **—dip·lo·mat·i·cal·ly** *adv.*

diplomatic corps *n.* The entire body of diplomatic personnel in residence at the capital of a nation.

diplomatic immunity *n.* Exemption from taxation and the ordinary processes of law afforded to diplomatic personnel in a foreign country.

dip·lo·mat·ics (dĭp′lə-măt′ĭks) *n. Used with a singular verb.* **1.** Diplomacy. **2.** The branch of paleography devoted to the study of ancient documents and the determination of their age and authenticity. [Sense 1, see **diplomatic**; sense 2, see **diploma.**]

di·plo·ma·tist (dĭ-plō′mə-tĭst) *n.* A diplomat.

dip·lont (dĭp′lŏnt′) *n. Biology.* An organism having somatic cells with diploid chromosomes. [DIPLO- + *-ont,* cell, from Greek *ōn* (stem *ont-*), present participle of *einai,* to be.]

di·plo·pi·a (dĭ-plō′pē-ə) *n. Pathology.* A disorder of vision that causes objects to appear double; double vision. [New Latin : DIPL(O)- + -OPIA.] **—di·plo·pic** (dĭ-plō′pĭk, -plĭp′ĭk) *adj.*

dip·lo·pod (dĭp′lə-pŏd′) *n.* Any of various segmented, cylindrical arthropods of the class Diplopoda, which includes the millipedes. [New Latin *Diplopoda* : DIPLO- + -POD.] **—dip·lo·pod** *adj.*

di·plo·sis (dĭ-plō′sĭs) *n.* The formation of the full (diploid) number of chromosomes found in a somatic cell by the fusion of gamete nuclei containing haploid sets in fertilization. [New Latin, from Greek *diplōsis,* a doubling, from *diploun,* to double, from *diploos,* double. See **diplo-.**]

dip·lo·tene (dĭp′lō-tēn) *n. Genetics.* A stage of the first prophase of meiosis during which crossing over occurs and the paired homologous chromosomes begin to separate. [DIPLO- + *-tene,* from Greek *tainia,* band.]

dip needle *n.* **1.** *Physics.* A magnetic needle balanced and pivoted to rotate freely in a vertical plane to indicate the local inclination of the earth's magnetic field. **2.** An instrument, the **inclinometer** *(see).*

dip·no·an (dĭp′nō-ən) *n.* Any of various fishes of the group Dipnoi, which includes the lungfishes, characterized by modified lungs that enable them to breathe atmospheric air.

∼adj. Of or belonging to the Dipnoi. [New Latin *Dipnoi,* from *dipnous,* having two apertures for breathing, from Greek *dipnoos* : DI- + *pnoē,* breath, from *pnein,* to breathe.]

dip·o·dy (dĭp′ə-dē) *n., pl.* **-dies.** A metrical unit in poetry consisting of two feet. [Late Latin *dipodia,* from Greek, from *dipous* (stem *dipod-*), two-footed : DI- + -POD.]

di·po·lar (dī′pō′lər) *adj.* Of or having a dipole.

di·pole (dī′pōl′) *n.* **1.** *Physics.* A pair of electric charges or magnetic poles, of equal magnitude but of opposite sign or polarity, sepa-

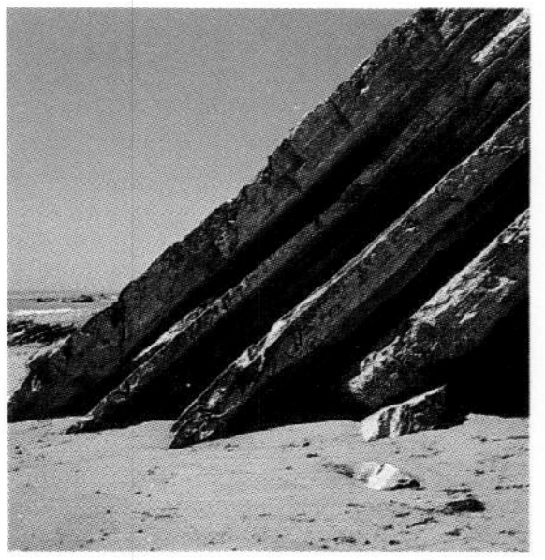

dip *In geological terms, a dip is where rock layers slope downward. The layers shown here dive into the sand at Refugio Beach, California.*

PRONUNCIATION KEY

ă, **pat**; ā, **pay**; âr, **care**;
ä, **father**, **are**; b, **bib**;
ch, **church**; d, **deed**; ĕ, **pet**;
ē, **be**; f, **fife**; g, **gag**; h, **hat**;
hw, **which**; ĭ, **pit**; ī, **pie**;
îr, **pier**; j, **judge**; k, **kick**;
l, **lid**, **needle**; m, **mum**;
n, **no**, **sudden**; ng, **thing**;
ŏ, **pot**; ō, **toe**; ô, **paw**, **for**;
oi, **noise**; ou, **out**; o͝o, **book**;
o͞o, **boot**; p, **pop**; r, **roar**;
s, **sauce**; sh, **ship**, **dish**;
t, **tight**; th, **thin**, **path**;
th, **this**, **bathe**; ŭ, **cut**; ûr, **fur**;
v, **valve**; w, **with**; y, **yes**;
z, **zebra**, **size**; zh, **vision**;
ə, **about**, **item**, **edible**,
gallop, **circus**, **peaceful**

IN FOREIGN WORDS:

à, *Fr.* **ami**; œ, *Fr.* **feu**, *Ger.* **schön**; ü, *Fr.* **tu**, *Ger.* **über**;
KH, *Ger.* **ich**, *Scot.* **loch**;
N, *Fr.* **bon**; y′, *Fr.* **Compiègne**

STRESS MARKS:

Primary stress: ′
in·cite′ (ĭn-sīt′)
Secondary stress: ′
in′sight′ (ĭn′sīt′)

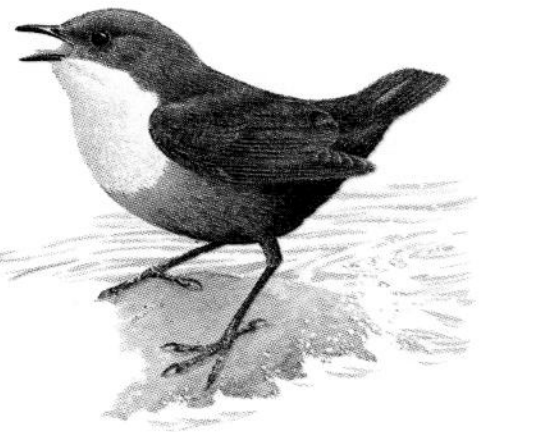

dipper *Between dives, dippers often perch on stones in the middle of streams. The birds hunt their food—insects and small fish—by plunging into the water in shallow rivers and walking along the bottom, their bodies tilted forward. This is the European dipper,* Cinclus cinclus.

rated by a small distance. **2.** *Electronics.* An antenna, usually fed from the center, consisting of two equal rods extending outward in a straight line. In this sense, also called "dipole antenna."

dipole moment *n.* **1.** The product of either charge in an electric dipole with the distance separating them. Also called "electric moment." **2.** The product of the strength of either pole in a magnetic dipole with the distance separating them. Also called "magnetic dipole moment," "magnetic moment."

dip·per (dĭp′ər) *n.* **1.** One that dips. **2.** A container used for dipping, such as a long-handled cup for taking up water. **3. Dipper.** Either of two star groups shaped like a ladle, the Big Dipper in Ursa Major or the Little Dipper in Ursa Minor. **4.** Any of several small diving birds of the genus *Cinclus.* Also called "water ouzel."

dip·py (dĭp′ē) *adj.* **-pier, -piest.** *Slang.* Foolish; not sensible. [20th century : origin obscure.]

di·pro·pel·lant (dī′prə-pĕl′ənt) *n.* A **bipropellant** *(see).*

dip·sas (dĭp′səs) *n., pl.* **-sades** (-sə-dēz′). A serpent whose bite was fabled to produce a great thirst. [Middle English, from Latin, from Greek, from *dipsa*†, thirst.]

dip slope *n.* A land surface whose degree and direction of slope corresponds roughly with the dip of the underlying rock strata.

dip·so (dĭp′sō′) *n., pl* **-sos.** *Slang.* An alcoholic; dipsomaniac.

dip·so·ma·ni·a (dĭp′sə-mā′nē-ə, -mān′yə) *n.* An insatiable, often periodic craving for alcoholic drink. [New Latin : Greek *dipsa*†, thirst + -MANIA.] **—dip·so·ma·ni·ac** *n. & adj.* **—dip·so·ma·ni·a·cal** (dĭp′-sə-mə-nī′ĭ-kəl) *adj.*

dip·stick (dĭp′stĭk′) *n.* A graduated rod for measuring the depth or amount of liquid in a container, as of oil in a crankcase.

dip·ter·al (dĭp′tər-əl) *adj.* **1.** *Architecture.* Built with two rows of columns. **2.** Variant of **dipterous.**

dip·ter·an (dĭp′tər-ən) *n.* Also **dip·ter·on** (-tə-rŏn′) A dipterous insect. [New Latin *Diptera,* plural of *dipterus,* DIPTEROUS.] **—dip·ter·an** *adj.*

dip·ter·ous (dĭp′tər-əs) *adj.* Also **dipteral. 1.** Of, pertaining to, or belonging to the Diptera, a large order of insects that includes the true flies and mosquitoes, characterized by a single pair of membranous wings and a pair of club-shaped balancing organs, the halteres. **2.** *Botany.* Having two winglike parts: *the dipterous fruit of the maple.* [New Latin *dipterus,* from Greek *dipteros,* having two wings : DI- + -PTEROUS.]

dip·tych (dĭp′tĭk) *n.* **1.** An ancient writing tablet having two leaves hinged together. **2.** A pair of painted or carved panels hinged together. [Late Latin *diptycha,* from Greek *diptukha,* from *diptukhos,* double-folded : DI- + *ptukhē,* a fold, from *ptussein,* to fold.]

di·quat (dī′kwät′) *n.* A strong, nonpersistent, yellow, crystalline herbicide, $C_{12}H_{12}Br_2N_2$, used to control water weeds. [DI- + QUAT(ERNARY).]

dir. director.

dire (dīr) *adj.* **direr, direst. 1.** Having dreadful or terrible implications or consequences; calamitous. **2.** Extreme; urgent: *in dire need.* **3.** *Informal.* Hard to bear; tiresome or unpleasant. [Latin *dīrus,* fearful, ill-omened.] **—dire·ly** *adv.* **—dire·ness** *n.*

di·rect (dĭ-rĕkt′, dī-) *v.* **-rected, -recting, -rects.** *—tr.* **1.** To conduct the affairs of; manage; regulate. **2.** To take charge of with authority; control; give commands to. **3. a.** To guide (musicians, especially a small group) while playing oneself. **b.** To conduct (musicians or a choir). **4.** To move (something or someone) toward a goal; aim; point. **5.** To give instructions to (someone) for finding a place. **6.** To address (mail) to a destination. **7.** To address (a speech, remark, or the like) to a person or audience. **8. a.** To give guidance and instruction to (actors, camera technicians, or the like) in the rehearsal and performance of a play or the making of a film. **b.** To supervise the performance of actors in. **c.** To supervise the creative aspects of the making of a (film). *—intr.* **1.** To give commands or directions. **2.** To supervise a performance, rehearsal, or the making of a film. —See Synonyms at **command, conduct.**
∼adj. **1.** Proceeding or lying in a straight course or line; not deviating or swerving. **2.** Straightforward; candid; frank. **3.** Without intervening persons, conditions, or agencies; immediate. **4.** By action of the voters, rather than through elected representatives or delegates. **5.** Of unbroken descent; lineal. **6.** Consisting of the exact words of the writer or speaker. **7.** Absolute; total: *direct opposites.* **8.** *Mathematics.* Varying in the same manner as another quantity; especially, increasing if another quantity increases or decreasing if it decreases. Compare **inverse. 9.** *Astronomy.* Designating a west-to-east motion of a planet or other celestial body in the same direction as the sun's movement among the stars. Compare **retrograde.**
∼adv. **1.** In a direct manner; straight; directly. **2.** Without going through a telephone operator: *dial direct.* [Middle English *directen,* from Latin *dīrigere* (past participle *dīrectus*), to arrange in distinct lines, direct : *dis-,* apart + *regere,* to guide.]

direct access *n.* *Computer Science.* **Random access** *(see).*

direct action *n.* The use of strikes, demonstrations, sabotage, and similar methods to exert pressure on a government, employer, or any other established authority. **—direct actionist** *n.*

di·rect-ac·tion (dĭ-rĕkt′ăk′shən, dī-) *adj.* Operating without intermediate ingredients, components, stages, or processes.

direct current *n. Abbr.* **dc, DC, D.C.** An electric current flowing in one direction.

direct drive *n.* A mechanism in which the drive shaft is directly connected to the part to be driven.

di·rec·ted angle (dĭ-rĕk′tĭd, dī-) *n.* An angle having an indicated positive sense.

directed distance *n.* A segment of a line having an indicated positive sense.

direct evidence *n. Law.* Evidence that bears directly on the fact in dispute, such as that of an eyewitness. Compare **circumstantial evidence.**

di·rec·tion (dĭ-rĕk′shən, dī-) *n.* **1.** The act or function of directing. **2.** Management, supervision, or guidance of some action or operation. **3.** The art or process of film or theatrical directing. **4.** A word or phrase in a musical score indicating how a particular passage is to be played or sung. **5.** *Usually* **directions.** An instruction or series of instructions for doing something. **6.** An order or command; an authoritative indication. **7. a.** The distance-independent relationship between two points that specifies the angular position of either with respect to the other; the relationship by which the alignment or orientation of any position with respect to any other position is established. **b.** A position to which motion or another position is referred. **c.** A line leading to a place or point. **d.** The line, course, or angle along which a person or thing moves. **e.** The destination of a person or thing. **8.** The statement, in degrees, of the angle measured between due north and a given line or course on a compass. Used to indicate the course of a ship, aircraft, or the like. **9.** A course or area of development or action; a tendency toward a particular end or goal. [Middle English, arrangement, management, from Old French, from Latin *dīrectiō* (stem *dīrectiōn-*), from *dīrigere,* to DIRECT.] **—di·rec·tion·less** *adj.*

di·rec·tion·al (dĭ-rĕk′shən-əl, dī-) *adj.* **1.** Of or indicating direction: *an automobile's directional lights.* **2.** *Electronics.* Capable of receiving or sending signals in one direction only. **3.** Of or relating to guidance in effort or behavior: *directional training.*
∼n. A directional signal. **—di·rec·tion·al·i·ty** *n.*

directional antenna *n.* An antenna adapted for receiving signals from or sending signals in a particular direction.

directional signal *n.* One of two flashing lights on an automotive vehicle that indicates the direction of a turn. Also called "directionals."

direction angle *n.* *Mathematics.* One of the three angles that a given line makes with the axes of a three-dimensional Cartesian coordinate system.

direction cosine *n.* *Mathematics.* The cosine of a direction angle of a given line.

direction finder *n. Abbr.* **DF** A device for determining the source of a transmitted signal, consisting mainly of a radio receiver and a coiled rotating antenna.

direction indicator *n.* A compass used in aircraft navigation to compare an intended course to the actual course.

direction ratio *n.* *Mathematics.* One of three numbers that are proportional to the direction cosines of a given line.

di·rec·tive (dĭ-rĕk′tĭv, dī-) *n.* An order or instruction, especially one issued by a central authority.
∼adj. Serving to direct, indicate, or point out; directing.

di·rect·ly (dĭ-rĕkt′lē, dī-) *adv.* **1.** In a direct line or manner; straight. **2.** Without anyone or anything intervening; immediately. **3.** Exactly; totally; absolutely. **4.** At once; instantly. —See Usage note at **immediately.**
∼conj. Chiefly British. As soon as: *We'll go directly she's ready.*

direct mail *n.* **1.** A method of advertising by which a business or organization approaches prospective customers or patrons directly through the mail. **2.** The advertising matter so sent.

direct method *n.* A method of teaching a foreign language using only the language being taught and introducing only a minimal amount of formal grammar.

direct object *n.* In English and some other languages, the word or words in a sentence designating the person or thing undergoing the action of a transitive verb and required to complete its syntactic function. The direct object in English is usually a noun, nominal clause or phrase, or pronoun, and generally follows the verb. In *The girl broke the dish,* the direct object is *the dish.* Compare **indirect object.**

Di·rec·toire (dē-rĕk-twâr′) *n.* The executive body in charge of the French government from 1795 to 1799. Also called "Directory."
∼adj. Of or in the ornate style characteristic of the period of the Directoire in France.

di·rec·tor (dĭ-rĕk′tər, dī-) *n. Abbr.* **dir. 1.** One who supervises, controls, or manages. **2.** A member of a board of persons that controls or governs the affairs of a business concern, institution, or the like. **3. a.** A person who supervises the creative aspects of a dramatic production and instructs the actors on stage. Compare **producer. b.** The person who supervises the creative aspects of the making of a film. **4.** The conductor of an orchestra or chorus. **5.** A surgical instrument used to control the direction and extent of an incision. **—di·rec·tor·ship** *n.*

di·rec·tor·ate (dĭ-rĕk′tər-ĭt, dī-) *n.* **1.** The office or position of a director. **2.** A board of directors.

di·rec·to·ri·al (dĭ-rĕk′tôr′ē-əl, -tōr′ē-əl) *adj.* **1.** Of or pertaining to a director or directorate. **2.** Serving to direct; directive. **—di·rec·to·ri·al·ly** *adv.*

director's chair *n.* A type of light folding chair, usually of canvas on a wooden frame, as used typically by film directors.

di·rec·to·ry (dĭ-rĕk′tə-rē, dī-) *n., pl.* **-ries. 1.** One that directs. **2.** A book listing names, addresses, and telephone numbers of: **a.** Persons living in a particular area, usually listed alphabetically. **b.** A

specific group of persons or firms, listed according to a trade or service offered. **3.** A book of rules or directions, especially for use in church worship. **4.** A directorate.
∼*adj.* Serving to direct.

Di·rec·to·ry (dĭ-rĕk′tə-rē, dī-) *n.* The **Directoire** *(see).*

direct primary *n.* A preliminary election in which a party's candidates for public office are nominated by popular vote.

di·rec·tress (dĭ-rĕk′trĭs, dī-) *n.* A woman who is a director.

di·rec·trix (dĭ-rĕk′trĭks, dī-) *n. pl.* **-trixes** or **directrices** (dĭ′rĕk-trī′sēz). **1.** *Geometry.* **a.** The straight reference line used in generating a conic. **b.** The curve about which the generator moves in forming a cone, cylinder, or other surface. **2.** *Military.* The median line in the trajectory of fire. [New Latin, "directress," from Late Latin *dīrector,* DIRECTOR.]

direct speech *n.* Speech or writing that is reported in its exact original form. Compare **indirect speech.**

direct tax *n.* A tax, such as an income or property tax, levied directly on the taxpayer. Compare **indirect tax.**

dire·ful (dīr′fəl) *adj.* Dreadful; frightful; dire. **—dire·ful·ly** *adv.* **—dire·ful·ness** *n.*

dirge (dûrj) *n.* **1.** A funeral hymn or lament. **2.** *Ecclesiastical.* The office for the dead; a funeral service that is sung. [Middle English *dirige, derge,* from the first word in Medieval Latin *dīrige, Domine, Deus meus, in conspectu tuo viam meam,* "Direct, O Lord, my God, my way in thy sight" (an antiphon in the office of the dead, adopted from Psalms 5:9), from Latin, singular imperative of *dīrigere,* to DIRECT.] **—dirge·ful** *adj.*

dir·ham (də-răm′) *n.* **1. a.** The basic monetary unit of Morocco, divided into 100 centimes. **b.** The basic monetary unit of the United Arab Emirates, divided into 100 fils. See feature at **currency. 2. a.** A monetary unit equal to 1/20 of the dinar of Iraq. **b.** A monetary unit equal to 1/10 of the dinar of Kuwait. **c.** A monetary unit equal to 1/1000 of the dinar of Libya. **d.** A monetary unit equal to 1/100 of the riyal of Qatar. See feature at **currency. 3.** A coin of various North African and Middle Eastern countries. [Arabic *dirham,* from Greek *drakhmē,* DRACHMA.]

dir·i·gi·ble (dĭr′ə-jə-bəl, dĭ-rĭj′ə-bəl) *n.* An early steerable airship.
∼*adj.* Able to be guided or steered. [Latin *dīrigere,* to guide, DIRECT.] **—dir·i·gi·bil·i·ty** (dĭr′ə-jə-bĭl′ĭ-tē) *n.*

dir·i·ment (dĭr′ə-mənt) *adj.* Rendering totally void; nullifying. Used especially in common law in the phrase *diriment impediment of marriage* to signify any sufficient cause for voiding a marriage. [Latin *dīrimēns* (stem *dīriment-*), present participle of *dīrimere,* to take apart, separate, interrupt : *dis-,* apart + *emere,* to take, buy.]

dirk (dûrk) *n.* A dagger, especially as worn by Scottish Highlanders.
∼*tr.v.* **dirked, dirking, dirks.** To stab with a dirk. [Earlier *durk, dork,* probably related to or altered from German *Dolch,* dagger.]

dirn·dl (dûrnd′l) *n.* **1.** A full-skirted dress with a tight bodice, patterned after Tyrolean peasant wear. **2.** A gathered skirt in this style. [German, short for *Dirndlkleid* : *Dirndl,* diminutive of *Dirne,* girl, from Old High German *thiorna,* maid + *Kleid,* dress.]

dirt (dûrt) *n.* **1.** Earth or soil. **2.** A filthy or soiling substance, such as mud, dust, or excrement. **3.** Something or someone mean, contemptible, or vile. **4.** Obscene language. **5.** Malicious or scandalous gossip. **6.** Gravel, slag, or other material from which metal is extracted in mining. **7.** Earth, gravel, or the like that has been pressed down to create a road surface.
∼*adj.* Made of dirt: *a dirt track.* [Middle English *dirt,* variant of *drit,* excrement, mud, filth, from Old Norse *drit,* from Germanic *drit-* (unattested).]

dirt bike *n.* A lightweight motorbike designed for use on rough surfaces, as dirt roads or trails.

dirt-cheap (dûrt′chēp′) *adj. Informal.* Very cheap. **—dirt-cheap** *adv.*

dirt farmer *n. Informal.* A farmer who does all his own work.

dirt·y (dûr′tē) *adj.* **-ier, -iest. 1.** Soiled, as with dirt; grimy; unclean. **2.** *Informal.* Obscene or scatological. **3.** Contemptibly contrary to honor or rules; underhand; nasty: *a dirty trick.* **4.** Of a clouded or muddy appearance. Said especially of colors. **5.** Designating a nuclear weapon that produces an excessive amount of radioactive fallout. **6.** Stormy; rough: *dirty weather.* **7.** Tending to soil or make grubby: *dirty work.* **8.** Expressing hostility or ill-will: *a dirty look.*
∼*v.* **dirtied, -ying, -ies.** *—tr.* To make soiled; stain; tarnish. *—intr.* To become dirty. [Middle English *dritti, dirti,* from *drit,* DIRT.] **—dirt·i·ly** *adv.* **—dirt·i·ness** *n.*
Synonyms: *filthy, foul, grimy, nasty, soiled, squalid.*

dirty linen *n. Informal.* Potentially embarrassing private affairs, such as those of a married couple. Used chiefly in the phrase *wash one's dirty linen in public.*

dirty old man *n. Abbr.* **D.O.M. 1.** A man, usually middle-aged or elderly, who makes furtive and unwelcome sexual advances to women and children. **2.** Any man seen as entertaining lewd or lecherous thoughts.

dirty pool *n. Slang.* Unjust or dishonest conduct. [From POOL (gambling).]

dirty tricks *pl.n. Informal.* Underhand political activities; especially, dishonest practices used in an election campaign to discredit opponents or subvert the electoral process.

dirty word *n.* **1.** A swearword; an obscenity. **2.** Something disapproved of or regarded as objectionable.

dirty work *n. Informal.* **1.** Foul play; deceit. **2.** A difficult or distasteful chore or task, especially when delegated to a subordinate.

dis- *prefix.* Indicates: **1.** Negation, lack, invalidation, or deprivation; for example, **distrust, disuse. 2.** Reversal; for example, **disengage, disunite. 3.** Removal or rejection; for example, **discard, disbar. 4.** Intensification or completion of negative action; for example, **disrupt.** [In borrowed Latin and French compounds, Latin *dis-* (Old French *des-*) indicates: 1. Apart, asunder, aside, as in **digress, distrain.** 2. Away, abroad, in different directions, as in **dismiss, divulge, disseminate.** 3. Negation, deprivation, as in **diffident, disparage.** 4. Reversal, as in **dissimulate.** 5. Removal, as in **dismantle.** 6. Intensification or completion of divisive action, as in **disturb, dissever.** 7. Pejoration, as in **disaster.** Latin *dis-* (sometimes *di-*) is the preverbal form of *dis*†, apart, asunder.]

dis·a·bil·i·ty (dĭs′ə-bĭl′ə-tē) *n., pl.* **-ties. 1.** A disabled state or condition; incapacity. **2.** Something that disables; a handicap. **3.** A legal incapacity or disqualification.

dis·a·ble (dĭs-ā′bəl) *tr.v.* **-bled, -bling, -bles. 1.** To weaken or destroy the normal physical or mental abilities of; cripple; incapacitate. **2.** To render legally disqualified. **3. a.** To make (a machine, for example) inoperative. **b.** *Computer Science.* To suppress an interrupt feature. **—dis·a·ble·ment** *n.*

dis·a·bled (dĭs-ā′bəld) *adj.* Physically handicapped; especially, lacking full use of one's limbs.

dis·a·buse (dĭs′ə-byōōz′) *tr.v.* **-bused, -busing, -buses.** To free from a false impression or misconception; undeceive.

di·sac·cha·ride (dī-săk′ə-rīd′) *n. Chemistry.* Any of a class of carbohydrates, including lactose and sucrose, that yield two monosaccharides on hydrolysis.

dis·ac·cord (dĭs′ə-kôrd′) *n.* Lack of accord; disagreement.
∼*intr.v.* **disaccorded, -cording, -cords.** *Rare.* To disagree.

dis·ac·cus·tom (dĭs′ə-kŭs′təm) *tr.v.* **-tomed, -toming, -toms.** To cause to become unaccustomed.

dis·ad·van·tage (dĭs′əd-văn′tĭj, -vän′tĭj) *n.* **1.** An unfavorable condition or circumstance; handicap. **2.** Detriment.
∼*tr.v.* **disadvantaged, -taging, -tages.** To put at a disadvantage; set back.

dis·ad·van·taged (dĭs′əd-văn′tĭjd, -vän′tĭjd) *adj.* Subjected to severe economic and social disadvantage.

dis·ad·van·ta·geous (dĭs-ăd′vən-tā′jəs, dĭs′ăd-vən-) *adj.* Detrimental; unfavorable; harmful. **—dis·ad·van·ta·geous·ly** *adv.* **—dis·ad·van·ta·geous·ness** *n.*

dis·af·fect (dĭs′ə-fĕkt′) *tr.v.* **-fected, -fecting, -fects.** To cause to lose affection or loyalty; alienate.

dis·af·fect·ed (dĭs′ə-fĕk′tĭd) *adj.* No longer contented and loyal; alienated. **—dis·af·fect·ed·ly** *adv.*

dis·af·fec·tion (dĭs′ə-fĕk′shən) *n.* Absence or withdrawal of affection or loyalty.

dis·af·fil·i·ate (dĭs′ə-fĭl′ē-āt′) *v.* **-ated, -ating, -ates.** *—tr.* To disassociate (oneself or another) from an alliance. *—intr.* To sever an affiliation or association. **—dis·af·fil·i·a·tion** *n.*

dis·af·firm (dĭs′ə-fûrm′) *tr.v.* **-firmed, -firming, -firms. 1.** To deny or contradict. **2.** *Law.* **a.** To repudiate. **b.** To set aside; reverse. **—dis·af·fir·mance** (dĭs′ə-fûr′məns), **dis·af·fir·ma·tion** (dĭs′ăf-ər-mā′shən) *n.*

dis·ag·gre·gate (dĭs-ăg′rə-gĭt′, -gāt′) *intr.v.* **-gated, -gating, -gates.** To break up or break apart. **—dis·ag·gre·ga·tive** *adj.*

dis·a·gree (dĭs′ə-grē′) *intr.v.* **-greed, -greeing, -grees. 1.** To be different or inconsistent; fail to correspond. **2.** To have a different opinion; fail to agree; dissent. **3.** To dispute; quarrel. **4.** To cause adverse effects; be incompatible: *Something I ate disagreed with me.*

dis·a·gree·a·ble (dĭs′ə-grē′ə-bəl) *adj.* **1.** Unpleasant; offensive; distasteful. **2.** Quarrelsome; bad-tempered. **—dis·a·gree·a·ble·ness** *n.* **—dis·a·gree·a·bly** *adv.*

dis·a·gree·ment (dĭs′ə-grē′mənt) *n.* **1.** A failure or refusal to agree. **2.** Disparity; inconsistency. **3.** A conflict or difference of opinion.

dis·al·low (dĭs′ə-lou′) *tr.v.* **-lowed, -lowing, -lows. 1.** To refuse to allow. **2.** To reject as invalid, untrue, or improper. **—dis·al·low·a·ble** *adj.* **—dis·al·low·ance** *n.*

dis·am·big·u·ate (dĭs′ăm-bĭg′yōō-āt′) *tr.v.* **-ated, -ating, -ates.** To establish a single grammatical or semantic interpretation for (an ambiguous word or phrase). **—dis·am·big·u·a·tion** *n.*

dis·an·nul (dĭs′ə-nŭl′) *tr.v.* **-nulled, -nulling, -nuls.** To annul completely; make void; cancel. **—dis·an·nul·ment** *n.*

dis·ap·pear (dĭs′ə-pîr′) *intr.v.* **-peared, -pearing, -pears. 1. a.** To pass out of sight, either suddenly or gradually; vanish. **b.** To cease to be perceived by the senses: *the pain has disappeared.* **2.** To die out; become extinct. **3.** To become lost or absent, often in a mysterious or sinister way. **—dis·ap·pear·ance** *n.*

dis·ap·point (dĭs′ə-point′) *tr.v.* **-pointed, -pointing, -points. 1.** To fail to satisfy the hope, desire, or expectation of. **2.** To frustrate; thwart. [Middle English *disappointen,* to remove from office, dispossess, from Old French *desapointier* : *des-,* from Latin *dis-* (reversal) + *apointier,* to APPOINT.] **—dis·ap·point·er** *n.* **—dis·ap·point·ing·ly** *adv.*

dis·ap·point·ed (dĭs′ə-poin′tĭd) *adj.* Made unhappy by the failure of hopes or expectations; frustrated. **—dis·ap·point·ed·ly** *adv.*

dis·ap·point·ment (dĭs′ə-point′mənt) *n.* **1. a.** The act of disappointing. **b.** The condition or feeling of being disappointed. **c.** An instance of disappointing or being disappointed. **2.** A person, thing, or state of affairs that disappoints.

Disappointment, Cape. Projection into the Pacific Ocean on the north side of the Columbia River in southwestern Washington. It was named in 1788 by an English sea captain, John Meares, who rounded it while searching for the fabled River of the West and was "disappointed" because he could not enter the river.

PRONUNCIATION KEY

ă, pat; ā, pay; âr, care;
ä, father, are; b, bib;
ch, church; d, deed; ĕ, pet;
ē, be; f, fife; g, gag; h, hat;
hw, which; ĭ, pit; ī, pie;
îr, pier; j, judge; k, kick;
l, lid, needle; m, mum;
n, no, sudden; ng, thing;
ŏ, pot; ō, toe; ô, paw, for;
oi, noise; ou, out; ŏŏ, book;
ōō, boot; p, pop; r, roar;
s, sauce; sh, ship, dish;
t, tight; th, thin, path;
th, this, bathe; ŭ, cut; ûr, fur;
v, valve; w, with; y, yes;
z, zebra, size; zh, vision;
ə, about, item, edible, gallop, circus, peaceful

IN FOREIGN WORDS:

à, *Fr.* ami; œ, *Fr.* feu, *Ger.* schön; ü, *Fr.* tu, *Ger.* über; KH, *Ger.* ich, *Scot.* loch; N, *Fr.* bon; y′, *Fr.* Compiègne

STRESS MARKS:

Primary stress: ′
in·cite′ (ĭn-sīt′)
Secondary stress: ′
in′sight′ (ĭn′sīt′)

dis·ap·pro·ba·tion (dĭs-ăp′rə-bā′shən) *n.* Moral disapproval; condemnation.

dis·ap·prov·al (dĭs′ə-pro͞o′vəl) *n.* The act of disapproving; condemnation; censure.

dis·ap·prove (dĭs′ə-pro͞ov′) *v.* **-proved, -proving, -proves.** —*tr.* **1.** To have an unfavorable opinion of; censure; condemn. **2.** To refuse to approve. —*intr.* To regard something as wrong, especially morally wrong; have an unfavorable opinion. Used with *of.* **—dis·ap·prov·ing·ly** *adv.*

dis·arm (dĭs-ärm′) *v.* **-armed, -arming, -arms.** —*tr.* **1.** To deprive of weapons; divest of arms. **2.** To deprive of the means of attack or defense; render helpless or harmless. **3.** To overcome or allay the suspicion, hostility, or antagonism of; win the confidence of. **4.** To win the affection of; charm. —*intr.* **1.** To lay down arms. **2.** To reduce or abolish one's stock of weapons, armaments, or armed forces. **—dis·arm·er** *n.*

dis·ar·ma·ment (dĭs-är′mə-mənt) *n.* **1.** The act of laying down arms; especially, the reduction or abolition of military forces and armaments by a national government. **2.** The condition of being disarmed.

dis·arm·ing (dĭs-är′mĭng) *adj.* Tending to remove suspicion or hostility; winning; endearing. **—dis·arm·ing·ly** *adv.*

dis·ar·range (dĭs′ə-rānj′) *tr.v.* **-ranged, -ranging, -ranges.** To upset the arrangement of; disorder. **—dis·ar·range·ment** *n.*

dis·ar·ray (dĭs′ə-rā′) *n.* **1.** A state of disorder; disarrangement; confusion. **2.** Disordered or untidy dress.
~*tr.v.* **disarrayed, -raying, -rays.** To throw into confusion; upset.

dis·ar·tic·u·late (dĭs′är-tĭk′yə-lāt′) *v.* **-lated, -lating, -lates.** —*tr.* To separate at the joints; disjoint. —*intr.* To come apart at the joints; become disjointed. **—dis·ar·tic·u·la·tion** *n.* **—dis·ar·tic·u·la·tor** *n.*

dis·as·sem·ble (dĭs′ə-sĕm′bəl) *tr.v.* **-bled, -bling, -bles.** To take apart. **—dis·as·sem·bly** *n.*

dis·as·so·ci·ate (dĭs′ə-sō′shē-āt′, -sē-āt′) *tr.v.* **-ated, -ating, -ates.** To dissociate. —See Usage note at **dissociate. —dis·as·so·ci·a·tion** *n.*

dis·as·ter (dĭ-zăs′tər, -zäs′tər) *n.* **1. a.** An occurrence inflicting widespread destruction and distress. **b.** A grave misfortune. **2.** *Informal.* A total failure. **3.** *Obsolete.* An unfavorable influence of a celestial body. [French *désastre,* from Italian *disastro,* back-formation from *disastrato,* "ill-starred" : *dis-,* from Latin (pejorative) + *astro,* star, from Latin *astrum,* from Greek *astron.*]
Synonyms: *calamity, cataclysm, catastrophe, debacle, holocaust.*

disaster area *n.* **1.** An area where a major disaster has occurred; especially, one officially designated as such and thus eligible for government or international aid. **2.** *Informal.* An untidy or disordered place.

disaster dump *n. Computer Science.* A printout that occurs as a result of a nonrecoverable program error.

dis·as·trous (dĭ-zăs′trəs, -zäs′trəs) *adj.* Calamitous; ruinous. **—dis·as·trous·ly** *adv.* **—dis·as·trous·ness** *n.*

dis·a·vow (dĭs′ə-vou′) *tr.v.* **-vowed, -vowing, -vows.** To disclaim knowledge of, responsibility for, or association with; disown. **—dis·a·vow·al** *n.* **—dis·a·vow·er** *n.*

dis·band (dĭs-bănd′) *v.* **-banded, -banding, -bands.** —*tr.* To break up (a group or unit, such as an army); dissolve. —*intr.* To become disbanded; disperse. **—dis·band·ment** *n.*

dis·bar (dĭs-bär′) *tr.v.* **-barred, -barring, -bars.** To expel (a lawyer) from the legal profession by official action or procedure. **—dis·bar·ment** *n.*

dis·be·lief (dĭs′bĭ-lēf′) *n.* Refusal or reluctance to believe.

dis·be·lieve (dĭs′bĭ-lēv′) *v.* **-lieved, -lieving, -lieves.** —*tr.* To refuse to believe; reject. —*intr.* To withhold belief. Used with *in.* **—dis·be·liev·er** *n.* **—dis·be·liev·ing·ly** *adv.*
Usage: In standard English this verb is not a simple opposite to *believe,* but has the specific sense of resistance to or refusal of belief.

dis·branch (dĭs-brănch′, -bränch′) *tr.v.* **-branched, -branching, -branches. 1.** To cut or break a branch or branches from (a tree). **2.** To remove (a limb or branch).

dis·bud (dĭs-bŭd′) *tr.v.* **-budded, -budding, -buds. 1.** *Horticulture.* To remove buds from (a plant) to promote better blooms from remaining buds or to control the shape of the plant. **2.** To remove newly developing horns from (livestock).

dis·bur·den (dĭs-bûrd′n) *v.* **-dened, -dening, -dens.** —*tr.* **1.** To relieve of a burden; especially, to relieve (oneself) of a feeling of anxiety or guilt. **2.** To unload or remove (a burden). —*intr.* To remove or unload a burden. **—dis·bur·den·ment** *n.*

dis·burse (dĭs-bûrs′) *tr.v.* **-bursed, -bursing, -burses.** To pay out; expend, as from a fund. [Old French *desbourser* : *des-,* from Latin *dis-* (reversal) + *bourse,* purse, from Medieval Latin *bursa,* from Greek.] **—dis·burs·a·ble** *adj.* **—dis·burs·er** *n.*

dis·burse·ment (dĭs-bûrs′mənt) *n.* Also **dis·bur·sal** (-bûr′səl). **1.** The act of disbursing. **2.** Money paid out; expenditure.

disc (dĭsk) *n.* Also **disk. 1.** *Informal.* A phonograph record. **2.** Variant of **disk.**

dis·calced (dĭs-kălst′) *adj.* Barefoot. Said of certain orders of monks. [Latin *discalceātus* : *dis-,* not + *calceātus,* shod, from *calceus,* shoe.]

discant. Variant of **descant.**

dis·card (dĭs-kärd′) *v.* **-carded, -carding, -cards.** —*tr.* **1.** To throw away; reject; dismiss as useless or unwanted. **2.** *Card Games.* **a.** To throw out (an undesired card or cards) from one's hand. **b.** To play (a card other than a trump and different in suit from the card led). —*intr. Card Games.* To discard a card.
~*n.* (*usually* dĭs′kärd′). **1.** The act of discarding. **2.** A person or thing that is discarded; especially, the card or cards discarded in a card game. **—dis·card·er** (dĭs-kärd′ər) *n.*

disc brake *n.* Also **disk brake.** A type of brake that works by bringing hydraulically operated friction pads into contact with a disc that is fixed to, and rotates with, the road wheel of a motor vehicle.

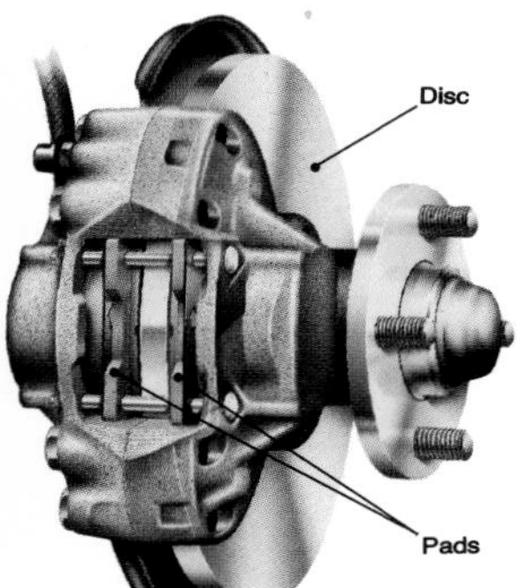

disc brake *In a car fitted with disc brakes, pressure on the brake pedal pushes the friction pads toward each other so that they rub on the disc between them. The disc is fixed to the wheel hub. The advantage of disc brakes over drum brakes is that disc brakes perform better during prolonged heavy braking. In a drum brake, the heat generated by such braking causes the drum to expand, resulting in the loss of efficiency known as "brake fade."*

dis·cern (dĭ-sûrn′, -zûrn′) *v.* **-cerned, -cerning, -cerns.** —*tr.* **1.** To perceive (something obscure or concealed); detect. **2.** To perceive as distinct; discriminate. —*intr.* To perceive differences; make distinctions. —See Synonyms at **see.** [Middle English *discernen,* from Old French *discerner,* from Latin *discernere,* to "separate by sifting," distinguish between : *dis-,* apart + *cernere,* to sift, separate, perceive.] **—dis·cern·er** *n.*

dis·cern·i·ble (dĭ-sûr′nə-bəl, dĭ-zûr′-) *adj.* Perceptible; distinguishable. —See Synonyms at **perceptible. —dis·cern·i·bly** *adv.*

dis·cern·ing (dĭ-sûr′nĭng, dĭ-zûr′-) *adj.* **1.** Astute; perceptive. **2.** Having or showing good taste or judgment. **—dis·cern·ing·ly** *adv.*

dis·cern·ment (dĭ-sûrn′mənt, dĭ-zûrn′-) *n.* **1.** The act or process of discerning. **2.** Keenness of discrimination; good judgment. —See Synonyms at **reason.**

dis·charge (dĭs-chärj′) *v.* **-charged, -charging, -charges.** —*tr.* **1.** To relieve of a burden or of contents; unload. **2.** To unload or empty (contents, such as ship's cargo). **3.** To release, as from confinement or hospital, or from duty. **4.** To dismiss from employment. **5.** To send or pour forth; emit. **6.** To shoot or fire (a projectile or weapon). **7.** To perform the obligations or demands of (an office, duty, or task). **8.** To acquit oneself of (a debt or promise); comply with the terms of. **9.** *Law.* **a.** To release (a defendant, for example). **b.** To set aside; dismiss; annul: *discharge a court order.* **10.** To remove (color) from cloth, as by chemical bleaching. **11.** *Electricity.* To cause electrical discharge in (a battery, for example). **12.** *Architecture.* **a.** To apportion (weight) evenly, as over a door. **b.** To relieve (a part) of excess weight by distribution of pressure. —*intr.* **1.** To get rid of a burden, load, or weight. **2.** To fire a projectile or weapon. **3.** To pour forth contents. **4.** To become blurred; run. Used of dye or dyed cloth. **5.** To undergo electrical discharge. —See Synonyms at **perform.**
~*n.* (dĭs′chärj′, dĭs-chärj′). **1.** The act of removing a load or burden; an unloading. **2.** The act of shooting or firing a projectile or weapon. **3.** A pouring forth; an emission; ejection. **4.** The amount or rate of emission or ejection. **5.** Something that is discharged, released, or emitted: *vaginal discharge.* **6.** A relieving from or elimination of an obligation, burden, or responsibility. **7.** Fulfillment or performance. **8. a.** Dismissal or release from employment, service, or confinement. **b.** A document certifying such release, especially from military service. **9.** A legal annulment or acquittal; a dismissal, as of a court order. **10.** *Electricity.* **a.** The release of stored energy in a capacitor by the flow of electric current between its terminals. **b.** The conversion of chemical energy to electric energy in a battery. **c.** A flow of electricity in a gas, especially a continuous luminous flow in a gas at low pressure. **d.** The elimination of net electric charge from any charged body. [Middle English *dischargen,* from Old French *deschargier,* from Vulgar Latin *discarricāre* (unattested), to unload : *dis-* (reversal) + *carricāre* (unattested), to load, CHARGE.] **—dis·charge·a·ble** *adj.* **—dis·charg·er** *n.*

discharge lamp *n.* A lamp that generates light by means of an internal electrical discharge in a gas.

discharge tube *n.* A closed insulating tube fitted with electrodes and containing a gas in which an electrical discharge is induced by a high applied potential difference.

dis·ci. Alternative plural of **discus.**

dis·ci·ple (dĭ-sī′pəl) *n.* **1. a.** A person who subscribes to the doctrines and teachings of another, especially of a great teacher or leader. **b.** Any active adherent, as of a movement or philosophy. **2.** *Often* **Disciple.** Any of Christ's personal followers, especially, any of the 12 Apostles. **3. Disciple.** A member of the Disciples of Christ. [Middle English *disciple,* Old English *discipul,* from Latin *discipulus,* pupil, from *discere,* to learn.] **—dis·ci·ple·ship** *n.*

Disciples of Christ *n.* A Christian denomination, founded in the United States in 1809, that accepts only the Bible as the rule of Christian faith and practice.

dis·ci·pli·nar·i·an (dĭs′ə-plə-nâr′ē-ən) *n.* A person who enforces or believes in strict discipline.

dis·ci·pli·nar·y (dĭs′ə-plə-nĕr′ē) *adj.* Also **dis·ci·pli·nal** (-plə-nəl, -plĭn′əl). Promoting or used for discipline.

dis·ci·pline (dĭs′ə-plĭn) *n.* **1.** Training that is expected to produce a particular character or pattern of behavior, especially that which is expected to produce moral or mental improvement. **2.** Controlled behavior resulting from such training; self-discipline. **3.** A systematic method of obtaining obedience: *military discipline.* **4.** A state of order based upon submission to rules and authority. **5.** Punishment intended to correct or train. **6.** In some religions, the mortification of the flesh as a penance. **7.** A set of rules or methods, such as those regulating the practice of a church or monastic order. **8.** A branch of knowledge or teaching.
~*tr.v.* **disciplined, -plining, -plines. 1.** To train by instruction and control; teach to obey rules or accept authority. **2.** To punish or penalize. **3.** To organize thoroughly; set in order: *a disciplined mind.* —See Synonyms at **teach, punish.** [Middle English, from Old French, from Latin *disciplīna,* instruction, knowledge, from *discipulus,* pupil, DISCIPLE.] **—dis·ci·plin·a·ble** *adj.* **—dis·ci·plin·er** *n.*

disc jockey *n.* Also **disk jockey.** A person who presents and comments on recordings of popular music, especially on the radio. Also called "DJ."

dis·claim (dĭs-klām′) v. **-claimed, -claiming, -claims.** —*tr.* **1.** To deny or renounce any claim to or connection with; disown. **2.** To deny the validity of; repudiate. **3.** *Law.* To renounce one's right or claim to. —*intr. Law.* To renounce a legal right or claim.

dis·claim·er (dĭs-klā′mər) n. **1.** A repudiation or denial of a claim. **2.** A statement denying responsibility for something.

dis·cla·ma·tion (dĭs′klə-mā′shən) n. Disavowal; renunciation.

dis·cli·max (dĭs-klī′măks′) n. A normally stable ecological community that has been altered by human or other influences, as a grassland community that has been turned into desert by overgrazing.

dis·close (dĭs-klōz′) tr.v. **-closed, -closing, -closes. 1.** To expose to view, as by removing a cover; uncover. **2.** To make known; divulge (a secret, for example). —See Synonyms at **reveal.** —**dis·clos·er** n.

disclosing tablet. A tablet used to show the presence of plaque on the teeth, reacting with it to produce a red stain.

dis·clo·sure (dĭs-klō′zhər) n. **1.** The act or process of disclosing. **2.** Something that is disclosed; a revelation.

dis·co (dĭs′kō′) n., pl. **-cos. 1.** A nightclub often having showy decor and special lighting effects and featuring live or recorded, electronically amplified music for dancing. **2. a.** Popular dance music marked by strong repetitive bass rhythms. **b.** A style of dancing done especially to disco music. ~*intr.v.* **-coed, -coing, -cos.** To dance to disco music. [Short for DISCOTHEQUE.]

disco– prefix. Indicates a phonograph record; for example, **discophile.** [From DISC.]

dis·cob·o·lus (dĭs-kŏb′ə-ləs) n., pl. **-li** (-lī′). A discus-thrower, or a statue of one, in ancient Greece or Rome. [Latin, from Greek *diskobolos : diskos,* quoit, DISK + *-bolos,* thrower, from *ballein,* to throw.]

dis·cog·ra·phy (dĭs-kŏg′rə-fē) n., pl. **-phies.** A catalogue of phonograph records; especially, a comprehensive list of the recordings made by a particular performer or of a particular composer's works. [French *discographie :* DISCO- + -GRAPHY.] —**dis·cog·ra·pher** n.

dis·coid (dĭs′koid′) adj. Also **dis·coi·dal** (dĭs-koid′l). **1.** Having the shape of a disk. **2.** *Botany.* Having disk flowers but no ray flowers. Said of the flower head of a tansy and similar composite plants. ~*n.* A disk or an object shaped like a disk. [Late Latin *dĭscoides,* disk-shaped, from Greek *diskoeidēs : diskos,* DISK + -OID.]

dis·col·or (dĭs-kŭl′ər) v. **-ored, -oring, -ors.** —*tr.* To alter or spoil the proper color of; stain. —*intr.* To become changed or spoiled in color.

dis·col·or·a·tion (dĭs-kŭl′ə-rā′shən) n. **1. a.** The act of discoloring. **b.** The condition of being discolored. **2.** A stain.

dis·com·bob·u·late (dĭs′kəm-bŏb′yə-lāt′) tr.v. **-lated, -lating, -lates.** *Slang.* To throw into a state of confusion; disconcert; upset. [Mock-Latin formation.]

dis·com·fit (dĭs-kŭm′fĭt) tr.v. **-fited, -fiting, -fits. 1.** To make uneasy or perplexed; disconcert; embarrass. **2.** To thwart the plans or purposes of; frustrate; foil. **3.** *Archaic.* To defeat in battle; rout; vanquish. [Middle English *discomfiten,* from Old French *desconfire* (past participle *disconfit*), to defeat, from Vulgar Latin *disconficere* (unattested) : Latin *dis-* (reversal) + *conficere,* to prepare, accomplish : *com-,* together + *facere,* to make.] —**dis·com·fi·ture** (dĭs-kŭm′fĭ-chŏŏr′) n.
Usage: Although *discomfit* was once used strictly in the sense of "to defeat or frustrate," it has also acquired the sense of "to disconcert or make uncomfortable" through confusion with the unrelated word *discomfort.*

dis·com·fort (dĭs-kŭm′fərt) n. **1.** The condition of being uncomfortable in body or mind; mild pain. **2.** Something that disturbs one's comfort; an annoyance. ~*tr.v.* **discomforted, -forting, -forts.** To make uneasy or uncomfortable. —See Usage note at **discomfit.**

dis·com·fort·a·ble (dĭs-kŭmf′tə-bəl, -kŭm′fər-tə-bəl) adj. *Rare.* Not comfortable; distressed or distressing.

dis·com·mend (dĭs′kə-mĕnd′) tr.v. **-mended, -mending, -mends.** *Formal.* **1.** To show or voice disapproval of. **2.** To bring into disfavor or ill regard. —**dis·com·mend·a·ble** adj.

dis·com·mode (dĭs′kə-mōd′) tr.v. **-moded, -moding, -modes.** *Formal.* To put to inconvenience; disturb. [French *discommoder :* Latin *dis-* (reversal) + *commode,* convenient (see **commode**).]

dis·com·pose (dĭs′kəm-pōz′) tr.v. **-posed, -posing, -poses. 1.** To disturb the composure or calm of; agitate; perturb. **2.** To put into a state of disorder; disarrange. —**dis·com·pos·ed·ly** (dĭs′kəm-pō′zĭd-lē) adv. —**dis·com·pos·ing·ly** adv.

dis·com·po·sure (dĭs′kəm-pō′zhər) n. Absence of composure; a state of agitation.

dis·con·cert (dĭs′kən-sûrt′) tr.v. **-certed, -certing, -certs. 1.** To upset the self-possession of; perturb; ruffle. **2.** To frustrate by throwing into disorder; upset; rout. [Obsolete French *disconcerter,* from Old French *desconcerter : des-,* from Latin *dis-* (reversal) + *concerter,* to bring into agreement, from Italian *concertare* (see **concert**).] —**dis·con·cert·ing·ly** adv.

dis·con·cert·ed (dĭs′kən-sûr′tĭd) adj. Deprived of one's composure; thrown into confusion or embarrassment. —**dis·con·cert·ed·ly** adv. —**dis·con·cert·ed·ness** n.

dis·con·form·i·ty (dĭs′kən-fôr′mə-tē) n., pl. **-ties.** *Geology.* A break in a stratigraphical sequence, caused by an interruption of sedimentation due to denudation. Compare **unconformity.**

dis·con·nect (dĭs′kə-nĕkt′) tr.v. **-nected, -necting, -nects. 1.** To

break or interrupt the connection of or between. **2.** To shut off the current in (an electrical appliance) by removing its connection with the power source. **3.** *Informal.* To cut off a power supply to the premises of: *If we don't pay the phone bill by Tuesday, we'll be disconnected.* —**dis·con·nec·tion** n.

dis·con·nect·ed (dĭs′kə-nĕk′tĭd) adj. **1.** Not connected; detached. **2.** Marked by a lack of logical connections; confused; incoherent. —**dis·con·nect·ed·ly** adv. —**dis·con·nect·ed·ness** n.

dis·con·so·late (dĭs-kŏn′sə-lĭt) adj. **1.** Too unhappy to be consoled; hopelessly sad. **2.** Cheerless; gloomy; dismal. [Middle English, from Medieval Latin *disconsōlātus :* Latin *dis-* (negative) + *consōlā-tus,* past participle of *consōlārī,* to CONSOLE.] —**dis·con·so·late·ly** adv. —**dis·con·so·late·ness, dis·con·so·la·tion** n.

dis·con·tent (dĭs′kən-tĕnt′) n. **1.** Absence of contentment; dissatisfaction. **2.** A sense of resentment and grievance. ~*adj.* Discontented. ~*tr.v.* **discontented, -tenting, -tents.** To cause dissatisfaction in; make discontented.

dis·con·tent·ed (dĭs′kən-tĕn′tĭd) adj. Restlessly unhappy; dissatisfied. —**dis·con·tent·ed·ly** adv. —**dis·con·tent·ed·ness** n.

dis·con·tin·u·ance (dĭs′kən-tĭn′yŏŏ-əns) n. **1.** The act of discontinuing or the condition of being discontinued; cessation. **2.** *Law.* The termination of an action by the plaintiff.

dis·con·tin·u·a·tion (dĭs′kən-tĭn′yŏŏ-ā′shən) n. Discontinuance; cessation.

dis·con·tin·ue (dĭs′kən-tĭn′yŏŏ) v. **-ued, -uing, -ues.** —*tr.* **1.** To cause to cease; put a stop to; terminate. **2.** To cease from; give up; abandon. **3.** *Law.* To terminate (an action) by discontinuance. **4.** To cease production of: *a sale of discontinued merchandise.* —*intr.* To come to an end. —**dis·con·tin·u·er** n.

dis·con·ti·nu·i·ty (dĭs′kŏn-tĭ-nŏŏ′ə-tē, -nyŏŏ′ə-tē) n., pl. **-ties. 1.** A lack of continuity, logical sequence, or cohesion. **2.** A break or gap. **3.** *Mathematics.* **a.** The property of being discontinuous. **b.** A point at which a function is defined but is not continuous. **c.** A point at which a function is undefined. **4.** *Geology.* A boundary across which the internal character of the earth changes abruptly, such as the Mohorovičić discontinuity. **5.** *Meteorology.* A **front** (see) or frontal zone.

dis·con·tin·u·ous (dĭs′kən-tĭn′yŏŏ-əs) adj. **1.** Marked by breaks or interruptions; intermittent. **2.** *Mathematics.* Possessing one or more discontinuities. —**dis·con·tin·u·ous·ly** adv. —**dis·con·tin·u·ous·ness** n.

dis·co·phile (dĭsk′ə-fīl′) n. A collector of or specialist in phonograph records. [DISCO- + -PHILE.]

dis·cord (dĭs′kôrd) n. **1.** Lack of agreement among persons, groups, or things; dissension. **2.** A confused or harsh mingling of sounds; a din. **3.** *Music.* **a.** The inharmonious combination of simultaneously sounded notes; dissonance. Compare **concord. b.** Any chord exemplifying this. ~*intr.v.* (dĭs-kôrd′), **discorded, -cording, -cords.** To fail to agree or harmonize; clash. [Middle English, from Old French *descorde,* from Latin *discordia,* strife, from *discors,* disagreeing : *dis-,* apart + *cor* (stem *cord-*), heart.]
Synonyms: clash, conflict, contention, dissension, strife, variance.

dis·cor·dant (dĭs-kôr′dənt) adj. **1.** Not in accord; conflicting. **2.** Disagreeable in sound; harsh or dissonant. —See Synonyms at **inconsistent.** —**dis·cor·dance, dis·cor·dan·cy** n. —**dis·cor·dant·ly** adv.

dis·co·theque, dis·co·thèque n. **1.** A usually small nightclub featuring dancing to live or recorded music. **2.** See **disco** (sense 1). [French : DISCO- + -THÈQUE, record library, by analogy with *bibliothèque,* library.]

dis·count (dĭs′kount′, dĭs-kount′) v. **-counted, -counting, -counts.** —*tr.* **1.** To deduct or subtract (a specified sum or percentage) from a cost or price. **2. a.** To buy or sell (a promissory note such as a treasury bill) after deducting the amount of interest that will accumulate before it matures. **b.** To advance money as a loan on (a promissory note not immediately payable) after deducting the interest. **3.** To reduce in cost, quantity, or value. **4.** To leave out of account as being untrustworthy or exaggerated; disregard; ignore. **5.** To anticipate and make allowance for. —*intr.* To lend money after deduction of interest. ~*n.* (dĭs′kount′). **1.** A reduction from the full or standard amount of a price or debt. **2.** The interest deducted in advance in purchasing, selling, or lending a promissory note such as a treasury bill. **3.** The rate of interest deducted in such a transaction. Also called "discount rate." **4.** The act or an instance of discounting a bill of exchange, treasury bill, or the like. ~*adj.* Selling at prices lower than those set by manufacturers. [Obsolete French *descompte, descompter,* from Medieval Latin *discompu-tāre :* Latin *dis-* (reversal) + *computāre,* to add, sum up, COMPUTE.] —**dis·count·a·ble** adj. —**dis·count·er** n.

dis·coun·te·nance (dĭs-koun′tə-nəns) tr.v. **-nanced, -nancing, -nances. 1.** To view or treat with disfavor. **2.** To embarrass; abash; disconcert. ~*n.* Disfavor; disapproval.

discount house n. A discount store.

discount store n. A store that sells merchandise, especially consumer goods, at a discount from the manufacturer's suggested retail price.

dis·cour·age (dĭs-kûr′ĭj) tr.v. **-aged, -aging, -ages. 1.** To deprive of confidence, hope, or spirit; dishearten; daunt. **2.** To hamper or hinder. **3.** To dissuade or deter. Used with *from.* **4.** To try to prevent by expressing disapproval or raising objections: *The report discourages smoking.* —**dis·cour·ag·er** *n.* —**dis·cour·ag·ing·ly** *adv.*

dis·cour·age·ment (dĭs-kûr′ĭj-mənt) *n.* **1. a.** The act of discouraging. **b.** The condition of being discouraged. **2.** Something that discourages; a deterrent. —See Synonyms at **despair.**

dis·course (dĭs′kôrs′, -kōrs′) *n.* **1.** Verbal expression in speech or writing. **2.** Verbal exchange; conversation. **3.** A formal and lengthy discussion of a subject, either written or spoken. **4.** *Archaic.* The process or power of reasoning.
~*v.* (dĭs-kôrs′, -kōrs′), **discoursed, -coursing, -courses.** —*intr.* **1.** To speak or write formally and at length. Used with *on* or *upon.* **2.** To engage in conversation or discussion; converse. —*tr. Archaic.* **1.** To narrate or discuss. **2.** To give forth (musical sounds); perform. —See Synonyms at **speak.** [Middle English *discours,* from Late Latin *discursus,* conversation, from Latin, "a running back and forth," from the past participle of *discurrere,* to run back and forth, speak at length : *dis-,* in different directions + *currere,* to run.] —**dis·cours·er** *n.*

dis·cour·te·ous (dĭs-kûr′tē-əs) *adj.* Lacking courtesy; impolite; rude. —**dis·cour·te·ous·ly** *adv.* —**dis·cour·te·ous·ness** *n.*

dis·cour·te·sy (dĭs-kûr′tə-sē) *n., pl.* **-sies. 1.** Lack of courtesy; rudeness. **2.** A discourteous act or statement.

dis·cov·er (dĭs-kŭv′ər) *tr.v.* **-ered, -ering, -ers. 1.** To obtain knowledge of; arrive at through search or study. **2.** To be the first to find, learn of, or observe. **3.** To learn of or experience for the first time: *discover the pleasures of music.* **4.** *Informal.* To find that (a previously unknown person) has marketable talents. **5.** *Archaic.* To reveal; expose. —**dis·cov·er·a·ble** *adj.* —**dis·cov·er·er** *n.*

dis·cov·ert (dĭs-kŭv′ərt) *adj. Law.* Having no husband, and therefore not subject to coverture. —**dis·cov·er·ture** *n.*

dis·cov·er·y (dĭs-kŭv′ə-rē) *n., pl.* **-ies. 1.** The act or an instance of discovering. **2. a.** Something that has been discovered. **b.** A person recently found to have a special talent. **3.** *Law.* The process whereby parties in an action are obliged to disclose any documents relevant to the case.

dis·cred·it (dĭs-krĕd′ĭt) *tr.v.* **-ited, -iting, -its. 1.** To damage in reputation; disgrace; dishonor. **2.** To cast doubt on; cause to be distrusted. **3.** To give no credence to; disbelieve. —See Synonyms at **degrade.**
~*n.* **1.** Loss of or damage to one's reputation; dishonor; disgrace. **2.** Lack or loss of trust or belief; doubt. **3.** Anything damaging to one's reputation or stature. —See Synonyms at **disgrace.**

dis·cred·it·a·ble (dĭs-krĕd′ĭ-tə-bəl) *adj.* Deserving of or resulting in discredit; blameworthy. —**dis·cred·it·a·bly** *adv.*

dis·creet (dĭs-krēt′) *adj.* **1.** Showing a judicious reserve in one's speech or behavior; especially, able to keep other people's secrets. **2.** Lacking ostentation or pretension; unobtrusive; modest. [Middle English, from Old French *discret,* from Medieval Latin *discrētus,* "showing good judgment," from Latin, past participle of *discernere,* to separate, DISCERN.] —**dis·creet·ly** *adv.* —**dis·creet·ness** *n.*

dis·crep·an·cy (dĭs-krĕp′ən-sē) *n., pl.* **-cies.** Also **dis·crep·ance** (-əns). **1.** Divergence or disagreement, as between facts or claims; inconsistency. **2.** An instance of such disagreement. —See Usage note at **difference.**

dis·crep·ant (dĭs-krĕp′ənt) *adj.* Marked by discrepancy; not consistent or matching; disagreeing. [Middle English *discrepaunt,* from Latin *discrepāns* (stem *discrepant-*), present participle of *discrepāre,* to sound different, vary : *dis-,* apart + *crepāre,* to rattle, sound.] —**dis·crep·ant·ly** *adv.*

dis·crete (dĭs-krēt′) *adj.* **1.** Constituting a separate thing; individual; distinct. **2.** Consisting of unconnected distinct parts. [Middle English, from Latin *discrētus,* separate. See **discreet.**] —**dis·crete·ly** *adv.* —**dis·crete·ness** *n.*

discrete variable *n.* A mathematical variable that assumes only whole numbers.

dis·cre·tion (dĭs-krĕsh′ən) *n.* **1.** The quality of being discreet; prudent or cautious reserve. **2.** Freedom to act or judge on one's own; latitude of choice and action: *the age of discretion.* —**at someone's discretion.** In accordance with the wishes or judgment of.

dis·cre·tion·ar·y (dĭs-krĕsh′ə-nĕr′ē) *adj.* Also **dis·cre·tion·al** (dĭs-krĕsh′ən-əl). **1.** Left to or regulated by one's own discretion or judgment. **2.** Based on consideration of a particular case, not on a general regulation: *a discretionary grant.* —**dis·cre·tion·ar·i·ly** *adv.*

dis·crim·i·nant (dĭs-krĭm′ə-nənt) *n. Mathematics.* A value or function related to a polynomial equation, giving information about the nature of the roots of the equation. It is the product of the squares of all the differences of the roots taken in pairs; for a quadratic equation $ax^2 + bx + c = 0$, the discriminant is $b^2 - 4ac$. [Latin *discrīmināns* (stem *discrīminant-*), present participle of *discrīmināre,* to DISCRIMINATE.]

dis·crim·i·nate (dĭs-krĭm′ə-nāt′) *v.* **-nated, -nating, -nates.** —*intr.* **1.** To make a clear distinction; differentiate. Often used with *between.* **2.** To act on the basis of prejudice. —*tr.* **1.** To perceive the distinguishing features of; recognize as distinct. **2.** To serve to mark; differentiate: *The ability to reason discriminates humans from animals.*
~*adj.* (dĭs-krĭm′ə-nĭt). Discriminating. [Latin *discrīmināre,* to divide, distinguish, from *discrīmen,* distinction.] —**dis·crim·i·nate·ly** *adv.*

dis·crim·i·nat·ing (dĭs-krĭm′ə-nā′tĭng) *adj.* **1.** Able or tending to draw fine distinctions; discerning. **2.** Fastidiously selective. **3.** Serving to differentiate; distinctive. **4.** Showing favoritism or

prejudice; differential, as a tariff may be. —**dis·crim·i·nat·ing·ly** *adv.*

dis·crim·i·na·tion (dĭs-krĭm′ə-nā′shən) *n.* **1.** The act of discriminating. **2.** The ability or power to see or make fine distinctions; discernment. **3.** Attitude, behavior, or treatment based on prejudice. **4.** *Electronics.* The use of a circuit to pass signals of one characteristic while rejecting others. See **discriminator.**

dis·crim·i·na·tive (dĭs-krĭm′ə-nā′tĭv, -ə-nə-tĭv) *adj.* **1.** Drawing distinctions; discriminating. **2.** Discriminatory. —**dis·crim·i·na·tive·ly** *adv.*

dis·crim·i·na·tor (dĭs-krĭm′ə-nā′tər) *n.* **1.** One that discriminates. **2.** *Electronics.* A device that converts a property of a signal, such as frequency or phase, into an amplitude variation.

dis·crim·i·na·to·ry (dĭs-krĭm′ə-nə-tôr′ē, -tōr′ē) *adj.* **1.** Marked by or showing prejudice; biased. **2.** Discriminating. —**dis·crim·i·na·to·ri·ly** *adv.*

dis·crown (dĭs-kroun′) *tr.v.* **-crowned, -crowning, -crowns.** To deprive of a crown; dethrone; depose.

dis·cur·sive (dĭs-kûr′sĭv) *adj.* **1.** Covering a wide field of subjects; rambling; digressive. **2.** Proceeding to a conclusion through reason rather than intuition. [Medieval Latin *discursīvus,* from Latin *discursus,* "a running back and forth." See **discourse.**] —**dis·cur·sive·ly** *adv.* —**dis·cur·sive·ness** *n.*

dis·cus (dĭs′kəs) *n., pl.* **-cuses** or **disci** (dĭs′ī). **1.** A disk, usually wooden with a metal rim and weighing about 4½ pounds, thrown for distance in athletic competitions. **2.** The field event in which this disk is thrown. **3.** A small, brilliantly colored South American freshwater fish, *Symphysodon discus,* that has a disk-shaped body and is popular in home aquariums. [Latin, DISK.]

dis·cuss (dĭs-kŭs′) *tr.v.* **-cussed, -cussing, -cusses. 1.** To discourse about in speech or writing; treat of. **2.** To consider (a matter) by speaking together about it; debate. **3.** To consume (food or drink) with relish. Used humorously. [Middle English *discussen,* from Late Latin *discutere* (past participle *discussus*), to investigate, discuss, from Latin, to break up, scatter : *dis-,* apart + *quatere,* to shake.] —**dis·cuss·er** *n.* —**dis·cuss·i·ble** *adj.*
Synonyms: argue, contend, debate, dispute.

dis·cus·sant (dĭs-kŭs′ənt) *n.* One who takes part in a discussion.

dis·cus·sion (dĭs-kŭsh′ən) *n.* **1.** The consideration of a subject by a group; an earnest conversation. **2.** A discourse by one person upon a topic; an exposition.

dis·dain (dĭs-dān′) *tr.v.* **-dained, -daining, -dains. 1.** To regard or treat with haughty contempt; despise. **2.** To consider unworthy of oneself; refuse with scorn.
~*n.* A feeling, attitude, or show of scornful superiority; aloof contempt: *a cold stare of disdain.* [Middle English *desdeynen,* from Old French *desdeignier,* from Vulgar Latin *disdignāre* (unattested), variant of Latin *dēdignārī,* to scorn : *dē-* (reversal) + *dignāre,* to deem worthy, from *dignus,* worthy.]

dis·dain·ful (dĭs-dān′fəl) *adj.* Feeling or showing disdain; scornful and haughty. —See Synonyms at **proud.** —**dis·dain·ful·ly** *adv.* —**dis·dain·ful·ness** *n.*

dis·ease (dĭ-zēz′) *n.* **1.** An abnormal condition of an organism or part, especially as a consequence of infection, inherent weakness, or environmental stress, that impairs normal physiological functioning. **2.** A condition or tendency, as of society, regarded as abnormal and pernicious. **3.** *Obsolete.* Lack of ease.

dis·eased (dĭ-zēzd′) *adj.* **1.** Affected with disease. **2.** Unhealthy; unsound; disordered.

dis·em·bark (dĭs′ĭm-bärk′) *v.* **-barked, -barking, -barks.** —*intr.* To go ashore from a ship. —*tr.* To put or cause to go ashore from a ship. —**dis·em·bar·ka·tion** *n.*

dis·em·bar·rass (dĭs′ĭm-băr′əs) *tr.v.* **-rassed, -rassing, -rasses.** To free from something embarrassing, bothersome, or encumbering; relieve. —**dis·em·bar·rass·ment** *n.*

dis·em·bod·ied (dĭs′ĭm-bŏd′ēd) *adj.* **1.** No longer connected with the body; ghostly. **2.** Unrelated to the real world.

dis·em·bod·y *tr.v.* **-ied, -ying, -ies. 1.** To free (the soul or spirit) from the body. **2.** To divest of reality. —**dis·em·bod·i·ment** *n.*

dis·em·bogue (dĭs′ĭm-bōg′) *v.* **-bogued, -boguing, -bogues.** —*intr.* To empty at the mouth. Used of a river. —*tr.* To discharge (waters) at the mouth. Used of a river. [Alteration of Spanish *desembocar* : *des-,* from Latin *dis-* (reversal) + *embocar,* to put into the mouth : *em-,* from Latin *in-,* in + *boca,* mouth, from Latin *bucca,* cheek.] —**dis·em·bogue·ment** *n.*

dis·em·bow·el (dĭs′ĭm-bou′əl) *tr.v.* **-eled, -eling, -els.** Also *chiefly British* **-elled, -elling.** To remove the bowels from. —**dis·em·bow·el·ment** *n.*

dis·em·broil (dĭs′ĭm-broil′) *tr.v.* **-broiled, -broiling, -broils.** To free from a condition of complexity or confusion; disentangle.

dis·en·chant (dĭs′ĭn-chănt′, -chänt′) *tr.v.* **-chanted, -chanting, -chants.** To free from enchantment or illusion; undeceive. —**dis·en·chant·er** *n.* —**dis·en·chant·ment** *n.*

dis·en·chant·ed (dĭs′ĭn-chănt′əd, -chänt′-) *adj.* Disappointed; disillusioned. Used with *with.*

dis·en·cum·ber (dĭs′ĭn-kŭm′bər) *tr.v.* **-bered, -bering, -bers.** To relieve of encumbrances. —**dis·en·cum·ber·ment** *n.*

dis·en·dow (dĭs′ĭn-dou′) *tr.v.* **-dowed, -dowing, -dows.** To deprive of endowments.

dis·en·fran·chise (dĭs′ĭn-frăn′chīz′) *tr.v.* **-ised, -ising, -ises.** Also **dis·fran·chise** (dĭs′frăn′chīz′). **1.** To deprive (an individual) of a right of citizenship, especially of the right to vote. **2.** To deprive (a company, for example) of a privilege or franchise. —**dis·en·fran-**

chise·ment, dis·fran·chise·ment n. —dis·en·fran·chis·er, dis·fran·chis·er n.

dis·en·gage (dĭs'ĭn-gāj') v. -gaged, -gaging, -gages. —tr. 1. To release from something that holds fast, connects, or entangles, especially in a mechanical device. 2. To unfasten; detach. 3. Archaic. To release from an engagement, pledge, or obligation. —intr. To become disengaged; get loose.

dis·en·gage·ment (dĭs'ĭn-gāj'mənt) n. 1. a. The act of disengaging. b. The condition of being disengaged. 2. Military. Withdrawal of forces from a particular military theater. 3. Freedom from obligation; ease of manner.

dis·en·tail (dĭs'ĭn-tāl') tr.v. -tailed, -tailing, -tails. Law. To release (an estate) from entail. —dis·en·tail·ment n.

dis·en·tan·gle (dĭs'ĭn-tăng'gəl) v. -gled, -gling, -gles. —tr. 1. To extricate from entanglement or involvement; free. 2. To clear up or resolve (a mystery, for example). —intr. To become disentangled. —dis·en·tan·gle·ment n.

dis·en·tomb (dĭs'ĭn-tōōm') tr.v. -tombed, -tombing, -tombs. To remove from or as if from a tomb. —dis·en·tomb·ment n.

dis·en·twine (dĭs'ĭn-twīn') v. -twined, -twining, -twines. —tr. To disentangle; untwine. —intr. To become untwined.

dis·e·qui·lib·ri·um (dĭs'ē-kwə-lĭb'rē-əm) n. Loss or lack of equilibrium or stability.

dis·es·tab·lish (dĭs'ĭ-stăb'lĭsh) tr.v. -lished, -lishing, -lishes. 1. To alter the status of (something established by authority or general acceptance). 2. To deprive (a church) of the status of an established church (see). —dis·es·tab·lish·ment n.

dis·es·teem (dĭs'ĭ-stēm') tr.v. -teemed, -teeming, -teems. To have little regard for; hold in disfavor. ~n. Lack of esteem.

dis·fa·vor (dĭs-fā'vər) n. 1. Unfavorable opinion or regard; disapproval. 2. The condition of being regarded with disapproval. 3. A disservice. ~tr.v. disfavored, -voring, -vors. 1. To view or treat with dislike or disapproval. 2. To withhold favor from.

dis·fea·ture (dĭs-fē'chər) tr.v. -tured, -turing, -tures. To spoil the features of; disfigure. —dis·fea·ture·ment n.

dis·fig·ure (dĭs-fĭg'yər) tr.v. -ured, -uring, -ures. To blemish or spoil the appearance or shape of. —dis·fig·ur·er n.

dis·fig·ure·ment (dĭs-fĭg'yər-mənt) n. Also dis·fig·u·ra·tion (-fĭg'yə-rā'shən). 1. a. The act of disfiguring. b. The condition of being disfigured. 2. A deformity; flaw.

disfranchise. Variant of disenfranchise.

dis·frock (dĭs-frŏk') tr.v. -frocked, -frocking, -frocks. To unfrock.

dis·gorge (dĭs-gôrj') v. -gorged, -gorging, -gorges. —tr. 1. To bring up and expel from the throat or stomach; vomit. 2. To discharge in a violent or confused manner; spew out. 3. To yield or return reluctantly. —intr. To discharge or pour forth contents. —dis·gorge·ment n.

dis·grace (dĭs-grās') n. 1. Loss of honor, respect, or reputation; shame. 2. The condition of being out of favor or badly thought of. 3. Something that brings shame, dishonor, or disfavor. 4. Informal. Something that is shocking in its poor quality or appearance. ~tr.v. disgraced, -gracing, -graces. 1. To bring shame or dishonor upon. 2. To cause (someone) to lose favor or reputation. —dis·grac·er n.

Synonyms: degradation, discredit, dishonor, disrepute, ignominy, infamy, obloquy, odium, opprobrium, scandal, shame.

dis·grace·ful (dĭs-grās'fəl) adj. Bringing or deserving disgrace; shameful. —dis·grace·ful·ly adv. —dis·grace·ful·ness n.

dis·grun·tle (dĭs-grŭnt'l) tr.v. -tled, -tling, -tles. To make discontented or cross; put in a disagreeable mood. [DIS- (intensive) + dialectal gruntle, to grumble, Middle English gruntlen, frequentative of grunten, to GRUNT.] —dis·grun·tled adj. —dis·grun·tle·ment n.

dis·guise (dĭs-gīz') tr.v. -guised, -guising, -guises. 1. To modify the appearance or manner of in order to prevent recognition. 2. To conceal or obscure by false pretenses; misrepresent. ~n. 1. a. The act of disguising. b. The condition of being disguised. 2. Something that serves to disguise, such as a mask, costume, or pretense. [Middle English disg(u)isen, from Old French desguisier : des-, from Latin dis- (reversal) + guise, manner, GUISE.] —dis·guis·er n.

dis·gust (dĭs-gŭst') tr.v. -gusted, -gusting, -gusts. 1. To be so unpleasant as to excite nausea in; sicken. 2. To offend the taste or moral sense of; repel. ~n. A strong feeling of distaste excited by something physically revolting or offensive to one's moral or aesthetic values. [Old French desgouster : des-, from Latin dis- (negative) + goust, taste, from Latin gustus.]

dis·gust·ed (dĭs-gŭs'tĭd) adj. Filled with disgust or irritated impatience. —dis·gust·ed·ly adv.

Usage: Three prepositions are used after disgusted in standard English. One is disgusted at someone's action or behavior, especially when one is giving an immediate reaction; one is disgusted with a person or his action, especially when one's attitude is being maintained over a period of time; and one may also be disgusted by someone or something.

dis·gust·ful (dĭs-gŭst'fəl) adj. 1. Causing disgust; repugnant. 2. Full of or marked by disgust. —dis·gust·ful·ly adv.

dis·gust·ing (dĭs-gŭs'tĭng) adj. Deeply offensive to one's taste or moral values; acutely repugnant. —dis·gust·ing·ly adv.

dish (dĭsh) n. 1. a. An open container, generally shallow and concave, for holding or serving food. b. Loosely, any container on which food is placed or served, such as a plate or bowl. c. The portion a dish holds. 2. A particular variety, preparation, or article of food. 3. a. A concavity or depression like that in a dish. b. The degree of such a concavity. 4. A large dish-shaped aerial, as in a radio telescope or radar apparatus. 5. Slang. A good-looking person, especially a woman. ~tr.v. dished, dishing, dishes. 1. To serve (food) in or from a dish, cooking pot, pan, or the like. Usually used with up or out. 2. To hollow out; make concave. 3. British Slang. To foil; ruin. 4. Informal. To give out; dispense; distribute. Used with out. —dish it out. Slang. To hand out abuse or punishment. —dish up. 1. To serve food or a meal. 2. Informal. To present (a proposal, for example) in an attractive manner. [Middle English dish, Old English disc, plate, bowl, platter, from West Germanic diskaz (unattested), from Latin discus, quoit, DISK.]

dis·ha·bille (dĭs'ə-bēl', -bē') n. Also des·ha·bille (dĕs'-). The state of being partially or very casually dressed; a state of undress. [French déshabillé, from the past participle of déshabiller, to undress : dés-, from Latin dis- (reversal) + habiller, to dress.] —dis·ha·bille adj.

dis·har·mo·ny (dĭs-här'mə-nē) n., pl. -nies. Lack of harmony; discord. —dis·har·mo·ni·ous (dĭs'här-mō'nē-əs) adj.

dish·cloth (dĭsh'klôth', -klŏth') n. A cloth used for washing dishes or wiping surfaces. Also called "dishrag."

dishcloth gourd n. 1. Any of several tropical vines of the genus Luffa; especially, L. cylindrica, cultivated for its cucumberlike fruits. 2. The fruit of any of these plants, the fibrous skeleton of which is used as a loofah (see).

dis·heart·en (dĭs-härt'n) tr.v. -ened, -ening, -ens. To shake or destroy the courage or resolution of; dispirit. —dis·heart·en·ing·ly adv. —dis·heart·en·ment n.

dished (dĭsht) adj. 1. Slanting toward one another at the bottom. Said of a pair of wheels. 2. Dish-shaped; concave.

di·shev·el (dĭ-shĕv'əl) tr.v. -eled, -eling, -els. Also chiefly British -elled, -elling. 1. To loosen and let fall (hair or clothing) in disarray. 2. To disarrange the hair or clothing of (a person). [Back-formation from DISHEVELED.] —di·shev·el·ment n.

di·shev·eled (dĭ-shĕv'əld) adj. 1. In a state of disarray; unkempt; untidy. [Middle English discheveled, from Old French deschevele, past participle of descheveler, to disarrange the hair : des-, from Latin dis-, apart + chevel, hair, from Latin capillus.]

dis·hon·est (dĭs-ŏn'ĭst) adj. 1. Disposed to lie, cheat, or deceive. 2. Involving deception or untruthfulness. 3. Obtained illegally or unfairly. —dis·hon·est·ly adv.

Synonyms: deceitful, lying, mendacious, shady, tricky, underhand, untruthful.

dis·hon·es·ty (dĭs-ŏn'ĭ-stē) n., pl. -ties. 1. Lack of honesty; inclination to deceive or cheat. 2. A dishonest act or statement.

dis·hon·or (dĭs-ŏn'ər) n. 1. Loss of honor, respect, or reputation; disgrace; shame. 2. Something that causes loss of honor. 3. An offense or insult. 4. Failure to pay a note or bill of exchange or to meet a commercial obligation. —See Synonyms at disgrace. ~tr.v. dishonored, -oring, -ors. 1. To deprive of honor; disgrace. 2. To offend the dignity of; slight. 3. To violate the chastity of. 4. To fail to pay (a note, for example). —dis·hon·or·er n.

dis·hon·or·a·ble (dĭs-ŏn'ər-ə-bəl) adj. 1. Characterized by or causing dishonor or discredit. 2. Lacking integrity; unprincipled. —dis·hon·or·a·ble·ness n. —dis·hon·or·a·bly adv.

dish·pan (dĭsh'păn') n. A flat-bottomed pan or basin for washing dishes.

dish·rag (dĭsh'răg') n. A dishcloth (see).

dish·tow·el (dĭsh'tou'əl) n. A towel for drying dishes. Also chiefly British "tea towel."

dish·ware (dĭsh'wâr') n. Dishes, as of china, used in serving food.

dish·wash·er (dĭsh'wŏsh'ər, -wô'shər) n. 1. An electric machine that washes dishes, cutlery, and utensils automatically. 2. A person who washes dishes; specifically, one employed to do this in a restaurant.

dish·wa·ter (dĭsh'wô'tər, -wŏt'ər) n. 1. Water in which dishes are being or have been washed. 2. Informal. An unpleasantly weak-tasting drink.

dish·y (dĭsh'ē) adj. -ier, -iest. Chiefly British Slang. Very attractive. [From DISH (attractive person).]

dis·il·lu·sion (dĭs'ĭ-lōō'zhən) tr.v. -sioned, -sioning, -sions. 1. To free or deprive of illusions or misconceptions. 2. To undermine or destroy the ideals of; disenchant. ~n. 1. The act of disillusioning. 2. The condition or fact of being disillusioned. —dis·il·lu·sion·ment n. —dis·il·lu·sive adj.

dis·il·lu·sioned (dĭs'ĭ-lōō'zhənd) adj. 1. No longer contented or satisfied. 2. No longer idealistic; cynical.

dis·in·cen·tive (dĭs'ĭn-sĕn'tĭv) n. Something that discourages or dissuades; a deterrent. —dis·in·cen·tive adj.

dis·in·cli·na·tion (dĭs'ĭn-klə-nā'shən) n. Lack of willingness or disposition; reluctance; aversion.

dis·in·cline (dĭs'ĭn-klīn') v. -clined, -clining, -clines. —tr. To make reluctant or unwilling. —intr. To be reluctant or unwilling.

dis·in·clined (dĭs'ĭn-klīnd') adj. Unwilling; reluctant.

dis·in·fect (dĭs'ĭn-fĕkt') tr.v. -fected, -fecting, -fects. To cleanse of disease-carrying microorganisms. —dis·in·fec·tion n.

dis·in·fec·tant (dĭs'ĭn-fĕk'tənt) n. An agent that disinfects by destroying, neutralizing, or inhibiting the growth of disease-carrying microorganisms. ~adj. Serving to disinfect.

dis·in·fest (dĭs'ĭn-fĕst') tr.v. -fested, -festing, -fests. To rid of vermin. —dis·in·fes·ta·tion n.

dis·in·fla·tion (dĭs′ĭn-flā′shən) *n.* The downward movement of inflated prices to a more normal level, without necessarily entailing a reduction in the level of economic activity.

dis·in·form (dĭs′ĭn-fôrm′, -fōrm′) *tr.v.* **-formed, -forming, -forms.** To supply with disinformation.

dis·in·for·ma·tion (dĭs-ĭn′fər-mā′shən) *n.* False or misleading information deliberately spread by a propaganda agency.

dis·in·gen·u·ous (dĭs′ĭn-jĕn′yōō-əs) *adj.* Not straightforward or candid; insincere; crafty. **—dis·in·gen·u·ous·ly** *adv.* **—dis·in·gen·u·ous·ness** *n.*

dis·in·her·it (dĭs′ĭn-hĕr′ĭt) *tr.v.* **-ited, -iting, -its.** To deprive of inheritance or the right to inherit, especially by excluding members of one's family. **—dis·in·her·i·tance** *n.*

dis·in·te·grate (dĭs-ĭn′tə-grāt′) *v.* **-grated, -grating, -grates.** *—intr.* **1.** To separate into components or fragments, especially after a physical shock. **2.** To weaken or collapse, especially in the face of difficulties. *—tr.* To cause (a body) to separate into components; destroy. —See Synonyms at **decay.** **—dis·in·te·gra·tor** *n.*

dis·in·te·gra·tion (dĭs-ĭn′tə-grā′shən) *n.* **1.** The process of disintegrating or the state of being disintegrated. **2.** *Physics.* The break-up of an atomic nucleus or an unstable elementary particle into smaller fragments, either spontaneously or as a result of bombardment with radiation. See **decay.**

dis·in·ter (dĭs′ĭn-tûr′) *tr.v.* **-terred, -terring, -ters.** **1.** To dig up or remove, as from a grave or tomb; exhume. **2.** To remove from obscurity; expose. **—dis·in·ter·ment** *n.*

dis·in·ter·est (dĭs-ĭn′trĭst, -ĭn′tər-ĭst) *n.* **1.** Freedom from selfish bias or self-interest; impartiality. **2.** *Nonstandard.* Lack of interest.

dis·in·ter·est·ed (dĭs-ĭn′trĭ-stĭd, -ĭn′tə-rĕs′tĭd) *adj.* **1.** Not influenced by self-interest; impartial: *disinterested praise.* **2.** *Nonstandard.* Uninterested; indifferent. **—dis·in·ter·est·ed·ly** *adv.* **—dis·in·ter·est·ed·ness** *n.*

Usage: Standard English attempts to maintain a clear distinction between *disinterested* meaning "impartial," "unbiased" and *uninterested* meaning "indifferent." The former implies a lack of self-interest, whereas the latter indicates a lack of any interest. In fact, the use of *disinterested* to mean "uninterested" came earlier than its sense of "impartial"; and conversely, the early use of *uninterested* was in the sense of "impartial." Both of these were recorded in the early 17th century.

dis·in·ter·me·di·a·tion (dĭs-ĭn′tər-me′dē-ā′shən) *n.* The process whereby savers bypass banks and savings and loan associations, lending their money directly to borrowers, such as the government, industry, and the like.

dis·in·tox·i·cate (dĭs′ĭn-tŏk′sĭ-kāt′) *tr.v.* **-cated, -cating, -cates.** To free from the effects of intoxication or from dependence on intoxicating agents. **—dis·in·tox·i·ca·tion** *n.*

dis·in·vest·ment (dĭs′ĭn-vĕst′mənt) *n. Economics.* A reduction of investment, especially through a failure to replace capital stock such as machinery.

dis·ject (dĭs-jĕkt′) *tr.v.* **-jected, -jecting, -jects.** To split or disperse with force; scatter. [Latin *disjicere* (past participle *disjectus*) : *dis-,* apart + *jacere,* to throw.]

dis·join (dĭs-join′) *v.* **-joined, -joining, -joins.** *—tr.* To undo the joining of; separate. *—intr.* To become disconnected. [Middle English, from Old French *desjoindre,* from Latin *disjungere* : DIS- + *jungere,* to JOIN.]

dis·joint (dĭs-joint′) *v.* **-jointed, -jointing, -joints.** *—tr.* **1.** To put out of joint; dislocate. **2.** To take apart at the joints; separate. **3.** To destroy the coherence or connections of. *—intr.* **1.** To come apart at the joints. **2.** To become dislocated. *~adj. Mathematics.* Having no elements in common. Said especially of sets. [Middle English *disjointen,* from Old French *desjoindre* (past participle *desjoint*), to DISJOIN.]

dis·joint·ed (dĭs-join′tĭd) *adj.* **1.** Separated at the joints. **2.** Out of joint; dislocated. **3.** Lacking order or coherence; disconnected. **—dis·joint·ed·ly** *adv.* **—dis·joint·ed·ness** *n.*

dis·junct (dĭs-jŭngkt′) *adj.* **1.** Separated; disconnected. **2.** *Music.* Pertaining to progression by intervals larger than major seconds. **3.** *Zoology.* Having the head, thorax, and abdomen separated by deep constrictions. Said of insects. *~n. Logic.* Any of the propositions in a disjunction. [Middle English *disjuncte,* from Latin *disjunctus,* past participle of *disjungere,* to DISJOIN.]

dis·junc·tion (dĭs-jŭngk′shən) *n.* Also **dis·junc·ture** (-chər) (for sense 1). **1.** The act of disjoining or the condition of being disjointed. **2.** *Logic.* A compound proposition that presents two or more alternative terms, with the assertion that only one is true. **3.** *Genetics.* Separation of homologous pairs of chromosomes during meiosis.

dis·junc·tive (dĭs-jŭngk′tĭv) *adj.* **1.** Serving to separate or divide. **2.** *Grammar.* **a.** Serving to establish a relationship of contrast or opposition. The conjunction *but* in the phrase *beautiful but smelly* is disjunctive. **b.** Able to stand in isolation; syntactically independent; for example, the word *honestly* in *Honestly, I don't know,* is disjunctive. **3.** *Logic.* **a.** Presenting two or more alternative propositions. Said of a compound proposition. **b.** Containing a disjunction as one premise. Said of a syllogism. *~n.* **1.** *Grammar.* A disjunctive word. **2.** *Logic.* A disjunction. **—dis·junc·tive·ly** *adv.*

disk (dĭsk) *n.* Also **disc.** **1.** A thin, flat, circular plate. **2.** Something resembling a disk, such as an astronomical body or an anatomical structure. **3.** *Botany.* The enlarged receptacle containing numerous tiny flowers in the flower head of many composite plants, such as the daisy and the coneflower. **4.** Variant of **disc** (sense 1). **5.** *Computer Science.* A round flat plate coated with a magnetic substance on which data may be stored. See **floppy disk, magnetic disk.** **6.** A circular grid in a phototype setting machine. *~tr.v.* **disked, disking, disks.** Also **disced, discing, discs.** To work (soil) with a disk harrow. [Latin *discus,* quoit < Greek *diskos* < *dikein,* to throw.]

disk crash *n. Computer Science.* A **crash** (*see*) involving a disk.

disk drive *n. Computer Science.* A device with read/write heads used for retrieving information from or storing information on a magnetic disk or tape.

dis·kette (dĭ-skĕt′) *n.* A **floppy disk** (*see*).

disk flower *n.* Any of the tiny tubular flowers forming the center of the flower head of certain composite plants, such as the daisy. Compare **ray flower.**

disk harrow *n.* A harrow equipped with a series of disks set on edge or at an angle on one or more axles.

disk jockey *n.* Variant of **disc jockey.**

disk pack *n. Computer Science.* A computer storage device consisting of several magnetic disks that can be used and stored as a unit.

dis·like (dĭs-līk′) *tr.v.* **-liked, -liking, -likes.** To regard with distaste or aversion; find unpleasant. *~n.* An attitude or feeling of distaste or aversion.

dis·lo·cate (dĭs′lō-kāt′, dĭs-lō′kāt′) *tr.v.* **-cated, -cating, -cates.** **1.** To put out from the usual or proper relationship with contiguous parts; displace; shift. **2.** *Pathology.* To displace (a limb or organ) from the normal position; especially, to displace (a bone) from its joint. **3.** To throw into confusion or disorder; upset.

dis·lo·ca·tion (dĭs′lō-kā′shən) *n.* **1.** The act of dislocating or the state or condition of being dislocated. **2.** *Geology.* A **fault** (*see*). **3.** *Crystallography.* A line or plane in a crystal in which there is a deviation from the regular repeating order of the crystal lattice. An *edge dislocation* is a straight line marking the edge of an incomplete plane of atoms. A *screw dislocation* is a line about which atoms are arranged in helices.

dis·lodge (dĭs-lŏj′) *v.* **-lodged, -lodging, -lodges.** *—tr.* To remove or force out from a previously occupied position. *—intr.* To move or go from a dwelling or former position. **—dis·lodg·ment, dis·lodge·ment** *n.*

dis·loy·al (dĭs-loi′əl) *adj.* Lacking in loyalty. —See Synonyms at **faithless. —dis·loy·al·ly** *adv.*

dis·loy·al·ty (dĭs-loi′əl-tē) *n., pl.* **-ties.** **1.** The quality of being disloyal; faithlessness. **2.** A disloyal act.

dis·mal (dĭz′məl) *adj.* **1.** Causing dismay or depression; dreary; drab. **2.** Causing dread or dismay; ghastly. **3.** *Informal.* Incompetent; inadequate: *a dismal effort.* *~n.* **1.** *dismals. Rare.* Low spirits: *in the dismals.* **2.** *Southern U.S.* An area of swampland. [Middle English, unlucky days (two days in each month that were considered unpropitious), from Medieval Latin *dies malī* : Latin *diēs,* plural of *diēs,* day + *malī,* plural of *malus,* evil.] **—dis·mal·ly** *adv.* **—dis·mal·ness** *n.*

Dis·mal Swamp (dĭz′məl). Swampy area in southeastern Virginia and northeastern North Carolina. Thought to have once covered *c.* 5,700 square kilometers (2,200 square miles), the heavily forested swamp has been reduced to less than 1,554 square kilometers (600 square miles) by drainage, The swamp was surveyed (1763) by George Washington, a member of the company formed to drain it.

dis·man·tle (dĭs-măn′tl) *tr.v.* **-tled, -tling, -tles.** **1.** To strip (a house, for example) of furnishings or equipment. **2.** To take apart; disassemble. **3.** To tear down; destroy. **4.** To strip of clothing or covering. **—dis·man·tle·ment** *n.*

dis·mast (dĭs-măst′, -mäst′) *tr.v.* **-masted, -masting, -masts.** *Nautical.* To remove or break off the mast or masts of.

dis·may (dĭs-mā′) *tr.v.* **-mayed, -maying, -mays.** **1.** To fill with dread or apprehension; make anxious or afraid. **2.** To discourage or trouble greatly; dishearten. *~n.* **1.** A feeling of discouragement or disappointment. **2.** A loss of courage or confidence in the face of trouble or danger; consternation. [Middle English *dismayen,* from Old French *desmayer* (attested only in past participle *dismaye*) : *des-,* from Latin *dis-* (intensive) + *esmayer,* to frighten, be frightened, from Vulgar Latin *exmagāre* (unattested), to deprive of power, from Germanic.]

dis·mem·ber (dĭs-mĕm′bər) *tr.v.* **-bered, -bering, -bers.** **1.** To cut, tear, or pull off the limbs of. **2.** To divide into pieces. **—dis·mem·ber·er** *n.* **—dis·mem·ber·ment** *n.*

dis·miss (dĭs-mĭs′) *tr.v.* **-missed, -missing, -misses.** **1.** To discharge, as from employment. **2.** To direct or allow to leave: *dismiss troops.* **3.** To rid one's mind of; dispel. **4.** To reject; repudiate: *dismiss an allegation.* **5.** To refuse to consider seriously: *They dismissed her great invention as a toy.* **6.** *Law.* To put (a claim or action) out of court without further hearing. [Middle English *dismissen,* from Medieval Latin *dismittere* (past participle *dismissus*), variant of Latin *dīmittere* : *dīs-,* away + *mittere,* to send.] **—dis·miss·i·ble** *adj.* **—dis·miss·ive** *adj.*

dis·miss·al (dĭs-mĭs′əl) *n.* Also **dis·mis·sion** (-mĭsh′ən). **1. a.** The act of dismissing. **b.** The condition of being dismissed. **2.** An order or notice of discharge.

dis·mount (dĭs-mount′) *v.* **-mounted, -mounting, -mounts.** *—intr.* To get off or down, as from a horse or bicycle; alight. *—tr.* **1.** To remove (a thing) from its support, setting, or mounting. **2.** To unseat, as from a horse. **3.** To take apart (a mechanism). *~n.* The act of dismounting.

Dis·ney (dĭz'nē), **Walter Elias,** known as "Walt" (1901–66). U.S. film producer and animator. He founded a film empire in the 1920's and 1930's with his creation of the cartoon characters Mickey Mouse and Donald Duck. He produced feature-length cartoon films, nature documentaries, and adventure films. In 1955 he opened Disneyland, a vast amusement park with attractions based on the characters and settings of his films, in Anaheim, California. His films include *Snow White and the Seven Dwarfs* (1938), *Fantasia* (1940), and *Mary Poppins* (1964).

dis·o·be·di·ence (dĭs'ə-bē'dē-əns) n. The condition or fact of not obeying; deliberate failure to obey; insubordination. —**dis·o·be·di·ent** *adj.* —**dis·o·be·di·ent·ly** *adv.*

dis·o·bey (dĭs'ə-bā') v. **-beyed, -beying, -beys.** —*intr.* To refuse or fail to follow an order or rule. —*tr.* To refuse or fail to obey. —**dis·o·bey·er** n.

dis·o·blige (dĭs'ə-blĭj') tr.v. **-bliged, -bliging, -bliges. 1.** To refuse or neglect to act in accord with the wishes of. **2.** *Regional.* To inconvenience. —**dis·o·blig·ing·ly** *adv.*

di·so·di·um phosphate (dī'sō'dē-əm) n. A sodium phosphate, Na_2HPO_4.

dis·or·der (dĭs-ôr'dər) n. **1.** A lack of order or regular arrangement; confusion. **2.** A breach of civic order or peace; public disturbance. **3.** Imperfect functioning of part of the body or mind. **4.** A breakdown, as in a system. ~*tr.v.* **disordered, -dering, -ders. 1.** To throw into disorder; muddle. **2.** To disturb the normal physical or mental health of; derange.

dis·or·dered (dĭs-ôr'dərd) adj. **1.** In a condition of disorder; disarranged. **2.** Physically or mentally ill; deranged.

dis·or·der·ly (dĭs-ôr'dər-lē) adj. **1.** Lacking regular or logical order or arrangement; irregular; unsystematic. **2.** Undisciplined; unruly; riotous. **3.** *Law.* Disturbing the public peace or decorum: *drunk and disorderly.* —**dis·or·der·li·ness** n.

disorderly conduct n. *Law.* Any of various petty offenses of a kind likely to cause a breach of the peace.

disorderly house n. *Law.* Any house, such as a house of prostitution, whose inmates regularly violate the public order or decency.

dis·or·gan·ize (dĭs-ôr'gə-nīz') tr.v. **-ized, -izing, -izes.** To destroy the organization, systematic arrangement, or unity of; throw into confusion. —**dis·or·gan·i·za·tion** n. —**dis·or·gan·iz·er** n.

dis·o·ri·ent (dĭs-ôr'ē-ĕnt', dĭs-ōr'-) tr.v. **-ented, -enting, -ents. 1. a.** To cause to lose one's sense of direction or location, as by removing from a familiar environment. **b.** *Psychology.* To cause to lose one's awareness of time, place, or self in relation to one's environment. **2.** To confuse; perplex. —**dis·o·ri·en·ta·tion** n.

dis·o·ri·en·tate (dĭs-ôr'ē-ĕn-tāt', dĭs-ōr'-) tr.v. **-tated, -tating, -tates.** To disorient.

dis·own (dĭs-ōn') tr.v. **-owned, -owning, -owns. 1.** To refuse to acknowledge or accept as one's own. **2.** To renounce; repudiate.

dis·par·age (dĭs-păr'ĭj) tr.v. **-aged, -aging, -ages. 1.** To speak of slightingly; belittle. **2.** To reduce in esteem; discredit. —See Synonyms at **decry.** [Middle English *disparagen,* to degrade, disgrace, humble, from Old French *desparager,* to degrade someone of his rank" : *des-,* from Latin *dis-* (privative) + *parage,* rank, from *per,* PEER.] —**dis·par·ag·er** n. —**dis·par·ag·ing·ly** *adv.*

dis·par·age·ment (dĭs-păr'ĭj-mənt) n. **1.** The act of disparaging; detraction. **2.** A lowering of dignity or esteem; discredit. **3.** Something that lowers dignity or esteem.

dis·pa·rate (dĭs'pər-ĭt, dĭs-păr'ĭt) adj. Completely distinct or different in kind; entirely dissimilar. [Latin *disparātus,* past participle of *disparāre,* to separate : *dis-,* apart + *parāre,* to prepare.] —**dis·pa·rate·ly** *adv.* —**dis·pa·rate·ness** n.

dis·par·i·ty (dĭs-păr'ə-tē) n., pl. **-ties. 1.** The condition or fact of being unequal in age, rank, degree, or other measure; difference. **2.** Unlikeness; incongruity; dissimilarity.

dis·pas·sion (dĭs-păsh'ən) n. Freedom from passion, bias, or emotion; objectivity.

dis·pas·sion·ate (dĭs-păsh'ən-ĭt) adj. Devoid of or unaffected by passion, emotion, or bias; impartial; calm: *dispassionate judgment.* —See Synonyms at **fair.** —**dis·pas·sion·ate·ly** *adv.* —**dis·pas·sion·ate·ness** n.

dis·patch, des·patch (dĭs-păch') tr.v. **-patched, -patching, -patches. 1.** To send off to a specific destination or on specific business. **2.** To complete or dispose of promptly. **3.** To put to death summarily. ~*n.* **1.** The act of dispatching or sending off. **2.** A putting to death. **3.** Efficient speed or promptness; expeditious performance. **4.** An official communication sent with speed; especially, a report of military operations. **5.** A news item sent to a newspaper, as by a correspondent. [Spanish *despachar* or Italian *dispacciare,* perhaps from Old French *despeechier,* to set free, unshackle : *des-,* from Latin *dis-* (reversal) + *(em)peechier,* to hinder, from Late Latin *impedicāre,* to entangle : Latin *in-* + *pedica,* shackle.]

dis·patch·er (dĭs-păch'ər) n. **1.** One that dispatches. **2.** A person who sends out trains, buses, trucks, or cars according to a schedule. **3.** *Computer Science.* A routine that controls the order in which input and output devices obtain access to the processing system.

dis·pel (dĭs-pĕl') tr.v. **-pelled, -pelling, -pels.** To rid of by or as if by driving away or scattering; dispense with: *"the effect of his tone was to dispel her shyness"* (Henry James). [Middle English *dispellen,* from Latin *dispellere* : *dis-,* away + *pellere,* to push, drive, strike.]

dis·pen·sa·ble (dĭs-pĕn'sə-bəl) adj. **1.** Capable of being dispensed with; unimportant. **2.** Able to be dispensed, administered, or dis-

tributed. **3.** Subject to exemption in particular cases, as a sin may be; condonable. —**dis·pen·sa·bil·i·ty, dis·pen·sa·ble·ness** n.

dis·pen·sa·ry (dĭs-pĕn'sə-rē) n., pl. **-ries. 1.** An office in a hospital or other institution from which medical supplies and preparations are dispensed. **2.** A public institution where medical aid is dispensed.

dis·pen·sa·tion (dĭs'pən-sā'shən, dĭs'pĕn-) n. **1.** The act of dispensing or giving out; distribution; apportionment. **2.** Something that is dispensed or given out. **3.** A specific arrangement or system by which something is dispensed or administered. **4.** Any exemption or release from an obligation or rule, granted by or as if by an authority. **5. a.** An exemption from a church law, a vow, or other similar obligation granted in a particular case by an ecclesiastical authority. **b.** The document containing this exemption. **6.** *Theology.* **a.** The divine ordering of worldly affairs. **b.** A religious system or code of commands considered to have been divinely revealed or appointed: *the Muslim dispensation.* —**dis·pen·sa·tion·al** adj.

dis·pen·sa·to·ry (dĭs-pĕn'sə-tôr'ē, -tōr'ē) adj. Of, pertaining to, or granted by dispensation. ~*n., pl.* **dispensatories. 1.** A book in which the preparation, uses, and contents of medicines are described; a pharmacopoeia. **2.** *Archaic.* A dispensary.

dis·pense (dĭs-pĕns') v. **-pensed, -pensing, -penses.** —*tr.* **1.** To deal out or distribute in parts or portions. **2.** To prepare and give out (medicines) according to a doctor's prescription. **3.** To administer (justice, for example). **4.** To exempt, as from a duty or religious obligation. —*intr.* To grant dispensation or exemption. —**dispense with. 1.** To manage without; forgo. **2.** To do away with; make unnecessary. —See Usage note at **distribute.** [Middle English *dispensen,* from Medieval Latin *dispensāre,* to grant dispensation to, exempt, condone, from Latin, to pay out, distribute, frequentative of *dispendere,* to weigh out : *dis-,* away + *pendere,* to weigh.]

dis·pens·er (dĭs-pĕn'sər) n. One that dispenses or gives out; specifically: **1.** A device that dispenses goods in measured amounts or single units: *a paper-cup dispenser.* **2.** A person who dispenses medicines.

dis·per·sal (dĭs-pûr'səl) n. The act or process of dispersing or the condition of being dispersed; distribution.

dis·per·sant (dĭs-pûr'sənt) n. A liquid or gas in which something is dispersed, such as the liquid used as a propellant in an aerosol can.

dis·perse (dĭs-pûrs') v. **-persed, -persing, -perses.** —*tr.* **1.** To scatter in various directions; distribute widely. **2.** To cause to vanish or evaporate; dispel. **3.** To disseminate (knowledge, for example). **4.** To separate (light or other radiation) into components with different wavelengths. —*intr.* To move or scatter in different directions. [Middle English *dispersen,* from Old French *disperser,* from Latin *dispergere* (past participle *dispersus*), to scatter on all sides : *dis-,* in different directions + *spargere,* to strew, scatter.] —**dis·pers·ed·ly** (dĭs-pûr'sĭd-lē) *adv.* —**dis·pers·er** n. —**dis·pers·i·ble** adj.

disperse system n. Any continuous medium containing dispersed entities of any size or state.

dis·per·sion (dĭs-pûr'zhən, -shən) n. **1. a.** The state of being dispersed. **b.** The act or process of dispersing. **2.** *Statistics.* The degree of scatter of data, usually about some mean or median value. **3.** *Physics.* The separation of a complex wave into component parts according to some characteristic, such as frequency or wavelength; for example, separation of visible light into its color components by refraction or diffraction. **4.** *Chemistry.* A suspension, such as smog or homogenized milk, of solid, liquid, or gaseous particles, of colloidal size or larger, in a liquid, solid, or gaseous medium. **5. Dispersion.** The Diaspora (*see*).

dis·per·sive (dĭs-pûr'sĭv, -zĭv) adj. **1.** Tending to become dispersed. **2.** Tending to produce dispersion.

dis·per·soid (dĭs-pûr'soid') n. *Chemistry.* A colloid in which one substance is dispersed in another. Also used adjectivally: *a dispersoid sol.*

dis·pir·it (dĭs-pîr'ĭt) tr.v. **-ited, -iting, -its.** To lower in spirit; dishearten. [DI(S)- (negative) + SPIRIT.]

dis·pir·it·ed (dĭs-pîr'ĭt-ĭd) adj. Characterized by low spirits; disheartened; dejected. —**dis·pir·it·ed·ly** *adv.* —**dis·pir·it·ed·ness** n.

dis·place (dĭs-plās') tr.v. **-placed, -placing, -places. 1.** To change the place or position of; move from the usual place. **2.** To take the place of; supplant. **3.** To discharge from an office or position. **4.** To cause a displacement of (a body, for example). —See Synonyms at **replace.** —**dis·place·a·ble** adj. —**dis·plac·er** n.

displaced person n. *Abbr.* **DP, D.P.** A person living in a foreign country who has been driven from his or her homeland, especially by war or political unrest.

dis·place·ment (dĭs-plās'mənt) n. **1. a.** The act of displacing. **b.** The condition of being displaced. **2.** *Chemistry.* A reaction in which one kind of atom or group is removed from a molecule and replaced by another. **3.** *Physics.* **a.** The weight or volume of a fluid displaced by a floating body, used especially as a measurement of the weight or bulk of ships. **b.** A vector, or the magnitude of a vector, from the initial position to a subsequent position assumed by a body. **4.** *Psychology.* **a.** The shifting of a feeling, such as anger, from an appropriate to an inappropriate object. **b.** Engagement in inappropriate or irrelevant behavior during situations of extreme emotion or conflict. Often used adjectivally: *displacement activity.*

displacement ton n. *Nautical.* A unit for measuring the displacement of a ship afloat, equivalent to one long ton or about 35 cubic feet of salt water.

dis·play (dĭs-plā′) tr.v. **-played, -playing, -plays. 1.** To hold up to view; make visible; expose; exhibit. **2.** To make manifest or noticeable; show evidence of. **3.** To exhibit ostentatiously; show off; flaunt. **4.** To spread out; unfurl: *a peacock displaying its tail.* **5.** *Printing.* To give prominence to (printed letters or words, for example), as by using large type. **—See Synonyms at show.** ~n. **1.** The act of displaying; exhibition. **2.** Anything that is exhibited or displayed. **3.** Vulgar ostentation. **4.** *Printing.* **a.** An arrangement or style of type designed to give prominence to printed matter. **b.** Printed matter that is set off prominently. **c.** An advertisement designed to catch the eye, as distinguished from a classified advertisement. Also used adjectivally: *display advertisements.* **5.** *Zoology.* A type of behavior characterized by gestures that act as specific signals in courtship and aggression, shown particularly by birds and fishes. **6. a.** An electronic device for representing text, numbers, or diagrams visually. **b.** The material represented on such a device. [Middle English *displayen,* to unfold, unfurl, exhibit, from Old French *despleier,* from Medieval Latin *displicāre,* from Latin, to scatter : *dis-* (reversal) + *plicāre,* to fold.]

dis·played (dĭs-plād′) adj. *Heraldry.* Standing erect with wings extended.

dis·please (dĭs-plēz′) v. **-pleased, -pleasing, -pleases.** —tr. To cause annoyance or vexation to; offend. —intr. To cause annoyance or offense. **—dis·pleas·ing·ly** adv.

dis·pleas·ure (dĭs-plĕzh′ər) n. **1.** The condition or fact of being displeased or dissatisfied; annoyance; anger. **2.** *Archaic.* Discomfort; uneasiness. **3.** *Archaic.* An annoying or injurious offense. ~tr.v. **displeasured, -uring, -ures.** *Archaic.* To displease.

dis·port (dĭs-pôrt′, -pōrt′) v. **-ported, -porting, -ports.** —intr. To play; frolic. —tr. To occupy (oneself) with diversion or amusement. ~n. Diversion; play; sport. [Middle English *disporten,* from Old French *desporter,* "to carry away," divert : *des-,* apart + *porter,* to carry, PORT.]

dis·pos·a·ble (dĭs-pō′zə-bəl) adj. **1.** Designed to be disposed of after use. **2.** Available for use. ~n. Something intended to be disposed of after use. **—dis·pos·a·bil·i·ty** n.

disposable income n. The residue of one's income that is available for use after all direct taxes have been paid.

dis·pos·al (dĭs-pō′zəl) n. **1.** A particular order, distribution, or arrangement. **2.** A particular method of attending to or settling matters. **3.** The transference of something by gift or sale. **4.** A throwing out or away. **5.** An apparatus or device for disposing of something, such as household waste. Also used adjectivally: *a disposal unit.* **6.** The liberty or power to dispose of or use someone or something: *funds at our disposal.*

dis·pose (dĭs-pōz′) v. **-posed, -posing, -poses.** —tr. **1.** To place in a particular order; arrange. **2.** To put (business affairs, for example) into correct, definitive, or conclusive form. **3.** To make willing or receptive; incline. Often used in the passive. —intr. To settle or decide a matter. **—dispose of. 1.** To attend to; arrange; settle. **2.** To transfer or part with, as by giving or selling. **3.** To get rid of; throw away. **4.** To eat or drink (food or liquid). ~n. *Obsolete.* **1.** Disposal. **2.** Disposition; demeanor. [Middle English *disposen,* from Old French *disposer,* reshaped (after *poser,* to POSE), from Latin *dispōnere,* to place here and there, arrange : *dis-,* in different directions + *pōnere,* to put.] **—dis·pos·er** n.

dis·po·si·tion (dĭs′pə-zĭsh′ən) n. **1.** One's customary manner of emotional response; temperament: *"She had a lively, playful disposition, which delighted in anything ridiculous"* (Jane Austen). **2.** A tendency or inclination, especially when habitual: *a disposition to heavy drinking.* **3. a.** The act or manner of disposing. **b.** The condition or fact of being disposed. **4.** The power or liberty to control, direct, or dispose.

   Synonyms: *character, nature, personality, temperament.*

dis·pos·sess (dĭs′pə-zĕs′) tr.v. **-sessed, -sessing, -sesses.** To deprive (someone) of the possession of something, especially property. **—dis·pos·ses·sion** n. **—dis·pos·ses·sor** n. **—dis·pos·ses·so·ry** adj.

dis·po·sure (dĭs-pō′zhər) n. *Rare.* Disposal.

dis·praise (dĭs-prāz′) tr.v. **-praised, -praising, -praises.** To express disapproval of; disparage; censure. ~n. Reproach; censure. [Middle English *dispreisen,* from Old French *despreisier,* from Vulgar Latin *dispretiāre* (unattested), variant of Latin *dēpretiāre,* to DEPRECIATE.] **—dis·prais·er** n. **—dis·prais·ing·ly** adv.

Dis·prin (dĭs′prĭn) n. A trademark for a preparation of aspirin, calcium carbonate, and anhydrous citric acid, taken, in the form of water-soluble tablets, for the relief of pain.

dis·prize (dĭs-prīz′) tr.v. **-prized, -prizing, -prizes.** *Archaic.* To hold in low esteem. [Middle English *disprisen, dispreisen,* to DISPRAISE.]

dis·proof (dĭs-prōōf′) n. **1.** The act of disproving or refuting. **2.** Evidence that disproves or refutes.

dis·pro·por·tion (dĭs′prə-pôr′shən) n. **1.** The absence of due proportion; disparity. **2.** An instance of a disproportionate relation, as in size. ~tr.v. **disproportioned, -tioning, -tions.** To make disproportionate.

dis·pro·por·tion·ate (dĭs′prə-pôr′shən-ĭt, -pōr′shən-ĭt) adj. Also **dis·pro·por·tion·al** (dĭs′prə-pôr′shən-əl, -pōr′shən-əl). Not proportionate; out of proportion, as in relative size, shape, or amount.

~intr.v. **-ated, -ating, -ates.** *Chemistry.* To undergo disproportionation. **—dis·pro·por·tion·ate·ly** adv. **—dis·pro·por·tion·ate·ness** n.

dis·pro·por·tion·a·tion (dĭs′prə-pôr′shə-nā′shən, -pôr′shə-) n. *Chemistry.* A type of chemical reaction in which one molecule of reactant is reduced and another is oxidized.

dis·prove (dĭs-prōōv′) tr.v. **-proved, -proving, -proves.** To prove to be false, invalid, or in error; refute. **—dis·prov·a·ble** adj. **—dis·prov·al** n.

dis·put·a·ble (dĭs-pyōō′tə-bəl, dĭs-pyōō-) adj. Capable of being disputed or challenged; debatable. **—dis·put·a·bil·i·ty** n. **—dis·put·a·bly** adv.

dis·pu·tant (dĭs-pyōō′tənt, dĭs′pyōō-tənt) adj. Engaged in argument or dispute. ~n. A person who disputes; debater.

dis·pu·ta·tion (dĭs′pyōō-tā′shən) n. **1.** The act of disputing; a debate. **2.** A formal academic debate or an oral defense of a thesis.

dis·pu·ta·tious (dĭs′pyōō-tā′shəs) adj. Argumentative; contentious. **—dis·pu·ta·tious·ly** adv. **—dis·pu·ta·tious·ness** n.

dis·pute (dĭs-pyōōt′) v. **-puted, -puting, -putes.** —tr. **1.** To argue about; debate. **2.** To question the truth or validity of; doubt. **3.** To strive to win (a prize, for example); contend for. **4.** To strive against; oppose; resist. —intr. **1.** To argue; discuss; debate. **2.** To quarrel vehemently. **—See Synonyms at discuss.** ~n. (*also* dĭs′pyōōt′). **1.** A verbal controversy; an argument; a debate. **2.** A quarrel. **—See Synonyms at argument.** [Middle English *disputen,* from Old French *desputer,* from Late Latin *disputāre,* from Latin, to reckon, discuss : *dis-,* separately + *putāre,* to clean, prune, settle an account, hence to reckon, think.] **—dis·put·er** n.

   Usage: Traditionally, the stress is on the second syllable, for both the verb and the noun. In recent years, however, many people have begun to put the stress on the first syllable in the case of the noun, but there is a great deal of inconsistency; for example, the phrase *in dispute′* usually retains the stress on the second syllable, even in the speech of people who often say *dís′pute.*

dis·qual·i·fi·ca·tion (dĭs-kwŏl′ə-fĭ-kā′shən) n. **1.** The act of disqualifying or the condition of being disqualified. **2.** Something that disqualifies.

dis·qual·i·fy (dĭs-kwŏl′ə-fī′) tr.v. **-fied, -fying, -fies. 1.** To render unfit or unqualified; disable. **2.** To declare ineligible or unqualified. **3.** To deprive of a legal right, power, or privilege: *disqualified from driving for 12 months.* **4.** To debar from a sports event, as for misconduct.

dis·qui·et (dĭs-kwī′ĭt) tr.v. **-eted, -eting, -ets.** To deprive of peace or rest; trouble. ~n. The absence of mental peace or rest; restlessness; anxiety. **—dis·qui·et·ing** adj. **—dis·qui·et·ing·ly** adv.

dis·qui·e·tude (dĭs-kwī′ĭ-tōōd′, -tyōōd′) n. A state of worry or uneasiness; anxiety.

dis·qui·si·tion (dĭs′kwə-zĭsh′ən) n. A formal discourse or treatise, often in writing; dissertation. [Latin *disquīsītiō* (stem *disquīsītiōn-*), enquiry, from *disquīrere,* to enquire diligently : *dis-* (intensive) + *quaerere,* to search for.]

Dis·rae·li (dĭz-rā′lē), **Benjamin,** 1st Earl of Beaconsfield, known as "Dizzy" (1804–81). British statesman. The grandson of a Venetian Jew, he became a Christian in 1817. In 1837 he entered Parliament and from 1842 led the Young England group of Conservatives. He was three times Chancellor of the Exchequer and in 1867 was responsible for the Reform Bill that gave household suffrage in the boroughs and extended the county franchise. Disraeli became prime minister in 1868 but lost office in the autumn to Gladstone and the Liberals. He returned to power in 1874. He bought Britain a major share in the Suez Canal, proclaimed Queen Victoria Empress of India (1876), and annexed Cyprus. He established the Conservative Party as a political force upholding the monarchy, the Anglican Church, and the empire.

dis·rate (dĭs-rāt′) tr.v. **-rated, -rating, -rates.** To reduce in rating or rank.

dis·re·gard (dĭs′rĭ-gärd′) tr.v. **-garded, -garding, -gards. 1.** To pay no attention or heed to; fail to consider; ignore. **2.** To treat without proper respect or attentiveness. ~n. Lack of thoughtful attention or due regard, especially when willful. **—dis·re·gard·er** n. **—dis·re·gard·ful** adj.

dis·rel·ish (dĭs-rĕl′ĭsh) tr.v. **-ished, -ishing, -ishes.** To have distaste for; dislike. ~n. Distaste; aversion.

dis·re·mem·ber (dĭs′rĭ-mĕm′bər) v. **-bered, -bering, -bers.** *Regional.* —tr. To fail to remember. —intr. To forget.

dis·re·pair (dĭs′rĭ-pâr′) n. The condition of being in need of repairs; a state of neglect; dilapidation: *a house in disrepair.*

dis·rep·u·ta·ble (dĭs-rĕp′yə-tə-bəl) adj. **1.** Lacking a good reputation; not esteemed. **2.** Not respectable in character or appearance. **3.** Disgraceful; discreditable. **—dis·rep·u·ta·bil·i·ty, dis·rep·u·ta·ble·ness** n. **—dis·rep·u·ta·bly** adv.

dis·re·pute (dĭs′rĭ-pyōōt′) n. Also *archaic* **dis·rep·u·ta·tion** (dĭs-rĕp′yə-tā′shən). The absence or loss of reputation; discredit; disgrace. **—See Synonyms at disgrace.**

dis·re·spect (dĭs′rĭ-spĕkt′) n. Lack of respect, esteem, or courteous regard; rudeness. ~tr.v. **disrespected, -specting, -spects.** To show a lack of respect for.

dis·re·spect·a·ble (dĭs′rĭ-spĕk′tə-bəl) adj. Lacking respectability; not worthy of respect. **—dis·re·spect·a·bil·i·ty** n.

dis·re·spect·ful (dĭs′rĭ-spĕkt′fəl) adj. Having or demonstrating a lack of respect; rude; discourteous. **—dis·re·spect·ful·ly** *adv.* **—dis·re·spect·ful·ness** *n.*

dis·robe (dĭs-rōb′) *v.* **-robed, -robing, -robes.** *—tr.* To remove the clothing from. *—intr.* To undress oneself. **—dis·robe·ment** *n.* **—dis·rob·er** *n.*

dis·rupt (dĭs-rŭpt′) *tr.v.* **-rupted, -rupting, -rupts. 1.** To upset the order of; throw into confusion or disorder. **2.** To interrupt or impede the progress, movement, or procedure of. **3.** To break or burst; rupture. [Latin *disrumpere* (past participle *disruptus*), to break asunder : *dis-*, asunder + *rumpere,* to break.] **—dis·rupt·er, dis·rup·tor** *n.*

dis·rup·tion (dĭs-rŭp′shən) *n.* **1.** The act of disrupting or the state of being disrupted. **2. Disruption.** The breaking away of the Free Church from the Established Church of Scotland in 1934.

dis·rup·tive (dĭs-rŭp′tĭv) *adj.* Pertaining to, causing, or produced by disruption. **—dis·rup·tive·ly** *adv.* **—dis·rup·tive·ness** *n.*

dis·sat·is·fac·tion (dĭs-săt′ĭs-făk′shən) *n.* **1.** The condition or feeling of being displeased or not satisfied; discontent. **2.** Anything that causes discontent.

dis·sat·is·fac·to·ry (dĭs-săt′ĭs-făk′tə-rē) *adj.* Unsatisfactory.

dis·sat·is·fied (dĭs-săt′ĭs-fīd′) *adj.* Affected by a sense of inadequacy, discontent, or displeasure, or by an insufficiency of something; not content. **—dis·sat·is·fied·ly** *adv.*

dis·sat·is·fy (dĭs-săt′ĭs-fī′) *tr.v.* **-fied, -fying, -fies.** To fail to meet the expectations or fulfill the desires of; disappoint.

dis·seat (dĭs-sēt′) *tr.v.* **-seated, -seating, -seats.** *Archaic.* To unseat.

dis·sect (dĭ-sĕkt′, dī′sĕkt′) *tr.v.* **-sected, -secting, -sects. 1.** To cut open or apart (plant or animal tissue), especially for scientific study or in surgery. **2.** To examine, analyze, or criticize in minute detail: *dissected her motives.* **3.** *Geology.* To carve up (a land form, especially a plateau) by erosion. Used of a river. [Latin *dissecāre* (past participle *dissectus*), to cut apart : *dis-*, apart + *secāre,* to cut.] **—dis·sec·ti·ble** *adj.* **—dis·sec·tor** *n.*

dis·sect·ed (dĭ-sĕk′tĭd, dī-) *adj. Botany.* Divided into numerous narrow segments or lobes: *dissected leaves.*

dis·sec·tion (dĭ-sĕk′shən, dī-) *n.* **1.** The act or process of dissecting. **2.** Something that has been dissected, such as tissue under study. **3.** A detailed examination or analysis.

dis·seize (dĭs-sēz′) *tr.v.* **-seized, -seizing, -seizes.** Also **dis·seise.** *Law.* To dispossess (a person) of property unlawfully. [Middle English *disseisen,* from Norman French *disseisir,* variant of Old French *dessaisir* : *des-*, from Latin *dis-* (reversal) + *saisir,* to SEIZE.] **—dis·sei·zor** (dĭs-sē′zər, -zôr′) *n.*

dis·sei·zee (dĭs′sē-zē′, dĭs-sē′zē′) *n.* Also **dis·seisee.** *Law.* A person who is disseized.

dis·sei·zin (dĭs-sē′zĭn) *n.* Also **dis·sei·sin, dis·sei·sure, dis·sei·zure** (dĭs-sē′zhər). *Law.* Wrongful usurpation of the powers and privileges of ownership; ejection of the lawful holder of a freehold. [Middle English *dysseysyne,* from Norman French *disseisine,* variant of Old French *dessaisine* : *des-*, from Latin *dis-* (reversal) + SEIZIN.]

dis·sem·blance (dĭ-sĕm′bləns) *n.* **1.** The act of dissembling or disguising; dissimulation. **2.** *Archaic.* Absence of resemblance; dissimilarity.

dis·sem·ble (dĭ-sĕm′bəl) *v.* **-bled, -bling, -bles.** *—tr.* **1.** To disguise the real nature of; hide with a false appearance or semblance: *dissemble one's fears with laughter.* **2.** To make a false show of; feign. *—intr.* To conceal one's real motives, nature, or feelings under a pretense. —See Synonyms at **pretend.** [Middle English *dissemblen,* from Old French *dessembler,* to be different (influenced by *dissimuler,* to pretend, dissimulate) : *des-*, from Latin *dis-* (reversal) + *sembler,* to be like, appear, seem.] **—dis·sem·bler** *n.* **—dis·sem·bling·ly** *adv.*

dis·sem·i·nate (dĭ-sĕm′ə-nāt′) *v.* **-nated, -nating, -nates.** *—tr.* **1.** To scatter widely, as in sowing seed; distribute; disperse. **2.** To spread abroad (information, for example); promulgate widely. *—intr. Rare.* To become diffused; spread. [Latin *dissēmināre* : *dis-*, in different directions + *sēmināre,* to sow, from *sēmen,* seed.] **—dis·sem·i·na·tion** *n.* **—dis·sem·i·na·tive** *adj.* **—dis·sem·i·na·tor** *n.*

dis·sem·i·nule (dĭ-sĕm′ə-nyo͞ol′) *n.* A plant part, such as a seed, fruit, or spore, that propagates and spreads the species. [DISSEMIN(ATE) + -ULE.]

dis·sen·sion (dĭ-sĕn′shən) *n.* Disagreement or quarreling caused by a difference of opinion. —See Synonyms at **discord.** [Middle English *dissencioun,* from Old French *dissension,* from Latin *dissensiō* (stem *dissensiōn-*), from *dissentīre,* to DISSENT.]

dis·sent (dĭ-sĕnt′) *intr.v.* **-sented,-senting, -sents. 1.** To think or feel differently; disagree; differ. **2.** To refuse to conform to the authority or doctrine of an established church. **3.** To withhold assent or approval. —See Synonyms at **object** (verb).
∼n. **1.** Difference of opinion or feeling; disagreement. **2.** The refusal to conform to the authority or doctrine of an established church; nonconformity. [Middle English *dissenten,* from Latin *dissentīre* : *dis-*, apart + *sentīre,* to feel.] **—dis·sent·ing·ly** *adv.*

dis·sent·er (dĭ-sĕn′tər) *n.* **1.** One who dissents. **2.** *Often* **Dissenter.** One who refuses to accept the doctrines or usages of an established or national church; especially, a Protestant who dissents from the Church of England. Compare **conformist.**

dis·sen·ti·ent (dĭ-sĕn′shənt) *adj.* Dissenting, especially from the view or policies of a majority.
∼n. One who dissents. **—dis·sen·tience** *n.*

dis·sen·tious (dĭ-sĕn′shəs) *adj.* Given to dissension.

dis·sep·i·ment (dĭ-sĕp′ə-mənt) *n.* A membranous or calcareous partition between organs or parts; septum. [Latin *dissaepīmentum,* partition, from *dissaepīre,* to separate, divide : *dis-*, apart + *saepīre,* to fence in, enclose, from *saepes,* fence, hedge.] **—dis·sep·i·men·tal** *adj.* **—dis·sep·i·men·tal·ly** *adv.*

dis·ser·tate (dĭs′ər-tāt′) *intr.v.* **-tated, -tating, -tates.** Also **dis·sert** (dĭ-sûrt′), **-serted, -serting, -serts.** *Rare.* To discourse formally, learnedly, or at some length. [Latin *dissertāre,* frequentative of *disserere,* to discuss (translation of Greek *dialegesthai,* to discuss, converse, "pick out," "separate"; see **dialogue**) : *dis-*, apart + *serere,* to connect, join (in speech), discuss.] **—dis·ser·ta·tor** *n.*

dis·ser·ta·tion (dĭs′ər-tā′shən) *n.* A lengthy and formal treatise or discourse, especially one written by a candidate for a higher university degree; thesis.

dis·serve (dĭs-sûrv′) *tr.v.* **-served, -serving, -serves.** To treat badly; do a disservice to; harm.

dis·ser·vice (dĭs-sûr′vĭs) *n.* A harmful action; an ill turn.

dis·sev·er (dĭ-sĕv′ər) *v.* **-ered, -ering, -ers.** *—tr.* **1.** To separate; sever. **2.** To divide into parts; break up. *—intr.* To become separated or disunited. [Middle English *dis(s)everen,* from Old French *des(s)evrer,* from Late Latin *dissēparāre* : Latin *dis-* (intensive) + *sēparāre,* to SEPARATE.] **—dis·sev·er·ance, dis·sev·er·ment** *n.*

dis·si·dence (dĭs′ə-dəns) *n.* Disagreement, as of opinion or belief; difference; dissent.

dis·si·dent (dĭs′ə-dənt) *adj.* Disagreeing, as in opinion or belief; differing; dissenting.
∼n. One who disagrees; especially, a citizen of a one-party state who is in fundamental disagreement with the prevailing politics or ideology. [Latin *dissidēns* (stem *dissident-*), present participle of *dissidēre,* "to sit apart," dissent : *dis-*, apart + *sedēre,* to sit.]

dis·sil·i·ent (dĭ-sĭl′ē-ənt) *adj.* Bursting apart, as some seed pods do when ripe. [Latin *dissiliens, dissilient,* present participle of *dissilire,* to burst apart : *dis-*, apart + *salire,* to leap.]

dis·sim·i·lar (dĭ-sĭm′ə-lər) *adj.* Distinct; unlike; different. **—dis·sim·i·lar·ly** *adv.*

dis·sim·i·lar·i·ty (dĭ-sĭm′ə-lăr′ə-tē) *n., pl.* **-ties. 1.** The quality of being distinct or unlike; difference. **2.** A point of distinction or difference. —See Usage note at **difference.**

dis·sim·i·late (dĭ-sĭm′ə-lāt′) *v.* **-lated, -lating, -lates.** *—tr.* **1.** To make dissimilar or unlike. **2.** *Linguistics.* To cause to undergo dissimilation. *—intr.* **1.** To become dissimilar. **2.** *Linguistics.* To undergo dissimilation. [DIS- + (AS)SIMILATE.]

dis·sim·i·la·tion (dĭ-sĭm′ə-lā′shən) *n.* **1.** The act or process of making or becoming dissimilar. **2.** *Linguistics.* The process by which one of two similar phonemes is displaced or changed by the other, as in the English form *marble* from French *marbre.*

dis·si·mil·i·tude (dĭs′ĭ-mĭl′ə-to͞od′, -tyo͞od′) *n.* **1.** Lack of resemblance; difference. **2.** A point of difference; a dissimilarity. [Middle English, from Latin *dissimilitūdō,* from *dissimilis,* different : *dis-*, not + *similis,* like, SIMILAR.]

dis·sim·u·late (dĭ-sĭm′yə-lāt′) *v.* **-lated, -lating, -lates.** *—tr.* To disguise (one's intentions, for example) under a feigned appearance. *—intr.* To conceal one's true feelings or intentions. **—dis·sim·u·la·tion** *n.* **—dis·sim·u·la·tive** *adj.* **—dis·sim·u·la·tor** *n.*

dis·si·pate (dĭs′ə-pāt′) *v.* **-pated, -pating, -pates.** *—tr.* **1.** To drive away or dispel by or as if by dispersing; rout; scatter. **2.** To spend or use up; waste; squander. *—intr.* **1.** To vanish by dispersion; scatter. **2.** *Physics.* To lose (energy) through conversion into another form, especially into heat. **3.** To indulge excessively in the pursuit of pleasure or debauchery. [Middle English *dissipaten,* from Latin *dissipāre,* to disperse, squander.] **—dis·si·pat·er, dis·si·pa·tor** *n.* **—dis·si·pa·tive** *adj.*

dis·si·pat·ed (dĭs′ə-pā′tĭd) *adj.* **1.** Unrestrained in the pursuit of pleasure; dissolute. **2.** Wasted; squandered. **—dis·si·pat·ed·ly** *adv.* **—dis·si·pat·ed·ness** *n.*

dis·si·pa·tion (dĭs′ə-pā′shən) *n.* **1. a.** The act of dissipating. **b.** The condition of being dissipated; dispersion. **2.** Wasteful consumption or expenditure. **3.** Dissolute indulgence in pleasure; intemperance. **4.** Amusement; diversion.

dis·so·cia·ble (dĭ-sō′shə-bəl, -shē-ə-bəl) *adj.* Capable of being dissociated; separable. **—dis·so·cia·bil·i·ty, dis·so·cia·ble·ness** *n.* **—dis·so·cia·bly** *adv.*

dis·so·ci·ate (dĭ-sō′shē-āt′, -sē-āt′) *v.* **-ated, -ating, -ates.** *—tr.* **1.** To remove from association; separate: *"Marx never dissociated man from his social environment"* (Sidney Hook). **2.** *Chemistry.* To cause to undergo dissociation. **3.** *Psychology.* To cause to undergo dissociation. *—intr.* **1.** To cease associating; part. **2.** *Chemistry.* To undergo dissociation. **3.** *Psychology.* To undergo dissociation. [Latin *dissociāre* : *dis-* (reversal) + *sociāre,* to join, associate, from *socius,* companion.] **—dis·so·ci·a·tive** *adj.*

Usage: *Dissociate* is traditionally used as the opposite of *associate,* but *disassociate* is increasing in use. Less commonly, *disassociation* is used for *dissociation.*

dis·so·ci·a·tion (dĭ-sō′sē-ā′shən, -shē-ā′shən) *n.* **1. a.** The act of dissociating. **b.** The condition of being dissociated; separation. —See Usage note at **dissociate. 2.** *Chemistry.* The chemical process, especially a reversible process, by means of which a change in physical condition, as in pressure, temperature, or the action of a solvent, causes a molecule to split into simpler groups of atoms, single atoms, or ions. **3.** *Psychology.* The separation of a belief or attitude, or a group of related psychological activities, from the rest of the personality so that they function independently, as in cases of multiple ("split") personalities. —See Usage note at **dissociate.**

dis·sol·u·ble (dĭ-sŏl′yə-bəl) *adj.* Capable of being dissolved; solu-

PRONUNCIATION KEY

ă, pat; ā, pay; âr, care; ä, father, are; b, bib; ch, church; d, deed; ĕ, pet; ē, be; f, fife; g, gag; h, hat; hw, which; ĭ, pit; ī, pie; îr, pier; j, judge; k, kick; l, lid, needle; m, mum; n, no, sudden; ng, thing; ŏ, pot; ō, toe; ô, paw, for; oi, noise; ou, out; o͝o, book; o͞o, boot; p, pop; r, roar; s, sauce; sh, ship, dish; t, tight; th, thin, path; *th*, this, bathe; ŭ, cut; ûr, fur; v, valve; w, with; y, yes; z, zebra, size; zh, vision; ə, about, item, edible, gallop, circus, peaceful

IN FOREIGN WORDS:

à, *Fr.* **ami; œ,** *Fr.* **feu,** *Ger.* **schön; ü,** *Fr.* **tu,** *Ger.* **über; KH,** *Ger.* **ich,** *Scot.* **loch; N,** *Fr.* **bon; y′,** *Fr.* **Compiègne**

STRESS MARKS:

Primary stress: ′
in·cite′ (ĭn-sīt′)
Secondary stress: ′
in′sight′ (ĭn′sīt′)

ble. [Latin *dissolūbilis,* from *dissolvere,* to DISSOLVE.] **—dis·sol·u·bil·i·ty, dis·sol·u·ble·ness** *n.*

dis·so·lute (dĭs′ə-lo͞ot′) *adj.* Lacking in moral restraint; debauched. [Middle English, from Latin *dissolūtus,* loose, licentious, past participle of *dissolvere,* to DISSOLVE.] **—dis·so·lute·ly** *adv.* **—dis·so·lute·ness** *n.*

dis·so·lu·tion (dĭs′ə-lo͞o′shən) *n.* **1.** Decomposition into fragments or constituent parts; disintegration. **2.** Termination or extinction by deconcentration or dispersion. **3.** Extinction of life; death. **4.** Annulment or termination of a formal or legal bond, tie, or contract. **5.** Formal dismissal of an assembly or legislature. **6.** Reduction to a liquid form; liquefaction. **—dis·so·lu·tive** *adj.*

dis·solve (dĭ-zŏlv′) *v.* **-solved, -solving, -solves.** *—tr.* **1.** To cause to pass into solution. **2.** To reduce to liquid form; melt. **3.** To break into component parts; cause to disintegrate or disappear. **4.** To bring to an end by or as if by breaking up; terminate. **5.** To dismiss (a meeting or parliament, for example). **6.** To cause to give way emotionally or psychologically; upset. **7.** To cause to lose definition; blur; confuse. **8.** *Law.* To render null; abrogate; annul. *—intr.* **1.** To pass into solution; be mixed or dispersed in another substance. **2.** To become liquid; melt. **3.** To break up or disperse. **4.** To disintegrate or disappear. **5.** To collapse emotionally or psychologically. **6.** To lose clarity or definition; fade away. **7.** To change scenes in a film or television program by having one scene fade out while the next appears behind it and grows clearer as the first dims. —See Synonyms at **melt.**
~n. A scene transition in a film or on television, made by dissolving. [Middle English *dissolven,* from Latin *dissolvere* : *dis-,* apart + *solvere,* to loosen, untie.] **—dis·solv·a·ble** *adj.* **—dis·solv·er** *n.*

dis·sol·vent (dĭ-zŏl′vənt) *adj.* Capable of dissolving.
~n. A solvent.

dis·so·nance (dĭs′ə-nəns) *n.* **1.** A harsh or disagreeable combination of sounds; discord. **2.** An absence of agreement or consistency; disparity. **3.** *Music.* A combination of notes conventionally considered to suggest unrelieved tension and to require resolution. Compare **consonance. 4.** *Psychology.* An aversive state that arises when an individual is aware of inconsistency or conflict within himself.

dis·so·nant (dĭs′ə-nənt) *adj.* **1.** Harsh or inharmonious in sound; discordant. **2.** Disagreeing or at variance: *"Jerome's new presumption, so dissonant from his former meekness"* (Horace Walpole). **3.** *Music.* Constituting or producing a dissonance. [Middle English, from Old French *dissonant,* from Latin *dissonāns* (stem *dissonant-*), present participle of *dissonāre,* to disagree in sound, be inharmonious : *dis-,* apart + *sonāre,* to sound.] **—dis·so·nant·ly** *adv.*

dis·suade (dĭ-swād′) *tr.v.* **-suaded, -suading, -suades.** To discourage or deter (a person) from a purpose or course of action by persuasion or exhortation. Used with *from.* [Latin *dissuādēre* : *dis-* (reversal) + *suādēre,* to advise, persuade.] **—dis·suad·er** *n.*

dis·sua·sion (dĭ-swā′zhən) *n.* The act or an instance of dissuading; exhortation against a course of action. [Latin *dissuāsiō* (stem *dissuāsiōn-*), from *dissuādēre,* to DISSUADE.] **—dis·sua·sive** *adj.* **—dis·sua·sive·ly** *adv.* **—dis·sua·sive·ness** *n.*

dis·syl·la·ble (dĭs′sĭl′ə-bəl, dĭ-sĭl′-, dĭ′sĭl′-) *n.* Also **di·syl·la·ble** (dī′-sĭl′-ə-bəl, dĭ-sĭl′-) A word with two syllables. **—dis·syl·lab·ic** (dĭs′-ĭ-lăb′ĭk, dĭ′sĭ-) *adj.*

dis·sym·me·try (dĭs-sĭm′ə-trē) *n., pl.* **-tries. 1.** Lack or absence of symmetry. **2.** Mirror-image symmetry, as of a left hand and a right hand. **—dis·sym·met·ric** (dĭ′sĭ-mĕt′rĭk), **dis·sym·met·ri·cal** *adj.* **—dis·sym·met·ri·cal·ly** *adv.*

dist. 1. distance; distant. **2.** distinguished. **3.** district.

dis·taff (dĭs′tăf′, -täf′) *n., pl.* **-taffs** or *rare* **-taves** (-tāvz′). **1.** A rod or stick with a cleft end in which is held the unspun flax, wool, or tow from which thread is drawn in spinning. **2.** A woman's work and concerns. **3.** Women in general. [Middle English *distaf,* Old English *distæf,* "flax staff" : *dis-,* bunch of flax, akin to Middle Low German *dise* (see **dizen**) + STAFF.]

distaff side *n.* The female line or maternal branch of a family. Also called "spindle side." Compare **spear side.**

dis·tal (dĭs′təl) *adj. Anatomy.* Located far from the origin, point of attachment, or median line of the body: *The fingers are at the distal end of the arm.* Compare **proximal.** [DIST(ANT) + -AL.] **—dis·tal·ly** *adv.*

dis·tance (dĭs′təns) *n. Abbr.* **dist. 1.** The fact or condition of being apart in space or time. **2.** *Geometry.* **a.** A nonnegative number designating the magnitude of a path along a straight line or curve. **b.** The length of a line segment joining two points. **c.** The length of the perpendicular from a given point to a given line or plane. **3. a.** The space between any two locations or points. **b.** The interval separating any two specified instants in time. **4. a.** The degree of deviation or difference that separates two things in relationship. **b.** The extent to which difference has arisen between two points in a trend or course: *The campaign moved some distance from its original objectives.* **5.** A stretch of linear space without designation of limit. **6. a.** A point removed in space or time. **b.** A position of being uninvolved or apart: *always kept himself at a distance.* **7.** Chilliness of manner; aloofness. **8.** The scheduled duration of a race, boxing match, or other sporting contest. Used chiefly in the phrases *go the distance* and *last the distance.* **—keep one's distance.** To remain reserved or aloof.
~tr.v. **distanced, -tancing, -tances. 1.** To place or keep at a distance. **2.** To cause to appear at a distance. **3.** To leave behind, as in a race; outrun; outstrip. [Middle English *distaunce,* from Old French *destance,* from Latin *distantia,* from *distāns,* DISTANT.]

dis·tant (dĭs′tənt) *adj. Abbr.* **dist. 1.** Separate or apart in space or time. **2.** Far removed in space or time. **3.** Located at, coming from, or going to a distance. **4.** Far apart in relationship; remote: *a distant cousin.* **5.** Far removed from the present situation: *distant thoughts.* **6.** Aloof or chilly in manner; reserved. [Middle English *distaunt,* from Old French, from Latin *distāns* (stem *distant-*), present participle of *distāre,* to be remote : *dis-,* apart + *stāre,* to stand.] **—dis·tant·ly** *adv.*
Usage: *distant, far, far-off, faraway, remote, removed.* These adjectives mean to be widely apart in space or, less often, in time. *Distant* can be used (with a figure) to indicate a specific separation, or it can indicate an indefinite but sizeable interval. *Far* implies a wide but indefinite interval, principally in space. *Far-off* and *faraway* imply a wider interval in either time or space. *Remote* not only means faraway but suggests isolation from the speaker's locality or point in time. *Removed* implies distinct separation in place, time, kind, or character with respect to the speaker.

dis·taste (dĭs-tāst′) *n.* Dislike or aversion. Often used with *for.*
~tr.v. **distasted, -tasting, -tastes.** *Archaic.* **1.** To feel repugnance for; dislike. **2.** To offend; displease.

dis·taste·ful (dĭs-tāst′fəl) *adj.* Unpleasant; disagreeable. **—dis·taste·ful·ly** *adv.* **—dis·taste·ful·ness** *n.*

dis·tem·per[1] (dĭs-tĕm′pər) *n.* **1. a.** An infectious virus disease occurring in certain mammals, especially dogs, characterized by loss of appetite, a catarrhal discharge from the eyes and nose, and often partial paralysis and death. **b.** Any of various similar mammalian diseases. **2.** Any illness or disease of the body or mind; an ailment. **3.** Ill humor; testiness. **4.** Disorder or disturbance, especially of a social or political nature.
~tr.v. **distempered, -pering, -pers.** *Archaic.* To upset or disturb; disorder. [Middle English *distemperen,* to upset the proper balance of the humors, vex, be ill, from Old French *destemprer,* from Medieval Latin *distemperāre* : Latin *dis-* (reversal) + *temperāre,* to mingle in due proportion, TEMPER.]

distemper[2] *n.* **1.** A process of painting in which pigments are mixed with water and a glue-size or casein binder, used for flat wall decoration or for scenic and poster painting. **2. a.** The paint used in this process. **b.** Any of various heavily pigmented matt paints, such as whitewash, that can be thinned with water. **3.** A painting done in distemper. **4.** *British.* **Calcimine** *(see).*
~tr.v. **distempered, -pering, -pers. 1.** To mix (powdered pigments or colors) with water and size. **2.** To paint using distemper. [Middle English *distemperen,* to dilute, mix, from Medieval Latin *distemperāre* : *dis-* (intensive) + *temperāre,* to mingle, TEMPER.]

dis·tend (dĭs-tĕnd′) *v.* **-tended, -tending, -tends.** *—intr.* To become bloated and swollen from or as if from internal pressure; swell out. *—tr.* **1.** To cause to expand by or as if by internal pressure; dilate. **2.** To stretch out; extend in all directions. [Middle English *distenden,* from Latin *distendere* : *dis-,* apart + *tendere,* to stretch.]

dis·ten·si·ble (dĭs-tĕn′sə-bəl) *adj.* Capable of being distended. **—dis·ten·si·bil·i·ty** *n.*

dis·ten·tion (dĭs-tĕn′shən) *n.* Also **dis·ten·sion.** The act of distending or the condition of being distended. [Middle English *distensioun,* from Latin *distentiō* (stem *distensiōn-*), from *distendere* (past participle *distentus*), to DISTEND.]

dis·tich (dĭs′tĭk) *n., pl.* **-tichs.** In poetry, a couplet, especially one used in a Latin or Greek elegy. [Latin *distichon,* from Greek *distikhon,* neuter of *distikhos,* having two rows or verses : DI- + *stikhos,* row, line, verse.]

dis·ti·chous (dĭs′tĭ-kəs) *adj. Botany.* Arranged in two vertical rows or ranks on opposite sides of an axis. Said of leaves. [Late Latin *distichus,* with two rows, from Greek *distikhos.* See **distich.**] **—dis·ti·chous·ly** *adv.*

dis·till (dĭ-stĭl′) *v.* **-tilled, -tilling, -tills.** Also *chiefly British* **dis·til, -tilled, -tilling, -tils.** *—tr.* **1.** To subject (a substance) to distillation. **2.** To extract (a distillate) by distillation. **3.** To purify or refine by or as if by distillation. **4.** To separate or extract (an essential idea or characteristic, for example) from its context, as if by distillation. **5.** To exude or give off (a substance) in drops or small quantities. *—intr.* **1.** To undergo or be produced by distillation. **2.** To fall or exude in drops or small quantities. [Middle English *distillen,* to trickle, drip, distill, from Old French *distiller,* from Latin *dēstillāre, distillāre* : *dē-,* down + *stillāre,* to drip, from *stilla*†, drop.] **—dis·till·a·ble** *adj.*

dis·til·late (dĭs′tə-lāt′, -lĭt, dĭ-stĭl′ĭt) *n.* **1.** The liquid condensed from vapor in distillation. **2.** Anything regarded as an essence or purified form. Also called "distillation."

dis·til·la·tion (dĭs′tə-lā′shən) *n.* **1.** Any of various heat-dependent processes used to purify or separate a fraction of a mixture; especially, the vaporization of a liquid mixture with subsequent collection of components by differential cooling to condensation. **2.** A distillate.

distillation column *n.* A tall cylindrical metal shell fitted inside with perforated horizontal plates used to promote separation of miscible liquids ascending in the shell as vapor.

dis·till·er (dĭ-stĭl′ər) *n.* **1.** One that distills, as a condenser. **2.** A producer or maker of alcoholic drinks by the process of distillation.

dis·till·er·y (dĭ-stĭl′ə-rē) *n., pl.* **-ies.** An establishment or plant for distilling, especially alcoholic liquors, such as whiskey or gin.

dis·tinct (dĭ-stĭngkt′) *adj.* **1.** Not identical; individual; discrete. **2.** Not similar; different; unlike. **3.** Easily perceived by the senses or intellect; clear. **4.** Well-defined; unmistakable; unquestionable:

PRONUNCIATION KEY

ă, pat; ā, pay; âr, care; ä, father, are; b, bib; ch, church; d, deed; ĕ, pet; ē, be; f, fife; g, gag; h, hat; hw, which; ĭ, pit; ī, pie; îr, pier; j, judge; k, kick; l, lid, needle; m, mum; n, no, sudden; ng, thing; ŏ, pot; ō, toe; ô, paw, for; oi, noise; ou, out; o͝o, book; o͞o, boot; p, pop; r, roar; s, sauce; sh, ship, dish; t, tight; th, thin, path; *th,* this, bathe; ŭ, cut; ûr, fur; v, valve; w, with; y, yes; z, zebra, size; zh, vision; ə, about, item, edible, gallop, circus, peaceful

IN FOREIGN WORDS:

à, *Fr.* ami; œ, *Fr.* feu, *Ger.* schön; ü, *Fr.* tu, *Ger.* über; KH, *Ger.* ich, *Scot.* loch; N, *Fr.* bon; y′, *Fr.* Compiègne

STRESS MARKS:

Primary stress: ′
in·cite′ (ĭn-sīt′)
Secondary stress: ′
in′sight′ (ĭn′sīt′)

a distinct improvement. —See Synonyms at **evident.** [Middle English, separated, different, from Old French, from Latin *distinctus,* past participle of *distinguere,* to DISTINGUISH.] —**dis·tinct·ly** *adv.* —**dis·tinct·ness** *n.*

Usage: *Distinct* and *distinctive* are seldom interchangeable. *Distinct* has the meaning "unmistakable" or "clear" in most of its uses; *distinctive* has the meaning "distinguishing," "setting something apart from others." The contrast can be seen in such phrases as *a distinct smell,* where the smell is pronounced, compared with a *distinctive smell,* where the smell is uniquely identifiable.

dis·tinc·tion (dĭ-stĭngk′shən) *n.* **1.** The action of distinguishing; differentiation. **2.** The condition or fact of being dissimilar or distinct; a difference. **3.** A distinguishing factor, attribute, or characteristic. **4.** Excellence or eminence, as of performance, character, or reputation: *a man of distinction.* **5. a.** Recognition of achievement or superiority: *She graduated with distinction.* **b.** An honor conferred in recognition of achievement or superiority. —See Usage note at **difference.**

dis·tinc·tive (dĭ-stingk′tĭv) *adj.* **1.** Serving to identify; distinguishing: *distinctive tribal tattoos.* **2.** Characteristic: *distinctive habits.* **3.** *Linguistics.* Serving to distinguish meaning. Said of a phonological feature. —See Synonyms at **characteristic.** —See Usage note at **distinct.** —**dis·tinc·tive·ly** *adv.* —**dis·tinc·tive·ness** *n.*

dis·tin·gué (dēs′tăng-gā′, dĭs′-, dĭ-stăng′gā) *adj.* Distinguished in appearance, manner, or bearing. [French, "distinguished."]

dis·tin·guish (dĭ-stĭng′gwĭsh) *v.* **-guished, -guishing, -guishes.** —*tr.* **1.** To recognize as being different or distinct. **2.** To perceive distinctly; discern; make out. **3.** To detect or recognize; pick out. **4.** To make noticeable or different; set apart; characterize. **5.** To cause to be eminent or recognized. Usually used reflexively: *He distinguished himself in the exam.* —*intr.* To perceive or indicate differences; discriminate. Usually used with *among* or *between.* [Middle English *distinguen,* from Old French *distinguer* (present stem *distinguiss-*), from Latin *distinguere,* to separate, distinguish.] —**dis·tin·guish·a·ble** *adj.* —**dis·tin·guish·a·bly** *adv.*

dis·tin·guished (dĭ-stĭng′gwĭsht) *adj. Abbr.* **dist. 1.** Characterized by excellence or distinction; eminent; renowned. **2.** Having an air of distinction and dignity in conduct or appearance.

Distinguished Conduct Medal *n. Abbr.* **D.C.M.** A British military decoration for distinguished conduct in the field.

Distinguished Flying Cross *n. Abbr.* **DFC, D.F.C. 1.** A U.S. military decoration awarded for heroism or extraordinary achievement in aerial combat. **2.** A similar British decoration awarded to officers of the Royal Air Force.

Distinguished Service Cross *n. Abbr.* **DSC, D.S.C. 1.** A U.S Army decoration awarded for exceptional heroism in combat. **2.** A British decoration awarded to officers of the Royal Navy for gallantry in action.

Distinguished Service Medal *n. Abbr.* **DSM, D.S.M. 1.** A U.S. military decoration awarded for distinguished performance in a duty of great responsibility. **2.** A British decoration awarded to noncommissioned officers and men in the Royal Navy and Royal Marines for distinguished conduct in war.

Distinguished Service Order *n. Abbr.* **D.S.O.** A British military decoration for gallantry in action.

dis·tort (dĭ-stôrt′) *tr.v.* **-torted, -torting, -torts. 1.** To twist out of a proper or natural relation of parts; misshape; contort. **2.** To cast false light on; alter misleadingly; misrepresent. **3.** To cause to work in a twisted or disordered manner; pervert. **4.** To alter the original or ideal form of (an electronic signal, sound wave, or the like). [Latin *distorquēre* (past participle *distortus*) : *dis-,* apart, aside + *torquēre,* to twist.] —**dis·tort·er** *n.*

Usage: *distort, twist, deform, contort, warp, gnarl.* These verbs mean to change the form or character of something, usually to its disadvantage. *Distort* applies to physical change in shape, as by bending, wrenching, or exaggerating certain features; to verbal or pictorial misrepresentation; and to alteration or perversion of meaning of something spoken or written. *Twist* has similar application but intensifies the idea of marked and deliberate change. *Deform* refers only to physical change that disfigures and usually deprives the object of attractiveness or capacity for normal functioning. *Contort* implies violent physical change that produces unnatural or grotesque effects. *Warp* can refer to physical turning or twisting out of shape, or, figuratively, to turning something, such as the human mind or judgment, from a true course. *Gnarl* usually refers to making twisted or knotty in a physical sense.

dis·tor·tion (dĭ-stôr′shən) *n.* **1. a.** The act or an instance of distorting. **b.** A product of distorting; a distorted feature: *The newspaper article was full of distortions.* **2.** The condition of being distorted. **3.** *Optics.* A distorted image resulting from imperfections in an optical system, such as a lens. **4. a.** An undesired change in the waveform of an electronic signal, sound wave, or the like. **b.** Any consequence of such a change; especially, diminished clarity in reception or reproduction. **5.** *Psychoanalysis.* The modification of unconscious impulses into acceptable forms by conscious or dreaming perception. —**dis·tor·tion·al** *adj.*

distr. distributor.

dis·tract (dĭ-străkt′) *tr.v.* **-tracted, -tracting, -tracts. 1.** To cause to turn away from the original focus of attention or interest; sidetrack; divert. **2.** To pull in conflicting emotional directions; unsettle; bewilder. [Middle English *distracten,* from Latin *distrahere* (past participle *distractus*), to pull apart, draw away, perplex : *dis-,* apart, aside + *trahere,* to draw.] —**dis·tract·ing·ly** —**dis·trac·tive·ly** *adv.* —**dis·trac·tive** *adj.*

dis·tract·ed (dĭ-străk′tĭd) *adj.* **1.** Having the attention diverted or not paying attention. **2.** Suffering conflicting emotions; confused. **3.** Distraught; made mad; *distracted by grief.* —See Synonyms at **forgetful.** —**dis·tract·ed·ly** *adv.*

dis·tract·er, dis·trac·tor (dĭ-străk′tər) *n.* One of the incorrect answers presented as a choice in a multiple-choice test.

dis·trac·tion (dĭ-străk′shən) *n.* **1.** The act of distracting or the condition of being distracted; a diversion from an original focus. **2.** Anything that compels attention or distracts; especially, an amusement. **3.** Extreme mental or emotional disturbance; obsession: *"I loved Dora Spenlow to distraction!"* (Charles Dickens).

dis·train (dĭ-strān′) *v.* **-trained, -training, -trains.** *Law.* —*tr.* To seize and hold (property) to compel payment or reparation, as of debts. —*intr.* To seize a person's goods in order to compel payment of his debts to the distrainer; levy a distress. Often used with *upon.* [Middle English *distreinen,* to seize, compel, detain, from Old French *destreindre* (present stem *destreign-*), from Medieval Latin *distringere,* to seize, compel, from Latin, to draw apart, detain, hinder : *dis-,* apart + *stringere,* to draw tight.] —**dis·train·a·ble** *adj.* —**dis·train·ment** *n.* —**dis·trai·nor, dis·train·er** *n.*

dis·train·ee (dĭs′trā-nē′) *n. Law.* One whose property has been distrained.

dis·traint (dĭ-strānt′) *n. Law.* The act or process of distraining; a distress. [From DISTRAIN (by analogy with *restraint, restrain*).]

dis·trait (dĭ-strāt′) *adj.* **1.** Inattentive; distracted. **2.** Agitated; worried. [Middle English, from Old French *destrait,* past participle of *destraire,* to DISTRACT.]

dis·traught (dĭ-strôt′) *adj.* **1.** Extremely anxious or agitated; harried; frantic with worry. **2.** Crazed; mad. [Middle English, alteration of *distract,* distracted, from Latin *distractus,* past participle of *distrahere,* to perplex, DISTRACT.]

dis·tress (dĭ-strĕs′) *tr.v.* **-tressed, -tressing, -tresses. 1.** To cause anxiety or suffering to; worry or upset. **2.** To bring into difficult circumstances, especially difficult financial circumstances. **3.** *Archaic.* To constrain by harassment; force. **4.** *Law.* To hold the property of (a person) against the payment of debts; distrain upon. ~*n.* **1.** Anxiety or suffering; sorrow; unhappiness. **2.** Severe strain resulting from exhaustion, accident, or the like. **3.** The condition of being in need of immediate assistance: *a person in distress; a ship in distress.* Also used adjectivally: *a distress signal.* **4.** *Law.* **a.** The seizing of goods belonging to a debtor, as security or in reparation; the act of distraining. **b.** The goods thus seized. [Middle English *distressen, destressen,* from Old French *destresser,* from *destresse,* "narrow passage," strait, constraint, from Vulgar Latin *districtia* (unattested), narrowness, from Latin *districtus,* past participle of *distringere,* to "draw tight," detain, hinder. See **distrain.**] —**dis·tress·ing·ly** *adv.*

dis·tressed (dĭ-strĕst′) *adj.* **1.** Upset or worried; made anxious; made to suffer. **2.** Impoverished; poor in comparison to one's former circumstances. **3.** Deliberately treated to give an impression of age and wear. Said of furniture and leather.

dis·tress·ful (dĭ-strĕs′fəl) *adj.* **1.** Causing distress. **2.** Experiencing distress. —**dis·tress·ful·ly** *adv.* —**dis·tress·ful·ness** *n.*

dis·trib·u·tar·y (dĭ-strĭb′yə-tĕr′ē) *n., pl.* **-ies.** A branch of a river that flows away from the main stream and does not return to it; especially, such a branch in the delta of a large river. Compare **tributary.**

dis·trib·ute (dĭ-strĭb′yo͞ot) *tr.v.* **-uted, -uting, -utes. 1.** To divide and dispense in portions; parcel out. **2.** To deliver or pass out: *distribute leaflets.* **3.** To spread or diffuse over an area. Often used in the passive: *a widely distributed species.* **4.** To separate into groups or categories; arrange or classify. **5.** *Logic.* To use (a term) so as to include all individuals or entities of a given class. **6.** *Printing.* To separate (type) and replace in the proper boxes. [Middle English *distributen,* from Latin *distribuere* : *dis-,* apart + *tribuere,* to allot, grant (see **tribute**).]

Usage: *distribute, divide, dispense, dole, deal, ration.* These verbs mean to give something as a portion or share. *Distribute* is the least specific. *Divide* implies giving out portions determined by plan and purpose, often equal parts or portions based on what is due or deserved. *Dispense* stresses even more the sense of careful determination of portions according to what is considered due or proper. *Dole* (usually followed by *out*) implies careful and scant measurement of portions; often it applies to distribution of charity or something given reluctantly. *Deal* suggests orderly and equitable distribution, piece by piece. *Ration* refers to equitable division of scarce items, often necessities, by a system that limits individual portions.

dis·trib·ut·ed (dĭ-strĭb′yə-tĭd) *adj.* Characterized by a particular statistical distribution.

dis·tri·bu·tion (dĭs′trə-byo͞o′shən) *n.* **1.** The act of distributing or the condition of being distributed; an apportionment. **2.** Something distributed; an allotment. **3.** The act of dispersing or the condition of being dispersed; a diffusion. **4.** The geographical occurrence or range of an organism. **5.** Division into categories; classification. **6.** *Law.* The division of an estate or property among rightful heirs. **7.** *Commerce.* The process of getting goods from the manufacturer to the consumer, including marketing, handling of orders, and transport of goods. **8.** Any spatial or temporal array of objects or events: *the distribution of theaters on Broadway.* **9.** *Symbol* + *Statistics* The particular way in which numbers representing a given characteristic are distributed among the members of a group, usually arranged according to frequency. See **frequency distribution.** **—dis·tri·bu·tion·al** *adj.*

dis·trib·u·tive (dĭ-strĭb′yə-tĭv) *adj.* **1.** Of or pertaining to distribution. **2.** Serving to distribute. **3.** *Grammar.* Referring to each individual or entity of a group separately rather than collectively; for example, *every* in the sentence *Every employee attended the meeting.* **4.** *Mathematics.* Of, pertaining to, or designating an operation having the same effect whether performed before or after another operation; for example, multiplication is *distributive* with respect to addition; that is, $a \times (b + c) = (a \times b) + (a \times c)$.
~*n.* A distributive word or term. **—dis·trib·u·tive·ly** *adv.* **—dis·trib·u·tive·ness** *n.*

distributive education *n.* An educational program in which students receive both classroom instruction and on-the-job training.

dis·trib·u·tor, dis·trib·ut·er (dĭ-strĭb′yə-tər) *n. Abbr.* **distr. 1.** One that distributes: *film distributors.* **2.** One that markets or sells a commodity; especially, a wholesaler. **3.** In the ignition system of an internal-combustion engine, a device for applying electric current in proper sequence to the spark plugs. **4.** *Computer Science.* The electronic circuitry that acts as an intermediate link between a computer's accumulator and drum storage.

dis·trict (dĭs′trĭkt) *n. Abbr.* **dist.** A division of an area or geographical unit either created arbitrarily, as for administrative purposes, or existing as a division by virtue of a characteristic: *an electoral district; a residential district; the District of Columbia.* —See Synonyms at **area.**
~*tr.v.* **districted, -tricting, -tricts.** To mark off or divide into districts. [French, from Medieval Latin *districtus,* (area of) jurisdiction, distraint, from Latin, past participle of *distringere,* to detain, hinder. See **distrain.**]

district attorney *n. Abbr.* **D.A.** The state's prosecuting officer in a given judicial district.

district court *n.* **1.** A U.S. Federal trial court serving a judicial district. **2.** In some states, a state court of general jurisdiction.

District of Co·lum·bi·a (kə-lŭm′bē-ə). *Abbr.* **D.C.** Federal area in the eastern United States, whose area is coextensive with Washington, the nation's capital. It is on the Potomac River.

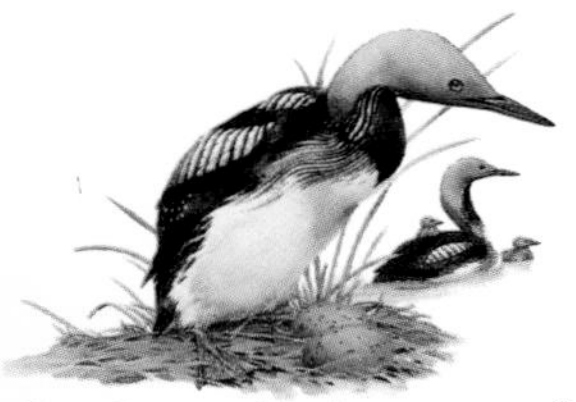

diver *Because their legs are set well back on their bodies, divers are clumsy on land. But the same feature helps to make them powerful underwater swimmers. They spend most of their time in the water, coming ashore only to nest. This is the black-throated diver of Europe,* Gavia arctica.

dis·trust (dĭs-trŭst′) *n.* Lack of trust; doubtfulness or misgiving; suspicion.
~*tr.v.* **distrusted, -trusting, -trusts.** To lack confidence in; doubt or suspect.

dis·trust·ful (dĭs-trŭst′fəl) *adj.* Doubting; suspicious. **—dis·trust·ful·ly** *adv.* **—dis·trust·ful·ness** *n.*

dis·turb (dĭ-stûrb′) *tr.v.* **-turbed, -turbing, -turbs. 1.** To break up or destroy the tranquillity or settled state of. **2.** To trouble emotionally or mentally; upset or alarm. **3.** To intrude upon; interrupt: *disturb one's sleep.* **4.** To disarrange; put out of order. **5.** To put (oneself) out; inconvenience (oneself): *She need not have disturbed herself on my account.* [Middle English *destourben,* from Old French *destorber,* from Latin *disturbāre* : *dis-* (intensive) + *turbāre,* to throw into disorder, disturb, from *turba,* confusion, probably from Greek *turbē,* disorder.] **—dis·turb·er** *n.* **—dis·turb·ing·ly** *adv.*

dis·tur·bance (dĭ-stûr′bəns) *n.* **1.** The act of disturbing or the condition of being disturbed. **2.** Something that disturbs; an interruption; intrusion. **3.** A commotion, brawl, or riot; especially, a public breach of the peace. **4.** Unbalance or disorder, as of the mind. **5.** A variation in a normal course or condition. **6.** *Law.* The infringement of or interference with another's incorporeal property interests, such as easements, tenancies, franchises, or the like. **7.** *Meteorology.* A **depression** *(see),* usually one of low intensity.

dis·turbed (dĭ-stûrbd′) *adj.* Mentally unbalanced; emotionally unstable.

di·sul·fide (dī-sŭl′fīd′) *n.* A chemical compound containing two sulfur atoms combined with other elements or radicals. Also called "bisulfide."

di·sul·fi·ram (dī-sŭl′fə-răm′) *n.* A drug used in the treatment of chronic alcoholism. It acts by producing unpleasant effects, such as nausea and vomiting, when taken with alcohol. [From tetraethyl-triu*ram disulf*ide.]

dis·un·ion (dĭs-yo͞on′yən) *n.* **1.** The state of being disunited; separation. **2.** Lack of unity; discord. **—dis·un·ion·ist** *n. & adj.*

dis·u·nite (dĭs′yo͞o-nīt′) *v.* **-nited, -niting, -nites.** —*tr.* **1.** To disrupt the union of; separate. **2.** To estrange; put at odds. —*intr.* To become separate.

dis·u·ni·ty (dĭs-yo͞o′nə-tē) *n., pl.* **-ties.** Lack of unity; dissension.

dis·use (dĭs-yo͞os′) *n.* The state of not being used or of being no longer in use; desuetude. **—dis·used** *adj.*

dis·u·til·i·ty (dĭs′yo͞o-tĭl′ə-tē) *n.* The negative or harmful aspects of something; disadvantage.

disyllable. Variant of **dissyllable.**

dit (dĭt) *n.* The oral representation of the dot in radio and telegraphic codes, as in Morse code. Compare **dah.** [Imitative.]

ditch (dĭch) *n.* A long narrow trench or furrow dug in the ground, as for irrigation or drainage, or as a boundary line.
~*v.* **ditched, ditching, ditches.** —*intr.* **1.** To make or repair ditches. **2.** To make a forced landing on water. —*tr.* **1.** To dig or make a ditch in. **2.** To surround with a ditch. **3. a.** To drive (a vehicle) into a ditch. **b.** To derail (a train). **c.** To bring (an aircraft) down on water in an emergency. **4.** *Slang.* To throw aside; discard; desert. [Middle English *dich,* Old English *dīc*†, moat, ditch.] **—ditch·er** *n.*

ditch·water (dĭch′wô′tər, -wŏt′ər) *n.* Foul, stagnant water, such as that found in ditches.

di·the·ism (dī-thē′ĭz-əm) *n.* **1.** A belief in two supreme gods. **2.** The belief that good and evil govern the world as two supreme principles.

dith·er (dĭth′ər) *n.* **1.** *Chiefly British.* A state of nervous indecision or uncertainty. **2.** A state of agitation, excitement, or confusion.
~*intr.v.* **dithered, -ering, -ers. 1.** To be in a dither. **2.** To quiver or tremble, as with excitement. [Earlier *didder,* Middle English *didderen,* to DODDER.] **—dith·er·er** *n.* **—dith·er·ing, dith·er·y** *adj.*

dith·y·ramb (dĭth′ĭ-răm′, -rămb′) *n.* **1.** A frenzied and impassioned choric hymn and dance of ancient Greece, in honor of Dionysus. **2.** An irregular poetic expression suggestive of the ancient Greek dithyramb. **3.** Any piece of writing or speech in a frenzied and impassioned style. [Latin *dīthyrambus,* from Greek *dithurambos,* of non-Indo-European origin; akin to *thriambos,* TRIUMPH, and *iambos,* IAMB.] **—dith·y·ramb·ic** *adj.*

dit·ta·ny (dĭt′n-ē) *n., pl.* **-nies. 1.** An aromatic Cretan plant, *Origanum dictamnus,* with pink flowers, formerly believed to have magical powers. **2.** The **gas plant** *(see).* [Middle English *ditane, ditene,* from Old French *ditan, ditain,* from Medieval Latin *di(p)tamnus,* variant of Latin *dictamnus,* from Greek *diktamnon,* perhaps after *Diktē,* mountain in Crete.]

dit·to (dĭt′ō) *n., pl.* **-tos.** *Abbr.* **do. 1.** The aforesaid; the above; the same as before. Used to avoid repetition and indicated by a pair of small *ditto marks* (″) placed under the word that would otherwise be repeated. **2.** A duplicate or copy.
~*adv.* As before; likewise.
~*tr.v.* **dittoed, -toing, -tos.** To duplicate or repeat.
~*interj.* Used to express agreement. [Italian dialectal (Tuscan) *ditto,* "said," from Latin *dictus,* past participle of *dīcere,* to say.]

dit·ty (dĭt′ē) *n., pl.* **-ties.** A simple song. [Middle English *dite, ditti,* from Old French *ditie,* "composition," from Latin *dictātum,* "thing dictated," from *dictāre,* to dictate, compose, frequentative of *dīcere,* to say.]

ditty bag *n.* A bag used by sailors to carry small items such as sewing implements. [Possibly from obsolete *dutty,* coarse calico, from Hindi *dhōtī,* loincloth, DHOTI.]

ditty box *n.* A box used like a ditty bag.

Di·u (dē′o͞o). Island and seaport, now part of the Indian territory of Goa, Daman, and Diu.

di·u·re·sis (dī′yo͞o-rē′sĭs) *n.* Excessive discharge of urine. [New Latin, from Late Latin *diūrēticus,* DIURETIC.]

di·u·ret·ic (dī′yo͞o-rĕt′ĭk) *adj.* Tending to increase the production and discharge of urine.
~*n.* A diuretic drug. [Middle English *diuretik,* from Late Latin *diūrēticus,* from Greek *diourētikos,* from *diourein,* to pass urine : *dia-,* through + *ourein,* to urinate, from *ouron,* urine.]

di·ur·nal (dī-ûr′nəl) *adj.* **1.** Pertaining to or occurring in a day or each day; daily. **2.** Occurring or active during the daytime rather than at night. Said especially of animals. Compare **nocturnal. 3.** Opening during daylight hours and closing at night. Said of flowers. [Middle English, from Latin *diurnālis,* from *diurnus,* of a day, daily : *diēs,* day + *-urnus,* adjective suffix.] **—di·ur·nal·ly** *adv.*

diurnal parallax *n. Astronomy.* **Parallax** *(see)* caused by the earth's daily rotation, defined by the angle subtended at a celestial body by the radius of the earth. Also called "geocentric parallax."

diurnal rhythm *n.* A **circadian rhythm** *(see).*

div. 1. *Mathematics.* divergence. **2.** divided; division; divisor. **3.** dividend. **4.** divorced.

di·va (dē′və) *n., pl.* **-vas** or *Italian* **-ve** (-vā). An operatic prima donna. [Italian, "goddess," from Latin, feminine of *dīvus,* god.]

di·va·gate (dī′və-gāt′, dĭv′ə-) *intr.v.* **-gated, -gating, -gates. 1.** To wander or drift about. **2.** To ramble; digress. [Late Latin *dīvagārī* : Latin *dis-,* apart + *vagārī,* to wander, from *vagus,* wandering, VAGUE.] **—di·va·ga·tion** *n.*

di·va·lent (dī-vā′lənt) *adj.* Having a valence of two; bivalent.

di·van (dĭ-văn′, dī′văn′ *for sense 1;* dĭ-văn′, -vän′, dī-văn′ *for senses 2, 3, 4, 5*) *n.* Also **di·wan** (dĭ-wän′) (for senses 2, 5). **1. a.** A long backless couch, especially one against a wall with pillows. **b.** A low bed without a headboard or footboard. **2.** In Muslim countries: **a.** A council that constitutes or is a part of the government. **b.** A room where such a council is held; a court of justice; a council chamber. **3.** Any council. **4.** Formerly, a coffee house or smoking room furnished with divans. **5.** In the Middle East, a book of poems by one author. [French, from Turkish *dīvān,* from Persian *dīvān*†, register, account, hence office of accounts, council of state.]

di·var·i·cate (dī-văr′ə-kāt′, dĭ-) *intr.v.* **-cated, -cating, -cates.** To diverge at a wide angle; branch off; spread apart. Used especially of branches.
~*adj.* (dī-văr′ə-kĭt, -kāt′, dĭ-). *Biology.* Branching or spreading widely from a point or axis; diverging. [Latin *dīvāricāre,* to spread apart : *dis-,* apart + *vāricāre,* to straddle, from *vāricus,* with the feet spread apart, from *vārus,* bent, knock-kneed.] **—di·var·i·cate·ly** *adv.*

di·var·i·ca·tion (dī-văr′ə-kā′shən, dĭ-) *n.* **1.** The act of divaricating; a branching off. **2.** A divergence of opinion. **3.** The point at which branching occurs.

di·var·i·ca·tor (dī-văr′ə-kāt′ər, dĭ-) *n.* **1.** A muscle that effects the opening and closing of the shell in brachiopods. **2.** A surgical instrument used to divide tissue into two separate parts.

dive (dīv) *v.* **dived** or **dove** (dōv), **dived, diving, dives.** —*intr.* **1. a.** To plunge headfirst into water, often as a sport. **b.** To go toward the bottom of a body of water: *dive for pearls.* **c.** To submerge under power. Used of a submarine. **d.** To fall head down through the air. **e.** To descend nose down at an acceleration usually

exceeding that of free fall. Used of an airplane. **f.** To engage in the sport of skydiving. **g.** To drop sharply and rapidly; plummet. **2. a.** To rush headlong, usually downward or out of sight: *dived into an alley.* **b.** To plunge one's hand into something: *dived into my handbag for a coin.* **3.** To lunge; throw oneself. Used with *at* or *for*: *We dived for the best seats.* **4.** To plunge or rush with great enthusiasm or vigor. Used with *in* or *into*: *The children all dived in and helped themselves to the food.* —*tr.* To cause (an aircraft or a submarine, for example) to dive.
~*n.* **1. a.** A headlong plunge into water, especially one executed deliberately. **b.** A nearly vertical descent at an accelerated speed through water, air, or space. **c.** A quick, pronounced drop. **2.** *Slang.* A disreputable or run-down bar or nightclub. **3.** *Slang.* A knockout feigned by prearrangement between boxers. Used chiefly in the phrase *to take a dive.* [Middle English *diven, duven,* to dive, to submerge, Old English *dȳfan* (transitive), to dip, immerse, and *dūfan* (intransitive), to sink, dive.]

dive-bomb (dīv′bŏm′) *tr.v.* **-bombed, -bombing, -bombs.** *Aviation.* To release a bomb at the end of a steep dive toward the target. **—dive-bomber** *n.*

div•er (dī′vər) *n.* **1.** One that dives. **2.** One who dives for something or goes underwater for work or pleasure, especially one equipped with breathing apparatus and weighted clothing. **3. a.** Any of several aquatic birds of the family Gaviidae, having black-and-white plumage and small, pointed wings and noted for their ability to dive deeply under water in search of prey. **b.** Any of various other diving birds, especially the loon.

di•verge (dĭ-vûrj′, dī-) *v.* **-verged, -verging, -verges.** —*intr.* **1.** To tend in different directions from a common point. **2.** To differ in opinion or manner. **3.** To depart from a set course or norm; deviate. **4.** *Mathematics.* To fail to approach a limit. Compare **converge.** —*tr.* To cause to diverge; deflect. —See Synonyms at **separate.** [Late Latin *dīvergere,* to turn aside : Latin *dis-,* apart + *vergere,* to bend, turn.]

di•ver•gence (dĭ-vûr′jəns, dī-) *n.* Also **di•ver•gen•cy** (-jən-sē), *pl.* **-cies.** *Abbr.* **div. 1. a.** The act of diverging. **b.** The state of being divergent. **c.** The degree by which things diverge. **2.** Departure from a norm; deviation. **3.** Difference, as of opinion. **4.** *Mathematics.* **a.** The property or manner of diverging; failure to approach a limit. **b.** The scalar product of the del operator and a vector function. In this sense, compare **curl. 5.** *Meteorology.* A condition characterized by a net horizontal outflow of air from a region, often compensated for by a descending air current, usually accompanied by fine dry weather. —See Usage note at **difference.**

di•ver•gent (dĭ-vûr′jənt, dī-) *adj.* **1. a.** Drawing apart from a common point; diverging. **b.** Causing divergence of radiation. **2.** Departing from convention; deviant. **3.** Differing from each other: *divergent opinions.* **4.** *Mathematics.* Failing to approach a limit; not convergent. **—di•ver•gent•ly** *adv.*

divergent thinking *n.* *Psychology.* A type of thinking characterized by breadth of vision and the use of imagination to arrive at a variety of possible solutions to a problem. Compare **convergent thinking.**

di•vers (dī′vərz) *adj.* Various; several; sundry. [Middle English *divers(e).* See **diverse.**]

di•verse (dĭ-vûrs′, dī-, dī′vûrs) *adj.* **1.** Distinct in kind; disparate; unlike. **2.** Having variety in form; diversified; multiform. [Middle English *divers(e),* from Old French *divers,* from Latin *dīversus,* contrary, diverse, from the past participle of *dīvertere,* to turn aside, DIVERT.] **—di•verse•ly** *adv.* **—di•verse•ness** *n.*

di•ver•si•form (dĭ-vûr′sə-fôrm′, dī-) *adj.* Having a variety of forms; variform. [DIVERSE + -FORM.]

di•ver•si•fy (dĭ-vûr′sə-fī′, dī-) *v.* **-fied, -fying, -fies.** —*tr.* **1.** To make diverse; give variety to; vary. **2. a.** To extend (activities) into various different disparate fields in order to increase profits, spread the risk of loss, or the like. Used of a business enterprise. **b.** To distribute (investments) among several companies in order to reduce the risk of loss. —*intr.* To engage in a wide range of activities. Used especially of a business enterprise. [Middle English *diversifien,* from Old French *diversifier,* from Medieval Latin *dīversificāre* : Latin *dīversus,* DIVERSE + *facere,* to make.] **—di•ver•si•fi•a•ble** *adj.* **—di•ver•si•fi•ca•tion** *n.*

di•ver•sion (dĭ-vûr′zhən, -shən, dī-) *n.* **1.** An act or instance of diverting; a turning aside. **2.** Something that distracts the mind and relaxes or entertains. **3.** In military strategy, a maneuver that draws the attention of the enemy away from the planned point of attack. **4.** A detour created for traffic. **—di•ver•sion•ar•y** *adj.*

di•ver•sion•ist (dĭ-vûr′zhən-ĭst, -shən-ĭst, dī-) *n.* *Politics.* One engaged in diversionary, disruptive, or subversive activities, especially from within and against a Communist state. **—di•ver•sion•ist** *adj.*

di•ver•si•ty (dĭ-vûr′sə-tē, dī-) *n., pl.* **-ties. 1. a.** The fact or quality of being diverse; difference. **b.** A point or respect in which things differ. **2.** Variety; multiformity: *a healthy diversity in one's diet.*

di•vert (dĭ-vûrt′, dī-) *v.* **-verted, -verting, -verts.** —*tr.* **1.** To turn aside from a usual course or direction; deflect. **2.** To distract. **3.** To amuse or entertain. —*intr.* To turn aside. [Middle English *diverten,* to turn aside, digress, escape, from Old French *divertir,* from Latin *dīvertere,* to turn aside : *dis-,* aside + *vertere,* to turn.] **—di•vert•er** *n.* **—di•vert•ing•ly** *adv.*

diverticular disease *n.* A condition in which diverticula in the colon are associated with lower abdominal pain.

di•ver•tic•u•li•tis (dī′vûr-tĭk′yə-lī′tĭs) *n.* *Pathology.* Inflammation of a diverticulum.

di•ver•tic•u•lo•sis (dī′vûr-tĭk′yə-lō′sĭs) *n.* A condition characterized by the presence of numerous diverticula in the colon. [DIVERTICU-L(UM) + -OSIS.]

di•ver•tic•u•lum (dī′vûr-tĭk′yə-ləm) *n., pl.* **-la** (-lə). A pouch or sac branching out from a hollow organ or structure, especially the intestine. Diverticula may occur as abnormal structures formed at weak points in the intestinal wall. [New Latin, from Latin *dēverticulum,* bypath, from *dēvertere,* to turn aside : *dē-,* away + *vertere,* to turn.] **—di•ver•tic•u•lar** *adj.*

di•ver•ti•men•to (dĭ-vĕr′tĭ-mĕn′tō) *n., pl.* **-ti** (-tē). *Music.* A chiefly 18th-century form of instrumental chamber music having several short movements. [Italian, "diversion," "amusement," from *divertire,* to DIVERT.]

di•ver•tisse•ment (dē-vĕr-tēs-mäN′) *n.* **1.** A short ballet or other performance given as an interlude in the opera or theater. **2. a.** *Music.* A divertimento. **b.** A fantasia composed using well-known melodies. **3.** A diversion; an amusement. [French, from *divertir,* to DIVERT.]

Di•ves (dī′vēz) *n.* A man of wealth. [Middle English, from Latin *Dīvēs,* the rich man in the parable of Lazarus, Luke 16:19–31, from *dīvēs,* rich, costly.]

di•vest (dĭ-vĕst′, dī-) *tr.v.* **-vested, -vesting, -vests. 1.** To strip, as of clothes. **2.** To deprive, as of rights or property; dispossess. **3.** *Law.* To devest. —See Synonyms at **strip.** [Alteration of DEVEST.]

di•vide (dĭ-vīd′) *v.* **-vided, -viding, -vides.** —*tr.* **1. a.** To separate into parts, sections, groups, or branches. **b.** To sector into units of measurement; graduate. **c.** To separate and group according to kind; classify. **2. a.** To separate into opposing factions; disunite: *The issue of unemployment divided the party.* **b.** *British.* To cause (Members of Parliament) to vote by separating into groups for and against a motion. **3.** To separate from; cut off; serve as a boundary between. **4.** To apportion among a number; share out. **5.** *Mathematics.* **a.** To subject to the process of division. **b.** To be an exact divisor of. —*intr.* **1. a.** To become separated into parts. **b.** To branch out. Used of a river, for example. **c.** To form into factions; take sides. **d.** *British.* To vote by being divided. **2.** To perform the mathematical operation of division. —See Synonyms at **separate.** —See Usage note at **distribute.**
~*n.* **1.** A dividing point or line. **2.** A ridge of land forming a watershed. **3.** See **Great Divide.** [Middle English *dividen,* from Latin *dīvidere.*] **—di•vid•a•ble** *adj.*

di•vid•ed (dĭ-vī′dĭd) *adj.* *Abbr.* **div. 1.** Separated into parts or pieces. **2.** In disagreement; disunited. **3.** Pulled by conflicting interests or activities. **4.** Having the lanes for opposing traffic separated. Said of a highway. **5.** *Botany.* Having indentations extending to the midrib or base and forming distinct divisions: *divided leaves.*

div•i•dend (dĭv′ə-dənd′) *n.* *Abbr.* **div. 1.** *Mathematics.* A quantity to be divided. **2. a.** A pro rata share of net profits distributed to a shareholder in a company. **b.** A share of profits received by a member of a cooperative society or by a policyholder in a mutual insurance society. **c.** A pro rata payment to a creditor of a person adjudged bankrupt. **3.** A benefit; bonus: *Our decision to buy a computer paid handsome dividends.* —See Synonyms at **bonus.** [French, from Latin *dīvidendum,* "thing to be divided," neuter gerundive of *dīvidere,* to DIVIDE.]

di•vid•er (dĭ-vī′dər) *n.* **1. a.** One that divides. **b.** A screen or other partition. **2. dividers.** A device resembling a compass with two points, used for dividing lines and transferring measurements.

div•i•div•i (dĭv′ē-dĭv′ē) *n., pl.* **-is. 1.** A tropical American tree, *Caesalpina coriaria,* having compound leaves and long pods. **2.** The dried pods of this tree, yielding an extract used in tanning leather. [Spanish *dividivi,* from Cariban.]

div•i•na•tion (dĭv′ə-nā′shən) *n.* **1.** The art or act of foretelling events or revealing occult knowledge by means of augury or alleged supernatural agency. **2.** Inspired insight; intuition. **3.** That which has been divined; a prophecy. **—di•vin•a•to•ry** (dĭ-vĭn′ə-tôr′ē, -tōr′ē) *adj.*

di•vine¹ (dĭ-vīn′) *adj.* **-viner, -vinest. 1. a.** Being or having the nature of a deity. **b.** Of, pertaining to, emanating from, or being the expression of a deity. **c.** In the service or worship of a deity or god; sacred; holy. **2.** Superhuman; godlike. **3.** Supremely good; magnificent. **4.** *Informal.* Heavenly; perfect.
~*n.* A clergyman, religious, or priest, especially one knowledgeable in theology. [Middle English, from Old French *devin,* from Latin *dīvīnus,* from *dīvus,* divine, god.] **—di•vine•ly** *adv.* **—di•vine•ness** *n.*

divine² *v.* **-vined, -vining, -vines.** —*tr.* **1.** To know, foresee, predict, or come to conjecture, as by inspiration, intuition, or reflection. **2.** To locate (water, minerals, or the like) with a divining rod or pendulum.
~*intr.* **1.** To practice divination. **2.** To guess. —See Synonyms at **foretell.** [Middle English *divinen,* from Old French *deviner,* from Latin *dīvīnāre,* from *dīvīnus,* soothsayer, "(one) inspired by the gods," DIVINE (adjective).] **—di•vin•er** *n.*

Divine Liturgy *n.* The Eastern Orthodox Eucharistic ceremony.

Divine Office *n.* *Roman Catholic Church.* The prayers and readings for the daily canonical hours; the offices and prayers in the breviary.

divine right *n.* **1.** The right of a monarch to rule, supposed to have come directly from God and to be independent of the will or consent of his subjects. Also called "divine right of kings." **2.** *Informal.* Any right or claim regarded by its holder as incontestable.

Divine Service *n.* A public service in a Christian church for the worship of God.

PRONUNCIATION KEY

ă, pat; ā, pay; âr, care;
ä, father, are; b, bib;
ch, church; d, deed; ĕ, pet;
ē, be; f, fife; g, gag; h, hat;
hw, which; ĭ, pit; ī, pie;
îr, pier; j, judge; k, kick;
l, lid, needle; m, mum;
n, no, sudden; ng, thing;
ŏ, pot; ō, toe; ô, paw, for;
oi, noise; ou, out; ŏŏ, book;
ōō, boot; p, pop; r, roar;
s, sauce; sh, ship, dish;
t, tight; th, thin, path;
th, this, bathe; ŭ, cut; ûr, fur;
v, valve; w, with; y, yes;
z, zebra, size; zh, vision;
ə, about, item, edible,
gallop, circus, peaceful

IN FOREIGN WORDS:

à, *Fr.* ami; œ, *Fr.* feu, *Ger.* schön; ü, *Fr.* tu, *Ger.* über; KH, *Ger.* ich, *Scot.* loch; N, *Fr.* bon; y′, *Fr.* Compiègne

STRESS MARKS:

Primary stress: ′
in•cite′ (ĭn-sīt′)
Secondary stress: ′
in′sight′ (ĭn′sīt′)

diving beetle *n.* Any of various predatory aquatic beetles of the family Dytiscidae, having streamlined bodies and flattened hind legs.

diving bell *n.* A large vessel for underwater work, open on the bottom and supplied with air under pressure.

diving board *n.* A flexible board or platform from which a dive may be executed, secured at one end and projecting over water at the other. Also called "springboard."

diving duck *n.* Any duck that dives to the bottom of a river or lake to feed. Diving ducks include the pochard, scaup, and goldeneye. Compare **dabbler.**

diving suit *n.* A heavy waterproof suit with a large detachable helmet supplied with air, used for underwater work.

divining rod *n.* A forked branch or stick that allegedly indicates subterranean water or minerals by bending downward when held over a source. Also called "dowsing rod."

di·vin·i·ty (dǐ-vǐn′ə-tē) *n., pl.* **-ties. 1.** The state or quality of being divine; especially, the state of being a deity. **2. a.** Divinity. God; the godhead. **b.** A god or goddess; a deity. **3.** Theology.

di·vis·i·ble (dǐ-vǐz′ə-bəl) *adj.* Capable of being divided, especially of being divided evenly with no remainder. —**di·vis·i·bil·i·ty** *n.* —**di·vis·i·bly** *adv.*

di·vi·sion (dǐ-vǐzh′ən) *n. Abbr.* **div. 1. a.** The act or process of dividing. **b.** The state of being divided. **2.** The act or process of sharing out; distribution. **3.** Something that serves to divide or keep separate, such as a boundary or partition. **4.** One of the parts, sections, or groups into which something is divided. **5. a.** An area of governmental, judicial, or business activity organized as an administrative or functional unit. **b.** A territorial section marked off, as for political, governmental, or policing purposes. **6.** *Military.* **a.** The major autonomous administrative and tactical unit of an army that is larger than a regiment but smaller than a corps. It is the smallest self-contained unit of an army that can engage independently in prolonged combat. **b.** A corresponding unit in any of the other armed forces. **7.** *Botany.* A major taxonomic category corresponding approximately to a phylum. **8. a.** Variance of opinion; disagreement. **b.** A splitting into factions; disunion. **9.** *British.* The physical separation of members of Parliament into groups according to their stand on an issue put to vote. Also used adjectivally: *the division bell.* **10.** *Mathematics.* The operation of determining how many times one quantity is contained in another. Compare **multiplication. 11.** A type of plant propagation in which a part separated from the parent grows into a new plant. **12.** *Sports.* Any of various competitive categories in a particular sport, organized according to age, ability, sex, or the like. [Middle English *divisioun,* from Old French *division,* from Latin *dīvīsiō* (stem *dīvīsiōn-*), from *dīvidere* (past participle *dīvīsus*), to DIVIDE.] —**di·vi·sion·al** *adj.*

di·vi·sion·ism (dǐ-vǐzh′ə-nǐz′əm) *n.* A branch of neo-impressionism in which colors are divided into their primary components and arranged in dabs so that the eye organizes the shape. Compare **pointillism.** —**di·vi·sion·ist** *n. & adj.*

division lobby *n. Chiefly British.* See **lobby** (sense 3).

division sign *n.* The symbol (÷) placed between two quantities to indicate the division of the first by the second.

di·vi·sive (dǐ-vī′sǐv) *adj.* Creating discord or dissension. —**di·vi·sive·ly** *adv.* —**di·vi·sive·ness** *n.*

di·vi·sor (dǐ-vī′zər) *n. Abbr.* **div. 1.** The quantity by which another quantity, the dividend, is to be divided. **2.** A number that divides another number exactly; a factor.

di·vorce (dǐ-vôrs′, -vōrs′) *n.* **1. a.** The dissolution of a marriage by the legal judgment of a court, or in some societies, by established custom. **b.** The legal declaration of such a dissolution. **2.** A complete or radical separation of things formerly closely connected. ~*v.* **divorced, -vorcing, -vorces.** —*tr.* **1.** To dissolve the marriage bond between. **2.** To end one's marriage to (one's spouse) by legal divorce. **3.** To separate or detach; disunite. —*intr.* To become divorced. —See Synonyms at **separate.** [Middle English, from Old French, from Latin *dīvortium,* separation, divorce, fork in a road, from *dīvortere, dīvertere,* to turn aside, separate, DIVERT.]

di·vor·cé (dǐ-vôr-sā′, -sē′, -vôr′sā, -sē′, -vōr′-) *n.* A divorced man. [French, masculine past participle of *divorcer,* to divorce, from Old French.]

di·vor·cée (dǐ-vôr-sā′, -sē′, -vōr-, -vôr′sā′, -sē′, -vōr′-) *n.* A divorced woman. [French, "divorced."]

di·vorce·ment (dǐ-vôrs′mənt, -vōrs′-) *n.* A complete separation of things.

div·ot (dǐv′ət) *n.* **1.** A piece of turf torn up by a golf club in striking a ball, or by a horse's hoof. **2.** *Scottish.* A thin square of turf or sod, used especially for roofing. [Scottish *deva(i)t, dewot, duvat†.*]

di·vulge (dǐ-vŭlj′) *tr.v.* **-vulged, -vulging, -vulges. 1.** To disclose (something previously kept secret); reveal; make known. **2.** *Archaic.* To proclaim publicly. —See Synonyms at **reveal.** [Middle English *divulgen,* from Latin *dīvulgāre,* to spread abroad among the people : *dis-,* abroad + *vulgāre,* to make common, publish, from *vulgus,* multitude, public. See **vulgar.**] —**di·vul·gence, di·vulge·ment** *n.* —**di·vulg·er** *n.*

di·vul·sion (dǐ-vŭl′shən) *n.* A tearing apart; a violent separation. [Latin *divulsiō* (stem *divulsiōn-*), from *dīvellere* (past participle *dīvulsus*), to tear apart : *dis-,* apart + *vellere,* to tear, pluck.] —**di·vul·sive** *adj.*

div·vy (dǐv′ē) *n., pl.* **-vies.** *Informal.* A share or portion. ~*tr.v.* **divvied, -vying, -vies.** *Informal.* To divide. Usually used with *up.* [Short for DIVIDEND.]

diwan. 1. Variant of **dewan. 2.** Variant of **divan.**

Dix (dǐks), **Dorothea Lynde** (1802–87). U.S. social reformer. She was a pioneer in the movement for specialized treatment for the insane. Her work in Massachusetts and elsewhere led to the founding of government hospitals for the insane in many states.

Dix·ie (dǐk′sē). The Southern states of the United States that joined the Confederacy during the Civil War. Also called "Dixie Land." [Perhaps from *dixie,* a 10-dollar bill issued by a New Orleans bank prior to the Civil War, with a large *Dix* printed on each side, from French *dix,* ten.]

Dix·ie·land (dǐk′sē-lǎnd′) *n.* A style of instrumental jazz based on the traditional New Orleans style of jazz with a relatively fast, strongly accented two-beat rhythm and group improvisation, but having a more regular melodic structure.

di·zen (dī′zən, dǐz′ən) *tr.v.* **-ened, -ening, -ens.** *Archaic.* To deck out, especially vulgarly, in fine clothes or adornments; bedizen. [Earlier *disen,* to dress a distaff with flax, perhaps from Low German *dise†,* bunch of flax on a distaff.] —**di·zen·ment** *n.*

di·zy·got·ic (dī′zī-gŏt′ĭk) *adj.* Derived from two separate and separately fertilized ova. Said especially of fraternal twins.

diz·zy (dǐz′ē) *adj.* **-zier, -ziest. 1.** Having a sensation of whirling or feeling a tendency to fall; giddy. **2.** Bewildered or confused. **3. a.** Producing or tending to produce giddiness or a whirling sensation: *the dizzy heights of success.* **b.** Characterized by giddiness; reeling: *a dizzy spell.* **4.** *Informal.* Scatterbrained; silly; foolish. ~*tr.v.* **dizzied, -zying, -zies.** To make dizzy; confuse; bewilder. [Middle English *dusie,* foolish, giddy, from Old English *dysig,* foolish, stupid.] —**diz·zi·ly** *adv.* —**diz·zi·ness** *n.*

DJ *n., pl.* **DJ's** or **DJs.** A disc jockey *(see).*

Djakarta. See **Jakarta.**

djellaba. Variant of **jellaba.**

Dji·bou·ti or **Ji·bu·ti** (jĭ-bōō′tē). Formerly (1967–77) **French Territory of the A·fars and Is·sas** (ə-färs′; ĭ′səs). Small, arid country on the northeast coast of Africa, on the Gulf of Aden. The population, mostly Muslim, is concentrated in the port of Djibouti, which was developed by the French when the area became the colony of French Somaliland in 1888. It became independent in 1977. Area, 22,000 square kilometers (8,492 square miles). Population, 400,000. Capital, Djibouti. See map at **Ethiopia.**

Dji·las (jĭl′əs), **Milovan** (1911–). Yugoslav politician and writer. He was a member of Tito's resistance group in World War II and served in the postwar Communist government, but was demoted for criticizing the regime. His writings include *The New Class* (1957), *Land Without Justice* (1958), and *Conversations with Stalin* (1962).

djinni, djinny. Variants of **jinni.**

Djokjakarta. See **Jogjakarta.**

dk. 1. dark. **2.** deck. **3.** dock.

dl deciliter.

D/L demand loan.

D layer *n. Meteorology.* The weakly ionized layer of the ionosphere, approximately 50 to 90 kilometers (30 to 55 miles) above the earth. Also called "D region."

D line *n. Physics.* One of two closely spaced lines in the yellow region of the spectrum of sodium, used as a standard for optical measurement. The lines occur at wavelengths of 589.6 and 589.0 nanometers.

D.Lit., D.Litt. Doctor of Letters; Doctor of Literature. [Latin *Doctor Lit(t)erarum.*]

dm decimeter.

DM 1. *Chemistry.* adamsite. **2.** Deutsche mark.

DMA *Computer Science.* direct memory access.

DMSO dimethylsulfoxide.

D. Mus. Doctor of Music.

DMZ demilitarized zone.

dn. down.

DNA *n.* Deoxyribonucleic acid, a nucleic acid that is the chief constituent of chromosomes, can replicate itself, and is responsible for transmitting genetic information, in the form of genes, from parents to offspring. It consists of a double helix of two long chains of linked **nucleotides** *(see),* connected to each other by hydrogen bonds between the bases adenine and thymine or cytosine and guanine.

DNB Dictionary of National Biography.

Dnie·per (nē′pər). *Russian* **Dne·pr** (dnyĕ′pər). River in west-central Russia, Belarus, and Ukraine. It flows from the Valdai Hills 2,286 kilometers (1,420 miles) to the Black Sea and is the third-longest river in Europe. Kiev is the biggest city on its banks. The river is an important source of hydroelectric power.

Dnie·ster (nēs′tər). River in Ukraine and Moldova. It flows in a winding course 1,411 kilometers (877 miles) from the Carpathian Mts. to the Black Sea near Odessa.

do¹ (dōō) *v.* **did** (dǐd), **done** (dŭn), **doing, does** (dŭz). Present tense, first person, do; second person, **do** or (for singular) *archaic* **doest** (dōō′əst), **dost** (dŭst); third person singular, **does** or *archaic* **doeth** (dōō′əth), **doth** (dŭth); third person plural, **do.** Used as an auxiliary in the past or present tense followed by the infinitive without *to,* or, in reply to a question or suggestion, with this infinitive understood. Its function can be: **1.** To indicate the tense of the infinitive in questions, negative statements, and inverted phrases: *Do you understand? I did not sleep well. Little did she suspect.* **2.** To intensify or emphasize: *Do be still!* **3.** To represent an antecedent verb and thus avoid its repetition: *She tries as hard as they do. Jane arrived late, and so did I.* **4.** To serve as an extra word, in verse or poetic prose,

which improves the sound but does not change the sense of a line, or to express certain nuances of irony or humor: *Well, I do declare.* —*tr.* **1.** To perform or execute (an action, procedure, or piece of work): *She did the driving. Have you done your homework?* **2.** To carry out; fulfill what is involved in: *We did all that was necessary.* **3.** To produce or make (a piece or amount of work): *did a portrait.* In this sense, often used in place of verbs such as *write, paint,* or *compose.* **4. a.** To bring about; achieve: *It won't do any good.* **b.** To effect (an improvement): *That hat doesn't do anything for her.* **5.** To attend to; deal with, or treat in an appropriate way: *do the dinner dishes; I must get the car done.* In this sense, often used in place of a wide variety of common verbs. **6.** To render or give: *do justice to her abilities.* **7.** To work at as an occupation or study. **8.** To work out the details of; solve: *do a crossword puzzle.* **9.** To present (a play or dramatic reading, for example); perform; stage. **10.** To have the role of; play. **11. a.** To travel over (a specified distance): *do a mile in four minutes; do 40 miles to the gallon.* **b.** To travel at or be capable of attaining (a specified speed). **12.** To travel about; visit; tour: *do Europe in five weeks.* **13.** To meet the needs of sufficiently; be suitable or convenient for; suffice: *This room will do us very nicely.* **14.** To groom or beautify (the hair, for example). **15.** To translate: *Homer's Iliad, done into English verse.* **16.** *Informal.* To serve (a term of imprisonment). **17.** *Informal.* **a.** To imitate; mimic. **b.** To behave in a manner that is characteristic of: *did a Houdini and escaped through the bars.* **18.** *Slang.* To cheat or swindle: *do someone out of an inheritance.* —*intr.* **1.** To behave or conduct oneself; act: *Do as you are told. You would do well to leave.* **2.** To act effectively or energetically; strive: *Do or die.* **3.** To get along; fare: *doing well at school.* **4.** To be suitable; serve the purpose: *This coat will do for another season.* **5.** To be sufficient or appropriate in a given situation: *That will do!* **6.** *Informal.* To happen; take place: *Was there anything doing in town yesterday?* —**do away with. 1.** To dispose of; eliminate. **2.** To destroy; kill. —**do by.** To behave with respect to; deal with. —**do for.** *Informal.* To care or provide for; take care of. —**do in.** *Slang.* **1.** To tire completely; exhaust. **2.** To kill. —**do over.** *Informal.* To redecorate. —**do up.** *Informal.* **1.** To groom or adorn lavishly. **2.** To wrap and tie (a package). **3.** To tie up or arrange (the hair) so that it is off the neck. **4.** To fasten; button or zip up. —**do with.** To be glad to have; need or want: *I could do with a drink.* —**do without.** To manage easily without; be able to dispense with. —**have to do with. 1.** To have a relation to or relationship with. **2.** To be concerned with; have as subject matter: *a book having to do with religion.* —**make do.** To manage with whatever one has or whatever is available.
—*n., pl.* **do's** or **dos** (dōōz). **1.** *Informal.* An entertainment; a party. **2.** *Informal.* A hoax or swindle; a cheat. **3.** A statement of what should be done: *do's and don'ts.* **4.** *Archaic.* Duty. Used chiefly in the phrase *to do one's do.* [Do, did, done, dost, does (or doth), didst; Middle English don, did(d)e, idon, dost, does (regularly doth), diddest, Old English dōn, dyde, gedōn, dēst, dēth (plural dōth), dydest, from Germanic; akin to Greek *tithēnai,* to place, Sanskrit *dádhāmi,* to put.]

Usage: The use of *don't* (*She just don't care*) for *doesn't* is nonstandard in both American and British English, but it is an extremely widespread form in regional dialects.

do² (dō) *n. Music.* The first tone of the diatonic scale in solfeggio. [Italian, variant of *du,* perhaps inverted variant of *ut.* See **gamut.**]

do. ditto.

D.O. 1. Doctor of Optometry. **2.** Doctor of Osteopathy.

D.O.A. *Medicine.* dead on arrival.

do·a·ble (dōō'ə-bəl) *adj.* Able to be done.

doat. Variant of **dote.**

dob·bin (dŏb'ĭn) *n.* A horse, especially a workhorse. [From *Dobbin,* alteration of *Robin,* pet form for the name *Robert.*]

Do·bell's solution (dō'bĕlz') *n.* An aqueous solution of sodium borate, sodium bicarbonate, glycerol, and phenol, used as an antibacterial agent for the mucous membranes of the nose and throat. [After Horace B. *Dobell* (1828–1917), British doctor.]

Do·ber·man pin·scher (dō'bər-mən pĭn'shər) *n.* A fairly large dog of a breed originating in Germany, having a smooth, short, usually black coat with rust-red markings and often used for guard or police work. [German *Dobermann,* after Ludwig *Dobermann,* 19th-century German dog breeder + *Pinscher,* terrier, probably from English PINCH (in allusion to its cropped ears and docked tail).]

do·bra (dō'brə) *n.* The basic monetary unit of São Tomé and Príncipe, equal to 100 centimos. See feature at **currency.** [Portuguese, ultimately from Latin *duplus,* double.]

dob·son (dŏb'sən) *n.* The larva of the dobson fly. Usually called "hellgrammite." [Probably from the family name *Dobson.*]

dobson fly *n.* An insect, *Corydalus cornutus,* having four large, many-veined wings and long, pincerlike mandibles. See **hellgrammite.**

doc (dŏk) *n. Informal.* A doctor.

doc. document.

do·cent (dō'sənt, dō-sĕnt') *n.* A teacher or lecturer at certain universities who is not a full faculty member. [Obsolete German *Docent,* from Latin *docēns* (stem *docent-*), present participle of *docēre,* to teach.]

Do·ce·tism (dō-sē'tĭz'əm, dō'sə-tĭz'əm) *n.* The doctrine, espoused by a sect considered heretical in the early Christian Church, that Christ had no human body and only appeared to suffer and die on the cross. [Late Latin *Docētae,* the sect advocating this doctrine, from Late Greek *Dokētai,* from Greek *dokein,* to seem, appear.] —**Do·ce·tic** *adj.* —**Do·ce·tist** *n. & adj.*

do·cile (dŏs'əl, -sīl') *adj.* **1.** Submissive to another's will; easily handled. **2.** Yielding to handling or treatment; easily shaped or formed: "*Metal is so docile that it will submit to any formal conception a sculptor may have*" (Herbert Read). **3.** Capable of being taught; ready and willing to learn. —See Synonyms at **obedient.** [Latin *docilis,* from *docēre,* to teach.] —**doc·ile·ly** *adv.* —**do·cil·i·ty** (dō-sĭl'ə-tē, dō-) *n.*

dock¹ (dŏk) *n. Abbr.* **dk. 1.** The area of water between two piers or alongside a pier that receives a ship for loading, unloading, or repairs. **2.** A pier or wharf. **3.** *Often* **docks.** A group of piers, often enclosed, on a protected basin or other waterway serving as a general landing area for ships or boats. **4.** A platform at which trucks or trains discharge or pick up freight.
—*v.* **docked, docking, docks.** —*tr.* **1.** To maneuver (a vessel) into or next to a dock. **2.** *Aerospace.* To couple (two or more spacecraft, for example) in space. —*intr.* **1.** To move or come into a dock. **2.** To join with another spacecraft while in space. [Middle Low German and Middle Dutch *docke,* probably from Vulgar Latin *ductia* (unattested), conduit, aqueduct, from Latin *dūcere,* to lead.]

dock² *n.* **1.** The solid or bony part of an animal's tail. **2.** The tail of an animal after it has been cut short.
—*tr.v.* **docked, docking, docks. 1.** To cut short or cut off (an animal's tail, for example). **2.** To deduct a part from (someone's salary or wages). **3.** To withhold or cut an amount, as of wages or salary, from. [Middle English *dok,* trimmed hair (of a tail), perhaps Old English *docca* (attested only in *fingerdocca,* finger muscle), from Germanic *dukk-* (unattested), bundle. See also **doxy.**]

dock³ *n.* An enclosed place where the defendant stands or sits in a criminal court. —**in the dock.** On trial or under intense scrutiny. [Flemish *docke, dok†,* cage, pen.]

dock⁴ *n.* Any of various weedy plants of the genus *Rumex,* having large leaves and clusters of small greenish or reddish flowers. [Middle English *dock, docke,* Old English *docce.*]

dock·age (dŏk'ĭj) *n.* **1.** A charge for docking vessels. **2.** Facilities for docking vessels. **3.** The docking of ships.

dock·er¹ (dŏk'ər) *n.* One that docks something, as the tail of an animal.

docker² *n.* A worker at a dock who loads and unloads ships; a longshoreman.

dock·et (dŏk'ĭt) *n.* **1.** A label on or ticket affixed to a package listing the contents or directions for assembling or operating. **2.** *Law.* **a.** A brief record of the proceedings in a court of justice. **b.** The book containing such records. **3. a.** A list of the cases awaiting action in a court. **b.** Any list of things to be done; an agenda. **4.** *Archaic.* A summary or other brief statement of the contents of a document; an abstract.
—*tr.v.* **docketed, -eting, -ets. 1.** To provide with a brief identifying statement. **2.** To enter in a docket. **3.** To label or ticket (a parcel). [Middle English *doggette†.*]

dock·hand (dŏk'hănd') *n.* A dockworker; a longshoreman.

dock·land (dŏk'lănd') *n. British. Often* **docklands.** The district surrounding a city's docks.

dock·work·er (dŏk'wûr'kər) *n.* A longshoreman.

dock·yard (dŏk'yärd') *n.* **1.** An area with facilities for building, repairing, or dry-docking ships. **2.** *British.* A government shipyard; a navy yard.

doc·tor (dŏk'tər) *n.* **1.** *Abbr.* **D.** A person who holds the highest academic degree awarded by a college or university in any specified discipline: *a Doctor of Music.* **2.** *Abbr.* **Dr.** A person qualified to practice medicine; especially, a physician, surgeon, a dentist, or veterinarian. **3.** *Abbr.* **Dr.** The title used in addressing a person who holds the degree of doctor. **4. a.** A Doctor of the Church. **b.** *Obsolete.* Any learned person; a teacher. **5.** A person who repairs things or remedies an undesirable situation. **6.** Any device designed to repair a defect or do a special task. **7.** Any of several brightly colored artificial flies used in fly fishing: *a silver doctor.* —**the Doctor.** Any of several local winds in different parts of the world that mitigate extreme, unhealthy weather conditions, as the harmattan of West Africa.
—*v.* **doctored, -toring, -tors.** *Informal.* —*tr.* **1.** To give medical treatment to. **2.** To repair, especially in a makeshift manner. **3.** To change or falsify (evidence or data) so as to make it favorable to oneself or one's cause. **4.** To add ingredients to (food) either to improve its taste or to make it poisonous. —*intr.* To practice medicine. [Middle English, Church Father, theologian, canonist, medical doctor, scholar, from Old French *docteur,* from Medieval Latin *doctor,* from Latin, teacher, from *docēre,* to teach.]

doc·tor·al (dŏk'tər-əl) *adj.* Of, belonging, or pertaining to an academic doctor: *doctoral robes; a doctoral thesis.*

doc·tor·ate (dŏk'tər-ĭt) *n.* The degree or status of a doctor as conferred by a university.

Doctor of Philosophy *n. Abbr.* **Ph.D., D.Ph., D.Phil.** The highest academic degree granted in most arts and sciences. Compare **Bachelor of Arts, Master of Arts.**

Doctor of the Church *n.* One of the saints recognized by the Church as being especially important in the development of Christian doctrine, traditionally any of the four Doctors of the Western Church, St. Ambrose, St. Augustine, St. Jerome, and St. Gregory, or the four Doctors of the Eastern Church, St. Athanasius, St. Basil, St. Gregory of Nyssa, and St. John Chrysostom.

doc·tri·naire (dŏk'trə-nâr') *adj.* Having or showing an inflexible

dog

DESCENDANTS OF THE WOLF

Bred for work, looks, and company

The 400 or so breeds of domestic dog are each probably descended from the wolf, which was domesticated about 10,000 years ago by the first Neolithic settlers. The dog displayed a propensity for dependence on man and it was this quality, its intelligence, and its sociability that made it suitable for selective breeding. The combinations of characteristics obtained by breeding are valued for sport, work, companionship, or merely decoration.

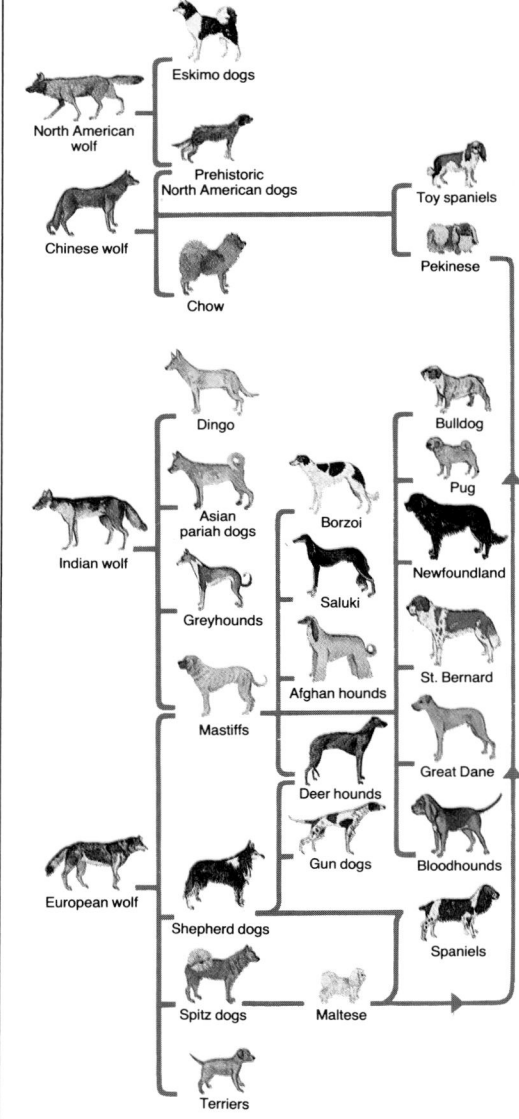

FAMILY TREE *This is only a rough guide to the descent of modern breeds—a great deal of random crossbreeding took place before distinct breeds were established. The dingo may be the only purebred dog in the world today, that is, the only dog directly descended from a single race of wolf. Early man took it from Asia to Australia, where it reverted to the wild.*

---

commitment to a particular theory or principle, and seeking to apply it without regard to practicality or individual circumstances; excessively and impractically dogmatic. —See Synonyms at **dictatorial.**
~*n.* One who adopts a doctrinaire approach; an impractical, dogmatic theorist. —**doc·tri·nair·ism** *n.* —**doc·tri·nar·i·an** *n.*
doc·tri·nal (dŏk′trə-nəl; *British* dŏk-trī′nəl) *adj.* Belonging to, characterized by, or concerning doctrine. —**doc·tri·nal·ly** *adv.*
doc·trine (dŏk′trĭn) *n.* **1.** Something that is taught; a principle or

body of principles taught or advocated in instruction. **2.** A principle or system of principles presented for acceptance or belief, as by a religious, political, scientific, or philosophic group; dogma; received theory. [Middle English, from Old French, from Latin *doctrīna,* teaching, learning, from *doctor,* teacher, DOCTOR.]
doc·u·dra·ma (dŏk′yə-drä′mə, -drăm′ə) *n.* A television or film presentation of political, social, or historical events or circumstances made like a documentary but recreating events in a fictionalized way, as by using actors to portray the protagonists.
doc·u·ment (dŏk′yə-mənt) *n.* **1.** *Abbr.* **doc.** A paper, such as a deed, letter, or report, that gives evidence or information, especially of an official or legal nature. **2.** A record; historical or sociological evidence: *The archaeologists' discoveries are a fascinating document of Viking civilization.* **3.** Anything serving as evidence or proof, as a material substance bearing a revealing symbol or mark.
~*tr.v.* **documented, -menting, -ments. 1.** To furnish with a document or documents. **2.** To support (an assertion or claim, for example) with documentary evidence or decisive information. **3.** To support (statements in a book, for example) with written references or citations; annotate. **4.** To record or provide evidence of. [Middle English, precept, instruction, from Old French, from Latin *documentum,* lesson, example, warning, from *docēre,* to teach.]
doc·u·men·tal·ist (dŏk′yə-mĕn′tl-ĭst′) *n.* A specialist who conserves and studies documents.
doc·u·men·ta·ry (dŏk′yə-mĕn′tə-rē) *adj.* Also **doc·u·men·tal** (-mĕnt′l). **1.** Consisting of, concerning, or based upon documents. **2.** Presenting facts objectively without inserting fictional matter, as in a book, newspaper account, or film.
~*n., pl.* **documentaries.** A television or film presentation of political, social, or historical events or circumstances, often consisting of news film accompanied by narration.
doc·u·men·ta·tion (dŏk′yə-mĕn-tā′shən) *n.* **1.** The supplying of documents or supporting references or records. **2.** The documents or references supplied. **3.** The process or science of gathering, classifying, and storing information.
dod·der¹ (dŏd′ər) *intr.v.* **-dered, -dering, -ders. 1.** To shake or tremble, as from old age; totter. **2.** To progress in a feeble, unsteady manner. [17th century : variant of obsolete *dadder,* Middle English *dadiren,* perhaps from Scandinavian; akin to Norwegian *dudra,* to quiver.]
dod·der² *n.* Any of various parasitic vines of the genus *Cuscuta,* having slender, twining yellow or reddish stems with a few minute, scalelike leaves, and small whitish flowers. [Middle English *doder,* perhaps from Low German; akin to Middle Low German *dod(d)er.*]
dod·dered (dŏd′ərd) *adj.* Lacking the top branches as a result of age or decay. [Alteration of *doddard : dod,* to lop off, Middle English *dodent* + -ARD.]
dod·der·ing (dŏd′ər-ĭng) *adj.* Also **dod·der·y** (dŏd′ər-ē). Feebleminded or unsteady from age; senile.
do·dec·a·gon (dō-dĕk′ə-gŏn′) *n.* A polygon having 12 sides and 12 angles. [Greek *dōdekagōnon : dōdeka, duōdeka,* twelve : *duo,* two + *deka,* ten + -GON.] —**do·de·cag·o·nal** (dō′dĕ-kăg′ə-nəl) *adj.*
do·dec·a·he·dron (dō′dĕk-ə-hē′drən) *n., pl.* **-drons** or **-dra** (-drə). A polyhedron with 12 plane surfaces. A *regular dodecahedron* has faces that are equal regular pentagons. [Greek *dōdekaedron : dōdeka,* twelve (see **dodecagon**) + -HEDRON.] —**do·dec·a·he·dral** *adj.*
Do·dec·a·nese (dō-dĕk′ə-nēs′, -nēz′). *Greek* **Dho·dhe·ká·ni·sos** (thō′thə-kä′nē-sôs′). Group of Greek islands in the southeast Aegean, forming part of the southern Sporades. The name means "12 islands," and there are 12 main ones, including Cos and Rhodes, and several islets. The city of Rhodes is the administrative center, and the islands are noted for tourism and sponge-diving.
do·dec·a·no·ic acid (dō′dĕk-ə-nō′ĭk) *n.* **Lauric acid** *(see).*
do·dec·a·phon·ic (dō′dĕk-ə-fŏn′ĭk) *adj.* Pertaining to, composed in, or consisting of 12-tone music. [Greek *dōdeka,* twelve (see **dodecagon**) + PHONIC.] —**do·dec·a·phon·ist** *n.* —**do·dec·a·phon·ism, do·dec·a·phon·y** (dō-dĕk′ə-fō′nē, dō′də-kăf′ə-nē) *n.*
do·dec·a·syl·la·ble (dō-dĕk′ə-sĭl′ə-bəl) *n.* A metrical line of 12 syllables.
dodge (dŏj) *v.* **dodged, dodging, dodges.** —*tr.* **1.** To avoid (a blow, for example) by moving or shifting quickly aside. **2.** To evade (an obligation or issue, for example) by cunning, trickery, or deceit. —*intr.* **1.** To move aside quickly, as to avoid a blow; shift or twist suddenly. **2.** To practice trickery or cunning; prevaricate.
~*n.* **1.** An act of dodging; a quick move or shift. **2.** A clever or evasive plan or device; stratagem. **3.** An ingenious method of doing something; shortcut. —See Synonyms at **artifice.** [16th century : origin obscure.]
Dodge (dŏj), **Mary Elizabeth Mapes** (1831–1905). U.S. author and editor. She is best known for her book *Hans Brinker, or the Silver Skates* (1865). As editor of *St. Nicholas Magazine* (1873–1905), she was an important influence on children's literature.
dodge ball *n.* A game in which the players stand in a circle and try to hit another player or players inside the circle with a large ball.
Dodge City. City of southwestern Kansas, on the Arkansas River. Laid out in 1872 on the old Santa Fe Trail, it soon became a wild and rowdy cow town. Wyatt Earp and Bat Masterson were among its famous residents. Boot Hill, an early cowboy burial ground, is a popular tourist attraction.
dodg·er (dŏj′ər) *n.* **1.** A person who dodges or evades. **2.** A shifty or dishonest person; a cheat; trickster. **3.** A shelter on the bridge of a ship providing protection against rain and sea-spray. **4.** *British Re-*

gional. Food. **5.** A small printed handbill. **6.** *Southern U.S.* A corn-dodger.

Dodg·son (dŏj′sən), **Charles Lutwidge,** known as "Lewis Carroll" (1832–98). English author of *Alice's Adventures in Wonderland* (1865) and *Through the Looking-Glass and What Alice Found There* (1872). A leading mathematician, he was ordained a deacon in the Church of England (1861) and was a pioneering portrait photographer. The Alice stories were written to amuse Alice Liddell, the daughter of the dean of Christ Church, Oxford. His other works include the nonsense poem *The Hunting of the Snark* (1876).

dodg·y (dŏj′ē) *adj.* **-ier, -iest.** *Chiefly British Informal.* **1.** Risky or dangerous. **2.** Unreliable; deceitful. **3.** Not in good health or condition; likely to give way under stress.

do·do (dō′dō) *n., pl.* **-does** or **-dos. 1.** A large flightless bird, *Raphus cucullatus,* of the island of Mauritius in the Indian Ocean, that has been extinct since the late 17th century. **2.** *Informal.* One whose ideas, dress, or manner of living are hopelessly out-of-date. [Portuguese *doudo,* from *doudo*†, stupid (from its clumsy appearance).]

Do·do·ma (dō-dō′mä). Capital of Tanzania since 1975. It is in the center of the country, and transfer of the government secretariat from the old capital, Dar es Salaam, was completed in 1983.

doe (dō) *n., pl.* **does** or **doe. 1.** The female of a deer or related animal. **2.** The female of certain other animals, such as the hare or kangaroo. [Middle English *do,* Old English *dā*†.]

Doenitz, Karl. See **Dönitz.**

do·er (do͞o′ər) *n.* **1.** A person who does something. **2.** A particularly active and energetic person who is able to achieve things.

does. Present tense, third person singular of **do.**

doe·skin (dō′skĭn′) *n.* **1.** The skin of a doe, deer, or goat. **2.** Leather made from this. **3.** A fine, soft, smooth woolen fabric.

does·n't (dŭz′ənt). Contraction of *does not.* —See Usage note at **do.**

do·est. *Archaic.* Second person singular, present tense of **do.** Used with *thou.*

do·eth. *Archaic.* Third person singular, present tense of **do.**

doff (dôf, dŏf) *tr.v.* **doffed, doffing, doffs. 1.** To remove or take off: *doff one's clothes.* **2.** To lift or remove (one's hat) in salutation. **3.** To throw out or away; discard. [Middle English *doffen,* from *don off* : *don,* to DO + OFF.]

dog (dôg, dŏg) *n.* **1.** A domesticated carnivorous mammal, *Canis familiaris,* developed in a wide variety of breeds and probably originally derived from several wild species. **2.** Any of various other animals of the family Canidae, such as the dingo. **3.** A male canine animal, especially of a domesticated breed or of the fox. **4.** Any of various other animals, such as the prairie dog. **5. a.** *Informal.* A fellow: *you lucky dog.* **b.** A contemptible, worthless fellow. **c.** *Informal.* A dashing fellow; a playboy. **6.** *Slang.* **a.** An uninteresting or unattractive person. **b.** A hopelessly inferior product or creation. **7. dogs.** *Informal.* Greyhound races. Preceded by *the.* **8. dogs.** *Slang.* The feet. **9.** A firedog; an andiron. **10. a.** Any of various hooked or U-shaped mechanical devices used for gripping or holding heavy objects. **b.** A pawl or other device engaging a gear or ratchet wheel. **11.** *Astronomy.* A **sun dog** *(see).* **—go to the dogs.** *Informal.* To go to ruin; degenerate. **—put on the dog.** *Informal.* To make an ostentatious display of elegance, wealth, or culture; feign refinement.

~adj. Inferior; not genuine: *dog Latin.*

~adv. Totally; completely. Used in combination: *dog-tired.*

~tr.v. **dogged, dogging, dogs. 1. a.** To follow after like a dog; pursue relentlessly. **b.** To trouble persistently; hound. **2.** To hold or fasten with a mechanical dog. [Middle English *dog, dogge,* Old English *docga*†.]

dog·bane (dôg′bān′, dŏg′-) *n.* Any of several plants of the genus *Apocynum,* mostly of tropical or subtropical regions, having bell-shaped white or pink flowers. [Said to be poisonous to dogs.]

dog·ber·ry (dôg′bĕr′ē, dŏg′-) *n., pl.* **-ries. 1.** A wild gooseberry, *Ribes cynosbati,* of eastern North America, bearing large, prickly berries. **2.** Any of several other plants or shrubs bearing berrylike fruit. **3.** The fruit of any of these plants.

dog·cart (dôg′kärt′, dŏg′-) *n.* **1.** A vehicle drawn by one horse and accommodating two persons seated back to back. **2.** A small cart pulled by dogs.

dog·catch·er (dôg′kăch′ər, dŏg′-) *n.* One appointed or elected to impound stray dogs.

dog collar *n.* **1.** A collar for a dog. **2.** *Informal.* A clerical collar. **3.** See **choker** (sense 2a).

dog days *pl.n.* **1.** In the Northern Hemisphere, the hot, sultry period between mid-July and September. **2.** A period of inactivity. [Translation of Late Latin *diēs canīculārēs,* "Dog Star days" (so called because Sirius rises and sets with the sun during this time).]

doge (dōj) *n.* The elected chief magistrate of the former republics of Venice and Genoa. [French, from Italian (Venetian dialect), from Latin *dux,* leader, from *dūcere,* to lead.]

dog-ear (dôg′îr′, dŏg′-) *n.* Also **dog's-ear** (dôgz′îr′, dŏgz′-). A turned-down corner of the page of a book. **—dog-ear** *tr.v.*

dog-eared (dôg′îrd′, dŏg′-) *adj.* **1.** Having pages with the corners turned down. Said of a book. **2.** Worn from overuse.

dog-eat-dog (dôg′ēt-dôg′, dŏg′ēt-dŏg′) *adj.* Ruthlessly competitive or acquisitive: *a dog-eat-dog society.*

dog·face (dôg′fās′, dŏg′-) *n.* *Slang.* An infantryman in the U.S. Army in World War II.

dog fennel *n.* **1.** Any of various strong-smelling plants of the genus *Anthemis,* such as the **stinking mayweed** *(see).* **2.** A weedy plant, *Eupatorium capillifolium,* of the southeastern United States, having divided leaves and long clusters of greenish flowers.

dog·fight (dôg′fīt′, dŏg′-) *n.* **1.** A violent fight between or as if between dogs; a brawl. **2.** An aerial battle, especially between fighter planes.

dog·fish (dôg′fĭsh′, dŏg′-) *n., pl.* **-fishes** or collectively **dogfish. 1.** Any of various small sharks, chiefly of the families Scyliorhinidae (*spotted dogfish*), Squalidae (*spiny dogfish*), and Triakidae (*smooth dogfish,* or *smooth hounds*). **2.** The **bowfin** *(see).*

dog·ged (dô′gĭd, dŏg′ĭd) *adj.* Not yielding readily; tenacious; stubborn and persistent: *dogged self-assertion.* See Synonyms at **obstinate. —dog·ged·ly** *adv.* **—dog·ged·ness** *n.*

dog·ger·el (dô′gər-əl, dŏg′ər-) *n.* Verse of a loose, irregular rhythm or of a trivial nature and poor quality. **—dog·ger·el** *adj.* [Middle English *dogerel,* poor, worthless, perhaps from *dogge,* DOG.]

dog·ger·y (dô′gə-rē, dŏg′ə-) *n., pl.* **-ies. 1.** Surly behavior; meanness. **2.** Undesirable elements; riffraff. **3.** A cheap bar or saloon.

dog·gish (dô′gĭsh, dŏg′ĭsh) *adj.* **1.** Pertaining to or suggestive of a dog. **2.** Surly. **3.** *Informal.* Showily stylish. **—dog·gish·ly** *adv.*

dog·go (dô′gō, dŏg′ō) *adv.* *Slang.* Quiet and out of sight. Used chiefly in the phrase *lie doggo.* [Probably from DOG.]

dog·gone (dôg′gŏn′, -gôn′, dŏg′-) *adj.* Damn. Used euphemistically. [Euphemistic for *God damn (it).*] **—dog·gone** *interj.*

dog·gy, dog·gie (dô′gē, dŏg′ē) *n., pl.* **-gies.** A dog, especially a small one.

~adj. **doggier, -giest. 1.** Of or like a dog. **2.** Liking and caring for dogs.

doggy bag, doggie bag *n.* *Informal.* A bag for leftover food that a diner in a restaurant may take home. [As if saving it for a pet.]

dog·house (dôg′hous′, dŏg′-) *n.* A small house or shelter for a dog. **—in the doghouse.** *Slang.* In disfavor; in trouble.

do·gie (dō′gē) *n.* Also **do·gy,** *pl.* **-gies.** *Western U.S.* A motherless or stray calf. [19th century : origin obscure.]

dog in the manger *n.* One who prevents others from enjoying what he himself has no use for. [From a fable of Aesop.]

dog·leg (dôg′lĕg′, dŏg′-) *n.* Something that has a sharp bend; especially, a golf hole in which the fairway is abruptly angled.

~intr.v. **-legged, -legging, -legs.** To move along a dogleg course: *The fairway doglegs to the left.* **—dog·leg·ged** (dôg′lĕg′ĭd, -lĕgd′, dŏg′-) *adj.*

dog·ma (dôg′mə, dŏg′-) *n., pl.* **-mas** or **-mata** (-mə-tə). **1.** *Theology.* A doctrine or system of doctrines proclaimed true by a religious sect: *Christian dogma.* **2.** A principle, belief, or statement of an idea or opinion, especially one that is authoritatively, sometimes arrogantly, asserted as absolute truth: *party dogma.* **3.** A system of such principles or beliefs. [Latin, from Greek, opinion, belief, public decree, from *dokein,* to seem, think.]

dog·mat·ic (dôg-măt′ĭk, dŏg-) *adj.* Also **dog·mat·i·cal** (-ĭ-kəl). **1.** Pertaining to or characteristic of dogma. **2.** Characterized by an authoritative, arrogant assertion of unproved or unprovable principles. —See Synonyms at **dictatorial.** [Late Latin *dogmaticus,* from Greek *dogmatikos,* from *dogma* (stem *dogmat-*), DOGMA.] **—dog·mat·i·cal·ly** *adv.*

dog·mat·ics (dôg-măt′ĭks, dŏg-) *n.* *Used with a singular verb.* The study of religious dogmas, especially those of the Christian church. Also called "dogmatic theology."

dog·ma·tism (dôg′mə-tĭz′əm, dŏg′-) *n.* Dogmatic assertion of opinion or belief.

dog·ma·tist (dôg′mə-tĭst, dŏg′-) *n.* **1.** An arrogantly assertive person. **2.** One who expresses or sets forth dogma.

dog·ma·tize (dôg′mə-tīz′, dŏg′-) *v.* **-tized, -tizing, -tizes.** *—intr.* To express oneself dogmatically in writing or speech. *—tr.* To proclaim as dogma. **—dog·ma·ti·za·tion** *n.*

dog·nap (dôg′năp′, dŏg′-) *tr.v.* **-napped, -napping, -naps** or **-naped, -naping, -naps.** To steal (a dog), especially in order to sell it to a research laboratory. [DOG + KID(NAP).] **—dog·nap·per** *n.*

do-good·er (do͞o′go͝od′ər) *n.* *Informal.* A person who does charitable work or supports good causes, often considered as naively idealistic or unrealistic. **—do-good·ism** *n.*

dog paddle, doggy paddle *n.* A stroke in which the swimmer's arms are bent in front of him and paddle (as a dog's forepaws do in swimming), while the legs kick vigorously in alternation.

dog rose *n.* A prickly wild rose, *Rosa canina,* native to Europe and Asia, having scentless pink or white flowers.

dog's age *n.* *Informal.* A long time.

dogs·bod·y (dôgz′bŏd′ē, dŏgz′-) *n., pl.* **-ies.** *Chiefly British Slang.* A person who is required to perform dreary tasks that others consider beneath them: *a general dogsbody.* [Originally naval slang, midshipman, from *dog's body,* slang for *pease pudding.*]

dog's-ear. Variant of **dog-ear.**

dog·sled (dôg′slĕd′, dŏg′-) *n.* A sled pulled by dogs.

dog's life *n.* *Informal.* An unhappy, slavish existence.

dog's mercury *n.* An ill-smelling Eurasian weed, *Mercurialis perennis,* having small greenish flowers and creeping rhizomes.

dog's-tail (dôgz′tāl′, dŏgz′-) *n.* Any grass of the genus *Cynosurus,* native to Europe; especially, *C. cristatus,* having spikelets in a densely crowded, narrow cluster.

Dog Star *n.* **1.** The star **Sirius** *(see).* **2.** The star **Procyon** *(see).*

dog's tongue (dôgz′tŭng′, dŏgz′-) *n.* A plant, **hound's-tongue** *(see).*

dog tag *n.* **1.** A metal identification disk attached to a dog's collar. **2.** An identification tag worn by soldiers in duplicate on a chain around the neck.

dog-tired (dôg′tīrd′, dŏg′-) *adj.* Extremely tired; exhausted.

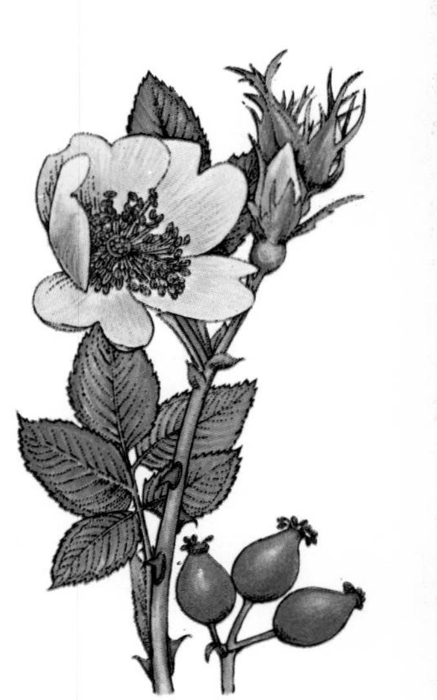

dog rose *This wild ancestor of the garden rose was the symbol of Tudor kings of England. But it is thought to get its name from an ancient Greek belief that it would cure a person who had been bitten by a mad dog.*

PRONUNCIATION KEY

ă, pat; ā, pay; âr, care;
ä, father, are; b, bib;
ch, church; d, deed; ĕ, pet;
ē, be; f, fife; g, gag; h, hat;
hw, which; ĭ, pit; ī, pie;
îr, pier; j, judge; k, kick;
l, lid, needle; m, mum;
n, no, sudden; ng, thing;
ŏ, pot; ō, toe; ô, paw, for;
oi, noise; ou, out; o͝o, book;
o͞o, boot; p, pop; r, roar;
s, sauce; sh, ship, dish;
t, tight; th, thin, path;
th, this, bathe; ŭ, cut; ûr, fur;
v, valve; w, with; y, yes;
z, zebra, size; zh, vision;
ə, about, item, edible,
gallop, circus, peaceful

IN FOREIGN WORDS:

à, *Fr.* ami; œ, *Fr.* feu, *Ger.* schön; ü, *Fr.* tu, *Ger.* über; KH, *Ger.* ich, *Scot.* loch; N, *Fr.* bon; y′, *Fr.* Compiègne

STRESS MARKS:

Primary stress: ′
in·cite′ (ĭn-sīt′)
Secondary stress: ′
in′sight′ (ĭn′sīt′)

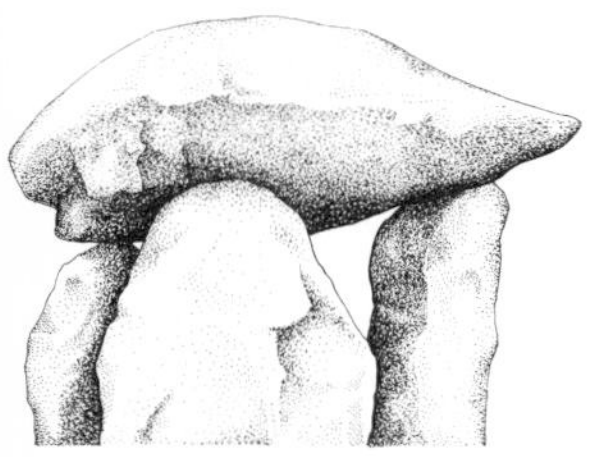

dolmen *Originally, these Neolithic burial chambers—formed by a ring of upright stones, topped by a capstone—were covered with earth. But many have been bared by erosion.*

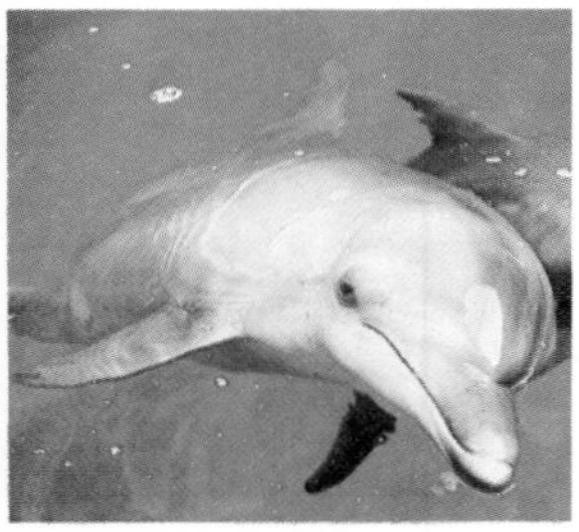

dolphin *A small whale with a beaklike snout, the dolphin has the largest brain relative to its size of any animal after man. The common dolphin,* Delphinus delphis *(above), lives in temperate and tropical seas and can swim at nearly 50 kilometers (30 miles) per hour.*

PRONUNCIATION KEY

ă, pat; ā, pay; âr, care;
ä, father, are; b, bib;
ch, church; d, deed; ĕ, pet;
ē, be; f, fife; g, gag; h, hat;
hw, which; ĭ, pit; ī, pie;
îr, pier; j, judge; k, kick;
l, lid, needle; m, mum;
n, no, sudden; ng, thing;
ŏ, pot; ō, toe; ô, paw, for;
oi, noise; ou, out; o͝o, book;
o͞o, boot; p, pop; r, roar;
s, sauce; sh, ship, dish;
t, tight; th, thin, path;
th, this, bathe; ŭ, cut; ûr, fur;
v, valve; w, with; y, yes;
z, zebra, size; zh, vision;
ə, about, item, edible, gallop, circus, peaceful

IN FOREIGN WORDS:

à, *Fr.* ami; œ, *Fr.* feu, *Ger.* schön; ü, *Fr.* tu, *Ger.* über; KH, *Ger.* ich, *Scot.* loch; N, *Fr.* bon; y', *Fr.* Compiègne

STRESS MARKS:

Primary stress: ′
in·cite′ (ĭn-sīt′)
Secondary stress: ′
in′sight′ (ĭn′sīt′)

dog·tooth (dôg′to͞oth′, dŏg′-) *n., pl.* **teeth** (-tēth). Also **dog tooth** (for sense 1). **1.** A canine tooth; an eyetooth. **2.** *Architecture.* A medieval architectural ornament consisting of four leaflike projections radiating from a raised center.
dogtooth check, dog's-tooth check *n.* **Hound's-tooth check** *(see).*
dogtooth violet *n.* Any of several plants of the genus *Erythronium,* especially *E. americanum,* of North America, having leaves with reddish blotches and nodding, lilylike yellow or purple flowers and sometimes grown as garden ornamentals. Also called "adder's-tongue," "trout lily."
dog·trot (dôg′trŏt′, dŏg′-) *n.* A steady trot like that of a dog.
dog violet *n.* A Eurasian violet, *Viola canina,* having blue-and-yellow flowers.
dog·watch (dôg′wŏch′, dŏg′-) *n. Nautical.* Either of two short periods of watch duty, from 4 to 6 p.m. or from 6 to 8 p.m.
dog·wood (dôg′wo͝od′, dŏg′-) *n.* **1.** A tree, *Cornus florida,* of eastern North America, having small greenish flowers surrounded by showy white or sometimes pink bracts that resemble petals. Also called "flowering dogwood." **2.** Any of various shrubs of the genus *Cornus,* such as the European dogwood, *C. sanguinea,* which has red stems, white flowers, and black berries.
Do·ha (dō′hə, -hä). Capital of Qatar. Since 1949 oil revenues have converted it from a tiny fishing village to a large city.
doi·ly, doy·ly (doi′lē) *n., pl.* **-lies.** Also **doy·ley,** *pl.* **-leys.** A small ornamental mat made of lace, linen, paper, or other material and used on plates or to protect or adorn furniture. [After *Doyly* or *Doily,* a London draper, *c.* 1712.]
do·ing (do͞o′ĭng) *n.* **1.** The act of performing something: *a job not worth the doing.* **2.** Events or activities, especially of a social nature.
do-it-your·self (do͞o′ĭt-yər-sĕlf′) *adj. Informal.* Of, relating to, or designed to be done by an amateur or as a hobby: *do-it-yourself home repairs; a do-it-yourself stereo kit.* **—do-it-your·self·er** *n.*
do·jo (dō′jō) *n.* A school for training in Japanese arts of self-defense, such as judo and karate. [Japanese : *do,* art + *-jo,* ground.]
dol (dŏl) *n.* A unit used to measure pain, or by inference analgesia, based on application of heat to the skin. See **dolorimetry.** [Latin *dolor,* pain, DOLOR.]
dol. **1.** *Music.* dolce. **2.** dollar.
do·lab·ri·form (dō-lăb′rə-fôrm′) *adj.* Also **do·lab·rate** (-rāt′). *Biology.* Having the shape of the head of an ax. [Latin *dolābra,* pickax, from *dolāre,* to hew + -FORM.]
Dol·by (dōl′bē) *adj.* Of or designating circuitry that reduces noise inherent in the tape recording process. During quiet passages the level of the incoming signal is increased; the compensating decrease during playback reduces noise (tape hiss) to below audibility. [The Dolby System (trademark) invented *c.* 1966 by R.M. *Dolby* (1933–), U.S. electronic engineer.]
dol·ce (dōl′chā′) *adv. Abbr.* **dol.** *Music.* Gently and sweetly. Used as a direction. [Italian, "sweet," from Latin *dulcis.*] **—dol·ce** *adj.*
dol·ce far nien·te (dōl′chā făr nyĕn′tā) *n. Italian.* Delicious inactivity. [Literally, "sweet doing nothing."]
Dol·ce lat·te (dl′chā lä′tā) *n.* A trademark for a smooth, blue-veined Italian cheese. [Italian, "sweet milk."]
dol·ce vi·ta (dōl′chā vē′tä) *n.* A life of comfort or luxury. [Italian, "sweet life."]
dol·drums (dōl′drəmz′, dôl′-, dŏl′-) *n. Used with a singular verb.* **1. a.** Ocean regions near the equator, characterized by calms or light winds. **b.** The calms characteristic of these areas. **2.** A period of inactivity, listlessness, or depression. **3.** A condition of stagnation or recession: *The automotive industry is in the doldrums.* In all three senses, usually preceded by *the.* [Dialect, perhaps ultimately from Old English *dol,* dull (probably influenced in form by TANTRUM).]
dole[1] (dōl) *n.* **1.** The distribution or dispensing of goods, especially of money, food, or clothing as charity. **2.** A gift or share of money, food, or clothing distributed as charity. **3.** *Chiefly British.* The distribution by the government of relief payments to the unemployed. **4.** *Archaic.* One's fate. **—on the dole.** *Chiefly British.* Receiving regular relief payments from the government.
~tr.v. **doled, doling, doles.** To distribute, especially in small portions. Usually used with *out: doled out the rations.* —See Usage note at **distribute.** [Middle English *dol(e),* part, division, Old English *dāl,* share, portion.]
dole[2] *n. Archaic.* Grief; sorrow; dolor. [Middle English *dol,* from Old French *dol, duel,* from Late Latin *dolus,* pain, grief, from Latin *dolēre,* to feel pain, grieve for.]
dole·ful (dōl′fəl) *adj.* Filled with grief; mournful; melancholy. —See Synonyms at **sad.** **—dole·ful·ly** *adv.* **—dole·ful·ness** *n.*
dol·er·ite (dŏl′ə-rīt′) *n.* A basic, medium-grained, intrusive igneous rock, mainly composed of feldspar, pyroxene, and sometimes olivine. Also called "diabase." [Greek *doleros,* deceitful, from *dolos,* bait, trick (so named from the difficulty in analyzing it) + -ITE.]
dol·i·cho·ce·phal·ic (dŏl′ə-kō-sə-făl′ĭk) *adj.* Also **dol·i·cho·ceph·a·lous** (-sĕf′ə-ləs). Having a relatively long head; designating a skull that is longer than it is broad, with a cephalic index of 75 or less. Compare **brachycephalic, mesocephalic.** [New Latin *dolichocephalus* : Greek *dolikhos,* long + -CEPHALOUS.] **—dol·i·cho·ceph·a·lism** (dŏl′ə-kō-sĕf′ə-lĭz′əm), **dol·i·cho·ceph·a·ly** (dŏl′ə-kō-sĕf′ə-lē) *n.*
dol·i·cho·cran·i·al (dŏl′ə-kō-krā′nē-əl) Also **dol·i·cho·cran·ic** (-nĭk) *adj.* Dolichocephalic. **—dol·i·cho·cran·y** *n.*
do·li·ne, do·li·na (də-lē′nə, dō-) *n.* A saucer-shaped or shallow funnel-shaped hollow in the ground, large enough to be cultivable, formed by dissolution of limestone. [Slavonic *dolina,* valley.]
doll (dŏl) *n.* **1. a.** A child's toy representing a baby or other human being. **b.** A dummy used by a ventriloquist. **2.** A pretty child. **3.** *Slang.* An attractive woman. **4.** *Informal.* Any person regarded with fond familiarity. **5.** *Slang.* A pep pill, sleeping pill, or other drug in capsule or tablet form.
~v. **dolled, dolling, dolls.** *Informal.* *—intr.* To dress up or adorn oneself smartly, as for a special occasion. Used with *up.* *—tr.* To dress up smartly, especially for ostentation. Used with *up.* [From *Doll,* pet name for *Dorothy.*]
dol·lar (dŏl′ər) *n. Abbr.* **dol.** *Symbol* **$** **1. a.** The basic monetary unit of the United States, equal to 100 cents. **b.** The basic monetary unit, equal to 100 cents, of numerous countries, including Australia, Canada, Ethiopia, Guyana, Hong Kong, Liberia, Malaysia, New Zealand, Singapore, Trinidad and Tobago, Western Samoa, and Zimbabwe. **2.** A coin or note worth one dollar. See feature at **currency.** [Low German *daler,* from German *Taler,* taler, short for *Joachimstaler,* a coin made with metal from *Joachimsthal,* Jachymov, town in the Erzgebirge Mountains, Czechoslovakia.]
dol·lar-a-year (dŏl′ər-ə-yîr′) *adj.* Designating U.S. Federal employees who receive token payment for patriotic service: *a dollar-a-year government consultant.*
dol·lar·bird (dŏl′ər-bûrd′) *n.* A bird, *Eurystomus orientalis,* of southeast Asia and Australia, having a round white spot on each wing.
dollar cost averaging *n.* The periodic investment of a fixed dollar amount in the stock market regardless of prevailing prices.
dollar diplomacy *n.* **1.** A foreign policy aimed at furthering the commercial interests and political influence of the United States by encouraging the investment of U.S. capital in foreign countries. **2.** A policy designed to safeguard such investments.
dol·lar·fish (dŏl′ər-fĭsh′) *n., pl.* **-fishes** or collectively **dollarfish.** Any of several rounded silvery fishes, such as the **moonfish** *(see).*
dollar sign *n.* The symbol ($) for a dollar or dollars when placed before a numeral. Also called "dollar mark."
dol·lop (dŏl′əp) *n. Informal.* **1.** A large lump or portion, as of mashed potatoes or ice cream. **2.** A small quantity of liquid, as of whiskey. **3.** A small amount: *not a dollop of truth to the story.* [19th century (earlier sense, tuft) : perhaps from Scandinavian.]
doll·house (dŏl′hous′) *n.* A small-scale model of a house, used as a child's toy.
dol·ly (dŏl′ē) *n., pl.* **-lies.** **1.** A doll. Used by or to children. **2.** A low mobile platform that rolls on casters, used for moving heavy loads. **3.** A similar wheeled apparatus used to move a motion-picture or television camera about a set. **4.** A small locomotive for use in a railroad yard, building site, or the like. **5.** A tool used to hold one end of a rivet while the opposite end is being hammered to form a head. **6.** A small piece of wood or metal placed on the head of a pile to prevent damage while the pile is being driven.
~intr.v. **dollied, -lying, -lies.** To move the dolly on which a motion-picture or television camera is mounted toward or away from the scene of action. Often used with *back, in,* or *out.* [From DOLL.]
dolly bird *n. Chiefly British Informal.* A pretty, flashily dressed young woman.
Dol·ly Var·den (dŏl′ē värd′n) *n.* **1.** A woman's large hat, trimmed with flowers. **2.** A colorfully spotted trout, *Salvelinus malma,* of northwestern North America. [After *Dolly Varden,* a character who wore such a hat in Charles Dickens's *Barnaby Rudge.*]
dol·ma (dôl′mə, -mä) *n.* Also **dol·ma·des** (dôl-mä′dēz′). A dish of Turkish origin, consisting of vine leaves stuffed with various mixtures. [Turkish, from *dolaman,* wrapping.]
dol·man (dŏl′mən) *n.* **1.** A long Turkish outer robe. **2.** A woman's cloak or coat with capelike arm pieces. **3.** A jacket, usually elaborately decorated, often worn like a cape as part of a hussar's uniform. [French, from German *Dolman,* from Turkish *dolaman,* wrapping, from *dolamak,* to wind.]
dolman sleeve *n.* A full sleeve that is very wide at the armhole and narrow at the wrist. [See **dolman.**]
dol·men (dŏl′mən) *n.* Any prehistoric megalithic structure consisting of two or more vertical stones supporting a horizontal one, typically forming a chamber. Also called "cromlech." Compare **menhir.** [French, probably coined from Breton *tol,* table, from Old Breton, from Latin *tabula,* TABLE + *men,* stone, from Celtic *magino-* (unattested); compare **menhir.**]
dol·o·mite (dŏl′ə-mīt′) *n.* **1.** A light-tinted, especially yellowish, brownish, or white mineral, essentially $CaMg(CO_3)_2$, used as a furnace refractory, construction, and ceramic material, and in fertilizers. **2.** A type of limestone consisting largely of the mineral dolomite. Also called "dolomitic limestone," "magnesian limestone." [French, after Déodat de *Dolomieu* (1750–1801), French geologist.] **—dol·o·mit·ic** (dŏl′ə-mĭt′ĭk) *adj.*
Dol·o·mites (dŏl′ə-mīts). *Italian* **Do·lo·mi·ti** (dō′lə-mē′tē). Dolomitic limestone mountain range in the Alps of northeast Italy, rising to 3,342 meters (10,965 feet) at Marmolada. Cortina d'Ampezzo is its principal tourist resort.
do·lor (dō′lər) *n.* Also *British* **do·lour.** *Poetic.* Sorrow; grief. [Middle English *dolour,* pain, suffering, grief, from Old French, from Latin *dolor,* from *dolēre,* to feel pain, grieve.]
dol·or·im·e·try (dŏl′ə-rĭm′ə-trē) *n.* A technique for measuring the intensity of pain perception ranging from unpleasant to unbearable, by applying heat to the skin. [DOLOR + -METRY.]
do·lo·ro·so (dō′lə-rō′sō) *adj. Music.* Mournful; plaintive.
~adv. Music. With a mournful or plaintive tempo or quality. Used as a direction. [Italian, from Latin *dolōrōsus,* DOLOROUS.]
do·lor·ous (dō′lə-rəs, dŏl′-) *adj.* **1.** Sorrowful; sad. **2.** Painful; distressing. [Middle English, from Late Latin *dolōrōsus,* from Latin

dolor, DOLOR.] —**do·lor·ous·ly** *adv.* —**do·lor·ous·ness** *n.*
dol·phin (dŏl′fĭn, dôl′-) *n.* **1.** Any of various marine mammals, chiefly of the family Delphinidae, related to the whales but generally smaller and having a beaklike snout; especially, the common, widely distributed species *Delphinus delphis.* Sometimes called "porpoise." **2.** Either of two marine fishes, *Coryphaena hippurus* or *C. equisetis,* having iridescent coloring. **3.** A post, bollard, or the like, for mooring a boat. [Middle English *dolphin, dalphin,* from Old French *daufin, dalfin,* from Vulgar Latin *dalfīnus* (unattested), from Latin *delphīnus,* from Greek *delphis* (stem *delphin-*).]
dolt (dōlt) *n.* A stupid person; a blockhead. [Perhaps from obsolete *dol,* a variant of DULL.] —**dolt·ish** *adj.* —**dolt·ish·ly** *adv.* —**dolt·ish·ness** *n.*
Dom (dŏm; *Portuguese* dōN) *n.* **1.** A title formerly bestowed in Portugal and Brazil on a man of high rank. Compare **don. 2.** *Roman Catholic Church.* A title used before the names of monks of certain orders, especially Benedictines. [Portuguese, from Latin *dominus,* lord.]
Dom. Dominican.
–dom *suffix.* Indicates: **1.** The condition of being; for example, **boredom. 2.** The domain, position, or rank of; for example, **dukedom. 3.** The people who comprise a group, or their general character; for example, **officialdom.** [Middle English *-dom,* Old English *-dōm.*]
do·main (dō-mān′) *n.* **1.** A territory or range of rule or control; realm. **2.** A sphere of interest, special knowledge, or action; field: *the domain of history.* **3.** *Physics.* Any of numerous contiguous regions in a ferromagnetic material in which the direction of spontaneous magnetization is uniform and different from that in neighboring regions. Also called "magnetic domain." **4.** *Law.* **a.** The ownership and right of disposal of property. **b.** The right of **eminent domain** (see). **5.** *Mathematics.* **a.** The set of possible values of an independent variable of a function. Also called "region." Compare **range. b.** Any open connected set that contains at least one point. [French *domaine,* from Old French *demaine,* from Latin *dominium,* property, ownership rights, from *dominus,* lord.]
do·maine (də-mān′, dō-, dō-mĕn′) *n.* A vineyard: *domaine-bottled wine.* [French, "domain."]
dome (dōm) *n.* **1.** A generally hemispherical roof or vault. **2. a.** Any object or structure resembling the shape of this, such as a **geodesic dome** (see). **b.** A natural formation resembling a dome: *the dome of the sky.* **3.** *Poetic.* A large, stately building. **4.** *Slang.* The head. **5.** *Crystallography.* A form of crystal in which two similarly inclined faces intersect in a line parallel to the horizontal axis. **6.** *Geology.* **a.** A **pericline** (see). **b.** A **salt dome** (see).
~*v.* **domed, doming, domes.** —*tr.* **1.** To cover with or as if with a dome. **2.** To shape like a dome. —*intr.* To assume the shape of a dome. [French *dôme,* from Italian *duomo,* (domed) cathedral, from Latin *domus,* house.] See **feature,** next page.
dome car *n.* A railroad passenger car with an elevated glassed-in section for scenic viewing.
domesday. Variant of **doomsday.**
Domes·day Book (dōomz′dā′, dōmz′-) *n.* Also **Dooms·day Book.** The written record of a census and survey of English landowners and their property, made by order of William the Conqueror in 1085–86.
do·mes·tic (də-mĕs′tĭk) *adj.* **1.** Of or pertaining to the family or household: *domestic chores.* **2.** Fond of home life and competent in household management. **3.** Tame; domesticated. Said of animals. **4.** Of or pertaining to a country's internal affairs: *domestic politics.* **5.** Produced in or indigenous to a particular country: *domestic wine.*
~*n.* **1.** A household servant. **2. domestics.** Household linens. [French *domestique,* from Latin *domesticus,* from *domus,* house.] —**do·mes·ti·cal·ly** *adv.*
do·mes·ti·cate (də-mĕs′tĭ-kāt′) *v.* **-cated, -cating, -cates.** Also **do·mes·ti·cize** (də-mĕs′tə-sīz′), **-cized, -cizing, -cizes.** —*tr.* **1.** To train to live with and be of use to man; tame. **2.** To bring into cultivation. **3.** To cause to feel comfortable at home; make domestic. **4.** To accommodate to an environment. —*intr.* To become domestic. [DOMESTIC + -ATE.] —**do·mes·ti·ca·tion** *n.*
do·mes·tic·i·ty (dō′mə-stĭs′ə-tē) *n., pl.* **-ties. 1.** The quality or condition of being domestic. **2.** Home life or devotion to it. **3. domesticities.** Household affairs.
domestic science *n.* The study of skills pertaining to cookery, dressmaking, and household management; home economics.
do·mi·cal (dō′mĭ-kəl, dŏm′ĭ-) *adj.* Also **do·mic** (dō′mĭk, dŏm′ĭk). Pertaining to, having, or shaped like a dome. —**do·mi·cal·ly** *adv.*
dom·i·cile (dŏm′ə-sīl′, -səl, dō′mə-) *n.* Also **dom·i·cil** (-səl). **1.** A residence; home. **2.** One's legal residence.
~*v.* **domiciled, -ciling, -ciles.** Also **dom·i·cil·i·ate** (dŏm′ə-sĭl′ē-āt′, dō′mə-) **-ated, -ating, -ates.** —*tr.* To establish (a person or oneself) in a residence. —*intr.* To reside or dwell. [Middle English, from Old French, from Latin *domicilium,* habitation, abode.] —**dom·i·cil·i·ar·y** (dŏm′ə-sĭl′ē-ĕr′ē) *adj.*
dom·i·nance (dŏm′ə-nəns) *n.* Also **dom·i·nan·cy** (-nən-sē). The condition or fact of being dominant; ascendancy.
dom·i·nant (dŏm′ə-nənt) *adj.* **1. a.** Exercising the most influence or control. **b.** Seeking or tending to exert control or occupy a pre-eminent position. **2.** Providing a view from above; in a commanding position. **3.** Most noticeable or prevalent. **4.** *Genetics.* Producing the same phenotypic effect whether paired with an identical or a dissimilar gene. Compare **recessive. 5.** *Ecology.* Designating or pertaining to the species that is most abundant in a habitat and that

may determine the presence and type of other species. **6.** *Music.* Pertaining to or based upon the fifth note of a diatonic scale.
~*n.* **1.** *Genetics.* A dominant gene or characteristic. **2.** *Ecology.* A dominant species. **3.** *Music.* The fifth note of a diatonic scale. [Old French, from Latin *domināns* (stem *dominant-*), present participle of *dominārī,* to DOMINATE.] —**dom·i·nant·ly** *adv.*
Synonyms: *paramount, predominant, pre-eminent, preponderant.*
dominant wavelength *n.* The wavelength of the light that, when combined in specific proportions with an achromatic standard light, matches a given color.
dom·i·nate (dŏm′ə-nāt′) *v.* **-nated, -nating, -nates.** —*tr.* **1.** To control, govern, or exert influence over by superior authority or power. **2.** To occupy the pre-eminent or most noticeable position in or over: *A large painting dominated the room.* **3.** To overlook from a height. —*intr.* To be dominant in position or authority. [Latin *dominārī,* to be lord and master, from *dominus,* master, lord.] —**dom·i·na·tive** *adj.* —**dom·i·na·tor** *n.*
dom·i·na·tion (dŏm′ə-nā′shən) *n.* **1.** The act of dominating or the condition of being dominated; rule; control. **2. dominations.** In medieval angelology, the fourth of the nine orders of angels. Also called "dominions." See **angel.**
dom·i·neer (dŏm′ə-nîr′) *v.* **-neered, -neering, -neers.** —*tr.* To rule over arbitrarily or arrogantly; tyrannize. —*intr.* To exercise control tyrannically. [Dutch *domineren,* from French *dominer,* from Latin *dominārī,* to DOMINATE.]
dom·i·neer·ing (dŏm′ə-nîr′ĭng) *adj.* Tending to domineer; overbearing. —**dom·i·neer·ing·ly** *adv.*
Do·min·go (dō-mĭng′gō, də-), **Placido** (1941–). Spanish tenor. He emigrated to Mexico as a child and made his debut at the Metropolitan Opera, New York, in 1968. He is one of the world's leading operatic tenors.
Dom·i·nic (dŏm′ə-nĭk), **Saint** (c. 1170–1221). Spanish churchman and founder of the Dominican order. He became prior at Osma Cathedral in Castile and backed the crusade of Simon IV de Montfort (c. 1160–1218) against the heretical Albigenses in southern France. He founded his order in 1216, and his zeal earned him a reputation as "the burner and slayer of heretics." His pursuit of them was ruthlessly followed by the Dominican-dominated Spanish Inquisition.
Dom·i·ni·ca (dŏm′ə-nē′kə, də-mĭn′ĭ-kə). Island country of the West Indies. The largest of the Windward Islands, it was named by Columbus for the day when he made landfall there, *Dies Dominica,* Sunday, November 3, 1493. After alternating between British and French rule, it became British in 1783. In 1978 it became an independent Commonwealth republic. Following devastating hurricanes in 1979 and 1980, government development of tourism and light industry is taking place to reduce dependence on the export of bananas. Area, 751 square kilometers (290 square miles). Population, 82,000. Capital, Roseau. See map at **Latin America.**
do·min·i·cal (də-mĭn′ĭ-kəl) *adj.* **1.** Of or associated with the Lord (Christ). **2.** Pertaining to Sunday as the Lord's day. [Medieval Latin *dominicālis,* from Latin *dominicus,* of a lord, from *dominus,* lord.]
dominical letter *n.* One of the first seven letters of the alphabet applied to Sundays in order to determine the ecclesiastical calendar for a given year, the letter being the one that corresponds with the first Sunday in January when the first seven days of the month are lettered in order; for example, if the first Sunday is January 2, *B* will be the dominical letter for the year.
Do·min·i·can (də-mĭn′ĭ-kən) *adj.* **1.** *Abbr.* **Dom.** Of, pertaining to, or designating the order of preaching friars established in 1216 by St. Dominic. **2.** Of or pertaining to the Dominican Republic. **3.** Of or pertaining to Dominica.
~*n.* **1.** *Abbr.* **Dom.** A friar of the order of Saint Dominic. **2.** A native or inhabitant of the Dominican Republic. **3.** A native or inhabitant of Dominica.
Do·min·i·can Republic (də-mĭn′ĭ-kən). Mountainous country on

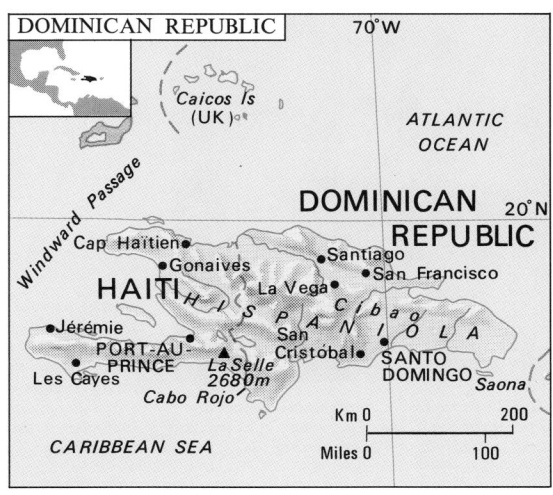

the eastern section of the West Indian island of Hispaniola, where Columbus landed in 1492. The present republic was established in 1844. This has been prone to economic and political instability and civil strife, and U.S. forces have intervened twice (1916–24, 1965–66). The dictator General Rafael Trujillo came to power in 1930. He was assassinated (1961) and succeeded by Joaquin Balaguer. A year later the leftist Juan Bosch was elected president—only to be deposed by a military coup (1963). A leftist revolt was put down with U.S. help in 1965. Sugar is the main industry and supplies 33 percent of the country's exports. However, after hurricane damage in 1979, tourism and mining are being developed rapidly. Gold, silver, and bauxite are also exported. Area, 48,734 square kilometers (18,811 square miles). Population, 7,200,000. Capital, Santo Domingo.

dom·i·nie (dŏm′ə-nē′, dō′mə-) *n.* **1.** *Chiefly Scottish.* A schoolmaster. **2.** A clergyman of the Dutch Reformed Church. **3.** *Informal.* Any minister. [From obsolete *domine,* form of address to ministers and schoolmasters, from Latin *dominē,* vocative of *dominus,* lord, master.]

do·min·ion (də-mĭn′yən) *n.* **1.** Control or the exercise of control; rule; sovereignty. **2.** A territory or sphere of influence or control; realm; domain. **3.** *Often* **Dominion.** A term formerly applied to any of the larger self-governing nations within the British Commonwealth, such as Canada or Australia. **4.** *Law.* Dominium. **5.** **dominions.** An order of angels, dominations. [Middle English *dominioun,* from Old French *dominion,* from Medieval Latin *dominiō* (stem *dominiōn-*), from Latin *dominium,* property, ownership rights, lordship, from *dominus,* lord, master.]

Dominion Day *n.* July 1, a national holiday in Canada, the anniversary of the Dominion's formation in 1867.

do·min·i·um (də-mĭn′ē-əm) *n. Law.* Ownership of property, especially of land, and the right to its disposition. Also called "dominion." [Latin, property, DOMINION.]

---

dome

THE DOME, ARCHITECTURE'S CROWNING GLORY
How Roman builders enclosed space and height

A dome is a rounded roof, hemispherical in shape or nearly so, that adds lofty grandeur and spaciousness to the interior of a building. Its base may be a circle, an ellipse, or a polygon. It was developed by Roman builders from the barrel vault, a tunnel formed by extending an arch. Stout walls and flying buttresses were used to support the great weight of the Roman domes. One outstanding example remains, surmounting the Pantheon, Rome's only building to survive from the time of the empire with its main structure intact. The stepped dome, 43 meters (142 feet) across and more than 22 meters (71 feet) high, has a substructure built with relieving arches to distribute the massive weight. The Emperor Hadrian had the elaborate brick Pantheon with its concrete dome built (A.D. 120–124) as a temple.

It was the Byzantines who found the secret of raising a dome without huge supporting walls. In Constantinople, now Istanbul, the dome of Santa Sophia (completed in 557) is on four pendentives (below right). These are built like a dome with the top cut off, leaving a circular base on which to build the dome itself.

Filippo Brunelleschi's pointed dome on Florence Cathedral, built 1420–46, takes the dome to its culmination. It rests on an octagonal drum, on which the buttresses are only small. Reinforcing the bottom of the dome, at its spread point, is a timber and chain link hoop.

FLORENCE CATHEDRAL *Brunelleschi's triumphant octagonal dome, rising above a masonry drum and culminating in a graceful cupola, towers over the city. It is a lasting monument to the brilliance of Renaissance builders.*

THE PANTHEON *The dome of the Pantheon in Rome climbs to an oculus, or opening, 8 meters (27 feet) across, which throws light onto the Corinthian columns and marble-veneered walls. The interior is not the original; it was renewed in 1747.*

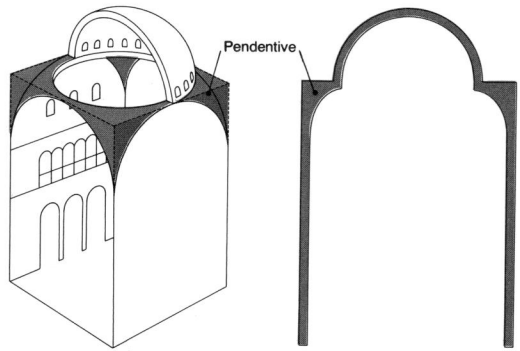

Pendentive

SANTA SOPHIA *At the church of Santa Sophia, now a mosque, Byzantine builders raised the spectacular dome on four pendentives. These are borne on four colossal corner pillars and constructed like a dome but with the topmost part missing, leaving a circular base on which to build the dome itself. The brick dome is 32 meters (107 feet) in diameter. It is shallower than a hemisphere and built with 40 ribs with 40 windows between them. Inside the mosque, the light pouring through this ring of windows creates the uncanny illusion that the dome is floating on air. Two huge arches between the pendentives increase the feeling of height and space.*

dom·i·no[1] (dŏm′ə-nō′) *n., pl.* **-noes** or **-nos. 1. a.** A hooded robe worn with an eye mask at a masquerade. **b.** The mask itself, worn with such a robe. **2.** A person wearing such a robe or mask. [French, probably from Latin *dominus,* lord, but the reason for the name is unknown.]

domino[2] *n., pl.* **-noes. 1.** A small, rectangular block, the face of which is divided into halves, used in games of dominoes. Each half is marked by one to six dots or is blank. **2. dominoes.** *Used with a singular verb.* Any of several games played with a set of usually 28 dominoes. [French, obscurely from DOMINO (hooded robe).]

Dom·i·no (dŏm′ə-nō′), **Fats,** born Antoine Domino (1928–). U.S. singer, pianist, and songwriter. His songs, popular especially in the 1950's, include *Ain't That A Shame, I'm In Love Again,* and *Blue Monday.*

domino effect *n.* A cumulative effect produced when one event sets off a chain of similar events.

domino theory *n.* A theory that one event, if allowed to happen, will inevitably lead to a succession of similar events, as a row of upright dominoes will fall if the first one is knocked down; especially, the theory that if one vulnerable nation, as in Southeast Asia, were to come under Communist domination, the neighboring nations would naturally follow.

Do·mi·nus (dō′mĭ-no͝os′, dŏm′ə-nəs) *n. Abbr.* **D.** *Latin.* The Lord. Used with reference to God or Christ.

Do·mi·tian (də-mĭsh′ən), full name **Titus Flavius Domitianus Augustus** (A.D. 51–96). Roman emperor. He succeeded his brother Titus in 81 and completed the conquest of Britain. After 89 his government became dictatorial, and with the senate firmly in his control, he instigated a reign of terror. He was murdered in his bedchamber by a freedman with the connivance of his wife.

don[1] (dŏn) *n.* **1. Don.** *Abbr.* **D.** Sir. A title formerly placed before the Christian name of a Spaniard of high rank, now used generally as a courtesy title. **2.** A Spanish gentleman. **3.** *British.* **a.** A head, tutor, or fellow of a college at Oxford or Cambridge. **b.** Any university lecturer. [Spanish, from Latin *dominus,* lord, master.]

don[2] *tr.v.* **donned, donning, dons.** To put on; dress in. [Contraction of *do on.*]

Don (dŏn). River in western Russia. It flows 1,930 kilometers (1,224 miles) south to the Sea of Azov.

do·ña (dō′nyä) *n.* **1.** A Spanish gentlewoman. **2. Doña.** A title of courtesy placed before a woman's Christian name in Spanish-speaking countries. [Spanish, "lady," from Latin *domina.* See **dame.**]

do·nate (dō′nāt′, dō-nāt′) *tr.v.* **-nated, -nating, -nates.** To present as a gift, especially to a fund or cause; contribute. [Back-formation from DONATION.] **—do·na·tor** *n.*

Do·na·tel·lo (dŏn′ə-tĕl′ō), born Donato di Niccolò di Betto Bardi (1386–1466). Florentine sculptor who was a pioneer of the Renaissance style, breaking all traditions with his natural, lifelike figures, such as the marble sculptures of *St. Mark* and *St. George.* Michelangelo is reputed to have been so impressed with *St. Mark* that he asked the statue why it did not speak to him.

do·na·tion (dō-nā′shən) *n.* **1.** The act of making a gift, especially to a fund or cause. **2.** A gift or grant; contribution. [Middle English *donacioun,* from Old French, from Latin *dōnātiō* (stem *dōnātiōn-*), from *dōnātus,* past participle of *dōnāre,* to give, from *dōnum,* gift.]

Do·na·tist (dŏn′ə-tĭst, dō′nə-) *n.* A member of a schismatic Christian sect that arose in North Africa in the 4th century A.D. [Medieval Latin *Dōnātista,* from *Dōnātus,* probably the bishop of Carthage in the fourth century.] **—Do·na·tism** *n.* **—Do·na·tist** *adj.*

do·na·tive (dō′nə-tĭv, dŏn′ə-) *n.* **1.** A gift or donation. **2.** A benefice that can be bestowed by its founder or patron without reference to the diocesan authorities.
~*adj.* Constituting such a benefice. [Latin *dōnātīvum,* neuter of *dōnātīvus,* of a donation, from *dōnātus.* See **donation.**]

Donau. See **Danube.**

Don·bas (dŏn′bäs). Also **Do·nets Basin** (də-nĕts′). Major industrial region in the lower Dnieper, Donets, and Don valleys, eastern Ukraine and southeast Russia. It produces coal and has extensive chemical industries based on local salt deposits. Donetsk and Rostov are the main centers.

done (dŭn). Past participle of **do.**
~*adj.* **1.** Finished. **2.** Cooked adequately. **3.** Socially acceptable: *not done in polite society.* **—done for. 1.** Doomed. **2.** Dead or dying. **3.** Exhausted.
~*interj.* Used to express agreement when concluding a deal.

do·nee (dō-nē′) *n.* **1.** A recipient of a gift. **2.** *Medicine.* The recipient of an organ transplanted from a donor. [DON(OR) + -EE.]

Don·e·gal (dŏn′ĭ-gôl′, dŭn′-). Mountainous county on the northwest Atlantic coast of the Republic of Ireland. Its chief occupations are sheep and cattle rearing and potato farming. Donegal tweed and linen are also produced. Its county town is Lifford.

do·ner kebab (dō′nər) *n.* A kebab made from meat, mostly mutton, sliced from a large compressed loaf that turns on an upright spit.

Do·nets (də-nĕts′). River, *c.* 1,045 kilometers (650 miles) long, mainly in Ukraine. It flows generally southeast to join the lower Don River near Rostov.

Do·netsk (də-nĕtsk′). Industrial city in southeast Ukraine, founded in the 1870's.

dong (dŏng) *n.* Symbol **D 1.** The basic monetary unit of Vietnam, equal to 100 sau. **2.** A coin or note worth one dong. See feature at **currency.** [Vietnamese.]

Dö·nitz or **Doe·nitz** (dœ′nĭts), **Karl** (1891–1981). German admiral. He developed the highly effective "pack" system of U-boat attacks in World War II. In 1943 he became grand admiral and commander in chief of the navy. Hitler nominated Dönitz as his successor, and he was briefly chancellor on Hitler's death. At the Nuremberg trials in 1946 he was sentenced to 10 years' imprisonment.

Do·ni·zet·ti (dŏn′ə-zĕt′ē), **Gaetano** (1797–1848). Italian composer of some 75 operas. His best-known work is *Lucia di Lammermoor* (1835).

don·jon (dŏn′jən, dŭn′-) *n.* The fortified main tower of a castle; a keep. Also called "dungeon." [Variant of DUNGEON.]

Don Ju·an (dŏn′ wän′) *n.* **1.** A man obsessed with seducing women. **2.** A libertine; profligate. [After *Don Juan,* legendary Spanish nobleman and libertine.]

don·key (dŏng′kē, dŭng′-, dông′-) *n., pl.* **-keys. 1.** The domesticated ass, probably descended from the wild ass *Equus asinus.* **2.** An obstinate, sluggish, or stupid person. [Perhaps from DUN (dark) + diminutive suffix *-ey* (influenced by MONKEY).]

donkey engine *n.* A small auxiliary steam engine used for hoisting or pumping, especially aboard ship.

donkey jacket *n.* A workman's thick jacket, usually with a piece of plastic or leather over each shoulder. [Alluding to the donkey as an animal associated with drudgery.]

donkey's years *n. British Informal.* A very long time. [Perhaps alteration of *donkey's ears,* hence, very long.]

don·key·work (dŏng′kē-wûrk′, dŭng′-, dông′-) *n.* **1.** The laborious, uninteresting part of an operation. **2.** Monotonous work; drudgery.

Don·lea·vy (dŏn-lē′vē), **James Patrick** (1926–). Irish-American novelist. Born in New York City, he later settled in Ireland. *The Ginger Man* (1955) won acclaim for his comic and irreverent style. Other works include *The Beastly Beatitudes of Balthazar B* (1968).

don·na (dŏn′ə; *Italian* dôn′nä) *n.* **1.** An Italian gentlewoman or lady. **2. Donna.** A title of courtesy placed before a woman's Christian name in Italian-speaking countries. [Italian, "lady," from Latin *domina.* See **dame.**]

Donne (dŭn), **John** (*c.* 1572–1631). English poet and divine, one of the great metaphysical poets. In 1601 he married a 16-year-old girl without her father's consent and was briefly imprisoned. He joined the Anglican Church and took holy orders (1615), becoming chaplain to King James before being appointed dean of St. Paul's (1621). Among his poems are *The Ecstasie, Hymn to God the Father,* and *La Corona.*

don·nish (dŏn′ĭsh) *adj.* Resembling or characteristic of a university don; bookish; pedantically erudite.

don·ny·brook (dŏn′ē-bro͝ok′) *n.* A brawl or uproar; a free-for-all. [After *Donnybrook* fair, held yearly at *Donnybrook,* near Dublin, at which such uproars were common.]

do·nor (dō′nər) *n.* **1.** One who contributes something, such as money to a cause or fund. **2. a.** One who donates blood, tissue, or an organ for use in a transfusion or transplant. **b.** One that provides semen for artificial insemination. **3.** *Chemistry.* The atom in a coordinate bond that supplies both electrons. Compare **acceptor. 4.** *Physics.* An impurity atom added to a semiconductor to increase the n-type conductivity. Compare **acceptor.** [Middle English, from Anglo-French *donour,* from Old French *doneur,* from Latin *dōnātor,* from *dōnātus.* See **donation.**]

do-no·thing (do͞o′nŭth′ĭng) *adj.* Offering no initiative for change, especially in politics.
~*n.* A person who is idle or lazy. **—do-no·thing·ism** *n.*

Don Qui·xo·te (dŏn′kē-hō′tē, kwĭk′sət) *n.* An impractical idealist bent on righting incorrigible wrongs. [After *Don Quixote,* hero of a satirical chivalric romance by Cervantes, published 1605–15.]

don't (dōnt). Contraction of *do not.* —See Usage note at **do.**

don't know *n.* One who has not yet arrived at a definite viewpoint, as in replying to an opinion poll, questionnaire, or the like.

donut. Variant of **doughnut.**

doo·dad (do͞o′dăd′) *n. Informal.* **1.** An unnamed gadget or trinket. **2.** Any article whose name one has forgotten or does not know. [20th century : origin obscure.]

doo·dle (do͞od′l) *v.* **-dled, -dling, -dles.** *Informal.* —*intr.* To scribble mechanically or absent-mindedly. —*tr.* To draw (figures) while preoccupied.
~*n. Informal.* A figure, design, or scribble drawn or written absent-mindedly. [17th century (originally, simpleton) : perhaps from Low German; current sense perhaps related to dialect *doodle*†, to fritter away time.]

doo·dle·bug (do͞od′l-bŭg′) *n.* **1. a.** An insect, the **ant lion** *(see),* in its larval stage. **b.** Loosely, any of various other similar insect larvae. **3.** A divining rod. **3.** A small vehicle. [Perhaps English dialect *doodle,* to waste time (see **doodle**) + BUG.]

doo·hick·ey (do͞o′hĭk′ē) *n., pl.* **-eys.** *Informal.* A doodad. [Perhaps DOO(DAD) + HICKEY.]

Doo·lit·tle (do͞o′lĭt′əl), **Hilda,** pen name "H.D." (1886–1961). U.S. poet, who lived in Europe after 1911. Friendships with Ezra Pound, Marianne Moore, and William Carlos Williams launched her career as an imagist poet.

Doolittle, James Harold, known as "Jimmy" (1896–). U.S. army officer and aviator. He first became involved in the development of military aviation in World War I and later set many speed records resulting from his work on technological improvements in aircraft and design. In World War II he led a daring bombing raid on Tokyo and other Japanese cities (1942).

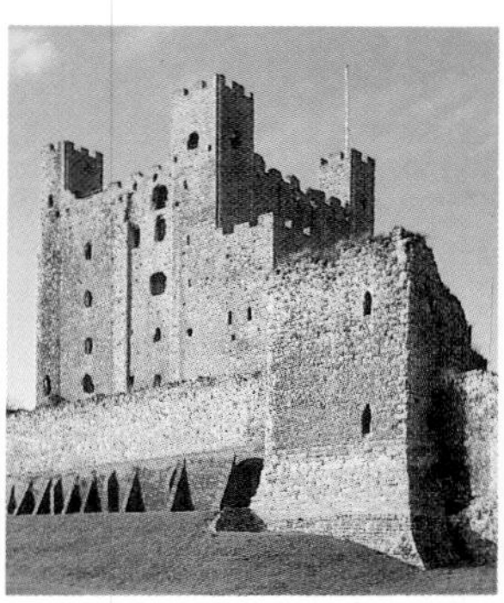

donjon *The principal tower, or donjon, of Rochester Castle in Kent, England. The castle was built in 1130.*

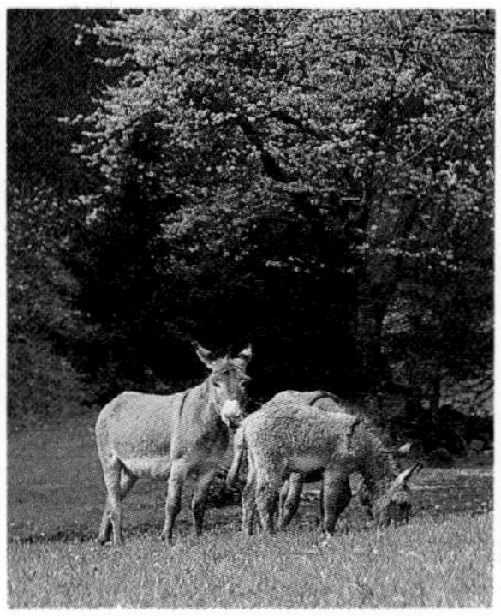

donkey *The donkey is descended from the African wild ass, which man domesticated more than 5,000 years ago as the first pack animal. Sure-footed and hardy, it can walk for long periods in hot and difficult conditions with a minimum of food and water.*

PRONUNCIATION KEY

ă, pat; ā, pay; âr, care;
ä, father, are; b, bib;
ch, church; d, deed; ĕ, pet;
ē, be; f, fife; g, gag; h, hat;
hw, which; ĭ, pit; ī, pie;
îr, pier; j, judge; k, kick;
l, lid, needle; m, mum;
n, no, sudden; ng, thing;
ŏ, pot; ō, toe; ô, paw, for;
oi, noise; ou, out; o͝o, book;
o͞o, boot; p, pop; r, roar;
s, sauce; sh, ship, dish;
t, tight; th, thin, path;
th, this, bathe; ŭ, cut; ûr, fur;
v, valve; w, with; y, yes;
z, zebra, size; zh, vision;
ə, about, item, edible, gallop, circus, peaceful

IN FOREIGN WORDS:

à, *Fr.* ami; œ, *Fr.* feu, *Ger.* schön; ü, *Fr.* tu, *Ger.* über; KH, *Ger.* ich, *Scot.* loch; N, *Fr.* bon; y', *Fr.* Compiègne

STRESS MARKS:

Primary stress: ′
in·cite′ (ĭn-sīt′)
Secondary stress: ′
in′sight′ (ĭn′sīt′)

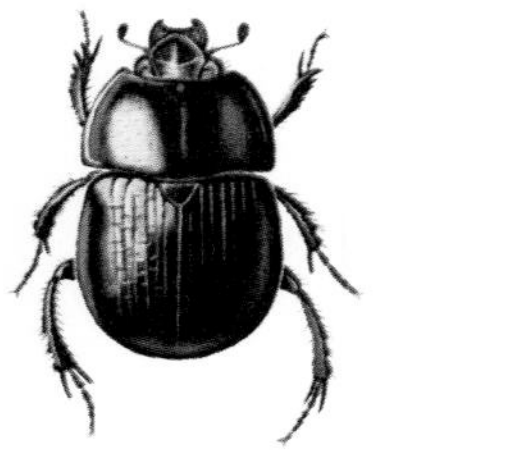

dorbeetle *A ground-living beetle that buries manure in holes beneath a patch of dung, as food for its larvae, and thus disperses the manure into the soil. The common dor (above) is one of a worldwide group of insects known as dung beetles.*

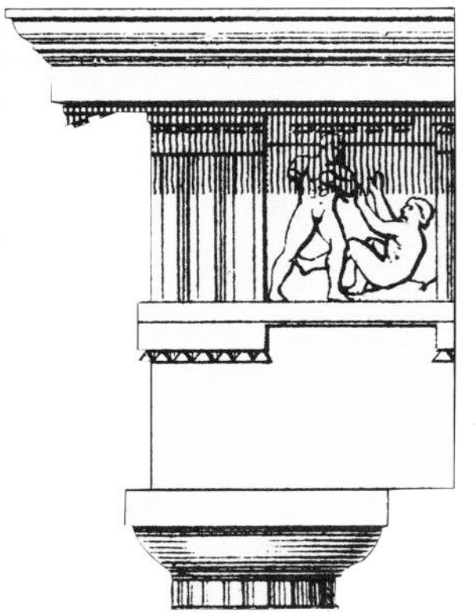

Doric order *The design of the Greek Doric order has its origins in early timber buildings. The grooved panels in the frieze (triglyphs) resemble in stylized form the ends of wooden roof beams.*

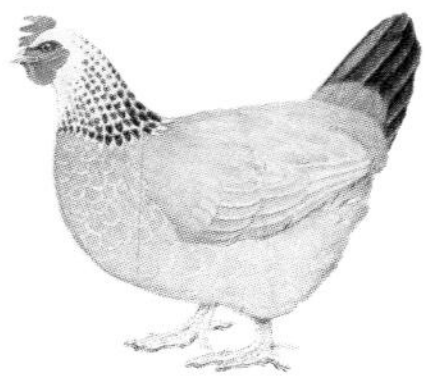

Dorking chicken *Unlike most birds, which have four toes, the Dorking chicken has five. Dorkings are good table birds, and young roosters can weigh up to about 6.4 kilograms (14 pounds).*

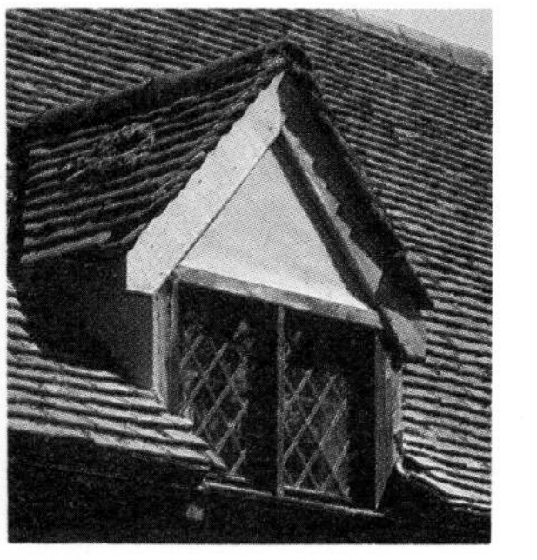

dormer *A dormer window projecting from a roof at Lavenham, Suffolk, in England.*

doom (do͞om) *n.* **1.** A predestined end in ruin or tragedy; a terrible fate. **2.** Disaster; ruin; extinction. **3.** The Last Judgment. **4.** *Archaic.* Condemnation to a severe penalty.
~*tr.v.* **doomed, dooming, dooms.** To condemn or destine to ruination or death. [Middle English *doom,* Old English *dōm.*]

doom palm. Variant of **doum palm.**

dooms·day (do͞omz′dā′) *n.* Also **domes·day** (do͞omz′dā′, dōmz′-). **1.** The day of the Last Judgment. **2.** Any dreaded day of judgment or reckoning. [Middle English *domesday,* Old English *dōmes dæg* : *dōmes,* genitive of *dōm,* DOOM + *dæg,* DAY.]

Doomsday Book. Variant of **Domesday Book.**

doom·watch (do͞om′wŏch′) *n.* A state of watching for and warning of impending disaster; especially, vigilance to protect the environment from possible destruction. **—doom·watch·er** *n.*

door (dôr, dōr) *n.* **1.** Any movable structure used to close off the entrance to a room, building, vehicle, cupboard, or the like, typically consisting of a panel of wood, glass, or metal that swings on hinges. **2.** The entranceway to a room, building, or passage. **3.** Any means of approach or access. **4.** The room or building to which a door belongs: *three doors down the hall.* **—at one's door** (or **doorstep**). Within one's sphere of responsibility: *They laid the blame at our door.* [Middle English *dor,* Old English *dor, duru,* gate, door.]

door·bell (dôr′bĕl′, dōr′-) *n.* A buzzer or bell outside a door, used as a signal for admission.

door·jamb (dôr′jăm′, dōr′-) *n.* Either of the two vertical pieces framing a doorway and supporting the lintel. Also called "doorpost."

door·keep·er (dôr′kē′pər, dōr′-) *n.* **1.** A person employed to guard an entrance or gateway. **2.** *Roman Catholic Church.* One of the **minor orders** *(see).*

door·knob (dôr′nŏb′, dōr′-) *n.* A knob-shaped handle for opening and closing a door.

door·man (dôr′măn′, -mən, dōr′-) *n., pl.* **-men** (-mĕn′, -mĭn). A man employed to stand watch at the entrance of a hotel, apartment house, or other large building.

door·mat (dôr′măt′, dōr′-) *n.* **1.** A mat placed before a doorway for wiping the shoes. **2.** *Informal.* A person who unprotestingly allows himself to be mistreated by others.

door·nail (dôr′nāl′, dōr′-) *n.* A large-headed nail formerly used as a stud on doors. **—dead as a doornail.** Undoubtedly dead.

door prize *n.* A prize awarded by lottery to the holder of a ticket purchased at or before a function.

door·sill (dôr′sĭl′, dōr′-) *n.* The threshold of a doorway.

door·step (dôr′stĕp′, dōr′-) *n.* A step leading to a door.

door·stop (dôr′stŏp′, dōr′-) *n.* **1.** A wedge inserted beneath a door to hold it open at a desired position. **2.** A weight or spring that prevents a door from slamming. **3.** A rubber-tipped projection attached to a wall to protect it from the impact of an opening door.

door-to-door (dôr′tə-dôr′, dōr′tə-dōr′) *adj.* **1.** Calling at every dwelling in a particular area. **2.** Moving directly from one place to another, especially from a place of collection or purchase to a specific address for delivery. **—door-to-door** *adv.*

door·way (dôr′wā′, dōr′-) *n.* The entrance to a room or building.

door·yard (dôr′yärd′, dōr′-) *n.* A yard in front of the door of a house.

do·pa (dō′pə) *n.* An intermediate compound in the synthesis of catecholamines from the amino acid tyrosine. It is needed for certain brain functions and the form L-dopa is used to treat Parkinson's disease. [From German, from *d*i*o*xy*p*henyl*a*lanine.]

do·pa·mine (dō′pə-mēn′) *n.* A catecholamine that is an intermediate in the synthesis of noradrenalin and possibly acts as a neurotransmitter. [DOPA + AMINE.]

dop·ant (dō′pənt) *n.* A small quantity of a substance, such as phosphorus, added to another substance, such as a semiconductor, to alter the latter's properties. [DOP(E) + -ANT.]

dope (dōp) *n.* **1.** Any viscid substance or liquid; especially: **a.** A lubricant, such as axle grease. **b.** An absorbent material used in manufacturing dynamite. **c.** Any of various preparations resembling varnish formerly used to protect, waterproof, and tauten the cloth surfaces of airplane wings. **2.** *Informal.* **a.** A drug, especially a narcotic. **b.** Any illegal drug, such as marijuana. **3.** *Slang.* A very stupid person. **4.** *Slang.* Factual information, especially of a confidential nature.
~*tr.v.* **doped, doping, dopes. 1.** To add or apply dope to. **2.** *Informal.* To administer a narcotic to; drug. **3.** *Electronics.* To add an impurity to (a semiconductor). **4.** *Informal.* To work out (an outcome or puzzle) by calculation and guesswork. Often used with *out.* [Dutch *doop,* sauce, from *doopen,* to dip, mix, from Middle Dutch *dōpen.*]

dope sheet *n. Slang.* A publication giving information on the horses running in the day's races.

dope·ster (dōp′stər) *n.* One who analyzes and forecasts future events, as in sports or politics.

do·pey, do·py (dō′pē) *adj.* **-ier, -iest.** *Slang.* **1.** Dazed or lethargic, as if drugged. **2.** Stupid; silly.

dop·pel·gäng·er, dop·pel·gang·er (dŏp′əl-găng′ər, dŏp′əl-gĕng′ər) *n.* **1.** A ghostly double of a living person, especially one that haunts its own fleshly counterpart. **2.** Loosely, a double of a person. [German, "double-goer."]

Dop·pler effect (dŏp′lər) *n.* An apparent change in the frequency of sound or electromagnetic waves occurring when the source and observer are in motion relative to one another, the frequency increasing when the source and observer approach one another and decreasing when they move apart. Also called "Doppler shift." See **red shift.** [After Christian *Doppler* (1803–53), Austrian physicist, who discovered the effect for sound waves.]

Doppler radar *n.* A radar system that uses the Doppler effect to measure velocity.

dor (dôr) *n.* Any of various insects that fly with a droning sound, such as a dorbeetle. [Middle English *dorre, dore,* Old English *dora,* bumblebee (probably imitative).]

Dor. Dorian; Doric.

do·ra·do (də-rä′dō) *n., pl.* **-dos.** A large marine fish, *Coryphaena hippurus.* See **dolphin.**

Do·ra·do (də-rä′dō) *n.* A constellation of the Southern Hemisphere near Reticulum and Pictor, containing a portion of the larger **Magellanic Cloud** *(see).*

dor·bee·tle (dôr′bēt′l) *n.* An Old World dung beetle, *Geotrupes stercorarius,* that flies with a droning sound.

Dor·cas society (dôr′kəs) *n.* A women's auxiliary group, often sponsored by a church, that provides clothes for the poor. [After *Dorcas,* a Christian woman of the 1st or 2nd century A.D.]

Dor·ches·ter (dôr′chĭs-tər, -chĕs′-). Market town in the south of England, the administrative center of Dorset. Thomas Hardy, born nearby, made it the model for Casterbridge in his *Wessex Tales.*

Dor·dogne (dôr-dōn′). River in southwest France. It flows 467 kilometers (290 miles) from the Auvergne Mts. to form the Gironde estuary with the Garonne River, crossing Dordogne department on the way. Its lower banks are lined with vineyards.

Do·ré (dô-rā′), **(Paul) Gustave** (1833–83). French engraver and lithographer who illustrated Dante, La Fontaine, Balzac, and scenes of London poverty. His drawings of eerie fantasy inspired a vogue for illustrated books. He illustrated Balzac's *Droll Stories,* La Fontaine's *Fables,* and Dante's *Divine Comedy.*

Do·ri·an (dôr′ē-ən, dōr′) *n. Abbr.* **Dor.** A member of a Hellenic people that invaded Greece around 1100 B.C. and remained culturally and linguistically distinct within the Greek world, especially in Sparta, Corinth, and Argos.
~*adj.* **1.** Of or pertaining to the Dorians. **2.** *Music.* Of or designating a mode represented by the white notes of the scale D to D on the piano keyboard.

Dor·ic (dôr′ĭk, dōr′-) *n. Abbr.* **Dor. 1.** One of the four main dialects of Ancient Greece spoken chiefly in the Peloponnese, in various Aegean islands, and in Magna Graecia. Compare **Aeolic, Arcado-Cyprian, Attic-Ionic. 2.** Any broad dialect of English; especially, the dialect of northeast Scotland.
~*adj. Abbr.* **Dor. 1.** Belonging to, characteristic of, or designating the Doric dialect. **2.** In the style of or designating the Doric order. **3.** Rustic. Said of a dialect. [Latin *Dōricus,* from Greek *Dōrikos,* from *Dōris,* area of Ancient Greece, the traditional home of the Dorians.]

Doric order *n.* The oldest and simplest of the three orders of classical Greek architecture, characterized by heavy, fluted columns having plain, saucer-shaped capitals, no base, and a bold, simple cornice. Compare **Corinthian order, Ionic order.**

Dor·king (dôr′kĭng) *n.* A domestic fowl of a breed having a heavy body and raised chiefly for table use. [After *Dorking,* Surrey, England, where it was bred.]

dorm (dôrm) *n. Informal.* A dormitory in a school or college.

dor·mant (dôr′mənt) *adj.* **1.** Asleep or lying as if asleep; not awake or active. **2. a.** Latent but capable of being activated. **b.** Temporarily inactive. **3.** Designating a volcano that has not erupted within recorded history but is thought not to be extinct. **4.** *Biology.* In a relatively inactive or resting condition in which some processes are slowed down or suspended. **5.** *Heraldry.* Lying in a sleeping position, with head on paws: *a lion dormant.* —See Synonyms at **inactive, latent.** [Middle English *dormaunt,* from Old French *dormant,* from the present participle of *dormir,* to sleep, from Latin *dormīre.*] **—dor·man·cy** *n.*

dor·mer (dôr′mər) *n.* **1.** A window set vertically in a small gable projecting from a sloping roof. Also called "dormer window." **2.** The gable holding such a window. [Old French *dormeor,* "bedroom window," from *dormir,* to sleep. See **dormant.**]

dor·mi·to·ry (dôr′mə-tôr′ē, -tōr′ē) *n., pl.* **-ries. 1.** A room providing sleeping quarters for a number of persons. **2.** A hall of residence in a college or university. **3.** A suburb or small town, many of whose inhabitants commute to work in a nearby urban center. Also used adjectivally: *a dormitory town.* [Latin *dormītōrium,* from *dormītōrius,* of sleep, from *dormītus,* past participle of *dormīre,* to sleep.]

dor·mouse (dôr′mous′) *n., pl.* **-mice** (-mīs′). **Any of various small Old World rodents of the family Gliridae, especially *Glis glis,*** of Europe and Asia Minor. [Middle English *dormowse*†.]

dor·my, dor·mie (dôr′mē) *adj. Golf.* Ahead of an opponent by as many holes as remain to be played. [19th century : origin obscure.]

dor·nick[1] (dôr′nĭk) *n.* A coarse damask cloth. [Middle English *dornewick,* first manufactured in *Doornik* (French *Tournai*), city in Belgium.]

dornick[2] *n. Regional.* A small chunk of rock; a stone. [Origin obscure.]

dorp (dôrp) *n. South African.* A small township; village. [Dutch; akin to THORP.]

Dorpat. See **Tartu.**

dor·sad (dôr′săd′) *adv. Anatomy.* In the direction of the back. [DORS(O)- + -AD (toward).]

dor·sal (dôr′səl) adj. 1. Anatomy. Of, toward, on, in, or near the back. 2. Botany. Of or on the surface of an organ directed away from the main axis. [Late Latin dorsālis, from Latin dorsuālis, from dorsum, back.] —**dor·sal·ly** adv.

dorsal fin n. The main unpaired fin on the dorsal surface of fishes or certain marine mammals.

Dor·set (dôr′sĭt). Also **Dor·set·shire** (-shĭr′, -shər). A county in southwest England. Agriculture is the main occupation, with sheep rearing on the downs and dairy cattle and crops in the lowlands. Tourism flourishes on the coast. Thomas Hardy portrayed the area in his Wessex Tales. Its administrative center is Dorchester.

Dorset Down n. A domestic sheep of a hornless breed with a brown face and legs, and fine-textured wool.

Dorset Horn n. A domestic sheep of a breed having large horns and fine-textured wool.

dor·si·ven·tral (dôr′sĭ-vĕn′trəl) adj. 1. Having distinct upper and lower surfaces, as most leaves do. 2. Dorsoventral.

dorso–, dorsi–, dors– prefix. Indicates the dorsal area; for example, **dorsoventral, dorsiventral, dorsad.** [Latin dorsum, back.]

dor·so·ven·tral (dôr′sō-vĕn′trəl) adj. Extending from a dorsal to a ventral surface. [DORSO- + VENTRAL.]

dor·sum (dôr′səm) n., pl. **-sa** (-sə). Anatomy. 1. The back. 2. Any part of an organ analogous to the back: the dorsum of the hand. [Latin, back.]

Dort·mund (dôrt′mənd). Industrial city and port at the end of the Dortmund-Ems Canal, in the Ruhr region of Germany. Other canals connect it to the Weser and Elbe rivers. Dortmund became part of the Hanseatic League in the 13th century and was ceded to Prussia in 1815.

Dort·mund-Ems Canal (dôrt′mənd-ĕmz′). An important industrial waterway in Germany. It is some 270 kilometers (168 miles) long and links the Ruhr with the Ems River and the North Sea.

dor·ty (dôr′tē) adj. **-tier, -tiest.** Scottish. Sullen; bad-tempered. [From Scottish dort, sullenness.]

do·ry¹ (dôr′ē, dōr′ē) n., pl. **-ries.** A small, narrow, flat-bottomed fishing boat with high sides and a sharp prow. [18th century : origin obscure.]

dory² n., pl. **-ries.** 1. Any of various marine fishes of the family Zeidae; especially, the **John Dory** (see). 2. A fish, the **walleye** (see). [Middle English dorre, from Old French doree, gilded (from its metallic shine), from the feminine past participle of dorer, to gild, from Late Latin dēaurāre : Latin dē-, thoroughly + aurum, gold.]

dos-à-dos (dō-zà-dō′) n., pl. **dos-à-dos** (-dōz′; French -dō′). Also **do-si-do** (dō′sē-dō′) (for sense 2), pl. **-dos.** 1. A sofa or carriage that accommodates two people seated back to back. 2. a. A movement in square dancing in which two dancers approach each other and circle back to back, then return to their original positions. b. The call given for such a movement. ~adj. Bound together back to back with one central board. Said of two books. [French, "back to back."]

dos·age (dō′sĭj) n. 1. The administration of a therapeutic agent in prescribed amounts. 2. The amount administered. 3. A dose of ionizing radiation. 4. A dose added to wine.

dose (dōs) n. 1. Abbr. **d., D.** A prescribed quantity of a therapeutic agent prescribed to be taken at one time or at stated intervals. 2. Informal. An amount, especially of something unpleasant, to which one is subjected: You need a dose of hard work. 3. An ingredient added to wine to impart flavor or strength. Also called "dosage." 4. Physics. The energy imparted to a unit mass of matter by ionizing radiation. Also called "absorbed dose." 5. The recommended upper limit of absorbed dose that a person should receive in a particular period. Also called "maximum permissible dose." 6. Slang. A venereal infection. ~tr.v. **dosed, dosing, doses.** 1. To give (someone) a dose, as of medicine. 2. To give or prescribe (medicine) in doses. 3. To treat (wine) with an ingredient, such as syrup, during bottling. [French, from Late Latin dosis, from Greek, a giving, dose, from didonai, to give.] —**dos·er** n.

do·sim·e·ter (dō-sĭm′ə-tər) n. A device that measures and indicates the amount of x-rays or other radiation absorbed by matter, or the intensity of a radioactive source. [DOS(E) + -METER.]

do·sim·e·try (dō-sĭm′ə-trē) n. Medicine. The accurate measurement of doses, especially of radiation for cancer treatment. [DOS(E) + -METRY.]

Dos Pas·sos (dəs păs′əs), **John Roderigo** (1896–1970). U.S. novelist. His writing combines narrative, stream-of-consciousness passages, and newspaper quotations. His best-known work is the trilogy called collectively U.S.A. (1930–36).

doss (dŏs) n. British Slang. 1. A makeshift or crude bed. 2. A sleep. ~intr.v. **dossed, dossing, dosses.** British Slang. To bed down; sleep. Often used with down. [Variant of earlier dorse, from Latin dorsum, back.]

dos·sal, dos·sel (dŏs′əl) n. 1. An ornamental hanging of rich fabric, as behind an altar or at the sides of a chancel. 2. An ornamental covering for the back of a chair or throne. In this sense, also called "dosser." [Medieval Latin dossāle, neuter of dossālis, of the back, from Late Latin dorsālis, DORSAL.]

dos·ser¹ (dŏs′ər) n. 1. A large pack basket; pannier. 2. A dossal. [Middle English doser, from Old French dossier, from Medieval Latin dorsārium, from Latin dorsum, back.]

dosser² n. British Slang. 1. A vagrant. 2. An idle person. [From DOSS.]

dos·si·er (dŏs′ē-ā′, dôs′yā′) n. A collection of papers or documents pertaining to a particular person or subject; a file. [French, from Old French, bundle of papers having a label on the back, from dos, back, from Latin dorsum.]

dost. Archaic. Second person singular present tense of **do.** Used with thou.

Dos·to·yev·sky (dŏs′tə-yĕf′skē), **Fyodor Mikhailovich** (1821–81). Russian novelist, whose works combine religious mysticism with profound psychological and social insight; he is often considered a forerunner of the existentialists. In 1849 he was found guilty of revolutionary activities and sent to a penal colony in Siberia for four years. The experience produced Notes from The House of the Dead (1862). His four great novels are Crime and Punishment (1866), The Idiot (1868), The Possessed (1871–72), and The Brothers Karamazov (1879–80).

dot¹ (dŏt) n. 1. a. A tiny round mark made by or as if by a pointed instrument; a spot; a point. b. Such a mark used in orthography, such as the dot above an i. 2. A tiny amount; speck. 3. In Morse and similar codes, a short sound or signal used in combination with the dash and written as a dot to represent letters, numbers, or punctuation. Compare **dit.** 4. Mathematics. a. A decimal point. b. A symbol of multiplication. 5. Music. a. A dot after a note or rest indicating an increase in time value by half. b. A dot above or below a note indicating that it should be played or sung staccato. —**on the dot.** Informal. Absolutely punctual; on time. ~v. **dotted, dotting, dots.** —tr. 1. To mark with a dot or dots. 2. To form or make with dots. 3. To cover at intervals with or as if with dots. —intr. To make a dot or dots. [16th century : perhaps from Old English dott, head of a boil, perhaps akin to Old English titt, teat, TIT.] —**dot·ter** n. —**dot·ted** adj.

dot² (dŏt; French dō) n. A woman's marriage portion; dowry. [French, from Latin dōs (stem dōt-), dowry.] —**do·tal** (dōt′l) adj.

do·tage (dō′tĭj) n. 1. a. Senility. b. Feeble-mindedness. 2. Foolish or excessive fondness. [Middle English, from doten, to DOTE.]

do·tard (dō′tərd) n. A senile person. [Middle English, from doten, to DOTE.]

dote, doat (dōt) intr.v. **doted** or **doated, doting** or **doating, dotes** or **doats.** 1. To lavish excessive love or fondness. Used with on or upon. 2. To be foolish or feeble-minded, especially as a result of senility. [Middle English doten, from Middle Dutch, to be silly.] —**dot·er** n.

doth. Archaic. Third person singular present tense of **do.**

dot product n. Mathematics. The **scalar product** (see). [So called because it is written x•y.]

dot·se·quen·tial (dŏt′sĭ-kwĕn′shəl) adj. Pertaining to or designating a color-television system in which the primary colors red, green, and blue are transmitted as dots in sequence and exhibited in the same sequence to produce a complete color image.

dot·ted line (dŏt′əd) n. A line of dots, on a legal document for example, where a signature is placed to indicate formal agreement or ratification.

dotted swiss n. A crisp cotton fabric, embellished with woven, flocked, or embroidered dots.

dot·ter·el (dŏt′ər-əl) n. Also **dot·trel** (dŏt′rəl). A small Eurasian plover, Eudromias morinellus, having a gray breast and a chestnut-brown belly. [Middle English, dotard, plover (apparently referring to its supposed stupidity) : DOTE + suffix -rel, as in wastrel.]

dot·tle, dot·tel (dŏt′l) n. The plug of tobacco left in the bowl of a pipe after it has been smoked. [From DOT (in the obsolete sense "lump").]

dot·ty (dŏt′ē) adj. **-tier, -tiest.** Informal. 1. Daft; crazy; eccentric. 2. Infatuated. Used with about. [Variant of Scottish dottle, silly, from Middle English doten, to DOTE.] —**dot·ti·ness** n.

Dou·ai (dōō′ā). Formerly **Dou·ay.** Industrial town in Nord department, France. A college for English Catholics was established here in 1568, where the Old Testament of the **Douay Bible** (see) was published in 1610.

Dou·a·la, Du·a·la (dōō-ä′lə). Chief seaport and largest town of Cameroon. It is one of West Africa's major industrial centers, with brewing, flour-milling, textile, food-processing, and timber industries.

Dou·ay Bible, Dou·ai Bible (dōō′ā). Abbr. **D.Bib., D.V.** An English translation of the Latin Vulgate Bible by Roman Catholic scholars. Also called "Douay Version."

dou·ble (dŭb′əl) adj. Abbr. **dbl.** 1. Of a size, strength, number, or amount that is exactly or roughly twice as great as is usual: a double dose. 2. Composed of two like parts; in a pair: double doors. 3. Composed of two unlike parts; combining two; dual: a double meaning. 4. Accommodating or designed for two: a double sleeping bag. 5. a. Acting two parts: a double agent. b. Characterized by duplicity; deceitful: speak with a double tongue. 6. Botany. Having many more than the usual number of petals, usually in a crowded or overlapping arrangement: a double chrysanthemum. 7. Music. Producing pitches one octave lower than the notes written on the score: a double bass. ~n. Abbr. **dbl.** 1. Something increased twofold; a double quantity or amount. 2. a. An exact likeness or copy of a thing or person. b. An apparition; wraith. 3. An actor's understudy. 4. a. A sharp turn in running, as of a hunted animal or a river; reversal. b. An evasive reversal or shift in argument. 5. a. In darts, the space between the two outer rings on a dartboard. b. A score made from a dart that lands in this space. 6. A bet on two horses in different races, any winnings from the first being placed on the second.

dormouse A largely tree-dwelling European rodent that may get its name from its habit of becoming "dormant" and sleeping through the winter in a nest below ground.

Dorset Horn Breeding in any season, the Dorset Horn is a fast-growing sheep that can lamb three times in two years.

7. *Bridge.* **a.** A bid indicating strength to one's partner; a request for a bid. **b.** A bid doubling one's opponent's bid, thus increasing the penalty for failure to fulfill the contract. **c.** A hand justifying such a bid. —**at** (or **on**) **the double. 1.** *Military.* In double time. **2.** *Informal.* Immediately.
~*v.* **doubled, -bling, -bles.** —*tr.* **1.** To make twice as great. **2.** To be twice as much as. **3.** To fold in two. **4.** *Bridge.* To challenge (an opponent's bid) with a double. **5.** *Music.* To duplicate (another part or voice) an octave higher or lower or in unison. **6.** *Nautical.* To sail around: *double a cape.* —*intr.* **1.** To be increased twofold. **2.** To turn sharply backward; reverse one's direction. Often used with *back: double back on one's trail.* **3.** To serve in an additional capacity: *The firefighter doubled as a carpenter in her spare time.* **4.** To replace an actor in the execution of a given action or in the actor's absence: *doubled for the star in the chase scene.* **5.** *Bridge.* To announce a double. —**double up. 1.** To bend in two: *doubled up with laughter.* **2.** To share the same living or sleeping accommodations. **3.** To cause to double up. **4.** To stake (the winnings from one horse race) on a second race.
~*adv.* **1. a.** To twice the extent; doubly. **b.** To twice the amount: *win double your money back.* **2.** Two together: *sleeping double.* **3.** In two: *bent double; fold the paper double.* —**see double.** To see two images of a single object, usually as a result of visual aberration. [Middle English, from Old French, from Latin *duplus,* twofold, double.] —**dou·ble·ness** *n.* —**dou·bler** *n.*

doub·le-act·ing (dŭb′əl-ăk′tĭng) *adj.* Designating a steam engine in which the pistons are pressurized at either end of the cylinders. Compare **single-acting.**

double agent *n.* A spy working overtly for one country or organization while secretly working for a rival country or organization.

double bar *n.* A double vertical or heavy black line drawn through a staff to indicate the end of any of the main sections of a musical composition.

dou·ble-bar·reled (dŭb′əl-băr′əld) *adj.* **1.** Having two barrels mounted side by side: *a double-barreled shotgun.* **2.** Serving two purposes; twofold; ambiguous.

double bass *n.* The largest member of the violin family, shaped like a cello, played with a bow or, especially in jazz, plucked, and having a deep range of about three octaves. Also called "bass," "bass fiddle," "contrabass," "string bass."

double bassoon *n.* The **contrabassoon** (see).

double bed *n.* A bed wide enough to accommodate two people.

double bill *n.* A bill, as at the movies or a concert, in which there are two main features.

double bind *n.* **1.** *Psychology.* A sense of impasse caused by contradictory injunctions, especially when these are uttered by the same authority. A child hearing *"You're a bad girl!"* and *"Be a good girl!"* is in a double bind, because the first statement may function subconsciously as an order. **2.** A situation that cannot be resolved; a dilemma.

double-blind (dŭb′əl-blīnd′) *adj.* Of, designating, or pertaining to an experiment in which neither the experimenter nor the subjects know, at the time of testing, which are the items or substances being tested and which are the controls. Compare **single-blind.** See **control experiment.**

double boiler *n.* A cooking utensil consisting of an upper removable pan that fits into a lower pan. Water simmering in the lower pan gently cooks the contents of the upper pan.

double bond *n.* A chemical bond that characterizes unsaturated organic molecules in which two atoms are linked by two covalent bonds.

dou·ble-breast·ed (dŭb′əl-brĕs′tĭd) *adj.* **1.** Fastened by lapping one half over the other, and usually having a double row of buttons with a single row of buttonholes: *a double-breasted jacket.* **2.** Having a jacket of this type: *a double-breasted suit.*

double check *n.* A careful reinspection or re-examination to ensure accuracy or efficiency; verification.

dou·ble-check (dŭb′əl-chĕk′) *v.* **-checked, -checking, -checks.** —*tr.* To inspect or examine again; verify. —*intr.* To make a double check.

double chin *n.* A fold of fatty flesh beneath the chin.

dou·ble-coat·ed (dŭb′əl-kō′tĭd) *adj.* Designating a mammal such as a rat or dog having two layers of hair, one longer than the other, which may give a two-tone color effect.

double coconut *n.* **1.** A tall palm tree, *Lodoicea maldivica* (or *L. seychellarum*), of the Seychelles Islands, having broad, fanlike foliage and large fruit. **2.** The two-lobed fruit of this tree, containing one enormous seed, the largest of any plant, sometimes weighing 22 kilograms (48 pounds) each. Also called "coco-de-mer."

double concerto *n.* *Music.* A concerto composed for two solo instruments.

double cream *n.* Thick cream with a high fat content.

dou·ble-cross (dŭb′əl-krôs′, -krōs′) *tr.v.* **-crossed, -crossing, -crosses.** To deceive or betray by acting in contradiction to an agreed course of action. —See Synonyms at **deceive.**
~*n.* An instance of such betrayal; treachery. —**dou·ble-cross·er** *n.* —**dou·ble-cross·ing** *adj.*

double dagger *n.* In writing and printing, a reference mark (‡). Also called "dagger," "diesis."

double date *n.* A date in which two couples participate. —**dou·ble-date** *v.*

Dou·ble·day (dŭb′əl-dā′), **Abner** (1819–93). U.S. army officer and reputed inventor of baseball. As a young man in Cooperstown, New York, he was known as a team sports organizer, and in the late 1800's he was presumed to be the originator of baseball, although later investigations indicate that a game very similar to baseball predates him. A West Point graduate (1842), he had a distinguished military career, which included commanding a division at Gettysburg.

dou·ble-deal·ing (dŭb′əl-dē′lĭng) *adj.* Characterized by duplicity; deceitful; treacherous.
~*n.* An act of treachery or duplicity. —**dou·ble-deal·er** *n.*

dou·ble-deck·er (dŭb′əl-dĕk′ər) *n.* **1.** A bus with two decks or tiers for passengers. **2.** *Informal.* A sandwich having three slices of bread and two layers of filling.

double decomposition *n.* A chemical reaction between two compounds in which the first and second parts of one reactant are united, respectively, with the second and first parts of the other reactant. Also called "metathesis."

dou·ble-dig·it (dŭb′əl-dĭj′ĭt) *adj.* Relating to percentage rates between 10 and 99 percent: *double-digit inflation.*

dou·ble-dot·ted (dŭb′əl-dŏt′ĭd) *adj. Music.* Having two dots added so as to increase the time value by three quarters. Said of a note.

double dribble *n. Basketball.* An illegal dribble in which a player uses both hands simultaneously to dribble the ball or begins to dribble the ball a second time after having come to a complete stop.

double Dutch *n.* Sometimes **double dutch.** Language that cannot be understood; gibberish.

dou·ble-edged (dŭb′əl-ĕjd′) *adj.* **1.** Having two cutting edges: *a double-edged sword.* **2.** Capable of being effective or interpreted in two ways: *double-edged praise.*

dou·ble en·ten·dre (dŭb′əl än-tän′drə; *French* dōō-blän-tän′dr′) *n.* **1.** A word or phrase having a double meaning, especially when the second meaning is risqué. **2.** The use of such expressions. [From obsolete French, "double meaning."]

double entry *n.* A method of bookkeeping in which a transaction is entered both as a debit to one account and a credit to another account, so that the totals of debits and credits are equal. Compare **single entry.**

dou·ble-faced (dŭb′əl-fāst′) *adj.* **1.** Having two faces, aspects, or sides. **2.** Characterized by duplicity; hypocritical. **3.** Finished on both sides. Said of fabric.

double fault *n.* In tennis, the serving of two faults in succession, resulting in the loss of a point.

double feature *n.* A motion-picture program consisting of two full-length films.

double glazing *n.* Glazing consisting of two panes of glass separated by an air space, used to provide protection against heat loss and noise. —**dou·ble-glaze** *v.*

Double Gloucester *n.* A type of mild, orange-colored cheese.

dou·ble-head·er (dŭb′əl-hĕd′ər) *n.* **1.** Two games or events held in succession on the same program, especially in baseball. **2.** A train pulled by two locomotives.

double helix *n. Biochemistry.* The structure of a DNA molecule, consisting of two spiral chains of polynucleotides coiled around the same axis.

double indemnity *n.* A clause in an insurance policy that provides for payment of double the face value of the contract in case of accidental death.

double integration *n. Mathematics.* Two separate integrations performed on an integrand containing two independent variables. In each integration one of the independent variables is kept constant.

dou·ble-joint·ed (dŭb′əl-join′tĭd) *adj.* Having unusually flexible joints permitting connected parts, such as limbs or fingers, to be bent at unusual angles.

double knit *n.* A jerseylike fabric knitted on a machine equipped with two sets of needles so that a double thickness of fabric is produced in which the two sides of the fabric are interlocked.

dou·ble-knit (dŭb′əl-nĭt′) *adj.* Of or made of double knit.

double negative *n.* **1.** A syntactic construction that employs two negatives, especially to express a single negation. **2.** A similar construction in which the repetition of negation produces an affirmative.

Usage: There are several constructions in English in which two negative forms are used together in the same clause to express a single "positive" or "negative" meaning. The most commonly used type, illustrated by *He never said nothing* (to mean "He said nothing"), is not an acceptable standard form. However, its use is widespread in regional dialects as an emphatic expression of negation and it has considerable literary precedent in earlier periods of English. Within standard English, certain types of double negative are acceptable: when the negatives do "cancel out," or "make a positive," as in *I can't not go* (that is, I have to go); to express understatement, as in *He's a not unattractive man;* between main and subordinate clauses of certain kinds, as in *I shouldn't be surprised if he doesn't go;* and as a means of reinforcement later in the sentence, as in *He wouldn't surrender, not even after several appeals.*

dou·ble-park (dŭb′əl-pärk′) *v.* **-parked, -parking, -parks.** —*tr.* To park (a vehicle) alongside another vehicle already parked parallel to the curb. —*intr.* To park a vehicle in such a manner.

double pneumonia *n.* Pneumonia afflicting both lungs.

dou·ble-quick (dŭb′əl-kwĭk′) *adj.* Very quick; rapid.
~*n.* A marching cadence, **double time** (see).
~*intr.v.* **double-quicked, -quicking, -quicks.** To double-time. —**dou·ble-quick** *adv.*

dou·ble-reed (dŭb′əl-rēd′) *adj.* Pertaining to or designating any of a

Douglas fir *One of the world's best timber trees, the Douglas fir is also known as the Oregon fir; it grows to 100 meters (330 feet) in height. It is named after David Douglas, the plant collector who introduced its seeds into Britain in 1827.*

group of wind instruments, such as the oboe, that have a mouthpiece formed of two joined reeds that vibrate against each other.

double refraction *n. Optics.* **Birefringence** *(see).*

dou·bles (dŭb′əlz) *n. Used with a singular verb.* A game, especially of tennis, having two players on each side.

double salt *n. Chemistry.* A salt consisting, or regarded as consisting, of a molecular combination of two simple salts.

dou·ble-space (dŭb′əl-spās′) *v.* **-spaced, -spacing, -spaces.** *—intr.* To type so that there is a full line space between lines. *—tr.* To type (copy) in this way.

dou·ble-speak (dŭb′əl-spēk′) *n.* Complicated and ambiguous language, often meaning the opposite of what is said; double talk.

double standard *n.* **1.** A set of inconsistent ethical principles in which something regarded as reprehensible in one person or in some circumstances may be condoned or approved in others. **2.** A set of principles permitting greater opportunity or liberty to one than to another, especially the granting of greater sexual freedom to men than to women.

double star *n.* A **binary star** *(see).*

dou·blet (dŭb′lĭt) *n.* **1.** A close-fitting jacket, with or without sleeves, worn by men between the 15th and 17th centuries: *doublet and hose.* **2.** A counterfeit gem made of a piece of colored glass covered with crystal or with a thin face of real gemstone. **3. a.** A pair of similar things. **b.** One of a pair. **c.** *Physics.* A multiplet with two members. **4.** *Linguistics.* One of two words derived from the same source by different routes of transmission, such as *fragile* and *frail.* **5. doublets.** A throw of two dice in which the same number of dots appears on the upper face of each. [Middle English, from Old French, from *double,* DOUBLE.]

double take *n.* A delayed reaction to an unusual remark or circumstance, often used in an exaggerated form as a comic device.

double talk *n.* **1.** Meaningless speech that consists of nonsense syllables mixed with intelligible words; gibberish. **2.** Ambiguous or evasive language.

dou·ble-team (dŭb′əl-tēm) *tr.v.* **-teamed, -teaming, -teams.** *Sports.* To guard or cover an offensive player with two defensive players simultaneously.

dou·ble-think (dŭb′əl-thĭngk′) *n.* The belief in two contradictory ideas or points of view at the same time, usually leading to a double standard.

double time *n. Abbr.* **d.t. 1.** A marching pace of 180 three-foot steps per minute. Also called "double-quick." **2.** *Music.* Duple time. **3.** *Military.* A regulation running pace.

dou·ble-time (dŭb′əl-tīm′) *v.* **-timed, -timing, -times.** *—tr.* To march (troops) in double time. *—intr.* **1.** To march in double time. **2.** To jog or run.

dou·ble-tongu·ing (dŭb′əl-tŭng′ĭng) *n.* The playing of a series of notes on a wind instrument by rapidly covering and uncovering the air passage with the tongue. Compare **single-tonguing, triple-tonguing.** **—double-tongue** *v.*

dou·ble·tree (dŭb′əl-trē′) *n.* A crossbar on a wagon or coach to which two whiffletrees are attached for harnessing two animals abreast.

dou·ble-u (dŭb′əl-yōō′) *n.* The letter *w.*

double vision *n.* The simultaneous perception of two images of the same object as a result of poor coordination of the muscles that move the eyeball.

double wedding *n.* A wedding of two couples at the same time.

dou·bloon (dŭ-blōōn′) *n.* An obsolete Spanish gold coin. [Spanish *doblón,* augmentative of *dobla,* Spanish coin, from Latin *dupla,* feminine of *duplus,* DOUBLE.]

dou·blure (dōō-blōōr′) *n.* An ornamental lining, as of vellum or leather, on the inside face of a book cover. [French, lining, from Old French, from *doubler,* to double, line, from Latin *duplāre,* to double, from *duplus,* DOUBLE.]

dou·bly (dŭb′lē) *adv.* **1.** To a double degree; twice. **2.** In a twofold manner.

doubt (dout) *v.* **doubted, doubting, doubts.** *—tr.* **1.** To be uncertain or skeptical about; be undecided about. **2.** To tend to disbelieve; distrust. **3.** *Archaic.* To suspect; fear: *I doubt that Thackeray did not write the Latin epitaph*" (A. Trollope). *—intr.* To be undecided, unconvinced, or skeptical.

~n. **1. a.** *Often* **doubts.** A lack of conviction or certainty. **b.** An instance of this; a point about which one is uncertain or skeptical. **2.** An uncertain condition or state of affairs: *an outcome still in doubt.* —See Synonyms at **uncertainty.** **—beyond doubt.** Unquestionably; definitely. **—no doubt. 1.** Certainly. **2.** Probably. **—without doubt.** Certainly. —See Usage note at **doubtless.** [Middle English *d(o)uten,* from Old French *douter,* from Latin *dubitāre,* to waver, vibrate.] **—doubt·er** *n.*

Usage: Doubt (and *doubtful*) may be followed by *whether, that,* or *if.* In positive statements intended to convey real uncertainty, *whether* is the usual choice, especially in formal contexts (*I doubt whether they can win*). *If* is acceptable but is less formal. The use of *that* in such contexts has been criticized as being "weak" in meaning, but it is quite widely used informally. In negative or interrogative constructions, where there is clear denial of doubt, *that* is appropriate (*Do you doubt that he will come?; I don't doubt that you're right*). See also Usage note at **but.**

doubt·ful (dout′fəl) *adj.* **1.** Subject to or tending to give rise to doubt; uncertain; unclear. **2.** Experiencing doubt. **3.** Of uncertain outcome; undecided. **4.** Questionable; suspect: *a governor with a*

doubtful past. —See Usage note at **doubt.** **—doubt·ful·ly** *adv.* **—doubt·ful·ness** *n.*

Synonyms: arguable, debatable, dubious, questionable.

doubting Thomas *n.* One who habitually expresses or feels doubts and requires concrete proof. [After St. Thomas, the apostle who doubted Christ's resurrection until he had proof.]

doubt·less (dout′lĭs) *adj.* Certain; assured: *doubtless of ultimate victory.*

~adv. **1.** Certainly. **2.** Presumably; probably. **—doubt·less·ly** *adv.*

Usage: Doubtless and *no doubt* are relatively weak in expressing certainty, because they can also indicate mere presumption or probability (*He's doubtless been caught in the traffic*) or concession (*No doubt you're right*). In contrast, *undoubtedly* and *without doubt* express only certainty and conviction (*You are undoubtedly/without doubt correct*).

douce (dōōs) *adj. British Regional.* Sedate; sober; gentle. [Middle English, sweet, pleasant, from Old French, from Latin *dulcis,* sweet.]

dou·ceur (dōō-sûr′) *n.* Money given as a tip, gratuity, or bribe. [French, "sweetness," from Late Latin *dulcor,* from Latin *dulcis,* sweet.]

douche (dōōsh) *n.* **1.** A stream of water or air applied to a part or cavity of the body for cleansing or medicinal purposes. **2.** The application of a douche. **3.** A syringe or other instrument for applying a douche.

~v. **douched, douching, douches.** *—tr.* To cleanse or treat by means of a douche. *—intr.* To be cleansed or treated by a douche. [French, douche, shower, from Italian *doccia,* conduit pipe, douche, probably from *doccione,* tube, from Latin *ductiō* (stem *ductiōn-*), a leading away, from *ductus,* past participle of *dūcere,* to lead.]

dough (dō) *n.* **1.** A soft, thick mixture of flour or meal, liquids, and various dry ingredients that is baked as bread, pastry, or the like. **2.** Any similar pasty mass. **3.** *Slang.* Money. [Middle English *dogh,* Old English *dāg;* from Germanic.]

dough·boy (dō′boi′) *n.* **1.** Bread dough that is rolled thin and cut into various shapes, then fried in deep fat, or that is made into a dumpling and boiled. **2.** *Informal.* An infantryman in World War I. [Sense 2, origin obscure.]

dough·nut, do·nut (dō′nŭt′, -nət) *n.* **1.** A small, ring-shaped or round cake made of rich, light dough that is fried in deep fat. **2.** Anything shaped like a ring; especially, a **torus** *(see).*

dough·ty (dou′tē) *adj.* **-tier, -tiest.** Characterized by courage; stouthearted; valiant. —See Synonyms at **brave.** [Middle English *doughty,* Old English *dohtig, dyhtig,* from Germanic.] **—dough·ti·ly** *adv.* **—dough·ti·ness** *n.*

dough·y (dō′ē) *adj.* **-ier, -iest.** Having the consistency or appearance of dough.

Doug·las (dŭg′ləs). Capital of the Isle of Man. Its buildings include the House of Keys (the parliament) and the Manx Museum. Douglas was the first seaport in the British Isles to be fitted with radar (1948).

Doug·las (dŭg′ləs), **Stephen Arnold** (1813-61). U.S. legislator. A congressman (1843-47) and senator (1847-61), he drafted the Kansas-Nebraska Act (1854), which gave settlers the right to determine whether their territory would be free or slaveholding. His short, thickset stature and political skills earned him the nickname "the Little Giant." Douglas's senatorial campaign of 1858 featured a famous series of debates with Abraham Lincoln. He ran unsuccessfully for president in 1860.

Douglas fir *n.* A tall evergreen timber tree, *Pseudotsuga menziesii,* of northwestern North America, having short needles and egg-shaped cones. Also called "Oregon fir." [After David *Douglas* (1798-1834), Scottish botanist.]

Doug·las-Home (dŭg′ləs-hyōōm′), **Alexander Frederick, Baron Home of the Hirsel** (1903-). British politician. He was elected as a Conservative M.P. in 1931. He lost his seat at the 1945 elections but was returned again in 1950. In 1951 he succeeded his father as the 14th Earl of Home. In 1963 he renounced his hereditary peerage in order to become prime minister and returned to the Commons as Sir Alec Douglas-Home. He was foreign secretary from 1970 to 1974, when he returned to the House of Lords as a life peer.

Douma. Variant of **Duma.**

doum palm, doom palm (dōōm) *n.* An African palm tree, *Hyphaene thebaica,* having a trunk that branches into two, fanlike foliage, and fruit that tastes like gingerbread. Also called "gingerbread palm." [From Arabic *dawm.*]

dour (dōōr, dour) *adj.* **1.** Silently ill-humored; gloomy. **2.** Marked by intractable sternness or harshness; forbidding. —See Synonyms at **glum.** [Middle English, perhaps from Latin *dūrus,* hard.]

doura, dourah. Variants of **durra.**

dou·rine (dōō-rēn′) *n.* A contagious disease of horses, asses, and mules, caused by the microorganism *Trypanosoma equiperdum,* which is transmitted during copulation. [French, from Arabic *darina,* to be dirty.]

Dou·ro (dō′rōō). Spanish **Due·ro** (dwä′rō). River in Portugal and Spain. It flows 722 kilometers (480 miles) from the Sierra de Cebollera, forming part of the Spanish and Portuguese border.

dou·rou·cou·li (dōō′rōō-kōō′lē) *n., pl.* **-lis.** Also **dou·ro·cou·li** (dōō′rō-). Any of various nocturnal monkeys of the genus *Aotus,* of Central and South America, having very large, round eyes. [Native South American name.]

douse¹, dowse (dous) *v.* **doused** or **dowsed, dousing** or **dowsing, douses** or **dowses.** *—tr.* **1.** To plunge into liquid; immerse. **2.** To

douroucouli *This large-eyed Central and South American primate is the only species of monkey to be active at night rather than day.*

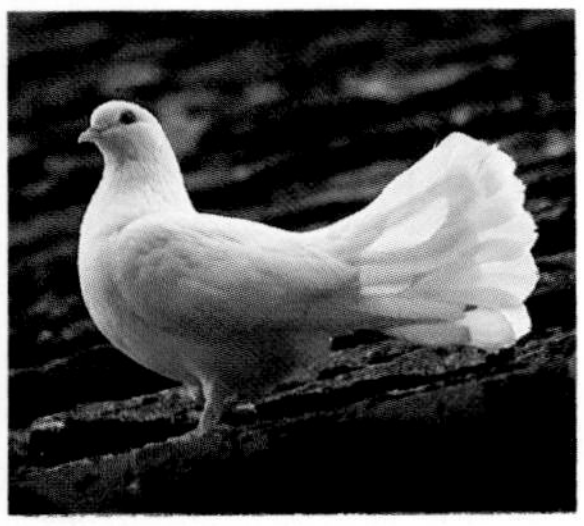

dove Doves pair for life, and both sexes help to rear the young—a habit that may explain their use as a symbol of peace. This is a white fantail dove.

wet thoroughly; drench. —*intr.* To become thoroughly wet; soak. ~*n.* A drenching. [16th century : *douse*†, to strike, smite.] —**dous·er** *n.*

douse² *tr.v.* **doused, dousing, douses.** To put out (a light or fire); extinguish. [Perhaps from earlier sense (to strike, smite) of DOUSE (immerse).]

douse³ *tr.v.* **doused, dousing, douses.** *Nautical.* **1.** To lower (a sail). **2.** To close (a porthole). [Perhaps from Low German; akin to Middle Dutch *dossen,* to beat, strike.]

douse⁴ (douz). Variant of **dowse** (to use a divining rod).

DOVAP (dō′văp′) *n. Electronics.* A system for determining the velocity and position of a long-range missile using the **Doppler effect** *(see).* [*Do*ppler *v*elocity *a*nd *p*osition.]

dove¹ (dŭv) *n.* **1.** Any of various birds of the family Columbidae, which also includes the pigeons; especially, an undomesticated species, such as the **mourning dove** *(see).* **2.** A gentle or innocent child or woman. Used especially as a term of endearment. **3.** A messenger of peace or deliverance from care by allusion to the dove of Genesis 8:8–12. **4.** One advocating a policy of conciliation or moderation. **5.** *Sometimes* **Dove.** The Holy Spirit. **6.** A warm pale gray or grayish-brown color. **7. Dove.** The constellation **Columba** *(see).* [Middle English *do(u)ve,* Old English *dūfe* (unattested), from Germanic.] —**dove** *adj.*

dove² (dōv). Alternate past tense of **dive.**

dove·cote (dŭv′kōt′, -kŏt′) *n.* Also **dove·cot** (-kŏt′). A roost for domesticated pigeons.

dove·kie (dŭv′kē) *n.* Also **dove·key,** *pl.* **-keys.** A sea bird, the **little auk** *(see).* [Diminutive of DOVE.]

Do·ver¹ (dō′vər). Port in Kent, southeast England, the only one of the Cinque Ports that still has a major dock. It is the United Kingdom's principal ferry and hovercraft terminus for the continent, with Calais only 35 kilometers (22 miles) away. The Norman castle that overlooks the town has in its precincts a Roman lighthouse that was used to guide the legions across the Channel.

Dover². The capital (since 1777) of Delaware, in the central part of the state. It was founded in 1683 on William Penn's orders and laid out in 1717. Nearby Dover Air Force Base is important to the city's economy.

Dover, Strait of. A stretch of water between England and France, connecting the English Channel with the North Sea. Its narrowest point, 34 kilometers (21 miles) between Dover and Cap Gris Nez, is the route taken by Channel swimmers. The first successful such crossing was made in 1875.

Dover sole *n.* A European sole, *Solea solea,* valued as a food fish.

Do·ver's powder (dō′vərz) *n.* A powdered drug, made essentially of ipecac and opium, formerly used to relieve pain and induce perspiration. [After Thomas *Dover* (1660–1742), English physician.]

dove·tail (dŭv′tāl′) *n.* **1.** In carpentry, a fan-shaped tenon that forms a tight interlocking joint when fitted into a corresponding mortise. **2.** A joint formed by interlocking one or more such tenons and mortises. In this sense, also called "dovetail joint."
~*v.* **dovetailed, -tailing, -tails.** —*tr.* **1.** To cut into or join by means of dovetails. **2.** To connect or combine precisely or harmoniously. —*intr.* To combine or interlock into a unified whole. [From its supposed resemblance to a dove's tail.]

dow·a·ger (dou′ə-jər) *n.* **1.** A widow who holds a title or property derived from her dead husband. Often used in combination with the title. **2.** An elderly woman of means or status. [Old French *douagiere,* from *douage,* dower, from *douer,* to portion, endow, from Latin *dōtāre,* from *dōs* (stem *dōt-*), dowry.]

dow·dy (dou′dē) *adj.* **-dier, -diest.** Lacking in stylishness or neatness; shabby; old-fashioned: *dowdy clothes.*
~*n., pl.* **dowdies.** A dowdy woman; frump. [From Middle English *doude*†, slut.] —**dow·di·ly** *adv.* —**dow·di·ness** *n.*

dow·el (dou′əl) *n.* **1.** A usually round pin that fits tightly into a corresponding hole to fasten or align two adjacent pieces of wood or stone. **2.** A round stick or rod from which dowels are cut. In this sense, also called "doweling." **3.** A piece of wood driven into a wall to act as an anchor for nails.
~*tr.v.* **doweled** or **-elled, doweling** or **-elling, -els. 1.** To fasten or align with dowels. **2.** To equip with dowels. [Middle English *dowle,* from Middle Low German *dovel,* peg, block, nail.]

dow·er (dou′ər) *n.* **1.** The part or interest of a deceased man's real estate allotted by law to his widow for her lifetime. Also *archaic* "dowry." **2.** A marriage portion, **dowry** *(see).* **3.** A natural endowment or gift.
~*tr.v.* **dowered, -ering, -ers.** To assign a dower to; endow. [Middle English *dowere,* from Old French *douaire,* from Medieval Latin *dōtārium,* from Latin *dōs* (stem *dōt-*), dowry.]

dower house *n.* A smaller house, often near a manor house, intended for occupation by a dowager.

dow·itch·er (dou′ĭ-chər) *n.* Either of two shore birds, *Limnodromus griseus* or *L. scolopaeus,* of northern regions, having brownish plumage and a long, straight bill. [Of Iroquoian origin.]

Dow-Jones Averages (dou′jōnz′) *n.* A trademark used for an index of the relative price of selected industrial, transportation, and utility stocks based on a formula developed and periodically revised by Dow Jones & Company, Inc. [After C.H. *Dow* (1851–1902) and E.D. *Jones* (1856–1920), U.S. economists.]

Dow·land (dou′lənd), **John** (1562–1626). Anglo-Irish composer, born in Dublin. He was the most celebrated lute player of his time and served the king of Denmark and Charles I of England. His *Songs or Ayres* (1597–1603) were known throughout Europe.

down¹ (doun) *adv. Abbr.* **dn. 1. a.** From a higher to a lower place or position. **b.** Downstairs. **c.** Toward, to, or on the ground, floor, or bottom. **d.** Toward a point further away. **e.** So as to be no longer erected or displayed: *took the decorations down.* **f.** So as to remain in the stomach: *can't keep her food down.* **2. a.** Into a lower posture. **b.** In or into a prostrate position. **3.** Out of one's grasp. **4.** Toward or in the south or in a southerly direction. **5. a.** Away from somewhere considered central or as a center of activity, such as a capital city. **b.** Away from a town: *down in the country; down on the farm.* **6.** To the source: *tracking a rumor down.* **7. a.** Toward or at a low or lower point on a scale. **b.** Lower in price, standing, or the like. **8.** To or in a quiescent or subdued state. **9. a.** To or in a low status, as of subjection or disgrace. **b.** Reduced to a specified condition: *down to begging from passers-by.* **c.** Progressing through all relevant stages toward the lowest stage: *down through the ranks.* **10.** *Sports.* Being a specified number of points behind a competitor: *went two goals down in the second half.* **11.** Seriously; vigorously: *get down to work.* **12.** From earlier times or people. **13 a.** To a reduced, lessened, or diluted form: *worn down; watered down.* **b.** To a reduced but more concentrated or finer consistency: *boiling down a sauce.* **14.** In writing; on paper: *taking a statement down.* **15.** In partial payment at the time of purchase: *twenty dollars down.* **16.** Into a state of silence or inaudibility: *shouted her down.* **17.** In a condition of inaction or malfunction: *The computer is down.* **18.** *Nautical.* Having the rudder to windward. —**down with.** Used to express disapproval or urge the removal of someone or something.
~*adj.* **1. a.** Moving or directed downward: *a down escalator.* **b.** In a low position; not up. **c.** At a reduced level. **2. a.** Ill; sick: *He's down with the flu.* **b.** Low in spirit; depressed: *feel down.* **3.** Being a deposit: *a down payment.* **4.** *Physics.* Designating a type of quark with minus one-third electronic charge, a baryon number of one-third, and no strangeness or charm. —**down on.** *Informal.* Hostile or negative toward; out of patience with.
~*prep.* **1.** In a descending direction along, upon, into, or through. **2.** Along the course of. **3.** Toward the mouth of a river.
~*n.* **1.** A downward movement; descent. **2.** A period of ill fortune or depression; *She had her ups and downs.*
~*v.* **downed, downing, downs.** —*tr.* **1.** To bring, put, strike, or throw down. **2.** To swallow hastily; gulp. —*intr.* To go or come down; descend. [Middle English *doun,* Old English *dūne,* short for *adūne,* reduced form of *ofdūne,* "from the hill" : *of,* OFF + *dūne,* dative of *dūn,* hill.]

Usage: As a general rule, *down* is used for travel in a southerly direction, and *up* for travel to the north.

down² *n.* **1.** Fine, soft, fluffy feathers forming the first plumage of a young bird and underlying the contour feathers in certain adult birds. **2.** *Botany.* A covering of soft, short fibers, as on some leaves. **3.** Any soft, silky, or feathery substance, such as the first growth of human beard. [Middle English *doun, downe,* from Old Norse *dūnn.*]

down³ *n.* **1.** *Usually* **downs. a.** An expanse of rolling, grassy upland, especially in southern England. **b.** The temperate grasslands of New Zealand and Australia. **2.** *Often* **Down.** Any of several breeds of sheep having short wool, developed in the downs of England. [Middle English *doun, dun,* hill, Old English *dūn.*]

Down (doun). County in Northern Ireland, stretching from the Mourne Mts. to the Irish Sea. Downpatrick is the county town.

down-and-out (doun′ən-out′) *n.* **1.** A destitute person. **2.** A person who is incapacitated. —**down-and-out** *adj.*

down·beat (doun′bēt′) *n. Music.* **1.** The downward stroke made by a conductor to indicate the first beat of a measure. Compare **upbeat. 2.** The first beat of a bar.
~*adj. Informal.* **1.** Depressed; pessimistic. **2.** Casual; relaxed and unconcerned.

down-bow (doun′bō′) *n. Music.* A stroke made by drawing a bow from handle to tip across the strings of a violin or other bowed instrument. Compare **up-bow.**

down·cast (doun′kăst′, -käst′) *adj.* **1.** Depressed; dejected; sad. **2.** Directed downward.
~*n.* **1.** A ventilation shaft in a mine. **2.** A **downthrow** *(see).* —See Synonyms at **sad.**

down·court (doun-kôrt′, -kŏrt′) *adv. & adj. Sports.* To, into, or in the far end of the court, especially in basketball.

Down East or **down East** *n.* New England, especially Maine.

Down Easter or **down-East·er** (doun-ē′stər) *n.* A native of New England, especially Maine.

down·er (dou′nər) *n. Slang.* **1.** A depressant or sedative drug, such as a barbiturate or tranquilizer. Compare **upper. 2.** A depressing experience.

down·fall (doun′fôl′) *n.* **1. a.** A sudden loss of wealth, rank, reputation, or happiness; ruin. **b.** Something causing this. **2.** A fall of rain or snow, especially a heavy or unexpected one.

down·fall·en (doun′fô′lən) *adj.* Fallen, as from prominence; ruined.

down·field (doun-fēld′) *adv. & adj. Sports.* To, into, or in the defensive team's end of the field.

down·grade (doun′grād′) *n.* A descending slope in a road. —**on the downgrade.** Declining, as in influence, reputation, or wealth; losing status.
~*tr.v.* **downgraded, -grading, -grades. 1.** To lower the status and salary of. **2.** To lower or minimize the importance or reputation of.

down·haul (doun′hôl′) *n. Nautical.* A rope or set of ropes for hauling down or securing a sail or spar.

down·heart·ed (doun′här′tĭd) *adj.* Low in spirit; depressed; discouraged. —**down·heart·ed·ly** *adv.* —**down·heart·ed·ness** *n.*

PRONUNCIATION KEY

ă, pat; ā, pay; âr, care; ä, father, are; b, bib; ch, church; d, deed; ĕ, pet; ē, be; f, fife; g, gag; h, hat; hw, which; ĭ, pit; ī, pie; îr, pier; j, judge; k, kick; l, lid, needle; m, mum; n, no, sudden; ng, thing; ŏ, pot; ō, toe; ô, paw, for; oi, noise; ou, out; ŏŏ, book; ōō, boot; p, pop; r, roar; s, sauce; sh, ship, dish; t, tight; th, thin, path; *th,* this, bathe; ŭ, cut; ûr, fur; v, valve; w, with; y, yes; z, zebra, size; zh, vision; ə, about, item, edible, gallop, circus, peaceful

IN FOREIGN WORDS:

à, *Fr.* ami; œ, *Fr.* feu, *Ger.* schön; ü, *Fr.* tu, *Ger.* über; KH, *Ger.* ich, *Scot.* loch; N, *Fr.* bon; y′, *Fr.* Compiègne

STRESS MARKS:

Primary stress: ′
in·cite′ (ĭn-sīt′)
Secondary stress: ′
in′sight′ (ĭn′sīt′)

down·hill (doun'hĭl') *adv.* Down the slope of a hill; in a downward direction. **—go downhill.** To decline, as in quality or performance. ~*adj.* (doun'hĭl'). **1.** Sloping downward; descending. **2.** Designating a skiing race run downhill. **3.** Placed lower on a slope. Said of a ski, skier's foot, or the like. **4.** Leading to failure or deterioration. **5.** Progressively easier. ~*n.* **1.** A downward slope. **2.** A skiing event in which competitors race one at a time down a slope against the clock.

down·home (doun'hōm') *adj.* Of, relating to, or characteristic of the rural southern United States or its people, as in simplicity, informality, or earthiness.

Down·ing Street (dou'nĭng) *n.* The British prime minister or government. [From the location of the prime minister's residence at No. 10 Downing Street, off Whitehall, in Westminster, London.]

down·load (doun'lōd') *tr.v.* **-loaded, -loading, -loads.** *Computer Science.* To transmit (programs or data) from a main computer to a smaller computer or terminal. [*downline* + *load.*]

down·play (doun'plā') *tr.v.* **-played, -playing, -plays.** To play down; minimize the importance or significance of.

down·pour (doun'pôr', -pōr') *n.* A heavy fall of rain.

down·range (doun'rānj') *adv.* In a direction away from the launch site and along the flight line of a missile test range. ~*adj.* (doun'rānj'). Designating the area and airspace along the flight line of a missile test range.

down·right (doun'rīt') *adj.* **1.** Thoroughgoing; unequivocal. **2.** Forthright; candid. ~*adv.* Thoroughly; absolutely.

down·shift (doun'shĭft') *intr.v.* **-shifted, -shifting, -shifts.** To shift a motor vehicle to a lower gear. **—down·shift** *n.*

Downs, North and South (dounz). Two roughly parallel ranges of chalk hills in southeast England. The North Downs run through Surrey and Kent to the white cliffs of Dover; the South Downs through Sussex to Beachy Head. Both are sheep-rearing areas.

down·spout (doun'spout') *n.* A pipe that carries water from a roof or gutter down to a drain or into the ground.

Down's syndrome (dounz) *n.* A type of mental retardation caused by a chromosome abnormality, giving rise to certain characteristic physical features, notably an oblique slant of the eyes. In nontechnical usage also called "mongolism." **—See usage note at mongolism.** [After John Langdon-*Down* (died 1896), English physician who classified it.]

down·stage (doun'stāj') *adv.* Toward or at the front of a stage. ~*adj.* (doun'stāj'). Pertaining to the front part of a stage. ~*n.* (doun'stāj'). The front half of a stage.

down·stairs (doun'stârz') *adv.* **1.** Down the stairs. **2.** To or on a lower floor. ~*adj.* (doun'stârz'). Located on a lower or main floor. ~*n.* (doun'stârz'). *Used with a singular verb.* The lower or main floor.

down·stream (doun'strēm') *adj.* **1.** In the direction of a river's or stream's current. **2.** *Finance.* Closer to the point of sale than to the point of production or manufacture. Compare **upstream.** ~*adv.* (doun'strēm'). Down a stream.

down·swing (doun'swĭng') *n.* **1.** A swing downward, especially in golf. **2.** A declining trend, as in popularity or prosperity.

down·throw (doun'thrō') *n.* *Geology.* The net downward movement of rocks on one side of a fault plane. Also used adjectively: *the downthrow side.* Also called "downcast."

down·tick (doun'tĭk') *n.* A transaction in a stock market security below the price of the previous transaction.

down·time (doun'tīm') *n.* **1.** The period of time when a factory or its machinery is inactive. **2.** Time during which a computer is inoperative because of a technical malfunction.

down-to-earth (doun'tə-ûrth') *adj.* Realistic; sensible.

down·town (doun'toun') *adv.* To, toward, or in the lower part or the business center of a city or town. ~*adj.* (doun'toun'). Of, pertaining to, or located in such an area. ~*n.* (doun'toun'). The business center or lower part of a city or town. Compare **uptown.**

down·trod·den (doun'trŏd'n) *adj.* **1.** Oppressed; tyrannized. **2.** Trampled down.

down·turn (doun'tûrn') *n.* A tendency downward, especially in business or economic activity.

down under *n. Informal.* Australia or New Zealand. ~*adv.* In or to Australia or New Zealand.

down·ward (doun'wərd) *adv.* Also **down·wards** (-wərdz), **down·ward·ly** (-wərd-lē). **1.** From a higher to a lower place, point, level, or condition. **2.** From an earlier to a more recent time. ~*adj.* **1.** Descending from a higher to a lower place, point, level, or condition. **2.** Descending from a source or origin.

downward mobility *n.* The movement of an individual or group to a lower social status.

down·warp (doun'wôrp') *n. Geology.* A small-scale downward movement of the earth's crust, producing no folding or faulting. **—down·warp·ing** *n.*

down·wind (doun'wĭnd') *adv.* In the direction in which the wind is blowing; leeward. **—down·wind** *adj.*

down·y (dou'nē) *adj.* **-ier, -iest.** **1.** Made of, filled with, or covered with down. **2. a.** Resembling down. **b.** Covered with something resembling down. **3.** Quietly soft; soothing.

downy mildew *n.* A disease of plants caused by fungi of the order Peronosporales and characterized by gray, velvety patches of spores on the lower surfaces of leaves.

dow·ry (dour'ē) *n., pl.* **-ries.** **1.** Money or property brought by a bride to her husband at marriage. Also called "dower." **2.** *Archaic.* A widow's inheritance, formerly a **dower** *(see).* **3.** A sum of money formerly required of a postulant when entering certain orders of nuns. **4.** A natural endowment or gift. [Variant of DOWER.]

dowse[1] (douz) *intr.v.* **dowsed, dowsing, dowses.** Also **douse, doused, dousing, douses.** **1.** To use a divining rod or pendulum to find underground water or minerals. **2.** To use apparently paranormal powers to make discoveries. [17th century : origin obscure.] **—dows·er** *n.*

dowse[2] (dous). Variant of **douse** (to drench).

dowsing rod *n.* A **divining rod** *(see).*

Dowson (dou'sən), **Ernest Christopher** (1867–1900). English poet. Alcoholic and debt-ridden, Dowson died of tuberculosis at 32. His poems include *Non Sum Qualis.*

Dow theory (dou) *n.* A theory of stock market forecasting based on the activity of the market itself. [After Charles H. *Dow* (1851–1902), U.S. economist.]

dox·as·tic (dŏk-săs'tĭk) *adj. Logic.* Of or pertaining to belief. [Greek *doxastikos,* having an opinion or belief, from *doxa,* belief.]

dox·ol·o·gy (dŏk-sŏl'ə-jē) *n., pl.* **-gies.** A liturgical formula of praise to God. See **Gloria in excelsis Deo, Gloria Patri.** [Medieval Latin *doxologia,* from Greek, laudation : *doxa,* opinion, judgment + -LOGY.] **—dox·o·log·i·cal** (dŏk'sə-lŏj'ə-kəl) *adj.* **—dox·o·log·i·cal·ly** *adv.*

dox·y (dŏk'sē) *n., pl.* **-ies.** *Slang.* **1.** A prostitute. **2.** A paramour. [16th century : (cant) origin obscure.]

dox·y·cy·cline (dŏk-sĭ-sī'klēn') *n.* A broad-spectrum antibiotic, $C_{22}H_{24}N_2O_8$, derived from tetracycline. [D(E)- + OX(Y)- + (TETRA)-CYCLINE.]

doy·en (doi-ĕn', doi'ən; *French* dwä-yăN') *n.* The eldest or senior member of a group, as of a diplomatic corps or literary circle. [French, from Late Latin *decānus,* chief of ten, a kind of officer, from Greek *dekanos,* from *deka,* ten.]

doy·enne (doi-ĕn'; *French* dwä-yĕN') *n.* A woman who is a doyen.

Doyle (doil), **Sir Arthur Conan** (1859–1930). British writer, the creator of Sherlock Holmes. He trained as a doctor but gave up medicine in 1890 after his first Sherlock Holmes book, *A Study in Scarlet.* He was knighted in 1902, the year he published his most celebrated piece of detective fiction, *The Hound of the Baskervilles.*

doyley, doyly. Variants of **doily.**

D'Oy·ly Carte (doi'lē kärt'), **Richard** (1844–1901). English theater impresario. He presented Gilbert and Sullivan's operettas and built the Savoy Theatre (1881) for the performance of their works.

doz. dozen.

doze (dōz) *intr.v.* **dozed, dozing, dozes.** To sleep lightly and intermittently; nod sleepily; nap. **—doze off.** To fall into a light sleep. ~*n.* A short, light sleep; nap. [Originally transitive, to make dull, drowse, probably of Scandinavian origin; akin to Danish *døse.*] **—doz·er** *n.*

doz·en (dŭz'ən) *n., pl.* **dozen** (for sense 1) or **-ens** (for sense 2). *Abbr.* **doz., dz.** **1.** A set of 12. **2. dozens.** *Informal.* An indefinite number; a great many. **—daily dozen.** Physical exercises performed regularly in the morning. ~*adj.* Twelve. [Middle English *dozeine,* from Old French, from *doze,* twelve, from Latin *duodecim* : *duo,* two + *decem,* ten.] **—doz·enth** *adj.*

do·zy (dō'zē) *adj.* **-zier, -ziest.** Drowsy; half asleep. **—doz·i·ly** *adv.* **—do·zi·ness** *n.*

DP, D.P. displaced person.

D.Ph., D.Phil. Doctor of Philosophy.

dpt. **1.** department. **2.** deponent.

dr dram.

dr. **1.** debit. **2.** debtor. **3.** drachm. **4.** drachma. **5.** drawer.

Dr. **1.** doctor. **2.** Drive (in street names).

drab[1] (drăb) *adj.* **drabber, drabbest.** **1.** Faded and dull in appearance. **2.** Of a commonplace character; dreary. **3. a.** Of a dull light brown. **b.** Of a light olive brown or khaki color. ~*n.* **1.** Cloth of a light dull brown, grayish brown, or unbleached natural color; especially, a heavy woolen or cotton fabric. **2.** Moderate to grayish or light grayish yellowish brown or light olive brown. **3.** Monotony. [Variant of obsolete *drap,* cloth, from Old French. See **drape.**] **—drab·ly** *adv.* **—drab·ness** *n.*

drab[2] *n.* **1.** A slovenly woman. **2.** A prostitute. ~*intr.v.* **drabbed, drabbing, drabs.** To consort with prostitutes. [Perhaps from Low German; compare Dutch *drab,* dregs.]

drab·bet (drăb'ət) *n. British.* A yellowish-brown twilled linen. [From DRAB (cloth).]

drab·ble (drăb'əl) *v.* **-bled, -bling, -bles.** **—intr.** To draggle; become wet and muddy. **—tr.** To bedraggle. [Middle English *drabelen,* of Low German origin, akin to Low German *drabbelen,* to paddle in water or mire.]

dra·cae·na (drə-sē'nə) *n.* Any of several tropical plants of the genera *Dracaena* and *Cordyline,* some species of which are cultivated as house plants for their decorative foliage. [New Latin *Dracaena,* from Late Latin, from Greek *drakaina,* feminine of *drakōn,* serpent, DRAGON.]

drachm (drăm) *n. British. Abbr.* **dr.** **1.** A dram. **2.** A drachma. [Middle English, from Old French, from Late Latin *dragma,* from Greek *drakhmē,* DRACHMA.]

drach·ma (drăk'mə) *n., pl.* **-mas** or **-mae** (-mē). *Abbr.* **d., D. dr.** **1. a.** The basic monetary unit of Greece, equal to 100 lepta. **b.** A coin worth one drachma. See feature at **currency.** **2.** A silver coin

Downing Street *The front door of 10 Downing Street, official residence of the British Prime Minister.*

dragon

THE UNIVERSAL MONSTER
Different roles for the dragon in myths from east and west

Every civilization creates its own legendary heroes. But most have had at least one beast in common: the dragon. Curiously, dragons are described remarkably consistently all over the world, as giant snakelike creatures with claws. Some are winged as well—like the red dragon of Wales—and some breathe fire. Christianity associated the monsters with the devil, and in Babylonian, Egyptian, and ancient Jewish legends, dragons symbolized chaos. But in Japan, the imperial family once traced its descent from a sea god called the Dragon King; and China and Scandinavia often saw dragons as guardians of treasure.

ST. GEORGE AND THE DRAGON *England's patron saint, St. George, saves a terrified maiden from death in a painting done by a 19th-century Czech artist, Josef Manes. The legend of the chivalrous Christian hero depicts the dragon as the embodiment of all evil, the devil incarnate.*

MARK OF THE BEAST *A fearsome but benevolent guardian dragon glares from a Chinese robe made during the Ch'ing dynasty (1644–1912). The beast's five-clawed limbs mark it as an exclusively imperial protector; commoners were restricted, on pain of death, to four-clawed designs.*

of ancient Greece. **3.** A unit of weight of ancient Greece. [Latin, from Greek *drakhmē.*]

Dra·co (drā′kō) *n.* A constellation in the polar region of the Northern Hemisphere near Cepheus and Ursa Major. Also called "Dragon." [Latin *dracō,* DRAGON.]

dra·co·ni·an (drā-kō′nē-ən) *adj.* Also **dra·con·ic** (drā-kŏn′ĭk). **1.** *Often* **Draconian.** Designating an ancient Athenian law or code reputed to be of extreme severity. **2.** Harsh; rigorous: *draconian measures; a draconian penalty.* [After *Draco,* Athenian statesman and lawgiver, whose code (621 B.C.) punished even the most trivial offenses by death.] —**dra·con·i·cal·ly** *adv.*

dra·con·ic[1] (drā-kŏn′ĭk) *adj.* Of or pertaining to a dragon. [Latin *dracō* (stem *dracōn-*), DRAGON.]

draconic[2]. Variant of **draconian.**

draff (drăf) *n.* Also *chiefly British* **draught.** Refuse from brewing or distilling; dregs; lees of malt. [Middle English *draf,* Old English *dræf* (unattested).]

draft (drăft, dräft) *n.* **1. a.** A current of air in an enclosed area. **b.** A current of air induced by artificial means. **c.** A device in a flue controlling the circulation of air. **2. a.** A pull or traction of a load. **b.** That which is pulled or drawn. **c.** *British.* The traction power or duty of a locomotive. **3.** The depth of a vessel's keel below the water line. **4. a.** A gulp, swallow, or inhalation. **b.** The amount taken in by a single act of drinking or inhaling. **c.** A measured portion, dose. **5.** The drawing of a liquid, as from a cask or keg. **6. a.** The drawing in of a fishnet. **b.** The catch. **7. a.** A preliminary version of a plan, document, picture, or the like. **b.** A representation of something to be constructed. **8.** A documentary instruction to transfer money. **9.** A demand, as on resources or a person's goodwill. **10. a.** The transfer of soldiers from one unit to another or to a special duty. **b.** The soldiers transferred. **11. a.** Conscription for military service. **b.** Those conscripted for military service. **12.** *Masonry.* A narrow line chiseled on a stone to guide the stonecutter in leveling its surface. **13.** *Metallurgy.* A slight taper given a die to facilitate the removal of a casting. **14.** *Commerce.* An allowance made for loss of weight in merchandise. —**on draft.** Tapped from the keg; not bottled.

~*tr.v.* **drafted, drafting, drafts.** Also *chiefly British* **draught. 1. a.** To draw up a preliminary version of or plan for. **b.** To compose. **2.** *Military.* **a.** To attach or assign to a different unit. **b.** To conscript. **3.** To enlist the services of (a person) for a special purpose. Often used with *in.* **4.** To chisel a line on (a stone) to guide the cutter.

~*adj.* Also *chiefly British* **draught. 1.** Suited for or used for drawing heavy loads. **2.** Drawn from a cask or tap. [Middle English *draught,* a pulling, a drawing, perhaps from Old Norse *drāttr.*] —**draft·er** *n.*

draft board *n.* A local board of civilians in charge of the selection of men for compulsory military service.

draft·ee (drăf-tē′, dräf-) *n.* One conscripted for military service.

draft·ing (drăf′tĭng, dräf′-) *n.* The systematic representation and dimensional specification of mechanical and architectural structures. Also called "mechanical drawing."

drafts·man (drăfts′mən, dräfts′-) *n., pl.* **-men** (-mĭn). **1.** One who draws plans or designs. **2.** One who draws up documents. **3.** One who excels in drawing. [Drafts, genitive of DRAFT + MAN.] —**drafts·man·ship** *n.*

draft·y (drăf′tē, dräf′-) *adj.* **-ier, iest.** Having or exposed to drafts of air. —**draft·i·ly** *adv.* —**draft·i·ness** *n.*

drag (drăg) *v.* **dragged, dragging, drags.** —*tr.* **1. a.** To pull or draw along the ground by force; haul. **b.** To cause to trail along the ground. **2. a.** To search or sweep the bottom of (a body of water), as with a grappling hook or dragnet. **b.** To bring up or catch by such means. **3. a.** To take forcibly away from, to, or into. **b.** To take (a reluctant person) somewhere. **4.** To move with great reluctance, weariness, or difficulty. **5.** To break (land) with a harrow. **6.** To prolong unnecessarily or tediously. Used with *out.* **7.** To introduce gratuitously into a discussion. Used with *in.* **8.** To extract (a confession, for example) from a stubbornly reticent person. **9.** To follow (an animal or a trail). Used of hunting hounds. —*intr.* **1.** To trail along the ground. **2.** To move slowly or with effort. **3.** To lag behind. **4.** To pass or proceed slowly, tediously, or laboriously. **5.** To search or dredge the bottom of a body of water. **6.** *Slang.* To draw on a cigarette.

~*n.* **1.** The act of dragging. **2.** Something that is dragged along the ground, such as a harrow or an implement for spreading manure. **3.** A device for dragging under water, such as a grappling hook, dredge, or dragnet. **4.** A heavy sledge or cart for conveying loads. **5.** A large four-horse coach with seats inside and on top. **6.** Something that retards motion, such as a sea anchor. **7. a.** A person or thing that holds one back or hinders progress; drawback. **b.** *Slang.* Something or someone that is obnoxiously tiresome or boring: *What a drag!* **8.** The degree of resistance involved in dragging or hauling. **9.** *Aviation.* The retarding force exerted on a moving body by a fluid medium. **10.** *Billiards.* A backspin given to the cue ball to prevent it from continuing onward after hitting another ball. **11.** A

dragonfly *One of the fastest-moving insects, it can swoop across fields at up to 55 kilometers (35 miles) per hour.*

slow, laborious motion or movement. **12.** *Hunting.* Something that provides an artificial scent. Also used adjectivally: *drag hounds.* **13.** *Slang.* A puff on a cigarette, pipe, or cigar. **14.** *Slang.* **a.** A **dragster** *(see).* **b.** A race for dragsters. **15.** *Slang.* Women's clothing worn by a man. Sometimes used adjectively: *a drag show.* [Middle English *draggen,* from Old English *dragan* or Old Norse *draga.*]

drag anchor *n. Nautical.* A **sea anchor** *(see).*

dra·gée (drȧ-zhāʹ) *n.* **1.** A tiny round, hard sweet used for decorating cakes. **2.** A small, often medicated, sweet. **3.** A sweet made of fruit and nuts and coated in hard icing. [French, "sweetmeat," from Old French *drageet.*]

drag·gle (drăgʹəl) *v.* **-gled, -gling, -gles.** —*tr.* To make wet and dirty by dragging in mud. —*intr.* **1.** To become muddy by being trailed. **2.** To follow slowly; lag; straggle. [Frequentative of DRAG.]

drag·gle-tail (drăgʹəl-tāl′) *n. Archaic.* A bedraggled or slatternly woman.

drag·gle-tailed (drăgʹəl-tāld′) *adj.* Bedraggled.

drag·gy (drăgʹē) *adj.* **-gier, -giest. 1.** Dull and listless. **2.** *Slang.* Obnoxiously tiresome.

drag·line (drăgʹlīn′) *n.* **1.** A line used for dragging. **2.** A kind of dredging machine.

drag link *n.* A link for transmitting rotary motion between cranks on two parallel but slightly offset shafts, such as the rod connecting the lever of the steering gear to the steering arm in an automobile.

drag·net (drăgʹnĕt′) *n.* **1. a.** A net for dragging the bottom of lakes or rivers in the search for an object. **b.** A net for catching small game. **2.** The system of interrelated police procedures used in the apprehension of criminal suspects.

drag·o·man (drăgʹə-mən) *n., pl.* **-mans** or **-men** (-mĭn). Formerly, an interpreter or guide in countries where Arabic, Turkish, or Persian was spoken. [Middle English *drogman,* from Old French *drugeman,* from Medieval Latin *dragumannus,* from Middle Greek *dragoumanos,* from Arabic *targumān,* from Aramaic *tūrgemānā,* from Akkadian *targumānu,* "interpreter," from *ragāmu,* to call, akin to Mishnaic Hebrew *targūm,* TARGUM.]

drag·on (drăgʹən) *n.* **1. a.** A fabulous monster, represented usually as a gigantic reptile breathing fire and having a lion's claws, the tail of a serpent, wings, and a scaly skin. **b.** A figure or other representation of this creature. **2.** *Archaic.* A large snake or serpent. **3.** A fiercely vigilant or intractable older woman. **4.** Any of various lizards, such as one of the genus *Draco,* or the **Komodo dragon** *(see).* **5.** A plant, the **green dragon** *(see).* **6. Dragon.** The constellation Draco *(see).* Preceded by *the.* **7. Dragon.** Satan; the Devil. Preceded by *the old.* [Middle English *drago(u)n,* from Old French *dragon,* from Latin *dracō* (stem *dracōn-*), dragon, serpent, from Greek *drakōn,* serpent.]

drag·on·et (drăgʹə-nĭt) *n.* Any of various small, often brightly colored marine fishes of the family Callionymidae, having a slender body and a flattened head. [Middle English, from DRAGON.]

drag·on·fly (drăgʹən-flī′) *n., pl.* **-flies.** Any of various large insects of the order Odonata, having two pairs of narrow, iridescent, netveined wings and a long, slender body. Sometimes called "darning needle," "devil's darning needle."

drag·on·head (drăgʹən-hĕd′) *n.* Any of several plants of the genera *Dracocephalum* or *Physostegia,* having terminal spikes of rose-pink or purplish flowers.

drag·on·nade (drăgʹə-nād′) *n.* **1.** *History.* An act of persecution of the Huguenots in France in the reign of Louis XIV, consisting of the quartering of dragoons on their property. **2.** Any subjection by military force.
~*tr.v.* To subject to military persecution. [French, from *dragon,* DRAGOON.]

drag·on·root (drăgʹən-rōōt′, -rŏot′) *n.* A plant, the **green dragon** *(see).*

dragon's blood *n.* **1.** A red, resinous substance obtained from the fruit of certain palm trees, such as *Daemonorops draco,* and from the stems of various species of *Dracaena,* formerly used in the manufacture of varnishes and lacquers. **2.** Any of several similar resins.

dragon's teeth *pl.n. Informal.* Obstacles, such as pointed concrete stakes, placed in the ground to hinder the progress of tanks and other military vehicles.

dragon tree *n.* A tree, *Dracaena draco,* of the Canary Islands, having a thick trunk, clusters of sword-shaped leaves, and orange fruit. [Its resin was once thought to be the same substance as the blood in a dragon's veins.]

dra·goon (drə-gōōn′, drȧ-) *n.* **1.** A heavily armed trooper in some European armies of the 17th and 18th centuries. **2.** A type of domestic fancy pigeon.
~*tr.v.* **dragooned, -gooning, -goons. 1.** To persecute by the use of troops. **2.** To coerce; harass. [French *dragon,* carbine, "firebreather," from Old French, DRAGON.]

drag race *n.* A race between specially modified cars to determine which can accelerate faster from a standstill.

drag rope *n.* **1.** A rope used for dragging military equipment. **2.** The rope that trails from a hot-air balloon and is used for braking or mooring.

drag·ster (drăgʹstər) *n.* A car specially modified for drag races.

drail (drāl) *n.* A fishhook weighted with lead and dragged through the water. [Probably a variant of TRAIL.]

drain (drān) *v.* **drained, draining, drains.** —*tr.* **1.** To draw off (a liquid) by a gradual process. **2.** To cause liquid substance to go out from; empty; dry. **3.** To drink all the contents of. **4. a.** To consume totally; exhaust. **b.** To deplete. **c.** To fatigue or spend emotionally or physically. —*intr.* **1.** To flow off or go out of. **2.** To become empty or dry by the drawing off of liquid. **3.** To discharge surface waters in a given tract of land or region, through natural drainage channels. —See Usage note at **deplete.**
~*n.* **1.** A pipe or channel by which liquid is drawn off, especially one carrying off rainwater, sewage, and the like. **2.** *Surgery.* A device, such as a tube, inserted into the opening of a wound or cavity to facilitate discharge of fluid. **3.** The action or process or an instance of depletion or exhaustion. **4.** *Electronics.* The electrode in a field-effect transistor into which the majority carriers flow from the interelectrode space. —**down the drain.** *Informal.* Wasted; lost. [Middle English *dreinen,* Old English *drēahnian,* from Germanic.] —**drain·a·ble** *adj.*

drain·age (drāʹnĭj) *n.* **1.** The action or a given method of draining. **2.** A natural or artificial system of drains. **3.** That which is drained off. **4.** *Medicine.* The draining of fluids from wounds or body cavities.

drainage basin *n.* The area drained by a river system.

drain·er (drāʹnər) *n.* One that drains, especially a device to hold objects being drained; specifically, a rack to hold tableware for drying.

drain·pipe (drān′pīp′) *n.* A pipe for carrying off rainwater or sewage.

drake¹ (drāk) *n.* A male duck. [Middle English, perhaps from Low German, from West Germanic *drako* (unattested), male.]

drake² *n.* **1.** A mayfly used as fishing bait. Also called "drake fly." **2.** *History.* A type of small cannon. [Middle English *drake,* dragon, drake fly, Old English *draca,* from West Germanic *drako* (unattested), from Latin *dracō,* DRAGON.]

Drake (drāk), **Sir Francis** (*c.* 1540–1596). English admiral and navigator, the first Englishman to circumnavigate the world (1580). In 1587, when war with Spain loomed, Drake attacked Cádiz, destroying about 30 Spanish ships. He was vice admiral of the fleet that destroyed the Spanish Armada (1588).

Dra·kens·berg Mountains (dräʹkənz-bûrg′). The principal mountain range in southern Africa, extending from Cape Province through the Transvaal and Natal.

Drake Strait or **Passage.** Strait in Antarctica, extending *c.* 805 kilometers (500 miles) between the South Pacific Ocean and the South Atlantic Ocean south of Cape Horn.

dram (drăm) *n.* **1.** *Abbr.* **dr** **a.** A unit of weight in the U.S. Customary System, an avoirdupois unit equal to 27.344 grains or 0.0625 ounce. **b.** A unit of apothecary weight, equal to 60 grains. **2. a.** A small draft: *a dram of whiskey.* **b.** A bit: *not a dram of sympathy.* [Middle English *dragme, drame,* dram, drachma, from Old French, from Medieval Latin *dragma,* from Latin *drachma,* DRACHMA.]

dram. dramatic.

dra·ma (dräʹmə, drămʹə) *n.* **1.** A prose or verse composition written for or as if for performance by actors; a play. **2.** The dramatic art or a particular dramatic repertory: *Elizabethan drama.* **3. a.** A situation or succession of events in real life having the dramatic progression or emotional content characteristic of a play. **b.** A histrionic scene. **4.** The quality or condition of being dramatic. [Late Latin *drāma,* from Greek *drama,* deed, action on the stage, drama, from *dran,* to do.]

Dram·a·mine (drămʹə-mēn′) *n.* A trademark for dimenhydrinate, used to treat travel sickness.

dra·mat·ic (drə-mătʹĭk) *adj. rare* **dra·mat·i·cal** (-ĭ-kəl). *Abbr.* **dram. 1.** Of or pertaining to drama or the theater. **2.** Resembling a drama in emotional content or progression. **3.** Striking in appearance or forcefully effective. [Late Latin *drāmaticus,* from Greek *dramatikos,* from *drama* (stem *dramat-*), DRAMA.] —**dra·mat·i·cal·ly** *adv.*

dramatic irony *n.* Irony occurring as in a drama, when the implications of words uttered are understood by the audience but not by the characters in the play. Also called "irony."

dramatic monologue *n.* A literary work, especially in verse, in which a figure reveals his or her character in a monologue addressed by the reader or to another person.

dra·mat·ics (drə-mătʹĭks) *n. Used with a singular or plural verb.* **1.** The art of acting. **2.** The study or art and practice of staging plays. **3.** Dramatic or histrionic behavior.

dram·a·tis per·so·nae (drămʹə-tĭs pər-sōʹnē, dräʹmə-tĭs) *pl.n.* **1.** *Used with a plural verb.* The characters in a play or story. **2.** *Used with a singular verb.* A list of these characters, printed at the beginning of the text. [New Latin, "characters of the drama."]

dram·a·tist (drămʹə-tĭst, dräʹmə-) *n.* A playwright.

dramatization (drămʹə-tə-zāʹshən, dräʹmə-) *n.* **1.** The act of dramatizing, especially of transforming a novel or similar work into a play or drama. **2.** A dramatic version of something.

dram·a·tize (drămʹə-tīz′, dräʹmə-) *v.* **-tized, -tizing, -tizes.** —*tr.* **1.** To adapt for presentation as a drama. **2.** To present or view in a dramatic or melodramatic way; exaggerate. **3.** To bring home strikingly; emphasize. —*intr.* **1.** To be adaptable to dramatic form. **2.** To indulge in dramatic or melodramatic behavior.

dram·a·turge (drămʹə-tûrj′, dräʹmə-) *n.* A playwright. [French, from Greek *dramatourgos,* contriver, dramatist : *drama* (stem *dramat-*), DRAMA + *ergon,* work, deed.]

dram·a·tur·gy (drămʹə-tûrʹjē, dräʹmə-) *n.* The art of the theater. —**dram·a·tur·gic, dram·a·tur·gi·cal** *adj.*

drank. Past tense of **drink.**

dr ap apothecaries' dram.

drape (drāp) *v.* **draped, draping, drapes.** —*tr.* **1.** To dress or hang with or as if with cloth in loose folds. **2.** To arrange or let fall in

dragon tree *An ornamental tree of the Canary Islands that can grow 18 meters (60 feet) tall and 6 meters (20 feet) across. It yields an orange fruit and a red gum once used in medicine.*

loose folds. **3.** To hang or rest limply: *I draped my legs over the chair.* —*intr.* To fall or hang in loose folds.
~*n.* **1.** A drapery. **2.** A curtain. **3.** The way in which cloth falls or hangs. [Middle English *drapen,* to weave, from Old French *draper,* from *drap,* cloth, from Late Latin *drappus,* from Celtic.]

drap·er (drā'pər) *n. British.* A dealer in cloth or clothing and haberdashery. [Middle English, from Norman French, from Old French *drap,* DRAPE.]

drap·er·y (drā'pə-rē) *n., pl.* **-ies. 1.** Cloth or clothing arranged in loose folds; especially, clothing draped on figures in sculpture and painting. **2.** *Often* **draperies.** Curtains, usually of heavy fabric, that drape. **3.** Cloth; fabric. **4.** *British.* The business or premises of a draper.

dras·tic (drăs'tĭk) *adj.* **1.** Violently effective. **2.** Especially severe; extreme. [Greek *drastikos,* active, efficient, from *drān,* to do.] —**dras·ti·cal·ly** *adv.*

drat (drăt) *tr.v.* **dratted, dratting, drats.** *Informal.* To damn. Used interjectionally to express annoyance. [Short for earlier *'od rot,* euphemism for *God rot.*]

Drau. See **Drava.**

draught. *Chiefly British.* Variant of **draft.**

draughts (drăfts, dräfts) *n. Chiefly British. Used with a singular verb.* The game of **checkers** *(see).* [Middle English *draughtes,* plural of DRAUGHT, in obsolete sense, a chess move.]

Dra·va, Dra·ve (drä'və). German **Drau** (drou). River in east-central Europe. It flows 724 kilometers (450 miles) from the Carnic Alps in northern Italy to join the Danube near Osijek, Croatia.

dr avdp avoirdupois dram.

drave. *Archaic.* Past tense of **drive.**

Dra·vid·i·an (drə-vĭd'ē-ən) *n.* **1.** A large family of languages spoken mainly in southern India and northern Sri Lanka, and including Tamil, Telegu, Malayalam, and Kanarese. **2.** A member of any of the peoples that speak one of the Dravidian languages; especially, a member of the aboriginal population of southern India. ~*adj.* Also **Dra·vid·ic** (-vĭd'ĭk). Of or pertaining to Dravidian or the Dravidians. [Sanskrit *Drāviḍaḥ,* a Dravidian. See also **Tamil.**]

draw (drô) *v.* **drew** (dro͞o), **drawn, drawing, draws.** —*tr.* **1.** To pull (something) toward or after one. **2.** To pull or move (something) in a given direction or to a given position. **3. a.** To remove or take out: *draw a book from the shelf.* **b.** To extract (a tooth). **c.** To take or pull out, as from a scabbard or holster. **4.** To cause to flow forth: *a pump drawing water.* **5.** To suck or take in (air or liquid). **6.** To displace (a specified depth of water) in floating: *a boat drawing 18 inches.* **7.** To cause to move, as by leading. **8.** To induce to act. **9.** To attract. **10. a.** To extract from evidence at hand; formulate: *draw conclusions.* **b.** To bring (a fact, for example) to someone's attention. **c.** To take from a source; derive. **11. a.** To earn; bring in: *draw interest.* **b.** To withdraw (money). **c.** To use (a check, for example) when paying. **12.** To evoke; elicit. **13.** To force (a card) to be played. **14.** To take or accept as a chance: *draw lots.* **15.** To get or receive by chance. **16.** To end (a game) in a draw. **17.** To distort; contract. **18. a.** To stretch taut. **b.** To bend (a bow) by pulling back the string. **19.** To shape (wire or candles, for example). **20.** To eviscerate. **21. a.** To describe (a line or figure) with a pencil or similar instrument. **b.** To draft or sketch (a picture). **22.** To portray by lines, words, or imitative actions. **23.** To compose or write up (a will or contract, for example) in proper form. **24.** To close or open (a curtain). **25.** In billiards, to cause (a ball) to spin backward after impact with another ball. —*intr.* **1.** To proceed; move. **2.** To describe forms and figures; sketch. **3.** To be an attraction. **4.** To take in a draft of air: *The flue isn't drawing.* **5.** To use or call upon part of a fund or store. Used with *on* or *upon.* **6.** To cause suppuration. **7.** To steep in the manner of tea. **8.** To pull out a weapon for use. —**draw a blank. 1.** To be unsuccessful; lose. **2. a.** To fail to find something. **b.** To forget something completely. —**draw and quarter. 1.** To execute (a prisoner) by tying each limb to a horse and driving the horses in different directions. **2.** To disembowel and dismember after hanging. —**draw away.** To move ahead (as of a competitor in a race). —**draw back. 1.** To step backward. **2.** To hesitate to carry something out; withdraw from something. —**draw down.** To deplete by consuming or spending: *drew down our oil reserves.* —**draw in. 1.** To entice or involve. **2. a.** To become shorter. Used of days. **b.** To become longer. Used of nights. —**draw on. 1.** To approach; move along. **2.** To bring on; cause. **3.** To use as a source of supply. —**draw oneself up.** To straighten oneself up, as when provoked or annoyed. —**draw out. 1.** To cause to converse easily. **2.** To cause to behave in a relaxed or natural way. **3.** To prolong; drag out. —**draw straws.** To decide by a lottery with straws of uneven length. —**draw the line.** To set a limit, as of acceptable behavior. —**draw up. 1.** To write up in set form; draft; compose. **2.** To pull up to a halt.
~*n.* **1.** An act of drawing. **2. a.** A raffle or lottery. **b.** The random choosing of tickets, numbers, contestants, or the like in a raffle, lottery, or sporting competition. **c.** Something chosen in or as if in a lottery. **3.** A special advantage; edge: *She had the draw on her opponent.* **4.** A contest ending in a tie. **5.** *Informal.* A person, event, or other spectacle that attracts large numbers of people. **6.** A natural drainage basin; gully. [Draw, drew, drawn; Middle English *drawen, drow, drawen,* Old English *dragan, drōh, dragen,* to drag, draw, from Germanic.]

draw·back (drô'băk') *n.* **1.** A disadvantage or inconvenience. **2.** A refund or remittance, such as a discount on duties or taxes for

goods destined for re-export or for the manufacture of goods that are to be exported.

draw·bar (drô'bär') *n.* **1.** A bar across the rear of a tractor to which machinery may be attached. **2.** A railroad coupler.

draw·bore (drô'bôr', -bōr') *n.* A hole bored in a tenon such that a pin driven into the hole will tighten the joint.

draw·bridge (drô'brĭj') *n.* A bridge that can be raised or drawn aside either to prevent access or to permit passage beneath it.

draw·down (drô'doun') *n.* **1.** A lowering of the water level in a reservoir. **2.** The act, process, or result of depleting.

draw·ee (drô'ē') *n.* A person or organization, such as a bank, on whom an order for the payment of money is drawn.

draw·er (drô'ər; drôr *for sense* 2; drôrz *for sense* 3) *n.* **1.** One who draws, specifically: **a.** A draftsman. **b.** *Abbr.* **dr.** A person who draws an order for the payment of money. **2.** A boxlike compartment in furniture that can be drawn out on slides. **3. drawers.** Underpants.

draw·ing (drô'ĭng) *n.* **1.** The act or an instance of drawing. **2.** The art of depicting forms or figures on a surface by means of lines. **3.** A portrayal of a form or figure in lines on a surface.

drawing account *n.* An account recording cash payments to a partner or employee to cover expenses or as advances on commissions.

drawing board *n.* **1.** A flat rectangular board to which paper or canvas may be affixed for making drawings. **2.** *Informal.* The basic planning stages. Used chiefly in the phrase *back to the drawing board.*

drawing pin *n. British.* A **thumbtack** *(see).*

drawing room *n.* **1.** A formal reception room. **2.** Formerly, a ceremonial reception. **3.** A private room on a railroad sleeping car. [Originally, a room to which one retired for rest, short for *withdrawing room.*]

draw·knife (drô'nīf') *n., pl.* **-knives** (-nīvz'). A woodcutting knife with a handle at each end of the blade, used to shave a surface with a drawing motion. Also called "drawshave," "spokeshave."

drawl (drôl) *v.* **drawled, drawling, drawls.** —*intr.* **1.** In the speech of certain dialects, for example, to lengthen or add vowels or to make diphthongs of vowels. **2.** To speak in a slow and lazy manner. —*tr.* To utter with a drawl.
~*n.* The speech or manner of speaking of one who drawls: *a Southern drawl.* [16th century : probably cant, from Low German.] —**drawl·er** *n.*

drawn. Past participle of **draw.**
~*adj.* **1.** Pulled out of a sheath. Said of a sword. **2.** Haggard, as from fatigue or ill health. **3.** Eviscerated, as is an oven-ready chicken. **4.** Resulting in a draw. Said of a game.

drawn butter *n.* The clarified butter that separates from the salt and curds after melting, often used with herbs as a sauce.

drawn work *n.* A type of needlework done by drawing out threads from the fabric, usually linen, which is being worked, and adding other embroidery. Also called "drawn thread work."

draw·plate (drô'plāt') *n.* A die with conical holes through which wire is drawn to regulate its thickness.

draw poker *n.* A kind of poker in which each player is dealt five cards face down and may then discard and get replacements for a specified number of cards after the first round of betting.

draw sheet *n.* A bed sheet that can be removed easily from under an invalid.

draw·string (drô'strĭng') *n.* A cord or ribbon run through a hem or casing and pulled to tighten or close an opening. Also used adjectivally: *a drawstring purse.*

draw·tube (drô'to͞ob', -tyo͞ob') *n.* A tube that slides within another tube to form a telescopic unit.

dray (drā) *n.* A low, heavy cart, typically without sides, used especially by brewers for haulage. [Middle English *draye,* probably Old English *dræge,* dragnet, from *dragan,* to DRAW.]

dray·age (drā'ĭj) *n.* **1.** Transport by dray. **2.** A charge for transport by dray.

dray horse *n.* A horse for hauling heavy loads; a draft horse.

dray·man (drā'mən) *n., pl.* **-men** (-mĭn). A driver of a dray.

dread¹ (drĕd) *v.* **dreaded, dreading, dreads.** —*tr.* **1.** To be in terror of; fear greatly. **2.** To anticipate with alarm, anxiety, or reluctance. **3.** To hold in awe or reverence. —*intr.* To be very afraid.
~*n.* **1.** Profound fear; terror. **2.** Anxious or fearful anticipation. **3.** Awe; reverence. **4.** The object of fear, awe, or reverence. —See Synonyms at **fear.**
~*adj.* **1.** Terrifying; fearsome; dreadful. **2.** Awesome; revered. [Middle English *dreden,* Old English *drǣdan†.*]

dread² *n.* A man who wears dreadlocks; a Rastafarian. —**dread** *adj.*

dread·ful (drĕd'fəl) *adj.* **1.** Extremely unpleasant; distasteful or shocking. **2.** *Informal.* Used as an intensive: *a dreadful rush.* **3.** Inspiring dread; terrible. —**dread·ful·ly** *adv.* —**dread·ful·ness** *n.*

dread·locks (drĕd'lŏks') *pl.n.* A matted, manelike hairstyle consisting of numerous twisted and waxed strands, characteristically worn by Rastafarian men. —**dread·lock** *adj.*

dread·nought (drĕd'nôt') *n.* A heavily armed battleship.

dream (drēm) *n.* **1.** A series of images, ideas, and emotions occurring involuntarily to the mind in certain stages of sleep. **2.** A daydream; reverie. **3.** A state of abstraction; a trance. **4.** A wild fancy or hope. **5.** An aspiration; an ambition. **6.** Anything extremely beautiful, fine, or pleasant. —**like a dream.** Smoothly; successfully.
~*v.* **dreamed** or **dreamt** (drĕmt), **dreaming, dreams.** —*intr.* **1.** To

experience a dream or dreams in sleep. **2.** To daydream. **3.** To have a deep aspiration; hope for something. Used with *of.* **4.** To consider something feasible or practical; conceive even remotely. Used in the negative with *of: I wouldn't dream of stopping you.* —*tr.* **1.** To experience an image sequence of in sleep. **2.** To conceive of; imagine. **3.** To pass idly or in reverie. Used with *away.* —**dream up.** To invent; concoct. [Middle English *drem, dreem,* Old English *drēam,* joy, gladness, music, from Germanic.]

dream·boat (drēm′bōt′) *n. Informal.* A person who is one's romantic ideal.

dream·er (drē′mər) *n.* **1.** One who dreams. **2.** A person who daydreams; an escapist. **3.** A person habitually inclined to interpret experience imaginatively without strict regard to practical concerns; a visionary.

dream·land (drēm′lănd′) *n.* An ideal or imaginary land.

dream·scape (drēm′skāp′) *n.* A dreamlike scene or illustration having surreal qualities. [*dream* + land*scape.*]

dream·y (drē′mē) *adj.* **-i·er, -i·est. 1.** Resembling a dream; vague. **2.** Given to daydreams or reverie. **3.** Soothing; quiet; serene. **4.** *Informal.* Inspiring delight; wonderful. —**dream·i·ly** *adv.* —**dream·i·ness** *n.*

drear·y (drîr′ē) *adj.* **-i·er, -i·est.** Also *poetic* **drear** (drîr). **1.** Gloomy; dismal. **2.** Boring; dull. **3.** Discouraging; depressing. —See Synonyms at **boring.** [Middle English *dreri,* Old English *drēorig,* bloody, grievous, sad, from *drēor,* blood.] —**drear·i·ly** *adv.* —**drear·i·ness** *n.*

dreck, drek (drĕk) *n. Slang.* Trash, especially inferior merchandise made to cheat the buyer. [Yiddish *drek* or German *Dreck,* from Middle High German *drec.*]

dredge¹ (drĕj) *n.* **1.** Any of various machines equipped with scooping or suction devices used in deepening or clearing harbors and waterways and in underwater mining. **2.** A boat or barge equipped with such a machine. **3.** An implement consisting of a net on a frame, used for gathering shellfish. —*v.* **dredged, dredging, dredges.** —*tr.* **1.** To clean, deepen, or widen with a dredge. **2.** To bring up with a dredge. Used with *up.* —*intr.* To use a dredge. —**dredge up.** To come up with; unearth. [15th century (Scottish); perhaps from Low German.]

dredge² *tr.v.* **dredged, dredging, dredges.** To coat (food, for example) by sprinkling with a powder, such as flour or sugar. [From obsolete *dredge,* sweetmeat, from Old French *dragie†,* DRAGÉE.]

dredg·er¹ (drĕj′ər) *n.* A barge or boat equipped with a dredge.

dredger² *n.* A container with a perforated lid used for coating food with a powder, such as flour.

dree (drē) *tr.v.* **dreed, dreeing, drees.** *Scottish & Archaic.* To endure. [Revived (by Sir Walter Scott) from Old English *drēogan.*]

D region *n. Meteorology.* The **D layer** *(see).*

dregs (drĕgz) *pl.n.* **1.** The sediment of a liquid; lees. **2.** The basest or least desirable portion. **3. dreg.** A small amount; residue. —**the dregs.** *Informal.* A contemptible individual or group. [Middle English *dreg* (singular), from Old Norse *dregg.*] —**dreg·gy** (drĕg′ē) *adj.*

Drei·bund (drī′bo͞ont′) *n.* An alliance of three powers, especially the Triple Alliance of Germany, Austria-Hungary, and Italy formed in 1882. [German, "triple bund."]

dreich (drēKH) *adj. Scottish.* Dreary; bleak. [Middle English *dreig,* enduring, Old English *drēog* (unattested), from *drēogan,* to endure.]

drei·del, drei·dl (drād′l) *n.* **1.** A toy similar to a top with four sides marked by Hebrew letters. **2.** A game of chance played by children at Hanukah. [Yiddish *dreydl,* from *dreyen,* to turn, from Middle High German *drœjen,* from Old High German *drāen.*]

Drei·ser (drī′sər, -zər), **Theodore** (1871-1945). U.S. novelist. His exposure of the seamier side of American life earned him charges of immorality, especially for his first novel, *Sister Carrie* (1900). He wrote *An American Tragedy* (1925), filmed as *A Place in the Sun.*

drench (drĕnch) *tr.v.* **drenched, drenching, drenches. 1.** To wet throughly; saturate. **2.** To administer a dose of liquid medicine to (an animal). —*n.* **1.** The act of drenching. **2.** A large dose of liquid medicine. [Middle English *drenchen,* to drown, from Old English *drencan,* to give to drink, soak.] —**drench·er** *n.*

Dres·den (drĕz′dən). City on the Elbe River in eastern Germany. It was once the capital of Saxony and in the 17th and 18th centuries was a center for the arts. It was badly damaged in 1760 during the Seven Years' War and was almost completely destroyed by Allied bombing in 1945. The famous Dresden china industry was moved to Meissen in 1710. The city now manufactures machine tools, electronics, and chemicals.

Dresden china *n.* Meissen ware *(see).* [From DRESDEN.]

dress (drĕs) *v.* **dressed, dressing, dresses.** —*tr.* **1.** To put clothes on; clothe. **2.** To trim; adorn. Sometimes used with *up.* **3.** To arrange a display in: *dress a shop window.* **4.** To arrange (troops) in ranks; align. **5.** To apply bandages or other therapeutic materials to (a wound). **6.** To arrange (the hair or a hairpiece); comb and set in a style. **7.** To groom (an animal); curry. **8.** To improve (land) by adding fertilizer, lime, or the like. **9.** To protect (seeds) with a fungicide. **10.** To clean (fish or fowl) for cooking or sale. **11.** To put a finish on (stone, fabric, or other material). **12.** To prepare (hides) in leather-making. —*intr.* **1.** To put on clothes. **2.** To wear clothes. **3.** To wear formal clothes. **4.** To get into proper alignment. —**dress down. 1.** To scold; reprimand. **2.** To wear more casual clothes than usual. —**dressed to kill.** *Informal.* Dressed with conspicuous elegance. —**dress up. 1.** To wear formal clothes, or cloth-

ing more formal than usual, as for a special occasion. **2.** To wear fancy dress. **3.** To arrange in ranks. —*n.* **1.** Clothing; apparel. **2.** A one-piece, skirted outer garment for women and children. **3.** An outer covering or appearance. **4.** *Obsolete.* A setting right; redress. —*adj.* **1.** For or pertaining to a dress. **2. a.** Suitable for a formal occasion: *a dress coat; dress uniform.* **b.** Requiring formal clothing: *a dress dinner.* [Middle English *dressen,* to place, put, prepare, from Old French *drecier, dresser,* from Vulgar Latin *directiāre* (unattested), from Latin *dīrigere* (past participle *dīrectus*), to DIRECT.]

dres·sage (drə-säzh′, drĕ-) *n.* **1.** The guiding of a horse through a series of complex maneuvers by slight movements of the hands, legs, and body weight. **2.** The training of a horse in deportment and obedience. **3.** A part of an equestrian competition in which such skills are tested. [French, preparation, from *dresser,* to DRESS.]

dress circle *n.* A section of seats in a theater or opera house, usually the first tier above the stalls or ground floor. [Originally reserved for persons in formal dress.]

dress code *n.* A set of rules, as in a school, indicating the approved manner of dress.

dress·er¹ (drĕs′ər) *n.* **1.** One that dresses. **2.** A wardrobe assistant, as for an actor; valet. **3.** One who dresses well or in some specified way. **4.** A tool used for dressing stone, leather, or other materials.

dresser² *n.* **1.** A chest of drawers with a mirror. **2.** A cupboard or set of shelves for the open display of dishes or kitchen utensils. [Middle English *dressour,* kitchen sideboard on which food was prepared, from Old French *dreceur,* from *drecier,* to prepare, DRESS.]

dress·ing (drĕs′ĭng) *n.* **1.** The act of one that dresses. **2.** A therapeutic material applied to a wound. **3.** A sauce for certain dishes, such as salads. **4.** Manure, lime, or the like, used to dress soil. **5.** Stiffening used in the finishing of fabrics. **6.** The various processes collectively by which hides are turned into leather. **7.** Stuffing for poultry, fish, or the like. **8.** Fungicide used to coat seeds.

dress·ing-down (drĕs′ĭng-doun′) *n.* A severe scolding.

dressing gown *n.* A light coatlike garment, usually worn for lounging or before dressing.

dressing room *n.* A room in a theater or home in which one may change clothes or apply make-up.

dressing table *n.* A piece of bedroom furniture, usually consisting of a low chest of drawers with a mirror.

dress·mak·er (drĕs′mā′kər) *n.* One who makes women's clothes and household articles, such as curtains, made of fabric. —*adj.* Having soft rather than tailored lines. Said of women's clothing. —**dress·mak·ing** *n.*

dress parade *n.* A military parade in dress uniform.

dress rehearsal *n.* A final, uninterrupted run-through, as of a play complete with costumes and stage properties.

dress shield *n.* A piece of waterproof material worn under the armpit to prevent perspiration from staining the clothing.

dress shirt *n.* A man's shirt that is suitable for wear with a necktie.

dress suit *n.* A man's formal suit.

dress·y *adj.* **-i·er, -i·est. 1.** Having a penchant for smart clothing. **2.** Smart; stylish. **3.** Suitable for more formal occasions: *too dressy to wear to the office.* —**dress·i·ly** *adv.* —**dress·i·ness** *n.*

drew. Past tense of **draw.**

Drew (dro͞o), **John** (1827-62). U.S. actor, born in Ireland. Noted for his performances in Shakespearean comedies and society dramas, he organized a famous stock company in Philadelphia with his wife, **Louisa Lane Drew** (1820-97). Their eldest son, **John Drew** (1853-1927), was a romantic actor noted for his versatility in comedy.

drey (drā) *n.* A squirrel's nest. [17th century : origin obscure.]

Drey·fus (drā′fəs, drī′-), **Alfred** (1859-1935). Jewish captain in the French army. He was convicted of treason (that is, of passing secrets to the Germans) by a secret court martial (1894) and sentenced to solitary confinement for life on Devil's Island. Émile Zola and other friends of Dreyfus who suspected that anti-Semites had victimized him campaigned on his behalf, and in 1898 it was disclosed that the evidence against him had been forged. In 1906 Dreyfus was officially cleared, reinstated as a major, and awarded the Legion of Honor.

drib·ble (drĭb′əl) *v.* **-bled, -bling, -bles.** —*intr.* **1.** To flow or fall in drops or an unsteady stream; trickle. **2.** To drool; slobber. **3.** *Sports.* To dribble a ball. —*tr.* **1.** To let flow or fall in drops or an unsteady stream. **2.** *Sports.* To move (a ball) by repeated light hits or kicks, as in basketball or soccer. —*n.* **1.** A trickle; a drip. **2.** A small quantity; a bit. **3.** *Sports.* The act of moving a ball by dribbling. [Frequentative of obsolete *drib,* variant of DRIP.] —**drib·bler** *n.*

drib·let (drĭb′lĭt) *n.* **1.** A tiny falling drop of liquid. **2.** A small amount or portion. [From obsolete *drib,* drop, from *drib,* to dribble, variant of DRIP.]

dribs and drabs (drĭbz′ən drăbz′) *pl.n.* Small and sporadic amounts. [From obsolete *drib,* a drop (see **driblet**) + *drab,* reduplication of *drib.*]

dri·er¹ (drī′ər) *n.* Also **dry·er. 1.** One that dries. **2.** A substance added to paint, varnish, or ink to speed drying.

drier². Alternate comparative of **dry.**

driest. Alternate superlative of **dry.**

drift (drĭft) *v.* **drifted, drifting, drifts.** —*intr.* **1.** To be carried along by or as if by currents of air or water. **2.** To proceed without resistance; move unhurriedly and smoothly. **3. a.** To move through life

with no particular goal. **b.** To progress without a set aim. **4. a.** To wander from a set course or point of attention; stray. **b.** To vary from or oscillate randomly about a fixed setting, position, or mode of operation. **5.** To be piled up in banks or heaps by the force of a current of wind or water. Used especially of snow. **6.** To continue in motion for a while after a switching off of power. *—tr.* **1.** To carry along by or as if by a current; cause to drift. **2.** *Western U.S.* To drive (livestock) slowly or far afield, especially for grazing.
~n. **1.** The act or condition of drifting. **2.** Something moving along on a current of air or water. **3. a.** A bank or pile, as of sand or snow, heaped up by currents of air or water. **b.** Any bank or mass, as of flowers. **4.** *Geology.* **a.** Rock debris transported and deposited by or from ice, especially by or from a glacier or ice sheet. **b.** *British.* Any superficial, unconsolidated deposit above a solid rock layer. **5. a.** A trend or general bearing; direction. **b.** General meaning or purport; tenor. **6. a.** Lateral displacement or deviation of a ship, aircraft, projectile, or the like from a planned course, especially as a result of wind, ocean current, or other disturbance in the medium of travel. **b.** Variation or random oscillation about a fixed setting, position, or mode of behavior. **7.** The rate of flow of a water current. **8. a.** A tool for ramming or driving something down. **b.** A tapered steel pin for enlarging and aligning holes. **9.** *Mining.* **a.** A horizontal or nearly horizontal passageway running through or parallel to a vein. **b.** A secondary passageway between two main shafts or tunnels. **10.** A drove or herd, especially of swine. **11.** *Linguistics.* Gradual change in a language or group of languages. —See Synonyms at **tendency**. [Middle English, a driving, snowdrift, a drove, both from Old Norse *drift,* snowdrift, and from Middle Dutch *drift,* herd, course.] **—drift·y** *adj.*

drift·age (drĭf′tĭj) *n.* **1.** Deviation from a set course caused by drifting. **2.** Anything that has been carried along or deposited by air or water currents.

drift anchor *n.* A sea anchor *(see).*

drift·er (drĭf′tər) *n.* **1.** One that drifts, especially: **a.** One who moves from place to place or from job to job. **b.** A vagabond. **c.** One who is passive and makes no attempt to control the course of his life. **2.** A fishing boat with a net that drifts with the current. **3.** A large sail on a ship used when there is little wind.

drift ice *n.* Loose pieces of ice floating on the sea that drift with the current or wind and so cause no danger to passing ships.

drift net *n.* A type of large fishing net with weights at the bottom and floats at the top that drifts with the tide.

drift transistor *n.* A transistor with a good high-frequency response in which the impurity concentration in the base region varies smoothly from a high level at the emitter-base junction to a low level at the base-collector junction.

drift tube *n. Physics.* A hollow tube formerly used as an electrode in a linear accelerator, inside which electrons, accelerated between electrodes by a radio-frequency field, drift (move at a constant velocity) toward the next electrode.

drift velocity *n. Physics.* The average velocity of a carrier moving in an applied electric field, especially in a semiconductor.

drift·wood (drĭft′wo͝od′) *n.* **1.** Wood floating in or washed up by a tide. **2.** A collection of worthless or trivial elements.

drill[1] (drĭl) *n.* **1. a.** An implement with cutting edges or a pointed end for boring holes in hard materials, usually by a rotating abrasion or by repeated blows. Also called "drill bit." **b.** A hand-held tool, electrically or manually powered, for rotating such an implement. **c.** A **drill press** *(see).* **2.** Disciplined, repetitious exercise as a means of teaching and perfecting a skill or procedure, especially as part of military training. **3.** A specific task or exercise designed to develop a skill or familiarity with a procedure. **4.** *Informal.* An appropriate procedure. **5.** Any of several marine gastropod mollusks of the genera *Urosalpinx, Ocenebra,* and related genera, that drill holes into the shells of bivalve mollusks; especially, *U. cinerea,* a species destructive to oysters.
~v. **drilled, drilling, drills.** *—tr.* **1.** To make a hole in (a hard material) with a drill. **2. a.** To instruct thoroughly and by repetition in a skill or procedure. **b.** To infuse knowledge of or skill in by repetitious instruction. **3.** *Slang.* To riddle with bullets. *—intr.* **1.** To make a hole with a drill. **2.** To sink a shaft, as when searching for oil. **3.** To perform an exercise; complete a drill. —See Synonyms at **teach.** [Probably Dutch *dril* (noun), from Middle Dutch, from *drillen*† (verb).]

drill[2] *n.* **1.** A trench or furrow in which seeds are planted. **2.** A row of planted seeds. **3.** A machine or implement for planting seeds in holes or furrows.
~tr.v. **drilled, drilling, drills.** **1.** To sow (seeds) in rows. **2.** To plant (a field) in drills. [18th century : perhaps special use of obsolete *drill*†, rivulet.]

drill[3] *n.* Strong cotton or linen twill of varying weights, generally used for work clothes. Also called "drilling." [Shortening of *drilling,* variant of German *drillich,* from Old High German *drilīch,* from Latin *trilīx,* triple-twilled : *tri-,* three + *līcium,* thread (see **trellis**).]

drill[4] *n.* A monkey, *Mandrillus leucophaeus,* of western Africa, related to and resembling the mandrill. [West African name.]

drill bit *n.* A boring tool, a **drill** *(see).*

drill instructor *n.* A noncommissioned officer who instructs recruits in military drill and discipline.

drill·mas·ter (drĭl′măs′tər, -mäs′tər) *n.* **1.** A military drill instructor. **2.** An instructor given to severely rigorous training.

drill press *n.* A powered vertical drilling machine, used mainly on metals, in which the drill is pressed to the metal by a hand lever or automatically. Also called "drill."

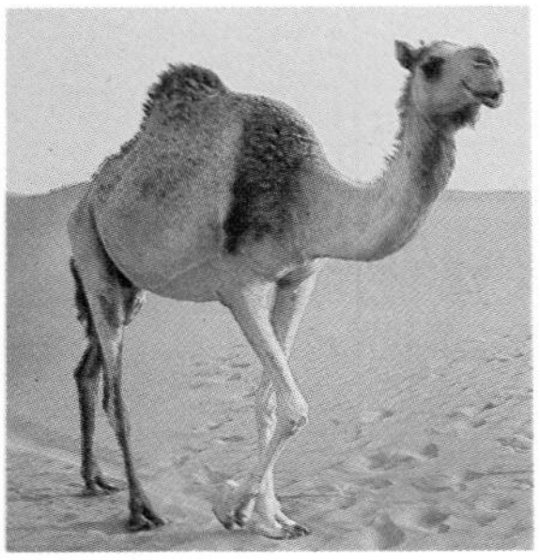

dromedary *The dromedary—an Arabian camel often bred for racing—has only one hump to the Bactrian camel's two. The hump stores fat and acts as the camel's food reserve.*

drill·ship (drĭl′shĭp′) *n.* A ship equipped for ocean floor drilling.

drill·stock (drĭl′stŏk′) *n.* The part of a drilling tool or machine that holds the shank of a drill or bit.

drink (drĭngk) *v.* **drank** (drăngk) or *archaic* **drunk** (drŭngk), **drunk** or *obsolete* **drunken** (drŭng′kən), **drinking, drinks.** *—tr.* **1. a.** To take into the mouth and swallow (a liquid). **b.** To swallow the liquid contents of (a vessel). **2.** To soak up (liquid or moisture); absorb; imbibe. **3.** To take in eagerly through the senses or intellect; receive with pleasure. Often used with *in.* **4.** To bring to a specified state by drinking alcoholic liquors: *drank himself into a stupor.* **5.** To drink something in response to (a toast) or in honor of (someone's health). *—intr.* **1.** To swallow liquid. **2.** To imbibe alcoholic liquids, especially excessively or habitually. **3.** To salute a person or occasion with a toast. Used with *to.* **—drink off.** To swallow in a single draft. **—drink up.** To finish off the contents of one's glass.
~n. **1.** Any liquid that is fit for drinking; a beverage. **2.** An alcoholic beverage, such as a cocktail. **3. a.** An amount of liquid swallowed, such as a cupful or glassful. **b.** A liquid that is absorbed, as for example, by a plant. **4.** Alcoholic drinks collectively. **5.** Excessive or habitual indulgence in alcoholic drink. **6.** *Slang.* A body of water; the sea. Preceded by *the.* [Drink, drank or drunk, drunk or drunken; Middle English *drinken, drank* or *dronk, drunke* or *drunken,* Old English *drincan, dranc* or *druncon* (plural), *druncen,* from Germanic.]

Usage: Standard English recognizes only *drank* for the past tense form of this verb, and *drunk* for the past participle. Sentences such as *I drunk it* are common in some dialects, but are nonstandard. The adjectival form *drunk* is generally used after a verb *(I was drunk),* whereas *drunken* is generally used before a noun *(a drunken driver). Drunk* is sometimes heard before a noun, but it is generally avoided in writing.

drink·a·ble (drĭng′kə-bəl) *adj.* Suitable for drinking; potable.
~n. A beverage. Usually used in the plural.

drink·er (drĭng′kər) *n.* **1.** One who drinks. **2.** One who enjoys alcoholic drinks; especially, one who drinks to excess: *a hard drinker.*

drinking fountain *n.* A device equipped with a nozzle that provides a stream of drinking water for public use.

dri·og·ra·phy (drī-ŏg′rə-fē) *n.* A lithographic printing process using special inks that eliminate the need for water on nonprinting areas of the plate. [DRY + -GRAPHY.] **—dri·o·graph·ic** (drī′ə-grăf′ĭk) *adj.*

drip (drĭp) *v.* **dripped** or *rare* **dript** (drĭpt), **dripping, drips.** *—intr.* **1.** To fall in drops. **2.** To shed drops. *—tr.* To let fall in or as if in drops.
~n. **1.** The process of forming and falling in drops; trickling. **2.** Liquid or moisture that falls in drops. **3.** The sound made by dripping liquid. **4.** A projection on a cornice or sill that protects the area below from rainwater. **5.** *Slang.* An insipid or tiresomely dull person. **6.** A drip feed. [Middle English *drippen,* perhaps from Middle Danish *drippe,* from Germanic.]

drip-dry (drĭp′drī′) *adj.* Made of a fabric that, when wet, will dry to a smooth finish without having to be ironed, merely by hanging.
~intr.v. **drip-dried, -drying, -dried.** To dry without excessive wrinkling.

drip feed *n. Medicine.* **1.** The administration of blood, plasma, saline, or sugar solutions, usually intravenously, a drop at a time. **2. a.** The machine or tubes by which these substances are administered. **b.** The substance administered. Also called "drip." **—drip-feed** (drĭp′fēd′) *tr.v.*

drip irrigation *n.* A form of irrigation in which water is applied to plants in small amounts at regular intervals.

drip pan *n.* Also **dripping pan.** A pan for catching the drippings from roasting meat.

drip·ping (drĭp′ĭng) *n.* **1.** The act or sound of something that drips. **2.** *Usually* **drippings.** The fat and juice exuded from roasting meat.
~adj. Very wet.
~adv. Completely; thoroughly. Used in the phrase *dripping wet.*

drip·py (drĭp′ē) *adj.* **-pier, -piest.** **1.** *Slang.* Mawkishly sentimental; insipid. **2.** Tending to drip.

drip·stone (drĭp′stōn′) *n.* **1.** A drip made of stone, as on a cornice over a door or window. Also called "hood mold." **2.** Calcium carbonate in the form of stalactites or stalagmites.

drive (drīv) *v.* **drove** (drōv) or *archaic* **drave** (drāv), **driven** (drĭv′ən), **driving, drives.** *—tr.* **1.** To push, propel, or press onward forcibly; urge forward. **2.** To force to work, usually excessively; overwork. **3.** To force or thrust into or from a particular act or state. **4.** *Sports.* To throw, strike, or cast (a ball, for example) hard or rapidly. **5.** To force to go through or penetrate. **6.** To create or produce (a hole) by penetrating forcibly. **7. a.** To guide, control, or direct (a vehicle). **b.** To lead or control (a draft animal, for example). **8.** To convey or transport in a vehicle. **9.** To supply the motive force to and cause to function. **10.** To carry through vigorously to a conclusion. **11. a.** To chase (game or an enemy) into the open or into a trap. **b.** To search (an area) for game or an enemy in this manner. **12.** To excavate (a mine or tunnel) horizontally. *—intr.* **1.** To move along or advance quickly as if pushed by an impelling force. **2.** To rush, dash, or advance violently against an obstruction. **3.** To hit, throw, or impel a ball or other missile forcibly. **4. a.** To operate a motor vehicle. **b.** To be able or licensed to drive a motor vehicle. **5.** To go or be transported in a car or other vehicle. **6.** To make an effort to reach or achieve a particular objective; aim. **—drive at.** To mean to do or say; imply. **—drive home.** **1.** To force in completely.

2. To cause to be evident or obvious through force or emphasis.
∼*n.* **1.** The act of driving. **2. a.** *Abbr.* **Dr.** A road, usually short and residential. **b.** A private road connecting a house, garage, or other building with the street. Also called "driveway." **3.** A trip or journey in a vehicle. **4. a.** The means or apparatus for transmitting motion to a machine or machine part. **b.** The means by which power in a motor vehicle is used to propel it: *four-wheel drive.* **c.** The means or apparatus for controlling and directing a motor vehicle: *right-hand drive.* **5.** An organized effort to accomplish some purpose, such as raising money; a campaign. **6.** Energy; push; aggressiveness; initiative. **7.** *Psychology.* A strong motivating tendency or instinct, especially of sexual or aggressive origin, that prompts activity toward a particular end. **8.** A massive and sustained military offensive. **9.** *Sports.* **a.** The hitting, knocking, or thrusting of a ball very swiftly. **b.** A stroke or thrust by which a ball is driven. **10. a.** A rounding-up and driving of cattle to new pastures or to market. **b.** A similar gathering and driving of logs down a river. **c.** The cattle or logs thus driven. **11.** A device for reading and writing on magnetic tape or disks. [Drive, drove or drave, driven; Middle English *driven, drof* or *draf, driven,* Old English *drīfan, drāf, drifon,* from Germanic.] **—driv·a·ble** *adj.* **—driv·a·bil·i·ty** *n.*

drive-in (drīv′ĭn′) *n.* A retail establishment, such as a restaurant or motion-picture theater, designed to permit customers to remain in their cars. Also used adjectivally: *a drive-in bank.*

driv·el (drĭv′əl) *v.* **-eled** or **-elled, -eling** or **-elling, -els.** *—intr.* **1.** To slobber; drool. **2.** To flow like spittle or saliva. **3.** To talk stupidly or childishly. *—tr.* **1.** To allow to flow from the mouth. **2.** To say (something) stupidly.
∼*n.* **1.** Stupid, childish, or senseless talk; twaddle. **2.** Saliva flowing from the mouth; slaver. [Middle English *drivelen, drevelen,* Old English *dreflian.*] **—driv·el·er** *n.*

drive·line (drīv′līn′) *n.* The components of an automotive vehicle that connect the transmission with the driving axles and include the universal joint and drive shaft.

driv·en (drĭv′ən) *adj.* **1.** Motivated by or as if by some inner compulsion. **2.** Carried along and piled into drifts by the wind.

drive-on (drīv′ôn′ *adj.* Designating a ship, ferry, or the like onto which motor vehicles can be driven.

driv·er (drī′vər) *n.* **1.** One who drives, especially: **a.** A chauffeur. **b.** A coachman. **c.** *British.* The operator of a train or bus. **d.** A drover on a cattle drive. **2.** An employer who demands hard work of subordinates. **3.** A tool or device used for driving, such as a hammer or mallet. **4.** Any machine part that transmits motion or force to another part. **5.** A wooden-headed golf club with a long shaft, used for making long shots from the tee. **6.** *Nautical.* A **spanker** *(see).* **—driv·er·less** *adj.*

driver ant *n.* Any of various rapacious tropical Old World ants of the subfamily Dorylinae, that move about in huge groups.

driver's license *n.* An official document that authorizes the holder to drive a motor vehicle on public roads.

driver's seat *n.* **1.** The seat occupied by the driver of a vehicle. **2.** *Informal.* Any position of control, authority, or superiority.

drive shaft *n.* A rotating shaft that transmits mechanical power to a point or region of application.

drive·way (drīv′wā′) *n.* A private road connecting a house, garage, or other building with the street.

driv·ing (drī′vĭng) *adj.* **1. a.** Violent, intense, or forceful. **b.** Rhythmic: *a driving beat.* **2.** Capable of eliciting work or participation from others; energetic; dynamic: *a driving force.*

driving test *n.* A practical and theoretical test of competence that all drivers of motor vehicles must pass before being allowed to drive unaccompanied on public roads.

driving wheel *n.* **1.** A wheel, especially a gear wheel, that communicates motive power in machinery. **2.** The large wheel in a steam locomotive.

driz·zle (drĭz′əl) *v.* **-zled, -zling, -zles.** *—intr.* To rain gently in fine, mistlike drops. *—tr.* **1.** To let fall in fine drops or particles. **2.** To moisten with fine drops.
∼*n.* A fine, gentle, continuous rain. [Perhaps a frequentative of Middle English *dresen,* to fall, Old English *drēosan.*] **—driz·zly** *adj.*

drogue (drōg) *n.* **1.** A **sea anchor** *(see).* **2.** A drogue parachute. **3.** A funnel- or cone-shaped device towed behind an aircraft as a target. **4.** A funnel-shaped device at the end of the hose of a tanker aircraft, used as a stabilizer and receptacle for the probe of a receiving aircraft. **5.** A device for indicating wind direction, a **windsock** *(see).* [18th century : origin obscure.]

drogue parachute *n.* **1.** A parachute used in decelerating a fast-moving object, especially a small parachute used to slow down a re-entering spacecraft or satellite prior to deployment of the main parachute. **2.** A small parachute used to pull a main parachute from its storage pack.

droit (droit; *French* drwȧ) *n.* **1.** A legal right. **2.** That to which one has legal right. [Old French, from Late Latin *dīrectum,* from *dīrectus,* right, correct, from Latin, past participle of *dīregere,* to DIRECT.]

droit de sei·gneur (drwȧ′də sān-yœr′) *n., pl.* **droits de seigneur** *(pronounced as singular).* Also **droit du seigneur** (dü). **1.** The supposed right of a feudal lord to have sexual intercourse with the bride of a vassal on her wedding night. **2.** Any excessive proprietary claim. [French, "right of the lord."]

droll (drōl) *adj.* Amusingly odd; whimsically comical.
∼*n. Archaic.* A buffoon. [French *drôle,* from noun, buffoon, from Middle Dutch *drol*†, "little man."] **—drol·ly** *adv.* **—droll·ness** *n.*

droll·er·y (drō′lə-rē) *n., pl.* **-ies.** **1.** A droll quality; quaint comedy. **2.** A droll way of acting, talking, or behaving. **3. a.** The act of joking; clowning. **b.** Something droll, such as a story.

-drome *suffix.* Indicates: **1.** A racecourse or a place for running; for example, **velodrome.** **2.** A large field or arena; for example, **airdrome.** [Old French, from Latin *-dromos,* from Greek *dromos,* race, course.]

drom·e·dar·y (drŏm′ə-dĕr′ē, drŭm′-) *n., pl.* **-ies.** The one-humped domesticated camel, *Camelus dromedarius,* widely used as a beast of burden in northern Africa and western Asia. Also called "Arabian camel." Compare **Bactrian camel.** [Middle English *dromedarie,* from Old French *dromedaire,* from Late Latin *dromedārius,* from Greek *dromas* (stem *dromad-*), dromedary, runner.]

drom·ond (drŏm′ənd, drŭm′-) *n.* Also **drom·on** (-ən). A large medieval sailing galley. [Middle English *dromon(d),* from Old French *dromon,* from Late Latin *dromō* (stem *dromōn-*), a kind of fast ship, from Late Greek *dromōn,* from *dromos,* a running, race, course.]

-dromous *suffix.* Indicates running or moving; for example, **catadromous.** [New Latin *-dromus,* from Greek *-dromos,* from *dromos,* a running, race, course.]

drone¹ (drōn) *n.* **1.** A male bee, especially a honeybee, characteristically stingless, performing no work, and producing no honey. Its only function is to mate with the queen bee. **2.** An idle person who lives off the efforts of others; a sponger or parasite. **3.** A pilotless aircraft operated by remote control. [Middle English *drane, drone,* Old English *drān, drœn.*]

drone² *v.* **droned, droning, drones.** *—intr.* **1.** To make a continuous low, dull, humming sound. **2.** To speak in a monotonous tone. *—tr.* To utter in a monotonous low tone: *"the mosquitoes droned their angry chant"* (Somerset Maugham). **—drone on.** To talk boringly and at length.
∼*n.* **1.** A continuous low humming or buzzing sound. **2.** Any of the pipes of a bagpipe tuned to produce a single note. Also called "drone pipe." **3.** *Music.* A single sustained note. [From DRONE (bee), imitative.]

dron·go (drŏng′gō) *n., pl.* **-gos** or **goes.** **1.** Any of various tropical Old World birds of the family Dicruridae, characteristically having glossy black plumage and a forked tail. **2.** *Australian & New Zealand Informal.* A dull-witted person. [Malagasy.]

drool (dro͞ol) *v.* **drooled, drooling, drools.** *—intr.* **1.** To let saliva run from the mouth; dribble. **2.** *Informal.* To make an extravagant show of appreciation. **3.** *Informal.* To talk nonsense. *—tr.* To let run from the mouth.
∼*n.* **1.** Saliva; drivel. **2.** *Informal.* Silly talk; nonsense. [Variant of DRIVEL.]

droop (dro͞op) *v.* **drooped, drooping, droops.** *—intr.* **1.** To bend or hang downward; sag. **2.** To sag in dejection, exhaustion, or lifelessness. *—tr.* To let bend or hang down.
∼*n.* The act or condition of drooping. [Middle English *droupen,* from Old Norse *drūpa,* from Germanic.] **—droop·i·ly, droop·ing·ly** *adv.* **—droop·y** *adj.*

droop nose *n.* An aircraft nose that can be inclined downward to increase runway visibility on takeoff and landing. Also called "droop snoot."

drop (drŏp) *n.* **1.** The smallest quantity of liquid heavy enough to fall in a spherical or pear-shaped mass; a globule. **2.** A minute quantity of any substance. **3. drops.** Liquid medicine administered in such quantity. **4.** A trace or hint of something abstract. **5. a.** Anything shaped or hanging like a drop. **b.** A small globular candy. **6. a.** An act of dropping or allowing to fall. **b.** An act of falling or being dropped; a rapid descent. **7.** A swift decline or decrease, as in quality, quantity, or intensity. **8. a.** The vertical distance from a higher to a lower level. **b.** The distance through which something falls or drops. **9.** A sheer incline, such as the face of a cliff; a steep slope. **10. a.** A delivery of goods, as by a carrier or parachute. **b.** A parachute jump. **11.** Something arranged to fall or be lowered, specifically: **a.** An unframed curtain that forms part of the scenery on a stage. **b.** A theater curtain that can be lowered or raised. Also called "drop curtain." **c.** A trapdoor on a gallows. **12.** A slot through which something is deposited in a receptacle. **13.** *Electronics.* A connection made available for a terminal unit on a transmission line. **14.** A place where secret letters, illicit goods, or the like are deposited for someone else to collect. **—a drop in the bucket** (or **ocean**). A tiny amount in relation to what is available or required. **—at the drop of a hat.** Immediately and willingly. **—get** (or **have**) **the drop on.** To get or have a distinct advantage over.
∼*v.* **dropped** or *archaic* **dropt, dropping, drops.** *—intr.* **1.** To fall in drops. **2.** To fall from a higher to a lower place or position. **3.** To become less in number, intensity, volume, or other measure; decrease; decline. **4.** To descend from one level to another. **5.** To fall or sink into a state of exhaustion or death. **6.** To pass or slip into some specified state or condition. **7.** To cease; come to an end. **8.** To crouch. Used of a hunting dog. *—tr.* **1.** To let fall by releasing hold of. **2.** To let fall in drops. **3.** To cause to become less; decrease; reduce. **4.** To cause to fall, as by hitting or shooting. **5.** To give birth to. Used of animals. **6.** To say or offer casually. **7.** To write and send off (a note, for example) at leisure. **8.** To cease consideration or treatment of; have done with. **9.** To terminate an association or relationship with. **10. a.** To leave out (a letter, for example) in speaking or writing. **b.** In knitting, to let (a stitch) fall accidentally from the needle before it has been worked. **11.** To leave out of a team. **12.** To leave or set down at a particular place. Often used with *off.* **13.** To parachute. **14.** To lower the level of

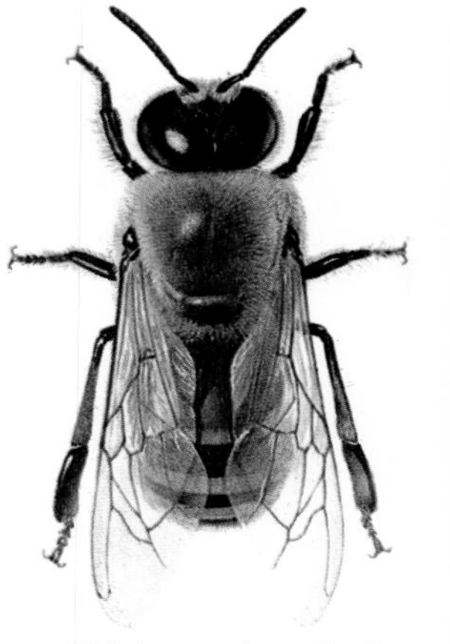

drone *Male bees, or drones, hatch from unfertilized eggs; their only function is to fertilize the queen bee, so that she can lay fertilized eggs that produce female worker bees. The workers feed all the bees in the hive, allowing the drones to starve to death when their usefulness is over.*

PRONUNCIATION KEY

ă, pat; ā, pay; âr, care;
ä, father, are; b, bib;
ch, church; d, deed; ĕ, pet;
ē, be; f, fife; g, gag; h, hat;
hw, which; ĭ, pit; ī, pie;
îr, pier; j, judge; k, kick;
l, lid, needle; m, mum;
n, no, sudden; ng, thing;
ŏ, pot; ō, toe; ô, paw, for;
oi, noise; ou, out; o͝o, book;
o͞o, boot; p, pop; r, roar;
s, sauce; sh, ship, dish;
t, tight; th, thin, path;
th, this, bathe; ŭ, cut; ûr, fur;
v, valve; w, with; y, yes;
z, zebra, size; zh, vision;
ə, about, item, edible, gallop, circus, peaceful

IN FOREIGN WORDS:

ȧ, *Fr.* ami; œ, *Fr.* feu, *Ger.* schön; ü, *Fr.* tu, *Ger.* über; KH, *Ger.* ich, *Scot.* loch; N, *Fr.* bon; y′, *Fr.* Compiègne

STRESS MARKS:

Primary stress: ′
in·cite′ (ĭn-sīt′)
Secondary stress: ′
in′sight′ (ĭn′sīt′)

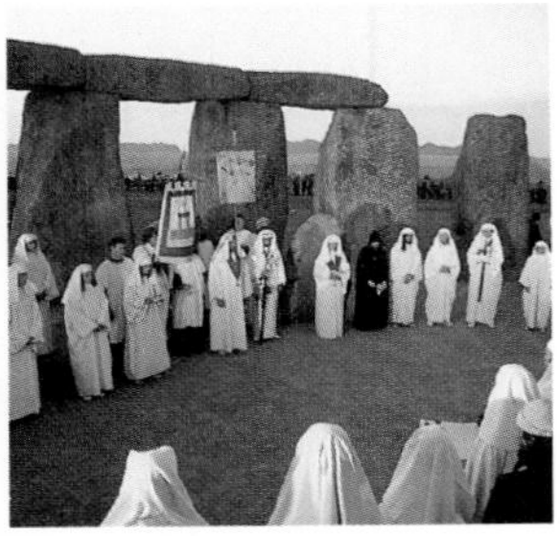

druids *A modern convocation of druids—priests of an ancient Celtic religion—celebrates the summer solstice at Stonehenge, in England.*

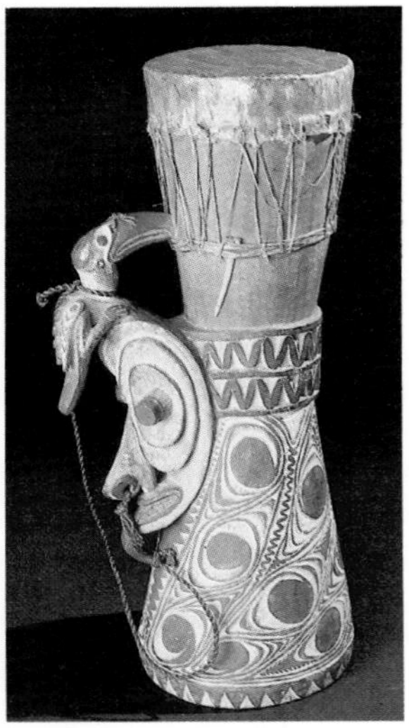

drum *A percussion instrument, usually consisting of a hollow cylinder closed off by a resonating surface at one or both ends. This native drum from New Guinea is made of skin stretched over a wooden frame.*

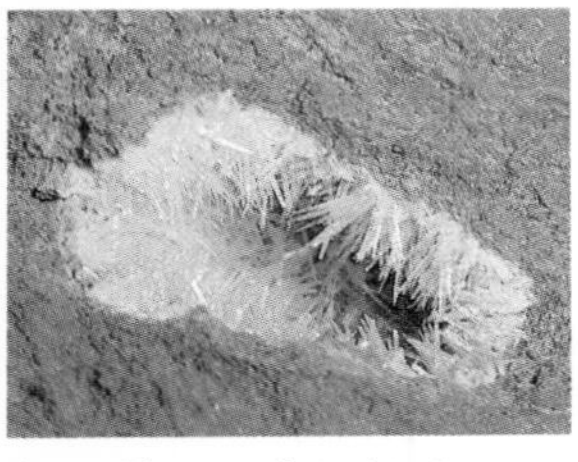

druse *The crystals in this druse, or cavity, are formed of limestone, the same mineral as the surrounding rock.*

(the voice). **15.** To lose (a game or contest, for example). **16.** To lower (the hem of a garment). **17.** *Slang.* To take orally (a drug, such as LSD). **—drop behind.** To fall behind or back. **—drop by** (or **in**). To stop in for a short visit. [Middle English *drop(e),* Old English *dropa,* from Germanic.]

drop cloth *n.* A sheet, as of cloth or plastic, for protection against spills or dripping, used especially by painters.

drop curtain *n.* **1.** An unframed curtain that forms part of the scenery on a stage. **2.** A theater curtain that can be lowered or raised.

drop·forge (drŏp′fôrj′, -fōrj′) *tr.v.* **-forged, -forging, -forges.** To forge (a metal) between dies by the force of a drop hammer.

drop hammer *n.* A machine used to forge or stamp metal, consisting of an anvil or base aligned with a hammer that is forced down upon the molten metal. Also called "drop forge," "drop press."

drop-head (drŏp′hĕd′) *n. British.* The canvas roof of a car, which can be folded back.

drop kick *n. Football.* A kick made by dropping the ball to the ground and kicking it just as it starts to rebound. **—drop-kick** (drŏp′kĭk′) *v.*

drop leaf *n.* A wing on a table, hinged for folding down when not in use. **—drop-leaf** (drŏp′lēf) *adj.*

drop·let (drŏp′lĭt) *n.* A tiny drop.

drop letter *n.* A letter mailed and picked up at or delivered from the same post office.

drop·light (drŏp′līt′) *n.* A hanging lamp that can be lowered and raised on its cord.

drop off *intr. v.* **1.** To decrease; lessen in quantity, volume, or the like. **2.** *Informal.* To fall asleep.

drop-off (drŏp′ôf′, -ŏf′) *n.* **1.** A very steep slope. **2.** A noticeable decrease.

drop out *intr. v.* **1.** To withdraw from participation in a group or organization, such as a game, club, or school. **2.** To refuse to participate in conventional society, by deliberately avoiding employment, for example.

drop·out (drŏp′out′) *n.* **1.** A person who quits school. **2. a.** A person who drops out of a given social group, environment, or from established society. **b.** A person who abandons something attempted: *a contact-lens dropout.* **3.** *Computer Science.* A segment of magnetic tape on which expected information is absent.

drop·per (drŏp′ər) *n.* **1.** One that drops. **2.** A small tube with a suction bulb at one end for drawing in a liquid and releasing it in drops. In this sense, also called "eyedropper."

drop·ping (drŏp′ĭng) *n.* **1.** That which has fallen in drops. **2. droppings.** The dung of certain animals, such as sheep or mice.

drop shipment *n.* Goods shipped by a manufacturer or seller directly to a retailer or customer but invoiced to the wholesaler.

drop shot *n.* **1.** In racquet games such as tennis or badminton, a shot that causes the ball to drop immediately after clearing the net or hitting the front wall. **2.** Shot made by percolating molten metal through a sieve and then dropping it in water.

drop·sonde (drŏp′sŏnd′) *n.* A **radiosonde** *(see)* that is dropped by parachute.

drop·sy (drŏp′sē) *n.* Pathological accumulation of diluted lymph in body tissues and cavities. [Middle English, shortened from *hydropsy,* from earlier *ydropesie,* from Old French, from Latin *hydrōpisis,* from Greek *hudrōpisis,* from *hudrōps,* from *hudōr,* water.] **—drop·si·cal** *adj.* **—drop·si·cal·ly** *adv.*

dropt. *Archaic.* Past tense and past participle of **drop.**

drop tank *n.* A fuel tank, carried externally by an aircraft, that can be jettisoned in flight.

drop·wort (drŏp′wûrt′) *n.* **1.** A plant, *Filipendula vulgaris* (or *F. hexapetala*), native to Eurasia, having finely divided leaflets and clusters of small white flowers. **2.** Any of various water plants of the genus *Oenanthe,* having white flowers borne in an umbel.

drosh·ky (drŏsh′kē) *n., pl.* **-kies.** Also **dros·ky** (drŏs′kē). An open, four-wheeled, horse-drawn carriage formerly common in Russia. [Russian *drozhki,* diminutive of *drogi,* wagon, plural formation from *droga,* beam of the wagon.]

dro·soph·i·la (drō-sŏf′ə-lə) *n., pl.* **-las** or **-lae** (-lē). A small fly of the genus *Drosophila*; especially, the fruit fly *D. melanogaster,* used extensively in genetic studies. [New Latin : Greek *drosos*†, dew + *-philos,* loving, -PHILOUS.]

dross (drôs, drŏs) *n.* **1.** Waste product or impurities formed on the surface of molten metal during smelting. **2. a.** Worthless or waste material. **b.** Stultifying rubbish: *reading the dross in the tabloids.* [Middle English *dros,* Old English *drōs,* dregs.] **—dross·i·ness** *n.* **—dross·y** *adj.*

drought (drout) *n.* Also **drouth** (drouth). **1.** A long period with no rain, especially during a planting season. **2.** A dearth of anything; scarcity. [Middle English *drought,* Old English *drūgath,* from *drȳge,* DRY.] **—drought·y** *adj.*

drove[1]. Past tense of **drive.**

drove[2] (drōv) *n.* **1.** A flock or herd being driven in a body. **2.** A large mass of people moving or acting as a body. **3.** A stonemason's broad-edged chisel used for rough-hewing. Also called "drove chisel." **4.** A stone surface dressed with a drove.
~*tr.v.* **droved, droving, droves.** **1.** *British.* To herd (animals). **2.** To dress (stone) with a drove. [Middle English *drove,* Old English *drāf,* from *drīfan,* to DRIVE.]

drov·er (drō′vər) *n.* A driver of cattle or sheep.

drown (droun) *v.* **drowned, drowning, drowns.** —*intr.* To die by suffocating in water or other liquid. —*tr.* **1.** To kill by submerging and suffocating in water or other liquid. **2.** To drench thoroughly or cover with a liquid. **3.** To deaden one's awareness of, as by immersion: *drowned her troubles in drink.* **4.** To overwhelm and blur (a sound) by a louder sound. Often used with *out.* [Middle English *dr(o)unen,* perhaps from Scandinavian; akin to Old Norse *drukna,* to be drowned.]

drown-proof·ing (droun′pro͞of′ĭng) *n.* A technique for staying afloat for a long period by making use of controlled breathing and one's natural buoyancy.

drowse (drouz) *v.* **drowsed, drowsing, drowses.** —*intr.* To be half-asleep; doze. —*tr.* **1.** To make drowsy: *"on a half-reaped furrow sound asleep, / drowsed with the fume of poppies"* (John Keats). **2.** To pass (time) drowsing. Used with *away.*
~*n.* A sleepy condition. [Back-formation from DROWSY.]

drow·sy (drou′zē) *adj.* **-sier, -siest.** **1.** Dull with sleepiness. **2.** Produced or characterized by sleepiness. **3.** Inducing sleepiness; soporific. **4.** Lethargic; lazy. [Perhaps akin to Old English *drūsian,* to be sluggish, and *drēosan,* to fall.] **—drow·si·ly** *adv.* **—drow·si·ness** *n.*

drub (drŭb) *v.* **drubbed, drubbing, drubs.** —*tr.* **1.** To thrash with a stick. **2.** To force or drive (an idea, for example). Used with *into* or *out of.* **3.** To defeat emphatically. **4.** To stamp (the feet). —*intr.* **1.** To beat the ground; stamp. **2.** To pound; throb.
~*n.* A blow with a stick. [Arabic *ḍáraba,* to beat.] **—drub·ber** *n.*

drub·bing (drŭb′ĭng) *n.* **1.** A severe thrashing. **2.** A total defeat.

drudge (drŭj) *n.* Also **drudg·er** (drŭj′ər). A person who does tedious, menial, or unpleasant work.
~*intr.v.* **drudged, drudging, drudges.** To do the work of a drudge. [Perhaps akin to DRAG.] **—drudg·ing·ly** *adv.*

drudg·er·y (drŭj′ə-rē) *n., pl.* **-ies.** Tedious, menial, or unpleasant work. —See Synonyms at **work.**

drug (drŭg) *n.* **1.** A substance used as medicine in the treatment of disease. **2.** A narcotic, especially one that is addictive. **3.** *Obsolete.* A chemical or dye. **—drug on the market.** A commodity for which there is no demand.
~*tr.v.* **drugged, drugging, drugs.** **1.** To administer a drug to. **2.** To poison or mix (food or drink, for example) with drugs. **3.** To stupefy or dull with or as if with a drug. [Middle English *drogge,* from Old French *drogue*†, chemical material.]

drug addict *n.* A person addicted to a narcotic drug such as heroin.

drug·get (drŭg′ĭt) *n.* **1.** A heavy felted fabric of wool or wool and cotton, having characteristic colored designs, used for floor covering. **2.** A coarse rug made of this fabric, made in India. **3.** A fabric woven wholly or partly of wool, formerly used for clothing. [16th century : from French *droguett.*]

drug·gist (drŭg′ĭst) *n.* **1.** A pharmacist. **2.** One who owns or operates a drugstore.

drug·store (drŭg′stôr′, -stōr′) *n.* A shop where prescriptions are made up and toiletries and other articles, such as confectionery, are sold.

dru·id (dro͞o′ĭd) *n. Often* **Druid.** **1.** A member of an order of priests in ancient Britain and Gaul, who appear in Welsh and Irish legend as prophets and mystics. **2.** A member of any of several modern mystical movements believing in one universal source of wisdom emanating from the sun. [Latin *druides,* druids, from Gaulish, perhaps "soothsayers," from Celtic *derwos* (unattested), true, or from Celtic *dru-* (unattested), tree (their rites being associated with the oak).] **—dru·id·ic, dru·id·i·cal** *adj.* **—dru·id·ism** *n.*

drum[1] (drŭm) *n.* **1.** A percussion instrument consisting of a hollow cylinder or hemisphere with a membrane stretched tightly over one or both ends, played by beating with the hands or sticks. **2.** A sound produced by such an instrument. **3.** Something resembling a drum in shape or structure, especially: **a.** A metal cylinder or spool, wound with cable, wire, or heavy rope. **b.** A cylindrical or barrel-like metal container. **4.** A cylindrical device in a computer on which data is stored. Also called "magnetic drum." **5.** *Anatomy.* The **eardrum** *(see).* **6.** *Architecture.* **a.** A cylindrical block or section forming the shaft of a stone pillar. **b.** A circular or polygonal wall or other structure, such as that supporting a dome. **7.** Any of various marine and freshwater fishes of the family Sciaenidae, which make a drumming sound. Also called "drumfish." **8.** A drumlin.
~*v.* **drummed, drumming, drums.** —*intr.* **1.** To play the drum. **2.** To thump or tap rhythmically or continually. **3.** To produce a booming, reverberating sound as certain birds do, by beating the wings. —*tr.* **1.** To perform (a piece or tune) on or as if on a drum. **2.** To summon by or as if by beating a drum. **3.** To force (knowledge, information, or instructions) upon a person by constant repetition. Used with *into.* **—drum out.** To expel or dismiss in disgrace, originally to the beat of a drum. **—drum up.** To obtain, create, or work up (business or support, for example) by canvassing, soliciting, or advertising. [Shortened from obsolete *dromslade,* drum, drummer, from Low German *trommelslag,* drumbeat : *trommel,* drum (akin to TRUMP) + *slag,* beat (akin to SLAY).]

drum[2] *n. Scottish & Irish.* A long, narrow ridge or hill.

drum·beat (drŭm′bēt′) *n.* The sound produced by beating a drum.

drum·beat·er (drŭm′bē′tər) *n.* One who supports a cause, especially vehemently. **—drum·beat·ing** *n.*

drum brake *n.* A type of brake consisting of two shoes that are forced against the inside of the brake drum of a vehicle when the brake is applied.

drum·fire (drŭm′fīr′) *n.* **1.** Heavy, continuous gunfire. **2.** A sound suggestive of this.

drum·fish (drŭm′fĭsh′) *n.* A fish, the **drum** *(see).*

drum·head (drŭm′hĕd′) *n.* **1.** The membrane stretched over the open end of a drum. **2.** *Nautical.* The circular top part of a capstan, used to hold bars for turning.

drumhead court-martial *n.* A court-martial held for the summary trial of an offense committed during military operations. [So called because it was sometimes held around a drumhead.]

drum·lin (drŭm′lĭn) *n.* A streamlined hill or ridge composed of glacial drift. Also called "drum." [Irish Gaelic *druim,* ridge, from Old Irish *druim*† + -LIN(G).]

drum major *n.* A person who leads a marching band or a corps of drums, often twirling a baton.

drum majorette *n.* **1.** A young woman who leads a marching band. **2.** A young woman who twirls a baton at the head of a marching band.

drum·mer (drŭm′ər) *n.* **1.** One who plays a drum, as in a band. **2.** A travelling salesman.

drum·roll (drŭm′rōl′) *n.* **1.** A roll on a drum. **2.** The sound of a drumroll.

drum·stick (drŭm′stĭk′) *n.* **1.** A stick for beating a drum. **2.** The lower part of the leg of a cooked fowl.

drunk (drŭngk). Past participle and *archaic* past tense of **drink.**
~*adj.* **1.** Intoxicated with alcoholic drink to the point of impairment of physical and mental faculties; inebriated. **2.** Overcome by strong feeling: *drunk with power.* —See Usage note at **drink.**
~*n.* **1.** A drunken person; especially, a drunkard. **2.** A bout of drinking; spree; binge.

drunk·ard (drŭng′kərd) *n.* One who is habitually drunk.

drunk·en (drŭng′kən). *Obsolete.* Alternate past participle of **drink.**
~*adj.* **1.** Delirious with or as with strong drink; intoxicated. **2.** Habitually intoxicated; chronically drunk: *a drunken wastrel.* **3.** Pertaining to or occurring during intoxication: *drunken driving.* —See Usage note at **drink.** **—drunk·en·ly** *adv.* **—drunk·en·ness** *n.*

drunk·o·me·ter (drŭng′kə-mē′tər, drŭng-kŏm′ə-tər) *n.* A device for determining the alcoholic content of the blood by analysis of the breath.

dru·pa·ceous (dro͞o-pā′shəs) *adj. Botany.* **1.** Pertaining to or consisting of a drupe: *drupaceous fruit.* **2.** Producing drupes: *a drupaceous tree.*

drupe (dro͞op) *n. Botany.* A fleshy fruit, such as the peach, plum, or cherry, having a single hard stone that encloses a seed. Also called "stone fruit." [New Latin *drupa,* from Latin *drūpa, druppa,* overripe olive, from Greek *druppa,* from *drupepēs,* "ripened on a tree," overripe : *drus,* tree + *peptein,* to cook, to ripen.]

dru·pel (dro͞op′əl) *n.* A collection of small drupes forming an aggregate fruit in plants such as the raspberry.

drupe·let (dro͞op′lĭt) *n. Botany.* A small drupe, such as one of the many subdivisions of the raspberry or the blackberry.

druse (dro͞oz) *n.* A small rock cavity lined with tiny, perfectly formed crystals of the minerals making up the rock. Compare **geode.** [German *Druse,* "weathered ore," from Old High German *druos*†, bump, gland.] **—drus·y** *adj.*

Druse, Druze (dro͞oz) *n.* A member of a sect in Syria, Israel, and Lebanon, whose primarily Muslim religion contains some elements of Christianity. [Arabic *Durūz,* plural of *darazi,* a Druse, after Ismail al-*Darazi* (died 1019), Muslim religious leader.] **—Druse, Dru·si·an, Dru·se·an** *adj.*

dry (drī) *adj.* **drier** or **dryer, driest** or **dryest. 1.** Free from liquid or moisture; not wet, damp, or moistened. **2.** Having or characterized by little or no rain: *a dry climate.* **3.** Marked by the absence of natural or normal moisture: *a dry month.* **4.** Not under water: *dry land.* **5.** Having all or almost all the water or liquid drained away, evaporated, or exhausted: *a dry river.* **6.** No longer yielding liquid, especially milk: *a dry cow.* **7.** Lacking a mucous or watery discharge: *a dry cough.* **8.** Needing or desiring drink; thirsty. **9. a.** Of or pertaining to solid rather than liquid substances or commodities. **b.** Not requiring water for use: *a dry shampoo.* **c.** Eaten without butter or other accompaniment: *dry toast.* **10.** Not sweet, as a result of the decomposition of sugar during fermentation. Said of wines. **11.** Having a large proportion of spirits to other ingredients. Said of a cocktail, such as a martini. **12. a.** Plain; bare; bald; unadorned. **b.** Lacking interest or stimulation: *a dry book.* **13.** Matter-of-fact; cold. **14.** Humorous or sarcastic in a shrewd, impersonal way: *dry wit.* **15.** *Informal.* **a.** Prohibiting or opposed to the sale or consumption of alcoholic beverages. **b.** *British.* Prohibiting the sale of alcoholic drinks on Sunday: *a dry county.* **16.** *British Informal.* Uncompromisingly conservative.
~*v.* **dried, drying, dries.** —*tr.* **1.** To make dry; free from moisture. **2.** To preserve (meat or other foods, for example) by extracting the moisture. —*intr.* To become dry or lose moisture. **—dry out. 1.** To dry completely. **2.** *Informal.* To treat for alcoholism or drug addiction. **3.** To undergo such treatment. **—dry up. 1. a.** To become intellectually unproductive. **b.** To forget one's lines in a dramatic performance. **2.** *Slang.* To stop talking; shut up. Often used in the imperative.
~*n., pl.* **drys, dries. 1.** *Informal.* A prohibitionist. **2.** *British Informal.* An uncompromisingly conservative person. [Middle English *dry, drye,* Old English *drȳge.*] **—dri·ly, dry·ly** *adv.* **—dry·ness** *n.*

dry·ad (drī′əd, -ăd′) *n., pl.* **-ads.** *Sometimes* **Dryad.** *Greek Mythology.* A nature divinity inhabiting or presiding over forests and trees; a wood nymph. [Latin *dryas* (stem *dryad-*), from Greek *druas,* from *drus,* tree.] **—dry·ad·ic** *adj.*

dryad's saddle *n.* A large, edible bracket fungus, *Polyporus squamosus,* that has a yellowish upper surface covered in brown scales, found growing on deciduous trees.

dry·as·dust (drī′əz-dŭst′) *n.* A dull, pedantic speaker or writer. [After Dr. Jonas *Dryasdust,* a fictitious character to whom Sir Walter Scott dedicated some of his novels.] **—dry-as-dust** *adj.*

dry battery *n.* An electric battery consisting of two or more dry cells.

dry-bone ore (drī-bōn′) *n. Mining.* **Smithsonite** *(see).*

dry-bulb thermometer (drī′bŭlb′) *n.* An ordinary thermometer used with a wet-bulb thermometer in a psychrometer to measure the relative humidity of the atmosphere.

dry cell *n.* A primary cell having an electrolyte in the form of moist paste. Compare **wet cell.** [Its contents are not spillable.]

dry-clean (drī′klēn′) *tr.v.* **-cleaned, -cleaning, -cleans.** To clean (clothing or fabrics) with chemical solvents such as trichlorethylene. **—dry-clean·er** *n.* **—dry-clean·ing** *n.*

dry-cure (drī′kyo͝or′) *tr.v.* **-cured, -curing, -cures.** To preserve (meat) by salting and drying.

Dry·den (drīd′n), **John** (1631–1700). English poet, dramatist, and critic, and the first poet laureate (1668). He commemorated Oliver Cromwell in *Heroic Stanzas* (1659), then on the restoration of Charles II in 1660 hailed the return of the monarchy in *Astraea Redux.* In the 1680's he wrote satirical and didactic poems on which his reputation rests, the most notable being *Absalom and Achitophel* (1681). Dryden was converted to Roman Catholicism (1686) and refused to take the oaths when William and Mary took the throne; as a result the poet laureateship was taken away from him.

dry distillation *n.* **Destructive distillation** *(see).*

dry dock *n.* A large floating or stationary dock in the form of a basin from which the water can be emptied, used for maintaining, repairing, and altering a ship below the water line.

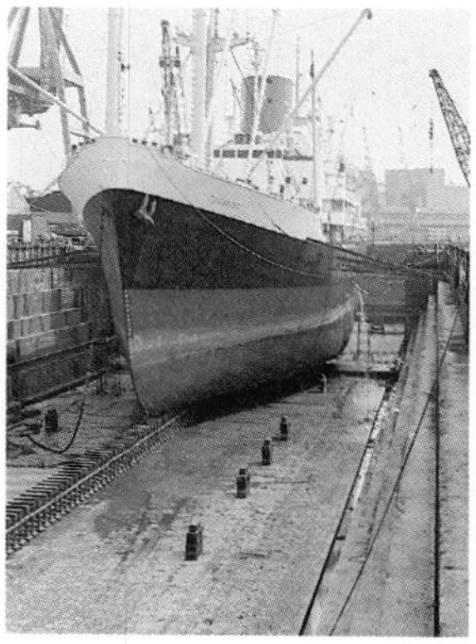

dry dock *A cargo ship being repaired at the dry dock in Avonmouth near Bristol, England. When repairs are completed, the dock is flooded and the ship towed out through gates at one end.*

dry-dock (drī′dŏk′) *v.* **-docked, -docking, -docks.** —*tr.* To place in a dry dock. —*intr.* To go into a dry dock. Used of a ship.

dry·er[1] (drī′ər) *n.* **1.** Any apparatus that removes moisture by heating or another process: *a grain dryer; a hair dryer; a clothes dryer.* **2.** Variant of **drier** (one that dries).

dryer[2]. Alternate comparative of **dry.**

dryest. Alternate superlative of **dry.**

dry-eyed (drī′īd′) *adj.* Not weeping: *dry-eyed mourners.*

dry farming *n.* A type of farming practiced in arid areas without irrigation by maintaining a fine surface tilth or mulch that protects the natural moisture of the soil from evaporation. **—dry farm** *n.* **—dry-farm** *v.* **—dry farmer** *n.*

dry fly *n.* An artificial fly used in fishing that floats on the water's surface when cast. Compare **wet fly.**

dry gangrene *n.* Gangrene that develops as a result of arterial obstruction and is characterized by mummification of the dead tissue and asepsis.

dry goods *pl.n.* **1.** Goods not containing liquid, such as flour, grain, or the like. **2.** Textiles, clothing, and related articles of trade. Also called "soft goods."

dry ice *n.* Solid carbon dioxide, which evaporates directly to gas at –78.5°C (–110°F) at normal atmospheric pressure and is used primarily as a refrigerant.

drying oil *n.* Any of various oily organic liquids, such as linseed oil, soyabean oil, or dehydrated castor oil, that form a tough plastic layer on exposure to air in thin films and are used as binders in paints and varnishes.

dry kiln *n.* A heated chamber in which cut timber is dried and seasoned.

dry law *n.* A law prohibiting the sale of alcoholic beverages.

dry measure *n.* A system of units for measuring dry quantities such as grains, fruits, and vegetables.

dry nurse *n.* A nurse employed to care for an infant without breastfeeding it. **—dry-nurse** *v.*

dry·o·pith·e·cine (drī′ō-pĭth′ə-sēn′) *n.* An extinct ape of the genus *Dryopithecus,* known from Old World fossil remains of the Miocene and Pliocene epochs, and believed to be an ancestor of the chimpanzees, gorillas, and man. [From New Latin *Dryopithecus* : Greek *drus,* tree + *pithēkos,* ape.] **—dry·o·pith·e·cine** *adj.*

dry point *n.* **1.** A technique of intaglio engraving in which a hard steel needle is used to incise lines in the metal plate, with the burr at the side of the furrows retained. **2.** An engraving or print made with this technique.

dry rot *n.* **1.** A fungous disease of timber that causes it to become brittle and crumble into powder. **2.** Any plant disease in which the plant tissue remains relatively dry while fungi invade and ultimately decay bulbs, fruit, or woody tissue. Compare **soft rot. 3.** A basidiomycete fungus *Serpula* (or *Merulius*) *lacrymans* that causes dry rot. **4.** Any deterioration that has gone undetected.

dry run *n.* **1.** *Military.* A test exercise in bombing, attacking, or other combat skills without the use of live ammunition. **2.** A trial run; rehearsal.

dry-salt (drī′sôlt′) *tr.v.* **-salted, -salting, -salts.** To preserve (meat or hides, for example) by salting and drying. **—dry-salt·er** *n.*

dry-shod (drī′shŏd′) *adv.* Without wetting the shoes or feet. **—dry-shod** *adj.*

dry socket *n.* A painful inflamed condition of a tooth socket after the tooth has been extracted.

dry steam *n.* Steam that does not contain drops of water.

dry-stone (drī′stōn′) *adj.* Made with stones piled on top of each other without mortar: *a dry-stone wall.*

dry wall *n.* A wall or section of a wall constructed of a prefabricated material, such as wallboard.

PRONUNCIATION KEY

ă, pat; ā, pay; âr, care;
ä, father, are; b, bib;
ch, church; d, deed; ĕ, pet;
ē, be; f, fife; g, gag; h, hat;
hw, which; ĭ, pit; ī, pie;
îr, pier; j, judge; k, kick;
l, lid, needle; m, mum;
n, no, sudden; ng, thing;
ŏ, pot; ō, toe; ô, paw, for;
oi, noise; ou, out; o͝o, book;
o͞o, boot; p, pop; r, roar;
s, sauce; sh, ship, dish;
t, tight; th, thin, path;
th, this, bathe; ŭ, cut; ûr, fur;
v, valve; w, with; y, yes;
z, zebra, size; zh, vision;
ə, about, item, edible,
gallop, circus, peaceful

IN FOREIGN WORDS:

à, *Fr.* ami; œ, *Fr.* feu, *Ger.* schön; ü, *Fr.* tu, *Ger.* über; KH, *Ger.* ich, *Scot.* loch; N, *Fr.* bon; y′, *Fr.* Compiègne

STRESS MARKS:

Primary stress: ′
in·cite′ (ĭn-sīt′)
Secondary stress: ′
in′sight′ (ĭn′sīt′)

d.s. 1. *Music*. dal segno. 2. *Commerce*. days after sight. 3. document signed.

D.S. *Music*. dal segno.

DSC, D.S.C. Distinguished Service Cross.

D.Sc. Doctor of Science.

DSM, D.S.M. Distinguished Service Medal.

D.S.O. Distinguished Service Order.

d.s.p. died without issue. [Latin *decessit sine prole*.]

DST, D.S.T. daylight-saving time.

d.t. double time.

DTL *Electronics*. diode transistor logic.

D.T.'s (dē'tēz') *pl.n. Informal.* **Delirium tremens** (*see*).

Du. 1. duke (title). 2. Dutch.

du·ad (dōo'ăd', dyōo'-) *n. Rare.* A unit of two objects; pair. [Greek *duas* (stem *duad*-), the number two, a pair, from *duo*, two.]

du·al (dōo'əl, dyōo'-) *adj.* 1. Composed of two parts; double; twofold: *dual controls on a car.* 2. Pertaining or relating to two. 3. *Grammar.* Designating or pertaining to a number category that indicates two persons or things, as in Greek, Sanskrit, or Old English. Compare **plural**.
~*n. Grammar.* 1. The dual number. 2. A word or expression in the dual number. [Latin *duālis*, from *duo*, two.] —**du·al·ly** *adv.*

Duala. See **Douala**.

dual-control *adj.* Having an auxiliary set of foot-operated controls. Said of a motor vehicle.

du·al·ism (dōo'ə-lĭz'əm, dyōo'-) *n.* 1. The condition of being twofold; duality. 2. *Philosophy.* The view that the world consists of or is explicable as two fundamental types of substance, such as mind and matter. Compare **monism, pluralism.** 3. *Psychology.* The view that there is a phenomenal distinction between mental and physical processes. 4. *Theology.* **a.** The concept that the world is ruled by the antagonistic forces of good and evil. **b.** The concept that humankind has two basic natures, the physical and the spiritual. **c.** The concept that there are two personalities in Christ, the human and the divine. —**du·al·ist** *n.*

du·al·is·tic (dōo'ə-lĭs'tĭk, dyōo'-) *adj.* 1. Pertaining to or having the nature of dualism. 2. Dual. —**du·al·is·ti·cal·ly** *adv.*

du·al·i·ty (dōo-ăl'ə-tē, dyōo-) *n.* The quality or character of being twofold; dichotomy.

du·al-pur·pose (dōo'əl-pûr'pəs, dyōo'-) *adj.* Having two functions or designed to serve two purposes.

dub¹ (dŭb) *tr.v.* **dubbed, dubbing, dubs.** 1. To tap lightly on the shoulder with a sword by way of conferring knighthood. 2. To honor with a new title or description; style. 3. To name facetiously or playfully; nickname. 4. To strike, cut, or rub (timber or leather, for example) so as to make even or smooth. 5. To dress (a fowl). 6. *Slang.* To execute (a golf stroke, for example) poorly; bungle.
~*n. Slang.* An awkward person or player. [Late Old English *dubbian* (unattested), from Norman French *(a)dubert*, provide with armor, equip, arrange.]

dub² *v.* **dubbed, dubbing, dubs.** —*tr.* 1. To thrust at; poke. 2. To beat (a drum). —*intr.* 1. To make a thrust. 2. To beat on a drum. ~*n.* 1. The act of dubbing. 2. A drumbeat. 3. *Music.* **a.** The basic Jamaican reggae backing rhythm, as played on bass and drums, with little or no melodic line. **b.** The purest form of instrumental reggae based on this, relying on studio effects over a heavy drum and bass. [Perhaps from Low German *dubben*, to hit, strike.]

dub³ *tr.v.* **dubbed, dubbing, dubs.** 1. To make a new recording from the original of (a record or tape) in order to make changes, cuts, or additions. 2. To insert a new sound track, often a synchronized translation of the original dialogue, into (a film). 3. To insert (sound) into a film or tape. Often used with *in*.
~*n.* The new sounds so added. [Short for DOUBLE.]

dub⁴ *n. British Regional.* A muddy, stagnant pool; a puddle. [Middle English (Scottish and northern) : perhaps from Scandinavian.]

Du·bai (dōo-bī'). *Arabic* **Du·bayy.** The second largest of the United Arab Emirates. Its capital, Dubai, containing most of the population, is on the Persian Gulf, and its Port Rashid is the chief seaport of the Emirates. The traditional occupations of smuggling and fishing have declined since the discovery of oil both onshore and offshore in the 1960's. Oil is now the major export.

du Bar·ry (dōo băr'ē, dyōo'ē), **Marie Jeanne Bécu, Comtesse** (1743–93). Mistress of Louis XV of France. She made a marriage of convenience with the Comte du Barry in 1769. She remained Louis's lover until his death (1774).

dub·bin (dŭb'ĭn) *n.* Also **dub·bing** (-ĭng). An application of tallow and oil for dressing leather. [From DUB (to dress, trim).]

Dub·ček (dōob'chĕk), **Alexander** (1921–92). Czech politician and first secretary of the Czechoslovak Communist Party in 1968. He introduced liberal reforms, relaxing censorship and pursuing an independent foreign policy. He called his policy "socialism with a human face." In 1968 Soviet authorities arrested Dubček and forced his resignation. Restrictions on his movements lasted until 1987. By 1989 he had fully returned to public life.

du·bi·e·ty (dōo-bī'ə-tē, dyōo'-) *n., pl.* **-ties.** Also **du·bi·os·i·ty** (dōo'bē-ŏs'ə-tē, dyōo'-). 1. The quality of being dubious. 2. A matter of doubt; an uncertainty. —See Synonyms at **uncertainty.** [Late Latin *dubietās* (stem *dubietat*-), from Latin *dubius*, DUBIOUS.]

du·bi·ous (dōo'bē-əs, dyōo'-) *adj.* 1. Fraught with uncertainty or doubt; not yet determined; undecided. 2. Arousing doubt as to validity, quality, or propriety; questionable: *a remark in dubious taste.* 3. Reluctant to concur; skeptical; doubtful. —See Synonyms at **doubtful.** [Latin *dubius*, dubious, fluctuating, moving in two di-

rections, from *duo*, two.] —**du·bi·ous·ly** *adv.* —**du·bi·ous·ness** *n.*

du·bi·ta·ble (dōo'bĭ-tə-bəl, dyōo'-) *adj.* Subject to doubt or question; uncertain. [Latin *dubitābilis*, from *dubitāre*, to DOUBT.] —**du·bi·ta·bly** *adv.*

du·bi·ta·tion (dōo'bĭ-tə-tā'shən, dyōo'-) *n. Archaic.* Doubt.

du·bi·ta·tive (dōo'bĭ-tā'tĭv, dyōo'-) *adj.* Feeling or expressing doubt or hesitancy; doubting. —**du·bi·ta·tive·ly** *adv.*

Dub·lin¹ (dŭb'lĭn). *Irish* **Baile Átha Cliath** (blä'klē'ə). Seaport and capital city of the Republic of Ireland, on the Liffey River. Danes settled here in the 9th century. They were driven out by the Anglo-Normans in 1170, and a year later Henry II established English rule, which was to last for more than 700 years. Dublin prospered in the 18th century as the second-largest city of the British Empire. Violence and disorder in the 19th century led in 1905 to the formation of the Sinn Fein movement, which urged home rule. Despite the failure of the Easter Rising of 1916, the first Sinn Fein parliament was convened in 1919 under the presidency of Eamon De Valera. St. Patrick's, the principal cathedral of the Church of Ireland, was founded in 1190. Jonathan Swift was dean from 1713 to 1745 and is buried there. The city's industries include engineering, flour milling, glassmaking, and brewing. —**Dub·lin·er** *n.*

Dublin². A county in Leinster, Republic of Ireland. More than 70 percent of the population is concentrated in the city of Dublin, the county town and commercial center.

Du Bois (dōo bois'), **William Edward Burghardt** (1868–1963). U.S. sociologist, educator, and author. A founder of the NAACP, he edited several journals, including *Crisis* (1909–32), and wrote many books, such as *The Negro* (1915) and *Color and Democracy* (1945), which promoted the cause of blacks in America and African colonies.

Du·bon·net (dōo'bə-nā'; *French* dü-bô-nĕ') *n.* A trademark for a fortified French sweet wine, often used as an apéritif.

Du·bos (dōo-bôs', -bō'), **René Jules** (1901–82). U.S. bacteriologist, born in France. He conducted pioneer research on natural antibiotics and later studied tuberculosis and environmental factors in disease. He wrote many influential books, including his Pulitzer Prize winner *So Human an Animal* (1963).

Du·brov·nik (dōo-brôv'nĭk). *Italian* **Ra·gu·sa** (rə-gōo'zə). A seaport on the Dalmatian coast of Croatia, founded in the 7th century by Greek refugees. Later settled by Slavs, it flourished as a virtually independent trading republic. It was ceded to Austria in 1815 and passed to Yugoslavia in 1918. It is now a tourist center.

Du·buf·fet (dōo'bə-fā'), **Jean Philippe Arthur** (1901–85). French artist. A painter, sculptor, and printmaker, he developed *art brut*, "raw art," to express the vitality and immediacy absent from some academic art. Many of his paintings consist of characters etched into a rough surface made of gravel, ashes, or sand bound with glue.

Du·buque (də-byōok'). A city of eastern Iowa, on the Mississippi River. The town developed first as a mining town, then as a lumbering and milling center. Today it is a trade, industrial, and rail center and a river port for an agricultural and dairy area.

du·cal (dōo'kəl, dyōo'-) *adj.* Of or pertaining to a duke, duchy, or dukedom. [French, from Late Latin *ducālis*, from Latin *dux* (stem *duc*-), leader, DUKE.] —**du·cal·ly** *adv.*

duc·at (dŭk'ət) *n.* 1. Any of various gold coins formerly used in European countries. 2. *Slang.* An admission ticket. [Middle English, from Old French, from Old Italian *ducato*, from Medieval Latin *ducātūs*, DUCHY (word used on one of the early ducats).]

du·ce (dōo'chä) *n. Italian.* 1. A leader or commander; chief. 2. **Duce.** The title of Benito Mussolini as the leader of Fascist Italy.

Du·champ (dōo-shän'), **Marcel** (1887–1968). French painter. He became a leader of the Dada movement in New York and was the first to exhibit "ready-made" objects, such as a urinal (entitled *Fountain*) to show that all things were art, or that all art is junk. His major work was *The Bride Stripped Bare by Her Bachelors, Even* (1923), a painting and construction on glass.

duch·ess (dŭch'ĭs) *n. Abbr.* **D.** 1. The wife or widow of a duke. 2. A woman holding title to a duchy in her own right. [Middle English *duchesse*, from Old French, from Medieval Latin *ducissa*, from Latin *dux* (stem *duc*-), leader, DUKE.]

duch·y (dŭch'ē) *n., pl.* **-ies.** A territory formerly ruled by a duke or duchess; a dukedom. [Middle English *duchie*, from Old French *duche*, from Medieval Latin *ducātūs*, from Latin *dux* (stem *duc*-), leader, DUKE.]

duck¹ (dŭk) *n., pl.* **ducks** or collectively **duck.** 1. Any of various wild or domesticated aquatic birds of the family Anatidae, characteristically having a broad, flat bill, short legs, and webbed feet. 2. The female of one of these birds, as distinguished from a drake. 3. The flesh of this bird used as food. 4. *Slang.* A person, especially a peculiar one. 5. *British Informal.* Dear. Used as a familiar term of address. In this sense, also "ducks," "ducky." [Middle English *doke*, Old English *dūce* (unattested), from *dūcan* (unattested), to dive, DUCK.]

duck² *v.* **ducked, ducking, ducks.** —*tr.* 1. To lower quickly, especially so as to avoid something: *He ducked his head as he went below deck.* 2. To evade; dodge. 3. To push suddenly under water. —*intr.* 1. To lower the head or body. 2. To move swiftly, especially so as to escape being seen. 3. To submerge the head or body briefly in water. 4. In bridge, to lose a trick deliberately.
~*n.* 1. A quick lowering of the head or body. 2. A plunge into water; a dip. [Middle English *douken*, Old English *dūcan* (unattested), to dive, from West Germanic *dukjan* (unattested).] —**duck·er** *n.*

duck³ *n.* 1. A very durable, closely woven heavy cotton or linen

duck *The Aylesbury duck (above) is a farmyard breed reared for the table. Aylesbury ducklings gain weight fast, but the breed lays poorly.*

fabric. **2. ducks.** Clothing made of this fabric; especially, white trousers. [Dutch *doek,* from Middle Dutch *doek, doec,* akin to Old Norse *dūkr†.*]

duck⁴ *n.* An amphibious military vehicle used during World War II. [Variant of *DUKW,* its code designation.]

duck-billed platypus (dŭk'bĭld') *n.* An aquatic, egg-laying mammal, *Ornithorhynchus anatinus,* native to Tasmania and southeastern Australia, that has webbed feet and a large, ducklike bill. Also called "duckbill," "platypus," "ornithorhyncus," and in Australia "water mole."

duck blind *n.* A structure of wood or canvas, often camouflaged with reeds and grasses, behind which a duck hunter can hide and shelter from winds while awaiting a flight of ducks.

duck-board (dŭk'bôrd', -bōrd') *n.* A board or set of wooden slats laid across wet or muddy ground or flooring.

duck hawk *n.* The peregrine falcon *(see).*

ducking stool *n.* A device formerly used in Europe and New England for punishment, consisting of a chair on which an offender was tied and ducked into water. Compare **cucking stool.**

duck-ling (dŭk'lĭng) *n.* A young duck.

duck-pin (dŭk'pĭn') *n.* **1.** A bowling pin, shorter and squatter than a tenpin. **2. duckpins.** *Used with a singular verb.* A bowling game played with duckpins and small balls. [From its squat appearance.]

ducks and drakes *n.* The game of skimming flat stones along the surface of water so they bounce. **—make ducks and drakes of** or **play ducks and drakes with.** To squander; waste.

duck soup *n. Slang.* Something easy to accomplish.

duck-tail (dŭk'tāl') *n.* A hairstyle in which the hair is swept back at the sides turning up at the back like a duck's tail. Also called "D.A."

duck-weed (dŭk'wēd') *n.* Any of various small, free-floating, stemless aquatic plants of the genera *Lemna* or *Wolffia,* having a rounded, lanceolate, or oval thallus that may be a modified leaf or stem.

duck-y (dŭk'ē) *adj.* **-i-er, -i-est. 1.** *Slang.* Excellent; fine. Often used ironically. **2.** *Informal.* Sweet; adorable. *~n., pl.* **duckies.** Dear. Used as a familiar term of address. [From DUCK (darling).]

duct (dŭkt) *n.* **1.** Any tubular passage through which a substance, especially a fluid, is conveyed. **2.** A bodily passage, especially one for secretion. **3.** A passage in plants into which substances such as resins are secreted. **4.** Any channel through which pipes or cables pass. *~tr.v.* **ducted, ducting, ducts.** To convey through a duct. [Latin *ductus,* a leading, a conducting, from the past participle of *dūcere,* to lead.]

duc-tile (dŭk'tĭl) *adj.* **1.** Capable of being drawn into wire or hammered thin. Said of metal. **2.** Capable of being easily molded or shaped; plastic. **3.** Readily persuaded or influenced; tractable. **—See Synonyms at flexible.** [Middle English, from Old French, from Latin *ductilis,* from *ductus,* DUCT.] **—duc·til·i·ty** *n.*

duct-less gland (dŭkt'lĭs) *n.* An endocrine gland *(see).*

duct-ule (dŭk'tōōl', -tyōōl') *n.* A small duct.

dud (dŭd) *n. Informal.* **1.** A bomb, shell, or cartridge that fails to explode when it should. **2.** Someone or something disappointingly ineffective or unsuccessful. **3. duds. a.** Clothes; clothing. **b.** Personal belongings. *~adj.* Useless; worthless. [Middle English *dudde†,* article of clothing, thing.]

dude (dōōd, dyōōd) *n.* **1.** *Informal.* A city-dweller, especially an Easterner who vacations on a Western ranch. **2.** *Informal.* A conspicuously overdressed man; a dandy. **3.** *Slang.* A fellow; chap. [19th century : probably from dialect German *Dude,* fool.]

du-deen, du-dheen (dōō-dēn') *n. Irish.* A short-stemmed clay pipe. [Irish *dūidín,* diminutive of *dúd,* pipe.]

dude ranch *n.* A resort modeled on a Western ranch, featuring camping, horseback riding, and other outdoor activities.

dudg-eon¹ (dŭj'ən) *n.* A sullen, angry, or indignant mood: *"Slamming the door in Meg's face, Aunt March drove off in high dudgeon"* (Louisa May Alcott). [16th century : origin obscure.]

dudgeon² *n.* **1.** *Obsolete.* A kind of wood used in making knife handles. **2.** *Archaic.* **a.** A dagger having a hilt made from this wood. **b.** The hilt of a dagger. [Middle English *dogeon,* from Norman French *digeon†.*]

due (dōō, dyōō) *adj.* **1.** Payable immediately or on demand. **2.** Owed as a debt; owing: *the sum still due.* **3.** Owed by right, convention, or courtesy; fitting or appropriate: *due esteem.* **4.** Meeting special requirements; sufficient; adequate: *due cause to honor him.* **5.** Expected or scheduled; especially, appointed to arrive. **—due to. 1.** Attributable to; caused by. **2.** Because of. *~n.* **1.** Something that is owed or deserved. **2. dues.** A charge or fee, as for membership in a club or organization. *~adv.* **1.** Straight; directly: *due west.* **2.** *Archaic.* Duly. [Middle English, from Old French *deu,* from Vulgar Latin *dēbūtus* (unattested), "owed," from Latin *dēbitus,* past participle of *dēbēre,* to owe.]

Usage: The traditional view is that, since *due* is an adjective, it can be used only after a linking verb *(His hesitation was due to fear)* or after a noun when the construction is used adjectivally *(His hesitation, due to fear, made him late).* Criticism focuses on the use of *due to* to introduce an adverbial phrase in sentences where *owing to, because of, on account of,* or *through* are more appropriate: *He hesitated due to fear; Due to his bad leg, he didn't come downstairs.*

Stylists have attacked this usage as illiterate for over 100 years. Nevertheless, it is widely employed in informal speech and writing and is increasingly to be encountered in formal contexts (as in *Due to circumstances beyond our control).*

due bill *n.* A written acknowledgment of indebtedness to a particular party, but not payable to his order or transferable by endorsement.

du-el (dōō'əl, dyōō'-) *n.* **1.** A prearranged combat between two persons, fought according to formal procedure with deadly weapons, typically to settle a point of honor. **2.** Any struggle for ascendancy between two contending persons, animals, groups, or ideas. *~intr. v.* **dueled** or **-elled, -eling** or **-elling, -els.** To fight a duel. [Medieval Latin *duellum,* from Latin, archaic form of *bellum,* war.] **—du·el·er, du·el·ist** *n.*

du-el-lo (dōō-ĕl'ō, dyōō-) *n.* **1.** The art of the duel. **2.** The code of rules by which duels were fought. [Italian, from Latin *duellum,* war. See **duel.**]

du-en-de (dōō-ĕn'dā') *n. Spanish.* **1.** Powerful or magical attraction; magnetism. **2.** A demon or ghost.

du-en-na (dōō-ĕn'ə, dyōō-) *n.* **1.** An elderly woman retained by a Spanish or Portuguese family to act as governess and companion to the daughters. **2.** Any chaperone. [Spanish *dueña,* from Latin *domina,* lady, feminine of *dominus,* lord, master.]

due process *n.* An established course for judicial proceedings or other governmental activities designed to safeguard the legal rights of the individual.

Duero. See **Douro.**

du-et (dōō-ĕt', dyōō-) *n.* **1.** A musical composition written for two voices or two instruments. **2.** The two performers presenting such a composition. **3.** Any verbal exchange between two people. **4.** Any closely related pair of individuals. [Italian *duetto,* diminutive of *duo,* duet, from Latin, two.] **—du·et·tist** *n.*

duff¹ (dŭf) *n.* A pudding, usually containing dried fruit, boiled in a cloth bag or steamed: *plum duff.* [Northern English dialectal variant of DOUGH.]

duff² *n.* **1.** Decaying leaves and branches covering a forest floor. **2.** Fine coal; coal dust; slack. [Perhaps from DUFF (dough).]

duff³ *n. Slang.* The buttocks. [Perhaps from DUFF (pudding).]

duf-fel, duf-fle (dŭf'əl) *n.* **1.** A blanket fabric made of low-grade woolen cloth with a nap on both sides. **2.** Clothing and other personal gear carried by a camper. [Dutch, from *Duffel,* town near Antwerp, Belgium.]

duffel bag *n.* A large cloth bag of canvas or duck for carrying personal belongings, originally used by soldiers and sailors.

duf-fer (dŭf'ər) *n.* **1.** *Informal.* An incompetent or slow-witted person. **2.** *Slang.* A peddler of cheap merchandise. **3.** Something worthless or useless. [Probably from Scottish *Duffart, doofart,* stupid fellow, worthless person.]

duffle coat *n.* Also **duffel coat.** A short, heavy woolen coat, usually having a hood and fastened with toggles.

Du-fy (dü-fē') **Raoul** (1877-1953). French painter and textile designer. He produced many brightly colored racing and seaside scenes and the vast panel *La Fée Electricité* for the Paris Exhibition of 1938.

dug¹ (dŭg) *n.* An udder, breast, or teat of a female mammal. [16th century : origin obscure.]

dug². Past tense and past participle of **dig.**

du-gong (dōō'gŏng) *n.* A herbivorous marine mammal, *Dugong dugon,* of tropical coastal waters of the Old World, having flipperlike forelimbs and a deeply notched tail fin. [Variant of Malay *dūyong.*]

dug-out (dŭg'out') *n.* **1.** A boat or canoe made by hollowing out a log. **2.** *Military.* A pit dug into the ground or on a hillside and used as a shelter. **3.** A long sunken shelter at the side of a baseball field where the players stay while not on the field.

Du-ha-mel (dōō'ə-mĕl', dyōō'-) **Georges** (1884-1966). French novelist and dramatist. From his experience as a surgeon in World War I he wrote *Civilisation* (1918), which won the Goncourt Prize. His most successful play was *In the Shadow of Statues* (1914).

dui. Alternate plural of **duo.**

dui-ker, duy-ker (dī'kər) *n.* **1.** Any of various small African antelopes, chiefly of the genus *Cephalophus,* having short, backward-pointing horns. Also called "duikerbok." **2.** *South African.* Any of several cormorants of the genus *Phalacrocorax.* [Afrikaans, "diver," from Dutch *duiken,* to dive, from Middle Dutch *dūken,* from West Germanic *dukjan* (unattested), to DUCK.]

Duis-burg (dōōs'bûrg'). A river port in North Rhine-Westphalia, West Germany. It is at the junction of the Rhine and the Ruhr.

dū jūn. Variant of **tuchun.**

Du-kas (dōō-kä', dyōō-), **Paul** (1865-1935). French composer. Before he died he burned many of his compositions, leaving little work. He is best remembered for the symphonic scherzo *The Sorcerer's Apprentice* (1897).

duke (dōōk, dyōōk) *n. Abbr.* **D., Du. 1.** A nobleman with the highest hereditary rank; especially, in Britain, a man of the highest grade of the peerage. **2.** A prince who rules an independent duchy. **3.** A type of cherry intermediate between a sweet and a sour cherry. [Middle English, from Old French *duc,* from Latin *dux* (stem *duc-*), leader, from *dūcere,* to lead.]

duke-dom (dōōk'dəm, dyōōk'-) *n.* **1.** The state or territory ruled by a duke; a duchy. **2.** The office, rank, or title of a duke.

dukes (dōōks, dyōōks) *pl.n. Slang.* The fists: *Put up your dukes!* [From *Duke of Yorks,* rhyming slang for *forks* (fingers).]

duiker *There are ten species of this African antelope that gets its name from the way it dives for cover into the undergrowth—duiker is the Afrikaans word for diver. Duikers feed at night, mainly on plants, but occasionally on carrion. The stripes of the forest-dwelling zebra duiker (above) help it to blend with the shadows cast by forest foliage.*

Du·kho·bors, Dou·kho·bors (do͞o'kə-bôrz') *pl.n.* The members of a Christian religious sect of Russia, many of whom migrated to Canada in the 1890's to escape persecution. [Russian *dukhoborets,* "spirit-wrestlers" : *dukh,* spirit + *borets,* wrestler, from *borot',* to struggle.]

dul·cet (dŭl'sĭt) *adj.* **1.** Pleasing to the ear; gently melodious; soothing. **2.** *Archaic.* Sweet to the taste.
~n. An organ stop pitched an octave higher than the dulciana. [Learned respelling of Middle English *doucet,* from Old French, from *doux* (feminine *douce*), sweet, from Latin *dulcis.*]

dul·ci·an·a (dŭl'sē-ăn'ə) *n.* An organ stop with a sweet, somewhat thin tone suggestive of a stringed instrument. [New Latin, from Medieval Latin, bassoon, perhaps from Latin *dulcis,* sweet.]

dul·ci·fy (dŭl'sĭ-fī') *tr.v.* **-fied, -fying, -fies.** *Rare.* **1.** To make agreeable or gentle; mollify. **2.** To sweeten. [Late Latin *dulcificāre,* to sweeten : Latin *dulcis,* sweet. + *facere,* to do.] **—dul·ci·fi·ca·tion** *n.*

dul·ci·mer (dŭl'sə-mər) *n.* **1.** A musical instrument with wire strings of graduated lengths stretched over a sound box, played with two padded hammers or by plucking. **2.** An instrument used in folk music consisting of a long, fretted fingerboard and three strings. It is usually laid across the knees and plucked. [Middle English *dowcemere,* from Old French *doulcemer, doulcemele* : probably Latin *dulcis,* sweet + *melos,* song, from Greek.]

Dul·ci·ne·a (dŭl'sĭ-nē'ə, dŭl-sĭn'ē-ə) *n. Sometimes* **dulcinea. 1.** An idealized woman. **2.** A female sweetheart. [After *Dulcinea del Toboso,* Don Quixote's idealized sweetheart in Cervantes' *Don Quixote.*]

Dulheggia. Variant of **Dhul-Hijja.**

du·li·a (do͞o'lē-ə, dyo͞o'-) *n. Theology.* Special reverence accorded to saints in the Roman Catholic and Eastern Orthodox Churches. Compare **hyperdulia, latria.**

Dulkaada. Variant of **Dhul-Qadah.**

dull (dŭl) *adj.* **duller, dullest. 1.** Lacking mental agility; slow to learn; stupid. **2.** Lacking responsiveness or alertness; insensitive. **3.** Dispirited; depressed. **4.** Not brisk or rapid; sluggish. **5.** Not sharp or keen; blunt. **6.** Not intensely or keenly felt: *a dull ache.* **7.** Arousing no interest or curiosity; unexciting; boring. **8.** Not bright or vivid; dim: *a dull brown.* **9.** Cloudy; gloomy. **10.** Muffled; indistinct. —See Synonyms at **stupid.**
~v. **dulled, dulling, dulls.** *—tr.* **1.** To make less sharp; blunt. **2.** To make less bright or distinct. **3.** To make (the senses, for example) less keen or receptive. *—intr.* To become dull. [Middle English *dul, dulle,* from Middle Low German *dul.*] **—dull·ish** *adj.* **—dull·ness, dul·ness** *n.* **—dul·ly** *adv.*

dull·ard (dŭl'ərd) *n.* A mentally dull person; dolt.

Dul·les (dŭl'əs), **John Foster** (1888–1959). U.S. politician. In 1953 he became secretary of state under President Eisenhower and pursued a policy of active opposition to the U.S.S.R.

dull-wit·ted (dŭl'wĭt'əd) *adj.* Slow to comprehend; stupid. **—dull-wit·ted·ness** *n.*

du·lo·sis (do͞o-lō'sĭs, dyo͞o-) *n.* A practice of certain ants in which members of one species make those of another species perform the work of the colony. Also called "helotism." **—du·lot·ic** (do͞o-lŏt'ĭk, dyo͞o-) *adj.*

dulse (dŭls) *n.* A coarse, reddish-brown seaweed, *Rhodymenia palmata,* sometimes eaten as a vegetable. [Irish Gaelic *duileasg,* from Old Irish *duilesc,* "seaweed."]

Du·luth (də-lo͞oth'). A city of northeastern Minnesota, at the western end of Lake Superior. Huge amounts of grain, iron ore, and bulk cargo are shipped on lake freighters and, since the opening of the St. Lawrence Seaway (1959), on oceangoing vessels.

du·ly (do͞o'lē, dyo͞o'-) *adv.* **1.** In a proper manner; rightfully; fittingly: *duly consecrate a church.* **2.** At the expected time; punctually. [Middle English, from DUE.]

Du·ma, Dou·ma (do͞o'mə) *n.* A Russian national parliament, convened and dissolved four times between 1905 and 1917. [Russian *duma,* thought, council, from Gothic *dōms,* judgment.]

Du·mas (do͞o-mä', dyo͞o-), **Alexandre,** also called "Dumas père" (1802–70). French novelist and dramatist, father of Alexandre, Dumas fils. Among his most famous works are *The Three Musketeers* (1844) and *The Count of Monte Cristo* (1845).

Dumas, Alexandre, also called "Dumas fils" (1824–95). French novelist and dramatist. His first play, *La Dame aux Camélias* (1852), a frank treatment of the love affair of a courtesan, caused a sensation. Verdi used the story for *La Traviata.*

du Mau·ri·er (do͞o môr'ē-ā'), **Dame Daphne** (1907–89). British novelist. Her works include *Jamaica Inn* (1936) and *Rebecca* (1938), which were both made into successful films.

du Maurier, George Louis Palmella Busson (1834–86). British novelist and illustrator, born in France of a French father and English mother. He was an illustrator for *Punch* magazine and wrote the novel *Trilby* (1894).

dumb (dŭm) *adj.* **dumber, dumbest. 1.** Lacking the power or faculty of speech; mute. **2.** Temporarily speechless with shock or fear. **3.** Unwilling to speak. **4.** Not producing or accompanied by speech or sound. **5.** Inarticulate; unable to express opinions. **6.** *Informal.* Ignorant or stupid. **7.** *Nautical.* Not self-propelling. [Middle English *dumb,* Old English *dumb*†.] **—dumb·ly** *adv.* **—dumb·ness** *n.*
Synonyms: *mute, speechless, voiceless.*

dumb·bell (dŭm'bĕl') *n.* **1.** A weight lifted for muscular exercise, consisting of a short bar with a metal ball at each end. **2.** *Slang.* A dull, stupid person; dolt. [Sense 1 : originally the weight resembled the device used for ringing a church bell, but without the bell.]

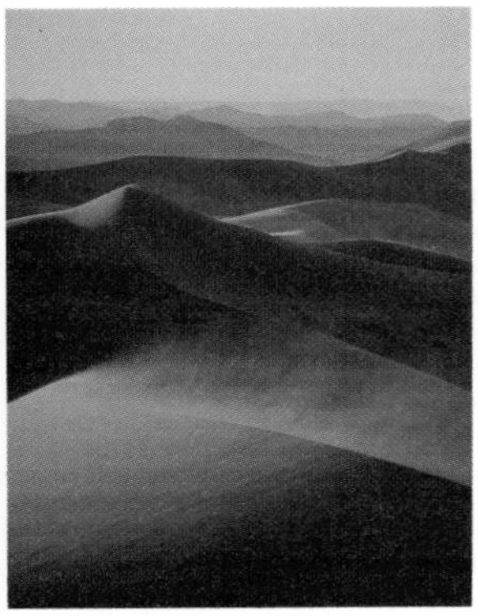

dune *A crescent-shaped sand dune, called a barchan, rises out of the wasteland of the Namib Desert in Namibia. Barchans, formed by wind action like all dunes, can move up to 30 meters (100 feet) in a year.*

dumb cane *n.* A tropical plant, *Dieffenbachia,* with an acrid juice that temporarily inhibits speech when a part of the plant is chewed.

dumb·found, dum·found (dŭm'found') *tr.v.* **-founded, -founding, -founds.** To strike dumb with astonishment or amazement; stun; nonplus. —See Synonyms at **surprise.** [DUMB + (CON)FOUND.]

dumb show *n.* **1.** A part of a dramatic performance unaccompanied by speech; a pantomime. **2.** Communication by means of gestures.

dumb·struck (dŭm'strŭk') *adj.* Temporarily unable to speak through shock or surprise.

dumb·wait·er (dŭm'wā'tər) *n.* **1.** A small elevator used to convey food or other goods from one floor to another. **2.** A portable serving table. **3.** *Chiefly British.* A revolving tray in the middle of the table.

dum·dum bullet (dŭm'dŭm') *n.* A small-arms bullet with a soft nose designed to expand upon contact, inflicting a gaping wound. Also called "spread-on-impact bullet." [After *Dum Dum,* military arsenal near Calcutta, where it was first made (*c.* 1897).]

Dum·fries (dŭm-frēs'). A market town in Dumfries and Galloway Region, Scotland. It was the county town of the former county of Dumfriesshire (or Dumfries).

Dumfries and Gal·lo·way (găl'ə-wā'). An administrative region bordering the Solway Firth, southwest Scotland. It is chiefly agricultural, the main crops being cereals and root vegetables.

dum·my (dŭm'ē) *n., pl.* **-mies. 1.** An imitation of a real or original object, intended to be used as a practical substitute. **2.** A figure imitating the human form, especially: **a.** A model used in designing and displaying clothes. **b.** A stuffed or pasteboard figure used as a target. **c.** A figure of a person or animal manipulated by a ventriloquist. **3.** *Military.* A blank round. **4.** *Informal.* **a.** A mute person. Usually considered offensive. **b.** A blockhead; dolt. **5.** *Informal.* Someone who does not take part or contribute actively. **6.** A person or agency secretly in the service of another; a front. **7.** *Printing.* **a.** A model of a work being published, indicating its general appearance and dimensions. **b.** A model page with text and illustrations pasted into place to direct the printer; a layout. **8. a.** In the game of bridge, the partner who exposes his hand to be played by the declarer. **b.** The hand thus exposed. **c.** In the game of whist, an imaginary fourth hand. **9.** In football, a feigned pass or swerve to defeat an opponent.
~adj. **1.** Simulating something but lacking its function; artificial: *a dummy pocket.* **2.** Silent; mute. **3.** Secretly serving another. **4.** Played with a dummy. Said of a card game.
~tr.v. **dummied, -mying, -mies.** *Printing.* To make a dummy of (a publication or page). Often used with *up.* [Earlier *dummie, dumbie,* dumb person, from DUMB.]

dummy variable *n.* A mathematical variable that can be arbitrarily replaced by another.

du·mor·ti·er·ite (do͞o-môr'tē-ə-rīt', dyo͞o-) *n.* A greenish-blue aluminum borosilicate mineral, used in spark-plug porcelain and in special refractories. [French, after Eugène *Dumortier,* 19th-century French paleontologist who discovered it.]

dump (dŭmp) *v.* **dumped, dumping, dumps.** *—tr.* **1.** To release or throw down in a large mass; drop heavily. **2.** To empty (material) out of a container or vehicle. **3.** To empty out (a container or vehicle), as by overturning or tilting. **4.** To get rid of (rubbish, for example); dispose of. **5.** To discard or reject (a burden or a problem, for example) unceremoniously. **6.** To place (goods) on the market, especially in a foreign country, in large quantities and at a lower price than in the country of origin, especially below cost price. **7.** To reproduce (data stored internally in a computer) onto an external storage medium, such as a printout. **8.** To put into temporary storage. *—intr.* **1.** To fall or drop abruptly, especially in a mass. **2.** To discharge cargo or contents; unload.
~n. **1.** A place where refuse is dumped. **2.** A storage place for goods or supplies; depot. **3.** An unordered accumulation; pile. **4.** An instance or the result of dumping data stored in a computer. **5.** *Slang.* A poorly maintained or disreputable place. [Middle English *dompen, dumpen,* to drop, fall, plunge, probably of Scandinavian origin; akin to Norwegian *dumpa,* to fall suddenly.] **—dump·er** *n.*

dump bin *n.* A freestanding container in a retail store, used to display goods that are being specially promoted.

dump·ling (dŭmp'lĭng) *n.* **1.** A small ball of dough cooked with stew or soup. **2.** Sweetened dough wrapped around an apple or other fruit, baked and served as a dessert. **3.** *Informal.* A short, chubby person. [16th century : origin obscure.]

dumps (dŭmps) *pl.n. Informal.* A gloomy, melancholy state of mind: *down in the dumps.* [Dutch *domp,* haze, exhalation, "hazy or gloomy state of mind," from Middle Dutch *domp, damp.* See **damp.**]

dump truck *n.* A heavy-duty truck having a bed that tilts backward to dump loose material.

dump·y¹ (dŭm'pē) *adj.* **-ier, -iest.** Short and stout; squat. [From archaic *dump,* a shapeless mass, lump, perhaps a back-formation from DUMPLING.] **—dump·i·ly** *adv.* **—dump·i·ness** *n.*

dumpy² *adj.* **-ier, -iest.** *Rare.* Depressed or discontented.

dumpy level *n.* A surveyor's instrument having a short telescope fixed rigidly to a horizontally rotating table.

dun¹ (dŭn) *tr.v.* **dunned, dunning, duns.** To importune (a debtor) persistently for payment.
~n. **1.** One who importunes debtors for payment; a debt collector. **2.** An importunate demand for payment. [Shortened from obsolete *dunkirk,* privateer, originally, ship from DUNKIRK, France.]

dun² *n.* **1.** A color ranging from almost neutral brownish gray to dull grayish brown. **2.** A dun-colored fishing fly. **3.** A dun-colored horse. **4.** The dun-colored subimaginal stages of a mayfly. —*adj.* **dunner, dunnest. 1.** Dull; gloomy. **2.** Grayish brown. [Middle English *dun,* Old English *dunn.*]

Du·na, Dunaj, Dunărea, Dunav. See **Danube.**

Dun·bar (dŭn-bär′), **William** (*c.* 1460–*c.* 1520). Scottish poet. He was probably a Franciscan who became attached to the court of James IV of Scotland. Most of his poems were allegories, such as *The Thistle and the Rose* (1503) and *The Dance of the Seven Deadly Sins* (*c.* 1508).

Dun·bar·ton (dŭn-bär′tən). Also **Dun·bar·ton·shire** (-shîr′, -shər). Former county in western Scotland, now part of Strathclyde Region.

Dun·can I (dŭng′kən) (died 1040). King of Scotland (1034–40). He succeeded his grandfather, Malcolm II Mackenneth. According to the legend used by Shakespeare in *Macbeth,* Duncan was slain by Macbeth at Pitvagenny, near Elgin, on August 14, 1040.

Duncan, Isadora (1878–1927). U.S. dancer. She met the choreographer Michel Fokine in Russia in 1905 and abandoned the traditional ballet costume for bare feet and Greek draperies. She danced to symphonic music not composed for dance, such as that of Wagner, Schubert, and Beethoven. Her championship of free movement made her a forerunner of modern dance. She was killed when her long scarf caught in the wheel of her car and strangled her.

dunce (dŭns) *n.* A dull-witted or stupid person. [Originally *Duns men,* a contemptuous reference to the disciples of John DUNS SCOTUS, used by their philosophical opponents.]

dunce cap *n.* Also **dunce's cap.** A cone-shaped paper cap, formerly placed upon the head of a slow or lazy pupil.

Dun·dalk (dŭn-dôk′, -dôlk′). County town of County Louth, Republic of Ireland. It was here, in 1315, that Edward Bruce declared himself king of Ireland. He was killed nearby three years later. Its port exports beef, cattle, and grain.

Dun·dee (dŭn-dē′). A city on the Firth of Tay, Scotland. It has been a royal burgh since 1190 and is linked with the south by rail over the Tay Bridge, rebuilt in 1888, and by a road bridge opened in 1966. Dundee manufactures linen, canvas, jute, and confectionery and serves the North Sea oilfields.

Dundee cake *n.* A rich fruit cake decorated with almonds.

dun·der·head (dŭn′dər-hĕd′) *n.* A numskull; dunce. [Perhaps "one stunned by a thunderstroke" : Dutch *donder,* thunder, from Middle Dutch + HEAD.] —**dun·der·head·ed** *adj.*

dun diver *n.* A young male or a female goosander.

dun·drear·ies (dŭn-drîr′ēz) *pl.n.* Long side whiskers with a clean-shaven chin. Also called "Dundreary whiskers." [After Lord *Dundreary,* a character in the play *Our American Cousin* (1855) by Tom Taylor (1817–80), British dramatist.]

dune (dōōn, dyōōn) *n.* A hill or ridge of wind-blown sand, especially one barren of vegetation. Also called "sand dune." [French, from Old French, from Middle Dutch *dūne.*]

dune buggy *n.* A small, light motor vehicle, generally having a rear-engine chassis and a molded fiber-glass frame without doors and roof, and usually equipped with a modified engine and oversize tires for driving on sand dunes.

Dunes State Park. See **Indiana Dunes National Lakeshore.**

dung (dŭng) *n.* **1.** The excrement of animals. **2.** Manure. **3.** Anything foul or abhorrent.
—*tr.v.* **dunged, dunging, dungs.** To fertilize with manure. [Middle English *dung,* from Old English *dung,* akin to Old Norse *dyngja,* heap, from Germanic *dung-* (unattested).] —**dung·y** *adj.*

dun·ga·ree (dŭng′gə-rē′) *n.* **1.** A sturdy, usually blue denim fabric. **2. dungarees.** Overalls or trousers made from this fabric. [Hindi *dungrī,* from *Dungri,* name of a district of Bombay where it originated.]

dung beetle *n.* Any of various beetles of the family Scarabaeidae, that form balls of dung on which they feed and in which they lay their eggs.

dun·geon (dŭn′jən) *n.* **1.** A dark, often underground chamber or cell used to confine prisoners. **2.** A donjon (*see*). [Middle English *donjon,* from Old French, "keep of the lord's castle," from Medieval Latin *dominiō,* lordship, from Latin *dominus,* lord, master.]

dung fly *n.* Any of various flies of the genus *Scatophaga* whose larvae feed in dung.

dung·hill (dŭng′hĭl′) *n.* **1.** A heap of animal excrement or manure. **2.** A foul, degraded place or condition.

dun·ite (dōō′nīt′, dŭn′īt′) *n.* An igneous rock consisting mainly of olivine.

dunk (dŭngk) *v.* **dunked, dunking, dunks.** —*tr.* **1.** To plunge into liquid; immerse. **2.** To dip (a doughnut, for example) into coffee or other liquid before eating it. **3.** *Basketball.* To slam (a ball) through the basket from above. —*intr.* **1.** To go under water; submerge oneself briefly. **2.** *Basketball.* To dunk a basketball.
—*n.* **1.** The act or an instance of dunking. **2.** *Basketball.* A shot made by jumping and slamming the ball down through the basket. [Pennsylvania Dutch *dunke,* from Middle High German *dunken, tunken,* from Old High German *dunkōn.*] —**dunk·er** *n.*

Dun·ker (dŭng′kər) *n.* Also **Dun·kard** (-kərd). A member of the German Baptist Brethren, a sect of German-American Baptists opposed to military service and the taking of legal oaths. [Pennsylvania Dutch, from *dunke,* DUNK (referring to their baptismal rite by triple immersion).]

Dun·kirk (dŭn′kûrk′). French **Dun·kerque** (dœN-kĕrk′). Port in Nord department, France. It grew around a 7th-century church

built on the Dunes of St. Eloi giving it its name—"Church in the Dunes." It was ceded to Cromwell in 1658 and sold to Louis XIV by Charles II in 1662. In 1940, during World War II 330,000 Allied troops were evacuated from the town's beaches in the face of enemy fire. Industries include oil refining, shipbuilding, and sugar refining.

dunk shot *n.* See **dunk** (sense 2).

dun·lin (dŭn′lĭn) *n., pl.* **-lins** or collectively **dunlin.** A brown and white sandpiper, *Erolia* or *Calidris*) *alpina,* of northern regions. Also formerly called "stint." [DUN (color) + -LIN(G), diminutive suffix.]

Dun·lop (dŭn′lŏp′, dŭn-lŏp′) *n.* A Scottish cheese, similar in flavor to Cheddar but paler in color.

Dunlop, John Boyd (1840–1921). Scottish inventor of the pneumatic rubber tire. He settled in Belfast as a veterinary surgeon and made the first pneumatic tire for his son's tricycle in 1887. The Dunlop Company began commercial production in 1890.

dun·nage (dŭn′ĭj) *n.* **1.** Loose packing material protecting a ship's cargo from damage during transport. **2.** *Informal.* Personal belongings or baggage. [Middle English *dennage, donage,* perhaps from Middle Low German *dünne,* thin, hence "loose, light stuff."]

Dunne (dŭn), **Finley Peter** (1867–1936). U.S. humorist. He is best known for his series of books featuring Mr. Dooley, an Irish saloonkeeper who comments satirically on current events, political leaders, and all aspects of the contemporary scene in a thick Irish brogue.

dun·nock (dŭn′ək) *n.* The **hedge sparrow** (*see*).

Duns Sco·tus (dŭnz skō′təs), **Joannes,** also known as "the Subtle Doctor" (*c.* 1265–*c.* 1308). Scottish Franciscan monk and theologian, who wrote *On the First Principle.* He disputed Aquinas's harmony of faith and reason and formed a school of scholasticism, known as Scotism.

Dun·stan (dŭn′stən), **Saint** (*c.* 910–988). English monk and archbishop of Canterbury (960–88). He was born near Glastonbury and became abbot of the monastery there in 943. He was exiled to Flanders by King Edwy, but King Eadgar recalled him as bishop of Winchester in 957 and two years later made him archbishop of Canterbury.

du·o (dōō′ō, dyōō′ō) *n., pl.* **-os** (-ōz) or **dui** (dōō′ē, dyōō′ē) (for senses 1, 2). **1.** *Music.* A duet. **2.** *Music.* Two performers singing or playing together. **3.** Two people in close association; a pair. —See Synonyms at **couple.** [Italian, "two," from Latin.]

duo– *prefix.* Indicates two; for example, **duologue.** [Latin, from *duo,* two.]

du·o·dec·i·mal (dōō′ō-dĕs′ə-məl, dyōō′-) *adj.* **1.** Of, pertaining to, or based on the number 12: *the duodecimal system.* **2.** Of or pertaining to twelfths.
—*n.* A twelfth. [From Latin *duodecimus,* twelfth, from *duodecim,* twelve : DUO- + *decem,* ten.] —**du·o·dec·i·mal·ly** *adv.*

du·o·dec·i·mo (dōō′ō-dĕs′ə-mō′, dyōō′-) *n., pl.* **-mos. 1.** The page size of a book, formed by folding a single printer's sheet into 12 leaves. **2.** A book composed of pages of this size. Also called "twelvemo." Also written *12mo., 12°.*
—*adj.* Having pages of this size. [Latin, ablative of *duodecimus,* twelfth, from *duodecim,* twelve. See **duodecimal.**]

du·o·den·a·ry (dōō′ō-dĕn′ə-rē, dyōō′-) *adj.* Of or pertaining to the number 12; duodecimal.

du·o·de·ni·tis (dōō′ə-də-nī′tĭs, dyōō′-) *n.* Inflammation of the duodenum. [New Latin : DUODEN(UM) + -ITIS.]

du·o·de·num (dōō′ə-dē′nəm, dyōō′-, dōō-ŏd′n-əm, dyōō-) *n., pl.* **-odena** (-ŏd′n-ə) or **-nums.** The portion of the small intestine starting at the lower end of the stomach and extending to the jejunum. [Middle English, from Medieval Latin, short for *intestinum duodenum digitōrum,* "intestine of twelve digits" (translation of the Greek *dodekadaktulon,* "twelve fingers long," the duodenum), from Latin *duodēni,* twelve each, from *duodecim,* twelve. See **duodecimal.**] —**du·o·de·nal** (dōō′ə-dē′nəl, dyōō′-, dōō-ŏd′n-əl, dyōō-) *adj.*

du·o·logue, du·o·log (dōō′ə-lŏg′, dyōō′-) *n.* A play, or part of a play, in which only two actors have speaking roles.

du·op·so·ny (dōō-ŏp′sə-nē, dyōō′-) *n., pl.* **-nies.** *Economics.* A stock-market condition wherein two rival buyers exert a controlling influence on numerous sellers. [DUO- + Greek *opsōnia,* purchasing of victuals, catering, from *opsōnes,* victualer, caterer : *opson,* food, relish, delicacy (see **opsonin**) + *ōnē,* buying.]

du·o·tone (dōō′ō-tōn′, dyōō′-) *n.* *Printing.* **1.** A process for printing halftone illustrations in two tones of the same color or black and one color. **2.** A picture in duotone.
—*adj.* *Printing.* Having a two-toned effect or appearance.

dup. duplicate.

du·pat·ta (dōō·pŭt′ə) *n.* A long scarf worn by Indian women. [Hindi.]

dupe (dōōp, dyōōp) *n.* **1.** A person who is easily deceived or used. **2.** A person who mainly acts as the tool of another person or a power: *a dupe of Communism.*
—*tr.v.* **duped, duping, dupes.** To deceive easily; fool. —See Synonyms at **deceive.** [French, from dialect French *dupe,* dupe, probably jocular use of *dupe,* hoopoe (from the supposed stupid appearance of the bird), contraction of *de huppe* : *de,* of + *huppe,* HOOPOE.] —**dup·a·bil·i·ty** *n.* —**dup·a·ble** *adj.*

dup·er·y (dōō′pə-rē, dyōō′-) *n., pl.* **-ies. 1.** The action of duping. **2.** The state of being duped: *"we must think so as to avoid dupery"* (William James). [French *duperie,* from *dupe,* DUPE.]

du·ple (dōō′pəl, dyōō′-) *adj.* **1.** Double; consisting of two. **2.** *Music.* Having two beats in a bar. [Latin *duplus,* twofold, double.]

Dürer

MESSENGER OF THE RENAISSANCE

Dürer carried the Italian artistic revolution to northern Europe

Albrecht Dürer, son of a German goldsmith, introduced the Renaissance art of Italy to northern Europe. He was born in Nuremberg in 1471 and was apprenticed to a painter and engraver in 1486. He twice visited Italy—with profound consequences for him and for northern art.

Emulating the Renaissance artists' skillful use of perspective and search for truth in nature, Dürer embarked on two series of woodcuts, *The Apocalypse* (1498) and the *Great Passion* (1510). He was artist, printer, and publisher of *The Apocalypse.* From 1500, he produced brilliant engravings on copper, including *The Dream, Adam and Eve* (1504), and *St. Jerome in his Study* (1514). His major painting, an altarpiece, is *The Feast of the Rose Garlands* (1506).

Dürer was a true Renaissance man and a recognized master of the age, with striking achievements in many spheres—woodcut designs, paintings, engravings, drawings, and theoretical books on geometry and perspective, fortification, and human proportions. His art exudes power and energy and shows a wealth of detail that is dramatic, elaborate, and inventive, but never overpowers the strong and accurate outlines of the individual subjects.

On a journey to the Netherlands in 1520–1, Dürer caught a fever in swamps where he had gone to draw a dead whale. He never recovered his health fully and died in 1528.

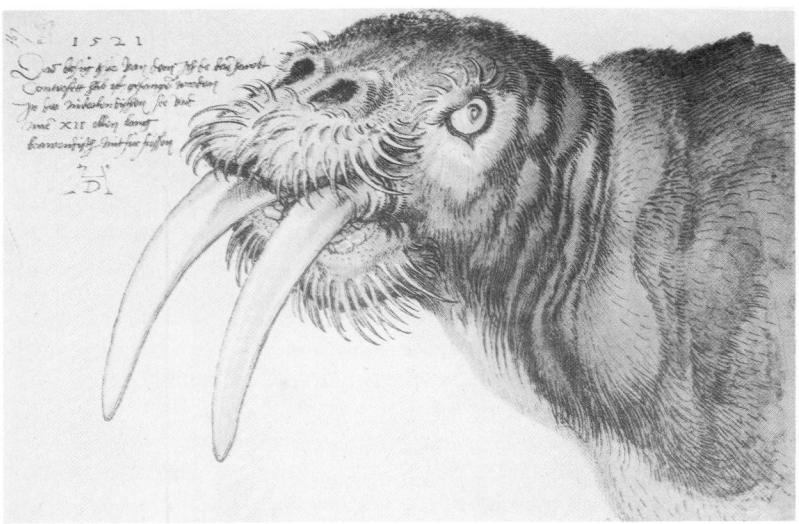

MIRROR OF NATURE *Dürer's search for truth in nature was inspired by the Italian painters. He did this brilliantly detailed head of a walrus in 1521. Two other similar watercolors are among his most famous works:* A Hare, *and* Great Piece of Turf *(both 1502).*

du·plet (dōō′plət, dyōō′-) *n* **1.** *Music.* A pair of notes having equal time value, played in the time of three. **2.** *Electronics.* A pair of electrons shared by two atoms, forming a valence bond.

du·plex (dōō′plĕks′, dyōō′-) *adj.* **1.** Twofold. **2.** *Engineering.* Having two identical units operating in a single frame, each capable of operating independently. **3.** *Electronics.* Able to transmit two messages simultaneously in the same or opposite directions over a single wire. Compare **multiplex, simplex.** ~*n.* **1.** A duplex apartment or house. **2.** A DNA or RNA molecule having a double strand. [Latin, twofold, double.] —**du·plex·i·ty** *n.*

duplex apartment *n.* An apartment having rooms on two adjoining floors connected by an inner staircase.

duplex house *n.* A house divided into two living units.

du·pli·cate (dōō′plĭ-kĭt, dyōō′-) *adj. Abbr.* **dup.** **1.** Identically copied from an original. **2.** Existing or growing in two corresponding parts; double. **3.** *Card Games.* Designating a manner of play in which all partnerships play the same hands and compare scores at the end. ~*n. Abbr.* **dup.** **1.** An identical copy; facsimile. **2.** Anything that corresponds exactly to something else, especially an original; a double. **3.** A duplicate card game. ~*tr.v.* (dōō′plĭ-kāt′, dyōō′-) **duplicated, -cating, -cates. 1.** To make an identical copy of; reproduce; imitate. **2.** To double; make twofold. **3.** To do or effect again or similarly, possibly without real need: *duplicating the process.* [Middle English, from Latin *duplicātus,* past participle of *duplicāre,* to make twofold, from *duplex,* twofold, DUPLEX.] —**du·pli·cate·ly** *adv.*

du·pli·ca·tion (dōō′plĭ-kā′shən, dyōō′-) *n.* **1. a.** The act or procedure of duplicating. **b.** The condition of being duplicated. **2.** A duplicate; replica. —**du·pli·ca·tive** *adj.*

du·pli·ca·tor (dōō′plĭ-kā′tər, dyōō′-) *n.* A machine that reproduces printed or written material, especially one designed for large-quantity reproduction using ink and a master plate or stencil.

du·plic·i·ty (dōō-plĭs′ə-tē, dyōō-) *n., pl.* **-ties.** Deliberate deceptiveness in behavior or speech; double-dealing. [Middle English *duplicite,* from Old French, from Late Latin *duplicitās* (stem *duplicitat-*),

from Latin *duplex* (stem *duplic-*), twofold, DUPLEX.]

Du Pont (dōō pŏnt′, dyōō-), **Eleuthère Irénée** (1771–1834). U.S. manufacturer, born in France. Trained in the royal gunpowder works, he came to the United States in 1800 and in 1802 began manufacturing improved gunpowder at his works near Wilmington, Delaware. Within a few years he established an extensive business for his company, which exists to this day.

Dur. Durham.

du·ra·ble (dōō′rə-bəl, dyōōr′-) *adj.* Able to withstand the effects of time, especially wear and tear or decay; lasting. ~*n.* A manufactured product that does not require frequent replacing, such as a domestic appliance or item of furniture: *consumer durables.* [Middle English, from Old French, from Latin *dūrābilis,* from *dūrāre,* to last, endure.] —**du·ra·bil·i·ty, du·ra·ble·ness** *n.*

durable goods *pl.n.* Durables.

durable press *n.* **1.** A chemical process in which fabrics are permanently shaped and treated for wrinkle resistance. **2.** A fabric treated by durable press.

du·ral (dōō′rəl, dyōōr′-) *adj.* Pertaining to the dura mater.

Du·ral·u·min (dōō-răl′yə-mĭn, dyōō-) *n.* A trademark for an alloy of aluminum containing copper, manganese, magnesium, iron, and silicon. It is resistant to corrosion by acids and sea water.

du·ra ma·ter (dōō′rə mā′tər, dyōōr′-) *n* A tough fibrous membrane that covers the brain and the spinal cord. [Middle English, from Medieval Latin *dūra mater (cerebrī),* "hard mother (of the brain)" (translation from Arabic *umm al-dimāgh aṣ-ṣafīqah*) : Latin *dūra,* feminine of *dūrus,* hard + *mater,* mother.]

du·ra·men (dōō-rā′mən, dyōō-) *n. Botany.* Heartwood (*see*). [New Latin, from Latin, hardness, from *dūrāre,* to harden, from *dūrus,* hard.]

dur·ance (dōōr′əns, dyōōr′-) *n.* Forced confinement; imprisonment. [Middle English *duraunce,* duration, "prison term," from Old French *durance,* from *durer,* to last, from Latin *dūrāre.*]

Dur·and (dyōō-rănd′), **Asher Brown** (1796–1886). U.S. artist. He was a founder of the Hudson River School, which specialized in romantic depictions of the American landscape. In his famous paintings of the Hudson River and the Catskill Mts. Durand adopted the then unusual practice of painting directly from nature.

Du·ran·go (dōō-răng′gō). A city in north-central Mexico, the capital of Durango state. It is in a mining, agricultural, and commercial area. Durango was founded *c.* 1563 and was an important political and religious center in the early history of Mexico.

Du·ran·te (də-răn′tē), **Jimmy** (1893–1980). U.S. comedian and entertainer. Often remembered for his hoarse voice, ample nose, and time-worn hat, he was successful in nightclubs, Broadway shows such as *Red Hot and Blue* (1936), motion pictures, including *Music for Millions* (1944), and television.

du·ra·tion (dōō-rā′shən, dyōō-) *n.* **1.** Continuance or persistence in time. **2.** The period of time during which something exists or persists. —**for the duration.** For an indefinite period. [Medieval Latin *dūrātiō* (stem *dūrātiōn-*), from Latin *dūrāre,* to last.]

durative (dōōr′ə-tĭv, dyōō′-) *adj. Grammar.* Designating a verb aspect that expresses continuing action, as in Russian.

Durazzo. See **Durrës.**

Dur·ban (dûr′bən). The largest city and main seaport of Natal, South Africa. Its harbor handles more foreign trade than Cape Town, exporting coal, manganese and chrome ores, sugar, oranges, pineapple, and maize and importing machinery for the Rand goldfields. Durban is also a major resort.

dur·bar (dûr′bär′) *n.* **1. a.** A state reception, often accompanied by a military display, given formerly by an Indian prince or by a British governor in India. **b.** The reception hall. **2.** The court of an Indian prince or ruler. [Hindi *darbār,* from Persian, "court" : *dar,* door + *bār,* admission, audience, time.]

Dü·rer (dōōr′ər, dyōōr′-), **Albrecht** (1471–1528). German painter and engraver. He began as an apprentice to his goldsmith father in Nuremberg. He carried the classicism of the Italian Renaissance into northern European painting.

du·ress (dōō-rĕs′, dyōō-, dōōr′ĭs, dyōōr′-) *n.* **1.** Constraint by threat; coercion: *confessed under duress.* **2.** *Law.* **a.** Coercion illegally applied. **b.** Forcible confinement. [Middle English *duresse,* hardness, restraint, confinement, from Old French *dure(s)ce,* hardness, from Latin *dūritia,* from *dūrus,* hard.]

Dur·ga (dōōr′gə) *n. Hinduism.* The goddess Devi considered as a fierce though benevolent protectress of heroes and an upholder of virtue.

Dur·ham¹ (dûr′əm). *Abbr.* **Dur.** County in northeast England stretching from the Pennines to the North Sea. Coal mining, though in decline, dominates the coastal plain. Other industries include light engineering and chemicals.

Durham². Principal city and administrative center of Durham, England. The city is dominated by its magnificent Norman cathedral; its castle, founded by William the Conqueror in 1072, is now part of the University of Durham, established in 1832.

Durham³. City in north-central North Carolina. It is in the heart of a tobacco-growing region.

Durham⁴. Any of a breed of beef cattle, a **shorthorn** (*see*). [Originally bred in DURHAM (county).]

du·ri·an (dōōr′ē-ən) *n.* **1.** A tree, *Durio zibethinus,* of southeastern Asia, bearing edible fruit. **2.** The fruit of this tree, having a hard, prickly rind and soft pulp with an offensive odor but a pleasant taste. [Malay.]

dur·ing (dōōr′ĭng, dyōōr′-) *prep.* **1.** Throughout the course or duration of. **2.** Within the time of; at some time in. [Middle English (after Old French *durant,* "lasting"), from *duren,* to last, from Old French *durer,* from Latin *durāre.*]

Durk·heim (dûr′kĕm′), **Emile** (1858–1917). French social scientist, a founder of modern sociology. He applied anthropological information and statistics to the study of society.

dur·mast (dûr′măst′, -mäst′) *n.* A European oak, *Quercus petrea,* having tough, elastic wood and sessile acorns. Also called "sessile oak." [Probably alteration of *dun mast* : DUN (grayish brown) + MAST (nut, acorn).]

du·ro (dŏŏ′rō) *n., pl.* **-ros.** The silver dollar of Spain and Spanish America. [Spanish *(peso) duro,* "hard (peso)," from Latin *dūrus,* hard.]

du·roc, Du·roc (dŏŏ-rŏk′, dyŏŏ-) *n.* A large red pig of a breed developed during the 19th century in the United States. [After *Duroc,* a horse owned by the developer of the breed.]

dur·ra, dou·ra, dou·rah (dŏŏr′ə) *n.* A cereal grain, *Sorghum vulgare durra,* of Asia and northern Africa, much cultivated in dry regions. Also called "Guinea corn," "Indian millett." [Arabic *dhurah,* grain.]

Dur·rell (dûr′əl), **Gerald** (1925–). British naturalist and writer, born in India, the brother of Lawrence. In 1958 he founded the Jersey Wildlife Preservation Fund, which runs a zoo on the island for endangered species. His stories include *The Overloaded Ark* (1953) and *My Family and Other Animals* (1956).

Durrell, Lawrence George (1912–90). British writer, born in India of Irish parents. His best-known work is the Alexandria Quartet: *Justine* (1957), *Balthazar* (1958), *Mountolive* (1958), and *Clea* (1960).

Dü·ren·matt (dŏŏr′ən-mät′), **Friedrich** (1921–90). Swiss novelist and dramatist. His plays include *The Visit* (1956), *Romulus* (1949), and *The Physicists* (1962). His novels include *The Judge and His Hangman* (1952) and *The Quarry* (1953).

Dur·rës (dŏŏr′əs). Italian **Du·raz·zo** (dŏŏ-rät′sō). Chief seaport of Albania and its former capital. A Greek city of the 7th century B.C. and important Roman port and bishopric (449), it was later held by Normans, Byzantines, Sicilians, Greeks, Serbs, and Turks until Albanian independence in 1913. A tourist center, Durrës also produces foodstuffs, tobacco, clothing, and ships.

durst. *Archaic.* Past tense of **dare.**

du·rum (dŏŏr′əm, dyŏŏr-) *n.* A hardy wheat, *Triticum durum,* grown mainly in the Mediterranean region and used chiefly in making macaroni, spaghetti, and similar products. Also called "durum wheat." [New Latin, from Latin, neuter of *dūrus,* hard.]

dur·zi (dûr′zē) *n.* An Indian tailor. [Hindi, from Persian *darzi,* from *darz,* sewing.]

Duse (dŏŏ′zā), **Eleonora** (1858–1924). Italian actress. The greatest interpretative actress of her day, she was most highly acclaimed as the heroine in the plays of her contemporaries Gabriele D'Annunzio and Henrik Ibsen. She fascinated critics and audiences around the world with her penetrating, insightful performances.

dusk (dŭsk) *n.* The darker stage of evening twilight.
~ *adj.* Tending to darkness.
~ *v.* **dusked, dusking, dusks.** *Poetic.* —*intr.* To become dark or dusky. —*tr.* To darken. [Middle English *dosc, dusk,* dusky, from Old English *dox,* dark, dusky.]

dusk·y (dŭs′kē) *adj.* **-ier, -iest. 1.** Dark; shadowy. **2.** Rather dark in color, especially in skin color. **3.** Gloomy. —See Usage note at **dark.** —**dusk·i·ly** *adv.* —**dusk·i·ness** *n.*

dusky grouse *n.* A bird, the **blue grouse** (see).

Düs·sel·dorf (dŏŏs′əl-dôrf′). City in North Rhine-Westphalia, in western Germany. It is a port on the Rhine River serving the Ruhr and Wupper industrial areas. Its industries include iron, steel, car assembly, and chemicals.

dust (dŭst) *n.* **1. a.** Matter composed of fine particles, such as earth or pollen. **b.** Small particles of matter that are fine enough to be carried by the wind. **2. a.** Clouds of such matter. **b.** A state of confusion. Used in such phrases as *let the dust settle.* **3.** Such matter regarded as the result of disintegration. **4. a.** Earth, especially when regarded as the substance of the grave: *"Dust thou art, and shalt to dust return"* (Milton). **b.** The remains of a dead person. **5.** The surface of the ground. Preceded by *the.* **6.** A debased or despised condition. Used especially in the phrase *in the dust.* **7.** Something of no worth. **8.** *British.* Ashes, household dirt, or rubbish. **9.** Disturbance; fuss. **10.** *Informal.* A lung condition caused by dust, **pneumoconiosis** (see). —**bite the dust. 1.** To fail or be defeated. **2.** To fall dead.
~ *v.* **dusted, dusting, dusts.** —*tr.* **1.** To remove dust from by wiping, brushing, or beating. **2.** To sprinkle with a powdery substance. **3.** To strew like dust: *Freckles dusted her nose.* **4.** To remove as dust: *dusted the crumbs off.* **5.** To restore to use. Used with *off.* **6.** *Archaic.* To cover with dust. —*intr.* **1.** To clean by removing dust. **2.** To cover itself with dust. Used of a bird. [Middle English *dust, doust,* Old English *dūst.*]

dust-bath (dŭst′băth′, -bäth′) *n.* The action of a bird working dust into its feathers so as to clean them or possibly help rid itself of parasites.

dust-bin (dŭst′bĭn′) *n. British.* A large cylindrical container for household rubbish.

dust bowl *n.* In semiarid regions, a barren area produced by excessive wind erosion of the soil, especially after the removal of vegetation by overgrazing or badly managed cultivation. The topsoil is removed, and the area swept by severe dust storms. —**the Dust Bowl.** Such an area that developed in the 1930's in the south-central United States, stretching through west Kansas, Oklahoma, Texas, Colorado, and into New Mexico.

dust cover *n.* **1.** A removable or hinged plastic cover used to protect a turntable. **2.** See **dust jacket** (sense 1).

dust devil *n.* A small transient whirlwind that swirls dust, debris, and sand up into the air.

dust·er (dŭs′tər) *n.* **1.** One that dusts. **2.** A cloth used to remove dust. **3.** A device for sifting or scattering a powdered substance. **4.** A smock worn to protect one's clothing from dust. **5.** A woman's loose housecoat.

dust·ing powder (dŭs′tĭng) *n* A fine powder, such as talcum powder, used on the skin.

dust jacket *n. Abbr.* **dj 1.** A removable paper cover used to protect the binding of a book. Also called "book jacket," "dust cover," "jacket." **2.** A cardboard sleeve in which a phonograph record is packaged.

dust·man (dŭst′mən) *n., pl.* **-men** (-mĭn). *British.* A man employed to remove trash.

dust·pan (dŭst′păn′) *n.* A short-handled, shovellike pan into which dust is swept.

dust shot *n.* The smallest-sized firing shot.

dust storm *n.* In a semiarid or arid region, a severe windstorm that sweeps clouds of dust across an extensive area.

dust-up (dŭst′ŭp′) *n. Informal.* An argument, especially one involving violence; a scuffle.

dust·y (dŭs′tē) *adj.* **-ier, -iest. 1.** Covered or filled with dust. **2.** Consisting of or resembling dust; powdery. **3.** Tinged with gray; subdued; dull. **4.** Dry; uninteresting. **5.** *British.* Not satisfactory or helpful: *a dusty answer.* —**dust·i·ly** *adv.* —**dust·i·ness** *n.*

dusty miller *n.* Any of various plants having leaves and stems covered with dustlike down, such as the **beach wormwood** and the **rose campion** (both of which see).

Dutch (dŭch) *adj. Abbr.* **D., Du. 1.** Of or pertaining to the Netherlands, its inhabitants, or their language. **2.** *Archaic.* German.
~ *n. Abbr.* **D., Du. 1.** Used with a plural verb. **a.** The people of the Netherlands. Preceded by *the.* **b.** *Archaic.* The Germans. **2. a.** The West Germanic language of the Netherlands. Sometimes called "Low Dutch." **b.** The German language. Now used only in the term *High Dutch.* **3. Pennsylvania Dutch** (see). —**in Dutch.** *Informal.* In trouble; in disfavor.
~ *adv.* So that each person pays his own way: *go Dutch for lunch.*

Dutch auction *n. Informal.* An auction in which the auctioneer opens with a high price and lowers it until a buyer is found.

Dutch bargain *n. Informal.* A transaction settled while both parties are drinking.

Dutch barn *n.* A barn with open sides and a curved roof.

Dutch cap *n.* **1.** A woman's lace cap with turned-back triangular flaps on each side. **2.** A type of contraceptive, a **diaphragm** (see).

Dutch cheese *n.* **Cottage cheese** (see).

Dutch clover *n.* The **white clover** (see).

Dutch courage *n. Informal.* Courage from drinking liquor.

Dutch doll *n.* A jointed wooden doll.

Dutch door *n.* A door divided in half horizontally so that either part may be left open or closed.

Dutch East Indies. See **Indonesia.**

Dutch elm disease *n.* A disease of elm trees caused by a fungus, *Ceratocystis ulmi,* and resulting in eventual death of the tree due to the water-conducting vessels becoming clogged with gums produced by the fungus.

Dutch Guiana. See **Surinam.**

Dutch hoe *n.* A hoe having a crosspiece attached to two prongs, used with a pushing motion.

dutch·man (dŭch′mən) *n., pl.* **-men** (-mĭn). Something used to conceal faulty construction. [Playful use of DUTCHMAN.]

Dutch·man (dŭch′mən) *n., pl.* **-men** (-mĭn). **1.** A native or inhabitant of the Netherlands. **2.** A person of Dutch descent. **3.** *Archaic.* A German.

Dutch·man's-breech·es (dŭch′mənz-brĭch′ĭz) *n. Used with a singular or plural verb.* A woodland plant, *Dicentra cucullaria,* of eastern North America, having finely divided leaves and yellowish-white flowers with two spurs. [From its breeches-shaped blossoms.]

Dutch metal *n.* An alloy of copper and zinc used in thin sheets as a cheap imitation of gold leaf. Also called "Dutch foil," "Dutch gold," "Dutch leaf." [Originally imported from Holland.]

Dutch oven *n.* **1.** A large, heavy pot or kettle, usually of cast iron and with a tight lid, used for slow cooking. **2.** A metal utensil open on one side and equipped with shelves, that is placed before an open fire for baking or roasting food. **3.** A wall oven in which food is baked by means of preheated brick walls.

Dutch rush *n.* A horsetail, *Equisetum hyemale,* with unbranched overwintering stems.

Dutch treat *n. Informal.* An outing, as for dinner or a film, for which each person pays his own expenses.

Dutch uncle *n. Informal.* A stern and candid critic or adviser.

Dutch West Indies. See **Netherlands Antilles.**

du·te·ous (dŏŏ′tē-əs, dyŏŏ′-) *adj. Formal.* Obedient; dutiful. [From DUTY.] —**du·te·ous·ly** *adv.* —**du·te·ous·ness** *n.*

du·ti·a·ble (dŏŏ′tē-ə-bəl, dyŏŏ′-) *adj.* Subject to import tax.

du·ti·ful (dŏŏ′tĭ-fəl, dyŏŏ′-) *adj.* **1.** Filled with or motivated by a sense of duty. **2.** Showing or proceeding from a sense of duty. —See Synonyms at **obedient.** —**du·ti·ful·ly** *adv.* —**du·ti·ful·ness** *n.*

du·ty (dŏŏ′tē, dyŏŏ′-) *n., pl.* **-ties. 1.** An act or a course of action that is exacted of one by law or social custom, or by one's position or

Dutchman's-breeches *A woodland plant of North America, so called because its flowers resemble the traditional Dutch garment.*

religion. **2. a.** Moral obligation. **b.** The compulsion felt to meet such obligation. **3. a.** A service assigned to or demanded of one, especially in the armed forces. **b.** A function; an allocated task. **4.** A tax charged by a government, on imports, transactions, transference of estates, or the like. **5.** *Engineering.* **a.** The work capability of a machine under specified conditions. **b.** A measure of efficiency expressed as work per unit energy input. **6.** *Agriculture.* The amount of water required to irrigate a given area for the cultivation of some crop. —**off duty.** Not engaged in one's assigned work; not at work. —**on duty.** At one's post or work; engaged in one's work. [Middle English *duete,* from Norman French, from Old French *deu,* DUE.]

duty-bound (dōo′tē-bound′, dyōo′-) *adj.* Obliged by a moral, legal, or other duty.

du·ty-free (dōo′tē-frē′, dyōo′-) *adj.* Exempt from customs duties. —*n. Informal.* A duty-free item of merchandise. —**du·ty-free** *adv.*

duty-free shop *n.* A shop, especially one at an airport or port, that sells duty-free goods such as tobacco, spirits, or perfume.

du·um·vir (dōo-ŭm′vər, dyōo-) *n., pl.* **-virs** or **-viri** (-və-rē′). A member of a duumvirate. [Latin, variant of *duovir* : *duo,* two + *vir,* man.]

du·um·vi·rate (dōo-ŭm′vər-ĭt, dyōo-) *n.* **1.** Any of various two-man governments in the Roman Republic. **2.** Any government or authority consisting of two men.

Du·va·lier (dōo′väl-yā′), **François,** also known as "Papa Doc" (1907–71). Haitian dictator. He was elected president of Haiti in 1957, and in 1964 he declared himself president for life. Duvalier executed opponents without trial and deprived the population of civil rights and education. His practice of voodooism led some uneducated Haitians to believe that he possessed supernatural powers.

Duvalier, Jean-Claude, also known as "Baby Doc" (1951–). Dictator of Haiti, son of François. He succeeded his father as president for life in 1971 but fled the country in 1986 after widespread civil unrest.

du·vet (dōo-vā′, dyōo-) *n.* A soft, light quilt filled with down, feathers, or a similar synthetic material and used in place of a sheet and blankets. [French, down, from Old French *duvet,* alteration of *dumet,* diminutive of *dum,* alteration (probably influenced by PLUME) of *dun,* from Old Norse *dūnn.*]

du·ve·tyn, du·ve·tine, du·ve·tyne (dōo′və-tēn′, dyōo′-, dōo′və-tēn′, dyōo′-) *n.* A soft, napped fabric with a twill weave, made of wool, cotton, rayon, or silk. [French *duvetine,* from DUVET.]

duyker. Variant of **duiker.**

D.V. 1. Deo volente. **2.** Douay Version (of the Bible).

dvan·dva (dvän′dvä′) *n.* A compound expression consisting of two elements typically belonging to the same part of speech and being of equal importance in determining the meaning of the compound; for example, a **fighter-bomber** is both a fighter and a bomber. Compare **bahuvrihi.** [Sanskrit, repeated nominative (exemplifying this compound) of *dva,* couple, pair.]

Dvi·na, Northern (dvē′nə). *Russian* **Se·ver·na·ya Dvina** (sā′vər-nə-yə). River in northwest Russia. It flows 750 kilometers (466 miles) northwest to Dvina Bay on the White Sea.

Dvina, Western. *Russian* **Za·pad·na·ya Dvina** (zä′pəd-nə-yə). River in Belarus, Latvia, and western Russia. It flows 1,030 kilometers (640 miles) from the Valdai Hills to the Gulf of Riga.

D.V.M. Doctor of Veterinary Medicine.

Dvo·řák (dvôr′zhäk), **Antonin** or **Anton** (1841–1904). Czech composer. He incorporated folk tunes into his music, especially in the *Slavonic Dances.* His last symphony, the Ninth, "From the New World" (1893), was composed in the United States where he was director of the National Conservatory in New York (1892–95).

D/W dock warrant.

dwarf (dwôrf) *n., pl.* **dwarfs** or **dwarves** (dwôrvz). **1. a.** A very small person, specifically, a person afflicted with dwarfism. Compare **midget. b.** An atypically small animal or plant. **2.** A diminutive, often ugly, manlike creature of fairy tales and legend. **3.** A dwarf star. —*v.* **dwarfed, dwarfing, dwarfs.** —*tr.* **1.** To check the natural growth or development of; stunt: *"the oaks were dwarfed from lack of moisture"* (John Steinbeck). **2.** To cause to appear small by comparison: *an old church dwarfed by the new office buildings.* —*intr.* To become stunted or grow smaller. —*adj.* **1.** Diminutive; undersized; stunted. **2.** *Biology.* Much smaller than the usual or typical kind: *dwarf gourami; dwarf zinnias.* [Middle English *dwerf, dwergh,* Old English *dweorg, dweorh,* from Germanic *dwerg-* (unattested).]

dwarf bean *n.* A variety of **string bean** *(see).*

dwarf cornel *n.* A woody plant, *Cornus canadensis,* of northern North America, having inconspicuous greenish flowers surrounded by white, petallike bracts, and scarlet fruit.

dwarf·ism (dwôr′fĭz′əm) *n.* A condition of arrested growth having various causes; especially: **1.** Achondroplasia *(see).* **2.** A deficiency of or failure to respond to growth hormone.

dwarf star *n.* A main-sequence star having relatively high density, small mass, and average or below average luminosity. Also called "dwarf." Compare **giant star.** See **white dwarf.**

dwell (dwĕl) *intr.v.* **dwelt** (dwĕlt) or **dwelled, dwelling, dwells. 1.** *Formal.* To live as a resident; reside. **2.** To exist in some place or state. **3. a.** To fasten one's attention; reflect on at length or in detail, especially in speech or writing. Used with *on* or *upon.* **b.** To emphasize or stress something: *dwelt on the importance of health care.* **c.** *Music.* To hold or sustain a note or phrase: *dwell on high C.*

—*n.* **1.** A short regular pause in the motion of a mechanical part of the constant-radius portion of a cam that causes it. **2.** *Computer Science.* A programmed time delay of variable duration. [Middle English *dwellen,* to delay, linger, remain, reside, Old English *dwellan,* deceive, hinder, delay (meaning influenced by Old Norse *dvelja,* "sojourn," "dwell").]

dwell·er (dwĕl′ər) *n.* A person or animal that lives in a specified place. Used in combination: *cave-dweller, city-dweller.*

dwell·ing (dwĕl′ĭng) *n. Formal.* A place of residence; a house; an abode.

dwelling house *n.* A building intended for occupation; a residence.

dwel·ling-place (dwĕl′ĭng-plās′) *n.* A dwelling.

dwin·dle (dwĭnd′l) *v.* **-dled, -dling, -dles.** —*intr.* To become gradually less until little remains; waste away; diminish. —*tr.* To make smaller or less; cause to shrink. —See Synonyms at **decrease.** [Frequentative of obsolete *dwine,* to waste away, diminish, languish, Middle English *dwinen,* Old English *dwīnan.*]

d.w.t. deadweight tonnage.

Dy The symbol for the element dysprosium.

dy·ad (dī′ăd′) *n.* **1.** Two units regarded as a pair. **2.** *Biology.* One pair of chromosomes separated from a tetrad in meiosis. **3.** *Chemistry.* A divalent atom or radical. **4.** A mathematical operator represented as a pair of vectors juxtaposed without multiplication. —*adj.* Made up of two units. [From Greek *duas* (stem *duad-*), pair, from *duo,* two.]

dy·ad·ic (dī-ăd′ĭk) *adj.* **1.** Twofold. **2.** Of or relating to a dyad. —*n. Mathematics.* The direct product *(B·C) AD* of two dyads *AB* and *CD.*

Dy·ak, Day·ak (dī′ăk′) *n.* **1.** A member of any of various Indonesian peoples of Borneo and the Sulu Sea islands **2.** The language of the Dyaks. [Malay *Dayak,* "upcountry," from *darat,* land.]

dyarchy. Variant of **diarchy.**

dyb·buk (dĭb′ək) *n.* In Jewish folklore, a malevolent spirit that enters the body of a person and controls his actions. [Yiddish, devil, from Hebrew *dibbūq,* from *dābhaq,* to cling.]

dye (dī) *n.* **1. a.** Any substance used to color materials. **b.** A liquid containing such a substance: *a vat of dye.* **2.** A color imparted by or as if by dyeing. —*v.* **dyed, dyeing, dyes.** —*tr.* **1.** To color (a material) with or as if with a dye, especially by soaking in a coloring solution. **2.** To add (color) with a dye. —*intr.* To take on or impart color. [Middle English *deie,* Old English *dēah, dēag†,* hue, tinge.] —**dy·er** *n.*

dyed-in-the-wool (dīd′ĭn-thə-wŏol′) *adj.* **1.** Dyed before being woven into cloth. **2.** Inflexible, especially in opinions, views, or the like; out-and-out.

Dy·er (dī′ər), **Mary** (died 1660). Quaker martyr in Massachusetts, born in England. She first came to America *c.* 1635. While on a visit to England in the 1650's she became a Quaker, and after her return to Boston in 1657, she was arrested and banished, returning twice (1659, 1660) to aid imprisoned Quakers. She was ultimately condemned for sedition and hanged.

dyer's greenweed *n.* A small broomlike shrub, *Genista tinctoria,* native to Eurasia, having clusters of yellow flowers. Also called "dyer's broom," "woadwaxen," "woodwaxen." [So called because it yields a green dye.]

dyer's rocket *n.* A plant, *Reseda luteola,* native to Europe, having long spikes of small, yellowish-green flowers and yielding a yellow dye. Also called "weld."

dy·er's-weed (dī′ərz-wēd′) *n.* Any of various plants yielding coloring matter used as a dye.

dye·stuff (dī′stŭf′) *n.* Any substance used as or yielding a dye. [Probably translation of German *Farbstoff.*]

dye·wood (dī′wŏod′) *n.* Any wood from which dyestuffs are obtained.

Dy·fed (dĭv′ĕd) County in southwest Wales, the largest of the Welsh counties, bordering the Irish Sea. Agriculture and stock rearing are widespread. Its administrative center is Carmarthen.

dy·ing (dī′ĭng) *adj.* **1.** About to die. **2.** Drawing to an end; declining. **3.** Done or uttered just before death. **4.** Of or pertaining to death: *one's dying day.*

dyke. Variant of **dike.**

Dyl·an (dĭl′ən), **Bob,** born Robert Allen Zimmerman (1941–). U.S. singer and songwriter. His protest songs with their plaintive surrealism made him a notable figure in popular music in the 1960's.

dy·nam·ic (dī-năm′ĭk) *adj.* Also **dy·nam·i·cal** (-ĭ-kəl). **1.** Of or pertaining to energy, force, or motion in relation to force. **2.** Characterized by or tending to produce continuous change or advance. **3.** Energetic and enterprising; forceful. **4.** Of or pertaining to variation of intensity or volume, as in musical sound. **5.** Designating a computer memory that needs periodic updates. —See Synonyms at **active.** —*n.* A social or psychological system or drive that underlies any relationship between individuals: *the parent-child dynamic.* [French *dynamique,* from Greek *dunamikos,* powerful, from *dunamis,* power, from *dunasthai,* to be able.] —**dy·nam·i·cal·ly** *adv.*

dynamical geology *n.* **Geodynamics** *(see).*

dynamic psychology *n.* A method in psychology that emphasizes the fluidity and energy of mental life and the motives of the individual that condition it.

dy·nam·ics (dī-năm′ĭks) *n.* **1.** *Used with a singular verb. Physics.* A branch of mechanics comprising the study of the relationship between motion and the forces affecting the motion of physical systems. Also called "kinetics." Compare **kinematics, statics. 2.** *Used* with a plural verb. The forces that produce motion and change in any field or system. **3.** *Used with a plural verb.* Variation in volume, force, or intensity, especially in musical sound. **4.** *Psychology.* **a.** *Used with a singular verb.* The action, fluidity, and energy of mental life. **b.** *Used with a plural verb.* The motives, needs, and drives of an individual or group.

dy·na·mism (dī′nə-mĭz′əm) n. **1.** Any of various theories or philosophical systems that explain the universe in terms of an immanent force or in terms of natural forces and their interplay. **2.** A process or mechanism responsible for the development or motion of a system. **3.** The quality of being dynamic. [French *dynamisme* : DYNAM(O)- + -ISM.] —**dy·na·mist** n. —**dy·na·mis·tic** adj.

dy·na·mite (dī′nə-mīt′) n. **1.** A powerful explosive composed of nitroglycerin or ammonium nitrate dispersed in an absorbent material such as wood pulp and an antacid such as calcium carbonate. **2.** *Informal.* **a.** Someone or something that is potentially dangerous or violent. **b.** Someone or something outstandingly fine. **3.** *Slang.* Heroin.
~tr.v. **dynamited, -miting, -mites. 1.** To blow up, shatter, or destroy with or as if with dynamite. **2.** To charge with dynamite. [Swedish *dynamit* : DYNAM(O)- + -ITE.] —**dy·na·mit·er** n.

dy·na·mo (dī′nə-mō′) n., pl. **-mos. 1.** A generator, especially one for producing direct current. **2.** *Informal.* An extremely energetic and forceful person. [Short for *dynamo(electric) machine,* translation of German *dynamoelektrische Maschine.*]

dynamo– prefix. Indicates power; for example, **dynamoelectric.** [Greek *dunamo-,* from *dunamis,* power, from *dunasthai,* to be able.]

dy·na·mo·e·lec·tric (dī′nə-mō′ə-lĕk′trĭk) adj. Also **dy·na·mo·e·lec·tri·cal** (-trĭ-kəl). Relating to the conversion of mechanical energy into electrical energy, or vice versa.

dy·na·mom·e·ter (dī′nə-mŏm′ə-tər) n. Any of several instruments used to measure force or power. [French *dynamomètre* : DYNAMO- + -METER.]

dy·na·mom·e·try (dī′nə-mŏm′ə-trē) n. Measurement by means of a dynamometer. —**dy·na·mo·met·ric** (dī′-nə-mō-mĕt′rĭk), **dy·na·mo·met·ri·cal** adj.

dy·na·mo·tor (dī′nə-mō′tər) n. A rotating electric machine with two armatures, used to convert alternating to direct current. [DYNA(MO)- + MOTOR.]

dy·nast (dī′năst′, -nəst) n. A lord or ruler; especially, a hereditary ruler. [Latin *dynastēs,* from Greek *dunastēs,* lord, master, from *dunasthai,* to be able.]

dy·nas·ty (dī′nə-stē) n., pl. **-ties. 1.** A succession of rulers from the same family or line. **2.** A family or group that maintains power or supremacy in a particular field for a considerable length of time. [French *dynastie,* from Greek *dunasteia,* domination, lordship, from *dunastēs,* ruler, DYNAST.] —**dy·nas·tic** (dī-năs′tĭk) adj. —**dy·nas·ti·cal·ly** adv.

dy·na·tron (dī′nə-trŏn′) n. Electronics. A tetrode with grid and anode potentials so arranged that anode current decreases when the anode potential increases. [DYNA(MO)- + -TRON.]

dyne (dīn) n. Physics. A centimeter-gram-second unit of force, equal to the force required to impart an acceleration of one centimeter per second per second to a mass of one gram. [French, from Greek *dunamis,* power. See **dynamic.**]

Dy·nel (dī-nĕl′). A trademark for a copolymer of vinyl chloride and acrylonitrile, used to make fire-resistant, insect-resistant, and easily dyed textile fiber.

dy·node (dī′nōd′) n. An electrode used in certain electron tubes to provide secondary emission. [DYN(AMO)- + -ODE.]

dys– prefix. Indicates diseased, painful, difficult, faulty, or bad; for example, **dysentery, dyslexia.** [Middle English *dis-,* from Old French, from Latin *dys-,* from Greek *dus-.*]

dys·cra·si·a (dĭs-krā′zhē-ə, -zhə) n. Rare. Loosely, a morbid state or condition resulting from the presence of abnormal material in the blood. [New Latin, from Medieval Latin, disease, distemper, "disproportionate mixture of the humors," from Greek *duskrasia* : DYS- + *krasis,* mixing.]

dys·en·ter·y (dĭs′ən-tĕr′ē) n. An infection of the lower intestinal tract producing pain, fever, and severe diarrhea, often with blood and mucus. [Middle English *dissenterie,* from Latin *dysenteria,* from Greek *dusenteria* : DYS- + *enteron,* intestine.] —**dys·en·ter·ic** adj.

dys·func·tion (dĭs-fŭngk′shən) n. Disordered or impaired functioning, as of a bodily system or organ.

dys·gen·ic (dĭs-jĕn′ĭk) adj. Pertaining to or causing the deterioration of hereditary qualities. [DYS- + -GENIC.]

dys·gen·ics (dĭs-jĕn′ĭks) n. Used with a singular verb. The biological study of the factors producing racial degeneration. Also called "cacogenics."

dys·graph·i·a (dĭs-grăf′ē-ə) n. Impairment of the ability to write. [New Latin : DYS- + -graphia, -graphy.]

dys·lex·i·a (dĭs-lĕk′sē-ə) n. A learning disorder causing impairment of the ability to read; incomplete alexia. Also called "word blindness." [New Latin : DYS- + Greek *lexis,* speech, from *legein,* to speak.] —**dys·lec·tic** (dĭs-lĕk′tĭk) adj. & n. —**dys·lex·ic** adj. & n.

dys·lo·gis·tic (dĭs′lō-jĭs′tĭk) adj. Conveying censure; disapproving. [DYS- + (EU)LOGISTIC.] —**dys·lo·gis·ti·cal·ly** adv.

dys·men·or·rhe·a, dys·men·or·rhoe·a (dĭs-mĕn′ə-rē′ə) n. Difficult or painful menstruation. [New Latin : DYS- + Greek *mēn* (stem *mēno-*), month + -RRHEA.]

dys·pa·reu·ni·a (dĭs′pə-rōō′nē-ə) n. Pain or difficulty experienced during sexual intercourse.

dys·pep·sia (dĭs-pĕp′shə, -sē-ə) n. Disturbed digestion; indigestion. [Latin, from Greek *duspepsia* : DYS- + *-pepsia,* digestion.]

dys·pep·tic (dĭs-pĕp′tĭk) adj. Also **dys·pep·ti·cal** (-tĭ-kəl). **1.** Pertaining to or having dyspepsia. **2.** Morose; gloomy.
~n. One who suffers from dyspepsia. —**dys·pep·ti·cal·ly** adv.

dys·pha·gi·a (dĭs-fā′jē-ə) n. Difficulty in swallowing. [New Latin : DYS- + -PHAGIA.] —**dys·phag·ic** (dĭs-făj′ĭk) adj.

dys·pha·sia (dĭs-fā′zhə, -zhē-ə) n. Impairment of speech and verbal comprehension, especially when associated with brain injury. [New Latin : DYS- + -PHASIA.] —**dys·pha·sic** (dĭs-fā′zĭk) adj.

dys·phe·mism (dĭs′fə-mĭz′əm) n. **1.** The substitution of an unpleasant or derogatory term for an inoffensive one. **2.** The term thus substituted. [DYS- + EUPHEMISM.]

dys·pho·ni·a (dĭs-fō′nē-ə) n. Difficulty in speaking, usually resulting in hoarseness. [New Latin : DYS- + Greek *-phōnia,* -PHONY.] —**dys·phon·ic** (dĭs-fŏn′ĭk) adj.

dys·pho·ri·a (dĭs-fôr′ē-ə, -fōr′ē-ə) n. An emotional state characterized by anxiety, depression, and restlessness. [New Latin, from Greek *dusphoria,* distress, from *dusphoros,* hard to bear : DYS- + -PHOROUS.] —**dys·phor·ic** (dĭs-fôr′ĭk, -fōr′ĭk) adj.

dys·pla·sia (dĭs-plā′zhə, -zē-ə) n. Abnormal development of tissues, organs, or cells. [New Latin : DYS- + Greek *plasis,* formation, from *plassein,* to mold.] —**dys·plas·tic** (dĭs-plăs′tĭk) adj.

dysp·ne·a (dĭsp-nē′ə) n. A sense of difficulty in breathing, often associated with lung or heart disease. [New Latin, from Greek *duspnoia,* from *duspnoos,* short of breath : DYS- + *-pnoos,* from *pnoē,* breathing, from *pnein,* to breathe.] —**dysp·ne·ic** adj.

dys·pro·si·um (dĭs-prō′zē-əm) n. Symbol **Dy** A soft, silvery rare-earth metal used in nuclear research. Atomic number 66, atomic weight 162.50, melting point 1,407°C, boiling point 2,335°C, specific gravity 8.536, valence 3. [New Latin, from Greek *dusprositos,* difficult to approach : DYS- + *prositos,* approachable, from *prosienai,* to approach : *pros-,* toward + *ienai,* to go.]

dys·tel·e·ol·o·gy (dĭs′tĕl-ē-ŏl′ə-jē, dĭs′tē-lē-) n. **1.** The doctrine of purposelessness in nature. Compare **teleology. 2.** Purposelessness in natural structures, as manifested by the existence of vestigial or nonfunctional organs or parts. [German *Dysteleologie* : DYS- + New Latin *teleologia,* TELEOLOGY.] —**dys·tel·e·o·log·i·cal** adj. —**dys·tel·e·ol·o·gist** n.

dys·thy·mi·a (dĭs-thī′mē-ə) n. Psychiatry. **1.** A form of neurosis characterized by depression, anxiety, obsessions, and compulsive behavior. **2.** Any condition caused by malfunction of the thymus during childhood. [New Latin, from Greek: DYS- + *thumos,* mind.]

dys·to·cia (dĭs-tōk′yə) n. Difficult birth. [New Latin : DYS- + -tocia, from Greek *tokos,* offspring.]

dys·to·pi·a (dĭs-tō′pē-ə) n. An imaginary place where everything is as bad as it could possibly be. Compare **utopia.** [DYS- + (UTOPIA) (coined by J.S. Mill).]

dys·tro·phy (dĭs′trə-fē) n. Also **dys·tro·phi·a** (dĭs-trō′fē-ə). **1.** Defective nutrition characterized by wasting of the tissues. **2.** Any disorder caused by defective nutrition. See **muscular dystrophy.** [New Latin *dystrophia* : DYS- + -TROPHY.] —**dys·troph·ic** adj.

dys·u·ri·a (dĭs-yōōr′ē-ə) n. Painful or difficult urination. [New Latin, from Greek *dusouria* : DYS- + -URIA.] —**dys·u·ric** adj.

dz. dozen.

dzo (zō) n., pl. **dzos** or collectively **dzo.** Also **zo** (zō) pl. **zos** or collectively **zo.** Any of a cross between a Tibetan yak and a cow, or between a bull and a female yak. [Tibetan.]

Dzun·gar·i·a (zŭn-gâr′ē-ə, dzŭn-). A vast arid region of northwestern China. Wheat, barley, oats, and sugar beets are grown, and cattle, sheep, and horses raised. There are deposits of coal, iron, gold, and oil.

PRONUNCIATION KEY

ă, pat; ā, pay; âr, care; ä, father, are; b, bib; ch, church; d, deed; ĕ, pet; ē, be; f, fife; g, gag; h, hat; hw, which; ĭ, pit; ī, pie; îr, pier; j, judge; k, kick; l, lid, needle; m, mum; n, no, sudden; ng, thing; ŏ, pot; ō, toe; ô, paw, for; oi, noise; ou, out; ŏŏ, book; ōō, boot; p, pop; r, roar; s, sauce; sh, ship, dish; t, tight; th, thin, path; *th*, this, bathe; ŭ, cut; ûr, fur; v, valve; w, with; y, yes; z, zebra, size; zh, vision; ə, about, item, edible, gallop, circus, peaceful

IN FOREIGN WORDS:

à, Fr. ami; œ, Fr. feu, Ger. schön; ü, Fr. tu, Ger. über; KH, Ger. ich, Scot. loch; N, Fr. bon; y', Fr. Compiègne

STRESS MARKS:

Primary stress: ′
in·cite′ (ĭn-sīt′)
Secondary stress: ′
in′sight′ (ĭn′sīt′)

E

eagle *Found in the wilder parts of much of the Northern Hemisphere, the golden eagle hunts for birds, small animals, and carrion over a territory of up to 250 square kilometers (100 square miles). With its powerful wings, up to 2 meters (6½ feet) across, the eagle can carry off prey as heavy as a fox.*

PRONUNCIATION KEY

ă, pat; ā, pay; âr, care;
ä, father, are; b, bib;
ch, **church**; d, deed; ĕ, pet;
ē, be; f, fife; g, gag; h, hat;
hw, which; ĭ, pit; ī, pie;
îr, pier; j, **judge**; k, kick;
l, lid, needle; m, mum;
n, no, sudden; ng, thing;
ŏ, pot; ō, toe; ô, paw, for;
oi, noise; ou, out; ŏŏ, book;
ōō, boot; p, pop; r, roar;
s, sauce; sh, ship, dish;
t, tight; th, thin, path;
th, this, bathe; ŭ, cut; ûr, fur;
v, valve; w, with; y, yes;
z, zebra, size; zh, vision;
ə, about, item, edible,
gallop, circus, peaceful

IN FOREIGN WORDS:

à, *Fr.* ami; œ, *Fr.* feu, *Ger.*
schön; ü, *Fr.* tu, *Ger.* über;
KH, *Ger.* ich, *Scot.* loch;
N, *Fr.* bon; y', *Fr.* Compiègne

STRESS MARKS:

Primary stress: ′
in·cite′ (ĭn-sīt′)
Secondary stress: ′
in′sight′ (ĭn′sīt′)

---

e, E (ē) *n., pl.* **e's** or *rare* **es, E's** or **Es. 1.** The fifth letter of the modern English alphabet. See feature at **alphabet. 2.** Any of the speech sounds represented by this letter. **3. E.** *Music.* **a.** The third tone in the scale of C major. **b.** The key or a scale in which E is the tonic. **c.** A written or printed note representing E. **d.** A string, key, or pipe tuned to the pitch of E. **4.** The fifth in a series.

e, E, e., E. *Note:* As an abbreviation or symbol, *e* may be a small or a capital letter, with or without a period. Established forms or those generally preferred precede the definition. When no form is given, all four forms are in general use in that sense. **1. E.** earl. **2. E** earth. **3.** east; eastern. **4. e** electron. **5. E** energy. **6. e., E.** engineer; engineering. **7. E, E.** English. **8. E** excellent. **9. E** illumination. **10. E** irradiance; irradiant. **11. e** *Mathematics.* The base of the natural system of logarithms, having a numerical value of approximately 2.718... .

each (ēch) *adj. Abbr.* **ea.** Every single person or thing considered individually: *Each man cast a vote.*
~*pron.* Every one of a group of objects, persons, or things considered individually; each one. Usually regarded as singular: *Each presented his gift.*
~*adv.* For or to each one; apiece: *ten dollars each.* [Middle English *ech, œlc,* Old English *ǣlc;* akin to Old High German *eogilīh,* from West Germanic *aiwō galikaz* (unattested), "ever alike."]
Usage: When the subject of a sentence begins with *each,* it is traditionally held to be grammatically singular, and the verb and following pronouns must be singular as well: *Each of the pitchers has* (not *have*) *his* (not *their*) *good curve ball.* When *each* follows a plural subject, however, the verb and following pronouns generally remain in the plural: *The boys each have their jobs to do.* The expression *each and every* is likewise followed by a singular verb and singular pronoun in formal style: *Each and every driver knows what his or her job is supposed to be.* —See also Usage note at **everyone.**

each other *pron.* **1.** Each the other. Used as a compound reciprocal pronoun: *They met each other* (each met the other). **2.** One another.
Usage: According to some traditional grammarians, *each other* is used of two, *one another* of more than two. This distinction has been ignored by many of the best writers, however, and many traditionalists find these examples acceptable: *The four partners regarded each other with suspicion. A husband and wife should confide in one another.* When speaking of an ordered series of events or stages, only *one another* can be used: *The Caesars exceeded one another* (not *each other*) *in cruelty* means that each Caesar was crueler than the last. • *Each other* cannot be used as the subject of a clause in formal writing. Instead of *We know what each other are thinking,* one should write *Each of us knows what the other is thinking.* Instead of *The men know that each other are coming,* write *Each of the men knows that the other is coming.* Instead of *We are all each other has,* write *Each of us is all the other has.* • The possessive forms of *each other* and *one another* are written *each other's* and *one another's: The boys wore each other's* (not *each others'*) *coats. They had forgotten one another's* (not *one anothers'*) *names.*

Edger. See **Edgar.**

Eads (ēdz), **John Buchanan** (1820–87). U.S. engineer. He built the triple-arch steel bridge (opened 1874) that spans the Mississippi River at St. Louis.

ea·ger¹ (ē′gər) *adj.* **-gerer, -gerest. 1.** Intensely desirous of something; impatiently expectant. **2.** Showing intense desire or impatient expectancy: *an eager search for a familiar face in the crowd.* **3.** Very willing. [Middle English *egre,* sharp, keen, eager, from Old French *aigre,* from Latin *ācer* (stem *acr-*), keen, sharp.] —**ea·ger·ly** *adv.* —**ea·ger·ness** *n.*
Synonyms: anxious, avid, earnest, fervid, keen, zealous.

eager². Variant of **eagre.**

eager beaver *n. Informal.* An industrious, overzealous person.

ea·gle (ē′gəl) *n.* **1.** Any of various large birds of prey of the family Accipitridae, including members of the genera *Aquila, Haliaeetus,* and other genera, characterized by a powerful hooked bill, long broad wings, and strong, soaring flight. See **golden eagle. 2.** A representation of an eagle used as an emblem, insignia, seal, or the

like. **3.** A former gold coin of the United States having a face value of ten dollars. **4.** A score in golf of two below par on a hole. [Middle English *egle,* from Old French *egle, aigle,* from Latin *aquila†.*]

ea·gle-eyed (ē′gəl-īd′) *adj.* **1.** Having keen eyesight. **2.** Highly observant.

eagle owl *n.* A large Eurasian owl, *Bubo bubo,* having brownish plumage and prominent ear tufts.

ea·glet (ē′glĭt) *n.* A young eagle.

ea·gle-wood (ē′gəl-wŏŏd′) *n.* See **aloes** (sense 2).

ea·gre, ea·ger (ē′gər, ā′gər) *n.* A tidal flood, a bore *(see).* [Perhaps ultimately from Old English *ēagor,* flood tide.]

Ea·kins (ā′kĭns), **Thomas** (1844–1916). U.S. artist. His portraits and starkly realistic paintings have contributed to his reputation as one of the foremost U.S. painters of all time, although he won little recognition in his own day. He used his knowledge of anatomy in his masterpiece, *The Surgical Clinic of Professor Gross* (1875), which scandalized the public when it was first exhibited.

eal·dor·man (ôl′dər-mən) *n., pl.* **-men** (-mĭn). The chief official or governor of a shire in Anglo-Saxon England. [Old English *ealdormann,* prince. See **alderman.**]

Eames (ēmz), **Charles** (1907–78). U.S. designer. He designed an innovative series of chairs that were featured in the Museum of Modern Art's first one-designer furniture exhibit (1946). Originally using molded plywood and aluminum tubing, he later incorporated plastics and coated wire meshes into his popular chairs.

-ean. Variant of **-ian.**

ear¹ (îr) *n.* **1.** *Anatomy.* **a.** The vertebrate organ of hearing, responsible, in general, for maintaining equilibrium as well as sensing sound, and divided in humans into the **external ear,** the **middle ear,** and the **internal ear** *(all of which see).* **b.** The part of this organ that is externally visible. **2.** An analogous organ in some invertebrates, such as insects. **3.** The sense of hearing. **4.** Aural sensitivity, as to differences in musical pitch or to speech sounds: *a good ear for foreign languages.* **5.** Attention; especially, favorable attention; heed: *"I shall beg your patient ear a little longer"* (Izaak Walton). **6.** Anything resembling or suggestive of the shape or position of the external ear, such as a tuft of feathers on the head of some owls or a projecting handle on a vase. **7.** A small box appearing in either of the upper corners of the front page of a newspaper, often containing an advertisement. —**all ears.** Acutely attentive: *If you want to tell your story, we're all ears.* —**by the ears.** Involved in a quarrel; at odds. —**fall on deaf ears.** To be ignored: *His advice fell on deaf ears.* —**have** (or **keep**) **an ear to the ground.** To give attention to or watch the trend of events and opinions. —**have the ear of.** To have one's advice or requests heeded by; be able to influence. —**in one ear and out the other.** Heard but without influence or effect. —**play by ear.** To perform music without reference to or memorization of a score. —**play it by ear.** *Informal.* To act without plan; improvise. —**turn a deaf ear.** To be unwilling to listen or pay heed. —**up to one's** (or **the**) **ears.** Deeply involved or committed: *up to one's ears in debt.* —**wet behind the ears.** Inexperienced or immature. [Middle English *ere,* Old English *ēare,* from Germanic; akin to Latin *auris,* Greek *ous.*] —**ear·less** *adj.*

ear² *n.* The seed-bearing spike of a cereal plant such as wheat.
~*intr.v.* **eared, earing, ears.** To form or grow ears. Used of cereal plants. [Middle English *ere, er,* Old English *ēar,* from Germanic.]

ear·ache (îr′āk′) *n.* Pain in the ear.

ear·bash (îr′băsh′) *v.* **-bashed, -bashing, -bashes.** *Australian Slang.* —*tr.* To talk incessantly to. —*intr.* To talk incessantly.

ear·drop (îr′drŏp′) *n.* **1.** A pendent earring. **2. eardrops.** Medicinal drops for inserting in the ear.

ear·drum (îr′drŭm′) *n. Anatomy.* The **tympanic membrane** *(see).*

eared (îrd) *adj.* **1.** Having ears or earlike projections. **2.** Having a specified kind or number of ears. Often used in combination: *a crop-eared puppy.*

eared seal *n.* Any of various seals of the family Otariidae, which includes the sea lions and fur seals, characterized by external ears, oarlike front flippers, and hind flippers that can be turned forward for walking on land. Compare **earless seal.**

ear·flap (îr′flăp′) *n.* Either of two cloth or fur appendages to a cap that may be turned down over the ears. Also called "earlap."

ear·ful (îr′fŏŏl′) *n. Informal.* **1.** A quantity of information or gossip. **2.** A severe reprimand.

Ear·hart (âr′härt′) **Amelia** (1898–1937). U.S. aviator. In May 1932 she became the first woman to fly solo across the Atlantic and in January 1935 the first to make a solo flight from Hawaii to California. Two years later she tried to fly around the world, but the plane crashed in the Pacific, and she and her navigator were never found.

ear·ing (îr′ĭng) *n. Nautical.* A short line attaching an upper corner of a sail to the yard. [Perhaps from EAR (part of body).]

earl (ûrl) *n. Abbr.* **E.** A British peer next in rank above a viscount and below a marquis. [Middle English *erl,* Old English *eorl,* warrior, chief, nobleman; akin to Old Saxon *erl,* Old Norse *jarl*†.]

ear·lap (îr′lăp′) *n.* An earflap.

earl·dom (ûrl′dəm) *n.* **1.** The rank or title of an earl. **2.** The territory under the jurisdiction of an earl.

earless seal *n.* Any of various seals of the family Phocidae, which includes the typical seals, having rudimentary hind limbs and no external ears. Compare **eared seal.**

ear lobe *n.* The soft, fleshy tissue at the lowest portion of the external ear.

ear·ly (ûr′lē) *adj.* **-lier, -liest. 1.** Near the beginning of a given series, period of time, or course of events: *in the early evening.* **2.** In or belonging to a distant or remote period or stage of development; primitive: *Early man discovered fire.* **3.** Occurring, developing, or appearing before the expected or usual time. **4.** Occurring in the near future: *Experts are hoping for an early settlement of the dispute.* ~*adv.* **1.** Near the beginning of a given series, period of time, or course of events. **2.** Before the expected or arranged time: *They left early.* —**early on.** Near the beginning of a given period or course of events. [Middle English *erly, erliche,* Old English *ǣrlīce,* from *ǣr,* ERE.] —**ear·li·ness** *n.*

   Usage: The phrase *earlier on* is criticized on the grounds that the *on* is neither necessary nor compatible in meaning with *earlier* (which is backward in time, not onward).

early bird *n.* A person who habitually arises early or arrives before others.

Early Bird *n.* Any of a number of communication satellites that provide telephone channels between Europe and the United States. The first was launched into stationary orbit in 1965.

ear·ly-clos·ing day (ûr′lē-klō′zĭng) *n. British.* A day, usually Wednesday or Thursday, on which many shops close after lunchtime to satisfy legal requirements.

Early English *n.* A style of architecture prevalent in England from the late 12th to the late 13th centuries, characterized by pointed arches, lancet windows, and simple tracery.

ear·ly-warn·ing system (ûr′lē-wôr′nĭng) *n.* A system designed to give warning of some forthcoming danger, such as an enemy attack or an earthquake.

ear·mark (îr′märk′) *n.* **1.** An identifying mark on the ear of a domestic animal. **2.** Any identifying feature or characteristic. ~*tr.v.* **earmarked, -marking, -marks. 1.** To mark the ear of (a domestic animal) for identification. **2.** To place an identifying or distinctive mark on. **3.** To reserve or set aside for some purpose: *earmark goods for special customers.*

ear·muff (îr′mŭf′) *n.* Either of a pair of fur or warm cloth ear coverings often attached to an adjustable headband and worn to protect the ears against cold.

earn¹ (ûrn) *tr.v.* **earned, earning, earns. 1.** To gain or deserve (a salary, wages, or other reward) for one's service, labor, or performance. **2. a.** To acquire or deserve as a result of one's behavior: *He has earned the disapproval of his peers.* **b.** To make liable to: *His incompetence earned him a severe scolding.* **3.** To produce (interest or return) as profit. [Middle English *ernen,* Old English *earnian,* to earn, merit; akin to *esne,* laborer.] —**earn·er** *n.*

earn² *intr.v.* **earned, earning, earns.** *Obsolete.* To yearn. [Variant of YEARN.]

ear·nest¹ (ûr′nĭst) *adj.* **1.** Seriously determined; eager; zealous: *an earnest attempt.* **2.** Showing deep sincerity or feeling; serious: *an earnest gesture of good will.* **3.** Of an important or vital nature; not trivial or petty: *an earnest conference affecting world peace.* —See Synonyms at **eager, serious.** —**in earnest.** With a purposeful or serious intent. [Middle English *ernest,* Old English *eornost,* zeal, seriousness.] —**ear·nest·ly** *adv.* —**ear·nest·ness** *n.*

earnest² *n.* **1.** Money paid in advance as part payment to bind a contract or bargain. Also called "earnest money." **2.** A token of something to come; a promise or assurance. [Middle English *ernest, ernes,* from Old French *erres,* plural of *erre,* pledge, earnest money, from Latin *arra, arrha,* short for *arrabō, arrhabō,* pledge, from Greek *arrabōn,* from Hebrew *'ērābhôn,* security, pledge, from *'ārabh,* he pledged.]

earn·ings (ûr′nĭngz) *pl.n.* Something earned, especially: **1.** The salary or wages of a person. **2.** The profits of a business enterprise. **3.** Gains from investment.

Earp (ûrp), **Wyatt Berry Stapp** (1848–1929). U.S. frontier figure, buffalo hunter, and gambler. In Tombstone, Arizona, he came into conflict with Ike Clanton and his gang, which led to the gunfight at the O.K. Corral on October 26, 1881.

ear·phone (îr′fōn′) *n.* A device that converts electric signals, as from a telephone or radio receiver, to audible sound and that is worn or held in contact with the ear.

ear·piece (îr′pēs′) *n.* **1.** The part of something, as a telephone handset, that is held next to the ear. **2.** One of the two parts of the frame that supports eyeglasses by passing around the ears.

ear·pierc·ing (îr′pîr′sĭng) *adj.* Loud and shrill enough to hurt the ears; deafening.

ear·plug (îr′plŭg′) *n.* A small wad, as of cotton or wax, placed in the ear to exclude noise or water.

ear·ring (îr′rĭng, îr′ĭng) *n.* An ornament or jewel worn on or hanging from the ear lobe.

ear shell *n.* The shell of the abalone.

ear·shot (îr′shŏt′) *n.* The range within which sound can be heard; hearing distance.

ear·split·ting (îr′splĭt′ĭng) *adj.* Loud and shrill enough to hurt the ears; deafening.

earth (ûrth) *n.* **1. a.** *Abbr.* **E** *Often* **Earth.** The third planet from the

---

ear

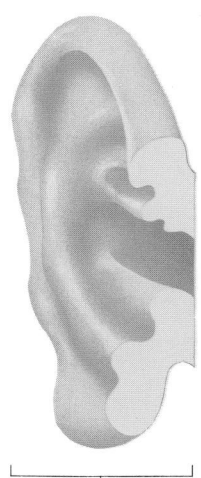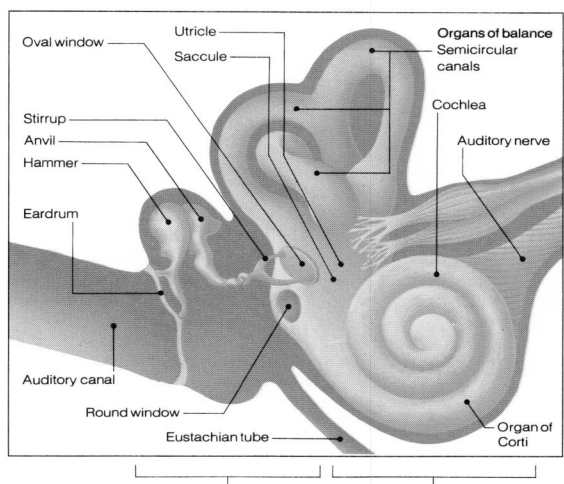

AN ORGAN WITH TWO FUNCTIONS: HEARING AND BALANCE
How the human ear transmits sound and motion to the brain

Oval window · Utricle · Saccule · Organs of balance · Semicircular canals · Cochlea · Stirrup · Anvil · Hammer · Auditory nerve · Eardrum · Auditory canal · Round window · Eustachian tube · Organ of Corti

EXTERNAL EAR · MIDDLE EAR · INNER EAR

The ear is designed to convert sounds into electrical impulses and transmit them to the brain for interpretation. Sounds are waves of vibration that spread in all directions from the source, a vibrating object. People with normal hearing can detect sounds at frequencies from 20 to 20,000 Hz (hertz, that is, cycles per second), but some can hear sounds as low as 15 Hz, or higher than 20,000 Hz. The external ear is shaped to receive sound waves and direct them into the auditory canal, a tube about 25 millimeters (1 inch) long. It is lined with hairs, and glands that secrete waxy cerumen, to trap dust and dirt.

The auditory canal acts as a resonance chamber, that is, it increases the amplitude, or loudness, of sound waves directed into it, funneling them toward the eardrum. This is a thin membrane that, as long as the pressure on either side of it is equal, vibrates like a drum skin in sympathy with the frequency of the sound waves striking it. Sudden changes in pressure in aircraft during takeoff and landing briefly cause deafness and pain; swallowing opens the Eustachian tube that links the middle ear with the throat, and equalizes the pressure.

Fixed to the center of the eardrum is the hammer, the first of three tiny bones called the ossicles, which bridge the middle ear. The other ossicles are the anvil and the stirrup. They convert the large but weak sound waves from the eardrum into smaller, but more powerful, waves that are transmitted through the footplates of the stirrup to the oval window. This membrane, which separates the middle from the inner ear, is similar to, but smaller than, the eardrum and vibrates in sympathy with it.

The sound vibrations from the oval window vibrate the fluid within the cochlea, a shell-like spiral tube, about 30 millimeters (1½ inches) long, in the inner ear. The round window, a

membrane at the end of the cochlea, bulges out when the oval window bulges in, and vice versa. The vibrations passing along the cochlea stimulate the basilar membrane that winds around within it. The membrane in turn stimulates the hairlike receptor cells of the organ of Corti that lies upon it. Groups of receptor cells lying on different parts of the membrane respond to different frequencies: low-pitched sounds are detected by the cells at the membrane's upper end; high-pitched sounds are detected by cells at the lower end.

The organ of Corti when stimulated acts like a microphone, converting sound vibrations into electrical impulses whose voltage is higher the lower the note. Nerve fibers from each of its receptor cells communicate with the brain by way of the auditory nerve, enabling the brain's auditory centers to interpret the differences in frequency and amplitude as differences in pitch and loudness.

The inner ear also contains the organs of balance. The three semicircular canals, each lying at right angles to the others, sense rotary motion and changes in speed. As the head moves, corresponding movement of the fluid in the canals stimulates their receptor cells, which send corresponding impulses along the nerve pathways to the reflex centers of the brain.

Each end of each canal meets the utricle, which, together with the adjoining saccule, senses the position of the head in space. Both contain hairlike receptor cells responsive to gravity. Those of the utricle point upward when the head is upright and are increasingly stimulated as the body turns upside-down. Those of the saccule point sideways and are increasingly stimulated as the head tilts to one side. As the head moves, the stimulated receptor cells trigger the transmission of impulses to the brain.

sun, having a sidereal period of revolution about the sun of 365.26 days at a mean distance of 92.96 million miles, an axial rotation period of 23 hours 56.07 minutes, an average radius of 3,963 miles, and a mass of 13.17×10^{24} pounds. **b.** The land surface of the world as distinguished from the oceans and air. **2.** The softer, friable part of land; soil, especially productive soil. **3.** The dwelling place of mortal men as distinguished from heaven and hell; the temporal world. **4.** All of the human inhabitants of the world: *The earth received the news with joy.* **5.** Worldly affairs; temporal matters as distinguished from spiritual concerns: *the temptations of the earth.* **6.** The material body of the human being considered as made of dust or clay. **7.** In ancient thought, one of the four **elements** (see). **8.** The lair of a burrowing animal. **9.** *Chiefly British Informal.* A large or excessive amount of money: *charged us the earth.* **10.** *Chiefly British. Electricity.* The ground of an electrical circuit. **11.** *Chemistry.* Any of several metallic oxides that are difficult to reduce, such as alumina or zirconia, formerly regarded as elements. **12.** *Geology.* A loose, fine-grained amorphous deposit such as fuller's earth or diatomaceous earth. See **alkaline earth, rare earth.** —**down to earth.** Without sentimentality or frills; sensible and realistic. —**on earth.** Used as an intensive: *Where on earth have you been all this time?* —**run to earth. 1.** To pursue (a fox, for example) to its lair; hunt down. **2.** *Informal.* To find; track down. ~*v.* **earthed, earthing, earths.** —*tr.* **1.** To cover or heap up (plants) with soil for protection. **2.** To chase into an underground lair. **3.** *Chiefly British.* To ground (an electrical device or circuit). —*intr.* To burrow or hide in the ground, as a hunted fox does. [Middle English *erthe,* Old English *eorthe,* from Germanic.]

earth·born (ûrth′bôrn′) *adj.* **1.** Springing from or born on the earth. **2.** Human; mortal.

earth·bound, earth-bound (ûrth′bound′) *adj.* **1. a.** Attached or confined to or by the earth and earthly interests. **b.** Unimaginative; ordinary. **2.** Heading for the earth: *an earthbound meteor.*

earth closet *Chiefly British. n.* An outhouse in which excreted matter is covered with earth.

earth·en (ûr′thən, -thən) *adj.* **1.** Made of dirt, soil, or earth: *an earthen fortification.* **2.** Made of baked clay: *an earthen vase.*

earth·en·ware (ûr′thən-wâr′, ûr′thən-) *n.* **1.** A variety of coarse, porous baked clay. **2.** Ware made from clay, such as dishes, pots, and tableware. ~*adj.* Made of earthenware.

earth·light (ûrth′līt′) *n.* **Earthshine** (see).

earth·ling (ûrth′lǐng) *n.* **1.** One who inhabits the earth; a human being, especially as opposed to an extraterrestrial being. **2.** A person devoted to worldly things.

earth·ly (ûrth′lē) *adj.* **1.** Of the earth, specifically: **a.** Not heavenly or divine; secular. **b.** Terrestrial. **2.** Conceivable; feasible; possible: *no earthly meaning whatever.* —**earth·li·ness** *n.*

Usage: *earthly, terrestrial, worldly, mundane, earthy.* These adjectives all indicate relationship to the earth but are not always interchangeable. *Earthly* is used principally in opposition or contrast to *heavenly. Terrestrial* is in opposition to *celestial* or specifies earth distinguished from other planets or land distinguished from water. *Worldly,* in opposition to spiritual, describes the actions and

---

Earth

THE LAYERS OF THE EARTH

Earthquakes reveal the mystery of the earth's core

Although the earth's interior cannot be studied directly, the measurement of earthquake waves as they bend through it has revealed three major layers.

The outermost layer of the planet is the crust (upper layer) beneath which lies the mantle (middle layer) and the core (lower layer). The place of contact between the crust and mantle is called the Mohorovičić discontinuity (Moho for short). As earthquake waves cross from the crust to the mantle, they increase in speed by 15 percent.

The crust is divided into two types, the oceanic and continental, and the mantle is divided into upper and lower regions with a transition zone between. Around the solid inner core there is a fluid outer core, in which the circulation of electrical currents causes the earth's magnetic field.

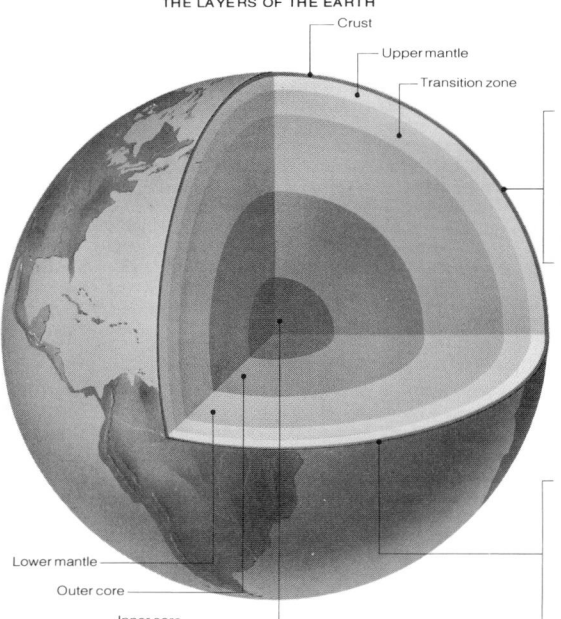

THE LAYERS OF THE EARTH

The earth's crust was once part of the mantle, but it separated over many millions of years. It is less dense than the mantle. The mantle, less dense than the core, is mainly silicates of iron and magnesium. The core is probably iron and iron sulfide.

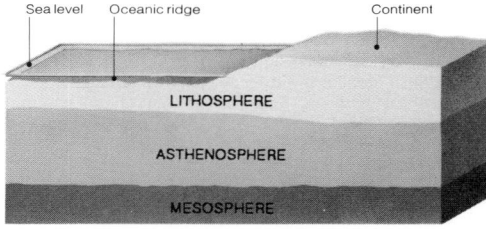

DIVISIONS OF THE CRUST

Continental crust is much thicker than oceanic crust and is thickest beneath mountain ranges. The depth of the Moho varies—from 5 kilometers (3 miles) beneath the seabed to 70 kilometers (45 miles) beneath high mountains.

SOLID AND SEMIFLUID LAYERS

An alternative division of the earth, based on its physical rather than its chemical properties, shows the solid lithosphere, which comprises the crust and upper mantle, lying above the semifluid asthenosphere and the solid mesosphere.

Planet location guide

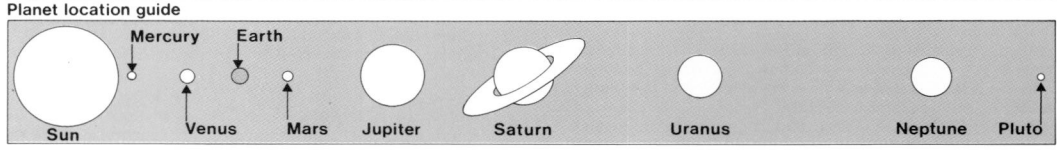

earthquake

VIOLENT SHIFTS IN THE EARTH'S CRUST
Clashes between the earth's plates can cause devastation

Every year there are about one million earthquakes around the world. Some of these tremors are so slight that they can be detected only by the most sensitive seismographs; others can unleash the destructive energy of a nuclear bomb.

Earthquakes are caused by movement of the plates that form the earth's crust. Where the plates meet there are fractures in the earth's surface. Pushed by slow convection currents from within the earth's molten interior, the plates grind against each other, building up tension and producing sudden violent shocks. Along the lines where these plates are pushing into one another the risk of severe shocks is greater, but where they are moving apart, which usually occurs on the ocean floor, molten rock pours up through the widening fracture.

Earthquakes coincide most often with plate margins along three main belts. One of these encircles the Pacific and is called the Ring of Fire. It is bordered roughly by the west coast of the American continent, Asia, Indonesia, New Zealand, and the Antarctic. It is joined by the second belt, which stretches west through China along the Himalayas and across Iran to the north and south of the Mediterranean.

The third of these danger zones lies under the oceans. When earthquakes are generated on the seabed, they can set up the monstrous waves that are misnamed tidal waves but should correctly be known by their Japanese name of tsunami.

EARTHQUAKES OF THE TWENTIETH CENTURY

Date	Place	Magnitude	Deaths
1906	San Francisco	8.3	503
1908	Italy	7.5	83,000
1920	China	8.6	180,000
1923	Japan	8.3	140,000–200,000
1927	China	8.3	200,000
1935	Pakistan	7.5	20,000–60,000
1960	Chile	8.5	4,000–5,000
1963	Yugoslavia	6.0	1,000
1964	Alaska	8.4	131
1968	Iran	7.4	12,000
1970	Peru	7.7	66,794
1976	China	8.2	240,000
1977	Romania	7.5	1,541
1978	Iran	7.7	15,000
1979	Ecuador	7.9	800
1980	Algeria	7.7	4,500
1980	Italy	7.2	3,000
1985	Mexico	8.1	7,200
1988	Armenia	6.8	55,000
1989	Northern California	6.9	62
1990	Iran	7.7	40,000

By measuring the size of an earthquake's shock waves, scientists can determine its magnitude—the amount of energy released at its focus. This is measured on the Richter scale devised by Californian scientist Charles Richter in 1935. Some of the most powerful shocks have occurred in sparsely populated areas and so caused less loss of life than other earthquakes of smaller magnitude.

DAMAGE TO BUILDINGS *Ground movement in an earthquake is usually slight. It is the sudden vibration that causes damage, and buildings are very vulnerable—as a photograph taken after the 1964 Alaskan earthquake shows (left). Unless they are protected by special foundations, modern concrete buildings do not survive the shock any better than timber structures.*

---

concerns of people, especially as they pertain to this life (distinguished from afterlife); the term is associated with the pursuit of pleasure, wealth, or success. *Mundane* likewise refers to what is secular rather than spiritual or eternal and especially to the more ordinary, routine aspects of life on the earth. *Earthy,* in opposition to spiritual, suggests what is down to earth, especially the satisfaction of material wants and the more primitive human instincts.

earth·man (ûrth'măn') *n., pl.* **-men** (-mĕn'). An inhabitant of the earth; an earthling. Used chiefly in science fiction.

earth mother *n.* **1.** A mother goddess considered as the giver of life. **2.** A woman combining maternal and sensual qualities.

earth·mov·er (ûrth'mōō'vər) *n.* A piece of heavy machinery, as a bulldozer, for excavating or moving large amounts of soil, dirt, or earth.

earth·nut (ûrth'nŭt') *n.* **1. a.** An Old World plant, *Conopodium denudatum,* having edible, nutlike tubers. **b.** The tuber of this plant. Also called "pignut." **2.** Any of various other plants having similar edible tubers or underground parts.

earth·quake (ûrth'kwāk') *n.* A series of shock waves in the earth's crust or upper mantle, caused by sudden release of strains accumulated along geologic faults and by volcanic action, and resulting in movements in the earth's surface. Also called "seism."

earth·rise (ûrth'rīz') *n.* The rise of the earth above the moon's horizon, as seen from the lunar surface or from a satellite.

earth satellite *n.* A satellite that orbits the earth.

earth science *n.* Any of several essentially geologic sciences concerned with the origin, structure, and physical phenomena of the earth.

earth·shak·ing (ûrth'shā'kĭng) *adj.* Of enormous consequence or fundamental importance.

earth·shat·ter·ing (ûrth'shăt'ər-ĭng) *adj.* Earthshaking.

earth·shine (ûrth'shīn') *n.* The sunlight reflected from the earth's

surface that illuminates the part of the moon not directly lit by the sun. Also called "earthlight."

earth·star (ûrth'stär') *n.* A fungus of the genus *Geastrum,* related to the puffballs and having an outer covering that splits open in a starlike form.

earth station *n.* An on-ground terminal linked to a spacecraft or satellite by an antenna and associated electronic equipment for the purpose of transmitting or receiving messages, tracking, or control.

earth·ward (ûrth'wərd) *adj.* Heading toward the earth; earthbound. *~adv.* Toward the earth. **—earth·wards** *adv.*

earth wax *n.* **Ozocerite** *(see).*

earth·work (ûrth'wûrk') *n.* **1.** *Often* **earthworks.** An earthen embankment, especially when used as a military fortification. **2.** *Engineering.* Excavation and embankment of earth, as in the building of a railroad. —See Synonyms at **bulwark.**

earth·worm (ûrth'wûrm') *n.* Any of various terrestrial annelid worms of the class Oligochaeta, and especially of the family Lumbricidae, that burrow into and help aerate and enrich soil.

earth·y (ûr'thē) *adj.* **-ier, -iest.** **1.** Consisting of or resembling earth or soil. **2.** Pertaining to or characteristic of this world; worldly. **3.** Crude or coarse; unrefined: *earthy humor.* **4.** Uninhibited; hearty. —See Usage note at **earthly.** **—earth·i·ness** *n.*

ear trumpet *n.* A horn-shaped instrument formerly used to direct sound into the ear of a partially deaf person.

ear·wax (îr'wăks') *n.* The waxlike secretion of certain glands lining the canal of the outer ear; cerumen.

ear·wig (îr'wĭg') *n.* Any of various insects of the order Dermaptera, such as the European species *Forficula auricularia,* having pincerlike appendages protruding from the rear of the abdomen. *~tr.v.* **earwigged, -wigging, -wigs.** To attempt to influence by insinuation or subterfuge. [Middle English *erwigge,* Old English *ēarwicga,* "ear insect" (thought to be able to penetrate a person's head

earthstar *An inedible fungus with an outer skin that splits and folds back into a starlike shape a few days after it breaks through the soil. This species is* Geastrum triplex, *which grows in beech woods during summer and autumn.*

earwig *A nocturnal and widely distributed insect easily identified by the pincerlike claws at the end of its body. The claws are thought to be defensive, but it is not known whether they inflict damage on the insect's enemies. Earwigs feed on carrion, leaves, and roots and often hide by day in small crevices—the origin, perhaps, of the mistaken belief for which they were named: that they like to crawl into the ears of humans.*

Easter egg *Painted and beribboned eggs are a traditional Easter gift in central Europe.*

Easter Island *These long-faced statues dominate the landscape of Easter Island, named because its first European explorers, the Dutch, landed on Easter Day 1722. Some of the statues are more than 9 meters (30 feet) tall and weigh up to 90 tons. All are made from the island's volcanic rock and the earliest date from about* A.D. *1100.*

through the ear) : EAR + *wicga,* insect.]

ease (ēz) *n.* **1.** The condition of being without discomfort; freedom from pain, worry, or agitation. **2.** Freedom from constraint, embarrassment, or awkwardness; poise; naturalness: *the ease of his approach to a stranger.* **3. a.** Freedom from difficulty, hard work, or great effort: *He could take his ease only after he had met the deadline.* **b.** Readiness in performance; facility: *play tennis with ease.* **4.** A state of rest or relaxation. **5.** Freedom from financial difficulty; affluence. **—at ease.** *Military.* In a position of rest, with the feet apart. —See Synonyms at **rest.**
∼*v.* **eased, easing, eases.** —*tr.* **1.** To free from pain, worry, agitation, or trouble; soothe; comfort: *The good news eased her mind considerably.* **2.** To alleviate or lighten (discomfort); mitigate; lessen: *took aspirin to ease his headache.* **3.** To slacken the strain, pressure, tension, or stress of; loosen. Often used with *away, down, up,* or *off*: *ease off a cable.* **4.** To reduce the difficulty of. **5.** To move or fit into place or position slowly and carefully: *ease the patient onto the stretcher.* —*intr.* To lessen in discomfort, effort, difficulty, pressure, or the like. Often used with *up* or *off.* [Middle English *ese,* from Old French *aise,* comfort, convenience, from Latin *adjacēns,* nearby, adjacent, from *adjacēre,* to lie near : *ad-,* near to + *jacēre,* to lie, from *jacere,* to throw.]

ease·ful (ēz'fəl) *adj.* Affording or characterized by comfort and peace; restful. **—ease·ful·ly** *adv.* **—ease·ful·ness** *n.*

ea·sel (ē'zəl) *n.* A frame, usually in the form of an upright tripod, upon which something may be displayed or which may support an artist's canvas. [Dutch *ezel,* "as," from Middle Dutch *esel,* from Common Germanic *asiluz* (unattested), from Latin *asinus.*]

ease·ment (ēz'mənt) *n.* **1.** The act of easing or the condition of being eased. **2.** Something that affords ease or comfort. **3.** *Law.* A right afforded a person to make limited use of another's land, as a right of way.

eas·i·ly (ē'zə-lē) *adv.* **1.** Without difficulty or stress: *a problem easily solved.* **2.** Without doubt or question; certainly: *easily the best play this season.* **3.** In all likelihood; well: *That might easily have been a mistake.*

eas·i·ness (ē'zē-nĭs) *n.* **1.** The condition or quality of being easy to accomplish, acquire, or the like. **2.** Ease of manner; nonchalance; poise.

east (ēst) *n. Abbr.* **e, E, e., E. 1. a.** The direction of the earth's axial rotation. **b.** The cardinal point on the mariner's compass 90° clockwise from north and directly opposite west. **2.** An area or region lying in the east. **3. a.** One of the four positions occupied by players in a game of bridge. **b.** The player occupying this position. **—the East. 1.** The eastern part of the earth, especially Asia and its neighboring islands; the Orient. **2.** The region of the United States east of the Alleghenies and north of the Mason-Dixon line. **3.** The formerly Communist countries of Eastern Europe.
∼*adj.* **1.** To, toward, of, facing, or in the east. **2.** Coming from or originating in the east, as a wind. **3. East.** Officially or conventionally designating the eastern part of a country, continent, or other geographic area: *East Germany.*
∼*adv.* In, from, or toward the east. [Middle English *e(a)st,* Old English *ēast,* from Germanic.]

East An·gli·a (ăng'glē-ə). Region in the east of England consisting of Norfolk, Suffolk, and parts of Cambridgeshire and Essex. It was once an Anglo-Saxon kingdom. Its main crops are wheat, barley, and sugar beets, and some of the best agricultural land in England is found in the low, flat land. In the Middle Ages wool made it an area of great wealth. **—East An·gli·an** *n. & adj.*

East Asia. See **Far East, the.**

East Berlin. See **Berlin.**

east·bound (ēst'bound') *adj.* Going toward the east.

east by north *n.* The direction or point on the mariner's compass halfway between due east and east-northeast. It is 78° 45' east of due north.

east by south *n.* The direction or point on the mariner's compass halfway between due east and east-southeast. It is 101° 15' east of due north.

East Caribbean dollar *n.* The basic monetary unit of Dominica, Grenada, St. Lucia, and St. Vincent & the Grenadines.

East China Sea. Shallow section of the western Pacific Ocean. Bounded by China, South Korea, Taiwan, and the Ryukyu and Kyushu islands, it is a rich fishing ground.

East End. A densely populated working-class and immigrant area of London containing industrial and dock areas. **—East End·er** *n.*

Eas·ter (ē'stər) *n.* **1.** A festival in the Christian Church commemorating the Resurrection of Christ, celebrated on the first Sunday following the full moon that occurs on or just after March 21. **2.** The Sunday on which the festival of Easter is held. Also called "Easter Day," "Easter Sunday." [Middle English *ester, estre,* Old English *ēastre* (usually in plural *ēastron*); probably from *Eostre,* Germanic goddess whose festival occurred in the spring.]

Easter egg *n.* A chocolate egg, decorated hen's egg, or egg-shaped ornament offered as a gift at Easter.

Easter Island. Volcanic island in the South Pacific Ocean, 3,700 kilometers (2,300 miles) west of Chile, of which it is a part, discovered on Easter Day, 1722, by the Dutch navigator Jakob Roggeven. It is famous for its colossal heads (up to 9 meters or 30 feet high) carved from tufa from the Rano Roraku volcano and its wooden tablets with their ideographic scripts, which may be the work of the ancestors of the island's Polynesian inhabitants.

Easter lily *n.* Any of various white-flowered lilies that bloom around Easter, especially *Lilium longiflorum.* This species is also called "Bermuda lily."

east·er·ly (ē'stər-lē) *adj.* **1.** Situated in or toward the east. **2.** From the east. Said of wind.
∼*n., pl.* **easterlies.** A storm or wind from the east. **—east·er·ly** *adv.*

Easter Monday *n.* The Monday following Easter Sunday.

east·ern (ē'stərn) *adj. Abbr.* **e, E, e., E. 1.** Situated toward, in, or facing the east. **2.** Coming from the east. Said of wind. **3.** Native to or growing in the east. **4.** *Often* **Eastern.** Of, pertaining to, or characteristic of eastern regions or the East. **5. Eastern.** Of, pertaining to, or characteristic of the eastern part of the earth, especially Asia and its neighboring islands; Oriental: *Eastern philosophy.* **6. Eastern.** Of or pertaining to the Eastern Churches, especially the Eastern Orthodox Church as distinguished from the Roman Catholic Church. [Middle English *esterne,* Old English *ēasterne.*]

Eastern Bloc. The countries associated under the **Warsaw Pact** *(see).*

Eastern Church *n.* **1.** The Church of the Roman Empire in the east, as distinguished from the Western Church, and including the patriarchates of Constantinople, Antioch, Alexandria, and Jerusalem. Also called "Greek Church." **2.** Any of the churches that have developed from this, especially: **a.** The Eastern Orthodox Church. **b.** Any of the Uniat Churches following the rites of the Eastern Orthodox Church.

Eastern Empire. See **Byzantine Empire.**

east·ern·er (ē'stər-nər) *n. Often* **Easterner.** A native or inhabitant of the east, especially of the eastern United States.

Eastern Europe. 1. Political region of Europe comprising Albania, Bosnia and Hercegovina, Bulgaria, Croatia, Czechoslovakia, East Germany (until 1990), Hungary, Poland, Romania, Slovenia, Yugoslavia, and the republics of the former U.S.S.R. west of the Ural Mts. After World War II, Communist regimes friendly to the U.S.S.R. were set up in several European countries. The U.S.S.R. refused Marshall Plan aid, forced its satellites to do the same, and founded Comecon (1949–91) to coordinate economic planning for the region. The U.S.S.R. also set up the Warsaw Pact (1955–91). In the late 1980s many Eastern European countries began to reject Soviet economic and military domination and adopt free-market economies and multi-party rule. **2.** Geographic region of Europe between the temperate Atlantic lands and the central Eurasian landmass. Northeastward, winters are progressively harsh, and only the Adriatic and Black Sea coasts are above the freezing point in January. Eastern Europe generally has less than 750 millimeters (30 inches) of rain a year. Some 45 percent of Eastern Europe is cultivated and 20 percent is grazing land. Potatoes, sugar beets, and cereal grains are grown on the best land. Bohemia is noted for hops, the Balkan basins for cotton and tobacco, and the Adriatic coast for citrus fruits and olives, while parts of the south produce grapes and wines. Poland, Czechoslovakia, Russia, Ukraine, and Hungary are the most industrialized countries of the region.

Eastern European Mutual Assistance Treaty *n.* The **Warsaw Pact** *(see).*

Eastern Ghats. See **Ghats.**

Eastern Hemisphere. The part of the earth, approximately half, that is east of the Greenwich meridian and includes the continents of Europe, Africa, Asia, and Australia.

east·ern·most (e'stərn-mōst') *adj.* Farthest east.

Eastern Orthodox Church *n.* The body of modern churches, including the Greek and Russian Orthodox, derived from the church of the Byzantine Empire and acknowledging the primacy of the patriarch of Constantinople. Also called "Eastern Church," "Greek Church," "Orthodox Church."

Eastern Roman Empire. See **Byzantine Empire.**

Eastern Samoa. See **American Samoa.**

Eastern Standard Time *n. Abbr.* **EST, E.S.T.** One of the four standard time zones of North America, based on the local time at the 75th meridian west of Greenwich, England, five hours behind Greenwich Mean Time.

Eas·ter·tide (ē'stər-tīd') *n.* **1.** The Easter season, extending in different churches from Easter to Ascension Day, Whitsunday, or Trinity Sunday. **2.** The week following Easter Sunday.

East Germanic *n.* A subdivision of the Germanic languages, represented only by Gothic.

East Germany. Until 1990 the **German Democratic Republic,** a people's republic in Eastern Europe. Formed from the Soviet-occupied zone of Germany following World War II, it became an independent Communist state. Economic austerity, curbs on civil liberties, and the Sovietization of industry and agriculture led to riots and discontent (crushed by Soviet forces in 1953) and mass migration to West Germany. The Berlin Wall, erected in 1961 by the East German government, effectively put a stop to the migration. The wall began to be dismantled in 1989, and East Germany was united with West Germany in 1990. East Germany's industries include shipbuilding, machinery, chemicals, textiles, and precision instruments, and prior to unification were planned in close cooperation with the U.S.S.R. Lignite is the region's chief mineral. As a member of Comecon, East Germany conducted nearly half of its foreign trade with the U.S.S.R. and over three quarters within the Communist bloc. Area 108,178 square kilometers (41,757 square miles). Population 16,700,000. Capital, East Berlin. See also **Germany. —East German** *n. & adj.* See map at **Germany.**

East Greek *n.* A principal dialectal division of Ancient Greek, com-

prising Mycenaean Greek, Arcado-Cyprian, Attic-Ionic, and Aeolic.

East India Company *n.* Any of several European companies organized in the 17th and 18th centuries to trade with the East Indies;
especially, the company chartered to do so by the British government in 1600.

East In·di·a·man (ĭn′dē-ə-mən) *n., pl.* **East In·di·a·men** (-mĭn). A
large, full-rigged merchant ship that was formerly used in trade
with the East Indies.

East In·dies (ĭn′dēz). *Abbr.* **E.I.** Name formerly applied to India, the
Malay Peninsula, and the Malay Archipelago. Subsequently it included only the Malay Archipelago or the Dutch East Indies (the
islands of the Malay Archipelago that became Indonesia after
World War II).

east·ing (ē′stĭng) *n.* **1.** *Nautical.* **a.** The distance sailed by a ship on
an easterly course. **b.** The longitudinal distance from a given meridian on an easterly course. **2.** An easterly direction.

East Lo·thi·an (lō′thē-ən). Former county, now part of Lothian Region, southeastern Scotland.

East·man (ēst′mən), **George** (1854–1932). U.S. businessman and
inventor. He invented a dry-plate process of film development, the
roll of film, the Kodak camera, and a process for color photography. In 1892 he founded the Eastman Kodak Company in Rochester, New York.

east-north-east (ēst′nôrth-ēst′; *Nautical* -nôr-ēst′) *n. Abbr.* **ENE**
The direction or point on the mariner's compass halfway between
due east and northeast. It is 67° 30′ east of due north.
—*adj.* Situated toward, facing, or in this direction.
—*adv.* In, from, or toward this direction.

East Pakistan. See **Bangladesh.**

East River. Narrow tidal strait, 26 kilometers (16 miles) long and
183 to 1,200 meters (600 to 4,000 feet) wide, connecting Upper New
York Bay and Long Island Sound. It separates the boroughs of
Manhattan and the Bronx from Brooklyn and Queens.

East Slavic *n.* The eastern division of the Slavic languages, consisting of Russian, Ukrainian, and Belorussian.

east-south-east (ēst′south-ēst′) *n. Abbr.* **ESE** The direction or point
on the mariner's compass halfway between due east and southeast.
It is 112° 30′ east of due north.
—*adj.* Situated toward, facing, or in this direction.
—*adv.* In, from, or toward this direction.

East St. Lou·is (sānt lōō′ĭs). City in southwestern Illinois, on the
Mississippi River opposite St. Louis. It is an important manufacturing and railway center; its industries include a large aluminum
works, and meat-packing and oil-refining plants.

East Sus·sex (sŭs′ĭks). County in southeastern England consisting
of the eastern parts of the former county of Sussex and bordering
on the English Channel.

east·ward (ēst′wərd) *adj.* Toward, facing, or in the east.
—*n.* An eastward direction, point, or region.
—*adv.* Toward the east. —**east·ward·ly** *adv.* —**east·wards** *adv.*

eas·y (ē′zē) *adj.* **-ier, -iest. 1.** Capable of being accomplished or ac-

EASTERN EUROPE

quired with ease; posing no difficulty: *"How easy is success to those who will only be true to themselves"* (Anthony Trollope). **2.** Free from worry, anxiety, trouble, or pain: *"Now as I was young and easy under the apple boughs"* (Dylan Thomas). **3.** Conducive to rest or comfort; pleasant and relaxing. **4.** Relaxed; easygoing; informal: *an easy, sociable manner.* **5.** Not strict or severe; lenient: *an easy teacher.* **6. a.** Readily persuaded or influenced; compliant. **b.** Not hard to trick or victimize: *an easy target for swindlers.* **7.** Not strained, hurried, or forced; moderate: *walked at an easy pace.* **8.** *Economics.* **a.** Less in demand and therefore readily obtainable: *Commodities are easier.* **b.** Plentiful and therefore obtainable at low interest rates: *easy credit.* **9.** *Informal.* Easily, often dishonestly obtained: *easy money.* —*adv.* **1.** In a relaxed manner: *breathe easy.* **2.** In an easy manner; easily: *Success came too easy to them.* **3.** In a cautious manner; carefully: *Go easy on this icy road.* **4.** Without being harshly penalized: *If he wasn't put in jail, he got off easy. Informal.* —**go easy on.** To exercise moderation in one's approach to: *Go easy on the new recruits.* —**take it easy.** *Informal.* **1.** To refrain from exertion; relax. **2.** To refrain from anger or violence; stay calm. [Middle English *esy,* from Old French *aisie,* past participle of *aisier,* to put at ease, from *aise,* EASE.]

Usage: *Easy* is used in standard English as an adverb in only a few idiomatic or informal constructions, such as *easy come easy go, easier said than done,* and *take things easy.* The usual adverbial form is *easily,* as in *The handle turns easily.*

easy chair *n.* A large, comfortable, well-upholstered chair.
eas·y·go·ing, eas·y-go·ing (ē′zē-gō′ĭng) *adj.* **1. a.** Living without intense worry; placid. **b.** Lazy and careless. **c.** Lax in moral attitudes. **2.** Undemanding: *an easygoing life.* **3.** Having or moving at an even gait. Said of a horse.
easy mark *n.* A person who is easily persuaded or taken advantage of.
easy street *n. Slang.* A condition of financial security or independence: *A substantial inheritance put them on easy street.*
eat (ēt) *v.* **ate** (āt; *British & Regional* ĕt), **eaten** (ēt′n), **eating, eats.** —*tr.* **1. a.** To take into the mouth, chew, and swallow (food). **b.** To consume the edible parts of: *eat a chop.* **c.** To take regularly as food. **2.** To consume, ravage, or destroy by or as if by eating. Usually used with *away* or *up.* **3.** To erode or corrode. **4.** *Slang.* To bother or annoy: *What's eating him?* —*intr.* **1.** To consume food; have or take a meal or meals. **2.** To exercise a gradual consuming or eroding effect. Used with *into: eating into our resources.* —**eat crow.** *Informal.* To be forced to accept a humiliating defeat. —**eat one's heart out.** To feel bitter, hopeless anguish or longing. —**eat one's words.** To retract something that one has said. —**eat out.** To eat in a restaurant or public place. —**eat out of someone's hand.** To be manipulated or dominated by another. —**eat up.** *Slang.* To absorb enthusiastically or avidly: *He eats up old movies.* [Eat, ate, eaten; Middle English *eten, et, eten,* Old English *etan, æt, eten.*]
eat·a·ble (ē′tə-bəl) *adj.* Fit to be eaten; edible. —*n. Usually* **eatables.** Something to be eaten; food.

Usage: *Eatable* and *edible* are sometimes interchangeable in the sense of "fit to be eaten," but usually there is a difference. *Eatable* refers to the extent to which food has been well prepared and is palatable. *Edible* refers to the extent to which it is possible to treat a substance as food. Food that is edible may on occasion be uneatable because of its condition. The colloquial use of *inedible* as a synonym for *uneatable* in such contexts is often heard.

eat·er (ē′tər) *n.* One that eats: *She's a light eater.*
eat·er·y (ē′tə-rē) *n., pl.* **-ies.** *Informal.* A place for eating, such as a cafeteria.
eat·ing (ē′tĭng) *n.* Food with respect to its flavor or quality: *The peaches were not only beautiful, they were good eating.* —*adj.* Suitable for eating raw: *eating apples.*
eats (ēts) *pl.n. Slang.* Food.
eau de co·logne (ō′ də kə-lōn′) *n., pl.* **eaux de cologne** (ō′, ōz′). A toilet water, **cologne** (see).
eau de nile (ō′ də nēl′, nīl′) *n., pl.* **eaux de nile** (ō′, ōz′). A pale green. [French, "water of (the) Nile."]
eau de vie (ō′ də vē′) *n., pl.* **eaux de vie** (ō′, ōz′). Brandy. [French, "water of life."]
eaves (ēvz) *pl.n.* The projecting overhang at the lower edge of a roof. [Middle English *eves,* Old English *yfes, efes,* eaves, edge, border; probably akin to OVER.]
eaves·drop (ēvz′drŏp′) *intr.v.* **-dropped, -dropping, -drops.** To listen secretly to the private conversation of others. Used with *on.* [Back-formation from *eavesdropper,* Middle English *evesdropper,* from *evesdrop,* water from the eaves, probably from Old English *yfesdrype.*] —**eaves·drop·per** *n.*
E_B The symbol for binding energy.
ebb (ĕb) *n.* **1. a.** The drawing back of the tide from the shore. **b.** An ebb tide. **2.** A fading away or diminishing; a decline: *"insistence upon rules of conduct marks the ebb of religious fervor"* (A.N. Whitehead). —*intr.v.* **ebbed, ebbing, ebbs. 1.** To draw back from the shore. Used of a tide. **2.** To fade or diminish. Often used with *away.* [Old English *ebbian* (verb); *ebba* (noun), from West Germanic *abhigo* (unattested); akin to Gothic *ibuks,* moving backward.]
ebb tide *n.* **1.** The receding tide between high water and a succeeding low water. Also called "ebb." **2.** The period during which the tide is receding. Compare **flood tide.**
EBCDIC (ĕb′sĭ-dĭk′) *n.* A code for representing alphanumeric infor-

mation. [E(XTENDED) + B(INARY) + C(ODED) + D(ECIMAL) + I(N-TERCHANGE) + C(ODE).]
Eb·lis (ĕb′lĭs). The principal evil spirit or devil of Islamic mythology. [Arabic *Iblīs,* from Greek *diabolos,* slanderer. See **devil.**]
E-boat (ē′bōt′) *n.* A German torpedo boat in World War II. [From *enemy boat.*]
eb·on (ĕb′ən) *adj. Poetic.* **1.** Made of ebony. **2.** Black. [Middle English *eban, ebenus,* from Old French, from Medieval Latin *ebanus,* from Greek *ebenos* (the tree), from Semitic.]
eb·on·ite (ĕb′ə-nīt′) *n.* **Hard rubber** *(see),* especially when it is colored black. [EBON + -ITE.]
eb·on·ize (ĕb′ə-nīz′) *tr.v.* **-ized, -izing, -izes.** To finish with an ebony stain. —**eb·on·i·za·tion** *n.*
eb·on·y (ĕb′ə-nē) *n., pl.* **-ies. 1.** Any of several chiefly tropical trees of the genus *Diospyros;* especially, *D. ebenum,* of southern Asia, having hard, dark-colored heartwood. **2.** The wood of such a tree, used in cabinetmaking and for piano keys. **3.** Black. —*adj.* **1.** Made of or suggesting ebony. **2.** Black. [Middle English, from Late Latin *ebeninus,* (made) of ebony, from Greek *ebeninos,* from *ebenos,* ebony tree, EBON.]
e·brac·te·ate (ē-brăk′tē-āt′) *adj. Botany.* Without bracts. [New Latin *ebracteatus* : EX- (out, without) + BRACTEATE.]
E·bro (ē′brō). Longest river completely in Spain. It rises in the Cantabrian Mts. in Santander province and flows 925 kilometers (575 miles) southeast to the Mediterranean. It is navigable by seagoing vessels as far as Tortosa, 32 kilometers (20 miles) inland.
e·bul·lient (ĭ-bool′yənt, ĭ-bŭl′-) *adj.* **1.** Overflowing with excitement, enthusiasm, or exuberance. **2.** Boiling. Said of a liquid. [Latin *ēbulliēns* (stem *ēbullient-*), present participle of *ēbullīre,* to boil over : *ex-,* completely + *bullīre,* to boil.] —**e·bul·lience** (ĭ-bool′yəns, ĭ-bŭl′-), **e·bul·lien·cy** (-yən-sē) *n.* —**e·bul·lient·ly** *adv.*
e·bul·li·os·co·py (ĭ-bool′ē-ŏs′kə-pē, ĭ-bŭl′-) *n.* A method of determining the molecular weight of a substance, based on measurements of the extent to which the boiling point of a solvent is altered by its presence in solution. [Latin *ēbullīre,* to boil over (see **ebullient**) + -SCOPY.] —**e·bul·li·o·scop·ic** (ĭ-bool′ē-ə-skŏp′ĭk, ĭ-bŭl′-) *adj.*
eb·ul·li·tion (ĕb′ə-lĭsh′ən) *n.* **1.** The bubbling or effervescence of a liquid; a boiling. **2.** A sudden, violent outpouring, as of emotion or unrest: *"did not . . . give way to any ebullitions of private grief"* (W.M. Thackeray). [Late Latin *ēbullītiō* (stem *ēbullītiōn-*), from Latin *ēbullīre,* to boil over. See **ebullient.**]
eb·ur·na·tion (ĕb′ər-nā′shən, ē′bər-) *n. Pathology.* The degeneration of bone into a hard, ivorylike mass, such as occurs at the articulating surfaces of bones in osteoarthritis. [Latin *eburnus,* (made) of ivory, from *ebur,* IVORY.]
E.C. Established Church.
e·cad (ē′kăd′, ĕk′ăd′) *n. Biology.* An organism or group of organisms that differs from other members of its species as a result of environmental conditions. [EC(OLOGY) + -AD.]
é·car·té (ā′kär-tā′) *n.* **1.** A card game for two players. **2.** In ballet, a position with an arm and a leg extended on the same side of the body. [French, past participle of *écarter,* to discard.]
ec·bol·ic (ĕk-bŏl′ĭk) *adj.* Stimulating childbirth or abortion. —*n.* A drug or other agent that stimulates childbirth or abortion. [Greek *ekbolē,* a throwing out, ejection, from *ekballein* : *ek-,* out + *ballein,* to throw.]
ec·ce ho·mo (ĕk′sē hō′mō, ĕk′ē) *n.* A picture depicting Christ wearing the crown of thorns. [Latin, "Behold the Man," words used by Pontius Pilate to present Christ crowned with thorns to his accusers. John 19:5.]
ec·cen·tric (ĕk-sĕn′trĭk, ĭk-) *adj.* **1.** Departing or deviating from the conventional norm, especially in an odd or amusing way: *an eccentric recluse.* **2.** Deviating from a circular form, as in an elliptical orbit. **3.** Not situated at or in the center. **4.** Not having the same center. Said of figures such as circles, cylinders, and spheres. Compare **concentric.** —See Synonyms at **strange.** —*n.* **1.** One that deviates markedly from a normal, conventional, or expected course or pattern; an odd or erratic person or thing. **2.** *Machinery.* A disk or wheel having its axis of revolution displaced from its center so that it is capable of imparting reciprocating motion. [Middle English *excentryke,* not having the same center (said of planets), from Late Latin *eccentricus,* from Greek *ekkentros* : *ex-,* out + *kentron,* point, center, from *kentein,* to prick.] —**ec·cen·tri·cal·ly** *adv.*
ec·cen·tric·i·ty (ĕk′sĕn-trĭs′ə-tē) *n., pl.* **-ties. 1. a.** Deviation from the normal, conventional, or expected. **b.** An instance of such deviation: *Storing old newspapers in the attic was one of his eccentricities.* **2. a.** The quality of being eccentric. **b.** The degree of being off-center or not concentric. **3.** *Machinery.* The distance between the center of an eccentric and its axis; the throw. **4.** *Mathematics.* The ratio of the distance of any point on a conic section from a focus to its distance from the corresponding directrix.
Synonyms: idiosyncrasy, quirk.
ec·chy·mo·sis (ĕk′ĭ-mō′sĭs) *n.* **1.** The passage of blood from ruptured blood vessels into subcutaneous tissue as a result of bruising, marked by a purple discoloration of the skin. **2.** The resultant skin discoloration. [New Latin, from Greek *ekkhumōsis,* from *ekkhumousthai,* to pour out : *ex-,* out of + *khumos,* juice, from *khein,* to pour.] —**ec·chy·mot·ic** (ĕk′ĭ-mŏt′ĭk) *adj.*
Ec·cles (ĕk′əlz). Town in Greater Manchester, England, on the Irwell River and the Manchester Ship Canal. Its industries include textiles, machinery, and chemicals.

Eccles cake n. British. A round or oval cake with a case of sugared flaky pastry and a currant filling. [After ECCLES in Greater Manchester, England.]

ec·cle·si·a (ĭ-klē'zhē-ə, -zē-ə, -zhə) n., pl. **-siae** (-zhē-ē', -zē-ē'). 1. The political assembly of citizens of an ancient Greek state. 2. A church or congregation. [Latin ecclēsia, from Greek ekklēsia, duly summoned assembly, from ekkalein, to call out, summon : ex-, out + kalein, to call.] —**ec·cle·si·al** adj.

Ec·cle·si·as·tes (ĭ-klē'zē-ăs'tēz') n. Abbr. **Eccles.** A book of the Old Testament traditionally attributed to Solomon. [Latin Ecclēsiastēs, from Greek ekklēsiastēs, member of the assembly of citizens, from ekklēsia, ECCLESIA.]

ec·cle·si·as·tic (ĭ-klē'zē-ăs'tĭk) adj. Ecclesiastical. ~n. A clergyman; a priest.

ec·cle·si·as·ti·cal (ĭ-klē'zē-ăs'tĭ-kəl) adj. Abbr. **eccles.** Of or pertaining to a church, especially as an organized institution; clerical. —**ec·cle·si·as·ti·cal·ly** adv.

ecclesiastical calendar n. The calendar of feasts celebrated by the Christian Church, in which the year begins on the first Sunday of Advent.

ec·cle·si·as·ti·cism (ĭ-klē'zē-ăs'tə-sĭz'əm) n. 1. Ecclesiastical principles, practices, and activities. 2. Excessive adherence to ecclesiastical principles and forms.

Ec·cle·si·as·ti·cus (ĭ-klē'zē-ăs'tĭ-kəs) n. A book of the Apocrypha. Also called "Wisdom of Jesus, the Son of Sirach."

ec·cle·si·ol·a·try (ĭ-klē'zē-ŏl'ə-trē) n. Worship of the church, especially extreme devotion to its principles or traditions. [From ECCLESI(A) + -LATRY.] —**ec·cle·si·ol·a·ter** (ĭ-klē'zē-ŏl'ə-tər) n.

ec·cle·si·ol·o·gy (ĭ-klē'zē-ŏl'ə-jē) n. 1. The study of the Christian Church as an institution. 2. The study of ecclesiastical art, especially in relation to the architecture and decoration of churches. —**ec·cle·si·o·log·i·cal** (ĭ-klē'zē-ə-lŏj'ĭ-kəl) adj. —**ec·cle·si·ol·o·gist** (ĭ-klē'zē-ŏl'ə-jĭst) n.

ec·crine (ĕk'rĭn, -rīn', -rēn') adj. 1. Secreting externally; especially, pertaining to an eccrine gland or its secretion. 2. **Exocrine** (see). [From Greek ekkrinein, to secrete : ex-, out + krinein, to separate.]

eccrine gland n. Any of the small sweat glands distributed over the body's surface.

ec·crin·ol·o·gy (ĕk'rə-nŏl'ə-jē) n. The study of eccrine secretions and secretory organs. [ECCRINE + -LOGY.]

ec·dem·ic (ĕk-dĕm'ĭk, ĭk-) adj. Designating diseases that do not normally occur in a given population but that have been brought in, as by immigrants or travelers; not endemic. [Greek ek-, out, outside + epidemic, people (by analogy with epidemic).]

ec·dys·i·ast (ĕk-dĭz'ē-ăst', -əst) n. A striptease artist. Used humorously. [From ECDYSIS; coined by H.L. MENCKEN.]

ec·dy·sis (ĕk'də-sĭs) n., pl. **-ses** (-sēz'). The shedding of an outer integument or layer of skin, as by insects, crustaceans, and snakes. [New Latin, from Greek ekdusis, a stripping, from ekduein, to take off : ex- (reversal) + duein, to get into, put on, enter.]

ec·dy·sone (ĕk'dĭ-sōn') n. A hormone secreted by insects and crustaceans that stimulates growth and molting. [ECDYS(IS) + -ONE.]

e·ce·sis (ĭ-sē'sĭs, ĭ-kē'-) n. The successful establishment of an organism in a new environment. [Greek oikēsis, habitation, from oikein, to dwell, from oikos, house.]

ECG electrocardiogram; electrocardiograph.

ec·hard (ĕk'härd') n. Ecology. Soil water not available for absorption by plants. [Greek ekhein, to hold, hold back + ardein†, to water, irrigate.]

ech·e·lon (ĕsh'ə-lŏn') n. 1. a. A formation of troops in which parallel units are arranged to the left or right of the rear unit in a steplike fashion. b. A similar formation of groups, units, or individuals. c. A similar formation or arrangement of vessels or aircraft. 2. A subdivision of a military or naval force: command echelon. 3. A level of responsibility or authority in a hierarchy. 4. Optics. A specialized form of diffraction grating consisting of parallel glass plates of successively varying sizes, used to determine wavelengths, especially of extremely fine structures. ~v. **echeloned, -loning, -lons.** —tr. To arrange in an echelon. —intr. To form, march, or move in an echelon. [French échelon, "rung of a ladder," from Old French eschelon, from eschile, ladder, from Latin scālae, ladder, stairs.]

ech·e·ve·ri·a (ĕch'ə-və-rē'ə) n. Any of various tropical American plants of the genus Echeveria, having thick, succulent leaves often clustered in a rosette and commonly cultivated as house plants. [New Latin Echeveria, after M. Echeveri, 19th-century Mexican botanical illustrator.]

e·chid·na (ĭ-kĭd'nə) n., pl. **-nas** or **-nae** (-nē') Any of several burrowing, egg-laying mammals of the genera Tachyglossus and Zaglossus, of Australia, Tasmania, and New Guinea, having a spiny coat, a slender snout, and a sticky tongue used for catching ants and termites. Also called "spiny anteater." [New Latin, from Latin, viper, from Greek ekhidna.]

ech·i·nate (ĕk'ə-nāt') adj. Biology. Bearing or covered with spines; prickly; spiny. [Latin echinātus, from echinus, hedgehog. See echino-.]

echino-, echin– prefix. Indicates prickly or covered with spines; for example, **echinoderm, echinoid.** [New Latin, from Latin echinus, hedgehog, sea urchin, from Greek echinos.]

e·chi·no·coc·co·sis (ĭ-kī'nə-kə-kō'sĭs) n., pl. **-ses** (-sēz'). Also **e·chi·no·coc·ci·a·sis** (-kə-kī'ə-sĭs) pl. **-ses** (-sēz') Infestation with echinococci; especially, **hydatid disease** (see). [ECHINOCC(US) + -OSIS.]

e·chi·no·coc·cus (ĭ-kī'nə-kŏk'əs) n., pl. **-cocci** (-kŏk'sī', -kŏk'ī')

Any of several parasitic tapeworms of the genus Echinococcus, the larvae of which infect mammals and form large, spherical cysts, causing serious or fatal disease. [New Latin Echinococcus : ECHINO- + COCCUS.]

e·chi·no·derm (ĭ-kī'nə-dûrm') n. Any of numerous radially symmetrical marine invertebrates of the phylum Echinodermata, which includes the starfishes, sea urchins, and sea cucumbers, having a calcareous skeleton just beneath the skin that is often covered with spines. [ECHINO- + -DERM.] —**e·chi·no·der·mal** (ĭ-kī'nə-dûr'məl), **e·chi·no·der·ma·tous** (ĭ-kī'nə-dûr'mə-təs) adj.

e·chi·noid (ĭ-kī'noid') n. Any echinoderm of the class Echinoidea, which includes the sand dollars and sea urchins. [ECHIN(O)- + -OID.]

e·chi·nus (ĭ-kī'nəs) n., pl. **-ni** (-nī'). Architecture. A curved molding just below the abacus of a Doric capital. [Latin, "hedgehog," "sea urchin" (from the shape). See echino-.]

ech·o (ĕk'ō) n., pl. **-oes.** 1. a. Repetition of a sound by reflection of sound waves from a surface. b. The sound produced in this manner. c. An electronic sound effect repeating a recorded sound. 2. Any repetition or imitation of something, as of the opinions, speech, or dress of another: The dress is an echo of Edwardian fashion. 3. One who imitates another, as in opinions, speech, or dress. 4. A sympathetic response. 5. A consequence or repercussion: Her assassination had political echoes. 6. The repetition of certain sounds or syllables in poetry. 7. Music. The soft repetition of a note or phrase. 8. A signal to a partner at bridge or whist that the same suit is to be continued. 9. Electronics. A reflected wave received by a radio or radar. ~v. **echoed, -oing, -oes.** —tr. 1. To repeat by or as if by an echo; send back the sound of: The canyon echoed her cry. 2. To repeat or imitate: followers echoing the thoughts of the leader. 3. To be reminiscent of; resemble: events echoing those of a century ago. —intr. 1. To be repeated by or as if by an echo. 2. To resound with or emit an echo; reverberate: woods echoing with hunting cries. [Middle English echo, ecko, from Old French echo, from Latin echo, from Greek ēkhō.] —**ech·o·er** n. —**ech·o·ey** adj.

Ech·o (ĕk'ō). Greek Mythology. A nymph whose unrequited love for Narcissus caused her to pine away until only her voice remained.

ech·o·car·di·og·ra·phy (ĕk'ō-kär'dē-ŏg'rə-fē) n. Medicine. A diagnostic technique that uses ultrasound waves to investigate the action of the beating heart and to depict this on a screen. —**ech·o·car·di·o·graph** (ĕk'ō-kär'dē-ə-grăf') n. —**ech·o·car·di·o·graph·ic** (ĕk'ō-kär'dē-ə-grăf'ĭk) adj.

echo chamber n. A room fitted with wall panels that reflect sound, used for making acoustic measurements and recordings requiring echo effects.

echo check n. An error-control technique in which the receiving terminal or computer returns the original message to verify its correct reception.

ech·og·ra·phy (ĕk-ŏg'rə-fē) n. Investigation of the internal organs of the body using ultrasound waves, which are reflected from the tissues.

e·cho·ic (ĭ-kō'ĭk) adj. 1. Being or resembling an echo. 2. Imitative of sounds; onomatopoeic. —**e·cho·i·cal·ly** adv.

ech·o·ism (ĕk'ō-ĭz'əm) n. The formation of words in imitation of sounds; onomatopoeia.

ech·o·la·li·a (ĕk'ō-lā'lē-ə) n. Psychology. Involuntary repetition of words or phrases just spoken by others, occurring in some mental and language disorders. [ECHO + Greek lalia, talk, from lalos, talkative.] —**ech·o·la·lic** (ĕk'ō-lā'lĭk) adj.

ech·o·lo·ca·tion (ĕk'ō-lō-kā'shən) n. 1. The ability of an animal that emits high-frequency sounds, such as a bat or dolphin, to orient itself by means of the reflected sound waves. 2. Electronics. Ranging by acoustical echo analysis.

ech·o·prax·i·a (ĕk'ō-prăk'sē-ə) n. Psychology. Pathological imitation of the actions of another person, occurring as a symptom of certain mental disorders. —**ech·o·prac·tic** (ĕk'ō-prăk'tĭk) adj.

echo sounder n. A device for measuring the depth of water by sending a high-frequency pulse to the bottom and measuring the time taken for the echo to return. —**echo sounding** n. See feature, next page.

ech·o·vi·rus (ĕk'ō-vī'rəs) n. Any virus of a group originally isolated from the intestinal tract and thought to cause nonspecific meningitis, many illnesses causing symptoms of the common cold, and various gastrointestinal and respiratory-tract infections. [Enteric Cytopathic Human Orphan + VIRUS.]

echt (ĕkt, ĕкнt) adj. Genuine or typical. [German.]

Eck (ĕk), **Johann Maier von** (1486–1543). German theologian. When Luther published his 95 theses in 1517, Eck became his principal opponent and went to Rome to bring back the papal bull condemning him in 1520.

Eck·hart (ĕk'härt'), **Johannes,** also known as "Meister Eckhart" (c. 1260–c. 1328). German theologian and mystic. He was considered the most accomplished scholar and preacher of his day but in 1326 was accused of heresy.

é·clair (ā-klâr', ā'klâr') n. A tube-shaped cream puff that is filled with whipped cream or custard and usually iced with chocolate. [French, "lightning," from Old French esclair, from esclairier, to light, flash, from Vulgar Latin exclāriāre (unattested), variant of Latin exclārāre : ex-, completely + clārāre, to brighten, clarify, from clārus, bright, clear.]

e·clamp·si·a (ĭ-klămp'sē-ə) n. Pathology. Coma and convulsions arising from any of several conditions during or immediately after

echidna A primitive egg-laying mammal, the echidna feeds on ants that it digs from the ground with its powerful claws. Echidnas are native to Australia and New Guinea.

TRACING THE HAZARDS AND TREASURES OF THE OCEANS
Pictures of fish, rocks, and wrecks beneath the sea are drawn from echoes

Dramatic losses of shipping, caused by the iceberg that sank the *Titanic* in 1912 and by the German U-boats in World War I, intensified work on devices to locate underwater dangers. By 1918 Allied warships were using echo-sounding equipment. It sent a pulse of sound down through the water and measured the time that passed before its echo bounced back from the seabed or from an obstacle. Such depth detectors were widely used in the 1930's. During World War II, sideways scanning was developed to locate objects near the surface. Since 1940 the system's American name "sonar" has replaced the British name "asdic."

Today, pinpointing of direction and distance has become precise, and fine detail of an object is re-vealed. Detection is possible over a range of 10 kilo-meters (6 miles); beyond that the returning signal cannot be distinguished from the background noise of the sea itself. Sonar equipment is used in military vessels and also to aid navigation in deep-sea vessels, to locate shoals of fish, to survey oil pipeline routes, and to search for wrecks of archeological interest.

HYDROSEARCH SYSTEM *The display screen of a hydro-search echo-sounding device shows a submarine resting on the ocean floor. Such devices are capable of a high degree of detail: the submarine's conning tower and peri-scope are visible in close-up in the panel on the right of the display screen.*

A transducer, set in a ship's hull, sends out and receives sound waves. It translates the returning waves into electrical pulses that form the patterns on the display screen

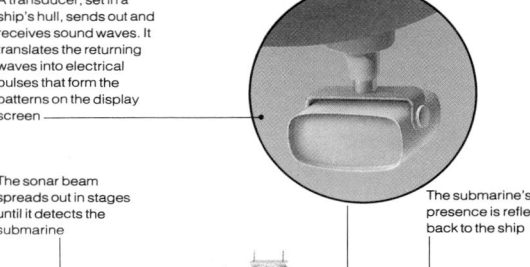

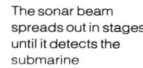

The sonar beam spreads out in stages until it detects the submarine

The submarine's presence is reflected back to the ship

Shoal of fish

Weed-covered rock

CHROMOSCOPE SYSTEM *Shoals of fish are located using the chromoscope, a Japanese echo-sounding device. The pattern on the screen (below) is made up of dots whose colors—from white, through deepening shades of yellow, to red—indicate the density of the ob-ject being scanned: the deeper the shade, the denser the object located. The dense red and yellow areas indi-cate objects covered with seaweed, and the small white area to the right represents a shoal of fish. Areas of the picture can be enlarged. Such sound-ers may be so accurate that they can be used to detect and identify individ-ual fish.*

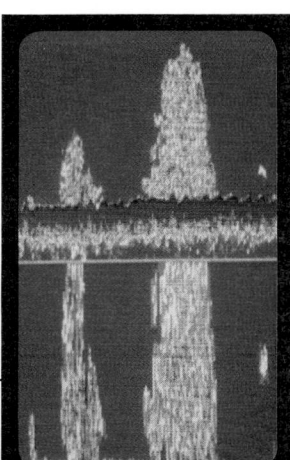

SCANNING THE DEPTHS *An echo sounder works by means of a transducer, a device that converts electricity into sound waves. It transmits pulses that travel at about 1,460 meters (4,800 feet) per second until they hit the seabed or an obstacle. This reflects them as echoes to the transducer. The time that elapses between transmitting a pulse and receiving its echo is recorded by an electrical circuit, displayed on a screen or on electrically sensitive paper, and measured to find the range.*

---

pregnancy. [New Latin, from Greek *eklampsis,* a shining forth, brightness, from *eklampein,* to shine forth : *ex-,* out + *lampein,* to shine.] —**e·clamp·tic** (ĭ-klămp'tĭk) *adj.*

é·clat (ā-klä', ā'klä') *n.* **1.** Great brilliance, as of performance or achievement. **2.** Conspicuous success or acclaim. [French, explo-sion, from *éclater,* to burst, explode, from Old French *esclater,* from Germanic *slītan* (unattested), to tear, SLIT.]

e·clec·tic (ĭ-klĕk'tĭk) *adj.* **1.** Choosing what appears to be the best from diverse sources, systems, or styles. **2.** Consisting of compo-nents selected from diverse sources.
~*n.* One who follows an eclectic method. [Greek *eklektikos,* from *eklektos,* selected, from *eklegein,* to single out : *ex-,* out + *legein,* to choose.] —**e·clec·ti·cal·ly** *adv.*

e·clec·ti·cism (ĭ-klĕk'tə-sĭz'əm) *n.* **1.** An eclectic system or method. **2.** Free selection, as of ideas, from diverse sources.

e·clipse (ĭ-klĭps') *n.* **1. a.** The partial or complete obscuring, relative to a designated observer, of one celestial body by another. **b.** The period of time during which such an obscuring occurs. **2.** Any tem-porary or permanent dimming or cutting off of light. **3.** Any falling into obscurity; an overshadowing or decline.
~*tr.v.* **eclipsed, eclipsing, eclipses. 1.** To cause an eclipse or ob-scuring of; darken. **2.** To obscure or overshadow the importance, fame, or reputation of; reduce in importance by comparison. [Mid-dle English *eclipse,* from Old French, from Latin *eclīpsis,* from Greek *ekleipsis,* cessation, abandonment, from *ekleipein,* to leave out, abandon : *ek-, ex-,* out + *leipein,* to leave.]

eclipsing binary *n. Astronomy.* A binary star one component of which is regularly eclipsed by the other because its orbital plane lies in or near the line of sight. Also called "eclipsing variable."

e·clip·tic (ĭ-klĭp'tĭk) *n. Astronomy.* **1.** The apparent path of the sun relative to the stars; the intersection plane of the earth's solar orbit with the celestial sphere. **2.** A great circle on a terrestrial globe inclined at an approximate angle of 23° 27' to the equator. [Middle English *ecliptik,* from Late Latin *eclīpticus,* from Latin, of an eclipse, from Greek *ekleiptikos,* from *ekleipein,* to abandon. See **eclipse.**] —**e·clip·tic** *adj.*

ec·lo·gite (ĕk'lə-jīt') *n.* A coarse-grained basic rock consisting of a greenish mixture of pyroxene, quartz, and feldspar with large red garnet inclusions. [Greek *eklogē,* selection (see **eclectic**) + -ITE.]

ec·logue (ĕk'lôg', -lŏg') *n.* A bucolic poem, typically a pastoral dia-logue. [French *éclogue,* from Old French *eglogue,* from Latin *ecloga,* "selection," from Greek *eklogē,* from *eklegein,* to single out. See **eclectic.**]

e·clo·sion (ĭ-klō'zhən) *n.* The emergence of an adult insect from a pupal case or of an insect larva from an egg. [French *éclosion,* from *éclore,* to open, be hatched, from Vulgar Latin *exclaudere* (unat-tested), variant of Latin *exclūdere,* to shut out : EX- + *claudere,* to shut, close.]

eco– *prefix.* Indicates ecology; for example, **ecosystem.** [From ECOLOGY.]

ec·o·cide (ĕk'ō-sīd', ē'kō-) *n.* Deliberate or avoidable destruction of the natural environment, as by pollutants. [ECO- + -CIDE.]

e·col·o·gy (ĭ-kŏl′ə-jē) n. Abbr. **ecol. 1. a.** The science of the relationships between organisms and their environments. Also called "bionomics." **b.** The relationship between organisms and their environment. **2. a.** The study of the relationships between people and their environment. **b.** The relationship between a human group and its environment. In this sense, also called "human ecology." [German *Ökologie* : Greek *oikos*, house + -LOGY.] —**ec·o·log·i·cal** (ĕk′ə-lŏj′ĭ-kəl, ē′kə-) adj. —**ec·o·log·ic** (-lŏj′ĭk) adj. —**ec·o·log·i·cal·ly** adv. —**e·col·o·gist** (ĭ-kŏl′ə-jĭst) n.

e·con·o·met·rics (ĭ-kŏn′ə-mĕt′rĭks) n. Used with a singular verb. The application of statistical techniques to economics in the study of problems, the analysis of data, and the development of theory. [ECONO(MICS) + -METRIC.] —**e·con·o·met·ric, e·con·o·met·ri·cal** adj. —**e·con·o·me·tri·cian** (ĭ-kŏn′ə-mə-trĭsh′ən), **e·con·o·met·rist** (-mĕt′rĭst) n.

ec·o·nom·ic (ĕk′ə-nŏm′ĭk, ē′kə-) adj. **1.** Of or pertaining to the production, development, and management of material wealth, as of a country, household, or business enterprise. **2.** Of or pertaining to economics. **3.** Of or pertaining to matters of finance. **4.** Chiefly British. Financially self-sustaining or self-justifying. **5.** Economical. **6.** Of or pertaining to the necessities of life; utilitarian. —See Usage note at **economical**.

ec·o·nom·i·cal (ĕk′ə-nŏm′ĭ-kəl, ē′kə-) adj. **1.** Not wasteful or extravagant; prudent in management of resources. **2.** Operating or designed in a way that avoids waste or excessive costs. —See Synonyms at **sparing**. —**ec·o·nom·i·cal·ly** adv.

Usage: **Economical** can only be used in the context of "saving," "not being wasteful": *an economical way of life. Economic* is the only form to use when referring to the field of economics *(economic issues; economic growth).* On the other hand, *economic* is also sometimes found as an alternative to *economical* in the sense of "saving" (as in *It's not economic to have a home freezer unless you buy in bulk).* In such pairs as *economic prices* and *economical prices,* the former is the more likely to mean "prices that do not lose money" (for the producer), while the latter is the more likely to mean "prices that save money" (for the consumer).

economic geography n. The study of the distribution and use of economic resources throughout the world.

ec·o·nom·ics (ĕk′ə-nŏm′ĭks, ē′kə-) n. Abbr. **econ. 1.** Used with a singular verb. The social science that deals with the production, distribution, and consumption of commodities and the theory and operation of financial systems. **2.** Used with a plural verb. **a.** An economic basis. **b.** Relevant financial considerations.

e·con·o·mist (ĭ-kŏn′ə-mĭst) n. Abbr. **econ.** A specialist in economics.

e·con·o·mize (ĭ-kŏn′ə-mīz′) v. **-mized, -mizing, -mizes.** —intr. To be frugal; reduce expenses. —tr. To use or manage in an economical way; save. —**e·con·o·mi·za·tion** n.

e·con·o·miz·er (ĭ-kŏn′ə-mī′zər) n. **1.** One that economizes. **2.** A device, as in power stations or steam engines, that uses some of the waste heat from a boiler flue to preheat the feed water.

e·con·o·my (ĭ-kŏn′ə-mē) n., pl. **-mies.** Abbr. **econ. 1.** The careful or thrifty use or management of resources, as of income, materials, or labor. **2.** An example of this; a saving. **3. a.** The management of the resources of a country, community, or business. **b.** A system for the management and development of such resources: *an agricultural economy.* **4.** The economic system of a country or area: *Floods disrupted the economy of the region.* **5.** Artistic restraint or avoidance of ornamentation. **6.** The functional arrangement of elements within a structure or system: *the economy of an organism.* **7.** Theology. The divine plan or system for the government of the world or for a specific period or nation. **8.** Economy class.
~adj. Allowing a saving to be made, as through bulk purchase: *economy size; an economy car.* [Old French *economie,* management of a household, from Latin *oeconomia,* from Greek *oikonomia,* from *oikonomos,* manager of a household : *oikos,* house + *-nomos,* managing (see **-nomy**).]

economy class n. The least expensive and least luxurious category of airline seating and service.

é·cor·ché (ā′kôr-shā′) n. A picture of the body or part of the body with the skin removed so as to show the appearance of the muscles. [French, "skinned."]

ec·o·spe·cies (ĕk′ō-spē′shēz, -sēz, ē′kō-) n. A taxonomic species considered in terms of its ecological characteristics and usually including several ecotypes. [ECO- + SPECIES.]

ec·o·sphere (ĕk′ō-sfîr′, ē′kō-) n. The regions of the universe, particularly on the earth, that are capable of supporting life.

é·cos·saise (ā′kô-sĕz′) n. Music. **1.** A piece of music with a dance-like rhythm in ²/₄ time. **2.** A lively dance to an écossaise. [French, "Scottish (dance)."]

ec·o·sys·tem (ĕk′ō-sĭs′təm, ē′kō-) n. An ecological community together with its physical environment, considered as a unit. [ECO- + SYSTEM.]

ec·o·tone (ĕk′ə-tōn′, ē′kə-) n. An ecological community of mixed vegetation formed by the overlapping of adjoining communities. [ECO- + Greek *tonos,* tension, TONE.]

ec·o·type (ĕk′ō-tīp′, ē′kō-) n. The smallest taxonomic subdivision of an ecospecies, consisting of subspecies or varieties adapted to a particular set of environmental conditions. [ECO- + TYPE.]

ec·ru (ĕk′rōō, ā′krōō) n. A grayish to pale yellow or light grayish yellowish brown. [French *écru* : *é-* (intensive) + *cru,* crude, raw.] —**ec·ru** adj.

E.C.S.C. European Coal and Steel Community.

ec·sta·sy (ĕk′stə-sē) n., pl. **-sies. 1.** A state of exalted delight. **2.** A state of any emotion experienced very intensely: *an ecstasy of anger.* **3. a.** The trance, frenzy, or rapture associated with mystic or prophetic exaltation. **b.** Psychology. An emotional state, associated with religious or sexual experience or with drug taking, characterized by exuberant behavior and loss of self-control. [Middle English *extasie,* from Old French, from Late Latin *extasis, ecstasis,* from Greek *ekstasis,* from *existanai,* to displace, drive out of one's senses : *ex-,* out + *histanai,* to place.]
Synonyms: bliss, delight, euphoria, exaltation, rapture, transport.

ec·stat·ic (ĕk-stăt′ĭk, ĭk-) adj. **1.** Of, relating to, induced by, or inducing ecstasy. **2.** In a state of ecstasy; enraptured.
~n. One subject to ecstasies. —**ec·stat·i·cal·ly** adv.

ECT, E.C.T. electroconvulsive therapy.

ec·thy·ma (ĕk-thī′mə) n. An inflammatory skin disease characterized by ulcerating pustules that penetrate to the lower layer of the skin and cause scarring when they heal. [New Latin, from Greek *ekthuma,* pustule, from *ekthuein,* to break out : *ek-,* out + *thuein,* to seethe.]

ecto– prefix. Indicates outside or external part or surface; for example, **ectoderm, ectoplasm.** [Greek *ekto-,* from *ektos,* outside (after *entos,* inside), from *ek, ex,* out.]

ec·to·derm (ĕk′tə-dûrm′) n. The outermost of the three primary germ layers of an embryo, developing into the epidermis, nervous tissue, and, in vertebrates, sense organs. Also called "exoderm."

eclosion *A lesser vine hawk moth emerges from its pupa case. The process is known as eclosion.*

---

eclipse

BLOTTING OUT THE SUN AND MOON

When earth and moon cast their shadows on each other

Eclipses are of two kinds—solar and lunar. Although the sun and moon appear almost the same size in the sky, the sun has 400 times the moon's diameter—but it is also nearly 400 times farther away. So when the moon passes between sun and earth, it blots out some or all of the sun, producing a partial or total solar eclipse. At a total eclipse, the solar atmosphere flashes into view, and the spectacle is magnificent. When the three bodies line up exactly but the moon is at its farthest from the earth, the moon appears too small to hide the sun, and a ring (annulus) of the sun is seen around the dark body of the moon; this is an annular eclipse.

Because the moon's shadow is only just long enough to reach the earth, it can blot out the sun completely for only a short time. At any one point on the earth's surface a total eclipse can never last for more than 7 minutes 40 seconds, and then only near the equator; farther to the north or south the duration of the eclipse will be shorter.

Lunar eclipses occur when the earth passes between the sun and the moon; the moon then passes through the cone of shadow cast by the earth. Direct sunlight is no longer reaching the moon, which turns a dim, coppery color until it emerges from the shadow. Usually the moon does not vanish completely, since some sunlight is bent or refracted onto its surface by the ring of atmosphere around the earth. A total lunar eclipse may last for 1 hour 40 minutes. A lunar eclipse can be seen from any point on the earth where the moon is above the horizon.

If the plane of the moon's orbit coincided exactly with the earth's there would be a solar and lunar eclipse every month. But, as the moon's orbit is offset by about 5 degrees, the three bodies align only occasionally—at most seven times a year.

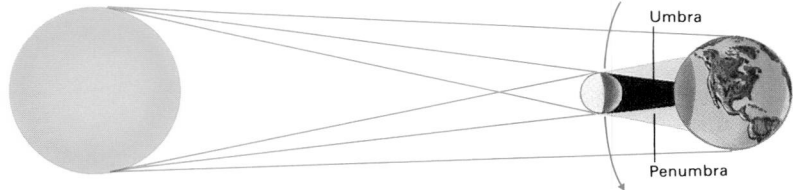

Umbra

Penumbra

ECLIPSE OF THE SUN *During a total eclipse of the sun, the main cone of the shadow that falls on the earth is the umbra. Only there will the eclipse be total. The shadow of the partial eclipse to either side is the penumbra.*

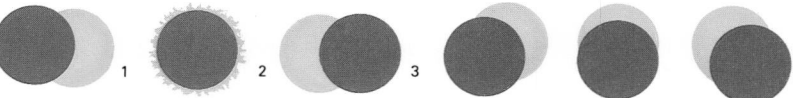

1 2 3

TOTAL ECLIPSE *The moon and sun approach totality (1), arrive at totality (2), and leave totality (3) in a matter of minutes.*

PARTIAL ECLIPSE *When the sun, earth, and moon are almost, but not exactly, in line, the eclipse is only partial anywhere on earth.*

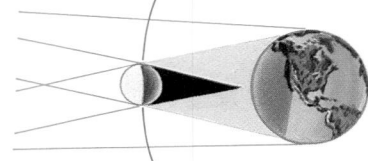

ANNULAR ECLIPSE *An eclipse is called annular (above and right) when the moon throws its shadow on the earth from the farthest part of its orbit. From earth, a circle of sun is visible around the moon (above and right).*

Compare **endoderm, mesoderm.** [ECTO- + -DERM.]

ec·tog·e·nous (ĕk-tŏj′ə-nəs) *adj.* Also **ec·to·gen·ic** (ĕk′tə-jĕn′ĭk). Able to live and develop outside a host. Said of certain pathogenic microorganisms. [ECTO- + -GENOUS.]

ec·to·mere (ĕk′tə-mîr′) *n. Biology.* A blastomere that develops into ectoderm. [ECTO- + -MERE.]

ec·to·morph (ĕk′tə-môrf′) *n.* A lean, slightly muscular human build with a large surface area of skin in relation to body weight. Compare **endomorph, mesomorph.** [ECTO- + -MORPH.] —**ec·to·mor·phic** (ĕk′tə-môr′fĭk) *adj.* —**ec·to·mor·phy** (ĕk′tə-môr′fē) *n.*

-ectomy *suffix.* Indicates removal of a part by surgery; for example, **tonsillectomy.** [New Latin *-ectomia* : Greek *ek-, ex-,* out + -TOMY.]

ec·to·par·a·site (ĕk′tə-păr′ə-sīt′) *n.* A parasite, such as a flea, that lives on the exterior of another organism.

ec·to·pi·a (ĕk-tŏ′pē-ə) *n. Pathology.* **1.** Misplacement of an organ or part, which may be congenital or due to injury. **2.** The occurrence of something in an unusual position. [New Latin, from Greek *ektopos,* away from a place : *ex-,* out of + *topos,* place (see **topic**).] —**ec·top·ic** (ĕk-tŏp′ĭk) *adj.*

ectopic beat *n. Pathology.* An **extrasystole** (see).

ectopic pregnancy *n. Pathology.* Gestation outside the uterus, often in a Fallopian tube.

ec·to·plasm (ĕk′tə-plăz′əm) *n.* **1.** *Biology.* A portion of the cytoplasm distinguishable in some cells as a relatively rigidly gelled outer layer just beneath the cell membrane. Compare **endoplasm.** **2.** The specter or emanation allegedly conjured up by a spiritualistic medium. [ECTO- + -PLASM.] —**ec·to·plas·mic** (ĕk′tə-plăz′mĭk) *adj.*

ec·to·sarc (ĕk′tə-särk′) *n.* The relatively clear outermost layer of protoplasm of certain protozoans, such as the amoeba. [ECTO- + Greek *sarx* (stem *sark-*), flesh.]

E·CU (ā-kōō′) *n., pl.* **ECU's.** A notional unit used for pricing goods within the European Economic Community independently of the currencies of individual member countries. [From *European Currency Unit.*]

é·cu (ā-kyōō′) *n., pl.* **écus** (*pronounced as singular*). Any of various old French gold or silver coins. [French, from Old French *escu,* from Latin *scūtum,* shield (from the shield stamped on the coin).]

Ec·ua·dor (ĕk′wə-dôr′). *Abbr.* **Ecua.** Country in northwestern South America. The Spanish occupied Quito, part of the Inca empire, in 1534, and the region became part of the viceroyalty of Peru and later of New Granada. By 1830 Ecuador had become an independent republic. Ecuador consists of a coastal plain in the west separated from Oriente in the Amazon Basin by the Andes. The Galapagos Islands, 1,000 kilometers (600 miles) offshore in the Pacific, belong to Ecuador. The country is South America's second largest oil producer, an important member of OPEC, and the world's largest producer of balsa. Area, 283,561 square kilometers (109,483 square miles). Population, 10,600,000. Capital, Quito. —**E·cua·do·ri·an, E·cua·do·re·an** (ĕk′wə-dôr′ē-ən) *n. & adj.*

ec·u·men·i·cal (ĕk′yə-mĕn′ĭ-kəl) *adj.* Also **ec·u·men·ic** (-mĕn′ĭk). **1.** Universal; worldwide. **2.** Of or pertaining to the worldwide Christian church. **3.** Concerned with promoting unity among the churches. [Late Latin *oecūmenicus,* from Greek *oikoumenikos,* of the whole world, from *oikoumenē,* the inhabited world, from *oikein,* to inhabit, from *oikos,* house.] —**ec·u·men·i·cal·ism** *n.* —**ec·u·men·i·cal·ly** *adv.*

ecumenical council *n.* **1.** Any of several councils of the early

edelweiss *The distinctive stars are formed by petallike white woolly bracts surrounding small yellow flowers.*

Christian church. **2.** *Roman Catholic Church.* A general council of bishops.

ecumenical patriarch *n.* A **patriarch** (see) of the Eastern Orthodox Church.

ec·u·me·nism (ĕk′yə-mə-nĭz′əm, ĭ-kyōō′mə-, ĕk′yə-mĕn′ĭz′-) *n.* **1.** A movement or doctrine promoting unity among the Christian churches. **2.** A movement or doctrine promoting worldwide unity among religions through greater cooperation and improved understanding.

ec·ze·ma (ĕk′sə-mə, ĕg′zə-, ĭg-zē′-) *n.* A noncontagious inflammation of the skin, marked mainly by redness, itching, and the outbreak of lesions that discharge serous matter and become encrusted and scaly. [New Latin, from Greek *ekzema,* eruption : *ex-,* out + *zema,* fermentation, boiling, from *zeein,* to boil.] —**ec·zem·a·tous** (ĕg-zĕm′ə-təs, -zē′mə-təs, ĭg-) *adj.*

-ed¹ *suffix.* Used to form the past tense of most verbs; for example, **removed.** [Middle English *-ede,* Old English *-ode, -ede, -ade.*]

-ed² *suffix.* Used to form the past participle of most verbs; for example, **hoped.** [Middle English *-ed,* Old English *-od, -ed, -ad.*]

-ed³ *suffix.* Indicates possessing, characterized by, or provided with; for example, **forked, gray-haired.** [Middle English *-ede, -de,* Old English *-ede.*]

ed. **1.** edited; edited by; edition; editor. **2.** education.

e·da·cious (ĭ-dā′shəs) *adj.* Gluttonous; voracious. [Latin *edax* (stem *edāc-*), gluttonous, from *edere,* to eat.] —**e·dac·i·ty** (ĭ-dăs′ə-tē), **e·da·cious·ness** *n.*

E·dam (ē′dəm, ē′dăm′) *n.* A mild yellow Dutch cheese pressed into balls and usually covered with red wax. [After *Edam,* northwestern Netherlands, town in which it is made.]

e·daph·ic (ĭ-dăf′ĭk) *adj.* Of or pertaining to soil, especially as it affects living organisms. [Greek *edaphos,* ground, foundation, floor.] —**e·daph·i·cal·ly** *adv.*

E.D.C. European Defense Community.

Ed·da (ĕd′ə) *n.* **1.** A collection of Old Norse poems called the *Elder* or *Poetic Edda,* assembled in the 12th or early 13th century. **2.** A manual of Icelandic poetry called the *Younger* or *Prose Edda,* compiled a generation later. [Old Norse *edda;* perhaps from *óthr,* poetry.]

Ed·ding·ton (ĕd′ĭng-tən), **Sir Arthur Stanley** (1882–1944). British astronomer and physicist. He was one of the earliest exponents of the theory of relativity (his *Mathematical Theory of Relativity* appeared in 1923).

ed·do (ĕd′ō) *n., pl.* **-does.** A plant, **taro** (see). [From an African word akin to Twi *ode,* yam.]

ed·dy (ĕd′ē) *n., pl.* **-dies.** **1.** A current, as of water or air, moving contrary to the direction of the main current, especially in a circular motion. **2.** A current that runs contrary to the main current or tradition, as of life, art, or philosophy; a byway. ~*v.* **eddied, -dying, -dies.** —*intr.* To move against the main current, as in an eddy. —*tr.* To cause to move against the main current, as in an eddy. —See Synonyms at **turn.** [Middle English *ydy,* probably from Old English *ed-,* back, again; akin to Old Norse *idha,* "that which flows back," whirlpool, from *idh-,* again.]

Ed·dy (ĕd′ē), **Mary Baker** (1821–1910). U.S. religious leader. She founded the Church of Christ, Scientist.

eddy current *n. Electricity.* An induced electric current in the iron core of an electromagnet, transformer, or the like, causing a loss of energy. Also called "Foucault current."

Ed·dy·stone Rocks (ĕd′ē-stōn′). Group of rocks dangerous to shipping, in the English Channel, 23 kilometers (14 miles) southwest of Plymouth. It has been the site of a lighthouse since 1698.

e·del·weiss (ā′dəl-vīs′, -wīs′) *n.* A plant, *Leontopodium alpinum,* of mountainous regions, especially Alpine regions, having leaves covered with whitish down and small flowers surrounded by conspicuous whitish bracts. [German *Edelweiss,* "noble white."]

e·de·ma, oe·de·ma (ĭ-dē′mə) *n., pl.* **-mas** or **-mata** (-mə-tə). **1.** *Pathology.* An excessive accumulation of serous fluid in the tissues. **2.** *Botany.* Extended swellings in plant organs caused primarily by an excessive accumulation of water. [New Latin, from Greek *oidēma,* tumor, swelling, from *oidein,* to swell.] —**e·dem·a·tous** (ĭ-dĕm′ə-təs) *adj.*

E·den (ēd′n) *n.* **1.** In the Bible, the first home of Adam and Eve; the earthly Paradise. Also called "Garden of Eden." **2.** Any delightful place or dwelling; a paradise. **3.** A state of bliss or ultimate happiness. [Middle English, from Late Latin *Ēden,* from Greek *Ēden,* from Hebrew *'ēdhen,* "(the place of) delight."]

E·den (ēd′n), **Robert Anthony, Earl of Avon** (1897–1977). British Conservative politician; foreign secretary 1935–38, 1940–45, and 1951–55, prime minister 1955–57. He entered Parliament in 1923 and in the 1930's was a determined opponent of Hitler and Mussolini. Convinced that Egypt's leader, Gamal Nasser, was a threat to world peace, he supported the 1956 Anglo-French invasion of Egypt in collusion with Israel; but international hostility to this policy forced a cease-fire. Domestic criticism and ill health caused his resignation.

e·den·tate (ē-dĕn′tāt′) *adj. Biology.* **1.** Lacking teeth. **2.** Of or belonging to the order Edentata, which includes mammals, such as anteaters, armadillos, and sloths, having few or no teeth. ~*n.* A member of the Edentata. [Latin *edentātus,* toothless, from the past participle of *edentāre,* to take out the teeth : *ex-,* out + *dēns* (stem *dent-*), tooth.]

e·den·tu·lous (ē-dĕn′chə-ləs) *adj.* Lacking teeth. [See **edentate, -ulous.**]

Map labels:
ECUADOR 80° W
PACIFIC OCEAN
COLOMBIA
Ibarra
Otavalo
Equator
QUITO
PICHINCHA
Latacunga
Cotopaxi 5896m
ECUADOR
Chimborazo 6310m
Ríobamba
Guayaquil
Playas
G. de Guayaquil
Cuenca
Loja
PERU
ANDES
Km 0 200 400
Miles 0 100 200

E·der·le (ā'dər-lē), **Gertrude Caroline** (1906–). U.S. swimmer. On August 26, 1926, she became the first woman to swim the English Channel, setting a new record of 14 hours and 31 minutes.

E·des·sa (ĭ-dĕs'ə). *Modern Greek* **E·dhes·sa** (ə-thä'sə). Town in Macedonia, northern Greece. In ancient times it was Macedonia's capital, known as Aegea. It is a commercial and industrial center also serving as a market town for the wine, fruit, and tobacco grown in the district.

Ed·gar (ĕd'gər) or **Ead·gar** (ĕd'gär), known as "the Peaceful" (*c.* 943–75). King of the English, son of Edmund I. After a revolt against his brother, Edwy, king of the English, he became king of the Mercians and Northumbrians and king of the English when Edwy died in 959.

Edgar the Aeth·e·ling (ăth'ə-lĭng) (*c.* 1050–*c.* 1130). English prince, grandson of Edmund Ironside. He was chosen king of the English when Harold was slain in the Battle of Hastings (1066) but submitted to the rule of William the Conqueror. After unsuccessful attempts to regain his kingdom, he led the English expedition that deposed Donald III of Scotland and placed his nephew, also called Edgar, on the Scottish throne.

edge (ĕj) *n.* **1. a.** The usually thin, sharpened side of the blade of a cutting instrument, weapon, or tool. **b.** The degree of sharpness of a cutting blade. **c.** A penetrating or incisive quality: "*His simplicity sets off the satire, and gives it a finer edge*" (William Hazlitt). **2.** Keenness, as of desire or enjoyment; zest. **3.** A rim, brink, or crest, as of a cliff or ridge of hills. **4. a.** The line at the outside of a surface. **b.** The part of a surface nearest this line: *lying at the edge of the road.* **c.** A point close to an action or state: *on the edge of divorce.* **5.** The line of intersection of two surfaces of a solid: *the edge of a cube.* **6.** A margin of superiority; an advantage: *a slight edge over the opposition.* —See Synonyms at **border.** —**on edge.** **1.** Highly tense or nervous; irritable. **2.** Eagerly anticipatory; impatient. —**set one's teeth on edge.** *Informal.* **1.** To give one an unpleasant nervous reaction or sensation, as of tingling. **2.** To provoke strong feelings of irritation or annoyance. —**take the edge off.** To soften or dull the pleasure, excitement, pain, or force of: *ate an apple to take the edge off her appetite.* ~*v.* **edged, edging, edges.** —*tr.* **1.** To give an edge to; sharpen. **2.** To put a border or edging on. **3.** To advance or push gradually: *The dog edged the ball toward the child with its nose.* **4. a.** To be the edge of. **b.** To be at the edge of. **5.** To cut the edge of (a lawn, for example). **6.** To dig the edge of (a ski) into the snow surface. —*intr.* To move gradually or hesitantly: *She edged toward the door.* [Middle English *egge,* Old English *ecg,* edge, point, sword; akin to Latin *acer,* sharp.]

edg·er (ĕj'ər) *n.* A tool for trimming the edge of a lawn.

edge tool *n.* A tool, such as a chisel, having a cutting edge.

edge·wise (ĕj'wīz') *adv.* Also **edge·ways** (-wāz'). **1.** With the edge foremost. **2.** On, by, with, or toward the edge. —**get a word in edgewise.** To manage to interrupt a talkative speaker.

Edge·worth (ĕj'wûrth'), **Maria** (1767–1849). Irish writer, born in England. Her most famous novel, *Castle Rackrent* (1800), a tale of ordinary Irish life, broke away from the romantic tradition of the 18th-century Gothic novel and helped to establish a realist tradition in English literature.

edg·ing (ĕj'ĭng) *n.* Something that forms or serves as an edge; a trimming; a border.

edg·y (ĕj'ē) *adj.* **-ier, -iest.** **1.** On edge; tense; nervous. **2.** With a sharp edge. —**edg·i·ly** *adv.* —**edg·i·ness** *n.*

edh, eth (ĕth) *n.* **1.** A letter (ð) appearing in Old and Middle English, Old Saxon, Old Norse, and modern Icelandic. In the Scandinavian languages it represents the interdental voiced fricative (transliterated as *dh* in the etymologies) and is distinguished from the voiceless thorn. In Old English the distinction between edh and thorn (both transliterated as *th*) was not observed. **2.** The letter in the International Phonetic Alphabet representing the interdental voiced fricative, as in *the, other.*

Edhessa. See **Edessa.**

ed·i·ble (ĕd'ə-bəl) *adj.* **1. a.** Capable of being eaten. **b.** Fit to eat; nonpoisonous. **2.** Ready to be eaten. —See Usage note at **eatable.** ~*n.* Often **edibles.** Something fit to be eaten; food. —See Usage note at **eatable.** [Late Latin *edibilis,* from Latin *edere,* to eat.] —**ed·i·bil·i·ty, ed·i·ble·ness** *n.*

e·dict (ē'dĭkt') *n.* **1.** An official decree or proclamation issued by an authority. **2.** A formal command or decree. [Latin *ēdictum,* from *ēdīcere,* to speak out, proclaim : *ex-,* out + *dīcere,* to speak.]

ed·i·fi·ca·tion (ĕd'ə-fĭ-kā'shən) *n.* Intellectual, moral, or spiritual improvement; enlightenment: "*I am now writing this book for the edification of the world*" (Laurence Sterne).

ed·i·fice (ĕd'ə-fĭs) *n.* **1.** A building, especially one of imposing appearance or size. **2.** Something with an elaborate structure: *an edifice of regulations.* [Middle English, from Old French, from Latin *aedificium,* from *aedificāre,* to build : *aedēs,* building, house + *fac(e)re,* to make.]

ed·i·fy (ĕd'ə-fī') *tr.v.* **-fied, -fying, -fies.** To instruct or enlighten so as to encourage moral or spiritual improvement. [Middle English *edifien,* from Old French *edifier,* from Latin *aedificāre,* to build, instruct. See **edifice.**] —**ed·i·fi·ca·to·ry** (ĭ-dĭf'ə-kə-tôr'ē, -tōr'ē) *adj.* —**ed·i·fi·er** *n.*

Ed·in·burgh (ĕd'n-bûr'ə) Capital of Scotland and the administrative center of the Lothian region. The city, once known as Auld Reekie because of the cloud of smoke that hung over low-lying areas, includes printing, publishing, brewing, whiskey distilling,

confectionery, and chemicals among its industries. Edinburgh is the home of an international festival of the arts, held annually. It takes its name from Edwin, king of Northumbria in the 7th century.

Edinburgh, Duke of. See Prince **Philip.**

E·dir·ne (ĕ-dîr'nĕ). Formerly **A·dri·a·no·ple** (ā'drē-ə-nō'pəl). Capital of Edirne province in European Turkey. It was expanded in the 2nd century A.D. by the Roman emperor Hadrian and was taken by the Goths in 378 and later by the Bulgarians before becoming the residence of the Turkish sultans from 1365 to 1453. Ceded to Greece after World War I, it was returned to Turkey once more in 1923.

Ed·i·son (ĕd'ə-sən), **Thomas Alva** (1847–1931). U.S. inventor. He held more than 1,300 U.S. and foreign patents for his inventions, most of them concerned with electricity. Among his first inventions were the carbon telephone transmitter (1877), the phonograph (1878), and the incandescent lamp with a carbon filament (1879). In New York he installed (1880) an experimental electric railway and (1881–82) the first central electric power plant in the world.

ed·it (ĕd'ĭt) *tr.v.* **-ited, -iting, -its.** **1. a.** To make (written material) suitable for publication or presentation. **b.** To prepare an edition of for publication: *edit a collection of short stories.* **2.** To supervise the publication of (a newspaper or magazine, for example). **3.** To omit or eliminate; delete. Usually used with *out.* **4.** To integrate the component parts of (a film, electronic tape, or sound track) by cutting, combining, and splicing. ~*n.* An instance of editing: *I gave his article a preliminary edit.* [Back-formation from EDITOR.]

e·di·tion (ĭ-dĭsh'ən) *n. Abbr.* **ed., edit.** **1.** *Printing.* **a.** The entire number of copies of a publication printed from a single typesetting or other form of reproduction. Compare **printing.** **b.** A single copy from this group. **c.** A version of an earlier publication having substantial changes or additions. **2. a.** Any of the various forms in which something is issued or produced, as publications, music, or stamps. **b.** Any of the forms in which a publication is produced: *a leather-bound edition.* **c.** One closely similar to an original; a version: *The boy was a smaller edition of his father.* **3.** An issue of a work identified by its editor or publisher: *the Oxford edition of Shakespeare.* **4.** All the copies of a single print run of a newspaper: *the morning edition.* [Old French, from Latin *ēditiō* (stem *ēditiōn-*), a bringing forth, publication, from *ēdere* (past participle *ēdictus*), to bring forth, publish : *ex-,* out + *dāre,* to give.]

e·di·ti·o prin·ceps (ĭ-dĭsh'ē-ō prĭn'sĕps') *n., pl.* **editiones principes** (ĭ-dĭsh'ē-ō'nēz prĭn'sə-pēz'). A first printed edition of a work. [Latin, "first edition."]

ed·i·tor (ĕd'ə-tər) *n. Abbr.* **ed., edit.** **1.** A person who edits a written work or musical composition for publication or public presentation. **2.** A person who supervises the policies or production of a publication or broadcast. **3.** A person in charge of a department of a publication: *a sports editor.* **4.** One who writes editorials. **5. a.** A person responsible for the editing of a film, sound track, or the like. **b.** A device for editing film, consisting basically of a splicer and viewer. **6.** *Computer Science.* A routine that performs editing functions. [Late Latin, publisher, from Latin *ēdere,* to bring forth, publish. See **edition.**] —**ed·i·tor·ship** *n.*

ed·i·to·ri·al (ĕd'ə-tôr'ē-əl, -tōr'ē-əl) *n.* **1.** An article in a newspaper or magazine expressing the opinion of its editors or publishers. **2.** A commentary on radio or television expressing the opinion of the station or network. ~*adj.* **1.** Of, concerning, or prepared by an editor or editors. **2.** Having the nature of an editorial in expressing opinion: *editorial comments.* —**ed·i·to·ri·al·ly** *adv.*

ed·i·to·ri·al·ize (ĕd'ə-tôr'ē-ə-līz', -tōr'ē-ə-līz') *intr.v.* **-ized, -izing, -izes.** **1.** To express an opinion in or as if in an editorial. **2.** To present a supposedly objective report in a way intended to implant an opinion. —**ed·i·to·ri·al·i·za·tion** *n.* —**ed·i·to·ri·al·iz·er** *n.*

editor in chief *n., pl.* **editors in chief.** The editor having final responsibility for the operations and policies of a publication.

Ed·mon·ton (ĕd'mən-tən). Capital of Alberta, western Canada, on the North Saskatchewan River. It is an industrial center in an agricultural and oil- coal-, and gas-producing region.

Ed·mund I (ĕd'mənd) (*c.* 921–46). King of the English. He succeeded his half brother, Athelstan, in 939. He expelled the Danish rulers Olaf and Ragnald from Northumbria in 944 and in the following year received the homage of the king of Scotland in return for Cumbria.

Edmund I·ron·side (ī'ərn-sīd') (*c.* 981–1016). King of the English, succeeding his father, Ethelred the Unready (1016). He led the resistance against Canute's invasion (1015), but when he became king most of the nobles supported Canute and he was forced to partition the country.

Edmund, Saint (*c.* 840–70). King of East Anglia. He was born in Germany and adopted by Offa, king of East Anglia, as his heir. He was killed, either during a battle against the Danes at Hoxne or shortly afterward. He is buried at the town named after him, Bury St. Edmunds.

Edo. See **Tokyo.**

E·dom (ē'dəm). Ancient country between the Dead Sea and the Gulf of Aqaba, now forming parts of Jordan and Israel. According to the Old Testament, the original inhabitants, the Edomites, were descended from Esau. —**E·dom·ite** *n.*

EDP electronic data processing.

EDTA (ē'dē'tē'ā') *n. Chemistry.* A colorless crystalline compound, [(HOOCCH$_2$)$_2$NCH$_2$]$_2$, used as a chelating agent in inorganic chemistry and biochemistry and as an antidote to metal poisoning. [From *ethylene diaminetetra-acetic acid*.]

ed·u·ca·ble (ĕj′ə-kə-bəl) *adj.* Capable of being educated. [EDUC(ATE) + -ABLE.]

ed·u·cate (ĕj′ə-kāt′) *v.* **-cated, -cating, -cates.** —*tr.* **1.** To provide with knowledge or training, especially through formal schooling; teach. **2.** To provide with specialized training for a particular purpose: *educated him for the priesthood.* **3.** To provide with information; inform. **4.** To stimulate or develop the mental or moral growth of; enlighten. **5.** To discipline, train, or develop (a taste or skill, for example). —*intr.* To teach or instruct a person or group: *Their purpose is to educate through the use of visual aids.* —See Synonyms at **teach.** [Middle English *educaten,* from Latin *ēducāre,* to bring up, educate. See **educe.**]

ed·u·cat·ed (ĕj′ə-kā′tĭd) *adj.* **1.** Having an education, especially one above the average. **2.** Showing evidence of having been taught or instructed; cultivated; cultured. **3.** Based primarily on experience and some factual knowledge: *an educated guess.*

ed·u·ca·tion (ĕj′ə-kā′shən) *n. Abbr.* **ed., educ. 1.** The act or process of imparting knowledge or skill; systematic instruction; teaching. **2.** The obtaining of knowledge or skill through such a process; learning. **3. a.** The knowledge or skill obtained or developed by such a process. **b.** A program of instruction of a specified kind or level: *a classical education.* **4.** The field of study that is concerned with teaching and learning; the theory of teaching; pedagogy. **5.** An enlightening experience: *His visit to India was an education.*

ed·u·ca·tion·al (ĕj′ə-kā′shə-nəl) *adj. Abbr.* **educ. 1.** Of or pertaining to education: *educational psychology.* **2.** Serving to educate; instructive: *an educational film.* —**ed·u·ca·tion·al·ly** *adv.*

ed·u·ca·tion·al·ist (ĕj′ə-kā′shə-nə-lĭst) *n.* Also **ed·u·ca·tion·ist** (-shə-nĭst). An educational theorist.

educational television *n.* **1. Public television** (see). **2.** A video system that provides instructional material.

ed·u·ca·tive (ĕj′ə-kā′tĭv) *adj.* Serving to educate or instruct.

ed·u·ca·tor (ĕj′ə-kā′tər) *n.* **1.** One trained in teaching; a teacher. **2.** A specialist in the theory and practice of education.

e·duce (ĭ-dōōs′, ĭ-dyōōs′) *tr.v.* **educed, educing, educes. 1.** To draw or bring out; elicit; evoke. **2.** To infer or work out from given facts; deduce. [Latin *ēdūcere* : *ex-,* out + *dūcere,* to lead.] —**e·duc·i·ble** *adj.*

e·duct (ē′dŭkt′) *n.* A substance that has been separated from another substance without chemical change. Compare **product.** [Latin *ēductus,* "drawn out," past participle of *ēducere.* See **educe.**]

e·duc·tion (ĭ-dŭk′shən) *n.* **1.** An act or the process of educing. **2.** The result of educing; an inference. **3.** The exhaust phase of an internal-combustion engine. [Middle English *educcion,* from Late Latin *ēductiō,* from Latin *ēdūcere,* to EDUCE.]

Ed·ward I (ĕd′wərd) (1239-1307). King of England (1272-1307). Son of Henry III. His reign was marked by successful military campaigns against Wales and victory against the Scots at Falkirk (1298). His Model Parliament of 1295 is sometimes looked upon as the first full English parliament.

Edward II (1284-1327). King of England (1307-27). Son of Edward I. The Scots defeated Edward's army at Bannockburn (1314). In 1326 the rebellion of the Earl of March led to Edward's capture and deposition (1327). He was imprisoned in Berkeley Castle and almost certainly murdered there.

Edward III (1312-77). King of England (1327-77). Son of Edward II. During the Hundred Years' War with France his armies won victories at Crécy (1346) and Poitiers (1356).

Edward IV (1442-83). King of England (1461-70, 1471-83). Son of Richard, Duke of York. As leader of the Yorkist faction in the Wars of the Roses, Edward defeated the Lancastrians at Mortimer's Cross (1461) and was proclaimed king. In 1470 the Earl of Warwick raised a rebellion against him and Edward fled to France. Henry VI, whom he had deposed, was restored to the throne, but a year later Edward returned, defeated the Lancastrians at Tewkesbury, and regained the throne. Henry VI was put to death, possibly on Edward's orders.

Edward V (1470-83). King of England (1483). Son of Edward IV. On Edward's accession to the throne at the age of 13, he was confined to the Tower of London with his younger brother Richard, Duke of York. There they were murdered, possibly on the orders of their uncle the Duke of Gloucester (later Richard III) or possibly by Henry Stafford or by Henry VII. Skeletons of boys aged about 13 and 10 were unearthed in the Tower in 1674.

Edward VI (1537-53). King of England (1547-53). Son of Henry VIII and Jane Seymour. He came to the throne at the age of 9 and died of tuberculosis at the age of 15.

Edward VII (1841-1910). King of Great Britain and Ireland (1901-10). Son of Queen Victoria, he became a popular figure as Prince of Wales. His personal popularity in France helped create the conditions for the Entente Cordiale (1904).

Edward VIII (1894-1972). King of Great Britain and Ireland (1936). Son of George V. On succeeding to the throne he precipitated a constitutional crisis by his determination to marry Mrs. Wallis Warfield Simpson, an American divorcée. Opposition from Church and government caused him to abdicate after a reign of 325 days. Thereafter, as the Duke of Windsor, he lived with his wife in France, except for the years 1940 to 1945, when he was the governor of the Bahamas. He died in Paris but was buried in Windsor, in England.

Edward, Prince of Wales (1330-76). Eldest son of Edward III, he played a valiant part in the Hundred Years' War, especially at Crécy (1346) and Poitiers (1356), where he led the English forces that captured John II of France. He was named the Black Prince by the French, presumably because of his black armor.

Ed·ward·i·an (ĕd-wôr′dē-ən, ĕd-wär′-) *adj.* **1.** Of, pertaining to, or characteristic of the reign or person of any of several kings of England named Edward. **2.** Of, pertaining to, or characteristic of the reign or person of King Edward VII, especially with respect to the lighthearted elegance considered typical of his reign. —*n.* A person living during the reign of one of these kings.

Edward the Confessor (died 1066). King of the English (1042-66). Son of Ethelred the Unready, and later stepson of Canute. Edward devoted much of his time to religious work, including the rebuilding of Westminster Abbey. He was canonized in the 12th century.

Edward the Elder (died 924). King of Wessex (899-924). Son of Alfred the Great. He fought the Danes and the Viking invaders and by 918 ruled all of England south of the Humber.

-ee[1] *suffix.* Indicates: **1.** The recipient or object of a specified action; for example, **addressee, endorsee. 2.** One who is in a specified condition; for example, **refugee. 3.** One who is carrying out or has carried out a specified act; for example, **escapee.** [Middle English *-e,* from Old French *-e,* from the past participial ending *-e,* from Latin *-ātus,* -ATE.]
Usage: The suffix *-ee* has generally been used to indicate a person to whom something has been done or upon whom some right has been conferred: *appointee; grantee.* It has come to be used also with reference to a person in a specified condition (*absentee; refugee; amputee*) or even a person performing a particular action (*escapee; standee*).

-ee[2] *suffix.* Indicates: **1.** A particular type of, especially when small; for example, **bootee. 2.** Something resembling or suggestive of; for example, **goatee.** [Originally *-ie,* variant of -Y.]

e.e. errors excepted.

E.E. electrical engineer; electrical engineering.

E.E. & M.P. Envoy Extraordinary and Minister Plenipotentiary.

EEC *n.* The **European Economic Community** (see).

EEG electroencephalogram; electroencephalograph.

eel (ēl) *n., pl.* **eels** or collectively **eel. 1.** Any of various long, snakelike marine or freshwater fishes of the order Anguilliformes (or Apodes); especially, *Anguilla rostrata,* of eastern North America, and *A. anguilla,* of Europe, characteristically migrating from fresh water to the Sargasso Sea to spawn. **2.** Any of several similar or related fishes. [Middle English *ele,* Old English *ǣl,* from Common Germanic *ǣlaz†* (unattested).]

eel·grass (ēl′grăs′, -gräs′) *n.* **1.** Any of several submerged aquatic plants of the genus *Zostera,* of coastal areas, having narrow, grasslike leaves and growing in dense masses. **2.** Any of several similar or related plants, such as **tape grass** (see).

eel·pout (ēl′pout′) *n., pl.* **-pouts** or collectively **eelpout.** Any of various marine fishes of the family Zoarcidae, having an elongated body and a large head. The European species *Zoarces viviparus* produces live young. [Middle English *elepout* (unattested), Old English *ǣlepūte* : EEL + POUT (fish).]

eel·worm (ēl′wûrm′) *n.* Any of various often parasitic nematode worms, such as the **vinegar eel** (see).

e'en[1] (ēn) *n. Poetic.* Evening.

e'en[2] *adv. Poetic.* Even.

-eer *suffix.* Indicates: **1.** One who works with or is concerned with; for example, **auctioneer, volunteer, profiteer, racketeer. 2.** One who makes or composes; for example, **balladeer.** [Old French *-ier,* from Latin *-ārius,* -ARY.]

e'er (âr) *adv. Poetic.* Ever.

ee·rie, ee·ry (îr′ē) *adj.* **-rier, -riest. 1.** Inspiring fear or dread without being openly threatening; peculiarly unsettling: *heard an eerie noise in the attic.* **2.** Supernatural in aspect or character; uncanny; mysterious. —See Synonyms at **weird.** [Middle English *eri,* fearful, cowardly, Old English *earg,* cowardly, timid, from Common Germanic *arg-* (unattested).] —**ee·ri·ness** *n.*

EEZ Economic Exclusion Zone.

ef-. Variant of **ex-**[1].

eff. efficiency.

ef·fa·ble (ĕf′ə-bəl) *adj. Archaic.* Capable of being expressed in words. [Latin *effābilis,* from *effārī,* to speak out : *ex-,* out + *fārī,* to speak.]

ef·face (ĭ-fās′) *tr.v.* **-faced, -facing, -faces. 1.** To rub or wipe out; obliterate; erase. **2.** To make faded or indistinct as if by rubbing out. **3.** To conduct (oneself) inconspicuously or humbly: *"When the two women went out together, Anna deliberately effaced herself and played to the dramatic Molly"* (Doris Lessing). —See Synonyms at **erase.** [Old French *effacer,* "to remove the face" : *ef-,* out, from Latin *ex-* + *face,* FACE.] —**ef·face·a·ble** *adj.* —**ef·face·ment** *n.* —**ef·fac·er** *n.*

ef·fect (ĭ-fĕkt′) *n.* **1.** Something brought about by a cause or agent; a result: *"Fortunately in England, at any rate, education produces no effect whatsoever"* (Oscar Wilde). **2.** The way in which something acts upon or influences an object: *the effect of a drug on the nervous system.* **3.** The final or comprehensive result; an outcome. **4.** The power or capacity to achieve the desired result; efficacy; influence. **5.** The condition of being in full force or execution; being; realization: *The law will come into effect tomorrow.* **6.** An impression produced by an artifice or manner of presentation: *an effect of spaciousness.* **7.** The basic meaning or tendency of something said or written; purport: *He said he approved, or something to that effect.*

EEC (European Economic Community)

THE EEC—FIRST STEP TOWARD A FEDERAL STATE OF EUROPE
How the Community regulates policy and law

EUROPEAN COMMISSION

The heads of the Commission, the European Commissioners, formally adopt draft proposals for new Community laws drawn up by their officials. When a draft proposal has been adopted, it is submitted to the Council, which circulates it to other Community bodies. Once the Commission has received comments on the draft, including those from COREPER, it is resubmitted to the Council, if necessary after being revised

The EEC (European Economic Community), or Common Market, was established in 1957 under the Treaty of Rome. The signatories—France, Belgium, the Netherlands, Italy, Luxembourg, and the Federal Republic of Germany—undertook to establish a common customs tariff and trade policy; freedom of movement of labor and capital; common agricultural, transport, and social policies; and to ensure free competition. A common agricultural policy was in operation by 1962 and a full customs union and freedom of movement for workers were established by 1968. Expansion of membership has been rapid. The United Kingdom, the Republic of Ireland, and Denmark joined in 1973, Greece in 1981; steps taken in the early 1980's led to the admission of Spain and Portugal. Conflicts in national trading interests have so far prevented full economic union, which, as a step toward full political union, was the Community's founding aim.

1 Draft proposal   **4** Revised proposal

COREPER

The Committee of Permanent Representatives, COREPER, consists of senior officials of ambassador rank representing the governments of the member states. They do the detailed work of the Council

COUNCIL OF MINISTERS

The Council of Ministers sends the draft proposal to other Community bodies and delegates its own study of the draft to COREPER. The Council may adopt the draft as Community law, request the Commission to amend it, reject it, or simply take no decision. The Council can adopt its own version, rather than the one proposed by the Commission, only by unanimous agreement

2

3

5

The Council issues laws in the form of: directives, which the member states must implement through their national law-making systems; regulations, which automatically have full force in all member states; and decisions, addressed to a member state, a company, or an individual, which are binding in every respect

ECOSOC

The Economic and Social Committee, ECOSOC, consists of representatives of employers and trade unions and a third group that includes other professional interests such as farmers and consumers. The Commission is not required to amend proposals for new laws in the light of ECOSOC's comments, but it may do so

EUROPEAN PARLIAMENT

The Parliament, the only directly elected institution, is purely consultative. The Commission must submit draft proposals to it, and its opinions must be noted—but not necessarily acted upon. However, it has power over part of the budget and can question the Commission and the Council on their handling of Community matters

6

EUROPEAN ECONOMIC COMMUNITY

Most Community laws are applied to people living in the twelve member states, through their national legal system, in the same way as national laws. Community laws take precedence over national laws

7

EUROPEAN COURT OF JUSTICE

The European Court is the final arbiter on Community law, but it is not an appeal court that can overrule a national court. It may, if requested by a national court, give an interpretation of Community law that the national court is then bound to apply. The Court may amend Community rules if they are incompatible with Community law. It can hear cases brought by member states or individuals against the Community institutions and by the institutions against the member states. It cannot impose fines or prison sentences to enforce its decision

---

8. A scientific law, hypothesis, or phenomenon: *the Faraday effect; photovoltaic effect.* **9. effects.** Physical belongings; goods. **10. effects. a. Sound effects** *(see).* **b. Special effects** *(see).* —See Synonyms at **assets.** —**for effect.** In order to impress or influence. —**in effect. 1.** In fact; actually. **2.** In essence; virtually. —**take effect.** To become operative; gain active force. ~*tr.v.* **effected, -fecting, -fects. 1.** To produce as a result. **2.** To cause to occur; bring about. —See Synonyms at **perform.** —See Usage note at **affect¹.** [Middle English, from Old French, from Latin *effectus,* past participle of *efficere,* to accomplish, perform, work out : *ex-,* out + *facere,* to do.] —**ef·fect·er** *n.* —**ef·fect·i·ble** *adj.*

Synonyms: consequence, outcome, result, sequel, upshot.

ef·fec·tive (ĭ-fĕk′tĭv) *adj.* **1.** Having the intended or expected effect; serving the purpose. **2.** Producing or adapted to produce the desired impression or response; striking: *an effective speech.* **3.** Operative; in effect: *The law is effective immediately.* **4.** Real and actual rather than supposed. **5.** Prepared for use or action in warfare: *We have eight effective troop divisions.* **6.** *Electricity.* Designating an alternating quantity, such as current, having a value equal to the square root of the mean of the squares of the instantaneous values over one cycle. ~*n.* **1.** A member of a military force or a piece of equipment that is ready for action. **2.** The total number of men prepared and available for military action. —**ef·fec·tive·ness** *n.*

Usage: The adjectives *effective, efficacious, effectual,* and *efficient* overlap in meaning but should be distinguished: *effective* and *effectual* may imply proven capacity for doing the job in question, and *efficacious* may suggest having the potential to do it. *Efficient* implies proven capability based on productiveness in operation and especially stresses ability to perform well and economically.

ef·fec·tive·ly (ĭ-fĕk′tĭv-lē) *adv.* **1.** In an effective way. **2.** In effect; for all practical purposes.

ef·fec·tor (ĭ-fĕk′tər) *n.* **1.** A nerve ending that activates either gland secretion or muscular contraction. **2.** A cell or organ, such as a muscle or gland, specialized to respond to nervous stimulation.

ef·fec·tu·al (ĭ-fĕk′chōō-əl) *adj.* **1.** Producing or sufficient to produce a desired effect; fully adequate. **2.** Valid or legally binding. —See Usage note at **effective.** —**ef·fec·tu·al·i·ty** (ĭ-fĕk′chōō-ăl′ə-tē), **ef·fec·tu·al·ness** *n.* —**ef·fec·tu·al·ly** *adv.*

ef·fec·tu·ate (ĭ-fĕk′chōō-āt′) *tr.v.* **-ated, -ating, -ates.** To cause; bring about; effect. [Medieval Latin *effectuāre,* from Latin *efficere,* to accomplish, EFFECT.] —**ef·fec·tu·a·tion** *n.*

ef·fem·i·nate (ĭ-fĕm′ə-nĭt) *adj.* **1.** Having qualities associated with women rather than those regarded as befitting a man; unmanly. Said of a man. **2.** Characterized by weakness or lack of force; not dynamic or vigorous. [Middle English *effeminat,* from Latin *effēminātus,* past participle of *effēmināre,* "to make a woman out of," to make effeminate : *ex-,* out of + *fēmina,* woman.] —**ef·fem·i·na·cy** (ĭ-fĕm′ə-nə-sē) *n.* —**ef·fem·i·nate·ly** *adv.* —**ef·fem·i·nate·ness** *n.*

ef·fen·di (ĭ-fĕn′dē) *n.* **1.** Used in Turkey and the Middle East as a term of respectful address, equivalent to *Sir.* **2.** An educated or respected man in the Ottoman Empire. [Turkish *efendi,* "master," from Medieval Greek *aphentē,* vocative of *aphentēs,* lord, master, from Greek *authentēs.* See **authentic.**]

ef·fer·ent (ĕf′ər-ənt) *adj.* Directed or conducting away from an organ or section; especially, designating nerves that carry impulses from the central nervous system to an effector. Compare **afferent.** ~*n.* An efferent organ or part. [French *efférent,* from Latin *efferēns* (stem *efferent-*), present participle of *efferre,* to carry away : *ex-,* away from + *ferre,* to carry.]

ef·fer·vesce (ĕf′ər-vĕs′) *intr.v.* **-vesced, -vescing, -vesces. 1.** To emit small bubbles of gas, as a carbonated or fermenting liquid does. **2.** To appear and come out of a liquid in bubbles; bubble forth. **3.** To show high spirits; be lively or vivacious. [Latin *effervēscere,* to boil over : *ex-* (intensive) + *fervēscere,* to start to boil, from *fervēre,* to be hot, boil.]

ef·fer·ves·cent (ĕf′ər-vĕs′ənt) *adj.* **1.** Emitting a profusion of small

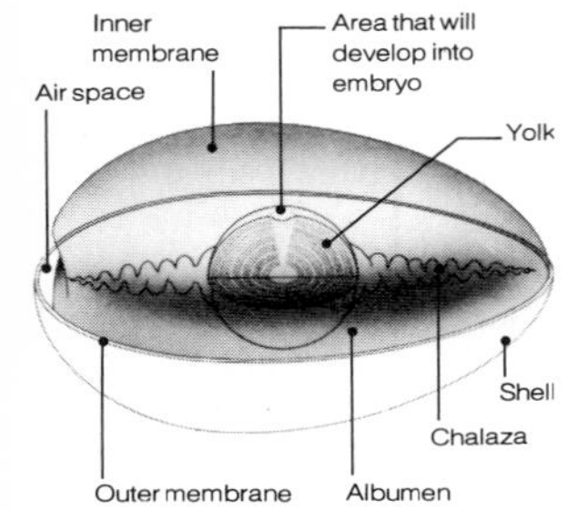
Inner membrane
Area that will develop into embryo
Air space
Yolk
Shell
Chalaza
Outer membrane
Albumen

egg *The embryo inside a bird's egg develops from a tiny disk of cytoplasm on top of the yolk. The watery albumen (the white of the egg) and the yolk are its main sources of nourishment; the twisted strands of albumen, the chalazae, keep the embryo disk upright.*

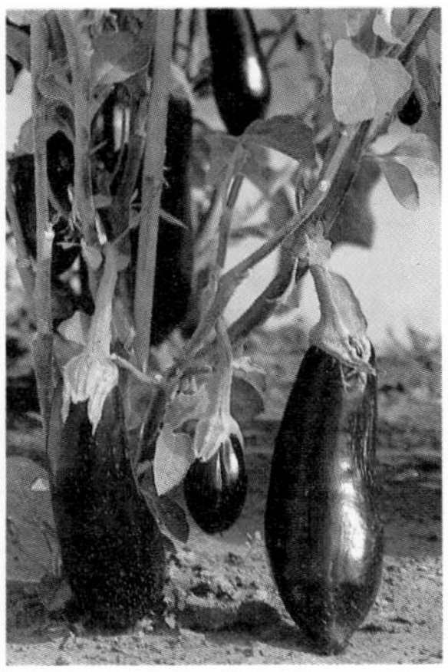

eggplant *The fruit of this tender annual plant, which is native to tropical Asia, is eaten as a vegetable. The variety shown here is "Long Purple."*

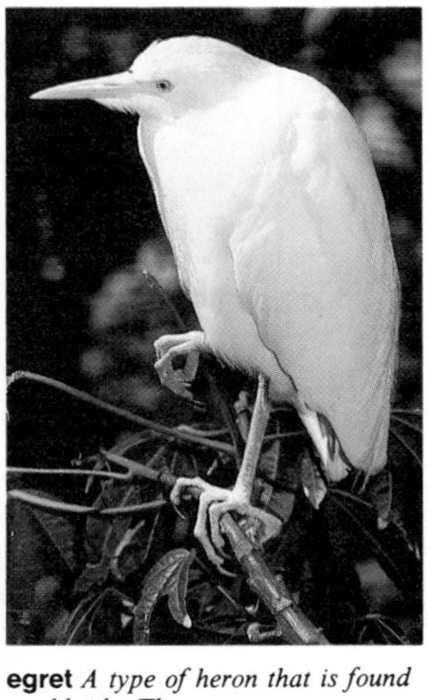

egret *A type of heron that is found worldwide. The great egret produces feathers that were once used to decorate hats. The smaller cattle egret (above) feeds on insects disturbed by the hoofs of grazing animals.*

bubbles of gas; bubbling. **2.** Produced by bubbles of gas: *an effervescent hiss.* **3.** High-spirited; vivacious. **—ef·fer·ves·cence** *n.*

ef·fete (ĭ-fēt′) *adj.* **1.** Exhausted of vitality, force, or effectiveness; depleted of vigor: *effete romanticism.* **2.** Characterized by unproductive self-indulgence, self-absorption, or decadence: *effete manners.* **3.** Unable to produce further offspring or fruit; barren. Said of animals or plants. [Latin *effētus,* worn out by childbearing : *ex-,* out + *fētus,* childbearing, offspring.] **—ef·fete·ly** *adv.* **—ef·fete·ness** *n.*

ef·fi·ca·cious (ĕf′ĭ-kā′shəs) *adj.* Capable of producing the desired effect. —See Usage note at **effective.** [Latin *efficāx* (stem *efficāc-*), effective, from *efficere,* to EFFECT.] **—ef·fi·ca·cious·ly** *adv.* **—ef·fi·ca·cious·ness** *n.*

ef·fi·ca·cy (ĕf′ĭ-kə-sē) *n.* Power or capacity to produce a desired effect; effectiveness. [Latin *efficācia,* from *efficāx,* EFFICACIOUS.]

ef·fi·cien·cy (ĭ-fĭsh′ən-sē) *n., pl.* **-cies. 1. a.** The quality or property of being efficient. **b.** The degree to which this quality is exercised. **2.** *Abbr.* **eff.** The ratio of the effective or useful output to the total input in any system; especially, the ratio of the energy delivered by a machine to the energy supplied for its operation, often expressed as a percentage. **3.** *Informal.* An efficiency apartment.

efficiency apartment *n.* A small, usually furnished apartment with a kitchenette and a private bathroom.

ef·fi·cient (ĭ-fĭsh′ənt) *adj.* **1.** Having a direct effect; causative. **2. a.** Acting or producing effectively with a minimum of waste, expense, or unnecessary effort. **b.** Exhibiting a high ratio of output to input. —See Usage note at **effective.** [Middle English, from Old French, from Latin *efficiēns* (stem *efficient-*), present participle of *efficere,* to EFFECT.] **—ef·fi·cient·ly** *adv.*

efficient cause *n.* That which renders a thing what it is; that which causes an effect. [Translation of Latin *causa efficiens.*]

ef·fi·gy (ĕf′ə-jē) *n., pl.* **-gies. 1.** A painted or sculptured representation of a person, as on a stone wall or monument. **2.** A crude image or dummy fashioned in the likeness of a person, often as an expression of mockery or hatred. **—hang** (or **burn**) **in effigy.** To hang (or burn) the effigy of a hated person in public. [Middle English *effigie,* from Latin *effigiēs,* likeness, image, from *effingere,* to form, portray : *ex-,* out of + *fingere,* to fashion, shape.]

ef·flo·resce (ĕf′lə-rĕs′) *intr.v.* **-resced, -rescing, -resces. 1.** To blossom; flower; bloom. **2.** *Chemistry.* **a.** To become a powder by losing water of crystallization. **b.** To become covered with a powdery deposit, as by evaporation. [Latin *efflōrēscere,* to blossom out : *ex-,* out + *flōrēscere,* inceptive of *flōrēre,* to blossom, from *flōs* (stem *flōr-*), flower.]

ef·flo·res·cence (ĕf′lə-rĕs′əns) *n.* **1.** A state or time of flowering. **2. a.** A gradual process of developing; blossoming. **b.** The highest point; culmination. **3.** *Chemistry.* **a.** The process of efflorescing. **b.** The deposit that results from this process. **c.** A growth of salt crystals on surfaces, such as those of wells, due to evaporation of salt-laden water. **—ef·flo·res·cent** *adj.*

ef·flu·ence (ĕf′lo͞o-əns) *n.* **1.** The act or an instance of flowing out. **2.** Something that flows out or forth; an emanation.

ef·flu·ent (ĕf′lo͞o-ənt) *adj.* Flowing out or forth.
∼*n.* **1.** Something that flows out or forth. **2.** A stream flowing out of a lake or other body of water. **3.** An outflow of a sewer, storage tank, irrigation canal, or other channel. **4.** Liquid waste resulting from an industrial process. **5.** Radioactive waste from a nuclear power station. [Middle English, from Latin *effluēns* (stem *effluent-*), present participle of *effluere,* to flow out : *ex-,* out + *fluere,* to flow.]

ef·flu·vi·um (ĭ-flo͞o′vē-əm) *n., pl.* **-via** (-vē-ə) or **-ums. 1.** An outflow or rising vapor of invisible or barely visible gas or particles. **2.** Foul-smelling vapor or fumes emanating from decaying matter. **3.** An imaginary outflow of imponderable radiation or invisible vapor; an aura. [Latin, from *effluere,* to flow out. See **effluent.**] **—ef·flu·vi·al** *adj.*

ef·flux (ĕf′lŭks′) *n.* Also **ef·flux·ion** (ĭ-flŭk′shən). **1.** An outward flowing; an emanating. **2.** Something that flows out or forth; an emanation. [Latin *efflūxus,* past participle of *effluere,* to flow out. See **effluent.**]

ef·fort (ĕf′ərt) *n.* **1.** The use of physical or mental energy to do something; exertion. **2.** A difficult or tiring exertion of the strength or will: *It was an effort to get up.* **3.** An attempt; especially, an earnest attempt: *Please make an effort to arrive on time.* **4.** Something done or produced through exertion; an achievement or creation: *His most recent symphony is his finest effort so far.* **5.** *Physics.* Force applied against inertia. [Old French *effort, esfort,* from *esforcier,* to force (reflexive *s'esforcier,* to exert oneself), from Vulgar Latin *exfortiāre* (unattested), to show strength : Latin *ex-,* out + *fortis,* strong.] **—ef·fort·ful** *adj.*
Synonyms: *endeavor, exertion, strain.*

ef·fort·less (ĕf′ərt-lĭs) *adj.* Calling for, requiring, or showing little or no effort. **—ef·fort·less·ly** *adv.* **—ef·fort·less·ness** *n.*

ef·front·er·y (ĭ-frŭn′tə-rē) *n., pl.* **-ies.** Impudent and insulting boldness; presumptuous self-assertion; audacity. —See Synonyms at **temerity.** [French *effronterie,* from *effronté,* shameless, from Vulgar Latin *exfrontātus* (unattested), from Late Latin *effrōns* (stem *effront-*), shameless, "barefaced" : *ex-,* out of + *frōns,* forehead (see **front**).]

ef·ful·gent (ĭ-fo͝ol′jənt, ĭ-fŭl′-) *adj.* Shining forth brilliantly; resplendent. [Latin *effulgēns* (stem *effulgent-*), present participle of *effulgēre,* to shine out : *ex-,* out + *fulgēre,* to shine.] **—ef·ful·gence** *n.*

ef·fuse (ĭ-fyo͞os′) *adj. Botany.* Spreading out loosely on a surface. Said especially of flower inflorescences.
∼*v.* (ĭ-fyo͞oz′) **effused, -fusing, -fuses.** —*tr.* To pour or spread out; disseminate. —*intr.* **1.** To spread out. **2.** To exude. **3.** To flow out. [Latin *effūsus,* past participle of *effundere,* to pour out : *ex-,* out + *fundere,* to pour.]

ef·fu·si·om·e·ter (ĭ-fyo͞o′zē-ŏm′ĭ-tər) *n.* An apparatus for determining molecular weights by measuring the rate of effusion of gases.

ef·fu·sion (ĭ-fyo͞o′zhən) *n.* **1. a.** The act or an instance of pouring forth. **b.** Something that is poured forth. **2.** An unrestrained outpouring of feeling, as in speech or writing: *"The devout effusions of sacred eloquence"* (Edmund Burke). **3.** *Pathology.* **a.** The seeping of serous, purulent, or bloody fluid into a body cavity. **b.** The effused fluid. **4.** *Physics.* The flow of gas through an aperture under pressure in circumstances in which the diameter of the aperture is small compared to the mean distance between the gas molecules.

ef·fu·sive (ĭ-fyo͞o′sĭv) *adj.* **1.** Irrepressibly demonstrative. **2.** Unrestrained in emotional expression; gushing. **3.** *Geology.* Poured out in a molten state and then solidified. Said of igneous rock. —See Synonyms at **talkative. —ef·fu·sive·ly** *adv.* **—ef·fu·sive·ness** *n.*

Ef·ik (ĕf′ĭk) *n., pl.* **-iks** or collectively **Efik. 1.** A member of a people of southeastern Nigeria. **2.** The Ibibio language of this people. **—Ef·ik** *adj.*

eft (ĕft) *n.* A newt; especially, the reddish-orange immature terrestrial form of a North American species, *Diemictylus viridescens.* [Middle English *evete,* Old English *efeta*†, lizard.]

E.F.T.A. European Free Trade Association.

eft·soons (ĕft-so͞onz′) *adv.* Also **eft·soon** (-so͞on′). *Archaic.* **1.** Soon afterward. **2.** Once again. [Middle English *eftsōne,* Old English *eftsōna* : *eft,* again + *sōna,* SOON.]

e.g. for example. —See Usage note at **i.e.** [Latin *exempli gratia.*]

Eg. Egypt; Egyptian.

e·gad (ĭ-găd′) *interj.* Used as a mild oath expressing surprise or enthusiasm. [Euphemism for *oh God* or *ah God.*]

e·gal·i·tar·i·an (ĭ-găl′ə-târ′ē-ən) *adj.* **1.** Advocating the doctrine of equal political, economic, and legal rights for all citizens. **2.** Pertaining to or arising from this doctrine.
∼*n.* One who holds or advances egalitarian opinions. [French *égalitaire,* from *égalité,* equality, from Latin *aequālitās,* from *aequālis,* EQUAL.] **—e·gal·i·tar·i·an·ism** *n.*

e·gest (ē-jĕst′) *tr.v.* **egested, egesting, egests.** To discharge or excrete from the body. [Latin *ēgerere* (past participle *ēgestus*), to carry out, expel : *ex-,* out + *gerere,* to carry.] **—e·ges·tion** *n.* **—e·ges·tive** *adj.*

e·ges·ta (ē-jĕs′tə) *pl.n.* Egested matter, especially excrement. [Latin *ēgesta,* neuter plural of Latin *ēgestus.* See **egest.**]

egg[1] (ĕg) *n.* **1.** Any of the female reproductive cells of various animals, consisting usually of an embryo surrounded by nutrient material with a protective covering, and often deposited externally. **2.** A female gamete; ovum. **3.** The oval, thin-shelled ovum of a bird, especially a domestic fowl, used as food. **4.** Something having the characteristic shape of a hen's egg. **5.** *Slang.* A fellow; a person: *a good egg.* **—have egg on one's face.** To be humiliated or embarrassed. **—put** (or **have**) **all one's eggs in one basket.** To risk everything on a single venture, method, or act.
∼*tr.v.* **egged, egging, eggs.** To mix or cover with beaten egg, as in cooking. [Middle English *egge,* from Old Norse *egg.*]

egg[2] *tr.v.* **egged, egging, eggs.** To encourage or incite with taunts, dares, or similar verbal appeals; urge; spur. Used with *on.* [Middle English *eggen,* Old English *eggian,* from Old Norse *eggja.*]

egg-and-dart (ĕg′ən-därt′) *n.* A decorative molding common in classical architecture and in cabinetwork that consists of a series of egg-shaped figures alternating with dart-, anchor-, or tongue-shaped figures.

egg-and-spoon race (ĕg′ən-spo͞on′) *n.* A running race in which competitors must carry an egg in a spoon without dropping it.

egg·beat·er (ĕg′bē′tər) *n.* A kitchen utensil with rotating blades for beating eggs, whipping cream, or mixing cooking ingredients.

egg·cup (ĕg′kŭp′) *n.* A small cup-shaped holder for a boiled egg.

eg·ger, eg·gar (ĕg′ər) *n.* Any of various moths of the family Lasiocampidae, of which the larvae often construct tentlike webs. [From EGG, from its egg-shaped cocoon.]

egg·head (ĕg′hĕd′) *n. Slang.* An intellectual; highbrow: *a lecture that attracted every egghead in town.* [Said to be originally applied to an intellectual who supported (1952) the U.S. Presidential candidate Adlai Stevenson, with reference to Stevenson's baldness.]

egg·nog (ĕg′nŏg′) *n.* A drink consisting of milk and beaten eggs, commonly mixed with rum, brandy, or wine. Also called "nog." [EGG + NOG (original sense "ale").]

egg·plant (ĕg′plănt′, -plänt′) *n.* **1. a.** A tropical Old World plant, *Solanum melongena,* cultivated for its edible fruit. **b.** The glossy, ovoid fruit of the eggplant. Also called "aubergine." **2.** A blackish purple.

egg roll *n.* A cylindrical case of egg dough filled with minced vegetables and often seafood or meat and fried.

egg·shell (ĕg′shĕl′) *n.* **1.** The thin, brittle exterior covering of a bird's egg. **2.** A pale yellow to yellowish white.
∼*adj.* **1.** Of or being a paint surface that has a mat rather than a glossy sheen. **2.** Very brittle and thin, as certain china. **3.** Pale yellow to yellowish white.

egg timer *n.* A small device, usually in the shape of an hourglass, for timing the boiling of an egg.

egg tooth *n.* A structure in embryo birds and reptiles that is used to pierce the eggshell. In birds it is a projection on the beak and in reptiles a temporary tooth.

egg white *n.* The albumen of an egg.

egis. Variant of **aegis.**

eg·lan·tine (ĕg′lən-tīn′, -tēn′) *n.* A rose, the **sweetbrier** *(see).* [Middle English *eglentyn,* from Old French *aiglantine,* from *aiglent,* from Vulgar Latin *aquilentum* (unattested), "prickly," irregularly from Latin *aculeus,* diminutive of *acus,* needle.]

Eg·mont (ĕg′mŏnt′), **Lamoral, Count van** (1522–68). Flemish general and statesman who served in the army of Philip II of Spain. He is the Egmont of Goethe's tragedy of the same name and also of Beethoven's *Egmont* overture.

e·go (ē′gō, ĕg′ō) *n.* **1.** The conscious subject, as designated by the first person singular pronoun; the self. **2.** *Psychoanalysis.* The personality component that is conscious, most immediately controls behavior, and is most in touch with external reality. See **id, super-ego. 3.** *Informal.* **a.** A sense of self-esteem. **b.** Conceit; egotism. [New Latin, from Latin, I.]

e·go·cen·tric (ē′gō-sĕn′trĭk, ĕg′ō-) *adj.* **1.** Thinking or acting with the view that one's self is the center, object, and norm of all experience. **2.** Self-centered; selfish. **3.** *Philosophy.* Real or valid only as perceived or conceived by the individual mind.
~*n.* An egocentric person. —**e·go·cen·tric·i·ty** (ē′gō-sĕn-trĭs′ə-tē, ĕg′ō-) *n.*

ego ideal *n.* **1.** *Psychoanalysis.* An individual's conception of the person he would wish to be, based on identification with persons admired during his development. **2.** Self-idealization.

e·go·ism (ē′gō-ĭz′əm, ĕg′ō-) *n.* **1.** The quality of thinking or acting with only oneself and one's own interests in mind; preoccupation with one's own welfare and advancement. **2.** *Ethics.* **a.** The doctrine that morality has its foundations in self-interest. **b.** The belief that self-interest is the just and proper motive for all human conduct. **3.** Conceit; egotism.

e·go·ist (ē′gō-ĭst, ĕg′ō-) *n.* **1.** One devoted to his own interests and advancement; an egocentric person. **2.** *Ethics.* An adherent of egoism. **3.** An egotist. [French *égoiste,* from EGO.] —**e·go·is·tic** (ē′-gō-ĭs′tĭk, ĕg′ō-), **e·go·is·ti·cal** (-tĭ-kəl) *adj.* —**e·go·is·ti·cal·ly** *adv.*

e·go·ma·ni·a (ē′gō-mā′nē-ə, -mān′yə) *n.* Obsessive or pathological preoccupation with the self; extreme egotism. [New Latin : EGO + -MANIA.] —**e·go·ma·ni·ac** (ē′gō-mā′nē-ăk′, ĕg′ō-) *n.* —**e·go·ma·ni·a·cal** (ē′gō-mə-nī′ə-kəl, ĕg′ō-) *adj.*

e·go·tism (ē′gə-tĭz′əm, ĕg′ə-) *n.* **1.** An inordinately large sense of self-importance; egoism. **2.** The tendency to speak or write of oneself excessively and boastfully. [EGO + -ISM (by analogy with nouns such as NEPOTISM).]

e·go·tist (ē′gə-tĭst, ĕg′ə-) *n.* **1.** A conceited, boastful person. **2.** A person who acts selfishly; an egoist. —**e·go·tis·tic** (ē′gə-tĭs′tĭk, ĕg′-ə-), **e·go·tis·ti·cal** (-tĭ-kəl) *adj.* —**e·go·tis·ti·cal·ly** *adv.*

ego trip *n. Slang.* **1.** An experience that boosts or gratifies the ego. **2.** An act of self-aggrandizement or self-indulgence.

e·go-trip (ē′gō-trĭp′, ĕg′ō-) *intr.v.* **-tripped, -tripping, trips.** *Slang.* To seek personal gratification, as by self-aggrandizement or self-indulgence.

e·gre·gious (ĭ-grē′jəs, -jē-əs) *adj.* Outstandingly bad; blatant; outrageous. [Latin *ēgregius,* "standing out from the herd" : *ex-,* out of + *grex* (stem *greg-*), herd, flock.] —**e·gre·gious·ly** *adv.* —**e·gre·gious·ness** *n.*

e·gress (ē′grĕs′) *n.* **1.** The act of going out; emergence. **2.** The path or opening by means of which one goes out; an exit. **3.** The right of going out: *deny egress.* **4.** *Astronomy.* The emergence of a celestial body from eclipse or occultation. Also called "emersion." [Latin *ēgressus,* from the past participle of *ēgredī,* to go out : *ex-,* out + *gradī,* to go, step.]

e·gret (ē′grĭt, ĕg′rĭt) *n.* Any of several usually white wading birds of the genera *Bubulcus, Casmerodius, Leucophoyx,* and related genera, characteristically having long, showy, drooping plumes during the breeding season. [Middle English *egrete,* from Old French *aigrette,* from Old Provençal *aigreta,* from *aigron,* heron, from Germanic.]

E·gypt (ē′jĭpt). *Abbr.* **Eg.** A country of northeastern Africa, bordering the Mediterranean. It is mainly desert and includes the Sinai peninsula, the upland Eastern desert, and the low-lying Western Desert, with its population concentrated along the fertile Nile Valley. Early Egyptian history is generally divided into 31 dynasties. The Old Kingdom, the third to the sixth dynasties, from *c.* 2700 to *c.* 2200 B.C., reached its peak when the pyramids of Giza were built. Under a succession of vigorous rulers of the early New Kingdom (*c.* 1570–*c.* 1200 B.C.), notably Thutmosis I and Thutmosis II, the kingdom extended its frontiers into Syria and Mesopotamia. The temples of Luxor and Karnak and the famous tomb of Tutankhamun were built during that period. By the end of the 20th dynasty, decline had set in and the Egyptian empire was conquered by the Assyrians in the 7th century B.C. and twice by the Persians. Liberated from Persian rule by Alexander the Great, the kingdom passed at his death to his general Ptolemy, whose descendants ruled until the suicide of Cleopatra VII in 30 B.C. After Egypt was conquered by the Romans, communications were improved and irrigation of the land gave the country a century of renewed wealth. In A.D. 642 it fell to the Arabs and was absorbed into the Islamic world. Other conquerers included the Fatimids (968), who founded Cairo, and Saladin, who restored Egypt to Baghdad in 1171. It was ruled by the Mamelukes from 1250 and was under Turkish rule from 1517 until 1798, when Napoleon made it a French protectorate (until 1801). By the mid-19th century British and French interests in Egypt had intensified, and the opening of the Suez Canal in 1869 gave Egypt international prominence. Britain dominated Egyptian

Egypt

"THE GIFT OF THE NILE"

On rich floodplains, Egyptians created a civilization lasting nearly 3,000 years

The Greek historian Herodotus said that Egypt was given to the Egyptians by the Nile. Along the river's narrow fertile strip, they built one of the world's earliest and greatest civilizations.

It emerged about 3000 B.C. Hieroglyphics, the early Egyptian system of writing, date from about the same time. Until the conquest of Egypt by Alexander the Great in 332 B.C., the country was ruled by a succession of more than 200 kings in 31 dynasties. The kings were regarded as gods.

The Egyptians believed in an afterlife and, to preserve their dead for it, developed mummification. They buried the dead with possessions needed for the afterlife.

The most remarkable Egyptian achievements were in architecture. Using ramps, levers, rollers, and huge numbers of men, they constructed pyramids, tombs, and temples that remain among the wonders of the world.

The Great Pyramid at Giza, just outside Cairo, built as a tomb for Cheops (or Khufu) in about 2650 B.C., contains over two million 2.5-ton blocks and covers 13 acres.

MODEL HOUSE *Complete with pots and food, the house above was made in about 1900 B.C. to be buried with its owner. The style—one or two rooms set in a courtyard—was standard for the wealthier Egyptians. A stairway leads to the roof, which was used for sleeping, baking, and storing food.*

NOBLE AND HIS WIFE *This statue (left), made about 1450 B.C., portrays a couple in conventionally stiff poses clad in wigs and linen skirts. The detailed features suggest that the faces are lifelike, if idealized, portraits.*

HOW THEY FARMED *A carving shows a farmer's plow of about 2000 B.C.—a wooden share, perhaps tipped with metal, a long shaft, and a yoke set on the necks of the two draft animals. Farmers plowed after the annual retreat of the Nile's floodwaters, which left a new, rich layer of silt for growing wheat and barley.*

A RIVER OUTING *A nobleman, Sennufer, and his wife are rowed on the Nile, while a slave serves food and drink. The scene—in traditional style, with heads in profile and shoulders squared to the front—is a mural in Sennufer's tomb, one of hundreds of noblemen's tombs in the ancient capital of Thebes (now Luxor). Above it there is an inscription in hieroglyphics.*

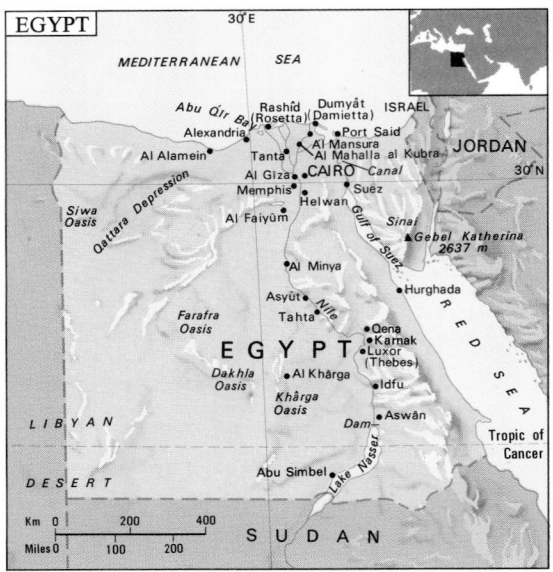

EGYPT

politics, despite nominal Ottoman sovereignty, and made Egypt a protectorate at the outbreak of World War I. It became a sovereign state in 1922. Corruption brought an end to its monarchy with the military coup and the abdication of King Farouk in 1952. Egypt became a republic in 1953. Under Col. Gamal Nasser the Suez Canal was nationalized in 1956, precipitating the Suez crisis and invasion by Israeli and Anglo-French forces, who later withdrew on orders from the United Nations. From 1958 to 1961 Egypt combined with Syria as the United Arab Republic. In 1967 Egypt fought the Six-Day War against Israel and lost the Sinai peninsula. Under President Anwar el-Sadat the country fought another Arab-Israeli war (1973) and signed the Camp David peace treaty with Israel (1979). Sadat was assassinated by Muslim fanatics (1981), and Vice President Hosni Mubarak succeeded him. Despite the lack of water, the Aswan High Dam and other modern irrigation systems have greatly increased the production of cotton (the chief cash crop), rice, millet, corn, sugar cane, fruit, and vegetables. Since the 1950's heavy industries (iron, steel, and engineering) have been introduced and are now supplied with power from the Aswan High Dam. Area, 1,001,449 square kilometers (386,559 square miles). Population, 52,400,000. Capital, Cairo.

E·gyp·tian (ĭ-jĭp′shən) *adj. Abbr.* **Eg.** **1.** Of or pertaining to Egypt, its people, or its culture. **2.** *Obsolete.* Of or pertaining to Gypsies. *~n.* **1.** A native or citizen of Egypt. **2.** The extinct Hamitic language spoken by the ancient Egyptians. **3.** *Obsolete.* A Gypsy.

Egyptian clover *n.* A plant, **berseem** (see).

Egyptian cotton *n.* A long-staple, fine cotton grown chiefly in northern Africa.

E·gyp·tol·o·gy (ē′jĭp-tŏl′ə-jē) *n.* The study of the language, culture, and artefacts of the ancient Egyptian civilization. **—E·gyp·to·log·i·cal** (ĭ-jĭp′tə-lŏj′ĭ-kəl) *adj.* **—E·gyp·tol·o·gist** *n.*

eh (ā, ĕ) *interj.* **1.** Used interrogatively: *Eh? What was that?* **2.** Used in asking for confirmation: *He is a shrewd one, eh?*

EHF extremely high frequency.

Eh·ren·burg (âr′ən-bŏŏrg′), **Ilya Gregorievich** (1891–1967). Russian writer who was awarded the Stalin Prize twice, for *The Fall of Paris* (1941) and *The Storm* (1948). In the West he is best known for his novel *The Thaw* (1954), which described repression under Stalin's regime.

Ehr·lich (âr′lĭKH), **Paul** (1854–1915). German bacteriologist who discovered arsenic compounds that were used to treat syphilis before the discovery of antibiotics. He shared the Nobel Prize in physiology and medicine with Ilya Metchnikoff (1845–1916) in 1908.

EHV extra high voltage.

E.I. East Indian; East Indies.

Eich·mann (īKH′män′), **Adolf** (1906–62). German official of the Nazi S.S. As head of the Gestapo's Jewish section after 1939, he was chiefly responsible for the murder of millions of Jews in occupied Europe. Arrested by the Allies in 1945, he escaped and fled to South America. He was captured by the Israeli secret service in Argentina (1960), taken to Jerusalem, tried, and executed (1962).

ei·der (ī′dər) *n.* Any of several sea ducks of the genus *Somateria* and related genera, especially *S. mollissima*, of northern regions, the females of which are the source of eiderdown. The males have predominantly black and white plumage. [Icelandic *ædhur* (genitive *ædhar*), from Old Norse *ædhr.*]

ei·der-down (ī′dər-doun′) *n.* **1.** The downy breast feathers of the female eider duck, used as stuffing for quilts and pillows. **2.** A quilt stuffed with eiderdown. **3.** A warm, napped fabric. [Probably from German *Eiderdaune,* from Icelandic *ædhardúnn* : *ædhar,* genitive of *ædhur,* EIDER + *dúnn,* DOWN.]

eider *The soft down plucked from the breast of the female eider is used to stuff pillows and quilts. Eiders breed in colonies in northern regions. The males are distinguished from the females by their distinctive black and white plumage.*

ei·det·ic (ī-dĕt′ĭk) *adj.* **1.** Especially vivid but unreal. Said of images experienced especially in childhood. **2.** Of or pertaining to vivid mental images: *an eidetic memory.* *~n.* One who experiences vivid mental images. [German *eidetisch,* from Greek *eidētikos,* relating to images or knowledge, from *eidēsis,* knowledge, from *eidos,* form, shape.] **—ei·det·i·cal·ly** *adv.*

ei·do·lon (ī-dō′lən) *n., pl.* **-lons** or **-la** (-lə). **1.** A phantom; an apparition. **2.** An image of an ideal. [Greek *eidōlon,* from *eidos,* form, shape.]

Eif·fel Tower (ī′fəl, ĕ-fĕl′) *n.* An iron tower on the left bank of the Seine in Paris, now standing 300 meters (984 feet) high, designed by the French engineer Alexandre Gustave Eiffel (1823–1923) and originally erected for the Paris Exhibition of 1889.

eigen– *prefix.* Indicates proper or characteristic; for example, **eigenvalue.** [German, "own."]

ei·gen·func·tion (ī′gən-fŭngk′shən) *n. Physics.* An allowed function for a system as determined by wave mechanics, enabling a meaningful solution to be obtained from the Schrödinger wave equation.

ei·gen·val·ue (ī′gən-văl′yōō) *n. Physics.* Any of a set of allowed energies of a particle in a system as determined by wave mechanics.

Ei·ger (ī′gər). Mountain (3,970 meters; 13,025 feet) in the Bernese Oberland, central Switzerland. Its steep north face was not conquered until 1938.

eight (āt) *n.* **1. a.** The cardinal number that is one more than seven. **b.** A symbol representing this, such as 8, VIII, or viii. **2.** A set made up of eight persons or things. **3. a.** The eighth in a series. **b.** A playing card marked with eight pips. **4.** Eight parts: *cut in eight.* **5.** A size, as in clothing, designated as eight. **6. a.** An eight-oared racing shell. **b.** A rowing crew of eight people. **7.** Eight hours after midnight or midday; eight o'clock. **8.** A **figure eight** (see). [Middle English *eighte, eihte,* Old English *eahta.*] **—eight** *adj.* **—eight-fold** (āt′fōld′) *adj. & adv.*

eight ball *n.* A black pool ball bearing the number eight that may place a player at a disadvantage. **—behind the eight ball.** *Slang.* In an unfavorable, disadvantageous, or uncomfortable position.

eight·een (ā-tēn′) *n.* **1. a.** The cardinal number that is one more than 17. **b.** A symbol representing this, such as 18, XVIII, or xviii. **2.** A set made up of 18 persons or things. **3.** The eighteenth in a series. **4.** A size, as in clothing, designated as eighteen. [Middle English *eightetene, eihtene,* Old English *eahtatīene* : EIGHT + -TEEN.] **—eight·een** *adj.*

eight·een·mo (ā-tēn′mō′) *n., pl.* **-mos.** A size of a page or a book, **octodecimo** (see). [EIGHTEEN + -MO.] **—eight·een·mo** *adj.*

eight·eenth (ā-tēnth′) *n.* **1.** The ordinal number 18 in a series. **2.** One of 18 equal parts. **—eight·eenth** *adj. & adv.*

eighth (ātth, āth) *n.* **1.** The ordinal number eight in a series. **2.** One of eight equal parts. **—eighth** *adj. & adv.*

eighth note *n. Music.* A note having one eighth the time value of a whole note.

eight·i·eth (ā′tē-ĭth) *n.* **1.** The ordinal number 80 in a series. **2.** One of 80 equal parts. **—eight·i·eth** *adj. & adv.*

eight·some reel (āt′səm) *n.* A Scottish dance in which eight people take part.

eight·vo (āt′vō′) *n., pl.* **-vos.** A size of a page or a book, **octavo** (see). [EIGHT + (OCTA)VO.] **—eight·vo** *adj.*

eight·y (ā′tē) *n., pl.* **-ies. 1. a.** The cardinal number that is ten more than seventy. **b.** A symbol representing this, such as 80 or LXXX. **2.** The eightieth in a series. **3.** A set made up of 80 persons or things. **4.** A size, as in clothing, designated as 80. **5. eighties. a.** The range of numbers from 80 to 89, considered as a range of age, price, temperature, or the like. **b.** The years numbered 80-89 in a century. Also used adjectively: *an eighties fashion.* [Middle English *eigh(te)ty,* Old English *eahtatig* : *eahta,* EIGHT + -*tig,* -TY (ten).] **—eight·y** *adj.*

Eijk·man (īk′män′), **Christiaan** (1858–1930). Dutch physician. He was awarded the Nobel Prize in physiology and medicine with F.G. Hopkins (1929) for his work on the causes of beriberi.

eikon. Variant of **icon.**

Eilat. See **Elat.**

–ein. Variant of **-in.**

Eind·ho·ven (īnt′hō′vən). Industrial town of North Brabant province in the Netherlands. It manufactures electrical goods, motor vehicles, textiles, plastics, and cigars.

ein·korn (īn′kôrn′) *n.* A one-seeded wheat, *Triticum monococcum,* grown in arid regions. [German *Einkorn* : *ein,* one, from Old High German *ein* + *Korn,* corn, grain, from Old High German *korn.*]

Ein·stein (īn′stīn′), **Albert** (1879–1955). U.S. physicist, born in Germany. His special and general theories of relativity revolutionized man's thinking about the nature of space and time. Einstein showed that the mass of a body is a measure of its energy content. He expressed his findings in the equation known as Einstein's law. Einstein was awarded the Nobel Prize in physics (1921) for his work in explaining the photoelectric effect.

ein·stein·i·um (īn-stī′nē-əm) *n. Symbol* **Es** A synthetic transuranic element first produced by neutron irradiation of uranium in a thermonuclear explosion. It has 12 known isotopes with half-lives ranging between 1.2 minutes and 270 days and mass numbers from 245 to 256. Atomic number 99. [New Latin, after Albert EINSTEIN.]

Einstein shift *n. Astronomy.* A small displacement toward the red in a star's spectrum, predicted by Einstein's general theory of relativity and caused by the interaction between the radiation and a gravitational field.

Einstein's law *n.* **1.** The law that $E = mc^2$, where E is the energy associated with a mass *m* and *c* is the speed of light. Also called "Einstein's equation." **2.** The law that the energy of an electron emitted in the photoelectric effect is $h\nu - \Phi$, where ν is the frequency of the incident radiation, Φ is the work function of the electron emitter, and *h* is the Planck constant.

Eire. See **Ireland.** [Irish Gaelic *Éire,* from Old Irish *Ériu.* See **Erin.**]

eirenic, eirenical. Variants of **irenic.**

ei·ren·i·con, i·ren·i·con (ī-rĕn'ĭ-kŏn', -kən) *n.* A proposal that attempts to create harmony between conflicting viewpoints. [Greek, from *eirēnikos,* relating to peace, from *eirēnē,* peace.]

ei·se·ge·sis (ī'sə-jē'sĭs) *n., pl.* **-ses** (-sēz'). An explanation or analysis, especially of a Biblical text, using one's own ideas. Compare **exegesis.** [19th century : from Greek *eis,* into + *-egesis,* as in EXEGESIS (with which the term was coined to contrast).]

Ei·sen·how·er (ī'zən-hou'ər), **Dwight David** (1890-1969). U.S. general and 34th President of the United States (1953–61). In 1943 he was made supreme commander of the Allied Expeditionary Forces, and he launched the D-Day invasion of Europe in 1944. In 1950 he was made supreme commander of NATO but resigned when he won the Republican Presidential nomination in 1952.

Ei·sen·stein (ī'zən-stīn'), **Sergei Mikhailovich** (1898–1948). Russian film director whose work included *Strike* (1924), *Battleship Potemkin* (1925), and *October* (1927), a film about the Bolshevik revolution. His first sound film was *Alexander Nevsky* (1938). His last film, *Ivan the Terrible,* was intended to be a trilogy, but he died after completing only the first two parts.

ei·stedd·fod (ī-stĕ*th*'vôd', ā-stĕ*th*'-) *n., pl.* **-fods** or **-fodau** (ī-stĕ*th*'vô'-dī'). Any of various annual assemblies of or competitions between Welsh poets and musicians. [Welsh, "session," "a sitting" : *eistedd,* to sit, from *sedd,* seat + *-fod,* from *bod,* to be.]

ei·ther (ē'*th*ər, ī'*th*ər) *pron.* One or the other: *Choose either.*
~*conj.* Used before the first of two or more stated alternatives, the following alternatives being signaled by *or*: *Either we go now, or we remain here forever.*
~*adj.* **1.** One or the other; any one of two: *Wear either coat.* **2.** One and the other; each: *She wore rings on either hand.*
~*adv.* Likewise; any more so; also. Used as an intensive following negative statements: *If you don't order a dessert, I won't either.* [Middle English *aither, either,* Old English *ǣgther, ǣghwæther.*]
Usage: *Either* is normally used to mean "one of two," although it is sometimes used of three or more: *either corner of the triangle.* When referring to more than two, *any* or *any one* is preferred. • *Either* takes a singular verb: *Either plant grows in the shade.* Sometimes it is used informally with a plural verb, especially when followed by *of* and a plural: *I doubt whether either of them are available.* But such use is usually considered unacceptable in formal writing. • In *either . . . or* constructions, the two conjunctions should be followed by parallel elements. The following is held to be incorrect: *You may either have the ring or the bracelet* (properly, *You may have either the ring or the bracelet).* The following is also incorrect: *He can take either the examination offered to all applicants or ask for a personal interview* (properly, *He can either take . . .*). • When all the elements in an *either . . . or* construction are singular, the verb is singular: *Either Mary's father or Tom's mother is coming.* When one element is singular and the other plural, it is sometimes suggested that the verb should agree with whichever element is closest to it: *Either Kim or the boys are going* but *Either the boys or Kim is going.* Some traditionalists, however, insist that such constructions should be avoided entirely and that substitutes such as *Either Kim is going, or the boys are* must be found for them. There is no generally accepted rule in these cases. See also Usage notes at **everyone** and **neither.**

ei·ther-or (ē'*th*ər-ôr', ī'*th*ər-) *adj.* Requiring a choice between two exclusive alternatives: *an either-or situation.*

e·jac·u·late (ĭ-jăk'yə-lāt') *v.* **-lated, -lating, -lates.** —*tr.* **1.** To eject or discharge abruptly; especially, to discharge (semen) in orgasm. **2.** To utter suddenly and passionately; exclaim. —*intr.* To discharge semen.
~*n.* (-lĭt). Semen ejaculated in orgasm. [Latin *ējaculārī* (past participle *ējaculātus*) : *ex-,* out + *jaculārī,* to throw, shoot, from *jaculum,* dart, from *jacere,* to throw.] **—e·jac·u·la·tor** *n.*

e·jac·u·la·tion (ĭ-jăk'yə-lā'shən) *n.* **1.** The act of ejaculating. **2.** An abrupt discharge of fluid; especially, an emission of seminal fluid. **3. a.** A sudden, emphatic utterance; an exclamation. **b.** A brief, pious utterance or prayer.

e·jac·u·la·to·ry (ĭ-jăk'yə-lə-tôr'ē, -tōr'ē) *adj.* Also **e·jac·u·la·tive** (-lā'-tĭv, -lə-tĭv). **1.** Of or pertaining to ejaculation. **2.** Pertaining to or constituting a sudden, brief utterance; exclamatory.

e·ject (ĭ-jĕkt') *v.* **ejected, ejecting, ejects.** —*tr.* **1.** To throw out forcefully; expel. **2.** To compel to leave; evict. **3.** To emit. —*intr.* To make an emergency exit by ejection capsule or seat. [Middle English *ejecten,* from Latin *ēicere* (past participle *ējectus*) : *ex-,* out + *jacere,* to throw.]
Synonyms: *evict, expel, throw out.*

e·jec·ta (ĭ-jĕk'tə) *pl.n.* Ejected matter, as that from an erupting volcano. [New Latin, from Latin *ējectus,* ejected. See **eject.**]

e·jec·tion (ĭ-jĕk'shən) *n.* **1.** The act of ejecting or the condition of being ejected. **2.** Ejected matter.

ejection seat *n.* Also **ejector seat.** A seat designed to eject an occupant, as the pilot, clear of an aircraft and enable him to parachute to the ground in an emergency.

e·ject·ment (ĭ-jĕkt'mənt) *n.* **1.** The act of ejecting; eviction; dispossession. **2.** *Law.* An action to regain possession of real estate held by another.

e·jec·tor (ĭ-jĕk'tər) *n.* **1.** A person or thing that ejects. **2.** A device in a gun that ejects the empty shell after each firing.

Ekaterinburg. See **Sverdlovsk.**

eke¹ (ēk) *tr.v.* **eked, eking, ekes.** **1.** To supplement with great effort; strain to fill out: *He eked out his income by working at night.* **2.** To earn with great effort or strain. Used with *out*: *eke out a living.* **3.** To cause (a limited resource) to last longer by careful management: *They eked out their emergency rations for a whole week.* [Middle English *eken,* Old English *ēacan,* to increase.]

eke² *adv. Archaic.* Also. [Middle English *ec, eke,* Old English *ēac.*]

EKG electrocardiogram; electrocardiograph.

e·kis·tics (ĭ-kĭs'tĭks) *n. Used with a singular verb.* The science of human settlements, including town or community planning and design. [Greek *oikistikē,* feminine of *oikistikos,* of settlements, from *oikizein,* to settle, from *oikos,* house. See **ecumenical.**] **—e·kis·tic, e·kis·ti·cal** *adj.* **—ek·is·ti·cian** (ĕk'ĭ-stĭsh'ən) *n.*

e·kue·le (ā-kwā'lā) *n., pl.* **ekuele.** The basic monetary unit of Equatorial Guinea, equal to 100 centimos. See feature at **currency.** [Native word in Equatorial Guinea.]

el¹ (ĕl) *n.* The letter *l.*

el² *n. Informal.* An elevated railway.

el. elevation.

e·lab·o·rate (ĭ-lăb'ər-ĭt) *adj.* **1.** Planned or executed with painstaking attention to numerous parts or details. **2.** Rich in detail; complicated; ornate.
~*v.* (-ə-rāt') **elaborated, -rating, -rates.** —*tr.* **1.** To work out with care and detail; develop thoroughly. **2.** To produce by effort; create. **3.** To add more detail to; make more complex; enrich. **4.** *Physiology.* To convert (food, for example) into a more complex chemical state for use by the body. —*intr.* To express oneself at greater length or in greater detail; provide further information. Often used with *on* or *upon.* [Latin *ēlabōrātus,* past participle of *ēlabōrāre,* "to work out" : *ex-,* out + *labōrāre,* to work, from *labor,* work.] **—e·lab·o·rate·ly** *adv.* **—e·lab·o·rate·ness** *n.* **—e·lab·o·ra·tion** (ĭ-lăb'ə-rā'shən) *n.* **—e·lab·o·ra·tor** *n.*

Elagabalus. See **Heliogabalus.**

E·laine (ĭ-lān). One of two women in Arthurian legend who loved Lancelot: **a.** One who died of unrequited love for him. **b.** One who was the mother of Galahad by Lancelot.

El A·la·mein (ĕl ăl'ə-mān'). Railway junction on the coast road of northern Egypt. It gave its name to a decisive battle of World War II when the British Eighth Army defeated the German Afrika Corps.

E·lam (ē'ləm). Also **Su·si·a·na** (sōō'zē-ä'nə, -ā'nə). Ancient country now in Iran. It was established east of the Tigris *c.* 3000 B.C., and Susa, its capital, later became a capital of the Persian Achaemenid Empire. The Elamites were thought to be descended from Shem, the son of Noah.

E·lam·ite (ē'lə-mīt') *n.* Also **E·lam·it·ic** (ē'lə-mĭt'ĭk) (for sense 2). **1.** A native or inhabitant of Elam. **2.** An unclassified language spoken by the ancient Elamites. In this sense, also called "Susian." **—E·lam·ite, E·lam·it·ic** *adj.*

é·lan (ā-läɴ, ā-län') *n.* **1.** Enthusiastic vigor and liveliness. **2.** Style; flair: *played the violin with élan.* [French *élan,* from Old French *eslan,* a rush, dash, from *eslancer,* to throw out : *es-,* out, from Latin *ex-* + *lancer,* to throw, from Late Latin *lanceāre,* to throw a lance, from Latin *lancea,* LANCE.]

e·land (ē'lənd) *n.* Either of two large African antelopes, *Taurotragus oryx* or *T. derbianus,* having a light-brown or grayish coat, a shoulder hump, and spirally twisted horns. [Afrikaans, from Dutch *eland,* elk, from late Middle Dutch *elen, elant,* from (obsolete) German *elen, elend,* from (Old) Lithuanian *ellenis,* stag.]

eland *The largest antelope in the world, the giant eland,* Taurotragus derbianus, *stands up to 1.8 meters (6 feet) tall at the shoulder and can weigh nearly a ton. It was once common in central and southern Africa, but its numbers have been reduced by hunting.*

élan vi·tal (vē-täl') *n.* The vital force hypothesized by Henri Bergson as a source of causation and evolution in nature. See **Bergsonism.** [French, "vital ardor."]

el·a·pid (ĕl'ə-pĭd) *n.* Any of various venomous snakes of the family Elapidae, which includes the cobras and coral snakes.
~*adj.* Of or belonging to the Elapidae. [New Latin *Elapidae,* from Medieval Greek *elaps* (stem *elapid-*), variant of Greek *elops,* a fish.]

e·lapse (ĭ-lăps') *intr.v.* **elapsed, elapsing, elapses.** To pass; slip by. Used of time.
~*n.* Passage of time: *returned to school after an elapse of 10 years.* [Latin *ēlābī* (past participle *ēlapsus*) : *ex-,* away + *lābī,* to slip, glide.]

elapsed time *n.* The measured duration of an event; especially, the actual time spent in transit, as in flight, by a moving body.

e·las·mo·branch (ĭ-lăz'mə-brăngk') *n.* Any of numerous fishes of the subclass Elasmobranchii within the class Chondricthyes, characterized by a cartilaginous skeleton and including the sharks, rays, and skates. [New Latin *Elasmobranchii,* "plate-gilled ones" : Greek *elasmos,* metal plate, from *elaunein,* to drive, beat + -BRANCH.] **—e·las·mo·branch** *adj.*

e·las·mo·saur (ĭ-lăz'mə-sôr', -sōr') *n.* Also **e·las·mo·sau·rus** (ĭ-lăz'-mə-sôr'əs, -sōr'əs) An extinct marine reptile that had a very long neck. [New Latin *elasmosaurus,* from Greek *elasmos,* metal plate (see **elasmobranch**) + *sauros,* lizard.]

e·las·tance (ĭ-lăs'təns) *n. Electricity.* The reciprocal of capacitance, measured in reciprocal farads (darafs).

e·las·tic (ĭ-lăs'tĭk) *adj.* **1.** *Physics.* **a.** Returning or capable of returning to an initial form or state after deformation. **b.** Conserving total kinetic energy of translation. Said of certain collisions. **2.** Capable

of adapting to change or a variety of circumstances; flexible: *an elastic schedule.* **3.** Quick to recover, as from disappointment, depression, or adversity; resilient: *an elastic spirit.* **4.** Springy; firm. **5.** Made of or containing elastic: *elastic thread.*
~*n.* **1. a.** A flexible stretchable fabric made with interwoven strands of rubber or an imitative synthetic fiber. **b.** Something, as a garter, made of this fabric. **2.** A rubber band *(see).* [New Latin *elasticus,* from Late Greek *elastikos,* from Greek *elastos, elatos,* beaten, from *elaunein,* to drive.] —**e·las·ti·cal·ly** *adv.*

elastic band *n.* A rubber band *(see).*

elastic collision *n.* A collision of particles in which the total kinetic energy of translation is conserved.

e·las·tic·i·ty (ĭ-lăs′tĭs′ə-tē, ē′lăs-) *n., pl.* **-ties. 1.** The condition or property of being elastic; resilience; flexibility. **2.** *Physics.* **a.** The property of returning to an initial form or state following deformation. **b.** The degree to which this property is exhibited.

e·las·ti·cized (ĭ-lăs′tə-sīzd′) *adj.* Made with elastic thread.

e·las·ti·ciz·er (ĭ-lăs′tə-sī′zər) *n.* An additive that increases the elasticity of a solid propellant to prevent cracking of the propellant grain in the combustion chamber.

elastic limit *n.* The maximum stress that can be applied to a body or substance without causing a permanent deformation.

e·las·tin (ĭ-lăs′tĭn) *n. Biochemistry.* A protein that is the principal component of *elastic tissue,* found in the walls of arteries, the dermis of the skin, and other elastic structures. [ELAST(IC) + -IN.]

e·las·to·mer (ĭ-lăs′tə-mər) *n.* Any of various polymers having the elastic properties of natural rubber. [Greek *elastos,* ELASTIC + -MER(E).]

E·las·to·plast (ĭ-lăs′tə-plăst′) *n.* A trademark for an adhesive surgical dressing.

E·lat, Ei·lat (ā-lät′). Israeli port on the Gulf of Aqaba, the country's only outlet to the Red Sea.

e·late (ĭ-lāt′) *tr.v.* **elated, elating, elates.** To raise the spirits of; excite feelings of pride or optimism in; encourage.
~*adj.* Elated; joyful; lively. [Latin *ēlātus* (past participle of *efferre,* to carry out, lift up) : *ex-,* out + *-lātus,* "carried."]

e·lat·ed (ĭ-lā′tĭd) *adj.* In high spirits; lively and joyful. —**e·lat·ed·ly** *adv.* —**e·lat·ed·ness** *n.*

el·a·ter (ĕl′ə-tər) *n.* **1.** An elaterid beetle. **2.** *Botany.* An elongated, often spirally thickened filament occurring in the spore-bearing structures of liverworts and other bryophytes, thought to aid spore dispersal. [New Latin, from Greek *elatēr,* driver, from *elaunein,* to drive.]

el·a·ter·id (ĭ-lăt′ər-ĭd) *n.* Any of numerous beetles of the family Elateridae, which includes the click beetles. [New Latin *Elateridae,* from *elater,* elongated filament, ELATER.] —**el·a·ter·id** *adj.*

el·a·te·ri·um (ĕl′ə-tîr′ē-əm) *n.* A sediment produced from the squirting cucumber and containing a crystalline substance used as a purgative. [Latin, from Greek *elatērion,* squirting cucumber, from *elatērios,* purgative, from *elaunein,* to drive.]

e·la·tion (ĭ-lā′shən) *n.* An exalted feeling arising typically from a sense of triumph, achievement, or relief.

E layer *n.* A region, or any of various layers in the region, of the ionosphere, occurring between about 90 kilometers (55 miles) and 150 kilometers (95 miles) above the earth and influencing long-distance communications by strongly reflecting radio waves in the range from one to three megahertz. Also called "E region," "Heaviside layer," "Kennelly-Heaviside layer." [*E* (arbitrary designation) + LAYER.]

El·ba (ĕl′bə). Largest island (223 square kilometers; 86 square miles) in the Tuscan Archipelago, part of Italy's Livorno province. Napoleon I spent a year in exile on Elba (1814–15).

Elbe (ĕl′bə, ĕlb). *Czech* **La·be** (lä′bĕ). River in central Europe. It rises on the south side of the Riesengebirge in northeastern Bohemia, Czechoslovakia, and flows 1,167 kilometers (725 miles) into Germany, passing Dresden and Magdeburg, and flowing through Hamburg and into the North Sea at Cuxhaven.

el·bow (ĕl′bō′) *n.* **1. a.** The joint or bend of the arm between the forearm and the upper arm. **b.** The bony outer projection of this joint. **c.** The part of a garment that covers this joint. **2.** A joint, as of a bird or quadruped, corresponding to the human elbow. **3.** Something having a bend or angle similar to an elbow, especially: **a.** A length of pipe with a sharp bend in it. **b.** A sharp bend in a river or a road. —**at one's elbow.** Close at hand; nearby. —**bend (or lift) an elbow.** *Informal.* To drink alcohol; especially, to drink too much. —**up to the elbows in** (or **with**). Busily occupied with; engrossed in.
~*v.* **elbowed, -bowing, -bows.** —*tr.* **1. a.** To push, jostle, or shove with or as if with the elbows. **b.** To make (one's way) by such pushing, jostling, or shoving. **2.** To knock or hit with one's elbow. —*intr.* To push, jostle, or shove one's way. [Middle English *elbowe,* Old English *elnboga,* "bow of the forearm" : ELL + BOW.]

elbow grease *n. Informal.* The vigorous exertion of energy, especially in strenuous physical effort.

el·bow·room (ĕl′bō-rōōm′, -rŏŏm′) *n.* **1.** Room enough to move around or function in. **2.** Adequate scope or leeway.

El·brus or **El·bruz, Mount** (ĕl-brōōz′). Highest mountain in Europe, lying in the Caucasus range. It consists of two extinct volcanic peaks, one to the west rising to 5,633 meters (18,481 feet).

el Cid (ĕl sĭd′), born Rodrigo (or Ruy) Díaz de Vivar (c. 1060–99). Spanish soldier and national hero. He fought against the Moors in the service of Ferdinand I and Sancho II of Castile, but was banished from Castile in 1081 by Alfonso VI, who feared him as a rival.

He then fought for the Moorish rulers of Saragossa against Christians and Moors and in 1094 conquered the kingdom of Valencia, which he ruled until his death. His exploits were recounted in the anonymous 12th-century epic *The Song of the Cid.*

eld·er¹ (ĕl′dər) *n.* **1.** An older person. **2.** An ancestor; a predecessor; a forefather. **3.** An older, influential man of a family, tribe, or community. **4. a.** One of the governing officers of a church. **b.** A member of the higher order of priesthood in the Mormon Church.
~*adj.* Born before; older; especially, being the older of two members of a family. [Middle English *eldre,* Old English *ieldra, eldra.*] —**el·der·ship** *n.*
Usage: *Elder* and *eldest* refer only to people; *older* and *oldest* apply also to things. There is also a difference in construction: *elder* is not followed by *than,* and neither *elder* nor *eldest* can be used without *the* when following a verb, as in *John is the elder* (but *John is older/John is older than Mary*).

eld·er² *n.* **1.** Any of various shrubs or small trees of the genus *Sambucus,* having clusters of small white flowers and red or blackish berrylike fruits. Also called "elderberry." **2.** Any of several similar trees or shrubs. [Middle English *eller, eldre,* Old English *ellaern, ellen.*]

el·der·ber·ry (ĕl′dər-bĕr′ē) *n., pl.* **-ries. 1.** The small, edible fruit of an elder, used to make wine or preserves. **2.** A shrub or tree producing such fruit; an elder.

eld·er·ly (ĕl′dər-lē) *adj.* Rather old. —See Synonyms at **old.** —**el·der·li·ness** *n.*

elder statesman *n.* An elderly person, usually a retired statesman, who acts as an unofficial adviser on national problems.

eld·est (ĕl′dĭst) *adj.* Oldest. Said of a person. —See Usage note at **elder.** [Middle English *eldest,* Old English *ieldesta, eldesta.*]

El Do·ra·do (ĕl′ də-rä′dō) *n.* **1.** A legendary kingdom or city in Spanish America rich in precious metals and jewels, sought after by 16th-century explorers. **2.** Any place of fabulous wealth or opportunity. [Spanish, "the gilded (one)" : *el,* the, from Latin *ille,* that + *dorado,* past participle of *dorar,* to gild, from Latin *deaurāre* : *de-,* thoroughly + *aurum,* gold.]

E·le·a (ē-lē′ə). Ancient Greek colony in southern Italy, site of the founding of the Eleatic school of philosophy.

El·ea·nor of Aq·ui·taine (ĕl′ə-nər, -nôr′; ăk′wə-tān′) (c. 1122–1204). Queen consort of Louis VII of France and subsequently of Henry II of England. Her marriage to Louis VII was annulled in 1152. She then married Henry, adding to his lands of Normandy and Anjou her vast possessions in Aquitaine. She bore him three daughters and five sons, including the future English kings Richard I and John.

Eleanor of Cas·tile (kă-stēl′) (died 1290). Queen consort of Edward I of England, daughter of Ferdinand III of Castile. She died in 1290, and in her memory Edward had crosses erected at 12 stages of her funeral procession from Nottinghamshire to London.

El·e·at·ic (ĕl′ē-ăt′ĭk) *adj.* Of or characteristic of Elea or the school of philosophy founded there in the 6th and 5th centuries B.C. by Xenophanes and Parmenides.
~*n.* An adherent of the Eleatic school, which held immutable being to be the only knowable reality and change and sensory perceptions to be illusory. —**El·e·at·i·cism** (ĕl′ē-ăt′ĭ-sĭz′əm) *n.*

elec. electric; electrical; electrician; electricity.

el·e·cam·pane (ĕl′ĭ-kăm-pān′) *n.* A tall, coarse plant, *Inula helenium,* native to Eurasia, having rayed yellow flowers. [Middle English *elycampane,* from Old French *enule campane,* from Medieval Latin *enula campāna* : *enula,* from Latin *inula,* elecampane, from Greek *helenion* + *campāna,* variant of Latin *campānea,* feminine of *campāneus,* of the field, from *campus,* field (see camp).]

e·lect (ĭ-lĕkt′) *v.* **elected, electing, elects.** —*tr.* **1. a.** To select by vote for an office, usually by a majority or plurality over other candidates. **b.** To select by vote for membership. **2.** To choose; decide in favor of: *elect to pursue an arts course.* **3.** *Theology.* To predestine for salvation. Used in the passive. —*intr.* To make a choice, especially with deliberation; decide. —See Synonyms at **choose.**
~*adj.* **1.** Chosen deliberately; singled out. **2.** Elected but not yet installed in office. Used in combination: *the governor-elect.* **3.** *Theology.* Selected by the divine will for salvation.
~*n.* **1.** A person who is chosen or selected. **2.** *Theology.* Those selected by the divine will for salvation. Preceded by *the.* **3.** Used with a plural verb. An exclusive group. [Middle English *electen,* from Latin *ēligere* (past participle of *ēlectus,* to pick out, select : *ex-,* out + *legere,* to gather, choose.]

elect. electric; electrical; electrician; electricity.

e·lec·tion (ĭ-lĕk′shən) *n.* **1.** The act or power of choosing. **2. a.** The act or process of choosing by vote among candidates to fill an office or position, especially a political one. **b.** The fact of being so chosen. **3.** *Theology.* Predestined salvation.

e·lec·tion·eer (ĭ-lĕk′shə-nîr′) *intr.v.* **-eered, -eering, -eers.** To work actively for a particular candidate or political party, as by canvassing.
~*n.* One who electioneers. —**e·lec·tion·eer·ing** *n. & adj.*

e·lec·tive (ĭ-lĕk′tĭv) *adj.* **1.** Of or pertaining to a selection by vote. **2.** Filled or obtained by election: *elective office.* **3.** Having the power or authority to elect; electoral. **4.** Permitting or involving a choice; optional: *Cosmetic surgery is usually elective.*
~*n.* An academic course or subject that is optional rather than obligatory. —**e·lec·tive·ly** *adv.*

e·lec·tor (ĭ-lĕk′tər) *n.* **1.** A person who elects; a qualified voter. **2.** A member of the Electoral College of the United States. **3.** *Usually*

Elector. Any of the German princes in the Holy Roman Empire who were entitled to elect the emperor.

e·lec·tor·al (ĭ-lĕk′tər-əl) *adj.* **1.** Of, pertaining to, or composed of electors. **2.** Of or pertaining to election.

Electoral College *n.* A popularly elected body of electors chosen to elect the President and Vice President of the United States.

e·lec·tor·ate (ĭ-lĕk′tər-ĭt) *n.* **1.** A body of qualified voters. **2.** In certain countries, a district or division of voters. **3.** The dignity or territory of an elector of the Holy Roman Empire.

E·lec·tra[1], **E·lek·tra** (ĭ-lĕk′trə). In Greek legend, the daughter of Clytemnestra and Agamemnon. She avenged the murder of Agamemnon with the help of her brother Orestes, who killed their mother and her lover, Aegisthus.

Electra[2] *n.* A star in the constellation Pleiades. [After *Electra,* daughter of Atlas.]

Electra complex *n. Psychoanalysis.* Unconscious sexual desire of a daughter for her father, generally manifesting itself first between the ages of three and five. Compare **Oedipus complex.**

e·lec·tret (ĭ-lĕk′trĭt) *n.* A solid dielectric that exhibits persistent dielectric polarization. [ELECTR(ICITY) + (MAGN)ET.]

e·lec·tric (ĭ-lĕk′trĭk) *adj.* Also **e·lec·tri·cal** (-trĭ-kəl). *Abbr.* **elec., elect. 1.** Of, pertaining to, producing, derived from, produced by, powered by, or operated by electricity. **2. a.** Emotionally exciting; thrilling. **b.** Exceptionally tense; charged with emotion. ~*n.* **electric.** An electrically powered machine, especially a vehicle. [New Latin *electricus,* "like amber," because amber produces sparks when rubbed, from Latin *ēlectrum,* amber, from Greek *ēlektron*†.] —**e·lec·tri·cal·ly** *adv.*

Usage: Electric is used of anything producing or powered by electricity: *electric light, electric chair. Electrical* has a looser connection with the physical power of electricity, being mainly used to characterize general concepts associated with the subject or the people and activities involved in its study: *electrical engineer; electrical design.*

electrical engineering *n. Abbr.* **E.E.** The study of the design and application of circuitry and equipment for power generation and distribution, machine control, and communications. —**electrical engineer** *n.*

electric blanket *n.* A blanket heated by means of internal electric wiring.

electric blue *n.* A metallic blue.

electric chair *n.* **1.** A chair used to restrain and electrocute a person sentenced to death. **2.** The punishment of death by electrocution. **3.** Execution by means of electrocution.

electric charge *n. Electricity.* **Charge** (see).

electric constant *n. Symbol* ϵ_0 The permittivity of free space, having the value 8.854×10^{-12} farad per meter. Also called "absolute permittivity."

electric current *n. Electricity.* **Current** (see).

electric displacement *n.* The product of the electric field strength and the absolute permittivity. Also called "electric flux density."

electric eel *n.* A long, eellike freshwater fish, *Electrophorus electricus,* of northern South America, having organs capable of producing a powerful electric discharge.

electric eye *n.* A **photoelectric cell** *(see),* especially when used as a sensor for an automatic switch.

electric fence *n.* A fence, usually consisting of a single strand of wire, that is charged with electricity.

electric field *n.* A region of space characterized by the existence of a force that is experienced by a stationary charged particle placed at any point within it.

electric field strength *n.* The strength of an electric field equal to the force experienced by a stationary charge within the field divided by the charge. It is measured in volts per meter.

electric flux *n.* The integral over a designated surface of the component of electric displacement normal to the surface.

electric flux density *n.* Electric displacement.

electric furnace *n.* An industrial or laboratory furnace heated by an electric arc, electric induction, or electric resistance.

electric guitar *n.* A guitar that transmits sounds to an amplifier by means of an electronic pickup placed under the strings.

e·lec·tri·cian (ĭ-lĕk′trĭsh′ən, ē′lĕk-) *n. Abbr.* **elec., elect.** A person whose occupation is the installation, maintenance, repair, or operation of electrical equipment and circuitry.

e·lec·tric·i·ty (ĭ-lĕk′trĭs′ə-tē, ē′lĕk-) *n. Abbr.* **elec., elect. 1.** The class of physical phenomena arising from the existence and interactions of positively and negatively charged particles. **2.** The physical science of such phenomena. **3.** Electric current used or regarded as a source of power. **4.** Intense emotional excitement.

electric lamp *n.* A lamp that uses electricity to produce light.

electric light *n.* **1.** An electric lamp. **2.** Light that is produced electrically.

electric moment *n.* The **dipole moment** *(see)* of an electric dipole.

electric motor *n.* A device for converting electrical energy directly

---

electric motor

THE PRINCIPLE OF THE ELECTRIC MOTOR

How magnets and electric current produce continuous rotary motion

An electric motor utilizes the basic principle of magnetism—that like poles repel, whereas unlike poles attract: two north magnetic poles or two south poles will repel each other; a north pole and a south pole will attract each other. In a motor, current is passed through a coil of wire, which sets up a magnetic field.

This field is made to interact with another magnetic field producing rotary motion as the magnetic poles attract or repel each other. Thus in a simple electric motor (below) at least two coils are wound around the poles of an armature that is mounted on an axle between the poles of a stationary magnet. When a direct

current is supplied to the coils, they effectively become magnets and the armature turns on its axle to align its north pole with the stationary magnet's south pole. A commutator then changes the polarity of the armature, which turns further to align its new north pole with the stationary magnet's south pole.

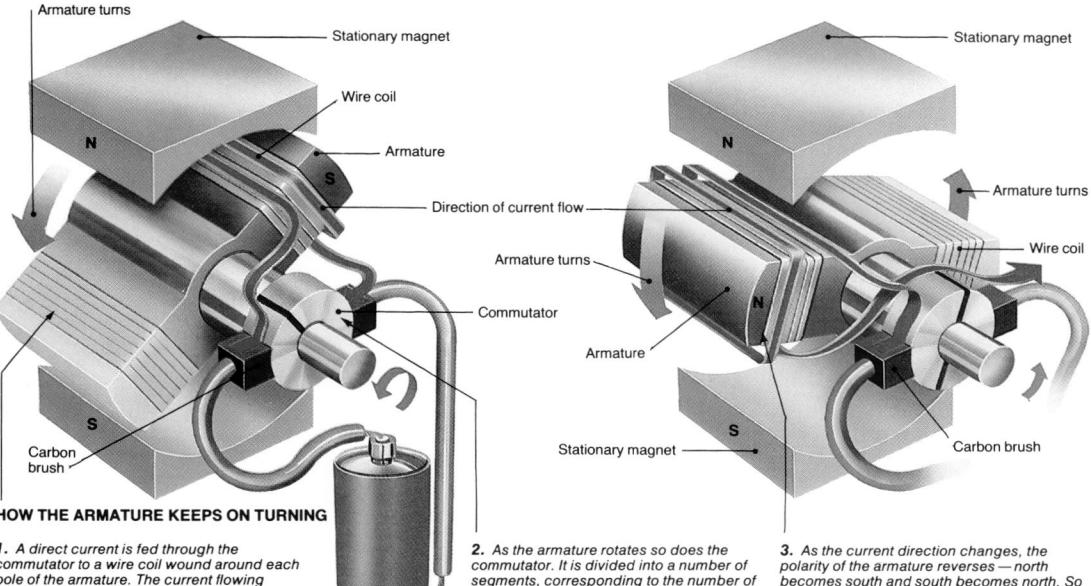

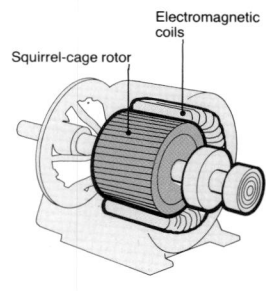

HOW THE ARMATURE KEEPS ON TURNING

1. A direct current is fed through the commutator to a wire coil wound around each pole of the armature. The current flowing through the coils creates a magnetic polarity in the armature, which turns as its north and south poles are attracted by the opposing poles of the stationary magnet — north to south, south to north

2. As the armature rotates so does the commutator. It is divided into a number of segments, corresponding to the number of coils, and rotates against the carbon brushes that supply the current. As the segments in turn touch the carbon brushes, contact is made with different coils in turn and the current changes direction

3. As the current direction changes, the polarity of the armature reverses — north becomes south and south becomes north. So the new north is repelled by the stationary north. It continues its circular motion, now attracted by the south pole on the stationary magnet

INDUCTION MOTOR *The rotary induction motor (above) works on the principle of electromagnetic conduction: whenever a conductor moves through a magnetic field, a current is induced in it. The rotor of the motor is a cylinder of metal bars that is known as a squirrel cage. Surrounding the cage are the coils of an electromagnet. When alternating current is fed to the coils, a rotating magnetic field is set up. It induces a second magnetic field, in the squirrel cage, which then 'chases" the rotating field.*

into mechanical energy by electromagnetic induction, having a fixed part (the stator), which produces a magnetic field, and a rotating coil or conductor (the rotor), which moves under the influence of an induced force. See **induction motor, synchronous motor, linear motor.**

electric needle *n.* A cutting instrument used in surgery and powered by a high-frequency current.

electric organ *n.* **1.** *Music.* An organ operated by electricity. **2.** A group of cells in some fishes, such as the electric eel and electric ray, that generate electricity.

electric ray *n.* Any of various fishes of the family Torpedinidae, having a rounded body and a pair of electric organs capable of producing a fairly strong electric discharge. Also called "numbfish."

e·lec·tri·fy (ĭ-lĕk′trə-fī′) *tr.v.* **-fied, -fying, -fies. 1.** To produce electric charge on or in (a conductor). **2. a.** To wire or otherwise equip (a building, for example) for the use of electric power. **b.** To convert (a railway system, for example) to enable it to operate by electricity. **c.** To provide with electric power. **3.** To thrill, startle greatly, or shock. [ELECTRI(C) + -FY.] **—e·lec·tri·fi·a·ble** *adj.* **—e·lec·tri·fi·ca·tion** *n.* **—e·lec·tri·fi·er** *n.*

e·lec·tro (ĭ-lĕk′trō) *n., pl.* **-tros. 1.** Electroplate *(see).* **2.** Electrotype *(see).*

electro-, electr- *prefix.* Indicates: **1.** Electric; for example, **electromagnet, electrode. 2.** Electrically; for example, **electrocute, electrograph. 3.** Electrolysis; for example, **electrolyte.** [New Latin, from Latin *ēlectrum,* amber, from Greek *ēlektron.* See **elector.**]

e·lec·tro·a·cous·tics (ĭ-lĕk′trō-ə-kōō′stĭks) *n. Used with a singular verb.* The science of the interaction or interconversion of electric and acoustic phenomena. **—e·lec·tro·a·cous·tic** *adj.* **—e·lec·tro·a·cous·ti·cal·ly** *adv.*

e·lec·tro·a·nal·y·sis (ĭ-lĕk′trō-ə-năl′ə-sĭs) *n., pl.* **-ses** (-sēz′). Chemical analysis using electrolytic techniques. **—e·lec·tro·an·a·lyt·ic** (ĭ-lĕk′trō-ăn′ə-lĭt′ĭk), **e·lec·tro·an·a·lyt·i·cal** (-ĭ-kəl) *adj.*

e·lec·tro·car·di·o·gram (ĭ-lĕk′trō-kär′dē-ə-grăm′) *n. Abbr.* **ECG, EKG.** The curve traced by an electrocardiograph, used to diagnose heart disease.

e·lec·tro·car·di·o·graph (ĭ-lĕk′trō-kär′dē-ə-grăf′, -grăf′) *n. Abbr.* **ECG, EKG** An instrument used to record electric potentials associated with the electric currents that initiate the heartbeat. **—e·lec·tro·car·di·o·graph·ic** (ĭ-lĕk′trō-kär′dē-ə-grăf′ĭk) *adj.* **—e·lec·tro·car·di·og·ra·phy** (ĭ-lĕk′trō-kär′dē-ŏg′rə-fē) *n.*

e·lec·tro·chem·i·cal series (ĭ-lĕk′trō-kĕm′ĭ-kəl) *n.* The **electromotive series** *(see).*

e·lec·tro·chem·is·try (ĭ-lĕk′trō-kĕm′ĭ-strē) *n.* The science of the interaction or interconversion of electric and chemical phenomena. **—e·lec·tro·chem·i·cal** *adj.* **—e·lec·tro·chem·i·cal·ly** *adv.* **—e·lec·tro·chem·ist** *n.*

e·lec·tro·co·ag·u·la·tion (ĭ-lĕk′trō-kō-ăg′yə-lā′shən) *n. Medicine.* The use of a high-frequency electric current to coagulate tissue so that bloodless incisions can be made during operations.

e·lec·tro·con·vul·sive therapy (ĭ-lĕk′trō-kən-vŭl′sĭv) *n. Abbr.* **ECT, E.C.T.** Treatment of certain mental disorders by passing an electric current through the brain to cause a convulsion.

e·lec·tro·cute (ĭ-lĕk′trə-kyōōt′) *tr.v.* **-cuted, -cuting, -cutes.** To kill with electricity; especially, to execute (a condemned criminal) by means of a high-voltage electric current. [ELECTRO- + (EXE)CUTE.] **—e·lec·tro·cu·tion** *n.*

e·lec·trode (ĭ-lĕk′trōd′) *n.* **1.** A solid electric conductor through which an electric current enters or leaves a medium such as an electrolyte, a nonmetallic solid, a molten metal, a gas, or a vacuum. **2.** A collector or emitter of electric charge or electric-charge carriers, as in a semiconductor device. [ELECTR(O)- + -ODE.]

e·lec·tro·de·pos·it (ĭ-lĕk′trō-dĭ-pŏz′ĭt) *tr.v.* **-ited, -iting, -its.** To deposit (a dissolved or suspended substance) on an electrode by electrolysis.
~*n.* The substance so deposited. **—e·lec·tro·dep·o·si·tion** (ĭ-lĕk′trō-dĕp′ə-zĭsh′ən, -dē′pə-zĭsh′ən) *n.*

e·lec·tro·di·al·y·sis (ĭ-lĕk′trō-dī-ăl′ə-sĭs) *n., pl.* **-ses** (-sēz′). Dialysis at a rate speeded by the application of an electric potential across the dialysis membrane, used especially to remove electrolytes from a colloidal suspension.

e·lec·tro·dy·nam·ics (ĭ-lĕk′trō-dī-năm′ĭks) *n. Used with a singular verb.* The physics of the relationship between electric, magnetic, and mechanical phenomena. **—e·lec·tro·dy·nam·ic** *adj.*

e·lec·tro·dy·na·mom·e·ter (ĭ-lĕk′trō-dī′nə-mŏm′ə-tər) *n.* An instrument that uses the interaction of the magnetic fields of fixed and moving sets of coils to measure current, voltage, or power.

e·lec·tro·en·ceph·a·lo·gram (ĭ-lĕk′trō-ĕn-sĕf′ə-lə-grăm′) *n. Abbr.* **EEG** A graphic record of the electrical activity of the brain as recorded by an electroencephalograph. Also called "encephalogram."

e·lec·tro·en·ceph·a·lo·graph (ĭ-lĕk′trō-ĕn-sĕf′ə-lə-grăf′, -grăf′) *n. Abbr.* **EEG** An instrument that records the electrical activity of the brain. **—e·lec·tro·en·ceph·a·lo·graph·ic** (ĭ-lĕk′trō-ĕn-sĕf′ə-lə-grăf′ĭk) *adj.* **—e·lec·tro·en·ceph·a·log·ra·phy** (ĭ-lĕk′trō-ĕn-sĕf′ə-lŏg′rə-fē) *n.*

e·lec·tro·form (ĭ-lĕk′trə-fôrm′) *tr.v.* **-formed, -forming, -forms.** To produce or reproduce by electrodeposition in a mold. [ELECTRO- + -FORM.]

e·lec·tro·gen·e·sis (ĭ-lĕk′trō-jĕn′ə-sĭs) *n.* The production of electrical activity, especially that produced in living tissue. **—e·lec·tro·gen·ic** (ĭ-lĕk′trō-jĕn′ĭk) *adj.*

e·lec·tro·graph (ĭ-lĕk′trə-grăf′, -grăf′) *n.* **1.** Any electrically pro-

duced graph or tracing. **2.** Equipment used to produce such graphs or tracings in facsimile transmission. **3.** A visual record of the composition of a metal surface obtained by placing the surface on a paper soaked in an electrolyte and passing a current from the surface through the paper to an electrode placed on the other side of the paper. [ELECTRO- + -GRAPH.]

e·lec·tro·ki·net·ics (ĭ-lĕk′trō-kĭ-nĕt′ĭks) *n. Used with a singular verb.* The electrodynamics of heating effects and of current distribution in electric networks. **—e·lec·tro·ki·net·ic** *adj.*

e·lec·tro·lu·mi·nes·cence (ĭ-lĕk′trō-lōō′mə-nĕs′əns) *n.* **1.** The direct conversion of electric energy to light by a solid phosphor subjected to an alternating electric field. **2.** The emission of light caused by electric discharge in a gas. **—e·lec·tro·lu·mi·nes·cent** *adj.*

e·lec·trol·y·sis (ĭ-lĕk′trŏl′ə-sĭs, ē′lĕk-) *n.* **1.** Chemical change, especially decomposition, produced in an electrolyte by an electric current. **2.** Destruction of living tissue, as of hair roots, by an electric current. [ELECTRO- + -LYSIS.]

e·lec·tro·lyte (ĭ-lĕk′trə-līt′) *n.* A substance that dissociates into ions in solution or when fused, thereby becoming electrically conducting. [ELECTRO- + -LYTE.]

e·lec·tro·lyt·ic (ĭ-lĕk′trə-lĭt′ĭk) *adj.* **1. a.** Of or pertaining to electrolysis. **b.** Produced by electrolysis. **2.** Of or pertaining to an electrolyte.

electrolytic cell *n.* **1.** A cell containing an electrolyte through which an externally generated electric current is passed by a system of electrodes in order to produce an electrochemical reaction. **2.** A cell containing an electrolyte in which an electrochemical reaction produces an electromotive force.

electrolytic gas *n.* A gas formed by the electrolysis of water, consisting of two parts of hydrogen and one part of water.

e·lec·tro·lyze (ĭ-lĕk′trə-līz′) *tr.v.* **-lyzed, -lyzing, -lyzes.** To decompose by electrolysis. [Back-formation from ELECTROLYSIS.]

e·lec·tro·mag·net (ĭ-lĕk′trō-măg′nĭt) *n.* A magnet consisting essentially of a soft-iron core wound with a current-carrying coil of insulated wire, the current in which produces the magnetization of the core.

e·lec·tro·mag·net·ic (ĭ-lĕk′trō-măg-nĕt′ĭk) *adj.* Of or exhibiting electromagnetism. **—e·lec·tro·mag·net·i·cal·ly** *adv.*

electromagnetic field *n.* The field of force associated with an accelerating electric charge, having both electric and magnetic components and containing a definite amount of electromagnetic energy.

electromagnetic interaction *n.* A form of interaction between particles that are charged as a result of their electric or magnetic fields or the exchange of virtual photons between them. Compare **strong interaction, weak interaction, gravitational interaction.**

electromagnetic pump *n.* A pump for moving liquid metals in which the pipe containing the liquid metal is placed between the poles of an electromagnet and a current is passed through the liquid metal.

electromagnetic radiation *n.* Radiation consisting of an electric field and a magnetic field perpendicular to each other and to the direction of propagation. The speed of propagation in a vacuum is 2.9979 x 10⁸ meters per second.

electromagnetic spectrum *n.* The entire range of radiation extending in frequency approximately from 10^{21} hertz to 0 hertz (or, in corresponding wavelengths, from 10^{-13} meter to infinity) and including, in order of decreasing frequency, gamma rays, x-rays, ultraviolet radiation, visible light, infrared radiation, microwaves, and radio waves.

electromagnetic unit *n.* Any of a system of units for electricity and magnetism based on a system of equations in which the magnetic constant is taken as unity and by means of which the abampere is defined as the fundamental unit of current.

electromagnetic wave *n.* A wave propagating as a periodic disturbance of the electromagnetic field and having a frequency in the electromagnetic spectrum.

e·lec·tro·mag·net·ism (ĭ-lĕk′trō-măg′nə-tĭz′əm) *n.* **1.** Magnetism arising from an accelerating electric charge. **2.** The physics of electricity and magnetism.

e·lec·tro·me·chan·i·cal (ĭ-lĕk′trō-mĭ-kăn′ĭ-kəl) *adj.* Of or designating a mechanical device that is operated by electricity. **—e·lec·tro·me·chan·i·cal·ly** *adv.*

e·lec·trom·er·ism (ĭ-lĕk′trŏm′ə-rĭz′əm, ē′lĕk-) *n. Chemistry.* A form of tautomerism in which the isomers differ in the way in which electric charge is distributed in their molecules. [ELECTRO- + (ISO)MERISM.]

e·lec·tro·met·al·lur·gy (ĭ-lĕk′trō-mĕt′ə-lûr′jē) *n.* The use of electricity to purify metals or to reduce metallic compounds to metals. **—e·lec·tro·met·al·lur·gi·cal** (ĭ-lĕk′trō-mĕt′ə-lûr′jĭ-kəl) *adj.*

e·lec·trom·e·ter (ĭ-lĕk′trŏm′ə-tər, ē′lĕk-) *n.* An instrument for detecting or measuring potential differences, electric charge, or, indirectly, electric current by means of mechanical forces exerted between electrically charged bodies. [ELECTRO- + -METER.]

e·lec·tro·mo·tive (ĭ-lĕk′trō-mō′tĭv) *adj.* Of, pertaining to, or producing electric current.

electromotive force *n. Abbr.* **emf, EMF** The energy per unit charge that is converted reversibly from chemical, mechanical, and other forms of energy into electrical energy in a conversion device such as a battery or dynamo. It is measured in volts.

electromotive series *n.* A series of metals, with hydrogen included, arranged in order of their electrode potentials. The series represents the order in which metals replace one another from their salts, those high in the series replacing those lower down. The series of the commoner metals is Na, Mg, Al, Zn, Fe, Co, Ni, Sn, Pb, H, Cu, Hg, Ag, Au. Also called "electrochemical series."

e·lec·tro·my·o·gram (ĭ-lĕk′trō-mī′ə-grăm′) n. A record of the electrical activity of a muscle obtained using an electromyograph.

e·lec·tro·my·o·graph (ĭ-lĕk′trō-mī′ə-grăf′, -grăf′) n. An instrument that records the electrical activity of a muscle by means of electrodes inserted into the muscle fiber. —**e·lec·tro·my·og·ra·phy** (ĭ-lĕk′trō-mī-ŏg′rə-fē) n.

e·lec·tron (ĭ-lĕk′trŏn′) n. Abbr. **e** A subatomic particle in the lepton family having a rest mass of 9.1096 × 10⁻²⁸ gram and a unit negative electric charge of approximately 1.602 × 10⁻¹⁹ coulomb. [ELECTR(O)- + -ON.]

electron camera n. A device forming part of a television camera in which an optical image is converted into an electrical signal.

e·lec·tro·neg·a·tive (ĭ-lĕk′trō-nĕg′ə-tĭv) adj. 1. Having a negative electric charge. 2. Tending to attract electrons to form a chemical bond. —**e·lec·tro·neg·a·tiv·i·ty** (ĭ-lĕk′trō-nĕg′ə-tĭv′ə-tē) n.

electron gun n. An electron-emitting electrode and associated elements, especially in a cathode-ray tube, that produce a beam of accelerated electrons.

e·lec·tron·ic (ĭ-lĕk′trŏn′ĭk, ē′lĕk-) adj. 1. Of or pertaining to electrons. 2. Of, pertaining to, based on, operated by, or otherwise involving the controlled conduction of electrons or other charge carriers, especially in a vacuum, gas, or semiconducting material. 3. Of or pertaining to electronics. —**e·lec·tron·i·cal·ly** adv.

electronic data processing n. Abbr. **EDP** Data processing in which electronic computers are used to manipulate the information.

electronic music n. 1. Music produced entirely or in part by manipulating natural or artificial sounds with tape recorders or other electronic devices. 2. Music consisting of sounds produced by oscillating electronic signals.

e·lec·tron·ics (ĭ-lĕk′trŏn′ĭks, ē′lĕk-) n. Used with a singular verb. 1. The science and technology of electronic phenomena. 2. The commercial industry of electronic devices and systems.

electron lens n. Any of various devices that use an electric or a magnetic field to focus a beam of electrons.

electron micrograph n. A micrograph made by an electron microscope.

electron microscope n. Any of a class of microscopes that use a beam of electrons rather than visible light to produce magnified images, especially of objects having dimensions smaller than the wavelengths of visible light, with linear magnification up to or exceeding a million (10⁶). See **scanning electron microscope.**

electron multiplier n. A vacuum tube in which a single electron produces a large number of secondary electrons by collision with an anode, the process generally being repeated through a number of stages to achieve great amplification.

electron optics n. Used with a singular verb. The science of the control of electron motion by electron lenses in systems or under conditions analogous to those involving or affecting visible light.

electron pair n. 1. Any two electrons functioning or regarded as functioning in concert; especially, two electrons shared by two atoms joined by a covalent chemical bond. 2. The combination of an electron and a positron as produced by a high-energy photon. Also called "pair." See **pair production.**

electron probe microanalysis n. Chemistry. A method of analyzing tiny quantities (as little as 10⁻¹³ gram) of material by bombarding the specimen with a finely focused beam of electrons and examining the resulting x-ray emission spectrum.

electron spin resonance n. Abbr. **ESR** Chemistry. A method of examining the molecular structure of paramagnetic substances by subjecting them to high-frequency radiation in a strong magnetic field. Changes in the spin of unpaired electrons in the molecules cause radiation to be absorbed at certain characteristic frequencies.

electron telescope n. An astronomical telescope that converts infrared radiation emitted by the planets into an optical image.

electron tube n. A sealed enclosure, either highly evacuated or containing a controlled quantity of gas, in which electrons can be made sufficiently mobile to act as the principal carriers of current between at least one pair of electrodes, often under the control of one or more additional electrodes.

electron volt n. Abbr. **eV** A unit of energy equal to the energy acquired by an electron falling through a potential difference of one volt, approximately 1.602 × 10⁻¹⁹ joule.

e·lec·tro·phil·ic (ĭ-lĕk′trō-fĭl′ĭk) n. Chemistry. Designating an atom, molecule, or ion that behaves as an electron acceptor. [ELECTRO- + -PHIL(E) + -IC.]

e·lec·tro·pho·re·sis (ĭ-lĕk′trō-fə-rē′sĭs) n. The motion of charged particles, especially colloidal particles, through a relatively stationary liquid under the influence of an applied electric field provided, in general, by immersed electrodes. Also called "cataphoresis." [ELECTRO- + -PHORESIS.]

e·lec·troph·o·rus (ĭ-lĕk′trŏf′ər-əs, ē′lĕk-) n., pl. **-ori** (-ə-rī′). An apparatus for generating static electricity, consisting of a disk that is given a negative charge by friction and a metal plate that is charged by induction when in contact with the disk. [ELECTRO- + -PHOROUS.]

e·lec·tro·plate (ĭ-lĕk′trə-plāt′) tr.v. **-plated, -plating, -plates.** To coat or cover with a thin layer of metal by electrodeposition.
~n. 1. An article that has been electroplated. 2. Electroplated articles collectively. Also called "electro."

e·lec·tro·pos·i·tive (ĭ-lĕk′trō-pŏz′ə-tĭv) adj. 1. Having a positive

electric charge. 2. Tending to release electrons to form a chemical bond.

e·lec·tro·scope (ĭ-lĕk′trə-skōp′) n. An instrument used to detect the presence, the sign, and in some configurations the magnitude of an electric charge by the mutual attraction or repulsion of metal foils. [ELECTRO- + -SCOPE.]

e·lec·tro·stat·ic (ĭ-lĕk′trō-stăt′ĭk) adj. 1. **a.** Of or pertaining to stationary electric charges. **b.** Produced or caused by such charges. 2. Of or pertaining to electrostatics. —**e·lec·tro·stat·i·cal·ly** adv.

electrostatic generator n. Any of various devices, including the electrophorus, the Wimshurst machine, and especially the **Van de Graaff generator** (see), that generate high voltages by accumulating large quantities of electric charge.

electrostatic precipitation n. The removal of particles suspended in a gas by electrostatic charging and subsequent precipitation onto a collector in a strong electric field.

e·lec·tro·stat·ics (ĭ-lĕk′trō-stăt′ĭks) n. Used with a singular verb. The branch of physics dealing with electrostatic phenomena.

electrostatic unit n. Abbr. **esu** Any of a system of units for electricity and magnetism based on a system of equations in which the electric constant is defined as unity and by means of which a fundamental unit of charge is defined.

e·lec·tro·stric·tion (ĭ-lĕk′trō-strĭk′shən) n. A change in the dimensions of a dielectric as the result of an applied electric field.

e·lec·tro·sur·ger·y (ĭ-lĕk′trō-sûr′jə-rē) n. Surgery using electrical methods, as in cauterization.

e·lec·tro·ther·a·peu·tics (ĭ-lĕk′trō-thĕr′ə-pyo͞o′tĭks) n. Used with a singular verb. The branch of medicine concerned with the use of electrotherapy. —**e·lec·tro·ther·a·peu·tic** adj.

e·lec·tro·ther·a·py (ĭ-lĕk′trō-thĕr′ə-pē) n. Medical therapy using electric currents, especially for stimulating muscles and nerves. —**e·lec·tro·ther·a·pist** n.

e·lec·tro·ther·mal (ĭ-lĕk′trō-thûr′məl) adj. Of or involving both electricity and heat; especially, producing heat electrically.

e·lec·trot·o·nus (ĭ-lĕk′trŏt′ə-nəs, ē′lĕk-) n. Physiology. The alteration in excitability and conductivity of a nerve caused by the passage of an electric current. [ELECTRO- + TONUS.] —**e·lec·tro·ton·ic** (ĭ-lĕk′trō-tŏn′ĭk) adj.

e·lec·tro·type (ĭ-lĕk′trə-tīp′) n. 1. A duplicate metal plate used in letterpress printing, made by electroplating a lead or plastic mold of the original plate. Also called "electro." 2. The process of making such a plate.
~tr.v. **electrotyped, -typing, -types.** To make an electrotype of. —**e·lec·tro·typ·er** n. —**e·lec·tro·typ·ic** (ĭ-lĕk′trə-tĭp′ĭk) adj.

e·lec·tro·va·lence (ĭ-lĕk′trō-vā′ləns) n. Also **e·lec·tro·va·len·cy** (-lən-sē). 1. Valence characterized by the transfer of electrons from atoms of one element to atoms of another. 2. The number of electric charges lost or gained by an atom in such a transfer. —**e·lec·tro·va·lent** adj.

electrovalent bond n. Chemistry. An **ionic bond** (see).

e·lec·trum (ĭ-lĕk′trəm) n. An alloy of varying proportions of silver and gold, especially one used in ancient metallurgy. [Middle English electrum, from Latin ēlectrum, amber, from Greek.]

e·lec·tu·ar·y (ĭ-lĕk′cho͞o-ĕr′ē) n., pl. **-ies.** A drug mixed with sugar and water or honey into a pasty mass suitable for oral administration. [Middle English electuarie, from Late Latin ēlectuārium, something that melts in the mouth.]

el·ee·mos·y·nar·y (ĕl′ĭ-mŏs′ə-nĕr′ē, ĕl′ē-ə-) adj. 1. Of or pertaining to alms or the giving of alms; charitable. 2. Dependent upon or supported by alms. 3. Contributed as alms or charity. [Medieval Latin eleēmosynārius, from Late Latin eleēmosyna, ALMS.]

el·e·gance (ĕl′ə-gəns) n. 1. **a.** Refinement and grace in movement, appearance, or manners. **b.** Tasteful opulence in form, decoration, or presentation. 2. Something that is elegant.

el·e·gant (ĕl′ə-gənt) adj. 1. Characterized by or exhibiting elegance; refined; graceful. 2. Scientifically exact and simple: an elegant mathematical proof. [Old French, from Latin ēlegāns (stem ēlegant-), choice, fine, from ēligere, to choose out, select : ex-, out + legere, to choose.] —**el·e·gant·ly** adv.

el·e·gi·ac (ĕl′ə-jī′ăk′, ĭ-lē′jē-ăk′) adj. 1. **a.** Pertaining to an elegy. **b.** Expressing sorrow; mournful. 2. Composed in classical distichs, having the first line a dactylic hexameter and the second a pentameter: an elegiac couplet. [French élégiaque, from Late Latin elegīacus, from Greek elegeiakos, from elegeia, ELEGY.]

el·e·gist (ĕl′ə-jĭst) n. The composer of an elegy or elegies.

el·e·git (ĭ-lē′jĭt) n. Law. A writ of execution against a debtor by which the plaintiff may enter the debtor's land until the debtor can settle his debt. [Latin ēlēgit, "he has chosen" (the first word in a phrase often used in such writs), from ēligere, to choose out. See **elegant.**]

el·e·gize (ĕl′ə-jīz′) v. **-gized, -gizing, -gizes.** —intr. To compose an elegy. —tr. To compose an elegy upon or for.

el·e·gy (ĕl′ə-jē) n., pl. **-gies.** 1. A poem composed in elegiac distichs. 2. A mournful poem; especially, a poem composed to lament one who is dead. 3. A mournful musical composition. [French élégie, from Latin elegīa, from Greek elegeia, from elegos, lament, probably from Phrygian.]

Elektra. Variant of **Electra** (daughter of Agamemnon).

el·e·ment (ĕl′ə-mənt) n. Abbr. **elem.** 1. **a.** A fundamental, essential, or irreducible constituent of a composite entity. **b.** A part of a larger unit, especially one with special characteristics, such as a military or social grouping. **c.** A factor affecting a decision, condition, or the like: a stubborn element in his personality. 2. **a.** A basic

electrostatic generator When the handle is turned on this 18th-century electrostatic generator, the silk cloth rubs against the glass cylinder, producing static electricity by friction.

elephant *A lone African bull elephant by a watering hole in Manyara National Park, Tanzania. Its larger ears and humped back differentiate it from the Indian species.*

elephant seal *Bull elephant seals like this one may be up to 6 meters (20 feet) long and weigh nearly 4 tons. They fight one another in the breeding season to win a harem of cow seals. The elephant seal's name comes not just from its size but also from the short trunk that hangs over the bull's mouth.*

assumption or proposition. **b. elements.** The first principles of a subject: *elements of geometry.* **3.** *Mathematics.* **a.** A member of a set. **b.** A point, line, or plane. **c.** A part of a geometric configuration, such as an angle in a triangle. **d.** The generatrix of a geometric figure. **e.** Any of the terms in the rectangular array of terms that constitute a matrix or determinant. **4.** *Chemistry & Physics.* A substance composed of atoms having an identical number of protons in each nucleus. **5.** *Astronomy.* A numerical quantity used in describing the orbit of a planet or satellite. **6.** Earth, air, fire, or water regarded as a fundamental constituent of the universe in ancient and medieval cosmologies. **7. elements.** The forces that collectively constitute the weather; especially, cold, wind, rain, or other harsh conditions. **8.** An environment naturally occupied, preferred, or regarded as being preferred by an individual. **9.** A very small amount; a hint: *an element of doubt as to his success.* **10.** The resistance wire in an electrical appliance such as a stove or heater. **11. elements.** The bread and wine of the Eucharist. [Middle English, from Old French, from Latin *elementum,* rudiment, first principle, perhaps from Etruscan.]

el·e·men·tal (ĕl′ə-mĕnt′l) *adj.* **1.** Of, pertaining to, or being an element. **2.** Fundamental or essential; basic. **3.** Resembling a force of nature in power or effect. **—el·e·men·tal·ly** *adv.*

el·e·men·ta·ry (ĕl′ə-mĕn′tə-rē, -trē) *adj. Abbr.* **elem. 1.** Fundamental, essential, or irreducible. **2. a.** Rudimentary; simple. **b.** Of, involving, or introducing the fundamental or simplest aspects of a subject: *an elementary text.* **—el·e·men·tar·i·ly** (ĕl′ə-mĕn-târ′ə-lē) *adv.* **—el·e·men·ta·ri·ness** *n.*

elementary particle *n.* **1.** Any of the four stable particles, the photon, the electron, the neutrino, and the proton, regarded as indivisible. **2.** Any member of the lepton, meson, or baryon family that may decay into a stable particle or particles. Also called "fundamental particle."

elementary school *n.* A school attended for the first six to eight years of a child's school career. Also called "grade school," "grammar school."

el·e·mi (ĕl′ə-mē) *n., pl.* **-mis.** Any of various oily resins derived from certain tropical trees, especially *Canarium luzonicum,* of the Philippines, used in making varnishes and inks. [Spanish *elemí,* from Arabic *elemī,* dialectal variant of *al-lāmi,* the elemi.]

e·len·chus (ĭ-lĕng′kəs) *n., pl.* **-chi** (-kī′, -kē′). **1.** *Logic.* A refutation that disproves an opponent's conclusion or establishes a proposition contrary to his. **2.** A syllogistic refutation. [Latin, from Greek *elenkhos,* refutation, from *elenkhein,* to refute.]

e·lenc·tic (ĭ-lĕngk′tĭk) *adj. Logic.* Refuting by proving the opposite. Compare **deictic.** [Greek *elenktikos,* from *elenkhein,* to refute. See **elenchus.**]

el·e·phant (ĕl′ə-fənt) *n.* **1.** Either of two very large herbivorous mammals, *Elephas maximus,* of south-central Asia, or *Loxodonta africana,* of Africa, having thick, almost hairless skin, a long, flexible prehensile trunk, upper incisors forming long, curved tusks, and, in the African species, large, fan-shaped ears. **2.** Any of several animals related to the elephant, including some species now extinct. [Middle English *elifaunt, elephan,* from Old French *olifant, elifant,* from Vulgar Latin *olifantus* (unattested), from Latin *elephantus,* from Greek *elephas* (stem *elephant-*), ivory, elephant, probably of non-Indo-European origin.]

elephant bird *n.* A large, extinct, flightless bird of the genus *Aepyornis,* remains of which have been found in Madagascar.

Elephant Butte Dam. A dam across the Rio Grande in southwestern New Mexico, 1,674 feet long and over 300 feet high, forming Elephant Butte Reservoir.

el·e·phant-ear (ĕl′ə-fənt-îr′) *n.* Also **el·e·phant's-ear** (ĕl′ə-fənts-). **1.** A plant, *Colocasia antiquorum,* native to the East Indies, having edible tubers and large leaves resembling an elephant's ears. **2.** A similar or related plant, such as the taro.

el·e·phan·ti·a·sis (ĕl′ə-fən-tī′ə-sĭs) *n.* A chronic, often extreme enlargement and hardening of the cutaneous and subcutaneous tissue, especially of the legs and the scrotum, resulting from lymphatic obstruction, and usually caused by a nematode worm, *Wuchereria bancrofti.* See **filariasis.** [Latin *elephantiāsis* : Greek *elephas,* ELEPHANT (so called because the affected skin resembles an elephant's hide) + -IASIS.]

el·e·phan·tine (ĕl′ə-făn′tēn′, -tīn′, ĕl′ə-fən-) *adj.* **1.** Of or pertaining to an elephant. **2.** Oversized and unwieldy.

elephant seal *n.* Either of two large seals, *Mirounga angustirostris* or *M. leonina,* of Pacific coastal waters of North and South America, having a trunklike proboscis. Also called "sea elephant."

elephant shrew *n.* Any insectivorous African mammal of the family Macroscelididae, having a long pointed nose and large ears.

El·eu·sin·i·an mysteries (ĕl′yo͞o-sĭn′ē-ən) *pl.n.* The ancient religious rites of spring celebrated at Eleusis in Greece in honor of the goddess Demeter.

E·leu·sis (ĭ-lo͞o′sĭs). A town in east-central Greece 16 kilometers (10 miles) east of Athens, site of the Eleusinian mysteries and the birthplace of Aeschylus.

el·e·vate (ĕl′ə-vāt′) *tr.v.* **-vated, -vating, -vates. 1.** To raise to a higher place or position; lift up. **2.** To increase the amplitude, intensity, or volume of. **3.** To promote to a higher rank. **4.** To raise to a higher moral, cultural, or intellectual level. **5.** To lift the spirits of; elate. **6.** *Roman Catholic Church.* To raise (the host or chalice) after the consecration at Mass. —See Synonyms at **lift.** [Middle English *elevaten,* from Latin *ēlevāre* : *ex-,* up + *levāre,* to lighten, raise.] **—el·e·va·to·ry** (el′ə-və-tôr′ē, -tōr′ē) *adj.*

el·e·vat·ed (ĕl′ə-vā′tĭd) *adj.* **1.** Raised above a given level. **2.** Exalted; high; lofty: *an elevated tone.* —See Synonyms at **high.**

elevated railway *n.* A railway that operates on a raised structure in order to permit passage of vehicles or pedestrians beneath it.

el·e·va·tion (ĕl′ə-vā′shən) *n. Abbr.* **el., elev. 1.** The act of elevating or the condition of being elevated. **2.** An elevated place or position. **3.** The height to which something is elevated above a reference point, especially above the ground. **4.** Loftiness of thought or feeling. **5.** A scale drawing of the side, front, or rear of a given structure. **6.** *Geography & Astronomy.* **Altitude** *(see).* **7.** *Surveying.* The angular distance between the plane through a point and an object above it. **8. a.** A leap, as by a dancer, in which the performer appears to be suspended in midair. **b.** The ability of a performer to execute an elevation.

el·e·va·tor (ĕl′ə-vā′tər) *n.* **1. a.** A platform or enclosure raised and lowered in a vertical shaft to transport freight or passengers. **b.** The platform or enclosure with its operating equipment, motor, cables, and accessories. **2.** A mechanism, used for hoisting material, that usually consists of buckets or scoops attached to a conveyor. **3.** A granary equipped with devices for hoisting and discharging grain. **4.** A movable control surface, usually attached to the horizontal stabilizer of an aircraft, used to produce up or down motion.

e·lev·en (ĭ-lĕv′ən) *n.* **1. a.** The cardinal number that is one more than ten. **b.** A symbol representing this, such as 11, XI, or xi. **2.** A set made up of eleven persons or things. **3.** The eleventh in a series. **4.** A size, as in clothing, designated as eleven. **5.** Eleven hours after midnight or midday; eleven o'clock. **6.** In sports, especially soccer, cricket, and hockey, a team of eleven players. [Middle English *ellevene, enlevene,* Old English *endleofan,* from Germanic : *aninaz* (unattested), ONE + *-lif* (unattested), probably "left" (that is, one left over after ten).] **—e·lev·en** *adj.*

e·lev·en-plus (ĭ-lĕv′ən-plŭs′) *n.* Formerly, an examination taken by children around the age of 11 in British state schools for admission to grammar school.

e·lev·ens·es (ĭ-lĕv′ən-zĭz) *pl.n. Used with a singular verb. British.* A snack, often accompanied by coffee or tea, taken at about 11 o'clock in the morning.

e·lev·enth (ĭ-lĕv′ənth) *n.* **1.** The ordinal number 11 in a series. **2.** One of 11 equal parts. **—e·lev·enth** *adj. & adv.*

eleventh hour *n.* The latest possible time. [By allusion to the parable (Matthew 20:1–16) in which the workers hired at the eleventh hour received the same wages as those hired earlier.]

el·e·von (ĕl′ə-vŏn′) *n.* An airplane control surface combining the functions of an elevator and an aileron. [*Elev*ator + ailer*on.*]

elf (ĕlf) *n., pl.* **elves** (ĕlvz). **1.** In folklore, a small, manlike creature, usually represented as mischievous and having magical powers. **2.** A mischievous child. **3.** A dwarf. [Middle English *elf,* Old English *ælf,* from Germanic.]

elf·in (ĕl′fĭn) *adj.* **1.** Pertaining to or of the nature of an elf; elfish. **2.** Having physical characteristics associated with elves, especially smallness, delicacy, and slightly pointed features. [Probably from Middle English *elvene,* genitive plural of ELF.]

elf·ish (ĕl′fĭsh) *adj.* Also **elv·ish** (ĕl′vĭsh). **1.** Of or pertaining to elves; elfin. **2.** Supernatural; weird. **3.** Mischievous. **—elf·ish·ly** *adv.* **—elf·ish·ness** *n.*

elf·lock (ĕlf′lŏk′) *n.* A tangled lock of hair.

El·gar (ĕl′gär′), **Sir Edward William** (1857–1934). English composer. His works include the *Enigma Variations* (1899), two symphonies (1908, 1911), a violin concerto (1910), and a cello concerto (1919). The song *Land of Hope and Glory* is set to the first of his five *Pomp and Circumstance* marches, written between 1901 and 1930.

El·gin Marbles (ĕl′gĭn) *pl.n.* Ancient Greek sculptures from the frieze of the Parthenon and other buildings on the Acropolis in Athens, taken to England by the 7th Earl of Elgin and now in the British Museum.

El Gre·co (ĕl grĕk′ō), born Domenicos Theotocopoulos and called in Spanish "the Greek" (*c.* 1541–1614). Spanish painter born in Greece. He excelled chiefly at religious subjects, such as the masterpieces *Christ Stripped of his Garments* (1579) and the *Assumption* (1613).

e·lic·it (ĭ-lĭs′ĭt) *tr.v.* **-ited, -iting, -its. 1.** To bring or draw out (something latent). **2.** To evoke; call forth. [Latin *ēlicere* (past participle *ēlicitus*) : *ex-,* out + *lacere,* to allure, deceive (see **delight**).] **—e·lic·i·ta·tion** *n.* **—e·lic·i·tor** *n.*

e·lide (ĭ-līd′) *v.* **elided, eliding, elides.** —*tr.* **1.** To omit or slur over (a vowel or syllable) in pronunciation. **2.** To run together; confuse; blur. —*intr.* To be omitted or slurred over. [Latin *ēlīdere,* to strike out : *ex-,* out + *laedere,* to strike, hurt (see **lesion**).]

el·i·gi·ble (ĕl′ĭ-jə-bəl) *adj.* **1.** Qualified for an office, position, or other function. **2.** Worthy of choice, acceptance, adoption, or the like. **3.** Qualified and desirable, especially for marriage: *an eligible bachelor.* [Middle English, from Old French, from Late Latin *ēligibilis,* from Latin *ēligere,* to choose, ELECT.] **—el·i·gi·bil·i·ty** *n.* **—el·i·gi·ble** *n.* **—el·i·gi·bly** *adv.*

E·li·jah (ĭ-lī′jə). Also **E·li·as** (ĭ-lī′əs). Hebrew prophet of the 9th century B.C.

e·lim·i·nate (ĭ-lĭm′ə-nāt′) *tr.v.* **-nated, -nating, -nates. 1.** To get rid of; remove. **2. a.** To leave out or omit from consideration; reject. **b.** To exclude from a contest by defeating; knock out. **3.** *Mathematics.* To remove (an unknown quantity) by combining equations. **4.** *Physiology.* To excrete (waste products). **5.** To murder. Used euphemistically. [Latin *ēlīmināre,* "to drive outside the threshold" : *ex-,* out + *līmen* (stem *līmin-*), threshold (see **limen**).] **—e·lim·i·na·**

tion *n.* —**e·lim·i·na·tive** (ĭ-lĭm′ə-nā′tĭv), **e·lim·i·na·to·ry** (-nə-tôr′ē, -tōr′ē) *adj.* —**e·lim·i·na·tor** *n.*

El·i·ot (ĕl′ē-ət), **George,** pen name of Mary Ann Evans (1819–80). English novelist of the 19th-century realist tradition. Her writings include *Adam Bede* (1859), *The Mill on the Floss* (1860), *Silas Marner* (1861), and *Romola* (1862–63). Most critics consider *Middlemarch* (1871–72) to be her masterpiece.

Eliot, Thomas Stearns, known as "T.S. Eliot" (1888–1965). English poet, playwright, and critic, born in the United States. He went to London in 1914 and became a British citizen in 1927. His early poems, *Prufrock and Other Observations* (1917) and *The Waste Land* (1922), depicted the spiritual desolation of the postwar world. In 1927 he was converted to Anglo-Catholicism, and his new faith found expression in his later poetry, notably *Ash Wednesday* (1930) and *The Four Quartets* (1935–42). His most famous verse dramas are *Murder in the Cathedral* (1935), *The Family Reunion* (1939), and *The Cocktail Party* (1950). He won the Nobel Prize for literature in 1948.

Elisabethville. See **Lubumbashi.**

e·li·sion (ĭ-lĭzh′ən) *n.* **1.** The action of eliding. **2.** The omission of an unstressed vowel or syllable, as in scanning a line of verse. **3.** An omission. [Latin *ēlīsiō* (stem *ēlīsiōn-*), from *ēlīdere* (past participle *ēlīsus*), to ELIDE.]

e·lite, é·lite (ĭ-lēt′, ā-lēt′) *n.* **1. a.** The best, most skilled, or most privileged members of a given social group. **b.** A narrow and powerful clique. **2.** A size of type on a typewriter, allowing 12 characters to an inch. [French *élite,* from Old French *eslite,* feminine past participle of *eslire,* to choose, from Vulgar Latin *exlegere* (unattested), variant of Latin *ēligere,* to ELECT.] —**e·lite** *adj.*

e·lit·ism, é·lit·ism (ĭ-lē′tĭz′əm, ā-lē′-) *n.* **1. a.** Belief in the right to power of an elite. **b.** Rule or domination by an elite. **2.** A sense of being part of a superior or privileged group: *intellectual elitism.* —**e·lit·ist** *adj. & n.*

e·lix·ir (ĭ-lĭk′sər) *n.* **1.** A sweetened aromatic preparation of alcohol and water, serving as a vehicle for medicine. **2.** A medicinal potion thought to have generalized curative or restorative powers. **3.** *Alchemy.* **a.** A substance believed to have the power to transmute base metals to gold. Also called "philosopher's stone." **b.** A substance believed to have the power to cure all human disorders. Also called "panacea." **c.** A substance believed to maintain life indefinitely. Also called "elixir of life." The three substances were often regarded as one. **4.** The quintessence or underlying principle of something. [Middle English *elixir,* from Medieval Latin, from Arabic *al-iksīr,* "the elixir" : *al-,* the + *iksīr,* probably from Greek *xērion,* dry powder medicine, from *xēros,* dry.]

E·liz·a·beth[1] (ĭ-lĭz′ə-bəth). The mother of John the Baptist and wife of Zacharias, and a kinswoman of Mary. Luke 1.

Elizabeth[2], born Elizabeth Bowes-Lyon, now the Queen Mother (1900–). Queen consort of King George VI and the mother of Elizabeth II. She was the daughter of the 14th Earl of Strathmore and Kinghorne and is sometimes called Elizabeth of Glamis. She married the future king in April, 1923, when he was George, Duke of York.

Elizabeth I (1533–1603). Queen of England (1558–1603), daughter of Henry VIII and Anne Boleyn. In 1558 she succeeded the Catholic Mary I on the throne and re-established the Protestant religion in England. She survived several plots to murder her and place the Catholic Mary, Queen of Scots, on the throne. Elizabeth, who never married, kept Mary imprisoned from 1568 until her execution in 1587. In 1588 Philip of Spain began a Catholic crusade against Protestant England. The defeat of the Spanish Armada in that year was a mark of England's rising status.

Elizabeth II (1926–). Queen of Great Britain and Northern Ireland (1952–), daughter of George VI. In 1947 she married Philip Mountbatten, Duke of Edinburgh. While she was in Kenya, on a Commonwealth tour, George VI died, on February 6, 1952. Her coronation took place on June 2, 1953. National celebrations marked her silver jubilee in 1977.

E·liz·a·be·than (ĭ-lĭz′ə-bē′thən, -bĕth′ən) *adj.* Of, pertaining to, or characteristic of the reign of Elizabeth I of England.
~*n.* One living during the reign of Elizabeth I.

Elizabethan sonnet *n.* A **Shakespearean sonnet** *(see).*

elk (ĕlk) *n., pl.* **elks** or collectively **elk. 1.** A large deer, *Alces alces,* of northern regions, having large, palmate antlers, and called "moose" in North America. **2.** A North American deer, the **wapiti** *(see).* **3.** A light, pliant leather of horsehide or calfskin, tanned and finished to resemble elk hide. [Middle English *elke,* from Old Norse *elgr.*]

elk·hound (ĕlk′hound′) *n.* A hunting dog of a breed developed in Scandinavia, having a grayish coat and a tail curled up over the back. Also called "Norwegian elkhound."

ell[1] (ĕl) *n.* **1.** A wing of a building at right angles to the main structure. **2.** A pipe or tube with a right-angle bend. [From its resemblance to the shape of the capital letter *L.*]

ell[2] *n.* An English linear measure equal to 45 inches, or 114 centimeters, formerly used in measuring cloth. [Middle English *elle, eln,* Old English *eln,* forearm, ell (originally about the length from the elbow to tip of the middle finger).]

el·lag·ic acid (ĭ-lăj′ĭk) *n.* A yellow crystalline compound, $C_{14}H_6O_8$, that is obtained from tannins. [French *ellagique,* from *ellag,* backward spelling of *galle,* plant gall, from Latin *galla.*]

Ellas. See **Greece.**

Elles·mere Island (ĕlz′mîr′). Most northerly part of Canada. An island in Northwest Territories, it is separated from Greenland by a narrow passage. Ellesmere Island has a small Eskimo population and a number of scientific stations.

Ellice Islands. See **Tuvalu.**

El·ling·ton (ĕl′ĭng-tən), **Edward Kennedy,** known as "Duke" (1899–1974). U.S. jazz musician and composer. He began his career in Washington, D.C., as a jazz pianist and in 1918 formed his own dance band. His best-loved compositions include *Mood Indigo* (1930), *Sophisticated Lady* (1933), and *Don't Get Around Much Anymore* (1942). He also wrote a number of longer suites for concert performances, among them *Black, Brown, and Beige* (1943) and *Liberian Suite* (1947).

el·lipse (ĭ-lĭps′) *n.* **1.** A plane curve formed by: **a.** A conic section taken neither parallel to an element nor parallel to the axis of the intersected cone. **b.** The locus of points the sum of the distances of each of which from two fixed points is the same constant. **2.** Ellipsis. [Back-formation from ELLIPSIS; when an ellipse is formed from a conic section the angle made by the base of the cone and the intersecting plane is less than, or "falls short of," the angle made by the intersecting plane, which forms a parabola.]

el·lip·sis (ĭ-lĭp′sĭs) *n., pl.* **-ses** (-sēz′). **1.** *Grammar.* The omission of a word or phrase necessary for a complete syntactic construction but not necessary for understanding, as *Coming!* for *I am coming.* **2.** The use of ellipsis, especially as a literary device. **3.** A mark or series of marks (. . . or ***) used in writing or printing to indicate an omission, especially of letters or words. [Latin *ellīpsis,* from Greek *elleipsis,* a falling short, defect, from *elleipein,* to leave in or behind, leave out : *en-,* in + *leipein,* to leave.]

el·lip·soid (ĭ-lĭp′soid′) *n.* A geometric surface whose plane sections are all either ellipses or circles. [ELLIPS(E) + -OID.] —**el·lip·soid, el·lip·soid·al** (ĭ-lĭp′soid′l, ĕl′ĭp-) *adj.*

el·lip·tic (ĭ-lĭp′tĭk) *adj.* Also **el·lip·ti·cal** (-tĭ-kəl). **1. a.** Of, pertaining to, or having the shape of an ellipse. **b.** Resembling or having the shape of a flattened circle. **2.** *Grammar.* Containing or characterized by ellipsis; having a word or words omitted. **3.** Expressing ideas in a compressed way that leaves much to be supplied by the understanding of the reader or hearer: *an elliptical style.* [Greek *elleiptikos,* defective, from *elleipein,* to fall short. See **ellipsis.**] —**el·lip·ti·cal·ly** *adv.*

elliptical polarization *n. Physics.* A type of polarization in which the radiation is composed of two plane-polarized waves at right angles, having different amplitudes, and having a phase difference of 90°. The end of the electric or magnetic vector describes an ellipse as the wave progresses.

elliptic geometry *n.* A form of non-Euclidean geometry, **Riemannian geometry** *(see).*

el·lip·tic·i·ty (ĭ-lĭp′tĭs′ə-tē, ĕ′lĭp-) *n.* **1.** Deviation from perfect circular or spherical form toward elliptic or ellipsoidal form. **2.** The degree of such deviation, expressed as the ratio of the length of the major axis to that of the minor axis.

El·lis (ĕl′ĭs), **(Henry) Havelock** (1859–1939). English writer and psychologist. His monumental *Studies in the Psychology of Sex* was published in seven volumes (1897–1928).

Ellis Island. Small island in Upper New York Bay, the reception center for immigrants to the United States from 1892 to 1943.

Ells·worth Land (ĕlz′wûrth′). Situated at the base of the Antarctic Peninsula, it contains the Ellsworth Mts., with Vinson Massif, at 5,140 meters (16,864 feet), the highest peak in the continent.

Ellul. Variant of **Elul.**

elm (ĕlm) *n.* **1.** Any of various deciduous trees of the genus *Ulmus,* widely planted as shade trees and characteristically having coarsely toothed leaves with one side longer than the other. **2.** The wood of an elm. [Middle English *elm,* Old English *elm.*]

elm *The English elm (above)—once common in America and Britian—has had its ranks severely reduced by Dutch elm disease. The species' botanical name is* Ulmus procera.

el·o·cu·tion (ĕl′ə-kyōō′shən) *n.* **1.** The art of public speaking, emphasizing gesture and vocal production and delivery. **2.** Style or manner of speaking, especially in public. [Middle English *elocucion,* from Latin *ēlocūtiō* (stem *ēlocūtiōn-*), from *ēloquī* (past participle *ēlocūtus*), to speak out : *ex-,* out + *loquī,* to speak.] —**el·o·cu·tion·ar·y** (ĕl′ə-kyōō′shə-nĕr′ē) *adj.* —**el·o·cu·tion·ist** *n.*

E·lo·him (ĕ-lō′hĭm, ĕl′ō-hēm′). The Hebrew name for God most frequently encountered in the Old Testament. Compare **Yahweh.** [Hebrew *'Elōhim,* plural of *'Elōah,* God, perhaps enlarged from *'Ēl,* God.]

E·lo·hist (ĕ-lō′hĭst, ĕl′ō-hĭst) *n.* The author of the passages of the Hexateuch in which the name *Elohim* is used to designate God rather than the name *Yahweh.* —**El·o·his·tic** (ĕl′ō-hĭs′tĭk) *adj.*

e·lon·gate (ĭ-lông′gāt′, ĭ-lŏng′-) *v.* **-gated, -gating, -gates.** —*tr.* To lengthen or extend. —*intr.* To grow in length.
~*adj.* **1.** Lengthened; extended. **2.** Slender; tapered. [Late Latin *ēlongāre* : Latin *ex-,* out + *longus,* long.]

e·lon·ga·tion (ĭ-lông′gā′shən, ĭ-lŏng′-, ē′lông-, ē′lŏng-) *n.* **1.** The act of elongating or the condition of being elongated. **2.** Something that elongates; an extension. **3.** *Physics.* The amount of elongation, usually expressed as a percentage of original length. **4.** *Astronomy.* The difference in celestial longitude between the sun and the moon or a planet.

e·lope (ĭ-lōp′) *intr.v.* **eloped, eloping, elopes. 1.** To run away with a lover, especially with the intention of getting married, usually without parental consent. **2.** To run away; abscond. [Norman French *aloper,* legal term applied to a wife who ran away with her lover, from Middle English *alopen* (unattested), past participle of *alepen* (unattested), to run away : *a-* (away) + *lepen,* to run, leap, Old English *hlēopan.*] —**e·lope·ment** *n.* —**e·lop·er** *n.*

el·o·quence (ĕl′ə-kwəns) *n.* **1.** Persuasive and fluent discourse.

PRONUNCIATION KEY

ă, pat; ā, pay; âr, care;
ä, father, are; b, bib;
ch, church; d, deed; ĕ, pet;
ē, be; f, fife; g, gag; h, hat;
hw, which; ĭ, pit; ī, pie;
îr, pier; j, judge; k, kick;
l, lid, needle; m, mum;
n, no, sudden; ng, thing;
ŏ, pot; ō, toe; ô, paw, for;
oi, noise; ou, out; ŏŏ, book;
ōō, boot; p, pop; r, roar;
s, sauce; sh, ship, dish;
t, tight; th, thin, path;
th, this, bathe; ŭ, cut; ûr, fur;
v, valve; w, with; y, yes;
z, zebra, size; zh, vision;
ə, about, item, edible,
gallop, circus, peaceful

IN FOREIGN WORDS:

à, *Fr.* ami; œ, *Fr.* feu, *Ger.* schön; ü, *Fr.* tu, *Ger.* über; KH, *Ger.* ich, *Scot.* loch; N, *Fr.* bon; y′, *Fr.* Compiègne

STRESS MARKS:

Primary stress: ′
in·cite′ (ĭn-sīt′)
Secondary stress: ′
in′sight′ (ĭn′sīt′)

2. The ability or power to persuade with discourse.

el·o·quent (ĕl′ə-kwənt) *adj.* **1.** Persuasive, fluent, and graceful in speech or writing. **2.** Vividly or movingly expressive, as of an emotion: *"Each face eloquent of polite misgiving"* (Evelyn Waugh). [Middle English, from Old French, from Latin *ēloquēns* (stem *ēloquent-*), present participle of *ēloquī,* to speak out. See **elocution.**] **—el·o·quent·ly** *adv.* **—el·o·quent·ness** *n.*

El Pas·o (ĕl păs′ō). A city of western Texas, on the Rio Grande just across the Mexican border.

El Sal·va·dor (ĕl săl′və-dôr′). The smallest and most densely populated state in mainland Latin America. Its colonizers, the Aztecs, were conquered by Spain in *c.* 1526. A civil war between left-wing guerrillas and the government (1979–1992) ended in a signed peace agreement. The country is chiefly agricultural, producing coffee, cotton, and hardwoods. The predominantly Roman Catholic population is of mixed European and Indian descent. Area, 21,041 square kilometers (8,122 square miles). Population, 4,800,000. Capital, San Salvador. See map at **Central America.**

Ely *Once a beacon for travelers through the surrounding fens, the tower of Ely Cathedral still commands the landscape for miles around as it has done for more than 800 years.*

else (ĕls) *adj.* **1.** Other; different: *somebody else.* **2.** In addition; additional; more: *Would you like anything else?*
∼*adv.* **1.** In a different time, place, or manner; differently: *How else could it be done?* **2.** If not; otherwise: *Be careful, or else you will make a mistake.* **—or else.** Or there will be unpleasant consequences. Used as a threat: *Behave yourself or else!* [Middle English *elles,* Old English *elles,* otherwise, else; akin to Latin *alius,* Greek *allos.*]

Usage: The possessive forms of constructions using this word are written *anyone else's, someone else's,* and so on. *Who else's,* whether used singly or in combination with a noun *(Who else's car was stolen?),* is felt to be an awkward construction, and stylists try to avoid it by using some phrase such as *Who else had a car stolen? Whose else* is often heard, especially governed by the verb *be*: *Whose else should it have been?* The use of *else* as a coordinating conjunction is common in informal speech *(Run, else you'll be late!),* but *or else* is recommended as the general rule.

else·where (ĕls′hwâr′) *adv.* To or in a different or other place: *The book isn't on the desk; you'll have to look elsewhere.*

ELT English language teaching.

El·ton (ĕl′tən), **Charles Sutherland** (1900–). British biologist, a founder of the modern science of ecology. His most important writings include *Animal Ecology* (1927) and *The Pattern of Animal Communities* (1966).

el·u·ant, el·u·ent (ĕl′yo͞o-ənt) *n. Chemistry.* A substance used as a solvent in the process of elution. [Latin *ēluere,* to wash out : *ē-, ex-,* out + *luere,* to wash.]

e·lu·ci·date (ĭ-lo͞o′sə-dāt′) *v.* **-dated, -dating, -dates.** *—tr.* To make clear or plain; clarify. *—intr.* To clarify something. —See Synonyms at **explain.** [Late Latin *ēlūcidāre* : Latin *ex-,* completely + *lūcidus,* bright, clear, from *lūcēre,* to shine.] **—e·lu·ci·da·tion** *n.* **—e·lu·ci·da·tive** (ĭ-lo͞o′sə-dā′tĭv) *adj.* **—e·lu·ci·da·tor** *n.*

e·lude (ĭ-lo͞od′) *tr.v.* **eluded, eluding, eludes. 1.** To avoid or escape from, as by cunning, daring, or artifice; evade: *elude capture.* **2.** To escape understanding or detection by; baffle: *The meaning of her glance eluded him.* —See Synonyms at **escape.** [Latin *ēlūdere,* "to take away from (someone) at play," to cheat, deceive : *ex-,* away + *lūdere,* to play, from *lūdus,* play.] **—e·lu·sion** (ĭ-lo͞o′zhən) *n.*

E·lul, El·lul (ĕ-lo͞ol′, ĕl′o͞ol) *n.* The 12th month of the year in the Hebrew calendar. See feature at **alphabet.** [Hebrew *'Elūl,* from Akkadian *ulūlu, elūlu,* "(time when the harvest is) brought in."]

e·lu·sive (ĭ-lo͞o′sĭv) *adj.* **1.** Tending to elude grasp, perception, or comprehension: *an elusive goal.* **2.** Difficult to define or describe: *an elusive charm.* **—e·lu·sive·ly** *adv.* **—e·lu·sive·ness** *n.*

e·lute (ē-lo͞ot′) *tr.v.* **eluted, eluting, elutes.** *Chemistry.* To remove (a mixture or a component from a mixture) by means of a solvent. [Latin *ēluere* (past participle *ēlutus*), to wash out. See **eluant.**] **—e·lu·tion** *n.*

e·lu·tri·ate (ĭ-lo͞o′trē-āt′) *tr.v.* **-ated, -ating, -ates.** To purify, separate, or remove (ore, for example) by washing, settling, and decanting. [Latin *ēlūtriāre,* from *ēluere,* to wash out. See **eluvium.**] **—e·lu·tri·a·tion** *n.*

e·lu·vi·al (ĭ-lo͞o′vē-əl) *adj.* Of, pertaining to, or consisting of eluvium.

e·lu·vi·a·tion (ĭ-lo͞o′vē-ā′shən) *n.* Internal movement of substances in solution or in suspension from the upper and middle layers of soil by water percolating downward or horizontally. Leaching is a form of eluviation. [ELUVI(UM) + -ATION.]

e·lu·vi·um (ĭ-lo͞o′vē-əm) *n.* Residual deposits of soil, dust, and rock particles produced by the action of the wind. [New Latin, from Latin *ēluere,* to wash out : *ex-,* out + *luere,* to wash.]

el·ver (ĕl′vər) *n.* A young or immature eel. [Variant of *eelfare,* originally "the passage of young eels up a river" : EEL + FARE.]

elves. Plural of **elf.**

elvish. Variant of **elfish.**

E·ly (ē′lē). A city on the Ouse River, in Cambridgeshire, England. The city is dominated by its cathedral, dating back to the 11th century and housing many Saxon relics.

Ely, Isle of. Region of Cambridgeshire in east-central England. The region has extensive fens, now drained and devoted to the cultivation of sugar beets and vegetables. The name *Isle* comes from the high ground amid the fens; the name *Ely* supposedly refers to the eels formerly found in the fens.

E·ly·sée (ā′lē-zā′) *n.* The residence of the president of France, in Paris on the Champs Elysées.

E·ly·sian (ĭ-lĭzh′ən) *adj.* **1.** Pertaining to or suggestive of Elysium. **2.** Blissful; delightful.

E·ly·si·um (ĭ-lĭz′ē-əm, ĭ-lĭzh′əm) *n.* **1.** *Greek Mythology.* The abode of the blessed after death. Also called "Elysian Fields." **2.** A place or condition of ideal happiness. [Latin *Ēlysium,* from Greek *Ēlusion† (pedion),* Elysian (fields).]

E·ly·tis (ĭ-lē′tĭs), **Odysseus,** born Odysseus Alepoudelis (1911–). Greek poet educated in Athens and Paris. His works include *Axion Esti* (1959), *Orientations* (1940), *The Light Tree* (1971), and *Maria Nefeli* (1978). In 1979 he received the Nobel Prize for literature.

el·y·tron (ĕl′ə-trŏn′) *n., pl.* **-tra** (-trə). Either of the leathery or chitinous forewings of a beetle or related insect, serving to encase the thin, membranous hind wings used in flight. [New Latin, from Greek *elutron,* covering, sheath.] **—el·y·troid** (ĕl′ə-troid′) *adj.*

em (ĕm) *n.* **1.** The letter *m.* **2.** *Printing. Abbr.* **m, M** The square of the body size of any type, used as a unit of measure; especially, that of a pica M. Originally, an em was equivalent to the space occupied by the letter M in any given font.
∼*adj. Printing.* Designating a dash or space equal to the width of an em.

'em (əm) *pron. Informal.* Them. [Originally from Middle English *hem,* Old English *him, heom,* dative and accusative plural of *hē,* HE; but now felt as a shortened form of *them.*]

em-[1]. Variant of **en-** (put into).

em-[2]. Variant of **en-** (into).

e·ma·ci·ate (ĭ-mā′shē-āt′) *tr.v.* **-ated, -ating, -ates.** To make abnormally thin, as by starvation or illness. [Latin *ēmaciāre* : *ex-,* completely + *maciāre,* to make thin, from *macer,* thin.] **—e·ma·ci·a·tion** *n.*

em·a·lan·ge·ni. Plural of **lilangeni.**

em·a·nate (ĕm′ə-nāt′) *v.* **-nated, -nating, -nates.** *—intr.* To come forth or proceed, as from a source or origin; issue; originate. *—tr.* To send forth; emit. [Latin *ēmānāre,* to flow out : *ex-,* out + *mānāre,* to flow.] **—em·a·na·tive** *adj.*

em·a·na·tion (ĕm′ə-nā′shən) *n.* **1.** An act or instance of emanating; a coming or flowing forth. **2. a.** Something that emanates or issues from a source; an effluence. **b.** *Chemistry.* A gaseous product of radioactive disintegration.

e·man·ci·pate (ĭ-măn′sə-pāt′) *tr.v.* **-pated, -pating, -pates. 1.** To free from oppression, bondage, or restraint; liberate. **2.** To free from constraints imposed by social or moral conventions. Often used in the passive. **3.** In Roman law, to release (a child) from the control of his parents. [Latin *ēmancipāre,* "to release from slavery or tutelage" : *e-,* out of, EX- + *mancipium,* ownership, purchase, from *manceps* (stem *mancip-*), purchaser.] **—e·man·ci·pa·tive** *adj.* **—e·man·ci·pa·tor** *n.*

e·man·ci·pat·ed (ĭ-măn′sə-pā′tĭd) *adj.* **1.** No longer subject to official authority or control. **2.** No longer subscribing to accepted moral and social conventions: *an emancipated woman.*

e·man·ci·pa·tion (ĭ-măn′sə-pā′shən) *n.* **1.** The act of emancipating. **2.** The condition of being emancipated; freedom; liberation.

e·mar·gi·nate (ĭ-mär′jə-nĭt, -nāt′) *adj.* Having a notched tip. Said of a leaf or petal. [Latin *ēmarginātus,* past participle of *ēmargināre,* to take the edge away : *ex-,* away + *margō* (stem *margin-*), MARGIN.]

e·mas·cu·late (ĭ-măs′kyə-lāt′) *tr.v.* **-lated, -lating, -lates. 1.** To remove the male organs of; castrate. **2.** To deprive of vigor or character; make weak or ineffectual.
∼*adj.* (-lĭt, -lāt′). **1.** Emasculated. **2.** Weak; ineffectual. [Latin *ēmasculāre* : *ex-* (removal) + *masculus,* male, manly.] **—e·mas·cu·la·tion** *n.* **—e·mas·cu·la·tive, e·mas·cu·la·to·ry** (ĭ-măs′kyə-lə-tôr′ē, -tōr′ē) *adj.* **—e·mas·cu·la·tor** *n.*

em·balm (ĕm-bäm′, ĭm-) *tr.v.* **-balmed, -balming, -balms. 1.** To prevent the decay of (a corpse) by treatment with preservatives. **2.** To save from oblivion; preserve the memory of. [Middle English *embaumen, embalmen,* from Old French *embaumer, embasmer* : *en-,* to put on + *basme,* BALM.] **—em·balm·er** *n.* **—em·balm·ment** *n.*

em·bank (ĕm-băngk′, ĭm-) *tr.v.* **-banked, -banking, -banks.** To confine, support, or protect with a bank or embankment.

em·bank·ment (ĕm-băngk′mənt, ĭm-) *n.* **1.** The act of embanking. **2.** A mound of earth or stone built to hold back water or to support a road or railway.

em·bar·go (ĕm-bär′gō, ĭm-) *n., pl.* **-goes. 1.** An order by a government prohibiting the movement of merchant ships into or out of its ports. **2.** A governmental suspension of foreign trade or of foreign trade in a particular commodity. **3.** An injunction forbidding the acceptance of particular freight for shipment. **4.** Any prohibition.
∼*tr.v.* **embargoed, -going, -goes. 1.** To impose an embargo upon. **2.** To commandeer for state use. [Spanish, from *embargar,* to impede, restrain, from Vulgar Latin *imbarricāre* (unattested), "to place behind bars" : Latin *in-,* in + *barra* (unattested), BAR.]

em·bark (ĕm-bärk′, ĭm-) *v.* **-barked, -barking, -barks.** *—tr.* **1.** To cause to board a vessel or aircraft. **2.** To enlist (a person) or invest (money) in an enterprise. *—intr.* **1.** To go aboard a vessel or aircraft, especially at the start of a journey. **2.** To set out on a venture; commence. Used with *on* or *upon.* [Old French *embarquer,* from Late Latin *imbarcāre* : *in-,* in + *barca,* BARK.] **—em·bar·ka·tion** (ĕm′bär-kā′shən), **em·bark·ment** *n.*

em·bar·ras de ri·chesses (äɴ′bä-rä′ də-rē-shĕs′) *n.* An abundance of possible choices so great as to perplex. [French, "embarrassment of riches."]

em·bar·rass (ĕm-băr′əs, ĭm-) *tr.v.* **-rassed, -rassing, -rasses. 1.** To cause to feel self-conscious or ill at ease; disconcert. **2.** To involve in or hamper with financial difficulties. Usually used in the passive.

3. To beset with difficulties; impede. **4.** To complicate. [French *embarrasser*, from Spanish *embarazar*, from Italian *imbarazzare*, from *imbarrare*, "to put in bars," impede : *in-*, in, from Latin + *barra* (unattested), BAR.] —**em·bar·rass·ing·ly** *adv.*

em·bar·rass·ment (ĕm-băr′əs-mənt, ĭm-) *n.* **1.** The state of being embarrassed. **2.** Something that embarrasses. **3.** A state of financial difficulty. **4.** An overabundance. Used chiefly in the phrase *an embarrassment of riches.*

em·bas·sy (ĕm′bə-sē) *n., pl.* **-sies.** **1.** The position, function, or duties of an ambassador. **2.** A mission to a foreign government headed by an ambassador. **3.** An ambassador and his staff. **4.** The official headquarters of an ambassador and his staff. [Middle English, from Old French *ambassee*, from Old Italian *ambasciata*, from Old Provençal *ambaissada*, from *ambaissa* (unattested), service, from Medieval Latin *ambactia*. See ambassador.]

em·bat·tle[1] (ĕm-băt′l, ĭm-) *tr.v.* **-tled, -tling, -tles.** **1.** To prepare or array for battle. **2.** To prepare to struggle or resist. **3.** To fortify. [Middle English *embatailen*, from Old French *embataillier* : *en-*, in + *bataille*, to battle, from *bataille*, BATTLE.]

embattle[2] *tr.v.* **-tled, -tling, -tles.** To furnish with battlements for defense. [Middle English *embatailen* : *en-*, in + *batailen*, to build, fortify, from Old French *bataillier*, from *bataille*, battlement, BATTLE.]

em·bat·tled (ĕm-băt′əld, ĭm-) *adj.* Involved in an argument, contest, or struggle.

em·bay (ĕm-bā′, ĭm-) *tr.v.* **-bayed, -baying, -bays.** **1.** To put or force (a vessel) into a bay; shelter or detain in a bay. **2.** To enclose in or as if in a bay. **3.** To form into a bay.

em·bay·ment (ĕm-bā′mənt, ĭm-) *n.* **1.** A bay or baylike indentation in a coastline. **2.** The formation of a bay.

em·bed (ĕm-bĕd′, ĭm-) *v.* **-bedded, -bedding, -beds.** Also **im·bed** (ĭm-). **-*tr.*** **1.** To fix firmly in a surrounding mass. **2.** To enclose snugly or firmly. **3.** To fix in the memory. **4.** To include (a subordinate clause, for example) in a sentence. **-*intr.*** To become embedded.

em·bel·lish (ĕm-bĕl′ĭsh, ĭm-) *tr.v.* **-lished, -lishing, -lishes.** **1.** To make more beautiful, as by ornamentation; adorn. **2.** To add fanciful or fictitious details to (a statement or narrative). **3.** To provide with a musical embellishment. [Middle English *embelisshen*, from Old French *embellir* (present stem *embelliss-*) : *en-* (causative) + *bel*, beautiful, from Latin *bellus*.]

em·bel·lish·ment (ĕm-bĕl′ĭsh-mənt, ĭm-) *n.* **1.** The act of embellishing. **2.** The state of being embellished. **3.** Something that serves to embellish; ornamentation. **4.** *Music.* A note or group of notes, as a trill, that embellishes a melody.

em·ber (ĕm′bər) *n.* **1.** A small piece of live coal or wood, as in a dying fire. **2. embers.** The smoldering coal or ash of a dying fire. **3. embers.** What is left of a once intense feeling. [Middle English *embre, emere,* Old English *ǣmerge,* embers, ashes.]

Ember day *n.* Any of three days out of each calendar season observed by special prayer and formerly by fasting in some Christian churches, falling on the Wednesday, Friday, and Saturday after the first Sunday of Lent, after Whitsunday, after September 14, and after December 13. [Middle English *Ymber Daye,* Old English *Ymbrendæg,* "recurring day" : *ymbryne,* "a running around," circuit : *ymbe,* around + *ryne,* a running + *dæg,* DAY.]

Ember week *n.* A week in which Ember days fall.

em·bez·zle (ĕm-bĕz′əl, ĭm-) *v.* **-zled, -zling, -zles.** **-*tr.*** To take (money or property) for one's own use in violation of a trust. **-*intr.*** To embezzle money or property. [Middle English *embesilen,* from Norman French *enbesiler* : Old French *en-* (intensive) + *besiller*†, to do away with, destroy.] —**em·bez·zle·ment** *n.* —**em·bez·zler** *n.*

em·bit·ter (ĕm-bĭt′ər, ĭm-) *tr.v.* **-tered, -tering, -ters.** **1.** To arouse bitter feelings in; make resentful or hostile. **2.** To make (a trouble or quarrel, for example) more distressing; aggravate. —**em·bit·ter·ment** *n.*

em·blaze (ĕm-blāz′, ĭm-) *tr.v.* **-blazed, -blazing, -blazes.** **1.** To set on fire. **2.** To cause to glow or glitter.

em·bla·zon (ĕm-blā′zən, ĭm-) *tr.v.* **-zoned, -zoning, -zons.** **1.** To ornament with heraldic devices or armorial bearings. **2.** To depict according to heraldic convention. **3.** To make resplendent with brilliant colors or other ornamentation. **4.** To proclaim or display conspicuously; celebrate. [EM- + BLAZON.] —**em·bla·zon·er** *n.* —**em·bla·zon·ment** *n.*

em·bla·zon·ry (ĕm-blā′zən-rē, ĭm-) *n.* **1.** The art of emblazoning according to heraldic convention. **2.** Heraldic devices collectively.

em·blem (ĕm′bləm) *n.* **1.** An object or a depiction of an object that comes to represent something else, usually by suggesting its nature or history; a pictorial symbol. **2.** A distinctive badge, design, or device. **3.** A typical representation or embodiment; a personification. [Middle English *emblem,* from Latin *emblēma,* inlaid work, from Greek, insertion, from *emballein,* to throw in, insert : *en-,* in + *ballein,* to throw.]

em·blem·at·ic (ĕm′blə-măt′ĭk) *adj.* Also **em·blem·at·i·cal** (-ĭ-kəl). **1.** Of, pertaining to, or serving as an emblem. **2.** Symbolic. —**em·blem·at·i·cal·ly** *adv.*

em·blem·a·tize (ĕm-blĕm′ə-tīz′) *tr.v.* **-tized, -tizing, -tizes.** Also **em·blem·ize** (ĕm′blə-mīz′) **-ized, -izing, -izes.** To represent with or as if with an emblem; symbolize.

em·ble·ments (ĕm′blə-mənts) *pl.n. Law.* The annual crops or profits of land cultivated by a tenant farmer. [Middle English *emblay-ment,* from Old French *emblaement,* land sown with wheat, from *blé,* wheat, corn.]

em·bod·i·ment (ĕm-bŏd′ĭ-mənt, ĭm-) *n.* **1.** The act of embodying or the condition of being embodied. **2.** One that embodies something: *"The flag is the embodiment, not of sentiment, but of history"* (Woodrow Wilson).

em·bod·y (ĕm-bŏd′ē, ĭm-) *tr.v.* **-bodied, -bodying, -bodies.** **1.** To invest with or as if with bodily form; make corporeal; incarnate. **2.** To express (a feeling or concept, for example) in tangible or concrete form: *The painting embodies the artist's horror of war.* **3.** To be a typical and concrete example or manifestation of; personify: *dedicated men who embodied the tradition of public service.* **4.** To include in a larger whole; incorporate.

em·bold·en (ĕm-bōl′dən, ĭm-) *tr.v.* **-ened, -ening, -ens.** To foster boldness in; encourage.

em·bo·lec·to·my (ĕm′bə-lĕk′tə-mē) *n., pl.* **-mies.** The surgical removal of an embolus. [EMBOL(US) + -ECTOMY.]

em·bol·ic (ĕm-bŏl′ĭk, ĭm-) *adj. Pathology.* Of or pertaining to an embolus or an embolism.

em·bo·lism (ĕm′bə-lĭz′əm) *n.* **1.** Obstruction or occlusion of a blood vessel by an embolus. **2.** The insertion of a period of time into a calendar; intercalation. [Middle English *embolisme,* from Medieval Latin *embolismus,* from Late Latin, insertion, from Greek *embolismos,* from *emballein,* "to throw in," insert. See emblem.] —**em·bo·lis·mic** (ĕm′bə-lĭz′mĭk) *adj.*

em·bo·lus (ĕm′bə-ləs) *n., pl.* **-li** (-lī′). An air bubble, detached clot, mass of bacteria, or other foreign body that obstructs a blood vessel. [New Latin, from Latin, piston, from Greek *embolos,* "something inserted," stopper, from *emballein,* to throw in, insert. See emblem.]

em·bo·ly (ĕm′bə-lē) *n. Embryology.* The development of a gastrula from a blastula by invagination. [Greek *embolē,* insertion, entrance, from *emballein,* to insert. See emblem.]

em·bon·point (äN′bôN-pwäN′) *n.* A well-fed appearance; plumpness. [French, from Old French, from *en bon point,* in good condition.]

em·bos·om (ĕm-bŏoz′əm, -bŏo′zəm, ĭm-) *tr.v.* **-omed, -oming, -oms.** **1.** *Archaic.* To clasp to or hold in the bosom; embrace. **2.** To envelop or enclose protectively; shelter.

em·boss (ĕm-bôs′, -bŏs′, ĭm-) *tr.v.* **-bossed, -bossing, -bosses.** **1.** To represent, mold, or carve (a design) in relief. **2.** To raise (an inscription, for example) in relief on paper, metal, or the like. **3.** To cover with or as if with bosses: *"The whole buoy was embossed with barnacles"* (Herman Melville). **4.** To ornament lavishly; adorn. [Middle English *embosen,* from Old French *embocer* (unattested), "to put a knob in" : *en-,* in + *boce,* BOSS (knob).] —**em·boss·er** *n.* —**em·boss·ment** *n.*

em·bou·chure (ŏm′bŏo-shŏor′) *n.* **1. a.** The mouth of a river. **b.** The opening out of a valley into a plain. **2. a.** The mouthpiece of a wind instrument. **b.** The manner in which the lips and tongue are applied to such a mouthpiece. [French, from Old French *emboucher,* "to put in one's mouth" : *en-,* in + *bouche,* mouth, from Latin *bucca,* puffed-out cheek.]

em·bowed (ĕm-bōd′, ĭm-) *adj.* **1.** Bent or curved like a bow. **2.** *Architecture.* **a.** Arched. **b.** Protruding in an outward curve so as to form a recess.

em·bow·el (ĕm-bou′əl, ĭm-) *tr.v.* **-eled, -eling, -els** or *chiefly British* **-elled, -elling, -els.** To disembowel.

em·bow·er (ĕm-bou′ər, ĭm-) *tr.v.* **-ered, -ering, -ers.** To enclose in or as if in a bower; surround, as with sheltering foliage.

em·brace[1] (ĕm-brās′, ĭm-) *v.* **-braced, -bracing, -braces.** **-*tr.*** **1.** To clasp or hold to one with the arms, usually as a display of affection. **2. a.** To encircle or surround. **b.** To twine around. **3.** To include, comprise, or contain; encompass. **4.** To take up (a cause or doctrine, for example); adopt. **5.** To avail oneself of; accept eagerly: *embrace an opportunity.* **6.** To take in with the eyes or mind. **7.** To submit to with dignity or fortitude: *embrace misfortune.* **-*intr.*** To join in an embrace; hug affectionately: *They embraced, then said good-by.* **-See Synonyms at include.** **~*n.*** **1.** An act of embracing; an affectionate hug. **2.** An enclosure or encirclement. **3.** Eager acceptance. [Middle English *embracen,* from Old French *embracer,* from Vulgar Latin *imbracchiāre* (unattested) : Latin *in-* + *bracchium,* arm, from Greek *brakhiōn.*] —**em·brace·a·ble** *adj.* —**em·brace·ment** *n.* —**em·brac·er** *n.*

embrace[2] *tr.v.* **-braced, -bracing, -braces.** *Law.* To try to influence (a judge or jury) by corrupt means. [Back-formation from EMBRACER.] —**em·brac·er·y** (ĕm-brā′sə-rē, ĭm-) *n.*

em·brac·er, em·brace·or (ĕm-brā′sər, ĭm-) *n. Law.* One guilty of attempting to influence a court illegally. [Middle English *embracer,* from Old French *embraseor,* instigator, from *embraser,* "to set on fire," instigate : *en-,* in + *brese,* embers.]

em·branch·ment (ĕm-brănch′mənt, ĕm-bränch′-, ĭm-) *n.* **1.** A branching out or off, as of a mountain range or river. **2.** A subdivision; a ramification.

em·bra·sure (ĕm-brā′zhər, ĭm-) *n.* **1.** *Architecture.* An opening in a wall for a door or window, slanted so that its interior dimensions are larger than those of its exterior. **2.** An opening for a gun in a wall or parapet. [French, from *embraser,* to set on fire, fire a gun. See embracer.]

em·bro·cate (ĕm′brə-kāt′) *tr.v.* **-cated, -cating, -cates.** To moisten and rub (a painful part of the body) with a liniment or lotion. [Medieval Latin *embrocāre,* from Late Latin *embrocha,* lotion, from

embrasure *Light from a window brightens a recess, or embrasure, inside a 13th-century tower in Pembroke Castle, Wales.*

Greek *embrokhē,* from *embrekhein,* to moisten with a lotion : *en-,* in + *brekhein,* to wet.]

em·bro·ca·tion (ĕm′brə-kā′shən) *n.* A liniment.

em·broi·der (ĕm-broi′dər, ĭm-) *v.* **-dered, -dering, -ders.** —*tr.* **1.** To ornament (fabric) with needlework. **2.** To work (a design) into fabric with a needle and thread. **3.** To embellish (a narrative, for example) with fictitious details or exaggerations. —*intr.* To make embroidery. [Middle English *embroderen,* from Norman French *enbrouder* : Old French *en-,* in + *brouder, brosder,* to embroider, from (unattested) Frankish *brusdan.*] —**em·broi·der·er** *n.*

em·broi·der·y (ĕm-broi′də-rē, ĭm-) *n., pl.* **-ies. 1.** The art, act, or practice of embroidering. **2.** Ornamentation on fabric done in needlework. **3.** A piece of embroidered fabric. **4.** Fictitious or exaggerated detail added, as to a narrative.

em·broil (ĕm-broil′, ĭm-) *tr.v.* **-broiled, -broiling, -broils. 1.** To involve in argument, conflict, or difficulties: *embroiled in a diplomatic scandal.* **2.** To throw (a situation, for example) into confusion or disorder; entangle. [French *embrouiller* : Old French *en-,* in + *brouiller,* to mix, confuse, probably from *breu,* broth, from Germanic.] —**em·broil·ment** *n.*

em·brown (ĕm-broun′, ĭm-) *tr.v.* **-browned, -browning, -browns.** To make brown or dusky; darken.

embrue. Variant of **imbrue.**

em·bry·ec·to·my (ĕm′brē-ĕk′tə-mē) *n., pl.* **-mies.** The surgical removal of an extrauterine embryo. [EMBRY(O) + -ECTOMY.]

em·bry·o (ĕm′brē-ō′) *n., pl.* **-os. 1.** *Biology.* **a.** An organism in its early stages of development, especially before it has reached a distinctively recognizable form. **b.** Such an organism at any time before full development, birth, or hatching. **2. a.** The fertilized egg of a vertebrate animal following cleavage. **b.** In man, the prefetal product of conception up to the beginning of the third month of pregnancy. **3.** *Botany.* The minute, rudimentary plant contained within a seed or archegonium. **4. a.** A rudimentary or initial stage. **b.** Something at a rudimentary or undeveloped stage: *the embryo of an idea.*
~*adj.* Incipient; rudimentary. [Medieval Latin *embryo* (stem *embryon-*), from Greek *embruon,* "something that grows in the body" : *en-,* in + *bruein,* to grow.]

em·bry·o·gen·e·sis (ĕm′brē-ō-jĕn′ə-sĭs) *n.* Also **em·bry·og·e·ny** (-ŏj′ə-nē). The development and growth of an embryo. —**em·bry·o·gen·ic** (ĕm′brē-ō-jĕn′ĭk), **em·bry·o·ge·net·ic** (-jə-nĕt′ĭk) *adj.*

em·bry·ol·o·gy (ĕm′brē-ŏl′ə-jē) *n.* **1.** The science dealing with the formation, early growth, and development of living organisms. **2.** The embryonic structure and development of a particular organism. —**em·bry·o·log·ic** (ĕm′brē-ə-lŏj′ĭk), **em·bry·o·log·i·cal** (-ĭ-kəl) *adj.* —**em·bry·o·log·i·cal·ly** *adv.* —**em·bry·ol·o·gist** *n.*

em·bry·on·ic (ĕm′brē-ŏn′ĭk) *adj.* Also **em·bry·on·al** (ĕm′brē-ə-nəl) (for sense 1). **1.** Of, pertaining to, or in the state of being an embryo. **2.** Still at an early stage of development; rudimentary.

embryo sac *n.* The large oval cell in which the embryo develops in seed plants.

em·bus (ĕm-bŭs′, ĭm-) *v.* **-bused** or **-bussed, -busing** or **-bussing, -buses** or **-busses.** —*tr.* To transport (troops, for example) by bus. —*intr.* To board a bus.

em·cee (ĕm-sē′) *n. Informal.* A **master of ceremonies** (see).
~*v.* **emceed, -ceeing, -cees.** *Informal.* —*tr.* To serve as master of ceremonies of. —*intr.* To act as master of ceremonies. [From *master* of ceremonies.]

-eme *suffix.* Indicates an irreducible unit of linguistic structure; for example, **morpheme, phoneme.** [French *-ème,* abstracted from *phonème,* PHONEME.]

emeer. Variant of **emir.**

e·mend (ĭ-mĕnd′) *tr.v.* **emended, emending, emends. 1.** To correct and improve (a text) by critical editing. **2.** *Archaic.* To free from faults. —See Usage note at **amend.** [Middle English *emenden,* from Latin *ēmendāre* : *ex-* (removal) + *mendum,* fault.]

e·men·date (ē′mĕn-dāt′, ĭ-mĕn′-) *tr.v.* **-dated, -dating, -dates.** To emend (a text). —**e·men·da·tor** *n.*

e·men·da·tion (ĭ-mĕn′dā′shən, ē′mĕn-) *n.* **1.** The act of emending. **2.** An alteration that improves something; especially, a textual correction, as in a literary work. —**e·men·da·to·ry** (ĭ-mĕn′də-tôr′ē, -tōr′ē) *adj.*

em·er·ald (ĕm′ər-əld, ĕm′rəld) *n.* **1.** A brilliant, transparent green beryl used as a gemstone. **2.** A brilliant green color.
~*adj.* **1.** Of, pertaining to, or similar to an emerald. **2.** Of a brilliant green color. [Middle English *emeraude,* from Old French *esmeraude,* from Vulgar Latin *smaralda* (unattested), variant of Latin *smaragdus,* SMARAGDITE.]

Emerald Isle. The island of Ireland.

e·merge (ĭ-mûrj′) *intr.v.* **emerged, emerging, emerges. 1.** To rise up or come forth from or as if from immersion. **2.** To become evident or known. **3.** To issue, as from obscurity or difficulties: *They emerged from the war changed men.* **4.** To come into existence. [Latin *ēmergere* : *ex-,* out of + *mergere,* to dip, immerse.]

e·mer·gence (ĭ-mûr′jəns) *n.* **1.** The act or process of emerging. **2.** *Botany.* A superficial outgrowth of plant tissue, such as a thorn, containing no conducting tissues. **3.** *Philosophy.* The unpredicted appearance of new characteristics or phenomena in the course of biological or social evolution.

e·mer·gen·cy (ĭ-mûr′jən-sē) *n., pl.* **-cies. 1.** An unexpected situation or sudden occurrence of a serious and urgent nature that demands immediate action. **2.** A pressing need, as after a flood, for relief or help: *a state of emergency.*

embroidery *An embroidered sampler by Hannah Taylor, made in 1774 in Newport, Rhode Island. Before printed embroidery patterns became available, samplers included a variety of stitches as demonstrations, or samples, of their creator's skill.*

e·mer·gent (ĭ-mûr′jənt) *adj.* **1.** Coming into existence, view, or attention; issuing forth. **2.** Newly independent. Said of a state.
~*n. Botany.* An emersed plant.

emergent evolution *n.* A theory holding that completely new types of organisms, modes of behavior, and consciousness appear at certain stages of the evolutionary process, usually as a result of an unpredictable rearrangement of the pre-existing elements.

e·mer·i·tus (ĭ-mĕr′ə-təs) *adj.* Retired but retaining an honorary title corresponding to that held immediately before retirement: *a professor emeritus.*
~*n., pl.* **emeriti** (-tī′). One who is emeritus. [Latin *ēmeritus,* past participle of *ēmererī,* to earn by service : *ex-,* out of + *merērī, merēre,* to earn, deserve.]

e·mersed (ĭ-mûrst′) *adj. Botany.* Rising above the surface of the water. Said of the leaves or stems of aquatic plants.

e·mer·sion (ĭ-mûr′zhən, -shən) *n.* **1.** The act of emerging; emergence. **2.** *Astronomy.* **Egress** (see). [Latin *ēmergere* (past participle *ēmersus*), to EMERGE.]

Em·er·son (ĕm′ər-sən), **Ralph Waldo** (1803–82). U.S. poet and essayist. A Unitarian pastor from 1829 to 1832, he subsequently became a writer and lecturer. *Nature* (1836) was an early manifesto of transcendentalist belief in the mystical unity of nature. His essays are regarded as landmarks in the development of American thought and literary expression. —**Em·er·son·i·an** (ĕm′ər-sō′nē-ən) *n. & adj.*

em·er·y (ĕm′ə-rē, ĕm′rē) *n.* A fine-grained impure form of corundum used for grinding and polishing. [Middle English *emery,* from Old French *emeri, esmeril,* from Vulgar Latin *smericulum* (unattested), from Medieval Greek *smēri,* variant of Greek *smuris†,* emery powder.]

emery board *n.* A small, flat strip of cardboard or thin wood coated with powdered emery, used to file the nails.

emery paper *n.* Paper coated with powdered emery, used as a fine abrasive.

emery wheel *n.* An abrasive wheel containing emery powder in a resinous binder, rotated by a motor, and used for smoothing or grinding.

em·e·sis (ĕm′ə-sĭs) *n.* Vomiting. [New Latin, from Greek, from *emein,* to vomit.]

e·met·ic (ĭ-mĕt′ĭk) *adj.* Causing vomiting.
~*n.* An emetic agent or medicine. [Latin *emeticus,* from Greek *emetikos,* inclined to vomit, from *emetos,* vomiting, from *emein,* to vomit.] —**e·met·i·cal·ly** *adv.*

em·e·tine (ĕm′ə-tēn′) *n.* A bitter-tasting, crystalline alkaloid, $C_{29}H_{40}O_4N_2$, derived from ipecac root, and used as an emetic. [French *émétine* : *émétique,* causing vomiting, from Latin *emeticus* (see **emetic**) + -INE.]

emf, EMF electromotive force.

-emia, -aemia, -hemia *suffix.* Indicates blood; for example, **leukemia.** [New Latin, from Greek *-aimiā,* from *haima,* blood.]

em·i·grant (ĕm′ĭ-grənt) *n.* One who emigrates. —**em·i·grant** *adj.*

em·i·grate (ĕm′ĭ-grāt′) *intr.v.* **-grated, -grating, -grates.** To leave one country or region, especially one's native country or region, to settle in another. —See Usage note at **migrate.** [Latin *ēmigrāre,* to move away from : *ex-,* away + *migrāre,* to move.] —**em·i·gra·tion** *n.*

é·mi·gré (ĕm′ĭ-grā′) *n.* An emigrant, especially one who has fled his country during a political upheaval. [French, past participle of *émigrer,* to emigrate, from Latin *ēmigrāre.* See **emigrate.**]

E·mi·li·a-Ro·ma·gna (ā-mēl′yä-rō-män′yä). Formerly **Emilia.** Region in northern Italy comprising the fertile lowlands of the Po River and part of the Apennines in the south.

em·i·nence (ĕm′ə-nəns) *n.* Also **em·i·nen·cy** (-nən-sē) *pl.* **-cies. 1.** A position of great distinction or superiority in achievement, rank, or character. **2.** A rise of ground; a hill. **3. Eminence.** A title of or form of address for a cardinal of the Roman Catholic Church. Used with *His* or *Your.* —See Synonyms at **fame.**

é·mi·nence grise (ā′mē-näns′ grēz′) *n., pl.* **éminences grises** (*pronounced as singular*). A person who exercises power behind the scenes through his influence with prominent people. Also called "gray eminence." [French, "gray eminence" (that is, cardinal), after the French monk Père Joseph (François Le Clerc du Tremblay, 1577–1638), who served as Cardinal Richelieu's secretary.]

em·i·nent (ĕm′ə-nənt) *adj.* **1. a.** Outstanding in performance or character; distinguished: *an eminent historian.* **b.** Of high rank or station. **2.** Towering or standing out above others; prominent. **3.** Remarkable or noteworthy: *a man esteemed for his eminent achievements.* [Middle English, from Old French, from Latin *ēminēns* (stem *ēminent-*), present participle of *ēminēre,* to stand out : *ex-,* out + *minēre,* to stand, project.]
Usage: Similarity in sound often leads to a confusion in spelling between *eminent* and *imminent,* but there is no overlap of meaning. *Eminent* means "prominent, outstanding"; *imminent* means "impending, about to occur."

eminent domain *n. Law.* The right of a government to appropriate private property for public use, usually with compensation to the owner.

em·i·nent·ly (ĕm′ə-nənt-lē) *adv.* Extremely; especially. Used as an intensive: *eminently suitable.*

e·mir, e·meer, a·mir, a·meer (ĭ-mîr′, ä-mîr′) *n.* **1.** A prince, chieftain, or governor, especially in the Middle East. **2.** An honorary title given to the descendants of Muhammad. [French *émir,* from Spanish *emir,* from Arabic *'amīr,* commander, from *amara,* he commanded.]

e·mir·ate (ĭ-mîr′ĭt, ä-mîr′-, -āt′) *n.* **1.** The office or jurisdiction of an emir. 2. A country ruled over by an emir.

em·is·sar·y (ĕm′ə-sĕr′ē) *n., pl.* **-ies. 1.** A messenger or agent sent to represent or advance the interests of a person or state. **2.** An agent with a secret mission. [Latin *ēmissārius,* from *ēmittere* (past participle *ēmissus*), to send out, EMIT.]

e·mis·sion (ĭ-mĭsh′ən) *n.* **1.** The action of emitting. **2.** Something that is emitted, such as the exhaust from an automobile engine. **3. a.** *Physics.* A discharge, as of electrons or radiation. **b.** The amount or rate of this discharge. **4.** An issue, as of paper money or shares. [Latin *ēmittere* (past participle *ēmissus*), to EMIT.]

emission nebula *n.* A nebula that absorbs ultraviolet radiation from stars and re-emits it as visible light.

emission spectrum *n.* The spectrum of bright lines, bands, or continuous radiation characteristic of and determined by a specific emitting substance subjected to a specific kind of excitation. Compare **absorption spectrum.**

e·mis·sive (ĭ-mĭs′ĭv) *adj.* **1.** Sending forth; emitting. **2.** Sent forth; emitted.

em·is·siv·i·ty (ĕm′ə-sĭv′ə-tē) *n.* The ratio of the radiation intensity emitted from a surface to the radiation intensity at the same wavelength emitted from a blackbody at the same temperature.

e·mit (ĭ-mĭt′) *tr.v.* **emitted, emitting, emits. 1.** To give off or send out (liquid, gas, or radiation, for example). **2.** To utter: *"she emitted her small strange laugh"* (Edith Wharton). **3.** To issue with authority; especially, to put (paper currency or shares in a company, for example) into circulation. [Latin *ēmittere,* to send out : *ex-,* out + *mittere,* to send.]

e·mit·ter (ĭ-mĭt′ər) *n.* **1.** An object that emits something. **2.** *Electronics.* The region in a transistor from which charge carriers flow into the base.

Emmanuel. Variant of **Immanuel.**

em·men·a·gogue (ĭ-mĕn′ə-gôg′, -gŏg′) *n.* A medicine that induces or hastens the menstrual flow. [Greek *emmēna,* the menses, from *emmēnos,* monthly : *en-,* in + *mēnē, mēn,* month + -AGOGUE.]

Em·men·thal¹, Em·men·tal (ĕm′ən-täl′). Valley of the upper Emme River in Bern canton, Switzerland, famous for its cheese. **—Em·men·thal·er** *n. & adj.*

Emmenthal², Emmental *n.* A hard cheese with holes. It is made in Emmenthal.

em·mer (ĕm′ər) *n.* A slender-eared Eurasian wheat, *Triticum dicoccum,* cultivated as a cereal grain and livestock feed. [German *Emmer,* from Old High German *amaro.* See **yellowhammer.**]

em·met (ĕm′ĭt) *n. Archaic.* An ant. [Middle English *emete,* from Old English *ǣmete.*]

Em·met (ĕm′ĭt), **Robert** (1778–1803). Irish revolutionary nationalist who in July, 1803, took part in a bungled uprising against British rule. A few weeks later he was captured in Dublin and hanged.

em·me·tro·pi·a (ĕm′ə-trō′pē-ə) *n.* The condition of the normal eye when parallel rays are focused exactly on the retina and vision is perfect. [New Latin : Greek *emmetros,* in measure : *en-,* in + *metron,* measure + -OPIA.] **—em·me·trop·ic** (ĕm′ə-trŏp′ĭk) *adj.*

Em·my (ĕm′ē) *n., pl.* **-mys** or **-mies.** One of the statuettes presented annually by the Academy of Television Arts and Sciences for outstanding television performances and productions. [Alteration of *Immy,* nickname for *image orthicon tube.*]

e·mol·lient (ĭ-mŏl′yənt) *adj.* Having softening and soothing qualities, especially for the skin.
~n. **1.** An agent that softens or soothes the skin. **2.** Anything that assuages or mollifies. [Latin *ēmolliēns* (stem *ēmollient-*), present participle of *ēmollīre,* to soften, soothe : *ex-,* completely + *mollīre,* to soften, from *mollis,* soft.]

e·mol·u·ment (ĭ-mŏl′yə-mənt) *n.* Profit derived from one's office or employment; payment for services rendered. [Middle English, from Latin *ēmolumentum,* originally "miller's fee for grinding grain," from *ēmolere,* to grind out : *ex-,* out + *molere,* to grind.]

e·mote (ĭ-mōt′) *intr.v.* **emoted, emoting, emotes.** *Informal.* To express emotion or sentiment, especially in an effusive and theatrical manner. [Back-formation from EMOTION.] **—e·mot·er** *n.*

e·mo·tion (ĭ-mō′shən) *n.* **1. a.** A complex and usually strong subjective response, as love or fear. **b.** Such a response involving physiological changes as a preparation for action. **2.** A state of agitation or disturbance: *controlled her emotions with effort.* **3.** The part of the consciousness that involves feeling or sensibility: *a choice determined by emotion rather than reason.* —See Synonyms at **feeling.** [French *émotion,* earlier *esmocion,* from Old French *esmovoir,* to excite, from Vulgar Latin *exmovēre* (unattested), variant of Latin *ēmovēre,* to move out, stir up, excite : *ex-,* out + *movēre,* to move.]

e·mo·tion·al (ĭ-mō′shə-nəl) *adj.* **1.** Of or pertaining to emotion. **2.** Readily affected with or stirred by emotion. **3.** Capable of stirring the emotions: *an emotional appeal.* **4.** Revealing emotion; agitated. **—e·mo·tion·al·i·ty** (ĭ-mō′shə-năl′ə-tē) *n.* **—e·mo·tion·al·ly** *adv.*

e·mo·tion·al·ism (ĭ-mō′shə-nə-lĭz′əm) *n.* **1.** An inclination to encourage or yield to emotion: *the emotionalism of adolescents.* **2.** Undue display of emotion. **3.** An ethical or aesthetic attitude basing conduct or value on emotion. **—e·mo·tion·al·ist** *n.* **—e·mo·tion·al·is·tic** (ĭ-mō′shə-nə-lĭs′tĭk) *adj.*

e·mo·tion·al·ize (ĭ-mō′shə-nə-līz′) *tr.v.* **-ized, -izing, -izes.** To impart an emotional character to.

e·mo·tion·less (ĭ-mō′shən-lĭs) *adj.* Devoid of apparent emotion.

e·mo·tive (ĭ-mō′tĭv) *adj.* Pertaining to, expressing, or tending to excite emotion; especially, likely to arouse an ill-considered or irrational response. **—e·mo·tive·ly** *adv.* **—e·mo·tive·ness, e·mo·tiv·i·ty** (ē′mō-tĭv′ə-tē) *n.*

e·mo·tiv·ism (ĭ-mō′tĭv-ĭz′əm) *n. Philosophy.* The doctrine that ethical propositions are neither true nor false statements, but expressions of emotion. Compare **descriptivism, prescriptivism. —e·mo·tiv·ist** *n. & adj.*

Emp. 1. emperor; empress. **2.** empire.

empale. Variant of **impale.**

empanel. Variant of **impanel.**

em·path·ic (ĕm-păth′ĭk, ĭm-) *adj.* Also **em·pa·thet·ic** (ĕm′pə-thĕt′ĭk). Of, pertaining to, or characterized by empathy. **—em·path·i·cal·ly, em·pa·thet·i·cal·ly** *adv.*

em·pa·thize (ĕm′pə-thīz′) *intr.v.* **-thized, -thizing, -thizes.** To feel or experience empathy. Often used with *with.*

em·pa·thy (ĕm′pə-thē) *n.* **1.** Understanding so intimate that the feelings, thoughts, and motives of one person are readily comprehended by another. **2.** The attribution of feelings aroused by an object in nature or art to the object itself, as when one speaks of a painting full of love. [EN- (in) + -PATHY (translation of German *Einfühlung,* "a feeling in"), after Greek *empatheia,* passion.]

Em·ped·o·cles (ĕm-pĕd′ə-klēz′) (*fl.* 5th century B.C.). Greek philosopher, poet, physician, and statesman, born in Sicily. He taught that all matter is composed of particles of fire, water, earth, and air. More important for the future of physics was his belief that all change is caused by motion.

em·pen·nage (ĕm′pə-nĭj, ŏm′pə-näzh′) *n. Aeronautics.* The **tail** *(see).* [French, originally "the feathers on an arrow," from *empenner,* to put feathers on an arrow : *en-,* in + *penne,* feather, from Latin *pinna.*]

em·per·or (ĕm′pər-ər) *n.* **1.** *Abbr.* **Emp.** The male ruler of an empire, having power either absolute or subject to constitutional restrictions. **2. a.** Any of several brightly colored butterflies of the family Nymphalidae, such as *Asterocampa clyton,* having orange-tawny wings with dark markings. Also called "emperor butterfly." **b.** Any of several moths of the family Saturniidae; especially, an Old World species, *Saturnia pavonia,* having distinctively patterned wings. Also called "emperor moth." [Middle English *emperour,* from Old French *empereor,* from Latin *imperātor,* emperor, commander, from *imperāre* (past participle *imperātus*), "to prepare against (an occasion)," hence to command : *in-,* against + *parāre,* to prepare.] **—em·per·or·ship** *n.*

emperor moth *The feathery antennae of the male emperor moth—varieties of which are found all over Europe and Asia—can detect the scent of a female from more than half a mile away. The cocoon of the moth's caterpillar has a ring of spines at its exit, like a lobster pot in reverse, preventing predators from entering.*

emperor penguin *n.* A large penguin, *Aptenodytes forsteri,* of Antarctic regions, having yellow-orange patches on the neck.

em·per·y (ĕm′pə-rē) *n., pl.* **-ies. 1.** Absolute dominion or jurisdiction; sovereignty. **2.** *Archaic.* The domain of an emperor. [Middle English *emperie,* from Old French, EMPIRE.]

em·pha·sis (ĕm′fə-sĭs) *n., pl.* **-ses** (-sēz′). **1.** Special importance or significance placed upon or imparted to something: *put too much emphasis on being neat.* **2.** Stress applied to a syllable, word, or passage by the use of vocal expression, gesture, italics, or other indication. **3.** Force or intensity of expression, feeling, or action. **4.** Sharpness or vividness of outline; prominence. [Latin, from Greek, reflection, meaning, significance, from *emphainein,* to exhibit, indicate : *en-,* in + *phainein,* to show.]

em·pha·size (ĕm′fə-sīz′) *tr.v.* **-sized, -sizing, -sizes.** To impart emphasis to; stress.

em·phat·ic (ĕm-făt′ĭk) *adj.* **1.** Expressed or performed with emphasis. **2.** Bold and definite in expression or action; positive. **3.** Standing out in a striking and clearly defined way; definite: *an emphatic victory.* **4.** Designating an English verb form using the auxiliary verb *do* to make a strong assertion. **5.** *Phonetics.* Having a hard constrictive velarized quality, as certain Arabic consonants do. [Late Latin *emphaticus,* from Greek *emphatikos,* exhibited, hence emphatic, from *emphainein,* to exhibit. See **emphasis.**] **—em·phat·i·cal·ly** *adv.*

em·phy·se·ma (ĕm′fə-sē′mə) *n.* **1.** An abnormal condition of the lungs marked by dilation of the air sacs resulting in labored breathing. **2.** A distention of connective tissues due to retention of air. [New Latin, from Greek *emphusēma,* swelling, inflation, from *emphusan,* to blow in : *en-,* in + *phusan,* to blow, from *phusai,* bellows.] **—em·phy·sem·a·tous** (ĕm′fə-sĕm′ə-təs) *adj.*

em·pire (ĕm′pīr′) *n. Abbr.* **Emp. 1.** A political unit, usually larger than a kingdom and often comprising a number of territories or nations, ruled by a single supreme authority. **2.** The territory included in such a unit. **3. a.** Imperial dominion. **b.** The period during which such dominion exists. **4.** An extensive enterprise under a unified authority: *a publishing empire.* [Middle English *empire,* from Old French *empire, emperie,* from Latin *imperium,* dominion, empire, from *imperāre,* to command. See **emperor.**]

Em·pire (ŏm-pîr′, ĕm′pīr′) *adj.* Of, pertaining to, or characteristic of a neoclassic style, as in clothing or the decorative arts, prevalent in France during the first part of the 19th century. [After the 1st *Empire* of France (1804–15).]

empire builder *n.* A person who seeks to increase his influence, power, or control by constantly acquiring new operations or staff. **—empire building** *n.*

em·pir·ic (ĕm-pîr′ĭk, ĭm-) *n.* One who believes that practical experience is the sole source of knowledge. [Latin *empiricus,* from Greek *empeirikos,* from *empeirā,* experience, from *empeiros,* experienced in : *en-,* in + *peira,* experiment, trial.]

em·pir·i·cal (ĕm-pîr′ĭ-kəl, ĭm-) *adj.* **1.** Relying upon or derived from observation or experiment: *empirical methods; an empirical conclu-*

PRONUNCIATION KEY

ă, pat; ā, pay; âr, care; ä, father, are; b, bib; ch, church; d, deed; ĕ, pet; ē, be; f, fife; g, gag; h, hat; hw, which; ĭ, pit; ī, pie; îr, pier; j, judge; k, kick; l, lid, needle; m, mum; n, no, sudden; ng, thing; ŏ, pot; ō, toe; ô, paw, for; oi, noise; ou, out; o͝o, book; o͞o, boot; p, pop; r, roar; s, sauce; sh, ship, dish; t, tight; th, thin, path; *th,* this, bathe; ŭ, cut; ûr, fur; v, valve; w, with; y, yes; z, zebra, size; zh, vision; ə, about, item, edible, gallop, circus, peaceful

IN FOREIGN WORDS:

à, *Fr.* ami; œ, *Fr.* feu, *Ger.* schön; ü, *Fr.* tu, *Ger.* über; KH, *Ger.* ich, *Scot.* loch; N, *Fr.* bon; y', *Fr.* Compiègne

STRESS MARKS:

Primary stress: ′ in·cite′ (ĭn-sīt′)
Secondary stress: ′ in′sight′ (ĭn′sīt′)

emu *Standing up to 1.8 meters (6 feet) tall and weighing more than 45 kilograms (100 pounds), the emu is a flightless bird of the Australian grasslands. It can run up to 50 kilometers (30 miles) per hour.*

enamel *Blue and red areas of glasslike enamel decorate a 19th-century thimble from Russia.*

sion. **2.** Guided by practical experience and not theory, especially in medicine. **—em·pir·i·cal·ly** *adv.*

empirical formula *n.* A type of chemical formula that indicates the ratio of the elements rather than the total number of atoms in a molecule. Compare **molecular formula, structural formula.**

em·pir·i·cism (ĕm-pîr′ə-sĭz′əm, ĭm-) *n.* **1. a.** The view that experience, especially of the senses, is the only source of knowledge. **b.** *Philosophy.* The doctrine based on this view. Compare **rationalism. 2. a.** The employment of empirical methods, as in an art or science. **b.** An empirical conclusion. **3.** The practice of medicine that is based upon practical experience rather than scientific theory. **—em·pir·i·cist** *n.*

em·place (ĕm-plās′, ĭm-) *tr.v.* **-placed, -placing, -places.** To put in place or position.

em·place·ment (ĕm-plās′mənt, ĭm-) *n.* **1.** A prepared position, such as a mounting or platform, for military equipment and guns. **2.** The act of setting in position; placement. **3.** Position; location. [French, place, situation, from (obsolete) *emplacer,* to place in (a position) : *em-,* in + *placer,* to PLACE.]

emplane. Variant of **enplane.**

em·ploy (ĕm-ploi′, ĭm-) *tr.v.* **-ployed, -ploying, -ploys. 1.** To use in some process or effort; put to service. **2.** To devote or apply (one's time or energies, for example) to some activity. **3. a.** To engage the services of; put to work. **b.** To provide with a job and livelihood.
~n. **1.** The state of being employed. **2.** *Archaic.* Occupation. [Middle English *emploien,* from Old French *employer, emplier,* from Latin *implicāre,* to infold, involve : *in-,* in + *plicāre,* to fold.] **—em·ploy·a·bil·i·ty** *n.* **—em·ploy·a·ble** *adj.*

em·ploy·ee (ĕm-ploi′ē, ĭm-, ĕm′ploi-ē′) *n.* A person who works for another in return for financial or other compensation.

em·ploy·er (ĕm-ploi′ər, ĭm-) *n.* A person or concern that employs persons for wages or a salary.

em·ploy·ment (ĕm-ploi′mənt, ĭm-) *n.* **1. a.** The act of employing; a putting to use. **b.** The state of being employed. **2.** The work in which one is engaged; business or profession. **3.** The purpose for which something is used. **4.** An activity to which one devotes time.

em·po·ri·um (ĕm-pôr′ē-əm, -pōr′ē-əm, ĭm-) *n., pl.* **-riums** or **-poria** (-pôr′ē-ə, -pōr′ē-ə). **1.** A large retail shop, such as a department store, carrying a wide variety of merchandise. **2.** A place, town, or city that is an important trade center; a marketplace. [Latin, from Greek *emporion,* market, from *emporos,* merchant, traveler : *en-,* in + *poros,* path, journey.]

em·pow·er (ĕm-pou′ər, ĭm-) *tr.v.* **-ered, -ering, -ers. 1.** To invest with legal power; authorize. **2.** To enable or permit. **—em·pow·er·ment** *n.*

em·press (ĕm′prĭs) *n. Abbr.* **Emp. 1.** A female sovereign of an empire. **2.** The wife or widow of an emperor. [Middle English *emperesse,* from Old French, feminine of *empereor,* EMPEROR.]

em·prise, em·prize (ĕm-prīz′, ĭm-) *n.* **1.** Chivalrous daring or prowess. **2.** An undertaking, especially one of a chivalrous or adventurous nature. [Middle English *emprise,* from Old French, from the feminine past participle of *emprendre,* to undertake, from Vulgar Latin *imprendere* (unattested) : Latin *in-,* in + *prendere, prehendere,* to take, seize.]

emp·ty (ĕmp′tē) *adj.* **-tier, -tiest. 1.** Void of content; containing nothing: *an empty bottle.* **2.** Having no occupants or inhabitants; vacant: *an empty chair.* **3.** Having no load or cargo: *an empty truck.* **4.** Lacking force or power: *an empty threat.* **5.** Lacking purpose or substance; meaningless: *an empty life.* **6.** Idle: *empty hours.* **7.** Vacuous; inane: *an empty mind.* **8.** Needing nourishment; hungry. **9.** Devoid; destitute. Used with *of*: *empty of pity.*
~v. **emptied, -tying, -ties.** *—tr.* **1.** To remove the contents of; make empty: *empty one's pockets.* **2.** To transfer or pour off: *empty the ashes into a pail.* **3.** To unburden; relieve. Used with *of*: *empty oneself of doubt.* *—intr.* **1.** To become empty. **2.** To discharge or flow. Used with *into*: *The river empties into a bay.*
~n., pl. **empties.** An empty container: *returned the empties to the store.* [Middle English *empty, emptie,* Old English *ǣmettig, ǣmtig,* empty, unoccupied, from *ǣmetta,* rest, leisure.] **—emp·ti·ly** *adv.* **—emp·ti·ness** *n.*

Synonyms: *bare, barren, blank, vacant, vacuous, void.*

emp·ty-hand·ed (ĕmp′tē-hăn′dĭd) *adj.* **1.** Bearing no gift, possessions, or the like: *They arrived empty-handed.* **2.** Having received or gained nothing.

emp·ty-head·ed (ĕmp′tē-hĕd′ĭd) *adj.* Lacking sense or discretion; foolish; scatterbrained.

Empty Quarter. See **Rub al Khali.**

empty set *n. Mathematics.* A set that has no members. Also called "null set."

em·pur·ple (ĕm-pûr′pəl, ĭm-) *tr.v.* **-pled, -pling, -ples.** To color or tinge with purple.

em·py·e·ma (ĕm′pī-ē′mə) *n., pl.* **-mata** (-mə-tə). Pus in a body cavity, especially the pleural cavity. [Medieval Latin, from Greek *empūēma,* from *empuein,* to suppurate.] **—em·py·e·mic** *adj.*

em·py·re·al (ĕm′pī-rē′əl, ĕm-pîr′ē-əl, ĭm-) *adj.* **1.** Empyrean. **2.** Of or pertaining to the sky; celestial. **3.** Formed of pure fire or light; fiery. **4.** Heavenly; sublime. [Middle English *imperyale,* from Late Latin *empyrius, empyreus,* from Greek *empurios, empuros,* fiery : *en-,* in + *pur,* fire.]

em·py·re·an (ĕm′pī-rē′ən, ĕm-pîr′ē-ən, ĭm-) *n.* **1.** The highest reaches of heaven, believed by the ancients to be a realm of pure fire and by early Christians to be the abode of God and the angels. **2.** The sky; space.
~adj. Of or pertaining to the empyrean of ancient belief. [Late Latin *empyreus,* EMPYREAL.]

EMS European Monetary System.

e·mu (ē′myo͞o) *n., pl.* **emus.** A large, flightless Australian bird, *Dromaius novaehollandiae,* related to and resembling the cassowary. [Portuguese *ema,* perhaps from Moluccan *eme.*]

emu electromagnetic unit.

em·u·late (ĕm′yə-lāt′) *tr.v.* **-lated, -lating, -lates. 1.** To strive to equal or excel, especially through imitation. **2.** To compete with or rival successfully: *Korea emulates Japan in its single-minded productivity.* **3.** *Computer Science.* To imitate one system with another so that both accept the same data, execute the same programs, and achieve the same results. —See Synonyms at **rival.** [Latin *aemulārī,* from *aemulus,* EMULOUS.] **—em·u·la·tive** *adj.* **—em·u·la·tive·ly** *adv.* **—em·u·la·tor** *n.*

em·u·la·tion (ĕm′yə-lā′shən) *n.* **1.** Effort or ambition to equal or surpass another. **2.** Imitation of another.

em·u·lous (ĕm′yə-ləs) *adj.* **1.** Eager or ambitious to equal or surpass another. **2.** Characterized or prompted by a spirit of rivalry. [Latin *aemulus,* imitating, probably related to *imitārī,* to IMITATE.] **—em·u·lous·ly** *adv.* **—em·u·lous·ness** *n.*

e·mul·si·fy (ĭ-mŭl′sə-fī′) *tr.v.* **-fied, -fying, -fies.** To make into an emulsion. [EMULSI(ON) + -FY.] **—e·mul·si·fi·ca·tion** *n.* **—e·mul·si·fi·er** *n.*

e·mul·sion (ĭ-mŭl′shən) *n.* **1. a.** A suspension of small globules of one liquid in a second liquid with which the first will not mix, such as milk fats in milk. **b.** Any milklike liquid. **2.** A light-sensitive coating, usually of silver halide grains in a thin gelatin layer, on photographic film, paper, or glass. **3.** Emulsion paint. [New Latin, from Latin *ēmulgēre* (past participle *ēmulsus*), to drain out, milk out : *ex-,* out + *mulgēre,* to milk.] **—e·mul·sive** *adj.*

emulsion paint *n.* A type of paint in which the pigment is dispersed in an oil that forms an emulsion with water.

e·mul·soid (ĭ-mŭl′soid′) *n. Chemistry.* A type of colloid in which small droplets of a liquid are dispersed throughout a solid continuous phase. [*Emul*sion + coll*oid.*]

e·munc·to·ry (ĭ-mŭngk′tə-rē) *adj.* Serving to carry waste matter out of the body; excretory.
~n., pl. **emunctories.** An emunctory organ or passage. [Middle English *emunctorie,* from Medieval Latin *ēmunctōrius,* from Latin *ēmungere* (past participle *ēmunctus*), to blow the nose : *ex-,* completely + *mungere,* to blow the nose.]

en (ĕn) *n.* **1.** The letter *n.* **2.** *Printing. Abbr.* **n, N** A space equal to half the width of an **em** *(see).*
~adj. Printing. Designating a dash or space that is equal to the width of an en.

en-[1] *prefix.* Also **em-** before *b, p,* and sometimes *m.* Indicates: **1.** To put into or on; for example, **encompass, enthrone. 2.** To go into or on; for example, **entrain. 3.** To cover, surround, or imbue with; for example, **enrobe, empurple. 4.** To provide with; for example, **empower. 5.** To cause to be in a specified state or condition; for example, **endanger, enslave.** [Middle English, from Old French, from Latin *in-, im-.*]

en-[2] *prefix.* Also **em-** before *b, m, p,* or *ph.* Indicates in, into, or within; for example, **enzootic, empathy.** [Middle English *en-,* from Latin, from Greek. In borrowed Greek compounds, *en-* also becomes *el-* before *l,* as in **ellipsis.**]

-en[1] *suffix.* Indicates: **1.** To be, become, or cause to be; for example, **cheapen, redden. 2.** To cause to have or gain; for example, **lengthen, hearten.** [Middle English *-nen, -nien,* Old English *-nian.*]

-en[2] *suffix.* Indicates made of, composed of, or resembling; for example, **wooden, earthen, ashen.** [Middle English *-en,* Old English *-en.*]

en·a·ble (ĕn-ā′bəl) *tr.v.* **-bled, -bling, -bles. 1. a.** To supply with the means, knowledge, or opportunity to be or do something. **b.** To make feasible or possible. **2.** To give legal power, capacity, or sanction to; permit.

enabling act *n. British.* A law passed to give certain powers to a person or organization, as a governmental department.

en·act (ĕn-ăkt′) *tr.v.* **-acted, -acting, -acts. 1.** To give effect to (legislation); decree by legislative process; pass. **2.** To act out, as on a stage; represent. **—en·act·a·ble** *adj.* **—en·ac·tor** *n.*

en·ac·tive (ĕn-ăk′tĭv) *adj.* Having the capacity or force to enact.

en·act·ment (ĕn-ăkt′mənt) *n.* **1.** The act of enacting. **2.** The state of being enacted. **3.** A law or statute.

en·am·el (ĭ-năm′əl) *n.* **1.** A smooth, glassy, usually opaque protective or decorative coating baked on metal, glass, or ceramic ware. **2.** An object with an enameled surface, as a piece of cloisonné. **3.** A paint that dries to a hard, glossy surface. **4.** A glossy, hard coating resembling enamel: *nail enamel.* **5.** *Anatomy.* The hard, calcium-containing substance covering the exposed portion of a tooth.
~tr.v. **enameled** or **-elled, -eling** or **-elling, -els. 1.** To coat, inlay, or decorate with enamel. **2.** To give a glossy or brilliant surface to. **3.** To adorn with or as if with bright colors. [Middle English *enamelen,* from Norman French *enameller, enamailler* : *en-,* in + *amail,* enamel, from Old French *esmail,* from Germanic.] **—en·am·el·er, en·am·el·ist** *n.*

en·am·el·ing (ĭ-năm′ə-lĭng) *n.* **1.** The art, craft, or occupation of a person who enamels. **2.** A coating or decoration of enamel.

en·am·el·ware (ĭ-năm′əl-wâr′) *n.* Articles coated with enamel.

en·am·or (ĭ-năm′ər) *tr.v.* **-ored, -oring, -ors.** Also *chiefly British* **en·am·our, -oured, -ouring, -ours.** To inspire with love; charm; captivate: *enamored of his surroundings.* [Middle English *enamouren,* from Old French *enamourer* : *en-*, in + *amour*, love, from Latin *amor*, from *amāre*, to love.]

en·an·ti·o·mer (ĕn-ăn′tē-ə-mər) *n.* An enantiomorph. [Greek *enantios*, opposite (see **enantiomorph**) + -MER.] —**en·an·ti·o·mer·ic** (ĕn-ăn′tē-ə-mĕr′ĭk) *adj.*

en·an·ti·o·morph (ĕn-ăn′tē-ə-môrf′) *n. Chemistry.* Either of a pair of crystals that are similar in form but cannot be superimposed, one crystal being the mirror image of the other. [Greek *enantios*, opposite : *en-*, in + *antios*, opposite, from *anti*, over against + -MORPH.] —**en·an·ti·o·morph·ism** (ĕn-ăn′tē-ə-môr′fĭz′əm) *n.* —**en·an·ti·o·mor·phous** (-môr′fəs), **en·an·ti·o·mor·phic** (-môr′fĭk) *adj.*

en·ar·thro·sis (ĕn′är-thrō′sĭs) *n., pl.* **-ses** (-sēz′). *Anatomy.* A ball-and-socket joint. [New Latin, from Greek *enarthrōsis*, from *enarthros*, jointed : *en-*, in + *arthron*, joint.]

e·nate (ē′nāt′, ĭ-nāt′) *adj.* Also **e·nat·ic** (ĭ-năt′ĭk) (for sense 2). **1.** Growing outward. **2.** Related on the mother's side. ~*n.* A relative on one's mother's side. [Latin *ēnātus*, past participle of *ēnāscī*, to be born from : *ex-*, out of + *nāscī*, to be born.]

en bloc (äN blŏk′) *adv.* All together; collectively; as a whole or single unit. [French, "in (a) block."]

en bro·chette (äN′ brô-shĕt′) *adj.* Broiled or roasted on a skewer. [French, "on (a) skewer."]

en brosse (äN brôs′) *adj.* Standing stiffly upright as a result of being cut very short. Said of hair. [French, "in (a) brush."]

enc. enclosed; enclosure.

en·cae·nia (ĕn-sēn′yə, -sē′nē-ə, ĭn-) *n.* An annual commemoration held at universities, especially in England, honoring founders and benefactors. [Latin, feast of dedication, from Greek *enkainia* (plural) : *en-*, in + *kainos*, new.]

en·cage (ĕn-kāj′, ĭn-) *tr.v.* **-caged, -caging, -cages.** To confine in or as if in a cage.

en·camp (ĕn-kămp′, ĭn-) *v.* **-camped, -camping, -camps.** —*intr.* To set up or live in a camp. —*tr.* To provide quarters for in a camp.

en·camp·ment (ĕn-kămp′mənt, ĭn-) *n.* **1.** The act of setting up a camp. **2.** A camp or campsite.

en·cap·su·late (ĕn-kăp′sə-lāt′, ĭn-) *v.* **-lated, -lating, -lates.** Also **in·cap·su·late** (ĭn-). —*tr.* **1.** To encase in or as if in a capsule. **2.** To summarize very concisely. —*intr.* To become encapsulated. —**en·cap·su·la·tion** *n.*

en·case (ĕn-kās′, ĭn-) *tr.v.* **-cased, -casing, -cases.** Also **in·case** (ĭn-). To enclose in or as if in a case. —**en·case·ment** *n.*

en·cash (ĕn-kăsh′, ĭn-) *tr.v.* **-cashed, -cashing, -cashes.** *British.* To cash (a check). —**en·cash·a·ble** *adj.* —**en·cash·ment** *n.*

en·caus·tic (ĕn-kô′stĭk, ĭn-) *adj.* Pertaining to a painting process in which colored beeswax is applied and fixed with heat. ~*n.* **1.** The art of painting in this way. **2.** An encaustic painting. [Latin *encausticus*, from Greek *enkaustikos*, from *enkaiein*, to burn in : *en-*, in + *kaiein*, to burn.]

-ence, -ency *suffix.* Indicates action, state, quality, or condition; for example, **competence, patience.** [Middle English *-ence*, from Old French, from Latin *-entia*, from *-ēns*, present participial suffix.]

en·ceinte¹ (äN-săNt′) *adj.* Being with child; pregnant. [French, from Old French, from Vulgar Latin *incienta* (unattested), from Latin *inciens*.]

enceinte² *n.* **1.** An encircling fortification around a fort, castle, or town. **2.** The structures or area protected by such a fortification. [French, from Latin *incinta*, feminine past participle of *incingere*, to gird in : *in-*, in + *cingere*, to gird.]

en·ce·phal·ic (ĕn′sə-făl′ĭk) *adj.* **1.** Of or pertaining to the brain. **2.** Located within the cranial cavity.

en·ceph·a·li·tis (ĕn-sĕf′ə-lī′tĭs) *n.* Inflammation of the brain. Also called "brain fever," "phrenitis." —**en·ceph·a·lit·ic** (ĕn-sĕf′ə-lĭt′ĭk) *adj.*

encephalitis le·thar·gi·ca (lə-thär′jĭ-kə) *n.* A viral epidemic encephalitis often held to be associated with some forms of influenza and marked by apathy, double vision, and extreme muscular weakness. Also called "lethargic encephalitis," "sleeping sickness." [New Latin, "lethargic encephalitis."]

encephalo-, encephal– *comb. form.* Indicates the brain; for example, **encephalogram, encephalitis.** [New Latin, from Greek *(muelos)* *enkephalos*, "(marrow) in the head," the brain : *en-*, in + *kephalē*, head.]

en·ceph·a·lo·gram (ĕn-sĕf′ə-lə-grăm′) *n.* **1.** An x-ray picture of the brain taken by encephalography. **2.** An **electroencephalogram** (see).

en·ceph·a·log·ra·phy (ĕn-sĕf′ə-lŏg′rə-fē) *n.* A technique for recording the structure of the brain by tracing electrical activity, detecting ultrasonic pulses, or introducing air to provide a contrast medium for x-rays. —**en·ceph·a·lo·graph** (ĕn-sĕf′ə-lə-grăf′) *n.* —**en·ceph·a·lo·graph·ic** (ĕn-sĕf′ə-lə-grăf′ĭk) *adj.*

en·ceph·a·lo·ma (ĕn-sĕf′ə-lō′mə) *n., pl.* **-mas** or **-mata** (-mə-tə). A tumor of the brain. [ENCEPHAL(O)- + -OMA.]

en·ceph·a·lo·my·e·li·tis (ĕn-sĕf′ə-lō-mī′ə-lī′tĭs) *n.* Acute inflammation of the brain and the spinal cord.

en·ceph·a·lon (ĕn-sĕf′ə-lŏn′) *n., pl.* **-la** (-lə). The brain of a vertebrate. [New Latin, from Greek *enkephalon, enkephalos*. See **en·cephalo-**.]

en·ceph·a·lop·a·thy (ĕn-sĕf′ə-lŏp′ə-thē) *n., pl.* **-thies.** Any of various diseases that affect the brain. [ENCEPHALO- + -PATHY.] —**en·ceph·a·lo·path·ic** (ĕn-sĕf′ə-lō-păth′ĭk) *adj.*

en·chain (ĕn-chān′, ĭn-) *tr.v.* **-chained, -chaining, -chains.** **1.** To bind with or as if with chains; fetter: *Superstition enchains the mind.* **2.** To hold fast; rivet (the attention, for example). [Middle English

encheynen, from Old French *enchaeiner* : *en-*, in + *chaeine*, CHAIN.] —**en·chain·ment** *n.*

en·chant (ĕn-chănt′, -chänt′, ĭn-) *tr.v.* **-chanted, -chanting, -chants.** **1.** To cast under a spell; bewitch. **2.** To delight completely; charm; enrapture. [Middle English *enchanten*, Old French *enchanter*, from Latin *incantāre*, to chant (magic words) : *in-* (intensive) + *cantāre*, frequentative of *canēre*, to sing.]

en·chant·er (ĕn-chăn′tər, -chän′tər, ĭn-) *n.* One that enchants; especially, a sorcerer or magician.

enchanter's nightshade *n.* Any of several plants of the genus *Circaea*, especially *C. lutetiana*, having small white flowers and bristly, clinging fruit.

en·chant·ing (ĕn-chăn′tĭng, -chän′tĭng, ĭn-) *adj.* Having the power to enchant; delightful: *a children's book with enchanting illustrations.* —**en·chant·ing·ly** *adv.*

en·chant·ment (ĕn-chănt′mənt, -chänt′mənt, ĭn-) *n.* **1. a.** An act of enchanting. **b.** The state of being enchanted. **2.** Something that enchants; an irresistible charm or allure. **3.** A magic spell.

en·chant·ress (ĕn-chăn′trĭs, -chän′trĭs, ĭn-) *n.* **1.** A woman of unusual allure or fascination. **2.** A sorceress.

en·chase (ĕn-chās′, ĭn-) *tr.v.* **-chased, -chasing, -chases.** **1.** To set (a gem, for example) in some material. **2.** To set with or as if with gems. **3.** To decorate or ornament (a surface) by inlaying, engraving, or chasing. [Middle English *enchasen*, from Old French *enchasser* : *en-*, in + *chasse*, case, from Latin *capsa*, box.]

en·chi·la·da (ĕn′chə-lä′də) *n.* A dish consisting of a tortilla rolled and stuffed usually with a mixture containing meat or cheese and served with a sauce spiced with chili. [American Spanish, feminine past participle of *enchilar*, to put chili in : *en-*, in, from Latin *in-* + *chile*, CHILI.]

en·chi·rid·i·on (ĕn′kī-rĭd′ē-ən) *n., pl.* **-ons** or **-ridia** (-rĭd′ē-ə). A handbook; a manual. [Late Latin, from Greek *enkheiridion* : *en-*, in + *-kheiridion*, diminutive of *kheir*, hand.]

en·chon·dro·ma (ĕn′kŏn-drō′mə) *n., pl.* **-mas** or **-mata** (-mə-tə). A benign cartilaginous tumor that occurs at the growing zone of a bone, between the end and the shaft. [EN- + CHONDR(O)- + -OMA.]

en·cho·ri·al (ĕn-kôr′ē-əl, -kōr′ē-əl, ĭn-) *adj.* Also **en·chor·ic** (-kôr′ĭk, -kōr′ĭk). Belonging or native to a particular region or people. Said especially of demotic writing. [Greek *enkhōrios*, indigenous, native : *en-*, in + *khōra*, country, place.]

-enchyma *suffix.* Indicates cellular tissue; for example, **collenchyma.** [New Latin, from (PAR)ENCHYMA.]

en·ci·pher (ĕn-sī′fər, ĭn-) *tr.v.* **-phered, -phering, -phers.** To put (a message) into cipher. —**en·ci·pher·er** *n.* —**en·ci·pher·ment** *n.*

en·cir·cle (ĕn-sûr′kəl, ĭn-) *tr.v.* **-cled, -cling, -cles.** **1.** To form a circle around; surround. **2.** To move or go around; make a circuit of. —**en·cir·cle·ment** *n.*

Enc·ke's comet (ĕng′kēz) *n.* A comet with a period of 3.3 years, decreasing by 2½ hours each revolution. First observed in 1786, it is the most studied of all comets. [After Johann *Encke* (1791–1865), German astronomer.]

encl. enclosed; enclosure.

en clair (äN klâr′) *adj.* In ordinary uncoded language. [French, "in (the) clear."] —**en clair** *adv.*

en·clasp (ĕn-klăsp′, -kläsp′, ĭn-) *tr.v.* **-clasped, -clasping, -clasps.** To hold in or as if in a clasp; embrace.

en·clave (ĕn′klāv′, ŏn′-) *n.* **1.** A country or part of a country lying wholly within the boundaries of another. Compare **exclave.** **2.** A distinctly bounded area enclosed within a larger area. **3.** An area, as of a city, in which a particular group of people lives or works: *an enclave of artists.* [French, from Old French *enclaver*, to enclose, from Vulgar Latin *inclāvāre* (unattested), to lock in with a key : Latin *in-*, in + *clāvis*, key.]

en·clit·ic (ĕn-klĭt′ĭk, ĭn-) *adj. Linguistics.* Having no independent accent in a sentence and forming an accentual and sometimes also graphemic unit with the preceding word. Said of a word or particle; for example, *'em* in informal English *Give 'em the works* or *-que* in Latin *Senatus populusque Romanus* ("The senate and people of Rome"). Compare **proclitic.** ~*n.* An enclitic word or particle. [Late Latin *encliticus*, from Greek *enklitikos*, "leaning (on the preceding word for accent)," from *enklinein*, to lean on : *en-*, in + *klinein*, to lean.]

en·close (ĕn-klōz′, ĭn-) *tr.v.* **-closed, -closing, -closes.** Also **in·close** (ĭn-). **1.** To surround on all sides; fence in; close in. **2. a.** To place within a container. **b.** To insert in the same envelope or package with the main letter. **3.** To contain, especially so as to shelter or hide: *"every one of those darkly clustered houses encloses its own secret"* (Charles Dickens). —See Usage note at **inclose.** [Middle English *enclosen*, from Old French *enclore* (past participle *enclose*), from Vulgar Latin *inclaudere* (unattested), variant of Latin *inclūdere*, to INCLUDE.]

en·clo·sure (ĕn-klō′zhər, ĭn-) *n. Abbr.* **enc., encl.** **1.** The act of enclosing. **2.** The state of being enclosed or shut up: *The house smelled stale from prolonged enclosure.* **3.** An area that is enclosed. **4.** Something that encloses, such as a wall or fence. **5.** Something, as a letter, that is enclosed in an envelope or package: *The note from his little daughter was a welcome and unexpected enclosure.*

en·code (ĕn-kōd′, ĭn-) *tr.v.* **-coded, -coding, -codes.** **1.** To put (a message) into code. **2.** *Computer Science.* To convert (a character) into an equivalent combination of bits. —**en·cod·er** *n.*

en·co·mi·ast (ĕn-kō′mē-ăst′) *n.* A person who delivers or writes encomiums; a eulogist. [Greek *enkōmiastēs*, from *enkōmiazein*, to praise, from *enkōmion*, ENCOMIUM.]

en·co·mi·as·tic (ĕn-kō'mē-ăs'tĭk) adj. Also en·co·mi·as·ti·cal (-tĭ-kəl). Pertaining to, containing, or being an encomium. —en·co·mi·as·ti·cal·ly adv.

en·co·mi·um (ĕn-kō'mē-əm) n., pl. -ums or -mia (-mē-ə). 1. Warm or glowing praise. 2. A formal expression of praise; a tribute. [Latin encōmium, from Greek enkōmion (epos), "(speech) in praise of a conqueror," from enkōmios, belonging to revels : en-, in + kōmos, celebration, revel (see comedy).]

en·com·pass (ĕn-kŭm'pəs, ĭn-) tr.v. -passed, -passing, -passes. 1. To form a circle or ring about; surround. 2. To enclose; envelop. 3. To comprise; include. 4. To succeed in completing or perfecting; accomplish: an assignment that only the most skilled could encompass. —en·com·pass·ment n.

en·core (ŏn'kôr', -kōr') n. 1. A demand by an audience for an additional performance. 2. An additional performance in response to such a demand.
~tr.v. encored, -coring, -cores. 1. To demand an encore of (a performer). 2. To demand as an encore.
~interj. Used to demand an additional performance. [French, still, yet, again, probably from Latin hinc ad hōram, from that to this hour : hinc, from here, from hic, this + ad, to + hōram, accusative of hōra, hour, from Greek hōra.]

en·coun·ter (ĕn-koun'tər, ĭn-) n. 1. A meeting, especially when casual and unplanned. 2. A hostile confrontation; clash.
~v. encountered, -tering, -ters. —tr. 1. To meet or come upon, especially casually or unexpectedly. 2. To confront in battle or contention. 3. To come up against; be faced with or exposed to: encounter numerous obstacles. —intr. To meet, especially in conflict. [Middle English encountre, from Old French encontre, from encontrer, to meet, from Vulgar Latin incontrāre (unattested) : Latin in-, in + contrā, opposite, against.]

encounter group n. A typically unstructured therapy group in which individuals seek to increase their sensitivity and responsiveness, reveal their feelings, and relate to others openly and intimately, as by verbalizing freely.

en·cour·age (ĕn-kûr'ĭj, ĭn-) tr.v. -aged, -aging, -ages. 1. To inspire to continue on a chosen course; impart courage or confidence to; embolden; hearten. 2. To give support to; foster. —See Synonyms at urge. [Middle English encoragen, from Old French encorager : en- (causative) + corage, COURAGE.] —en·cour·age·ment n.

en·cour·ag·ing (ĕn-kûr'ə-jĭng, ĭn-) adj. Permitting one to be confident or hopeful. —en·cour·ag·ing·ly adv.

en·croach (ĕn-krōch', ĭn-) intr.v. -croached, -croaching, -croaches. 1. To intrude gradually or insidiously upon the domain, possessions, or rights of another; trespass. Used with on or upon. 2. To advance beyond proper or prescribed limits. [Middle English encroachen, from Old French encrochier, "to catch in a hook," seize : en-, in + croc, hook, from (unattested) Frankish krōk.]

en·croach·ment (ĕn-krōch'mənt, ĭn-) n. The act or an instance of encroaching. —See Synonyms at breach.

en·crust (ĕn-krŭst', ĭn-) tr.v. -crusted, -crusting, -crusts. Also in·crust (ĭn-). 1. To cover or surmount with a crust or crustlike layer. 2. To adorn, as with jewels. [Probably from French incruster, from Latin incrustāre : in- (causative) + crusta, CRUST.] —en·crust·a·tion (ĕn'krŭ-stā'shən) n.

en·cryp·tion (ĕn-krĭp'shən, ĭn-) n. A process for scrambling access codes to computer programs to prevent illicit entry into and control of the system.

en·cum·ber (ĕn-kŭm'bər, ĭn-) tr.v. -bered, -bering, -bers. 1. To weigh down unduly; lay too much upon. 2. To hinder, impede, or clutter, as with useless articles or unwanted additions. 3. To handicap or burden, as with obligations or legal claims. —See Synonyms at hinder. [Middle English encombren, from Old French encombrer, to block up : en-, in + combre, hindrance, from Gaulish comboros† (unattested).]

en·cum·brance (ĕn-kŭm'brəns, ĭn-) n. 1. One that encumbers; a burden, impediment, or obstacle. 2. Law. A lien or claim upon property, such as a mortgage. —See Synonyms at obstacle.

en·cum·branc·er (ĕn-kŭm'brən-sər, ĭn-) n. Law. A person who holds an encumbrance, as on another's property.

ency., encyc., encycl. encyclopedia.

-ency. Variant of -ence.

en·cyc·li·cal (ĕn-sĭk'lĭ-kəl, ĭn-) adj. Intended for general or wide circulation. Said of letters.
~n. Roman Catholic Church. A papal letter on a specific subject addressed officially to the clergy or to the hierarchy of a particular country. [Late Latin encyclicus, from Greek enkuklios, in a circle, circular : en-, in + kuklos, circle.]

en·cy·clo·pe·di·a, en·cy·clo·pae·di·a (ĕn-sī'klə-pē'dē-ə, ĭn-) n. Abbr. ency., encyc., encycl. A comprehensive, often multivolume reference work containing articles on a wide range of subjects or on numerous aspects of a particular field, usually arranged alphabetically. [Medieval Latin encyclopaedia, general education course, from Greek enkuklopaideiā, a mistaken transcription of enkuklios paideia, general education : enkuklios, circular, general (see encyclical) + paideia, education, training, from pais (stem paid-), child.]

en·cy·clo·pe·dic, en·cy·clo·pae·dic (ĕn-sī'klə-pē'dĭk, ĭn-) adj. 1. Of, pertaining to, or characteristic of an encyclopedia. 2. Embracing many subjects; comprehensive. —en·cy·clo·pe·di·cal·ly adv.

en·cy·clo·pe·dism, en·cy·clo·pae·dism (ĕn-sī'klə-pē'dĭz'əm, ĭn-) n. Encyclopedic learning.

en·cy·clo·pe·dist, en·cy·clo·pae·dist (ĕn-sī'klə-pē'dĭst, ĭn-) n. 1. A person who writes for or compiles an encyclopedia. 2. Encyclopedist. Any of the writers of the French Encyclopédie (1751–72), including its editors, Diderot and d'Alembert.

en·cyst (ĕn-sĭst', ĭn-) v. -cysted, -cysting, -cysts. —tr. To enclose in a cyst. —intr. To take the form of or become enclosed in a cyst. —en·cyst·ment, en·cys·ta·tion (ĕn'sĭ-stā'shən) n.

end (ĕnd) n. 1. Either extremity of something that has length. 2. The outside or extreme edge or limit of a space, form, or area; a boundary. 3. The point in time at which an action, event, or phenomenon ceases or is completed; a conclusion: the end of a day. 4. A result; an outcome: The end of the negotiations was agreement. 5. The termination of life or existence; death. 6. An ultimate extent; limit: soon reached the end of her patience. 7. a. That toward which one strives; a goal: "The end of Poetry is to produce excitement in coexistence with an overbalance of pleasure" (William Wordsworth). b. The reason or object by virtue of which something exists or takes place. 8. Often ends. A remainder, leftover, scrap, or remnant: My desk is littered with odds and ends. 9. a. A share of a responsibility or obligation; part: Try to keep up your end of the bargain. b. A particular area or phase of an enterprise or undertaking: He is involved with the packaging end of the business. 10. Football. a. Either of the players in the outermost position at the line of scrimmage. b. The position played by an end. —See Synonyms at boundary, intention. —at a loose ends. Aimless; unoccupied. —make (both) ends meet. To manage to live within one's means. —no end. Informal. A great deal: no end of stories to tell. —the end. Informal. An extremely exasperating person or situation.
~v. ended, ending, ends. —tr. 1. To bring to an end; finish; conclude. 2. To form the end or concluding part of. 3. To bring about the extinction of; destroy. 4. To be the finest of (a kind); surpass: a prize to end all prizes. —intr. 1. To come to an end; cease. 2. To die. —See Synonyms at complete. —end it all. Informal. To commit suicide. —end up. 1. To conclude. 2. To find or put oneself in a specified state, position, or the like: We ended up laughing.
~adj. At a position on the end; final; concluding: end man; end point. [Middle English ende, Old English ende, from Germanic.]

end-. Variant of endo-.

endamoeba. Variant of entamoeba.

en·dan·ger (ĕn-dān'jər, ĭn-) tr.v. -gered, -gering, -gers. To expose to danger or harm; imperil. —en·dan·ger·ment n.

endangered species n. A species in danger of extinction.

end·ar·ter·ec·to·my (ĕn'där-tə-rĕk'tə-mē) n., pl. -mies. Medicine. The surgical excision of the lining of an artery that has become clogged with atherosclerotic buildup. [END(O)- + ARTER(Y) + -ECTOMY.]

end·brain (ĕnd'brān') n. Anatomy. The telencephalon (see).

en·dear (ĕn-dîr', ĭn-) tr.v. -deared, -dearing, -dears. To cause to inspire affection or warm sympathy. —en·dear·ing·ly adv.

en·dear·ment (ĕn-dîr'mənt, ĭn-) n. 1. The act of endearing. 2. An expression of affection; a loving word or caress.

en·deav·or (ĕn-dĕv'ər, ĭn-) n. Also chiefly British en·deav·our. 1. A conscientious or concerted effort toward a given end; an earnest attempt. 2. Often endeavors. Earnest striving. —See Synonyms at effort.
~intr.v. endeavored, -oring, -ors. Also chiefly British endeavour -oured, -ouring, -ours. To make an earnest attempt; strive. Usually used with an infinitive: endeavor to stay solvent. [Middle English endevour, from endeveren, to exert oneself, from the phrase putten in dever, to put in duty, make it one's duty : IN + dever, duty, from Old French devoir, DEVOIR.] —en·deav·or·er n.

en·dem·ic (ĕn-dĕm'ĭk, ĭn-) adj. Also en·de·mi·al (-dē'mē-əl), en·dem·i·cal (-dĕm'ĭ-kəl). 1. Prevalent in or peculiar to a particular group or locality: "Disorder in some sense appears to be endemic in all societies" (Crane Brinton). 2. Ecology. Native or confined to a certain region; having a comparatively restricted distribution. 3. Medicine. Peculiar to and recurring in a particular locality. Said of a disease.
~n. Ecology. An endemic plant or animal. [French endémique, from Greek endēmios, endēmos, dwelling in a place, indigenous : en-, in + dēmos, people.] —en·dem·i·cal·ly adv. —en·dem·ism (ĕn-dĕm'ĭz'əm, ĭn-) n.

En·der·by Land (ĕn'dər-bē). Area in Antarctica, on the Indian Ocean. Discovered in 1831, it is claimed by Australia.

en·der·mic (ĕn-dûr'mĭk, ĭn-) adj. Medicine. Acting by absorption through the skin. Said of lotions and similar preparations. [EN- + -DERM + -IC.]

end·game (ĕnd'gām') n. The final stage of a game; especially, the final stage of chess, when only a few pieces survive.

end·ing (ĕn'dĭng) n. 1. A conclusion or termination. 2. The concluding part, especially of a book, play, or film; a finale: a happy ending. 3. The letter, letters, sound, or sounds added to a word or word part, especially to make a derivative or inflectional form.

en·dive (ĕn'dīv', ŏn'dēv') n. 1. A plant, Cichorium endivia, cultivated for its crown of crisp, succulent leaves, used in salads. 2. A variety of the common chicory, Cichorium intybus, cultivated to produce a narrow, pointed cluster of whitish leaves used in salads. [Middle English, from Old French, from Medieval Latin endiva, variant of Latin entubus, entibus, chicory, from Greek entubioi, perhaps from Egyptian tybi, January, because the plant grows in this month.]

end leaf n. An endpaper (see).

end·less (ĕnd'lĭs) adj. 1. Being or seeming to be without an end; infinite; boundless. 2. Incessant; interminable: an endless conversa-

endocrine gland

CHEMICAL ORDERS TO THE BODY

How hormones travel to where they are needed

Bodily changes such as growth, digestion, and cell reproduction are controlled by the brain just as much as is the voluntary decision to stand up or sit down. Such changes are responses to messages sent by the brain—not sent along the nerve pathways, however, but delivered by chemicals known as hormones.

Various organs and tissues secrete hormones in response to chemical instructions from the brain, but the chief producers are the endocrine glands. They are called ductless glands because unlike most glands, for example the sweat glands, whose secretions are carried through ducts opening on the skin surface, endocrine glands pump their hormones directly into the bloodstream. The blood carries them to the places—target tissues—they are intended to affect.

Hormones released by the six main sets of glands in the endocrine system control the inner rhythms of the body. The pituitary, at the base of the brain, is the master gland. It produces hormones that act purely as messengers to stimulate hormone production in other endocrine glands. It also secretes a hormone that controls body growth.

Hormones produced by the thyroid gland control heat and energy production. The parathyroid glands secrete a hormone that maintains calcium levels; the thymus gives infants a defense against infection. Adrenalin, from the adrenals, boosts energy production during stress, and insulin, produced by the islets of Langerhans in the pancreas, is essential for the efficient utilization of sugar. The sex glands, or gonads, produce sex hormones, for example, the estrogens responsible for the menstrual cycle in women.

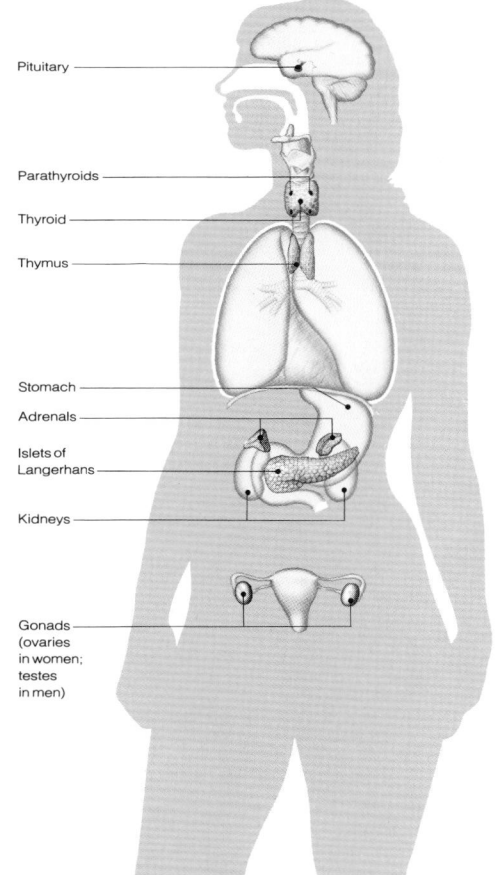

Pituitary

Parathyroids

Thyroid

Thymus

Stomach

Adrenals

Islets of
Langerhans

Kidneys

Gonads
(ovaries
in women;
testes
in men)

ENDOCRINE GLANDS AND TISSUES *As well as the six main endocrine glands, various tissues secrete hormones. Secretions in the stomach regulate digestion, and secretions in the kidneys control the production of red blood cells.*

tion. **3.** Formed with the ends joined; continuous: *an endless chain.* —**end·less·ly** *adv.* —**end·less·ness** *n.*

end man *n.* A man in a minstrel show who sits at one end of the company and banters with the interlocutor.

end matter *n.* Material, often including an index, appendix, bibliography, or notes, that follows the main part of a book. Also called "back matter." Compare **front matter.**

end·most (ĕnd′mōst′) *adj.* Being at or closest to the end; last.

endo-, end– *prefix.* Indicates inside or within; for example, **endocarp, endomorph.** [Greek, from *endon,* within.]

en·do·blast (ĕn′də-blăst′, -bläst′) *n.* Also **en·to·blast** (ĕn′tə-). In embryology, the inner layer of the blastoderm that becomes the endoderm at gastrulation. Also called "hypoblast." [ENDO- + -BLAST.] —**en·do·blas·tic** (ĕn′də-blăs′tĭk) *adj.*

en·do·car·di·tis (ĕn′dō-kär-dī′tĭs) *n.* Inflammation of the endocardium. [ENDOCARD(IUM) + -ITIS.] —**en·do·car·dit·ic** (ĕn′dō-kär-dĭt′ĭk) *adj.*

en·do·car·di·um (ĕn′dō-kär′dē-əm) *n., pl.* **-dia** (-dē-ə). The thin, endothelial, serous membrane that lines the interior of the heart. [New Latin : ENDO- + Greek *kardia,* heart.] —**en·do·car·di·al** *adj.*

en·do·carp (ĕn′də-kärp′) *n. Botany.* The often hard or leathery inner layer of the pericarp of many fruits. [ENDO- + -CARP.]

en·do·cen·tric (ĕn′dō-sĕn′trĭk) *adj. Grammar.* Designating a construction with the same grammatical function in combination as at least one of its constituents; for example, *five gold rings* is an endocentric construction, since the entire noun phrase functions grammatically in the same way as its head noun, *rings.* Compare **exocentric.** [ENDO- + -CENTRIC.]

en·do·cra·ni·um (ĕn′dō-krā′nē-əm) *n., pl.* **-nia** (-nē-ə). The outermost layer of the dura mater.

en·do·crine (ĕn′də-krĭn, -krēn′, -krīn′) *adj.* Also **en·do·cri·nal** (ĕn′də-krī′nəl, -krē′nəl), **en·do·crin·ic** (ĕn′də-krĭn′ĭk), **en·doc·ri·nous** (ĕn-dŏk′rə-nəs). **1.** Secreting internally. **2.** Of or pertaining to any of the ductless or endocrine glands. ~*n.* An endocrine gland. [ENDO- + Greek *krīnein,* to separate, "secrete."]

endocrine gland *n.* Any of the ductless glands, such as the thyroid or adrenal, the secretions of which pass directly into the bloodstream from the cells of the gland. Also called "ductless gland." See **hormone.**

en·do·cri·nol·o·gy (ĕn′də-krə-nŏl′ə-jē) *n.* The study of the endocrine glands, their secretions, and their diseases. —**en·do·cri·no·log·ic** (ĕn′də-krĭn′ə-lŏj′ĭk), **en·do·cri·no·log·i·cal** (-ĭ-kəl) *adj.* —**en·do·cri·nol·o·gist** (ĕn′də-krə-nŏl′ə-jĭst) *n.*

en·do·derm (ĕn′də-dûrm′) *n.* Also **en·to·derm** (ĕn′tə-). The innermost of the three primary germ layers of an embryo, developing into the lining of the intestinal tract and its derivatives. [ENDO- + -DERM.] —**en·do·der·mal** (ĕn′də-dûr′məl) *adj.*

en·do·der·mis (ĕn′də-dûr′mĭs) *n. Botany.* The innermost layer of the cortex, found in all roots and in the stems of certain plants, which controls the passage of water. [ENDO- + Greek *derma,* skin, DERMA.]

en·do·don·tics (ĕn′də-dŏn′tĭks) *n.* Also **en·do·don·tia** (-shə, -shē-ə). *(Used with a singular verb).* The branch of dentistry dealing with diseases of the tooth pulp. [ENDO- + -ODONT + -ICS.] —**en·do·don·tic** *adj.* —**en·do·don·tist** *n.*

en·do·en·zyme (ĕn′dō-ĕn′zīm′) *n.* **1.** An enzyme that acts upon inner chemical bonds in a chain molecule. **2.** An enzyme that acts inside the cell that produces it.

en·do·er·gic (ĕn′dō-ûr′jĭk) *adj. Physics.* Of or involving absorption of energy. Said of nuclear reactions. [ENDO- + *-ergic,* from Greek *ergon,* work.]

en·dog·a·my (ĕn-dŏg′ə-mē) *n.* **1.** *Anthropology.* Marriage within a particular group, caste, class, or tribe in accordance with set custom or law. Compare **exogamy. 2.** *Biology.* **a.** The fusion of gametes from closely related parents. **b.** Pollination between two flowers of the same plant. [ENDO- + -GAMY.] —**en·dog·a·mous** *adj.*

en·dog·e·nous (ĕn-dŏj′ə-nəs) *adj.* **1.** Produced from within. **2.** *Biology.* Originating within an organ or part. [ENDO- + -GENOUS.] —**en·dog·e·nous·ly** *adv.* —**en·dog·e·ny** *n.*

en·do·lymph (ĕn′də-lĭmf′) *n.* The fluid in the cochlear duct of the labyrinth of the ear.

en·do·me·tri·o·sis (ĕn′dō-mē′trē-ō′sĭs) *n.* The presence of endometrium, which is normally confined to the uterus, in other parts of the pelvic cavity, such as the ovaries, resulting in localized monthly pain.

en·do·me·tri·um (ĕn′dō-mē′trē-əm) *n., pl.* **-tria** (-trē-ə). The mucous membrane lining the uterus. [ENDO- + METR(O)- (uterus) + -IUM.] —**en·do·me·tri·al** *adj.*

en·do·morph (ĕn′də-môrf′) *n.* **1.** *Mineralogy.* A mineral found as an inclusion in another, as rutile or tourmaline may be found in quartz. Compare **perimorph. 2.** *Physiology.* A person of a type having a relatively fat body with prominent abdominal parts and weak muscular and skeletal development. Compare **ectomorph, mesomorph.** [ENDO- + -MORPH.]

en·do·mor·phic (ĕn′də-môr′fĭk) *adj.* **1.** *Mineralogy.* **a.** Of or pertaining to an endomorph. **b.** Created through endomorphism. **2.** *Physiology.* Of, pertaining to, or characteristic of an endomorphic individual. —**en·do·mor·phy** *n.*

en·do·morph·ism (ĕn′də-môr′fĭz′əm) *n. Geology.* The metamorphism of igneous rock as it cools, resulting from contact with and assimilation of the wall rock.

en·do·par·a·site (ĕn′dō-păr′ə-sīt′) *n.* An organism, such as a tape-

endomorph *One mineral enclosed within another: in this case, crystals of lead set in rock from the Dolomites.*

worm, that lives parasitically within another organism. —**en·do·par·a·sit·ic** (ĕn'dō-păr'ə-sĭt'ĭk) adj.

en·do·phyte (ĕn'də-fīt') n. A plant, such as any of certain fungi, growing within another plant. [ENDO- + -PHYTE.] —**en·do·phyt·ic** (ĕn'də-fĭt'ĭk) adj.

en·do·plasm (ĕn'də-plăz'əm) n. The inner, less viscous portion of the cytoplasm distinguishable within some cells. Compare **ectoplasm**. [ENDO- + -PLASM.] —**en·do·plas·mic** (ĕn'də-plăz'mĭk) adj.

endoplasmic reticulum n. Abbr. **ER** A system of membrane-bounded sacs in the cytoplasm of cells that functions in intracellular transport.

en·do·ra·di·o·sonde (ĕn'dō-rā'dē-ō-sŏnd') n. A microelectronic device that is introduced into the body by swallowing to record physiological data.

end organ n. Anatomy. The expanded functional termination of a sensory or motor nerve.

en·dor·phin (ĕn-dôr'fĭn, ĭn-) n. Any of a group of hormonelike substances with pain-killing and tranquilizing properties that are secreted by the brain. [ENDO- + -orphin, as in morphine.]

en·dorse (ĕn-dôrs', ĭn-) tr.v. **-dorsed, -dorsing, -dorses.** Also **in·dorse** (ĭn-). **1.** To write one's signature on the back of (a check or money order, for example) as evidence of the legal transfer of its ownership, especially in return for the cash or credit indicated on its face. **2. a.** To place (one's signature) on a contract or other document to indicate approval of its contents or terms. **b.** To allow one's name and reputation to be used to publicize (a product) in return for payment. **3.** To acknowledge (receipt of payment) by signing a bill, draft, or other document. **4.** To give approval of or support to; sanction. —See Synonyms at **approve**. —See Usage note at **indorse**. [Middle English endosen, from Old French endosser, "to put on the back of" : en-, to put on + dos, back, from Latin dorsum.] —**en·dors·a·ble** adj. —**en·dors·er, en·dor·sor** n.

en·dor·see (ĕn-dôr'sē', ĭn-, ĕn'dôr-sē') n. One to whom ownership of a negotiable document is transferred by endorsement.

en·dorse·ment (ĕn-dôrs'mənt, ĭn-) n. **1.** An act of endorsing. **2.** Something that endorses or validates, such as a signature or voucher. **3.** Approbation; sanction; support. **4.** An amendment to a contract, such as an insurance policy, permitting a change in the original terms.

endorsement in blank n. A blank endorsement (see).

en·do·scope (ĕn'də-skōp') n. An instrument for examining the interior of a bodily canal or hollow organ. [ENDO- + -SCOPE.] —**en·do·scop·ic** (ĕn'də-skŏp'ĭk) adj. —**en·do·scop·i·cal·ly** adv. —**en·dos·co·pist** (ĕn-dŏs'kə-pĭst) n. —**en·dos·co·py** (-pē) n.

en·do·skel·e·ton (ĕn'dō-skĕl'ə-tən) n. An internal supporting skeleton characteristic of vertebrates. Compare **exoskeleton**. —**en·do·skel·e·tal** adj.

en·dos·mo·sis (ĕn'dŏz-mō'sĭs, ĕn'dŏs-) n. The flow of a solvent through a semipermeable membrane from a surrounding fluid; especially, the flow of water through a cell membrane into a cell or organism. Compare **exosmosis**. [END(O)- + OSMOSIS.] —**en·dos·mot·ic** (ĕn'dŏz-mŏt'ĭk, ĕn'dŏs-) adj. —**en·dos·mot·i·cal·ly** adv.

en·do·some (ĕn'də-sōm') n. A discrete darker area within a nucleus, especially the nucleolus.

en·do·sperm (ĕn'də-spûrm') n. Botany. The nutritive tissue surrounding and absorbed by the embryo in flowering plants. [ENDO- + -SPERM.] —**en·do·sper·mic** (ĕn'də-spûr'mĭk) adj.

en·do·spore (ĕn'də-spôr', -spōr') n. An asexual spore formed within the cells of certain bacteria and acting as a resting stage.

en·do·spo·ri·um (ĕn'də-spôr'ē-əm, -spōr'ē-əm) n. The **intine** (see). [New Latin, from ENDO- + SPORE.]

en·dos·te·um (ĕn-dŏs'tē-əm) n., pl. **-tea** (-tē-ə). The membrane that lines the marrow cavity of a long bone. [New Latin : END(O)- + Greek osteon, bone.] —**en·dos·te·al** adj.

en·do·the·ci·um (ĕn'dō-thē'sē-əm, -shē-əm) n., pl. **-cia** (-sē-ə, -shē-ə). Botany. The inner tissue of an anther or a moss capsule. [New Latin : ENDO- + Greek thēkion, diminutive of thēkē, chest.] —**en·do·the·ci·al** adj.

en·do·the·li·o·ma (ĕn'dō-thē'lē-ō'mə) n., pl. **-mas** or **-mata** (-mə-tə). Any of various tumors derived from endothelial tissue. [ENDOTHELI(UM) + -OMA.]

en·do·the·li·um (ĕn'dō-thē'lē-əm) n., pl. **-lia** (-lē-ə). A thin layer of flat cells that lines serous cavities, lymph vessels, and blood vessels. [New Latin : ENDO- + Greek thēlē, nipple.] —**en·do·the·li·al, en·do·the·li·oid** (-lē-oid') adj.

en·do·ther·mic (ĕn'dō-thûr'mĭk) adj. Also **en·do·ther·mal** (-məl). Characterized by or causing the absorption of heat. Said especially of chemical reactions. Compare **exothermic**. [ENDO- + THERM + -IC.] —**en·do·ther·mi·cal·ly** adv.

en·do·tox·in (ĕn'dō-tŏk'sĭn) n. A toxin produced within a microorganism and released upon destruction of the cell in which it is produced. [ENDO- + TOXIN.] —**en·do·tox·ic** adj.

en·do·tra·che·al (ĕn'dō-trā'kē-əl) adj. Within the trachea.

en·dow (ĕn-dou', ĭn-) tr.v. **-dowed, -dowing, -dows. 1.** To provide with property, income, or a source of income. **2.** To invest with specified qualities or characteristics. Used with **with**. [Middle English endowen, from Norman French endouer : Old French en- (intensive) + douer, to provide with a dowry, from Latin dōtāre, from dōs (stem dōt-), dowry.]

en·dow·ment (ĕn-dou'mənt, ĭn-) n. **1.** An act of endowing. **2.** Funds or property donated to an institution, individual, or group as a source of income. **3.** A natural gift or quality; an attribute, such as beauty or talent.

~adj. Designating or involving a form of life insurance in which the policy matures within a specific period after issuance and becomes a claim payable to the insured at that time, or to his beneficiary upon the death of the insured before that time.

end·pa·per (ĕnd'pā'pər) n. Either of two folded sheets of heavy paper having one half pasted to the inside front or back cover of a book and the other half pasted to the base of the first or last page to form a flyleaf. Also called "end leaf."

end·plate (ĕnd'plāt') n. Physiology. A flattened motor nerve terminal that transmits nerve impulses to muscle.

end·play (ĕnd'plā') tr.v. **-played, -playing, -plays.** In bridge, to force (an opponent) to play a particular card during a late trick. —**end·play** n.

end·point (ĕnd'point') n. **1.** Chemistry. The point at which a titration is complete, with neither reactant in excess. **2.** Either of two points marking the end of a line segment. **3.** Any completion point.

end product n. The final conclusion of a series or process; specifically, the finished product of a manufacturing or similar process.

end·stopped (ĕnd'stŏpt') adj. Having a punctuation mark or distinct pause at the end of a line. Said of verse.

en·due (ĕn-dōō', -dyōō', ĭn-) tr.v. **-dued, -duing, -dues.** Also **in·due** (ĭn-). **1.** To provide with some specified quality or trait. Used with **with. 2. a.** To put on; dress in. **b.** To clothe. [Sense 1, Middle English enduen, endeuen, from Old French endure, to lead in, induct (meaning influenced by Middle English endowen, to endow), from Latin indūcere, to INDUCE. Sense 2, Middle English induen, from Latin induere, to don.]

en·dur·ance (ĕn-dōōr'əns, -dyōōr'əns, ĭn-) n. **1.** The act, quality, or power of withstanding hardship or stress. **2.** The state or fact of persevering. **3.** Continuing existence; survival.

en·dure (ĕn-dōōr', -dyōōr', ĭn-) v. **-dured, -during, -dures.** —tr. **1.** To carry on through despite hardships; undergo: endure an Arctic winter. **2.** To bear with tolerance; put up with: endure insults. —intr. **1.** To continue in existence; remain; last: buildings that endure for centuries. **2.** To suffer patiently without yielding; persevere; hold out. —See Synonyms at **bear**. [Middle English enduren, from Old French endurer, from Late Latin indūrāre, "to harden one's heart against," bear, from Latin, to harden : in- (intensive) + dūrāre, to harden, from dūrus, hard.] —**en·dur·a·bil·i·ty** n. —**en·dur·a·ble** adj. —**en·dur·a·bly** adv.

en·dur·ing (ĕn-dōōr'ĭng, -dyōōr'ĭng, ĭn-) adj. **1.** Lasting; durable. **2.** Chronic; unresolved: an enduring problem. **3.** Long-suffering. —**en·dur·ing·ly** adv. —**en·dur·ing·ness** n.

end·wise (ĕnd'wīz') adv. Also **end·ways** (-wāz'). **1.** On end. **2.** With the end foremost. **3.** Lengthwise. **4.** End to end. —**end·wise** adj.

En·dym·i·on (ĕn-dĭm'ē-ən) n. Greek Mythology. A handsome young man who was loved by the moon goddess Selene and whose youth was preserved by eternal sleep. [Latin, from Greek Endumiōn, "diver" (so called perhaps because Endymion was originally a sun god), from enduein, to dive into : en-, into + dueint, to dive, sink, set (as the sun).]

ENE east-northeast.

-ene suffix. Chemistry. Indicates unsaturation of an organic compound, especially one having a double bond; for example, **ethylene**. [Greek -ēnē, feminine patronymic suffix.]

en·e·ma (ĕn'ə-mə) n., pl. **-mas** or **enemata** (ĕn'ə-mä'tə). **1.** The injection of liquid into the rectum for cleansing, laxative, or other therapeutic purposes. **2.** The fluid injected as an enema. [Late Latin, from Greek, from enienai, to throw in, inject : en-, in + hienai, to send, throw.]

en·e·my (ĕn'ə-mē) n., pl. **-mies. 1. a.** One who shows malice or hostility toward another; a foe. **b.** One who opposes the purposes or interests of another; an opponent. **2. a.** A hostile, usually armed power or force, such as a nation. **b.** A member or unit of such a force. **3.** Something destructive or injurious in its effects: Fear is our chief enemy. ~adj. Of or pertaining to a hostile power or force. [Middle English enemi, from Old French, from Latin inimīcus : in-, not + amīcus, friend.]

en·er·get·ic (ĕn'ər-jĕt'ĭk) adj. Possessing, exerting, or displaying energy; vigorous. —See Synonyms at **active**. [Greek energētikos, active, from energein, to be active, from energos, active. See **energy**.] —**en·er·get·i·cal·ly** adv.

en·er·get·ics (ĕn'ər-jĕt'ĭks) n. **1.** Used with a plural verb. The energy changes in a particular physical system: the energetics of a chemical reaction. **2.** Used with a singular verb. The physics of energy and of transformations of energy.

en·er·gid (ĕn'ər-jĭd) n. Biology. A unit that consists of a nucleus surrounded by cytoplasm but that does not constitute a cell. [ENERG(Y) + -ID.]

en·er·gize (ĕn'ər-jīz') v. **-gized, -gizing, -gizes.** —tr. **1.** To give energy to; charge. **2.** To power (a device, such as the winding of an electric motor) with electricity. —intr. To release or put out energy. —**en·er·giz·er** n.

en·er·gu·men (ĕn'ər-gyōō'mən) n. **1.** One believed to be possessed by an evil spirit; a demoniac. **2.** A zealot; a fanatic. [Late Latin energūmenus, from Greek energoumenos, worked on, "possessed," from energein, to be active, effect, from energos, active. See **energy**.]

en·er·gy (ĕn'ər-jē) n., pl. **-gies. 1. a.** Vigor or power as shown in action, exertion, or performance. **b.** Vitality and intensity of expression. **2.** The capacity for action or accomplishment: lacked energy to finish the job. **3.** Often **energies**. Power exercised with vigor and determination: devote one's energies to a worthy cause.

4. a. *Physics. Abbr.* **E** The work that a physical system is capable of doing in changing from its actual state to a specific reference state, the total including, in general, contributions of **potential energy, kinetic energy,** and **rest energy** (*all of which see*). **b.** The capacity to activate systems, as machines, or to generate light and heat: *solar energy.* **c.** Energy-generating fuels or sources collectively. Also used adjectively: *the energy crisis.* —See Synonyms at **strength.** [Late Latin *energīa,* from Greek *energeia,* coined by Aristotle from *energēs, energos,* active, at work : *en-,* at + *ergon,* work.]

energy band *n. Physics.* A range of allowed energies of electrons in a solid.

energy density *n.* The energy per unit area or volume of a surface or region of space.

energy gap *n.* The discrepancy between the amount of fuel needed to satisfy current levels of energy consumption and the actual quantities likely to be available in the future.

energy level *n. Physics.* **1.** The energy characteristic of a stationary state of a quantum mechanical system. **2.** The stationary state of a quantum mechanical system.

en·er·vate (ĕn′ər-vāt′) *tr.v.* **-vated, -vating, -vates.** To deprive of strength or vitality; weaken. —See Usage note at **deplete.** ~*adj.* (ĭ-nûr′vĭt). Deprived of strength or vitality; devitalized. [Latin *ēnervāre,* "to remove the sinews from" : *ex-* (removal) + *nervus,* sinew, nerve.] —**en·er·va·tion** (ĕn′ər-vā′shən) *n.* —**en·er·va·tor** (ĕn′ər-vā′tər) *n.*

en·face (ĕn-fās′, ĭn-) *tr.v.* **-faced, -facing, -faces.** To write, stamp, or print on the face of (a check or other document). —**en·face·ment** *n.*

en fa·mille (än′ fə-mē′) *adv.* In or with the family; at home and without ceremony. [French, "in (the) family."]

en·fant ter·ri·ble (äN-fäN′ tĕ-rē′bl′) *n., pl.* **enfants terribles** (*pronounced as singular*). **1.** A child who habitually causes embarrassment by his conduct or remarks. **2.** A person whose startlingly unconventional behavior and ideas are a source of consternation or dismay to a cause, group, or profession. [French, "terrible child."]

en·fee·ble (ĕn-fē′bəl, ĭn-) *tr.v.* **-bled, -bling, -bles.** To make feeble; deprive of strength. [Middle English *enfeblen,* from Old French *enfebler* : *en-* (causative) + *feble,* FEEBLE.] —**en·fee·ble·ment** *n.* —**en·fee·bler** *n.*

en·fet·ter (ĕn-fĕt′ər, ĭn-) *tr.v.* **-tered, -tering, -ters.** To bind in fetters; enchain; enslave.

En·field rifle (ĕn′fēld′) *n.* Any of several rifles of varying calibers used formerly by British and American troops, especially the .30 or .303 bolt-action breechloading model. Also called "Enfield." [After *Enfield,* England, where it was first made.]

en·fi·lade (ĕn′fə-lād′, -läd′) *n.* **1.** The firing of a gun or guns so as to sweep the length of a target such as a column of troops. **2.** A position or emplacement under enfilade. ~*tr.v.* **enfiladed, -lading, -lades.** To rake with gunfire. [French, "series," from *enfiler,* to thread, from Old French : *en-,* in + *fil,* thread, from Latin *fīlum.*]

en·fleu·rage (ŏN′flə-räzh′, -räj′) *n.* A process used in the making of perfume to extract essential oils from plant material, such as leaves or petals, by placing the material in contact with an odorless fat that absorbs the essential oil. The essential oil is subsequently extracted from the fat by a solvent. [French, from *enfleurer,* to cause to take in the fragrance of flowers : Old French *en-,* in + *fleur, flor,* flower, from Latin *flōs* (stem *flōr-*).]

en·flu·rane (ĕn-floor′ăn′, ĭn-) *n.* A nonexplosive anesthetic, $C_3H_2ClF_5O$. [EN- + FLU(O)- + (ETH)ANE.]

en·fold (ĕn-fōld′, ĭn-) *tr.v.* **-folded, -folding, -folds.** Also **in·fold** (ĭn-). **1.** To cover with or as if with folds; wrap up: *The fog seemed to enfold the whole village.* **2.** To hold within limits; enclose. **3.** To embrace. **4.** To form or shape into folds. —**en·fold·er** *n.*

en·force (ĕn-fôrs′, -fōrs′, ĭn-) *tr.v.* **-forced, -forcing, -forces. 1.** To compel observance of or obedience to: *enforce a regulation.* **2.** To impose (specified action or behavior); compel. **3.** To give force to; stress; underline; reinforce. [Middle English *enforcen,* from Old French *enforcier,* from Vulgar Latin *infortiāre* (unattested), to make strong : Latin *in-* (causative) + *fortis,* strong.] —**en·force·a·ble** *adj.* —**en·force·ment** *n.* —**en·forc·er** *n.*

en·fran·chise (ĕn-frăn′chīz′, ĭn-) *tr.v.* **-chised, -chising, -chises. 1.** To endow with the rights of citizenship, especially the right to vote. **2.** To give (a town, for example) the right to political representation. **3.** To bestow a franchise upon. **4.** To free, as from slavery. [Middle English *enfraunchisen,* from Old French *enfranchir* (present stem *enfranchiss-*) : *en-* (causative) + *franche, franc,* free (see **franchise**).]

eng (ĕng) *n.* A phonetic symbol (ŋ) representing in some pronunciation alphabets the velar nasal consonantal sound of *ng,* as in br*ing* or l*o*ng, or of *n,* as in li*n*k. Also called "agma."

eng. 1. engine. **2.** engineer; engineering.

Eng. England; English.

En·ga·dine (ĕng′gə-dēn′). Swiss part of the upper Inn Valley, in Grisons (or Graubünden) canton. It has several winter sports centers, including St. Moritz.

en·gage (ĕn-gāj′, ĭn-) *v.* **-gaged, -gaging, -gages.** —*tr.* **1.** To obtain or contract for the services of; employ: *engage a carpenter.* **2.** To contract for the use of; reserve: *engage a room.* **3.** To obtain and hold the attention of; engross: *The project engaged her interest for months.* **4.** To require the use of; occupy: *Studying engages most of a student's time.* **5.** To pledge; especially, to promise to marry; betroth. Usually used in the passive: *She is engaged to Harry.* **6.** To meet in or bring into conflict: *We have engaged the enemy.* **7.** To cause to interlock or mesh. **8.** To please or attract; win. **9.** To occupy or involve. Often used with *in: engage someone in idle chatter.* **10.** *Archaic.* To give or take as security; attach. —*intr.* **1.** To involve oneself or become occupied; participate. Usually used with *in: engage in conversation.* **2.** To assume an obligation; pledge; agree. **3.** To enter into conflict or battle. **4.** To become meshed or interlocked. [Middle English *engagen,* from Old French *engager,* from Vulgar Latin *inwadiāre* : *in-,* in + *wadiāre* (unattested), to pledge, GAGE.] —**en·gag·er** *n.*

en·ga·gé (äN′gä-zhā′) *adj.* Actively committed, as to a political cause. [French, "committed."]

en·gaged (ĕn-gājd′, ĭn-) *adj.* **1. a.** Employed, occupied, or busy. **b.** *British.* In use. Said of a telephone line. **2.** Contracted for; pledged. **3.** Bound by a promise to marry; betrothed: *an engaged couple.* **4.** *Architecture.* Partly sunk, built into, or attached to another part, as columns on a wall.

en·gage·ment (ĕn-gāj′mənt, ĭn-) *n.* **1.** An act of engaging or the state or period of being engaged. **2.** A promise of marriage; betrothal. **3.** A person or thing that engages. **4.** A promise, pledge, or obligation; especially, a commitment to appear at a certain time, as for business or social activity; an appointment. **5. a.** Employment, especially for a specific time. **b.** The period of employment. **6.** A battle or encounter. **7.** The condition of being in gear.

en·gag·ing (ĕn-gā′jĭng, ĭn-) *adj.* Tending to attract; charming; pleasing. —**en·gag·ing·ly** *adv.*

en garde (äN gärd′) *interj.* Used to warn a fencer to assume the first position preparatory to a match. [French, "on guard."]

Eng·els (ĕng′əlz, ĕng′gəlz), **Friedrich** (1820–95). German political theorist and socialist philosopher. He met Karl Marx in Paris in 1844 and published *The Condition of the Working Classes in England.* *The Communist Manifesto* was published in 1848. Engels settled in England in 1850 and played an important part in the founding of the First and Second Internationals. *Anti-Dühring* (1878) and *The Origin of the Family, Private Property, and the State* (1884) were major contributions to the development of Communist theory.

en·gen·der (ĕn-jĕn′dər, ĭn-) *v.* **-dered, -dering, -ders.** —*tr.* **1.** To bring into existence; give rise to; produce. **2.** To procreate; propagate. —*intr.* **1.** To come into existence; be born; be produced. [Middle English *engenderen,* from Old French *engenderer,* from Latin *ingenerāre* : *in-,* in + *generāre,* to GENERATE.]

engin. engineering.

en·gine (ĕn′jĭn) *n. Abbr.* **eng. 1. a.** A machine that converts some form of energy into mechanical motion. **b.** Such a machine distinguished from an electric, spring-driven, or hydraulic motor by its consumption of a fuel. **c.** Any mechanical appliance, instrument, or tool. **2.** A locomotive. **3.** *Archaic.* An agent, instrument, or means of accomplishment. [Middle English *engin,* from Old French, skill, invention, from Latin *ingenium,* inborn talent, skill.]

engine block *n.* The metal block containing the cylinders of an internal-combustion engine. Also called "block."

engine driver *n. Chiefly British.* A person who drives a locomotive; engineer.

en·gi·neer (ĕn′jə-nîr′) *n. Abbr.* **e., E., eng. 1.** A person trained in, skilled at, or professionally engaged in a branch of engineering: *a mining engineer.* **2.** A person who skillfully or shrewdly manages an enterprise: *He was the engineer of the treaty that ended the war.* **3.** A person who operates an engine, especially a railroad locomotive. **4.** A person who oversees, services, or repairs engines or systems or appliances run by engines: *a central-heating engineer.* **5.** A soldier employed or trained in engineering as applied to military purposes. ~*tr.v.* **engineered, -neering, -neers. 1.** To plan, construct, and manage as an engineer; act as engineer of or for. **2.** To plan, manage, and put through by skillful acts or contrivance; maneuver: *"Claudius's murder was engineered by his wife Agrippina"* (Robert Graves). [Middle English *enginer,* from Old French *enginneor,* from Medieval Latin *ingeniātor,* contriver, from *ingeniāre,* to contrive, from Latin *ingenium,* talent. See **engine.**]

en·gi·neer·ing (ĕn′jə-nîr′ĭng) *n. Abbr.* **e., E., eng., engin. 1.** The application of scientific principles to such practical ends as the design, construction, and operation of efficient and economical structures, equipment, and systems. **2.** The profession of or the work performed by an engineer. **3.** Skillful management; maneuvering or contrivance.

en·gine·ry (ĕn′jĭn-rē) *n.* **1.** Machines and tools; machinery. **2.** Engines or instruments of war.

en·gird (ĕn-gûrd′, ĭn-) *tr.v.* **-girt** (-gûrt′) or **-girded, -girding, -girds.** Also **en·gir·dle** (-gûrd′l) **-dled, -dling, -dles.** To surround with or as if with a girdle; encircle.

en·gla·cial (ĕn-glā′shəl, ĭn-) *adj.* Located or occurring within a glacier: *an englacial stream.* —**en·gla·cial·ly** *adv.*

Eng·land (ĭng′glənd) *n.* Largest political division of the United Kingdom, settled by the Celts, subsequently conquered by the Romans, Angles, Saxons, Jutes, Danes, and finally the Normans. A major trading nation, its main ports are London, Liverpool, and Southampton. Though heavily agricultural, England became a leading manufacturing nation after the Industrial Revolution of the mid-18th century. Foreign competition and the loss of cheap imports from its former empire have contributed to a decline in the 20th century. England's chief industries today include shipbuilding, coal mining, motor vehicle production, iron and steel, electronics, aircraft building, petroleum, chemicals, and tourism. Area, 130,357 square kilometers (50,331 square miles). Capital, London. See also **Great Britain.**

Eng·lish (ĭng'glĭsh) *adj.* **1. a.** Of, pertaining to, or characteristic of England and its inhabitants. **b.** Of a type or style predominant in England: *English breakfast.* **2.** Of, belonging to, or spoken or written in the English language. **3.** Loosely, British. **~***n. Abbr.* **E, E., Eng. 1.** *Used with a plural verb.* **a.** The people of England collectively. **b.** Loosely, the British. **2.** The West Germanic language of the English, divided historically into Old English, Middle English, and Modern English and now spoken in the British Isles, the United States, and numerous other countries. **3.** The English language as spoken or written at a specified time, in a specified region, or by a specified person or group of people: *Australian English; Shakespeare's English.* **4.** A translation into or an equivalent in the English language. **5.** A course or individual class in the study of English literature, language, or composition. **6.** *Printing.* A size of type, 14-point. **7.** *Often* **english.** The spin given to a ball by striking it on one side or releasing it with a sharp twist.

English bond *n.* A common masonry bond consisting of alternate rows of headers and stretchers.

English Channel. *French* **La Manche** (lä mänsh'). One of the world's busiest shipping lanes, lying between England and France. It is 560 kilometers (350 miles) long, 160 kilometers (100 miles) wide at the west end between Ushant and the Scilly Isles, and 34 kilometers (21 miles) wide at the Strait of Dover at the east end.

English Civil War *n.* In England, the war between Charles I and Parliament. Hostilities commenced in 1642 and Charles finally surrendered at Newark (1646). A Royalist uprising in 1648 prompted the second part of the Civil War and led to the execution of the king

---

English Civil War

THE KING WHO LOST HIS HEAD
The English Civil War broke the monarch's power

The first English Civil War (1642–46) broke the power of the throne and established the parliamentary rule that exists today. Growing confidence among the merchant classes steeled Parliament to challenge Charles I's unshakable belief in the divine right of kings. Charles needed Parliament only to raise taxes, and for 11 years, from 1629–40, he ruled without it.

In 1639, the Archbishop of Canterbury, William Laud, tried to force the Reformed prayer book on Scotland. The Scots rebelled. Charles called Parliament to raise money to fight them. The House agreed—on condition that he approved the Grand Remonstrance, a document denying his right to dismiss Parliament and rule without it. The king refused. His bid to arrest the Parliamentary leaders failed and he prepared for war, raising his standard in November 1642.

After initial successes by the Royalist troops, called Cavaliers, parliamentary troops—the Roundheads—led by Oliver Cromwell, were the victors at Marston Moor (1644) and at Naseby (1645). Finally, in May 1646, Charles surrendered to the Scots. No settlement was reached despite negotiations and further fighting (the second Civil War). Cromwell's army was again victorious. Charles was tried by Parliament, found guilty of murder and treason, and executed on January 30, 1649.

For nine years, Cromwell ruled as dictator. But after his death, the monarchy was restored. Charles I's son became King Charles II in 1660, but he had to accept that Parliament was the supreme arm of government.

EXECUTION OF A KING *On January 30, 1649, Charles I placed his head on the block in Whitehall, London. He died still believing that he had a divine right to rule England as he wished. That night, Oliver Cromwell looked at the royal corpse in St. James's Palace and muttered: "Cruel necessity."*

---

in 1649. A commonwealth was established and the Civil War was concluded by the subjection of Ireland (1649–50) and the defeat of Charles's heir at Dunbar in 1650. Also called the "Great Rebellion."

English daisy *n.* See **daisy** (sense 2).

English finish *n.* A smooth, nonglossy finish for paper.

English flute *n.* A musical instrument, the **recorder** *(see).*

English horn *n.* A double-reed woodwind instrument similar to but larger than the oboe and pitched lower by a fifth. Also called "cor anglais."

Eng·lish·man (ĭng'glĭsh-mən) *n., pl.* **-men** (-mĭn). **1.** A native or inhabitant of England. **2.** Loosely, a British man.

Englishman's tie *n. Nautical.* A **fisherman's knot** *(see).* Also called "Englishman's knot."

English muffin *n.* A flat round of yeast dough that has been baked on a griddle and is usually split and toasted before eating.

English setter *n.* A dog of a breed developed in England, having a silky white coat usually with black or brownish markings.

English sheepdog *n.* The **Old English sheepdog** *(see).*

English sonnet *n.* A **Shakespearean sonnet** *(see).*

English sparrow *n.* The **house sparrow** *(see).*

English walnut *n.* **1.** A Eurasian tree, *Juglans regia,* cultivated in southern Europe and California. **2.** The large edible nut of the English walnut tree.

Eng·lish·wom·an (ĭng'glĭsh-wŏŏm'ən) *n., pl.* **-women** (-wĭm'ĭn). **1.** A woman who is a native or inhabitant of England. **2.** Loosely, a British woman.

en·glut (ĕn-glŭt', ĭn-) *tr.v.* **-glutted, -glutting, -gluts.** To gulp down; swallow greedily. [EN- + GLUT.]

en·gorge (ĕn-gôrj', ĭn-) *tr.v.* **-gorged, -gorging, -gorges. 1.** To devour greedily. **2.** To gorge; glut. **3.** To congest or fill to excess, as with blood or other fluid. Usually used in the passive. [French *engorger : en-,* in + *gorge,* throat, GORGE.] **—en·gorge·ment** *n.*

en·graft (ĕn-grăft', -gräft', ĭn-) *tr.v.* **-grafted, -grafting, -grafts.** Also **in·graft** (ĭn-). **1.** To graft (a shoot or bud) onto or into another plant. **2.** To implant firmly; incorporate. **—en·graft·ment** *n.*

en·grail (ĕn-grāl', ĭn-) *tr.v.* **-grailed, -grailing, -grails. 1.** To indent (the edge of something) with small curves. **2.** To decorate the edge of by adding a series of curved indentations. [Middle English *engrelen,* from Old French *engresler : en-,* in + *gresle,* hail (the indentations were imagined to resemble hailstones).]

en·grain (ĕn-grān', ĭn-) *tr.v.* **-grained, -graining, -grains. 1.** To treat, dye, or color so as to suggest the grain of wood. **2.** Variant of **ingrain.** [Middle English *engreinen,* from Old French *engrainer,* to dye in grain, from *en graine,* in grain : *en-,* in + *graine,* cochineal dye, kermes, from Latin *grāna,* plural of *grānum,* GRAIN.]

en·gram, en·gramme (ĕn'grăm') *n.* A persistent protoplasmic alteration hypothesized to occur on stimulation of living neural tissue and to account for memory. Also called "memory engram," "neurogram." [EN- + -GRAM.] **—en·gram·mat·ic** (ĕn'grə-măt'ĭk), **en·gram·mic** (ĕn-grăm'ĭk) *adj.*

en·grave (ĕn-grāv', ĭn-) *tr.v.* **-graved, -graving, -graves. 1.** To carve, cut, or etch (a design or letters) into a material. **2. a.** To carve, cut, or etch (a design or letters) into a block or surface used for printing. **b.** To carve a design on (a printing block or plate). **c.** To print from a block or plate made by such a process. **3.** To impress deeply; fix permanently. [EN- + GRAVE (to carve).] **—en·grav·er** *n.*

en·grav·ing (ĕn-grā'vĭng, ĭn-) *n.* **1.** The art or technique of one that engraves. **2.** An engraved surface for printing. **3.** A print made from an engraved plate or block. See feature page 562.

en·gross (ĕn-grōs', ĭn-) *tr.v.* **-grossed, -grossing, -grosses. 1.** To occupy the complete attention of; absorb wholly. **2.** To acquire most or all of (a commodity); monopolize (a market). Compare **forestall. 3. a.** To write or transcribe in a large, clear hand. **b.** To prepare the text of (an official document) by an officially prescribed process, such as handwriting or printing. [Senses 1 and 2, Middle English *engrossen,* from Norman French *engrosser,* from *en gros,* in large quantity, wholesale. Sense 3, Middle English, from Norman French *engrosser,* from *en grosse,* in large handwriting.] **—en·gross·er** *n.*

en·grossed (ĕn-grōst', ĭn-) *adj.* Having one's attention completely occupied; totally absorbed.

en·gross·ing (ĕn-grō'sĭng, ĭn-) *adj.* Occupying one's complete attention; wholly absorbing. **—en·gross·ing·ly** *adv.*

en·gross·ment (ĕn-grōs'mənt, ĭn-) *n.* **1.** The state of being completely absorbed, occupied, or monopolized. **2.** A document, such as a deed or will, that has been engrossed.

en·gulf (ĕn-gŭlf', ĭn-) *tr.v.* **-gulfed, -gulfing, -gulfs.** Also **in·gulf** (ĭn-). **1.** To surround completely. **2.** To swallow up or overwhelm by or as if by flowing over and enclosing: *engulfed by bad luck.* **—en·gulf·ment** *n.*

en·hance (ĕn-hăns', -häns', ĭn-) *tr.v.* **-hanced, -hancing, -hances. 1.** To increase or make greater, as in value, cost, beauty, or reputation; augment. **2.** To increase the clarity of (a photograph, especially one taken from space or the air) by using a computer to improve contrast. **—See Synonyms at improve.** [Middle English *enhauncen,* from Norman French *enhauncer,* variant of Old French *enhaucer,* from Vulgar Latin *inaltiāre* (unattested), to raise : Latin *in-* (intensive) + *altus,* high.] **—en·hance·ment** *n.* **—en·hanc·er** *n.* **—en·hanc·ive** *adj.*

enhanced radiation *n.* Radiation released by certain nuclear devices in the form of neutrons and gamma rays, able to destroy life but having a reduced nuclear blast and thus causing limited damage to the nonliving environment.

en·hanced radiation bomb *n.* A neutron bomb (*see*).

en·har·mon·ic (ĕn'här-mŏn'ĭk) *adj. Music.* 1. Of, pertaining to, or being an ancient Greek scale consisting of quartertones. 2. Of, pertaining to, or being a note of the same pitch but different written representation, as C and D♭, on all instruments such as pianos that are tuned to the tempered scale. [Late Latin *enharmonicus,* from Greek *enarmonikos,* "in harmony" : *en-,* in + *harmonia,* HARMONY.] —**en·har·mon·i·cal·ly** *adv.*

e·nig·ma (ĭ-nĭg'mə) *n.* 1. An obscure riddle. 2. An obscure piece of speech or writing. 3. Someone or something that is puzzling, ambiguous, or inexplicable. [Latin *aenigma,* from Greek *ainigma,* from *ainissesthai,* to speak in riddles, hint, from *ainos,* tale, story.]

en·ig·mat·ic (ĕn'ĭg-măt'ĭk) *adj.* Also **en·ig·mat·i·cal** (-ĭ-kəl). Of or resembling an enigma; puzzling: *an enigmatic smile.* —**en·ig·mat·i·cal·ly** *adv.*

en·isle (ĕn-īl', ĭn-) *tr.v.* **-isled, -isling, -isles.** 1. To make into an island. 2. To set apart from others; isolate.

E·ni·we·tok (ĕn'ə-wē'tŏk'). An uninhabited coral atoll in the Ralik Chain of the Marshall Islands, west-central Pacific Ocean. Atomic tests were conducted here from 1948 to 1954.

en·jamb·ment, en·jambe·ment (ĕn-jăm'mənt, -jămb'mənt, ĭn-, än'zhäNb-mäN') *n.* The continuation of a sentence or idea from one line or couplet of a poem to the next. [French, from Old French *enjamber,* to straddle : *en-,* in + *jambe,* leg (see **jamb**).] —**en·jambed** (ĕn-jămd', ĭn-) *adj.*

en·join (ĕn-join', ĭn-) *tr.v.* **-joined, -joining, -joins.** 1. To require or direct with authority and emphasis; command; impose. 2. To urge or order (a person) to do something. 3. To prohibit or forbid, especially by legal action: *The court enjoined him from visiting his children.* —See Synonyms at **command.** [Middle English *enjoinen,* from Old French *enjoindre,* from Latin *injungere,* to join to, impose : *in-,* in, to + *jungere,* to join.] —**en·join·er** *n.* —**en·join·ment** *n.*

en·joy (ĕn-joi', ĭn-) *tr.v.* **-joyed, -joying, -joys.** 1. To experience joy in or receive pleasure from; relish: *They enjoy good food and the companionship of friends.* 2. To have the use of or benefit from: *She enjoyed a generous allowance.* 3. To have as one's lot; experience: *His parents enjoy excellent health.* 4. To have sexual intercourse with. —See Synonyms at **like.** —**enjoy oneself.** To have a pleasant time. [Middle English *enjoien,* from Old French *enjoïr* : *en-,* in + *joïr,* to rejoice, from Latin *gaudēre.*] —**en·joy·er** *n.*

en·joy·a·ble (ĕn-joi'ə-bəl, ĭn-) *adj.* Giving or capable of giving enjoyment; pleasurable; agreeable. —**en·joy·a·ble·ness** *n.* —**en·joy·a·bly** *adv.*

en·joy·ment (ĕn-joi'mənt, ĭn-) *n.* 1. The act or state of experiencing joy or pleasure in something. 2. The use or possession of something, as: **a.** Something beneficial or pleasurable. **b.** A legal right: *enjoyment of the right to vote.* 3. Something that is enjoyed. 4. Pleasure; joy. —See Synonyms at **pleasure.**

en·keph·a·lin (ĕn-kĕf'ə-lĭn) *n.* A chemical occurring naturally in the brain and having effects similar to those of morphine. [ENCEPHALO- + -IN.]

en·kin·dle (ĕn-kĭnd'l, ĭn-) *tr.v.* **-dled, -dling, -dles.** 1. To set on fire; light; kindle. 2. To incite; arouse. 3. To make luminous and glowing. —**en·kin·dler** *n.*

enl. 1. enlarged. 2. enlisted.

en·lace (ĕn-lās', ĭn-) *tr.v.* **-laced, -lacing, -laces.** Also **in·lace** (ĭn-). 1. To wrap or wind about with or as if with a lace or laces; encircle. 2. To interlace; entangle; entwine. —**en·lace·ment** *n.*

en·large (ĕn-lärj', ĭn-) *v.* **-larged, -larging, -larges.** —*tr.* 1. **a.** To make larger; add to: *We enlarged the kitchen.* **b.** To make (a photographic print) larger than the original print or larger than the standard size. 2. To give greater scope to; expand: *Travel enlarged the child's experience.* 3. To set free; liberate. —*intr.* 1. To become larger; grow. 2. To speak or write at greater length or in greater detail: *He enlarged on his plans.* —See Synonyms at **increase.** [Middle English *enlargen,* from Old French *enlargier* : *en-,* in + *large,* LARGE.]

en·large·ment (ĕn-lärj'mənt, ĭn-) *n.* 1. An act or process of enlarging or the state of being enlarged. 2. Something, such as an addition, expansion, or increase, that enlarges something else. 3. A reproduction or copy larger than the original; especially, an optically magnified print of a photographic negative.

en·larg·er (ĕn-lär'jər, ĭn-) *n.* An optical instrument for producing enlarged photographic prints by projecting an image of the negative onto sensitive paper.

en·light·en (ĕn-līt'n, ĭn-) *tr.v.* **-ened, -ening, -ens.** 1. **a.** To give knowledge or truth to. **b.** To endow with spiritual understanding. 2. To acquaint (someone) with information; inform. 3. To free (someone) from prejudice or false belief. —**en·light·en·er** *n.*

en·light·en·ment (ĕn-līt'n-mənt, ĭn-) *n.* 1. An act or means of enlightening. 2. The state of being enlightened. 3. *Buddhism.* A state marked by spiritual insight and freedom from illusory appearances. 4. **Enlightenment.** A philosophical movement of the 18th century, concerned with the critical examination of previously accepted doctrines and institutions from the point of view of rationalism. —See Synonyms at **knowledge.**

en·list (ĕn-lĭst', ĭn-) *v.* **-listed, -listing, -lists.** —*tr.* 1. To persuade to enter the armed forces. 2. To engage the assistance or cooperation of; secure on one's behalf. —*intr.* 1. To enter the armed forces voluntarily. 2. To participate actively in some cause or enterprise. [EN- + LIST (roster).] —**en·list·ment** *n.*

enlisted man *n.* A man or woman who has enlisted in the armed forces without an officer's commission or warrant.

en·liv·en (ĕn-lī'vən, ĭn-) *tr.v.* **-ened, -ening, -ens.** 1. To make lively or spirited; animate; invigorate. 2. To brighten; cheer. [EN- + LIVE (adjective).] —**en·liv·en·er** *n.* —**en·liv·en·ment** *n.*

en masse (ŏn măs', äN mäs') *adv.* In one group or body; all together. [French : *en,* in + *masse,* MASS (body).]

en·mesh (ĕn-mĕsh', ĭn-) *tr.v.* **-meshed, -meshing, -meshes.** Also **in·mesh** (ĭn-), **im·mesh** (ĭ-mĕsh'). 1. To entangle, involve, or catch in or as if in a net. 2. To cover with net or mesh.

en·mi·ty (ĕn'mə-tē) *n., pl.* **-ties.** Deep-seated hatred, as between rivals or opponents; antagonism. [Middle English *enemite,* from Old French *enemiste,* from Vulgar Latin *inimīcītās* (unattested), from Latin *inimīcus,* ENEMY.]

Synonyms: animosity, animus, antagonism, antipathy, rancor.

en·ne·ad (ĕn'ē-ăd') *n.* Any group or set of nine. [Greek *enneas* (stem *ennead-*), nine.]

en·ne·a·he·dron (ĕn'ē-ə-hē'drən) *n., pl.* **-drons** or **-dra** (-drə). *Mathematics.* A solid that has nine faces. [Greek *ennea,* nine + -HEDRON.]

en·no·ble (ĕn-nō'bəl, ĭn-) *tr.v.* **-bled, -bling, -bles.** 1. To invest with nobility; bring honor or glory to. 2. To raise to the rank of nobleman; confer nobility upon. [Middle English *ennoblen,* from Old French *ennoblir* : *en-,* in + NOBLE.] —**en·no·ble·ment** *n.*

en·nui (ŏn-wē', ŏn'wē) *n.* Listlessness and dissatisfaction resulting from lack of interest; boredom: *gossiping to relieve their ennui.* [French, from Old French *enui,* from Latin *in odiō,* "in hate," odious : *in,* in + *odium,* hate.]

E·noch[1] (ē'nŏk, ē'nŏk'). The eldest son of Cain. Genesis 4:17. [Late Latin, from Greek *Enōkh,* from Hebrew *Ḥanōkh,* "consecrated," "initiated," from *hānakh,* he initiated.]

Enoch[2]. The father of Methuselah. Genesis 5:21.

e·nol (ē'nôl', ē'nōl') *n.* An organic compound containing a hydroxyl group bonded to a carbon atom that in turn is doubly bonded to another carbon atom. See **keto-enol tautomerism.** [-ENE + -OL.] —**e·nol·ic** (ē-nŏl'ĭk) *adj.*

e·no·lase (ē'nə-lās', -lāz') *n.* An enzyme present in muscle tissue that acts in carbohydrate metabolism. [ENOL + -ASE.]

enology. Variant of **oenology.**

e·nor·mi·ty (ĭ-nôr'mə-tē) *n., pl.* **-ties.** 1. The quality of passing all moral bounds; excessive wickedness; outrageousness. 2. A monstrous offense or evil; an outrage.

e·nor·mous (ĭ-nôr'məs) *adj.* 1. Very great in size, extent, number, or degree; immense: *swam in an enormous pool.* 2. *Archaic.* Very wicked; heinous. [Middle English *enorme,* from Latin *ēnormis,* unusual, immense : *ex-,* out of + *norma,* pattern, rule.] —**e·nor·mous·ly** *adv.* —**e·nor·mous·ness** *n.*

Synonyms: colossal, gargantuan, gigantic, huge, immense, mammoth, tremendous, vast.

E·nos (ē'nəs, ē'nŏs'). A son of Seth. Genesis 4:26. [Greek *Enōs,* from Hebrew *Enōsh,* "man."]

e·nough (ĭ-nŭf') *adj.* 1. Sufficient to meet a need or satisfy a desire; adequate: *enough food for two.* 2. Used in requests to stop: *That's enough, now!*
~*pron.* An adequate quantity or number: *He ate enough for two.*
~*adv.* 1. To a satisfactory amount or degree; sufficiently. 2. Very; fully; quite: *We were glad enough to leave.* 3. Tolerably; rather: *She sang well enough, but the show was a failure.* 4. Used as an intensive following certain adverbs: *funnily enough; sure enough; oddly enough.* [Middle English *ynough, inough,* Old English *genōg,* from Germanic.]

e·nounce (ĭ-nouns') *tr.v.* **enounced, enouncing, enounces.** 1. To declare publicly; state; announce. 2. To pronounce; enunciate. [French *énoncer,* from Latin *ēnūntiāre,* to ENUNCIATE.] —**e·nounce·ment** *n.*

e·now (ĭ-nou') *adj. Archaic.* Enough. —**e·now** *adv.*

en pas·sant (äN' pä-säN') *adv.*) In passing; by the way.
~*n.* The capture of a chess pawn after an initial move of two squares by an enemy pawn in a position to make a capture on the first of the two squares so crossed. [French.]

en·phy·tot·ic (ĕn'fī-tŏt'ĭk) *adj.* Designating or characterizing a plant disease that causes a relatively constant amount of damage each year. [EN- + -PHYT(E) + -OTIC.]

en·plane (ĕn-plān', ĭn-) *intr.v.* **-planed, -planing, -planes.** Also **em·plane** (ĕm-, ĭm-). To board an airplane.

enquire. Variant of **inquire.**

enquiry. Variant of **inquiry.**

en·rage (ĕn-rāj', ĭn-) *tr.v.* **-raged, -raging, -rages.** To put in a rage; infuriate; anger.

en·rapt (ĕn-răpt', ĭn-) *adj.* 1. Enraptured. 2. Enthralled.

en·rap·ture (ĕn-răp'chər, ĭn-) *tr.v.* **-tured, -turing, -tures.** To move to rapture; overwhelm with delight.

en·rich (ĕn-rĭch', ĭn-) *tr.v.* **-riched, -riching, -riches.** 1. To make rich or richer. 2. **a.** To add to in quality or quantity; improve. **b.** To make fuller, more meaningful, or more rewarding: *Reading enriches the vocabulary.* 3. To add fertilizer to (soil) to increase productivity. 4. To add nutrients to (foodstuffs) during processing. 5. To add to the beauty or character of; embellish or adorn: *The carved moldings enriched the walls.* 6. *Physics.* To increase the ratio of radioactive isotopes in (a sample); especially, to increase the ratio of amount of fissionable uranium 235 in (natural uranium) so that it can be used as a nuclear fuel. 7. *Chemistry.* To increase the amount of a particular substance in (a mixture or solution). [Middle English *enrichen,* from Old French *enricher* : *en-* (causative) + *riche*, RICH.] **—en·rich·er** *n.*

en·rich·ment (ĕn-rĭch′mənt, ĭn-) *n.* **1. a.** The act of enriching. **b.** The state of being enriched. **2.** Something that enriches: *added butter to the sauce as an enrichment.*

en·robe (ĕn-rōb′, ĭn-) *tr.v.* **-robed, -robing, -robes. 1.** To put a robe on. **2.** To dress richly as if in a robe.

en·roll, en·rol (ĕn-rōl′, ĭn-) *v.* **-rolled, -rolling, -rolls** or **-rols. —tr. 1.** To enter the name of in a register, record, or roll. **2.** To put on record; record. **3.** To roll or wrap up. **4.** To cause (a person) to become a member. —*intr.* **1.** To place one's name on a roll or register. **2.** To become a member. [Middle English *enrollen*, from Old French *enroller* : *en-*, in + *rolle*, ROLL.]

en·roll·ment, en·rol·ment (ĕn-rōl′mənt, ĭn-) *n.* **1. a.** The action of enrolling. **b.** The state or process of being enrolled. **c.** The number enrolled. **2.** A record or entry.

en·root (ĕn-rōōt′, -rŏŏt′, ĭn-) *tr.v.* **-rooted, -rooting, -roots.** To establish firmly by or as if by roots; implant.

en route (ŏn rōōt′, ĕn, äN) *adv.* On the route; on or along the way. [French.]

ens (ĕnz) *n., pl.* **entia** (ĕn′shē-ə, -shə). *Philosophy.* **1.** Existence or being as an abstract concept. **2.** An entity as opposed to an attribute. [Medieval Latin, from Latin, irregular present participle of *esse*, to be.]

Ens. ensign.

en·san·guine (ĕn-săng′gwĭn, ĭn-) *tr.v.* **-guined, -guining, -guines. 1.** To cover or stain with or as if with blood. **2.** To color or stain a crimson red.

en·sconce (ĕn-skŏns′, ĭn-) *tr.v.* **-sconced, -sconcing, -sconces. 1.** To settle (oneself) securely or comfortably: *ensconced in an armchair.* **2.** To place, fix, or conceal in a secure place. [EN- + SCONCE (fortification), originally meaning to take shelter, as behind a fortification.]

en·sem·ble (ŏn-sŏm′bəl) *n.* **1.** A unit or group of complementary parts that contribute to a single effect. **2.** A coordinated outfit or costume. **3.** A set, as of furniture. **4.** A group of musicians, singers, dancers, or actors who perform together. **5. a.** Music for two or more vocalists or instrumentalists. **b.** The musicians who perform in an ensemble. **c.** The quality of performance of a musical ensemble, especially as judged in regard to unity and balance of style and technique: *The individual players were all virtuosos, but the ensemble was poor.* Also used adjectively: *ensemble playing.* **6.** *Physics.* A large collection of atoms, or a collection of assemblies of atoms, used in statistical mechanics to calculate the thermodynamic properties of a system. [French, "together," from Vulgar Latin *insemul* (unattested), from Latin *insimul*, at the same time : *in-*, in + *simul, semul*, at the same time.]

en·shrine (ĕn-shrīn′, ĭn-) *tr.v.* **-shrined, -shrining, -shrines.** Also **in·shrine** (ĭn-). **1.** To enclose in or as if in a shrine: *a book enshrining their ideals.* **2.** To cherish as sacred. **—en·shrine·ment** *n.*

en·shroud (ĕn-shroud′, ĭn-) *tr.v.* **-shrouded, -shrouding, -shrouds.** To shroud or cover; veil or conceal.

en·si·form (ĕn′sə-fôrm′) *adj.* Sword-shaped, as the leaf of an iris or gladiolus. [French *ensiforme*, from Latin *ēnsis*, sword + -FORM.]

en·sign (ĕn′sən; *also* ĕn′sīn′ *for senses 1, 2, 3, 5*) *n.* **1. a.** A national flag displayed on ships and aircraft, often with the special insignia of a branch or unit of the armed forces: *the naval ensign.* **b.** *British.* A flag, usually on a ship, incorporating the Union Jack in the top left-hand corner. **2.** A standard or banner, as of a military unit. **3.** *Archaic.* A standard-bearer. **4. a.** *Abbr.* **Ens.** A commissioned officer of the lowest rank in the U.S. Navy or Coast Guard. **b.** Formerly, a commissioned officer of the lowest rank in the British infantry. **5. a.** A badge; emblem. **b.** A sign; token. [Middle English *ensigne*, from Old French *enseigne*, from Latin *insignia*, INSIGNIA.]

en·si·lage (ĕn′sə-lĭj) *n.* **1.** The process of storing and fermenting green fodder in a silo. **2.** Fodder thus preserved; silage. ~*tr.v.* **ensilaged, -laging, -lages.** To ensile.

en·sile (ĕn-sīl′, ĭn-) *tr.v.* **-siled, -siling, -siles. 1.** To store (fodder) in a silo for preservation. **2.** To convert (green fodder) into silage.

en·slave (ĕn-slāv′, ĭn-) *tr.v.* **-slaved, -slaving, -slaves.** To make a slave of; reduce to slavery, bondage, or dependence. **—en·slave·ment** *n.* **—en·slav·er** *n.*

en·snare (ĕn-snâr′, ĭn-) *tr.v.* **-snared, -snaring, -snares.** Also **in·snare** (ĭn-). To catch in or as if in a snare; trap. **—en·snare·ment** *n.*

en·soul (ĕn-sōl′, ĭn-) *tr.v.* **-souled, -souling, -souls. 1.** To endow with a soul. **2.** To unite with the soul.

en·sphere (ĕn-sfîr′, ĭn-) *tr.v.* **-sphered, -sphering, -spheres.** Also **in·sphere** (ĭn-). **1.** To enclose in or as if in a sphere. **2.** To give spherical form to.

en·sta·tite (ĕn′stə-tīt′) *n.* A variety of orthorhombic pyroxene having a magnesium silicate base, mainly $Mg_2Si_2O_6$, usually found embedded in igneous rocks. [German *Enstatit* : Greek *enstatēs*, adversary (from its refractory nature) : *en-*, in, at, near + *-statēs*, standing + -ITE.]

en·sue (ĕn-sōō′, ĭn-) *intr.v.* **-sued, -suing, -sues. 1.** To follow immediately afterward; take place subsequently. **2.** To follow as a consequence; result. —See Synonyms at **follow.** [Middle English *ensuen*, from Old French *ensuivre* (stem *ensu-*), from Vulgar Latin *insequere* (unattested), variant of Latin *insequī*, to follow after or on : *in-*, in, onward + *sequī*, to follow.]

en suite (äN swēt′) *adv.* As part of a unit or set: *a master bedroom en suite with bathroom.* [French, "in sequence."]

en·sure (ĕn-shōōr′, ĭn-) *tr.v.* **-sured, -suring, -sures.** To make sure or certain; make secure; guarantee.

–ent *suffix.* **1.** Indicates performing, promoting, or causing a specified action; for example, **effervescent, absorbent. 2.** Indicates one that performs, promotes, or causes a specified action; for example, **referent.** [Middle English *-ent*, from Old French, from Latin *-ens* (stem *-ent-*). Compare *-ant.*]

E.N.T. *Medicine.* ear, nose, and throat.

en·tab·la·ture (ĕn-tăb′lə-chŏŏr′, -chər, ĭn-) *n. Architecture.* **1.** The upper section of a classical order, resting on the capital and including the architrave, frieze, and cornice. **2.** Any raised, horizontal architectural feature. [Obsolete French, from Italian *intavolatura*, from *intavolare*, to put on the table : *in-*, in, from Latin + *tavola*, table, from Latin *tabula*, board, TABLE.]

en·ta·ble·ment (ĕn-tā′bəl-mənt, ĭn-) *n.* The platform supporting a statue, above the base and the dado. [French, from Old French : *en-*, in + TABLE.]

en·tail (ĕn-tāl′, ĭn-) *tr.v.* **-tailed, -tailing, -tails. 1.** To have as a necessary accompaniment or consequence. **2.** To limit the inheritance of (property) to a specific, unalterable succession of heirs.

---

engraving

ENGRAVING: PRINTING PICTURES FROM A METAL PLATE

An art form that was also used to mass-produce original works of art

In Europe, engraving pictures on metal plates began in the 15th century, probably in the Rhineland. Until the advent of photography four centuries later it was used to mass-produce original drawings and paintings and to illustrate books. Great artists—including Dürer, Rembrandt, Goya, and Picasso—have used the technique to produce original works of art.

In line engraving, the artist draws on a plate of metal, usually copper, using a sharp tool. The plate is then inked and wiped clean, leaving ink in the engraved furrows. A damp piece of paper is laid on the plate, and both are rolled through a heavy press. The paper is forced into the furrows, picking up the ink; on the finished print the engraved lines stand up in relief.

In drypoint, the burr at the side of the furrow is left, rather than being scraped off, and is used together with the line itself to add character to the drawing. This produces a broad soft line rather than a thin clean one.

Etching is done on a plate coated with an acid-resistant ground. The artist's needle exposes the copper, and the plate is then put in an acid bath, which eats away the exposed parts.

Aquatint is a form of etching in which dots give gradations of light and dark. It uses a porous ground that the acid penetrates to form tiny dots. Tone is controlled by the length of time different areas are exposed to the acid.

Mezzotint is a process that was widely used to reproduce paintings in the 18th century. The plate surface is covered with innumerable minute pits by a tool called a rocker, and so prints as a uniform velvety black. Whites and grays are achieved by burnishing the metal surface.

DÜRER *An engraving by Albrecht Dürer of a peasant couple dancing, dated 1514. In his lifetime (1471-1528), Dürer's works of art included 250 woodcuts and more than 100 engravings. He drew the sketches for his woodcuts, but they were cut into the woodblock by skilled artisans. The engravings, however, are entirely Dürer's own work, and he created them as individual works of art. A number of his engravings are portraits of peasants who were regular marketgoers to his local market square at Nuremberg, in Germany, and the fairs at Frankfurt.*

∼*n.* (ĕn'tāl', ĕn-tāl', ĭn-). **1. a.** The act of entailing, especially property. **b.** The state of being entailed. **2.** An entailed estate. **3.** A predetermined order of succession, as to an estate or to an office. **4.** Something transmitted as if by unalterable inheritance. [Middle English *entaillen, entailen* : EN- + *taille,* TAIL (limitation).] —**en·tail·ment** *n.*

en·ta·moe·ba (ĕn'tə-mē'bə) *n., pl.* **-bas** or **-bae** (-bē). Also **en·da·moe·ba** (ĕn'də-). Any of several parasitic amoebas of the genus *Entamoeba;* especially, *E. histolytica,* causing dysentery and ulceration of the colon and liver. [New Latin *Entamoeba* : ENT(O)- + AMOEBA.]

en·tan·gle (ĕn-tăng'gəl, ĭn-) *tr.v.* **-gled, -gling, -gles. 1.** To twist together so that disengagement is difficult; make tangled; snarl. **2.** To complicate; confuse. **3.** To involve inextricably, as in complications or difficulties. —**en·tan·gler** *n.*

en·tan·gle·ment (ĕn-tăng'gəl-mənt, ĭn-) *n.* **1. a.** The act of entangling. **b.** The state of being entangled. **2.** Something that entangles, as a dangerous or compromising relationship, especially a sexual one. **3.** A military barrier of barbed wire.

en·ta·sis (ĕn'tə-sĭs) *n., pl.* **-ses** (-sēz'). *Architecture.* A slight bulge in a column, introduced to avoid the illusion of concavity that a straight column would give. [New Latin, from Greek, from *enteinein,* to stretch tight : *en-* (intensive) + *teinein,* to stretch.]

En·teb·be (ĕn-tĕb'ē). Town in Uganda, situated on Lake Victoria, south of Kampala. At its airport in 1976 an Israeli airborne commando force rescued all but 3 of 110 hostages after the hijacking of an Air France plane by Palestinian guerrillas.

en·tel·e·chy (ĕn-tĕl'ə-kē, ĭn-) *n., pl.* **-chies. 1.** In the philosophy of Aristotle, the condition of a thing whose essence is fully realized; actuality as distinguished from potentiality. **2.** In various philosophical systems, a vital force urging an organism toward self-fulfillment: *"Courage is the affirmation of one's essential nature, one's inner aim or entelechy"* (Paul Tillich). [Late Latin *entelechia,* from Greek *entelekheia,* complete reality : *entelēs,* complete, full : *en-,* in + *telos,* perfection, end + *ekhein,* to have.]

en·tente (ŏn-tŏnt', äN-täNt') *n.* **1.** An agreement, usually unformalized, between two or more governments or powers for cooperative action or policy. **2.** The coalition resulting from an entente. [French, "understanding," from Old French *entendre,* to understand, INTEND.]

en·ter (ĕn'tər) *v.* **-tered, -tering, -ters.** —*tr.* **1.** To come or go into. **2.** To penetrate; pierce. **3.** To introduce; insert. **4.** To become an element in or a part of. **5.** To begin (an age or phase); embark upon: *He was entering a period of crisis.* **6. a.** To obtain admission to (a school, for example). **b.** To secure the admission of. **c.** To enroll. **7. a.** To submit or register as an entry in an exhibition or competition: *enter dahlias in a flower show.* **b.** To become a participant or a contestant in. **8.** To take up (a profession or career); embrace: *Their son entered the priesthood.* **9.** *Law.* **a.** To place formally before a court or upon the records: *enter a plea.* **b.** To go upon or into (real property) as a trespasser or with felonious intent. See **breaking and entering. c.** To go upon in order to take possession of (real property, especially land). **10.** To record, as in a register or on a list. **11.** To make known; register: *enter a protest.* —*intr.* **1.** To come or go in; make an entry. **2.** To gain entry; penetrate. **3.** To become a member of a group. **4.** To come on-stage in a theater: *Enter stage left.* —**enter into. 1.** To participate in; take an active interest in. **2.** To be a component of; form a part of. **3.** To consider; delve into. **4.** To become party to (a contract). **5.** To empathize with; be in sympathy with. —**enter on** (or **upon**). **1.** To set out upon; embark upon. **2.** To take legal possession of (real property, especially land). **3.** To begin to consider or deal with (a subject). [Middle English *entren,* from Old French *entrer,* from Latin *intrāre,* from *intrā,* within.]

en·ter·ic (ĕn-tĕr'ĭk, ĭn-) *adj.* Also **en·ter·al** (ĕn'tər-əl). Of, pertaining to, or affecting the intestine. [Greek *enterikos,* from *enteron,* ENTERON.]

enteric fever *n. Pathology.* **Typhoid fever** *(see).*

en·ter·i·tis (ĕn'tə-rī'tĭs) *n.* Inflammation of the intestinal tract. [New Latin : ENTER(O)- + -ITIS.]

entero-, enter- *prefix.* Indicates the intestine; for example, **enterostomy, enteritis.** [New Latin, from Greek *enteron,* intestine.]

en·ter·o·bi·a·sis (ĕn'tə-rō-bī'ə-sĭs) *n.* Infestation of the intestine with pinworms. Also called "oxyuriasis." [New Latin *enterobius (vermicularis),* pinworm (see **entero-**) + -IASIS.]

en·ter·o·gas·trone (ĕn'tə-rō-găs'trōn') *n.* A hormone liberated by the small intestine (duodenum) that inhibits secretion of gastric juice by the stomach. [ENTERO- + GASTR(O)- + (HORM)ONE.]

en·ter·o·ki·nase (ĕn'tə-rō-kī'nās', -nāz') *n.* An enzyme found in intestinal juice that converts trypsinogen to trypsin. [ENTERO- + KINASE.]

en·ter·on (ĕn'tə-rŏn') *n.* The intestine, especially that of an embryo or coelenterate. [New Latin, from Greek, intestine, entrails.]

en·ter·os·to·my (ĕn'tə-rŏs'tə-mē) *n., pl.* **-mies.** Surgical formation of an opening into the intestine through the abdominal wall. [ENTERO- + -STOMY.] —**en·ter·os·to·mal** *adj.*

en·ter·ot·o·my (ĕn'tə-rŏt'ə-mē) *n., pl.* **-mies.** Surgical incision into the intestine. [ENTERO- + -TOMY.]

en·ter·o·vir·us (ĕn'tə-rō-vī'rəs) *n.* Any virus, such as the polio virus, that enters the body through and multiplies in the gastrointestinal tract, and then usually invades the central nervous system.

en·ter·prise (ĕn'tər-prīz') *n.* **1.** An undertaking, especially of some scope, complication, and risk. **2. a.** Commercial or economic activity; business: *private enterprise.* **b.** A business or company. **3.** Industrious effort, especially when directed toward making money. **4.** Readiness to venture; boldness; initiative. [Middle English, from Old French *entreprise,* from the feminine past participle of *entreprendre,* to undertake : *entre-,* between, from Latin *inter-* + *prendre,* to take, from Latin *prendere, prehendere.*] —**en·ter·pris·er** *n.*

en·ter·pris·ing (ĕn'tər-prī'zĭng) *adj.* Showing imagination, initiative, and readiness to undertake new ventures. —**en·ter·pris·ing·ly** *adv.*

en·ter·tain (ĕn'tər-tān') *v.* **-tained, -taining, -tains.** —*tr.* **1.** To hold the attention of; especially, to perform for the pleasure of; amuse. **2.** To extend hospitality toward: *entertain friends for dinner.* **3. a.** To mull over; contemplate: *entertain an idea.* **b.** To hold in mind; harbor: *entertain illusions.* **4.** *Sports.* To play at home against (an opposing team, for example). —*intr.* **1.** To have guests, as for dinner or a party. **2.** To provide entertainment. [Middle English *entertinen,* to maintain, from Old French *entretenir,* from Vulgar Latin *intertenēre* (unattested), "to hold between" : Latin *inter-,* between + *tenēre,* to hold.]

en·ter·tain·er (ĕn'tər-tā'nər) *n.* **1.** A person who performs, as by singing or dancing, as a profession. **2.** Someone who entertains.

en·ter·tain·ing (ĕn'tər-tā'nĭng) *adj.* Serving to entertain; agreeably diverting; amusing. —**en·ter·tain·ing·ly** *adv.*

en·ter·tain·ment (ĕn'tər-tān'mənt) *n.* **1.** The act of entertaining. **2.** The art, profession, or field of entertaining. **3.** Something that entertains; especially, a performance or show designed to amuse or divert. **4.** The pleasure afforded by being entertained; amusement. **5.** Hospitality extended toward guests.

en·thal·py (ĕn'thăl'pē, ĕn-thăl'-) *n.* A thermodynamic function of a system, equivalent to the internal energy plus the product of the pressure and the volume. Also called "heat content." [Greek *enthalpein,* to heat in : *en-,* in + *thalpein*†, to warm, heat.]

en·thrall, en·thral (ĕn-thrôl', ĭn-) *tr.v.* **-thralled, -thralling, -thralls** or **-thrals. 1.** To hold spellbound; captivate; charm. **2.** To reduce to thralldom; enslave. [Middle English *enthrallen* : EN- + THRALL.] —**en·thrall·ment** *n.*

en·throne (ĕn-thrōn', ĭn-) *tr.v.* **-throned, -throning, -thrones. 1.** To seat on a throne. **2.** To invest with sovereign power or with the authority of high office. **3.** To raise to a lofty position; revere; exalt. —**en·throne·ment** *n.*

en·thuse (ĕn-thōōz', ĭn-) *v.* **-thused, -thusing, -thuses.** *Informal.* —*tr.* To stimulate enthusiasm in. —*intr.* To show enthusiasm. [Back-formation from ENTHUSIASM.]

en·thu·si·asm (ĕn-thōō'zē-ăz'əm, ĭn-) *n.* **1. a.** Keen interest or excitement. **b.** Eagerness; zeal. **c.** Ardent fondness. **2.** A subject or activity that inspires a lively interest. **3.** *Archaic.* **a.** Ecstasy arising from supposed possession by a god. **b.** Fanatical religious ardor. —See Synonyms at **passion.** [Late Latin *enthūsiasmus,* from Greek *enthousiasmos,* inspiration, from *enthousiazein,* to be inspired by a god, from *enthous, entheos,* possessed, inspired : *en-,* in + *theos,* god.]

en·thu·si·ast (ĕn-thōō'zē-ăst', ĭn-) *n.* **1.** A person filled with enthusiasm; especially, one ardently preoccupied with a particular subject: *a baseball enthusiast.* **2.** *Archaic.* A religious zealot, fanatic, or visionary. —See Synonyms at **fanatic.** —**en·thu·si·as·tic** (ĕn-thōō'zē-ăs'tĭk, ĭn-) *adj.* —**en·thu·si·as·ti·cal·ly** *adv.*

en·thy·meme (ĕn'thə-mēm') *n. Logic.* A syllogism with one of the premises implicit or unexpressed because it is thought to be self-evident. [Latin *enthȳmēma,* from Greek *enthumēma,* from *enthumeisthai,* "to have in mind," consider : *en-,* in + *thūmos,* mind.]

en·ti·a. Plural of **ens.**

en·tice (ĕn-tīs', ĭn-) *tr.v.* **-ticed, -ticing, -tices.** To attract by arousing hope or desire; lure. —See Synonyms at **lure.** [Middle English *enticen,* from Old French *enticier,* from Vulgar Latin *intītiāre* (unattested), to set on fire : Latin *in-,* in + *tītiō*†, firebrand.] —**en·tice·ment** *n.* —**en·tic·er** *n.* —**en·tic·ing·ly** *adv.*

en·tire (ĕn-tīr', ĭn-) *adj.* **1.** Having no part missing or excepted; whole: *an entire set of the encyclopedia; the entire country.* **2.** Without reservation or limitation; total; complete: *entire freedom; my entire approval; his entire attention.* **3.** All in one piece; unbroken; intact: *The ship was still entire after the typhoon.* **4.** Of one piece; continuous. **5.** Not castrated. **6.** *Botany.* Not indented or toothed, as the margin of a leaf.
∼*n.* **1.** The whole of something; entirety. **2.** An uncastrated horse. [Middle English *entier,* from Old French, from Latin *integrum,* accusative of *integer,* intact.] —**en·tire·ness** *n.*

en·tire·ly (ĕn-tīr'lē, ĭn-) *adv.* **1.** Wholly; completely. **2.** Solely or exclusively.

en·tire·ty (ĕn-tī'rə-tē, -tīr'tē, ĭn-) *n., pl.* **-ties. 1.** The state or condition of being entire or complete; completeness. **2.** Something that is entire; a whole. **3.** The entire amount or extent; the sum total.

en·ti·tle (ĕn-tīt'l, ĭn-) *tr.v.* **-tled, -tling, -tles. 1.** To give a name or title to; designate: *a novel entitled "Summer."* **2. a.** To give (a person) the right to do or have something; qualify. **b.** To give to or prove a legal right to or claim on something. [Middle English *entitlen,* from Old French *entiteler,* from Late Latin *intitulāre* : *in-,* in + *titulus,* TITLE.] —**en·ti·tle·ment** *n.*

en·ti·ty (ĕn'tə-tē) *n., pl.* **-ties. 1.** The fact of existence; being. **2.** Something that exists independently and apart from other things. **3.** A particular and discrete unit: *Persons and corporations are equivalent entities under the law.* [Medieval Latin *entitās,* from Latin *ēns* (stem *ent-*), irregular present participle of *esse,* to be.]

ento- *prefix.* Indicates within, inside; for example, **entozoa.** [New Latin, from Greek *entos,* within.]

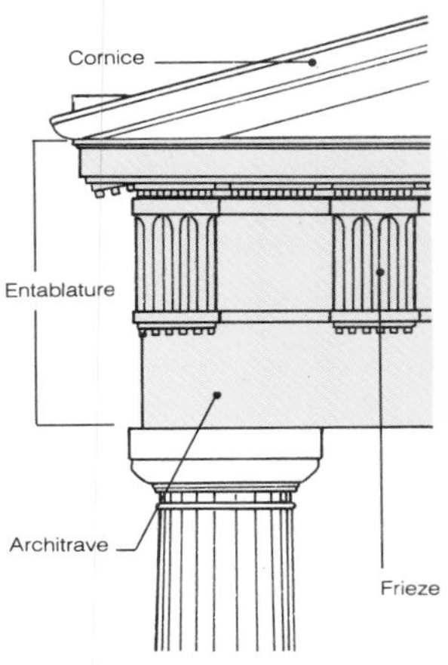

entablature *In classical architecture, the entablature is the collective name for the horizontal parts of a building above the supporting columns. It consists of three elements: the architrave; the frieze; and the cornice.*

PRONUNCIATION KEY

ă, pat; ā, pay; âr, care;
ä, father, are; b, bib;
ch, church; d, deed; ĕ, pet;
ē, be; f, fife; g, gag; h, hat;
hw, which; ĭ, pit; ī, pie;
îr, pier; j, judge; k, kick;
l, lid, needle; m, mum;
n, no, sudden; ng, thing;
ŏ, pot; ō, toe; ô, paw, for;
oi, noise; ou, out; ŏŏ, book;
ōō, boot; p, pop; r, roar;
s, sauce; sh, ship, dish;
t, tight; th, thin, path;
th, this, bathe; ŭ, cut; ûr, fur;
v, valve; w, with; y, yes;
z, zebra, size; zh, vision;
ə, about, item, edible,
gallop, circus, peaceful

IN FOREIGN WORDS:

à, *Fr.* ami; œ, *Fr.* feu, *Ger.* schön; ü, *Fr.* tu, *Ger.* über; KH, *Ger.* ich, *Scot.* loch; N, *Fr.* bon; y', *Fr.* Compiègne

STRESS MARKS:

Primary stress: '
in·cite' (ĭn-sīt')
Secondary stress: '
in'sight' (ĭn'sīt')

entoblast. Variant of **endoblast.**

entoderm. Variant of **endoderm.**

entom. entomological; entomology.

en·tomb (ĕn-tōōm′, ĭn-) tr.v. **-tombed, -tombing, -tombs. 1.** To place in or as if in a tomb or grave; bury. **2.** To serve as a tomb for. [Middle English entoumben, from Old French entomber : en-, in + tombe, tomb, from Late Latin tumba, TOMB.] **—en·tomb·ment** n.

entomo– prefix. Indicates insect; for example, **entomology, entomophagous.** [French, from Greek entomon, insect, "one whose body is cut into segments," from entomos, cut up, from entemnein, to cut in, cut up : en-, in + temnein, to cut.]

entomol. entomology.

en·to·mol·o·gize (ĕn′tə-mŏl′ə-jīz′) intr.v. **-gized, -gizing, -gizes.** To study or collect insects.

en·to·mol·o·gy (ĕn′tə-mŏl′ə-jē) n. Abbr. **entom., entomol.** The scientific study of insects. [ENTOMO- + -LOGY.] **—en·to·mo·log·i·cal** (ĕn′tə-mə-lŏj′ĭ-kəl) adj. **—en·to·mo·log·i·cal·ly** adv. **—en·to·mol·o·gist** (-mŏl′ə-jĭst) n.

en·to·moph·a·gous (ĕn′tə-mŏf′ə-gəs) adj. Feeding on insects; insectivorous. [ENTOMO- + -PHAGOUS.]

en·to·moph·i·lous (ĕn′tə-mŏf′ə-ləs) adj. Pollinated by insects. [ENTOMO- + -PHILOUS.] **—en·to·moph·i·ly** n.

en·tou·rage (ŏn′tōō-räzh′) n. **1.** A group of attendants, followers, or associates. **2.** One's environment or surroundings. [French, from entourer, to surround, from Old French entour, surroundings : en-, in + tour, circuit, TOUR.]

en·to·zo·a (ĕn′tə-zō′ə) pl.n. Singular **-zoan** (-zō′ən) or **-zoon** (-zō′ŏn′). Various animals, such as tapeworms, that live within other animals, usually as parasites. [New Latin : ENTO- + -ZOA.] **—en·to·zo·ic** adj.

en·tr'acte (ŏn′träkt′, än-träkt′) n. **1.** The interval between two successive acts of a theatrical performance. **2.** An entertainment, especially a piece of music, provided during this interval. [French, "between act."]

en·trails (ĕn′trālz′, -trəlz) pl.n. **1.** The internal organs, especially the intestines; viscera. **2.** The inner parts of something. [Middle English entrailles, from Old French, from Medieval Latin intrālia, variant of Latin interānea, from the neuter plural of interāneus, internal, from inter, within.]

en·train¹ (ĕn-trān′, ĭn-) tr.v. **-trained, -training, -trains.** To pull or draw along after itself. [Old French entrainer : en-, in + trainer, to draw (see train).]

entrain² v. **-trained, -training, -trains.** —tr. To put on a train. —intr. To board a train. **—en·train·ment** n.

en·trance¹ (ĕn′trəns) n. **1.** The act or an instance of entering; especially, the entry of an actor into the performing area. **2.** Any passage, opening, doorway, or the like where one can enter. **3.** The permission, power, or liberty to enter; admission. Also used adjectivally: entrance money. **4.** The point in a script or musical score at which a performer is to begin. [Middle English entraunce, from Old French entrance, from entrer, to ENTER.]

en·trance² (ĕn-trăns′, -träns′, ĭn-) tr.v. **-tranced, -trancing, -trances. 1.** To put into a trance. **2.** To fill with great pleasure, wonder, or enchantment; fascinate: a child entranced by his own reflection. **—en·trance·ment** n. **—en·tranc·ing·ly** adv.

en·trant (ĕn′trənt) n. **1.** One who enters; especially, one who enters a competition: There were ten entrants in the beauty contest. **2.** A new member, as of a profession, organization, university, or the like. [French, from the present participle of entrer, to ENTER.]

en·trap (ĕn-trăp′, ĭn-) tr.v. **-trapped, -trapping, -traps. 1.** To catch in or as if in a trap. **2.** To lure into danger, difficulty, or self-incrimination. [Old French entraper : en-, in + trape, trap.] **—en·trap·ment** n.

en·treat (ĕn-trēt′, ĭn-) v. **-treated, -treating, -treats.** Also **in·treat** (ĭn-). —tr. **1.** To ask (someone) earnestly; beseech; implore; beg. **2.** To ask for (something) earnestly; petition for. —intr. To make an earnest request or petition; plead. **—See Synonyms at beg.** [Middle English entreten, to deal with, plead with, from Old French entraitier : en-, in + traitier, traiter, to TREAT.] **—en·treat·ing·ly** adv. **—en·treat·ment** n.

en·treat·y (ĕn-trē′tē, ĭn-) n., pl. **-ies.** An earnest treaty; a plea.

en·tre·chat (ŏn′trə-shä′, än′trə-shä′) n. A leap in ballet during which the dancer crosses his feet a number of times, often beating them together. [French, earlier entrecha(se), by folk etymology (influenced by chasse, chase) from Italian (capriola) intrecciata, "interlaced (caper)," from the feminine past participle of intrecciare, to interlace, entwine : in-, in, from Latin + treccia, tress, akin to Old French tresse, TRESS.]

en·tre·côte (ŏn′trə-kōt′) n. A cut of steak taken from between the ribs. [French, "between the ribs."]

en·trée, en·tree (ŏn′trā′, ŏn-trā′) n. **1. a.** The power, permission, or liberty to enter; admittance. **b.** Access by special privilege to a place normally inaccessible. **2. a.** A dish served between the fish course and the main meat course, or immediately before the main course, especially in an elaborate or formal dinner. **b.** The main course, especially in an ordinary or simple meal. [French, ENTRY.]

en·tre·mets (ŏn′trə-mā′, än′-) n., pl. **entremets** (-māz′, -mā′). A side dish or dishes; especially, a dish served between principal courses or as a dessert. [French, earlier entremes : Old French entre-, between + mes, dish, MESS.]

en·trench (ĕn-trĕnch′, ĭn-) v. **-trenched, -trenching, -trenches.** Also **in·trench** (ĭn-). —tr. **1.** Military. **a.** To provide with a trench or trenches for the purpose of draining, fortifying, defending, or supporting. **b.** To set up (a base, for example) in a defensible position. **2.** To establish firmly or securely: entrenched prejudices. —intr. **1.** To dig a trench or trenches. **2.** To adopt a safe or strongly defended position. **3.** To encroach or trespass.

en·trench·ment (ĕn-trĕnch′mənt, ĭn-) n. Also **in·trench·ment** (ĭn-). **1.** The act of entrenching or the condition of being entrenched. **2.** A fortification; especially, a series of banked trenches.

en·tre nous (ŏn′trə nōō′, än′trə) adv. Between ourselves; confidentially. [French.]

en·tre·pôt (ŏn′trə-pō′, än′-) n. **1.** A place where goods are stored or deposited and from which they are distributed. **2.** A trading or market center. [French, from entreposer, to put in, to store : Old French entre-, in, between, from Latin inter- + poser, to put, POSE.]

en·tre·pre·neur (ŏn′trə-prə-nûr′, -nōōr′, -nyōōr′) n. A person who organizes, operates, and assumes the risk for business ventures. [French, from Old French, from entreprendre, to undertake. See enterprise.] **—en·tre·pre·neur·i·al** adj.

en·tre·sol (ŏn′trə-sŏl′, -sōl′, än′-) n. A floor just above the ground floor; mezzanine. [French, "between floors."]

en·tro·py (ĕn′trə-pē) n., pl. **-pies. 1.** A measure of the capacity of a system to undergo spontaneous change, thermodynamically specified by the relationship $dS = dQ/T$, where dS is an infinitesimal change in the measure for a system absorbing an infinitesimal quantity of heat dQ at thermodynamic temperature T. **2.** The tendency of the energy of a closed system, including that of the universe itself, to become less available to do work with the passage of time. **3.** A measure of the randomness, disorder, or chaos in a system specified in statistical mechanics by the relationship $S = k \ln P + c$, where S is the value of the measure for a system in a given state, P is the probability of occurrence of that state, k is the Boltzmann constant, and c is an arbitrary constant. [German Entropie : Greek en-, in + tropē, a turning, change.]

en·trust (ĕn-trŭst′, ĭn-) tr.v. **-trusted, -trusting, -trusts.** Also **in·trust** (ĭn-). **1.** To give over to another for care, protection, or performance: entrusted the task to his aides. **2.** To commit something trustfully to; place a trust upon: entrusted his aides with the task. **—See Synonyms at commit.**

en·try (ĕn′trē) n., pl. **-tries. 1.** The act or an instance of entering. **2.** The right to enter: It was difficult to gain entry to the club. **3. a.** The inclusion or insertion of an item in a diary, register, list, or other record. **b.** An item thus entered: I made no entries in the journal for a week. **4.** An item in a reference book, such as an article in an encyclopedia or a word, term, or phrase defined or identified in a dictionary, together with the text related to it. **5. a.** One registered as a participant in a competition. **b.** All such participants collectively. **6.** The entrance on-stage or manner of entering of an actor. **7.** Law. The act of taking possession of land or property by entering. **8.** A passage or opening where one can enter. [Middle English entre, from Old French entree, from Vulgar Latin intrāta (unattested), from the feminine past participle of Latin intrāre, to ENTER.]

en·try·way (ĕn′trē-wā′) n. A passage or opening serving as an entrance.

en·twine (ĕn-twīn′, ĭn-) v. **-twined, -twining, -twines.** Also **in·twine** (ĭn-). —tr. To twine or twist around or about: Ivy entwined the pillar. —intr. To twine or twist together.

en·twist (ĕn-twĭst′, ĭn-) tr.v. **-twisted, -twisting, -twists.** Also **in·twist** (ĭn-). To twist together; entwine.

e·nu·cle·ate (ĭ-nōō′klē-āt′, ĭ-nyōō′-) tr.v. **ated, -ating, -ates. 1.** In surgery, to remove (a tumor or eyeball, for example) from its enveloping cover or sac. **2.** Biology. To remove the nucleus of (a cell). **3.** Archaic. To explain or elucidate. ~adj. (-ĭt, -āt′). Lacking a nucleus. [Latin ēnucleāre, to take out the kernel : ex-, out + nucleus, kernel, NUCLEUS.] **—e·nu·cle·a·tion** n. **—e·nu·cle·a·tor** n.

e·nu·mer·ate (ĭ-nōō′mə-rāt′, ĭ-nyōō′-) tr.v. **ated, -ating, -ates. 1.** To count off or name one by one; list: Let me enumerate all the good reasons for going. **2.** To determine the number of; count. [Latin ēnumerāre, to count out : ex-, out + numerus, number.] **—e·nu·mer·a·tive** (-rā′tĭv, -mər-ə-tĭv, -nyōō′-) adj.

e·nu·mer·a·tion (ĭ-nōō′mə-rā′shən, ĭ-nyōō′-) n. **1.** The act of enumerating. **2.** A detailed list of items.

e·nu·mer·a·tor (ĭ-nōō′mə-rā′tər, ĭ-nyōō′-) n. **1.** One that enumerates. **2.** British. A person involved in the distribution and collection of census forms.

e·nun·ci·ate (ĭ-nŭn′sē-āt′) v. **-ated, -ating, -ates.** —tr. **1.** To pronounce or articulate (speech sounds); especially, to pronounce with clarity or in another specified manner. **2.** To state or set forth precisely or systematically: enunciate a doctrine. **3.** To announce; proclaim. —intr. To pronounce words, especially distinctly. [Latin ēnuntiāre, ēnunciāre : ex-, out + nuntiāre, to announce, from nuncius, nuntius, message, messenger.] **—e·nun·ci·a·ble** (ĭ-nŭn′sē-ə-bəl), **e·nun·ci·a·tive** (-ā′tĭv, -ə-tĭv), **e·nun·ci·a·to·ry** (-tôr′ē, -tōr′ē) adj. **—e·nun·ci·a·tive·ly** adv. **—e·nun·ci·a·tor** n.

e·nun·ci·a·tion (ĭ-nŭn′sē-ā′shən) n. **1.** The act or manner of enunciating; especially, the manner in which a speaker articulates words or speech sounds. **2.** An announcement, declaration, or similar official statement. **—See Synonyms at diction.**

enure. Variant of **inure.**

en·u·re·sis (ĕn′yə-rē′sĭs) n. Involuntary urination. [New Latin, from Greek enourein, to urinate in : en-, in + ourein, to urinate, from ouron, urine.] **—en·u·ret·ic** (ĕn′yə-rĕt′ĭk) n. & adj.

env. envelope.

en·vel·op (ĕn-vĕl′əp, ĭn-) *tr.v.* **-oped, -oping, -ops.** **1.** To enclose, cover, or obscure with or as if with a covering or wrapping. **2.** To serve as a covering or wrapping for. **3.** To surround or enfold: *enveloped in the cheerful atmosphere.* **4.** To attack (an enemy's flank). [Middle English *enveloupen,* from Old French *enveloper* : *en-,* in + *veloper,* to wrap up (see **develop**).] —**en·vel·op·er** *n.* —**en·vel·op·ment** *n.*

en·ve·lope (ĕn′və-lōp′, ŏn′-) *n. Abbr.* **env. 1.** Something that envelops; an enclosing or surrounding cover, coat, or wrapping. **2.** A flat, folded paper container for a letter or similar object, usually rectangular and having a gummed sealing flap. **3.** *Biology.* Any enclosing covering, membrane, or structure. **4.** The bag containing the gas in a balloon. **5.** *Mathematics.* **a.** A curve that is a tangent to all the curves of a family of curves. **b.** A surface that is a tangent to a family of surfaces. **6.** The glass or metal casing of an electronic valve or similar device. [French *enveloppe,* from Old French *envelope,* from *enveloper,* to **ENVELOP**.]

en·ven·om (ĕn-vĕn′əm, ĭn-) *tr.v.* **-omed, -oming, -oms. 1.** To put venom into or on; make poisonous or noxious. **2.** To fill with malice; embitter. [Middle English *envenimen,* from Old French *envenimer* : **IN** + **VENOM**.]

en·vi·a·ble (ĕn′vē-ə-bəl) *adj.* **1.** Arousing strong envy. **2.** Highly desirable but rare: *"the enviable English quality of being able to be mute without unrest"* (Henry James). —**en·vi·a·bly** *adv.*

en·vi·ous (ĕn′vē-əs) *adj.* **1.** Feeling, expressing, or characterized by envy. **2.** *Obsolete.* Eager to emulate; emulous. —**en·vi·ous·ly** *adv.* —**en·vi·ous·ness** *n.*

en·vi·ron (ĕn-vī′rən, ĭn-) *tr.v.* **-roned, -roning, -rons.** To encircle; surround. [Middle English *environen,* from Old French *environer,* from *environ,* around : *en-,* in + *viron,* circle, from *virer,* to turn, **VEER**.]

en·vi·ron·ment (ĕn-vī′rən-mənt, ĭn-) *n.* **1.** Something that surrounds; surroundings. **2.** The aggregate of circumstances surrounding an organism or group of organisms, specifically: **a.** The combination of external or extrinsic physical conditions that affect and influence the growth and development of organisms. **b.** The complex of social and cultural conditions affecting the nature of an individual or community. Compare **heredity.** —**en·vi·ron·men·tal** (ĕn-vī′rən-mĕnt′l, ĭn-) *adj.* —**en·vi·ron·men·tal·ly** *adv.*

en·vi·ron·men·tal·ism (ĕn-vī′rən-mĕn′tə-lĭz′əm, ĭn-) *n.* **1.** The theory that environment rather than heredity is the primary influence on intellectual growth and cultural development. **2.** Belief that the natural environment should be protected.

en·vi·ron·men·tal·ist (ĕn-vī′rən-mĕn′tə-lĭst, ĭn-) *n.* **1.** A person who seeks to protect the natural environment. **2.** An adherent of the theory of environmentalism.

en·vi·rons (ĕn-vī′rənz, ĭn-) *pl.n.* **1.** The surrounding area, especially of a city; the suburbs; the outskirts. **2.** Surroundings; environment.

en·vis·age (ĕn-vĭz′ĭj, ĭn-) *tr.v.* **-aged, -aging, -ages.** To conceive of, especially as a future possibility. [French *envisager* : **IN** + **VISAGE**.]

en·vi·sion (ĕn-vĭzh′ən, ĭn-) *tr.v.* **-sioned, -sioning, -sions.** To picture in the mind; foresee.

en·voi, en·voy (ĕn′voi, ŏn′-) *n.* A short concluding stanza of certain French verse forms, such as the ballade, originally serving as a postscript dedicating the poem to a patron and later as a pithy summation of the poem. [Middle English *envoie,* from Old French *envoy,* "a sending away," conclusion, from *envoier,* to send. See **envoy** (messenger).]

en·voy¹ (ĕn′voi, ŏn′-) *n.* **1.** A messenger or other agent sent on a mission. **2.** A representative of a government or faction sent on a special diplomatic mission. [French *envoyé,* one who is sent, from the past participle of *envoyer,* to send, from Old French *envoier, enveier,* from Late Latin *inviāre,* to put on the way : Latin *in-,* in + *via,* way.]

envoy². Variant of **envoi.**

en·vy (ĕn′vē) *n., pl.* **-vies. 1. a.** A feeling of discontent and resentment aroused by contemplation of another's possessions, qualities, or achievements, with a strong wish that they were one's own. **b.** A more moderate feeling aroused by admiration rather than resentment. **2. a.** A possession of another that is strongly desired. **b.** One who possesses what another strongly desires: *She was the envy of her friends.* **3.** *Obsolete.* Malevolence. —*v.* **envied, -vying, -vies.** —*tr.* To feel envy for; regard with envy. —*intr.* To be filled with envy. [Middle English *envie,* from Old French, from Latin *invidia,* from *invidēre,* to look at with malice : *in-,* in, upon + *vidēre,* to see.] —**en·vi·er** *n.* —**en·vy·ing·ly** *adv.*

en·wind (ĕn-wīnd′, ĭn-) *tr.v.* **-wound** (-wound′), **-winding, -winds.** To wind around or about; encircle.

en·wrap (ĕn-răp′, ĭn-) *tr.v.* **-wrapped, -wrapping, -wraps. 1.** To wrap up; enclose; enfold. **2.** To engross.

En·zed (ĕn-zĕd′) *n. Australian & New Zealand Informal.* **1.** New Zealand. **2.** A New Zealander. [From the initials *N.Z.*]

en·zo·ot·ic (ĕn′zō-ŏt′ĭk) *adj.* Affecting or peculiar to animals of a specific area or limited district. Said of diseases. —*n.* An enzootic disease. [**EN-** (within) + **ZO(O)-** + **-OTIC**.]

en·zyme (ĕn′zīm′) *n.* Any of numerous proteins or conjugated proteins produced by living organisms and functioning as biochemical catalysts. [German *Enzym,* from Medieval Greek *enzumos,* leavened : Greek *en-,* in + *zumē,* leaven.] —**en·zy·mat·ic** (ĕn′zī-măt′ĭk) *adj.* —**en·zy·mic** (ĕn′zī′mĭk) *adj.*

en·zy·mol·o·gy (ĕn′zī-mŏl′ə-jē) *n.* The biochemistry of enzymes. —**en·zy·mol·o·gist** *n.*

eo- *prefix.* Indicates: **1.** An early period of time; for example, **Eo-**

cene. 2. An early form or representative; for example, **eohippus.** [Greek *ēō-,* from *ēōs,* dawn.]

e.o. ex officio.

E·o·cene (ē′ə-sēn′) *adj.* Of, pertaining to, or designating the geologic time, rock system, and fossils of the second oldest of the five epochs of the Tertiary period of the Cenozoic era, extending from the end of the Paleocene to the beginning of the Oligocene and characterized by the rise of mammals. —*n.* The Eocene epoch. Preceded by *the.* [**EO-** + **-CENE.**]

e·o·hip·pus (ē′ō-hĭp′əs) *n.* An extinct, small, herbivorous mammal of the genus *Hyracotherium* (or *Eohippus*), of the Eocene epoch, having four-toed front feet and three-toed hind feet, and related ancestrally to the horse. [New Latin : **EO-** + Greek *hippos,* horse.]

EOKA. See **Cyprus, Republic of.**

e·o·lith (ē′ə-lĭth′) *n. Archaeology.* Any of the stone artefacts allegedly characterizing the Eolithic period. [**EO-** + **-LITH.**]

E·o·lith·ic (ē′ə-lĭth′ĭk) *adj. Archaeology.* Of or pertaining to the postulated earliest period of human culture preceding the Lower Paleolithic. —*n.* The Eolithic period. Preceded by *the.* [**EO-** + **-LITHIC.**]

e.o.m. end of month.

e·on, ae·on (ē′ŏn′, ē′ən) *n.* **1.** An indefinitely long period of time; age. **2.** *Geology.* The longest division of geologic time, containing two or more eras. [Late Latin *aeōn,* age, from Greek *aiōn.*]

e·on·ism (ē′ə-nĭz′əm) *n.* **Transvestism** *(see)* when practiced by a man. [After Charles *Éon* de Beaumont (1728–1810), French transvestite.]

E·os (ē′ŏs′). *Greek Mythology.* The goddess of the dawn, identified with the Roman goddess Aurora. [Greek *Ēōs,* from *ēōs,* dawn.]

e·o·sin (ē′ə-sĭn) *n.* Also **e·o·sine** (-sĭn, -sēn′). A red crystalline powder, $C_{20}H_8Br_4O_5$, used in textile dyeing, histology, and the manufacture of inks. [Greek *ēōs,* dawn + **-IN.**]

e·o·sin·o·phil (ē′ə-sĭn′ə-fĭl′) *n.* Also **e·o·sin·o·phile** (-fīl′). *Physiology.* A type of leukocyte with a lobed nucleus that stains with an eosin dye. —**e·o·sin·o·phil·ic** (ē′ə-sĭn′ə-fĭl′ĭk), **e·o·si·noph·i·lous** (ē′ə-sə-nŏf′ə-ləs) *adj.*

-eous *suffix.* Having the nature of or akin to; for example, **gaseous, beauteous.** [Latin *-eus.*]

e·pact (ē′păkt′, ĕp′ăkt′) *n.* **1.** The excess of time, about 11 days, of the solar year over the lunar year. **2.** The age of the moon at the beginning of the calendar year. **3.** The excess of time of a calendar month over a lunar month. [Old French *epacte,* from Late Latin *epacta,* from Greek *epaktai (hēmerai),* "(days) brought in," from *epaktos,* brought in from abroad, from *epagein,* to lead on, bring in : *epi-,* on + *agein,* again to lead.]

ep·arch (ĕp′ärk′) *n.* **1.** The chief administrator of an eparchy. **2.** *Greek Orthodox Church.* A bishop or metropolitan. [Greek *eparkhos,* commander, governor : *epi-,* on, over + **-ARCH.**] —**e·par·chi·al** (ī-pär′kē-əl) *adj.*

ep·ar·chy (ĕp′är′kē) *n., pl.* **-chies. 1.** An administrative subdivision of modern Greece. **2.** *Greek Orthodox Church.* An ecclesiastical district; a diocese.

ep·au·let, ep·au·lette (ĕp′ə-lĕt′, ĕp′ə-lĕt′) *n.* A shoulder ornament; especially, either of two fringed straps on certain military uniforms. [French *épaulette,* diminutive of *épaule,* shoulder, from Old French *espaule,* from Latin *spatula.* See **spatula.**]

é·pée, e·pee (ā-pā′, ĕp′ā′) *n.* **1.** A fencing sword with a bowl-shaped guard and a long, narrow, fluted blade that has no cutting edge and tapers to a blunted point. **2.** The art of fencing with the épée. [French, from Latin *spatha,* sword, blade. See **spatula.**] —**é·pée·ist** *n.*

ep·ei·rog·e·ny (ĕp′ī-rŏj′ə-nē) *n.* Also **ep·ei·ro·gen·e·sis** (ə-pī′rō-jĕn′ə-sĭs). The deformation of the crust of the earth by which continents and oceanic basins, or parts of these, are formed. [Greek *ēpeiros,* continent + **-GENY.**] —**e·pei·ro·gen·ic** (ī-pī′rō-jĕn′ĭk) *adj.*

e·pen·the·sis (ĭ-pĕn′thə-sĭs) *n., pl.* **-ses** (-sēz′). *Linguistics.* The insertion of an extra sound into the pronunciation of a word, especially before an *l* or *r* sound, either as a process of phonetic development or as a feature of nonstandard speech; for example, the nonstandard pronunciation of *umbrella* as (ŭm′bə-rĕl′ə). [Late Latin, from Greek, from *epentithenai,* to insert : *epi-,* in, in addition to + *entithenai,* to put in : *en-,* in + *tithenai,* to place.] —**ep·en·thet·ic** (ĕp′ən-thĕt′ĭk) *adj.*

e·pergne (ī-pûrn′, ā-pârn′) *n.* A large silver or glass centerpiece for a table consisting of a frame with extended arms or branches supporting holders, as for flowers, fruit, or candies. [Probably from French *épargne,* saving, from *épargner,* to save, from Old French *espargnier,* from Germanic *sparōjan* (unattested), to **SPARE.**]

É·per·nay (ā′pĕr-nā′). Town in northeastern France, on the Marne River. After Rheims it is the most important center for the production of champagne.

ep·ex·e·ge·sis (ĕp′ĕk′sə-jē′sĭs) *n., pl.* **-ses** (-sēz′). **1.** The addition of explanatory material to clarify something immediately preceding it. **2.** The additional material itself. [Greek *epexēgēsis,* from *epexēgeisthai,* to explain in detail : *epi-,* in addition to + *exēgeisthai,* to explain (see **exegesis**).] —**ep·ex·e·get·ic** (ĕp′ĕk′sə-jĕt′ĭk), **ep·ex·e·get·i·cal** (-ĭ-kəl) *adj.*

Eph. Ephesians (New Testament).

e·phah, e·pha (ē′fə, ĕ′fə) *n.* A unit of dry measure equal to slightly more than a bushel, used by the ancient Hebrews. [Hebrew *'ephāh,* probably from Egyptian *'pt.*]

e·phebe (ĕf′ēb′, ĭ-fēb′) *n.* In ancient Greece, a youth in military training who is between eighteen and twenty years of age. [Latin *ephēbus,* from Greek *ephēbos* : *epi-,* at + *hēbē,* youth.] **—e·phe·bic** (ĭ-fē′bĭk) *adj.*

e·phed·ra (ĭ-fĕd′rə, ĕf′ĭ-drə) *n.* Any gymnosperm shrub of the genus *Ephedra,* found in Eurasia and the United States. [New Latin, from Greek, from *ephedros,* "a sitting upon" : *ep-,* EPI- + *hedra,* seat.]

e·phed·rine (ĭ-fĕd′rĭn, ĕf′ə-drēn′) *n.* A white, odorless, powdered or crystalline alkaloid, $C_{10}H_{15}NO$, isolated from shrubs of the genus *Ephedra* or made synthetically, used to treat allergies and asthma and as a vasoconstrictor. [New Latin *Ephedra,* genus name of ma-huang, from Latin *ephedra,* horsetail, from Greek *ephedros,* sitting upon : *epi-,* upon + *hedra,* seat + -INE.]

e·phem·er·a (ĭ-fĕm′ər-ə) *n., pl.* **-as** or **-erae** (-ə-rē′) or **ephemera** (for sense 2). **1.** Something short-lived or transitory. **2. ephemera.** Printed matter of passing interest, as periodicals, handbills, and topical pamphlets. [From the plural of EPHEMERON.]

e·phem·er·al (ĭ-fĕm′ər-əl) *adj.* **1.** Lasting for a brief time; short-lived; transitory. **2.** Living or lasting only one day, as certain flowers or adult insects do. —See Synonyms at **transient.**

~*n.* An ephemeral thing or organism. [Greek *ephēmeros* : *epi-,* on + *hēmera,* day.] **—e·phem·er·al·i·ty** (ĭ-fĕm′ə-răl′ə-tē) *n.* **—e·phem·er·al·ly** *adv.*

e·phem·er·id (ĭ-fĕm′ər-ĭd) *n.* An insect of the order Ephemeroptera, which comprises the mayflies. [New Latin *Ephemeridae,* former name of the order, from Greek *ephēmeros,* EPHEMERAL.]

e·phem·er·is (ĭ-fĕm′ər-ĭs) *n., pl.* **ephemerides** (ĕf′ə-mĕr′ə-dēz′). **1.** A table giving the coordinates of one or a number of celestial bodies at a number of specific times during a given period. **2.** A publication that presents a collection of such tables; an astronomical almanac. [Late Latin *ephēmeris,* diary, from Greek, from *ephēmeros,* EPHEMERAL.]

ephemeris time *n.* A highly accurate astronomical system for the measurement of time based on the period of the earth's orbit, but in practice relying on lunar observations and an accurate lunar ephemeris to calculate corrections to be applied to clocks. The unit is the ephemeris second, equal to 1/31,556,925.9747 of the tropical year for epoch 1900 January 0.

e·phem·er·on (ĭ-fĕm′ə-rŏn′) *n., pl.* **-era** (-ər-ə) or **-ons.** A short-lived thing or organism. [New Latin, from Greek *ephemeron,* mayfly, from the neuter of *ephemēros,* EPHEMERAL.]

E·phe·sian (ĭ-fē′zhən) *adj.* Of or pertaining to Ephesus or its people.

~*n.* A native or inhabitant of Ephesus.

E·phe·sians (ĭ-fē′zhənz) *n. Used with a singular verb. Abbr.* **Eph.** A book of the New Testament consisting of the Apostle Paul's epistle to the Christians of Ephesus.

Eph·e·sus (ĕf′ə-səs). Ancient Greek city of Asia Minor, in what is now western Turkey, near the mouth of the Kücük Menderes. Its great Temple of Artemis, one of the Seven Wonders of the World, was destroyed by the Goths (A.D. 262).

eph·od (ĕf′ŏd′, ē′fŏd′) *n.* An embroidered vestment worn by ancient Hebrew priests. [Hebrew *ēphōdh.*]

eph·or (ĕf′ôr′, -ər) *n., pl.* **-ors** or **-ori** (-ə-rī′). Any of a body of five elected officials exercising a supervisory power over the kings of ancient Sparta. [Latin *ephorus,* from Greek *ephoros,* from *ephoran,* to oversee : *epi-,* over + *horan,* to see.]

E·phra·im[1] (ē′frē-əm, ē′frəm). The younger son of Joseph. Genesis 41:52. [Hebrew, perhaps "meadows."]

Ephraim[2] *n.* A tribe of Israel descended from the younger son of Joseph.

E·phra·im·ite (ē′frē-ə-mīt′, ē′frə-) *n.* A member of the tribe of Ephraim. **—E·phra·im·ite** *adj.*

epi– *prefix.* Indicates: **1.** On, upon; for example, **epiphyte. 2.** Over, above; for example, **epicenter. 3.** Around, covering; for example, **epicardium. 4.** To, toward, close to, next to; for example, **epicalyx. 5.** Besides, in addition; for example, **epiphenomenon. 6.** After; for example, **epigenesis. 7.** Among; for example, **epizootic.** [Greek *epi-* (before a vowel, *ep-*), from *epi,* upon, over, at, after.]

ep·i·blast (ĕp′ə-blăst′, -bläst′) *n.* The outer layer of a gastrula. **—ep·i·blas·tic** (ĕp′ə-blăs′tĭk) *adj.*

e·pib·o·ly (ĭ-pĭb′ə-lē) *n. Zoology.* A process in the development of the embryo in which the part of the blastula that was nearest the nucleus of the ovum grows over and encloses the part farthest from the nucleus and eventually forms the ectoderm. [Greek *epibolē,* a throwing on, from *epiballein,* to throw on : *epi-,* on + *ballein,* to throw.] **—ep·i·bol·ic** (ĕp′ə-bŏl′ĭk) *adj.*

ep·ic (ĕp′ĭk) *n.* **1.** An extended narrative poem, such as *Beowulf* or the *Iliad,* celebrating episodes of a people's heroic tradition, typically developed by oral composition within a standard formulaic diction and set of metrical and narrative conventions, a final version being transcribed after the introduction of writing. **2.** The genre represented by such poems; epos. **3.** A formal poem, such as the *Aeneid,* composed in literary imitation of these conventions. **4.** A story, film, or the like thought to embody the qualities characteristic of epic poetry. **5.** An event or series of events regarded as a fit subject for an epic: *the epic of man's first journey to the moon.*

~*adj.* **1.** Of or designating an epic: *an epic poem.* **2.** Occurring in or characteristic of epics: *an epic simile.* **3. a.** Suitable for or typical of an epic. **b.** Large-scale in grandeur, scope, or theme; heroic. [Latin *epicus,* from Greek *epikos,* from *epos,* song, word.]

ep·i·ca·lyx (ĕp′ĭ-kā′lĭks, -kăl′ĭks) *n., pl.* **-calyxes** or **-calyces** (-kā′lə-sēz′, -kăl′ə-sēz′). *Botany.* A set of bracts close to and resembling a calyx. Also called "calycle."

ep·i·can·thic fold (ĕp′ĭ-kăn′thĭk) *n.* A fold of skin of the upper eyelid that tends to cover the inner corner of the eye, characteristic of many Mongolian peoples and found in certain congenital conditions, such as Down's syndrome. Also called "epicanthus."

ep·i·car·di·um (ĕp′ĭ-kär′dē-əm) *n., pl.* **-dia** (-dē-ə). The inner layer of the pericardium that is in actual contact with the heart. [New Latin : EPI- + Greek *kardia,* heart.]

ep·i·carp (ĕp′ĭ-kärp′) *n. Botany.* An **exocarp** *(see).* [French *épicarpe* : EPI- + -CARP.]

ep·i·ce·di·um (ĕp′ə-sē′dē-əm) *n., pl.* **-dia** (-dē-ə). A funeral hymn or dirge. [Latin *epicēdium,* from Greek *epikēdeion,* from the neuter of *epikēdeios,* of a funeral : *epi-,* at + *kēdos,* sorrow, grief.]

ep·i·cene (ĕp′ə-sēn′) *adj.* **1. a.** Belonging to or having the characteristics of both the male and the female: *an epicene statue; an epicene angel.* **b.** Effeminate; effete. **c.** Sexless; neuter. **2.** *Linguistics.* Designating a noun that may be applied to both the male and the female without a change in form, as Greek *pais,* child (*ho pais,* the boy; *hē pais,* the girl).

~*n.* **1.** *Linguistics.* An epicene noun. **2.** An epicene person or object. [Middle English *epicene,* from Latin *epicoenus,* from Greek *epikoinos,* common to many, promiscuous : *epi-,* to + *koinos,* common.]

ep·i·cen·ter (ĕp′ə-sĕn′tər) *n.* **1.** The part of the earth's surface directly above the focus of an earthquake. **2.** A focal point. [New Latin *epicentrum* : EPI- + Latin *centrum,* CENTER.]

ep·i·cle·sis (ĕp′ĭ-klē′sĭs) *n., pl.* **-ses** (-sēz′). A prayer in the Mass calling on the Holy Spirit to turn the bread and wine into the body and blood of Christ. [Greek, invocation : *epi-,* EPI- + *klēsis,* prayer, from *kalein,* to call.]

ep·i·cot·yl (ĕp′ĭ-kŏt′l) *n. Botany.* The part of the stem of a seedling or embryonic plant that is above the cotyledons and below the first true leaves. [EPI- + COTYL(EDON).]

ep·i·cri·sis (ĕp′ĭ-krī′sĭs) *n., pl.* **-ses** (-sēz′). *Pathology.* A crisis that occurs after the primary crisis of a disease.

ep·i·crit·ic (ĕp′ĭ-krĭt′ĭk) *adj.* Pertaining to or designating sensory nerve fibers that make possible acute sensitivity to temperature and touch. Compare **protopathic.** [Greek *epikritikos,* decisive, from *epikritos,* decided on, from *epikrinein,* to decide.]

ep·i·cure (ĕp′ĭ-kyŏŏr′) *n.* **1.** A person with refined taste in food and wine. **2.** *Archaic.* A person devoted to sensuous pleasure and luxurious living. [After EPICURUS, who supposedly advocated sensuous pleasure as the highest good.]

Ep·i·cu·re·an (ĕp′ĭ-kyŏŏ-rē′ən) *adj.* **1.** Of or associated with the philosophy of Epicurus. **2. epicurean.** Devoted to the pursuit of pleasure; fond of good food, comfort, and ease; hedonistic. **3. epicurean.** Suited to the tastes of an epicure: *an epicurean repast.* —See Synonyms at **sensuous.**

~*n.* **1.** A follower of Epicurus. **2. epicurean.** An epicure.

Ep·i·cu·re·an·ism (ĕp′ĭ-kyŏŏ-rē′ə-nĭz′əm) *n.* Also **Ep·i·cur·ism** (ĕp′ĭ-kyŏŏ-rĭz′əm). **1.** The philosophy advanced by Epicurus. **2. epicureanism.** The beliefs, tastes, or way of life of an epicure.

E·pi·cu·rus (ĕp′ĭ-kyŏŏr′əs) (*c.* 341–270 B.C.). Greek philosopher, born at Samos. From his philosophy the word "Epicurean" was derived to describe a life of indulgent pleasure seeking, but his hedonism exalted the avoidance of pain rather than the satisfying of desires and was governed by a strict code of social behavior.

ep·i·cy·cle (ĕp′ə-sī′kəl) *n.* **1.** In Ptolemaic cosmology, a small circle, the center of which moves on the circumference of a larger circle at whose center is the earth and the circumference of which describes the orbit of a planet around the earth. **2.** A small circle that moves around the circumference of a larger circle, either on the inside or outside. [Middle English, from Old French or Late Latin, from Greek : *epi-,* EPI- + *kuklos,* circle.] **—ep·i·cy·clic** (ĕp′ə-sī′klĭk, -sĭk′lĭk) *adj.*

epicyclic train *n.* A system of gears in which at least one wheel axis revolves about another. It usually consists of a large annulus wheel with internal teeth, a small coaxial wheel with external teeth, and one or more planetary gears engaging with both of them.

ep·i·cy·cloid (ĕp′ə-sī′kloid′) *n.* The curve described by a point fixed on the circumference of a circle as it rolls on the outside of the circumference of a fixed coplanar circle. [EPICYCL(E) + -OID.] **—ep·i·cy·cloid·al** (ĕp′ə-sī-kloid′l) *adj.*

epicycloidal wheel *n.* A planetary wheel in an epicyclic train.

Ep·i·dau·rus (ĕp′ə-dôr′əs). Ancient town of Greece, near the eastern shore of the Peloponnese; the site of the best-preserved ancient Greek theater.

ep·i·deic·tic (ĕp′ə-dīk′tĭk) *adj.* Intended for rhetorical effect or display. [Greek, from *epideiknunai,* to display, show off : *epi-,* EPI- + *deiknunai,* to show.]

ep·i·dem·ic (ĕp′ə-dĕm′ĭk) *adj.* **1.** Spreading rapidly and extensively among many individuals in an area. Said especially of contagious diseases. **2.** Resembling or characteristic of a rapidly spreading disease: *Street crime has reached epidemic proportions.*

~*n.* **1.** An outbreak of a contagious disease that spreads rapidly and widely. **2.** A temporary, widespread popularity, as of a fashion or a fad. **3.** A rapid spread, growth, or development. [French *épidémique,* from *épidémie,* from Old French *espydymie,* from Late Latin *epidēmia,* from Greek *epidēmia (nosos),* "(illness) prevalent among people," from *epidēmos,* prevalent, common : *epi-,* on, "among" + *dēmos,* people.] **—ep·i·dem·i·cal·ly** *adv.*

ep·i·de·mi·ol·o·gy (ĕp′ə-dē′mē-ŏl′ə-jē, -dĕm′ē-ŏl′ə-jē) *n.* The study of epidemics and the causes and distribution of epidemic diseases. [Late Latin *epidēmia,* an EPIDEM(IC) + -LOGY.] **—ep·i·de·mi·o·log·**

PRONUNCIATION KEY

ă, pat; ā, pay; âr, care;
ä, father, are; b, bib;
ch, church; d, deed; ĕ, pet;
ē, be; f, fife; g, gag; h, hat;
hw, which; ĭ, pit; ī, pie;
îr, pier; j, judge; k, kick;
l, lid, needle; m, mum;
n, no, sudden; ng, thing;
ŏ, pot; ō, toe; ô, paw, for;
oi, noise; ou, out; ŏŏ, book;
ōō, boot; p, pop; r, roar;
s, sauce; sh, ship, dish;
t, tight; th, thin, path;
th, this, bathe; ŭ, cut; ûr, fur;
v, valve; w, with; y, yes;
z, zebra, size; zh, vision;
ə, about, item, edible,
gallop, circus, peaceful

IN FOREIGN WORDS:

à, *Fr.* ami; œ, *Fr.* feu, *Ger.* schön; ü, *Fr.* tu, *Ger.* über;
KH, *Ger.* ich, *Scot.* loch;
N, *Fr.* bon; y′, *Fr.* Compiègne

STRESS MARKS:

Primary stress: ′
in·cite′ (ĭn-sīt′)
Secondary stress: ′
in′sight′ (ĭn′sīt′)

i·cal (ĕp′ə-dē′mē-ə-lŏj′ĭ-kəl, ĕp′ə-dĕm′ē-), **ep·i·de·me·o·log·ic** (-ĭk) *adj.* —**ep·i·de·mi·ol·o·gist** *n.*

ep·i·der·mis (ĕp′ə-dûr′mĭs) *n.* **1.** *Zoology.* **a.** The outer, protective layer of the skin in vertebrates. **b.** A single outer layer of cells in invertebrates. **2.** *Botany.* The outermost layer of cells or protective covering of a plant or plant part. [Late Latin, from Greek : *epi-,* over + *derma,* skin.] —**ep·i·der·mal** (ĕp′ə-dûr′məl), **ep·i·der·mic** (-mĭk), **ep·i·der·moid** (-moid′) *adj.*

ep·i·di·a·scope (ĕp′ə-dī′ə-skōp′) *n.* An optical device for projecting onto a screen the images of opaque objects or transparencies. Compare **diascope, episcope.** [EPI- + DIA- + -SCOPE.]

ep·i·did·y·mis (ĕp′ə-dĭd′ə-mĭs) *n., pl.* **-mides** (-mə-dēz′). A long, narrow, flattened convoluted tube that is part of the spermatic duct system, connecting the testicle to the vas deferens. [New Latin, from Greek : *epi-,* at, near + *didumos,* testicle.] —**ep·i·did·y·mal** *adj.*

ep·i·dote (ĕp′ə-dōt′) *n.* A natural yellow, green, or black mineral consisting mainly of a silicate of calcium, aluminum, and iron, commonly found in metamorphic rock. [French *épidote,* from Greek *epididonai,* to give additionally, increase (so called because two sides of the mineral's base are longer than the other two) : *epi-,* in addition + *didonai,* to give.] —**ep·i·dot·ic** (ĕp′ə-dŏt′ĭk) *adj.*

ep·i·du·ral (ĕp′ə-dŏŏr′əl, -dyŏŏr′əl) *adj.* On or administered outside the dura mater.

~*n.* **1.** An injection of anesthetic into the outer lining of the spinal cord. **2.** Anesthesia resulting from such an injection. Also called "epidural anesthesia." [EPI- + DURA (MATER) + -AL.]

ep·i·fo·cal (ĕp′ə-fō′kəl) *adj. Geology.* Of, occurring at, or pertaining to an epicenter.

ep·i·gas·tri·um (ĕp′ĭ-găs′trē-əm) *n., pl.* **-tria** (-trē-ə). The upper middle region of the abdomen. [New Latin, from Greek *epigastrion* : *epi-,* above + *gastrium,* diminutive of *gastēr,* stomach.] —**ep·i·gas·tric** (ĕp′ĭ-găs′trĭk) *adj.*

ep·i·ge·al (ĕp′ə-jē′əl) *adj.* Also **ep·i·ge·an** (-ən), **ep·i·ge·ous** (-əs). **1.** *Botany.* Characterized by germination in which the cotyledons appear above the surface of the ground. Compare **hypogeal. 2.** *Biology.* Living or occurring on or near the surface of the ground. [Greek *epigaios,* on the earth : *epi-,* on + *gaia, gē,* earth.]

ep·i·gene (ĕp′ə-jēn′) *adj.* **1.** Formed, originating, or occurring on or just below the surface of the earth. **2.** Foreign; not natural to the material in which found. Said of crystals. [French *épigène,* from Greek *epigenēs,* arising after, from *epigignesthai,* to be born after : *epi-,* after + *gignesthai,* to be born.]

ep·i·gen·e·sis (ĕp′ə-jĕn′ə-sĭs) *n.* **1.** *Biology.* The generally accepted theory that the individual is developed by structural elaboration of the unstructured egg rather than by a simple enlarging of a preformed entity. Compare **preformation. 2.** *Geology.* Change in the mineral characteristics of a rock due to outside influence. [EPI- + GENESIS.] —**ep·i·ge·net·ic** (ĕp′ə-jə-nĕt′ĭk) *adj.*

e·pig·e·nous (ĭ-pĭj′ə-nəs) *adj. Botany.* Developing or growing on an upper surface, as fungi on leaves. [EPI- + -GENOUS.]

ep·i·glot·tis (ĕp′ĭ-glŏt′ĭs) *n., pl.* **-tises** or **-glottides** (-glŏt′ə-dēz′). An elastic cartilage, located at the root of the tongue, that folds over the glottis to prevent food from entering the windpipe during the act of swallowing. [New Latin, from Greek *epiglōttis* : *epi-,* over + *glōttis,* GLOTTIS.]

ep·i·gone (ĕp′ĭ-gōn′) *n.* Also **ep·i·gon** (-gŏn′). A second-rate imitator or follower, as of an artist or philosopher. [From Greek *Epigonoi,* sons of the Seven against Thebes who imitated their fathers by attacking Thebes, from the plural of *epigonos,* born after : EPI- + *gonos,* child.] —**ep·i·gon·ic** (ĕp′ĭ-gŏn′ĭk) *adj.*

ep·i·gram (ĕp′ĭ-grăm′) *n.* **1.** A short poem expressing a single thought or observation with terseness and wit. **2.** A concisely and cleverly worded statement making a pointed observation and often concluding with a satirical twist. **3.** Discourse or expression by means of such statements. —See Synonyms at **saying.** [Old French *epigramme,* from Latin *epigramma,* from Greek, inscription, from *epigraphein,* to write on : *epi-,* on + *graphein,* to write.]

ep·i·gram·mat·ic (ĕp′ĭ-grə-măt′ĭk) *adj.* **1.** Of or having the nature of an epigram. **2.** Full of or given to the use of epigrams. —See Synonyms at **concise.** —**ep·i·gram·mat·i·cal·ly** *adv.*

ep·i·gram·ma·tize (ĕp′ĭ-grăm′ə-tīz′) *v.* **-tized, -tizing, -tizes.** —*tr.* To express (a thought or sentiment) in an epigram or epigrams. —*intr.* To speak or write in epigrams. —**ep·i·gram·ma·tist** (ĕp′ĭ-grăm′ə-tĭst) *n.*

ep·i·graph (ĕp′ĭ-grăf′, -gräf′) *n.* **1.** An inscription, as on a statue or building. **2.** A motto or quotation, as at the beginning of a book or chapter, usually intended to give an idea of its theme. [Greek *epigraphē,* from *epigraphos,* written on, from *epigraphein,* to write on. See **epigram.**] —**ep·i·graph·ic** (ĕp′ĭ-grăf′ĭk), **ep·i·graph·i·cal** *adj.* —**ep·i·graph·i·cal·ly** *adv.*

e·pig·ra·phy (ĭ-pĭg′rə-fē) *n.* **1.** Inscriptions collectively. **2. a.** The study of inscriptions. **b.** The interpretation of ancient inscriptions. Compare **paleography.** —**e·pig·ra·pher, e·pig·ra·phist** *n.*

e·pig·y·ny (ĭ-pĭj′ə-nē) *n. Botany.* A condition in which the petals, sepals, and male organs of flowers are above the female organs so that the ovary is enclosed by and fused with the tip of the flower stalk. [EPI- + -GYNY.] —**e·pig·y·nous** *adj.*

ep·i·lep·sy (ĕp′ə-lĕp′sē) *n.* Any of various disorders characterized by sudden recurring attacks of motor, sensory, or psychic malfunction with or without unconsciousness or convulsive movements. See **grand mal, petit mal.** [Old French *epilepsie,* from Late Latin *epilēpsia,* from Greek, from *epilambanein* (stem *epilab-*), to seize upon : *epi-,* upon + *lambanein,* to take hold of.] —**ep·i·lep·tic** (ĕp′ə-lĕp′tĭk) *n.* & *adj.*

ep·i·lep·toid (ĕp′ə-lĕp′toid′) *adj.* Resembling epilepsy or any of its symptoms. [EPILEPT(IC) + -OID.]

ep·i·logue, ep·i·log (ĕp′ə-lôg′, -lŏg′) *n.* **1. a.** A short poem or speech spoken directly to the audience following the conclusion of a play. **b.** The performer or performers who speak this. **2.** A short addition or concluding section at the end of a literary work, often dealing with the future of its characters. **3.** *British.* A short religious program at the end of a day's broadcasting. [Middle English *epiloge,* from Old French *epilogue,* from Latin *epilogus,* from Greek *epilogos,* from *epilegein,* to say more, to add : *epi-,* in addition + *legein,* to say.]

e·pim·er·ism (ĭ-pĭm′ə-rĭz′əm) *n. Chemistry.* A form of optical isomerism in which isomers can form about asymmetric atoms. [EPI- + (ISO)MERISM.] —**ep·i·mer·ic** (ĕp′ə-mĕr′ĭk) *adj.*

ep·i·mys·i·um (ĕp′ə-mĭz′ē-əm, -mĭzh′ē-əm) *n., pl.* **-mysia** (-mĭz′ē-ə, -mĭzh′ē-ə). The fibrous sheath enclosing a muscle. [New Latin : EPI- + Greek *mus,* muscle.]

ep·i·nas·ty (ĕp′ə-năs′tē) *n., pl.* **-ties.** A downward bending of leaves or other plant parts, resulting from greater growth of the upper side than of the lower side. [EPI- + -NASTY.] —**ep·i·nas·tic** (ĕp′ə-năs′tĭk) *adj.*

ep·i·neph·rine, ep·i·neph·rin (ĕp′ə-nĕf′rĭn) *n.* **1.** An adrenal hormone that stimulates autonomic nerve action. **2.** A white to brownish crystalline compound, $C_9H_{13}NO_3$, isolated from the adrenal glands of certain mammals or synthesized and used as a heart stimulant, vasoconstrictor, and in the treatment of asthma. Also called "adrenalin." [EPI- + NEPHR(O)- + -INE.]

ep·i·neu·ri·um (ĕp′ə-nŏŏr′ē-əm, -nyŏŏr′ē-əm) *n., pl.* **-neuria** (-nŏŏr′ē-ə, -nyŏŏr′ē-ə). The connective tissue sheath surrounding the bundles of fibers that make up a nerve. [EPI- + NEUR(O)- + -IUM.] —**ep·i·neu·ri·al** *adj.*

e·piph·a·ny (ĭ-pĭf′ə-nē) *n., pl.* **-nies. 1.** A revelatory manifestation of a divine being. **2.** A spiritual event in which the essential nature of something appears to the subject, as in a sudden flash of recognition. **3.** A revelation or experience of insight. [Greek *epiphaneia,* manifestation, appearance, from *epiphanēs,* appearing, manifest, from *epiphainein,* to manifest : *epi-,* to + *phainein,* to show.]

E·piph·a·ny (ĭ-pĭf′ə-nē) *n.* A Christian festival held on January 6 in celebration of the manifestation of the divine nature of Christ to the Gentiles as represented by the Magi.

ep·i·phe·nom·e·nal·ism (ĕp′ə-fĭ-nŏm′ə-nə-lĭz′əm) *n. Philosophy.* The doctrine that mental activities are simply epiphenomena of the neural processes of the brain and have no causal influence.

ep·i·phe·nom·e·non (ĕp′ə-fĭ-nŏm′ə-nŏn′) *n., pl.* **-na** (-nə). **1.** A secondary phenomenon accompanying and resulting from another. **2.** *Pathology.* An unusual additional condition in the course of a disease, not necessarily connected with the disease. —**ep·i·phe·nom·e·nal** (ĕp′ə-fĭ-nŏm′ə-nəl) *adj.*

e·piph·y·sis (ĭ-pĭf′ə-sĭs) *n., pl.* **-ses** (-sēz′). *Anatomy.* **1.** A part of a bone that is separated from the shaft by cartilage until growth is complete. **2.** The **pineal body** *(see).* [New Latin, from Greek *epiphusis,* a growth upon : *epi-,* upon + *phusis,* growth, from *phuein,* to grow.] —**ep·i·phys·i·al, ep·i·phys·e·al** (ĕp′ə-fĭz′ē-əl) *adj.*

ep·i·phyte (ĕp′ə-fīt′) *n.* A plant, such as any of certain orchids or ferns, that grows on another plant or object upon which it depends for mechanical support but not as a source of nutrients. Also called "air plant," "aerophyte." [EPI- + -PHYTE.] —**ep·i·phyt·ic** (ĕp′ə-fĭt′ĭk), **ep·i·phyt·i·cal** *adj.*

ep·i·phy·tot·ic (ĕp′ə-fī-tŏt′ĭk) *adj.* Of, pertaining to, or designating a sudden or abnormally destructive outbreak of a plant disease, usually over an extended geographic area.

~*n.* An outbreak of such a disease. [EPI- + PHYT(O)- + -OTIC.]

Epis. 1. Episcopal; Episcopalian. **2.** Epistle.

Episc. Episcopal; Episcopalian.

e·pis·co·pa·cy (ĭ-pĭs′kə-pə-sē) *n., pl.* **-cies. 1.** An episcopate. **2.** The system of church government in which bishops are the chief ministers. [From EPISCOPATE.]

e·pis·co·pal (ĭ-pĭs′kə-pəl) *adj.* **1.** Of or pertaining to a bishop. **2.** Of, having, or advocating church government by bishops. **3. Episcopal.** *Abbr.* **Epis., Episc.** Of, pertaining to, or belonging to the Protestant Episcopal Church. [Middle English, from Old French, from Late Latin *episcopālis,* from *episcopus,* bishop, from Greek *episkopos,* overseer : *epi-,* over + *skopos,* watcher, seer.]

Episcopal Church *n.* **1.** The **Protestant Episcopal Church** *(see).* **2.** Any of the branches of the Anglican Communion outside England, especially that in Scotland.

e·pis·co·pa·li·an (ĭ-pĭs′kə-pā′lē-ən, -pāl′yən) *adj.* **1.** Of or advocating church government by bishops. **2. Episcopalian.** *Abbr.* **Epis., Episc.** Of, pertaining to, or belonging to the Protestant Episcopal Church. —**e·pis·co·pa·li·an** *n.*

e·pis·co·pal·ism (ĭ-pĭs′kə-pə-lĭz′əm) *n.* The belief that the power to govern the church should rest with bishops.

e·pis·co·pate (ĭ-pĭs′kə-pĭt, -pāt′) *n.* **1.** The position or term of office of a bishop. **2.** The area of jurisdiction of a bishop; a diocese. **3.** Bishops collectively. [Late Latin *episcopātus,* from *episcopus,* bishop. See **episcopal.**]

ep·i·scope (ĕp′ə-skōp′) *n.* An optical device for projecting onto a screen an enlarged image of an opaque object. Compare **epidiascope.** [EPI- + -SCOPE.]

e·pi·si·ot·o·my (ĭ-pē′zē-ŏt′ə-mē) *n., pl.* **-mies.** A surgical incision into the tissues around the vagina during childbirth to enlarge the

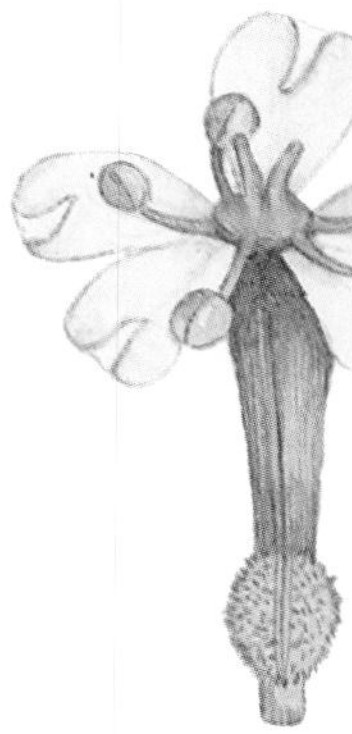

epigyny *In most flowers, the ovary of the plant is set above the base of the petals. In the flower head (above) of* Scandix pecten-veneris, *or shepherd's needle, however, the ovary is contained in the oval hairy bulge below the petals. Botanists describe plants with this rarer structure as epigynous.*

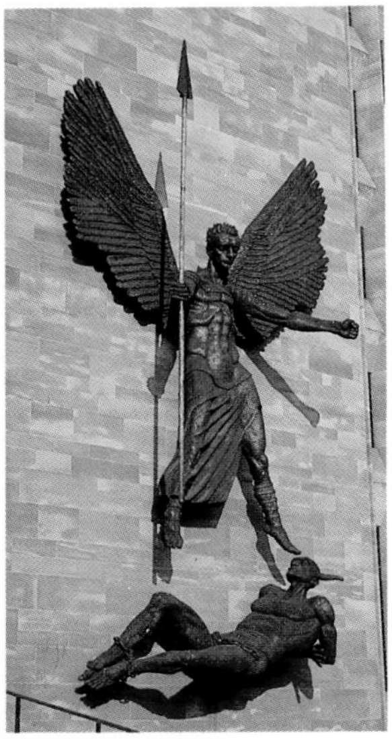

Epstein sculpture Saint Michael and the Devil, *on the east front of Coventry Cathedral, England.*

PRONUNCIATION KEY

ă, pat; ā, pay; âr, care;
ä, father, are; b, bib;
ch, church; d, deed; ĕ, pet;
ē, be; f, fife; g, gag; h, hat;
hw, which; ĭ, pit; ī, pie;
îr, pier; j, judge; k, kick;
l, lid, needle; m, mum;
n, no, sudden; ng, thing;
ŏ, pot; ō, toe; ô, paw, for;
oi, noise; ou, out; o͝o, book;
o͞o, boot; p, pop; r, roar;
s, sauce; sh, ship, dish;
t, tight; th, thin, path;
th, this, bathe; ŭ, cut; ûr, fur;
v, valve; w, with; y, yes;
z, zebra, size; zh, vision;
ə, about, item, edible, gallop, circus, peaceful

IN FOREIGN WORDS:

à, *Fr.* ami; œ, *Fr.* feu, *Ger.* schön; ü, *Fr.* tu, *Ger.* über; KH, *Ger.* ich, *Scot.* loch; N, *Fr.* bon; y', *Fr.* Compiègne

STRESS MARKS:

Primary stress: ′
in·cite′ (ĭn-sīt′)
Secondary stress: ′
in′sight′ (ĭn′sīt′)

opening and make delivery easier. [Greek *epision,* pubic area + -TOMY.]

ep·i·sode (ĕp′ə-sōd′) *n.* **1.** An incident or series of related events in the course of a continuous experience: *an episode from her childhood.* **2.** A portion of a narrative that relates an event or series of connected events and forms a coherent story in itself; an incident: *an episode of a picaresque novel.* **3.** A separately presented portion of a serialized novel, play, radio or television drama, or the like; an installment. **4.** A section of a classical Greek tragedy that occurs between two choric songs. **5.** *Music.* A passage between statements of a main subject or theme, as in a rondo or fugue. —See Synonyms at **occurrence.** [Greek *epeisodion,* "addition," from *epeisodios,* coming in besides : *epi-,* besides + *eisodios,* coming in : *eis,* into + *hodos,* way, road.]

ep·i·sod·ic (ĕp′ə-sŏd′ĭk) *adj.* Also **ep·i·sod·i·cal** (-ĭ-kəl). **1.** Of, pertaining to, or resembling an episode. **2.** Composed of a series of episodes: *an episodic narrative.* **3.** Not in a continuous sequence; disjointed. **4.** Occasional, sporadic, or unpredictable: *Their efforts were episodic.* —**ep·i·sod·i·cal·ly** *adv.*

ep·i·spas·tic (ĕp′ə-spăs′tĭk) *adj.* Causing blisters.
~*n.* A blistering agent; a vesicatory. [Greek *epispastikos,* drawing after (because blisters were thought to be humors drawn toward the skin), from *epispatos,* drawn, from *epispan,* to draw after one, attract : *epi-,* after + *span,* to draw (see **spasm**).]

Epist. Epistle.

e·pis·ta·sis (ĭ-pĭs′tə-sĭs) *n., pl.* **-ses** (-sēz′). **1.** *Genetics.* A nonreciprocal interaction between nonalternative forms of genes in which one gene suppresses the expression of another affecting the same part of an organism. **2.** *Medicine.* Matter that rises to the surface of a bodily discharge. [New Latin, from Greek, stoppage, stopping, from *ephistanai,* to place upon, stop : *epi-,* upon + *histanai,* to place, set.] —**ep·i·stat·ic** (ĕp′ə-stăt′ĭk) *adj.*

ep·i·stax·is (ĕp′ə-stăk′sĭs) *n., pl.* **-ses** (-sēz′). *Pathology.* A nosebleed. [New Latin, from Greek, "dropping," from *epistazein,* to let fall in drops upon : *epi-,* upon + *stazein,* to drip.]

e·pis·te·mol·o·gy (ĭ-pĭs′tə-mŏl′ə-jē) *n., pl.* **-gies.** **1.** The division of philosophy that investigates the nature and origin of knowledge. **2.** A theory of the nature of knowledge. [Greek *epistēmē,* knowledge, understanding, from *epistanai,* "to stand upon," understand : *epi-,* upon + *histanai,* to stand, place + -LOGY.] —**e·pis·te·mo·log·i·cal** (ĭ-pĭs′tə-mə-lŏj′ĭ-kəl) *adj.* —**e·pis·te·mo·log·i·cal·ly** *adv.* —**e·pis·te·mol·o·gist** (-mŏl′ə-jĭst) *n.*

e·pis·tle (ĭ-pĭs′əl) *n.* **1.** A letter, especially a formal one. **2.** *Usually* **Epistle.** *Abbr.* **Epis., Epist. a.** Any of the letters written by any of various Apostles or their helpers to early Christians and included in the New Testament. **b.** An excerpt from any of these letters, read as part of a religious service. **3.** A verse letter of the genre invented by Horace and imitated by poets of the 17th and 18th centuries. **4.** A prefatory dedication in the form of a letter. [Middle English, from Old French, from Latin *epistola,* from Greek *epistolē,* from *epistellein,* to send to : *epi-,* to + *stellein,* to send.]

e·pis·tler (ĭ-pĭs′lər) *n.* Also **e·pis·to·ler** (ĭ-pĭs′tə-lər). **1.** A writer of epistles. **2.** *Usually* **Epistler.** The person who reads the Epistle in a religious service.

e·pis·to·lar·y (ĭ-pĭs′tə-lĕr′ē) *adj.* **1.** Of or associated with letters or letter writing. **2.** In the form of a letter or series of letters. Said of a literary work. **3.** Carried on by or made up of letters: *an epistolary friendship.* [Latin *epistolāris,* from *epistola,* EPISTLE.]

ep·i·style (ĕp′ə-stīl′) *n. Architecture.* An **architrave** *(see).* [Latin *epistylium,* from Greek *epistulion* : *epi-,* upon + *stulos,* pillar.]

ep·i·taph (ĕp′ə-tăf′, -täf′) *n.* **1.** An inscription on a tombstone or monument in memory of the one or ones buried there. **2.** A brief literary piece summarizing or epitomizing a deceased person. **3.** A final view, opinion, or judgment on someone or something past: *an epitaph on her ex-husband.* [Middle English *epitaphe,* from Old French, from Latin *epitaphium,* funeral oration, from Greek *epitaphion,* neuter of *epitaphios,* "over a tomb" : *epi-,* over + *taphos,* tomb.] —**ep·i·taph·ic** (ĕp′ə-tăf′ĭk) *adj.*

e·pit·a·sis (ĭ-pĭt′ə-sĭs) *n., pl.* **-ses** (-sēz′). The part of a play, especially in classical Greek drama, in which the plot develops toward its dénouement. [Greek, a stretching over, intensification, from *epiteinein,* to stretch over : *epi-,* over + *teinein,* to stretch.]

ep·i·tax·i·al (ĕp′ə-tăk′sē-əl) *adj.* **1.** Designating a thin layer on the surface of a crystal, especially one that has the same structure as the underlying crystal. **2.** Designating a transistor made by depositing such a layer of semiconductor on a crystal support. [EPI- + -TAXY + -AL.] —**ep·i·tax·y** (ĕp′ə-tăk′sē) *n.*

ep·i·tha·la·mi·um (ĕp-ə-thə-lā′mē-əm) *n., pl.* **-ums** or **-mia** (-mē-ə). A lyric ode in honor of a marriage. [Latin, from Greek *epithalamion,* from the neuter of *epithalamios,* belonging to a wedding : *epi-,* at + *thalamos,* bridal chamber (see **thalamus**).]

ep·i·the·li·o·ma (ĕp′ə-thē′lē-ō′mə) *n., pl.* **-mata** (-mə-tə) or **-mas.** A benign or malignant tumor derived from the epithelium. [New Latin : EPITHEL(IUM) + -OMA.] —**ep·i·the·li·om·a·tous** (ĕp′ə-thē′lē-ŏm′ə-təs) *adj.*

ep·i·the·li·um (ĕp′ə-thē′lē-əm) *n., pl.* **-ums** or **-lia** (-lē-ə). Membranous tissue, usually in a single layer, composed of closely arranged cells separated by very little intercellular substance and forming the covering of most internal surfaces and organs and the outer surface of an animal body. [New Latin : EPI- + Greek *thēlē,* nipple.] —**ep·i·the·li·al** *adj.*

ep·i·thet (ĕp′ə-thĕt′) *n.* **1.** A term used to characterize the nature of a person or thing: *"Moderate" is a much misused epithet in politics.* **2.** An adjective or descriptive phrase that comes to form part of or to substitute for a person's name or title: *"The Lion-Hearted" is an epithet for Richard I.* **3.** An abusive or contemptuous word or phrase used to describe a person: *Her sarcastic smile made "Your Honor" an epithet.* [Latin *epitheton,* from Greek, "an addition," from *epitithenai,* to put on, add : *epi-,* on + *tithenai,* to place, put.] —**ep·i·thet·ic** (ĕp′ə-thĕt′ĭk), **ep·i·thet·i·cal** (-ĭ-kəl) *adj.*

e·pit·o·me (ĭ-pĭt′ə-mē) *n.* **1.** A summary of a book, article, event, or the like; an abridgment; an abstract. **2.** One that is perfectly and strikingly representative or expressive of an entire class or type; an embodiment: *Keats was the epitome of the Romantic poet.* [Latin *epitomē,* from Greek, from *epitemnein,* to cut upon the surface, cut short : *epi-,* upon + *temnein,* to cut.]

e·pit·o·mize (ĭ-pĭt′ə-mīz′) *tr.v.* **-mized, -mizing, -mizes.** **1.** To make an epitome of; sum up. **2.** To typify (an entire class, type, or quality); represent or express the essence of: *A baby epitomizes innocence.*

ep·i·zo·ic (ĕp′ə-zō′ĭk) *adj.* Living or growing on the exterior of a living animal: *epizoic fungi.* [EPI- + -ZOIC.]

ep·i·zo·ot·ic (ĕp′ə-zō-ŏt′ĭk) *adj.* **1.** Attacking a large number of animals within a short time. Said of a disease. **2.** Prevalent among a group of animals. Said of a disease.
~*n.* An epizootic disease. [EPI- + ZO(O)- + -OTIC.]

e plu·ri·bus u·num (ē′ plo͝or′ə-bəs yo͞o′nəm, o͞o′nəm) *n.* One out of many. The motto of the United States. [Latin.]

E.P.N.S. electroplated nickel silver.

ep·och (ĕp′ək, ē′pŏk′) *n.* **1.** A period of history; especially, one characterized by remarkable events or by the predominance of a particular person, group, or state of affairs; an era. **2.** A point in time or progress that marks the beginning of such a period; a milestone; a breakthrough: *The addition of sound marked an epoch in film history.* **3.** *Geology.* A unit of geologic time that is a division of a period. **4.** *Astronomy.* An instant in time that is arbitrarily selected as a reference point. [New Latin *epocha,* from Greek *epokhē,* pause.]

ep·och·al (ĕp′ə-kəl, -ŏk′əl) *adj.* **1.** Of, pertaining to, or characteristic of an epoch. **2.** Epoch-making.

ep·och-mak·ing (ĕp′ək-mā′kĭng, ē′pək-) *adj.* Highly significant or important; momentous.

ep·ode (ĕp′ōd′) *n.* **1.** The last strophe of the triad (strophe, antistrophe, and epode) that forms the basic compositional unit of the lyric ode. **2.** A lyric composition of a type invented by Archilochus and used by Horace, characterized by couplets of a long line followed by a shorter one. [Latin *epōdos,* from Greek *epōidos,* "a singing after," from *epaidein,* to sing after : *epi-,* after + *aidein,* to sing.]

ep·o·nym (ĕp′ə-nĭm′) *n.* A real or mythical person whose name is or is thought to be the source of the name of a city, country, era, institution, or the like: *"Romulus" is the eponym of Rome.* [Greek *epōnumos,* EPONYMOUS.] —**ep·o·nym·ic** (ĕp′ə-nĭm′ĭk) *adj.*

e·pon·y·mous (ĭ-pŏn′ə-məs) *adj.* Of, pertaining to, or designating a person after whom something, such as a city, era, book, or play, is named or thought to be named: *In the movie "Ben Hur" the eponymous hero was played by a famous actor.* [Greek *epōnumos* : *epi-,* to + *onoma,* name.]

e·pon·y·my (ĭ-pŏn′ə-mē) *n.* The derivation of the name of a city, country, era, institution, or the like, from that of a person.

ep·o·pee (ĕp′ə-pē′) *n.* **1.** Epic poetry, especially as a literary genre. **2.** An epic poem. [French *épopée,* from Greek *epopoiia,* from *epopoios,* epic poet : *epos,* word, EPIC + *poiein,* to make (see **poet**).]

ep·os (ĕp′ŏs′) *n.* **1.** Oral epic poetry. **2.** An epic poem. [Latin, from Greek, word, poem.]

ep·ox·y (ĕp′ŏk′sē, ĭ-pŏk′-) *adj.* Of, composed of, or containing a substance with a molecular structure in which an oxygen atom is joined to two different groups that are themselves joined to other groups.
~*n., pl.* **-ies.** Any of various usually thermosetting resins characterized by toughness, strong adhesion, and high corrosion and chemical resistance, used especially in surface coatings and adhesives. Also called "epoxy resin." [EP(I)- + OXY-.]

Ep·ping (ĕp′ĭng). Town in Essex, now virtually a northeast suburb of London. It is famous for Epping Forest (2,270 hectares; 5,600 acres), formerly a royal hunting park.

ep·si·lon (ĕp′sə-lŏn′, -lən) *n.* The fifth letter in the Greek alphabet, written Ε, ε. Transliterated in English as *E, e.* See feature at **alphabet.** [Greek *e psilon,* "simple *e,*" from *psilos,* mere, simple.]

Ep·som (ĕp′səm). Town in Surrey, England, now part of the municipal borough of Epsom and Ewell. The Derby is run annually at Epsom Downs, a racecourse here.

Epsom salts *pl.n.* Hydrated **magnesium sulfate** *(see)* used especially as a cathartic and to reduce swellings. [After EPSOM, where it was originally obtained from a mineral spring.]

Ep·stein (ĕp′stīn′), **Sir Jacob** (1880–1959). British sculptor, born in New York of Russian-Polish parents. He studied in Paris with Rodin before settling in England (1905). He became famous for his massive subjects in bronze and stone, among them the marble *Venus* (1917), a bronze *Christ* (1919), and the alabaster *Adam* (1939).

Ep·stein-Barr virus (ĕp′stīn-bär′) *n.* The virus that is believed to cause infectious mononucleosis. [After M.A. *Epstein* (1921–) and Y.M. *Barr* (1932–), British pathologists who discovered it.]

eq. **1.** equal. **2.** equation. **3.** equivalent.

eq·ua·ble (ĕk′wə-bəl, ē′kwə-) *adj.* **1.** Unvarying; uniform: *an equable climate.* **2.** Not easily disturbed; serene: *an equable temperament.* —See Synonyms at **steady.** [Latin *aequābilis,* from *aequāre,*

to make even, from *aequus,* level, even, EQUAL.] **—eq·ua·bil·i·ty** (ĕk′wə-bĭl′ə-tē), **eq·ua·ble·ness** *n.* **—eq·ua·bly** *adv.*

e·qual (ē′kwəl) *adj. Abbr.* **eq. 1.** Having the same capability, quantity, or effect as another: *equal strength.* **2.** *Mathematics.* Related by a reflexive, symmetrical, and transitive relationship; broadly, alike or in agreement in a specific sense with respect to specific properties. **3.** Having the same privileges, status, or rights: *equal before the law.* **4.** Fairly and evenly available or granted: *equal rights.* **5.** Fairly and evenly balanced: *an equal contest.* **6. a.** Having the requisite qualities, as strength, ability, or determination, to accomplish a task or cope with a situation: *"Elizabeth found herself quite equal to the scene"* (Jane Austen). **b.** Adequate in extent, amount, or degree: *money equal to their needs.* **7.** *Archaic.* Impartial; just; equitable: *equal laws.* **8.** *Archaic.* Tranquil; equable. —See Synonyms at **same.**

∼*n.* A person or thing that is equal to another, especially: **1.** One who is equal in rank or status. **2.** A worthy substitute or rival: *I am his equal in every respect.*

∼*tr.v.* **equaled** or **equalled, equaling** or **equalling, equals. 1.** To be equal to, especially in amount or value. **2.** To do, make, or produce something equal to: *He equaled the world record for the mile.* **—equal out.** To reach a point of equilibrium; become equal. [Latin *aequālis,* from *aequus*†, even, level.]

Usage: The main problem is whether *equal* can be used along with *more* and *most.* Purists point out that if two things are equal, then one cannot be more equal than the other. But a sentence such as *There is a more equal distribution of wealth* is possible, with *equal* having the sense "more equitable" or "more nearly equal." *Most* is less often encountered but is still possible in such sentences as *That's the most equal division of opinion I have ever seen.* • *Equally* gives rise to two problems. It is often used with *as: Equally as interesting is his new book* would be reduced in careful usage to either *Equally interesting . . .* or *As interesting. . . .* It is usual to use *as* when a comparison is explicit, and *equally* when it is not: *His new book is equally interesting, His new book is as interesting as his earlier books,* but not *His new book is equally interesting as his earlier books.* When comparisons are made like those in the sentence *The device is equally useful inside and outside the house, equally . . . and* demonstrates more respect for careful usage than the informal *equally . . . or.*

e·qual-ar·e·a projection (ē′kwəl-âr′ē-ə) *n.* A map projection reproducing the same area ratios as exist on the earth's surface. Also called "homolographic projection."

e·qual·i·ty (ĭ-kwŏl′ə-tē) *n. pl.* **-ties. 1.** The state or an instance of being equal; especially, the state of enjoying equal rights in political, economic, and social affairs. **2.** A mathematical statement, usually an equation, that one thing equals another. [Middle English *equalite,* from Old French, from Latin *aequālitās,* from *aequālis,* EQUAL.]

e·qual·ize (ē′kwə-līz′) *v.* **-ized, -izing, -izes.** —*tr.* **1.** To make equal. **2.** To make uniform. —*intr.* To constitute or induce equality, equilibrium, or balance.

e·qual·iz·er (ē′kwə-lī′zər) *n.* **1.** One that equalizes. **2.** A device for equalizing pressure or strain. **3.** *Electronics.* A tone control system for frequency distortion in audio systems. **4.** *Slang.* A weapon, especially a revolver.

e·qual·ly (ē′kwə-lē) *adv.* **1.** In an equal or even manner. **2.** To an equal degree: *applies equally to children and adults.* **3.** In the same manner or way; likewise: *I taught and equally learned from my students.* —See Usage note at **equal.**

Equal Rights Amendment *n. Abbr.* **ERA** A proposed amendment to the U.S. Constitution to guarantee equal rights under the law to both sexes.

equal sign *n.* Also **equals sign.** The symbol (=) used, especially in an equation, to indicate that one thing is logically or mathematically equal to another.

equal temperament *n. Music.* The tuning of keyboard instruments, as pianos, to produce octaves of 12 equal semitones. Also called "temperament."

e·qua·nim·i·ty (ē′kwə-nĭm′ə-tē, ĕk′wə-) *n.* The quality or characteristic of being calm and even-tempered; composure. [Latin *aequanimitās,* from *aequanimis,* even-tempered : *aequus,* even, EQUAL + *animus,* mind.] **—e·quan·i·mous** (ĭ-kwŏn′ə-məs) *adj.*

Synonyms: *composure, sang-froid, serenity.*

e·quate (ĭ-kwāt′) *v.* **equated, equating, equates.** —*tr.* **1.** To make, treat, or regard as equal or equivalent: *Many people equate wisdom with old age.* **2.** To reduce to a standard or average; equalize or stabilize; balance: *equate profit and loss.* **3.** To show or state the equality of; express in or as if in an equation. —*intr.* To be or seem to be equal; correspond; accord: *She equates easily with our conception of classic beauty.* [Middle English *equaten,* from Latin *aequāre,* from *aequus,* EQUAL.]

e·qua·tion (ĭ-kwā′zhən, -shən) *n. Abbr.* **eq. 1.** The process or act of equating or state of being equated. **2.** The state of being equal; a balanced state. **3.** *Mathematics.* A linear array of mathematical symbols separated into left and right sides that are designated at least conditionally equal by an equal sign. **4.** Broadly, a concept of equivalence or balance between a variety of factors: *Salaries have risen dramatically, but on the other side of the equation there has been a comparable rise in output.* **5.** *Chemistry.* A symbolic representation of a chemical reaction as a linear array of symbols for the reacting atomic and molecular species, separated into left and right sides by an equal sign, arrow, or opposing arrows. **6.** A complex of variable factors or considerations that must be taken into account, especially a **personal equation** *(see).* **—e·qua·tion·al** *adj.* **—e·qua·tion·al·ly** *adv.*

e·qua·tor (ĭ-kwā′tər) *n.* **1. a.** *Often* **Equator.** The great circle circumscribing the earth's surface, the reckoning datum of latitudes and the dividing boundary of Northern and Southern hemispheres, formed by the intersection of a plane passing through the earth's center perpendicular to its axis of rotation. **b.** A similar great circle drawn on the surface of a celestial body at right angles to the axis of rotation. **2.** The **magnetic equator** *(see).* **3.** *Astronomy.* The **celestial equator** *(see).* [Middle English, from Medieval Latin *(circulus) aequator (diei et noctis),* (circle) equalizing (day and night), from Latin *aequāre,* to EQUATE.]

e·qua·to·ri·al (ē′kwə-tôr′ē-əl, -tōr′ē-əl, ĕk′wə-) *adj.* **1.** Of or pertaining to the equator. **2.** Characteristic of or existing at or near the earth's equator: *equatorial climate; equatorial rain forests.* **3.** Lying in the same plane on the equator: *an equatorial orbit.* **4.** Having a support with two perpendicular axes, one of which is parallel to the earth's rotational axis. Said of a telescope.

∼*n. Astronomy.* An equatorial telescope. **—e·qua·to·ri·al·ly** *adv.*

Equatorial Gui·nea (gĭn′ē). Formerly **Span·ish Guinea** (spăn′ĭsh). Country of West Africa consisting of a mainland territory and several islands. Most of the people are subsistence farmers, but cocoa, coffee, and hardwoods are exported. The country gained independence from Spain in 1968. Area, 28,051 square kilometers (10,828 square miles). Population, 400,000. Capital, Malabo.

eq·uer·ry (ĕk′wə-rē) *n., pl.* **-ries. 1.** An attendant to the British royal household. **2.** An officer charged with supervision of the horses belonging to a royal or noble household. [Earlier *escurie,* from obsolete French *escuirie*†, stable, mistakenly associated with Latin *equus,* horse.]

e·ques·tri·an (ĭ-kwĕs′trē-ən) *adj.* **1.** Of or pertaining to horsemanship or horseback riding. **2.** Depicted or represented on horseback: *an equestrian statue of an emperor.* **3.** Of, pertaining to, or composed of knights, horsemen, or cavalry: *equestrian troops.*

∼*n.* One who rides a horse or performs on horseback. [Latin *equester,* from *equus,* horse.]

e·ques·tri·enne (ĭ-kwĕs′trē-ĕn′) *n.* A female equestrian.

equi– *prefix.* Indicates equality; for example, **equiangular.** [Middle English *equi-,* from Latin *aequi-,* from *aequus,* EQUAL.]

e·qui·an·gu·lar (ē′kwē-ăng′gyə-lər, ĕk′wē-) *adj.* Having all angles equal.

e·qui·dis·tant (ē′kwə-dĭs′tənt, ĕk′wə-) *adj.* Equally distant. **—e·qui·dis·tance** *n.* **—e·qui·dis·tant·ly** *adv.*

e·qui·lat·er·al (ē′kwə-lăt′ər-əl, ĕk′wə-) *adj.* Having all sides or faces equal.

∼*n.* **1.** A side exactly equal to others. **2.** A geometric figure having equal sides. **—e·qui·lat·er·al·ly** *adv.*

e·quil·i·brant (ĭ-kwĭl′ə-brənt) *n.* A force capable of balancing a system of forces to produce equilibrium. [EQUILIBR(ATE) + -ANT.]

e·quil·i·brate (ĭ-kwĭl′ə-brāt′) *v.* **-brated, -brating, -brates.** —*intr.* To be in or bring about equilibrium. —*tr.* To maintain in or bring into equilibrium. [Latin *aequilibrāre,* to balance, from *aequilībris,* in perfect balance, from *aequilibrium,* EQUILIBRIUM.] **—e·quil·i·bra·tion** *n.*

e·quil·i·bra·tor (ĭ-kwĭl′ə-brā′tər) *n.* A device that brings about and helps maintain equilibrium.

e·quil·i·brist (ĭ-kwĭl′ə-brĭst) *n.* A person who performs feats of balance, such as tightrope walking. [French *équilibriste,* from Latin *aequilībrium,* EQUILIBRIUM.]

e·qui·lib·ri·um (ē′kwə-lĭb′rē-əm, ĕk′wə-) *n.* **1.** A condition in which all acting influences are cancelled by others, resulting in a stable, balanced, or unchanging state. **2.** *Physics.* The condition of a system in which the resultant of all acting forces is zero and the sum of all torques about any axis is zero. **3.** *Chemistry.* The state of a reaction in which its forward and reverse reactions occur at equal rates so that the concentration of the reactants does not change with time. **4.** Mental or emotional balance; psychological stability. [Latin *aequilībrium,* even balance : EQUI- + *libra,* balance.]

e·qui·mo·lec·u·lar (ē′kwə-mə-lĕk′yə-lər, ĕk′wə-) *adj.* Designating solutions, substances, or the like that contain equal numbers of molecules.

e·quine (ē′kwīn′, ĕk′wīn′) *adj.* **1.** Of, pertaining to, or characteristic of a horse. **2.** Of or belonging to the family Equidae, which includes the horses, asses, and zebras.

∼*n.* A member of the Equidae. [Latin *equīnus,* from *equus,* horse.]

e·qui·noc·tial (ē′kwə-nŏk′shəl, ĕk′wə-) *adj.* **1.** Pertaining to or occurring at an equinox. **2.** Pertaining to the celestial equator. **3.** *Botany.* Having or characterizing flowers that open and close at specific times.

∼*n.* **1.** *Meteorology.* A violent storm of wind and rain reputed to occur at or near the time of the equinox. **2.** The equinoctial circle. [Middle English *equinoxial,* from Old French, from Latin *aequinoctiālis,* from *aequinoctium,* EQUINOX.]

equinoctial circle *n.* The **celestial equator** *(see).* Also called "equinoctial," "equinoctial line."

e·qui·nox (ē′kwə-nŏks′, ĕk′wə-) *n.* **1.** Either of two points on the celestial sphere at which the ecliptic intersects the celestial equator. **2.** Either of the two times during a year when the sun crosses the celestial equator and when the length of day and night are approximately equal: the **vernal equinox** and the **autumnal equinox** *(both of which see).* [Middle English *equinox,* from Old French, from Medieval Latin *aequinoxium,* variant of Latin *aequinoctium* : EQUI- + *nox* (stem *noct-*), night.]

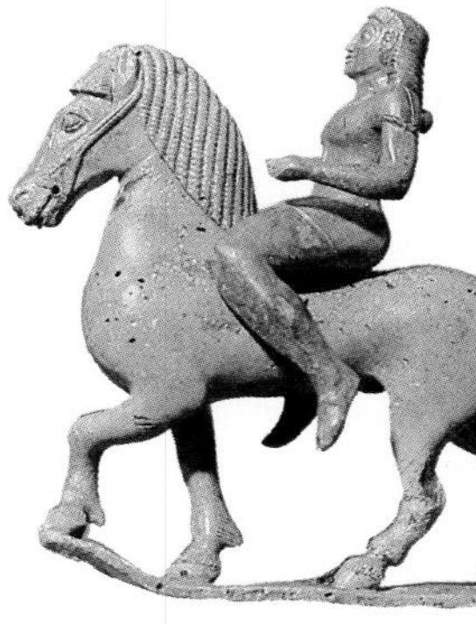

equestrian *A horse and rider, shown here in a Peloponnesian bronze statue that was made in about 550 B.C.*

e·quip (ĭ-kwĭp′) tr.v. **equipped, equipping, equips. 1.** To supply with material necessities such as tools, gear, provisions, or furnishings. **2.** To prepare in an intellectual, emotional, or spiritual way: *His training equipped him for such problems.* **3.** To dress or array. [Old French *eschiper, e(s)quiper,* to put to sea, embark, from Germanic.]

eq·ui·page (ĕk′wə-pĭj) n. **1.** Equipment or furnishings, especially of a military unit or ship; accouterments. **2. a.** A carriage that is elegantly equipped, as with caparisoned horses and liveried footmen. **b.** Any carriage. **3.** *Archaic.* A retinue, as of a person of royalty or nobility. **4.** *Archaic.* A set of articles, such as a dinner service or collection of jewelery.

e·quip·ment (ĭ-kwĭp′mənt) n. **1.** The act of equipping or the state of being equipped. **2.** Something material with which a person, organization, or thing is equipped; especially, the tools, apparatus, or the like required for a particular job or purpose: *camping equipment.* **3.** A person's intellectual or emotional resources.

e·qui·poise (ē′kwə-poiz′, ĕk′wə-) n. **1.** Equality in distribution, as of weight, relationship, or emotional forces; balance; equilibrium. **2.** A counterpoise; a counterbalance.
~tr.v. **equipoised, -poising, -poises.** To counterbalance.

e·qui·pol·lence (ē′kwə-pŏl′əns, ĕk′wə-) n. Also **e·qui·pol·len·cy** (-ən-sē). Equality, as in effectiveness or validity; equivalence.

e·qui·pol·lent (ē′kwə-pŏl′ənt, ĕk′wə-) adj. **1.** Equal in power, effectiveness, significance, or the like. **2.** *Logic.* Expressing the same thing; validly derived from each other. Said of two propositions. **3.** Equivalent.
~n. An equivalent. [Middle English *equipollent,* from Old French, from Latin *aequipollēns* (stem *aequipollent-*) : EQUI- + *pollēns,* present participle of *pollēre†,* to be powerful.]

e·qui·pon·der·ate (ē′kwə-pŏn′də-rāt′, ĕk′wə-) tr.v. **-ated, -ating, -ates. 1.** To counterbalance. **2.** To give equal balance or weight to. [Medieval Latin *aequiponderāre* : EQUI- + Latin *ponderāre,* to weigh.]

e·qui·po·ten·tial (ē′kwə-pə-tĕn′shəl, ĕk′wə-) adj. **1.** Having equal potential. **2.** *Physics.* Having the same potential at every point: *an equipotential surface.*

eq·ui·se·tum (ĕk′wə-sē′təm) n. Any of the flowerless, seedless plants of the genus *Equisetum,* which includes the horsetails. [New Latin, from Latin *equisaetum,* the horsetail : *equus,* horse + *saeta,* bristle, SETA.]

eq·ui·ta·ble (ĕk′wə-tə-bəl) adj. **1.** Exhibiting or characterized by equity; impartial or reasonable in judgment or treatment; fair; just. **2.** *Law.* Concerned with or valid in equity as distinguished from statute and common law. —See Synonyms at **fair.** [French *équitable,* from Old French, from *equite,* EQUITY.] —**eq·ui·ta·ble·ness** n. —**eq·ui·ta·bly** adv.

eq·ui·tant (ĕk′wə-tənt) adj. *Botany.* Overlapping at the base to form a flat, fanlike arrangement, as the leaves of some irises do. [Latin *equitāns* (stem *equitant-*), present participle of *equitāre,* to ride, from *eques* (stem *equit-*), horseman, from *equus,* horse.]

eq·ui·ta·tion (ĕk′wə-tā′shən) n. The art or practice of riding a horse; horsemanship. [Old French, from Latin *equitātiō* (stem *equitātiōn-*), riding, from *equitāre,* to ride. See **equitant.**]

eq·ui·ty (ĕk′wə-tē) n., pl. **-ties. 1.** The state, ideal, or quality of being just, impartial, and fair. **2.** Something that is just, impartial, and fair. **3.** The residual value of a business or property beyond any mortgage thereon and liability therein. **4.** *Law.* **a.** An organized body of legal rules based ultimately on principles of natural justice and applied either to cover cases not foreseen by common or statute law or to modify the rigor of common or statute law. **b.** An equitable right or claim. **5.** *Law.* Equity of redemption. **6.** **Equity.** *British.* The actors' trade union. [Middle English *equite,* from Old French, from Latin *aequitās* (stem *aequitāt-*), from *aequus,* EQUAL.]

equity of redemption n. *Law.* The right of one who has mortgaged his property to redeem that property upon payment of the sum due within a reasonable amount of time after the due date. Also called "equity."

equity stock n. **Common stock** (see).

equiv. equivalent.

e·quiv·a·lence (ĭ-kwĭv′ə-ləns) n. Also **e·quiv·a·len·cy** (-lən-sē) pl. **-cies. 1.** The state or condition of being equivalent; equality. **2.** *Mathematics.* A reflexive, symmetric, and transitive relation between elements of a set that establishes any two elements in the set as equivalent or nonequivalent. In this sense, also called "equivalence relationship." **3.** *Logic.* **a.** The relationship between two propositions having the same truth-value. **b.** The relationship between two propositions such that for one to be true and the other false gives rise to a contradiction. Compare **biconditional.**

e·quiv·a·lent (ĭ-kwĭv′ə-lənt; ē′kwə-vā′lənt, ĕk′wə- *for sense 4 only*) adj. Abbr. **eq., equiv. 1. a.** Equal in substance, degree, value, force, or meaning. **b.** Having similar or identical effects. **2.** Virtually the same; tantamount. Used with *to: This request was equivalent to an order.* **3.** *Mathematics.* Capable of being put into a one-to-one relationship. Said of two sets. **b.** Broadly, having identical corresponding parts. **c.** Equal. **4.** *Chemistry.* Having the same ability to combine. **5.** *Logic.* Exhibiting equivalence. Said of propositions. —See Synonyms at **same.**
~n. Abbr. **eq., equiv. 1.** Something that is equivalent. **2.** *Chemistry.* Equivalent weight. [Middle English, from Old French, from Late Latin *aequivalēns* (stem *aequivalent-*), present participle of *aequivalēre,* to be equal in value : EQUI- + *valēre,* to be strong, be worth.] —**e·quiv·a·lent·ly** adv.

equivalent weight n. The number of parts by weight of any element combining with or replacing the equivalent of half the atomic weight of oxygen or one atomic weight of hydrogen. Also called "combining weight," "equivalent."

e·quiv·o·cal (ĭ-kwĭv′ə-kəl) adj. **1.** Capable of two interpretations; ambiguous: *an equivocal statement.* **2.** Of uncertain nature; indeterminate: *an equivocal result.* **3.** Misleading; evasive. **4.** Of questionable integrity: *an equivocal sort of man.* [Late Latin *aequivocus* : EQUI- + Latin *vōx* (stem *vōc-*), voice.] —**e·quiv·o·cal·ly** adv. —**e·quiv·o·cal·ness** n.

e·quiv·o·cate (ĭ-kwĭv′ə-kāt′) intr.v. **-cated, -cating, -cates.** To use equivocal language intentionally; hedge. [Middle English *equivocaten,* from Medieval Latin *aequivocāre,* from Late Latin *aequivocus,* EQUIVOCAL.] —**e·quiv·o·ca·tion** n. —**e·quiv·o·ca·tor** n.

e·qui·voque, e·qui·voke (ĕk′wə-vōk′, ē′kwə-) n. **1.** A play on words; a pun. **2.** A double meaning. [French *équivoque,* from adjective, EQUIVOCAL.]

E·quu·le·us (ĭ-kwōō′lē-əs) n. A constellation in the equatorial region of the Northern Hemisphere near Delphinus and Pegasus. [Latin, diminutive of *equus,* horse.]

Er The symbol for the element erbium.

ER endoplasmic reticulum.

-er¹ suffix. **1.** Indicates: **a.** Someone who or something that performs the specified action; for example, **helper, blender. b.** Someone performing or involved with a specified occupation or function; for example, **photographer, bookkeeper. c.** Geographic origin or residence; for example, **Vermonter, northerner. d.** Nature or appearance; for example, **two-seater. 2.** Used to form informal versions of certain words; for example, **homer** instead of **home run.** [Middle English *-er, -ere,* Old English *-ere,* from Common Germanic *-ārjaz* (unattested), from Latin *-ārius.* See **-ary.**]

-er², -r suffix. Used to form the comparative degree of adjectives and adverbs; for example, **whiter, slower.** [Middle English *-ere, -re,* Old English *-re, -ra.*]

e·ra (îr′ə, ĕr′ə) n. **1.** A period of time that utilizes a specific point in history as the basis of its chronology: *After 1492 a new era in the history of mankind began.* **2.** A period of time that is distinctive or notable because of its new or different aspects, events, or personages: *the era of the computer.* **3.** The beginning or onset of such a period of time; a turning point or milestone; an epoch. **4.** *Geology.* The longest division of geologic time comprising one or more periods. [Late Latin *aera,* era, from Latin, "counters for calculating," a number used as a basis for calculating, an era from which time is reckoned, from *aes* (stem *aer-*), brass, copper, money.]

ERA Equal Rights Amendment.

e·ra·di·ate (ĭ-rā′dē-āt′) v. **-ated, -ating, -ates.** —tr. To send out (radiation); radiate. —intr. To emanate. [EX- + RADIATE.] —**e·ra·di·a·tion** n.

e·rad·i·cate (ĭ-răd′ĭ-kāt′) tr.v. **-cated, -cating, -cates. 1.** To get rid of completely; remove totally: *The goal was to eradicate corruption.* **2.** To pull or tear up by or as if by the roots; uproot. —See Synonyms at **abolish.** [Latin *ērādicāre,* to pluck up by the roots, to root out : *ē,* out, from *ex-* + *rādix* (stem *rādic-*), root.] —**e·rad·i·ca·ble** adj. —**e·rad·i·ca·tion** n. —**e·rad·i·ca·tive** (ĭ-răd′ĭ-kā′tĭv, -kə-tĭv) adj. —**e·rad·i·ca·tor** n.

e·rase (ĭ-rās′) tr.v. **erased, erasing, erases. 1.** To remove; rub, wipe, scrape, or blot out; efface. **2. a.** To remove (a sound recording) from magnetic tape. **b.** To remove a sound recording from (magnetic tape). **3.** To remove (information) from a computer memory. **4.** To destroy all traces of: *a civilization erased by time.* [Latin *ērādere* (past participle *ērāsus*), to scrape out, scrape off : *ex-,* out + *rādere,* to scrape.] —**e·ras·a·ble** adj.

> **Synonyms:** blot, cancel, delete, efface, expunge.

e·ras·er (ĭ-rā′sər) n. Something used for erasing writing, especially a piece of rubber.

e·ra·sion (ĭ-rā′zhən, -shən) n. **1.** An act of erasing. **2.** *Surgery.* The removal of diseased tissue, especially bone, by scraping.

Er·a·sis·tra·tus of Ce·os (ĕr′ə-sĭs′trə-təs; sē′ŏs′) (fl. 3rd century B.C.). Greek physician who described with great accuracy (derived from surgery and post-mortem examinations) many vital organs, especially the heart and liver. He also correctly distinguished between motor and sensory nerves.

E·ras·mus (ĭ-răz′məs), **Desiderius** (c.1466-1536). Dutch scholar and humanist who worked to revive classical texts from antiquity and to restore simple Christian faith by the study of the Scriptures. His books *In Praise of Folly* (1509) and *The Handbook of a Christian Knight* (1503) exposed the worldliness of the medieval church.

E·ras·tian·ism (ĭ-răs′chə-nĭz′əm, ĭ-răs′tē-ə-) n. A doctrine attributed to the Swiss theologian Thomas Erastus (1524-83) advocating the submission of the church to civil authority in all matters. —**E·ras·tian** adj. & n.

e·ra·sure (ĭ-rā′shər) n. **1.** An act of erasing. **2.** Something that has been erased; a deletion.

Er·a·to (ĕr′ə-tō′). *Greek Mythology.* The Muse of lyric poetry. [Latin *Eratō,* from Greek, from *eratos,* loved, from *eran,* to love, akin to *erōs†,* love.]

Er·a·tos·the·nes of Cy·re·ne (ĕr′ə-tŏs′thə-nēz′; sī-rē′nē). (c. 276-c. 194 B.C.). Greek astronomer. He was the first man known to have measured the circumference of the earth, by measuring the sun's position at the summer solstice at different places.

er·bi·um (ûr′bē-əm) n. *Symbol* **Er** A soft, malleable, silvery rare-earth element, used in metallurgy, nuclear research, and to color glass and porcelain. Atomic number 68, atomic weight 167.26, melting point 1,497° C, boiling point 2,900° C, specific gravity 9.051, valence 3. [New Latin, after *Ytterby,* Sweden, where it was discovered.]

ere (âr) *prep. Archaic.* Previous to; before.
~*conj. Archaic.* **1.** Before. **2.** Sooner than; rather than. [Middle English *ar, er,* Old English *ǣr,* before.]

Er·e·bus (ĕr′ə-bəs). *Greek Mythology.* The dark region beneath the earth through which the dead must pass before they reach Hades. [Latin, from Greek *Erebos.*]

Erebus, Mount. Volcanic mountain (3,794 meters; 12,447 feet) on Ross Island, in the Ross Sea, eastern Antarctica. It was discovered in 1841 by the British explorer James C. Ross.

e·rect (ĭ-rĕkt′) *adj.* **1.** Directed or pointing upward; standing upright; vertical: *erect posture.* **2.** Being in a stiff, rigid condition: *every hair erect.* **3.** *Physiology.* In erection. Said of parts of the body. **4.** *Archaic.* Wide-awake; alert.
~*v.* **erected, erecting, erects.** —*tr.* **1.** To raise (a building, for example); construct: *erect a skyscraper.* **2.** To raise upright; set on end; lift up: *erect a Christmas tree for decorating.* **3.** To put together; fashion; assemble: *erect a child's model airport; erect a theory.* **4.** To set up; establish: *erect a dynasty.* **5.** To transform and exalt: *He erected the editorial into an art form.* **6.** *Geometry.* To construct (an altitude, for example) from or upon a given base. —*intr. Physiology.* To become rigid and upright by filling with blood. [Middle English, from Latin *ērectus,* past participle of *ērigere,* to raise up, set up, erect : *ē-,* out, up, from *ex-* + *regere,* to direct, to set.] **—e·rect·ly** *adv.* **—e·rect·ness** *n.*

e·rec·tile (ĭ-rĕk′təl, -tīl′) *adj.* **1.** Capable of being erected or raised upright. **2.** *Physiology.* Of or pertaining to vascular tissue, such as that of the penis and the clitoris, that is capable of filling with blood and becoming rigid. **—e·rec·til·i·ty** (ĭ-rĕk′tĭl′ə-tē) *n.*

e·rec·tion (ĭ-rĕk′shən) *n.* **1.** The act of erecting. **2.** The state of being erected. **3.** Something erected; especially, a construction or edifice. **4.** *Physiology.* **a.** The firm and enlarged condition of erectile tissue when filled with blood. **b.** The process of filling with blood. **c.** An erect penis.

e·rec·tor, e·rect·er (ĭ-rĕk′tər) *n.* **1.** One that erects. **2.** *Anatomy.* A muscle that causes or maintains the erection of a body part.

E region *n.* A layer of the ionosphere, the **E layer** *(see).*

er·e·mite (ĕr′ə-mīt′) *n.* A person who isolates himself from society, especially as a religious recluse. [Middle English *(h)ermite,* HERMIT.] **—er·e·mit·ic** (ĕr′ə-mĭt′ĭk), **er·e·mit·i·cal** (-ĭ-kəl) *adj.*

e·rep·sin (ĭ-rĕp′sĭn) *n.* A mixture of peptidases in the small intestine that breaks down proteins into amino acids. [Probably Latin *ēr(ipere),* to snatch away : *ē-,* away, from *ex-* + *rapere,* to snatch.]

er·e·thism (ĕr′ə-thĭz′əm) *n.* Abnormal irritability and sensibility to stimulation in any part of the body. [French *éréthisme,* from Greek *erethismos,* irritation, annoyance, from *erethizein, eretheint†,* to irritate, stir.] **—er·e·this·mic** (ĕr′ə-thĭz′mĭk) *adj.*

erg[1] (ûrg) *n.* A centimeter-gram-second unit of energy or work equal to the work done by a force of one dyne acting over a distance of one centimeter. [Greek *ergon,* work.]

erg[2] (ârg, ûrg) *n.* An area of shifting sand dunes in the Sahara desert. [Arabic *'irj.*]

er·go (ûr′gō, âr′-) *conj.* Consequently; therefore.
~*adv.* Consequently; hence. [Latin *ergō,* therefore.]

er·go·cal·cif·er·ol (ûr′gō-kăl-sĭf′ə-rôl′, -rōl′) *n.* **vitamin D_2** *(see).* [ERGO(T) + CALCIFEROL.]

er·go·graph (ûr′gə-grăf′, -gräf′) *n.* A device for determining the work capacity and rate of fatigue of a muscle or group of muscles by measuring the extent of movement. [Greek *ergon,* work (see **erg**) + -GRAPH.]

er·gom·e·ter (ûr-gŏm′ə-tər) *n.* An apparatus for measuring the amount of work done by a group of muscles under control conditions. [Greek *ergon,* work (see **erg**) + -METER.] **—er·go·met·ric** (ûr′gə-mĕt′rĭk) *adj.*

er·go·nom·ics (ûr′gə-nŏm′ĭks) *n.* The study of the application of biology and engineering to the relationship between workers and their environment. Also called "biotechnology."

er·gos·ter·ol (ûr-gŏs′tə-rôl′, -rōl′) *n.* A plant sterol, $C_{28}H_{44}O$, converted by ultraviolet radiation to vitamin D_2. [ERGO(T) + STEROL.]

er·got (ûr′gət, -gŏt′) *n.* **1.** Any fungus of the genus *Claviceps,* especially *C. purpurea,* infecting various cereal plants, and forming black sclerotia, or compact masses of branching filaments, that replace many of the seeds of the host plant. **2.** The disease caused by such a fungus. **3.** The dried sclerotia of such a fungus, usually obtained from rye seed, and used as a source of several medicinally important alkaloids and as the basic source of lysergic acid. [French, "cock's spur," which the fungus resembles, from Old French *argor, argot†.*]

er·got·ism (ûr′gə-tĭz′əm) *n.* Poisoning by ergot-infected grain, notably rye, characterized by gangrene of the extremities and in some cases convulsions and mental disturbance.

Er·hard (ĕr′härt′) **Ludwig** (1897–1977). Chancellor of West Germany (1963–66). As minister for economic affairs (1949–63), he was the chief architect of the so-called German economic miracle.

er·i·ca (ĕr′ĭ-kə) *n.* Any shrub of the genus *Erica,* which includes the heathers and heaths. [Latin, from Greek *ereikē,* heath.]

Er·ic·son or **Er·ic·sson** (ĕr′ĭk-sən), **Leif** (*fl.* 1000). Norse navigator. According to Norse sagas, on his return from Greenland in 1000 he was blown off course to an unknown land, called Vinland after the vines supposedly growing there. It is thought to lie somewhere between Newfoundland and Virginia.

Er·ic the Red (ĕr′ĭk) (*fl.* 10th century). Norse chieftain who in *c.* 982 sailed west and discovered Greenland. Four years later he established a small colony of about 500 people there.

E·rid·a·nus (ĭ-rĭd′n-əs) *n.* A constellation located in the Southern Hemisphere near Orion and Fornax and containing the star Achernar. [Greek *Ēridanos,* a mythical river associated with the myth of Phaethon.]

E·rie (îr′ē). The fourth-largest of the Great Lakes, between central Canada and the United States.

Erie Canal. An artificial waterway, 580 kilometers (360 miles) long, extending across central New York State from Albany to Buffalo and connecting the Hudson River with Lake Erie. The canal was opened in 1825, but shipping volume declined in the 1860's with the rise of the railroads for long-distance hauling. Much of the canal is now part of the New York State Barge Canal System.

Er·in (ĕr′ĭn). *Poetic.* Ireland. [Middle English *Erin,* from Old Irish *Ērinn,* dative of *Ēriu,* Ireland.]

E·rin·y·es (ĭ-rĭn′ē-ēz′) *pl.n. Greek Mythology.* The Furies. [Latin *Erīnyes,* from Greek *Erinues,* plural of *Erinus†,* a Fury.]

e·ris·tic (ĭ-rĭs′tĭk) *adj.* **1.** Of or relating to argument, controversy, or discord. **2.** Given to argument or dispute, especially when specious; disputatious.
~*n.* **1.** One given to or expert in argument or dispute. **2.** The art or practice of debate. [Greek *eristikos,* eager for strife, from *erizein,* to strive, wrangle, from *eris,* strife, discord.]

Er·i·tre·a (ĕr′ĭ-trē′ə). Province of Ethiopia, mainly desert, bordering the Red Sea. In 1890 it was proclaimed an Italian colony and was used as the stepping-off point for Italy's conquest of Ethiopia in 1935–36. After World War II it was administered by Britain, was federated with Ethiopia in 1952, and by 1962 had become an integral part of Ethiopia. Since then Eritrean rebels have been fighting to win back their independence. **—Er·i·tre·an** *n. & adj.*

erk (ûrk) *n. British Slang.* **1.** A rating in the navy or an aircraftman in the Royal Air Force. **2.** A person one dislikes. [20th century : perhaps a corruption of *A.C.* (aircraftman).]

Er·len·mey·er flask (ûr′lən-mī′ər, âr′-) *n.* A conical laboratory flask with a narrow neck and flat, broad bottom. [Originated by Emil *Erlenmeyer* (1825–1909), German chemist.]

erl·king (ûrl′kĭng′, ârl′-) *n.* An evil spirit of Germanic mythology and folklore, typically represented as abducting children to the land of death. [Partial translation of German *Erlkönig,* "king of alders," coined by Herder in a misunderstanding of Danish *ellerkonge,* variant of *elverkonge,* elf-king : *elver,* elf + *konge,* king.]

er·mine (ûr′mĭn) *n.* **1.** A weasel, *Mustela erminea,* of northern regions, having brownish fur that in winter turns to white with a black tail tip. **2.** The valuable white fur of the ermine, used for ornament, as on the robes of peers or judges. **3.** A stylized representation of ermine fur in heraldry. [Middle English *ermin,* from Old French, from Medieval Latin *(mūs) Armenius,* "Armenian (mouse)."]

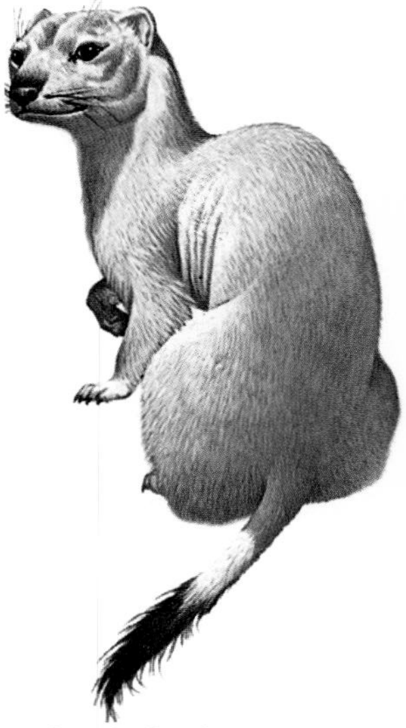

ermine *The fur of the stoat—a member of the weasel family native to the cooler regions of the Northern Hemisphere—changes from brown to white in winter. The fur, and the animal, are then known as ermine.*

erne, ern (ûrn) *n.* Any of several sea eagles, especially *Haliaeetus albicella,* of the Old World. [Middle English *ern,* eagle, Old English *earn.*]

Ernst (ĕrnst), **Max** (1891–1976). German painter and sculptor. In 1922 he moved to Paris and became a leading figure in the surrealist movement and an exponent of collage and photomontage.

e·rode (ĭ-rōd′) *v.* **eroded, eroding, erodes.** —*tr.* **1.** To wear down or wear away by or as if by the action of water, ice, wind, or the like. **2.** To destroy gradually; undermine: *His status has been eroded.* **3.** To eat away; corrode. **4.** To make or form by wearing away. —*intr.* To become eroded or worn. [Latin *ērōdere,* to gnaw off, eat away : *ē-,* off, from *ex-* + *rōdere,* to gnaw.]

e·rog·e·nous (ĭ-rŏj′ə-nəs) *adj.* Also **er·o·gen·ic** (ĕr′ə-jĕn′ĭk). Arousing sexual desire; especially, indicating or pertaining to parts of the body sensitive to sexual stimulation: *erogenous zones.* [Greek *erōs†,* desire, sexual love + -GENOUS.]

Er·os[1] (ĕr′ŏs′, îr′-). *Greek Mythology.* The god of love, son of Aphrodite. [Latin *Erōs,* from Greek *erōs†,* love, desire.]

Eros[2] *n. Psychoanalysis.* **1.** The sum of all self-preservative, as contrasted with self-destructive, instincts. **2.** Sexual drive; libido. [From EROS.]

e·rose (ĭ-rōs′) *adj.* Irregularly notched, toothed, or indented, as if gnawed; jagged: *erose leaves.* [Latin *ērōsus,* past participle of *ērōdere,* to ERODE.]

e·ro·sion (ĭ-rō′zhən) *n.* **1.** The state of being eroded or the process of eroding. **2.** *Geology.* The group of natural processes, including weathering, dissolution, abrasion, and corrosion, all involving transport of material, by which earthy or rocky material is removed from the earth's surface.

e·ro·sive (ĭ-rō′sĭv) *adj.* Causing erosion.

e·rot·ic (ĭ-rŏt′ĭk) *adj.* **1.** Of, concerning, or tending to arouse sexual love or desire: *erotic literature.* **2.** Dominated by sexual love or desire. [Greek *erōtikos,* of or caused by love, from *erōs†* (stem *erōt-*), love, desire.] **—e·rot·i·cal·ly** *adv.*

e·rot·i·ca (ĭ-rŏt′ĭ-kə) *pl.n.* Literature or art concerning sex or intended to arouse sexual desire. [New Latin, from Greek *erōtika,* plural of *erōtikos,* EROTIC.]

e·rot·i·cism (ĭ-rŏt′ə-sĭz′əm) *n.* Also **er·o·tism** (ĕr′ə-tĭz′əm). **1.** Erotic quality or character. **2. a.** Sexual excitement. **b.** Abnormally persistent sexual excitement. **3.** The use of erotic themes in literature and art, especially to a degree that amounts to preoccupation.

er·o·tol·o·gy (ĕr′ə-tŏl′ə-jē) *n.* **1.** The study of sexual phenomena. **2.** Erotic art and literature; erotica.

e·ro·to·ma·ni·a (ĭ-rō′tə-mā′nē-ə, -mān′yə, ĭ-rŏt′ə-) *n.* Abnormally strong sexual desire. [New Latin : Greek *erōs†* (stem *erōt-*), love + -MANIA.]

err (ûr, ĕr) *intr.v.* **erred, erring, errs.** **1.** To make an error or mistake; be incorrect: *We erred on the side of caution.* **2.** To violate accepted moral standards; sin. **3.** *Archaic.* To go astray. [Middle English *erren,* to wander about, from Old French *errer,* from Latin *errāre.*] —**err·ing·ly** *adv.*

er·ran·cy (ĕr′ən-sē) *n., pl.* **-cies.** A state or instance of erring; especially, the condition of being in doctrinal error.

er·rand (ĕr′ənd) *n.* **1.** A short trip taken to convey a message or perform a particular task. **2.** The purpose or object of such a trip: *His errand was to mail a letter.* [Middle English *erend,* business, message, from Old English *ǣrende,* message, from Germanic *arundjam* (unattested).]

er·rant (ĕr′ənt) *adj.* **1.** Roving, especially in search of adventure: *knights errant.* **2.** Straying from the proper course or standards; erring. [Middle English *erraunt,* from Old French *errant,* present participle of both *errer,* to travel, to look for an adventure, from Vulgar Latin *iterāre* (unattested), from Late Latin *itinerārī,* to ITINERATE, and *errer,* to ERR.] —**er·rant·ly** *adv.*

er·rant·ry (ĕr′ən-trē) *n.* The condition of being errant; especially, the conduct or attitudes characteristic of a knight errant.

er·rat·ic (ĭ-răt′ĭk) *adj.* **1.** Without a fixed or regular course; straying; wandering: *an erratic route to the capital.* **2.** Deviating from the customary course in conduct or opinion; unconventional; eccentric: *erratic behavior.* **3.** Lacking consistency, regularity, or uniformity. —*n.* *Geology.* A piece of rock differing from surrounding rocks, having been moved from its original position, especially by glacial action. [Middle English *erratik,* from Old French *erratique,* from Latin *errāticus,* wandering, from *errāre,* to wander.] —**er·rat·i·cal·ly** *adv.*

er·ra·tum (ĭ-rä′təm, ĭ-rā′-) *n., pl.* **-ta** (-tə). An error in printing or writing, especially such an error noted in a list of corrections appended to a book. [Latin *errātum,* neuter past participle of *errāre,* to wander, ERR.]
     Usage: The use of *errata* as if it were singular (*an errata . . . the errata is . . . .*) is considered unacceptable in standard English. This rule applies even when *errata* is being used in the collective sense of "a list of errors."

er·rhine (ĕr′īn) *adj.* Promoting nasal discharge. —*n.* An errhine medicine. [Greek *errhinos* : *en-,* in + *rhis* (stem *rhin-*), nose.]

er·ro·ne·ous (ĭ-rō′nē-əs) *adj.* Containing or derived from error; mistaken; false. [Middle English, from Old French *erroneus* or Latin *errōneus,* wandering, from *errāre,* to wander, ERR.] —**er·ro·ne·ous·ly** *adv.* —**er·ro·ne·ous·ness** *n.*

er·ror (ĕr′ər) *n.* **1.** An act, assertion, or belief that unintentionally deviates from what is correct, right, or true. **2.** The condition of having mistaken beliefs or false knowledge. **3.** The act or an instance of deviation from an accepted code of behavior. **4.** A mistake: *a clerical error.* **5.** The difference between a computed or measured value and a correct value. **6. a.** In tennis, a failure to return the ball during play. **b.** In baseball, a defensive fielding or throwing misplay by a player when a play should have resulted in an out or prevented an advance by a base runner. [Middle English *errour,* from Old French, from Latin *error,* from *errāre,* to ERR.]
     Synonyms: *blunder, mistake, oversight, slip.*

er·satz (ĕr′zäts, ĕr-zäts′) *adj.* **1.** Substitute; artificial: *ersatz mink.* **2.** Being an inferior imitator or imitation of a specified person or thing: *an ersatz Dickens.* —See Synonyms at **artificial.** —*n.* A substitute; especially, an inferior imitation. [German, from *Ersatz,* compensation, replacement, from *ersetzen,* to replace, from Old High German *irsezzen* : *ir-* (perfective prefix) + *sezzen,* to set.]

Erse (ûrs) *n.* The Gaelic language; **Irish Gaelic** or **Scottish Gaelic** (both of which see). —*adj.* Of or pertaining to the Scottish or Irish Celts or their language. [Middle English (Scottish) *Erisch,* variant of IRISH.]

erst·while (ûrst′hwīl′) *adj.* Former. —*adv.* *Archaic.* Formerly.

er·u·bes·cence (ĕr′ə-bĕs′əns, ĕr′yə-) *n.* A reddening of the skin; a blush. [Latin *ērubēscentia,* from *ērubēscēns* (stem *ērubēscent-*), present participle of *ērubēscere,* to blush, to grow red : *ē-,* out, "completely," from *ex-* + *rubēscere,* to grow red, from *rubēre,* to be red.] —**er·u·bes·cent** *adj.*

e·ruct (ĭ-rŭkt′) *v.* **eructed, eructing, eructs.** —*intr.* To belch. —*tr.* **1.** To belch (gas from the stomach). **2.** To emit (fumes) violently. Used of a volcano. [Latin *ēructāre* : *ē-,* out, from *ex-* + *ructāre,* to belch.]

e·ruc·ta·tion (ĭ-rŭk′tā′shən, ē′rŭk-) *n.* **1.** The act or an instance of eructing or belching. **2.** Matter belched forth.

er·u·dite (ĕr′yə-dīt′, ĕr′ə-) *adj.* **1.** Deeply learned. **2.** Characterized by erudition. [Middle English *erudit,* from Latin *ērudītus,* past participle of *ērudīre,* "to take the roughness out of," polish, teach : *ē-,* out of, from *ex-* + *rudis,* rough, RUDE.] —**er·u·dite·ly** *adv.* —**er·u·dite·ness** *n.*

er·u·di·tion (ĕr′yə-dĭsh′ən, ĕr′ə-) *n.* Deep and extensive knowledge, especially when derived from books; profound learning. —See Synonyms at **knowledge.**

e·rum·pent (ĭ-rŭm′pənt) *adj.* Bursting through or as if through a surface or covering. [Latin *ērumpens* (stem *ērumpent-*), present participle of *ērumpere,* to ERUPT.]

e·rupt (ĭ-rŭpt′) *v.* **erupted, erupting, erupts.** —*intr.* **1.** To emerge violently from limits or restraint; explode. **2.** To become violently active and discharge lava. Used of a volcano. **3.** To force out or suddenly release something enclosed or pent up: *The geyser erupts periodically.* **4.** To give sudden and forceful expression to an emotion: *The crowd erupted in fury.* **5. a.** To pierce the gum. Used of a tooth. **b.** To appear on the skin. Used of a skin blemish. —*tr.* To eject (steam or lava, for example) violently. [Latin *ērumpere* (past participle *ēruptus*), to erupt, to break out, to burst : *ē-,* out, from *ex-* + *rumpere,* to break.] —**e·rup·tive** *adj.* —**e·rup·tive·ly** *adv.*

e·rup·tion (ĭ-rŭp′shən) *n.* **1.** An act, process, or instance of erupting; especially, the discharge of lava from a volcano, or of water or mud from a geyser. **2.** A sudden, often violent outburst. **3. a.** A rash or blemish on the skin. **b.** The passage of a tooth through the gum.

-ery, -ry *suffix.* Used to form nouns from verbs or other nouns to indicate: **1.** A place for a specified business or activity; for example, **bakery, hatchery.** **2.** A specified class of persons; for example, **Jewry.** **3.** A collection or class of objects of a specified type; for example, **jewelry, cutlery.** **4.** A specified craft, study, or practice; for example, **cookery, husbandry.** **5. a.** Certain specified characteristics; for example, **snobbery.** **b.** A specified kind of behavior; for example, **knavery.** **6.** A specified condition or status; for example, **slavery.** [Middle English *-erie,* from Old French : *-er, -ier,* from Latin *-ārius* (see *-ary*) + *-ie,* from Latin *-ia* (see *-ia*).]

e·ryn·go (ĭ-rĭng′gō) *n., pl.* **-goes.** Any of several plants of the genus *Eryngium,* such as the sea holly, having spiny leaves and dense clusters of small bluish flowers. [Latin *ēryngion,* from Greek *ērun-gion,* diminutive of *ērungos,* eryngo, sea holly, possibly from *ēr,* ear, spring, in the sense "spring flower."]

er·y·sip·e·las (ĕr′ə-sĭp′ə-ləs, îr′-) *n.* An acute disease of the skin and subcutaneous tissue caused by a streptococcus and marked by spreading inflammation. Also called "St. Anthony's fire." [Middle English *erisipila, herisipila,* from Latin *erysipelas,* from Greek *erusi-pelas,* "red skin" : *eruthros,* red + *-pelas,* skin.] —**er·y·si·pel·a·tous** (ĕr′ə-sĭ-pĕl′ə-təs, îr′-) *adj.*

er·y·sip·e·loid (ĕr′ə-sĭp′ə-loid′, îr′-) *n.* An infectious disease of the hands characterized by red lesions and caused by the bacterium *Erysipelothrix rhusiopathiae,* found in infected meat or fish. [ERYSIPEL(AS) + -OID.]

er·y·the·ma (ĕr′ə-thē′mə) *n.* A redness of the skin, due to dilation of the blood capillaries, that may be caused by toxins in the blood, heat, infection, or injury. [New Latin, from Greek *eruthēma,* from *eruthainein,* to be red, from *eruthros,* red.] —**er·y·them·a·tous** (ĕr′ə-thĕm′ə-təs, -thē′mə-təs), **er·y·the·mat·ic** (-thĭ-măt′ĭk), **er·y·the·mic** (-thē′mĭk) *adj.*

e·ryth·rism (ĭ-rĭth′rĭz′əm) *n.* Unusual redness of pigmentation as of hair or plumage. [ERYTHR(O)- + -ISM.] —**er·y·thris·mal** (ĕr′ə-thrĭz′-məl) *adj.*

e·ryth·rite (ĭ-rĭth′rīt′) *n.* A reddish mineral, the hydrated arsenate of cobalt, used in coloring glass. [ERYTHR(O)- + -ITE.]

erythro-, erythr– *prefix.* Indicates red; for example, **erythrocyte, erythrite.** [From Greek *eruthros,* red.]

e·ryth·ro·blast (ĭ-rĭth′rə-blăst′, -blăst′) *n.* Any of the nucleated cells in bone marrow that develop into erythrocytes. [ERYTHRO- -BLAST.] —**e·ryth·ro·blas·tic** (ĭ-rĭth′rə-blăs′tĭk) *adj.*

e·ryth·ro·cyte (ĭ-rĭth′rə-sīt′) *n.* The nonnucleated, disk-shaped blood cell containing the red pigment hemoglobin, which transports oxygen and carbon dioxide around the body. It is responsible for the color of the blood. Also called "red blood cell." [ERYTHRO- + -CYTE.] —**e·ryth·ro·cyt·ic** (ĭ-rĭth′rə-sĭt′ĭk) *adj.*

e·ryth·ro·cy·tom·e·ter (ĭ-rĭth′rə-sī-tŏm′ə-tər) *n.* An apparatus for counting the number of erythrocytes in a blood sample. [ERYTHROCYT(E) + -METER.]

e·ryth·ro·my·cin (ĭ-rĭth′rə-mī′sĭn) *n.* An antibiotic agent from cultures of the bacterium *Streptomyces erythreus,* effective especially against Gram-positive bacteria. [ERYTHRO- + -MYCIN.]

Erz·ge·bir·ge (ĕrts′gə-bîr′gə). A mountain range on the border between Czechoslovakia and Germany. Rich in mineral resources, including uranium, lead, zinc, tin, copper, and wolframite, it is an important industrial area. The highest point is Klínovec (1,245 meters; 4,800 feet), in Czechoslovakia.

Es The symbol for the element einsteinium.

-es¹ *suffix.* Indicates the plural form, for which it is used in nouns ending in a sibilant or an affricate and in some nouns ending in a vowel or a postconsonantal *y;* for example, **trusses, switches, cargoes, ladies.** Compare **-s** (in nouns). [Middle English *-es, -s, -s* (plural).]

-es² *suffix.* Indicates the third person singular form of the present indicative, for which it is used in most verbs ending in a sibilant, an affricate, a vowel, or a postconsonantal *y;* for example, **guesses, rushes, does, defies.** Compare **-s** (in verbs). [Middle English *-es, -s, -s* (third person singular indicative suffix).]

E·sa·ki diode (ĭ-sä′kē) *n.* *Electronics.* A **tunnel diode** (see).

E·sau (ē′sô′). The son of Isaac and Rebecca, who sold his birthright to his brother Jacob. Genesis 25:25. [Late Latin *Ēsau,* from Greek, from Hebrew *'Ēsāw,* "hairy."]

ESCA (ē′ĕs′sē′ā′) *n.* A technique for analyzing or investigating chemical compounds by irradiating them with x-rays and monitoring the characteristic energy spectrum of electrons emitted. [*Electron spectroscopy for chemical analysis.*]

es·ca·lade (ĕs′kə-lād′, -lād′) *n.* The act of scaling a fortified wall or rampart, especially during an assault. [French, from Italian *scalata,* from *scalare,* to climb, from *scala,* ladder, from Late Latin *scāla,* from Latin *scālae,* steps.] —**es·ca·lade** *v.*

es·ca·late (ĕs′kə-lāt′) v. **-lated, -lating, -lates.** —*tr.* To increase, enlarge, or intensify; especially, to increase the scale or intensity of (a conflict). —*intr.* To increase in intensity or extent. [Back-formation from ESCALATOR.] —**es·ca·la·tion** n.

es·ca·la·tor (ĕs′kə-lā′tər) n. **1.** A moving stairway consisting of steps attached to a continuously circulating belt, for moving passengers up and down between floors. Also called "moving staircase." **2.** An escalator clause. [Originally a trademark : perhaps *escal*ade + *elevator*.]

escalator clause n. A provision in a contract stipulating an increase or decrease, as in wages, benefits, or prices, under certain conditions, such as changes in the cost of living or in production costs. Also called "escalator."

es·cal·lo·ni·a (ĕs′kə-lō′nē-ə) n. Any evergreen shrub of the South American genus *Escallonia*, cultivated for its red or white flowers. [After *Escallon*, 18th-century Spanish traveler who discovered it.]

escallop. Variant of **scallop.**

es·ca·pade (ĕs′kə-pād′) n. **1. a.** An act of breaking loose from restraint. **b.** A flight from confining rules. **2.** A carefree or reckless adventure; a fling or a caper. [French, from Old French, from Old Italian *scappata*, from the feminine past participle of *scappare*, to escape, from Vulgar Latin *excappāre* (unattested), to ESCAPE.]

es·cape (ĭ-skāp′) v. **-caped, -caping, -capes.** Also archaic **scape** (skāp), **scaped, scap·ing, scapes.** —*intr.* **1.** To break loose from confinement; get free: *The prisoner escaped.* **2.** To issue from confinement or an enclosure; leak or seep out. **3.** To succeed in avoiding capture, danger, or harm. **4.** To grow beyond a cultivated area or a condition of cultivation. Used of plants. —*tr.* **1. a.** To break loose from; get free of. **b.** To succeed in avoiding (capture, danger, or harm). **2. a.** To elude the comprehension of: *The meaning of this cryptic note escapes me.* **b.** To elude the attention, memory, or detection of: *The mistake escaped my notice.* **3.** To issue involuntarily from: *A regretful sigh escaped her lips.* —*n.* **1.** The act or an instance of escaping. **2.** A means of escaping. **3. a.** Temporary freedom from worry, care, or unpleasantness. **b.** A means of obtaining this: *Television is his escape from worry.* **4.** A gradual and accidental pouring out or leaking from an enclosure, as a container; leakage: *an escape of gas.* **5.** A cultivated plant that has become established away from cultivation. —*adj.* **1.** Affording a means of escape, especially in an emergency: *an escape hatch.* **2.** Providing a legal basis for avoiding liability or responsibility: *an escape clause.* [Middle English *escapen*, from Old North French *escaper*, "to take off one's cloak," to emerge from restraint, escape, from Vulgar Latin *excappāre* (unattested) : *ex-*, out, off + Late Latin *cappa*, cloak, hood (see cape).] —**es·cap·a·ble** adj. —**es·cap·er** n.

Synonyms: avoid, elude, eschew, evade, shun.

es·cap·ee (ĭ-skā′pē′, ĕs′kā-) n. One that has escaped; especially, an escaped prisoner.

es·cape·ment (ĭ-skāp′mənt) n. **1.** A mechanism consisting in general of an escape wheel and anchor, used especially in timepieces to control the wheel movement and to provide periodic energy impulses to a pendulum or balance. **2.** The mechanism in a typewriter that controls the lateral movement of the carriage. **3.** An escape. **4.** A means of escape.

escape velocity n. The minimum velocity that a body, such as a space rocket, must attain to overcome the gravitational attraction of another body, such as the earth.

escape wheel n. The rotating notched wheel periodically engaged and disengaged by the anchor in the escapement of a timepiece.

es·cap·ism (ĭ-skā′pĭz′əm) n. The habit or tendency of seeking escape from unpleasant realities in self-deceiving fantasy or entertainment. —**es·cap·ist** adj. & n.

es·cap·ol·o·gist (ĕs′kā-pŏl′ə-jĭst, ĭ-skā′-) n. A person who escapes from confinement, usually as a form of public entertainment. —**es·cap·ol·o·gy** n.

es·car·got (ĕs′kär-gō′) n., pl. **-gots** (-gō′). An edible snail, especially when cooked. [French, a snail, from Old French, from Old Provençal *escaragol*†.]

es·carp (ĭ-skärp′) n. **1.** A steep slope or cliff; an escarpment. **2.** The inner wall of a ditch or trench dug around a fortification. —*tr.v.* **escarped, -carping, -carps.** To cut or erode so as to form a steep slope. [French *escarpe*, from Old French, from Italian *scarpa*, SCARP.]

es·carp·ment (ĭ-skärp′mənt) n. **1.** A steep slope or long cliff resulting from erosion or faulting and separating two relatively level areas of differing elevations. **2.** The steeper slope of an asymmetrical ridge, especially one formed when gently dipping rock strata are denuded differentially. **3.** A steep slope in front of a fortification.

Escaut. See **Scheldt.**

-escence suffix. Indicates a beginning or continuing state; for example, *opalescence*, *luminescence*. [Old French, from Latin *-ēscentia*, from *-ēscēns* (stem *-escent-*), -ESCENT.]

-escent suffix. Indicates beginning to be or exhibit; for example, *luminescent*, *phosphorescent*. [Old French, from Latin *-ēscēns* (stem *-escent-*), present participial suffix of *-ēscere*, chiefly inceptives of verbs in *-ēre*. See -ent.]

esch·a·lot (ĕsh′ə-lŏt′) n. A shallot. [French *eschalote*, from obsolete French *eschalotte*, SHALLOT.]

es·char (ĕs′kär′) n. A dry scab or slough formed on the skin as a result of a burn or by the action of a corrosive or caustic substance. [Middle English *escare*, scab, SCAR.]

es·cha·rot·ic (ĕs′kə-rŏt′ĭk) adj. Producing or capable of producing an eschar. —*n.* An escharotic substance or drug.

es·cha·tol·o·gy (ĕs′kə-tŏl′ə-jē) n. The branch of theology that is concerned with the ultimate or last things, such as death, judgment, heaven, and hell. [Greek *eskhatos*, last, extreme + -LOGY.] —**es·chat·o·log·i·cal** (ĭ-skăt′l-ŏj′ĭ-kəl, ĕs′kə-tə-lŏj′-) adj. —**es·cha·tol·o·gist** n.

es·cheat (ĭs-chēt′) n. **1.** The reversion of land held under feudal tenure to the manor in the absence of legal heirs or claimants. **2.** The reversion of property to the state in the absence of legal heirs or claimants. **3.** Land or property that has reverted in the absence of legal heirs or claimants. —*v.* **escheated, -cheating, -cheats.** —*intr.* To revert to the state by escheat. —*tr.* To cause (property) to revert to the state by escheat. [Middle English *eschete*, from Old French *eschete*, *escheoite*, from *escheoit*, past participle of *escheoir*, to fall out, from Vulgar Latin *excadēre* (unattested) : Latin *ex-*, out + *cadere*, to fall.] —**es·cheat·a·ble** adj.

es·cheat·age (ĭs-chē′tĭj) n. The right of the state to acquire property by escheat.

es·chew (ĭs-chōō′) tr.v. **-chewed, -chewing, -chews. 1.** To take care to avoid; shun. **2.** To abstain from. —See Synonyms at **escape.** [Middle English *eschewen*, *eschiuen*, from Old French *eschiver*, *eschiuver*, to shun, to avoid, from Vulgar Latin *scivāre* (unattested), from Germanic *skiuhwan* (unattested), from *skiuhwaz* (unattested), SHY.] —**es·chew·al** n.

Es·cof·fier (ĕs′kō-fyā′), **Auguste** (c. 1846–1935). French chef. His reputation as "the king of chefs and the chef of kings" was made chiefly in England.

es·co·lar (ĕs′kə-lär′) n., pl. **-lars** or collectively **escolar.** Any of several slender carnivorous fishes of the family Gempylidae, of warm marine waters. Also called "snake mackerel." [Spanish, "scholar" (from the spectaclelike rings around its eyes), from Late Latin *scholāris*, SCHOLAR.]

Es·co·ri·al, El (ĕ-skôr′ē-əl). Granite palace and monastery near Madrid in Spain, one of the world's great architectural monuments. It was begun by Juan Bautista de Toledo in 1563 and completed by Juan de Herrera (1530–97) in 1584.

es·cort (ĕs′kôrt′) n. **1.** One or more persons accompanying another to give guidance or protection or as a mark of honor. **2.** One or more guards, often armed, traveling with important persons or goods. **3.** A man who is the companion of a woman, especially on a social occasion. **4. a.** One or more vehicles accompanying another vehicle to guide, protect, or honor its passengers. **b.** A warship or plane or a group of warships or planes used to defend or protect other craft from enemy attack. **5.** The state of being accompanied by an escort. —*tr.v.* (ĭ-skôrt′, ĕ-skôrt′, ĕs′kôrt′) **escorted, -corting, -corts.** To accompany as an escort. —See Synonyms at **accompany.** [French *escorte*, from Old French *(e)scorte*, from Old Italian *scorta*, guide, an escorting, from the feminine past participle of *scorgere*, to show, to guide, from Vulgar Latin *excorrigere* (unattested), to conduct, guide, escort : Latin *ex-*, out + *corrigere*, to set right, CORRECT.]

escort agency n. An agency that provides male or female partners for social outings.

e·scribe (ĭ-skrīb′) tr.v. **escribed, escribing, escribes.** To draw (a circle or other curve) touching one side of a triangle or other plane figure and the extensions of the two adjacent sides. [EX- (out) + Latin *scribere*, to write.]

es·cri·toire (ĕs′krĭ-twär′) n. A writing desk, especially one consisting of a stand or chest of drawers surmounted by smaller drawers or compartments that are concealed by a hinged lid that when opened provides a writing surface. [French, from Old French *escriptoire*, a study, from Medieval Latin *scriptorium*, SCRIPTORIUM.]

es·crow (ĕs′krō′, ĕ-skrō′) n. **1. a.** A written agreement, such as a deed or bond, put into the custody of a third party and not in effect until certain conditions are fulfilled by the grantee. **b.** Money or property held in this way. **2.** The condition of being ineffective until certain conditions are fulfilled: *a deed held in escrow.* [Old French *escroe*, strip of parchment, scroll, from Frankish *scrōda* (unattested), piece.]

es·cu·do (ĕs-skōō′dō) n., pl. **-dos. 1. a.** The basic monetary unit of Portugal, equal to 100 centavos. **b.** The basic monetary unit of Cape Verde, equal to 100 centavos. **2.** A coin worth one escudo. See feature at **currency.** [Portuguese and Spanish, "shield," from Latin *scūtum*, shield.]

es·cu·lent (ĕs′kyə-lənt) adj. Suitable for eating; edible. —*n.* Something edible, as a vegetable. [Latin *esculentus*, from *esca*, food, from *edere*, to eat.]

es·cutch·eon (ĭ-skŭch′ən) n. Also **scutch·eon** (skŭch′ən). **1.** A shield or shield-shaped emblem bearing a coat of arms. **2.** An ornamental or protective shield-shaped object, as a movable plate covering a keyhole or a plate on which a door knocker is mounted. **3.** Nautical. The ornamented plate in the middle of a ship's stern inscribed with the ship's name and home port. [Middle English *escochon*, from Old French *escuchon*, *escusson*, from Vulgar Latin *scūtiō* (unattested), from Latin *scūtum*, shield.] —**es·cutch·eoned** adj.

Es·dra·e·lon (ĕz′drə-ē′lən). One of the most fertile plains in Israel. It stretches about 40 kilometers (25 miles) from the coastal lowland near Mt. Carmel to the Jordan River valley.

Es·dras (ĕz′drəs) n. *Abbr.* **Esd. 1.** Either of the first two books of the

escapement *A facsimile of Galileo's escapement, the mechanism that regulates the action of a traditional clock or watch.*

Apocrypha, I Esdras and II Esdras, called in the Douay Bible III Esdras and IV Esdras. **2.** Either of two books of the Douay Bible Old Testament, I Esdras and II Esdras, corresponding to the books Ezra and Nehemiah in the King James Bible and other versions.

ESE east-southeast.

-ese *suffix.* Indicates: **1.** A native or inhabitant; for example, **Sudanese. 2.** A language or dialect; for example, **Japanese. 3.** A literary style or diction; for example, **journalese.** In this sense, usually used derogatorily. [Old French *-eis* and Italian *-ese*, from Latin *-ēnsis*, "originating in."]

es·er·ine (ĕs′ə-rēn′) *n. Biochemistry.* **Physostigmine** *(see).* [*Eser-*, native African name + -INE.]

es·ker (ĕs′kər) *n.* Also **es·kar** (ĕs′kär, -kər). A long, narrow ridge of sand and gravel deposited by a stream flowing between a valley glacier and the valley wall, or in a tunnel under a retreating glacial ice sheet. Also called "os." [Irish *eiscir*, ridge, from Old Irish *escir*†.]

Es·ki·mo (ĕs′kə-mō′) *n., pl.* **-mos** or collectively **Eskimo.** Also **Es·qui·mau** *pl.* **-maux** (-mōz′). *Abbr.* **Esk. 1.** A member of a people native to the Arctic coastal regions of North America and to parts of Greenland and northeastern Siberia. **2.** The language spoken by this people.
~*adj.* Also **Esquimau.** *Abbr.* **Esk.** Of, pertaining to, or concerning the Eskimos or their language. [Earlier *Esquimawes*, perhaps from Micmac *eskameege*, to eat raw fish : Proto-Algonquian *ašk-* (unattested), "raw" + *-amekw-* (unattested), "fish."]

Es·ki·mo-Al·e·ut (ĕs′kə-mō-ăl′ē-ōōt′) *n.* A family of languages spoken chiefly among peoples native to the Arctic coastal regions of North America, Greenland, the Aleutian Islands, and the northeastern tip of Siberia.

Eskimo dog *n.* A large dog of a breed used in Arctic regions as a sled dog, having a thick coat and a plumed tail.

e·soph·a·gus, oe·soph·a·gus (ĭ-sŏf′ə-gəs) *n., pl.* **-gi** (-jī′). A muscular, membranous tube for the passage of food from the pharynx to the stomach. [Middle English *ysophagus*, from Greek *oisophagos*, gullet.] —**e·soph·a·ge·al** (ĭ-sŏf′ə-jē′əl) *adj.*

es·o·ter·ic (ĕs′ə-tĕr′ĭk) *adj.* **1.** Intended for, limited to, or understood by only a small group: *an esoteric cult.* Compare **exoteric. 2.** Difficult to understand; abstruse: *The theory remained esoteric despite efforts to popularize it.* **3.** Not publicly disclosed; confidential. [Late Latin *esōtericus*, from Greek *esōterikos*, from *esōterō*, comparative of *esō*, within.] —**es·o·ter·i·cal·ly** *adv.*

ESP (ĕ′ĕs-pē′) *n.* Extrasensory perception.

esp. especially.

es·pa·drille (ĕs′pə-drĭl′) *n.* A light shoe having a rope or fiber sole and a canvas upper part. [French, variant of *espardille*, from Provençal *espardilho*, diminutive of *espart*, esparto, from Latin *spartum*, ESPARTO.]

es·pal·ier (ĭ-spăl′yər, -yā′) *n.* **1.** A tree or shrub that is trained to grow flat against a wall, often in a symmetrical pattern. **2.** A framework, as a trellis, on which an espalier is grown.
~*tr.v.* **espaliered, -iering, -iers.** To train (a plant) on an espalier. [French, from Italian *spalliera*, applied to shoulder supports, hence stakes of that height, from *spalla*, shoulder, from Latin *spatula*, broad piece, flat piece. See **spatula.**]

es·par·to (ĭ-spär′tō) *n., pl.* **-tos.** A tough, wiry grass, *Stipa tenacissima*, of Spain and northern Africa, yielding a fiber used in making paper and as cordage. [Spanish, from Latin *spartum*, from Greek *sparton*, rope, cable, esparto.]

es·pe·cial (ĭ-spĕsh′əl) *adj.* **1.** Outstanding; exceptional: *of especial value.* **2.** Pertaining uniquely to one person, group, or thing; particular: *her own especial quality.* —See Usage note at **special.** [Middle English, from Old French, from Latin *speciālis*, from *speciēs*, a view, appearance.]

es·pe·cial·ly (ĭ-spĕsh′ə-lē) *adv. Abbr.* **esp.** To an extent or degree deserving of special emphasis; particularly.

Es·pe·ran·to (ĕs′pə-răn′tō, -rän′tō) *n.* An artificial international language, invented in 1887, characterized by a vocabulary based on word roots common to many European languages, a single, unvarying ending for each principal part of speech, and a regularized system of conjugation and inflection. [After Dr. *Esperanto* ("one who hopes"), pen name of Lazarus Ludwig Zamenhof (1859–1917), Polish philologist.]

es·pi·al (ĭ-spī′əl) *n.* **1.** The act of catching sight of something. **2.** The act of watching, especially in secret. **3.** The fact of being seen or noticed. [Middle English *espiaille*, from Old French, from *espier*, to watch, to SPY.]

es·pi·o·nage (ĕs′pē-ə-näzh′, -näj′, -nĭj) *n.* The practice of spying or using spies to obtain secret information about the activities and plans of another government or rival group. [French *espionnage*, from Old French, from *espionner*, to spy, from *espion*, spy, from Old Italian *spione*, from *spia*, from Germanic.]

es·pla·nade (ĕs′plə-näd′, -nād′) *n.* **1.** A flat, open, often paved stretch of ground used as a promenade; especially, such a promenade along the shore. **2.** A level area in front of a fortification. [French, from Italian *spianala*, from *spianare*, to level, from *explānāre*, to flatten, EXPLAIN.]

es·pou·sal (ĭ-spou′zəl) *n.* **1.** An espousing or adoption, as of an idea or cause. **2. a.** A betrothal. **b.** A wedding.

es·pouse (ĭ-spouz′) *tr.v.* **-poused, -pousing, -pouses. 1.** To take in marriage; marry. **2.** To give (a woman) in marriage. **3.** To adopt and support (a cause, belief, or the like). [Middle English *espousen*, from Old French *espouser*, from Late Latin *spōnsāre*, from Latin

spondēre (past participle *spōnsus*), to promise solemnly.]

es·pres·so (ĭ-sprĕs′ō) *n., pl.* **-sos.** A strong coffee brewed by forcing steam or hot water under pressure through long-roasted, powdered beans. [Italian *(caffè) espresso*, "pressed out (coffee)," from the past participle of *esprimere*, to press out, express, from Latin *exprimere* : *ex-*, out + *premere*, to PRESS.]

es·prit (ĕ-sprē′) *n.* **1.** Spirit. **2.** Liveliness of mind and expression; wit. [French, from Latin *spīritus*, SPIRIT.]

esprit de corps (də kôr′, kōr′) *n.* A spirit of devotion and enthusiasm among members of a group for one another, their group, and its purposes. [French, "spirit of (the) body."]

esprit d'es·cal·ier (dĕs′kăl-yā′) *n.* A witty retort that occurs to one too late. [French, "spirit of (the) stairs."]

es·py (ĭ-spī′) *tr.v.* **-pied, -pying, -pies.** To catch sight of; glimpse (something distant or partly obscured): *"Through one of the rents of his gown, you espied a fat capon hung round the monk's waist"* (Henry James). —See Synonyms at **see.** [Middle English *(e)spien*, from Old French *espier*, to SPY.]

Esq. Esquire (title).

-esque *suffix.* Indicates possession of a specified manner or quality; for example, **statuesque, Kafkaesque.** [French, from Italian *-esco*, from Germanic *-iskaz* (unattested). See also **-ish.**]

Es·qui·line (ĕs′kwə-līn′). One of the seven hills of Rome.

Esquimau. Variant of **Eskimo.**

es·quire (ĕs′kwīr′, ĭ-skwīr′) *n.* **1.** A candidate for knighthood in medieval times, serving a knight as attendant and shield-bearer; a squire. **2.** Formerly, a member of the English gentry ranking just below a knight. **3.** Esquire. *Abbr.* **Esq.** Used as a title of courtesy after a man's full name: *Martin Chuzzlewit, Esq.* [Middle English *esquier*, *esquire*, from Old French *esquier*, *escuier*, squire, "shield-carrier," from Late Latin *scūtārius*, from Latin *scūtum*, shield.]
Usage: The term *Esquire*, and its abbreviation *Esq.*, traditionally reserved for men, is now sometimes used in correspondence addressed to women, especially female attorneys: *Jane Roe, Esq.*

ESR electron spin resonance.

ess (ĕs) *n.* The letter *s.*

-ess *suffix.* Indicates a female; for example, **heiress, lioness.** [Middle English *-esse*, from Old French *-esse*, from Late Latin *-issa*, from Greek.]
Usage: The use of this suffix is changing in the wake of changing attitudes to feminine roles in society. Originally the suffix simply indicated female gender and had no additional overtones; a *poetess* was simply a female poet. These days several *-ess* forms are considered pejorative. Strongly disliked are *Negress* and *Jewess*; less pejorative are *authoress*, *poetess*, *sculptress*, and the like. Several words, such as *waitress*, *actress*, and *heiress*, remain relatively unaffected, but even these can become a focus of contention on occasion. See also Usage note at **person.**

Ess. Essex.

es·say (ĕ-sā′, ĕs′ā′) *tr.v.* **-sayed, -saying, -says. 1.** To make an attempt at; try, especially in a tentative manner. **2.** To subject to a test; try out.
~*n.* (ĕs′ā′, ĕ-sā′ *for senses 1, 3;* ĕs′ā′ *for sense 2*). **1.** An attempt; an endeavor. **2. a.** A short literary composition on a single subject, usually presenting the personal views of the author. **b.** An academic composition by a student on a set subject. **3.** A testing or trial. [Middle English, from Old French *essaier*, *assaier*, from *essai*, *assai*, a trial, from Vulgar Latin *exagiāre* (unattested), to weigh out, from Late Latin *exagium*, a weighing, from Latin *exigere*, to weigh out, examine. See **exact.**] —**es·say·er** *n.*

es·say·ist (ĕs′ā′ĭst) *n.* A writer of essays.

Es·sen (ĕs′ən). Industrial city on the Ruhr River, North Rhine-Westphalia, in Germany. In the second half of the 19th century it became one of Germany's leading manufacturing towns.

es·sence (ĕs′əns) *n.* **1.** The quality or qualities of a thing that give it its identity; the intrinsic or indispensable properties of a thing: *"Government and Law, in their very essence, consist of restrictions on freedom"* (Bertrand Russell). **2.** The most important ingredient; the crucial element. **3.** *Philosophy.* The inherent, unchanging nature of a thing or class of things, as distinguished from its attributes or its existence. **4. a.** An extract of a substance that retains its fundamental or most desirable properties in concentrated form. **b.** Such an extract in a solution of alcohol. **c.** A perfume or scent. **d.** A flavoring. **5.** An embodiment or personification: *the essence of kindness.* **6.** A spiritual or incorporeal entity. —**of the essence.** Of supreme importance: *Speed is of the essence if we are to finish the job on time.* [Middle English *essence*, *essencia*, from Old French *essence*, from Latin *essentia*, from *esse*, to be.]

Es·sene (ĕs′ēn′, ĭ-sēn′) *n.* A member of an ascetic Jewish sect that existed in ancient Palestine from the 2nd century B.C. to the 3rd century A.D. —**Es·se·ni·an** (ĕ-sē′nē-ən), **Es·sen·ic** (ĕ-sĕn′ĭk) *adj.*

es·sen·tial (ĭ-sĕn′shəl) *adj.* **1.** Constituting or part of the essence of something: *the essential simplicity of the idea.* **2.** Of basic importance; indispensable: *essential ingredients.* **3.** Constituting or containing an essence of a plant, liquid, or other substance. —See Synonyms at **necessary.**
~*n.* A fundamental, necessary, or indispensable part, item, or principle. [Middle English, from Late Latin *essentiālis*. See **essence, -ial.**] —**es·sen·ti·al·i·ty** (ĭ-sĕn′shē-ăl′ə-tē), **es·sen·tial·ness** *n.* —**es·sen·tial·ly** *adv.*

essential amino acid *n.* Any of eight amino acids that must be included in the human diet, since they cannot be synthesized by the body.

essential oil *n.* A volatile oil, usually having the characteristic odor or flavor of the plant from which it is obtained, used to make perfumes and flavorings.

Es·sex (ĕs'ĭks). *Abbr.* **Ess.** Originally an early kingdom of Anglo-Saxon England, it was settled by Saxons, probably early in the 6th century. It is now a county in southeastern England; its administrative center is Chelmsford.

Essex, Robert Devereux, 2nd Earl of (1566–1601). English courtier and man of arms. He was a favorite at the court of Elizabeth I but imperiled his position by marrying Sir Philip Sidney's widow in 1590 and scheming to overthrow the queen's principal adviser, Lord Burghley. His part in a rising of the people of London led to his arrest and execution for treason.

es·so·nite (ĕs'ə-nīt') *n.* Also **hes·son·ite** (hĕs'-). A reddish-brown variety of garnet. Also called "cinnamon stone." [French, from Greek *hēssōn,* inferior to, less than (it is less hard than true hyacinth), from *hēka,* a little, slightly.]

EST, E.S.T. Eastern Standard Time.

est. 1. established. 2. *Law.* estate. 3. estimate; estimated.

-est¹ *suffix.* Indicates the superlative degree of adjectives and adverbs; for example, **greatest, earliest.** [Middle English *-est,* Old English *-est, -ost,* from Common Germanic *-istaz* (unattested).]

-est², -st *suffix.* Indicates the archaic second person singular form of the present and past indicative tenses, with the pronoun *thou;* for example, **comest, didst.** [Middle English *-est,* Old English *-est, -ast.*]

es·tab·lish (ĭ-stăb'lĭsh) *tr.v.* **-lished, -lishing, -lishes.** Also *archaic* **stab·lish** (stăb'lĭsh). 1. To settle (a person) permanently or securely in a position or condition; install. 2. To found or set up on a lasting basis: *establish a business.* 3. To bring about; create: *establish order.* 4. To introduce or institute (laws, for example). 5. To turn (a church or religion) into a national institution. 6. **a.** To gain recognition for or acceptance of: *The book established his reputation.* **b.** To make familiar to a reader or audience: *establish a character.* 7. To prove the validity or truth of: *establish the facts.* 8. *Card Games.* To gain control of (a suit) so that all remaining tricks can be won. —See Synonyms at **confirm.** [Middle English *establissen,* from Old French *establir* (stem *establiss-*), from Latin *stabilīre,* to make firm, from *stabilis,* firm.] **—es·tab·lish·er** *n.*

established church. A church that is officially recognized and given support as a national institution by a government.

es·tab·lish·ment (ĭ-stăb'lĭsh-mənt) *n.* 1. The act of establishing. 2. The condition or fact of being established. 3. **a.** An institution, such as a business, club, or hotel. **b.** The premises of such an institution. **c.** The permanent staff of such an institution. **d.** An organized group, such as a government, political party, or military force. 4. **a.** A place of residence. **b.** Those living and working in it. 5. An established church. 6. **Establishment. a.** The people and institutions, such as prominent politicians, financiers, the armed forces, and the civil service, that collectively constitute the power structure of a given society and are regarded as exerting a strongly conservative influence. **b.** A powerful group that tacitly controls a specified field of activity, usually in a conservative manner: *the literary Establishment.*

es·tab·lish·men·tar·i·an (ĭ-stăb'lĭsh-mĕn-târ'ē-ən) *adj.* 1. Of or pertaining to an established church. 2. Advocating the introduction or continuance of an established church. **—es·tab·lish·men·tar·i·an** *n.* **—es·tab·lish·men·tar·i·an·ism** *n.*

es·ta·mi·net (ĕ-stä'mē-nā') *n.* A small café. [French.]

es·tan·cia (ĕ-stäns'yä) *n.* A large estate or cattle ranch in Latin America. [American Spanish, from Spanish, room, enclosure, from Vulgar Latin *stantia* (unattested), a standing (thing), from Latin *stāns* (stem *stant-*), present participle of *stāre,* to stand.]

es·tate (ĭ-stāt') *n.* 1. **a.** A sizable piece of rural land, usually with a large house. **b.** Such a piece of land used for the cultivation of crops such as tobacco or rubber; plantation. 2. *British.* An area developed for a specific use, such as housing or factories: *an industrial estate.* 3. The whole of one's possessions; especially, all of the property and debts left by a deceased or bankrupt person. 4. *Law. Abbr.* **est.** The nature and extent of an owner's rights with respect to his property and its use. 5. A stage in one's development or maturation: *"When that I reached a man's estate"* (Shakespeare). 6. **a.** A condition of life, wealth, or status; rank. **b.** High rank or status: *gentlemen of estate.* 7. A class of citizens, as the nobility, that formerly possessed distinct political rights. Often called Estates of the Realm. [Middle English *estat,* state, condition, from Old French, STATE.]

estate agent *n. British.* One who handles the advertising and sale of buildings and land.

estate car *n. British.* A station wagon *(see).*

Es·tates-Gen·er·al (ĭ-stāts'jĕn'ər-əl) *n.* The **States-General** *(see).* [Translation of French *états généraux.*]

Es·te (ĕs'tā). Distinguished Italian family, celebrated as patrons of art. The line was founded by Oberto, who was invested with the fief of Este by the emperor Otto I. His descendants were the rulers of Ferrara (1240-1597) and of Modena (1288–1796).

es·teem (ĭ-stēm') *tr.v.* **-teemed, -teeming, -teems.** 1. To regard as of a high order; think of with respect; prize: *Oysters were much esteemed as a delicacy.* 2. To judge to be; regard as; consider. —See Synonyms at **appreciate.**
~n. 1. Favorable regard; respect: *He is held in high esteem.* 2. *Archaic.* Judgment; opinion. —See Synonyms at **regard.** [Middle

English *estemen,* from Old French *estimer,* from Latin *aestimāre,* to ESTIMATE.]

es·ter (ĕs'tər) *n.* Any of a class of organic compounds derived from an acid by the replacement of hydrogen by an alkyl radical. Esters, which are analogous to inorganic salts, are formed by reaction of acids with alcohols. [German *Ester,* short for *Essigäther,* "vinegar ether" : *Essig,* vinegar, from Middle High German *ezzich,* from Old High German *ezzīh,* from Latin *acētum* + *Äther,* from Latin *aethēr,* ETHER.]

es·ter·ase (ĕs'tə-rās', -rāz') *n.* An enzyme that catalyzes the hydrolysis of an ester.

Es·ter·há·zy (ĕs'tər-hä'zē), **Nikolaus Joseph, Prince Esterházy von Galantha** (1714–90). Member of a princely Hungarian family, famous for his association with Haydn, whom he appointed musical director at the Esterházy seat of Eisenstadt in 1766.

es·ter·i·fy (ĕ-stĕr'ə-fī') *v.* **-fied, -fying, -fies.** *Chemistry.* —*intr.* To change to an ester. —*tr.* To change (a compound) into an ester.

Es·ther (ĕs'tər) *n.* A book of the Old Testament recounting the story of Esther, the Jewish queen of Persia who saved her people from massacre.

es·the·sia (ĕs-thē'zhə, -zhē-ə) *n.* The ability to receive sense impressions. [Back-formation from ANESTHESIA.]

esthete. Variant of **aesthete.**

esthetic. Variant of **aesthetic.**

esthetician. Variant of **aesthetician.**

estheticism. Variant of **aestheticism.**

esthetics. Variant of **aesthetics.**

es·ti·ma·ble (ĕs'tə-mə-bəl) *adj.* 1. Capable of being estimated or evaluated; calculable. 2. Deserving of esteem; admirable. **—es·ti·ma·ble·ness** *n.* **—es·ti·ma·bly** *adv.*

es·ti·mate (ĕs'tə-māt') *tr.v.* **-mated, -mating, -mates.** 1. To calculate approximately the cost, quantity, or extent of. 2. To form a tentative opinion about; evaluate: *"While an author is yet living we estimate his powers by his worst performance"* (Samuel Johnson). —See Synonyms at **calculate.**
~n. (-mĭt). *Abbr.* **est.** 1. A tentative evaluation or rough calculation. 2. **a.** A preliminary calculation of the cost of work to be undertaken. **b.** The statement of such a calculation. 3. A judgment based upon one's impressions; an opinion. [From Latin *aestimāre†.*] **—es·ti·ma·tive** (ĕs'tə-mā'tĭv, -mə-tĭv) *adj.* **—es·ti·ma·tor** *n.*
Synonyms: *appraise, assay, assess, evaluate, rate.*

es·ti·ma·tion (ĕs'tə-mā'shən) *n.* 1. The act or an instance of estimating. 2. An opinion reached by estimating; a judgment. 3. Favorable regard; esteem.

estival. Variant of **aestival.**

estivate. Variant of **aestivate.**

estivation. Variant of **aestivation.**

Es·to·ni·a (ĕ-stō'nē-ə). Republic in eastern Europe, on the Baltic Sea. In 1940 it was incorporated into the U.S.S.R. and became a constituent republic. It regained independence in 1991. Area, 45,100 square kilometers (17,000 square miles). Population, 1,573,000. Capital, Tallinn.

Es·to·ni·an, Es·tho·ni·an (ĕ-stō'nē-ən) *n.* 1. A native or inhabitant of Estonia. 2. The Finno-Ugric language of Estonia. **—Es·to·ni·an, Es·tho·ni·an** *adj.*

es·top (ĕ-stŏp') *tr.v.* **-topped, -topping, -tops.** 1. *Law.* To prohibit, preclude, or impede by estoppel. 2. *Archaic.* To stop up. [Middle English *estoppen,* from Old French *estoper, estouper,* from Late Latin *stuppāre,* to stop up. See **stop.**] **—es·top·page** (ĕ-stŏp'ĭj) *n.*

es·top·pel (ĕ-stŏp'əl) *n. Law.* A restraint on a person to prevent him from contradicting his own previous assertion. Also called "conclusion." [Old French *estoupail, estouppail,* from *estouper,* to ESTOP.]

estr-, estro-, oestr-, oestro- *prefix.* Indicates estrus; for example, **estrogen.**

es·tra·di·ol, oes·tra·di·ol (ĕs'trə-dī'ôl', -ōl') *n.* An estrogenic hormone, $C_{18}H_{24}O_2$, used in treating estrogen deficiency. [ESTR(US) + -OL.]

es·trange (ĭ-strānj') *tr.v.* **-tranged, -tranging, -tranges.** 1. To remove from an accustomed place or relation. 2. To alienate the affections of; make hostile or unsympathetic. [Old French *estranger, estrangier,* from Medieval Latin *extrāneāre,* from Latin *extrāneus,* STRANGE.] **—es·trange·ment** *n.* **—es·trang·er** *n.*

es·tray (ĭ-strā') *n.* 1. *Law.* A stray domestic animal. 2. *Archaic.* A stray person, animal, or thing.
~intr.v. **estrayed, -traying, -trays.** *Archaic.* To stray. [Norman French *estray,* from Old French *estraie,* stray, wandering, from *estraier,* to STRAY.]

Es·tre·ma·du·ra¹ (ĕs'trə-mə-door'ə). Former province of central Portugal, comprising the lower Tagus River valley, one of the country's richest farming areas. Lisbon, the national capital, is the chief town. **—Es·tre·ma·du·ran** *n. & adj.*

Estremadura². See **Extremadura.**

es·tri·ol, oes·tri·ol (ĕs'trī'ôl', -ōl', ĕ-strī'-) *n.* An estrogenic hormone, $C_{18}H_{24}O_3$, that is obtained commercially from the urine of pregnant animals and used in treating estrogen deficiency. [ES-(TRUS) + TRI- -OL.]

es·tro·gen, oes·tro·gen (ĕs'trə-jən) *n.* Any of several steroid hormones produced chiefly by the ovary and responsible for promoting estrus and the development and maintenance of female secondary sex characteristics. [ESTR(US) + -GEN.] **—es·tro·gen·ic** (ĕs'trə-jĕn'ĭk) *adj.*

es·trone, oes·trone (ĕs'trōn') *n.* An estrogenic hormone, $C_{18}H_{22}O_2$, isolated from the urine of pregnant females for use in treating estrogen deficiency. [ESTR(US) + -ONE.]

es·trous, oes·trus (ĕs'trəs) *adj.* **1.** Of or pertaining to estrus. **2.** Being in heat.

estrous cycle, oestrus cycle *n.* The series of chemical and physiological changes in female mammals from the onset of one period of estrus to the onset of the next.

es·trus, oes·trus (ĕs'trəs) *n.* A regularly recurring period of ovulation and sexual excitement in female mammals other than humans; heat. [New Latin, from Latin *oestrus,* frenzy, from Greek *oistros.*]

es·tu·a·rine (ĕs'chōō-ə-rīn', -rēn') *adj.* Of, pertaining to, or found in an estuary.

es·tu·ar·y (ĕs'chōō-ĕr'ē) *n., pl.* **-ies. 1.** The part of the wide lower course of a river where its current is met by the tides. **2.** An arm of the sea that extends inland to meet the mouth of a river. [Latin *aestuārium,* estuary, tidal channel, from *aestus,* heat, swell, surge, tide.] **—es·tu·ar·i·al** (ĕs'chōō-âr'ē-əl) *adj.*

esu electrostatic unit.

e·su·ri·ent (ĭ-sŏŏr'ē-ənt, ĭ-zŏŏr'-) *adj.* Hungry; greedy. [Latin *ēsuriēns* (stem *ēsurient-*), present participle of *ēsurīre,* to want food, to be hungry, desiderative of *edere* (past participle *ēsus*), to eat.] **—e·su·ri·ence** (ĕ-sŏŏr'ē-əns, ĭ-zŏŏr'-), **e·su·ri·en·cy** (-ən-sē) *n.*

-et *suffix.* Indicates smallness or lesser status; for example, **baronet, pullet.** [Middle English *-et,* from Old French *-et,* from Common Romance *-itta, -etto* (both unattested).]

e·ta (ā'tə, ē'tə) *n.* The seventh letter in the Greek alphabet, written H, η. Transliterated in English as *e.* See feature at **alphabet.** [Late Latin *ēta,* from Greek, from a Phoenician source, akin to Hebrew *hēth,* HETH.]

e.t.a. estimated time of arrival.

é·ta·gère, e·ta·gere (ā'tä-zhâr') *n.* A piece of furniture with open shelves for ornaments or bric-a-brac. [French, from Old French *estagiere, estage,* floor of a building, position. See **stage.**]

et al. and others [Latin *et alii.*]

etc. et cetera.

et cet·er·a, et·cet·er·a (ĕt-sĕt'ər-ə, -sĕt'rə) *adv. Abbr.* **etc.** And further unspecified things of the same class; and so forth. [Latin, "and other (things)" : *et,* and + *cētera,* the rest, from the neuter plural of *cēterus,* remaining.]

Usage: The use of *et cetera* and its abbreviation *etc.* is principally appropriate to informal writing or to special areas such as technical reporting or business correspondence. It is not appropriate to formal writing in general.

et·cet·er·as (ĕt-sĕt'ər-əz, -sĕt'rəz) *pl.n.* Other incidental items not mentioned individually.

etch (ĕch) *v.* **etched, etching, etches.** *—tr.* **1.** To wear away (metal or glass, for example) with or as if with acid. **2.** To make (a pattern) on a metal plate or other surface with acid. **3.** To cut or engrave. **4.** To impress or imprint (an event, for example) clearly in the mind. *—intr.* To practice etching. [Dutch *etsen,* from German *ätzen,* to etch, to bite, to feed, from Old High German *ezzen,* to feed.] **—etch·er** *n.*

etch·ing (ĕch'ĭng) *n.* **1.** The art of preparing etched plates from which designs and pictures are printed. **2.** A design etched on a plate. **3.** An impression made from an etched plate.

e.t.d. estimated time of departure.

e·ter·nal (ĭ-tûr'nəl) *adj.* **1.** Without beginning or end; existing outside time: *eternal God.* **2.** Having a beginning but without interruption or end: *an eternal flame.* **3.** Unaffected by time; timeless: *eternal truths.* **4.** Seemingly endless; interminable: *tired of your eternal complaining.* **5.** Of or relating to existence after death: *went to their eternal rest.* —See Synonyms at **continual, infinite.**
~n. **1.** Something eternal. **2.** **Eternal.** God. [Middle English, from Old French, from Late Latin *aeternālis,* from Latin *aeternus,* eternal.] **—e·ter·nal·i·ty** (ē'tûr-năl'ə-tē), **e·ter·nal·ness** *n.* **—e·ter·nal·ly** *adv.*

e·ter·nal·ize (ĭ-tûr'nə-līz') *tr.v.* **-ized, -izing, -izes.** To eternize.

e·terne (ĭ-tûrn') *adj. Archaic.* Eternal. [Middle English, from Old French, from Latin *aeternus,* ETERNAL.]

e·ter·ni·ty (ĭ-tûr'nə-tē) *n., pl.* **-ties. 1.** The totality of time without beginning or end; infinite time. **2.** The state or quality of being eternal; everlastingness. **3. a.** The endless period of time following death. **b.** The afterlife; immortality. **4.** *Informal.* A very long or seemingly very long time. [Middle English *eternite,* from Old French, from Latin *aeternitās* (stem *aeternitāt-*), from *aeternus,* ETERNAL.]

e·ter·nize (ĭ-tûr'nīz') *tr.v.* **-nized, -nizing, -nizes. 1.** To make eternal. **2.** To make perpetually famous; immortalize. [Old French *eterniser,* from ETERNE.]

e·te·sian (ĭ-tē'zhən) *adj.* Recurring annually. Said of prevailing northerly summer winds of the Mediterranean. [Latin *etēsius,* from Greek *etēsios,* from *etos,* year.]

eth. Variant of **edh.**

eth-, etho- *suffix.* Indicates the presence of an ethyl group or derivation from ethane; for example, **ethoxide.**

-eth¹, -th *suffix.* Indicates the archaic third person singular form of the present indicative tense; for example, *leadeth, praiseth.* [Middle English *-eth,* Old English *-eth, -th.*]

-eth² Variant of **-th** (in ordinal numbers).

eth·an·am·ide (ĕth-ăn'ə-mīd') *n.* **Acetamide** *(see).*

eth·ane (ĕth'ān') *n.* A colorless, odorless gas, C_2H_6, occurring as a constituent of natural gas and used as a fuel and refrigerant. [ETH(YL) + -ANE.]

eth·ane·di·o·ic acid (ĕth'ān-dī-ō'ĭk) *n.* An organic acid, **oxalic acid** *(see).*

eth·ane·di·ol (ĕth'ān-dī'ôl', -ōl') *n.* An alcohol, **ethylene glycol** *(see).*

eth·a·no·ic acid (ĕth'ə-nō'ĭk) *n.* **Acetic acid** *(see).*

Eth·el·red or **Aeth·el·red** (ĕth'əl-rĕd'), known as "the Unready" (c. 968–1016). King of the English (978–1016). Most of his reign was spent unsuccessfully resisting Danish invasions. He was driven from London (1013) and fled to Normandy, but he returned a year later to be restored to the throne.

eth·ene (ĕth'ēn') *n. Chemistry.* **Ethylene** *(see).* [ETH(YL) + -ENE.]

e·ther (ē'thər) *n.* Also **ae·ther** (for sense 3). **1.** Any of a class of organic compounds in which two hydrocarbon groups are linked by an oxygen atom. **2.** A volatile, highly flammable liquid, $C_4H_{10}O$, derived from the distillation of ethanol with sulfuric acid and widely used in industry and as an anesthetic. Also called "diethyl ether," "ethyl ether," "ethoxyethane." **3.** The regions of space beyond the earth's atmosphere; the heavens. **4.** *Physics.* An all-pervading, infinitely elastic, massless medium formerly postulated as the medium of propagation of electromagnetic waves. [Middle English, from Latin *aethēr,* the upper or bright air, ether, from Greek *aithēr.*] **—e·ther·ic** (ĭ-thĕr'ĭk, ĭ-thîr'-) *adj.*

e·the·re·al, ae·the·re·al (ĭ-thîr'ē-əl) *adj.* **1.** Marked by lightness and insubstantiality; intangible. **2.** Highly refined; delicate. **3. a.** Of the celestial spheres; heavenly: *"Him the almighty power/Hurl'd headlong flaming from th' Ethereal Sky"* (Milton). **b.** Unearthly; spiritual. **4.** *Chemistry.* Of, pertaining to, or dissolved in ether. [Latin *aetherius, aethereus,* from Greek *aitherios,* from *aithēr,* ETHER.] **—e·the·re·al·i·ty** (ĭ-thîr'ē-ăl'ə-tē), **e·the·re·al·ness** *n.* **—e·the·re·al·ly** *adv.*

e·the·re·al·ize (ĭ-thîr'ē-ə-līz') *v.* **-ized, -izing, -izes.** *—tr.* To make or treat as being ethereal; spiritualize. *—intr.* To become ethereal. **—e·the·re·al·i·za·tion** *n.*

e·ther·i·fy (ĭ-thĕr'ə-fī') *tr.v.* **-fied, -fying, -fies.** To convert (an alcohol) into an ether. **—e·ther·i·fi·ca·tion** *n.*

e·ther·ize (ē'thə-rīz') *tr.v.* **-ized, -izing, -izes. 1.** To subject to the fumes of ether; anesthetize. **2.** *Chemistry.* To etherify. **—e·ther·i·za·tion** *n.* **—e·ther·iz·er** *n.*

eth·ic (ĕth'ĭk) *n.* **1.** A principle of right or good conduct. **2.** A body of such principles: *the work ethic.* [Middle English *et(h)ik,* the science of ethics, from Old French *ethique,* from Late Latin *ēthica* and Latin *ēthicē,* from Greek *ēthikē,* from *ēthikos,* ethical, from *ēthos,* moral custom.]

eth·i·cal (ĕth'ĭ-kəl) *adj.* **1.** Of, pertaining to, or dealing with ethics: *an ethical dilemma.* **2.** In accordance with the accepted principles of right and wrong governing the conduct of a profession. **3.** Designating a medicinal preparation dispensed solely on a doctor's prescription. —See Synonyms at **moral. —eth·i·cal·ly** *adv.* **—eth·i·cal·ness, eth·i·cal·i·ty** (ĕth'ĭ-kăl'ə-tē) *n.*

eth·ics (ĕth'ĭks) *pl.n.* **1.** *Used with a singular verb.* **a.** The study of the general nature of morals and of the specific moral choices to be made by the individual in his relationship with others. Also called "moral philosophy." **b.** The moral sciences as a whole, including moral philosophy and customary, civil, and religious law. **2.** The rules or standards governing the conduct of the members of a profession: *medical ethics.* **3.** The moral quality of a course of action; propriety: *I question the ethics of his decision.*

E·thi·op (ē'thē-ŏp') *n.* Also **E·thi·ope** (-ōp'). *Archaic.* An Ethiopian. [Latin *Aethiops,* from Greek *Aithiops,* "burnt face" : *aithein,* to burn + *ōps,* face.]

E·thi·o·pi·a (ē'thē-ō'pē-ə). Formerly **Abyssinia.** Country in eastern Africa. An ancient kingdom, it converted to Christianity in the 4th century A.D. In 1974, following widespread famine, Emperor Haile Selassie was deposed by a Communist military junta, and the crown was abolished (1975). The annexation of the province of Eritrea (1962) was followed by civil war. In the 1980's the country suffered drought and warfare. Area, 1,221,900 square kilometers (471,653 square miles). Population, 49,200,000. Capital, Addis Ababa.

E·thi·o·pi·an (ē'thē-ō'pē-ən) *adj.* **1.** Of or pertaining to Ethiopia, its languages, or its people. **2.** *Ecology.* Of or designating the zoogeographic region that includes Africa south of the Sahara and most of Arabia. Also called "Ethiopian region." **3.** *Archaic.* Black African. *~n.* **1.** A native or inhabitant of Ethiopia. **2.** *Archaic.* A member of the ancient Greek classification of dark-skinned Africans from the lands beyond Egypt; a Negro.

E·thi·op·ic (ē'thē-ŏp'ĭk, -ō'pĭk) *n.* The Semitic language of ancient Ethiopia that is still used as a liturgical language in the Christian church in Ethiopia. Also called "Geez." **—E·thi·op·ic** *adj.*

eth·moid (ĕth'moid') *adj.* Also **eth·moid·al** (ĕth-moid'l). Of or designating a light spongy bone located between the eye sockets that forms part of the walls of the superior nasal cavity. *~n.* The ethmoid bone. [French *ethmoïde,* from Old French, from Greek *ēthmoeidēs,* perforated (the bone contains many perforations) : *ēthmos,* strainer, from *ēthein,* to strain, to sift + -OID.]

eth·narch (ĕth'närk') *n.* The ruler of a province or a people. [Greek *ethnarkhēs,* ruler of the people : ETHN(O)- + *arkhos,* -ARCH.] **—eth·nar·chy** *n.*

eth·nic (ĕth'nĭk) *adj.* Also **eth·ni·cal** (-nĭ-kəl). **1. a.** Of, pertaining to, or designating a social group within a cultural and social system that claims or is accorded special status on the basis of complex, often variable traits including religious, linguistic, ancestral, or physical characteristics. **b.** Pertaining to the study and classification of such groups. **2. a.** Broadly, characteristic of a religious, ra-

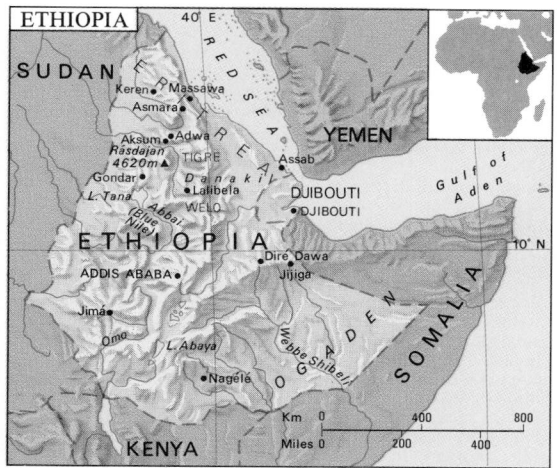

ETHIOPIA

cial, national, or cultural group. **b.** Characteristic of traditional folk styles of food, dress, or other customs. **c.** *Informal.* Quaint; picturesque. **3.** Of or pertaining to a people not Christian or Jewish; heathen.
~*n.* **ethnic.** *Informal.* A member of a particular ethnic group. [Late Latin *ethnicus,* heathen, foreign, from Greek *ethnikos,* of a national group, foreign, from *ethnos,* people, nation.] —**eth·ni·cal·ly** *adv.*

eth·nic·i·ty (ĕth-nĭs′ə-tē) *n.* **1.** The condition of belonging to a particular ethnic group. **2.** Ethnic pride.

ethnic minority *n.* An ethnic group living in a society where members of a different race or culture predominate.

ethno-, ethn– *prefix.* Indicates race, culture, or people; for example, **ethnocentrism.** [French, from Late Greek, from Greek *ethnos,* people.]

eth·no·bot·a·ny (ĕth′nō-bŏt′n-ē) *n.* The branch of botany relating to the use of plants in religion, folk medicine, and the like. —**eth·no·bot·a·nist** *n.*

eth·no·cen·trism (ĕth′nō-sĕn′trĭz′əm) *n.* **1.** Belief in the superiority of one's own ethnic group. **2.** Overriding concern with race. [ETHNO- + CENTR(O)- + -ISM.] —**eth·no·cen·tric** *adj.*

eth·nog·ra·phy (ĕth-nŏg′rə-fē) *n., pl.* **-phies. 1.** The descriptive anthropology of ethnic groups, especially technologically primitive societies. **2.** Ethnology. [French *ethnographie* : ETHNO- + -GRAPHY.] —**eth·nog·ra·pher** *n.* —**eth·no·graph·ic** (ĕth′nə-grăf′ĭk), **eth·no·graph·i·cal** (-ĭ-kəl) *adj.* —**eth·no·graph·i·cal·ly** *adv.*

eth·nol·o·gy (ĕth-nŏl′ə-jē) *n.* The anthropological study of socioeconomic systems and cultural heritage, especially of cultural origins and of factors influencing cultural growth and change, usually in technologically primitive societies. [ETHNO- + -LOGY.] —**eth·no·log·ic** (ĕth′nə-lŏj′ĭk), **eth·no·log·i·cal** (-ĭ-kəl) *adj.* —**eth·no·log·i·cal·ly** *adv.* —**eth·nol·o·gist** *n.*

eth·no·mu·si·col·o·gy (ĕth′nō-myōō′zĭ-kŏl′ə-jē) *n.* The study of the music and musical traditions of ethnic groups. —**eth·no·mu·si·col·o·gist** *n.*

etho–. Variant of **eth-.**

e·thol·o·gy (ĭ-thŏl′ə-jē, ē-thŏl′-) *n.* The scientific study of animal behavior in the natural environment. [Latin *ēthologia,* the art of depicting character, from Greek *ēthologia* : *ēthos,* ETHOS + -LOGY.] —**eth·o·log·i·cal** (ĕth′ə-lŏj′ĭ-kəl, ē′thə-) *adj.* —**e·thol·o·gist** *n.*

e·thos (ē′thŏs′) *n.* **1.** The disposition, character, or attitude peculiar to a specific people, culture, or group that distinguishes it from other peoples or groups; fundamental values or spirit; mores. **2.** The essential character of a period, movement, work of art, mode of expression, or the like: *the revolutionary ethos.* [New Latin, from Greek *ēthos,* custom, usage, trait.]

eth·ox·ide (ĭ-thŏk′sīd′) *n. Chemistry.* A salt formed by the reaction of a metal with alcohol, HOC₂H₅. Also called "ethylate." $\mathrm{HOC_2H_5}$

eth·ox·y·eth·ane (ĕth′ŏk′sē-ĕth′ān′) *n.* An organic compound, **ether** *(see).*

eth·yl (ĕth′əl) *n.* A univalent organic radical, $\mathrm{C_2H_5}$. [ETH(ER) + -YL.] —**eth·yl·ic** (ĕ-thĭl′ĭk) *adj.*

ethyl acetate *n.* A colorless, volatile, flammable liquid, $\mathrm{CH_3COOC_2H_5}$, used in perfumes, flavorings, lacquers, pharmaceuticals, and rayon, and as a general solvent.

ethyl alcohol *n.* **Alcohol** *(see).*

eth·yl·a·mine (ĕth′ə-lə-mēn′) *n.* A colorless, volatile liquid, $\mathrm{C_2H_5NH_2}$, used in petroleum refining, detergents, and organic synthesis.

eth·yl·ate (ĕth′ə-lāt′) *tr.v.* **-ated, -ating, -ates.** *Chemistry.* To introduce the ethyl group into (a compound).
~*n.* An ethoxide. [ETHYL + -ATE.] —**eth·yl·a·tion** *n.*

ethyl carbamate *n.* A chemical compound, **urethane** *(see).*

ethyl chloride *n.* A chemical compound, $\mathrm{C_2H_5Cl}$, a gas at ordinary temperatures and a colorless, volatile, flammable liquid when compressed, used as a solvent, refrigerant, and in the manufacture of tetraethyl lead.

eth·yl·ene (ĕth′ə-lēn′) *n.* **1.** A colorless, flammable gas, $\mathrm{C_2H_4}$, de-

rived from natural gas and petroleum and used as a source of many organic compounds, in welding and cutting metals, to color citrus fruits, and as an anesthetic. **2.** The bivalent organic radical $\mathrm{C_2H_4}$. Also called "ethene." [ETHYL + -ENE.]

ethylene glycol *n.* A colorless, syrupy alcohol, $\mathrm{C_2H_6O_2}$, used as an antifreeze in cooling and heating systems. Also called "ethanediol."

ethyl ether *n. Chemistry.* **Ether** *(see).*

ethyl mercaptan *n. Chemistry.* See **mercaptan.**

eth·yne (ē′thīn′, ĕth′īn′) *n.* A gaseous hydrocarbon, **acetylene** *(see).*

e·ti·o·late (ē′tē-ə-lāt′) *v.* **-lated, -lating, -lates.** —*tr.* **1.** To cause (a plant) to develop without normal green coloring by preventing exposure to sunlight; blanch; whiten. **2.** To cause (a person) to lose healthy coloring and become weak. **3.** To cause to lose vigor, body, force, or the like. —*intr.* **1.** To become blanched or whitened and abnormally elongated, as when grown without sunlight. **2.** To lose healthy coloring and become weak. [French *étioler,* from *eteule,* a stalk, from Old French *estuble,* from Latin *stipula,* stalk, straw, stubble.] —**e·ti·o·la·tion** *n.*

e·ti·ol·o·gy, ae·ti·ol·o·gy (ē′tē-ŏl′ə-jē) *n.* **1.** The study of causes or origins. **2.** The branch of medicine that deals with the causes of disease. **3. a.** The assignment of a cause, origin, or reason for something. **b.** The cause of a disease or disorder as determined by medical diagnosis. [Late Latin *aetiologia,* from Greek *aitiologia,* a giving the cause of : *aita,* responsibility, cause + -LOGY.] —**e·ti·o·log·ic** (ē′tē-ə-lŏj′ĭk), **e·ti·o·log·i·cal** (-ĭ-kəl) *adj.* —**e·ti·o·log·i·cal·ly** *adv.* —**e·ti·ol·o·gist** *n.*

et·i·quette (ĕt′ə-kĕt′, -kĭt) *n.* A code of behavior prescribed or conventionally accepted as correct or polite, as at court, among a profession, or in society at large. [French *etiquette,* prescribed routine, label, ticket, from Old French *estiqu(i)er,* to attach, from Middle Dutch *steken.*]
Synonyms: *decorum, propriety, protocol.*

Et·na (ĕt′nə). Europe's highest active volcano (3,340 meters; 10,958 feet), near the east coast of Sicily. It is first known to have erupted in 475 B.C.

E·ton (ē′tn). Town in Buckinghamshire on the Thames River. It is the home of Britain's most famous public school, Eton College, founded by King Henry VI in 1440.

Eton collar *n.* A broad, stiff white collar worn overlapping the lapels of a jacket.

Eton jacket *n.* A waist-length jacket that has wide lapels and is cut square at the hips.

E·to·sha Game Park (ē-tō′shə). Largest game reserve in southern Africa. Lying in northwest Namibia, it covers 22,270 square kilometers (8,600 square miles) and includes Etosha Pan, a dried-up salt lake.

é·tri·er (ā′trē-ā′) *n.* A short rope ladder used in mountaineering. [French, "stirrup."]

E·tru·ri·a (ĭ-trŏŏr′ē-ə). Ancient country in Italy, now Tuscany and part of Umbria. It was the center of the civilization of the Etruscans, but by the end of the 5th century B.C. it succumbed to Rome.

E·tru·ri·an (ĭ-trŏŏr′ē-ən) *n.* Etruscan. —**E·tru·ri·an** *adj.*

E·trus·can (ĭ-trŭs′kən) *adj.* Of, pertaining to, or characteristic of Etruria, its inhabitants, or their language or culture.
~*n.* **1.** A person who lived in ancient Etruria. **2.** The pre-Roman, now extinct language of the Etruscans, of undetermined linguistic affiliation. See feature, next page.

et seq. and the following. [Latin *et sequens, et sequentia.*]

–ette *suffix.* Indicates: **1.** Small or diminutive; for example, **kitchenette. 2.** An imitation of or a substitute for; for example, **leatherette. 3.** Female or feminine; for example, **usherette.** [Middle English *-ette,* from Old French, feminine of -ET.]

e·tude (ā′tōōd′, ā′tyōōd′, ā-tüd′) *n.* **1.** A piece of music composed as an exercise for the development of a given point of technique. **2.** A composition embodying some point of technique but intended for performance. [French *étude,* study, from Old French *estudie,* STUDY.]

é·tui (ā-twē′) *n., pl.* **étuis** (ā-twēz′). A case for holding small articles, such as needles or toiletries. [French, from Old French *estui,* container, prison, from *estuier,* to shut up, guard, probably from Vulgar Latin *estudiāre* (unattested), to take care of, from Latin *studium,* STUDY.]

et·y·mo·log·i·cal (ĕt′ə-mə-lŏj′ĭ-kəl) *adj.* Also **et·y·mo·log·ic** (-lŏj′ĭk). *Abbr.* **etym., etymol.** Of or pertaining to etymology, or based upon the principles of etymology. —**et·y·mo·log·i·cal·ly** *adv.*

et·y·mol·o·gist (ĕt′ə-mŏl′ə-jĭst) *n.* A specialist in the principles of etymology and their application.

et·y·mol·o·gize (ĕt′ə-mŏl′ə-jīz′) *v.* **-gized, -gizing, -gizes.** —*tr.* To trace and state the etymology of (a word or words). —*intr.* To give or suggest the etymology of a word or words.

et·y·mol·o·gy (ĕt′ə-mŏl′ə-jē) *n., pl.* **-gies.** *Abbr.* **etym., etymol. 1.** The origin and historical development of a word or word part, as evidenced by study of its basic elements, earliest known use, and changes in form and meaning; semantic derivation and evolution. **2.** An account of the history of a specific word. **3.** The branch of linguistics that studies the derivation of words. [Learned respelling of Middle English *ethimologie,* from Old French, from Medieval Latin *ethimologia,* from Latin *etymologia,* from Greek *etumologiā* : *etumon,* ETYMON + -LOGY.]

et·y·mon (ĕt′ĭ-mŏn′) *n., pl.* **-mons** or **-ma** (-mə). **1.** The earlier form of a word or word part in the same language or in an ancestor language. **2.** A word or morpheme from which compounds and derivatives are formed. **3.** A foreign word from which a particular

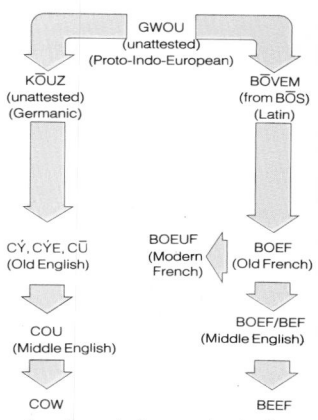

etymology *A diagram showing how the words "cow" and "beef" developed from a common origin. Major changes only are shown; a full etymological account would include how the words were used and how the meanings changed in the various languages.*

loan word is derived. [Latin, origin of a word, from Greek *etumon,* true sense of a word, etymology, from *etumos,* true, real.]

Eu The symbol for the element europium.

eu– *prefix.* Indicates: **1.** Well, pleasant, or beneficial; for example, **euphony. 2.** Derivative of a specified substance; for example, **eucaine. 3.** True; truly so; for example, **eubacteria.** [Middle English *eu-,* from Latin, from Greek, from *eus,* good.]

Etruscan

THE BURIED TREASURE OF THE ETRUSCANS
The civilization that flourished in Italy before the Romans

The Etruscans, who dominated central Italy from the 8th to the 5th century B.C., are known from archaeological remains and the writings of Roman historians. More than 8,000 inscriptions exist in the Etruscan language. Most are personal names and not all have been fully deciphered, but the alphabet is of Greek derivation.

It was trade with Greece as well as their own industry, in metalware for example, that made the Etruscans wealthy and powerful. Their navy was one of the strongest in the Mediterranean.

The Etruscan state (Etruria) was not close-knit but a loose association of city settlements. The people lived in brick houses with stone foundations, and they built extensive underground tombs whose walls bore colorful paintings. Oriental motifs in the paintings may have come from Greece. The tombs contained fine gray pottery (called Bucchero) and metalwork. Etruscan metalwork was widely exported.

The Etruscans' power declined from the 4th century B.C. as the Romans overcame them.

POWER BASE *The core of Etruria was central Italy (blue on the map), but at their peak, about 600 B.C., the Etruscans dominated most of the peninsula.*

BRONZE AMAZON *The lid of an Etruscan burial chest (left) made about 500 B.C. bears a bronze statuette of a mounted Amazon—one of the race of women warriors from Asia Minor whose deeds are legendary.*

FUNERAL WRESTLING *A wall painting found in a tomb at Tarquinia shows professional wrestlers about to fight for a prize of gold and silver bowls during funeral games. These were held after prominent Etruscans had died. The combatants are naked, in the style of Greek wrestlers.*

---

eu·bac·te·ri·a (yōō′băk-tîr′ē-ə) *pl.n.* A large and diverse group of bacteria characterized by rigid cell walls; true bacteria.

Eu·boe·a (yōō-bē′ə). *Modern Greek* **Év·voia** (ĕv′yä). Island in the Aegean Sea. The largest of the Greek islands after Crete, it produces sheep, goats, cattle, grapes, olives, and wheat.

eu·caine (yōō-kān′) *n.* A crystalline substance, $C_{15}H_{21}NO_2$, formerly used as a local anesthetic. [EU- + -CAINE.]

eu·ca·lyp·tol (yōō′kə-lĭp′tŏl′, -tōl′) *n.* Also **eu·ca·lyp·tole** (-tōl′). A colorless oily liquid, $C_{10}H_{18}O$, derived from eucalyptus oil and used in pharmaceuticals, flavoring, and perfumery. Also called "cineol." [EUCALYPT(US) + -OL.]

eu·ca·lyp·tus (yōō′kə-lĭp′təs) *n., pl.* **-tuses** or **-ti** (-tī′) Any of numerous tall trees of the genus *Eucalyptus,* mostly native to Australia, cultivated for their aromatic leaves that yield eucalyptus oil, for their wood valued as timber, and for ornament. [New Latin : EU- + Greek *kaluptos,* covered (from the flower, which is covered before it opens), from *kaluptein,* to cover, hide.]

eucalyptus oil *n.* An oil derived from the leaves of the eucalyptus, used as a flavoring and as an expectorant and antiseptic.

eu·car·y·ote, eu·kar·y·ote (yōō-kăr′ē-ōt′, -ət) *n. Biology.* An organism in which the genetic material is enclosed by a membrane to form a nucleus. Eucaryotes include all organisms except bacteria, blue-green algae, and viruses. Compare **procaryote.** [EU- + -*karyote,* irregularly from Greek *karuon,* kernel, nucleus. See KARYO-.] —**eu·car·y·ot·ic** (yōō-kăr′ē-ōt′ĭk) *adj.*

Eu·cha·rist (yōō′kər-ĭst) *n.* **1. a.** The Christian sacrament instituted at the Last Supper in which bread and wine are consecrated and then eaten and drunk as a memorial of Christ's death. Also called "Communion," "Holy Communion." **b.** The consecrated elements of bread and wine used in this sacrament. **2.** *Christian Science.* Spiritual communion with God. [Middle English *eukarist,* from Old French *eucariste,* from Late Latin *eucharistia,* from Greek *eukharistia,* gratitude, from *eukharistos,* grateful : *eu-,* well, good + *kharizesthai,* to show favor, from *kharis,* favor, grace.] —**Eu·cha·ris·tic** (yōō′kə-rĭs′tĭk), **Eu·cha·ris·ti·cal** (-tĭ-kəl) *adj.*

eu·chre (yōō′kər) *n.* **1.** A card game in which each player is dealt five cards and the player making the trump is required to take at least three tricks to win. **2.** The action of euchring an opponent. ~*tr.v.* **euchred, -chring, -chres. 1.** To prevent (an opponent) from taking three tricks in euchre. **2.** *Informal.* To deceive by sly or underhand means; cheat: *euchred them out of their savings.* [Origin unknown.]

eu·chro·ma·tin (yōō-krō′mə-tĭn) *n.* The chromosome material that stains most deeply with basic dyes when the cell is dividing and represents the major genes involved in protein synthesis. Compare **heterochromatin.**

Eu·clid (yōō′klĭd) (fl. 300 B.C.). Greek mathematician. His most important contribution to mathematics was the use of the deductive principles of logic as the basis of his geometry, deriving statements from clearly defined axioms.

Eu·clid·e·an, Eu·clid·i·an (yōō-klĭd′ē-ən) *adj.* Of or pertaining to Euclid's geometric principles.

Euclidean algorithm *n.* A method of finding the greatest common divisor of two numbers by dividing one by the other, the second by the remainder, the remainder by the second remainder, and so on until an exact division is reached, when the last divisor is the greatest common divisor of the two numbers.

Euclidean geometry *n.* Geometry based on the postulates of Euclid; especially, the parallel postulate that for a point outside a line only one other line can be drawn through the point parallel to the first line.

eu·de·mon, eu·dae·mon (yōō-dē′mən) *n.* A benevolent spirit.

eu·de·mo·ni·a, eu·dae·mo·ni·a (yōō′də-mō′nē-ə, -mōn′yə) *n.* **1.** Happiness or well-being. **2.** In Aristotelian philosophy, an active, rational life. [Greek *eudaimonia,* from *eudaimōn,* lucky, with a good spirit : *eu-,* good + *daimōn,* spirit.]

eu·de·mon·ism, eu·dae·mon·ism (yōō-dē′mə-nĭz′əm) *n.* A system of ethics that evaluates the morality of actions in terms of their capacity to produce happiness. —**eu·de·mon·ist** *n.* —**eu·de·mon·is·tic** (yōō-dē′mə-nĭs′tĭk), **eu·de·mon·is·ti·cal** *adj.*

eu·di·om·e·ter (yōō′dē-ŏm′ə-tər) *n. Chemistry.* A graduated glass apparatus used to study gas reactions by volume changes. [From Greek *eudios,* "clear-skied" : EU- + *dios,* genitive of *Zeus,* god of the heavens + METER; the apparatus was originally used to measure the amount of oxygen present in the air, believed to be greater in clear weather.] —**eu·di·o·met·ric** (yōō′dē-ə-mĕt′rĭk), **eu·di·o·met·ri·cal** *adj.* —**eu·di·om·e·try** *n.*

eu·gen·ic (yōō-jĕn′ĭk) *adj.* **1.** Of or pertaining to eugenics. **2.** Pertaining or adapted to the production of good offspring. —**eu·gen·i·cal·ly** *adv.*

eu·gen·i·cist (yōō-jĕn′ə-sĭst) *n.* Also **eu·gen·ist** (yōō-jĕ′nĭst, yōō′jə-nĭst). An advocate of or specialist in eugenics.

eu·gen·ics (yōō-jĕn′ĭks) *n. Used with a singular verb.* The study of the hereditary improvement of the human race by controlled selective breeding. Compare **euthenics.** [Greek *eugenēs,* well-born : EU- + -GEN.]

Eu·gé·nie (yōō′zhä-nē′) (1826–1920). French empress, born in Spain and the consort of Napoleon III from her marriage to him in 1853 until his overthrow in 1870. She acted as regent during Napoleon's absences from France and is believed to have had much influence on events that led to the Franco-Prussian War of 1870. She fled to England after Napoleon's capture at Sedan in September, 1870.

eu·ge·nol (yōō'jə-nôl', -nōl') *n.* A colorless aromatic oil, $C_{10}H_{12}O_2$, the chief constituent of oil of cloves. [New Latin *Eugenia*, genus of the clove, after *Eugene*, Prince of Savoy (1633–1736) + -OL.]

eu·gle·na (yōō-glē'nə) *n.* Any of various minute unicellular freshwater organisms of the genus *Euglena*, characterized by the presence of chlorophyll, a reddish eyespot, and a single anterior flagellum. [New Latin : EU- + Greek *glēnē*, eyeball.]

eu·glob·u·lin (yōō-glŏb'yə-lĭn) *n.* A globulin that is soluble in dilute salt solutions and insoluble in distilled water.

eu·he·mer·ism (yōō-hē'mə-rĭz'əm, -hĕm'ə-rĭz'əm) *n.* **1.** A theory attributing the origin of the gods to the deification of historical heroes. **2.** A theory linking mythology or folklore with real persons or events. [After *Euhemerus* (c. 300 B.C.), Greek philosopher.] —**eu·he·mer·ist** *n.* —**eu·he·mer·is·tic** (yōō-hē'mə-rĭs'tĭk, yōō-hĕm'ə-) *adj.* —**eu·he·mer·is·ti·cal·ly** *adv.*

eu·he·mer·ize (yōō-hē'mə-rĭz', -hĕm'ə-rĭz') *tr.v.* **-ized, -izing, -izes.** To explain or interpret (myths) euhemeristically.

eu·la·chon (yōō'lə-kŏn') *n., pl.* **-chons** or collectively **eulachon.** The **candlefish** (*see*). [Chinook *ulâkân.*]

Eu·ler (oi'lər), **Leonhard** (1707–83). Swiss mathematician. His fame rests mainly on his pioneering development of the methods of calculus and on the differential equation named after him.

Euler's formula *n. Mathematics.* **1.** The formula $v + f - e = 2$ relating the numbers of vertices *(v),* faces *(f),* and edges *(e)* of a polyhedron. **2.** The formula $e^{i\theta} = cos\theta + i\, sin\theta$ for complex numbers.

eu·lo·gi·a (yōō-lō'jē-ə, -jə) *n.* Blessed bread distributed to the congregation after the liturgy in the Greek Orthodox Church. [Greek, "blessing."]

eu·lo·gize (yōō'lə-jīz') *tr.v.* **-gized, -gizing, -gizes. 1.** To write or deliver a eulogy about or for. **2.** To praise highly; extol. —**eu·lo·gist, eu·lo·giz·er** *n.*

eu·lo·gy (yōō'lə-jē) *n., pl.* **-gies. 1.** A public speech or written tribute extolling the virtues of a person or thing; especially, an oration honoring one recently deceased. **2.** Great praise or commendation. [Middle English *euloge*, from Medieval Latin *eulogium*, probably variant of *eulogia*, from Greek, praise, eulogy : EU- + -LOGY.] —**eu·lo·gis·tic** (yōō'lə-jĭs'tĭk) *adj.*

Eu·men·i·des (yōō-mĕn'ə-dēz') *pl.n. Greek Mythology.* The **Furies** *(see).* [Latin, from Greek, "well-minded (ones)," euphemism for the Furies, from *eumenēs*, kindly, well-disposed : *eu-*, well + *menos*, spirit.]

eu·nuch (yōō'nək) *n.* **1.** A castrated man; especially, one of those who were employed as harem attendants or functionaries in certain Oriental courts and under the Roman emperors. **2.** An ineffectual or powerless man: *an artistic eunuch.* [Middle English *eunuke,* from Latin *eunūchus,* from Greek *eunoukhos,* "bed-watcher," eunuch : *eunē†,* bed + *ekhein,* to have, to hold.]

eu·on·y·mus (yōō-ŏn'ə-məs) *n.* Any of various trees, shrubs, or vines of the genus *Euonymus,* many of which are cultivated for their decorative foliage or fruits. [New Latin, from Latin *euōnymus,* spindle, tree, from Greek *euōnumos,* of good name : *eu-,* good + *onoma,* name.]

eu·pat·rid (yōō-păt'rĭd, -pā'trĭd) *n., pl.* **-ridae** (-păt'rĭ-dē', -pā'trĭ-dē') or **-rids.** A member of the hereditary aristocracy of ancient Athens. [Greek *eupatridēs,* of noble family : *eu-,* well + *patēr* (stem *patr-*), father + *-idēs,* patronymic suffix.] —**eu·pat·rid** *adj.*

eu·pep·si·a (yōō-pĕp'sē-ə, -shə) *n.* Good digestion. [New Latin, from Greek, from *eupeptos,* EUPEPTIC.]

eu·pep·tic (yōō-pĕp'tĭk) *adj.* **1.** Pertaining to or having good digestion. **2.** Conducive to digestion. **3.** Cheerful. [Greek *eupeptos,* having good digestion : *eu-,* well + *peptein,* to digest, cook.] —**eu·pep·ti·cal·ly** *adv.*

eu·phau·si·id (yōō-fô'zē-ĭd) *n.* Any small, shrimplike crustacean of the order Euphausiacea. See **krill.**

eu·phe·mism (yōō'fə-mĭz'əm) *n.* **1.** The substitution of an inoffensive term for one considered offensively explicit. **2.** The term thus substituted: *"Euphemisms such as 'slumber room' . . . abound in the funeral business"* (Jessica Mitford). [Greek *euphēmismos,* from *euphēmizein,* to speak with good words, from *euphēmia,* use of good words : *eu-,* good + *phēmē,* speech, saying.] —**eu·phe·mist** *n.* —**eu·phe·mis·tic** (yōō'fə-mĭs'tĭk) *adj.* —**eu·phe·mis·ti·cal·ly** *adv.*

eu·phe·mize (yōō'fə-mīz') *v.* **-mized, -mizing, -mizes.** —*tr.* To speak of or refer to euphemistically. —*intr.* To speak with euphemisms.

eu·pho·ni·ous (yōō-fō'nē-əs) *adj.* Characterized by euphony; agreeable to the ear. —**eu·pho·ni·ous·ly** *adv.*

eu·pho·ni·um (yōō-fō'nē-əm) *n.* A brass wind instrument similar to the tuba but having a somewhat higher pitch and a mellower sound. [Greek *euphōnos,* sweet-voiced. See **euphony.**]

eu·pho·nize (yōō'fə-nīz') *tr.v.* **-nized, -nizing, -nizes.** To make euphonious. —**eu·pho·ni·za·tion** *n.*

eu·pho·ny (yōō'fə-nē) *n., pl.* **-nies. 1.** Agreeable sound, especially in the phonetic quality of words. **2.** *Phonetics.* The tendency to change speech sounds for the sake of easier pronunciation. [French *euphonie,* from Late Latin *euphōnia,* from Greek, from *euphōnos,* sweet-voiced, euphonious : *eu-,* good + *phōnē,* sound.] —**eu·phon·ic** (yōō-fŏn'ĭk) *adj.*

eu·phor·bi·a (yōō-fôr'bē-ə) *n.* A plant of the genus *Euphorbia,* which includes the spurges and poinsettia. [New Latin, from Latin *euphorbea,* from *Euphorbus,* Greek physician of the 1st century A.D.]

eu·pho·ri·a (yōō-fôr'ē-ə, -fōr'ē-ə) *n.* **1.** A feeling of great happiness or well-being; bliss. **2.** *Psychiatry.* An exaggerated sense of well-being in pathological cases involving sympathetic delusions. —See Synonyms at **ecstasy.** [New Latin, from Greek, from *euphoros,* easy to bear, well-borne : *eu-,* well + *pherein,* to bear.] —**eu·phor·ic** (yōō-fôr'ĭk, -fōr'ĭk) *adj.*

eu·pho·ri·ant (yōō-fôr'ē-ənt, -fōr'ē-ənt) *adj.* Tending to produce euphoria.
~*n.* An agent that produces euphoria.

eu·phot·ic (yōō-fŏt'ĭk, -fō'tĭk) *adj.* Pertaining to, designating, or characterizing the uppermost layer of a body of water that receives sufficient light for photosynthesis and the growth of green plants. [EU- + PHOTIC.]

eu·phra·sy (yōō'frə-sē) *n. Archaic.* A plant of the genus *Euphrasia;* eyebright. [Middle English *eufrasie,* from Medieval Latin *eufrasia,* from Greek *euphrasia,* good cheer, from *euphrainein,* to cheer, gladden : *eu-,* good + *phrēn,* mind.]

Eu·phra·tes (yōō-frā'tēz). River in southwestern Asia, formed by the confluence of the Murad and Kara rivers and flowing for 2,740 kilometers (1,700 miles) from central Turkey through Syria into Iraq, where it joins with the Tigris River to form the Shatt al Arab. The Euphrates is too shallow for heavy craft.

eu·phroe (yōō'frō') *n.* **1.** *Nautical.* A perforated batten through which the lines of a crowfoot are passed to suspend an awning. **2.** A piece of wood having holes through which a tent rope, for example, is passed, and by means of which tension on the rope can be adjusted. [Dutch *juffrouw,* maiden, euphroe, from Middle Dutch *joncfrouwe.*]

Eu·phros·y·ne (yōō-frŏz'ə-nē). *Greek Mythology.* One of the three **Graces** *(see.)* [Latin *Euphrosynē,* from Greek *Euphrosunē,* "mirth," from *euphrōn,* of good mind, cheerful : *eu-,* good + *phrēn,* mind.]

eu·phu·ism (yōō'fyōō-ĭz'əm) *n.* **1.** An affectedly elegant style of speech or writing used by imitators of John Lyly in the late 16th and early 17th centuries, characterized by elaborate alliteration, antitheses, and similes. **2.** Broadly, affected elegance of language: *"Among his contemporaries, Willie's euphuisms only raised a laugh"* (Aldous Huxley). [After *Euphues,* a character in two works by John Lyly, from Greek *euphuēs,* shapely, well-grown : *eu-,* well + *phuein,* to grow, to bring forth.] —**eu·phu·ist** *n.* —**eu·phu·is·tic** (yōō'fyōō-ĭs'tĭk) *adj.* —**eu·phu·is·ti·cal·ly** *adv.*

eu·plas·tic (yōō-plăs'tĭk) *adj.* Healing readily.

eu·ploid (yōō'ploid') *n.* An organism or cell whose chromosome number is an exact multiple of the haploid number characteristic of the species. [EU- + (HA)PLOID.] —**eu·ploid** *adj.* —**eu·ploi·dy** *n.*

eup·ne·a, eup·noe·a (yōōp-nē'ə) *n.* Normal, unlabored breathing. [New Latin, from Greek *eupnoia,* from *eupnoos,* breathing well : *eu-,* good + *pnoē, pnoiē,* a breathing, from *pnein,* to breathe.]

Eur. Europe; European.

Eu·rail·pass (yōō-rāl'păs', -päs') *n.* A season ticket, sold only outside Europe, allowing extended rail travel in most countries of continental western Europe.

Eur·a·sia (yōō-rā'zhə). The landmass that comprises the continents of Europe and Asia.

Eur·a·sian (yōō-rā'zhən, -shən) *adj.* **1.** Of, pertaining to, or originating in Eurasia. **2.** Of mixed European and Asian ancestry. ~*n.* A person of mixed European and Asian ancestry.

Eur·at·om, EUR·AT·OM (yōō-răt'əm) *n.* The European Atomic Energy Commission.

eu·re·ka (yōō-rē'kə) *interj.* Used to express triumph upon finding or discovering something. [Greek *heurēka,* "I have found (it)" (see **Archimedes**), perfect indicative of *heuriskein,* to find.]

eurhythmic. Variant of **eurythmic.**

eurhythmics. Variant of **eurythmics.**

eurhythmy. Variant of **eurythmy.**

Eu·rip·i·des (yōō-rĭp'ĭ-dēz') (c. 480–406 B.C.). Greek dramatist who ranks with Sophocles and Aeschylus as one of the great writers of classical tragedy. He wrote over 90 plays; among those that survive are *Alcestis, Hippolytus, The Trojan Women, Electra, Medea,* and *Iphigenia in Tauris.*

eu·ri·pus (yōō-rī'pəs) *n., pl.* **-pi** (-pī'). A sea channel characterized by turbulent and unpredictable currents in either direction. [Latin, from Greek *euripos,* strait, place where the current is violent : *eu-,* well (euphemistic) + *ripē,* rush, force, from *rīptein,* to throw.]

eu·ro (yōō'rō) *n., pl.* **-ros.** A kangaroo, the **wallaroo** *(see).* [Native word in Australia.]

Euro– *prefix.* Indicates: **1.** Europe, especially Western Europe, or European; for example, **Eurodollar. 2.** The European Economic Community; for example, **Eurocrat.**

Eu·ro·bond (yōō'rō-bŏnd') *n.* A bond of a United States corporation issued in Europe. [EURO- + BOND.]

Eu·ro·com·mu·nism (yōō'rō-kŏm'yə-nĭz'əm). *n.* The variety of Communist theory and practice favored by most of the Communist parties in Western Europe, characterized by a more liberal outlook than and nonalignment with the Communist parties of the former Eastern bloc of Europe and Asia. —**Eu·ro·com·mu·nist** *n.* & *adj.*

Eu·ro·crat (yōō'rə-krăt', yōō'rō-) *n. Informal.* A senior official in the administration of the European Economic Community. Sometimes used derogatorily. [EURO- + (BUREAU)CRAT.]

Eu·ro·cur·ren·cy (yōō'rō-kûr'ən-sē) *n., pl.* **-cies.** Any of various national currencies used for trade and exchange dealings in Europe and elsewhere.

Eu·ro·dol·lar (yōō'rō-dŏl'ər) *n.* A United States dollar on deposit with a bank abroad, especially in Europe.

Eu·ro·mar·ket (yōō'rō-mär'kĭt) *n.* Also **Eu·ro·mart** (-märt'). The European Economic Community.

eucalyptus An evergreen tree native to Australia. There are over 500 species of eucalyptus, some of which produce an oil used in cough medicines. The cider gum tree, Eucalyptus gunnii (above), can grow to 30 meters (100 feet).

Eu·ro·pa (yoō-rō′pə). *Greek Mythology.* A Phoenician princess abducted to Crete by Zeus, in the guise of a white bull.

Eu·rope (yoōr′əp). *Abbr.* **Eur.** The world's second-smallest major land area, after Oceania. It has only 7 percent of the globe's land, but with 15 percent of the world's people it is the second most populous continent after Asia. Europe includes part of the world's largest country, Russia, and also its smallest sovereign state, the Vatican City. After World War II, the U.S.S.R. dominated Eastern Europe, also known as the Eastern, or Communist, Bloc, where the countries had centrally planned economies. The nations of Western Europe, with capitalist or mixed economies, have largely looked to the United States for military alliance. Area, 10,498,000 square kilometers (4,053,000 square miles), including Russia west of the Ural Mts.

Eu·ro·pe·an (yoōr′ə-pē′ən) *adj. Abbr.* **Eur.** **1.** Of, pertaining to, or derived from the continent of Europe, its peoples, cultures, or languages. **2.** Indigenous to or native to Europe. **3.** Of or pertaining to the European Economic Community.
~*n.* **1.** A native or inhabitant of Europe. **2.** One of European ancestry. **3.** A citizen of a country belonging to the European Economic Community, especially with reference to the extent of the person's support for the Community: *good Europeans.* **4.** *South African.* A white native of South Africa.

European Communities *pl.n.* A union of three communities that share a common administrative organization: the European Coal and Steel Community, the European Economic Community, and the European Atomic Energy Commission (Euratom).

European Court of Justice *n.* A court in Luxembourg that deals with cases involving the laws of the European Economic Community.

European Economic Community *n. Abbr.* **EEC** An association of member countries (Belgium, France, Federal Republic of Germany, Luxembourg, the Netherlands, and Italy, founder members; subsequently joined by the United Kingdom, the Republic of Ireland, Denmark, Greece, Spain, and Portugal). Founded by the Treaty of Rome (1957) as a customs union and to promote economic and political cooperation. Also called "European Community," "Common Market." See feature page 539.

Eu·ro·pe·an·ism (yoōr′ə-pē′ə-nĭz′əm) *n.* **1.** A political movement promoting a policy of unity among European countries, especially the European Economic Community. **2.** Support for such a policy; a favorable attitude toward the European Economic Community. **—Eu·ro·pe·an·ist** *n.*

Eu·ro·pe·an·ize (yoōr′ə-pē′ə-nīz′) *tr.v.* **-ized, -izing, -izes. 1.** To make European in culture, political institutions, or customs. **2.** To introduce the institutions and regulations of the European Economic Community into (a country). **—Eu·ro·pe·an·i·za·tion** (yoōr′-ə-pē′ə-nə-zā′shən) *n.*

European Parliament *n.* The legislative assembly of the European Economic Community.

European plan *n.* A system of hotel tariffs in which a guest pays for his room and services separately from his payment for meals. Compare **American plan.**

European Recovery Program *n.* An American program to provide economic aid to European nations following World War II that was initiated by General George C. Marshall.

eu·ro·pi·um (yoō-rō′pē-əm) *n. Symbol* **Eu** A silvery-white, soft rare-earth element occurring in monazite and bastnaesite. It is used as a laser dopant, phosphor, and in research to absorb neutrons. Atomic number 63, atomic weight 151.96, melting point 826°C, boiling point 1,439°C, specific gravity 5.259, valences 2, 3. [New Latin, from EUROPE.]

Eu·ro·vi·sion (yoōr′ə-vĭzh′ən) *n.* The television network of the European Broadcasting Union, through which news and programs are exchanged or relayed.

Eu·rus (yoōr′əs). *Greek Mythology.* The god of the east or southeast wind. [Latin, from Greek *Euros*, possibly from *heuein*, to burn, to singe.]

eury– *prefix.* Indicates wide or broad; for example, **eurypterid.** [New Latin, from Greek *euru-*, from *eurus*, wide.]

Eu·ry·a·le (yoō-rī′ə-lē). *Greek Mythology.* One of the three Gorgons.

Eu·ryd·i·ce (yoō-rĭd′ə-sē). *Greek Mythology.* The wife of Orpheus, who was permitted by Pluto to follow her husband out of Hades provided that he refrain from looking back at her; Orpheus did look back, and Eurydice was doomed to return to the dead. [Latin, from Greek *Eurudikē*, "wide justice" : *euru-*, EURY- + *dikē*, justice, custom, law.]

eu·ry·ha·line (yoōr′ə-hā′lĭn′, -hăl′ĭn′) *adj.* Able to tolerate wide variations in salt concentration. Said of aquatic animals such as eels. Compare **stenohaline.**

eu·ryp·ter·id (yoō-rĭp′tər-ĭd) *n.* Any of various large, extinct aquatic arthropods of the order Eurypterida, existing from the Ordovician to the Permian period. [New Latin *Eurypterida*, from *Eurypterus* (genus) : EURY- + -PTEROUS.]

eu·ry·ther·mal (yoōr′ə-thûr′məl) *adj.* Also **eu·ry·ther·mic** (-mĭk), **eu·ry·ther·mous** (-məs). Adaptable to a wide range of temperatures. Said of an organism.

eu·ryth·mic, eu·rhyth·mic (yoō-rĭth′mĭk) *adj.* **1.** Harmonious in rhythm or proportions. **2.** Of or pertaining to eurythmics.

eu·ryth·mics, eu·rhyth·mics (yoō-rĭth′mĭks) *n. Used with a singular verb.* The choreographic art of interpreting music through rhythmical, free-style, graceful movement of the body.

eu·ryth·my, eu·rhyth·my (yoō-rĭth′mē) *n.* **1.** Harmony of propor-

tions in architecture. **2.** Rhythmical or graceful movements. **3.** A system of rhythmical body movements in harmony with the rhythm of the spoken word, used in a form of dance training.

eu·ry·top·ic (yoōr′ə-tŏp′ĭk) *adj.* Capable of existing in a wide range of environmental conditions. Said of plant and animal species.

eu·spo·ran·gi·ate (yoō′spə-răn′jē-ĭt, -āt′) *adj.* Of or designating ferns in which the sporangium develops from a group of cells. Compare **leptosporangiate.**

Eu·sta·chi·an tube (yoō-stā′shən, -shē-ən, -stā′kē-ən) *n.* A bony and cartilaginous tube that connects the tympanic cavity with the nasal part of the pharynx and equalizes pressure on either side of the eardrum. [After Bartolommeo *Eustachio* (c. 1524–74), Italian anatomist.]

eu·stat·ic (yoō-stăt′ĭk) *adj.* Of or pertaining to overall changes in sea level, as produced by large-scale geologic changes such as movement of the ocean floor or melting of ice caps.

eu·tec·tic (yoō-tĕk′tĭk) *adj.* **1.** Of, pertaining to, or formed at the lowest possible temperature of solidification for any mixture of specific constituents. Said especially of alloys. **2.** Exhibiting the constitution or properties of a solid so formed.
~*n.* **1.** A eutectic mixture, solution, or alloy. **2.** The temperature at which a eutectic forms. [Greek *eutēktos,* easily melted : *eu-,* well + *tēktos,* melted, from *tēkein,* to melt.]

Eu·ter·pe (yoō-tûr′pē). *Greek Mythology.* The Muse of lyric poetry and music.

eu·tha·na·sia (yoō′thə-nā′zhə, -zhē-ə) *n.* The action of inducing the painless death of a person from motives of compassion. Also called "mercy killing." [Greek : *eu-,* good + *thanatos,* death.]

eu·then·ics (yoō-thĕn′ĭks) *n. Used with a singular verb.* The study of the improvement of human functioning and well-being by adjustment of environment. Compare **eugenics.** [Greek *euthenein,* to flourish, thrive.]

eu·the·ri·an (yoō-thîr′ē-ən) *adj.* Of, pertaining to, or designating mammals of the subclass Eutheria, characterized by the formation of a placenta and including all mammals except the monotremes and marsupials. [New Latin *Eutheria* : Greek *eu-,* well + *thēria,* plural of *thērion,* beast.] **—eu·the·ri·an** *n.*

eu·troph·ic (yoō-trŏf′ĭk, -trō′fĭk) *adj.* Designating a body of water in which the increase of mineral and organic nutrients has reduced the dissolved oxygen, producing an environment that favors plant life over animal life. [Probably from German *Eutroph,* from Greek *eutrophos,* well-nourished, from *eutrophein,* to thrive : *eu-,* well + *trephein,* to nourish.] **—eu·troph·i·ca·tion** (yoō-trŏf′ĭ-kā′shən, yoō-trō′fĭ-) *n.*

eux·e·nite (yoōk′sə-nīt′) *n.* A lustrous blackish-brown mineral consisting of cerium, erbium, niobium, titanium, uranium, and yttrium. [German *Euxenit,* from Greek *euxenos,* kind to strangers (it contains many rare or "strange" elements) : *eu-,* good + *xenos,* stranger.]

eV electron volt.

EVA extravehicular activity.

e·vac·u·ant (ĭ-văk′yoō-ənt) *adj.* Causing evacuation of an organ, especially of the bowels.
~*n.* An evacuant medicine or agent; a purgative or emetic.

e·vac·u·ate (ĭ-văk′yoō-āt′) *v.* **-ated, -ating, -ates.** —*tr.* **1. a.** To cause to be empty by removing the contents. **b.** To create a vacuum in. **2.** To excrete or discharge (waste matter), especially from the bowels. **3.** *Military.* **a.** To relinquish possession or occupation of (a town, fortress, or encampment, for example). **b.** To withdraw or send away (troops or inhabitants) from a threatened area. **4.** To withdraw or depart from; vacate. —*intr.* **1.** To withdraw from or vacate any place or area, especially a threatened area. **2.** To discharge waste matter from the body. [Latin *ēvacuāre,* to empty out, to evacuate : *ē-,* out, from *ex-* + *vacuus,* empty.] **—e·vac·u·a·tion** *n.* **—e·vac·u·a·tor** *n.*

e·vac·u·ee (ĭ-văk′yoō-ē′) *n.* A person withdrawn or sent away from a threatened or dangerous area.

e·vade (ĭ-vād′) *v.* **evaded, evading, evades.** —*tr.* **1.** To escape or avoid by cleverness or deceit: *evade arrest.* **2.** To avoid fulfilling, answering, or performing: *evade responsibility.* **3.** To baffle or elude: *The accident evades explanation.* —*intr.* To use cleverness or deceit in avoiding or escaping. —See Synonyms at **escape.** [Old French *evader,* from Latin *ēvādere,* to evade, go out, escape : *ē-,* out, from *ex-* + *vādere,* to go.] **—e·vad·a·ble** *adj.* **—e·vad·er** *n.*

e·vag·i·nate (ĭ-văj′ə-nāt′) *tr.v.* **-nated, -nating, -nates.** *Medicine.* To cause (a body part) to turn inside out by eversion of an inner surface. [Latin *ēvāgināre,* to unsheath : *ē-* (indicating removal), from *ex-* + *vāgīna,* sheath.] **—e·vag·i·na·tion** *n.*

e·val·u·ate (ĭ-văl′yoō-āt′) *tr.v.* **-ated, -ating, -ates. 1.** To ascertain or fix the value or worth of. **2.** To examine and judge; appraise; estimate. **3.** *Mathematics.* To calculate or set down the numerical value of; express numerically. —See Synonyms at **estimate.** [Back-formation from *evaluation,* from French *évaluation,* from Old French, from *evaluer,* to evaluate : *e-,* out, from Latin *ex-* + VALUE.] **—e·val·u·a·tion** *n.*

ev·a·nesce (ĕv′ə-nĕs′) *intr.v.* **-nesced, -nescing, -nesces.** To dissipate like vapor; disappear gradually; fade away; vanish. [Latin *ēvānēscere,* to vanish : *ē-,* completely, from *ex-* + *vānēscere,* to pass away, from *vānus,* empty, vain.] **—ev·a·nes·cence** *n.*

ev·a·nes·cent (ĕv′ə-nĕs′ənt) *adj.* Vanishing or likely to vanish; transitory; fleeting: *"Seeking permanence in the midst of what was only perpetually evanescent"* (Malcolm Lowry). —See Synonyms at **transient.** **—ev·a·nes·cent·ly** *adv.*

---

e·van·gel (ĭ-văn'jəl) n. **1.** Usually **Evangel**. The Christian gospel; especially, any of the four Gospels of the New Testament. **2.** Glad tidings. **3.** An evangelist. [Middle English evangelie, from Old French evangile, from Late Latin evangelium, from Greek euangelion, good news, reward for bringing good news, from euangelos, bringing good news : eu-, good + angelos, messenger.]

e·van·gel·i·cal (ē'văn-jĕl'ĭ-kəl, ĕv'ən-) adj. Also **e·van·gel·ic** (-jĕl'ĭk). **1.** Of, pertaining to, or in accordance with the Christian gospel, especially the four Gospels of the New Testament. **2.** Often **Evangelical**. Protestant. **3.** Of, pertaining to, or being a Protestant group emphasizing the authority of the gospel and the importance of personal conversion and faith in Christ as one's own savior. **4. Evangelical.** Pertaining or belonging to the Evangelical Church in Germany. **5.** Pertaining or belonging to the Low Church party in the Church of England. **6.** Characterized by evangelism; zealous. ~n. A member of an evangelical church or party. —**e·van·gel·i·cal·ly** adv.

e·van·gel·i·cal·ism (ē'văn-jĕl'ĭ-kə-lĭz'əm, ĕv'ən-) n. **1.** Evangelical beliefs or doctrines. **2.** Adherence to a church or party professing such beliefs or doctrines.

e·van·gel·ism (ĭ-văn'jə-lĭz'əm) n. **1.** The zealous preaching and dissemination of the gospel, as through missionary work. **2.** Militant zeal for any cause.

e·van·gel·ist (ĭ-văn'jə-lĭst) n. **1.** Usually **Evangelist**. Any of the authors of the four New Testament Gospels: Matthew, Mark, Luke, or John. **2.** One who practices evangelism; especially, a Protestant preacher or missionary. **3.** In the Mormon Church, a patriarch (see). —**e·van·gel·is·tic** (ĭ-văn'jə-lĭs'tĭk) adj. —**e·van·gel·is·ti·cal·ly** adv.

e·van·gel·ize (ĭ-văn'jə-līz') v. **-ized, -izing, -izes.** —tr. **1.** To preach the gospel to. **2.** To convert to Christianity. —intr. To preach the gospel; be an evangelist. —**e·van·gel·i·za·tion** n. —**e·van·gel·iz·er** n.

Ev·ans (ĕv'ənz), **Sir Arthur John** (1851-1941). British archaeologist. His excavations in Crete, mostly at Knossos, unearthed a Bronze Age civilization that he named Minoan, after the legendary King Minos.

Evans, Dame Edith (1888-1976). English actress. After winning acclaim for her performance as Cressida in 1912, she joined the Old Vic and thereafter played a wide variety of roles, of which her most famous was Lady Bracknell in The Importance of Being Earnest. Her films include Look Back in Anger (1959).

Evans, Mary Ann. See George Eliot.

Evans, Walker (1903-75). U.S. photographer. His best-known works are studies of Victorian architecture and photographs of the rural South during the Depression. He collaborated with James Agee on the book Let Us Now Praise Famous Men (1941).

Ev·ans·ton (ĕv'ən-stən). A city in northeastern Illinois, on Lake Michigan. It is mainly residential with some industries, including publishing and food processing. Northwestern University is here.

Ev·ans·ville (ĕv'ənz-vĭl'). A city of extreme southwestern Indiana, on the Ohio River. It is the shipping and commercial center for a coal, oil, and farm region. Its manufactures include heavy machinery and pharmaceuticals.

e·vap·o·ra·ble (ĭ-văp'ər-ə-bəl) adj. Capable of being evaporated. —**e·vap·o·ra·bil·i·ty** n.

e·vap·o·rate (ĭ-văp'ə-rāt') v. **-rated, -rating, -rates.** —tr. **1. a.** To convert or change into a vapor, especially at a temperature below the boiling point. **b.** To draw off in the form of vapor. **2.** To draw moisture from, leaving only the dry solid portion. **3.** To deposit (a metal) on a substrate by vacuum sublimation. —intr. **1. a.** To change into vapor. **b.** To pass off in or as vapor. **2.** To produce vapor. **3.** To disappear; vanish: His fears evaporated. [Middle English evaporaten, from Latin ēvapōrāre (past participle ēvapōrātus), "to go out in vapor," evaporate : ē-, out of, from ex- + vapor, steam, vapor.] —**e·vap·o·ra·tion** n. —**e·vap·o·ra·tive** (ĭ-văp'ə-rā'tĭv, -ər-ə-tĭv) adj. —**e·vap·o·ra·tor** n.

evaporated milk n. Concentrated, unsweetened milk processed by evaporating some of the water from whole milk. Compare **condensed milk.**

e·vap·o·rite (ĭ-văp'ə-rīt') n. A sedimentary rock or mineral, such as rock salt or gypsum, that has been formed by evaporation of salt water.

e·va·sion (ĭ-vā'zhən) n. **1.** The act of avoiding, evading, or escaping. **2.** A means of evading; a subterfuge. **3.** An excuse or equivocal answer. [Middle English evasioun, from Old French evasion, from Late Latin ēvāsiō (stem ēvāsiōn-), from Latin ēvāsus, past participle of ēvādere, to EVADE.]

e·va·sive (ĭ-vā'sĭv, -zĭv) adj. **1.** Characterized by or exhibiting evasion. **2.** Intentionally vague or ambiguous; equivocal: an evasive statement. —**e·va·sive·ly** adv. —**e·va·sive·ness** n.

eve (ēv) n. **1.** Often **Eve**. The evening or day preceding a special day, such as a saint's day or holiday: Saint Agnes' Eve; New Year's Eve. **2.** The period immediately preceding a certain event: the eve of war. **3.** Poetic. Evening. [Middle English eve, variant of EVEN (evening).]

Eve (ēv). In the Bible, the first woman and wife of Adam. Genesis 3:20.

e·vec·tion (ĭ-věk'shən) n. Astronomy. Solar perturbation of the lunar orbit. [Latin ēvectiō (stem ēvectiōn-), a going up, from ēvectus, past participle of ēvehere, to carry out : ē-, out, upward, from ex- + vehere, to carry.] —**e·vec·tion·al** adj.

Eve·lyn (ĕv'lĭn, ēv'-), **John** (1620-1706). English writer and one of the founders of the Royal Society. He is best known for his Diary, which covers most of his life and is rich in information about 17th-century England.

e·ven¹ (ē'vən) adj. **1. a.** Having a horizontal surface; flat: an even floor. **b.** Having no irregularities, roughness, or indentations; smooth. **2.** Having the same plane or line; at the same height or depth; parallel; level: The picture is even with the window. **3.** Having no variations or fluctuations; uniform; steady; regular: an even rate of speed. **4.** Of uniform thickness; uniformly distributed: an even application of varnish. **5.** Tranquil; calm; placid: an even temper. **6.** Equally matched or balanced: an even contest. **7.** Equal or identical in degree, extent, or amount: even amounts of wine and water. **8.** Having equal probability. Said of alternatives, possibilities, or events: an even chance of winning or losing. **9. a.** Having an equal score: The teams are even. **b.** Being equal for each opponent. Said of a score. **10.** Neither owing nor being owed; having nothing due: Give him five dollars, and you will be even. **11.** Having exacted full revenge. **12. a.** Mathematics. Exactly divisible by 2. **b.** Characterized or indicated by a number exactly divisible by 2. Compare **odd**. **13. a.** Having an even number in a series. **b.** Having an even number of members. **14.** Having an exact amount, extent, or number: an even pound. —See Synonyms at **level, steady.** ~adv. **1.** Used to stress something that might not be expected: He even drove us home. **2.** At the same time as; just: Even as we watched, the building collapsed. **3.** In spite of; notwithstanding: Even with his head start, I soon overtook him. **4. a.** To a higher degree or extent; yet; still. Used as an intensive: an even worse condition. **b.** Indeed; in fact; moreover. Used as an intensive: unhappy, even weeping. **5.** To a degree that extends as specified: loyal even unto death. **6.** Archaic. The same as; identical with: It is I, even I. —**break even.** Informal. To have neither losses nor gains. —**get even.** To exact one's full measure of revenge. ~v. **evened, evening, evens.** —tr. **1.** To make even, smooth, or level. **2.** To settle or balance (accounts, debts, or the like); square. Often used with off or up. —intr. To become even or smooth. Used with off, out, or up. [Middle English even, Old English ef(e)n, even, level, from Common Germanic ibnaz (unattested).] —**e·ven·ly** adv. —**e·ven·ness** n.

even² n. Archaic. Evening. [Middle English eve, even, Old English æfen.]

e·ven·fall (ē'vən-fôl') n. Poetic. The beginning of evening; twilight.

e·ven·hand·ed (ē'vən-hăn'dĭd) adj. Dealing equitably with all; impartial. —**e·ven·hand·ed·ly** adv. —**e·ven·hand·ed·ness** n.

eve·ning (ēv'nĭng) n. Abbr. **evg. 1.** The period of decreasing daylight during the decline and setting of the sun between afternoon and night. **2. a.** The period between the termination of one's daily activities and bedtime. **b.** This period occupied in a given manner: an evening at home. **3.** Any latter period or time of decline: in the evening of his life. [Middle English evening, Old English æfnung, evening, from æfnian, to become evening, from æfen, evening.]

evening dress n. **1.** Clothing, especially formal clothing, such as a man's dinner jacket, worn for evening social events. **2.** A woman's formal dress, usually low, that is worn especially in the evening. In this sense, also called "evening gown."

Evening Prayer n. An evening prayer service that is read or sung; especially, evensong in the Anglican Church or vespers in the Roman Catholic Church.

evening primrose n. Any of various North American plants of the genus Oenothera, characteristically having four-petaled yellow flowers that open in the evening and containing an oil with a high concentration of essential fatty acids.

eve·nings (ēv'nĭngs) adv. Regularly or habitually in the evening: They read evenings.

evening star n. A planet that crosses the local meridian before midnight, especially Mercury or Venus when either is prominent in the west shortly after sunset. Also, especially referring to Venus, formerly called "Vesper."

evening stock n. A plant, Mathiola bicornis, native to Eurasia, having fragrant purple flowers that bloom at night. Also called "night-scented stock."

e·vens (ē'vəns) adj. British. **1.** Standing to win exactly the sum staked. Said of a bet. **2.** Being offered at these odds. Said of a horse or other racing animal. —**e·vens** adv.

e·ven·song (ē'vən-sông', -sŏng') n. **1.** The service of Evening Prayer in the Anglican Church, often a choral service. **2.** A vesper service. **3.** A song sung in the evening. **4.** Archaic. Evening.

e·vent (ĭ-věnt') n. **1.** An occurrence, incident, or experience, especially one of some significance. **2.** The actual outcome or final result. **3.** One of the items in a calendar or program of sports. **4.** An important social occasion. **5.** Physics. A coincidence of two or more points at a particular position in space at a particular instant of time, regarded as the fundamental observational entity in relativity theory. —See Synonyms at **occurrence.** —**at all events** or **in any event.** In any case; whatever the circumstances. —**in the event. 1.** If it should happen; in case: what to do in the event of an accident. **2.** Chiefly British. As it turned out; as things happened: In the event I'd had nothing to fear after all. [Latin ēventus, a coming out, event, from the past participle of ēvenīre, to come out, happen : ē-, out, from ex- + venīre, to come.]

e·ven·tem·pered (ē'vən-těm'pərd) adj. Not easily disturbed; equable.

e·vent·ful (ĭ-věnt'fəl) adj. **1.** Full of or rich in events: an eventful week. **2.** Important; momentous: an eventful decision. —**e·vent·ful·ly** adv. —**e·vent·ful·ness** n.

Evert, Chris *Born in Florida in December 1954, Chris Evert turned professional when she reached her 18th birthday and won the women's singles championship at Wimbledon in 1974, 1976, and 1981.*

PRONUNCIATION KEY

ă, pat; ā, pay; âr, care; ä, father, are; b, bib; ch, church; d, deed; ĕ, pet; ē, be; f, fife; g, gag; h, hat; hw, which; ĭ, pit; ī, pie; îr, pier; j, judge; k, kick; l, lid, needle; m, mum; n, no, sudden; ng, thing; ŏ, pot; ō, toe; ô, paw, for; oi, noise; ou, out; o͝o, book; o͞o, boot; p, pop; r, roar; s, sauce; sh, ship, dish; t, tight; th, thin, path; *th*, this, bathe; ŭ, cut; ûr, fur; v, valve; w, with; y, yes; z, zebra, size; zh, vision; ə, about, item, edible, gallop, circus, peaceful

IN FOREIGN WORDS:

à, *Fr.* ami; œ, *Fr.* feu, *Ger.* schön; ü, *Fr.* tu, *Ger.* über; KH, *Ger.* ich, *Scot.* loch; N, *Fr.* bon; y', *Fr.* Compiègne

STRESS MARKS:

Primary stress: ′
in·cite′ (ĭn-sīt′)
Secondary stress: ′
in′sight′ (ĭn′sīt′)

event horizon *n. Astronomy.* The spherical surface marking the boundary of a black hole, being the place at which the escape velocity is equal to the speed of light, so that no electromagnetic radiation or information can leave the black hole.

e·ven·tide (ē′vən-tīd′) *n. Poetic.* Evening. [Middle English *eventide,* Old English *ǣfentīd* : *ǣfen,* EVEN (evening) + *tīd,* time, season.]

e·ven·tu·al (ĭ-vĕn′cho͞o-əl) *adj.* **1.** Occurring at an unspecified time in the future; ultimate: *his eventual death.* **2.** Occurring or having occurred after some time has elapsed. **3.** *Archaic.* Dependent on circumstance; possible; contingent. —See Synonyms at **last.** [From EVENT.]

e·ven·tu·al·i·ty (ĭ-vĕn′cho͞o-ăl′ə-tē) *n., pl.* **-ties.** Something that may occur; a contingency; a possibility.

e·ven·tu·al·ly (ĭ-vĕn′cho͞o-ə-lē) *adv.* **1.** Finally; as the last step in a process. **2.** After a long delay.

e·ven·tu·ate (ĭ-vĕn′cho͞o-āt′) *intr.v.* **-ated, -ating, -ates.** To result ultimately: *Their debate eventuated in peaceable agreement.* **—e·ven·tu·a·tion** *n.*

ev·er (ĕv′ər) *adv.* **1. a.** At all times; always; constantly. Sometimes used in combination: *his ever-patient sister.* **b.** Repeatedly: *ever complaining.* **2.** At any time: *Have you ever seen a circus?* **3.** Used to add emphasis, especially in questions: *How could you ever treat him so?* **4.** *Chiefly British Informal.* To a great degree; very much. Used as an intensive: *I'm ever so relieved.* **5.** *Informal.* Certainly; without doubt: *Happy? Is she ever!* **—for ever and a day.** Always; forever. [Middle English *ever,* Old English *ǣfre.*]

Ev·er·est (ĕv′ər-ĭst, ĕv′rĭst) *n.* The ultimate or highest point of achievement or ambition: *The marathon is a runner's Everest.*

Everest, Mount. The world's highest mountain (8,848 meters; 29,028 feet) in the central Himalayas, on the border of Nepal and Tibet. In Tibet it is called Chomolungma ("Mother Goddess of the World"); it takes its English name from the surveyor general of India, Sir George Everest (1790–1866). The summit was first reached by Sir Edmund Hillary and Tenzing Norgay on May 28, 1953.

ev·er·glade (ĕv′ər-glād′) *n.* A tract of marshland, usually under water and covered in places with tall grass; a swamp. [Perhaps EVER ("interminable") + GLADE (open space).]

Ev·er·glades (ĕv′ər-glādz′). Swampy region of 13,000 square kilometers (5,000 square miles) at the southern tip of Florida. It is abundant in crocodiles, alligators, egrets, and bald eagles. Its national park is the third largest in the United States.

ev·er·green (ĕv′ər-grēn′) *adj.* **1. a.** Having foliage that persists and remains green throughout the year: *evergreen trees.* **b.** Persisting and remaining green throughout the year: *evergreen foliage.* Compare **deciduous. 2.** Retaining freshness and popularity over a long period: *an evergreen musical.*
∼*n.* **1.** An evergreen tree or shrub. **2.** Something that retains freshness and popularity over a long period.

ev·er·last·ing (ĕv′ər-lăs′tĭng, -lä′stĭng) *adj.* **1.** Lasting forever; eternal. **2.** Continuing indefinitely or for a long period of time; perpetual. **3.** Lasting too long; tedious: *his everlasting complaints.* **4.** Retaining color and form for a long time when cut or dried, as certain plants do.
∼*n.* **1. Everlasting.** God. Preceded by *the.* **2.** Eternal duration; eternity. **3.** Any of various everlasting plants, such as *Helichrysum bracteatum.*

ev·er·more (ĕv′ə-môr′, -mōr′) *adv.* **1.** Forever. Obsolete except in the phrase *for evermore.* **2.** Constantly; always.

e·vert (ĭ-vûrt′) *tr.v.* **everted, everting, everts.** To turn (the cervix, intestines, or other part of the body) inside out or outward. [Latin *ēvertere,* to turn out, overturn : *ē-,* out, from *ex-* + *vertere,* to turn.] **—e·ver·sion** (ĭ-vûr′zhən, -shən) *n.* **—e·ver·si·ble** (ĭ-vûr′sə-bəl) *adj.*

Ev·ert (ĕv′ərt), **Christine,** known as "Chris" (1954–). U.S. tennis player. She was U.S. women's singles champion (1975–78, 1980, 1982) and captured the Wimbledon singles title in 1974, 1976, and 1981.

e·ver·tor (ĭ-vûr′tər) *n.* A muscle that acts to turn a part outward or inside out.

eve·ry (ĕv′rē) *adj.* **1.** Each and all single members of an aggregate; each without exception: *every student in the class.* **2.** Each particular member of a series. Used where a qualification is involved: *every third seat; every two hours.* **3.** Each thing or all possible things without exception; no matter which or when: *arrive late at every party.* **4.** The utmost, most earnest, or most extensive: *gave him every care.*
∼*adv.* More or less; periodically. Used as an intensive with idioms indicating indefinite or occasional recurrence: *every once in a while.* **—every bit.** *Informal.* In all ways; quite; equally: *He is every bit as mean as she is.* **—every other. 1.** Each alternate; each second: *Leave every other door unmarked.* **2.** *Informal.* Almost each: *Every other cup is chipped.* **—every so often.** From time to time; occasionally: *They met on the street every so often.* **—every which way. 1.** *Informal.* In complete disorder; chaotic. **2.** In every sequence or direction. [Middle English *every, everich, everulch,* Old English *ǣfre ǣlc,* "ever each," every, each one : *ǣfre,* EVER + *ǣlc,* EACH.]

Usage: *Every* takes a singular verb: *Every person has to get what he wants.* There is rarely a problem over agreement with the verb, but there is some variability over agreement with a pronoun later in the sentence, especially when the speaker does not wish to select a pronoun such as *he* or *she. Every person knows what they have to do* may therefore be heard, alongside the more careful (but also more awkward) *Every person knows what he or she has to do* and the simpler (but, to some, sexist) use of *he,* as above. • The phrase *each and every* has attracted occasional criticism as a redundant expression, *each and every day* being felt to be equivalent to *each day* or *every day.* But the extra emphasis conveyed by this phrase seems sufficient to explain its continued use in both formal and informal styles. —See also Usage note at **each** and **everyone.**

eve·ry·bod·y (ĕv′rē-bŏd′ē) *pron.* Every person; everyone. —See Usage note at **everyone.**

eve·ry·day (ĕv′rē-dā′) *adj.* **1.** Suitable for ordinary days or routine occasions: *an everyday suit.* **2.** Commonplace; usual; ordinary: *everyday worries.*

Usage: This is written as a single word only when it is used as an adjective, as in *an everyday happening.* In other circumstances, it is written as two words: *I go there every day.* In speech, the stress pattern is usually different, with *day* being more strongly stressed in the latter sense.

eve·ry·man (ĕv′rē-măn′) *n. Often* **Everyman.** The common, typical, or ordinary man, with all his weaknesses and failings. [After the central character in the medieval morality play *Everyman.*]

eve·ry·one (ĕv′rē-wŭn′) *pron.* Every person; everybody.

Usage: There are a large number of words and expressions in English that are singular in form but felt to be plural in sense, so that speakers are uncertain as to whether to use a singular or plural pronoun in referring back to them. For example, strict grammarians have long insisted that it is correct to say *everyone took his coat,* not *their coat* or *their coats,* and that we must say *no one is happy when he is abandoned,* and not *when they are abandoned.* Yet speakers persist in using the plural pronouns, and the most thoughtful grammarians, like Fowler, have recognized that there is no entirely happy solution to the problem. • The constructions affected fall into three classes. First, there are words formed with the word elements *-one* and *-body,* such as *anyone, somebody, everyone, nobody,* together with the two-word form *no one.* Second, there are the words *either, each, none,* and *any,* either used alone, as in *each found his seat,* or together with a noun, as in *each of the boys has his notebook* and *none of the books has its cover intact.* Finally, there are the words *whoever, whatever,* and *whichever,* either used as indefinite pronouns, as in *whoever talks out of turn will have his name sent to the office,* or together with a noun, as in *whichever nation is attacked first will find itself at a disadvantage.* • The traditional rule is that only a singular pronoun can be used in referring back to these constructions, as in the preceding examples of correct usage. But the rule as stated creates grammatical complications. For one thing, a pronoun outside the sentence containing the element it refers to *cannot* be in the singular. Thus, it is simply not English to say: *Everybody left in a hurry. He took his coat with him.* Nor can one say: *No one could be seen. He must have been hiding behind a rock.* Constructions with *whoever* are exceptions. One says: *Whoever is elected will take office in January. I am sure he will do a good job.* Writers who do not want to risk a violation of the traditional rule will have to find other ways of expressing the meaning. One may rephrase so as to get the pronoun into the same sentence as its antecedent, saying, for example, *Everybody left carrying his raincoat with him.* One may also substitute other words, for example the plural *all,* as in *All the guests left. They took their coats with them.* • *Each* presents some special problems. When it precedes the noun, a following pronoun is correctly singular: *Each of the actors has learned his* (not *their*) *part.* When *each* follows the noun, however, the pronoun is generally plural: *The actors have each learned their parts* (not *his part*). It should also be noted that *none* has for centuries been used by the best writers as if it were a plural form, taking both plural verb and plural pronouns: *None of them have learned their parts* must be considered an entirely acceptable variant of *None of them has learned his part.* Only the mixture of singular verb and plural pronoun would be considered incorrect, as in *None of them has learned their parts.* • The traditional rule may also be politically offensive to many speakers. When referring back to a group consisting of both men and women, strict grammarians have insisted that the masculine singular *him* or *his* be used as a "neutral" form; one is thus required to say *Every one of the actors and actresses has learned his part.* Since the last century, however, feminists and their allies have objected to this presumption. The writer who finds the singular *he* and *his* distasteful in these cases has the choice of flying in the face of traditional grammar and using *they* and *their* or of using the somewhat clumsier variants *his and her* (or *her and his*); attempts to introduce new pronouns like *s/he* appear unlikely to win general acceptance. The entire matter is properly outside the scope of grammar. In the end, as Fowler put it, "everyone must decide for himself (or for himself and herself, or for themselves)." —See also Usage note at **each** and **neither.**

eve·ry·place (ĕv′rē-plās′) *adv. Informal.* Everywhere.

Usage: *Everyplace* and *every place* used adverbially for *everywhere* are appropriate principally to informal writing or speech: *Everyplace* (or *every place*) *I go, I see her* (in formal writing, preferably *everywhere I go*). *Every place,* as a combination of adjective and noun, is, of course, standard English: *I searched in every place he suggested.*

eve·ry·thing (ĕv′rē-thĭng′) *pron.* **1.** All things or factors that exist or pertain to a given instance; the entirety or totality: *everything in this room.* **2.** All relevant items or factors: *Tell him everything.* **3.** The most important fact or consideration, especially for success or happiness; the principal concern: *Her children mean everything to her.* **4.** All aspects of something; life in general: *Everything went wrong.*

5. Every desirable or necessary quality or possession: *The paintings in his collection are everything to him.*
eve·ry·where (ĕv′rē-hwâr′) *adv.* In or to any or every place; in all places.
~*n.* Any or every place; all places: *Music lovers came from everywhere to hear the concert.*
Usage: The only acceptable word is *everywhere* (not *everywheres*). The use of *that* with *everywhere* (*everywhere that I go*) is superfluous. —See also Usage note at **everyplace.**
evg. evening.
e·vict (ĭ-vĭkt′) *tr.v.* **evicted, evicting, evicts.** **1.** To expel (a tenant, for example) by legal process; put out. **2.** To force out; eject; dispossess: *"We have allowed the Communists to evict us from our rightful estate"* (John F. Kennedy). **3.** To recover (property, for example) by a superior claim or legal process. —See Synonyms at **eject.** [Middle English *evicten,* from Latin *ēvincere* (past participle *ēvictus*), to conquer, overcome : *ē-,* completely, from *ex-* + *vincere,* to conquer.] **—e·vic·tion** *n.* **—e·vic·tor** *n.*
ev·i·dence (ĕv′ə-dəns) *n.* **1.** The data on which a judgment or conclusion may be based or by which proof or probability may be established: *fossilized evidence of climatic change.* **2.** Something that serves to indicate or suggest: *His reaction was evidence of guilt.* **3.** *Law.* The documentary or verbal statements and the material objects admissible as testimony in a court of law. **—in evidence. 1.** Present and plainly visible; conspicuous: *He was very much in evidence at the convention.* **2.** As legal evidence: *The lawyer handed the clerk the documents in evidence.*
~*tr.v.* **evidenced, -dencing, -dences. 1.** To indicate clearly; exemplify or prove. **2.** To support by testimony; attest. [Middle English, from Old French, from Late Latin *ēvidentia,* from Latin *ēvidēns,* EVIDENT.]
ev·i·dent (ĕv′ə-dənt) *adj.* Easily recognized or understood; clear and obvious. [Middle English, from Old French, from Latin *ēvidēns* (stem *ēvident-*), evident, clear : *ē-,* completely, from *ex-* + *vidēns,* present participle of *vidēre,* to see.]
Synonyms: *apparent, distinct, manifest, obvious, plain.*
ev·i·den·tial (ĕv′ə-dĕn′shəl) *adj.* Pertaining to, providing, or having the nature of evidence. **—ev·i·den·tial·ly** *adv.*
ev·i·dent·ly (ĕv′ə-dənt-lē, -dĕnt′lē) *adv.* **1.** Obviously; perceptibly; clearly: *He was quite evidently dead.* **2.** Apparently or seemingly; probably: *She's evidently going to be late.*
e·vil (ē′vəl) *adj.* **1.** Morally bad or wrong; wicked and malevolent: *an evil tyrant.* **2.** Causing an undesirable condition, such as ruin, injury, or pain; harmful or injurious: *an evil suggestion.* **3.** Characterized by or boding misfortune; foreboding; ominous: *evil omens.* **4.** Actually or purportedly bad or blameworthy; infamous: *an evil reputation.* **5.** Characterized by anger or spite; malicious: *an evil temper.* **6.** Very unpleasant; objectionable: *an evil smell.*
~*n.* **1.** Something that is destructive, corruptive, or injurious, whether from natural circumstances or by human ignorance, error, or design: *"The evil that men do lives after them"* (Shakespeare). **2. a.** Something that is morally bad or wrong; wickedness; sin: *was eulogized as a person who had done no evil to those around him.* **b.** Something that causes or constitutes misfortune, suffering, injury, or difficulty: *The use of addictive drugs is one of the greatest evils of our times.* **3.** Something that is undesirable because of its injurious nature or effect: *the evils of war; the lesser of two evils.* **4.** *Archaic.* A disease.
~*adv. Archaic.* In an evil manner. [Middle English *evel, ivel,* Old English *yfel.*] **—e·vil·ly** *adv.* **—e·vil·ness** *n.*
e·vil·do·er (ē′vəl-do͞o′ər) *n.* A person who does evil; a perpetrator of evil. **—e·vil·do·ing** *n.*
evil eye *n.* **1. a.** A look or a stare superstitiously believed to cause injury or misfortune to others. **b.** The power supposedly possessed by certain people to bring misfortune to others with such looks. **2.** The power of evil personified as an all-watching eye and warded off since ancient times by symbols, amulets, and beads themselves representing an eye.
e·vil-mind·ed (ē′vəl-mīn′dĭd) *adj.* Having evil thoughts, opinions, or intentions. **—e·vil-mind·ed·ly** *adv.* **—e·vil-mind·ed·ness** *n.*
Evil One *n.* The Devil. Preceded by *the.*
e·vince (ĭ-vĭns′) *tr.v.* **evinced, evincing, evinces.** To show or demonstrate clearly or convincingly; manifest; exhibit: *evince surprise.* [Latin *ēvincere,* to conquer, to prove. See **evict.**] **—e·vinc·i·ble** *adj.*
e·vis·cer·ate (ĭ-vĭs′ə-rāt′) *v.* **-ated, -ating, -ates.** —*tr.* **1.** To remove the entrails of; disembowel: *The cook eviscerated the chicken.* **2.** To take away a vital or essential part of. **3.** *Medicine.* **a.** To remove the contents of (an eyeball). **b.** To remove an organ, such as an eye, from (a patient). —*intr. Medicine.* To protrude through an incision after an operation.
~*adj.* (-ər-ĭt, -ə-rāt′). Disemboweled. [Latin *ēviscerāre,* "to remove the viscera from," to disembowel : *ē-,* indicating removal, from *ex-* + VISCERA.] **—e·vis·cer·a·tion** *n.*
ev·i·ta·ble (ĕv′ə-tə-bəl) *adj.* Avoidable. [Latin *ēvītabilis,* from *ēvītāre,* to avoid : *ē-,* away, from *ex-* + *vītāre*†, to shun.]
ev·o·ca·tion (ĕv′ə-kā′shən, ē′və-) *n.* The act of calling forth or conjuring up: *an evocation of childhood memories.*
e·voc·a·tive (ĭ-vŏk′ə-tĭv) *adj.* Tending or having the power to evoke. **—e·voc·a·tive·ly** *adv.*
ev·o·ca·tor (ĕv′ə-kā′tər, ē′və-) *n.* **1.** One that evokes. **2.** A naturally occurring substance that induces undifferentiated embryonic tissue to develop in a particular way.
e·voc·a·to·ry (ĭ-vŏk′ə-tôr′ē, -tōr′ē) *adj.* Evocative.
e·voke (ĭ-vōk′) *tr.v.* **evoked, evoking, evokes. 1.** To summon or call forth (memories, for example); reawaken; inspire. **2.** To produce or elicit (a reaction, emotion, or response): *evoke curiosity.* **3.** To cause (a spirit, for example) to appear; call up; conjure up. [Latin *ēvocāre,* to call forth, to call out, summon : *ē-,* out, from *ex-* + *vocāre,* to call.] **—ev·o·ca·ble** (ĕv′ə-kə-bəl, ĭ-vō′kə-) *adj.*
ev·o·lute (ĕv′ə-lo͞ot′, ē′və-) *n.* The locus of the centers of curvature of a given curve. [Back-formation from EVOLUTION.]
ev·o·lu·tion (ĕv′ə-lo͞o′shən, ē′və-) *n.* **1.** A gradual process in which something changes into a significantly different and usually more complex or more sophisticated form. **2.** *Biology.* **a.** The theory that groups of organisms may change with the passage of time so that new species differing morphologically and physiologically from their ancestors are formed. See **natural selection. b.** The historical development of a related group of organisms; phylogeny. **3.** The gradual process of the development or growth of something, as of a social institution, geographic division, or system of thought. **4.** *Often* **evolutions.** A turning movement that is part of a larger pattern, as: **a.** A wheeling motion in a dance. **b.** A tactical or parade-ground maneuver. **5.** A yielding or throwing off of gas, vapor, or heat. **6.** *Mathematics.* The extraction of a root of a quantity. In this sense, compare **involution.** [Latin *ēvolūtiō,* an opening, an unrolling, from *ēvolūtus,* past participle of *ēvolvere,* to roll out, to open, EVOLVE.] See feature, next page.
ev·o·lu·tion·al (ĕv′ə-lo͞o′shə-nəl, ē′və-) *adj.* Evolutionary.
ev·o·lu·tion·ar·y (ĕv′ə-lo͞o′shə-nĕr′ē, ē′və-) *adj.* **1.** Of, pertaining to, or resulting from evolution: *a continuous evolutionary process.* **2.** In accord with the theory of biological evolution. **3.** Developing or evolving as a slow or historical process; gradually changing or progressing.
ev·o·lu·tion·ism (ĕv′ə-lo͞o′shə-nĭz′əm, ē′və-) *n.* **1.** A theory of biological evolution, especially that formulated by Charles Darwin. Compare **creationism. 2.** Advocacy of or belief in an evolutionary process. **—ev·o·lu·tion·ist** *n.*
e·volve (ĭ-vŏlv′) *v.* **evolved, evolving, evolves.** —*tr.* **1.** To develop or achieve gradually; devise or formulate. **2.** *Biology.* To develop by evolutionary processes. **3.** To yield, give, or throw off (gas, vapor, or heat, for example); set free. —*intr.* **1.** To be part of or subject to the process of natural, temporal, or biological evolution, as in an organism or rock stratum. **2.** To be developed, disclosed, or unfolded: *The plot evolves in many subtle ways.* **3.** To undergo change or transformation; develop. [Latin *ēvolvere,* to roll out, unfold : *ē-,* out, from *ex-* + *volvere,* to roll.] **—e·volv·a·ble** *adj.* **—e·volve·ment** *n.*
e·vul·sion (ĭ-vŭl′shən) *n.* A pulling out; a forcible extraction. [Latin *ēvulsiō* (stem *ēvulsiōn-*), a pulling out, from *ēvulsus,* past participle of *ēvellere,* to pull out : *ē-,* out, from *ex-* + *vellere,* to pull.]
Évvoia. See **Euboea.**
ev·zone (ĕv′zōn′) *n.* An infantryman of a special corps of the Greek army. [Modern Greek *euzōnos,* from Greek, well-girdled, active : *eu-,* well + *zōnē,* girdle.]
ewe (yo͞o) *n.* A female sheep, especially when full-grown. [Middle English *ewe,* Old English *ēowu.*]
E·we (ā′wā′, ā′vā′) *n.* **1.** A member of a Negroid people of Togo, Ghana, and parts of Benin. **2.** The language of this people, belonging to the Niger-Congo family of languages.
ewe-neck (yo͞o′nĕk′) *n.* A defect in a horse or dog in which the neck is thin and has a concave arch. **—ewe-necked** *adj.*
ew·er (yo͞o′ər) *n.* A large, wide-mouthed pitcher or jug. [Middle English, from Norman French, from Old North French *eviere,* from Vulgar Latin *aquāria* (unattested), from Latin *āquārius,* relating to water, from *aqua,* water.]
ex[1] (ĕks) *prep. Abbr.* **x. 1.** *Finance.* Not including or participating in; without: *ex dividend; ex rights.* **2.** *Commerce.* Free of charge to the purchaser until removed from a particular place or thing. [Latin *ex,* out of, from.]
ex[2] *n. Informal.* A former wife, husband, or lover.
ex–[1], **ef–** *prefix.* Indicates: **1.** Removal out of or from; for example, **explant. 2.** Former; for example, *ex-president.* [Middle English, from Old French, from Latin. In borrowed Latin compounds *ex-* indicates: 1. out or out of, as in **expire.** 2. away from or removed away from, as in **expropriate.** 3. up, as in **elevate.** 4. completely or intensively, as in **execute.** 5. opposing, as in **execrate.** *Ex-* becomes *ef-* before *f.* [Latin *ex-,* from *ex,* out, out of.]
ex–[2] *prefix.* Indicates out of; for example, **exergue.** [In borrowed Greek compounds *ex-* indicates: 1. out of, as in **exegesis.** 2. away from, as in **exorcise.** Greek *ex-,* from *ex,* out of.]
ex. 1. examination. **2.** example. **3.** except; excepted; exception. **4.** exchange. **5.** executive. **6.** express. **7.** extra.
Ex. Exodus (Old Testament).
ex·ac·er·bate (ĭg-zăs′ər-bāt′, ĭk-săs′-) *tr.v.* **-bated, -bating, -bates. 1.** To increase the severity of (a pain, emotion, disease, problem, or the like). **2.** To embitter or irritate (a person). [Latin *exacerbāre,* to aggravate, make harsh : *ex-,* completely + *acerbus,* bitter, harsh.] **—ex·ac·er·ba·tion** *n.*
ex·act (ĭg-zăkt′) *adj.* **1. a.** Accurate in every respect: *an exact copy.* **b.** Specific in every detail: *exact instructions.* **2.** Precise in quantity, weight, or the like, as opposed to approximate: *the exact amount.* **3.** Precise in technique or movement: *an exact measuring device.* **4.** Designating a science based on verifiable facts. **5.** Identical; very same: *the exact place.* **6.** Meticulously observing or adhering to a standard.
~*tr.v.* **exacted, -acting, -acts. 1.** To demand and enforce (payment

ewer *A jug used to bring water to a washbasin for washing the hands before faucets became common. This ewer was made in 1828 at the Tucker factory in Philadelphia.*

THE AMAZING VARIETY OF LIFE ON EARTH

A fan of life forms developed in the course of 2.5 billion years

Single-celled life forms probably appeared in earth's oceans more than 2.5 billion years ago. They gradually evolved into organisms made up, like sponges, of groups of semi-independent cells, which evolved in turn into multicellular animals such as jellyfish and worms. Creatures with external skeletons, the ancestors of lobsters, crabs, and snails, flourished during the Cambrian period, but by the start of the Ordovician period shell-skinned fish, jawless like lampreys, had developed a notochord, a primitive spine. Their vertebrate descendants dominated the Devonian, the period when the lobefins first moved from water to land, using their fleshy fins as legs. Their relatives, the first amphibians, found shores dense with fernlike psilophytes, descendants of seaweeds evolved during the pre-Cambrian period. The Carboniferous saw the emergence of seed-bearing plants and the reptiles, the first true land animals. Tortoises and turtles are the descendants of the first reptiles, the anapsids. Mammals evolved from the synapsids, also descended from the reptiles. Catastrophic geological and climatic changes at the end of the Permian may have caused many fish and amphibians to become extinct. Archeopteryx, the first-known bird, was descended from the diapsids, which were also the ancestors of the dinosaurs. Dinosaurs were successful until the end of the Cretaceous period, during which flowering plants developed. Then, changes in geology and climate may have affected evolution again. The Cenozoic era saw an explosion of species. Mammals branched into egg-layers, marsupials that carry their young in pouches, and placental mammals whose young grow to an advanced stage in the maternal uterus. The primates, a forest group of placental mammals, became adept coordinators of hand and eye. It was from a primate that man evolved.

or performance of something, for example); extort. **2.** To call for; require. [Latin *exactus,* past participle of *exigere,* "to drive out," require, examine : *ex-,* out + *agere,* to lead, drive.] **—ex·act·a·ble** *adj.* **—ex·act·ness** *n.* **—ex·ac·tor, ex·act·er** *n.*

ex·act·a (ĭg-zăk′tə) *n.* A method of betting, as on a horse race, in which the bettor must pick those finishing in first and second place in exactly that sequence. [American Spanish *quiniela exacta,* exact quinella.]

ex·act·ing (ĭg-zăk′tĭng) *adj.* **1.** Making severe or unremitting demands: *an exacting taskmaster.* **2.** Requiring great care, effort, or attention: *an exacting task.* —See Synonyms at **burdensome, severe.** **—ex·act·ing·ly** *adv.* **—ex·act·ing·ness** *n.*

ex·ac·tion (ĭg-zăk′shən) *n.* **1.** The act of exacting. **2.** Something that is exacted, such as a sum of money or act of obedience.

ex·act·i·tude (ĭg-zăk′tə-to͞od′, -tyo͞od′) *n.* The state or quality of being exact.

ex·act·ly (ĭg-zăkt′lē) *adv.* **1.** In an exact manner; accurately. **2.** In all respects; just: *Do exactly as you please.*
∼*interj.* Used to express agreement.

ex·ag·ger·ate (ĭg-zăj′ə-rāt′) *v.* **-ated, -ating, -ates.** —*tr.* **1.** To enlarge (something) disproportionately; increase to an abnormal degree. **2.** To make (something) appear greater than is actually the case; magnify beyond the truth. —*intr.* To distort through overstatement. [Latin *exaggerāre,* to pile up, exaggerate : *ex-,* completely + *aggerāre,* to pile up, from *agger*†, pile, heap.] **—ex·ag·ger·a·tive** (ĭg-zăj′ə-rā′tĭv, -ər-ə-tĭv), **ex·ag·ger·a·to·ry** (-rə-tôr′ē, -tōr′ē) *adj.* **—ex·ag·ger·a·tor** *n.*

ex·ag·ger·at·ed (ĭg-zăj′ə-rā′tĭd) *adj.* **1.** Unduly emphasized or magnified; going beyond truth, fact, or reality. **2.** Physically enlarged; abnormally or disproportionately developed. **—ex·ag·ger·at·ed·ly** *adv.*

ex·ag·ger·a·tion (ĭg-zăj′ə-rā′shən) *n.* **1.** The act of exaggerating. **2.** An instance of exaggerating; an overstatement.

ex·alt (ĭg-zôlt′) *tr.v.* **-alted, -alting, -alts.** **1.** To raise in position, character, or status; elevate: *"Do away with masters, exalt the will of the people"* (D.H. Lawrence). **2.** To glorify, praise, or honor. **3.** To increase the effect or intensity of; heighten. [Middle English *exalten,* from Old French *exalter,* from Latin *exaltāre,* to lift up, exalt : *ex-,* up + *altus,* high.] **—ex·alt·er** *n.*

ex·al·ta·tion (ĕg′zôl-tā′shən) *n.* **1.** The act of exalting. **2.** The state of being exalted; elevation. **3.** A state or feeling of intense, often excessive exhilaration and well-being; elation. —See Synonyms at **ecstasy.**

ex·alt·ed (ĭg-zôl′tĭd) *adj.* **1.** Elevated in rank, character, or status. **2.** Lofty; noble: *"That provision should be made for continuing the race of . . . so exalted . . . a Being as man — I am far from denying"* (Laurence Sterne). **3.** Exaggeratedly favorable: *had an exalted view of their own importance.* **—ex·alt·ed·ly** *adv.* **—ex·alt·ed·ness** *n.*

ex·am (ĭg-zăm′) *n. Informal.* An examination.

ex·a·men (ĭg-zā′mən) *n. Roman Catholic Church.* A usually daily examination of one's conscience. [Latin *exāmen,* consideration, examination, from *exigere,* to EXAMINE.]

ex·am·i·nant (ĭg-zăm′ə-nənt) *n.* **1.** One who examines. **2.** One who is examined; examinee.

ex·am·i·na·tion (ĭg-zăm′ə-nā′shən) *n. Abbr.* **ex., exam.** **1.** The act of examining or the state or result of being examined. **2.** An instance of examining; a thorough inspection or scrutiny. **3.** A set of questions or exercises testing knowledge or skills; a written, practical, or oral test. **4.** Formal interrogation; official inquiry. **—ex·am·i·na·tion·al** *adj.*

ex·am·ine (ĭg-zăm′ĭn) *tr.v.* **-ined, -ining, -ines.** **1.** To inspect or scrutinize (a person, thing, or situation) in detail; observe or analyze carefully. **2.** To test the state of health of. **3.** To test the qualifications, aptitude, or knowledge of (a candidate) by means of an examination. **4.** To interrogate or question formally to elicit facts, information, or the like. **5.** To consider or test introspectively; reflect upon: *"The time has come, God knows, for us to examine ourselves"* (James Baldwin). —See Synonyms at **ask.** [Middle English *examinen,* from Old French *examiner,* from Latin *exāmināre,* to weigh accurately, examine, from *exāmen,* a weighing, consideration, from *exigere,* to examine : *ex-,* out + *agere,* to lead.] **—ex·am·in·a·ble** *adj.* **—ex·am·in·er** *n.*

ex·am·in·ee (ĭg-zăm′ə-nē′) *n.* One who is examined.

ex·am·ple (ĭg-zăm′pəl, -zäm′pəl) *n. Abbr.* **ex.** **1.** One that is representative of a group as a whole; a sample; a specimen. **2.** Someone or something that serves as a model or pattern for imitation or duplication; an exemplar. **3.** A previous case or situation that is the same as or similar to one at hand; a precedent. **4.** One that serves as a warning, such as a punishment or a punished person. **5.** An illustrative problem or exercise with its solution. **—for example.** Serving as an illustration, a model, or an instance. [Middle English *exaumple,* from Old French *example, essample,* from Latin *exemplum,* "(something) taken out," example, sample, from *eximere,* to take out : *ex-,* out + *emere,* to take.]
Synonyms: *case, illustration, instance, sample, specimen.*

ex·an·i·mate (ĭg-zăn′ə-mĭt) *adj.* Lifeless; dead.

ex·an·the·ma (ĕg′zăn-thē′mə) *n., pl.* **-mata** (-mə-tə) or **-mas.** Also **ex·an·them** (ĭg-zăn′thəm). **1.** A skin eruption accompanying a disease or fever. **2.** A disease, such as measles or scarlet fever, accompanied by a skin eruption. [New Latin, from Late Latin *exanthēma,* from Greek, "a blooming out," eruption, from *exanthein,* to bloom out, burst forth : *ex-,* out + *anthein,* to bloom, from *anthos,* flower.] **—ex·an·the·mat·ic** (ĭg-zăn′thə-măt′ĭk), **ex·an·them·a·tous** (ĕg′-zăn-thĕm′ə-təs) *adj.*

ex·a·rate (ĕk′sə-rāt′) *adj. Zoology.* Designating pupae whose wings and legs are free and able to make limited movements. [Latin *exarātus,* "plowed up" (apparently referring to the pupa's method of shedding its larval skin), past participle of *exarāre* : EX- + *arāre,* to plow.]

ex·arch[1] (ĕk′särk′) *n.* **1.** The ruler of a province in the Byzantine Empire. **2.** *Eastern Orthodox Church.* **a.** The deputy of a patriarch. **b.** A bishop ranking immediately below a patriarch. **c.** The head of certain independent churches. [Late Latin *exarchus,* from Greek *exarkhos,* leader, from *exarkhein,* to initiate, lead out : *ex-,* out + *arkhein,* to rule, lead.] **—ex·arch·al** (ĭk-sär′kəl) *adj.*

exarch[2] *adj. Botany.* Having vascular tissue in which the first-formed xylem is external to that formed later. [EX- (outside) + Greek *arkhē,* beginning, origin.]

ex·ar·chate (ĕk′sär′kĭt) *n.* Also **ex·ar·chy** (-kē) *pl.* **-chies.** The office, rank, jurisdiction, or province of an exarch.

ex·as·per·ate (ĭg-zăs′pə-rāt′) *tr.v.* **-ated, -ating, -ates.** **1.** To make very angry or irritated; tax the patience of; provoke; irk. **2.** To increase the gravity or intensity of (a passion or pain, for example). [Latin *exasperāre,* to exasperate, irritate, make rough : *ex-,* entirely + *asperāre,* to make rough, from *asper,* rough.] **—ex·as·per·at·ed·ly** *adv.* **—ex·as·per·at·ing·ly** *adv.*

ex·as·per·a·tion (ĭg-zăs′pə-rā′shən) *n.* **1.** An act or instance of exasperating. **2.** The state of being exasperated; extreme annoyance or irritation.

exc. **1.** excellent. **2.** except; excepted; exception.

Exc. Excellency.

Ex·cal·i·bur (ĭk-skăl′ə-bər) *n.* King Arthur's sword. [Middle English *Excalibur,* from Old French *Escalibor,* from Medieval Latin *Caliburnus,* from Welsh *Caledvwlch,* from Celtic *kaleto-* (unattested), hard.]

ex ca·the·dra (ĕks′ kə-thē′drə) *adj. & adv.* With the authority derived from one's office or position. Said especially of official or papal pronouncements. [Latin : *ex,* from + CATHEDRA.]

ex·cau·date (ĕk-skô′dāt′) *adj. Zoology.* Tailless; without a tail.

ex·ca·vate (ĕk′skə-vāt′) *v.* **-vated, -vating, -vates.** —*tr.* **1.** To make a cavity or hole in; dig out; hollow out. **2.** To form (a tunnel, for example) by such hollowing out; dig. **3.** To remove (soil) by digging or scooping out. **4.** To expose or uncover by digging, especially in search of historical or archaeological information. —*intr.* To engage in digging, hollowing out, or removing. [Latin *excavāre,* to hollow out : *ex-,* out + *cavāre,* to hollow, from *cavus,* hollow.]

ex·ca·va·tion (ĕk′skə-vā′shən) *n.* **1.** The act or process of excavating. **2.** A cavity formed by excavating. —See Synonyms at **hole.** **—ex·ca·va·tion·al** *adj.*

ex·ca·va·tor (ĕk′skə-vā′tər) *n.* **1.** One that excavates. **2.** A power-operated digging machine; especially, a tractor with endless chain treads and digging attachments.

ex·ceed (ĭk-sēd′) *tr.v.* **-ceeded, -ceeding, -ceeds.** **1.** To be greater than; surpass. **2.** To go beyond the prior or proper limits of. —See Synonyms at **excel.** [Middle English *exceden,* from Old French *exceder,* from Latin *excēdere,* to depart, to go out, surpass : *ex-,* out + *cēdere,* to go.]

ex·ceed·ing (ĭk-sē′dĭng) *adj.* Extreme; extraordinary.
∼*adv. Archaic.* Exceedingly.

ex·ceed·ing·ly (ĭk-sē′dĭng-lē) *adv.* To an advanced or unusual degree; extremely.

ex·cel (ĭk-sĕl′) *v.* **-celled, -celling, -cels.** —*tr.* To be or do better than; surpass: *excels the rest of the class in English.* —*intr.* To be better or do better than others; be superior to others: *a musician who excels in the performance of the classics.* [Middle English *excellen,* from Latin *excellere,* to excel, raise up.]
Synonyms: *exceed, outdo, outstrip, surpass, transcend.*

ex·cel·lence (ĕk′sə-ləns) *n.* **1.** The state, quality, or condition of excelling; superiority. **2.** Something in which a person or thing excels. **3. Excellence.** Excellency. [From EXCEL.]

Ex·cel·len·cy (ĕk′sə-lən-sē) *n., pl.* **-cies.** *Abbr.* **Exc.** A title of or form of address for certain high officials, such as ambassadors, bishops, or governors. Usually used with *His, Her,* or *Your.*

ex·cel·lent (ĕk′sə-lənt) *adj.* **1.** *Abbr.* **E, exc.** Being of the highest or finest quality; exceptionally good of its kind: *We had an excellent dinner.* **2.** *Archaic.* Surpassing; superior. [Middle English, from Old French, from Latin *excellēns* (stem *excellent-*), present participle of *excellere,* to EXCEL.] **—ex·cel·lent·ly** *adv.*

ex·cel·si·or (ĭk-sĕl′sē-ər) *n.* Slender, curved wood shavings used for packing, stuffing, or the like. [Latin, comparative of *excelsus,* high, from the past participle of *excellere,* to EXCEL.]

ex·cept (ĭk-sĕpt′) *prep. Abbr.* **ex., exc** With the exclusion of; but: *After the party all the guests left except for one. All the eggs except one broke.*
∼*conj.* **1.** If it were not for the fact that; only: *He would buy the suit except that it costs too much.* **2.** Otherwise than; with any purpose or manner other than. Usually used with an adverb, a clause, or a phrase: *He would not open his mouth except to yell.* **3.** *Archaic.* Unless.
∼*v.* **excepted, -cepting, -cepts.** —*tr.* To leave out; exclude or excuse. —*intr.* To object. Usually used with *to* or *against.* [Middle English, from Latin *exceptus,* past participle of *excipere,* to take out, except : *ex-,* out + *capere,* to take.]
Usage: *Except,* in the sense of *with the exclusion of, other than,* or *but,* is usually construed as a preposition (as it is defined above)

excavator *This giant electrically powered excavator is used to mine coal near Erfstadt in West Germany. Each tooth on the wheel is a claw-edged bucket.*

PRONUNCIATION KEY

ă, pat; ā, pay; âr, care;
ä, father, are; b, bib;
ch, church; d, deed; ĕ, pet;
ē, be; f, fife; g, gag; h, hat;
hw, which; ĭ, pit; ī, pie;
îr, pier; j, judge; k, kick;
l, lid, needle; m, mum;
n, no, sudden; ng, thing;
ŏ, pot; ō, toe; ô, paw, for;
oi, noise; ou, out; o͝o, book;
o͞o, boot; p, pop; r, roar;
s, sauce; sh, ship, dish;
t, tight; th, thin, path;
th, this, bathe; ŭ, cut; ûr, fur;
v, valve; w, with; y, yes;
z, zebra, size; zh, vision;
ə, about, item, edible, gallop, circus, peaceful

IN FOREIGN WORDS:

à, *Fr.* ami; œ, *Fr.* feu, *Ger.* schön; ü, *Fr.* tu, *Ger.* über; KH, *Ger.* ich, *Scot.* loch; N, *Fr.* bon; y′, *Fr.* Compiègne

STRESS MARKS:

Primary stress: ′
in·cite′ (ĭn-sīt′)
Secondary stress: ′
in′sight′ (ĭn′sīt′)

rather than as a conjunction. When a pronoun follows *except* in this sense, therefore, it is in the objective case: *No one except me knew it. Every member of the original cast was signed except her.* In this sense *except* is much more common than *excepting,* in modern usage. *Excepting* appears principally in negative constructions: *All money received, not excepting bonuses, must be reported.*

ex·cept·ing (ĭk-sĕp′tĭng) *prep.* Excluding; except. —See Usage note at **except.**

　~*conj. Archaic.* Except; unless.

ex·cep·tion (ĭk-sĕp′shən) *n. Abbr.* **ex., exc.** **1.** The act of excepting or state of being excepted; exclusion. **2.** One that is excepted; a case that does not conform to normal rules or general principles: *We all want to be liked—and I am no exception.* **3.** An objection or criticism; opposition: *open to exception.* **4.** *Law.* **a.** A formal objection taken in the course of an action or proceeding. **b.** A restricting clause or provision in a contract or similar document. —**take exception.** To object or take offense; take issue. Usually used with *to: I take exception to your remarks.*

ex·cep·tion·a·ble (ĭk-sĕp′shə-nə-bəl) *adj.* Open or liable to objection or exception. —See Usage note at **exceptional.** —**ex·cep·tion·a·bly** *adv.*

ex·cep·tion·al (ĭk-sĕp′shə-nəl) *adj.* **1.** Being an exception; uncommon or extraordinary. **2.** Unusually skillful, accomplished, or intelligent; gifted. —**ex·cep·tion·al·ly** *adv.*

　Usage: Exceptional and exceptionable are not interchangeable. *Exceptionable* has the meaning of "objectionable" or "debatable" — something to which exception can be taken. *Exceptional* has the meaning of "uncommon" or "extraordinary."

ex·cep·tive (ĭk-sĕp′tĭv) *adj.* **1.** Of, being, or containing an exception. **2.** *Archaic.* Tending to object or criticize; captious.

ex·cerpt (ĕk′sûrpt′, ĕg′zûrpt′) *n.* A passage or scene selected from a speech, book, film, or play; an extract.

　~*tr.v.* (ĭk-sûrpt′, ĭg-zûrpt′) **excerpted, -cerpting, -cerpts.** To select, quote, or take out (a passage or scene) from a book, speech, play, film, or the like. [Latin *excerptum,* "something picked out," excerpt, from the neuter past participle of *excerpere,* to pick out, excerpt : *ex-,* out + *carpere,* to pick, pluck.]

ex·cess (ĭk-sĕs′, ĕk′sĕs′) *n.* **1.** The state of exceeding what is normal or sufficient. **2.** An amount or quantity beyond what is requisite; a superfluity. **3.** The amount or degree by which one quantity exceeds another; a remainder. **4.** Lack of moderation and self-restraint; overindulgence: *youthful excess.* **5.** *Chemistry.* An amount of a reagent that is present in a greater quantity than that necessary to complete a given reaction. —**in excess of.** Greater than; more than. —**to excess.** To an extreme degree or extent; too much.

　~*tr.v.* **excessed, -cessing, -cesses.** To eliminate the job or position of.

　~*adj.* **1.** Being more than is required, usual, or permitted. **2.** Due; not having previously been paid in full: *excess postage.* [Middle English, from Old French *exces,* from Latin *excessus,* past participle of *excēdere,* to EXCEED.]

excess baggage *n.* **1.** Baggage, as on airplanes, in excess of the amount carried free, for which the passenger pays an extra charge. **2.** Something that is useless or hampers.

ex·ces·sive (ĭk-sĕs′ĭv) *adj.* Exceeding a reasonable degree of propriety, necessity, or the like; extreme; inordinate: *excessive charges.* —**ex·ces·sive·ly** *adv.*

　Synonyms: exorbitant, extravagant, extreme, immoderate, inordinate, unreasonable.

exch. **1.** exchange. **2.** exchequer.

ex·change (ĭks-chānj′) *v.* **-changed, -changing, -changes.** —*tr.* **1.** To give and receive in a reciprocal manner; interchange: *exchange ideas.* **2.** To relinquish (one thing) for another; give over. **3.** To replace (something unsatisfactory) with something else: *exchange defective goods.* **4.** To provide or transfer (goods or services, for example) in return for something of equal value. **5.** In chess, to capture (an opponent's piece) immediately after sacrificing a piece, usually of similar value. —*intr.* To transfer something and receive something equivalent in return; reciprocate; swap.

　~*n. Abbr.* **ex., exch.** **1.** An act or instance of exchanging. **2.** One that is exchanged. **3.** A usually short and often lively or caustic conversation: *a noisy exchange.* **4.** A **telephone exchange** *(see).* **5.** A place where things are exchanged; especially, a center where securities and commodities are bought and sold: *a stock exchange.* **6.** A system of payments using instruments such as negotiable drafts instead of money. **7.** The fee or percentage charged for participating in such a system of payment. **8.** **Rate of exchange** *(see).* **9.** The amount of difference in the actual value of two or more currencies, or between values of the same currency at two or more places. **10.** *Usually* **exchanges.** The instruments, as checks or drafts, presented to a clearing house for settlement or exchange. **11.** In chess, the capture in successive moves of pieces, usually equivalent in value, by each of the two players. **12.** *Physics.* The transfer of a real or virtual particle between two other particles, such as nucleons, caused by an exchange of real or virtual particles between them. **2.** A force that aligns the magnetic dipole moments of atoms in a ferromagnetic material. [Middle English *eschaungen,* from Norman French *eschaunge,* from Old French *eschangier,* from Vulgar Latin *excambiāre* (unattested) : Late Latin *ex-,* showing change + *cambiāre,* to exchange.] —**ex·chang·er** *n.*

ex·change·a·ble (ĭks-chān′jə-bəl) *adj.* Able to be exchanged; remittable. —**ex·change·a·bil·i·ty** *n.*

exchange force *n. Physics.* **1.** A force between two elementary particles, such as nucleons, caused by an exchange of real or virtual particles between them. **2.** A force that aligns the magnetic dipole moments of atoms in a ferromagnetic material.

exchange rate *n.* **Rate of exchange** *(see).*

ex·cheq·uer (ĕks′chĕk′ər, ĭks-chĕk′-) *n.* **1. Exchequer.** The department of the British and some other governments in charge of the collection and care of the national revenue. **2.** *Abbr.* **exch.** A treasury, as of a nation or an organization. **3.** *Informal.* The total of one's financial resources; funds. [Middle English *escheker,* from Norman French, from Old French *eschequier,* chessboard, a counting table usually covered with a checkered cloth, from *eschec,* CHECK (at chess).]

ex·ci·mer (ĕk′sə-mər, ĭk-sī′mər) *n. Chemistry.* A dimer formed by the association of excited and unexcited molecules, which in the ground state would remain dissociated. [*Excited* di*mer.*]

ex·cip·i·ent (ĭk-sĭp′ē-ənt) *n.* An inert substance used as a diluent or vehicle for a drug. [Latin *excipiēns* (stem *excipient-*), present participle of *excipere,* to EXCEPT.]

ex·cis·a·ble (ĭk-sī′zə-bəl) *adj.* Subject to excise.

ex·cise¹ (ĕk′sīz′) *n.* **1.** An indirect tax levied on the production, sale, or consumption of certain commodities, such as tobacco or alcohol, within a country. Also called "excise tax." **2.** A license fee paid to allow a person to pursue certain types of employment or amusement, such as operating a gambling casino. **3.** In Britain, the branch of the civil service that is responsible for the collection of excise tax.

　~*tr.v.* **-cised, -cising, -cises.** To levy an excise on. [Obsolete Dutch *excijs,* from Middle Dutch, probably from Old French *acceis,* from Vulgar Latin *accēnsum* (unattested) : Latin *ad-,* against, to + *cēnsus,* tax, CENSUS.]

ex·cise² (ĕk-sīz′) *tr.v.* **-cised, -cising, -cises.** **1.** To delete (a passage of text). **2.** To remove by or as if by cutting; especially, to remove (an organ or part) surgically. [Latin *excīdere* (past participle *excīsus*), to cut out : *ex-,* out + *caedere,* to cut.] —**ex·ci·sion** (ĭk-sĭzh′ən) *n.*

ex·cise·man (ĕk′sīz′mən, ĭk-sīz′-) *n., pl.* **-men** (-mĭn). *British.* An officer who collects excise taxes or enforces excise laws.

ex·cit·a·ble (ĭk-sī′tə-bəl) *adj.* **1. a.** Capable of being excited. **b.** Easily excited; sensitive or volatile. **2.** Capable of responding to stimuli. Said especially of nerves. —**ex·cit·a·bil·i·ty, ex·cit·a·ble·ness** *n.* —**ex·cit·a·bly** *adv.*

ex·ci·tant (ĭk-sī′tənt) *adj.* Also **ex·ci·ta·tive** (-sī′tə-tĭv), **ex·ci·ta·to·ry** (-tə-tôr′ē, -tōr′ē). Capable of exciting or stimulating. —**ex·ci·tant** *n.*

ex·ci·ta·tion (ĕk′sī-tā′shən) *n.* **1.** The act or process of exciting something. **2.** An agent or means used to excite or stimulate. **3.** The state or condition of being excited. **4.** The stimulus-induced response of an organ or tissue, especially that of a nerve cell. **5.** The electric current producing a magnetic field in an electromagnetic device, as in a motor, generator, or transformer.

ex·cite (ĭk-sīt′) *tr.v.* **-cited, -citing, -cites.** **1.** To stir to activity; put into motion. **2.** To elicit (a reaction or emotion, for example); induce: *excite a response.* **3. a.** To affect with a feeling of agitated elation or delight. **b.** To arouse strong feeling in; provoke: *She excited him to anger.* **c.** To stir the sexual passions of; arouse. **4.** *Biology.* To produce increased activity in (an organism or part); stimulate. **5.** *Physics.* **a.** To increase the energy of. **b.** To raise (an atom, molecule, nucleus, or electron) to a higher energy level than the ground state. **c.** To supply current to (the coils of a motor or generator) to create a magnetic field. **d.** To supply a signal to (a transistor circuit). —See Synonyms at **provoke.** [Middle English *exciten,* from Old French *exciter,* from Latin *excitāre,* to excite, arouse, frequentative of *exciēre* (past participle *excitus*), to call or bring out : *ex-,* out + *ciēre, cīre,* to call, put in motion.]

ex·cit·ed (ĭk-sī′tĭd) *adj.* **1.** In a state of agitated elation or sexual arousal. **2.** Caused by or characterized by excitement: *an excited hush.* **3.** *Physics.* At an energy level higher than the ground state. —**ex·cit·ed·ly** *adv.*

ex·cite·ment (ĭk-sīt′mənt) *n.* **1.** The state or condition of being excited; agitation. **2.** Something that excites.

ex·cit·er (ĭk-sī′tər) *n.* **1.** One that excites. **2.** An auxiliary generator used to provide field current for a larger generator or alternator. **3.** *Electronics.* An oscillator for generating the carrier frequency of a transmitter.

ex·cit·ing (ĭk-sī′tĭng) *adj.* Creating excitement or agitation; rousing. —**ex·cit·ing·ly** *adv.*

ex·ci·ton (ĕk′sī-tŏn′, ĕk′sī′-) *n.* An electrically neutral excited state of a crystal, often regarded as a bound state of an electron and a hole. [EXCIT(ATION) + -ON.]

ex·ci·tor (ĭk-sī′tər) *n.* Any nervous or chemical agent that induces activity in an organism.

excl. excluding; exclusive.

ex·claim (ĭk-sklām′) *v.* **-claimed, -claiming, -claims.** —*intr.* To cry out or speak suddenly or vehemently, as from surprise or emotion. —*tr.* To cry out or utter suddenly or vehemently. [Old French *exclamer,* from Latin *exclāmāre,* to call out, exclaim : *ex-,* out + *clāmāre,* to call.] —**ex·claim·er** *n.*

ex·cla·ma·tion (ĕk′sklə-mā′shən) *n.* **1.** An abrupt, forceful utterance. **2.** An outcry.

exclamation point *n.* **1.** A punctuation mark (!) used after an exclamation. **2.** An exclamation point used as a symbol, as in mathematics or logic.

ex·clam·a·to·ry (ĭk-sklăm′ə-tôr′ē, -tōr′ē) *adj.* Constituting, containing, relating to, or using exclamation.

ex·claus·tra·tion (ĕk'sklô-trā'shən) n. The release from vows and return to the outside world of a monk or nun. [Medieval Latin *exclaustrātiō* (stem *exclaustrātiōn-*), a putting outside the cloister. See ex-, cloister.]

ex·clave (ĕks'klāv') n. A portion of a country that is isolated from the main part and that exists as an enclave in alien territory: *Cabinda, in Zaire, is an exclave of Angola.* Compare **enclave.** [EX- + (EN)CLAVE.]

ex·clo·sure (ĭk-sklō'zhər) n. An area, as in a forest, fenced off to prevent intrusion.

ex·clude (ĭk-sklōōd') tr.v. -cluded, -cluding, -cludes. 1. To prevent or keep from entering a place, group, or the like; bar; reject. 2. To avoid noticing or considering; leave out; disregard. 3. To eject; expel. [Middle English *excluden*, from Latin *exclūdere* : *ex-*, out + *claudere*, to shut.] —ex·clud·a·bil·i·ty n. —ex·clud·a·ble, ex·clud·i·ble adj. —ex·clud·er n.

ex·clu·sion (ĭk-sklōō'zhən) n. 1. The act of excluding; rejection. 2. The state of being excluded. [Latin *exclūsiō* (stem *exclūsiōn-*), from *exclūsus*, past participle of *exclūdere*, to EXCLUDE.] —ex·clu·sion·ar·y (ĭk-sklōō'zhə-něr'ē) adj.

ex·clu·sion·ist (ĭk-sklōō'zhə-nĭst) n. One who favors or practices excluding others from rights or privileges. —ex·clu·sion·ism n. —ex·clu·sion·ist adj.

exclusion principle n. The principle that no two particles of a given type, such as electrons, protons, or neutrons, can occupy a particular quantum state. Also called "Pauli exclusion principle."

ex·clu·sive (ĭk-sklōō'sĭv) adj. Abbr. **excl.** 1. Pertaining to, characterized by, or requiring exclusion. 2. a. Not divided or shared with others: *exclusive publishing rights.* b. Available through only one retail outlet. 3. Single or independent; sole: *your exclusive function.* 4. Regarded as unrelated or autonomous; separate; incompatible: *mutually exclusive roles in life.* 5. Concentrated on the matter at hand; undivided; undistracted. 6. Not including the specified limits or items: *paragraphs 8 to 17 exclusive.* 7. a. Admitting only certain people to membership, participation, or the like; select. b. Catering to a wealthy clientele; expensive; chic: *exclusive shops.* 8. *Logic.* Designating a disjunction that is valid if one but not both of its elements is true. —exclusive of. Not including or considering: *exclusive of other factors.*
~n. 1. A news item granted to or obtained by only one person or source. 2. An exclusive right or privilege, as to market a product. —ex·clu·siv·i·ty (ĕk'sklōō-sĭv'ə-tē) n. —ex·clu·sive·ly adv. —ex·clu·sive·ness n.

ex·cog·i·tate (ĕk-skŏj'ə-tāt') tr.v. -tated, -tating, -tates. 1. To think out in great detail. 2. To devise; contrive. [Latin *excōgitāre*, to find out by thinking : *ex-*, out + *cōgitāre*, to COGITATE.] —ex·cog·i·ta·tion n. —ex·cog·i·ta·tive (ĕk-skŏj'ə-tā'tĭv, -tə-tĭv) adj.

ex·com·mu·ni·ca·ble (ĕks'kə-myōō'nĭ-kə-bəl) adj. Liable to, meriting, or punishable by excommunication.

ex·com·mu·ni·cate (ĕks'kə-myōō'nĭ-kāt') tr.v. -cated, -cating, -cates. 1. To cut off from the rites, privileges, or fellowship of a church by ecclesiastical authority; exclude from religious membership. 2. To exclude from membership or participation in a group. ~n. (-kĭt). A person who has been excommunicated.
~adj. (-kĭt, -kāt'). Excommunicated. [Middle English *excommunicaten*, from Late Latin *excommūnicāre* (past participle *excommūnicātus*), to put out of the (church) community : Latin *ex-*, out + *commūnicāre*, to COMMUNICATE.] —ex·com·mu·ni·ca·tive (ĕks'kə-myōō'nĭ-kā'tĭv, -kə-tĭv), ex·com·mu·ni·ca·to·ry (-kə-tôr'ē, -tōr'ē) adj. —ex·com·mu·ni·ca·tor n.

ex·com·mu·ni·ca·tion (ĕks'kə-myōō'nĭ-kā'shən) n. 1. The act of excommunicating. 2. The state of being excommunicated; exclusion. 3. The formal ecclesiastical censure or motion by which one is excommunicated.

ex·co·ri·ate (ĭk-skôr'ē-āt', ĭk-skōr'-) tr.v. -ated, -ating, -ates. 1. To censure strongly; denounce severely; upbraid. 2. To tear or wear off the skin of; abrade; chafe. [Middle English *excoriaten*, from Latin *excoriāre* (past participle *excoriātus*), to strip of its skin : *ex-*, removal from + *corium*, skin, hide, leather.]

ex·co·ri·a·tion (ĭk-skôr'ē-ā'shən, ĭk-skōr'-) n. 1. a. The act of excoriating. b. The state of being excoriated. 2. The raw skin surface resulting from abrasion or scraping; a sore.

ex·cre·ment (ĕk'skrə-mənt) n. Waste material expelled from the body; especially, fecal matter. [Latin *excrēmentum*, from *excrētus*, past participle of *excernere*, to sift out : *ex-*, out + *cernere*, to sift.] —ex·cre·men·tal (ĕk'skrə-měn'təl) adj.

ex·cres·cence (ĭk-skrěs'əns) n. 1. An abnormal, disfiguring outgrowth or enlargement: *"a weird horny excrescence that had detached itself from the ceremonious big toe"* (John Cowper Powys). 2. A normal outgrowth or appendage, such as a beard or toenail. [Middle English, from Latin *excrēscentia*, from *excrēscēns*, present participle of *excrēscere*, to grow out : *ex-*, out + *crēscere*, to grow.]

ex·cres·cen·cy (ĭk-skrěs'ən-sē) n., pl. -cies. 1. The state of being excrescent. 2. An excrescence.

ex·cres·cent (ĭk-skrěs'ənt) adj. 1. Growing out abnormally, excessively, or superfluously. 2. *Linguistics.* Designating a speech sound added without any grammatical or etymological basis; epenthetic. —ex·cres·cent·ly adv.

ex·cre·ta (ĭk-skrē'tə) pl.n. Waste matter, such as sweat, urine, or feces, excreted from the body. [New Latin, from Latin *excrēta*, from the neuter plural past participle of *excernere*, to sift out. See excrement.] —ex·cre·tal adj.

ex·crete (ĭk-skrēt') tr.v. -creted, -creting, -cretes. To eliminate (waste matter) from the blood, tissues, or organs. [Latin *excernere* (past participle *excrētus*), to sift out. See excrement.]

ex·cre·tion (ĭk-skrē'shən) n. 1. The process or act of excreting undigested food residues or metabolic wastes. 2. The matter so excreted.

ex·cre·to·ry (ĕk'skrə-tôr'ē) adj. Also ex·cre·tive (ĭk-skrē'tĭv). 1. Of or pertaining to excretion. 2. Having the function of excreting: *excretory organs.*

ex·cru·ci·ate (ĭk-skrōō'shē-āt') tr.v. -ated, -ating, -ates. 1. To inflict severe pain on; torture. 2. To inflict great mental pain on; torment. [Latin *excruciāre*, to torment : *ex-*, completely + *cruciāre*, to torment, crucify, from *crux* (stem *cruc-*), CROSS.] —ex·cru·ci·a·tion n.

ex·cru·ci·at·ing (ĭk-skrōō'shē-ā'tĭng) adj. 1. Intensely painful; agonizing: *an excruciating headache.* 2. Marked by great intensity. —ex·cru·ci·at·ing·ly adv.

ex·cul·pate (ĕk'skəl-pāt', ĭk-skŭl'-) tr.v. -pated, -pating, -pates. To clear of a charge; prove guiltless or blameless; exonerate. [Medieval Latin *exculpāre* : Latin *ex-* (removal away from) + *culpa*, guilt, blame (see culpa).] —ex·cul·pa·ble adj. —ex·cul·pa·tion (ĕk'skəl-pā'shən) n.

ex·cul·pa·to·ry (ĭk-skŭl'pə-tôr'ē, -tōr'ē) adj. Proving or tending to prove guiltless; exculpating.

ex·cur·rent (ĭk-skûr'ənt) adj. 1. a. Running or flowing in an outward direction. b. Having an outward flow. Said of a duct, tube, or anatomical passage. 2. *Botany.* a. Having a single, undivided trunk with lateral branches, as do many coniferous trees. b. Extending beyond the apex of a leaf, as a midrib or vein does. [Latin *excurrens* (stem *excurrent-*), present participle of *excurrere*, to run out. See excursion.]

ex·cur·sion (ĭk-skûr'zhən) n. 1. A usually short journey made with the intention of returning to the starting point; an outing. 2. a. A pleasure tour, as in a bus or train, especially one of limited duration and at a special low fare. b. The people on such a tour. 3. A rambling from the main topic; a digression. 4. *Obsolete.* A military raid; a sortie. 5. a. A movement from a mean position or axis in an oscillating or alternating motion. b. The distance traversed in such a movement. 6. An explosion of fissionable material in a nuclear reactor, caused by an uncontrollable chain reaction of neutrons. [Latin *excursiō* (stem *excursiōn-*), from *excursus*, past participle of *excurrere*, to run out : *ex-*, out + *currere*, to run.]

ex·cur·sion·ist (ĭk-skûr'zhə-nĭst) n. A person who goes on an excursion.

ex·cur·sive (ĭk-skûr'sĭv) adj. 1. Given to digression; rambling: *an excursive lecturer.* 2. Unmethodical; desultory: *excursive reading habits.* [From Latin *excursus.* See excursion.] —ex·cur·sive·ly adv. —ex·cur·sive·ness n.

ex·cur·sus (ĭk-skûr'səs) n., pl. -suses or excursus. 1. A lengthy, appended exposition of a topic or point, as in a text. 2. A digression. [Latin, from the past participle of *excurrere*, to run out. See excursion.]

ex·cus·a·to·ry (ĭk-skyōō'zə-tôr'ē, -tōr'ē) adj. Tending or serving to excuse; apologetic.

ex·cuse (ĭk-skyōōz') tr.v. -cused, -cusing, -cuses. 1. To grant pardon to; forgive: *She excused him for his clumsiness.* 2. To make allowance for (a shortcoming); overlook: *I hope you'll excuse my mistake.* 3. To serve as justification for; vindicate: *Her brilliance does not excuse her rudeness.* 4. To free, as from an obligation or duty; exempt: *The sick child was excused from basketball practice.* 5. ᴛo give (someone) permission to leave; dismiss or release. 6. To refrain from exacting; remit: *excuse taxes.* —See Synonyms at forgive. —excuse me. 1. Used, sometimes ironically, as an apology. 2. Used to request someone to move out of the way. 3. Used to request someone to repeat what he has just said. —excuse oneself. 1. To request forgiveness; seek indulgence or apologize. 2. To request exemption, as from an obligation or duty. 3. To request permission to leave.
~n. (ĭk-skyōōs') 1. A plea or explanation offered to elicit pardon. 2. The reason or ground for excusing. 3. An act of excusing; forgiveness or indulgence. 4. A note explaining an absence. 5. *Informal.* One that falls short of certain standards or expectations: *He is a poor excuse for a poet.* [Middle English *excusen*, from Old French *excuser*, from Latin *excūsāre* : *ex-*, removal from + *causa*, accusation, CAUSE.] —ex·cus·a·ble adj. —ex·cus·a·ble·ness n. —ex·cus·a·bly adv. —ex·cus·er n.

Usage: The expression *excuse away* has no meaning beyond that of *excuse* (unlike *explain away,* which has a different meaning from *explain*): *His behavior cannot be excused* (not *excused away*).

ex·di·rec·to·ry (ĕks'dĭ-rěk'tə-rē, ĕks'dī-) adj. British. Unlisted in the telephone directory and not procurable by inquiry.

ex dividend adj. Abbr. **ex div.** Finance. Without claim on the current dividend.

ex·e·at (ĕk'sē-ăt') n. British. 1. Official permission to be absent from classes or from residence in an institution. 2. Official permission from a bishop for a clergyman to leave the diocese. [Latin, "let him go out."]

ex·e·cra·ble (ĕk'sĭ-krə-bəl) adj. 1. Detestable; abominable; abhorrent. 2. Extremely inferior; very bad. [Middle English, from Old French, from Latin *ex(s)ecrābilis*, from *ex(s)ecrārī*, to EXECRATE.] —ex·e·cra·bly adv.

ex·e·crate (ĕk'sĭ-krāt') tr.v. -crated, -crating, -crates. 1. To inveigh against; denounce. 2. To abominate; abhor. 3. *Archaic.* To invoke a curse upon; curse. [Latin *ex(s)ecrārī*, to curse, execrate : *ex-*, opposing + *sacrāre*, to be sacred, from *sacer*, sacred.] —ex·e·cra·tive *adj.* —**ex·e·cra·tor** *n.* —**ex·e·cra·to·ry** (ĕk'sĭ-krə-tôr'ē, -tōr'ē) *adj.*

ex·e·cra·tion (ĕk'sĭ-krā'shən) *n.* **1.** The act of execrating. **2.** A curse. **3.** Detestation; abhorrence. **4.** That which is execrated; something that is loathed.

ex·ec·u·tant (ĭg-zĕk'yə-tənt) *n.* One who performs or carries out; especially, a musical performer.

ex·e·cute (ĕk'sĭ-kyo͞ot') *tr.v.* **-cuted, -cuting, -cutes. 1.** To carry out; put into effect: *execute a law.* **2.** To perform; do. **3.** To produce (a work of art, for example) in accordance with a prescribed design. **4.** To make valid, as by signing and sealing; legalize: *execute a deed.* **5.** To perform or carry out what is required by: *execute a will.* **6.** To subject to capital punishment. —See Synonyms at **perform.** [Middle English *executen,* from Old French *executer,* from Medieval Latin *executāre,* from Latin *ex(s)equī* (past participle *ex(s)ecūtus*), to execute, follow to the end : *ex-,* completely + *sequī,* to follow.] —**ex·e·cut·a·ble** *adj.* —**ex·e·cut·er** *n.*

ex·e·cu·tion (ĕk'sĭ-kyo͞o'shən) *n.* **1.** The act of executing. **2.** The state of being executed. **3.** The manner, style, or result of performance. **4.** A putting or being put to death as a legal penalty. **5.** *Law.* **a.** The carrying into effect of a court judgment. **b.** A writ empowering an officer to enforce a judgment. **6.** *Law.* The validating of a legal document by the performance of certain formalities, such as signing or sealing. **7.** Effective, punitive, or destructive action.

ex·e·cu·tion·er (ĕk'sĭ-kyo͞o'shə-nər) *n.* **1.** One who administers capital punishment. **2.** One who puts another to death.

ex·ec·u·tive (ĭg-zĕk'yə-tĭv) *n. Abbr.* **ex., exec. 1.** A person or group having administrative or managerial authority in an organization. **2.** The branch of government charged with putting into effect a country's laws and with the administration of its functions. **3.** The chief officer of a government, state, or political division.
~*adj. Abbr.* **ex., exec. 1.** Of, pertaining to, capable of, or suited for carrying out plans, duties, or the like. **2.** Of or pertaining to the branch of government charged with the execution and administration of a nation's laws. Compare **legislative, judicial. 3.** Of, pertaining to, or suitable for an executive: *an executive suite.*

executive officer *n.* **1.** A person holding executive power in an organization. **2.** The officer second in command of a military unit smaller than a division. **3.** The officer second in command of a naval unit.

executive routine *n. Computer Science.* A set of coded instructions given to a computer in order to use it to develop or control other routines.

executive secretary *n.* A secretary having administrative duties and responsibilities.

executive session *n.* A legislative session, usually one closed to the public.

ex·ec·u·tor (ĭg-zĕk'yə-tər; *also* ĕk'sĭ-kyo͞o'tər *for sense 1*) *n.* **1.** A person who carries out or performs something. **2.** *Law.* A person who is appointed by a testator to execute his will. —**ex·ec·u·to·ri·al** (ĭg-zĕk'yə-tôr'ē-əl, -tōr'ē-əl) *adj.* —**ex·ec·u·tor·ship** *n.*

ex·ec·u·to·ry (ĭg-zĕk'yə-tôr'ē, -tōr'ē) *adj.* **1.** Administrative. **2.** Operative; in effect. **3.** *Law.* Intended to go into effect, or having the potential of becoming effective at some future time; contingent.

ex·ec·u·trix (ĭg-zĕk'yə-trĭks) *n., pl.* **-trixes** or **executrices** (ĭg-zĕk'-yə-trī'sēz'). *Law.* A woman who is appointed by a testator to execute his will.

ex·e·dra (ĕk'sĭ-drə, ĭk-sē'-) *n., pl.* **-drae** (-drē'). **1.** In classical architecture, a portico with a curved continuous bench where discussions were held. **2.** A usually curved outdoor bench of masonry with a high back. [Latin, from Greek *exedra,* out(door) seat, bench : *ex-,* out + *hedra,* seat.]

ex·e·ge·sis (ĕk'sə-jē'sĭs) *n., pl.* **-ses** (-sēz'). Critical explanation or analysis; especially, interpretation of the Scriptures. Compare **eisegesis.** [New Latin, from Greek *exēgēsis,* from *exēgeisthai,* to show the way, expound : *ex-,* out of + *hēgeisthai,* to lead.]

ex·e·gete (ĕk'sə-jēt') *n.* Also **ex·e·get·ist** (ĕk'sə-jēt'ĭst). A person skilled in exegesis. [Greek *exēgētes,* from *exēgeisthai,* to expound. See **exegesis.**]

ex·e·get·ic (ĕk'sə-jĕt'ĭk) *adj.* Also **ex·e·get·i·cal** (-ĭ-kəl). Of or pertaining to exegesis; analytic. —**ex·e·get·i·cal·ly** *adv.*

ex·e·get·ics (ĕk'sə-jĕt'ĭks) *n. Used with a singular verb.* The science of exegesis. Compare **hermeneutics.**

ex·em·plar (ĭg-zĕm'plär', -plər) *n.* **1.** One that is worthy of being copied; a model. **2.** One considered typical or representative; an example; a specimen. **3.** An original, whether real or ideal; an archetype. **4.** A copy, as of a book, especially one that provided the basis for other copies. —See Synonyms at **ideal.** [Middle English, from Old French *exemplaire,* from Late Latin *exemplārium,* from Latin *exemplum,* EXAMPLE.]

ex·em·pla·ry (ĭg-zĕm'plə-rē) *adj.* **1.** Worthy of being imitated; commendable: *exemplary behavior.* **2.** Serving as a model or archetype. **3.** Serving as an illustration; typical. **4.** Serving as a warning: *exemplary punishment.* —**ex·em·plar·i·ly** (ĕg'zĕm-plâr'ə-lē) *adv.* —**ex·em·pla·ri·ness** *n.*

exemplary damages *pl.n.* **Punitive damages** *(see).*

ex·em·pli·fi·ca·tion (ĭg-zĕm'plə-fĭ-kā'shən) *n.* **1.** The act of exemplifying. **2.** One that exemplifies; an example. **3.** *Law.* An official and certified copy of a document from public records.

ex·em·pli·fi·ca·tive (ĭg-zĕm'plə-fĭ-kā'tĭv) *adj.* Serving to exemplify; providing an example.

ex·em·pli·fy (ĭg-zĕm'plə-fī') *tr.v.* **-fied, -fying, -fies. 1. a.** To illustrate by example. **b.** To serve as an example of. **2.** *Law.* To make a certified copy of (a document from public records). [Middle English *exemplifien,* from Old French *exemplifier,* from Medieval Latin *exemplificāre* : Latin *exemplum,* EXAMPLE + *facere,* to make.] —**ex·em·pli·fi·a·ble** *adj.* —**ex·em·pli·fi·er** *n.*

ex·em·pli gra·ti·a (ĭg-zĕm'plē grä'tē-ä', grā'shē-ə, -shə) *adv. Abbr.* **e.g.** For the sake of example; for example. [Latin.]

ex·em·plum (ĭg-zĕm'pləm) *n., pl.* **-pla** (-plə). **1.** A short moral story or fable used to illustrate an argument, especially in medieval sermons. **2.** Any illustrative example. [Latin, example.]

ex·empt (ĭg-zĕmpt') *tr.v.* **-empted, -empting, -empts.** To free from an obligation or duty required of others.
~*adj.* Freed from or not liable to something to which others are subject: *Nobody is exempt from blame.* Often used in combination: *a tax-exempt benefit.*
~*n.* One who is exempted from an obligation. [Middle English *exempten,* from Latin *eximere* (past participle *exemptus*), to take out, exempt. See **example.**] —**ex·empt·i·ble** *adj.*

ex·emp·tion (ĭg-zĕmp'shən) *n.* **1. a.** An act of exempting. **b.** The state of being exempt; immunity. **2. a.** Something that exempts. **b.** Something that is exempted, especially from taxable income.

ex·en·ter·ate (ĭg-zĕn'tə-rāt') *tr.v.* **-ated, -ating, -ates. 1.** To disembowel; eviscerate. **2.** *Surgery.* To remove the contents of (an organ). [Latin *exenterāre* (past participle *exenterātus*), to disembowel : *ex,* from, out of + Greek *enteron,* insides, intestines.] —**ex·en·ter·a·tion** *n.*

ex·e·qua·tur (ĕk'sĭ-kwā'tər, -kwä'tər) *n.* **1.** An official document recognizing a consul or commercial agent, granted by the country to which he is assigned. **2.** Authorization by a secular authority for the publication of ecclesiastical documents or for the performance by a bishop of his duties. [Latin, "let him perform," third person singular present subjunctive of *exequī,* to EXECUTE.]

ex·e·quies (ĕk'sĭ-kwēz) *pl.n.* Funeral rites. [Middle English *exequies,* from Old French, from Latin *exsequiae,* funeral ceremonies, from *ex(s)equī,* to follow, EXECUTE.]

ex·er·cise (ĕk'sər-sīz') *n.* **1.** An act of employing or putting into play; use: *"the demand for orthodoxy is stifling to any free exercise of intellect"* (Bertrand Russell). **2.** The discharge of a duty, function, or office. **3.** Activity that requires physical or mental exertion, especially when performed to develop or maintain fitness. **4. a.** A lesson, composition, problem, or the like, designed to increase one's skill, discipline, or fitness in some capacity: *a piano exercise.* **b.** A written task assigned to school pupils. **5.** *Military.* A program of practice maneuvers undertaken as part of military training. **6.** Any of the various events in gymnastics. **7. exercises.** A ceremony, either religious or secular, including speeches, awards, and other traditional rites: *graduation exercises.*
~*v.* **exercised, -cising, -cises.** —*tr.* **1.** To put into play or operation; employ. **2.** To bring to bear; exert: *"the desire to be re-elected exercises a strong brake on independent courage"* (John F. Kennedy). **3.** To subject to forms of practice or exertion in order to train, strengthen, or condition; put through exercises: *exercise the memory; exercise a platoon.* **4.** To carry out the functions of; execute; perform: *exercise the role of disciplinarian.* **5.** To absorb the attentions of; especially, to worry, upset, or make anxious: *He was greatly exercised by his wife's illness.* —*intr.* To take exercise or do exercises. [Middle English, from Old French *exercice,* from Latin *exercitium,* exercise, from *exercitus,* past participle of *exercēre,* to drive on, drill, practice : *ex-,* out of, from + *arcēre,* to enclose, restrain.] —**ex·er·cis·a·ble** *adj.*

ex·er·cis·er (ĕk'sər-sī'zər) *n.* **1.** A person who exercises or performs exercises. **2.** A device for exercising the body.

ex·er·ci·ta·tion (ĭg-zûr'sə-tā'shən) *n.* **1.** Exercise, as of a particular faculty or power: *intellectual exercitation.* **2.** Practice, as of an art, with a view to improvement: *rhetorical exercitation.* **3.** A display of oratorical skill: *the exercitations of Demosthenes.* [Middle English *exercitacioun,* from Latin *exercitātiō* (stem *exercitātiōn-*), from *exercitāre,* to exercise often, frequentative of *exercēre* (past participle *exercitus*), to EXERCISE.]

ex·er·gon·ic (ĕk'sər-gŏn'ĭk) *adj. Physics.* Designating a reaction, especially a nuclear reaction, that releases energy. [EX- (out) + Greek *ergon,* energy, work + -IC.]

ex·ergue (ĕk'sûrg', ĕg'zûrg') *n.* **1.** The space on the reverse of a coin or medal, usually below the central design. **2.** The inscription in an exergue, often showing the date and place of engraving. [French, from New Latin *exergum* : Greek *ex-,* out of + *ergon,* work.] —**ex·ergu·al** (ĕk-sûr'gəl) *adj.*

ex·ert (ĭg-zûrt') *tr.v.* **-erted, -erting, -erts. 1.** To put forth (strength or effort, for example). **2.** To bring to bear; exercise: *exert influence.* **3.** To cause (oneself) to make strenuous efforts. **4.** To make use of; employ: *took every opportunity to exert their authority.* [Latin *ex(s)erere* (past participle *ex(s)ertus*), to stretch out : *ex-,* out + *serere,* to join, put in a row, unite.]

ex·er·tion (ĭg-zûr'shən) *n.* An act or instance of exerting, especially a strenuous effort. —See Synonyms at **effort.**

Ex·e·ter (ĕk'sə-tər). County town of Devon, in southwestern England on the Exe River. It was a Roman fortress town, Isca Damnoniorum. Exeter's cathedral is a fine example of Gothic architecture.

ex·e·unt (ĕk'sē-ənt, -o͝ont'). Used as a stage direction to indicate that two or more actors leave the stage. [Latin, "they go out."]

exeunt om·nes (ŏm'nēz'). Used as a stage direction to indicate that all actors leave the stage. [Latin, "they all go out."]

ex·fo·li·ate (ĕks-fō'lē-āt') *v.* **-ated, -ating, -ates.** —*tr.* **1.** To remove (skin or bark, for example) in flakes or scales; peel. **2.** To cast off in scales, flakes, or the like. —*intr.* To come off or separate in scales,

PRONUNCIATION KEY

ă, pat; ā, pay; âr, care;
ä, father, are; b, bib;
ch, church; d, deed; ĕ, pet;
ē, be; f, fife; g, gag; h, hat;
hw, which; ĭ, pit; ī, pie;
îr, pier; j, judge; k, kick;
l, lid, needle; m, mum;
n, no, sudden; ng, thing;
ŏ, pot; ō, toe; ô, paw, for;
oi, noise; ou, out; o͝o, book;
o͞o, boot; p, pop; r, roar;
s, sauce; sh, ship, dish;
t, tight; th, thin, path;
th, this, bathe; ŭ, cut; ûr, fur;
v, valve; w, with; y, yes;
z, zebra, size; zh, vision;
ə, about, item, edible,
gallop, circus, peaceful

IN FOREIGN WORDS:

à, *Fr.* ami; œ, *Fr.* feu, *Ger.* schön; ü, *Fr.* tu, *Ger.* über; KH, *Ger.* ich, *Scot.* loch; N, *Fr.* bon; y', *Fr.* Compiègne

STRESS MARKS:

Primary stress: '
in·cite' (ĭn-sīt')
Secondary stress: '
in'sight' (ĭn'sīt')

flakes, sheets, or layers. [Latin *exfoliāre,* to strip of leaves : *ex-,* removal from + *folium,* leaf.] **—ex·fo·li·a·tion** *n.* **—ex·fo·li·a·tive** (ĕks-fōʹlē-āʹtĭv, -ə-tĭv) *adj.*

ex gra·ti·a (ĕks grāʹshē-ə, -shə) *adj.* Given without legal obligation; given as a favor: *an ex gratia payment.* [Latin, "from favor."]

ex·ha·lant (ĕks-hāʹlənt, ĕk-sāʹ-) *adj.* Performing or functioning in exhalation.

ex·ha·la·tion (ĕksʹhə-lāʹshən, ĕkʹsə-) *n.* **1.** An act of exhaling. **2.** Something that is exhaled, as air or vapor.

ex·hale (ĕks-hālʹ, ĕk-sālʹ) *v.* **-haled, -haling, -hales.** *—intr.* **1. a.** To breathe out. **b.** To emit air or vapor. **2.** To be given off or emitted. *—tr.* **1.** To blow forth or breathe out (vapor, smoke, or the like). **2.** To give off; emit. **3.** To draw out or off; evaporate. [Middle English *exalen,* from Old French *exhaler,* from Latin *exhālāre,* to breathe out : *ex-,* out + *hālāre,* to breathe.] **—ex·hal·a·ble** *adj.*

ex·haust (ĭg-zôstʹ) *v.* **-hausted, -hausting, -hausts.** *—tr.* **1.** To let out or draw off (air or fumes). **2. a.** To draw out the contents of; drain. **b.** To draw off; drain: *exhaust the oil from a storage tank.* **3.** To create a vacuum or partial vacuum in (a container). **4.** To use up; consume: *exhaust one's money.* **5.** To wear out completely; tire. **6.** To drain of resources or properties; deplete: *cotton crops that exhausted the soil.* **7.** To study or deal with comprehensively: *exhaust a topic.* *—intr.* To escape or pass out, as steam. —See Usage note at **deplete.**

~n. **1. a.** The escape or release of gas or vapor, as from an engine. **b.** The fumes or gases released. **2.** A device or part, such as a pipe, through which waste material is emitted. **3.** An apparatus for drawing out noxious air or waste material by means of a partial vacuum.

~adj. **1.** Designating a part of an engine through which expanded steam or the products of combustion pass: *exhaust valve; exhaust manifold.* **2.** Of, pertaining to, or designating the expanded steam or products of combustion of an engine or any phase of the engine's cycle relating to their extraction: *exhaust gas; exhaust stroke.* [Latin *exhaurīre* (past participle *exhaustus*), to draw out, exhaust : *ex-,* out + *haurīre,* to draw up.] **—ex·haust·er** *n.* **—ex·haust·i·bil·i·ty** *n.* **—ex·haust·i·ble** *adj.* **—ex·haust·ing·ly** *adv.*

ex·haus·tion (ĭg-zôsʹchən) *n.* **1.** The act or an instance of exhausting. **2.** The state of being exhausted. **3.** A state of great weariness; extreme fatigue.

ex·haus·tive (ĭg-zôʹstĭv) *adj.* **1.** Dealing with or taking account of all aspects; comprehensive; thorough. **2.** Tending to exhaust. **—ex·haus·tive·ly** *adv.* **—ex·haus·tive·ness** *n.*

ex·haust·less (ĭg-zôstʹlĭs) *adj.* Impossible to exhaust; inexhaustible. **—ex·haust·less·ness** *n.*

ex·hib·it (ĭg-zĭbʹĭt) *v.* **-ited, -iting, -its.** *—tr.* **1.** To show; display. **2. a.** To present for the public to view. **b.** To enter or show in an exhibition or contest. **3.** To give an instance or evidence of; demonstrate: *The specimen exhibits a cancerous condition.* **4.** *Law.* To submit (objects or documents) as evidence in a court; introduce officially. *—intr.* To put something on display; have an exhibition. —See Synonyms at **show.**

~n. **1.** An act of exhibiting. **2.** Something that is exhibited. **3.** *Law.* Something, such as a document, formally introduced as evidence in court. [Middle English *exhibiten,* from Latin *exhibēre* (past participle *exhibitus*), to hold forth, exhibit : *ex-,* out + *habēre,* to hold.] **—ex·hib·i·tive** *adj.* **—ex·hib·i·tive·ly** *adv.*

ex·hi·bi·tion (ĕkʹsə-bĭshʹən) *n.* **1.** An act of exhibiting: *Don't make an exhibition of yourself.* **2.** Something exhibited. **3.** A display for the public, as of art objects, industrial achievements, or agricultural products. **4.** *British.* A scholarship given to a student by a public school or university.

ex·hi·bi·tion·er (ĕkʹsə-bĭshʹə-nər) *n. British.* A student who has received an exhibition.

ex·hi·bi·tion·ism (ĕkʹsə-bĭshʹə-nĭzʹəm) *n.* **1.** The act or practice of behaving in an ostentatious way in order to attract attention. **2.** *Psychology.* Compulsive exposure of the sexual organs in public. **—ex·hi·bi·tion·ist** *n. & adj.* **—ex·hi·bi·tion·is·tic** *adj.*

ex·hib·i·tor (ĭg-zĭbʹə-tər) *n.* One that exhibits; especially, a person or group exhibiting articles in a show.

ex·hil·a·rant (ĭg-zĭlʹər-ənt) *adj.* Exhilarating.

~n. A stimulant or euphoriant.

ex·hil·a·rate (ĭg-zĭlʹə-rātʹ) *tr.v.* **-rated, -rating, -rates.** **1.** To make cheerful; elate. **2.** To invigorate; stimulate. [Latin *exhilarāre* : *ex-,* completely + *hilarāre,* to make happy, from *hilaris,* cheerful, happy, from Greek *hilaros.*] **—ex·hil·a·ra·tion** *n.* **—ex·hil·a·ra·tive** *adj.* **—ex·hil·a·ra·tor** *n.*

ex·hil·a·rat·ing (ĭg-zĭlʹə-rāʹtĭng) *adj.* **1.** Cheering; gladdening. **2.** Invigorating; stimulating. **—ex·hil·a·rat·ing·ly** *adv.*

ex·hort (ĭg-zôrtʹ) *v.* **-horted, -horting, -horts.** *—tr.* To urge or incite by strong argument, advice, or appeal; admonish earnestly. *—intr.* To make urgent appeal. —See Synonyms at **urge.** [Middle English *exhorten,* from Old French *exhorter,* from Latin *exhortārī* : *ex-,* completely + *hortārī,* to encourage.] **—ex·hor·ta·tive** (ĭg-zôrʹtə-tĭv), **ex·hor·ta·to·ry** (-tôrʹē, -tōrʹē) *adj.* **—ex·hort·er** *n.*

ex·hor·ta·tion (ĕgʹzôr-tāʹshən, ĕkʹsôr-) *n.* **1.** An act of exhorting. **2.** The practice of exhorting. **3.** A speech or discourse intended to advise, incite, or encourage.

ex·hume (ĭg-zo͞omʹ, -zyo͞omʹ, ĭk-so͞omʹ, -syo͞omʹ) *tr.v.* **-humed, -huming, -humes.** **1.** To remove (a dead body) from a grave; disinter. **2.** To bring to light; uncover: *exhume ancient superstitions.* [French *exhumer,* from Medieval Latin *exhumāre* : Latin *ex-,* out of + *humus,* earth.] **—ex·hu·ma·tion** (ĕgʹzo͞o-māʹshən, ĕgʹzyo͞o-, ĕkʹso͞o-, ĕkʹsyo͞o-) *n.* **—ex·hum·er** *n.*

ex hy·poth·e·si (ĕksʹ hī-pŏthʹə-sīʹ) *adv.* Following from the premise of the argument; in accordance with the stated hypothesis. [New Latin, "according to the hypothesis."]

ex·i·gen·cy (ĕkʹsə-jən-sē) *n., pl.* **-cies.** Also **ex·i·gence** (-jəns). **1.** The state or quality of being exigent. **2.** A situation demanding swift attention; emergency. **3.** *Often* **exigencies.** Urgent requirement; pressing need.

ex·i·gent (ĕkʹsə-jənt) *adj.* **1.** Requiring immediate attention or remedy; urgent. **2.** Excessively demanding; exacting. [Latin *exigēns* (stem *exigent-*), present participle of *exigere,* to demand.] **—ex·i·gent·ly** *adv.*

ex·i·gi·ble (ĕkʹsə-jə-bəl) *adj.* Able to be exacted; demandable; requirable. [French, from *exiger,* to demand, from Latin *exigere.*]

ex·ig·u·ous (ĭg-zĭgʹyo͞o-əs, ĭk-sĭgʹ-) *adj.* Scanty; meager. [Latin *exiguus,* from *exigere,* to weigh exactly, demand. See **exact.**] **—ex·i·gu·i·ty** (ĕkʹsə-gyo͞oʹə-tē), **ex·ig·u·ous·ness** *n.* **—ex·ig·u·ous·ly** *adv.*

ex·ile (ĕgʹzīlʹ, ĕkʹsīlʹ) *n.* **1. a.** Enforced removal from one's native country by authoritative decree; banishment. **b.** Self-imposed separation from one's country. **2. a.** The state or circumstance of being in exile. **b.** The period of time in exile. **3.** One who is separated or has been banished from his country.

~tr.v. **exiled, -iling, -iles.** To send (a person) into exile. —See Synonyms at **banish.** [Middle English *exil,* from Old French, from Latin *exilium,* from *exul,* one who is exiled.] **—ex·il·ic** (ĕg-zĭlʹĭk, ĕk-sĭlʹ-), **ex·il·ian** (ĕg-zĭlʹyən, -zĭlʹē-ən, ĭk-sĭlʹyən, -sĭlʹē-ən) *adj.*

ex in. *Finance.* Without interest. [Latin *ex,* without + *in*terest.]

ex·ine (ĕkʹsēnʹ, -sīnʹ) *n.* The outer wall of a spore or pollen grain. Also called "exosporium." [Latin *ex(timus),* outermost + -INE.]

ex·ist (ĭg-zĭstʹ) *intr.v.* **-isted, -isting, -ists.** **1.** To have being or actuality; be. **2. a.** To have life; live. **b.** To continue to live; survive, especially in difficult or reduced circumstances. **3.** To be present under certain circumstances or in a specified place; occur: *Tapeworms exist in human intestines.* [Latin *ex(s)istere,* to exist, come forth : *ex-,* out + *sistere,* to take a position, stand firm.]

ex·is·tence (ĭg-zĭsʹtəns) *n.* **1.** The fact or state of existing; being. **2.** The fact or state of continued being; life; survival. **3. a.** All that exists. **b.** A thing that exists; an entity. **4.** A mode or manner of existing: *a meager existence.* **5.** Occurrence; specific presence: *the existence of life on other planets.*

ex·is·tent (ĭg-zĭsʹtənt) *adj.* **1.** Having life or being; existing. **2.** Occurring or present at the moment; current. —See Synonyms at **real.**

~n. One that exists.

ex·is·ten·tial (ĕgʹzĭ-stĕnʹshəl, ĕkʹsĭ-) *adj.* **1.** Of, pertaining to, or dealing with existence. **2.** Based on experience; empirical. **3.** Of or pertaining to existentialism. **4.** *Logic.* Of, pertaining to, or designating a proposition that implies or specifies the existence of at least one of its elements. **—ex·is·ten·tial·ly** *adv.*

ex·is·ten·tial·ism (ĕgʹzĭ-stĕnʹshə-lĭzʹəm, ĕkʹsĭ-) *n.* A body of ethical thought, current in the 20th century, centering on the uniqueness and isolation of individual experience in a universe indifferent or even hostile to man, regarding human existence as unexplainable, and emphasizing man's freedom of choice and responsibility for the consequences of his acts. **—ex·is·ten·tial·ist** *adj. & n.*

ex·it[1] (ĕgʹzĭt, ĕkʹsĭt). Used as a stage direction for a specified actor to leave the stage. [Latin, "He (or she) goes out."]

exit[2] *n.* **1.** The departure of a performer from the stage. **2. a.** The act of going away or out. **b.** Death; demise. **3.** A way out; a door or passage through which one can leave.

~intr.v. **exited, -iting, -its.** To go away or out. [Latin *exitus,* exit, departure, from the past participle of *exīre,* to go out : *ex-,* out + *īre,* to go.]

ex·i·tance (ĕkʹsə-təns) *n.* A measure of the ability of a surface to emit radiation. See **luminous exitance, radiant exitance.** [Latin *exitus,* departure, emission + -ANCE.]

exit permit *n.* In South Africa, a permit to emigrate without the right to return.

ex li·bris (ĕks lĭʹbrĭs, lēʹ-) *n., pl.* **ex libris.** *Abbr.* **ex lib.** A bookplate. [Latin, "from the books."]

ex-li·brist (ĕks-lĭʹbrĭst, -lēʹbrĭst) *n.* One who collects bookplates. **—ex-li·brism** *n.*

Ex·moor (ĕksʹmo͝orʹ). A thinly populated moorland in southwestern England, forming much of Exmoor National Park. The moor contains a number of prehistoric earthworks.

Exmoor pony *n.* A pony of a hardy, sure-footed breed that originated in the Exmoor region of England and has short ears, large eyes, and a bay, brown, or dun coat.

Exmoor pony *One of nine breeds of pony that roam the mountains and moors of the British Isles. It stands about 12 hands high at the shoulder (a hand is about 10 centimeters, or 4 inches) and is distinguished from its close relative, the Dartmoor pony, by its longer and larger head.*

ex ni·hi·lo (ĕks nēʹə-lōʹ, nīʹə-lōʹ) *adj. & adv.* Out of nothing. [Latin.]

exo– *prefix.* Indicates outside, external, or beyond; for example, **exocarp, exoskeleton.** [Greek *exō,* outside, from *ex,* out of.]

ex·o·bi·ol·o·gy (ĕkʹsō-bī-ŏlʹə-jē) *n.* **1.** A branch of biology that deals with the search for and study of extraterrestrial living organisms. Also called "astrobiology." **2.** A branch of biology that deals with the effects of extraterrestrial space on living organisms. In this sense, also called "space biology."

ex·o·carp (ĕkʹsō-kärpʹ) *n. Botany.* The outermost layer of the pericarp of fruit. Also called "epicarp." [EXO- + -CARP.]

ex·o·cen·tric (ĕkʹsō-sĕnʹtrĭk) *adj. Grammar.* Designating a construction that serves a grammatical function different from that of any of its constituents; for example, *toward the icy summit* is an exocentric construction, since while it functions adverbially, none of its constituent words does. Compare **endocentric.**

Ex·o·cet (ĕkʹsō-sĕtʹ) *n.* A trademark for a versatile guided missile steered by a preset guidance system until it is near the target, after

which it is guided by radar signals. [French, from New Latin *exocoeta (volans),* the (flying) fish, from Greek *exōkoitos,* name of a fish believed to sleep out of the water at night : *exō,* out of + *koitos,* bed.]

ex·o·crine (ĕk'sə-krĭn, -krēn', -krīn') *adj.* **1.** Having or secreting through a duct. Said of a gland. **2.** Of or pertaining to the secretion of a gland having a duct. [EXO- + Greek *krinein,* to separate.]

Exod. Exodus (Old Testament).

ex·o·derm (ĕk'sō-dûrm') *n.* An embryonic germ layer, the **ectoderm** *(see).* [EXO- + -DERM.]

ex·o·der·mis (ĕk'sə-dûr'mĭs) *n. Botany.* A layer of protective cells in roots, lying just beneath the epidermis.

ex·o·don·tia (ĕk'sə-dŏn'shə, -shē-ə) *n.* Dentistry involving the extraction of teeth. [New Latin : EX- + *-odontia,* from -ODONT.] **—ex·o·don·tist** *n.*

ex·o·dus (ĕk'sə-dəs) *n.* **1.** A movement away; a departure, usually of a large number of people. **2. Exodus.** The departure of the Israelites from Egypt. Preceded by *the.* [Late Latin, from Greek *exodos,* a going out, a way out : *ex-,* out + *hodos,* way.]

Exodus *n. Abbr.* **Ex., Exod.** The second book of the Old Testament, which recounts the Exodus of the Israelites.

ex·o·en·zyme (ĕk'sō-ĕn'zīm') *n.* **1.** An enzyme that acts on the terminal chemical bonds in a chain molecule. **2.** An enzyme, such as a digestive enzyme, that functions outside a cell.

ex·o·er·gic (ĕk'sō-ûr'jĭk) *adj. Physics.* Exergonic.

ex of·fi·ci·o (ĕks' ə-fĭsh'ē-ō') *adj. Abbr.* **e.o., ex off.** By virtue of office or position. [Latin.] **—ex officio** *adv.*

ex·og·a·my (ĕk-sŏg'ə-mē) *n.* **1.** The custom of marrying outside the tribe, family, clan, or other social unit. Compare **endogamy. 2.** *Biology.* Reproduction by the fusion of gametes that are not closely related. [EXO- + -GAMY.] **—ex·o·gam·ic** (ĕk'sə-găm'ĭk), **ex·og·a·mous** (ĕk-sŏg'ə-məs) *adj.*

ex·og·e·nous (ĕk-sŏj'ə-nəs) *adj.* **1.** *Biology.* Derived or developed from outside the body, as substances derived from diet rather than metabolism are. **2.** *Botany.* Characterized by the addition of layers of woody tissue. **3.** Having a cause external to the body. Said of diseases. **4.** Having an outside origin: *exogenous political unrest.* [French *exogène,* having additional layers : EXO- + -GEN.] **—ex·o·gen·ic** (ĕk'sə-jĕn'ĭk) *adj.* **—ex·og·e·nous·ly** *adv.*

ex·o·in·tine (ĕk'sō-ĭn'tĭn, -tēn', -tīn') *n.* The middle layer of a spore or pollen grain, between the intine and the exine. Also called "mesosporium."

ex·on·er·ate (ĭg-zŏn'ə-rāt') *tr.v.* **-ated, -ating, -ates. 1.** To free from a charge; declare blameless; exculpate. **2.** To free from a responsibility, obligation, or task; exempt. [Middle English *exoneraten,* from Latin *exonerāre* (past participle *exonerātus*), to free from a burden : *ex-,* removal from + *onus* (stem *oner-*), load, burden.] **—ex·on·er·a·tion** *n.*

ex·o·nu·mi·a (ĕk'sō-nōō'mē-ə, -nyōō'mē-ə) *n.* The study and collection of small items, such as tickets or labels, that are not traditionally classified as numismatic objects. [EXO- (outside, beyond) + *-numia,* from Latin *nummus,* coin.]

ex·o·nym (ĕk'sə-nĭm') *n.* Any of the names of a city, river, or the like, in a language other than the language of the region or country in which that place or geographic feature is located; for example, *Londres* is an exonym of *London.* [EX(O)- + -ONYM.]

ex·oph·thal·mic goiter (ĕk'sŏf-thăl'mĭk) *n.* A disease caused by the excessive production of thyroid hormone and characterized by an enlarged thyroid gland, protrusion of the eyeballs, a rapid heartbeat, weight loss, and nervous excitability. Also called "Graves' disease." [From EXOPHTHALMOS.]

ex·oph·thal·mos (ĕk'sŏf-thăl'məs) *n.* Also **ex·oph·thal·mi·a** (-mē-ə), **ex·oph·thal·mus** (-məs). Abnormal protrusion of the eyeballs. [New Latin, from Greek, with prominent eyes : *ex-,* out of + *ophthalmos,* eye.]

ex·or·bi·tant (ĭg-zôr'bə-tənt) *adj.* Beyond reasonable limits or bounds; immoderate. **—See Synonyms at excessive.** [Middle English, from Old French, from Late Latin *exorbitāns,* present participle of *exorbitāre,* to deviate : Latin *ex-,* out of + *orbita,* route, ORBIT.] **—ex·or·bi·tance** *n.* **—ex·or·bi·tant·ly** *adv.*

ex·or·cise, ex·or·cize (ĕk'sôr-sīz', ĕk'sər-) *tr.v.* **-cised, -cising, -cises** or **-cized, -cizing, -cizes. 1.** To expel (an evil spirit) by or as if by incantation or prayer. **2.** To free from evil spirits. [Middle English *exorcisen,* from Old French *exorciser,* from Late Latin *exorcīzāre,* from Greek *exorkizein,* to exorcise (an evil spirit) with an oath : *ex-,* away + *horkos†,* oath.] **—ex·or·cis·er** *n.*

ex·or·cism (ĕk'sôr-sĭz'əm, ĕk'sər-) *n.* **1.** The act of exorcising. **2.** A formula used in exorcising. **—ex·or·cist** *n.*

ex·or·di·um (ĭg-zôr'dē-əm, ĭk-sôr'-) *n., pl.* **-ums** or **-dia** (-dē-ə). An introductory part, especially of a speech or treatise. [Latin, from *exōrdīrī,* to begin : *ex-,* completely + *ōrdīrī,* to begin.] **—ex·or·di·al** *adj.*

ex·o·skel·e·ton (ĕk'sō-skĕl'ə-tən) *n.* The external protective or supporting structure of many invertebrates, such as insects and crustaceans. Compare **endoskeleton.**

ex·os·mo·sis (ĕk'sŏz-mō'sĭs) *n.* The flow of a solvent through a semipermeable membrane into a surrounding fluid; especially, the flow of water through a cell membrane into the external medium. Compare **endosmosis.** [EX(O)- + OSMOSIS.] **—ex·os·mot·ic** (ĕk'sŏz-mŏt'ĭk) *adj.*

ex·o·sphere (ĕk'sə-sfîr') *n.* The outermost portion of the atmosphere, estimated to begin 300 to 600 miles above the earth and characterized by the ability of constituent molecules with appropri-

ate velocities to escape from the earth without colliding with other molecules. [EXO- + -SPHERE.]

ex·o·spore (ĕk'sō-spôr', -spōr') *n. Botany.* The outermost layer of a spore in some algae and fungi. [EXO- + SPORE.]

ex·o·spo·ri·um (ĕk'sō-spôr'ē-əm, -spōr'ē-əm) *n.* Exine *(see).*

ex·os·to·sis (ĕk'sō-stō'sĭs) *n., pl.* **-ses** (-sēz'). A bony tumor on the surface of a bone. [New Latin, from Greek *exostōsis : ex-,* out of + *osteon,* bone.]

ex·o·ter·ic (ĕk'sə-tĕr'ĭk) *adj.* **1.** Not confined to an inner circle of disciples or initiates. **2.** Comprehensible to or suited to the general public; popular. Compare **esoteric. 3.** Pertaining to the outside; external. [Latin *exōtericus,* external, from Greek *exōterikos,* from *exōterō,* comparative of *exō,* outside, from *ex,* out.]

ex·o·ther·mic (ĕk'sō-thûr'mĭk) *adj.* Also **ex·o·ther·mal** (-məl). Characterized by or causing the release of heat. Compare **endothermic.** [EXO- + THERM(O)- + -IC.]

ex·ot·ic (ĭg-zŏt'ĭk) *adj.* **1.** From another part of the world; not indigenous; foreign. **2.** Having the charm of the unfamiliar; strikingly and intriguingly unusual, different, or beautiful. **—See Synonyms at fantastic.**
~*n.* Something that is exotic, such as an alien plant, animal, or disease. [Latin *exōticus,* from Greek *exōtikos,* from *exō,* outside, from *ex,* out.] **—ex·ot·i·cal·ly** *adv.* **—ex·ot·i·cism** (ĭg-zŏt'ĭ-sĭz'əm), **ex·ot·ic·ness** *n.*

ex·ot·i·ca (ĭg-zŏt'ĭ-kə) *pl.n.* Exotic things, as in a collection. [Latin, neuter plural of *exōticus,* EXOTIC.]

ex·o·tox·in (ĕk'sō-tŏk'sĭn) *n.* A toxin excreted by a microorganism into a surrounding medium and recoverable from a culture without destruction of the producing agent. See **toxin.**

exp exponential.

ex·pand (ĭk-spănd') *v.* **-panded, -panding, -pands.** *—tr.* **1.** To open up or out; spread out; unfold. **2.** To increase the dimensions of; cause to swell; distend. **3.** To increase the scope of; extend; develop. **4.** *Mathematics.* To write (a quantity) as a sum of terms, as a continued product, or as another extended form. *—intr.* **1.** To open up; unfold. **2.** To become larger or wider. **3.** To speak or write at length; expatiate. **4.** To become expansive. **—See Synonyms at increase.** [Middle English *expanden,* from Latin *expandere : ex-,* out + *pandere,* to spread.] **—ex·pand·a·ble** *adj.*

ex·pand·ed (ĭk-spăn'dĭd) *adj.* **1.** *Printing.* Wider than normal in proportion to its height; extended. Said of type. Compare **condensed. 2.** Puffed into a foamlike texture by the addition of gas during solidification. Said of a plastic or similar material used in packaging or insulating.

expanded metal *n.* An open metal mesh used for reinforcing brittle materials and in fencing.

ex·pand·er, ex·pan·dor (ĭk-spăn'dər) *n.* **1.** *Electronics.* A device for expanding the range of output voltages for a given range of input voltages according to a specific law. **2.** A device for exercising and developing body muscles: *a chest expander.*

expanding universe theory *n.* **1.** A theory that interprets the shifts of the lines in the spectra of galaxies as resulting from a Doppler effect, with the result that all galaxies are assumed to be retreating from each other at speeds proportional to the distance separating them and that the universe is expanding. **2.** The cosmological theory in which violent eruption from a point source leads to the formation of elementary particles, the subsequent formation of hydrogen and helium, and the dispersion of the galaxies that develop from this matter. Compare **steady-state theory.** See **big-bang theory.**

ex·panse (ĭk-spăns') *n.* **1.** A wide and open extent, as of land, sky, or water. **2.** Expansion. [Latin *expansum,* from the neuter participle of *expandere,* to EXPAND.]

ex·pan·si·ble (ĭk-spăn'sə-bəl) *adj.* Capable of expanding or of being expanded. **—ex·pan·si·bil·i·ty** *n.*

ex·pan·sile (ĭk-spăn'səl, -sīl') *adj.* Of, pertaining to, or adapted for expansion.

ex·pan·sion (ĭk-spăn'shən) *n.* **1.** The act or process of expanding. **2.** The state of being expanded. **3.** A part or form produced by expanding. **4.** The extent or amount by which something has expanded. **5.** An enlargement, increase, or extension, as of business, currency, or territory. **6.** Increase in the dimensions of a body. **7.** *Mathematics.* **a.** A quantity written in an extended form, such as a series. **b.** The process of obtaining this form. **8.** An expanse. **—ex·pan·sion·ar·y** (ĭk-spăn'shə-nĕr'ē) *adj.*

expansion bolt *n.* A bolt having an attachment that expands as the bolt is driven into a surface.

ex·pan·sion·ism (ĭk-spăn'shə-nĭz'əm) *n.* The practice or policy of territorial or economic expansion, as by a nation. **—ex·pan·sion·ist** *n. & adj.* **—ex·pan·sion·is·tic** (ĭk-spăn'shə-nĭs'tĭk) *adj.*

ex·pan·sive (ĭk-spăn'sĭv) *adj.* **1.** Capable of expanding or tending to expand. **2.** Wide; sweeping; comprehensive. **3.** Disposed to be open and outgoing. **4.** *Psychology.* Marked by euphoria and delusions of grandeur. **5.** Grand in scale: *expansive living.* **—ex·pan·sive·ly** *adv.* **—ex·pan·sive·ness** *n.*

ex parte (ĕks pär'tē) *adj. & adv.* **1.** *Law.* From or on one side only. **2.** One-sided; partisan. [Latin.]

ex·pa·ti·ate (ĭk-spā'shē-āt') *intr.v.* **-ated, -ating, -ates. 1.** To speak or write at length on a subject; dilate. Often used with *on* or *upon.* **2.** *Archaic.* To wander freely. [Latin *ex(s)patiārī,* to spread out, digress, expatiate : *ex-,* out + *spatiārī,* to walk, to spread, from *spatium,* SPACE.] **—ex·pa·ti·a·tion** *n.* **—ex·pa·ti·a·to·ry** (ĭk-spā'shə-tôr'ē, -tōr'ē) *adj.*

ex·pa·tri·ate (ĕks-pā′trē-āt′) v. -ated, -ating, -ates. —tr. **1.** To banish (a person) from his native land; exile. **2.** To banish (oneself) from one's native land. —intr. To leave one's homeland, and often renounce one's citizenship, to reside in another country. —See Synonyms at **banish.**
~n. (-ĭt, -āt′). An expatriated person; an exile.
~adj. (-āt′, -ĭt). Expatriated. [Medieval Latin expatriāre : Latin ex-, out of + patria, native land, from pater (stem patr-), father.] —**ex·pa·tri·a·tion** n.

ex·pect (ĭk-spĕkt′) tr.v. -pected, -pecting, -pects. **1.** To look forward to the probable occurrence or appearance of. **2.** To consider likely or certain. **3.** To consider reasonable or due: I expect an apology. **4.** To consider obligatory; require. **5.** Informal. To presume; suppose. —See Usage note at **anticipate.** [Latin ex(s)pectāre, to look out (for), expect : ex-, out + spectāre, to look at, frequentative of specere, to see, look at.]
   Synonyms: anticipate, await, foresee, hope.

ex·pec·tan·cy (ĭk-spĕk′tən-sē) n., pl. -cies. Also **ex·pec·tance** (-təns). **1.** The act or state of expecting; expectation. **2.** The state of being expected. **3. a.** Something expected. **b.** An expected amount calculated on the basis of statistical probability: a life expectancy of seventy years.

ex·pec·tant (ĭk-spĕk′tənt) adj. **1.** Having or marked by expectation: an expectant pause. **2.** Awaiting the birth of a child: an expectant mother. **3.** Waiting in confident expectation. Used with of: expectant of praise.
~n. A person who is expecting something. —**ex·pec·tant·ly** adv.

ex·pec·ta·tion (ĕk′spĕk-tā′shən) n. **1. a.** The act or state of expecting. **b.** Eager anticipation: The child's eyes were bright with expectation. **2.** The state of being expected. **3. expectations.** Prospects, especially of inheritance. **4.** Something expected or hoped for. **5.** The expected value of a random variable, especially the **mean** (see). —See Usage note at **prospect.**

ex·pec·ta·tive (ĭk-spĕk′tə-tĭv) adj. Of, pertaining to, or characterized by expectation.

ex·pect·ing (ĭk-spĕk′tĭng) adj. Informal. Awaiting the birth of a child; pregnant.

ex·pec·to·rant (ĭk-spĕk′tər-ənt) adj. Promoting or facilitating the secretion or expulsion of phlegm or other matter from the mucous membrane of the air passages.
~n. An expectorant medicine.

ex·pec·to·rate (ĭk-spĕk′tə-rāt′) v. -rated, -rating, -rates. —tr. **1.** To eject from the mouth; spit. **2.** To cough up and eject by spitting. —intr. **1.** To spit. **2.** To clear out the chest and lungs by coughing up and spitting out matter. [Latin expectorāre, to drive from the breast : ex-, from, out of + pectus (stem pector-), breast.] —**ex·pec·to·ra·tion** n.

ex·pe·di·en·cy (ĭk-spē′dē-ən-sē) n., pl. -cies. Also **ex·pe·di·ence** (-dē-əns). **1.** Appropriateness to the purpose at hand. **2.** Adherence to what is personally advantageous; self-interest. **3.** An expedient.

ex·pe·di·ent (ĭk-spē′dē-ənt) adj. **1.** Appropriate to the purpose at hand. **2.** Serving to promote one's own interests; politic though perhaps unprincipled.
~n. **1.** Something that answers an immediate purpose; a means to an end. **2.** A contrivance adopted to meet an urgent need. [Middle English, from Old French, from Latin expediēns (stem expedient-), present participle of expedīre, to free, make ready. See **expedite.**] —**ex·pe·di·ent·ly** adv.

ex·pe·di·en·tial (ĭk-spē′dē-ĕn′shəl) adj. Of, pertaining to, or concerned with what is expedient. —**ex·pe·di·en·tial·ly** adv.

ex·pe·dite (ĕk′spə-dīt′) tr.v. -dited, -diting, -dites. **1.** To speed up the progress of; help along; assist; facilitate. **2.** To perform quickly and efficiently. **3.** To issue officially; dispatch. —See Synonyms at **speed.** [Latin expedīre (past participle expedītus), to free the feet, to extricate.] —**ex·pe·dit·er, ex·pe·di·tor** n.

ex·pe·di·tion (ĕk′spə-dĭsh′ən) n. **1. a.** A journey undertaken by an organized group of people with a definite objective, such as exploration. **b.** The people on such a journey. **2. a.** A long march or voyage made by military forces to a scene of battle. **b.** The force sent out, with vehicles and equipment. **3.** Speed in performance; promptness. [Middle English expedicioun, from Old French expedition, from Latin expedītiō (stem expedītiōn-), from expedītus, past participle of expedīre, to extricate. See **expedite.**]

ex·pe·di·tion·ar·y (ĕk′spə-dĭsh′ə-nĕr′ē) adj. Of, pertaining to, or being an expedition, especially a military expedition.

ex·pe·di·tious (ĕk′spə-dĭsh′əs) adj. Acting or done with speed and efficiency. —See Synonyms at **fast.** —**ex·pe·di·tious·ly** adv. —**ex·pe·di·tious·ness** n.

ex·pel (ĭk-spĕl′) tr.v. -pelled, -pelling, -pels. **1.** To force or drive out; eject forcefully. **2.** To discharge, as from the body or a receptacle: expelled a huge sigh of relief. **3.** To dismiss, as from a school, by official decision; turn out. —See Synonyms at **eject.** [Middle English expellen, from Latin expellere : ex-, out + pellere, to drive.] —**ex·pel·la·ble** adj. —**ex·pel·ler** n.

ex·pel·lant, ex·pel·lent (ĭk-spĕl′ənt) adj. Expelling or tending to expel; expulsive.
~n. A medicine used to expel substances or organisms from the body, especially worms from the intestines.

ex·pend (ĭk-spĕnd′) tr.v. -pended, -pending, -pends. **1.** To put out or lay out; spend. **2.** To use up; consume. [Middle English expenden, from Latin expendere, to pay out : ex, out + pendere, to weigh, pay.]

ex·pend·a·ble (ĭk-spĕn′də-bəl) adj. **1.** Subject to use or consump-

tion. **2.** Liable to being sacrificed in the interests of gaining an objective, especially a military one.
~n. Something that is expendable.

ex·pen·di·ture (ĭk-spĕn′də-chər, -choor′) n. **1.** The act or process of expending; outlay. **2. a.** The amount expended. **b.** An expense. —See Synonyms at **price.**

ex·pense (ĭk-spĕns′) n. **1. a.** Cost; charge. **b.** Outlay of money: He was put to considerable expense. **c.** A sacrifice; a price: "Every attempt at a system is made at the expense of facts" (Bernard Berenson). **2. expenses. a.** Charges incurred while performing one's job. **b.** Informal. Money allotted for payment of such charges. **3.** Something requiring the expenditure of money: Educating his children was an enormous expense. **4.** Archaic. An act of expending; expenditure. —See Synonyms at **price.**
~tr.v. -pensed, -pensing, -penses. **1.** To charge with expenses. **2.** To write off as an expense. [Middle English, from Old French espense, from Late Latin expensa, from the feminine past participle of Latin expendere, to EXPEND.]

expense account n. An account of expenses for travel, entertainment, or the like, incurred by an employee in the course of his work and repaid by his employer.

ex·pen·sive (ĭk-spĕn′sĭv) adj. **1.** Involving a large expenditure; high-priced; costly. **2.** Involving considerable loss or sacrifice: an expensive mistake. —See Synonyms at **costly.** —**ex·pen·sive·ly** adv. —**ex·pen·sive·ness** n.

ex·pe·ri·ence (ĭk-spîr′ē-əns) n. **1.** The apprehension of an object, thought, or emotion through the senses or mind: the experience of art. **2.** Active participation in events or activities, leading to the accumulation of knowledge or skill. **3.** The knowledge or skill so derived. **4.** An event or series of events participated in or lived through, especially one that makes a powerful impression on the mind or senses. **5.** The totality of such events in the past of an individual or group.
~tr.v. experienced, -encing, -ences. To participate in or partake of personally; undergo: experience a feeling of loneliness. [Middle English, from Old French, from Latin experientia, from experiēns, present participle of experīrī, to try, test.]

ex·pe·ri·enced (ĭk-spîr′ē-ənst) adj. **1.** Skilled through frequent use or practice. **2.** Knowledgeable from long or wide experience: an experienced teacher.

experience table n. A table compiled from life-insurance statistics to indicate life expectancy.

ex·pe·ri·en·tial (ĭk-spîr′ē-ĕn′shəl) adj. Pertaining to or derived from experience. —**ex·pe·ri·en·tial·ly** adv.

ex·pe·ri·en·tial·ism (ĭk-spîr′ē-ĕn′shə-lĭz′əm) n. Philosophy. The doctrine that knowledge is derived only from experience.

ex·per·i·ment (ĭk-spĕr′ə-mənt) n. **1.** A test made to demonstrate a known truth, to examine the validity of a hypothesis, or to determine the efficacy of something previously untried: a laboratory experiment. **2.** The process of conducting an experiment. **3.** An act or approach that is original or unusual: Presenting a classical opera with the singers in modern dress was an experiment.
~intr.v. (-mĕnt′) experimented, -menting, -ments. To conduct an experiment or experiments; try or test. [Middle English, from Old French, from Latin experimentum, from experīrī, to try, test. See **experience.**] —**ex·per·i·ment·er** n. —**ex·per·i·men·ta·tion** (ĭk-spĕr′ə-mĕn-tā′shən) n.

ex·per·i·men·tal (ĭk-spĕr′ə-mĕnt′l) adj. **1. a.** Pertaining to or based upon experiment. **b.** Given to experimenting. **2.** Provisional; tentative. **3.** Founded upon experience; empirical. —**ex·per·i·men·tal·ly** adv.

ex·per·i·men·tal·ism (ĭk-spĕr′ə-mĕnt′l-ĭz′əm) n. The use of empirical or experimental methods in determining the validity of an idea. —**ex·per·i·men·tal·ist** n.

ex·pert (ĕk′spûrt′) n. A person with a high degree of skill in or knowledge of a certain subject.
~adj. (ĕk′spûrt′, ĭk-spûrt′). Having or demonstrating impressive skill, dexterity, or knowledge. [Middle English, from Old French, from Latin expertus, past participle of experīrī, to try.] —**ex·pert·ly** adv. —**ex·pert·ness** n.

ex·per·tise (ĕk′spər-tēz′, -tēs′) n. **1.** Expert advice or opinion. **2.** Specialized knowledge; expertness. [French, survey, evaluation, from Old French, expertness, from EXPERT.]

ex·pi·a·ble (ĕk′spē-ə-bəl) adj. Capable of being expiated.

ex·pi·ate (ĕk′spē-āt′) v. -ated, -ating, -ates. —tr. To make atonement for; redress. —intr. To make expiation. [Latin expiāre : ex-, completely + piāre, to appease, atone, from pius, devout.] —**ex·pi·a·tor** n.

ex·pi·a·tion (ĕk′spē-ā′shən) n. **1.** The act of expiating; atonement. **2.** The means of redress or atonement; amends. —**ex·pi·a·to·ry** (ĕk′spē-ə-tôr′ē, -tōr′ē) adj.

ex·pi·ra·tion (ĕk′spə-rā′shən) n. **1.** A coming to a close; a termination; an ending. **2.** The act or sound of breathing out.

ex·pi·ra·to·ry (ĭk-spīr′ə-tôr′ē, -tōr′ē) adj. Of, pertaining to, or involving the expiration of air from the lungs.

ex·pire (ĭk-spīr′) v. -pired, -piring, -pires. —intr. **1.** To come to an end; terminate: His membership expired. **2.** To breathe one's last breath; die. **3.** To breathe out; exhale. —tr. **1.** To breathe out. **2.** Archaic. To give off (moisture, for example); exude. [Middle English expiren, from Old French exspirer, from Latin ex(s)pīrāre, to breathe out, to expire : ex-, out + spīrāre, to breathe.]

ex·pir·ee (ĕk′spī-rē′, ĭk-spī′-) n. Formerly, a British convict who had been transported to Australia and whose sentence had expired.

ex·pi·ry (ĭk-spīr′ē) *n., pl.* **-ries.** An expiration, especially of a contract or agreement. [From EXPIRE.]

ex·plain (ĭk-splān′) *v.* **-plained, -plaining, -plains.** *—tr.* **1.** To make plain or comprehensible; remove obscurity from; elucidate: *explain a puzzle.* **2.** To define; explicate; expound: *He explained his plan.* **3.** To offer reasons for or a cause of; answer for; justify: *explain an error.* *—intr.* To give an explanation. **—explain away.** To minimize, excuse, or nullify by explanation. **—explain oneself.** To clarify the meaning of what one has said or the motives for one's actions. [Middle English *explanen,* from Latin *explānāre,* to explain, to spread out : *ex-,* completely + *plānus,* plain, flat.] **—ex·plain·a·ble** *adj.*

Synonyms: *elucidate, explicate, expound, interpret.*

ex·pla·na·tion (ĕk′splə-nā′shən) *n.* **1.** The act or process of making plain or comprehensible; elucidation; clarification: *His plan requires explanation.* **2.** That which serves to explain or to account for something: *He always has a ready explanation.* **3.** A mutual clarification of misunderstandings; a reconciliation.

ex·plan·a·tive (ĭk-splăn′ə-tĭv) *adj.* Explanatory.

ex·plan·a·to·ry (ĭk-splăn′ə-tôr′ē, -tōr′ē) *adj.* Serving or intended to explain. **—ex·plan·a·to·ri·ly** *adv.*

ex·plant (ĕks-plănt′, -plänt′) *tr.v.* **-planted, -planting, -plants.** To take (living tissue) from the natural site of growth and place in a medium or culture.
∼n. (ĕks′plănt′, -plänt′). Material explanted. **—ex·plan·ta·tion** (ĕks′plăn-tā′shən) *n.*

ex·ple·tive (ĕk′splə-tĭv) *n.* **1.** An exclamation or oath, especially one that is profane or obscene. **2. a.** A word or phrase added to a line of verse or a sentence in order to ease syntax or rhythm but not to add any meaning. **b.** A word that stands in place of and anticipates a following word or phrase; for example, the word *it* is an expletive in the sentence *It is nice to see you.*
∼adj. Also **ex·ple·to·ry** (ĕk′splə-tôr′ē, -tōr′ē). Added or inserted in order to fill out something, such as a metrical line or a sentence. [Late Latin *explētīvus,* from Latin *explētus,* past participle of *explēre,* to fill out : *ex-,* out + *plēre,* to fill.]

ex·pli·ca·ble (ĕk′splĭ-kə-bəl, ĭk-splĭk′ə-) *adj.* Capable of being explained; explainable.

ex·pli·cate (ĕk′splĭ-kāt′) *tr.v.* **-cated, -cating, -cates. 1.** To make clear the meaning of; explain. **2.** To devise or elaborate (a theory). —See Synonyms at **explain.** [Latin *explicāre,* to unfold, explicate : *ex-* (reversal) + *plicāre,* to fold.] **—ex·pli·ca·tor** *n.*

ex·pli·ca·tion (ĕk′splĭ-kā′shən) *n.* **1.** An explanation. **2.** Exhaustive exposition and elucidation. **3.** Critical exposition and interpretation, as of literary texts.

ex·pli·ca·tive (ĕk′splĭ-kā′tĭv, ĭk-splĭk′ə-) *adj.* Also **ex·pli·ca·to·ry** (ĕk′splĭ-kə-tôr′ē, -tōr′ē, ĭk-splĭk′ə-). Serving to explain; explanatory.

ex·plic·it[1] (ĭk-splĭs′ĭt) *adj.* **1.** Expressed fully and with precision; clearly defined; specific. **2. a.** Forthright and unreserved in expression; outspoken: *They were explicit in their criticism.* **b.** Describing sexual acts in detail. Used euphemistically. **3.** Designating a function having an equation $y = f(x)$, in which y can be expressed directly in terms of x. Compare **implicit.** [French *explicite,* from Latin *explicitus,* past participle of *explicāre,* to EXPLICATE.] **—ex·plic·it·ly** *adv.* **—ex·plic·it·ness** *n.*

ex·pli·cit[2] (ĕk′splĭ-kĭt, -sĭt) *n.* A word formerly used to indicate the close of a manuscript or book. [Late Latin, short for *explicitus (est liber),* "(the book is) unrolled," from Latin *explicitus,* EXPLICIT.]

ex·plode (ĭk-splōd′) *v.* **-ploded, -ploding, -plodes.** *—intr.* **1.** To release mechanical, chemical, or nuclear energy in an explosion. **2.** To burst and be destroyed by explosion. **3.** To burst forth or break out suddenly: *explode into action.* **4.** To fly into a sudden rage. **5.** To increase suddenly, sharply, and without control. *—tr.* **1.** To cause to explode or burst violently and noisily; detonate. **2.** To expose as false, unreliable, or irrelevant; confute: *explode a hypothesis.* [Latin *explōdere,* to drive out by clapping : *ex-,* out + *plauderet†,* to clap.] **—ex·plod·er** *n.*

exploded view *n.* An illustration or diagram of a construction that shows its parts separately but in positions that indicate their proper relationships to the whole.

ex·ploit (ĕk′sploit′, ĭk-sploit′) *n.* An act or deed, especially a brilliant or heroic feat.
∼tr.v. (ĭk-sploit′, ĕk′sploit′) **exploited, -ploiting, -ploits. 1. a.** To employ to the greatest possible advantage; utilize: *exploit an advantage.* **b.** To turn to maximum commercial advantage. **2.** To make use of selfishly or unethically; take advantage of: *exploit peasant labor.* [Middle English *esploit, expleit,* from Old French *exploit, esplait,* achievement, from Gallo-Romance *explictum* (unattested), from Latin *explicitus,* EXPLICIT.] **—ex·ploit·a·ble** *adj.* **—ex·ploit·a·tive** (ĭk-sploi′tə-tĭv), **ex·ploit·ive** (-sploi′tĭv) *adj.* **—ex·ploit·er** *n.*

ex·ploi·ta·tion (ĕk′sploi-tā′shən) *n.* **1.** The act of exploiting. **2.** The utilization of another person for selfish purposes.

ex·plo·ra·tion (ĕk′splə-rā′shən) *n.* The act or an instance of exploring; an investigation or search.

ex·plore (ĭk-splôr′, -splōr′) *v.* **-plored, -ploring, -plores.** *—tr.* **1.** To investigate systematically; examine: *explore every possibility.* **2.** To search into or range over (a country) for the purpose of discovery. **3.** *Medicine.* To examine for diagnostic purposes. *—intr.* **1.** To make an examination; study. **2.** To travel through an unfamiliar region with a view to learning about it. [Latin *explōrāre,* to search out, explore : *ex-,* out + *plōrāre,* to cry aloud (see **deplore**).] **—ex·plor·a·to·ry** (ĭk-splôr′ə-tôr′ē, -splōr′ə-tōr′ē) *adj.*

ex·plor·er (ĭk-splôr′ər, -splōr′ər) *n.* **1.** One who explores; especially, one who explores a geographic area. **2.** An implement or tool used for exploring; a probe. **3. Explorer.** Any of a series of early U.S. satellites, the first of which confirmed the existence of the Van Allen belts, others being used for scientific study, as of the atmosphere, the earth's magnetic field, solar radiation, and x-rays from space.

ex·plo·sion (ĭk-splō′zhən) *n.* **1.** A sudden rapid violent release of mechanical, chemical, or nuclear energy from a confined region; especially, such a release that generates a radially propagating shock wave accompanied by a loud, sharp report, flying debris, heat, light, and fire. **2.** The loud, sharp sound accompanying such a release. **3.** Anything regarded as having the characteristics or destructive potential of such a release. **4.** A sudden and often vehement outburst, as of emotion: *an abrupt explosion of rage.* **5.** A sudden and great increase: *the population explosion.* **6.** *Phonetics.* **Plosion** *(see).* [Latin *explōsiō* (stem *explōsiōn-*), from *explōsus,* past participle of *explōdere,* to EXPLODE.]

ex·plo·sive (ĭk-splō′sĭv, -zĭv) *adj.* **1.** Pertaining to or involving an explosion. **2.** Tending or liable to explode. **3.** Liable to give rise to conflict or argument: *an explosive topic.* **4.** *Phonetics.* Pertaining to plosion; plosive.
∼n. **1.** A substance, especially a prepared chemical, that explodes or causes explosion. **2.** *Phonetics.* A **plosive** *(see).* [Old French *explosif,* from Latin *explōsus.* See **explosion.**] **—ex·plo·sive·ly** *adv.* **—ex·plo·sive·ness** *n.*

ex·po (ĕk′spō) *n., pl.* **-pos.** *Informal.* An exhibition, as of industrial products. [Short for EXPOSITION.]

ex·po·nent (ĭk-spō′nənt, ĕk′spō′-) *n.* **1.** One that defines, expounds, or interprets. **2.** One that speaks for, represents, or advocates: *an exponent of international cooperation.* **3.** An interpretive artist, especially one highly skilled in a particular musical instrument. **4.** *Mathematics.* A number or symbol, as 3 in $(x+y)^3$, placed to the right of and above another number, symbol, or expression, denoting the number of times the number, symbol, or expression is to be multiplied by itself. In this sense, also called "power."
∼adj. Giving an explanation or analysis; explanatory. [Latin *expōnēns* (stem *expōnent-*), present participle of *expōnere,* to EXPOUND.]

ex·po·nen·tial (ĕk′spə-nĕn′shəl) *adj.* **1.** *Mathematics.* **a.** Containing, involving, or expressed as an exponent. **b.** *Abbr.* **exp** Expressed in terms of a designated exponent of *e,* the base of natural logarithms. **2.** Of or pertaining to an exponent.
∼n. An exponential function. **—ex·po·nen·tial·ly** *adv.*

exponential growth *n. Ecology.* Optimal growth of numbers in a population, where the rate of increase is proportional to the number of individuals and thus becomes increasingly fast until some factor, such as lack of food, limits further increase.

exponential series *n. Mathematics.* The series $e^x = 1 + x + x^2/2! + x^3/3! \ldots + x^n/n!$ When $x = 1$, $e = 2.718$.

ex·po·ni·ble (ĭk-spō′nə-bəl) *adj.* Requiring or admitting of explanation. Said especially of an obscure logical proposition. [Medieval Latin *expōnibilis,* from Latin *expōnere,* to EXPOUND.]

ex·port (ĭk-spôrt′, -spōrt′, ĕk′spôrt′, -spōrt′) *v.* **-ported, -porting, -ports.** *—tr.* **1. a.** To sell (goods or services) to a foreign country. **b.** To send or carry (goods) abroad, especially for sale or trade. Compare **import. 2.** To encourage or propagate (an idea, for example) abroad: *export revolution.* *—intr.* To send or carry goods abroad, especially for sale or trade.
∼n. (ĕk′spôrt′, -spōrt′). **1.** The act of exporting: *the export of heavy machinery.* **2.** Something that is exported. [Latin *exportāre,* to carry out or away : *ex-,* out + *portāre,* to carry.] **—ex·port** (ĕk′spôrt′, -spōrt′) *adj.* **—ex·port·a·bil·i·ty** *n.* **—ex·port·a·ble** *adj.* **—ex·port·er** *n.*

ex·por·ta·tion (ĕk′spôr-tā′shən, ĕk′spōr-) *n.* **1.** The act, process, or business of exporting. **2.** Something that is exported.

ex·pose (ĭk-spōz′) *tr.v.* **-posed, -posing, -poses. 1. a.** To lay open to something undesirable or injurious; make vulnerable: *expose a child to an unnecessary risk.* **b.** To lay open or introduce to something beneficial or positive: *She was exposed to music before she had even learned to talk.* **2.** To subject (a photographic film or plate) to the action of light. **3.** To make visible or known; make manifest: *Cleaning exposed the grain of the wood.* **4.** To disclose or unmask (a crime or criminal, for example); lay bare; make known. **5.** *Roman Catholic Church.* To leave (the Host) displayed on the altar for veneration. **6.** To abandon (an infant, for example) without food or shelter. —See Synonyms at **reveal, show. —expose oneself.** To engage in exhibitionism. [Middle English *exposen,* from Old French *exposer,* from Latin *expōnere,* to expose, EXPOUND.] **—ex·pos·er** *n.*

ex·po·sé (ĕk′spō-zā′) *n.* **1.** An exposure or revelation of something discreditable or scandalous. **2.** Something, as a book, that contains an exposé. **3.** A detailed account or statement of the facts; an exposition. [French, from the past participle of *exposer,* to EXPOSE.]

ex·posed (ĭk-spōzd′) *adj.* **1.** Open to view; not hidden. **2.** Unsheltered or uncovered: *an exposed layer of rock.* **3.** Open to attack, criticism, or danger; vulnerable; susceptible.

ex·po·si·tion (ĕk′spə-zĭsh′ən) *n.* **1.** A setting forth of meaning or intent. **2.** A precise statement or definition; an explication; an elucidation. **3.** *Music.* The first part of a sonata or fugue that introduces the themes. **4.** The part of a play or story that introduces the theme and chief characters. **5.** The act of exposing or the condition of being exposed. **6.** A public exhibition or show, as of artistic or industrial products. **7.** *Roman Catholic Church.* The displaying of

PRONUNCIATION KEY

ă, pat; ā, pay; âr, care; ä, father, are; b, bib; ch, church; d, deed; ĕ, pet; ē, be; f, fife; g, gag; h, hat; hw, which; ĭ, pit; ī, pie; îr, pier; j, judge; k, kick; l, lid, needle; m, mum; n, no, sudden; ng, thing; ŏ, pot; ō, toe; ô, paw, for; oi, noise; ou, out; o͝o, book; o͞o, boot; p, pop; r, roar; s, sauce; sh, ship, dish; t, tight; th, thin, path; *th*, this, bathe; ŭ, cut; ûr, fur; v, valve; w, with; y, yes; z, zebra, size; zh, vision; ə, about, item, edible, gallop, circus, peaceful

IN FOREIGN WORDS:

à, *Fr.* ami; œ, *Fr.* feu, *Ger.* schön; ü, *Fr.* tu, *Ger.* über; KH, *Ger.* ich, *Scot.* loch; N, *Fr.* bon; y′, *Fr.* Compiègne

STRESS MARKS:

Primary stress: ′ in·cite′ (ĭn-sīt′)
Secondary stress: ′ in′sight′ (ĭn′sīt′)

the Host on the altar for public veneration. **8.** *Archaic.* Exposure. [Middle English *exposicioun,* from Old French *exposition,* from Latin *expositiō* (stem *expositiōn-*), from *expositus,* past participle of *expōnere,* to EXPOUND.] **—ex·pos·i·tive** (ĭk-spŏz′ə-tĭv), **ex·pos·i·to·ry** (-tôr′ē, -tōr′ē) *adj.* **—ex·pos·i·tor** *n.*

ex post fac·to (ĕks′ pōst′ făk′tō) *adj.* Formulated, enacted, or operating retroactively. Said especially of a law. [Medieval Latin *ex postfacto,* "from what is done afterward."]

ex·pos·tu·late (ĭk-spŏs′chə-lāt′) *intr.v.* **-lated, -lating, -lates.** To reason earnestly with someone in an effort to dissuade or correct; remonstrate. —See Synonyms at **object.** [Latin *expostulāre,* to demand strongly : *ex-,* entirely + *postulāre,* to demand.] **—ex·pos·tu·la·tor** *n.* **—ex·pos·tu·la·to·ry** (ĭk-spŏs′chə-lə-tôr′ē, -tōr′ē), **ex·pos·tu·la·tive** (-lā′tĭv, -lə-tĭv) *adj.*

ex·pos·tu·la·tion (ĭk-spŏs′chə-lā′shən) *n.* The act or an instance of expostulating; remonstrance.

ex·po·sure (ĭk-spō′zhər) *n.* **1.** The act or an instance of exposing. **2. a.** The condition of being exposed, as to influences or danger: *The exposure of children to drugs is a matter of grave concern.* **b.** Lack of protection from harsh weather conditions, especially cold: *die of exposure.* **3.** The fact or state of being presented to public view, as before an audience: *The candidates for election sought maximum television exposure.* **4.** A position in relation to climatic or weather conditions or points of the compass: *a room with a southern exposure.* **5. a.** The act of exposing sensitized photographic film or plate. **b.** A film or plate so exposed. **c.** The amount of radiant energy needed to expose a photographic film. **d.** A part of a film for individual pictures: *A 35-millimeter film often has 36 exposures.* **e.** The time, shutter speed, or aperture, or a combination of two or all three, that is used in exposing film.

exposure meter *n.* A photoelectric instrument that measures light intensity in a given area and in photographic use indicates the proper exposure for a particular shutter speed and type of film. Also called "light meter."

ex·pound (ĭk-spound′) *v.* **-pounded, -pounding, -pounds.** *—tr.* **1.** To give a detailed statement of; set forth. **2.** To elucidate or explain; interpret. *—intr.* To make a detailed statement; explain a point of view: *He was expounding on his favorite sport.* —See Synonyms at **explain.** [Middle English *expoun(d)en,* from Old French *espondre,* from Latin *expōnere,* to put forth, expose : *ex-,* out + *pōnere,* to place, put.] **—ex·pound·er** *n.*

ex·press (ĭk-sprĕs′) *tr.v.* **-pressed, -pressing, -presses. 1.** To make known or set forth in words; state; utter: *express one's wishes.* **2.** To manifest or communicate, as by a gesture; show; exhibit: *His posture expressed his exhaustion.* **3.** To make (one's opinions, for example) known: *expressed his feelings forcefully.* **4.** To convey or represent through words or other artistic means: *His poems express a sense of wonder.* **5.** To represent by a sign or symbol; symbolize: *The ∞ sign expresses infinity.* **6.** To squeeze or press out (juice from a fruit, for example). **7.** To send by special courier or rapid transport. —See Synonyms at **vent. —express oneself.** To communicate one's thoughts or feelings through words, gestures, or artistic activity.
~*adj. Abbr.* **ex., exp. 1.** Definitely and unmistakably stated; explicit: *an express wish.* **2.** Particular; specific: *an express purpose.* **3. a.** Sent out with or moving at high speed. **b.** Direct, rapid, and usually nonstop: *express mail.* **c.** Of, pertaining to, or appropriate for rapid travel.
~*adv.* By express delivery or transport.
~*n. Abbr.* **ex., exp. 1. a.** A means of transport, as a train, that travels rapidly and makes few or no stops. **b.** A company that deals in such transport. **2. a.** A special courier. **b.** A message delivered by special courier. **3. a.** A rapid, efficient system for the delivery of goods and mail. **b.** Goods and mail conveyed by such a system. **4.** An express rifle. [Middle English *expressen,* from Old French *expresser,* from Vulgar Latin *expressāre* (unattested), to press out, express : Latin *ex-,* out + *pressāre,* to press, from *premere* (past participle *pressus*), to press.] **—ex·press·er** *n.* **—ex·press·i·ble** *adj.*

ex·press·age (ĭk-sprĕs′ĭj) *n.* **1.** The conveyance of goods by express. **2.** The amount charged for such conveyance.

ex·pres·sion (ĭk-sprĕsh′ən) *n.* **1.** The act of expressing, conveying, or representing in words, art, music, or movement; a manifestation: *the expression of an idea.* **2.** That which communicates, indicates, embodies, or symbolizes something; a symbol; a sign; a token. **3.** *Mathematics.* Any symbolic mathematical form, such as an equation. **4. a.** The means by which something is expressed: *expression through music.* **b.** The quality of expressing feelings, attitudes, or the like through means such as tone or gesture: *His playing lacked expression.* **5.** The manner in which one expresses oneself, especially in speaking, depicting, or performing. **6.** A particular word or phrase: *a slang expression.* **7.** The outward manifestation of an inner mood or disposition: *Her tears were an expression of her grief.* **8.** A facial aspect or look that conveys a special feeling: *an expression of scorn in his eyes.* **9.** *Genetics.* **Penetrance** *(see).* **10.** The act of removing a liquid from a solid by squeezing.

ex·pres·sion·ism (ĭk-sprĕsh′ə-nĭz′əm) *n.* A movement in the fine arts during the first half of the 20th century that originated in Europe and tried to convey the quality of emotional experience rather than representing the physical world. In painting, this was achieved by the use of exaggeration and distortion, strong colors, and simplified outlines. **—ex·pres·sion·ist** *n.* & *adj.* **—ex·pres·sion·is·tic** (ĭk-sprĕsh′ə-nĭs′tĭk) *adj.*

ex·pres·sion·less (ĭk-sprĕsh′ən-lĭs) *adj.* **1.** Lacking expression. **2.** Having a fixed facial expression that shows or reveals no emotion. **—ex·pres·sion·less·ly** *adv.*

ex·pres·sive (ĭk-sprĕs′ĭv) *adj.* **1.** Pertaining to, related to, or characterized by expression: *expressive hands.* **2.** Serving to express or indicate: *His actions are expressive of frustration.* **3.** Full of expression; significant: *an expressive glance.* **—ex·pres·sive·ly** *adv.* **—ex·pres·sive·ness** *n.*

ex·pres·siv·i·ty (ĕk′sprĕ-sĭv′ə-tē) *n.* **1.** The quality of being expressive. **2.** *Genetics.* The degree to which a particular gene can affect the phenotype of an organism.

ex·press·ly (ĭk-sprĕs′lē) *adv.* **1.** In an express or definite manner; explicitly: *I expressly order you to leave.* **2.** Especially; particularly: *These chocolates are expressly for you.*

express rifle *n.* A hunting rifle having low trajectory, high velocity, and a long point-blank range.

express train *n.* A passenger or freight train that travels at high speed and makes a minimum of stops.

ex·press·way (ĭk-sprĕs′wā′) *n.* A major divided highway designed for fast travel.

ex·pro·pri·ate (ĕks-prō′prē-āt′) *tr.v.* **-ated, -ating, -ates. 1.** To deprive (a person) of ownership or property. **2.** To take away or transfer (ownership or property, for example) from an owner; especially, to acquire for public use. [Medieval Latin *expropriāre* : Latin *ex-* (removal away from) + *proprius,* one's own.] **—ex·pro·pri·a·tion** *n.* **—ex·pro·pri·a·tor** *n.* **—ex·pro·pri·a·to·ry** (ĕks-prō′prē-ə-tôr′ē, -tōr′ē) *adj.*

ex·pugn·a·ble (ĭk-spyo͞o′nə-bəl) *adj.* Capable of being defeated or taken by force. [Latin *expugnabilis* : *expugnāre,* to take by storm + *abilis,* -ABLE.]

ex·pul·sion (ĭk-spŭl′shən) *n.* The act of expelling or the state of being expelled. **—ex·pul·sive** (ĭk-spŭl′sĭv) *adj.*

ex·punc·tion (ĭk-spŭngk′shən, -spŭng′shən) *n.* The act of expunging or the condition of being expunged; deletion. [Latin *expunctus,* past participle of *expungere,* to EXPUNGE + -ION.]

ex·punge (ĭk-spŭnj′) *tr.v.* **-punged, -punging, -punges. 1.** To omit, erase, strike out, or obliterate (a word or sentence, for example). **2.** To eliminate physically; annihilate. —See Synonyms at **erase.** [Latin *expungere,* to prick out, erase : *ex-,* out + *pungere,* to prick.] **—ex·pung·er** *n.*

ex·pur·gate (ĕk′spər-gāt′) *tr.v.* **-gated, -gating, -gates. 1.** To amend (a text) by removing obscene or objectionable passages, especially prior to publication. **2.** To cleanse; purge. [Latin *expurgāre,* to purge out, purify : *ex-,* out + *purgāre,* to purge.] **—ex·pur·ga·tion** *n.* **—ex·pur·ga·tor** *n.* **—ex·pur·ga·to·ry** (ĭk-spûr′gə-tôr′ē, -tōr′ē), **ex·pur·ga·to·ri·al** (ĭk-spûr′gə-tôr′ē-əl, -tōr′ē-əl) *adj.*

ex·qui·site (ĕk′skwĭ-zĭt, ĭk-skwĭz′ĭt) *adj.* **1.** Beautifully made or designed: *an exquisite chalice.* **2.** Of such beauty or delicacy as to arouse delight: *an exquisite sunset.* **3.** Acutely perceptive or discriminating: *an exquisite sense of color.* **4.** Intense; keen: *an exquisite pain.*
~*n.* One who is excessively sensitive and fastidious in dress, manners, or taste; a dandy; a fop. [Middle English *exquisit,* from Latin *exquīsītus,* chosen, exquisite, from the past participle of *exquīrere,* to search out : *ex-,* out + *quaerere,* to seek.] **—ex·qui·site·ly** *adv.* **—ex·qui·site·ness** *n.*

ex·san·gui·nate (ĕks-săng′gwə-nāt′) *tr.v.* **-nated, -nating, -nates.** To drain of blood. [From Latin *exsanguinātus,* bloodless : *ex-,* without + *sanguis* (stem *sanguin-*), blood (see **sanguine**).] **—ex·san·gui·na·tion** *n.*

ex·san·guine (ĕks-săng′gwĭn) *adj.* Also **ex·san·gui·nous** (-gwĭ-nəs). Lacking blood; anemic. [Latin *exsanguis,* deprived of blood : *ex-,* without + *sanguis* (stem *sanguin-*), blood (see **sanguine**).]

ex·scind (ĭk-sĭnd′) *tr.v.* **-scinded, -scinding, -scinds.** To excise or cut out; extirpate. [Latin *exscindere* : *ex-,* out + *scindere,* to cut.]

ex·sect (ĭk-sĕkt′) *tr.v.* **-sected, -secting, -sects.** To cut out. [Latin *exsecāre* (past participle *exsectus*) : *ex-,* out + *secāre,* to cut.] **—ex·sec·tion** *n.*

ex·sert (ĭk-sûrt′) *tr.v.* **-serted, -serting, -serts.** To thrust out or forth; cause to protrude.
~*adj.* Also **ex·sert·ed** (-sûr′tĭd). *Biology.* Thrust outward or protruding, as stamens protruding beyond the petals. [Latin *ex(s)erere* (past participle *ex(s)ertus*), to EXERT.] **—ex·ser·tion** *n.*

ex·ser·vice (ĕks′sûr′vĭs) *adj.* **1.** Having formerly served in the armed forces. **2.** Formerly belonging to the armed forces.

ex·ser·vice·man (ĕks′sûr′vĭs-măn′) *n., pl.* **-men** (-mĕn′). One who has formerly served in the armed forces.

ex·sic·cate (ĕk′sĭ-kāt′) *v.* **-cated, -cating, -cates.** *—tr.* To make dry; remove the moisture from; dehydrate. *—intr.* To dry up. [Latin *exsiccāre,* to dry out : *ex-,* out + *siccāre,* to dry, from *siccus,* dry.] **—ex·sic·ca·tion** *n.* **—ex·sic·ca·tive** (ĕk′sĭ-kā′tĭv) *adj.* **—ex·sic·ca·tor** *n.*

ex·stip·u·late (ĕks-stĭp′yə-lĭt, -lāt′) *adj. Botany.* Having no stipules. [From EX- + STIPULE.]

ext. 1. extension. **2.** exterior. **3.** external. **4.** extra.

ex·tant (ĕk′stənt, ĕk-stănt′) *adj.* Still in existence; not destroyed, lost, or extinct: *extant manuscripts; extant species of mammals.* —See Synonyms at **living.** [Latin *ex(s)tāns* (stem *ex(s)tant-*), present participle of *ex(s)tāre,* to stand out, exist, be prominent : *ex-,* out + *stāre,* to stand.]

ex·tem·po·ra·ne·ous (ĭk-stĕm′pə-rā′nē-əs) *adj.* **1.** Done, made, spoken, or otherwise performed with little or no preparation or practice; impromptu: *an extemporaneous recital.* **2.** Delivered without notes or text: *an extemporaneous sermon.* **3.** Provided, made, or

Expression in repose

"Grin face"

"Play face"

Pout

expression *Chimpanzees, like humans, can convey a wide range of emotions through their faces. The "grin face," with bared upper teeth, is a reaction to a threat and may express a mixture of anger, fear, and surprise; the "play face," with upper teeth hidden, is a friendly invitation to play; and the pout is an expression of interest or curiosity.*

adapted as an expedient; improvised; makeshift. [Late Latin *extemporāneus,* from Latin *ex tempore,* EXTEMPORE.] —**ex·tem·po·ra·ne·ous·ly** *adv.* —**ex·tem·po·ra·ne·ous·ness** *n.*

Synonyms: *ad lib, impromptu, improvised, unpremeditated, unrehearsed.*

ex·tem·po·rar·y (ĭk-stĕm′pə-rĕr′ē) *adj.* Extemporaneous. [Latin *ex tempore,* EXTEMPORE.] —**ex·tem·po·rar·i·ly** (ĭk-stĕm′pə-râr′ə-lē) *adv.*

ex·tem·po·re (ĭk-stĕm′pə-rē) *adv.* **1.** Without preparation; impromptu. **2.** Without notes or text: *speak extempore.* **3.** By improvising. [Latin *ex tempore* : *ex-,* out of + *tempore,* ablative of *tempus,* time (see **temporal**).] —**ex·tem·po·re** *adj.*

ex·tem·po·rize (ĭk-stĕm′pə-rīz′) *v.* **-rized, -rizing, -rizes.** —*tr.* To perform, utter, or do (something) extempore. —*intr.* To perform, utter, or do something extempore; improvise. —**ex·tem·po·ri·za·tion** *n.* —**ex·tem·po·riz·er** *n.*

ex·tend (ĭk-stĕnd′) *v.* **-tended, -tending, -tends.** —*tr.* **1.** To open or straighten out to full length; unbend: *extend the leg.* Compare **flex.** **2.** To stretch out or spread to fullest length: *The ladder was fully extended.* **3. a.** To exert (oneself) vigorously or to full capacity. **b.** To cause (a horse, for example) to move at full gallop. **4. a.** To enlarge the area or scope of; expand: *extend our boundaries.* **b.** To expand the influence, range, or meaning of; make more comprehensive or inclusive: *extend his responsibilities.* **5.** To offer to give or grant; afford: *extend one's greetings.* **6.** *Finance.* To cause to be longer; especially, to prolong the time of payment of (a debt, for example). **7. a.** To increase in quantity or bulk by adding a cheaper substance. **b.** To adulterate. —*intr.* **1.** To be or become extended. **2.** To stretch or reach, as in a certain direction or for a certain time: *His influence extended to other continents.* —See Synonyms at **increase.** —See Usage note at **prolong.** [Middle English *extenden,* from Latin *extendere* : *ex-,* out + *tendere,* to stretch.] —**ex·tend·i·bil·i·ty** *n.* —**ex·tend·i·ble** *adj.*

ex·tend·ed (ĭk-stĕn′dĭd) *adj.* **1.** Stretched or pulled out. **2.** Continued for a long period of time. **3.** Enlarged or extensive; widespread: *extended television coverage.* —**ex·tend·ed·ly** *adv.*

extended family *n.* A family unit consisting of parents, children, and other close relatives, such as grandparents or aunts and uncles, who live together. Compare **nuclear family.**

ex·tend·er (ĭk-stĕn′dər) *n.* A substance added to another substance to modify, dilute, or adulterate.

ex·ten·si·ble (ĭk-stĕn′sə-bəl) *adj.* **1.** Capable of being extended or protruded. **2.** Extensile. [Latin *extensus,* past participle of *extendere,* to EXTEND.] —**ex·ten·si·bil·i·ty** *n.*

ex·ten·sile (ĭk-stĕn′səl, -sīl′) *adj.* Capable of being stretched out or protruded, especially without breaking; extensible.

ex·ten·sion (ĭk-stĕn′shən) *n. Abbr.* **ext. 1. a.** The act of extending or the condition of being extended. **b.** That which is extended. **2.** The amount, degree, or range to which something extends or can extend; compass. **3. a.** The act of straightening or extending a limb. **b.** The position assumed by an extended limb. **4.** *Medicine.* The application of traction to a fractured or dislocated limb to restore the normal position. **5.** A part added to or extended from a main structure to form an addition: *an extension to a hospital.* **6.** An additional telephone connected to the main line. **7. a.** A granting of extra time, especially for the repayment of a debt or compliance with a legal formality. **b.** The period of this extra time. **8.** The property of an object by which it occupies space; spatial magnitude. **9.** *Logic.* The class of objects designated by a specific term or concept; denotation. Compare **intension.** **10.** A program of instruction offered, as by a university or college, to outside or part-time students. **11.** *Mathematics.* A set that includes a given and similar set as a subset. [Middle English *extensioun,* from Old French *extension,* from Late Latin *extensiō* (stem *extensiōn-*), from Latin *extensus,* past participle of *extendere,* to EXTEND.]

ex·ten·si·ty (ĭk-stĕn′sə-tē) *n.* **1.** The attribute of sensation that enables one to perceive space or size. **2.** The quality of having extension or being extensive.

ex·ten·sive (ĭk-stĕn′sĭv) *adj.* **1.** Having a great extent; vast; broad: *an extensive meadow.* **2.** Having a wide range; inclusive; comprehensive: *an extensive library.* **3.** Considerable in amount: *Extensive capital was invested.* **4.** Pertaining to or characterized by extension. **5.** Designating or pertaining to the agricultural cultivation of vast areas of land with a minimum of labor or expense. Compare **intensive.** **6.** *Physics.* **a.** Having a value that is the sum of the values for subdivisions of a thermodynamic system. Said of volume, for example. **b.** Designating a property or measurement that is dependent on mass. In this sense, compare **intensive.** —**ex·ten·sive·ly** *adv.* —**ex·ten·sive·ness** *n.*

ex·ten·som·e·ter (ĕk′stĕn-sŏm′ə-tər) *n.* An instrument used to measure minute deformations in a test specimen of a material. [EXTENS(ION) + -O- + -METER.]

ex·ten·sor (ĭk-stĕn′sər) *n.* A muscle that extends or stretches a limb. Compare **flexor.** [New Latin, from Latin *extensus,* past participle of *extendere,* to EXTEND.]

ex·tent (ĭk-stĕnt′) *n.* **1.** The range over which something extends; scope; comprehensiveness. **2. a.** The dimensions to which something is extended; magnitude; spread. **b.** The distance over which a thing extends or the space it occupies. **3.** Any extensive space or area: *an extent of desert.* **4.** A certain degree, usually specified: *to a great extent; to some extent.* [Middle English *extente,* from Norman French, from Medieval Latin *extenta,* from Latin, feminine past participle of *extendere,* to EXTEND.]

ex·ten·u·ate (ĭk-stĕn′yo͞o-āt′) *tr.v.* **-ated, -ating, -ates. 1.** To lessen or attempt to lessen the magnitude of (guilt or an offense) by providing partial excuses. **2.** To cause to appear less serious or blameworthy: *circumstances extenuating the error.* [Latin *extenuāre,* to thin out, lessen : *ex-,* out + *tenuāre,* to make thin, from *tenuis,* thin.] —**ex·ten·u·a·tive** (ĭk-stĕn′yo͞o-ā′tĭv) *adj. & n.* —**ex·ten·u·a·to·ry** (-ə-tôr′ē, -tōr′ē) *adj.*

ex·ten·u·at·ing (ĭk-stĕn′yo͞o-ā′tĭng) *adj.* Serving to lessen, excuse, or qualify guilt or blame: *extenuating circumstances.*

ex·ten·u·a·tion (ĭk-stĕn′yo͞o-ā′shən) *n.* **1.** The act of extenuating or the condition of being extenuated; partial justification. **2.** That which serves to extenuate; a partial excuse.

ex·te·ri·or (ĭk-stîr′ē-ər) *adj. Abbr.* **ext. 1.** Outer; external. **2.** Originating or acting from the outside. **3.** Suitable for use outside: *an exterior paint.* **4.** Not situated or placed inside a building; outdoor. **5.** Outwardly apparent: *an exterior affability.*
∼*n. Abbr.* **ext. 1.** A part or surface that is outside. **2.** An external or outward appearance; an aspect: *a friendly exterior.* **3.** A representation, as a picture or photograph, of an outdoor scene. [Latin, comparative of *exterus,* outward, outside.] —**ex·te·ri·or·i·ty** (ĭk-stîr′ē-ôr′ə-tē, -ŏr′ə-tē) *n.* —**ex·te·ri·or·ly** *adv.*

exterior angle *n.* **1.** The angle between any side of a polygon and an extended adjacent side. **2.** Any of the four angles that do not include a region of the space between two lines intersected by a transversal.

ex·te·ri·or·ize (ĭk-stîr′ē-ə-rīz′) *tr.v.* **-ized, -izing, -izes. 1.** To externalize. **2.** *Surgery.* To bring (an organ or part) out of the abdominal cavity. —**ex·te·ri·or·i·za·tion** *n.*

ex·ter·mi·nate (ĭk-stûr′mə-nāt′) *tr.v.* **-nated, -nating, -nates.** To get rid of by destroying completely; extirpate: *a spray to exterminate insects.* [Latin *extermināre,* to drive out : *ex-,* out of + *termināre,* to limit, end.] —**ex·ter·mi·na·tion** *n.* —**ex·ter·mi·na·tive** (ĭk-stûr′mə-nā′tĭv, -nə-tĭv), **ex·ter·mi·na·to·ry** (-nə-tôr′ē, -tōr′ē) *adj.*

extermination camp *n.* In World War II, a Nazi concentration camp in which large numbers of people, especially Jews, were executed. Also called "death camp."

ex·ter·mi·na·tor (ĭk-stûr′mə-nā′tər) *n.* One that exterminates; especially, one whose occupation is the extermination of vermin.

ex·tern, ex·terne (ĕk′stûrn′) *n.* A person associated with but not officially residing in an institution, especially a nonresident doctor on a hospital staff. [Old French *externe,* from Latin *externus,* EXTERNAL.]

ex·ter·nal (ĭk-stûr′nəl) *adj. Abbr.* **ext. 1. a.** Pertaining to, existing or visible on, or connected with the outside or an outer part; exterior. **b.** Pertaining to the outside of the body: *for external use only.* **2.** Affecting or capable of affecting the outside: *an external application.* **3.** *Philosophy.* Existing independently of the mind; objective; phenomenal: *external objects.* **4.** Acting or coming from the outside: *external pressures.* **5.** Of or pertaining to the outward appearance; superficial. **6.** Of or pertaining to foreign affairs or foreign countries; international.
∼*n. Abbr.* **ext. 1.** An exterior part or surface. **2. externals.** External circumstances; appearances. [Middle English, from Latin *externus,* from *exterus,* outward.] —**ex·ter·nal·ly** *adv.*

ex·ter·nal-com·bus·tion engine (ĭk-stûr′nəl-kəm-bŭs′chən) *n.* An engine, such as a steam engine, in which the fuel is burned outside the engine cylinder.

external ear *n.* The portion of the ear including the auricle (or pinna) and the passage leading to the eardrum.

ex·ter·nal·ism (ĭk-stûr′nə-lĭz′əm) *n.* **1.** *Philosophy.* The doctrine that only objects perceived by the senses are capable of being judged real; phenomenalism. **2.** Devotion to externals or to matters of form or procedure, as in religion. —**ex·ter·nal·ist** *n.*

ex·ter·nal·i·ty (ĕk′stər-năl′ə-tē) *n., pl.* **-ties. 1.** The condition or quality of being external or externalized. **2.** *Philosophy.* The quality of being external to the perceiving subject.

ex·ter·nal·ize (ĭk-stûr′nə-līz′) *tr.v.* **-ized, -izing, -izes. 1.** To make external. **2.** To project (a feeling or opinion) onto others or one's environment; rationalize: *tending to externalize his insecurity.* **3.** To express (personal feelings or problems, for example) freely, especially in words. —**ex·ter·nal·i·za·tion** *n.*

ex·ter·o·cep·tor (ĕk′stə-rō-sĕp′tər) *n.* A sense organ receiving and responding to external stimuli. [New Latin : Latin *exter, exterus,* EXTER(IOR) + -O- + (RE)CEPTOR.] —**ex·ter·o·cep·tive** (ĕk′stə-rō-sĕp′tĭv) *adj.*

ex·ter·ri·to·ri·al (ĕks′tĕr′ə-tôr′ē-əl, -tōr′ē-əl) *adj.* Beyond the territorial limits; extraterritorial. —**ex·ter·ri·to·ri·al·i·ty** (ĕks′tĕr′ə-tôr′ē-ăl′ə-tē, -tōr′ē-ăl′ə-tē) *n.* —**ex·ter·ri·to·ri·al·ly** *adv.*

ex·tinct (ĭk-stĭngkt′) *adj.* **1.** Extinguished or inactive, as a fire or volcano might be. **2.** No longer existing in living form; having died out: *extinct birds such as the dodo and moa.* **3.** Lacking a claimant; void: *an extinct title.* **4.** No longer in use; superseded: *an extinct custom.* —See Usage note at **dead.** [Middle English, from Latin *ex(s)tinctus,* past participle of *ex(s)tinguere,* to EXTINGUISH.]

ex·tinc·tion (ĭk-stĭngk′shən) *n.* **1.** The act of extinguishing or making extinct. **2.** The fact or condition of being extinguished or extinct. **3.** *Physics.* A reduction in the intensity of light or other radiation passing through a medium, caused by absorption or scattering. **4.** The absorption of light from a planet or star by the earth's atmosphere. **5.** Complete destruction; annihilation. —**ex·tinc·tive** (ĭk-stĭngk′tĭv) *adj.*

ex·tin·guish (ĭk-stĭng′gwĭsh) *tr.v.* **-guished, -guishing, -guishes. 1.** To put out (a fire or light); quench. **2.** To put an end to (hope, for example); destroy. **3.** *Law.* **a.** To settle or discharge (a debt).

PRONUNCIATION KEY

ă, pat; ā, pay; âr, care;
ä, father, are; b, bib;
ch, church; d, deed; ĕ, pet;
ē, be; f, fife; g, gag; h, hat;
hw, which; ĭ, pit; ī, pie;
îr, pier; j, judge; k, kick;
l, lid, needle; m, mum;
n, no, sudden; ng, thing;
ŏ, pot; ō, toe; ô, paw, for;
oi, noise; ou, out; o͝o, book;
o͞o, boot; p, pop; r, roar;
s, sauce; sh, ship, dish;
t, tight; th, thin, path;
th, this, bathe; ŭ, cut; ûr, fur;
v, valve; w, with; y, yes;
z, zebra, size; zh, vision;
ə, about, item, edible,
gallop, circus, peaceful

IN FOREIGN WORDS:

à, *Fr.* ami; œ, *Fr.* feu, *Ger.* schön; ü, *Fr.* tu, *Ger.* über; KH, *Ger.* ich, *Scot.* loch; N, *Fr.* bon; y′, *Fr.* Compiègne

STRESS MARKS:

Primary stress: ′
in·cite′ (ĭn-sīt′)
Secondary stress: ′
in′sight′ (ĭn′sīt′)

b. To nullify. [Latin *ex(s)tinguere* : *ex-*, out + *stinguere*, to quench.] —**ex·tin·guish·a·ble** *adj.* —**ex·tin·guish·ment** *n.*

ex·tin·guish·er (ĭk-stĭng′gwĭ-shər) *n.* One that extinguishes, especially: **a.** A small metal cone on a long handle that is used for snuffing out candles. **b.** A **fire extinguisher** (*see*). [French : Latin *ex-*, out + *stinguere* (*see*).]

ex·tir·pate (ĕk′stər-pāt′) *tr.v.* **-pated, -pating, -pates. 1.** To pull up by or as if by the roots; root out. **2.** To destroy wholly; exterminate. **3.** To remove by surgery. —See Synonyms at **abolish**. [Latin *ex(s)tirpāre*, to pluck up by the roots : *ex-*, out + *stirps*, root, stem (see **stirps**).] —**ex·tir·pa·tion** *n.* —**ex·tir·pa·tive** *adj.* —**ex·tir·pa·tor** *n.*

ex·tol, ex·toll (ĭk-stōl′) *tr.v.* **-tolled, -tolling, -tols** or **-tolls.** To praise lavishly; laud or eulogize. —See Synonyms at **praise**. [Middle English *extollen*, to lift up, from Latin *extollere* : *ex-*, up + *tollere*, to lift, raise.] —**ex·tol·ler** *n.* —**ex·tol·ment** *n.*

ex·tort (ĭk-stôrt′) *tr.v.* **-torted, -torting, -torts. 1.** To obtain (money or information, for example) from another by coercion, intimidation, or the wrong use of an official position. **2.** To exact; wring. [Latin *extorquēre* (past participle *extortus*), to twist out : *ex-*, out + *torquēre*, to twist.] —**ex·tort·er** *n.* —**ex·tor·tive** *adj.*

ex·tor·tion (ĭk-stôr′shən) *n.* **1.** The act or an instance of extorting. **2.** The criminal offense of using one's official position or power to obtain property, funds, or patronage to which one is not entitled. **3.** An exorbitant price. **4.** Something extorted. —**ex·tor·tion·ar·y** (ĭk-stôr′shə-nĕr′ē) *adj.* —**ex·tor·tion·ist, ex·tor·tion·er** *n.*

ex·tor·tion·ate (ĭk-stôr′shə-nĭt) *adj.* **1.** Exorbitant; excessive. **2.** Characterized by extortion. —**ex·tor·tion·ate·ly** *adv.*

ex·tra (ĕk′strə) *adj.* **Abbr. ex., ext. 1.** More or beyond what is usual, normal, expected, or necessary; additional: *extra pay.* **2.** Better than ordinary; superior: *extra fineness.* **3.** Liable to an additional charge: *Salad is extra.*
~*n.* **1.** Something more than what is usual or necessary: *I put out a second blanket as an extra.* **2.** Something, such as an accessory on a car, for which an additional charge is made. **3.** A special edition of a newspaper. **4.** An additional or alternate worker. **5.** An actor hired to play a minor part, as in a crowd scene. **6.** Something of exceptional quality.
~*adv.* Exceptionally; unusually: *extra dry.* [Probably short for EXTRAORDINARY, by analogy with similar French and German shortenings.]

extra– *prefix.* Indicates outside a boundary or scope; for example, **extragalactic.** *Note:* Many compounds other than those entered here may be formed with *extra-*. In forming compounds, *extra-* is often joined with the following element without a space or hyphen: *extracurricular.* However, if the second element begins with a capital letter or with the letter *a*, it is separated with a hyphen: *extra-Biblical, extra-alimentary.* [Middle English, from Latin *extrā, extra-alimentary*, outside, above, beyond, without, short for *extera*, ablative feminine of *exterus*, outward.]

ex·tra-base hit (ĕk′strə-bās′) *n. Baseball.* A double, a triple, or a home run.

ex·tra·ca·non·i·cal (ĕk′strə-kə-nŏn′ĭ-kəl) *adj.* Not included in any ecclesiastical canon of Scripture; noncanonical.

ex·tra·cel·lu·lar (ĕk′strə-sĕl′yə-lər) *adj.* Located or occurring outside a cell. —**ex·tra·cel·lu·lar·ly** *adv.*

ex·tract (ĭk-străkt′) *tr.v.* **-tracted, -tracting, -tracts. 1.** To draw out or forth forcibly; pull out: *extract a tooth.* **2.** To obtain despite resistance, as by contrivance or extortion: *extract a promise.* **3.** To obtain from a substance by chemical or mechanical action, as by pressure, distillation, or evaporation: *extract juice from an orange.* **4. a.** To remove (a literary passage, for example) for separate consideration or publication. **b.** To remove and separate. **5.** *Mathematics.* To determine or calculate (the root of a number). **6.** To derive.
~*n.* (ĕk′străkt′). **1.** Something drawn or pulled out. **2.** A passage from a literary work; an excerpt. **3.** A concentrated preparation of the essential constituents of a food, flavoring, or other substance: *vanilla extract.* [Middle English *extracten*, from Latin *extrahere* (past participle *extractus*), to draw out : *ex-*, out + *trahere*, to draw.] —**ex·tract·a·ble, ex·tract·i·ble** *adj.*

ex·trac·tion (ĭk-străk′shən) *n.* **1.** The act of extracting or the condition of being extracted. **2.** Something obtained by extracting; an extract. **3.** Origin; descent; lineage: *of Asian extraction; of noble extraction.*

ex·trac·tive (ĭk-străk′tĭv) *adj.* **1.** Used in or obtained by extraction. **2.** Capable of being extracted.
~*n.* **1.** Something that may be extracted. **2.** The insoluble portion of an extract.

ex·trac·tor (ĭk-străk′tər) *n.* One that extracts, especially a device such as a forceps used for extracting teeth or delivering a baby.

ex·tra·cur·ric·u·lar (ĕk′strə-kə-rĭk′yə-lər) *adj.* **1.** Carried on outside the curriculum or regular course of study in school or college life. **2.** Outside the usual duties of a job or profession.

ex·tra·dit·a·ble (ĕk′strə-dī′tə-bəl) *adj.* Subject to or making one liable to extradition: *an extraditable crime.*

ex·tra·dite (ĕk′strə-dīt′) *tr.v.* **-dited, -diting, -dites. 1.** To surrender (an alleged criminal) to another authority, such as the government of a foreign country, for trial. **2.** To obtain (an alleged criminal held by another authority) for trial. —See Synonyms at **banish**. [Back-formation from EXTRADITION.]

ex·tra·di·tion (ĕk′strə-dĭsh′ən) *n.* The legal surrender of an alleged criminal to the jurisdiction of another state, country, or government for trial. [French : Latin *ex-*, out + *trāditiō* (stem *trāditiōn-*), a surrendering (see **tradition**).]

ex·tra·dos (ĕk′strə-dŏs′, -dō′, ĕk-strā′dŏs′) *n., pl.* **extrados** (-dōz′, -dŏs′) or **-doses.** *Architecture.* The upper or exterior curve of an arch. [French : Latin *extrā*, outside (see **extra-**) + French *dos*, back, from Latin *dorsum.*]

ex·tra·ga·lac·tic (ĕk′strə-gə-lăk′tĭk) *adj.* Located or originating beyond the galaxy.

ex·tra·ju·di·cial (ĕk′strə-jōō-dĭsh′əl) *adj.* **1.** Outside the authority of a court. **2.** Outside usual judicial proceedings. —**ex·tra·ju·di·cial·ly** *adv.*

ex·tra·mar·i·tal (ĕk′strə-măr′ə-təl) *adj.* Of or pertaining to a spouse's relationships, usually sexual, outside marriage; adulterous.

ex·tra·mun·dane (ĕk′strə-mŭn-dān′, -mŭn′dān′) *adj.* Occurring or existing outside the physical world or universe.

ex·tra·mu·ral (ĕk′strə-myŏor′əl) *adj.* **1.** Occurring or situated outside the walls or boundaries, as of a fortress or city: *extramural skirmishes.* **2.** Connected with a university or college but taking place outside. Said especially of nonresident students or their studies.

ex·tra·ne·ous (ĭk-strā′nē-əs) *adj.* **1.** Coming from outside; foreign: *extraneous interference.* **2.** Present but not essential or vital; accidental. **3.** Irrelevant. —See Synonyms at **extrinsic**. [Latin *extrāneus*, strange, from *extrā*, outward.] —**ex·tra·ne·ous·ly** *adv.* —**ex·tra·ne·ous·ness** *n.*

ex·tra·nu·cle·ar (ĕk′strə-nōō′klē-ər, -nyōō′klē-ər) *adj. Biology.* Located or occurring outside the nucleus.

ex·traor·di·nar·y (ĭk-strôr′də-nĕr′ē, ĕk′strə-ôr′-) *adj.* **1.** Beyond what is ordinary, usual, or commonplace: *extraordinary authority.* **2.** Exceeding the ordinary degree, amount, or extent; exceptional; remarkable: *an extraordinary feat.* **3.** Used, held, or appointed for a special service or occasion: *an extraordinary general meeting; an ambassador extraordinary.* —**ex·traor·di·nar·i·ly** (ĭk-strôr′də-nâr′ə-lē, ĕk′strə-ôr′də-) *adv.*

extraordinary ray *n.* The plane-polarized ray of light that is produced by a doubly refracting crystal and does not obey the laws of refraction. Compare **ordinary ray**.

ex·trap·o·late (ĭk-străp′ə-lāt′) *v.* **-lated, -lating, -lates.** —*tr.* **1.** *Mathematics.* To estimate (a value or values of a function) for values of the argument not used in the process of estimation; broadly, to infer (a value or values) from known values. **2.** To infer or estimate (unknown information) from known information. —*intr.* To engage in the process of extrapolating. [EXTRA- + (IN-TER)POLATE.] —**ex·trap·o·la·tion** *n.* —**ex·trap·o·la·tive** (ĭk-străp′ə-lā′tĭv, -lə-tĭv) *adj.*

ex·tra·sen·so·ry (ĕk′strə-sĕn′sə-rē) *adj.* **1.** Outside the normal range or bounds of the senses. **2.** Perceptible by supernatural means. **3.** Supernatural.

extrasensory perception *n.* **Abbr. ESP** Powers of perception of occurrences or objects that are not perceptible by the ordinary senses.

ex·tra·sys·to·le (ĕk′strə-sĭs′tə-lē) *n. Medicine.* A generally premature heartbeat caused by a heart impulse generated outside the sinoatrial node.

ex·tra·ter·res·tri·al (ĕk′strə-tə-rĕs′trē-əl) *adj.* Originating, located, or occurring outside the earth or its atmosphere.

ex·tra·ter·ri·to·ri·al (ĕk′strə-tĕr′ə-tôr′ē-əl, -tōr′ē-əl) *adj.* **1.** Located outside territorial boundaries. **2.** Of or pertaining to persons exempt from the legal jurisdiction of the country in which they reside. —**ex·tra·ter·ri·to·ri·al·ly** *adv.*

ex·tra·ter·ri·to·ri·al·i·ty (ĕk′strə-tĕr′ə-tôr′ē-ăl′ə-tē, -tōr′ē-ăl′ə-tē) *n.* **1.** Exemption from local legal jurisdiction, such as is granted to foreign diplomats. **2.** The jurisdiction of a country over its nationals abroad.

ex·tra·u·ter·ine (ĕk′strə-yōō′tər-ĭn, -tə-rīn′) *adj.* Located or occurring outside the uterus: *extrauterine pregnancy.*

ex·trav·a·gance (ĭk-străv′ə-gəns) *n.* Also **ex·trav·a·gan·cy** (-gən-sē) *pl.* **-cies. 1.** The quality of being extravagant; immoderation, especially in expenditure. **2.** An immoderate expense or display. **3.** Something costly and self-indulgent. **4.** An instance of excess, as in behavior.

ex·trav·a·gant (ĭk-străv′ə-gənt) *adj.* **1.** Given to lavish or imprudent expenditure; prodigal. **2.** Exceeding reasonable bounds; excessive: *extravagant demands.* **3.** Extremely abundant; profuse: *extravagant vegetation.* **4.** Unreasonably high; exorbitant: *That boutique charges extravagant prices.* —See Synonyms at **excessive**. [Middle English *extravagaunt*, from Old French *extravagant*, from Medieval Latin *extrāvagāns* (stem *extrāvagant-*), present participle of *extrāvagārī*, to wander beyond : Latin *extrā*, beyond + *vagārī*, to wander, akin to *vagus*, VAGUE.] —**ex·trav·a·gant·ly** *adv.* —**ex·trav·a·gant·ness** *n.*

ex·trav·a·gan·za (ĭk-străv′ə-găn′zə) *n.* **1.** A light orchestral composition marked by freedom and diversity of form, often with burlesque elements. **2.** An elaborate, spectacular entertainment. **3.** An instance of extravagant behavior or activity. [Italian *(e)stravaganza*, from *(e)stravagant*, extravagant, from Medieval Latin *extrāvagāns*, EXTRAVAGANT.]

ex·trav·a·sate (ĭk-străv′ə-sāt′) *v.* **-sated, -sating, -sates.** —*tr. Pathology.* To force the flow of (blood or lymph) out into surrounding tissue. —*intr. Pathology.* To exude into the surrounding tissues. Used of blood or lymph. [EXTRA- + VAS + -ATE.] —**ex·trav·a·sa·tion** *n.*

ex·tra·vas·cu·lar (ĕk′strə-văs′kyə-lər) *adj.* Located or occurring outside a blood vessel or the vascular system.

ex·tra·ve·hic·u·lar activity (ĕk′strə-vē-hĭk′yə-lər) *n. Abbr.* **EVA** Activity or maneuvers performed by an astronaut outside a spacecraft in space.

extraversion. Variant of **extroversion.**

extravert. Variant of **extrovert.**

Ex·tre·ma·du·ra or **Es·tre·ma·du·ra** (ĕs′trə-mə-dōōr′ə). Region of west-central Spain comprising Badajoz and Cáceres provinces. Long a generally poor farming area, it is being developed with irrigation, and is also noted for its cork-oak forests and pigs. —**Ex·tre·ma·du·ran** *n. & adj.*

ex·treme (ĭk-strēm′) *adj.* **1.** Outermost or farthest; most remote in any direction: *the extreme edge of the field.* **2.** Final; last. **3.** Being in or attaining the greatest or highest degree; very intense: *extreme pleasure; extreme degradation.* **4.** Extending far beyond the norm; radical: *an extreme conservative.* **5.** Of the greatest severity; drastic: *extreme measures.* —See Synonyms at **excessive.**
~*n.* **1.** The greatest or utmost degree or point: *eager in the extreme.* **2.** Either of the two ends of a state or condition considered as a measurable or approximately measurable continuum: *the extremes of boiling and freezing; the extremes of wealth and poverty.* **3.** An extreme condition. **4.** A drastic or immoderate expedient: *driven to extremes.* **5.** *Mathematics.* The first or last term of a ratio or series. **6.** *Logic.* The major or minor term of a syllogism. [Middle English, from Old French, from Latin *extrēmus.*] —**ex·treme·ly** *adv.* —**ex·treme·ness** *n.*

extremely high frequency *n. Abbr.* **EHF** A radio-frequency band with a range of 30,000 to 300,000 megahertz.

extreme unction *n. Roman Catholic Church.* The sacrament in which a priest anoints and prays for one in danger of death.

ex·trem·ist (ĭk-strē′mĭst) *n.* A person who advocates or resorts to extreme measures, especially in politics; a radical. —See Synonyms at **fanatic.**
~*adj.* Belonging or pertaining to extremists. —**ex·trem·ism** *n.*

ex·trem·i·ty (ĭk-strĕm′ə-tē) *n., pl.* **-ties. 1.** The outermost or farthest point or portion; an end; an edge. **2.** The greatest or utmost degree: *the extremity of despair.* **3.** Grave danger, necessity, or distress. **4.** The moment at which the end, as of life, is imminent. **5.** A bodily limb or appendage. **6.** A hand or foot.

ex·tri·cate (ĕk′strĭ-kāt′) *tr.v.* **-cated, -cating, -cates. 1.** To release from an entanglement or difficulty; disengage. **2.** To cause to be liberated or emitted: *extricate gas from a solution.* [Latin *extrīcāre :* *ex-,* out + *trīcae†,* perplexities.] —**ex·tri·ca·ble** *adj.* —**ex·tri·ca·tion** *n.*

ex·trin·sic (ĭk-strĭn′sĭk, -zĭk) *adj.* **1.** Not forming an essential part of a thing; extraneous; inessential. **2.** Not inherent; accessory; accidental. **3.** Originating from the outside; external. [Late Latin *extrinsecus,* outer, from Latin, outwardly : *exterus,* EXTERIOR + *secus,* alongside.] —**ex·trin·si·cal·ly** *adv.*
    Synonyms: alien, extraneous, foreign.

ex·trorse (ĕk-strôrs′) *adj. Botany.* Facing outward; turned away from the axis. Said especially of anthers. [Late Latin *extrōrsus,* outward : *extrā,* outside + *introrsus,* INTRORSE.]

ex·tro·ver·sion, ex·tra·ver·sion (ĕk′strə-vûr′zhən, -shən) *n.* **1. a.** Interest in and aptitude for dealing with the external world and other people as opposed to or to the neglect of oneself or one's inner feelings. **b.** A disposition toward extroversion. Compare **introversion. 2.** A turning inside out, as of an organ or part. [From *extro-,* variant of EXTRA- + Latin *versus,* past participle of *vertere,* to turn.] —**ex·tro·ver·sive** (ĕk′strə-vûr′sĭv, -zĭv) *adj.* —**ex·tro·ver·sive·ly** *adv.*

ex·tro·vert, ex·tra·vert (ĕk′strə-vûrt′) *n.* **1.** A person whose behavior is characterized by extroversion. **2.** An outgoing, gregarious, lively person. Compare **introvert.** [From *extro-,* variant of EXTRA- + Latin *vertere,* to turn.] —**ex·tro·vert·ed** (ĕk′strə-vûr′tĭd) *adj.*

ex·trude (ĭk-strōōd′) *v.* **-truded, -truding, -trudes.** —*tr.* **1.** To push or thrust out. **2.** To shape (metal or plastic, for example) by forcing through a die. —*intr.* To protrude or project. [Latin *extrūdere,* to thrust out : *ex-,* out + *trūdere,* to thrust.]

ex·tru·sion (ĭk-strōō′zhən) *n.* **1.** The act or process of extruding. **2.** Material that has been extruded. **3.** *Geology.* **a.** The movement of magma through volcanic craters and fissures in the earth's crust, forming igneous rocks. **b.** The igneous rocks so formed. [Medieval Latin *extrūsiō* (stem *extrūsiōn-*), from Latin *extrūsus,* past participle of *extrūdere,* to EXTRUDE.]

ex·tru·sive (ĭk-strōō′sĭv, -zĭv) *adj.* **1.** Tending to extrude. **2.** *Geology.* Derived from magma that has cooled and solidified on the earth's surface. Said of rock.

ex·u·ber·ant (ĭg-zōō′bər-ənt) *adj.* **1.** Full of unrestrained high spirits; abandonedly joyous. **2.** Lavish; effusive; overflowing. **3.** Growing or producing abundantly; luxuriant. [Middle English, from Old French, from Latin *exūberāns* (stem *exūberant-*), present participle of *exūberāre,* to EXUBERATE.] —**ex·u·ber·ance** (ĭg-zōō′bər-əns) *n.* —**ex·u·ber·ant·ly** *adv.*

ex·u·ber·ate (ĭg-zōō′bə-rāt′) *intr.v.* **-ated, -ating, -ates. 1.** To be exuberant. **2.** *Archaic.* To abound or overflow. [Latin *exūberāre : ex-,* completely + *ūberāre,* to be fruitful, from *ūber,* fertile.]

ex·u·date (ĕks′yōō-dāt′) *n.* An exuded substance; an exudation. [From EXUDE.]

ex·u·da·tion (ĕks′yōō-dā′shən) *n.* **1.** The act or an instance of exuding. **2.** Something that is exuded; exudate: *an exudation of sweat.* —**ex·u·da·tive** (ĕks′yōō-dā′tĭv) *adj.*

ex·ude (ĭg-zōōd′, ĭk-sōōd′) *v.* **-uded, -uding, -udes.** —*intr.* To ooze forth; come gradually through an opening: *Sap exudes from the pine.* —*tr.* **1.** To discharge or emit gradually. **2.** To give off copiously; make (a quality) felt: *"he exuded about as much menace as boiled haddock"* (S.J. Perelman). [Latin *ex(s)ūdāre,* to sweat out, exude : *ex-,* out + *sūdāre,* to sweat, ooze.]

ex·ult (ĭg-zŭlt′) *intr.v.* **-ulted, -ulting, -ults.** To rejoice greatly; be jubilant or triumphant: *exulted in their victory.* [Latin *ex(s)ultāre,* frequentative of *exsilīre,* to leap up, rejoice : *ex-,* up + *salīre,* to leap.] —**ex·ul·ta·tion** (ĕk′səl-tā′shən, ĕg′zəl-), **ex·ul·tan·cy** (ĭg-zŭl′tən-sē) *n.* —**ex·ult·ing·ly** *adv.*

ex·ul·tant (ĭg-zŭl′tənt) *adj.* Joyful; jubilant; triumphant. —**ex·ul·tant·ly** *adv.*

ex·ur·ban·ite (ĕk-sûr′bə-nīt′, ĕg-zûr′-) *n.* A person living in a community, usually a well-to-do town, beyond the suburbs of a major city. [EX- + (SUB)URBANITE.]

ex·ur·bi·a (ĕk-sûr′bē-ə, ĕg-zûr′-) *n.* A semirural residential area situated beyond the suburbs of a city and inhabited principally by well-to-do people. [EX- + (SUB)URBIA.]

ex·u·vi·ae (ĭg-zōō′vē-ē′) *pl.n.* The cast-off skins or coverings of various animals, especially of the larvae and nymphs of insects. [Latin, stripped-off clothing, spoils, from *exuere,* to take off.] —**ex·u·vi·al** *adj.*

ex·u·vi·ate (ĭg-zōō′vē-āt′) *v.* **-ated, -ating, -ates.** —*tr.* To shed (a covering, such as a skin). —*intr.* To shed or cast off exuviae. [From EXUVIAE.] —**ex·u·vi·a·tion** *n.*

-ey¹. Variant of **-y** (existence or possession).

-ey². Variant of **-y** (smallness).

ey·as (ī′əs) *n.* A nestling hawk or falcon, especially one to be trained for falconry. [Middle English, variant (by incorrect division of *an ias* for *a nias*) of *niyas,* from Old French *niais,* bird taken from the nest, from Vulgar Latin *nidax* (unattested), from Latin *nīdus,* nest.]

eye (ī) *n.* **1.** An organ of vision or of light sensitivity. **2. a.** The vertebrate organ of vision; either of a pair of hollow structures located in fixed bony sockets of the skull, functioning together or independently, each having a lens capable of focusing incident light

---

eye

THE MIRACLE OF SIGHT
How the eyes and brain work together

Much of the knowledge we absorb is gathered by the eyes—two small spheres each 25 millimeters (1 inch) across. In common with those animals that rely on their eyes for hunting and collecting food, man has binocular vision. Both eyes can focus on one target, a help in judging distance.

In contrast, animals such as cows and rabbits have eyes that function independently on each side of the head, so that they can keep an all-around watch for danger.

The human eye depends on the brain. For example, the eye does not take in a scene or an object at one glance but sees it as a rapid series of images.

It is the brain that, in effect, blends the successive frames of a film into a continuous vision. And it is the brain that stores, organizes, and assesses visual impressions and compares them with past experiences.

Most people receive positive evidence of the brain's role in sight only when they dream. For they "see" pictures with their eyes closed. Those people who have been born blind dream in terms of other sensory stimuli: touch, sound, and even smell.

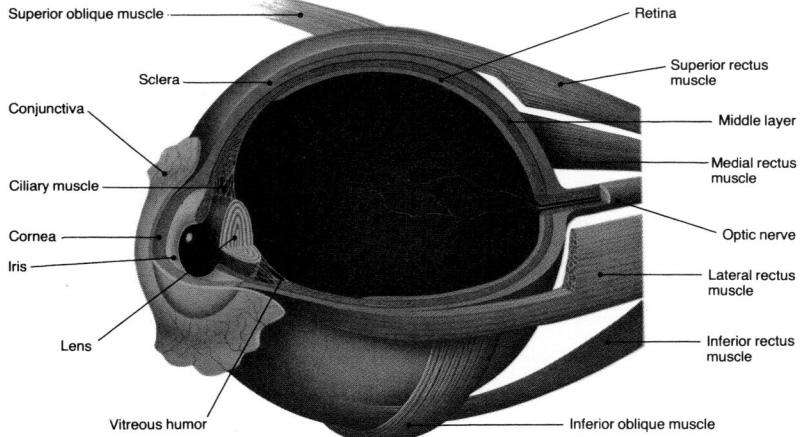

STRUCTURE OF THE EYE *The eye functions much as a camera, with a lens at the front and a light-sensitive screen, the retina, at the rear. The intervening space contains a transparent jelly, the vitreous humor, which together with the outer layer, or sclera, helps the eyeball to hold its shape.*

Light enters through the cornea, a transparent domed window at the front of the eyeball. The size of the pupil, an aperture in the center of the iris, controls the amount of light that is then focused by the lens onto the retina as an upside-down image.

Contractions of the ciliary muscle control the shape and power of the lens. The retina, which is nourished by the blood vessels of the middle layer, contains more than 130 million light-receptor cells. These convert light into nerve impulses that are transmitted right side up by the optic nerve to the brain, where they are interpreted.

The conjunctiva, a transparent membrane, lines the eyelids and partly covers the eyeball. Muscles attached to the eye control its movements—sideways, up and down, and rotating.

on an internal photosensitive retina from which nerve impulses are sent to the brain. **b.** The external, visible portion of this organ together with its associated structures, such as the eyelids, eyelashes, and eyebrows. **c.** The pigmented iris of this organ. **3.** The faculty of seeing; vision. **4.** The ability to discriminate or appreciate; discernment: *a good eye for fashion.* **5. a.** A look; gaze. **b.** A way of regarding something; a point of view: *You're wrong, at least in my eyes.* **6.** Something suggestive of an eye in appearance, such as an opening in a needle, a marking on a peacock feather, or a hole in cheese. **7.** A loop, such as one for attaching a hook. **8.** *Botany.* **a.** A bud on a twig or tuber: *the eye of a potato.* **b.** The often differently colored center of the corolla of some flowers. **9.** *Meteorology.* The circular area of relative calm at the center of a cyclone. **10.** Something construed as a center or focal point: *Corruption is the eye of the problem.* **11.** Keen observation; attention: *Keep an eye on the baby while I'm out.* **12.** A photosensitive device, such as a photoelectric cell. **13.** *Informal.* A detective. **—all eyes.** Alert; observant. **—an eye for an eye.** Punishment requiring that the offender suffer what he has caused another to suffer. [A Biblical phrase: ". . . life shall go for life, eye for eye, tooth for tooth, hand for hand, foot for foot" (Deuteronomy 19:21; also Exodus 21:2).] **—catch someone's eye.** *Informal.* To attract someone's attention. **—give someone the eye.** To look at admiringly or invitingly. **—have an eye to.** **1.** To be on the lookout for. **2.** To have as an aim. **—have eyes only for.** To be attentive solely to; be interested exclusively in: *She has eyes only for you.* **—in one's mind's eye.** Pictured, remembered, or clearly imagined in the mind. **—in the eye of the wind.** *Nautical.* In the direction opposite to that of the wind; close to the wind. **—keep one's eyes peeled (or skinned).** To be constantly vigilant and observant. **—make eyes at.** To glance or gaze at flirtatiously. **—my eye.** *Slang.* In no way; not at all. **—see eye to eye.** To be in complete agreement. **—turn a blind eye to.** To ignore deliberately (a prohibited action that one witnesses, for example). **—up to one's eyes.** Fully occupied; overwhelmed, as with work. **—with an eye to.** With a view to: *saving money with an eye to future need.* **~***tr.v.* **eyed, eyeing** or **eying, eyes.** **1.** To concentrate the eyes on; stare at. **2.** To watch attentively: *The hungry child eyed my sandwich.* [Middle English *eie, eighe,* Old English *ēage.*]

eye-ball (ī'bôl') *n.* **1.** The ball-shaped portion of the eye enclosed by the socket and eyelids. **2.** The eye. **—eyeball to eyeball.** *Informal.* Face to face. **~***tr.v.* **eyeballed, -balling, -balls.** *Informal.* **1.** To stare steadily at, especially in a menacing way. **2.** To confront (a rival, for example) in an uncompromising way.

eye bank *n.* A place at which corneas taken from human bodies immediately after death are stored and preserved for subsequent transplantation to individuals with corneal defects.

eye bath *n.* An eyecup.

eye-bolt (ī'bōlt') *n.* A bolt having a looped head designed to receive a hook or rope.

eye-bright (ī'brīt') *n.* Any of several plants of the genus *Euphrasia;* especially, *E. officinalis,* native to the Old World, having small white and purplish flowers and formerly used in the preparation of eye lotions.

eye-brow (ī'brou') *n.* **1.** The bony ridge extending over the eye. **2.** The arch of short hairs covering this ridge.

eyebrow pencil *n.* A cosmetic in pencil form used for extending, redrawing, or darkening the eyebrows.

eye-catch-ing (ī'kăch'ĭng) *adj.* Attracting the eye; striking.

eye contact *n.* Direct visual contact with the eyes of another person.

eye-cup (ī'kŭp') *n.* A small cup with a rim contoured to fit the outside of the eye, used for applying a liquid medicine or wash to the eye.

eyed (īd) *adj.* **1.** Having an eye or eyes, as a sail might. **2.** Having eyes of a specified number or kind. Used in combination: *one-eyed; blue-eyed.* **3.** Having markings that resemble eyes.

eye dialect *n.* The use of misspellings, such as *wimmin* for *women,* to represent dialectal or nonstandard speech.

eye-drop-per (ī'drŏp'ər) *n.* A dropper for administering liquid eye medicines.

eye-ful (ī'fōōl') *n.* **1.** An amount of something that covers the eye: *an eyeful of salt water.* **2.** *Informal.* All that the eye can encompass at one time; a good look. **3.** *Informal.* A sight to please the eyes; especially, a good-looking person.

eye-glass (ī'glăs', ī'gläs') *n.* **1. a.** **eyeglasses.** A pair of lenses used to correct faulty vision; glasses. **b.** A monocle. **2.** An eyepiece. **3.** An eyecup.

eye-hole (ī'hōl') *n.* **1.** The socket of the eye. **2.** A peephole. **3.** An eye for the insertion of a rope, pin, hook, or the like.

eye-hook (ī'hōōk') *n.* A hook attached to a ring at the end of a rope or chain.

eye-lash (ī'lăsh') *n.* **1.** Any of a row of short hairs fringing the edge of the eyelid. **2.** A row of these hairs.

eye-let (ī'lĭt) *n.* **1. a.** A small hole or perforation, usually rimmed with metal, cord, fabric, or leather, used for fastening with a cord or hook. **b.** A metal ring designed to reinforce such a hole; a grommet. **2. a.** A small hole edged with fine embroidered stitches as part of a design. **b.** A piece of embroidery so worked. Also called "eyelet embroidery." **c.** Cloth that is ornamented with machine-produced eyelet embroidery. **d.** A small hole created in knitted or crocheted material and lace by combining and separating different stitches. **3.** An aperture or peephole. **4.** A small eye. **~***tr.v.* **eyeletted, -letting, -lets.** To make eyelets in. [Middle English *oilet,* from Old French *oillet,* diminutive of *oil,* eye, from Latin *oculus,* eye.]

eye-let-eer (ī'lə-tîr') *n.* A pointed instrument for piercing eyelets in cloth; a bodkin; a stiletto.

eye-lid (ī'lĭd') *n.* Either of two folds of skin and muscle that can be closed over the exposed portion of the eyeball.

eye-lin-er (ī'lī'nər) *n.* A cosmetic preparation that is applied close to the eyelashes to accentuate the eyes.

eye-o-pen-er (ī'ō'pə-nər) *n.* **1.** A revelation, usually a startling or shocking one. **2.** A drink of liquor taken especially when one wakes up.

eye-piece (ī'pēs') *n.* The lens or lens group closest to the eye in a microscope, telescope, or other optical instrument; an ocular.

eye rhyme *n.* A false rhyme consisting of words, as *lint* and *pint,* with similar spellings but different sounds.

eye-shade (ī'shād') *n.* A visor made of tinted plastic or a similar opaque material, worn to protect the eyes from glare.

eye shadow *n.* A cosmetic available in various colors or tints and applied to the eyelids to enhance the eyes.

eye-shot (ī'shŏt') *n.* The range of vision; view; sight.

eye-sight (ī'sīt') *n.* **1.** The faculty of sight; vision. **2.** The range of vision; view.

eyes-on-ly (īz'ōn'lē) *adj.* Of, pertaining to, or being top-secret: *an eyes-only memorandum.*

eye-sore (ī'sôr', ī'sōr') *n.* Something ugly or offensive to look at.

eye splice *n.* *Nautical.* A loop formed at the end of a rope by turning it back and splicing in the end strands.

eye-spot (ī'spŏt') *n.* **1.** A light-sensitive, pigmented area in certain algae, protozoans, and other primitive animals. **2.** A rounded, eye-like marking, as on the tail of a peacock.

eye-stalk (ī'stôk') *n.* A movable, stalklike structure bearing at its tip one of the eyes of a crab, shrimp, or similar crustacean.

eye-strain (ī'strān') *n.* Aching and fatigue of the eyes, often accompanied by headache, resulting from prolonged close work, uncorrected errors of vision, or an imbalance of the eye muscles.

eye-tooth (ī'tōōth') *n., pl.* **eyeteeth** (ī'tēth'). A canine *(see)* of the upper jaw. **—give one's eyeteeth for.** To be willing to give up a great deal to acquire something much desired. [So called because it lies immediately under the eye.]

eye-wash (ī'wŏsh', ī'wôsh') *n.* **1.** A medicated solution applied as a wash for the eyes. **2.** Misleading, evasive, or meaningless speech or writing.

eye-wink (ī'wĭngk') *n.* **1.** A wink of the eye. **2.** An instant. **3.** *Obsolete.* A glance.

eye-wit-ness (ī'wĭt'nəs) *n.* A person who has seen a particular event or act and can describe it, as in court.

eyot (āt, ā'ət) *n.* Also **ait** (āt). *British.* A small island, especially in a river. [Middle English *eigt, eyt, eit,* Old English *iggath, ȳgett,* from *īeg, ȳg,* ISLAND + *-ett, -ath,* diminutive suffix.]

Eyre, Lake (âr). Largest lake in Australia, lying in central South Australia. It is salty and shallow and in the hot, arid summers of the Australian interior can dry up. At 16 meters (52 feet) below sea level, it is Australia's lowest point.

eyrie. Variant of **aerie.**

ey-rir (ā'rîr') *n., pl.* **aurar** (ou'rär', œ'rär'). A coin equal to ¹⁄₁₀₀ of the krona of Iceland. See feature at **currency.** [Icelandic, from Old Norse, an ounce, probably from Latin *aureus,* gold coin, from *aurum,* gold.]

Ezek. Ezekiel (Old Testament).

E·ze·ki·el[1] (ĭ-zē'kē-əl). A major Hebrew prophet of the 6th century B.C., author of the Old Testament Book of Ezekiel. [Greek *Iezekiel,* from Hebrew *Y'hezkēl,* "may God strengthen."]

Ezekiel[2] *n. Abbr.* **Ezek.** The Old Testament book bearing the name of the prophet Ezekiel.

Ez·ra[1] (ĕz'rə). A Hebrew high priest of the 5th century B.C. [Hebrew, "help."]

Ezra[2] *n.* A book of the Old Testament bearing the name of the priest Ezra. Also called "Esdras" in the Douay Bible.

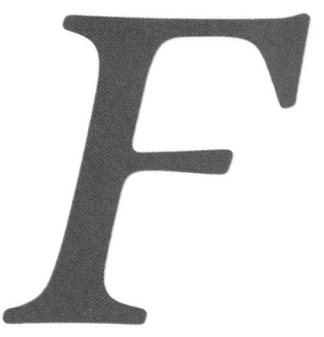

F

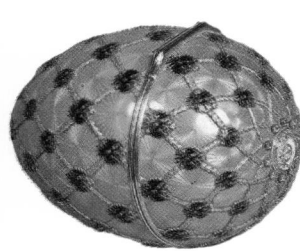

Fabergé egg *This golden egg set with enamel and diamonds was made by the Russian jeweler and goldsmith in 1897 in honor of the coronation of the czar, Nicholas II. Standing only 12.5 centimeters (5 inches) high, it contains a minute replica of the imperial coach used at the coronation.*

f, F (ĕf) *n., pl.* **f's** or **F's. 1.** The sixth letter of the modern English alphabet. **2.** Any of the speech sounds represented by this letter. **3. F. a.** The fourth tone in the scale of C major. **b.** The key or a scale in which F is the tonic. **c.** A written or printed note representing F. **d.** A string, key, or pipe tuned to the pitch of F. **4.** Something shaped like the letter F. **5.** The sixth in a series.

f, F, f., F. *Note:* As an abbreviation or symbol, *f* may be a small or a capital letter, with or without a period. Established forms or those generally preferred precede the definition. When no form is given, all four forms are in general use in that sense. **1.** F Fahrenheit. **2.** F farad. **3. f.** farthing. **4. F.** February. **5. F, F.** fellow (of a university or other institution). **6.** female. **7. f., F.** *Grammar.* feminine. **8. f** *Physics.* femto-. **9. f., F.** *Metallurgy.* fine. **10. F** The symbol for the element fluorine. **11. f., F.** folio. **12. f.** following. **13. F** *Physics.* force. **14. f, F** *Music.* forte. **15. f.** *Sports.* foul. **16. f.** franc. **17. F.** French. **18. F.** Friday. **19. F** A failing grade in academic work. **20.** *Genetics.* A filial generation, F_1 being the first generation resulting from a given cross, F_2 the second generation resulting from crossing within the F_1 generation, and so on.

fa (fä) *n. Music.* The fourth tone of the diatonic scale in solmization. [Middle English, from Medieval Latin, short for *famuli*, servants, word sung to this note in a hymn to St. John the Baptist (see **gamut**), plural of Latin *famulus*, servant. See **family**.]

FA 1. field artillery. **2.** fine art. **3.** football association.

F.A. 1. fine art. **2.** football association.

F.A.A. Federal Aviation Administration.

Fab·er·gé (făb′ər-zhā′), **Peter Carl** (1846–1920). Russian goldsmith who made ornate decorative objects for European royalty. He was famous for his jeweled eggs containing surprise gifts.

Fa·bi·an (fā′bē-ən) *adj.* **1.** Using or characterized by a cautious strategy of gradual social progress and avoidance of direct confrontation with the state. **2.** Of or relating to the Fabian Society. *~n.* A member or supporter of the Fabian Society. [Latin *Fabiānus*, after Quintus *Fabius* Maximus (died 203 B.C.), known as *Cunctator* ("Delayer"), Roman general who defeated Hannibal by avoiding direct conflict.] **—Fa·bi·an·ism** *n.* **—Fa·bi·an·ist** *n. & adj.*

Fabian Society *n.* An organization founded in Great Britain in 1883 to promote the gradual spread of democratic socialism.

fa·ble (fā′bəl) *n.* **1.** A concise narrative making an edifying, moral, or cautionary point and often employing as characters animals that speak and act like human beings. **2. a.** A story or myth about legendary persons and exploits. **b.** Such stories and myths collectively. **c.** A literary genre consisting of such stories. **3.** A falsehood; a lie. *~v.* **fabled, -bling, -bles.** *—tr.* To recount as if true. *—intr. Archaic.* To compose fables. [Middle English, from Old French, from Latin *fābula*, narration, account, story, from *fārī*, to speak.] **—fa·bler** *n.*

fa·bled (fā′bəld) *adj.* **1.** Made known or famous by fable; legendary. **2.** Existing only in fable; fictitious.

fab·li·au (făb′lē-ō′) *n., pl.* **-liaux** (-lē-ō′, -ōz′). A medieval verse tale that is characterized by comic and ribald treatment of themes drawn from life, such as Chaucer's "Miller's Tale." [French, from Old French (Picardy dialect) *fabliaux*, plural of *fablel*, diminutive of *fable*, FABLE.]

Fa·bre (fä′brə), **Jean Henri** (1823–1915). French entomologist and man of letters. He conducted important research on bees and wasps, grasshoppers and crickets, and beetles, describing the importance of instincts to insect behavior. He also wrote many popular books on science.

fab·ric (făb′rĭk) *n.* **1.** Any material structure consisting of connected parts; a framework. **2.** A structure consisting of human relations or of relations between ideas, expressions, emotions, or the like: *"the pattern of her mind, the whole fabric of her nature"* (James Thurber). **3.** A method or style of construction. **4. a.** Any cloth produced by joining fibers, as by knitting, weaving, or felting. **b.** The texture or quality of such cloth. **5.** The walls, roof, and floor of a building. [Middle English, from Old French *fabrique*, from Latin *fabrica*, workshop, a trade, from *faber*, workman, artisan.]

fab·ri·cate (făb′rĭ-kāt′) *tr.v.* **-cated, -cating, -cates. 1.** To prepare, make, or fashion. **2.** To construct by putting together finished parts; assemble. **3.** To invent (a story); devise (a deception). [Middle English *fabricaten*, from Latin *fabricārī* (past participle *fabricātus*), to fabricate, build, from *fabrica*, workshop. See **fabric**.] **—fab·ri·ca·tor** *n.*

fab·ri·ca·tion (făb′rĭ-kā′shən) *n.* **1. a.** Something, such as a deliberately false statement, that is made up or fabricated. **b.** The action of inventing a false statement or of forging a document. **2.** The process of fabricating; manufacture.

fab·u·list (făb′yə-lĭst) *n.* **1.** A composer of fables, especially of moral tales. **2.** An inventor or teller of falsehoods. [French *fabuliste*, from Latin *fābula*, FABLE.]

fab·u·lous (făb′yə-ləs) *adj.* **1.** Of the nature of a fable or myth; legendary. **2.** Told of or celebrated in fables or legends. **3.** Barely credible; astonishing: *fabulous riches.* **4.** *Informal.* Extremely pleasing or successful; apparently: *We had a fabulous time at the carnival.* [Middle English, from Latin *fābulōsus*, from *fābula*, FABLE.] **—fab·u·lous·ly** *adv.* **—fab·u·lous·ness** *n.*

fac. facsimile.

fa·çade, fa·cade (fə-säd′) *n.* **1.** *Architecture.* A face of a building; especially, a front face that is given distinguishing treatment. **2.** The face or front part of anything; especially, an artificial or false appearance or aspect. [French, from Italian *facciata*, from *faccia*, face, from Vulgar Latin *facia* (unattested), FACE.]

face (fās) *n.* **1.** The surface of the front of the head from the top of the forehead to the base of the chin and from ear to ear. Also used adjectivally: *face cream.* **2.** The arrangement or expression of the features of this part of the head; the countenance. **3.** An exaggerated facial expression; a grimace. **4. a.** The outward appearance, aspect, or look: *The face of the city has changed.* **b.** An assumed bearing; a front: *We must put a good face on things.* **5.** Value or standing in the eyes of others; dignity; prestige: *The country feared it would lose face.* **6.** *Informal.* Effrontery; impudence. **7.** The most significant or prominent surface of any object, especially: **a.** The surface presented to view; the front: *the face of a building.* **b.** The outer surface: *the face of the earth.* **c.** A steep side of a hill or mountain. **d.** The upper or marked side; the most meaningful surface: *the face of a clock.* **e.** The side of an instrument or device that is applied or makes contact: *the face of a golf club.* **f.** Either side of a coin; especially, a side bearing the representation of a head. **8.** *Geometry.* A planar surface bounding a solid. **9.** Any of the surfaces of a rock or crystal. **10.** *Military.* Any of the sides of a formation of men or of a fortified position. **11.** The appearance and geologic surface features of an area of land; topography. **12.** The exposed working surface of an ore, as coal, in a mine. **13.** A typeface (*see*). **—face to face. 1.** In each other's presence; in direct communication: *We finally spoke face to face.* **2.** Directly confronting. Used with *with: His illness brought him face to face with death.* **—fly in the face of.** To defy openly. **—in the face of. 1.** Despite the opposition of; notwithstanding. **2.** Considering the fact of; in view of. **—laugh in someone's face.** To be openly disrespectful or contemptuous toward someone. **—on the face of it.** From its appearance alone; apparently. **—put one's face on.** *Informal.* To put on make-up. **—set one's face against.** To oppose resolutely. **—show one's face.** To make an appearance. **—to someone's face.** In someone's physical presence; directly, boldly, and frankly: *She accused the offender to his face.* *~v.* **faced, facing, faces.** *—tr.* **1.** To turn or be turned or situated in the direction of. **2.** To be opposite; have the front directly opposite to; front: *a window facing the south.* **3. a.** To realize; be cognizant of: *facing facts.* **b.** To confront or deal with boldly or bravely: *"What this generation must do is face its problems"* (John F. Kennedy). **4.** To be certain to encounter; have in store: *The unskilled youth faces a difficult life.* **5.** To cause (a soldier or formation of troops) to change direction sharply by giving a command. **6.** To turn (a playing card) so that the face is up. **7.** To furnish with a surface or cover of a different material: *bronze faced with gold foil.* **8.** To provide the edge or edges of (a cloth or garment) with finishing or trimming. **9.** To treat or dress the surface of (a material);

smooth. —*intr.* **1.** To be turned or placed with the front toward a specified direction. **2.** To turn the face in a specified direction. **—face down.** To overcome or prevail over by a stare or a resolute manner. **—face out.** To endure to the end. **—face up to. 1.** To recognize the existence or importance of. **2.** To confront bravely. [Middle English, from Old French, from Vulgar Latin *facia* (unattested), from Latin *faciēs,* form, shape, face, from *facere,* to make, form.] **—face·a·ble** *adj.*

face-ache (fās'āk') *n.* *British.* Neuralgia of a cranial nerve; specifically, trigeminal neuralgia.

face card *n.* A playing card bearing a jack, queen, or king. Also called "court card."

face-cen·tered (fās'sĕn'tərd) *adj.* Designating a crystal or crystal lattice in which there is a lattice point at the center of each face of each unit cell. Compare **body-centered.**

face·cloth (fās'klôth', -klŏth') *n.* A washcloth.

faced (fāst) *adj.* **1.** Having a face or faces. **2.** Having a specified number or kind of faces. Used in combination: *two-faced; red-faced.*

face-hard·en (fās'härd'n) *tr.v.* **-ened, -ening, -ens.** To harden the surface of (a metal).

face·less (fās'lĭs) *adj.* **1.** Without a face. **2.** Anonymous; hard to identify: *faceless bureaucrats.*

face lifting *n.* Also **face-lift** (fās'lĭft') **1.** A cosmetic plastic-surgery operation for tightening facial tissues and improving the appearance of facial skin. **2.** A restyling or modernizing of an outward appearance.

face off *intr.v.* To start play in hockey, lacrosse, and other games by releasing the puck or ball between two opposing players.

face-off (fās'ôf', -ŏf') *n.* **1.** A method of starting play in hockey, lacrosse, and other games in which an official drops the puck or ball between two opposing players who contend for its control. **2.** A confrontation.

face pack *n.* A cosmetic preparation used for cleansing and toning the complexion, usually consisting of a thick paste that is washed or peeled off when dry. Also called "face mask," "pack."

face·plate (fās'plāt') *n.* **1.** A disk that is attached to the headstock of a lathe to hold flat or irregularly shaped work. **2.** A planometer *(see).*

fac·er (fā'sər) *n.* **1.** A person or thing that faces; especially, a device used in smoothing or dressing metal, stone, or other material. **2.** *Chiefly British.* An unexpected blow or defeat.

face-sav·ing (fās'sā'vĭng) *n.* Preserving prestige or respect in the face of potential embarrassment or humiliation. **—face-sav·er** (fās'sā'vər) *n.*

fac·et (fās'ĭt) *n.* **1.** Any of the flat polished surfaces cut on a gemstone. **2.** A small planar or rounded smooth surface on a bone or tooth. **3.** Any of the lenslike divisions of a compound eye, as of an insect. **4.** An aspect or phase: *The four principal characters are facets of the author's personality.*
~*tr.v.* **faceted** or **facetted, -eting** or **-etting, -ets.** To cut facets in (a gemstone). [French *facette,* diminutive of FACE.]

fa·ce·ti·ae (fə-sē'shē-ē') *pl.n.* Witty or coarsely humorous writings and sayings; pleasantries. [Latin *facētiae,* plural of *facētia,* a jest, from *facētus,* FACETIOUS.]

fa·ce·tious (fə-sē'shəs) *adj.* Playfully and often unsuitably jocular; flippant: *a facetious remark.* [Old French *facetieux,* from *facetie,* a jest, from Latin *facētia,* from *facētus†,* elegant, fine, facetious.] **—fa·ce·tious·ly** *adv.* **—fa·ce·tious·ness** *n.*

face value *n.* **1.** The value printed or written on a bill, bond, coin, or the like. **2.** The apparent value or significance: *He accepted their professed loyalty at face value.*

facia. Variant of **fascia.**

fa·cial (fā'shəl) *adj.* Of or concerning the face.
~*n.* A treatment for the face, usually consisting of a massage and the application of cosmetic creams. [Medieval Latin *faciālis.* See **face, -al.**] **—fa·cial·ly** *adv.*

facial nerve *n.* The seventh cranial nerve, which supplies motor fibers to the muscles of the face and carries sensory fibers from the tastebuds and salivary glands.

-facient *suffix.* Indicates a bringing about or causing to become; for example, **absorbefacient, abortifacient.** [Latin *faciēns* (stem *facient-*), present participle of *facere,* to do.]

fa·ci·es (fā'shē-ēz') *n.,* pl. **facies. 1.** The general aspect or outward appearance, as of a given growth of flora. **2.** *Medicine.* A patient's facial expression, especially if typical of a certain disorder or disease. **3.** *Geology.* The total characteristics of a rock, including appearance, composition, and fossil content, as used to distinguish rocks of the same age, according to the lateral differences. [New Latin, from Latin *faciēs,* shape, form, FACE.]

fac·ile (fās'əl) *adj.* **1.** Done or achieved with little effort or difficulty; easy. **2.** Working, acting, or speaking effortlessly; fluent: *a facile speaker.* **3.** Arrived at without due care, effort, or examination; superficial; glib. **4.** Easy and relaxed in manner. **5.** *Archaic.* Yielding; compliant. [French, from Latin *facilis,* from *facere,* to do.] **—fac·ile·ly** *adv.* **—fac·ile·ness** *n.*

fa·cil·i·tate (fə-sĭl'ə-tāt') *tr.v.* **-tated, -tating, -tates.** To free from difficulties or obstacles; make easier; aid; assist. [French *faciliter,* from Italian *facilitare,* from *facile,* easy, from Latin *facilis,* FACILE.] **—fa·cil·i·ta·tion** (fə-sĭl'ə-tā'shən) *n.*

fa·cil·i·ty (fə-sĭl'ə-tē) *n.,* pl. **-ties. 1.** Ease in moving, acting, or doing; aptitude. **2.** Ready skill derived from practice or familiarity: *"the workman's quick facility with his hands"* (Sherwood Anderson). **3.** *Often* **facilities.** The means or equipment to facilitate an action or process; provision: *the facilities of a library; sports facilities.* **4.** *Archaic.* An agreeable, pliable disposition. **5. facilities.** *Informal.* The available toilet arrangements. [French *facilité.* See **facile, -ity.**]

fac·ing (fā'sĭng) *n.* **1. a.** A piece of material sewn to the edge of a dress, coat, or other garment as lining or decoration. **b.** Fabric used for this. **c. facings.** Fabric of contrasting color used to trim the collar, cuffs, or similar parts of the jacket of a military uniform. **2.** An outer layer or coating of different material applied to a surface for protection or decoration: *a stone wall with wood facing.*

fac·sim·i·le (făk-sĭm'ə-lē) *n. Abbr.* **fac., facsim. 1.** An exact copy or reproduction, as of a document. **2. a.** A method of transmitting images by converting the information into an electronic signal for transmission by cable or radio. **b.** An image so transmitted.
~*adj.* **1.** Of or used to produce facsimiles. **2.** Exactly reproduced; duplicate.
~*tr.v.* **facsimiled, -leing** (-lē-ĭng), **-les.** To make a facsimile of. [Latin *fac simile,* make (it) similar : *fac,* imperative of *facere,* to make, do + *simile,* neuter of *similis,* SIMILAR.]

fact (făkt) *n.* **1.** Something known with certainty. **2.** Something asserted as certain. **3.** Something that has been objectively verified. **4.** Something having real, demonstrable existence. **5.** *Law.* **a.** An act considered with regard to its legality. Used chiefly in the phrases *before* or *after the fact.* **b.** The aspect of a case at law comprising events determined by evidence as distinguished from interpretation of law: *The jury made a finding of fact.* **—as a matter of fact.** Actually; interestingly enough. **—in (point of) fact.** In reality; in truth; actually. [Latin *factum,* a deed, from *factus,* past participle of *facere,* to do.]

fact-find·ing (făkt'fīn'dĭng) *n.* The discovery or determination of facts or accurate information.
~*adj.* Engaged in or designed to ascertain facts: *a fact-finding committee.* **—fact-find·er** *n.*

fac·tion (făk'shən) *n.* **1.** A group of persons forming a cohesive, usually contentious minority within a larger group. **2.** Internal dissension; conflict within an organization or nation: *"And whereas our own beloved country . . . is now afflicted with faction and civil war"* (Lincoln). [Old French, from Latin *factiō* (stem *factiōn-*), an acting (together), a making, from *factus,* past participle of *facere,* to do, make.]

fac·tion·al (făk'shə-nəl) *adj.* Of, characterized by, or causing a contentious faction or factions; partisan. **—fac·tion·al·ism** *n.*

fac·tious (făk'shəs) *adj.* **1.** Produced or characterized by contentious faction. **2.** Creating or promoting faction; divisive: *"The . . . injustice with which a factious spirit has tainted our public administration"* (James Madison). —See Usage note at **insubordinate. —fac·tious·ly** *adv.* **—fac·tious·ness** *n.*

fac·ti·tious (făk-tĭsh'əs) *adj.* **1.** Produced artificially rather than by natural process; contrived: *speculators responsible for the factitious value of some stocks.* **2.** Lacking authenticity or genuineness; sham: *a factitious smile.* [Latin *factīcius,* made by art, from *facere,* to make, do.] **—fac·ti·tious·ly** *adv.* **—fac·ti·tious·ness** *n.*

fac·ti·tive (făk'tə-tĭv) *adj. Grammar.* Of or constituting a transitive verb that in some constructions takes an objective complement to modify its direct object. For example, the verb *elect* is factitive in *They elected him chairman.* [New Latin *factitivus,* from Latin *factus,* done. See **fact.**] **—fac·ti·tive·ly** *adv.*

fact of life *n.* **1.** A fact or situation that must be faced in a realistic manner. **2. facts of life.** The facts about human reproduction and sexuality.

fac·tor (făk'tər) *n.* **1. a.** One who acts for someone else; especially, one who buys and sells on commission; an agent. **b.** *Scottish.* An estate manager; a steward. **c.** A person or company that accepts trade debts as security for short-term loans. **2.** An element that actively contributes to an accomplishment, result, or process: *Cloudy weather was a factor in our decision to stay home.* **3.** *Mathematics.* One of two or more quantities having a designated product: *2 and 3 are factors of 6.* **4.** A gene. No longer in technical usage.
~*v.* **factored, -toring, -tors.** —*tr.* To separate into factors or components. —*intr.* To act as a factor; do business as a factor. [Middle English *factour,* from Old French *facteur,* from Latin *factor,* maker, doer, from *factus,* FACT.] **—fac·tor·ship** *n.*

fac·tor·a·ble (făk'tər-ə-bəl) *adj.* Capable of being expressed as a product of factors. Said especially of mathematical expressions.

fac·tor·age (făk'tər-ĭj) *n.* **1.** The business of a factor. **2.** The commission or fee paid to a factor.

fac·to·ri·al (făk-tôr'ē-əl, -tōr'ē-əl) *n.* The product of all the positive integers from 1 to a given number. For example, 4 factorial, usually written 4!, is the product 1·2·3·4 = 24.
~*adj.* Of or relating to a factor or factorial.

fac·tor·ize (făk'tə-rīz') *tr.v.* **-ized, -izing, -izes.** To resolve (a mathematical expression) into factors. **—fac·tor·i·za·tion** (făk'tə-rə-zā'shən) *n.*

factor of safety *n.* The ratio of the stress required to break a material, part, or structure to the calculated maximum working stress to which it will be subjected in use. Also called "safety factor."

fac·to·ry (făk'tə-rē) *n.,* pl. **-ries.** A building or group of buildings in which goods are manufactured; a plant. [Medieval Latin *factōria,* establishment for factors, from *factor,* FACTOR.]

factory farming *n.* A method of farming employing industrial methods, such as the automated feeding of livestock, to increase production and reduce labor costs. **—factory farm** *n.*

factory ship *n.* A whaling or fishing vessel that has equipment for processing its catch on board.

faience *This faience plaque from ancient Egypt depicts the hippopotamus goddess Thoueris. Egyptian faience usually consisted of a ground-quartz or rock-crystal base under a glasslike glaze. The plaque's vivid color was obtained by adding a copper compound to the glaze.*

fac·to·tum (făk-tō′təm) *n., pl.* **-tums.** An employee or assistant who serves in a wide range of capacities. [Medieval Latin *factōtum,* from Latin *fac tōtum,* do everything : *fac,* imperative of *facere,* to do + *tōtum,* everything, the whole, from *tōtus,* all.]

fac·tu·al (făk′cho͞o-əl) *adj.* **1.** Of the nature of fact; actual; real. **2.** Of or containing facts. **—fac·tu·al·ly** *adv.*

fac·tu·al·ism (făk′cho͞o-ə-lĭz′əm) *n.* Devotion or adherence to fact. **—fac·tu·al·ist** *n.*

fac·ture (făk′chər) *n.* **1.** The process or manner of making something. **2.** That which is made.

fac·u·la (făk′yə-lə) *n., pl.* **-lae** (-lē′). Any of various large bright spots or streaks on the sun's photosphere, most conspicuous at the solar edge or near sunspots. [Latin, diminutive of *fax*† (stem *fac-*), flame, torch.]

fac·ul·ta·tive (făk′əl-tā′tĭv) *adj.* **1.** Of or associated with a mental faculty or faculties. **2.** Capable of occurring or not occurring; contingent. **3.** Granting permission or authority. **4.** Not obligatory; optional. **5.** *Biology.* Capable of existing in very different environmental conditions, as certain microorganisms that can live with or without oxygen. Compare **obligate. —fac·ul·ta·tive·ly** *adv.*

fac·ul·ty (făk′əl-tē) *n., pl.* **-ties. 1.** An inherent power or ability: *"Her strength lay in her extraordinary faculty for . . . observation"* (J.B. Priestly). **2.** Any of the powers or capacities possessed by the human mind: *The blow deprived him of his faculties.* **3.** The ability to perform well in a given activity; skill. **4.** *Archaic.* An occupation; a trade. **5. a.** Any of the divisions or comprehensive branches of learning at a college or university: *the faculty of law.* **b.** The teachers within such a division. **c.** The teachers of a school, college, or university. **6.** All of the members of a learned profession: *the medical faculty.* **7.** Authorization granted by authority; conferred power. [Middle English *faculte,* from Old French, from Latin *facultās* (stem *facultāt-*), power, capability, from Old Latin *facul,* easy.]

fad (făd) *n.* **1.** A fashion in dress, behavior, or speech that enjoys brief popularity. **2.** The object of this fashion. [19th century : originally dialect, perhaps from *fidfad,* shortening of FIDDLE-FADDLE.] **—fad·dist** *n.*

FAD (ĕf′ā-dē′) *n. Biochemistry.* A derivative of riboflavin that is a coenzyme in many oxidation-reduction reactions. [*F*lavin *a*denine *d*inucleotide.]

fad·dish (făd′ĭsh) *adj.* **1.** Of the nature of a fad: *a faddish fondness for the latest hats.* **2.** Given to fads. **—fad·dish·ly** *adv.* **—fad·dish·ness** *n.*

fade (fād) *v.* **faded, fading, fades.** *—intr.* **1.** To lose brightness, loudness, or brilliance gradually; dim. **2.** To lose freshness; wither. **3.** To lose strength or vitality; decline in energy; wane. **4.** To disappear slowly or gradually; die out; vanish. Often used with *out* or *away: All hope of reaching the camp by nightfall soon faded away.* **5.** To lose power gradually. Used of brakes. **6.** To move back from the scrimmage line. Used of a football quarterback. *—tr.* **1.** To cause to fade. **2.** *Slang.* To meet the bet of (an opposing player) in a dice game.

~n. **1.** An act or instance of fading. **2.** A dissolve in motion pictures or television. [Middle English *faden,* from Old French *fader,* from *fade,* faded, vapid, from Vulgar Latin *fatidus* (unattested), probably a blend of Latin *fatuus,* insipid, foolish, FATUOUS, and *vapidus,* VAPID.] **—fade·less** *adj.* **—fade·less·ly** *adv.*

fade in *intr.v.* To appear gradually. Used of a motion-picture or television image or of a sound. *—tr.* To make (an image or sound) appear gradually.

fade-in (fād′ĭn′) *n.* **1.** The gradual coming or bringing into full visibility of an image in motion pictures or television. **2.** The gradual coming or bringing into audibility of a sound, as in broadcasting.

fade out *intr.v.* To disappear gradually. Used of a motion-picture or television image or of a sound. *—tr.v.* To make (an image or sound) disappear gradually.

fade-out (fād′out′) *n.* **1.** The gradual disappearance of a motion-picture or television image or of a sound. **2.** A reduction in strength in or temporary loss of a radio or television signal. **3.** A gradual decline or disappearance.

fad·ing (fā′dĭng) *n.* **1.** A waning; a decline: *the gradual fading of imperial power.* **2.** Fluctuation in the strength of received radio signals because of variations in the transmission medium.

fa·do (fä′do͞o) *n., pl.* **-dos.** A plaintive, usually sentimental Portuguese folk song. [Portuguese, fado, "fate," from Latin *fātum,* FATE.]

faecal. Variant of **fecal.**

faeces. Variant of **feces.**

Fa·en·za (fä-ĕn′zə). Town in the Emilia-Romagna district of northern Italy, on the Lamone River. Since the 12th century the pottery faience has been made here.

fa·er·ie (fā′ə-rē, fâr′ē) *n.* Also **fa·er·y** *pl.* **-ies.** *Archaic.* **1.** A fairy. **2.** The land or realm of the fairies.

~adj. Also **fa·er·y. 1.** *Archaic.* Of or like a fairy or fairies. **2.** Enchanted; visionary; fanciful. [Variant (in Spenser's *The Faerie Queen,* 1590–96) of FAIRY.]

Faer·oe or **Far·oe Islands** (fâr′ō). *Danish* **Fær·ø·er·ne** (fâr′û′ər-nə). Group of 22 volcanic islands belonging to Denmark, lying in the North Atlantic Ocean between Iceland and the Shetland Islands. Seventeen are inhabited; on the largest of them, Streymoy, is the islands' capital, Tórshavn. The economy is based on fish and wool. See map at **Western Europe.**

Faeroese. Variant of **Faroese.**

Faf·nir (fäv′nər, -nîr′). The dragon in Norse mythology that guarded the treasure of the Nibelungs and was slain by Sigurd. [Old Norse *Fafnir.*]

fag[1] (făg) *n.* **1.** *Informal.* **a.** Fatiguing or tedious work; drudgery. **b.** A drudge. **2.** *British.* A schoolboy at some English public schools who is required to perform menial tasks for a pupil in a higher class.

~v. **fagged, fagging, fags.** *—intr.* **1.** *Informal.* To work to exhaustion; become weary from toil. **2.** *British.* To serve as the fag of another pupil. *—tr.* **1.** *Informal.* To exhaust from long work or vigorous activity; weary; fatigue. Often used with *out: was fagged out at the end of three hours on the tennis court.* **2.** *British.* To use (a boy) as a fag. [16th century (to droop, hang down, flag) : origin obscure.]

fag[2] *n. Slang.* A cigarette. [Short for FAG END.]

fag[3] *n. Slang.* A male homosexual. Usually used derogatorily. [Short for FAGGOT.] **—fag·gy** *adj.*

fag end *n.* **1.** The frayed end of a length of cloth or rope. **2.** An inferior remnant or last part of anything; that which remains of something exhausted of its quality or utility. **3.** *Slang.* A cigarette stub. [Middle English *fagge*†.]

Fa·gin (fā′gən) *n.* A man who trains children to steal. [After *Fagin,* an old man in Dickens's *Oliver Twist* who trains children to be pickpockets.]

fag·ot, fag·got (făg′ət) *n.* **1.** A bundle of twigs, sticks, or branches bound together. **2.** A bundle of pieces of iron or steel to be welded or hammered into bars. **3.** A ball or cube of chopped meat, usually pig's offal, bread, and herbs, served baked or fried. **4.** *Slang.* A male homosexual. Usually used derogatorily.

~tr.v. **fagoted, -oting, -ots.** Also **faggot. 1.** To collect or bind into a fagot or fagots; bundle. **2.** To decorate with fagoting. [Middle English, from Old French, from Italian *fagotto,* from Vulgar Latin *facus* (unattested), back-formation from Greek *phakelos*†. Sense 4, from earlier derogatory sense applied abusively to women (compare **baggage**).]

fag·ot·ing, fag·got·ing (făg′ə-tĭng) *n.* **1.** A method of decorating cloth by pulling out horizontal threads and tying the remaining vertical threads into hourglass-shaped bunches. **2.** A method of joining hemmed edges by crisscrossing thread over an open seam.

fah-fee, fa-fi (fä′fē′) *n.* In South Africa, an illegal gambling game popular among black city-dwellers. It is a form of roulette in which a bet is placed on any number from 1 to 36, often chosen on the basis of dreams. [20th century : origin obscure.]

Fahr. Fahrenheit.

Fahr·en·heit (făr′ən-hīt′) *adj. Abbr.* **F, Fahr.** Of or pertaining to a temperature scale that registers the freezing point of water as 32° and the boiling point as 212° under standard atmospheric pressure. Fahrenheit temperatures are related to Celsius temperatures by the equation $F = 1.8C + 32$. [After Gabriel FAHRENHEIT.]

Fahrenheit, Gabriel Daniel (1686–1736). German physicist resident in Holland. He developed the use of mercury in thermometry and devised the temperature scale that bears his name.

fa·ience (fī-äns′, fā-, fä-yäɴs′) *n.* A kind of fine glazed pottery, usually decorated with colorful glazes. [French, short for *(vaisselle de) Faïence,* "(vessel of) Faenza."]

fail (fāl) *v.* **failed, failing, fails.** *—intr.* **1.** To prove deficient or lacking; perform ineffectively or inadequately. **2.** To be unsuccessful in attempting to do or become something. **3. a.** To receive a mark or grade, usually an academic grade, below the acceptable minimum. **b.** To fall below an acceptable standard. **4.** To prove insufficient in quantity or duration; give out. **5.** To decline in strength or effectiveness; wane; fade away. **6.** To cease functioning properly. **7.** To become bankrupt or insolvent. *—tr.* **1.** To disappoint or prove undependable to: *Our sentries failed us.* **2.** To abandon; forsake: *His strength failed him.* **3.** To omit or neglect. Used with an infinitive: *The defendant failed to appear in court.* **4. a.** To receive a mark or grade below the acceptable minimum in (a course, examination, or the like). **b.** To fall below an acceptable standard in (a test, for example). **5. a.** To give a mark or grade of failure to (a student). **b.** To decide that (a candidate or student) has not reached an acceptable standard.

~n. A failure to reach an acceptable standard. **—without fail.** Certainly; definitely. [Middle English *failen, faillen,* from Old French *faillir,* from Vulgar Latin *fallīre* (unattested), from Latin *fallere*†, to deceive, disappoint, fail.]

fail·ing (fā′lĭng) *n.* **1.** The act of a person or thing that fails; a failure. **2.** A minor fault or weakness; a shortcoming; a defect. **—**See Synonyms at **fault.**

~prep. In the absence of; unless there is: *Failing a rainstorm, the game will be played this afternoon.*

faille (fāl, fīl) *n.* A slightly ribbed, woven fabric of silk, cotton, or rayon. [French, from Old French *faille*†.]

fail-safe (fāl′sāf′) *adj.* **1.** Capable of compensating automatically for a failure. Said of a mechanical device. **2.** Capable of returning to a safe condition in the event of a malfunction. **3.** Acting to stop a military attack on the occurrence of any of a variety of predetermined conditions.

~n. A fail-safe mechanism.

fail·ure (fāl′yər) *n.* **1.** The condition or fact of not achieving the desired end or ends: *the failure of an experiment.* **2. a.** One that fails. **b.** *Informal.* An unsuccessful or generally ineffectual person. **3.** The condition or fact of being insufficient or lacking; a falling short: *the failure of the sugar-cane harvest.* **4.** A cessation of proper functioning or performance: *an electric power failure.* **5.** Nonperformance of what is requested or expected; omission: *failure to re-*

port a change of address. **6.** The act or fact of failing to pass a course, examination, or test, or to reach an acceptable standard. **7.** A decline in strength or effectiveness; a weakening. **8.** The act or fact of becoming bankrupt or insolvent. [Variant of earlier *failer,* from Norman French *failer,* from Old French *faillir,* to FAIL.]

fain (fān) *adv. Archaic.* Preferably; gladly.
~*adj. Archaic.* **1.** Ready; willing. **2.** Obliged or required. [Middle English, from *fain,* joyful, happy, Old English *fægen.*]

fai·né·ant (fā′nā-äN′) *adj.* Given to doing nothing; idle; lazy.
~*n.* An irresponsible idler. [French, folk etymological variant (influenced by *fait,* does + *néant,* nothing) of Old French *faignant,* idler, present participle of *faindre,* to be idle, FEIGN.]

faint (fānt) *adj.* **fainter, faintest. 1.** Lacking strength or vigor; feeble. **2.** Lacking conviction, boldness, or courage; timid. **3.** Barely perceptible; indistinct; dim. **4.** Ready to fall into a faint; suddenly dizzy and weak.
~*n.* An abrupt, usually brief loss of consciousness, generally associated with failure of normal blood circulation.
~*intr.v.* **fainted, fainting, faints. 1.** To fall into a faint; swoon. **2.** *Archaic.* To weaken in purpose or spirit; languish. [Middle English *feint, faint,* faint, feigned, from Old French, past participle of *faindre,* to FEIGN.] **—faint·er** *n.* **—faint·ly** *adv.* **—faint·ness** *n.*

faint·est (fān′tĭst) *n. Informal.* The least idea: *I haven't the faintest.*

faint·heart (fānt′härt′) *n.* A faint-hearted person; a coward. [Back-formation from FAINT-HEARTED.]

faint-heart·ed (fānt′här′tĭd) *adj.* Deficient in conviction or courage; cowardly; timid. **—faint-heart·ed·ly** *adv.* **—faint-heart·ed·ness** *n.*

faints, feints (fānts) *pl.n.* The impure spirits produced in the first and last stages of the distillation of liquors. [From FAINT.]

fair¹ (fâr) *adj.* **fairer, fairest. 1.** Visually beautiful or admirable; lovely: *a fair maiden.* **2.** Of light color, as: **a.** Blond: *fair hair.* **b.** Pale or white; not ruddy: *fair skin.* **3.** Clear and sunny; free of clouds or storms: *fair skies.* **4.** Free of blemishes; unstained; clean: *one's fair name.* **5.** Regular and even: *a fair edge.* **6.** Free of obstacles; open: *fair sailing.* **7.** Promising; likely; propitious: *in a fair way to succeed.* **8.** Free of favoritism or bias; impartial: *a fair judge.* **9.** Just to all parties; equitable: *a fair compromise.* **10.** Consistent with rules, standards, logic, or ethics: *a fair tactic.* **11.** Moderately good; mildly satisfying: *a fair job of redecorating.* **12.** Courteous; agreeable: *fair manners.* **13.** Superficially true or good; specious: *They coaxed us with fair words.* **14.** Favorable: *a fair wind for sailing.* **15.** *Informal.* Considerable: *a fair distance.* **16.** *Baseball.* Designating or falling into the area of the playing field bounded by the foul lines. —See Synonyms at **average, beautiful.**
~*adv.* **1.** In a fair manner; correctly; properly: *playing fair.* **2.** Directly; squarely; straight: *a blow caught fair in the stomach.* **—fair and square.** Justly and honestly. **—look fair to.** To be likely to.
~*n. Archaic.* **1.** Loveliness; beauty. **2.** A person or thing that is fair; especially, a beautiful or beloved woman.
~*v.* **faired, fairing, fairs.** —*tr.* To make (timber, a surface, or a joint) smooth, even, or regular. —*intr. Regional.* To become cloudless or mild: *The weather should fair by morning.* [Middle English *fair, fager,* Old English *fæger,* from Germanic.] **—fair·ness** *n.*
Synonyms: *dispassionate, equitable, impartial, just, objective, straightforward, unbiased, unprejudiced.*

fair² *n.* **1.** A gathering held at a specified time and place for the buying and selling of goods; a market. **2.** A regional event, usually held annually, with displays of farm and home products and various competitions and entertainments: *a state fair.* **3. a.** An exhibition presented by representatives of a particular trade in order to facilitate business. **b.** A large exhibition presented jointly by a number of nations, each of which maintains a public building containing educational, artistic, and trade exhibits: *world's fair.* **4.** An event, usually for the benefit of a charity or public institution, including entertainment and the sale of goods; a bazaar: *a church fair.* **5.** *Chiefly British.* An amusement park. [Middle English *feire,* from Old French, from Late Latin *fēria,* from Latin *fēriæ,* holiday.]

fair ball *n. Baseball.* A batted ball that first strikes the ground or leaves the playing field beyond first or third base within the foul lines or that is within the foul lines as it bounces past first or third base or that comes to rest or is touched by a fielder in front of first or third base within the foul lines.

Fair·banks (fâr′băngks′). Town in central Alaska, on the Chena River. Although it was the scene of a gold rush in 1902, its mining now has little commercial value.

Fairbanks, Douglas Elton, born Douglas Ulman (1883–1939). U.S. silent screen actor famed for swashbuckling heroics in romantic adventures. His better-known films include *The Mark of Zorro* (1920), *The Three Musketeers* (1921), and *Robin Hood* (1922). His son, **Douglas Elton Fairbanks, Jr.** (1909–), was also a swashbuckling film adventurer, adding a debonair quality to the Fairbanks tradition. He starred in *The Prisoner of Zenda* (1937) and *Sinbad the Sailor* (1947).

fair copy *n.* A copy of a document made after all corrections and revisions have been completed.

fair game *n.* **1.** Game, such as deer or pheasant, that it is lawful to pursue and kill. **2.** Something deserving criticism or ridicule; something that it is legitimate to attack.

fair·ground (fâr′ground′) *n.* An open space where fairs are held.

fair·ing¹ (fâr′ĭng) *n.* An auxiliary structure or the external surface of an aircraft, car, or vessel serving to reduce drag. [From FAIR (to make smooth).]

fairing² *n. British.* A gift, especially one bought or given at a fair.

fair·ish (fâr′ĭsh) *adj.* **1.** Moderately fair. **2.** Of moderately good size or quality.

fair isle *n.* **1.** A knitting technique of working yarns of many different colors in stocking stitch to produce geometric designs such as those that originated in Fair Isle in the Shetlands. **2. a.** The multicolored pattern formed by this technique. **b.** Material or garments worked in fair isle. **—fair-isle** (fâr′īl′) *adj.*

Fair Isle. The southernmost of the Shetland Islands, Scotland. It is known for its knitted woolen garments with distinctive colored patterns and for its bird sanctuary.

fair·lead (fâr′lēd′) *n.* Also **fair·lead·er** (-lē′dər). *Nautical.* A device such as a ring or block of wood with a hole in it through which rigging is passed to hold it in place or prevent it from snagging or chafing.

fair·ly (fâr′lē) *adv.* **1. a.** In a fair or just manner; equitably. **b.** Legitimately; suitably. **2.** Actually; completely; fully: *The walls fairly shook with his bellowing.* **3.** Moderately; rather: *a fairly good dinner.* **4.** Clearly; distinctly.

fair-mind·ed (fâr′mīn′dĭd) *adj.* Just and impartial in judgment; unprejudiced. **—fair-mind·ed·ness** *n.*

fair play *n.* Conformance to the established rules or ethics of a sport, business, or other activity.

fair sex *n.* Women collectively. Preceded by *the.*

fair-spo·ken (fâr′spō′kən) *adj.* Civil, courteous, and gentle in speech.

fair trade *n.* Trade that conforms to a fair-trade agreement.

fair-trade (fâr′trād′) *tr.v.* **-trad·ed, -trad·ing, -trades.** To sell (a commodity) at a price consistent with a fair-trade agreement.

fair-trade agreement *n.* A commercial agreement under which distributors sell products of a given kind at no less than a minimum price set by the manufacturer.

fair·way (fâr′wā′) *n.* **1.** A stretch of ground free of obstacles to movement. **2.** The part of a golf course covered with short grass and extending from the tee to the putting green. **3.** *Nautical.* **a.** A navigable deep-water channel in a river harbor or along a coastline. **b.** The usual course taken by vessels through a harbor or coastal waters.

fair-weath·er (fâr′wĕth′ər) *adj.* **1.** Suitable or used only during fair weather. **2.** Only engaging in an activity during good weather. Used derogatorily : *fair-weather cyclists.* **3.** Present and dependable only in good times; failing in times of trouble: *fair-weather friends.*

fair·y (fâr′ē) *n., pl.* **-ies. 1.** A tiny supernatural being in human form, typically female and depicted as clever, mischievous, and capable of assisting or harassing humans. **2.** *Slang.* A male homosexual. **—away with the fairies.** *Chiefly Scottish.* Abstracted or eccentric in behavior.
~*adj.* **1.** Of or associated with fairies. **2.** Resembling a fairy; fanciful, graceful, or delicate. [Middle English *fairie,* from Old French *faerie, faierie,* enchantment, from *fae,* fairy, from Latin *fāta,* the Fates, plural of *fātum,* FATE.]

fairy godmother *n.* A benefactress or sometimes a benefactor; especially, one who appears unexpectedly to help in a crisis. [After similar characters in such well-known tales as *Cinderella.*]

fairy gold *n.* **1.** In fairy tales, a gift or theft of gold from fairyland, which turns to dust before the eyes or overnight. **2.** Anything likened to this in elusiveness; a disappointing illusion.

fair·y·land (fâr′ē-lănd′) *n.* **1.** The imaginary land of the fairies. **2.** Any charming, enchanting place; a wonderland.

fairy lights *pl.n. Chiefly British.* Small colored lights used for decoration, as on Christmas trees or in window displays.

fairy ring *n.* A circle of darker luxuriant grass corresponding to an area of underground mycelial growth, the periphery of which is seasonally marked by an overground growth of mushrooms. [The circle is superstitiously believed to be produced by dancing fairies.]

fairy shrimp *n.* Any of various transparent freshwater crustaceans of the order Anostraca that characteristically swim on their backs.

fairy tale *n.* **1.** A story about fairies. **2.** A fanciful tale of legendary deeds and romance, usually intended to please children. **3.** A fictitious, highly fanciful story or explanation.

fair·y-tale (fâr′ē-tāl′) *adj.* Suitable for or like a fairy tale; especially, so delightful as to be like a fantasy: *a fairy-tale wedding.*

Fai·sal (fī′səl), **Ibn Abdul Aziz al-Saud** (1905–75). King of Saudi Arabia. He succeeded to the throne on the abdication of his brother King Saud in 1964. During his reign, government oil profits were used to increase industrialization, education, and health in Saudi Arabia. He was assassinated by his nephew.

fait ac·com·pli (fā′tä-kôN-plē′, fĕt′ä-) *n., pl.* **faits accomplis** (*pronounced as singular*). An accomplished and presumably irreversible deed or fact. [French, "accomplished fact."]

faith (fāth) *n.* **1. a.** A confident belief in the truth, value, or trustworthiness of a person, idea, or thing. **b.** Reliance; trust. **2.** Belief that does not rest on logical proof or material evidence: *faith in miracles.* **3.** Loyalty to a person or thing; allegiance: *keeping faith with one's supporters.* **4.** Belief and trust in God and in the doctrines expressed in the Scriptures or other sacred works; religious conviction. **5.** A system of religious beliefs: *the Muslim faith.* **6.** Any set of principles or beliefs: *"Realism had been his literary faith from his earliest days"* (Alfred Kazin). —See Synonyms at **trust.** [Middle English *feith, feth,* from Old French *feid, feit,* from Latin *fidēs.*]

faith cure *n.* A cure of an ailment held to be accomplished through religious faith.

faith·ful (fāth′fəl) *adj.* **1.** Adhering strictly to the person, cause, or idea to which one is bound; dutiful and loyal. **2.** Worthy of trust or

PRONUNCIATION KEY

ă, pat; ā, pay; âr, care;
ä, father, are; b, bib;
ch, church; d, deed; ĕ, pet;
ē, be; f, fife; g, gag; h, hat;
hw, which; ĭ, pit; ī, pie;
îr, pier; j, judge; k, kick;
l, lid, needle; m, mum;
n, no, sudden; ng, thing;
ŏ, pot; ō, toe; ô, paw, for;
oi, noise; ou, out; o͝o, book;
o͞o, boot; p, pop; r, roar;
s, sauce; sh, ship, dish;
t, tight; th, thin, path;
th, this, bathe; ŭ, cut; ûr, fur;
v, valve; w, with; y, yes;
z, zebra, size; zh, vision;
ə, about, item, edible, gallop, circus, peaceful

IN FOREIGN WORDS:

ä, *Fr.* ami; œ, *Fr.* feu, *Ger.* schön; ü, *Fr.* tu, *Ger.* über; KH, *Ger.* ich, *Scot.* loch; N, *Fr.* bon; y′, *Fr.* Compiègne

STRESS MARKS:

Primary stress: ′
in·cite′ (ĭn-sīt′)
Secondary stress: ′
in′sight′ (ĭn′sīt′)

credence; consistently reliable: *a faithful guide.* **3.** Consistent with truth or actuality; accurate; exact: *a faithful reproduction.* **4.** Not having sexual relations with anyone other than one's spouse or lover. **—the faithful. 1.** The practicing members of a religious faith, especially of Christianity or Islam. **2.** The steadfast adherents of any faith or cause. **—faith·ful·ly** *adv.* **—faith·ful·ness** *n.*

Synonyms: *constant, dependable, devoted, loyal, steadfast, true.*

faith healer *n.* One who attempts to effect faith cures; one who tries to heal by prayer and religious faith.

faith·less (fāth'lĭs) *adj.* **1.** Untrue to duty or obligation; breaking faith; disloyal. **2.** Lacking confidence or trust in a given person or cause. **3. a.** Without religious faith. **b.** Without faith in Christianity; heathen. **4.** Unworthy of faith or trust; unreliable. **—faith·less·ly** *adv.* **—faith·less·ness** *n.*

Synonyms: *disloyal, false, fickle, inconstant, perfidious, traitorous, undependable, unfaithful.*

fake[1] (fāk) *adj.* **1.** Having a false or misleading appearance; fraudulent. **2.** Counterfeit: *a fake Rubens.*

~n. **1.** A person, act, or thing that is not genuine or authentic; a sham; a counterfeit. **2.** *Sports.* A feint or aborted change of direction intended to mislead one's opponents.

~v. **faked, faking, fakes.** *—tr.* **1.** To contrive and present as genuine; counterfeit. **2.** To simulate; pretend; feign. *—intr.* **1.** To engage in faking. **2.** *Sports.* To perform a fake. —See Synonyms at **pretend.** [19th century (thieves' slang) : from obsolete *feak,* to beat, from German *fezen,* to polish, beat, rebuke.]

fake[2] *n. Nautical.* One loop of a coiled rope or cable.

~tr.v. **faked, faking, fakes.** *Nautical.* To coil (a rope or cable). [Middle English *faken*†.]

fak·er (fā'kər) *n.* **1.** A person who fakes or who produces fakes. **2.** One who practices fraud; a swindler. **—fak·er·y** *n.*

fa·kir (fə-kîr', fā'kər) *n.* Also **fa·keer** (fə-kîr'). **1.** A Muslim religious mendicant. **2.** A Hindu ascetic or religious mendicant; especially, one who performs feats of magic or endurance. [Arabic *faqīr,* from *faqura,* he was poor.]

falconry *A jessed peregrine—one fitted with a short strap to its leg for tethering—being launched from a falconer's gauntlet to hunt grouse in Scotland.*

fa·la·fel, fe·la·fel (fə-lä'fəl) *n.* **1.** Ground, spiced chickpeas or fava beans shaped into balls and fried. **2.** A sandwich filled with falafel. [Arabic.]

Fa·laise (fə-lāz'). Market town in Normandy, northern France, and birthplace of William the Conqueror. In the Normandy campaign of 1944 the British captured Falaise, thus opening the way for the Allied armies to liberate northern France.

Fa·lange (fā'lănj', fə-lănj') *n.* A fascist organization constituting the official ruling party of Spain under General Franco. [Spanish, from *falange,* phalanx, from Latin *phalanx* (stem *phalang-*), PHALANX.] **—Fa·lan·gist** (fə-lan'jĭst, fā'lăn'-) *n.*

fal·ba·la (făl'bə-lə) *n.* A flounce, frill, or ruffle. [18th century : French, from dialectal *ferbelà*†, akin to FURBELOW.]

fal·cate (făl'kāt') *adj.* Also **fal·cat·ed** (făl'kā'tĭd). *Biology.* Curved and tapering to a point at either end; sickle-shaped. [Latin *falcātus,* from *falx*† (stem *falc-*), sickle.]

fal·chion (fôl'chən, -shən) *n.* **1.** A short, broad sword with a convex cutting edge and a sharp point, used in medieval times. **2.** *Archaic.* Any sword. [Middle English *fauchoun,* from Old French *fauchon,* from Vulgar Latin *falciō* (stem *falciōn-*) (unattested), from Latin *falx* (stem *falc-*), sickle.]

fal·ci·form (făl'sə-fôrm') *adj.* Curved or sickle-shaped; falcate. [Latin *falx* (stem *falc-*), sickle (see **falcate**) + -FORM.]

fal·con (făl'kən, fôl'-, fô'-) *n.* **1. a.** Any of various birds of prey of the family Falconidae, and especially of the genus *Falco,* having long, pointed, powerful wings adapted for swift flight. **b.** Any of several species of these birds or related birds such as hawks, trained to hunt small game. **c.** In falconry, a female bird of this type. **2.** A small cannon of the 15th to 17th century. [Middle English *faucoun,* from Old French *faucon,* from Late Latin *falcō* (stem *falcōn-*).]

fal·con·er (făl'kə-nər, fôl'-, fô'-) *n.* **1.** A person who breeds and trains falcons. **2.** One who hunts with falcons.

fal·co·net (făl'kə-nĕt', fôl'-, fô'-) *n.* **1.** A small or young falcon. **2.** Any of several small falcons of the genus *Microhierax,* chiefly of tropical Asia.

fal·con-gen·tle (făl'kən-jĕn'təl, fôl'-, fô'-) *n.* A female falcon, especially a peregrine falcon. [Middle English *faucoun gentil,* from Old French *faucon gentil,* "noble falcon" : *faucon,* FALCON + *gentil,* noble (see **gentle**).]

fal·con·ry (făl'kən-rē, fôl'-, fô'-) *n.* **1.** The sport of hunting with falcons. **2.** The art of training falcons for hunting.

falderal, falderol. Variants of **folderol.**

fald·stool (fôld'stōōl') *n.* **1.** A small, usually cushioned stool at which worshipers kneel to pray; especially, one on which the British sovereign kneels at the coronation. **2.** A portable, backless chair or stool used by a bishop when not occupying his throne or when presiding away from his own cathedral. **3.** *Anglican Church.* A desk at which the litany is recited. [Partial translation of Medieval Latin *faldistolium,* folding stool, from Germanic.]

Falk·land Islands (fôk'lənd). *Spanish* **Is·las Mal·vi·nas** (ēz'läz mäl-vē'nəs). Group of 202 small islands *c.* 480 kilometers (300 miles) east of the Strait of Magellan in the South Atlantic Ocean. The two largest islands are East Falkland and West Falkland. The capital is Port Stanley (also called Stanley). The islands have been a British crown colony since 1833 but are claimed by Argentina. In 1982 Argentine forces seized the islands and were expelled by a British military expedition. The colony includes the dependencies of South Georgia, 1,290 kilometers (800 miles) southeast of East Falkland, and the South Sandwich Islands, 760 kilometers (470 miles) southeast of South Georgia. See map at **Argentina.**

fall (fôl) *v.* **fell** (fĕl), **fallen** (fô'lən), **falling, falls.** *—intr.* **1.** To move under the influence of gravity; especially, to drop without restraint. **2.** To drop oneself from an erect to a less erect position: *He stumbled and fell.* **3.** To be severely wounded or to be killed in battle. **4.** To collapse from lack of structural support: *Several buildings fell during the earthquake.* **5.** To come to rest; strike bottom; land: *The aircraft fell in an uninhabited region.* **6.** To hang down: *Her hair fell in ringlets.* **7.** To be cast down; be averted: *Her eyes fell.* **8.** To assume an expression of disappointment: *Her face fell when she heard the report.* **9.** To be conquered or seized: *The city fell after a long siege.* **10.** To lose power; be defeated or overthrown: *During periods of crisis, governments may fall.* **11.** To follow a downward direction; slope: *The plain falls gently toward the coast.* **12.** To undergo a reduction in amount, degree, or value; diminish: *The air pressure is falling.* **13.** To diminish in pitch or volume: *His voice fell to a whisper.* **14.** To decline in rank, status, or importance. **15.** To yield to temptation; err or sin. **16.** To pass into a specified condition: *The crowd fell silent.* **17.** To arrive and pervade: *A hush fell on the crowd.* **18.** To occur at a specified time: *Christmas falls on a Tuesday this year.* **19.** To occur at a specified place: *The stress falls on the last syllable.* **20.** To come or be allotted by chance or distribution: *The greatest task fell to him.* **21.** To be given by right or stipulation: *The estate fell to the eldest surviving son.* **22.** To divide naturally. Used with *into: The specimens fall into three categories.* **23.** To be directed; come to rest: *His gaze fell on a small book in the corner.* **24.** To be uttered as if involuntarily; slip out: *A murmur of impatience fell from his lips.* **25.** To be born. Used chiefly of lambs. *—tr.* To cut down (a tree); fell. **—fall among.** To come casually into the company of. **—fall away. 1.** To decline; languish; weaken. **2.** To withdraw friendship or support; part company. **3.** To slope downward. **—fall back. 1.** To give ground; recede; retreat. **2.** To move backward. **—fall back on** (or **upon**). **1.** To retreat to. **2.** To resort to. **—fall behind. 1.** To lag behind; fail to keep up with. **2.** To be in arrears. **3.** To move behind. **—fall down.** *Informal.* To prove unsuccessful; fail or lag in performance. **—fall flat.** *Informal.* To fail completely to achieve the intended effect. **—fall for.** *Informal.* **1.** To become infatuated with; fall suddenly in love with. **2.** To be tricked or deceived by. **—fall foul** (or **afoul**). *Nautical.* **1.** To collide. Used of vessels. **2.** To become entangled. Used of rigging. **—fall foul of.** To incur the displeasure of; come into conflict with. **—fall in.** *Military.* To take one's place in a formation; form ranks. **—fall in with. 1.** To agree. **2.** To meet by chance; join. **—fall on** (or **upon**). To attack suddenly; ambush. **—fall short. 1.** To fail to attain a specified amount, level, or degree. **2.** To prove inadequate or lacking. **—fall through. 1.** To fail; collapse; miscarry. **2.** To fail to occur. **—fall to. 1.** To begin an activity energetically. **2.** To shut or move into place unaided. **—fall under. 1.** To occur in the class of; be listed or located within. **2.** To succumb to; come under the influence or power of.

~n. **1.** The act or an instance of falling; a dropping down; a free descent. **2.** A sudden drop from a relatively erect to a less erect position: *He had a bad fall.* **3.** That which has fallen: *The field was covered with a fall of hail.* **4. a.** The amount of what has fallen: *a fall of two inches of rain.* **b.** The distance that something falls: *a fall of three stories.* **5.** *Often* **Fall.** Autumn. **6.** *Often* **falls.** A waterfall; a cascade. **7.** A downward movement or slope: *the fall of a river toward its mouth.* **8.** Any of several hanging articles of dress, especially: **a.** A veil hung from a woman's hat and down her back. **b.** An ornamental cascade of lace or trimming attached to a dress, usually at the collar. **c.** A woman's hairpiece with long, free-hanging hair. **9.** A capture, overthrow, or collapse: *the fall of a government.* **10.** A reduction in value, amount, or degree. **11.** A decline in status, rank, or importance. **12.** A loss of virtue or moral innocence; a yielding to sin. **13.** *Usually* **Fall.** *Theology.* Adam's sin of disobeying God by eating the forbidden fruit in the Garden of Eden and the consequent loss of innocence and grace of all his descendants. Preceded by *the.* **14.** In wrestling: **a.** The act of throwing or forcing an opponent down on his back. **b.** Any of various maneuvers used for this. **15.** *Nautical.* A break or rise in the level of a deck. **16. falls.** *Nautical.* The apparatus used to hoist and transfer cargo or lifeboats. **17.** The end of a cable, rope, or chain that is pulled by the power source in hoisting. **18. a.** The birth of an animal; especially, the birth of a lamb. **b.** All of the animals born at one birth; a litter. **—ride for a fall.** To court danger or disaster. [Fall, fell, fallen; Middle English *fallen, fell, fallen,* Old English *feallan, fēol, feallan,* from Germanic *fallan* (unattested).]

Fal·la (fä'yə), **Manuel de** (1876–1946). Spanish composer and pianist. He was influenced by Debussy and Ravel and blended elements of their music with his own ebullient style, as in *Nights in the Gardens of Spain* (1916). His music later became starker, as in the ballet for Diaghilev, *The Three-Cornered Hat* (1919).

fal·la·cious (fə-lā'shəs) *adj.* **1.** Containing or based on a fallacy: *a fallacious syllogism.* **2.** Deceptive in appearance or meaning; misleading: *fallacious evidence.* **3.** Not real or sound; delusive: *fallacious signs of a change in the weather.* **—fal·la·cious·ly** *adv.* **—fal·la·cious·ness** *n.*

fal·la·cy (făl'ə-sē) *n., pl.* **-cies. 1.** An idea or opinion founded on mistaken logic or perception; a false notion. **2.** An argument or thesis that is inconsistent with logic or fact and thus renders the conclusion invalid. **3.** The quality of being in error; incorrectness of reasoning or belief. **4.** The quality of being deceptive. [Latin *fallā-*

PRONUNCIATION KEY

ă, pat; ā, pay; âr, care; ä, father, are; b, bib; ch, church; d, deed; ĕ, pet; ē, be; f, fife; g, gag; h, hat; hw, which; ĭ, pit; ī, pie; îr, pier; j, judge; k, kick; l, lid, needle; m, mum; n, no, sudden; ng, thing; ŏ, pot; ō, toe; ô, paw, for; oi, noise; ou, out; ŏŏ, book; ōō, boot; p, pop; r, roar; s, sauce; sh, ship, dish; t, tight; th, thin, path; *th*, this, bathe; ŭ, cut; ûr, fur; v, valve; w, with; y, yes; z, zebra, size; zh, vision; ə, about, item, edible, gallop, circus, peaceful

IN FOREIGN WORDS:

à, *Fr.* ami; œ, *Fr.* feu, *Ger.* schön; ü, *Fr.* tu, *Ger.* über; KH, *Ger.* ich, *Scot.* loch; N, *Fr.* bon; y', *Fr.* Compiègne

STRESS MARKS:

Primary stress: ' **in·cite'** (ĭn-sīt')
Secondary stress: ' **in'sight'** (ĭn'sīt')

cia, deceit, trick, from *fallāx* (stem *fallāc-*), deceitful, from *fallere,* to deceive. See **fail.**]

fal·lal (fă-lăl′, făl′ăl′) *n.* A trifling, showy article of dress; a piece of finery; frippery.
~*adj. Archaic.* Affected; foppish. [18th century : perhaps akin to FALBALA.]

fallen arch *n.* A collapse of the normally arch-shaped instep of the foot that results in a flat foot.

fall guy *n. Slang.* **1.** One who takes the responsibility or blame, as for another's dereliction or delinquency; a scapegoat. **2.** An easy victim, as of a confidence trick.

fal·li·ble (făl′ə-bəl) *adj.* **1.** Capable of erring. **2.** Tending or likely to err. [Middle English, from Medieval Latin *fallibilis,* from Latin *fallere,* to deceive. See **fail.**] —**fal·li·bil·i·ty** (făl′ə-bĭl′ə-tē), **fal·li·ble·ness** *n.* —**fal·li·bly** *adv.*

falling band *n.* A wide collar of linen or lace turned down over the shoulders, worn during the 17th century.

fall·ing-out (fô′lĭng-out′) *n., pl.* **fallings-out** or **falling-outs.** A personal disagreement that has resulted in a broken or more distant relationship; an estrangement; a breach.

falling sickness *n.* Epilepsy. Not in technical usage.

falling star *n.* Any object, such as a meteoroid, rendered visible as a bright streak in the sky by falling and being ignited by atmospheric friction.

fall line *n.* **1.** *Geography.* An imaginary line marking a drop in land level or height, formulated by connecting the waterfalls of nearly parallel rivers. **2. Fall Line.** The line between the Piedmont Plateau and the Atlantic coastal plain where the Appalachians slope sharply. **3.** *Skiing.* The natural line of descent between two points on a slope.

fall off *intr.v.* **1.** To lessen in intensity, volume, number, or the like: *Ticket sales are falling off.* **2.** *Nautical.* To change course to leeward.

fall·off (fôl′ôf′, -ŏf′) *n.* A decline or decrease: *a falloff in sales.*

Fal·lo·pi·an tube (fə-lō′pē-ən) *n.* Either of a pair of slender ducts along which eggs pass from the ovaries to the womb in the female reproductive system of humans and other mammals. [After Gabriel FALLOPIUS.]

Fal·lo·pi·us (fə-lō′pē-əs), **Fal·lo·pi·o** (-pē-ō′), **Gabriel** (1523–62). Italian anatomist who discovered the Fallopian tubes, which connect the ovaries with the uterus in females.

fall out *intr.v.* **1.** *Military.* To leave ranks; withdraw from formation. **2.** To quarrel; become estranged. **3.** To happen; occur.

fall·out (fôl′out′) *n.* **1. a.** The slow descent of minute particles of radioactive debris in the atmosphere following a nuclear explosion in which radioactive material escapes into the atmosphere. **b.** The particles so descending. **c.** Such particles collectively. **2.** An incidental result or side effect: *the technological fallout of the space program; political fallout.*

fal·low (făl′ō) *adj.* **1. a.** Plowed and tilled but left unseeded during a growing season: *a fallow field.* **b.** Uncultivated. Said of land. **2. a.** Not pregnant: *a fallow mare.* **b.** Marked by the absence of pregnancy. —**lie fallow.** To go unexercised or unrealized.
~*n.* **1.** Land that has been plowed but left unseeded during a growing season. **2.** The process of leaving plowed land unseeded during a growing season.
~*tr.v.* **fallowed, -lowing, -lows. 1.** To make (land) fallow by plowing. **2.** To plow (land) by way of preparing it for sowing. [Middle English *falow, falwe,* Old English *fealh†,* arable land.] —**fal·low·ness** *n.*

fallow crop *n.* A crop that tends to nourish soil and is rotated with a more demanding crop to maintain productivity of the soil.

fallow deer *n.* Either of two Eurasian deer, *Dama dama* or *D. mesopotamica,* having a yellowish-red coat spotted with white in summer, and broad, flattened antlers in the male. [From obsolete *fallow,* reddish-yellow, from Middle English *falwe,* sallow, Old English *fealu.*]

Fall River (fôl). An industrial city in southeastern Massachusetts, at the mouth of the Taunton River. It was once the foremost U.S. cotton textile center. Lizzie Borden lived in Fall River and was tried here (1892) for the murder of her father and stepmother.

Fal·mouth (făl′məth). A resort town on Cape Cod, in southeastern Massachusetts. It was settled *c.* 1660 and was once a whaling and shipbuilding center. The town includes Woods Hole, site of a major oceanographic institute.

false (fôls) *adj.* **falser, falsest. 1.** Contrary to fact or truth; without grounds; incorrect. **2.** Fallacious; specious: *false logic.* **3.** Untruthful. **4. a.** Without meaning or sincerity; deceiving; sham: *false promises.* **b.** Misplaced and unjustified: *false modesty.* **c.** Deceptive; belying appearances: *a false start.* **5.** Not keeping faith; treacherous: *a false lover.* **6.** Not real or natural; artificial; synthetic: *false fur.* **7.** Resembling but not accurately or properly designated as such. Often used in plant names: *false hellebore.* **8.** *Music.* Of incorrect pitch. —See Synonyms at **faithless.** —**play someone false.** To betray. [Middle English *fals,* from Old French, from Latin *falsus,* past participle of *fallere,* to deceive. See **fail.**] —**false·ly** *adv.* —**false·ness** *n.*

false alarm *n.* **1.** An emergency alarm set off unnecessarily, whether by accident or intentionally; especially, a fire alarm where no fire exists. **2.** *Informal.* Any seeming crisis, signal, or warning that is groundless or abortive.

false arrest *n. Law.* An unlawful or unjustifiable arrest.

false bottom *n.* **1.** A partition that seems to be the bottom of a trunk, case, chest, or other receptacle but under which is another

compartment. **2.** A base, as of a glass or bowl, that by its shape gives a false idea of the capacity of the vessel.

false brome *n.* Either of two grasses, *Brachypodium sylvaticum* or *B. pinnatum,* having long awns like the true brome grasses.

false colors *pl.n.* **1.** The flag or symbol of another country when used for deception, as by pirates on the high seas. **2.** Misleading representation; pretense.

false dawn *n.* **1.** Faint light observed low in the sky before dawn, caused by **zodiacal light** (*see*). **2.** An apparent arrival or advent that turns out to be short-lived and premature.

false friend *n.* A word in another language that is identical or almost identical to a word in one's own but that has a quite different meaning, as the French word *éventuel,* meaning "possible," and the German *Gift,* "poison."

false fruit *n.* A pseudocarp (*see*).

false-heart·ed (fôls′här′tĭd) *adj.* Having a deceitful nature; disloyal; treacherous.

false hellebore *n.* A species of **hellebore** (*see*).

false·hood (fôls′hŏŏd′) *n.* **1.** Contradiction to or disparity with truth or fact; that which is groundless or specious; an inaccuracy. **2.** The act of deceiving; lying. **3.** An untrue statement; a deception; a lie.

false imprisonment *n. Law.* Unlawful arrest or detention of a person, such as that enforced without a warrant or with an illegal one.

false indigo *n.* **1.** A shrub, *Amorpha fruticosa,* of eastern North America, having compound leaves with numerous leaflets and long clusters of purplish flowers. **2.** A plant, *Baptista australis,* of the southeastern United States, having compound leaves and purplish flowers.

false keel *n.* A protective strip fixed below a ship's main keel.

false position *n.* **1.** A situation in which a person's actions or motives, however good or well-intentioned, will be misconstrued or seen as wrong. **2.** A situation in which a person will be forced to act against his principles.

false pretenses *pl.n.* Misrepresentations of fact for an ulterior motive.

false rib *n.* In human beings, any of the ten lower ribs that do not unite directly with the sternum.

false step *n.* **1.** A slip; a stumble. **2.** A social blunder; a faux pas.

false teeth *pl.n.* Removable artificial teeth for one or both jaws.

fal·set·to (fôl-sĕt′ō) *n., pl.* **-tos.** A singing voice, typically male, marked by artificially produced notes in an upper register beyond its normal range.
~*adj.* Having the quality of falsetto: *a falsetto tone.*
~*adv.* In falsetto. [Italian, diminutive of *falso,* false, from Latin *falsus,* FALSE.]

false·work (fôls′wûrk′) *n.* A temporary supporting framework for a structure during construction or demolition.

fals·ies (fôl′sēz) *pl.n. Informal.* Pads or padding worn inside, or as part of, a brassiere to exaggerate the dimensions of the breasts.

fal·si·fy (fôl′sə-fī′) *v.* **-fied, -fying, -fies.** —*tr.* **1.** To state untruthfully; misrepresent. **2.** To alter (a document) in order to deceive. **3.** To counterfeit; forge. **4.** *Philosophy.* To show to be false. —*intr.* To make untrue statements; lie. [Middle English *falsifien,* from Old French *falsifier,* from Medieval Latin *falsificāre* : Latin *falsus,* FALSE + *facere,* to make.] —**fal·si·fi·a·bil·i·ty** (fôl′sə-fī′ə-bĭl′ə-tē) *n.* —**fal·si·fi·a·ble** (fôl′sə-fī′ə-bəl) *adj.* —**fal·si·fi·ca·tion** (fôl′sə-fī-kā′shən) *n.* —**fal·si·fi·er** *n.*

fal·si·ty (fôl′sə-tē) *n., pl.* **-ties. 1.** The condition of being false. **2.** Something false; an untruth; a lie or falsehood.

Fal·staff·i·an (fôl-stăf′ē-ən) *adj.* Resembling or characteristic of Falstaff, a fat, merry, ribald, and boastful knight in Shakespeare's *Henry IV: Parts I and II* and *The Merry Wives of Windsor.*

falt·boat (fält′bōt′) *n.* A small boat consisting of canvas stretched over a collapsible frame and resembling a kayak. Also called "foldboat." [Partial translation of German *Faltboot,* folding boat, from *falten,* to fold, from Old High German *falden.*]

fal·ter (fôl′tər) *intr.v.* **-tered, -tering, -ters. 1.** To waver in confidence; hesitate. **2.** To speak hesitatingly; stammer. **3. a.** To move ineptly or haltingly; stumble; stagger. **b.** To operate unsteadily or ineffectively. —See Synonyms at **hesitate.**
~*n.* **1.** An unsteadiness in speech or action. **2.** A faltering sound. [Middle English *falteren†.*] —**fal·ter·ing·ly** *adv.*

fam. 1. familiar. **2.** family.

F.A.M. Free and Accepted Masons.

Fa·ma·gu·sta (fä′mə-gŏŏ′stə). Port on Famagusta Bay, an inlet of the Mediterranean, in eastern Cyprus. It is an ancient fishing and trading town, with remains of medieval walls.

fame (fām) *n.* **1.** Great reputation and recognition, usually favorable; public esteem; renown. **2.** Reputation. **3.** *Archaic.* Rumor.
~*tr.v.* **famed, faming, fames.** *Archaic.* To make famous by talking of. [Middle English, from Old French, from Latin *fāma,* talk, reputation.]
Synonyms: *eminence, glory, notoriety, renown, repute.*

famed (fāmd) *adj.* Having great fame; publicly acclaimed; celebrated; famous.

fa·mil·ial (fə-mĭl′yəl) *adj.* **1.** Of or pertaining to a family. **2.** *Genetics.* Passed on in a family; hereditary: *a familial trait.*

fa·mil·iar (fə-mĭl′yər) *adj. Abbr.* **fam. 1.** Of frequent instance or occurrence; often encountered; common: *a familiar sight.* **2.** Having fair knowledge of something; acquainted. Used with *with: familiar with those roads.* **3.** Of established friendship; close; intimate: *be on familiar terms.* **4.** Natural and unstudied; informal: *He lectured in a*

fallow deer *The antlers of a young fallow deer buck (above) have a soft covering, called velvet, which is shed in the autumn as the breeding season approaches.*

familiar style. **5.** Presuming upon acquaintance; taking liberties. **6.** *Archaic.* Familial. —See Synonyms at **common.**
~*n.* **1.** A close friend or associate. **2.** A spirit, often taking animal form, thought to attend a witch or wizard. **3.** *Roman Catholic Church.* One who performs domestic service in the household of a bishop. [Middle English, familial, from Old French *familier,* from Latin *familiāris,* from *familia,* FAMILY.] —**fa·mil·iar·ly** *adv.*
 Synonyms: *chummy, close, fraternal, intimate.*
fa·mil·iar·i·ty (fə-mĭl′yăr′ə-tē, -ē-ăr′ə-tē) *n., pl.* **-ties. 1.** Substantial or reasonable acquaintance with something; moderate understanding; knowledge. Used with *with.* **2.** Established friendship; candor; intimacy. **3.** Presumption; undue liberty; boldness. **4.** *Often* **familiarities.** Actions or behavior presuming intimacy, especially sexual advances; liberties.
fa·mil·iar·ize (fə-mĭl′yə-rīz′) *tr.v.* **-ized, -izing, -izes. 1.** To make generally known, recognized, or familiar; popularize. **2.** To make (oneself or another) acquainted. —**fa·mil·iar·i·za·tion** (fə-mĭl′yər-ī-zā′shən) *n.* —**fa·mil·iar·iz·er** *n.*

fam·i·ly (făm′ə-lē, făm′lē) *n., pl.* **-lies.** *Abbr.* **fam. 1. a.** The fundamental social or mating group among human beings and animals. **b.** Two or more adults and the children living with them. **2. a.** One's spouse and children. **b.** One's children. **c.** One's parents and siblings. **3.** Persons related by blood or marriage; relatives; kin. **4.** Lineage; especially, upper-class lineage. **5.** All the members of a household; those who share a home. **6. a.** A group of like things; a class. **b.** A special or particular world of something; a kingdom; a fellowship: *the family of man.* **7.** *Biology.* A taxonomic category ranking below an order and above a genus. **8.** *Linguistics.* A language group derived from the same parent language. **9.** A locally independent unit of the Mafia. **10.** A set of related curves or surfaces that are given by different values of a constant in a single equation. For example, different values of *r* in the equation $x^2 + y^2 = r^2$ generate a family of concentric circles.
~*adj.* **1.** Of or pertaining to a family: *a family reunion.* **2.** Suitable or intended for children and their parents: *a family show.* —**in the family way.** *Informal.* Pregnant. [Middle English *familie,* from

---

family tree

CHARTING A FAMILY'S HISTORY
Two billion ancestors in 30 generations

In each generation the number of any person's direct ancestors—their parents, grandparents, great-grandparents, and so on—doubles. So, theoretically, over 30 generations everyone has, amazingly, more than 2 billion ancestors.

A family tree can be necessary to establish the transmission of property or title from one generation to another. Some cultures use a matrilineal line, which traces descent through the mother. Most, however, use

patrilineage, which traces descent through the father. Since Roman times it has been customary in the West to trace descent through the male line.

The legally enforced registration of births, marriages, and deaths, introduced in many countries during the 19th century, has made it reasonably simple to trace ancestors back over the last three or four generations. Research is also made easier by census returns, wills, parish registers, and records of service in the

armed forces. The British royal family can trace its ancestors back through 53 generations and 1,500 years to Cerdic, a Saxon invader who became king of the West Saxons; he died in 534.

The largest family tree known to exist was compiled by Nellaray Holt of Union Gap in Washington State, over a period of 16 years. It is the record of a family called Borton, which contains 6,820 names and goes back to 1562.

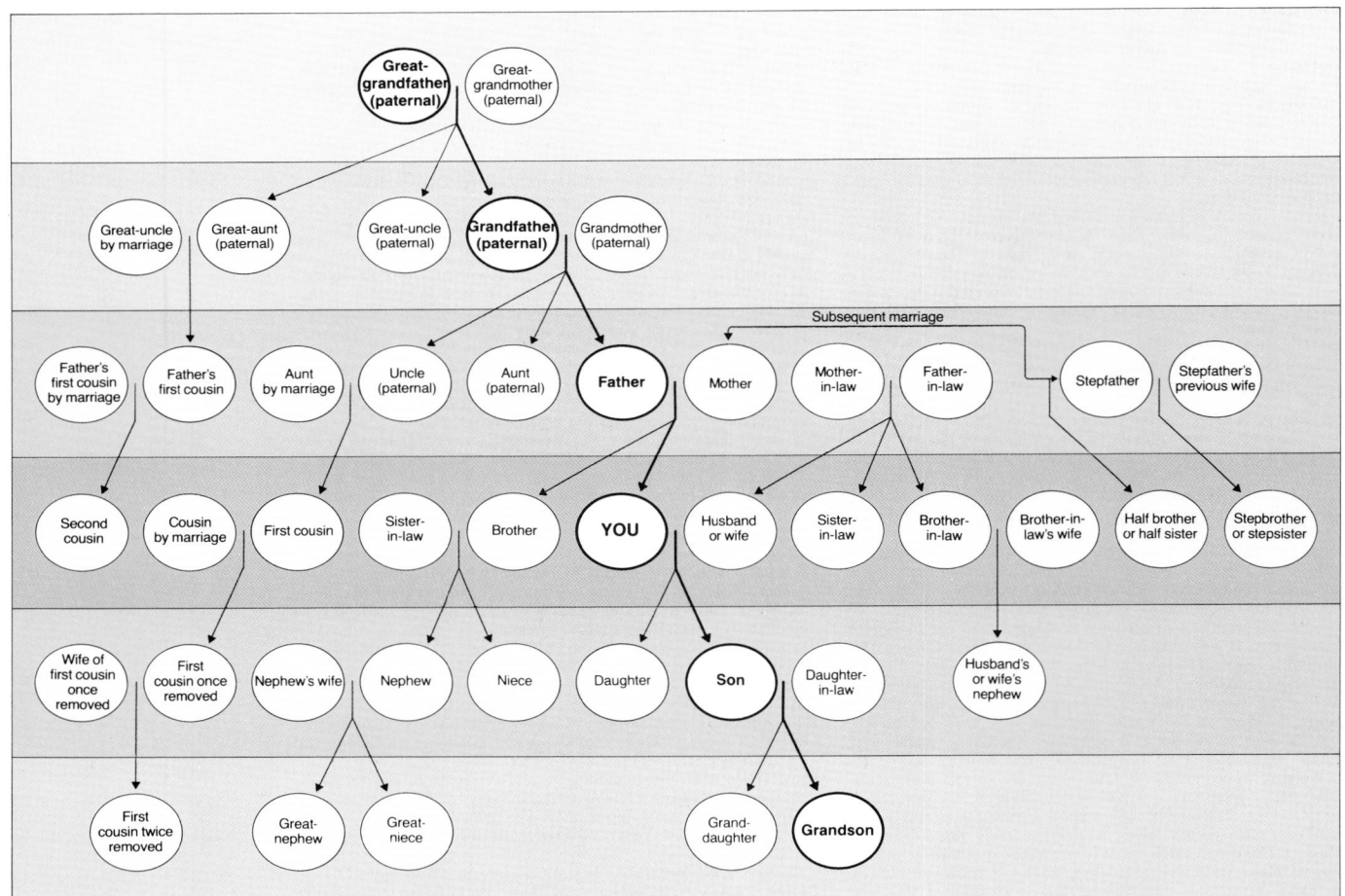

HOW YOU ARE RELATED TO THE REST OF YOUR FAMILY *In large families, relationships can become complicated—particularly if some members have remarried and had a second family of children. This chart gives the terms used to refer to relatives. For simplicity, it follows the male side of the family only. The terms used for the female side are the same except that great-grandparents, grandparents, uncles, and aunts are referred to as ma-* *ternal rather than paternal. Terms most often confused are second cousin and first cousin once removed. Your second cousin is the child of the first cousin of one of your parents. He is the same generation as yourself. A first cousin once removed is the child of your own first cousin; he is a generation later than you. "Once removed" means removed by one generation.*

Latin *familia,* family, household, servants of a household, from *famulus*†, servant.]

family Bible *n.* A Bible with special pages to record a family's births, deaths, and marriages.

family circle *n.* A section of less expensive theater seats.

family doctor *n.* A **general practitioner** *(see).*

family man *n.* **1.** A man who is devoted to his family, especially his wife and children, and who enjoys domestic life. **2.** A man who has a wife and children.

family name *n.* **1. a.** A surname. **b.** A surname considered as standing for the whole family and its honor. **2.** A first or middle name, often a former surname, given to many members of a family.

family planning *n.* **1.** The regulation of the number of children conceived and the intervals between them by some means of contraception. **2.** Contraception.

family tree *n.* **1.** A genealogical diagram of a family. **2.** The ancestors and descendants collectively of a family.

fam·ine (făm′ĭn) *n.* **1.** A drastic and wide-reaching shortage of food. **2.** A drastic shortage of anything; a dearth. **3.** *Archaic.* Severe hunger; starvation. **4.** Extreme appetite, as of a starving person. [Middle English *famine,* from Old French, from Vulgar Latin *famina* (unattested), from Latin *fames*†, hunger.]

fam·ish (făm′ĭsh) *v.* **-ished, -ishing, -ishes.** *Archaic.* —*tr.* **1.** To cause to endure severe hunger; starve. **2.** To cause to die from hunger; starve to death. —*intr.* **1.** To endure severe hunger; starve. **2.** To die from hunger; starve to death. [Middle English *famishen,* extended form of *famen,* from Old French *afamer,* from Vulgar Latin *affamāre* (unattested) : Latin *ad-,* toward + *fames*†, hunger.] **—fam·ish·ment** *n.*

fam·ished (făm′ĭsht) *adj.* Extremely hungry; starving.

fa·mous (fā′məs) *adj.* **1.** Generally recorded in history or currently renowned; publicly acclaimed; celebrated. **2.** *Informal.* First-rate; excellent. **3.** *Archaic.* Infamous; notorious. [Middle English, from Old French *fameus,* from Latin *famōsus,* from *fāma,* FAME.] **—fa·mous·ly** *adv.* **—fa·mous·ness** *n.*

fam·u·lus (făm′yə-ləs) *n., pl.* **-li** (-lī′). An attendant or servant, especially of a medieval magician or scholar. [German *Famulus,* from Latin *famulus*†, servant.]

fan¹ (făn) *n.* **1.** A hand-waved implement for creating a current of air or a breeze; especially, one in the form of a flat, fixed or collapsible device, usually round or approximately semicircular, and made of a light material such as silk, paper, or fine ivory. **2.** Anything resembling a fan, especially in being shaped like a semicircle or segment of a circle, such as an arrangement of seats in an auditorium. **3.** Any device for creating air movement, such as: **a.** An array of thin, rigid blades attached to a central hub. **b.** A machine that rotates one or more such arrays on electrically powered shafts in order to move air, as for cooling or to exhaust an enclosure. **4.** A machine that throws grain and chaff into the air so that the latter will be blown away. **5.** A small rudderlike vane that keeps the sails of a windmill at right angles to the wind.
~*v.* **fanned, fanning, fans.** —*tr.* **1.** To cause a current of or move (air) with or as if with a fan. **2.** To direct a current of air or a breeze upon, especially in order to cool: *fan one's face.* **3.** To stir up; activate: *fan resentment.* **4.** To open out (a hand of cards, for example) to a fan shape. **5. a.** To fire (an automatic gun) in a continuous sweep while keeping one's finger on the trigger. **b.** To fire (a nonautomatic gun) rapidly by chopping the hammer with the palm. **6.** To winnow; separate (grain) from chaff by air or wind. **7.** *Baseball.* To strike out (a batter). —*intr.* **1.** To spread like a fan. Used with *out.* **2.** *Baseball.* To strike out. [Middle English *fan(ne),* Old English *fann,* from Latin *vannus.*]

fan² *n. Informal.* An ardent devotee or admirer, as of a sport, athletic team, or famous person. [Short for FANATIC.]

Fan·a·ga·lo (făn′ə-gə-lō′) *n.* Also **Fan·a·ka·lo** (-kə-lō′). A pidgin language spoken in southern Africa, containing elements of Zulu, English, and Afrikaans. [From *fana ga lo,* "like this" (a common phrase in the language) : Zulu *fana,* be like + *ka,* "of" (possessive prefix) + *lo,* this.]

fa·nat·ic (fə-năt′ĭk) *n.* A person possessed by an excessive and irrational zeal, especially for a religious or political cause. Sometimes used humorously: *an opera fanatic.*
~*adj.* Variant of **fanatical.** [Latin *fānāticus,* of a temple, inspired by a god, mad, from *fānum,* temple.]
Synonyms: *enthusiast, extremist, zealot.*

fa·nat·i·cal (fə-năt′ĭ-kəl) *adj.* Also **fa·nat·ic** (-năt′ĭk). **1.** Possessed or driven by excessive or irrational zeal. **2.** Pertaining to or characteristic of a fanatic. **—fa·nat·i·cal·ly** *adv.*

fa·nat·i·cism (fə-năt′ə-sĭz′əm) *n.* Excessive, irrational zeal; extreme or unscrupulous dedication; monomania.

fan belt *n.* A belt that transfers torque from the crankshaft of an internal-combustion engine to the shaft of the cooling fan and the dynamo or alternator.

fan·cied (fan′sēd) *adj.* **1.** Produced by the fancy; imaginary; unreal. **2.** Supposed: *this fancied insult.* **3.** Expected to do well or to win.

fan·ci·er (făn′sē-ər) *n.* **1.** A person who has a special enthusiasm for something and who makes a hobby of his interest: *a fancier of antiques.* **2.** A person who breeds plants or animals: *a pigeon fancier.* **3.** A person given to reverie or whimsy; a dreamer.

fan·ci·ful (făn′sĭ-fəl) *adj.* **1.** Created in the fancy; unreal; wishful; dubious: *a fanciful story.* **2.** Showing invention or whimsy in design; imaginative; curious: *a fanciful pattern.* **3.** Indulging in imagination and fancy: *a fanciful novelist.* —See Synonyms at **fantastic.** **—fan·ci·ful·ly** *adv.* **—fan·ci·ful·ness** *n.*

fan·cy (făn′sē) *n., pl.* **-cies.** **1. a.** The light invention or play of the mind through which whims, visions, fantasies, or the like are summoned up; imagination, especially in a conscious or direct sense; caprice. **b.** In the literary theory of Coleridge, an aspect of the faculty of memory that merely combines images, in contrast with true creative imagination. **2.** An associative image; fantastical invention. **3.** A notion not derived from evidence; an unfounded opinion; a delusion. **4.** A capricious idea; a whim; an impulse. **5.** *Informal.* A capricious or sudden liking; a frivolous inclination. **6.** Taste or preference; critical sensibility. **7.** The art, hobby, or profession of breeding fancy animals. —See Synonyms at **caprice.** **—the fancy.** **1.** *Archaic.* **a.** The sport of boxing. **b.** The followers and patrons of this sport. **2. a.** Any sport or hobby. **b.** The followers and patrons of a sport or hobby.
~*adj.* **fancier, -ciest.** **1.** Decorative and ornamental rather than plain: *fancy socks.* **2.** Fanciful; illusory or vain. **3.** Characterized by skill or some other quality that is felt to be more ostentatious than worthwhile: *fancy speeches.* Used derogatorily. **4.** Out of the ordinary; superior; fine. **5.** Excessive or exorbitant; inordinate: *a fancy bid.* **6.** Bred for unusual qualities or special points. Said of birds and other animals.
~*tr.v.* **fancied, -cying, -cies.** **1.** To visualize; imagine; picture: *"And she tried to fancy what the flame of a candle looks like after the candle is blown out"* (Lewis Carroll). **2.** To suppose; surmise. **3.** To take to or like; be fond of. **4.** *Informal.* **a.** To desire; want. **b.** To desire sexually; be physically attracted to. **5.** *Informal.* To have an unduly good or inflated opinion of (oneself): *He fancies himself as a musician.* **6.** To consider (a racehorse, for example) as likely to win or be successful. **7.** To breed (pigeons or rabbits, for example) for unusual qualities or special points. —See Synonyms at **like.**
~*interj.* Used to express surprise. Often used with *that.* [Middle English *fantsy,* short for *fantasie,* fancy, FANTASY.] **—fan·ci·ly** *adv.* **—fan·ci·ness** *n.*

fancy dress *n.* Special clothes, such as a uniform or a masquerade costume, worn for a party or similar entertainment. **—fan·cy-dress** (făn′sē-drĕs′) *adj.*

fan·cy-free (făn′sē-frē′) *adj.* Carefree; without commitment or restriction; unattached.

fancy goods *pl.n.* Ornamental items; small decorative goods.

fancy man *n.* **1.** A boyfriend; a lover. **2.** A pimp. In both senses, used derogatorily.

fan·cy·work (făn′sē-wûrk′) *n.* Any decorative needlework, such as crochet, embroidery, or needlepoint.

fan·dan·gle (făn-dăng′gəl) *n.* **1.** Elaborate ornamentation. **2.** Nonsense; foolishness. [Perhaps alteration (influenced by *newfangle*) of FANDANGO.]

fan·dan·go (făn-dăng′gō) *n., pl.* **-gos.** **1.** An animated Spanish or Latin-American dance in triple time. **2.** A piece of music for such a dance. [Spanish *fandango*†.]

fan·fare (făn′fâr′) *n.* **1.** A loud flourish or ceremonial sounding of trumpets or other brass instruments. **2.** *Informal.* A clamorous or spectacular public display, ceremony, or reaction; a stir. [French (imitative).]

fan·fa·ron·ade (făn′fər-ə-nād′) *n.* **1.** Any vaunting or blustering manner or behavior. **2.** A fanfare. [French *fanfarronade,* from Spanish *fanfarronada,* from *fanfarrón* (imitative).]

fang (făng) *n.* **1.** A long, pointed tooth, especially: **a.** Any of the hollow, grooved teeth with which a venomous snake injects its venom. **b.** Any of the teeth of a carnivorous animal with which it seizes and tears its prey. **c.** Either of the sharp upper incisors of the true vampire bats. **2.** A similar structure, such as a chelicera of a venomous spider. **3. fangs.** *Informal.* The teeth. [Middle English *fang,* prey, spoils, Old English *fang,* plunder, from Germanic *fang-* (unattested), to catch.] **—fanged** *adj.*

fan heater *n.* A **convector heater** *(see)* in which a fan blowing air over heated wires causes heat to be transferred by forced convection.

fan-in (făn′ĭn′) *n. Computer Science.* The number of inputs available to a given function or logic stage.

fan·kle (făng′kəl) *tr.v.* **fan·kled, -kling, -kles.** *Scottish.* To entangle.
~*n. Scottish.* A muddle. [From *fank,* coil of rope, variant of *fang,* obsolete variant of VANG.]

fan·light (făn′līt′) *n.* **1.** *Architecture.* A half-circle window, often with sash bars arranged like the ribs of a fan. Also called "fan window." **2.** *British.* A transom.

fan mail *n.* Letters, usually of praise, to a public figure from his devotees or admirers.

fan·ny (făn′ē) *n., pl.* **-nies.** *Slang.* The buttocks. [20th century : origin obscure.]

fan·on (făn′ən) *n. Ecclesiastical.* **1.** A capelike garment formerly worn only by a pope when celebrating Solemn High Mass. **2.** Formerly, any of various embroidered cloths, such as a maniple, a piece of silk attached to a bishop's crosier, or a cover for the offerings brought by worshipers. [Middle English *fanoun,* from Old French *fanon,* from Frankish *fanon* (unattested).]

fan-out (făn′out′) *n. Computer Science.* The number of circuits fed input signals from an output terminal.

fan palm *n.* Any palm tree having leaves with a short axis and consequently fanlike. Compare **feather palm.**

fan·tail (făn′tāl′) *n.* **1.** Any of a breed of domestic pigeons having a rounded, fan-shaped tail. **2.** Any of several birds of the genus *Rhi-*

fan *This fan would have been used by a French lady of the mid-18th century. It is now in the Victoria and Albert Museum, London.*

fanlight *Named after their resemblance to fans, fanlights were often installed over doorways to improve the lighting in hallways and corridors.*

fantail *Many varieties of the fantail have been bred from the wild rock dove, mostly for show or to grace ornamental dovecotes. There are 175 species worldwide.*

fan vaulting *One of the marvels of English Perpendicular architecture, fan vaulting is so called because its intricately carved beams resemble a lady's fan. This 14th-century ceiling is in the cloister of Gloucester Cathedral, England.*

pidura, of eastern Asia and Australia, having a long, fan-shaped tail. **3.** A goldfish of a breed having a wide, fanlike double tail fin. **4.** A tail, end, or part having a fanlike shape. **5.** The stern overhang of a ship. **6.** Something shaped like a fantail, as a flat jet of flame in certain types of burners. **—fan·tailed** *adj.*

fan-tan (făn′tăn′) *n.* **1.** A Chinese betting game in which the players lay wagers on the number of beans, coins, or other counters that will remain when a hidden pile of them has been divided by four. **2.** A card game in which sevens and their equivalent are played in sequence and the first to discard all his cards is the winner. [Cantonese *fan t'an,* "repeated division" : *fan,* times, division + *t'an,* distribution, division.]

fan·ta·sia (făn-tā′zhə, -zhē-ə, făn′tə-zē′ə) *n.* **1.** An improvised musical composition structured according to the composer's fancy. **2.** A medley of familiar musical themes with variations and interludes. **3.** A poem or other work that is highly imaginative or fanciful. [Italian, fantasy, from Latin *phantasia,* FANTASY.]

fan·ta·sist (făn′tə-sĭst) *n.* Someone, especially an author or artist, who creates fantasies or fantasias.

fan·ta·size (făn′tə-sīz′) *v.* **-sized, -sizing, -sizes.** *—tr.* To portray in the mind; imagine; picture; fancy. *—intr.* To indulge in fantasies.

fan·tast (făn′tăst′) *n.* A visionary; a dreamer. [German *Fantast, Phantast,* from Medieval Latin *phantasta,* from Greek *phantastēs,* a boaster, one who is ostentatious, from *phantazein,* to make visible. See **fantasy.**]

fan·tas·tic (făn-tăs′tĭk) *adj.* Also **fan·tas·ti·cal** (-tĭ-kəl) (for senses 1, 2, 3, 4). **1.** Bizarre in form, conception, or appearance; strange; wondrous; fanciful. **2. a.** Unbelievable; preposterous. **b.** Existing in the fancy; unreal; illusory. **3.** Unrestrainedly fanciful; extravagant: *fantastic hopes.* **4.** Capricious or fitful: *in a fantastic mood.* **5.** *Informal.* **a.** Wonderful or remarkable. **b.** Very large; great.
~n. **fantastic.** *Archaic.* A person who is unrestrainedly fanciful or eccentric in behavior or appearance. [Middle English *fantastik,* from Old French *fantastique,* from Medieval Latin *fantasticus,* from Late Latin *phantasticus,* imaginary, from Greek *phantastikos,* able to produce the appearance of, from *phantazein,* to make visible. See **fantasy.**] **—fan·tas·ti·cal·i·ty** (făn-tăs′tĭ-kăl′ə-tē), **fan·tas·ti·cal·ness** *n.* **—fan·tas·ti·cal·ly** *adv.*
Synonyms: *bizarre, exotic, fanciful, grotesque.*

fan·ta·sy, phan·ta·sy (făn′tə-sē, -zē) *n., pl.* **-sies. 1.** The realm of vivid imagination, reverie, depiction, illusion, and the like; the natural conjurings of mental invention and association; the visionary world; make-believe. **2.** A mental image, especially a disordered and weird image; an illusion; a phantasm. **3.** A capricious or whimsical idea or notion; a conceit. **4. a.** Literary or dramatic fiction characterized by highly fanciful or supernatural elements. **b.** An example of such fiction. **5.** *Psychology.* An imagined event or condition fulfilling a wish. Also used adjectivally: *a fantasy world.* **6.** *Music.* A fantasia. **7.** A coin, such as a commemorative coin, that is not intended for use as legal tender.
~tr.v. **fantasied, -sying, -sies.** To imagine; visualize. [Middle English *fantasie,* fancy, fantasy, from Old French, from Latin *phantasia,* from Greek, appearance, perception, faculty of imagination, from *phantazein,* to make visible, from *phainein,* to show.]

Fan·tin-La·tour (făN-tăN′ lə-to͝or′), **Ignace Henri Joseph Théodore** (1836–1904). French painter noted for his meticulous still-life paintings of flowers and portrait groups.

fan·toc·ci·ni (făn′tə-chē′nē) *pl.n.* **1.** Puppets animated by moving wires; marionettes. **2.** Plays with marionettes; puppet shows. [Italian, plural of *fantoccino,* diminutive of *fantoccio,* puppet, doll, augmentative of *fante,* child, servant, short for *infante,* from Latin *infāns* (stem *infant-*), INFANT.]

fan·tod (făn′tŏd′) *n.* **1.** Irritable behavior. **2. fantods.** A state of restlessness. [19th century : origin obscure.]

fan vaulting *n. Architecture.* An intricate style of traceried vaulting, common in late English Gothic, in which ribs arch out like a fan from a single point such as a capital or corbel.

fan window *n. Architecture.* A **fanlight** *(see).*

fan worm *n.* Any bristle worm of the family Sarbellidae, living in tubes of mud on the seashore and having fans of feathery tentacles that protrude from the tube when it is covered by the tide.

fan·zine (făn-zēn′) *n.* A magazine for fans of a particular person, hobby, or interest, such as science fiction. [*fan* + *magazine.*]

FAO Food and Agriculture Organization.

FAQ fair average quality.

far (fär) *adv.* **farther** (fär′*th*ər) or **further** (fûr′*th*ər), **farthest** (fär′*th*ĭst) or **furthest** (fûr′*th*ĭst). **1.** To, from, or at considerable distance, time, degree, or position. **2.** To or at a specific distance, time, degree, or position: *Just how far are you taking this argument?* **3.** To a considerable degree; much. Used chiefly in comparisons: *"It is a far, far better thing I do"* (Charles Dickens). **—as far as.** To the distance, extent, or degree that: *as far as I know.* **—by far.** To a considerable or evident degree. **—far and away.** By a considerable margin: *He's far and away the better skier.* **—far and wide.** All over; everywhere. **—far be it from me.** May I never; I neither hope nor dare: *Far be it from me to insult you.* **—far from.** Not at all; by no means: *Far from being annoyed about it, she was very glad.* **—far gone. 1.** In a very poor state; much deteriorated. **2.** So advanced as to be irreversible. **3.** Drunk. Used humorously. **—from far.** From a great distance. **—go far. 1.** To be successful; accomplish a great deal: *That boy will go far.* **2.** To provide for much or many; last a long time. **—so far. 1.** Up to the present moment. **2.** To a limited extent: *You can only go so far on two dollars.* **—so far as.** To the extent that: *so far as I can tell.* **—so far so good.** Used to express satisfaction with current progress while anticipating further difficulties.
~adj. **farther** or **further, farthest** or **furthest. 1.** At a considerable distance: *a far country.* **2.** More distant; opposite: *the far corner.* **3.** Extensive or lengthy: *a far trek.* **4.** Politically extreme: *the far right.* —See Synonyms at **distant.** [Middle English *fer,* Old English *feor(r),* far, distant, remote.]

far·ad (făr′əd, -ăd′) *n. Abbr.* **F** A unit of capacitance equal to the capacitance of a capacitor having a charge of 1 coulomb on each plate and a potential difference of 1 volt between the plates. [After Michael FARADAY.]

far·a·day (făr′ə-dā′) *n.* The quantity of electricity that is capable of depositing or dissolving 1 gram equivalent weight of a substance in electrolysis, approximately 9.6494×10^4 coulombs. [After Michael FARADAY.]

Far·a·day (făr′ə-dā′), **Michael** (1791–1867). British chemist and physicist, discoverer of electromagnetism. In 1831 he discovered the connection between electricity and magnetism, producing an electric current by rotating a copper disk between the poles of a magnet. He also investigated the process of electrolysis.

fa·rad·ic (fə-răd′ĭk) *adj.* Also **far·a·da·ic** (făr′ə-dā′ĭk). Of, pertaining to, or using an intermittent asymmetric alternating electric current produced by an induction coil. [After Michael FARADAY.]

far·a·di·za·tion (făr′ə-də-zā′shən) *n.* Also **far·a·dism** (făr′ə-dĭz′əm). Medical therapy by application of faradic currents to stimulate nerve and muscle activity.

far·a·dize (făr′ə-dīz′) *tr.v.* **-dized, -dizing, -dizes.** *Medicine.* To treat (an organ or part) with faradic currents.

far·an·dole (făr′ən-dōl′) *n.* **1.** A spirited circle dance of Provençal derivation. **2.** The music for this dance. [French, from Provençal *farandoulo*†.]

far·a·way (făr′ə-wā′) *adj.* **1.** Very distant; beyond immediate contact; remote: *faraway lands.* **2.** Bemused or abstracted; dreamy: *a faraway smile.* —See Synonyms at **distant.**

farce (färs) *n.* **1.** A theatrical composition in which broad improbabilities of plot and characterization are used for humorous effect. **2.** Something ludicrous; an empty show; a mockery: *"childish family portraits, with their farce of sentiment and smiling lies"* (Thackeray).
~tr.v. **farced, farcing, farces. 1.** To intersperse or fill out (one's speech or a play) with jokes or witticisms. **2.** *Obsolete.* To stuff (a bird, for example) for roasting. [Middle English *farse,* stuffing, from Old French *farce,* stuffing, farce, from *farcir,* from Latin *farcīre,* to stuff, hence to pad out with interludes.]

far·ceur (fär-sœr′) *n.* Also **farc·er** (fär′sər). **1.** An actor in a farce. **2.** A writer of farces. **3.** A comic; a joker. [French, from Old French, author or actor of farce, from *farce,* FARCE.]

far·ci (fär-sē′) *adj.* Stuffed. Said of food. [French, past participle of *farcir.*]

far·ci·cal (fär′sĭ-kəl) *adj.* **1.** Pertaining to farce. **2.** Resembling farce; ludicrous; absurd. **—far·ci·cal·i·ty** (fär′sĭ-kăl′ə-tē), **far·ci·cal·ness** *n.* **—far·ci·cal·ly** *adv.*

far·cy (fär′sē) *n. Veterinary Medicine.* Chronic cutaneous **glanders** *(see).* [Middle English *farsi(n),* from Old French *farcin,* from Late Latin *farcīmen,* farcy, from Latin, sausage, from *farcīre,* to stuff. See **farce.**]

farcy bud *n. Veterinary Medicine.* A craterlike ulcer characteristic of farcy.

fard·ed (fär′dĭd) *adj.* Painted with cosmetics. [Past participle of obsolete *fard,* from Old French *farder,* to paint (the face) with cosmetics, from Germanic.]

far·del (fär′dəl) *n. Archaic.* A pack; a load; a burden. [Middle English, from Old French, diminutive of *farde,* package, from Vulgar Latin *fardum* (unattested), from Arabic *fardah, farde,* load.]

fare (fâr) *intr.v.* **fared, faring, fares. 1.** To get along: *How did he fare with his project?* **2.** To turn out; go. Used impersonally: *How does it fare with you?* **3.** *Rare.* To be entertained with food and drink. **4.** *Archaic.* To travel; wander.
~n. **1.** A transportation charge, as for a bus or taxi. **2.** A passenger transported for a fee. **3.** Food and drink: *modest fare.* **4.** *Archaic.* The condition of things. [Middle English *faren,* to travel, go, fare, Old English *faran,* from Germanic.] **—far·er** *n.*

Far East. Also **East Asia.** The countries of China, Japan, North and South Korea, and Mongolia and, sometimes, Indochina, Malaysia, and Indonesia. **—Far-East·ern** *adj.*

fare·well (fâr-wĕl′) *interj.* May you fare well; Godspeed; good-by.
~n. **1.** An acknowledgment at parting; a good-by. **2.** A leave-taking; a departure.
~adj. (fâr′wĕl′). Pertaining to parting or leave-taking: *a farewell party.* [Middle English *fare wel!* : *fare,* go, fare, imperative of *faren,* to FARE + WELL.]

far-fetched (fär′fĕcht′) *adj.* Strained or improbable in nature or relevance: *a far-fetched alibi.*

far-flung (fär′flŭng′) *adj.* **1.** Widely distributed; wide-ranging: *far-flung reporters.* **2.** Remote; distant.

fa·ri·na (fə-rē′nə) *n.* **1.** Fine meal prepared from cereal grain and various other plant products and often used as a cooked cereal or in puddings. **2.** Starch, especially that prepared from potato flour. [Latin *farīna,* ground corn, meal, from *far,* a kind of grain.]

far·i·na·ceous (făr′ə-nā′shəs) *adj.* **1.** Made from, rich in, or consisting of starch. **2.** Having a mealy or powdery texture. **3.** Made from or with pasta. [Late Latin *farīnāceus*, mealy : Latin *farīna*, FARINA + -ACEOUS.]

far·i·nose (făr'ə-nōs') *adj.* **1.** Similar to or yielding farina. **2.** *Biology.* Covered with short hairs resembling mealy dust or powder. [Late Latin *farīnōsus*, mealy, from Latin *farīna*, FARINA.]

far·kle·ber·ry (făr'kəl-bĕr'ē) *n., pl.* **-ries.** A shrub or small tree, *Vaccinium arboreum*, of the southeastern United States, having leathery leaves and hard black berries. [*Farkle-†* + BERRY.]

farm (färm) *n.* **1.** A tract of agricultural land on which livestock or crops are raised. **2.** Any land or water area devoted to the raising, breeding, or production of a specified type of animal or vegetable life: *a trout farm.* **3.** A minor-league baseball club affiliated with a major-league club for the training of recruits and the maintenance of temporarily unneeded players. **4.** A country rest home for alcoholics or psychiatric patients. **5.** *Obsolete.* **a.** The system of leasing out the rights of collecting and retaining taxes in a certain district. **b.** A district so leased.
~*v.* **farmed, farming, farms.** —*tr.* **1. a.** To cultivate or produce a crop or raise livestock on (land). **b.** To cultivate or produce (a crop). **c.** To breed (livestock). **2.** To have the right to operate or supervise and retain profits from (a business or tax district, for example). **3.** To let to a concessionaire the rights to operate or supervise and retain profits from (a business or tax district, for example). Used with *out.* **4.** To offer the services of (a worker) for a fee or rent. **5.** To send (work) from a central point to be done elsewhere. Used with *out: farm out typing.* **6.** To assign (a baseball player) to a minor-league team. Used with *out.* —*intr.* To engage in farming; be a farmer. [Middle English *ferme*, lease, rent, from Old French, from Medieval Latin *firma*, fixed payment, from Latin *firmāre*, to fortify, fix, confirm, from *firmus*, firm.]

farm·er (fär'mər) *n.* **1.** One who owns, operates, or works on a farm. **2.** *Archaic.* One who has paid for and holds a concession on the rights of collecting and retaining taxes.

Far·mer (fär'mər), **Fannie Merritt** (1857–1915). U.S. cookery expert. Prevented from attending college by a paralytic stroke, she turned to studying cooking, first at home and then at the Boston Cooking School, which she directed from 1891 until 1902, when she opened her own school. She edited the *Boston Cooking School Cook Book* (1896), which has been revised many times over the years as *The Fannie Farmer Cookbook.*

farmer's lung *n.* An occupational lung disease characterized by chronic breathlessness and caused by an allergic reaction to fungal spores in hay that has not been properly dried.

farm hand *n.* A farm laborer.

farm·house (färm'hous') *n., pl.* **-houses** (-hou'zĭz). **1.** The farmer's dwelling on a farm. **2.** A type of large loaf of white bread.

farm·stead (färm'stĕd') *n.* **1.** A farm, including its land and buildings. **2.** That part of a farm including and surrounding the farmhouse.

farm·yard (färm'yärd') *n.* An area surrounded by or adjacent to farm buildings.

Farne Islands (färn). Group of islets of dolerite rock in the North Sea off Northumberland. The islands are a bird sanctuary.

Far·ne·se (fär-nā'zē), **Alessandro, Duke of Parma** (1545–92). Italian general, nephew of King Philip II of Spain. He fought the Turks at the Battle of Lepanto (1571) in which the Holy League under John of Austria destroyed the Ottoman navy.

far·ne·sol (fär'nə-sôl', -sŏl') *n.* A compound, $C_{15}H_{26}O$, extracted from the flowers and essential oils of various plants, and used in perfumery. [New Latin *farnesiana*, from *Acacia farnesiana* (a plant whose flowers yield the compound), after Odoardo *Farnese*, 17th-century Italian cardinal + -OL.]

Farns·worth (färnz'wûrth'), **Philo Taylor** (1906–71). U.S. engineer and inventor. As early as 1927 he was demonstrating his working model of a television set. His "dissector tube" separated an image into electronic particles that could be transmitted over a distance, then re-formed to produce a replica of the original.

far·o (fâr'ō) *n.* A card game in which the players lay bets on the top card of the dealer's pack. [Variant of PHARAOH; perhaps the name originally applied to the king of hearts.]

Fa·ro (fä'rōō). Atlantic port and southernmost town of Portugal, capital of the Algarve.

Faroe. See **Faeroe Islands.**

Far·o·ese, Faer·o·ese (fâr'ō-ēz', -ēs') *n., pl.* **Faroese** or **Faeroese.** **1.** A member of a Germanic people inhabiting the Faeroe Islands. **2.** The North Germanic language spoken by the inhabitants of the Faeroe Islands.
~*adj.* Of or pertaining to the Faeroe Islands, the Faroese people, or their language.

far-off (fär'ôf', -ŏf') *adj.* Remote in space or time; distant; faraway. —See Synonyms at **distant.**

fa·rouche (fə-rōōsh') *adj.* **1.** Sullenly shy. **2.** Wild. [Old French *faroche*, from Medieval Latin *forasticus*, from Latin *foras*, out of doors.]

Fa·rouk I (fə-rōōk') (1920–65). The last king of Egypt (1936–52). The defeat of the Egyptian army in the first Arab-Israeli war (1948–49) and Farouk's extravagant lifestyle alienated the people. In July 1952 his administration was overthrown by the Free Officers led by Gen. Muhammad Naguib and a junior officer, Gamal Abdul Nasser. Farouk was forced to abdicate.

far-out (fär'out') *adj. Slang.* **1.** Extremely unconventional. **2.** Excellent; marvelous.

far point *n.* The farthest point at which an object can be seen distinctly by the eye at rest.

far·ra·go (fə-rā'gō, -rä'gō) *n., pl.* **-gos.** A medley; a conglomeration; a mixture: *"This is a farrago of absurdity"* (Virginia Woolf). [Latin *farrāgo*, mixed fodder for cattle, from *far* (stem *farr*-), a grain.] —**far·rag·i·nous** (fə-răj'ə-nəs) *adj.*

Far·ra·gut (făr'ə-gət), **David Glasgow** (1801–70). U.S. naval officer. During the Civil War, he commanded Union ships on daring, pivotal missions, including the capture of New Orleans (1862) and the taking of Mobile Bay (1864), during which he uttered his famous rallying cry, "Damn the torpedoes—full speed ahead!"

far-reach·ing (fär'rē'chĭng) *adj.* Having a wide range, influence, or effect; extending far.

Far·rell (făr'əl), **Eileen** (1920–). U.S. soprano. Gifted with a voice of enormous power and clarity of tone, she began her career in radio and debuted in New York at Carnegie Hall (1950). Her first appearance with the Metropolitan Opera was in 1960.

Farrell, James Thomas (1904–79). U.S. novelist. His naturalistic works often decried the economic and social conditions that produced emotional and material poverty. He is best known for his trilogy (1932–35) about Studs Lonigan, a poor Irish Catholic from the South Side of Chicago.

far·ri·er (făr'ē-ər) *n. Chiefly British.* One who shoes horses or treats them medically. [Old French *ferrier*, blacksmith, from Latin *ferrārius*, from *ferrum*, iron.]

far·row¹ (făr'ō) *n.* **1.** A litter of pigs. **2.** The act of giving birth to a litter of pigs.
~*v.* **farrowed, -rowing, -rows.** —*tr.* To give birth to (a litter of pigs). —*intr.* To produce a farrow. [Perhaps Middle English *faren* (plural), Old English *fearh*, little pig.]

farrow² *adj.* Not pregnant; barren. Said of a cow. [Middle English (Scottish dialect) *fer(r)ow*, from Middle Dutch *verwe-* (unattested), cow past the age of bearing.]

far-see·ing (fär'sē'ĭng) *adj.* **1.** Prudent; foresighted. **2.** Able to see far; keen-sighted.

far-sight·ed (fär'sī'tĭd) *adj.* **1. a.** Able to see objects better from a distance than from short range. **b.** Hyperopic. See **hyperopia.** **2.** Planning prudently for the future; foresighted. —**far-sight·ed·ly** *adv.* —**far-sight·ed·ness** *n.*

far·ther (fär'thər) *adv.* **1.** To or at a more distant or more remote point in space or time. **2.** In addition.
~*adj.* **1.** Remoter; more distant. **2.** Additional. [Middle English *ferther*, variant of *further*, FURTHER.]
Usage: According to many traditional grammarians, the etymological distinction between *farther* ("more far") and *further* ("more to the fore") should be preserved. In that case *farther* should be used only for physical distance, as in *They went farther down the road. Further* should be used in most other senses, especially when referring to degree, quantity, or time: *further in debt; further steps must be taken; a further reason.* In some cases either word is acceptable; one may say either *further from the truth* or *farther from the truth.* It should be noted that writers since Shakespeare have often ignored the distinction between the two words.

far·ther·most (fär'thər-mōst') *adj.* Farthest.

far·thest (fär'thĭst) *adj.* Most remote or distant.
~*adv.* To or at the most distant or remote point in space or time. —See Usage note at **farther.** [Middle English *ferthest*, from *ferther*, FARTHER.]

far·thing (fär'thĭng) *n. Abbr.* **f. 1.** A former British bronze coin worth one quarter of an old penny. It was abolished as legal tender in 1961. **2.** The sum of one quarter of an old penny. **3.** Something of little value. [Middle English *ferthing*, Old English *fēorthing* : *fēortha*, FOURTH + -ING.]

far·thin·gale (fär'thĭng-gāl') *n.* **1.** A hoop or series of hoops extending horizontally from the waist, worn beneath a woman's skirts in the 16th and 17th centuries. **2.** The skirt worn over this device. [Variant of Old French *verdugale, vertugalle*, from Spanish *verdugado*, from *verdugo*, rod, stick, shoot of a tree, from *verde*, green, from Latin *virdis*, from *virēre*, to be green.]

farthingale chair *n.* A type of chair, used in the 16th and 17th centuries in England, having no arms, a straight, low back, and a high seat.

Fas. See **Fès.**

f.a.s., F.A.S. free alongside ship.

fasc. fascicle.

fas·ces (făs'ēz') *pl.n.* **1.** A bundle of rods bound together around an ax with the blade projecting, carried before magistrates of ancient Rome as an emblem of authority. **2.** This emblem used as a symbol of the Fascists in modern Italy. [Latin, plural of *fascis*, bundle.]

fas·ci·a (făsh'ē-ə, fā'shē-ə; fā'shə *for sense 5*) *n., pl.* **-ciae** (făsh'ē-ē', fā'shē-ē'). Also **fa·ci·a** (for sense 4). **1.** *Anatomy.* A sheet of fibrous tissue beneath the surface of the skin, enveloping the body, enclosing muscles or muscular groups, and separating muscular layers. **2.** A broad and distinct band of color, especially that on an insect or plant. **3.** *Architecture.* A flat horizontal band or member between moldings; especially, such a member in a classical entablature. **4.** The board above a shop or other business on which the name or nature of the business is displayed. **5.** *Chiefly British.* A dashboard, as of an automobile. [New Latin, from Latin, band, bandage, fillet.] —**fas·ci·al** *adj.*

fas·ci·ate (făsh'ē-āt') *adj.* Also **fas·ci·at·ed** (-ā'tĭd). **1.** *Botany.* Abnormally flattened or compressed, as certain stems are. **2.** *Zoology.*

Marked by broad bands of color, as certain insects. [New Latin *fasciatus* : FASCI(A) + -ATE.]

fas·ci·a·tion (făsh′ē-ā′shən) *n.* **1.** The act of binding up or fastening, as with bandages or bands. **2.** The manner in which something is bound up or fastened. **3.** *Botany.* An abnormal flattening or compression of stems or leaf stalks.

fas·ci·cle (făs′ĭ-kəl) *n.* Also **fas·ci·cule** (-kyo͞ol′) (for sense 2). *Abbr.* **fasc. 1.** A small bundle. **2.** One of the separately published parts or installments of a book. **3.** *Botany.* A bundlelike cluster, especially of leaves, branches, roots, or fibers. **4.** *Anatomy.* A fasciculus. [Latin *fasciculus,* diminutive of *fascis,* a bundle.] **—fas·ci·cled** *adj.*

fas·cic·u·late (fə-sĭk′yə-lĭt, -lāt′) *adj.* Also **fas·cic·u·lar** (-lər), **fas·cic·u·lat·ed** (-lā′tĭd). Of, pertaining to, or resembling a fascicle. **—fas·cic·u·late·ly** *adv.* **—fas·cic·u·la·tion** (fə-sĭk′yə-lā′shən) *n.*

fas·cic·u·lus (fə-sĭk′yə-ləs) *n., pl.* **-li** (-lī′). A bundle of anatomical fibers; especially, a bundle of nerve fibers having common functions and connections. [New Latin, from Latin, FASCICLE.]

fas·ci·nate (făs′ə-nāt′) *tr.v.* **-nated, -nating, -nates. 1.** To be an object of intense interest to; attract irresistibly. **2.** To hold motionless; spellbind or mesmerize. **3.** *Obsolete.* To bewitch; cast under a spell. [Latin *fascināre,* to enchant, bewitch, from *fascinus,* a bewitching amulet in the shape of a phallus.]

fas·ci·nat·ing (făs′ə-nā′tĭng) *adj.* Arousing unflagging interest, as by charm or beauty; captivating. **—fas·ci·nat·ing·ly** *adv.*

fas·ci·na·tion (făs′ə-nā′shən) *n.* **1.** The power of fascinating. **2.** The condition of being fascinated. **3.** A fascinating quality.

fas·ci·na·tor (făs′ə-nā′tər) *n.* **1.** One that fascinates. **2.** A woman's head scarf made of net or lace.

fas·cine (fă-sēn′, fə-) *n.* A bundle of sticks bound together and used for various engineering purposes, especially the construction of fortresses, earthworks, or reinforced trenches. [French, from Latin *fascīna,* from *fascis,* bundle.]

fas·ci·o·li·a·sis (fə-sē′ə-lī′ə-sĭs, fə-sī′-) *n.* Infestation with parasitic flukes of the family Fasciolidae; especially, infestation of the liver and bile ducts with the liver fluke *Fasciola hepatica.* [New Latin *Fasciolidae* (family name), from Latin *fasciola,* augmentative of *fascia,* band, fillet (see **fascia**) + -IASIS.]

fas·cism (făsh′ĭz′əm) *n.* **1.** A philosophy or system of government that advocates or exercises a dictatorship of the extreme right, typically through the merging of state and business leadership, together with an ideology of belligerent nationalism. **2. Fascism.** The governmental system of Italy under Benito Mussolini from 1922 to 1943. [Italian *fascismo,* from *fascio,* bundle, group, assemblage, from Latin *fascis,* bundle.]

fas·cist (făsh′ĭst) *n.* **1.** A person who advocates or practices fascism. **2.** *Often* **Fascist.** A person who belongs to a party or organization that promotes fascism. **3.** *Informal.* Any right-wing or authoritarian person. [Italian *fascista,* from *fascio,* bundle, group. See **fascism.**] **—fas·cist, fa·scis·tic** (fə-shĭs′tĭk) *adj.*

Fa·scis·ti (fə-shĭs′tē; *Italian* fä-shē′stē) *pl.n.* The members of the Italian political organization led by Benito Mussolini. [Italian, plural of *fascista,* FASCIST.]

fash (făsh) *n. Scottish.* Trouble; worry; inconvenience.
∼*tr.v.* **fashed, fashing, fashes.** *Scottish.* To trouble; annoy. [Obsolete French *fascher,* to annoy, from Vulgar Latin *fastidicare* (unattested), from Latin *fastidium,* aversion, disdain, from *fastus,* disdain.]

fash·ion (făsh′ən) *n.* **1.** The current style or custom, as in dress or behavior; the mode for the present: *out of fashion.* **2.** Something that is in the current mode. **3.** Fashionable or style-conscious people in general; the social elite. **4.** The way in which something is formed; a configuration; an aspect: *"as he prayed, the fashion of his countenance was altered"* (Luke 9:29). **5.** A kind or variety; a sort. **6.** A manner of performing; a way: *Do it in this fashion.* —See Synonyms at **habit. —after** (or **in**) **a fashion.** In some way or other; to some extent: *She sings after a fashion.*
∼*tr.v.* **fashioned, -ioning, -ions. 1. a.** To make into a particular shape or form: *"And wilt thou have me fashion into speech/The love I bear thee"* (Elizabeth Barrett Browning). **b.** To train or influence into a particular state or character. **2.** To make suitable; adapt, as to a purpose or occasion. **3.** *Obsolete.* To contrive. [Middle English *facioun,* from Old French *facon,* from Latin *factiō* (stem *factiōn-*), "a making," from *factus,* past participle of *facere,* to make, do.]
Synonyms: *mode, style, vogue.*

fash·ion·a·ble (făsh′ə-nə-bəl) *adj.* **1.** Conforming to the current style; in fashion. **2.** Frequented by or associated with persons of fashion. **—fash·ion·a·ble·ness** *n.* **—fash·ion·a·bly** *adv.*

fash·ion·mon·ger (făsh′ən-mŭng′gər, -mŏng′gər) *n.* A person much concerned with following, setting, or spreading fashions.

fashion plate *n.* **1.** An illustration of current styles in dress. **2.** A person who consistently wears the latest fashions.

Fass·bin·der (făs′bĭn′dər), **Rainer Werner** (1946–82). German film director. His films, both realistic and despairing, include *Fear Eats the Soul* (1974), *Fox* (1975), *Despair* (1978), and *Lola* (1982).

fast¹ (făst, fäst) *adj.* **faster, fastest. 1.** Acting, moving, or capable of moving quickly; swift; rapid. **2.** Accomplished in relatively little time: *a fast visit.* **3.** Indicating a time somewhat ahead of the actual time: *My wrist watch is fast.* **4. a.** Adapted to or suitable for rapid movement: *a fast road.* **b.** Showing rapidity of movement: *a fast game.* **5.** Disposed to flout conventional or moral standards; especially, sexually active: *a fast life.* **6.** Resistant. Often used in combination: *acid-fast.* **7.** Firmly fixed or fastened; not readily moved, removed, or loosened. **8.** Fixed firmly in place; secure: *"O that I past changing were/Fast in thy paradise"* (George Herbert). **9.** Loyal; constant; firm. **10.** Permanent; resisting fading: *fast dyes.* **11.** Deep; sound: *a fast sleep.* **12.** *Photography.* **a.** Compatible with a high shutter speed: *a fast lens.* **b.** Designed for short exposure; highly sensitive: *fast film.*
∼*adv.* **1.** Firmly; securely; tightly. **2.** Deeply; soundly: *fast asleep.* **3.** Quickly; rapidly. **4.** In a dissipated, immoderate way: *living fast.* **5.** *Archaic.* Close by; near. **—play fast and loose.** To behave without integrity or consideration. [Middle English *fast,* Old English *fæst,* from Germanic.]
Synonyms: *accelerated, expeditious, fleet, hasty, quick, rapid, speedy, swift.*

fast² *intr.v.* **fasted, fasting, fasts.** To abstain from eating all or certain foods, especially as a religious discipline or as a means of protest.
∼*n.* The act or a period of fasting. [Middle English *fasten,* Old English *fæstan,* to hold fast, to observe, to abstain from food, from Germanic.]

fast·back (făst′băk′, fäst′-) *n.* A car having a straight or slightly curved sloping back.

fast·ball (făst′bôl′, fäst′-) *n. Baseball.* A pitch that is thrown at the pitcher's maximum speed.

fast-breed·er reactor (făst′brē′dər, fäst′-) *n.* A fast nuclear reactor that produces more fissionable material than it consumes.

fast buck *n. Informal.* Money easily made: *earn a fast buck.*

fast day *n.* A day reserved for fasting; especially, a day thus reserved by ecclesiastical authority.

fas·ten (făs′ən, fä′sən) *v.* **-tened, -tening, -tens.** —*tr.* **1.** To attach; join; connect: *fasten the button to the skirt.* **2. a.** To make fast or secure. **b.** To close, as by shutting or fixing firmly in place. **3.** To fix or direct (the gaze, attention, or the like) steadily: *"My eyes fastened themselves upon the old scarlet letter"* (Hawthorne). **4.** To place; attribute: *Don't fasten the blame on him.* —*intr.* **1.** To become attached, fixed, or joined. **2.** To take firm hold; cling fast. Usually used with *on* or *upon.* [Middle English *fastnen,* Old English *fæstnian,* to settle, establish, make fast.] **—fas·ten·er** *n.*

fas·ten·ing (făs′ə-nĭng, fä′sə-) *n.* **1.** The act or a method of making something fast. **2.** Something used to fasten, as a lock or hook.

fast-food (făst′fo͞od′, fäst′-) *adj.* Specializing in foods prepared and served quickly: *a fast-food restaurant.*

fas·tid·i·ous (fă-stĭd′ē-əs, fə-) *adj.* **1.** Careful in all details; exacting; meticulous. **2.** Difficult to please; overcritical. **3.** Easily disgusted; squeamish. —See Synonyms at **meticulous.** [Middle English, disdainful, distasteful, loathsome, from Latin *fastīdiōsus,* from *fastīdium,* a loathing, from *fastus,* disdain.] **—fas·tid·i·ous·ly** *adv.* **—fas·tid·i·ous·ness** *n.*

fas·tig·i·ate (fă-stĭj′ē-ĭt, -āt′, fə-) *adj.* Also **fas·tig·i·at·ed** (-ā′tĭd). **1.** Tapering to a point; forming a cone or similar shape. **2.** *Botany.* Erect and almost parallel, as certain branches are. [Medieval Latin *fastīgiātus,* high, lofty, from Latin *fastīgium,* top, summit, height.]

fas·tig·i·um (fă-stĭj′ē-əm) *n.* The period of maximum development of a disease. [New Latin, from Latin, extremity.]

fast·ness (făst′nĭs, fäst′-) *n.* **1. a.** A fortified place; a stronghold or fortress. **b.** A remote and secret place. **2.** The condition or quality of being fast, especially: **a.** Firmness; security. **b.** Rapidity; swiftness. **c.** Colorfastness.

fast neutron *n.* A neutron produced during nuclear fission that has kinetic energy in excess of O.l MeV, having lost little energy in collisions.

fast one *n. Slang.* A deceptive or unfair action done to gain an advantage. Used chiefly in the phrase *pull a fast one.*

fast reactor *n.* A nuclear reactor that uses little or no moderator, the fission resulting from fast neutrons.

fast talk *n. Informal.* Rapid deceptive patter, as that aimed at persuading someone to buy something not really wanted. **—fast-talk** (făst′tôk′, fäst′-) *v.* **—fast-talk·er** *n.*

fat (făt) *n.* **1. a.** The glyceride ester of a **fatty acid** *(see).* **b.** Any of various soft solid or semisolid organic compounds comprising the glyceride esters of fatty acids and associated phosphatides, sterols, alcohols, hydrocarbons, ketones, and related compounds. **c.** A mixture of such compounds occurring widely in organic tissue, especially in the subcutaneous connective tissue of animals and in the seeds, nuts, and fruits of plants. **d.** Loosely, organic tissue containing such substances. **e.** A solidified animal or vegetable oil. See **oil. 2.** Plumpness; obesity. **3.** The best or most desirable part of something. **—chew the fat.** *Slang.* To have a leisurely conversation.
∼*adj.* **fatter, fattest. 1.** Having much or too much fat or flesh; plump or obese. **2.** Full of fat or oil; oily; greasy. **3.** Abounding in desirable elements: *Fat pine yields much resin.* **4.** Fertile or productive; rich: *"It was a fine, green, fat landscape"* (R.L. Stevenson). **5.** Having an abundance or amplitude; well-stocked: *a fat larder.* **6.** Yielding profit or plenty; lucrative: *a fat promotion.* **7.** Thick; broad; large: *a fat plank.* **8.** *Slang.* Small; meager: *a fat chance.*
∼*v.* **fatted, fatting, fats.** —*tr.* To make fat. —*intr.* To become fat. [Middle English, Old English *fǣtt,* from Germanic.] **—fat·ly** *adv.* **—fat·ness** *n.*
Synonyms: *chubby, corpulent, fleshy, obese, plump, portly, pudgy, rotund, stout.*

Fa·tah (fä-tä′) *n.* Also **Al Fa·tah** (äl′ fä-tä′) A Palestinian nationalist organization, founded in 1956, the largest grouping in the PLO. [Arabic, "opening."]

fa·tal (fāt′l) *adj.* **1.** Causing or capable of causing death; mortal. **2.** Causing ruin or destruction; disastrous: *"Such doctrines, if true,*

PRONUNCIATION KEY

ă, pat; ā, pay; âr, care;
ä, father, are; b, bib;
ch, church; d, deed; ĕ, pet;
ē, be; f, fife; g, gag; h, hat;
hw, which; ĭ, pit; ī, pie;
îr, pier; j, judge; k, kick;
l, lid, needle; m, mum;
n, no, sudden; ng, thing;
ŏ, pot; ō, toe; ô, paw, for;
oi, noise; ou, out; o͝o, book;
o͞o, boot; p, pop; r, roar;
s, sauce; sh, ship, dish;
t, tight; th, thin, path;
th, this, bathe; ŭ, cut; ûr, fur;
v, valve; w, with; y, yes;
z, zebra, size; zh, vision;
ə, about, item, edible,
gallop, circus, peaceful

IN FOREIGN WORDS:

à, *Fr.* ami; œ, *Fr.* feu, *Ger.* schön; ü, *Fr.* tu, *Ger.* über; KH, *Ger.* ich, *Scot.* loch; N, *Fr.* bon; y′, *Fr.* Compiègne

STRESS MARKS:

Primary stress: ′
in·cite′ (ĭn-sīt′)
Secondary stress: ′
in′sight′ (ĭn′sīt′)

would be absolutely fatal to my theory" (Charles Darwin). **3.** Of decisive importance; fateful. **4.** Controlling destiny. **5.** *Obsolete.* Destined; inevitable. [Middle English, fated, fatal, from Old French, from Latin *fātālis,* from *fātum,* FATE.]
Synonyms: *deadly, lethal, mortal.*

fa·tal·ism (fāt′l-ĭz′əm) *n.* **1.** The doctrine that all events are predetermined by fate and therefore unalterable by man. **2.** The acceptance of this doctrine; submission to fate. —**fa·tal·ist** *n.* —**fa·tal·is·tic** (fāt′l-ĭs′tĭk) *adj.* —**fa·tal·is·ti·cal·ly** *adv.*

fa·tal·i·ty (fā-tăl′ə-tē, fə-) *n., pl.* **-ties. 1. a.** A death that results from an unexpected occurrence: *fatalities from road accidents.* **b.** One who is killed as a result of such an occurrence. **c.** An occurrence or accident that results in a death. **2.** The ability to cause death or disaster; a lethal quality. **3.** The condition or quality of being governed or determined by fate. **4.** A dictate or determination by fate. **5.** A liability to disaster: *the fatality of his decision.*

fatality rate *n.* **Death rate** (see).

fa·tal·ly (fāt′l-ē) *adv.* **1.** So as to cause death, ruin, or disaster; mortally. **2.** According to the decree of fate; inevitably.

Fatal Sisters *pl.n.* The Fates. Preceded by *the.*

fa·ta mor·ga·na (fä′tə môr-gä′nə) *n.* A **mirage** (see). [Italian, Morgan le Fay (the mirage was attributed to her witchcraft).]

fat·back (făt′băk′) *n.* The strip of fat taken from the upper part of a side of pork and usually dried and salt-cured.

fat cat *n. Slang.* A wealthy and highly privileged person; especially, a heavy contributor to a political party.

fate (fāt) *n.* **1.** The supposed force, principle, or power that predetermines events. **2.** The inevitable event or events predestined by this force. **3.** A final result or consequence; an outcome. **4.** An unfavorable destiny; doom. [Middle English, from Old French, from Latin *fātum,* from the neuter past participle of *fārī,* to speak.]

fat·ed (fā′tĭd) *adj.* **1.** Governed by fate; predetermined: *his fated lot.* **2.** Condemned to death or destruction; doomed.

fate·ful (fāt′fəl) *adj.* **1.** Affecting one's destiny or future; crucially important: *the fateful final examination.* **2.** Controlled by or as if by fate; predetermined. **3.** Bringing death or disaster; fatal. **4.** Portentous; ominous: *a fateful sign.* —**fate·ful·ly** *adv.* —**fate·ful·ness** *n.*

Fa·teh·pur Si·kri (fä′tə-pōōr′ sē′krə). City in the state of Uttar Pradesh in northern India. It was the capital of the Mogul Empire, under Akbar, from its foundation in 1569 until 1584, but in the 17th century it was deserted because of an inadequate water supply. It is now carefully preserved as a virtually unaltered Mogul city.

Fates (fāts). *Greek & Roman Mythology.* The three goddesses who govern human destiny. Preceded by *the.* See **Atropos, Clotho,** and **Lachesis.** Also called the "Fatal Sisters," "Moirae," "Parcae."

fath, fath. fathom.

fat·head (făt′hĕd′) *n. Slang.* A stupid person; a dolt.

fat hen *n. Chiefly British.* A plant, **pigweed** (sense 2) *(see).*

fa·ther (fä′thər) *n.* **1.** A male parent. **2.** A male who functions in a paternal capacity with regard to another; especially, a man who adopts a child. **3.** Any male ancestor; especially, the founder of a line of descent; a forefather. **4.** A man who creates, founds, or originates something: *Chaucer is considered by many to be the father of English poetry.* **5. Father. a.** God. **b.** The first member of the Trinity. **6.** Any elderly or venerable man. Used as a title of respect. **7.** A member of the senate in ancient Rome. **8.** *Sometimes* **Father.** Any of the authoritative early writers in the Christian Church who formulated doctrines and codified religious observances. **9.** *Often* **Father.** *Abbr.* **Fr.** A priest or other clergyman or dignitary in the Roman Catholic or Anglican churches. Often used as a title of respect with or without the clergyman's name. **10.** *British.* The member holding the longest tenure in a profession, society, or similar organization. **11.** A leader of a council, branch of a union, or similar organization: *the city fathers; father of the chapel.*
~*tr.v.* **fathered, -thering, -thers. 1.** To beget. **2.** To act or serve as a father to. **3.** To create, found, or originate. **4.** To acknowledge as one's work; accept responsibility for. **5. a.** To attribute the paternity, creation, or origin of. Used with *on* or *upon.* **b.** To assign falsely or unjustly; foist. Used with *on* or *upon: You father undue significance upon my words.* [Middle English *fader,* Old English *fæder,* from Germanic *fadēr* (unattested).]

Father Christmas *n. Chiefly British.* **Santa Claus** (see).

father confessor *n.* **1.** A priest who hears confessions. **2.** Any person in whom one confides.

father figure *n.* An older person who acts in a fatherly way or is looked up to as being stable and dependable.

fa·ther·hood (fä′thər-hŏŏd′) *n.* The condition of being a father; paternity.

fa·ther-in-law (fä′thər-ĭn-lô′) *n., pl.* **fathers-in-law.** The father of one's husband or wife.

fa·ther·land (fä′thər-lănd′) *n.* **1.** A person's native country. **2.** The land of one's forebears.

fa·ther·ly (fä′thər-lē) *adj.* **1.** Pertaining to, characteristic of, or appropriate to a father. **2.** Showing the affection of a father.
~*adv.* In a fatherly manner. —**fa·ther·li·ness** *n.*

Father's Day *n.* An annual day of honoring fathers and fatherhood, observed on the third Sunday in June.

Father Time *n.* Time personified as an old man with a long beard carrying a scythe and an hourglass.

fath·om (fă*th*′əm) *n., pl.* **fathoms** or **fathom.** *Abbr.* **fath, fath., fm. 1.** A unit of length equal to 6 feet (1.829 meters), and used principally in the measurement and specification of marine depths. **2.** A unit of volume equal to 6 cubic feet (0.17 cubic meters).
~*tr.v.* **fathomed, -oming, -oms. 1.** To determine the depth of; sound. **2.** To get to the bottom of; penetrate to the meaning of: *"Her simplicity fathomed what clever people falsified"* (Virginia Woolf). [Middle English *fadme,* Old English *fæthm,* a measure of length equal to two arms; akin to Old Norse *fathmr,* embrace.] —**fath·om·a·ble** *adj.*

Fa·thom·e·ter (fă-*th*ŏm′ə-tər) *n.* A trademark for a sonic depth finder.

fath·om·less (fă*th*′əm-lĭs) *adj.* **1.** Too deep to be fathomed or measured; unfathomable. **2.** Too abstruse or complicated to be understood.

fa·tid·ic (fə-tĭd′ĭk) *adj.* Also **fa·tid·i·cal** (-ĭ-kəl). Pertaining to or characterized by prophecy; prophetic. [Latin *fātidicus : fātum,* FATE + *dīcere,* to say.]

fat·i·ga·ble (făt′ĭ-gə-bəl) *adj.* Subject to weariness; easily tired. [Late Latin *fatīgābilis,* from Latin *fatīgāre,* to FATIGUE.]

fa·tigue (fə-tēg′) *n.* **1.** Physical or mental weariness or exhaustion resulting from exertion. **2.** Tiring effort or activity; labor. **3.** *Physiology.* The decreased capacity or complete inability of an organism, organ, or part to function normally because of excessive stimulation or prolonged exertion. **4.** Weakness in metal, wood, or other material resulting from prolonged stress. **5.** Manual or menial labor, such as barracks cleaning, assigned to soldiers, often as a punishment: *a weekend on fatigue.* Also called "fatigue duty." **6. fatigues.** Clothing designated or permitted for work and field duty.
~*v.* **fatigued, -tiguing, -tigues.** —*tr.* **1.** To tire out; exhaust. **2.** To weaken (a metal, for example) by prolonged stress. —*intr.* **1.** To be or become exhausted or tired out. **2.** To become weakened as a result of stress. Used of metals and other materials. [French, from Old French, from *fatiguer,* to fatigue, from Latin *fatīgāre†.*]

fa·tigued (fə-tēgd′) *adj.* Exhausted. —See Synonyms at **tired.**

Fa·ti·ha, Fa·ti·hah (fä′tē-hä′) *n. Islam.* The first sura of the Koran, used as a prayer. [From Arabic, "opening."]

Fat·i·ma or **Fat·i·mah** (făt′ə-mə) (died A.D. 632). The daughter of the prophet Muhammad, she married Ali, one of the first to embrace Islam. She is considered by Muslims to be one of the Four Perfect Women.

Fát·i·ma (făt′ə-mə). Small hamlet in west-central Portugal and site of the national shrine of Our Lady of the Rosary of Fátima. Apparitions of the Virgin Mary were reputedly seen here in 1917.

Fat·i·mid[1] (făt′ə-mĭd) *n.* A member of a Muslim dynasty that ruled over parts of northern Africa and Egypt between A.D. 909 and 1171. —**Fat·i·mid, Fat·i·mite** (făt′ə-mīt′) *adj.*

Fatimid[2] *n.* A person descended from Fatima, the daughter of Muhammad. —**Fat·i·mid, Fat·i·mite** *adj.*

fat·ling (făt′lĭng) *n.* A young animal, such as a lamb or calf, fattened for slaughter.

fat mouse *n.* Any of various African mice of the genus *Steatomys,* eaten as a delicacy in Africa because of their high content of fat.

fat·so (făt′sō) *n., pl.* **-soes.** *Slang.* A fat person. [FAT + -s (plural suffix) + -o.]

fat-sol·u·ble (făt′sŏl′yə-bəl) *adj.* Soluble in fats or fat solvents, such as ether; lipid-soluble. Said of certain vitamins.

fat·stock (făt′stŏk′) *n. Used with a singular or plural verb.* Livestock that have been fattened up for market.

fat·ten (făt′n) *v.* **-tened, -tening, -tens.** —*tr.* **1.** To make plump or fat. Often used with *up.* **2.** To fertilize (land). **3.** To increase the amount or substance of; swell. —*intr.* To grow fat or fatter. —**fat·ten·er** *n.*

fat·tish (făt′ĭsh) *adj.* Somewhat fat; chubby. —**fat·tish·ness** *n.*

fat·ty (făt′ē) *adj.* **-tier, -tiest. 1. a.** Containing fat. **b.** Containing excessive amounts of fat. **2.** Characteristic of fat; especially, greasy. **3.** Derived from or chemically related to fat.
~*n., pl.* **-ties.** *Informal.* A fat person. Often used in direct address. —**fat·ti·ly** *adv.* —**fat·ti·ness** *n.*

fatty acid *n.* Any of a large group of monobasic acids having the general formula $C_nH_{2n+1}COOH$; especially, any of a commercially important subgroup obtained from animals and plants, characteristically saturated or unsaturated aliphatic compounds with an even number of carbon atoms, the most abundant of which contain 16 or 18 carbon atoms and include palmitic, stearic, and oleic acids.

fatty degeneration *n.* Deterioration in the functioning of a tissue or organ, such as the liver or heart, due to the abnormal deposition within it of large amounts of fat.

fa·tu·i·ty (fə-tōō′ə-tē, -tyōō′ə-tē) *n., pl.* **-ties. 1.** Stupidity accompanied by an air of pride or self-satisfaction. **2.** A fatuous act, remark, or sentiment. **3.** Futility; vanity. [Old French *fatuite,* from Latin *fatuitās* (stem *fatuitāt-*), from *fatuus,* FATUOUS.]

fat·u·ous (făch′ōō-əs) *adj.* **1.** Complacently or unconsciously stupid; asinine; inane. **2.** Delusive; self-deceiving: *fatuous hopes.* —See Synonyms at **foolish.** [Latin *fatuus†,* silly, fatuous, absurd.] —**fat·u·ous·ly** *adv.* —**fat·u·ous·ness** *n.*

fau·bourg (fō′bŏŏrg′, fō-bōŏr′) *n.* A suburb, district, or quarter of a town, especially in a French-speaking country. [Middle English *fabour,* from Old French *faubourg,* variant (influenced by *faux,* false) of *forsbo(u)rc,* "(something) outside the city" : *fors,* outside of, from Latin *forīs,* out, outside + *borc,* fortified place, town, from Late Latin *burgus,* from Germanic.]

fau·cal (fô′kəl) *adj.* **1.** *Anatomy.* Of or relating to the fauces. **2.** *Phonetics.* Produced in or near the fauces. Said of a sound.

fau·ces (fô′sēz′) *pl.n. Anatomy.* The space between the mouth and pharynx bounded by the soft palate, the base of the tongue, and the palatine arches. [Latin *faucēs†*, throat.]

fau·cet (fô′sĭt) *n.* A device for drawing a flow of a liquid from a pipe, drum, or other reservoir; tap. [Middle English *faucet*, from Old French *fausset*, plug, from *fausser*, to break into, from Late Latin *falsāre*, to falsify, from Latin *falsus*, FALSE.]

faugh (fô) *interj.* Used to express contempt, disgust, or dismissal. [Imitative.]

fauld (fôld) *n.* A skirt-shaped piece of armor protecting the area between the waist and the top of the thighs. [Variant of FOLD.]

Faulk·ner (fôk′nər), **William,** originally spelled Falkner (1897–1962). U.S. novelist. Raised in Oxford, Mississippi, he drew on the history, legends, and social problems of his native South. His early work includes *Sartoris, The Sound and the Fury* (both 1929), and *As I Lay Dying* (1930). He consolidated his reputation with *Sanctuary* (1931) and *Absalom, Absalom!* (1936). In 1949 he was awarded the Nobel Prize.

fault (fôlt) *n.* **1.** Something that prevents perfection, as: **a.** A flaw, blemish, or defect. **b.** A mistake; an error. **c.** An offense, transgression, or minor vice. **2.** Responsibility for such a mistake or offense; culpability. **3.** *Geology.* A break in the continuity of a rock formation, caused by a shifting or dislodging of the earth's crust, in which adjacent surfaces are differentially displaced parallel to the plane of fracture. Also called "dislocation." **4.** *Electricity.* A defect in a circuit or wiring caused by imperfect connections, poor insulation or grounding, or shorting. **5.** *Sports.* **a.** A bad service, as in tennis. **b.** A penalty incurred in show jumping when a horse hits or refuses to jump a fence. **6.** In hunting, the loss of the scent by a dog or dogs. **7.** *Obsolete.* A lack or deficiency. —See Synonyms at **blemish.** —**at fault. 1.** Deserving of blame; guilty. **2.** Confused and puzzled. **3.** In hunting, unable to recapture the scent of the game. —**find fault.** To seek, find, and complain about faults; carp. —**to a fault.** Excessively.
~*v.* **faulted, faulting, faults.** —*tr.* **1.** To find a fault in; criticize or blame. **2.** *Geology.* To produce a fault in; fracture. —*intr.* **1.** To commit a fault or error. **2.** *Geology.* To shift so as to produce a fault. [Middle English *faute*, from Old French, from Vulgar Latin *fallita* (unattested), feminine past participle of Latin *fallere*, to fail, deceive. See **fail.**]
   Synonyms: *foible, frailty, vice, weakness.*

fault·find·er (fôlt′fīn′dər) *n.* One who seeks out faults; a chronic complainer.

fault·find·ing (fôlt′fīn′dĭng) *n.* Petty criticism; carping.
~*adj.* Disposed to find trivial faults; captious.

fault·less (fôlt′lĭs) *adj.* **1.** Without fault; blameless. **2.** Without a fault; flawless. —**fault·less·ly** *adv.* —**fault·less·ness** *n.*

fault plane *n. Geology.* The plane along which the break or shear of a geologic fault occurs.

fault·y (fôl′tē) *adj.* **-ier, -iest. 1.** Containing a fault or faults; imperfect or defective. **2.** *Obsolete.* Deserving of blame; guilty. —**fault·i·ly** *adv.* —**fault·i·ness** *n.*

faun (fôn) *n. Roman Mythology.* Any of a group of rural deities represented as having the body of a man and the horns, ears, tail, and sometimes legs of a goat. [Middle English *faun*, from Latin *Faunus*, FAUNUS.]

fau·na (fô′nə) *n., pl.* **-nas** or **-nae** (-nē′). **1.** Animals collectively; especially, the animals of a particular region or time. **2.** A descriptive list of animals. [New Latin, from Latin *Fauna*, sister of FAUNUS.]

Fau·nus (fô′nəs). *Roman Mythology.* A god of nature and fertility, worshiped by shepherds and farmers, and identified with the Greek Pan. [Latin *Faunus†*.]

Fau·ré (fô-rā′), **Gabriel Urbain** (1845–1924). French composer and organist. His compositions include *Requiem* (1888), the song cycle *La Bonne Chanson* (1891–92), and the opera *Pénélope* (1913).

Faust (foust). Also **Faust·us** (fou′stəs, fô′-). A magician and alchemist, hero of several poetic and dramatic works, who sells his soul to the devil in exchange for power and knowledge. [German, after Johann *Faust*, 16th-century magician and astrologer.] —**Faust·i·an** (fou′stē-ən) *adj.*

faute de mieux (fōt′ də myœ′) *adv.* For want of anything better: *wanted to go to Europe but visited home faute de mieux.*
~*adj.* Accepted or undertaken for want of anything better. [French.]

fau·teuil (fô′tĭl; *French* fō-tœ′ē) *n.* **1.** *British.* A stall in a theater. **2.** An armchair. [French, from Old French *faudestuel, faldestoel,* folding stool, from Germanic.]

fauv·ism (fō′vĭz′əm) *n. Often* **Fauvism.** An art movement originating in Paris in 1905 as a revolt against impressionism, characterized by simplified form and the use of vivid colors. Its members included Dufy, Matisse, and Rouault. [From French *fauve,* wild beast (term applied to Matisse, Vlaminck, and other members of the group because of their use of violent colors).] —**fauve** (fōv) *n. & adj.* —**fauv·ist** *n. & adj.*

faux-na·ïf (fō′nä-ēf′) *adj.* Seeming or pretending to be ingenuous and unsophisticated.
~*n.* One who pretends to be ingenuous and unsophisticated. [French, "false naïve."]

faux pas (fō pä′) *n., pl.* **faux pas** (fō päz′). A social blunder; a breach of etiquette. [French, "false step."]

fa·va bean (fä′və) *n.* A broad bean (see). [Italian *fava,* from Latin *faba,* bean + BEAN.]

fault

THE EARTH'S FAULTY SURFACE

How rocks are distorted by underground movement

A fault is a fracture in the earth's crust where two blocks of rock are moving against each other. The fracture is caused by stresses arising from movements in the earth's crust. There are three main types of fault—normal dip-slip and reverse dip-slip (characterized by vertical movement), and strike-slip (characterized by horizontal movement).

Movement of the two blocks of fractured rock is slow; they pass each other at about 10 millimeters (²⁄₅ inch) or less a year. But occasionally two blocks get stuck, movement ceases, and tension builds up. Eventually a sudden movement makes up for lost time. These sudden displacements along faults are the most frequent causes of earthquakes.

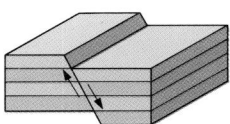
NORMAL FAULT *One side is displaced downward along a fault plane (inclined) at an angle of more than 45°, as in the Utah–Nevada region of the United States. It is also called a gravity fault.*

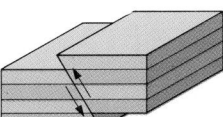
REVERSE FAULT *Produced by shortening or compression within the crust. One block is forced over another along a fault plane, as in the Highland Boundary Fault in Scotland.*

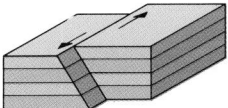
STRIKE-SLIP FAULT *The movement of rock blocks is horizontal, as in the San Andreas Fault in California.*

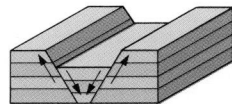
RIFT VALLEY *This occurs when the rocks between two faults drop, as in the Great Rift Valley of East Africa.*

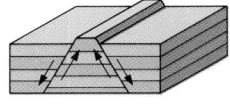
HORST *The opposite of a rift valley, a horst is created when land on either side of a central block sinks. This is how the Vosges Mountains in France were formed.*

fa·ve·o·late (fə-vē′ə-lāt′) *adj.* Pitted with cavities or cells; honeycombed. [New Latin *faveolus,* diminutive of Latin *favus†,* honeycomb.]

fa·vo·ni·an (fə-vō′nē-ən) *adj.* **1.** Of the west wind. **2.** Mild; benign. [Latin *Favōniānus,* from *Favōnius†,* west wind.]

fa·vor (fā′vər) *n.* Also chiefly *British* **fa·vour. 1. a.** A gracious, kind, or friendly attitude. **b.** An act that reveals such an attitude; an act of kindness: *Will you do me a favor?* **c.** *Often* **favors.** An act requiring sacrifice or special generosity. **2. a.** Friendly regard shown by a group or a superior. **b.** The state of being held in such regard. **3.** Approval or support; sanction. **4.** Partiality; favoritism. **5.** *Usually* **favors.** Sexual privileges, as granted by a woman. **6. a.** Something given as a token of love, loyalty, affection, or remembrance. **b.** A small, decorative gift given to each guest at a party or ball. **7.** Advantage; benefit: *a balance in our favor.* **8.** *Obsolete.* A communication, especially a letter. **9.** *Obsolete.* **a.** The aspect or appearance. **b.** A countenance; a visage; a face. **c.** Any part of the face; a feature. —**in favor of. 1.** In support of; approving. **2.** To the advantage of. **3.** Inscribed or made out to, as a check. **4.** Preferring: *She turned down my suggestion in favor of yours.*
~*tr.v.* **favored, -voring, -vors.** Also chiefly *British* **fa·vour, -voured, -vouring, -vours. 1.** To perform a kindness for; oblige. **2.** To regard with approval; like. **3.** To be partial to; indulge a liking for: *He favors garish ties.* **4.** To be or tend to be in support of. **5.** To make easier or more possible; facilitate. **6.** To resemble in appearance: *"Annie May favors her Father and his people who were small and lightly built"* (James Agee). **7.** To treat with care; be gentle with: *The soldier favored his wounded leg.* [Middle English *favour,* from Old French, from Latin *favor,* from *favēre,* to favor, be favorable.] —**fa·vor·er** *n.* —**fa·vor·ing·ly** *adv.*

fa·vor·a·ble (fā′vər-ə-bəl, fāv′rə-) *adj.* **1.** Advantageous; helpful. **2.** Propitious; encouraging. **3.** Manifesting approval; commendatory. **4.** Embodying or conceding that which was desired or re-

quested: *a favorable reply.* **5.** Indulgent or partial. —**fa·vor·a·ble·ness** *n.* —**fa·vor·a·bly** *adv.*
    Synonyms: *auspicious, benign, conducive, propitious.*
fa·vored (fā′vərd) *adj.* **1.** Treated or thought of with kindness or liking; indulged; privileged. **2.** Having special talents, gifts, or beauty. **3.** Having a physical appearance of a specified kind. Used chiefly in the combinations *well-favored* and *ill-favored.*
fa·vor·ite (fā′vər-ĭt, fāv′rĭt) *n.* **1. a.** A person or thing liked or preferred above all others. **b.** A person especially indulged by a superior. **2.** *Sports.* A competitor regarded as most likely to win.
    ~*adj.* Liked or preferred above all others; regarded with special favor. [Obsolete French *favorit,* from Italian *favorito,* past participle of *favorire,* to favor, from *favore,* favor, from Latin *favor,* FAVOR.]
favorite son *n.* A man nominated as a presidential candidate, often merely as an honorary gesture, by the delegates from his own constituency at a national political convention.
fa·vor·it·ism (fā′vər-ə-tĭz′əm, fāv′rə-) *n.* **1.** A display of privileged treatment or partiality, especially when unjust, toward a favored person or group. **2.** The state of being held in special favor.
fav·rile glass (fəv-rēl′) *n.* **Tiffany glass** *(see).* [Former trademark (1894) for Tiffany glass, based on *fabrile,* "of a craftsman," from Old French, from Latin *fabrīlis,* from *faber,* artificer.]
fa·vus (fā′vəs) *n.* A chronic fungous infection of the scalp and nails. [New Latin, from Latin, honeycomb. See **faveolate.**]
Fawkes (fôks), **Guy** (1570–1606). English conspirator in the Gunpowder Plot. Fawkes, a Roman Catholic, took part in a plot to blow up King James I and the English Parliament on November 5, 1605, to avenge the persecution of Roman Catholics in England. He was found in a cellar with the gunpowder, was tortured, and disclosed his accomplices. He was hanged in 1606. Guy Fawkes Day is widely celebrated each November 5 by burning effigies of Fawkes on bonfires.
fawn¹ (fôn) *intr.v.* **fawned, fawning, fawns. 1.** To attempt to please or exhibit affection, as in the manner of a dog wagging its tail and whining. Used with *on* or *upon.* **2.** To seek favor or attention by flattery and obsequious behavior. Often used with *on* or *upon.* [Middle English *faunen,* Old English *fagnian, fægnian,* to rejoice, from *fægen,* FAIN.] —**fawn·er** *n.* —**fawn·ing·ly** *adv.*
fawn² *n.* **1.** A young deer, especially one less than a year old. **2.** Light yellowish brown to light grayish brown. [Middle English *foun, fawn,* from Old French *foun, feon,* offspring of an animal, from Vulgar Latin *fētō,* from Latin *fētus,* offspring, a giving birth.] —**fawn** *adj.*
fawn lily *n.* Any of several North American plants of the genus *Erythronium,* especially *E. grandiflorum,* of western North America, having nodding yellow flowers.
fax (făks) *n.* A facsimile.
fay¹ (fā) *v.* **fayed, faying, fays.** —*tr.* To join (beams, for example) closely or tightly. —*intr.* To be fitted or joined tightly. [Middle English *feien,* Old English *fēgan.*]
fay² *n.* A fairy, sprite, or elf.
    ~*adj.* Pertaining to or resembling a fairy or elf. [Middle English *faie,* one possessing magical powers, from Old French *faie, fae,* from Latin *fāta,* the Fates, plural of *fātum,* FATE.]
fay³ *n.* Obsolete. Faith. Used in oaths: *"sirrah, by my fay, it waxes late"* (Shakespeare). [Middle English *fai, fei,* FAITH.]
fay·al·ite (fā′ə-līt′) *n.* A yellowish to black mineral, mostly Fe₂SiO₄, of the olivine group. [German *Fayalit : Fayal,* German form for *Faial* (island in the Azores where it was first found) + -ITE.]
faze (fāz) *tr.v.* **fazed, fazing, fazes.** To disrupt the composure of; bother; disconcert. [Variant of FEEZE.]
fa·zen·da (fə-zěn′də) *n., pl.* **-das.** In Brazil, a hacienda, estate, or plantation, especially a coffee plantation. [Portuguese, from Latin *facienda,* things to be done, neuter plural gerundive of *facere,* to do.]
fb, f.b. fullback.
F.B.A. Fellow of the British Academy.
FBI, F.B.I. Federal Bureau of Investigation.
fc foot-candle.
f.c. *Printing.* follow copy.
fcap., fcp. foolscap.
FCC Federal Communications Commission.
F clef *n. Music.* A **bass clef** *(see).*
F.D. 1. Fidei Defensor. **2.** fire department.
FDA Food and Drug Administration.
FDIC Federal Deposit Insurance Corporation.
FDR Franklin Delano Roosevelt.
Fe The symbol for the element iron [Latin *ferrum*].
fe·al·ty (fē′əl-tē) *n., pl.* **-ties. 1.** The obligation of loyalty owed by a vassal to his feudal lord. **2.** Faithfulness; allegiance. —See Synonyms at **fidelity.** [Middle English *fealtye, feute,* from Old French *fealte, feau(l)te,* from Latin *fidēlitās* (stem *fidēlitāt-*), faithfulness, from *fidēlis,* faithful, from *fidēs,* faith.]
fear (fîr) *n.* **1.** A feeling of alarm or disquiet caused by the expectation of danger, pain, disaster, or the like; terror; dread; apprehension. **2.** An instance or manifestation of such a feeling. **3.** A state or condition of alarm or dread: *The prisoners spent the night in fear.* **4.** Extreme reverence or awe, as toward a supreme power. **5.** A ground for dread or apprehension; a possibility of danger. —**for fear of.** So as to prevent or avoid: *She tiptoed for fear of waking the children.* —**for fear that.** Lest; in case: *He hurried home for fear that he might miss his guests.* —**no fear of.** No chance or possibility of: *There's no fear of that happening.* —**without fear or favor.** Impartially; without bias.

~*v.* **feared, fearing, fears.** —*tr.* **1.** To be afraid or frightened of. **2.** To be anxious or apprehensive about. **3.** To be in awe of; revere. **4. a.** To suspect: *I fear you are wrong.* **b.** To be sorry: *I fear I have some bad news for you.* —*intr.* **1.** To be afraid, frightened, or terrified. **2.** To feel anxious or apprehensive. Used with *for.* [Middle English *fer,* Old English *fǣr,* danger, sudden calamity, from Germanic.] —**fear·er** *n.*
    Synonyms: *alarm, dread, fright, panic, terror, trepidation.*
fear·ful (fîr′fəl) *adj.* **1.** Causing or capable of causing fear; frightening; terrifying. **2.** Experiencing fear; frightened. **3.** Feeling anxious or apprehensive. **4.** Feeling reverence, dread, or awe. **5.** *Informal.* Very bad; dreadful: *a fearful blunder.* —**fear·ful·ness** *n.*
fear·ful·ly (fîr′fə-lē) *adv.* **1.** In a fearful manner. **2.** *Informal.* Extremely; very: *I'm fearfully sorry.*
fear·less (fîr′lĭs) *adj.* Having no fear; unafraid; brave. —See Synonyms at **brave.** —**fear·less·ly** *adv.* —**fear·less·ness** *n.*
fear·nought, fear·naught (fîr′nôt′) *n.* **1.** A heavy, thick, often rough woolen material used in making overcoats. **2.** A garment made of this cloth.
fear·some (fîr′səm) *adj.* **1.** Causing or capable of causing fear; frightening; awesome. **2.** Afraid; frightened; fearful; timid. —**fear·some·ly** *adv.* —**fear·some·ness** *n.*
fea·sance (fē′zəns) *n. Law.* The execution of an obligation or duty. [Norman French *fesance,* from *faire,* to do, from Latin *facere.*]
fea·si·ble (fē′zə-bəl) *adj.* **1.** Capable of being accomplished or brought about; practicable; possible: *a feasible outline for the project.* **2.** Capable of being utilized or dealt with successfully; suitable. **3.** Logical; likely: *He gave a feasible excuse for his absence.* —See Synonyms at **possible.** [Middle English *faisible, fesable,* from Old French *faisible,* from *faire* (present stem *fais-*), to do, from Latin *facere.*] —**fea·si·bil·i·ty** (fē′zə-bĭl′ə-tē), **fea·si·ble·ness** *n.* —**fea·si·bly** *adv.*
feast (fēst) *n.* **1. a.** A large, elaborately prepared meal, usually for many persons and often with entertainment; a banquet. **b.** Any large, sumptuous, or delicious meal. **2.** A periodic religious festival in commemoration of an event or in honor of a god or saint. **3.** Something giving great pleasure or satisfaction: *a feast for the mind.*
    ~*v.* **feasted, feasting, feasts.** —*tr.* **1.** To give a feast for; entertain or feed sumptuously. **2.** To provide with pleasure; delight; gratify: *"Augustus too feasted his eyes on the same plate of fruit"* (Virginia Woolf). —*intr.* **1.** To partake of a feast. **2.** To eat with great enjoyment. Used with *on: The boys feasted on the fish they caught.* **3.** To experience something with gratification or delight. [Middle English

---

Fauvism

THE WILD BEASTS

An exuberant use of color that outraged the critics

Fauvism was a brief, vigorous reaction by French artists in the early 20th century against the conservatism of the artistic establishment. Its main proponent was Matisse, its main weapon was color. To Matisse, color transmitted intensity of feeling. The style got its name when a group of painters, which included Maurice Vlaminck and André Derain, had embraced Matisse's approach and exhibited works at the Salon d'Automne in Paris in 1905.

One critic, seeing a Renaissance-style sculpture among them, remarked: "Donatello among the wild beasts *(les fauves)!*" The name stuck. But the group had no real coherence or direction. It broke up by 1908, having left its mark on German expressionism and cubism.

LONDON BRIDGE, *1906 Derain displays the bold slabs of strong color that typified the work of Fauvists. They aimed to portray the world with all the immediacy of primitive or untutored artists.*

feather *One of the jay's wing coverts: the interlocking feathers that give the bird's wings their smooth, aerodynamic surface. They cover the bases of the main flight feathers (remiges), which give the bird lift and propel it through the air. Fossil evidence suggests that birds evolved feathers millions of years before they developed flight—their original function was simply to provide warmth.*

feather palm *The feather palm gets its name from its feathery leaves, seen here on a group of the palms near a Tunisian oasis.*

feste, from Old French, from Latin *fēsta,* neuter plural (taken as feminine singular) of *fēstus,* joyous, festal.] **—feast·er** *n.*

Feast of Dedication *n.* A Jewish holiday, **Chanukah** *(see).*

Feast of Lanterns *n.* **1.** A Chinese festival, held at the first full moon of the new year, at which colored lanterns are displayed. **2.** A Japanese festival, **Bon** *(see).* **3.** A Hindu festival in October or November, lasting five days and dedicated to the goddess of wealth.

Feast of Lights *n.* A Jewish holiday, **Chanukah** *(see).*

Feast of Tabernacles *n.* A Jewish holiday, **Succoth** *(see).*

Feast of Weeks *n.* A Jewish holiday, **Shavuot** *(see).*

feat[1] (fēt) *n.* **1.** Any act or deed; especially, an act of courage. **2.** Any act or product of skill, endurance, imagination, or strength; an achievement. [Middle English *fete,* from Old French *fait, fet,* from Latin *factum,* something done, from the neuter past participle of *facere,* to do.]

feat[2] *adj.* **feater, featest.** *Archaic.* **1.** Adroit; dexterous; skillful. **2.** Neat; trim. [Middle English *fete,* adroit, skillful, from Old French *fait,* from Latin *factum,* deed. See **feat**[1].] **—feat·ly** *adv.*

feath·er (fĕth'ər) *n.* **1.** Any of the light, flat structures constituting the plumage of birds, consisting of numerous slender, closely arranged parallel barbs forming a vane on either side of a tapering hollow shaft. **2. feathers.** Plumage. **3. feathers.** *Informal.* Clothing; attire. **4.** A tuft or fringe of hair resembling a feather, as on the legs or tail of some dogs. **5.** Character, kind, or nature: *Birds of a feather flock together.* **6.** Something small, trivial, or inconsequential. **7. a.** A strip, wedge, or flange used as a strengthening part. **b.** A wedge or key that fits into a groove to make a joint. **8.** The vane of an arrow, made of real or imitation feathers. **9.** A feather-shaped flaw, as in a gem or precious stone. **10.** The wake made by a submarine periscope. **11.** The act of feathering the blade of an oar in rowing. **—a feather in one's cap.** A distinctive achievement; an act or deed to one's credit. **—in fine** (or **good**) **feather.** In excellent form, health, or humor. **—in full feather. 1.** Having plenty of money. **2.** Elaborately dressed or equipped.
~v. **feathered, -ering, -ers.** *—tr.* **1.** To cover, dress, or decorate with or as if with feathers. **2.** To fit (an arrow) with a feather; fletch. **3. a.** To thin, reduce, or fringe the edge of by cutting, shaving, or wearing away. **b.** To shorten and taper (hair) by cutting and thinning. **4.** To connect with a tongue-and-groove joint. **5.** To turn (an oar blade) horizontal to the surface of the water between strokes. **6.** *Aeronautics.* To alter the pitch of (a propeller) so that the blade chords are parallel with the line of flight. *—intr.* **1.** To grow feathers or become feathered. **2.** To move, spread, or grow in a manner suggestive of feathers. **3.** To feather an oar. **4.** *Aeronautics.* To feather a propeller. **5.** To quiver through the whole body. Used of a hound when hunting. **—feather one's nest.** To grow wealthy by making use of property or funds left in one's trust. [Old English *fether.*] **—feath·er·less** *adj.*

feather bed *n.* A mattress stuffed with feathers or down.

feath·er·bed (fĕth'ər-bĕd') *v.* **-bedded, -bedding, -beds.** *—intr.* **1.** To employ more workers than are actually needed for a given purpose. **2.** To be so employed. *—tr.* To pamper or spoil.

feath·er·brain (fĕth'ər-brān') *n. Informal.* A silly, flighty, or empty-headed person. Also called "featherhead," "featherpate." **—feath·er·brained** *adj.*

feather duster *n.* A brush consisting of a bunch of feathers fastened to the end of a stick, used for dusting delicate objects or clearing away cobwebs.

feath·ered (fĕth'ərd) *adj.* **1.** Having feathers; covered or adorned with feathers. **2.** *Aeronautics.* Having the propeller blade chords parallel to the line of flight.

feath·er·edge (fĕth'ər-ĕj') *n.* **1.** A thin fragile edge; especially, a tapering edge of a board. **2.** A **deckle edge** *(see).* **—feath·er·edged** *adj.*

feather grass *n.* Any of various grasses of the genus *Stipa,* having clusters of featherlike spikelets.

feath·er·ing (fĕth'ər-ĭng) *n.* **1.** Plumage. **2.** The feathers fitted to an arrow. **3.** A fringe of long hair on an animal's coat, especially that on a dog's leg. **4.** *Architecture.* The cusps in Gothic tracery.

feather palm *n.* Any palm tree having pinnate leaves forming featherlike fronds. Compare **fan palm.**

feather star *n.* Any of numerous crinoids of the genus *Antedon* and related genera, having a free-moving, stalkless adult stage with branched, feathery arms.

feath·er·stitch (fĕth'ər-stĭch') *n.* An embroidery stitch that produces a decorative zigzag line. **—feath·er·stitch** *v.*

feath·er-veined (fĕth'ər-vānd') *adj.* Having veins branching from either side of a midrib. Said of leaves.

feath·er·weight (fĕth'ər-wāt') *n.* **1.** A boxer or wrestler weighing between 119 and 126 pounds or 54 and 57 kilograms. **2.** A person or thing of little weight or size. **3.** An insignificant person or thing.
~adj. **1.** Of or pertaining to featherweights: *a featherweight match.* **2.** Unimportant; trivial; superficial.

feath·er·y (fĕth'ə-rē) *adj.* **1.** Covered with or consisting of feathers. **2.** Resembling or suggestive of a feather or feathers, as in form or lightness. **—feath·er·i·ness** *n.*

fea·ture (fē'chər) *n.* **1. features.** The make-up or appearance of the face or its parts. **2.** Any of the distinct parts of the face, such as the nose, mouth, or eyes. **3.** Any prominent or distinctive aspect, quality, or characteristic: *Indecision was a strong feature of his character.* **4. a.** The main presentation at a motion-picture theater. **b.** A full-length fictional motion picture, especially as opposed to a documentary. **5.** A prominent or extra article or story in a newspaper or periodical. **6.** Anything advertised as especially attractive or as an inducement, such as an item on sale at a discount in a department store. **7.** *Archaic.* Form; shape; appearance.
~v. **featured, -turing, -tures.** *—tr.* **1.** To give special attention to; make prominent, display, or publicize. **2.** To have or include as a prominent part or characteristic: *The film featured many well-known actors.* **3.** To draw or otherwise portray the features of. **4.** *Informal.* To picture mentally; imagine. *—intr.* **1.** To be a feature. **2.** To be a prominent or distinct part or characteristic. [Middle English *feture,* from Old French *feture, faiture,* form, from Latin *factūra,* a making, formation, from *factus,* past participle of *facere,* to do, make.]

fea·tured (fē'chərd) *adj.* **1.** Given special attention or publicity; made prominent: *a featured role in a movie.* **2.** Having a specified kind of facial features. Often used in combination: *small-featured; sharp-featured.*

fea·ture-length (fē'chər-lĕngkth', -lĕngth') *adj.* Of normal or full length: *a feature-length film.*

fea·ture·less (fē'chər-lĭs) *adj.* With no distinguishing characteristics; unremarkable.

Feb. February.

febri– *prefix.* Indicates fever; for example, **febrifuge.** [Latin *febris,* FEVER.]

fe·bric·i·ty (fĭ-brĭs'ə-tē) *n.* The condition of having a fever. [Medieval Latin *febricitās* (stem *febricitāt-*), from Latin *febris,* FEVER.]

feb·ri·fa·cient (fĕb'rə-fā'shənt) *n.* A substance that causes a fever. *~adj.* Causing fever. [Latin *febris,* FEVER + -FACIENT.]

fe·brif·ic (fĭ-brĭf'ĭk) *adj.* **1.** Causing fever. **2.** Having a fever; feverish. [Latin *febris,* FEVER + -FIC.]

feb·ri·fuge (fĕb'rə-fyo͞oj') *n.* Any agent that reduces a fever. *~adj.* Fever-reducing. [French *fébrifuge,* from New Latin *febrifugus* : Latin *febris,* FEVER + *fugāre,* to drive away, from *fugere,* to flee.]

feb·rile (fĕb'rəl, fē'brəl; *British* fē'brīl') *adj.* Of or pertaining to fever; feverish. [French *fébrile,* from Latin *febris,* FEVER.]

Feb·ru·ar·y (fĕb'ro͞o-ĕr'ē, fĕb'yo͞o-) *n., pl.* **-ies** or **-ys.** *Abbr.* **Feb.** The second month of the year according to the Gregorian calendar. February has 28 days, 29 in leap years. See feature at **calendar.** [Middle English *feveryer,* from Old French *feverier,* from Late Latin *febrārius,* from Latin *februārius,* from *februa,* festival of purification held on February 15, of Sabine origin.]

fe·cal, fae·cal (fē'kəl) *adj.* Of, pertaining to, or constituting feces.

fe·ces, fae·ces (fē'sēz) *pl.n.* Waste excreted from the bowels; excrement. [Middle English, from Latin, plural of *faex* (stem *faec-*), dregs.]

fe·cit (fā'kĭt, fē'sĭt) *n. Abbr.* **fec.** *Latin.* He (or she) made (or did) it. Used before or after an artist's name on a work of art.

feck·less (fĕk'lĭs) *adj.* **1.** Lacking purpose or vitality; feeble; ineffective. **2.** Careless; irresponsible. [Scottish *feck,* efficacy, short for EFFECT + -LESS.] **—feck·less·ly** *adv.* **—feck·less·ness** *n.*

fec·u·lent (fĕk'yə-lənt) *adj.* Full of foul matter, dregs, or sediment; foul; fetid. [Middle English *feculent,* from Latin *faeculentus,* from *faex* (stem *faec-*), FECES.] **—fec·u·lence** *n.*

fe·cund (fē'kənd, fĕk'ənd) *adj.* **1.** Capable of producing offspring or vegetation; fertile; productive; fruitful. **2.** Marked by intellectual productivity. [Middle English *fecound,* from Old French *fecond,* from Latin *fēcundus,* perhaps akin to *fēlix,* happy.]

fe·cun·date (fē'kən-dāt', fĕk'ən-) *tr.v.* **-dated, -dating, -dates. 1.** To make fecund or fruitful. **2.** To impregnate; fertilize. [Latin *fēcundāre,* from *fēcundus,* FECUND.]

fe·cun·di·ty (fĭ-kŭn'də-tē) *n.* **1.** The quality or power of producing abundantly; fertility. **2.** The capacity for or power of producing young, especially in abundance; productiveness. **3.** Productive or creative power: *the fecundity of his mind.*

fed. Past tense and past participle of **feed.**

Fed (fĕd) *n. Informal.* **1.** An agent or representative of the federal government. **2.** The Federal Reserve Board.

Fed., fed. federal; federated; federation.

Fe·da·yee (fē-dä'yē') *n., pl.* **-yeen** (-yēn'). An Arab commando, especially one operating against Israel. [Arabic *fedā'yūn,* commandos, from *fidā'ī,* one who sacrifices himself for his country, from *fidā',* redemption.]

fed·er·al (fĕd'ər-əl) *adj. Abbr.* **Fed., fed. 1.** Of, pertaining to, or designating a form of government in which states, provinces, or other political units recognize the sovereignty of a central authority while retaining certain residual powers of government. **2.** Of or pertaining to the central government of a federation, as distinct from the governments of its constituent political units. **3.** Of, pertaining to, or formed by a treaty or compact between constituent political units: *"Our connection had been federal only, and was now dissolved by the commencement of hostilities"* (Thomas Jefferson). **4.** *Often* **Federal. a.** Of, pertaining to, or designating the central government of the United States or Canada. **b.** Of, pertaining to, or characterizing the U.S. Federalist Party or Federalism. **c.** Of, pertaining to, or supporting the Federal government during the Civil War; pro-Union. **5. Federal.** Pertaining to or characteristic of a style of architecture, furniture, and decoration produced in the United States (1783–1815) and characterized by adaptations of classical forms often combined with typically American motifs.
~n. **1.** A supporter of federation or federal government. **2. Federal. a.** A Federalist. **b.** A supporter of the Union during the U.S. Civil War; especially, a Union soldier. [Latin *foedus* (stem *foeder-*), league, treaty, compact.] **—fed·er·al·ly** *adv.*

Federal Bureau of Investigation *n. Abbr.* **FBI, F.B.I.** An agency of the U.S. Justice Department responsible for investigating violations of federal law.

Federal Capital Territory. See **Australian Capital Territory.**

Federal Communications Commission *n. Abbr.* **FCC** A U.S. government agency responsible for the supervision and regulation of wire, radio, and television communication.

Federal Deposit Insurance Corporation *n. Abbr.* **FDIC** An independent U.S. government agency primarily responsible for insuring bank depositors against loss.

Federal District *n.* An area in certain federal countries that is reserved as the site of the national capital, such as the District of Columbia. Also called "Federal Territory."

fed·er·al·ism (fĕd′ər-ə-lĭz′əm) *n.* **1. a.** The doctrine or system of federal government. **b.** The advocacy of such a government. **2. Federalism.** The doctrine of the Federalist Party.

fed·er·al·ist (fĕd′ər-ə-lĭst) *n.* **1.** An advocate of federalism. **2. Federalist.** A member or supporter of the Federalist Party. **—fed·er·al·ist, fed·er·al·is·tic** (fĕd′ər-ə-lĭs′tĭk) *adj.*

Federalist Party *n.* Also **Federal Party.** A U.S. political party founded in 1787 that favored a strong central government.

fed·er·al·ize (fĕd′ər-ə-līz′) *tr.v.* **-ized, -izing, -izes. 1.** To unite in a federal union. **2.** To subject to the authority of a federal government; put under federal control. **—fed·er·al·i·za·tion** *n.*

Federal Republic of Germany. See **Germany, West Germany.**

Federal Reserve System *n. Abbr.* **FRS** A U.S. banking system consisting of 12 Federal Reserve banks, each serving member banks in a Federal Reserve District and supervised by the Federal Reserve Board, appointed by the President.

fed·er·ate (fĕd′ə-rāt′) *v.* **-ated, -ating, -ates.** *—tr.* To join or bring together in a league, federal union, or similar association. *—intr.* To unite in a federal union.

~adj. (fĕd′ər-ĭt). United under a central government; federated. [Latin *foederāre,* from *foedus* (stem *foeder-*), league, treaty.] **—fed·er·a·tive** (fĕd′ə-rā′tĭv, fĕd′ər-ə-) *adj.*

fed·er·a·tion (fĕd′ə-rā′shən) *n. Abbr.* **fed. 1.** The act of federating; especially, a joining together of states in a league or federal union. **2.** A league or association formed by federating, especially a political unit or country so formed, in which the central government is relatively powerful. Compare **confederation.**

fe·do·ra (fĭ-dôr′ə, -dōr′ə) *n.* A soft felt hat with a brim that can be turned up or down and a fairly low crown creased lengthwise. [From *Fédora* (1882), play by Victorien Sardou (1831–1908), French playwright.]

fed up *adj.* **1.** Out of patience; irritated: *I'm fed up with your nagging.* **2.** Bored; having had too much.

fee (fē) *n.* **1. a.** A charge fixed by an institution or by law: *tuition fees; the fee for a fishing license.* **b.** Any fixed charge. **2.** A payment for professional or special service: *a tax consultant's fee.* **3.** A tip; a gratuity. **4.** *Law.* An inherited or heritable estate in land. See **fee simple, fee tail. 5. a.** In feudal law, an estate in land granted by a lord to his vassal on condition of homage and service. In this sense, also called "feoff," "feud," "feudality," "fief." **b.** The land so held. —See Synonyms at **price. —hold in fee.** To have absolute and legal possession of.

~tr.v. **feed, feeing, fees.** To give a fee to. [Middle English *fe,* inherited estate, payment, from Old French *fe, fief,* from Frankish *fehu-ōd* (unattested), cattle, property; akin to FIEF, FEUD (estate).]

fee·ble (fē′bəl) *adj.* **-bler, -blest. 1. a.** Lacking strength; weak; especially, frail or infirm: *a feeble old woman.* **b.** Indicating weakness: *a feeble walk.* **2.** Lacking vigor or force; inadequate; ineffective: *a feeble attempt.* **3.** Barely discernible; faint; slight: *a feeble cry.* —See Synonyms at **weak.** [Middle English *feble,* from Old French *feble, fieble, fleible,* from Latin *flēbilis,* to be wept over, lamentable, from *flēre,* to weep.] **—fee·ble·ness** *n.* **—fee·bly** *adv.*

fee·ble-mind·ed (fē′bəl-mīn′dĭd) *adj.* **1.** Mentally deficient; subnormal in intelligence. **2.** Dull-witted; stupid; foolish. **3.** Irresolute; indecisive. **—fee·ble-mind·ed·ly** *adv.* **—fee·ble-mind·ed·ness** *n.*

feed (fēd) *v.* **fed** (fĕd), **feeding, feeds.** *—tr.* **1. a.** To give food to; supply with nourishment: *feed the children.* **b.** To provide as food or nourishment: *feed fish to a cat.* **2. a.** To serve as food for: *The turkey is large enough to feed a dozen.* **b.** To produce food for: *The valley feeds an entire county.* **3. a.** To supply or maintain a flow of (a material to be consumed, utilized, or worked upon): *feed ammunition to a gun crew.* **b.** To supply with fuel: *Leaking oil fed the flames.* **4. a.** To minister to; gratify: *The story fed their appetite for the morbid.* **b.** To support or promote: *feed suspicions.* **5.** *Sports.* To pass the ball or puck to (a teammate), especially in order to score. *—intr.* To eat. Used chiefly of animals. **—feed on** (or **upon**). **1.** To consume as food. **2.** To draw support or satisfaction from: *His ego feeds on flattery.*

~n. **1.** An act or instance of feeding. **2. a.** Food for animals or birds; fodder. **b.** The allowance of fodder given at one time. **3.** *Informal.* A meal. **4. a.** Material or an amount of material supplied to a machine. **b.** The act of supplying this material. **5. a.** The apparatus that supplies material to a machine. **b.** The aperture through which such material enters a machine. **—off one's feed.** *Slang.* Temporarily without appetite. [Feed, fed, fed; Middle English *feden, fed, fedde,* Old English *fēdan, fēdde, fēdd,* from Germanic.]

feed back *tr.v.* To return by feedback. *—intr.v.* To return as feedback.

feed·back (fēd′băk′) *n.* **1. a.** The return of a portion of the output of any process or system to the input, especially when used to maintain the output within predetermined limits. See **positive feedback, negative feedback. b.** The portion of the output so returned. **c.** Control of a system or process by such means: *"When feedback is possible and stable, its advantage . . . is to make performance less dependent on the load"* (Norbert Wiener). **d.** The high-pitched whistle produced in a public-address system that occurs when sound from the loudspeaker is picked up by the microphone. **2.** Any information about the result of a process; a response: *The magazine likes to get feedback from its readers.*

feedback inhibition *n.* A biological control mechanism that causes excessive accumulation of the end product of a biochemical pathway to inhibit the action of an enzyme near the beginning of the pathway.

feed·bag (fēd′băg′) *n.* A bag that fits over a horse's muzzle and holds feed. Also called "nosebag."

feed·er (fē′dər) *n.* **1. a.** One that supplies food. **b.** One that is fed, especially an animal that is being fattened. **2.** One that feeds materials into a machine for further processing. **3.** Something that contributes to the operation, maintenance, or supply of something else, as: **a.** A tributary. **b.** A secondary bus, road, airway, or railroad line linking a small community with a main bus, road, airway, or railroad line. **4.** *Electricity.* Any of the medium-voltage lines used to distribute electric power from a substation to consumers or smaller substations.

~adj. Being or functioning as a feeder: *a feeder airline.*

feed·lot (fēd′lŏt′) *n.* An area where animals are fattened up for market.

feed·pipe (fēd′pīp′) *n.* A pipe through which water or some other fluid is introduced into a system, such as the pipe through which feedwater is fed into a boiler.

feed·stock (fēd′stŏk) *n.* Raw materials fed into a machine or chemical plant for processing.

feed·wa·ter (fēd′wô′tər, -wŏt′ər) *n.* The clean, air-free water that is fed into a boiler or some other equipment or system.

feel (fēl) *v.* **felt** (fĕlt), **feeling, feels.** *—tr.* **1. a.** To perceive through the sense of touch. **b.** To perceive as a localized physical sensation: *feel a sharp pain.* **c.** To perceive as a nonlocalized physical sensation: *feel the cold.* **2. a.** To touch. **b.** To examine by touching. **c.** To test carefully; explore with caution: *feel one's way in a new job.* **3. a.** To experience (an emotion): *I felt great shame.* **b.** To be aware of; sense: *She felt his annoyance.* **c.** To suffer from; experience the impact of: *feel the loss of someone.* **d.** To be emotionally convinced of: *feel it in one's bones.* **4.** To believe or consider: *His answer was felt to be evasive.* *—intr.* **1.** To experience sensations of touch. **2.** To give or produce sensation or feeling, especially through the sense of touch: *The sheets felt smooth.* **3. a.** To perceive oneself to be: *I feel so stupid.* **b.** To have or experience a specified physical or emotional sensation: *I feel tired. He felt very sad.* **4.** To search or be guided by or as if by the sense of touch: *feeling for the light switch in the dark.* **5.** To have compassion or sympathy. Used with *with* or *for*: *I feel for him in his troubles.* **6. a.** To be emotionally moved: *feel strongly about the election.* **b.** To be guided by sentiment or emotion: *"We all do no end of feeling and we mistake it for thinking"* (Mark Twain). **—feel like.** *Informal.* To be in the mood for; have a desire for. **—feel (like) oneself.** To sense oneself as being in a normal state of health or spirits: *I don't feel quite myself today.* **—feel out.** To try cautiously or indirectly to ascertain the viewpoint of (a person) or the nature of (a situation). **—feel up to.** To feel capable of or ready for.

~n. **1. a.** The sensation experienced by touching or feeling: *the feel of a rose petal.* **b.** The act or an instance of touching or feeling: *have a feel under the chair for the pen.* **2.** The sense of touch: *rough to the feel.* **3.** The nature, condition, or quality of something perceived physically or emotionally: *the feel of a sports car; get the feel of one's audience.* [Feel, felt, felt; Middle English *felen, felde, feld,* Old English *fēlan, fēlde, fēld,* from West Germanic.]

Usage: *Feel* (verb) is followed by an adjective when the sense relates to a person's perception of his condition of being: *I was sick last week but now I feel different; today I feel strong.* The adjectives *different* and *strong* describe the subject in such examples. In other senses of *feel* an adverb is possible in the position following the verb, as, for example, when *feel* means to have an opinion, conviction, or the like: *She feels strongly about equal rights for women. He used to agree with her position, but he feels differently now.* Here *strongly* and *differently* modify the verb with respect to degree and condition.

feel·er (fē′lər) *n.* **1.** One that feels. **2.** A remark, hint, question, or the like, designed to elicit the attitude or intention of others. **3.** A sensory or tactile organ, such as an antenna, tentacle, or barbel.

feel·ing (fē′lĭng) *n.* **1. a.** The sensation involving perception by touch. **b.** A sensation perceived by touch. **c.** Any physical sensation. **2.** Any affective state of consciousness, such as that resulting from emotions, sentiments, or desires: *a feeling of excitement.* **3.** An awareness; an impression: *a feeling that one is being followed.* **4. a.** An emotional state or disposition; emotion: *expressed deep feeling.* **b.** A tender emotion; love; fondness. **5. a.** Refined sensibility, often approaching sentimentality: *a man of feeling.* **b. feelings.** Emotional responses; tendency to feel wounded, moved, offended, or the like: *hurt one's feelings.* **6.** Opinion based on emotional reaction rather than on reason. **7.** An impression produced by a person, place, thing, or event. **8. a.** An appreciative regard and understanding. Used with *for*: *a feeling for propriety.* **b.** A bent; an aptitude. Used with *for*: *a feeling for carpentry.* —See Synonyms at **opinion.**

~adj. **1. a.** Having the ability to react or feel emotionally; sentient;

PRONUNCIATION KEY

ă, pat; ā, pay; âr, care;
ä, father, are; b, bib;
ch, church; d, deed; ĕ, pet;
ē, be; f, fife; g, gag; h, hat;
hw, which; ĭ, pit; ī, pie;
îr, pier; j, judge; k, kick;
l, lid, needle; m, mum;
n, no, sudden; ng, thing;
ŏ, pot; ō, toe; ô, paw, for;
oi, noise; ou, out; o͝o, book;
o͞o, boot; p, pop; r, roar;
s, sauce; sh, ship, dish;
t, tight; th, thin, path;
th, this, bathe; ŭ, cut; ûr, fur;
v, valve; w, with; y, yes;
z, zebra, size; zh, vision;
ə, about, item, edible,
gallop, circus, peaceful

IN FOREIGN WORDS:

à, *Fr.* ami; œ, *Fr.* feu, *Ger.* schön; ü, *Fr.* tu, *Ger.* über; KH, *Ger.* ich, *Scot.* loch; N, *Fr.* bon; y′, *Fr.* Compiègne

STRESS MARKS:

Primary stress: ′
in·cite′ (ĭn-sīt′)
Secondary stress: ′
in′sight′ (ĭn′sīt′)

sensitive. **b.** Easily moved emotionally. **2.** Having sensibility; sympathetic. **3.** Expressive of sensibility; indicating emotion: *a feeling glance.* **—feel·ing·ly** *adv.*

Synonyms: *emotion, passion.*

fee simple *n., pl.* **fees simple.** *Law.* An estate in land of which the inheritor has unqualified ownership and power of disposition.

feet. Plural of **foot.** **—feet of clay.** A weakness or flaw in someone who is apparently faultless. [Biblical allusion to the "great image" described in Daniel (2:31–34): "a stone . . . smote the image upon his feet that were iron and clay, and brake them to pieces."] **—find one's feet.** To become settled or accustomed, as in a new environment. **—have** (or **keep**) **both feet on the ground.** To be or remain practical and down-to-earth. **—land on one's feet.** To recover quickly from a setback or mishap. **—on one's feet. 1.** Well after an illness. **2.** Progressing or thriving. Said of a project, business, or the like. **—run** (or **rushed**) **off one's feet.** Very busy; frantic. **—stand on one's own (two) feet.** To be or become independent. **—sweep one off one's feet. 1.** To fill with enthusiasm. **2.** To cause to fall in love; enchant; enrapture. **—vote with one's feet.** To express one's disapproval of a regime, employer, policy, or the like by resigning, physically distancing oneself, or emigrating.

fee tail *n., pl.* **fees tail.** *Law.* An estate in land limited in inheritance to a specified individual, group, or class of heirs.

feeze (fēz, fāz) *n. Regional.* **1.** A heavy impact. **2.** A state of vexation.
~*tr.v.* **feezed, feezing, feezes.** *Regional.* **1.** To drive off; put to flight. **2.** To faze; disconcert. [Middle English *fese,* from *fesen,* to drive off, Old English *fēsian*†.]

Feif·fer (fī'fər), **Jules** (1927–). U.S. cartoonist. Since 1956 he has been producing his satiric strips that feature the struggles between the individual and the state, between the races, and between the sexes. He has also written plays and screenplays.

feign (fān) *v.* **feigned, feigning, feigns.** *—tr.* **1. a.** To give a false appearance of; pretend; sham: *jump into bed and feign sleep.* **b.** To represent falsely; pretend to: *feign authorship of a novel.* **2.** To invent; make up; fabricate: *feign an experience.* **3.** To imitate: *feign another's handwriting.* *—intr.* To pretend; dissemble. —See Synonyms at **pretend.** [Middle English *feinen,* from Old French *faindre, feindre* (present stem *fei(g)n-*), from Latin *fingere,* to form, shape, alter.]

feigned (fānd) *adj.* **1.** Not real; simulated: *"those who, with a feigned modesty, condemn as useless what they write"* (John Locke). **2.** Made-up; fictitious. **—feign·ed·ly** (fā'nĭd-lē) *adv.*

Fei·ning·er (fī'nĭng-ər), **Lyonel** (1871–1956). U.S. painter and illustrator. After studying in Berlin, Hamburg, and Paris, he spent many years in Europe, returning to the United States in 1937. His delicately geometric works often feature sailboats or skyscrapers.

feint[1] (fānt) *n.* **1.** A misleading movement or feigned attack designed to draw defensive action away from an intended target or objective. **2.** A pretense intended to mislead; a stratagem. —See Synonyms at **artifice.**
~*intr.v.* **feinted, feinting, feints.** To make a feint. [French *feinte,* from Old French, from the past participle of *feindre,* to FEIGN.]

feint[2] *n. Printing.* The finest line used in the printing of ruled paper. [Variant of FAINT.]

feints. Variant of **faints.**

feist (fīst) *n.* Also **fice** (fīs). *Regional.* A small dog of mixed ancestry; mongrel. [Shortening and variation of obsolete *fisting (dog),* from obsolete *fist,* to break wind, from Middle English *fisten,* Old English *fistan* (unattested).]

feis·ty (fī'stē) *adj.* **-tier, -tiest. 1.** *Regional.* Touchy; excitable; quarrelsome. **2.** Spirited, tough, or frisky. [From FEIST.]

felafel. Variant of **falafel.**

feld·spar (fĕld'spär', fĕl'-) *n.* Also **fel·spar** (fĕl'-). Any of a group of abundant rock-forming minerals occurring in most igneous and many sedimentary and metamorphic rocks and consisting of a silicate of aluminum with one or two of the following metals: potassium, sodium, calcium, and rarely barium. [Partial translation of obsolete German *Feldspath,* "field spar" : *Feld,* field + *Spath,* spar.]

feld·spath·ic (fĕld-spăth'ĭk, fĕl-) *adj.* Of, relating to, or containing feldspar. [From obsolete German *Feldspath,* feldspar: *Feld,* field (see **feldspar**) + *Spath,* spar, from Middle High German *spat.*]

fe·li·cif·ic (fē'lə-sĭf'ĭk) *adj.* Producing or bringing about happiness. [Latin *fēlīx* (stem *fēlīc-*), favorable, fertile + -FIC.]

fe·lic·i·tate (fĭ-lĭs'ə-tāt') *tr.v.* **-tated, -tating, -tates. 1.** To wish happiness to; congratulate. **2.** *Archaic.* To make happy.
~*adj. Obsolete.* Made happy. [Latin *fēlīcitāre,* to make happy, from *fēlīx* (stem *fēlīc-*), happy, FELICIFIC.] **—fe·lic·i·ta·tor** *n.*

fe·lic·i·ta·tion (fĭ-lĭs'ə-tā'shən) *n. Usually* **felicitations.** Congratulations.

fe·lic·i·tous (fĭ-lĭs'ə-təs) *adj.* **1. a.** Well-chosen; apt; appropriate: *a felicitous comparison.* **b.** Having an appropriate and agreeable manner or style: *a felicitous writer.* **2.** Marked by well-being or good fortune: *a felicitous life.* —See Synonyms at **fit. —fe·lic·i·tous·ly** *adv.* **—fe·lic·i·tous·ness** *n.*

fe·lic·i·ty (fĭ-lĭs'ə-tē) *n., pl.* **-ties. 1. a.** Great happiness; bliss. **b.** An instance of this. **2.** Something that causes or produces happiness. **3. a.** An appropriate and pleasing manner or style: *felicity of speech.* **b.** An instance of this. [Middle English *felicite,* from Old French, from Latin *fēlīcitās* (stem *fēlīcitāt-*), from *fēlix* (stem *fēlīc-*), happy, FELICIFIC.]

fe·lid (fē'lĭd) *n.* A feline. **—fe·lid** *adj.*

fe·line (fē'līn') *adj.* **1.** Of or belonging to the family Felidae, which includes the lions, tigers, jaguars, and wild and domestic cats. **2.** Resembling or suggestive of a cat, as in suppleness, slyness, or stealthiness.
~*n.* A feline animal. [Latin *fēlīnus,* from *fēlēs*†, cat.] **—fe·line·ly** *adv.* **—fe·line·ness, fe·lin·i·ty** (fĭ-lĭn'ə-tē) *n.*

fell[1] (fĕl) *tr.v.* **felled, felling, fells. 1.** To cause to fall; cut or knock down: *fell a tree; fell an opponent.* **2.** To sew or finish (a seam) with the raw edges flattened, turned under, and stitched down.
~*n.* **1.** The timber cut down in one season. **2.** A felled seam. [Middle English *fellen,* Old English *fellan, fyllan,* to strike down, fell.] **—fell·a·ble** *adj.*

fell[2] *adj.* **1.** Of an inhumanly cruel nature; fierce; unsparing: *fell hordes.* **2.** Able to destroy; lethal: *a fell blow.* **3.** Dire; sinister: *by some fell chance.* **4.** *Scottish.* Sharp and biting: *a fell word.* **—at one fell swoop.** All at once. [Middle English *fel,* from Old French, from Medieval Latin *fellō,* wicked person, FELON.] **—fell·ness** *n.*

fell[3] *n.* The hide of an animal; a skin; a pelt. [Middle English *fel,* Old English *fell.*]

fell[4] *n. British Regional.* **1.** An upland stretch of open country; a moor. **2.** The highest point of a fell. [Middle English, from Old Norse *fjall,* hill; probably akin to Old Saxon *felis,* rock.]

fell[5]**.** Past tense of **fall.**

fel·la (fĕl'ə) *n.* Also **fel·ler** (fĕl'ər). *Informal.* **1.** A man or boy. **2.** A boyfriend or lover. **3.** A husband.

fel·lah (fĕl'ə, fə-lä') *n., pl.* **fellahin** or **fellaheen** (fĕl'ə-hēn', fə-lä'hēn'). A peasant or agricultural laborer in an Arab country, as Syria. [Arabic *fellāḥ,* dialectal variant of *fallāḥ,* from *falaḥa,* to cultivate, till.]

fell·er[1] (fĕl'ər) *n.* **1.** One that fells. **2.** A sewing machine attachment for felling seams.

feller[2]**.** Variant of **fella.**

Fel·li·ni (fə-lē'nē), **Federico** (1920–). Italian film director. His films combine social satire with elements of fantasy. His successes include *La Dolce Vita (The Sweet Life)* (1960) and *Satyricon* (1969). *Amarcord* (1974) won an Academy Award in 1975.

fell·mon·ger (fĕl'mŭng'gər, -mŏng'gər) *n. British.* One who sells hides or prepares hides for making leather. **—fell·mon·ger·ing, fell·mon·ger·y** *n.*

fel·low (fĕl'ō) *n.* **1. a.** A man or boy. **b.** *Informal.* A boyfriend or lover. **c.** *Informal.* A husband. **2. a.** Anybody in general; any human being. **b.** A person considered to be worthless or unimportant. **3.** A companion; a comrade; an associate. **4. a.** A person similar to oneself in rank, position, or background; an equal; a peer. **b.** Either of a pair; a counterpart; a mate. **5.** *Abbr.* **F, F.** A member of a learned society or similar association. **6.** *Abbr.* **F, F.** A graduate student appointed to a position granting financial aid for a period of research. **7.** *British.* **a.** An incorporated senior member of certain colleges and universities. **b.** A member of the governing body of certain colleges and universities.
~*adj.* Being of the same kind, group, occupation, society, or locality; having in common certain characteristics or interests: *fellow workers.* [Middle English *felawe,* Old English *fēolaga,* from Old Norse *fēlagi,* partner, fellow, one who lays down money : *fē,* cattle, money + *lag,* a laying down.]

fellow creature *n.* A kindred creature; especially, another member of the human race.

fellow feeling *n.* **1.** Sympathetic awareness of others; rapport. **2.** Common interests or opinions.

fellow man *n., pl.* **fellow men.** Also **fel·low·man** (fĕl'ō-măn') *pl.* **-men** (-mĕn'). **1.** All humanity regarded as united in shared experience. **2.** Any person regarded as related to one through the general human experience.

fellow servant *n. Law.* Any of a group of employees working together under such circumstances that the employer cannot be expected to protect against or be liable for harm to one employee caused by the negligence of another.

fel·low·ship (fĕl'ō-shĭp') *n.* **1. a.** The condition of being together or of sharing similar interests or experiences, as do members of a profession, religion, or nationality; companionship. **b.** The companionship of individuals in a congenial atmosphere and on equal terms. **2. a.** A union of friends or equals sharing similar interests; a club; a brotherhood. **b.** A church association. **3. a.** Friendship; comradeship. **b.** Mutual concern and trust among Christians. **4. a.** A scholarship or grant awarded to a graduate student in a college or university. **b.** The state of having been awarded such a scholarship or grant. **c.** A foundation established for the awarding of such a scholarship or grant.

fellow traveler *n.* One who sympathizes with the tenets and program of an organized group without actually joining it; especially, a supporter of the Communist Party.

fel·ly (fĕl'ē) *n., pl.* **-lies.** Also **fel·loe** (fĕl'ō). **1.** The rim of a wheel supported by spokes. **2.** A section of such a rim. [Middle English *fely,* Old English *felg,* from West Germanic *felgam* (unattested).]

fe·lo-de-se (fĕl'ō-də-sā', -sē') *n., pl.* **fe·lo·nes-de-se** (fə-lō'nēz-) or **fe·los-de-se** (fĕl'ōz-). *Law.* **1.** The act of suicide. **2.** One who commits suicide. [Medieval Latin, "felon of himself" : *felō, fellō,* FELON + *dē,* of + *sē,* ablative of *suī,* himself, oneself, from Latin.]

fel·on[1] (fĕl'ən) *n.* **1.** *Law.* A person who has committed a felony. **2.** *Archaic.* An evil person.
~*adj. Archaic.* Evil; cruel. [Middle English *feloun,* from Old French *felon,* from Medieval Latin *fellō* (stem *fellōn-*), from Vulgar Latin *fellō*† (unattested).]

felon[2] *n.* A purulent infection at the end of a finger near or around

PRONUNCIATION KEY

ă, pat; ā, pay; âr, care;
ä, father, are; b, bib;
ch, church; d, deed; ĕ, pet;
ē, be; f, fife; g, gag; h, hat;
hw, which; ĭ, pit; ī, pie;
îr, pier; j, judge; k, kick;
l, lid, needle; m, mum;
n, no, sudden; ng, thing;
ŏ, pot; ō, toe; ô, paw, for;
oi, noise; ou, out; o͝o, book;
o͞o, boot; p, pop; r, roar;
s, sauce; sh, ship, dish;
t, tight; th, thin, path;
th, this, bathe; ŭ, cut; ûr, fur;
v, valve; w, with; y, yes;
z, zebra, size; zh, vision;
ə, about, item, edible,
gallop, circus, peaceful

IN FOREIGN WORDS:

å, *Fr.* ami; œ, *Fr.* feu, *Ger.* schön; ü, *Fr.* tu, *Ger.* über;
KH, *Ger.* ich, *Scot.* loch;
N, *Fr.* bon; y', *Fr.* Compiègne

STRESS MARKS:

Primary stress: '
in·cite' (ĭn-sīt')
Secondary stress: '
in'sight' (ĭn'sīt')

the nail or the bone. [Middle English *feloun,* from Old French, possibly from Latin *fel,* bile, venom.]

fe·lo·ni·ous (fə-lō′nē-əs) *adj.* **1.** *Law.* **a.** Of or pertaining to a felony. **b.** Characterized by or of the nature of a felony: *felonious intent.* **2.** *Archaic.* Evil; wicked. **—fe·lo·ni·ous·ly** *adv.* **—fe·lo·ni·ous·ness** *n.*

fel·on·ry (fĕl′ən-rē) *n.* **1.** Felons collectively. **2.** *Australian.* Formerly, the convict population of a penal settlement.

fel·o·ny (fĕl′ə-nē) *n., pl.* **-nies.** *Law.* **1.** Any of several crimes, such as murder, rape, or burglary, considered more serious than a misdemeanor and punishable by a more stringent sentence. Compare **misdemeanor. 2.** Any of several crimes in early English law that were punishable by forfeiture of land or goods and by possible loss of life or a bodily part.

fel·site (fĕl′sīt′) *n.* A fine-grained igneous rock, chiefly feldspar and quartz. [FELS(PAR) + -ITE.] **—fel·sit·ic** (fĕl-sĭt′ĭk) *adj.*

felspar. Variant of **feldspar.**

felt[1] (fĕlt) *n.* **1.** A fabric of matted, compressed animal fibers, such as wool or fur, sometimes mixed with vegetable or synthetic fibers. **2.** Any fabric or material resembling this. **3.** Something made of felt or a similar material.
~*adj.* **1.** Made of felt. **2.** Pertaining or similar to felt.
~*v.* **felted, felting, felts.** *—tr.* **1.** To make into felt. **2.** To cover with felt. *—intr.* To become like felt; mat together. [Middle English *felt,* Old English *felt,* from West Germanic.]

felt[2]. Past tense and past participle of **feel.**

felt·ing (fĕl′tĭng) *n.* **1.** The practice or process of making felt. **2.** The materials from which felt is made. **3.** Felted fabric.

fe·luc·ca (fə-lo͞o′kə, -lŭk′ə) *n.* A narrow, swift vessel, chiefly of the Mediterranean, propelled by lateen sails or oars or both. [Italian *feluc(c)a,* from obsolete Spanish *faluca,* from Arabic *fulk,* ship.]

fel·wort (fĕl′wûrt′, -wôrt′) *n.* Any of several plants of the genera *Gentianella* or *Swertia;* especially, *G. amarella,* having small, purplish flowers. [Middle English *feldwort,* Old English *feldwyrt* : *feld,* FIELD + *wyrt,* WORT.]

fem. 1. female. 2. feminine.

FEM field-emission microscope; field-emission microscopy.

fe·male (fē′māl′) *adj. Abbr.* **f, F, f., F., fem. 1.** Of, pertaining to, or designating the sex that produces ova. **2.** Characteristic of or appropriate to this sex; feminine. **3.** Consisting of members of this sex. **4.** *Botany.* **a.** Pertaining to or designating an organ, such as a pistil or ovary, that functions in producing seeds or spores after fertilization. **b.** Bearing pistils but not stamens: *female flowers.* **5.** Designating or having a part, such as a slot or receptacle, designed to receive a complementary male part, such as a plug or prongs.
~*n. Abbr.* **f, F, f., F., fem. 1.** A member of the sex that produces ova. **2.** Anything or anyone female. **3.** A woman or girl, as distinguished from a man or boy. **4.** *Botany.* A plant having only pistillate flowers. [Middle English, variant (influenced by *male)* of *femelle,* from Old French, from Latin *fēmella,* diminutive of *fēmina,* woman, female.] **—fe·male·ness** *n.*

female impersonator *n.* A male entertainer who dresses up as a woman.

feme (fĕm, fēm) *n.* **1.** *Law.* A wife. **2.** *Obsolete.* A woman. [Norman French, from Latin *fēmina,* woman, FEMALE.]

feme cov·ert (fĕm′ kŭv′ərt, fēm′) *n. Law.* A married woman.

feme sole (fĕm′ sōl′, fēm′) *n. Law.* A single woman, whether divorced, widowed, or never married.

fem·i·ne·i·ty (fĕm′ə-nē′ə-tē) *n.* Womanliness; femininity.

fem·i·nie (fĕm′ə-nē) *n. Archaic.* Women collectively; womankind. [Middle English, from Old French, from Latin *fēmina,* FEMALE.]

fem·i·nine (fĕm′ə-nĭn) *adj. Abbr.* **f., F., fem. 1.** Of or belonging to the female sex. Said especially of members of the human species. **2.** Characterized by or possessing qualities generally attributed to or considered appropriate to a woman; womanly: *"an artist of feminine and receptive temperament"* (Havelock Ellis). **3.** Effeminate; womanish. **4.** *Grammar.* Indicating or belonging to the gender that includes words and grammatical forms associated chiefly with femaleness: *the feminine pronoun "she"; a feminine noun.* Compare **masculine, neuter.**
~*n. Abbr.* **f., F., fem.** *Grammar.* **1.** The feminine gender. **2.** A word or form belonging to that gender. [Middle English, from Old French, from Latin *fēminīnus,* from *fēmina,* FEMALE.] **—fem·i·nine·ly** *adv.* **—fem·i·nine·ness** *n.*

feminine ending *n.* **1.** The termination of a line or verse in an unaccented syllable. **2.** *Grammar.* A final syllable or ending that marks or forms words in the feminine gender; for example, the ending *-ess* added to *lion* to form *lioness.*

feminine rhyme *n.* **1.** A rhyme of two syllables in which the second syllable is unstressed; for example, *follow* and *hollow; brightly* and *nightly.* **2.** A rhyme of three syllables in which only the first syllable is stressed; for example, *edible* and *incredible.* Compare **masculine rhyme.**

fem·i·nin·i·ty (fĕm′ə-nĭn′ə-tē) *n., pl.* **-ties. 1.** The quality or condition of being feminine; womanhood; womanliness. **2.** Women collectively.

fem·i·nism (fĕm′ə-nĭz′əm) *n.* **1.** A social movement that seeks to change the traditional role and image of women, to eliminate sexism, and to heighten appreciation of the experiences and qualities unique to the female sex. See **Women's Liberation Movement. 2.** The doctrine of this movement. **—fem·i·nist** *n. & adj.*

fem·i·nize (fĕm′ə-nīz′) *v.* **-nized, -nizing, -nizes.** *—tr.* To make feminine. *—intr.* To become feminine. **—fem·i·ni·za·tion** (fĕm′ə-nĭ-zā′shən) *n.*

femme (fĕm) *n.* A woman who plays the female role in a lesbian relationship.

femme fa·tale (fĕm′ fə-tăl′, -täl′, făm′) *n., pl.* **femmes fatales** *(pronounced as singular).* A woman whose sexual attractiveness leads a man into compromising or dangerous situations. [French.]

fem·o·ral (fĕm′ər-əl) *adj.* Of or pertaining to the thigh or the femur: *femoral artery.* [Latin *femur* (stem *femor-*), FEMUR.]

femto- *prefix. Symbol* **f** Indicates one quadrillionth (10^{-15}); for example, **femtometer.** [Danish or Norwegian *femten,* fifteen, from Old Norse *fimmtān.*]

fem·to·joule (fĕm′tə-jo͞ol′, -joul′) *n. Abbr.* **fJ** 10^{-15} joule.

fem·tom·e·ter (fĕm-tŏm′ə-tər) *n. Abbr.* **fm** 10^{-15} meter.

fe·mur (fē′mər) *n., pl.* **-murs** or **femora** (fĕm′ər-ə). **1. a.** The proximal bone of the lower or hind limb in vertebrates, situated between the pelvis and knee in humans. Also called "thighbone." **b.** The thigh. **2.** The usually stout third segment of an insect's leg. [Latin *femur*†, thigh.]

fen[1] (fĕn) *n.* Low, flat, swampy land; a bog; a marsh. [Middle English *fen,* Old English *fenn,* from Germanic.] **—fen·ny** *adj.*

fen[2] *n., pl.* **fen.** A coin that is equal to $1/100$ of the yuan of China. Also called "jiao." See feature at **currency.** [Mandarin Chinese *fēn,* division, part.]

fence (fĕns) *n.* **1.** A structure serving as an enclosure, barrier, or boundary, usually made of posts or stakes joined together by boards, wire, or rails. **2.** *Archaic.* Something intended as a means of defense; a protection. **3.** The art or practice of swordplay; fencing. **4. a.** One who receives and sells stolen goods. **b.** A place where such goods are received and sold. **5.** An attachment on a machine or tool that directs, regulates, and limits its action. **—on the fence.** *Informal.* Undecided as to which of two sides to support, especially in order to protect one's own interests; neutral. **—mend one's fences.** To restore good relations.
~*v.* **fenced, fencing, fences.** *—tr.* **1.** To surround or close in by means of a fence. **2.** To separate or close off by means of a fence. **3.** *Archaic.* To defend or ward off. **4.** To sell (stolen goods) to a fence. *—intr.* **1.** To practice or demonstrate the art of fencing. **2.** To engage in the art of skillful conversation or debate. **3.** To avoid giving direct answers; be evasive. **4.** To act as a fence for stolen goods. [Middle English *fens,* short for *defens,* DEFENSE.]

fenc·er (fĕn′sər) *n.* **1.** A person who fences, as with a foil; a swordsman. **2.** A person who erects or repairs fences.

fence·row (fĕns′rō′) *n.* The uncultivated land alongside a fence.

fen·ci·ble (fĕn′sə-bəl) *n.* Formerly, a soldier enlisted for home service only. [Middle English, aphetic variant of DEFENSIBLE.]

fenc·ing (fĕn′sĭng) *n.* **1.** The art, practice, or sport of using a foil, épée, or saber; swordplay. **2.** The art or practice of skillful conversation or debate; repartee. **3.** Evasiveness in answering questions or giving information. **4. a.** Material, such as wire, stakes, rails, and the like, used in the construction of fences. **b.** Fences collectively. **c.** The work, skill, or business of erecting or repairing fences.

fend (fĕnd) *v.* **fended, fending, fends.** *—tr. Archaic.* To defend. *—intr.* To resist. **—fend for oneself.** To provide for oneself; survive without help; manage alone. **—fend off.** To turn aside; deflect; parry. [Middle English *fenden,* shortening of *defenden,* to DEFEND.]

fend·er (fĕn′dər) *n.* **1.** One that fends or wards off. **2.** A shaped metal structure or a portion of the automotive body over each wheel of an automotive vehicle. **3.** A usually metal structure over the top of a bicycle or motorcycle wheel, placed so as to block thrown-up water and mud; mudguard. **4.** A device at the front end of a streetcar or locomotive designed to push aside obstructions. **5.** A metal device placed in front of a fireplace to keep hot coals and debris from falling out; a fireguard. **6.** *Nautical.* A device, such as a bundle of rope, a piece of timber, or an automobile tire, used on the side of a vessel or dock to absorb impact or friction.

fen·es·tel·la (fĕn′ə-stĕl′ə) *n., pl.* **-tellae** (-stĕl′ē′). **1.** A small niche in the wall of a church containing the piscina. **2.** *Architecture.* A small window. [Latin, diminutive of *fenestra,* window.]

fe·nes·tra (fĭ-nĕs′trə) *n., pl.* **-trae** (-trē′). **1.** *Anatomy.* A small opening; especially, either of two apertures in the medial wall of the middle ear. **2.** A windowlike opening. **3.** *Biology.* A transparent spot or marking, as on the wing of an insect. [New Latin, from Latin *fenestra*†, opening in the wall, window.]

fen·es·trat·ed (fĕn′ə-strā′tĭd) *adj.* Also **fen·es·trate** (fĕn′ə-strāt′, fĭ-nĕs′trāt′) (especially for sense 2). **1.** Having windows or windowlike openings. **2.** *Biology.* Having fenestrae. [Latin *fenestrātus,* past participle of *fenestrāre,* to provide with windows or openings, from *fenestra,* window, FENESTRA.]

fen·es·tra·tion (fĕn′ə-strā′shən) *n.* **1.** *Architecture.* The design and placement of windows in a building. **2.** An opening in a structure. **3.** In surgery, the cutting of an opening from the external auditory canal to the labyrinth of the internal ear to restore hearing.

Fe·ni·an (fē′nē-ən) *n.* **1. a. Fenians.** A legendary group of heroic Irish warriors of the 2nd and 3rd centuries A.D. Also called "Fianna." **b.** A member of this group. **2.** A member of a secret organization in the United States and Ireland in the mid-19th century, whose goal was the overthrow of British rule in Ireland. **3.** *Sometimes* **fenian.** Loosely, a supporter of the republican cause in Northern Ireland. [Sense 2 : from Old Irish *féne,* an ancient Irish people, confused with *fiann,* legendary group of warriors, after *Fíann,* legendary hero.] **—Fe·ni·an** *adj.* **—Fe·ni·an·ism** *n.*

felucca *Swift lateen-rigged feluccas still ply parts of the Mediterranean. This one was photographed on the Nile near Luxor in Egypt.*

fencing *Two fencers in combat, one lunging to strike the chest of his opponent with his foil.*

fen·nec (fĕn′ĭk) n. A nocturnal small fox, *Fennecus zerda,* of desert regions of northern Africa, having fawn-colored fur and large, pointed ears. [Arabic *fanak, fenek,* fox, small furry animal.]

fen·nel (fĕn′əl) n. **1. a.** A plant, *Foeniculum vulgare,* native to Eurasia, having finely dissected leaves, clusters of small yellow flowers, and aromatic seeds. **b.** The seeds or leaves of this plant, used for flavoring. **2.** A variety of this plant, **finochio** *(see).* **3.** Any of several similar or related plants. [Middle English *fenel,* Old English *fenol, finugle,* from Vulgar Latin *fēnoclum* (unattested), from Latin *fēniculum,* diminutive of *fēnum, faenum,* hay.]

fen·u·greek (fĕn′yōō-grēk′) n. **1.** A cloverlike Eurasian plant, *Trigonella foenum-graecum,* having white flowers and pungent, aromatic seeds used as flavoring. **2.** The seeds of this plant. [Middle English *fenigrek,* from Old French *fenugrec,* from Latin *fēnugraecum,* from *fēnum graecum,* "Greek hay" (from the use of the dried plant as fodder).]

fen·u·ron (fĕn′yə-rŏn′) n. A white compound, $C_9H_{12}N_2O$, used as a herbicide. [*fen-,* alteration of PHEN- + U(REA) + -ON.]

feoff (fĕf, fēf) tr.v. **feoffed, feoffing, feoffs.** To grant a feudal estate or fee to; enfeoff.
~n. A feudal estate, a **fee** *(see).* [Middle English *feoffen, feffen,* from Norman French *feoffer,* from Old French *fieffer,* from *fief,* FIEF.]

feoff·ee (fĕ-fē′, fē-fē′) n. A person to whom a feoffment is granted.

feoff·er, feof·for (fĕf′ər, fē′fər) n. A person who grants a feoffment.

feoff·ment (fĕf′mənt, fēf′-) n. A grant of lands as a fee.

-fer *suffix.* Indicates agency, bearing, or production; for example, **aquifer, conifer.** [Latin, from *ferre,* to carry, bear.]

fe·ral (fîr′əl, fĕr′-) adj. **1.** Existing in a wild or untamed state; especially, having reverted to such a state from domestication. **2.** Of or characteristic of a wild animal; savage. [Latin *fera,* wild animal, from *ferus,* wild.]

fer·bam (fûr′băm′) n. A black iron compound, $C_9H_{18}FeN_3S_6$, used as an agricultural fungicide. [*Fer*ric dimethyl-dithiocar*bam*ate.]

Fer·ber (fûr′bər), **Edna** (1887–1968). U.S. author. She wrote several best-selling novels, including her Pulitzer Prize winner *So Big* (1924), *Show Boat* (1926), and *Giant* (1952), a number of plays, and many magazine articles that examined and exalted the American spirit. Many of her works were made into successful movies.

fer-de-lance (fĕr′də-läns′, -läns′) n. A venomous tropical American snake, *Bothrops atrox,* having brown and grayish markings. [French, iron (head) of a lance.]

Fer·di·nand II (fûrd′n-änd′) (1578–1637). King of Bohemia (1617–37) and Hungary (1618–37) and Holy Roman Emperor (1619–37).

Ferdinand V, II, and III, also known as "Ferdinand the Catholic" (1452–1516). King of Castile as Ferdinand V (1474–1504), king of Aragon as Ferdinand II (1479–1516), and king of Naples as Ferdinand III (1504–16), joint ruler with his wife, Isabella I of Castile. He and Isabella sent Columbus to America in 1492.

fere (fîr) n. *Archaic.* **1.** A companion. **2.** A spouse. [Middle English *fere,* Old English *gefēra.*]

fer·e·to·ry (fĕr′ə-tôr′ē, -tōr′ē) n., pl. **-ries.** **1.** A shrine to hold the relics of saints. **2.** An area of a church in which such shrines are kept. [Middle English *fertre, feretory,* from Old French *fiertre,* from Latin *feretrum,* bier, from Greek *pheretron,* from *pherein,* to bear, carry.]

fe·ri·a (fîr′ē-ə, fĕr′-) n., pl. **-as** or **feriae** (fîr′ē-ē′, fĕr′-). *Ecclesiastical.* A day of the week on which no feast is observed. [From Medieval Latin *fēria,* from Late Latin, day of the week, from Latin *fēriae,* days of rest, holidays, festivals.] **—fe·ri·al** (fîr′ē-əl, fĕr′-) adj.

fe·rine (fîr′īn′) adj. Untamed; feral. [Latin *ferīnus,* from *fera,* wild animal. See **feral.**]

fer·i·ty (fĕr′ə-tē) n. **1.** The condition of being feral; existence in a wild state. **2.** The condition of being savage; ferocity. [Latin *feritās* (stem *feritāt-*), from *ferus,* wild. See **feral.**]

Fer·lin·ghet·ti (fûr′lĭng-gĕt′ē), **Lawrence** (1920–). U.S. poet. He was a leader of the 1950's beat movement that opposed social, moral, and literary conventions. His collections include *Pictures of the Gone World* (1955) and *Tyrannus Nix?* (1969).

Fer·mat (fĕr-mä′), **Pierre de** (1601–65). French mathematician. He formulated Fermat's theorem and the least-time law, Fermat's principle, to explain the diffraction of light.

fer·ma·ta (fĕr-mä′tə) n. *Music.* **1.** The holding or sustaining of a tone, chord, or rest beyond its indicated time value. **2.** The sign that indicates such a prolongation. [Italian, pause, stop, from the feminine past participle of *fermare,* to pause, stop, from Latin *firmāre,* to make firm, from *firmus,* firm.]

Fermat's principle n. *Physics.* The principle that the path taken by a ray of light through any system is always the one that takes the shortest possible time.

Fermat's theorem n. The theorem, postulated by Pierre de Fermat but never proven, that the equation $x^n + y^n = z^n$, where n is an integer, has no integral solutions for x, y, and z for any value of n greater than 2. Also called "Fermat's last theorem."

fer·ment (fûr′mĕnt′) n. **1.** Anything that causes fermentation, such as a yeast, bacterium, mold, or enzyme. **2.** Fermentation. **3.** A state of agitation; unrest; turbulence.
~v. (fər-mĕnt′) **fermented, -menting, -ments.** —tr. **1.** To produce by or as if by fermentation. **2.** To cause to undergo fermentation. **3.** To generate or stir up (trouble, for example). —intr. **1.** To undergo fermentation. **2.** To be turbulent; seethe. [Middle English, leaven, yeast, from Old French, from Latin *fermentum.*] **—fer·**

ment·a·bil·i·ty (fər-mĕn′tə-bĭl′ə-tē) n. **—fer·ment·a·ble** (fər-mĕn′tə-bəl) adj. **—fer·ment·er** n.

fer·men·ta·tion (fûr′mĕn-tā′shən) n. **1.** Any of a group of chemical reactions induced by living or nonliving ferments that split complex organic compounds into relatively simple substances; especially, the anaerobic conversion of sugar to carbon dioxide and alcohol by yeast, as in the making of alcoholic beverages. **2.** Unrest; commotion; agitation.

fer·men·ta·tive (fər-mĕn′tə-tĭv) adj. **1. a.** Causing fermentation. **b.** Capable of causing or undergoing fermentation. **2.** Pertaining to or of the nature of fermentation.

fer·mi (fĕr′mē, fûr′-) n. A unit of length equal to one femtometer (10^{-15} meter), used in nuclear physics. [After Enrico FERMI.]

Fer·mi (fĕr′mē), **Enrico** (1901–54). Italian-born physicist. He left Italy in 1938 to settle in the United States. That same year he was awarded a Nobel Prize for his work on artificial radioactivity caused by neutron bombardment. In 1942 Fermi produced the first controlled nuclear chain reaction in a squash court at the University of Chicago. He also helped develop the first atomic bomb.

Fer·mi-Dir·ac statistics (fĕr′mē-dĭ-răk′) n. *Physics.* A type of quantum statistics used for elementary particles that obey the exclusion principle (only two particles can occupy a given energy level). Compare **Bose-Einstein statistics.** [After Enrico FERMI and Paul DIRAC.]

fer·mi·on (fĕr′mē-ŏn′, fûr′-) n. A particle, such as an electron, proton, or neutron, having half-integral spin and obeying statistical rules requiring that not more than one in a set of identical particles may occupy a particular quantum state. Compare **boson.** [After Enrico FERMI.]

fer·mi·um (fĕr′mē-əm, fûr′-) n. *Symbol* **Fm** A synthetic transuranic metallic element having 10 isotopes with mass numbers ranging from 248 to 257 and corresponding half-lives ranging from 0.6 minute to approximately 100 days. Atomic number 100. [New Latin, after Enrico FERMI.]

fern (fûrn) n. Any of numerous flowerless, seedless pteridophytic plants of the class Filicinae, characteristically having fronds with divided leaflets, and reproducing by means of spores produced on the undersurface of the fronds. [Middle English *fern,* Old English *fearn.*]

Fer·nan·del (fâr′năn-dĕl′), born Fernand Joseph Désiré Contandin (1903–71). French comedian with a toothy grin. He starred in the 1950's *Don Camillo* film series. Other films include *Fric Frac* (1939), *The Red Inn* (1951), and *The Sheep Has Five Legs* (1954).

fern·er·y (fûr′nə-rē) n., pl. **-ies.** **1.** A place or container in which ferns are grown. **2.** A bed or collection of ferns.

fern seed pl.n. The minute spores of ferns, formerly believed to be seeds, and supposed to have the power of making one invisible.

fern·y (fûr′nē) adj. **-ier, -iest.** **1.** Abounding in ferns. **2.** Of, pertaining to, or characteristic of ferns.

fe·ro·cious (fə-rō′shəs) adj. **1.** Extremely savage; fierce. **2.** Extreme; intense: *a ferocious blizzard.* —See Synonyms at **cruel.** [Latin *ferōx* (stem *ferōc-*), wild, fierce.] **—fe·ro·cious·ly** adv. **—fe·ro·cious·ness** n.

fe·roc·i·ty (fə-rŏs′ə-tē) n., pl. **-ties.** The condition or quality of being ferocious.

-ferous *suffix.* Indicates bearing, producing, or containing; for example, **crystalliferous, umbelliferous.** [Middle English : -FER + -OUS.]

Fer·ra·ra (fə-rär′ə). Capital city of the province of the same name in the Emilia-Romagna region of northern Italy.

fer·rate (fĕr′āt′) n. A **ferrite** *(see).* [FERR(O)- + -ATE.]

fer·re·dox·in (fĕr′ĭ-dŏk′sĭn) n. Any of a group of red-brown iron-containing proteins that are strong reducing agents and function in electron transport in many organisms, as in photosynthetic plants. [Latin *ferrum,* iron + REDOX + -IN.]

fer·ret¹ (fĕr′ĭt) n. **1.** A domesticated, usually albino form of the Old World polecat, often trained to hunt rats or rabbits. **2.** A **black-footed ferret** *(see).*
~v. **ferreted, -reting, -rets.** —tr. **1.** To hunt (rats, for example) with a ferret. **2.** To drive out; expel: *ferret the troublemakers from the team.* **3.** To uncover and bring to light by intensive investigation. Used with *out:* *"piqued by the failure of all his endeavors to ferret out the assassins"* (Edgar Allan Poe). —intr. **1.** To hunt with a ferret or ferrets. **2.** To search about; rummage. [Middle English *feret, firette,* from Old French *fuiret, furet,* from Vulgar Latin *fūrittus* (unattested), little thief, from Latin *fūr,* thief. See **furtive.**] **—fer·ret·er** n. **—fer·ret·y** adj.

ferret² n. Also **fer·ret·ing** (fĕr′ĭ-tĭng). A narrow piece of tape used to bind or edge fabric. [Probably from Italian *fioretti,* floss silk, plural of *fioretto,* diminutive of *fiore,* flower, from Latin *flōs* (stem *flōr-*), flower.]

ferri– *prefix.* *Chemistry.* Indicates iron, especially with a valence of 3; for example, **ferricyanide.** [Latin *ferrum,* iron.]

fer·ri·age (fĕr′ē-ĭj) n. **1.** The act or business of ferrying. **2.** The toll charged for ferrying.

fer·ric (fĕr′ĭk) adj. Of, pertaining to, or containing iron; especially, containing iron with a valence of 3 or with a valence higher than in a corresponding ferrous compound. [FERR(O)- + -IC.]

ferric oxide n. A dark compound, Fe_2O_3, occurring naturally as hematite ore and rust, and used in pigments, metallurgy, polishing compounds, and magnetic tapes.

fer·ri·cy·an·ic acid (fĕr′ĭ-sī-ăn′ĭk, fĕr′ĭ-) n. A reddish-brown solid compound, $H_3[Fe(CN)_6]$.

fer·ri·cy·a·nide (fĕr′ĭ-sī′ə-nīd′, fĕr′ĭ-) *n.* Any of various salts derived from ferricyanic acid and used in making blue pigments.

fer·rif·er·ous (fə-rĭf′ər-əs, fĕ-) *adj.* Containing or yielding iron: *ferriferous rock.* [FERRI- + -FEROUS.]

fer·ri·mag·net·ic (fĕr′ĭ-măg-nĕt′ĭk, fĕr′ĭ-) *adj.* Pertaining to or characteristic of substances, such as certain ferrites and garnets, that have magnetic properties similar to ferromagnetic materials. Ferrimagnetic substances have weaker magnetism than ferromagnetic substances; their properties arise because the different types of atom in the crystal have unequal antiparallel magnetic moments. **—fer·ri·mag·net·ism** (fĕr′ĭ-măg′nə-tĭz′əm, fĕr′ĭ-) *n.*

Fer·ris wheel (fĕr′ĭs) *n.* Often **ferris wheel.** A large, upright, rotating wheel having suspended cars in which passengers ride for amusement. [Designed for the Chicago World's Fair in 1893 by George W.G. *Ferris* (1859–96), U.S. engineer.]

fer·rite (fĕr′īt′) *n.* **1.** Any of a group of nonmetallic, ceramiclike, usually ferromagnetic compounds of ferric oxide with other oxides; especially, such a compound with spinel crystalline structure, characterized by extremely high electrical resistivity and used in computer memory elements, permanent magnets, and various solid-state devices. Also called "ferrate." **2.** Iron having a body-centered cubic crystalline form, occurring commonly in steel, cast iron, and pig iron below 910°C. [FERR(O)- + -ITE.]

fer·ri·tin (fĕr′ĭ-tĭn) *n.* An iron-containing protein complex that is one of the forms in which iron is stored in the tissues. [FERRITE + -IN.]

ferro-, ferr– *prefix.* Indicates: **1.** Iron; for example, **ferromagnetic, ferrite. 2.** Iron in alloy; for example, **ferromanganese. 3.** Iron in its ferrous valence; for example, **ferrocyanide.** [Latin *ferrum,* iron.]

fer·ro·al·loy (fĕr′ō-ăl′oi′, -ə-loi′) *n.* Any of various alloys of iron and one or more other elements, such as manganese or silicon, used in the production of steel.

fer·ro·cene (fĕr′ō-sēn′, fĕr′ə-) *n.* A reddish crystalline compound, Fe(C₅H₅), the first known sandwich compound.

fer·ro·chro·mi·um (fĕr′ō-krō′mē-əm) *n.* An alloy of iron and chromium (50–70%) used in making chromium alloy steels.

fer·ro·con·crete (fĕr′ō-kŏn′krēt′, -kŏn-krēt′) *n.* **Reinforced concrete** *(see).*

fer·ro·cy·an·ic acid (fĕr′ō-sī-ăn′ĭk) *n.* A solid, white compound, H₄Fe(CN)₆.

fer·ro·cy·a·nide (fĕr′ō-sī′ə-nīd′) *n.* A salt derived from ferrocyanic acid, the sodium and potassium salts being used in making blue pigments, blueprint paper, and ferricyanide.

fer·ro·e·lec·tric (fĕr′ō-ĭ-lĕk′trĭk) *adj.* Of or pertaining to a crystalline dielectric that can be given a permanent electric polarization by application of an electric field.
~*n.* A ferroelectric substance. **—fer·ro·e·lec·tric·i·ty** (fĕr′ō-ĭ-lĕk′trĭs′ə-tē, fĕr′ō-ē′lĕk-) *n.*

fer·ro·mag·ne·sian (fĕr′ō-măg-nē′zhən, -shən) *adj.* Containing iron and magnesium. Said especially of certain minerals.

fer·ro·mag·net (fĕr′ō-măg′nĭt) *n.* **1.** A ferromagnetic substance; broadly, a substance with magnetic properties resembling those of iron. **2.** A **permanent magnet** *(see).*

fer·ro·mag·net·ism (fĕr′ō-măg′nə-tĭz′əm) *n.* A type of magnetism occurring in substances, such as iron, nickel, and cobalt, that exhibit extremely high magnetic permeability, the ability to acquire high magnetization and saturation in relatively weak magnetic fields, a large positive magnetic susceptibility, and magnetic hysteresis. **—fer·ro·mag·net·ic** (fĕr′ō-măg-nĕt′ĭk) *n.*

fer·ro·man·ga·nese (fĕr′ō-măng′gə-nēz′, -nēs′) *n.* An alloy of iron and manganese (70–80%).

fer·ro·sil·i·con (fĕr′ō-sĭl′ĭ-kən, -kŏn′) *n.* An alloy of iron and silicon (up to 15%) used in making alloy steels.

fer·ro·type (fĕr′ə-tīp′) *n.* **1.** A positive photograph made directly on an iron plate varnished with a sensitized film. Also called "tintype." **2.** The process by which such photographs are made.

fer·rous (fĕr′əs) *adj.* Of, pertaining to, or containing iron, especially with a valence of 2. [New Latin *ferrosus* : Latin *ferrum,* iron + -OUS.]

ferrous oxide *n.* A black powdery compound, FeO, used in the manufacture of steel, green heat-absorbing glass, and enamels.

ferrous sulfate *n.* A greenish crystalline compound, FeSO₄·7H₂O, used as a pigment, fertilizer, feed additive, and in the medical treatment of iron-deficiency anemia. Also called "green vitriol."

ferrous sulfide *n.* A black to brown sulfide of iron, FeS, used in making hydrogen sulfide.

fer·ru·gi·nous (fə-rōō′jə-nəs, fĕ-) *adj.* **1.** Of, containing, or similar to iron. **2.** Having the color of iron rust. [Latin *ferrūginus,* from *ferrūgō* (stem *ferrūgin-*), iron rust, from *ferrum,* iron.]

fer·rule, fer·ule (fĕr′əl, -ool′) *n.* **1.** A metal ring or cap attached to or near the end of a pole, cane, wooden handle, or the like, for reinforcement or to prevent splitting. **2.** A bushing used to secure a pipe joint.
~*tr.v.* **ferruled, -ruling, -rules.** To furnish with a ferrule. [Variant (influenced by Latin *ferrum,* iron) of earlier *verrel, virl,* from Middle English *verelle, virol,* from Old French *virelle, virole,* from Latin *viriola,* little bracelet, diminutive of *viriae,* bracelets.]

fer·ry (fĕr′ē) *n., pl.* **-ries. 1.** A commercial service for transporting people, vehicles, goods, or the like, across a body of water. **2.** A boat used in such transportation. **3.** The place of embarkation or disembarkation of a ferryboat. **4.** A franchise or legal right to operate such a service for a fee. **5.** The transporting of a vehicle, especially an aircraft, under its own power to its eventual user. **6.** A module for transporting astronauts from a spacecraft to the surface of a planet.
~*v.* **ferried, -rying, -ries.** —*tr.* **1.** To transport (a person or thing) across a body of water. **2.** To cross (a body of water) on or as if on a ferry. **3.** To deliver (a vehicle, especially an aircraft) under its own power to its eventual user. **4.** To transport (people or goods), especially to and fro over short distances. —*intr.* To cross a body of water on or as if on a ferry. [Middle English *fery, ferie,* probably from Old Norse *ferja.*]

fer·ry·boat (fĕr′ē-bōt′) *n.* A boat used to ferry passengers or goods.

fer·ry·man (fĕr′ē-mən) *n., pl.* **-men** (-mĭn). A person who owns, administers, or operates a ferry.

fer·tile (fûrt′l) *adj.* **1.** *Biology.* **a.** Capable of reproducing. **b.** Capable of growing and developing; able to mature: *fertile seeds.* **2.** *Botany.* Capable of producing spores, pollen, seeds, or fruit. **3.** Rich in material needed to sustain plant growth: *fertile soil.* **4.** Producing many offspring. **5.** Highly or continuously productive; prolific: *a fertile imagination.* **6.** *Physics.* Capable of being converted into fissionable material. [Middle English, from Old French, from Latin *fertilis,* from *ferre,* to bear, carry, produce.] **—fer·tile·ly** *adv.* **—fer·tile·ness** *n.*

fern

THE DOUBLE LIFE OF A FERN
Survivors from 370 million years ago

Ferns were among the first plants on earth to grow big aerial leaves that could photosynthesize sunlight in the way most plants do today. Fossil evidence shows that they appeared, along with the primitive club mosses and horsetails, during the Devonian period about 370 million years ago. Descendants of early ferns survive today, some as high as 15 meters (49 feet) in tropical rain forests. Their slender trunks produce new fronds only at the crowns.

There are at least 10,000—possibly 15,000 — species of fern. They grow best in a hot, damp climate but have spread to most regions of the earth. A fern's life cycle has two distinct stages: the main plant, which produces spores, not flowers; and a very small plant, which is the sexual stage and produces new main plants.

ADAPTABLE *Ferns have adapted to most climates. These plants flourish on a rugged Welsh hillside.*

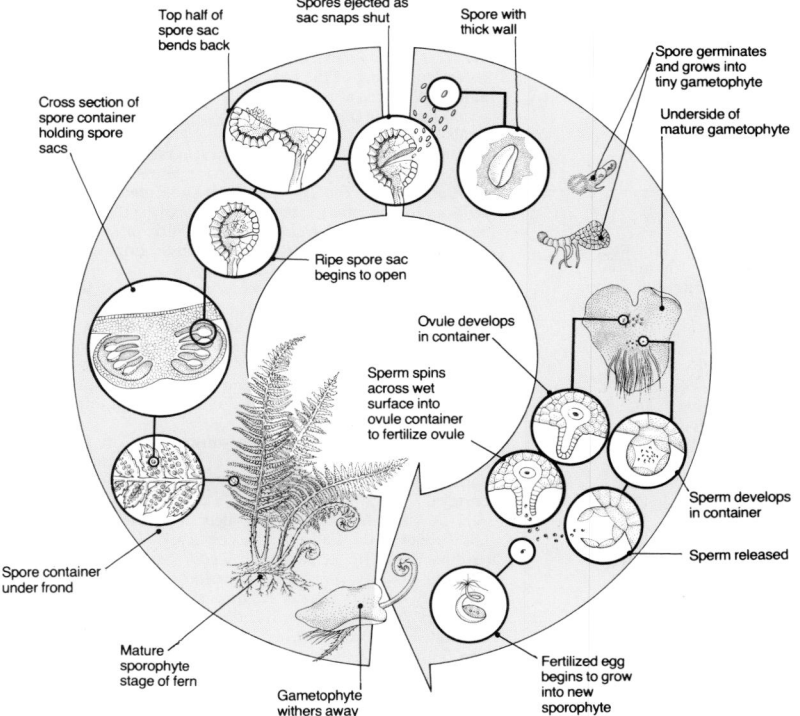

LIFE CYCLE *The fern exists in two stages, one tiny, the other large. The large stage, the sporophyte, produces spores in containers under its leaves. Each spore is ejected, lands in the soil, and forms the fern's tiny stage—a little heart-shaped plant called a gametophyte. The gametophyte stage is sexual: each gametophyte forms ovules and sperm cells. The sperm cells fertilize the ovules and give rise to a new generation of the large sporophyte plants.*

Fertile Crescent. The crescent-shaped area of relatively fertile land in the Middle East in ancient times. The area extended from Mesopotamia to Assyria, then westward to the Mediterranean and south through Palestine to the Nile Valley.

fer·til·i·ty (fər-tĭl′ə-tē) *n.* The state or quality of being fertile.

fertility cult *n.* The celebration of various ceremonies or magical rites, usually in primitive agricultural communities, with the aim of increasing crops, bringing rain, or the like.

fertility drug *n.* Any of various drugs, such as a **gonadotropin** *(see),* taken by infertile women to stimulate the release of an egg cell from the ovary and therefore increase the chances of pregnancy.

fertility rate *n.* The number of live births that occur in a year per thousand women of childbearing age.

fer·til·i·za·tion (fûrt′l-ĭ-zā′shən) *n.* **1.** The act or process of initiating biological reproduction. **2.** The process in which two gametes unite to form a zygote. **3.** The act or process of rendering fertile, especially by use of fertilizer.

fer·til·ize (fûrt′l-īz′) *v.* **-ized, -izing, -izes.** —*tr.* **1.** To cause fertilization of (an ovum, animal, or plant) by providing with sperm or pollen. **2.** To render fertile, especially by spreading fertilizer. —*intr.* To spread fertilizer. —**fer·til·iz·a·ble** *adj.*

fer·til·iz·er (fûrt′l-ī′zər) *n.* **1.** A person or agent that causes fertilization of an animal or plant. **2.** Any of a large number of natural and synthetic materials, including manure and nitrogen, phosphorus, and potassium compounds, spread on or worked into soil to increase its fertility.

fer·u·la (fĕr′yə-lə, fĕr′ə-) *n., pl.* **-las** or **-lae** (-lē′). **1.** A flat piece of wood, such as a stick; a ferule. **2.** Any plant of the genus *Ferula,* of Mediterranean regions, containing resins for which it is cultivated. [New Latin, from Latin, giant fennel. See **ferule.**]

fer·ule¹ (fĕr′əl, -ōōl′) *n.* A baton, cane, strap, or stick used in punishing children.
—*tr.v.* **feruled, -uling, -ules.** To punish or discipline with a ferule. [Latin *ferula†,* giant fennel, rod used to punish.]

ferule². Variant of **ferrule.**

fer·ven·cy (fûr′vən-sē) *n., pl.* **-cies.** The condition or quality of being fervent.

fer·vent (fûr′vənt) *adj.* **1.** Having or showing great emotion or warmth; passionate; ardent. **2.** Extremely hot; glowing. [Middle English, from Old French, from Latin *fervēns* (stem *fervent-*), present participle of *fervēre,* to boil, glow.] —**fer·vent·ly** *adv.* —**fer·vent·ness** *n.*

fer·vid (fûr′vĭd) *adj.* **1.** Intensely fervent or zealous; impassioned. **2.** Extremely hot; burning. —See Synonyms at **eager.** [Latin *fervidus,* glowing, from *fervēre,* to glow, boil.] —**fer·vid·ly** *adv.* —**fer·vid·ness** *n.*

fer·vor (fûr′vər) *n.* Also *chiefly British* **fer·vour. 1.** Intensity of emotion; fervency; zeal. **2.** Intense heat. —See Synonyms at **passion.** [Middle English *fervour,* from Old French, from Latin *fervor,* a boiling, from *fervēre,* to boil.]

Fès (fĕs). Also **Fez** (fĕz). *Arabic* **Fas** (fäs). City in northern Morocco, consisting of the old city (A.D. 808) and the new city (1276).

fes·cen·nine (fĕs′ə-nīn′, -nēn′) *adj.* Licentious; obscene. [Latin *Fescennīnus,* of the town *Fescennia* in Etruria, noted for licentious festivals and verses.]

fes·cue (fĕs′kyōō) *n.* **1.** Any of various grasses of the genus *Festuca,* often cultivated as pasturage and for lawns. **2.** A stick used as a pointer. [Middle English *festu,* from Old French, from Vulgar Latin *festūcum* (unattested), from Latin *festūca†,* stalk, stem.]

fess, fesse (fĕs) *n.* *Heraldry.* A wide horizontal band forming the middle section of an escutcheon. [Middle English *fesse,* from Old French, from Latin *fascia,* band, fillet.]

fess point *n.* *Heraldry.* The center point of an escutcheon.

-fest *suffix.* Indicates a gathering or occasion characterized by a specified activity; for example, *slugfest.* [From German *Fest,* feast, festival, from Middle High German *vest,* from Latin *fēstum,* neuter of *fēstus,* joyous, festal.]

fes·tal (fĕs′təl) *adj.* Of, pertaining to, or of the nature of a feast or festival; festive; joyous. [Old French, from Latin *fēsta,* FEAST.] —**fes·tal·ly** *adv.*

fes·ter (fĕs′tər) *v.* **-tered, -tering, -ters.** —*intr.* **1.** To generate pus; suppurate. **2.** To form an ulcer. **3.** To decay; rot. **4.** To be or become a source of irritation; rankle. —*tr.* To infect, inflame, or corrupt. —*n.* A small, festering sore or ulcer. [Middle English *festre,* Old French, from Latin *fistula,* FISTULA.]

fes·ti·na len·te (fĕ-stē′nä lĕn′tā). *Latin.* Make haste slowly.

fes·ti·val (fĕs′tə-vəl) *n.* **1.** An occasion for feasting or celebration; especially, a day or time of religious significance that recurs at regular intervals: *a harvest festival; the festival of Chanukah.* **2.** A series of related performances, exhibitions, competitions, or the like: *a film festival.* **3.** Conviviality; revelry. —*adj.* Festive. [Middle English, from Old French, from Medieval Latin *fēstivālis,* from *fēstīvus,* FESTIVE.]

fes·tive (fĕs′tĭv) *adj.* **1.** Of, pertaining to, or appropriate to a feast or festival. **2.** Merry; joyous: *a festive occasion.* [Latin *fēstīvus,* from *fēstus,* joyous.] —**fes·tive·ly** *adv.* —**fes·tive·ness** *n.*

fes·tiv·i·ty (fĕ-stĭv′ə-tē) *n., pl.* **-ties. 1.** A joyous feast, holiday, or celebration; a festival. **2.** The pleasure, joy, and gaiety of a festival or celebration. **3.** festivities. The proceedings or events of a festival or celebration; festive activity.

fes·toon (fĕ-stōōn′) *n.* **1.** A string or garland of leaves, flowers, ribbon, or the like, suspended in a loop or curve between two points.

2. A representation of this, as in sculpture or architecture. —*tr.v.* **festooned, -tooning, -toons. 1.** To decorate with or as if with a festoon or festoons. **2.** To form or make into a festoon or festoons. **3.** To join together by festoons. [French *feston,* from Italian *festone,* festal ornament, from *fēsta,* feast, festival, from Latin, plural of *fēstus,* joyous, festal.]

fes·toon·er·y (fĕ-stōō′nə-rē) *n., pl.* **-ies. 1.** An arrangement of or into festoons. **2.** Festoons collectively.

fest·schrift (fĕst′shrĭft′) *n., pl.* **-schriften** (-shrĭf′tən) or **-schrifts.** A volume of learned essays or articles contributed by colleagues and admirers as a tribute to a scholar. [German, "festival writing."]

fet·a, fet·ta (fĕt′ə) *n.* A white, crumbly Greek cheese made usually of goat's or ewe's milk and preserved in brine. [Modern Greek, short for *turi pheta,* "cheese slice" : *turi,* cheese + *pheta,* from Italian *fetta,* slice.]

FET field-effect transistor.

fe·tal, foe·tal (fēt′l) *adj.* Of, pertaining to, or having the nature of a fetus.

fetal alcohol syndrome *n.* A group of birth defects including retarded growth and cardiac abnormalities, occurring in infants born to alcoholic mothers.

fetal position *n.* A position of the body at rest in which the spine is curved, the head is bowed forward, and the arms and legs are drawn in toward the chest. [From its resemblance to the position of the fetus in the womb.]

fe·ta·tion, foe·ta·tion (fē-tā′shən) *n.* The development of a fetus; pregnancy. [FET(US) + -ATION.]

fetch¹ (fĕch) *v.* **fetched, fetching, fetches.** —*tr.* **1.** To go after and return with; get; bring. **2.** To cause to come or be drawn forth: *A bell fetched the receptionist.* **3. a.** To draw in (breath); inhale. **b.** To bring forth (a sigh, for example). **4.** *Informal.* To bring in (a price); sell for. **5.** To interest; attract: *How does this idea fetch you?* **6.** *Archaic.* To perform or make (a movement, step, or the like). **7.** *Informal.* To strike or deal (a blow, punch, or the like). **8.** *Nautical.* To arrive at; come to; reach. —*intr.* **1.** To go after and return with things. **2.** In hunting, to retrieve game. Often used as a command to a dog. **3.** *Nautical.* **a.** To hold a course. **b.** To turn about; veer. —**fetch and carry.** To do minor tasks. —**fetch up.** To reach a place and halt there; end up.
—*n.* **1.** An act or instance of fetching. **2.** A stratagem or trick. [Middle English *fecchen,* Old English *feccan, fetian.*] —**fetch·er** *n.*

fetch² *n.* An apparition of a living person; a doppelgänger. [18th century : origin obscure.]

fetch·ing (fĕch′ĭng) *adj. Informal.* Very attractive; charming; captivating. —**fetch·ing·ly** *adv.*

fete, fête (fāt, fĕt) *n.* **1.** A festival or elaborate feast. **2.** A bazaar or fair, usually held outdoors, to raise money for charity. **3.** Especially in Roman Catholic countries, the feast day of a saint, observed as a festival by those bearing the name of the saint.
—*tr.v.* **feted, feting, fetes.** Also **fête. 1.** To celebrate with a festival or party. **2.** To pay honor to, especially by entertaining. [French *fête,* from Old French *feste,* FEAST.]

fête cham·pê·tre (fĕt′ shän-pĕt′rə) *n., pl.* **fêtes champêtres** *(pronounced as singular).* An outdoor dinner, party, or similar entertainment. [French.]

fet·e·ri·ta (fĕt′ə-rē′tə) *n.* A variety of sorghum, *Sorghum vulgare caudatum,* grown in warm regions for its grain and as forage. [Arabic (Sudanese dialect).]

fet·id, foe·tid (fĕt′ĭd, fē′tĭd) *adj.* Having an offensive odor; foul-smelling; stinking: *fetid air swarming with mosquitoes.* [Middle English, from Latin *fetidus, foetidus,* from *fētēre, foetēre†,* to stink.] —**fet·id·ly** *adv.* —**fet·id·ness** *n.*

fet·ish, fet·ich (fĕt′ĭsh, fē′tĭsh) *n.* **1. a.** A material object believed among primitive cultures to have magical power. **b.** Belief in the power of such objects. **2.** An object, principle, activity, or the like that receives unreasonably excessive attention or reverence. **3.** *Psychology.* **a.** An abnormal sexual attraction to some object or part of the body not normally considered erogenous: *a foot fetish.* **b.** The object of this attraction. [French *fétiche,* from Portuguese *feitiço,* charm, sorcery, from Latin *factītius,* made by art, from *facere,* to make, do.]

fet·ish·ism (fĕt′ĭ-shĭz′əm, fē′tĭ-) *n.* **1.** The worship of or belief in fetishes. **2.** Excessive attention to or attachment for something. **3.** *Psychology.* A condition involving a fetish. —**fet·ish·ist** *n.* —**fet·ish·is·tic** (fĕt′ĭ-shĭs′tĭk, fē′tĭ-) *adj.*

fet·lock (fĕt′lŏk′) *n.* **1. a.** A projection on the lower part of the leg of a horse or related animal, above and behind the hoof. **b.** A tuft of hair on such a projection. **2.** The joint marked by this projection. In this sense, also called "fetlock joint." [Middle English *fitlok,* from Germanic; akin to Middle High German *vizzelach.*]

fe·tor, foe·tor (fē′tər, fē′tôr′) *n.* An exceptionally offensive odor; a strong stench. [Middle English *fetour,* from Latin *fētor, foetor,* from *fētēre, foetēre†,* to stink.]

fetta. Variant of **feta.**

fet·ter (fĕt′ər) *n.* **1.** A chain or shackle attached to the ankle to restrain movement. **2.** fetters. Anything that serves to restrict; a restraint.
—*tr.v.* **fettered, -tering, -ters. 1.** To put fetters on; shackle. **2.** To restrict the freedom of movement or thought of; confine; impede. [Middle English *feter,* Old English *fetor, feter,* from Germanic.]

fet·tle (fĕt′l) *tr.v.* **-tled, -tling, -tles.** *Metallurgy.* To line (the hearth of a reverberatory furnace) with loose sand or ore preparatory to pouring molten metal.

~n. 1. The material used to line a furnace in fettling. 2. Proper or sound condition; good spirits: *in fine fettle.* [Middle English *fetlen,* to shape, make ready, probably from Old English *fetel,* girdle, belt, from Germanic.]

fet·tling (fĕt'lĭng) *n.* The material, such as loose ore and sand, used to line a reverberatory furnace.

fet·tuc·ci·ne, fet·tu·ci·ni (fĕt'ə-chē'nē) *n. Used with a singular or plural verb.* Italian pasta in the form of narrow strips. [Italian *fettucine* (plural), diminutive of *fetta,* slice.]

fe·tus, foe·tus (fē'təs) *n., pl.* **-tuses.** The unborn young of a viviparous vertebrate; in human beings, the unborn young from the end of the eighth week to the moment of birth, as distinguished from the earlier embryo. [Middle English, from Latin *fētus,* pregnancy, offspring.]

Feucht·wang·er (foikHt'väng'ər), **Lion** (1884–1958). German novelist and dramatist. He wrote *The Ugly Duchess* (1923) and *Jud Süss* (1925). He was exiled in 1933 and settled in California in 1940.

feud[1] (fyōōd) *n.* 1. A bitter, prolonged state of hostility between two families, individuals, or clans; vendetta. 2. An often prolonged quarrel. ~*intr.v.* **feuded, feuding, feuds.** To carry on a feud. [Middle English *fede, feide,* from Old French, from Old High German *fēhida;* akin to Old English *fǣhthu,* enmity (see FOE, -TH).]

feud[2] *n.* A feudal estate, a **fee** (*see*). [Medieval Latin *feudum,* probably from Germanic.]

feu·dal (fyōōd'l) *adj.* 1. Of, pertaining to, or characteristic of feudalism. 2. Of or pertaining to lands held in fee or to the holding of such lands. [Medieval Latin *feudālis,* from *feudum,* FEUD (estate).] —**feu·dal·ly** *adv.*

feu·dal·ism (fyōōd'l-ĭz'əm) *n.* A political and economic system of medieval Europe, based on the relation of lord to vassal, in which land was held on condition of homage and service. —**feu·dal·ist** *n.* —**feu·dal·is·tic** (fyōōd'l-ĭs'tĭk) *adj.*

feu·dal·i·ty (fyōō-dăl'ə-tē) *n., pl.* **-ties.** 1. The state or quality of being feudal. 2. A feudal estate, a **fee** (*see*).

feu·dal·ize (fyōōd'l-īz') *tr.v.* **-ized, -izing, -izes.** To organize into a feudal system; make feudal. —**feu·dal·i·za·tion** *n.*

feu·da·to·ry (fyōō'də-tôr'ē, -tōr'ē) *n., pl.* **-ries.** 1. A person who holds a feudal fee; a vassal. 2. A feudal fee. ~*adj.* 1. Of, pertaining to, or characteristic of the feudal relationship between vassal and lord. 2. Owing feudal homage or allegiance. [Medieval Latin *feudātōrius,* from *feudātus,* past participle of *feudāre,* to enfeoff, from *feudum,* FEUD (estate).]

feud·ist (fyōō'dĭst) *n.* A person who feuds with another.

Feu·er·bach (foi'ər-bäkH'), **Ludwig Andreas** (1804–72). German philosopher. He explained history in materialistic terms, claiming that "Man is what he eats." In *The Essence of Christianity* (1841) he argued that God was a projection of man's inner self.

feuil·le·ton (fœ'yə-tôN') *n.* 1. The part of a French or other European newspaper devoted to light fiction, reviews, and similar articles. 2. An article appearing in a feuilleton, such as an installment of a serialized novel. [French, from *feuillet,* diminutive of *feuille,* leaf, from Old French *fueille, foille,* from Latin *folia,* plural of *folium,* leaf.] —**feuil·le·ton·ism** (fœ'yə-tō'nĭz'əm, -tôN'nĭz-əm) *n.* —**feuil·le·ton·ist** (-nĭst) *n.*

Feul·gen reaction (foil'gən) *n.* A staining reaction in which the presence of DNA is demonstrated by the appearance of purple color upon contact with a reagent containing fuchsin and sulfuric acid. [After R.J. *Feulgen* (1884–1955), German biochemist.]

fe·ver (fē'vər) *n.* 1. Abnormally high body temperature, usually associated with shivering and a fast pulse. 2. Any disease characterized by abnormally high body temperatures. 3. A condition of heightened activity or excitement; a ferment; agitation: *a fever of anticipation.* 4. A contagious, usually short-lived enthusiasm or eagerness. ~*tr.v.* **fevered, -vering, -vers.** To put into a fever. [Middle English *fever,* Old English *fēfor, fēfer,* from Latin *febris†.*]

fever blister *n.* A cold sore (*see*).

fe·ver·few (fē'vər-fyōō') *n.* An aromatic plant, *Chrysanthemum parthenium,* native to Eurasia, having clusters of buttonlike, white-rayed flowers. [Middle English *feverfu,* from Norman French *fevrefue* (unattested), from Latin *febrifugia* : *febris,* FEVER + *fugāre,* to drive away, from *fugere,* to run away.]

fe·ver·ish (fē'vər-ĭsh) *adj.* Also **fe·ver·ous** (-əs) (for sense 1). 1. a. Having a fever, especially a slight fever. b. Of, pertaining to, or resembling a fever. c. Causing or tending to cause fever. 2. In an agitated or restless state; intensely emotional or active. —**fe·ver·ish·ly** *adv.* —**fe·ver·ish·ness** *n.*

fever pitch *n.* An intense degree of excitement or agitation.

fever therapy *n.* Treatment of disease by means of artificially induced fever.

fever tree *n.* Any of several trees, such as certain species of eucalyptus or *Pinckneya pubens,* of the southeastern United States, having leaves or bark capable of reducing fever.

fe·ver·wort (fē'vər-wûrt', -wôrt') *n.* Any of several plants considered to have medicinal properties, such as the **horse gentian** and **boneset** (*both of which see*).

few (fyōō) *adj.* **fewer, fewest.** Amounting to or consisting of a small number. —**few and far between.** Scarce; in short supply. ~*n. Used with a plural verb.* 1. An indefinitely small number of persons or things; not many: *Bring me a few of your books.* 2. A limited number of people; the select. Usually preceded by *the: the discerning few.* —**a good few.** Several or many. —**have a few too many.** *Informal.* To consume too many alcoholic drinks. —**quite a few.** A lot; many.

~*pron. Used with a plural verb.* A small number of persons or things: *"many are called, but few are chosen"* (Matthew 22:14). [Middle English *fewe,* Old English *fēa, fēawe.*]

Usage: *Fewer* and *less* sometimes overlap in usage. *Fewer* is the preferred word when the reference is to numbers or to entities considered as individuals that can be counted or listed. *Less* is preferred when the reference is to collective quantity or to something abstract. Contrast *fewer workers, less production,* and *fewer opportunities, less opportunity.* Informally there is a tendency for *less* to be used in place of *fewer,* especially when there is an implicit contrast with *more: No less than 15 people telephoned. There are 15 less trains on the line now than there were last year.* Here formal English prefers *fewer.* However, even formal English will accept *less* when the contrast is explicit, as in *We want a few more cars and a few less buses* (where *a few fewer* would be unacceptable); or in expressions of measurement, even when plural, since the sense is collective: *less than 60 years old; less than 50 feet; less than $4,000.*

fey (fā) *adj.* 1. *Scottish.* a. Fated to die soon. b. Full of the sense of approaching death. 2. Having visionary power; clairvoyant. 3. Appearing as if under a spell; enchanted; touched. 4. Whimsical or fanciful. [Middle English *feie,* Old English *fǣge.*]

Fey·deau (fā'dō, fā-dō'), **Georges** (1862–1921). French playwright. He wrote many farcical comedies, including *The Lady From Maxim's* (1899) and *A Flea in Her Ear* (1907).

Feyn·man (fīn'mən), **Richard Phillips** (1918–86). U.S. physicist. He is best known for his work in quantum electrodynamics, especially the Feynman diagrams, which illustrate interactions between charged particles as an exchange of virtual photons. He shared the Nobel Prize in 1965.

fez (fĕz) *n., pl.* **fezzes.** A man's felt cap in the shape of a truncated cone, usually red with a black tassel hanging from the crown, worn chiefly in the eastern Mediterranean region. [French, from Turkish, perhaps after Fès.]

Fez. See **Fès.**

ff *Music.* fortissimo.

ff. 1. folios. 2. following.

Ffestiniog. See **Meirionydd.**

FFV Order of the First Families of Virginia.

FG fine grain.

f.g. *Sports.* field goal; field goals.

FH fire hydrant.

FHA Federal Housing Administration.

FHLBB Federal Home Loan Bank Board.

f.h.p. friction horsepower.

fi·a·cre (fē-ä'krə) *n.* A small hackney coach. [French, after the Hôtel de St. *Fiacre,* Paris.]

fi·an·cé (fē'än-sā', fē-än'sā') *n.* A man engaged to be married. [French, past participle of *fiancer,* to betroth, from Old French *fiancier,* from *fier,* to trust, from Vulgar Latin *fīdāre* (unattested), from Latin *fīdere.*]

fi·an·cée (fē'än-sā', fē-än'sā') *n.* A woman engaged to be married. [French, feminine of FIANCÉ.]

Fi·an·na (fē'ə-nə) *n.* Fenian (*see*).

Fi·an·na Fáil (fē'ə-nə foil') *n.* A major Irish political party founded in 1926 by Eamon De Valera with the aim of removing all British influence from Ireland. [Irish, "Fenians of the land" : *Fianna* (see **Fenian**) + *Fáil,* from *fál,* earth, sod.]

fi·as·co (fē-ăs'kō, -ä'skō) *n., pl.* **-coes** or **-cos.** A complete failure, especially a very embarrassing one. [French, from Italian (*far*) *fiasco,* "(to make) a bottle," an unexplained allusion, perhaps from Late Latin *flascō,* FLASK.]

fi·at (fē'ăt', fī'ăt', -ət) *n.* 1. An arbitrary order or decree. 2. Authorization; sanction. [Latin *fiat,* "let it be done," third person singular present subjunctive of *fierī,* to become, representing the passive of *facere,* to do.]

fiat money *n.* Paper money decreed legal tender, not backed by gold or silver, and not necessarily redeemable in coin.

fib (fĭb) *n.* An inconsequential lie. ~*intr.v.* **fibbed, fibbing, fibs.** To tell a fib. [17th century : perhaps shortened from obsolete *fible-fable,* nonsense, reduplication of FABLE.] —**fib·ber** *n.*

fi·ber (fī'bər) *n.* Also *chiefly British* **fi·bre.** 1. A slender, elongated structure; thread or strand. 2. Any of the elongated, thick-walled cells that give strength and support to plant tissue. 3. Any of the filaments constituting the intracellular matrix of connective tissue. 4. *Anatomy.* Any of various threadlike structures; especially, a **muscle fiber** or a **nerve fiber** (*both of which see*). 5. a. A natural or synthetic thread, as of cotton or nylon, capable of being spun into yarn. b. Material made of such filaments. 6. The essential substance: *"stirred the deeper fibers of my nature"* (Oscar Wilde). 7. Internal strength; character: *lacking in moral fiber.* [Middle English, from Old French *fibre,* from Latin *fibra†.*]

fi·ber·board (fī'bər-bôrd', -bōrd') *n.* 1. A building material composed of wood or other plant fibers bonded together and compressed into rigid sheets. 2. A sheet of this material.

Fi·ber·fill (fī'bər-fĭl') *n.* A trademark for a synthetic resin used as quilt filling.

Fi·ber·glas (fī'bər-glăs', -gläs') *n.* A trademark for a type of fiber glass.

fiber glass *n.* Spun filaments of glass made into yarn and textiles

feverfew *A pungently aromatic plant, feverfew grows wild in Europe and Asia. Now considered only a weed, it was so named because it was once thought to be effective in driving away fevers.*

or, when hardened with resin, used as a strong, lightweight construction material.

fiber optics *n.* *Used with a singular verb.* The optics of light transmission through very fine, flexible glass fibers by internal reflection. —**fi·ber-op·tic** (fī′bər-ŏp′tĭk) *adj.*

fi·ber·scope (fī′bər-skōp′) *n.* A flexible fiber-optic instrument used to view objects that would otherwise be inaccessible, especially tissues and organs in inaccessible parts of the body.

Fi·bo·nac·ci (fē′bə-nä′chē), **Leonardo** (*c.* 1170–*c.* 1240). Italian mathematician. In North Africa he learned the decimal system of numerals, which he published in his *Liber Abaci* (1202).

Fibonacci sequence *n.* A sequence of numbers (Fibonacci numbers), each of which is the sum of the two preceding numbers: 1, 1,

fiber optics

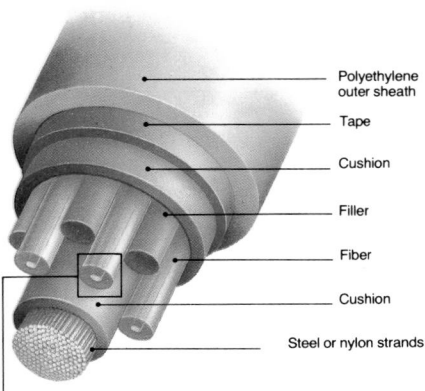

MAKING LIGHT THE SERVANT OF SCIENCE
See and be seen (and heard) along a glass thread

Fiber optics is a branch of engineering concerned with the transmission of light along flexible glass fibers and plays an increasing role in medicine and telecommunications.

The basic element in fiber optics is a glass thread less than a millimeter thick, along which light will travel by bouncing from side to side, however curved the fiber. The first use of fiber optics came in 1955. The technique has since been used to improve ways of seeing inside the body; light is shone in through the fibers and they return a clear image. In the 1960's, it was seen that fiber-optic cables could be used to carry telecommunications signals in much greater quantity and for longer distances than copper wires. In fiber-optic systems information is transmitted by means of coded laser beams.

Polyethylene outer sheath
Tape
Cushion
Filler
Fiber
Cushion
Steel or nylon strands

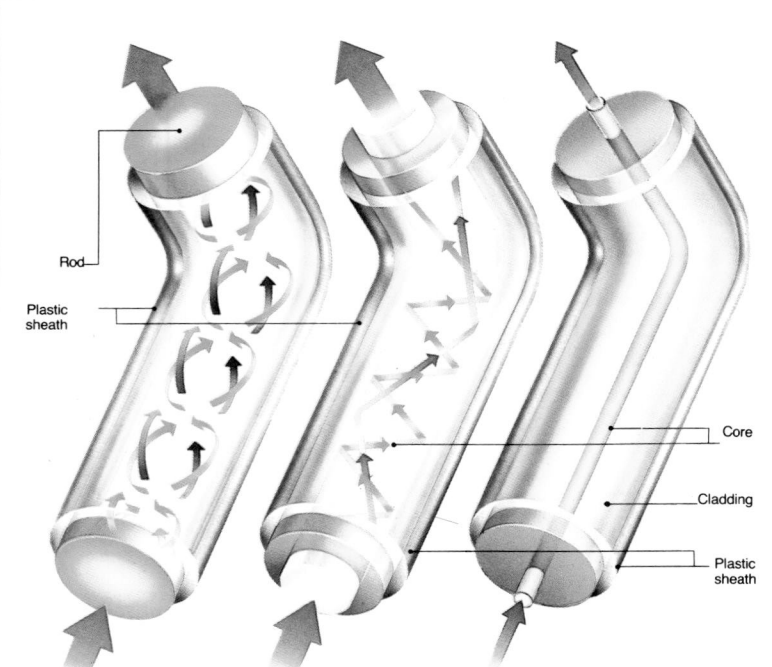

Rod
Plastic sheath
Core
Cladding
Plastic sheath

FIBER-OPTIC CABLE *The cable contains bundles of fine glass fibers in a protective sheath and with strengthening strands of steel or nylon at the center. A fiber may be a "graded-index" rod (left) that bends light by decreasing amounts from its center outward; or it may be a "stepped-index" rod (center and right) consisting of two types of glass, one outside the other, that bend light by different amounts.*

Light signals may be sent in quantity or singly. In multiple transmissions (left and center) a thick fiber carries up to 10,000 signals, but with some loss of quality. Single signals are transmitted along a minute stepped-index fiber (right) that is hard to make—it is only eight times wider than the wavelength of the infrared light used—but the signal is remarkably true.

2, 3, 5, 8, 13, 21 . . . . . . [After Leonardo FIBONACCI.]

fi·bri·form (fī′brə-fôrm′) *adj.* Similar in form or structure to a fiber.

fi·bril (fī′brəl, fīb′rəl) *n.* Also **fi·bril·la** (fī-brĭl′ə) *pl.* **-brillae** (-brĭl′ē). A small, slender fiber, such as a root hair or a constituent thread of a muscle fiber. [New Latin *fibrilla,* diminutive of Latin *fibra,* FIBER.] —**fi·bril·lar** (fī′brə-lər, fīb′rə-), **fi·bril·lar·y** (-lĕr′ē) *adj.*

fib·ril·la·tion (fīb′rə-lā′shən, fī′brə-) *n.* **1.** The forming of fibers. **2.** Uncoordinated twitching of individual muscle fibers with little or no movement of the muscle as a whole. **3.** *Pathology.* Fine, rapid fibrillar movements that replace the normal contraction of the heart muscle. [New Latin *fibrilla,* FIBRIL.]

fi·bril·li·form (fī-brĭl′ə-fôrm′, fī-brĭl′-) *adj.* Having the form of a fibril.

fi·bril·lose (fī′brə-lōs′, fīb′rə-) *adj.* Having or consisting of fibrils.

fi·brin (fī′brĭn) *n.* An elastic, insoluble protein derived from the interaction of fibrinogen with thrombin and forming a fibrous network in the coagulation of blood. [FIBR(O)- + -IN.]

fi·brin·o·gen (fī-brĭn′ə-jən) *n.* A protein in the blood plasma that is converted to fibrin by the action of thrombin in the presence of ionized calcium. [FIBRIN + -O-GEN.]

fi·bri·nol·y·sin (fī′brə-nŏl′ə-sĭn) *n.* An enzyme, **plasmin** *(see).* [FIBRIN + -O- + LYSIN.]

fi·bri·nol·y·sis (fī′brə-nŏl′ə-sĭs) *n.* The breakdown of blood clots, which involves the dissolution of fibrin by the enzyme plasmin. [FIBRIN + -O-LYSIS.]

fi·brin·ous (fī′brə-nəs) *adj.* Of, pertaining to, or having the nature of fibrin.

fibro-, fibr- *prefix.* Indicates: **1.** Fibrous tissue; for example, **fibrovascular, fibrosis. 2.** Fiber; for example, **fibrocement.** [Latin *fibra,* FIBER.]

fi·bro·blast (fī′brə-blăst′, -blăst′) *n.* A cell in connective tissue that is responsible for producing fibers. [FIBRO- + -BLAST.]

fi·bro·car·ti·lage (fī′brō-kär′tə-lĭj) *n.* A type of cartilage containing many fibers, as found in the intervertebral disks.

fi·bro·ce·ment (fī′brō-sĭ-měnt′) *n.* A building material made out of cement and asbestos mixed together and formed into sheets.

fi·broid (fī′broid′) *adj.* Resembling or composed of fibrous tissue. *~n.* A benign tumor of smooth muscle, especially in the uterine wall. [FIBR(O)- + -OID.]

fi·bro·in (fī′brō-ĭn) *n.* A white protein that is the essential component of raw silk and spider-web filaments. [French *fibroïne* : FIBRO- + -IN.]

fi·bro·ma (fī-brō′mə) *n., pl.* **-mas** or **-mata** (-mə-tə). Any benign tumor derived from fibrous tissue, such as a fibroid. [New Latin : FIBR(O)- + -OMA.] —**fi·brom·a·tous** (fī-brŏm′ə-təs, fī-brō′mə-) *adj.*

fi·bro·sis (fī-brō′sĭs) *n.* The formation of excess fibrous tissue in an organ, such as the lung, usually as a result of inflammation or injury. See **cystic fibrosis.** [New Latin : FIBR(O)- + -OSIS.]

fi·bro·si·tis (fī′brə-sī′tĭs, fīb′rə-) *n.* Inflammation of fibrous connective tissue, especially in the muscles and muscle sheaths of the back. [New Latin *fibrosus,* FIBROUS + -ITIS.]

fi·brous (fī′brəs) *adj.* Having, consisting of, or resembling fibers.

fi·bro·vas·cu·lar (fī′brō-văs′kyə-lər) *adj. Botany.* Having fibrous tissue and vascular tissue. Said of the vascular bundles in woody tissue.

fib·u·la (fīb′yə-lə) *n., pl.* **-lae** (-lē′) or **-las.** **1.** The outer and smaller of two bones of the human leg or the hind leg of an animal, in humans between the knee and ankle. **2.** A broochlike clasp used in the ancient world. [Latin *fībula,* perhaps from the root of *fīgere,* to fix.] —**fib·u·lar** *adj.*

-fic *suffix.* Indicates making, causing, or creating; for example, **morbific.** [New Latin *-ficus,* from Latin, from *facere,* to do, make.]

FICA Federal Insurance Contributions Act.

fice. Variant of **feist.**

fiche (fēsh) *n.* A microfiche *(see).*

Fich·te (fĭKH′tə), **Johann Gottlieb** (1762–1814). German philosopher. He argued that moral reason is the base of all reason, knowledge, and humanity. His philosophical works include *The Vocation of Man.* Fichte is considered one of the most important transcendental idealists.

fi·chu (fĭsh′ōō, fē-shōō′) *n.* A woman's triangular scarf of lightweight fabric, worn over the shoulders and crossed or tied in a loose knot at the breast. [French, from the past participle of *ficher,* to fix, attach, from Vulgar Latin *fīgicāre* (unattested), from Latin *fīgere,* to FIX.]

fick·le (fĭk′əl) *adj.* Changeable, especially with regard to affections or attachments; inconstant; capricious. —See Synonyms at **faithless.** [Middle English *fikel,* false, treacherous, Old English *ficol.*] —**fick·le·ness** *n.*

fic·tile (fĭk′təl, -tīl′) *adj.* **1.** Able to be molded; plastic. **2.** Formed of a moldable substance, such as clay or earth. **3.** Of or pertaining to earthenware or pottery. [Latin *fictilis,* from *fictus,* past participle of *fingere,* to touch, form, mold, shape.]

fic·tion (fĭk′shən) *n.* **1.** An event, statement, or occurrence that has been invented or feigned rather than having actually taken place. **2.** The act of producing such inventions; a feigning. **3.** A lie. **4. a.** A literary work whose content is produced by the imagination and is not necessarily based on fact. **b.** The category of literature comprising works of this kind, including novels and short stories. **5.** Something accepted as fact without any real justification, but merely for the sake of convenience: *a legal fiction.* [Middle English *ficcioun,* invention, from Old French *fiction,* from Latin *fictiō* (stem *fictiōn-*), a making, fashioning, from *fictus,* past participle of *fingere,* to touch, form, mold.] **—fic·tion·al** *adj.* **—fic·tion·al·ly** *adv.*

fic·tion·al·ize (fĭk'shə-nə-līz') *tr.v.* **-ized, -izing, -izes.** To treat as or make into fiction by changing details such as names and locations. **—fic·tion·al·i·za·tion** (fĭk'shə-nə-lĭ-zā'shən) *n.*

fic·ti·tious (fĭk-tĭsh'əs) *adj.* **1.** Of, pertaining to, or characterized by fiction; nonexistent; imaginary; unreal: *a fictitious event.* **2.** Purposefully deceptive; false; untrue: *a fictitious name.* **—fic·ti·tious·ly** *adv.* **—fic·ti·tious·ness** *n.*

fictitious force *n. Physics.* A force, such as centrifugal or Coriolis force, that arises because of the frame of reference of the observer and disappears on transformation to a more suitable frame.

fic·tive (fĭk'tĭv) *adj.* **1.** Of or pertaining to the creation of fiction. **2.** Pertaining to or characterized by fiction; fictitious; imaginary. **3.** Feigned; sham. **—fic·tive·ly** *adv.*

fid (fĭd) *n. Nautical.* **1.** A square bar used as a support for a topmast. **2.** A large, tapering pin used to open the strands of a rope prior to splicing. [17th century : origin obscure.]

fid. fidelity.

-fid *suffix.* Indicates a division or separation into parts or lobes; for example, **pinnatifid.** [Latin *-fidus,* from *findere,* to split.]

Fid. Def. Fidei Defensor.

fid·dle (fĭd'l) *n.* **1. a.** *Informal.* A **violin** *(see).* **b.** Any member of the violin family, including similarly designed medieval and Oriental instruments. **2.** *Nautical.* A guard rail used on a table during rough weather to prevent things from slipping off. **3.** *Informal.* Nonsensical trifling; stupidity. **4.** *British Informal.* An illegal or underhand practice or act: *a tax fiddle.* **—fit as a fiddle.** Very healthy. **—play second fiddle.** *Informal.* To be subordinate.

~v. **fiddled, -dling, -dles.** *—intr.* **1. a.** To move one's fingers or hands in a restless fashion; fidget. **b.** To putter or tamper with something: *Don't fiddle with my belongings.* **2.** To waste time. Usually used with *around* or *about.* **3.** *Informal.* To play a violin. *—tr. Informal.* **1.** To arrange or contrive, especially by slightly underhand methods. **2.** To waste or squander: *fiddled away the day.* **3.** To cheat or swindle. **4.** To play (a tune) on a violin. [Middle English *fithele, fidle,* Old English *fithele,* from West Germanic *fithula* (unattested), from Medieval Latin *vītula,* from Latin *vītulārī,* to celebrate a victory, from *Vītula,* goddess of joy and victory, probably of Sabine origin.]

fid·dle·back (fĭd'l-băk') *adj.* Shaped like the body of a violin: *a fiddleback chair.*

fid·dle-de-dee (fĭd'l-dē-dē') *interj.* Used to express mild annoyance or impatience. [Nonsensical formation from FIDDLE.]

fid·dle-fad·dle (fĭd'l-făd'l) *interj.* Used to express mild annoyance or impatience.

~n. Nonsense or petty matters.

~intr.v. **fiddle-faddled, -dling, -dles.** To fritter away one's time; dally. [Reduplication of FIDDLE.] **—fid·dle-fad·dler** *n.*

fid·dle·head (fĭd'l-hĕd') *n.* A curved, scroll-like ornamentation at the top of a ship's bow that resembles the neck of a violin.

fid·dler (fĭd'lər) *n. Informal.* A person who plays the violin.

fiddler crab *n.* Any of various burrowing crabs of the genus *Uca,* having one of the anterior claws much enlarged in the male. [So called from its large claw that it seems to hold like a fiddle.]

fid·dle·sticks (fĭd'l-stĭks') *interj.* Used to express mild annoyance or impatience.

fid·dling (fĭd'lĭng) *adj.* Unimportant; trifling; silly.

fid·dly (fĭd'lē) *adj.* **-dlier, -dliest.** Awkward or difficult to do, use, or handle, as because of smallness of size or extreme detail.

F.I.D.E. (fē'dā') *n.* The World Chess Federation. [*F*édération *I*nternationale *d*es *É*checs.]

Fi·de·i De·fen·sor (fī'dē-ī' dĭ-fĕn'sôr', fē'dā-ē' dā-fĕn'sôr') *n. Abbr.* **F.D., Fid. Def.** *Latin.* Defender of the Faith. Used as one of the titles of the British sovereign.

fi·de·ism (fē'dā-ĭz'əm) *n.* The belief or doctrine that knowledge of religious matters can be obtained only through revelation or faith and cannot be established by rational means. [Latin *fidēs,* faith + -ISM.]

fi·del·i·ty (fĭ-dĕl'ə-tē, fī-) *n., pl.* **-ties.** **1.** Faithfulness to obligations, duties, or observances; loyalty. **2.** Faithfulness or loyalty, as to a friend or cause; specifically, faithfulness to a spouse or lover. **3.** Correspondence with fact or a given quality, condition, or event; verity; truthfulness; accuracy. **4.** *Abbr.* **fid.** The degree to which an electronic system, such as a radio or record player, accurately reproduces at its output the essential characteristics of its input signal. [Middle English *fidelite,* from Old French, from Latin *fidēlitās* (stem *fidēlitāt-*), from *fidēlis,* faithful, from *fidēs,* faith.]

Synonyms: *allegiance, devotion, fealty, loyalty.*

fidg·et (fĭj'ĭt) *v.* **-eted, -eting, -ets.** *—intr.* **1.** To keep some part of one's body in continuous motion, as by shifting one's hands or feet; move nervously or restlessly. **2.** To play with or finger something nervously. Used with *with: The lecturer fidgeted with his notes.* *—tr.* To cause (someone) to fidget; make restless or nervous.

~n. **1. fidgets.** A condition of restlessness. **2.** One who fidgets. [Frequentative of obsolete *fidge,* variant of *fitch, fike,* from Middle English *fiken,* probably from Old Norse *fīkjast,* akin to Old English *fācian*†, to try to obtain.]

fidg·et·y (fĭj'ĭ-tē) *adj.* **1.** Habitually fidgeting; nervous; restless. **2.** Unnecessarily fussy. **—fidg·et·i·ness** *n.*

fi·du·cial (fĭ-do͞o'shəl, -dyo͞o'shəl, fī-) *adj.* **1.** Based on or pertaining to faith or trust. **2.** Pertaining to a legal trust; fiduciary. **3.** Regarded or employed as a standard of reference, as in measurement. [Late Latin *fīdūciālis,* from Latin *fīdūcia,* trust, from *fīdere,* to trust.] **—fi·du·cial·ly** *adv.*

fi·du·ci·ar·y (fĭ-do͞o'shē-ĕr'ē, fĭ-dyo͞o'-, fī-) *adj.* **1.** Of, pertaining to, or involving one who holds something in trust for another: *a fiduciary heir; a fiduciary contract.* **2. a.** Of, pertaining to, or designating a trustee or trusteeship. **b.** Held in trust. **3.** Of, pertaining to, or consisting of paper currency that is issued without being backed by gold.

~n., pl. **fiduciaries.** A person who stands in a special relation of trust, confidence, or responsibility in his obligations to others, such as a company director or an agent of a principal. [Latin *fīdūciārius,* from *fīdūcia,* trust. See **fiducial.**]

fie (fī) *interj.* **1.** Used to express distaste or shock. **2.** Used humorously to express pretended shock. [Middle English *fi,* from Old French, from Latin *fī,* expression of disgust at a bad smell.]

Fied·ler (fēd'lər), **Arthur** (1894–1979). U.S. conductor. He studied music in Berlin, then returned to his birthplace, Boston, to join the Boston Symphony Orchestra. In 1929 he founded the popular summer Esplanade Concerts and in 1930 became conductor of the Boston Pops, an institution famous for its performances on radio and public television.

fief (fēf) *n.* **1.** A feudal estate, a **fee** *(see).* **2.** A sphere of authority or influence. [French, from Old French *fie(f),* FEE.]

fief·dom (fēf'dəm) *n.* **1.** A fief. **2.** A person's sphere of influence or control.

field (fēld) *n. Abbr.* **fld.** **1.** A broad, level, open expanse of land; a meadow: *a field of buttercups.* **2.** An expanse of land, usually enclosed grassland, used for pasturage. **3.** A cultivated expanse of land, especially one devoted to a particular crop. **4.** A portion of land or a geologic formation containing a specified natural resource: *an oil field.* **5.** A large, flat surface used by aircraft for landing and taking off; an airfield. **6.** A background area, as on a flag, painting, or coin: *a blue insignia on a field of red.* **7.** *Heraldry.* The background area of a shield, or one of the divisions of the background. **8.** *Sports.* **a.** A delineated area on which a sports event, such as a baseball or football game, takes place. **b.** The portion of a playing field having specific dimensions on which the action of a game takes place: *The spectators were ordered to stay off the field.* **c.** All the contestants or participants in an event. **d.** All the contestants except those specified: *Her horse led the field in the stretch.* **e.** The body of horsemen following a pack of hounds. **9.** A group of rival candidates for selection: *chosen from a talented field of applicants.* **10. a.** An area of human activity or interest: *a field of endeavor.* **b.** A topic, subject, or area of academic interest or specialization. **c.** Profession, employment, or business: *Data processing is definitely not his field.* **11.** An area or setting of practical activity or application, especially as distinguished from one of academic study or theoretical research: *out in the field selling encyclopedias.* **12. a.** The scene of a battle. **b.** A battle while it is in progress. **c.** The land, especially when considered topographically, where a battle has been fought; a battlefield. **13.** *Mathematics.* A set with two binary operations, *addition* and *multiplication,* satisfying the conditions that the set is a commutative group with respect to addition, that the set with the zero omitted is a commutative group with respect to multiplication, and that multiplication is distributive over addition for all elements in the set. **14.** *Physics.* A region of space characterized by a physical property, such as gravitational or electromagnetic force or fluid pressure, having a determinable value at every point in the region. **15.** *Optics.* The usually circular area in which the image is rendered by the lens system of an optical instrument. **16.** *Computer Science.* **a.** A group of characters treated as a unit of information. **b.** The characters recorded in a vertical column on a punched card. **—keep** (or **hold**) **the field.** To continue in one's position in the face of adversity. **—leave the field.** *Informal.* To concede one's interest to another or others. **—play the field.** *Informal.* To maintain a broad range of options in personal or business matters, rather than making a specific commitment. **—take the field.** To begin or resume activity, as in military operations or in a sport.

~v. **fielded, fielding, fields.** *—tr.* **1.** *Sports.* **a.** To retrieve, catch, or stop (a ball): *The shortstop fielded the ground ball and threw the batter out.* **b.** To place (a team or player) in playing position. **c.** To be able to put (a team, for example) into a contest: *The coach fielded a strong team.* **2.** To handle adequately and be able to return in kind; cope with: *The mayor fielded the question very clumsily.* *—intr. Sports.* **1.** To retrieve, catch, or stop a ball. **2.** To play or take a turn as a fielder.

~adj. **1.** Of, pertaining or appropriate to, or carried out in a field or fields: *field work.* **2.** Growing or living in a field or fields: *field crops.* [Middle English *feld, field,* Old English *feld,* from West Germanic.]

Field (fēld), **Cyrus West** (1819–92). U.S. financier. In 1854 he conceived the idea of a transatlantic telegraph cable and was persistent in accomplishing his goal (1866) despite numerous setbacks. Later he was instrumental in organizing the elevated rapid-transit system of New York City.

Field, Marshall (1834–1906). U.S. merchant. Starting as a clerk in a Chicago dry-goods store, he eventually organized Marshall Field and Company, the largest wholesale and retail dry-goods establishment in the world from 1881 to 1906. He is especially noted for his philanthropy, giving land and money to such institutions as the Art Institute of Chicago and the University of Chicago.

field artillery *n. Abbr.* **FA** Artillery, with the exception of antiair-

fiddler crab *This crab, found on tidal mud flats in temperate and tropical parts of the world, takes its name from the way it moves its bright-red claw to and fro, in the manner of a violinist, to warn off attackers.*

PRONUNCIATION KEY

ă, pat; ā, pay; âr, care;
ä, father, are; b, bib;
ch, church; d, deed; ĕ, pet;
ē, be; f, fife; g, gag; h, hat;
hw, which; ĭ, pit; ī, pie;
îr, pier; j, judge; k, kick;
l, lid, needle; m, mum;
n, no, sudden; ng, thing;
ŏ, pot; ō, toe; ô, paw, for;
oi, noise; ou, out; o͝o, book;
o͞o, boot; p, pop; r, roar;
s, sauce; sh, ship, dish;
t, tight; th, thin, path;
th, this, bathe; ŭ, cut; ûr, fur;
v, valve; w, with; y, yes;
z, zebra, size; zh, vision;
ə, about, item, edible,
gallop, circus, peaceful

IN FOREIGN WORDS:

à, *Fr.* ami; œ, *Fr.* feu, *Ger.* schön; ü, *Fr.* tu, *Ger.* über; KH, *Ger.* ich, *Scot.* loch; N, *Fr.* bon; y', *Fr.* Compiègne

STRESS MARKS:

Primary stress: '
in·cite' (ĭn-sīt')
Secondary stress: '
in'sight' (ĭn'sīt')

craft artillery, light enough to be mounted for use in the field.
field battery *n.* A tactical artillery unit usually consisting of four or six field guns.
field coil *n.* An electric coil used to generate a magnetic field, as in a motor or direct-current generator.
field day *n.* **1.** A day spent outdoors engaged in a planned activity such as an athletic competition or nature study. **2.** A festive day, such as one on which a fair is held. **3.** *Informal.* An opportunity for expressing or asserting oneself with the fullest pleasure or triumph.
field-ef·fect transistor (fēld′ĭ-fĕkt′) *n. Abbr.* **FET** A transistor device in which a current flowing in a narrow channel between two regions (the source and the drain) is controlled by an electric field applied to a third region (the gate).
field emission *n.* The emission of electrons from the surface of a conductor, caused by a strong electric field at the surface distorting the potential barrier.
field-e·mis·sion microscope (fēld′ĭ-mĭsh′ən) *n. Abbr.* **FEM** An instrument for investigating metal surfaces, consisting of a sharply pointed piece of metal to which a high electric field is applied in a vacuum, so that electrons escaping by field emission are accelerated to a fluorescent screen where they produce a highly magnified image of the tip of the sample. **—field-e·mis·sion microscopy** *n.*
field·er (fēl′dər) *n. Sports.* **1.** A person who fields a ball. **2.** A person who plays a field position, especially in baseball or cricket.
fielder's choice *n.* A baseball play in which the batter reaches first base while a fielder is attempting to put out an advancing base runner.
field event *n.* A throwing or jumping event of a track meet as distinguished from a running event.
field·fare (fēld′fâr′) *n.* A European thrush, *Turdus pilaris,* having gray and brown plumage. [Middle English *feldefare,* probably late Old English *feldefare,* "field-goer" : FIELD + *faran,* to go.]
field glass *n. Often* **field glasses.** A portable binocular instrument used for magnifying and viewing distant objects.
field goal *n. Abbr.* **f.g.** **1.** *Football.* A score counting three points made on an ordinary down by place-kicking or drop-kicking the ball over the crossbar and between the goal posts. **2.** *Basketball.* A score counting two points made by throwing the ball through the basket in regulation play.
field gun *n.* A mobile piece of field artillery.
field hand *n.* A hired laborer or worker on a farm.
field hockey *n.* A form of **hockey** *(see)* played on a turf field.
field hospital *n.* A hospital set up on a temporary basis for soldiers serving in a remote area.
Field·ing (fēl′dĭng), **Henry** (1707–54). English novelist and dramatist. He wrote numerous plays and novels, many of them satirical, and topical comedies. His most successful novel was *Tom Jones* (1749); his other works include *Joseph Andrews* (1742).
field intensity *n.* The effectiveness of a field of force at any point as measured by the force exerted on a unit entity, as a unit charge or unit magnetic pole, subjected to the field at that point. Also called "field strength."
field-i·on microscope (fēld′ī′ən, -ŏn′) *n. Abbr.* **FIM** An instrument for investigating metal surfaces, consisting of a sharply pointed piece of metal to which a high electric field is applied in a low pressure of helium gas. Helium ions formed at the surface by field ionization are accelerated to a fluorescent screen, where they produce a highly magnified image of the tip of the sample. **—field-i·on microscopy** *n.*
field lens *n.* The lens that is farthest from the eye in a compound eyepiece.
field magnet *n.* A magnet used to provide a magnetic field in an electrical device such as a generator or motor.
field marshal *n. Abbr.* **F.M.** **1.** The highest-ranking officer in the British and Australian armies. **2.** An officer in some European armies usually ranking just below the commander in chief.
field mouse *n.* Any of various small, nocturnal, long-tailed mice of the genus *Apodemus,* inhabiting meadows and fields and often causing damage to crops. Also called "meadow mouse."
field mushroom *n.* A common edible fungus, *Agaricus campestris,* having a white cap and pink or brown gills. Also called "meadow mushroom."
field officer *n. Abbr.* **F.O.** *Military.* An officer, such as a major, lieutenant colonel, or colonel, ranking above a captain and below a brigadier general.
field of force *n.* A region of space throughout which the force produced by a single agent, such as an electric current, is operative. Also called "force field."
field of honor *n.* **1.** The scene of a duel involving a matter of personal honor. **2.** A battlefield.
field-piece (fēld′pēs′) *n.* A field gun.
Fields (fēldz), **Gracie,** born Grace Stansfield (1898–1979). British singer and comedienne. Her Lancashire humor and inimitable voice won her great popularity, especially during the Depression of the 1930's. Her most notable films include *Sally in Our Alley* (1931) and *Sing as We Go* (1934).
Fields, W.C., born William Claude Dukenfield (1880–1946). U.S. screen actor and comedian. He began making films in the early 1920's and quickly found fame as an offbeat misogynist, a screen character he based on his own genuine eccentricity.
fields·man (fēldz′mən) *n., pl.* **-men** (-mĭn). *Cricket.* A fielder.
field·stone (fēld′stōn′) *n.* A stone naturally occurring in fields, often used as a building material.
field strength *n.* **Field intensity** *(see).*
field-strip (fēld′strĭp′) *tr.v.* **-stripped, -stripping, -strips.** To disassemble (a weapon) for cleaning, repair, and inspection.
field theory *n.* The theory concerned with algebraic fields.
field trial *n.* **1.** A test for young, untried hunting dogs to determine their competence in pointing and retrieving. **2. field trials.** Tests to observe efficiency, durability, or performance, as of a special vehicle or invention or of a new product or plant variety.
field trip *n.* A group excursion or expedition for the purpose of firsthand observation, as to a museum, woods, or historical site.
field winding *n.* The electrically conducting winding of a field magnet that produces electrical excitation, especially of a motor or generator.
field·work (fēld′wûrk′) *n.* **1.** *Military.* A temporary fortification erected in the field. **2.** Work done or observations made in the field, as at a site of archaeological or geologic study, rather than in a library, laboratory, or other place of academic study. **—field·work·er** *n.*
fiend (fēnd) *n.* **1.** An evil spirit; a demon. **2. Fiend.** Satan; the Devil. **3.** A diabolically evil or wicked person. **4.** *Informal.* **a.** One who is addicted to a specified vice: *a dope fiend.* **b.** A person completely absorbed in or obsessed with a specified job or pastime: *a crossword-puzzle fiend.* [Middle English *fe(o)nd,* enemy, devil, fiend, Old English *fēond, fīond.*]
fiend·ish (fēn′dĭsh) *adj.* **1.** Pertaining to, similar to, or suggestive of a fiend; diabolical. **2. a.** Extremely difficult or grueling. **b.** Extremely clever but devious: *a fiendish maneuver.* **—fiend·ish·ly** *adv.* **—fiend·ish·ness** *n.*
fierce (fîrs) *adj.* **fiercer, fiercest.** **1.** Having a savage and violent nature; ferocious. **2.** Extremely severe or violent; terrible: *fierce thunder.* **3.** Intense or ardent; extreme: *fierce loyalty.* **4.** Very difficult or unpleasant. [Middle English *f(i)ers,* from Old French, from Latin *ferus,* wild.] **—fierce·ly** *adv.* **—fierce·ness** *n.*
fi·e·ri fa·ci·as (fī′ə-rī′ fā′shē-əs, fē′ə-rē′ fä′kē-äs′) *n. Law.* A writ of execution commanding a sheriff to lay a claim to and seize the goods and chattels of a debtor to fulfill a judgment against him. [Latin, "cause (it) to be done" (words used in such a writ).]
fier·y (fīr′ē, fī′ə-rē) *adj.* **-ier, -iest.** **1.** Consisting of or containing fire: *a fiery furnace.* **2.** Of, pertaining to, or resembling a fire: *a fiery sunset.* **3.** Torridly hot: *a fiery gust of the sirocco.* **4.** Flammable; liable to explode. Said of gas, a mine, or the like. **5.** Causing a hot, burning sensation; strong or highly spiced. Said of food or drink: *a fiery curry.* **6.** Emitting or appearing to emit sparks; glowing. **7. a.** Easily excited or emotionally volatile; tempestuous: *a fiery temper.* **b.** Showing passion or strong feeling: *a fiery outburst.* **8.** Inflamed. Said of the skin. [Middle English *fiery, firi,* from FIRE.] **—fier·i·ly** *adv.* **—fier·i·ness** *n.*
fiery cross *n.* **1.** Formerly, a wooden cross with charred or bloody ends used by the Scottish clans to summon forth men into battle. **2.** A burning cross used by the Ku Klux Klan as a symbol or emblem.
Fi·e·so·le (fē-ā′zə-lē′, -lā′) Ancient town founded by the Etruscans, near present-day Florence in Tuscany, Italy. It is a tourist spot because of its Etruscan and Roman museum.
fi·es·ta (fē-ĕs′tə) *n.* **1.** A religious feast or holiday; especially, a saint's day celebrated in Spanish-speaking countries. **2.** A celebration or festival. [Spanish, from Latin *fēsta,* neuter plural of *fēstus,* joyous, festive.]
FI·FA (fē′fə) *n.* The international governing body of soccer. [*F*édération *I*nternationale de *F*ootball *A*ssociation.]
fife (fīf) *n.* A musical instrument similar to a flute but higher in range, used primarily to accompany drums in military music.
~*v.* **fifed, fifing, fifes.** —*tr.* To play (a tune) on a fife. —*intr.* To play a fife. [German *Pfeife,* from Old High German *pfīffa,* from West Germanic *pīpa* (unattested), from Vulgar Latin *pīpa* (unattested), from Latin *pīpāre,* to chirp.]
fife rail *n.* A rail around the lower part of a ship's mast to which the belaying pins for the rigging are secured.
Fife Region (fīf). Unit of local administration in east-central Scotland, formerly the county of Fife. It borders on the North Sea between the Firth of Tay and the Firth of Forth. Fishing, arable farming, and coal mining make it one of the most prosperous regions in Scotland.
fif·teen (fĭf-tēn′) *n.* **1. a.** The cardinal number that is one more than fourteen. **b.** A symbol representing this, such as 15 or XV. **2.** A set made up of fifteen persons or things. **3.** The fifteenth in a series. **4.** A size, as in clothing, designated as fifteen. [Middle English *fiftene,* Old English *fīftȳne, fīftēne.*] **—fif·teen** *adj. & pron.*
Fifteen *n.* In British history, the **Jacobite Rebellion** *(see)* of 1715. Preceded by *the.*
fif·teenth (fĭf-tēnth′) *n.* **1.** The ordinal number 15 in a series. **2.** One of 15 equal parts. **3.** *Music.* **a.** An interval of two octaves. **b.** An organ stop pitched two octaves above the normal pitch. **—fif·teenth** *adj. & adv.*
fifth (fĭfth) *n.* **1.** The ordinal number five in a series. **2.** Any of five equal parts. **3. a.** A musical interval encompassing five diatonic tones, such as C, D, E, F, and G. **b.** The combination of the two tones constituting the extremities of such an interval. **c.** The dominant of a tonality. **4. a.** One fifth of a gallon of liquor. **b.** A bottle containing a fifth of liquor. [Middle English *fifthe, fifte,* Old English *fīfta.*] **—fifth** *adj. & adv.* **—fifth·ly** *adv.*
Fifth Amendment *n.* An amendment to the Constitution of the United States, ratified in 1791, that deals with the rights of accused

fig Ficus carica, *the fig tree, has been cultivated for its fruit in Europe and Asia since remote antiquity. The trees grow wild in the Middle East and western Asia between Syria and Afghanistan.*

PRONUNCIATION KEY

ă, pat; ā, pay; âr, care;
ä, father, are; b, bib;
ch, church; d, deed; ĕ, pet;
ē, be; f, fife; g, gag; h, hat;
hw, which; ĭ, pit; ī, pie;
îr, pier; j, judge; k, kick;
l, lid, needle; m, mum;
n, no, sudden; ng, thing;
ŏ, pot; ō, toe; ô, paw, for;
oi, noise; ou, out; o͝o, book;
o͞o, boot; p, pop; r, roar;
s, sauce; sh, ship, dish;
t, tight; th, thin, path;
th, this, bathe; ŭ, cut; ûr, fur;
v, valve; w, with; y, yes;
z, zebra, size; zh, vision;
ə, about, item, edible, gallop, circus, peaceful

IN FOREIGN WORDS:

à, *Fr.* ami; œ, *Fr.* feu, *Ger.* schön; ü, *Fr.* tu, *Ger.* über;
KH, *Ger.* ich, *Scot.* loch;
N, *Fr.* bon; y', *Fr.* Compiègne

STRESS MARKS:

Primary stress: ′
in·cite′ (ĭn-sīt′)
Secondary stress: ′
in′sight′ (ĭn′sīt′)

criminals by providing for due process of law, forbidding double jeopardy, and stating that no person may be forced to testify as a witness against himself.

fifth column *n.* **1.** A clandestine subversive organization working within a given country to further an invading enemy's military and political aims. **2.** Any subversive element working within an organization or institution. [First applied in 1936 to the Franco supporters in Madrid by Gen. Emilio Mola, who was leading four rebel columns of troops against that city.] **—fifth columnist** *n.*

fifth wheel *n.* **1.** A wheel or portion of a wheel placed horizontally over the forward axle of a carriage to provide support and stability during turns. **2.** An additional wheel carried on a four-wheeled vehicle as a spare. **3.** Any extra and unnecessary person or thing.

fif·ti·eth (fĭf′tē-ĭth) *n.* **1.** The ordinal number 50 in a series. **2.** Any of 50 equal parts. **—fif·ti·eth** *adj. & adv.*

fif·ty (fĭf′tē) *n.* **1. a.** The cardinal number that is ten more than forty. **b.** A symbol representing this, such as 50 or L. **2.** A set made up of fifty persons or things. **3.** The fiftieth in a series. **4.** A size, as in clothing, designated as fifty. **5.** A bill or coin having a denomination of fifty: *I'll take the money in fifties.* **6. fifties. a.** The numbers from 50 to 59, considered as a range of age, price, temperature, or the like. **b.** The years numbered 50 to 59 in a century. [Middle English *fifti,* Old English *fīftig.*] **—fif·ty** *adj. & pron.*

fif·ty-fif·ty (fĭf′tē-fĭf′tē) *adj. Informal.* **1.** Divided or shared in two equal portions: *a fifty-fifty split of the profits.* **2.** Even: *a fifty-fifty chance.* **—fif·ty-fif·ty** *adv.*

fig[1] (fĭg) *n.* **1.** Any of several trees or shrubs of the genus *Ficus;* especially, *F. carica,* native to the Mediterranean region and widely cultivated for its edible fruit. Also called "fig tree." **2.** The sweet, pear-shaped, many-seeded fruit of this tree. **3. a.** Any of several plants bearing similar edible fruit, such as the Hottentot fig, *Mesembryanthemum edule,* of southern Africa. See **fig marigold. b.** The fruit of such a plant. **4.** A trivial or contemptible amount; a jot; a whit: *"None of them . . . would have cared a fig the more for me"* (Hawthorne). [Middle English *fig(e),* from Old French *figue,* from Old Provençal *figa,* from Vulgar Latin *fīca* (unattested), from Latin *fīcus,* from the same Mediterranean source as Greek *sukon.* See also **syconium.**]

fig[2] *tr.v.* **figged, figging, figs.** *Informal.* **1.** To dress or furnish; array; furbish. Used with *out*: *all figged out.* **2.** To make (a horse) appear lively, usually by means of drugs. Used with *up* or *out.*
∼*n. Informal.* **1.** Dress; array: *in full fig.* **2.** Physical condition; shape: *in poor fig.* [Variant of obsolete *feague,* from German *fegen,* to polish, furbish. See **fake.**]

fig[3] *n.* An obscene gesture of contempt made by brandishing a fist with the thumb held between the first and second fingers. [French *(faire la) figue,* to make this gesture, from Italian *fica,* vulva, fig, from Vulgar Latin *fīca* (unattested), FIG (tree).]

fig. 1. figurative; figuratively. **2.** figure.

fig-bird (fĭg′bûrd′) *n.* An Australian oriole of the genus *Sphecotheres* that feeds on figs and other fruits.

fight (fīt) *v.* **fought** (fôt), **fighting, fights.** *—intr.* **1.** To participate in combat or battle. **2.** To make a strenuous effort; struggle: *fight against oppression.* **3.** To quarrel; argue. **4.** To participate in boxing or wrestling: *He fights professionally.* *—tr.* **1.** To contend with physically or in battle. **2.** To box or wrestle against in a ring. **3.** To contend with or struggle against: *fight prejudice.* **4.** To strive to prevent or undo the development or occurrence of: *fight a fire; fought temptation; fought back her tears.* **5. a.** To wage (a battle or war, for example). **b.** To engage in (a lawsuit, election, or other contest) against another. **6.** To do battle for; contend for: *"I now resolved that Calais should be fought to the death"* (Winston Churchill). **7.** To make (one's way) as if by fighting: *He fought his way to the top of his profession.* **8.** To set in combat with another: *fighting cocks.* **—fight off.** To defend against or drive back (a hostile force). **—fight it out.** To fight until something is settled or until one side is clearly the victor: *fight it out in public.* **—fight shy of.** To be reluctant to confront; avoid.
∼*n.* **1.** A battle waged between opposing groups; combat. **2.** A struggle, quarrel, or conflict. **3. a.** A physical conflict between two or more individuals; a brawl. **b.** A boxing or wrestling match; a bout. **4.** The power or inclination to fight; pugnacity. **5.** A struggle to achieve an objective. **—put up a fight.** To make a determined show of resistance. —See Synonyms at **conflict.** [Fight, fought, fought; Middle English *fighten, fa(u)ght, fo(u)ghten,* Old English *feohtan, feaht, fohten,* from Germanic.]

fight·er (fī′tər) *n.* **1.** One engaged in fighting. **2.** One employed to fight; a boxer. **3.** A pugnacious, unyielding, or determined person. **4.** *Military.* A fast, maneuverable combat aircraft used to engage enemy aircraft and to escort and defend bombers.

fight·er-bomb·er (fī′tər-bŏm′ər) *n.* An airplane capable of functioning both as a fighter and bomber.

fight·ing (fī′tĭng) *adj.* **1.** Ready to fight; equipped, prepared, or inclined to oppose. **2.** Liable to provoke conflict: *fighting words.* **—fighting fit.** Very fit; in peak condition.

fighting chance *n.* A slight chance to win, following a struggle.

fighting cock *n.* **1.** A cock bred for fighting. **2.** *Informal.* A quarrelsome person.

fighting fish *n.* Any of various small freshwater fishes of the genus *Betta,* of tropical Asia; especially, the **Siamese fighting fish** *(see).*

fighting fund *n. Chiefly British.* A fund set up to finance a campaign.

fig leaf *n.* **1.** A stylized representation of the leaf of a fig, used especially to conceal the genitalia on statues. **2.** A device intended to conceal something offensive or discreditable.

fig marigold *n.* Any of various plants of the genus *Mesembryanthemum,* native to southern Africa, having thick, fleshy leaves and variously colored flowers.

fig·ment (fĭg′mənt) *n.* **1.** Something imaginary; a fabrication. **2.** An arbitrary notion. [Middle English, from Latin *figmentum,* a formation, from *fingere,* to mold, fashion.]

fig tree *n.* A tree, the **fig** *(see).*

fig·ur·al (fĭg′yər-əl) *adj.* Consisting of or forming a pictorial composition or design of human or animal figures.

fig·u·rant (fĭg′yə-ränt′, -rănt′, -räN′) *n.* **1.** A member of a corps de ballet who does not perform solos. **2.** A stage performer without a speaking part. [French, from the present participle of *figurer,* to figure, represent, from Old French, from Latin *figūrāre,* to form, from *figūra,* FIGURE.]

fig·u·rate (fĭg′yər-ĭt, -yə-rāt′) *adj.* **1.** Having a definite or particular shape or form; figured. **2.** *Music.* Characterized by figuration; ornamented. [Latin *figūrātus,* past participle of *figūrāre,* to shape, from *figūra,* form, FIGURE.]

fig·u·ra·tion (fĭg′yə-rā′shən) *n.* **1.** The act of forming something into a particular shape. **2.** A shape, form, or outline. **3.** The act of representing with figures. **4.** A figurative representation, often symbolic or emblematic. **5.** *Music.* **a.** The continuous repetition of a pattern of notes or musical figures for decorative purposes. **b.** Ornamentation. **6.** The ornamentation of something with small designs.

fig·u·ra·tive (fĭg′yər-ə-tĭv) *adj. Abbr.* **fig. 1. a.** Based on or making use of figures of speech, especially metaphor; not literal; metaphorical: *figurative language.* **b.** Containing many figures of speech; ornate. **2.** Represented by a figure or figures; symbolic or emblematic. **3.** *Art.* **a.** Of or relating to representation by means of animal or human figures; figural. **b.** Representational rather than abstract. **c.** Designating a style of painting in which the subjects are recognizable but not conventionally depicted. **—fig·u·ra·tive·ly** *adv.* **—fig·u·ra·tive·ness** *n.*

fig·ure (fĭg′yər) *n. Abbr.* **fig. 1.** A written symbol representing anything other than a letter; especially, a number. **2. figures.** Mathematical calculation involving the use of such symbols: *She is good at figures.* **3. a.** An amount represented in numbers: *a large figure.* **b.** An estimate: *Can you give me a figure?* **4.** The outline, form, or silhouette of a thing. **5. a.** The shape or form of a human body, especially as regards weight and proportion: *a pear-shaped figure.* **b.** A slim, attractive body: *still hasn't lost her figure at 52.* **6.** An individual, especially a well-known personage. **7.** The impression an individual makes through behavior or appearance: *He cuts a dashing figure.* **8.** A person, animal, or object that symbolizes something: *She'll always be a mother figure to me.* **9.** A pictorial or sculptural representation, especially of the human body. **10. a.** A diagram. **b.** A design or pattern. **11.** An illustration printed from an engraved plate or block. **12.** A configuration or distinct group of steps in skating or a dance. **13.** *Music.* A brief melodic or harmonic unit often constituting the base for a larger musical phrase or structure. **14.** *Logic.* Any one of the forms that a syllogism can take, depending on the position of the middle term. **15.** A **figure of speech** *(see).* **16.** *Mathematics.* A geometric shape formed by lines, curves, or surfaces, either a *plane figure* in two dimensions or a *solid figure* in three. —See Synonyms at **form.**
∼*v.* **figured, -uring, -ures.** *—tr.* **1.** To calculate with numbers; tally or work out mathematically. **2. a.** To make a likeness of; depict. **b.** To symbolize; represent. **3.** To adorn with a design or figures. **4.** *Music.* To indicate the chordal structure of (a bass line of single notes) with a sequence of conventionalized numbers. **5.** *Informal.* To conclude, believe, or predict: *What do you figure will happen?* *—intr.* **1.** To calculate; compute. **2.** To be an element; be involved: *Your name didn't even figure in the conversation.* **3.** *Informal.* To make sense; add up: *That figures!* **—figure on** (or **upon**). *Informal.* **1.** To count on. **2.** To take into consideration; expect. **—figure out.** *Informal.* To solve; comprehend; work out. [Middle English, from Old French, from Latin *figūra,* form, shape, figure.]

fig·ured (fĭg′yərd) *adj.* **1.** Decorated with a design; patterned: *"My dress is richly figured"* (Amy Lowell). **2.** Represented, as in graphic art or sculpture; depicted.

figured bass *n. Music.* A **continuo** *(see).*

figure eight *n.* **1.** *Aeronautics.* A maneuver in which an aircraft flies a path tracing the outline of the number 8. **2.** A skating figure or dance pattern shaped like the number 8. **3.** Any of various forms having the shape of the number 8, such as a knot.

fig·ure-ground (fĭg′yər-ground′) *n. Psychology.* The organization of visual perception into a unified object standing out from a background. The organization of a visual field can change depending on the individual and the familiarity or regularity of parts of the field, or those parts of the field being attended to, and is used as the basis for many types of optical illusion.

fig·ure·head (fĭg′yər-hĕd′) *n.* **1.** A person given a position of nominal leadership but having no actual authority or responsibility. **2.** *Nautical.* A carved, decorative figure placed on the prow of a ship.

figure of speech *n.* An expression in which words are used, not in their literal sense, but to create a more forceful or dramatic image, as **metaphor, simile,** or **hyperbole** *(all of which see).*

fig·u·rine (fĭg′yə-rēn′) *n.* A small ornamental figure, as one carved or formed from wood, porcelain, glass, or metal; a statuette.

fig-bird *Figs are only part of the diet of the southern fig-bird,* Sphecotheres vieilloti, *which also feeds on other fruit and on berries.*

figurine *A porcelain figurine of the Chinese goddess of mercy, Guanyin. The crayfish on which she stands is an emblem of wealth and harmony.*

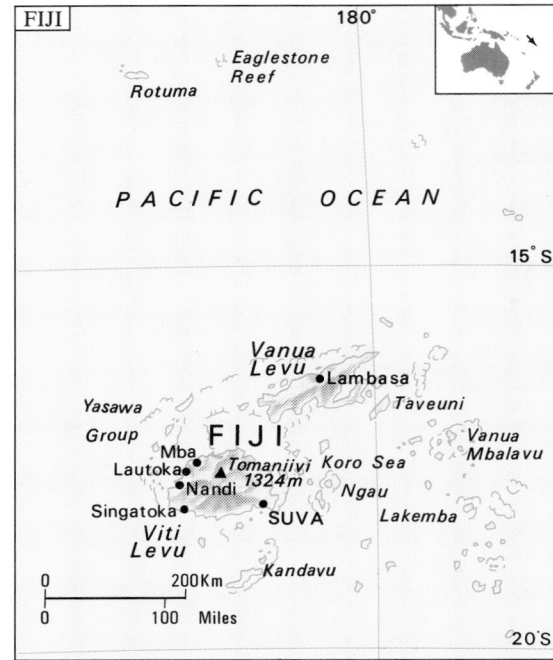

[French, from Italian *figurina*, diminutive of *figura*, figure, from Latin *figūra*, FIGURE.]

fig wasp *n.* A small wasp of the genus *Blastophaga*, which is the agent for caprification in figs.

fig-wort (fĭg'wûrt', -wôrt') *n.* Any of various plants of the genus *Scrophularia*, having loose, branching clusters of small greenish or purple flowers. [From FIG, alluding to swellings, as in scrofula, for which the plant was believed to be a remedy.]

Fi·ji¹ (fē'jē). Independent republic within the British Commonwealth, consisting of more than 330 islands and islets in the South Pacific Ocean. Some 106 of the larger islands are inhabited. The capital, Suva, is on the largest island, Viti Levu. The islands were discovered by the Dutch explorer Abel Tasman in 1643 and explored by Capt. William Bligh after he was set adrift by the *Bounty* mutineers (1789). Annexed by Great Britain in 1874, they remained a crown colony until 1970. Sugar is the most important crop. Area, 18,333 square kilometers (7,078 square miles). Population, 800,000.

Fi·ji² *n.* **1.** A Fijian. **2.** The language of the Fijians.

Fi·ji·an (fē'jē-ən) *adj.* Of Fiji or the Fiji Islands, or the people or language of these places.
    —*n.* **1.** A native of Fiji or the Fiji Islands, being of predominantly Melanesian stock with an admixture of Polynesian. **2.** The Oceanic language of Fiji or the Fiji Islands.

fi·la. Plural of **filum**.

filagree. Variant of **filigree**.

fil·a·ment (fĭl'ə-mənt) *n.* **1.** A fine or thinly spun thread, fiber, wire, or the like. **2.** *Biology.* A slender, threadlike appendage, part, or structure, especially: **a.** The slender stalk of a stamen on which the anther is borne. **b.** A chainlike series of cells, as in some algae and bacteria. **c.** The free barb of a down feather. **3. a.** *Electricity.* A fine wire heated electrically to incandescence in an electric lamp. **b.** *Electronics.* A high-resistance wire or ribbon forming the cathode in some thermionic valves. [Old French, from Medieval Latin *fīlamentum*, from Late Latin *fīlāre*, to wind threads, spin, from Latin *fīlum*, thread.] —**fil·a·men·tous** (fĭl'ə-mĕn'təs), **fil·a·men·ta·ry** (fĭl'ə-mĕn'tə-rē) *adj.*

fi·lar (fī'lər) *adj.* **1.** Of or pertaining to a thread or threads. **2.** Having fine threads across the field of view for measuring small distances, as in a microscope or telescope eyepiece. [Latin *fīlum*, thread.]

fil·a·ree (fĭl'ə-rē') *n.* A plant, the **alfilaria** (see). [Variant of American Spanish *alfilerillo*, ALFILARIA.]

fi·lar·i·a (fĭ-lâr'ē-ə) *n., pl.* **-iae** (-ē-ē'). Any of various parasitic nematode worms of the superfamily Filarioidea that infest man and other vertebrates. [New Latin *Filaria* (former genus name), "threadworm," from Latin *fīlum*, thread.] —**fi·lar·i·al, fi·lar·i·an** *adj.*

fi·la·ri·a·sis (fĭl'ə-rī'ə-sĭs) *n.* Infestation of the lymph glands with the filaria *Wuchereria bancrofti* or *Brugia malayi*, resulting in inflammation and **elephantiasis** (see). [New Latin : FILAR(IA) + -IASIS.]

fil·a·ture (fĭl'ə-chŏŏr', -chər) *n.* **1.** The act or process of spinning, drawing, or twisting into threads. **2.** The reeling of raw silk from cocoons. **3.** A reel used in this process. **4.** An establishment where this process is performed. [French, from Late Latin *fīlātus*, past participle of *fīlāre*, to draw out thread, spin. See **filament**.]

fil·bert (fĭl'bərt) *n.* **1.** A Eurasian shrub or tree, *Corylus maxima*, a species of hazel, cultivated for its edible nuts. **2.** The rounded, smooth-shelled nut of this shrub. **3.** Any hazelnut. [Middle English *filbert, philliberd*, from Norman French (*noix de*) *filbert*, "nut of St. Philbert" (died A.D. 684), Frankish abbot whose feast day on August 22 marks the ripening season of the nut.]

filch (fĭlch) *tr.v.* **filched, filching, filches.** To steal (something) in a furtive manner; pilfer. —See Synonyms at **rob**. [Middle English *filchen*†.] —**filch·er** *n.*

file¹ (fīl) *n.* **1.** A receptacle, such as a folder or box, that keeps loose objects, such as papers, cards, or any collection of small items, in useful order. **2.** A collection of objects kept thus; especially, a set of documents related to one subject, such as a particular client or case. **3. a.** A line of persons, animals, or things positioned one behind another. **b.** *Military.* A line of soldiers or vehicles so positioned. **4.** Any of the rows of squares that run vertically on a chessboard. **5.** A set of data with an identifying label held in a computer storage device. —**on file.** Catalogued or recorded in a file.
    —*v.* **filed, filing, files.** —*tr.* **1.** To put or keep (papers or cards, for example) in useful order; catalogue. **2. a.** To enter (a legal document, for example) on public record or official record. **b.** To submit (a complaint or legal petition, for example) to a relevant authority. **3.** To send or submit (copy) to a newspaper or other news agency. —*intr.* **1.** To march or walk in a line or lines. **2.** To submit a formal application, as for divorce. [Noun, sense 1: Old French *fil*, "thread," wire or string on which documents are strung, from Latin *fīlum*, thread. Noun, sense 3: Old French *file*, from *filer*, "to draw out thread," march in a line, from Late Latin *fīlāre*, to spin, from Latin *fīlum*, thread.] —**fil·er** *n.*

file² *n.* **1.** Any of several steel tools with hardened ridged surfaces, used in smoothing, polishing, grinding down, or boring. **2.** *Archaic British Slang.* A deceitful, cunning person.
    —*tr.v.* **filed, filing, files.** To smooth, polish, grind, bore, or remove with or as if with a file. [Middle English *file, fyle*, Old English *fēol, fīl*.] —**fil·er** *n.*

file clerk *n.* A person employed to maintain the files and records of an office.

file·fish (fīl'fĭsh') *n., pl.* **-fishes** or collectively **filefish.** Any of various chiefly tropical marine fishes of the family Balistidae, related to and resembling the triggerfishes. [Referring to the rough scales of some species.]

fi·let¹ (fĭ-lā', fĭl'ā') *n.* A net or lace with a simple pattern of squares. [French, from Old French *filé*, from Old Provençal *filat*, "made of threads," from *fil*, thread, from Latin *fīlum*.]

filet². Variant of **fillet**.

fi·let mi·gnon (fĭ-lā' mĭn-yŏn', fīl'ā mĕn-yôN') *n.* A small, round, very choice cut of beef from the center of the fillet. [French, "dainty fillet."]

fil·i·al (fĭl'ē-əl) *adj.* Of, pertaining to, or befitting a son or daughter. [Middle English, from Late Latin *fīliālis*, from Latin *fīlius*, son.] —**fil·i·al·ly** *adv.* —**fil·i·al·ness** *n.*

filial generation *n.* A set of offspring from a specific mating that follows the parental generation.

fil·i·ate (fĭl'ē-āt') *tr.v.* **-ated, -ating, -ates. 1.** *Rare.* To affiliate. **2.** *Law.* To assign paternity to (an illegitimate child, for example). [Medieval Latin *fīliāre*, to acknowledge as a son, from Latin *fīlius*, son.]

fil·i·a·tion (fĭl'ē-ā'shən) *n.* **1.** The condition or fact of being the child of a certain parent. **2.** A line of descent; derivation; lineage. **3. a.** The act or fact of forming a new branch, as of a society or language group; expansion or division. **b.** The branch thus formed; an offshoot. **4.** *Law.* Affiliation.

fil·i·beg (fĭl'ə-bĕg') *n.* A kilt. [Scottish Gaelic *féileadhbeag* : *féileadh*†, fold, kilt + *beag*, small, little, akin to Old Irish *becc*, small, from Common Celtic *biggo-* (unattested).]

fil·i·bus·ter (fĭl'ə-bŭs'tər) *n.* **1. a.** The use of obstructionist tactics, such as the making of prolonged speeches or the introduction of irrelevant material, for the purpose of delaying legislative action. **b.** An instance of the use of such tactics in a legislative body. **c.** A user of such tactics. **2.** An adventurer who engages in a private military action in a foreign country.
    —*v.* **filibustered, -tering, -ters.** —*intr.* **1.** To use obstructionist tactics, especially prolonged speeches, in a legislative body. **2.** To engage in a private military action in a foreign country. —*tr.* To use obstructionist tactics against (legislation, for example). [Originally "freebooter," from Spanish *filibustero*, from French *flibustier*, from Dutch *vrijbuiter*, pirate, "one who plunders freely" : *vrij*, free + *-buiter*, plunderer, from *buit*, BOOTY.] —**fil·i·bus·ter·er** *n.*

fil·i·cide (fĭl'ə-sīd') *n. Rare.* **1.** The act of killing one's child. **2.** One who kills his child. [Latin *fīlius*, son, or its derivative *fīlia*, daughter + -CIDE.] —**fil·i·cid·al** (fĭl'ə-sīd'l) *adj.*

fil·i·form (fĭl'ə-fôrm') *adj. Biology.* Resembling or having the form of a thread; threadlike. [Latin *fīlum*, thread + -FORM.]

fil·i·gree, fil·a·gree, fil·la·gree (fĭl'ə-grē') *n.* **1.** Delicate and intricate ornamental work made from gold, silver, or other fine twisted wire. **2.** Any intricate, delicate, or fanciful ornamentation.
    —*adj.* Resembling or made of filigree.
    —*tr.v.* **filigreed, -greeing, -grees.** To decorate with or as if with filigree. [Earlier *filigreen*, from French *filigrane*, from Italian *filigrana* : *fili-*, from Latin *fīlum*, thread + *grana*, grain, from Latin *grānum*.]

fil·ing (fī'lĭng) *n.* **1.** The act of using a file. **2.** A particle or shaving removed by a file.

filing cabinet *n.* A cabinet with drawers used for holding documents, files, or the like.

filing clerk *n.* A file clerk.

filefish *Filefish, which are found in warm seas all over the world, get their name from their sandpapery skin that is covered with tiny close-set spikes. This is the fringed filefish, a Caribbean species.*

filigree *Silver wire twisted into the delicate lacelike pattern known as filigree decorates these 19th-century thimble holders that contain miniature sewing kits.*

Fil·i·pi·no (fĭl'ə-pē'nō) *n., pl.* **-nos.** A native, citizen, or inhabitant of the Philippines.
~*adj.* Of or pertaining to the Philippines or Filipinos. [Spanish, from *(Islas) Filipinas,* the PHILIPPINE(S).]

fill (fĭl) *v.* **filled, filling, fills.** *—tr.* **1.** To put into as much as can be held; load completely; make full. **2.** To close or plug up (an opening, for example). **3.** To stop up a cavity in (a tooth). **4.** To produce a sensation of fullness in (the stomach, for example). **5.** To supply (an empty space) with material, such as writing, an inscription, or an illustration. **6.** To put someone into or elect to (an office or position); furnish with a holder or occupant. **7.** To occupy or hold (an office or position). **8. a.** To occupy the whole of: *fill one's time.* **b.** To pervade: *Cries filled the air.* **9.** To affect profoundly (the mind or thoughts, for example): *The prospect filled him with dread.* **10.** To add an inferior substance or substances to (a product) to increase bulk. **11. a.** To cause (a sail) to swell. **b.** To adjust (a yard) so that wind will cause a sail to swell. *—intr.* To become full. **—fill out. 1.** To make or become fuller, rounder, broader, or shapelier. **2.** To complete (a form, for example) by adding the necessary information. **—fill someone's shoes.** To assume someone's duties or position. **—fill the bill.** *Informal.* To serve a given purpose.
~*n.* **1.** That which is needed to make full, complete, or satisfied: *eat one's fill.* **2. a.** A built-up piece of land; an embankment. **b.** The material, such as earth, gravel, or sand, used for this. **—have one's fill.** To be thoroughly sated or weary. [Middle English *fillen,* Old English *fyllan.*]

fille de joie (fē' də zhwä') *n., pl.* **filles de joie** *(pronounced as singular).* A prostitute. [French, "daughter of joy."]

filled gold *n.* A base metal such as brass with a surface layer of bonded gold, used especially in jewelry.

fill·er (fĭl'ər) *n.* **1.** One who fills. **2.** Something added in order to augment weight or size or to fill space. **3.** A composition, especially a semisolid that hardens on drying, used to fill pores, cracks, or holes in a wood, plaster, or other construction surface prior to finishing. **4.** Tobacco used in a plug or to form the body of a cigar. **5.** A short item used to fill space in a newspaper, magazine, or other publication. **6.** Something, such as a news item or piece of music, used to fill time in a radio, television, or theatrical presentation. **7.** A device, such as a funnel, used to fill something. **8.** *Architecture.* Any element, such as a plate, used to fill the space between two supporting members.

fil·lér (fĭl'âr') *n., pl.* **-lérs** or collectively **fillér.** A coin equal to 1/100 of the forint of Hungary. See feature at **currency.** [Hungarian.]

fil·let (fĭl'ĭt; *usually* fĭ-lā', fĭl'ā' *for sense 2) n.* Also **fi·let** (for sense 2). **1.** A narrow strip of ribbon or similar material or a thin band of metal, often worn in the hair or around the head. **2. a.** A strip or compact piece of boneless meat or fish. **b.** A cut of beef taken from the underside of the loin. **c.** A cut of pork, veal, or lamb taken from the top of the hind leg. **3.** *Architecture.* **a.** A thin, flat molding used as separation between or ornamentation for larger moldings. **b.** A ridge between the indentations of a fluted column. **4. a.** A narrow decorative line impressed upon the cover of a book. **b.** A hand tool or wheel used in making such a line. **5.** *Heraldry.* A narrow horizontal band placed in the lower fourth area of the chief. **6.** *Anatomy.* A loop-shaped band of fibers, such as the lemniscus. **7.** A raised band or rim on a surface. **8.** A structure added to round off an angle; a fairing.
~*tr.v.* **filleted** (fĭl'ĭ-tĭd; *usually* fĭ-lād', fĭl'ād' *for sense 2*), **-leting** (fĭl'ĭ-tĭng; *usually* fĭ-lā'ĭng, fĭl'ā'ĭng *for sense 2*), **-lets** (fĭl'ĭts; *usually* fĭ-lāz', fĭl'āz' *for sense 2*). Also **fi·let** (for sense 2). **1.** To bind or decorate with or as if with a fillet. **2.** To slice, bone, or make into a fillet or fillets. [Middle English *filet,* from Old French, diminutive of *fil,* thread, from Latin *filum.*]

fill in *tr.v.* **1.** To place material in (a hole or space, for example) so as to occupy completely. **2.** To complete (a form, for example) by adding the necessary information. **3.** To occupy (time). **4.** To set down (information), as on a form: *Fill in your name and address.* **5.** *Informal.* To inform. Used with *on: Fill me in on what's happening.* *—intr.v.* To act as a substitute.

fill-in (fĭl'ĭn') *n. Informal.* **1.** One that fills a vacancy, gap, or temporary need. **2.** A summary of necessary or important information; a briefing.

fill·ing (fĭl'ĭng) *n.* **1.** Something used to fill a space or container. **2.** Any of various substances, such as amalgam or cement, used to fill a cavity in a tooth. **3.** An edible mixture used to fill sandwiches, cakes, and pastries. **4.** The horizontal threads that cross the warp in weaving; weft.
~*adj.* Tending to fill; especially, tending to cause a sensation of fullness in the stomach.

filling station *n.* A retail establishment at which vehicles are serviced, especially with gasoline, oil, water, and air. Also called "gas station," "service station."

fil·lip (fĭl'əp) *n.* **1.** A light blow or flick made by pressing a fingertip against the thumb and suddenly releasing it. **2.** A slight goad or incentive; a stimulus.
~*v.* **filliped, -liping, -lips.** *—tr.* **1.** To strike or propel with a fillip. **2.** To excite, arouse, or stimulate. *—intr.* To make a fillip. [15th century : imitative.]

Fill·more (fĭl'môr', -mōr'), **Millard** (1800–74). 13th U.S. President (1850–53). Assuming the Presidency on the death of Zachary Taylor (July 9, 1850), he struggled to keep the nation intact, signing the Compromise of 1850 and the Fugitive Slave Law. The latter act cost him the Whig Party renomination in 1852. Fillmore later campaigned unsuccessfully as a candidate for the Know-Nothing Party (1856).

fill up *tr.v.* **1. a.** To fill completely. **b.** To fill (the gas tank of a motor vehicle). **2.** To fill in (a form, for example). *—intr.v.* To become full.

fill-up (fĭl'ŭp') *n.* An act or instance of filling up.

fil·ly (fĭl'ē) *n., pl.* **-lies. 1.** A young female horse; a young mare. **2.** *Informal.* A lively and high-spirited girl. [Middle English *filli,* from Old Norse *fylja,* from Germanic *ful-* (unattested), FOAL.]

film (fĭlm) *n.* **1. a.** A thin covering or coating. **b.** A thin, generally flexible transparent sheet, as of plastic or rubber, used in wrapping or packaging. **2.** A thin skin or membranous coating. **3.** An abnormal, thin, opaque coating on the cornea in certain eye diseases. **4.** A thin sheet or strip of flexible cellulose material coated with a photosensitive emulsion, used to make photographic negatives or transparencies. **5. a.** A motion picture. **b.** Motion pictures collectively; the cinema. **6.** A haze or mist.
~*v.* **filmed, filming, films.** *—tr.* **1.** To cover with or as if with a film. **2.** To photograph (an event, scene, or person, for example) in the making of a motion picture. **3.** To turn (a novel, for example) into a motion picture. *—intr.* **1.** To become coated or obscured with or as if with a film. **2.** To make a motion picture. **3.** To be reproduced in a motion picture. [Middle English *film,* Old English *filmen,* from Germanic.]

film·go·er (fĭlm'gō'ər) *n.* One who regularly goes to see motion pictures.

film·ic (fĭl'mĭk) *adj.* Of, pertaining to, or resembling motion pictures. **—film·i·cal·ly** *adv.*

film·mak·ing (fĭlm'mā'kĭng) *n.* The production of motion pictures. **—film·mak·er** *n.*

fil·mog·ra·phy (fĭl-mŏg'rə-fē) *n., pl.* **-phies.** A list of the motion pictures that a given actor or director, for example, has made, or that have a similar subject.

film pack *n.* A pack of photographic sheet films that can be exposed in succession and withdrawn from the exposure position for storage at the rear of the pack.

film·set (fĭlm'sĕt') *tr.v.* **-set, -setting, sets.** *Printing.* To set (type matter) by means of photocomposition; photocompose. **—film·set·ter** *n.*

film·set·ting (fĭlm'sĕt'ĭng) *n.* **Photocomposition** *(see).*

film·strip (fĭlm'strĭp') *n.* A length of film containing photographs, diagrams, or other graphic matter prepared for still projection.

film·y (fĭl'mē) *adj.* **-ier, -iest. 1.** Resembling or consisting of film; transparent; gauzy. **2.** Covered by or as if by a film; blurred; hazy. **—film·i·ly** *adv.* **—film·i·ness** *n.*

filmy fern *n.* Any fern having fronds only one cell thick and consequently usually limited to very humid or shady habitats.

fil·o·plume (fĭl'ə-plo͞om', fī'lə-) *n.* A hairlike feather having few or no barbs, occurring between the contour feathers. [Latin *filum,* thread + PLUME.]

fi·lose (fī'lōs') *adj. Biology.* **1.** Threadlike. **2.** Having or ending in a threadlike part. [Latin *filum,* thread.]

fils[1] (fĭls) or **fil** (fĭl) *n., pl.* **fils.** A monetary unit equal to 1/1000 of the dinar of Bahrain, Iraq, Jordan, Kuwait, and South Yemen, 1/100 of the dirham of the United Arab Emirates, or 1/100 of the rial of Yemen. See feature at **currency.** [Arabic.]

fils[2] (fēs). *French.* Son. Used after a proper name to distinguish a son from a father with the same name. Compare **père.**

fil·ter (fĭl'tər) *n.* **1.** Any porous substance through which a liquid or gas is passed in order to remove suspended matter. **2. a.** A device containing or consisting of such a substance, especially when used to extract impurities from air, water, or the like. **b.** A filter tip. **3.** Any of various electric, electronic, acoustic, or optical devices used to reject signals, vibrations, or radiations of certain frequencies while passing others.
~*v.* **filtered, -tering, -ters.** *—tr.* **1.** To pass (a liquid or gas) through a filter. **2.** To remove by passing through a filter. *—intr.* **1.** To pass through or as if through a filter: *"The chapel was flooded by the dull scarlet of light that filtered through the lower blinds"* (James Joyce). **2.** To emerge gradually. Used of news, facts, or other information. **3.** To flow or proceed gradually: *People filtered into the room.* [Middle English *filtre,* a piece of felt (used to strain liquid), from Old French, from Medieval Latin *filtrum,* from Frankish *filtir* (unattested).] **—fil·ter·er** *n.*

fil·ter·a·ble (fĭl'tər-ə-bəl, fĭl'trə-) *adj.* Also **fil·tra·ble** (fĭl'trə-bəl). **1.** Capable of being filtered; especially, capable of being removed by filtering. **2.** Sufficiently minute to pass through a fine filter, thereby maintaining the infectivity of the filtrate. Said of certain viruses. **—fil·ter·a·bil·i·ty** (fĭl'tər-ə-bĭl'ə-tē, fĭl'trə-) *n.*

filter bed *n.* A layer of sand or gravel on the bottom of a reservoir or tank used to filter water or sewage.

filter feeder *n.* Any aquatic animal that uses a filtering mechanism to ingest minute food particles from the water.

filter paper *n.* Porous paper suitable for use as a filter.

filter pump *n.* A simple vacuum pump by which air is removed from a system by carrying it away in a narrow, fast jet of water.

filter tip *n.* **1.** A small tube of porous material attached to the end of a cigarette to remove part of the harmful substances from the smoke. **2.** A cigarette with such an attachment.

filth (fĭlth) *n.* **1. a.** Foul or dirty matter. **b.** Refuse. **2.** A dirty or corrupt condition; foulness. **3.** Material or language considered obscene, prurient, or immoral. [Middle English *filth, fulth,* Old English *fȳlth,* putrid matter.]

PRONUNCIATION KEY

ă, pat; ā, pay; âr, care;
ä, father, are; b, bib;
ch, church; d, deed; ĕ, pet;
ē, be; f, fife; g, gag; h, hat;
hw, which; ĭ, pit; ī, pie;
îr, pier; j, judge; k, kick;
l, lid, needle; m, mum;
n, no, sudden; ng, thing;
ŏ, pot; ō, toe; ô, paw, for;
oi, noise; ou, out; o͝o, book;
o͞o, boot; p, pop; r, roar;
s, sauce; sh, ship, dish;
t, tight; th, thin, path;
th, this, bathe; ŭ, cut; ûr, fur;
v, valve; w, with; y, yes;
z, zebra, size; zh, vision;
ə, about, item, edible,
gallop, circus, peaceful

IN FOREIGN WORDS:

à, *Fr.* ami; œ, *Fr.* feu, *Ger.* schön; ü, *Fr.* tu, *Ger.* über; KH, *Ger.* ich, *Scot.* loch; N, *Fr.* bon; y', *Fr.* Compiègne

STRESS MARKS:

Primary stress: '
in·cite' (ĭn-sīt')
Secondary stress: '
in'sight' (ĭn'sīt')

filth·y (fĭl′thē) *adj.* **-ier, -iest. 1.** Heavily soiled; very dirty. **2.** Obscene; scatological. **3.** Highly objectionable; vile; nasty. **4.** *Informal.* Very bad; unpleasant: *filthy weather.* —See Synonyms at **dirty.** —**filth·i·ly** *adv.* —**filth·i·ness** *n.*

fil·trate (fĭl′trāt′) *v.* **-trated, -trating, -trates.** —*tr.* To put through a filter. —*intr.* To go through a filter.
~*n.* The portion of filtered material that passes through the filter. [Medieval Latin *filtrāre,* from *filtrum,* FILTER.]

fil·tra·tion (fĭl-trā′shən) *n.* The act or process of filtering.

fi·lum (fī′ləm) *n., pl.* **-la** (-lə). Any threadlike anatomical structure; a filament. [Latin *fīlum,* thread.]

FIM field-ion microscope; field-ion microscopy.

fim·bri·a (fĭm′brē-ə) *n., pl.* **-briae** (-brē-ē′). A fringelike structure, as at the opening of the Fallopian tube in mammals. [Late Latin, fiber, fringe, from Latin *fimbriae*†, fibers, threads. See also **fringe.**]

fim·bri·ate (fĭm′brē-ĭt, -āt′) *adj.* Also **fim·bri·at·ed** (-ā′tĭd). Fringed, as the edge of a petal or the opening of a duct may be. [Late Latin *fimbriātus,* fringed, from FIMBRIA.] —**fim·bri·a·tion** *n.*

fin[1] (fĭn) *n.* **1.** A membranous appendage extending from the body of a fish or other aquatic animal, used for propelling, steering, or maintaining balance. **2.** Something resembling a fin in shape or function, such as a diver's flipper. **3.** A fixed or movable vane or airfoil used to stabilize an aircraft or missile in flight. **4.** An appendage on a boat, such as a submarine; especially, a **fin keel** *(see).* **5.** A projecting vane used for cooling, as on a radiator or engine cylinder. **6.** An ornamental projection, as on the rear wing of a car.
~*v.* **finned, finning, fins.** —*tr.* **1.** To equip with fins. **2.** To cut the fins from. —*intr.* To emerge with the fins above water. [Middle English *finne,* Old English *finn,* akin to Middle Low German *finne*†.]

fin[2] *n. Slang.* A five-dollar bill [Yiddish *finf,* five, from Middle High German *vimf,* from Old High German *funf, finf.*]

fin. 1. finance; financial. **2.** finish.

Fin. Finland; Finnish.

fin·a·ble, fine·a·ble (fī′nə-bəl) *adj.* Liable to a fine or fines.

fi·na·gle (fĭ-nā′gəl) *v.* **-gled, -gling, -gles.** *Informal.* —*tr.* **1.** To achieve by dubious or crafty methods; wangle. **2.** To trick or delude; deceive. —*intr.* To use crafty, deceitful methods. [Probably from dialectal *fainaigue*†, to cheat.] —**fi·na·gler** *n.*

fi·nal (fī′nəl) *adj.* **1. a.** Forming or occurring at the end; concluding; last. **b.** *Phonetics.* Occurring at the end of a word or syllable. **2.** Pertaining to or constituting the end result of a process or procedure; ultimate: *the final purpose.* **3.** Decisive; conclusive; unalterable: *The judges' decision is final.* **4.** *Grammar.* Indicating purpose: *a final clause.* —See Synonyms at **last.**
~*n.* Something that comes at or forms the end, especially: **1.** The last or one of the last of a series of sports contests or other competitions. **2.** The last examination of an academic course. **3.** The edition of a newspaper published last in the day. [Middle English, from Old French, from Latin *fīnālis,* from *fīnis*†, end.]

final cause *n. Philosophy.* The ultimate purpose of something.

fi·na·le (fĭ-năl′ē, -nä′lē) *n.* The concluding part of an entertainment or work, especially a musical composition. [Italian, "final," from Latin *fīnālis,* FINAL.]

fi·nal·ist (fī′nə-lĭst) *n.* A contestant in the final session of a competition.

fi·nal·i·ty (fī-năl′ə-tē, fĭ-) *n., pl.* **-ties. 1.** The condition or fact of being final; conclusiveness. **2.** A final, conclusive, or decisive act or utterance.

fi·nal·ize (fī′nə-līz′) *tr.v.* **-ized, -izing, -izes. 1.** To put into final form. **2.** To complete arrangements for. —**fi·nal·i·za·tion** (fī′nə-lĭ-zā′shən) *n.*

Usage: *Finalize* is widely used in official communications. Because of its bureaucratic associations, many people avoid using it, preferring *complete, conclude, make final,* or *put in final form.*

fi·nal·ly (fī′nə-lē) *adv.* **1.** At the final point; at the end; last. **2.** Decisively; irrevocably. **3.** After a considerable delay; eventually; at last. **4.** Ultimately; in the end. **5.** Used to introduce a concluding point of discussion: *Finally, we must consider . . .*

Final Solution *n.* **1.** The Nazi plan in World War II for the mass killing of European Jews. **2. final solution.** Any attempt at mass destruction of a people.

fi·nance (fĭ-năns′, fī-, fī′năns′) *n.* **1.** *Abbr.* **fin. a.** The science of the management of money and other assets. **b.** The disposition of public revenues by a government. **2. finances. a.** Monetary resources or funds, especially of a government or corporate body. **b.** The monetary affairs or arrangements of a person, company, or the like. **3.** The obtainment of funds; financing.
~*v.* **financed, -nancing, -nances.** —*tr.* To supply or raise the funds or capital for. —*intr.* **1.** To raise or supply funds. **2.** To manage finances. [Middle English *finaunce,* end, settlement, payment, from Old French *finance,* from *finer,* to end, settle, from *fin,* end, from Latin *fīnis*†.]

finance bill *n.* A legislative act designed to raise public revenues.

finance company *n.* A company offering loans to individuals, as for the purchase of goods or property.

fi·nan·cial (fĭ-năn′shəl, fī-) *adj. Abbr.* **fin.** Of or pertaining to finances or those who deal with finances. —**fi·nan·cial·ly** *adv.*

Synonyms: *fiscal, monetary, pecuniary.*

financial year *n.* A **fiscal year** *(see).*

fin·an·cier (fĭn′ən-sîr′, fĭ-năn′-, fī′năn-) *n.* One who is occupied with or expert in large-scale financial affairs. [French, from FINANCE.]

fin·back (fĭn′băk′) *n.* A whale, the **rorqual** *(see).*

finch (fĭnch) *n.* Any of various relatively small birds of the family Fringillidae, such as a goldfinch, cardinal, or canary, having a short, stout bill adapted for cracking seeds. [Middle English *finch,* Old English *finc,* from Germanic.]

find (fīnd) *v.* **found** (found), **finding, finds.** —*tr.* **1.** To come upon by accident; discover by chance. **2.** To come upon after a search: *find the cause of the trouble.* **3.** To come upon through experience or effort; obtain knowledge of; attain: *found contentment at last.* **4.** To succeed in reaching; arrive at: *The dart found the mark.* **5. a.** To learn by inquiry or research; determine; ascertain: *found the solution to the problem.* **b.** To learn accidentally. **6.** To consider; regard: *I find her charm irresistible.* **7.** To recover (something lost). **8.** To recover the use of; regain: *found his voice and responded.* **9.** To manage to obtain: *find money for food.* **10.** To declare as a verdict or conclusion. **11.** To furnish; supply. —*intr.* To come to a legal decision or verdict: *The jury found for the defendant.* —**find oneself. 1.** To discover what one truly wishes to be and do in life. **2.** To become aware of being in a condition or place. —**find out. 1.** To learn by accident or through inquiry. **2.** To discover the dishonesty, bad reputation, or deceit of (a person).
~*n.* **1.** An act of finding. **2.** That which is found; especially, a rare or valuable discovery. [Find, found, found; Middle English *finden, found, founden,* Old English *findan, fand* (plural *fundon*), *funden,* from Germanic.]

find·er (fīn′dər) *n.* **1.** One that finds. **2.** A **viewfinder** *(see).* **3.** *Astronomy.* A small telescope attached to the body of a larger one for locating an object to be observed with the larger telescope.

fin-de-siè·cle (făN′də-sē-ĕk′lə) *adj.* Of or characteristic of the last part of the 19th century, especially with reference to its artistic climate of effete sophistication. [French, "end of (the) century."]

find·ing (fīn′dĭng) *n.* **1.** Something that has been found. **2.** The result of a trial or legal inquiry: *a finding of accidental death.* **3.** *Usually* **findings.** A conclusion reached after examination or investigation. **4. findings.** Small tools and materials used by an artisan, as a jeweler.

fine[1] (fīn) *adj.* **finer, finest. 1.** Of superior quality, skill, or appearance; admirable. **2.** Most enjoyable; pleasant. **3.** Free from impurities: *fine copper.* **4.** *Abbr.* **f., F.** Containing pure metal in a specified proportion or amount: *gold 21 carats fine.* **5.** Cut or honed to great sharpness: *a blade with a fine edge.* **6. a.** Thin; slender. **b.** Not coarse in texture: *fine hair.* **7.** Showing workmanship of great care and delicacy: *fine china.* **8.** Consisting of extremely small particles; not coarse: *fine dust.* **9.** Subtle or precise: *a fine shade of meaning.* **10.** Able to make or detect subtle or precise effects; sensitive: *a fine eye for color.* **11.** Trained to the highest degree of physical efficiency; superbly conditioned: *a fine racehorse.* **12.** Of refined manners; elegant. **13.** Grand or elevated in a somewhat pompous way: *fine speeches.* **14.** Awful; terrible. Used ironically: *That's a fine position to be in.* **15.** Satisfactory or acceptable: *A cup of tea would be fine.* **16.** Having no clouds; clear; sunny: *a fine day.* **17.** *Informal.* Quite well; in satisfactory health: *I'm fine, and you?*
~*adv.* **1.** Finely. **2.** *Informal.* Very well: *doing fine.*
~*v.* **fined, fining, fines.** —*tr.* **1.** To make finer; refine. **2.** To taper or make smaller or thinner. **3.** To clarify (wine, for example). —*intr.* To become finer, purer, or cleaner. —**fine up.** *Australian.* To become fine. Said of weather. [Middle English *fin,* from Old French, from Latin *fīnis*†, the end (as in *fīnis honorum,* the height of honor).]

fine[2] *n.* **1.** A sum of money imposed as a penalty for an offense. **2.** *Law.* Formerly, a fee paid to a feudal lord by his tenant. **3.** *Obsolete.* Finish; end; termination. —**in fine. 1.** In conclusion; finally. **2.** In summation; in brief.
~*tr.v.* **fined, fining, fines.** To require the payment of a fine from; impose a fine on. [Middle English *fin,* a fine, a payment for completion, an end, from Old French, from Latin *fīnis*†, limit, end.]

fi·ne[3] (fē′nā) *n. Music.* The end. Used to indicate the end of a passage that has been repeated. [Italian, from Latin *fīnis*†, end.]

fine[4] (fēn) *n.* A cognac, **fine champagne** *(see).*

fineable. Variant of **finable.**

fine art *n.* **1.** Art produced or intended primarily for beauty alone rather than utility. **2.** *Often* **fine arts.** Any of the forms such art takes, including sculpture, painting, drawing, and often architecture, literature, drama, music, and the dance. **3.** An activity requiring or demonstrating considerable skill: *the fine art of freeway driving.* [Translation of French *beaux arts* (plural).]

fine cham·pagne (fēn′ shäN-pän′yə) *n. French.* A cognac made from grapes from the Grande Champagne and Petite Champagne districts in southwestern France. Also called "fine." [Contraction of *eau-de-vie de la Champagne,* "fine brandy from Champagne."]

fine-cut (fīn′kŭt′) *adj.* Finely and evenly shredded, as tobacco.

fine-draw (fīn′drô′) *tr.v.* **-drew** (-dro͞o′), **-drawn** (-drôn′), **-drawing, -draws. 1.** To mend or sew (a seam or tear) in such a way that the joint is invisible. **2.** To draw out (wire, for example) to a slender, threadlike state.

fine-drawn (fīn′drôn′) *adj.* **1.** Drawn out to a slender, threadlike state, as wire may be. **2.** Subtly or precisely fashioned, as an argument or theory may be. **3.** Delicately formed; suggestive of refinement: *fine-drawn features.*

fine-grained (fīn′grānd′) *adj.* Having a fine, smooth, even grain, as leather or wood.

fine·ly (fīn′lē) *adv.* **1.** In a fine manner; excellently; splendidly. **2.** To a fine point; discriminatingly. **3.** Delicately or subtly. **4.** In small pieces or parts: *finely chopped nuts.*

PRONUNCIATION KEY

ă, pat; ā, pay; âr, care;
ä, father, are; b, bib;
ch, church; d, deed; ĕ, pet;
ē, be; f, fife; g, gag; h, hat;
hw, which; ĭ, pit; ī, pie;
îr, pier; j, judge; k, kick;
l, lid, needle; m, mum;
n, no, sudden; ng, thing;
ŏ, pot; ō, toe; ô, paw, for;
oi, noise; ou, out; o͝o, book;
o͞o, boot; p, pop; r, roar;
s, sauce; sh, ship, dish;
t, tight; th, thin, path;
th, this, bathe; ŭ, cut; ûr, fur;
v, valve; w, with; y, yes;
z, zebra, size; zh, vision;
ə, about, item, edible,
gallop, circus, peaceful

IN FOREIGN WORDS:

à, *Fr.* ami; œ, *Fr.* feu, *Ger.* schön; ü, *Fr.* tu, *Ger.* über; KH, *Ger.* ich, *Scot.* loch; N, *Fr.* bon; y', *Fr.* Compiègne

STRESS MARKS:

Primary stress: ′
in·cite′ (ĭn-sīt′)
Secondary stress: ′
in′sight′ (ĭn′sīt′)

fine·ness (fīn'nĭs) n. 1. The condition or quality of being fine. 2. The proportion of pure metal, such as gold, in an alloy.

fine print n. Matter printed with small type; especially, parts of a contract or other agreement printed inconspicuously and often containing provisions or conditions that might easily be overlooked. Also called "small print."

fin·er·y[1] (fī'nə-rē) n. Elaborate adornment; fine clothing and accessories. [From FINE (excellent).]

finery[2] n., pl. **-ies.** A furnace or hearth where cast iron is made malleable. [French finerie, from finer, to REFINE.]

fines herbes (fēn' ûrbz', fēn' zĕrb') pl.n. Finely chopped herbs, such as parsley, chives, tarragon, and thyme, used as a seasoning. [French.]

fine-spun (fīn'spŭn') adj. 1. Spun or drawn out to extreme fineness or subtlety; elaborate and delicate. 2. Developed to excessive fineness; oversubtle.

fi·nesse (fĭ-nĕs') n. 1. Restraint and delicacy of performance or behavior. 2. Subtlety or tact in maneuvering; craftiness. 3. In bridge and whist, the playing of a card in a suit in which one holds a nonsequential higher card, either to induce an opponent to play an intermediate card that one's partner can then top, or to win the trick economically. 4. Any stratagem in which one appears to decline an advantage. —See Synonyms at **artifice, tact.**
~v. **finessed, -nessing, -nesses.** —tr. 1. To accomplish with finesse. 2. To handle with a deceptive or evasive strategy. 3. To play (a card) as a finesse. —intr. 1. To employ finesse. 2. To make a finesse in a card game. [Old French, delicacy, fineness, from fin, FINE.]

fine structure n. 1. Physics. Structure in spectral lines caused by the magnetic moments of orbiting electrons. Under high resolution certain lines can be resolved into two or more closely spaced lines. See **hyperfine structure.** 2. Biology. Ultrastructure (see).

fine-toothed comb (fīn'tootht', -toothd') n. A comb with thin, closely spaced teeth. —**go over with a fine-toothed comb.** To examine in exhaustive detail.

fine-tune (fīn'toon', -tyoon') tr.v. **-tuned, -tuning, -tunes.** 1. To make small adjustments to the tuning of (a radio receiver, car engine, or the like) to obtain efficient or improved operation. 2. To make small adjustments or changes to. —**fine-tun·er** n.

fin·foot (fīn'foot') n., pl. **-foots** or collectively **finfoot.** Any of various aquatic, tropical, or subtropical cranelike birds of the family Heliornithidae, having lobed toes and pale brown plumage. Also called "sungrebe."

fin·ger (fīng'gər) n. 1. Any of the five digits of the hand; especially, any one other than the thumb. 2. The part of a glove designed to cover such a digit. 3. Something resembling a finger, such as a peninsula. 4. The length or width of a finger. 5. Informal. A measure of spirits, a quantity approximately one fingerbreadth deep in a glass. 6. Machinery. Any small projecting machine part. —**burn one's fingers.** To suffer as a result of meddlesome, inquisitive, or incautious behavior. —**have a finger in the pie.** To be involved, especially in a meddlesome way, in a matter. —**put one's finger on.** To identify or point out with precision. —**put the finger on.** Slang. 1. To inform on. 2. To designate, as an intended victim. —**snap one's fingers at.** 1. To treat contemptuously. 2. To disobey or ignore defiantly. —**twist (or wrap) around one's little finger.** Informal. To dominate utterly and effortlessly.
~v. **fingered, -gering, -gers.** —tr. 1. To touch with the fingers; handle. 2. Music. To mark (a score) with indications of which fingers are to play the notes. 3. Music. To play (an instrument) by using the fingers in a particular order or way. 4. Slang. a. To inform on. b. To designate as an intended victim. —intr. 1. To handle something with the fingers. 2. To use the fingers, especially in playing an instrument. 3. To be played by using the fingers in a specified way: His clarinet fingers like yours. [Middle English finger, Old English finger, from Germanic.] —**fin·ger·er** n.

fin·ger·board (fīng'gər-bôrd', -bōrd') n. A strip of wood on the neck of a stringed instrument against which the strings are pressed in playing.

finger bowl n. A small bowl or basin to hold water for rinsing the fingers at the table.

fin·ger·breadth (fīng'gər-brĕdth', -brĕtth') n. Also **finger's breadth.** The breadth of one finger; approximately ³/₄ of an inch.

fin·gered (fīng'gərd) adj. 1. Having a finger or fingers. 2. Having a specified number or kind of fingers. Used in combination: four-fingered; rosy-fingered.

fin·ger·ing[1] (fīng'gər-ĭng) n. 1. The technique used in playing a musical instrument with the fingers. 2. The indication on a score of which fingers are to be used in playing.

fingering[2] n. Fine knitting wool. [From obsolete fingram, probably from French fin grain, fine grain.]

finger lake n. A long, narrow lake formed when glacial debris impedes drainage of a U-shaped glaciated valley.

Finger Lakes. A group of 11 long, narrow glacial lakes in west-central New York. Cayuga and Seneca are the longest and deepest lakes. The region is a grape- and truck-farming area, with many resorts and state parks.

fin·ger·ling (fīng'gər-lĭng) n. 1. A young or small fish; especially, a young salmon or trout. 2. Any small object or creature.

fin·ger·mark (fīng'gər-märk') n. A mark left on a surface by a dirty or greasy finger.

fin·ger·nail (fīng'gər-nāl') n. A thin, horny, transparent plate covering the upper surface of the tip of each finger.

fin·ger·paint (fīng'gər-pānt') v. **-painted, -painting, -paints.** —intr. To engage in finger painting. —tr. To make by finger painting.

finger painting n. 1. The technique of painting by applying colors to moistened paper with the fingers. 2. A painting so made.

fin·ger·plate (fīng'gər-plāt') n. A plate of metal, plastic, or the like fixed to a door near the handle to protect it from fingermarks.

finger post n. A guidepost resembling a pointing finger.

fin·ger·print (fīng'gər-prĭnt') n. An impression of the curves formed by the system of ridges on the skin surface of the end of a finger; especially, such an impression made in ink for purposes of identification.
~tr.v. **fingerprinted, -printing, -prints.** To take an ink impression of a fingerprint or the fingerprints of.

fin·ger·stall (fīng'gər-stôl') n. A protective covering worn on an injured finger. Also called "stall."

finger tip, fin·ger·tip (fīng'gər-tĭp') n. The extreme end or tip of a finger. —**have at one's finger tips.** 1. To have readily or instantly available. 2. To have a thorough knowledge of.

finger wave n. A wave set into damp hair using only the fingers.

fin·i·al (fīn'ē-əl) n. 1. Architecture. An ornament fixed to the peak of a gable, arched structure, or the like. 2. Any ornamental terminating part, such as the screw on top of a piece of furniture. [Middle English finial, from adjective, "final," variant of FINAL.]

fin·i·cal (fīn'ĭ-kəl) adj. Fastidious; finicky. [Probably originally university slang, irregularly from FINE (delicate).] —**fin·i·cal·i·ty** (fīn'-ĭ-kăl'ə-tē), **fin·i·cal·ness** n. —**fin·i·cal·ly** adv.

fin·ick·y (fīn'ĭ-kē) adj. Also **fin·ick·ing** (fīn'ĭ-kĭng). Highly fastidious in tastes or standards; hard to please; fussy. [From FINICAL.]

fin·ing (fī'nĭng) n. 1. The process of clarifying wines or other liquors. 2. **finings.** A substance, such as isinglass, used in this process.

fi·nis (fĭn'ĭs, fī'nĭs) n. The end. Formerly used to indicate the end of a book or film. [Middle English, from Latin finis.]

fin·ish (fīn'ĭsh) v. **-ished, -ishing, -ishes.** —tr. 1. To arrive at or attain the end of: finish a race. 2. To bring to an end; terminate; accomplish: finish a task. 3. To consume all of; use up: finish a pie. 4. To put the final touches to; bring to a desired or required state; perfect: finish a painting. 5. To give (wood or cloth, for example) a desired surface texture. 6. To complete the education of, especially with training in artistic tastes and social graces. 7. To vanquish; destroy; kill: finish an enemy. 8. To bring about the ruin of; overcome: The stock-market crash finished him. —intr. 1. To come to a conclusion; end; stop. 2. To reach the end of a task, course, or relationship. —**finish off.** 1. To bring to a final conclusion. 2. To kill (a wounded person, for example). 3. To ruin completely (a failing venture, for example). —**finish up.** To end. Often used with by or a participle: I finished up paying the whole bill. —**finish with.** 1. To have no further use for. 2. To end a relationship with (someone). —See Synonyms at **complete.**
~n. Abbr. **fin.** 1. a. The final part or conclusion of something; end: a close finish in the race. b. The reason for one's ruin; downfall. 2. Something that completes, concludes, or perfects. 3. a. The last treatment or coating of a surface. b. The surface texture thus produced. 4. The material used in surfacing or finishing something: a wax finish. 5. Completeness, thoroughness, or smoothness of execution; perfection. 6. Polish or refinement in speech, manners, and the like. 7. High-grade lumber used to finish the interior of a building. 8. Sports. The ability to perform well at the end of a contest. [Middle English finishen, from Old French fenir, finir (stems feniss-, finiss-), from Latin finīre, to limit, complete, from finis, end.] —**fin·ish·er** n.

fin·ished (fīn'ĭsht) adj. 1. Skilled; accomplished; perfected. 2. Smooth and polished, as wood. 3. Having all hopes destroyed; undone; ruined.

finishing school n. A private school that trains girls in the social graces for life in society.

finishing touch n. A final act or decorative addition that achieves a desired total effect.

Fin·is·tère (fīn'ə-stâr'). A department in Brittany, occupying the most westerly tip of France.

Fin·is·terre, Cape (fīn'ə-stâr'). Rugged, steep promontory at the tip of an Atlantic peninsula forming the westernmost point of Spain. It takes its name from the Latin phrase finis terrae, "land's end."

fi·nite (fī'nīt') adj. 1. a. Having boundaries; limited. b. Capable of being bounded, enclosed, or encompassed. 2. Being neither infinite nor infinitesimal. 3. Mathematics. a. Bounded in an interval. Said of a quantity defined in an interval. b. Incapable of being put into one-to-one correspondence with a part of itself. Said of a set. c. Real or complex, as distinguished from ideal. Said of a number. 4. Existing, persisting, or enduring for a limited time only; impermanent; transient. 5. Grammar. Limited by person, number, tense, and mood; not an infinitive, gerund, or participle. Said of verbs.
~n. Finite entities collectively. Preceded by the. [Middle English finit, from Latin finītus, past participle of finīre, to limit, FINISH.] —**fi·nite·ly** adv. —**fi·nite·ness** n.

fin·i·tude (fīn'ə-tood', -tyood', fī'nə-) n. The quality or condition of being finite.

fink (fĭngk) n. Slang. 1. A hired strikebreaker. 2. A person who informs against another. 3. A person who is despised or regarded with contempt.
~intr.v. **finked, finking, finks.** Slang. 1. To inform. Used with on. 2. To withhold support or participation. Used with out: He promised to help, but finked out. [20th century : origin obscure.]

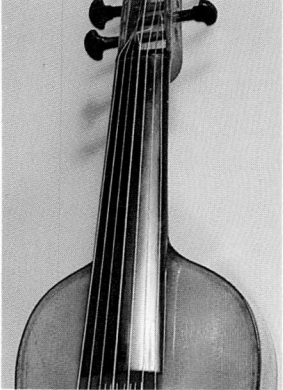

fingerboard Board at the neck of a stringed instrument such as a violin or guitar, where the musician stops the strings with his fingers to raise the pitch of notes. This is the board of a viola d'amore, made by the Parisian instrument maker Jean Nicolas Lambert in 1772.

FINLAND

fin keel *n.* A short keel usually made of metal, with ballast on the lower edge, used chiefly on racing yachts.

Fin·land (fĭn′lənd). *Abbr.* **Fin.** *Finnish* **Suo·mi** (swô′mē). Republic of northern Europe. It has been independent since 1919, when it gained its freedom from Russia, having been a grand duchy since the early 19th century. After World War II Finland was forced to cede part of the Karelian Isthmus and other land totaling 12 percent of its area to the U.S.S.R. Finland is largely a barren, ice-scoured "shield," covered by more than 70,000 lakes and vast forests. Its forest-based industries account for more than half its exports. The chief port and capital is Helsinki. Area, 337,009 square kilometers (130,085 square miles). Population, 5,000,000.

Finland, Gulf of. Eastern arm of the Baltic Sea. About 460 kilometers (285 miles) long, with a maximum width of 120 kilometers (75 miles), it separates Finland's southern coast from Estonia. It is an important shipping lane, whose chief ports are St. Petersburg and Helsinki, but it is frozen from December to March.

Fin·land·i·za·tion (fĭn′lən-dĭ-zā′shən, -dī-zā′shən) *n.* The adoption of a neutral or conciliatory policy in relations with a powerful neighboring country as practiced by Finland with respect to the former U.S.S.R.

Finn (fĭn) *n.* **1.** A native or inhabitant of Finland. Also called "Finlander." **2.** One who speaks Finnish or a Finnic language. [Swedish *Finne* (superseding Old English *Finnas,* Finns), from Germanic *Finnar* (unattested).]

fin·nan had·die (fĭn′ən hăd′ē) *n.* Also **fin·nan haddock.** Smoked haddock. [Earlier *findon haddock,* from earlier *findhorn haddock,* after the river *Findhorn* in Scotland.]

finned (fĭnd) *adj.* Having a fin, fins, or finlike parts.

Fin·ney (fĭn′ē), **Albert** (1936–). British actor. Following his early successes in the theater, he made a number of films, including *Saturday Night and Sunday Morning* (1960), *Tom Jones* (1963), and *Charlie Bubbles* (1968).

Finn·ic (fĭn′ĭk) *adj.* Of or pertaining to Finland or the Finns.
~*n.* A branch of Finno-Ugric that includes Finnish, Estonian, and Lapp.

Finn·ish (fĭn′ĭsh) *adj. Abbr.* **Fin.** Of or pertaining to Finland, its language, or its people.
~*n.* The Finno-Ugric language of the Finns.

Fin·no-U·gric (fĭn′ō-ōō′grĭk, -yōō′grĭk). Also **Fin·no-U·gri·an** (-ōō′-grē-ən, -yōō′grē-ən). A subfamily of the Uralic language group including Finnish and Hungarian.
~*adj.* **1.** Pertaining to the Finns and the Ugrians. **2.** Pertaining to the languages of the Finns and the Ugrians.

fin·ny (fĭn′ē) *adj.* **-nier, -niest. 1.** Having a fin or fins. **2.** Resembling a fin; finlike. **3.** Of, pertaining to, or full of fish.

fi·no (fē′nō) *n., pl.* **-nos.** The driest variety of sherry. [Spanish, "fine."]

fi·no·chi·o, fi·noc·chio (fĭ-nō′kē-ō) *n.* A variety of fennel, *Foeniculum vulgare dulce,* whose thickened leafstalks are eaten as a vegeta-

ble. Also called "Florence fennel," "sweet fennel." [Italian *finocchio,* from Vulgar Latin *fēnuculum* (unattested), fennel, from Latin *fēniculum,* diminutive of *fēnum,* hay.]

fin rot *n.* A bacterial disease of fish marked by the progressive deterioration of the fin tissue.

fiord. Variant of **fjord.**

fip·ple (fĭp′əl) *n.* **1.** A wooden block that forms a flue at the mouth end of certain musical wind instruments. **2.** A similar object in an organ pipe. [17th century : origin obscure.]

fipple flute *n.* A flute with a fipple, such as a recorder.

fir (fûr) *n.* **1.** Any of various evergreen coniferous trees of the genus *Abies,* having flat needles and erect cones. **2.** Any of several similar or related trees, such as the **Douglas fir** *(see).* **3.** The wood of any of these trees. [Middle English *fir(re),* Old English *furh,* probably from Old Norse *fyri-,* from Germanic.] —**fir·ry** *adj.*

Fir·bank (fûr′băngk′), **(Arthur Annesley) Ronald** (1886–1926). British novelist. His work, set in the Edwardian period, reflects his eccentricity and has a witty and impressionistic style. It includes the novels *Caprice* (1916) and *Valmouth* (1919).

fire (fīr) *n.* **1.** A rapid, persistent chemical reaction that releases heat and light; especially, the exothermic combination of a combustible substance with oxygen. **2. a.** A quantity of combustible material, such as wood or coal, undergoing this reaction and used for heating, cooking, or the like. **b.** *Chiefly British.* Combustible material intended to undergo this reaction; kindling: *lay a fire.* **c.** A destroying or consuming of an object by fire. **3.** A heating appliance powered by gas or electricity. **4. a.** Intensity, as of feeling; ardor, especially in love or rage. **b.** Enthusiasm or energy. **5.** Luminosity or brilliance, as of a cut and polished gemstone. **6.** The result of inspiration; vividness; brilliance: *the fire of his verse.* **7.** A sensation of heat or burning, such as that produced by fever or by drinking alcoholic liquor. **8.** A torment, trial, or tribulation. **9. a.** The discharge of firearms; firing. **b.** The bullets, shells, or similar projectiles discharged. **10.** A rapid succession of questions, criticisms, or the like. **11.** In ancient thought, one of the four elements. —**between two fires.** Being attacked from two sources or sides simultaneously. —**catch** (or **take**) **fire. 1.** To become ignited. **2.** To become excited or enthusiastic. —**hang fire. 1.** To fail to fire or be slow in firing, as a gun. **2.** To be delayed, as an event or decision. —**on fire. 1.** Ignited; burning; ablaze. **2.** Filled with enthusiasm or excitement. —**open fire. 1.** To commence shooting. **2.** To commence asking questions or making criticisms. —**play with fire.** To take part in a dangerous or risky activity; be foolhardy. —**set fire to** or **set on fire. 1.** To ignite. **2.** To make excited; inflame. —**under fire. 1.** Exposed or subjected to armed attack. **2.** Exposed or subjected to criticism or censure.
~*v.* **fired, firing, fires.** —*tr.* **1.** To cause to burn; ignite. **2. a.** To add fuel to (something burning). **b.** To maintain or intensify a fire in (a boiler, for example). **c.** To be the fuel for (a central heating system, for example). **3.** To bake in a kiln: *fire a flowerpot.* **4.** To dry or cure by heat: *fire tobacco.* **5. a.** To arouse the emotions of; make enthusiastic or ardent: *He was fired by patriotism.* **b.** To stimulate (enthusiasm, for example). **6.** To cause to glow. **7.** To detonate or discharge (a firearm, explosives, or a projectile): *fire a rifle; fire a rocket.* **8.** To cauterize (an animal's wound). **9.** *Informal.* To project or hurl suddenly and forcefully: *fire a ball at a batter; fire questions at a witness.* **10.** *Informal.* To discharge from a position; dismiss: *fire an employee.* —*intr.* **1. a.** To become ignited; flame up. **b.** To allow internal combustion to occur. Said of the cylinders in an engine. **2.** To become excited or ardent; feel deeply. **3.** To tend a fire. **4.** To have a specified reaction to being fired in a kiln: *This bowl will fire beautifully.* **5.** To become yellowed, brown, or blotchy before reaching maturity: *The drought caused the grain to fire.* **6.** To discharge; go off: *The mortar fired toward the enemy.* **7.** To detonate or shoot a weapon: *He fired at the enemy.* **8.** *Informal.* To project or hurl a missile. —**fire away.** To bombard someone, as with projectiles or questions. —**fire up. 1.** To inspire with enthusiasm. **2.** To become excited or emotional. [Middle English *fir, fur, feir, fire,* Old English *fȳr,* from West Germanic *fūir* (unattested).]

fire alarm *n.* **1.** A warning of the outbreak of a fire. **2.** A device, such as a bell or siren, used in announcing the outbreak of a fire.

fire-and-brim·stone (fīr′ən-brĭm′stōn′) *adj.* **1.** Characteristic or suggestive of hellfire. **2.** Extremely zealous in warning of divine punishment awaiting sinners. [From the Biblical *fire and brimstone,* which God often used to destroy sinners. Revelation 20:10.]

fire ant *n.* Any of several ants of the genus *Solenopsis;* especially, *S. geminata* or *S. saevissima,* of the southern United States and tropical America, that can inflict a painful bite.

fire·arm (fīr′ärm′) *n.* Any weapon capable of firing a missile; especially, a pistol or rifle using an explosive charge as a propellant.

fire·back (fīr′băk′) *n.* **1.** An iron plate, usually ornamental, at the back of a fireplace. **2.** A pheasant of the genus *Lophura,* of southeastern Asia.

fire·ball (fīr′bôl′) *n.* **1.** Any brilliantly burning sphere; especially, a flash of **ball lightning** *(see).* **2.** An exceptionally bright meteor. **3.** A highly luminous, intensely hot, spherical cloud of dust, gas, and vapor generated by a nuclear explosion. **4.** *Slang.* A highly energetic person.

fire beetle *n.* Any of various tropical American click beetles of the genus *Pyrophorus,* especially *P. noctilucus,* having brightly luminous spots.

fire·bird (fīr'bûrd') *n.* Any of various birds, as the Baltimore oriole, having bright scarlet or orange plumage.

fire blight *n.* A destructive disease of apples, pears, and related plants, caused by a bacterium, *Erwinia amylovora.*

fire bomb *n.* An **incendiary bomb** *(see).* —**fire-bomb** (fīr'bŏm') *v.*

fire·box (fīr'bŏks') *n.* A chamber in which fuel is burned; especially, the furnace of a steam locomotive.

fire·brand (fīr'brănd') *n.* **1.** A piece of burning wood. **2.** A person who stirs up trouble or kindles a revolt.

fire·brat (fīr'brăt') *n.* A small, wingless insect, *Thermobia domestica,* frequenting warm areas of buildings.

fire·break (fīr'brāk') *n.* A strip of cleared or plowed land used to stop the spread of a fire. Also called "fireguard," "fire line."

fire·brick (fīr'brĭk') *n.* A refractory brick, especially of fire clay, used for lining furnaces, fireboxes, chimneys, or fireplaces.

fire brigade *n.* **1.** An organized body of firefighters. **2.** A body of reinforcements or helpers called in to help in an emergency.

fire bug *n.* The **harlequin bug** *(see).*

fire·bug (fīr'bŭg') *n. Informal.* A person who deliberately sets fire to property; a pyromaniac.

fire clay *n.* A type of heat-resistant clay used to make firebricks, crucibles, and other objects exposed to high temperatures.

fire company *n.* **1.** An organized body of firefighters. **2.** A business firm that sells fire insurance.

fire control *n. Abbr.* **FC** The control of the delivery of gunfire on military targets.

fire·crack·er (fīr'krăk'ər) *n.* A small explosive charge in a cylinder of heavy paper, used to make noise.

fire·crest (fīr'krĕst') *n.* A small European warbler, *Regulus ignicapillus,* having a crown with yellow, black, and white stripes.

fire·cure (fīr'kyŏŏr') *tr.v.* **-cured, -curing, -cures.** To cure (tobacco, for example) by exposing it to the heat and smoke of a wood fire.

fire·damp (fīr'dămp') *n.* **1.** A combustible gas, chiefly methane, occurring naturally in coal mines and forming explosive mixtures with air. **2.** The explosive mixture itself. Compare **damp.**

fire department *n. Abbr.* **F.D.** A department, especially of a municipal government, whose purpose is to prevent and put out fires and to conduct emergency evacuations and resuscitations.

fire·dog (fīr'dôg', -dŏg') *n.* An andiron *(see).*

fire door *n.* An internal door in a building with a strong spring that makes it self-closing, designed to stop the spread of fire by eliminating through drafts.

fire·drake (fīr'drāk') *n.* A fiery dragon of Germanic mythology. [Middle English *firdrake,* Old English *fȳr-draca* : *fȳr,* FIRE + *draca,* dragon, DRAKE.]

fire drill *n.* A practice exercise in the use of firefighting equipment or the exit procedure to be followed in case of a fire.

fire·eat·er (fīr'ē'tər) *n.* **1.** A performer who pretends to swallow fire. **2.** A vigorous or pugnacious person.

fire engine *n.* Any of various large motor vehicles that carry firefighters and equipment to a fire and that support extinguishing operations, as by pumping water or raising ladders.

fire escape *n.* Any structure or device, as a metal ladder or an outside stairway attached to a building, erected for emergency exit in the event of fire.

fire extinguisher *n.* A portable apparatus containing water or chemicals that can be discharged in a jet to extinguish a small fire.

fire·fight·er (fīr'fī'tər) *n.* A person employed by a fire department to fight fires. —**fire-fight·ing** *adj. & n.*

fire·fly (fīr'flī') *n., pl.* **-flies.** Any of various nocturnal beetles of the family Lampyridae, characteristically having luminous abdominal organs that produce a flashing light.

fire·guard (fīr'gärd') *n.* **1.** A metal screen placed in front of an open fireplace to catch sparks. Also called "fire screen." **2.** A **firebreak** *(see).*

fire hall *n. Chiefly Canadian.* A fire station.

fire·house (fīr'hous') *n.* A **fire station** *(see).*

fire hydrant *n.* A **hydrant** *(see).*

fire insurance *n.* Insurance against the damage or loss of property as a result of fire or lightning.

fire irons *pl.n.* The equipment used to tend a fireplace, including tongs, a shovel, and a poker.

Fire Island A narrow barrier island, 52 kilometers (32 miles) long, off the southern coast of Long Island, southeastern New York. It has many resort communities, a state park, and the Fire Island National Seashore, which includes the Sunken Forest with its unusual plant and animal life.

fire·less cooker (fīr'lĭs) *n.* An insulated container that when preheated retains sufficient heat to cook food.

fire·light (fīr'līt') *n.* The light from a fire, as in a fireplace or at a campsite.

fire line *n.* A strip of cleared land, a **firebreak** *(see).*

fire·lock (fīr'lŏk') *n.* A **flintlock** *(see).*

fire·man (fīr'mən) *n., pl.* **-men** (-mĭn). **1.** A firefighter. **2.** A man who tends a boiler or furnace; a stoker. **3. a.** A man who tends the boiler of a steam locomotive. **b.** A locomotive engineer's assistant. **4.** An enlisted man in the U.S. Navy engaged in the operation of the engineering machinery. **5.** *Baseball.* A relief pitcher.

Firenze. See **Florence.**

fire opal *n.* An opal with brilliant flamelike yellow, orange, and red colors. Also called "girasol."

fire·pan (fīr'păn') *n.* A metal grate or brazier for holding fire.

fire·place (fīr'plās') *n.* **1.** An open recess for holding a fire at the base of a chimney; a hearth. **2.** A structure, usually of stone or brick, for holding an outdoor fire.

fire·plug (fīr'plŭg') *n.* A **hydrant** *(see).*

fire·pow·er (fīr'pou'ər) *n.* The capacity, as of a weapon, military unit, or ship, for discharging ammunition.

fire·proof (fīr'prŏŏf') *adj.* Capable of withstanding or resisting damage by fire.
~*tr.v.* **fireproofed, -proofing, -proofs.** To make fireproof.

fir·er (fīr'ər) *n.* **1.** One that kindles, builds, or tends a fire. **2.** A firearm considered with respect to the speed or technique of its firing. Often used in combination: *rapid-firer.*

fire·rais·er (fīr'rā'zər) *n. British.* An arsonist. —**fire-rais·ing** *n.*

fire sale *n.* A sale of commodities damaged by fire.

fire screen *n.* **1.** An ornamental screen placed in front of a fireplace that is not in use. **2.** A **fireguard** *(see).*

fire ship *n.* A vessel loaded with explosives and combustible material and set adrift among enemy ships to destroy them.

fire·side (fīr'sīd') *n.* **1.** The area immediately surrounding a fireplace or hearth. **2.** Home.

fire station *n.* A building for firefighting equipment and firefighters. Also called "firehouse."

fire·stone (fīr'stōn') *n.* **1.** A flint or other stone used to strike a spark of fire. **2.** A fire-resistant stone, as certain sandstones, used as a construction material.

fire·storm (fīr'stôrm') *n.* A violent storm caused by hot air rising from an area that is on fire, typically following a heavy bombing attack, characterized by very high winds rushing in to replace the rising air.

fire·thorn (fīr'thôrn') *n.* Any of various thorny shrubs of the genus *Pyracantha,* native to Asia, and often cultivated for their evergreen foliage and showy reddish or orange berries.

fire·trap (fīr'trăp') *n.* A building susceptible to catching fire easily or difficult to escape from in the event of fire.

fire wall *n.* A fireproof wall used to prevent the spread of a fire.

fire warden *n.* An official responsible for the prevention or putting out of fires, especially in forested areas.

fire·watch·er (fīr'wŏch'ər) *n. British.* One who keeps a lookout for fires started by bombs. —**fire-watch·ing** *n.*

fire·wa·ter (fīr'wô'tər, -wŏt'ər) *n. Slang.* Strong liquor, especially when of poor quality. [Translation of an Algonquian term such as Ojibwa *iškotēwābō.*]

fire·weed (fīr'wēd') *n.* **1.** A species of willow herb, *Epilobium angustifolium,* having terminal clusters of pinkish-purple flowers. **2.** A weedy North American plant, *Erechtites hieracifolia,* having small white or greenish flowers. **3.** Any of various other plants often appearing as the first vegetation in burned-over areas.

fire·wood (fīr'wŏŏd') *n.* Wood used as fuel.

fire·work (fīr'wûrk') *n.* **1.** Any of various devices using combinations of explosives and combustibles to generate colored lights, smoke, and noise for amusement. **2. fireworks.** A display of such devices. **3. fireworks.** An exciting or spectacular display, as of musical or literary virtuosity. **4. fireworks.** A temperamental outburst.

fir·ing (fīr'ĭng) *n.* **1.** Fuel for fires. **2.** The application of fire or heat, as in the hardening or glazing of ceramics.

firing line *n.* **1.** The line of positions from which fire is directed against a target. **2.** A position in which one is exposed to criticism or attack.

firing party *n. British.* A detachment of soldiers chosen to fire a salute at a military funeral. Also called "firing squad."

firing pin *n.* The part of the bolt or breech of a firearm that strikes the primer and explodes the charge of the projectile.

firing squad *n.* **1.** A detachment assigned to shoot persons condemned to death. **2.** A firing party.

fir·kin (fûr'kĭn) *n.* **1.** A small wooden barrel or keg, used especially for storing butter, cheese, or lard. **2.** Any of several British units of capacity, usually equal to about 9 gallons (41 liters). [Middle English *ferdekin, ferken,* a cask, one-fourth of a barrel, probably from Middle Dutch *vierdelkijn* (unattested), "little quarter," diminutive of *vierdel,* fourth part.]

firm¹ (fûrm) *adj.* **firmer, firmest. 1.** Unyielding to pressure; rigid or solid to the touch. **2.** Not easily moved or detached; securely fixed in place. **3.** Showing determination or resolution; unshakable. **4.** Constant; steadfast: *a firm ally.* **5.** Fixed formally; definite; final: *a firm offer.* **6.** Unfluctuating; steady. Said of prices. **7.** Strong and sure: *a firm handshake.* ~*v.* **firmed, firming, firms.** —*tr.* To make firm. —*intr.* **1.** To become firm. **2.** To begin to rise again after a decline. Used of prices. ~*adv.* Resolutely; unwaveringly: *stand firm; hold firm.* [Middle English *ferm,* from Old French *ferme,* from Latin *firmus.*] —**firm·ly** *adv.* —**firm·ness** *n.*

firm² *n.* **1.** A commercial partnership of two or more people. **2.** The name or designation under which a firm transacts business. [Italian *firma,* signature, name of a business establishment or partnership, from *firmare,* to sign, "confirm by signature," from Late Latin *firmāre,* to confirm, from Latin, to strengthen, from *firmus,* FIRM.]

fir·ma·ment (fûr'mə-mənt) *n.* The vault or expanse of the heavens; the sky. [Middle English, from Old French, from Late Latin *firmāmentum* (translation of Greek *stereōma,* heavenly vault, translation of Hebrew *rāqī'a*), from Latin, a strengthening, support, from *firmāre,* to make firm, from *firmus,* FIRM.] —**fir·ma·men·tal** (fûr'mə-mĕnt'l) *adj.*

firmer chisel (fûr'mər) *n.* A chisel or gouge with a thin blade, used to shape and finish wood. Also called "firmer." [French *fermoir,*

fireworks *The Chinese invented these gunpowder-based devices in about the tenth century* A.D. *Modern fireworks are even more spectacular because of new ingredients such as magnesium, first used in the nineteenth century.*

variant (influenced by *fermer,* to make firm) of Old French *formoir,* from *former,* to form, shape, from Latin *fōrmāre,* from *fōrma,* FORM.]

firm·ware (fûrm′wâr′) *n.* **1.** A computer program that is stored in a read-only memory so that it cannot be accidentally overwritten or erased. **2.** An electronic device incorporating such programs. Compare **software, hardware.**

firn (fîrn) *n.* Snow that has been partially consolidated by thawing and freezing but not yet converted to glacial ice. [German *Firn,* "last year's (snow)," from (Swiss dialect) *firn,* of last year, from Old High German *firni,* old.]

first (fûrst) *adj.* **1.** Coming, counted, or located before all others. **2.** Occurring or acting prior to all others; earliest. **3.** Ranking above all others; foremost in position, quality, or importance: *the king's first secretary; matters of the first importance.* **4.** *Music.* Highest in pitch or foremost in carrying melody: *first soprano; first trumpet.* **5.** Of or pertaining to the transmission gear, or corresponding gear ratio, used to produce the range of lowest drive speeds in a motor vehicle. —*adv.* **1.** Before anything else. **2.** Before or above all others in time or rank. **3.** For the first time: *since you first came.* **4.** Preferably; rather: *I'd die first.* —*n.* **1.** The ordinal number one in a series. **2.** The one coming, counted, occurring, or ranking before or above all others. **3.** The beginning; the outset: *from the first; at first.* **4.** *Music.* The voice or instrument highest in pitch or foremost in carrying melody. **5.** The transmission gear or corresponding gear ratio used to produce the range of lowest drive speeds in a motor vehicle. **6.** The winner or winning position in a contest. **7.** An innovation or breakthrough: *a first for the human race.* **8. firsts.** The best grade or quality of merchandise. [Middle English *first,* Old English *fyrst,* from Germanic *furistaz* (unattested), superlative of *fur-, for-* (unattested).]

---

fish

INHABITANTS OF A WATERY PLANET
Species that have adapted to almost every ecological niche

Fish are the most numerous vertebrates. The 20,000 or so species range from the 8-millimeter (5/16-inch) dwarf pygmy goby to the whale shark, which has been known to reach a length of 18 meters (59 feet). Seventy percent of the earth's surface is covered by water and most of the water, whether salt or fresh, is inhabited by fish. Although cold-blooded, fish live in temperatures from 38°C (100°F) down to freezing.

There are three classes of fish: the primitive, jawless agnatha, of which lampreys and hagfish are the only survivors; the sharklike fish with cartilaginous skeletons; and the bony fish, which include almost all fish species. Despite their differences, fish share several features. They are streamlined and slimy to allow them to slip through the water easily; they have gills and fins; and they almost all lay eggs.

BONY FISH

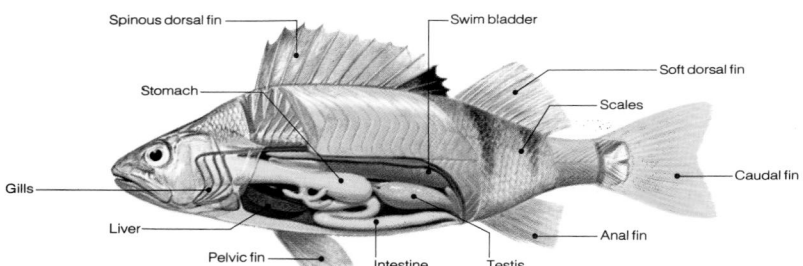

The bony fish (Osteichthyes) are divided into fleshy-finned and ray-finned fish, the latter including 95 percent of all fish species. Early bony fish evolved lungs. These remain in some archaic species, such as the lungfish, but in most the lung has become a swim bladder that buoys up the body. Bony fish have scales, and fertilization of the eggs takes place outside the body.

CARTILAGINOUS FISH

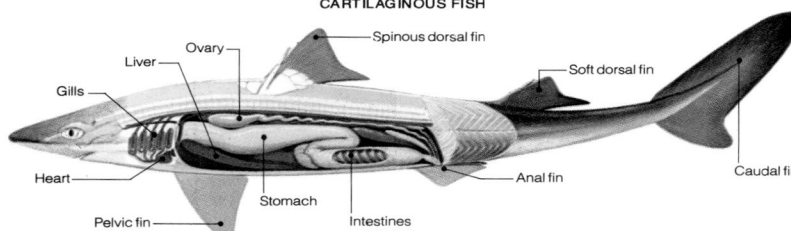

Cartilaginous fish (Chondrichthyes)—sharks, rays, and chimaeras—are survivors of an earlier stage of evolution. They have skeletons of tough gristle instead of bone. They have no swim bladders and most move constantly to prevent themselves from sinking. The skin consists of rough denticles that are modified in the mouth to form sawlike teeth set in rows that move forward continuously to replace worn sets. Fertilization takes place inside the female. The male has copulatory organs—claspers—on the inside of the pelvic fin. Many species bear live young.

Usage: First and *last* usually precede a numeral in expressions such as *the first two chapters* and *the last four chapters,* with reference to a single book or the like. An alternative and older form, illustrated by *the two first chapters* and *the four last pages,* is used only where low numerals or numbers are involved.

first aid *n.* Emergency treatment administered to injured or sick persons before professional medical care is available.

first base *n.* **1.** *Baseball.* **a.** The first of the bases in the infield, counterclockwise from home plate. **b.** The fielding position played by the first baseman. **2.** *Informal.* The first step toward achievement or success: *The reform bill never got to first base.*

first baseman *n. Baseball.* The infielder stationed at or near first base.

first-born (fûrst′bôrn′) *adj.* First in order of birth; born first. —*n.* A first-born child.

first class *n.* **1.** The first, highest, or best group of a particular category. **2.** The most luxurious and most expensive class of accommodation on a train or other means of transport. **3.** A class of mail given priority for handling and delivery.

first-class (fûrst′klăs′, -kläs′) *adj.* **1.** Indicating the first, highest, or best group of a particular category. **2.** Of the foremost excellence or highest quality; first-rate: *a first-class mind.* —*adv.* **1.** In first-class accommodations. **2.** By first-class mail.

first cousin *n.* See **cousin.**

first-day cover (fûrst′dā′) *n.* An envelope bearing stamps postmarked on their day of issue.

first-de·gree burn (fûrst′dĭ-grē′) *n.* A mild burn that produces redness of the skin but no blistering.

first floor *n.* **1.** The ground floor of a building. **2.** *British.* The floor immediately above the ground floor.

first-foot (fûrst′fŏŏt′) *n. British.* The first person to enter a house at New Year. —*intr.v.* **first-footed, -footing, -foots.** *British.* To be the first person to enter a house at New Year.

first fruit *n.* Also **first fruits. 1.** The first product of a season's harvest. **2.** The first result or profit of an undertaking.

first-gen·er·a·tion (fûrst′jĕn′ə-rā′shən) *adj.* Of, pertaining to, or being the offspring of immigrant parents: *a first-generation American.*

first-hand (fûrst′hănd′) *adj.* Received from the original source: *firsthand information.* —*adv.* From the original source; directly. [Originally, *at (the) first hand.*]

First International *n.* See **International** (sense 1a).

first lady *n.* **1.** *Sometimes* **First Lady.** The wife or hostess of the chief executive of a country, state, or city. **2.** The foremost woman of a specified profession or art: *the first lady of the ballet.*

first lieutenant *n.* A commissioned officer in the U.S. Army, Air Force, or Marine Corps ranking above a second lieutenant and below a captain.

first-ling (fûrst′lĭng) *n.* **1.** The first of a kind or category. **2.** The first-born offspring.

first-ly (fûrst′lē) *adv.* **1.** Before anything else. **2.** Before all others. **3.** In the first place; to begin with.

Usage: Firstly may be used in a sequence: *firstly, secondly, thirdly,* and so on. However, it has fallen into disuse among many writers, who prefer this sequence: *first, secondly, thirdly.* Another alternative, since all these ordinals can be used adverbially, is *first, second, third.*

first mate *n.* A ship's officer ranking immediately below the captain. Also called "first officer."

first name *n.* A person's given, personal, or Christian name. —**on first-name terms.** Friendly enough to use first names.

first night *n.* The official opening performance of a play, opera, or the like.

first-night·er (fûrst′nī′tər) *n.* One attending a first night.

first offender *n.* One found guilty of an offense who has no previous convictions.

first papers *pl.n.* The documents first filed by a person applying for U.S. citizenship.

first person *n.* **1.** A category of linguistic forms, such as verbs and pronouns, designating the speaker or writer of the sentence in which they appear. **2.** Any of these forms as *I* or *we.* **3.** A discourse or literary style in which the narrator recounts his or her own experiences and impressions using such forms: *a novel written in the first person.*

first principles *pl.n.* The basic premises from which any intellectual argument proceeds.

first-rate (fûrst′rāt′) *adj.* Foremost in quality or rank.

first refusal *n.* The right to be the first to be offered something.

first sergeant *n.* In the U.S. Army, the highest-ranking noncommissioned officer of a company or other military unit.

first strike *n.* An aggressive rather than retaliatory attack with nuclear weapons, intended to reduce or destroy an enemy's ability to strike back. Also used adjectivally: *first-strike missiles.*

first-string (fûrst′strĭng′) *adj.* **1.** Being a regular team member rather than a reserve or substitute: *the first-string quarterback.* **2.** First-rate; of high importance or quality.

first thing *adv.* At the earliest possible moment.

first water *n.* **1.** The highest degree of quality or value in gems or pearls. **2.** The foremost rank or quality: *a pianist of the first water.*

First World *n.* The industrialized nations of the world, including Western Europe, North America, Australia and New Zealand, and Japan, and sometimes thought to include the Soviet bloc.

First World War *n.* World War I (see).

firth (fûrth) *n.* In Scotland, a long, narrow inlet of the sea; a fjord. [Middle English *ford, furth,* from Old Norse *fjörthr,* FIORD.]

fisc (fĭsk) *n.* The treasury of a kingdom or country. [Old French, from Latin *fiscus†,* woven basket, money basket used by tax collectors, treasury.]

fis·cal (fĭs'kəl) *adj.* **1.** Of or pertaining to the treasury or finances of a nation or branch of government; especially, of or pertaining to matters of taxation. **2.** Of or pertaining to finances in general: *a fiscal agent.* —See Synonyms at **financial.** ~*n.* A **procurator fiscal** (see). [Old French, from Latin *fiscālis,* from *fiscus†,* treasury, basket.] —**fis·cal·ly** *adv.*

fiscal drag *n.* The limitation of economic growth caused by taxation affecting a higher proportion of taxpayers as inflation reduces the real value of money.

fiscal year *n. Abbr.* **FY** A 12-month period for which an organization plans the use of its funds. The fiscal year of the U.S. government begins October 1. Also called "financial year."

Fisch·er (fĭsh'ər), **Bobby,** born Robert James Fischer (1943–). U.S. chess player. He won world champion (1972–74).

fish¹ (fĭsh) *n., pl.* **fishes** or collectively **fish. 1.** Any of numerous cold-blooded aquatic vertebrates of the superclass Pisces, characteristically having fins, gills, and a streamlined body, and including: **a.** Any of the class Osteichthyes, having a bony skeleton. **b.** Any of the class Chondrichthyes, having a cartilaginous skeleton, and including the sharks, rays, and skates. **c.** The flesh of such animals for use in cooking. **2.** Any aquatic vertebrate of the class Agnatha, lacking jaws, and including the lampreys and hagfishes. **3.** Loosely, any of various unrelated aquatic animals, such as a jellyfish, cuttlefish, or crayfish. **4.** *Informal.* A person likened to a fish for lacking some human attribute or advantage: *a cold fish.* **5. Fish.** The constellation and sign of the Zodiac **Pisces** (see). ~*v.* **fished, fishing, fishes.** —*intr.* **1.** To catch or try to catch fish. **2.** To search or hunt for something in or under water: *fish for sponges.* **3.** To look for something by feeling around: *fished for the map in the glove compartment.* **4.** To seek to elicit information, compliments, or the like. —*tr.* **1.** To catch or try to catch fish in: *fish a lake.* **2.** To pull out or up in the manner of one who fishes. Used with *out* or *from: fished the keys out of her purse.* [Middle English *fish, fisk,* Old English *fisc,* from Germanic.]

Usage: This word has two plural forms: *fish* and *fishes. Fish* is the more widely used, referring to fish viewed collectively (*the fish in the sea*). *Fishes* is used to refer to individual species or members of a group: *The fishes pass through the hole one at a time.*

fish² *n., pl.* **fishes.** A piece of wood or an iron plate used to join or strengthen a beam, bar, or the like. ~*tr.v.* **fished, fishing, fishes.** To join, reinforce, or mend with a fish. [French *ficher,* to fix, from Vulgar Latin *figicare* (unattested), from Latin *figere.*]

fish and chips *pl.n.* Fried fillets of fish and French-fried potatoes.

fish·bolt (fĭsh'bōlt') *n.* A bolt used in a fish joint.

fish·bowl (fĭsh'bōl') *n.* **1.** A transparent bowl in which live fish are kept. **2.** A location or situation that is lacking in privacy.

fish cake *n.* A fried cake, patty, or ball of chopped fish, often mixed with potato or rice.

fish crow *n.* A crow, *Corvus ossifragus,* of the coast and rivers of the eastern United States.

fish eagle *n.* The **osprey** (see).

fish·er (fĭsh'ər) *n.* **1. a.** One that fishes. **b.** A fisherman. **2. a.** A carnivorous mammal, *Martes pennanti,* of northern North America, having thick, dark brown fur. Also called "pekan." **b.** The fur of this animal.

fish·er·man (fĭsh'ər-mən) *n., pl.* **-men** (-mĭn). **1.** One who fishes as an occupation or sport. **2.** A commercial fishing vessel.

fisherman's bend *n.* A knot used to secure the end of a line to a ring or spar, made by two turns with the end passing back under both.

fisherman's knot *n.* A knot used to join two lines, made by securing either end to the opposite standing part by an overhand knot. Also called "Englishman's tie."

fish·er·y (fĭsh'ə-rē) *n., pl.* **-ies. 1. a.** The industry or occupation of catching, processing, or selling fish and fish products. **b.** A place where fish are processed and sold. **2.** An area where commercial fishing is carried on; a fishing ground. **3.** A hatchery for fish. **4.** The legal right to fish in specific waters or areas.

Fish·es (fĭsh'ĭz) *pl.n.* The constellation and sign of the zodiac **Pisces** (see).

fish-eye lens (fĭsh'ī') *n. Photography.* A lens with a large curvature used to take pictures over a very wide field of view but producing a somewhat distorted image of the sides.

fish farm *n.* A place in which food fish are bred commercially in tanks or ponds.

fish·gig (fĭsh'gĭg') *n.* Also **fiz·gig** (fĭz'-). A pronged instrument for spearing fish. Also called "gig." [Variant (influenced by FISH) of earlier *fisgig,* from Spanish *fisga†.*]

fish hawk *n.* The **osprey** (see).

fish·hook (fĭsh'hŏŏk') *n.* A barbed metal hook used for catching fish.

fish·ing (fĭsh'ĭng) *n.* The sport or occupation of catching fish.

fishing rod *n.* A rod of wood, steel, or fiber glass used with a line for catching fish.

fish joint *n.* A joint formed by bolting fishplates to either side of two rails or beams.

fish kettle *n.* A long, oval-shaped saucepan with a lid and usually a detachable grid that fits inside, for poaching or steaming whole fish.

fish ladder *n.* A set of pools one above the other that enables fish to pass over a dam or similar obstacle when swimming upstream.

fish louse *n.* Any of various small, rounded parasitic crustaceans of the subclass Branchiura that live attached to fish.

fish·meal (fĭsh'mēl') *n.* A nutritive mealy substance produced from fish and used as animal feed and fertilizer.

fish·mon·ger (fĭsh'mŭng'gər, -mŏng'gər) *n. Chiefly British.* One who sells fish.

fish·net (fĭsh'nĕt') *n.* **1.** A meshed openwork fabric. **2.** A net for catching fish, often fitted with floats or a supporting frame. ~*adj.* Meshed or woven together like a fish net: *fishnet tights.*

fish·plate (fĭsh'plāt') *n.* Any of the connecting metal plates bolted along the side of two rails or beams placed end to end, used especially in the laying of railroad track.

fish·pond (fĭsh'pŏnd') *n.* A small body of water stocked with fish.

Fish River Canyon. A spectacular canyon formed by the Fish River in southern Namibia, second in size only to the Grand Canyon of the Colorado River in Arizona. Its maximum depth is approximately 600 meters (2,000 feet).

fish·tail (fĭsh'tāl') *adj.* Resembling or suggestive of the tail of a fish in shape or movement. ~*intr.v.* **fishtailed, -tailing, -tails.** To swing the rear end of a motor vehicle or aircraft from side to side while moving forward. ~*n.* **1.** A fishtailing maneuver. **2.** An attachment for a Bunsen burner that produces a thin, broad flame.

fish·wife (fĭsh'wīf') *n., pl.* **-wives** (-wīvz'). **1.** A woman who sells fish. **2.** A coarse, abusive woman.

fish·y (fĭsh'ē) *adj.* **-ier, -iest. 1.** Resembling or suggestive of fish, as in taste or smell. **2.** Cold or expressionless: *a fishy stare.* **3.** *Informal.* **a.** Unlikely; questionable. **b.** Giving rise to suspicion; dubious. —**fish·i·ly** *adv.* —**fish·i·ness** *n.*

fissi– *prefix.* Indicates a split or cleft shape; for example, **fissipalmate.** [Latin *fissus,* past participle of *findere,* to cleave, split.]

fis·sile (fĭs'əl, -īl') *adj.* **1.** Capable of being split. **2.** *Physics.* Fissionable, especially by neutrons of all energies. [Latin *fissilis,* from *fissus,* split. See **fissi-.**] —**fis·sil·i·ty** (fĭ-sĭl'ə-tē) *n.*

fis·sion (fĭsh'ən) *n.* **1.** The act or process of splitting into parts. **2.** *Physics.* A nuclear reaction in which any of certain heavy atomic nuclei split into fragments, usually two fragments of comparable mass, releasing a large amount of energy. Also called "nuclear fission." Compare **fusion. 3.** *Biology.* An asexual reproductive process in which a unicellular organism splits into two or more independently maturing daughter cells. [Latin *fissiō* (stem *fissiōn-*), from *fissus,* past participle of *findere,* to split.]

fis·sion·a·ble (fĭsh'ə-nə-bəl) *adj.* Capable of undergoing fission; especially, capable of being induced to undergo nuclear fission by slow neutrons. Said of isotopes.

fission bomb *n.* A bomb in which the explosion is produced by nuclear fission; an atomic bomb.

fission reactor *n.* A nuclear reactor that produces energy by controlled nuclear fission of a radioactive fuel.

fis·si·pal·mate (fĭs'ə-păl'māt') *adj.* Having lobed or partially webbed separated toes, as the feet of certain birds.

fis·sip·a·rous (fĭ-sĭp'ər-əs) *adj.* Reproducing by biological fission. [FISSI- + -PAROUS.]

fis·si·ped (fĭs'ə-pĕd') *adj.* Having the toes separated from one another, as certain carnivorous mammals. ~*n.* A carnivorous mammal having such toes, such as a dog or cat. [Late Latin *fissipēs* : FISSI- + -PED.]

fis·sure (fĭsh'ər) *n.* **1.** A narrow crack or cleft, as in a rock face. **2.** A schism; a split. **3.** *Anatomy.* A groove or furrow, as in the liver or brain, that divides an organ into lobes or separates it into areas. **4.** *Pathology.* A cleft in the skin or mucous membrane resulting from disease. **5.** A crack in the surface of a tooth. ~*v.* **fissured, -suring, -sures.** —*tr.* To cause a fissure in; split. —*intr.* To form fissures; become cleft; crack. [Middle English, fracture, opening, from Old French, from Latin *fissūra,* from *fissus.* See **fission.**]

fist (fĭst) *n.* **1.** The hand closed tightly with the fingers bent against the palm. **2.** *Informal.* A grasping hand; a clutch: *Don't let him get his fists on this.* **3.** A printer's mark, an **index** (see). ~*tr.v.* **fisted, fisting, fists. 1.** To hit with the fist. **2.** *Nautical.* To grasp or handle: *fisting a slippery anchor chain.* [Middle English *fist, fust,* Old English *fȳst,* from Germanic.]

fist·fight (fĭst'fīt') *n.* A fight with the fists.

fist·ful (fĭst'fŏŏl') *n., pl.* **-fuls.** A handful.

fist·ic (fĭs'tĭk) *adj.* Of or pertaining to fighting with the fists; pugilistic.

fist·i·cuffs (fĭs'tĭ-kŭfs') *pl.n.* **1.** A fistfight. **2.** *Boxing.* [Earlier *fisty cuff* : *fisty,* from FIST + CUFF (a blow).] —**fist·i·cuff·er** *n.*

fis·tu·la (fĭs'chŏŏ-lə) *n., pl.* **-las** or **-lae** (-lē'). An abnormal duct or passage from an abscess, cavity, or hollow organ to the body surface or to another hollow organ. [Middle English, from Latin *fistula†,* pipe, tube, fistula.]

fis·tu·lous (fĭs'chŏŏ-ləs) *adj.* **1.** Of or resembling a fistula. **2.** Tubular and hollow; needlike. **3.** Made of or containing tubular parts.

fit¹ (fĭt) *v.* **fitted** or **fit, fitted, fitting, fits.** —*tr.* **1.** To be the proper size and shape for. **2.** To be appropriate or suitable to; be in keeping with. **3.** To modify or adapt so as to be of the desired size or

fisherman's bend *This knot is used for securing a hauling rope to an anchor ring. The double turn on the rope reduces the risk from chafing.*

type. **4.** To be in conformity with; correspond to; suit: *Let the punishment fit the crime.* **5.** To render competent or qualified; prepare. **6.** To equip or furnish. Used with *up* or *out.* **7.** To provide a place or time for. Used with *in* or *into.* **8.** To insert so as to be properly in place; install: *fit a new gearbox.* —*intr.* **1.** To conform as to size and shape. **2.** To be appropriate or suitable. **3.** To correspond or agree, as with the circumstances of a given situation. Often used with *in* or *into.*

~*adj.* **fitter, fittest. 1.** Suited, adapted, or adequate to a given circumstance, end, or design. **2.** Appropriate; proper; fitting. **3.** Rightly deserving or entitled: *not fit to live.* **4.** Ready; disposed: *fit to drop from exhaustion.* **5.** Physically sound, especially as a result of regular exercise.

~*n.* **1.** Adjustment or alteration to a given pattern or standard. **2.** The manner in which clothing fits. **3.** The degree of precision with which surfaces or parts are adjusted or adapted to each other at a joint or edge. **4.** *Slang.* The needle and other equipment of a narcotics user.

~*adv. Informal.* In a manner likely to lead to a specified outcome: *They were laughing fit to burst.* [Middle English, probably from the past participle of *fitten*†, to marshal troops, (hence) to arrange.] **—fit·ly** *adv.* **—fit·ness** *n.*

Synonyms: *appropriate, apt, felicitous, fitting, happy, proper, suitable.*

Usage: When *fit* is used to mean "to cause to fit," only *fitted* is used as the past tense: *The tailor fitted* (not *fit*) *the suit in a few minutes.* In other uses either *fitted* or *fit* is correct as the past tense of *fit: The suit fitted* (or *fit*) *me well the last time I tried it on.*

fit² *n.* **1.** *Medicine.* **a.** A seizure or convulsion, especially one due to epilepsy. **b.** A sudden attack, as of coughing. **2.** A sudden outburst or display of some specified emotion: *a fit of jealousy.* **3.** A sudden period of vigorous activity. **—by** (or **in**) **fits and starts.** With irregular intervals of action and inaction; intermittently; spasmodically. [Middle English *fit,* hardship, painful experience, Old English *fitt*†, conflict.]

fit³ *n. Archaic.* A section of a poem or ballad; a canto. [Middle English *fit,* Old English *fit(t)*†.]

fitch (fĭch) *n.* The Old World polecat or its fur. [Middle Dutch *fisse*†.]

fit·ful (fĭt′fəl) *adj.* Occurring in or characterized by intermittent bursts of activity; irregular. —See Synonyms at **periodic. —fit·ful·ly** *adv.* **—fit·ful·ness** *n.*

fit·ted (fĭt′ĭd) *adj.* **1.** Cut for a close fit: *a fitted shirt.* **2.** Cut and laid so as to fit a floor area exactly: *a fitted carpet.* **3.** Forming a fixed, integral part of a structure: *fitted wardrobes.*

fit·ter (fĭt′ər) *n.* **1.** One who alters or adjusts garments. **2.** One who installs or adjusts parts of machines or other equipment.

fit·ting (fĭt′ĭng) *adj.* Suitable; appropriate: *The host offered a few fitting expressions of welcome.* —See Synonyms at **fit.**

~*n.* **1.** The act of trying on clothes whose fit is being adjusted. **2.** A small, detachable part for a machine or an apparatus. **3.** *British.* **fittings.** Movable furnishings or accessories. Compare **fixture. 4.** The work of a fitter. **—fit·ting·ly** *adv.* **—fit·ting·ness** *n.*

Fitz·Ger·ald (fĭts-jĕr′əld), **Edward** (1809–83). British poet and translator. His English version of the *Rubáiyát of Omar Khayyám* (1859) is by far the best known.

Fitzgerald, Ella (1918–). U.S. jazz singer. Her first worldwide hit came in 1938 with "A-tisket, A-tasket." Often called the First Lady of Jazz, she is considered the greatest of all female jazz singers.

Fitzgerald, Francis Scott Key, known as F. Scott Fitzgerald (1896–1940). U.S. novelist and short-story writer. After the success of his first novel, the autobiographical *This Side of Paradise* (1920), he married Zelda Sayre (1900–47). In the 1920's he lived on the French Riviera, where he wrote his best-known novel, *The Great Gatsby* (1925).

Fiume. See **Rijeka.**

five (fīv) *n.* **1. a.** The cardinal number that is one more than four. **b.** A symbol representing this, such as 5, V, or v. **2.** A set made up of five persons or things. **3. a.** The fifth in a series. **b.** A playing card marked with five pips. **4.** Five parts: *cut in five.* **5.** A size, as in clothing, designated as five. **6.** A bill or coin having a denomination of five. **7.** Five hours after midnight or midday. [Middle English *fif, five,* Old English *fīf.*] **—five** *adj. & pron.*

five-and-ten-cent store (fīv′ən-tĕn′sĕnt′) *n.* A large variety store selling inexpensive merchandise such as household items and toys. Also called "dime store," "five-and-dime."

five-fin·ger (fīv′fĭng′gər) *n.* Any of several plants having compound leaves with five leaflets, such as the **cinquefoil** *(see).*

five-finger exercise *n.* **1.** A piano exercise to develop fingering technique. **2.** A simple task.

five·fold (fīv′fōld′) *adj.* **1.** Consisting of five parts. **2.** Five times as many or as much. **—five·fold** *adv.*

Five Nations *n.* See **Iroquois.**

five-o'clock shadow (fīv′ə-klŏk′) *n.* The beard stubble visible on the face of a clean-shaven man by early evening.

five·pins (fīv′pĭnz′) *n. Used with a singular verb.* An indoor bowling game common in Canada, using five pins. Also called "fivepin bowling."

fiv·er (fī′vər) *n. Informal.* **1.** A five-dollar bill. **2.** *British.* A five-pound note.

fives (fīvz) *n. Used with a singular verb.* A British form of handball, often played doubles and on a four-walled court. [17th century : plural of FIVE (perhaps originally played by two teams of five each).]

Five-Year Plan (fīv′yîr′) *n.* A program for national economic development over a five-year period, administered by a socialist government. [Translation of Russian *pyatilyetnii plan, pyatilyetka.*]

fix (fĭks) *v.* **fixed, fixing, fixes.** —*tr.* **1. a.** To place or fasten securely; attach: *fix the notice to the wall.* **b.** To set or implant permanently: *fix something in one's memory.* **2.** To put into a stable or unalterable form, as: **a.** *Chemistry.* To make (a substance) nonvolatile or solid. **b.** *Biology.* To convert (nitrogen) into stable, biologically assimilable compounds. **c.** To kill, harden, and preserve (a specimen) for microscopic study. **d.** To prevent discoloration of (a photographic image) by washing or coating with a chemical preservative. **3.** To set (one's jaw, for example) firmly. **4.** To immobilize; rivet: *fixed to the spot.* **5. a.** To direct (the gaze, for example) steadily; concentrate. **b.** To give (a person, for example) a penetrating look. **6.** To establish definitely; specify: *fix a time.* **7.** To ascribe; allot: *fixing the blame.* **8.** To restore to proper condition or functioning; set right; repair. **9.** To arrange; adjust: *Just let me fix my hair.* **10.** *Informal.* To make ready (a meal, for example); put together; prepare. **11.** To spay or castrate (an animal). **12.** *Informal.* **a.** To take revenge upon; get even with. **b.** To deal with (a troublesome person). **c.** To put a stop to (something troublesome). **13.** To determine (a location, for example) with precision. **14.** *Informal.* To influence or arrange the outcome of (a contest, for example) by unlawful means. —*intr.* **1.** To become fixed, firm, or secure. **2.** *Regional.* To make plans or preparations; get ready: *We're fixing to leave town.* **—be fixed for.** *Informal.* To be in a specified position with regard to: *How are we fixed for time?* **—fix on** (or **upon**). To decide or agree on. **—fix up.** *Informal.* **1.** To set right; repair. **2.** To provide; equip. **3.** To assemble or prepare. **4.** To arrange: *The travel agent fixed up a tour for us.*

~*n.* **1.** A difficult or embarrassing position; a predicament. **2.** The position, as of a ship or aircraft, as determined by observations or radio. **3.** *Informal.* A contest whose outcome has been fraudulently predetermined. **4.** *Slang.* An intravenous injection of heroin or a similar drug. [Middle English *fixen,* partly from Medieval Latin *fīxāre,* to fix, from Latin *fīgere* (past participle *fīxus*), to fasten, partly from Old French *fix,* fixed, from Latin *fīxus,* past participle of *fīgere.*] **—fix·a·ble** *adj.*

fix·ate (fĭk′sāt′) *v.* **-ated, -ating, -ates.** —*tr.* **1.** To make fixed, stable, or stationary. **2.** To focus one's eyes or concentrate one's attention on. **3.** *Psychology.* **a.** To cause (the libido) to be arrested at an immature stage of psychosexual development. **b.** To cause (a person) to become attached to someone or something in an immature or neurotic fashion. —*intr.* **1.** To focus or concentrate one's attention. **2.** *Psychology.* To become fixated; form a fixation.

fix·a·tion (fĭk-sā′shən) *n.* **1.** The act or process of fixing or fixating. **2.** *Psychology.* A strong attachment to a person or thing; especially, such an attachment formed in childhood or infancy and persisting in immature or neurotic behavior.

fix·a·tive (fĭk′sə-tĭv) *adj.* Acting to fix; tending to make permanent.

~*n.* Something that fixes, protects, or preserves, especially: **1.** A liquid preservative applied to works of art, such as water-color paintings or charcoal drawings. **2.** A fluid, such as alcohol, used to preserve and harden fresh tissue for microscopic examination. **3.** A substance mixed with perfume to prevent rapid evaporation.

fixed (fĭkst) *adj.* **1.** Firmly in position; stationary; unmovable. **2.** *Chemistry.* **a.** Nonvolatile: *fixed oils.* **b.** In a stable combined form: *fixed nitrogen.* **3.** Not subject to change or variation; constant: *a fixed routine.* **4.** Officially established; unchangeable: *fixed prices.* **5.** No longer developing: *The language became fixed in the 17th century.* **6.** Firmly, often dogmatically held to: *a fixed notion.* **7.** *Informal.* Illegally prearranged as to outcome. **—fix·ed·ly** (fĭk′sĭd-lē) *adv.* **—fix·ed·ness** *n.*

fixed assets *pl.n.* The capital assets of a commercial enterprise, as equipment or a factory.

fixed head *n.* A fixed device for reading or imprinting information on a single track of magnetic tape, as in a tape recorder.

fixed idea *n.* An idea, especially an incorrect idea, held persistently despite contrary evidence or rational refutation; an idée fixe.

fixed oil *n.* A nonvolatile oil; especially, a fatty oil from a plant as distinguished from an essential oil.

fixed point *n.* **1.** *Physics.* A reference temperature used in defining a practical temperature scale at standard pressure, usually a boiling, melting, or triple point of some pure substance, such as water, helium, or gold. **2.** *Mathematics.* A point that is not changed by a given transformation.

fixed-point (fĭkst′point′) *adj. Mathematics.* Designating or pertaining to a system of representing numbers by a single string of digits, with the position of a digit in the string determining the power of the base of the number system. Compare **floating-point.**

fixed-point theorem *n. Mathematics.* The principle that for all points within a closed cell, as a circle, polygon, sphere, or polyhedron, any transformation that takes all points of the set into points of the same set will leave at least one point fixed.

fixed star *n.* A star so distant from the earth that its movements can be measured only over long periods of time. The term was used originally to distinguish such stars from wandering stars (planets).

fix·er (fĭk′sər) *n.* **1.** A fixative agent used in developing photographic prints. **2.** *Informal.* One who arranges; especially, one who makes fraudulent arrangements in an attempt to change the normal outcome of a contest, political process, or the like.

fix·ings (fĭk′sĭngz) *pl.n. Informal.* Accessories; trimmings.
fix·i·ty (fĭk′sə-tē) *n., pl.* **-ties. 1.** The quality or condition of being fixed; immutability; stability. **2.** Something that is fixed.
fix·ture (fĭks′chər) *n.* **1.** Something securely fixed in place. **2.** Something attached as a permanent appendage, apparatus, or appliance: *plumbing fixtures.* **3.** *Law.* A chattel considered to belong to or be part of a property. **4.** A person or thing long associated with, established in, or restricted to a position or function. [Variant of obsolete *fixure* (influenced by MIXTURE), Late Latin *fixūra,* from Latin *fīxus.* See **fix.**]
fiz·gig[1] (fĭz′gĭg′) *n.* **1.** *Archaic.* A frivolous, giddy woman. **2.** A firework that produces a hissing or sputtering sound. [Earlier *fisgigg* : probably obsolete *fise,* breaking wind, fart, probably from Scandinavian + GIG (carriage, original sense, "frivolous woman").]
fizgig[2]. Variant of **fishgig.**
fizz (fĭz) *intr.v.* **fizzed, fizzing, fizzes. 1.** To make a hissing or bubbling sound. **2.** To effervesce. Used of drinks.
~*n.* **1.** A hissing or bubbling sound. **2.** Effervescence. **3.** An effervescent drink, especially lemonade or champagne. [Imitative.]
fiz·zle (fĭz′əl) *intr.v.* **-zled, -zling, -zles. 1.** To make a hissing or sputtering sound. **2.** *Informal.* To fail or die out, especially after a hopeful beginning. Usually used with *out.*
~*n.* **1.** A fizzling sound. **2.** *Informal.* A failure; a fiasco. [Probably frequentative of obsolete *fist,* to break wind. See **feist.**]
fjeld (fyĕld) *n.* A high, barren plateau in the Scandinavian countries. [Danish, from Old Norse *fjall,* mountain.]
fjord, fiord (fyôrd, fyōrd) *n.* A long, narrow, deep inlet of the sea bordered by steep slopes. Fjords are submerged U-shaped glaciated valleys found especially along the coasts of Norway and Alaska. [Norwegian, from Old Norse *fjörthr,* from Germanic; akin to FIRTH, FORD.]
fl fluid.
fL foot-lambert.
FL Florida (used with a Zip Code).
fl. 1. floor. **2.** *Latin.* floruit (flourished). **3.** fluid.
Fla. Florida.
flab (flăb) *n.* Loose, unwanted fatty tissue on the body. [Back-formation from FLABBY.]
flab·ber·gast (flăb′ər-găst′, -gäst′) *tr.v.* **-gasted, -gasting, -gasts.** To confound or overwhelm with astonishment; astound. —See Synonyms at **surprise.** [18th century (slang) : perhaps humorous blend of FLABBY + AGHAST.]
flab·by (flăb′ē) *adj.* **-bier, -biest. 1.** Lacking firmness; loose and yielding to the touch; flaccid: *flabby skin.* **2.** Obese. **3.** Lacking force or vitality; feeble; ineffectual. [Variant of *flappy,* from FLAP.] **—flab·bi·ly** *adv.* **—flab·bi·ness** *n.*
fla·bel·late (flə-bĕl′ĭt, -āt′) *adj.* Also **fla·bel·li·form** (flə-bĕl′ə-fôrm′). *Biology.* Fan-shaped. [Latin *flābellum,* fan. See **flabellum.**]
fla·bel·lum (flə-bĕl′əm) *n., pl.* **-bella** (-bĕl′ə). **1.** A fan-shaped biological structure. **2.** A fan used in certain religious ceremonies. [Latin *flābellum,* small fan, diminutive of *flābrum* (usually in plural *flābra*), gust of wind, from *flāre,* to blow.]
flac·cid (flăk′sĭd, flăs′ĭd) *adj.* Lacking firmness; soft and limp; flabby: *"His mouth, pink and flaccid, trembled sometimes like the underlip of a cow"* (H.E. Bates). [French *flaccide,* from Latin *flaccidus,* from *flaccus*†, hanging, flabby.] **—flac·cid·i·ty** (flăk-sĭd′ə-tē, flə-sĭd′-), **flac·cid·ness** *n.* **—flac·cid·ly** *adv.*
flack. Variant of **flak.**
flac·on (flăk′ən, -ŏn′) *n.* A small stoppered bottle, as for perfume. [French, from Old French *fla(s)con,* FLAGON.]
flag[1] (flăg) *n.* **1.** A piece of cloth or bunting varying in size, color, and design, used as a symbol, standard, signal, and especially as a national emblem. **2.** *Chiefly British.* A small paper badge given to contributors to a charity. **3.** A ship carrying the flag of an admiral; a flagship. **4.** The masthead of a newspaper. **5.** A distinctively shaped or marked tail, as of a dog or deer. **6.** In musical notation, a cross stroke added to a note that is less than a quarter note in value. **—fly the flag.** *Informal.* To represent one's country in a particular field or activity with exuberance and pride.
~*tr.v.* **flagged, flagging, flags. 1.** To decorate with a flag or flags. **2.** To signal or communicate (a message) with or as if with a flag. **3.** To mark with a symbol for purposes of identification. **—flag down.** To signal (a vehicle) to stop. [16th century : perhaps from obsolete *flag*†, hanging limp, drooping.] **—flag·ger** *n.* See feature, pages 634–637.
flag[2] *n.* Any of various plants having long bladelike leaves, especially the sweet flag (*Acorus calamus*). [Middle English *flagge*†, rush, reed.]
flag[3] *intr.v.* **flagged, flagging, flags. 1.** To hang limply; droop. **2.** To become tired; decline in vigor. **3.** To decline in interest; grow dull. [16th century : akin to obsolete *flag*†, drooping.]
flag[4] *n.* **1.** A slab of flagstone used for paving. **2.** *Geology.* **Flagstone** *(see).*
~*tr.v.* **flagged, flagging, flags.** To pave with flags. [Middle English *flagge,* piece of turf, sod, probably from Old Norse *flaga,* slab of stone.]
flag captain *n.* The captain of a flagship.
Flag Day *n.* An annual holiday on June 14 celebrating the adoption in 1777 of the official U.S. flag.
flag·el·lant (flăj′ə-lənt, flə-jĕl′ənt) *n.* One who whips; especially, one who scourges himself by way of religious discipline or for sexual stimulation. [Latin *flagellāns* (stem *flagellant-*), present participle of *flagellāre,* to FLAGELLATE.] **—flag·el·lant** *adj.*
flag·el·late (flăj′ə-lāt′) *tr.v.* **-lated, -lating, -lates.** To whip or flog; scourge.
~*adj.* (-lĭt, -lāt′, flə-jĕl′ĭt). **1.** Having a flagellum or flagella, as do unicellular animals of the class Flagellata (or Mastigophora). **2.** Resembling or having the form of a flagellum; whiplike.
~*n.* (-lĭt, -lāt′, flə-jĕl′ĭt). A flagellate organism. [Latin *flagellāre,* to whip, scourge, from *flagellum,* diminutive of *flagrum,* whip.] **—flag·el·la·tion** (flăj′ə-lā′shən) *n.*
fla·gel·li·form (flə-jĕl′ə-fôrm′) *adj.* Long, thin, and tapering; whipshaped: *flagelliform appendages.* [Latin *flagellum,* small whip (see **flagellate**) + -FORM.]
fla·gel·lin (flə-jĕl′ĭn) *n.* A protein that is a constituent of flagella. [FLAGELL(A) + -IN.]
fla·gel·lum (flə-jĕl′əm) *n., pl.* **-gella** (-jĕl′ə). *Biology.* A long, threadlike appendage; especially, one of the whiplike extensions of certain cells or unicellular organisms, usually functioning in locomotion. [New Latin, from Latin, small whip. See **flagellate.**] **—fla·gel·lar** *adj.*
flag·eo·let (flăj′ə-lĕt′, -lā′) *n.* **1.** A small flutelike instrument having a cylindrical mouthpiece, four fingerholes, and two thumbholes. **2.** A haricot bean. [French, diminutive of Old French *flajol,* from Vulgar Latin *flabeolum* (unattested), flute, from Latin *flāre,* to blow.]
Flagg (flăg), **James Montgomery** (1877–1960). U.S. painter, illustrator, and author. After studying in England and France, he returned to his native New York and began a highly successful career as an artist. He is best known for his series of World War I recruitment posters.
flag·ging[1] (flăg′ĭng) *adj.* **1.** Drooping; languid. **2.** Declining; weakening. **—flag·ging·ly** *adv.*
flagging[2] *n.* A pavement laid with flagstones.
fla·gi·tious (flə-jĭsh′əs) *adj.* **1.** Guilty of or addicted to extremely brutal or cruel crimes; vicious. **2.** Shockingly evil; infamous; scandalous; heinous. [Middle English *flagicious,* from Latin *flāgitiōsus,* from *flāgitium,* noisy protest against one's conduct, scandal, shameful act, from *flāgitāre,* to demand fiercely.] **—fla·gi·tious·ly** *adv.* **—fla·gi·tious·ness** *n.*
flag·man (flăg′mən) *n., pl.* **-men** (-mĭn). One who signals with or carries a flag.
flag of convenience *n.* A flag of a country that offers ship owners financial and in some cases legal advantages to register their ships in that country.
flag officer *n.* A naval or coast guard officer holding the rank of rear admiral, vice admiral, or admiral.
flag of truce *n.* A white flag brought or displayed to an enemy as an invitation to a conference or a signal of surrender.
flag·on (flăg′ən) *n.* **1.** A vessel for holding liquor, as wine, usually made of metal or pottery and having a handle and spout and often a lid. **2.** The quantity of liquid contained in a flagon. [Middle English *flagon, flakon,* from Old French *fla(s)con,* from Late Latin *flascō* (stem *flascōn-*), bottle, FLASK.]
flag·pole (flăg′pōl′) *n.* A pole on which a flag is hoisted; a flagstaff.
flag rank *n.* The rank of a flag officer.
fla·grant (flā′grənt) *adj.* **1.** Outstanding or conspicuous in being wrong or evil; notorious; shocking: *a flagrant miscarriage of justice.* **2.** *Obsolete.* Flaming; blazing. —See Usage note at **blatant.** [Latin *flagrāns* (stem *flagrant-*), present participle of *flagrāre,* to burn, blaze.] **—fla·gran·cy, fla·grance** *n.* **—fla·grant·ly** *adv.*
***Synonyms:** glaring, gross, rank.*
flag·ship (flăg′shĭp′) *n.* **1.** A ship bearing the flag of a fleet or squadron commander. **2.** The best or largest ship operated by a passenger line. **3.** The leading member of a group or chain.
Flag·stad (flăg′stăd′), **Kirsten** (1895–1962). Norwegian soprano, celebrated for her performances of Wagner's heroines, such as Brünnhilde in *Der Ring des Nibelungen* and Kundry in *Parsifal.*
flag·staff (flăg′stăf′, -stäf′) *n., pl.* **-staffs** or **-staves** (-stāvz′). A flagpole.
Flag·staff (flăg′stăf′, -stäf′). A city of northern Arizona, near the San Francisco Peaks. It is a tourist center for a region containing ruined Indian pueblos, state parks, lakes, and pine forests.
flag·stone (flăg′stōn′) *n.* **1.** A flat, natural or artificial stone used in paving. **2.** *Geology.* Hard, fine-grained sedimentary rock easily split into layers or large slabs, usually a sandstone or sandy limestone. In both senses, also called "flag." [FLAG (stone) + STONE.]
flag·wav·ing (flăg′wā′vĭng) *n.* A display of patriotic fervor.
Fla·her·ty (flă′ər-tē, flă′-), **Robert Joseph** (1884–1951). U.S. film director and explorer. His films, including *Nanook of the North* (1921) and *Moana* (1926), were the first major documentaries. They greatly influenced documentary filmmaking.
flail (flāl) *n.* A manual threshing device consisting of a long wooden handle or staff with a shorter free-swinging stick attached to its end.
~*v.* **flailed, flailing, flails.** —*tr.* **1.** To thresh using a flail. **2.** To beat, thrash, or strike with or as if with a flail. —*intr.* To move about erratically; thrash about: *arms flailing.* [Middle English *fleil, flail,* from Old English *flegil* (unattested) and Old French *flaiel,* both from Latin *flagellum,* diminutive of *flagrum,* whip.]
flair (flâr) *n.* **1.** A natural talent or aptitude; a bent; a knack: *a flair for interior decorating.* **2.** Instinctive discernment; keenness: *"Boswell, with his usual flair, arrived in Florence at a most exciting time"* (Frederick A. Pottle). **3.** A natural and exuberant sense of style. [French, "sense of smell," from Old French, from *flairer,* to scent, smell, from Vulgar Latin *flāgrāre* (unattested), from Latin *frāgrāre,* to emit a smell.]

fjord *A glacial valley invaded by the sea. This one is in Norway. Fjords are usually deep—sometimes more than 1,200 meters (4,000 feet) in places—but often have a shallow mouth.*

PRONUNCIATION KEY
ă, pat; ā, pay; âr, care; ä, father, are; b, bib; ch, church; d, deed; ĕ, pet; ē, be; f, fife; g, gag; h, hat; hw, which; ĭ, pit; ī, pie; îr, pier; j, judge; k, kick; l, lid, needle; m, mum; n, no, sudden; ng, thing; ŏ, pot; ō, toe; ô, paw, for; oi, noise; ou, out; o͝o, book; o͞o, boot; p, pop; r, roar; s, sauce; sh, ship, dish; t, tight; th, thin, path; *th,* this, bathe; ŭ, cut; ûr, fur; v, valve; w, with; y, yes; z, zebra, size; zh, vision; ə, about, item, edible, gallop, circus, peaceful

IN FOREIGN WORDS:
ȧ, *Fr.* ami; œ, *Fr.* feu, *Ger.* schön; ü, *Fr.* tu, *Ger.* über; KH, *Ger.* ich, *Scot.* loch; N, *Fr.* bon; y′, *Fr.* Compiègne

STRESS MARKS:
Primary stress: ′
in·cite′ (ĭn-sīt′)
Secondary stress: ′
in′sight′ (ĭn′sīt′)

flak, flack (flăk) *n.* **1.** Antiaircraft artillery. **2.** The bursting shells fired from such artillery. **3.** *Slang.* Excessive criticism; abuse. [German *Flak,* short for *Fl(ieger)a(bwehr)k(anone),* "aircraft defense gun."]

flake¹ (flāk) *n.* **1.** A flat, thin piece or layer; a chip. **2.** A small piece of something that has been peeled, rubbed, or sliced off: *flakes of fish.* **3.** A small, crystalline particle of snow. **4.** *Slang.* An eccentric or oddly humorous person; oddball. ~*v.* **flaked, flaking, flakes.** —*tr.* **1.** To break flakes from; take off in flakes; chip. **2.** To cover, mark, or overlay with or as if with flakes; fleck. **3.** To form into flakes: *Flake the almonds with a sharp knife.* —*intr.* To come off in flakes; chip off. —**flake out.** *Slang.* To fall asleep or collapse from fatigue or exhaustion. [Middle English, from Scandinavian, akin to Norwegian *flak.*] —**flak·er** *n.*

flake² *n.* **1.** A frame or platform for drying fish or produce. **2.** A scaffold lowered over the side of a ship to support workmen. [Middle English *fleke,* from Old Norse *fleki, flaki.*]

flake white *n.* A pigment made of flakes of white lead.

flak jacket *n.* A bulletproof jacket or vest.

flak·y (flā'kē) *adj.* **-ier, -iest. 1.** Made of or resembling flakes. **2.** Forming or tending to form flakes or thin, crisp fragments. **3.** *Slang.* Eccentric; crazy. —**flak·i·ly** *adv.* —**flak·i·ness** *n.*

flaky pastry *n.* A type of pastry resembling puff pastry but less rich and firm in texture.

flam¹ (flăm) *n. Informal.* **1.** A lie or hoax; a deception. **2.** Nonsense; drivel. [Short for FLIMFLAM.]

flam² *n.* A drumbeat produced by two almost simultaneous strokes. [Perhaps imitative.]

flam·bé (fläm-bā', flän-bā') *adj.* Served flaming in ignited liquor, as brandy. Said of food. ~*tr.v.* **flambéd, -béing, -bés.** To drench with a liquor, as brandy, and ignite. [From French, past participle of *flamber,* to flame, from Old French *flambe,* flame.]

flam·beau (flăm'bō') *n., pl.* **-beaux** (-bōz') or **-beau. 1.** A flaming torch. **2.** A large ornamental candlestick. [French, from Old French, from *flambe, flamble,* "small flame," from Latin *flammula,* diminutive of *flamma,* FLAME.]

flam·boy·ant (flăm-boi'ənt) *adj.* **1.** Given to or characterized by elaborate ostentation; showy: *a flamboyant dresser.* **2.** Richly colored; vivid; resplendent. **3.** *Architecture.* Pertaining to or designating a style of 15th- and 16th-century French Gothic architecture characterized by waving lines and flamelike forms. —See Synonyms at **ornate.** ~*n.* A tree, the **royal poinciana** *(see).* [French, from Old French, present participle of *flamboyer, flambeiier,* to blaze, from *flambe, flamble,* small flame. See **flambeau.**] —**flam·boy·ance, flam·boy·an·cy** *n.* —**flam·boy·ant·ly** *adv.*

flame (flām) *n.* **1. a.** The zone of burning gases and fine suspended matter associated with the combustion of a substance. **b.** Broadly, a hot, luminous mass of burning gas or vapor, typically tongue-shaped and flickering. **2.** *Often* **flames.** The condition of active, blazing combustion: *burst into flames.* **3.** Something flamelike in motion, brilliance, intensity, or shape. **4.** A violent or intense passion; a burning emotion. **5.** A reddish orange. **6.** *Informal.* A sweetheart: *an old flame.* —See Synonyms at **blaze.** ~*v.* **flamed, flaming, flames.** —*intr.* **1.** To burn brightly; give off flames or a flame; blaze. Often used with *up.* **2.** To color or glow suddenly. **3. a.** To display a violent or intense emotion: *flaming with indignation.* **b.** To burst out with violent and intense expression: *The people's anger flamed up.* —*tr.* **1.** To burn, ignite, or scorch. **2.** *Obsolete.* To inflame. [Middle English *flaume, flam(m)e,* from Old French *flam(m)e,* from Latin *flamma.*] —**flam·y** *adj.*

---

flags of the world

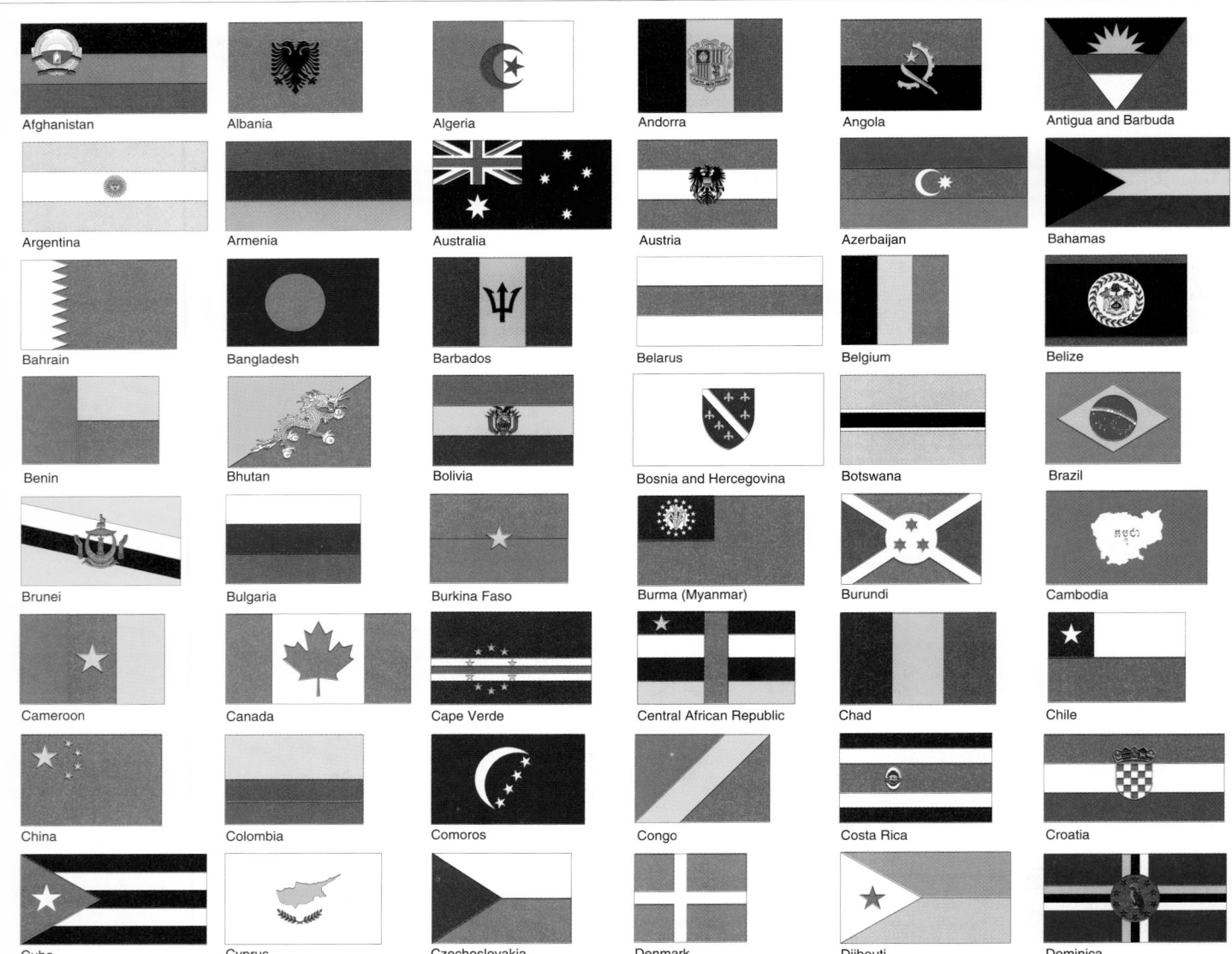

Afghanistan

Albania

Algeria

Andorra

Angola

Antigua and Barbuda

Argentina

Armenia

Australia

Austria

Azerbaijan

Bahamas

Bahrain

Bangladesh

Barbados

Belarus

Belgium

Belize

Benin

Bhutan

Bolivia

Bosnia and Hercegovina

Botswana

Brazil

Brunei

Bulgaria

Burkina Faso

Burma (Myanmar)

Burundi

Cambodia

Cameroon

Canada

Cape Verde

Central African Republic

Chad

Chile

China

Colombia

Comoros

Congo

Costa Rica

Croatia

Cuba

Cyprus

Czechoslovakia

Denmark

Djibouti

Dominica

flame cell *n.* A hollow cell in flatworms and certain other invertebrates that contains cilia and functions as an organ of excretion.

flame gun *n.* A portable gas or oil burner used to destroy weeds.

fla·men (flā′mən) *n., pl.* **-mens** or **flamines** (flăm′ə-nēz′). A priest or servant of a Roman deity. [Middle English *flamin,* from Latin *flāmen;* akin to Sanskrit *Brahmán,* BRAHMA.]

fla·men·co (flə-mĕng′kō) *n., pl.* **-cos. 1.** A dance style of the Andalusian Gypsies characterized by forceful, often improvised rhythms. **2.** The guitar music that usually accompanies this dance style. ~*adj.* Of or pertaining to such dancing or music: *a flamenco guitar.* [Spanish *flamenco,* Gypsy living in Andalusia, resembling a Gypsy, Flemish, from Middle Dutch *Vlāming,* FLEMING.]

flame-out (flām′out′) *n.* Failure of a jet aircraft engine in flight.

flame-proof (flām′prōof′) *adj.* **1.** Able to withstand direct contact with flame; specifically, able to be used over a gas flame. Compare **ovenproof. 2.** Insulated to prevent sparks from igniting any surrounding gas. Said of electrical apparatus. —**flame·proof** *v.*

flame-re·tard·ant (flăm′rĭ-tär′dənt) *adj.* Resistant to catching fire. —**flame-re·tard·ant** *n.*

flame test *n. Chemistry.* A simple qualitative test for the presence of certain metals by in which the sample is held in a flame and the characteristic colors produced are observed. A blue flame, for example, indicates the presence of copper.

flame-throw·er (flăm′thrō′ər) *n.* A weapon that projects ignited incendiary fuel, such as napalm, in a steady stream.

flame tree *n.* Any of several trees with red or orange flowers, such as *Butea frondosa,* of India and Burma, or *Brachychiton acerifolium,* of Australia.

flam·ing (flā′mĭng) *adj.* **1.** On fire; in flames; ablaze. **2.** Brilliant; splendid; flamelike. **3.** Intense; passionate: *a flaming accusation.* **4.** Arrant; flagrant. —**flam·ing·ly** *adv.*

fla·min·go (flə-mĭng′gō) *n., pl.* **-gos** or **-goes. 1.** Any of several large, gregarious wading birds of the family Phoenicopteridae, of tropical regions, having reddish or pinkish plumage, long legs, a long, flexible neck, and a bill turned downward at the tip. **2.** Moderate pinkish orange. [Perhaps Portuguese *flamengo,* from Provençal *flamenc,* probably from its bright plumage) : *flama,* flame, from Latin *flamma,* FLAME + *-enc,* from Germanic *-ing,* suffix denoting "belonging to."]

Fla·min·i·an Way (flə-mĭn′ē-ən). Great Roman road, the chief transport route between Rome and the Adriatic. Construction was begun by Gaius Flaminius in *c.* 220 B.C. and the original road ran to Ariminum (Rimini), a distance of *c.* 208 miles (335 kilometers).

flam·ma·ble (flăm′ə-bəl) *adj.* Easily ignitable and capable of burning with rapidity; inflammable. [Latin *flammāre,* to blaze, from *flamma,* FLAME.] —**flam·ma·bil·i·ty** (flăm′ə-bĭl′ə-tē) *n.* —**flam·ma·ble** *n.*

   Usage: *Flammable* and *inflammable* have the same meaning, "highly combustible." The prefix *in-* is an intensive here, and not an expression of negation, so that *inflammable* really means *inflame* + *-able.* Something that cannot be burned is *nonflammable.* Because of the widespread use of the prefix *in-* with a negative meaning, however (*invisible, incapacity*), *inflammable* is sometimes mistakenly interpreted as "noncombustible." For this reason *flammable* is the preferred term in technical writing and in contexts where people are being warned. In figurative usage only *inflammable* is used: *an inflammable nature* or *temper.*

flan (flăn, flän) *n.* **1.** An open tart with a sweet or savory filling, often containing eggs, cheese, or cream. **2.** A metal disk to be stamped as a coin; a blank. [French, from Old French *fla(o)n,* from Germanic.]

flanch¹ (flănch) *n.* Also **flaunch** (flônch). A slope of cement or simi-

continued

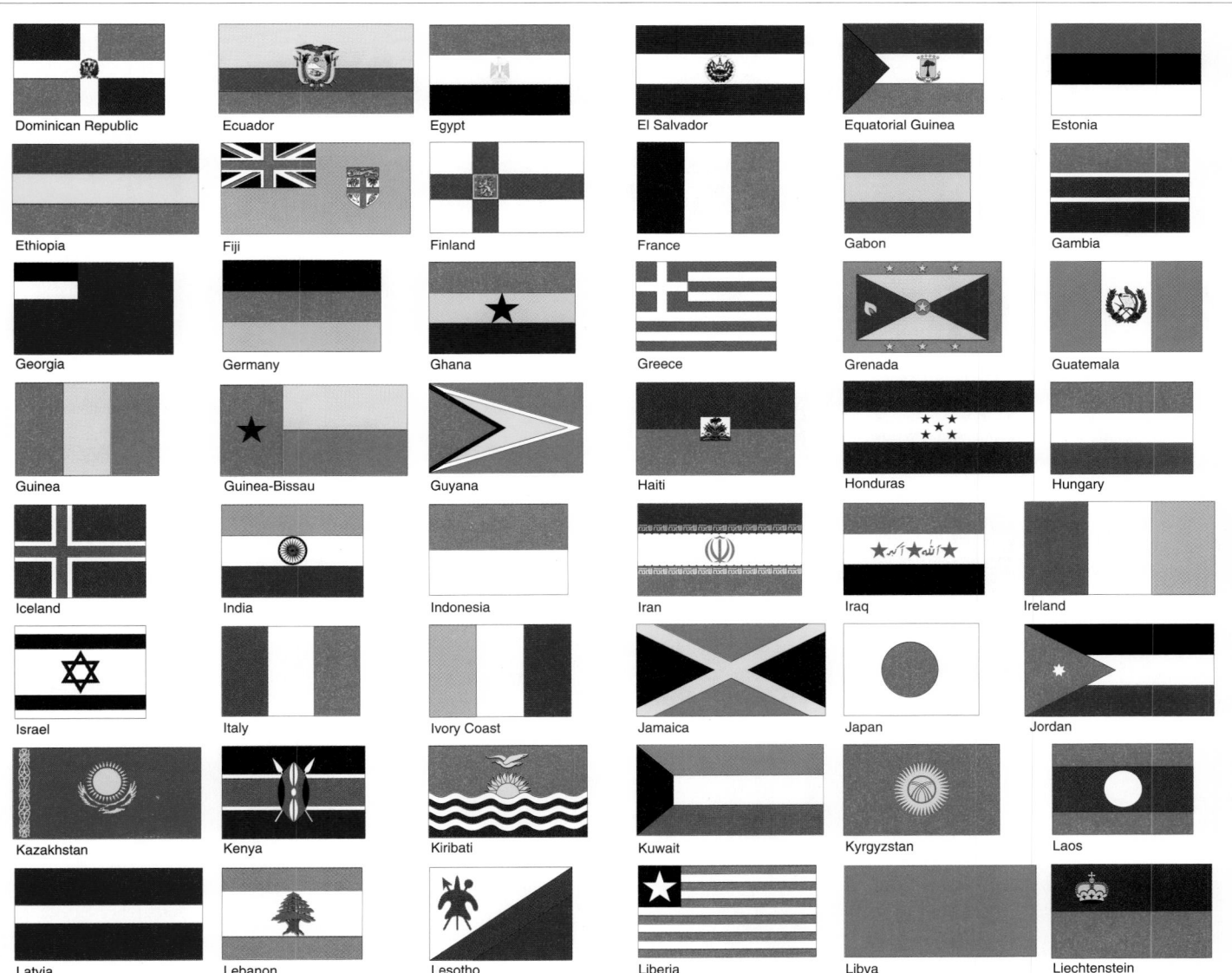

Dominican Republic · Ecuador · Egypt · El Salvador · Equatorial Guinea · Estonia

Ethiopia · Fiji · Finland · France · Gabon · Gambia

Georgia · Germany · Ghana · Greece · Grenada · Guatemala

Guinea · Guinea-Bissau · Guyana · Haiti · Honduras · Hungary

Iceland · India · Indonesia · Iran · Iraq · Ireland

Israel · Italy · Ivory Coast · Jamaica · Japan · Jordan

Kazakhstan · Kenya · Kiribati · Kuwait · Kyrgyzstan · Laos

Latvia · Lebanon · Lesotho · Liberia · Libya · Liechtenstein

lar material surrounding a structure such as a chimney top to drain off rainwater.
~*v.* **flanched, flanching, flanches.** Also **flaunch, flaunched, flaunching, flaunches.** —*tr.* To provide with a flanch. —*intr.* To have a flanch. [Variant of FLANGE.]

flanch² *n.* Either of two inward-curving segments at each side of a heraldic field. [18th century : perhaps from Old French *flanchir*, from *flanche,* variant of *flanc,* FLANK.]

Flan·ders (flăn′dərz). Former county of the Low Countries, west of the Scheldt River. It included the present East and West Flanders provinces of Belgium, the Nord and Pas-de-Calais departments of France (where it is known as French Flanders), and a small part of Zeeland province in the Netherlands. During the Middle Ages the county was the center of the rich Flemish cloth industry. The area saw heavy fighting in both World Wars.

Flanders poppy *n.* The **corn poppy** *(see).*

flâ·ne·rie (flän-rē′, flä′nə-rē′) *n.* Aimless idling; dawdling. [French.]

flâ·neur (flä-nœr′) *n.* An aimless idler. [French.]

flange (flănj) *n.* A protruding rim, edge, rib, or collar, as on a wheel or a pipe shaft, used to strengthen an object, hold it in place, or attach it to another object.
~*tr.v.* **flanged, flanging, flanges.** To furnish with a flange. [17th century : perhaps from obsolete *flange,* to widen, from Old French *flangir,* variant of *flanchir.* See **flanch, flank.**]

flank (flăngk) *n.* **1. a.** The section of flesh between the last rib and the hip; a side. **b.** A cut of meat from this section of an animal. **2.** The side of the thigh. **3.** A side or lateral part: *the flank of a mountain.* **4. a.** The right or left side of a military formation: *attack on both flanks.* **b.** The right or left side of a bastion.
~*tr.v.* **flanked, flanking, flanks. 1.** To protect or guard the flank of. **2.** To menace, attack, or maneuver around the flank of. **3.** To be placed or situated at the flank or side of. **4.** To put something on each side of. [Middle English *fla(u)nke,* from Old French *flanc,* from Frankish *hlanca* (unattested), side.]

flank·er (flăng′kər) *n.* **1.** One that flanks. **2.** A division of soldiers guarding the flank of a marching column. **3.** A fortification attached to the side or flank of another part. **4.** *Informal.* An unscrupulous trick. **5.** *Football.* A flankerback.

flank·er·back (flăng′kər-băk′) *n. Football.* An offensive back stationed wide of his team's formation and just behind the line of scrimmage. Also called "flanker."

flan·nel (flăn′əl) *n.* **1.** A soft woven cloth of wool or of a blend of wool and cotton or synthetics. **2.** Flannelette. **3. flannels.** Clothing, especially trousers, made of flannel.
~*tr.v.* **flanneled** or **-nelled, -neling** or **-nelling, -nels. 1.** To wash, clean, or rub with flannel. **2.** To wrap in flannel. [Middle English, probably from *flanen* or similar material, from Welsh *gwlanen,* "woolen cloth," from *gwlân,* wool.] —**flan·nel·ly** *adj.*

flan·nel·board (flăn′əl-bôrd′, -bōrd′) *n.* A piece of board covered in flannel or similar material to which paper or cloth cutouts may be attached, as in making a collage or as a visual aid in teaching.

flannel bush *n.* A shrub or small tree, *Fremontia californica,* of California and northern Mexico, having downy, lobed leaves and showy yellow flowers.

flan·nel·ette (flăn′ə-lĕt′) *n.* A cotton cloth processed to resemble flannel.

Flan·ner (flăn′ər), **Janet** (1892–1978). U.S. journalist. Raised in Indianapolis, she traveled extensively after 1918 and spent most of her life abroad. She is best known for her "Letters from Paris," which she wrote for the *New Yorker* and signed with the pen name Genêt.

flap (flăp) *v.* **flapped, flapping, flaps.** —*tr.* **1.** To wave (wings or

flags *continued*

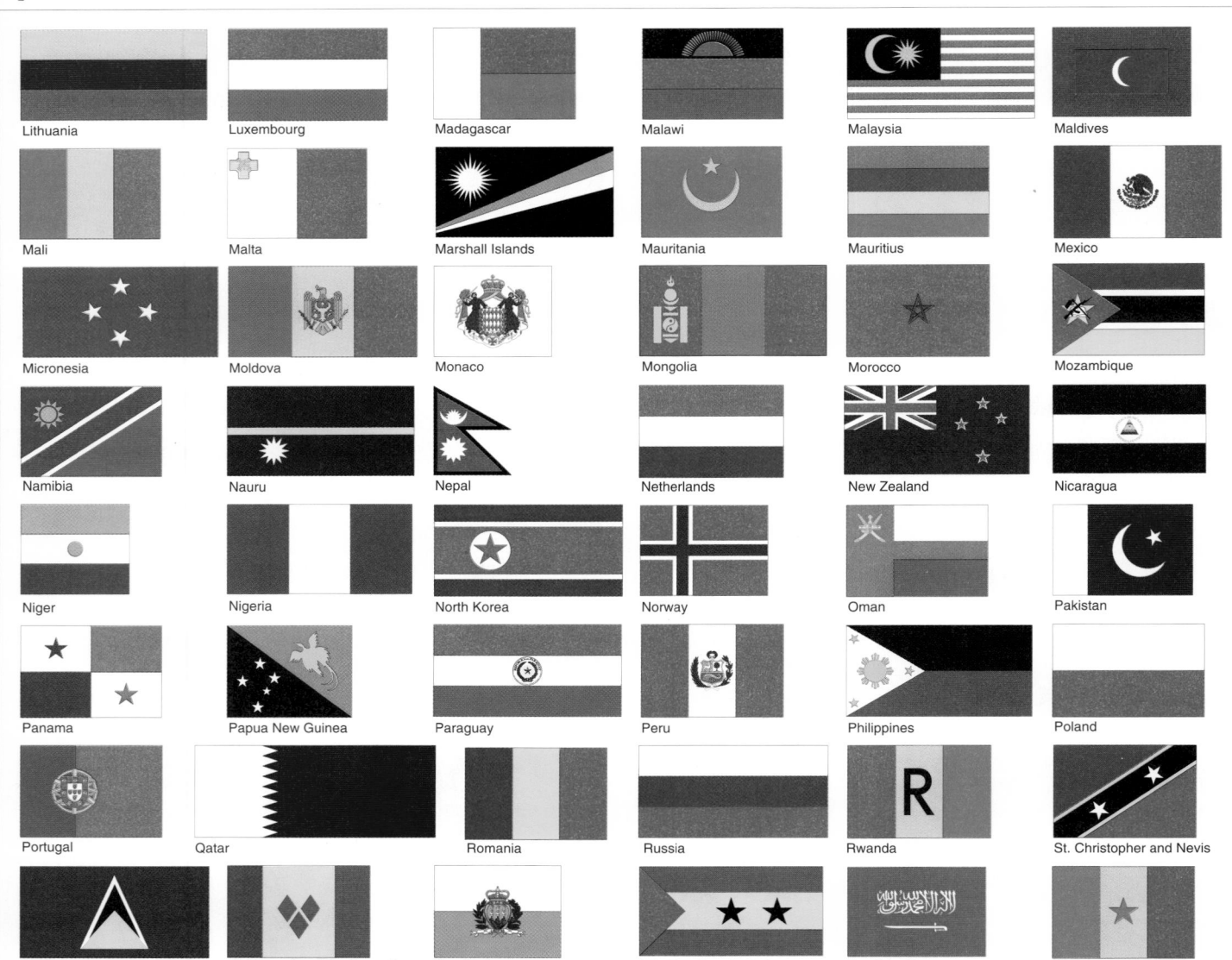

Lithuania • Luxembourg • Madagascar • Malawi • Malaysia • Maldives

Mali • Malta • Marshall Islands • Mauritania • Mauritius • Mexico

Micronesia • Moldova • Monaco • Mongolia • Morocco • Mozambique

Namibia • Nauru • Nepal • Netherlands • New Zealand • Nicaragua

Niger • Nigeria • North Korea • Norway • Oman • Pakistan

Panama • Papua New Guinea • Paraguay • Peru • Philippines • Poland

Portugal • Qatar • Romania • Russia • Rwanda • St. Christopher and Nevis

St. Lucia • St. Vincent and the Grenadines • San Marino • São Tomé and Principe • Saudi Arabia • Senegal

arms, for example) up and down; beat. **2.** To cause to wave or undulate; agitate. **3.** To hit with something broad and flat; slap. **4.** *Phonetics.* To produce (an r sound) while bringing the tongue rapidly in contact with the alveolar ridge. —*intr.* **1.** To wave about while fixed at one edge or corner to something stationary; flutter. **2.** To wave arms or wings up and down; beat the air. **3.** To fly by beating the air with the wings. **4.** *Informal.* To become agitated or nervous. ~*n.* **1.** A flat covering piece usually intended to double over and protect or seal something, as on an envelope, pocket, or hat. **2.** The action of waving or fluttering; flapping. **3.** The sound of flapping. **4.** A blow given with something flat; a slap. **5.** *Aeronautics.* A variable control surface on the trailing edge of an aircraft wing, used primarily to increase lift or drag. **6.** *Surgery.* Tissue that has been partially detached and used in plastic surgery to fill an adjacent defect or to cover the cut end of a bone after amputation. **7.** *Phonetics.* A flapped (r) sound. **8.** *Informal.* A condition of agitated distress. [Middle English *flappe,* slap, from *flappen,* to beat.]

flap·doo·dle (flăp'dōōd'l) *n. Slang.* Foolish talk; nonsense. [Origin obscure.]

flap·jack (flăp'jăk') *n.* A pancake. [FLAP (to toss) + *Jack* (name).]

flap·pa·ble (flăp'ə-bəl) *adj. Slang.* Easily excited or upset.

flap·per (flăp'ər) *n.* **1.** One that flaps, such as a device for swatting flies. **2.** A flipper or similar broad, flexible part. **3.** *Informal.* A young woman, especially one in the 1920's who flaunted her disdain for conventional dress and behavior.

flare (flâr) *v.* **flared, flaring, flares.** —*intr.* **1.** To flame up with a bright, wavering light; blaze unsteadily. **2.** To burst into intense, short-lived flame. Often used with *up.* **3.** To widen gradually, as a skirt or vase might. **4.** *Metallurgy.* To give off burning gas. Used of a molten metal. —*tr.* **1.** To cause (something) to flare. **2.** To signal with flares. **3.** To burn off (gas given off at a wellhead). Used with *off.* ~*n.* **1.** A brief, wavering blaze of light. **2.** A device that can be fired into the sky to produce a bright light for signaling, illumination, or identification. **3.** An outbreak, as of emotion or activity. **4.** A gradual widening: *trousers with a slight flare.* **5.** *Photography.* A lens reflection or the resultant film fogging. **6.** Reddening of the skin due to infection, irritation, or an allergic reaction. **7.** *Astronomy.* A localized outburst of radiation from the surface of the sun. —See Synonyms at **blaze.** [Origin unknown.]

flare-back (flâr'băk') *n.* A flame produced in the breech of a gun by ignition of residual gases.

flare star *n. Astronomy.* A star that shows sudden, short-lived increases in brightness. Flares can increase the luminosity of a star by several magnitudes for a few minutes.

flare up *intr.v.* **1.** To display sudden intense emotion or passion. **2. a.** To break out suddenly or undergo a sudden increase in intensity. Used of wars, quarrels, or the like. **b.** To become active suddenly, causing reddening of the skin: *Her rash has flared up again.*

flare-up (flâr'ŭp') *n.* **1.** A sudden outbreak of flame or light. **2.** An outburst or eruption: *a flare-up of anger.* **3.** An intensification of something hitherto mild or dormant: *a flare-up of old antagonisms.*

flash (flăsh) *v.* **flashed, flashing, flashes.** —*intr.* **1.** To appear or emerge suddenly in or as if in bright flame. **2.** To appear or be perceived for an instant only. **3.** To be lighted intermittently; sparkle; scintillate. **4.** To move rapidly. **5.** To be suddenly perceived by the mind or sight. **6.** To flow rapidly; rush. Used of water. **7.** *Informal.* To expose oneself indecently. —*tr.* **1. a.** To cause (light) to appear suddenly or in intermittent bursts. **b.** To cause to shine or reflect light briefly: *flashed his light at the intruders.* **c.** To cause to burst into flame. **d.** To reflect (light). **e.** To reflect light from (a

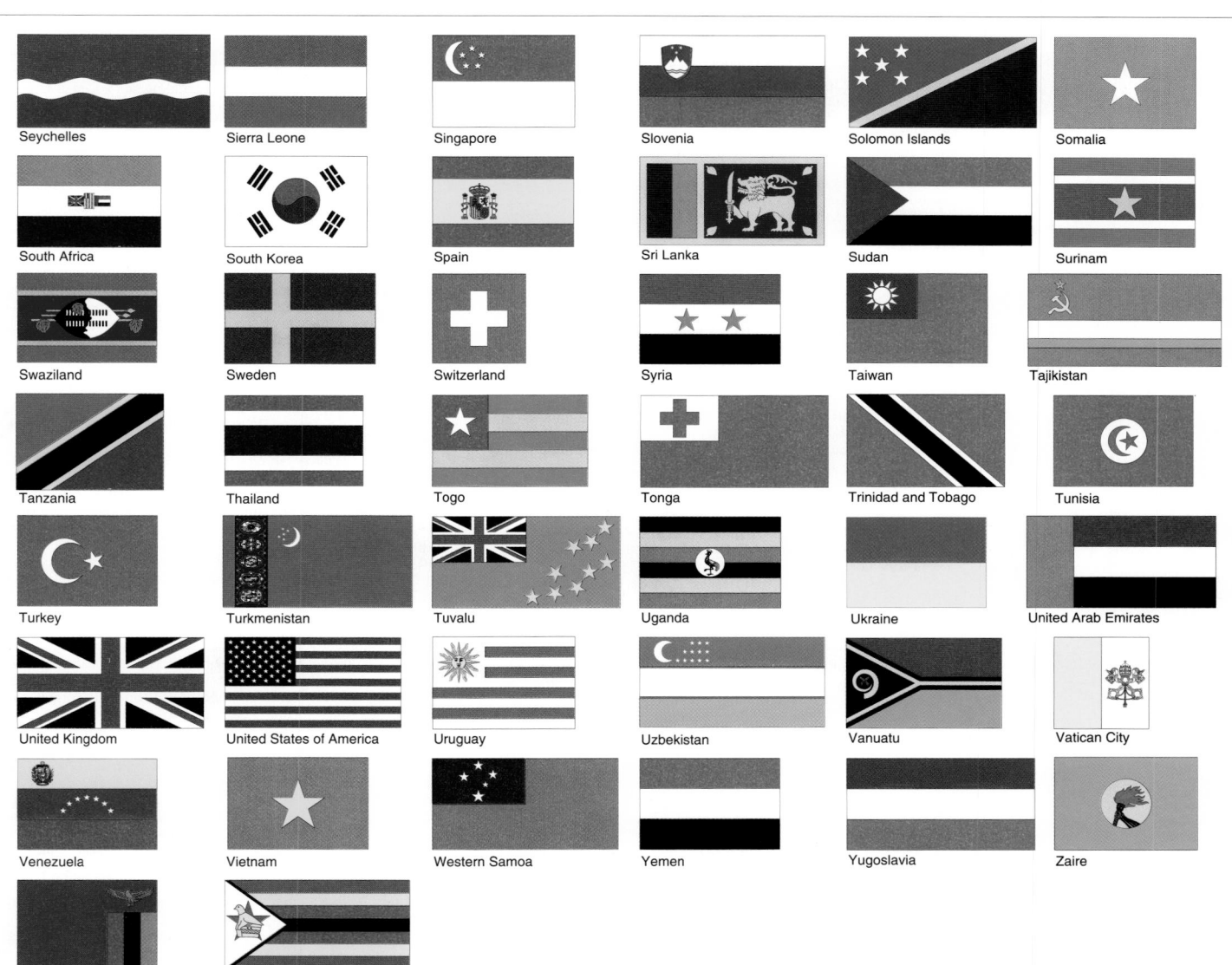

Seychelles	Sierra Leone	Singapore	Slovenia	Solomon Islands	Somalia
South Africa	South Korea	Spain	Sri Lanka	Sudan	Surinam
Swaziland	Sweden	Switzerland	Syria	Taiwan	Tajikistan
Tanzania	Thailand	Togo	Tonga	Trinidad and Tobago	Tunisia
Turkey	Turkmenistan	Tuvalu	Uganda	Ukraine	United Arab Emirates
United Kingdom	United States of America	Uruguay	Uzbekistan	Vanuatu	Vatican City
Venezuela	Vietnam	Western Samoa	Yemen	Yugoslavia	Zaire
Zambia	Zimbabwe				

surface). **2. a.** To expose to a flash or flashes of light. **b.** To expose to a flash of radiation. **3.** To display as if by a flash of light: *Her eyes flashed hatred at me.* **4. a.** To send (a message) with light signals. **b.** To signal to (another driver) with a flash of one's car headlights. **5. a.** To communicate (information) at great speed. **b.** To display (a picture, for example) rapidly on a screen. **6.** To reveal (something concealed) briefly: *The police officer flashed her badge.* **7.** *Informal.* To display ostentatiously; flaunt. **8. a.** To fill suddenly with a rush of water. **b.** To sweep away (a boat, for example) on a rush of water. **9.** To cover (glass) with a thin layer of metal or different-colored glass, for example. **10.** To cause (a liquid) to boil and evaporate through direct contact with a hot surface. **11.** To provide (a roof, for example) with flashing.
~*n.* **1.** A sudden, brief, intense display of light. **2.** A sudden manifestation of a quality, such as insight or wit. **3.** A split second; an instant: *in a flash.* **4.** A brief, important news dispatch or transmission. Also called "newsflash." **5. a.** Instantaneous illumination for photography. **b.** Any equipment or device, such as a flash bulb, flash gun, or flash lamp, used to produce such illumination. **6.** In a motion picture, a brief display of a scene. **7.** *Informal.* A sudden brief display: *He gave me a flash of his wallet.* **8.** *Chiefly British.* A patch of colored cloth on a military uniform for identification. **9.** A patch of coloring on an animal's coat. **10.** *Archaic.* A sudden heavy onrush of water deliberately released to take a boat over a shallow stretch of water. —See Synonyms at **blaze, moment.** —**flash in the pan. 1.** An explosion of the gunpowder in the pan of a flintlock rifle that does not set off the charge. **2.** Someone or something that has merely transitory interest, success, or appeal.
~*adj.* **1.** Happening suddenly or very quickly: *flash freezing.* **2.** *Informal.* Ostentatious or showy: *a flash car.* **3.** Counterfeit; bogus. **4.** Of or pertaining to gamblers and followers of racing and boxing. **5.** Of or pertaining to thieves, confidence men, and underworld figures. [Middle English *flashen,* to splash, burst into flame (imitative).]

Usage: *flash, gleam, glance, glint, sparkle, glitter, glisten, shimmer, glimmer, twinkle, spark, scintillate.* These verbs mean to send forth or reflect light. *Flash* refers to a sudden and brilliant but short-lived outburst of light. *Gleam* implies light of moderate brightness, either transient or constant and often appearing against a dark background. *Glance* refers most often to light reflected obliquely. *Glint* refers to emitted or reflected light in flashes. *Sparkle* suggests a rapid succession of flashes of high brilliance, and *glitter* a similar succession of even greater intensity. *Glisten* usually refers to lustrous, reflected light, and *shimmer* to the reflection of soft, undulating light. *Glimmer* is applied to emission or reflection of subdued, fleeting light. *Twinkle* refers to the intermittent emission of soft, wavering light, and *spark* to the production of brief flashes of light or fire. *Scintillate* is applied to what flashes as if throwing off sparks in a continuous stream.

flash back *intr.v.* To interrupt a story in order to portray or recount an incident or scene from the past; cut back.

flash·back (flăsh′băk′) *n.* In a novel, motion picture, or other narrative, a depiction of events belonging to an earlier part of the story or a reversion to previously depicted events.

flash·board (flăsh′bôrd′, -bōrd′) *n.* Boarding that extends above a dam to increase the depth of water held.

flash bulb *n.* A glass bulb filled with finely shredded aluminum or magnesium foil that is ignited by electricity to produce a short-duration, high-intensity light flash for taking photographs. Also called "photoflash."

flash burn *n.* A burn resulting from brief exposure to intense radiation.

flash card *n.* Any of a set or integrated series of cards used for brief, usually successive display; especially, such a card used by a teacher as a visual aid in spelling or other exercises.

flash·cube (flăsh′kyo͞ob′) *n.* A small cube that contains four flash bulbs and that rotates automatically when a picture is taken with a camera to which it is attached.

flash·er (flăsh′ər) *n.* **1.** One that flashes. **2.** A device that automatically switches an electric lamp off and on, such as a car's direction indicator. **3.** *Informal.* A person who exposes himself indecently.

flash flood *n.* A sudden, violent flood after a heavy rain.

flash gun *n.* A photographic apparatus that holds and electrically triggers a flash bulb.

flash·ing (flăsh′ĭng) *n.* Sheet metal or weather stripping used to reinforce and weatherproof the joints and angles of a roof.

flash lamp *n.* An electric lamp for producing a high-intensity light of very short duration for use in photography.

flash·light (flăsh′līt′) *n.* **1.** A small, portable lamp usually powered by batteries and encased in a metal or plastic cylinder. **2.** A brief, brilliant flood of light from a photographic lamp. **3.** A bright, flashing beam or light, as of a beacon or signal lamp.

flash·o·ver (flăsh′ō′vər) *n.* An unintended electric arc, as between two pieces of apparatus.

flash photolysis *n.* A technique for studying the spectra and reactions of short-lived free radicals by subjecting a sample, usually a gas in a glass or quartz tube, to a brief intense pulse of light and recording an absorption spectrum using a separate continuous light source.

flash point *n.* **1.** The lowest temperature at which the vapor of a combustible liquid can be made to ignite momentarily in air. **2.** The point at which a situation or person erupts or may erupt, as into violence.

flash tube *n.* A gas discharge tube used in an electronic flash to produce a brief, intense pulse of light.

flash unit *n.* **1.** An electronic flash system containing both power supply and flash tube in a single compact unit. **2. a.** A flash gun. **b.** A flash gun and reflector.

flash·y (flăsh′ē) *adj.* **-ier, -iest. 1.** Giving a momentary or superficial impression of brilliance. **2.** Cheap-looking and showy; tastelessly ostentatious. —**flash·i·ly** *adv.* —**flash·i·ness** *n.*

flask (flăsk, fläsk) *n.* **1.** A small bottle or other container with a narrow neck and usually a cap, especially: **a.** A pocket-sized, flat-shaped container for holding liquor. **b.** A container or case for carrying gunpowder or shot. **c.** A vial or round long-necked bottle for laboratory use. **2.** A frame for holding a sand mold in a foundry. [Old French *flasque, flaske,* from Late Latin *flascō, flasca,* probably from Germanic *flaska-* (unattested).]

flask·et (flăs′kĭt, flä′skĭt) *n.* **1.** A long, shallow basket. **2.** A small flask. [Old North French *flasquet,* diminutive of Old French *flasque,* FLASK.]

flat¹ (flăt) *adj.* **flatter, flattest. 1.** Having no curves; of zero curvature. **2.** Extending or lying completely in a plane, especially a horizontal plane; planar. **3. a.** Having a smooth, even, level surface. **b.** Not hilly; generally level: *a flat landscape.* **c.** Lying closely against another surface: *clasped it flat against his chest.* **d.** Extended or leveled after being rolled up, folded, or the like. **4.** Not deep or high; shallow; low: *a flat box.* **5.** Lying prone; prostrate. **6.** Unequivocal; unqualified; absolute: *a flat refusal.* **7.** Fixed; unvarying: *a flat rate.* **8.** Neither more nor less; to the exact measure: *ten minutes flat.* **9.** Uninteresting; dull: *The party was rather flat.* **10. a.** Lacking zest or animation. **b.** Having lost a characteristic effervescence; dead; stale. Said of beverages. **11. a.** Deflated. Said of a tire. **b.** Electrically discharged. Said of a battery or accumulator. **12.** Commercially inactive; sluggish: *a flat market.* **13.** Unmodulated; monotonous: *a flat voice.* **14. a.** Executed with an even thickness of paint; lacking relief. **b.** Lacking contrast in tint or shading; uniform. Said of a painting or photograph. **15.** Mat; not glossy. Said of a paint. **16.** *Music.* **a.** Below the intended pitch. **b.** Designating a key with one or more flats in the signature. **c.** Being half a step lower than the corresponding natural key: *the key of B flat.* Compare **sharp. 17.** Designating the vowel *a* as pronounced in *bad* or *cat.* **18.** With low heels. Said of shoes. **19.** Having little or no arch. Said of a foot. **20.** *Chiefly British.* Designating horse races run over level ground without obstacles. —See Synonyms at **level.**
~*adv.* **1. a.** Horizontally; level with the ground. **b.** Prostrate. **2.** So as to be flat. **3.** Directly; completely: *He went flat against the rules.* **4.** *Music.* Below the intended pitch: *sing flat.* —**fall flat.** To fail: *Our plans fell flat.* —**flat out.** *Informal.* **1.** With the utmost effort or vigor. **2.** In a direct manner; bluntly. **3.** At top speed.
~*n.* **1.** A flat surface or part. **2. a.** *Often* **flats.** A stretch of level ground: *the salt flats.* **b.** Low-lying, partly flooded ground such as tideland. **c.** A shallow; a shoal. **3.** Stage scenery on a movable wooden frame. **4.** The inner side of the extended hand. **5.** A shallow frame or box for seeds or seedlings. **6.** A shoe with a flat heel. **7.** A flatcar. **8.** A deflated tire. **9.** *Music.* **a.** A sign (♭) affixed to a note to indicate that it is to be lowered by half a tone below its natural pitch. **b.** A note that is lowered in this way: *B flat.* In this sense, compare **sharp.**
~*tr.v.* **flatted, flatting, flats. 1.** To make flat; flatten. **2.** *Music.* To lower (a note) by a semitone. [Middle English, from Old Norse *flatr,* from Germanic.] —**flat·ly** *adv.* —**flat·ness** *n.*

flat² *n.* **1.** *Chiefly British.* An apartment on one floor of a building. **2.** *Archaic.* A story in a house.
~*tr.v.* **flatted, flatting, flats.** *Chiefly British.* To divide (a building) into separate flats. [Variant (influenced by the adjective) of obsolete *flet,* interior of a house, Middle English *flet,* Old English *flett,* floor, ground, hall.]

flat-bed press (flăt′bĕd′) *n.* A printing press in which the type is supported by a flat surface (bed) and the paper is applied to the type either by a flat platen (in older models) or by a cylinder against which the bed moves.

flat·boat (flăt′bōt′) *n.* A boat with a flat bottom and square ends, used for transporting goods on inland waterways.

flat·car (flăt′kär′) *n.* A railroad freight car without sides or roof.

flat·fish (flăt′fĭsh′) *n., pl.* **-fishes** or collectively **flatfish.** Any of numerous chiefly marine fishes of the order Pleuronectiformes (or Heterosomata), which includes the sole, halibut, and turbot.

flat·foot (flăt′fo͝ot′) *n., pl.* **-feet** (-fēt′) (for sense 1) or **-foots** (for sense 2). **1.** A condition in which the arch of the foot is flattened so that the entire sole makes contact with the ground. **2. a.** *Informal.* A person with flat feet. **b.** *Slang.* A police officer.

flat-foot·ed (flăt′fo͝ot′ĭd) *adj.* **1.** Of or suffering from flatfoot. **2.** *Informal.* Without reservation; forthright; uncompromising: *a flat-footed denial.* **3.** *Informal.* Clumsy; graceless. **4.** *Informal.* Uninspired; tedious. **5.** *Informal.* Unprepared; unable to react quickly: *caught him flat-footed.* —**flat-foot·ed·ly** *adv.* —**flat-foot·ed·ness** *n.*

flat·head (flăt′hĕd′) *n.* A food fish of the family Platycephalidae, of Pacific waters, having a tapering body and a large, flat head covered with spines and ridges.

flat·i·ron (flăt′ī′ərn) *n.* An externally heated iron for pressing clothes.

flat knot *n.* A **reef knot** *(see).*

flat·let (flăt′lĭt) *n.* *Chiefly British.* A small apartment.

PRONUNCIATION KEY

ă, pat; ā, pay; âr, care;
ä, father, are; b, bib;
ch, church; d, deed; ĕ, pet;
ē, be; f, fife; g, gag; h, hat;
hw, which; ĭ, pit; ī, pie;
îr, pier; j, judge; k, kick;
l, lid, needle; m, mum;
n, no, sudden; ng, thing;
ŏ, pot; ō, toe; ô, paw, for;
oi, noise; ou, out; o͝o, book;
o͞o, boot; p, pop; r, roar;
s, sauce; sh, ship, dish;
t, tight; th, thin, path;
th, this, bathe; ŭ, cut; ûr, fur;
v, valve; w, with; y, yes;
z, zebra, size; zh, vision;
ə, about, item, edible, gallop, circus, peaceful

IN FOREIGN WORDS:

à, *Fr.* ami; œ, *Fr.* feu, *Ger.* schön; ü, *Fr.* tu, *Ger.* über; KH, *Ger.* ich, *Scot.* loch; N, *Fr.* bon; y', *Fr.* Compiègne

STRESS MARKS:

Primary stress: ′
in·cite′ (ĭn-sīt′)
Secondary stress: ′
in′sight′ (ĭn′sīt′)

flat spin *n.* **1.** *Aeronautics.* A spin around a nearly horizontal axis. **2.** *Slang.* A state of great agitation.

flat·ten (flăt′n) *v.* **-tened, -tening, -tens.** —*tr.* **1.** To make flat or flatter. **2.** To knock down; lay low. **3.** *Informal.* To humiliate or subdue. —*intr.* **1.** To become flat or more nearly flat. **2.** To become flat, horizontal, or prostrate. Used with *out.* **3.** *Aeronautics.* To bring an aircraft into a horizontal position. Used with *out.* **—flat·ten·er** *n.*

flat·ter¹ (flăt′ər) *v.* **-tered, -tering, -ters.** —*tr.* **1.** To compliment excessively and often insincerely, especially in order to win favor; court; blandish. **2.** To please or gratify; feed the vanity of: *"What really flatters a man is that you think him worth flattering"* (G.B. Shaw). **3. a.** To portray favorably. **b.** To show off becomingly or advantageously. **4.** To persuade (oneself) that something one wants to believe is the case: *"many flattered themselves that I had turned out a failure"* (John Stuart Mill). —*intr.* To practice flattery. [Middle English *flateren,* from Old French *flat(t)er,* "to caress with the hand," smooth, flatter, from Frankish *flat* (unattested), flat, flat part of a person's hand.] **—flat·ter·er** *n.* **—flat·ter·ing·ly** *adv.*

flatter² *n.* **1.** A flat-faced swage or hammer used by blacksmiths. **2.** A die plate for flattening metal into strips, as in the manufacture of watch springs.

flat·ter·y (flăt′ə-rē) *n., pl.* **-ies.** **1.** The act or practice of flattering. **2.** Excessive, false, or sycophantic praise.

Flattery, Cape. A headland in northwestern Washington, at the entrance to Juan de Fuca Strait. It was discovered in 1778 by Capt. James Cook.

flat·ting (flăt′ĭng) *n.* The process of rolling sheet metal.

flat·tish (flăt′ĭsh) *adj.* Somewhat flat.

flat·top (flăt′tŏp′) *n. Informal.* **1.** A U.S. aircraft carrier. **2.** A man's short haircut with a flat, brushlike crown.

flat·u·lence (flăch′ōō-ləns) *n.* Also **flat·u·len·cy** (-lən-sē). **1.** The presence of excessive gas in the digestive tract. **2.** Windy, high-flown speech; pomposity.

flat·u·lent (flăch′ōō-lənt) *adj.* **1. a.** Of, suffering from, or caused by flatulence. **b.** Inducing flatulence. **2.** Inflated with self-importance; pompous and pretentious: *flatulent oratory.* [French, from New Latin *flatulentus,* from Latin *flātus,* a breaking wind. See **flatus.**] **—flat·u·lent·ly** *adv.*

fla·tus (flā′təs) *n.* Gas generated in the stomach or intestines. [Latin *flātus,* a breaking wind, a blowing, from the past participle of *flāre,* to blow.]

flat·ware (flăt′wâr′) *n.* **1.** Tableware that is fairly flat and fashioned usually of a single piece, such as plates and saucers. **2.** Table utensils such as knives, forks, and spoons. Compare **hollowware.**

flat·wise (flăt′wīz′) *adv.* Also **flat·ways** (-wāz′). With the flat side down or in contact with a surface.

flat·worm (flăt′wûrm′) *n.* Any wormlike animal of the phylum Platyhelminthes; a **platyhelminth** *(see).*

Flau·bert (flō-bâr′), **Gustave** (1821–80). French novelist. His novels include *Madame Bovary* (1856), *Salammbô* (1862), and *La Tentation de Saint Antoine* (1874). *Trois Contes* (1877) established him as a master of the short story. **—Flau·bert·i·an** (flō-bâr′tē-ən) *adj.*

flaunch. Variant of **flanch.**

flaunt (flônt) *v.* **flaunted, flaunting, flaunts.** —*tr.* **1.** To exhibit ostentatiously; show off: *She flaunted her engagement ring.* **2.** *Nonstandard.* To flout. —*intr.* **1.** To parade oneself ostentatiously or pertly; show oneself off. **2.** To be gaudily in evidence. **3.** To wave proudly, as a flag does. —See Synonyms at **show.** [16th century : origin obscure.] **—flaunt·er** *n.* **—flaunt·ing·ly** *adv.*

Usage: Although they are similar in form, *flaunt* and *flout* have distinctly different senses. *Flaunt* means "to show off," while *flout* means "to treat with contempt." Thus a soldier who *flaunts* his new uniform is proud of it and is not likely to *flout* the regulations ordering him to wear it. The substitution of *flaunt* for *flout,* though frequent in modern usage, is not generally considered acceptable in formal contexts.

flau·tist (flô′tĭst, flou′-) *n.* A **flutist** *(see).* [Italian *flautista,* from *flauto,* FLUTE.]

fla·ves·cent (flə-vĕs′ənt) *adj.* Turning yellow; yellowish. [Latin *flāvēscens,* present participle of *flāvēscere,* to turn yellow, inceptive of *flāvēre,* to be yellow, from *flāvus,* yellow.]

fla·vin (flā′vĭn) *n.* Also **fla·vine** (flā′vēn′). **1.** Any of various water-soluble yellow pigments derived from riboflavin, including **FAD** and **FMN** *(both of which see),* found in plant and animal tissue as prosthetic groups of flavoprotein. **2.** A compound, $C_{10}H_6N_4O_2$, that is the nucleus of various natural yellow pigments. [Latin *flāvus,* yellow + -IN.]

flavin adenine dinucleotide *n.* **FAD** *(see).*

fla·vine (flā′vēn′) *n.* **1.** A brownish-red crystalline powder, $C_{14}H_{15}N_3Cl_2$, used as an antiseptic. **2.** Variant of **flavin.**

flavin mononucleotide *n.* **FMN** *(see).*

fla·vone (flā′vōn′) *n.* A crystalline compound, $C_{15}H_{10}O_2$, the parent substance of a number of important yellow pigments. [Latin *flāvus,* yellow + -ONE.]

fla·von·oid (flā′və-noid′) *n.* Any of a large group of plant pigments, including the anthocyanins. [FLAVON(E) + -OID.]

fla·vo·pro·tein (flā′vō-prō′tēn′, -tē-ĭn) *n.* Any of a class of enzymes containing flavin bound to protein and acting as dehydrogenation catalysts in biological reactions. [Latin *flāvus,* yellow + PROTEIN.]

fla·vor (flā′vər) *n.* Also *chiefly British* **fla·vour.** **1.** Distinctive taste; savor: *a flavor of smoke in bacon.* **2.** An ineffable quality felt to be characteristic of a specified thing: *the flavor of the Orient.* **3.** A seasoning; a flavoring. **4.** *Archaic.* Aroma. **5.** *Physics.* Any of various types of quark. Symmetry between quarks and leptons requires at least six flavors, these quarks being designated as up, down, charmed, strange, top, and bottom.
~*tr.v.* **flavored, -voring, -vors.** Also *chiefly British* **fla·vour, -voured, -vouring, -vours.** To give flavor to. [Middle English *flavour,* aroma, variant (influenced by *savour*) of Old French *flaor,* from Vulgar Latin *flātor* (unattested), from Latin *flātus,* blowing, breeze, from the past participle of *flāre,* to blow.] **—fla·vor·er** *n.* **—fla·vor·ous, fla·vor·some** *adj.* **—fla·vor·less** *adj.*

fla·vor·ful (flā′vər-fəl) *adj.* Full of flavor; savory; tasty. **—fla·vor·ful·ly** *adv.*

fla·vor·ing (flā′vər-ĭng) *n.* A substance that imparts flavor, such as an extract or spice.

flaw¹ (flô) *n.* **1.** An imperfection; a blemish or defect. **2.** *Law.* A defect in a legal document, proceeding, or piece of evidence that renders it invalid. **3.** A small fissure; a crack. —See Synonyms at **blemish.**
~*v.* **flawed, flawing, flaws.** —*tr.* To make defective; mar. —*intr.* To become defective. [Middle English *flawe, flai,* flake, fragment, from Old Norse *flaga,* slab or layer of stone.] **—flaw·less** *adj.* **—flaw·less·ly** *adv.* **—flaw·less·ness** *n.*

flaw² *n.* **1.** A brief gust or blast of wind; a squall. **2.** A brief spell of stormy weather. [Probably from Middle Low German *vlāge* or Middle Dutch *vlāghe,* a push, attack, storm.] **—flaw·y** *adj.*

flax (flăks) *n.* **1.** Any of several plants of the genus *Linum;* especially, a widely cultivated species, *L. usitatissimum,* having blue flowers, seeds that yield linseed oil, and slender stems from which a fine, light-colored textile fiber is obtained. **2.** The textile fiber obtained from this plant, from which linen is made. **3.** Any of several plants resembling flax. **4.** Grayish yellow. [Middle English *flax, flex,* Old English *fleax, flæx.*] **—flax·y** *adj.*

flax·en (flăk′sən) *adj.* **1.** Made of or resembling flax. **2.** Having the color of flax fiber; pale yellow.

Flax·man (flăks′mən), **John Henry** (1755–1826). British sculptor and book illustrator. A designer of friezes and portrait medallions for Wedgwood, he also established a reputation as a neoclassical artist with illustrations for the *Odyssey* and *Iliad* (1792).

flax·seed (flăks′sēd′) *n.* The seed of flax, the source of linseed oil and of emollient medicinal preparations.

flay (flā) *tr.v.* **flayed, flaying, flays.** **1. a.** To skin (an animal). **b.** To strip off the skin of (a person), as by whipping. **2.** To strip of money or goods, especially by fraud; fleece. **3.** To assail with stinging criticism. [Middle English *flen,* Old English *flēan.*] **—flay·er** *n.*

F layer *n.* **1.** The highest zone of the ionosphere, extending continuously at night from approximately 120 to 250 miles (195 to 400 kilometers). **2.** Either of two layers into which this zone is divided during the day, especially in summer, usually designated F_1 and F_2, and extending respectively from 90 to 150 miles (145 to 240 kilometers) and from 150 miles (240 kilometers) upward. Also called "F region," "Appleton layer." [*F* (arbitrary designation) + LAYER.]

fld. field.

flea (flē) *n.* **1.** Any of various small, wingless, bloodsucking insects of the order Siphonaptera that have legs adapted for jumping and are parasitic on warm-blooded animals. **2.** Any of various small crustaceans that resemble or move like fleas, such as the **water flea** *(see).* **—a flea in one's ear.** A sharp, stinging rebuke or pointed, annoying hint. [Middle English *fle,* Old English *flēa(h),* from Germanic.]

flea·bag (flē′băg′) *n.* **1.** A bed or sleeping bag. **2.** A cheap, disreputable hotel or lodging place.

flea·bane (flē′bān′) *n.* Any of various plants of the genus *Erigeron,* having variously colored, daisylike flowers, such as the **horseweed** *(see).* [From its supposed ability to drive away fleas.]

flea beetle *n.* Any of various small beetles of the family Chrysomelidae that have hind legs enlarged for jumping.

flea·bite (flē′bīt′) *n.* **1. a.** The bite of a flea. **b.** The little red mark caused by a flea's bite. **2.** A trifling loss or inconvenience.

flea-bit·ten (flē′bĭt′n) *adj.* **1.** Covered with fleas or fleabites. **2.** *Informal.* Shabby; mean; wretched. **3.** Having a pale coat with reddish-brown flecks. Said of horses.

flea collar *n.* A collar containing an insecticide, worn by dogs and cats to kill fleas and ticks.

flea market *n.* A shop or open market selling antiques, used household goods, curios, and the like.

flea·pit (flē′pĭt′) *n. British Slang.* A cheap or squalid theater.

flea·wort (flē′wûrt′) *n.* Any of various plants reputed to repel fleas, such as *Senecio integrifolius,* which has yellow, daisylike flowers, and a species of plantain, *Plantago psyllium.*

flèche (flĕsh) *n.* **1.** *Architecture.* A slender spire, especially one on a church above the intersection of the nave and transepts. Also called "spirelet." **2.** *Architecture.* An outward-pointing parapet on a fortified wall. **3.** Any of the points on a backgammon board. **4.** In fencing, a lunging attack. [French, "arrow," from Old French, from Frankish *fliugika* (unattested).]

flé·chette (flā-shĕt′) *n.* A steel missile or dart dropped from an aircraft, as used in World War I. [French, from FLÈCHE.]

fleck (flĕk) *n.* **1.** A tiny mark or spot, such as a freckle. **2.** A small bit or flake. **3.** A small patch of color or light.
~*tr.v.* **flecked, flecking, flecks.** To spot or streak. [Probably from Middle English *flecked,* spotted, dappled, from Old Norse *flekkōttr,* from *flekkr,* spot, stain.]

flec·tion (flĕk′shən) *n.* Also *chiefly British* **flex·ion.** **1.** The act or

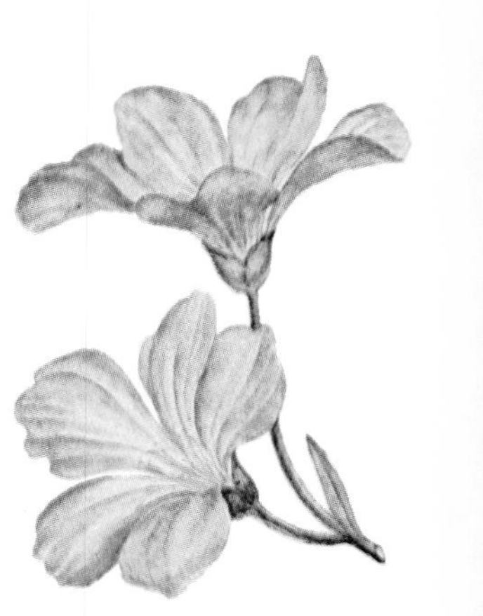

flax *Pale-blue flowers of the flax plant,* Linum usitatissimum. *Flax flowers through the summer and its stems, soaked and combed, once provided the fiber for linen. The word linen comes from* lin, *the Old English name for flax.*

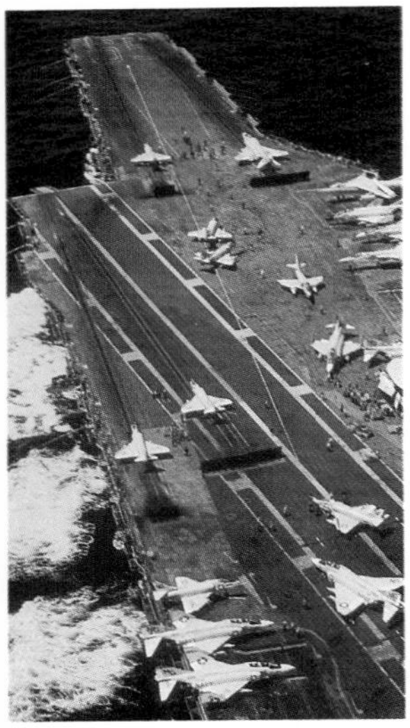

flight deck *Modern aircraft carriers have an angled flight deck. This British invention allows aircraft to be parked on each side while others are taking off or landing. The deck shown here is on the U.S.S.* Enterprise.

PRONUNCIATION KEY

ă, pat; ā, pay; âr, care;
ä, father, are; b, **bib**;
ch, **church**; d, **deed**; ĕ, pet;
ē, be; f, **fife**; g, **gag**; h, **hat**;
hw, **which**; ĭ, pit; ī, pie;
îr, pier; j, **judge**; k, **kick**;
l, lid, needle; m, **mum**;
n, no, sudden; ng, thing;
ŏ, pot; ō, toe; ô, paw, for;
oi, noise; ou, **out**; o͝o, book;
o͞o, boot; p, **pop**; r, **roar**;
s, sauce; sh, **ship**, dish;
t, **tight**; th, **thin**, path;
th, **this**, bathe; ŭ, cut; ûr, **fur**;
v, valve; w, **with**; y, **yes**;
z, zebra, size; zh, vision;
ə, about, item, edible, gallop, circus, peaceful

IN FOREIGN WORDS:

à, *Fr.* ami; œ, *Fr.* **feu**, *Ger.* schön; ü, *Fr.* **tu**, *Ger.* über; KH, *Ger.* **ich**, *Scot.* loch; N, *Fr.* bon; y', *Fr.* Compiègne

STRESS MARKS:

Primary stress: ′
in·cite′ (ĭn-sīt′)
Secondary stress: ′
in′sight′ (ĭn′sīt′)

process of bending or flexing. **2.** A bent part; a curve; a bend. **3.** *Grammar.* Inflection. [Latin *flexiō* (stem *flexiōn-*), a bending, from *flexus,* past participle of *flectere,* to bend, FLEX.] **—flec·tion·al** *adj.*

fled. Past tense and past participle of **flee.**

fledge (flĕj) *v.* **fledged, fledging, fledges.** *—tr.* **1.** To take care of (a young bird) until it is ready to fly. **2.** To cover with or as if with feathers. **3.** To provide (an arrow) with feathers; feather; fletch. *—intr.* To grow the plumage necessary for flight. [Probably from obsolete *fledge,* feathered, from Middle English *flegge,* Old English *flycge.*]

fledg·ling, fledge·ling (flĕj′lĭng) *n.* **1.** A young bird that has recently acquired its flight feathers. **2.** One that is young and inexperienced. Also used adjectivally: *a fledgling republic.*

fledg·y (flĕj′ē) *adj.* **-ier, -iest.** Covered with feathers; feathery. **—fledg·i·ness** *n.*

flee (flē) *v.* **fled** (flĕd), **fleeing, flees.** *—intr.* **1.** To run away, as from trouble or danger. **2.** To withdraw abruptly; rush off: *She fled to her bedroom.* **3.** To pass swiftly away; vanish: *time fleeing.* *—tr.* To run away from; shun: *The child forgot her lines and fled the auditorium in embarrassment.* [Middle English *flen, fleon,* Old English *flēon,* from Germanic. (The past tense *fled* and past participle *fled* are from Middle English *fledde* and *fledd,* which superseded the strong forms inherited from Old English.)] **—fle·er** *n.*

fleece (flēs) *n.* **1.** The coat of wool of a sheep or similar animal. **2.** The yield of wool shorn from a sheep at one time. **3.** A soft, woolly covering or mass. **4.** Fabric with a soft, deep pile.
~tr.v. **fleeced, fleecing, fleeces.** **1.** To shear the fleece from. **2.** To defraud of money or property; swindle. **3.** To cover with or as if with fleece. [Middle English *flees, fles,* Old English *flēos,* from Germanic.] **—fleec·er** *n.*

fleec·y (flē′sē) *adj.* **-ier, -iest.** Of, like, or covered with fleece: *"a thick fleecy sky threatened snow"* (Edith Wharton). **—fleec·i·ly** *adv.* **—fleec·i·ness** *n.*

fleer (flîr) *v.* **fleered, fleering, fleers.** *—tr.* To sneer at; scoff; scorn. *—intr.* To smirk or laugh in contempt or derision.
~n. A scoffing or taunting look or gibe. [Middle English *flerien,* to laugh mockingly, jeer, from Scandinavian; akin to Norwegian and Swedish dialectal *flira,* to laugh, Danish dialectal *flire,* to giggle. See **flimflam.**] **—fleer·ing·ly** *adv.*

fleet[1] (flēt) *n.* **1. a.** A number of warships operating together under one command. **b.** The entire navy of a state. **2.** Any group of craft or vehicles, such as taxis or fishing boats, owned or operated as a unit. [Middle English *flete,* Old English *flēot,* from *flēotan,* to float.]

fleet[2] *adj.* **fleeter, fleetest.** **1.** Moving swiftly; rapid or nimble. **2.** *Archaic.* Fleeting. **—**See Synonyms at **fast.**
~v. **fleeted, fleeting, fleets.** *—intr.* **1.** To move or pass swiftly. **2.** To glide away; fade; vanish. *—tr.* **1.** To pass (time) quickly. **2.** *Nautical.* To alter the position of (tackle, rope, or the like). [Probably from Middle English *fleten,* to flow, glide swiftly, Old English *flēotan,* to float, drift.] **—fleet·ly** *adv.* **—fleet·ness** *n.*

fleet[3] *n. British Regional.* A small inlet or creek. [Middle English *flete,* Old English *flēot.*]

Fleet Admiral *n.* The officer having the highest rank in the U.S. and some other navies. See **Admiral of the Fleet.**

fleet-foot·ed (flēt′fo͝ot′ĭd) *adj.* Capable of running fast.

fleet·ing (flē′tĭng) *adj.* Passing quickly; very brief. **—**See Synonyms at **transient.** **—fleet·ing·ly** *adv.* **—fleet·ing·ness** *n.*

Fleet Street *n.* **1.** A thoroughfare of central London along which many British newspaper publishers are located. **2.** British journalism.

Flem·ing (flĕm′ĭng) *n.* **1.** A native of Flanders. **2.** A Belgian who speaks Flemish. Compare **Walloon.** [Middle English, from Old Norse *Flæmingi,* from Middle Dutch *Vlāming,* from *Vlām-,* FLANDERS.]

Fleming, Sir Alexander (1881–1955). British bacteriologist, discoverer of penicillin. Fleming was unable to isolate or identify the antibiotic, but this was later achieved by H.W. Florey and E.B. Chain, with whom Fleming shared the Nobel Prize in medicine in 1945.

Fleming, Ian Lancaster (1908–64). British writer. His most famous character, the superspy James Bond, first appeared in 1953.

Fleming, Sir John Ambrose (1849–1945). British electrical engineer. He was a pioneer in the development of electric lighting, the telephone, and wireless telegraphy in England. In 1904 he devised the first electron tube, which he called a "thermionic valve."

Flem·ish (flĕm′ĭsh) *adj. Abbr.* **Flem.** Of or pertaining to Flanders, the Flemings, or their language.
~n. Abbr. **Flem.** **1.** The West Germanic language, very similar to Dutch, that is one of Belgium's two official languages. **2.** *Used with a plural verb.* The Flemings. Preceded by *the.* [Middle English, from Old Norse *Flæmskr,* from Middle Dutch *Vlāmish,* from *Vlām-,* FLANDERS.]

Flemish bond *n.* In masonry, a bond consisting of alternate headers and stretchers in each course.

flench. Variant of **flense.**

flense (flĕns) *tr.v.* **flensed, flensing, flenses.** Also **flench** (flĕnch), **flenched, flenching, flenches.** To strip the blubber or skin from (a whale, for example). [Danish *flense.*] **—flens·er** *n.*

flesh (flĕsh) *n.* **1.** The soft tissue of the body; especially, skeletal muscle as opposed to bone and viscera. **2.** The meat of animals as distinguished from the edible tissue of fish or sometimes poultry. **3.** The pulpy, usually edible part of a fruit or vegetable. **4.** Excess tissue; fat; plumpness. **5.** The surface or skin of the human body. **6. a.** The body as distinguished from the mind or soul. **b.** Man's physical or carnal nature. **c.** Sensual appetites. **7. a.** Mankind: *"The glory of the Lord shall be revealed, and all flesh shall see it together"* (Isaiah 40:3). **b.** All living animals. **8.** One's family; kin. **9.** Yellowish pink to pale grayish brown. **—in the flesh.** **1.** Alive. **2.** In person; present.
~v. **fleshed, fleshing, fleshes.** *—tr.* **1.** To encourage (a hunting dog or falcon) to participate in the chase by feeding it flesh from a kill; blood. **2.** To inure to battle or bloodshed. **3.** To fill out or give substance to (a framework or plan, for example). Used with *out.* **4.** To plunge or thrust (a weapon) into flesh. **5.** To clean (a hide) of adhering flesh. *—intr.* To gain weight; become plump or fleshy. Usually used with *out.* [Middle English *flesh, fleish,* Old English *flǣsc,* from Germanic.]

flesh and blood *n.* **1.** Human nature or physical existence, together with its weaknesses. **2.** One's blood relatives; kin.

flesh·er (flĕsh′ər) *n.* **1.** A person who fleshes hides. **2.** An instrument for fleshing hides. **3.** *Scottish.* A butcher.

flesh fly *n.* Any of various flies of the genus *Sarcophaga,* the larvae of which are parasitic in animal tissue or feed on carrion.

flesh·ings (flĕsh′ĭngz) *pl.n.* **1.** Flesh-colored tights, as those worn by actors. **2.** Bits of flesh removed from a hide in cleaning.

flesh·ly (flĕsh′lē) *adj.* **-lier, -liest.** **1.** Of or pertaining to the body; corporeal. **2.** Inclined to or concerned with carnality; sensual. **3.** Not spiritual; worldly. **4.** Tending to plumpness; fleshy. **—flesh·li·ness** *n.*

flesh·pot (flĕsh′pŏt′) *n.* **1.** *Archaic.* A pot for cooking meat. **2. fleshpots. a.** Sensual gratification; self-indulgence. **b.** A place in which such gratification is obtained.

flesh wound *n.* A wound that penetrates the flesh but does not damage bones or vital organs.

flesh·y (flĕsh′ē) *adj.* **-ier, -iest.** **1.** Pertaining to, consisting of, or resembling flesh. **2.** Having much flesh; corpulent; plump. **3.** Not fibrous; firm and pulpy. Said of fruit, leaves, or the like. **—**See Synonyms at **fat.** **—flesh·i·ness** *n.*

fleshy fruit *n.* A fruit, such as a drupe or berry, whose pericarp is soft and pulpy as opposed to hard and dry.

fletch (flĕch) *tr.v.* **fletched, fletching, fletches.** To feather (an arrow); fledge. [Perhaps from FLETCHER.]

fletch·er (flĕch′ər) *n.* One who makes arrows. [Middle English *fleccher,* from Old French *flech(i)er,* from *fleche,* arrow, from Frankish *fliugika* (unattested).]

Fletch·er (flĕch′ər), **John** (1579–1625). English dramatist and poet. With Francis Beaumont he wrote a number of romantic tragicomedies, including *Philaster* (1610) and *The Maid's Tragedy* (1611).

flet·ton (flĕt′n) *n.* A common type of brick made by compressing ground clay, mixed with a minimum of water, in a steel mold before firing. [After *Fletton,* Cambridgeshire, England, near the source of the clay originally used for this brick.]

fleur de coin (flœr′ də kwăN′) *adj.* In mint condition. Said of a coin. [French, "flower of the minting die."]

fleur-de-lis, fleur-de-lys (flûr′də-lē′, flo͝or′-) *n., pl.* **fleurs-de-lis, fleurs-de-lys** (flûr′də-lēz′, flo͝or′-). Also *archaic* **flow·er-de-luce** (flou′ər-də-lo͞os′), *pl.* **flowers-de-luce.** **1.** *Heraldry.* A device consisting of a stylized three-petaled iris flower, used as the armorial emblem of the kings of France. **2.** An iris; especially, a white-flowered form of *Iris germanica.* [Middle English, from Old French *flor de lis,* lily flower : *flo(u)r,* FLOWER + *de,* of + *lis,* LILY.]

fleur·on (flûr′ŏn′, flo͝or′-) *n.* A crescent-shaped piece of puff pastry used as a garnish in cooking. [French, from Old French *floron,* from *flor, flour, flur,* FLOWER.]

flew[1]. Past tense of **fly** (to move through the air).

flew[2]. Variant of **flue** (fishing net).

flews (flo͞oz) *pl.n.* The pendulous corners of the upper lip of certain dogs, such as the bloodhound. [16th century : origin obscure.]

flex (flĕks) *v.* **flexed, flexing, flexes.** *—tr.* **1. a.** To bend (something pliant or elastic). **b.** To bend (a joint). **c.** To bend (a joint) repeatedly. **2.** To contract (a muscle). Compare **extend.** *—intr.* To bend: *"His hands flexed nervously as he spoke"* (Mary McCarthy).
~n. British. Flexible insulated electric wire. [Latin *flectere*† (past participle *flexus*), to bend.]

flex·a·gon (flĕk′sə-gŏn′) *n.* A folded paper construction capable of being flexed along its folds to reveal different combinations of faces. [FLEX + -GON.]

flex·i·ble (flĕk′sə-bəl) *adj.* Also **flex·ile** (flĕk′səl, -sīl′). **1.** Capable of being bent or flexed; pliable. **2.** Susceptible to influence or persuasion; tractable. **3.** Responsive to change; adaptable. **4.** Capable of variation or modification. **—flex·i·bil·i·ty** (flĕk′sə-bĭl′ə-tē), **flex·i·ble·ness** *n.* **—flex·i·bly** *adv.*

Synonyms: *adaptable, ductile, plastic, pliable, pliant, supple.*

flexible sandstone *n.* **Itacolumite** *(see).*

flex·ion (flĕk′shən) *n.* **1.** *Anatomy.* **a.** The act of bending a limb or joint. **b.** The condition of being bent. **2.** A part that is bent. **3.** *Chiefly British.* Variant of **flection.** [Variant of FLECTION.] **—flex·ion·al** *adj.* **—flex·ion·less** *adj.*

flex·og·ra·phy (flĕk-sŏg′rə-fē) *n. Printing.* **1.** A system of rotary printing used especially for printing on metal or plastic sheets. **2.** Anything printed by this method. [From Latin *flexus,* past participle of *flectere,* to bend + -GRAPHY.] **—flex·o·graph·ic** (flĕk′sə-grăf′ĭk) *adj.* **—flex·o·graph·i·cal·ly** *adv.*

flex·or (flĕk′sər) *n.* A muscle that acts to bend a joint. Compare

extensor. [New Latin, from Latin *flexus,* past participle of *flectere,* to FLEX.]

flex·time (flĕks′tīm′) *n.* An arrangement by which employees may vary their own starting and finishing hours within agreed limits while maintaining a fixed average number of hours per working day. [FLEX(IBLE) + TIME.]

flex·u·ous (flĕk′sho͞o-əs) *adj.* Also **flex·u·ose** (-ōs′). Bending or winding alternately from side to side; sinuous. [Latin *flexuōsus,* from *flexus.* See **flex.**] **—flex·u·ous·ly** *adv.*

flex·ure (flĕk′shər) *n.* **1.** A bend, curve, or turn, such as a bend in a tubular organ: *the hepatic flexure of the colon.* **2.** A bending or flexing; flexion. **—flex·ur·al** *adj.*

fley (flā) *v.* **fleyed, fleying, fleys.** *Chiefly Scottish.* *—tr.v.* **1.** To frighten. **2.** To cause to run away in fright; scare off. *—intr.* To be frightened; take fright. [Middle English *flayen, fleien,* to put to flight, frighten, Old English *flȳgan.*]

flib·ber·ti·gib·bet (flĭb′ər-tē-jĭb′ĭt) *n.* A silly, scatterbrained, or garrulous person, especially a young girl. [Earlier *flibbergib, flipergebet*† (imitative of foolish talk).]

flick[1] (flĭk) *n.* **1.** A light, quick blow, jerk, or touch, as with a whip or fingernail. **2.** The sound accompanying such a movement; a snap. **3.** A light splash, dash, or streak.
~*v.* **flicked, flicking, flicks.** *—tr.* **1.** To touch or hit with a light, quick movement. **2.** To cause to move with a light movement, usually of the hand or finger; snap. **3.** To remove with a light, quick movement. *—intr.* **1.** To look through reading matter inattentively or very quickly. Used with *through.* **2.** To twitch or flutter. [Middle English (imitative).]

flick[2] *n. Slang.* A motion picture. [Back-formation from FLICKER.]

flick·book (flĭk′bo͝ok′) *n.* A booklet consisting of a series of images that give the illusion of continuous movement when the edges of the pages are observed quickly. Also called "flipbook."

flick·er[1] (flĭk′ər) *v.* **-ered, -ering, -ers.** *—intr.* **1.** To give off inconstant, fitful light; burn unsteadily. **2.** To shine or blaze momentarily, as lightning does. **3.** To move waveringly; flutter. *—tr.* To cause to flicker.
~*n.* **1.** An inconstant or wavering light: *"a flicker like green fire in his eyes"* (J.R.R. Tolkien). **2.** A brief or slight sensation, as of an emotion: *a flicker of hope.* **3.** A tremor or flutter. [Middle English *flikeren, flekeren,* to flutter, flicker, Old English *flicorian*†, to flutter, hover.]

flicker[2] *n.* Any of several large North American woodpeckers of the genus *Colaptes,* especially *C. auratus,* the common flicker, having a brown back and a white rump. [Imitative of its call.]

flick knife *n. British.* A **switchblade** *(see).*

flied. Past tense and past participle of **fly** (to hit a fly ball).

fli·er, fly·er (flī′ər) *n.* **1. a.** One that flies. **b.** An aircraft pilot; an aviator. **2.** A step in a straight as opposed to winding staircase. Compare **winder. 3.** *Informal.* A daring financial venture. **4.** An advertising pamphlet or circular.

flight[1] (flīt) *n.* **1. a.** The motion of an object in or through a medium, especially through the earth's atmosphere or through space, that is characterized by lack of contact with any other object, especially with the earth. **b.** An instance of such motion: *the flight of a spacecraft.* **c.** The duration of or distance covered in a flight. **2. a.** The act or process of flying; locomotion through the air by means of wings. **b.** The ability to engage in such motion. **3.** Any swift passage or movement. **4. a.** A journey in an aircraft, especially a scheduled airline trip. **b.** The aircraft making such a trip: *Your flight leaves in 15 minutes.* **5.** A group, especially of birds or aircraft, flying together. **6.** A number of military aircraft forming a subdivision of a squadron. **7.** An effort that transcends the usual restraints; a soaring: *a flight of fancy.* **8.** A flight feather. **9.** A series of stairs rising from one landing to another. **10.** A series or line of hurdles, gates, canal locks, or the like. **11.** The flared tail of an arrow or dart, usually made of feathers or plastic, that is designed to give stability. **12.** In archery, a thin, light arrow designed for long-range shooting. Also called "flight arrow." **13.** In angling, a device that whirls the bait rapidly in trolling.
~*v.* **flighted, flighting, flights.** *—intr.* To migrate or fly in flocks. *—tr. Sports.* To cause (a ball or dart, for example) to float in an unpredictable trajectory: *a flighted delivery.* [Middle English *flight,* Old English *flyht*; akin to FLY (verb).]

flight[2] *n.* A running away; an escape. **—put to flight.** To drive or frighten away; repel; rout. **—take (to) flight.** To run or fly away; withdraw rapidly; flee. [Middle English *flight,* Old English *flyht* (unattested); akin to FLEE.]

flight attendant *n.* An attendant who assists passengers in an airplane.

flight bag *n.* A lightweight, flexible piece of luggage with zippered outside pockets.

flight check *n.* A proficiency check in an airborne aircraft of the pilot, crew members, or a piece of equipment.

flight deck *n.* **1.** The upper deck of an aircraft carrier, used as a runway. **2.** The forward compartment in a large aircraft, used by the pilot, copilot, and flight engineer.

flight engineer *n.* The crew member responsible for the mechanical performance of an aircraft flight.

flight feather *n.* Any of the comparatively large, stiff feathers of a bird's wing or tail that are necessary for flight. Also called "flight."

flight·less (flīt′lĭs) *adj.* Incapable of flying. Said of certain birds and insects.

flight lieutenant *n.* An officer in the British and certain other air forces ranking between a squadron leader and a flying officer and equivalent in rank to a captain in the army.

flight path *n.* The precise route taken or due to be taken through the air by an aircraft or spacecraft.

flight plan *n.* A detailed statement of an aircraft's expected departure time, route, and so on.

flight recorder *n.* An electronic device that records details of an aircraft's performance during flight. Also called "black box."

flight surgeon *n.* An air force medical officer who specializes in aviation medicine.

flight·y (flī′tē) *adj.* **-ier, -iest. 1.** Given to capricious behavior; fickle or unstable. **2.** Given to flirting. **3.** Easily excited; skittish. Said of a horse. [Originally "swift," from FLIGHT.] **—flight·i·ly** *adv.* **—flight·i·ness** *n.*

flim·flam (flĭm′flăm′) *n. Informal.* **1.** Nonsense; humbug. **2.** A deception; a swindle.
~*tr.v.* **flimflammed, -flamming, -flams.** *Informal.* To swindle or dupe. [Reduplication (imitative) of an unknown Scandinavian word akin to Old Norse *flim,* mockery, Danish dialectal *flire,* to giggle, from Germanic *fli-* (unattested).] **—flim·flam·mer** *n.* **—flim·flam·mer·y** *n.*

flim·sy (flĭm′zē) *adj.* **-sier, -siest. 1.** Light, thin, and insubstantial. **2.** Lacking solidity or strength: *a flimsy building.* **3.** Lacking plausibility; unconvincing: *a flimsy theory.*
~*n., pl.* **flimsies. 1.** Thin paper usually used to make multiple copies. **2.** Something written on such paper. [17th century : origin obscure.] **—flim·si·ly** *adv.* **—flim·si·ness** *n.*

flinch (flĭnch) *intr.v.* **flinched, flinching, flinches. 1.** To betray fear, pain, or surprise with an involuntary gesture such as a start; wince. **2.** To draw away; retreat. —See Synonyms at **recoil.**
~*n.* An act or instance of flinching. [Old French *flenchir, flainchir,* from Germanic.] **—flinch·er** *n.* **—flinch·ing·ly** *adv.*

flin·ders (flĭn′dərz) *pl.n.* Bits; fragments; splinters. [Middle English *flenderis,* from Scandinavian; akin to Norwegian *flindra,* splinter.]

Flin·ders (flĭn′dərz). River in northern Queensland, Australia. It rises in the Eastern Highlands and flows 837 kilometers (520 miles) northwest to the Gulf of Carpentaria.

Flinders, Matthew (1774–1814). British navigator and hydrographer. In 1795 he sailed to New South Wales and subsequently made a thorough study of the Australian coast. Among his scientific works is *A Voyage to Terra Australis* (1814).

Flinders Ranges. Mountain chain between Lake Torrens and Lake Frome, in South Australia. About 420 kilometers (260 miles) long, it has valuable deposits of uranium and copper.

fling (flĭng) *v.* **flung** (flŭng), **flinging, flings.** *—tr.* **1.** To throw violently or carelessly; hurl. **2.** To put or send suddenly or unexpectedly: *The army was flung into battle.* **3.** To throw (oneself) into some activity with abandon and energy. **4.** To throw (an opponent or rider, for example) to the ground. **5.** To toss aside; discard: *fling propriety away.* **6.** To speak or shout (words) in a passionate way. *—intr.* To move quickly, violently, or impulsively: *She flung out of the room in a rage.* —See Synonyms at **throw.**
~*n.* **1.** An act of flinging or hurling; a throw. **2.** A brief period of indulging one's impulses; a spree. **3.** A dance in which the arms and legs are flung about; especially, the **Highland fling** *(see).* **4.** *Informal.* A brief attempt: *Have a fling at it.* [Fling, flung, flung; Middle English *flingen, flung* (more often *flang*), *flungen,* from Scandinavian; akin to Old Norse *flengja,* to flog.]

flink·ite (flĭng′kīt′) *n.* A brownish-green mineral form of magnesium arsenate. [German *Flinkit,* after Gustav *Flink* (1849–1931), Swedish mineralogist.]

flint (flĭnt) *n.* **1.** A very hard, fine-grained quartz that sparks when struck with steel. **2.** A piece of flint fashioned into a tool by human beings of the Stone Age. **3. a.** A piece of flint used to produce a spark. **b.** A small solid cylinder of a spark-producing alloy, used in lighters to ignite the fuel. **4.** Anything likened to flint in hardness: *a jaw of flint.* [Middle English *flint,* Old English *flint,* from Germanic.]

Flint (flĭnt). A city in southern Michigan, on the Flint River. A fur-trading post was established here in 1819. Since 1902 the city has been a major automobile-manufacturing center.

flint glass *n.* A soft, fusible, lustrous, brilliant lead-oxide optical glass with high refraction and low dispersion. Also called "lead glass." Compare **crown glass.**

flint·lock (flĭnt′lŏk′) *n.* **1.** An obsolete gunlock in which a flint embedded in the hammer produces a spark that ignites the charge. **2.** A firearm having such a gunlock. Also called "firelock."

Flint·shire (flĭnt′shîr′, -shər). A former county in Wales, in the northeast on the Dee estuary. Since 1974 it has been part of the county of Clwyd.

flint·y (flĭn′tē) *adj.* **-ier, -iest. 1.** Containing or composed of flint. **2.** Unyielding or unfeeling; stony. **—flint·i·ly** *adv.* **—flint·i·ness** *n.*

flip (flĭp) *v.* **flipped, flipping, flips.** *—tr.* **1.** To throw or flick with a brisk motion, especially of the finger and thumb; toss. **2.** To toss (a coin, for example) in the air, imparting a spin. **3.** To reverse or turn over quickly and effortlessly. *—intr.* **1.** To strike at something quickly or lightly, as with a fillip. **2.** To move suddenly or jerkily. **3.** *Slang.* **a.** To be overwhelmed by excitement or enthusiasm: *They flipped when they saw the new car.* **b.** To fly into a rage. **c.** To lose one's mind; go mad. Often used with *out.* **4.** To look through or read something, such as a book, very quickly or inattentively. Used with *through.*
~*n.* **1.** An act of flipping, especially: **a.** A fillip or tap. **b.** A quick,

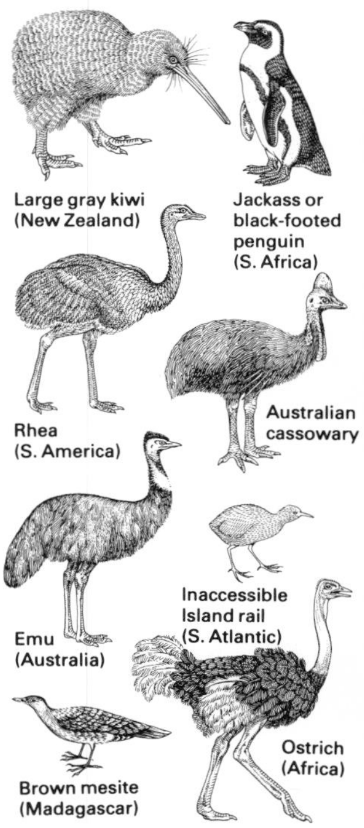
Large gray kiwi
(New Zealand)
Jackass or
black-footed
penguin
(S. Africa)
Rhea
(S. America)
Australian
cassowary
Emu
(Australia)
Inaccessible
Island rail
(S. Atlantic)
Brown mesite
(Madagascar)
Ostrich
(Africa)

flightless birds *Some birds have lost the ability to fly, simply because they live in regions where flight is of no advantage to them — on islands where there are no predators, for example. They all have vestigial wings, though the kiwi's are so small that the bird appears to be wingless. Some flightless birds have developed to great size, such as the ostrich, which stands about 2.5 meters (8 feet) tall and is the largest living bird.*

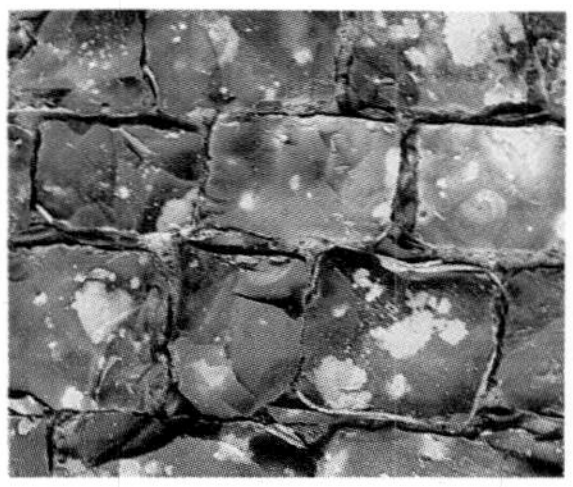

flint *Widely used as a building material, flint is often chipped, to form a regular surface, as in this picture. The stone is split to reveal a dark, shiny face.*

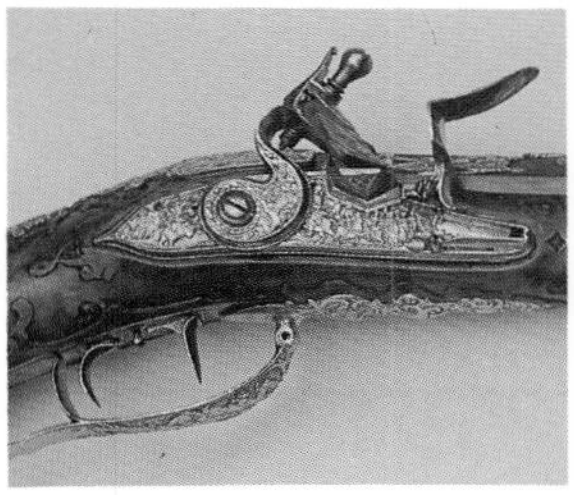

flintlock *The striking mechanism used on firearms from the mid-17th century until the invention of percussion-ignited shells in the 19th century. When the gun was fired, the flint clamped in the hammer struck a spark from a steel plate to ignite the charge.*

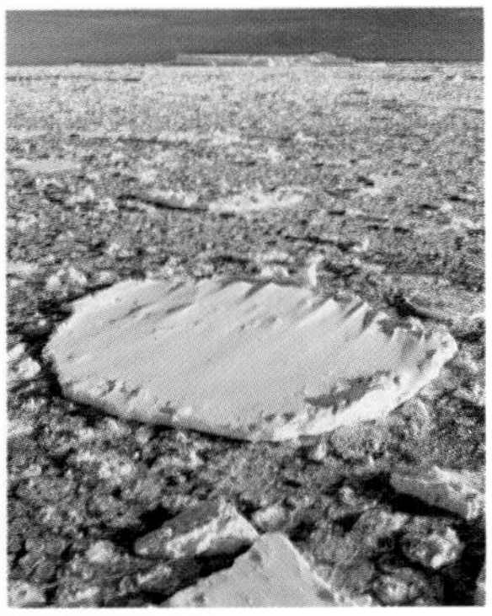

floe *Open pack ice in the sea off Antarctica, with larger floes known as "pancake ice."*

jerky movement. **c.** A somersault. **2.** A mixed drink made with any of various alcoholic beverages, usually including beaten eggs.
~*adj. Informal.* Disrespectful; impertinent: *a flip attitude.* [Perhaps from FILLIP.]

flip·book (flĭp′bo͝ok′) *n.* A **flickbook** *(see).*

flip-flop (flĭp′flŏp′) *n.* **1.** The movement or sound of repeated flapping: *the flip-flop of sandals on a tile floor.* **2.** A simple sandal, a **thong** *(see).* **3.** *Electronics.* An electronic circuit having two stable states, either of which can be assumed depending on the input signal. Flip-flops are used in computers to store a single bit of information. **4.** A backward somersault or handspring. **5.** *Informal.* A reversal, as of opinion: *The senator did a complete flip-flop on arms reduction.* [Reduplication of FLIP.] **—flip-flop** *v. & adv.*

flip·pant (flĭp′ənt) *adj.* **1. a.** Marked by disrespectful and insensitive levity; pert. **b.** Clever in a shallow or superficial way. **2.** *Archaic.* Talkative; voluble. [Probably FLIP + -ANT.] **—flip·pan·cy** *n.* **—flip·pant·ly** *adv.*

flip·per (flĭp′ər) *n.* **1.** One that flips. **2.** A wide, flat limb, as of a seal, whale, or other aquatic animal, adapted especially for swimming. **3.** A rubber foot covering with a flat, flexible portion that widens as it extends forward from the toes to increase propulsion in swimming. **4.** *Slang.* A hand.

flip side *n.* The reverse side, as of a phonograph record.

flirt (flûrt) *v.* **flirted, flirting, flirts.** *—intr.* **1.** To amuse oneself in playful amorousness; play lightly or teasingly at courtship. **2.** To deal with something playfully, triflingly, or coyly; toy: *The bullfighter flirted with death. We flirted with the idea of buying a new car.* **3.** To move abruptly or jerkily. *—tr.* **1.** To toss or flip suddenly; flick. **2.** To move quickly; jerk or wave briskly: *The dancer flirted her fan.*
~*n.* **1.** One given to flirting. **2.** An abrupt, jerking movement. [16th century ("sudden pull or twist," brisk movement, as of a bird's tail, flighty woman, hence current senses) : imitative.]

flir·ta·tion (flûr-tā′shən) *n.* **1.** The practice of flirting; coquetry. **2.** A casual, playful romance. **3.** Any brief involvement.

flir·ta·tious (flûr-tā′shəs) *adj.* **1.** Given to flirting. **2.** Full of playful allure: *a flirtatious glance.* **—flir·ta·tious·ly** *adv.* **—flir·ta·tious·ness** *n.*

flit (flĭt) *intr.v.* **flitted, flitting, flits. 1.** To move about rapidly and nimbly. **2.** To move quickly from one situation or location to another. **3.** *British Informal.* To move house; relocate.
~*n.* **1.** A fluttering or darting movement. **2.** *British Informal.* A hasty escape or departure, as to avoid payment of rent. Used especially in the phrase *do a moonlight flit.* [Middle English *flitten,* to transport, convey, from Old Norse *flytja,* to convey.] **—flit·ter** *n.*

flitch (flĭch) *n.* **1.** A salted and cured side of bacon. **2.** A longitudinal cut from the trunk of a tree. **3.** Any of several planks secured together to form a single beam. [Middle English *fliche,* side of animal salted and cured, Old English *flicce,* from Germanic.]

flit·ter (flĭt′ər) *intr.v.* **-tered, -tering, -ters.** To flit about; flutter. [Frequentative of FLIT.]

flit·ter·mouse (flĭt′ər-mous′) *n., pl.* **-mice** (-mīs′). A **bat** *(see).* [Translation of German *Fledermaus.*]

fliv·ver (flĭv′ər) *n.* An old or cheap car. [Origin unknown.]

float (flōt) *v.* **floated, floating, floats.** *—intr.* **1. a.** To remain suspended within or on the surface of a fluid without sinking. **b.** To be suspended unsupported in space without falling. **2.** To move from position to position, especially at random; drift. **3.** To move easily and lightly as if suspended: *"Miss Golightly . . . floated round in their arms light as a scarf"* (Truman Capote). **4.** *Finance.* To find a level in relation to other currencies solely in response to the law of supply and demand: *The dollar should be allowed to float.* *—tr.* **1.** To cause to remain suspended without sinking or falling. **2.** To flood (land), as for irrigation. **3. a.** To launch or establish (a business enterprise, for example). **b.** To set (an idea, rumor, or the like) in circulation. **4.** To offer (shares, bonds, or the like) for sale. **5.** To make the surface of (plaster, for example) level or smooth. **6.** To seek support for (a scheme or idea). **7.** *Finance.* To allow (the exchange value of a currency) to find its real level freely in relation to other currencies.
~*n.* **1.** Something that floats, as: **a.** A raft. **b.** A buoy. **c.** A life belt. **d.** A cork or other floating object on a fishing line. **e.** A pontoon for amphibious aircraft. **f.** A hollow ball attached to a lever to regulate the water level in a tank. **g.** An air-filled or gas-filled organ or sac that enables an organism to remain suspended in water. **2. a.** An exhibit carried through the streets in a parade. **b.** A large, flat vehicle bearing such an exhibit. **3.** A tool for smoothing the surface of plaster or cement. **4.** A soft drink with ice cream floating in it. **5.** Any of the blades on a paddle wheel. **6.** *Finance.* The amount of money representing debts still outstanding. **7. floats.** Footlights in a theater. [Middle English *floten,* Old English *flotian.*] **—float·a·ble** *adj.* **—float·y** *adj.*

floatage. Variant of **flotage.**

floatation. Variant of **flotation.**

float·er (flō′tər) *n.* **1.** One that floats. **2.** One who wanders from place to place or job to job; drifter. **3.** An employee who is reassigned from job to job or shift to shift within an operation. **4.** One who votes illegally in a number of polling places. **5.** An insurance policy that protects movable property such as jewelry or artwork.

float glass *n.* Flat plate glass made by floating molten glass on molten lead or some other liquid and allowing the glass to harden.

float·ing (flō′tĭng) *adj.* **1.** Buoyed on or suspended in or as if in a fluid. **2.** Not secured in place; unattached. **3.** Inclined to move about; drifting; errant. **4.** *Finance.* **a.** Available for use; in circulation. Said of capital. **b.** Short-term and usually unfunded. Said of a debt. **c.** Freed to rise and fall in value in relation to other currencies. Said of a currency.

floating dock *n.* A structure that can be submerged to permit the entry and docking of a ship and then raised to lift the ship from the water for repairs. Also called "floating dry dock."

floating island *n.* **1.** A solid mass of soil and vegetation floating in water. **2.** A dessert of soft custard with beaten egg whites or whipped cream floating on its surface.

floating kidney *n. Medicine.* **1.** An abnormal condition in which one or both kidneys are mobile and descend into the pelvis. **2.** Such a kidney.

float·ing-point (flō′tĭng-point′) *adj. Mathematics.* Designating or pertaining to a system of expressing numbers by two separate numbers, one giving the value of the digits and the other the power of the number base. For example, 2,3 is 2×10^3 (or 2,000) in base 10. Compare **fixed-point.**

floating rib *n.* Any of the four lower ribs of man that, unlike the other ribs, are not attached at the front to the breastbone.

floc (flŏk) *n.* A flocculent mass as formed in certain serological precipitin tests. [Latin *floccus,* tuft of wool.]

floc·cu·late (flŏk′yə-lāt′) *v.* **-lated, -lating, -lates.** *—tr.* **1.** To cause (soil or chemical precipitates, for example) to form lumps or masses. **2.** To cause (clouds) to form fluffy masses. *—intr.* To turn into lumpy or fluffy masses. [From FLOCCULE.] **—floc·cu·la·tion** *n.*

floc·cule (flŏk′yo͞ol) *n.* Any small, loosely held mass or aggregate of fine particles suspended in or precipitated from a solution. [From FLOCCULUS.]

floc·cu·lent (flŏk′yə-lənt) *adj.* **1.** Having a fluffy or woolly appearance. **2.** *Chemistry.* Made up of or containing woolly masses. **3.** *Biology.* Flaky, waxy, and woollike, as is the secretion covering some insects. [Latin *floccus,* tuft + -ULENT.] **—floc·cu·lence** *n.* **—floc·cu·lent·ly** *adv.*

floc·cu·lus (flŏk′yə-ləs) *n., pl.* **-li** (-lī′). **1.** A small, fluffy mass. **2.** *Anatomy.* Either of two small lobes on the lower posterior border of each lobe of the cerebellum. **3.** *Astronomy.* Any of various masses of gases appearing as bright or dark patches on the sun's surface. Also called "plage." [New Latin, diminutive of Latin *floccus,* tuft of wool.]

floc·cus (flŏk′əs) *n., pl.* **flocci** (flŏk′ī′, flŏk′sī′). **1.** The downy or woolly covering of the young of certain birds. **2.** A woolly tuft of hairs or filaments. [Latin, FLOCK.]

flock[1] (flŏk) *n.* **1.** A group of animals, such as birds or sheep, that live, travel, or feed together. **2.** A group of people under the leadership of one person; especially, the members of a church or congregation. **3.** A large crowd or number.
~*intr.v.* **flocked, flocking, flocks.** To congregate or travel in a flock or crowd: *flock to the January sales.* [Middle English *flok,* Old English *flocc,* from Germanic *flugnaz* (unattested).]

flock[2] *n.* **1.** A tuft, as of fiber or hair. **2.** Waste wool or cotton used for stuffing furniture and mattresses. **3.** An inferior grade of wool added to cloth for extra weight. **4.** Pulverized wool applied to paper, cloth, or metal to produce a texture or pattern. **5.** A floccule.
~*tr.v.* **flocked, flocking, flocks. 1.** To stuff with flock. **2.** To texture or pattern with flock. [Middle English *flok,* probably from Old French *floc,* from Latin *floccus.*]

Flod·den (flŏd′n). Hillside in Northumberland, England, where on September 9, 1513, the English routed the Scots. James IV and more than 10,000 men were slain.

floe (flō) *n.* **1.** A large, flat mass of ice formed on the surface of a body of water. **2.** A segment separated from such an ice mass. [Probably from Norwegian *flo,* layer, slab, from Old Norse *flō,* stratum, coating.]

flog (flŏg, flôg) *tr.v.* **flogged, flogging, flogs. 1.** To beat severely with a whip or rod. **2.** *Slang.* To exert (oneself) strenuously. **3.** *Chiefly British Slang.* To sell. **4.** To criticize severely. [Perhaps shortened from Latin *flagellāre,* to whip, from *flagellum,* diminutive of *flagrum,* whip.] **—flog·ger** *n.*

flong (flŏng, flông) *n. Printing.* Papier-mâché or a paperlike substance used in making a stereotype mold. [From French *flan,* FLAN.]

flood (flŭd) *n.* **1.** An overflowing of water onto land that is normally dry; a deluge. **2.** Flood tide. **3.** Any abundant flow or outpouring: *choke back a flood of tears.* **4.** *Archaic.* A sea. **5.** *Informal.* A floodlight. **—in flood.** At an abnormally high level. Said of a river. **—the Flood.** The universal deluge recorded in the Bible as having occurred during the life of Noah. Genesis 7.
~*v.* **flooded, flooding, floods.** *—tr.* **1.** To cover or submerge with a flood; inundate. **2.** To fill with an abundance or an excess. **3.** To hinder the operation of (a carburetor) by supplying too much fuel: *I flooded the engine.* *—intr.* **1.** To become inundated or submerged. **2.** To pour or flow in or as if in a flood: *Applications flooded in.* [Middle English *flod, flud,* Old English *flōd,* from Germanic.]

flood·gate (flŭd′gāt′) *n.* **1.** A gate used to control the flow of a body of water. Also called "water gate." **2.** *Often* **floodgates.** Anything that restrains a flood or onrush.

flood·light (flŭd′līt′) *n.* **1.** Artificial light in an intensely bright and broad beam, as that used to illuminate a sports field. **2.** A lamp or lighting unit that produces such a beam.
~*tr.v.* **floodlighted** or **-lit** (-lĭt′), **-lighting, -lights.** To illuminate with a floodlight.

flood plain *n.* A plain bordering a river subject to flooding.

flood tide *n.* The incoming or rising tide. Compare **ebb tide.**
floor (flôr, flōr) *n. Abbr.* **fl.** **1.** The surface of a room on which one stands. **2.** The lower or supporting surface of any structure. **3.** A minimum or base; a lower limit, especially of wages or prices. **4.** The ground or lowermost surface, together with accumulated layers of detritus, as of a forest or ocean. **5.** A level area on which a specified activity takes place: *a dance floor; a factory floor; a threshing floor.* **6.** The lower part of a room, such as a legislative chamber or stock exchange, where business is conducted. **7. a.** The right to address an assembly, as granted under parliamentary procedure: *be given the floor.* **b.** The body of assembly members: *a motion from the floor.* **8. a.** A story or level of a building. **b.** The occupants of such a story or level. —*tr.v.* **floored, flooring, floors.** **1.** To provide with a floor. **2.** To knock or press to the floor or ground: *The wrestler floored his opponent.* **3.** *Informal.* To stun; overwhelm. **4.** To press (the accelerator of a motor vehicle) to the floor. [Middle English *flor,* Old English *flōr,* from Germanic.] —**floor'er** *n.*
floor·age (flôr'ĭj, flōr'-) *n.* A stretch of floor; floor space.
floor·board (flôr'bôrd', flōr'bōrd') *n.* Any of the boards forming a floor.
floor exercise *n. Sports.* An event in competitive gymnastics that consists of various tumbling maneuvers performed on a mat.
floor·ing (flôr'ĭng, flōr'-) *n.* **1. a.** Floors collectively. **b.** A floor. **2.** Material, such as wood or tiles, used in making floors.
flooring saw *n.* A saw with a curved toothed edge used for cutting through floorboards.
floor manager *n.* A person who supervises or directs something, as at a political convention, from the floor.
floor plan *n.* A scale diagram of a room or building drawn as if seen from above.
floor show *n.* A series of entertainments presented in a nightclub, hotel, or the like.
floor·walk·er (flôr'wô'kər, flōr'-) *n.* An employee of a department store who supervises sales personnel and assists customers in a designated area of the store.
floo·zy, floo·zie (flōo'zē) *n., pl.* **-zies.** *Slang.* A slovenly or vulgar woman; especially, a cheap prostitute. [Origin unknown.]
flop (flŏp) *v.* **flopped, flopping, flops.** —*intr.* **1.** To move or fall heavily and clumsily. **2.** To swing or move about in a loose, noisy way; flap. **3.** *Informal.* To fail. **4.** *Slang.* To go to bed. Often used with *out.* —*tr.* To cause to fall down suddenly and noisily. —*n.* **1.** The action of flopping. **2.** The sound of flopping; a dull thud. **3.** *Informal.* An utter failure. [Variant of FLAP.] —**flop'per** *n.*
flop·house (flŏp'hous') *n., pl.* **-houses** (-hou'zĭz). A cheap hotel for indigent transients.
flop·py (flŏp'ē) *adj.* **-pier, -piest.** Tending to flop; loose and flexible. —*n. Computer Science.* A floppy disk. —**flop'pi·ness** *n.*
floppy disk *n. Computer Science.* A thin flexible plastic disk with a magnetic coating used to store computer data. Also called "magnetic disk," "floppy," "diskette."
flo·ra (flôr'ə, flōr'ə) *n., pl.* **-ras** or **florae** (flôr'ē, flōr'ē). **1.** Plants collectively; especially, the plants of a particular region or time. **2.** A systematic compilation describing plants. **3. Intestinal flora** *(see).* [From FLORA.]
Flo·ra (flôr'ə, flōr'ə). *Roman Mythology.* The goddess of flowers. [Latin *Flōra,* from *flōs* (stem *flōr-*), flower.]
flo·ral (flôr'əl, flōr'-) *adj.* Of, pertaining to, consisting of, or suggestive of a flower or flowers. —**flo'ral·ly** *adv.*
floral envelope *n.* The perianth of a flower, which surrounds the stamens and pistil; the sepals and petals collectively.
Flor·ence (flôr'əns, flōr'-). *Italian* **Fi·ren·ze** (fē-rĕnt'sä). City in the Tuscany region of north-central Italy, on the Arno River at the foot of the Apeninnes. Originally an Etruscan settlement, then a Roman town on the Cassian way, Florence was one of the most powerful and artistically brilliant city-states of the Italian Renaissance, when it was under the rule of the Medici family. Giotto, Michelangelo, Leonardo, Raphael, Dante, and Donatello were all active in the city.
Florence fennel *n.* A variety of fennel, **finochio** *(see).*
Flor·en·tine (flôr'ən-tēn', -tīn', flōr'-) *adj.* **1.** Of or pertaining to the city of Florence. **2.** Of or pertaining to the style of art and architecture that flourished in Renaissance Florence. **3.** *Often* **florentine.** Cooked or served with spinach. Said of eggs and other dishes. —*n.* **1.** A native or inhabitant of Florence. **2.** *Often* **florentine.** A large rich pastry containing nuts and preserved fruit and coated with chocolate on one side. [Latin *Flōrentīnus,* from *Flōrentia,* FLORENCE.]
flo·res·cence (flô-rĕs'əns, flō-, flə-) *n.* The condition, time, or period of blossoming. [New Latin *florescentia,* from Latin *flōrēscēns,* present participle of *flōrēscere,* to begin to bloom, inceptive of *flōrēre,* to bloom, from *flōs* (stem *flōr-*), FLOWER.] —**flo·res'cent** *adj.*
flo·ret (flôr'ĭt, flōr'-) *n.* A small flower, usually part of a dense cluster; especially, one of the disk or ray flowers of a composite plant, such as a daisy. [Middle English *flouret,* from Old French *florete,* diminutive of *flo(u)r,* FLOWER.]
Flo·rey (flôr'ē, flōr'ē), **Howard Walter, Baron** (1898–1968). Australian pathologist. Working with Sir Ernest Chain, he isolated and purified the antibiotic penicillin, discovered by Sir Alexander Fleming in 1928. Florey, Chain, and Fleming shared the Nobel Prize in medicine in 1945.
flo·ri·at·ed, flo·re·at·ed (flôr'ē-ā'tĭd, flōr'-) *adj.* Decorated with floral designs; flowery or flowerlike. [Latin *flōs* (stem *flōr-*), flower.]

flo·ri·bun·da (flôr'ə-bŭn'də, flōr'-) *n.* Any of several hybrid roses bearing numerous single or double flowers. [New Latin, feminine of *floribundus,* blossoming freely, from Latin *flōs* (stem *flōr-*), FLOWER.]
flo·ri·cul·ture (flôr'ĭ-kŭl'chər, flōr'-) *n.* The cultivation of flowering plants. [Latin *flōs* (stem *flōr-*), flower + CULTURE.] —**flo·ri·cul·tur·al** (flôr'ĭ-kŭl'chər-əl, flōr'-) *adj.* —**flo·ri·cul·tur·ist** *n.*
flor·id (flôr'ĭd, flōr'-) *adj.* **1.** Flushed with rosy color; ruddy. **2.** Heavily adorned or embellished; flowery: *"their style is clear, masculine, and smooth, but not florid"* (Jonathan Swift). **3.** *Archaic.* Healthy; blooming. —See Synonyms at **ornate.** [French *floride,* from Latin *flōridus,* from *flōrēre,* to bloom, from *flōs* (stem *flōr-*), FLOWER.] —**flo·rid·i·ty** (flə-rĭd'ə-tē), **flor·id·ness** *n.* —**flor·id·ly** *adv.*
Flor·i·da (flôr'ə-də, flōr'-). *Abbr.* **Fla.** State of the United States occupying a long peninsula between the Atlantic Ocean and the Gulf of Mexico. It was admitted to the Union in 1845. Florida's wide, sandy beaches and hot climate make it one of the country's leading tourist regions. Its southern swamps form the Everglades National Park. Florida is the leading producer of citrus fruits in the United States. Tallahassee is the capital. —**Flo·rid·i·an** (flə-rĭd'ē-ən), **Flor·i·dan** (flôr'ə-dən, flōr'-) *adj. & n.*
Florida, Straits of. Sea passage, *c.* 145 kilometers (90 miles) wide, between the Florida Keys and Cuba. It connects the Atlantic Ocean with the Gulf of Mexico.
Florida Keys. Chain of small, sandy coral and limestone islands and reefs *c.* 240 kilometers (150 miles) off southern Florida, from south of Miami Beach to Key West. The subtropical keys are popular tourist resorts. The world's longest overwater highway links the islands with 42 bridges.
flo·rif·er·ous (flô-rĭf'ər-əs, flō-) *adj.* Bearing flowers; especially, flowering abundantly. [Latin *flōrifer : flōs* (stem *flōr-*), FLOWER + -FEROUS.]
flo·ri·gen (flôr'ə-jən, flōr'-) *n.* A hypothetical plant hormone thought to be produced in the leaves and transmitted to the growing points where it causes the initiation of flower buds. [Latin *flōs* (stem *flōr-*), flower + -GEN.]
flor·in (flôr'ĭn, flōr'-) *n. Abbr.* **fl.** **1. a.** A former British coin worth two shillings (ten pence). **b.** The sum of two shillings (ten pence). **2.** A monetary unit, the **guilder** *(see).* See feature at **currency.** **3. a.** A gold coin first issued in Florence in 1252. **b.** Any of several obsolete European gold coins similar to the Florentine florin. [Middle English *flore(i)n,* from Old French *florin,* from Italian *fiorino,* from *fiore,* flower, from Latin *flōs* (stem *flōr-*), FLOWER.]
flo·rist (flôr'ĭst, flōr'-) *n.* A person whose business is the growing or selling of flowers and ornamental plants. [Latin *flōs* (stem *flōr-*), FLOWER + -IST.]
flo·ris·tic (flô-rĭs'tĭk, flō-) *adj.* Of or pertaining to flowers, flora, or floristics. [Back-formation from FLORISTICS.] —**flo·ris·ti·cal·ly** *adv.*
flo·ris·tics (flô-rĭs'tĭks, flō-) *n. Used with a singular verb.* The study of the types and numerical distribution of the plant species in a particular area. [FLOR(A) + (STAT)ISTICS.]
-florous *suffix.* Indicates number or kind of flowers; for example, **tubuliflorous.** [Late Latin *-flōrus,* from Latin *flōs* (stem *flōr-*), FLOWER.]
flo·ru·it (flôr'ōō-ĭt, -yōō-ĭt, flōr'-) *n. Abbr.* **fl.** The period during which a person, or sometimes a group, movement, or the like, was most active or flourishing. [Latin, he (or she) flourished, from *flōrēre,* to bloom, FLOURISH.]
floss (flôs, flŏs) *n.* **1. a.** Short fibers or waste silk from the cocoon of a silkworm. **b.** The fluffy mass of fibers from cotton or similar plants. **2.** A soft, loosely twisted thread used in embroidery. **3.** A soft, silky, fibrous substance, such as the styles and stigmas of corn. **4. Dental floss** *(see).* —*v.* **flossed, flossing, flosses.** —*tr.* To clean between (teeth) with dental floss. —*intr.* To use dental floss. [Possibly from French *floche,* from Old French *flosche†,* down.]
floss·y (flô'sē, flŏs'ē) *adj.* **-ier, -iest.** **1.** Made of or resembling floss; downy; silky. **2.** *Slang.* Ostentatiously stylish; flashy.
flo·tage, float·age (flō'tĭj) *n.* **1.** Flotation. **2.** Floating objects or material.
flo·ta·tion, float·a·tion (flō-tā'shən) *n.* **1.** The act, process, or condition of floating or launching. **2.** *Finance.* **a.** An act or instance of launching or financing a business venture by selling an issue of shares or bonds. **b.** The raising of a loan by such an issue. **3.** Any of several processes in which different materials, notably minerals, are separated by agitation of a pulverized mixture of the material with water, oil, and chemicals that cause differential wetting of the suspended particles, the unwetted particles being carried by air bubbles to the surface for collection. [Alteration of earlier *floatation* (FLOAT + -ATION), after *rotation.*]
flo·til·la (flō-tĭl'ə) *n.* **1. a.** A fleet of small ships. **b.** A small fleet of ships. **2.** Any group resembling a small fleet: *a flotilla of taxis.* [Spanish, diminutive of *flota,* fleet, from Old French *flote,* from Old Norse *floti,* raft, fleet.]
flot·sam (flŏt'səm) *n.* **1.** Any wreckage or cargo that remains afloat after a ship has sunk. Compare **jetsam.** **2.** Any discarded odds and ends. **3.** Unemployed and vagrant people; drifters. **4.** Miscellaneous articles. [Earlier *flotsen, flotson,* from Norman French *floteson,* from *floter,* to float, from Vulgar Latin *flottāre* (unattested), from Germanic.]
flounce¹ (flouns) *n.* A strip of gathered or pleated material secured on its upper edge to another surface, as on a garment or curtain. —*tr.v.* **flounced, flouncing, flounces.** To trim with a flounce or

flounces. [Variant of obsolete *frounce*, Middle English *frounce*, a wrinkle, crease, from Old French *fronce*, from *froncir*, to wrinkle, from Frankish *hrunkjan* (unattested).]

flounce² *intr.v.* **flounced, flouncing, flounces.** To move with exaggerated motions expressive of displeasure or impatience.
~*n.* The act of flouncing. [Possibly of Scandinavian origin.]

floun·der¹ (floun'dər) *intr.v.* **-dered, -dering, -ders. 1.** To move clumsily and with difficulty, as if trying to regain balance. **2.** To proceed clumsily and in confusion.
~*n.* The act of floundering. [Probably blend of FOUNDER and BLUNDER (and influenced by FLOUNCE, to move jerkily).]

flounder² *n., pl.* **-ders** or collectively **flounder. 1.** A European flatfish, *Platichthys flesus,* that has a grayish-brown mottled body and is an important food fish. **2.** Any other flatfish of the families Bothidae and Pleuronectidae. [Middle English, from Norman French *floundre,* probably from Scandinavian.]

flour (flour) *n.* **1.** A soft, fine, powdery substance obtained by grinding and sifting the meal of a grain, especially wheat. **2.** Any similar soft, fine powder.
~*tr.v.* **floured, flouring, flours. 1.** To cover or coat with flour. **2.** To make into flour. [Middle English *flour, flur,* finer meal, farina, FLOWER.] —**flour·y** *adj.*

flour·ish (flûr'ĭsh) *v.* **-ished, -ishing, -ishes.** —*intr.* **1.** To grow well or luxuriantly: *Most flowers flourish in full sunlight.* **2.** To fare well; thrive; prosper. **3.** To be active; especially, to be at the peak of one's activity, fame, or the like. See **floruit. 4.** To make bold, sweeping movements; wave vigorously: *The flag flourished in the wind.*
~*tr.* To wield, wave, or exhibit dramatically: *flourish a baton.*
~*n.* **1.** An act or instance of ostentatiously waving or brandishing: *The swordsman made a flourish.* **2.** An embellishment or ornamentation, as in handwriting or literary composition. **3.** A dramatic action or gesture. **4.** A musical fanfare or similar passage. **5.** *Obsolete.* A period or state of thriving or of being in flower. [Middle

English *florishen,* from Old French *florir* (stem *floriss-*), to bloom, from Vulgar Latin *florīre* (unattested), from Latin *flōrēre,* from *flōs* (stem *flōr-*), flower.] —**flour·ish·er** *n.*

flout (flout) *v.* **flouted, flouting, flouts.** —*tr.* To show contempt for, especially in one's actions; scorn: *flout convention.* —*intr.* To be scornful; jeer. —See Usage note at **flaunt.**
~*n.* A contemptuous action or remark; an insult. [Probably extended use of Middle English *flouten,* to play the flute, from Old French *flauter,* from *flaute,* FLUTE.] —**flout·er** *n.* —**flout·ing·ly** *adv.*

flow (flō) *v.* **flowed, flowing, flows.** —*intr.* **1.** To move or run freely in the manner characteristic of a fluid. **2.** To circulate, as the blood in the body does. **3.** To discharge in a stream; pour forth. **4.** To move or proceed smoothly and steadily as if in an uninterrupted stream: *The traffic flowed across the bridge.* **5.** To proceed with ease: *The conversation flowed.* **6.** To appear smooth, harmonious, or graceful: *the building's flowing lines.* **7.** To rise. Used of the tide. **8.** To arise; derive: *Several conclusions flow from this hypothesis.* **9.** To abound or be plentiful. **10.** To hang loosely and gracefully: *The cape flowed from his shoulders.* **11.** To undergo plastic deformation without cleavage or breaking, as slate might. —*tr.* **1.** To release as a stream. **2.** To cause to flow. **3.** To flood.
~*n.* **1. a.** The smooth motion characteristic of fluids. **b.** The act of flowing. **2.** A stream. **3. a.** A continuous output or outpouring; a flood: *a flow of ideas.* **b.** A continuous movement or circulation: *the flow of traffic.* **4.** The amount that flows in a given period of time. **5.** The incoming or rise of the tide. **6.** Continuity and smoothness of appearance. **7.** Menstrual discharge. [Middle English *flouen,* Old English *flōwan,* from Germanic.] —**flow·ing·ly** *adv.*

flow·age (flō'ĭj) *n.* **1.** The act of flowing or overflowing. **2.** The state of being flooded. **3.** A liquid that flows or overflows. **4.** The gradual plastic deformation of a solid body, as by stress.

flow chart *n.* A schematic representation of a sequence of operations, as in a manufacturing process or a computer program. Also called "flow diagram," "flow sheet."

flow·er (flou'ər) *n.* **1. a.** The reproductive structure of an angiosperm plant, characteristically having specialized male and female organs (stamens and a pistil) enclosed in an outer envelope of petals and sepals, all borne on a receptacle. **b.** Any such structure having showy or colorful parts; a blossom. **2.** Any similar reproductive organ of other plants, as gymnosperms and mosses. **3. a.** A plant cultivated or conspicuous for its blossoms. **b.** The condition of being in blossom: *in flower.* **4.** That which is produced by any natural process; an outgrowth: *"His attitude was simply a flower of his general good-nature"* (Henry James). **5.** The period of highest development; peak. **6.** The highest or brightest example; the best representative of something: *the flower of our generation.* **7.** An embellishment. **8.** *Usually* **flowers.** *Chemistry.* A fine powder produced by condensation or sublimation.
~*v.* **flowered, -ering, -ers.** —*intr.* **1.** To produce a flower or flowers; blossom; bloom. **2.** To develop fully; reach a peak. —*tr.* To decorate with flowers or with a floral pattern. [Middle English *flo(u)r,* from Old French *flo(u)r,* from Latin *flōs* (stem *flōr-*).] —**flow·er·less** *adj.*

flow·er·age (flou'ər-ĭj) *n.* **1.** Flowers collectively. **2.** The process or state of flowering.

flow·er·bed (flou'ər-bĕd') *n.* A plot of earth, as in a garden or park, in which flowers are grown.

flow·er-de-luce. *Archaic.* Variant of **fleur-de-lis.**

flow·ered (flou'ərd) *adj.* **1.** Having flowers. **2.** Decorated with flowers or a floral pattern: *flowered wallpaper.*

flow·er·er (flou'ər-ər) *n.* A plant that flowers in a specified way or at a specified time: *a late flowerer.*

flow·er·et (flou'ər-ĭt) *n.* A small flower. [Middle English *flourette,* from Old French *flo(u)rete,* diminutive of *flo(u)r,* FLOWER.]

flower girl *n.* **1.** A girl or woman who sells flowers in the street. **2.** A little girl who carries flowers in a wedding procession.

flower head *n.* A dense cluster of very small flowers at the tip of the plant stem.

flow·er·ing (flou'ər-ĭng) *adj.* Capable of producing decorative flowers. Said of plants, especially trees.

flowering currant *n.* An ornamental shrub, *Ribes sanguineum,* native to North America but widely cultivated for its drooping clusters of small pink flowers, which appear before the leaves.

flowering dogwood *n.* See **dogwood.**

flowering maple *n.* Any of several tropical shrubs of the genus *Abutilon;* especially, *A. hybridum,* having lobed leaves resembling those of the maple and variously colored flowers.

flowering plant *n.* An **angiosperm** (see).

flowering quince *n.* See **japonica** (sense 1).

flow·er·peck·er (flou'ər-pĕk'ər) *n.* Any small bird of the family Dicaeidae, of Australia and southeast Asia.

flow·er·pot (flou'ər-pŏt') *n.* A pot in which plants are grown.

flower power *n. Informal.* **1.** The goal or ethos of a youth cult prevalent in the 1960's, advocating peace and love. A flower was used to symbolize the ideals of the *flower children* or *flower people* involved. **2.** The cult itself.

flow·er·y (flou'ə-rē) *adj.* **-ier, -iest. 1.** Abounding in or bedecked with flowers. **2.** Suggestive of flowers: *a flowery perfume.* **3.** Having a floral pattern. **4.** Full of figurative and ornate expressions; highly embellished. —**flow·er·i·ness** *n.*

flow meter *n.* An apparatus for monitoring, measuring, or recording fluid flow, especially of a gaseous fuel.

flown. Past participle of **fly** (to move through the air).

---

flower

THE REPRODUCTIVE PROCESSES OF FLOWERS
How flowers are fertilized by pollen grains

Flowers are the reproductive parts of seed-bearing plants (angiosperms). The central part of the flower consists of the sexual organs—the male pollen-producing stamen and the female pistil, which contains the ovules. Pollen is generally transmitted by wind or insects to other flowers; self-pollination occurs in some species, but in most it is prevented because the stamen and pistil mature at different times.

In insect-pollinated plants the flower is surrounded by the perianth—the sepals, which protect the flower in bud, and the petals, which are colored and scented to attract insects. Most wind-pollinated flowers have no perianths.

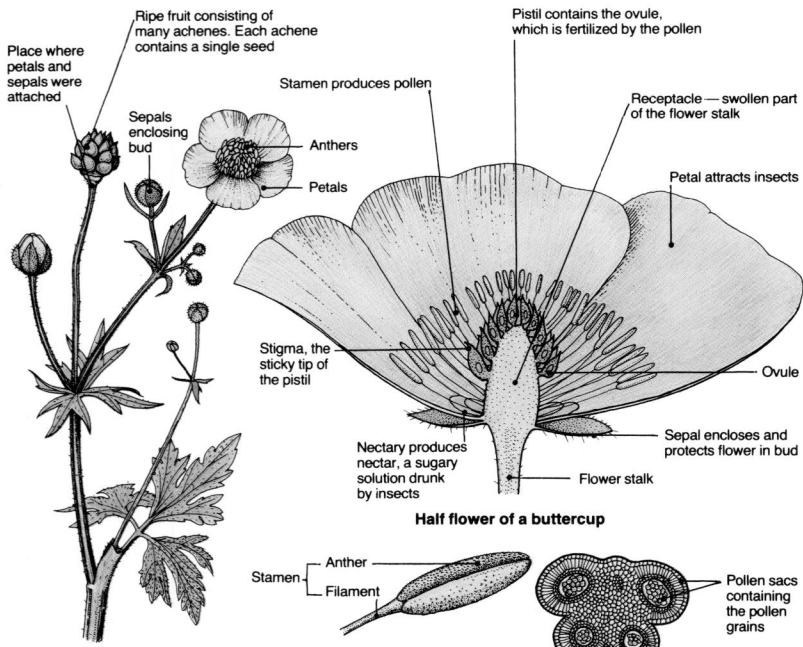

Ripe fruit consisting of many achenes. Each achene contains a single seed

Place where petals and sepals were attached

Sepals enclosing bud

Stamen produces pollen

Anthers

Petals

Pistil contains the ovule, which is fertilized by the pollen

Receptacle — swollen part of the flower stalk

Petal attracts insects

Stigma, the sticky tip of the pistil

Ovule

Nectary produces nectar, a sugary solution drunk by insects

Sepal encloses and protects flower in bud

Flower stalk

Half flower of a buttercup

Stamen — Anther — Filament

Pollen sacs containing the pollen grains

Meadow buttercup

Close-up of stamen and cross section of anther containing pollen

MEADOW BUTTERCUP *The reproductive processes of the buttercup are typical of all flowers, except that some are pollinated by the wind instead of by insects. Sacs in the anther burst to release pollen grains. These stick first to the anther and then to* an insect when it settles on the flower. When the insect lands on another flower, pollen grains stick to the stigmas at the tip of the pistils. A tube grows from the grain to the ovule and fertilizes it, initiating its change into a seed.

flow sheet *n.* A flow chart (see).

fl. oz. fluid ounce.

flu (flⁿ) *n. Informal.* Influenza.

fluc·tu·ant (flŭk′chⁿ-ənt) *adj.* Varying; fluctuating; unstable. [Latin *fluctuāns* (stem *fluctuant-*), present participle of *fluctuāre*, to FLUCTUATE.]

fluc·tu·ate (flŭk′chⁿ-āt′) *v.* **-ated, -ating, -ates.** *—intr.* **1.** To vary irregularly. **2.** To waver; vacillate. **3.** To rise and fall like waves; undulate. *—tr.* To cause to fluctuate. —See Synonyms at **swing.** [Latin *fluctuāre,* from *fluctus,* a flowing, from the past participle of *fluere,* to flow.] **—fluc·tu·a·tion** *n.*

flue¹ (flⁿ) *n.* **1.** A pipe, tube, or channel through which hot air, gas, steam, or smoke may pass, as in a boiler or a chimney. **2. a.** A flue pipe. **b.** The air passage in such a pipe. [Origin unknown.]

flue² *n.* Fluffy waste, as from a textile. [Flemish *vluwe,* from French *velu,* velvety, from Old French, shaggy. See **velvet.**]

flue³, flew *n.* Any of several kinds of fishing net. [Middle English *flue,* from Middle Dutch *vlūwe.*]

flu·ent (flⁿ′ənt) *adj.* **1. a.** Expressing oneself readily and effortlessly: *a fluent speaker.* **b.** Effortless; flowing; polished: *speak fluent French.* **2.** Flowing smoothly and easily; graceful: *fluent curves.* **3.** Flowing or capable of flowing; fluid; liquid. [Latin *fluēns* (stem *fluent-*), present participle of *fluere,* to flow.] **—flu·en·cy** *n.* **—flu·ent·ly** *adv.*

flue pipe *n.* An organ pipe sounded by means of a current of air striking a lip in the side of the pipe and causing the air within to vibrate. Also called "flue." Compare **reed pipe.**

flue stop *n.* An organ stop controlling a set of flue pipes. Compare **reed stop.**

fluff (flŭf) *n.* **1.** Light, feathery down or nap. **2.** Something having a light, soft, or frothy consistency or appearance. **3.** Something of little consequence; a trifle. **4.** *Informal.* An error or lapse of memory in the reading, recitation, or delivery of lines, as by an actor or announcer. *~v.* **fluffed, fluffing, fluffs.** *—tr.* **1.** To make light and puffy by shaking or patting into a soft, loose mass: *fluff a pillow.* **2.** *Informal.* To misread or forget (one's lines). **3.** *Informal.* To mar or ruin by making a mistake or blunder. *—intr.* **1.** To become soft and puffy or feathery. **2.** *Informal.* To make an error; especially, to forget or botch one's lines. [Probably variant of FLUE (down).]

fluff·y (flŭf′ē) *adj.* **-ier, -iest. 1.** Of, like, or covered with fluff or down. **2.** Light and airy; soft: *fluffy curls.* **—fluff·i·ly** *adv.* **—fluff·i·ness** *n.*

flü·gel·horn (flⁿ′gəl-hôrn′, flü′-) *n.* A bugle with valves, similar to the cornet but having a wider bore. [German : *Flügel,* wing, flank (from its use to summon flanks during a battle), from Middle High German *vlügel* + *Horn,* horn.]

flu·id (flⁿ′ĭd) *n.* *Abbr.* **fl, fl.** A substance that has a low resistance to flow and the tendency to assume the shape of its container; a liquid or a gas. *~adj. Abbr.* **fl, fl. 1.** Characteristic of a fluid; especially, flowing easily. **2.** Used in the measurement of fluids. **3.** Readily reshaped; pliable. **4.** Smooth and effortless; flowing. **5.** Likely or tending to change; not stable: *The political situation remains fluid and uncertain.* **6.** Convertible into cash: *fluid assets.* [Middle English, from Old French *fluide,* from Latin *fluidus,* from *fluere,* to flow.] **—flu·id·i·ty** (flⁿ-ĭd′ə-tē), **flu·id·ness** *n.* **—flu·id·ly** *adv.*

fluid dram *n.* One-eighth of a **fluid ounce** (see).

flu·id·ex·tract (flⁿ′ĭd-ĕk′străkt′) *n.* A concentrated alcohol solution of a vegetable drug containing the equivalent of one gram in powdered form of the active principle in each milliliter.

flu·id·ic (flⁿ-ĭd′ĭk) *adj.* Of, pertaining to, or operated by fluids.

flu·id·ics (flⁿ-ĭd′ĭks) *n. Used with a singular verb.* The technology of fluids used as nonmoving, nonelectrical components of control and sensing systems.

flu·id·ize (flⁿ′ĭ-dīz′) *tr.v.* **-ized, -izing, -izes.** To convert (a solid) into a fine, flowing powder that can be conveyed in a stream of gas. **—flu·id·i·za·tion** *n.*

fluid mechanics *n. Used with a singular verb.* The branch of engineering concerned with the study and applications of fluid flow. Also called "hydraulics."

fluid ounce *n. Abbr.* **fl. oz. 1.** A unit of volume or capacity in the U.S. Customary System, used in liquid measure, equal to 29.6 cubic centimeters (1.804 cubic inches). **2.** A unit of volume or capacity in the British Imperial System, used in liquid and dry measure, equal to 28.41 cubic centimeters (1.734 cubic inches).

fluke¹ (flⁿk) *n., pl.* **fluke** (for sense 2) or **flukes. 1.** A flatworm, a **trematode** (see); especially, any of various parasitic species. See **liver fluke. 2.** Any of various flatfishes; especially, a **flounder** (see). [Middle English *fluke, flok,* Old English *flōc,* from Germanic.]

fluke² *n.* **1.** The triangular blade at the end of either arm of an anchor, designed to catch in the ground. **2.** A barb or barbed head, as on an arrow or harpoon. **3.** Either of the two horizontally flattened divisions of the tail of a whale or related animal. [Probably from FLUKE (fish or worm, from its shape).]

fluke³ *n.* **1.** A stroke of good luck. **2.** A chance occurrence. **3.** An accidentally good or successful stroke in billiards or pool. *~v.* **fluked, fluking, flukes.** *—tr.* To get, make, or do by chance. *—intr.* To produce a fluke. [19th century : origin obscure.]

fluk·y, fluk·ey (flⁿ′kē) *adj.* **-ier, -iest.** *Informal.* **1.** Resulting from mere chance. **2.** Constantly shifting; uncertain; variable: *a fluky wind.* [From FLUKE (chance shot).]

flume (flⁿm) *n.* **1.** A narrow defile or gorge, usually with a stream flowing through it. **2.** An artificial channel or chute for a stream of water, as for furnishing power or conveying logs. *~tr.v.* **flumed, fluming, flumes. 1.** To divert (water) by means of a flume. **2.** To transport (logs, for example) by the use of a flume. [Earlier, "river," from Middle English *flum,* from Old French, from Latin *flūmen,* from *fluere,* to flow.]

flum·mer·y (flŭm′ə-rē) *n., pl.* **-ies. 1. a.** Any of several soft, light, bland foods, such as a custard or blancmange. **b.** Originally, a soft gelatinous food made by straining boiled oatmeal, to which fruit, honey, or the like, could be added. **2.** Meaningless flattery; mere nonsense; humbug. [Welsh *llymru†.*]

flum·mox (flŭm′əks) *tr.v.* **-moxed, -moxing, -moxes.** *Slang.* To confuse; perplex. [Origin unknown.]

flung. Past tense and past participle of **fling.**

flunk (flŭngk) *v.* **flunked, flunking, flunks.** *Informal.* *—intr.* To fail an examination or course of study. *—tr.* **1.** To fail (an examination or course). **2.** To give (someone) a failing mark. **—flunk out.** To be expelled from an educational institution or course because of failure to meet required standards. [19th century : origin obscure.]

flun·ky (flŭng′kē) *n., pl.* **-kies.** Also **flun·key,** *pl.* **-keys. 1.** A liveried manservant or valet; a lackey. **2.** An obsequious or fawning person; a toady. **3.** A person who does menial or trivial work. [Originally Scottish (dialectal) *flunky†.*] **—flun·ky·ism** *n.*

flu·or (flⁿ′ôr′, flⁿ′ər) *n.* Fluorite. [New Latin, from Latin, a flowing, fluid (from its use as a flux in smelting), from *fluere,* to flow.]

flu·o·resce (flⁿ′ə-rĕs′, flⁿ-rĕs′) *v.* **-resced, -rescing, -resces.** *—intr.* To undergo, produce, or show fluorescence. *—tr.* To cause to produce fluorescence. [Back-formation from FLUORESCENCE.]

flu·o·res·ce·in (flⁿ′ə-rĕs′ē-ĭn, flⁿ-rĕs′-) *n.* An orange-red compound, $C_{20}H_{12}O_5$, that exhibits intense fluorescence in alkaline solution. It is used to dye sea water for spotting or tracing operations and as a chemical indicator.

flu·o·res·cence (flⁿ′ə-rĕs′əns, flⁿ-rĕs′-) *n.* **1.** The emission of electromagnetic radiation, especially of light, resulting from irradiation with other electromagnetic radiation or with particles, and persisting only as long as the stimulating radiation is continued. **2.** The radiation so emitted. Compare **bioluminescence, phosphorescence.** [FLUOR + -ESCENCE.]

flu·o·res·cent (flⁿ′ə-rĕs′ənt, flⁿ-rĕs′-) *adj.* Exhibiting or capable of exhibiting fluorescence.

fluorescent lamp *n.* A lamp that produces light by fluorescence; especially, a glass tube the inner wall of which is coated with a material that fluoresces when bombarded by a gaseous discharge within the tube. See feature, next page.

flu·o·ri·date (flⁿr′ĭ-dāt′, flôr′-, flōr′-) *tr.v.* **-dated, -dating, -dates.** To add a fluorine compound to (a water supply, for example) for the purpose of preventing tooth decay. [Back-formation from *fluoridation* : FLUORID(E) + -ATION.] **—flu·o·ri·da·tion** *n.*

flu·o·ride (flⁿr′ə-rīd′, flôr′ĭd′) *n.* Any binary compound of fluorine with another element. [FLUOR(O)- + -IDE.]

flu·o·rine (flⁿr′ə-rēn′, -rĭn, flôr′ə-, -ĭn) *n.* *Symbol* **F** A pale yellow, highly corrosive, highly poisonous, gaseous halogen element, the most electronegative and most reactive of all the elements. It is used in a wide variety of industrially important compounds. Atomic number 9, atomic weight 18.9984, freezing point –219.62°C, boiling point –188.14°C, specific gravity of liquid 1.108, valence 1. [French, from New Latin *fluor,* generic name for a group of minerals used as fluxes, FLUOR.] **—flu·o·ri·nate** (flⁿr′ə-rə-nāt′, flôr′ə-) *v.* **—flu·o·ri·na·tion** *n.*

flu·o·rite (flⁿr′ə-rīt′, flôr′ĭt′) *n.* A white or colorless mineral, CaF_2, often tinged green, blue, violet, yellow, or brown by impurities. The colored varieties are fluorescent in ultraviolet radiation. Also called "fluorspar."

fluoro–, fluor– *prefix.* Indicates: **1.** *Chemistry.* Fluorine in compound; for example, **fluorosis. 2.** Fluorescence; for example, **fluoroscope.** [From FLUORINE and FLUORESCENCE.]

flu·o·ro·car·bon (flⁿr′ə-rō-kär′bən, flôr′ō-) *n.* Any of various inert organic compounds derived from hydrocarbons with fluorine replacing all or part of the hydrogen, used as aerosol propellants, refrigerants, solvents, lubricants, and in making plastics and resins.

flu·o·rom·e·ter (flⁿr′ə-rŏm′ə-tər, flôr′ō-rŏm′-) *n.* Any instrument for detecting and measuring fluorescence. [FLUORO- + -METER.] **—flu·o·rom·e·try** *n.*

flu·o·ro·scope (flⁿr′ə-skōp′, flôr′ər-ə-) *n.* A suitably mounted fluorescent screen on which the contents or internal structure of an object, the human body, or the like, may be continuously viewed as shadows formed by differential transmission of x-rays through the object. Also called "radioscope." *~tr.v.* **fluoroscoped, -scoping, -scopes.** To examine the interior of (an object) with a fluoroscope. [FLUORO- + -SCOPE.] **—flu·o·ro·scop·ic** (flⁿr′ə-skŏp′ĭk, flôr′ə-) *adj.* **—flu·o·ro·scop·i·cal·ly** *adv.*

flu·o·ros·co·py (flⁿr′ə-rŏs′kə-pē, flôr′ō-rŏs′-) *n.* Examination with the use of a fluoroscope.

flu·o·ro·sis (flⁿr′ə-rō′sĭs, flôr′ō-rō′-) *n.* An abnormal condition caused by excessive intake of fluorides, as in drinking water, characterized chiefly by mottling of the teeth. [New Latin : FLUOR(O)- + -OSIS.]

flu·o·rou·ra·cil (flⁿr′ə-rō-yⁿr′ə-sĭl, flôr′ō-) *n.* A drug, $C_4H_3FN_2O_2$, used in the treatment of cancer of the breast and digestive system.

flu·or·spar (flⁿr′ər-spär′, flôr′-) *n.* Fluorite. [FLUOR(O)- + SPAR.]

flur·ry (flûr′ē) *n., pl.* **-ries. 1.** A sudden gust of wind. **2.** A sudden

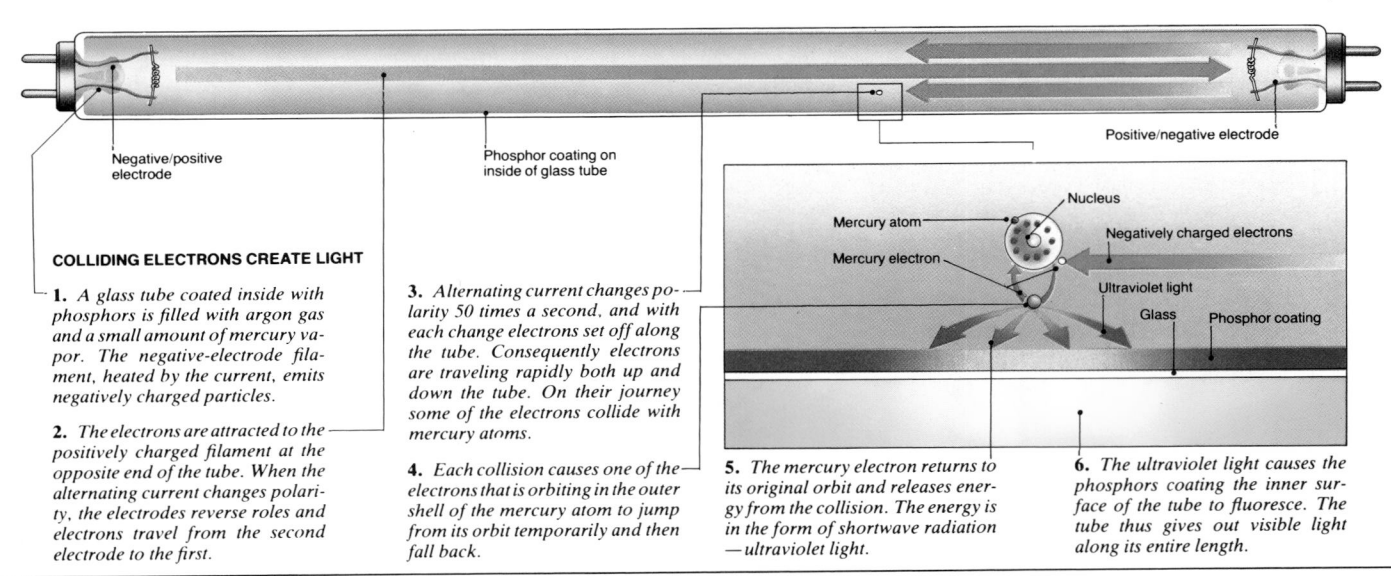

COMBINING GAS AND ELECTRICITY TO PRODUCE LIGHT
An economical lamp that gives a bright light

A fluorescent lamp contains, at low pressure, a gas—typically neon, sodium vapor, or mercury vapor—that produces light (though not always visible light) when excited by an electric current. In a domestic fluores-cent lamp, a tube is filled with mercury vapor, which emits ultraviolet light when bombarded by electrons. The ultraviolet light is converted into visible light by a coating of phosphors (fluorescent chemicals) on the inside of the tube. The fluorescent lamp is much more efficient than the ordinary tungsten-filament electric light bulb: it gives about four times as much light for the same amount of electricity.

COLLIDING ELECTRONS CREATE LIGHT

1. *A glass tube coated inside with phosphors is filled with argon gas and a small amount of mercury vapor. The negative-electrode filament, heated by the current, emits negatively charged particles.*

2. *The electrons are attracted to the positively charged filament at the opposite end of the tube. When the alternating current changes polarity, the electrodes reverse roles and electrons travel from the second electrode to the first.*

3. *Alternating current changes polarity 50 times a second, and with each change electrons set off along the tube. Consequently electrons are traveling rapidly both up and down the tube. On their journey some of the electrons collide with mercury atoms.*

4. *Each collision causes one of the electrons that is orbiting in the outer shell of the mercury atom to jump from its orbit temporarily and then fall back.*

5. *The mercury electron returns to its original orbit and releases energy from the collision. The energy is in the form of shortwave radiation —ultraviolet light.*

6. *The ultraviolet light causes the phosphors coating the inner surface of the tube to fluoresce. The tube thus gives out visible light along its entire length.*

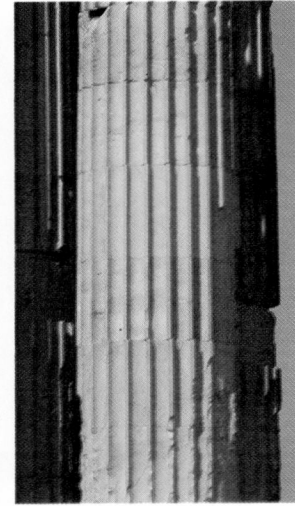

fluting *Rounded grooves carved in architectural columns, as here at the Temple of Zeus, in Athens, Greece.*

fly *A large and worldwide group of two-winged insects. The larvae of many species of fly feed on decaying plant and animal matter. The adults of some—such as mosquitoes and tsetse flies—are bloodsuckers and can transmit diseases to humans.*

burst of confusion, excitement, or bustling activity; a stir. **3.** A light shower of snow or rain. **~v. flurried, -rying, -ries.** *—tr.* To agitate, confuse, or make nervous; fluster. *—intr.* To become agitated or confused. [From obsolete *flurr,* to whirl up, scatter, probably an expressive formation on analogy with HURRY.]

flush¹ (flŭsh) *v.* **flushed, flushing, flushes.** *—intr.* **1.** To turn red in the face from fever, embarrassment, or strong emotion; color; blush. **2.** To flow suddenly and abundantly; spread out quickly; flood. **3.** To glow, especially with a reddish color. **4. a.** To be cleaned by a rapid, brief gush of water. **b.** To function by means of a flushing mechanism. Used of a toilet. *—tr.* **1.** To cause to redden or glow. **2.** To excite or elate, as with a feeling of pride or accomplishment. Usually used in the passive: *flushed with victory.* **3. a.** To wash, empty, or purify with a sudden, rapid flow of water or other liquid. **b.** To remove or dispose of by flushing. **~n.** **1.** A blush or glow: *a flush of red on a cloud.* **2.** A brief but copious flow or gushing, as of water. **3.** Redness of the skin, as with fever. **4.** A feeling of animation or exhilaration; a rush of emotion. **5.** A freshness, development, or growth. **~adj. flusher, flushest.** **1. a.** Having surfaces in the same plane; even; level. **b.** Arranged with adjacent sides, surfaces, or edges touching. **2.** Abundant; plentiful. **3.** *Informal.* Having an abundant supply of money; prosperous; affluent. **4.** Lively; vigorous; lusty. **5.** Having a healthy reddish color; blushing; glowing. **6.** *Printing.* Having the copy lined up evenly at the margins with no indentations. **—See Synonyms at level.** **~adv.** **1.** So as to be even, in one plane, or aligned with a margin. **2.** Squarely; solidly: *The ball hit him flush on the face.* [Probably from FLUSH (to take flight, dart out).] **—flush·ness** *n.*

flush² *n.* In poker or similar games, a hand in which all the cards are of the same suit, rated above a straight and below a full house. See **royal flush, straight flush.** [Probably from Old French *flus, flux,* from Latin *fluxus,* a flow, FLUX.]

flush³ *v.* **flushed, flushing, flushes.** *—tr.* **1.** To frighten (a game bird, for example) from cover. **2.** To cause to leave a place of concealment. Used with *out: used tear gas to flush out the terrorists.* *—intr.* To dart out or fly from cover; take flight. [Middle English *flusshen,* perhaps from (unattested) Old English *flyscan* (imitative).]

Flush·ing (flŭsh´ĭng). Former village of eastern Long Island, part of Queens, New York City. Flushing Meadow was the site of two world's fairs (1939–40 and 1964–65) and temporary headquarters of the United Nations (1946–49). The U.S. Open tennis tournament has been held here since 1978.

flus·ter (flŭs´tər) *v.* **-tered, -tering, -ters.** *—tr.* To make nervous, confused, or agitated. *—intr.* To become nervous or excited, as from confusion or bewilderment. **~n.** A state of agitation, confusion, or excitement; flurry; flap. [Middle English *flostren,* possibly from Scandinavian, akin to Icelandic *flaustra,* to bustle.]

flute (flōōt) *n.* *Abbr.* **fl.** **1.** A high-pitched instrument of the woodwind family, tubular in shape and with fingerholes and keys on the side and a reedless mouthpiece either at the end, as in the recorder, or on the side, as in the transverse flute. **2.** An organ stop whose flue pipe produces a flutelike tone. **3.** *Architecture.* Any of the long parallel grooves, usually with rounded inner surfaces, incised in the shaft of a column as a decorative motif. **4.** A groove similar to a flute, as on the leg of a chair. **~v. fluted, fluting, flutes.** *—tr.* **1.** To play (a tune) on a flute. **2.** To sing, whistle, or otherwise produce (a flutelike sound). **3.** To make flutes in (a column or piece of cloth, for example). *—intr.* **1.** To play a flute. **2.** To sing, whistle, or utter with a flutelike sound. [Middle English *floute, floite,* from Old French *flaute, fleute* (probably imitative); the initial consonant cluster was probably influenced by FLAGEOLET and Latin *flāre,* to blow.] **—flut·y** *adj.*

flut·ed (flōō´tĭd) *adj.* **1.** Decorated with parallel grooves, as a column or ruffle. **2.** Having a sound like that of a flute; high-pitched and clear.

flut·er (flōō´tər) *n.* **1. a.** One who makes flutings. **b.** A device used in making flutings. **2.** A flutist.

flut·ing (flōō´tĭng) *n.* **1.** A decorative motif consisting of a series of long, rounded, parallel grooves, such as those incised in the surface of a column. **2.** The grooves formed by narrow pleats in cloth, as in a ruffle.

flut·ist (flōō´tĭst) *n.* One who plays a flute.

flut·ter (flŭt´ər) *v.* **-tered, -tering, -ters.** *—intr.* **1.** To wave or flap lightly and rapidly in an irregular manner: *The curtains fluttered in the breeze.* **2. a.** To fly by a quick, light flapping of the wings. **b.** To flap the wings without flying. **3.** To move or fall in a manner suggestive of tremulous flight: *"Her arms rose, fell, and fluttered with the rhythm of the song"* (Evelyn Waugh). **4.** To vibrate or beat rapidly or erratically: *His heart fluttered wildly.* **5.** To move quickly in a nervous, restless, or excited fashion; flit. **6.** To be excited, flustered, or nervous. *—tr.* **1.** To cause to flutter; wave; flap: *fluttering her eyelashes.* **2.** To make excited or nervous; confuse; fluster. **~n.** **1.** An act of fluttering; a quick flapping. **2.** A condition of nervous excitement or agitation. **3.** A brief state of excitement, surprise, or bewilderment; commotion; flurry. **4.** *Medicine.* Abnormally rapid beating of the heart. **5.** *Electronics.* A distortion in reproduced sound due to frequency deviations created by faulty recording or reproduction techniques. **6.** *British Informal.* A small bet. [Middle English *floteren,* to flutter, be tossed by waves, Old English *floterian.*] **—flut·ter·er** *n.* **—flut·ter·y** *adj.*

flutter kick *n.* A swimming kick in which the legs are held horizontally and alternately moved up and down in rapid strokes without bending the knees.

flutter tonguing *n.* The technique of vibrating the tongue rapidly to produce a trill-like sound on a wind instrument.

flu·vi·al (flōō´vē-əl) *adj.* **1.** Of, pertaining to, or inhabiting a river or stream. **2.** Formed or produced by the action of flowing water.

[Middle English, from Latin *fluviālis,* from *fluvius,* river, from *fluere,* to flow.]

flu·vi·o·ma·rine (flo͞o'vē-ō-mə-rēn') *adj. Geology.* Pertaining to deposits formed by the joint action of the sea and a river. [Latin *fluvius,* river, from *fluere,* to flow + MARINE.]

flux (flŭks) *n.* **1. a.** A flow or flowing. **b.** A continued flow or flood. **2.** *Physics.* **a.** The rate of flow across a unit area of a fluid, electromagnetic energy, or particles such as neutrons. **b.** Flux density. **3.** *Medicine.* The discharge of large quantities of fluid material from the body, such as watery feces in diarrhea. **4.** Continuous change: *a state of flux.* **5.** *Chemistry & Metallurgy.* A substance that aids, induces, or otherwise actively participates in a flowing, as: **a.** A mineral added to a furnace charge to promote fusing of metals or to prevent the formation of oxides. **b.** A substance applied in soldering and brazing to portions of a surface to be joined, acting on application of heat to prevent oxide formation and to facilitate the flowing of solder. **c.** Any readily fusible glass or enamel used as a base in ceramic work.
~*v.* **fluxed, fluxing, fluxes.** —*tr.* **1.** To melt; fuse. **2.** To apply a flux to. —*intr.* **1.** To become fluid. **2.** To flow; stream. [Middle English, from Old French, from Latin *fluxus,* from the past participle of *fluere,* to flow.]

flux density *n. Physics.* The strength of a magnetic or electric field or the like per unit area.

flux·ion (flŭk'shən) *n.* **1.** Continual change. **2.** Something that flows; a discharge or issue. **3.** *Mathematics. Archaic.* **a.** A derivative. **b. fluxions.** Differential calculus. [Old French, from Latin *fluxiō* (stem *fluxiōn-*), from *fluxus,* FLUX.] —**flux·ion·al, flux·ion·ar·y** (flŭk'shə-nĕr'ē) *adj.* —**flux·ion·al·ly** *adv.*

fly[1] (flī) *v.* **flew** (flo͞o), **flown** (flōn), **flying, flies.** —*intr.* **1.** To engage in flight, especially: **a.** To move through the air with the aid of wings. **b.** To travel by air. **c.** To pilot an aircraft. **2.** To glide through the air sustained by winglike parts. **3. a.** To rise in the air or be carried through the air by the wind. **b.** To float or flutter in the air. **4.** To be sent or driven through the air with great speed or force. **5. a.** To rush; run. **b.** To flee; escape or try to escape. **c.** To hasten; spring: *He flew to my defense.* **6.** To pass by swiftly, as time or youth might. **7.** To be dissipated rapidly; vanish unaccountably, as money might. **8.** *Past tense and past participle* **flied.** *Baseball.* To hit a fly ball. **9.** To react explosively; burst: *He flew into a rage.* **10.** To shoot forth: *Sparks flew in all directions from the torch.* —*tr.* **1. a.** To cause to fly, hover, or float in the air. **b.** To keep (a flag) aloft. **2. a.** To pilot (an aircraft). **b.** To transport or dispatch in an aircraft. **c.** To pass over in an aircraft: *fly the ocean.* **d.** To travel by air using (a particular airline). **3.** To shun; run away from; flee from. —**fly at.** To attack suddenly, either physically or verbally. —**fly blind.** To fly an aircraft relying wholly on instruments, as in bad visibility. —**fly high. 1.** To be in the clouds; be elated. **2.** To prosper; be successful. —**fly in the face** (or **teeth**) **of.** To resist or defy openly. —**fly off the handle.** To lose control of one's temper. —**fly the coop.** To get away; escape. —**let fly. 1.** To emit, send forth, or direct with force or violence. **2.** To release pent-up feelings of anger. Used with *at.* —**make the fur** (or **feathers**) **fly.** To cause a commotion or upset with an insult or by provoking a fight.
~*n., pl.* **flies. 1.** An overlapping fold of cloth that hides a zipper, buttons, or other fastening, as in a pair of trousers. **2.** A cloth flap that covers an entrance or forms a roof extension for a tent or wagon. **3.** A flyleaf. **4.** A fly ball. **5.** The length of a flag from the staff to the outer edge. **6.** The outer edge of a flag. **7.** A flywheel or similar mechanism. **8.** *Printing.* A person or device that carries the printed sheets from the press and places them in a flat pile. **9. flies.** The area directly over the stage of a theater and behind the proscenium, containing the overhead lights, drop curtains, and equipment for raising and lowering sets. **10.** *British.* A one-horse carriage, formerly hired out. —**on the fly.** In flight; on the run; in a hurry. [Fly, flew, flown; Middle English *flien, flew, flowen,* Old English *flēogan, flēah* (plural *flugon*), *flogen,* from Germanic.]

fly[2] *n., pl.* **flies. 1.** Any of numerous two-winged insects of the order Diptera; especially, any of the family Muscidae, which includes the **housefly** *(see).* **2.** Any of various other flying insects, such as the caddis fly. **3.** A fishing lure simulating a fly. —**fly in the ointment.** *Informal.* Something that detracts from the pleasure, value, or effectiveness of something; a jarring or negative factor. [Biblical allusion: "Dead flies cause the ointment of the apothecary to send forth a stinking savor. . ." (Ecclesiastes 10:1).] —**fly on the wall.** One who is in a position to observe others while not being seen himself. [Middle English *flie,* Old English *flēoge,* from Germanic.]

fly[3] *adj. British Informal.* Alert; clever; sharp. [Probably from FLY (to go swiftly).]

fly agaric *n.* A poisonous mushroom, *Amanita muscaria,* usually having a red or orange cap with white patches. Also called "fly amanita." [From its use as a fly poison.]

fly ash *n.* Fine ash carried into the air during combustion.

fly·a·way (flī'ə-wā') *adj.* **1.** Blown or appearing to be blown by the wind; fluttering or streaming. **2.** Flighty; frivolous; giddy.
~*n.* One that is restless, flighty, or elusive.

fly ball *n. Baseball.* A ball that is batted in a high arc, usually to the outfield.

fly·blow (flī'blō') *n.* The egg or larva of a blowfly, usually deposited on food.
~*tr.v.* **flyblew** (-blo͞o'), **-blown** (-blōn'), **-blowing, -blows. 1.** To deposit (the eggs of a blowfly) in. **2.** To taint; contaminate.

fly·blown (flī'blōn') *adj.* **1.** Contaminated with flyblows. **2. a.** Spoiled; tainted; corrupt. **b.** Seedy; shabby.

fly book *n.* A case in which artificial flies for fishing are carried.

fly·boy (flī'boi') *n. Slang.* An air force pilot.

fly-by (flī'bī') *n., pl.* **-bys.** A flight passing close to a specific target or position; especially, a maneuver in which a spacecraft passes sufficiently close to a planet to make relatively detailed observations without landing.

fly-by-night (flī'bī-nīt') *adj. Informal.* **1.** Unreliable with regard to business dealings; shady. **2.** Dubious and temporary.
~*n.* **1.** One who cheats his creditors, as by absconding in the night. **2.** Something of a dubiously transitory nature.

fly·catch·er (flī'kăch'ər) *n.* **1.** Any of various birds of the Old World family Muscicapidae that feed on insects, usually catching them in flight. **2.** Any similar bird of the American family Tyrannidae. In this sense, also called "tyrant flycatcher."

fly-drive (flī'drīv') *n.* An organized vacation providing air travel to a destination and a rented car on arrival. —**fly-drive** *adj. & adv.*

flyer. Variant of **flier.**

fly-fishing (flī'fĭsh'ĭng) *n.* Angling using artificial flies for bait. —**fly-fish** *v.* —**fly-fish·er** *n.* —**fly-fish·er·man** *n.*

fly front *n.* A garment front that has a fly concealing the fastenings.

fly·ing (flī'ĭng) *adj.* **1.** Moving through the air with or as if with wings. **2.** Brief; hurried: *a flying visit.* **3.** Concerned with or used in aviation: *a flying jacket.* **4.** *Nautical.* Not secured by spars or stays. Said of sails.
~*n.* **1.** Flight in an aircraft. **2.** The piloting of an aircraft.

flying boat *n.* A large seaplane that is kept afloat by its hull rather than by pontoons.

flying bomb *n.* A **robot bomb** *(see).*

flying buttress *n. Architecture.* An arched masonry prop that springs from a pier or other support and abuts against another part of the structure to receive thrust. Also called "arc-boutant."

flying circus *n.* **1.** A squadron of fighter planes in World War I. **2.** An exhibition of stunt flying; an aerobatics display. **3.** The aircraft and team of men involved in such an exhibition.

flying colors *pl.n..* Triumph; outstanding success: *pass an exam with flying colors.*

flying dragon *n.* The flying lizard.

Flying Dutchman *n.* **1.** A legendary mariner condemned to sail the seas against the wind until Judgment Day. **2.** His spectral ship, said to appear in storms near the Cape of Good Hope.

flying field *n.* An airfield.

flying fish *n.* Any of various marine fishes of the family Exocoetidae, having enlarged pectoral or pelvic fins capable of sustaining them in brief, gliding flight over the water.

flying fox *n.* **1.** Any of various fruit bats of the genus *Pteropus,* chiefly of tropical Africa, Asia, and Australia, having a foxlike muzzle and ears. **2.** Any of several similar or related mammals.

flying frog *n.* A tree-dwelling frog, *Rhacophorus reinwardtii,* of southeastern Asia, having toes connected by broad webbing and capable of gliding considerable distances.

flying gurnard *n.* Any of various chiefly tropical marine fishes of the family Dactylopteridae, having winglike, much enlarged pectoral fins, and capable of gliding flight over the water.

flying jib *n. Nautical.* A light sail that extends beyond the jib and is attached to an extension of the jib boom.

flying lemur *n.* Either of two mammals, *Cynocephalus volans* or *C. variegatus,* of tropical Asia, that are sustained in gliding leaps by a wide, fur-covered membrane extending from each side of the body. Also called "gliding lemur," "colugo."

flying lizard *n.* Any of various small tropical Asian lizards of the genus *Draco,* capable of gliding by spreading the winglike membranes on each side of the body. Also called "flying dragon."

flying machine *n.* A machine designed for flight; especially, any of the early experimental types of aircraft.

flying mare *n.* In wrestling, a throw in which one grabs the opponent's wrist or head, turns around quickly, and flips him over one's shoulder onto the ground.

flying officer *n. Abbr.* **F.O.** An officer in the British and certain other air forces ranking between a flight lieutenant and a pilot officer and equivalent in rank to a lieutenant in the army and a sublieutenant in the navy.

flying phalanger *n.* Any of several small marsupials of the family Phalangeridae, especially one of the genus *Petaurus,* of Australia, New Guinea, and Tasmania, capable of gliding through the air sustained by large folds of skin between the forelegs and hind legs. Also called "gliding possum."

flying saucer *n.* Any of various unidentified flying objects typically described as luminous disks and alleged to have come from outer space.

flying snake *n.* A tree-dwelling snake of the genus *Chrysopelea,* of southern Asia and the East Indies, that can glide for short distances by flattening its belly scales.

flying squad *n. Chiefly British.* A small mobile group, especially of policemen equipped with motor vehicles, capable of moving very swiftly into action when summoned or alerted.

flying squirrel *n.* Any of various nocturnal squirrels of the genera *Pteromys, Glaucomys,* and related genera, having membranes between the forelegs and hind legs that enable them to glide.

flying start *n.* **1.** The crossing of the starting line of a race at full speed. **2.** Any quick or promising start. **3.** An advantage over one's rivals at the outset.

flying wing *n.* **1.** An aircraft in which a single large streamlined

fly agaric *This poisonous Northern Hemisphere fungus, with its white-speckled red cap, is found in damp woods from August to November.*

flycatcher *The spotted flycatcher,* Muscicapa striata *(above), breeds in summer mostly in Europe and parts of Asia, but it spends the northern winter in tropical and southern Africa. It feeds almost exclusively on insects, especially flies, which it catches on the wing.*

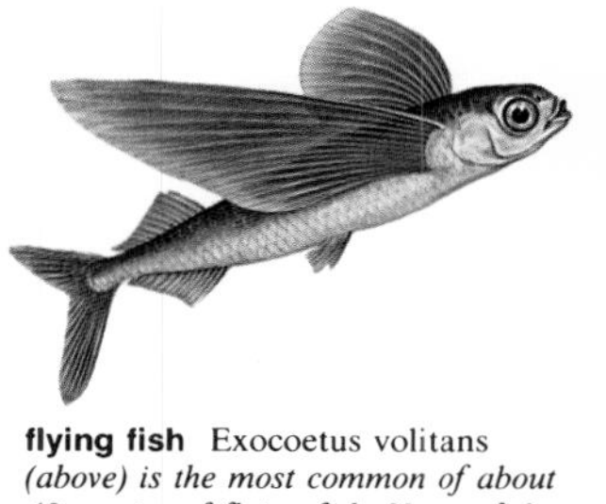

flying fish Exocoetus volitans *(above) is the most common of about 40 species of flying fish. None of the species grows to larger than 45 centimeters (18 inches). Flying fish, which live in warm seas, do not actually fly. Instead they glide through the air on winglike fins, after building up speed underwater and launching themselves with powerful beats of their tails.*

fly-tying

MAKING AN IMITATION TO DECEIVE A FISH

To many fishermen fly-tying is part of the art of fishing

Fly-fishermen use artificial flies to imitate any one of thousands of insects that might tempt a trout to feed. Lacy-winged flies, of which the mayfly is one of the best known, and caddis (or sedge) flies are the insects most usually imitated.

As any insect grows to maturity through various stages, and male and female often vary, the number of possible imitations runs to hundreds of thousands. In addition, the factors that tempt fish to feed change with place and time of year.

Imitation flies are made from fur, feathers, tinsel, raffia, and any other material that will help them to resemble natural flies. Many fishermen consider tying their own flies successfully to be part of the art of fishing. In dry-fly fishing the fly rests on the water to tempt, for example, feeding trout. The wet fly is made to imitate an insect in its subaquatic stage and is allowed to sink.

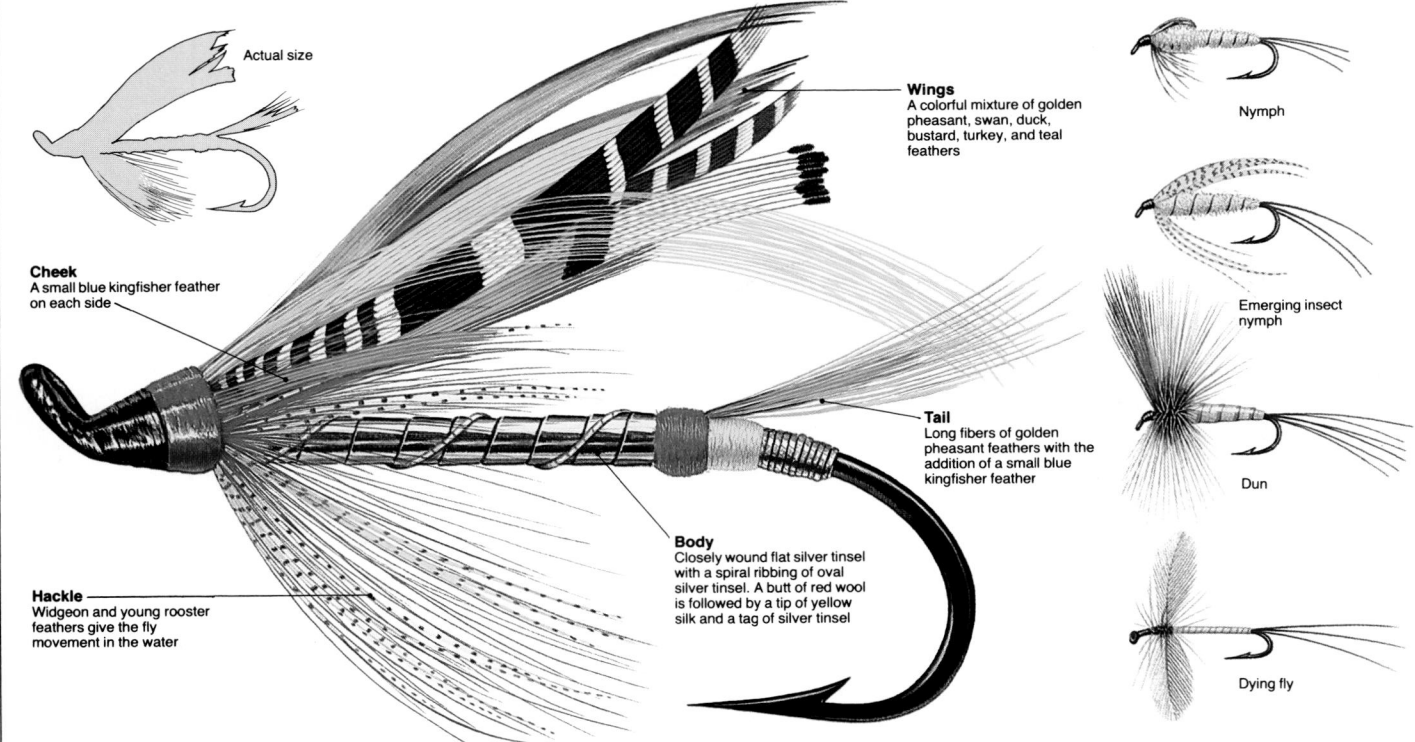

Actual size

Cheek
A small blue kingfisher feather on each side

Wings
A colorful mixture of golden pheasant, swan, duck, bustard, turkey, and teal feathers

Tail
Long fibers of golden pheasant feathers with the addition of a small blue kingfisher feather

Body
Closely wound flat silver tinsel with a spiral ribbing of oval silver tinsel. A butt of red wool is followed by a tip of yellow silk and a tag of silver tinsel

Hackle
Widgeon and young rooster feathers give the fly movement in the water

Nymph

Emerging insect nymph

Dun

Dying fly

SALMON FLY *The Silver Wilkinson is a popular salmon fly that bears no resemblance to any real insect. Because salmon do not feed on their way upriver to spawn, sal-* *mon flies are made to excite the fishes' attention and provoke them to attack. Trout flies are intended to be realistic imitations.*

LIFE CYCLE *The mayfly egg, laid on the surface, sinks to the bed and becomes a larva (nymph). The nymph surfaces for the winged dun to emerge.*

wing incorporating the fuselage constitutes the principal portion of the airframe. **2.** In Canadian football, a backfield man who moves to various positions behind the line of scrimmage.

fly-leaf (flī′lēf′) *n., pl.* **-leaves** (-lēvz′). A blank leaf at the beginning or end of a book, between the lining paper and the first or last signature. See **endpaper.**

fly net *n.* A net covering used to keep flies off or out.

Flynn (flĭn), **Errol** (1909–59). Australian-born actor, noted for his swashbuckling roles in such films as *Captain Blood* (1935), *The Adventures of Robin Hood* (1938), and *Too Much Too Soon* (1958).

fly-o-ver (flī′ō′vər) *n.* **1.** A flight of aircraft at low altitude over a particular area, usually as a military or ceremonial display. **2.** *British.* An overpass on a highway.

fly-pa-per (flī′pā′pər) *n.* A ribbon of paper coated with a sticky, sometimes poisonous substance used to catch flies.

fly-past (flī′păst′, -päst′) *n. British.* A flyover (sense 1).

fly-poi-son (flī′poi′zən) *n.* A poisonous plant, *Amianthium muscaetoxicum,* of the southeastern United States, having narrow basal leaves and a terminal cluster of small white or greenish flowers.

fly-speck (flī′spĕk′) *n.* **1.** A small, dark speck or stain made by the excrement of a fly. **2.** A minute spot. —*tr.v.* **flyspecked, -specking, -specks.** To mark or befoul with flyspecks.

fly swatter *n.* A swatter used to kill flies or other insects.

fly-trap (flī′trăp′) *n.* **1.** A trap for catching flies. **2.** A plant, as the Venus's-flytrap, that traps insects.

fly-ty-ing (flī′tī′ĭng) *n.* The art or hobby of making artificial fishing flies out of materials such as colored feathers or tinsel.

fly-weight (flī′wāt′) *n.* **1.** In professional boxing, a boxer of the lightest weight class, weighing 112 pounds (51 kilograms) or less. **2.** In amateur boxing, a boxer weighing 48 to 51 kilograms (106 to 112 pounds).

fly-wheel (flī′hwēl′) *n.* A heavy rotating wheel used to minimize speed variation in a machine subject to fluctuation in drive and load.

fm, FM frequency modulation.

Fm The symbol for the element fermium.

fm. fathom.

F.M. field marshal.

FMN (ĕf′ĕm-ĕn′) *n.* A derivative of riboflavin that functions, as FAD does, as a coenzyme in many oxidation-reduction reactions. [*F*lavin *m*ono*n*ucleotide.]

fn. footnote.

f-num-ber (ĕf′nŭm′bər) *n.* The ratio of focal length to the effective aperture diameter in a lens or lens system. Also called "f-stop." [*F*, symbol for *focal length.*]

F.O. 1. field officer. **2.** flying officer. **3.** Foreign Office.

foal (fōl) *n.* The young offspring of a horse or other equine animal, especially when under a year old. —*v.* **foaled, foaling, foals.** —*tr.* To give birth to (a foal). —*intr.* To give birth to a foal. [Middle English *fole,* Old English *fola,* from Germanic.]

foam (fōm) *n.* **1.** A mass of gas bubbles; especially, a light, bubbly gas and liquid mass formed by agitating a liquid containing certain soaps or detergents. **2. a.** Frothy saliva from the mouth. **b.** The frothy sweat of a horse or other equine animal. **3.** *Poetic.* The sea. **4.** Any of various light, bulky materials used as thermal or mechanical insulators in packaging, furniture, and the like, made by injecting a gas into a material such as latex or polystyrene. Also used adjectivally: *foam plastic.* **5.** Any of various chemical substances used in fire extinguishers. —*v.* **foamed, foaming, foams.** —*intr.* **1.** To produce or come forth in foam; froth. **2.** *Informal.* To be extremely angry. —*tr.* To cause to foam. [Middle English *fom,* saliva, foam, Old English *fām.*] —**foam·ing·ly** *adv.*

foam rubber *n.* A light, firm, spongy rubber made by beating air into latex with subsequent curing and used as an upholstery material and insulating medium.

foam·y (fō′mē) *adj.* **-ier, -iest. 1.** Pertaining to or resembling foam. **2.** Consisting of or covered with foam. —**foam·i·ly** *adv.* —**foam·i·ness** *n.*

fob¹ (fŏb) *n.* **1.** A small pocket at the front waistline of a man's trousers or in the front of a vest, used to hold a watch or coins. **2.** A short chain or ribbon attached to a pocket watch and worn hanging in front of the vest or waist. **3.** An ornament or seal attached to a watch chain. [17th century (originally cant) : probably akin to German (dialectal) *Fuppe*†, pocket.]

fob² *tr.v.* **fobbed, fobbing, fobs. 1.** To put off or appease by deceitful or evasive means. Used with *off.* **2.** To dispose of (goods) by fraud or deception; palm off. Used with *off.* **3.** *Archaic.* To deceive; cheat. [Middle English *fobben*†.]

f.o.b., F.O.B. free on board.

fo·cal (fō′kəl) *adj.* **1.** Of or pertaining to a focus. **2.** Placed at or measured from the focus. **—fo·cal·ly** *adv.*

focal infection *n.* An infection localized in a specific part of the body.

fo·cal·ize (fō′kə-līz′) *v.* **-ized, -izing, -izes.** *—tr.* To adjust or bring to a focus. *—intr.* To come or be brought to a focus. **—fo·cal·i·za·tion** *n.*

focal length *n. Physics.* The distance of the focal point from the surface of a mirror or from the center of a lens. Also called "focal distance," "focus."

focal plane *n.* A plane in which the image from a lens, mirror, or optical instrument is in focus.

focal point *n.* **1.** A point on the axis of symmetry of an optical system, as of a mirror or lens, to which parallel incident rays converge or from which they appear to diverge after reflection or transmission. Also called "principal focus." **2.** A center of activity or interest; a focus.

Foch (fôsh, fŏsh), **Ferdinand** (1851–1929). French marshal who in World War I was largely responsible for halting the German advance at the Marne (1914) and for the Allied victory at Ypres (1915). In 1918, as Allied commander, he launched the July advance that pushed the Germans back to the Rhine and ended the war.

fo'c's'le. Variant of **forecastle.**

fo·cus (fō′kəs) *n., pl.* **-cuses** or **-ci** (-sī′). **1.** A point at which something converges or from which something diverges. **2.** *Physics.* **a.** A point in an optical system to which rays converge or from which they appear to diverge; a focal point. **b.** Focal length. **c.** The distinctness or clarity with which an optical system renders an image. **d.** Adjustment for distinctness or clarity. **3.** Something, as a place, person, or issue, on which attention converges or around which activity centers. **4.** A condition in which something can be clearly perceived: *couldn't get the problem into focus.* **5.** *Pathology.* The region of a localized bodily infection. **6.** *Geology.* The point of origin of an earthquake. **7.** *Geometry.* A point that together with a directrix determines a conic section. **—in focus.** Sharply or clearly defined; distinct. **—out of focus.** Not distinct; blurred or cloudy.
~v. **focused** or **focussed, -cusing** or **-cussing, -cuses** or **-cusses.** *—tr.* **1. a.** To produce a clear image of (photographed material, for example) by adjustment of a projection lens or other optical equipment. **b.** To adjust the setting of (a lens, for example) to produce a clear image. **2.** To direct (attention or effort, for example) toward a particular point or purpose. *—intr.* **1.** To converge at a point of focus; be focused. **2.** To bring objects into focus. [Latin *focus,* fireplace, hearth (the center of the home).]

fod·der (fŏd′ər) *n.* **1.** Feed for livestock, especially hay, straw, and other plants. **2.** Raw material, as for artistic creation. **3.** People viewed as raw material for the achievement of a specified commercial, political, or military end: *cannon fodder.*
~tr.v. **foddered, -dering, -ders.** To feed (animals) with fodder. [Middle English *fodder,* Old English *fōdor,* from Germanic.]

foe (fō) *n.* **1.** A personal enemy: *tried to win over his political foes.* **2.** An enemy in war. **3.** An adversary; opponent: *My representative in Congress is a foe of tax reform.* **4.** Something that serves to oppose, injure, or impede. [Middle English *fo,* Old English *gefā,* from *gefāh,* at feud with, hostile, from Germanic.]

foehn. Variant of **föhn.**

foe·man (fō′mən) *n., pl.* **-men** (-mĭn). A foe in battle; enemy.

foetal. Variant of **fetal.**

foetid. Variant of **fetid.**

foetor. Variant of **fetor.**

foetus. Variant of **fetus.**

fog¹ (fôg, fŏg) *n.* **1.** Condensed water vapor droplets with particles of dust and smoke in suspension, occurring in cloudlike masses close to the ground and limiting visibility to less than one kilometer (0.6 mile). **2.** Any mass of floating material, such as dust or smoke, that forms an obscuring haze. **3.** A state of bewilderment. **4.** In photography, a dark blur on a developed negative.
~v. **fogged, fogging, fogs.** *—tr.* **1.** To cover or envelop with fog. **2.** To cause to be clouded or obscured; blur. **3.** To make uncertain or unclear; bewilder. **4.** In photography, to obscure or dim (a negative) with a dark blur. *—intr.* **1.** To be covered or enveloped with fog. Often used with *up* or *over.* **2.** To be blurred or obscured. **3.** In photography, to be dimmed or obscured with a dark blur. Used of a print or negative. [Perhaps a back-formation from earlier *foggy,* murky, moist, boggy, from FOG (rank grass).]

fog² *n.* **1.** A second growth of grass on a field that has been mowed or grazed. **2.** Tall, thick grass left standing after cutting or grazing. [Middle English *fogge, fog,* perhaps from Scandinavian.]

fog bank *n.* An opaque mass of fog sharply defined in contrast to surrounding, clearer air; especially, such a fog occurring at sea.

fog·bound (fôg′bound′, fŏg′-) *adj.* **1.** Immobilized by heavy fog. **2.** Clouded or obscured by fog.

fog·bow (fôg′bō′, fŏg′-) *n.* A faint white or yellowish arc-shaped light, similar to a rainbow, often seen opposite the sun in a fog bank. Also called "seadog."

fog·dog (fôg′dôg′, fŏg′dŏg′) *n.* A bright spot in a fog bank.

fog·gy (fô′gē, fŏg′ē) *adj.* **-gier, -giest. 1.** Full of, surrounded by, or suggestive of fog. **2.** Clouded, obscured, or blurred by or as if by fog. **3.** In photography, obscured or dimmed by a fog or dark blur. **—fog·gi·ly** *adv.* **—fog·gi·ness** *n.*

fog·horn (fôg′hôrn′, fŏg′-) *n.* **1.** A horn used by ships and coastal installations to sound warning signals, typically of long, deep tones, in fog or darkness. **2.** A loud, booming voice.

fo·gy (fō′gē) *n., pl.* **-gies.** Also **fo·gey** *pl.* **-geys.** A person of old-fashioned habits and outmoded attitudes: *an old fogy.* [Origin obscure.] **—fo·gy·ish** *adj.*

föhn, foehn (fœn, fān) *n.* A warm dry wind coming off the leeward side of a mountain range, especially off the northern slopes of the Alps. [German, from Old High German *phōnno,* from Latin *Favōnius*†, the west wind. See **favonian.**]

foi·ble (foi′bəl) *n.* **1.** A minor weakness or failing of character; a small personal fault. **2.** The weaker section of a sword blade, from the middle to the tip. In this sense, compare **forte.** —See Synonyms at **fault.** [Obsolete French, variant of *faible,* weak, FEEBLE.]

foie gras (fwä′ grä′) *n.* **Pâté de foie gras** *(see).*

foil¹ (foil) *tr.v.* **foiled, foiling, foils. 1.** To prevent from being successful; thwart. **2.** To obscure or confuse (a trail or scent) so as to evade pursuers. —See Synonyms at **frustrate.**
~n. **1.** *Archaic.* A foiling; a repulse; setback. **2.** The trail or scent of a hunted animal, especially one that confuses its pursuer. [Originally to trample, tread upon, Middle English *foilen,* perhaps from Norman French *fuler* (unattested), variant of Old French *fouler,* to FULL (cloth).]

foil² *n.* **1.** A thin, flexible leaf or sheet of a metal. **2.** A thin layer of bright metal placed under a displayed gem or piece of jewelry to lend it brilliance. **3.** A person or thing that by strong contrast underlines or enhances the distinctive characteristics of another. **4.** The metal coating applied to the back of a plate of glass to form a mirror. **5.** *Architecture.* A leaflike design or space worked in stone or glass, found especially in Gothic window tracery. **6.** An **airfoil** *(see).* **7.** A **hydrofoil** *(see).* **8. Aluminum foil** *(see).*
~tr.v. **foiled, foiling, foils. 1.** To back or cover with a thin, pliant sheet of metal. **2.** To serve as a foil to; set off by contrast. **3.** *Architecture.* To ornament (windows or walls) with foils. [Middle English *foil(le), foile,* thin sheet of metal, leaf, from Old French, from Latin *folium.*]

foil³ *n.* **1.** A fencing sword with a flat guard for the hand and a thin blade with a blunt point to prevent injury. **2.** *Often* **foils.** The art or act of fencing with foils. [Origin unknown.]

foils·man (foilz′mən) *n., pl.* **-men** (-mĭn). One who fences with a foil; fencer.

foin (foin) *intr.v.* **foined, foining, foins.** *Archaic.* To thrust with a pointed weapon.
~n. Archaic. A lunge or thrust with a pointed weapon. [Middle English *foinen,* from *foin,* a thrust, a three-pronged fork for spearing fish, from Old French *foin, foisne,* from Latin *fuscina*†, trident.]

Fo·ism (fō′ĭz′əm) *n.* Chinese Buddhism. [Mandarin Chinese *fó,* Buddha, from Sanskrit *Buddha,* BUDDHA.] **—Fo·ist** *n. & adj.*

foi·son (foi′zən) *n. Archaic.* **1.** A plentiful harvest; a good crop. **2.** Abundance; plenty. [Middle English *foisoun,* from Old French *foison,* power, abundance, from Vulgar Latin *fusiō* (unattested), from Latin *fūsiō* (stem *fūsiōn-*), an outpouring, effusion, from *fūsus,* past participle of *fundere,* to pour.]

foist (foist) *tr.v.* **foisted, foisting, foists. 1.** To pass off as genuine, valuable, or worthy; palm off. **2.** To impose (someone or something unwanted) upon another by coercion or trickery. **3.** To insert fraudulently or deceitfully. [Original sense, to introduce a palmed dice surreptitiously, from Dutch (dialectal) *vuisten,* from *vuist,* fist.]

Fo·kine (fō-kēn′), **Michel** (1880–1942). Russian dancer and choreographer. Working with Diaghilev's Ballets Russes in Paris from 1909, he was partly responsible for revitalizing the ballet through his choreography for such revolutionary works as Stravinsky's *Firebird* (1910) and *Petruskha* (1912). After 1923 he worked in the United States.

Fok·ker (fŏk′ər), **Anthony Hermann Gerard** (1890–1939). Dutch aircraft engineer. In 1912 he opened an aircraft factory in Germany that supplied the Germans with some of the most advanced planes of World War I. He revolutionized aerial warfare in 1915 by synchronizing a machine gun to fire through the propeller of a plane.

fol. folio.

fo·late (fō′lāt′) *n.* **Folic acid** *(see).* [FOL(IC ACID) + -ATE.]

fold¹ (fōld) *v.* **folded, folding, folds.** *—tr.* **1.** To bend over or double up so that one part lies on another part: *fold a newspaper.* **2.** To make compact by successively bending over parts. Sometimes used with *up.* **3.** To bring from an extended to a closed position: *On alighting, the hawk folded its wings.* **4.** To place together and intertwine: *fold one's arms.* **5.** To bend, clasp, or entwine. **6.** To surround with the arms; enfold; embrace. **7.** To wrap; envelop. **8.** In cooking, to mix in (an ingredient) by slowly and gently turning one part over another. **9.** *Geology.* To form (rock) into folds. *—intr.* **1.** To become folded or be capable of being folded: *a folding bed.* **2.** *Informal.* To close for lack of funds; fail financially. **3.** *Informal.* To weaken or collapse, as from exertion or laughter. Usually used with *up.* **4.** *Geology.* To form folds. Used of stratified rocks.
~n. **1.** The act or an instance of folding. **2.** A part or section that has been folded over another. **3.** The space or hollow at the junc-

PRONUNCIATION KEY

ă, pat; ā, pay; âr, care;
ä, father, are; b, **bib**;
ch, **church**; d, **deed**; ĕ, pet;
ē, be; f, **fife**; g, **gag**; h, **hat**;
hw, **which**; ĭ, pit; ī, pie;
îr, pier; j, **judge**; k, **kick**;
l, lid, needle; m, **mum**;
n, no, sudden; ng, **thing**;
ŏ, pot; ō, toe; ô, paw, for;
oi, noise; ou, **out**; o͝o, **book**;
o͞o, **boot**; p, **pop**; r, roar;
s, sauce; sh, **ship, dish**;
t, **tight**; th, **thin, path**;
th, **this**, bathe; ŭ, cut; ûr, **fur**;
v, valve; w, **with**; y, yes;
z, zebra, size; zh, vision;
ə, about, item, edible, gallop, circus, peaceful

IN FOREIGN WORDS:

à, *Fr.* ami; œ, *Fr.* feu, *Ger.* schön; ü, *Fr.* tu, *Ger.* über;
KH, *Ger.* **ich**, *Scot.* loch;
N, *Fr.* bon; y′, *Fr.* Compiègne

STRESS MARKS:

Primary stress: ′
in·cite′ (ĭn-sīt′)
Secondary stress: ′
in′sight′ (ĭn′sīt′)

tion of two folded parts. **4.** A hollow or dale in hilly country. **5.** *Geology.* A bend in rock strata. **6.** A coil, as of rope or a snake. **7.** *Anatomy.* A crease apparently formed by folding, as of a membrane; a plica. [Middle English *folden, falden,* Old English *faldan, fealdan,* from Germanic.]

fold[2] *n.* **1.** A fenced enclosure for domestic animals, especially sheep. **2.** The sheep enclosed in such a pen. **3.** A flock of sheep. **4.** Any group of people bound together by common beliefs and aims, or by mutual loyalty; especially, the members of a church. —*tr.v.* **folded, folding, folds.** To place or keep (sheep) in a fold. [Middle English *fold,* Old English *fald, falod,* akin to Middle Low German *valt*†.]

-fold *suffix.* Indicates: **1.** Division into a specified number of parts; for example, *fivefold.* **2.** Multiplication by a specified number; for example, *fiftyfold.* [Middle English, from Old English *-f(e)ald.*]

fold·a·way (fōld'ə-wā') *adj.* Designating a piece of furniture, especially a bed, that can be folded up when not in use.

fold·boat (fōld'bōt') *n.* A **faltboat** *(see).* [Translation of German *Faltboot.*]

fold·er (fōl'dər) *n.* **1.** One that folds. **2.** A sheet of cardboard or thick paper folded in the center and used as a holder for loose paper. **3.** A folded sheet of printed matter.

fol·de·rol (fŏl'də-rŏl') *n.* Also **fal·de·ral** (făl'də-răl'), **fal·de·rol** (făl'də-rŏl'). **1.** Foolish talk or procedure; nonsense. **2.** A worthless trifle; gewgaw. [From *fol-de-rol* and *fal-deral,* a meaningless refrain in some old songs.]

fold-out (fōld'out') *n. Printing.* A **gatefold** *(see).*

fo·li·a. Plural of **folium.**

fo·li·a·ceous (fō'lē-ā'shəs) *adj.* **1.** Of, relating to, or resembling the leaf of a plant. **2.** Having leaves or leaflike structures. **3.** Consisting of thin laminated layers, as do certain rocks. [Latin *foliāceus,* from *folium,* leaf, FOLIUM.]

fo·li·age (fō'lē-ĭj) *n.* **1.** The leaves of growing plants; plant leaves collectively. **2.** An ornamental representation of leaves, branches, or flowers. [Middle English *foilage,* from Old French *feuillage, foillage,* from *feuille, foille,* leaf, from Latin *folium.*] —**fo·li·aged** *adj.*

foliage plant *n.* A plant cultivated chiefly for its ornamental leaves.

fo·li·ar (fō'lē-ər) *adj.* Of or pertaining to a leaf or leaves. [French *foliaire,* from Latin *folium,* leaf, FOLIUM.]

fo·li·ate (fō'lē-ĭt, -āt') *adj.* **1.** Of or pertaining to leaves. **2.** Shaped like a leaf. **3.** Having a specified number or kind of leaves or layers. Used in combination: *trifoliate; perfoliate.*
—*v.* (fō'lē-āt') **foliated, -ating, -ates.** —*tr.* **1.** To hammer or cut (metal) into thin plates, leaf, or foil. **2. a.** To coat (glass) with metal foil. **b.** To furnish or adorn with metal foil. **3.** *Architecture.* To decorate (an arch, for example) with foils. **4.** To number the leaves of (a book). In this sense, compare **paginate.** —*intr.* **1.** To produce foliage; put forth leaves. **2.** To become split into thin layers. [Latin *foliātus,* bearing leaves, from *folium,* leaf, FOLIUM.]

fo·li·a·tion (fō'lē-ā'shən) *n.* **1.** *Botany.* The state of being in leaf or putting forth leaves. **2.** Decoration with foliage. **3.** *Architecture.* The decoration of an archway, window, or other opening with cusps and foils, as in Gothic tracery. **4. a.** The act or process of foliating metal. **b.** The foliating of glass. **5.** The process of numbering consecutively the leaves of a book. [Latin *folium,* leaf, FOLIUM.]

fo·lic acid (fō'lĭk) *n.* A yellowish-orange compound, $C_{19}H_{19}N_7O_6$, a member of the vitamin B complex, occurring in green plants, fresh fruit, liver, and yeast, and used medicinally to treat pernicious anemia. Also called "folate," "vitamin B_c." [Latin *fol(ium),* leaf, FOLIUM + -IC.]

fo·lie à deux (fō-lē' ä dœ', fŏl'ē) *n.* The simultaneous presence of symptoms of mental illness in two closely attached people, usually a married couple or siblings. [French, "madness of two."]

fo·li·ic·o·lous (fō'lē-ĭk'ə-ləs) *adj.* Thriving on or parasitic to leaves. [Latin *folium,* leaf + -COLOUS.]

fo li·o (fō'lē-ō') *n., pl.* **-os.** *Abbr.* **f., F., fol.** **1.** A large sheet of paper folded once in the middle, making two leaves or four pages of a book or manuscript. **2. a.** The largest common size of book or manuscript, usually about 38 centimeters (15 inches) in height and made up of such folded sheets. **b.** A book or manuscript of this size. **3.** A leaf of a book numbered only on the front side. **4.** A page number in a book; especially, one assigned to a page during the printing process. **5.** *Accounting.* A page in a ledger or two facing pages assigned a single number. **6.** *Law.* A specific number of words used as a unit for measuring the length of the text of a document.
—*adj.* **1.** Of or pertaining to a folio: *folio pages.* **2.** Presented in the form of a folio: *a folio edition.*
—*tr.v.* **folioed, -oing, -os.** To number consecutively the pages of (a book). [Medieval Latin, ablative (used for page references, "at leaf *x*") of Latin *folium,* leaf, FOLIUM.]

fo·li·o·late (fō'lē-ə-lāt') *adj. Botany.* Having or consisting of leaflets. Usually used in combination: *bifoliolate.* [From earlier *foliole,* leaflet, from French, from New Latin *foliolum,* diminutive of Latin *folium,* leaf, FOLIUM.]

fo·li·ose (fō'lē-ōs') *adj.* **1.** *Botany.* Bearing numerous leaves or leaflets; leafy. **2.** Of, pertaining to, or resembling a leaf or leaves. [Latin *foliōsus,* from *folium,* leaf, FOLIUM.]

fo·li·ot (fō'lē-ət) *n.* A clock escapement of the earliest type, consisting of a bar adjusted by weights placed along its length. [French, from Old French, probably from *folier,* to play the fool, from *fol,* foolish. See **fool.**]

fo·li·um (fō'lē-əm) *n., pl.* **-lia** (-lē-ə). **1.** *Geology.* A thin layer or stratum occurring especially in metamorphic rock. **2.** *Geometry.* A plane cubic curve having a single loop, a node, and two ends asymptotic to the same line. In this sense, also called "folium of Descartes." [New Latin, from Latin, leaf.]

folk (fōk) *n., pl.* **folk** or **folks.** **1.** *Often* **folks.** People of a specified group or kind: *city folk.* **2. folks.** *Informal.* **a.** The members of one's family or childhood household; one's relatives. **b.** One's parents. **3. folks.** *Informal.* People in general: *Folks will talk.* **4.** An ethnic group; a people or race. **5.** *Informal.* Folk music.
—*adj.* Of, occurring in, or originating among the common people; especially, untutored or unrefined: *folk painting.* [Middle English *folk,* Old English *folc,* the people, nation, tribe, from Germanic *folkam* (unattested).]

folk dance *n.* **1.** A traditional dance originating among the rural areas of a nation or region. **2.** The music accompanying such a dance. **3.** A social gathering at which such dances are performed. —**folk dancing** *n.*

Folke·stone (fōk'stən). Residential town and resort in Kent, southeastern England. Its harbor is a leading departure point for cross-Channel ferry services to France.

Fol·ke·ting, Fol·ke·thing (fōl'kə-tĭng) *n.* The parliament of Denmark, consisting of a single chamber. [Danish : *folk,* the people, FOLK + *ting,* assembly, from Old Norse *thing.*]

folk etymology *n.* **1.** A change in form of a word or phrase resulting from an incorrect popular notion of the origin or meaning of the term or from the influence of a more familiar term mistakenly taken to be analogous. **2.** A word or phrase that is a product of this modification, as *sparrowgrass* from *asparagus.* **3.** A popular but mistaken view of the origin of a word, as if *hybrid* were to be taken to derive from *high-bred.* —**folk-et·y·mo·log·i·cal** (fōk'ĕt'ə-mə-lŏj'ĭ-kəl) *adj.*

folk·lore (fōk'lôr', -lōr') *n.* **1.** The traditional orally transmitted beliefs, practices, and tales of a people. **2.** The comparative study of folk knowledge and culture. **3.** A body of widely accepted but specious notions about a place, group, or institution: *the folklore of Hollywood.* —**folk·lor·ic** *adj.* —**folk·lor·ist** *n.*

folk mass *n.* A mass in which folk music is used instead of liturgical music for part of the service.

folk medicine *n.* Medicine as practiced among primitive peoples, usually involving the use of natural remedies, as herbs.

folk·moot (fōk'mo͞ot') *n.* Also **folk·mote** (-mōt'). A general assembly of the people of a town, district, or shire in medieval England. [Old English *folcmōt* : *folc,* FOLK + *mōt,* meeting, assembly.]

folk music *n.* **1.** Music and song originating among the common people of a nation or region and characterized by a tradition of oral transmission and usually anonymous authorship. **2.** Contemporary music and song using elements of the style of traditional folk music.

folk rock *n.* A variety of popular music that combines elements of rock 'n' roll and folk music.

folk singer *n.* A singer of folk songs. —**folk singing** *n.*

folk song *n.* **1.** A song belonging to the folk music of a people or area, characterized chiefly by directness and simplicity of expression and often sung or performed in several versions. **2.** A song of known authorship composed in imitation of such songs.

folk·sy (fōk'sē) *adj.* **-sier, -siest.** *Informal.* **1.** Simple and unpretentious in social behavior. **2.** Affectedly rustic or simple. **3.** Characterized by congeniality and affability. —**folk·si·ness** *n.*

folk tale *n.* A story or legend forming part of an oral tradition and passed on from generation to generation.

folk·way (fōk'wā') *n.* A way of thinking or acting practiced by the members of a group as part of their shared culture.

folk weave *n.* A type of cloth with a loose or rough weave.

fol·li·cle (fŏl'ĭ-kəl) *n.* **1.** *Anatomy.* An approximately spherical group of cells containing a cavity, such as a sac from which a hair grows or any of the cavities in the ovary containing ova. **2.** *Botany.* A single-chambered fruit, such as that of larkspur, that splits along only one seam to release its seeds. [Latin *folliculus,* little bag, diminutive of *follis,* bellows.] —**fol·lic·u·lar** (fə-lĭk'yə-lər), **fol·lic·u·late** (fə-lĭk'yə-lĭt), **fol·lic·u·lat·ed** (fə-lĭk'yə-lā'tĭd) *adj.*

fol·li·cle-stim·u·lat·ing hormone (fŏl'ĭ-kəl-stĭm'yə-lā'tĭng) *n. Abbr.* **FSH** A gonadotropic hormone of the anterior pituitary gland that stimulates the growth of follicles in the ovary and induces the formation of sperm in the testis.

fol·li·cu·li·tis (fə-lĭk'yə-lī'tĭs) *n.* Inflammation of a follicle, especially of a hair follicle. [Latin *folliculus,* FOLLICLE + -ITIS.]

fol·lies (fŏl'ēz) *n. Used with a singular verb.* An elaborate, richly costumed theatrical revue consisting of a series of musical or dance skits. [Plural of FOLLY.]

fol·low (fŏl'ō) *v.* **-lowed, -lowing, -lows.** —*tr.* **1.** To come or go after; move behind and in the same direction as. **2.** To go after with or as if with the intention of overtaking; pursue. **3.** To come or go with; accompany; attend. **4.** To move along the course of; take (a course or direction): *We followed a path to the shore.* **5.** To accept the guidance or leadership of; have as a model; emulate. **6.** To adhere to the cause or principles of; advocate: *follow outdated doctrines.* **7.** To be governed by; obey; comply with: *We follow the rules.* **8. a.** To occur after (a specified event) in a temporal sequence. **b.** To occupy a position that occurs after (a specified position) in a hierarchy, list, or other ordering: *Captain follows major in rank.* **9.** To succeed to the place or position of: *Elizabeth II followed George VI.* **10.** To engage in; work at (a trade or occupation). **11.** To occur or be evident as a consequence of: *Your conclusion does not follow your premise.* **12.** To be attentive to; listen to or

PRONUNCIATION KEY

ă, pat; ā, pay; âr, care; ä, father, are; b, bib; ch, church; d, deed; ĕ, pet; ē, be; f, fife; g, gag; h, hat; hw, which; ĭ, pit; ī, pie; îr, pier; j, judge; k, kick; l, lid, needle; m, mum; n, no, sudden; ng, thing; ŏ, pot; ō, toe; ô, paw, for; oi, noise; ou, out; o͝o, book; o͞o, boot; p, pop; r, roar; s, sauce; sh, ship, dish; t, tight; th, thin, path; *th,* this, bathe; ŭ, cut; ûr, fur; v, valve; w, with; y, yes; z, zebra, size; zh, vision; ə, about, item, edible, gallop, circus, peaceful

IN FOREIGN WORDS:

à, *Fr.* ami; œ, *Fr.* feu, *Ger.* schön; ü, *Fr.* tu, *Ger.* über; KH, *Ger.* ich, *Scot.* loch; N, *Fr.* bon; y', *Fr.* Compiègne

STRESS MARKS:

Primary stress: ' in·cite' (ĭn-sīt')
Secondary stress: ' in'sight' (ĭn'sīt')

watch closely: *I was too sleepy to follow the sermon.* **13.** To grasp the meaning or logic of; keep up with the reasoning of: *Do you follow my argument?* **14.** To inform oneself of the course or progress of: *follow the stock market.* **15.** To be a keen and knowledgeable fan of (a sport, team, or the like). —*intr.* **1.** To come, move, or take place after some other person or thing in order or time. **2.** To occur or be evident as a consequence; result; ensue: *If you ignore your diet, trouble will follow.* **3.** To grasp the meaning or reasoning of what is said; understand. **—as follows.** As is now to be given or explained; as listed or explained below. **—follow out.** To comply with fully; carry out. **—follow suit. 1.** *Card Games.* To play a card of the same suit as the one led. **2.** To act after another's example. ∼*n.* A billiards shot in which the cue ball is struck in such a way that it follows the path of the object ball after impact. [Middle English *fol(o)wen,* Old English *folgian* and *fylgan,* from Germanic *fulg-* (unattested).]

Synonyms: *ensue, result, succeed, supervene.*

Usage: *As follows* is a fixed phrase in standard English and does not change along with the number of the noun that precedes it. *His reply was as follows* is found alongside *His replies were as follows. As follow* in this last example would be unacceptable.

fol·low·er (fŏl′ō-ər) *n.* **1.** One that comes or occurs after another. **2.** One who is keenly interested in a sport, team, fashion, or the like; devotee. **3.** An attendant, servant, or subordinate. **4.** One who subscribes to the teachings or methods of another; adherent. **5.** A machine element moved by another machine element. **6.** *Archaic.* A male admirer of a woman.

fol·low·ing (fŏl′ō-ĭng) *adj. Abbr.* **f., ff., foll. 1.** Coming next in time or order: *in the following chapter.* **2.** Now to be enumerated: *The following men will report for duty.* **3.** Blowing in the same direction as the course of a ship or aircraft. Said of a wind.
∼*n.* A group or gathering of admirers, adherents, or disciples: *a lecturer with a large following.* **—the following. 1.** What is to be mentioned or listed next: *Please buy the following.* **2.** What is now to be said or specified: *Listen closely to the following.*

follow through *intr.v.* **1.** *Sports.* To continue a stroke or shot to natural completion after hitting the ball. **2.** To carry an act, project, or train of thought to completion; pursue fully.

fol·low-through (fŏl′ō-thrōō′) *n.* **1.** The carrying of a stroke to natural completion after the ball has been hit, as in tennis, golf, or baseball. **2.** The concluding part of a stroke, after the ball has been hit. **3.** The completion of a sequence of acts or processes.

follow up *tr.v.* **1.** To carry to completion; follow through. **2.** To increase the effectiveness of by further action. —*intr.v.* To take further action: *I followed up on your comment by working harder.*

fol·low-up (fŏl′ō-ŭp′) *n.* **1.** The act or an instance of repeating or adding to previous action so as to increase effectiveness. **2.** The means, such as a letter, procedure, or visit, used to increase or reinforce the effectiveness of previous action. Also used adjectivally: *a follow-up letter.* **3.** A newspaper article giving further information on a previously published item of news.

fol·ly (fŏl′ē) *n., pl.* **-lies. 1.** The condition or quality of being foolish; a lack of good sense, understanding, or foresight. **2. a.** Any act or instance of foolishness. **b.** A costly undertaking having an absurd or ruinous outcome. **3.** *Archaic.* Action or behavior considered immoral or criminal. **4.** An ornamental building or structure built purely for decoration. **5.** *Obsolete.* Evil; wickedness. [Middle English *folie,* from Old French, from *fol,* foolish, from Latin *follis,* bellows. See **fool.**]

Fol·som (fŏl′səm) *adj.* Of or relating to an early North American culture of the Pleistocene period flourishing east of the Rocky Mountains and notable chiefly for the use of leaf-shaped flint implements. [After *Folsom,* New Mexico.]

Fo·mal·haut (fō′məl-hôt′) *n.* The brightest star in the constellation Piscis Austrinus, 24 light-years from earth. [Arabic *fum'l-ḥūt,* "mouth of the fish."]

fo·ment (fō-mĕnt′) *tr.v.* **-mented, -menting, -ments. 1.** To promote the growth or arousal of (discontent or strife); stir up; instigate. **2.** To treat (the skin) by fomentation. [Middle English *fomenten,* from Old French *fomenter,* from Late Latin *fōmentāre,* from Latin *fōmentum,* warm application, short for *fovementum* (unattested), from *fovēre,* to warm, cherish.] **—fo·ment·er** *n.*

fo·men·ta·tion (fō′mən-tā′shən) *n.* **1.** The act or an instance of promoting discontent, rebellion, or strife; instigation. **2. a.** A warm, moist medicinal compress; poultice. **b.** The therapeutic application of warmth and moisture.

fo·mite (fō′mīt′) *n.* An inanimate object or substance that serves to transfer infectious organisms from one individual to another. Also called "fomes." [Back-formation from New Latin *fomites,* plural of Latin *fomes,* tinder.]

fond[1] (fŏnd) *adj.* **fonder, fondest. 1.** Affectionate; tender: *a fond embrace.* **2.** Having a tender interest or affection or great liking. Used with *of*: *"He was fond of the fine arts, fond of long words, and fond of me"* (Mary McCarthy). **3.** Immoderately or irrationally affectionate; infatuated; doting. **4.** Cherished; dear: *my fondest hopes.* **5.** *Archaic.* Naively credulous; foolish. [Middle English *fonned,* foolish, probably from *fon*†, a fool.] **—fond·ly** *adv.*

fond[2] *n.* **1.** A foundation; basis. **2.** The background of a design in lace. [French, from Latin *fundus,* bottom.]

Fon·da (fŏn′də), **Henry** (1905–82). U.S. actor. He made his film debut in *The Farmer Takes a Wife* (1935). He went on to become a Hollywood star with such films as *Young Mr. Lincoln* (1939), *The Grapes of Wrath* (1940), and *Twelve Angry Men* (1957). He received an Academy Award in 1982 for his part in *On Golden Pond.* His daughter **Jane** (1937–) made her first major film appearance in *Barbarella* (1968). Later films included *Klute* (1971) and *Coming Home* (1978). Her brother **Peter** (1939–) starred in *Easy Rider* (1969).

fon·dant (fŏn′dənt; *French* fôN-däN′) *n.* **1.** A sweet, creamy sugar paste eaten as a candy or used in icings or as a filling for other candies. **2.** A candy made of or containing fondant. [French, from the present participle of *fondre,* to melt (it melts quickly in the mouth), from Latin *fundere,* to pour, melt.]

fon·dle (fŏnd′l) *v.* **-dled, -dling, -dles.** —*tr.* To handle or stroke with affection; caress lovingly with the hands. —*intr.* To show fondness or affection by caressing. [Frequentative of obsolete *fond,* to show fondness for.]

fond·ness (fŏnd′nĭs) *n.* **1.** Warm affection; tender liking. **2.** Strong preference; inclination; relish. **3.** *Archaic.* Naive trustfulness; credulity. —See Synonyms at **love.**

fon·due, fon·du (fŏn-dōō′, -dyōō′) *n.* **1.** A hot dish made of melted cheese and wine into which pieces of bread or meat are dipped. **2. a.** A dish made with pieces of beef that are cooked individually on skewers in hot oil at table and eaten with a variety of sauces. **b.** A similar dish made with pieces of fruit or vegetable dipped in a hot sauce and eaten. [French, feminine past participle of *fondre,* to melt. See **fondant.**]

font[1] (fŏnt) *n.* **1.** A basin, usually mounted on a stone pedestal, holding baptismal water in a church. **2.** A receptacle for holy water; stoup. **3.** The oil reservoir in an oil-burning lamp. **4.** *Archaic.* A fountain or spring. **5.** Any source of abundance; fount: *a font of knowledge.* [Middle English, Old English *font, fant,* from Latin *fōns* (stem *font-*), spring, fountain.] **—font·al** *adj.*

font[2] *n. Printing.* A complete set of type of one size and face. [Old French, casting, from *fondre,* to melt, cast. See **fondant.**]

Fon·taine·bleau (fŏn′tən-blō′). Town in France, 59 kilometers (37 miles) southeast of Paris. From the 10th century it was a residence of the French kings, chiefly because of the good hunting ground offered by the Forest of Fontainebleau. Its magnificent palace, an outstanding example of French Renaissance architecture, was built by Francis I in the 16th century and decorated by Il Rosso, Francesco Primaticcio, and other members of the so-called Fontainebleau School.

fon·ta·nel, fon·ta·nelle (fŏn′tə-nĕl′) *n.* Any of the soft membranous gaps between the incompletely formed cranial bones of fetuses and infants. Also called "soft spot." [Middle English *fontinel,* a hollow, from Old French *fontenele,* diminutive of *fontaine,* FOUNTAIN.]

Fon·tanne (fŏn-tăn′), **Lynn** (1887–1983). U.S. actress; born in England. After making her acting debut in London (1905), she moved to the United States (1910), where she won fame as the lead in *Dulcy* (1921). The next year she married Alfred Lunt, creating one of America's premier husband-and-wife acting teams.

Fon·teyn (fŏn-tān′), **Dame Margot,** born Margaret Hookham (1919–91). British ballerina. She joined the Sadler's Wells Company (subsequently the Royal Ballet Company) in 1934. The beauty of her line, her musicality, and her dramatic interpretation of roles made her famous, especially in partnership with Rudolph Nureyev.

Foochow. See **Fuzhou.**

food (fōōd) *n.* **1.** Any material, usually of plant or animal origin, containing or consisting of essential nutrients, such as carbohydrates, fats, proteins, vitamins, or minerals, that is taken in and assimilated by an organism to maintain life and growth. **2.** A specified kind of nourishment: *breakfast food; plant food.* **3.** Nourishment eaten in solid form, as distinguished from liquid nourishment: *good food and wine.* **4.** Anything that nourishes or sustains in a way suggestive of physical nourishment: *food for thought.* [Middle English *fode,* Old English *fōda,* from Germanic.]

food chain *n.* A succession of organisms in an ecological community, each of which feeds on a lower member and is in turn eaten by a higher member. See feature, next page.

food fish *n.* Any edible fish, such as a cod, flounder, or herring, that is used commercially as a source of human food.

food poisoning *n.* **1.** Poisoning caused by eating food contaminated by bacteria, especially bacteria of the genus *Salmonella,* and characterized, with varying severity, by vomiting, diarrhea, prostration, and sometimes shock. See **salmonellosis. 2.** Poisoning caused by eating foods containing natural toxins.

food processor *n.* An appliance consisting of a container with interchangeable blades that processes food, as by mincing, shredding, slicing, or mixing, at very high speed.

food stamp *n.* A stamp or coupon issued by the government and sold or given to low-income persons to be redeemed for food.

food·stuff (fōōd′stŭf′) *n.* **1.** Any substance suitable for food; especially, a crude product suitable for food after processing. **2.** Any substance, such as protein or fat, that forms part of a variety of foods.

food web *n.* A group of organisms in an ecological community that forms a complex of interconnected food chains.

fool[1] (fōōl) *n.* **1.** One who shows himself, by words or actions, to be deficient in judgment, sense, or understanding; a stupid or thoughtless person. **2.** One who acts unwisely on a given occasion: *I was a fool to refuse the job.* **3.** Formerly, a member of a royal or noble household who entertained the court with jests, mimicry, and the like; jester; buffoon. **4.** One who has been or can be easily deceived or imposed upon; dupe: *They made a fool of me.* **5.** *Obso-*

font *A medieval Gothic font from Fosdyke in Lincolnshire, England.*

NATURE'S COMPLEX CHAIN OF REGENERATION
The intricate pattern of life on a forest floor

All living things in a particular environment are part of a food chain. A typical community of organisms, such as that found on the floor of a deciduous forest, includes producers, consumers, and decomposers.

The producers are green plants, which use light to make food from carbon dioxide and water. The plants are then eaten by herbivorous animals (primary consumers), which in turn are eaten by carnivores (sec-

ondary consumers). Finally, decomposers and scavengers break down the remains of the dead organisms and waste materials, releasing substances that enrich the soil and are used by the producers.

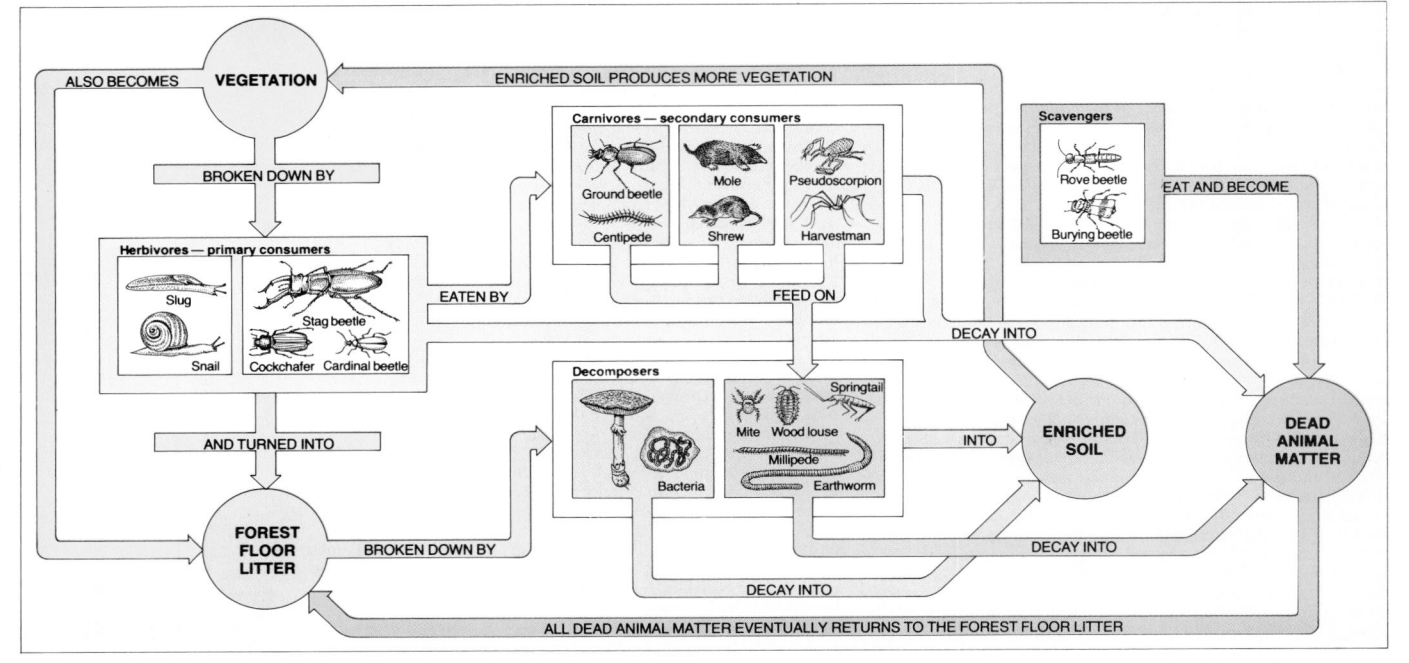

lete. A feeble-minded person; an idiot. **6.** *Informal.* A person with extreme fondness or enthusiasm for a specified activity or person: *a fool for weightlifting.* **—no** (or **nobody's**) **fool.** A shrewd or wise person. **—play** (or **act**) **the fool. 1.** To act in an irresponsible or foolish manner. **2.** To behave in a playful or comical manner.
~*v.* **fooled, fooling, fools.** —*tr.* To deceive or misinform, especially for amusement or to gain an advantage; trick; dupe. —See Synonyms at **deceive.** —*intr.* **1.** To act or speak in jest; play; joke; be amusing. **2.** To act, speak, argue, or contend without but as if with serious or harmful intent: *They thought he might shoot, but he was only fooling.* **—fool around** (or **about**). *Informal.* **1.** To engage in or amuse oneself with useless or trifling activity. **2.** To trifle; not treat seriously. Used with *with.* **3.** To behave irresponsibly. **—fool with.** To toy or tamper aimlessly with; meddle with. [Middle English *fol(e),* a fool, foolish, from Old French *fol,* from Latin *follis,* bellows, windbag.]
fool² *n. Chiefly British.* A dessert of crushed, stewed, or puréed fruit mixed with cream or custard and served cold. [Perhaps a specialized use of FOOL.]
fool·er·y (fōō′lə-rē) *n., pl.* **-ies. 1.** Foolish behavior or speech; playfulness or facetiousness. **2.** An instance of this; a jest or trick.
fool·har·dy (fōōl′här′dē) *adj.* **-dier, -diest.** Unwisely bold or adventurous; rash. —See Synonyms at **reckless.** [Middle English *folhardi,* from Old French *folhardi* : *fol,* foolish (see **fool**) + *hardi,* HARDY.] **—fool·har·di·ly** *adv.* **—fool·har·di·ness** *n.*
fool·ish (fōō′lĭsh) *adj.* **1.** Lacking good sense or judgment; silly: *foolish remarks.* **2.** Resulting from stupidity or misinformation; ill-advised; unwise: *a foolish decision.* **3.** Ridiculous; inane: *a foolish grin.* **4.** Abashed; embarrassed: *I feel foolish telling you this.* **5.** *Archaic.* Insignificant; worthless: *"We have a trifling foolish banquet"* (Shakespeare). **—fool·ish·ly** *adv.* **—fool·ish·ness** *n.*
  Synonyms: *absurd, fatuous, inane, ludicrous, preposterous, ridiculous, silly.*
fool·proof (fōōl′prōōf′) *adj.* **1.** Designed so as to be proof against or resistant to human incompetence, error, or misuse: *a foolproof detonator.* **2.** Always effective; infallible: *a foolproof scheme.*
fools·cap (fōōlz′kăp′) *n. Abbr.* **fcp., fcap.** A sheet of writing or printing paper approximately 33 x 41 centimeters (13 x 16 inches). [From the watermark of a fool's cap with bells originally marking this type of paper.]
fool's errand *n.* A fruitless errand or undertaking.
fool's gold *n.* A mineral, such as pyrite, found in gold-colored veins or nuggets and sometimes mistaken for gold.
fool's paradise *n.* A state of delusive contentment or false hope.

fool's-pars·ley (fōōlz′pär′slē) *n.* A poisonous plant, *Aethusa cynapium,* native to Eurasia, having finely divided leaves, clusters of small white flowers, and an unpleasant smell.
foot (fōōt) *n., pl.* **feet** (fēt) or **foot** (for sense 8). **1.** The lower extremity of the vertebrate leg that is in direct contact with the ground in standing or walking. **2.** A structure used for locomotion or attachment in an invertebrate animal, such as the muscular organ extending from the ventral side of a mollusk. **3.** *Botany.* The lower part of some plants or plant structures. **4.** Something resembling or suggestive of a foot in position or function, especially: **a.** The bottom or lowest part of anything standing vertically or considered in its vertical dimension: *the foot of a mountain; the foot of a page.* **b.** The termination of the leg on a table or chair. **c.** The end or final section of an order or series; rear: *the foot of a parade.* **d.** The inferior part or rank: *the foot of the class.* **5.** The lower end of an object or the end opposite the head, as of a bed or table. **6.** The part of a stocking, sock, boot, or the like that encloses the foot. **7.** A manner of moving; a step: *He walks with a light foot.* **8.** Foot soldiers; infantry. **9.** The attachment on a sewing machine that clamps down and guides the cloth. **10.** *Prosody.* A metric unit consisting of a stressed or unstressed syllable or syllables. **11.** *Symbol* ′ *Abbr.* **ft** A unit of length in the U.S. Customary and British Imperial systems equal to ⅓ yard, or 12 inches, and equivalent to 0.3048 meter. **—have one foot in the grave.** To be very old or very ill and so be unlikely to live for much longer. **—my foot.** Used to express contemptuous disbelief. **—on foot.** Walking or standing; not riding or traveling in a vehicle. **—put one's best foot forward.** *Informal.* To make a good beginning or favorable first impression. **—put one's foot down.** *Informal.* To assert one's will emphatically. **—put one's foot in one's mouth.** *Informal.* To make an embarrassing or tactless blunder. **—under foot. 1.** At one's feet; on the ground or floor. **2.** Obstructing free movement; in the way.
~*v.* **footed, footing, foots.** —*intr.* **1.** To go on foot; walk. Often used with *it.* **2.** To dance. Often used with *it.* —*tr.* **1.** To go by foot on or through; pace; tread. **2.** To provide (a stocking, for example) with a foot. **3.** To add (a column of numbers) and write the total at the bottom; total. Used with *up: Foot up the bill.* **4.** *Informal.* To pay: *Can you foot the bill?* [Foot, feet; Middle English *fot, fet,* Old English *fōt, fēt,* from Germanic.]
  Usage: *Foot* and *feet,* as units of measure, are employed typically in the following: *a four-foot plank; a plank four feet long* (or *four feet in length*); *a man six feet tall; a ledge two feet below.*
foot·age (fōōt′ĭj) *n.* **1.** The length or extent of something as expressed in feet. **2.** A portion of cinematic film; especially, an

amount of film depicting a specified event or kind of action: *news footage*. **3.** *Mining.* **a.** Payment calculated on the number of feet mined. **b.** The amount of payment thus calculated.

foot-and-mouth disease (fŏŏt'n-mouth') *n.* An acute, highly contagious, usually nonfatal viral disease of cattle and other cloven-hoofed animals such as pigs, sheep, and goats, characterized by fever and the eruption of vesicles around the mouth and hoofs.

foot·ball (fŏŏt'bôl') *n.* **1. a.** A game played by two teams of 11 players each on a rectangular, 100-yard-long field with goal lines and posts at either end, the object being to gain possession of the ball and advance it in running or passing plays across the opponent's goal line. **b.** The inflated oval ball used in this game. **2.** *Chiefly British.* **a. Soccer** (see). Also used adjectivally: *football supporter; Football League.* **b. Rugby football** (see). **c.** The ball used in such games. **3.** Any problem or issue that is passed about among groups or persons without being settled: *Unemployment has become a political football.* —**foot·ball·er** *n.*

foot·bath (fŏŏt'băth', -bäth') *n., pl.* **-baths.** **1.** A small bath used for washing or disinfecting the feet. **2.** An act of washing the feet.

foot·board (fŏŏt'bôrd', -bōrd') *n.* **1.** A board or small raised platform on which to support or rest the feet, as in a carriage. **2.** An upright board across the foot of a bedstead.

foot·boy (fŏŏt'boi') *n.* A youth employed as a servant or page.

foot brake *n.* A brake operated by pressure of the foot on a pedal, as in a car.

foot·bridge (fŏŏt'brĭj') *n.* A narrow bridge designed to carry only pedestrians.

foot·can·dle (fŏŏt'kănd'l) *n. Abbr.* **fc** *Physics.* The illumination of a surface one foot distant from a source of one candela, equal to one lumen per square foot. Also called "candle-foot."

foot·ed (fŏŏt'ĭd) *adj.* **1.** Having a foot or feet. **2.** Having a specified kind or number of feet. Used in combination: *web-footed.*

foot·er (fŏŏt'ər) *n.* A person or thing measuring a specified number of feet in height or length. Used in combination: *a six-footer.*

foot·fall (fŏŏt'fôl') *n.* **1.** A footstep. **2.** The sound of a footstep.

foot fault *n.* A fault against the server, as in tennis, called for failure to keep both feet behind the base line when serving. —**foot-fault** (fŏŏt'fôlt') *v.*

foot·gear (fŏŏt'gîr') *n.* Sturdy footwear, such as shoes or boots.

foot·hill (fŏŏt'hĭl') *n.* A low hill near the base of a mountain or mountain range.

foot·hold (fŏŏt'hōld') *n.* **1.** A place affording support for the foot in climbing or standing. **2.** A firm or secure position enabling one to proceed with confidence.

foot·ing (fŏŏt'ĭng) *n.* **1.** A secure placement of the feet in standing or moving. **2.** A place on which one can stand or move securely. **3.** A surface or the condition of a surface with respect to the ease with which one may walk or run on it: *poor footing on the track.* **4.** *Architecture.* The supporting base or groundwork of a structure, as for a monument or wall. **5.** A basis; foundation: *a business on a good footing.* **6.** A social or business relationship; standing. **7.** The sum of a column of figures.

foot·lam·bert (fŏŏt'lăm'bərt) *n. Abbr.* **fL** *Physics.* A unit of luminance equal to 1/π candela per square foot.

foot·le (fŏŏt'l) *intr.v.* **-led, -ling, -les.** *Informal.* **1.** To waste time; trifle. Used with *around* or *about.* **2.** To talk nonsense. —*n. Informal.* Foolishness; nonsense. [Probably a variant of dialectal *footer,* probably from French *foutre,* to copulate with, from Old French, from Latin *futuere.*]

foot·less (fŏŏt'lĭs) *adj.* **1.** Without feet. **2.** Without basis; groundless. **3.** Without skill; inept. —**foot·less·ly** *adv.*

foot·lights (fŏŏt'līts') *pl.n.* **1.** Lights placed in a row along the front of a stage floor. **2.** The theater as a profession; the stage.

foot·ling (fŏŏt'lĭng) *adj. Informal.* **1.** Foolish; trifling; insignificant. **2.** Stupid; inept. [Present participle of FOOTLE.]

foot·lock·er (fŏŏt'lŏk'ər) *n.* A small trunk for storing personal belongings and small items, especially one kept at the foot of the bed.

foot·loose (fŏŏt'lōōs') *adj.* Having no attachments or ties; free to do as one pleases.

foot·man (fŏŏt'mən) *n., pl.* **-men** (-mĭn). **1.** A male servant employed in the house to wait at table, attend to the door, and run various errands. **2.** A metal stand or trivet used in a fireplace for keeping things hot. **3.** *Archaic.* A foot soldier; infantryman.

foot·mark (fŏŏt'märk') *n.* A footprint.

foot·note (fŏŏt'nōt') *n.* **1.** *Abbr.* **fn.** A note placed at the bottom of a page of a book or manuscript or at the end of a chapter that comments on or cites a reference for a designated part of the text. **2.** Something said or done after the more important work has been completed; an afterthought. —*tr.v.* **footnoted, -noting, -notes.** To furnish with footnotes.

foot·pace (fŏŏt'pās') *n.* **1.** A walking pace. **2.** A raised platform in a room, as for a lecturer; dais.

foot·pad (fŏŏt'păd') *n. Archaic.* A highwayman or street robber who goes about on foot. [FOOT + earlier *pad,* path, probably from Middle Dutch, path.]

foot·path (fŏŏt'păth', -päth') *n., pl.* **-paths** (-păthz', -päthz', -păths', -päths'). A narrow path for persons on foot; especially, one along the side of a road.

foot·pound (fŏŏt'pound') *n. Abbr.* **ft-lb** A unit of work equal to the work done by a force of one pound weight acting through a distance of one foot in the direction of the force.

foot·pound·al (fŏŏt'pound'l) *n.* A unit of work equal to the work done by a force of one poundal acting through a distance of one foot in the direction of the force.

foot-pound-sec·ond (fŏŏt'pound'sĕk'ənd) *adj. Abbr.* **fps** Of, designating, or characteristic of a system of units based on the foot, the pound, and the second as the fundamental units of length, mass, and time.

foot·print (fŏŏt'prĭnt') *n.* **1.** An outline or indentation left by a foot on a surface. **2.** In telecommunications, the area of the earth's surface where adequate reception of a signal from a communications satellite in a geostationary orbit may be obtained. Also called "groundprint."

foot·rest (fŏŏt'rĕst') *n.* A low stool, metal bar, or other support on which to rest the feet.

foot·rope (fŏŏt'rōp') *n. Nautical.* **1.** A rope attached to the lower border of a sail. **2.** A rope, rigged beneath a yard, for men to stand on during the reefing or furling of sail.

foot·rot (fŏŏt'rŏt') *n.* **1.** An inflammatory infection of the feet in certain hoofed animals, especially cattle or sheep, often resulting in loss of the hoof. **2.** Any of various plant diseases caused by fungi that attack the base of the stem or trunk and bring about the eventual death of the plant. **3.** *Informal.* **Athlete's foot** (see).

foot rule *n.* A rigid measure one foot (304 millimeters) long.

foots (fŏŏts) *pl.n.* The sediment that forms during the refining of oils and other liquids; dregs. [A plural of FOOT.]

foot·sie, foot·sy (fŏŏt'sē) *n. Informal.* A flirting game in which a couple touch feet or legs, usually in secret, as under a table. Used especially in the phrase *play footsie.* [From FOOT.]

foot·slog (fŏŏt'slŏg') *intr.v.* **-slogged, -slogging, -slogs.** *Informal.* To walk, tramp, or march, especially over a long distance. —**foot·slog·ger** *n.* —**foot·slog·ging** *n.*

foot soldier *n.* A soldier who fights on foot; infantryman.

foot·sore (fŏŏt'sôr', -sōr') *adj.* Having sore or tired feet from much walking. —**foot·sore·ness** *n.*

foot·stalk (fŏŏt'stôk') *n. Biology.* A supporting stalk, such as a peduncle or pedicel.

foot·stall (fŏŏt'stôl') *n.* **1.** The pedestal or plinth of a pillar. **2.** The stirrup on a sidesaddle.

foot·step (fŏŏt'stĕp') *n.* **1.** A step with the foot. **2.** The distance covered by one step: *a footstep away.* **3.** The sound of a foot stepping. **4.** A footprint. **5.** A step up or down: *the footsteps of a stairway.* —**follow in someone's footsteps.** To carry on the work or tradition of a predecessor.

foot·stone (fŏŏt'stōn') *n.* A marking stone placed at the foot of a grave.

foot·stool (fŏŏt'stōōl') *n.* A low stool for supporting the feet.

foot·wall (fŏŏt'wôl') *n.* The mass of rock underlying the mineral deposit in a mine.

foot·way (fŏŏt'wā') *n.* A walk or path for pedestrians.

foot·wear (fŏŏt'wâr') *n.* Covering for the feet, as shoes, boots, or slippers.

foot·work (fŏŏt'wûrk') *n.* **1.** The manner in which the feet are employed, as in dancing, boxing, fencing, or tennis. **2.** Skillful maneuvering to attain one's ends: *fancy footwork.*

foot·worn (fŏŏt'wôrn', -wōrn') *adj.* **1.** Footsore. **2.** Having been worn down by feet, as a path or carpet.

foo yong (fōō' yŭng') *n.* In Chinese cooking, an omelet made with green peppers, bean sprouts, and onion. [Cantonese *foo yong (dan),* Mandarin *fú róng (dàn),* hibiscus (egg) (from the fancied resemblance between the omelet and the large showy flower).]

fop (fŏp) *n.* A vain, affected man who is preoccupied with his clothes and manners; a dandy. [Middle English *fop, foppe,* a fool, perhaps akin to *fobben,* to cheat, FOB.]

fop·per·y (fŏp'ə-rē) *n., pl.* **-ies.** The dress or manner of a fop.

fop·pish (fŏp'ĭsh) *adj.* Of, pertaining to, or characteristic of a fop; dandified. —**fop·pish·ly** *adv.* —**fop·pish·ness** *n.*

for (fôr; *unstressed* fər) *prep.* **1.** Directed or sent to: *a letter for me.* **2.** Directed or inclined toward: *an eye for pretty girls.* **3.** As a result of; out of: *crying for joy.* **4.** To the extent of: *The road is paved for one mile.* **5.** Through the length or duration of: *sit still for an hour.* **6.** In order to go to: *leave for Scotland.* **7.** With an aim or view to: *We swim for fun.* **8.** In order to have or find: *look for a bargain.* **9.** In order to serve in or as: *train for the ministry.* **10.** In or to the amount of: *a bill for fifty dollars.* **11.** At the price of: *buy a dog for ten dollars.* **12.** In response to; as requital of: *good for bad.* **13.** Considering the nature or usual character of: *very warm for April.* **14.** Appropriate or suitable to: *a time for rejoicing.* **15.** At or on an appointed time or occasion: *an appointment for three o'clock.* **16.** Notwithstanding; despite: *For all his experience, he is inefficient.* **17.** Intended to be used as: *Books are for reading.* **18.** With a desire or longing toward: *The puppy whimpered for his supper.* **19.** So as to obtain: *work for a salary.* **20.** In honor of: *a dinner for the ambassador.* **21.** In place of: *use artificial flowers for real ones.* **22.** In its effect on: *Fresh air is good for you.* **23.** In favor, defense, or support of: *vote for the candidate of one's choice.* **24.** Accompanying; paired with: *one rotten apple for every good one.* **25.** As against; as measured or compared with: *pound for pound.* **26.** As being: *We mistook her for the waitress.* **27.** In order to retain, conserve, or save: *Run for your life!* **28.** As the duty or task of; up to: *It is for the judge to rule.* **29. a.** To the advantage of: *I built up the business for my daughter.* **b.** In order to help or remedy: *took pills for his headache.* **30.** Conducive to or resulting in: *motives for action.* **31.** Because of the fact or existence of; on account of: *If it weren't for the rain, we*

could go. **32.** Allocated to: *one for you, two for me.* **—for to.** *Archaic & Regional.* In order to.
~conj. Because; since. [Middle English *for,* Old English *for* (the conjunction develops from Old English phrases such as *for thon the,* "for the (reason) that").]

for– *prefix.* Indicates: **1.** Completely; to exhaustion; excessively; for example, **forspent, forlorn. 2.** Prohibition; abstention; for example, **forswear, forbid.** [Old English *for-, fær-*; akin to Latin *per-,* Greek *peri-.*]

fo·ra. Alternate plural of **forum.**

for·age (fôr′ĭj, fŏr′-) *n.* **1.** Food for domestic animals, such as horses, cows, and sheep; fodder. Also used adjectivally: *forage crop.* **2.** The act of looking or searching for such food. **3.** The act of looking or searching for supplies of any kind.
~v. **foraged, -aging, -ages.** *—intr.* **1.** To search for food or provisions. **2.** To make a raid, as for food, supplies, or anything needed or desired. **3.** To hunt or search about. *—tr.* **1.** To wander or rummage through, especially in search of provisions. **2.** To raid; plunder. **3.** To provide with fodder; feed. **4.** To secure by searching about. [Middle English, from Old French *fo(ur)rage,* from *feurre,* fodder, from Germanic.] **—for·ag·er** *n.*

forage cap *n.* A brimless, close-fitting military cap with a central dent running lengthwise.

fo·ra·men (fə-rā′mən) *n., pl.* **-ramina** (-răm′ə-nə) or **-mens.** An opening or perforation in a bone or through a membranous anatomical structure. [New Latin, from Latin *forāmen,* an opening, from *forāre,* to bore.] **—fo·ram·i·nal** (fə-răm′ə-nəl) *adj.*

foramen mag·num (măg′nəm) *n.* The large orifice in the base of the skull through which the spinal cord passes and becomes continuous with the medulla oblongata. [New Latin, "large orifice."]

foramen o·val·e (ō-văl′ē, -vā′lē, -vä′lē) *n.* An opening in the septum between the right and left atria in the heart of a fetus. [New Latin, oval opening.]

for·a·min·i·fer·an (fôr′ə-mĭn′ə-fər-ən, fŏr′-) *n.* Also **for·am** (fôr′əm, fŏr′-), **for·a·min·i·fer** (fôr′ə-mĭn′ə-fər, fŏr′-). Any of the unicellular microorganisms of the order Foraminifera, characteristically having a calcareous shell with perforations through which numerous pseudopodia protrude. [New Latin *Foraminifera* : *forāmen,* opening, FORAMEN + -FER.] **—fo·ram·i·nif·er·ous** (fə-răm′ə-nĭf′ər-əs), **fo·ram·i·nif·er·al** *adj.*

for·as·much as (fôr′əz-mŭch′ əz) *conj.* Inasmuch as; since.

for·ay (fôr′ā′, fŏr′ā′) *n.* **1.** A sudden raid or military advance. **2.** A venture or initial attempt in some field. **3.** *Chiefly British.* An outing or expedition with the object of finding certain animals or plants in their natural surroundings: *a fungus foray.*
~v. **forayed, -aying, -ays.** *—intr.* To make a raid. *—tr.* To make a raid against; plunder. [Middle English *forrai,* from *forraien,* to foray, back-formation from *forreour,* raider, plunderer, from Old French *forrier,* from Vulgar Latin *fodrārius* (unattested), from Germanic.]

forb (fôrb) *n.* Any herbaceous plant other than a grass, especially one growing in a field or meadow. [Greek *phorbē,* fodder, from *pherbein*†, to feed, graze.]

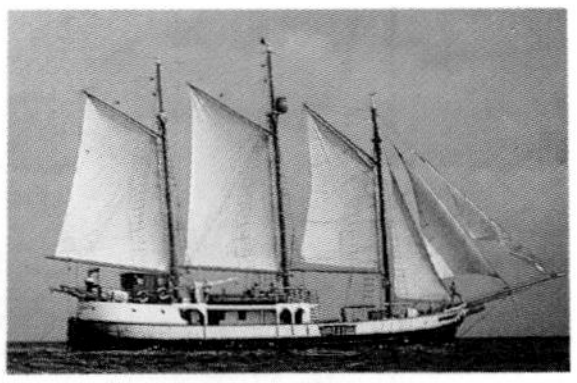

fore-and-aft rig *The sails in a fore-and-aft rig lie along the length of a ship, not across it, enabling the vessel to sail closer to the wind. Fore-and-aft sails, which are typically quadrilateral and triangular, were probably first used on Arab ships in the Mediterranean in the ninth century* A.D.

for·bear[1] (fôr-bâr′) *v.* **-bore** (-bôr′, -bōr′), **-borne** (-bôrn′, -bōrn′), **-bearing, -bears.** *—tr.* **1.** To refrain from; keep oneself from: *forbear replying.* **2.** To desist from; cease. **3.** *Archaic.* To endure; tolerate. *—intr.* **1.** To hold back; refrain. **2.** To be tolerant or patient. [Middle English *forberen,* Old English *forberan,* to bear, endure, from Germanic.] **—for·bear·er** *n.*

forbear[2]. Variant of **forebear.**

for·bear·ance (fôr-bâr′əns) *n.* **1.** The act of refraining from something; abstinence. **2.** Tolerance and restraint in the face of provocation; patience. **3.** *Law.* The act of a creditor who refrains from enforcing a debt when it falls due. —See Synonyms at **mercy, patience.**

for·bear·ing (fôr-bâr′ĭng) *adj.* Tolerant; patient.

for·bid (fər-bĭd′, fôr-) *tr.v.* **-bade** (-băd′, -bād′) or **-bad** (-băd′), **-bidden** (-bĭd′n) or **-bid, -bidding, -bids. 1.** To command (someone) not to do something: *I forbid you to go.* **2.** To prohibit; interdict: *Smoking is forbidden.* **3.** To have the effect of preventing; preclude. **—God forbid.** Let it not happen; I do not wish it to happen. [Middle English *forbidden, forbeden,* Old English *forbēodan,* from Germanic.] **—for·bid·dance** *n.* **—for·bid·der** *n.*

Usage: The standard English constructions with this verb are the infinitive (*I forbid you to go*) and the *-ing* form of the verb (*I forbid your going*), which is a little more formal. The use of *from* with *forbid* (*I forbid you from going*) is not standard. See also **prevent, prohibit.**

for·bid·den (fər-bĭd′n, fôr-) *adj. Physics.* Of or pertaining to secondary quantum effects: *forbidden spectral lines.*

Forbidden City. Name given to the ancient imperial residence and seat of central government within the Inner or Tatar City, Beijing (Peking), China. Now a vast museum, it comprises two sets of three imperial palaces and some smaller palaces, laid out within a walled enclosure.

forbidden fruit *n.* Anything desirable but forbidden; especially, illicit sexual pleasure. [Alluding to the fruit forbidden to Adam in the garden of Eden (Genesis 2:17).]

for·bid·ding (fər-bĭd′ĭng, fôr-) *adj.* **1.** Tending or threatening to impede progress. **2.** Unfriendly; disagreeable. **3.** Grim; ominous.

for·bye, for·by (fôr-bī′) *prep. Scottish.* Besides.
~adv. In addition. [Middle English : FOR- + BY.]

force (fôrs, fōrs) *n.* **1.** Capacity to do work or cause physical change; strength; power. **2.** Power made operative against resistance; exertion: *use force in driving a nail.* **3.** Violence or the threat of violence used against a person or thing. **4.** Intellectual power or vigor, as of a statement. **5.** A capacity for influencing the mind or behavior; efficacy. **6.** Anything or anyone possessing such capacity: *forces of evil.* **7.** A body of persons or other resources organized or available for a specified purpose: *a work force.* **8. a.** A group organized for military, police, or hostile purposes: *an armed force.* **b. forces.** The armed forces of a country; the navy, army, and air force. **9.** *Law.* Legal validity; efficacy. **10.** *Symbol* **F** *Physics.* A vector quantity that tends to produce an acceleration of a body in the direction of its application. —See Synonyms at **strength. —in force. 1.** In full strength. **2.** In effect; operative: *a rule no longer in force.* **—join forces.** To unite; combine efforts.
~tr.v. **forced, forcing, forces. 1.** To compel to perform an action; coerce. **2.** To obtain by the use of force or coercion: *force a confession.* **3.** To produce by effort: *force a tear from one's eye.* **4.** To move (something) against resistance; push: *force open the barricaded door.* **5.** To move, open, or clear by force: *force one's way through a crowd.* **6.** To break down or open by force: *force a lock.* **7.** To rape. **8.** To inflict or impose: *force one's will on someone.* **9.** To place undue strain upon; push beyond normal capacity or use: *force one's voice.* **10.** To cause to grow or mature by artificially accelerating the normal processes: *force flowers in a greenhouse.* **11.** *Baseball.* **a.** To put (a runner) out by tagging the base to which he must advance. **b.** To allow (a run) to be scored by walking a batter when the bases are loaded. [Middle English, from Old French, from Vulgar Latin *fortia* (unattested), from Latin *fortis,* strong.] **—force·a·ble** *adj.* **—forc·er** *n.*

Synonyms: *coerce, compel, constrain, necessitate, oblige.*

forced (fôrst, fōrst) *adj.* **1.** Enforced; compulsory; involuntary: *forced labor.* **2.** Produced under strain; not spontaneous: *forced laughter.* **3.** Effected in an emergency: *a forced landing.* **—forc·ed·ly** (fôr′sĭd-lē, fōr′-) *adv.* **—forc·ed·ness** *n.*

forced march *n.* A long march made at a rigorously fast pace over a longer distance than normal.

force feed *n.* A system that supplies lubricants under pressure, as to a car engine.

force-feed (fôrs′fēd′, fōrs′-) *tr.v.* **-fed** (-fĕd′), **-feeding, -feeds. 1.** To force to ingest food; feed forcibly. **2.** To force to assimilate ideas, information, or the like. **—force-feed·ing** *n.*

force field *n.* A **field of force** *(see).*

force·ful (fôrs′fəl, fōrs′-) *adj.* Characterized by or full of force; effective; persuasive. **—force·ful·ly** *adv.* **—force·ful·ness** *n.*

force ma·jeure (fôrs′ mä-zhûr′, fōrs′) *n.* An unexpected or uncontrollable event that upsets one's plans or releases one from obligations, especially legal obligations. [French, "superior force."]

force·meat (fôrs′mēt′, fōrs′-) *n.* Finely chopped spiced meat or poultry, used in stuffing or as a garnish. [From *force,* variant of FARCE (to stuff).]

force of habit *n.* Automatic behavior, as from long practice or frequent repetition.

force-out (fôrs′out′, fōrs′-) *n. Baseball.* An out made by tagging a base to which a runner must advance.

for·ceps (fôr′səps) *n., pl.* **forceps. 1.** An instrument resembling a pair of pincers or tongs, used for grasping, manipulating, or extracting; especially, such an instrument used by surgeons or dentists. **2.** A pincerlike clasping organ at the posterior end of the abdomen in certain insects, such as earwigs. [Latin *forceps,* fire tongs, pincers.]

force pump *n.* A pump with a solid piston and valves used to raise a liquid or expel it under pressure.

for·ci·ble (fôr′sə-bəl, fōr′-) *adj.* **1.** Effected through the use of force: *a forcible entry.* **2.** Characterized by force; forceful; persuasive. **—for·ci·ble·ness** *n.* **—for·ci·bly** *adv.*

for·ci·pate (fôr′sə-pāt′) *adj.* Shaped like a forceps. [Latin *forceps, forcip-,* pincers + -ATE.]

ford (fôrd, fōrd) *n.* A shallow place in a body of water, such as a river, where a crossing can be made on foot or in a vehicle.
~tr.v. **forded, fording, fords.** To cross (a body of water) at a ford. [Middle English *ford,* Old English *ford.*] **—ford·a·ble** *adj.*

Ford (fôrd, fōrd), **Ford Madox** (1873–1939). British novelist and editor. He collaborated with Joseph Conrad on *The Inheritors* (1901) and *Romance* (1903) and wrote novels, verse, and criticism. He founded the *English Review* (1908) and the *Transatlantic Review* (1924).

Ford, Gerald Rudolph, born Leslie Lynch King, Jr. (1913–). 38th president of the United States. He was elected to the House of Representatives in 1949. In 1973 he became vice president to Richard Nixon, and a year later, after Nixon's resignation over the Watergate scandal, he became president. He was defeated by Jimmy Carter (1976).

Ford, Henry (1863–1947). U.S. automobile manufacturer. He founded the Ford Motor Company in 1903 and produced the first of the legendary Model T's in 1908. With assembly-line production he was turning out two million cars a year by 1924, at prices that made them accessible to the general public. His grandson, **Henry II** (1917–87) became president of the company in 1945.

Ford, John[1] (*c.* 1586–*c.* 1640). English dramatist. He collaborated with other dramatists, notably Dekker and Webster, and wrote works of his own, including *'Tis Pity She's a Whore* (1633) and *Perkin Warbeck* (1634).

Ford, John[2], born Sean O'Feeney (1895–1973). U.S. director of 125 feature films. His best-known films, starring John Wayne, include *Stagecoach* (1939) and *The Man Who Shot Liberty Valance* (1962). Other films include *The Informer* (1935), *The Grapes of Wrath* (1940), *How Green Was My Valley* (1941), and *The Quiet Man* (1952), all of which won Academy Awards.

for·do, fore·do (fôr-dōō′, fōr-) *tr.v.* **-did** (-dĭd′), **-done** (-dŭn′), **-do·ing, -does** (-dŭz′). *Archaic.* **1.** To kill. **2.** To bring to ruin. **3.** To exhaust utterly. [Middle English *fordon,* Old English *fordōn* : FOR- (indicating destruction) + *dōn,* to DO.]

fore (fôr, fōr) *adj.* Located at or toward the front; anterior.
~*n.* **1.** Something at or toward the front. **2.** The front part. **3.** The bow of a ship. —**to the fore.** In, into, or toward a position of prominence.
~*adv.* Toward or at the bow of a ship; forward.
~*prep.* Also **'fore.** *Archaic.* Before. Frequently used in oaths: *Fore God, Sir, you are mistaken!*
~*interj. Golf.* Used to warn those ahead that a ball is about to be driven in their direction. [Middle English *fore,* probably from adverb, "beforehand," Old English *for(e).*]

fore– *prefix.* Indicates: **1.** Before in time; for example, **forebode, foresight. 2.** The front or front part; for example, **foredeck, foreskin.** [Middle English *for-, fore-,* Old English *fore,* from *fore* (adverb), in front, beforehand.]

fore and aft *adv.* **1.** From the bow to the stern of a ship; lengthwise of a ship. **2.** In, at, or toward both ends of a ship.

fore-and-aft (fôr′ən-ăft′, -äft′, fōr′-) *adj.* Parallel with the keel of a ship.

fore-and-aft·er (fôr′ən-ăf′tər, -äf′tər, fōr′-) *n.* A sailing ship, such as a ketch or schooner, carrying a fore-and-aft rig.

fore-and-aft rig *n.* A ship rig with quadrilateral and triangular fore-and-aft sails. Compare **square rig.** —**fore-and-aft-rigged** *adj.*

fore-and-aft sail *n.* A sail set parallel with the keel of a vessel as opposed to being hung from a horizontal bar (yard) across the mast as in a **square rig** *(see).*

fore·arm[1] (fôr-ärm′, fōr-) *tr.v.* **-armed, -arming, -arms.** To prepare or arm in advance of some confrontation.

fore·arm[2] (fôr′ärm′, fōr′-) *n.* The part of the arm between the wrist and elbow.

fore·bear, for·bear (fôr′bâr′, fōr′-) *n.* A forefather; ancestor. [Middle English (Scottish dialect) *forebear* : FORE- + *bear,* "be-er," from *been,* to BE.]

fore·bode (fôr-bōd′, fōr-) *tr.v.* **-boded, -boding, -bodes. 1.** To indicate the threatening likelihood of; give warning of; portend. **2.** To have a premonition of (a future misfortune). —See Synonyms at **foretell.**

fore·bod·ing (fôr-bō′dĭng, fōr-) *n.* **1.** A dark sense of impending evil; premonition. **2.** An evil omen; portent. —See Synonyms at **apprehension.**
~*adj.* Ominous. —**fore·bod·ing·ly** *adv.*

fore·brain (fôr′brān′, fōr′-) *n.* **1.** The anterior region of the embryonic brain from which the telencephalon and diencephalon develop. Also called "prosencephalon." **2.** The segment of the adult brain that develops from the embryonic forebrain and includes the cerebrum, thalamus, and hypothalamus.

fore·cast (fôr′kăst′, -kăst′, fōr′-) *v.* **-cast** or **-casted, -casting, -casts.** —*tr.* **1.** To estimate or calculate in advance, especially: **a.** To predict (weather conditions) by analysis of meteorological data. **b.** To predict (the behavior of the economy, financial markets, or the like) by the analysis of economic and financial data. **2.** To serve as an advance indication of; foreshadow. —*intr.* To make an estimation in advance. —See Synonyms at **foretell.**
~*n.* **1.** A prediction, as of the weather. **2.** A conjecture concerning the future. [Middle English *forecasten,* to devise beforehand : FORE- + CAST.] —**fore·cast·er** *n.*

fore·cas·tle (fōk′səl, fôr′kăs′əl, -kä′səl, fōr′-) *n.* Also **fo'c's'le** (fōk′səl). **1.** The section of the upper deck of a ship located at the bow, in front of the foremast. **2.** A raised deck at the bow of a merchant ship where the crew is housed.

fore·close (fôr-klōz′, fōr-) *v.* **-closed, -closing, -closes.** —*tr.* **1.** *Law.* **a.** To deprive (a mortgagor) of the right to redeem mortgaged property, as when he has failed in his payments; repossess the mortgaged property of. **b.** To bar the right to redeem (a mortgage). **2.** To shut out; bar. **3.** To settle or resolve beforehand. **4.** To hinder; deter; thwart. —*intr.* To foreclose a mortgage. Often used with *on.* [Middle English *forclosen,* to shut out, preclude, from Old French *forclore* (past participle *forclos*) : *fors,* outside, from Latin *forīs* + *clore,* from Latin *claudere,* to CLOSE.] —**fore·clos·a·ble** *adj.*

fore·clo·sure (fôr-klō′zhər, fōr-) *n.* The act of foreclosing; especially, a legal proceeding by which a mortgage is foreclosed.

fore·course (fôr′kôrs′, fōr′kôrs′) *n.* A foresail.

fore·court (fôr′kôrt′, fōr′kōrt′) *n.* **1.** A courtyard in front of a building. **2.** The part of a playing court nearest the net or wall, as in tennis or handball.

fore·date (fôr-dāt′, fōr-) *tr.v.* **-dated, -dating, -dates.** To antedate.

fore·deck (fôr′dĕk′, fōr′-) *n.* The forward part of a deck, usually the main deck.

foredo. Variant of **fordo.**

fore·doom (fôr-dōōm′, fōr-) *tr.v.* **-doomed, -dooming, -dooms.** To doom or condemn beforehand. —**fore·doom** (fôr′dōōm′, fōr′-) *n.*

fore·fa·ther (fôr′fä′*th*ər, fōr′-) *n.* An ancestor.

forefend. Variant of **forfend.**

fore·fin·ger (fôr′fĭng′gər, fōr′-) *n.* The **index finger** *(see).*

fore·foot (fôr′fŏŏt′, fōr′-) *n., pl.* **-feet** (-fēt′). **1.** Either of the front

feet of a quadruped. **2.** *Nautical.* The part of a ship at which the prow joins the keel.

fore·front (fôr′frŭnt′, fōr′-) *n.* **1.** The foremost part or area of something. **2.** The position of most importance, prominence, or responsibility.

foregather. Variant of **forgather.**

fore·go[1] (fôr-gō′, fōr-) *tr.v.* **-went** (-wĕnt′), **-gone** (-gôn′, -gŏn′), **-going, -goes** (-gōz′). To precede or go before, as in time or place. —**fore·go·er** *n.*

forego[2]. Variant of **forgo.**

fore·go·ing (fôr-gō′ĭng, fōr-, fôr′gō′ĭng, fōr′-) *adj.* Just past; preceding; previously said or written.

fore·gone (fôr′gôn′, -gŏn′, fōr′-) *adj.* Having gone or been completed previously; departed; past. [Past participle of FOREGO.]

foregone conclusion *n.* An end or result regarded as inevitable.

fore·ground (fôr′ground′, fōr′-) *n.* **1.** The part of a view or sight that is nearest to the viewer. **2.** The part of a picture, as in a painting or photograph, that is represented as nearest to the viewer. **3.** The most important or prominent position.

fore·gut (fôr′gŭt′, fōr′-) *n.* The anterior part of the digestive tract, which in vertebrates extends from the buccal cavity to the bile duct and in arthropods comprises the buccal cavity, esophagus, crop, and gizzard.

fore·hand (fôr′hănd′, fōr′-) *adj.* **1. a.** Made with the hand moving palm forward: *a forehand tennis stroke.* **b.** Pertaining to the side of the body on which a forehand stroke is played. **2.** Foremost; leading. **3.** *Archaic.* Taking place beforehand; prior.
~*n.* **1. a.** A forehand stroke, as in tennis. **b.** The side of the body on which a forehand stroke is played. **2.** The part of a horse in front of the rider. —**fore·hand** *adv.*

fore·hand·ed (fôr′hăn′dĭd, fōr′-) *adj.* **1.** Forehand, as in tennis. **2.** Looking or planning ahead. **3.** Having ample financial resources; well-off. —**fore·hand·ed·ness** *n.*

fore·head (fôr′ĭd, fōr′hĕd′, fōr′-) *n.* The part of the head or face between the eyebrows, the normal hairline, and the temples.

for·eign (fôr′ĭn, fŏr′-) *adj.* **1.** Located away from one's native country: *a foreign city.* **2.** Of, characteristic of, or from a country other than one's own: *a foreign custom.* **3.** Conducted or involved with other nations or governments; not domestic: *foreign trade.* **4.** Situated in an abnormal or improper place: *a foreign body in one's eye.* **5.** Outside of a scope, range, or essential nature; alien: *Lying is quite foreign to her nature.* **6.** Not to the point; extraneous; irrelevant. **7.** *Law.* Subject to the jurisdiction of another political unit. —See Synonyms at **extrinsic.** [Middle English *forein,* from Old French *forein, forain,* from Late Latin *forānus,* from Latin *forās,* out of doors, abroad.] —**for·eign·ness** *n.*

foreign affairs *pl.n.* **1.** A country's relationships and dealings with other countries. **2.** Events that take place in another country.

foreign aid *n.* Financial and practical assistance given by one country to another, especially by a technologically advanced country to a less developed one. Also called "aid."

foreign bill *n.* A draft for a sum of money to be paid in another country. Also called "foreign bill of exchange," "foreign draft."

foreign correspondent *n.* A journalist or reporter who sends news reports or commentary from a foreign country for publication or broadcasting.

for·eign·er (fôr′ə-nər, fŏr′-) *n.* A person from a foreign country.

foreign exchange *n.* **1.** The transaction of international monetary business, as between governments or businessmen of different countries. **2.** Negotiable bills drawn in one country to be paid in another country.

Foreign Legion *n.* A French military unit composed of volunteers of any nationality.

foreign minister, Foreign Minister *n.* The government minister in charge of dealings between his own government and those of foreign countries.

foreign mission *n.* **1.** A group sent to a foreign country for missionary service, as in religion or medicine. **2.** A group sent to a foreign country for diplomatic service.

Foreign Office *n. Abbr.* **F.O.** The official government department in several countries that is in charge of foreign affairs.

foreign policy *n.* The diplomatic policy of a nation in its interactions with other nations.

fore·judge, for·judge (fôr-jŭj′, fōr-) *v.* **-judged, -judging, -judges.** —*tr.* To judge beforehand; prejudge. —*intr.* To judge something or someone beforehand.

fore·knowl·edge (fôr-nŏl′ĭj, fōr-) *n.* Knowledge or awareness of something prior to its existence or occurrence; prescience.

fore·la·dy (fôr′lā′dē, fōr′-) *n., pl.* **-dies.** A forewoman.

fore·land (fôr′lənd, -lănd′, fōr′-) *n.* **1.** A projecting land mass; promontory; cape. **2.** Land or territory lying to the fore, as bordering land or land at the edge of a body of water.

fore·leg (fôr′lĕg′, fōr′-) *n.* Either of the front legs of a quadruped.

fore·limb (fôr′lĭm′, fōr′-) *n.* An anterior appendage, such as a leg, wing, or flipper in a vertebrate.

fore·lock[1] (fôr′lŏk′, fōr′-) *n.* A lock of hair that grows or falls on the forehead; especially, the part of a horse's mane that falls forward between the ears.

forelock[2] *n.* A cotter pin; linchpin.

fore·man (fôr′mən, fōr′-) *n., pl.* **-men** (-mĭn). **1.** A man who has charge of a group of workers, as at a factory. **2.** The chairman and spokesman of a jury. —**fore·man·ship** *n.*

fore·mast (fôr′məst, -măst′, -mäst′, fōr′-) *n.* The forward mast on any sailing vessel with two or more masts, with the exception of the ketch and the yawl.

fore·milk (fôr′mĭlk′, fōr′-) *n.* Colostrum (see).

fore·most (fôr′mōst′, fōr′-) *adj.* Ahead of all others, especially in position or rank; paramount. —See Synonyms at **chief.** ~*adv.* In the front or first position. [Variant (influenced by FORE-) of Middle English *formest, formost,* Old English *formest,* superlative of *forma,* first.]

fore·name (fôr′nām′, fōr′-) *n.* A first name.

fore·named (fôr′nāmd′, fōr′-) *adj.* Named earlier; aforesaid.

fore·noon (fôr′nōōn′, fōr′-, fôr-nōōn′, fōr-) *n.* **1.** The period of time between sunrise and noon; daylight morning hours. **2.** The latter part of the morning.

fo·ren·sic (fə-rĕn′sĭk, -zĭk) *adj.* **1.** Pertaining to or employed in legal proceedings or argumentation. **2.** Pertaining to a forensic science, such as pathology: *a forensic laboratory.* **3.** Of or employed in debate or argument; rhetorical. [Latin *forēnsis,* of a market or forum, public, from *forum,* forum.] —**fo·ren·si·cal·ly** *adv.*

forensic medicine *n.* The application of medical science to interpret or establish the facts in civil or criminal law cases. Also called "medical jurisprudence."

fo·ren·sics (fə-rĕn′sĭks, -zĭks) *n.* Used with a singular verb. The study or practice of formal debate; argumentation.

fore·or·dain (fôr′ôr-dān′, fōr′-) *tr.v.* **-dained, -daining, -dains.** To appoint, determine, or ordain beforehand; predestine. —**fore·or·dain·ment** *n.* —**fore·or·di·na·tion** (fôr-ôr′də-nā′shən, fōr-) *n.*

fore·part (fôr′pärt′, fōr′-) *n.* The first or foremost part.

fore·paw (fôr′pô′, fōr′-) *n.* Either of the front feet of a land mammal that does not have hoofs.

fore·peak (fôr′pēk′, fōr′-) *n.* The section of the hold of a ship that is within the angle made by the bow.

fore·per·son (fôr′pûr′sən, fōr′-) *n.* A foreman or forewoman.

fore·play (fôr′plā′, fōr′-) *n.* Sexual stimulation that precedes sexual intercourse.

fore·quar·ter (fôr′kwôr′tər, fōr′-) *n.* **1.** The front section of a side of meat. **2. forequarters.** The forelegs, shoulders, and adjacent parts of an animal, especially a horse.

fore·reach (fôr-rēch′, fōr-) *v.* **-reached, -reaching, -reaches.** —*tr.* **1.** To get ahead of; pass, especially in a sailing vessel. **2.** To get the advantage over; excel. —*intr.* To move up; gain ground, especially upon a sailing vessel.

fore·run (fôr-rŭn′, fōr′-) *tr.v.* **-ran** (-răn′), **-run, -running, -runs. 1.** To run in advance or in front of. **2.** To be the precursor of; foreshadow. **3.** To forestall; prevent.

fore·run·ner (fôr′rŭn′ər, fōr′-) *n.* **1.** Someone who or something that precedes, as in time; predecessor. **2.** An ancestor; forebear. **3.** Someone who or something that provides advance notice of the coming of others; harbinger; precursor.

fore·said (fôr′sĕd′, fōr′-) *adj.* Previously named or said; aforesaid.

fore·sail (fôr′səl, -sāl′, fōr′-) *n.* Nautical. **1.** The principal square sail hung to the foremast of a square-rigged vessel. Also called "fore-course." **2.** The principal triangular sail hung to the mast of a fore-and-aft-rigged vessel. **3.** The triangular sail hung to the forestay of a cutter or sloop. **4. foresails.** The sails on the foremast or before the mast.

fore·see (fôr-sē′, fōr-) *tr.v.* **-saw** (-sô′), **-seen** (-sēn′), **-seeing, -sees.** To see or know beforehand; anticipate; envision: *"many families, foreseeing the approach of the distemper, laid up stores of provisions"* (Defoe). —See Synonyms at **expect.** —**fore·see·a·ble** *adj.* —**fore·se·er** *n.*

fore·shad·ow (fôr-shăd′ō, fōr-) *tr.v.* **-owed, -owing, -ows.** To present an often ominous indication or suggestion of beforehand; portend.

fore·sheet (fôr′shēt′, fōr′-) *n.* **1.** A rope used in trimming a foresail. **2. foresheets.** The space near the bow of an open boat.

fore·shock (fôr′shŏk′, fōr′-) *n.* A minor tremor that precedes an earthquake.

fore·shore (fôr′shôr′, fōr′shōr′) *n.* **1.** The part of a shore covered at high tide. **2.** The part of a shore between the water and occupied or cultivated land.

fore·short·en (fôr-shôrt′n, fōr-) *tr.v.* **-ened, -ening, -ens. 1.** In drawing or painting, to represent the long axis of (an object or form) by contracting its lines so as to produce an illusion of depth or distance. **2.** To shorten beforehand; curtail.

fore·show (fôr-shō′, fōr-) *tr.v.* **-showed, -shown** (-shōn′) or **-showed, -showing, -shows.** To show in advance; prognosticate.

fore·side (fôr′sīd′, fōr′-) *n.* The front or upper side.

fore·sight (fôr′sīt′, fōr′-) *n.* **1.** The ability to foresee. **2.** The act of looking forward. **3.** Concern or prudence with respect to the future. —**fore·sight·ed** *adj.* —**fore·sight·ed·ly** *adv.* —**fore·sight·ed·ness** *n.*

fore·skin (fôr′skĭn′, fōr′-) *n.* The loose fold of skin that covers the glans of the penis. Also called "prepuce."

fore·speak (fôr-spēk′, fōr-) *tr.v.* **-spoken** (-spō′kən), **-speaking, -speaks. 1.** To speak of in advance; predict. **2.** To arrange for or engage in advance.

forespent. Variant of **forspent.**

for·est (fôr′ĭst, fŏr′-) *n.* **1. a.** A large area covered by a dense growth of trees, together with other plants. **b.** The trees themselves. **2.** Something that resembles a forest in density, quantity, or profusion: *a forest of skyscrapers.* **3.** Law. A defined area of land formerly set aside in England as a royal hunting ground. ~*tr.v.* **forested, -esting, -ests.** To plant trees on; transform into a forest. [Middle English, from Old French, from the Late Latin ex-

---

pression *forestis (silva),* outside (forest), referring originally to the royal forest or game preserve of Charlemagne, probably from Latin *forīs,* outside, outdoors.] —**for·est·al, fo·res·tial** (fə-rĕs′chəl) *adj.* —**for·es·ta·tion** (fôr′ə-stā′shən, fōr′-) *n.*

fore·stall (fôr-stôl′, fōr-) *tr.v.* **-stalled, -stalling, -stalls. 1.** To prevent, delay, or take precautionary measures against beforehand. **2.** To deal with or think of beforehand; anticipate. **3.** To prevent or hinder normal sales of by buying up merchandise, discouraging others from bringing their goods to market, or encouraging an increase in prices of goods already on the market. Compare **engross.** —See Synonyms at **prevent.** [Middle English *forestallen,* to forestall, obstruct, from *forestal,* the crime of waylaying or ambushing on the highway, Old English *foresteall,* waylaying, interception : *fore-,* in front of + *steall,* position, place.] —**fore·stall·er** *n.* —**fore·stall·ment** *n.*

fore·stay (fôr′stā′, fōr′-) *n.* A stay extending from the head of the foremast to the bowsprit of a ship.

fore·stay·sail (fôr′stā′səl, -sāl′, fōr′-) *n.* A triangular sail set on the forestay.

for·est·er (fôr′ĭ-stər, fōr′-) *n.* **1.** A person trained in forestry. **2.** One that inhabits a forest. **3.** Any of various chiefly tropical moths of the genus *Ino,* many of which are a brilliant green.

For·est·er (fôr′ĭ-stər, fōr′-), **Cecil Scott** (1899–1966). British novelist. He is best known for his *Captain Horatio Hornblower* series, sea adventures set in Napoleonic times. His other books include *Payment Deferred* (1926) and *The African Queen* (1935).

Forest Hills. Residential section of central Queens borough in New York City. Until 1978 the U.S. Open Championship tennis matches were held at the West Side Tennis Club here.

for·est·land (fôr′ĭst-lănd′, fōr′-) *n.* A section of land covered with forest.

forest ranger *n.* An officer in charge of protecting or managing a public forest or section of a public forest.

for·est·ry (fôr′ĭ-strē, fōr′-) *n.* **1.** The science and art of cultivating, maintaining, and developing forests. **2.** The management of forestland. **3.** Forestland.

foreswear. Variant of **forswear.**

fore·taste (fôr′tāst′, fōr′-) *n.* An advance taste, experience, or realization: *a foretaste of doom.* ~*tr.v.* (fôr-tāst′, fōr-, fôr′tāst′, fōr′-) **foretasted, -tasting, -tastes.** To have an advance realization of; anticipate.

fore·tell (fôr-tĕl′, fōr-) *v.* **-told** (-tōld′), **-telling, -tells.** —*tr.* To tell of or indicate beforehand; prophesy; predict. —*intr.* To tell beforehand. Often used with *of: foretell of disaster.* —**fore·tell·er** *n.*

   Synonyms: *augur, bode, divine, forebode, forecast, portend, predict, presage, prophesy.*

fore·thought (fôr′thôt′, fōr′-) *n.* **1.** Deliberation, consideration, or planning beforehand. **2.** Preparation or thought for the future; prudent anticipation. —**fore·thought·ful** *adj.* —**fore·thought·ful·ly** *adv.* —**fore·thought·ful·ness** *n.*

fore·time (fôr′tīm′, fōr′-) *n.* Archaic. Former time; the past.

fore·to·ken (fôr-tō′kən, fōr-) *tr.v.* **-kened, -kening, -kens.** To foreshadow; presage. ~*n.* (fôr′tō′kən, fōr′-). An advance warning.

fore·top (fôr′tŏp′, -təp, fōr′-) *n.* **1.** A platform at the top of a ship's foremast. **2.** A forelock, especially of a horse.

fore·top·gal·lant (fôr′tŏp-găl′ənt, fōr′-, fôr′tə-, fōr′tə-) *adj.* Nautical. Of or relating to the mast directly above the foremast.

fore·top·gal·lant·mast (fôr′tŏp-găl′ənt-măst′, -mäst′, fôr′tə-, fōr′tə-) *n.* The mast above the fore-topmast.

fore·top·mast (fôr′tŏp′məst, fōr′-, fôr′təp-măst′, -mäst′, fōr′təp-) *n.* The mast that is above the foretop.

fore·top·sail (fôr′tŏp′səl, fōr′-, fôr′təp-, fōr′təp-) *n.* The sail hung from the fore-topmast.

for·ev·er (fôr-ĕv′ər, fər-) *adv.* **1.** For everlasting time; eternally. **2.** At all times; incessantly.

for·ev·er·more (fôr-ĕv′ər-môr′, -mōr′, fər-) *adv.* Forever.

fore·warn (fôr-wôrn′, fōr-) *tr.v.* **-warned, -warning, -warns.** To warn clearly in advance. —See Synonyms at **warn.**

fore·went. Past tense of **forego** (to go before).

fore·wing (fôr′wĭng′, fōr′-) *n.* Either of a pair of anterior wings, as in certain insects.

fore·wom·an (fôr′wŏŏm′ən, fōr′-) *n., pl.* **-women** (-wĭm′ĭn). **1.** A woman who has charge of a group of workers, as at a factory. **2.** The chairwoman and spokeswoman for a jury.

fore·word (fôr′wûrd′, -wərd, fōr′-) *n.* A preface or introductory note, especially at the beginning of a book. [Translation of German *Vorwort.*]

foreworn. Variant of **forworn.**

fore·yard (fôr′yärd′, fōr′-) *n.* Nautical. The lowest yard on a foremast.

for·feit (fôr′fĭt) *n.* **1.** Something surrendered as punishment for a crime, offense, error, or breach of contract; a penalty or fine. **2.** Something given up or surrendered for a breach of rules or a mistake in a game. **3.** A forfeiture. **4.** Often **forfeits.** A game in which forfeits are required. ~*adj.* Surrendered or alienated for a crime, offense, error, or breach of contract. ~*tr.v.* **forfeited, -feiting, -feits. 1.** To surrender or be forced to surrender as a forfeit. **2.** To subject to forfeiture. [Middle English *forfet,* forfeit, transgression, from Old French *forfet,* from *for(s)faire,* to commit a crime : *fors-,* beyond (here, beyond what is permitted),

---

forge *A blacksmith's workshop and the furnace or hearth where the metal is heated are both known as forges. In front of the hearth in this picture is the quenching trough, which contains water to cool the metal being worked or the smith's tools.*

from Latin *forīs,* outside + *faire,* to do, act, from Latin *facere.*] **—for·feit·a·ble** *adj.* **—for·feit·er** *n.*

for·fei·ture (fôr′fĭ-cho͝or′, -chər) *n.* **1.** The act of surrendering something as a forfeit. **2.** Something that is forfeited.

for·fend, fore·fend (fôr-fĕnd′, fōr-) *tr.v.* **-fended, -fending, -fends. 1.** To keep or ward off; avert. **2.** *Archaic.* To forbid. **3.** To defend or protect. [Middle English *forfenden,* to forbid, prevent : FOR- (prohibition) + FEND.]

for·fi·cate (fôr′fĭ-kĭt, -kāt′) *adj.* Deeply forked, as is the tail of certain birds. [Latin *forfex* (stem *forfic-*), a pair of scissors + -ATE.]

for·gath·er, fore·gath·er (fôr-găth′ər, fōr-) *intr.v.* **-ered, -ering, -ers. 1.** To gather together; assemble. **2.** To have a chance encounter; meet by accident. **3.** To keep company or consort. Used with *with.* [Originally Scottish : FOR- + GATHER.]

for·gave. Past tense of **forgive.**

forge[1] (fôrj, fōrj) *n.* **1.** A furnace or hearth where metals are heated or wrought; smithy. **2.** A workshop where pig iron is transformed into wrought iron.

∼*v.* **forged, forging, forges.** *—tr.* **1.** To form (metal) by heating in a forge and beating or hammering into shape. **2.** To give form or shape to; bring about, especially by dint of effort or application: *forge a friendship.* **3.** To fashion or reproduce for fraudulent purposes; fake; counterfeit. *—intr.* **1.** To work at a forge or smithy. **2.** To make a forgery or counterfeit. [Middle English, from Old French, from Vulgar Latin *faurga* (unattested), from Latin *fabrica,* smithy, artisan's workshop, from *faber,* smith.] **—forg·er** *n.*

forge[2] *intr.v.* **forged, forging, forges. 1.** To advance gradually but steadily. Often used with *ahead.* **2.** To advance with an abrupt increase of speed. Often used with *ahead.* [Perhaps a variant of FORCE, which has been used in the same senses.]

for·ger·y (fôr′jə-rē, fōr′-) *n., pl.* **-ies. 1.** The crime of producing something counterfeit or forged. **2.** Something counterfeit, forged, or fraudulent.

for·get (fər-gĕt′, fôr-) *v.* **-got** (-gŏt′), **-gotten** (-gŏt′n) or **-got, -getting, -gets.** *—tr.* **1.** To be unable to remember or call to mind. **2.** To lack concern for; treat with inattention; neglect: *forget one's family.* **3.** To leave behind unintentionally. **4.** To fail to mention; pass over. **5.** To banish from one's thoughts: *forget a disgrace.* *—intr.* **1.** To cease remembering. **2.** To fail or neglect to become aware at the proper moment: *forget about paying one's taxes.* **—forget oneself.** To lose one's proper sense of decorum or self-restraint. [Middle English *forgeten,* Old English *forgietan,* from Germanic.] **—for·get·ta·ble** *adj.* **—for·get·ter** *n.*

for·get·ful (fər-gĕt′fəl, fôr-) *adj.* **1.** Tending or likely to forget. **2.** Neglectful; thoughtless; careless: *forgetful of one's duties.* **—for·get·ful·ly** *adv.* **—for·get·ful·ness** *n.*

Synonyms: *absent-minded, abstracted, distracted, heedless, oblivious, unmindful.*

for·get-me-not (fər-gĕt′mē-nŏt′, fôr-) *n.* **1.** Any of various plants of the genus *Myosotis,* having small blue flowers. Also called "scorpion grass." **2.** Any of several similar or related plants. [Translation of Old French *ne m'oubliez mie.*]

forg·ing (fôr′jĭng, fōr′-) *n.* Something that is forged.

for·give (fər-gĭv′, fôr-) *v.* **-gave** (-gāv′), **-given** (-gĭv′ən), **-giving, -gives.** *—tr.* **1.** To excuse for a fault or offense; pardon. **2.** To renounce anger or resentment against; cease to blame. **3.** To absolve from payment of. *—intr.* To grant forgiveness. [Middle English *foryeven, forgiven,* Old English *forgiefan* (translation of Medieval Latin *perdōnāre,* to pardon).] **—for·giv·a·ble** *adj.* **—for·giv·er** *n.*

Synonyms: *condone, excuse, pardon.*

for·give·ness (fər-gĭv′nĭs, fôr-) *n.* **1.** The act of forgiving. **2.** The willingness to forgive. **3.** Pardon.

for·go, fore·go (fôr-gō′, fōr-) *tr.v.* **-went** (-wĕnt′), **-gone** (-gôn′, -gŏn′), **-going, -goes. 1.** To relinquish; give up; forsake. **2.** To abstain from; do without. —See Synonyms at **relinquish.** [Middle English *forgon, forgan,* Old English *forgān,* originally to pass on, pass away : FOR- (exclusion) + *gān,* to go.] **—for·go·er** *n.*

for·got. Past tense and alternate past participle of **forget.**

for·got·ten. Past participle of **forget.**

for·int (fôr′ĭnt′) *n.* **1.** The basic monetary unit of Hungary, equal to 100 fillér. **2.** A coin worth one forint. See feature at **currency.** [Hungarian, from Italian *fiorino,* FLORIN.]

forjudge. Variant of **forejudge.**

fork (fôrk) *n.* **1.** An implement or piece of equipment with two or more prongs used for raising, carrying, piercing, or digging. **2.** A utensil with prongs for serving or eating food. **3.** Any device, piece of machinery, or the like with two or more prongs. **4. a.** A bifurcation or separation into two or more branches or parts. **b.** The point at which such a bifurcation or separation occurs: *a fork in a road.* **c.** Either of the branches of such a bifurcation or separation: *take the right fork.* **5.** A simultaneous attack on two chessmen by one.

∼*v.* **forked, forking, forks.** *—tr.* **1.** To raise, carry, pitch, or pierce with a fork. **2.** To give the shape of a fork to. **3.** To launch an attack on (two chessmen) with one chessman. *—intr.* **1.** To make a fork; divide into two or more branches. **2.** To take one branch at a fork in a road, river, or the like. **3.** *Informal.* To hand over; pay. Used with *out, over,* or *up*: *forked over their savings to buy a TV.* [Middle English *forke,* Old English *force, forca,* fork (for digging), from Latin *furca*†, two-pronged fork, fork-shaped prop.]

forked (fôrkt, fôr′kĭd) *adj.* **1.** Containing or characterized by a fork: *a forked river.* **2.** Shaped like or similar to a fork: *forked lightning; a forked tail.* **3.** Ambiguous; equivocal; deceitful: *a forked tongue.*

fork·ful (fôrk′fo͝ol′) *n., pl.* **forkfuls** or **forksful.** As much as a fork will hold or lift.

fork lift *n.* A small industrial vehicle with a power-operated pronged platform that can be raised and lowered for insertion under a load to be lifted and carried.

for·lorn (fôr-lôrn′, fər-) *adj.* **1.** Wretched or pitiful in appearance or condition. **2.** Suffering extreme want; destitute. **3.** Deserted; abandoned. **4.** Nearly hopeless; desperate. **5.** Very unhappy; miserable. **6.** Bereft: *forlorn of hope.* [Middle English *forloren,* past participle of *forlēsen,* to forfeit, lose, abandon, Old English *forlēosan.*] **—for·lorn·ly** *adv.* **—for·lorn·ness** *n.*

forlorn hope *n.* **1.** A hopeless or arduous undertaking. **2.** A misguided or vain hope. **3.** An advance guard of men sent on a hazardous mission. [Variant by folk etymology of Dutch *verloren hoop,* "lost troop" : *verloren,* past participle of *verliezen,* to lose + *hoop,* "heap," band, troop.]

form (fôrm) *n.* **1. a.** Shape or outward appearance. **b.** The contour, structure, or pattern of something as distinguished from its substance or content. **2.** The body or outward appearance of a person or animal, especially considered separately from the face or head. **3.** *Philosophy.* The essence of something as distinguished from its matter. **4. a.** The way or mode in which a thing exists, acts, or manifests itself: *Help appeared in the form of a lifeboat.* **b.** Kind; type; variety: *Ice is a form of water.* **c.** A group of organisms that differ in color, size, or some other aspect from other members of the same species. **5.** Procedure as determined or governed by regulation or custom: *know the form.* **6.** Manners as governed by etiquette, decorum, or custom: *good form.* **7. a.** Performance or condition considered with regard to acknowledged criteria: *true to form.* **b.** Mental or physical state, especially when good. **8. a.** Fitness, as of an athlete or animal, with regard to health or training. **b.** The record, as of a racehorse or greyhound, of training and races run; details of previous performances. **9.** A fixed order of words or procedures, as used in a ceremony or other regulated social situation. Also used adjectivally: *a form letter.* **10.** A document with blanks for the insertion of details or information: *an entry form.* **11.** Style or manner of presenting ideas or concepts in literary or musical composition or in organized discourse. **12.** The design, structure, or pattern of a work of art. **13.** A model for making a mold. **14.** A copy of the human figure used for modeling clothes. **15.** Linotype that has been assembled and locked up in a chase for printing. **16.** In Britain and some other countries, a class or all the children in the same year in a school: *sixth form.* **17. a.** A **linguistic form** *(see).* **b.** The external aspect of words with regard to their inflections, pronunciation, or spelling: *verb forms.* **18.** *Chiefly British.* A backless bench. **19.** The resting place of a hare.

∼*v.* **formed, forming, forms.** *—tr.* **1.** To give form to; shape; mold. **2. a.** To shape or mold into a particular form. **b.** To make; bring into being. **3.** To fashion, train, or develop by instruction or precept: *form the mind.* **4.** To come to have; develop; acquire: *form a habit.* **5.** To constitute or compose an element, part, or characteristic of. **6.** To develop in the mind; conceive: *form an opinion.* **7.** To produce (a tense, for example) by assuming an inflection: *form the pluperfect.* **8.** To make (a word) by derivation or composition. **9.** To put in order; draw up; arrange. *—intr.* **1.** To become formed or shaped. **2.** To be created; come into being; arise. **3.** To assume a specified form, shape, or pattern. Often used with *up.* [Middle English *forme, fourme,* from Old French, from Latin *fōrma,* form, contour, shape.]

Synonyms: *contour, figure, outline, profile, shape.*

-form *suffix.* Indicates having the form of; for example, **cuneiform, cruciform.** [New Latin *-formis,* from Latin *-fōrmis,* from *fōrma,* FORM.]

for·mal (fôr′məl) *adj.* **1. a.** Pertaining to the external, extrinsic aspect of something as distinguished from its substance or material. **b.** Pertaining to structure rather than content: *formal logic.* **2.** *Philosophy.* Being or pertaining to the essential form or constitution of something. **3.** Following or adhering to accepted forms, conventions, or regulations: *a formal requirement.* **4.** Done in proper, regular, or official form: *a formal reprimand.* **5.** Characterized by strict or meticulous observation of forms; ceremonial; proper. **6.** Stiff or cold; ceremonious: *a formal manner.* **7.** Done for the sake of form only; having the outward appearance but wanting in substance: *a purely formal greeting.*

∼*n.* **1.** An occasion or ceremony requiring formal attire. **2.** Formal attire. [Middle English, from Old French, from Latin *fōrmālis,* of or for form, from *fōrma,* FORM.] **—for·mal·ly** *adv.*

for·mal·de·hyde (fôr-măl′də-hīd′) *n.* A colorless, gaseous compound, HCHO, used to manufacture melamine and phenolic resins, fertilizers, dyes, and, in aqueous solution, as a preservative and disinfectant. [German *Formaldehyd* : FORM(IC ACID) + ALDEHYDE.]

For·ma·lin (fôr′mə-lĭn) *n.* A trademark for a 37 percent by weight solution of formaldehyde in water with some methanol, used especially for preserving biological specimens.

for·mal·ism (fôr′mə-lĭz′əm) *n.* **1.** Rigorous or excessive adherence to recognized forms, especially as opposed to content. **2.** The mathematical or logical structure of a scientific argument, especially as distinguished from its content. **3.** In the philosophy of mathematics, the doctrine that mathematics has no subject matter or content and is purely the study of symbols and their rule-governed configurations and manipulation. **—for·mal·ist** *n.* **—for·mal·is·tic** (fôr′mə-lĭs′tĭk) *adj.*

for·mal·i·ty (fôr-măl′ə-tē) *n., pl.* **-ties. 1.** The quality or condition of

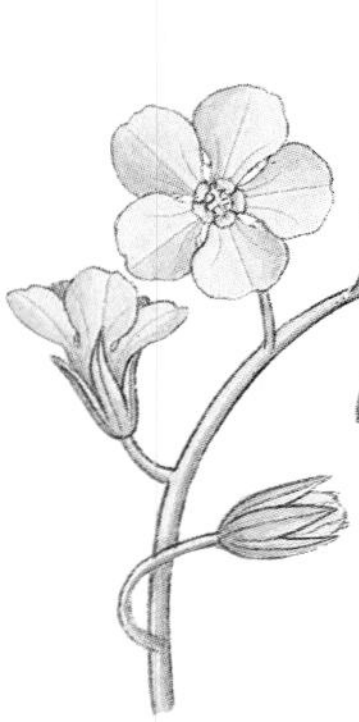

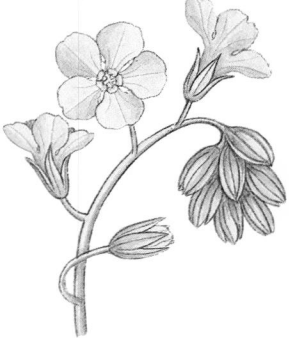

forget-me-not *The 19th-century poet Samuel Taylor Coleridge gave this Eurasian and North American wildflower its common English name. In his poem* The Keepsake, *published in 1802, he described it as "That blue and bright-eyed flowerlet of the brook, Hope's gentle gem, the sweet forget-me-not." This is the common forget-me-not,* Myosotis arvensis.

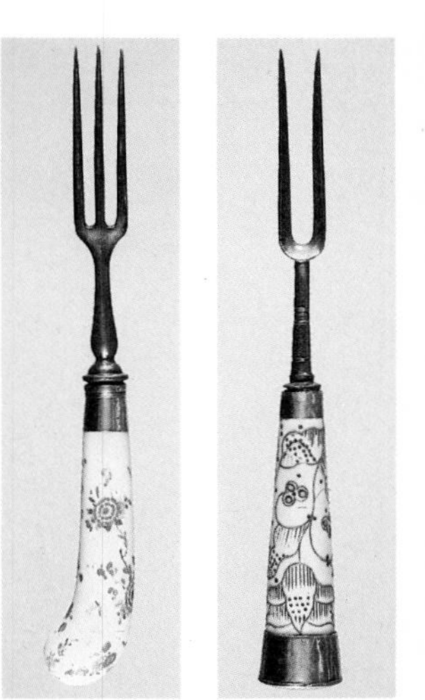

fork *Knives and spoons are very ancient eating utensils. But forks are much more recent; in Britain, for example, they were not in common use until about 1700. Early forks were two-pronged, like the ivory-handled one shown here on the right, which dates from 1685. The three-pronged porcelain-handled fork on the left was made between 1750 and 1775.*

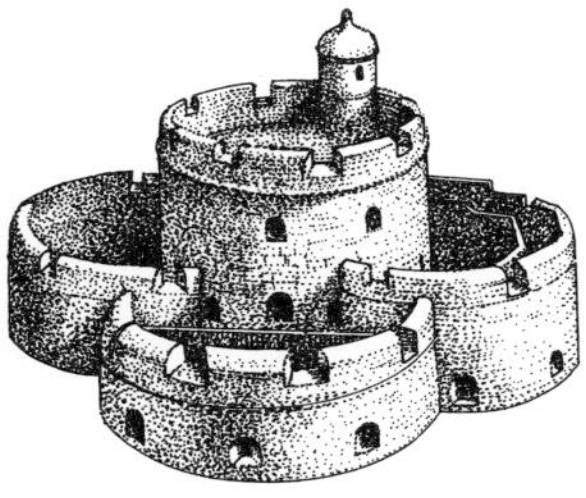

fort *The English king Henry VIII built a chain of coastal forts, like this one at St. Mawes, Cornwall. The cloverleaf design of the outer walls was intended to deflect cannon shot.*

being formal. **2.** Rigorous or ceremonious adherence to established forms, rules, or customs. **3.** An established form, rule, or custom. **4.** Something done for the sake of form, custom, or decorum.

for·mal·ize (fôr'mə-līz') *tr.v.* **-ized, -izing, -izes. 1.** To give a definite form or shape to. **2. a.** To render formal. **b.** *Logic.* To translate into logical symbolism. **3.** To give formal endorsement to. **—for·mal·i·za·tion** *n.*

formal logic *n.* The study of the properties of propositions by abstraction and analysis of their form rather than their content, especially by the use of rules and symbols. See **symbolic logic.**

form·am·id·ase (fôr-măm'ĭ-dās', -dāz') *n.* An enzyme that participates in the catabolism of the amino acid tryptophan. [FORM(IC ACID) + AMID(E) + -ASE.]

For·man (fôr'mən), **Miloš** (1932–). Czech film director, known for his use of comedy and disturbing realism. His films include *A Blonde in Love* (1965) and *One Flew Over the Cuckoo's Nest* (1975).

for·mant (fôr'mənt) *n.* Any of several frequency regions of relatively great intensity in a sound spectrum, which together determine the characteristic quality of a vowel sound, musical instrument, or other sound source. [German *Formant,* from Latin *fōrmāns* (stem *fōrmant-*), present participle of *fōrmāre,* to form, from *fōrma,* FORM.]

for·mat (fôr'măt') *n.* **1.** A plan for the organization and arrangement of a production, such as a television program. **2.** The material form or layout of a publication. **3.** The way in which data are arranged in a computer storage device.
~*tr.v.* **-matted, -matting, -mats.** To put into a particular format; especially, to arrange (data) in a suitable format for use in a computer. [French, from German *Format,* from Latin *fōrmātus,* past participle of *fōrmāre,* to form, from *fōrma,* FORM.]

for·mate (fôr'māt') *n.* A salt or ester of formic acid. [FORM(IC ACID) + -ATE.]

for·ma·tion (fôr-mā'shən) *n.* **1.** The process of forming or producing. **2.** Something that is formed. **3.** The manner or style in which something is formed. **4.** A specific arrangement, configuration, or deployment, as of troops, aircraft in flight, dancers, or the like. Also used adjectivally: *formation dancing.* **5.** *Geology.* The primary unit of lithostratigraphy, consisting of a succession of strata useful for mapping or description. **6.** *Ecology.* A plant community, such as a savanna, that extends over a large area. **—for·ma·tion·al** *adj.*

for·ma·tive (fôr'mə-tĭv) *adj.* **1.** Forming or capable of forming. **2.** Susceptible of transformation by growth and development. **3.** Pertaining to formation, growth, or development: *a formative stage.* **4.** Pertaining to the formation or inflection of words.
~*n.* The element of a word that is not contained in the base and that gives the word a suitable form.

form class *n.* A set of linguistic forms that share one or more morphological or syntactic features, such as a plural or past tense form.

form drag *n.* A component of the drag on a body moving through a fluid that is dependent on the shape of the body.

form·er[1] (fôr'mər) *n.* **1.** One that forms. **2.** A tool or device that gives something a particular shape or form.

for·mer[2] (fôr'mər) *adj.* **1.** Occurring earlier in time; pertaining to a period previous to the one specified. **2.** Coming before in place or order. **3.** Being the first mentioned of two.
~*n.* The first mentioned of two. Used with *the.* [Middle English, earlier, from *forme,* first, from Old English *forma.*]

Usage: *Former* is applicable only to the first of two in an enumeration. When reference to the first of three or more is intended, either *first* or *first-named* is possible, but often a repetition of the name of the person or thing involved is an aid to clarity.

for·mer·ly (fôr'mər-lē) *adv.* At a former time; previously.

form·fit·ting (fôrm'fĭt'ĭng) *adj.* Closely fitted to the body.

for·mic (fôr'mĭk) *adj.* **1.** Of or pertaining to ants. **2.** Of, derived from, or containing formic acid. [Latin *formīca,* ant.]

For·mi·ca (fôr-mī'kə) *n.* A trademark for any of various high-pressure laminated plastic sheets of melamine and phenolic materials used especially for chemical and heat-resistant surfaces.

formic acid *n.* A colorless caustic fuming liquid, HCOOH, used in dyeing and finishing textiles and paper and in the manufacture of fumigants, insecticides, and refrigerants. [From FORMIC (from its natural occurrence in ants).]

for·mi·car·y (fôr'mĭ-kĕr'ē) *n., pl.* **-ies. 1.** A nest of ants; an anthill. **2.** A glass-sided box containing a colony of ants kept for observational purposes. [Medieval Latin *formīcārium,* from Latin *formīca,* ant.]

for·mi·cate (fôr'mĭ-kāt') *intr.v.* **-cated, -cating, -cates. 1.** To swarm with or as if with ants. **2.** To crawl like ants. [Latin *formīcāre,* to swarm like ants, from *formīca,* ant. See **formic.**]

for·mi·ca·tion (fôr'mĭ-kā'shən) *n.* A spontaneous abnormal sensation of ants or other insects running over the skin.

for·mi·civ·o·rous (fôr'mĭ-sĭv'ər-əs) *adj.* Feeding on ants. [Latin *formica,* ant + -VOROUS.]

for·mi·da·ble (fôr'mə-də-bəl) *adj.* **1.** Arousing fear, dread, or alarm. **2.** Admirable or awe-inspiring. **3.** Difficult to surmount, defeat, or undertake; awesome. [Middle English, from Old French, from Latin *formīdābilis,* from *formīdāre,* to dread, from *formīdō,* fright, fear.] **—for·mi·da·bil·i·ty, for·mi·da·ble·ness** *n.* **—for·mi·da·bly** *adv.*

form·less (fôrm'lĭs) *adj.* Having no specified form; shapeless.

form letter *n.* A usually impersonal letter in a standardized format that may be sent to different people or to large numbers of people.

Formosa. See **Taiwan.**

For·mo·sa Strait (fôr-mō'sə). Arm of the Pacific Ocean between Taiwan and the coast of Fujian province, China. It links the East China and South China seas.

for·mu·la (fôr'myə-lə) *n., pl.* **-las** or **-lae** (-lē'). **1.** An established form of words or symbols for use in a ceremony or procedure. **2.** An utterance of conventional notions or beliefs; a hackneyed expression; cliché. **3.** *Chemistry.* **a.** A symbolic representation of the composition or of the composition and structure of a chemical compound. **b.** The chemical compound so represented. **4.** A prescription of ingredients in fixed proportion; recipe. **5.** A mathematical statement, especially an equation, of a rule, principle, answer, or other logical relation. **6.** A method, procedure, or specified combination of actions tending toward an end or result: *a formula for success; a peace formula.* **7.** A category of racing car defined by its engine size, weight, and fuel capacity. **8.** A specially prepared liquid food for infants. [Latin *fōrmula,* diminutive of *fōrma,* FORM.] **—for·mu·la·ic** (fôr'myə-lā'ĭk) *adj.*

for·mu·la·rize (fôr'myə-lə-rīz') *tr.v.* **-rized, -rizing, -rizes.** To formulate. **—for·mu·la·ri·za·tion** *n.*

for·mu·lar·y (fôr'myə-lĕr'ē) *n., pl.* **-ies. 1.** A book or other collection of formulas. **2.** A statement expressed in formulas. **3.** A formula. **4.** A book containing the names of pharmaceutical substances, their uses, and the means by which they are prepared.
~*adj.* **1.** Using or containing formulas. **2.** Pertaining to formulas.

for·mu·late (fôr'myə-lāt') *tr.v.* **-lated, -lating, -lates. 1.** To state as a formula. **2.** To express in systematic terms or concepts. **3.** To devise; invent. **4.** To prepare according to a specific formula. **—for·mu·la·tion** *n.* **—for·mu·la·tor** *n.*

formula weight *n.* **Molecular weight** *(see).*

for·mu·lism (fôr'myə-lĭz'əm) *n.* Adherence to or dependence upon formulas. **—for·mu·lis·tic** (fôr'myə-lĭs'tĭk) *adj.*

for·mu·lize (fôr'myə-līz') *tr.v.* **-lized, -lizing, -lizes.** To formulate. **—for·mu·li·za·tion** *n.* **—for·mu·liz·er** *n.*

form word *n.* A **function word** *(see).*

for·myl (fôr'mĭl) *n.* The univalent radical CHO. [FORM(IC ACID) + -YL.]

For·nax (fôr'năks') *n.* A constellation in the Southern Hemisphere near Sculptor and Eridanus. [Latin *fornāx,* furnace, oven.]

for·ni·cate[1] (fôr'nĭ-kĭt, -kāt') *adj.* Also **for·ni·cat·ed** (-kā'tĭd). *Biology.* Arched or vaulted. [Latin *fornicātus,* from *fornix* (stem *fornic-*), vault, arch.]

for·ni·cate[2] (fôr'nĭ-kāt') *intr.v.* **-cated, -cating, -cates.** To commit fornication. [Late Latin *fornicārī,* from *fornix* (stem *fornic-*), vault, arch, in the late republican period a vaulted underground dwelling in Rome where poor people and prostitutes lived, hence (especially in early Christian writings) a brothel.] **—for·ni·ca·tor** *n.*

for·ni·ca·tion (fôr'nĭ-kā'shən) *n.* **1.** Voluntary sexual intercourse between two unmarried persons. **2.** Voluntary sexual intercourse between a married person and an unmarried person.

for·nix (fôr'nĭks) *n., pl.* **-nices** (-nə-sēz'). **1.** *Anatomy.* Any vaultlike structure; especially the *fornix cerebri,* an arched band of white matter in the brain between the hippocampus and hypothalamus. **2.** A vaulted space. [New Latin, from Latin, vault, arch.]

for·sake (fôr-sāk', fər-) *tr.v.* **-sook** (-so͝ok'), **-saken** (-sā'kən), **-saking, -sakes. 1.** To give up; renounce. **2.** To leave altogether; desert; abandon. [Forsake, forsook, forsaken; Middle English *forsaken, forsok, forsaken,* to object to, reject, from Old English *forsacan, forsōc, forsacen.*]

for·sooth (fôr-so͞oth', fər-) *adv. Archaic.* In truth; indeed. [Middle English *for soth,* Old English *forsōth* : FOR + SOOTH.]

for·spent, fore·spent (fôr-spĕnt', fər-) *adj. Archaic.* Worn out with exertion; exhausted.

For·ster (fôr'stər), **Edward Morgan,** known as E.M. Forster (1879–1970). British novelist and essayist. Following his first novel, *Where Angels Fear to Tread* (1905), he wrote such classics as *A Room with a View* (1908), *Howards End* (1910), and his masterpiece, *A Passage to India* (1924).

for·ster·ite (fôr'stə-rīt') *n.* A white or yellow olivine mineral, Mg_2SiO_4. [After Johann *Forster* (1729–98), Prussian naturalist.]

for·swear, fore·swear (fôr-swâr', fōr-) *v.* **-swore** (-swôr', -swōr'), **-sworn** (-swôrn', -swōrn'), **-swearing, -swears.** —*tr.* **1.** To renounce or forsake unalterably. **2.** To disavow or repudiate unalterably. **3.** To perjure (oneself). —*intr.* To swear falsely; commit perjury. [Middle English *forsweren,* from Old English *forswerian,* to swear falsely : *for-,* wrongly + *swerian,* to SWEAR.]

for·syth·i·a (fôr-sĭth'ē-ə, fər-) *n.* Any shrub of the genus *Forsythia,* native to Asia, cultivated for its early-blooming yellow flowers. [After William *Forsyth* (1737–1804), English botanist.]

fort (fôrt, fōrt) *n. Abbr.* **ft.** A fortified place or position stationed with troops; fortification; bastion. **—hold the fort.** To manage or cope, especially in a difficult situation, while acting as a substitute for someone else. [Middle English, from Old French *fort,* from *fort(e),* strong, from Latin *fortis.*]

for·ta·lice (fôr'tə-lĭs) *n.* A minor defensive structure or position; a small fort. [Middle English, from Medieval Latin *fortalitia,* from Latin *fortis,* strong.]

Fort-de-France (fôr'də-fräNs'). Capital of Martinique. It is a tourist resort and exports sugar, bananas, and rum.

forte[1] (fôrt, fōrt, fôr'tā) *n.* **1.** Something in which a person excels; strong point. **2.** The strong part of a sword blade, between the middle and the hilt. Compare **foible.** [Old French *fort,* from adjective, "strong." See **fort.**]

for·te[2] (fôr'tā) *adv. Abbr.* **f, F** *Music.* Loudly; forcefully. Used as a direction.

~*n. Music.* A note, passage, or chord played forte.
~*adj. Music.* Loud; forceful. [Italian, "strongly," from adjective, "strong," from Latin *fortis.*]

for·te·pi·an·o (fôr′tā-pē-ăn′ō, -ä′nō) *adv. Music.* Loudly and then softly. Used as a direction
~*adj. Music.* Loud and then soft. [Italian : *forte,* loud + *piano,* soft.]

for·te·pi·an·o (fôr′tā-pē-ăn′ō) *n.* The pianoforte of the 18th and 19th centuries, as distinct from the modern piano.

Fort Fred·er·i·ca National Monument (frĕd′ə-rē′kə). Ruins of an early British fort, on St. Simon Island in southeastern Georgia.

forth (fôrth, fōrth) *adv.* **1.** Forward in time, place, or order; on; onward. **2.** Out into view, as from confinement or concealment. **3.** Away from a specified place; abroad.
~*prep. Archaic.* Out of; forth from. [Middle English *forth,* Old English *forth.*]

Forth, Firth of (fôrth, fōrth). The estuary of the Forth River, Scotland, forming an arm of the North Sea. It is *c.* 80 kilometers (50 miles) long and some 30 kilometers (18 miles) wide at its entrance. It is a major seaway with several ports, including Edinburgh's port, Leith, and the Rosyth naval base. Three bridges span the firth: the Forth Bridge (1936), the Forth Road Bridge (1964), one of the longest suspension bridges in Europe, and the Forth Railway Bridge (1890), the world's first cantilever bridge.

forth·com·ing (fôrth-kŭm′ĭng, fōrth-) *adj.* **1.** About to appear; approaching; coming: *the forthcoming elections.* **2.** Available when required or as promised. **3.** Responsive; open; informative. **—forth·com·ing·ness** *n.*

forth·right (fôrth′rīt′, fōrth′-) *adj.* Straightforward; frank; candid: *a forthright appraisal.*
~*adv.* **1.** Unhesitatingly; frankly. **2.** *Archaic.* At once; directly; immediately. **—forth·right·ly** *adv.* **—forth·right·ness** *n.*

forth·with (fôrth-wĭth′, -wĭth′, fōrth-) *adv.* At once; immediately; without delay. —See Usage note at **immediately.**

for·ti·eth (fôr′tē-ĭth) *n.* **1.** The ordinal number 40 in a series. **2.** Any of 40 equal parts. **—for·ti·eth** *adj. & adv.*

for·ti·fi·ca·tion (fôr′tə-fĭ-kā′shən) *n. Abbr.* **ft.** **1.** The act, science, or art of fortifying. **2.** Something that serves to defend, strengthen, or fortify; especially, a military defensive work.

fortified wine *n.* An alcoholic drink, such as sherry or port, made from wine to which extra alcohol, usually in the form of brandy, has been added.

for·ti·fy (fôr′tə-fī′) *v.* **-fied, -fying, -fies.** —*tr.* **1.** To strengthen and secure (a position) with fortifications. **2.** To add strength to (a structure) by reinforcement; reinforce. **3.** To impart physical strength to; invigorate: *The coffee fortified her.* **4.** To give moral or mental strength to; encourage: *He fortified his troubled spirit by praying.* **5.** To corroborate; confirm; support. **6.** To strengthen or increase the content of (a substance), as by adding extra alcohol to wine or vitamins to food: *milk fortified with vitamin D.* —*intr.* To prepare defensive works; build fortifications. [Middle English *fortifien,* from Old French *fortifier,* from Late Latin *fortificāre,* from Latin *fortis,* strong.] **—for·ti·fi·a·ble** *adj.* **—for·ti·fi·er** *n.*

for·tis (fôr′tĭs) *adj. Phonetics.* Pronounced with tension and strong articulation. Said of certain consonants such as *f* and *p.* Compare **lenis.**
~*n. Phonetics.* A fortis consonant. [New Latin, from Latin *fortis,* strong.]

for·tis·si·mo (fôr-tĭs′ə-mō′) *adv. Abbr.* **ff** *Music.* Very loudly. Used as a direction.
~*n., pl.* **fortissimos.** *Music.* A fortissimo note, passage, or chord. [Italian, from Latin *fortissimus,* superlative of *fortis,* strong.] **—for·tis·si·mo** *adj.*

for·ti·tude (fôr′tə-to͞od′, -tyo͞od′) *n.* Strength of mind that allows one to endure pain or adversity with courage. —See Synonyms at **courage.** [Middle English, from Latin *fortitūdō,* from *fortis,* strong.] **—for·ti·tu·di·nous** (fôr′tə-to͞od′n-əs, -tyo͞od′n-əs) *adj.*

Fort Knox (nŏks). U.S. military reservation, occupying 44,550 hectares (110,000 acres) in northern Kentucky. Most of the country's reserves of gold bullion are stored in the steel and concrete vaults of the depository built here in 1936–37.

Fort Lamy. See **N'djamena.**

Fort Lar·a·mie National Historic Site (lăr′ə-mē). Area in southwestern Wyoming, site of a trading post on the Oregon Trail.

Fort Lau·der·dale (lô′dər-dāl′). City and resort on the Atlantic coast of southeastern Florida. It is built on the site of a fort established in 1837 during the Seminole War.

Fort Leav·en·worth (lĕv′ən-wûrth′). A military post in northeastern Kansas on the Missouri River. It was established in 1827 to protect travelers on the Santa Fe Trail. The oldest U.S. military prison (1874) is here.

Fort Ma·tan·zas National Monument (mə-tăn′zəs). Site of historic Spanish ruins in St. Augustine, northeastern Florida.

Fort Mc·Hen·ry (mək-hĕn′rē). A former military post in Baltimore harbor. In the War of 1812 it was bombarded (September 13–14, 1814) by the British, but it resisted the attack, inspiring Francis Scott Key's poem "The Star-Spangled Banner." The restored fort is now a national monument.

Fort Mon·roe (mən-rō′). A fort in southeastern Virginia, at the entrance to Chesapeake Bay and Hampton Roads. The English built fortifications here in 1609 and 1727. The present six-sided fort (1819–34), surrounded by a moat, is the only one of its kind left in the United States.

fort·night (fôrt′nīt′) *n.* A period of 14 days and nights; two weeks. [Middle English *fourtenight,* Old English *fēowertīene niht* : FOURTEEN + NIGHT.]

fort·night·ly (fôrt′nīt′lē) *adj.* Happening or appearing once in or every two weeks.
~*adv.* Once in two weeks; every fortnight.
~*n., pl.* **fortnightlies.** A publication issued every two weeks.

Fort Pu·las·ki National Monument (pə-lăs′kē). Site of a brick fortification on an island in southeastern Georgia, built in 1829–47 and captured by Union troops in April 1862.

FORTRAN, For·tran (fôr′trăn′) *n.* A computer programming language for problems that can be expressed in algebraic terms. [*For*mula *tran*slation.]

for·tress (fôr′trĭs) *n.* A fortified place, especially a large and permanent military stronghold, often including a town; a fort.
~*tr.v.* **fortressed, -tressing, -tresses.** To strengthen or fortify with or as if with a fortress; fortify. [Middle English *forteresse,* from Old French, from Vulgar Latin *fortaritia* (unattested), from Latin *fortis,* strong.]

Fort Sum·ter (sŭm′tər). Fortification, built 1829–60, at the entrance to Charleston harbor, South Carolina. It was the site of the opening engagement of the Civil War (April 12–14, 1861). Confederate forces took the fort after a 34-hour bombardment and retained control until April 1865.

for·tu·i·tous (fôr-to͞o′ə-təs, fôr-tyo͞o′-) *adj.* Happening by accident or chance; unplanned. [Latin *fortuitus,* from *forte,* by chance, ablative of *fors,* chance.] **—for·tu·i·tous·ly** *adv.* **—for·tu·i·tous·ness** *n.*
Usage: *Fortuitous* is often confused with *fortunate.* What is *fortuitous* happens by chance or accident or without plan; *fortunate* and *lucky* are not thus restricted in meaning. What is *fortuitous* can also be *fortunate* or *lucky,* but to employ *fortuitous* in the sense of those terms, without clear indication in the context of chance or accident, is loose usage. The following example, in which there is no such indication, is considered unacceptable: *The meeting proved fortuitous; I came away with a much better idea of my role.*

for·tu·i·ty (fôr-to͞o′ə-tē, fôr-tyo͞o′-) *n., pl.* **-ties.** **1.** An accidental occurrence. **2.** The quality or condition of being fortuitous.

For·tu·na (fôr-to͞o′nə, -tyo͞o′nə). The Roman goddess of fortune. [Latin *Fortūna,* from *fortūna,* FORTUNE.]

for·tu·nate (fôr′chə-nĭt) *adj.* **1.** Occurring by good fortune or favorable chance; bringing something good and unforeseen; auspicious. **2.** Having unusual good fortune; lucky. **—for·tu·nate·ly** *adv.*

for·tune (fôr′chən) *n.* **1.** A hypothetical, often personified force or power that favorably or unfavorably governs the events of one's life: *Fortune is on our side.* **2.** The good or bad luck that is to befall someone; destiny; fate: *It is my fortune to be a failure.* **3.** Luck, especially when good; success: *Fortune accompanied his endeavors.* **4. a.** A person's condition or standing in life determined by material possessions or money. **b.** Extensive amounts of material possessions or money. **c.** A large sum of money. **5.** Material or financial success; prosperity. [Middle English, fortune, chance, luck, from Old French, from Latin *fortūna,* chance, fate, (good or bad) luck, from *fors*†, chance, luck.]

fortune cookie *n.* A small cookie made from a thin layer of dough folded and baked around a slip of paper bearing a prediction of fortune or a maxim.

fortune hunter *n.* A person who seeks to become wealthy, especially through marriage.

for·tune·tell·er (fôr′chən-tĕl′ər) *n.* A person who, usually for a fee, will undertake to predict future events in a person's life. **—for·tune·tell·ing** *n. & adj.*

Fort Van·cou·ver National Historic Site (văn-ko͞o′vər). Area in southwestern Washington State, site of a Hudson's Bay Company post (1825–49) and later of a U.S. Army fort.

Fort Wayne (wān). A city of northeastern Indiana. The French built a trading post here *c.* 1680. Today the city is a major railroad, shipping, distribution, and manufacturing center.

Fort Worth (wûrth). City in northern Texas. An army post was established here in 1847, and the settlement became a railroad town and a center for meatpacking and later an oil refining center. Since 1945 it has been dominated by the aircraft industry.

for·ty (fôr′tē) *n., pl.* **-ties.** **1. a.** The cardinal number that is ten more than thirty. **b.** A symbol representing this, such as 40 or XL. **2.** A set made up of forty persons or things. **3.** The fortieth in a series. **4.** A size, as in clothing, designated as forty. **5. forties. a.** The range of numbers from 40 to 49, considered as a range of age, price, temperature, or the like. **b.** The years numbered 40 to 49 in a century. Also used adjectivally: *a forties film.* **—for·ty** *adj. & pron.*

for·ty-five (fôr′tē-fīv′) *n.* **1.** A .45-caliber pistol. **2.** A phonograph record, a **single** *(see).*

Forty-Five *n.* In British history, the later **Jacobite Rebellion** *(see)* of 1745. Preceded by *the.*

for·ty-nin·er (fôr′tē-nī′nər) *n.* One who took part in the 1849 California gold rush.

forty winks *n. Informal. Used with a singular verb.* A short nap.

fo·rum (fôr′əm, fōr′-) *n., pl.* **-rums** or **fora** (fôr′ə, fōr′ə). **1.** The public square or marketplace of an ancient Roman city that was the assembly place for judicial and other public activity. **2. a.** Any public meeting place for open discussion. **b.** A meeting for open discussion. **c.** Any medium for open discussion, such as a magazine or radio or television program. **3.** A court of law; a tribunal. **4. Forum.** The forum in ancient Rome. [Middle English, from Latin, forum, place out-of-doors.]

PRONUNCIATION KEY

ă, pat; ā, pay; âr, care; ä, father, are; b, bib; ch, church; d, deed; ĕ, pet; ē, be; f, fife; g, gag; h, hat; hw, which; ĭ, pit; ī, pie; îr, pier; j, judge; k, kick; l, lid, needle; m, mum; n, no, sudden; ng, thing; ŏ, pot; ō, toe; ô, paw, for; oi, noise; ou, out; o͝o, book; o͞o, boot; p, pop; r, roar; s, sauce; sh, ship, dish; t, tight; th, thin, path; *th,* this, bathe; ŭ, cut; ûr, fur; v, valve; w, with; y, yes; z, zebra, size; zh, vision; ə, about, item, edible, gallop, circus, peaceful

IN FOREIGN WORDS:

à, *Fr.* ami; œ, *Fr.* feu, *Ger.* schön; ü, *Fr.* tu, *Ger.* über; KH, *Ger.* ich, *Scot.* loch; N, *Fr.* bon; y′, *Fr.* Compiègne

STRESS MARKS:

Primary stress: ′ **in·cite′** (ĭn-sīt′)
Secondary stress: ′ **in′sight′** (ĭn′sīt′)

for·ward (fôr'wərd) *adj.* **1. a.** At, near, or belonging to the front; fore: *the forward part of a train.* **b.** Toward the front of a ship: *a forward cabin.* **c.** Lying ahead or in the line of motion. **2. a.** Going, tending, or moving toward a position in front: *a forward thrust of a sword; a forward fall down a flight of stairs.* **b.** *Sports.* Going, tending, or moving toward an opponent's goal. **3. a.** Ardently inclined; eager; anxious. **b.** Presumptuous; impudent; bold: *a forward manner.* **4.** Progressive, especially technologically, politically, or economically: *a forward new nation; a forward concept.* **5.** Mentally, physically, socially, or biologically advanced; precocious: *a forward child.* **6.** Prompt; eager. **7.** For the future; completed or made in advance: *My broker does not intend to bid on forward contracts for corn.* —See Synonyms at **shameless**.
~*adv.* Also **for·wards** (for sense 1). **1.** Toward or tending to the front; frontward: *step forward.* **2.** In or toward the future; at a future time; onward: *I look forward to seeing you.* **3.** Into view or prominence; forth; out: *Neighbors came forward to help.*
~*n. Abbr.* **fwd.** *Sports.* **1.** A player in certain games, such as basketball or soccer, who is part of the front line and usually plays in an attacking position. **2.** The position itself.
~*tr.v.* **forwarded, -warding, -wards. 1.** To send on (letters, for example) to a subsequent destination or address. **2.** To advance; promote; advocate. **3.** To prepare (a book) for the finisher by supplying with a paper cover. [Middle English *for(e)ward*, Old English *foreweard* : FORE- + -WARD.]

for·ward·er (fôr'wər-dər) *n.* One that forwards; especially, a forwarding agent.

forwarding agent *n.* An agent, agency, or other business that facilitates and assures the passage of received goods to their destination; a forwarder of goods.

for·ward-look·ing (fôr'wərd-lŏŏk'ĭng) *adj.* **1.** Having advanced and enlightened views; progressive. **2.** Careful of and concerned with the future.

for·ward·ly (fôr'wərd-lē) *adv.* **1.** At or toward the front; forward. **2.** In a bold or forward manner; presumptuously. **3.** With dispatch or eagerness; promptly.

for·ward·ness (fôr'wərd-nĭs) *n.* **1.** The condition or state of being forward; readiness; zeal; eagerness. **2.** An advanced state of development or progress; precocity. **3.** Overeagerness to promote oneself; audacity; boldness.

forward pass *n. Football. Abbr.* **fp** A pass thrown in the direction of the opponent's goal.

for·wards (fôr'wərdz) *adv.* Forward (sense 1).

for·went. Past tense of **forgo.**

for·why (fôr-hwī') *adv. Obsolete.* For what reason; why.
~*conj. Obsolete.* Because; since. [Middle English *forwhy*, Old English *for hwȳ* : FOR + *hwȳ*, instrumental of *hwæt*, WHAT.]

for·worn, fore·worn (fôr-wôrn', -wōrn') *adj. Archaic.* Worn-out. [Past participle of obsolete *forwear*, from Middle English *forweren*, to hollow out : FOR- (destruction) + WEAR.]

forzando. Variant of **sforzando.**

Fos·bur·y flop (fŏz'bĕr'ē flŏp') *n.* A technique in modern high-jumping whereby the jumper goes over the bar headfirst with the back toward the ground and the face up. [After Richard *Fosbury*, U.S. Olympic champion (Mexico, 1968).]

fos·sa¹ (fŏs'ə) *n., pl.* **fossae** (fŏs'ē'). *Anatomy.* A hollow or depression, as in a bone. [Latin, ditch, trench, from the feminine past participle of *fodere*, to dig.]

fossa² *n.* **1.** A carnivorous Madagascan mammal, *Cryptoprocta ferox*, of the family Viverridae, having a long tail, short legs, and a pointed snout. **2.** Any animal of the genus *Fossa*, which includes the Madagascan civets. [Malagasy.]

fosse, foss (fŏs) *n.* A ditch; especially, a moat around a fortification. [Middle English, from Old French, from Latin *fossa.*]

fos·sick (fŏs'ĭk) *v.* **-sicked, -sicking, -sicks.** *Chiefly Australian.* —*intr.* **1.** To search for gold, especially by reworking washings or waste piles. **2.** To rummage or search, especially for a possible profit. —*tr.* To search for by or as if by rummaging. [Perhaps variant of dialectal *fussick*, to bustle about, from FUSS.] —**fos·sick·er** *n.*

fos·sil (fŏs'əl) *n.* **1.** A remnant or trace of an organism of a past geologic age, as a skeleton, footprint, or leaf imprint, embedded in the earth's crust. **2.** One that is outdated or antiquated; especially, a person with outmoded ideas. **3.** An obsolete word or word element used only in an idiom, as *fro* in *to and fro.*
~*adj.* **1.** Of or pertaining to a fossil or fossils. **2.** Derived from fossils: *Coal is a fossil fuel.* [Latin *fossilis*, dug up, from *fossus*, past participle of *fodere*, to dig.]

fossil fuel *n.* A carbon or hydrocarbon fuel, such as coal, petroleum, or natural gas, derived from the decomposition of organisms of an earlier geologic period.

fos·sil·if·er·ous (fŏs'ə-lĭf'ər-əs) *adj.* Containing fossils. [FOSSIL + -FEROUS.]

fos·sil·ize (fŏs'ə-līz') *v.* **-ized, -izing, -izes.** —*tr.* **1.** To convert into a fossil. **2.** To make outmoded, rigid, or fixed; antiquate. —*intr.* **1.** To become a fossil. **2.** To become outmoded, rigid, or fixed. —**fos·sil·i·za·tion** *n.*

fos·so·ri·al (fŏ-sôr'ē-əl, -sōr'ē-əl) *adj. Zoology.* Adapted for or used in burrowing or digging. [Medieval Latin *fossorius*, from Latin *fossus*, past participle of *fodere*, to dig.]

fos·ter (fô'stər, fŏs'tər) *tr.v.* **-tered, -tering, -ters. 1.** To bring up, rear, or nurture; especially, to bring up (a child that is not one's own or one's adopted child). **2.** To promote the development or growth of; encourage; cultivate: *fostered his love of music.* **3.** To nurse; cherish: *foster a secret hope.* **4.** *Chiefly British.* To place (a child) in a foster home.
~*adj.* Receiving, sharing, or affording parental care and nurture although not related through legal or blood ties: *a foster child; a foster home.* [Middle English *fostren*, Old English *fōstrian*, to provide with food, nourish, from *fōstor*, food.] —**fos·ter·age** *n.*

Fos·ter (fô'stər, fŏs'tər), **Stephen Collins** (1826–64). U.S. songwriter. Among the popular quasi-folk songs he composed are "The Old Folks at Home," "My Old Kentucky Home," and "Swanee River."

fos·ter·ling (fô'stər-lĭng, fŏs'tər-) *n.* A foster child.

Foth·er·ing·hay (fŏth'ər-ĭng-gā', fŏth'rĭng-). Small village in Northamptonshire in central England, on the Nene River. Its 12th-century castle, now marked only by a mound and a few railings, was the birthplace of Richard III and the scene of the imprisonment and execution in 1587 of Mary, Queen of Scots.

Fou·cault (fōō-kō'), **Jean Bernard Léon** (1819–68). French physicist. In 1851 he demonstrated the rotation of the earth with the Foucault pendulum. He also measured the velocity of light and showed that it travels more slowly in water. He is credited with inventing the gyroscope in 1852.

Foucault current *n.* An **eddy current** *(see).* [After J.B.L. FOU-CAULT.]

Foucault pendulum *n.* A simple pendulum suspended so that the plane of motion is not fixed, set into motion along a meridian, and appearing to turn clockwise in the Northern Hemisphere or counterclockwise in the Southern Hemisphere, demonstrating the axial rotation of the earth. [Demonstrated by J.B.L. FOUCAULT.]

fou·droy·ant (fōō-droi'ənt, fōō'drwä-yän') *adj.* **1.** Dazzling; stunning. **2.** Designating a disease occurring suddenly and with great severity. [French, present participle of *foudroyer*, to strike (as with lightning), from Old French *foudroier*, from *foudre*, lightning, from Latin *fulgur*, from *fulgēre*, to shine.]

fought. Past tense and past participle of **fight.**

foul (foul) *adj.* **fouler, foulest. 1.** Offensive to the senses; disgusting; revolting. **2.** Having an offensive odor; fetid; rank; smelly. **3.** Spoiled; rotten; putrid. Said especially of food. **4.** Full of dirt or mud; dirty; filthy. **5.** Immoral; wicked; detestable. **6.** Vulgar; obscene; profane: *foul language.* **7.** *Archaic.* Ugly; unattractive. **8.** *Informal.* Terrible; disagreeable; displeasing: *a foul party.* **9.** Unpleasant; bad; unfavorable. Often said of weather: *a foul day.* **10.** Not according to accepted standards or rules; unfair; dishonorable: *win by foul means.* **11.** *Sports.* Contrary to the rules of a game or sport. **12.** Covered with barnacles, weed, or the like. Said of a ship's bottom. **13.** Entangled; twisted: *a foul anchor.* **14.** Clogged or obstructed by something; blocked: *a foul ventilator shaft.* —See Synonyms at **dirty**.
~*n.* **1.** Anything that is dirty or foul. **2.** *Sports.* An infraction or violation of the rules of play. **3.** An entanglement or collision. **4.** A clogging or obstructing.
~*adv.* In a foul manner.
~*v.* **fouled, fouling, fouls.** —*tr.* **1.** To make dirty or foul; soil; pollute; sully. **2.** To bring into dishonor; disgrace; besmirch. **3.** To clog or obstruct; block. **4.** To entangle or catch. Used of a rope. **5.** To encrust (a ship's hull) with foreign matter, such as barnacles. **6.** *Sports.* To commit a foul against. **7.** To deposit excrement on. —*intr.* **1.** To become foul. **2.** *Sports.* To commit a foul. **3.** To become entangled or twisted: *The anchor fouled on a rock.* **4.** To become clogged or obstructed. —**foul out. 1.** *Baseball.* To make an out by hitting a foul ball that is caught before it touches the ground. **2.** *Sports.* To be put out of play by exceeding the number of permissible fouls. [Middle English *foul*, Old English *fūl*, from Germanic.] —**foul·ly** *adv.*

fou·lard (fōō-lärd') *n.* **1.** A lightweight twill or plain-woven fabric of silk or silk and cotton, usually having a small printed design. **2.** An article, especially a handkerchief or scarf, made of this fabric. [French *foulard*†.]

foul ball *n. Baseball.* A batted ball that touches the ground outside of fair territory.

foul line *n.* **1.** *Baseball.* Either of two straight lines extending from the rear of home plate to the boundary of the playing field to indicate the area in which a fair ball can be hit. **2.** *Basketball.* A line from which a player makes a foul shot. **3.** *Sports.* Any boundary limiting the playing area, especially in bowling and tennis.

foul-mouthed (foul'mouthd', -moutht') *adj.* Using obscene or scurrilous language.

foul·ness (foul'nĭs) *n.* **1.** The state or condition of being foul. **2.** Foul matter; filth; trash; waste. **3.** Obscenity; vulgarity; wickedness.

foul play *n.* **1.** Malicious or treacherous action, especially when involving violence. **2.** Conduct that is unsportsmanlike.

foul shot *n. Basketball.* An unguarded throw to the basket from the foul line awarded to a fouled player and scored as one point if successful.

foul tip *n. Baseball.* A pitched ball that is slightly deflected off the bat into the foul zone.

foul up *tr.v.* **1.** To make dirty; contaminate. **2.** To entangle, choke, or obstruct. **3.** To cause to go wrong because of mistakes, poor judgment, or unforeseen difficulties.

foul-up (foul'ŭp') *n. Informal.* **1.** A condition of confusion caused by poor judgment, mistakes, or unforeseen difficulties. **2.** Mechanical trouble.

Fosbury flop *The modern high-jumping technique, named after American Olympic champion Richard Fosbury, who first popularized it.*

found¹ (found) v. **founded, founding, founds.** —tr. **1.** To originate or establish (a business or college, for example); create; set up. **2.** To establish the foundation of (a building); lay a base for. **3.** To base (an argument or story, for example). Used with *on* or *upon.* —intr. To have a foundation or base. Used with *on* or *upon.* [Middle English *founden,* from Old French *fonder,* from Latin *fundāre,* to lay the foundation for, from *fundus,* bottom.]

found² tr.v. **founded, founding, founds. 1.** To melt (a material such as metal) and pour into a mold. **2.** To make (objects) in this fashion; cast. [Middle English *founden,* from Old French *fondre,* from Latin *fundere,* to pour, melt.]

found³. Past tense and past participle of **find.**

foun·da·tion (foun-dā′shən) n. **1.** The act of founding or state of being founded; especially, the establishment of an institution with provision for future maintenance. **2. a.** The basis on which a thing stands, is founded, or is supported; an underlying support. **b.** *Often* **foundations.** The part of a building or other structure that is below the ground and on which it rests or is supported. **c.** The grounds or basis for a claim, argument, story, or the like. **3.** Funds for the perpetual support of an institution, such as a school; an endowment. **4.** An institution supported by such a fund; an endowed institution. **5.** A foundation garment. **6.** A cosmetic used as a base for facial make-up. —See Synonyms at **base.** —**foun·da·tion·al** *adj.*

foundation garment n. A woman's supporting undergarment, such as a corset or girdle.

foundation stone n. A stone, usually bearing a commemorative inscription, normally laid at a ceremony marking the beginning of a building's construction.

found·er¹ (foun′dər) n. **1.** One who founds an institution, business, movement, or the like; one who initiates or lays the basis. **2.** One who casts metal: *a bell founder.*

foun·der² (foun′dər) v. **-dered, -dering, -ders.** —intr. **1.** To stumble; especially, to stumble and as a consequence go lame. Used of horses. **2.** To fail utterly; collapse or break down; give way. **3.** *Nautical.* To sink below the water. **4.** To cave in; fall in; sink. Used of ground or buildings. **5.** *Veterinary Medicine.* To be afflicted with founder. Used of horses. **6.** To become ill from overeating. Used of livestock. —tr. To cause to founder.
~n. *Veterinary Medicine.* A disease of horses, **laminitis** (*see*). [Middle English *foundren,* to fall to the ground, from Old French *fondrer,* to submerge, from Vulgar Latin *fundorāre* (unattested), from Latin *fundus,* bottom.]

founders' shares pl.n. Shares issued to the founders or original subscribers of a company and often carrying special privileges.

found·ing father (foun′dĭng) n. **1. Founding Father.** A member of the American Constitutional Convention of 1787. **2.** One considered as having an important role as an innovator or originator: *one of the founding fathers of socialism.*

found·ling (found′lĭng) n. A child deserted by parents whose identity is not known. [Middle English, probably from *founden,* past participle of *finden,* to **find.**]

foun·dry (foun′drē) n., pl. **-dries. 1.** An establishment in which metal castings are made. **2. a.** The art or operation of casting metals. **b.** The castings made in a foundry.

foundry proof n. A proof taken from composed type for a final check before plates are made.

fount¹ (fount) n. **1.** A fountain. **2.** Any source. Used especially in the phrase *a fount of wisdom.* **3.** A reservoir for liquids; especially, one for ink in a fountain pen. [Probably a back-formation from **FOUNTAIN.**]

fount² n. *Chiefly British.* A type font.

foun·tain (foun′tən) n. **1.** A spring; especially, the source of a stream. **2.** A source; point of origin. **3. a.** An artificially created jet or stream of water. **b.** A device that produces and contains such a jet or stream: *a drinking fountain.* **4.** A reservoir, tank, or chamber containing a supply of something, such as ink or oil, that can be siphoned off as needed. **5.** A soda fountain (*see*). [Middle English *fountaine,* spring, from Old French *fontaine,* from Late Latin *fontāna,* from *fontānus,* of a spring, from *fons* (stem *font-*), spring.]

foun·tain·head (foun′tən-hĕd′) n. **1.** A spring that is the source or head of a stream. **2.** A principal source or origin.

Fountain of Youth n. A legendary spring believed to have the power of rejuvenation, sought by Ponce de León and other explorers in Florida and the West Indies.

fountain pen n. A pen filled from an external source and containing an ink reservoir that automatically feeds the nib.

four (fôr, fōr) n. **1. a.** The cardinal number that is one more than three. **b.** A symbol representing this, such as 4, IV, or iv. **2.** A set made up of four persons or things. **3.** The fourth in a series. **4.** Four parts: *cut in four.* **5.** A size, as in clothing, designated as four. **6.** Four hours after midnight or midday. **7. a.** A racing boat for four oarsmen. **b.** Its crew. [Middle English, from Old English *fēower;* akin to German *vier,* Latin *quattuor,* Greek *tettares,* and Sanskrit *catur.*] —**four** *adj. & pron.*

four-ball (fôr′bôl′, fōr′-) n. A golf match between two pairs of players with only the score of the better-playing partner of each pair being counted at the end of the game.

four·chette (fōōr-shĕt′) n. **1.** A narrow, forked strip of material joining the front and back sections of the fingers of gloves. **2.** *Anatomy.* The fold of skin forming the posterior margin of the vulva. **3.** *Anatomy.* A **furcula** (*see*). [French, "fork," from Old French *forchete,*

diminutive of *forche,* fork, pitchfork, from Latin *furca,* (two-pronged) **FORK.**]

four-col·or (fôr′kŭl′ər) adj. Designating a color printing or photographic process in which three primary colors and black (used in combination) are transferred by four different plates or filters to a surface, reproducing the colors of the subject matter.

four-di·men·sion·al (fôr′dĭ-mĕn′shən-əl, fōr′-) adj. Exhibiting or being specified by four dimensions, especially the three spatial dimensions and single temporal dimension of relativity theory.

Four·drin·i·er (fōōr-drĭn′ē-ər) adj. Designating a papermaking machine used to produce paper in a continuous roll or web. [After Henry (1766–1854) and Sealy (died 1847) *Fourdrinier,* English papermakers.]

four-eyed fish (fôr′īd′, fōr′-). Either of two freshwater fishes, *Anableps anableps* or *A. microlepis,* of tropical America, having bulging eyes divided longitudinally, with the upper part adapted for aerial vision, the lower part for underwater vision.

four flush n. In poker, a five-card hand having four cards in the same suit.

four-flush (fôr′flŭsh′, fōr′-) intr.v. **-flushed, -flushing, -flushes. 1.** To bluff in poker with a four-flush hand. **2.** *Slang.* To bluff.

four-flush·er (fôr′flŭsh′ər, fōr′-) n. *Slang.* A person who cannot or does not substantiate his pretensions; bluffer; faker.

four·fold (fôr′fōld′, fōr′-) adj. **1.** Having four units or aspects; quadruple. **2.** Being four times as much or as many as some understood figure. ~adv. (fôr′fōld′, fōr′-). In quadrupled measure.

four-foot·ed (fôr′fōōt′ĭd, fōr′-) adj. Having four feet.

Four Freedoms pl.n. Four basic human freedoms, freedom of speech and religion and freedom from want and fear. Preceded by *the.*

four·gon (fōōr-gôN′) n., pl. **-gons** (-gôN′, -gôNz′). A wagon used mainly for carrying baggage. [French.]

four·hand·ed (fôr′hăn′dĭd, fōr′-) adj. **1.** Involving or requiring four players, as some games do. **2.** Designed to be played by four hands, as a piano duet: *a four-handed waltz.* **3.** Having four extremities functioning like hands; quadrumanous.

Four-H Club (fôr′āch′, fōr′-) n. A youth organization sponsored by the Department of Agriculture and offering instruction in agriculture and home economics. [From its four goals to improve head, heart, hands, and health.] —**Four-H'er** (fôr′ā′chər, fōr′-) n.

four hundred n. *Often* **Four Hundred.** The wealthiest and most exclusive social set. Preceded by *the.* [Term introduced (1892) by Ward McAllister (1827–95), New York socialite, to describe members of "true" New York society.]

Fou·ri·er (fōōr′ē-ā′), **François Marie Charles** (1772–1837). French utopian socialist philosopher. He believed that social harmony could be achieved through "phalanxes," small self-sustaining communal groups of people who would live in communal "phalansteries." Work would be shared according to each person's natural abilities and preferences. —**Fou·ri·er·ism** (fōōr′ē-ə-rĭz′əm) n. —**Fou·ri·er·ist, Fou·ri·er·ite** (fōōr′ē-ə-rīt′) n. & adj.

Fourier, Jean Baptiste Joseph, Baron (1768–1830). French mathematician and physicist. He made valuable contributions to scientific knowledge, especially in the field of heat theory.

Fourier analysis n. *Mathematics.* A method of analyzing a periodic function into its harmonic components, the sum of which form a Fourier series. [After J.B.J. **FOURIER.**]

Fourier series n. An infinite series of sine and cosine functions, capable if uniformly convergent of approximating a wide variety of mathematical functions. [Devised by J.B.J. **FOURIER.**]

four-in-hand (fôr′ĭn-hănd′, fōr′-) n. **1.** A vehicle drawn by four horses and driven by one person. **2.** A team of four horses. **3.** A tie tied in a slipknot with the ends left hanging and overlapping. ~adj. Designating or pertaining to a four-in-hand.

four-leaf clover (fôr′lēf′, fōr′-) n. Also **four-leaved clover** (-lēvd′). A clover leaf having four leaflets instead of the normal three, considered to be an omen of good luck.

four-let·ter word (fôr′lĕt′ər, fōr′-) n. Any of several short English words generally regarded as vulgar or obscene.

four-mast·ed (fôr′măs′tĭd, -mä′stĭd, fōr′-) adj. *Nautical.* Having four masts. —**four-mast·er** n.

four-o'clock (fôr′ə-klŏk′, fōr′-) n. Any of several plants of the genus *Mirabilis;* especially, *M. jalapa,* native to tropical America, and widely cultivated for its tubular, variously colored flowers that open in the late afternoon. Also called "marvel-of-Peru."

four·pence (fôr′pəns, fōr′-) n. *British.* **1.** A sum of money equal to four pence or four old pennies. Used chiefly before the decimalization of British currency. **2.** Formerly, a small silver coin of this value.

four-post·er (fôr′pō′stər, fōr′-) n. A bed having tall corner posts to support curtains or a canopy. Also called "four-poster bed."

four·ra·gère (fōōr′ə-zhâr′) n. **1.** An ornamental braided cord usually looped around the left shoulder. **2.** Such a cord awarded to an entire military unit. [French, from the feminine of *fourrager,* of forage, from *fourrage,* forage, from Old French *forage,* **FORAGE.**]

four·score (fôr′skôr′, fōr′-) adj. Eighty; four times twenty.

four·some (fôr′səm, fōr′-) n. **1.** Any group of four persons; especially, two couples. **2. a.** A game, such as a golf match, played by four persons, two on each side. **b.** The players in such a game. ~adj. Consisting of or involving a group of four. [Middle English *four-sum,* from Old English *fēowra sum,* one of four : *fēowra,* genitive of *fēower,* **FOUR** + *sum,* one, **SOME.**]

four-poster *This large square bedstead with its canopy on four upright posts is at Crathes Castle, Scotland.*

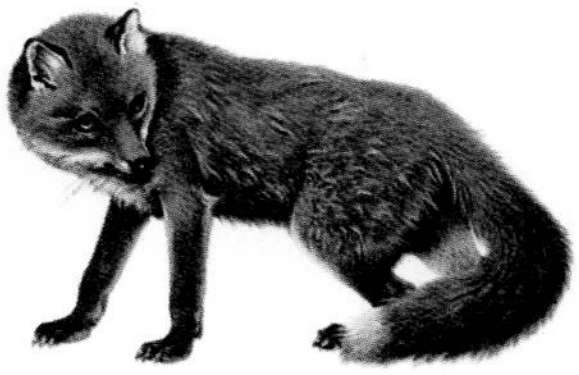

fox *The red fox of Eurasia,* Vulpes vulpes, *breeds once a year, usually in January. Its cubs are born in late March or early April.*

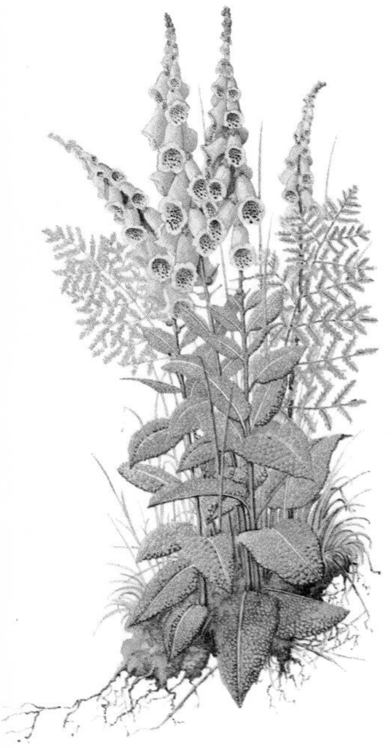

foxglove *This perennial herb,* Digitalis purpurea, *grows wild throughout Europe and Asia on banks and hillsides. Digitalin, a drug extracted from its leaves, is used by doctors as a heart stimulant.*

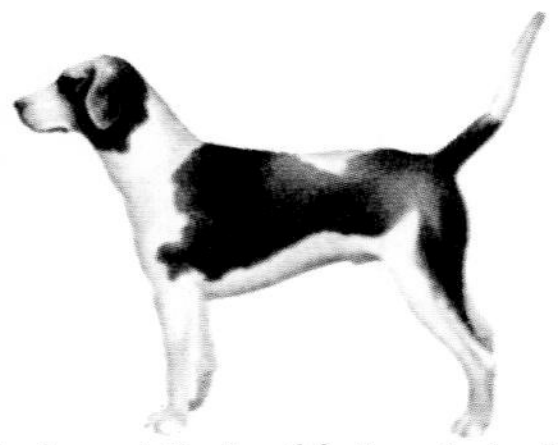

foxhound *Packs of foxhounds, bred for stamina and their acute sense of smell, are used as hunting dogs to find and chase foxes. They are rarely kept as pets. There are two breeds: the English foxhound (above) and the lighter American foxhound, developed from English dogs first taken across the North Atlantic in 1650.*

four·square (fôr′skwâr′, fōr′-) *adj.* **1.** Unyielding; firm. **2.** Forthright; honest; frank.
~adv. Squarely; forthrightly.

four-stroke (fôr′strōk′, fōr′-) *adj.* Designating an internal-combustion engine in which the pistons make four strokes for each explosion. Compare **two-stroke.**

four·teen (fôr-tēn′, fōr-) *n.* **1. a.** The cardinal number that is one more than 13. **b.** A symbol representing this, such as 14 or XIV. **2.** A set made up of 14 persons or things. **3.** The 14th in a series. **4.** A size, as in clothing, designated as 14. [Middle English *fourtene,* from Old English *fēowertīene.*] **—four·teen** *adj. & pron.*

four·teenth (fôr-tēnth′, fōr-) *n.* **1.** The ordinal number 14 in a series. **2.** One of 14 equal parts. **—four·teenth** *adj. & adv.*

fourth (fôrth, fōrth) *n.* **1.** The ordinal number four in a series. **2.** Any of four equal parts. **3.** *Music.* **a.** In a diatonic scale, a tone four degrees above or below any given tone. **b.** The interval between two such tones. **c.** The harmonic combination of these tones. **d.** In a scale, the subdominant. **4.** The fourth forward gear of a motor vehicle. **5. Fourth.** The Fourth of July. [Middle English *fourthe,* earlier *ferthe, furthe,* Old English *fēortha, fēowertha.*] **—fourth** *adj. & adv.* **—fourth·ly** *adv.*

fourth-class (fôrth′klăs′, -kläs′, fōrth′-) *adj.* Designating a class of mail consisting of merchandise or certain printed matter weighing over eight ounces and not sealed against inspection.
~adv. As or by fourth-class mail.

fourth dimension *n.* Time regarded as a dimension, that together with the three spatial dimensions is required to specify completely the location of any event in a space-time continuum.

fourth estate *n. Sometimes* **Fourth Estate.** The public press; journalism or journalists generally. [Formerly used jocularly to refer to something outside the (three) Estates of the Realm.]

Fourth International *n.* See **International.**

Fourth of July *n.* Independence Day.

four-wheel drive (fôr′hwēl′, fōr′-) *n. Abbr.* **f.w.d.** An automotive drive mechanism in which all four wheels are connected to the source of driving power.

fo·ve·a (fō′vē-ə) *n., pl.* **-veae** (-vē-ē′). **1.** A shallow cuplike depression or pit in a bone or other organ. **2.** The fovea centralis. [New Latin, from Latin *fovea,* small pit, possibly from Etruscan.] **—fo·ve·al, fo·ve·ate** *adj.*

fovea cen·tra·lis (sĕn-trā′lĭs) *n.* A small depression in the retina of the eye, constituting the area of most distinct vision. Also called "fovea."

fowl (foul) *n., pl.* **fowls** or collectively **fowl. 1.** Any of various birds of the order Galliformes; especially, the common, widely domesticated chicken, *Gallus gallus.* **2.** Any bird used as food or hunted as game. **3.** The edible flesh of such a bird. **4.** *Archaic.* Any bird.
~intr.v. **fowled, fowling, fowls.** To hunt, trap, or shoot wild fowl. [Middle English *foul,* Old English *fugol.*] **—fowl·er** *n.*

fowl cholera *n.* An acute, infectious, often fatal intestinal disease of domestic poultry and wild birds, caused by a bacterium, *Pasteurella multocida,* and characterized by enteritis, submucous hemorrhage, and vascular congestion.

Fow·ler (fou′lər), **Henry Watson** (1858–1933). British lexicographer. He collaborated with his brother, **Francis Fowler** (1870–1918), on a number of English dictionaries and edited the *Concise Oxford Dictionary* (1911). His best-known work is *Modern English Usage* (1926; revised 1965).

Fowles (foulz), **John** (1926–). British novelist. Though *The Magus* (1966) was his first novel, it was not published until after *The Collector* (1963). His other works include *The French Lieutenant's Woman* (1969), *Daniel Martin* (1977), and *Mantissa* (1982).

fowl·ing (fou′lĭng) *n.* The hunting of wild fowl.

fowling piece *n.* A light shotgun for shooting birds and small animals.

fowl pox *n.* A viral infection of poultry and other birds, characterized by wartlike nodules on the skin and cankers in the digestive and upper respiratory tracts.

fox (fŏks) *n.* **1.** Any of various carnivorous mammals of the genus *Vulpes* and related genera, related to the dogs and wolves, and characteristically having upright ears, a pointed snout, and a long, bushy tail. **2.** The fur of a fox. **3.** A crafty, sly, or clever person. **4.** *Archaic.* A sword. **5.** *Nautical.* Small cordage made by twisting together two or more strands of tarred yarn.
~v. **foxed, foxing, foxes.** *—tr.* **1. a.** To trick or fool by ingenuity or cunning; outwit. **b.** To baffle or confuse. **2.** *Archaic.* To make drunk; intoxicate. **3.** To make (beer) sour by fermenting. **4.** To repair (a shoe) by adding a new upper. *—intr.* **1.** To act deceitfully or craftily; pretend. **2.** To turn sour in fermenting. Used of beer. [Middle English, from Old English.]

Fox (fŏks), **Charles James** (1749-1806). English Whig statesman. He entered parliament in 1768 and in 1782 was appointed Britain's first foreign secretary. An ardent promoter of liberal causes, he supported American independence, parliamentary reform, and the French Revolution, but he was dismissed from the Privy Council in 1798 for opposing war with France.

Fox, George (1624–91). Founder of the Society of Friends (Quakers). Originally a shoemaker's apprentice, he became a traveling preacher in 1647. His stand against the established church won him many supporters, but he was frequently imprisoned for his beliefs.

foxed (fŏkst) *adj.* Discolored with yellowish-brown stains, as an old book or print may be. [From the resemblance of the stain to the color of a fox.]

fox·fire (fŏks′fīr′) *n.* A phosphorescent glow, especially that produced by certain fungi found on rotting wood. [Middle English, perhaps from the silvery quality of some fox fur.]

fox·glove (fŏks′glŭv′) *n.* **1.** Any of several plants of the genus *Digitalis;* especially, *D. purpurea,* native to Europe, having a long cluster of large, tubular, pinkish-purple flowers, and leaves that are the source of the medicinal drug digitalis. **2.** Any of several similar or related plants. [Middle English *foxes-glove,* Old English *foxes glōfa,* "fox's glove" (the reason for association with the fox is not known).]

fox·hole (fŏks′hōl′) *n.* A shallow pit dug by a soldier for immediate individual refuge against enemy fire.

fox·hound (fŏks′hound′) *n.* A dog developed for fox hunting; especially, a short-haired hound of either of two breeds, the *English foxhound* and the *American foxhound.*

fox hunt *n.* The hunting of a fox with hounds.

fox-hunt·ing (fŏks′hŭn′tĭng) *n.* The sport of hunting a fox with hounds, usually by people on horseback.

fox·ing (fŏk′sĭng) *n.* A brownish discoloration of paper or a book, caused by damp.

fox squirrel *n.* A squirrel, *Sciurus niger,* of the United States, having rusty or grayish fur.

fox·tail (fŏks′tāl′) *n.* **1.** Any of several grasses of the genus *Alopecurus,* having dense, silky or bristly flowering spikes. **2.** Any of several similar or related plants.

fox terrier *n.* A small dog having a white coat with dark markings, bred in both wire-haired and smooth-coated varieties.

fox·trot (fŏks′trŏt′) *n.* **1.** A ballroom dance in 2/4 or 4/4 time, composed of a variety of slow and fast steps. **2.** The music or a piece of music for this dance.
~intr.v. **fox·trotted, -trotting, -trots.** To dance a foxtrot. [From the short steps attributed to the comparatively short-legged fox.]

fox·y (fŏk′sē) *adj.* **-ier, -iest. 1.** Suggestive of a fox; sly; cunning; clever. **2.** Having a reddish-brown color. **3.** Discolored, as by decay; stained; foxed. **4.** Having the distinctive sharp flavor of some American grapes. Said of wine. **5.** *Informal.* Sexually attractive: *a foxy lady.* —See Synonyms at **sly. —fox·i·ly** *adv.* **—fox·i·ness** *n.*

foy (foi) *n. Chiefly Scottish.* A farewell entertainment, feast, drink, or gift, as at the end of a harvest or on the eve of a wedding. [Dialectal Dutch *fooi,* feast given for farm laborers after harvest, from Middle Dutch *foye, voye,* "voyage," feast given at parting, from Old French *voie,* way, journey, from Latin *via.*]

foy·er (foi′ər, foi′ā′, fwä′yā′) *n.* **1.** The entrance hall, lobby, or anteroom of a public building, such as a theater, hotel, or concert hall. **2.** The entrance hall or vestibule of a private dwelling. [French, hearth, home, foyer, from Medieval Latin *focārius,* from Latin *focus,* hearth, fireplace.]

Foyle, Lough (foil). Sea lough on the western border of Northern Ireland with the Republic of Ireland.

fp 1. forward pass. **2.** freezing point.

fpm, f.p.m. feet per minute.

FPO fleet post office.

fps foot-pound-second.

f.p.s. 1. feet per second. **2.** frames per second. **3.** foot-pound-second.

Fr The symbol for the element francium.

fr. 1. franc. **2.** from.

Fr. 1. father (clergyman). **2.** France; French. **3.** frater. **4.** Frau. **5.** friar.

Fra (frä) *n.* Brother. Used as a title for an Italian monk or friar. [Italian, short for *frate,* "brother," from Latin *frāter.*]

frab·jous (frăb′jəs) *adj. Informal.* Delightful; wonderful. [Coined by Lewis Carroll, perhaps based on *fair* and *joyous.*]

fra·cas (frā′kəs, frăk′əs; *British* frăk′ä′) *n., pl.* **fracas.** A disorderly uproar; a noisy quarrel; brawl. [French, from Italian *fracasso,* from *fracassare,* probably a blend of Latin *frangere,* to break, and *quassāre,* to shatter.]

frac·tion (frăk′shən) *n.* **1.** A small part of something; a scant portion: *a fraction of the populace.* **2.** A disconnected piece of something; a fragment; scrap; bit. **3.** *Mathematics.* An indicated quotient of two quantities. **4.** *Chemistry.* A component separated by a fractional process; a product of fractionation. **5.** The breaking of the host in the Eucharist. [Middle English *fraccioun,* from Late Latin *fractiō* (stem *fractiōn-*), act of breaking (especially bread), from Latin *fractus,* past participle of *frangere,* to break.]

frac·tion·al (frăk′shə-nəl) *adj.* **1.** Of, pertaining to, or constituting a fraction or fractions. **2.** Very small; insignificant; infinitesimal. **3.** Being in fractions or pieces; broken; fragmentary. **4.** Designating a chemical process in which components of a mixture are separated on the basis of differences in their physical properties: *fractional crystallization.* **—frac·tion·al·ly** *adv.*

fractional currency *n.* Any currency in a denomination less than the standard monetary unit.

fractional distillation *n.* **1.** Distillation in which the purity of the product is increased by bringing the vapor into contact with the condensed liquid in a countercurrent system. **2.** Distillation in which the product is collected in a series of separate fractions.

frac·tion·ate (frăk′shə-nāt′) *tr.v.* **-ated, -ating, -ates.** To separate (a chemical compound) into components by a fractional process, as by distillation or crystallization. **—frac·tion·a·tion** *n.* **—frac·tion·a·tor** *n.*

frac·tion·ize (frăk′shə-nīz′) *v.* **-ized, -izing, -izes.** *—tr.* To divide into fractions. *—intr.* To divide something into fractions. **—frac·tion·i·za·tion** *n.*

frac·tious (frăk′shəs) *adj.* **1.** Inclined to make trouble; unruly: *He was very fractious when drunk.* **2.** Having a peevish nature; irritable. [From FRACTION, in the sense of "breaking."] **—frac·tious·ly** *adv.* **—frac·tious·ness** *n.*
frac·to·cu·mu·lus cloud (frăk′tō-kyōōm′yə-ləs) *n.* A low, ragged cumulus cloud. [Latin *fractus,* broken (past participle of *frangere*) + CUMULUS.]
frac·to·stra·tus cloud (frăk′tō-strā′təs, -străt′əs) *n.* A low, ragged stratus cloud. [Latin *fractus,* broken (see **fractocumulus cloud**) + STRATUS.]
frac·ture (frăk′chər) *n.* **1. a.** The act or process of breaking. **b.** The condition of being broken. **2.** A break, rupture, tear, or crack, as in bone or cartilage, as: a *comminuted fracture,* a fracture in which the bone is broken into several pieces; a *compound* or *open fracture,* a fracture with an open wound, often with the broken bone exposed; an *impacted fracture,* a fracture in which the broken ends have been forced into each other; a *simple* or *closed fracture,* a fracture with no break in the skin. **3.** *Mineralogy.* **a.** The characteristic manner in which a mineral breaks. **b.** The characteristic appearance of a broken mineral.
∼*v.* **fractured, -turing, -tures.** *—tr.* To break; crack. *—intr.* To undergo a fracture. —See Synonyms at **break.** [Middle English, from Old French, from Latin *fractūra,* from *fractus,* broken. See **fraction.**]
frae (frā) *prep. Scottish.* From. [Middle English *fra,* from Old Norse *frā.*]
fraenulum. Variant of **frenulum.**
fraenum. Variant of **frenum.**
frag·ile (frăj′əl, -īl′) *adj.* **1.** Easily broken or damaged; brittle. **2.** Physically weak; frail. **3.** Suggesting fragility; delicate. **4.** Tenuous; flimsy: *a fragile claim to fame.* [Old French, from Latin *fragilis,* from *frangere,* to break.] **—frag·ile·ly** *adv.* **—fra·gil·i·ty** (frə-jĭl′ə-tē), **frag·ile·ness** *n.*
***Synonyms:** breakable, brittle, delicate, frail.*
frag·ment (frăg′mənt) *n.* **1.** A part broken off or detached from a whole. **2.** Something incomplete or unconnected; an odd bit or piece: *a fragment of conversation.* **3.** An extant part of an unfinished or lost text.
∼*v.* (frăg′mĕnt′) **fragmented, -menting, -ments.** *—tr.* To break or separate (something) into fragments. *—intr.* To break into pieces. [Middle English, from Latin *fragmentum,* from *frangere,* to break.]
frag·men·tal (frăg-mĕnt′l) *adj.* **1.** Fragmentary. **2.** *Geology.* Consisting of broken material moved from its place of origin.
frag·men·tar·y (frăg′mən-tĕr′ē) *adj.* Consisting of fragments or disconnected parts; broken. **—frag·men·tar·i·ly** (frăg′mən-târ′ə-lē) *adv.* **—frag·men·tar·i·ness** *n.*
frag·men·ta·tion (frăg′mən-tā′shən, frăg′mĕn-) *n.* **1.** The act or process of breaking into fragments. **2.** The scattering of the fragments of an exploding grenade, bomb, or shell; dispersion.
∼*adj.* Exploding into lethal high-velocity fragments of metal: *a fragmentation grenade.*
fragmentation bomb *n.* An aerial antipersonnel bomb that scatters shrapnel over a wide area.
frag·ment·ed (frăg′mĕn′tĭd) *adj.* Broken into fragments.
frag·ment·ize (frăg′mən-tīz′) *v.* **-ized, -izing, -izes.** *—tr.* To break (something) into fragments. *—intr.* To fragment.
Fra·go·nard (frăg′ə-när′), **Jean Honoré** (1732-1806). French painter and engraver. He is best known for his rococo paintings depicting lovers in exotic settings, cupids, nymphs, and other romantic figures.
fra·grance (frā′grəns) *n.* **1.** The state or quality of being fragrant. **2.** A sweet or pleasant odor; perfume. —See Synonyms at **smell.**
fra·grant (frā′grənt) *adj.* Having a pleasant odor; sweet-smelling; perfumed. [Middle English, from Old French, from Latin *fragrāns* (stem *fragrant-*), present participle of *fragrāre,* to emit an odor (good or bad), to reek.]
frail[1] (frāl) *adj.* **frailer, frailest. 1.** Having a delicate constitution; physically weak; not robust. **2.** Slight; weak; not strong or substantial. **3.** Easily broken or destroyed; vulnerable; fragile; uncertain. **4.** Morally weak; easily led astray or into evil. —See Synonyms at **fragile, weak.** [Middle English *frele, frail,* from Old French *frele, fraile,* from Latin *fragilis,* FRAGILE.] **—frail·ly** *adv.* **—frail·ness** *n.*
frail[2] *n.* **1.** A rush basket for holding fruit, especially dried fruit. **2.** The quantity of fruit, such as raisins or figs, contained in a frail, usually from 23 to 34 kilograms (50 to 75 pounds). [Middle English *fraiel,* from Old French *fraiel*†.]
frail·ty (frāl′tē) *n., pl.* **-ties. 1.** The condition or quality of being frail; weakness, especially of resolution. **2.** A fault arising from weakness; a failing: *human frailties.* —See Synonyms at **fault.**
fraise (frāz) *n.* **1.** A barrier or defense of pointed, inclined stakes or of barbed wire. **2.** A ruff for the neck, worn in the 16th century. **3.** A tool for enlarging a small circular hole. **4.** A tool for cutting teeth on a wheel, especially on a watch wheel. [French, "mesentery of a calf or lamb," originally "outer covering," "casing," from Old French *fraiser,* to remove the outer covering (used especially of beans), from Vulgar Latin *frēsāre* (unattested), from Latin *(faba) frēsa,* ground (bean), from *frēsus,* past participle of *frendere,* to grind with the teeth.]
frak·tur (fräk-tōōr′) *n.* A style of letter formerly used in German manuscripts and printing. [German *Fraktur,* from Latin *fractūra,* a breaking (from the curlicues that appear to break up the word), FRACTURE.]
fram·be·sia (frăm-bē′zhə) *n. Pathology.* **Yaws** *(see).* [New Latin, from French *framboise,* raspberry (from the appearance of the excrescences), from Old French, variant (influenced by *fraise,* strawberry) of Frankish *brām-besi* (unattested), "brambleberry."]
fram·boise (frăɴ-bwäz′) *n.* A clear French brandy distilled from raspberries. [French, "raspberry." See **frambesia.**]
frame (frām) *v.* **framed, framing, frames.** *—tr.* **1.** To construct by putting together the various parts of; build. **2.** To formulate or conceive; fashion; design; draw up. **3.** To arrange or adjust for a purpose; compose. **4. a.** To put into words; phrase: *frame a reply.* **b.** To form (words) silently with the lips. **5.** To provide with or as if with a surrounding or bordering frame; enclose or encircle. **6.** *Slang.* **a.** To rig evidence or events so as to incriminate (a person) falsely. **b.** To fix (a contest, for example) so as to ensure a desired fraudulent outcome: *frame a prizefight.* *—intr.* **1.** *Archaic.* To resort; proceed. **2.** *Obsolete.* To manage or contrive to do something.
∼*n.* **1.** Something composed of parts fitted and joined together; a structure, as: **a.** A basic or skeletal structure designed to give shape or support: *the frame of a house.* **b.** An open structure or rim for encasing, holding, or bordering something: *a window frame; a picture frame; glasses frames.* **c.** The human body. **d.** A **cold frame** *(see).* **e.** A climbing apparatus as used in a gymnasium or children's playground. **2.** A machine built upon or utilizing a frame. **3.** The general structure of something; system; order: *the frame of government.* **4. a.** Any of the transverse ribs of a ship's hull from the gunwale to the keel or the bilge, consisting of either a *square frame,* perpendicular to the keel's vertical plane, or a *cant frame,* at an oblique angle to it. **b.** A transverse stiffening rib in the fuselage of an aircraft. **5. a.** In billiards, a rigid triangular device for arranging the balls at the beginning of a game; a rack. **b.** The balls so arranged. **6. a.** A round or period of play in some games, such as bowling or billiards. **b.** *Baseball.* An inning. **7. a.** A single exposure on a roll of motion-picture film. **b.** A single scene in a cartoon strip. **8.** The total area of a television picture formed by a single traverse of the scanning spot. **9.** In electronics, computer science, and telecommunications, a cycle of regularly recurring pulses in a train of pulses. **10.** A slat or slats, serving as a base for building honeycombs, that is part of the structure of a man-made beehive. **11.** *Slang.* A frame-up. **12.** *Obsolete.* Shape; form. [Middle English *framen, framien,* to be advantageous, benefit, form, construct, Old English *framian,* to benefit, avail.] **—fram·er** *n.*
frame aerial *n.* A **loop aerial** *(see).*
frame house *n.* A house constructed with a wooden framework and usually covered with wooden boards.
frame of mind *n.* Mental state or attitude; mood.
frame of reference *n.* **1.** *Physics.* A set of coordinate axes in terms of which position or movement may be specified, or with reference to which physical laws may be mathematically stated. **2.** A set or system of ideas, as of philosophical or religious doctrine, in terms of which other ideas are interpreted or assigned meaning.
frame-up (frām′ŭp′) *n. Informal.* **1.** A prearranged or fraudulent scheme; a fix. **2.** A conspiracy to throw guilt on an innocent person; a scheme involving falsified charges or evidence.
frame·work (frām′wûrk′) *n.* **1.** A structure for supporting, defining, or enclosing something; especially, skeletal erections and supports used as the basis for something being constructed. **2.** Any outlying erection or work platform that allows access to something being constructed or worked on in some way; a rig; scaffolding. **3.** A basic arrangement, form, or system; a design.
fram·ing (frā′mĭng) *n.* A frame, framework, or system of frames.
franc (frăngk) *n. Abbr.* **f., fr. 1.** The basic monetary unit of France, Belgium, Switzerland, and numerous other countries, especially former French colonies. It is equal to 100 centimes. **2.** A coin worth one franc. See feature at **currency.** [Middle English *frank,* from Old French *franc,* from the Latin legend *Francorum rex,* "king of the Franks," on gold coins struck during the reign of Jean le Bon (1350–64).]
France (frăns, fräns). *Abbr.* **Fr.** Republic on the western seaboard of Europe. It is the continent's oldest state and largest country excluding Russia. It was settled by the Franks, a Germanic people from across the Rhine, after the retreat of the Romans, who had conquered the Celtic Gauls in 57–71 B.C. The country enjoys all three European climates—maritime, continental, and Mediterranean. Its richest resource is its soil; 90 percent of the land is productive, either as arable land, permanent pasture, or forest. France is the world's second-largest producer of wine, after Italy, and is self-sufficient in meat and cereals. It is also heavily industrialized, and tourism is a major industry. Area, 547,026 square kilometers (211,208 square miles). Population, 56,100,000. Capital, Paris. [Middle English *France,* from Old French *France,* from Late Latin *Francia,* country of the Franks, from *Francus,* a FRANK.] See map, next page.
France (frăns, fräns, fräɴs), **Anatole,** born Jacques Anatole France Thibault (1844–1924). French novelist. He was a great short-story writer and literary satirist. His works include *Thaïs* (1890), *L'Ile des Pingouins* (1908), and *La Révolte des Anges* (1914). He won the Nobel Prize in 1921.
Francesca, Piero della. See **Piero della Francesca.**
Fran·ces·ca de Ri·mi·ni (frăn-chĕs′kə də rĭm′ĭ-nē) (died *c.* 1285). Italian noblewoman. Unhappy in her arranged marriage to an Italian nobleman, she fell in love with her husband's brother, Paolo Malatesta. When her husband discovered the affair, he murdered both Francesca and her lover. This tragic love story is recounted in Dante's *Inferno* and several plays and operas.

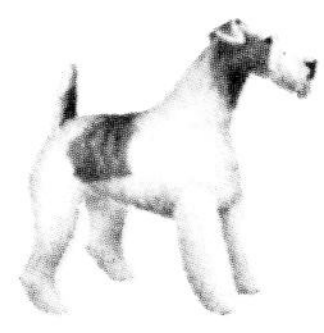

fox terrier *Fox terriers were bred as short-legged sporting dogs, small enough to get into a fox's earth or lair and drive it out into the open. This is a wire-haired fox terrier.*

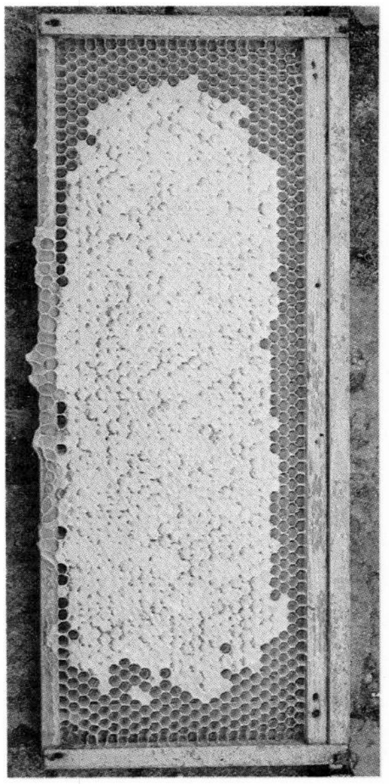

frame *A manmade honeycomb frame.*

PRONUNCIATION KEY

ă, pat; ā, pay; âr, care;
ä, father, are; b, bib;
ch, church; d, deed; ĕ, pet;
ē, be; f, fife; g, gag; h, hat;
hw, which; ĭ, pit; ī, pie;
îr, pier; j, judge; k, kick;
l, lid, needle; m, mum;
n, no, sudden; ng, thing;
ŏ, pot; ō, toe; ô, paw, for;
oi, noise; ou, out; ŏŏ, book;
ōō, boot; p, pop; r, roar;
s, sauce; sh, ship, dish;
t, tight; th, thin, path;
th, this, bathe; ŭ, cut; ûr, fur;
v, valve; w, with; y, yes;
z, zebra, size; zh, vision;
ə, about, item, edible,
gallop, circus, peaceful

IN FOREIGN WORDS:

à, *Fr.* ami; œ, *Fr.* feu, *Ger.* schön; ü, *Fr.* tu, *Ger.* über; KH, *Ger.* ich, *Scot.* loch; ɴ, *Fr.* bon; y′, *Fr.* Compiègne

STRESS MARKS:

Primary stress: ′
in·cite′ (ĭn-sīt′)
Secondary stress: ′
in′sight′ (ĭn′sīt′)

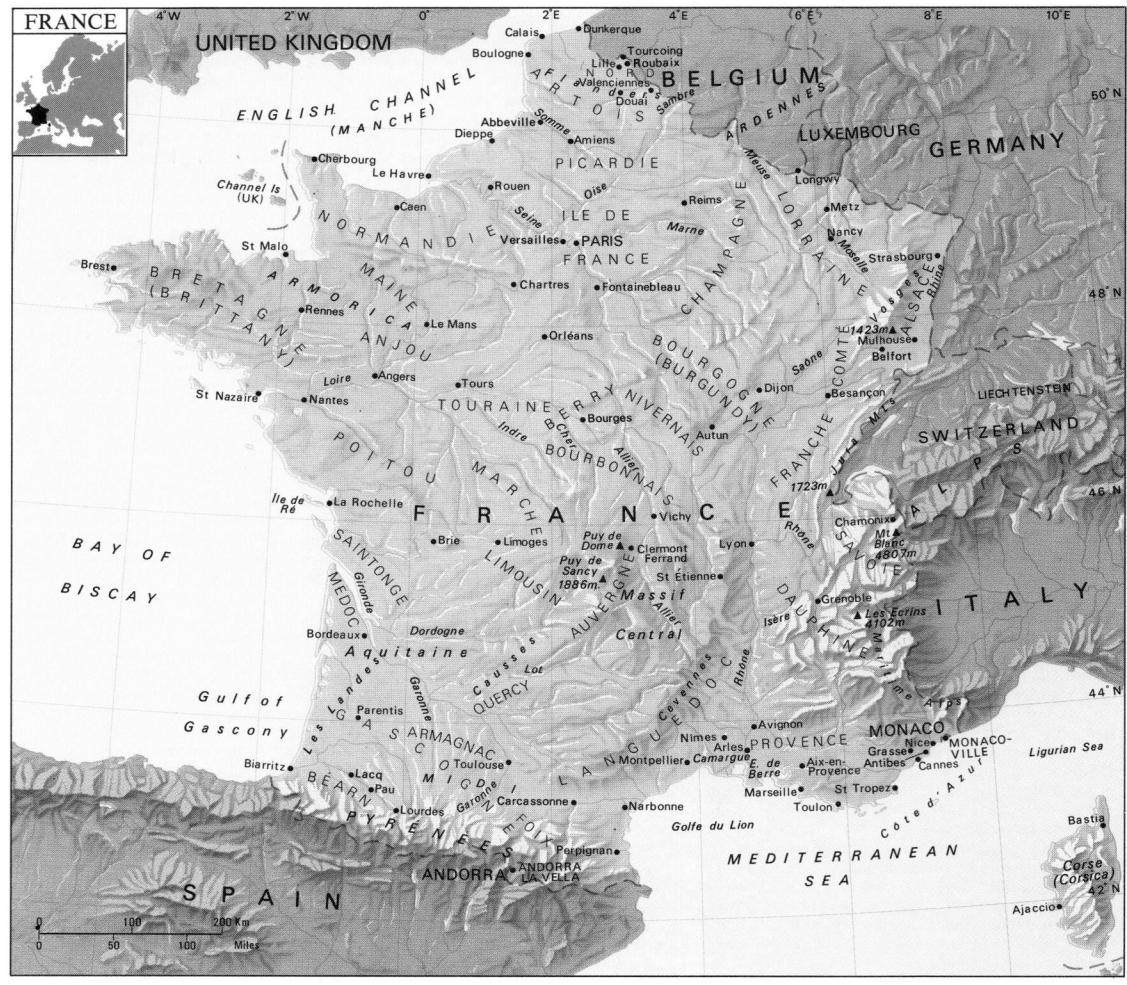

fran·chise (frăn′chīz′) *n.* **1.** A privilege or right granted a person or a group by a government, state, or sovereign, especially: **a.** The constitutional or statutory right to vote; suffrage. **b.** Formerly, legal immunity from certain burdens, servitude, or other restrictions. **2.** Authorization granted by a manufacturer to a distributor or dealer to sell his products. **3.** The territory or limits within which some privilege, right, or immunity may be exercised. —See Synonyms at **right.**
~*tr.v.* **franchised, -chising, -chises.** To endow with a franchise. [Middle English *fraunchise,* freedom, privilege, from Old French *franchise,* from *franc* (feminine *franche*), free, FRANK.]

Fran·cis·can (frăn-sĭs′kən) *n.* A member of a religious mendicant order founded by St. Francis of Assisi in 1209 and now divided into three independent branches. Often called "Gray Friar."
~*adj.* Of or pertaining to St. Francis of Assisi or to the order founded by him.

Fran·cis Jo·seph (frăn′sĭs, frăn′-; jō′zəf, -səf) (1830–1916). *German* **Franz Jo·sef** (frănts′ yō′zĕf′). Austrian emperor. His reign (1848–1916) began at the height of the 1848 Revolution and was marked by a succession of crises. To ease tensions within his empire, he created the Dual Monarchy (1867) with Austria and Hungary. He was defeated by the Prussians (1866) but later allied with the German Empire (1879) and with Italy (1882) to form the Triple Alliance. Following the assassination (1914) of his nephew, Archduke Francis Ferdinand, by a Serbian nationalist, he issued an ultimatum to Serbia that was to lead to World War I.

Francis of As·si·si (ə-sē′zē, -sē) Saint (c. 1182–1226). Founder of the Franciscan order. He served for a time as soldier, but in 1206 devoted himself to a life of poverty. In 1210 he received papal permission to found his holy order, and he and his followers took Christ's teaching as far as North Africa and the Holy Land. His *Canticle to the Sun* (1225–26) testifies to his love of nature. He was canonized in 1228 and in 1980 was declared patron saint of ecology.

Francis of Sales (sălz, säl), Saint (1567–1622). French ecclesiastic. In his many spiritual works, including *Introduction to a Devout Life* (1609), he maintained that spiritual perfection is possible not just for religious contemplatives but also for people involved in secular pursuits. He is the patron saint of writers.

Francis Xa·vi·er (ză′vē-ər, zăv′ē-), Saint (1506–52). Spanish Jesuit missionary. He was cofounder, with St. Ignatius Loyola, of the Jesuit order. Known as the Apostle of the Indies, he established

missions in the East Indies, Japan, and Ceylon.

fran·ci·um (frăn′sē-əm) *n. Symbol* **Fr** An extremely unstable radioactive metallic element, having 20 known isotopes, the most stable of which is Fr 223 with a half-life of 21 minutes. Atomic number 87, valence 1. [New Latin, from FRANCE.]

Franck (frängk, frängk), **César Auguste** (1822–90). Belgian composer and organist. He traveled to Paris in 1834 and became one of the most influential musical figures in mid-19th-century France. Though he composed mainly for the organ, his works also include an orchestral symphony and some oratorios.

Fran·co (fräng′kō, fräng′-), **Francisco** (1892–1975). Spanish dictator. As military governor of the Canary Islands, he helped direct the uprising of July 1936 and later that year became head of the Nationalist government and rebel armed forces. Following the defeat of the Republicans in the Spanish Civil War (1939), he ruled Spain until his death, when he was succeeded by a restored Bourbon monarchy.

Franco– *prefix.* Indicates France or French; for example, **Francophile, Francophobe.** [Medieval Latin *Francus,* a Frenchman, from Late Latin, a FRANK.]

fran·co·lin (frăng′kə-lĭn) *n.* **1.** Any of various Old World birds of the genus *Francolinus,* related to and resembling the quails and partridges. **2.** Any of various related birds, such as the Chinese francolin, *Excalfactoria.* [French, from Italian *francolino†.*]

Fran·co·phile (frăng′kə-fīl′) *n.* Also **Fran·co·phil** (-fĭl′). An admirer of France, its people, and its customs. [FRANCO- + -PHILE.] —**Fran·co·phile** *adj.*

Fran·co·phobe (frăng′kə-fōb′) *n.* One who fears or dislikes France, its people, or its customs. [FRANCO- + -PHOBE.] —**Fran·co·phobe** *adj.*

Fran·co·phone (frăng′kə-fōn′) *adj.* French-speaking.
~*n.* A French-speaking person. [FRANCO- + -PHONE.]

Fran·co-Prus·sian War (frăng′kō-prŭsh′ən) *n.* The war of 1870–71 between Prussia and France.

franc ti·reur (frän′ tē-rœr′) *n., pl.* **francs tireurs** (*pronounced as singular*). A soldier or guerrilla who is not a member of a regular military force. [French, literally "free shooter."]

fran·gi·ble (frăn′jə-bəl) *adj.* Easily broken; breakable. [Middle English, from Old French, from Medieval Latin *frangibilis,* from Latin *frangere,* to break.] —**fran·gi·bil·i·ty, fran·gi·ble·ness** *n.*

fran·gi·pan·i (frăn′jə-păn′ē, -pä′nē) *n.* Also **fran·gi·pane** (frăn′-

jə-pān′) (for senses 2, 3). **1.** Any of various tropical American shrubs of the genus *Plumeria,* having milky juice and showy, fragrant, variously colored flowers. **2.** A perfume derived from or similar in scent to these flowers. **3.** A creamy pastry filling flavored with almonds. [French *frangipane,* from *(gants de) frangipane,* (gloves with) frangipani, after the Marquis *Frangipani* of Rome, who invented a perfume for scenting gloves in the 16th century.]

Fran·glais (frän-glā′) *n.* French as used with numerous English words, word endings, and other borrowings from English. [Blend of French *Français,* French, and *Anglais,* English.]

frank (frăngk) *adj.* **franker, frankest. 1.** Open and sincere in expression; straightforward. **2.** Clearly manifest; undisguised; evident: *frank enjoyment.* **3.** *Rare.* Liberal in giving; generous. **4.** *Obsolete.* Free; open.
~*tr.v.* **franked, franking, franks. 1. a.** To put an official mark on (a letter, for example) to ensure free delivery through special official privilege. **b.** To send (mail) free of charge. **2.** To place a stamp or mark on (a letter or parcel) to show the payment of postage. **3.** To place a postmark on. **4.** To enable (a person) to come and go easily; especially, to allow to go free of charge.
~*n.* **1.** A mark or signature placed on a letter or parcel to indicate the right to send it free of postage. **2.** A franked letter or parcel. [Middle English, free, generous, from Old French *franc,* free, from Medieval Latin *francus,* from Late Latin *Francus,* FRANK (in Frankish Gaul full freedom was the right only of the conquering people or those under their protection).] —**frank·ly** *adv.* —**frank·ness** *n.*
Synonyms: candid, ingenuous, open, outspoken.

Frank (frăngk) *n.* A member of one of the Germanic tribes of the Rhine region in the early Christian era; especially, one of the Salian Franks who conquered Gaul about 500 A.D. and established an extensive empire that reached its greatest power in the 9th century. [Middle English *Franc,* from Old English *Franca* and Old French *Franc,* from Late Latin *Francus,* from Germanic.]

Frank (frăngk, frängk), **Anne** (1929–45). A Jewish girl who fled Germany with her family in 1933 to escape Nazi persecution, she was trapped in Amsterdam by the German invasion (1941). The family hid in a sealed room from 1942 until her arrest in 1944. She died in Bergen-Belsen concentration camp. The diary of her years in hiding was published in 1947; the house in Amsterdam is preserved as a museum.

Frank·en·stein monster (frăng′kən-stīn′) *n.* Also **Frank·en·stein's monster** (-stīnz′). **1.** Any agency or creation that slips from the control of and ultimately destroys its creator. **2.** A monster having the appearance of a man; specifically, the monster created by the protagonist of Mary Shelley's novel *Frankenstein* (1818), which brought about the ruin of its creator. Also called "Frankenstein."

Frank·en·thal·er (frăng′kən-thô′lər, -thôl′ər), **Helen** (1928–). U.S. artist. An abstract expressionist painter, she has used brilliant colors and innovative techniques to create graceful, stirring works, including *Mountains and Sea* (1952), *Arcadia* (1962), and *The Human Edge* (1967).

Frank·fort (frăngk′fərt). The capital of Kentucky, on the Kentucky River in the north-central part of the state. In the heart of the Bluegrass Country, Frankfort has diversified manufactures and is a trade and shipping center for an area yielding tobacco, livestock, and limestone.

Frank·furt am Main (frăngk′fərt äm mīn′, frängk′foŏrt). Industrial city, financial center, and river port in Hesse, in western Germany. From 1816 to 1866, the city was the virtual capital of Germany and the seat of the Federal Diet (parliament).

Frankfurt an der O·der (än′ dĕr ō′dər). Town in eastern Germany, on the Oder River at the Polish border. It is an industrial center and agricultural market.

frank·furt·er, frank·fort·er (frăngk′fər-tər) *n.* Also **frank·furt, frank·fort** (frăngk′fərt). A smoked sausage of pork, beef, or beef and pork made in long, reddish links. [From FRANKFURT (AM MAIN), where it was originally made.]

Frank·furt·er (frăngk′fər-tər), **Felix** (1882–1965). U.S. jurist; Supreme Court Justice (1939–62); born in Austria. A founder of the American Civil Liberties Union (1920), he was appointed to the U.S. Supreme Court (1939) and, despite his liberal background, maintained that overliberal interpretations of the Constitution, particularly the First Amendment, could be detrimental to society.

frank·in·cense (frăng′kĭn-sĕns′) *n.* An aromatic gum resin obtained from African and Asian trees of the genus *Boswellia* and used chiefly as incense. Also called "olibanum." [Middle English *frank encens,* from Old French *franc encens : franc,* free, superior, FRANK + *encens,* INCENSE.]

Frank·ish (frăng′kĭsh) *adj.* Of or pertaining to the Franks or their language.
~*n.* The West Germanic language of the Franks.

frank·lin (frăng′klĭn) *n.* In England during the late medieval period, a freeholder not of noble birth but with extensive property; a country gentleman. [Middle English *frankelein,* from Medieval Latin *francālānus,* from *francālis,* (feudal estate) held without dues, from *francus,* free, FRANK.]

Frank·lin (frăng′klĭn). District within the Northwest Territories, Canada. It comprises the islands of the Canadian Arctic Archipelago and the Boothia and Melville peninsulas. It was named after the British Arctic explorer Sir John Franklin (1786–1847).

Franklin, Benjamin (1706–90). U.S. statesman, philosopher, physicist, and journalist. Following the success of his *Poor Richard's Almanac,* he entered politics and played a major part in the American Revolution. He negotiated French support for the colonists, promoted the Declaration of Independence (1776), and signed the Treaty of Paris (1783). He is remembered for his work on the drafting of the Constitution and his development of the lightning rod.

frank·lin·ite (frăng′klə-nīt′) *n.* A blackish, slightly magnetic mineral of zinc, iron, and manganese that is a valuable source of zinc. [After *Franklin,* New Jersey, where it is mined.]

frank·pledge (frăngk′plĕj′) *n.* **1.** In old English law, a system in which units or tithings composed of ten households were formed, in each of which members were held responsible for one another's conduct. **2.** A member of such a group, bound in pledge for his neighbors. **3.** The tithing itself. [Middle English *fraunkiplegge,* from Norman French *frauncplege : Old French *franc,* free, FRANK + Old French *plege,* PLEDGE.]

fran·tic (frăn′tĭk) *adj.* **1.** Emotionally distraught, as from fear, pain, worry, or passion; desperate; overwrought. **2.** Uncontrolled; wildly excited; frenzied. **3.** *Archaic.* Mad; insane. [Middle English *frantik, frenetik,* FRENETIC.] —**fran·ti·cal·ly, fran·tic·ly** *adv.* —**fran·tic·ness** *n.*

Franz Josef. See **Francis Joseph.**

Franz Jo·sef Land (frănts′ jō′səf, fränts′ yō′zĕf′). Also **Fridt·jof Nan·sen Land** (frĭt′yôf nän′sən). Arctic archipelago north of Novaya Zemlya. It was claimed by the U.S.S.R. in 1926 and is its most northerly territory. The 87 islands are mostly ice-covered all year and are inhabited mainly by polar bears, arctic foxes, walrus, and seals. The only human inhabitants are scientists at Soviet weather stations. The group was first explored by an Austrian expedition in 1873 and was named after the Austrian emperor. The group's alternate name, Fridtjof Nansen Land, comes from the Norwegian explorer who led an expedition to the archipelago (1895–99).

trap (frăp) *tr.v.* **trapped, trapping, traps.** *Nautical.* **1.** To make secure by lashing: *frap a sail.* **2.** To tighten; take up the slack of. [Middle English *frapen,* to strike, from Old French *fraper,* possibly from Frankish *hrappan†* (unattested).]

frap·pé (fră-pā′, frăp) *n., pl.* **trappés. 1.** A frozen, fruit-flavored mixture similar to sherbet and served as a dessert or appetizer. **2.** A beverage, usually a liqueur, poured over crushed ice. **3.** A milk shake containing ice cream. [French, from the past participle of *frapper,* "to strike," chill, from Old French *fraper,* to strike. See **trap.**] —**frap·pé** *adj.*

Fras·ca·ti (frä-skä′tē). Town in southern Italy c. 16 kilometers (10 miles) east of Rome. It is the site of the ruins of Cicero's villa and is also known for its dry white wine.

Fra·ser (frā′zər, -zhər). Chief river of British Columbia, Canada. It rises in the Rocky Mts. near the border with Alberta and flows c. 1,370 kilometers (850 miles) northwest and then south and west to the Strait of Georgia at Vancouver. The river is a major salmon-spawning ground, and its delta is a fertile agricultural region. Logging is important along its upper course.

Fraser, Simon (1776–1862). Canadian fur trader and explorer. He worked for the North West Company and explored the river named after him in British Columbia.

frat (frăt) *n. Informal.* A college fraternity.

fra·ter[1] (frā′tər) *n. Abbr.* **Fr.** A brother, as in a religious order or a fraternity. [Medieval Latin *frāter,* from Latin.]

frater[2] *n.* A refectory in a medieval monastery. [Middle English, from Old French *fraitur,* aphetic variant of *refreitor,* from Medieval Latin *refectorium,* REFECTORY.]

fra·ter·nal (frə-tûr′nəl) *adj.* **1. a.** Of or pertaining to brothers. **b.** Brotherly. **2.** Pertaining to or constituting a fraternity. **3.** *Biology.* Of, pertaining to, or being a twin or twins developed from separately fertilized ova. —See Synonyms at **familiar.** [Middle English, from Medieval Latin *frāternālis,* from Latin *frāternus,* from FRATER (brother).] —**fra·ter·nal·ism** *n.* —**fra·ter·nal·ly** *adv.*

fra·ter·ni·ty (frə-tûr′nə-tē) *n., pl.* **-ties. 1.** A body of men, such as a religious order or a guild, associated for some common purpose or interest. **2.** A group of men linked together by similar backgrounds, predilections, or occupations: *the fraternity of birdwatchers.* **3.** A chiefly social organization of male college students, usually designated by Greek letters. Compare **sorority. 4.** The relationship of a brother or brothers; brotherhood. **5.** Brotherliness. [Middle English *fraternite,* from Old French, from Latin *frāternitās* (stem *frāternitāt-*), from *frāternus,* FRATERNAL.]

frat·er·nize (frăt′ər-nīz′) *intr.v.* **-nized, -nizing, -nizes. 1.** To associate with others in a brotherly or congenial way. **2.** To mix intimately with the people of an enemy or conquered country, often in violation of military law. [French *fraterniser,* from Medieval Latin *frāternizāre,* from Latin *frāternus,* FRATERNAL.] —**frat·er·ni·za·tion** *n.* —**frat·er·niz·er** *n.*

frat·ri·cide (frăt′rə-sīd′) *n.* **1.** The killing of one's brother or sister. **2.** One who has killed his brother or sister. [Middle English (sense 2 only), from Old French (both senses), from Latin *frātricīda* (the person) and *frātricīdium* (the act) : *frāter,* FRATER + -CIDE.] —**frat·ri·cid·al** (frăt′rə-sīd′l) *adj.*

Frau (frou) *n., pl.* **Frauen** (frou′ən). *Abbr.* **Fr. 1.** A married woman in a German-speaking country or district. Used as a title corresponding to *Mrs.* **2.** *Informal.* A German woman. [German *Frau,* from Middle High German *vrouwe,* from Old High German *frouwa.*]

fraud (frôd) *n.* **1.** A deception deliberately practiced in order to secure unfair or unlawful gain. **2.** A piece of trickery; a swindle. **3. a.** One that defrauds; a cheat. **b.** One who assumes a false pose; an impostor. **c.** Something that is not what it appears or is claimed to be; a sham. [Middle English *fraude,* from Old French, from Latin *fraus*† (stem *fraud-*).]

fraud·u·lent (frô′jə-lənt) *adj.* **1.** Engaging in fraud; deceitful. **2.** Characterized by, constituting, or gained by fraud: *a fraudulent contract.* [Middle English, from Old French, from Latin *fraudulentus,* from *fraus,* FRAUD.] **—fraud·u·lence** *n.* **—fraud·u·lent·ly** *adv.*

fraught (frôt) *adj.* **1.** Filled or attended; charged. Used with *with: an occasion fraught with peril.* **2.** *Informal.* **a.** Causing anxiety or difficulty. **b.** Anxious or harassed. **3.** *Archaic.* Laden; freighted. [Middle English, past participle of *fraughten,* to load a ship, from Middle Dutch *vrachten,* from *vracht,* freight.]

Fräu·lein (froi′līn′, frou′-) *n., pl.* **Fräulein.** *Abbr.* **Frl. 1.** An unmarried girl or woman in a German-speaking country or district. Used as a title corresponding to *Miss.* **2.** *Chiefly British.* A German governess. [German, from Middle High German *vrouwelīn,* diminutive of *vrouwe,* wife, FRAU.]

Fraun·ho·fer (froun′hō′fər), **Joseph von** (1787–1826). German physicist. His development of optical lenses led to important discoveries in spectroscopy.

Fraunhofer lines *pl.n.* A set of several hundred dark lines appearing against the bright background of the continuous solar spectrum, produced by the absorption of light by cooler gases in the sun's outer atmosphere at frequencies corresponding to the atomic transition frequencies of these gases. [After J. von FRAUNHOFER.]

frax·i·nel·la (frăk′sə-nĕl′ə) *n.* The **gas plant** *(see).* [New Latin, diminutive of Latin *fraxinus,* ash tree (from the resemblance of its leaves to those of the ash).]

fray[1] (frā) *n.* **1.** A scuffle or brawl. **2.** A heated dispute or contest. [Middle English, fright, commotion, conflict, from *fraien,* to frighten, short for *afraien, affraien,* from Old French *affreer,* to AFFRAY.]

fray[2] *v.* **frayed, fraying, frays.** *—tr.* **1.** To unravel, wear away, or tatter (the edges of fabric, for example) by rubbing. **2.** To strain; chafe: *nerves frayed by noise.* *—intr.* To become tattered, unraveled, or threadbare along the edges.

∼n. A frayed or threadbare spot, as on fabric. [Middle English *fraien,* from Old French *fraier,* from Latin *fricāre,* to rub.]

Fray Ben·tos (frā bĕn′təs). River port in southwestern Uruguay, on the Uruguay River. It was founded in 1859 and has long been an important meat-packing center, noted for corned beef.

Fra·zer (frā′zər), **Sir James George** (1854–1941). British anthropologist and writer. His most famous work, *The Golden Bough* (1890), examined the development of human thought with reference to magic, religion, and science.

Fra·zier (frā′zhər), **Joe** (1944–). U.S. boxer. He was Olympic heavyweight champion (1964) and later won the world professional heavyweight title (1970), but lost it to George Foreman (1973).

fra·zil (frā′zəl, frăz′əl) *n.* Ice fragments, often sharp and pointed, that occur in turbulent water in which sheets of ice cannot form. [Canadian French *frasil;* akin to French *fraisil,* cinders.]

fraz·zle (frăz′əl) *v.* **-zled, -zling, -zles.** *Informal.* *—tr.* **1.** To fray; chafe. **2.** To wear out the nerves or strength of. *—intr.* To become frazzled or worn out.

∼n. **1.** A frayed or tattered condition. **2.** A condition of nervous exhaustion: *The racket the children made wore me to a frazzle.* [Probably a blend of FRAY (wear) and dialectal *fazzle,* to fray, from Middle English *faselen,* from *fasel,* fringe, frayed edge, diminutive of *fas,* fringe, Old English *fæs,* from Germanic *fas-* (unattested).]

F.R.B. Federal Reserve Board.

F.R.C.P. Fellow of the Royal College of Physicians.

F.R.C.S. Fellow of the Royal College of Surgeons.

freak[1] (frēk) *n.* **1.** A thing or occurrence that is very unusual or irregular: *A freak of nature produced the midsummer snowstorm.* Also used adjectivally: *a freak wind; a freak accident.* **2.** An abnormally formed organism; especially, a person or animal regarded as a curiosity or monstrosity. **3.** A sudden capricious turn of the mind; whim. **4.** *Slang.* **a.** A drug user or addict: *a speed freak.* **b.** A person with a great enthusiasm or liking for a particular subject, interest, or activity: *a baseball freak.* **5.** *Slang.* An unconventional or intentionally bizarre person.

∼v. **freaked, freaking, freaks.** *Slang.* *—intr.* **1.** To become highly excited and emotional about something. **2.** To become emotionally or mentally unstable or outlandishly uninhibited in behavior. Often used with *out.* **3.** To undergo a hallucinatory experience, especially as a result of taking drugs. Often used with *out.* *—tr.* To cause to freak or freak out. [16th century : of dialect origin.] **—freak·i·ly** *adv.* **—freak·i·ness** *n.* **—freak·y** *adj.*

freak[2] *n.* A fleck or streak of color.

∼tr.v. **freaked, freaking, freaks.** To speckle or streak with color. [Originally *freaked,* probably formed by Milton, probably variant (influenced by STREAK) of obsolete *freckt,* from FRECKLE.]

freak·ish (frē′kĭsh) *adj.* **1.** Unusual; outlandish; abnormal. **2.** Pertaining to or characteristic of a freak. **3.** Capricious. **—freak·ish·ly** *adv.* **—freak·ish·ness** *n.*

freck·le (frĕk′əl) *n.* A small brown mark or precipitation of pigment in the skin, often brought out by the sun.

∼v. **freckled, -ling, -les.** *—tr.* To dot with freckles or spots of color. *—intr.* To become dotted with freckles. [Middle English *frakles* (plural), variant of *fraknes,* from Old Norse *freknur* (plural).] **—freck·ly** *adj.*

Fred·er·ick I (frĕd′ər-ĭk, frĕd′rĭk), known as "Barbarossa" (Redbeard) (*c.* 1123–90). Holy Roman Emperor (1155–90). On his accession he asserted imperial power against the papacy in an attempt to enforce his feudal rights in Italy, but was crushingly defeated at Legnano (1176). He drowned while leading the Third Crusade.

Frederick II, known as "the Great" (1712–86). King of Prussia (1740–86). In a brilliant military career he elevated Prussia to a position of great power in Germany. He pursued a policy of enlightened despotism, laying the foundations of the Prussian military state.

Fred·er·icks·burg (frĕd′rĭks-bûrg′). City of northern Virginia, midway between Washington, D.C., and Richmond. Noted for its fine old houses, it was the site of a Civil War battle (1862) in which Gen. Robert E. Lee's Confederate forces routed the Union troops of Gen. Ambrose E. Burnside.

Fred·er·ic·ton (frĕd′ər-ĭk-tən, frĕd′rĭk-). Capital of New Brunswick, eastern Canada, in the south-central part of the province on the St. John River. The city was founded by Loyalists in 1783. Shoes and wood products are manufactured here.

free (frē) *adj.* **freer, freest. 1.** At liberty; not bound or constrained. **2.** Discharged from arrest or detention. **3.** Not under obligation or necessity. **4. a.** Politically independent. Said of a country or nation. **b.** Governed by consent and possessing civil liberties: *a free society.* **c.** Immune to arbitrary interference by government or others: *a free press.* **5. a.** Not affected or restricted by a given condition or circumstance. Used with *from* or *of*: *free from need.* Often used in combination: *trouble-free.* **b.** Not subject to a given condition; exempt. Often used in combination: *duty-free.* **c.** Not containing; without. Often used in combination: *fat-free; sugar-free.* **6. a.** Not subject to external constraint: *free criticism.* **b.** Not subject to external physical restraint: *free fall.* **c.** Graceful; easy: *free gestures.* **d.** Not fixed, attached, or tied: *the free end of a rope.* **7. a.** Not strict or literal: *a free translation.* **b.** Not following formal rules or conventions: *free verse.* **c.** Not subject to any melodic or rhythmic patterns; completely improvised: *free jazz.* **8. a.** Costing nothing; gratuitous: *a free ticket.* **b.** Public; open to all: *free education.* **c.** Not paying the usual fee: *a free patient.* **9. a.** Unoccupied; available for use: *a free shelf.* **b.** Not busy; available: *a free afternoon; free to see you now.* **c.** Unobstructed; clear: *a free lane.* **10.** Guileless; frank: *"The Moor is of a free and open nature"* (Shakespeare). **11.** Taking undue liberties; forward. **12.** Liberal or lavish: *free with his money.* **13.** Uninhibited; racy: *much free talking and flirting at the party.* **14.** Uncommitted; independent: *a free woman.* **15.** *Chemistry & Physics.* **a.** Unconstrained; unconfined: *free expansion.* **b.** Not fixed in position; capable of relatively unrestricted motion: *a free electron.* **c.** Not chemically bound; uncombined: *free oxygen.* **d.** Involving no collisions or interactions: *a free path.* **16.** *Nautical.* Favorable. Said of a wind. **17.** *Phonetics.* Designating a vowel in an open syllable unchecked by a consonant; for example, *o* in *go* is a free vowel. **18.** *Botany.* Not joined to one another or to other organs. Said especially of flower parts, as petals.

∼adv. **1.** In a free manner; freely. **2.** Without charge. **—make free with.** To take liberties with. **—run free.** *Nautical.* To sail with the wind aft.

∼tr.v. **freed, freeing, frees. 1.** To set at liberty; release. **2.** To rid or release. Used with *of* or *from: a people freed from fear.* **3.** To disengage; untangle: *free a rope.* [Middle English *fre(e),* Old English *frēo,* from Germanic *frijaz* (unattested).] **—free·ly** *adv.* **—free·ness** *n.*

Usage: In its sense "unaffected or unrestricted by a given condition," *free* takes both *from* and *of. Of* is found in the context of finance (*free of charge; free of tax*) and where the general sense is one of removing a problem or restriction: *The room has been disinfected and is now free of germs. From* tends to be used where the general sense is one of actively preventing a problem from developing: *kept the garden free from weeds.*

free agent *n.* A person unconstrained by ties of emotion, contract, or other commitments; especially, a professional athlete who is free to sign a contract with any sports team.

free alongside ship *adj. Abbr.* **f.a.s., F.A.S.** Delivered to the pier or dock at no extra charge. Said of cargo going by sea.

free-and-eas·y (frē′ən-ē′zē) *adj.* Also **free and easy.** Informal in manner and unconcerned with strict niceties.

free-as·so·ci·ate (frē′ə-sō′shē-āt′, -sē-āt′) *intr.v.* **-ated, -ating, -ates.** To engage in free association.

free association *n.* **1.** A spontaneous, logically unconstrained association of ideas and feelings. **2.** A psychoanalytic technique in which a patient's articulation of such associations is encouraged in order to elicit repressed thoughts and emotions.

free·bie, free·bee (frē′bē) *n. Slang.* A free gift; something provided without payment. [From FREE.]

free·board (frē′bôrd′, -bōrd′) *n.* **1.** *Nautical.* The distance between the water line and the uppermost full deck. **2.** The distance between the ground and the undercarriage of an automobile.

freeboard deck *n.* The uppermost deck that is officially considered completely watertight.

free·boot (frē′bo͞ot′) *intr.v.* **-booted, -booting, -boots.** To act as a freebooter; plunder. [Back-formation from FREEBOOTER.]

free·boot·er (frē′bo͞o′tər) *n.* A person who pillages and plunders; especially, a pirate; buccaneer. [Partial cognate translation of Dutch *vrijbuiter,* from *vrijbuit,* free booty : *vrij,* FREE + *buit,* BOOTY.]

free·born (frē′bôrn′) *adj.* **1.** Born as a free person. **2.** Pertaining to or befitting a person born free.

free capital *n.* **1.** Capital available for investment. **2.** Capital not earmarked for a specific use.

PRONUNCIATION KEY

ă, pat; ā, pay; âr, care;
ä, father, are; b, bib;
ch, church; d, deed; ĕ, pet;
ē, be; f, fife; g, gag; h, hat;
hw, which; ĭ, pit; ī, pie;
îr, pier; j, judge; k, kick;
l, lid, needle; m, mum;
n, no, sudden; ng, thing;
ŏ, pot; ō, toe; ô, paw, for;
oi, noise; ou, out; o͝o, book;
o͞o, boot; p, pop; r, roar;
s, sauce; sh, ship, dish;
t, tight; th, thin, path;
th, this, bathe; ŭ, cut; ûr, fur;
v, valve; w, with; y, yes;
z, zebra, size; zh, vision;
ə, about, item, edible,
gallop, circus, peaceful

IN FOREIGN WORDS:

à, *Fr.* ami; œ, *Fr.* feu, *Ger.* schön; ü, *Fr.* tu, *Ger.* über;
KH, *Ger.* ich, *Scot.* loch;
N, *Fr.* bon; y′, *Fr.* Compiègne

STRESS MARKS:

Primary stress: ′
in·cite′ (ĭn-sīt′)
Secondary stress: ′
in′sight′ (ĭn′sīt′)

Free Church *n. Chiefly British.* **1.** Any non-Anglican Protestant Church; a Nonconformist church. **2.** Any church that is not the established church of a state or that is free of state control. **—Free-Church** (frē'chûrch') *adj.*

free city *n.* **1.** A sovereign city-state, such as those established in Germany and Italy in the Middle Ages. **2.** A city governed as an autonomous political unit under international auspices.

free companion *n.* A mercenary of the Middle Ages.

free company *n.* A company of free companions.

freed·man (frēd'mən) *n., pl.* **-men** (mĭn). A man who has been freed from bondage; an emancipated slave.

free·dom (frē'dəm) *n.* **1.** The condition of being free of restraints. **2.** The condition of not being subject to slavery, oppression, or imprisonment. **3. a.** Political independence. **b.** Possession of civil rights; immunity from the arbitrary exercise of authority. **4.** Exemption from unpleasant or onerous conditions. Used with *from: freedom from fear and want.* **5.** The capacity to exercise choice; free will. **6.** Facility or ease, as of movement. **7.** Originality of style or conception. **8.** Frankness. **9. a.** Boldness; impertinence. **b.** An instance of improper boldness; a liberty. **10.** Unrestricted use or access. **11.** The right of enjoying all of the privileges of membership or citizenship: *the freedom of the city.* [Middle English *fredom,* Old English *frēodōm : frēo,* FREE + -DOM.]

freedom fighter *n.* One who takes militant action against an established government, usually one of an authoritarian nature.

freedom of the seas *n. International Law.* **1.** The doctrine that ships of any nation may travel through international waters unhampered. **2.** The right of neutral shipping in wartime to trade at will except where blockades are established.

freed·wom·an (frēd'wŏŏm'ən) *n., pl.* **-women** (-wĭm'ĭn). A woman freed from bondage.

free electron *n.* An electron that is not bound to an atom, such as an electron in a conductor that is available to move in a current.

free energy *n.* **1.** A thermodynamic quantity that is the difference between the internal energy and the product of the thermodynamic temperature and entropy of a system. Also called "Helmholtz free energy." **2.** A thermodynamic quantity that is the difference between the enthalpy and the product of the thermodynamic temperature and entropy of a system. In this sense, also called "Gibbs free energy."

free enterprise *n.* The freedom of private businesses to operate competitively for profit, with minimal government regulation.

free fall *n.* **1.** The fall of a body within the atmosphere without a drag-producing device such as a parachute. **2.** The unconstrained motion of a body in a gravitational field.

free flight *n.* Flight, as of an aircraft or spacecraft, after termination of powered flight.

free-float·ing (frē'flō'tĭng) *adj.* **1.** Not attached or fixed to any specific base or source. **2.** Not committed to any particular viewpoint or course of action; independent.

free-for-all (frē'fər-ôl') *n.* A brawl, argument, or competition in which everyone present takes part.

free form *n. Linguistics.* A morpheme capable of standing alone and retaining meaning. Compare **bound form.**

free-form (frē'fôrm') *adj.* Designating a form in music, art, literature, or the like that is free of stylistic conventions.

free gift *n.* An object given away with or accompanying without extra charge a purchased object. Often used as an inducement to purchase, especially in mail-order selling.

free hand *n.* Full liberty to do or decide as one sees fit.

free-hand (frē'hănd') *adj.* Drawn by hand without the aid of tracing or guiding instruments: *a freehand sketch.*
~*adv.* By hand without mechanical aids.

free-hand·ed (frē'hăn'dĭd) *adj.* Openhanded; generous; unstinting. **—free-hand·ed·ly** *adv.* **—free-hand·ed·ness** *n.*

free-heart·ed (frē'här'tĭd) *adj.* Unreserved; open; generous; liberal. **—free-heart·ed·ly** *adv.* **—free-heart·ed·ness** *n.*

free-hold (frē'hōld') *n.* **1.** *Law.* **a.** An estate held in fee simple, fee tail, or for life. **b.** The tenure by which such an estate is held. Compare **leasehold. 2.** Loosely, outright ownership of land. **3.** A lease of an office or a dignity for life. [Middle English *frehold* (translation of Norman French *frauc tenement,* "free or frank holding") : FREE + HOLD.] **—free-hold** *adj.* **—free-hold·er** *n.*

free kick *n.* In various types of football, an unhindered kick awarded to a team for an infringement of the rules by the opposing team.

free-lance (frē'lăns', -läns') *n.* Also **free-lanc·er** (frē'lăn'sər, -län'sər). **1.** A person, especially a writer or an artist, who sells his services to employers without a long-term commitment to any one of them. **2.** One who remains uncommitted to a party and proceeds as an independent. **3.** A medieval mercenary; a free companion.
~*v.* **freelanced, -lancing, -lances.** —*intr.* To work as a freelance. —*tr.* To produce and sell as a freelance.
~*adj.* Pertaining to or produced by a freelance.
~*adv.* On a freelance basis.

free-liv·ing (frē'lĭv'ĭng) *adj.* **1.** Given to self-indulgence. **2.** *Biology.* Living or moving independently; not part of a parasitic or symbiotic relationship.

free-load (frē'lōd') *intr.v.* **-loaded, -loading, -loads.** *Slang.* To act as a freeloader; sponge.

free-load·er (frē'lō'dər) *n. Slang.* One who takes advantage of the generosity or hospitality of others; a sponger.

free love *n.* The practice of sexual relations without marriage and without formal or legal obligations.

free·man (frē'mən) *n., pl.* **-men** (-mĭn). **1.** A person not in slavery or serfdom. **2.** One who possesses the rights or privileges of a citizen.

free·mar·tin (frē'märt'n) *n.* A sterile or otherwise sexually deficient female calf born as the twin of a bull calf. [17th century : origin obscure.]

free·ma·son (frē'mā'sən) *n.* **1.** A member of a guild of skilled itinerant masons of the Middle Ages. **2. Freemason.** A member of the Free and Accepted Masons, an international secret society. In this sense, also called "Mason." [Originally, perhaps a mason not subject to guild control and so free to work anywhere.]

free·ma·son·ry (frē'mā'sən-rē) *n.* **1.** Tacit fellowship and sympathy among a number of people. **2. Freemasonry. a.** The institutions, precepts, and rites of the Freemasons. **b.** The Freemasons. In this sense, also called "Masonry."

free on board *adj. Abbr.* **f.o.b., F.O.B. 1.** In international commerce, designating goods delivered and insured at the seller's expense until arriving at the port of shipment named by the buyer. **2.** Delivered on board or into a carrier without charge.

free port *n.* **1.** A port open on equal terms to all commercial vessels. **2.** An area in which imported goods can be held or processed before re-export, free of customs duties.

fre·er¹ (frē'ər) *n.* One who frees.

fre·er². Comparative of **free.**

free radical *n.* An atom or group of atoms containing at least one unpaired electron and having a short lifetime before reacting to form a stable molecule.

free·si·a (frē'zhē-ə, -zhə, -zē-ə) *n.* Any of several widely cultivated plants of the genus *Freesia,* native to southern Africa, having one-sided clusters of fragrant, variously colored flowers. [New Latin, after Friedrich H.T. *Freese* (died 1876), German physician.]

free silver *n.* The free coinage of silver, especially at a fixed ratio to gold.

free soil *n.* U.S. territory in which slavery was prohibited before the Civil War.

free-soil (frē'soil') *adj.* **1.** Prohibiting slavery: *free-soil states.* **2.** Opposing the extension of slavery prior to the Civil War. **3. Free-Soil.** Pertaining to or designating a U.S. political party founded in 1848 to oppose the extension of slavery into U.S. Territories and the admission of slave states into the Union.

free speech *n.* The right to express any opinion in public.

free-spo·ken (frē'spō'kən) *adj.* Candid in expression; outspoken; frank. **—free-spo·ken·ness** *n.*

fre·est. Superlative of **free.**

free-stand·ing (frē'stăn'dĭng) *adj.* Standing independently; free of support or attachment.

Free State. A U.S. state prohibiting slavery prior to the Civil War.

free-stone (frē'stōn') *n.* **1.** A stone, such as some sandstones or limestones, fine-grained and even-textured enough to be cut easily in any direction without shattering or splitting. **2.** A fruit, especially a peach, having a stone that does not adhere to the pulp. In this sense, compare **clingstone.**
~*adj.* Having a stone that does not adhere to the pulp.

free-style (frē'stīl') *n.* **1.** In swimming, a race in which any stroke may be used. The **crawl** *(see)* is usually chosen because of the speed achieved with this stroke. **2.** In various sports, a contest or style of performing in which any movements are allowed. Also used adjectivally: *freestyle wrestling.* **—free-style** *adv.*

free-swim·ming (frē'swĭm'ĭng) *adj. Zoology.* Able to swim freely; not sessile or attached: *the free-swimming larva of the oyster.* **—free-swim·mer** *n.*

free-think·er (frē'thĭng'kər) *n.* One who has rejected authority and dogma, especially in his religious thinking, in favor of rational inquiry and speculation. **—free-think·ing** *adj. & n.*

free thought *n.* Freethinking; unorthodox thought.

free throw *n. Basketball.* A foul shot *(see).*

free-throw line (frē'thrō') *n. Basketball.* The foul line *(see).*

Free·town (frē'toun'). Capital of Sierra Leone. Situated on the Sierra Leone peninsula, with an exceptional natural harbor, it is also one of West Africa's chief ports. The town was founded by freed slaves sent from North America in 1787 by the Sierra Leone Company.

free trade *n.* Trade between nations or states without protective customs tariffs or other restrictions.

free verse *n.* Verse that does not follow a conventional metrical or stanzaic pattern and has either an irregular rhyme or no rhyme. [Translation of French *vers libre.*]

free-way (frē'wā') *n.* **1.** A highway with several lanes and no intersections or stoplights; expressway. **2.** A highway without tolls.

free-wheel (frē'hwēl') *n.* **1.** A transmission device in a motor vehicle that allows the drive shaft to continue turning when its speed is greater than that of the engine shaft. **2.** A device in the rear-wheel hub of a bicycle that permits the wheel to turn without pedal action. Also used adjectivally: *a freewheel bicycle.*
~*intr.v.* **freewheeled, -wheeling, -wheels.** To live or move freely, aimlessly, or irresponsibly.

free-wheel·ing (frē'hwē'lĭng) *adj.* **1.** Pertaining to or equipped with a freewheel. **2.** *Informal.* **a.** Free of restraints or rules in organization, methods, or procedure. **b.** Heedless; carefree.

free will *n.* **1.** The power or discretion to choose; free choice. **2.** The belief that man's choices ultimately are or can be voluntary, and are not determined by external causes. Compare **determinism**. [Translation of Late Latin *liberum arbitrium*.]

free world *n. Sometimes* **Free World.** The portion of the world marked by democratic and capitalistic or socialistic systems rather than by Communist or totalitarian systems.

freeze (frēz) *v.* **froze** (frōz), **frozen** (frō′zən), **freezing, freezes.** —*intr.* **1. a.** To pass from the liquid to the solid state by loss of heat. **b.** To acquire a surface of ice from cold. Often used with *over.* **2.** To become inoperative owing to frost or the formation of ice: *The pipes froze.* **3.** To become hard from cold, as laundry or the ground. **4.** To undergo freezing and thawing successfully: *Raspberries don't freeze well.* **5. a.** To be at that degree of temperature at which ice forms. Used impersonally: *It may freeze tonight.* **b.** To be uncomfortably cold. Used impersonally: *It's freezing in here.* **6.** To be harmed, ruined, or killed by cold or frost: *The crops froze.* **7.** To feel the cold acutely: *I'm freezing.* **8.** To become fixed, stuck, or attached by or as if by frost: *The bolt had frozen in place.* **9.** To become motionless, as from fear, horror, or shyness. **10.** To become icily silent in manner. Often used with *up: She froze up at the rebuke.* —*tr.* **1. a.** To convert into ice. **b.** To cause ice to form upon. **c.** To cause to become solid, congeal, or stiffen from extreme cold. **2.** To preserve by subjecting to freezing temperatures. **3.** To damage, kill, or make inoperative by cold or by the formation of ice. **4. a.** To make very cold; chill. **b.** To chill with an icy or formal manner. **5.** To make rigid and inflexible. **6.** To fix (prices or wages) at a given or current level. **7.** To prohibit further manufacture or use of. **8.** To prevent or restrict the exchange, liquidation, or granting of by law: *The banks have agreed to freeze investment loans.* **9. a.** *Surgery.* To anesthetize by freezing. **b.** Loosely, to apply a local anesthetic to. **10. a.** To stop (a moving film) at a particular frame. **b.** To repeat a frame in (a moving film) to give the impression of arrested movement. **11.** To stop (a process or action) at a particular point in development. —**freeze in one's tracks.** To stop short and remain motionless, as with fear. —**freeze out.** *Informal.* To shut out or bar, as from a business or a social group, by boycotting, snubbing, or cold treatment.

~*n.* **1. a.** An act of freezing. **b.** The state of being frozen. **2.** A spell of cold weather; a frost. [Freeze, froze, frozen; Middle English *fresen, frose, frosen,* variant (influenced by present tense) of *froren,* from Old English *frēosan, frēas, froren,* from Germanic.]

freeze-dry (frēz′drī′) *tr.v.* **-dried, -drying, -dries.** To preserve by freeze-drying.

freeze-dry·ing (frēz′drī′ĭng) *n.* Preservation, as of foodstuffs or histological specimens, by rapid freezing and drying in a high vacuum.

freeze-etch·ing (frēz′ĕch′ĭng) *n.* A method of preparing a specimen for examination under an electron microscope whereby the specimen is frozen and then fractured with a knife so that a shadowed replica of the surface can be made.

freeze-frame (frēz′frām′) *n.* The capacity in film projection systems to stop a moving film at a particular frame. Also used adjectivally: *freeze-frame capacity.*

freez·er (frē′zər) *n.* **1.** One that freezes. **2.** A thermally insulated cabinet, compartment, or room that maintains a subfreezing temperature for the rapid freezing and storing of perishable food. Also called "deepfreeze."

freeze-up (frēz′ŭp′) *n. Informal.* **1.** A period of intensely cold weather. **2.** The freezing over of lakes and rivers.

freez·ing (frē′zĭng) *adj.* Extremely cold. ~*adv.* Used as an intensive: *freezing cold.*

freezing mixture *n.* A mixture of two substances, usually ice and salt, that gives a temperature of less than 0°C.

freezing point *n. Abbr.* **fp 1.** The temperature at which a liquid solidifies. **2.** The temperature at which the solid and liquid phases of a substance are in equilibrium at atmospheric pressure.

free zone *n.* An area at a port or city where goods may be received and held without the payment of duty.

F region *n.* A region of the ionosphere, the **F layer** *(see).*

Freiburg. See Fribourg.

Frei·burg im Breis·gau (frī′bûrg ĭm brīs′gou′, frī′bo͝ork′). City in Baden-Württemberg in Germany, on the western edge of the Black Forest. The city, seat of a university (founded 1457), is a tourist center, with some light manufacturing, notably of textiles, paper, and musical and optical instruments.

freight (frāt) *n. Abbr.* **frt. 1. a.** Goods carried by a vessel or aircraft; lading. **b.** Goods transported as cargo by a commercial carrier, as distinguished from luggage and mail. **2.** A charge or burden. **3.** The commercial transportation of goods. **4.** The charge for transporting goods by cargo carrier. **5.** *Chiefly British.* The cargo of a ship or airplane.

~*tr.v.* **freighted, freighting, freights. 1.** To convey commercially as cargo. **2.** To load with goods to be transported. **3.** To load; charge. [Middle English *fraught, freight,* from Middle Dutch *vrecht, vracht,* cargo, fee for a transport vessel.]

freight·age (frā′tĭj) *n.* **1.** The commercial transportation of goods. **2.** The charge for such transportation. **3.** Cargo.

freight car *n.* A railroad car designed for carrying freight.

freight·er (frā′tər) *n.* **1.** A ship or aircraft for carrying freight. **2.** A shipper of cargo.

freight train *n.* A railroad train made up of freight cars.

Fre·man·tle (frē′măn′tl). Chief port of Western Australia, now part of the city of Perth. It is one of the oldest European settlements in Australia.

frem·i·tus (frĕm′ə-təs) *n., pl.* **fremitus.** *Pathology.* A palpable vibration, as felt by the hand placed on the chest during coughing or speaking. [Latin, noise, roar, from the past participle of *fremere,* to roar.]

Fré·mont (frē′mŏnt′), **John Charles** (1813–90). U.S. explorer, soldier, and politician. He explored the West and Northwest, mapping much of the region and earning himself wide repute as an adventurer. During the Mexican War he twice captured Los Angeles (1847). After a stint as a U.S. senator (1850–51) and a bid for the Presidency (1856), he resumed his volatile military career.

fre·na. Alternate plural of **frenum.**

french (frĕnch) *tr.v.* **frenched, frenching, frenches. 1.** To cut into thin strips before cooking. **2.** To trim fat or bone from (a chop, for example).

French (frĕnch) *adj. Abbr.* **F., Fr.** Of, pertaining to, or characteristic of France or its people, language, or culture.

~*n. Abbr.* **F., Fr. 1.** The Romance language spoken by the people of France, western Switzerland, and southern Belgium, and in various former French possessions. **2.** *Used with a plural verb.* The people of France. Preceded by *the.* [Middle English *french,* Old English *frencisc,* FRANKISH.]

French, Daniel Chester (1850–1931). U.S. sculptor. Largely self-taught, he created notable works of sculpture such as *The Minute Man* (1875). His best-known work, the seated marble figure of Abraham Lincoln at the Lincoln Memorial in Washington, D.C., has inspired countless visitors since its dedication in 1922.

French, John Denton Pinkstone, 1st Earl of Ypres (1852–1925). British field marshal. He led the British Expeditionary Force to Europe at the outbreak of World War 1, but following its near annihilation in the first two battles of Ypres he resigned his command (1915).

French and Indian War. A war (1754–63) that was fought in North America between England and France, who had the support of Indian allies.

French bread *n.* Bread made with water, flour, and yeast and baked in long, crusty loaves.

French bulldog *n.* A small compact dog of a breed developed in France from toy English bulldogs and native breeds.

French Canada. The region of Canada dominated by French-Canadians; especially, Quebec.

French-Ca·na·di·an (frĕnch′kə-nā′dē-ən) *n.* Also **French Canadian. 1.** A Canadian of French descent. **2.** The French language as spoken in Canada. —**French-Ca·na·di·an** *adj.*

French chalk *n.* Chalk made of a soft, white variety of talc, used by tailors for marking fabrics, and by dry cleaners for removing grease.

French chop *n.* A rib chop with the meat and fat trimmed from the end of the rib.

French Community. Association of France and its territories and some former colonies, established in 1958 by the constitution of the Fifth Republic. It is made up of the French Republic, comprising metropolitan France (mainland France and Corsica) and the overseas departments and territories, and several independent African republics. It is a loose association, designed to promote members' cooperation in military, economic, and cultural affairs.

French cuff *n.* A wide cuff that is folded back to make a double cuff and fastened with a cufflink.

French curve *n.* A flat instrument with curved edges and scroll-shaped cutouts, used by draftsmen for drawing irregular curves and as a guide in connecting a set of individual points with a smooth curve.

French door *n.* A door of light construction with glass panes often extending the full length, and usually hung in pairs.

French dressing *n.* A seasoned oil-and-vinegar salad dressing.

French Equatorial Africa. A former French territory in west-central Africa, known before 1910 as the French Congo. It consisted of Gabon, Middle Congo (now Congo), Chad, and Ubangi-Shari (now the Central African Republic); its capital was Brazzaville. When each constituent voted to become independent in 1958, the territory broke up, and in 1960 the four new republics became members of the French Community.

French fries *pl.n.* Also **french fries.** Thin strips of potatoes fried in deep fat.

French-fry (frĕnch′frī′) *tr.v.* **-fried, -frying, -fries.** To fry (potato strips, for example) in deep fat.

French Gui·an·a (gē-ăn′ə, -ä′nə). French overseas department on the Atlantic coast of northeastern South America. It became a permanent French colony in 1817 and in 1946 was given the status of an overseas department. Devil's Island, just off the coast, was formerly the site of a penal colony. The capital is Cayenne. See map at **Guyana.**

French Guinea. See **Guinea.**

French harp *n. Informal.* A mouth organ; harmonica.

French heel *n.* A curved moderately high heel on a woman's shoe.

French horn *n.* A valved brass wind instrument with a circular shape, tapering from a narrow mouthpiece to a flaring bell at the other end, and producing a mellow tone.

French ice cream *n.* An ice cream rich in egg yolks and cream.

French·i·fy (frĕn′chə-fī′) *v.* **-fied, -fying, -fies.** —*tr.* To give a French character or quality to. —*intr.* To assume French ways or characteristics.

French India. A former overseas territory of France in India, including the settlements of Chandernagore, Pondicherry (the capital), and Yanaon on the east coast and Mahé on the west, with a combined area of 500 square kilometers (193 square miles). The territory was returned to India (1949–54).

French Indochina. Part of Southeast Asia formerly controlled by France, mostly until 1954. Set up in 1887, it included Cochin China, Annam and Tonkin (which now make up Vietnam), and Cambodia (now Kampuchea). Laos was added in 1893.

French kiss *n. Slang.* A kiss in which the tongue enters the partner's mouth. —**French-kiss** (frěnch'kǐs') *v.*

French knitting *n.* A technique of braiding yarn around pins attached to the top of a cotton reel. The finished work is pulled through the center of the reel as a knitted tube, which is then rolled up and sewn into mats.

French knot *n.* A decorative stitch made by looping the thread two or more times around the needle, which is then inserted into the fabric.

French leave *n.* An unauthorized or unannounced departure or absence. [From an 18th-century French custom of leaving without bidding good-by to the host or hostess.]

French-man (frěnch'mən) *n., pl.* **-men** (-mĭn). **1.** A native or citizen of France. **2.** A French ship.

French marigold *n.* A widely cultivated plant, *Tagetes patula,* native to Mexico, having divided leaves and yellow flowers with reddish markings.

French Morocco. A former French protectorate established over most of the area of present-day Morocco in 1912, and now part of the kingdom of Morocco.

French mulberry *n.* A species of **beautyberry** *(see).*

French navy *n.* Lightish navy blue.

French North Africa. A term formerly used to designate Algeria, French Morocco, and Tunisia collectively.

French pastry *n.* Any of a wide variety of rich and elaborate pastries prepared in individual portions.

French polish *n.* **1.** A wood varnish consisting of a solution of shellac dissolved in methanol. **2.** The finish produced on a piece of furniture by this varnish.

French-pol·ish (frěnch'pŏl'ĭsh) *tr.v.* **-polished, -polishing, -polishes.** To apply French polish to (a surface).

French Polynesia. A French overseas territory consisting of *c.* 130 tropical islands scattered over some 4 million square kilometers (1.5 million square miles) of the eastern Pacific Ocean. The capital, Papeete, is on Tahiti. The island groups became a French colony in 1880 and in 1958 opted to become an overseas territory within the French Community. Tourism and copra export are the mainstays of the economy. See map at **Pacific Ocean.**

French provincial *n.* A style of architecture or furniture characteristic of the provinces in 17th- and 18th-century France.

French Revolution *n.* A revolt in France against the monarchy and aristocracy lasting from 1789 to 1799, when Napoleon gained control.

French roll *n.* A woman's hairstyle with the hair pulled back from the face and worn in a vertical cylindrical roll at the back of the head. Also called "French pleat."

French roof *n. Architecture.* A curb roof resembling the mansard and having nearly perpendicular slopes.

French seam *n.* A seam stitched first on the right side and then turned in and stitched on the wrong side so that the raw edges are enclosed in the seam.

French Somaliland. See **Djibouti.**

French Southern and Antarctic Territories. An overseas territory of France comprising Adélie Land in Antarctica and several islands south of 38° S. The islands are the Kerguelen and Crozet groups and Amsterdam (formerly Nouvelle Amsterdam) and Saint-Paul islands. The only population of the territory, administered from Paris, is the staff of the hospital and office on Amsterdam and scientific and meteorological research workers scattered over the territory.

French Sudan. See **Mali.**

French toast *n.* Sliced bread soaked in a milk and egg batter and lightly fried.

French To·go·land (tō'gō-lănd'). A former United Nations Trust Territory in western Africa, administered by France (1946–60). See **Togo.**

French vermouth *n.* A dry vermouth.

French West Africa. Former federation of French colonies in Africa. Established in 1895, it included Senegal, French Guinea, the Ivory Coast, and French Sudan (Mali) and was administered as one colony from Dakar. Later Dahomey, Upper Senegal-Niger, Mauritania, and Upper Volta were incorporated. The federation was dissolved in 1958 and the territories, with the exception of French Guinea, became independent republics within the French Community.

French West Indies. Unofficially, the French overseas departments of Guadeloupe and Martinique, in the Caribbean.

French window *n.* A door with one large or several small glass panes, or a casement window extending to floor level, usually hung in pairs and often giving access to a garden or balcony.

French·wom·an (frěnch'wŏŏm'ən) *n., pl.* **-women** (-wĭm'ĭn). A woman who is a native or citizen of France.

French·y (frěnch'ē) *adj.* **-ier, -iest.** *Informal.* Displaying French characteristics.

~*n., pl.* **Frenchies.** *Slang.* A French person.

Fre·neau (frĭ-nō') **Philip Morin** (1752–1832). U.S. author and sailor. Before the American Revolution he penned several satirical

VIOLENT CLIMAX OF AN AGE OF UNREST
Liberty, Equality, and Fraternity at the cost of Terror

The French Revolution of 1789–99 was part of an age of social uprising involving America and Europe from about 1770 to the 1840's. Its roots lay in the strain of long wars and heavy taxation imposed by the autocratic Louis XIV (died 1715). An absolute monarchy and an entrenched nobility and clergy formed too rigid a system to allow the changes needed by a rising middle class, a burgeoning population, and a peasantry restless under feudal obligations.

The immediate cause of violence was to try to eradicate the national debt by increasing taxes. When the States General, the national assembly, met in May 1789 to resolve the crisis, it was bombarded with demands for more basic changes. In response, the commons, the middle-class majority in the Third Estate of the national assembly, claimed supremacy, declared itself to be the National Assembly, and prepared to draft France's first constitution. The king, Louis XVI, grudgingly agreed.

On July 14, Parisian mobs supporting the commons stormed the Bastille, a prison that symbolized absolutism. Riots spread among the peasants across the nation. The Assembly proclaimed a new era of liberty and equality. Louis withheld agreement, and both he and his wife, Marie Antoinette, were seized. The royal couple managed to flee, only to be caught and forced to accede in June 1791.

In 1792 the Assembly sought to spread revolution by war and attacked Austria and Prussia. Soon most of Europe was involved in the revolutionary wars, and there was much bloodshed in France. Fearing betrayal, revolutionaries imprisoned the king and ordered elections for a National Convention. In September hundreds of royalists were murdered.

The Convention established a republic and on January 21, 1793, the king was executed. War was declared against Holland, Spain, and Britain. Then to protect its reforms, the Convention, dominated by Maximilian Robespierre, initiated a Reign of Terror in which 300,000 were arrested and 17,000 executed by the guillotine. Eventually, the Convention, fearful for their own lives, turned against Robespierre himself and executed him.

The Convention proceeded to draw up a new constitution and established a five-man Directory in October 1795 to govern France. The Directory was split by corruption, intrigue, and a fatal dependence on the army to maintain order. This internal conflict led to a coup d'état, in September 1797, directed against those who wished to restore constitutional monarchy. However, in 1799 Napoleon Bonaparte returned from fighting in Egypt and overthrew the Directory. He established the Consulate and thereby ended the Revolution.

DEATH OF THE KING *Louis XVI, as much a victim of his time as he was a poor ruler, was unable to stem the flow of revolutionary violence. In 1793 the Republicans executed him by the guillotine.*

pamphlets and his most critically acclaimed poems. During the war he served in the navy and was captured by the British, an experience recounted in *The British Prison Ship: A Poem* (1781).

fre·net·ic (frə-nĕt'ĭk) *adj.* Frantic; frenzied. [Middle English *frenetik,* frenzied, insane, from Old French *frenetique,* from Latin *phrenēticus,* from Greek *phrenitikos,* from *phrenitis,* brain disease, insanity, from *phrēn,* mind.] —**fre·net·i·cal·ly** *adv.*

fren·u·lum, fraen·u·lum (frĕn'yə-ləm) *n., pl.* **-la** (-lə). **1.** A bristly structure on the hind wing of certain moths and other insects that holds the forewing and hind wing together during flight. **2.** A small **frenum** *(see).* [New Latin, diminutive of FRENUM.]

fre·num, frae·num (frē'nəm) *n., pl.* **-nums** or **-na** (-nə). A membranous fold that supports or restricts the movement of a part, such as the fold under the tongue. [Latin, "bridle."]

fren·zied (frĕn'zēd) *adj.* Characterized by, affected with, or filled with frenzy; frantic. —**fren·zied·ly** *adv.*

fren·zy (frĕn'zē) *n., pl.* **-zies. 1.** A seizure of violent agitation or wild excitement, often accompanied by manic activity. **2.** Temporary madness or delirium: *"I struggled with the frenzy, though I felt it must tear me in pieces"* (Mary Renault). **3.** An extravagant idea;

mania; craze. Used with *for*: *"man had a frenzy for getting away from any control"* (D.H. Lawrence).
~*tr.v.* **frenzied, -zying, -zies.** To drive into a frenzy. [Middle English *frenesie,* from Old French, from Medieval Latin *phrenēsia,* from Latin *phrenēsis,* from *phrēn,* mind, from Greek.]

fresco *A detail from* The Annunciation of the Virgin *by Pontormo (1494–1557). In fresco painting, mineral and earth colors are applied quickly on fresh plaster or mortar before it dries.*

Fre·on (frē′ŏn′) *n.* A trademark for any of various nonflammable gaseous or liquid fluorocarbons that are used mainly as working fluids in refrigeration and air conditioning and as aerosol propellants.
freq. **1.** frequentative. **2.** frequently.
fre·quence (frē′kwəns) *n.* Frequency. [Middle English, multitude, from Latin *frequentia,* from *frequens,* crowded.]
fre·quen·cy (frē′kwən-sē) *n., pl.* **-cies. 1.** *Mathematics & Physics.* The number of times a specified phenomenon occurs within a specified interval, as: **a.** The number of repetitions of a complete sequence of values of a periodic function per unit variation of an independent variable. **b.** The number of complete cycles of a periodic process occurring per unit time. **c.** The number of repetitions per unit time of a complete waveform, as of an electric current. **2.** *Statistics.* **a.** The number of measurements in an interval of a frequency distribution. **b.** The ratio of the number of times an event occurs in a series of trials of a chance experiment to the number of trials of the experiment performed. **3.** The property or condition of occurring repeatedly at short intervals. **4.** The number of times that something regularly recurs. [Latin *frequentia,* crowd, from *frequēns,* FREQUENT.]
frequency band *n.* A band of frequencies. See **band.**
frequency curve *n. Statistics.* A graphic representation of a frequency distribution obtained by plotting the variable property along the x-axis divided into intervals and the numbers of members along the y-axis. If there is a finite number of intervals of significant size and if the points are joined by straight lines, the resulting diagram is a frequency polygon.
frequency distribution *n. Statistics.* The way in which some property is distributed among members of a set, according to the numbers of members having particular values of the property. It is obtained by dividing the variable (property) into intervals and specifying the number of members of the set having a value of the property lying within each interval.
frequency modulation *n. Abbr.* **fm, FM** *Electronics.* The encoding of a carrier wave by variation of its frequency in accordance with an input signal. Compare **amplitude modulation.**
frequency polygon *n.* A graphic representation of a frequency distribution consisting of a set of points each obtained by plotting class frequency as ordinate and class mark as abscissa, together with line segments joining points of adjacent classes.
fre·quent (frē′kwənt) *adj.* Occurring or appearing quite often or at close intervals.
~*tr.v.* (frē-kwĕnt′, frē′kwənt) **frequented, -quenting, -quents.** To pay frequent visits to; be often in, at, or in the company of. [Middle English, profuse, ample, from Old French, from Latin *frequēns* (stem *frequent-*), full, frequent.] **—fre·quent·er** (frē-kwĕn′tər) *n.* **—fre·quent·ly** *adv.* **—fre·quent·ness** *n.*

friarbird *Also called the leatherhead, the friarbird is native to Australia, using its long bill to suck nectar from flowers. It gets its name from a bald patch on its head that resembles a friar's tonsure.*

fre·quen·ta·tion (frē′kwĕn-tā′shən, frē′kwən-) *n.* The act or practice of frequenting a place.
fre·quen·ta·tive (frē-kwĕn′tə-tĭv) *adj. Abbr.* **freq.** *Grammar.* Expressing or denoting repeated action.
~*n. Abbr.* **freq.** A frequentative verb or verb form.
fres·co (frĕs′kō) *n., pl.* **-coes** or **-cos. 1.** The art of painting by applying pure pigments dissolved in water onto fresh lime plaster. **2.** A painting executed on plaster.
~*tr.v.* **frescoed, -coing, -coes.** To paint on fresh plaster. [Italian, from phrases such as *(in) fresco,* (on the) fresh (plaster), from West Germanic *friskaz* (unattested), FRESH.] **—fres·co·er, fres·co·ist** *n.*
fresh (frĕsh) *adj.* **fresher, freshest. 1.** New to one's experience; not encountered before. **2.** Novel; different; original: *a fresh slant.* **3.** Recently made, produced, or harvested; not stale, spoiled, or withered: *fresh bread.* **4.** Not preserved, as by canning, smoking, drying, or freezing: *fresh vegetables.* **5.** Not saline or salty: *fresh water.* **6.** Not yet used or soiled; clean: *a fresh sheet of paper.* **7.** Additional; new: *a fresh start.* **8.** Bright and clear; not dull or faded: *a fresh color; a fresh memory.* **9.** Having the glowing, unspoiled appearance of youth or health: *a fresh complexion.* **10.** Untried; inexperienced: *fresh recruits.* **11.** Having just arrived; straight: *fresh from Paris.* **12. a.** Revived or reinvigorated; refreshed: *got up fresh as a daisy after her afternoon nap.* **b.** Charged with energy; frisky. **13.** Revivifying; cool and invigorating: *fresh morning air.* **14.** Fairly strong; brisk: *a fresh wind.* **15.** Having recently calved and therefore with milk. Said of a cow. **16.** *Informal.* Bold and saucy; impudent: *scolded for such a fresh answer.*
~*adv.* Recently; newly. Usually used in combination: *fresh-baked bread.*
~*n.* **1.** The early and fresh part: *the fresh of the day.* **2.** A freshet. [Middle English, from Old French *freis* (feminine *fresche*), from West Germanic *friskaz* (unattested).] **—fresh·ly** *adv.* **—fresh·ness** *n.*
fresh breeze *n.* A wind whose speed is approximately 31 to 39 kilometers or 19 to 24 miles per hour, force 5 on the Beaufort scale.
fresh·en (frĕsh′ən) *v.* **-ened, -ening, -ens.** *—intr.* **1.** To become fresh. Often used with *up.* **2.** To make oneself clean and fresh. Used with *up*: *freshen up after a day's work.* **3.** To become brisk; increase in strength. Used of a wind. **4.** To lose saltiness. Used of water. **5.** To calve and therefore produce milk. *—tr.* To impart a fresh quality to; make fresh. **—fresh·en·er** *n.*
fresh·et (frĕsh′ĭt) *n.* **1.** A sudden surge of water down a small stream resulting from a heavy rainstorm or a thaw. **2.** A stream of fresh water that empties into a body of salt water. [FRESH + -ET.]
fresh gale *n.* A wind whose speed is approximately 63 to 74 kilometers or 39 to 46 miles per hour, force 8 on the Beaufort scale.
fresh·man (frĕsh′mən) *n., pl.* **-men** (-mĭn). **1.** A first-year student, as in high school or college. **2.** A beginner; novice.
fresh·wa·ter (frĕsh′wô′tər, -wŏt′ər) *adj.* **1.** Pertaining to, living in, or consisting of fresh water. **2.** Unaccustomed to the seas: *a freshwater sailor.* **3.** Located away from the sea; inland.
fres·nel (frā-nĕl′) *n.* A unit of frequency equal to 10^{12} hertz. [After A.J. *Fresnel* (1788–1827), French physicist.]
Fres·nel lens (frā-nĕl′) *n.* An optical lens made up of a number of smaller lenses arranged to give a short focal length. [After A.J. *Fresnel* (see **fresnel**).]
fret[1] (frĕt) *v.* **fretted, fretting, frets.** *—tr.* **1.** To cause to be uneasy; distress; vex. **2. a.** To gnaw or wear away. **b.** To produce a hole or worn spot in; chafe; corrode. **3.** To form (a passage or channel) by erosion. **4.** To disturb the surface of (water or a stream); agitate. *—intr.* **1.** To be vexed or troubled; worry. **2.** To be worn or eaten away; become corroded. **3.** To move agitatedly; be ruffled.
~*n.* **1.** An act or instance of fretting. **2.** A hole, worn spot, or path made by abrasion or erosion. **3.** A state of irritation, annoyance, or worry. [Middle English *freten,* to devour, irritate, Old English *fretan,* from Germanic *fra-*†, FOR- + *etan*†, to EAT.]
fret[2] *n.* Any of several guide ridges, usually of metal, set across the fingerboard of a guitar or other stringed instrument.
~*tr.v.* **fretted, fretting, frets.** To provide with frets. [15th century : origin obscure.]
fret[3] *n.* **1.** An ornamental design contained within a band or border, consisting of repeated, symmetrical, and often geometric figures. **2.** Such an ornamental design made in relief, often with numerous small openings.
~*tr.v.* **fretted, fretting, frets.** To provide with a fret or frets. [Middle English, from Old French *frete*†, trellis, embossed work.]
fret·ful (frĕt′fəl) *adj.* Inclined to fret; peevish; plaintive. **—fret·ful·ly** *adv.* **—fret·ful·ness** *n.*
fret·saw (frĕt′sô′) *n.* A narrow-bladed saw having fine teeth, used in producing ornamental work in thin wood or metal.
fret·work (frĕt′wûrk′) *n.* **1.** Ornamental work consisting of three-dimensional frets; geometric openwork. **2.** Such ornamental work represented graphically in monochrome or contrasting colors.
Freud (froid), **Sigmund** (1856–1939). Austrian psychiatrist. After long experience working with hysterical and neurologically disturbed patients, he developed the theory of psychoanalysis. When first publicized in the 1880's, his ideas attracted hostility, but by 1910 they had gained general recognition, and works such as *The Interpretation of Dreams* (1899) and *The Ego and the Id* (1923) have had a profound influence on 20th-century thought. He fled to London (1938) to escape Nazi persecution.
Freud·i·an (froi′dē-ən) *adj.* **1.** Pertaining to or in accordance with the psychoanalytic theories of Sigmund Freud. **2.** *Informal.* Psychologically telling or revealing.
~*n.* **1.** One who actively applies the psychoanalytic methods or theories of Freud in conducting psychotherapy. **2.** One who studies or applies the psychoanalytic theories of Freud for interpretation or explanation, as in historical or literary criticism.
Freudian slip *n.* A slip of the tongue or pen, or some other unintentional act, that seems to reveal an individual's real state of mind.
Frey (frā). Also **Freyr** (frâr). *Norse Mythology.* The god who dispenses peace, good weather, prosperity, and bountiful crops.
Frey·a, Frey·ja (frā′ə). *Norse Mythology.* The sister of Frey and the goddess of love and beauty.
Fri. Friday.
fri·a·ble (frī′ə-bəl) *adj.* Readily crumbled. [French, from Latin *friābilis,* crumbling, from *friāre,* to crumble.] **—fri·a·bil·i·ty, fri·a·ble·ness** *n.*
fri·ar (frī′ər) *n. Abbr.* **Fr.** A member of a Roman Catholic order, such as the Dominicans or Franciscans, that was originally mendicant. [Middle English *frere,* from Old French, from Latin *frāter* (stem *frātr-*), brother.]
fri·ar·bird (frī′ər-bûrd′) *n.* Any of various birds of the genus *Philemon,* of Australia and adjacent regions, having a partly naked head. Also called "leatherhead." [From its bare head, likened to a friar's tonsure.]
friar's lantern *n.* **ignis fatuus** *(see).*
fri·ar·y (frī′ə-rē) *n., pl.* **-ies.** A monastery of friars.
frib·ble (frĭb′əl) *v.* **-bled, -bling, -bles.** *—tr.* To waste (time, for example). *—intr.* To waste time; trifle.
~*n.* **1.** A frivolity; trifle. **2.** A frivolous person. [17th century (imitative).] **—frib·bler** *n.*
Fri·bourg (frē-bo͝or′, frī′bûrg′). *German* **Frei·burg** (frī′bo͝ork′). Mainly French-speaking canton of northern Switzerland. It occupies the west of the Swiss plateau and is a rich agricultural region noted for its cheeses, including Gruyère.
fric·an·deau (frĭk′ən-dō′) *n., pl.* **-deaux** (-dōz′). A cut of veal, usually rump or shoulder, that has been larded and braised or roasted with vegetables. [French, from *fricasser,* to FRICASSEE.]
fric·as·see (frĭk′ə-sē′) *n.* Poultry or meat cut into pieces and stewed in a thick gravy.
~*tr.v.* **fricasseed, -seeing, -sees.** To prepare as a fricassee.

[French *fricassée*, feminine past participle of *fricasser†*, to fry.]

fric·a·tive (frĭk'ə-tĭv) *adj. Phonetics.* Produced by the forcing of breath through a constricted passage, as are such consonantal sounds as (f) and (v), (s) and (z), (sh) and (zh), (th) and (*th*). —*n. Phonetics.* A fricative consonant. Also called "spirant." [New Latin *fricativus*, from *fricāre*, to rub.]

Frick (frĭk), **Henry Clay** (1849–1919). U.S. industrialist. He made his fortune primarily in the steel business and worked closely with Andrew Carnegie until 1899. His mansion in New York City, together with his art collection and an endowment of 15 million dollars, was willed to the public and is now a museum.

fric·tion (frĭk'shən) *n.* **1.** The rubbing of one object or surface against another. **2.** Conflict, as of dissimilar ideas, persons, or interests obliged to coexist; clashing. **3.** *Physics.* A force tangential to the common boundary of two bodies in contact that resists the motion or tendency to motion of one relative to the other. **4.** A massage of the body or scalp for therapeutic purposes. [French, from Latin *frictiō* (stem *frictiōn-*), from *frictus*, past participle of *fricāre*, to rub.] —**fric·tion·al** *adj.* —**fric·tion·al·ly** *adv.*

friction clutch *n.* A clutch in which axial pressure with resultant friction between the clutch faces, rather than the interlocking of mated parts, transmits torque.

friction drive *n.* A transmission system in which motion is transmitted from one part to another by the surface friction of rolling contact rather than by toothed gears.

friction match *n.* A match that ignites when struck on an abrasive surface.

friction tape *n.* A sturdy moisture-resistant adhesive tape used chiefly to insulate electrical conductors.

Fri·day (frī'dē, -dā') *n. Abbr.* **Fri.** The day of the week following Thursday; the fifth day of the working week. [Middle English *fridai*, Old English *frīgedæg*, "day of *Frīg* (wife of Odin)," a translation of Late Latin *Veneris dies*, day of (the planet) Venus, based on Greek *Aphroditēs hēmera*, Aphrodite's day. See **Frigg**.]

fridge (frĭj) *n. Informal.* A refrigerator.

Fridtjof Nansen Land. See **Franz Josef Land**.

Frie·dan (frĭ-dăn'), **Betty Naomi** (1921–). U.S. social reformer and feminist. In 1963 she published *The Feminine Mystique,* debunking the popular notion that women could find fulfillment only in homemaking and raising children. She founded the National Organization for Women (NOW) in 1966.

Fried·man (frēd'mən), **Milton** (1912–). U.S. economist. He set out his philosophy of monetary control and government nonintervention in *Capitalism and Freedom* (1962). Several Western governments have pursued his policies after the stagnation and inflation of the mid-1970's. He was awarded a Nobel Prize (1976).

fried cake *n.* A small pastry, such as a doughnut, fried in deep fat.

Frie·drich (frē'drĭKH), **Caspar David** (1774–1840). German painter. His mysterious landscapes are characteristic of the romantic movement. His later works symbolize man's insignificance in relation to the elements, as in *Wreck of the Hope* (1822).

friend (frĕnd) *n.* **1.** A person whom one knows, likes, and trusts. **2.** Any associate or acquaintance. Often used as a form of address: *my honorable friend.* **3.** A favored companion: *Man's best friend is his dog.* **4.** One with whom one is allied in a struggle or cause; a comrade. **5.** One who supports, sympathizes with, or patronizes a group, cause, or movement. **6. Friend.** A member of the Society of Friends; a Quaker. Also used by Quakers as a term of address. —**be friends with.** To be a friend of. —**make friends with.** To enter into friendship with. —*tr.v.* **friended, friending, friends.** *Archaic.* To befriend. [Middle English *friend,* Old English *frēond,* from Germanic.]

friend at court *n.* An influential person whom one knows and who will be able to advance one's interests.

friend·less (frĕnd'lĭs) *adj.* Without friends.

friend·ly (frĕnd'lē) *adj.* **-li·er, -li·est. 1.** Of, pertaining to, or befitting a friend. **2.** Favorably disposed; not antagonistic; amicable. **3.** Warm; welcoming. —*adv.* Also **friend·li·ly** (frĕnd'lə-lē). In the manner of a friend; amicably. —*n., pl.* **friendlies.** One that is friendly; especially, one fighting on or favorable to one's own side. —**friend·li·ness** *n.*

Friendly Islands. See **Tonga.**

friend·ship (frĕnd'shĭp') *n.* **1.** The condition or relation of being friends. **2.** Friendly feeling toward another; friendliness.

frier. Variant of **fryer.**

Frie·sian¹ (frē'zhən) *n. Chiefly British.* A **Holstein** (see).

Friesian². Variant of **Frisian.**

Fries·land (frēz'lənd, -lănd'). *Dutch* **Vries·land** (vrēz'-). Province in the northern Netherlands. It includes the West Frisian Islands and land reclaimed from the Ijsselmeer. The district is chiefly a beef-producing and dairying area, and the Friesian breed of cow that originated here is highly prized worldwide.

frieze¹ (frēz) *n. Architecture.* **1.** A plain or decorated horizontal part of an entablature between the architrave and cornice. **2.** Any decorative horizontal band, as along the upper part of a wall in a room. [French *frise,* from Old French, from Medieval Latin *frisium, frigium,* fringe, embroidered cloth, from Latin *Phrygium,* of Phrygia, a place noted for its embroidery.]

frieze² *n.* A coarse woolen cloth with an uncut nap. Also called "frisé." [Middle English *frise,* from Old French, from Middle Dutch *vriese,* perhaps from *Vriese,* from Latin *Frīsiī,* **Frisian.**]

frig·ate (frĭg'ĭt) *n.* **1.** A high-speed, medium-sized sailing war vessel of the 17th, 18th, and 19th centuries. **2.** A British warship intermediate between a corvette and a destroyer. **3.** A U.S. warship intermediate between a cruiser and a destroyer. **4.** *Archaic.* Any fast, light vessel. [French *frégate,* from Italian *fregata†.*]

frigate bird *n.* Any of various large, tropical sea birds of the genus *Fregata,* which characteristically snatch food from other birds in flight. Also called "man-o'-war bird."

Frigg (frĭg). Also **Frig·ga** (frĭg'ə). *Norse Mythology.* The consort of Odin and goddess of married lore and the hearth. [Old Norse, from Germanic *frijaz* (unattested), noble, FREE.]

fright (frīt) *n.* **1.** Sudden, intense fear, as of something immediately threatening; alarm. **2.** *Informal.* Something extremely unsightly, alarming, or strange. —See Synonyms at **fear.** —**take fright.** To become frightened. —*tr.v.* **frighted, frighting, frights.** *Archaic.* To frighten. [Middle English *fright,* Old English *fryhto, fyrhto,* from Germanic *furht-* (unattested), afraid.]

fright·en (frīt'n) *tr.v.* **-ened, -ening, -ens. 1.** To make suddenly afraid; alarm or startle. **2.** To drive or force by arousing fear. Used with *away, into, off,* or *out: He was frightened into confessing.* [From FRIGHT.] —**fright·en·er** *n.*

Synonyms: alarm, panic, scare, terrify, terrorize.

fright·ened (frīt'nd) *adj.* **1.** Afraid. **2.** Timid.

fright·en·ing (frīt'nĭng) *adj.* Causing fright or sudden alarm. —**fright·en·ing·ly** *adv.*

fright·ful (frīt'fəl) *adj.* **1.** Causing disgust or shock; horrifying. **2.** Causing fright; terrifying. **3.** *Informal.* **a.** Excessive; extreme: *a frightful liar.* **b.** Disagreeable; distressing: *frightful weather.* —**fright·ful·ly** *adv.* —**fright·ful·ness** *n.*

frig·id (frĭj'ĭd) *adj.* **1.** Extremely cold. **2.** Lacking warmth of feeling; stiff and formal in manner: *a frigid refusal to a request.* **3. a.** Disliking sexual intercourse. Usually said of women. **b.** Unable to experience orgasm in sexual intercourse. Used of females. [Latin *frīgidus,* from *frīgēre,* to be cold, from *frīgus,* cold.] —**fri·gid·i·ty** (frĭ-jĭd'ə-tē), **frig·id·ness** *n.* —**frig·id·ly** *adv.*

Frigid Zone *n.* The area within the Arctic Circle or that within the Antarctic Circle.

frig·o·rif·ic (frĭg'ə-rĭf'ĭk) *adj.* Causing coldness; chilling. [Latin *frīgorificus : frīgus* (stem *frīgor-*), FRIGID + -FIC.]

fri·jol (frē-hōl', frē'hōl') *n., pl.* **trijoles** (frē-hō'lēz). Also **fri·jo·le** (frē-hō'lē). A bean cultivated and used for food, especially in Mexico and in the southwestern United States. [Spanish, variant of *fresol,* from Latin *phaseolus,* diminutive of *phasēlus,* kidney bean, from Greek *phasēlos†.*]

frill (frĭl) *n.* **1. a.** A ruffled, gathered, or pleated border or projection, such as a fabric edge used to trim clothing. **b.** A similar curled paper strip used, for example, for decorating the bone of a piece of meat. **2.** *Zoology.* A ruff of hair or feathers or a similar membranous projection about the neck of an animal or bird. **3.** *Photography.* A wrinkling of the edge of a film. **4.** *Usually* **frills.** *Informal.* Something superfluous; an embellishment: *plain home cooking and no frills; cheap, no-frills flights to London.* —*v.* **frilled, frilling, frills.** —*tr.* **1.** To make into a ruffle or frill. **2.** To add a ruffle or frill to. —*intr. Photography.* To become wrinkled along the edge. [16th century : origin obscure.]

frilled lizard *n.* An Australian lizard, *Chlamydosaurus kingi,* having a broad membrane extending from the neck and throat that can be extended like a ruff when the mouth is opened.

frill·y (frĭl'ē) *adj.* **-i·er, -i·est. 1.** Decorated with or having a frill or frills. **2.** Similar to or suggesting a frill or frills. **3.** *Informal.* Superfluously ornamental.

Friml (frĭm'əl), **(Charles) Rudolf** (1879–1972). U.S. composer, born in Czechoslovakia. He wrote some 33 light operas, including *The Firefly* (1912), *Rose Marie* (1924), and *The Vagabond King* (1925).

fringe (frĭnj) *n.* **1.** A decorative border or edging of hanging threads, cords, or strips, often attached to a separate band. **2.** Hair combed over the forehead and cut near eyebrow level. **3.** Anything placed or growing along an edge. **4.** A marginal or peripheral part; an edge: *the fringes of the crowd.* **5.** Artistic activities that are considered to lie outside the mainstream or that are deliberately unconventional or uncommercial. Also used adjectivally: *fringe theater.* **6.** Those members of a group or political party holding extreme views. **7.** *Optics.* Any of the light or dark bands produced by the diffraction or interference of light. —*tr.v.* **fringed, fringing, fringes. 1.** To decorate with a fringe. **2.** To grow or occur along the edge of; border: *"deep and sullen pools fringed with tall rushes"* (H. Rider Haggard). [Middle English *frenge,* from Old French, from Vulgar Latin *frimbia* (unattested), from Late Latin *fimbria.* See **fimbria.**] —**fring·y** *adj.*

fringe benefit *n.* An employment benefit given in addition to one's wages or salary.

fringed orchis *n.* Any of various orchids of the genus *Habenaria,* having variously colored flowers with a fringed lip.

frin·gil·lid (frĭn-jĭl'ĭd) *adj.* Of or belonging to the family Fringillidae, which includes relatively small birds, such as the finches, sparrows, and buntings. —*n.* A member of the Fringillidae. [New Latin *Fringillidae : Fringilla* (type genus), from Latin *fringilla†,* finch + -ID.]

fringing reef *n.* A coral reef along a coast.

frip·per·y (frĭp'ə-rē) *n., pl.* **-ies. 1.** Pretentious finery; excessively ornamented dress. **2.** Pretentious elegance; ostentation. **3.** Trivia. —*adj.* Pretentious and trivial. [French *friperie,* from Old French

fritillary *The fritillary butterflies are named after their resemblance to the checkered flowers of the* Fritillaria *genus, native to the Northern Hemisphere. The high brown fritillary, shown here, lives mostly on the edges of woodlands. Its caterpillars feed only on violets.*

frog *Unlike the toad, whose skin is dry to the touch, the common frog has a soft, moist skin. The frog's skin can become darker or lighter in color to match its surroundings.*

freperie, from *frepe, felpe,* frill, from Medieval Latin *faluppa*†, fiber.]

Fris. Frisian.

Fris·bee (frĭz′bē) *n.* A trademark for a concave disk made of light plastic that is thrown in the air with a spinning motion as a game.

Frisch (frĭsh), **Karl von** (1886–1982). Austrian zoologist. He is best known for his discovery of the "dance" of the bees, by which the location of flowers is communicated. In 1973 he shared the Nobel Prize for physiology and medicine with Konrad Lorenz (1903–89) and Nikolaas Tinbergen (1907–88).

Frisch, Max Rudolf (1911–91). Swiss writer. In his plays and novels, including *I'm not Stiller* (1954), *Homo Faber* (1957), and *Andorra* (1961), he explored the existential plight of the modern, complicated individual in a society that stereotypes its members and defeats those who attempt to change it.

fri·sé (frē-zā′) *n.* A fabric, **frieze** *(see).* [French, from the past participle of *friser,* to curl, FRIZZ.]

frisette. Variant of **frizette.**

Fris·i·a (frĭz′ē-ə). Ancient country of the Frisians. In the 8th century it included what is now northern Belgium, the Netherlands, and Germany west of the Weser River.

Fri·sian (frĭzh′ən, frē′zhən) *adj.* Also **Frie·sian** (frē′zhən). *Abbr.* **Fris., Frs.** Of the Frisian Islands, Friesland, or Frisia.
∼*n.* Also **Frie·sian.** *Abbr.* **Fris., Frs. 1.** A native or inhabitant of the Frisian Islands or Friesland. **2.** The Germanic language spoken by the Frisian people.

Frisian Islands. Group of *c.* 30 low, sandy islands in the North Sea off northwestern Europe. The West Frisians belong to the Netherlands, the East Frisians to Germany, and the North Frisians are divided between Germany and Denmark. There are few permanent inhabitants, although there are numerous summer homes. See also **Friesland.**

frisk (frĭsk) *v.* **frisked, frisking, frisks.** —*intr.* To move about briskly and playfully, as a puppy does; gambol; frolic. —*tr.* To search (a person) for something concealed, especially weapons, by passing the hands quickly over clothes or through pockets.
∼*n.* **1.** An energetic, playful movement; a gambol; caper. **2.** An act of frisking, as for concealed weapons. [From obsolete *frisk,* lively, from Old French *frisque,* from Common Germanic *friskaz* (unattested), FRESH.] **—frisk·er** *n.*

fris·ket (frĭs′kĭt) *n.* A light frame with a windowed sheet of parchment that protects areas of the paper not to be printed in a hand printing press. [French *frisquette*†.]

frisk·y (frĭs′kē) *adj.* **-ier, -iest.** Energetic, lively, and playful. [From obsolete *frisk,* lively. See **frisk.**] **—frisk·i·ly** *adv.* **—frisk·i·ness** *n.*

fris·son (frē-sôɴ′) *n.* A pleasurable shiver caused by excitement or thrilling danger. [French, shiver.]

frit (frĭt) *n.* **1.** The fused or partially fused materials used in making glass. **2.** A vitreous substance used in making porcelain or glazes.
∼*tr.v.* **fritted, fritting, frits.** To make into frit. [Italian *fritta,* from the feminine past participle of *friggere,* to fry, from Latin *frīgere,* to FRY.]

frit fly *n.* Any of several small flies of the family Chloropidae; especially, *Oscinella frit,* having larvae that are destructive to cereal plants, particularly oats. [19th century : origin obscure.]

frith (frĭth) *n. Scottish.* An estuary. [Variant of FIRTH.]

frit·il·lar·y (frĭt′l-ĕr′ē) *n., pl.* **-ies. 1.** Any of various bulbous plants of the genus *Fritillaria,* having nodding, variously colored, often spotted or checkered bell-shaped flowers. In this sense, also called "snakeshead." **2.** Any of various butterflies of the family Nymphalidae, having brownish wings marked with black or silvery spots. [New Latin *Fritillaria,* from Latin *fritillus*†, dice box, a reference to the checkered markings.]

frit·ter¹ (frĭt′ər) *tr.v.* **-tered, -tering, -ters. 1.** To reduce wastefully or squander little by little. Usually used with *away*: *He frittered his money away on expensive cars.* **2.** To break, tear, or cut into bits; shred. [Probably from obsolete *fritter,* to break in pieces, perhaps related to Middle High German *vetze,* rags.]

fritter² *n.* A small cake made of batter, often containing fruit, vegetables, meat, or fish, sautéed or fried in deep fat. [Middle English *friture,* from Old French, from Vulgar Latin *frīctūra* (unattested), from Latin *frīctus,* past participle of *frīgere,* to FRY.]

Fri·u·li (frē-ōō′lē). A historic region and former duchy of northeastern Italy, part of which now extends into Yugoslavia.

Fri·u·li·an (frē-ōō′lē-ən) *n.* **1.** A member of a people inhabiting Friuli in northeastern Italy. **2.** The Rhaeto-Romanic dialect spoken by these people.

friv·ol (frĭv′əl) *v.* **-oled** or **-olled, -oling** or **-olling, -ols.** *Informal.* —*tr.* To squander. Used with *away.* —*intr.* To behave frivolously. [Back-formation from FRIVOLOUS.] **—friv·ol·er** *n.*

fri·vol·i·ty (frĭ-vŏl′ə-tē) *n., pl.* **-ties. 1.** The condition or quality of being frivolous. **2.** A frivolous act or thing.

friv·o·lous (frĭv′ə-ləs) *adj.* **1.** Unworthy of serious attention; insignificant; trivial. **2.** Marked by flippancy; silly. —See Synonyms at **playful.** [Middle English, from Latin *frīvolus*†.] **—friv·o·lous·ly** *adv.* **—friv·o·lous·ness** *n.*

fri·zette, fri·sette (frĭ-zĕt′) *n.* A curled fringe of hair, usually worn on the forehead by a woman. [French *frisette,* "little curl," from *friser,* to curl, FRIZZ.]

frizz¹, friz (frĭz) *v.* **frizzed, frizzing, frizzes.** —*tr.* To form (nap or hair, for example) into small, tight curls or tufts. —*intr.* To be formed into small, tight curls or tufts.
∼*n.* **1.** The condition of being frizzed. **2.** A tight curl or tight curls of hair or fabric. **3.** A hairstyle consisting of small, tight curls. [French *friser,* to curl, to shrivel up (as when fried), perhaps from *frire* (stem *fris-*), to FRY.] **—frizz·er** *n.*

frizz², friz *v.* **frizzed, frizzing, frizzes.** —*tr.* To fry or burn with a sizzling noise. —*intr.* To be fried or burned with a sizzling noise. [Perhaps from FRIZZLE (to fry).]

friz·zle¹ (frĭz′əl) *v.* **-zled, -zling, -zles.** —*tr.* **1.** To fry until crisp and curled: *frizzled the bacon.* **2.** To scorch or sear with heat. —*intr.* **1.** To fry or sear with a sizzling noise. **2.** To scorch. [Perhaps blend of FRY and SIZZLE.]

frizzle² *v.* **-zled, -zling, -zles.** —*tr.* To frizz (hair). —*intr.* To form tight curls.
∼*n.* A small, tight curl. [16th century : origin uncertain, earlier than FRIZZ (to form curls).]

friz·zly (frĭz′lē) *adj.* **-zlier, -zliest.** Tightly curled.

friz·zy (frĭz′ē) *adj.* **-zier, -ziest.** Tightly curled; frizzly. **—friz·zi·ly** *adv.* **—friz·zi·ness** *n.*

Frl. Fräulein.

fro (frō) *adv.* Away; back again. Used in the phrase *to and fro.*
∼*prep. Scottish.* From. [Middle English *fra, fro,* adverb and preposition, from Old Norse *frā.*]

Fro·bi·sher (frō′bĭ-shər), **Sir Martin** (*c.* 1535–94). English explorer. He made three voyages to the Canadian Arctic in 1576, 1577, and 1578, seeking the Northwest Passage.

Frobisher Bay. Arm of the North Atlantic Ocean, cutting deeply into Baffin Island, Canada. It is *c.* 240 kilometers (150 miles) long and 65 kilometers (40 miles) at its widest.

frock (frŏk) *n.* **1.** A long, loose outer garment, such as that worn by artists and craftsmen; a smock. **2.** A woolen garment formerly worn by sailors; jersey. **3.** A frock coat. **4.** A robe worn by monks, friars, and other clerics; habit. **5.** The state of being a priest or clergyman. **6.** A woman's or girl's dress.
∼*tr.v.* **frocked, frocking, frocks. 1.** To clothe in a frock. **2.** To invest with clerical office. [Middle English *frok,* from Old French *froc,* from Germanic *hrok-* (unattested).]

frock coat *n.* A man's dress overcoat with knee-length skirts, worn chiefly in the 19th century.

froe, frow (frō) *n.* A cleaving tool having a heavy blade set at right angles to the handle. [Origin uncertain.]

Froe·bel (frœ′bəl), **Friedrich Wilhelm August** (1782–1852). German educator who believed that school should be happy. His book *Education of Man* (1826) was profoundly influential. In 1837 he opened the first kindergarten, at Blankenburg.

frog¹ (frôg, frŏg) *n.* **1.** Any of numerous tailless, chiefly aquatic amphibians of the order Anura, and especially of the family Ranidae, characteristically having a smooth, moist skin, webbed feet, and long hind legs adapted for leaping. **2.** A spiked or perforated object placed in a container and used to support stems in a decorative floral arrangement. **3.** A recess or groove in one side or on opposite sides of a brick. **4.** *Informal.* Hoarseness in the throat. [Middle English *frogge,* Old English *frogga,* a pet form of *forse, frosc,* from Germanic.]

frog² *n.* A grooved iron or steel plate that guides the wheels of a train over an intersection in the track. [Origin obscure.]

frog³ *n.* **1.** A loop fastened to a belt to hold a tool or weapon. **2.** An ornamental looped braid or cord with a button or knot for fastening the front of a garment. [18th century : origin obscure.]

frog⁴ *n.* A wedge-shaped, horny prominence in the sole of a horse's hoof. [17th century : perhaps from FROG (animal), influenced by French *fourchette* and Italian *forchetta* (diminutives of *fourche, forca,* FORK, referring to the shape of the prominence).]

frog·eye (frôg′ī′, frŏg′ī′) *n.* A plant disease caused by fungi and characterized by rounded spots on the leaves.

frog·fish (frôg′fĭsh′, frŏg′-) *n., pl.* **-fishes** or collectively **frogfish.** Any of various anglerfishes of the family Antennariidae, of tropical and temperate seas, characteristically covered with fleshy or filamentous processes.

frogged (frôgd, frŏgd) *adj.* Decorated with ornamental frogs. Said of a garment, as a coat or uniform.

frog·ging (frô′gĭng, frŏg′ĭng) *n.* The ornamental loops of braid or cord on a garment; decorative frogs collectively.

frog·gy (frô′gē, frŏg′ē) *adj.* **-gier, -giest. 1.** Of, resembling, or characteristic of a frog. **2.** Full of frogs.

frog·hop·per (frôg′hŏp′ər, frŏg′-) *n.* Any of various jumping insects of the family Ceropidae, the nymphs of which secrete a protective spittlelike substance (cuckoo spit) around themselves. Also called "spittle insect," "spittlebug."

frog kick *n.* A swimming kick in which the legs are drawn up close beneath one, then thrust outward and together vigorously.

frog·man (frôg′măn′, -mən, frŏg′-) *n., pl.* **-men** (-mĕn′, -mĭn). A swimmer provided with breathing apparatus and other equipment, such as a rubber suit and flippers, to execute underwater maneuvers, especially military maneuvers.

frog·mouth (frôg′mouth′, frŏg′-) *n.* Any of various brown or gray nocturnal insectivorous birds of the genera *Podargus* and *Batrachostomus,* of southeastern Asia and Australia, having a wide mouth and a hooked bill.

frog·spawn (frôg′spôn′, frŏg′-) *n.* A transparent gelatinous mass interspersed with black dots, comprising many fertilized frogs' eggs or developing tadpoles, each surrounded by nutrient jelly.

frog spit *n.* Also **frog spittle. 1.** An insect secretion, **cuckoo spit** *(see).* **2.** A foamlike aggregation of small aquatic plants, such as green algae, on the surface of a pond.

frol·ic (frŏl′ĭk) n. **1.** Gaiety; merriment. **2.** A gay, carefree time. **3.** A prank, trick, or antic.
~intr.v. **frolicked, -icking, -ics. 1.** To behave playfully and uninhibitedly; romp. **2.** To engage in merrymaking, joking, or teasing. ~adj. Archaic. Merry; frisky; prankish. [Dutch vrolijk, from Middle Dutch vrolijc : vro, gay, happy + -lijc, -ly.] —**frol·ick·er** n.
frol·ic·some (frŏl′ĭk-səm) adj. Full of high-spirited fun; frisky.
from (frŭm, frŏm) prep. Abbr. **fr. 1.** Beginning at a specified place or time: walked home from the station; from six o'clock on. **2. a.** With a specified time or point as the first of two limits: from age four to age eight. **b.** With a specified lowest limit: real leather shoes from $20. **3.** With a person, place, or thing as the source, cause, or instrument: a note from the teacher. **4.** Out of: take a book from the shelf. **5.** Out of the jurisdiction, control, restraint, or possession of: escaped from jail; free from pain. **6.** So as not to be engaged in: keep someone from making a mistake. **7.** Measured by or with reference to: far away from home. **8.** As opposed to: know right from wrong. **9.** Because of: faint from hunger; crying from desperation. **10.** Beginning with or in a specified state: from rags to riches; from annoyance to fury. **11.** Belonging to: memories from childhood. **12.** On the basis of: judging from appearances. [Middle English from, fram, Old English from, fram.]
fromenty. Variant of **frumenty.**
Fromm (frŏm, frôm), **Erich** (1900–80). German-born American psychoanalyst.
frond (frŏnd) n. **1.** The usually compound leaf of a fern. **2.** A large compound leaf of certain other plants, such as a palm. **3.** A leaflike thallus, as of a seaweed or lichen. [Latin frōns† (stem frond-), branch, leaf.] —**frond·ed** adj.
Fronde (frŏnd, frônd; French frôNd) n. The French political movement that opposed Cardinal Mazarin and the court during the minority of Louis XIV in the mid-17th century.
fron·des·cent (frŏn-dĕs′ənt) adj. Bearing, resembling, or having a profusion of leaves or fronds; leafy. [Latin frondescens (stem frondescent-), present participle of frondescere, to become leafy, from frondēre, to put forth leaves, from frōns (stem frond-), leaf, FROND.] —**fron·des·cence** n.
fron·dose (frŏn′dōs′) adj. **1.** Bearing fronds. **2.** Resembling a frond or fronds; frondlike. [Latin frondōsus : frōns (stem frond-), FROND + -OSE.] —**fron·dose·ly** adv.
front (frŭnt) n. **1.** The forward part or surface, as of a building. **2.** The area, location, or position directly before or ahead. **3.** The position of leadership or superiority; forefront. **4.** The first part; beginning; opening. **5.** The forehead, especially of an animal or bird. **6.** Archaic. The entire face; countenance. **7.** Demeanor or bearing when faced with a particular situation: maintain a brave front. **8.** An outward or feigned aspect; a false appearance or manner. **9.** Land bordering a lake, river, or street: a house on the lake front. **10.** A promenade along a beach. **11.** The top forward part of a garment: spilled gravy down his front. **12.** A detachable part of a man's dress shirt covering the chest; a dickey. **13.** Military. **a.** The most forward line of a military combat force. **b.** An area of contact between opposing combat forces. **14.** Meteorology. The interface between air masses at different temperatures. Also called "discontinuity." **15.** A group or movement uniting various individuals or organizations for the achievement of a common purpose; coalition. **16.** An apparently respectable person, group, or business under whose cover secret or illegal activities are carried on. **17.** A field of activity: the economic front.
~adj. **1.** Of, pertaining to, aimed at, or located in the front. **2.** Phonetics. Produced with the front of the tongue in a forward position. Said of vowel sounds.
~v. **fronted, fronting, fronts.** —tr. **1.** To look out upon; face. **2.** To meet in opposition; confront. **3.** To provide a front for. **4.** To serve as a front for; head. —intr. **1.** To have a front; face. Usually used with on: Her property fronts on the main road. **2.** To act as a front. Used with for. [Middle English, from Old French, from Latin frōns† (stem front-), front, forehead.]
front. frontispiece.
front·age (frŭn′tĭj) n. **1.** The front part of a piece of property, such as a lot or building. **2.** The length of such a part. **3.** The land between a building and the street. **4.** The direction in which something faces. **5.** Land adjacent to something such as a street or body of water.
fron·tal¹ (frŭnt′l) adj. **1.** Of, pertaining to, directed toward, or situated at the front. **2.** Of or pertaining to a meteorological front. **3.** Of or pertaining to the forehead. —**fron·tal·ly** adv.
frontal² n. **1.** An ornamental drapery covering the front of an altar. **2.** The façade of a building. [Middle English frontel, from Medieval Latin frontellum, from Latin frōns (stem front-), FRONT.]
frontal bone n. A cranial bone consisting of a vertical portion corresponding to the forehead and a horizontal portion that forms the roofs of the orbital and nasal cavities.
frontal lobe n. The anterior portion of each cerebral hemisphere, extending back to the central sulcus.
frontal plane n. Anatomy. A plane parallel to the long axis of the body that is perpendicular to the sagittal plane.
front bench n. The front row of seats on either side of the House of Commons or a similar legislative body, traditionally reserved for government ministers and leading members of the opposition. —**front-bench** (frŭnt′bĕnch′) adj. —**front-bench·er** n.
front·court (frŭnt′kôrt′, -kōrt′) n. The offensive half of the court used by a team in basketball.

Fron·te·nac (frŏn′tə-năk′), **Louis de Buade, Comte de Palluau et de** (1620–98). French soldier and governor of New France (1672–82 and 1689–98). He held Quebec against the English in the early part of the French and Indian War.
front end n. Computer Science. A piece of software designed to make another piece of software easier to operate or understand.
front-end (frŭnt′ĕnd′) adj. **1.** Of or pertaining to the initial phase of a project. **2.** Computer Science. Designating or pertaining to a computer that is attached to another computer to relieve it of some of its basic tasks.
front-end load n. The amount deducted from early payments made to a mutual fund purchase plan that covers expenses such as sales commissions.
fron·te·nis (frŭn-tĕn′ĭs, frŏn-) n. A Latin-American tennis game played on a three-walled court. [American Spanish, blend of Spanish fronton, gable, jai alai court (from frenta, forehead, from Latin frons) and tenis, tennis (from English TENNIS).]
fron·tier (frŭn-tîr′) n. **1.** An international border, or the area along it. **2.** A region just beyond or at the edge of a settled area. **3.** The limit of what is known in a science or other branch of knowledge. —See Synonyms at **boundary.**
~adj. Of, pertaining to, or situated at a frontier. [Middle English frountier, from Old French frontiere, from front, FRONT.]
fron·tiers·man (frŭn-tîrz′mən) n., pl. **-men** (-mĭn). A man who lives on the frontier.
fron·tis·piece (frŭn′tĭs-pēs′) n. **1.** Abbr. **front.** An illustration that faces or immediately precedes the title page of a book, book section, or magazine. **2.** Architecture. A façade; especially, an ornamental façade. **3.** Architecture. A small ornamental pediment, as on top of a door or window. [Variant (influenced by PIECE) of earlier frontispice, from Old French, from Late Latin frontispicium, "examination of the front," building exterior : Latin frōns (stem front-), FRONT + specere, to look at.]
front·let (frŭnt′lĭt) n. **1.** An ornament or band worn on the forehead. **2.** The forehead of an animal or bird, especially when distinctively marked. **3.** Ecclesiastical. The ornamental border of a frontal. [Middle English, from Old French frontelet, diminutive of frontel, from Latin frontāle, from frōns (stem front-), FRONT.]
front-line (frŭnt′lĭn′) adj. **1.** Located or used at a military front. **2.** Of or relating to the most important or advanced position or activity in a field or undertaking.
front man n. **1.** A person who serves as nominal leader but lacks real authority. **2.** A person who acts as a front for groups or organizations carrying on secret or illegal activities.
front matter n. The material, such as the preface, frontispiece, and title page, preceding the text in a book. Compare **end matter.**
front office n. The policy-making members of an organization.
fron·to·gen·e·sis (frŭn′tō-jĕn′ə-sĭs) n. Development or intensification of a meteorological front. [New Latin : FRONT + -GENESIS.]
fron·tol·y·sis (frŭn-tŏl′ə-sĭs) n. The disintegration of a meteorological front. [New Latin : FRONT + -LYSIS.]
front-page (frŭnt′pāj′) adj. Receiving or worthy of coverage on the front page of a newspaper.
Front Range. Line of mountains running c. 480 kilometers (300 miles) through Wyoming and Colorado. It is the loftiest part of the U.S. Rocky Mts.; its highest elevation is Mt. Elbert (4,399 meters; 14,432 feet).
front-run·ner (frŭnt′rŭn′ər) n. A leading contender in a contest, election, or the like.
front·ward (frŭnt′wərd) adv. Also **front·wards** (-wərdz). At or toward the front.
front-wheel drive (frŭnt′hwēl′) n. Abbr. **f.w.d.** An automotive drive mechanism in which the drive is applied only to the front wheels.
frosh (frŏsh) n., pl. **frosh.** Informal. A freshman. [Shortening and alteration of FRESHMAN.]
frost (frôst, frŏst) n. **1.** A deposit or covering of minute ice crystals formed from frozen water vapor. **2.** The atmospheric conditions when the temperature is at or below the freezing point of water. **3.** The process of freezing. **4.** A cold or icy manner; aloofness. **5.** Informal. Something given a cold reception; fiasco; failure.
~v. **frosted, frosting, frosts.** —tr. **1.** To cover with frost. **2.** To damage or kill by frost. **3.** To cover (glass or metal) with a roughened or speckled decorative surface. **4.** To cover or decorate (a cake) with icing. —intr. To become covered with or as if with frost. [Middle English frost, Old English frost, forst, from Germanic.]
Frost (frôst, frŏst), **Robert Lee** (1874–1963). U.S. poet. From the age of 10 he spent much of his life in rural New England, and his work frequently uses aspects of this experience to explore man's relationship with nature. His collections include A Boy's Will (1913) and In the Clearing (1962).
frost·bite (frôst′bīt′, frŏst′-) n. Tissue destruction resulting from ice forming in the tissues, especially of the nose, fingers, toes, and ears.
~tr.v. **frostbit** (-bĭt′), **-bitten** (-bĭt′n), **-biting, -bites.** To injure or damage by freezing.
frost·bit·ten (frôst′bĭt′n, frŏst′-) adj. Affected by frostbite.
frost·ed (frô′stĭd, frŏs′tĭd) adj. **1.** Covered by frost. **2.** Covered or decorated with icing. **3.** Decorated with frosting, as glass. **4.** Subjected to frosting. **5.** Informal. Angry.
frost heave n. An uplifting of soil, a pavement, or a similar surface as a result of freezing below the surface.
frost·ing (frô′stĭng, frŏs′tĭng) n. **1.** Icing. **2.** A roughened surface imparted to glass or metal. **3.** The use of bleach to lighten strands of hair over the entire head and create a two-tone appearance.

frost Ice crystals, formed when the dew freezes, produce hoarfrost that gives plants a hoary, aged look.

frost line *n.* The limit to which frost penetrates the earth.
frost-re·sis·tant (frôst′rĭ-zĭs′tənt, frŏst′-) *adj.* Designating plants that are able to survive the period of winter frost.
frost·work (frôst′wûrk′, frŏst′-) *n.* **1.** The intricate patterns produced by frost, as on a windowpane. **2.** Similar ornamental patterns produced artificially, as on metal or glass.
frost·y (frô′stē, frŏs′tē) *adj.* **-ier, -iest. 1.** Producing or characterized by frost; freezing. **2.** Covered with or as if with frost. **3.** Silvery white; hoary. **4.** Cold in manner; haughty; distant. **—frost·i·ly** *adv.* **—frost·i·ness** *n.*

fruit bat *Sometimes known as flying foxes, fruit bats—which feed chiefly on fruit—are found in tropical and subtropical regions of Asia. Most species have good eyesight, unlike the smaller insect-eating bats that find their way by echolocation. This is a Malaysian fruit bat.*

froth (frôth, frŏth) *n.* **1.** A mass of bubbles in or on a liquid; foam. **2.** A salivary foam released as a result of disease or exhaustion. **3.** Anything unsubstantial or trivial.
~*v.* **frothed, frothing, froths.** —*tr.* **1.** To exude or expel in the form of foam. **2.** To cover with foam. **3.** To cause to foam. —*intr.* To exude or expel froth; foam. [Middle English, from Old Norse *frodha,* from Germanic *frudh-* (unattested).]
froth·y (frô′thē, frŏth′ē) *adj.* **-ier, -iest. 1.** Made of, covered with, or resembling froth; foamy. **2.** Playfully frivolous in character or content. **—froth·i·ly** *adv.* **—froth·i·ness** *n.*
frot·tage (frô-täzh′) *n.* **1.** A method of making a design by placing a piece of paper on top of an object and then rubbing over it, as with charcoal or a pencil. **2.** A design made by frottage. [French, rubbing, from *frotter,* to rub.]
frou-frou (fro͞o′fro͞o) *n.* **1.** A rustling sound, as of silk. **2.** Fussy or showy dress or ornamentation. [French (imitative).]
frow. Variant of **froe.**
fro·ward (frō′wərd, frō′ərd) *adj.* Stubbornly contrary and disobedient; obstinate. [Middle English *froward* : FRO + -WARD.] **—fro·ward·ly** *adv.* **—fro·ward·ness** *n.*
frown (froun) *v.* **frowned, frowning, frowns.** —*intr.* **1.** To wrinkle the brow, as in thought, worry, or displeasure. **2.** To regard with disapproval or distaste. Used with *on* or *upon*: *"The English frown on the use of tea bags"* (Craig Claiborne). —*tr.* **1.** To express (disapproval or distaste, for example) by wrinkling the brow. **2.** To wrinkle the brow so as to dismiss (a person or statement, for example): *frown objections away.*
~*n.* A wrinkling of the brow in thought, worry, or displeasure. [Middle English *frounen,* from Old French *froigner,* from Celtic, akin to Welsh *ffroen*†, nose.] **—frown·er** *n.* **—frown·ing·ly** *adv.*
frowst (froust) *n. Chiefly British.* A hot and stuffy atmosphere.
~*intr.v.* **frowsted, frowsting, frowsts.** To lounge in a hot and stuffy atmosphere. [Back-formation from FROWSTY.] **—frowst·er** *n.*
frowst·y (frou′stē) *adj.* **-ier, -iest.** *Chiefly British.* Having a hot and stuffy atmosphere. [Perhaps a variant of FROWZY.]
frow·zy, frow·sy (frou′zē) *adj.* **-zier, -ziest** or **-sier, -siest. 1.** Unkempt in appearance; slovenly; shabby. **2.** Having an unpleasant smell; musty. —See Synonyms at **sloppy.** [17th century : origin obscure.] **—frow·zi·ly** *adv.* **—frow·zi·ness** *n.*
froze. Past tense of **freeze.**
fro·zen (frō′zən). Past participle of **freeze.**
~*adj.* **1.** Made into, covered with, or surrounded by ice. **2.** Affected or killed by extreme cold. **3.** Preserved by freezing. **4.** Rendered immobile. **5.** Expressive of cold unfriendliness or disdain: *a frozen stare.* **6. a.** Fixed at an arbitrary level. Said of wages, profits, or the like. **b.** Incapable of being withdrawn, sold, or liquidated. Said of investments, assets, or the like. **—fro·zen·ness** *n.*
frozen food *n.* Food that has undergone quick freezing and that is intended to remain frozen until used.
FRS Federal Reserve System.
Frs. Frisian.
F.R.S. Fellow of the Royal Society.
frt. freight.

fruit fly *Fruit flies—members of a large and widely distributed family of insects—breed on fruit trees during the growing season, causing considerable damage to fruit harvests.*

fruc·tif·er·ous (frŭk-tĭf′ər-əs, fro͝ok-) *adj.* Bearing fruit. [Latin *frūctifer* : *frūctus,* FRUIT + -FEROUS.]
fruc·ti·fi·ca·tion (frŭk′tə-fĭ-kā′shən, fro͝ok′-) *n.* **1.** The producing of fruit. **2.** The fruit of a seed-bearing plant. **3.** A spore-bearing structure.
fruc·ti·fy (frŭk′tə-fī′, fro͝ok′-) *v.* **-fied, -fying, -fies.** —*tr.* To cause to produce fruit; make fruitful or productive. —*intr.* To bear fruit. [Middle English *fructifien,* from Old French *fructifier,* from Latin *frūctificāre* : *frūctus,* FRUIT + *facere,* to make, do.]
fruc·tose (frŭk′tōs′, fro͝ok′-) *n.* A very sweet sugar, $C_6H_{12}O_6$, occurring in many fruits and honey and used as a preservative for foodstuffs and as an intravenous nutrient. Also called "fruit sugar," "levulose." [Latin *frūctus,* FRUIT + -OSE.]
fruc·tu·ous (frŭk′cho͞o-əs, fro͝ok′-) *adj.* Fruitful; productive. [Middle English, from Old French, from Latin *frūctuōsus,* from *frūctus,* FRUIT.]
fru·gal (fro͞o′gəl) *adj.* **1.** Avoiding unnecessary expenditure of money; thrifty. **2.** Not plentiful and costing little: *a frugal lunch.* —See Synonyms at **sparing.** [Latin *frūgālis,* back-formation from *frūgālior,* comparative of *frūgī,* useful, worthy, dative of *frūx* (stem *frūg-*), fruit.] **—fru·gal·i·ty** (fro͞o-găl′ə-tē), **fru·gal·ness** *n.* **—fru·gal·ly** *adv.*
fru·giv·o·rous (fro͞o-jĭv′ər-əs) *adj.* Feeding on fruit; fruit-eating. [Latin *frūx* (stem *frūg-*), fruit + -VOROUS.]
fruit (fro͞ot) *n., pl.* **fruit** or **fruits. 1. a.** The ripened ovary or ovaries of a seed-bearing plant, containing the seeds and occurring in a wide variety of forms. **b.** Any other edible fleshy part of a plant that contains seeds but consists of other tissue, such as the receptacle, in addition to the ripened ovary; a pseudocarp or false fruit. **2. a.** Such parts collectively, considered as a type of food. **b.** A vegetable fruit, such as rhubarb. **c.** A part or amount of such a plant product, served as food. **3.** The spore-bearing structure of a plant that does not bear seeds. **4.** A plant crop or product. **5.** Result; issue; outcome: *the fruits of their labor.* **6.** Offspring; progeny. **7.** *Slang.* A male homosexual.
~*v.* **fruited, fruiting, fruits.** —*intr.* To produce fruit. —*tr.* To cause to produce fruit. [Middle English, from Old French, from Latin *frūctus,* enjoyment, use, produce, fruit, from the past participle of *fruī,* to enjoy, to eat fruit.]
fruit·age (fro͞o′tĭj) *n.* **1.** The process, time, or condition of bearing fruit. **2.** Fruit collectively. **3.** A result or effect.
fruit·ar·i·an (fro͞o-târ′ē-ən) *n.* One who lives entirely on fruit. [Formed by analogy with *vegetarian.*] **—fruit·ar·i·an** *adj.* **—fruit·ar·i·an·ism** *n.*
fruit bat *n.* Any of various fruit-eating bats of the family Pteropodidae, of tropical and subtropical regions of the Old World.
fruit·cake (fro͞ot′kāk′) *n.* **1.** A heavy spiced cake containing citron, nuts, raisins, and preserved fruits. **2.** *Informal.* A person whose behavior is considered strange or eccentric.
fruit cocktail *n.* A fruit cup.
fruit cup *n.* A mixture of fresh or preserved fruits cut into pieces and served as an appetizer or dessert.
fruit·er (fro͞o′tər) *n.* **1.** A tree that produces fruit. **2.** One who grows fruit. **3.** A ship that transports fruit.
fruit·er·er (fro͞o′tər-ər) *n. Chiefly British.* A fruit grower or retailer. [Middle English, from FRUITER (grower).]
fruit fly *n.* **1.** Any of various small flies of the family Drosophilidae, having larvae that feed on ripening or fermenting fruit; especially, a common species, *Drosophila melanogaster.* **2.** Any of various flies of the family Trypetidae (or Tephritidae), having larvae that hatch in and damage plant tissue.
fruit·ful (fro͞ot′fəl) *adj.* **1.** Producing fruit. **2.** Producing fruit or offspring in abundance; prolific. **3.** Conducive to productivity; leading to abundant crops: *a fruitful climate.* **4.** Producing results; profitable. **—fruit·ful·ly** *adv.* **—fruit·ful·ness** *n.*
fruiting body *n.* A specialized spore-producing structure, especially of a fungus.
fru·i·tion (fro͞o-ĭsh′ən) *n.* **1.** Enjoyment derived from use or possession; pleasure. **2.** The achievement of something desired or worked for; accomplishment; realization. **3.** The condition of bearing fruit. [Middle English *fruicioun,* from Old French *fruition,* from Late Latin *fruitiō* (stem *fruitiōn-*), from *fruī,* to enjoy, eat fruit.]
fruit·less (fro͞ot′lĭs) *adj.* **1.** Producing no fruit. **2.** Having negligible or no results; unproductive: *"In these fruitless searches he spent ten months"* (Samuel Johnson). **—fruit·less·ly** *adv.* **—fruit·less·ness** *n.*
fruit salad *n.* **1.** A salad containing fruit. **2.** *Slang.* Ribbons and decorations worn on the breast of a military uniform.
fruit salts *pl.n.* Mineral salts.
fruit sugar *n.* **Fructose** *(see).*
fruit tree *n.* Any tree that produces fruit.
fruit·y (fro͞o′tē) *adj.* **-ier, -iest. 1.** Of, containing, or relating to fruit. **2. a.** Tasting and smelling richly of fruit. **b.** Tasting of the grape. Said of a wine. **3.** Mellow; rich: *a fruity voice.* **4.** Exuding sentiment or unctuousness. **5.** *Slang.* **a.** Homosexual. **b.** Crazy; odd. **—fruit·i·ness** *n.*
fru·men·ta·ceous (fro͞o′mən-tā′shəs, fro͞o′mĕn-) *adj.* Resembling or consisting of grain, especially wheat. [Late Latin *frūmentāceus* : Latin *frūmentum,* grain, perhaps from *fruī,* to enjoy + -ACEOUS.]
fru·men·ty (fro͞o′mən-tē) *n.* Also **fur·men·ty** (fûr′-), **fro·men·ty** (frō′-). *British.* Hulled wheat boiled in milk and flavored with sugar and spices. [Middle English *frumente,* from Old French *frumentee,* from *frument,* grain, from Latin *frūmentum.* See **frumentaceous.**]
frump (frŭmp) *n.* A dull, plain, unfashionably dressed girl or woman. [Perhaps short for dialectal *frumple,* to wrinkle, from Middle English *fromplen,* from Middle Dutch *verrompelen* : *ver-,* for- + *rompelen,* to RUMPLE.] **—frump·ish, frump·y** *adj.* **—frump·ish·ly, frump·i·ly** *adv.* **—frump·ish·ness, frump·i·ness** *n.*
frus·trate (frŭs′trāt′) *tr.v.* **-trated, -trating, -trates. 1. a.** To prevent from accomplishing a purpose or fulfilling a desire; thwart. **b.** To cause feelings of discouragement or dissatisfaction in. **c.** To hinder from finding an outlet for sexual desire. **2.** To prevent the accomplishment or development of; nullify.
~*adj. Archaic.* Baffled or thwarted. [Middle English *frustraten,* from Latin *frūstrāre* (past participle *frūstrātus*), to disappoint, frustrate, from *frūstrā*†, in error, uselessly.] **—frus·trat·er** *n.* **—frus·trat·ing·ly** *adv.*
Synonyms: *balk, foil, thwart.*
frus·trat·ed (frŭs′trā′tĭd) *adj.* **1.** Suffering from feelings of annoyance or dissatisfaction through the frustration of one's aims or desires. **2.** Unsuccessful in some activity; unfulfilled.
frus·tra·tion (frŭ-strā′shən) *n.* **1.** The condition or an instance of being frustrated. **2.** One that frustrates. **3.** *Psychology.* **a.** Feelings of dissatisfaction caused by an inability to achieve personal or sexual fulfillment. **b.** Something that gives rise to such feelings.
frus·tule (frŭs′cho͞ol, -tyo͞ol) *n.* The hard, siliceous shell of a diatom. [French, from Latin *frustulum,* diminutive of *frustum,* piece.]
frus·tum (frŭs′təm) *n., pl.* **-tums** or **-ta** (-tə). A part of a solid, such as a cone or pyramid, between two parallel planes cutting the solid, especially the section between the base and a plane parallel to it. [Latin, piece, piece cut off.]
fru·tes·cent (fro͞o-tĕs′ənt) *adj.* Pertaining to, resembling, or assuming the form of a shrub; shrubby. [Latin *frutex,* bush (see **fruticose**) + -ESCENT.] **—fru·tes·cence** *n.*

fru·ti·cose (fro͞o′tĭ-kōs′) *adj.* Shrublike, especially in form. [Latin *fruticōsus,* from *frutex*† (stem *frutic-*), shrub, bush.]

fry[1] (frī) *v.* **fried, frying, fries.** —*tr.* To cook over direct heat in hot oil or fat. —*intr.* **1.** To undergo frying. **2.** *Informal.* To swelter. **3.** *Slang.* To undergo execution in the electric chair.
∼*n., pl.* **fries. 1.** A dish of any fried food. **2.** A social gathering featuring fried food: *a fish fry.* [Middle English *frien,* from Old French *frire,* from Latin *frīgere.*]

fry[2] *n., pl.* **fry. 1.** A small fish; especially, a recently hatched fish. **2.** The similar young of certain other animals. **3.** Individuals; people: *invited the young fry to a party.* See **small fry.** [Middle English, young offspring, perhaps from Norman French *frie,* from Old French *freier,* to spawn, rub, from Latin *fricāre,* to rub.]

Fry (frī), **Christopher,** born Christopher Harris (1907–). British playwright. He became a major figure in postwar drama with his verse plays, especially *A Phoenix Too Frequent* (1946) and *The Lady's Not for Burning* (1948).

Fry, Roger Eliot (1866–1934). British painter and critic. His exhibitions (1910–12) did much to promote recognition of the postimpressionist movement in Britain. His works include studies of Paul Cézanne (1927) and Henri Matisse (1930), *Vision and Design* (1920), and *Reflections on British Paintings* (1934).

Frye (frī), **H(erman) Northrop** (1912–91). Canadian literary critic. He wrote *Fearful Symmetry* (1947), a study of William Blake, and *Anatomy of Criticism* (1957).

fry·er, fri·er (frī′ər) *n.* **1.** One that fries, especially a deep pan or vessel that is suitable for frying food. **2.** A small, young chicken that is suitable for frying.

frying pan *n.* A shallow, long-handled pan used for frying food.

FSH follicle-stimulating hormone.

f-stop (ĕf′stŏp′) *n.* **1.** A camera lens aperture setting calibrated to a corresponding f-number. **2.** An **f-number** *(see).* [*F*ocal length *stop.*]

f-sys·tem (ĕf′sĭs′təm) *n.* A method of indicating the relative aperture of a camera lens based on the f-number.

ft foot.

ft. fort; fortification.

F.T.A. Future Teachers of America.

FTC Federal Trade Commission.

ft-c foot-candle.

FT Index (ĕf′tē′) *n.* The daily index of prices on the London stock exchange based on the average price of 30 selected shares. Called in full "Financial Times Industrial Ordinary Share Index." Compare **Dow-Jones average.**

ft-lb foot-pound.

fub·sy (fŭb′zē) *adj.* **-sier, -siest.** *British Regional.* Somewhat fat and squat. [From obsolete *fubs*†, a chubby person.]

Fu-chien. See **Fujian.**

Fu-chou. See **Fuzhou.**

Fuchs (fo͝oks), **Klaus Emil Julian** (1911–88). German-born physicist. He worked on atomic research in Britain during and after World War II and was imprisoned (1950–59) for passing secret information to the Soviet government.

fuch·sia (fyo͞o′shə) *n.* **1.** Any of various chiefly tropical shrubs of the genus *Fuchsia,* widely cultivated for their showy, drooping purplish, reddish, pink, or white flowers. **2.** The hardy or common fuchsia, *F. magellanica,* having flowers with scarlet sepals and purple-blue petals forming a bell. **3.** Strong, vivid purplish red. [New Latin, after Leonhard *Fuchs* (1501–1566), German botanist.]

fuch·sin, fuch·sine (fyo͞ok′sĭn, -sēn′) *n.* A dark-green synthetic aniline dyestuff, the hydrochloride of rosaniline, used to make a purple-red dye used to color textiles and leather and as a bacterial stain. Also called "magenta." [FUCHS(IA) + -IN.]

fu·coid (fyo͞o′koid′) *adj.* Of or belonging to the order Fucales, which includes brown algae such as wracks, kelps, and similar seaweeds.
∼*n.* **1.** A member of the Fucales. **2.** A fossilized cast or impression of a seaweed. [Perhaps FUC(US) + -OID.]

fu·cose (fyo͞o′kōs′) *n.* An aldose, $C_6H_{12}O_5$, present in the polysaccharides associated with several blood groups. [FUC(US) + -OSE.]

fu·co·xan·thin (fyo͞o′kō-zăn′thĭn) *n.* A brown carotenoid pigment, $C_{40}H_{60}O_6$, found in brown algae. [FUC(US) + XANTH(O)- + -IN.]

fu·cus (fyo͞o′kəs) *n.* Any of various brown algae of the genus *Fucus,* which includes many of the larger seaweeds found between high and low tide mark. [New Latin *Fucus,* from Latin *fūcus,* red dye, orchil, from Greek *phukos.* See **phyco-.**]

fud·dle (fŭd′l) *v.* **-dled, -dling, -dles.** —*tr.* To muddle with or as if with strong drink; intoxicate. —*intr.* To drink; tipple.
∼*n.* A state of intoxication or confusion. [16th century : origin obscure.]

fud·dy-dud·dy (fŭd′ē-dŭd′ē) *n., pl.* **-dies.** One who is old-fashioned and fussy. [20th century : origin obscure.] **—fud·dy-dud·dy** *adj.*

fudge (fŭj) *n.* **1.** A soft, rich candy made of sugar, butter, milk, and flavoring. **2.** Nonsense; humbug. **3.** A small section of a newspaper page in which last-minute copy may be inserted after the plate or type is on the printing press. **4.** The news item so inserted.
∼*interj.* Used to express disbelief, disappointment, or annoyance.
∼*v.* **fudged, fudging, fudges.** —*tr.* **1.** To make or repair in a clumsy way; botch. **2.** To evade (an issue, for example); dodge. **3.** To fake or falsify. —*intr.* **1.** To act or talk in an evasive or indecisive manner. **2.** To act dishonestly; cheat. [Perhaps from obsolete *fadge*†, to adjust, fit, fake, deceive.]

Fue·gi·an (fwā′jē-ən) *adj.* Of or relating to Tierra del Fuego, its inhabitants, or its culture.
∼*n.* An inhabitant of Tierra del Fuego.

fuehrer. Variant of **führer.**

fu·el (fyo͞o′əl) *n.* **1.** Anything consumed to produce energy, especially: **a.** A material such as coal, gas, or oil burned to produce heat. **b.** Fissionable material used in a nuclear reactor. **c.** Nutritive material metabolized by a living organism. **2.** Anything that maintains or heightens an activity or an emotion.
∼*v.* **fueled** or **-elled, -eling** or **-elling, -els.** —*tr.* **1.** To provide with fuel. **2.** To stimulate: *His insolence fueled her anger.* —*intr.* To take in fuel. [Middle English *feuel,* from Old French *fouaille,* from Vulgar Latin *focālia* (unattested), from Latin *focus*†, fire, hearth.] **—fu·el·er** *n.*

fuel cell *n.* An electrochemical cell in which the energy of a reaction between a fuel such as liquid hydrogen and an oxidant such as liquid oxygen is converted directly and continuously into the energy of direct electric current.

fuel element *n.* A can that contains the nuclear fuel in a nuclear reactor.

fuel injection *n.* Any of several methods or mechanical systems by which a fuel is vaporized and sprayed into the cylinders of an internal-combustion engine without the use of a carburetor.

fuel oil *n.* Any liquid or liquefiable petroleum product that ignites spontaneously at a temperature above 100°F, used to generate heat or power.

fug (fŭg) *n.* A hot, stuffy, and usually smoke-laden atmosphere. [19th century : origin obscure.] **—fug·gy** *adj.*

fu·ga·cious (fyo͞o-gā′shəs) *adj.* **1.** Passing away quickly; evanescent. **2.** *Botany.* Withering or dropping off early: *fugacious petals.* [Latin *fugāx* (stem *fugāc-*), swift, fleeting, from *fugere,* to flee.] **—fu·ga·cious·ly** *adv.* **—fu·ga·cious·ness** *n.*

fu·gac·i·ty (fyo͞o-găs′ĭ-tē) *n.* **1.** The state or quality of being fugacious. **2.** A property of a gas that is a measure of its ability to escape or expand, given by d $(\log_e f) = d\mu/RT$, where μ is the chemical potential, R is the gas constant, and T is the thermodynamic temperature.

Fu·gard (fo͞o′gärd′), **Athol** (1932–). South African playwright and actor. His plays, including *The Blood Knot* (1962), *Boesman and Lena* (1973), and *A Lesson from Aloes* (1981), examine the treatment of society's misfits and outcasts.

-fuge *suffix.* Indicates an expulsion or driving away; for example, **vermifuge.** [Latin *fugāre,* to put to flight, expel, from *fuga,* flight.]

fu·gi·tive (fyo͞o′jĭ-tĭv) *adj.* **1.** Running or having run away; fleeing, as from justice or the law. **2. a.** Passing quickly; fleeting: *fugitive hours.* **b.** Difficult to comprehend or retain; elusive. **c.** Given to change or disappearance; perishable. **3.** Having to do with topics of temporary interest; ephemeral. —See Synonyms at **transient.**
∼*n.* **1.** One who flees; a runaway; refugee. **2.** Anything fleeting or ephemeral. [Middle English *fugitif,* from Old French, from Latin *fugitīvus,* from adjective, "fleeing," from *fugitus,* past participle of *fugere,* to flee.] **—fu·gi·tive·ly** *adv.* **—fu·gi·tive·ness** *n.*

fu·gle (fyo͞o′gəl) *intr.v.* **-gled, -gling, -gles.** *Archaic.* To act as a fugleman. [Back-formation from FUGLEMAN.]

fu·gle·man (fyo͞o′gəl-mən) *n., pl.* **-men** (-mĭn). **1.** *Archaic.* A soldier who serves as a guide and model for his company. **2.** A leader; especially, a political leader. [German *Flügelmann,* soldier, "man on the wing" : *Flügel,* wing + *Mann,* man.]

fugue (fyo͞og) *n.* **1.** A polyphonic musical form or composition in which a theme or themes stated successively by a number of voices in imitation are developed contrapuntally. **2.** A pathological amnesiac condition during which the patient is apparently conscious of his actions but on return to normal has no recollection of them. [French *fugue* or Italian *fuga,* flight, from Latin, flight.] **—fu·gal** *adj.* **—fu·gal·ly** *adv.*

füh·rer, fueh·rer (fyo͝or′ər; *German* fü′rər) *n.* **1.** A leader; especially, one exercising the powers of a dictator. **2. Führer.** The title of Adolf Hitler as the leader of the German Nazis. [German *Führer,* from Middle High German *vüerer,* bearer, from *vüeren,* to lead, bear, from Old High German *fuoren,* to lead.]

Fu·jian or **Fu-chien** (fo͞o′jĕn′). Also **Fu·kien** (-kyĕn′). Province in southeastern China. It has some of Asia's finest scenery, with wooded mountains such as the Wuyi Shan, terraced rice paddies, orchards, and tea gardens. [Chinese, "happy establishment."]

Fu·ji·ya·ma (fo͞o′jē-yä′mə). Also **Fu·ji·san** (fo͞o′jē-sän′) or **Mount Fu·ji** (fo͞o′jē). Active volcano on the island of Honshu and the highest mountain (3,776 meters; 12,388 feet) in Japan. Its summit is a place of pilgrimage, and its snow-capped, strikingly symmetrical cone has long been a favorite subject of Japanese painters. The last major eruption took place in 1707.

-ful *suffix.* Indicates: **1.** Having the characteristics of; for example, **masterful. 2.** Tendency or ability; for example, **useful. 3.** The amount or number that will fill; for example, **armful.** [Middle English *-ful,* Old English *-ful, -full,* from *full,* FULL.]

Fu·la, Fu·lah (fo͞o′lə) *n., pl.* **-las** or **-lahs** or collectively **Fula** or **Fulah.** A mostly Muslim people of the western Sudan region of Africa, of mixed Hamitic and Negroid stock.

Fu·la·ni (fo͞o′lä′nē, fo͞o-lä′nē) *n., pl.* **-nis** or collectively **Fulani. 1.** A member of the Fula. **2.** The language of the Fula.

ful·crum (fo͝ol′krəm, fŭl′-) *n., pl.* **-crums** or **-cra** (-krə). **1.** The point or support on which a lever turns. **2.** A factor critically affecting an outcome, reaction, or the like: *Cost was the fulcrum of their decision.* [Latin, bedpost, support, from *fulcīre,* to prop up, support.]

ful·fill, ful·fil (fo͝ol-fĭl′) *tr.v.* **-filled, -filling, -fills** or **-fils. 1.** To realize (expectations or promise, for example); achieve. **2.** To carry out (an order or duty, for example). **3.** To measure up to; satisfy. **4.** To go

fuchsia *There are more than 100 species of fuchsia, most of which are native to Central and South America and New Zealand. They have brightly colored pendant flowers and are often grown in hanging baskets.*

PRONUNCIATION KEY

ă, pat; ā, pay; âr, care;
ä, father, are; b, bib;
ch, church; d, deed; ĕ, pet;
ē, be; f, fife; g, gag; h, hat;
hw, which; ĭ, pit; ī, pie;
îr, pier; j, judge; k, kick;
l, lid, needle; m, mum;
n, no, sudden; ng, thing;
ŏ, pot; ō, toe; ô, paw, for;
oi, noise; ou, out; o͝o, book;
o͞o, boot; p, pop; r, roar;
s, sauce; sh, ship, dish;
t, tight; th, thin, path;
th, this, bathe; ŭ, cut; ûr, fur;
v, valve; w, with; y, yes;
z, zebra, size; zh, vision;
ə, about, item, edible, gallop, circus, peaceful

IN FOREIGN WORDS:

à, *Fr.* ami; œ, *Fr.* feu, *Ger.* schön; ü, *Fr.* tu, *Ger.* über;
KH, *Ger.* ich, *Scot.* loch;
N, *Fr.* bon; y′, *Fr.* Compiègne

STRESS MARKS:

Primary stress: ′
in·cite′ (ĭn-sīt′)
Secondary stress: ′
in′sight′ (ĭn′sīt′)

to the end of (a period of time); finish or complete. —See Synonyms at **perform.** **—fulfill oneself.** To achieve personal fulfillment. [Middle English *fulfillen,* Old English *fullfyllan,* to fill full : *ful,* FULL + *fyllan,* to FILL.] **—ful·fill·er** *n.*

ful·fill·ment, ful·fil·ment (fo͝ol-fĭl′mənt) *n.* **1.** The act or process of fulfilling. **2.** The state or quality of being fulfilled; completion. **3.** Satisfaction gained from fully realizing one's personal aims or potential. **4.** The processing of orders in a direct mail operation, as for magazine subscriptions.

ful·gent (fŭl′jənt, fo͝ol′-) *adj.* Shining brilliantly. [Middle English, from Latin *fulgēns* (stem *fulgent-*), present participle of *fulgēre,* to flash, shine.] **—ful·gent·ly** *adv.*

ful·gu·rant (fŭl′gyər-ənt, fo͝ol′-) *adj.* **1.** Flashing like lightning. **2.** *Medicine.* Fulminant. [Latin *fulgurāns* (stem *fulgurant-*), present participle of *fulgurāre,* to FULGURATE.]

ful·gu·rate (fŭl′gyə-rāt′, fo͝ol′-) *v.* **-rated, -rating, -rates.** *—intr.* To give off or seem to give off flashes of lightning. *—tr. Medicine.* To destroy (tissue) by fulguration. [Latin *fulgurāre,* to flash, glow like lightning, from *fulgur,* lightning, from *fulgēre,* to flash, shine.]

ful·gu·ra·tion (fŭl′gyə-rā′shən, fo͝ol′-) *n.* **1.** The act of flashing like lightning or flashing with light. **2.** The destruction of unwanted tissue, such as warts, with electric current.

ful·gu·rite (fŭl′gyə-rīt′, fo͝ol′-) *n.* A tubular body of glassy rock produced by lightning striking loose unconsolidated sand or more solid rock. [Latin *fulgur,* lightning (see **fulgurate**) + -ITE.]

ful·gu·rous (fŭl′gyər-əs, fo͝ol′-) *adj.* **1.** Emitting flashes of lightning. **2.** Appearing or acting like lightning.

fu·lig·i·nous (fyo͞o-lĭj′ə-nəs) *adj.* **1.** Sooty. **2.** Colored by or as if by soot. [Late Latin *fūlīginōsus,* from Latin *fūlīgō* (stem *fūlīgin-*), soot.] **—fu·lig·i·nous·ly** *adv.*

full[1] (fo͝ol) *adj.* **fuller, fullest. 1.** Containing all that is normal or possible; filled: *a full bottle.* **2. a.** Not deficient or partial: *a full view of the stage.* **b.** Complete; no less than: *a full half hour.* **c.** Maximum: *its full length.* **d.** Whole; entire: *He realized the full implications of his act.* **e.** At the highest degree or at the greatest extent: *at full speed; in full color.* **3. a.** Having a great deal or many of. Used with *of*: *a room full of people.* **b.** Abounding in. Used with *of*: *full of enthusiasm.* **4. a.** Profoundly affected by an emotion. **b.** Deeply engrossed or preoccupied by; talking and thinking of nothing else. Used with *of*: *They were all full of the idea.* **5. a.** Very busy: *a full day.* **b.** Satisfying; fulfilling: *a full life.* **6. a.** Having all appropriate rights and responsibilities: *a full member.* **b.** Designating a relation or relationship based on descent from the same parents: *full brothers.* **7. a.** Rounded in shape; plump: *a full figure.* **b.** Of ample cut or generous proportions; wide: *full draperies.* **8.** Satiated, especially with food or drink; abundantly fed. **9. a.** Having depth and body; rich: *a full color.* **b.** Resonant: *the full tone of the cellos.* **10.** Full-bodied. Said of wines. **11.** Thoroughly documented and presented; detailed: *a full report.* **12.** Having the observable surface completely illuminated. Said of the moon. **13.** At the flood; high. Said of the tide. **14.** Extended by the wind. Said of sails.
~adv. **1.** To a complete extent; entirely. Often used in combination: *full-grown.* **2.** Exactly; directly: *full in the path of the ball.* **3.** Quite; equally: *full as wicked as I am.* **—full well.** Very well: *I know full well how you feel.*
~v. **fulled, fulling, fulls.** *—tr.* To make (a garment) full, as by pleating or gathering. *—intr.* To become full. Used of the moon.
~n. The maximum or complete size, amount, or development. **—at the full.** At the state or period of fullness. **—in full. 1.** To, for, or with the entire amount. **2.** With nothing left out; completely. **—to the full.** To the utmost extent; completely. [Middle English *ful(l),* Old English *full.*]

fulmar *The northern fulmar defends itself by squirting stinking oil—produced from its stomach—over an intruder. It nests on cliffs around the Arctic Circle and western Europe.*

full[2] *v.* **fulled, fulling, fulls.** *—tr.* To clean and increase the weight and bulk of (cloth) by washing, shrinking, and beating or pressing. *—intr.* To become heavier and more compact. Used of cloth. [Middle English *fullen,* from Old French *fouler,* from Vulgar Latin *fullāre* (unattested), from Latin *fullō*†, a fuller.]

full·back (fo͝ol′băk′) *n. Abbr.* **fb, f.b. 1. a.** *Football.* A backfield player whose position is behind the quarterback and halfbacks and who performs offensive blocking and line plunges and defensive linebacking. **b.** A similar player in field hockey, soccer, and rugby. **2.** The position played by a fullback.

full blood *n.* **1.** Relationship established through having the same parents. **2.** A person or animal of unmixed race or breed; a purebred.

full-blood·ed (fo͝ol′blŭd′ĭd) *adj.* Also **full-blood** (fo͝ol′blŭd′) (for sense 1). **1. a.** Of unmixed ancestry; purebred. **b.** Related through having the same parents. **2.** Vigorous; forceful. **3.** Thoroughgoing: *a full-blooded communist.*

full-blown (fo͝ol′blōn′) *adj.* **1.** In full blossom; fully open: *a full-blown tulip.* **2.** Fully developed or matured: *a full-blown beauty.*

full-bod·ied (fo͝ol′bŏd′ēd) *adj.* Having richness and intensity of flavor. Said of wines.

full brother *n.* See **brother.**

full cousin *n.* See **cousin.**

full-cream (fo͝ol′krēm′) *adj.* Designating or made with milk that has had none of the cream skimmed off.

full dress *n.* The attire appropriate for formal or ceremonial events.

full-dress (fo͝ol′drĕs′) *adj.* **1.** Requiring or consisting of full dress; formal: *a full-dress banquet.* **2.** Full-scale: *a full-dress investigation.*

full·er[1] (fo͝ol′ər) *n.* A person who fulls cloth. [Middle English *fullere,* Old English *fullere,* from Latin *fullō.* See **full** (to clean).]

fuller[2] *n.* **1.** A hammer used by a blacksmith for grooving or spreading iron. **2.** A groove made with this tool.
~tr.v. **fullered, -ering, -ers.** To make (a groove) with a fuller. [Perhaps from the name *Fuller.*]

Ful·ler (fo͝ol′ər), **(Richard) Buckminster** (1895–1983). U.S. designer and architect. His high-efficiency, low-pollution prefabricated geodesic domes were very popular, and his book *Operating Manual for Spaceship Earth* (1969) was influential in the environmentalist movement of the 1970's.

Fuller, (Sarah) Margaret (1810–50). U.S. author, critic, and reformer. An editor of the transcendentalist periodical *Dial* (1840) and the literary critic for the *New York Tribune* (1844–45), she was regarded as one of America's premier critics. On a European tour (1845–50), she married an Italian marquis, joined the ill-fated Roman Revolution, and wrote a history of that rebellion. While en route to the United States, she perished in a shipwreck.

fuller's earth *n.* A highly absorbent clay used in fulling woolen cloth, in talcum powders, as a filter, and as a catalyst.

fuller's teasel *n.* A European plant, *Dipsacus fullonum,* having bristly flower heads used by fullers to raise the nap on cloth. See **teasel.**

full face *adv.* Face on to an observer or a specified object.

full-fash·ioned (fo͝ol′făsh′ənd) *adj.* Knitted in a shape that conforms closely to body lines.

full-fledged (fo͝ol′flĕjd′) *adj.* **1.** Having fully developed adult plumage. **2.** Having reached full development; mature. **3.** Having full status or rank: *a full-fledged lawyer.*

full gainer *n.* A forward dive in which one executes a full back somersault before entering the water.

full house *n.* **1.** In poker, a hand containing three of a kind and a pair. **2.** A movie theater, concert hall, or the like in which every seat for a performance is taken. **3.** A winning set of numbers at bingo.

full-length (fo͝ol′lĕngkth′, -lĕngth′) *adj.* **1.** Showing, covering, or fitted to the entire length of someone or something: *a full-length mirror.* **2.** Of a normal or standard length; unabridged: *a full-length novel.*

full moon *n.* **1.** The phase of the moon when it is visible as a fully illuminated disk. **2.** The period of the month when this occurs. **3.** The fully illuminated moon.

full-mouthed (fo͝ol′mouth*d*′, -moutht′) *adj.* **1.** Having a complete set of teeth. Said of cattle and other livestock. **2.** Uttered loudly or noisily: *a full-mouthed oath.*

full nelson *n.* A wrestling hold in which both hands are first thrust under the opponent's arms from behind and then pressed against the back of his neck. Compare **half nelson.**

full·ness, ful·ness (fo͝ol′nĭs) *n.* The quality or state of being full. **—in the fullness of time.** At the proper, appointed time.

full-out (fo͝ol′out′) *adj.* **1.** Total; complete. **2.** *Printing.* Not indented; aligned with the margin. **—full-out** *adv.*

full-rigged (fo͝ol′rĭgd′) *adj.* Having three or more masts all square-rigged.

full rhyme *n.* A **perfect rhyme** *(see).*

full-scale (fo͝ol′skāl′) *adj.* **1.** Of the actual or full size; not reduced: *a full-scale model.* **2.** Carried out in a thoroughgoing manner and with a total commitment of effort: *a full-scale campaign.* **3.** Occurring on a large scale: *a full-scale disaster.*

full sister *n.* See **sister.**

full stop *n. Chiefly British.* A dot indicating the end of a sentence or an abbreviation; period.

full tilt *adv.* At high or top speed: *ran full tilt into the tree.*

full-time (fo͝ol′tīm′) *adj.* **1.** Of, pertaining to, or designating work requiring attendance throughout the working week. Compare **part-time. 2.** Performing an activity or job for the normal or required amount of time: *a full-time student.* **3.** Of or pertaining to an activity that requires a person's full attention. **—full-time** *adv.*

ful·ly (fo͝ol′ē) *adv.* **1.** Totally or completely. **2.** Adequately; sufficiently. **3.** At a conservative estimate; at least.

ful·mar (fo͝ol′mər, -mär′) *n.* **1.** A gull-like bird, *Fulmarus glacialis,* of Arctic regions, having smoky gray plumage. Also called "fulmar petrel." **2.** Any of several similar related birds. [Perhaps from Old Norse *fūlmār,* "foul gull" (probably referring to its smell) : *fūll,* foul + *mār,* gull, from Germanic *maiwa-* (unattested), gull, MEW.]

ful·mi·nant (fŭl′mə-nənt, fo͝ol′-) *adj.* **1.** Fulminating. **2.** *Pathology.* Occurring suddenly, rapidly, and with great intensity. Said of symptoms, especially of pain. [Latin *fulmināns* (stem *fulminant-*), present participle of *fulmināre,* to strike with lightning, FULMINATE.]

ful·mi·nate (fŭl′mə-nāt′, fo͝ol′-) *v.* **-nated, -nating, -nates.** *—intr.* **1.** To issue a thunderous verbal attack or denunciation; inveigh: *fulminate against political chicanery.* **2.** To explode or detonate with sudden violence. *—tr.* **1.** To thunder out or issue (a decree or denunciation, for example). **2.** To cause to explode.
~n. An explosive salt or ester of fulminic acid; especially, fulminate of mercury. [Middle English *fulminaten,* from Medieval Latin *fulmināre* (past participle *fulminātus*), to censure (in ecclesiastical decrees), from Latin, to strike with lightning, from *fulmen* (stem *fulmin-*), lightning.] **—ful·mi·na·tor** *n.* **—ful·mi·na·to·ry** (fŭl′mə-nə-tôr′ē, -tōr′ē, fo͝ol′-) *adj.*

fulminate of mercury *n.* A gray crystalline powder, $Hg(CNO)_2$, that explodes on impact when dry and is used as a high explosive.

fulminating powder *n.* An explosive powder that can be detonated by impact.

ful·mi·na·tion (fŭl′mə-nā′shən, fo͝ol′-) *n.* **1.** The act of fulminating. **2.** A thunderous denunciation or censure. **3.** A violent explosion.

ful·min·ic acid (fŭl-mĭn′ĭk, fo͝ol-) *n.* An unstable acid, HONC, that forms highly explosive salts and esters. [Latin *fulmen* (stem *fulmin-*), lightning. See **fulminate**.]

ful·some (fo͝ol′səm) *adj.* **1.** Offensively excessive, flattering, or insincere: *fulsome praise.* **2.** Offensive to the taste or sensibilities; loathsome; disgusting. **3.** *Archaic.* Copious or abundant in supply. [Middle English *fulsom,* abundant : *ful,* FULL + -SOME.] **—ful·some·ly** *adv.* **—ful·some·ness** *n.*

Usage: *Fulsome* is often misused, especially in the phrase *fulsome praise,* by those who think that the term is equivalent merely to *full* and *abundant.* In modern usage *full* and *abundant* are obsolete as senses of *fulsome,* which now combines the idea of fullness or abundance with that of excess or insincerity.

Ful·ton (fo͝ol′tən), **Robert** (1765–1815). U.S. engineer. He developed the first practical submarine and torpedo (1800) and is most famous as the inventor of the steamship. His first steamboat, the *Clermont,* made the round trip from New York City to Albany on the Hudson River in 62 hours (1806).

ful·vous (fo͝ol′vəs, fŭl′-) *adj.* Tawny yellowish-brown. [Latin *fulvus;* akin to *fulgēre,* to shine.]

fu·mar·ic acid (fyo͞o-măr′ĭk) *n.* An acid, $C_4H_4O_4$, found in various plants and produced synthetically, used mainly in resins, paints, and varnishes. [New Latin *Fumaria,* genus of fumitory, from Late Latin *fūmāria,* fumitory, from Latin *fūmus,* smoke.]

fu·ma·role (fyo͞o′mə-rōl′) *n.* A vent or small hole in a volcanic area from which hot smoke and gases arise. [Italian *fumarola,* from Late Latin *fūmāriolum,* smoke hole, from Latin *fūmārium,* smoke chamber, from *fūmus,* smoke.]

fu·ma·to·ri·um (fyo͞o′mə-tôr′ē-əm, -tōr′ē-əm) *n., pl.* **-ums** or **-toria** (-tôr′ē-ə, -tōr′ē-ə). An airtight fumigation chamber in which chemical vapors are used to destroy insects and fungi on plants. [New Latin, from Latin *fūmātus,* past participle of *fūmāre,* to smoke, from *fūmus,* smoke.]

fu·ma·to·ry (fyo͞o′mə-tôr′ē, -tōr′ē) *adj.* Of or pertaining to smoke or fumigating.

~n., pl. **fumatories.** A fumatorium. [New Latin *fumatorius,* from FUMATORIUM.]

fum·ble (fŭm′bəl) *v.* **-bled, -bling, -bles.** *—intr.* **1.** To touch or handle nervously or idly: *fumble with a necktie.* **2.** To grope awkwardly to find or to accomplish: *fumble for a key.* **3.** To proceed awkwardly and uncertainly; blunder: *fumble through a speech.* **4. a.** *Baseball.* To mishandle a ground ball. **b.** *Football.* To drop a ball that is in play. *—tr.* **1.** To catch, touch, or handle clumsily or idly. **2. a.** To feel or make (one's way) awkwardly. **b.** To make a botch of; bungle. **3. a.** *Baseball.* To mishandle (a ground ball). **b.** *Football.* To drop (a ball that is in play).

~n. **1.** The act of fumbling. **2.** An instance of fumbling. **3.** *Sports.* A ball that has been fumbled. [Low German *fummeln*†.] **—fum·bler** *n.*

fume (fyo͞om) *n.* **1.** *Often* **fumes.** An exhalation of smoke, vapor, or gas; especially, an irritating or disagreeable exhalation. **2.** A strong or acrid odor. **3.** A state of irritation or anger.

~v. **fumed, fuming, fumes.** *—tr.* **1.** To subject to or treat with fumes. **2.** To give off in or as if in fumes. *—intr.* **1.** To emit fumes. **2.** To rise or dissipate in vapor. **3.** To feel or show anger. [Middle English, from Old French *fum,* from Latin *fūmus,* smoke, steam.]

fume cupboard *n. British.* A cupboard or glass chamber in a laboratory within which operations involving chemicals that emit harmful vapors are performed or where such chemicals are stored.

fu·mi·gate (fyo͞o′mĭ-gāt′) *tr.v.* **-gated, -gating, -gates.** To subject to smoke or fumes, usually in order to exterminate vermin or insects. [Latin *fūmigāre* : *fūmus,* smoke, FUME + *agere,* to make, do.] **—fu·mi·gant** *n.* **—fu·mi·ga·tion** *n.* **—fu·mi·ga·tor** *n.*

fuming sulfuric acid *n.* A mixture of sulfuric acids made by dissolving sulfur trioxide in concentrated sulfuric acid. It is principally pyrosulfuric acid, $H_2S_2O_7$. Also called "oleum," "Nordhausen acid."

fu·mi·to·ry (fyo͞o′mə-tôr′ē, -tōr′ē) *n., pl.* **-ries. 1.** A climbing annual plant, *Fumaria officinalis,* native to Europe, having finely divided leaves and spurred purplish flowers. **2.** Any other plants of the genus *Fumaria.* [Middle English *fumetere,* from Old French *fumeterre,* from Medieval Latin *fūmus terrae,* "smoke of the earth" (its growth resembles a cloud of smoke over the ground) : Latin *fūmus,* smoke, FUME + *terrae,* genitive of *terra,* earth.]

fun (fŭn) *n.* **1.** A source of enjoyment or pleasure; amusing diversion: *Clowns are fun.* **2.** Enjoyment; pleasure; amusement: *have fun at the beach.* **3.** Excited, playful activity or altercation. **—for** (or **in**) **fun.** As a joke; playfully. **—like fun.** *Slang.* Absolutely not; of course not. **—make fun of.** To ridicule.

~intr.v. **funned, funning, funs.** To behave playfully; joke.

~adj. Informal. Providing fun; amusing: *a fun group of people.* [Perhaps from obsolete *fun,* to trick, from Middle English *fonnen,* to make fun of, from *fon, fonne,* a fool. See **fond.**]

fu·nam·bu·list (fyo͞o-năm′byə-lĭst) *n.* One who performs on a tightrope or a slack rope. [Probably from Latin *fūnambulus,* rope dancer : *fūnis*†, rope + *ambulāre,* to walk around.] **—fu·nam·bu·lism** *n.*

Fun·chal (fo͞on-shäl′). Popular winter resort city on Madeira island and capital of the Funchal overseas district of Portugal, comprising the Madeira archipelago.

func·tion (fŭngk′shən) *n.* **1.** The natural or proper action for which a person, office, thing, or organ is fitted or employed. **2. a.** Assigned duty or activity: *His functions include maintaining office records.* **b.** Specific occupation or role: *in her function as mayor.* **3.** An official ceremony or elaborate social occasion. **4.** Something closely related to another thing and dependent upon it for its existence, value, or significance. **5.** *Grammar.* The role or position of a linguistic element in a construction. **6.** *Mathematics.* **a.** A variable so related to another that for each value assumed by one there is a value determined for the other. **b.** A rule of correspondence between two sets such that there is a unique element in one set assigned to each element in the other.

~intr.v. **functioned, -tioning, -tions.** To have or perform a function; serve. [Latin *functiō* (stem *functiōn-*), activity, performance, from *functus,* past participle of *fungī,* to perform.]

func·tion·al (fŭngk′shə-nəl) *adj.* **1.** Of or pertaining to a function or functions. **2. a.** Designed for or adapted to a particular practical need or activity: *functional clothing for infants.* **b.** Stressing practical usefulness and function other than extraneous embellishment: *functional architecture.* **3.** Capable of performing; operative. **4.** *Pathology.* Pertaining to a disease having no apparent physiological or structural cause. **5.** *Mathematics.* Of, relating to, or indicating a function or functions. **—func·tion·al·ly** *adv.*

functional disease *n.* Any disease having no apparent physiological or structural cause. Compare **organic disease.**

functional group *n. Chemistry.* The group of atoms in a molecule that determines its chemical behavior; for example, -CHO is the functional group in aldehydes.

func·tion·al·ism (fŭngk′shə-nə-lĭz′əm) *n.* **1.** The doctrine or the application of the doctrine that the function of an object should determine its design and materials. **2.** Any doctrine or its application stressing purpose, practicality, and utility.

functional shift *n. Linguistics.* A shift in the syntactic function of a word without a change in its form, as when a noun serves as a verb.

func·tion·ar·y (fŭngk′shə-nĕr′ē) *n., pl.* **-ies.** A person who holds an office or a trust; an official.

function word *n. Linguistics.* A word that chiefly indicates a grammatical relationship in a sentence or phrase, as a preposition, conjunction, or auxiliary verb. Also called "form word."

fund (fŭnd) *n.* **1.** A source of supply; a stock: *a fund of good will.* **2. a.** A sum of money or other resources set aside for a specific purpose. **b. funds.** Available money; finances. **3. funds.** *British.* The permanent national debt, considered as securities. Preceded by *the.* **4.** An organization established to administer a fund.

~tr.v. **funded, funding, funds. 1.** To provide money for paying off the interest or principal of (a debt). **2.** To convert (a debt) into a long-term or floating debt with fixed interest payments. **3.** To place or accumulate in a fund. **4.** To furnish a fund or financing for: *fund cancer research.* [Blend of French *fond,* bottom, and *fonds,* stock, both from Latin *fundus,* bottom, landed property.]

fun·da·ment (fŭn′də-mənt) *n.* **1. a.** The buttocks. **b.** The anus. **2.** The natural features of a land surface unaltered by human beings. **3.** A foundation. **4.** A theoretical basis; an underlying principle. [Middle English *foundement,* foundation, lower part, from Old French *fondement,* from Latin *fundāmentum,* from *fundāre,* to lay the bottom for, from *fundus,* bottom.]

fun·da·men·tal (fŭn′də-mĕnt′l) *adj.* **1. a.** Having to do with the foundation; elemental; basic. **b.** Critical or central: *of fundamental importance.* **2.** Having to do with the origin; generative; primary: *fundamental research.* **3.** *Physics.* **a.** Of or pertaining to the component of lowest frequency of a periodic wave or quantity. **b.** Of or pertaining to the lowest possible frequency at which a system or element will vibrate naturally.

~n. **1.** Something that is an elemental part of a system, such as a principle or law; an essential. **2.** *Physics.* The lowest frequency of a periodically varying quantity or of a vibrating system. **3.** *Music.* The lowest or bass note of a chord, considered as the root of the chord. **—fun·da·men·tal·ly** *adv.*

fundamental constant *n. Physics.* The value of a physical quantity, such as the speed of light in a vacuum or the electronic charge, that is regarded as basic and constant under all circumstances. Also called "universal constant."

fun·da·men·tal·ism (fŭn′də-mĕnt′l-ĭz′əm) *n.* **1.** Belief in the Bible as factual historical record and incontrovertible prophecy, including such doctrines as the Creation, the Virgin Birth, and the Second Coming. **2. a.** *Often* **Fundamentalism.** A movement among Protestants based upon this belief. **b.** Adherence to this belief. **3.** Unswerving belief in a set of basic and unalterable principles of a religious or philosophical nature. **—fun·da·men·tal·ist** *n. & adj.* **—fun·da·men·tal·ist·ic** (fŭn′də-mĕnt′l-ĭs′tĭk) *adj.*

fundamental particle *n. Physics.* An **elementary particle** *(see).*

fundamental unit *n.* Any of a set of unrelated units used to measure different quantities, such as length, mass, and time, that form the basis of a system of units.

fun·di (fo͞on′dē) *n.* **1.** *East African.* A maintenance man or mechanic; a mechanical expert. **2.** *South African.* An expert or authority in any field; a pundit. [Swahili.]

fun·dus (fŭn′dəs) *n., pl.* **-di** (-dī′). *Anatomy.* The inner basal surface of an organ farthest away from the opening, as in the eye or uterus. [New Latin, from Latin, bottom.]

Fun·dy, Bay of (fŭn′dē). Arm of the Atlantic Ocean between the provinces of Nova Scotia and New Brunswick in eastern Canada. It is *c.* 270 kilometers (168 miles) long, with a maximum width of 80 kilometers (50 miles). The bay's tidal range, which can be as much as 21 meters (68 feet), is the greatest in the world.

fu·ner·al (fyo͞o′nər-əl) *n.* **1.** The ceremonies held in connection with the burial or cremation of the dead. **2.** A party accompanying a body to the grave; a funeral procession. **3.** *Informal.* A problem; a

PRONUNCIATION KEY

ă, pat; ā, pay; âr, care;
ä, father, are; b, bib;
ch, church; d, deed; ĕ, pet;
ē, be; f, fife; g, gag; h, hat;
hw, which; ĭ, pit; ī, pie;
îr, pier; j, judge; k, kick;
l, lid, needle; m, mum;
n, no, sudden; ng, thing;
ŏ, pot; ō, toe; ô, paw, for;
oi, noise; ou, out; o͝o, book;
o͞o, boot; p, pop; r, roar;
s, sauce; sh, ship, dish;
t, tight; th, thin, path;
th, this, bathe; ŭ, cut; ûr, fur;
v, valve; w, with; y, yes;
z, zebra, size; zh, vision;
ə, about, item, edible,
gallop, circus, peaceful

IN FOREIGN WORDS:

à, *Fr.* ami; œ, *Fr.* feu, *Ger.* schön; ü, *Fr.* tu, *Ger.* über;
KH, *Ger.* ich, *Scot.* loch;
N, *Fr.* bon; y′, *Fr.* Compiègne

STRESS MARKS:

Primary stress: ′
in·cite′ (ĭn-sīt′)
Secondary stress: ′
in′sight′ (ĭn′sīt′)

fungus

SIMPLE AND ANCIENT PLANTS

Different species give us food, diseases, and cures

Fungi are nonflowering plants that lack chlorophyll—the pigment that enables green plants to synthesize food from sunlight. For sustenance fungi rely instead on other plants and animals. Some 50,000 species are known, and there may be that many, or even more, still unidentified. Dating back some 500 million years, fungi include some of the simplest and most ancient plants.

Although some scientists consider slime molds to be fungi, their status is disputed and true fungi are divided into three groups:
- sac fungi (Ascomycetes), which include truffles, yeasts, powdery mildew, Dutch elm disease fungus, and blue-green molds (such as those that tint blue cheeses and form penicillin);
- club fungi (Basidiomycetes), which include mushrooms, puffballs, and various crop rusts;
- algal fungi (Phycomycetes), which include the white and gray molds such as those that grow on old bread and cause athlete's foot.

Fungi multiply by releasing spores, not seeds. When a spore germinates, it produces fine threads—hyphae—that form a microscopic branched system—a mycelium—to penetrate the food source. The hyphae secrete enzymes that digest the tissues of dead or living organisms. Hyphae may combine and coalesce to form large bodies such as the mushroom. In some species the hyphae spread in a circle underground and break the surface to make "fairy rings." Mature fungi grow spores by the billion. A mushroom 100 millimeters (4 inches) wide may produce 16 billion spores. In 28 grams (1 ounce) of soil there may be 2,500,000 fungal spores.

The best-known fungi are mushrooms, a term that technically includes toadstools, which is the popular name for inedible mushrooms. The only way to tell edible from inedible species is to identify each one individually.

HOW A MUSHROOM IS FORMED

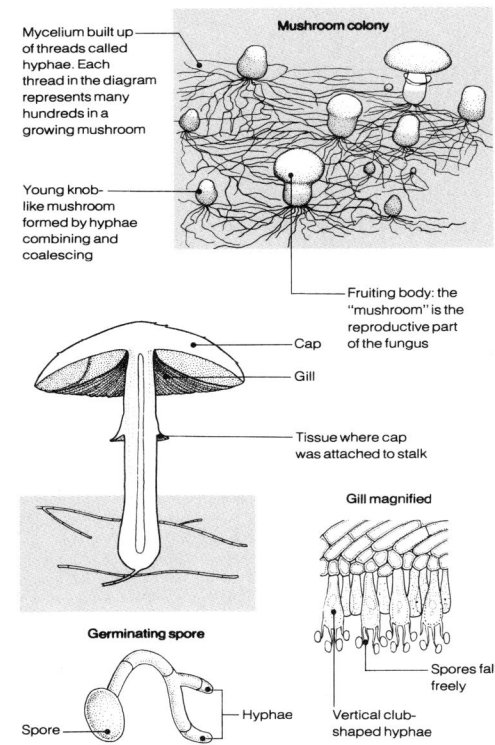

Mycelium built up of threads called hyphae. Each thread in the diagram represents many hundreds in a growing mushroom

Young knob-like mushroom formed by hyphae combining and coalescing

Mushroom colony

Fruiting body: the "mushroom" is the reproductive part of the fungus

Cap

Gill

Tissue where cap was attached to stalk

Gill magnified

Germinating spore

Spore

Hyphae

Spores fall freely

Vertical club-shaped hyphae

Like all fungi, mushrooms are formed of hyphae that grow from spores in the soil. The familiar stalk and cap are devices to ensure the spread of new spores. Hyphae combine to form the stalk, then radiate out into the cap. Beneath the cap grow thin, bladelike gills that produce and release the spores.

source of trouble or worry: *If he runs out of money, that's his funeral.* ~*adj.* Of or relating to a funeral. [Middle English *funerelles*, rites for a dead person, from Old French *funerailles*, from Medieval Latin *fūnerālia*, from Late Latin, neuter plural of *fūnerālis*, funereal, from Latin *fūnus†* (stem *fūner-*), funeral, death.]

funeral director *n.* An undertaker.

funeral home *n.* Also **funeral parlor.** An establishment in which the dead are prepared for burial or cremation and in which wakes and funerals may be held.

fu·ner·ar·y (fyōō'nə-rĕr'ē) *adj.* Of or suitable for a funeral or burial. [Latin *fūnerārius*, from *fūnus* (stem *fūner-*), FUNERAL.]

fu·ne·re·al (fyōō-nîr'ē-əl) *adj.* **1.** Of or suitable for a funeral: *a funereal wreath.* **2.** Suggesting gloom; mournful. [From Latin *fūnereus*, from *fūnus* (stem *fūner-*), FUNERAL.] —**fu·ne·re·al·ly** *adv.*

fun·gal (fŭng'gəl) *adj.* Of, pertaining to, or caused by a fungus; fungous.

fun·gi. Plural of **fungus.**

fun·gi·ble (fŭn'jə-bəl) *adj. Law.* Being of such a nature or kind that one unit or part may be exchanged or substituted for another equivalent unit or part in the discharging of an obligation. ~*n.* Something fungible, such as money or grain. [Medieval Latin *fungibilis*, serving a function, from *fungī*, to perform.]

fun·gi·cide (fŭn'jə-sīd', fŭng'gə-) *n.* A substance that destroys or inhibits the growth of fungi. [FUNG(US) + -CIDE.] —**fun·gi·cid·al** (fŭn'jə-sīd'l, fŭng'gə-) *adj.*

fun·gi·form (fŭn'jə-fôrm', fŭng'gə-) *adj.* Shaped like a mushroom. [FUNG(US) + -FORM.]

fun·gi·stat (fŭn'jə-stăt', fŭng'gə-) *n.* A substance that stops or is capable of stopping the growth of fungi.

fun·go (fŭng'gō) *n., pl.* **-goes.** *Baseball.* A practice fly ball hit to a fielder with a specially designed bat. [Origin unknown.]

fun·goid (fŭng'goid') *adj.* Resembling a fungus.

fun·gous (fŭng'gəs) *adj.* **1.** Of, pertaining to, resembling, or characteristic of a fungus; fungal. **2.** Caused by a fungus. [Middle English, from Latin *fungōsus*, from *fungus*, FUNGUS.]

fun·gus (fŭng'gəs) *n., pl.* **fungi** (fŭn'jī') or **-guses.** Any of numerous organisms of the divisions Eumycophyta (true fungi) or Myxomycophyta (slime fungi), which lack chlorophyll and are generally parasitic or saprophytic. They range from single cells to masses of filamentous hyphae that often produce specialized fruiting bodies and include the yeasts, molds, mildews, and toadstools. [Latin, probably from Greek *sp(h)ongos*, SPONGE.]

fu·ni·cle (fyōō'nĭ-kəl) *n. Botany.* The stalk connecting the ovule with the placenta in angiosperm ovaries. [Latin *fūniculus*, diminutive of *fūnis*, rope.]

fu·nic·u·lar (fyōō-nĭk'yə-lər, fə-) *adj.* **1.** Of, pertaining to, or resembling a rope or cord. **2.** Operated or moved by a cable. **3.** Of, pertaining to, or constituting a funiculus. ~*n.* A cable railway on a steep incline; especially, such a railway with simultaneously ascending and descending cars counterbalancing one another. Also called "funicular railway."

fu·nic·u·lus (fyōō-nĭk'yə-ləs, fə-) *n., pl.* **-li** (-lī'). **1.** *Anatomy.* A slender cordlike strand or band, especially: **a.** A bundle of nerve fibers in the nerve trunk; a fasciculus. **b.** One of the three major columns of white matter in each lateral half of the spinal cord. **c.** The umbilical cord. **2.** *Botany.* A funicle (see). [New Latin, from Latin *fūniculus*, diminutive of *fūnis*, rope.]

funk¹ (fŭngk) *n. Informal.* **1. a.** A state of cowardly fright; panic. **b.** A state of extreme depression. **2.** A cowardly, fearful person. ~*v.* **funked, funking, funks.** *Informal.* —*tr.* **1.** To try to avoid out of fright; shrink from. **2.** To frighten. —*intr.* To shrink in fright; cower. [Probably from obsolete Flemish *fonck*.]

funk² *n. Slang.* Funky music. [Back-formation from FUNKY.]

funk·y¹ (fŭng'kē) *adj.* **-ier, -iest.** Frightened; panicky.

funky² *adj.* **-ier, -iest.** *Slang.* **1.** Designating a type of popular music combining elements from jazz and blues and characterized by a slow, syncopated rhythm and a heavily repetitive bass line. **2.** Characterized by self-expression, originality, and modishness; trendy and unconventional: *funky clothes.* [Originally "smelly," from obsolete *funk*, tobacco smoke.] —**funk·i·ness** *n.*

fun·nel (fŭn'əl) *n.* **1.** A conical utensil with a small hole or narrow tube at the apex used to channel a substance into a small-mouthed container or to support a filter paper in filtration. **2.** Something having such a conical form. **3.** A shaft, flue, or chimney for the passage of smoke or fumes; especially, the smokestack of a ship or locomotive. ~*v.* **funneled, -neling, -nels.** Also *chiefly British* **-nelled, -nelling.** —*intr.* **1.** To assume the shape of a funnel. **2.** To move through or as if through a funnel: *Tourists funnel slowly through customs.* —*tr.* To cause to funnel. [Middle English *fonel*, from Provencal *fonilh*, from Latin *infundibulum*, from *infundere*, to pour in : *in-*, in + *fundere*, to pour.]

fun·nel-web spider (fŭn'əl-wĕb') *n.* Any large, black, poisonous spider of the family Agelemidae, constructing funnel-shaped webs.

fun·ny (fŭn'ē) *adj.* **-nier, -niest.** **1.** Causing laughter or amusement; humorous or witty. **2.** Strangely or suspiciously odd; curious. **3.** Tricky or deceitful. **4.** Dizzy or unwell. ~*n., pl.* **funnies.** *Informal.* **1.** A joke or witticism. **2. funnies.** Comic strips. [From FUN.] —**fun·ni·ly** *adv.* —**fun·ni·ness** *n.*

funny bone *n. Informal.* **1.** The point near the elbow where the ulnar nerve runs close to the surface and if accidentally knocked against the bone produces a tingling sensation; the **olecranon** (see). Also called "crazy bone." **2.** A sense of humor.

fun·ny book *n.* A comic book.
funny farm *n. Slang.* A mental hospital.
funny paper *n.* A newspaper section or supplement containing comic strips.
fur (fûr) *n.* **1.** The thick coat of hair covering the body of any of various animals, such as a fox, beaver, or cat. **2. a.** A dressed animal pelt, or part of one, used in the making of garments, trimmings, or decoration. **b.** Such pelts collectively. **c.** A synthetic fabric resembling dressed animal pelts. **3.** Any garment made of or lined with such pelts. **4.** Any coating of furlike material. **5.** A coating of whitish cellular debris on the tongue caused by stomach upset or smoking, for example. **6.** A grayish deposit, consisting mainly of calcium carbonate, deposited from hard water onto the internal surfaces of pipes, boilers, kettles, and the like. **—make the fur fly.** *Slang.* To cause or engage in a dispute or brawl.
~adj. Made of or lined with fur.
~v. **furred, furring, furs.** *—tr.* **1.** To cover or line with fur. **2.** To provide fur garments for. **3.** To cover with a furlike deposit: *intestinal disorders that fur the tongue.* **4.** To line (a wall or floor) with furring. *—intr.* To become coated with or as if with fur. [Middle English *furre,* from *furren,* to line with fur, from Old French *forrer,* from *forre,* lining, from Germanic.]
fur. furlong.
fu·ran (fyo͝or′ăn′, fyo͝o-răn′) *n.* Also **fur·fu·ran** (fûr′fə-răn′, fûr′fyə-). A colorless, volatile, liquid heterocyclic compound, C_4H_4O, that is derived from the dehydration of certain carbohydrates and is used in the synthesis of organic compounds, especially nylon. [FUR(FURAL) + -AN.]
fur·be·low (fûr′bə-lō′) *n.* **1.** A ruffle or flounce on a garment. **2.** Any small piece of showy ornamentation.
~tr.v. **furbelowed, -lowing, -lows.** To decorate with furbelows. [Alteration of FALBALA.]
fur·bish (fûr′bĭsh) *tr.v.* **-bished, -bishing, -bishes. 1.** To brighten by cleaning or rubbing; burnish. **2.** To restore to attractive or serviceable condition; renovate. [Middle English *furbishen,* from Old French *fo(u)rbir* (stem *fo(u)rbiss-*), from Germanic.] **—fur·bish·er** *n.*
fur·cate (fûr′kāt′) *intr.v.* **-cated, -cating, -cates.** To divide into branches; fork.
~adj. Forked. [Late Latin *furcātus,* from Latin *furca,* FORK.] **—fur·ca·tion** *n.*
fur·cu·la (fûr′kyə-lə) *n., pl.* **-lae** (-lē′). Also **fur·cu·lum** (fûr′kyə-ləm) *pl.* **-la** (-lə). A forked part or bone; especially, the wishbone of a bird. [New Latin, from Latin, diminutive of *furca,* FORK.]
fur·fur (fûr′fər) *n., pl.* **-fures** (-fyə-rēz′). *Sometimes* **furfures.** A skin scale, as in dandruff. [Latin *furfur*†, bran, scales.]
fur·fu·ra·ceous (fûr′fyə-rā′shəs) *adj.* **1.** Made of or covered with scaly particles, such as dandruff. **2.** Pertaining to or resembling bran. [Late Latin *furfurāceus* : FURFUR + -ACEOUS.]
fur·fur·al (fûr′fə-răl′, fûr′fyə-) *n.* A colorless mobile liquid, C_4H_3OCHO, used as a solvent for cellulose nitrate and in the manufacture of dyes and plastics. Also called "furfuraldehyde." [*furfur* + *al*dehyde.]
Fu·ries (fyo͝or′ēz). *Greek & Roman Mythology.* The three terrible, winged goddesses with serpents for hair, Alecto, Megaera, and Tisiphone, who pursue doers of unavenged crimes. Also called "Erinyes," "Eumenides." [Latin *Furiae,* plural of *furia,* FURY.]
fu·ri·o·so (fyo͝or′ē-ō′sō, -zō) *adv. Music.* In a tempestuous and headlong manner. Used as a direction. [Italian, from Latin *furiōsus,* FURIOUS.] **—fu·ri·o·so** *adj.*
fu·ri·ous (fyo͝or′ē-əs) *adj.* **1.** Full of or characterized by extreme anger; raging. **2.** Wild or frenetic in action or appearance: *the furious sea.* [Middle English, from Old French *furieus,* from Latin *furiōsus,* from *furia,* FURY.] **—fu·ri·ous·ly** *adv.* **—fu·ri·ous·ness** *n.*
furl (fûrl) *v.* **furled, furling, furls.** *—tr.* **1.** To take in and secure (a sail) to a yard or mast. **2.** To roll up (an umbrella, flag, or the like). *—intr.* **1.** To be rolled up. **2.** To disappear as if furled.
~n. **1.** The act of furling. **2.** A single roll or rolled section of something furled. [Old French *ferler, ferlier* : *fer(m),* firm, from Latin *firmus,* FIRM + *lier,* to bind, from Latin *ligāre.*]
fur·long (fûr′lông′, -lŏng′) *n. Abbr.* **fur.** A unit for measuring distance, equal to 201 meters, 1/8 mile, or 220 yards. [Middle English, from Old English *furlang* : *furh,* FURROW + *lang,* LONG. Originally the length of the furrow made on a square field of 10 acres.]
fur·lough (fûr′lō) *n.* **1.** A leave of absence; especially, a leave of absence from duty granted to enlisted personnel of the armed services. **2.** The papers authorizing a furlough.
~tr.v. **furloughed, -loughing, -loughs.** To grant a furlough to. [Dutch *verlof,* leave, permission, from Middle Dutch.]
furmenty. Variant of **frumenty.**
furn. furnished.
fur·nace (fûr′nĭs) *n.* **1.** An enclosure in which energy in a nonthermal form is converted to heat; especially, such an enclosure in which heat is generated by the combustion of a suitable fuel. **2.** Any intensely hot, enclosed place. **—tried in the furnace.** Severely tested. [Middle English *furna(i)s,* from Old French *fornais,* from Latin *fornāx* (stem *fornāc-*), oven.]
fur·nish (fûr′nĭsh) *tr.v.* **-nished, -nishing, -nishes. 1.** To equip with what is needed. **2.** To provide furniture and other accessories for. **3.** To provide; supply: *The dictionary furnished an apt quotation.* [Middle English *furnisshen,* from Old French *furnir* (stem *furniss-*), *fornir,* from Common Romance *fornir* (unattested), to supply, from Germanic.] **—fur·nish·er** *n.*
fur·nish·ings (fûr′nĭ-shĭngz) *pl.n.* **1.** The furniture, curtains, carpets, and similar articles used to decorate and furnish a home or office. **2.** Wearing apparel and accessories.
fur·ni·ture (fûr′nə-chər) *n.* **1.** The movable articles in a room or establishment that make it fit for living or working in. **2.** The necessary equipment for a factory, ship, or the like. **3.** *Printing.* Blank strips of wood or metal placed between and around type on a page to hold it in place. [Old French *fourniture,* from *fournir, furnir,* to FURNISH.]
fu·ror (fyo͝or′ôr′, -ōr′) *n.* Also *chiefly British* **fu·rore. 1.** Violent anger; frenzy. **2.** A general commotion; public disorder or uproar. **3.** A fashion adopted enthusiastically by the public; fad. [Latin, from *furere,* to rage. See **fury.**]
fu·ro·se·mide (fyo͞o-rō′sə-mīd′) *n.* A compound, $C_{12}H_{11}ClN_2O_5S$, used as a diuretic. [FUR(FURAL) + S(ULF)- + *emide,* alteration of AMIDE.]
furred (fûrd) *adj.* **1.** Bearing fur. **2.** Made, covered, or trimmed with fur. **3.** Wearing fur garments. **4.** Covered with a furlike deposit. **5.** Provided with furring, as a wall, ceiling, or floor.
fur·ri·er (fûr′ē-ər) *n.* One whose occupation is the dressing, designing, selling, or repairing of furs. [Middle English *furrer,* from Old French *forreor,* from *forrer,* to line with fur. See **fur.**]
fur·ri·er·y (fûr′ē-ə-rē) *n., pl.* **-ies. 1.** Fur garments and trimmings collectively. **2.** The business of a furrier.
fur·ring (fûr′ĭng) *n.* **1. a.** A trimming or lining made of fur. **b.** Fur trimmings and linings collectively. **2.** A furlike coating, as on the tongue or in a pipe. **3. a.** The act of preparing a wall, ceiling, or floor with strips of wood or metal to provide a level surface for the fixing of floorboards, plasterboard, or the like. **b.** Strips of material used for this. Also used adjectivally: *a furring strip.*
fur·row (fûr′ō) *n.* **1.** A long, narrow, shallow trench made in the ground by a plow or other implement. **2.** Any rut, groove, or narrow depression similar to this. **3.** A deep wrinkle in the skin, as on the forehead. **—plow a lonely furrow.** To pursue one's objectives alone and unaided.
~v. **furrowed, -rowing, -rows.** *—tr.* **1.** To make furrows in; plow. **2.** To form deep wrinkles in. *—intr.* To become furrowed or deeply wrinkled. [Middle English *for(o)we, furgh,* Old English *furh.*]
fur·ry (fûr′ē) *adj.* **-rier, -riest. 1.** Consisting of or decorated with fur. **2.** Covered with fur or a furlike coating. **3.** Resembling fur in thickness or softness. **—fur·ri·ness** *n.*
fur seal *n.* Any of several eared seals of the genera *Callorhinus* or *Arctocephalus,* having thick, soft underfur that is valued commercially.

fur seal *The thick underfur of fur seals distinguishes them from sea lions, which belong to the same family. The Kerguelen fur seal (above) breeds on remote islands in the seas of the Southern Hemisphere.*

fur·ther (fûr′*th*ər) *adj.* **1.** More distant in time or degree. **2.** Additional. **3.** More distant in space. —See Usage note at **farther.**
~adv. **1.** To a greater extent; more. **2.** In addition; furthermore; also. **3.** At or to a more distant point in space or time. —See Usage note at **farther.**
~tr.v. **furthered, -thering, -thers.** To help the progress of; advance. —See Synonyms at **advance.** [Middle English *further,* earlier, from Old English *furthor.*] **—fur·ther·er** *n.*
fur·ther·ance (fûr′*th*ər-əns) *n.* **1.** The act of furthering, advancing, or helping forward. **2.** One that furthers or assists.
fur·ther·more (fûr′*th*ər-môr′, -mōr′) *adv.* Moreover; in addition. —See Synonyms at **also.**
fur·ther·most (fûr′*th*ər-mōst′) *adj.* Most distant or remote.
fur·thest (fûr′*th*ĭst) *adj.* **1.** Most distant in time or degree. **2.** Most distant in space. —See Usage note at **farther.**
~adv. **1.** To the greatest extent or degree. **2.** At or to the most distant point in space or time. —See Usage note at **farther.** [Middle English, from FURTHER.]
fur·tive (fûr′tĭv) *adj.* **1.** Characterized by stealth; surreptitious. **2.** Suggesting hidden motives or purposes; shifty. —See Synonyms at **secret.** [French *furtif,* from Old French, from Latin *furtīvus,* from *furtum,* theft, from *fūr*†, thief.] **—fur·tive·ly** *adv.* **—fur·tive·ness** *n.*
Furt·wäng·ler (fo͝ort′vĕng′lər, -vĕng′glər), **Wilhelm** (1886–1954). German orchestral and operatic conductor. The conductor of the Berlin Philharmonic Orchestra from 1922 until his death except for a short interval in 1934, he was the leading interpreter of 19th-century romantic composers.
fu·run·cle (fyo͝or′ŭng′kəl) *n. Pathology.* A **boil** *(see).* [Latin *fūrunculus,* petty thief, vine knob that "steals" the sap from the main branches, boil, diminutive of *fūr,* thief.] **—fu·run·cu·lar** *adj.*
fu·run·cu·lo·sis (fyo͞o-rŭng′kyə-lō′sĭs) *n.* A skin complaint characterized by the simultaneous occurrence or continuing recurrence of furuncles. [Latin *fūrunculus,* FURUNCLE + -OSIS.]
fu·ry (fyo͝or′ē) *n., pl.* **-ries. 1.** Violent anger; rage. **2.** An outburst of violent rage. **3.** Violent, uncontrolled action; turbulence. **4.** One given to fits of violent anger. **5. Fury.** Any of the **Furies** *(see).* —See Synonyms at **anger.** [Middle English *furie,* from Old French, from Latin *furia,* from *furere*†, to rage.]
furze (fûrz) *n.* A spiny shrub, **gorse** *(see).* [Middle English *furse, firse,* Old English *fyrs.*]
fu·sain (fyo͞o-zān′, fyo͞o′zān′) *n.* **1.** Fine charcoal in stick form, made from the wood of a spindle tree. **2.** A sketch or drawing made with this. [French, from Vulgar Latin *fūsāgō* (unattested), spindle (formerly made from the wood of the spindle tree), from Latin *fūsus,* spindle. See **fuse.**]
fuse[1] (fyo͞oz) *n.* **1.** A length of readily combustible material that is lighted at one end to carry a flame to and detonate an explosive at the other. **2.** Variant of **fuze.**

PRONUNCIATION KEY
ă, pat; ā, pay; âr, care;
ä, father, are; b, bib;
ch, church; d, deed; ĕ, pet;
ē, be; f, fife; g, gag; h, hat;
hw, which; ĭ, pit; ī, pie;
îr, pier; j, judge; k, kick;
l, lid, needle; m, mum;
n, no, sudden; ng, thing;
ŏ, pot; ō, toe; ô, paw, for;
oi, noise; ou, out; o͝o, book;
o͞o, boot; p, pop; r, roar;
s, sauce; sh, ship, dish;
t, tight; th, thin, path;
th, this, bathe; ŭ, cut; ûr, fur;
v, valve; w, with; y, yes;
z, zebra, size; zh, vision;
ə, about, item, edible, gallop, circus, peaceful

IN FOREIGN WORDS:
à, *Fr.* ami; œ, *Fr.* feu, *Ger.* schön; ü, *Fr.* tu, *Ger.* über; KH, *Ger.* ich, *Scot.* loch; N, *Fr.* bon; y′, *Fr.* Compiègne

STRESS MARKS:
Primary stress: ′
in·cite′ (ĭn-sīt′)
Secondary stress: ′
in′sight′ (ĭn′sīt′)

~*tr.v.* **fused, fusing, fuses.** To provide or equip with a fuse. [Italian *fuso,* from Latin *fūsus*†, spindle.]

fuse² *v.* **fused, fusing, fuses.** —*tr.* **1.** To liquefy or reduce to a plastic state by heating; melt. **2.** To mix together by or as if by melting; blend. **3.** To fit a fuse to (an electric plug, for example). **4.** To stop (an electrical appliance, for example) from functioning by overloading the fuse. —*intr.* **1.** To become liquefied from heat. **2.** To become mixed or united by or as if by melting together: *Joy and sorrow fused into one.* **3.** To stop functioning when an electrical fuse has been overloaded. ~*n.* **1.** A device containing an element that protects an electric circuit by melting when overloaded, thereby opening the circuit. **2.** A circuit breaker fulfilling the same function. —See Synonyms at **mix.** [Latin *fundere* (past participle *fūsus*), to pour, melt.]

fuse box *n.* A box in which the fuses protecting a number of electrical circuits are housed.

fu·see, fu·zee (fyŏŏ-zē′) *n.* **1.** A friction match with a large head capable of burning in a wind. **2.** A grooved, cone-shaped pulley in old-style clocks. **3.** A fuse for detonating explosives. [French *fusée,* spindle-shaped figure, from Old French *fusee,* from *fus,* spindle, from Latin *fūsus.* See **fuse.**]

fu·se·lage (fyŏŏ′sə-läzh′, fyŏŏ′zə-) *n.* The central body of an aircraft that accommodates passengers, cargo, and crew, and to which the wings and tail assembly are attached. [French, from *fuseler,* to shape like a spindle, from *fuseau,* spindle, from Old French *fusel,* spindle, diminutive of *fus,* spindle, from Latin *fūsus.* See **fuse.**]

Fu·se·li (fyŏŏ′zə-lē) **Henry,** earlier Johann Heinrich Füssli (1741–1825). Swiss-born British artist. His works, including *The Nightmare* (1782) and illustrations of the works of Shakespeare and Milton, display a fantastic, macabre quality that was to influence the surrealists of the 1920's and 1930's.

fu·sel oil (fyŏŏ′zəl) *n.* A clear, colorless, poisonous, liquid mixture of amyl alcohols, obtained as a by-product of the fermentation of starch-containing and sugar-containing plant materials, and used as a solvent for fats, oils, resins, and waxes, and in the manufacture of explosives and pure amyl alcohols. [German *Fusel*†, bad liquor.]

fuse wire *n.* Thin metal wire, used in electrical fuses, that melts when a current passed through it exceeds a specific safe limit.

fu·si·ble (fyŏŏ′zə-bəl) *adj.* Capable of being fused or melted by heating. —**fu·si·bil·i·ty, fu·si·ble·ness** *n.*

fusible metal *n.* A metal alloy having a melting point below 300°F, used as solder and for safety plugs and fuses. Also called "fusible alloy."

fu·si·form (fyŏŏ′zə-fôrm′) *adj.* Tapering at each end; spindle-

---

Futurism

THE PACE OF LIFE CAPTURED IN ART

Futurism welcomed the new machine age and denounced all links with the past

Futurism aimed to reflect in the arts the dynamism of life as it was experienced in a world dominated by machines. Its main theme was movement and the rhythm of space and time. It was inaugurated by a manifesto published in Paris in 1909 by the Italian poet and playwright Marinetti, who glorified speed, aggression, patriotism, and war.

Despite its political bias, Futurism revitalized Italian art. Carra, Boccioni, Balla, and Severini joined Marinetti and published a "Manifesto of Futurist painting" (1910). Their "new form of beauty, the beauty of speed" was exemplified in their paintings, for example in Boccioni's *States of Mind: the Farewells* (1911) and Balla's *Rhythms of the Bow* (1912). Their abusive public meetings were a vital feature of the movement's style and had a profound effect later on the Dada circle.

A Russian version of Futurism emerged in 1910 with an almanac entitled "A Trap for Judges," which appeared in St. Petersburg. In 1912 Burliuk published "A Slap in the Face of Public Taste," which rejected the recognized masters of Russian literature, including Tolstoy and Pushkin, and wanted the language of the streets to be used for literature. Burliuk was soon joined by Mayakovsky, the renowned poet, playwright, and artist. When revolution came in 1917, the Russian Futurists embraced it as their own, and almost all were ready to serve the state. The early 1920's was a golden age of Russian art, with Mayakovsky, Lissitzky, and Kandinsky seeking to merge realism with total abstraction.

The Russian Futurists were notable for their inspired multimedia approach, experimenting in architecture, typography, film, theater, and literature. In literature, for example, Zamyatin's *We* was the forerunner of *Brave New World* and *1984.* However, the exuberance of the years immediately after the revolution was constricted with the advent of Stalin, and one of the most vital art movements of the 20th century was swamped by the Soviet Socialist Realism of the official propaganda machine. Although Mayakovsky in his photomontages was occasionally able to produce messages contrary to the aims of the regime, the restrictions under which he was forced to work contributed to his suicide in 1930.

MOTION PICTURES *Balla's painting,* Rhythms of the Bow, *focuses on the action of the musician. Balla had long been interested in photographic techniques and wished to emulate the ability of a film to record motion in one image.*

shaped. [Latin *fūsus,* spindle (see **fuse**) + -FORM.]

fu·sil (fyōō′zəl) *n.* A light flintlock musket. [French, musket, from Old French *fuisil,* fusil, steel for a tinderbox, from Vulgar Latin *focīle* (unattested), from Latin *focus,* fireplace. See **fuel.**]

fu·sile (fyōō′zəl, -zīl′) *adj.* Also **fu·sil** (-zəl). **1.** Formed by melting or casting. **2.** Capable of being fused. [Latin *fūsilis,* from *fūsus,* past participle of *fundere,* to melt, pour.]

fu·si·lier (fyōō′zə-lîr′) *n.* Also **fu·si·leer** (for sense 2). **1.** A soldier armed with a fusil. **2.** **Fusilier.** A soldier belonging to certain British army regiments. [French, from FUSIL.]

fu·sil·lade (fyōō′sə-läd′, -lād′, fyōō′zə-) *n.* **1.** A discharge of many firearms, simultaneously or in rapid succession. **2.** Any rapid outburst or barrage: *a fusillade of insults.*
~*tr.v.* **fusilladed, -lading, -lades.** To attack or shoot down with a fusillade. [French, from *fusiller,* to shoot, from FUSIL.]

fu·sion (fyōō′zhən) *n.* **1.** The act or procedure of liquefying or melting together by heat. **2.** The liquid or melted state induced by heat. **3.** A union resulting from fusing. **4.** The merging of different elements into a union. **5.** *Physics.* A nuclear reaction in which any of certain light atomic nuclei combine to form more massive nuclei with the simultaneous release of energy. In this sense, also called "nuclear fusion." Compare **fission.** [Latin *fūsiō* (stem *fūsiōn*-), from *fūsus,* past participle of *fundere,* to pour, melt.]

fusion bomb *n.* An atomic bomb that derives its energy output principally from fusion reactions among light nuclei; especially, a **hydrogen bomb** (*see*).

fu·sion·ism (fyōō′zhə-nĭz′əm) *n.* The theory, practice, or advocacy of forming coalitions of political groups or factions. —**fu·sion·ist** *n.*

fuss (fŭs) *n.* **1.** Needless or useless excited activity; commotion; bustle. **2. a.** A state of excessive and unwarranted concern over an unimportant matter. **b.** Objections; protests. **3.** A quarrel.
~*v.* **fussed, fussing, fusses.** —*intr.* **1.** To trouble or worry over trifles. **2.** To be excessively careful or solicitous. —*tr. Informal.* To disturb or vex with unimportant matters. [18th century (Anglo-Irish) : origin obscure.] —**fuss·er** *n.*

fuss·budg·et (fŭs′bŭj′ĭt) *n.* A person who fusses over trifles.

fuss·pot (fŭs′pŏt′) *n.* A fussbudget.

fuss·y (fŭs′ē) *adj.* **-ier, -iest. 1.** Given to fussing; easily upset: *"The bridegroom, fussy as a poodle, pops his eyes"* (Kenneth Tynan). **2.** Paying great attention to petty matters or details; fastidious. **3.** Calling for or requiring great attention to trivial details; meticulous. **4.** Full of superfluous details or trimmings; ornate. —**fuss·i·ly** *adv.* —**fuss·i·ness** *n.*

fus·ta·nel·la (fŭs′tə-nĕl′ə, fōō′stə-) *n.* A short, stiff skirt of white cloth worn by men in modern Greece. [Italian, from Modern Greek *phoustanella,* diminutive of *phoustani,* from Italian *fustagno,* coarse cloth, from Medieval Latin *fustāneus,* FUSTIAN.]

fus·tian (fŭs′chən) *n.* **1.** Any of several thick, twilled cotton fabrics with a short nap. **2.** Pretentious, pompous speech or writing.
~*adj.* **1.** Made of fustian. **2.** Pompous; ranting; bombastic. [Middle English, from Old French *fustai(g)ne,* from Medieval Latin *fustāneus,* cloth, perhaps after *Fostat,* a suburb of Cairo, Egypt.]

fus·tic (fŭs′tĭk) *n.* **1.** A tropical American tree, *Chlorophora tinctoria,* having wood yielding a yellow dyestuff. **2.** The wood of this tree. **3.** The dyestuff obtained from such wood. **4.** Any of various trees, such as sumacs, that yield a similar dye. [Middle English *fustik,* from Old French *fustoc,* from Arabic *fustuq,* from Greek *pistakē,* PISTACHIO.]

fus·ti·gate (fŭs′tĭ-gāt′) *tr.v.* **-gated, -gating, -gates.** To beat with a club. [Late Latin *fūstigāre* : Latin *fūstis*†, club + *agere,* to do.]

fus·ty (fŭs′tē) *adj.* **-tier, -tiest. 1.** Smelling of mildew or decay; musty; moldy. **2.** Old-fashioned; antiquated. [Middle English, from Old French *fuste,* barrel, stale odor of a barrel, from *fust,* barrel, tree trunk, club, from Latin *fūstis*†, club.] —**fus·ti·ly** *adv.* —**fus·ti·ness** *n.*

fut. *Grammar.* future.

fu·thark, fu·tharc (fōō′thärk′) *n.* Also **fu·thork, fu·thorc** (-thôrk′). The runic alphabet. [From the first six letters of the alphabet: *f, u, th* (thorn), *a* or *o, r, k.*]

fu·tile (fyōōt′l, fyōō′tīl′) *adj.* **1.** Having no useful result; ineffectual; useless; vain. **2.** Unproductive; frivolous; idle: *futile talk.* [Latin *futtilis, fūtilis,* untrustworthy, useless.] —**fu·tile·ly** *adv.* —**fu·tile·ness** *n.*

fu·til·i·tar·i·an (fyōō-tĭl′ə-târ′ē-ən) *adj.* Holding or based on the view that human endeavor is futile.
~*n.* One who holds such a view. [Blend of FUTILE and UTILITARIAN.]

fu·til·i·ty (fyōō-tĭl′ə-tē) *n., pl.* **-ties. 1.** The quality of being futile; uselessness; ineffectiveness. **2.** Lack of importance or purpose. **3.** Anything that is futile.

fu·ton (fōō′tŏn′) *n.* A Japanese mattress for sleeping on. [Japanese.]

fut·tock (fŭt′ək) *n. Nautical.* Any of the curved timbers that form a rib in the frame of a wooden ship. [Middle English *fottek,* perhaps variant of *fothok* (unattested) : FOOT + HOOK.]

futtock plate *n. Nautical.* Any of the iron plates attached to the top of a mast to hold the ends of the futtock shrouds.

futtock shroud *n. Nautical.* Any of the iron rods extending from the futtock plate, used to brace the base of a mast.

fu·ture (fyōō′chər) *n.* **1.** The indefinite period of time yet to be; time that is to come. **2.** That which will happen in time to come. **3.** The prospective or foreseen condition of a person or thing: *a student's future.* **4.** Prospects of advancement; chances of success: *a business with no future.* **5. futures.** Commodities or shares bought or sold at an agreed price for delivery in time to come. **6.** *Abbr.* **fut.** *Grammar.* **a.** The future tense. **b.** A verb in the future tense.
~*adj.* **1.** That is to be or come in the future. **2.** Of or relating to time to come. **3.** That will be as specified at a later time: *a future politician.* [Middle English, from Old French *futur,* from Latin *futūrus,* future participle of *esse,* to be.] —**fu·ture·less** *adj.*

future perfect *n. Grammar.* **1.** A verb tense expressing action completed by a specified time in the future. This tense is formed in English by combining *will have* or *shall have* with a past participle, as *will have counted* in *They will have counted all the votes by midnight.* **2.** A verb in the future perfect tense.

future shock *n.* The disorientation suffered by people bewildered by rapid changes in the social structure or technology of modern society. [After the book *Future Shock* (1970) by Alvin Toffler (born 1928), U.S. author.]

future tense *n.* A verb tense used to express action in the future, as *will see* in *I will see you tomorrow.*

Fu·tur·ism (fyōō′chə-rĭz′əm) *n.* An artistic movement originating in Italy in about 1909 and marked by an attempt to depict vividly the energetic and dynamic quality of contemporary life as influenced by the motion and force of modern machinery. —**Fu·tur·ist** *n.*

fu·tur·is·tic (fyōō′chə-rĭs′tĭk) *adj.* **1.** Futuristic. Of, pertaining to, or characteristic of Futurism. **2.** Suggesting the future; indicating advanced thinking: *futuristic design.*

fu·tur·ist·ics (fyōō′chə-rĭs′tĭks) *n. Used with a singular verb.* Futurology. —**fu·tur·ist** *n.*

fu·tu·ri·ty (fyōō-tōor′ə-tē, fyōō-tyōor′-, fyōō-chōor′-) *n., pl.* **-ties. 1.** The future. **2.** The condition or quality of being in or of the future. **3.** A future event or possibility. **4.** A futurity race.

futurity race *n.* A race, especially a horse race, for which entries are made well in advance, as at birth.

futurity stakes *pl.n.* **1.** The stakes awarded to the winner or winners in a futurity race. **2.** A futurity race.

fu·tur·ol·o·gy (fyōō′chə-rŏl′ə-jē) *n.* The study or prediction of the likely future state of the world and its inhabitants. —**fu·tur·ol·o·gist** *n.*

fuze, fuse (fyōōz) *n.* A mechanical or electrical mechanism used to detonate an explosive charge or device such as a bomb or grenade. [Variant of FUSE (detonator).]

fuzee. Variant of **fusee.**

Fu·zhou, Fu·chou, Foo·chow (fōō′jō′). Capital city of the southeastern province of Fujian in China, on the estuary of the Min Jiang. It is an ancient walled city, dating from at least the 2nd century B.C., and has been the capital of Fujian province since the 10th century. Since the mid-19th century it has been one of China's major naval stations and international trading ports.

fuzz¹ (fŭz) *n.* **1.** A mass of fine, light particles, fibers, or hairs; down: *the fuzz on a peach.* **2.** A blur.
~*v.* **fuzzed, fuzzing, fuzzes.** —*tr.* To cover with fuzz. —*intr.* To become blurred. [Perhaps back-formation from FUZZY.]

fuzz² *n. Slang.* The police; policemen collectively. Preceded by *the.* [20th century : origin obscure.]

fuzz·y (fŭz′ē) *adj.* **-ier, -iest. 1.** Covered with fuzz. **2.** Of or resembling fuzz. **3.** Not sharply delineated or focused; indistinct; blurred. **4.** Not clearly reasoned or expressed; confused. **5.** Frizzy or very tightly curled. Said of hair. [Perhaps from Low German *fussig,* spongy.] —**fuzz·i·ly** *adv.* —**fuzz·i·ness** *n.*

fwd. forward.

f.w.d. 1. four-wheel drive. **2.** front-wheel drive.

FY fiscal year.

-fy *suffix.* Indicates a making or forming into; for example, **reify, nitrify.** [Middle English *-fien,* from Old French *-fier,* from Latin *-ficāre,* from *-ficus,* -FIC.]

fyke (fīk) *n.* A long, bag-shaped net held open by hoops, used for catching fish. [Dutch *fuik,* from Middle Dutch *fūke*†.]

fyl·fot (fĭl′fŏt′) *n.* An ornamental figure identified with the swastika : [Middle English, device for filling the foot of a painted window : *fillen,* to FILL + FOOT.]

682

gable *A generally triangular portion of wall at the end of a pitched roof. The shaped gable above, on a house in Holland, is typical of Dutch architecture.*

g, G (jē) *n., pl.* **g's** or **G's. 1.** The seventh letter of the modern English alphabet. **2.** Any of the speech sounds represented by this letter. **3. G** *Music.* **a.** The fifth tone in the scale of C major. **b.** The key or a scale in which G is the tonic. **c.** A written or printed note representing G. **4.** Something shaped like the letter G. **5. G** *Slang.* One thousand dollars. **6.** The seventh in a series.

g, G, g., G. *Note:* As an abbreviation or symbol, *g* may be a small or a capital letter, with or without a period. Established forms or those generally preferred precede the definition. When no form is given, all four forms are in general use in that sense. **1. g** acceleration of gravity. **2. g.** gallon. **3. g., G.** gauge. **4. G** *Physics.* gauss. **5. g.** gelding. **6. g.** gender. **7. g.** genitive. **8. G.** German. **9. G** giga-. **10. g., G.** good. **11. g., G.** gourde. **12. g** gram. **13. G** *Physics.* gravitation constant. **14. g.** guide. **15. g., G.** guilder. **16. g., G.** guinea. **17. g., G.** gulf (ocean area).

Ga The symbol for the element gallium.

GA Georgia (used with a Zip Code).

Ga. Georgia.

gab (găb) *intr.v.* **gabbed, gabbing, gabs.** *Informal.* To talk easily or excessively about trivial matters; chatter.
—*n.* *Informal.* Idle talk; chatter: *bored by the gab at the dinner table.* [Perhaps from Scottish *gab,* mouthful, lump, mouth, variant of GOB (lump).] —**gab·ber** *n.*

gab·ar·dine (găb′ər-dēn′, găb′ər-dēn′) *n.* **1.** A worsted cotton, wool, or rayon twill used in making dresses, suits, and coats. **2.** A gaberdine. [Alteration of GABERDINE.]

gab·bart (găb′ərt) *n.* Also **gab·bard** (-ərd). *Scottish.* A flat-bottomed barge used to load and unload cargo offshore or to transport goods on inland waterways. [Modification of Old French *gab(b)arre,* from Old Provençal *gabarra,* probably from Late Latin *carabus,* a small, rawhide-covered boat, from Greek *karabos†,* horned beetle, crayfish, light ship.]

gab·ble (găb′əl) *v.* **-bled, -bling, -bles.** —*intr.* **1.** To speak rapidly or incoherently; jabber. **2.** To make rapid, repeated cackling noises, as a goose or duck does. —*tr.* To utter quickly or unintelligibly. —*n.* **1.** Rapid, incoherent, or meaningless speech. **2.** A jumble of cackling noises or meaningless utterances. [Middle Dutch *gabbelen* (imitative).]

gab·bro (găb′rō) *n., pl.* **-bros.** A coarse-grained, intrusive igneous rock composed chiefly of calcic plagioclase and pyroxene, sometimes with other minerals. Also called "norite." [Italian, from Latin *glaber,* smooth, bald.]

gab·by (găb′ē) *adj.* **-bier, -biest.** *Informal.* Tending to talk excessively.

gab·er·dine (găb′ər-dēn′, găb′ər-dēn′) *n.* **1.** A long, coarse garment, such as a cloak or frock, worn during the Middle Ages. **2.** *British.* A loose smock worn by laborers. **3.** Gabardine. [Earlier *gawbardine,* from Old French *gauvardine, gallevardine,* "pilgrim's frock," from Middle High German *wallevart,* pilgrimage : *wallen,* to roam, from Old High German *wallōn* + *vart,* journey, way, from *faran,* to go.]

gab·fest (găb′fĕst′) *n.* *Slang.* An informal gathering for the exchange of news and gossip.

Ga·bin (gä-băⁿ′), **Jean,** born Jean Alexis Moncorgé (1904–76). French film actor. He starred in *La Grande Illusion* (1937), and in other films played Georges Simenon's detective, Inspector Maigret.

ga·bi·on (gā′bē-ən, găb′ē-) *n.* **1.** A cylindrical wicker basket filled with earth and stones, formerly used in building fortifications. **2.** A similar cylinder, often of metal, used in constructing dams, foundations, and the like. [Old French *gabion,* from Old Italian *gabbione,* augmentative of *gabbia,* cage, from Latin *cavea,* a hollow, enclosure, from *cavus,* hollow.]

ga·bi·on·ade (gā′bē-ə-nād′, -näd′, găb′ē-) *n.* A fortification or defensive embankment or wall built with gabions. [French *gabionnade,* from Old Italian *gabbionata,* from *gabbione,* GABION.]

ga·ble (gā′bəl) *n.* *Architecture.* **1.** The triangular wall section at the ends of a pitched roof, bounded by the two roof slopes and the ridge. **2.** An end of a building having a gable in the roof section. Also called "gable end." **3.** A triangular architectural section, usually ornamental, as over a door or window. [Middle English *gable,*

gabyl, from Old French *gable,* probably from Old Norse *gafl.*] —**ga·bled** *adj.*

Ga·ble (gā′bəl), **(William) Clark** (1901–60). U.S. actor. He became known as "the King of Hollywood" after his success in *Gone With the Wind* (1939). He died shortly after making *The Misfits* (released 1961), in which he did his own stunt work.

gable roof *n.* A pitched roof that ends in a gable.

Ga·bon (gə-bōn′, gä-bôn′). Country in Equatorial Africa. European slavers reached the area *c.* 1470. The French dominated it in the 19th century, settling freed slaves at Libreville ("free town"), and in 1910 it became part of French Equatorial Africa. Dr. Albert Schweitzer founded the region's first hospital in 1913 at Lambaréné. Gabon became independent in 1960. French remains the official language. Area, 267,667 square kilometers (103,319 square miles). Population, 1,200,000. Capital and chief port, Libreville. —**Gab·o·nese** (găb′ə-nēz′) *n. & adj.*

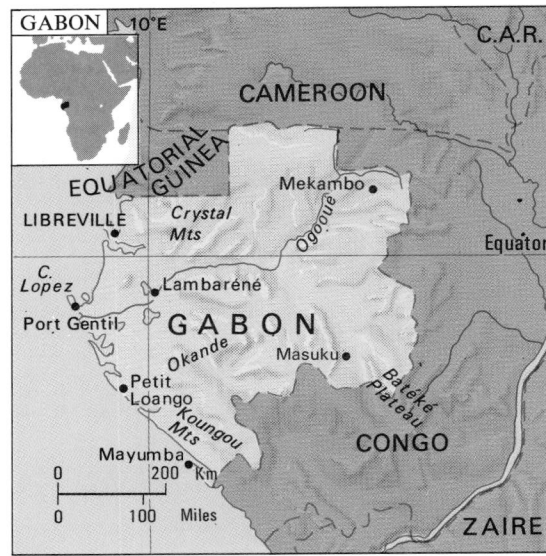

Ga·bor (gä′bôr, gə-bôr′), **Dennis** (1900–79). Hungarian-born British electrical engineer. He won the Nobel Prize in physics (1971) for his work on holography.

Gab·o·ro·ne (găb′ə-rō′nē). Capital of Botswana, near the border with South Africa.

Ga·bri·el (gā′brē-əl). An archangel who acts as the messenger of God in the Bible.

ga·by (gā′bē) *n., pl.* **-bies.** *Archaic & British Regional.* A simpleton. [18th century : origin obscure.]

gad¹ (găd) *interj.* Used to express surprise or as a mild oath. [Euphemistic for *God.*]

gad² *intr.v.* **gadded, gadding, gads. 1.** To roam about aimlessly or restlessly. **2.** To go about in search of pleasure or entertainment. Used with *about* or *around.*
—*n.* The action of gadding. Used only in the phrase *on the gad.* [Middle English *gadden,* probably back-formation from *gadeling,* companion, (hence) wanderer, Old English *gædeling.*] —**gad·der** *n.*

gad³ *n.* **1.** *Mining.* A spike or other pointed tool for working or breaking rock or ore. **2.** A goad, as for prodding cattle to make them move.
—*tr.v.* **gadded, gadding, gads. 1.** *Mining.* To break up (rock or ore,

for example) with a gad. **2.** To goad (cattle). [Middle English *gad(de)*, from Old Norse *gaddr*, rod, goad, spike.]

Gad¹ (găd). A son of Zilpah and Jacob. Genesis 30:11. [Hebrew *Gādh*, from *gādh*, fortune.]

Gad² *n.* The tribe of Israel descended from Gad.

gad·a·bout (găd'ə-bout') *n. Informal.* One who goes about seeking amusement or excitement.

Gad·a·rene (găd'ə-rēn') *adj.* Involving or taking part in a headlong rush; precipitate. [Late Latin, from Greek *gadarēnos*, referring to the Gadarene swine in the Bible (Matthew 8:28-33).]

Gaddafi, Muammar. See **Qaddafi.**

gad·fly (găd'flī') *n., pl.* **-flies. 1.** Any of various flies, especially of the family Tabanidae, that bite or annoy livestock and other animals. **2.** A person who is persistently critical, irritating, or provocative. **3.** Something that acts as a provocative stimulus. [GAD (goad, sting) + FLY.]

gadg·et (găj'ĭt) *n.* **1.** A small specialized mechanical or electronic device; a contrivance. —See Synonyms at **tool.** [19th century (nautical) : origin obscure.]

gadg·et·ry (găj'ĭ-trē) *n.* **1.** Gadgets collectively. **2.** The designing or constructing of gadgets.

Gadhelic. Variant of **Goidelic.**

ga·doid (gā'doid', găd'oid') *adj.* Also **ga·did** (gā'dĭd) *adj.* Of or belonging to the family Gadidae, which includes fishes such as the cod and the hake. —*n.* A member of the Gadidae. [New Latin *Gadus* (genus name), from Greek *gados†*, a kind of fish + -OID.]

gad·o·lin·ite (găd'l-ə-nīt') *n.* A rare blackish mineral silicate of iron, beryllium, and yttrium, 2BeO·FeO·Y₂O₃·2SiO₂. Also called "ytterbite." [After Johan *Gadolin* (1760-1852), Finnish chemist.]

gad·o·lin·i·um (găd'l-ĭn'ē-əm) *n. Symbol* **Gd** A silvery-white, malleable, ductile metallic rare-earth element obtained from monazite and bastnaesite. It has the highest neutron-absorption cross-section known and is useful in improving high-temperature characteristics of iron, chromium, and related metallic alloys. Atomic number 64, atomic weight 157.25, melting point 1,312°C, boiling point approximately 3,000°C, specific gravity 7.9, valence 3. [New Latin, after Johan *Gadolin* (1760-1852), Finnish chemist.]

ga·droon (gə-drōōn') *n.* **1.** *Architecture.* A band of convex molding ornamentally carved with beading or reeding. **2.** An ornamental band, especially as used in silverwork, embellished with fluting, reeding, or some other pattern. [French *godron*, from Old French *goderon*, perhaps diminutive of *godet*, drinking cup, from Middle Dutch *coddet†*, cylindrical piece of wood.]

Gads·den Purchase (gădz'dən). Strip of land, *c.* 77,000 square kilometers (33,000 square miles), in present-day southern New Mexico and Arizona. It was purchased (1853) from Mexico for 10 million dollars and named after James Gadsden (1788-1858), U.S. minister to Mexico who negotiated the sale.

gad·wall (găd'wôl') *n.* A widely distributed duck, *Anas strepera*, having grayish or brown plumage. [17th century : origin obscure.]

gad·zooks (găd-zōōks', -zōōks') *interj. Archaic.* Used to express surprise or annoyance. [17th century : GAD (God) + *zooks†*; perhaps originally *Gad's hooks*, "God's hooks," that is, the nails of the Crucifixion.]

Gae·a (jē'ə). Also **Gai·a** (gā'ə), **Ge** (jē, gē). *Greek Mythology.* The goddess of the earth, who bore and married Uranus and became the mother of the Titans and the Cyclopes. [Greek *Gaia*, personification of *gaia, gē*, earth.]

Gael (gāl) *n.* **1.** A Gaelic-speaking Celt of Scotland, Ireland, or the Isle of Man. **2.** A Scottish Highlander. [Scottish Gaelic *Gaidheal*, probably from Old Irish *goidel*, a Celt, from Old Welsh *Gwyddel*, Irishman, probably from *gwydd*, wild.]

Gael·ic (gāl'ĭk) *adj. Abbr.* **Gael.** Of or relating to the Gaels or their languages. —*n. Abbr.* **Gael. 1.** The Goidelic family of the Celtic languages. **2.** Any of the languages of the Gaels; Irish, Manx, or the language of the Scottish Highlanders. [Scottish Gaelic *Gaidhealach*, of the Gaels, and *Gaidhlig*, the Gaelic language, from *Gaidheal*, GAEL.]

Gaelic football *n.* A type of football similar to rugby that is chiefly played in Ireland.

Gael·tacht (gāl'tŭкнt) *n.* Any region in Ireland where the vernacular speech is Irish Gaelic.

gaff¹ (găf) *n.* **1.** An iron hook attached to a pole and used to land and maneuver large fish. **2.** *Nautical.* A spar used to extend the top edge of a fore-and-aft sail. **3.** A metal spur attached to the leg of a gamecock during a cockfight. **4.** *Slang.* Harshness of treatment; abuse. —*tr.v.* **gaffed, gaffing, gaffs. 1.** To hook or land (a fish) using a gaff. **2.** *Slang.* To alter or fix (dice, for example) in order to cheat. [Middle English *gaffe*, from Old French, from Old Provençal *gaf†*.]

gaff² *n. British Slang.* A public place of entertainment; especially, a cheap or disreputable music hall or theater. [18th century : origin obscure.]

gaffe (găf) *n.* A clumsy social error; a faux pas. [French, from *gaffer*, to hook, hence in seaman's slang, to blunder, from *gaffe*, hook, GAFF.]

gaf·fer (găf'ər) *n.* **1.** *Regional.* An old man or rustic. **2.** *British Informal.* A boss or foreman. **3.** An electrician who deals with lighting on a motion-picture or television set. [Contraction of GODFATHER.]

gaff-top·sail (găf'tŏp'səl, -sāl') *n. Nautical.* A light, triangular or quadrilateral sail set over a gaff.

gag (găg) *n.* **1.** Something forced into or put over the mouth to prevent the utterance of sound. **2.** Any obstacle to or censoring of free expression. **3.** A device placed in the mouth to keep it open, as in dentistry or surgery. **4.** *Informal.* **a.** A practical joke; a hoax. **b.** A comic effect or remark; a joke. —See Synonyms at **joke.** —*v.* **gagged, gagging, gags.** —*tr.* **1.** To prevent from uttering any sounds by using a gag. **2.** To repress or censor (free speech, the press, and the like). **3.** To keep (the mouth) open by using a gag. **4.** To block off or stop up (a pipe or valve, for example). **5.** To cause to choke or retch. —*intr.* **1.** To choke or retch from nausea. **2.** *Informal.* To make jokes or quips. [Middle English *gaggen*, to suffocate (probably imitative).]

ga·ga (gä'gä) *adj. Informal.* **1.** Senseless; crazy. **2.** Senile. [French, from *gaga*, foolish old man (imitative of stammering).]

Ga·ga·rin (gə-gä'rĭn), **Yuri Alexeevich** (1934-68). Russian cosmonaut. In 1961 he became the first man to travel in space. He died in an airplane crash.

gage¹ (gāj) *n.* **1.** Something deposited or given as security against an obligation; a pledge. **2.** Something, such as a glove, offered or thrown down as a pledge or challenge to fight. **3.** Any test or challenge. —*tr.v.* **gaged, gaging, gages.** *Archaic.* **1.** To pledge as security. **2.** To offer as a stake in a bet; wager. [Middle English, from Old French, from Germanic *wadhjam* (unattested).]

gage² *n.* Any of several varieties of plum, as the greengage.

gage³. Variant of **gauge.**

gag·ger (găg'ər) *n.* **1.** One that gags. **2.** A piece of iron used to keep the core in position in a foundry mold.

gag·gle (găg'əl) *intr.v.* **-gled, -gling, -gles.** To make gabbling sounds, as geese do; cackle. —*n.* **1.** A flock of geese. **2.** An often disorderly group, as of people; cluster. [Middle English *gagelen†*.]

gag·man (găg'măn') *n., pl.* **-men** (-mĕn'). A person who writes jokes or comedy routines for plays, films, or performers.

gag rein *n.* A horse's rein adjusted to make the bit more powerful.

gag rule *n.* A rule, as in a legislative body, limiting discussion or debate on a given issue. Also called "gag law."

gag·ster (găg'stər) *n.* A gagman.

gahn·ite (gä'nīt) *n.* A gray mineral, ZnO·Al₂O₃. Also called "zinc spinel." [German *Gahnit*, after Johan G. *Gahn* (1745-1818), Swedish chemist.]

Gaia. Variant of **Gaea.**

gai·e·ty, gay·e·ty (gā'ə-tē) *n., pl.* **-ties. 1.** A state of being cheerful or merry. **2.** Activity brought about by or inspiring joyousness; festivity; merriment. **3.** Gay color or showiness, as of dress; finery. [French *gaieté*, from Old French *gai*, GAY.]

Gail·lard Cut (gĭl-yärd'). Formerly **Cu·le·bra Cut** (kyōō-lā'brə). Excavation, 13 kilometers (8 miles) long, through a hill in the Canal Zone, Panama. It forms the southeastern part of the Panama Canal. U.S. Army engineer David Du Bose Gaillard (1859-1913) was in charge of the excavation work (completed 1908).

gail·lar·di·a (gə-lär'dē-ə) *n.* Any of several plants of the genus *Gaillardia*, of western North America, having yellow or reddish rayed flowers. [New Latin *Gaillardia*, after *Gaillard* de Marentonneau, 18th-century French botanist.]

gai·ly, gay·ly (gā'lē) *adv.* **1.** In a joyful, cheerful, or happy manner; merrily. **2.** With brightness; colorfully or showily: *gaily dressed.*

gain¹ (gān) *v.* **gained, gaining, gains.** —*tr.* **1.** To become the owner of; obtain; get. **2.** To acquire in competition or battle; win. **3.** To achieve through one's efforts or merits, or as a natural development: *gained recognition; gained widespread support.* **4.** To secure as a profit or through labor. **5.** To build up an increase of (weight or momentum, for example). **6.** To come to; arrive at; reach. **7.** To become fast by (the specified amount of time). Used of a timepiece: *My watch gains two minutes a day.* —*intr.* **1.** To become better or greater; advance or progress. **2.** To come nearer; get closer. Used with *on* or *upon.* **3.** To increase a lead. Used with *on, upon,* or *over.* **4.** To run fast. Used of a timepiece. —See Synonyms at **reach.** —*n.* **1.** Something earned, won, or otherwise acquired; a profit; an advantage; an increase. **2.** The act of acquiring something; attainment. **3.** *Electronics.* **a.** An increase in signal power. **b.** The ratio of output to input, as of output power to input power in an aerial or of output voltage to input voltage in an amplifier. [Old French *gaaignier, gaigner*, from Germanic *waithanjan* (unattested).]

gain² *n.* A notch or mortise cut into a board to receive another part. [17th century : origin obscure.]

gain·er (gā'nər) *n.* **1.** One that gains. **2.** A dive in which the diver leaves the board facing forward, does a backward somersault, and enters the water feet first.

gain·ful (gān'fəl) *adj.* Providing a gain; profitable. —**gain·ful·ly** *adv.* —**gain·ful·ness** *n.*

gain·ings (gā'nĭngz) *pl.n.* The amount of money earned; profits.

gain·say (gān-sā') *tr.v.* **-said** (-sĕd'), **-saying, -says. 1.** To declare false; deny. **2.** To be contrary to; oppose; contradict. —See Synonyms at **deny.** [Middle English *gaynsayen*, "to say against" : *gayn-*, against, Old English *gegn-* + SAY.] —**gain·say·er** *n.*

Gains·bor·ough (gānz'bûr'ō, -bər-ə), **Thomas** (1727-88). English landscape and portrait painter. His masterpieces include *The Blue Boy* (early 1770's) and *The Harvest Wagon* (1767).

'gainst, gainst (gĕnst, gănst) *prep. Poetic.* Against.

gait (gāt) *n.* **1.** A way of moving on foot; a particular fashion of walking or running. **2.** Any of the ways a horse or other four-legged animal may move by lifting the feet in different order or rhythm, as

gadwall *Found through much of the Northern Hemisphere, this duck eats roots and water plants in reed-fringed inland lakes.*

a canter, trot, or walk. [Middle English *gate, gait,* way, passage, from Old Norse *gata,* path, street.]

gait·ed (gā'tĭd) *adj.* Having a specified gait or number of gaits. Usually used in combination: *fast-gaited; a three-gaited mare.*

gai·ter (gā'tər) *n.* **1.** A leather or heavy cloth covering for the legs extending from the knee to the instep; a legging. **2.** An ankle-high shoe with elastic insets in the sides. **3.** An overshoe with a cloth top. [French *guêtre,* from Old French *guestre, guietre,* probably from Frankish *wrist* (unattested), instep.]

Gait·skell (gāt'skəl), **Hugh Todd Naylor** (1906–63). British politician. He became an M.P. (1945), Chancellor of the Exchequer (1950–51), and leader of the Labour Party (1955–63). He persuaded the party to abandon unilateral disarmament (1961).

gal (găl) *n. Informal.* A girl.

gal. gallon.

Gal. Galatians (New Testament).

galaxy

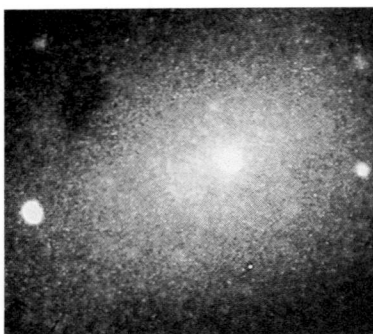
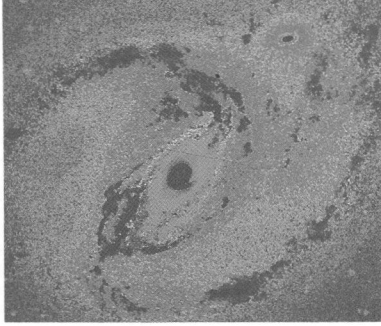
ga·la (gā'lə, găl'ə, gä'lə) *n.* **1.** A festive occasion or celebration; a festival. **2.** *British.* A competitive sports meeting, especially a swimming competition.
—*adj.* Characterized by or suitable to celebration; festive. [Italian, from Spanish, from Old French *gale,* pleasure, merrymaking, from *galer,* to make merry, live a gay life, from Gallo-Roman *walare* (unattested), from Frankish *wala* (unattested), well.]

ga·lac·ta·gogue (gə-lăk'tə-gôg', -gŏg') *n.* A substance that induces a flow of milk.
—*adj.* Inducing a flow of milk. [GALACT(O)- + -AGOGUE.]

ga·lac·tic (gə-lăk'tĭk) *adj.* **1.** Of or pertaining to a galaxy or galaxies. **2.** *Sometimes* **Galactic.** Of, pertaining to, occurring, or originating in the Milky Way. [Late Latin *galacticus,* from Greek *galaktikos,* from *gala* (stem *galakt-*), milk. See **galaxy.**]

galactic equator *n.* The great circle of the celestial sphere that lies in the plane bisecting the band of the Milky Way, inclined at an angle of approximately 62° to the celestial equator.

galactic nebula *n.* A nebula lying within the Milky Way Galaxy.

galactic noise *n.* Radio-frequency radiation originating within the Milky Way.

galactic year *n.* The **cosmic year** (see).

galacto–, galact– *prefix.* Indicates milk or milky; for example, **galactopoiesis, galactose.** [Greek *gala* (stem *galakt-*), milk.]

ga·lac·to·poi·e·sis (gə-lăk'tə-poi-ē'sĭs) *n.* The secretion and continued production of milk. [GALACTO- + -POIESIS.] —**ga·lac·to·poi·et·ic** (gə-lăk'tə-poi-ĕt'ĭk) *adj.*

ga·lac·tose (gə-lăk'tōs') *n.* A simple sugar, $C_6H_{12}O_6$, commonly occurring in **lactose** (see). [French : GALACT(O)- + -OSE.]

ga·lac·to·se·mi·a (gə-lăk'tə-sē'mē-ə) *n.* A congenital disease characterized by the inability to metabolize galactose, which consequently accumulates in the blood and if untreated causes mental retardation and stunted growth. [GALACTOSE + -EMIA.]

ga·la·go (gə-lä'gō, gə-lä'-) *n., pl.* **-gos.** A small primate, the **bush baby** (see). [New Latin *Galago,* perhaps from an African word *goigkh,* monkey.]

ga·lah (gə-lä') *n.* **1.** An Australian cockatoo, *Cacatua* (or *Kakatoe*) *roseicapilla,* having pale blue-gray plumage and a pink breast. **2.** *Australian Slang.* A fool; an idiot. [From a native Australian language.]

Gal·a·had (găl'ə-hăd') *n.* Any man considered to be noble, pure, or chivalrous. [After *Galahad,* a knight of King Arthur's Round Table who was known for his purity and who alone succeeded in the quest for the Holy Grail.]

ga·lan·gal (gə-lăng'gəl) *n.* **1.** A plant, *Alpinia officinarum,* of eastern Asia, having pungent, aromatic roots used medicinally and as seasoning. **2.** The dried roots of this plant. **3.** The **galingale** (see). [Originally a variant of GALINGALE.]

gal·an·tine (găl'ən-tēn') *n.* A dish of boned, stuffed poultry, meat, or fish cooked and served cold coated with aspic or its own jelly. [Middle English *galauntyne,* a sauce for fish and poultry, from Old French *galantine, galatine,* from Medieval Latin *galatīna, gelatīna,* probably from Latin *gelāre,* to freeze.]

ga·lan·ty show (gə-lăn'tē) *n.* A play performed by casting the shadows of miniature figures on a screen or wall. [Perhaps from Italian *galanti,* plural of *galante,* a gallant, from Old French *galant* (from the stories of gallantry portrayed in the show).]

Ga·lá·pa·gos Islands (gə-lä'pə-gəs, -lăp'ə-). *Spanish* **Ar·chi·pié·la·go de Co·lón** (är'chĭ-pyĕl'ə-gō de kə-lōn'). An Ecuadorian archipelago in the Pacific Ocean. The 15 large and many small volcanic islands lie *c.* 970 kilometers (600 miles) west of Ecuador. The population is concentrated on Isabela (Albemarle), the largest island, and San Cristóbal (Chatham). Most of the reptile life and over half the flora are unknown outside the islands, now a nature reserve. In 1835 Charles Darwin collected a wealth of scientific data here, which led to his theory of evolution. Giant tortoises once abounded on the islands, which take their name from the Spanish word *galpágo,* "tortoise." See map at **Pacific Ocean.**

gal·a·te·a (găl'ə-tē'ə) *n.* A durable cotton fabric, often striped, used in making clothing. [Originally used for children's sailor suits, after the *Galatea,* 19th-century British warship.]

Gal·a·te·a (găl'ə-tē'ə). *Greek Mythology.* An ivory statue of a maiden, brought to life by Aphrodite in answer to the pleas of the sculptor, Pygmalion, who had fallen in love with his creation.

Ga·la·ti·a (gə-lā'shə). Ancient country forming part of central Asia Minor. Chief city, Ancyra (modern Ankara, Turkey). —**Ga·la·tian** *adj. & n.*

Ga·la·tians (gə-lā'shənz) *n. Abbr.* **Gal.** A book of the New Testament consisting of an Epistle written to the Christians of Galatia by the apostle Paul in about A.D. 58. Called in full "Epistle to the Galatians."

galavant. Variant of **gallivant.**

ga·lax (gā'lăks') *n.* A plant, *Galax aphylla,* of the southeastern United States, having glossy, evergreen leaves and a cluster of small white flowers. [New Latin *Galax,* probably from Greek *galaxias,* the Milky Way, GALAXY (from its white flowers).]

gal·ax·y (găl'ək-sē) *n., pl.* **-ies. 1.** *Astronomy.* **a.** Any of numerous large-scale aggregates of stars, gas, and dust, having one of several more or less definite overall structures, containing an average of 100 billion (10^{11}) solar masses, and ranging in diameter from 1,500 to 300,000 light-years. **b.** *Often* **Galaxy.** The galaxy of which the earth's sun is a part, the **Milky Way** (see). Usually preceded by *the.* **2.** An assembly of brilliant, beautiful, or distinguished persons or things. [Middle English *galaxie,* the Milky Way, from Old French, from Latin *galaxiās,* from Greek *galaxias (kuklos),* "milky (circle)," from *gala,* milk.]

gal·ba·num (găl′bə-nəm, gôl′-) *n.* A bitter, aromatic gum resin extracted from an Asiatic plant, *Ferula galbaniflua,* or any of several related plants, and used in incense and medicinally as a counterirritant. [Middle English, from Latin, from Greek *khalbanē,* from Hebrew *ḥelbənāh.*]

Gal·braith (găl′brāth′), **John Kenneth** (1908–). Canadian-born U.S. economist. His works include *The Great Crash* (1955), *The Affluent Society* (1958), and *The New Industrial State* (1967). He was U.S. ambassador to India (1961–63).

gale[1] (gāl) *n.* **1. a.** A very strong wind. **b.** *Meteorology.* A wind whose speed is between 39 and 46 miles per hour, force 8 on the Beaufort scale. **2.** *Archaic.* A breeze. **3.** A forceful outburst, as of laughter. —See Synonyms at **wind.** [Probably short for *gale wind,* "bad wind," perhaps from Norwegian *galen,* bad, probably from Old Norse *galinn,* bewitched, enchanted, from *gala,* to sing, enchant, bewitch.]

gale[2] *n.* A plant, the **sweet myrtle** *(see).* [Middle English, *gale, gayl,* Old English *gagel,* akin to Middle Dutch *gaghel*†.]

ga·le·a (gā′lē-ə) *n., pl.* **-leae** (-lē-ē′). *Biology.* A helmet-shaped part, such as the upper petal of certain plants or part of the maxilla of an insect. [Latin, leather helmet, originally "cap made of weasel skin," from Greek *galeē,* weasel.]

ga·le·ate (gā′lē-āt′) *adj.* Also **ga·le·at·ed** (-ā′tĭd). *Biology.* **1.** Having a galea. **2.** Helmet-shaped. [Latin *galeātus,* from *galea,* GALEA.]

ga·le·i·form (gā′lē-ə-fôrm′, gə-lē′-) *adj.* Helmet-shaped. [French *galéiforme* : Latin *galea,* GALEA + -FORM.]

Ga·len (gā′lən). (A.D. *c.* 130–*c.* 200). Greek physician. He compiled Greek medical knowledge into treatises that formed the basis of European medicine until the Renaissance.

ga·le·na (gə-lē′nə) *n.* A gray mineral, essentially PbS, the principal ore of lead. Also called "lead glance." [Latin *galēna*†, lead ore.]

ga·len·ic (gə-lĕn′ĭk, gā-) *adj.* Also **ga·len·i·cal** (-ĭ-kəl). Designating a drug preparation of plant or animal origin. [After GALEN.] **—ga·len·ic, ga·len·i·cal** *n.*

Ga·len·ism (gā′lə-nĭz′əm) *n.* The medical system based on Galen's surviving treatises, including the notion of the four bodily humors. **—Ga·len·ic** (gə-lĕn′ĭk, gā-), **Ga·len·i·cal** (-ĭ-kəl) *adj.* **—Ga·len·ist** *adj. & n.*

ga·lère (gə-lâr′) *n. French.* A group or coterie, especially of undesirable people. [French, "galley."]

Ga·li·bi (gə-lē′bē, găl′ə-) *n., pl.* **-bis** or collectively **Galibi. 1.** A member of the Carib people of French Guiana. **2.** The language of this people. [Carib *galibi,* "strong man," akin to Cariban *caribe,* brave, CARIB.]

Ga·li·cia[1] (gə-lĭsh′ə, -lĭsh′ē-ə). Region and former kingdom in northwest Spain, on the Atlantic Ocean south of the Bay of Biscay. Colonized by the Goths in the 6th century, it became a subject of Castile in the 11th century.

Galicia[2]. *Polish* **Ha·licz** (hä′lĭch). *Russian* **Ga·lich** (gä′lĭch) or **Ga·li·tsi·ya** (gə-lē′tsē-yə). Historic region in Central Europe. It became an independent principality in 1087 but was conquered by the Russians in the 12th century. Absorbed by Poland in the 14th century, it became Austrian four centuries later. Following World War I it was returned to Poland, but after World War II East Galicia was ceded to the U.S.S.R.

Ga·li·cian (gə-lĭsh′ən) *adj.* **1.** Of or pertaining to Spanish Galicia, its people, or their language. **2.** Of or pertaining to Polish Galicia or its people.
~*n.* **1.** A native or inhabitant of Spanish or Polish Galicia. **2.** The Portuguese dialect spoken in Spanish Galicia.

Gal·i·le·an[1] (găl′ə-lē′ən) *adj.* Of or pertaining to Galilee or its people.
~*n.* **1.** A native or inhabitant of Galilee. **2.** A Christian. **3.** Jesus.

Gal·i·le·an[2] (găl′ə-lē′ən, -lā′ən) *adj.* Of, pertaining to, or in accordance with the work of Galileo.

gal·i·lee (găl′ə-lē′) *n.* A small chapel or porch at the western end of some medieval English churches and cathedrals. Also called "galilee porch." [Middle English *galile,* from Old French *galilee,* from Medieval Latin *galilaea,* from Latin *Galilaea,* GALILEE.]

Gal·i·lee (găl′ə-lē′). A region in northern Israel. The northernmost region of Palestine and of the ancient Jewish kingdom of Israel, Galilee was the province where Jesus Christ began his ministry. It became part of the newly founded state of Israel in 1949.

Galilee, Sea of. Biblical names **Sea of Ti·be·ri·as** (tī-bîr′ē-əs) or **Lake of Gen·nes·a·ret** (gə-nĕs′ə-rĕt′) or **Sea of Chin·ne·reth** (kĭn′ə-rĕth′). Lake in northern Israel. It is 21 kilometers (13 miles) long and lies in the Great Rift Valley, its surface being 209 meters (686 feet) below sea level.

Gal·i·le·o Gal·i·le·i (găl′ə-lā′ō găl′ə-lā′ē) (1564–1642). Italian astronomer and mathematician. He developed his own telescope (1609) and discovered four satellites of Jupiter and the nature of lunar illumination. His belief that Copernicus was right to claim that the sun was the center of our universe led to his persecution by the Inquisition (1633). He recanted but is said to have muttered under his breath "But it (the earth) does move."

gal·i·ma·ti·as (găl′ə-mā′shē-əs, -shəs, -măt′ē-əs) *n.* Nonsensical talk; gibberish. [French, perhaps originally students' jargon : Latin *gallus,* "cock," student who takes part in a discussion + Greek *-mathia,* knowledge, from *manthanein,* to learn.]

gal·in·gale (găl′ən-gāl′, găl′ĭng-) *n.* Any of various sedges of the genus *Cyperus;* especially, *C. longus,* of Europe, having rough-edged leaves, reddish spikelets, and aromatic roots. Also called "galangal." [Middle English, from Old French *galingal,* from Arabic *khalanjān,* from Chinese *gāo liáng jiāng,* good ginger from Gaozhou (present-day Maoming in Guangdong Province).]

galiot. Variant of **galliot.**

gal·i·pot (găl′ə-pŏt′, -pō′) *n.* The crude turpentine resin that is obtained from various pine species, especially the cluster pine, *Pinus pinaster,* of southern Europe, and is often seen as a hardened mass on the bark. [18th century : from French, of obscure origin.]

Galitsiya. See **Galicia** (Central Europe).

gall[1] (gôl) *n.* **1. a. Bile** *(see).* **b.** The gallbladder. **2.** Bitterness of feeling; rancor. **3.** Something bitter to endure: *the gall of disappointment.* **4.** Impudence; effrontery: *He had the gall to try to borrow money.* —See Synonyms at **temerity.** [Middle English *gall(e),* Old English *gealla,* from Germanic.]

gall[2] *n.* **1.** A skin sore caused by friction and abrasion: *a saddle gall.* **2. a.** Exasperation; irritation; vexation. **b.** The cause of such vexation.
~*v.* **galled, galling, galls.** —*tr.* **1.** To make (the skin) sore by abrasion; chafe. **2.** To damage or break the surface of by or as if by friction or abrasion; abrade: *the bark of saplings galled by improper staking.* **3.** To exasperate; vex. —*intr.* To become irritated, chafed, or sore. [Middle English *galle,* from Middle Low German; akin to Old English *gealla,* sore place, Old Norse *galli,* fault.]

gall[3] *n.* An abnormal swelling of plant tissue, caused by insects, microorganisms, or external injury. [Middle English *galle,* from Old French, from Latin *galla*†.]

gall. gallon.

Gal·la (găl′ə) *n., pl.* **-las** or collectively **Galla. 1.** A member of a pastoral Hamitic people of southern Ethiopia and Somalia. **2.** The language of this people, belonging to the Ethiopian or Cushitic group of the Afro-Asiatic languages.
~*adj.* Of or pertaining to this people or their language. [Perhaps from Arabic *ghalīẓ,* rough.]

gal·lant (găl′ənt *for senses 1, 3, 4;* gə-lănt′, -länt′, găl′ənt *for sense 2*) *adj.* **1.** Courageous; daring; valorous: *gallant soldiers.* **2. a.** Attentive to women; chivalrous; courteous. **b.** Amorous. **3.** Stately; majestic; noble: *"On my word, master, this is a gallant trout"* (Isaak Walton). **4.** Showy and gay in appearance, dress, or bearing; dashing. —See Synonyms at **brave.**
~*n.* (gə-lănt′, -länt′, găl′ənt). **1.** A fashionable young man. **2. a.** A man courteously attentive to women; a ladies' man. **b.** A woman's lover; a paramour.
~*v.* (gə-lănt′, -länt′) **gallanted, -lanting, -lants.** —*tr.* To woo, attend, or escort (a lady); pay court to. —*intr.* To play the gallant. [Middle English *galaunt,* from Old French *galant,* gorgeous, showy, brave, from the present participle of *galer,* to rejoice, from Gallo-Roman *walāre* (unattested), from Frankish *wala* (unattested), well.] **—gal·lant·ly** *adv.*

gal·lant·ry (găl′ən-trē) *n., pl.* **-ries. 1.** Nobility of spirit or action; great courage. **2. a.** Chivalrous attention toward women; courtliness; courteousness. **b.** Amorous attentiveness to a woman. **3.** An act or instance of gallantry in speech or behavior. **4.** *Archaic.* A bold or colorful display or appearance.

Gal·la·tin Range (găl′ə-tən). Section of the Rocky Mts. in northwestern Wyoming and southwestern Montana. The highest elevation is Electric Peak, rising to 3,402 meters (11,155 feet), in the northwestern corner of Yellowstone National Park.

gall·blad·der, gall blad·der (gôl′blăd′ər) *n.* A small, pear-shaped muscular sac located under the right lobe of the liver, in which bile secreted by the liver is stored.

Galle (gāl, găl). Formerly **Point de Galle** (point′ də gāl′, găl′). Seaport and commercial center of Sri Lanka. It was the country's main port under the Arabs and Portuguese and the capital under the Dutch until 1656.

gal·le·ass, gal·li·ass (găl′ē-əs) *n.* A large, heavily armed, three-masted Mediterranean galley of the 16th and 17th centuries. [Old French *galeasse,* from Old Italian *galeaza,* augmentative of *galea,* galley, from Medieval Latin, GALLEY.]

gal·le·on (găl′ē-ən) *n.* A large, three-masted sailing ship generally having two or more decks, used during the 15th and 16th centuries by Spain and other countries as a merchantman or warship. [Spanish *galeon,* from Old French *galion,* from *galie,* GALLEY.]

gal·ler·y (găl′ə-rē, găl′rē) *n., pl.* **-ies. 1.** A roofed promenade, especially one extending along the wall of a building, with its roof supported by pillars on the outer side; a colonnade. **2.** An elevated covered platform along the outer wall of a building; a long balcony. **3. a.** An enclosed narrow passageway, such as a hall or corridor. **b.** A long room or passage resembling such a corridor and used for a specified purpose: *a shooting gallery.* **4. a.** An upper floor projecting over the main floor of a theater, and usually providing cheaper seats than those in the orchestra. **b.** The seats in such a section. **c.** The audience occupying these seats. **d.** A similar projecting upper floor in a large building, as in a church, law court, or legislative assembly. **5.** A large audience or group of spectators, as in a stadium, grandstand, or legislative assembly. **6. a.** A building or hall in which sculpture, paintings, photographs, or other works of art are exhibited. **b.** A private institution that exhibits and sells works of art. **7.** An underground tunnel or other passageway, such as one dug for military or mining purposes, or found in animal burrows, insects' nests, and so on. **8.** *Nautical.* A platform or balcony at the stern or quarters of certain early sailing ships. **9.** A decorative upright trimming or molding along the edge of a table top, tray, or

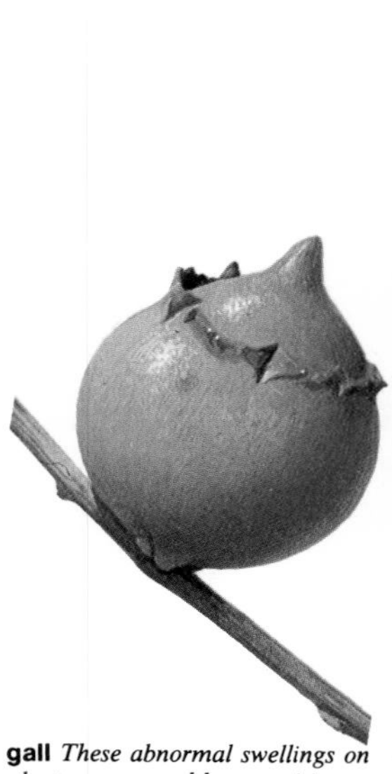

gall *These abnormal swellings on plants are caused by parasitic infections, often transmitted by insects. The gall shown here is an oak marble, caused by the larva of a tiny wasp.*

PRONUNCIATION KEY

ă, pat; ā, pay; âr, care;
ä, father, are; b, bib;
ch, church; d, deed; ĕ, pet;
ē, be; f, fife; g, gag; h, hat;
hw, which; ĭ, pit; ī, pie;
îr, pier; j, judge; k, kick;
l, lid, needle; m, mum;
n, no, sudden; ng, thing;
ŏ, pot; ō, toe; ô, paw, for;
oi, noise; ou, out; o͝o, book;
o͞o, boot; p, pop; r, roar;
s, sauce; sh, ship, dish;
t, tight; th, thin, path;
th, this, bathe; ŭ, cut; ûr, fur;
v, valve; w, with; y, yes;
z, zebra, size; zh, vision;
ə, about, item, edible,
gallop, circus, peaceful

IN FOREIGN WORDS:

à, *Fr.* ami; œ, *Fr.* feu, *Ger.* schön; ü, *Fr.* tu, *Ger.* über; KH, *Ger.* ich, *Scot.* loch; N, *Fr.* bon; y′, *Fr.* Compiègne

STRESS MARKS:

Primary stress: ′
in·cite′ (ĭn-sīt′)
Secondary stress: ′
in′sight′ (ĭn′sīt′)

shelf. **—play to the gallery.** **1.** To perform a play, scene, or role in a manner calculated to please the less sophisticated members of an audience who, in former times, were mainly congregated in the gallery. **2.** To try to gain the favor or applause of the general public, especially by crude or obvious means.
∼*tr.v.* **galleried, -lerying, -leries.** To provide with a gallery. [Middle English *galerie,* from Old French, portico, from Italian *galleria,* from Medieval Latin *galeria,* perhaps variant of *galilaea,* porch of a church, GALILEE.]

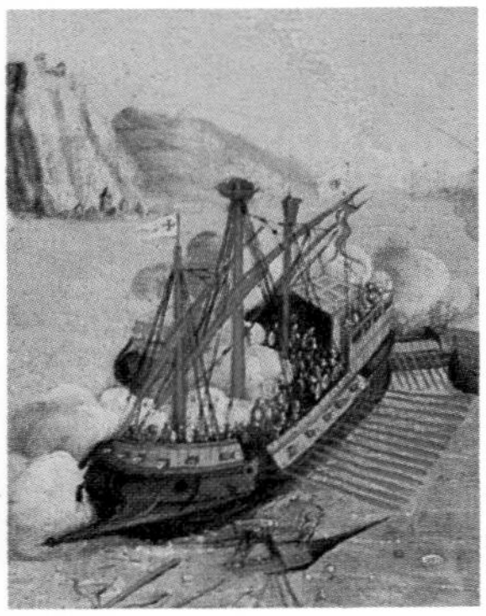

galley *A detail from* Battle of Lepanto, *a painting of one of the last major actions between galleys. In the battle, on October 7, 1571, the Muslim Ottoman Turks were decisively defeated by a Christian armada under Don John of Austria, losing all but 40 of their 300 war galleys.*

gallery forest *n.* A stretch of forest bordering a river and surrounded by treeless country.
gal·ley (găl′ē) *n., pl.* **-leys.** **1.** A large medieval ship of shallow draft that had a single deck, was propelled by sails and oars, and was used as a merchantman or warship in the Mediterranean. **2.** An ancient seagoing vessel propelled by oars. **3.** A large rowboat, such as one formerly used by British customs officers. **4.** The kitchen of a ship, boat, or airliner. **5.** *Printing.* **a.** A long tray, usually of metal, used for holding composed type. **b.** A galley proof. [Middle English *galeie, galy,* from Old French *galie, galee,* from Medieval Latin *galea,* from Medieval Greek *galea*†.]
galley proof *n. Printing.* A printer's proof taken from composed type before page composition to allow for the detection and correction of errors. Also called "galley."
galley slave *n.* **1.** A slave or convict forced to man an oar of a galley. **2.** A person forced to perform tedious or menial tasks; a drudge.
galley west *adv. Informal.* Out of shape; out of commission. Used in the phrase *to knock galley west.* [Perhaps alteration of dialectal *collywest,* askew, perhaps from *Collyweston,* village in Northamptonshire, England.]
gall·fly (gôl′flī′) *n., pl.* **-flies.** Any of various small insects, such as the gall midge or gall wasp, that deposit their eggs on plant stems or in the bark of trees, causing the formation of galls in which their larvae grow.
Gallia. See **Gaul.**
gal·li·am·bic (găl′ē-ăm′bĭk) *adj.* Designating or characteristic of a verse meter formed by two iambic dimeters. [Latin *galliambus,* song of the *Gallī* (priests of Cybele); see **iamb.**]
gal·liard (găl′yərd) *adj. Archaic.* Spirited; lively; gay.
∼*n.* **1.** A spirited dance popular in the 16th and 17th centuries. **2.** The music for this dance. [Middle English *galiard, gaillard,* valiant, lively, from Old French *gaillard,* from Gallo-Roman *galia* (unattested), strength, power.]
galliass. Variant of **galleass.**
gal·lic (găl′ĭk) *adj. Chemistry.* Of or pertaining to gallium. Used especially of chemical compounds that contain gallium with a valence of 3.
Gal·lic (găl′ĭk) *adj.* Of or pertaining to ancient Gaul or to modern France; French. [Latin *Gallicus,* Gaulish, from *Galli,* Gauls.]
gal·lic acid (găl′ĭk) *n.* A colorless crystalline compound, $C_7H_6O_5 \cdot H_2O$, derived from tannin and used in photography, as a tanning agent, and in ink and paper manufacture.
Gal·li·can (găl′ĭ-kən) *adj.* Pertaining to or characteristic of Gallicanism.
∼*n.* A supporter of Gallicanism. [Middle English, from Old French, from Medieval Latin *Gallicānus,* French, from Latin, Gaulish, from *Gallicus,* GALLIC.]
Gal·li·can·ism (găl′ĭ-kə-nĭz′əm) *n.* A movement originating among the French Roman Catholic clergy, favoring the restriction of papal control and the achievement by each nation of individual administrative autonomy. Compare **Ultramontanism.**
Gal·li·cism (găl′ĭ-sĭz′əm) *n.* **1.** A French phrase or idiom appearing in another language. **2.** A characteristic French trait.
Gal·li·cize (găl′ĭ-sīz′) *v.* **-cized, -cizing, -cizes.** *—intr.* To become like the French, as in speech, character, or custom. *—tr.* To make like the French, as in speech, character, or custom.
gal·li·gas·kins (găl′ĭ-găs′kĭnz) *pl.n.* **1.** Full-length, loosely fitting hose or breeches worn in the 16th and 17th centuries. **2.** Loose breeches or trousers. **3.** *Regional.* Leggings. [Earlier *gallogascaine, garragascoyne,* perhaps from Old French *garguesque, greguesque,* from Old Italian *grechesca,* "Grecian breeches," from the feminine of *grechesco,* Grecian, from *greco,* Greek, from Latin *Graecus,* GREEK.]
gal·li·mau·fry (găl′ə-mô′frē) *n., pl.* **-fries.** A jumble; a hodgepodge. [French *galimafrée,* from Old French *calimafree* : probably *galer,* to live a gay life (see **gallant**) + Picard *mafrer,* to eat voraciously, from Middle Dutch *maffelen*†.]
gal·li·na·ceous (găl′ə-nā′shəs) *adj.* **1.** Of, belonging to, or characteristic of the order Galliformes, which includes the common domestic fowl as well as the pheasants, turkeys, and grouse. **2.** Relating to or resembling the domestic fowl. [Latin *gallīnāceus,* of poultry, from *gallīna,* hen, feminine of *gallus,* cock.] **—gal·li·na·cean** (găl′ə-nā′shən) *n.*
gall·ing (gô′lĭng) *adj.* Causing acute irritation, humiliation, exasperation, or discomfort. **—gall·ing·ly** *adv.*
gal·li·nip·per (găl′ə-nĭp′ər) *n.* A large mosquito or similar insect capable of inflicting a painful bite. [Origin unknown.]

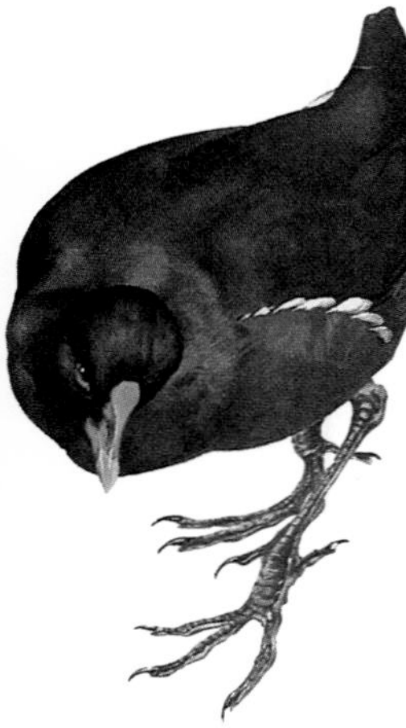

gallinule *This wading bird is found in most parts of the world except Australia, nesting beside freshwater ponds, lakes, and rivers. When alarmed, it can sink below the surface, leaving only its bill protruding like a snorkel. In the U.S.A. it is sometimes called marsh hen.*

gal·li·nule (găl′ə-no͞ol′, -nyo͞ol′) *n.* Any of various wading birds of the genera *Gallinula, Porphyrio,* or *Porphyrula,* frequenting swampy regions and characteristically having dark, iridescent plumage. [New Latin *Gallinula,* from Latin *gallīnula,* chicken, pullet, diminutive of *gallīna,* hen, feminine of *gallus,* cock.]
gal·li·ot, gal·i·ot (găl′ē-ət) *n.* **1.** A light, swift galley propelled by sails and oars, formerly used on the Mediterranean. **2.** A light, single-masted, flat-bottomed Dutch merchant ship or seagoing barge. [Middle English, from Old French *galiote,* from Italian *galeotta,* from Medieval Latin *galea,* GALLEY.]
Gal·lip·o·li (gə-lĭp′ə-lē). *Turkish* **Ge·li·bo·lu** (gĕl′ə-bə-lo͞o′). Seaport of European Turkey. It lies on the Gallipoli Peninsula in the Dardanelles, and in 1354 was the Ottoman Turks' first European conquest. From April 1915 to January 1916 the peninsula was the scene of unsuccessful and costly landings by Australian, New Zealand, French, and British troops in an attempt to clear the Dardanelles and thus the sea route to Russia. The devastated town was ceded to Greece in 1920 but was returned to Turkey in 1923.
gal·li·pot (găl′ə-pŏt′) *n.* A small glazed earthenware jar formerly used by pharmacists for medicaments. [Middle English *galy pott* : probably GALLEY + POT (originally imported from the Mediterranean by galleys).]
gal·li·um (găl′ē-əm) *n. Symbol* **Ga** A rare metallic element that is liquid near room temperature, expands on solidifying, and is found as a trace element in coal, bauxite, and other minerals. It is used in semiconductor technology and as a component of various low-melting alloys. Atomic number 31, atomic weight 69.72, melting point 29.78°C, boiling point 2,403°C, specific gravity 5.907 (20°C), valences 2, 3. [New Latin, from Latin *gallus,* cock (playful translation of the name of its discoverer, *Lecoq* de Boisbaudran, 1838–1912, French chemist). See **gallinaceous.**]
gallium arsenide *n.* A dark-gray crystalline compound, GaAs, used in transistors, solar cells, and semiconducting lasers.
gal·li·vant, gal·a·vant (găl′ə-vănt′) *intr.v.* **-vanted, -vanting, -vants.** **1.** To roam about aimlessly or frivolously; gad about. **2.** To consort frivolously with members of the opposite sex; flirt. [Perhaps alteration of GALLANT.]
gal·li·wasp (găl′ə-wŏsp′, -wôsp′) *n.* Any of several long-bodied lizards of the genera *Diploglossus* or *Celestus,* of Central America and the West Indies. [18th century : origin obscure.]
gall midge *n.* Any of various small, mosquitolike flies making up the family Cecidomyiidae, the larvae of which produce galls in plants.
gall mite *n.* Any of various mites of the family Eriophyidae that produce galls in plants.
gall·nut (gôl′nŭt′) *n.* A plant gall having a rounded form suggestive of a nut.
Gallo– *prefix.* Indicates Gaul or France; for example, **Gallo-Roman.** [Latin *Gallus,* a Gaul.]
galloglass. Variant of **gallowglass.**
Gal·lo·ma·ni·a (găl′ə-mā′nē-ə) *n.* A strong predilection for anything French. [French *gallomanie* : GALLO- + -MANIA.]
gal·lon (găl′ən) *n. Abbr.* **g., gal., gall.** **1.** A unit of volume or capacity in the U.S. Customary System, used in liquid measure, equal to 4 quarts, or 3.79 liters (231 cubic inches, or 0.83 of a British gallon). **2.** A unit of volume in the British Imperial system, used in liquid and dry measure, equal to 4.55 liters (277.420 cubic inches). [Middle English *gallun, gallon,* from Old North French, from Medieval Latin *gallēta,* jug, measure for wine, perhaps from Celtic.]
gal·lon·age (găl′ə-nĭj) *n.* The amount of something measured in gallons.
gal·loon (gə-lo͞on′) *n.* A narrow band or braid used as trimming, and commonly made of lace, metallic thread, or embroidery. [French *galon,* from Old French *galonner,* to decorate with ribbons, perhaps from Frankish *wōlōn,* to tie up with cord.]
gal·lop (găl′əp) *n.* **1.** The fastest gait of a horse or other quadruped, in which all four legs are off the ground at the same time. **2.** A ride taken at the gallop. **3.** A fast pace.
∼*v.* **galloped, -loping, -lops.** *—tr.* **1.** To cause to gallop. **2.** To transport at or as if at a gallop. *—intr.* **1.** To go at a gallop. Used of a horse or its rider. **2.** To move or progress rapidly: *galloped through the agenda.* [Middle English *galopen,* from Old French *galoper,* variant of Old North French *waloper,* from Frankish *walahlaupan* (unattested), "to run well" : *wala* (unattested), well + *hlaupan* (unattested), to jump, run.] **—gal·lop·er** *n.*
gallopade. Variant of **galop.**
gal·lop·ing (găl′ə-pĭng) *adj.* **1.** Of or resembling a gallop, especially in rhythm or rapidity. **2. a.** Developing at an accelerated rate and leading to death. Said of certain diseases, principally in nontechnical contexts. **b.** Increasing rapidly or uncontrollably: *galloping inflation.*
Gal·lo-Ro·man (găl′ō-rō′mən) *n.* **1.** A native or inhabitant of Roman Gaul. **2.** The Vulgar Latin spoken by the Romanized inhabitants of Gaul. **—Gal·lo-Ro·man** *adj.*
Gal·lo-Ro·mance (găl′ō-rō-măns′, -rō′măns′) *n.* The language supposed by scholars to have developed from the Vulgar Latin that was spoken in Gaul after the end of Roman rule, before the development of Old French. **—Gal·lo-Ro·mance** *adj.*

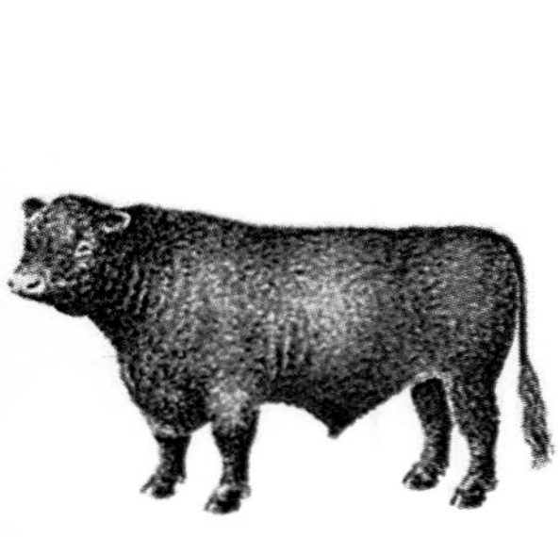

Galloway *A distinctive Scottish breed of beef cattle with a shaggy coat of black, gray-brown, or silvery hair and no horns.*

Gal·lo·way¹ (găl′ə-wā′) *n. Often* **galloway.** **1.** Any of a breed of hornless black cattle. **2.** Any of a breed of small hardy horses. [After GALLOWAY in Scotland, where they were originally bred.]
Gal·lo·way² (găl′ə-wā). Area in southwest Scotland. It comprises part of Dumfries and Galloway Region and part of Strathclyde.
gal·low·glass, gal·lo·glass (găl′ō-glăs′, -gläs′) *n.* Formerly, an armed retainer or mercenary in the service of an Irish chieftain. [Irish Gaelic *galloglach,* "foreign youth" : *gall,* foreigner + *oglach,* youth : *og,* young, from Old Irish *ōac* + *-lach,* abstract suffix.]
gal·lows (găl′ōz) *n., pl.* **gallows.** **1. a.** A device usually consisting of two upright beams supporting a crossbeam from which a noose is

suspended and used for execution by hanging. Also called "gallows tree." **b.** A similar structure used for supporting or suspending; especially, in Australia, a frame on which slaughtered cattle are hoisted. **2.** Execution on a gallows or by hanging. [Middle English *galwes, galawis,* plural of *galwe,* gallows, cross, from Old English *gealga.*]

gallows bird *n. Informal.* One who deserves to be hanged.

gallows humor *n.* Humorous treatment of a situation that is actually frightening or very grave.

gall·stone (gôl′stōn′) *n.* A small, hard pathological concretion of cholesterol, calcium salts, and bile pigments, formed in the gall-bladder or in a bile duct.

Gal·lup (găl′əp), **George Horace** (1901–84). U.S. statistician. Through his techniques of polling the public, he accurately predicted the result of the 1936 presidential election. Gallup polls have been used regularly ever since.

Gal·lup poll (găl′əp) *n.* A sampling of the views of a representative section of the population on a particular issue; especially, one taken to assess the relative popularity of different political parties or to forecast the outcome of an election.

gal·lus·es (găl′ə-sīz) *pl.n. Informal.* Suspenders for trousers. [Plural of *gallus,* variant of GALLOWS (obsolete sense "braces").]

gall wasp *n.* Any of various wasps of the family Cynipidae that produce distinctively shaped galls on oaks and other plants.

ga·loot (gə-lōot′) *n. Slang.* A clumsy, uncouth, or stupid person. [19th century (nautical slang) : origin obscure.]

gal·op (găl′əp) *n.* Also **gal·o·pade, gal·lo·pade** (găl′ə-pād′, -päd′). **1.** A lively dance in duple rhythm, popular in the 19th century. **2.** The music for this dance. [French, gallop, from Old French *galoper,* to GALLOP.]

ga·lore (gə-lôr′, -lōr′) *adj. Informal.* In great numbers; in abundance. Used after a noun: *dresses galore; opportunities galore.* [Irish Gaelic *go leór* : *go,* to, from Old Irish *co, cu*† + *leór,* sufficiency, enough, from Old Irish *lour.*]

ga·losh (gə-lŏsh′) *n.* **1.** *Usually* **galoshes.** A waterproof overshoe. **2.** *Obsolete.* A sturdy heavy-soled boot or shoe. [Middle English *galoche,* from Old French, probably from Late Latin *gallicula,* diminutive of Latin *gallica (solea),* "Gaulish (sandal)," from the feminine of *gallicus,* Gaulish, Gaelic, from *Galli,* Gauls.]

Gals·wor·thy (gôlz′wûr′thē), **John** (1867–1933). British novelist and playwright. He wrote the *The Forsyte Saga* (1906–21) and many other *Forsyte* novels and stories, and was awarded the Nobel Prize for literature (1932).

Gal·ton (gôl′tən), **Sir Francis** (1822–1911). British biologist. He showed that mental characteristics could be inherited and developed a method of identification by fingerprints.

ga·lumph (gə-lŭmpf′, -lŭmf′) *intr.v.* **-lumphed, -lumphing, -lumphs.** *Informal.* To move or jump about in a clumsy way. [19th century (coined by Lewis Carroll) : probably a blend of GALLOP + TRI-UMPH.]

galv. galvanized.

Gal·va·ni (găl-vä′nē), **Luigi** (1737–98). Italian physician. His experiments making frogs' legs twitch led him to believe, erroneously, that electricity was a fluid in nerve tissue. He gave his name to galvanism, electricity generated by chemical means.

gal·van·ic (găl-văn′ĭk) *adj.* **1.** Of or pertaining to direct-current electricity, especially when produced chemically. **2.** Having the effect of or produced as if by an electric shock. [French *galvanique,* from *galvanisme,* GALVANISM.] **—gal·van·i·cal·ly** *adv.*

galvanic cell *n. Electricity.* A primary cell (see).

galvanic couple *n. Electricity.* A voltaic couple (see).

galvanic pile *n. Electricity.* A voltaic pile (see).

gal·va·nism (găl′və-nĭz′əm) *n.* **1.** Direct-current electricity, especially when produced chemically. Also called "voltaism." **2.** A form of medical treatment using direct-current electricity. [French *galvanisme,* from Italian *galvanismo,* first described by Luigi GALVANI.]

gal·va·nize (găl′və-nīz′) *tr.v.* **-nized, -nizing, -nizes. 1.** To stimulate or shock with an electric current. **2.** To arouse to awareness or action; spur. **3.** To coat (iron or steel) with rust-resistant zinc by spraying, immersion, or electrolytic deposition. **—gal·va·ni·za·tion** *n.*

gal·va·nom·e·ter (găl′və-nŏm′ə-tər) *n.* A device for detecting or measuring small electric currents by means of mechanical effects produced by the current to be measured. [GALVAN(ISM) + -METER.] **—gal·va·no·met·ric** (găl′və-nō-mět′rĭk), **gal·va·no·met·ri·cal** *adj.* **—gal·va·nom·e·try** (găl′və-nŏm′ə-trē) *n.*

gal·van·o·scope (găl-văn′ə-skōp′, găl′və-nə-) *n.* A galvanometer used to detect the presence and direction of electric currents by the deflection of a magnetic needle. [GALVAN(ISM) + -SCOPE.] **—gal·van·o·scop·ic** (găl-văn′ə-skŏp′ĭk, găl′və-nə-) *adj.* **—gal·va·nos·co·py** (găl′və-nŏs′kə-pē) *n.*

Gal·ves·ton (găl′və-stən). A port city in southeastern Texas, on Galveston Island, at the entrance to Galveston Bay, an inlet of the Gulf of Mexico. The Spanish explorer Cabeza de Vaca may have been shipwrecked on the island in 1528. Settlement began in the 1830's. The city was damaged by hurricanes in 1900 and 1961.

Gal·way[1] (gôl′wā). County in Connacht in the west of the Republic of Ireland. The western section is mountainous; the eastern section is a rolling plain.

Galway[2]. Fishing port and the county town of County Galway in the Republic of Ireland. Situated at the mouth of the Corrib River, it is a well-known salmon-fishing center.

Galway, James (1939–). Irish flutist. He has been lead flutist with the London Symphony and Royal Philharmonic orchestras.

gal·yak (găl′yăk′) *n.* A flat, glossy fur made from the pelt of a stillborn lamb or kid. [Russian dialectal *galyak,* perhaps from Russian *golyĭ,* bald, naked.]

gam[1] (găm) *n.* **1.** A school or herd of whales. **2.** A social meeting, especially between whalers at sea. **~v. gammed, gamming, gams.** *—intr.* To come together socially, especially while at sea. *—tr.* To socialize with. [Perhaps short for GAMMON (deceptive talk).]

gam[2] *n. Slang.* A person's leg. [Probably from obsolete *gamb,* leg of an animal, from Old North French *gambe,* Late Latin *gamba,* hook, leg, from Greek *kampē,* a bend.]

Ga·ma (găm′ə, gä′mə), **Vasco da** (*c.* 1469–1524). Portuguese navigator. He discovered the sea route from Europe to India via the Cape of Good Hope (1497–98).

gam·a grass (găm′ə, gä′mə) *n.* A perennial grass, *Tripsacum dactyloides,* of southern North America, that is grown for fodder. [*Gama,* probably alteration of Spanish *grama,* from Latin *grāmen,* grass.]

ga·may (gă-mā′, găm′ā′) *n.* A variety of red grape used for making red wines, especially Beaujolais. [French, after *Gamay,* a hamlet in the wine-growing area of Beaune.]

gam·ba (găm′bə, găm′-) *n.* A viola da gamba (see). [Italian, leg, shortened from VIOLA DA GAMBA.]

gam·ba·do[1] (găm-bā′dō) *n., pl.* **-does** or **-dos.** Also **gam·bade** (-bād′, -bäd′). **1.** In dressage, a low leap of a horse in which all four feet are off the ground. **2.** A leaping or gamboling movement. [Spanish *gambada,* from Italian *gambata,* GAMBOL.]

gambado[2] *n., pl.* **-does** or **-dos. 1.** Either of a pair of protective leather gaiters attached to a saddle. **2.** A rider's legging or gaiter. [Italian *gamba,* leg (perhaps influenced by BASTINADO). See **gambol.**]

gam·be·son (găm′bə-sən, -zən) *n.* A sleeveless garment of leather or quilted material worn under armor in the Middle Ages. [Middle English *gambisoun,* from Old French *gambe(i)son,* from *gambais, wambais,* probably from Frankish *wamba* (unattested), belly, from Common Germanic *wambō* (unattested), WOMB.]

Gam·bet·ta (găm-bět′ə), **Léon** (1838–82). French politician. After the defeat of Napoleon III at the Battle of Sedan (1870), Gambetta helped set up the Third Republic, escaping from the siege of Paris by balloon. He virtually ruled France until its defeat by Germany (1871). He was premier (1881–82).

Gam·bi·a[1] (găm′bē-ə). River in West Africa. Rising in the Fouta Djallon Plateau of Guinea, it flows 1,126 kilometers (700 miles) through Senegambia to the Atlantic Ocean, and can take oceangoing vessels almost 320 kilometers (199 miles) inland.

Gambia[2]. Africa's smallest independent state. Lying in West Africa, it comprises the lower valley of the Gambia River. It is primarily agricultural, peanuts being the mainstay of the economy. The Portuguese reached the Gambia region in 1456, and British merchants were granted trading rights in 1588. The area became a British protectorate in 1894 and an independent republic within the Commonwealth in 1970. From 1981 to 1989 Gambia and Senegal formed the Confederation of Senegambia, which involved economic integration and cooperation in foreign policy. Area, 11,295 square kilometers (4,360 square miles). Population, 800,000. Capital, Banjul (formerly Bathurst). **—Gam·bi·an** *adj. & n.*

gam·bier, gam·bir (găm′bîr′) *n.* A resinous, astringent obtained from a woody vine, *Uncaria gambier* (or *gambir*), of south-central Asia, used medicinally and in tanning and dyeing. [Malay *gambir.*]

gam·bit (găm′bĭt) *n.* **1.** A chess opening in which one or more pawns are offered in exchange for a favorable position. **2.** An opening remark or maneuver, as in a conversation or series of negotiations. [Earlier *gamet,* from Italian *gambetto,* "a tripping up," from *gamba,* leg. See **gambol.**]

gam·ble (găm′bəl) *v.* **-bled, -bling, -bles.** *—intr.* **1. a.** To bet money on the outcome of a game, contest, or other event. **b.** To play a game of chance for money or other stakes. **2.** To take a risk in the hope of gaining an advantage; speculate: *I gambled on his willingness to help me.* *—tr.* **1.** To put up in gambling; wager. **2.** To expose to hazard; risk. **3.** To lose by gambling: *gambled away their future.*
~n. 1. A bet, wager, or other gambling venture. **2.** An act or undertaking of uncertain outcome; a risk. [Probably from earlier *gamel,* from *gamner,* gambler, from *gamene,* to gamble, Middle English *gamenen,* Old English *gamenian,* to sport, play, from *gamen,* amusement. See **game.**] **—gam·bler** *n.*

gam·boge (găm-bōj′, -bōōzh′) *n.* **1.** A brownish or orange resin obtained from any of several trees of the genus *Garcinia,* of south-central Asia, and yielding a golden-yellow pigment. Also called "cambogia." **2.** A strong yellow. [New Latin *gambogium, cambugium,* obtained from CAMBODIA.] **—gam·boge** *adj.*

gam·bol (găm′bəl) *intr.v.* **-boled** or **-bolled, -boling** or **-bolling, -bols.** To leap about playfully; frolic; skip.
~n. A skipping or frolicking about. [Earlier *gamba(u)de,* from Old French *gambade,* from Italian *gambata,* from *gamba,* leg, from Late Latin *gamba,* leg, hoof, from Greek *kampē,* bend.]

gam·brel (găm′brəl) *n.* **1.** The hock of a horse or other animal. **2.** A wooden or metal frame used by butchers for hanging carcasses by the legs. [Old North French *gamberel,* diminutive of *gambier,* gambrel, from *gambe,* leg, from Late Latin *gamba,* hoof, leg.]

gambrel roof *n.* **1.** A ridged roof with two slopes on each side, the lower slope having the steeper pitch. **2.** *British.* A hipped roof that is topped by a small gable with vertical ends.

game¹ (gām) *n.* **1.** A way of amusing oneself; diversion: *Until she sold her first story, she thought of writing simply as a game.* **2. a.** A sport or other competitive activity governed by specific rules: *the game of tennis.* **b.** A single instance of such an activity: *We lost the first game.* **c. games.** A series of events, especially sporting events, for which competitors gather: *the Olympic Games.* **d.** The rules governing a game: *Her grandfather taught her the game.* **3. a.** The total number of points required to win a game: *One hundred points is game in bridge.* **b.** The score accumulated at any given time in a game: *At half time, the game was 14 to 12.* **4.** The equipment needed for playing certain games: *pack the children's games in the car.* **5.** A particular style or manner of playing a game: *His bridge game is only adequate.* **6. a.** A calculated plan or action for attaining an end: *The negotiators played a stalling game.* **b.** A scheme, especially one of dubious legality: *We saw through his game.* **7. a.** Wild animals, birds, or fish hunted for food or sport. Also used adjectivally: *game birds.* **b.** The flesh of game, eaten as food. **8. a.** Something hunted or fit to be hunted; quarry. **b.** An object of ridicule, teasing, or scorn: *His arrogance makes him fair game.* **9.** *Mathematics.* A set of rules defining an abstract model of a strategic competition. See **game theory.** **10.** *Informal.* A vocation or business, especially a competitive one: *the publishing game.*
~*v.* **gamed, gaming, games.** —*tr.* *Archaic.* To waste or lose by gambling. —*intr.* To play for money or other stakes.
~*adj.* **gamer, gamest. 1.** Plucky and unyielding in spirit; resolute. **2.** *Informal.* Ready and willing: *Are you game for a swim?* —See Synonyms at **brave.** [Middle English *game(n)*, Old English *gamen*, amusement, sport, from Common Germanic *gam-* (unattested), to enjoy.]

game² *adj.* **gamer, gamest.** Crippled; lame: *had a game leg.* [Perhaps from French *gambi†*, crooked.]

game·cock (gām'kŏk') *n.* A rooster trained for cockfighting. Also called "fighting cock."

game fowl *n.* **1.** A bird sought after as game. **2.** Any of several breeds of domestic fowl bred especially for cockfighting.

game·keep·er (gām'kē'pər) *n.* A person employed to protect and maintain game birds and animals, especially on an estate or game preserve.

gam·e·lan (găm'ə-lăn') *n.* A type of orchestra common in Southeast Asia, consisting mainly of tuned metal or wooden chimes and other percussion instruments. [Javanese.]

game laws *pl.n.* Regulations for the protection of game animals, including birds and fish, that define the hunting season for each species and place restrictions on the method of capture and on the number of animals that may be taken.

game·ly (gām'lē) *adv.* With pluck; courageously.

game·ness (gām'nĭs) *n.* Courage; pluck.

game plan *n.* **1.** A strategy devised for winning a game, as in football. **2.** A strategy for reaching an objective.

game point *n.* A state in a game, especially tennis, in which one side or player will win after gaining the next point.

game show *n.* A television show in which contestants vie for prizes, usually by playing a competitive game.

games·man·ship (gāmz'mən-shĭp') *n.* The art or practice of winning a game or contest by methods that may be unsportsmanlike or devious but that do not actually break the rules.

game·some (gām'səm) *adj.* Frolicsome; playful; merry. —**game·some·ly** *adv.* —**game·some·ness** *n.*

game·ster (gām'stər) *n.* A habitual gambler.

gam·e·tan·gi·um (găm'ə-tăn'jē-əm) *n., pl.* **-gia** (-jē-ə). *Botany.* An organ or cell in which gametes are produced, especially in primitive plant forms. [GAMET(O)- + Greek *angeion*, vessel.] —**gam·e·tan·gi·al** *adj.*

gam·ete (găm'ēt', gə-mēt') *n.* A germ cell possessing the haploid number of chromosomes (half the number of chromosomes possessed by the somatic or body cells); especially, a mature sperm or egg capable of participating in fertilization. See **fertilization.** [New Latin *gameta*, from Greek *gametē*, wife, and *gametēs*, husband, both from *gamos*, marriage.]

game theory *n.* The mathematical analysis of abstract models of situations involving a conflict of interest with the object of determining the best strategy and anticipating the reactions of opponents. It has applications in linear programming, statistical decision making, operations research, and military and economic planning. Also called "theory of games."

gameto– *prefix.* Indicates gamete; for example, **gametophyte, gametophore.** [New Latin, from GAMETE.]

ga·me·to·cyte (gə-mē'tə-sīt') *n.* A cell from which gametes develop by meiotic division; a spermatocyte or an oocyte. [GAMETO- + -CYTE.]

ga·me·to·gen·e·sis (gə-mē'tə-jĕn'ə-sĭs) *n.* Also **gam·e·tog·e·ny** (găm'ə-tŏj'ə-nē). The production of gametes. Also called "maturation." [GAMETO- + -GENESIS.] —**ga·me·to·gen·ic** (gə-mē'tə-jĕn'ĭk), **gam·e·tog·e·nous** (găm'ə-tŏj'ə-nəs) *adj.*

ga·me·to·phore (gə-mē'tə-fôr', -fōr') *n.* *Botany.* A structure, as in mosses, on which gametangia are borne. [GAMETO- + -PHORE.] —**ga·me·to·phor·ic** (gə-mē'tə-fôr'ĭk, -fōr'ĭk) *adj.*

ga·me·to·phyte (gə-mē'tə-fīt') *n.* *Botany.* The generation or form that reproduces sexually in a plant characterized by alternation of generations. Compare **sporophyte.** [GAMETO- + -PHYTE.] —**ga·me·to·phyt·ic** (gə-mē'tə-fĭt'ĭk) *adj.*

game warden *n.* One who looks after game, especially in a preserve or park.

gamey. Variant of **gamy.**

gam·ic (găm'ĭk) *adj.* Of or requiring fertilization in reproduction; sexual. [Greek *gamos*, marriage. See **gamete.**]

gam·i·ly (gā'mə-lē) *adv.* In a game manner; gamely.

gam·in (găm'ĭn) *n.* A boy who roams about the streets; urchin. [French, perhaps from German *Gammel*, loud rejoicing, (hence) ungainly young man, good-for-nothing, from Old High German *gaman*, amusement, game, from Common Germanic *gam-* (unattested), to enjoy.]

gam·ine (gă-mēn') *n.* **1.** A girl who roams about the streets; urchin. **2.** An attractively boyish girl or young woman. [French, feminine of GAMIN.]

gam·ing (gā'mĭng) *n.* The playing of games of chance; gambling. Also used adjectivally: *the gaming laws; a gaming house.*

gam·ma (găm'ə) *n.* **1.** The third letter in the Greek alphabet, written γ. Transliterated in English as *g*, or as *n* before *g, k,* or *kh*. See feature at **alphabet. 2.** A gamma ray. [Greek *gamma*, from Semitic, akin to Hebrew *gīmel*, probably "camel."]

gam·ma·di·on (gə-mä'dē-ŏn', -măd'ē-ŏn') *n., pl.* **-dia** (-dē-ə). A cross composed of four capital Greek gammas, especially so as to form a swastika; a fylfot. [Medieval Greek, from Greek, from GAMMA.]

gamma globulin *n.* Any of several globulin fractions of blood serum, most of which are immunoglobulins, used to treat infectious diseases, as measles.

gamma iron *n.* An allotropic form of iron that exists between 910°C and 1400°C and is nonmagnetic.

gamma ray *n.* **1.** Electromagnetic radiation emitted by radioactive decay and having energies in a range overlapping that of the highest energy x-rays, extending up to several hundred thousand electron volts. **2.** Electromagnetic radiation with energy greater than several hundred thousand electron volts. **3.** A high-energy photon.

gam·mer (găm'ər) *n.* *Regional.* An elderly woman. [Probably contraction of GODMOTHER or GRANDMOTHER.]

gam·mon¹ (găm'ən) *n.* A victory in backgammon occurring before the loser has removed a single man.
~*tr.v.* **gammoned, -moning, -mons.** To defeat in backgammon by scoring a gammon. [Probably from Middle English *gamen*, GAME.]

gammon² *n. British Informal.* Misleading or nonsensical talk; blather.
~*v.* **gammoned, -moning, -mons.** *British Informal.* —*tr.* To mislead by deceptive talk. —*intr.* To talk gammon. [Perhaps from thieves' slang expressions *to give gammon, to keep in gammon,* to talk to and divert the attention of someone while another thief is robbing him, perhaps slang use of GAMMON (backgammon term).] —**gam·mon·er** *n.*

gammon³ *n.* **1.** A ham that has been cured or smoked. **2.** The lower or bottom part of a side of bacon. [Old North French *gambon*, from *gambe*, leg, from Late Latin *gamba*, hoof, leg, from Greek *kampē*, a bend.]

gammon⁴ *tr.v.* **-moned, -moning, -mons.** *Nautical.* To fasten (a bowsprit) to the stem of a ship. [Perhaps from GAMMON (cured ham, hence "the tying up of a ham").]

gam·my (găm'ē) *adj.* **-mier, -miest.** *British Slang.* Lame; injured: *a gammy leg.* [Dialectal variant of GAME (lame).]

gamo– *prefix.* Indicates: **1.** Sexual union; for example, **gamogenesis. 2.** Union or fusion; for example, **gamopetalous.** [Greek *gamos*, marriage.]

gam·o·gen·e·sis (găm'ə-jĕn'ə-sĭs) *n.* Sexual reproduction. [GAMO- + -GENESIS.] —**gam·o·ge·net·ic** (găm'ə-jə-nĕt'ĭk) *adj.* —**gam·o·ge·net·i·cal·ly** *adv.*

gam·o·pet·al·ous (găm'ə-pĕt'l-əs) *adj.* *Botany.* Having or designating a corolla with the petals fused or partially fused; sympetalous. [New Latin *gamopetalus*: GAMO- + PETALOUS.]

gam·o·phyl·lous (găm'ə-fĭl'əs) *adj.* *Botany.* Having or designating united leaves or leaflike parts. [GAMO- + -PHYLLOUS.]

gam·o·sep·al·ous (găm'ə-sĕp'ə-ləs) *adj.* *Botany.* Having the sepals united or partly united; synsepalous. [GAMO- + -SEPALOUS.]

–gamous *suffix.* Indicates marriage or sexual union; for example, **bigamous, dichogamous.** [Greek *gamos*, marriage.]

gamp (gămp) *n. British Informal.* A large, baggy umbrella. Used humorously. [After Mrs. Sarah *Gamp*, nurse in Charles Dickens' *Martin Chuzzlewit* (1844), who owns such an umbrella.]

gam·ut (găm'ət) *n.* **1.** A complete range; extent: *a face that expresses the gamut of emotion, from rage to peaceful contentment.* **2.** The entire series of recognized musical notes. [Middle English, contracted from Medieval Latin *gamma ut : gamma,* note one tone lower than the first note in Guido d'Arezzo's scale, from the Greek letter GAMMA + *ut* (now *do*), lowest note in Guido's scale. (The notes of the scale are named after syllables in a Latin hymn to St. John: *Ut queant laxis resonāre fibris Mira gestorum famuli tuorum, Solve polluti labii reatum, Sancte Iohannes.*)]

gam·y, gam·ey (gā'mē) *adj.* **-ier, -iest. 1.** Having the flavor or odor of game, especially of game that has been hung too long. **2.** Showing an unyielding spirit; plucky; hardy: *a gamy little mare.* **3.** Scandalous; risqué. —**gam·i·ness** *n.*

–gamy *suffix.* Indicates marriage or sexual union; for example, **allogamy.** [Greek *-gamia*, from *gamos*, marriage.]

gan (găn) *intr.v.* **ganned, ganning, gans.** *British Regional.* To go. [Old English *gangan*; see **gang** (group).]

Gand. See **Ghent.**

gan·der (găn′dər) *n.* **1.** A male goose. **2.** *Informal.* A simpleton; a halfwit. **3.** *Slang.* A quick look; a glance. [Middle English *gander*, Old English *gandra, ganra.*]

Gan·der (găn′dər). A town in northeastern Newfoundland, Canada. It has grown around Gander Airport, one of the world's largest air terminals, whose air-traffic controllers take over North America-bound aircraft from Europe in mid-Atlantic.

Gan·dhi (găn′dē, gän′-), **Indira** (1917–84). Indian politician. She followed her father, Jawaharlal Nehru, India's first prime minister, into politics and became prime minister in 1966. In 1975 she declared a state emergency following allegations of repression and corruption, and was defeated in the 1977 election. She was re-elected in 1980 but was assassinated in 1984.

Gandhi, Mohandas Karamchand, known as "Mahatma" (1869–1948). Indian politician. He went to South Africa in 1893 to defend the Asian community there and developed his policy of Satyagraha, passive resistance. He returned to India in 1914 and became leader of the home rule movement. The British frequently imprisoned him for acts of civil disobedience. Independence was achieved in 1947, and Gandhi won worldwide respect for the bloodless way his aims had been achieved. He was murdered by a fanatic for his commitment to Hindu-Muslim reconciliation. —**Gan·dhi·an** *adj.*

Gandhi, Rajiv (1945–91). Indian politician, prime minister (1984–89). The son of Indira Gandhi, he played no part in politics until the death of his brother Sanjay in 1981. After Mrs. Gandhi's assassination (1984), he was sworn in as prime minister. He called for a general election, which he won by a landslide majority. He was assassinated while campaigning for re-election.

gan·dy dancer (găn′dē) *n. Slang.* **1.** A railroad worker. **2.** An itinerant laborer. [From the rhythmic movements of the railroad laborer working with tools produced by the now defunct *Gandy Manufacturing Company* in Chicago.]

ga·nef, go·nef (gä′nəf) *n.* A thief, scoundrel, or rascal. [Yiddish *ganef, gannef,* from Hebrew *gannābh,* from *gānnabh,* he stole.]

gang¹ (găng) *n.* **1.** A group of people who associate regularly on a social basis. **2.** A group of criminals, juvenile delinquents, or hoodlums who band together for mutual protection and profit. **3.** A group of laborers organized together on one job or under one foreman: *a railroad gang.* **4.** A set, especially of matched tools: *a gang of chisels.* **5. a.** A herd, especially of buffalo or elk. **b.** A pack of wolves or wild dogs. —*v.* **ganged, ganging, gangs.** —*intr.* To band together as a group or gang. —*tr.* **1.** To group together into a gang. **2.** *Electronics.* To arrange (two or more components) so that they can be varied by a single control. —**gang up.** *Informal.* **1.** To make an attack as a group: *ganged up on him and thrashed him soundly.* **2.** To act together as a group: *Countries should gang up against terrorism.* [Originally "a going," "journey," "way," Middle English *gang,* Old English *gang,* from Germanic.]

gang² *intr.v.* **ganged, ganging, gangs.** *Scottish.* To go. [Old English *gangan;* see **gang** (group).]

gang·bust·er (găng′bŭs′tər) *n. Slang.* A law officer who fights to break up organized criminal groups. —**like gangbusters.** *Slang.* With great force or zeal.

gang·er (găng′ər) *n. Chiefly British.* A gang foreman.

Gan·ges (găn′jēz′). *Hindi* **Gan·ga** (gŭng′gä). River of India and Bangladesh. It flows 2,505 kilometers (1,557 miles) from the Himalayas to the Bay of Bengal and has the largest delta in the world. It is the Hindus' most sacred river.

gang hook *n.* A multiple fishhook consisting of two or more hooks joined shank to shank. [From GANG (set of tools).]

gang·land (găng′lănd′) *n. Informal.* The criminal underworld.

gan·gli·at·ed (găng′glē-ā′tĭd) *adj.* Also **gan·gli·ate** (-ĭt, -āt′). Having ganglia.

gan·gling (găng′glĭng) *adj.* Also **gang·ly** (-glē), **-lier, -liest.** Tall, thin, and ungraceful; rangy. [Irregularly from dialectal *gang,* to go, from, Middle English *gangen,* from Old English *gangan.*]

gan·gli·on (găng′glē-ən) *n., pl.* **-glia** (-glē-ə) or **-ons. 1.** *Anatomy.* A group of nerve cell bodies, such as one located outside the brain or spinal cord. **2.** A center of power, activity, or energy. **3.** *Pathology.* A harmless cystic lesion resembling a tumor, occurring in a tendon sheath or joint capsule. [Greek *ganglion,* cystlike tumor, hence nerve bundle, ganglion.] —**gan·gli·on·ic** (găng′glē-ŏn′ĭk) *adj.*

gang·plank (găng′plăngk′) *n.* A board or ramp used as a removable footway between a ship and a pier. [GANG (in obsolete sense "passage") + PLANK.]

gang·plow (găng′plou′) *n.* A plow equipped with several blades that make parallel furrows. [GANG (set of tools) + PLOW.]

gan·grel (găng′grəl) *n. British Regional.* A vagabond; a drifter. [Middle English, from *gangen,* to go, Old English *gangan.*]

gan·grene (găng′grēn′, găng-grēn′) *n.* **1.** Death and decay of tissue in a part of the body, usually a limb, due to failure of blood supply, injury, or disease. Compare **necrobiosis. 2. a.** Moral decay. **b.** Something causing or symptomatic of moral decay. —*v.* **gangrened, -grening, -grenes.** —*tr.* To affect with gangrene. —*intr.* To become affected with gangrene. [Old French *gangrine,* from Latin *gangraena,* from Greek *gangraina.*] —**gan·gre·nous** (găng′grə-nəs) *adj.*

gang saw *n.* A saw in which a group of blades fitted in a frame make parallel simultaneous cuts.

gang·ster (găng′stər) *n.* A member of an organized group of criminals; a racketeer. [GANG + -STER.]

gangue (găng) *n.* The worthless rock or other material in which valuable minerals are found. [French, from German *Gang,* course, lode, vein, from Old High German, a going.]

gang·way (găng′wā′) *n.* **1.** *Nautical.* **a.** A passage along either side of a ship's upper deck. **b.** A gangplank. **c.** An opening in the bulwark of a ship through which passengers may board. **2.** *British.* **a.** The aisle that runs lengthwise and divides the seating sections of the House of Commons, separating the front and back benches. **b.** An aisle between seating sections, as in a theater. **3.** *Mining.* The main level of a mine. —*interj.* Used to clear a passage through a crowd or obstructed area. [GANG (in obsolete sense "passage") + WAY.]

gan·is·ter, gan·nis·ter (găn′ə-stər) *n.* **1.** A silicon-rich sedimentary rock used for refractory furnace linings. **2.** A mixture of fire clay and ground quartz used to line furnaces. [Origin unknown.]

gan·ja (gän′jə, găn′-) *n.* A highly resinous form of marijuana, prepared by collecting only the flowering tops and leaves of carefully selected and cultivated plants. [Hindi *gānjhā,* from Sanskrit *grñja.*]

gan·net (găn′ĭt) *n.* Any of several large sea birds of the genus *Morus;* especially, *M. bassanus,* of northern coastal regions, having white plumage with black wing tips and a yellow crown. [Middle English *ganat, ganett,* Old English *ganot.*]

gan·oid (găn′oid′) *adj.* Of, pertaining to, or characteristic of certain bony fishes, such as the sturgeon and the gar, having armorlike scales consisting of bony plates covered with layers of dentine and enamel. —*n.* A ganoid fish. [New Latin *Ganoidei* (former designation), from French *ganoïde,* having a shiny surface : Greek *ganos,* brightness, joy, from *ganusthai,* to rejoice.]

gansey. Variant of **ganzie.**

Gan·su or **Kan·su** (găn′soo′). Province in north-central China. Much of its population is Muslim. Its capital is Lanzhou (Lanchow).

gant·let¹, gaunt·let (gônt′lĭt, gŏnt′-, gănt′-) *n.* A section of double railroad tracks where the two inner tracks are overlapped in order to afford passage at a narrow place without switching. —*tr.v.* **gantleted, -leting, -lets.** To overlap (railroad tracks) to form a gantlet. [Alteration (influenced by GAUNTLET) of earlier *gant(e)lope,* from Swedish *gatlopp,* from Old Swedish *gatulop,* "passageway" : *gata,* road, way + *lop,* course.]

gant·let². 1. Variant of **gauntlet** (glove). **2.** Variant of **gauntlet** (ordeal).

gant·line (gănt′līn′, -lĭn) *n.* A rope passed through a single block at the top of a mast or stackpole and used for hoisting. [Perhaps alteration of *girtline* : GIRT (girdle) + LINE.]

gan·try (găn′trē) *n., pl.* **-tries. 1.** A bridgelike frame over which a traveling crane moves. **2.** A similar spanning frame supporting a group of railroad signals over several tracks. **3.** *Aerospace.* A massive vertical structure used in assembling or servicing rockets. **4.** A support for a barrel lying on its side. [Probably dialectal variant of *gallon-tree.*]

Gan·y·mede¹ (găn′ə-mēd′). *Greek Mythology.* A Trojan prince of great beauty whom Zeus carried away to be cupbearer to the gods.

Ganymede² *n. Astronomy.* The third moon of Jupiter, one of the largest planetary satellites in the solar system. [After GANYMEDE.]

gan·zie, gan·sey (găn′zē) *n. Northern British.* A knitted woolen pullover. [Alteration of GUERNSEY (pullover).]

gaol. *Chiefly British.* Variant of **jail.**

gap (găp) *n.* **1.** An opening, as in a partition or wall; cleft. **2.** A break in a mountain range; a pass or gorge. **3.** A suspension of continuity; hiatus: *a gap in his report.* **4.** A conspicuous difference; disparity: *a gap between expenses and receipts.* **5.** *Electricity.* A space traversed by an electric spark; spark gap. **6.** *Computer Science.* An absence of information on a recording medium, often used to signal the end of a segment of information. **7.** *Electronics.* The distance between the head of a recording device and the surface of the recording medium. —*v.* **gapped, gapping, gaps.** —*tr.* To make a gap in. —*intr.* To be or become open. [Middle English *gap(pe),* from Old Norse *gap,* chasm.]

gape (gāp, găp) *intr.v.* **gaped, gaping, gapes. 1.** To open the mouth wide; yawn. **2.** To stare wonderingly, as with the mouth open. **3.** To become widely open or separated: *The curtains gaped when the wind blew.* —See Synonyms at **gaze.** —*n.* **1.** An act or instance of gaping. **2.** A large opening. **3.** *Zoology.* The width of the space between the open jaws or mandibles of a vertebrate. **4. gapes.** Used with a singular verb. A disease of birds, especially young domesticated poultry, caused by gapeworms and resulting in obstructed breathing. **5. gapes.** A fit of yawning. [Middle English *gapen,* Old Norse *gapa,* to open the mouth.]

gap·er (gā′pər) *n.* Any of various marine bivalve mollusks of the genera *Lutraria* and *Mya,* having oval shells that gape at both ends; especially, the **soft-shell clam** *(see).*

gape·worm (gāp′wûrm′, găp′-) *n.* Any of several nematode worms of the genus *Syngamus;* especially, *S. trachea,* infecting the trachea of certain birds and causing gapes.

gap·ing (gā′pĭng) *adj.* Deep and wide open; cavernous: *a gaping wound.* —**gap·ing·ly** *adv.*

gap-toothed (găp′tootht′, -toothd′) *adj.* Having wide gaps between the teeth.

gap·y (gā′pē) *adj.* Afflicted with the gapes, as a bird.

gar¹ (gär) *n.* **1.** Any of several ganoid fishes of the genus *Lepisosteus,* of fresh and brackish waters of North and Central America, having

gannet *An adult gannet reaches maturity in its third year, when its plumage is all white except for black wing tips and a buff-colored head. It has a wingspan of up to 1.8 meters (6 feet).*

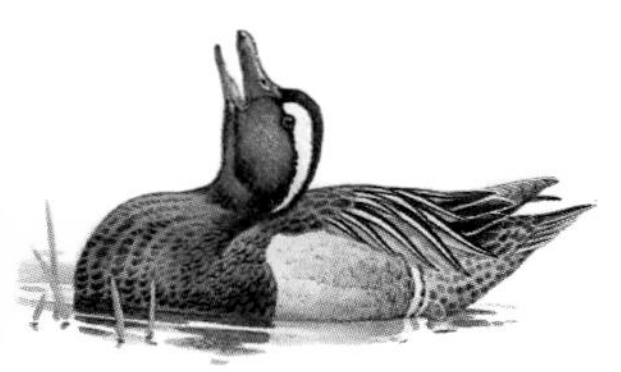

garganey *During courtship the male garganey throws back its head in a characteristic display. Garganeys migrate 5,000 kilometers (3,000 miles) from Africa to Europe to breed. They feed as they swim, dipping their heads underwater.*

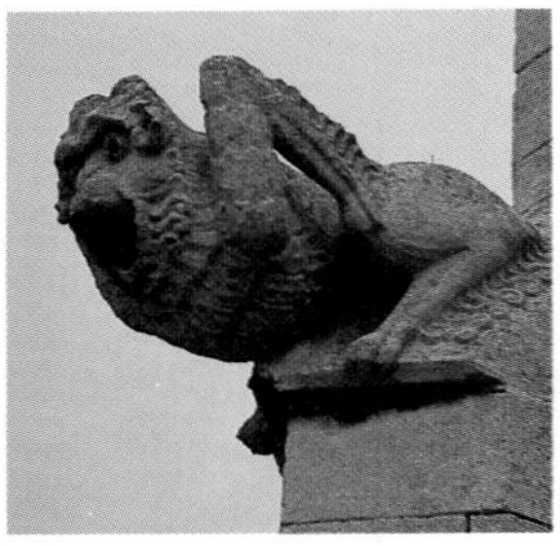

gargoyle *This grotesque figure peers down from the roof of a church at Thaxted, England.*

PRONUNCIATION KEY

ă, pat; ā, pay; âr, care;
ä, father, are; b, bib;
ch, church; d, deed; ĕ, pet;
ē, be; f, fife; g, gag; h, hat;
hw, which; ĭ, pit; ī, pie;
îr, pier; j, judge; k, kick;
l, lid, needle; m, mum;
n, no, sudden; ng, thing;
ŏ, pot; ō, toe; ô, paw, for;
oi, noise; ou, out; o͝o, book;
o͞o, boot; p, pop; r, roar;
s, sauce; sh, ship, dish;
t, tight; th, thin, path;
th, this, bathe; ŭ, cut; ûr, fur;
v, valve; w, with; y, yes;
z, zebra, size; zh, vision;
ə, about, item, edible, gallop, circus, peaceful

IN FOREIGN WORDS:

à, *Fr.* ami; œ, *Fr.* feu, *Ger.* schön; ü, *Fr.* tu, *Ger.* über; KH, *Ger.* ich, *Scot.* loch; N, *Fr.* bon; y', *Fr.* Compiègne

STRESS MARKS:

Primary stress: ′
in·cite′ (ĭn-sīt′)
Secondary stress: ′
in′sight′ (ĭn′sīt′)

an elongated body and a long snout. **2.** A similar or related fish, such as the needlefish. Also called "garfish," "garpike." [Short for GARFISH.]

gar² *tr.v.* **garred, garring, gars.** *Chiefly Scottish.* To cause or compel. [Middle English *gere,* from Old Norse *gera,* to make, do.]

ga·rage (gə-räzh′, -räj′) *n.* **1.** A building or wing of a building, as of a house, in which to park a car or cars. **2.** A commercial establishment where cars are repaired, serviced, or parked.
∼*tr.v.* **garaged, -raging, -rages.** To put or store in a garage. [French, from *garer,* to dock (ships), store in a garage, from Old French, to warn, protect, guard, from Frankish *warōn* (unattested).]

garage sale *n.* A sale of used household items or clothing held at the home of the seller. Also called "tag sale."

ga·ram ma·sa·la (gä′rəm mä-sä′lə) *n.* A mixture of spices used in Indian cooking.

garb (gärb) *n.* **1.** Clothing, especially if distinctive or unusual: *clerical garb.* **2.** An outward appearance; guise.
∼*tr.v.* **garbed, garbing, garbs.** To cover with or as if with clothing; dress; array. [Obsolete French *garbe,* graceful appearance, from Italian *garbo,* grace, elegance of dress, from Germanic.]

gar·bage (gär′bĭj) *n.* **1. a.** Food wastes, as from a kitchen. **b.** Refuse. **2.** Worthless matter; trash; rubbish: *rhetorical garbage.* **3.** *Computer Science.* Unwanted or incorrect information in a device's input, output, or storage. [Middle English, probably from Norman French *garbelage,* removal of discarded matter.]

gar·ban·zo (gär-bän′zō, -băn′zō) *n., pl.* **-zos.** A plant, the **chickpea** *(see),* or its edible seed. [Spanish *garbanzo,* alteration (influenced by *garroba,* carob) of Old Spanish *arvanço,* from Germanic, akin to Old High German *araweiz,* pea, Latin *ervum,* bitter vetch, probably of Asiatic origin.]

gar·ble (gär′bəl) *tr.v.* **-bled, -bling, -bles.** **1.** To unintentionally distort or confuse (an account or message) so that it becomes unintelligible. **2.** To deliberately distort (an account or message), especially by the selective omission of relevant data. **3.** *Archaic.* To sort out; cull.
∼*n.* The act or an instance of garbling. [Middle English *garbelen,* to sift, select, from Italian *garbellare,* from Arabic *gharbala,* from *ghirbāl,* sieve, from Late Latin *crībellāre,* to sift, from *crībellum,* diminutive of *crībrum,* sieve.] **—gar·bler** *n.*

gar·bo (gär′bō) *n., pl.* **-bos.** *Australian Informal.* A person employed to remove trash. [From *garbage.*]

Gar·bo (gär′bō), **Greta,** born Greta Gustavson or Gustaffson (1905–90). Swedish-born U.S. actress. She became a Hollywood star in 1926 but kept herself aloof and mysterious, retiring suddenly in 1941. Her films include Queen Christina (1933) and Camille (1936). She received a special Academy Award in 1954.

gar·board (gär′bôrd′, -bōrd′) *n. Nautical.* The first range or strake of planks laid next to the ship's keel. [Obsolete Dutch *gaarboord* : perhaps *garen,* to gather, contraction of Middle Dutch *gaderen* + Dutch *boord,* border, ship's side, from Middle Dutch *bort,* board.]

gar·boil (gär′boil′) *n. Archaic.* Confusion; uproar. [Old French *garbouil(le),* from Old Italian *garbuglio,* reduplicative formation (with *gar-* for *bar-*) from Latin *bullīre,* to boil, bubble.]

García Lorca, Federico. See **Lorca.**

García Márquez, Gabriel. See **Márquez.**

Gar·ci·la·so de la Ve·ga (gär-sē-lä′sô dā lā vā′gə) (1503–36). Spanish poet and soldier. The first and most influential major poet in the Golden Age of Spanish literature, he incorporated Italian meter into his poetry, a small but highly acclaimed body of work. At the age of 33, he was fatally wounded in battle.

gar·çon (gär-sôN′) *n., pl.* **-çons** (-sôN′). A waiter, especially in a French restaurant. [French, from old French *garçun,* servant.]

Gar·da, Lake (gär′də). Lake in northern Italy, the largest in the country. The sheltering Alps to the north and the mitigating effects of the lake give its shores an unusually temperate climate.

gar·den (gärd′n) *n.* **1.** A plot of land, often adjoining a house, used for the cultivation of grass, flowers, vegetables, or fruit. **2.** *Often* **gardens.** Grounds adorned with flowers, shrubs, and trees for public enjoyment. **3.** An open-air business establishment where refreshments are served: *a tea garden.* **4.** A fertile, well-cultivated region: *California is the garden of the United States.* **—lead someone up the garden path.** *Informal.* To mislead.
∼*v.* **gardened, -dening, -dens.** —*tr.* To cultivate (a plot of ground) as a garden. —*intr.* **1.** To tend a garden. **2.** To work as a gardener.
∼*adj.* **1.** Of, pertaining to, intended for, or found in a garden: *garden flowers.* **2.** Surrounded by gardens; provided with open areas and greenery: *a garden community.* **3.** Of, pertaining to, or being an apartment situated on the ground floor of a building and usually having access to a garden. [Middle English *gardyn,* from Old North French *gardin,* from Vulgar Latin *(hortus) gardīnus* (unattested), "enclosed (garden)," from *gardo* (unattested), fence, enclosure, from Frankish *gardo* (unattested).]

garden center *n.* A place where trees, plants, gardening tools, garden furniture, and similar items are sold.

garden city *n.* A town of limited size planned so as to provide a pleasant nonurban environment, with low-density housing and plenty of trees and open space.

garden cress *n.* A pungent-tasting plant, *Lepidium sativum,* that has fragrant white or pinkish flowers and is cultivated for use in salads.

gar·den·er (gärd′nər, gärd′n-ər) *n.* A person who works in or tends a garden for pleasure or profit.

garden heliotrope *n.* A widely cultivated species of valerian, *Valeriana officinalis,* having clusters of small purplish, pink, or white flowers.

gar·de·nia (gär-dēn′yə, -dē′nē-ə) *n.* **1.** Any of various shrubs and trees of the genus *Gardenia;* especially, *G. jasminoides,* native to China, having glossy, evergreen leaves and large, fragrant, usually white waxy flowers. This species is also called "Cape jasmine." **2.** The flower of this shrub. [New Latin *Gardenia,* after Dr. Alexander *Garden* (*c.* 1730–91), Scottish-born naturalist.]

gar·den·ing (gärd′nĭng, gärd′n-ĭng) *n.* The work or occupation of tending a garden or cultivating plants.

Garden of Eden *n.* **Eden** *(see).*

garden party *n.* A social gathering held on a lawn, at which refreshments are served.

garden suburb *n.* A planned, low-density residential suburb with gardens and community facilities.

garde·robe (gärd′rōb′) *n. Archaic.* **1. a.** A chamber for storing clothes; a wardrobe. **b.** The contents of a wardrobe. **2.** Any private chamber. [Middle English, from Old French : *garder, guarder,* to GUARD + *robe,* ROBE.]

Gard·ner (gärd′nər), **Erle Stanley** (1889–1970). U.S. author. While working as a lawyer in California, he began writing magazine detective stories, then full-length books. Most of them featured a wily attorney, Perry Mason, his secretary, Della Street, and adroit legal maneuvering to unmask the murderers.

Gar·field (gär′fēld′), **James Abram** (1831–81). 20th U.S. president (1881). After serving as a Civil War officer and as a U.S. congressman (1863–80), he won the controversial Republican nomination and the presidential election of 1880. On July 2, 1881, five months into his term, he was mortally wounded by Charles Guiteau (1841–82), a frustrated office seeker. Garfield died 11 weeks later.

gar·fish (gär′fĭsh′) *n., pl.* **-fishes** or collectively **garfish.** Either of two fishes, the **gar** or the **garpike** *(both of which see).* [Middle English *garfyssh,* probably "spear fish" : *gare, gore,* spear, Old English *gār* + FISH.]

gar·ga·ney (gär′gə-nē) *n., pl.* **-neys** or collectively **garganey.** An Old World duck, *Anas querquedula,* having a conspicuous white stripe over each eye and down the back of the head in the male. Also called "garganey teal." [Italian dialectal *gargenei* (imitative).]

Gar·gan·tu·a (gär-găn′cho͞o-ə). A giant king noted for his enormous physical and intellectual appetites, the hero of Rabelais' satires *Gargantua* and *Pantagruel.*

gar·gan·tu·an (gär-găn′cho͞o-ən) *adj. Often* **Gargantuan.** Of immense size or volume; gigantic; colossal; huge. **—**See Synonyms at **enormous.**

gar·get (gär′gĭt) *n.* Mastitis of domestic animals, especially cattle. [Perhaps specialized use of Middle English *garget, gargat,* throat; from Old French *garguette, gargate,* from Old Provençal *gargata,* probably from Latin *gurges,* throat.]

gar·gle (gär′gəl) *v.* **-gled, -gling, -gles.** —*intr.* **1.** To force exhaled air through a liquid held in the back of the mouth, with the head tilted back, in order to cleanse or medicate the mouth or throat. **2.** To produce the characteristic sound of gargling. —*tr.* **1.** To rinse or medicate (the mouth or throat) by gargling. **2.** To circulate or apply (a solution or medicine) by gargling. **3.** To utter with a gargling sound.
∼*n.* **1.** A medicated solution for gargling. **2.** An act of gargling. **3.** A gargling sound. [Old French *gargouiller,* from *gargouille, garoule,* throat, GARGOYLE.]

gar·goyle (gär′goil′) *n.* **1.** A roof spout carved to represent a grotesque human or animal figure, and projecting from a gutter to carry rainwater clear of the wall. **2.** Any grotesque ornamental figure or projection. **3.** A person of grotesque appearance. [Middle English *gargoyl,* from Old French *gargouille, gargoul,* "throat," from Latin *gurguliō,* windpipe.]

gar·i·bal·di (găr′ə-bôl′dē) *n.* **1.** A loose high-necked blouse styled after the red shirts of Garibaldi and his soldiers, fashionable among women in the mid-19th century. **2.** *British.* A type of cooky containing a layer of currants.

Ga·ri·bal·di (găr′ə-bôl′dē), **Giuseppe** (1807–82). Italian soldier and nationalist leader. He and his 1,000 volunteers, the Redshirts, captured Sicily and Naples (1860) to add to the kingdom of Italy.

gar·ish (gâr′ĭsh, găr′-) *adj.* **1. a.** Marred by strident color or excessive ornamentation; gaudy; tawdry. **b.** Loud and flashy: *garish make-up.* **2.** Glaring; dazzling: *"Hide me from Day's garish eye"* (Milton). [Formerly also *gaurish,* perhaps from obsolete *gaur,* to stare, Middle English *gauren*†.] **—gar·ish·ly** *adv.* **—gar·ish·ness** *n.*

gar·land (gär′lənd) *n.* **1.** A wreath, circlet, or festoon of flowers, leaves, or other material worn as a crown or collar, or hung as an ornament. **2.** A representation of a garland in metal or other material, for ornamentation or as a heraldic device. **3.** Something resembling a garland. **4.** A mark of victory or distinction; a prize. **5.** *Nautical.* A ring or collar of rope or wire used to hoist spars or prevent rubbing or fraying. **6.** An anthology, as of ballads or poems.
∼*tr.v.* **garlanded, -landing, -lands.** **1.** To embellish or deck with a garland. **2.** To serve as a garland for. [Middle English *gerlond, garland,* from Old French *gerlande, garlande,* "ornament made with gold threads," from Frankish *wiara, weara* (unattested), wire, thread.]

Gar·land (gär′lənd), **(Hannibal) Hamlin** (1860–1940). U.S. author. He spent most of his life in the farming country of the Middle West and used the harsh realities of the farmers' lives as the inspiration for his stories and novels. Garland is best known for his autobiographical work *Son of the Middle Border* (1917).

Garland, Judy, born Frances Gumm (1922–69). U.S. singer and actress. She made her stage debut at five and starred in *The Wizard of Oz* (1939). In 1939 she received a special Academy Award.

gar·lic (gär′lĭk) *n.* **1.** A plant, *Allium sativum,* related to the onion, having a bulb with a strong, distinctive odor and flavor. **2.** The bulb of this plant, divisible into separate cloves and used as a flavoring. [Middle English *garlec, garly,* Old English *gārlēac,* "spear leek" (from its spear-shaped leaves) : *gār,* spear + *lēac,* leek.]

gar·lick·y (gär′lĭ-kē) *adj.* Containing, tasting of, or smelling of garlic.

garlic mustard *n.* A weedy plant, *Alliaria officinalis* (or *petiolata*), native to Europe, having small white flowers and an odor of garlic. Also called "hedge mustard."

gar·ment (gär′mənt) *n.* Any article of clothing.
∼*tr.v.* **garmented, -menting, -ments.** To clothe; to dress. Usually used in the passive. [Middle English *gar(ne)ment,* from Old French *garnement,* "equipment," from *g(u)arnir,* to furnish, equip.]

garn (gärn) *interj. British Informal.* Used to express derision or disbelief. [Cockney pronunciation spelling of *go on.*]

gar·ner (gär′nər) *tr.v.* **-nered, -nering, -ners. 1.** To gather and store in or as if in a granary. **2.** To amass; acquire.
∼*n.* A granary. [Middle English *gerner, garner,* granary, from Old French *gernier, grenier,* from Latin *grānārium,* from *grānum,* grain.]

gar·net[1] (gär′nĭt) *n.* **1.** Any of several widespread silicate minerals, often embedded in igneous and metamorphic rocks, colored red, brown, black, green, yellow, or white and used both as gemstones and as abrasives. **2.** A dark to very dark red. [Middle English *gernet, granate,* from Old French *grenat,* dark red, garnet, pomegranate-colored, from *pome grenate,* POMEGRANATE.]

garnet[2] *n. Nautical.* A tackle for hoisting light cargo. [Middle English *garnett,* probably from Middle Dutch *garnaat, karnaat*†.]

gar·ni·er·ite (gär′nē-ə-rīt′) *n.* A mineral, $(Ni,Mg)_6(OH)_8Si_4O_8 \cdot H_2O$, apple-green in color and an important nickel ore. [Discovered by Jules *Garnier* (died 1904), French geologist.]

gar·nish (gär′nĭsh) *tr.v.* **-nished, -nishing, -nishes. 1.** To enhance the appearance of by adding decorative touches; especially, to embellish (food) by decorating it, as with a sprig of parsley or a slice of lemon. **2.** *Law.* To garnishee.
∼*n.* **1. a.** Ornamentation; embellishment. **b.** Something used to garnish food. **2.** An unwarranted fee, as one formerly extorted from a new prisoner in an English jail by a jailer. [Middle English *garnysshen,* to equip, adorn, from Old French *guarnir, garnir* (present stem *garniss-*), from Germanic.] **—gar·nish·er** *n.*

gar·nish·ee (gär′nĭ-shē′) *n. Law.* **1.** A debtor against whom a plaintiff has instituted a process of garnishment. **2.** A third party who has been warned that money or property in his control but due or belonging to the defendant has been attached.
∼*tr.v.* **garnisheed, -eeing, -ees.** *Law.* **1.** To attach (a debtor's pay, for example) by garnishment. **2.** To serve with a garnishment.

gar·nish·ment (gär′nĭsh-mənt) *n.* **1.** Ornamentation; embellishment. **2.** *Law.* **a.** A legal proceeding whereby money or property due or belonging to a debtor but currently in the possession of a third party, such as a trustee, is applied to the payment of the debt to the plaintiff. **b.** A court order directing a third party who owes a defendant money or holds property belonging to him, to withhold such money or property. Also called "trustee process."

gar·ni·ture (gär′nĭ-chər) *n.* Something that garnishes or decorates; embellishment. [Old French *garniture, garneture,* from *garnir,* to GARNISH.]

Ga·ronne (gä-rôn′). River of southwest France. It rises in the Spanish Pyrenees and flows 503 kilometers (312 miles) through Toulouse and Bordeaux to the Gironde estuary. Its main tributaries are the Lot, Tarn, and Ariège.

gar·pike (gär′pīk′) *n.* **1.** A fish, the **gar** *(see).* **2.** A marine fish, *Belone belone,* of European waters, having long toothed jaws and green bones. Also called "garfish."

gar·ret (găr′ĭt) *n.* A room on the top floor of a house, typically immediately under a pitched roof; an attic. [Middle English *garet(te),* turret, watchtower, from Old French *garite,* from *g(u)arir,* to defend, protect, from Germanic.]

gar·ret·eer (găr′ə-tîr′) *n.* A person who lives in a garret, especially a struggling artist.

Gar·rick (găr′ĭk), **David** (1717–79). English actor and theater manager. He was considered the foremost Shakespearean actor of his time.

gar·ri·son (găr′ĭ-sən) *n.* **1.** A military post, especially one permanently established. **2.** The troops stationed at such a post.
∼*tr.v.* **garrisoned, -soning, -sons. 1.** To assign (troops) to a military post. **2.** To supply (a post) with troops. **3.** To occupy as or convert into a garrison. [Middle English *gariso(u)n,* protection, fortress, from Old French *garison,* from *g(u)arir,* to protect, from Germanic.]

Gar·ri·son (găr′ĭ-sən), **William Lloyd** (1805–79). U.S. abolitionist. On January 1, 1831, he published the first issue of his militant weekly *The Liberator,* which he continued publishing until the passage of the Thirteenth Amendment in 1865. Garrison was best known for his fiery polemics and his demand, "I will be heard."

garrison cap *n.* A soft cloth cap without a visor, worn as a dress headgear chiefly by Army and Air Force personnel. Also called "overseas cap."

gar·rote, gar·rotte (gə-rŏt′, -rōt′) *n.* **1. a.** A former Spanish method of execution by strangulation or by breaking the neck with an iron collar screwed tight with a knoblike device. **b.** A collar used for this. **2.** Strangulation, especially in order to rob.
∼*tr.v.* **garroted** or **garrotted, -roting** or **-rotting, -rotes** or **rottes. 1.** To execute by garrote. **2.** To strangle or throttle, especially in order to rob. [Spanish, cudgel, probably from Old French *garrot,* earlier *guaroc,* club turning rod, from *garokier*†, to bend down, strangle.] **—gar·rot·er** *n.*

gar·ru·li·ty (gə-ro͞o′lə-tē) *n.* Talkativeness; chattiness: *"Its style is relaxed to the point of garrulity"* (Dwight Macdonald).

gar·ru·lous (găr′ə-ləs, găr′yə-) *adj.* **1.** Habitually talkative; loquacious. **2.** Wordy; prolix. —See Synonyms at **talkative.** [Latin *garrulus,* from *garrīre,* to chatter.] **—gar·ru·lous·ly** *adv.* **—gar·ru·lous·ness** *n.*

gar·ry·a (găr′ē-ə) *n.* Any evergreen shrub of the American genus *Garrya,* some species of which have long catkins and are grown for ornament. [New Latin, after Nicholas *Garry,* 19th-century English official of the Hudson's Bay Company.]

gar·ter (gär′tər) *n.* **1. a.** An elasticized band worn around the leg to support a sock or stocking. **b.** A suspender strap with a fastener attached to a girdle or belt for supporting hose. **c.** An elasticized band worn around the arm to keep the sleeve pushed up. **2. Garter. a.** The **Order of the Garter** *(see).* **b.** The badge of this order. **c.** Membership in this order.
∼*tr.v.* **gartered, -tering, -ters. 1.** To fasten and hold with a garter. **2.** To put a garter upon. [Middle English *garter, garder,* from Old North French *gartier,* from *garet,* bend of the knee, from Gaulish *garr-* (unattested), leg.]

garter belt *n.* An undergarment for women consisting of an adjustable belt with garters for the support of hose. Also *British* "suspender belt."

garter snake *n.* **1.** Any of various nonvenomous North American snakes of the genus *Thamnophis,* having longitudinal stripes. **2.** Any of several African snakes of the genus *Elaps,* marked with black and white bands.

garter stitch *n.* **1.** A knitting stitch formed by working each row in plain stitch only. **2. a.** The raised pattern formed by this technique. **b.** Material worked in garter stitch.

garth (gärth) *n.* **1.** A grassy quadrangle surrounded by cloisters. **2.** *Archaic.* A yard, garden, or paddock. [Middle English, from Old Norse *garthr,* yard.]

Gar·vey (gär′vē), **Marcus (Moziah) Aurelius** (1887–1940). Jamaican black nationalist active in America. The founder of the Universal Negro Improvement Association (1914), he moved to New York (1916) and became a highly influential leader who called for economic independence of blacks and a large-scale resettlement of blacks in Liberia.

gas (găs) *n., pl.* **gases** or **gasses. 1. a.** The state of matter distinguished from the solid and liquid states by very low density and viscosity, relatively great expansion and contraction with changes in pressure and temperature, the ability to diffuse readily, and the spontaneous tendency to become distributed uniformly throughout any container. **b.** A substance in this state. **c.** A substance in this state at room temperature and atmospheric pressure. **2.** A gaseous fuel such as **natural gas** *(see).* **3.** *Mining.* An explosive mixture of firedamp (methane) and air. **4.** A gaseous asphyxiant, irritant, or poison. **5.** A gaseous anesthetic. **6. a.** Gasoline. **b.** The speed control of a gasoline engine: *pressed the gas to the floor.* **7.** *Slang.* Idle or boastful talk. **8.** *Slang.* Something providing great fun and excitement: *The party was a real gas.* **—step on the gas. 1.** *Informal.* To accelerate in a motor vehicle. **2.** To go faster; hurry up.
∼*v.* **gassed, gassing, gases** or **gasses.** —*tr.* **1.** To supply with gas or gasoline. **2.** To treat chemically with gas. **3.** To disable or kill with gas. —*intr.* **1.** To give off gas. **2.** *Slang.* To talk excessively. **3.** *Informal.* To fill the tank of a motor vehicle with gasoline: *gassed up before leaving on our vacation.* [Dutch *gas,* an occult principle supposed to be present in all bodies, coined (by J.B. van Helmont, 1577–1644, Belgian chemist) from Greek *khaos,* CHAOS.]

gas·bag (găs′băg′) *n.* **1.** An expandable bag for holding gas. **2.** *Slang.* One given to empty chatter.

gas burner *n.* A nozzle or jet on a fitting through which combustible gas is released to burn.

gas chamber *n.* A sealed enclosure in which prisoners sentenced to death are killed by means of a poisonous gas.

gas chromatography *n.* Chromatography in which the substance to be analyzed is vaporized and diffused along with a carrier gas through a liquid or solid adsorbent for differential adsorption. See **gas-liquid chromatography.**

gas coal *n.* Coal containing a large amount of volatile hydrocarbons, suitable for converting into fuel gas.

gas·con (găs′kən) *n.* A boastful person; a braggart. [French, from Old French *gascon,* GASCON (from the traditional garrulity of the Gascons).]

Gas·con (găs′kən) *n.* **1.** A native of Gascony. **2.** The French dialect of the Gascons.
∼*adj.* Of or pertaining to Gascony or the Gascons.

gas·con·ade (găs′kə-nād′) *n.* Boastfulness; bravado; swagger.
∼*intr.v.* **gasconaded, -ading, -ades.** To boast or swagger.

gas constant *n. Symbol* **R.** The constant in the ideal gas law, equal to 8.3143 joules per kelvin per mole. Also called "universal gas constant."

Gas·co·ny (găs′kə-nē). *French* **Gas·cogne** (gȧs-kôn′yə). Ancient province in southwest France. It is bounded by the Garonne River,

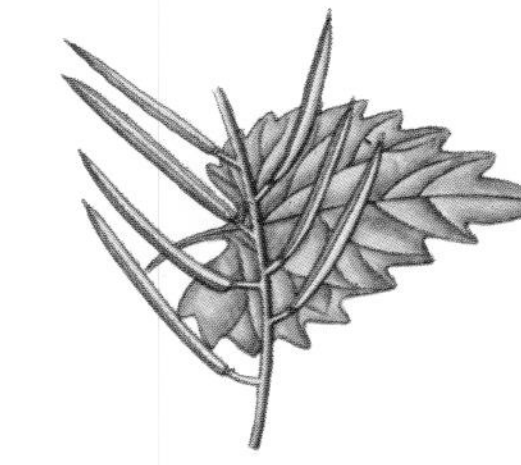

garlic mustard *Known also as hedge garlic, its leaves give off a strong smell of garlic when crushed.*

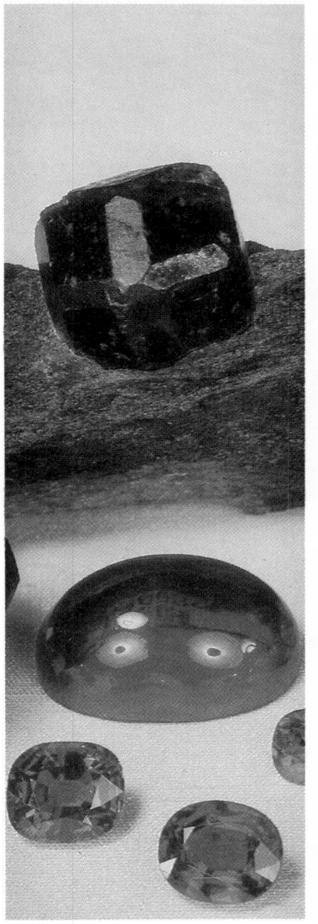

garnet *Garnet is the name given to a group of minerals that share a common crystalline structure and similar chemical composition. As jewelry, it was popular in Victorian times.*

the Pyrenees, and the Atlantic. In the 6th century it was settled by the Vascones (Basques), who later set up the duchy of Vasconia. This was united with neighboring Aquitaine in 1052.

gas-cooled reactor (găs'kōōld') *n.* A nuclear reactor in which heat is removed from the core by a gaseous coolant, usually carbon dioxide. See **advanced gas-cooled reactor.**

gas·e·lier, gas·o·lier (găs'ə-lîr') *n.* A chandelier having tubular branches with gas jets. [*gas* +chand*elier.*]

gas·e·ous (găs'ē-əs, găsh'əs) *adj.* **1.** Of, pertaining to, or existing as a gas. **2.** Lacking concreteness; tenuous.

gas equation *n.* An equation applying to ideal gases: $pV = nRT$, where p is the pressure, V the volume, n the amount of substance (number of moles), R the gas constant, and T the thermodynamic temperature. The equation approximately describes the behavior of real gases. Also called "ideal gas law."

gas fitter *n.* A workman who installs or repairs gas pipes, fixtures, or appliances.

gas gangrene *n.* Gangrene occurring in a wound infected with bacteria of the genus *Clostridium,* especially with *C. welchii* or *C. oedematiens,* and characterized by the presence of gas in the affected tissue and constitutional septic symptoms.

gash (găsh) *tr.v.* **gashed, gashing, gashes.** To make a long, deep cut in; slash deeply.
~*n.* **1.** A long, deep cut. **2.** A deep flesh wound. [Earlier *garsh, garse,* Middle English *garsen,* to cut, slash, from Old North French *garser,* probably from Late Latin *charaxāre,* from Greek *kharassein,* to carve, cut.]

gas·hold·er (găs'hōl'dər) *n.* A storage container for fuel gas, especially a large, telescoping, cylindrical tank. Also called "gasometer."

gas·i·form (găs'ə-fôrm') *adj.* In the form of gas; gaseous.

gas·i·fy (găs'ə-fī') *v.* **-fied, -fying, -fies.** —*tr.* **1.** To convert into gas. **2.** To produce gas from (wood or coal, for example). —*intr.* To become gas. —**gas·i·fi·a·ble** *adj.* —**gas·i·fi·ca·tion** *n.*

gas jet *n.* **1.** A gas burner. **2.** The flame of burning gas from a gas burner.

Gas·kell (găs'kəl), **Elizabeth Cleghorn,** born Elizabeth Cleghorn Stevenson (1810–65). English novelist. She wrote *Cranford* (1853), *North and South* (1855), and a biography of her friend Charlotte Brontë (1857).

gas·ket (găs'kĭt) *n.* **1.** Any of a wide variety of seals or packings used between matched machine parts or around pipe joints to prevent the escape of a gas or fluid. **2.** *Nautical.* A cord or canvas strap used to secure a furled sail to a yard boom or gaff. —**blow a gasket.** *Slang.* To explode with anger. [Perhaps variant of obsolete *gassit,* from French *garcette,* "little girl," rope, diminutive of *garce,* girl, from *gars,* boy.]

gas·kin (găs'kĭn) *n.* **1.** The part of the hind leg of a horse or related animal between the stifle and the hock. **2. gaskins.** *Obsolete.* Galligaskins. [Probably shortened from GALLIGASKINS.]

gas law *n.* A law, as Boyle's law or Charles's law, relating to the pressure, volume, and temperature of gases.

gas·light (găs'līt') *n.* **1.** Light produced by burning illuminating gas. **2.** A gas burner or lamp.

gas-liq·uid chromatography (găs'lĭk'wĭd) *n. Abbr.* **GLC** A form of gas chromatography in which the adsorbent medium is an inert solid coated with a liquid.

gas log *n.* A gas heater designed to look like a log for use in a fireplace.

gas main *n.* A major pipeline or conduit conveying gas to smaller pipes for distribution to consumers.

gas·man (găs'măn') *n., pl.* **-men** (-měn'). **1.** A person employed to read gas meters for the billing of consumers. **2.** A gas fitter.

gas mantle *n.* An incandescent mantle used in a gaslight.

gas mask *n.* A respirator covering the face and having a chemical air filter to protect against poisonous gases.

gas meter *n.* A device for measuring the rate of flow of a gas; especially, a device for measuring and recording the amount of fuel gas used by a domestic consumer.

gas·o·hol (găs'ə-hôl') *n.* A fuel consisting of a blend of ethanol and unleaded gasoline, especially a blend of 10 percent ethanol and 90 percent gasoline. [GAS(OLINE) + (ALC)OHOL.]

gas oil *n.* A mixture of hydrocarbons intermediate between paraffin and lubricating oil, obtained by distilling petroleum and used as fuel.

gasolier. Variant of **gaselier.**

gas·o·line, gas·o·lene (găs'ə-lēn', găs'ə-lēn') *n.* A volatile mixture of flammable liquid hydrocarbons derived chiefly from crude petroleum and used principally as a fuel for internal-combustion engines and as a solvent, illuminant, and thinner.

gas·om·e·ter (gă-sŏm'ə-tər) *n.* **1.** A gasholder (*see*). **2.** An apparatus for measuring the volume of gases. [French *gazomètre : gaz,* from GAS + -METER.]

gasp (găsp, gäsp) *v.* **gasped, gasping, gasps.** —*intr.* **1.** To draw in or catch the breath sharply, as from shock. **2.** To breathe convulsively or laboriously. **3.** *Informal.* To long; crave. Used with *for: gasping for a drink.* —*tr.* To utter between gasps. Often used with *out.*
~*n.* A short convulsive intake or catching of the breath. [Middle English *ga(y)spen,* from Old Norse *geispa.*]

Gaspar. See **Caspar.**

Gas·pé Peninsula (găs-pā'). A peninsula in eastern Quebec, Canada, between the mouth of the St. Lawrence River and Chaleur Bay. The peninsula has mountains, forests, and picturesque villages

along the coast and is noted for its hunting, fishing, and spectacular scenery.

gasp·er (găs'pər, gä'spər) *n.* **1.** One who gasps. **2.** *British Slang.* A cigarette.

gas plant *n.* A plant, *Dictamnus albus,* native to Eurasia, having aromatic foliage and white flowers and emitting a vapor capable of being ignited. Also called "burning bush," "dittany," "fraxinella."

gas poker *n.* A device resembling a hollow poker that is fitted with a gas jet and ignited to kindle a fire.

gas ring *n.* A device consisting of a set of gas jets arranged in a circle, as on a gas stove.

gas·ser (găs'ər) *n.* **1.** A well or drilling that yields natural gas. **2.** *Slang.* Something unusually entertaining; a gas.

gas station *n.* A filling station (*see*).

gas·sy (găs'ē) *adj.* **-sier, -siest. 1.** Containing, full of, or resembling gas. **2.** *Slang.* Bombastic; boastful.

gast (găst) *tr.v.* **gasted, gasting, gasts.** *Obsolete.* To scare. [Middle English *gasten,* Old English *gæstan.*]

gast·ar·bei·ter (găst'är'bī'tər) *n., pl.* **gastarbeiter.** An immigrant worker; especially a worker in West Germany of Italian, Yugoslav, or Turkish origin. [German, "guest worker."]

gas thermometer *n.* An apparatus for measuring temperature by determining the volume of a gas at constant pressure (*constant-pressure gas thermometer*) or by the pressure at constant volume (*constant-volume gas thermometer*).

gas-tight (găs'tīt') *adj.* Not permitting the escape or entry of gas.

gas·trec·to·my (gă-strĕk'tə-mē) *n., pl.* **-mies.** Surgical excision of part or all of the stomach. [GASTR(O)- + -ECTOMY.]

gas·tric (găs'trĭk) *adj.* Of, pertaining to, or near the stomach. [French *gastrique,* from New Latin *gastricus,* from Greek *gastēr,* (stem *gastr-*), belly, womb.]

gastric gland *n.* Any of various tubular glands in the mucous membrane lining the stomach that secrete gastric juice.

gastric juice *n.* The colorless, watery, acidic digestive fluid secreted by the gastric glands of the stomach and containing hydrochloric acid, pepsin, rennin, and mucin.

gastric ulcer *n.* An ulcer in the mucous membrane lining the stomach.

gas·trin (găs'trĭn) *n.* A hormone secreted by the gastric mucosa that stimulates production of gastric juice. [GASTR(O)- + -IN.]

gas·tri·tis (gă-strī'tĭs) *n.* Chronic or acute inflammation of the stomach. [New Latin : GASTR(O)- + -ITIS.]

gastro–, gastr– *prefix.* Indicates stomach; for example, **gastroscope, gastritis.** [Greek *gastēr* (stem *gastr-*), belly, womb.]

gas·troc·ne·mi·us (găs'trŏk-nē'mē-əs) *n.* The muscle that forms the major part of the calf of the leg. [New Latin, from Greek *gastroknēmē,* calf of the leg : GASTRO- (belly) + *knēmē,* shin, leg.]

gas·tro·en·ter·ic (găs'trō-ĕn-tĕr'ĭk) *adj.* Gastrointestinal.

gas·tro·en·ter·i·tis (găs'trō-ĕn'tə-rī'tĭs) *n.* Inflammation of the mucous membrane of the stomach and intestine.

gas·tro·en·ter·ol·o·gy (găs'trō-ĕn'tə-rŏl'ə-jē) *n.* The medical study of diseases of the stomach and the intestines. —**gas·tro·en·ter·o·log·i·cal** (găs'trō-ĕn'tər-ə-lŏj'ĭ-kəl) *adj.* —**gas·tro·en·ter·ol·o·gist** *n.*

gas·tro·en·ter·os·to·my (găs'trō-ĕn'tə-rŏs'tə-mē) *n., pl.* **-mies.** The surgical formation of a passage between the stomach and the small intestine.

gas·tro·in·tes·ti·nal (găs'trō-ĭn-tĕs'tə-nəl) *adj.* Of or pertaining to the stomach and intestines; gastroenteric.

gas·tro·lith (găs'trə-lĭth') *n.* A small, pathological stony mass formed in the stomach; a gastric calculus. [GASTRO- + -LITH.]

gas·trol·o·gy (gă-strŏl'ə-jē) *n.* The medical study of the stomach and its diseases. [GASTRO- + -LOGY.] —**gas·tro·log·i·cal** (găs'trə-lŏj'ĭ-kəl) *adj.* —**gas·trol·o·gist** *n.*

gas·tro·nome (găs'trə-nōm') *n.* Also **gas·tron·o·mer** (gă-strŏn'ə-mər). A connoisseur of good food and drink; a gourmet. [From GASTRONOMY.]

gas·tro·nom·ic (găs'trə-nŏm'ĭk) *adj.* Also **gas·tro·nom·i·cal** (-ĭ-kəl). Of or pertaining to gastronomes or gastronomy. —**gas·tro·nom·i·cal·ly** *adv.*

gas·tron·o·my (gă-strŏn'ə-mē) *n.* **1.** The art or science of good eating. **2.** Cooking, as of a particular region or country. [French *gastronomie,* from Greek *gastronomia :* GASTRO- + -NOMY.]

gas·tro·pod (găs'trə-pŏd') *n.* A mollusk of the class Gastropoda, as a snail, slug, cowry, or limpet, characteristically having a single, usually coiled shell and a ventral muscular foot serving as an organ of locomotion.
~*adj.* Of or belonging to the Gastropoda. [New Latin *Gastropoda,* "belly-footed creatures" (from their ventral disks used as feet) : GASTRO- + -POD.] —**gas·trop·o·dan** (gă-strŏp'ə-dən), **gas·trop·o·dous** *adj.*

gas·tro·scope (găs'trə-skōp') *n.* An instrument used for examining the interior of the stomach. [GASTRO- + -SCOPE.] —**gas·tro·scop·ic** (găs'trə-skŏp'ĭk) *adj.* —**gas·tros·co·pist** (gă-strŏs'kə-pĭst) *n.* —**gas·tros·co·py** (gă-strŏs'kə-pē) *n.*

gas·tros·to·my (gă-strŏs'tə-mē) *n., pl.* **-mies.** The surgical construction of a permanent opening from the external surface of the body into the stomach, usually for inserting a feeding tube. [GASTRO- + -STOMY.]

gas·trot·o·my (gă-strŏt'ə-mē) *n., pl.* **-mies.** A surgical incision into the stomach. [GASTRO- + -TOMY.]

gas·tro·trich (găs'trə-trĭk') *n.* Any minute aquatic animal of the phylum Gastrotricha, having a wormlike, ciliated body. [GASTRO- + -TRICH.]

gas·tro·vas·cu·lar (găs′trō-văs′kyə-lər) *adj.* Having both a digestive and a circulatory function. Said especially of the body cavity of a coelenterate.

gas·tru·la (găs′trə-lə) *n., pl.* **-las** or **-lae** (-lē′). An embryo at the stage following the blastula, consisting of a layer of cells differentiated into ectoderm, endoderm, and mesoderm and enclosing a cavity, the archenteron, which opens to the exterior by the blastopore. [New Latin, "small stomach" (from its shape), diminutive of Greek *gastēr* (stem *gastr-*), belly, womb.] —**gas·tru·lar** *adj.*

gas·tru·late (găs′trə-lāt′) *intr.v.* **-lated, -lating, -lates.** To form or become a gastrula. —**gas·tru·la·tion** *n.*

gas turbine *n.* An internal-combustion engine consisting essentially of an air compressor, a combustion chamber, and a turbine wheel, used especially for propulsion rather than fixed power generation.

gas well *n.* A well that yields natural gas.

gas·works (găs′wûrks′) *n. Used with a singular verb.* An industrial plant in which gas for heating and lighting is produced.

gat[1] (găt) *n.* **1.** A narrow passage extending inland from a shore. **2.** A tidal channel between offshore islands or shoals. [Probably from Dutch *gat,* "opening," from Middle Dutch, from Germanic *gatam* (unattested). See **gate**[1].]

gat[2] *n. Slang.* A pistol. [Short for GAT(LING GUN).]

gat[3] *Archaic.* Past tense of **get**.

gate[1] (gāt) *n.* **1.** A structure that may be swung, drawn, or lowered to block an entrance or passageway. **2. a.** An opening in a wall or fence for entrance or exit; a gateway. **b.** The structure surrounding such an opening, as the monumental or fortified entrance to a palace or walled town. **3. a.** Something that gives access: *the gate to fortune.* **b.** A place giving access to another region or country; especially, a mountain pass. **4.** A device for controlling the passage of water or gas through a dam, lock, or pipe. **5. a.** The number of spectators attending an event such as a football match: *the problem of falling gates.* **b.** The total admission receipts at such an event. In this sense, also called "gate money." **6.** Any of the numbered exits, as in an airport terminal, through which passengers proceed for embarkation. **7.** *Metallurgy.* The channel through which molten metal flows into the shaped cavity of a mold. **8.** *Electronics.* **a.** A circuit extensively used in computers that has an output dependent on some function of its input. **b.** Such a circuit having an output when any or all of a designated set of inputs are received within a given time interval. In this sense, also called "coincidence gate." **c.** A circuit designed to cut out part of a signal. **d.** The region or electrode that controls the current in a field-effect transistor. **9.** In photography, a device that holds a frame of film in place behind the lens. **10.** A slotted frame enabling the gearshift lever of a motor vehicle to be moved into different positions when engaging gears. ~*tr.v.* **gated, gating, gates. 1.** *British.* To punish (a student) by confining within the school or college gates after a certain hour or for a certain period of time. **2.** *Electronics.* To connect (one or more inputs) to a gate. [Middle English *gat,* g(e)ate, Old English *geat,* from Common Germanic *gatam* (unattested).]

gate[2] *n.* **1.** *Archaic & Regional.* A path or road; a way. **2.** *Regional.* A particular way of acting or doing; a manner. [Middle English, from Old Norse *gata,* path, passage.]

gâ·teau, ga·teau (gă-tō′) *n. pl.* **-teaux** (-tō′, -tōz′) or **-teaus.** A cake, especially a large, elaborate one. [French, "cake."]

gate-crash·er (gāt′krăsh′ər) *n. Informal.* A person who gains admittance, as to a party or concert, without being invited or without paying. —**gate-crash** *v.*

gate·fold (gāt′fōld′) *n.* A folded insert in a book or magazine whose full size exceeds that of the regular page. Also called "fold-out."

gate·house (gāt′hous′) *n.* **1.** A lodge at the entrance to the driveway of a country house or estate. **2.** A fortified room built over a gateway to a city or castle, formerly used as a prison. **3.** A building that houses the controls of a dam or lock.

gate·keep·er (gāt′kē′pər) *n.* A person in charge of a gate. Also called "gateman."

gate-leg table (gāt′lĕg′) *n.* A drop-leaf table with movable legs arranged in pairs.

gate·man (gāt′mən, -măn′) *n., pl.* **-men** (-mĭn, -mĕn′). A gatekeeper.

gate·post (gāt′pōst′) *n.* An upright post on which a gate is hung or against which a gate is closed.

gate·way (gāt′wā′) *n.* **1.** A structure, such as an arch, framing an entrance or passage that may be closed by a gate. **2.** A place or a thing that serves as an entrance or means of access: *a gateway to success.* **3.** *Computer Science.* A link that enables information to be exchanged between one computer network and another.

gath·er (gă*th*′ər) *v.* **-ered, -ering, -ers.** —*tr.* **1.** To cause to come together; convene. **2. a.** To accumulate gradually; amass. **b.** To harvest or pick: *gather flowers; gather in the crops.* **c.** To gain by a process of gradual increase: *The ship began to gather speed as it left the harbor.* **3. a.** To collect into one place; assemble. **b.** In bookbinding, to arrange (signatures) in sequence. **4.** To pick up and embrace. Used with *in* or *into: gathered the child into his arms.* **5. a.** To pull (cloth) along a thread so as to create small folds or puckers. **b.** To contract (the brow) so as to form wrinkles. **6.** To draw (a garment, for example) about or closer to something. **7.** To conclude or apprehend; infer: *I gather that a decision has not been reached.* **8. a.** To summon up; muster: *gather courage.* **b.** To collect (one's wits or powers). Often used with *together.* **9.** To attract as a center of attraction for: *a movement that is gathering support; books gathering dust.* —*intr.* **1.** To come together or assemble.

2. To accumulate. **3.** To grow or increase by degrees. **4.** To come to a head, as a boil does; fester. ~*n.* **1. a.** An act or instance of gathering. **b.** A quantity that is gathered. **2.** A small tuck or pucker in cloth. [Middle English *gad(e)ren,* Old English *gad(e)rian,* to put together, come together, from Germanic.] —**gath·er·er** *n.*

Synonyms: *accumulate, amass, assemble, collect, marshal, rally.*

gath·er·ing (gă*th*′ər-ĭng) *n.* **1.** Something gathered or amassed; a collection or accumulation. **2.** An assembly of persons; a meeting: *a cultural gathering.* **3.** A gather in cloth. **4.** A suppurated swelling; a boil or abscess.

Gat·ling gun (găt′lĭng) *n.* A machine gun having a cluster of barrels, each of which is fired as the cluster is turned. [Designed by Richard J. *Gatling* (1818–1903), American inventor.]

Gat·wick (găt′wĭk). Village in West Sussex, England. Lying 43 kilometers (27 miles) south of London, it is the site of one of London's principal airports.

gauche (gōsh) *adj.* **1.** Awkward in manner; lacking social grace; tactless; clumsy. **2.** *Chemistry.* Of or designating a conformation of a chemical compound in which two groups or atoms attached to two adjacent atoms are on the same side of the bond but one is displaced rotationally with respect to the other. —See Synonyms at **awkward.** [French, "left," originally "bent," "askew," from Old French *gauchir,* to turn aside, detour, probably altered from earlier *guenchir,* from Frankish *wenkjan* (unattested).] —**gauche·ly** *adv.* —**gauche·ness** *n.*

gau·che·rie (gō′shə-rē′, gōsh-rē′) *n.* **1.** An awkward or tactless action, manner, or expression. **2.** Tactlessness; awkwardness. [French, from *gauche,* left, GAUCHE.]

Gau·cher's disease (gō-shāz′) *n.* A metabolic disease in which fatty compounds accumulate in the liver, spleen, lymph nodes, and nervous system. [After Ernest *Gaucher* (1854–1918), French physician.]

gau·cho (gou′chō) *n., pl.* **-chos.** A cowboy of the South American pampas. [American Spanish, probably from Quechua *wáhcha,* poor person, vagabond.]

gaud (gôd) *n.* Something gaudy or showy. [Middle English *gaude, gawde,* jest, plaything, toy, from Old French *gaudir,* to rejoice, from Latin *gaudēre,* to delight in.]

gaud·er·y (gô′də-rē) *n., pl.* **-ies.** Showy things; finery.

Gau·dí (gou′dē), **Antonio** (1852–1926). Spanish architect. He worked mainly in Barcelona, developing a startling new style that paralleled developments in art nouveau and incorporated color and odd bits of material, such as rubble, bricks, and polychrome tiles. His most famous work is the Church of the Holy Family (1882–1930).

gaud·y[1] (gô′dē) *adj.* **-ier, -iest. 1.** Characterized by tasteless or showy colors; garish. **2.** Crude and showy. —See Synonyms at **ornate.** [From GAUD.] —**gaud·i·ly** *adv.* —**gaud·i·ness** *n.*

gaudy[2] *n., pl.* **-ies.** *British.* A feast; especially, an annual university dinner. [Latin *gaudium,* joy, from *gaudēre,* to rejoice.]

gauffer. Variant of **goffer.**

gauge, gage (gāj) *n. Abbr.* **g., G. 1. a.** A standard or scale of measurement. **b.** A standard dimension, quantity, or capacity. **2.** An instrument for measuring or testing. **3.** A means of estimating or evaluating; a test: *a gauge of character.* **4.** *Nautical.* The position of a vessel in relation to another vessel and the wind. **5. a.** The distance between the two rails of a railroad. **b.** The distance between two wheels on an axle. **6.** The diameter of a shotgun barrel as determined by the number of lead balls in a pound that exactly fit the barrel. **7.** The amount of plaster of Paris mixed with common plaster to speed its setting. **8.** Thickness or diameter, as of sheet metal or wire. **9.** The fineness of knitted cloth as determined by the number of loops per 1½ inches. **10.** The distance between nails securing tiles or slates to a roof. ~*tr.v.* **gauged, gauging, gauges** or **gaged, gaging, gages. 1.** To measure precisely. **2.** To determine the capacity, volume, or contents of. **3.** To evaluate or judge: *gauge ability.* **4.** To adapt to a specified measurement. **5.** To mix (plaster) in specific proportions. **6.** To chip or rub (bricks or stones) to size. ~*adj. Physics.* Measured above or below atmospheric pressure as the zero reference. Used with the noun: *7 bar gauge.* Compare **absolute** (pressure). [Middle English, from Old North French *gauget.*]

gaug·er (gā′jər) *n.* **1.** One that gauges. **2.** *Chiefly British.* **a.** A revenue officer who inspects bulk goods subject to duty. **b.** A collector of excise duties.

Gau·guin (gō-găɴ′), **(Eugène Henri) Paul** (1848–1903). French painter, regarded as a postimpressionist. In 1891 he settled in Tahiti and his paintings of the islanders show the influence of primitive art.

Gaul[1] (gôl). Latin name **Gal·li·a** (găl′ē-ə). The name given in antiquity to the region in Europe south and west of the Rhine, west of the Alps, and north of the Pyrenees, comprising approximately the territory of modern France and Belgium. [French *Gaule,* from Latin *Gallia,* from *Galli,* the Gauls.]

Gaul[2] *n.* **1.** A Celt of ancient Gaul. **2.** A Frenchman.

gau·lei·ter (gou′lī′tər) *n.* **1.** A governor of a district in Germany during the Nazi regime. **2.** A person similar to a gauleiter, as in point of view; petty tyrant. [German *Gau,* administrative district + *Leiter,* leader.]

Gaul·ish (gô′lĭsh) *n.* The Celtic language of ancient Gaul.

~*adj.* Of or pertaining to ancient Gaul or to its people, language, and culture.

Gaull·ism (gō'lĭz'əm, gô'-) *n.* **1.** The political movement supporting Charles de Gaulle as leader of the French government in exile during World War II. **2.** The body of political theory and practice characteristic of Charles de Gaulle and his followers. —**Gaull·ist** *adj. & n.*

gault (gôlt) *n. Geology.* **1.** *Often* **Gault.** A formation of Cretaceous origin in Britain, consisting of clay and marl and occurring between the Greensand formations. **2.** The clay and marl comprising this formation. **3.** A brick made from this type of clay. [16th century : origin obscure.]

gaul·the·ri·a (gôl-thîr'ē-ə) *n.* Any shrub of the genus *Gaultheria,* having aromatic evergreen foliage; especially, the **wintergreen** *(see).* [New Latin, after Jean-François *Gaultier,* 18th-century Canadian botanist.]

gaum (gôm) *tr.v.* **gaumed, gauming, gaums.** *Regional.* To smudge or smear. [Dialectal variant of GUM (verb).]

gaunt (gônt, gŏnt) *adj.* **gaunter, gauntest. 1.** Thin and bony; angular; lank. **2.** Emaciated and haggard; drawn. **3.** Bleak and desolate; barren. —See Usage note at **lean.** [Middle English *gawnt, gaunt, lean,* perhaps from Scandinavian; akin to Norwegian dialectal *gand†,* thin stick, lanky person.] —**gaunt·ly** *adv.* —**gaunt·ness** *n.*

gaunt·let¹, gant·let (gônt'lĭt, gänt'-) *n.* **1.** A protective glove worn as a part of medieval armor. **2.** A protective glove with a flaring cuff, used in manual labor, for driving, and in some sports. **3.** A challenge. Used chiefly in the phrases *fling* or *throw down the gauntlet.* [Middle English *gaunt(e)let,* from Old French *gantelet,* diminutive of *gant,* glove, from Frankish *want†* (unattested), mitten.]

gauntlet², gantlet *n.* **1.** Two lines of men facing each other and armed with sticks or other weapons with which they beat a person forced to run between them. **2.** A severe trial; ordeal: *The candidate was subjected to a gauntlet of searching questions from the journalists at the press conference.* [Earlier *gantlope.* See **gantlet** (railroad track).]

Usage: In the expression *run the gauntlet,* this spelling alternates with *gantlet. Gantlet* is the more common spelling in earlier American usage, and is still considered preferable by some authorities and mandatory by others, but *gauntlet* is acceptable in this expression to most users. *Gauntlet* is the term used in *fling* (or *throw*) *down the gauntlet,* to issue a challenge, and *take up the gauntlet,* to accept a challenge. *Run the gauntlet* (or *gantlet*) is sometimes confused with *run the gamut,* to cover an entire range.

gauntlet³. Variant of **gantlet** (railroad track).

gaur (gour, gou'ər) *n.* A large, dark-coated bovine mammal, *Bos gaurus,* of hilly areas of southeastern Asia. [Hindi *gaur,* from Sanskrit *gaura.*]

gauss (gous) *n. Abbr.* **G** The centimeter-gram-second electromagnetic unit of magnetic flux density, equal to one maxwell per square centimeter (10^{-4} tesla). [After Karl Friedrich GAUSS.]

Gauss (gous), **(Johann) Karl Friedrich** (1777–1855). German mathematician. His contributions to algebra, differential geometry, probability theory, and number theory were of vital importance. He also worked in astronomy and contributed to the invention of the telegraph.

Gauss·i·an distribution (gou'sē-ən) *n.* **Normal distribution** *(see).*

gauss·me·ter (gous'mē'tər) *n. Physics.* Any of various instruments used to measure magnetic flux density. [After Karl Friedrich GAUSS.]

Gau·tier (gō-tyā'), **Théophile** (1811–72). French author. A poet, critic, journalist, novelist, and playwright, he influenced French literature during its shift from romanticism to aestheticism and naturalism. Among his many works are *Young France* (1833), *Enamels and Cameos* (1852), and *The Dead Lover, Avatar* (1857).

gauze (gôz) *n.* **1. a.** A thin, transparent fabric with a loose open weave, used for curtains or clothing. **b.** A thin, open-woven cotton surgical dressing. **c.** A thin plastic or metal woven mesh. **2.** A mist or haze. [French *gaze,* probably after GAZA, where it was supposed to be made.]

gauz·y (gô'zē) *adj.* **-ier, -iest.** Of, pertaining to, or like gauze: *I bought a gauzy silk scarf.* —**gauz·i·ly** *adv.* —**gauz·i·ness** *n.*

ga·vage (gə-väzh', gä-) *n.* The introduction of material, especially nutritive material, into the stomach by means of a tube. [French, from *gaver,* to force down the throat, stuff, from Picard, from Old Latin *gaba†* (unattested), throat.]

gave. Past tense of **give.**

gav·el¹ (găv'əl) *n.* **1.** The mallet or hammer used by a presiding officer, a judge, or an auctioneer to signal for attention or order. **2.** A maul used by masons in fitting stones. —*tr.v.* **-eled** or **-elled, -eling** or **-elling, -els.** To cause or compel by using a gavel: *The judge gaveled the courtroom into silence.* [19th century : origin obscure.]

gavel² *n.* Tribute or rent in ancient and medieval England. [Middle English *gavel,* Old English *gafol,* tribute.]

gav·el·kind (găv'əl-kīnd') *n.* An English system of tenure, prevalent especially in Kent from Anglo-Saxon times until 1926, whereby land was held in exchange for rent rather than services and could be inherited by all qualified heirs rather than by primogeniture. [Middle English *gavelkynde,* Old English *gafolgecynd* (unattested), "tenure by payment of rent" : *gafol,* GAVEL (rent) + *cynd, gecynd,* KIND.]

ga·vi·al (gā'vē-əl) *n.* A large reptile, *Gavialis gangeticus,* of southern Asia, related to and resembling the crocodiles and having a long,

slender snout. Also called "gharial." [French, from Hindi *ghariyāl†.*]

ga·votte (gə-vŏt') *n.* **1.** A French dance resembling the minuet. **2.** Music for this dance, or in a similar style, in moderately quick ⁴⁄₄ time. [French, from Provençal *gavoto,* from *Gavot,* "mountaineer," "rustic," inhabitant of the Alps (where the dance originated), perhaps from *gava,* crop of a bird, frill, goiter, from Old Latin *gaba†* (unattested), throat.]

Ga·wain (gə-wān', gä'wān', gou'ən). A nephew of King Arthur and a knight of the Round Table.

Gawd (gôd) *interj. Slang.* Used as an expression of annoyance, surprise, or the like. [Cockney pronunciation spelling of *God.*]

gawk (gôk) *n.* An awkward or self-conscious person. —*intr.v.* **gawked, gawking, gawks.** *Informal.* To stare like a gawk; gape stupidly. [Perhaps alteration of obsolete *gaw,* to stare, gape, Middle English *gawen,* from Old Norse *gā,* to heed.]

gawk·y (gô'kē) *adj.* **-ier, -iest.** Awkward; ill-at-ease. —**gawk·i·ly** *adv.* —**gawk·i·ness** *n.*

gawp (gôp) *intr.v.* **gawped, gawping, gawps.** To gawk; gape. [Variant of earlier *gaup, galp,* Middle English *galpen,* to yawn, YELP.]

gay (gā) *adj.* **gayer, gayest. 1.** Showing or characterized by cheerfulness and light-hearted excitement; merry. **2.** Bright or brilliant, especially in color: *a gay, sunny room.* **3. a.** Homosexual. **b.** Of, pertaining to, or for homosexuals. **4.** Full of or given to social pleasures. **5.** Dissolute; licentious.
—*n.* A homosexual. [Middle English *gay, gai,* from Old French *gai,* from Old Provençal, probably from Gothic *gaheis* (unattested), akin to Old High German *gāhi†,* sudden, impetuous.] —**gay** *adv.* —**gay·ness** *n.*

Gay (gā), **John** (1685–1732). English poet and dramatist. A friend and protégé of Pope, he is best remembered for *The Beggar's Opera* (1728), a colorful satire that shocked many of his contemporaries by its candid portrayal of low life.

Ga·ya (gə-yä', gī'ə). City in central Bihar state, India. It is the capital and market center of a district that is famous for its strong Hindu and Buddhist associations and attracts many pilgrims.

ga·yal (gə-yäl') *n.* A domesticated bovine mammal, *Bos frontalis,* of India and Burma, having thick, pointed horns, a dark coat, and a tufted tail. [Bengali *gayāl,* probably from Sanskrit *gauḥ,* cow.]

gayety. Variant of **gaiety.**

Gay Gordons *n.* Used with a singular verb. A lively Scottish dance. [After the *Gordon Highlanders* (2nd Battalion, 92nd Highlanders).]

Gay-Lus·sac (gā-lü-säk'), **Joseph Louis** (1778–1850). French chemist and physicist. His experiments added considerably to knowledge of the way in which elements combine to form compounds. He discovered Gay-Lussac's law and isolated the element boron.

Gay-Lus·sac's law (gā'lü-säks') *n.* **1.** The principle that gases react in volumes that have a simple ratio to each other and to the volumes of gaseous products. **2. Charles's law** *(see).* [After J.L. GAY-LUSSAC.]

gayly. Variant of **gaily.**

Gay·nor (gā'nər), **Janet** (1906–84). U.S. actress. She started as an extra and became one of the most important movie stars of the late 1920's and early 1930's. For her performances in *Seventh Heaven, Street Angel,* and *Sunrise* she was awarded the first Academy Award as best actress (1928).

gaz. gazette; gazetteer.

Ga·za (gä'zə, găz'ə). *Arabic* **Ghaz·zah.** City in the Gaza Strip. Inhabited for more than 3,000 years, it was a major city of the Philistines, where Samson killed himself and his jailers by bringing down its temple (Judges 16).

ga·za·bo (gə-zā'bō) *n., pl.* **-bos** or **-boes.** *Slang.* A fellow; guy. [Origin unknown.]

ga·za·ni·a (gə-zā'nē-ə) *n.* Any South African plant of the genus *Gazania,* some species of which are grown for their ornamental yellow or orange flowers. [New Latin, irregularly from Teodoro *Gaza,* 15th-century Greek scholar.]

Gaza Strip. A territory between southwest Israel and the Mediterranean Sea. It was part of the British League of Nations mandate for Palestine (1920–48), but following the Arab-Israeli war of 1948–49 it came under Egyptian military rule. Apart from a brief Israeli occupation (November 1956–March 1957) it remained under Egyptian rule until taken in 1967 by the Israelis, who set up a military regime. The Camp David Accords of 1979 included provisions for its autonomy. A scene of sporadic unrest, the strip has several huge refugee camps.

gaze (gāz) *intr.v.* **gazed, gazing, gazes.** To look or stare steadily for some length of time, often in an absorbed or abstracted way. —*n.* A steady look. [Middle English *gazen,* probably from Scandinavian, akin to Swedish dialectal *gasa†.*] —**gaz·er** *n.*
Synonyms: gape, glare, ogle, peer, stare.

ga·ze·bo (gə-zā'bō, -zē'bō) *n., pl.* **-bos** or **-boes. 1.** A free-standing, roofed, often open-sided structure providing a shady resting place. **2.** A belvedere, especially one having a view. [Probably mock Latin formation from GAZE (with Latin future suffix *-ēbō,* as in *vidēbō, I shall see*).]

gaze·hound (gāz'hound') *n.* A dog that hunts its prey by sight rather than scent.

ga·zelle (gə-zĕl') *n.* Any of various small antelopes of the genus *Gazella* and related genera, of Africa and Asia, characteristically having a slender neck, and ringed, lyrate horns. [Old French, probably from Spanish *gacela,* from Arabic *ghazāl.*]

gazelle *The common name for an antelope group of animals native to Africa and Asia. This is a Grant's gazelle, an East African species distinguished by the white stripes running from each horn to the muzzle.*

ga·zette (gə-zĕt′) *n. Abbr.* **gaz. 1.** A newspaper. **2.** An official journal. **3.** *Chiefly British.* An announcement or report in an official journal. —*tr.v.* **gazetted, -zetting, -zettes.** *British.* To announce or publish in a gazette. *"Sham colonels gazetted"* (W.S. Gilbert). [French, from Italian *gazetta,* from Venetian *gazeta (de la novita),* (newspaper sold for) a small copper coin, from *gazeta,* a small copper coin, probably diminutive of *gaz(z)a,* magpie, from Latin *gaia,* from *gaius,* jay (perhaps imitative).]

gaz·et·teer (găz′ə-tîr′) *n. Abbr.* **gaz. 1.** A geographic dictionary or index. **2.** *Archaic.* A person who writes for a gazette or newspaper; journalist.

gaz·pa·cho (gə-spä′chō, gəz-pä′-) *n., pl.* **-chos.** A Spanish soup made from salad ingredients, such as tomatoes, peppers, garlic, and olive oil, and served chilled. [Spanish.]

ga·zump (gə-zŭmp′) *v.* **-zumped, -zumping, -zumps.** *British.* —*tr.* **1.** To go back on an agreement with (a prospective purchaser of a property) by raising a previously agreed price. **2.** To swindle. —*intr.* To raise the previously agreed price of a property. [20th century : origin obscure.] —**ga·zump·er** *n.*

G.B. Great Britain.
G.B.E. Grand Cross of the British Empire (in Britain).
GC gigacycle.
GCA *Aviation.* ground control approach.
G.C.B. Grand Cross of the Bath (in Britain).
g.c.d. greatest common divisor.
GCE, G.C.E. (jē′sē-ē′) *n., pl.* **GCE's, G.C.E.'s.** In Britain, the General Certificate of Education: either of two sets of public examinations that may be taken in a variety of subjects either at *O level* or *A level.* **2.** A certificate awarded for passing such an examination.
g.c.f. greatest common factor.
GCI *Aviation.* ground control intercept.
G clef *n.* The **treble clef** *(see).*
GCM Good Conduct Medal.
Gd The symbol for the element gadolinium.
G.D. grand duchess; grand duchy; grand duke.
Gdańsk (gə-dänsk′, -dănsk′). *German* **Dan·zig** (dăn′sĭg, dän′-). Polish port and industrial center on the Baltic Sea. A rich Hanseatic town from the 13th century, it was a free city 1466–1793 (under Polish sovereignty), 1807–14, and 1919–39. Hitler's claim to Danzig in 1939 led to the German invasion of Poland and World War II. Returned to Poland in 1945, the city was rebuilt and its shipyards are among the world's largest. Riots by shipworkers in 1970 led to government changes, and in 1980 Solidarity, Communist Poland's first independent trade union, was established here.
gde. gourde.
G.D.R. German Democratic Republic (East Germany).
gds. goods.
Gdy·nia (gə-dĭn′yə). *German* **Gding·en** (gə-dĭng′ən). Polish port and rail center on the Baltic Sea, 19 kilometers (12 miles) from Gdańsk.
Ge The symbol for the element germanium.
Ge. Variant of **Gaea.**
gean (gēn) *n. Chiefly British.* A wild cherry tree, *Prunus avium,* of Eurasia and North Africa, from which cultivated trees bearing sweet cherries have been derived. See **sweet cherry, wild cherry.** [French *guine†.*]
ge·an·ti·cline (jē-ăn′tĭ-klīn′) *n.* A large upward fold of the earth's crust. [Greek *gē,* earth + ANTICLINE.] —**ge·an·ti·cli·nal** (jē-ăn′tī-klī′nəl) *adj.*
gear (gîr) *n.* **1. a.** A toothed wheel, cylinder, or other machine element that meshes with another toothed element to transmit motion or to change speed or direction. **b.** A complete assembly that performs a specific function in a larger machine. **c.** A transmission configuration for a specific ratio of engine to axle torque in a motor vehicle. **2. a.** Equipment or tackle required for a particular activity or purpose; paraphernalia: *a plumber's gear.* **b.** *Informal.* Clothing and accessories, especially as worn by young people following fashion. **3.** The harness for a draft animal. **4.** The rigging of a ship. **5. a.** A sailor's personal effects. **b.** *Informal.* Personal belongings: *I keep my gear in that closet.* —**in** (or **out of**) **gear. 1.** Having a gear engaged (or not engaged). **2.** Performing (or not performing) well. —*v.* **geared, gearing, gears.** —*tr.* **1. a.** To provide with gears. **b.** To connect by gears. **c.** To put into gear. **2. a.** To adjust or adapt: *geared the speed to the conservative audience.* **b.** To prepare for action: *geared themselves up for the big game.* **3.** To provide with gear. —*intr.* **1.** To be or become in gear. **2.** To adjust so as to fit or blend. [Middle English *gere,* from Old Norse *gervi,* equipment, gear.]
gear·box (gîr′bŏks′) *n.* An automotive transmission.
gear·ing (gîr′ĭng) *n.* **1.** A system of gears and associated elements by which motion is transferred within a machine. **2.** The act or technique of providing with gears. **3.** *British.* The ratio of a company's fixed-interest debt to its equity capital.
gear·le·ver (gîr′lē′vər, -lĕv′ər) *n. British.* A gearshift.
gear·shift (gîr′shĭft′) *n.* A mechanism for changing from one gear to another in a transmission.
gear train *n.* A system of interconnected gears.
gear·wheel (gîr′hwēl′) *n.* A wheel with a toothed rim.
geck·o (gĕk′ō) *n., pl.* **-os** or **-oes.** Any of various usually small lizards of the family Gekkonidae, of warm regions, having toes with adhesive pads that enable them to climb on vertical surfaces. [Malay *ge′kok,* imitative of its cry).]
gee¹ (jē) *interj.* Gee whiz. [Euphemistic shortening of JESUS.]

gee² *n.* The gravitational acceleration at the earth's surface. [From the symbol *g* for gravitational acceleration.]
gee³ *n. Slang.* A thousand dollars. [Short for GRAND.]
gee⁴ *interj.* Used to encourage a horse or similar animal to turn to the right or go forward. Compare **haw.** —*intr.v.* **geed, geeing, gees.** To turn to the right. [Origin obscure.]
gee⁵ *n.* The letter *g.*
gee-gee (jē′jē) *n. Informal.* A horse. [Child's word for horse, from GEE (interjection).]
geek (gēk) *n. Slang.* **1.** A carnival performer whose act consists of biting the head off a live animal, such as a chicken or snake. **2.** Broadly, any person whose behavior is considered to be eccentric or freakish. [Perhaps variant of Scottish *geck,* fool, from Middle Low German.]
Gee·long (jĭ-lông′). Port in Victoria, Australia. It was founded in 1837 on the western shore of Corio Bay, 68 kilometers (42 miles) southwest of Melbourne.
gee·pound (jē′pound′) *n.* A unit of mass, the **slug** *(see).* [GEE (gravitational acceleration) + POUND (weight).]
geese. Plural of **goose.**
gee whiz, gee whizz *interj.* Used to express mild surprise or delight.
Ge·ez (gē-ĕz′, gā-) *n.* **Ethiopic** *(see).*
gee·zer (gē′zər) *n. Slang.* A man; especially, an eccentric old man. [Probably dialectal pronunciation of *guiser,* one in disguise, masquerader, from GUISE.]
ge·fil·te fish, ge·füll·te fish (gə-fĭl′tə) *n.* Chopped fish mixed with crumbs, eggs, and seasonings, cooked in stock and usually served chilled in the form of balls or oval-shaped cakes. [Yiddish, "filled fish."]
ge·gen·schein (gā′gən-shīn′) *n.* A faint, glowing spot in the sky exactly opposite the position of the sun. Also called "counterglow." [German *Gegenschein,* "opposite light" : *gegen,* against, + *Schein,* light.]
Ge·hen·na (gə-hĕn′ə) *n.* **1.** A place or state of burning, torment, or suffering. **2.** Hell. [Late Latin, from Greek *Geenna,* from Hebrew *Gê' Hinnôm,* Valley of Hinnom, a ravine outside ancient Jerusalem where refuse was dumped, (hence figuratively) hell.]
Geh·rig (gĕr′ĭg), **Henry Louis,** known as "Lou" (1903–42). U.S. baseball player. As a New York Yankee first baseman, he had a lifetime batting average of .340, was the American League's most valuable player four times, and, most remarkably, never missed a game in fourteen seasons, playing in 2,130 consecutive contests.
Gei·ger (gī′gər), **Hans** (1882–1945). German physicist. He is best known for his work with Ernest Rutherford at Manchester, which resulted in the invention of the Geiger counter.
Geiger counter *n.* An instrument consisting of a Geiger tube and associated electronic equipment, used to detect, measure, and record ionizing radiation and charged particles. Also called "Geiger-Müller counter." [After Hans GEIGER.]
Geiger tube *n.* A gas-filled tube containing a fine wire electrode inside a coaxial cylindrical electrode, between which a potential difference slightly below the breakdown voltage is maintained, so that production of a pair of ions in the gas by the passage of a charged particle or by ionizing radiation causes a breakdown throughout the volume of the tube. Also called "Geiger-Müller tube." [After Hans GEIGER.]
Gei·sel (gī′zəl), **Theodor Seuss,** pen name "Dr. Seuss" (1904–91). U.S. author and illustrator. He combined light, sometimes nonsense verse and prose with imaginative artwork to produce popular and highly acclaimed children's books, including *And to Think That I Saw It on Mulberry Street* (1937), *The Cat in the Hat* (1957), and *The Butter Battle Book* (1984).
gei·sha (gā′shə, gē′-) *n., pl.* **geisha** or **-shas.** A Japanese girl trained to provide entertainment, such as singing, dancing, or amusing talk, especially for men. [Japanese, "artist" : *gei,* art + *sha,* person.]
Geis·sler tube (gī′slər) *n. Physics.* An electric discharge tube having two electrodes separated by a narrow capillary, used as a source of visible or ultraviolet radiation. [After Heinrich *Geissler* (1815–79), German mechanic.]
geist (gīst) *n.* **1.** Reason or intelligence, especially that of an individual. **2.** Prevailing intellectual character. [German, "spirit."]
gel (jĕl) *n.* **1.** A colloid in which the disperse phase has combined with the continuous phase to produce a semisolid material, such as a jelly. **2.** *Informal.* A gelatin used in theatrical lighting. —*v.* **gelled, gelling, gels.** —*intr.* To form into a gel. —*tr.* To cause (a colloid) to become a gel. [Short for GELATIN.]
gel·a·ble (jĕl′ə-bəl) *adj.* Capable of gelling.
gel·a·da (jĕl′ə-də, gĕl′-, jə-lä′də, gə-) *n.* A baboon, *Theropithecus gelada,* of Ethiopia, having a dark coat with a bare reddish area on the chest, and a mane covering the shoulders. Also called "gelada baboon." [Perhaps from Arabic *qilādah,* mane.]
ge·län·de·sprung (gə-lĕn′də-shprōong′, -sprōong′) *n.* A jump in skiing made from a crouching position with the use of both poles. [German : *Gelände,* level land + *Sprung,* a jump.]
gel·a·tin, gel·a·tine (jĕl′ə-tĭn) *n.* **1.** A colorless or slightly yellow, transparent, brittle protein formed by boiling the specially prepared skin, bones, and connective tissue of animals and used in foods, drugs, and photographic film. **2.** Any of various similar substances. **3.** A jelly made with gelatin, used as a dessert or salad base. **4.** A thin, transparent colored membrane used in theatrical lighting. [French *gélatine,* from Italian *gelatina,* diminutive of *gelata,* jelly,

gecko *This striped gecko is a small member of a largely tropical lizard family, the Gekkonidae, and is active mainly at night.*

gem

CRYSTALLINE DELIGHT

Earth's most precious stones

Men and women have worn colored stones for decoration and as talismans for thousands of years. Valued for their color, translucency, durability, and scarcity, gems have been polished and cut to enhance their beauty since at least early Egyptian times. Today diamond, emerald, ruby, and sapphire are the most prized gems, with flawless fine-colored rubies and emeralds the rarest and most costly.

Other valuable rarities are alexandrite with its red-green color change, green demantoid garnet, and Imperial jade. There is a profusion of colors and lusters, ranging from subtle to dazzling, in the less rare aquamarine, garnet, jade, lapis lazuli, moonstone, opal, peridot, quartz family, spinel, topaz, tourmaline, turquoise, and zircon.

FIVE WAYS IN WHICH A JEWELER CAN CUT GEMS

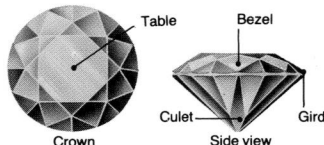 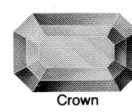   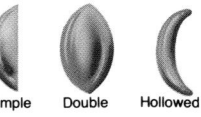

BRILLIANT CUT *Used for diamonds. Its precisely angled facets and perfect proportions both reflect and split light in a play of fiery brilliance.*

TRAP CUT *Intricate shaping of the pavilion, a spider's web of angled surfaces, enhances color and emphasizes flawlessness. Used for colored stones.*

ROSE CUT *An old-fashioned cut used mainly for small diamonds.*

TABLE CUT *The simple forerunner of the brilliant and trap cuts.*

SECTIONS OF CABOCHONS *The oldest of all cuts, polished round or oval domes. Ideal for opaque gems, such as lapis lazuli, or star rubies and sapphires.*

BRILLIANCY OF THE FINISHED STONE

DIAMOND *Supremely hard and lustrous, diamond retains its brilliant polish and fire for generations.*

RUBY *Rarest of the precious stones; chromium imparts the glowing and most prized "pigeon's blood" red.*

EMERALD *Also colored by chromium, emerald's velvety green is rarely flawless. A brittle gem, it may chip.*

SAPPHIRE *The hardest gem after diamond, it varies from pure blue to purple, pink, orange, gold, green, and white.*

NATURAL STATE OF GEMSTONES

 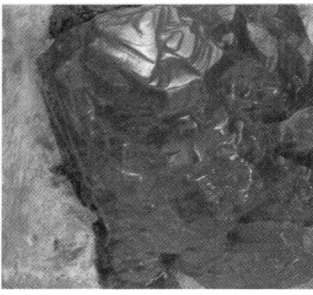 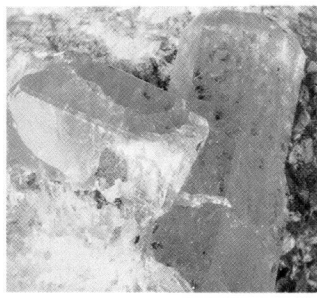 

DIAMOND *The hardest natural stone, a form of carbon crystallized under enormous pressure and in great heat.*

RUBY *Rich red rubies, formed in thermally altered limestones, are quarried from the Burma gem gravels.*

EMERALD *A silicate of beryllium and aluminum. The finest emeralds are mined from veins in shales in Colombia.*

SAPPHIRE *Like ruby, it is a variety of the aluminum oxide corundum. Sri Lanka is a famous source of all colors.*

---

from Vulgar Latin *gelāta* (unattested), from Latin, feminine past participle of *gelāre*, to freeze, congeal.]

ge·lat·i·nize (jə-lăt′n-īz′, jĕl′ə-tə-nīz′) *v.* **-nized, -nizing, -nizes.** —*tr.* **1.** To convert to gelatin or jelly. **2.** To coat with gelatin. —*intr.* To become gelatinous. —**ge·lat·i·ni·za·tion** *n.*

ge·lat·i·nous (jə-lăt′n-əs) *adj.* **1.** Thick and viscous; resembling jelly. **2.** Of, pertaining to, containing, or similar to gelatin. —**ge·lat·i·nous·ly** *adv.* —**ge·lat·i·nous·ness** *n.*

ge·la·tion (jə-lā′shən) *n.* **1.** Solidification by cooling or freezing. **2.** The process of forming a gel. [Latin *gelātiō* (stem *gelātiōn-*), from *gelāre*, to freeze, congeal.]

geld¹ (gĕld) *tr.v.* **gelded** or **gelt** (gĕlt), **gelding, gelds. 1.** To castrate (a horse or other animal). **2.** To emasculate; weaken. [Middle English *gelden*, from Old Norse *gelda*.]

geld² *n.* A tax paid to the crown by English landholders under Anglo-Saxon and Norman kings. [Medieval Latin (Domesday Book) *geldum*, from Old English *g(i)eld*, payment, tribute.]

geld·ing (gĕl′dĭng) *n. Abbr.* **g.** A castrated animal; especially, a castrated male horse. [Middle English, from Old Norse *geldingr*, from *gelda*, GELD (to castrate).]

Gelibolu. See **Gallipoli.**

gel·id (jĕl′ĭd) *adj.* Very cold; icy. [Latin *gelidus*, from *gelū*, cold, frost.] —**ge·lid·i·ty** (jə-lĭd′ə-tē), **gel·id·ness** *n.* —**gel·id·ly** *adv.*

gel·ig·nite (jĕl′ĭg-nīt′) *n.* A high explosive made by combining nitroglycerin with wood pulp and sodium or potassium nitrate. [From GELATIN + Latin *ign(is)*, fire + -ITE.]

Gell-Mann (gĕl′män′), **Murray** (1929–). U.S. physicist. In 1954 he introduced the concept of "strangeness" to explain the slow decay of certain particles and in 1961 postulated the existence of elementary particles he called "quarks." He was awarded the Nobel Prize in 1969.

gel·se·mi·um (jĕl-sē′mē-əm) *n.* **1.** Any shrub of the genus *Gelsemium*, such as *G. sempervirens*, yellow jasmine, of the southeastern United States. **2.** The powdered root of the yellow jasmine, which has sedative properties. [New Latin, from Italian *gelsomino*, JASMINE.]

gelt¹ (gĕlt) *n. Slang.* Money. [Yiddish *gelt* and German *Geld*, from Old High German *gelt*, recompense, reward.]

gelt². Alternate past tense and past participle of **geld.**

gem¹ (jĕm) *n.* **1.** A precious or semiprecious stone that has been cut and polished. **2. a.** Something that is valued for its beauty or per-

fection. **b.** A beloved or highly prized person: *a real gem.* **3.** A type of muffin.
~*tr.v.* **gemmed, gemming, gems.** To adorn with or as if with gems. [Middle English *gemme,* from Old French, from Latin *gemma,* bud, precious stone.]

gem² *adj. Chemistry.* Designating or pertaining to a chemical compound that has two identical atoms or groups attached to the same atom. Compare **vicinal.** [Shortened from GEMINATE.]

Ge·ma·ra (gə-mär'ə, -môr'ə) *n.* The second part of the Talmud, consisting chiefly of commentary on the Mishnah. [Aramaic *gemārā,* completion, from *gemār,* to complete.] —**Ge·ma·ric** (jə-mär'ĭk, -môr'ĭk) *adj.* —**Ge·ma·rist** *n.*

gem·i·nate (jĕm'ə-nāt') *v.* **-nated, -nating, -nates.** —*tr.* To arrange in pairs or to double. —*intr.* To occur in pairs.
~*adj.* (jĕm'ə-nĭt, -nāt'). Forming a pair; doubled. [Latin *gemināre,* from *geminus,* twin.] —**gem·i·na·tion** *n.*

Gem·i·ni (jĕm'ə-nī', -nē') *n.* **1.** *Astronomy.* A constellation in the Northern Hemisphere containing the stars Castor and Pollux. **2. a.** The third sign of the **zodiac** *(see).* Also called the "Twins." **b.** One born under this sign. **3.** Any of a series of U.S. space probes designed to gain experience of manual flight and practice docking methods. There were 12 Gemini flights (1964–66), the first two unmanned and the others each carrying two astronauts. [Latin, plural of *geminus,* twin.] —**Gem·i·ni·an** (jĕm'ə-nī'ən) *adj. & n.*

gem·ma (jĕm'ə) *n., pl.* **gemmae** (jĕm'ē'). An asexual reproductive structure, as in liverworts and mosses, consisting of a cell or group of cells capable of developing into a new individual; a bud. [Latin, bud, precious stone.]

gem·mate (jĕm'āt') *adj.* Having or reproducing by gemmae.
~*intr.v.* **gemmated, -mating, -mates.** To produce gemmae or reproduce by means of gemmae. [Latin *gemmāre,* to bud, from *gemma,* bud, GEMMA.] —**gem·ma·tion** *n.*

gem·mip·a·rous (jĕ-mĭp'ər-əs) *adj.* Reproducing by buds or gemmae. [New Latin *gemmiparus* : Latin *gemma,* bud, GEMMA + -PAROUS.]

gem·mu·la·tion (jĕm'yə-lā'shən) *n.* Production of or reproduction by gemmules.

gem·mule (jĕm'yōol) *n.* **1.** A small gemma or similar structure; especially, a reproductive structure in some sponges that remains dormant through the winter and later develops into a new individual. **2.** A hypothetical particle of heredity postulated in the theory of pangenesis *(see).* [French, from Latin *gemmula,* diminutive of *gemma,* GEMMA.]

gem·my (jĕm'ē) *adj.* **1.** Full of or set with gems. **2.** Like a gem; glittering.

gem·ol·o·gy, gem·mol·o·gy (jĕ-mŏl'ə-jē) *n.* The study of gemstones. —**gem·o·log·i·cal** (jĕm'ə-lŏj'ĭ-kəl) *adj.* —**gem·ol·o·gist** (jĕ-mŏl'ə-jĭst) *n.*

ge·mot, ge·mote (gə-mōt') *n.* A public meeting or local judicial assembly in England prior to the Norman Conquest. [Old English *gemōt* : *ge-,* perfective prefix + *mōt,* assembly, council.]

gems·bok (gĕmz'bŏk') *n.* An antelope, *Oryx gazella,* of arid regions of southern Africa, having long, sharp, straight horns and a black band along each flank. [Afrikaans, from Dutch *gemsbok,* "male chamois," from German *Gemsbock* : *Gemse,* chamois + *Bock,* he-goat, buck.]

gem·stone (jĕm'stōn') *n.* A precious or semiprecious stone that may be used as a gem when cut and polished.

ge·müt·lich (gə-müt'lĭкн) *adj.* Having a feeling of warmth or congeniality; friendly. [German, from *gemüt,* spirit.]

ge·müt·lich·keit (gə-müt'lĭкн-kīt') *n.* A feeling of warmth; congeniality. [German, from GEMÜTLICH.]

-gen, -gene *suffix.* Indicates: **1.** That which produces; producing; for example, *antigen.* **2.** Something produced; for example, *phosgene.* [French *-gène,* from Greek *-genēs,* born.]

gen (jĕn) *n. British Informal.* Relevant information.
~*tr.v.* **genned, genning, gens.** *British Informal.* To give (a person) relevant information on a subject. Used with *up.* [Probably from *general information.*]

gen. **1.** gender. **2.** general; generally. **3.** generator. **4.** generic. **5.** genitive. **6.** genus.

Gen. **1.** general (military rank). **2.** Genesis (Old Testament).

ge·nappe (jə-năp', zhə-) *n.* An exceptionally smooth worsted yarn used in the manufacture of fringes and braids. [After *Genappe,* Belgium, where it was originally made.]

gen·darme (zhän'därm', jän'-) *n.* **1.** A member of a national police organization in France and some countries formerly controlled by France, constituting a branch of the armed forces with responsibilities for internal defense, frontier and customs guard, traffic control, and general law enforcement in rural districts. **2.** A cavalryman belonging to any of various units organized under royal authority in France from the 15th century until 1789. **3.** *Informal.* A French policeman. **4.** *Slang.* A policeman. **5.** An isolated pinnacle on a mountain ridge forming an obstacle to climbers. [French, from *gens d'armes,* "men of arms."]

gen·dar·mer·ie, gen·dar·mer·y (zhän-där'mə-rē, jän-) *n.* **1.** A military police organization having general responsibility for public security and law enforcement in France and some countries formerly controlled by France. **2.** A headquarters of a body of gendarmes. **3.** A French royal cavalry corps, as variously organized at different times between the 15th century and 1789. [French, from GENDARME.]

gen·der (jĕn'dər) *n. Abbr.* **g., gen. 1.** *Grammar.* **a.** Any set of two or more categories, such as masculine, feminine, and neuter, into which words are divided according to sex, animation, psychological associations, or some other characteristic, and that determine agreement with or the selection of modifiers, referents, or grammatical forms. **b.** One category of such a set. See **common gender, grammatical gender, natural gender. c.** The classification of a word or grammatical form in such a category. **d.** The distinguishing form or forms used. **2. a.** Classification of sex. **b.** The sex of a person.
~*tr.v.* **gendered, -dering, -ders.** *Archaic.* To engender. [Middle English *gendre,* from Old French *gen(d)re,* kind, sort, from Latin *genus* (stem *gener-*), race, kind.]

gene (jēn) *n.* A hereditary unit located on a chromosome that determines a specific characteristic or function in an organism. Genes are capable of replication and recombination, exist in a number of different forms, called **alleles** *(see),* and can undergo mutation. [German *Gen,* short for *Pangen* : PAN- + -GEN.]

–gene. Variant of **-gen.**

ge·ne·al·o·gy (jē'nē-ăl'ə-jē, -ŏl'ə-jē, jĕn'ē-) *n., pl.* **-gies.** *Abbr.* **geneal. 1.** A record or table of the descent of a family, group, or person from an ancestor or ancestors; a family tree. **2.** Direct descent from an ancestor; lineage; pedigree. **3.** The study or investigation of ancestry and family histories. **4.** The study of the development of plants and animals from their earlier forms. [Middle English *genealogie,* from Old French, from Late Latin *genealogia,* from Greek : *genea,* race, generation + -LOGY.] —**ge·ne·a·log·i·cal** (jē'nē-ə-lŏj'ĭ-kəl, jĕn'ē-) *adj.* —**ge·ne·a·log·i·cal·ly** *adv.* —**ge·ne·al·o·gist** *n.*

gen·e·col·o·gy (jĕn'ĭ-kŏl'ə-jē, jēn'ĭ-) *n.* The study of the genetics of populations in relation to their environment. [GENE(TICS) + ECOLOGY.] —**gen·e·co·log·i·cal** (jē'nĭ-kə-lŏj'ĭ-kəl, jĕn'ĭ-) *adj.*

gene flow *n.* The introduction and movement of new allelic forms of genes in populations due to immigration and subsequent interbreeding.

gene frequency *n.* The frequency of occurrence of an allelic form of a gene in relation to that of other alleles of the same gene.

gene pool *n.* The total number of genes in an interbreeding population at a given time.

gen·e·ra. Plural of **genus.**

gen·er·a·ble (jĕn'ər-ə-bəl) *adj.* Capable of being generated. [Middle English *generabill,* from Latin *generābilis,* from *generāre,* to GENERATE.]

gen·er·al (jĕn'ər-əl, jĕn'rəl) *adj. Abbr.* **gen., genl. 1. a.** Relating to, concerned with, or applicable to the whole or to every member of a class or category: *a program to improve the general welfare.* **b.** *Medicine.* Pertaining to or involving the whole body. **2.** Affecting or characteristic of the majority of those involved; prevalent: *a general discontent.* **3.** Being usually the case; true or applicable in most instances but not all: *the general correctness of his decisions.* **4. a.** Not limited in scope, area, or application; not restricted: *a general rule to follow.* **b.** Not limited to or dealing with one class of things; diversified; miscellaneous: *general studies; a general store.* **5.** Involving only the main or more obvious features of something rather than details or particulars: *a general grasp of a subject.* **6.** Highest or superior in rank; chief within a particular sphere: *the general manager; secretary general.*
~*n.* **1.** *Abbr.* **Gen. a.** An officer in the U.S. Army, Air Force, or Marine Corps holding a rank above colonel; especially, an officer of the second-highest rank in the U.S. Army or Air Force and the highest rank in the Marine Corps. **b.** An officer of the British and Australian armies ranking between a field marshal and a lieutenant general and equivalent in rank to an admiral in the Navy and an air chief marshal in the Air Force. **c.** An officer of the highest rank in the Royal Marines. **2. a.** The head of certain Roman Catholic religious orders. **b.** The head of the Salvation Army. **3.** Something, such as a condition, principle, or fact, that embraces or is applicable to the whole. **4.** *Archaic.* The public: " *'twas caviare to the general"* (Shakespeare). —**in general.** Generally. [Middle English, from Old French, from Latin *generālis,* belonging to a kind or species, relating to all, from *genus* (stem *gener-*), birth, race, kind.] —**gen·er·al·ness** *n.*

general anesthetic *n.* An anesthetic that causes loss of sensation in the entire body and induces unconsciousness. Compare **local anesthetic.**

general assembly *n. Abbr.* **GA, G.A. 1. General Assembly.** The principal deliberative body of the United Nations, in which each member nation is represented and has one vote. **2.** The supreme governing body of some religious denominations, especially that of the Church of Scotland and other Presbyterian churches. **3.** Any of various legislative bodies, especially that of a U.S. state.

General Certificate of Education *n.* See **GCE.**

general confession *n.* **1.** In the services of the Anglican Church, a prayer of confession recited by the whole congregation. **2.** In the Roman Catholic Church, a confession in which the penitent considers his life in general rather than his recent past.

General Court *n.* **1.** A Colonial legislative body with judicial powers. **2.** The state legislature of Massachusetts and New Hampshire.

general court-martial *n.* A court-martial consisting of at least five officers for trying major offenses.

gen·er·al·cy (jĕn'ər-əl-sē) *n., pl.* **-cies.** The rank, appointment, authority, or tenure of a general.

general delivery *n.* **1.** A department of a post office that holds mail for addressees until it is called for. Also *chiefly British* "poste restante." **2.** Mail sent to general delivery.

general election *n.* An election at which all or most constituencies

gemsbok *Native to southern and eastern Africa, the gemsbok, a type of antelope, can survive long periods without water by eating moisture-filled tubers and roots. Once widely hunted, it is now an endangered species.*

genet *These stealthy woodland hunters are related to the mongoose. Several species of genet live in Africa and one species in Europe.*

return a representative to a legislative body.

general hospital *n.* A hospital that provides basic services for its patients without specializing in particular diseases.

gen·er·al·is·si·mo (jĕn′ər-ə-lĭs′ə-mō′) *n., pl.* **-mos.** The commander in chief of all the armed forces in certain countries, or, occasionally, of the armed forces of allied countries in a joint campaign. [Italian, superlative of *generale,* general, from Latin *generālis,* belonging to a kind, GENERAL.]

gen·er·al·ist (jĕn′ər-ə-lĭst) *n.* A person with broad general knowledge and skills in several disciplines, fields, or areas.

gen·er·al·i·ty (jĕn′ə-răl′ə-tē) *n., pl.* **-ties. 1.** The condition or quality of being general. **2.** An observation or principle having general application; a generalization. **3.** A statement or idea that is imprecise or vague. **4.** The greater portion or number; the majority.

gen·er·al·i·za·tion (jĕn′ər-ə-lə-zā′shən) *n.* **1.** An act or instance of generalizing. **2.** A general principle, statement, or idea having general application. **3.** *Psychology.* A process by which behavior prompted by a particular stimulus can also be prompted by a similar stimulus.

gen·er·al·ize (jĕn′ər-ə-līz′) *v.* **-ized, -izing, -izes.** *—tr.* **1. a.** To reduce to a general form, class, or law. **b.** To render indefinite or unspecific. **2. a.** To infer from many particulars. **b.** To draw inferences or a general conclusion from. **3. a.** To make generally or universally applicable. **b.** To popularize. *—intr.* **1. a.** To form a concept inductively. **b.** To form general notions or conclusions, especially after incomplete consideration of the facts. **2.** To speak or think in generalities; speak vaguely. **3.** *Medicine.* To spread through the body. Used of a usually localized disease.

gen·er·al·ized (jĕn′ər-ə-līzd′) *adj.* **1.** Generally prevalent. **2. a.** General; unspecific. **b.** Not well adapted to a specific environment or function; undifferentiated.

generalized order *n. Psychology.* An organized group whose group identity allows an individual to establish a personal identity by reference to it.

general knowledge *n.* Knowledge of a wide variety of facts from many fields.

gen·er·al·ly (jĕn′ər-ə-lē, jĕn′rə-) *adv. Abbr.* **gen. 1.** For the most part; widely: *generally known.* **2.** As a rule; usually; ordinarily. **3.** Viewing circumstances overall; not specifically: *generally speaking.*

general officer *n.* Any officer ranking above colonel.

general paresis *n.* A brain disease occurring as a late consequence of syphilis and characterized by mental deterioration, speech disturbances, and progressive muscular weakness. Also called "paresis."

General Post Office *n. Abbr.* **GPO 1.** Formerly in Britain, the central governmental department providing postal and telecommunications services. **2.** The main post office in a large city.

general practitioner *n. Abbr.* **G.P.** A physician in general practice who treats a variety of medical problems but sends patients requiring more specialized treatment to a hospital or a consultant. Also called "family doctor."

gen·er·al-pur·pose (jĕn′ər-əl-pûr′pəs, jĕn′rəl-) *adj.* Capable of being used or applied in many circumstances.

general relativity *n. Physics.* The later part of the theory of **relativity** *(see),* dealing with accelerated motion.

general semantics *n. Used with a singular verb.* A doctrine proposed by Alfred Korzybski (1879–1950) that presents a method of improving human behavior through a more critical use of words and symbols.

gen·er·al·ship (jĕn′ər-əl-shĭp′, jĕn′rəl-) *n.* **1.** The rank, office, or tenure of a general. **2.** Leadership or skill in the conduct of a war. **3.** Skillful management or leadership.

general staff *n. Abbr.* **GS, G.S.** *Military.* A group of officers, usually of the rank of major and above, who are charged with assisting senior officers in planning and supervising operations.

general strike *n.* A simultaneous strike by all workers of the unionized industries of a nation or area.

General Synod *n.* The governing body of the Church of England, composed of the diocesan bishops and elected clerical and lay representatives.

gen·er·ate (jĕn′ə-rāt′) *tr.v.* **-ated, -ating, -ates. 1. a.** To bring into existence; give rise to: *generate discussion.* **b.** To produce (electricity or heat, for example) as a result of a chemical or physical process. **2.** To engender (offspring); beget. **3.** To form (a geometric figure) by describing a curve or surface. **4.** *Computer Science.* To produce (a program) by instructing a computer to follow given parameters with a skeleton program. [Latin *generāre,* from *genus* (stem *gener-*), birth, race, kind.] **—gen·er·a·tive** (jĕn′ər-ə-tĭv, -ə-rā′-tĭv) *adj.*

gen·er·a·tion (jĕn′ə-rā′shən) *n.* **1.** The act or process of generating; especially, origination, production, or procreation. **2.** Offspring having a common parent or parents and constituting a single stage of descent. **3.** *Biology.* All the individuals produced during a particular phase of the life cycle that have the same method of reproduction. **4.** A class of objects derived from a preceding class: *the new generation of minicomputers.* **5. a.** A group of contemporaneous individuals. **b.** A group of individuals, usually contemporaneous, regarded as having a common cultural or social attribute: *music that inspired a whole generation of composers.* **6.** The average time interval between the birth of parents and the birth of their offspring. **7.** *Computer Science.* The technique of generating programs. **—gen·er·a·tion·al** *adj.*

generation gap *n.* The differences in outlook and attitude between people of different generations, especially between young people and their parents.

generative grammar *n. Linguistics.* An ordered set of rules intended to produce all and only the well-formed sentences of a language; specifically, **transformational-generative grammar** *(see).*

generative semantics *n. Used with a singular verb.* A theory based on the belief that syntactic and semantic structures are of the same nature and that the mind relates surface structure to meaning.

gen·er·a·tor (jĕn′ə-rā′tər) *n. Abbr.* **gen. 1.** One that generates. **2.** A machine that converts mechanical energy into electrical energy, as a dynamo in a power station. **3.** An apparatus that generates a vapor or gas. **4.** A generatrix. **5.** *Computer Science.* A routine that performs a generating function.

gen·er·a·trix (jĕn′ə-rā′trĭks) *n., pl.* **generatrices** (-rā′trə-sēz′, -ər-ə-trī′sēz′). A point, line, or plane that generates a geometric figure; especially, a straight line that generates a surface by moving in a given fashion.

ge·ner·ic (jə-nĕr′ĭk) *adj. Abbr.* **gen. 1.** Relating to or descriptive of an entire group or class; general. **2.** *Biology.* Of or relating to a genus. **3.** Not protected by trademark; nonproprietary.
∼*n.* A generic product, especially a drug. [French *générique,* from Latin *genus* (stem *gener-*), race, species, kind.] **—ge·ner·i·cal·ly** *adv.*

gen·er·os·i·ty (jĕn′ə-rŏs′ə-tē) *n., pl.* **-ties. 1.** The quality of being generous; liberality in giving or willingness to give. **2.** Nobility of thought or behavior; magnanimity. **3.** Amplitude; abundance. **4.** A generous act.

gen·er·ous (jĕn′ər-əs) *adj.* **1.** Willing to give or share; unselfish. **2.** Lacking pettiness or meanness in thought or behavior; magnanimous. **3.** Characterized by abundance; bountiful; ample. **4.** Having a rich bouquet and flavor. Said of wine. **5.** Fertile. Said of soil. [Old French *genereux,* from Latin *generōsus,* of noble birth, excellent, magnanimous, from *genus* (stem *gener-*), birth, race, kind.] **—gen·er·ous·ly** *adv.* **—gen·er·ous·ness** *n.*

gen·e·sis (jĕn′ə-sĭs) *n., pl.* **-ses** (-sēz′). The coming into being of something; origin. [Latin, from Greek, generation, birth, origin.]

Gen·e·sis (jĕn′ə-sĭs) *n. Abbr.* **Gen.** The first book of the Old Testament, recounting the creation of the world and the establishment and early history of Israel.

-genesis *suffix.* Indicates generation; for example, **biogenesis, paragenesis.** [New Latin, from Latin *genesis,* birth, GENESIS.]

gene-splic·ing (jēn′splī′sĭng) *n.* The process in which DNA fragments from one or more different organisms are combined and made to function within the cells of a host organism.

gen·et[1] (jĕn′ĭt, jə-nĕt′) *n.* Any of several Old World carnivorous mammals of the genus *Genetta,* having grayish or yellowish fur with dark spots and a long, ringed tail. [Middle English *genete,* from Old French, from Arabic *jarnayṭ.*]

genet[2]. Variant of **jennet.**

Ge·net (zhə-nā′), **Jean** (1910–86). French novelist and playwright. After many convictions for theft and homosexuality, he was released from a life sentence when many of France's leading intellectuals, led by Jean Cocteau, petitioned the president. His early works, such as *The Miracle of the Rose* (1946) and *A Thief's Journal* (1948), draw on his prison experiences. His later works tend toward the nihilistic and the absurd.

ge·net·ic (jə-nĕt′ĭk) *adj.* Also **ge·net·i·cal** (-ĭ-kəl). **1.** Of or pertaining to the origin or development of something. **2. a.** Of or pertaining to genetics or genes. **b.** Affecting or affected by genes: *a genetic disorder.* [From GENESIS.] **—ge·net·i·cal·ly** *adv.*

genetic code *n.* The information carried by DNA, which determines the nature of all the proteins made in the cell. The code is expressed by the sequence of nitrogenous bases in the DNA molecule, three consecutive bases (a codon) coding for a particular amino acid in the protein.

genetic drift *n.* The tendency for a genetic variant to become fixed in or lost from a population by chance rather than by natural selection. It most commonly occurs in small, isolated populations. Also called "Sewall Wright effect."

genetic engineering *n.* The modification of the structure of the chromosomes of living organisms, especially bacteria and viruses, in such a way as to benefit man. It has been employed in agriculture and medicine. See **biotechnology. —genetic engineer** *n.*

ge·net·i·cist (jə-nĕt′ə-sĭst) *n.* One who specializes in genetics.

ge·net·ics (jə-nĕt′ĭks) *n.* **1.** *Used with a singular verb.* The biology of heredity; especially, the study of the mechanisms of hereditary transmission and the variation of heritable characteristics. **2.** *Used with a singular or plural verb.* The genetic constitution of an individual, group, or class.

Ge·ne·va (jə-nē′və). *French* **Ge·nève** (zhə-nĕv′). *German* **Genf** (gĕnf). A city in Switzerland, on the southwest corner of Lake Geneva. It is the country's third-largest city and capital of Geneva canton. Many international organizations, such as the Red Cross, and agencies of the United Nations, including the World Health Organization, have their headquarters here.

Geneva, Lake. *French* **Lac Lé·man** (lăk lĕ′mən, lĕm′ən, lə-măn′). *German* **Gen·fer·see** (gĕn′fər-zā). Lake of Switzerland and France. Approximately 72 kilometers (45 miles) long and 13 kilometers (8 miles) at its widest point, it lies between southwest Switzerland and the Haute-Savoie department of France. The surface is subject to changes of level caused by variations in atmospheric pressure and wind direction.

Ge·ne·va bands (jə-nē′və) *pl.n.* Two strips of white cloth hanging from the collar of some clerical and academic robes. [Originally worn by Calvinist clergymen in Geneva.]

Geneva Convention *n.* Any of several agreements, the first of which was formulated in 1864 at an international convention held in Geneva, Switzerland, establishing rules for the wartime treatment of prisoners and the sick or wounded.

Geneva cross *n.* A red Greek or St. George's cross on a white ground, used as a symbol by the Red Cross and as a sign of neutrality.

Geneva gown *n.* A loose black academic or clerical gown with wide sleeves. [Originally worn by Calvinist clergymen in Geneva.]

Ge·ne·van (jə-nē′vən) *adj.* Also **Gen·e·vese** (jĕn′ə-vēz′, -vēs′). 1. Of or relating to Geneva, Switzerland. 2. Of or relating to Geneva during the time of John Calvin; Calvinist.
~*n.* Also **Genevese.** 1. A native or inhabitant of Geneva, Switzerland. 2. A follower of Calvin; a Calvinist.

Geneva Protocol *n.* A document drafted in 1925 that sought to ban the use of poison gas in warfare and to enforce sanctions against the aggressors in wars.

Genf. See **Geneva.**

Gen·ghis Khan (jĕng′gĭz kän, gĕng′-), **Chin·giz Khan** (chĭng′-), **Jen·ghiz Khan** (jĕng′-, gĕng′-), or **Jin·ghiz Khan** (jĭng′-), born Temujin (c. 1162–1227). Mongolian emperor. The son of a Mongol chieftain, he united the Mongolian tribes by conquest, and in 1206 took the title Genghis Khan (supreme ruler). By brilliant use of light cavalry, he annexed northern China, central Asia, Iran, and southern Russia. Though capable of horrific cruelty in battle, he was a far-sighted administrator and lawmaker.

gen·ial[1] (jēn′yəl) *adj.* 1. Having a pleasant or friendly disposition or manner; cordial and kindly. 2. Conducive to life or growth; mild. 3. *Obsolete.* Characteristic of or relating to genius. [Latin *geniālis,* of generation or birth, nuptial, hence festive, joyous, from *genius,* deity of generation and birth.] —**gen·ial·ly** *adv.* —**ge·ni·al·i·ty** (jē′-nē-ăl′ə-tē), **gen·ial·ness** *n.*

ge·ni·al[2] (jə-nī′əl) *adj. Anatomy.* Of or pertaining to the chin. [Greek *geneion,* chin, from *genus,* jaw.]

gen·ic (jē′nĭk, jĕn′ĭk) *adj.* Of, relating to, produced by, or being a gene or genes; genetic.

–genic *suffix.* Indicates: 1. Generation or production; for example, **antigenic.** 2. Suitability for; for example, **photogenic.** [From -GEN.]

ge·nic·u·late (jə-nĭk′yə-lĭt) *adj.* Also **ge·nic·u·lat·ed** (-lā′tĭd). 1. *Biology.* Bent at an abrupt angle like that of a bent knee. 2. Jointed so as to be capable of bending at an abrupt angle. [Latin *geniculātus,* with bent knee, curved, from *geniculum,* diminutive of *genu,* knee.] —**ge·nic·u·late·ly** *adv.* —**ge·nic·u·la·tion** *n.*

ge·nie (jē′nē) *n.* A supernatural creature who does one's bidding. [French *génie,* spirit, from Latin *genius,* guardian spirit, GENIUS.]

ge·ni·i. Alternate plural of **genius.**

gen·ip (jĕn′əp) *n.* 1. A tropical American tree, *Melicocca bijuga,* having small greenish-white flowers and small yellow fruit. 2. The sweet, edible fruit of the genip. 3. The genipap. [Spanish *genipa,* a kind of palm, probably of Carib origin.]

gen·i·pap (jĕn′ə-păp′) *n.* 1. An evergreen tree, *Genipa americana,* of the West Indies, having yellowish-white flowers and edible fruit. 2. The reddish-brown fruit of the genipap. Also called "genip," "marmalade box." [Portuguese *genipapo,* from Tupi.]

ge·nis·ta (jə-nĭs′tə) *n.* Any shrub of the European genus *Genista,* similar and related to the broom; especially, **dyer's greenweed** *(see).* [New Latin *Genista* (genus), from Latin, broom.]

genit. genitive.

gen·i·tal (jĕn′ə-təl) *adj.* 1. Of or relating to biological reproduction. 2. Of or pertaining to the genitals. 3. *Psychoanalysis.* Pertaining to or designating a stage at which a child's anal and oral impulses give way to more mature personal relationships. Compare **anal, oral.** [Middle English *genytal,* from Old French *genital,* from Latin *genitālis,* from *gignere* (past participle *genitus*), to beget, produce.]

genital herpes *n.* A recurrent viral infection of the genital region that may cause painful eruptions of the skin or be symptomless. See **herpes.**

gen·i·ta·li·a (jĕn′ə-tā′lē-ə, -tāl′yə) *pl.n.* The reproductive organs; especially, the external sex organs. [Latin *genitālia (membra),* genital (members), neuter plural of *genitālis,* GENITAL.]

gen·i·tals (jĕn′ə-təlz) *pl.n.* Genitalia.

gen·i·ti·val (jĕn′ə-tī′vəl) *adj. Grammar.* Of, pertaining to, or in the genitive case. —**gen·i·ti·val·ly** *adv.*

gen·i·tive (jĕn′ə-tĭv) *n. Abbr.* **g., gen., genit.** 1. The grammatical case in certain languages, usually expressed in English by a prepositional phrase with *of,* that denotes possession, measurement, or source. 2. A form or construction in this case.
~*adj. Abbr.* **g., gen., genit.** *Grammar.* Designating, pertaining to, or inflected in the genitive. [Middle English *genitif (case),* from Latin *(casus) genitīvus,* "case of production or origin" (translation of Greek *genikē ptōsis,* "case of race"), from *gignere* (past participle *genitus*), to beget, produce.]

gen·i·tor (jĕn′ə-tər) *n.* 1. One who begets or creates. 2. *Anthropology.* A natural father as distinguished from the socially responsible foster father in certain cultures. [Middle English *genytur,* from Latin *genitor,* from *gignere* (past participle *genitus*), to beget.]

gen·i·to·u·ri·nar·y (jĕn′ə-tō-yŏŏr′ə-nĕr′ē) *adj.* Of or pertaining to the genital and urinary organs or their functions. [GENIT(AL) + URINARY.]

gen·ius (jēn′yəs) *n., pl.* **-iuses** or **genii** (jē′nē-ī′) (for senses 4, 6).

1. **a.** Exceptional or transcendent intellectual and creative power. **b.** One who possesses such power. 2. **a.** A natural talent or inclination. Used with *to* or *for: She has a genius for acting.* **b.** One who has such a talent or inclination: *He is a genius at diplomacy.* 3. The prevailing spirit or character, as of a place, person, time, or group: *the genius of the Elizabethan poets.* 4. *Roman Mythology.* A tutelary deity or guardian spirit allotted to a person from birth. **b.** Any guiding spirit of a person or place. 5. A person who has great influence over another. 6. In Muslim legend, a jinni or demon. [Latin *genius,* deity of generation and birth, guardian spirit.]

ge·ni·us lo·ci (jē′nē-əs lō′sī′) *n.* 1. A guardian deity of a particular locality. 2. The distinctive atmosphere or particular character of a place. [Latin.]

ge·ni·zah (gə-nē′zə) *n.* A room adjacent to a synagogue where discarded books and sacred relics are stored. [Hebrew, "hiding place," from *gānaz,* to hide.]

genl. general.

Gennesaret, Lake of. See **Galilee, Sea of.**

Gen·o·a (jĕn′ō-ə). *Italian* **Ge·no·va** (jĕn′ə-və). Port on the Gulf of Genoa, Italy. The capital of Liguria and of Genoa province, it is Italy's chief seaport and handles over one third of the country's shipping. —**Gen·o·ese** (jĕn′ō-ēz′) *adj. & n.*

Gen·o·a cake (jĕn′ō-ə) *n.* A rich sponge cake, sometimes made with cherries. [After GENOA, Italy.]

Genoa jib *n. Nautical.* A large jib used on a racing yacht. [After GENOA, Italy.]

gen·o·cide (jĕn′ə-sīd′) *n.* The systematic, planned annihilation of a racial, political, or cultural group. [Greek *genos,* race + -CIDE.] —**gen·o·cid·al** (jĕn′ə-sīd′l) *adj.*

ge·nome (jē′nōm′) *n.* Also **ge·nom** (-nŏm′). *Biology.* A complete haploid set of chromosomes. [German *Genom : Gen,* GENE + (CHROMOS)OME.]

gen·o·type (jĕn′ə-tīp′, jē′nə-) *n.* 1. The genetic constitution of an organism, especially as distinguished from its physical appearance. Compare **phenotype.** 2. A group or class of organisms having the same genetic constitution. [Greek *genos,* race + TYPE.] —**gen·o·typ·ic** (jĕn′ə-tĭp′ĭk, jē′nə-), **gen·o·typ·i·cal** *adj.* —**gen·o·typ·i·cal·ly** *adv.* —**gen·o·ty·pic·i·ty** (jĕn′ə-tī-pĭs′ə-tē, jē′nə-) *n.*

–genous *suffix.* Indicates: 1. Generating or producing; for example, **androgenous.** 2. Generated by, produced by, or arising from; for example, **endogenous.** [From -GEN.]

Genova. See **Genoa.**

gen·re (zhän′rə) *n.* 1. Type; class. 2. **a.** A category of artistic composition, as of music, marked by a distinctive style, form, or content, especially a style of painting concerned with depicting scenes and subjects of common everyday life. **b.** A distinctive class or category of literary composition.
~*adj.* Of or relating to genre. [French, kind, from Old French *gen(d)re,* from Latin *genus* (stem *gener-*), race, kind.]

gen·ro (gĕn′rō′) *n., pl.* **-ros.** 1. In Japan, a group of elder statesmen, formerly advisers to the emperor. 2. Any of these elder statesmen. [Japanese *genrō.*]

gens (jĕnz, gĕnz) *n., pl.* **gentes** (jĕn′tēz′, gĕn′tās′). 1. The patrilineal clan forming the basic unit of the Roman tribe and having originally a common name, land, cult, and burial ground. 2. *Anthropology.* An exogamous patrilineal clan. [Latin *gēns,* clan.]

gent (jĕnt) *n. Informal.* A gentleman; a man. [Shortened from GENTLEMAN.]

Gent. See **Ghent.**

gen·ta·mi·cin (jĕn′tə-mī′sĭn) *n.* An antibiotic used to treat a wide variety of infections and applied by injection or in the form of a cream or drops. [Variant of earlier *gentamycin : genta-* (probably irregularly formed from *gentian violet,* referring to the color of the organism from which it is derived) + *-mycin,* as in STREPTOMYCIN.]

gen·teel (jĕn-tēl′) *adj.* 1. **a.** Striving to convey a manner or appearance of refinement and respectability. **b.** Marked by affected and somewhat prudish refinement. 2. Refined in manner; well-bred; polite. 3. Free from vulgarity or rudeness. 4. Fashionable; elegant: *"It was a genteel old-fashioned house, very quiet and orderly"* (Charles Dickens). —See Synonyms at **polite.** [Old French *gentil,* GENTLE.] —**gen·teel·ly** *adv.* —**gen·teel·ness** *n.*

gen·teel·ism (jĕn-tē′lĭz′əm) *n.* A word or expression thought by its user to be genteel.

gen·tian (jĕn′shən) *n.* 1. Any of numerous plants of the genus *Gentiana,* characteristically having showy blue, yellow, or red flowers. 2. The dried rhizome and roots of a yellow-flowered European gentian, *G. lutea,* sometimes used as a tonic. [Middle English *gencian,* from Old French *genciane,* from Latin *gentiāna,* probably after *Gentius,* king of Illyria (2nd century B.C.), supposed discoverer of the medicinal properties of the plant.]

gen·tia·nel·la (jĕn′shə-nĕl′ə, jĕn′shē-ə-) *n.* 1. An alpine plant, *Gentiana acaulis,* with ornamental blue flowers. 2. Any of several similar and related plants. [New Latin, diminutive of GENTIAN.]

gentian violet *n.* A purple dye used chiefly as a biological stain and bactericide. Also called "crystal violet."

gen·tile (jĕn′tīl′) *adj.* 1. Of or pertaining to the gens or to the tribal society based on it. 2. Of or relating to Gentiles. 3. *Grammar.* Of or pertaining to a noun or adjective designating a nation, place, or people; for example, *American* and *Italian* are gentile nouns.
~*n.* 1. A member of a gens. 2. A gentile noun or adjective. [Latin *gentīlis,* from *gēns,* clan, GENS.]

Gen·tile (jĕn′tīl′) *n.* 1. A person who is not of the Jewish faith or is of a non-Jewish nation. 2. A Christian as distinguished from a Jew.

gentian *One of the wildflowers most favored by herbalists. Gentians have been used for curing indigestion, bites and stings, dysentery and catarrh, and as a flavoring for bitter beer. This is the marsh gentian,* Gentiana pneumonanthe.

geological time scale

HOW WE GAUGE EARTH'S AGE
The planet's story, revealed by its rocks

The eras of the earth have been well established by isotope dating, in which the age of rocks is calculated from the amount of radioactive-decay products they are found to contain. Major divisions reflect changes in the positions of continents and the emergence of new forms of life.

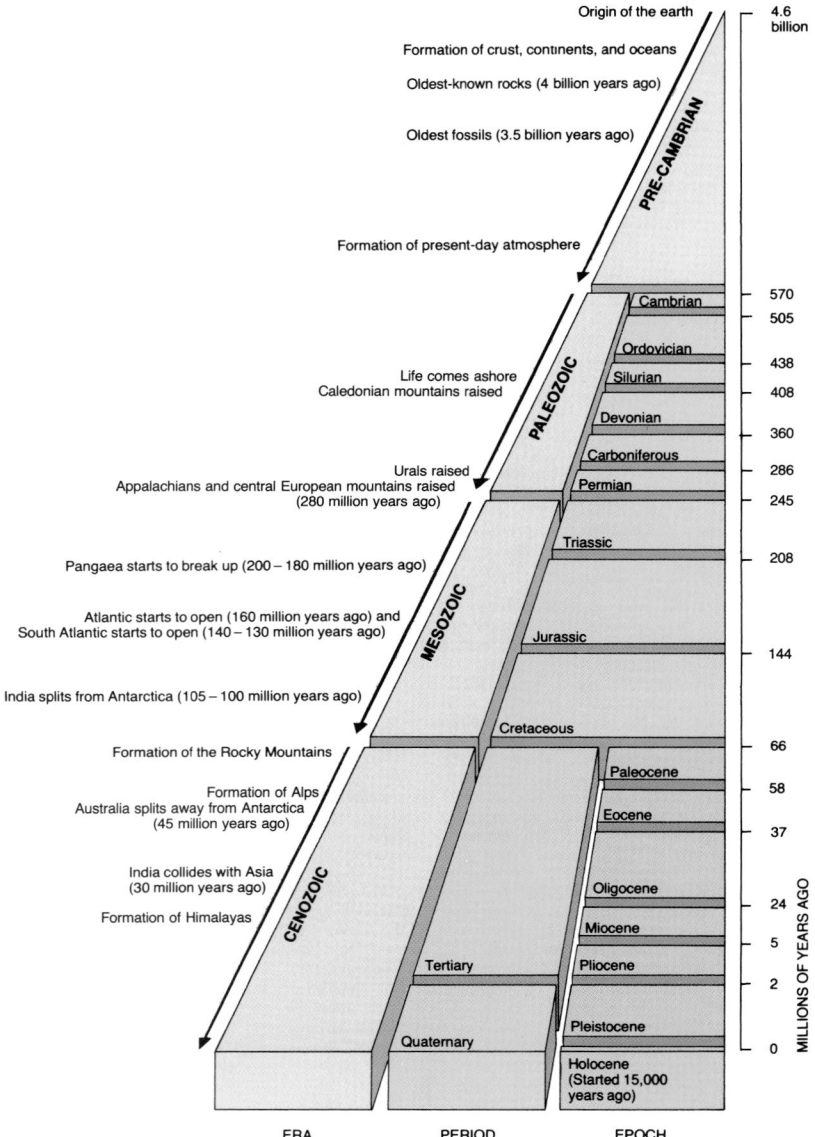

Origin of the earth	4.6 billion
Formation of crust, continents, and oceans	
Oldest-known rocks (4 billion years ago)	
Oldest fossils (3.5 billion years ago)	

PRE-CAMBRIAN

Formation of present-day atmosphere

PALEOZOIC

Cambrian	570
Ordovician	505
Silurian	438
Devonian	408
Carboniferous	360
Permian	286

Life comes ashore
Caledonian mountains raised

Urals raised
Appalachians and central European mountains raised (280 million years ago)

MESOZOIC

Triassic	245
	208
Jurassic	144
Cretaceous	

Pangaea starts to break up (200 – 180 million years ago)

Atlantic starts to open (160 million years ago) and South Atlantic starts to open (140 – 130 million years ago)

India splits from Antarctica (105 – 100 million years ago)

Formation of the Rocky Mountains

CENOZOIC

Formation of Alps
Australia splits away from Antarctica (45 million years ago)

India collides with Asia (30 million years ago)
Formation of Himalayas

Tertiary

Paleocene	66
Eocene	58
	37
Oligocene	24
Miocene	5
Pliocene	2
Pleistocene	0

Quaternary

| Holocene (Started 15,000 years ago) | |

MILLIONS OF YEARS AGO

ERA   PERIOD   EPOCH

ERAS OF THE WORLD *Eras (and periods) are defined by life forms. Fossils in pre-Cambrian rocks are very rare. The Paleozoic ("old life") saw the rise of invertebrates and amphibians. The Mesozoic ("middle life") was the age of reptiles. The Cenozoic ("recent life") is the age of mammals.*

---

gen·tle (jĕnt′l) *adj.* **-tler, -tlest. 1.** Considerate or kindly in disposition; tender and patient: *a gentle mother.* **2.** Not harsh, severe, or violent; mild: *a gentle scolding.* **3.** Easily managed or handled; docile; tame: *a gentle horse.* **4.** Gradual; not steep or sudden: *a gentle incline.* **5.** Moderate. **6.** Of good family; well-born. **7.** *Archaic.* Noble; chivalrous: *a gentle knight.* ~*n.* **1.** *Archaic.* One of gentle birth or station. **2.** The larva of a bluebottle. ~*tr.v.* **gentled, -tling, -tles. 1.** To make gentle; pacify; mollify. **2.** To tame (a horse, for example). [Middle English *gentil,* well-born, noble, graceful, from Old French, from Latin *gentīlis,* of the same clan, of noble birth, from *gēns,* clan.] —**gen·tly** *adv.*

gentle breeze *n.* A wind whose speed is between 12.9 and 19.3 kilometers, or 8 and 12 miles, per hour, force 3 on the Beaufort scale.

gen·tle·folk (jĕnt′l-fōk′) *pl.n.* Also **gen·tle·folks** (-fōks′). Persons of good family and breeding.

gen·tle·man (jĕnt′l-mən) *n., pl.* **-men** (-mĭn). **1.** A polite, gracious, or considerate man with high standards of propriety or correct behavior. **2.** A man of gentle or noble birth or superior social position. **3. a.** A man. **b. gentlemen.** A form of address for a group of men. Used both in speech and in writing. **4.** A manservant; valet. **5.** *British.* Formerly, a man higher than a yeoman in social position. **6.** A man of independent means who does not or need not work to support himself. [GENTLE + MAN (after French *gentilhomme*).] —**gen·tle·man·ly** *adj.*

Usage: *Gentleman* is used instead of *man* only in restricted contexts, and usually carries a nuance: *He's no gentleman* (meaning that he does not act in a well-mannered, considerate way). The form is used neutrally in direct address: *Ladies and gentlemen; We must now turn, gentlemen, to the second point on the agenda.* It is also preferred when referring to a person in his presence: *You had better ask this gentleman to wait outside* (where *man* would sound abrupt and rude).

gen·tle·man-at-arms (jĕnt′l-mən-ət-ärmz′) *n., pl.* **gen·tle·men-at-arms** (-mĭn-). Any of a corps of about 35 senior retired army officers who attend the British sovereign as a ceremonial guard on state occasions.

gentleman farmer *n., pl.* **gentlemen farmers.** A man who farms chiefly for pleasure rather than income or whose means permit him to be an absentee proprietor of his farming interests.

gentleman's agreement *n.* An agreement guaranteed only by the honor of the participants and not legally binding.

gentleman's gentleman *n.* A manservant; a valet.

gen·tle·ness (jĕnt′l-nĭs) *n.* **1.** The quality of being gentle. **2.** *Physics.* A property or quantum number of elementary particles, similar to charm. It is conserved in strong interactions.

gentle sex *n.* Women collectively.

gen·tle·wom·an (jĕnt′l-wŏŏm′ən) *n., pl.* **-women** (-wĭm′ĭn). **1.** A woman of gentle birth or superior social position. **2.** A polite, gracious, or considerate woman. **3.** A woman acting as a personal attendant to a lady of rank.

Gen·too (jĕn′tōō) *n., pl.* **-toos.** *Archaic.* A Hindu. [Portuguese *gentio,* "a pagan," from Late Latin *gentīlis,* pagan, GENTILE.]

gen·tri·fy (jĕn′trə-fī′) *tr.v.* **-fied, -fying, -fies.** To change the character of (restored property, especially in a working-class neighborhood) by an influx of middle-class or upper-class residents. [GENTRY + -FY.] —**gen·tri·fi·ca·tion** *n.*

gen·try (jĕn′trē) *n., pl.* **-tries. 1.** People of gentle birth, good breeding, or high social position. **2.** In Britain, the upper middle classes. **3.** People of a particular class or group: *another commuter from the suburban gentry.* [Middle English *gentri(se),* gentle birth, from Old French *genterise, gentelise,* from *gentil,* GENTLE.]

gen·u (jĕn′yōō) *n., pl.* **genua** (jĕn′yōō-ə). *Anatomy.* The knee. [New Latin, from Latin.]

gen·u·flect (jĕn′yə-flĕkt′) *intr.v.* **-flected, -flecting, -flects. 1.** To bend the knee in a kneeling or half-kneeling position, as in reverence. **2.** To exhibit a deferential or obsequious attitude or manner. [Late Latin *genuflectere* : Latin *genu,* knee + *flectere,* to bend.]

gen·u·flec·tion (jĕn′yə-flĕk′shən) *n.* Also *chiefly British* **gen·u·flex·ion.** The act of kneeling briefly by bending one knee, as in reverence.

gen·u·ine (jĕn′yōō-ĭn) *adj.* **1.** Actually possessing or produced by the alleged or apparent attribute, character, or source: *genuine sorrow; genuine leather.* **2.** Not spurious or counterfeit; authentic: *a genuine claim.* **3.** Free from hypocrisy or dishonesty; sincere: *genuine admiration.* **4.** Being of pure or original stock. —See Synonyms at **real.** [Latin *genuīnus,* perhaps originally "placed on the knees" (from the ancient custom that a father acknowledges a child by placing him or her on his knees), from *genu,* knee.] —**gen·u·ine·ly** *adv.* —**gen·u·ine·ness** *n.*

ge·nus (jē′nəs) *n., pl.* **genera** (jĕn′ər-ə). *Abbr.* **gen. 1.** *Biology.* A taxonomic category ranking below a family and above a species, used in taxonomic nomenclature followed by a Latin adjective or epithet to form the name of a species. **2.** *Logic.* A class of objects divided into subordinate species having certain common attributes. **3.** Any class, group, or kind with common attributes. **4.** *Mathematics.* A number denoting the topological complexity of a surface. A sphere has a genus of 0; a torus has a genus of 1. [Latin *genus,* birth, race, kind.]

–geny *suffix.* Indicates manner of origin or development; for example, **ontogeny.** [Greek *-geneia,* from *-genēs,* born.]

---

3. A pagan or heathen. **4.** Among Mormons, a person who is not a Mormon. ~*adj.* Of or pertaining to a Gentile. [Middle English *gentil, gentyle,* from Late Latin *gentīles,* pagans, heathens, from *gentīlis,* pagan, from Latin, of the same clan, from *gēns,* clan.]

gen·ti·lesse (jĕn′tə-lĕs′) *n. Archaic.* Refinement and courtesy resulting from good breeding. [Middle English, from Old French, from *gentil,* GENTLE.]

gen·til·i·ty (jĕn-tĭl′ə-tē) *n.* **1.** The condition of being genteel. **2.** The condition of being born to the gentry. **3.** Persons of gentle birth collectively; the gentry. **4.** The attempt to convey or maintain the appearance of refinement and respectability. —See Usage note at **culture.** [Middle English *gentilete,* from Old French, from Latin *gentīlitās* (stem *gentīlitāt-*), clanship, from *gentīlis,* belonging to a clan, GENTLE.]

geo– *prefix.* Indicates the earth; for example, **geotropism, geology.** [Greek *geō-,* from *gē,* earth.]

ge·o·cen·tric (jē'ō-sĕn'trĭk) *adj.* **1.** Pertaining to, measured from, or observed from the center of the earth. **2.** Having the earth as a center. **—ge·o·cen·tri·cal·ly** *adv.*

geocentric parallax *n. Astronomy.* **Diurnal parallax** *(see).*

ge·o·chem·is·try (jē'ō-kĕm'ĭ-strē) *n.* The science and study of the composition and chemical processes that take place in the earth's crust. **—ge·o·chem·i·cal** *adj.* **—ge·o·chem·ist** *n.*

ge·o·chro·nol·o·gy (jē'ō-krə-nŏl'ə-jē) *n.* The chronology of the earth's history as determined by geologic events. **—ge·o·chron·o·log·ic** (jē'ō-krŏn'ə-lŏj'ĭk), **ge·o·chron·o·log·i·cal** *adj.*

geod. 1. geodesy. **2.** geodesic. **3.** geodetic.

ge·ode (jē'ōd') *n.* A small, hollow, usually spheroidal nodule with crystals lining the inside wall. [Latin *geōdēs,* from Greek, earthlike : *gē,* earth + -ODE (resembling).]

ge·o·des·ic (jē'ə-dĕs'ĭk, -dēz'ĭk, -dē'sĭk, -dē'zĭk) *adj. Abbr.* **geod. 1.** *Mathematics.* Of or pertaining to the geometry of geodesics. **2.** Geodetic.
∼*n. Mathematics.* In three-dimensional Euclidean space, a curve whose principal normal at any point is the normal to the surface on which the curve occurs; the shortest line between two points on any mathematically derived surface.

geodesic dome *n.* A domed or vaulted structure of lightweight straight elements that form interlocking polygons.

ge·od·e·sy (jē-ŏd'ə-sē) *n. Abbr.* **geod.** The branch of mathematics concerned with the size and shape of the earth, including the techniques of measuring distance on the earth's surface and of determining exact geographic location. [French *geodesie,* from New Latin *geodaesia,* from Greek *geōdaisia,* "division of the earth" : GEO- + *daiesthai,* to divide.] **—ge·od·e·sist** *n.*

ge·o·det·ic (jē'ə-dĕt'ĭk) *adj.* Also **geo·det·i·cal** (-ĭ-kəl). *Abbr.* **geod. 1.** Of or pertaining to geodesy. **2.** Geodesic. **—ge·o·det·i·cal·ly** *adv.*

geo·duck (gōō'ē-dŭk') *n.* A very large edible clam, *Panope generosa,* of the Pacific coast of northwestern North America. [Chinook jargon *go-duck.*]

ge·o·dy·nam·ics (jē'ō-dī-năm'ĭks) *n. Used with a singular verb.* The study of the forces acting inside the earth's crust and the way in which they affect its formation, alteration, and disturbance. **—ge·o·dy·nam·ic** *adj.* **—ge·o·dy·nam·i·cist** *n.*

Geof·frey of Mon·mouth (jĕf'rē; mŏn'məth) (*c.* 1100–54). English writer. His *History of the Kings of Britain,* tracing an almost entirely fictitious line of descent from the Trojans to King Arthur, recorded British folk history and inspired the Arthurian writers and Shakespeare's *King Lear* and *Cymbeline.*

geog. 1. geographer. **2.** geographic. **3.** geography.

ge·og·no·sy (jē-ŏg'nə-sē) *n.* The scientific study of the organization and structure of the earth and its materials. [GEO- + Greek *-gnosia,* knowledge, -GNOSIS.]

ge·o·graph·ic (jē'ə-grăf'ĭk), **ge·o·graph·i·cal** (-ĭ-kəl) *adj. Abbr.* **geog. 1.** Pertaining to geography. **2.** Concerning the topography of a specific region. **—ge·o·graph·i·cal·ly** *adv.*

geographic mile *n.* A nautical mile.

ge·og·ra·phy (gē-ŏg'rə-fē) *n., pl.* **-phies.** *Abbr.* **geog. 1. a.** The study of the earth and its surface features, how they influence human distribution and activity, and how they in turn are affected by human activity. **b.** Broadly, the science of the distribution of all the components of the physical world. **2.** The geographic characteristics of an area. **3.** A book on geography. **4.** An ordered arrangement of constituent elements. [Latin *geōgraphia,* from Greek : GEO- + -GRAPHY.] **—ge·og·ra·pher** *n.*

ge·oid (jē'oid') *n.* **1.** The hypothetical surface of the earth formed from mean sea level and its continuation through the continents. **2.** A geometric figure similar to this surface. [German *Geoid,* from Greek *geoidēs,* earthlike : GE(O)- + -OID.]

geol. 1. geologic. **2.** geologist. **3.** geology.

geologic time *n.* The period of time covering the earth's geologic history.

geological time scale *n.* The division of geological time into chronological units. The last 570–600 million years are divided into the units **era, period, epoch,** and **age** *(all of which see).* The time before this is the **Precambrian** *(see).*

ge·ol·o·gize (jē-ŏl'ə-jīz') *intr.v.* **-gized, -gizing, -gizes.** To study geology or make geologic investigations.

ge·ol·o·gy (jē-ŏl'ə-jē) *n., pl.* **-gies.** *Abbr.* **geol. 1.** The scientific study of the origin, history, structure, and processes of the earth. **2.** The structure of a specific region of the earth's surface. **3.** A book on geology. **4.** The scientific study of the origin, history, and structure of the solid matter of a celestial body. [New Latin *geologia* : GEO- + -LOGY.] **—ge·o·log·ic** (jē'ə-lŏj'ĭk), **ge·o·log·i·cal** *adj.* **—ge·o·log·i·cal·ly** *adv.* **—ge·ol·o·gist, ge·ol·o·ger** *n.*

geom. 1. geometric. **2.** geometry.

geomagnetic equator *n.* The great circle on the earth's surface formed by the intersection of a plane passing through the earth's center perpendicular to the axis connecting the north and south magnetic poles. It is the geometric rationalization of the empirically defined **magnetic equator** *(see).*

ge·o·mag·ne·tism (jē'ō-măg'nə-tĭz'əm) *n.* **1.** The magnetism of the earth. **2.** The study of the earth's magnetic field. **—ge·o·mag·net·ic** (jē'ō-măg-nĕt'ĭk) *adj.* **—ge·o·mag·net·i·cal·ly** *adv.*

ge·o·man·cy (jē'ə-măn'sē) *n.* Divination by means of dust patterns, or of lines and figures. [Middle English, from Old French *geomancie,* from Medieval Latin *geōmantia,* from Late Greek *geōmanteia,* divination from signs obtained from the earth : GEO- + -MANCY.] **—ge·o·man·cer** *n.* **—ge·o·man·tic** (jē'ə-măn'tĭk) *adj.*

ge·o·me·chan·ics (jē'ō-mə-kăn'ĭks) *n. Used with a singular verb.* The study of the mechanics of rock and soil and its application in civil engineering.

ge·om·e·ter (jē-ŏm'ə-tər) *n.* **1.** A geometrician. **2.** A geometrid moth.

ge·o·met·ric (jē'ə-mĕt'rĭk) *adj.* Also **ge·o·met·ri·cal** (-rĭ-kəl). *Abbr.* **geom. 1.** Of or pertaining to geometry and its methods and principles. **2.** Using simple geometric forms in design and decoration. **—ge·o·met·ri·cal·ly** *adv.*

geometrical isomerism *n.* **Cis-trans isomerism** *(see).*

geometric isomer *n. Chemistry.* A type of **isomer** *(see).*

geometric mean *n.* The *n*th root, usually the positive *n*th root, of a product of *n* factors; for example, the geometric mean of 1, 3, and 9 is the cube root of 1 × 3 × 9.

geometric optics *n.* The study of reflection, refraction, and other optical phenomena using rays to represent the paths of light without reference to the wave properties of the light.

geometric progression *n.* A sequence of terms, such as 1, 3, 9, 27, 81, each of which is a constant multiple of the immediately preceding term. Also called "geometric sequence."

geometric series *n.* A sum in which the terms are members of a geometric progression.

ge·om·e·trid (jē-ŏm'ə-trĭd, jē'ə-mĕt'rĭd) *n.* Any of various moths of the family Geometridae, having caterpillars that move by looping the body in alternate contractions and expansions.
∼*adj.* Of or belonging to the Geometridae. [New Latin *Geometridae,* "land measurers" (from the movement of the caterpillars), from Latin *geōmetrēs,* geometrician, from Greek, from *geōmetrein,* to measure land. See **geometry.**]

ge·om·e·trize (jē-ŏm'ə-trīz') *v.* **-trized, -trizing, -trizes.** *—intr.* To study geometry. *—tr.* To apply the methods of geometry to (a physical theory, for example).

ge·om·e·try (jē-ŏm'ə-trē) *n., pl.* **-tries.** *Abbr.* **geom. 1. a.** The mathematics of the properties, measurement, and relationships of points, lines, angles, surfaces, and solids. **b.** A system of geometry: *Euclidean geometry.* **c.** A geometry restricted to a class of problems or objects: *solid geometry.* **2.** Configuration; arrangement. **3.** A surface shape. **4.** Any physical arrangement suggesting geometric forms or lines. [Middle English, from Old French *geometrie,* from Latin *geōmetria,* from Greek, from *geōmetrein,* to measure land : GEO- + *metrein,* to measure, from *metron,* measure.] **—ge·om·e·tri·cian** (jē-ŏm'ə-trĭsh'ən, jē'ə-mə-) *n.*

ge·o·mor·phic (jē'ə-môr'fĭk) *adj.* Of or like the earth, its shape, or its surface configuration. [GEO- + -MORPHIC.]

ge·o·mor·phol·o·gy (jē'ō-môr-fŏl'ə-jē) *n.* The scientific study of the configuration and evolution of land forms. **—ge·o·mor·pho·log·ic** (jē'ə-môr'fə-lŏj'ĭk), **ge·o·mor·pho·log·i·cal** *adj.* **—ge·o·mor·pho·log·i·cal·ly** *adv.*

ge·oph·a·gy (jē-ŏf'ə-jē) *n.* Also **ge·o·pha·gia** (jē'ə-fā'jə, -jē-ə). The practice of eating earthy substances, such as clay. [GEO- + -PHAGY.] **—ge·oph·a·gist** *n.*

ge·o·phys·ics (jē'ō-fĭz'ĭks) *n. Used with a singular verb.* The physics of the earth and of the processes that take place on and within it, sometimes including fields such as meteorology and climatology and also the physics of the moon and planets. **—ge·o·phys·i·cal** *adj.* **—ge·o·phys·i·cist** *n.*

ge·o·phyte (jē'ə-fīt') *n. Botany.* A perennial plant propagated by underground buds. [GEO- + -PHYTE.]

ge·o·pol·i·tics (jē'ō-pŏl'ə-tĭks) *n. Used with a singular verb.* **1.** The study of the relationship between politics and geography. **2.** A Nazi doctrine of expansion that concentrated on the reallocation of geographic, economic, and political boundaries. **—ge·o·po·lit·i·cal** (jē'ō-pə-lĭt'ĭ-kəl) *adj.*

ge·o·pon·ic (jē'ə-pŏn'ĭk) *adj.* **1.** Of or relating to agriculture or farming. **2.** Rustic; bucolic. [Greek *geōponikos,* from *geōponia,* tillage, from *geōponein,* to till land : GEO- + *ponein,* to toil, labor.]

ge·o·pon·ics (jē'ə-pŏn'ĭks) *n. Used with a singular verb.* The study or science of agriculture.

George I (jôrj) (1660–1727). Elector of Hanover (1698–1727), and king of Great Britain and Ireland (1714–27). As a Protestant he was offered the British throne in 1714, the Roman Catholic James Stuart having been excluded by Parliament. He left the running of the country to his Whig ministers, the chief of whom, Sir Robert Walpole, is regarded as Britain's first prime minister.

George II (1683–1760). King of Great Britain and Ireland and elector of Hanover (1727–60). His victory at the Battle of Dettingen (1743) was the last time that a British monarch led his troops in the field.

George III (1738–1820). King of Great Britain and Ireland (1760–1820) and of Hanover (1815–20). His attempts to interfere in government were instrumental in the loss of the American colonies (1776).

George IV (1762–1830). King of Great Britain and Ireland (1820–30) and of Hanover. As regent during his father's 30-year long mental and physical illness, he patronized art and fashion, but scandals involving his two marriages brought the monarchy into disrepute.

George V (1865–1936). King of Great Britain and Northern Ireland and emperor of India (1910–36). He changed the name of the royal house to Windsor during World War I.

George VI (1895–1952). King of Great Britain and Northern Ire-

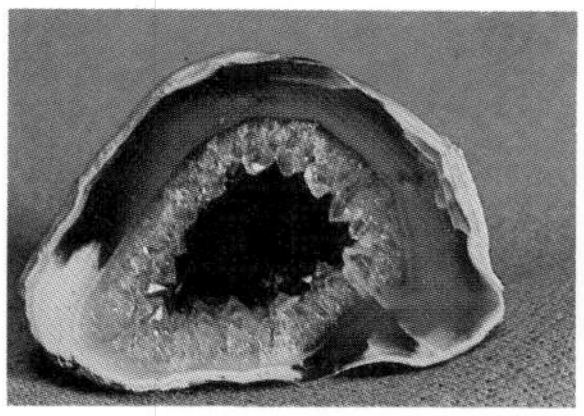

geode *A rounded nodule of stone containing a small cavity, usually lined with crystals. This geode is lined with amethyst.*

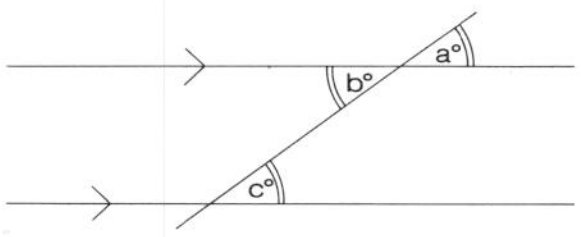

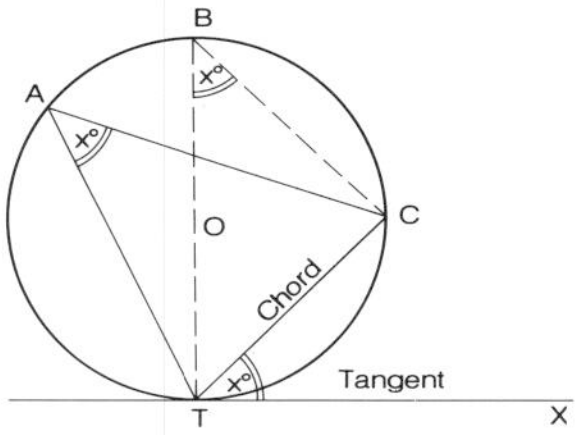

geometry *The study of the mathematical relationships between lines, angles, areas, and volumes—the discipline called geometry—is an essential tool of navigators, surveyors, engineers, and builders. The diagrams above illustrate some of the major theorems. When a straight line cuts a pair of parallel lines (upper drawing), the angles a, b, and c will be equal. In a circle (lower drawing), the angle between the chord TC and the tangent TX is equal to the angle at B, and lines drawn from the ends of the chord to any other point on the circle will contain the same angle. If the chord—like the line BT—passes through the center of the circle O, the angle between the lines (here, BC and CT) will be a right angle.*

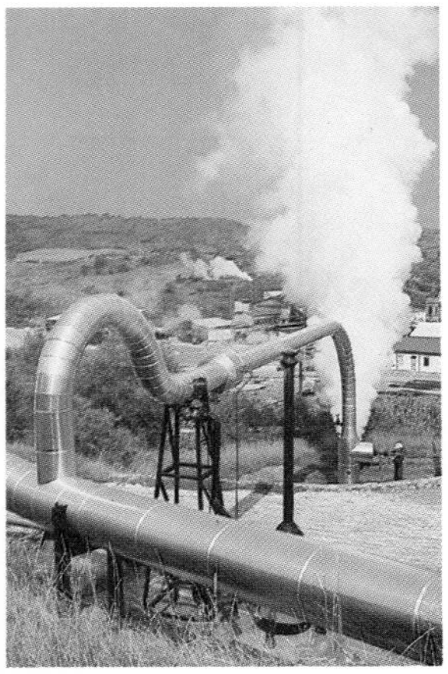

geothermal *Steam from underground springs, heated by the earth's molten interior, drives turbine generators at this geothermal power plant at Larderello, Italy.*

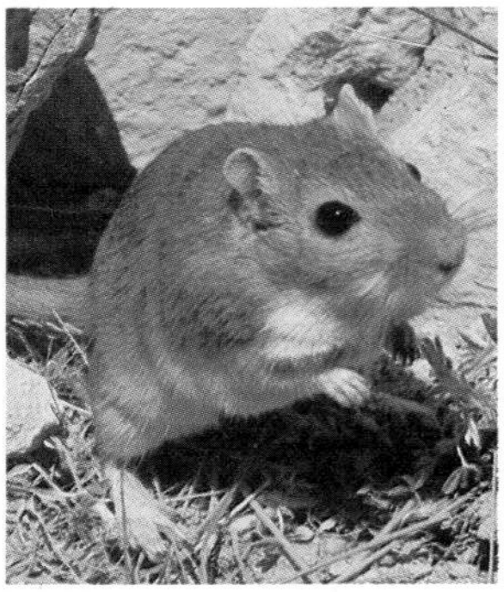

gerbil *There are about a dozen genera and almost 100 species of this burrowing rodent.*

PRONUNCIATION KEY

ă, **pat**; ā, **pay**; âr, **care**;
ä, **father**, **are**; b, **bib**;
ch, **church**; d, **deed**; ĕ, **pet**;
ē, **be**; f, **fife**; g, **gag**; h, **hat**;
hw, **which**; ĭ, **pit**; ī, **pie**;
îr, **pier**; j, **judge**; k, **kick**;
l, **lid**, **needle**; m, **mum**;
n, **no**, **sudden**; ng, **thing**;
ŏ, **pot**; ō, **toe**; ô, **paw**, **for**;
oi, **noise**; ou, **out**; o͝o, **book**;
o͞o, **boot**; p, **pop**; r, **roar**;
s, **sauce**; sh, **ship**, **dish**;
t, **tight**; th, **thin**, **path**;
th, **this**, **bathe**; ŭ, **cut**; ûr, **fur**;
v, **valve**; w, **with**; y, **yes**;
z, **zebra**, **size**; zh, **vision**;
ə, **about**, **item**, **edible**,
gallop, **circus**, **peaceful**

IN FOREIGN WORDS:

à, *Fr.* **ami**; œ, *Fr.* **feu**, *Ger.* **schön**; ü, *Fr.* **tu**, *Ger.* **über**; KH, *Ger.* **ich**, *Scot.* **loch**; N, *Fr.* **bon**; y', *Fr.* **Compiègne**

STRESS MARKS:

Primary stress: ′
in·cite′ (ĭn-sīt′)
Secondary stress: ′
in′sight′ (ĭn′sīt′)

land (1936–52) and emperor of India (1936–48). He acceded to the throne on the abdication of his brother Edward VIII and won enormous popularity by his dedication to his duties as a constitutional monarch, especially during World War II.

George, Lake. Glacial lake in the foothills of the Adirondack Mts., northeastern New York. It was the scene of many battles in the French and Indian War and the American Revolution. Today it is the center of an extensive resort area.

George Cross *n. Abbr.* **G.C.** A British civilian award for bravery.

George Town. Also **Pe·nang** (pə-năng′). City in northwest Malaysia. The capital of Penang state, it is the country's chief port, exporting tin, rubber, and copra. It became part of the British Straits Settlements in 1867, joining the Federation of Malaya in 1948.

George·town[1] (jôrj′toun′). Capital and chief port of Guyana, in the north at the mouth of the Demerara River.

Georgetown[2]. Capital of the Cayman Islands, on Grand Cayman, in the West Indies.

Georgetown[3]. Mainly residential section of western Washington, D.C. It was settled *c.* 1665, incorporated as a town in 1789, and annexed to Washington in 1878. Its beautiful old houses and gardens attract many tourists.

geor·gette (jôr-jĕt′) *n.* A sheer, strong silk or silklike crepe fabric with a dull surface, used for dresses, blouses, or trimming. Also called "georgette crepe." [Originally a trademark, after Madame *Georgette* de la Plante, a French modiste.]

George Wash·ing·ton Birthplace National Monument (wŏsh′-ĭng-tən, wôsh′-). Area in northeastern Virginia preserving the estate, called Wakefield, where the first president was born.

George Washington Car·ver National Monument (kär′vər). Site in southwestern Missouri containing the birthplace and boyhood home of the famed botanist and agricultural pioneer.

Geor·gia[1] (jôr′jə). *Abbr.* **Ga.** State of the southeast United States. Named after George II, it was founded in 1732, the last of the original 13 colonies. As a supporter of the Confederate cause, it suffered considerable damage in the Civil War. In the 20th century it has experienced many social and economic problems. Atlanta is the capital.

Georgia[2]. A republic bounded by the Caucasus Mountains and the Black Sea. An independent kingdom in the Middle Ages, it was invaded by the Mongols in 1234, divided between Persia and Turkey in 1555, and annexed by Russia in the 19th century. Independent in 1918, it joined the U.S.S.R. in 1922 and became a constituent republic in 1936. In 1991 it declared independence. Georgia is rich in minerals, especially manganese. Area, 69,967 square kilometers (26,911 square miles). Population, 5,535,000. Capital, T'bilisi.

Georgia, Strait of. Channel, *c.* 240 kilometers (150 miles) long, bordered on the west by Vancouver Island, on the east and northeast by the mainland of British Columbia, and on the southeast by Washington State. It links Puget Sound to Queen Charlotte Sound and is the gateway to the Inside (Inland) Passage to Alaska.

Geor·gian (jôr′jən) *adj.* **1.** Of, pertaining to, or characteristic of any of the reigns of the four Georges who ruled Great Britain from 1714 to 1830; especially, of or pertaining to the architectural style of this period, characterized by plain, symmetrical façades including many classical features. **2.** Of, pertaining to, or characteristic of the reign of King George V of Great Britain: *Georgian poetry.* **3.** Of or pertaining to the U.S. state of Georgia or to its inhabitants. **4.** Of or pertaining to the republic of Georgia or to its people or their language.
~*n.* **1.** A native or inhabitant of the state of Georgia. **2.** A native or inhabitant of the republic of Georgia. **3.** The Caucasian language of the republic of Georgia. **4.** A person belonging to or whose style is imitative of the period of any of the reigns of the Georges in Great Britain.

Georgian Bay. Large bay of Lake Huron in Ontario, Canada. Forty islands and part of the mainland comprise the Georgian Bay Islands National Park.

geor·gic (jôr′jĭk) *adj.* Of or pertaining to agriculture or rural life. ~*n.* **1. Georgics.** A poem by Virgil in four books, concerning agriculture and country life. **2.** A poem concerning farming or rural life. [Latin *Georgica,* from Greek *geōrgika,* cultivated lands, from neuter plural of *geōrgikos,* agricultural, from *geōrgos,* farmer, "(one) tilling the soil" : GEO- + *ergon,* work.]

ge·o·sci·ence (jē′ō-sī′əns) *n.* A science dealing with the earth, including geology, geophysics, oceanography, and applied sciences such as mining and engineering geology. Sometimes meteorology, climatology, and similar subjects are included.

ge·o·stat·ics (jē′ō-stăt′ĭks) *n. Used with a singular verb.* The study of the forces within the earth, as, for example, the pressure exerted by rock or soil. **—ge·o·stat·ic** *adj.*

ge·o·sta·tion·ar·y (jē′ō-stā′shə-nĕr′ē) *adj.* Of, pertaining to, or designating an artificial satellite that maintains a constant position above a point on the earth's equator.

ge·o·stroph·ic (jē′ə-strŏf′ĭk) *adj.* Of or pertaining to force caused by the earth's rotation: *a geostrophic wind.* [GEO- + Greek *strophē,* a turning, STROPHE.]

ge·o·syn·chro·nous (jē′ō-sĭng′krə-nəs, -sĭn′krə-nəs) *adj.* Of or pertaining to an artificial satellite that orbits the earth in the same direction as the earth's rotation and with an orbital period equal to the earth's rotation period.

ge·o·syn·cline (jē′ō-sĭn′klīn′) *n.* An extensive, usually linear depression in the earth's crust in which a succession of sedimentary strata has accumulated.

ge·o·tax·is (jē′ō-tăk′sĭs) *n. Biology.* The movement of an organism in response to the forces of gravity. **—ge·o·tac·tic** (jē′ō-tăk′tĭk) *adj.* **—ge·o·tac·ti·cal·ly** *adv.*

ge·o·tec·ton·ic (jē′ō-tĕk-tŏn′ĭk) *adj.* Of or relating to the mode of formation, shape, structure, and arrangement of the rock masses constituting the earth's crust.

ge·o·ther·mal (jē′ō-thûr′məl) *adj.* Also **ge·o·ther·mic** (-mĭk). Of or pertaining to the internal heat of the earth. **—ge·o·ther·mal·ly** *adv.*

geothermal power *n.* Heat originating in the earth's interior, as in volcanoes or geysers, and used as a source of energy.

ge·ot·ro·pism (jē-ŏt′rə-pĭz′əm) *n. Biology.* The response of a plant organ to gravity, as the downward growth of plant roots (*positive geotropism*). [GEO- + -TROPISM.] **—ge·o·tro·pic** (jē′ə-trō′pĭk, -trŏp′ĭk) *adj.* **—ge·o·tro·pi·cal·ly** *adv.*

ger. gerund.

Ger. 1. German. **2.** Germany.

ge·rah (gîr′ə) *n.* **1.** An ancient Hebrew unit of weight equal to 1/20 of a shekel. **2.** An ancient Hebrew coin. [Hebrew *gērāh,* "bean."]

ge·ra·ni·al (jə-rā′nē-ăl′) *n.* A perfume and flavoring ingredient, an isomer of **citral** *(see).* [GERANI(UM) + -AL (aldehyde).]

ge·ra·ni·ol (jə-rā′nē-ôl′, -ōl′) *n.* A fragrant pale yellow liquid, $C_{10}H_{18}O$, derived chiefly from the oils of geranium and citronella and used in cosmetics and flavorings. [GERANI(UM) + -OL (alcohol).]

ge·ra·ni·um (jə-rā′nē-əm) *n.* **1.** Any of various plants of the genus *Pelargonium,* native chiefly to southern Africa; especially, *P. domesticum,* widely cultivated for its rounded, often variegated leaves and showy clusters of red, pink, or white flowers. **2.** Any of various plants of the genus *Geranium,* having divided leaves and pink or purplish flowers. **3.** A strong to vivid red. [Latin, from Greek *geranion,* "small crane" (because the fruit resembles a crane's bill), from *geranos,* crane.]

ger·a·tol·o·gy (jĕr′ə-tŏl′ə-jē) *n.* The scientific study of the aging process and the problems and diseases associated with it. [Greek *gēras* (stem *gērat-*), old age + -LOGY.]

ger·bil (jûr′bəl) *n.* Any of various small, mouselike rodents of the genus *Gerbillus* and related genera, of arid regions of Africa and Asia Minor, having long hind legs and a long tail. [French *gerbille,* from New Latin *Gerbillus,* diminutive of *gerboa, jerboa,* JERBOA.]

ge·rent (jîr′ənt) *n.* A ruler or manager; an overseer. [Latin *gerēns* (stem *gerent-*), present participle of *gerere,* to carry, conduct, govern.]

ger·e·nuk (gĕr′ə-no͝ok′) *n.* An African gazelle, *Litocranius walleri,* having long legs, a long, slender neck, and backward-curving horns in the male. [Somali *garanug.*]

gerfalcon. Variant of **gyrfalcon.**

ger·i·at·ric (jĕr′ē-ăt′rĭk, jîr′-) *adj.* **1.** Of or pertaining to geriatrics. **2.** Of or pertaining to the aged or to their characteristic afflictions. ~*n.* An aged person, especially one requiring medical or social care. [Greek *gēras,* old age + -IATRIC.]

ger·i·at·rics (jĕr′ē-ăt′rĭks, jîr′-) *n. Used with a singular verb.* The branch of medicine concerned with the diagnosis and treatment of diseases of the elderly. **—ger·i·a·tri·cian** (jĕr′ē-ə-trĭsh′ən, jîr′-), **ger·i·at·rist** (jĕr′ē-ăt′rĭst, jə-rī′ə-trĭst) *n.*

Gé·ri·cault (zhā-rē-kō′), **Théodore** (1791–1824). French painter. His most famous work, *The Raft of the Medusa* (1819), portrayed an actual maritime disaster that had caused a political scandal.

germ (jûrm) *n.* **1.** A microorganism such as a bacterium or virus, especially one causing disease. **2.** *Biology.* A small organic structure or cell from which a new organism may develop. **3.** Something that may serve as the basis of further growth or development: *the germ of an idea.* [French *germe,* from Latin *germen,* offshoot, sprout, fetus.]

Usage: *Germ, microbe, bacteria, bacillus,* and *virus* are nouns denoting minute organisms or agents invisible to the unaided human eye, some of which are related to the production of disease. They are not interchangeable in careful usage except as indicated. *Germ* and *microbe* are nonscientific terms for such microorganisms; in popular usage they usually refer to disease-producing bodies. *Bacteria* (plural of *bacterium*) is the scientific term for a large group of microorganisms, only some of which produce disease. Many others are active in processes beneficial or not harmful to human, animal, and plant life. *Bacillus* is the scientific designation for a specific class of bacteria that includes some disease-producing microorganisms; only in loose popular usage is the term employed as the equivalent of any bacterium or any pathogenic bacterium. *Virus* is the technical term for any of a group of extremely small agents capable of producing certain diseases in human, animal, and plant life.

ger·man[1] (jûr′mən) *n.* **1.** An intricate dance for many couples. **2.** A party for dancing at which the german is featured. [Short for *German cotillion.*]

german[2] *adj.* **1.** Having the same parents or having the same grandparents on one side. Obsolete except as the second element in combinations: *cousin-german.* **2.** *Archaic.* Related; germane. [Middle English *germa(i)n,* from Old French *germain,* from Latin *germānus,* "from the same race," from *germen,* offshoot, fetus.]

Ger·man (jûr′mən) *adj. Abbr.* **G., Ger.** Of, pertaining to, or characteristic of Germany, its people, or their language.
~*n. Abbr.* **G., Ger. 1. a.** A native or citizen of Germany. **b.** A person of German descent. **c.** A person whose native language is

German. **2.** The West Germanic language spoken in Germany, Austria, and part of Switzerland. [Middle English *Germanes,* Teutons, Germans, from Latin *Germānus,* German, perhaps from Celtic *gair†,* neighbor.]

German cockroach *n.* A small cockroach, *Blatella germanica,* that is a common household pest.

German Democratic Republic. *Abbr.* **G.D.R.** See **Germany, East Germany.**

ger·man·der (jər-măn′dər) *n.* Any of various usually aromatic plants of the genus *Teucrium,* having purplish or reddish two-lipped flowers. [Middle English *germandre,* from Old French *germandree,* from Medieval Latin *germandra,* alteration of *gama(n)drea,* from Latin *chamadreos,* from Greek *khamaidrus,* "ground oak" : *khamai,* on the ground + *drus,* oak.]

ger·mane (jər-mān′) *adj.* Having a significant bearing upon a point at issue; pertinent: *The question you raised is not germane to the discussion.* —See Synonyms at **relevant.** [Middle English *germa(i)n,* having the same parents, GERMAN.]

ger·man·ic (jər-măn′ĭk) *n.* Of or pertaining to germanium. Said especially of compounds that contain germanium with a valence of 4. [GERMAN(IUM) + -IC.]

Ger·man·ic (jər-măn′ĭk) *adj.* **1. a.** Of, pertaining to, or characteristic of Germany or of the German people or their culture. **b.** Of or pertaining to Teutons. **c.** Of or pertaining to a Germanic-speaking people. **2.** Of, pertaining to, or constituting Germanic. —*n.* **1.** A branch of the Indo-European language family divided into North Germanic, West Germanic, and East Germanic. It includes English, Dutch, German, and the Scandinavian languages. **2.** The unrecorded ancestor language of this branch, **Proto-Germanic** *(see).*

Ger·man·ism (jûr′mə-nĭz′əm) *n.* **1.** An attitude, custom, or practice that seems characteristically German. **2.** A German idiom or phrasing that appears in another language. **3.** Esteem for Germany and emulation of German ways.

ger·man·ite (jûr′mə-nīt′) *n.* A mineral consisting of a complex sulfide of copper and arsenic with small amounts of germanium, gallium, and other metals. It is an ore of germanium and gallium. [GERMAN(IUM) + -ITE.]

ger·ma·ni·um (jər-mā′nē-əm) *n. Symbol* **Ge** A brittle, crystalline, gray-white metalloid element, widely used as a semiconductor, as an alloying agent and catalyst, and in certain optical glasses. Atomic number 32, atomic weight 72.59, melting point 937.4°C, boiling point 2,830°C, specific gravity 5.323 (25°C), valences 2, 4. [New Latin, from Latin *Germānia,* Germany, from Latin *Germānus,* GERMAN.]

Ger·man·ize (jûr′mə-nīz′) *v.* **-ized, -izing, -izes.** —*tr.* **1.** To give a German quality or character to; make German. **2.** *Archaic.* To translate into German. —*intr.* To adopt German customs or attitudes. —**Ger·man·i·za·tion** *n.* —**Ger·man·iz·er** *n.*

German measles *n.* A mild, contagious, eruptive disease caused by a virus spread in droplet sprays from the nose and throat. It is capable of causing congenital defects in infants born to mothers infected during the first three months of pregnancy. Also called "rubella."

Ger·man·o·phile (jər-măn′ə-fīl′) *n.* One who loves or admires Germany, the Germans, or German ways. [Latin *Germānus,* GERMAN + -PHILE.]

Ger·man·o·phobe (jər-măn′ə-fōb′) *n.* One who hates or has an obsessive fear of Germany, the Germans, or German ways. [Latin *Germānus,* GERMAN + -PHOBE.]

ger·ma·nous (jər-mā′nəs) *n.* Of or pertaining to germanium. Said especially of compounds containing germanium with a valence of 2.

German shepherd *n.* A large breed of dog with a thick brownish coat, often used as a guard dog, as a police dog, or as a guide dog for the blind. Also called "Alsatian."

German silver *n.* An alloy, **nickel silver** *(see).*

Ger·ma·ny (jûr′mə-nē), *Abbr.* **Ger.** German **Deutsch·land** (doich′-länt′). Official name: **Federal Republic of Germany.** Country in central Europe. Occupied from *c.* 500 B.C. by Germanic tribes, it had become part of the kingdom of the Franks by the time of Charlemagne. After the death of Charlemagne in 814, Germany became a loose federation of principalities. This federation was strengthened under the Saxon dynasty (919–1024). The third in this line of rulers, Otto I, was crowned Holy Roman Emperor by Pope John XII in 962. By the 14th century Germany's frontiers extended as far east as the Vistula. The 16th and 17th centuries, however, were dominated by religious strife and dynastic feuds culminating in the Thirty Years' War (1618–48), which left Germany divided into a predominantly Roman Catholic south and a Protestant north. In 1806 Napoleon finally broke up the empire and united the country. From 1815 Germany was a confederation, with Prussia being the dominant state. Prussia defeated Austria in 1866 and France in 1871, and Bismarck realized his dream of a united German Empire with the Prussian king as hereditary ruler. Rapid industrialization and colonial expansion took place in the late 19th and early 20th centuries; Germany's international aspirations were a major cause of World War I (1914–18). Following defeat in 1918, the empire was dissolved and the Weimar Republic established. By the end of the 1920's, the depressed economy facilitated Adolf Hitler's rise to power. His aggressive and expansionist foreign policy led to the outbreak of World War II in 1939 and defeat at the hands of the Allies in 1945. The subsequent split of the country into **East Germany** and **West Germany** lasted until 1990, when the

East German states joined with West Germany. Area, 356,000 square kilometers (137,000 square miles). Population, 79,100,000. Capital, Berlin. See map, next page.

germ cell *n.* A cell having reproduction as its principal function; especially, an egg or sperm cell.

ger·mi·cide (jûr′mə-sīd′) *n.* An agent that kills germs. [GERM + -CIDE.] —**ger·mi·cid·al** (jûr′mə-sīd′l) *adj.*

ger·mi·nal (jûr′mə-nəl) *adj.* **1.** Of, pertaining to, or having the nature of a germ cell. **2.** Of, in, or pertaining to the earliest stage of development; embryonic. [French, from Latin *germen* (stem *germin-*), offshoot, GERM.]

germinal disc *n. Biology.* A disklike region from which the embryo begins to develop in certain ova. Also called "blastodisc."

germinal epithelium *n.* The epithelium of the ovary or testis, containing cells that develop into ova or spermatozoa.

germinal vesicle *n. Biology.* The nucleus of an oocyte.

ger·mi·nant (jûr′mə-nənt) *adj.* Germinating; sprouting.

ger·mi·nate (jûr′mə-nāt′) *v.* **-nated, -nating, -nates.** —*intr.* **1.** *Biology.* To begin to grow; sprout. **2.** To come into being and develop: *His hatred germinated slowly.* —*tr.* **1.** *Biology.* To cause (seeds or spores) to sprout. **2.** To bring into being; produce. [Latin *germināre,* to sprout, from *germen* (stem *germin-*), sprout, GERM.] —**ger·mi·na·ble** (jûr′mə-nə-bəl), **ger·mi·na·tive** (jûr′mə-nā′tīv, -nə-tīv) *adj.* —**ger·mi·na·tion** *n.* —**ger·mi·na·tor** *n.*

Ger·mis·ton (jûr′mĭ-stən). Town in the Transvaal in South Africa. It has the world's largest gold refinery, serving the Witwatersrand mines.

germ layer *n.* Any of three cellular layers, the **ectoderm, endoderm,** or **mesoderm** *(all of which see),* into which most animal embryos differentiate.

germ plasm *n.* **1.** The protoplasm of an egg cell, especially that part containing the hereditary material. **2.** Germ cells collectively. **3.** The hereditary material postulated by Weismann and other 19th-century biologists, thought to be transmitted in the germ cells and to remain unchanged from one generation to the next.

germ theory *n.* **1.** The doctrine that infectious diseases are caused by the activity of microorganisms within the body. **2.** The theory that living organisms can only develop from other living organisms through the fusion and subsequent differentiation of germ cells.

germ warfare *n.* **Biological warfare** *(see).*

Ge·ron·i·mo (jə-rŏn′ə-mō′) (1829–1909). North American Indian chief. From 1871 to 1886 he led the Chiricahua Apaches in daring guerrilla campaigns against the U.S. and Mexican governments.

geronto–, geront– *prefix.* Indicates old people or old age; for ex-

---

germination

FROM DORMANT SEED TO LIVING PLANT

The varied conditions that are needed to start growth

Germination is the process by which a seed becomes a plant. Shortly before a seed is shed by its parent, it becomes dormant to await good growing conditions. Seeds remain able to sprout for some time, from a few weeks to an extreme of about 10,000 years in the case of an arctic lupine seed found frozen in the Yukon in 1966.

The conditions that revive a seed vary. Warmth, water, and oxygen are usually needed. Some seeds, such as peas, do not need water but require certain bacteria in the soil. Winter annuals respond to cold, not warmth.

THE GERMINATION OF A BEAN

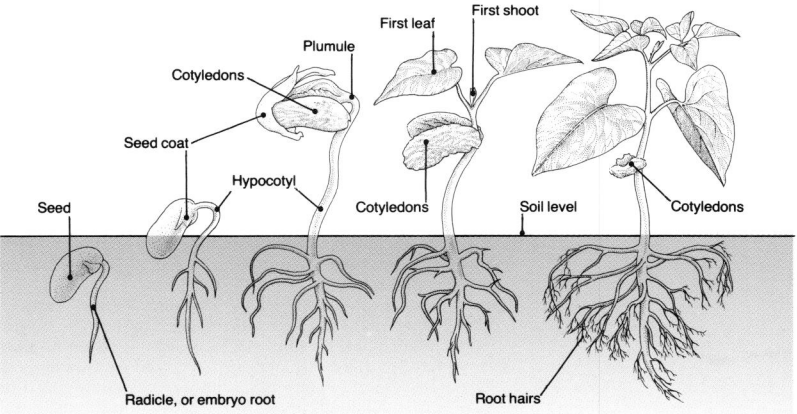

Generally, germination begins when air and water enter the seed through a tiny hole (micropyle) in the coat. The seed revives and begins to feed off its one or two seed leaves (cotyledons). The radicle, or embryo root, emerges and grows downward. It is followed by the plumule, or embryo shoot, which *grows upward. In some seeds the cotyledons remain below the soil, but in others they are carried above ground by a stemlike hypocotyl. The main shoot grows on above the cotyledons that wither when the food contained in them is exhausted. The plant then feeds itself.*

GERMANY

ample, **gerontology.** [French *géronto-,* from Greek *gerōn* (stem *geront-*), old man.]

ger·on·toc·ra·cy (jĕr′ən-tŏk′rə-sē) *n., pl.* **-cies. 1.** Government based on rule by old men. **2.** A governing group of old men. [French *gérontocratie* : GERONTO- + -CRACY.] **—ger·on·to·crat·ic** (jə-rŏn′tə-krăt′ĭk) *adj.*

ger·on·tol·o·gy (jĕr′ən-tŏl′ə-jē) *n.* The study of the diseases and other phenomena associated with old age. [GERONTO- + -LOGY.] **—ger·on·to·log·i·cal** (jə-rŏn′tə-lŏj′ĭ-kəl) *adj.* **—ger·on·tol·o·gist** *n.*

ger·ry·man·der (jĕr′ē-măn′dər, gĕr′-) *v.* **-dered, -dering, -ders.** *—intr.* To divide a constituency, county, or city into voting districts so as to give unfair advantage to one party in elections. *—tr.* To divide (a voting area) so as to give unfair advantage to one party in elections.

~*n.* An act or product of gerrymandering. [From Elbridge *Gerry,* 18th-century U.S. politician + (SALA)MANDER, from the shape of an election district formed (1812) in Massachusetts while Gerry was governor.]

Gersh·win (gûrsh′wĭn), **George,** born Jacob Gershvin (1898–1937). U.S. composer. A master of most forms of popular music of his day, he is best known for his experiments in orchestral jazz, notably

Rhapsody in Blue (1924) and the folk opera *Porgy and Bess* (1935), with lyrics by his brother Ira (1896–1983).

ger·und (jĕr′ənd) *n. Abbr.* **ger. 1.** In Latin, a verbal form that can be used as a noun in all singular cases except the nominative while conveying the meaning of the verb; for example, in the phrase *modus vivendi* ("a manner of living"), *vivendi* is a gerund formed from the verb *vivere,* to live. **2.** In English, the verbal form ending in *-ing* when used as a noun while conveying the meaning of the verb; for example, in the sentences *Cooking is an art* and *I don't like cooking, cooking* is a gerund formed from the verb *cook.* **3.** An analogous grammatical form in some other languages. [Late Latin *gerundium,* from Latin *gerundum, gerendum,* acting, carrying, gerund of *gerere,* to carry, act.] **—ge·run·di·al** (jə-rŭn′dē-əl) *adj.*

Usage: When a verb form ending in *-ing* is used as a noun it raises different problems of usage from when it is used as a verb (see also **participle**). The *-ing* form used as a noun (or *gerund,* as it is known in traditional grammar) is illustrated in *The inspector objected to my going.* In formal English, the possessive form of the item preceding the gerund is standard, and this involves the use of the apostrophe when the item is a noun, as in *He objected to John's going.* Informal English, on the other hand, often uses the neutral form, as in *He objected to me/John going.* Even in formal English the use of the possessive is sometimes very awkward or impossible, as in *His absence prevented anything* (not *anything's*) *being accomplished.* In such cases it is usually recommended that the construction be rephrased (for example, *prevented the accomplishment of anything*). Similarly, in cases where the addition of an *'s* would lead to ambiguity it is generally avoided: *He objected to his son leaving the room,* where *son's* might be confused with *sons.* It is also not used when there is an irregular plural noun: *the problems of mice* (not *mice's*) *damaging the wires.*

ge·run·dive (jə-rŭn′dĭv) *n.* **1.** In Latin, a verbal adjective with the construction of a future passive participle, suggesting appropriateness, necessity, or imminence; for example, in the sentence *Legibus parendum est* ("The laws must be obeyed" or "The laws are to be obeyed"), *parendum* is a gerundive. **2.** An analogous grammatical form or construction in some other languages. —*adj.* Pertaining to or like a gerund or gerundive. [Middle English *gerundif,* from Late Latin *gerundivus,* from *gerundium,* GERUND.]

Ge·ry·on (jîr′ē-ən, gĕr′-). *Greek Mythology.* A monster with three heads and upper bodies who was robbed of his herd of cattle and slain by Hercules.

Ge·sell (gĭ-zĕl′), **Arnold Lucius** (1880–1961). U.S. psychologist and pediatrician. He conducted research of normal child development and outlined the progressive stages of a child's life in many scholarly books, such as *Studies in Child Development* (1948), and three popular works, including *Infant and Child in the Culture of Today* (1943).

ges·so (jĕs′ō) *n.* **1.** A preparation of plaster of Paris and glue used as a base for low relief sculpting or as a surface for painting. **2.** A surface of this preparation. [Italian, gypsum, chalk, from Latin *gypsum,* GYPSUM.]

gest¹, geste (jĕst) *n. Archaic.* **1.** A feat or exploit; a notable deed. **2. a.** A verse romance or tale. **b.** A prose romance. [Middle English *geste, jeste,* from Old French, from Latin *gesta,* actions, exploits, from *gestus,* past participle of *gerere,* to act, carry.]

gest², geste (jĕst) *n. Archaic.* **1.** Mien or bearing. **2.** A gesture. [Old French *geste,* from Latin *gestus.* See **gesture.**]

ge·stalt, Ge·stalt (gə-shtält′, -stält′, -shtôlt′, -stôlt′) *n., pl.* **-stalts** or **-stalten** (-shtält′n, -stält′n, -shtôlt′n, -stôlt′n). **1.** A unified physical, psychological, or symbolic configuration having properties that cannot be derived from its parts. **2.** A complicated combination, as of experiences that constitute a relationship. [German *Gestalt,* form, shape, from Middle High German *gestalt,* from *ungestalt,* deformity, from Old High German *ungistalt,* ugly : *un-,* not + *gistalt,* past participle of *stellen,* to set, place.]

Gestalt psychology *n.* A school or doctrine of psychology holding that psychological phenomena are made up of irreducible gestalts. Also called "configurationism."

Ge·sta·po (gə-stä′pō, -shtä′pō) *n.* The German internal security police as organized under the Nazi regime. [German, short for *Ge(heime) Sta(ats)po(lizei),* "secret state police."]

Ges·ta Ro·ma·no·rum (jĕs′tə rō′mə-nôr′əm, -nôr′əm) *n.* An anthology of popular tales in Latin, collected in England in the late 13th or early 14th century and used as a source by preachers and by Chaucer and Shakespeare. [Latin, "deeds of the Romans."]

ges·tate (jĕs′tāt′) *v.* **-tated, -tating, -tates.** —*tr.* **1.** To carry (unborn young) within the uterus for a period following conception. **2.** To conceive and develop (a plan or idea, for example) in the mind. —*intr.* **1.** To carry unborn young for a period following conception; be pregnant. **2.** To develop slowly in the mind, as an idea or plot might. [Back-formation from GESTATION.]

ges·ta·tion (jĕ-stä′shən) *n.* **1.** The period between conception and birth during which an embryo grows and develops in the uterus; pregnancy. **2.** The development or duration of development of a plan or idea in the mind. [Latin *gestātiō* (stem *gestātiōn-*), from *gestāre,* frequentative of *gerere* (past participle *gestus*), to carry, bear.] —**ges·ta·to·ry** (jĕs′tə-tôr′ē, -tōr′ē) *adj.*

geste. **1.** Variant of **gest** (feat). **2.** Variant of **gest** (mien).

ges·tic (jĕs′tĭk) *adj.* Pertaining to movement of the body, especially in dancing. [From GEST (mien).]

ges·tic·u·late (jĕ-stĭk′yə-lāt′) *v.* **-lated, -lating, -lates.** —*intr.* To make animated and vigorous motions or gestures, especially as an expression complementing or substituting for speech. —*tr.* To say or express by gestures. [Latin *gesticulārī,* from *gesticulus,* diminutive of *gestus,* action, GEST.] —**ges·tic·u·la·tive** (jĕ-stĭk′yə-lā′tĭv, -lə-tĭv) *adj.* —**ges·tic·u·la·tor** *n.*

ges·tic·u·la·tion (jĕ-stĭk′yə-lā′shən) *n.* **1.** The act of gesticulating. **2.** A deliberate and vigorous motion or gesture. —**ges·tic·u·la·to·ry** (jĕ-stĭk′yə-lə-tôr′ē, -tōr′ē) *adj.*

ges·ture (jĕs′chər) *n.* **1.** A motion of the limbs or body made to express or help express thought or to emphasize speech. **2.** The use of gestures as a means of expression. **3.** An act or expression made as a sign, often formal, of intention or attitude: *a gesture of friendship; a mere gesture.* —*v.* **gestured, -turing, -tures.** —*intr.* To make gestures. —*tr.* To show, express, or direct by gestures. [Medieval Latin *gestūra,* bearing, carriage, from Latin *gestus,* past participle of *gerere,* to carry, act.] —**ges·tur·er** *n.*

Ge·sund·heit (gə-zŏŏnt′hīt′) *interj.* German. Used to wish good health to a person who has just sneezed.

get¹ (gĕt) *v.* **got** (gŏt) or *archaic* **gat** (găt), **got** or **gotten** (gŏt′n), **getting, gets.** —*tr.* **1.** To obtain or acquire. **2.** To procure; gain; secure. **3.** To go after; fetch; retrieve. **4.** To reach or make contact with by or as if by radio or telephone. **5.** To

earn; gain: *get a reward.* **6.** To receive or come into possession of: *get a present.* **7.** To buy. **8.** To incur: *get a tongue-lashing.* **9.** *Informal.* To meet with; suffer: *He got a few knocks, but he'll recover.* **10.** To catch; contract: *They all got chicken pox at once.* **11.** To have or reach by calculation: *If you add them, you'll get 1,000.* **12.** To have obtained or received and now possess. Used only in the form of the present perfect, and generally equivalent to *have: I've got a large collection of books.* **13.** To possess or gain understanding or mastery of by study: *I must get this by heart.* **14.** To understand; comprehend: *Do you get his point?* **15.** *Informal.* To register or catch, as by eye or ear: *I'm sorry, I didn't get your name.* **16.** *Informal.* To understand the meaning of a remark made by or the behavior of (a person): *I don't quite get you.* **17.** To put: *get your hat on.* **18.** To cause to become or to be in a specified condition: *He got the hook loose. Don't get your friends into trouble.* **19.** To cause to move,

---

gestation

HOW LONG TO MAKE A MAMMAL?

Factors that affect the gestation period

The period from a mammal's conception to its birth varies from the Virginia opossum's 12 days to an elephant's 22 months. The reasons are many. Size is a major factor. Another is the need to bear young when food is available. This may be why in some species, weasels for example, the embryo lies dormant for months before developing.

Animals whose young are born in the open—potential prey—carry their young longer than burrowers. Rabbits, for example, have a gestation period of 31 days before their young are born in the burrow. Hares, who give birth in the open, have a gestation period of 39 days and the young are more highly developed when they are born into this less protected environment.

Marsupials have gestation periods that are short in relation to their size. The young are highly developed at birth and continue their development in the maternal pouch.

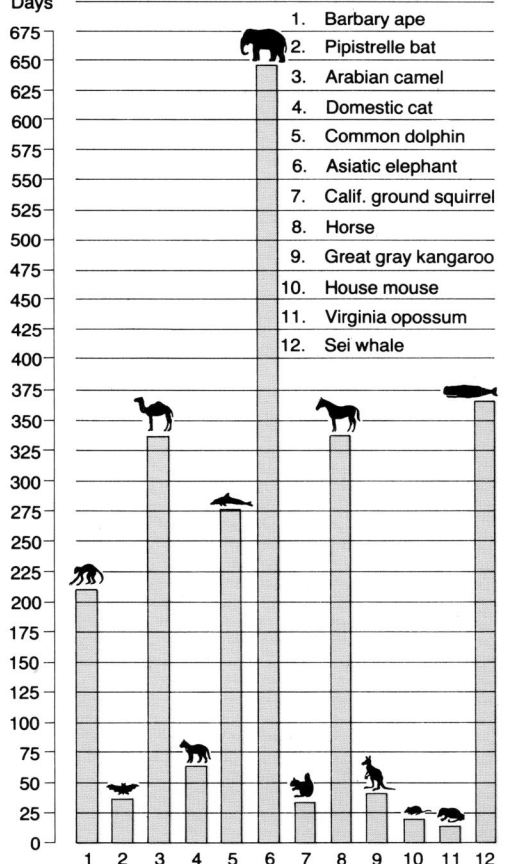

Days	
675	1. Barbary ape
650	2. Pipistrelle bat
625	3. Arabian camel
600	4. Domestic cat
575	5. Common dolphin
550	6. Asiatic elephant
525	7. Calif. ground squirrel
500	8. Horse
475	9. Great gray kangaroo
450	10. House mouse
425	11. Virginia opossum
400	12. Sei whale

GESTATION AND SIZE *There is generally a correlation between the length of a mammal's gestation period and its size. The human gestation period (average 267 days) is less than that of a horse and about the same as that of a dolphin.*

PRONUNCIATION KEY

ă, pat; ā, pay; âr, care;
ä, father, are; b, bib;
ch, church; d, deed; ĕ, pet;
ē, be; f, fife; g, gag; h, hat;
hw, which; ĭ, pit; ī, pie;
îr, pier; j, judge; k, kick;
l, lid, needle; m, mum;
n, no, sudden; ng, thing;
ŏ, pot; ō, toe; ô, paw, for;
oi, noise; ou, out; ŏŏ, book;
ōō, boot; p, pop; r, roar;
s, sauce; sh, ship, dish;
t, tight; th, thin, path;
th, this, bathe; ŭ, cut; ûr, fur;
v, valve; w, with; y, yes;
z, zebra, size; zh, vision;
ə, about, item, edible,
gallop, circus, peaceful

IN FOREIGN WORDS:

â, *Fr.* ami; œ, *Fr.* feu, *Ger.*
schön; ü, *Fr.* tu, *Ger.* über;
KH, *Ger.* ich, *Scot.* loch;
N, *Fr.* bon; y', *Fr.* Compiègne

STRESS MARKS:

Primary stress: ′
in·cite′ (ĭn-sīt′)
Secondary stress: ′
in′sight′ (ĭn′sīt′)

come, or go: *Get that dog out of here!* **20. a.** To bring: *I'll get him in here, and you can talk to him.* **b.** To gather: *get a few clothes together.* **21.** To induce or persuade; prevail upon: *I'll get my friend to show you his house.* **22.** To overpower; destroy: *Frost got our tomato crop.* **23.** To capture or catch: *The police got him.* **24.** *Slang.* To cause harm to; especially, to reciprocate by causing harm to: *I'll get you for that remark.* **25.** *Informal.* To strike or hit: *That blow got him on the chin.* **26. a.** In baseball, to put out: *The catcher got him sliding into home plate.* **b.** In football, to tackle; touch. **27.** *Slang.* To baffle; puzzle: *You've got me on that one!* **28.** *Slang.* To elicit a strong, usually negative reaction in: *Noisy eaters really get me.* **29.** To catch (a scheduled train or plane, for example). **30.** To have as an obligation; be constrained. Used only in the form of the present perfect and equivalent to *must*: *I have got to go.* —*intr.* **1.** To become, as by: **a.** Change: *get well again; get angry.* **b.** Movement: *get out of earshot.* **c.** Endeavor: *get to be chairman; get into Congress.* **2.** To move as specified: *get down from the ladder; get off the bus; get out.* **3.** To continue or proceed. Used with *back to, on,* or *on with*: *get back to work; get on with the job.* **4.** To arrive at or reach a particular point. Often used with *in, into,* or *to*: *The train gets in at midnight. We got to the end.* **5.** *Informal.* To start: *Get going!* **6.** *Regional & Informal.* To be off; depart: *Now get!* **7.** To work for gain or profit; make money: *He spends all his time getting and spending.* **—get about. 1.** *Informal.* To be active socially; go to many social events. **2.** To move around freely: *He no longer needs his crutches; he can get about without help.* **3.** To spread or travel. Used of a rumor or news. **—get across. 1.** To make understandable or clear: *Am I getting this across to you?* **2.** To be clear or understandable: *It's not getting across to him.* **3.** To communicate one's meaning or personality, as to an audience. **—get ahead.** To be successful; attain prosperity. **—get along. 1.** To be mutually congenial; be at harmony. **2.** To manage or fare with reasonable success: *He hasn't much money, but he gets along.* **3.** To advance, especially in years. **—get around. 1.** To avoid or circumvent (a problem, obstacle, or the like). **2.** *Informal.* To persuade or convince by wheedling or flattering. **3.** To consider or deal with after an initial delay: *I finally got around to writing the letter.* **—get at. 1.** To reach; find a way to: *It's under the desk and I can't get at it.* **2.** To lead up to or arrive at (a conclusion or meaning, for example): *Do you understand what I'm getting at?* **3.** To attack or try to attack and injure: *we went where they couldn't get at us.* **4.** *Informal.* To influence, especially by bribery. **—get away with.** *Informal.* To be successful in avoiding the discovery of (something done that deserves criticism or punishment). **—get back at.** *Informal.* To retaliate against or have revenge on: *He swears he'll get back at me.* **—get by.** To manage; survive; fare: *It will be a hard year, but we'll get by.* **—get down. 1.** To take cover; hide. **2.** To write (something) down. **3.** To depress or demoralize: *You mustn't let a small setback get you down.* **4.** To succeed in swallowing: *The pill was too big for him to get down.* **—get down to.** To begin doing; actively engage in: *They got down to some serious thinking.* **—get in. 1.** *Slang.* To gain the favor of. Used with *with*: *He wants to get in with that teacher.* **2.** To become involved in or part of. Used with *with*: *She wants to get in with a different crowd.* **3.** To be elected to office or accepted for membership. **—get into.** *Informal.* To develop an interest in or enthusiasm for: *I'm really getting into my new job.* **—get it. 1.** To comprehend; understand. **2.** *Informal.* To be punished or scolded. **—get nowhere.** To make no progress; have no success. **—get off. 1.** To send (a letter, for example). **2.** To escape, as from punishment or labor: *He got off scot-free.* **3.** To gain a release or lesser penalty for (a person). **4.** *Slang.* To get high, especially on a drug. **5.** *Slang.* To feel great pleasure or gratification. **—get off on.** *Slang.* **1.** To reach a state of euphoric consciousness through; get high on: *get off on acid.* **2.** To be stimulated or excited by; enjoy greatly: *get off on Mozart.* **—get on. 1.** To succeed; fare well. **2.** To advance. Used of time or aging: *It's getting on toward noon. He's getting on in years.* **3.** To be friendly or well disposed toward another or each other. Often used with *with.* **—get out of. 1.** To derive or draw: *He gets out of it what he can.* **2.** To avoid or get around. **—get over. 1.** To recover from (a sorrow or illness, for example). **2.** To overcome or rise above (a difficulty): *He'll soon get over his unfamiliarity with our procedures.* **3.** To complete (something, especially something unpleasant). Often used with *with*: *Let's get the shopping over with first.* **—get somewhere.** To make progress; achieve success. **—get there.** *Informal.* To attain one's goal. **—get through. 1.** To finish or complete. **2.** To undergo and survive: *I wonder if that tree will get through the winter.* **3.** To reach a destination, especially in the face of difficulties. **4.** To pass an examination. **5.** To succeed in making contact by telephone. Often used with *to.* **—get through to.** To make oneself or something understandable or apparent to. **—get to. 1.** To have the opportunity of or be able to: *I hope I get to go.* **2.** *Informal.* To happen to start; begin: *Then we got to remembering good times.* **3.** *Slang.* To impress or affect emotionally: *Her singing really gets to me.* **—get with it.** *Slang.* To become up to date.

~*n.* **1.** The act of begetting. **2.** Progeny; offspring. **3.** *Tennis.* A return on a shot that seems impossible to reach. [Get, got, got; Middle English *getten, gat, getten,* from Old Norse *geta, gat, getinn.*] **—get·a·ble, get·ta·ble** *adj.*

Usage: *Get* has a great number of uses, some of which are acceptable at all levels and some of which are generally felt to be informal (though never incorrect). Some uses better avoided in writing are: (1) The use of *get* in place of *be* or *become* in sentences as *He got arrested.* (2) The use of *get* or *get to* in place of *start* or *begin,* as in *When he gets (or gets to) reminiscing, he can't stop.* (3) The use of *have got to* in place of *must* in sentences like *I have got to go now.* • *Gotten* is a common past participle form, but it is not used when the senses involved are those of obligation or possession, as in *I've got to do it* and *I've got one in my hand. I've gotten to do it* means "I have succeeded in doing it," and *I've gotten a new car* means "I have just obtained a new car."

geyser *Superheated water and steam spurt into the air from Castle Geyser in Yellowstone National Park. The geyser gets its name from the ramparts around its vent, built from silica deposited by the mineral-rich water.*

get^2, gett *n.* A Jewish bill of divorce. [Hebrew *gēṭ.*]

get·a (gĕt′ə, gā′tə) *n., pl.* **geta** or **-as.** A wooden-soled shoe worn by the Japanese. [Japanese.]

get away *intr.v.* **1.** To escape. **2.** To leave; depart. **3.** To go away, as on a vacation. **4.** To start off in a race.

get·a·way (gĕt′ə-wā′) *n.* **1.** The act or an instance of escaping. **2.** A start, as of a race; takeoff.

~*adj.* Used for escape: *a getaway car.*

geth·sem·a·ne (gĕth-sĕm′ə-nē) *n.* Any instance or place of great suffering.

Geth·sem·a·ne (gĕth-sĕm′ə-nē). The garden outside Jerusalem that was the scene of the agony and arrest of Jesus. Matthew 26:36–56.

get out *intr.v.* **1.** To become public or known: *The news got out.* **2.** To go out or away; leave: *got out unharmed.* —*tr.v.* **1.** To publish (a newspaper, for example). **2.** To cause to go out or away. **3.** To say with an effort: *He stammered but managed to get the name out finally.*

get-out (gĕt′out′) *n. Informal.* An escape or means of avoiding difficulty: *A feigned headache was his get-out.* **—all get-out.** *Informal.* Used as a generalized superlative in comparisons: *cold as all get-out.*

get-rich-quick (gĕt′rĭch′kwĭk′) *adj.* Of, pertaining to, or being a plan or project designed to make money by rapid and often unscrupulous methods.

get·ter (gĕt′ər) *n.* **1.** One that gets. **2. a.** A material added in small amounts during a chemical or metallurgical process to absorb impurities. **b.** A substance, usually a metal, used to remove residual gas from a high-vacuum enclosure.

~*v.* **gettered, -tering, -ters.** —*tr.* **1.** To remove impurities from (a metal, for example) with a getter. **2.** To remove (gas) with a getter. —*intr.* To use a getter, as in removing impurities from a substance.

get together *intr.v.* To come together; assemble, especially socially: *Let's get together for a drink.* **—get it together.** *Slang.* **1.** To achieve personal fulfillment. **2.** To function with optimum efficiency in a particular sphere.

get-to·geth·er (gĕt′tə-gĕth′ər) *n. Informal.* **1.** A small party. **2.** A meeting or informal conference.

Get·ty (gĕt′ē), **J(ean) Paul** (1892–1976). U.S. financier and art collector. A millionaire by the age of 22, he turned his father's oil business into one of the world's largest financial empires.

Get·tys·burg (gĕt′ĭz-bûrg′). Town in southern Pennsylvania. It was here that the Union Army under Gen. George Meade defeated the Confederates under Gen. Robert E. Lee in July 1863 during the Civil War.

get up *intr.v.* **1.** To arise, as from bed or a stooping or prone position. **2.** To rise to one's feet. **3.** To increase in force or intensity: *The wind's getting up.* —*tr.v.* **1.** To study or revise. **2.** To act as the creator or organizer of: *get up a party; got up a petition against the new tax.* **3.** *Informal.* To dress or make up (oneself) elaborately. **4.** To bring into being in oneself; generate: *couldn't get up the indignation to protest.*

get-up (gĕt′ŭp′) *n.* **1.** An outfit or costume, especially one that is remarkable or bizarre. **2.** The arrangement and production style, as of a magazine or book.

get-up-and-go (gĕt′ŭp′ən-gō′) *n. Informal.* Energy and ambition; initiative and determination; drive.

ge·um (jē′əm) *n.* Any plant of the genus *Geum,* which includes **avens** and **herb bennet** *(both of which see).* [New Latin, from Latin *gaeum,* herb bennet.]

GeV *Physics.* Giga (10^9) electron volts. See **BeV.**

gew·gaw (gyo͞o′gô′) *n.* **1.** A decorative trinket; a bauble. **2.** Something that is decorative and showy but valueless. [Middle English : origin obscure.]

Ge·würz·tram·i·ner (gə-vo͝orts′trăm′ə-nər, -trä′mə-nər) *n.* A dry white table wine with a distinctive spicy flavor produced in Alsace.

gey·ser (gī′zər *for sense 1;* gē′zər, gī′- *for sense 2*) *n.* **1.** A natural hot spring that intermittently ejects a column of water and steam into the air. **2.** *British.* A domestic, usually gas-operated hot-water heater. [Icelandic *Geysir,* "gusher," the name of a hot spring in Iceland, from *geysa,* to gush, from Old Norse.]

gey·ser·ite (gī′zə-rīt′) *n.* An opaline, usually siliceous deposit formed around natural hot springs. It is a form of sinter.

Gha·li (gä′lē), **Boutros Boutros** (1922–). Egyptian diplomat. He serves as secretary-general of the United Nations (1992–).

Gha·na (gä′nə). Country in West Africa on the Gulf of Guinea. In 1472 European trading posts were established, and the territory subsequently became a center of the slave trade and the scene of bitter rivalries between British, Danish, French, and Dutch companies. In 1874 the south was established as the British colony of the Gold Coast, and the north was added by 1901. Together with the British section of Togo, the country became independent in 1957, and in 1960 it became a republic within the Commonwealth. Agriculture is important; cocoa, of which Ghana is one of the world's principal producers, is the major export. Area, 238,305 square kilometers (92,010 square miles). Population, 15,000,000. Capital, Accra. See map at **West African States.** —**Gha·na·ian** (gä-nä′ən), **Gha·ni·an** (gä′nē-ən) *adj. & n.*

gha·ri·al (gä′rē-əl) *n.* A reptile, the **gavial** (*see*).

ghar·ry, ghar·ri (găr′ē, gär′ē) *n., pl.* **-ries.** A small horse-drawn carriage in India. [Hindi *gāṛī.*]

ghast·ly (găst′lē, gäst′-) *adj.* **-lier, -liest. 1.** Terrifying; dreadful: *a ghastly accident.* **2.** Having a deathlike pallor: *"amid the dim and ghastly glare of a snowy night"* (Washington Irving). **3.** Extremely unpleasant or bad: *a ghastly little book.* ~*adv.* Dreadfully; horribly. [Middle English *gastlich,* Old English *gāstlīc,* spiritual, ghostly, ghastly, from *gāst,* soul, ghost.] —**ghast·li·ness** *n.*

    Synonyms: *grim, grisly, gruesome, lurid, macabre.*

ghat, ghaut (gôt, gät) *n.* In India: **1.** A mountain pass. **2.** A mountain chain. **3.** A flight of steps down to the bank of a river. **4.** An area beside a river, used for bathing. [Hindi *ghāt,* from Sanskrit *ghaṭṭa,* perhaps from *ghṛṣṭa,* rubbed.]

Ghats (gôts, gäts). Two coastal mountain ranges in India, forming the edges of the Deccan plateau. The Western Ghats extend approximately 1,500 kilometers (932 miles) along the west coast and rise to 2,698 meters (8,852 feet) at Anai Mudi. The Eastern Ghats extend approximately 1,400 kilometers (880 miles) along the east coast, rising to 2,637 meters (8,651 feet) at Doda Betta.

gha·zi (gä′zē) *n., pl.* **-zies. 1.** A Muslim warrior who has fought successfully against infidels. Often used as a title of honor. **2.** A high-ranking Turkish warrior. [Arabic *ghāzi,* participle of *ghazā,* he made war.]

Ghazzah. See **Gaza.**

ghee (gē) *n.* Clarified butter from the butterfat of buffalo or other milk. It is used in cooking, especially in India and neighboring countries. [Hindi *ghī,* from Sanskrit *ghṛta,* present participle of *ghṛ†,* to sprinkle.]

Ghent (gĕnt). *Flemish* **Gent** (gĕnt); *French* **Gand** (gän). A city and port in northwest-central Belgium, the capital of East Flanders.

ghe·rao (gə-rou′) *n.* In India, a coercive tactic adopted during industrial disputes whereby workers surround an employer and detain him on his own premises until he agrees to their demands. ~*tr.v.* **gheraoed, -raoing, -raoes.** To coerce (an employer) by using this technique. [Bengali, to surround, from Indic *gher-* (unattested), causative of *ghir-* (unattested), "to go around," from Dravidian.]

gher·kin (gûr′kĭn) *n.* **1.** A small cucumber, especially one used for pickling. **2.** A tropical American vine, *Cucumis anguria,* bearing prickly, edible fruit. **3.** The fruit of this vine. [Dutch *agurk(je),* from Low German *agurke,* from Lithuanian *agurkas,* from Polish *ogorek, ogurek,* from Medieval Greek *angourion,* probably from Greek *agouros,* youth, "unripe," from *aōros : a-,* not + *ōros,* time.]

ghet·to (gĕt′ō) *n., pl.* **-tos** or **-toes. 1.** A slum section of a city occupied predominantly by members of a minority group who live there because of social or economic pressure. **2.** A section or quarter in a European city to which Jews were formerly restricted. **3.** An area occupied by a group, institution, or the like, with a distinctive, and often exclusive, specified common trait: *a cultural ghetto.* [Italian *ghetto†.*]

Ghib·el·line (gĭb′ə-lēn′, -līn′, -lĭn) *n.* Any of the members of the aristocratic political faction who fought during the Middle Ages for German imperial control of Italy, in opposition to the Guelphs, who favored papal control. Compare **Guelph.** [Italian *Ghibellino,* from Middle High German *Waiblingen,* name of a Hohenstaufen estate.]

Ghi·ber·ti (gē-bĕr′tē), **Lorenzo** (*c.*1378–1455). Italian goldsmith and sculptor. He is best known for his series of bronze panels for the doors of the baptistry of Florence Cathedral, depicting scenes from the New and Old Testaments.

ghilgai. Variant of **gilgai.**

ghil·lie (gĭl′ē) *n., pl.* **-lies. 1.** A low-cut sports shoe with fringed laces, originally worn by the Scots. **2.** Variant of **gillie.** [Scottish Gaelic *gille,* boy, servant, GILLIE.]

ghost (gōst) *n.* **1.** The spirit of a dead person, supposed to haunt living persons or former habitats; a specter; a phantom; a wraith. **2.** *Archaic.* The animus or soul as opposed to the body. **3.** A returning or haunting memory or image. **4.** A slight trace or vestige of something; a hint; a semblance: *a ghost of a smile; a ghost of a chance.* **5. a.** A faint, false secondary image, such as: **a.** A displaced image in a mirror caused by reflection from the front of the glass. **b.** A displaced image in a photograph caused by the optical system of the camera. **c.** A secondary image on a television or radar screen caused by reflected waves. **d.** A false spectral line caused by imperfections in the diffraction grating. **6.** *Printing.* A variation or unevenness of color intensity on a surface intended to be solidly tinted, as the result of irregular distribution of ink. **7.** *Obsolete.* The Holy Ghost. **8.** *Informal.* A ghostwriter. **9.** A nonexistent publication listed in bibliographies. In this sense, also called "ghost edition." **10.** A ghost word. —**give up the ghost.** To die. ~*v.* **ghosted, ghosting, ghosts.** —*intr. Informal.* To work as a ghostwriter. —*tr.* **1.** To haunt. **2.** *Informal.* To write (a work) as a ghostwriter. [Middle English *gost, gast,* Old English *gāst,* from Germanic.]

ghost crab *n.* Any of several light-colored burrowing crabs of the genus *Ocypoda,* frequenting the tide line along sandy shores.

ghost dance *n.* Either of two religious dances practiced chiefly by certain North American Indians of the southwestern United States and California during the latter half of the 19th century to invoke a return of their former condition.

ghost gum *n.* Any of various Australian eucalyptus trees with a smooth, whitish trunk and branches.

ghost·ly (gōst′lē) *adj.* **-lier, -liest. 1.** Pertaining to or resembling a ghost or apparition; spectral; eerie. **2.** Pertaining to the spirit or to religion; spiritual. —**ghost·li·ness** *n.*

ghost moth *n.* Any of various moths of the family Hepialidae that have large, pale wings and are active at dusk. Also called "swift moth."

ghost town *n.* A town, especially a boom town of the West, that has now been completely abandoned.

ghost word *n.* A word that has come into a language through the perpetuation of a misreading of a manuscript, a typographical error, or a misunderstanding. For example, in *Ye Olde Sweete Shoppe, Ye* is a ghost word, the *y* having been a misreading of the runic letter thorn.

ghost·write (gōst′rīt′) *v.* **-wrote** (-rōt′), **-written** (-rĭt′n), **-writing, -writes.** —*intr.* To work as a ghostwriter. —*tr.* To write (something) as a ghostwriter.

ghost·writ·er (gōst′rī′tər) *n.* A person who is hired to write for another person who then takes credit of authorship. Also informally called "ghost."

ghoul (gōōl) *n.* **1.** One who delights in what is revolting, macabre, or loathsome. **2.** A grave robber. **3. a.** A malevolent ghost. **b.** An evil spirit or demon in Muslim folklore supposed to plunder graves and feed on corpses. [Arabic *ghūl,* from *ghāla,* he took suddenly.] —**ghoul·ish** *adj.* —**ghoul·ish·ly** *adv.* —**ghoul·ish·ness** *n.*

GHQ, G.H.Q. general headquarters.

ghyll. Variant of **gill** (stream or ravine).

gi gill (liquid measure).

Gi gilbert (unit of magnetomotive force).

GI (jē′ī′) *n., pl.* **GIs** or **GI's.** A serviceman in or ex-serviceman of any of the U.S. armed forces. ~*adj.* **1.** Pertaining to or characteristic of a GI. **2.** In conformity to or accordance with U.S. military regulations or procedures. **3.** Issued by an official U.S. military supply department. [Abbreviation of *general issue* or *government issue.*]

GI 1. general issue. **2.** Government Issue.

G.I. Government Issue.

Gia·co·met·ti (jä′kō-mĕt′ə), **Alberto** (1901–66). Swiss painter and sculptor. From 1922 to 1935 he experimented with cubism but later evolved a distinctive, elongated style of representing the human figure.

gi·ant (jī′ənt) *n.* **1. a.** A person or thing of extraordinary size or strength. **b.** A person of outstanding importance or achievement: *He is a giant in his field.* **2. a.** *Greek Mythology.* Any of a race of manlike beings of enormous strength and stature who warred with the Olympians, by whom they were finally destroyed. **b.** Any similar being in folklore or myth. ~*adj.* Of immense size; gigantic; huge. [Middle English *geant,* from Old French, from Vulgar Latin *gangante* (unattested), from Latin *gigās* (stem *gigant-*), from Greek *gigas†.*]

giant anteater *n.* See **anteater.**

giant axon *n.* A giant fiber (*see*).

giant chromosome *n.* A chromosome consisting of many parallel strands of chromatids that have failed to separate after duplication. Giant chromosomes, which occur in the salivary glands of *Drosophila* and other insects, are used to study gene activity.

gi·ant·ess (jī′ən-tĭs) *n.* A female giant.

giant fiber *n. Zoology.* A nerve fiber with a very large diameter found in many invertebrate animals that is capable of rapid conduction of impulses. Also called "giant axon."

giant hogweed *n., pl.* **giant hogweeds** or collectively **giant hogweed.** A very tall plant, *Heracleum mantegazzianum,* with clusters of small white flowers, found especially on waste ground.

gi·ant·ism (jī′ən-tĭz′əm) *n.* **1.** The condition of being a giant. **2.** *Pathology.* Gigantism (*see*).

gi·ant-kill·er (jī′ənt-kĭl′ər) *n.* An individual, such as a sportsman, that defeats an apparently more powerful opponent against all expectations.

giant panda *n.* See **panda.**

giant planet *n.* A planet with a large mass of low density. The giant planets are **Jupiter, Saturn, Neptune,** and **Uranus.**

giant powder *n.* A high explosive consisting of trinitroglycerin absorbed in kieselguhr.

Giant's Causeway. Promontory on the northern coast of County Antrim, Northern Ireland on the North Channel. It consists of thousands of basaltic columns formed by a flow of lava into the sea. Legend has it that it was once a bridge for giants to cross between Ireland and Scotland.

giant sequoia *n.* A very tall evergreen tree, *Sequoia gigantea,* of mountainous regions of southern California, having a massive trunk and light-colored, reddish wood. Also called "big tree," "wellingtonia." Compare **redwood.**

giant star *n.* Any of a class of highly luminous, exceptionally massive stars having relatively low density and lying above the main sequence. Compare **dwarf star.**

giaour (jour) *n.* A nonbeliever in the Muslim faith; especially, a Christian. [Turkish *giaur,* infidel, from Persian *gaur,* variant of *gäbr†,* fire worshiper.]

gi·ar·di·a·sis (jē-är-dī′ə-sĭs) *n.* A disease caused by infestations of the small intestine with the parasitic protozoan *Giardia lamblia* and characterized by diarrhea and nausea. [New Latin *giardia,* after A.M. *Giard* (died 1908), French biologist + -IASIS.]

gib¹ (gĭb) *n.* A plain or notched, often wedge-shaped piece of wood or metal designed to hold parts of a machine or structure in place or to provide a bearing surface, usually adjusted by a screw or key. ~*tr.v.* **gibbed, gibbing, gibs.** To apply a gib to. [18th century : origin obscure.]

gib² *n.* A male cat, especially one that has been castrated. [Perhaps from *Gib,* the nickname for *Gilbert.*]

Gi·ba·ra Bay (hē-bär'ə). Inlet of the Atlantic Ocean on the northeastern coast of Cuba. It is traditionally considered to be the site of Columbus's first landing in the New World (1492).

gib·ber¹ (jĭb'ər) *intr.v.* **-bered, -bering, -bers. 1.** To make rapid, chattering noises, as a monkey does. **2.** To prattle or chatter unintelligibly. ~*n.* Senseless talk or prate; gibberish. [Imitative.]

gib·ber² (jĭb'ər) *n. Australian.* A stone or rock, especially one polished by the wind. [From a native Australian language.]

gib·ber·el·lic acid (jĭb'ə-rĕl'ĭk) *n.* A substance, $C_{19}H_{22}O_6$, first isolated from a fungus, *Gibberella fujikuroi,* and occurring naturally in many plants, where it promotes elongation of the cells. [From GIB-BERELLIN.]

gib·ber·el·lin (jĭb'ə-rĕl'ĭn) *n.* Any of a class of natural plant growth substances, such as gibberellic acid, that promote elongation of the stems and leaves. [New Latin *Gibberella,* diminutive of Latin *gibber,* hunchbacked, akin to Latin *gibbus,* hump.]

gib·ber·ish (jĭb'ər-ĭsh) *n.* Nonsensical, rapid talk; prattle.

gib·bet (jĭb'ĭt) *n.* **1.** A gallows. **2.** An upright post with a crosspiece, forming a T-shaped structure from which executed criminals were hung for public viewing. ~*tr.v.* **gibbeted** or **gibbetted, -beting** or **-betting, -bets. 1.** To execute by hanging. **2.** To hang on a gibbet for public viewing. **3.** To expose to infamy or public ridicule. [Middle English *gibet,* from Old French, diminutive of *gibe,* staff, club, possibly from Frankish *gibb-*† (unattested), forked stick.]

gib·bon (gĭb'ən) *n.* Any of several apes of the genera *Hylobates* or *Symphalangus,* of tropical Asia, that live in trees and have a slender body and long arms. [French, perhaps from a native word in India.]

Gib·bon (gĭb'ən), **Edward** (1737–94). British historian. His principal work, *The History of the Decline and Fall of the Roman Empire* (1776–88), covers some 1,200 years of history and remains a monumental work of its kind.

Gib·bons (gĭb'ənz), **Grinling** (1648–1721). Dutch-born British sculptor. He excelled in the carving of fruit and flowers in wood and was commissioned by Sir Christopher Wren to work on the choir stalls and organ screen of St. Paul's Cathedral.

Gibbons, Orlando (1583–1625). English composer. Organist at the Chapel Royal from 1604, he was appointed organist of Westminster Abbey in 1623. His sacred and secular compositions include some beautiful madrigals.

gib·bos·i·ty (gĭ-bŏs'ə-tē) *n., pl.* **-ties. 1.** The condition of being gibbous. **2.** A rounded hump or protuberance; a swelling. **3.** *Pathology.* A sharply angled curvature of the spine, formerly commonly caused by tuberculosis.

gib·bous (gĭb'əs) *adj.* **1.** Rounded; convex; protuberant. **2.** More than half but less than fully illuminated. Said of the moon or a planet. **3.** Humpbacked. [Middle English, from Late Latin *gebbōsus,* humpbacked, from *gibbus,* hump (expressive).] **—gib·bous·ly** *adv.* **—gib·bous·ness** *n.*

Gibbs free energy (gĭbz) *n.* Gibbs function.

Gibbs function *n.* A measure of the thermodynamic free energy of a system, used for changes at constant pressure equal to the enthalpy minus the product of entropy and thermodynamic temperature. Also called "Gibbs free energy." [After Josiah Willard *Gibbs* (1839–1903), U.S. physicist and mathematician.]

gibbs·ite (gĭb'zīt') *n.* Hydrated aluminum oxide, $Al_2O_3 \cdot 3H_2O,$ a constituent of bauxite. [After George *Gibbs* (1776–1833), U.S. mineralogist.]

gibe (jīb) *v.* **gibed, gibing, gibes.** Also **jibe, jibed, jibing, jibes.** —*intr.* To make heckling or mocking remarks; scoff. Usually used with *at.* —*tr.* To reproach by taunting; deride. —See Synonyms at **ridicule.** ~*n.* A derisive remark; a taunt. [Perhaps from Old French *giber*†, to handle roughly.] **—gib·er** *n.* **—gib·ing·ly** *adv.*

Gib·e·on·ite (gĭb'ē-ə-nīt') *n.* Any of the inhabitants of Gibeon, a village of ancient Palestine, condemned by Joshua to serve as manual laborers for the Israelites. Joshua 9.

gib·lets (jĭb'lĭts) *pl.n.* The edible inside parts of a fowl, such as the heart, liver, or gizzard. [Middle English *gibelet,* from Old French, probably variant of *giberet* (unattested), diminutive of *gibier,* hunting, game, from Frankish *gabaiti* (unattested), hunting with falcons.]

Gib·ral·tar (jĭ-brôl'tər). British crown colony at the western entrance to the Mediterranean Sea. Linked by a sandy isthmus to the Spanish mainland, it rises to 427 meters (1,400 feet) at the Rock of Gibraltar. In ancient times it was the Calpe of the Greeks and the Romans, forming, with ancient Abyla on the African coast, the Pillars of Hercules, long thought to mark the western edge of the world. Successively ruled by the Moors and Castile, it was taken by Adm. George Rooke in 1704 and has remained a British possession since. In 1967 it was granted a measure of internal self-government. Following Spanish demands for decolonization (1967), a referendum was held; the population voted 12,138 to 44 in favor of the status quo. Gibraltar has few natural resources and relies chiefly on its strategic position as a port. Tourism is also important. Its name

is derived from Jabel-al-Tarik, after its Moorish conqueror of 711, Tarik. **—Gib·ral·tar·i·an** (jĭ'brôl-târ'ē-ən) *n. & adj.*

Gibraltar, Strait of. Channel between southern Spain and Morocco in northwest Africa. Some 58 kilometers (36 miles) long and 13 kilometers (8 miles) wide at its narrowest point, it links the Mediterranean Sea with the Atlantic Ocean.

Gib·ran (jə-brän'), **Khalil** (1883–1931). Lebanese poet. His major work in the English language, *The Prophet* (1923), expounds his philosophy with a vivid use of metaphor.

Gib·son Desert (gĭb'sən). The central section of the desert of western Australia, lying between the Great Sandy Desert and the Victoria Desert.

Gib·son girl (gĭb'sən) *n.* The ideal American girl of the 1890's as portrayed in sketches by the illustrator Charles Dana Gibson (1867–1944), typically dressed in a tailored shirtwaist with leg-of-mutton sleeves and a long skirt.

gid (gĭd) *n.* A disease of sheep caused by the presence in the brain of the larva of a tapeworm, *Taenia caenurus,* and resulting in a staggering gait. Also called "sturdy," "waterbrain." [Back-formation from GIDDY.]

gid·dy (gĭd'ē) *adj.* **-dier, -diest. 1. a.** Having a reeling, light-headed sensation; dizzy. **b.** Causing or capable of causing dizziness: *a giddy climb to the top of the tower.* **2.** Frivolous and lighthearted; flighty: *giddy young girls.* ~*v.* **giddied, -dying, -dies.** —*intr.* To become giddy. —*tr.* To make giddy. [Middle English *gidy,* mad, foolish, Old English *gydig,* possessed by a god, insane.] **—gid·di·ly** *adv.* **—gid·di·ness** *n.*

gid·dy·ap (gĭd'ē-ăp', -ŭp') *interj.* Also **gid·dap** (gĭ-dăp'). Used as a command to make an animal, especially a horse, move or go faster. [From *get up.*]

Gide (zhēd), **André** (1869–1951). French novelist and diarist. Much of his work examines the tensions between desire and duty, with particular reference to his own Christianity and homosexuality. His novels include *La Porte Étroite* (1909) and *Les Faux Monnayeurs* (1925). He was awarded the Nobel Prize for literature in 1947.

Gid·e·on (gĭd'ē-ən). A judge of Israel and conqueror of the Midianites. Judges 6–8. [Hebrew *Gidh'ōn,* "hewer," "feller," from *gādha,* "he cut down."]

Gideon Bible *n.* A Bible put in a public place, especially a hotel room, by a member of the Gideons, a Christian organization. [After GIDEON.]

gie (gē) *v.* **gied** or **gae** (gā), **gied** or **gien** (gēn), **gieing, gies.** *Scottish.* To give.

Giel·gud (gēl'gŏŏd, gēl'-), **Sir (Arthur) John** (1904–). British actor and director. He won popular acclaim with his performances in and productions of Shakespeare's plays.

gift (gĭft) *n.* **1.** Something that is bestowed voluntarily and without compensation; a present. **2.** The act, right, or power of giving: *The privilege is in the gift of the bishop.* **3.** A talent, endowment, aptitude, or power: *a gift for languages.* **4.** *Informal.* Something obtained very readily or cheaply. **—(the) gift of gab.** A talent for speaking easily or well. ~*tr.v.* **gifted, gifting, gifts. 1.** To present with a gift. **2.** *Chiefly British.* To bestow as a gift. **3.** To endow with; invest. [Middle English *gift, yift,* from Old Norse *gipt, gift.*]

gift certificate *n.* A certificate given as a present that can be exchanged at the store that issued it for goods to the amount stated on it.

gift·ed (gĭf'tĭd) *adj.* **1.** Endowed with natural ability, talent, or other assets; especially, endowed with exceptional intelligence: *a gifted child.* **2.** Revealing talent: *a gifted rendition of a song.* **—gift·ed·ly** *adv.* **—gift·ed·ness** *n.*

gift horse *n.* **—look a gift horse in the mouth.** To be suspicious of or to find fault with a gift or lucky chance. [Alluding to the practice of examining a horse's teeth to determine its age.]

gift of tongues *n.* An ecstatic utterance that is partly or wholly unintelligible to hearers, especially as practiced liturgically in certain Christian congregations. Also called "glossolalia." [By allusion to the Pentecostal miracle whereby the Apostles "were all filled with the Holy Ghost, and began to speak with other tongues, as the Spirit gave them utterance." Acts 2:4.]

gift-wrap (gĭft'răp') *tr.v.* **-wrapped, -wrapping, -wraps.** To wrap (a purchase or present) in fancy paper with elaborate trimmings.

gig¹ (gĭg) *n.* **1.** A light, two-wheeled vehicle drawn by one horse. **2. a.** A long, light ship's boat having oars, sails, or a motor and usually reserved for use by the ship's captain. **b.** A fast, light rowboat. [Middle English *gigg*†, giddy girl, something that whirls.]

gig² *n.* **1.** An arrangement of barbless hooks that is dragged through a school of fish to hook them in the bodies. **2.** A spear for fishing, a **fishgig** (*see*). ~*v.* **gigged, gigging, gigs.** —*tr.* **1.** To catch with a gig. **2.** *Regional.* To goad; prod. —*intr.* To fish with a gig. [Short for FISH-GIG.]

gig³ *n. Slang.* **1.** A job, engagement, or booking for musicians, especially pop or jazz musicians. **2.** A performance by pop or jazz musicians, as at a club or concert. ~*intr.v.* **gigged, gigging, gigs.** *Slang.* To perform a gig, as at a club or concert. [20th century : origin obscure.]

giga– *prefix. Abbr.* **G** Indicates one thousand million (10^9); for example, *gigavolt* (1,000,000,000 volts). [Greek *gigas,* GIANT.]

gi·gan·tic (jī-găn'tĭk) *adj.* **1.** Pertaining to or suitable for a giant. **2. a.** Exceedingly large of its kind: *a gigantic toadstool.* **b.** Very large or extensive: *a gigantic radio network.* **—See Synonyms at enor-**

gibbon *The common or lar gibbon—one of several Southeast Asian species of this ape—lives almost entirely in the trees. It is a remarkable acrobat, swinging from branch to branch in leaps of up to 15 meters (50 feet).*

mous. [Latin *gigās* (stem *gigant-*), GIANT.] —**gi·gan·ti·cal·ly** *adv.*

gi·gan·tism (jī-găn′tĭz′əm, jī′gən-) *n.* **1.** Excessive growth of the body or any of its parts as a result of oversecretion of the pituitary growth hormone during childhood. Also called "giantism." **2.** Abnormal size.

gi·gan·tom·a·chy (jī′găn-tŏm′ə-kē) *n.* Also **gi·gan·to·ma·chi·a** (jī-găn′tə-mā′kē-ə). **1.** *Greek Mythology.* The war of the giants against Zeus and the other Olympian gods. **2.** Any battle or contest on a massive scale. [Greek *gigantomakhia* : *gigas* (stem *gigant-*), GIANT + -MACHY.]

gig·gle (gĭg′əl) *intr.v.* **-gled, -gling, -gles.** To laugh with repeated short, high-pitched, convulsive sounds, as when nervous or when attempting to suppress mirth.
~*n.* A high-pitched, spasmodic laugh. [Imitative.] —**gig·gler** *n.* —**gig·gling·ly** *adv.*

gig·gly (gĭg′lē) *adj.* **-glier, -gliest.** Inclined to giggle.

gig·o·lo (jĭg′ə-lō′, zhĭg′-) *n., pl.* **-los. 1.** A young man who is kept as a lover by a woman, especially an older woman. **2.** A paid male escort or dancing partner. [French, from *gigolette*, dance-hall partner, from *giguer*, to dance, from *gigue*, leg, fiddle, from Old French, from Old High German *giga†*.]

gig·ot (jĭg′ət, zhē-gō′) *n.* **1.** A leg of mutton or lamb for cooking. **2.** A leg-of-mutton sleeve. Also called "gigot sleeve." [Old French, diminutive of *gigue*, leg, fiddle. See gigolo.]

gigue (zhēg) *n.* **1.** A dance, the jig *(see)*. **2.** *Music.* A lively piece of music in ⁶/₈, ⁹/₈, or ¹²/₈ time, often forming the final movement of the classical suite. [French, from English JIG.]

GI Joe *n. Informal.* A serviceman in the U.S. Army, especially during World War II.

Gi·jón (gē-hôn′, hē-). Port in northwestern Spain, on the Bay of Biscay, in Oviedo province in Asturias. It is an important industrial center.

Gi·la (hē′lə). River rising in the mountains of western New Mexico. It flows 1,014 kilometers (630 miles) across southern Arizona to the Colorado River at Yuma, on the border with California. Ancestors of the Pima and Papago Indians used irrigation to farm the river's valley.

Gila Cliff Dwellings National Monument. A park, 65 hectares (160 acres), in southwestern New Mexico, set aside to preserve Pueblo Indian dwellings built into the side of a cliff 46 meters (150 feet) high.

Gila monster *n.* A venomous lizard, *Heloderma suspectum*, of the southwestern United States and northern Mexico, having a stout body covered with black and orange or yellowish scales. [After the GILA River.]

gil·bert (gĭl′bərt) *n. Abbr.* **Gi** The centimeter-gram-second electromagnetic unit of magnetomotive force, equal to ¹⁰/₄π ampere-turn. [After William GILBERT.]

Gil·bert (gĭl′bərt), **William** (1544–1603). English physicist. His work on magnets led to his theory, broadly correct, that the earth is a magnet with its poles at the North and South poles. He also coined the term "electricity" and was a physician to Elizabeth I.

Gilbert, Sir William Schwenk (1836–1911). English librettist and humorist. He is best known for the Savoy operas he wrote with the composer Sir Arthur Sullivan.

Gilbert Islands. See Kiribati, Republic of.

gild¹ (gĭld) *tr.v.* **gilded** or **gilt** (gĭlt), **gilding, gilds. 1.** To cover with or as if with a thin layer of gold. **2.** To give an often deceptively attractive or improved appearance to; gloss or gloss over. **3.** *Archaic.* To smear with blood. —**gild the lily.** To adorn unnecessarily something that is already beautiful. [Middle English *gilden*, Old English *gyldan*.]

gild² Variant of **guild.**

gild·er¹ (gĭl′dər) *n.* A person whose work is gilding.

gilder² Variant of **guilder.**

gild·ing (gĭl′dĭng) *n.* **1.** The art or process of applying gilt to a surface. **2.** Gilt. **3.** Something used to give a superficially attractive appearance.

gi·let (zhē-lā′) *n.* A waistcoat. [French.]

gil·gai, ghil·gai (gĭl′gī′) *n.* In Australia, a cracked, uneven natural depression in the ground; a water hole. [From a native Australian language.]

gill¹ (gĭl) *n.* **1.** *Zoology.* The respiratory organ of fishes, larval amphibians, and numerous aquatic invertebrates, typically consisting of a membranous appendage well supplied with blood vessels for gaseous exchange. **2.** *Usually* **gills.** The wattle of a bird. **3.** *Usually* **gills.** *Informal.* The area around the chin and neck. **4.** *Botany.* Any of the thin, platelike, spore-producing structures on the underside of the cap of a mushroom or similar fungus. —**green around** (or **about) the gills.** Looking or feeling nauseated.
~*tr.v.* **gilled, gilling, gills. 1.** To catch (fish) in a gill net. **2.** To gut or clean (fish). [Middle English *gille*, probably from Old Norse *gil* (unattested).]

gill² (jĭl) *n. Abbr.* **gi 1.** A unit of volume or capacity in the U.S. Customary System, used in liquid measure, equal to 4 fluid ounces (¼ pint) or 23.656 milliliters. **2.** A unit of volume or capacity in the British Imperial System, used in dry and liquid measure, equal to 5 fluid ounces (¼ pint) or 28.423 milliliters. [Middle English *gille*, from Old French *gille, gelle*, from Late Latin *gillot*, water pot.]

gill³, ghyll (gĭl) *n. British Regional.* **1.** A swift-flowing mountain stream. **2.** A ravine. [Middle English *gille*, from Old Norse *gil*.]

gill bar (gĭl) *n.* Any of a series of skeletal structures in the pharyngeal wall of fishes that supports the tissue separating the gill slits.

gill books (gĭl) *pl.n.* The respiratory organs of king crabs, consisting of layers of thin vascular plates attached to the abdominal appendages.

Gil·les·pie (gĭ-lĕs′pē), **John Birks** known as **"Dizzy"** (1917–). U.S. jazz trumpeter. After 1944 he began to develop the style known as "bop."

Gil·lette (jə-lĕt′), **King Camp** (1855–1932). U.S. inventor and manufacturer. He was first a traveling salesman, but in the late 1890's developed a crude model of a razor using a thin, double-edged, disposable blade. His new product, manufactured by his company, soon became greatly popular.

gill fungus (gĭl) *n.* Any fleshy fungus having a cap with gills on the underside.

gil·lie, gil·ly, ghil·lie (gĭl′ē) *n., pl.* **-lies.** *Scottish.* A professional guide and servant for sportsmen, especially in fishing and deerstalking. [Scottish Gaelic *gille*, boy, servant, akin to Irish *giolla†*.]

gil·lion (jĭl′yən) *n. British.* One thousand million. [Blend of GIGA- + MILLION.]

gill net (gĭl) *n.* A fishing net set vertically in the water so that fish swimming into it are entangled by the gills in its mesh.

gill-o·ver-the-ground (gĭl′ō-vər-thə-ground′) *n.* A plant, the ground ivy *(see)*.

gill pouch (gĭl) *n.* Any of a series of paired pouches in the pharyngeal wall of chordate embryos that become the gill slits of aquatic vertebrates.

gill slit (gĭl) *n.* Any of several narrow, paired external openings connecting with the pharynx, present in all vertebrates during embryonic development, and characteristic of adult fishes and other aquatic vertebrates.

gil·ly·flow·er, gil·li·flow·er (gĭl′ē-flou′ər) *n.* **1.** The carnation or a similar plant of the genus *Dianthus*. **2.** Any of several plants having fragrant flowers, as the stock or wallflower. [Alteration (influenced by FLOWER) of Middle English *gilofre, gelofer*, from Old French *girofre, girofle*, from Medieval Latin *caryophylum*, clove, from Greek *karuophullon* : *karuon*, nut + *phullon*, leaf.]

Gil·son·ite (gĭl′sən-nīt′) *n.* A trademark for a natural black bitumen found in Utah and Colorado, used in the manufacture of acid, alkali, and waterproof coatings. Also called "uintaite." [After S.H. *Gilson*, of Salt Lake City, Utah.]

gilt¹ (gĭlt). Alternate past tense and past participle of **gild.**
~*adj.* **1.** Covered with gold or a substance simulating gold; gilded. **2.** Having the appearance of gold.
~*n. Abbr.* **gt. 1.** A thin layer of gold or something simulating gold that is applied in gilding. **2. a.** Shining brilliance; glitter. **b.** Superficial brilliance or gloss.

gilt² *n.* A young sow that has not yet produced a litter. [Middle English *gilt*, young sow, from Old Norse *gylta*, sow.]

gilt-edged (gĭlt′ĕjd′) *adj.* Also **gilt-edge** (-ĕj′). **1.** Having gilded edges, as the pages of a book. **2. a.** Of the highest quality or value: *gilt-edged securities.* **b.** Of a high degree of reliability.

gim·bals (gĭm′bəlz, jĭm′-) *pl.n.* A device consisting of two rings mounted on axes at right angles to each other so that an object such as a ship's compass will remain suspended in a horizontal plane between them regardless of their motion. [Plural of *gimbal*, from Old French *gemel*, GIMMAL.]

gim·crack (jĭm′krăk′) *n.* A cheap and showy object of little or no use; a knickknack.
~*adj.* Cheap and shoddy; flimsy. [Middle English *gibecrake†*, ornament, gimcrack.] —**gim·crack·er·y** *n.*

gim·el (gĭm′əl) *n.* The third letter of the Hebrew alphabet. See feature at **alphabet.** [Hebrew *gīmel*, "camel" (from the ancient form of the letter), akin to *gāmāl*, CAMEL.]

gim·let (gĭm′lĭt) *n.* **1.** A small hand tool for boring holes, having a spiraled shank, a screw tip, and a cross handle. **2.** A cocktail made with vodka or gin and sweetened lime juice, garnished with a slice of lime.
~*tr.v.* **gimleted, -leting, -lets.** To penetrate with or as if with a gimlet; puncture; pierce.
~*adj.* Piercing; penetrating: *gimlet eyes.* [Middle English, from Old French *guimbelet*, probably from Middle Dutch *wimmelkijn*, diminutive of *wimmel*, auger.]

gim·mal (gĭm′əl, jĭm′-) *n.* A ring made of two narrower rings interlocked. [Earlier *gemel*, from Old French, from Latin *gemellus*, diminutive of *geminus*, twin.]

gim·me (gĭm′ē). *Slang.* Contraction of *give me.*

gim·mick (gĭm′ĭk) *n.* **1.** A device employed, often illegally, to cheat, deceive, or trick, especially a mechanism for the secret control of a gambling wheel. **2.** A clever device or stratagem used to promote or publicize a project: *an advertising gimmick.* **3.** A significant feature that is obscured or misrepresented; catch. **4.** A trivial or unnecessary innovation, as a gadget, used to attract attention or interest. **5.** A small object whose name eludes one.
~*tr.v.* **gimmicked, -micking, -micks.** To add gimmicks to: *gimmicked up the dress with fringe and sequins.* [20th century (American) : origin obscure.] —**gim·mick·ry** *n.* —**gim·mick·y** *adj.*

gimp¹ (gĭmp) *n.* A narrow braid or cord of fabric, sometimes stiffened, used to trim or pipe clothes, curtains, or upholstered furniture. Also called "guimpe," "guipure."
~*tr.v.* **gimped, gimping, gimps.** To trim or edge with gimp. [Dutch *gimp†*.]

gimp² *n. Slang.* Spirit; courage. [20th century : origin obscure.]

gimp³ *n. Slang.* **1.** A limp or limping gait. **2.** A person who limps.
~*intr.v. Slang.* To limp. [Origin unknown.] —**gimp·y** *adj.*

Gila monster *This venomous lizard is found in the Arizona desert. It can survive without food or water for several months and grows to a length of almost 60 centimeters (2 feet).*

giraffe *Found in the savannah lands of Africa, the giraffe is the tallest living mammal. It can be nearly 6 meters (20 feet) tall and feeds mainly on thorn trees.*

girandole *The characteristically radiating design known as girandole is used here in a gold and emerald earring made in the 18th century in Spain or Portugal.*

gin¹ (jĭn) *n.* **1.** A strong alcoholic liquor distilled from grain, as rye or barley, and flavored with juniper berries. **2.** A liquor similar to gin but flavored with some other aromatic substance, as aniseed. [Shortened from Dutch *jenever,* from Middle Dutch *geniver, genever,* juniper, from Old French *geneivre,* from Latin *jūniperus,* JUNIPER.]

gin² (jĭn) *n.* **1.** Any of several machines or devices, as: **a.** A machine for hoisting or moving heavy objects. **b.** A **pile driver** *(see).* **c.** A snare or trap for game. **d.** A pump operated by a windmill. **2.** A **cotton gin** *(see).*
~*tr.v.* **ginned, ginning, gins. 1.** To remove the seeds from (cotton) with a cotton gin. **2.** To trap (game) in a gin. [Middle English *gin,* short for *engin,* ENGINE.]

gin³ (jĭn) *n.* A card game, **gin rummy** *(see).*

gin⁴ (jĭn) *n. Australian.* An aboriginal woman. [From a native Australian language.]

gin⁵ (gĭn) *prep. Scottish.* If. [Probably akin to *gif,* IF.]

gin and tonic (jĭn) *n.* A drink made with gin and quinine water with a garnish of a slice or wedge of lemon or lime.

gin·ger (jĭn′jər) *n.* **1. a.** A plant, *Zingiber officinale,* of tropical Asia, having yellowish-green flowers and a pungent, aromatic rootstock. **b.** The rootstock of this plant, often dried and powdered and used as a spice. **c.** The rootstock of this plant cooked in a heavy sugar syrup until glazed, used as a candy. **2.** Any of various plants of the family Zingiberaceae, having variously colored, often fragrant flowers. **3.** The **wild ginger** *(see).* **4.** A reddish yellow or yellowish brown. **5.** *Informal.* Liveliness; vigor.
~*tr.v.* **gingered, -gering, -gers. 1.** To spice with ginger. **2.** *Informal.* To make more lively. Often used with *up*: *She gingered up the party.* [Middle English *gingivere,* from Old English *gingifer* and Old French *gingivre, gingembre,* from Medieval Latin *gingiber, gingiver,* from Latin *zinziberi,* from Greek *ziggiberis,* from Prakrit *singabēra,* from Sanskrit *śṛṅgaveram* : *śṛṅga-,* horn + *vera-*†, body (so called from its shape).]

ginger ale *n.* An effervescent soft drink, pale orange or brown in color, that is flavored with ginger.

ginger beer *n.* An effervescent soft drink, popular in England, that is cloudy gray in color and flavored with fermented ginger.

gin·ger·bread (jĭn′jər-brĕd′) *n.* **1. a.** A dark molasses cake flavored with ginger. **b.** A soft molasses and ginger cooky cut in various shapes and sometimes elaborately decorated with colored icing. **2. a.** Elaborate ornamentation. **b.** Superfluous or tasteless embellishment, especially in architecture.
~*adj.* **1.** Made of gingerbread. **2.** Tastelessly elaborate. [Middle English *gingebred,* preserved ginger, alteration (influenced by *bred,* BREAD) of Old French *gingebras,* from Medieval Latin *gingibrātum,* from *gingiber,* GINGER.]

gingerbread palm *n.* A tree, the **doum palm** *(see).*

gingerbread tree *n.* An African tree, *Parinarium macrophyllum,* having large edible fruits and useful wood. Also called "gingerbread plum."

ginger group *n. Chiefly British.* A group of people within an association or organization that represent a challenging, progressive, or radical viewpoint. [From GINGER (verb).]

gin·ger·ly (jĭn′jər-lē) *adv.* **1.** With great care or delicacy. **2.** Cautiously; carefully; timidly.
~*adj.* Cautious; careful; timid. [Earliest sense "daintily," perhaps from Old French *gensor, genzor,* comparative of *gent,* pretty, of noble birth, from Latin *genitus,* past participle of *gignere,* to bring forth.] **—gin·ger·li·ness** *n.*

gin·ger·root (jĭn′jər-ro͞ot′, -ro͝ot′) *n.* The rootstock of the ginger plant.

gin·ger·snap (jĭn′jər-snăp′) *n.* A flat, brittle cooky sweetened with molasses and spiced with ginger.

gin·ger·y (jĭn′jə-rē) *adj.* **1.** Having the spicy flavor of ginger. **2.** Sharp and pungent; biting: *a gingery remark.* **3.** Reddish yellow or yellowish brown.

ging·ham (gĭng′əm) *n.* A yarn-dyed cotton fabric woven in stripes, checks, or plaids. [Dutch *gingang,* from Malay *ginggang, gĕnggang,* "interspace."]

gin·gi·li (jĭn′jə-lē) *n.* **1.** Oil extracted from sesame seeds. Also called "gingili oil." **2.** The sesame plant. [Hindi *jingali.*]

gin·gi·va (jĭn′jə-və, jĭn-jī′-) *n., pl.* **-vae** (-vē′). *Anatomy.* The **gum** *(see).*

gin·gi·val (jĭn′jə-vəl, jĭn-jī′-) *adj.* Of or having to do with the gums. [From Latin *gingīva*†, gum.]

gin·gi·vi·tis (jĭn′jə-vī′tĭs) *n.* Inflammation of the gums. [New Latin : Latin *gingīva*†, gum + -ITIS.]

gingko. Variant of **ginkgo.**

gin·gly·mus (jĭng′glə-məs, gĭng′-) *n., pl.* **-mi** (-mī′). *Anatomy.* A hinge joint, such as the elbow or knee joint, allowing movement in one plane only. [New Latin, from Greek *ginglumos,* hinge.]

gink (gĭngk) *n. Slang.* A man or boy, especially one considered odd in some way. [19th century (American) : origin obscure.]

gink·go (gĭng′kō) *n., pl.* **-goes.** Also **ging·ko,** *pl.* **-koes.** A gymnosperm tree, *Ginkgo biloba,* native to China, having fan-shaped leaves and fleshy, yellowish fruit and often planted for ornament. Also called "maidenhair tree." [Japanese *ginkyō,* from ancient Chinese *ngien hang* (Mandarin *yín xìng*), "silver apricot" : *ngien,* silver + *hang,* apricot.]

gin mill (jĭn) *n. Slang.* A saloon.

gin rummy (jĭn) *n.* A variety of rummy for two or more persons in which a person may win by matching all his cards or may end the game by melding when his unmatched cards add up to ten points or less. Also called "gin." [GIN (alcohol) + RUMMY, suggested by a play on RUM (alcohol).]

Gins·berg (gĭnz′bərg), **Allen** (1926–). U.S. poet. He became a celebrity in the 1960's for his part in campaigns on behalf of civil rights and against the Vietnam War. His books include *Howl* (1956), *Kaddish* (1960), and *Reality Sandwiches* (1963).

gin·seng (jĭn′sĕng′) *n.* **1.** Any of several plants of the genus *Panax;* especially, *P. schinseng,* of eastern Asia, or *P. quinquefolium,* of North America, having small greenish flowers and a forked root believed to have medicinal properties, especially the power to promote long life. **2.** The root of either of these plants. [Mandarin Chinese *rén shēn* : *rén,* man (because the forked root resembles a human being with limbs) + *shēn,* ginseng.]

gin sling (jĭn) *n.* An iced, often sweetened cocktail made from gin, lime or lemon juice, and water.

Gior·gio·ne (jôr-jō′nē), **Il,** originally Giorgio Barbarelli, also known as "Giorgio da Castelfranco" (*c.*1477–1511). Italian painter of the Venetian school. He left not a single signed and dated painting. Giorgione was one of the first to paint small canvases for private collectors.

Gior·gi system (jôr′jē) *n. Physics.* A system of units based on the meter, kilogram, second, and ampere in which the magnetic constant has the value $4\pi \times 10^{-7}$ henries per meter. [After Giovanni *Giorgi* (1871–1950), Italian physicist.]

Giot·to (jô′tō, jŏt′ō), in full, Giotto di Bondone (*c.* 1266–1337). Italian Florentine painter, architect, and sculptor. Among his most famous works is the fresco cycle *Lives of the Virgin and Christ* that decorates the walls of the Arena chapel at Padua. Other great fresco cycles are at Assisi and in Santa Croce, Florence.

gip. Variant of **gyp.**

Gipsy. Variant of **Gypsy.**

gi·raffe (jə-răf′, -räf′) *n.* An African ruminant mammal, *Giraffa camelopardis,* having a very long neck and legs, a tan coat with brown blotches, and short horns. It is the tallest living mammal. [Italian *giraffa,* from Arabic *zirāfah,* probably of African origin.]

Gi·ral·dus Cam·bren·sis (jĭ-răl′dəs kăm-brĕn′sĭs), also known as Gerald de Barri (*c.*1146–*c.*1223). Welsh churchman and historian. His writings provide a vivid picture of early medieval life in Wales and Ireland, especially the *Topographia Hibernica,* the *Expugnatio Hibernica,* and the *Itinerarium Cambriae.*

gir·an·dole (jĭr′ən-dōl′) *n.* **1. a.** A composition or structure in radiating form or arrangement, as a rotating display of fireworks. **b.** A branched candleholder, sometimes backed by a mirror. **2.** A piece of jewelry, such as an earring, having a large stone surrounded by small drops. [French *girandole,* from Italian *girandola,* from *girare,* to turn, from Latin *gȳrāre,* to GYRATE.]

gir·a·sol, gir·o·sol, gir·a·sole (jĭr′ə-sôl′, -sŏl′, -sōl′) *n.* A **fire opal** *(see).* [Italian *girasole* : *girare,* to turn (see **girandole**) + *sole,* sun, from Latin *sōl.*]

Gi·rau·doux (zhē-rō-do͞o′), **Jean** (1882–1944). French novelist and playwright. His literary career began with a novel, *Suzanne et le Pacifique* (1921), but he wrote principally for the stage. *La Guerre de Troie n'aura pas lieu* (1935) was his most famous play.

gird¹ (gûrd) *v.* **girded** or **girt** (gûrt), **girding, girds.** *—tr.* **1. a.** To encircle with a belt or band. **b.** To fasten or secure with a belt, cord, or the like. **c.** To surround: *an island girded by water.* **2. a.** To supply with something needed or desired; equip: *girded with the sword of knighthood.* **b.** To endow with an attribute: *girded with righteousness.* **3.** To make (oneself) ready for action. *—intr.* To make oneself ready for action. **—gird one's loins.** To prepare for a severe test, as of courage or strength. [Middle English *girden,* Old English *gyrdan.*]

gird² *v.* **girded, girding, girds.** *—tr. Obsolete.* To jeer at; mock. *—intr.* To make taunting remarks; jeer.
~*n. Obsolete.* A sarcastic remark. [Middle English *girden*†, to strike, cut, charge.] **—gird·er** *n.*

gird·er (gûr′dər) *n.* A horizontal beam, as of steel or wood, used as a main support for a vertical load.

gir·dle (gûrd′l) *n.* **1. a.** A belt, sash, or the like, worn at the waist. **b.** A band or structure that encircles like a belt. **2.** An elasticized, flexible corset worn over the waist and hips. **3.** A band made around the trunk of a tree by the removal of a strip of bark. **4.** The edge of a cut gem held by the setting. **5.** *Anatomy.* The **pelvic girdle** or **pectoral girdle** *(both of which see).*
~*tr.v.* **girdled, -dling, -dles. 1.** To encircle with or as if with a belt. **2.** To put a girdle on or around. **3.** To remove a band of bark completely from the circumference of (a tree), usually to kill it. [Middle English *girdel,* Old English *gyrdel.*]

gird·ler (gûrd′lər) *n.* **1.** One that girdles. **2.** Any of various insects that chew circular bands around twigs or stems in preparing nesting sites. **3.** One who makes girdles.

girl (gûrl) *n.* **1.** A female who has not yet attained womanhood. **2.** A female child. **3.** A single young woman. **4.** *Informal.* A woman: *invited the girls over for a game of bridge.* **5.** A daughter. **6.** A girlfriend. **7. a.** A female worker or employee. **b.** A female servant. [Middle English *girle, gerle, gurle*†.]

girl Friday *n. Informal.* A female employee, especially one having a great variety of responsibilities. [By analogy with MAN FRIDAY.]

girl·friend (gûrl′frĕnd′) *n.* **1.** A favorite female friend, especially one with whom a person is sexually or romantically involved. **2.** A female friend.

Girl Guide *n. Often* **girl guide.** A member of the Girl Guides Association.

Girl Guides Association *n.* A British youth organization founded in 1910 to promote character development and practical skills.

girl·hood (gûrl′ho͝od′) *n.* The state or time of being a girl.

girl·ie, girl·y (gûr′lē) *adj. Informal.* Containing or displaying pictures of naked or almost naked women that are intended to be sexually stimulating: *girlie magazines.*

girl·ish (gûr′lĭsh) *adj.* Pertaining to, characteristic of, or suitable for a girl. **—girl·ish·ly** *adv.* **—girl·ish·ness** *n.*

Girl Scout *n.* A member of the Girl Scouts, a youth organization founded in the United States in 1912 on the plan of the Girl Guides Association.

girn (gûrn) *intr.v.* **girned, girning, girns.** *Scottish.* To complain in a whining voice. [Middle English *girnen,* variant of *grinnen,* to grimace, whimper, GRIN.]

gi·ro (jîr′ō, zhîr′ō, jī′rō) *n., pl.* **-ros.** A centrally operated system of settling debts and transferring credits between different European banks or post offices. [German, from Italian, "circulation."] **—gi·ro** *adj.*

Gi·ronde¹ (jĭ-rŏnd′). France's largest department, in the southwest on the Bay of Biscay. It contains some of the country's finest vineyards, the districts of Médoc, Graves, and Sauternes having given their names to several famous wines. Bordeaux is the capital.

Gironde². Estuary in southwest France, formed by the Garonne and Dordogne rivers. Some 70 kilometers (45 miles) long, it is the seaway to the port of Bordeaux.

Gi·rond·ist (jə-rŏn′dĭst, zhĭ-) *n.* A member of a moderate republican political party of revolutionary France (1791–93). See **Jacobin.** [After GIRONDE, because the leaders of the party were deputies of that department.] **—Gi·rond·ist** *adj.*

girosol. Variant of **girasol.**

girt¹ (gûrt) *v.* **girted, girting, girts.** *—tr.* **1.** To gird; encircle or bind. **2.** To measure the girth of. *—intr.* To measure in girth. [Variant of GIRD.]

girt². Alternate past tense and past participle of **gird** (to encircle).

girth (gûrth) *n.* **1.** The distance around something; the circumference. **2.** The size of something; bulk. **3.** A strap encircling the body of; an animal, as a horse, to secure a load or saddle upon its back; cinch.
~*tr.v.* **girthed, girthing, girths. 1.** To measure the circumference of. **2.** To encircle. **3.** To secure with a girth. [Middle English *gerth,* from Old Norse *györth,* girdle.]

gi·sarme (gĭ-zärm′) *n.* A halberd with a long shaft and a two-sided blade, carried by medieval foot soldiers. [Middle English, from Old French *g(u)isarme,* from Old High German *getīsarn* : *getan*†, to weed + *īsarn,* iron, from Common Germanic *īsarna-* (unattested), IRON.]

Gis·card d'Es·taing (zhĭ-skär′ dĕ-stăng′), **Valéry** (1926–). French politician. He was first elected to the National Assembly at the age of 29 and twice held office as minister of finance (1962–66 and 1969–74). He was elected president of the republic as leader of the Independent Republicans in 1974 and was defeated in his attempt to be re-elected in 1981.

Gish (gĭsh), **Lillian** (*c.* 1896–). U.S. actress. She made her film debut in 1912 and won international acclaim in 1915 for her role in *The Birth of a Nation.* Her later films included *Way Down East* (1920) and *Duel in the Sun* (1946).

gis·mo, giz·mo (gĭz′mō) *n., pl.* **-mos.** *Slang.* A mechanical device or part whose name is forgotten, unknown, or not yet designated. [20th century : origin obscure.]

Gis·sing (gĭs′ĭng), **George Robert** (1857–1903). British novelist. His best-known works are *New Grub Street* (1891) and the semiautobiographical, imaginary journal, *The Private Papers of Henry Ryecroft* (1903).

gist (jĭst) *n.* **1.** The central idea of a matter, such as an argument or a speech; the essence: *The gist of what he was saying was that he flatly refused to help.* **2.** *Law.* The grounds for action in a suit. [Old French *(cest action) gist,* (this action) lies, from *gesir,* to lie, from Latin *jacēre,* from *jacere,* to throw.]

git (gĭt) *n. British Slang.* A silly or contemptible person. [Variant of GET (offspring, fool).]

give (gĭv) *v.* **gave** (gāv), **given** (gĭv′ən), **giving, gives.** *—tr.* **1. a.** To make a present of; bestow ownership of on: *gave her flowers for her birthday.* **b.** To deliver in exchange or in recompense; pay: *He will give you five dollars for the book.* **c.** To put temporarily at the disposal of; entrust to: *give them the cottage for a week.* **d.** To place in the hands of; pass: *Give me the scissors.* **2. a.** To convey or offer for conveyance; communicate: *Give him my best wishes.* **b.** To bestow, especially officially; confer: *give authority.* **c.** To accord or tender to another; grant: *give permission.* **3.** To supply, especially in common with others; donate: *give one's time.* **4. a.** To be a source of; afford: *His remark gave offense.* **b.** To cause to have or be subject to: *She gave him the measles.* **5.** To bring forth; produce or yield: *This cow gives three gallons of milk per day.* **6.** To provide (something required or expected): *Please give your name and address.* **7. a.** To inflict as punishment: *gave the naughty child a spanking.* **b.** To mete out as a remedy; administer: *gave the patient a prescription cough syrup.* **8. a.** To grant; concede: *I'll give you that point.* **b.** To allow: *give odds of five to one.* **c.** To relinquish; yield: *give ground.* **9.** To emit or utter: *give a sigh of contentment.* **10. a.** To assign as one's portion; allot: *give her five minutes to finish.* **b.** To select and cite for a particular time or purpose; designate: *give a departure date.* **11.** To award as due: *The judges gave him first prize for the best roses.* **12.** To ascribe to a particular cause or source; attribute: *give him the blame.* **13.** To grant as a supposition; acknowledge: *Given their superiority, we can't expect to win.* **14. a.** To cause to take place, especially for entertainment: *give a dinner party.* **b.** To proffer: *give a toast.* **c.** To offer to observation or view; manifest: *give promise of brilliance.* **d.** *Informal.* To offer by way of explanation: *Don't give me that old story!* **e.** To perform for an audience: *gave a series of concerts.* **f.** To perform by moving the body or a part of the body: *give a bow.* **g.** To engage in: *give battle.* **15.** To submit for consideration or acceptance; tender: *give an opinion.* **16.** To cause or be responsible for; lead or allow: *She gave me to think she loved me.* **17.** To apply entirely to a particular activity, pursuit, cause, or person; devote: *give oneself to one's work.* **18.** To undergo the loss of; sacrifice: *give a son to the war.* **19.** To propose as a toast to: *I give you the regiment.* *—intr.* **1.** To make gifts or donations: *Please give generously.* **2.** To be unable to hold up; yield or collapse: *The roof gave under the weight of the snow.* **3.** To afford a view of or access to something: *The French doors give onto a terrace.* **4.** *Informal.* To be happening; occur: *What gives?* **—give a good account of oneself.** To behave or perform creditably. **—give as good as one gets.** To respond to an attack with equal effect or force. **—give forth. 1.** To report; circulate. **2.** To emit. **—give in. 1.** To cease opposition; concede. **2.** To hand in; submit: *She gave in her report.* **—give off.** To send forth; emit: *Chemical changes that give off energy.* **—give or take.** Adding or subtracting: *I'll be there at five, give or take ten minutes.* **—give out. 1.** To let (something) be known: *gave out the good news.* **2.** To stop functioning; fail. **3.** To become used up; run out: *Our supply of firewood gave out.* **—give over. 1.** To relinquish the care of; hand over. **2.** To make available for a particular purpose or use; devote: *a week given over to indulgence.* **3.** To surrender completely and unrestrainedly; abandon: *gave herself over to her grief.* **4.** To stop; desist. **—give rise to.** To be the cause of; occasion. **—give someone one.** *Slang.* To hit with or as if with the fists; strike. **—give someone what for.** *Slang.* To punish, especially by blows or a sharp reproof. **—give up. 1.** To surrender: *Give yourself up to the police.* **2.** To leave off; stop: *give up smoking.* **3.** To part with; relinquish: *gave up all hope.* **4.** To abandon hope for: *give her up as lost.* **5.** To admit defeat. **—give way. 1. a.** To withdraw; retreat. **b.** To make room for or wait for the passage of: *give way to an oncoming car.* **2.** To collapse from or as if from physical pressure: *The ladder gave way.* **3.** To abandon oneself: *give way to hysteria.*
~*n.* **1.** The act or process of yielding, adapting, or bending under pressure. **2.** The quality or state of being resilient; springiness: *The mattress has lots of give.* [Give, gave, given; Middle English *given, gaf, given,* Old English *giefan, geaf, giefen.*]

give and take *intr.v.* To engage in give-and-take.

give-and-take (gĭv′ən-tāk′) *n.* **1.** The practice of compromise. **2.** Lively exchange of ideas or conversation.

give away *tr.v.* **1.** To make a gift of. **2.** To observe ceremonially the transfer of (a bride) from her family to her husband. **3.** To reveal or make known, often accidentally.

give·a·way (gĭv′ə-wā′) *n. Informal.* **1.** Something that betrays or exposes, often accidentally. **2.** Something offered at a bargain price. **3.** Something given away at no charge.

giv·en (gĭv′ən) *adj.* **1. a.** Specific: *a given date.* **b.** Issued on a specific date. Said of legal documents. **2.** Accepted as a fact; acknowledged; assumed. **3.** Habitually inclined. Used with *to*: *given to shyness.* **4.** Bestowed; presented.

given name *n.* A name given to a person at birth or at baptism; a Christian name.

Gi·za, Al (gē′zə). Town in Egypt. The capital of the Giza governate, it is on the west bank of the Nile River. Nearby is the Great Pyramid of Cheops (Khufu), one of the Seven Wonders of the Ancient World.

giz·zard (gĭz′ərd) *n.* **1.** An enlargement of the alimentary canal in birds, often having dense muscular walls and containing fine grit eaten to aid in breaking up hard food. **2.** A similar digestive organ of certain invertebrates, such as the earthworm. **3.** The **proventriculus** *(see)* of insects and crustaceans. **4.** *Informal.* The stomach. [Middle English *giser,* from Old French *giser, gezier,* from Vulgar Latin *gicerium* (unattested), from Latin *gigeria,* cooked entrails of poultry, perhaps from Persian *jigar.*]

Gk. Greek.

gla·bel·la (glə-bĕl′ə) *n., pl.* **-bellae** (-bĕl′ē). *Anatomy.* The smooth area between the eyebrows just above the nose, formed by part of the frontal bone. [New Latin, from Latin *glabellus,* hairless, from *glaber,* hairless, bald, GLABROUS.]

gla·brous (glā′brəs) *adj. Biology.* Having no hairs or down; smooth. [Latin *glaber,* hairless, bald.]

gla·cé (glă-sā′) *adj.* **1.** Having a glazed, glossy surface. **2.** Coated with a sugar glaze or icing.
~*tr.v.* **glacéed, -céing, -cés.** To coat with sugar glaze or icing. [French, past participle of *glacer,* to ice, glaze, from *glace,* ice, from Latin *glaciēs.*]

gla·cial (glā′shəl) *adj.* **1.** Of, pertaining to, or derived from a glacier or ice sheet. **2.** *Often* **Glacial.** Characterized or dominated by the existence of glaciers or ice sheets. Said especially of the Pleistocene. **3.** Extremely cold; icy: *glacial waters.* **4.** Having the appearance of ice. **5.** Lacking warmth and friendliness: *a glacial stare.* [Latin *glaciālis,* icy, from *glaciēs,* ice.] **—gla·cial·ly** *adv.*

glacial acetic acid *n.* **Acetic acid** *(see)* that is almost pure.

PRONUNCIATION KEY

ă, **pat**; ā, **pay**; âr, **care**;
ä, **father**, **are**; b, **bib**;
ch, **church**; d, **deed**; ĕ, **pet**;
ē, **be**; f, **fife**; g, **gag**; h, **hat**;
hw, **which**; ĭ, **pit**; ī, **pie**;
îr, **pier**; j, **judge**; k, **kick**;
l, **lid**, **needle**; m, **mum**;
n, **no**, **sudden**; ng, **thing**;
ŏ, **pot**; ō, **toe**; ô, **paw**, **for**;
oi, **noise**; ou, **out**; o͝o, **book**;
o͞o, **boot**; p, **pop**; r, **roar**;
s, **sauce**; sh, **ship**, **dish**;
t, **tight**; th, **thin**, **path**;
th, **this**, **bathe**; ŭ, **cut**; ûr, **fur**;
v, **valve**; w, **with**; y, **yes**;
z, **zebra**, **size**; zh, **vision**;
ə, **about**, **item**, **edible**, **gallop**, **circus**, **peaceful**

IN FOREIGN WORDS:

à, *Fr.* **ami**; œ, *Fr.* **feu**, *Ger.* **schön**; ü, *Fr.* **tu**, *Ger.* **über**;
KH, *Ger.* **ich**, *Scot.* **loch**;
N, *Fr.* **bon**; y′, *Fr.* **Compiègne**

STRESS MARKS:

Primary stress: ′
in·cite′ (ĭn-sīt′)
Secondary stress: ′
in′sight′ (ĭn′sīt′)

glacier *As the climate in the Himalayas of northern Nepal gradually becomes warmer, the Langtang glacier (above) is slowly shrinking. The melting ice exposes jumbled debris (moraines) eroded from the rock on the glacier's journey down the mountain.*

glacial epoch *n.* **1.** Any of several periods during the Pleistocene epoch up to 1,000,000 years ago, when much of the earth's surface was covered by glaciers. **2.** The Pleistocene epoch.

gla·ci·ate (glā′shē-āt′, -sē-) *v.* **-ated, -ating, -ates.** —*tr.* **1.** To subject to the effects of glaciers. **2.** To freeze. —*intr.* To become covered with glaciers or ice sheets. [Latin *glaciāre*, to freeze, from *glaciēs*, ice. See glacier.]

gla·ci·a·tion (glā′shē-ā′shən, -sē-) *n.* *Geology.* **1.** The formation, movement, and retreat of ice sheets and glaciers. **2.** The overall effects on a landscape produced by glacial action.

gla·cier (glā′shər, -zhər) *n.* **1.** A huge mass of ice, originating from compacted snow, moving slowly in a continuous stream down a valley under its own weight. **2.** An ice sheet that has spread out from a central mass and covers a large part of a continent. [French, from *glace*, ice, from Latin *glaciēs*.]

Glacier Bay National Park. An area of 1,135,555 hectares (2,803,840 acres) in southeastern Alaska, in the Panhandle near Juneau. The park has towering snow-covered mountains, spectacular glaciers, many of them flowing into the Pacific Ocean, and wildlife ranging from bears and mountain goats to whales and porpoises.

Glacier National Park. A park comprising 410,306 hectares (1,013,040 acres) in northwestern Montana, straddling the Continental Divide of the Rocky Mts. The primitive wilderness area includes glaciers, glacier-fed lakes, waterfalls, sheer rock precipices, extensive forests, and a wide variety of wildlife and wild flowers.

gla·ci·ol·o·gy (glā′shē-ŏl′ə-jē, -sē-) *n.* The scientific study of glaciers. [GLACIER + -LOGY.] —**gla·ci·o·log·ic** (glā′shē-ə-lŏj′ĭk, -sē-), **gla·ci·o·log·i·cal** *adj.* —**gla·ci·ol·o·gist** *n.*

gla·cis (glā-sē′, glăs′ē, glā′sĭs) *n.* **1.** A gentle slope; an incline. **2.** A slope extended in front of a fortification in such a way that approaching attackers are made particularly vulnerable to the defenders' fire. [French, from Old French *glacier*, to slide, from *glace*, ice, from Latin *glaciēs*.]

Glack·ens (glăk′ənz), **William James** (1870–1938). U.S. artist. He studied at the Pennsylvania Academy of Fine Arts and in Paris, where he was influenced by the works of Manet and Renoir. Glackens is particularly known for his landscapes and genre paintings, including *Parade, Washington Square.*

glad¹ (glăd) *adj.* **gladder, gladdest.** **1.** Experiencing or exhibiting joy and pleasure. **2.** Providing joy and pleasure: *a glad occasion.* **3.** Pleased; willing: *glad to help.* **4.** *Archaic.* Of a cheerful disposition.
~*tr.v.* **gladded, gladding, glads.** *Obsolete.* To gladden. [Middle English *glad*, joyful, happy, shining, Old English *glæd*, from Germanic.] —**glad·ly** *adv.* —**glad·ness** *n.*
Synonyms: *cheerful, happy, joyful, joyous, light-hearted.*

glad² *n.* *Informal.* A gladiolus.

glad·den (glăd′n) *v.* **-dened, -dening, -dens.** —*tr.* To make glad. —*intr.* *Archaic.* To become glad.

glade (glād) *n.* An open space in a wood or forest. [16th century : origin obscure.]

glad eye *n.* *Slang.* A provocative look: *He gave her the glad eye.*

glad hand *n.* *Informal.* **1.** A hearty and friendly handshake, welcome, or greeting. **2.** A hearty, often insincere and offensively familiar welcome or greeting.

glad-hand (glăd′hănd′) *v.* **-handed, -handing, -hands.** *Informal.* —*tr.* To extend a glad hand to. —*intr.* To extend a glad hand. —**glad-hand·er** *n.*

glad·i·ate (glăd′ē-āt′, -ĭt, glā′dē-) *adj.* Sword-shaped, as a leaf. [New Latin *gladiatus*, from Latin *gladius*, sword.]

glad·i·a·tor (glăd′ē-ā′tər) *n.* **1.** In ancient Rome, a professional combatant, slave, captive, or condemned prisoner trained to entertain the public by engaging in combat in the arena. **2.** A contender or debater, especially one chosen to represent his faction or party in public. **3.** A prizefighter. [Middle English, from Latin *gladiātor*, from *gladius*, sword.] —**glad·i·a·to·ri·al** (glăd′ē-ə-tôr′ē-əl, -tōr′-) *adj.*

glad·i·o·lus (glăd′ē-ō′ləs) *n., pl.* **-li** (-lī′, -lē′) or **-luses.** Also **glad·i·o·la** (-lə) (for sense 1). **1.** Any of various plants of the genus *Gladiolus*, native to tropical regions but widely cultivated elsewhere, having sword-shaped leaves and a spike of showy, variously colored flowers. Also called "sword lily." **2.** *Anatomy.* The large middle section of the sternum. [Latin, diminutive of *gladius*, sword.]

glad rags *pl.n.* *Informal.* One's best or most elegant clothes.

glad·some (glăd′səm) *adj.* **1.** Glad; joyful. **2.** Causing gladness. —**glad·some·ly** *adv.* —**glad·some·ness** *n.*

Glad·stone (glăd′stōn′, -stən) *n.* **1.** A light four-wheeled convertible carriage with two interior seats and places outside for a driver and footman. **2.** A Gladstone bag. [After W.E. GLADSTONE.]

Gladstone, William Ewart (1809–98). British statesman. He was Liberal prime minister four times (1868–74, 1880–85, 1886, and 1892–94). His first government passed a Land Act to protect Irish tenants, established national education in England, and introduced the secret ballot in parliamentary elections. During his second term of office the Reform Act of 1884 was passed. His third and fourth terms of office were taken up with unsuccessful attempts to gain support for a Home Rule Bill for Ireland.

Gladstone bag *n.* A piece of light hand luggage consisting of two hinged compartments. [After W.E. GLADSTONE.]

Glag·o·lit·ic (glăg′ə-lĭt′ĭk) *adj.* Also **Glag·o·lith·ic** (-lĭth′ĭk). Belonging to or written in an alphabet attributed to St. Cyril, formerly used in the writing of various Slavic languages but now limited to the Catholic liturgical books used by some communities along the Dalmatian coast. Compare **Cyrillic alphabet.** [New Latin *glagoliticus*, from Serbo-Croatian *glagolica*, the Glagolitic alphabet, from *glagól*, word; akin to Old Church Slavonic *glagolŭ*, word.]

glai·kit, glai·ket (glā′kĭt) *adj.* *Chiefly Scottish.* Foolish; emptyheaded. [15th century : origin obscure.]

glair, glaire (glâr) *n.* **1.** Raw egg white used in sizing or glazing. **2. a.** A sizing, glaze, or adhesive made of egg white. **b.** Any similar viscous substance.
~*tr.v.* **glaired, glairing, glairs.** To apply glair to. [Middle English *glaire*, from Old French, from Vulgar Latin *clāria ovi* (unattested), white of egg, from *clārus*, clear.]

glair·y (glâr′ē) *adj.* **-ier, -iest.** Also **glair·e·ous** (-ē-əs). **1.** Like glair. **2.** Coated with glair. —**glair·i·ness** *n.*

glaive (glāv) *n.* *Archaic & Poetic.* A sword; especially, a broadsword. [Middle English *glaive*, from Old French, from Latin *gladius*, sword.]

Gla·mor·gan (glə-môr′gən). Also **Gla·mor·gan·shire** (-shîr, -shər). A former county of southern Wales. Since the reorganization of local government in 1974, it has been fragmented to form parts of Mid Glamorgan, South Glamorgan, West Glamorgan, and Gwent.

glam·or·ize, glam·our·ize (glăm′ə-rīz′) *tr.v.* **-ized, -izing, -izes.** **1.** To make glamorous or add glamour to. **2.** To treat or portray in a romantic manner; romanticize, idealize, or glorify. —**glam·or·i·za·tion** *n.* —**glam·or·iz·er** *n.*

glam·or·ous, glam·our·ous (glăm′ər-əs) *adj.* Characterized by glamour. —**glam·or·ous·ly** *adv.* —**glam·or·ous·ness** *n.*

glam·our, glam·or (glăm′ər) *n.* **1.** Compelling charm, romance, and excitement, especially when delusively alluring: *the glamour of the foreign service.* **2.** Sophisticated or fashionable attractiveness, especially when aided by the use of cosmetics. Also used adjectively: *a glamour show.* **3.** *Archaic.* Magic; enchantment. [Scottish variant of GRAMMAR (from the association of learning with magic).]

glance¹ (glăns, gläns) *v.* **glanced, glancing, glances.** —*intr.* **1.** To strike a surface at such an angle as to be deflected: *A pebble glanced off the windshield.* **2.** To direct the gaze briefly: *glance at the menu.*

---

glaciation

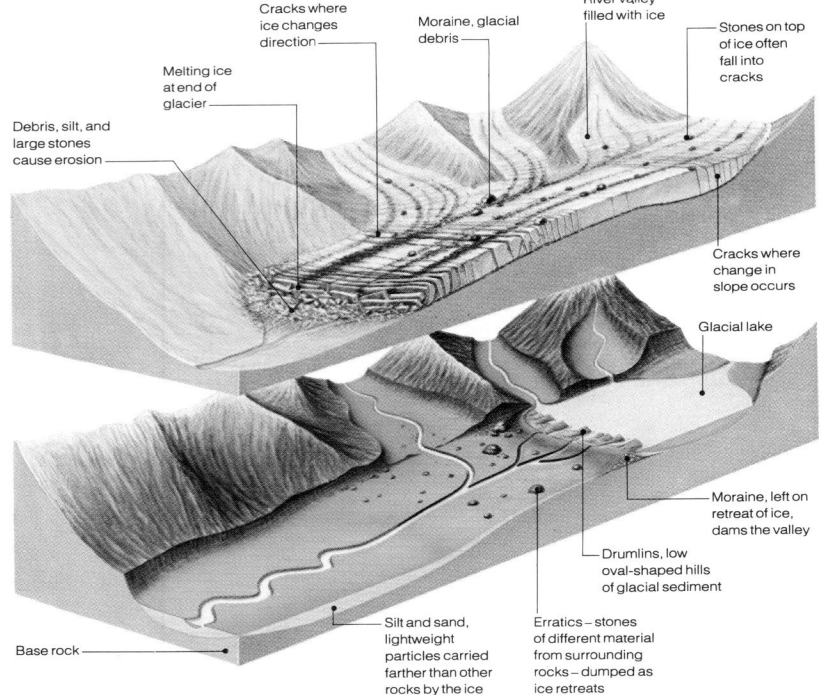

CHANGING THE SURFACE OF THE LAND
Ice that gouges and planes the earth's features

Glaciers are slow-moving rivers of ice formed by compacted snow. As they flow downhill, they alter landscapes in several ways, principally by erosion and by depositing moraines, or sediments, that remain when the glaciers melt. The effects of erosion range from the gouging of valleys (as in Scotland and Norway) to the planing of vast areas (as in Canada).

Moraines are ridge-shaped and occur at the sides and end of a glacier. They may become the dam for a lake or form islands such as Long Island, New York.

Cracks where ice changes direction

Moraine, glacial debris

River valley filled with ice

Stones on top of ice often fall into cracks

Melting ice at end of glacier

Debris, silt, and large stones cause erosion

Cracks where change in slope occurs

Glacial lake

Moraine, left on retreat of ice, dams the valley

Drumlins, low oval-shaped hills of glacial sediment

Silt and sand, lightweight particles carried farther than other rocks by the ice

Erratics – stones of different material from surrounding rocks – dumped as ice retreats

Base rock

EFFECTS IN MOUNTAINS *During the Ice Age, which ended 10,000 years ago, glaciers in mountains ground out steep valley heads known as cirques and wore V-shaped valleys into U-shapes. The moraines they deposited across valleys became dams behind which lakes formed.*

3. To shine briefly; glint. **4.** To refer to or touch upon briefly: *a survey of music history that glances at the styles of the major composers of each period.* —*tr.* **1.** To strike (a surface) at an angle; graze: *The baseball glanced the fence.* **2.** To cause to strike a surface at an angle: *glance a stone over the stream.* —See Usage note at **flash.**
~*n.* **1.** An oblique movement following impact; a deflection. **2.** A brief or cursory look: *The defendant darted surreptitious glances at the prosecutor and the jury.* **3.** A quick flash of light; a gleam: *the glance of a mirror struck by a ray of sunlight.* —**at a glance.** Immediately; with only a brief look: *I could tell at a glance that he was upset.* [Alteration of Middle English *glacen* (influenced by *glenten,* to shine, GLINT), from Old French *glacier,* to slide, from *glace,* ice, from Latin *glaciēs.*]

glance² *n.* Any of various minerals, usually sulfides, that have a brilliant luster: *silver glance.* [German *Glanz,* from Old High German *glanz,* bright.]

gland (glănd) *n.* **1. a.** *Anatomy.* An organ that synthesizes specific substances, such as hormones, and secretes them into the bloodstream or elsewhere. See **endocrine gland, exocrine. b.** Any of various nonsecretory or excretory organs that resemble such organs, as a lymph node. **2.** *Botany.* An organ or cell that secretes a substance. **3.** *Machinery.* A part that seals a casing to prevent fluid leakage at a point where a moving shaft comes out. [French *glande,* from Old French, glandular swelling, acorn, from Latin *glāns* (stem *gland-*), acorn.]

glan·ders (glăn′dərz) *n. Used with a singular or plural verb.* A contagious, often chronic, sometimes fatal disease of horses and other animals, caused by a bacillus, *Actinobacillus mallei,* and characterized by a nasal discharge and ulcers in the lungs, respiratory tract, and skin. [Old French *glandres,* plural of *glandre,* glandular swelling, from Latin *glandula,* diminutive of *glāns* (stem *gland-*), acorn.] —**glan·der·ous** *adj.*

glan·du·lar (glăn′jə-lər) *adj.* **1.** Of, pertaining to, affecting, or resembling a gland or its secretion. **2.** Functioning as a gland. **3.** Having glands. **4.** Resulting from abnormal gland function. **5.** Possessed as an essential characteristic; inherent. [French *glandulaire,* from *glandule,* small gland, from Latin *glandula,* glandular swelling.] —**glan·du·lar·ly** *adv.*

glandular fever *n. Pathology.* **Mononucleosis** *(see).*

glan·dule (glăn′jo͞ol) *n.* A small gland. [From Latin *glandula,* diminutive of *glāns* (stem *gland-*), gland.]

glans (glănz) *n., pl.* **glandes** (glăn′dēz′). *Anatomy.* **1.** The glans penis. **2.** The glans clitoridis. [Latin *glāns,* "acorn" (from its shape).]

glans cli·tor·i·dis (klĭ-tôr′ə-dĭs, -tōr′-, klī-) *n.* The small mass of erectile tissue at the tip of the clitoris. Also called "glans."

glans penis *n.* The head or tip of the penis. Also called "glans."

glare¹ (glâr) *v.* **glared, glaring, glares.** —*intr.* **1.** To stare fixedly and angrily. **2.** To shine intensely and blindingly: *The spotlight glared mercilessly on the lone skater.* **3.** To be conspicuous; stand out obtrusively. —*tr.* To express (an emotion) by staring fixedly and angrily: *glared his disapproval.* —See Synonyms at **gaze.**
~*n.* **1.** A fixed, angry stare: *The teacher gave the unruly student a glare.* **2.** An intense and blinding light: *the glare of the sun on the water.* **3.** Unwelcome attention: *The senator's wife detested the glare of publicity.* **4.** Showy brilliance; gaudiness: *the pomp and glare of rhetoric.* —See Synonyms at **blaze.** [Middle English *glaren,* probably from Middle Low German, to gleam.]

glare² *n.* A sheet or surface of slick, glassy ice. [Probably from GLARE (shine).]

glar·ing (glâr′ĭng) *adj.* **1.** Staring fixedly and angrily: *glaring eyes.* **2.** Shining intensely and blindingly: *The glaring sun.* **3.** Gaudy; garish. **4.** Painfully conspicuous; egregious: *a glaring error.* —See Synonyms at **flagrant.** —**glar·ing·ly** *adv.*

glar·y (glâr′ē) *adj.* **-ier, -iest.** Dazzlingly bright; glaring.

Gla·ser (glā′zər), **Donald Arthur** (1926–) U.S. physicist. He invented the bubble chamber for the study of subatomic particles, and for this he was awarded the Nobel Prize for physics in 1960. Since then he has undertaken important research into DNA.

Glas·gow (glăs′gō, -kō, gläs′-). The largest city in Scotland, a major port and the administrative center of Strathclyde Region, situated on the Clyde River in the west of the country. A cathedral city since the 12th century, Glasgow prospered in the 18th century through trade in sugar and tobacco with the Americas. A major industrial center, its traditional shipbuilding industry has suffered a decline but remains an important source of income.

glass (glăs, gläs) *n.* **1.** Any of a large class of materials with highly variable mechanical and optical properties that solidify from the molten state without crystallization and are typically based on silicon dioxide, boric oxide, aluminum oxide, or phosphorus pentoxide. They are generally transparent or translucent and are regarded physically as supercooled liquids rather than true solids. **2.** Objects made of glass collectively; glassware. **3.** Something made of glass, especially: **a.** A drinking vessel. **b.** A mirror. **c.** A barometer. **d.** A windowpane. **4. a.** A device, as a telescope, containing a lens or lenses and used as an aid to vision. **b. glasses.** A pair of lenses mounted in a light frame that passes over the nose and around the ears and that is used to correct faulty vision or to protect the eyes. Also called "spectacles," "eyeglasses." **6.** The quantity contained by a drinking vessel; a glassful: *drank a glass of grapefruit juice.* **7.** *Geology.* Hard, shiny rock that has no crystalline structure.
~*adj.* Of, pertaining to, or made of glass.
~*v.* **glassed, glassing, glasses.** —*tr.* **1.** To place within glass or a glass container. **2.** To provide with glass or glass parts. **3. a.** To see reflected, as in a mirror. **b.** To mirror; reflect. —*intr.* To become like glass. [Middle English *glas,* Old English *glæs,* from Germanic.]

glass blowing *n.* The art or process of shaping an object from molten glass by blowing air into it through a tube. —**glass blower** *n.*

glass cutter *n.* **1.** One who cuts or etches patterns on glass. **2.** A tool for cutting glass. —**glass cutting** *n.*

glass eel *n.* An eel in its transparent, postlarval stage.

glass electrode *n.* An instrument for measuring pH (acidity or alkalinity), consisting of a thin glass bulb containing a buffer solution with a platinum wire dipping into it. The bulb is placed in the solution to be investigated and the pH is indicated by the potential difference between the glass and the platinum.

glass eye *n.* An artificial eye made of glass.

glass·fish (glăs′fĭsh′, gläs′-) *n., pl.* **-fishes** or collectively **glassfish.** Any of various fishes of the family Centropomidae, of warm and tropical waters, having a transparent body and a cleft dorsal fin. Also called "glassperch."

glass·ful (glăs′fo͝ol′, gläs′-) *n., pl.* **-fuls.** The quantity contained in a glass.

glass harmonica *n.* An 18th-century musical instrument consisting of a set of graduated glass bowls that produce tones when a moistened finger is passed over their rims.

glass·house (glăs′hous′; gläs′-) *n.* **1.** A glassworks. **2.** *Chiefly British.* A greenhouse. **3.** *British Slang.* A military prison.

glass·ine (glă-sēn′) *n.* A nearly transparent, resilient, glazed paper resistant to the passage of air and grease.

glass jaw *n.* A jaw, specifically a boxer's jaw, that is very vulnerable to punches.

glass·mak·er (glăs′mā′kər, gläs′-) *n.* One who makes glass. —**glass·mak·ing** *n.*

glass·man (glăs′mən, -măn′, gläs′-) *n., pl.* **-men** (-mĭn, -mĕn′). **1.** One who sells glass. **2.** A glassmaker.

glass·pa·per (glăs′pā′pər, gläs′-) *n.* Strong paper in which small glass particles are embedded that is used to smooth surfaces, as of wood.
~*tr.v.* **glasspapered, -pering, -pers.** To smooth (a surface) with glasspaper.

glass·perch (glăs′pûrch′, gläs′-) *n.* A **glassfish** *(see).*

glass snake *n.* Any of several slender, limbless, snakelike lizards of the genus *Ophisaurus,* having a tail that breaks or snaps off readily. [From the brittleness of its tail.]

glass·ware (glăs′wâr′, gläs′-) *n.* Objects, especially tableware, made of glass.

glass wool *n.* Fine-spun fibers of glass used especially for insulation, in air filters, and for synthetic composite materials.

glass·work (glăs′wûrk′, gläs′-) *n.* **1. a.** The manufacture of glassware or glass. **b.** The cutting and fitting of glass panes; glaziery. **2.** Glassware. **3. glassworks.** *Used with a singular verb.* An establishment, as a workshop or factory, where glass is made. —**glass·work·er** *n.*

glass·wort (glăs′wûrt′, -wôrt′, gläs′-) *n.* **1.** Any of various plants of the genus *Salicornia,* growing in salt marshes and having fleshy stems and rudimentary, scalelike leaves. Also called "samphire." **2.** A plant, the **saltwort** *(see).* [Formerly used in making glass.]

glass·y (glăs′ē, glä′sē) *adj.* **-ier, -iest. 1.** Made of or resembling glass. **2.** Lifeless; expressionless: *a glassy stare.* —**glass·i·ly** *adv.* —**glass·i·ness** *n.*

Glas·ton·bur·y (glăs′tən-bĕr′ē). A market town in Somerset in the southwest of England. It is the traditional site of King Arthur's Isle of Avalon. Its ruined Benedictine abbey of St. Mary (*c.* 678) is built on the site of an earlier Celtic monastery.

Glau·ber's salts, Glau·ber's salt (glou′bərz) *n.* A hydrated sodium sulfate, $Na_2SO_4 \cdot 10H_2O$, used in paper and glass manufacturing and as a laxative. [After J.R. *Glauber* (1604–68), German chemist.]

glau·co·ma (glou-kō′mə, glô-) *n.* A disease of the eye characterized by high intraocular pressure, damaged optic disk, hardening of the eyeball, and partial or complete loss of vision. [Latin *glaucōma,* cataract, from Greek *glaukōma,* from *glaukos,* GLAUCOUS.] —**glau·co·ma·tous** (glou-kō′mə-təs, glô-) *adj.*

glau·co·nite (glô′kə-nīt′) *n.* A greenish mineral consisting essentially of a hydrous silicate of potassium and iron that is found most commonly in greensand and is used as a water softener and a fertilizer. [Greek *glaukon,* neuter of *glaukos,* GLAUCOUS + -ITE.] —**glau·co·nit·ic** (glô′kə-nĭt′ĭk) *adj.*

glau·cous (glô′kəs) *adj.* **1.** Grayish green or bluish green. **2.** *Botany.* Covered with a fine, whitish, powdery coating. [Latin *glaucus,* from Greek *glaukos†,* gleaming, bluish green or gray.]

glaur (glôr) *n. Scottish.* Mire or mud. [Middle English (Scottish and northern English); perhaps akin to Old Norse *leir,* mud.] —**glaur·y** *adj.*

glaze (glāz) *n.* **1. a.** A thin, smooth, shiny coating. **b.** The substance of which this coating is made. **2.** A coating of colored, opaque, or transparent material applied to ceramics before firing to produce a glassy, waterproof surface. **3.** A substance, as syrup or gelatin, applied to food, on which it solidifies to form a thin coating. **4.** A transparent coating applied to the surface of a painting to modify the color tones. **5.** A glassy film, as over the eyes. **6.** A thin, glassy coating of ice.
~*v.* **glazed, glazing, glazes.** —*tr.* **1.** To fit or furnish (a window, for example) with glass. **2.** To apply a glaze to: *glaze a doughnut; glaze pottery.* **3.** To give a smooth, lustrous surface to. —*intr.* **1.** To be or become glazed or glassy: *eyes glazing over from boredom.*

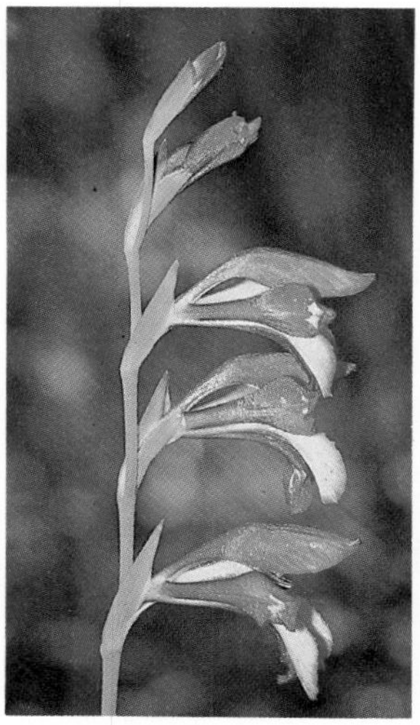

gladiolus *The many garden varieties of gladiolus originated in southern Africa but a wild gladiolus, the crimson-purple* Gladiolus illyricus *(above), does occur in scrub and open woods in Europe.*

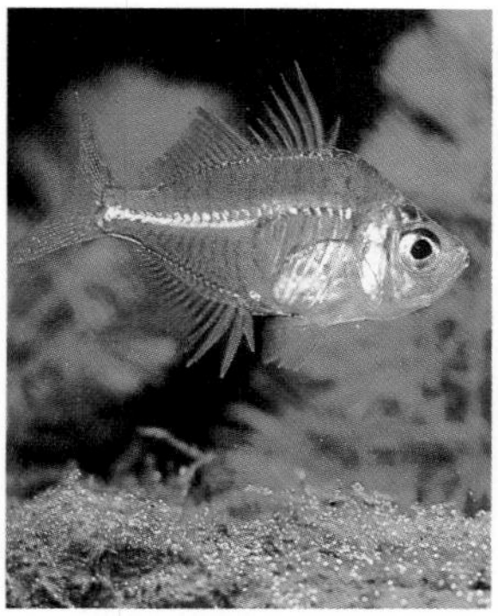

glassfish *The Siamese glassfish, or glassperch, is one of about 20 Indo-Pacific fish with transparent bodies. It reflects light in the manner of glass.*

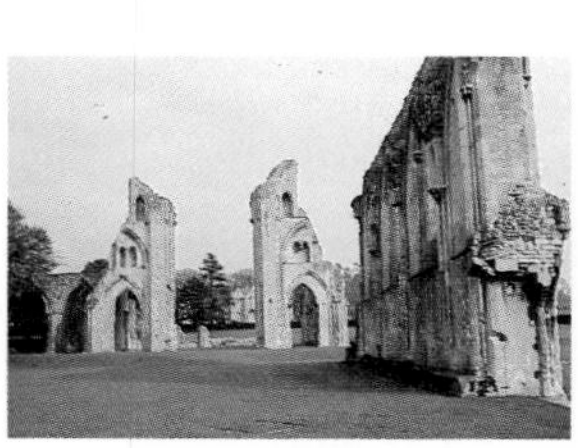

Glastonbury *This English abbey was destroyed by Henry VIII during the Dissolution of the Monasteries in 1539.*

2. To form a glaze. [Middle English *glasen,* to provide with glass or a glassy surface, from *glas,* GLASS.] —**glaz·er** *n.*

glaze ice *n. British.* A thin, glassy coating of ice; glaze.

gla·zier (glā'zhər) *n.* One who cuts and fits window glass. [Middle English *glasier,* from *glas,* GLASS.]

gla·zier·y (glā'zhə-rē) *n.* **1.** The cutting and fitting of window glass. **2.** Glasswork.

glaz·ing (glā'zīng) *n.* **1. a.** Glasswork. **b.** Glass set or made to be set in frames. **2. a.** A glaze. **b.** The act or process of applying a glaze.

Gla·zu·nov (glăz'ə-nôf', -nôv'), **Alexander Konstantinovich** (1865–1936). Russian composer. He was taught by Rimsky-Korsakov, with whom he completed Borodin's opera *Prince Igor.* He wrote eight symphonies and many chamber works.

GLC gas-liquid chromatography.

gld. guilder.

gleam (glēm) *n.* **1.** A fleeting beam or flash of light: *saw gleams of daylight through the cracks.* **2.** A steady but subdued shining; a glow: *the gleam of a steel blade.* **3.** A brief or dim manifestation or indication: *a gleam of intelligence.*
~*intr.v.* **gleamed, gleaming, gleams. 1.** To emit a gleam; flash or glow: *"It shone with gold and gleamed with ivory"* (Edith Hamilton). **2.** To be manifested or indicated briefly or faintly. —See Usage note at **flash.** [Middle English *gleem, glem,* Old English *glǣm,* from Germanic.]

gleam·er (glē'mər) *n.* **1.** One that gleams. **2.** Make-up applied to the face and lips to give a glossy appearance.

glean (glēn) *v.* **gleaned, gleaning, gleans.** —*intr.* To gather grain left behind in a field after the crop has been harvested. —*tr.* **1.** To gather (grain left behind in a field after harvesting). **2.** To collect (knowledge or information, for example) bit by bit: *Historians glean their knowledge from old records and documents.* [Middle English *glenen,* from Old French *glener,* from Late Latin *glennāre,* from Celtic *glend-no-* (unattested).] —**glean·er** *n.*

glean·ings (glē'nĭngz) *pl.n.* **1.** Knowledge or information collected bit by bit. **2.** The grain left behind in a field after the crop has been harvested.

Glea·son (glē'sən), **Herbert John,** known as "Jackie" (1916–87). U.S. entertainer. He first gained popularity in 1949 in the television series *The Life of Riley,* but is best known for his role as the bus driver Ralph Kramden in the weekly series *The Honeymooners,* which is still being rerun in many parts of the world.

gle·ba (glē'bə) *n., pl.* **-bae** (-bē). *Botany.* The inner, spore-bearing mass of puffballs and related fungi. [New Latin, from Latin *glēba, glǣba,* clod, GLEBE.]

glebe (glēb) *n.* **1.** *British.* A plot of land granted to a clergyman as part of his benefice during his tenure of office. **2.** *Archaic.* The soil or earth, especially when regarded as the source of vegetation; land. [Middle English, from Latin *glēba, glǣba,* clod.]

glede (glēd) *n. British Regional.* A predatory bird, the red kite, *Milvus milvus.* [Middle English *glede,* Old English *glida,* from Germanic; akin to GLIDE.]

glee (glē) *n.* **1.** Jubilant gaiety; merriment. **2.** An unaccompanied part song scored for three or more male voices that was popular in the 18th century. —See Synonyms at **mirth.** [Middle English *glē,* Old English *glēo,* merriment, play, music, from Germanic.]

glee club *n.* A group of singers who perform usually short pieces of choral music.

gleed (glēd) *n. British Regional.* A glowing coal; an ember. [Middle English *glede, gleed,* Old English *glēd.*]

glee·ful (glē'fəl) *adj.* Full of glee; merry. —**glee·ful·ly** *adv.* —**glee·ful·ness** *n.*

glee·man (glē'mən) *n., pl.* **-men** (-mĭn). *Archaic.* A medieval itinerant singer; a minstrel. [Middle English *gleeman,* Old English *glēoman* : *glēo,* GLEE + *mann,* MAN.]

gleet (glēt) *n.* **1.** Inflammation of the urethra resulting from chronic gonorrhea and characterized by mucopurulent discharge. **2.** The discharge that is characteristic of gleet. [Middle English *glet,* slime, mucus, from Old French *glete,* from Latin *glittus,* sticky.] —**gleet·y** *adj.*

gleg (glĕg) *adj. Scottish.* Alert and quick to respond. [Middle English *gleg,* clear-sighted, from Old Norse *glöggr.*]

glen (glĕn) *n.* A narrow, flat-bottomed, steep-sided valley. [Middle English *glen,* from Scottish Gaelic *gle(a)nn,* from Old Irish *glend†.*]

Glen-dow-er (glĕn'dou'ər), **Owen** (c. 1359–c. 1416). Welsh national leader. He led a revolt against the English in 1400 and by 1404 controlled most of Wales. In 1405 he summoned a Welsh parliament, but two defeats marked the end of his rebellion, and he ended his life in hiding.

glen·gar·ry (glĕn-găr'ē) *n., pl.* **-ries.** A brimless woolen cap that originated in Scotland, is creased lengthwise, and often has short ribbons at the back. Also called "glengarry bonnet." [After *Glengarry,* Scotland.]

Glenn (glĕn), **John Herschel, Jr.** (1921–). U.S. astronaut and politician. A highly decorated military aviator, he became a test pilot and was selected as one of America's first seven astronauts. On February 20, 1962, he became the first American to orbit the earth. He was elected a U.S. senator in 1976 and unsuccessfully sought the Democratic presidential nomination in 1984.

gle·noid cavity (glē'noid') *n. Anatomy.* The cavity at the top of the scapula that forms the socket of the shoulder joint, into which the head of the humerus fits. [From Greek *glēnoeidēs,* from *glēnē,* socket of a joint, eyeball.]

gley (glā) *n.* A sticky, bluish-gray soil layer formed under the influ-

ence of excessive moisture. [Ukrainian, CLAY.]

gli·a (glē'ə, glī'ə) *n.* **Neuroglia** *(see).*

gli·a·din (glī'ə-dĭn) *n.* Any of several simple proteins derived from rye or wheat gluten. [Italian *gliadina,* from Medieval Greek *glia, gloia,* glue.]

glib (glĭb) *adj.* **glibber, glibbest. 1. a.** Performed with a natural, offhand ease: *a glib conversation.* **b.** Showing little thought, preparation, or concern: *glib replies.* **2.** Marked by a quickness or fluency that often suggests or stems from insincerity or deception: *glib politicians.* [Probably from Low German *glibbrig,* from Middle Low German *glibberich,* slippery.] —**glib·ly** *adv.* —**glib·ness** *n.*

glide (glīd) *v.* **glided, gliding, glides.** —*intr.* **1.** To move in a smooth, effortless manner. **2.** To move silently and furtively. **3.** To occur or pass imperceptibly. **4. a.** To fly a glider. **b.** *Aeronautics.* To fly without propulsion. **5.** *Music.* To blend one note into the next; slur. **6.** *Phonetics.* To articulate a glide. **7.** *Physics.* To deform so that one crystal plane slips over another. Used of solids. —*tr.* To cause to glide.
~*n.* **1.** The act or an instance of gliding. **2.** *Music.* A slur. **3.** *Phonetics.* **a.** The transitional sound produced by passing from the articulatory position of one speech sound to that of another. **b.** A **semivowel** *(see).* [Middle English *gliden,* Old English *glīdan,* from Germanic.]

glide path *n.* The path of an aircraft when descending to land as marked out by a radio beam.

glid·er (glī'dər) *n.* **1.** One that glides. **2.** A light, engineless aircraft designed to glide after being towed aloft or launched from a catapult. **3.** A swinging couch suspended from a vertical frame. **4.** A device that aids gliding.

glid·ing (glī'dĭng) *n.* The practice or sport of flying gliders.

gliding lemur *n.* The **flying lemur** *(see).*

gliding possum *n.* The **flying phalanger** *(see).*

glim (glĭm) *n. Archaic Slang.* **1.** A source of light, such as a candle. **2.** An eye. [Perhaps shortened from GLIMMER.]

glim·mer (glĭm'ər) *n.* **1.** A dim or intermittent light; a flicker. **2.** A faint manifestation or indication; a glimpse: *a glimmer of hope.*
~*intr.v.* **glimmered, -mering, -mers. 1.** To emit a dim or intermittent light. **2.** To appear or be indicated faintly. —See Usage note at **flash.** [From Middle English *glimeren,* probably from Scandinavian, akin to Swedish *glimra.*]

glimpse (glĭmps) *n.* **1.** A brief, incomplete view or look. **2.** *Archaic.* A brief flash of light.
~*v.* **glimpsed, glimpsing, glimpses.** —*tr.* To obtain a brief, incomplete view of. —*intr.* To obtain a brief, incomplete view: *glimpsed at the headlines.* [Middle English *glimsen, glymsen,* from Germanic; akin to Middle High German *glimsen,* to gleam.]

Glin·ka (glĭng'kə), **Mikhail Ivanovich** (1803–57). Russian composer, often called "the Father of Russian music." His two most famous operas, which display Russian folk influences, are *A Life for the Czar* (1836) and *Russlan and Ludmilla* (1842).

glint (glĭnt) *n.* **1.** A momentary flash of light; a sparkle. **2.** A faint or fleeting manifestation; a trace. **3.** *Archaic.* A glance.
~*v.* **glinted, glinting, glints.** —*intr.* **1.** To gleam or flash. **2.** *Archaic.* To move abruptly; dart. —*tr.* To cause to gleam or flash. —See Usage note at **flash.** [From Middle English *glinten, glenten,* to shine, move quickly, from Scandinavian; akin to Swedish dialectal *glänta, glinta,* to shine.]

gli·o·ma (glī-ō'mə, glī-) *n., pl.* **-mas** or **-mata** (-mə-tə). A tumor that consists of neuroglia cells. [New Latin : GLIA + -OMA.]

glis·sade (glĭ-säd', -sād') *n.* **1.** A gliding ballet step. **2.** A controlled slide in a standing or sitting position used in descending a steep icy or snowy incline.
~*intr.v.* **glissaded, -sading, -sades.** To perform a glissade. [French, from Old French, sliding motion, from *glisser,* to slide, from *glier,* to glide, from Frankish *glīdan* (unattested).]

glis·san·do (glĭ-sän'dō) *n., pl.* **-di** (-dē) or **-dos.** *Music.* A rapid slide through a series of consecutive notes in a scalelike passage. [Probably pseudo-Italian formation from GLISSADE.]

glis·ten (glĭs'ən) *intr.v.* **-tened, -tening, -tens.** To shine by reflection; reflect or be reflected lustrously. —See Usage note at **flash.** ~*n.* A shine or sparkle. [Middle English *glistnen,* Old English *glisnian.*]

glis·ter (glĭs'tər) *intr.v.* **-tered, -tering, -ters.** To shine; glisten. ~*n.* Glitter; brilliance. [Middle English *glistren,* probably from Middle Dutch *glisteren.*]

glitch (glĭch) *n.* **1.** A minor malfunction, mishap, or technical problem. **2.** *Astronomy.* A temporary change in the frequency of emission of a pulsar. **2.** *Electronics.* A false or spurious electronic signal caused by a brief unwanted surge of electric power. [Perhaps from German *Glitsche,* a slip, slide.]

glit·ter (glĭt'ər) *n.* **1.** A sparkling light or brightness. **2. a.** Brilliant attractiveness. **b.** Showy splendor: *the glitter of show business.* **3.** Small pieces of light-reflecting decorative material.
~*intr.v.* **glittered, -tering, -ters. 1. a.** To sparkle brilliantly; glisten. **b.** To sparkle malevolently or coldly; flash: *eyes glittering at the prospect of revenge.* **2.** To be brilliantly and often deceptively attractive. —See Usage note at **flash.** [Middle English *gliteren,* from Old Norse *glitra.*] —**glit·ter·ing·ly** *adv.* —**glit·ter·y** *adj.*

glitz (glĭts) *n. Slang.* Excessive showiness; flashiness. [Yiddish, glitter.] —**glitz·y** *adj.*

gloam·ing (glō'mĭng) *n. Also archaic* **gloam** (glōm). Twilight; dusk. [Middle English *gloming* (Scottish dialect), Old English *glōmung,* from *glōm,* dusk; akin to GLOW.]

gloat (glōt) *intr.v.* **gloated, gloating, gloats.** To feel or express great, often malicious pleasure or self-satisfaction: *gloated over his opponent's defeat.*
∼*n.* **1.** The act of gloating. **2.** A feeling of great, often malicious pleasure or self-satisfaction. [Perhaps from Scandinavian; akin to Old Norse *glotta,* to smile scornfully.] **—gloat·ing·ly** *adv.*
glob (glŏb) *n.* **1.** A small drop; globule. **2.** A rounded, usually large lump or mass: *a glob of mashed potatoes.* [Middle English *globbe,* large mass, from Latin *globus,* GLOBE.]
glob·al (glō′bəl) *adj.* **1.** Of, pertaining to, or involving the entire earth; worldwide: *a global disarmament treaty.* **2.** Comprehensive; entire; total. **—glob·al·ly** *adv.*
glob·al·ism (glō′bə-lĭz′əm) *n.* **1.** Globalization. **2.** A policy promoting globalization. **—glob·al·ist** *n.*
glob·al·i·za·tion (glō′bə-lĭ-zā′shən) *n.* The act, process, or policy of making something worldwide in scope or application.
glob·al·ize (glō′bə-līz′) *tr.v.* **-ized, -izing, -izes.** To make global; make worldwide. **—glob·al·iz·er** *n.*
glo·bate (glō′bāt′) *adj.* Also **glo·bat·ed** (-bā′tĭd). Having the shape of a globe; globular. [Latin *globātus,* past participle of *globāre,* to form into a globe, from *globus,* GLOBE.]
globe (glōb) *n.* **1.** A body having the shape of a sphere; especially, a representation of the earth or heavens in the form of a hollow ball. **2. a.** The earth. **b.** A planet. **3.** An object resembling a globe; especially, a rounded container, as a glass sphere covering a light bulb. **4.** A sphere emblematic of sovereignty; an orb.
∼*v.* **globed, globing, globes.** —*intr.* To assume the shape of a globe. —*tr.* To form into a globe. [Middle English, from Old French, from Latin *globus.*]
globe amaranth *n.* A tropical Old World plant, *Gomphrena globosa,* cultivated for its variously colored flowers that retain their colors when dried.
globe artichoke *n.* An **artichoke** *(see).*
globe·fish (glōb′fĭsh′) *n., pl.* **-fishes** or collectively **globefish.** Any of various fishes, such as the ocean sunfish, having or capable of assuming a globular shape.
globe·flow·er (glōb′flou′ər) *n.* Any of several plants of the genus *Trollius,* having globe-shaped, usually yellow flowers.
globe thistle *n.* A tall thistle of the genus *Echinops,* native to south and central Europe and often planted in gardens for its large, spherical, usually blue flower heads.
globe·trot·ter (glōb′trŏt′ər) *n.* One who travels often and widely. **—globe·trot·ting** *n.* & *adj.*
glo·big·er·i·na (glō-bĭj′ə-rī′nə, -rē′nə) *n.* Any of the small marine protozoans of the genus *Globigerina,* having rounded spiny shells that accumulate in large numbers on the ocean floor to form a deposit. [New Latin : from Latin *globus,* GLOBE + *gerere,* to bear.]
glo·bin (glō′bĭn) *n.* A simple protein that is a constituent of hemoglobin. [Latin *globus,* GLOBE + -IN.]
glo·boid (glō′boid′) *adj.* Having a globelike shape; spheroid.
∼*n.* A globe-shaped object; a spheroid. [GLOB(E) + -OID.]
glo·bose (glō′bōs′) *adj.* Also **glo·bous** (-bəs). Spherical; globular. [Latin *globōsus,* from *globus,* GLOBE.] **—glo·bose·ly** *adv.* **—glo·bose·ness, glo·bos·i·ty** (glō-bŏs′ə-tē) *n.*
glob·u·lar (glŏb′yə-lər) *adj.* **1.** Having the shape of a globe or globule; spherical. **2.** Consisting of globules. **3.** Worldwide; global. **—glob·u·lar·ly** *adv.* **—glob·u·lar·ness** *n.*
globular cluster *n. Astronomy.* A roughly spherical cluster of stars.
glob·ule (glŏb′yo͞ol) *n.* A small, often minute spherical mass; especially, a small drop of liquid. [Latin *globulus,* diminutive of *globus,* GLOBE.]
glob·u·lif·er·ous (glŏb′yə-lĭf′ər-əs) *adj.* Composed of or producing globules. [GLOBUL(E) + -FEROUS.]
glob·u·lin (glŏb′yə-lĭn) *n.* Any of a class of simple proteins that are found extensively in blood, milk, muscle, and plant seeds and that are insoluble in pure water, soluble in dilute salt solution, and coagulable by heat. [GLOBUL(E) + -IN.]
glo·chid·i·um (glō-kĭd′ē-əm) *n., pl.* **-ia** (-ē-ə). Also **glo·chid** (glō′kĭd) (for sense 2). **1.** *Zoology.* A parasitic larva of certain freshwater mussels of the family Unionidae, having hooks for attaching to a host fish. **2.** *Botany.* Any of the barbed hairs or bristles on certain plants, such as the prickly pear and some ferns. [New Latin, from Greek *glōkhīs,* barb of an arrow.] **—glo·chid·i·ate** (glō-kĭd′ē-ĭt, -āt′) *adj.*
glock·en·spiel (glŏk′ən-spēl′, -shpēl′) *n.* A percussion instrument consisting of a series of metal bars tuned to the chromatic scale and played with two light hammers. [German *Glockenspiel,* "play of bells" : *Glocke,* bell, from Old High German *glocka* (imitative) + *Spiel,* play.]
glogg (glŏg) *n.* Also **glögg** (glœg). A hot punch, originally from Sweden, made of red wine and brandy and flavored with almonds, raisins, and orange peel.
glom·er·ate (glŏm′ər-ĭt, -ə-rāt′) *adj.* Formed into a compact, rounded mass; tightly clustered; conglomerate. [Latin *glomerātus,* past participle of *glomerāre,* to make into a ball, from *glomus* (stem *glomer-*), ball.]
glom·er·a·tion (glŏm′ə-rā′shən) *n.* A compact, rounded mass; a cluster; a conglomeration.
glom·er·ule (glŏm′ə-ro͞ol′, glŏm′yə-) *n.* **1.** *Botany.* A compact cluster of flowers borne on a single stem. **2.** *Anatomy.* A glomerulus. [New Latin *glomerulus,* from Latin *glomus* (stem *glomer-*), ball.] **—glo·mer·u·late** (glə-mĕr′yə-lĭt) *adj.*
glo·mer·u·lo·ne·phri·tis (glə-mĕr′yə-lō-nə-frī′tĭs) *n.* An inflammatory disease of the kidney affecting the glomeruli, occurring in acute and chronic forms. [New Latin : GLOMERULUS + NEPHRITIS.]
glo·mer·u·lus (glə-mĕr′yə-ləs, glō-) *n., pl.* **-li** (-lī′). *Anatomy.* **1.** A tuft of capillaries situated within the capsule at the end of a urine-secreting tubule in the vertebrate kidney. **2.** The twisted secretory portion of a sweat gland. Also called "glomerule." [New Latin, GLOMERULE.]
glo·mus (glō′məs) *n., pl.* **glomera** (glŏm′ər-ə, glō′mər-ə). *Anatomy.* A small body that forms a connection between fine arteries and veins. [New Latin, from Latin *glomus,* ball.]
gloom (glo͞om) *n.* **1.** Partial or total darkness; dimness. **2.** A partially or totally dark place, area, or location. **3. a.** An appearance or atmosphere of melancholy or depression. **b.** A state of melancholy or depression; dejection.
∼*v.* **gloomed, glooming, glooms.** —*intr.* **1.** To be or become dark, shaded, or obscure. **2.** To feel, appear, or act despondent, sad, or mournful. —*tr.* **1.** To make dark, shaded, or obscure. **2.** To make despondent; sadden. [Middle English *gloum(b)en*†, to look glum, become dark.]
gloom·y (glo͞o′mē) *adj.* **-ier, -iest.** **1.** Dismal, dark, or dreary. **2.** Showing or filled with gloom; despondent: *gloomy faces.* **3. a.** Causing or producing gloom or dejection; depressing: *gloomy news.* **b.** Marked by hopelessness; pessimistic: *gloomy predictions.* —See Synonyms at **glum.** **—gloom·i·ly** *adv.* **—gloom·i·ness** *n.*
glop (glŏp) *n. Slang.* A messy mixture, as of food. [Imitative of the sound of food being mixed.] **—glop·py** *adj.*
glo·ri·a (glôr′ē-ə, glōr′-) *n.* **1.** A halo, aureole, or nimbus. **2.** A lightweight fabric, chiefly of silk, wool, or cotton, used for umbrellas and dresses. [Late Latin *glōria,* from Latin, GLORY.]
Glo·ri·a (glôr′ē-ə, glōr′-) *n.* **1.** Any of the Christian prayers of praise beginning with the word *Gloria.* **2.** The music to which any of these is set. [Middle English, from Latin *glōria*†, glory.]
Gloria in ex·cel·sis De·o (ĭn ĭk-sĕl′sĭs dā′ō, dē′ō) *n.* A Latin doxology forming part of the Ordinary of the Mass, beginning with the words *Gloria in excelsis Deo.* Also called "greater doxology." [Late Latin, "Glory to God in the highest."]
Gloria Pa·tri (păt′rē, pä′trē) *n.* A short Latin prayer of praise to the Trinity, beginning with the words *Gloria Patri* and often sung or recited at the end of another prayer, as to conclude a psalm. Also called "lesser doxology." [Late Latin, "Glory to the Father."]
glo·ri·fi·ca·tion (glôr′ə-fĭ-kā′shən, glōr′-) *n.* **1.** The act of glorifying or the state of being glorified. **2.** *Informal.* An enhanced or exaggerated version of something.
glo·ri·fy (glôr′ə-fī′, glōr′-) *tr.v.* **-fied, -fying, -fies.** **1.** To give glory, honor, or high praise to; exalt. **2.** To cause to be or seem more glorious or excellent than is actually the case: *His description glorified the simple cottage into a mansion.* **3.** To give glory to, especially through worship. [Middle English *glorifien,* from Old French *glorifier,* from Late Latin *glōrificāre* : Latin *glōria,* GLORY + -FY.] **—glo·ri·fi·er** *n.*
glo·ri·ole (glôr′ē-ōl′, glōr′-) *n.* A halo, aureole, or nimbus; a gloria. [French, from Latin *glōriola,* diminutive of *glōria,* GLORY.]
glo·ri·ous (glôr′ē-əs, glōr′-) *adj.* **1.** Having or deserving glory; famous; illustrious. **2.** Conferring or advancing glory: *a glorious achievement.* **3.** Characterized by great beauty and splendor; magnificent: *a glorious sunset.* **4.** *Informal.* Very pleasant; delightful: *had a glorious visit.* **—glo·ri·ous·ly** *adv.* **—glo·ri·ous·ness** *n.*
Glorious Revolution. The period in British history (1688–89) during which King James II was deposed and his sister Mary and her husband William of Orange were invited to assume the throne as joint monarchs Mary II and William III. Also called "Bloodless Revolution."
glo·ry (glôr′ē, glōr′ē) *n., pl.* **-ries.** **1.** Exalted honor, praise, or distinction accorded by common consent; renown. **2.** Something that brings honor or renown: *the glory of her position as president of the corporation.* **3.** A highly praiseworthy asset: *Her hair is her crowning glory.* **4.** Adoration, praise, and thanksgiving offered in worship: *We sing Thy glory.* **5.** Majestic beauty and splendor; resplendence: *The sun set in a blaze of glory.* **6.** The splendor and bliss of heaven; a state of perfect happiness. **7.** A height of achievement, enjoyment, or prosperity: *Paris in its greatest glory.* **8.** A halo, nimbus, or aureole. —See Synonyms at **fame.**
∼*intr.v.* **gloried, -rying, -ries.** **1.** To rejoice triumphantly; exult: *petty generals who gloried in war.* [Middle English *glorie,* from Old French, from Latin *glōria*†, glory.]
glory hole *n. Informal.* A box, drawer, small space, or room in a house or on a ship where unwanted or unsorted articles are stored.
glo·ry-of-the-snow (glôr′ē-əv-*thə*-snō′, glōr′-) *n.* A small bulbous plant, *Chionodoxa luciliae,* native to Asia Minor, cultivated for its early-blooming blue flowers.
gloss[1] (glŏs, glôs) *n.* **1.** A surface shininess or luster. Also used adjectivally: *gloss paint.* **2.** A deceptive or superficially attractive appearance. **3.** A cosmetic applied to give shine or brilliance: *lip gloss.*
∼*v.* **glossed, glossing, glosses.** —*tr.* **1.** To give a bright sheen or luster to. **2.** To apply a gloss to. **3.** To make attractive or acceptable by deception or superficial treatment: *She praised the candidate, glossing over his many weaknesses.* —*intr.* To become shiny or lustrous. [Perhaps from Scandinavian; akin to Icelandic *glossi,* spark.]
gloss[2] *n.* **1.** A brief explanatory note or translation of a difficult or technical expression, often inserted in the margin or between lines of a text or manuscript. **2.** An expanded version of such notes; a

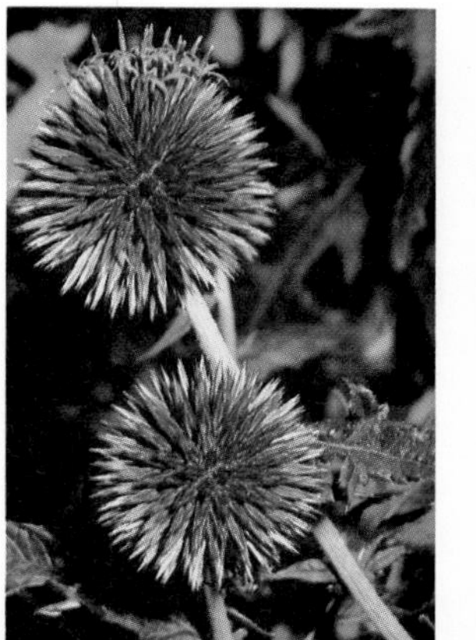

globe thistle *This hardy biennial or perennial flower is a member of the* Echinops *genus, which includes about 100 species native to Europe and Asia.*

glowworm *Several species of insect can glow in the dark; the female of the European firefly,* Lampyris noctiluca *(above), is perhaps the best known.*

gloxinia *A member of the* Sinningia *genus grown in temperate climates as a hothouse plant. This variety is "Pink Beauty."*

glossary. **3.** A purposely misleading interpretation or explanation. **4.** An extensive commentary, often accompanying a text or publication.
~*v.* **glossed, glossing, glosses.** —*tr.* **1.** To provide (a word, expression, or text) with a gloss or glosses. **2.** To give a false interpretation to. —*intr.* To make a gloss or glosses. [Middle English *glose,* from Old French, from Medieval Latin *glōsa,* from Latin *glōssa,* word that needs explanation, from Greek *glōssa,* tongue, language.] —**gloss·er** *n.*

gloss. glossary.

glos·sa (glŏs′ə, glô′sə) *n., pl.* **-sae** (-sē′, -sī′) or **-sas. 1.** *Anatomy.* The tongue. **2.** *Zoology.* A tonguelike structure in the labium of an insect. [Greek *glōssa,* tongue.]

glos·sal (glŏs′əl, glô′səl) *adj.* Of or pertaining to the tongue. [Greek *glōssa,* tongue. See **gloss** (explanation).]

glos·sa·ry (glŏs′ə-rē, glô′sə-) *n., pl.* **-ries.** *Abbr.* **gloss.** A collection of glosses, as a list of specialized terms with accompanying definitions. [Latin *glossārium,* from *glōssa,* GLOSS (explanation).] —**glos·sar·i·al** (glō-sâr′ē-əl, glô-) *adj.* —**glos·sar·i·al·ly** *adv.* —**glos·sa·rist** (glŏs′ər-ĭst, glô′sər-) *n.*

glos·sec·to·my (glŏ-sĕk′tə-mē, glô-) *n., pl.* **-mies.** The surgical removal of the tongue. [GLOSSO- + -ECTOMY.]

glos·seme (glŏs′ēm′, glô′sēm′) *n.* *Linguistics.* Any of the most basic elements of meaning in a language, as a morpheme or a unit of stress. [Greek *glōssēma.* See **glosso-, -eme.**] —**glos·se·mic** (glŏ-sē′mĭk, glô-) *adj.*

glos·si·tis (glŏ-sī′tĭs, glô-) *n.* Inflammation of the tongue. [GLOSSO- + -ITIS.]

glosso-, gloss– *prefix.* Indicates the tongue or language; for example, **glossitis, glossology.** [Greek *glōssa,* tongue. See **gloss** (explanation).]

glos·sog·ra·phy (glŏ-sŏg′rə-fē, glô-) *n.* The writing and compilation of glosses or glossaries. [Greek *glōssa,* tongue, language, GLOSS (explanation) + -GRAPHY.] —**glos·sog·ra·pher** *n.*

glos·so·la·li·a (glŏs′ə-lā′lē-ə, -lăl′yə, glô′sə-) *n.* **1.** Fabricated, incoherent, or nonsensical speech, especially as associated with certain schizophrenic syndromes. **2.** The **gift of tongues** *(see).* [New Latin *glossolalia,* from (New Testament) Greek *glōssais lalein,* "to speak with tongues" : *glossa,* tongue + *lalein,* to talk, babble.]

glos·sol·o·gy (glŏ-sŏl′ə-jē, glô-) *n. Obsolete. Linguistics.* [Greek *glōssa,* tongue, language, GLOSS (explanation) + -LOGY.] —**glos·sol·o·gist** *n.*

glos·so·phar·yn·ge·al nerve (glŏs′ō-făr′ĭn-jē′əl, -fə-rĭn′jē-əl, glô′sō-) *n.* The ninth cranial nerve, which supplies the tongue, soft palate, pharynx, and parotid salivary gland.

gloss·y (glŏs′ē, glô′sē) *adj.* **-ier, -iest. 1.** Having a smooth, shiny, lustrous surface: *glossy satin; glossy hair.* **2.** Superficially, artificially, and speciously attractive; slick: *We listened to the salesman's glossy pitch with amusement.*
~*n., pl.* **glossies. 1.** In photography, a print on smooth, shiny paper. Also called "glossy print." **2.** *Chiefly British.* An expensively produced magazine printed on high-quality glossy paper; slick. —**gloss·i·ly** *adv.* —**gloss·i·ness** *n.*

glost (glŏst, glôst) *n.* A lead glaze used for pottery. [Variation of GLOSS (sheen).]

glot·tal (glŏt′l) *adj.* **1.** Of or relating to the glottis. **2.** *Phonetics.* Articulated in the glottis. [From GLOTTIS.]

glottal stop *n. Phonetics.* A speech sound produced by a momentary complete closure of the glottis, followed by an explosive release.

glot·tis (glŏt′ĭs) *n., pl.* **-tises** or **glottides** (-ə-dēz′). **1.** The space between the vocal cords at the upper part of the larynx. **2.** The vocal structures of the larynx. [New Latin, from Greek *glōttis,* from *glōtta, glōssa,* tongue, language.]

glot·to·chro·nol·o·gy (glŏt′ō-krə-nŏl′ə-jē) *n. Linguistics.* The investigation by means of statistics of the historical relationships between various languages, including the approximate times when related languages began to diverge from one another. —**glot·to·chron·o·log·i·cal** (glŏt′ō-krŏn′ə-lŏj′ĭ-kəl) *adj.*

Glouces·ter (glŏs′tər, glôs′-). A city in the west of England, the administrative center of Gloucestershire, on the Severn River. Known as Glevum to the Romans, it became the capital of Mercia in Anglo-Saxon times. Its cathedral (founded 1100) contains fine examples of Norman work.

Glouces·ter·shire (glŏs′tər-shîr, -shər, glôs′-). A county in the west of England. It encompasses much of the Cotswolds to the east, the Forest of Dean to the west, and a central region formed by the valley of the Severn River. Agriculture is the main occupation. Gloucester is its administrative center.

glove (glŭv) *n.* **1. a.** A fitted covering for the hand, usually made of leather, wool, or cloth, having a separate sheath for the thumb and for each finger. **b.** A gauntlet. **2. a.** *Baseball.* An oversized padded leather covering for the hand that is used in catching balls; especially, such a glove with more finger sheaths than a catcher's or first baseman's mitt. **b.** A **boxing glove** *(see).* —**hand in glove.** In a close or harmonious relationship: *worked together hand in glove.* —**with gloves off.** Without moderation; mercilessly.
~*tr.v.* **gloved, gloving, gloves. 1.** To furnish with gloves. **2.** To cover with or as if with a glove. [Middle English *glove,* Old English *glōf,* from Germanic.]

glove box *n.* **1.** An enclosure with a window and two long rubber gloves sealed into the front that is used for handling toxic, corrosive, or radioactive substances. **2.** *Chiefly British.* A glove compartment.

glove compartment *n.* A small storage container in the dashboard of an automobile.

glove puppet *n.* A puppet that fits over the hand and is manipulated by the fingers.

glov·er (glŭv′ər) *n.* One who makes or sells gloves.

glow (glō) *intr.v.* **glowed, glowing, glows. 1. a.** To burn or shine brightly and steadily, especially without a flame: *embers glowing in the furnace.* **b.** To shine as if with intense heat. **c.** To have a feeling of suffusing warmth: *exercised until we glowed all over.* **2.** To have a bright, warm, usually reddish color: *cheeks glowing from the cold.* **3. a.** To have a healthy, ruddy complexion. **b.** To flush; blush: *We knew he was embarrassed because his face glowed.* **4.** To be exuberant or radiant, as with pride.
~*n.* **1. a.** A light produced by a body heated to luminosity; incandescence. **b.** A bright, warm, steady light. **2.** Brilliance or warmth of color, especially redness: *"the evening glow of the city streets when the sun has gone behind the tallest houses"* (Sean O'Faolain). **3.** A sensation of physical warmth. **4.** A warm feeling of passion or emotion; ardor. **5.** A glow discharge. —See Synonyms at **blaze.** [Middle English *glowen,* Old English *glōwan,* from Germanic.]

glow discharge *n.* A continuous luminous discharge of electricity through a gas at low pressure, as in neon or fluorescent lighting. Also called "glow."

glow·er (glou′ər) *intr.v.* **-ered, -ering, -ers.** To look or stare angrily or sullenly; frown.
~*n.* An angry, sullen, or threatening stare. [Middle English *glo(u)ren,* to shine, stare, probably from Scandinavian; akin to Norwegian dialectal *glora.*] —**glow·er·ing·ly** *adv.*

glow·ing (glō′ĭng) *adj.* **1.** Incandescent; luminous. **2.** Characterized by rich, warm coloration; especially, having a ruddy, healthy complexion. **3.** Ardently enthusiastic or favorable: *glowing praise.*

glow lamp *n.* A small electric light bulb, as in a night light, in which a glow discharge occurs between two small electrodes in a medium of neon or similar gas at low pressure.

glow plug *n.* A small heating element in a diesel-engine cylinder used to facilitate starting.

glow·worm (glō′wûrm′) *n.* The luminous larva or wingless, grublike female of a firefly, especially the European species, *Lampyris noctiluca.*

glox·in·i·a (glŏk-sĭn′ē-ə) *n.* Any of several tropical South American plants of the genus *Sinningia;* especially, *S. speciosa,* cultivated as a house plant for its showy, variously colored flowers. [New Latin, after Benjamin Peter *Gloxin,* 18th-century German botanist and physician.]

gloze (glōz) *v.* **glozed, glozing, glozes.** —*tr.* **1.** To minimize or underplay; gloss. Used with *over.* **2.** *Archaic.* To explain or comment on; gloss. —*intr. Archaic.* To use flattery or cajolery. [Middle English *glosen,* to gloss, falsify, flatter, from Old French *glosser,* from *glose,* GLOSS (explanation).]

glu·ca·gon (glōō′kə-gŏn′) *n.* A hormone produced by the pancreas that stimulates an increase in the amount of sugar in the blood, thus opposing the action of insulin. [GLUC(OSE) + Greek *agōn,* leading.]

Gluck (glŏŏk), **Christoph Willibald** (1714–87). German composer. He rid opera music of baroque ornamentation of the Italian style and began to write unified lyrical tragedy in a manner that foreshadowed Wagner. His best-known operas are *Orpheus and Eurydice* (1762) and *Alceste* (1767).

gluco-, gluc– *prefix.* Indicates glucose; for example, **gluconeogenesis.**

glu·co·cor·ti·coid (glōō′kō-kôr′tĭ-koid′) *n.* Any of a group of corticosteroids that control carbohydrate, fat, and protein metabolism and have anti-inflammatory properties.

glu·co·ne·o·gen·e·sis (glōō′kō-nē′ō-jĕn′ə-sĭs) *n.* The biochemical process in which glucose is formed from noncarbohydrate sources, such as amino acids.

glu·cos·a·mine (glōō-kŏs′ə-mēn′, -zə-mēn′) *n.* An amino sugar, $C_6H_{13}NO_5$, that is a constituent of heparin and other polysaccharides. [GLUCOSE + AMINE.]

glu·cose (glōō′kōs′, -kōz′) *n.* **1.** A white monosaccharide sugar, $C_6H_{12}O_6$, the most abundant form of which is **dextrose** *(see),* a major energy source for plants and animals. **2.** A colorless to yellowish syrupy mixture of dextrose, maltose, and dextrins with about 20 percent water, used in confectionery, alcoholic fermentation, tanning, and treating tobacco. [French, from Greek *gleukos,* sweet new wine, must.]

glu·co·side (glōō′kə-sīd′) *n.* A **glycoside** *(see),* the sugar component of which is glucose. —**glu·co·sid·ic** (glōō′kə-sĭd′ĭk) *adj.*

glue (glōō) *n.* **1.** An adhesive substance or solution; a viscous substance used to join or bond. **2.** An adhesive obtained by boiling animal **collagen** *(see)* and drying the residue. In this sense, also called "animal glue."
~*tr.v.* **glued, gluing, glues. 1.** To stick or fasten together with glue: *glued the parts of the picture frame together.* **2.** To fasten on something steadily and attentively: *Our eyes were glued to the stage.* [Middle English *gleu,* glue, birdlime, gum, from Old French *glu,* from Late Latin *glūs* (stem *glūt-*), from Latin *glūten.*] —**glu·er** *n.* —**glue·y** *adj.*

glum (glŭm) *adj.* **glummer, glummest. 1.** In low spirits; dejected. **2.** Gloomy; dismal. [Middle English *glomen, gloumen,* to look sullen, GLOOM.] —**glum·ly** *adv.* —**glum·ness** *n.*
Synonyms: *dour, gloomy, morose, mournful.*

glu·ma·ceous (gloō-mā′shəs) *adj.* Having or resembling a glume or glumes.

glume (gloōm) *n. Botany.* A chaffy basal bract on the spikelet of a grass. [New Latin *gluma,* from Latin *glūma,* husk.]

glu·on (gloō′ŏn′) *n. Physics.* A hypothetical elementary particle postulated to be exchanged between quarks to hold them together. There are eight types of gluon distinguished by different combinations of color and anticolor.

glut (glŭt) *v.* **glutted, glutting, gluts.** —*tr.* **1.** To fill beyond capacity; satiate. **2.** To flood (a market) with an excess of goods so that supply exceeds demand. —*intr.* To eat excessively. —See Synonyms at **satiate.**
~*n.* **1.** An oversupply. **2.** The act or process of glutting. [Middle English *glotten, glouten,* probably from Old French *gloutir,* to swallow, from Latin *gluttīre.*]

glu·ta·mate (gloō′tə-māt′) *n.* A salt of glutamic acid, especially a sodium salt, **monosodium glutamate** (*see*). [GLUTAM(IC) + -ATE.]

glu·tam·ic acid (gloō-tăm′ĭk) *n.* An amino acid, $C_5H_9NO_4$, present in all complete proteins, found widely in plant and animal tissue, and having an important role in nitrogen metabolism. [GLUT(EN) + AM(IDE) + -IC.]

glu·ta·mine (gloō′tə-mēn′) *n.* A white crystalline amino acid, $C_5H_{10}N_2O_3$, occurring in plant and animal tissue and produced commercially for use in medicine and biochemical research. [GLUT(EN) + AMINE.]

glu·ta·thi·one (gloō′tə-thī′ōn′) *n.* A peptide consisting of glutamic acid, cysteine, and glycine that functions as a coenzyme in various oxidation-reduction reactions. [GLUTA(MIC) + THI- + -ONE.]

glu·te·lin (gloōt′l-ĭn) *n.* Any of a group of simple proteins occurring in cereals and soluble only in dilute acids and bases. [Irregularly from GLUTEN + -IN.]

glu·ten (gloōt′n) *n.* A mixture of plant proteins occurring in cereal grains, chiefly wheat, and used as an adhesive and as a flour substitute. [Latin *glūten,* glue.] —**glu·ten·ous** *adj.*

gluten bread *n.* Bread made from flour with a high gluten content and low starch content.

glu·te·us (gloō′tē-əs, gloō-tē′-) *n., pl.* **glutei** (gloō′tē-ī′, gloō-tē′ī′). Any of three large muscles of the buttocks: **a.** *gluteus maximus,* which extends the thigh; **b.** *gluteus medius,* which rotates and abducts the thigh; **c.** *gluteus minimus,* which abducts the thigh. [New Latin, from Greek *gloutos,* buttock.] —**glu·te·al** *adj.*

glu·ti·nous (gloōt′n-əs) *adj.* Resembling or of the nature of glue; sticky; viscous. [Latin *glūtinōsus,* from *glūten,* glue.] —**glu·ti·nous·ly** *adv.* —**glu·ti·nous·ness, glu·ti·nos·i·ty** (gloōt′n-ŏs′ə-tē) *n.*

glut·ton[1] (glŭt′n) *n.* **1.** A person who eats or consumes immoderate amounts of food and drink. **2.** A person with an inordinate capacity to receive or withstand something: *a glutton for punishment.* [Middle English *glotoun,* from Old French *gluton, gloton,* from Latin *gluttō* (stem *gluttōn-*); akin to *gluttire,* to swallow, and *gluttus,* greedy.] —**glut·ton·ous** *adj.* —**glut·ton·ous·ly** *adv.*

glut·ton[2] *n.* A mammal, the **wolverine** (*see*). [From GLUTTON (eater), translation of German *Vielfrass,* "great eater."]

glut·ton·y (glŭt′n-ē) *n.* Excess in eating or drinking.

glyc·er·al·de·hyde (glĭs′ə-răl′də-hīd′) *n.* A sweet colorless solid, $C_3H_6O_3$, that is an intermediate compound in carbohydrate metabolism. [GLYCER(IN) + ALDEHYDE.]

gly·cer·ic acid (glĭ-sĕr′ĭk) *n.* A syrupy compound, $C_3H_6O_4$. [From GLYCERIN.]

glyc·er·ide (glĭs′ə-rīd′) *n.* An ester of glycerol and fatty acids. [GLYCER(IN) + -IDE.]

glyc·er·in, glyc·er·ine (glĭs′ər-ĭn) *n.* Glycerol. [French, from Greek *glukeros,* sweet.]

glyc·er·ol (glĭs′ə-rôl′, -rōl′, -rŏl′) *n.* A syrupy, sweet, colorless or yellowish liquid, $C_3H_8O_3$, obtained from fats and oils as a by-product of the manufacture of soaps and fatty acids. It is used as a solvent, antifreeze and antifrost fluid, plasticizer and sweetener, and in the manufacture of dynamite, cosmetics, liquid soaps, inks, and lubricants. [GLYCER(IN) + -OL.]

glyc·er·yl (glĭs′ər-əl) *n.* The trivalent radical of glycerol, CH_2CHCH_2. [GLYCER(IN) + -YL.]

gly·cin (glī′sĭn) *n.* Also **gly·cine** (-sēn′, -sīn). A poisonous compound, $C_8H_9NO_3$, used as a photographic developer. [From GLYCINE.]

gly·cine (glī′sēn′, -sīn) *n.* **1.** A white, very sweet crystalline amino acid, $C_2H_5NO_2$, the principal amino acid occurring in sugar cane, derived by alkaline hydrolysis of gelatin, and used in biochemical research and medicine. **2.** Variant of **glycin**. [GLYC(O)- + -INE.]

glyco-, glyc- *prefix.* Indicates: **1.** Sugar; for example, **glycine. 2.** Glycogen; for example, **glycogenesis.** [Greek *glukus,* sweet.]

gly·co·gen (glī′kə-jən) *n.* A carbohydrate, $(C_6H_{10}O_5)_n$. It is the main form in which carbohydrate is stored in animals and occurs primarily in the liver and muscles. Also called "animal starch," "liver starch." [GLYCO- + -GEN.] —**gly·co·gen·ic** (glī′kə-jĕn′ĭk) *adj.*

gly·co·gen·e·sis (glī′kə-jĕn′ə-sĭs) *n.* **1.** The formation of glycogen. **2.** The formation of sugar from glycogen. [GLYCO- + -GENESIS.] —**gly·co·ge·net·ic** (glī′kə-jə-nĕt′ĭk) *adj.*

gly·col (glī′kôl′, -kŏl′, -kōl′) *n.* **1.** Ethylene glycol (*see*). **2.** An alcohol with two hydroxyl groups. [GLYC(O)- + -OL.]

gly·col·ic acid (glī-kŏl′ĭk) *n.* A colorless crystalline compound, $C_2H_4O_3$, found in sugar beets, cane sugar, and unripe grapes, and used in leather dyeing and tanning and in pharmaceuticals, pesticides, adhesives, and plasticizers.

gly·co·lip·id (glī′kō-lĭp′ĭd) *n.* Any of a group of lipids that contain one or more sugar molecules.

gly·col·y·sis (glī-kŏl′ə-sĭs) *n.* The biochemical breakdown of glucose to lactic acid, with the production of energy in the form of ATP. [GLYCO- + -LYSIS.]

gly·co·pro·tein (glī′kō-prō′tēn′, -tē-ĭn) *n.* Any of several conjugated proteins that contain carbohydrates as prosthetic groups.

gly·co·side (glī′kə-sīd′) *n.* Any of a group of organic compounds, occurring abundantly in plants, that produce sugars and related substances on hydrolysis. A medically important example is digitalis. [*Glycose,* variant of GLUCOSE + -IDE.] —**gly·co·sid·ic** (glī′-kə-sĭd′ĭk) *adj.*

gly·co·su·ri·a (glī′kə-soōr′ē-ə, -shoōr′ē-ə) *n.* The excretion of excess quantities of sugar in the urine, as occurs in diabetes. [*Glycose,* variant of GLUCOSE + -URIA.] —**gly·co·su·ric** *adj.*

Glyn (glĭn), **Elinor Sutherland** (1864–1943). British author. She wrote many sensational and highly romantic novels in the early 1900's, including *Three Weeks* (1907), a steamy (for then) tale of illicit passion complete with tiger-skin rugs, and *It* (1927).

Glynde·bourne (glīnd′bôrn′, -bōrn′). An estate in East Sussex in southeast England. Since 1934 it has been the site of an annual opera festival.

gly·ox·a·line (glī-ŏk′sə-lēn′, -lĭn) *n.* A chemical compound, **imidazole** (*see*). [GLY(COL) + OXAL(IC ACID) + -INE.]

glyph (glĭf) *n.* **1.** *Architecture.* A vertical groove, especially in a Doric column or frieze. **2.** A symbolic figure, either engraved or incised; a hieroglyph. **3.** A symbol, as figures of people on a road sign, that imparts information nonverbally. [Greek *gluphē,* carving, from *gluphein,* to carve.] —**glyph·ic** *adj.*

glyp·tal (glĭp′təl) *n.* A synthetic resin used for surface coatings, made by copolymerizing dihydric alcohols and dibasic acids.

glyp·tic (glĭp′tĭk) *adj.* Of or pertaining to engraving or carving, especially on precious stones. [Greek *gluptikos,* from *gluptēs,* carver, from *gluphein,* to carve.]

glyp·tics (glĭp′tĭks) *n. Used with a singular verb.* The art of engraving or carving, especially on precious stones.

glyp·to·dont (glĭp′tə-dŏnt′) *n.* An extinct South American mammal of the genus *Glyptodon* and related genera that lived in the late Cenozoic period and resembled a giant armadillo. [New Latin : Greek *gluptos,* carved, from *gluphein,* to carve + -ODONT.]

glyp·to·graph (glĭp′tə-grăf′, -gräf′) *n.* An engraved inscription on a precious stone. [Greek *gluptos,* carved, from *gluphein,* to carve + -GRAPH.]

glyp·tog·ra·phy (glĭp-tŏg′rə-fē) *n.* The art or process of carving or engraving on precious stones. —**glyp·tog·ra·pher** *n.* —**glyp·to·graph·ic** (glĭp′tə-grăf′ĭk), **glyp·to·graph·i·cal** *adj.*

gm gram.

G.M. **1.** general manager. **2.** grand master.

G-man (jē′măn′) *n., pl.* **-men** (-mĕn′). An agent of the Federal Bureau of Investigation. [G(OVERNMENT) + MAN.]

GMAT Greenwich mean astronomical time.

GM counter (jē′ĕm′) *n.* A Geiger counter (*see*).

GMT, G.m.t. Greenwich mean time.

GM tube *n.* A Geiger tube (*see*).

gnarl (närl) *n.* A protruding knot on a tree.
~*tr.v.* **gnarled, gnarling, gnarls.** To knot and cause to be deformed; twist. —See Usage note at **distort.** [Back-formation from GNARLED.]

gnarled (närld) *adj.* **1.** Having gnarls; knotty or misshapen: *gnarled branches.* **2.** Crabbed in temperament; bad-tempered. **3.** Rugged and roughened, as from old age or hard work: *The gnarled hands of a carpenter.* [Probably variant of KNURLED.]

gnash (năsh) *v.* **gnashed, gnashing, gnashes.** —*tr.* **1.** To grind or strike (the teeth, for example) together. **2.** To bite or chew by grinding the teeth. —*intr.* To grind the teeth together.
~*n.* **1.** The grinding together of the teeth. **2.** An action or sound resembling a gnash. [Middle English *gnasten, gnaisten,* probably from Scandinavian, akin to Old Norse *gnast(r)an,* gnashing (probably imitative).]

gnat (năt) *n.* Any of numerous small, biting, winged insects, especially the common gnat, *Culex pipiens,* common in swarms over stagnant water. [Middle English *gnat,* Old English *gnæt.*]

gnat·catch·er (năt′kăch′ər) *n.* Any of several small New World birds of the genus *Polioptila* and related genera, having grayish and white plumage and a long tail.

gna·thal (nā′thəl, năth′əl) *adj.* Gnathic.

gnath·ic (năth′ĭk) *adj. Anatomy.* Of or relating to the jaw. [Greek *gnathos,* jaw.]

gna·thi·on (nā′thē-ŏn′, năth′ē-) *n. Anatomy.* The lowest point of the midline of the lower jaw. [New Latin, from Greek *gnathos,* jaw.]

gna·thite (nā′thīt′, năth′īt′) *n.* A jaw or jawlike appendage of an insect or other arthropod. [Greek *gnathos,* jaw + -ITE.]

-gnathous *suffix.* Indicates the jaw; for example, **prognathous.** [New Latin *-gnathus,* from Greek *gnathos,* jaw.]

gnaw (nô) *v.* **gnawed, gnawed** or **gnawn** (nôn), **gnawing, gnaws.** —*tr.* **1.** To bite, chew on, or erode with the teeth. **2.** To produce by gnawing: *gnaw a hole.* **3.** To erode or diminish gradually as if by gnawing: *waves gnawing the rocky shore.* **4.** To afflict or trouble persistently: *fear gnawing her.* —*intr.* **1.** To bite or chew persistently: *The dog gnawed at the bone.* **2.** To cause erosion or gradual diminishment. **3.** To cause persistent trouble or distress: *What I had done gnawed at my conscience.*

glyph *A representational carving. This is a scarab, or dung beetle, a sacred symbol in ancient Egypt. Egyptian representational writing carved on monuments came to be called "hieroglyphic" (sacred carving).*

gnat *Small flying insects, the females of which are bloodsucking. The name is often used loosely for other similar insects that do not bite.*

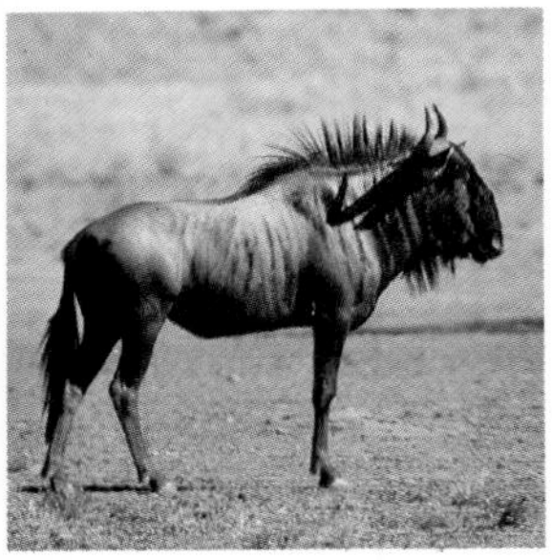

gnu *Also called wildebeest, the gnu—a type of antelope—is a native of the East African plains. Herds of up to 10,000 animals may gather in the dry season when grazing becomes scarce.*

~n. The action or an instance of gnawing. [Middle English *gnawen,* Old English *gnagan.*]
gnaw·ing (nôʹĭng) *adj.* Persistently troublesome or distressing: *a gnawing doubt.* **—gnaw·ing·ly** *adv.*
gneiss (nīs) *n. Geology.* A coarse-grained banded or foliated metamorphic rock in which the minerals are arranged in darker and lighter layers. [German *Gneis,* perhaps from Middle High German *gneiste,* spark, from Old High German *gneisto.*] **—gneiss·ic** (nīʹsĭk), **gneiss·oid** (nīʹsoid'), **gneiss·ose** (nīʹsōs') *adj.*
gnoc·chi (nyôʹkē) *pl.n.* Dumplings made of flour, semolina, or potato starch, boiled or baked and served with grated Parmesan cheese or with various sauces. [Italian, plural of *gnocco, nocchio,* "knot (of a tree)," "lump," from Germanic.]
gnome[1] (nōm) *n.* **1.** Any of a fabled race of dwarflike creatures, often portrayed as wizened old men, who live underground and guard treasure hoards. **2.** A shriveled old man. [French, from New Latin *gnomus*† (coined by Paracelsus).] **—gnom·ish** *adj.*
gnome[2] *n.* A pithy saying that expresses a general truth or fundamental principle; a maxim; an aphorism. [Greek *gnōmē,* intelligence, judgment, maxim, from *gignōskein,* to know.]
gno·mic (nōʹmĭk) *adj.* Of or of the nature of pithy sayings; aphoristic: *gnomic utterances.*
gno·mon (nōʹmŏn', -mən) *n.* **1.** An object, such as the projecting arm of a sundial, that casts a shadow used as an indicator. **2.** *Mathematics.* The figure that remains after a parallelogram has been removed from a similar but larger parallelogram with which it has a common corner. [Latin *gnōmōn,* from Greek, one who knows, indicator, interpreter, from *gignōskein,* to know.]
gno·mon·ic projection (nō-mŏnʹĭk) *n.* A type of azimuthal or zenithal map projection in which great circles of the earth are shown as straight lines and all straight lines are great circles.
gno·sis (nōʹsĭs) *n.* Intuitive apprehension of spiritual truths, an esoteric form of knowledge sought by the Gnostics. [Greek *gnōsis,* knowledge, from *gignōskein,* to know.]
-gnosis *suffix. Medicine.* Indicates knowledge or recognition; for example, **psychognosis.** [Latin, from Greek *-gnōsia,* from *gnōsis,* knowledge, GNOSIS.]
gnos·tic (nŏsʹtĭk) *adj.* **1.** Of, relating to, or possessing knowledge, especially spiritual knowledge. **2. Gnostic.** Of or pertaining to Gnostics or Gnosticism.
~n. **Gnostic.** A believer in Gnosticism.
Gnos·ti·cism (nŏsʹtĭ-sĭz'əm) *n.* The doctrines of certain early Christian sects, considered heretical, that valued inquiry into spiritual truth above faith, thought salvation attainable only by the few whose faith enabled them to transcend matter, and viewed Christ as noncorporeal.
gno·to·bi·ot·ics (nō'tō-bī-ŏtʹĭks) *n. Used with a singular verb.* The study of organisms in relation to the effects of known microorganisms on them. [New Latin : Greek *gnōtos,* known, past participle of *gignōskein,* to know + *bios,* life.] **—gno·to·bi·ot·ic** *adj.* **—gno·to·bi·ot·i·cal·ly** *adv.*
GNP gross national product.
gnu (no͞o, nyo͞o) *n.* Either of two large African antelopes, *Connochaetes gnou* or *C. taurinus,* having a drooping beard, a long, tufted tail, and curved horns in both sexes. Also called "wildebeest." [Xhosa *nqu.*]
go[1] (gō) *v.* **went** (wĕnt), **gone** (gôn, gŏn), **going, goes.** *—intr.* **1.** To move along; proceed: *going by bus; went fast.* **2.** To move to a particular place: *went to town.* **3.** To move from a place; depart: *Go before I really get mad.* **4. a.** To pursue a certain course, method, or procedure: *Instructions go from parent to child.* **b.** To resort to someone, as for aid: *went directly to the voters of her district.* **5.** To proceed to the performance of an activity: *went to eat.* **6.** Used in the form *be going* with the sense of *will* to indicate indefinite future intent or expectation: *He is going to learn to fly.* **7.** To engage in an activity. Used with a present participle: *go riding.* **8.** To function, move, or operate properly: *The car won't go.* **9.** To make a specified sound: *The glass went crack.* **10. a.** To be customarily located; belong: *The fork goes to the left of the plate.* **b.** To be capable of entering or being held: *Will the bike go into the trunk of your car?* **11.** To extend between two points or in a certain direction: *curtains going from the ceiling to the floor.* **12.** To give entry; lead: *a bulkhead going to the cellar.* **13.** To pass or be given into someone's possession: *Her jewelry went to her granddaughter.* **14.** To be allotted or awarded: *money to go for food.* **15.** To be a factor that contributes or leads: *It goes to show he was wrong.* **16. a.** To be compatible; harmonize: *The rug goes well with this room.* **b.** To match or fit. **c.** To occur with or together. **17.** To have a particular form or proceed in a particular sequence: *Is this the way the song goes?* **18.** To die. **19.** To come apart or break up. **20.** To become weak; fail: *His hearing began to go.* **21.** To be consumed or used up: *Our money is going fast.* **22.** To lose effect; disappear. **23.** To be given up or abolished: *Unnecessary expenditures must go.* **24.** To pass by; elapse: *Where did the time go?* **25.** To pass in a commercial transaction; be sold or auctioned off: *The house will go to the highest bidder.* **26.** To come to be in a specified condition; become: *go insane; go to sleep.* **27.** To be or continue to be in a specified condition: *go unchallenged.* **28.** To get along; fare: *How are things going?* **29.** To be as a general rule: *As cats go, this one is well behaved.* **30.** To carry out an action to a certain point or extent: *go too far; go to a lot of trouble.* **31.** To act, especially under guidance or on advice: *We have to go by the rules.* **32.** To pass from one person to another: *Measles went through the whole school. A rumor was going around the office.* **33.** To have a successful outcome: *made a huge effort to make the campaign go.* **34.** To attend regularly: *Does he go to school yet?* **35. a.** To be accepted or acceptable: *Anything goes.* **b.** To be the rule; be the only acceptable thing: *What I say goes.* **36.** To be contained: *5 goes into 25 five times.* **37.** To be known: *goes by a different name now.* **38.** *Informal.* To excrete waste from the bladder or bowels. *—tr.* **1.** To proceed along; follow: *We're not going the same way.* **2.** To make as a wager; bet: *He went $100 on the result.* **3.** To take part to the extent of: *go fifty-fifty on a deal.* **4.** To take on the responsibility of furnishing: *go bail for a client.* **—go about. 1.** To busy oneself with; undertake. **2.** To change direction in a sailing vessel; tack. **—go after.** To pursue in an effort to take; seek. **—go along.** To be in agreement; cooperate. **—go around** (or **round**). **1.** To move from one place to another. **2.** To be habitually in the company of, especially in public. Used with *with.* **3.** To be engaged in: *She goes around making a nuisance of herself.* **4.** To spread; circulate: *a rumor going around.* **5.** To satisfy a demand or requirement; be sufficient: *enough to go round.* **—go at. 1.** To attack verbally or physically. **2.** To work at diligently or energetically. **—go away.** To take a vacation away from home. **—go back.** To be established or be recorded in history; have existed in an earlier time. **—go back on.** To back down on; repudiate. **—go down. 1.** To be defeated; lose. **2.** To sink. Used of ships. **3.** To decrease in size, level, or weight: *The temperature went down.* **4.** *British.* To fall ill: *He went down with measles.* **5.** *British.* To travel away or graduate from a university. **6.** *British Slang.* To go to prison. **7.** To go below the horizon: *The sun went down.* **8.** To be renowned or remembered: *This occasion will go down in history.* **9.** *Slang.* To take place; happen: *Something big is going down.* **—go for. 1.** To try to obtain. **2.** *Informal.* To enjoy or appreciate: *goes for Chinese cooking.* **3.** To pass as; be thought of as. **4.** To make an attack on; assail. **5.** To apply to: *That goes for you too!* **6.** To find acceptable: *don't go for the plan.* **—go in. 1.** To be obscured by a cloud. Used of the sun and sometimes of the moon. **2.** To take part in a cooperative venture: *went in with the others to buy a present.* **—go in for.** *Informal.* **1.** To enjoy doing or participating in. **2.** To enter or participate in (a competition or contest). **—go into. 1.** To inquire about; investigate: *went into the reasons for our failure.* **2.** To take up or turn to as an occupation, study, or pastime. **—go it.** *Informal.* **1.** To move very fast. **2.** To participate energetically. **—go it alone.** To be independent; act by oneself. **—go off. 1.** To happen in a specified manner: *The dinner went off according to plan.* **2.** To be fired or shot; explode: *The gun went off.* **3.** To make a noise; sound: *The alarm clock went off.* **4.** To go away; leave. **—go on. 1.** To continue as before: *went on eating.* **2.** To happen; occur: *don't know what's going on.* **3.** To make one's entrance on the stage of a theater. **4.** To talk at length: *went on about his trip.* **5.** To use as evidence or a basis for further action: *You've got to give me more than that to go on.* **6.** Used as an interjection to express surprise or disbelief. **—go one better.** To surpass or outdo. **—go out. 1.** To stop burning or casting light; become extinguished. **2.** To cease to be popular; become unfashionable. **3.** To try to become a member of or a participant in: *went out for the basketball team.* **4.** In card games, to lay down all one's cards. **—go over. 1.** To check or examine. **2.** To be received in a specified manner: *a speech that went over well.* **—go through. 1.** To search or examine thoroughly. **2. a.** To suffer; undergo. **b.** To participate in; experience. **3.** To use up entirely: *went through his inheritance quickly.* **4.** To be voted for, as a plan or law; pass. **—go to one's head. 1.** To make excited or dizzy. **2.** To make vain or overconfident. **—go to pieces.** To lose one's self-control or health. **—go under. 1.** To lose consciousness. **2.** To be overwhelmed by difficulties. **—go with.** To be the regular romantic or sexual partner of.
~n., pl. **goes.** *Informal.* **1.** An attempt; try: *had a go at acting.* **2.** The act or an instance of going. **3.** A turn, as in a game. **4.** Energy; vitality. **—from the word go.** *Informal.* From the very beginning. **—no go.** *Informal.* Of no use; ineffective. **—on the go.** *Informal.* Perpetually busy; active.
~adj. Informal. Functioning correctly and ready for action: *All systems are go.* [Go, gone; Middle English *gon, gōn(e),* Old English *gān, gegān.* Went; Middle English *wente,* past tense of *wenden,* to turn, WEND.]
go[2] *n.* A Japanese game for two played with pebblelike counters on a board divided into 361 squares. [Japanese.]
GO general order.
go·a (gōʹə) *n.* A gazelle, *Procapra picticaudata,* of eastern Asia, the male of which has backward-curving horns. [Tibetan *dgoba.*]
Go·a (gōʹə). District on the west coast of India, formerly a Portuguese possession. Annexed by India in 1961, it now forms part of the territory of Goa, Daman, and Diu. The district centers on the port of Goa, which formerly controlled the spice trade with the East.
Goa, Da·man, and Di·u (də-mănʹ, dēʹo͞o). Territory of India, formed from three former Portuguese possessions on the west coast. Goa lies south of Bombay, Daman to the north, while Diu is an island off Gujarat. Though separated by long stretches of coastline, they share a common cultural background and were all annexed by India in 1961. Panaji (in Goa) is the capital.
goad (gōd) *n.* **1.** A long stick with a pointed end used for prodding animals. **2.** Something that prods or urges; a stimulus or irritating incentive.
~tr.v. **goaded, goading, goads.** To prod with or as if with a goad;

PRONUNCIATION KEY

ă, pat; ā, pay; âr, care; ä, father, are; b, bib; ch, church; d, deed; ĕ, pet; ē, be; f, fife; g, gag; h, hat; hw, which; ĭ, pit; ī, pie; îr, pier; j, judge; k, kick; l, lid, needle; m, mum; n, no, sudden; ng, thing; ŏ, pot; ō, toe; ô, paw, for; oi, noise; ou, out; o͝o, book; o͞o, boot; p, pop; r, roar; s, sauce; sh, ship, dish; t, tight; th, thin, path; *th,* this, bathe; ŭ, cut; ûr, fur; v, valve; w, with; y, yes; z, zebra, size; zh, vision; ə, about, item, edible, gallop, circus, peaceful

IN FOREIGN WORDS:

à, *Fr.* ami; œ, *Fr.* feu, *Ger.* schön; ü, *Fr.* tu, *Ger.* über; KH, *Ger.* ich, *Scot.* loch; N, *Fr.* bon; y', *Fr.* Compiègne

STRESS MARKS:

Primary stress: ʹ
in·citeʹ (ĭn-sītʹ)
Secondary stress: '
inʹsight' (ĭnʹsīt')

give impetus to; incite. [Middle English *gode,* Old English *gād,* from Germanic.]

go ahead *intr.v.* To start or continue, especially after an interruption; proceed.

go-a·head (gō′ə-hĕd′) *n. Informal.* Permission to proceed: *The manager gave the clerk the go-ahead to mark the suit down.*
~*adj. Informal.* **1.** Enterprising and adventurous: *The young entrepreneur had real go-ahead spirit.* **2.** Indicating permission to proceed: *a go-ahead sign.*

goal (gōl) *n.* **1.** The purpose toward which an endeavor is directed; objective: *Her goal was to attend graduate school.* **2.** The finishing point or line of a race. **3.** *Sports.* **a.** A structure or area into or over which players endeavor to advance a ball or puck. **b.** A successful attempt at advancing a ball or puck into or over a goal. **c.** The score awarded for such an act. —See Synonyms at **intention.** [Middle English *gol,* boundary, limit, probably from Old English *gǣl*† (unattested), obstacle.]

goal area *n.* In soccer, a rectangular area in front of the goal, 6 yards deep and 20 yards wide, in which goal kicks are taken.

goal·ie (gō′lē) *n. Informal.* A goalkeeper.

goal·keep·er (gōl′kē′pər) *n.* A player assigned to protect the goal in various sports.

goal kick *n.* In soccer, a free kick taken from the goal area, awarded to the defending team when the ball has been put out of play over the goal line by an attacking player.

goal line *n. Sports.* Either of two lines running the width of the playing area at each end of the field. In games such as soccer and hockey, the goals are located along the goal line, which also marks the boundary of the playing area; in games such as football, the ball must be carried over the goal line to score a touchdown.

goal·mouth (gōl′mouth′) *n. Sports.* The area between the goalposts just in front of the goal.

goal·post (gōl′pōst′) *n.* Either of a pair of posts joined with a crossbar and set at each end of a football or soccer field to form the goal.

goal·tend·er (gōl′tĕn′dər) *n.* A goalkeeper.

goal·tend·ing (gōl′tĕn′dĭng) *n.* **1.** The act of protecting the goal in various sports, as hockey. **2.** *Basketball.* An illegal play in which a player deflects a ball that is on the downward path to the basket or is already inside the rim of the cylinder, carrying the penalty of an automatic score for the offensive team.

go·an·na (gō-ăn′ə) *n.* Any of various monitor lizards of Australia. [Mispronunciation of IGUANA.]

Goa powder *n.* **Araroba** *(see).*

goat (gōt) *n.* **1.** Any of various horned, bearded ruminant mammals of the genus *Capra,* originally of mountainous regions of the Old World; especially, any of the domesticated forms of *C. hircus,* kept for milk, wool, and meat. **2. Goat.** *Astronomy.* The constellation and sign of the zodiac **Capricornus** *(see).* Usually preceded by *the.* **3.** A lecherous man. **4.** A silly person; a fool. **5.** A scapegoat. **—get someone's goat.** *Informal.* To make (someone) angry or annoyed. [Middle English *gote,* Old English *gāt.*]

goat antelope *n.* Any of various ruminant mammals, such as the mountain goat or the chamois, having characteristics of both goats and antelopes.

goat·ee (gō-tē′) *n.* A small chin beard trimmed to a point and resembling that of a goat. [From GOAT + -EE.]

goat·fish (gōt′fĭsh′) *n., pl.* **-fishes** or collectively **goatfish.** Any of various brightly colored fishes of the family Mullidae, of warm seas, having two sensory barbels on the chin. Also called "surmullet" or *British* "red mullet."

goat·herd (gōt′hûrd′) *n.* A person who looks after goats.

goat·ish (gō′tĭsh) *adj.* **1.** Of, pertaining to, or resembling a goat. **2.** Lecherous; lustful. **—goat·ish·ly** *adv.* **—goat·ish·ness** *n.*

goat moth *n.* A European moth, *Cossus cossus,* with large, pale brownish wings.

goats·beard, goat's-beard (gōts′bîrd′) *n.* **1.** A plant, *Tragopogon pratensis,* native to Europe, having grasslike leaves and yellow, dandelionlike flowers. **2.** A tall plant, *Aruncus dioicus,* having compound leaves and branching clusters of small white flowers.

goat·skin (gōt′skĭn′) *n.* **1.** The skin of a goat. **2.** Leather made from goatskin. **3.** A container, as for wine, made from goatskin.

goat's-rue (gōts′rōō′) *n.* **1.** A Eurasian plant, *Galega officinalis,* cultivated for its showy, variously colored flowers. **2.** A North American plant, *Tephrosia virginiana,* having yellow and pink flowers.

goat·suck·er (gōt′sŭk′ər) *n.* Any of various chiefly nocturnal birds of the family Caprimulgidae, which includes the nighthawk and the whippoorwill. [The bird was thought to suck goat's milk.]

go-away bird (gō′ə-wā′) *n.* Any of various touracos of the genus *Corythaixoides,* of Africa. [Imitative of its call.]

gob¹ (gŏb) *n.* **1.** A small piece or lump. **2.** A small mass or lump of spit or phlegm. **3.** *Often* **gobs.** *Informal.* A large quantity, as of money: *They have gobs of books in their library.*
~*intr.v.* **gobbed, gobbing, gobs.** *British Informal.* To spit. [Middle English *gobbe,* lump, mass, from Old French *gobe,* mouthful, lump, from *gober,* to swallow, gulp, from Gallo-Roman *gobb-* (unattested), from Celtic *gobbo-* (unattested), mouth, beak, GOB.]

gob² *n. Slang.* The mouth. [Perhaps from Scottish and Irish Gaelic *gob,* beak, mouth, from Celtic *gobbo-* (unattested).]

gob³ *n. Slang.* A sailor. [20th century : origin obscure.]

gob·bet (gŏb′ĭt) *n.* **1.** An extract from a text. **2.** A piece or chunk, especially of raw meat. [Middle English *gobet,* from Old French, diminutive of *gobe,* GOB (lump).]

gob·ble¹ (gŏb′əl) *v.* **-bled, -bling, -bles.** —*tr.* **1.** To devour in large, greedy gulps: *gobbled up his dinner.* **2.** To snatch greedily; grab: *All the remaining tickets were gobbled up within an hour.* —*intr.* To eat greedily or rapidly. [Frequentative of Middle English *gobben,* to drink greedily, probably from *gobbe,* lump, GOB.]

gobble² *intr.v.* **-bled, -bling, -bles.** To make the guttural, chortling sound of a male turkey. —*n.* The guttural, chortling sound made by a male turkey. [Imitative.]

gob·ble·de·gook, gob·ble·dy·gook (gŏb′əl-dē-gŏŏk′) *n.* **1.** Unclear, often verbose language. **2.** Gobbledegook that is associated with bureaucracy: *The current tax law is gobbledegook.* [From GOBBLE (to sound like a turkey), influenced by GOOK.]

gob·bler (gŏb′lər) *n.* A male turkey.

Go·be·lin (gō′bə-lĭn, gŏb′ə-, gō-blăN′) *n.* A tapestry of a kind woven at the Gobelin works in Paris, France, noted for its rich pictorial design.

go-be·tween (gō′bĭ-twēn′) *n.* One who acts as an intermediary or messenger between two sides.

Go·bi (gō′bē). A vast desert in northern China and southern Mongolia, encompassing an area of some 1,295,000 square kilometers (500,000 square miles). It lies on a plateau roughly 1,200 meters (4,000 feet) high and consists chiefly of sand and gravel plains broken by low rocky ranges and salt pans. It is mostly dry but has some small lakes. Its fringe of sparse pastureland is inhabited by Mongolian nomads.

gob·let (gŏb′lĭt) *n.* **1.** A drinking glass or similar vessel with a stem and base. **2.** *Archaic.* A drinking bowl without handles. [Middle English *gobelet,* from Old French, diminutive of *gobel,* cup, from Gallo-Roman *gobb-* (unattested), from Celtic *gobbo-* (unattested), mouth, beak, GOB.]

goblet cell *n. Biology.* Any of the pear-shaped cells in vertebrate epithelium that secrete the chief constituents of mucus.

gob·lin (gŏb′lĭn) *n.* A grotesque, elfin creature of folklore, thought to work mischief or evil. [Middle English *gobelin,* from Old French, from Middle High German *kobolt,* goblin.]

go·bo (gō′bō) *n., pl.* **-bos** or **-boes.** **1.** A screen around a microphone to reduce extraneous sound. **2.** A screen around a camera lens to block unwanted light. [20th century : origin obscure.]

gob·stop·per (gŏb′stŏp′ər) *n. British.* **1.** A large round, hard candy with layers of different colors. **2.** Loosely, any large mouth-filling candy.

go by *intr.v.* To pass: *Three minutes went by. Four buses went by.* ~*tr.v.* **1.** To estimate; judge: *go by appearances.* **2.** To be guided by; follow: *go by the instructions.*

go-by (gō′bī′) *n., pl.* **-bys.** *Informal.* An act of intentional avoidance; run-around: *Why did you give me the go-by?*

go·by (gō′bē) *n., pl.* **-bies** or collectively **goby.** Any of numerous usually small freshwater and marine fishes of the family Gobiidae, having the pelvic fins united to form a sucking disk. [Latin *gōbius,* variant of *cōbius,* from Greek *kōbios*†, GUDGEON.]

go-cart (gō′kärt′) *n.* **1.** A small wagon for children to ride in, drive, or pull. **2.** A handcart. **3.** A stroller. **4.** A small frame on casters designed to help support a child who is learning to walk.

god (gŏd) *n.* **1.** A being of supernatural powers or attributes, believed in and worshiped by a people; especially, a male deity thought to control some part of nature or reality or to personify some force or activity. **2.** An image of a supernatural being; idol. **3.** Something that is worshiped or idealized as a god: *Money was his god.* **4. a.** A man who is godlike in aspect or power. **b.** A man of great beauty. [Middle English *god,* Old English *god.*]

God (gŏd) *n.* **1. a.** A being conceived as the perfect, omnipotent, omniscient originator and ruler of the universe, the principal object of faith and worship in monotheistic religions. **b.** The force, effect, or a manifestation or aspect of this being. **c.** *Christian Science.* "Infinite Mind; Spirit; Soul; Principle; Life; Truth; Love" (Mary Baker Eddy). **2.** The single supreme agency postulated in some philosophical systems to explain the phenomena of the world, having a nature variously conceived in such terms as prime mover, an immanent vital force, or infinity.
~*interj.* Used as an oath or to express surprise, dismay, impatience, or the like, often in phrases such as *Oh God!* and *Thank God!*

Go·dard (gō-där′), **Jean Luc** (1930–). French film director, a leading figure of the 1960's "new wave." His films, which use experimental narrative techniques and reflect his Marxist views, include *A Married Woman* (1964), *Weekend* (1968), *Tout Va Bien* (1972), and *Slow Motion* (1980).

god·aw·ful (gŏd′ô′fəl) *adj. Slang.* Extremely trying; atrocious: *a brat with godawful manners.*

god·child (gŏd′chīld′) *n., pl.* **-children** (-chĭl′drən). A person who is sponsored at baptism by an adult.

God damn *interj.* Also **god·damn** (gŏd′dăm). Used as a profane oath, once a strong one invoking God's curses.

god·damned (gŏd′dămd′) *adj. Informal.* **1.** Very bad; atrocious: *I hate this goddamned weather.* **2.** Total; complete: *He's a goddamned idiot.*
~*adv. Informal.* Very; exceptionally: *a goddamned interesting play.*
~*interj. Informal.* Used to express surprise, frustration, and sometimes delight.

God·dard (gŏd′ərd), **Robert Hutchings** (1882–1945). U.S. physicist. He made and successfully launched the first liquid-fueled rocket.

god·daugh·ter (gŏd′dô′tər) *n.* A female godchild.

God·den (gŏd′n), **Rumer** (1907–). British novelist and short-story author. She spent many years in India and Kashmir, and her novels

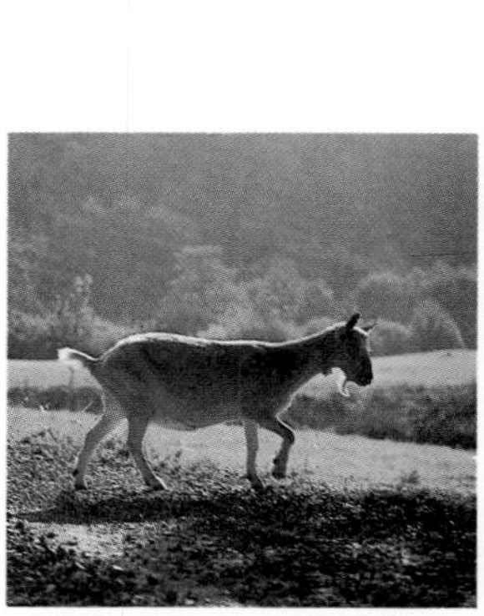

goat *Voracious eaters, goats will severely damage vegetation over a wide area if not tethered. They are widely kept as domestic animals, especially by the nomadic tribes of Africa and the Middle East.*

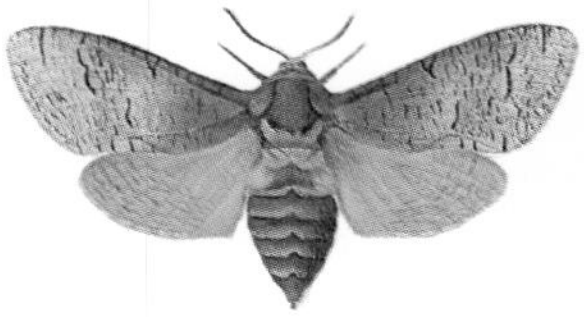

goat moth *The goat moth,* Cossus cossus*—varieties of which are found throughout Europe—is so called because the caterpillar gives off an odor similar to that of a male goat.*

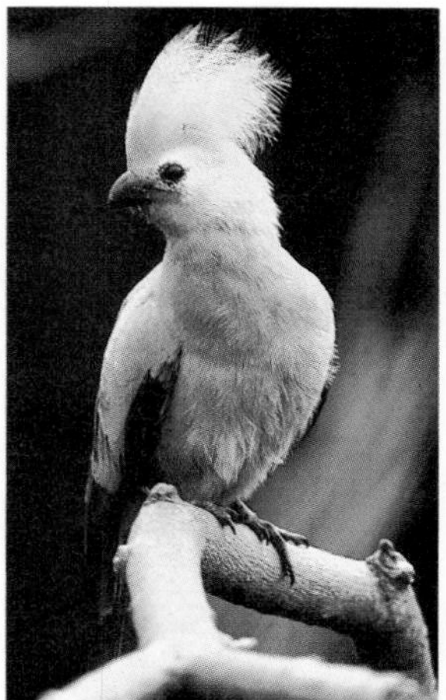

go-away bird *This African fruit eater gets its name from the call it makes when disturbed.*

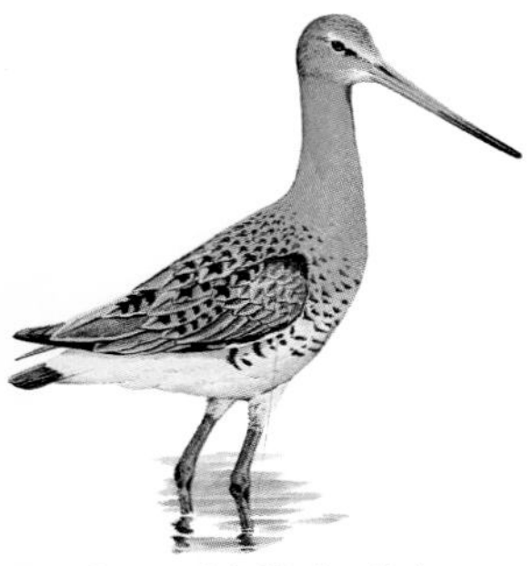

godwit *An adult black-tailed godwit,* Limosa limosa, *in its summer plumage. In winter the birds are brown-gray with pale undersides. Black-tailed godwits nest in May in grass-lined scraped hollows in the ground, and the young leave the nest only a few hours after hatching. They breed in northern Europe and Asia but migrate during the winter, some birds flying as far as Tasmania and New Zealand.*

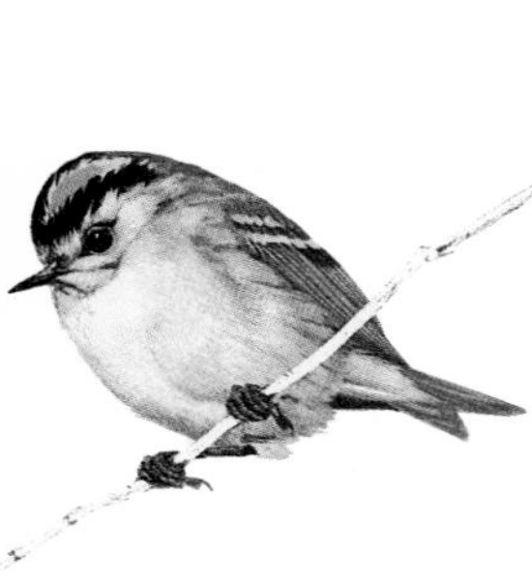

goldcrest *One of the smallest European birds, the goldcrest,* Regulus regulus, *grows to only 90 millimeters (3½ inches) in length. It usually nests in coniferous trees, laying up to ten eggs at a time, and is native to Europe and Asia.*

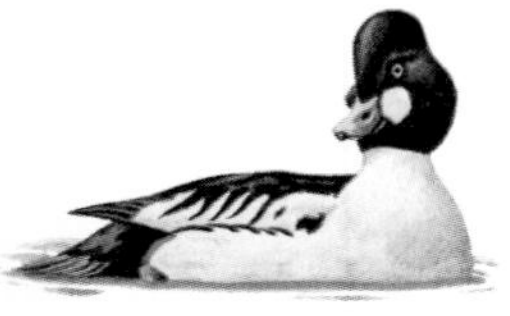

goldeneye *A winter visitor to the Gulf Coast and Florida as well as Mediterranean Europe. Goldeneye ducks form large flocks that rarely come ashore. They breed on lakes and ponds in northern regions. The male (above) can be recognized by its black-green head and white cheek patches.*

include *A Candle for St. Jude* (1948), *An Episode for Sparrows* (1955), and *The Diddakoi* (1972).

god·dess (gŏd′ĭs) *n.* **1.** A female being of supernatural powers or attributes, believed in and worshiped by a people. **2.** An image of a goddess; idol. **3.** A woman of great beauty or grace. **4.** A woman who is adored.

Gö·del (gœd′l), **Kurt** (1906–78). U.S. mathematician and logician, born in Czechoslovakia. He settled in the United States in 1940. In 1951 he was awarded the Albert Einstein award for outstanding achievement in the natural sciences.

Gödel's proof *n.* A mathematical proof that under a given consistency condition, any sufficiently strong formal axiomatic system must contain a proposition such that neither it nor its negation is provable and that any consistency proof for the system must use ideas and methods beyond those of the system itself. [After Kurt GÖDEL.]

go·de·tia (gō-dē′shə, -shē-ə) *n.* Any plant of the genus *Godetia,* some species and varieties of which are cultivated because of their showy, colorful flowers. [After C.H. *Godet* (died 1879), Swiss botanist.]

go-dev·il (gō′dĕv′əl) *n.* **1.** A jointed tool for cleaning an oil pipeline and disengaging obstructions. **2.** An iron dart dropped into an oil well to explode a charge of dynamite. **3.** A logging sled. **4.** A railroad handcar.

god·fa·ther (gŏd′fä′*th*ər) *n.* **1.** A man who sponsors a child at its baptism. **2.** *Slang. Often* **Godfather.** The head of a criminal organization, especially a Mafia family. **3.** A man who has a relationship to another that resembles the relationship of a godfather to his godchild: *The teacher had been godfather to many promising students.*

god-fear·ing (gŏd′fîr′ĭng) *adj.* Religious; devout.

god·for·sak·en (gŏd′fər-sā′kən) *adj.* **1.** Located in a dismal or remote area. **2.** Desolate; forlorn.

god·head (gŏd′hĕd′) *n.* **1.** Divinity; godhood. **2. Godhead. a.** God. **b.** The essential and divine nature of God regarded abstractly. Preceded by *the.* [Middle English *godhede* : GOD + *-hede,* variant of *-hode,* -HOOD.]

god·hood (gŏd′ho͝od′) *n.* The quality or state of being a god; divinity. [Middle English *godhode,* Old English *godhād* : GOD + -HOOD.]

Go·di·va (gə-dī′və), **Lady** (*fl.* 1040–80). English heroine, the wife of Leofric, Earl of Mercia. She was the benefactor of several monasteries, including one at Coventry in 1043. She is famous for the episode, probably legendary, in which, to secure a promise from her husband that he would reduce taxation in Coventry, she rode naked through the town on a white horse.

god·less (gŏd′lĭs) *adj.* **1.** Lacking reverence for God and God's laws; impious. **2.** Recognizing or worshiping no god. **—god·less·ly** *adv.* **—god·less·ness** *n.*

god·like (gŏd′līk′) *adj.* Resembling or of the nature of a god or God; divine.

god·ly (gŏd′lē) *adj.* **-lier, -liest. 1.** Having great reverence for God; divine. **2.** Divine. **—god·li·ness** *n.*

god·moth·er (gŏd′mŭ*th*′ər) *n.* A woman who sponsors a child at its baptism.

Go·dol·phin (gə-dŏl′fĭn), **Sidney, 1st Earl of** (1645–1712). English courtier and politician, the lifelong ally of John Churchill, 1st Duke of Marlborough. He first became an M.P. in 1668 and served in the administrations of Charles II, James II, William III, and Anne.

go·down (gō′doun′) *n.* In India and east Asia, a warehouse, especially one at a dock. [Portuguese *gudão,* from Malay *godong,* perhaps from Telugu *gidangi,* warehouse, from *kidu,* to lie.]

god·par·ent (gŏd′pâr′ənt) *n.* A godfather or godmother.

God's acre *n.* A churchyard or burial ground. [Translation of German *Gottesacker,* God's field.]

god·send (gŏd′sĕnd′) *n.* An unexpected boon or stroke of luck that comes just when it is most needed; a windfall. [Middle English *goddes sand,* God's message : GOD + *sand,* message, Old English *sand,* message, messenger.]

god·son (gŏd′sŭn′) *n.* A male godchild.

God slot *n. British Slang.* **1.** A religious program on radio or television. **2.** The period of time during which such a program is regularly broadcast.

God·speed (gŏd′spēd′) *n.* Success or good fortune. Used in the phrase *wish someone Godspeed.* [From the phrase *God speed,* may God prosper (someone).]

Godthåb. See **Nuuk.**

Go·du·nov (gŏ′də-nôf′, go͞od′ə-), **Boris** (*c.* 1550–1605). Russian statesman, czar of Russia (1598–1605). He was chief adviser to Ivan the Terrible, upon whose death in 1584 he became regent to Fyodor I and virtual dictator of Russia. He may have been implicated in the murder of Dimitry, Fyodor's younger brother and heir to the throne, in 1591. On Fyodor's death in 1598 he was chosen as czar.

God·win (gŏd′wĭn), **William** (1756–1836). British political theorist and novelist, husband of Mary Wollstonecraft and father-in-law of the poet Shelley. A staunch supporter of the French Revolution and an adherent of utilitarian principles in ethics, his most important work was the radical, pro-anarchist *Enquiry Concerning Political Justice* (1793).

God·win-Aus·ten, Mount (gŏd′wĭn-ô′stĭn). Also **Dap·sang** (dăp′-săng′) or **K2** (kā-to͞o′). The world's second-highest mountain (after Mt. Everest), in the Karakoram Range of northern India. It rises to 8,611 meters (28,250 feet) and is also known as K2 because it was the second Karakoram peak to be measured for height.

god·wit (gŏd′wĭt′) *n.* Any of various wading birds of the genus *Limosa,* having a long, slender, slightly upturned bill. [16th century : origin obscure.]

Goeb·bels (gœb′əls), **(Paul) Joseph** (1897–1945). German politician. After a brief career as a journalist and unsuccessful novelist, he joined the Nazi Party and by 1926 was appointed district party leader in Berlin. There he founded and edited the party's propaganda organ, *Der Angriff* ("Attack"). In 1928 he was elected to the Reichstag, and when Hitler was made chancellor (1933), he was appointed minister of propaganda. His venomous attacks on the Jews, his powerful oratory, and his use of radio and mass meetings made him the second most powerful man in the party. He played an important part in the "final solution" directed against the Jews and remained loyal to Hitler until April 1945, when he and his wife killed their children and committed suicide in Hitler's bunker.

go·er (gō′ər) *n.* **1.** A person who goes to or attends something regularly. Usually used in combination: *a theatergoer.* **2.** *Informal.* One that moves very fast. **3.** *Australian & New Zealand Informal.* An idea, project, or proposal that seems likely to be successful.

Goe·ring or **Gö·ring** (gœr′ĭng), **Hermann Wilhelm** (1893–1946). German politician and high-ranking Nazi official. He joined the National Socialist Party and took part with Hitler in the Munich putsch of 1923. In 1928 he was elected to the Reichstag, and when Hitler became chancellor (1933), he was appointed air minister. During World War II he was in command of the German air offensive until he lost favor with Hitler (1943) and was stripped of authority. He committed suicide before his sentence of death at the Nuremberg trials (1946) could be carried out.

Goe·thals (gō′thəlz), **George Washington** (1858–1928). U.S. army officer. He was appointed chief engineer of the Panama Canal project in 1907. Though forced to deal with unexpected engineering difficulties and problems of climate, disease, and low morale, he managed to complete the canal in just seven years.

Goe·the (gœ′tə), **Johann Wolfgang von** (1749–1832). German writer, scientist, and a major figure in world literature. Although trained as a lawyer, he devoted his life to his poetry, novels, and dramas. He first gained notice with the historical drama *Götz von Berlichingen* (1773) and the novel *The Sorrows of Young Werther* (1774). In 1775 he was invited to the ducal court at Weimar, where he spent the remainder of his life. His two greatest works were the novel *Wilhelm Meister,* completed in 1829, and the poetic drama *Faust,* the first part of which appeared in 1808 and the second part after his death.

goe·thite (gō′thīt′, gœ′tīt′) *n.* A brown mineral, essentially a hydrated oxide of iron, $Fe_2O_3 \cdot H_2O$, used as an iron ore. [Named in honor of Johann W. von GOETHE.]

go·fer (gō′fər) *n. Slang.* An employee who runs errands in addition to regular duties. [From the phrase *go for* (i.e., fetch something).]

gof·fer, gauf·fer (gŏf′ər, gô′fər) *tr.v.* **-fered, -fering, -fers. 1.** To press ridges or narrow pleats into (a frill, for example); flute or crimp. **2.** To emboss (the edges of paper or a book) with a repeating pattern.

~*n.* **1.** An iron used for goffering. **2. a.** Ridged or pleated ornamentation produced by goffering. **b.** An embossed pattern produced by goffering. [French *gaufrer,* to crimp lace, from Old French *gaufre,* honeycomb, waffle, from Middle Low German *wāfel.*]

Gog and Ma·gog (gŏg′; mā′gŏg′). In Biblical prophecy, the heathen nations to be led by Satan in a war against the Kingdom of God. Revelation 20:7–8.

go-get·ter (gō′gĕt′ər) *n. Informal.* An enterprising, forceful, and ambitious person.

gog·gle (gŏg′əl) *v.* **-gled, -gling, -gles.** —*intr.* **1.** To stare with wide and bulging eyes. **2.** To roll or bulge. Used of the eyes. —*tr.* To roll or bulge (the eyes).

~*n.* **1.** A stare or leer. **2. goggles. a.** Eye coverings that look like glasses but have shielding sidepieces and are worn as a protection, as against water, snow, wind, or dust. **b.** *Slang.* A pair of spectacles; glasses. [Middle English *gog(e)len,* to roll the eyes, perhaps from *gog-,* root expressive of up and down movement.] **—gog·gly** *adj.*

gog·gle·box (gŏg′əl-bŏks′) *n. British Slang.* A television set.

gog·gle-eyed (gŏg′əl-īd′) *adj.* Having prominent, bulging, or rolling eyes.

Gogh, Vincent van. See **van Gogh.**

go-go dancer (gō′gō′) *n.* A girl who dances in a lively, titillating manner, often on a platform, in a discothèque or cabaret. **—go-go dancing** *n.*

Go·gol (gō′gəl), **Nikolay Vasilyevich** (1809–52). Russian writer, one of the founders of the Russian realist tradition. He was of Cossack descent, and his first literary success was a collection of tales of the Ukraine, *Evenings on a Farm near Dikanka* (1832). His most famous play, *The Inspector General* (1836), revealed his talent for satirizing Russian officialdom, a talent that reached its highest expression in the novel *Dead Souls* (1842).

Goi·del (goid′l) *n.* A member of a Goidelic-speaking people. [Old Irish.]

Goi·del·ic, Goi·dhel·ic (goi-dĕl′ĭk) *n.* Also **Ga·dhel·ic** (gə-dĕl′ĭk, gă-). A group of Celtic languages comprising Irish Gaelic, Scottish Gaelic, and Manx.

~*adj.* Also **Gadhelic. 1.** Of or pertaining to the Gaels. **2.** Of, pertaining to, or characteristic of Goidelic. [Old Irish *Goidel,* Gael, Celt, from Old Welsh *gwyddel,* from *gwydd,* wild.]

go·ing (gō′ĭng) *n.* **1. a.** Departure: *comings and goings.* **b.** Demise;

death. **2.** The condition underfoot as it affects one's headway in walking or riding. **3.** *Informal.* Progress or existence considered with regard to the conditions to be coped with. **4.** The activity of attending something. Used in combination: *partygoing.*
~*adj.* **1.** Working; running: *in going order.* **2.** In full operation; flourishing: *a going concern.* **3.** Current; prevailing: *The going rates are low.* **4.** Available; to be found. Used after the noun: *the best products going.*

go·ing-o·ver (gō′ĭng-ō′vər) *n., pl.* **goings-over.** *Informal.* **1.** An examination; an inspection. **2.** A severe beating; a thrashing. **3.** A severe reprimand; scolding or rebuke.

go·ings-on (gō′ĭngz-ŏn′, -ôn′) *pl.n. Informal.* Events or behavior, especially when regarded as improper or mysterious.

goi·ter, goi·tre (goi′tər) *n. Pathology.* A chronic, noncancerous enlargement of the thyroid gland, visible as a swelling at the front of the neck, that may be due to underactivity or overactivity of the gland and may be associated with iodine deficiency. Also called "struma." See **exophthalmic goiter.** [French *goitre,* from Provençal *goitron,* from Vulgar Latin *gutturōnem* (unattested), from Latin *guttur*†, throat.] **—goi·trous** (goi′trəs) *adj.*

Go·lan Heights (gō′lən, -län′). Range of hills to the east of the Jordan River, disputed between Syria and Israel. Marking Syria's southern border after World War II, it was used from 1948 as a base from which to shell Israeli settlements. The heights were stormed by Israel during the last hours of the 1967 Middle East War and were subsequently colonized by Jewish settlers. They remain of vital strategic importance, and their administration is a key issue in Middle East peace negotiations.

Gol·con·da (gŏl-kŏn′də) *n.* A source of great riches, especially a mine. [After *Golconda,* India, city near Hyderabad, formerly noted for its diamonds.]

gold (gōld) *n.* **1.** *Symbol* **Au** A soft, yellow, corrosion-resistant element, the most malleable and ductile metal, occurring in veins and alluvial deposits and recovered by mining or by panning or sluicing. It is a good thermal and electrical conductor, is generally alloyed to increase its strength, and is used as an international monetary standard, in jewelry, for decoration, in dentistry, and as a plated coating on a wide variety of electrical and mechanical components. Atomic number 79, atomic weight 196.967, melting point 1,063.0°C, boiling point 2,966.0°C, specific gravity 19.32, valences 1, 3. **2. a.** Coins made of gold. **b.** A gold standard. **3.** Money; riches. **4.** A light olive-brown to dark yellow, or moderate, strong, to vivid yellow. **5.** Something regarded as having great value or goodness: *a heart of gold.* **6.** A gold medal.
~*adj.* **1.** Of, pertaining to, or containing gold. **2.** Of the color of gold. **3.** Redeemable or secured by gold: *a gold bond.* [Middle English *gold,* Old English *gold.*]

Gold·bach's conjecture (gōld′bäKHs′) *n. Mathematics.* The hypothesis that every even number greater than two is the sum of two prime numbers. It is generally thought to be true but so far is unproved. [After C. *Goldbach* (1690–1764), German mathematician.]

gold basis *n.* A gold standard as a basis for determining prices.

gold·beat·er's skin (gōld′bē′tərz) *n.* Treated animal membrane used to separate sheets of gold being hammered into gold leaf.

gold·beat·ing (gōld′bē′tĭng) *n.* The act, art, or process of beating sheets of gold into gold leaf. **—gold·beat·er** *n.*

Gold·berg (gōld′bərg), **Reuben Lucius,** known as "Rube" (1883–1970). U.S. cartoonist. He delighted his readers with several syndicated cartoon series and is perhaps best remembered for his drawings of zany and incredibly complex inventions that performed simple tasks. In 1948 he won a Pulitzer Prize for his political cartoons.

gold brick, gold·brick (gōld′brĭk′) *n.* **1.** A bar of gilded cheap metal that appears to be genuine gold. **2.** A fraudulent and worthless substitute. **3.** *Slang.* A person, especially a soldier, who avoids assigned duties or work; shirker.
~*intr.v.* **-bricked, -bricking, -bricks.** *Slang.* To be a shirker.

gold bug *n.* A North American beetle, *Metriona bicolor,* with a metallic luster.

gold certificate *n.* A monetary note formerly issued to the public by the U.S. Treasury and redeemable in gold but now issued to Federal Reserve Banks to certify conformity with their legal reserve requirements.

Gold Coast. The name of Ghana before the country's independence (1957). The term was first applied by European traders to its coastline on the Gulf of Guinea, where gold was brought for sale from the forests inland.

gold·crest (gōld′krĕst) *n.* A small Eurasian songbird, *Regulus regulus,* with yellow-green plumage and an orange or yellow crest.

gold digger *n. Informal.* A person, especially a woman, who seeks gifts and expensive pleasures from others.

gold dust *n.* Gold in powder form, such as that found in placer mining.

gold·en (gōl′dən) *adj.* **1.** Of, pertaining to, made of, or containing gold: *a golden ring.* **2. a.** Having the color of gold or a yellow color suggestive of gold: *golden hair.* **b.** Suggestive of gold, as in richness or splendor: *a golden voice.* **3.** Of the greatest value or importance; precious. **4.** Marked by peace, prosperity, and often creativeness: *a golden year.* **5.** Very favorable or advantageous; excellent: *a golden opportunity.* **6.** Having a promising future; seemingly assured of success. **7.** Of, pertaining to, being, or marking a 50th anniversary. **—gold·en·ly** *adv.* **—gold·en·ness** *n.*

golden age *n.* **1.** *Greek & Roman Mythology.* The first age of the world, an untroubled and prosperous era during which humankind lived in ideal happiness. **2.** A period when a nation or some wide field of endeavor reaches its height. Compare **iron age, silver age.**

golden ager *n.* An elderly person, especially one of retirement age.

golden Al·ex·an·ders (ăl′ĭg-zăn′dərz) *n. Used with a singular or plural verb.* A plant, *Zizia aurea,* of eastern North America, having clusters of small yellow flowers.

golden anniversary *n.* A 50th anniversary, symbolized by gold.

golden aster *n.* Any of various North American plants of the genus *Chrysopsis,* having yellow, rayed flowers.

golden bantam *n.* A variety of corn having large, bright-yellow kernels on a relatively small ear.

golden calf *n.* **1.** A golden image of a sacrificial calf fashioned by Aaron and worshiped by the Israelites. Exodus 32. **2.** Wealth as an object of worship; mammon.

golden chain *n.* A shrub, the **laburnum** *(see).*

golden club *n.* An aquatic plant, *Orontium aquaticum,* of the eastern United States, having small golden-yellow flowers covering a clublike spadix.

Golden Delicious *n.* A variety of eating apple having greenish-yellow skin and sweet flesh.

golden eagle *n.* An eagle, *Aquila chrysaetos,* of mountainous areas of the Northern Hemisphere, having dark plumage with yellowish feathers on the head and neck.

gol·den·eye (gōl′dən-ī′) *n.* Either of two ducks, *Bucephala clangula* or *B. islandica,* of northern regions, having a short black bill, a rounded head, yellow eyes, and black and white plumage. [From their golden-yellow eyes.]

Golden Fleece *n. Greek Mythology.* The magic fleece of the winged ram, stolen by Jason and the Argonauts.

Golden Gate Bridge. Suspension bridge near San Francisco, California. It crosses the strait that links San Francisco Bay with the Pacific Ocean. The bridge was completed in 1937, and its central span of 1,280 meters (4,200 feet) was then the longest in the world.

golden glow *n.* A tall plant, *Rudbeckia laciniata hortensis,* cultivated for its yellow, many-rayed, double flowers.

Golden Horde *n.* The Mongol army that swept over eastern Europe in the 13th century and established a suzerain in Russia. [Translation of Tatar *altūn ordū,* from the color of the tent of their commander, Batu Khan.]

Golden Horn. *Turkish* **Ha·liç** (hä-lēch′). Inlet of the Bosporus in northwestern Turkey. It has served as the harbor for Istanbul since ancient times.

golden mean *n.* **1.** The course between extremes; moderation. **2.** The golden section.

golden oldie *n.* A recording, motion picture, or other form of entertainment that was very popular in the past.

golden pheasant *n.* A pheasant, *Chrysolophus pictus,* of China and Tibet, having a long tail and brilliantly colored plumage.

golden retriever *n.* A dog of a breed of retriever having a dense, wavy, cream or yellow coat.

gold·en·rod (gōl′dən-rŏd′) *n.* Any of various plants of the chiefly North American genus *Solidago,* having clusters of small yellow flowers that bloom in late summer or autumn.

golden rule *n.* **1.** The maxim or teaching that one should behave toward others as one would have others behave toward oneself. Matthew 7:12. **2.** Any basic important principle.

golden samphire *n.* A plant, the **samphire** *(see).*

gold·en·seal (gōl′dən-sēl′) *n.* A woodland plant, *Hydrastis canadensis,* of eastern North America, having small greenish-white flowers and a yellow root formerly used medicinally.

golden section *n.* A ratio between the two dimensions of a plane figure or the two divisions of a line such that the smaller is to the larger as the larger is to the sum of the two, roughly a ratio of three to five. The proportion, which is used in the fine arts, is considered particularly aesthetically pleasing. Also called "golden mean."

golden wattle *n.* Any of several yellow-flowered Australian trees or shrubs of the genus *Acacia;* especially, *A. pycnantha.*

gold-ex·change standard (gōld′ĭks-chānj′) *n.* A monetary system in which a country maintains its currency at par with the currency of another country on the gold standard.

gold-filled (gōld′fĭld′) *adj.* Made of a hard base metal with an outer layer of gold.

gold·finch (gōld′fĭnch′) *n.* **1.** A small Old World bird, *Carduelis carduelis,* having brownish plumage with red, yellow, and black markings. **2.** Any of several small New World birds of the genus *Spinus;* especially, *S. tristis,* of which the male has yellow and black plumage.

gold·fish (gōld′fĭsh′) *n., pl.* **-fishes** or collectively **goldfish. 1.** A freshwater fish, *Carassius auratus,* native to eastern Asia, characteristically having brassy or reddish coloring, and bred in many ornamental forms as an aquarium fish. **2.** Any of various similar aquarium fishes, especially the golden **orfe** *(see).*

goldfish bowl *n.* **1.** A **fish bowl** *(see).* **2.** A place or condition of exposure to public view.

gold foil *n.* Gold rolled or beaten into thin sheets thicker than gold leaf.

gold·i·locks (gōl′dē-lŏks′) *n.* **1.** A European plant, *Linosyrus vulgaris,* having narrow leaves and clusters of small yellow flowers. **2.** A Eurasian woodland plant, *Ranunculus auricomus,* similar and related to the buttercup. [Obsolete *goldy,* golden, from GOLD + LOCK(S).]

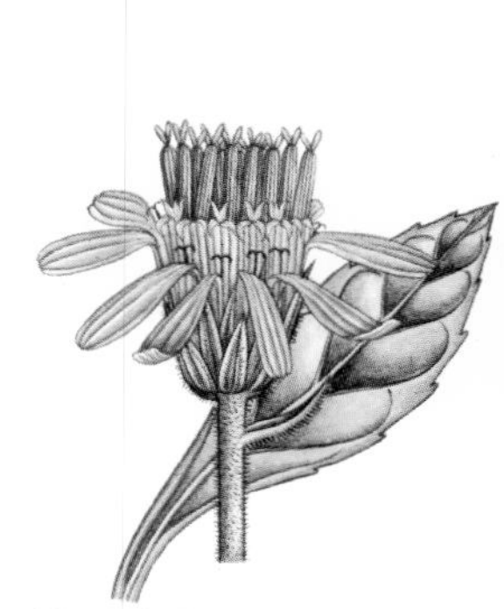

goldenrod *There are about 100 species of this herb, most of which are native to North America. The European goldenrod,* Solidago virgaurea *(above), was imported into Britain in Tudor times and used as a salve for wounds.*

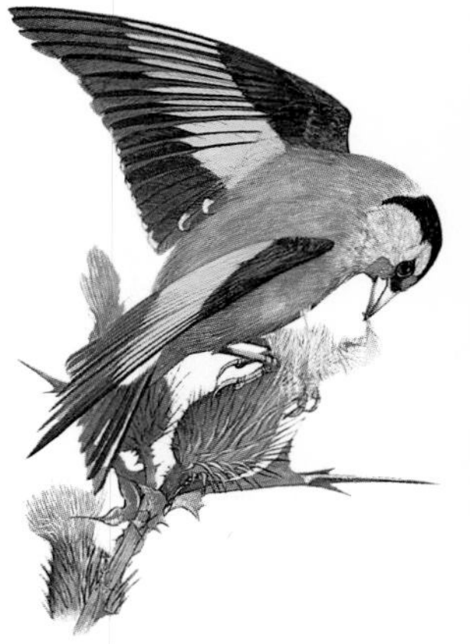

goldfinch *Among the smallest of finches,* Carduelis carduelis *(above) measures about 12 centimeters (4¾ inches) from head to tail. It feeds mainly on thistle seeds that it plucks with its pointed beak.*

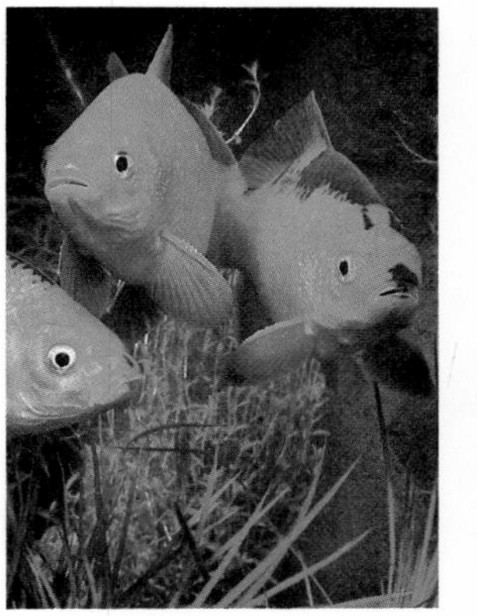

goldfish *The domesticated goldfish popular in aquariums and garden ponds was originally bred in China. Goldfish are descended from a grayish-yellow species of carp found in Europe and Asia.*

Gold·ing (gōl'dĭng), **William Gerald** (1911–). British novelist. He established his reputation with *Lord of the Flies* (1954). Later novels include *Pincher Martin* (1956), *Free Fall* (1959), and *The Scorpion God* (1971). He was awarded the Nobel Prize for literature (1983).

gold leaf *n.* Gold beaten into extremely thin sheets, used for gilding.

Gold·man (gōld'mən), **Emma** (1869–1940). U.S. anarchist agitator, born in Russia. In 1916 she was imprisoned for advocating birth control, in 1917 for opposing military conscription. In 1919 she was deported to Russia. She went to Spain during the Civil War and died in Canada in 1940. Her writings include *Anarchism and Other Essays* (1911) and *My Disillusionment in Russia* (1923).

gold medal *n.* A medal made of gold, or something looking like gold, awarded as a prize for coming in first in a race, competition, or the like. Compare **bronze medal, silver medal.**

gold mine *n.* **1.** A mine yielding gold ore. **2.** *Informal.* **a.** A source of great wealth or profit. **b.** An abundant source of something that is wanted: *a gold mine of information.*

gold-of-pleas·ure (gōld'əv-plĕzh'ər) *n.* A plant, *Camelina sativa*, native to Europe and Asia, having small yellow flowers and seeds rich in oil.

Gol·do·ni (gŏl-dō'nē), **Carlo** (1707–93). Italian comic playwright. He wrote over 250 plays, 150 of which are comedies, including *The Mistress of the Inn* (1753), *The Fan* (1764), and *The Accomplished Maid* (1756). He lived in Paris after 1762 and died there a pauper.

gold plate *n.* **1.** Vessels, dishes, and utensils made of gold. **2.** A covering of gold, usually produced by electroplating.

gold-plate (gōld'plāt') *tr.v.* **-plated, -plating, -plates.** To cover with gold plate, usually by electroplating.

gold point *n.* **1.** The point in foreign-exchange rates at which it is no more expensive to import or export gold bullion in settling international accounts than to buy or sell bills of exchange. Also called "specie point." **2.** *Physics.* The melting point of gold, used as a fixed point for temperature scales.

gold reserve *n.* The reserve of gold bullion held by a government or central bank to redeem its notes.

gold rush *n.* A rush of migrants to an area where gold has been discovered, such as that to California in 1849.

Gold·schmidt process (gōld'shmĭt') *n.* A process for extracting metals by reducing the oxide with aluminum. [After Hans *Goldschmidt* (1861–1923), German chemist.]

gold·smith (gōld'smĭth') *n.* **1.** An artisan who fashions objects in gold. **2.** A tradesman who deals in gold articles.

Gold·smith (gōld'smĭth'), **Oliver** (*c.* 1728–74). Irish writer. He settled in London in 1756 and published his first work, *Enquiry into the Present State of Polite Learning in Europe* (1759). The publication of the satirical essays *The Citizen of the World* (1762) established him as a man of letters. His most famous works are his novel *The Vicar of Wakefield* (1766), the pastoral poem *The Deserted Village* (1770), and the dramatic comedy *She Stoops to Conquer* (1773).

goldsmith beetle *n.* Either of two scarabaeid beetles, *Cotalpa lanigera* or *Cetonia aurata*, having metallic greenish-yellow coloring.

gold standard *n.* A monetary standard under which the basic unit of currency is equal in value to and exchangeable in principle for a given amount of gold.

gold·stone (gōld'stōn') *n.* An **aventurine** (see) with gold-colored inclusions.

gold·thread (gōld'thrĕd') *n.* A low-growing woodland plant, *Coptis trifolia*, having white flowers and slender yellow roots.

Gold·wyn (gōld'wĭn), **Samuel**, born Samuel Goldfish (1882–1974). Polish-born U.S. film producer. In 1916 he established his own Goldwyn Pictures Corporation and then merged with Louis B. Mayer in 1924 to become Metro-Goldwyn-Mayer. Goldwyn produced a number of major films, including *Guys and Dolls* (1955) and *Porgy and Bess* (1959). He won an Academy Award for *The Best Years of Our Lives* (1946).

go·lem (gō'lĕm, -ləm) *n.* *Jewish Folklore.* An artificially created human being endowed with life by supernatural means.

golf (gŏlf, gôlf, gŏf, gôf) *n.* A game played on a large outdoor obstacle course having a series of usually 9 or 18 holes spaced far apart, the object being to propel a small ball by the use of a club into each hole with as few strokes as possible.

~*intr.v.* **golfed, golfing, golfs.** To play golf. [Middle English *golf†* (Scottish dialect).] —**golf·er** *n.*

golf ball *n.* **1.** A small, hard, dimpled ball used in golf. **2.** *Informal.* A revolving metal sphere on which the type is carried in many electric typewriters. **3.** A typewriter equipped with such a sphere.

golf club *n.* **1.** Any of a set of clubs having a slender shaft and a head of wood or iron, used in golf. **2. a.** An organization of golfers usually having its own golf course and premises. **b.** Such premises.

golf course *n.* A large tract of land laid out for golf. Also called "golf links."

Gol·gi (gôl'jē), **Camillo** (1844–1926). Italian physician. He established the existence of a complex of vesicles present in cells, now known as the Golgi apparatus. For his work on the structure of the nervous system he was awarded, with Santiago Ramón y Cajal (1852–1934), the Nobel Prize for physiology and medicine (1906).

Golgi apparatus *n.* A stack of membranous vesicles present in living cells and believed to function in the formation of secretions within the cell. Also called "Golgi body," "Golgi complex." [After Camillo GOLGI.]

gol·go·tha (gŏl'gə-thə) *n.* **1.** A place of burial. **2.** A place or occasion of suffering or agony. [After GOLGOTHA.]

Gol·go·tha (gŏl'gə-thə). The hill of Calvary where Jesus was crucified. [Late Latin, from Greek, from Aramaic *gulgūltha*, skull (from the shape of the hill).]

gol·iard (gōl'yərd) *n.* Any of a class of wandering students in medieval Europe, who are supposed to have led a life of conviviality and debauchery and to have composed ribald and satirical Latin songs. [Middle English *goliard*, from Old French, glutton, trickster, from *gole*, throat, from Latin *gula*, gullet.] —**gol·iar·dic** (gŏl-yär'dĭk) *adj.*

Go·li·ath (gə-lī'əth). The giant Philistine warrior who was slain by David with a stone and sling. I Samuel 17:4–51.

goliath beetle *n.* Any of several very large, herbivorous, scarabaeid beetles; especially, the African species *Goliathus giganteus*, which can reach a length of 20 centimeters (8 inches).

goliath frog *n.* The largest known frog, *Rana goliath*, which occurs in Africa and can reach a length of 35 centimeters (14 inches).

gol·li·wog, gol·li·wogg (gŏl'ē-wŏg') *n.* A male doll with a black face and longish hair standing out from its head, usually made from soft material. [Originally the name of a doll designed by Florence Upton (died 1922) for a series of children's books by Bertha Upton (died 1912); possibly after POLLIWOG.]

golly *interj.* *Informal.* Used to express mild surprise or wonder. [Euphemism for GOD.]

GOM, G.O.M. Grand Old Man.

gombo. Variant of **gumbo.**

gom·broon (gŏm-brōon') *n.* A kind of Persian pottery. [After *Gombroon*, town in Iran.]

Gó·mez (gō'mĕz), **Juan Vicente** (*c.* 1857–1935). Venezuelan soldier and politician; president (1908–35). Once a cattle herdsman and almost illiterate, he gathered a guerrilla force around him that helped win the presidency for Cipriano Castro (*c.* 1858–1924). Castro made him vice president in 1899, but Gómez deposed him in 1908. He ruled by severe methods and established a police state. He also established the foundations of Venezuela's modern industrial economy.

Go·mor·rah (gə-môr'ə, -mŏr'ə). A city of ancient Palestine near Sodom.

Gom·pers (gŏm'pərz), **Samuel** (1850–1924). English-born U.S. labor leader who took part in the founding of the Federation of Organized Trades and Labor Unions (1881). When it was reorganized as the American Federation of Labor (1886), Gompers became its first president, an office he held until his death.

gom·pho·sis (gŏm-fō'sĭs) *n.* *Anatomy.* An immovable articulation consisting of a peg and rigid socket, such as a tooth and its bony socket. [New Latin, from Greek *gomphōsis*, from *gomphoun*, to fasten with bolts, from *gomphos*, bolt.]

Go·mul·ka (gō-mōōl'kə, -mŭl'kə), **Wladyslaw** (1905–82). Polish Communist leader. An active trade unionist, he was secretary of the Polish Workers' Central Committee (1943–49) and played a leading part in the resistance movement against the Germans. From 1945 to 1949 he was deputy premier of Poland but was purged for alleged "bourgeois nationalism" and sympathy with Tito. He was imprisoned without trial (1951–54) but readmitted to the party in 1956 and elected first secretary. He removed Stalinists from key positions, reduced the secret police terror, ended compulsory collectivization, and reached a compromise with the Church. In 1970 he resigned as first secretary in the wake of food riots.

go·mu·ti (gə-mōō'tē) *n.* **1.** A palm tree, *Arenga pinnata*, of southeast Asia, the sap of which yields sugar. **2.** The leaf fibers of this palm, used to make cord, rope, and the like. [Malay *gĕmuti*.]

–gon *suffix.* Indicates a figure having a specified number of sides and angles; for example, **nonagon**. [Greek *-gōnon*, from *-gonos*, -angled, from *gōnia*, angle.]

go·nad (gō'năd', gŏn'ăd') *n.* An organ in animals that produces gametes; especially, a testis or ovary. [New Latin, from Greek *gonos*, offspring, procreation, genitals.] —**go·nad·al, go·nad·ic** *adj.*

gon·a·do·trop·ic (gŏn'ə-dō-trŏp'ĭk, -trō'pĭk) *adj.* Also **gon·a·do·troph·ic** (-trŏf'ĭk, -trō'fĭk). Acting on or stimulating the gonads, as does a hormone.

gon·a·do·tro·pin (gŏn'ə-dō-trō'pĭn, -trŏp'ĭn) *n.* Also **gon·a·do·tro·phin** (-trō'fĭn). Any of several hormones that are secreted by the pituitary gland and stimulate activity of the ovaries and testes, as for example the **follicle-stimulating hormone** (see). Also called "gonadotropic hormone."

Gon·cha·rov (gŏn'chə-rôf'), **Ivan Alexandrovich** (1812–91). Russian novelist, famous for one novel, *Oblomov* (1858), a masterpiece of comedy.

Gon·court (gôn-kōōr'), **Edmond Louis Antoine de** (1822–96) and his brother **Jules Alfred Huot de** (1830–70). French writers and literary critics. They are best known for their journal, published in nine volumes (1887–96). Edmond's will provided for the foundation of the Goncourt Academy, which annually awards the Goncourt Prize for literature.

Gond (gŏnd) *n.* A member of a people of Dravidian stock of central India.

Gon·dar (gŏn'dər). Town in northwest Ethiopia. It was a capital of Ethiopia, flourishing from *c.* 1630 to *c.* 1860.

Gon·di (gŏn'dē) *n.* The Dravidian language of the Gonds.

gon·do·la (gŏnd'l-ə, gŏn-dō'lə) *n.* **1.** A narrow, lightweight barge having ends that curve up into a point and often a small cabin in the middle, propelled with a single oar from the stern, used on the canals of Venice. **2.** Any of various containers or vehicles suspended from a framework or larger vehicle, as: **a.** A cabin or basket suspended from a balloon or airship. **b.** A car or seat suspended

gondola *These long single-oared boats are the traditional form of transportation on the canals of Venice.*

from cables, as on a ski lift. **c.** A movable platform or container suspended from a building and used by builders and other workmen to gain access to outside walls and windows. **3.** An open, shallow freight car. Also called "gondola car." **4.** A flat-bottomed river boat. [Italian (Venetian dialect), *gondola†*, roll, rock.]

gon·do·lier (gŏnd′l-îr′) *n.* The boatman of a gondola.

Gond·wa·na (gŏnd-wä′nə). Region of north-central India noted for its rock system and fossil flora. [Sanskrit *gondavana*, "Gond forest" : *gonda*, fleshy navel, name applied to the GOND + *vana*, forest.]

Gond·wa·na·land (gŏnd-wä′nə-lănd′) *n.* A hypothetical southern portion of the earth's original land mass, Pangaea. Africa, South America, India, Arabia, Australia, Madagascar, New Guinea, the Malay Peninsula, Indonesia, and Antarctica are thought to have begun drifting apart, out of Gondwanaland, some 200 million years ago. See also **Laurasia.**

gone (gôn, gŏn). Past participle of **go.**
~*adj.* **1.** Past; bygone. **2.** Advanced beyond hope or recall. **3.** Dying or dead. **4.** Ruined; lost. **5.** *Informal.* **a.** Carried away; absorbed. **b.** Exhilarated; excited. **6.** Used up; exhausted. **7.** *Informal.* At a specified stage of a pregnancy: *four months gone.* —**gone on.** *Slang.* Infatuated with: *gone on the girl.*

gon·er (gôn′ər, gŏn′-) *n. Slang.* One who is ruined or doomed. [From GONE.]

gon·fa·lon (gŏn′fə-lŏn) *n.* A banner suspended from a crosspiece, especially as a standard in an ecclesiastical procession or as the ensign of a medieval Italian republic. [Italian *gonfalone*, standard, from Germanic.]

gon·fa·lon·ier (gŏn′fə-lə-nîr′) *n.* **1.** The bearer of a gonfalon. **2.** The chief magistrate in any of several medieval Italian republics.

gong (gông, gŏng) *n.* **1. a.** A hanging rimmed metal disk that produces a loud, sonorous tone when struck with a padded mallet. **b.** See **tam-tam. 2.** A usually saucer-shaped bell that is struck with a mechanically operated hammer. **3.** *British Slang.* A medal. [Malay *gŏng* (imitative).]

Gon·gor·ism (gŏng′gə-rĭz′əm) *n.* A florid, cluttered literary style. [Popularized by Luis de *Góngora y Argote* (1561–1627), Spanish poet.] —**Gon·go·ris·tic** (gŏng′gə-rĭs′tĭk) *adj.*

go·ni·a·tite (gō′nē-ə-tīt′) *n.* Any of various extinct cephalopod mollusks of the genus *Goniatites*, the fossil remains of which are common constituents of Devonian and Carboniferous rocks. [Greek *gōnia*, angle (referring to the angular sutures in some species).]

go·nid·i·um (gō-nĭd′ē-əm) *n., pl.* -**ia** (-ē-ə). **1.** An asexually produced reproductive cell that separates from the parent body, as in certain colonial algae. **2.** An algal cell in the thallus of a lichen, so called because they were once thought to be the reproductive cells of the lichen. [New Latin : GON(O)- + Greek *-idion*, diminutive suffix.]

gonif. Variant of **ganef.**

go·ni·om·e·ter (gō′nē-ŏm′ə-tər) *n.* **1.** An optical instrument for measuring crystal angles. **2.** A radio receiver and directional antenna used as a system to determine the angular direction of incoming radio signals. [Greek *gōnia*, angle + -METER.] —**go·ni·o·met·ric** (gō′nē-ō-mĕt′rĭk), **go·ni·o·met·ri·cal** *adj.*

go·ni·om·e·try (gō′nē-ŏm′ə-trē) *n.* The science of measuring angles. [Greek *gōnia*, angle + -METRY.]

go·ni·on (gō′nē-ŏn′) *n.* The point of the angle on either side of the lower jaw. [New Latin, from Greek *gōnia*, angle.]

go·ni·o·punc·ture (gō′nē-ō-pŭngk′chər) *n.* An operation for glaucoma in which fluid is drained from the eye by inserting a small knife through the cornea.

-gonium *suffix.* Indicates a reproductive cell or seed; for example, **oogonium.** [New Latin *gonium*, seed, cell, from Greek *gonos*, seed, procreation.]

gono-, gon- *prefix.* Indicates sexual, reproductive, or procreative; for example, **gonococcus, gonidium.** [New Latin *gono-*, from Greek, from *gonos*, offspring, seed, procreation.]

gon·o·coc·cus (gŏn′ə-kŏk′əs) *n., pl.* -**cocci** (-kŏk′sī′). The bacterium, *Neisseria gonorrhoeae*, that causes gonorrhea. [New Latin : GONO- + -COCCUS.]

gon·o·cyte (gō′nō-sīt′) *n.* **1.** An embryonic cell that develops into an ovum or a spermatozoon. **2.** An oocyte or spermatocyte. [GONO- + -CYTE.]

go-no-go (gō-nō′gō) *adj.* Of, pertaining to, or requiring the outcome of a parameter in order to stop or continue a course of action: *a go-no-go space launch.*

gon·o·phore (gŏn′ə-fôr′, -fōr′) *n.* A structure bearing or consisting of a reproductive organ or part, such as a reproductive cell or bud in a hydroid colony. [GONO- + -PHORE.] —**gon·o·phor·ic** (gŏn′ə-fôr′ĭk, -fōr′ĭk), **go·noph·o·rous** (gə-nŏf′ər-əs) *adj.*

gon·o·pore (gŏn′ə-pôr′, -pōr′) *n.* A reproductive aperture or pore, as in insects.

gon·or·rhe·a (gŏn′ə-rē′ə) *n.* An infectious disease of the genitourinary tract, rectum, and cervix, caused by the gonococcus, transmitted chiefly by sexual intercourse, and characterized by acute purulent urethritis with dysuria. [Late Latin *gonorrhoea*, from Greek *gonorrhoia* : GONO- + -RRHEA.] —**gon·or·rhe·al, gon·or·rhe·ic** *adj.*

-gony *suffix.* Indicates the production of; for example, **sporogony.** [Latin *-gonia*, from Greek, from *-goneia*, generation, from *gonos*, offspring, seed.]

Gon·za·ga (gən-zä′gə, -zăg′ə). Illustrious Italian princely house, whose members ruled Mantua from the 14th to the 18th century. The name comes from the village of Gonzaga, near Mantua, which

Francesco Gonzaga (1466–1519) made into a center of learning and the arts.

Gon·za·les (gən-zä′ləs), **Richard Alonzo**, known as "Pancho" (1928–). U.S. tennis player. He won the U.S. lawn and clay-court championships for two years in succession (1948–49) before turning professional. He was the world professional champion every year but one between 1954 and 1961.

goo (gōō) *n. Informal.* **1.** A sticky moist substance. **2.** Sentimental drivel. [Perhaps short for BURGOO.] —**goo·ey** *adj.* —**goo·i·ly** *adv.*

goo·ber (gōō′bər) *n. Regional.* A peanut *(see).* Also called "goober pea." [Angolese *nguba*.]

good (gōōd) *adj.* **better, best. 1. a.** Having positive or desirable qualities; not bad or poor. **b.** Virtuous; morally admirable; upright. **2. a.** Serving the end desired; suitable; serviceable: *a good outdoor paint.* **b.** Worthy of proper treatment; not to be spoiled or wasted: *don't ruin good work.* **3. a.** Not spoiled or ruined; able to be used: *The milk is still good.* **b.** In excellent condition; whole; sound: *a good tooth.* **c.** Handsome or fine in appearance: *a good figure.* **4.** Superior to the average: *a good student.* **5. a.** Of high quality: *good books.* **b.** Discriminating: *good taste.* **c.** Well-tested or trustworthy: *a good brand of tuna.* **6.** Suitable for special or formal occasions: *his good clothes.* **7. a.** Beneficial; salutary: *a good night's rest.* **b.** Undisturbed or comfortable: *The patient had a good night.* **8.** Competent; skilled: *a good machinist; good at math.* **9.** Complete; thorough: *a good workout.* **10. a.** Safe; sure: *a good investment.* **b.** Valid or sound: *a good reason.* **c.** Genuine; real: *a good check.* **d.** Applicable; relevant: *his claim to the money was good.* **11. a.** Ample; substantial; considerable: *a good income.* **b.** Bountiful: *a good table.* **12.** Full: *a good mile from here.* **13. a.** Pleasant; enjoyable: *having a good time at the party.* **b.** Propitious; favorable: *good weather; a good omen.* **14. a.** Benevolent; cheerful; kind: *a good soul.* **b.** Loyal; staunch: *a good Socialist.* **15. a.** Well-behaved; obedient: *a good child.* **b.** Socially correct; proper: *good manners.* **c.** Kindly; well-disposed: *She's good to her husband.* **16.** Fertile: *good land.* **17.** Well-established; well-bred; of a high class: *a good family.* **18.** Physically pleasurable or materially enjoyable: *the good things in life.* **19.** Large; substantial: *a good distance away.* **20.** Used to introduce meeting and leave-taking formulas: *good morning; good evening; good night.* —**as good as.** Practically; virtually; nearly: *as good as new.* —**good and.** *Informal.* Very; entirely: *good and tired.* —**good for. 1.** Able to serve or continue performing for a specified period of time: *good for another year.* **2.** Able to be counted upon for producing something specified: *good for a laugh.* **3.** Worth in exchange: *a ticket good for two trips.* —**make good. 1.** To fulfill a promise, commitment, or the like; make valid. **2.** To compensate for or replace. **3.** To prove; verify. **4.** *Informal.* To succeed; do well.
~*n.* **1. a.** That which is good. **b.** The good, valuable, or useful part or aspect: *get the good out of something.* **c.** Benefit; real advantage: *Some good may yet come of it.* **2.** Welfare; benefit; well-being: *for the common good.* **3.** Goodness; virtue; merit: *There is much good in him.* —**come to no good.** To come to a bad end; prove worthless. —**for good.** For all time to come; permanently; forever: *She came home to stay for good.* —**no good.** *Informal.* **1.** Worthless. **2.** Futile; useless: *It's no good trying to coax him.* —**to the good. 1.** To one's benefit; for the best. **2.** In an advantageous financial position.
~*adv. Nonstandard.* Well. [Middle English *god, gode,* Old English *gōd.*]

Usage: There is a clear distinction between the use of *good* and *well* following verbs. *Good* is an adjective that qualifies the subject of a linking verb, such as *be, feel, seem, smell, taste: It feels good; that tastes good. Well* is an adverb that qualifies the verb directly: *He dances well. He acts really well.* It is nonstandard to say or write *He dances good* or *He acts real good.*

good book *n. Often* **Good Book.** The Bible. Often preceded by *the.*

goodby, good-bye (gōōd′bī′) *interj.* Used to express farewell on parting.
~*n., pl.* **good-bys, good-byes. 1.** An expression of farewell. **2.** An act of leave-taking: *lingering over their good-bys.* [Contraction of *God be with you.*]

good faith *n.* Integrity; sincerity of intent: *a promise made in good faith.*

good fellow *n.* A genial, companionable person.

good-fel·low·ship (gōōd′fĕl′ō-shĭp′) *n.* Pleasant sociability; comradeship.

good-for-noth·ing (gōōd′fər-nŭth′ĭng) *n.* A person of little worth or usefulness.
~*adj.* Having little worth; useless.

Good Friday *n.* The Friday before Easter, observed by Christians in commemoration of the Crucifixion of Jesus.

good-heart·ed (gōōd′här′tĭd) *adj.* Kind and generous. —**good-heart·ed·ly** *adv.* —**good-heart·ed·ness** *n.*

Good Hope, Cape of. A promontory on the southwestern coast of Cape Province, in southern South Africa near Cape Town. It was circumnavigated by Bartolomeu Diaz (1488) and by Vasco da Gama (1497).

good-hu·mored (gōōd′hyōō′mərd) *adj.* Cheerful; amiable. —**good-hu·mored·ly** *adv.* —**good-hu·mored·ness** *n.*

goodie. Variant of **goody** (treat).

good·ish (gōōd′ĭsh) *adj.* **1.** Somewhat good. **2.** Somewhat large or big; goodly.

good-look·er (gōōd′lōōk′ər) *n. Informal.* A good-looking person, especially a woman.

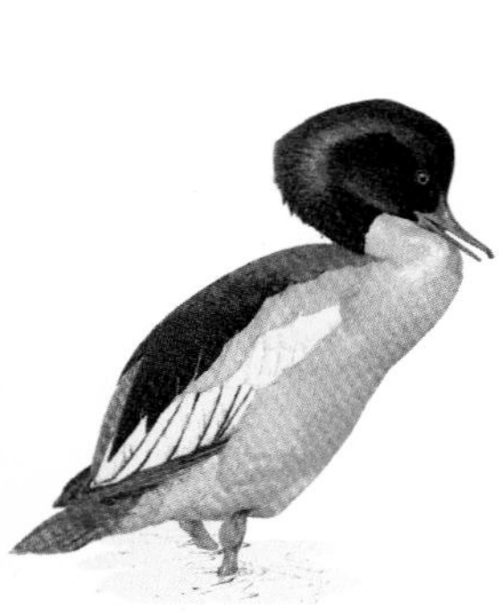

goosander *Mergus merganser, the goosander, is one of the few ducks that nest in tree holes. Common in the cooler regions of the Northern Hemisphere, it feeds largely on fish. It is an efficient swimmer, capable of staying underwater for more than a minute at a time.*

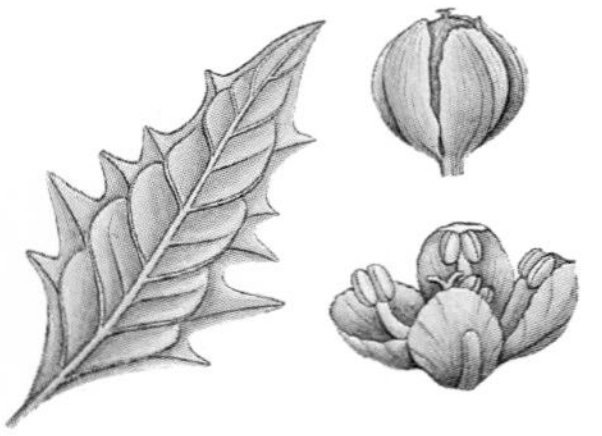

goosefoot *A plant that thrives in the nitrogen-rich soil near ponds and sewage farms. Its toothed leaf looks like a goose's foot. The red goosefoot,* Chenopodium rubrum, *is shown here.*

PRONUNCIATION KEY

ă, pat; ā, pay; âr, care;
ä, father, are; b, bib;
ch, church; d, deed; ĕ, pet;
ē, be; f, fife; g, gag; h, hat;
hw, which; ĭ, pit; ī, pie;
îr, pier; j, judge; k, kick;
l, lid, needle; m, mum;
n, no, sudden; ng, thing;
ŏ, pot; ō, toe; ô, paw, for;
oi, noise; ou, out; o͝o, book;
o͞o, boot; p, pop; r, roar;
s, sauce; sh, ship, dish;
t, tight; th, thin, path;
th, this, bathe; ŭ, cut; ûr, fur;
v, valve; w, with; y, yes;
z, zebra, size; zh, vision;
ə, about, item, edible,
gallop, circus, peaceful

IN FOREIGN WORDS:

à, *Fr.* ami; œ, *Fr.* feu, *Ger.* schön; ü, *Fr.* tu, *Ger.* über; KH, *Ger.* ich, *Scot.* loch; N, *Fr.* bon; y', *Fr.* Compiègne

STRESS MARKS:

Primary stress: ′
in·cite′ (ĭn-sīt′)
Secondary stress: ′
in′sight′ (ĭn′sīt′)

good-look·ing (go͝od′lo͝ok′ĭng) *adj.* Of a pleasing appearance; attractive; handsome.

good looks *pl.n.* Attractive appearance; handsomeness.

good·ly (go͝od′lē) *adj.* **-lier, -liest. 1.** Fairly large; considerable: *a goodly sum.* **2.** Of pleasing appearance; comely. **—good·li·ness** *n.*

good·man (go͝od′mən) *n., pl.* **-men** (-mĭn). *Archaic.* **1. a.** The male head of a household; the master. **b.** A husband. **2.** A courteous title of or form of address for a man not of gentle birth.

Good·man (go͝od′mən), **Benny,** originally Benjamin David Goodman (1909–86). U.S. clarinetist, known as the "King of Swing." In New York in 1935 he formed the Benny Goodman trio with Gene Krupa and Teddy Wilson; a year later Lionel Hampton made it a quartet. For at least 30 years Goodman maintained his reputation as one of the finest jazz musicians in the world.

good nature *n.* Cheerful, obliging disposition.

good-na·tured (go͝od′nā′chərd) *adj.* Having an easy-going, cheerful disposition. **—good-na·tured·ly** *adv.* **—good-na·tured·ness** *n.*

good·ness (go͝od′nĭs) *n.* **1.** The state or quality of being good; excellence; merit; worth. **2.** Virtuousness; moral rectitude. **3.** Kindness; benevolence; generosity. **4.** The good part of something; essence; strength.
~*interj.* Used as a euphemism for "god," often in phrases such as *Thank goodness* or *My goodness,* to express relief, surprise, or the like.

good offices *pl.n.* Favorable intervention, usually unobtrusive, on a person's behalf.

goods (go͝odz) *pl.n. Abbr.* **gds. 1.** Merchandise; wares. **2.** Portable personal property. **3.** *Chiefly British.* Merchandise to be transported; freight. Also used adjectivally: *a goods train.* **4.** *Economics.* Physical commodities, usually movable, and only consumed some time after production. Compare **services. 5.** *Used with a singular or plural verb.* Fabric; material. **—deliver the goods.** *Informal.* To produce what is expected; carry out a promise. **—get** (or **have**) **the goods on.** *Slang.* To obtain or have incriminating information or material against. **—the goods.** *Slang.* The real or genuine thing. [Plural of GOOD.]

Good Samaritan *n.* **1.** In a New Testament parable, the only passer-by to aid a man who had been beaten and robbed. Luke 10:30–37. **2.** A compassionate person who unselfishly helps another or others.

goods and chattels *pl.n.* Personal belongings.

Good Shepherd *n.* A name for Jesus. John 10:11–12.

good-sized (go͝od′sīzd′) *adj.* Of a fairly large size.

good-tem·pered (go͝od′tĕm′pərd) *adj.* Having an even or mild temper; not easily irritated. **—good-tem·pered·ly** *adv.* **—good-tem·pered·ness** *n.*

good turn *n.* An act or gesture that helps another person; a favor.

good·wife (go͝od′wīf′) *n., pl.* **-wives** (-wīvz′). *Archaic.* **1.** The female head of a household; the mistress. **2.** A courteous title of or form of address for a woman not of gentle birth.

good·will, good will (go͝od′wĭl′) *n.* **1.** Friendly or neighborly feeling; benevolence. Also used adjectivally: *a goodwill visit.* **2.** Cheerful acquiescence or willingness. **3.** *Accounting.* The good relationship of a business enterprise with its customers, regarded and assessed as an intangible asset.

Good·win Sands (go͝od′wĭn). Group of sandbanks in the Strait of Dover, lying *c.* 10 kilometers (6 miles) off the southeast coast of England. Shifting and partially exposed at low tide, they are extremely dangerous to shipping.

good·y[1], good·ie (go͝od′ē) *n., pl.* **-ies.** *Informal.* **1.** *Usually* **goodies.** Something attractive, interesting, or delectable; especially, something sweet to eat. **2.** A goody-goody. **3.** The virtuous character, as in a movie or play. Compare **baddy.**
~*adj. Informal.* Goody-goody.
~*interj.* Used to express childish delight.

goody[2] *n., pl.* **-ies.** *Archaic.* A polite title of or form of address for a married woman of humble rank. Often used with a surname. [Short for GOODWIFE.]

Good·year (go͝od′yîr′), **Charles** (1800–60). U.S. inventor. After experimenting for 10 years to find a method of raising the melting point of rubber, he accidentally came upon vulcanization when rubber mixed with sulfur dropped on a hot stove. The method was patented in 1844, but after failing to establish companies in Britain and France, Goodyear was imprisoned in Paris for debt in 1855 and died a pauper.

good·y-good·y (go͝od′ē-go͝od′ē) *adj.* Affectedly sweet or good; cloyingly sanctimonious.
~*n., pl.* **goody-goodies.** One who is affectedly good or virtuous.

goo·ey (go͞o′ē) *adj.* **-ier, -iest.** *Informal.* Thick and sticky. [From GOO.]

goof (go͞of) *n. Slang.* **1.** An incompetent, foolish, or stupid person. **2.** A careless mistake; slip.
~*v.* **goofed, goofing, goofs.** *Slang.* —*intr.* **1.** To make a silly mistake; blunder. **2.** To have aimless fun; fool about. Used with *about, around,* or *off.* —*tr.* **1.** To spoil; bungle. Often used with *up.* **2.** To give drugs to (a horse, for example); dope. **3.** To take or swallow (drugs). [Variant of dialect *goff,* from Old French *goffe,* awkward, from Medieval Latin *gufus*†, coarse.]

goof·ball (go͞of′bôl′) *n. Slang.* **1.** A barbiturate sleeping pill. **2.** An eccentric or deranged person.

goof-off (go͞of′ôf′, -ŏf′) *n.* One who shirks work or responsibility.

goof·y (go͞o′fē) *adj.* **-ier, -iest.** *Informal.* Silly; awkward; ridiculous: *a goofy hat.* **—goof·i·ly** *adv.* **—goof·i·ness** *n.*

goo·gol (go͞o′gôl′) *n.* The number 10 raised to the power 100 (10^{100}); the number 1 followed by 100 zeros. [Coined by Edward *Kasner* (1878–1955), U.S. mathematician.]

goo·gol·plex (go͞o′gôl-plĕks′) *n.* The number 10 raised to the power of one googol; the number 1 followed by 10^{100} zeros. [*googol* + du*plex.*]

gook (go͝ok, go͞ok) *n. Slang.* A dirty, sludgy, or slimy substance. [Possible alteration of GOO.]

Goo·la·gong Caw·ley (go͞o′lə-gông kô′lē), **Evonne** (1951–). Australian tennis player. She won the Wimbledon ladies' singles championship twice (1971 and 1980) and the doubles championship in 1974. Her record also includes three Australian singles championships (1974, 1975, and 1976).

goon (go͞on) *n.* **1.** *Slang.* A stupid or oafish person. **2.** *Informal.* A thug hired to commit acts of intimidation or violence. [From dialectal *gooney, gony*†, fool; popularized by the comic-strip character Alice the *Goon,* created by E.C. *Segar* (1894–1938).]

goo·ney bird (go͞o′nē) *n.* An albatross; especially, *Diomedea nigripes,* common on islands of the Pacific. [From dialectal *gooney,* fool. See **goon.**]

goop (go͞op) *n. Slang.* An ill-mannered person. [Coined by Gelett *Burgess* (1866–1951), U.S. humorist.]

goos·an·der (go͞os-ăn′dər) *n.* A duck, *Mergus merganser,* the male of which has a dark head and white body. [Probably GOOS(E) + Old Norse *önd* (stem *andar-*), duck.]

goose[1] (go͞os) *n., pl.* **geese** (gēs) or **gooses** (for sense 5). **1.** Any of various wild or domesticated water birds of the family Anatidae, and especially of the genera *Anser* and *Branta,* characteristically having a shorter neck than that of a swan and a shorter, more pointed bill than that of a duck. **2.** The female of such a bird, as distinguished from a gander. **3.** The flesh of such a bird, used as food. **4.** *Informal.* A silly person; simpleton. **5.** A tailor's pressing iron with a long curved handle. **—cook someone's goose.** *Informal.* To ruin someone's chances. [Goose, geese; Middle English *goos, gees,* Old English *gōs, gēs.*]

goose[2] *tr.v.* **goosed, goosing, gooses.** *Slang.* To jab (someone) between the buttocks with an upward thrust.
~*n., pl.* **gooses.** *Slang.* A jab between the buttocks. [Perhaps after GOOSE (bird), from the supposed resemblance of an upturned thumb to an outstretched goose's neck.]

goose barnacle *n.* Any of various barnacles of the genus *Lepas,* which are attached by a stalk to wood and other surfaces and have flattened shells. [So named from the belief that geese were born from barnacles.]

goose·ber·ry (go͞os′bĕr′ē, -bə-rē, go͞oz′-) *n., pl.* **-ries. 1.** A spiny shrub, *Ribes uva-crispa* (or *R. grossularia*), native to Eurasia, having lobed leaves, greenish flowers, and edible greenish or reddish berries. **2.** The fruit of this plant. **3.** Any of several plants bearing fruit similar to the gooseberry, such as the **Cape gooseberry** *(see).* [Perhaps GOOSE + BERRY.]

goose egg *n. Slang.* Zero, especially when written as a numeral to indicate that no points have been scored.

goose·fish (go͞os′fĭsh′) *n., pl.* **-fishes** or collectively **goosefish.** Any of several anglerfishes of the genus *Lophius,* such as *L. Americanus,* of Northern American Atlantic waters. Also called "monkfish."

goose flesh *n.* Momentary roughness of skin caused by erection of the papillae in response to cold or fear. Also called "goose bumps," "goose pimples."

goose·foot (go͞os′fo͝ot′) *n., pl.* **-foots.** Any of various usually weedy plants of the genus *Chenopodium,* having small greenish flowers. [From the shape of its leaves.]

goose grass *n.* A plant, **cleavers** *(see).*

goose·herd (go͞os′hûrd′) *n.* One who tends a flock of geese.

goose·neck (go͞os′nĕk′) *n.* **1.** A slender, curved object or part, such as the flexible shaft of a type of desk lamp. **2.** *Nautical.* A metal fitting joining a boom to a mast. **—goose·necked** *adj.*

goose step *n.* A military parade step performed by swinging each leg alternately sharply from the hips and keeping the knees locked.

goose-step (go͞os′stĕp′) *intr.v.* **-stepped, -stepping, -steps.** To execute or march in a goose step.

goos·y, goos·ey (go͞o′sē) *adj.* **-ier, -iest. 1.** Pertaining to or resembling a goose. **2.** *Informal.* Foolish; scatterbrained. **3.** *Informal.* Causing or affected with goose flesh.

G.O.P. Grand Old Party.

go·pher (gō′fər) *n.* **1.** Any of various short-tailed, burrowing mammals of the family Geomyidae, of North America, having fur-lined external cheek pouches. Also called "pocket gopher." **2.** A **ground squirrel** *(see),* especially one of the genus *Citellus.* **3.** Any of several burrowing tortoises of the genus *Gopherus;* especially, *G. polyphemus,* of the southeastern United States. In this sense, also called "gopher tortoise." [Shortening of earlier *magopher*†.]

gopher ball *n. Baseball.* A pitched ball that is hit for a home run.

gopher snake *n.* A **bull snake** *(see).*

go·pher·wood (gō′fər-wo͝od′) *n.* Also **gopher wood** (for sense 1). **1.** An unidentified wood, probably a kind of cypress, used in the construction of Noah's ark. Genesis 6:14. **2.** A tree, the **yellowwood** *(see).* [Hebrew *gōper.*]

go·ral (gôr′əl, gōr′-) *n.* Either of two goat antelopes, *Naemorhedus goral* or *N. cranbrooki,* of mountainous regions of eastern Asia, having short, ridged, backward-curving horns in both sexes. [Hindi *gūral, goral,* perhaps from Sanskrit *gaura,* gaur.]

Gor·ba·chev (gôr′bə-chôf′), **Mikhail Sergeevich** (1931–). Soviet politician and leader. The success of his pioneering agrarian reforms earned him a place on the Central Committee (1978). In 1980 he was elected to the Politburo, where he became an advocate of economic and administrative reform. In 1985 he was elected general secretary of the Communist Party, and in 1989 he was elected to the Soviet presidency. After a failed coup (1991) he first resigned as general secretary and then later that year he gave up the presidency.

gor·cock (gôr′kŏk′) *n.* The male of the red grouse. [From *gor-*† + COCK.]

Gor·di·an knot (gôr′dē-ən) *n.* **1.** An intricate knot tied by King Gordius of Phrygia and cut by Alexander the Great with his sword after hearing an oracle promise that whoever could undo it would be the next ruler of Asia. **2.** An exceedingly complicated problem or deadlock. **—cut the Gordian knot.** To solve a problem by resorting to prompt and bold measures.

Gor·di·mer (gôr′də-mər), **Nadine** (1923–). South African novelist and short-story writer, noted for her sensitive portrayals of interracial relationships. Among her best-known works are *The Soft Voice of the Serpent* (1953), *A Guest of Honor* (1970), and *July's People* (1981).

Gor·don (gôr′dn), **Charles George** (1833–85). British soldier who took part in the British capture of Peking (Beijing) in 1860. His later command of the Chinese army raised to put down the Taiping rebellion earned him the nickname of "Chinese Gordon." As governor general of Sudan, he died fighting the Mahdi when his garrison at Khartoum was overrun before a relief force could reach him.

Gordon setter *n.* A hunting dog of a breed originating in Scotland, having a silky black-and-tan coat. [After Alexander Gordon, the 4th Duke of *Gordon* (1743–1827).]

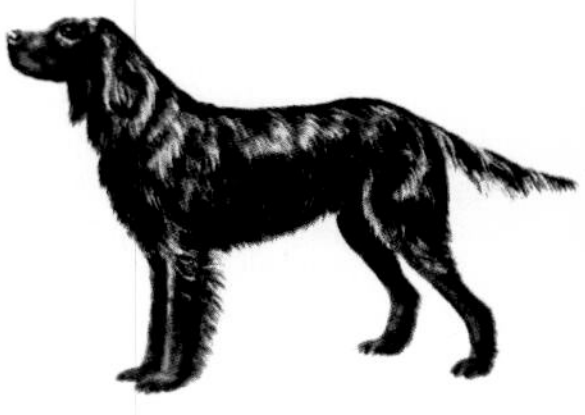

Gordon setter *This Scottish retriever was originally bred as a gun dog to collect game.*

gore[1] (gôr) *tr.v.* **gored, goring, gores.** To pierce or stab with a horn or tusk. [Middle English *gōren,* to pierce, from *gore,* spear, Old English *gār.*]

gore[2] *n.* **1.** A triangular or tapering piece of cloth used as a part of a garment, such as a skirt, or in an umbrella or sail. **2.** A small triangular piece of land.
∼*tr.v.* **gored, goring, gores. 1.** To make or provide with a gore or gores. **2.** To cut into a gore. [Middle English *gore,* Old English *gāra,* triangular piece of land; akin to Old English *gār,* spear (from the triangular shape of the spearhead).]

gore[3] *n* **1.** Blood, especially coagulated blood from a wound. **2.** *Informal.* Violence or killing, as in movie scenes. [Middle English *gore,* Old English *gor*†, dung, dirt.]

Go·ren (gôr′ən), **Charles Henry** (1901–91). U.S. contract bridge authority. A lawyer and avid bridge player, he developed a revolutionary point-count system and soon abandoned his law practice to devote his time completely to bridge. His writings on the subject include *Contract Bridge Complete* (1951) and numerous newspaper columns.

gorge (gôrj) *n.* **1.** A deep, narrow passage with precipitous rocky sides, enclosed between mountains, usually a river valley or former river valley. **2.** A narrow entrance or passageway from the rear into the bastion or other outwork of a fortification. **3. a.** The contents of a stomach. **b.** *Archaic.* The throat; gullet. **4.** An instance of gluttonous eating; a gorging. **5.** A mass obstructing a narrow passage: *The shipping lane was blocked by an ice gorge.* **—make one's gorge rise.** To make one feel strong revulsion or violent anger.
∼*v.* **gorged, gorging, gorges.** —*tr.* **1.** To stuff; satiate; glut. Usually used reflexively. **2.** To devour greedily. —*intr.* To eat gluttonously. —See Synonyms at **satiate.** [Middle English, throat, from Old French, from Vulgar Latin *gurga* (unattested), variant of Latin *gurges,* whirlpool, throat.] **—gorg·er** *n.*

gor·geous (gôr′jəs) *adj.* **1.** Dazzlingly brilliant; resplendent; magnificent. **2.** Strikingly beautiful or attractive. **3.** *Informal.* Wonderful; delightful. [Middle English *gorgeouse,* showy, splendid, from Old French *gorgias*†, stylish, fine, elegant.] **—gor·geous·ly** *adv.* **—gor·geous·ness** *n.*

gor·ger·in (gôr′jər-ən) *n. Architecture.* The necking of a column. [French, from *gorge,* throat, GORGE.]

gor·get (gôr′jĭt) *n.* **1.** A piece of armor protecting the throat. **2.** An ornamental collar. **3.** The scarflike part of a wimple covering the neck and shoulders. **4.** A band or patch of distinctive color on the throat of an animal, especially a bird. **5.** A surgical instrument used to remove stones from the bladder. [Middle English, from Old French, diminutive of *gorge,* throat, GORGE.]

Gor·gon (gôr′gən) *n.* **1.** *Greek Mythology.* Any of the three sisters Stheno, Euryale, and the mortal Medusa who had terrifying teeth and claws, snakes for hair, and eyes which, if looked into, turned the beholder into stone. **2. gorgon.** A repulsively ugly or terrifying woman. [Middle English, from Latin *Gorgō* (stem *Gorgōn-*), from Greek, from *gorgos*†, terrible.] **—Gor·go·ni·an** *adj.*

gor·go·nei·on (gôr′gə-nē′ən) *n., pl.* **-neia** (-nē′ə). A representation of a Gorgon's head, especially one of Medusa. [Greek, from the neuter of *gorgoneios,* of a Gorgon, from *Gorgō,* GORGON.]

gor·go·ni·an (gôr-gō′nē-ən) *n.* Any of various corals of the order Gorgonacea, having a flexible, often branching skeleton of horny material.
∼*adj.* Of or belonging to the Gorgonacea. [Latin *Gorgonia,* coral, from *Gorgō,* GORGON.]

gor·gon·ize (gôr′gə-nīz′) *tr.v.* **-ized, -izing, -izes.** To have a paralyzing effect upon; petrify, as with fear. [From GORGON.]

Gor·gon·zo·la (gôr′gən-zō′lə) *n.* A pungent, blue-veined, cream-colored Italian cheese made of pressed cow's milk.

go·ril·la (gə-rĭl′ə) *n.* **1.** A large anthropoid ape, *Gorilla gorilla,* of forests of equatorial Africa, having a stocky body and coarse, dark hair. **2.** A brutish or thuglike man. [New Latin (adopted 1847), from Greek *Gorillai*†, name of African tribe of hairy men.]

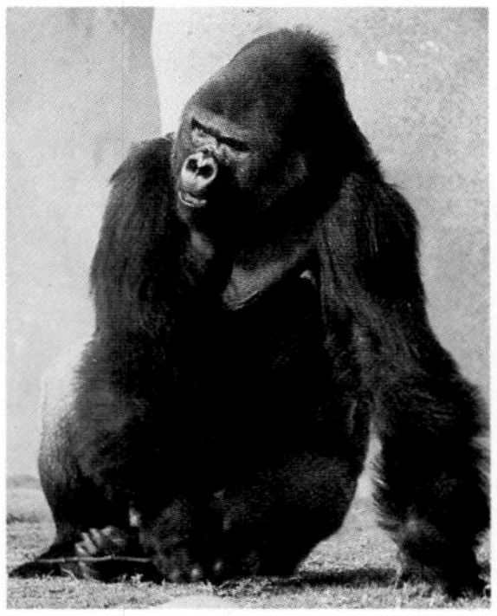

gorilla *Largely ground-dwelling, this African ape—which reaches 1.7 meters (5 feet 8 inches) in height—is, despite its fearsome appearance, a peaceful vegetarian.*

Göring, Hermann. See **Goering.**

Gor·ky or **Gor·ki** (gôr′kē). Former name of **Nizh·ny Nov·go·rod** (nĭzh′nē nôv′gə-rŏd′). The second-largest city in Russia, at the confluence of the Volga and Oka rivers. Under the czarist regime it was the site of historic trade fairs that continued until 1917. Maxim Gorky was born here, and the city was renamed in his honor in 1932. In 1991 the original name was restored.

Gorky or **Gorki, Maxim,** originally Alexey Maximovich Pyeshkov (1868–1936). Self-educated Russian writer, often considered the father of Soviet literature. His works include the play *The Lower Depths* (1902) and the novel *Mother* (1907).

gormand. Variant of **gourmand.**

gor·mand·ize (gôr′mən-dīz′) *v.* **-ized, -izing, -izes.** —*intr.* To eat gluttonously; gorge. —*tr.* To devour (food) gluttonously; gorge.
∼*n. Rare.* Variant of **gourmandise.** [From GOURMANDISE (obsolete sense "gluttony").] **—gor·mand·iz·er** *n.*

gorm·less (gôrm′ləs) *adj. British Informal.* Stupid; unable to deal with practical problems; blundering. [Variant of earlier *gaumless,* from dialect *gaum,* understanding, from Old English *gom, gome,* from Old Norse *gaumr,* heed.]

gorp (gôrp) *n.* A mixture of high-energy foods, such as dried fruit, nuts, and seeds, eaten as a snack. [Perhaps from slang *gorp,* to eat greedily.]

gorse (gôrs) *n.* Any of several spiny, thickset shrubs of the genus *Ulex*; especially, *U. europaeus,* native to Europe, having fragrant yellow flowers. Also called "furze," "whin." [Middle English *gorst, gors,* Old English *gorst, gors.*]

go·ry (gôr′ē, gōr′ē) *adj.* **-rier, -riest. 1.** Covered or stained with gore; bloody; bloodstained. **2.** Characterized by a great effusion of blood: *a gory battle.* **3.** Full of or characterized by bloodshed, slaughter, or acts of violence: *a gory narrative.* **—gor·i·ly** *adv.* **—gor·i·ness** *n.*

gosh (gŏsh) *interj. Informal.* Used to express mild surprise or delight. [Euphemistic variant of GOD.]

gos·hawk (gŏs′hôk′) *n.* **1.** A large hawk, *Accipiter gentilis,* having broad, rounded wings and gray or brownish plumage. **2.** Any of several similar or related hawks. [Middle English *goshawke,* Old English *gōshafoc* : *gōs,* GOOSE + *hafoc,* HAWK.]

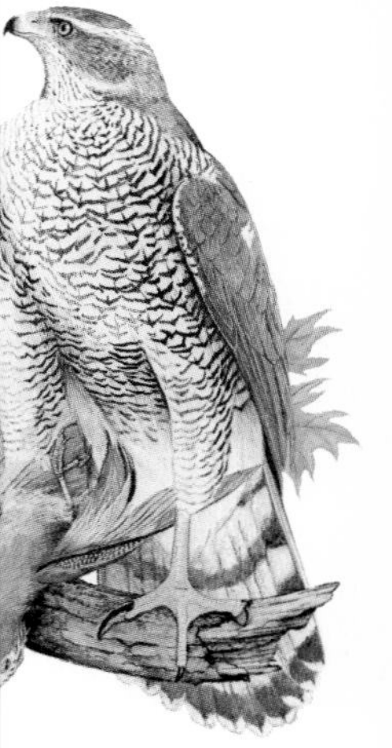

goshawk *An inhabitant of woodlands, the goshawk has short rounded wings and a long tail, enabling it to twist and turn at speed among trees to catch its prey. Because of its efficiency in catching large animals such as game birds and hares, it is often trained for falconry.*

Go·shen (gō′shən). Region of ancient Egypt on the eastern delta of the Nile, inhabited by the Israelites from the time of Joseph until the Exodus. Genesis 45:10.

gos·ling (gŏz′lĭng) *n.* **1.** A young goose. **2.** An inexperienced young person. [Middle English, earlier *gesling,* from Old Norse *gæslingr.* See **goose, -ling.**]

gos·pel (gŏs′pəl) *n.* **1.** *Sometimes* **Gospel.** The teachings of Jesus and the Apostles. **2. a. Gospel.** Any of the first four books of the New Testament describing the life, death, and resurrection of Jesus. **b.** A similar narrative. **3.** *Often* **Gospel.** A reading from any of these books included as part of a religious service. **4.** A teaching or doctrine of a religious teacher. **5.** A principle that is strongly advocated: *the gospel of hard work.* **6.** The infallibly accurate account of matters; the last word; *Don't take Freud as gospel.* Also used adjectivally: *the gospel truth.* **7.** Religious music of a style originated among blacks in the southern United States, characterized by evangelical lyrics and fervent singing, and much influenced by jazz. Also used adjectivally: *a gospel song.* [Middle English *gospel,* Old English *godspell,* "good news" (translation of Late Latin *evangelium,* EVANGEL) : *gōd,* GOOD + *spel,* news.]

gos·pel·er, gos·pel·ler (gŏs′pə-lər) *n.* **1.** One who teaches or professes faith in a gospel. **2.** A person who reads or sings the Gospel as part of a church service. [Middle English *gospeller,* Old English *godspellere,* from *godspellian,* to teach the gospel, from *godspell,* GOSPEL.]

gospel side, Gospel Side *n.* The left side of an altar or chancel. [So called from the practice in some churches of reading the Gospel and Epistle from different sides.]

gos·po·din (gŏs′pə-dēn′) *n., pl.* **-da** (-dä′). A courteous form of address used in the U.S.S.R. by Russians for non-Russians. [Russian, "master," "lord."]

gos·port (gŏs′pôrt′, -pōrt′) *n.* A flexible speaking tube used for communication between individual compartments or cockpits of an airplane. [After *Gosport,* England.]

gos·sa·mer (gŏs′ə-mər) *n.* **1.** A fine film of cobwebs often seen floating in the air or caught on bushes or grass. **2.** A soft, sheer, gauzy fabric. **3.** Anything delicate, light, or insubstantial.
∼*adj.* Also **gos·sa·mer·y** (-mə-rē). Light, thin, and delicate. [Middle English *gossomer, gosesomer* : perhaps *goos, gos,* GOOSE + *somer,* SUMMER (that is, early November (St. Martin's summer), when geese are eaten and gossamer is most in evidence).]

gos·san (gŏs′ən) *n. Geology.* An outcrop of quartz and iron oxides, often marking a sulfide ore. [Cornish *gossen,* from *gōs,* blood, from Old Cornish *guit* (referring to its russet color).]

Gosse (gŏs), **Sir Edmund William** (1849–1928). British critic and writer. He wrote essays and criticism and was chiefly responsible for introducing modern Scandinavian literature, especially that of Ibsen, to English readers. He is best known for his autobiographical work, *Father and Son,* published anonymously (1907).

gos·sip (gŏs′əp) *n.* **1. a.** Trifling, often groundless rumor, usually of a personal, sensational, or intimate nature. **b.** A friendly conversation on unimportant matters; chat. **c.** News of no great impor-

Gothic

PINNACLES OF CREATIVITY
Gothic architecture and carving marked a high point of European art

The term Gothic, now applied to four centuries of medieval European art, was originally coined during the Renaissance. The style reflected the intense religious formalism of the Middle Ages and was an attempt to express spiritual and mystical values while maintaining vitality and lightness.

The Gothic style was expressed predominantly architecturally, in cathedrals. Characteristic traits include stone tracery and ribs on walls and ceilings that serve to accentuate soaring pillars and high, pointed arches. The use of flying buttresses, which took from the walls and pillars much of the weight of the roof, enabled architects to lighten wall structure and incorporate huge stained-glass windows. The effect is of lightweight masonry shot through with light and color. Exteriors often had twin towers on the façade, lavishly decorated entrances, and rows of pinnacled flying buttresses.

The Gothic style made its appearance with the building of the abbey of Saint-Denis (1140–44), now a northern suburb of Paris, and reached a high point in Chartres Cathedral at the beginning of the 13th century. The style spread to Germany where Cologne Cathedral is a classic of Gothic style. In Britain an early example is Canterbury Cathedral, where, after a fire, the choir was rebuilt (1174–85) in a style inspired by the French Gothic cathedrals. English Gothic differed from the continental style in aiming for length rather than height. Because of this the building methods were different. French-style flying buttresses were not used. Later Gothic styles in Britain are termed Decorated (13th and 14th centuries) and Perpendicular (late 14th to 16th centuries). A unique feature of English Gothic architecture is fan vaulting. It was first used in the 14th century at Gloucester Cathedral.

The Gothic style also involved the development of sculpture. During the building of the abbey, Saint-Denis was a European center for metalworkers and stone sculptors, and their styles and techniques became international. Their hallmark was startling realism: portraits are lifelike, form is hinted at with exquisitely rendered draperies, and foliage is accurately recorded.

Stained glass and tapestry were also important art forms, as was painting, mainly in illuminated manuscripts, panels, and Italian frescoes. Gothic art culminated in the 1399 altarpiece by Melchior Broederlam at Dijon Cathedral and the manuscript prayer book, the *Très Riches Heures,* illuminated for the Duc de Berry in about 1411–16 by the Limbourg brothers. By then the Renaissance had begun in Italy.

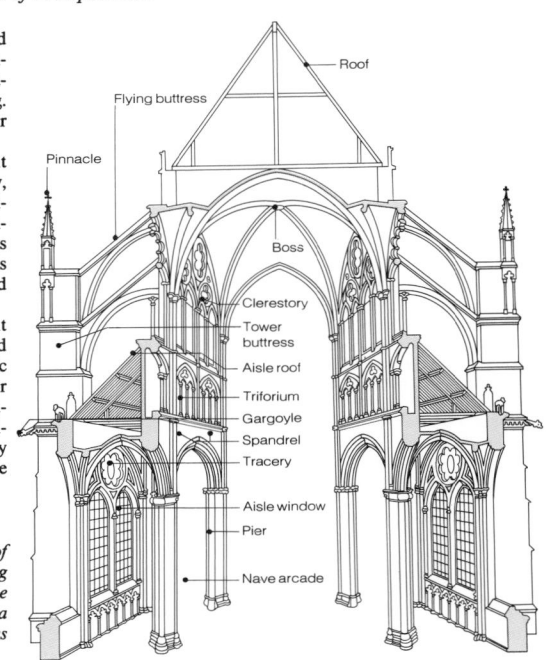

BUILT TO AMAZE *The Gothic cathedral was a web of stonework. Flying buttresses outside the building strengthened the structure, allowing the walls to be pierced by many windows and to soar past triforia and clerestories to high, pointed arches and cross vaulting delicately outlined by ribbed masonry.*

LIGHT AND SHADE *The high, vaulted nave of Amiens Cathedral, begun in 1220, shows a typical Gothic forest of pillars and interplay of light and shade.*

NOVEL REALISM *A 12th-century illumination for the Bible of Bury St. Edmunds shows Moses, Aaron, and the Numbering of the People with a novel realism.*

STONE MASTERPIECES *The faces and drapery in the 13th-century carved stone figures on Chartres Cathedral are masterpieces of Gothic sculpture.*

---

tance, as in a letter or article, written in a light style. **2.** A person who habitually talks about other people and their private affairs, especially in a disparaging way. **3.** *Archaic.* A close woman friend or companion. **4.** *Archaic.* A godparent.
~*intr.v.* **gossiped, -siping, -sips.** To engage in or spread gossip. —See Synonyms at **speak.** [Middle English *godsib,* godparent, godchild, close friend, Old English *godsibb* : *god,* GOD + *sibb,* kinsman.] —**gos·sip·er** *n.* —**gos·sip·y** *adj.*

gossip column *n.* A newspaper column that gives news of the private lives of famous people.

gos·sip·mong·er (gŏs′ĭp-mŭng′gər, -mŏng′gər) *n.* A person who spreads gossip.

gos·soon (gŏ-sōon′) *n. Irish.* A boy; especially, a servant boy. [French *garçon,* GARÇON.]

got. Past tense and past participle of **get.**

Gö·te·borg (yœ′tə-bôr′yə). Also **Goth·en·burg** (gŏth′ən-bûrg′, gŏt′n-). Chief port and second-largest city in Sweden, at the mouth of the Göta River on the southwest coast of the country and connected to Stockholm by the Göta Canal. The city has major oil refineries.

Goth (gŏth) *n.* **1.** A member of the Germanic people that originally occupied a region between the Baltic and the Black Sea, and that invaded the Roman Empire in the early centuries of the Christian era. See **Ostrogoth, Visigoth. 2.** An uncivilized or barbaric person. [Middle English *Gothes,* Goths, from Late Latin *Gothī* (singular *Gothus*), from Gothic *Gutans*† (unattested), tribal name.]

Goth. Gothic.

Goth·a (gō'tä). Town in central Germany. It was once the residence of the dukes of Saxe-Coburg-Gotha. The *Almanach de Gotha,* published here (1761–1944), was an annual record of Europe's royal and aristocratic houses.

Goth·am[1] (gŏth'əm). Village of southern Nottinghamshire in England whose early inhabitants, the Wise Men of Gotham, are reputed by legend to have feigned stupidity in order to discourage King John from establishing a residence here.

Gotham[2]. New York City. Used as a nickname. **—Goth·am·ite** *n.*

Gothenburg. See **Göteborg.**

Goth·ic (gŏth'ĭk) *adj. Abbr.* **Goth. 1. a.** Of or pertaining to the Goths or their language. **b.** Germanic; Teutonic. **2.** Of or pertaining to the Middle Ages; medieval. **3. a.** Of, pertaining to, or designating an architectural style prevalent in western Europe from the 12th to the 16th century, and characterized by pointed arches, rib vaulting, and flying buttresses. **b.** Of or pertaining to painting, sculpture, or other art forms prevalent in northern Europe from the 12th to the 16th century. **c.** Of or relating to an architectural style derived from medieval Gothic. **4.** *Sometimes* **gothic.** Of, pertaining to, or reminiscent of a literary style of fiction prevalent in the late 18th and early 19th centuries that emphasized the grotesque, mysterious, and desolate: *a Gothic novel.* **5.** *Sometimes* **gothic.** Barbarous; uncivilized; primitive; crude.
∼*n. Abbr.* **Goth. 1.** The extinct East Germanic language of the Goths. **2.** Gothic art or architecture. **3.** *Often* **gothic.** *Printing.* **a.** A typeface, **black letter** *(see).* **b.** A typeface, **sans serif** *(see).* **—Goth·i·cal·ly** *adv.*

Gothic arch *n. Architecture.* A pointed arch, especially one with a jointed apex.

Goth·i·cism (gŏth'ĭ-sĭz'əm) *n.* **1.** Use of, imitation of, or an instance of Gothic style, as in architecture, art, or literature. **2.** A barbarous or crude manner or style.

Goth·i·cize (gŏth'ĭ-sīz') *tr.v.* **-cized, -cizing, -cizes.** To make Gothic.

Got·land or **Goth·land** or **Gott·land** (gŏt'lənd). The largest Swedish island, in the Baltic Sea to the east of the mainland. By tradition it is the original homeland of the Goths.

GO TO *n. Computer Science.* An instruction in programming language for the computer to leave the current sequence of instructions for another sequence at another point in the program.

got·ten. Past participle of **get.**

Göt·ter·däm·mer·ung (gərt'ər-dĕm'ə-rŭng') *n.* **1.** *Germanic Mythology.* The process of destruction of the ancient gods by the forces of evil. Also called "Twilight of the Gods." **2.** Any failure or slow destruction of some heroic person, magnificent enterprise, or the like.

Göt·ting·en (gœt'ĭng-ən). City in Lower Saxony in central Germany, on the Leine Canal. It is famous for its university (founded 1734) and its influential Society of Sciences.

gouache (gwŏsh, gŏŏ-äsh') *n.* **1.** A method of painting using opaque water colors mixed with a preparation of gum. **2.** An opaque pigment prepared in such a way. **3.** A painting executed with such pigments. [French, from Italian *guazzo,* "puddle," from Latin *aquātiō,* watering, from *aquārī,* to bring water to, from *aqua,* water.]

Gou·da[1] (gou'də, gōō'-). Town in the South Holland province of the Netherlands, at the confluence of the Gouwe and Ijssel rivers. It has the largest market square in Holland.

Gouda[2] *n.* A mild, close-textured, pale yellow cheese made from whole or partially skimmed milk and often covered with a protective coating of wax. [Originally made in GOUDA.]

gouge (gouj) *n.* **1. a.** A chisel with a rounded, troughlike blade. **b.** A surgical instrument resembling this, used to cut and remove bone. **2.** A scooping or digging action, as with a gouge. **3.** A groove, hole, or indentation scooped with or as if with a gouge. **4.** *Informal.* **a.** An act of extortion or swindling. **b.** A large amount of money extorted. **5.** *Geology.* A deposit of clay, rock particles, or the like, in a fault or vein.
∼*tr.v.* **gouged, gouging, gouges. 1.** To cut or scoop out with or as if with a gouge: *gouge a pattern in the sand.* **2.** To force out: *gouged out his eyes.* **3.** *Informal.* **a.** To extort from. **b.** To swindle. [Middle English *gouge,* from Old French, from Late Latin *gubia,* perhaps from Celtic, akin to Old Irish *gulban*†.] **—goug·er** *n.*

gou·lash (gōō'läsh, -lăsh) *n.* A stew of beef, lamb, or veal and vegetables, highly seasoned with paprika. Also called "Hungarian goulash." [Hungarian *gulyás (hus),* "herdsman('s meat)," from *gulya,* herd.]

Goul·burn (gōl'bərn). City in New South Wales in southeast Australia. Founded in 1833, it has two cathedrals and is a marketing center that serves a prosperous agricultural region.

Gould (gōōld), **Glenn** (1932–82). Canadian pianist. He first played with the Toronto Symphony Orchestra when he was 14 and was acclaimed for his performances of Bach, Beethoven, and Brahms.

goun·dou (gōōn'dōō') *n. Medicine.* A condition occurring in the tropics as a complication of yaws, in which bony swellings occur on either side of the nose. [From a West African name.]

Gou·nod (gōō-nō'), **Charles François** (1818–93). French composer. He wrote symphonies, oratorios, and songs but is mainly remembered for the operas *Faust* (1859) and *Romeo and Juliet* (1867) and for his church music.

gou·ra·mi (gōō-rä'mē, gŏŏr'ə-mē) *n., pl.* **-mis** or collectively **gourami.** Any of various freshwater fishes of the family Anabantidae, of southeastern Asia, many species of which are brightly colored and popular in home aquariums. *Osphronemus goramy* has been widely introduced and bred as a food fish. [Malay *gurāmi.*]

gourd (gôrd, gōrd, gŏŏrd) *n.* **1.** Any of several vines of the family Cucurbitaceae, such as the **bottle gourd** *(see),* related to the pumpkin, squash, and cucumber, and bearing fruits with a hard rind. **2.** The fruit of such a vine, such as a calabash, often of irregular and unusual shape. **3.** The dried and hollowed-out shell of one of these fruits, used as a drinking vessel or utensil. **4.** A small gourd-shaped bottle. [Middle English *gourde,* from Old French, from Latin *cucurbita,* probably of Mediterranean origin.]

gourde (gŏŏrd) *n. Abbr.* **g., G., gde. 1.** The basic monetary unit of Haiti, equal to 100 centimes. See feature at **currency. 2.** A coin worth one gourde. [French, feminine of *gourd,* heavy, from Latin *gurdus*†, heavy, dull, stupid.]

gour·mand, gor·mand (gŏŏr'mənd; *French* gōōr-mäɴ') *n.* A person who delights in eating well and heartily. [Middle English *gourmaunt,* glutton, from Old French *gourmand, gourmant*†.]

gour·mand·ise (gŏŏr'mən-dēz') *n.* Also *rare* **gor·mand·ize** (gôr'-). A taste and relish for good food. [Middle English, from Old French *gourmandise,* from GOURMAND.]

gour·met (gŏŏr-mā'; *French* gōōr-mĕ') *n.* A connoisseur of fine food and drink. Also used adjectivally: *gourmet foods.* [French (influenced in sense by *gourmand*), from Old French *gromet, gourmet*†, wine-taster.]

gout (gout) *n.* **1.** *Pathology.* A disturbance of uric-acid metabolism, occurring predominantly in males, in which deposits of urates accumulate in the joints, especially those of the big toe, and cause arthritic attacks that may become chronic and produce deformity. **2.** A large blob or clot: *"and makes it bleed great gouts of blood"* (Oscar Wilde). [Middle English *goute,* from Old French, "drop" (from the belief that gout was caused by a flowing down of morbid humors), from Latin *gutta*†, drop.]

gout·weed (gout'wēd') *n.* A plant, **ground elder** *(see).*

gout·y (gou'tē) *adj.* **-ier, -iest. 1.** Of, relating to, or resembling gout. **2.** Suffering from or showing the effects of gout. **—gout·i·ly** *adv.* **—gout·i·ness** *n.*

gov. **1.** government. **2.** governor.

Gov. Governor.

gov·ern (gŭv'ərn) *v.* **-erned, -erning, -erns.** —*tr.* **1.** To control the actions or behavior of; guide; direct. **2.** To make and administer public policy for (a political unit); exercise sovereign authority in. **3.** To control the speed or magnitude of; regulate: *a valve governing fuel intake.* **4.** To keep under control; restrain. **5.** To decide; determine: *Chance usually governs the outcome of the game.* **6.** *Grammar.* **a.** To require (a noun or verb) to be in a particular case or mood. **b.** To require the use of (a specified case or mood). —*intr.* **1.** To exercise political authority. **2.** To have or exercise a predominating influence. [Middle English *governen,* from Old French *governer,* from Latin *gubernāre,* to direct, steer, from Greek *kubernan*†.] **—gov·ern·a·ble** *adj.*

gov·ern·ance (gŏv'ər-nəns) *n.* **1.** The act, process, or power of governing; government; authority. **2.** The system of government. **3.** The state of being governed.

gov·ern·ess (gŏv'ər-nĭs) *n.* **1.** A woman employed to educate and train the children of a private household. **2.** *Rare.* A woman who governs.

governing body *n.* A group of people responsible for the administration of a school, college, or similar institution.

gov·ern·ment (gŏv'ərn-mənt) *n. Abbr.* **gov., govt. 1.** The act or process of governing; especially, the administration of public policy in a political unit; political jurisdiction. **2.** The office, function, or authority of one who governs or a governing body. **3.** A system or policy by which a political unit is governed. **4.** Political science. **5.** A governing body or organization. **6.** An area within a single rule; a political unit. **7.** Influence; regulation; determination. **8.** *Grammar.* The affecting of a word's case or mood by another word. **—gov·ern·ment·al** *adj.* **—gov·ern·men·tal·ly** *adv.*

Government Issue *n. Abbr.* **GI, G.I.** Anything issued by the government or a government agency, such as U.S. Army equipment. **—government issue** *adj.*

gov·er·nor (gŭv'ər-nər, gŭv'nər) *n. Abbr.* **gov., Gov. 1.** A person who governs, especially: **a.** An official appointed to govern a colony or territory. **b.** The chief executive of a state in the United States. **2.** The manager or administrative head of an organization, business, or institution. **3.** A military commandant. **4.** *British Informal.* **a.** Used as a form of address, equivalent to *sir,* to a stranger, respected acquaintance, employer, or superior. **b.** One's father. **5.** *Machinery.* A feedback device on a machine or engine used to provide automatic control, as of speed, pressure, or temperature. [Middle English *governour,* from Old French *governeor,* from Latin *gubernātor,* from *gubernāre,* GOVERN.]

governor general *n., pl.* **governors general.** Also *Chiefly British* **gov·er·nor-gen·er·al** (gŭv'ər-nər-jĕn'ər-əl, gŭv'nər-, -jĕn'rəl) *pl.* **governors-general** or **governor-generals.** *Abbr.* **Gov. Gen. 1.** *Often* **Governor General.** The highest-ranking representative of the Crown in some Commonwealth countries or formerly in a British

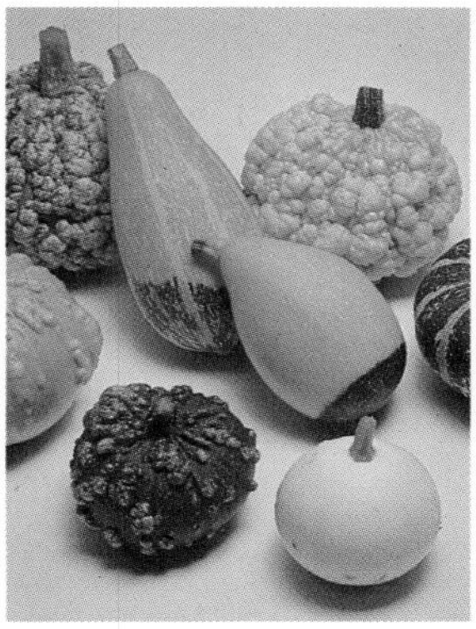

gourd *Gourds are fruit that are related to cucumbers and pumpkins. The dried shells of some species are used as containers for liquids. These are ornamental varieties.*

PRONUNCIATION KEY

ă, pat; ā, pay; âr, care;
ä, father, are; b, bib;
ch, church; d, deed; ĕ, pet;
ē, be; f, fife; g, gag; h, hat;
hw, which; ĭ, pit; ī, pie;
îr, pier; j, judge; k, kick;
l, lid, needle; m, mum;
n, no, sudden; ng, thing;
ŏ, pot; ō, toe; ô, paw, for;
oi, noise; ou, out; ŏŏ, book;
ōō, boot; p, pop; r, roar;
s, sauce; sh, ship, dish;
t, tight; th, thin, path;
th, this, bathe; ŭ, cut; ûr, fur;
v, valve; w, with; y, yes;
z, zebra, size; zh, vision;
ə, about, item, edible,
gallop, circus, peaceful

IN FOREIGN WORDS:

à, *Fr.* ami; œ, *Fr.* feu, *Ger.* schön; ü, *Fr.* tu, *Ger.* über;
KH, *Ger.* ich, *Scot.* loch;
ɴ, *Fr.* bon; y', *Fr.* Compiègne

STRESS MARKS:

Primary stress: '
in·cite' (ĭn-sīt')
Secondary stress: '
in'sight' (ĭn'sīt')

colony. **2.** A governor who has other, subordinate governors under his jurisdiction. **—gov·er·nor·gen·er·al·ship** n.

gov·er·nor·ship (gŭv′ər-nər-shĭp′) n. The office, term, or jurisdiction of a governor.

Gov. Gen. governor general.

govt. government.

gow·an (gou′ən) n. Scottish. A yellow or white wildflower, especially the daisy. [Dialect gollan, from Middle English, probably from Scandinavian; akin to Old Norse gullinn, golden.]

gowk (gôk) n. British Regional. A stupid person; fool. [Middle English gowke, from Old Norse gaukr, a cuckoo, from Germanic gaukaz (imitative).]

gown (goun) n. **1.** Any of various long, loose, flowing garments, such as a dressing gown or surgeon's protective coat. **2.** A long, usually formal, woman's dress. **3.** A distinctive outer robe worn on ceremonial occasions, as by scholars or clergymen. **4.** The academic community of a university town, as distinguished from the townspeople: town and gown. Compare **town.**
~tr.v. **gowned, gowning, gowns.** To dress in or invest with a gown. [Middle English goune, from Old French, from Late Latin gunna†, robe, fur.]

gowns·man (gounz′mən) n., pl. **-men** (-mĭn). One who wears a distinctive gown as a mark of profession or office.

Gow·on (gou′ən), **Yakubu** (1934–). Nigerian army officer and politician. Trained at the Sandhurst Military Academy in England, he took a commission in the Nigerian army (1954), becoming battalion commander (1966). After two coups (1966) he was appointed army commander in chief and head of the new military government. He led the federal forces in their successful war against the secessionist Biafran government (1967–70). He was deposed (1975).

Goy·a y Lu·ci·en·tes (goi′ə ē lо̄о̄-sē-ĕn′tĕs), **Francisco José de** (1746–1828). Spanish painter and etcher. His best portraits, including The Duchess of Alba, were done mostly in the 1790's, his so-called "silver period." The war against France inspired some of his most powerful work, including 65 etchings, The Disasters of the War (1810–14).

G.P. 1. general practitioner. **2.** Grand Prix.

G-par·i·ty (jē′păr′ə-tē) n. Physics. A quantum property of elementary particles that have zero strangeness and baryon number, conserved in strong interactions.

g.p.m. gallons per minute.

GPO 1. general post office. **2.** Government Printing Office.

g.p.s. gallons per second.

GPU, G.P.U. Government Political Administration (Russian Gosudarstvennoye Politicheskoye Upravlenie): a former administrative branch of the Soviet government functioning as a policing and security organization in succession to the **Cheka** (see) and corresponding in broad outline to the later **KGB** (see).

gr. 1. grade. **2.** gram. **3.** gross. **4.** group.

Gr. Greece; Greek.

Graaf·i·an follicle (grä′fē-ən) n. Anatomy. Any of the follicles in the mammalian ovary, containing a maturing ovum. [After Regnier de Graaf (1641–73), Dutch anatomist.]

grab¹ (grăb) v. **grabbed, grabbing, grabs.** —tr. **1.** To take or grasp suddenly; snatch; seize. **2.** To capture or restrain; arrest. **3.** To obtain or appropriate unscrupulously or forcibly. **4.** To consume hurriedly: He grabbed a bite to eat. **5.** Slang. To make an impression on; affect, especially in a positive or favorable way. —intr. To make a snatch: He grabbed for the gun.
~n. **1.** The act of grabbing; a sudden snatch. **2.** Anything grabbed. **3.** A mechanical device for gripping, for example, the jaws of an earth-moving machine. **—up for grabs.** Informal. Available for anyone to take. [Middle Dutch and Middle Low German grabben.] **—grab·ber** n.

grab² n. An Oriental coastal vessel with two or three masts. [Arabic ghurāb, raven, swift galley.]

grab bag n. **1.** A container filled with articles, such as party gifts, to be drawn at random. **2.** Any miscellaneous collection of often valuable items.

grab·ble (grăb′əl) intr.v. **-bled, -bling, -bles. 1.** To feel around with the hands; grope. **2.** To sprawl on the ground on all fours. [Dutch grabbelen, frequentative of Middle Dutch grabben, GRAB (to seize).]

grab·by (grăb′ē) adj. **-bier, -biest.** Inclined to grab; greedy. **—grab·bi·ness** n.

gra·ben (grä′bən) n. A usually elongated depression of the earth's crust between two parallel faults. [German Graben, trench, from Old High German grabo, from graban, to dig.]

grab rope n. A rope for steadying oneself, as on a gangplank or an open deck.

Grac·chus (grăk′əs), **Tiberius Sempronius** (c. 163–133 B.C.) and **Caius Sempronius** (c. 153–121 B.C.), known as "the Gracchi." Roman statesmen. Tiberius was elected tribune of the people in 133. He passed a law to redistribute land but was killed in the same year during a riot. In 123 Caius was elected tribune, and when he proposed granting Roman citizenship to Latins, he too was killed in riots.

grace (grās) n. **1.** Seemingly effortless beauty or charm of movement, form, or proportion. **2.** A characteristic, quality, or accomplishment pleasing for its charm or refinement: social graces. **3.** Skill at avoiding the inept or clumsy course; a sense of fitness or propriety. **4. a.** A disposition to be generous or helpful; goodwill. **b.** Mercy; clemency. **5. a.** A favor rendered by one who need not do so. **b.** Kindly feeling; indulgence. **6.** Temporary immunity from

penalties, granted after a deadline has been passed: a period of grace before a new law is enforced. **7.** Theology. **a.** Divine love and protection bestowed freely upon mankind. **b.** The state of being protected or sanctified by the favor of God. **c.** An excellence or power granted by God; an unmerited gift from God. **8.** A short prayer of blessing or thanksgiving said before or after a meal. **9.** Usually **Grace.** A title of or form of address for a duke, duchess, or archbishop. Used with His, Her, or Your. **10.** Music. A musical embellishment, such as an appoggiatura. **—fall from grace.** To lose the esteem in which one was formerly held, usually as a result of some misconduct. **—in someone's good** (or **bad**) **graces.** In (or out of) favor with; well (or unfavorably) regarded by. **—with (a) good** (or **bad**) **grace.** In a willing (or grudging) manner.
~tr.v. **graced, gracing, graces. 1.** To honor or favor. **2.** To give beauty, elegance, or charm to. **3.** Music. To embellish with grace notes. [Middle English, from Old French, from Latin grātia, pleasure, favor, thanks, from grātus, favorable, pleasing.]

Grace, Princess. See Grace **Kelly.**

grace cup n. **1.** A cup used at the end of a meal, usually after grace, for the final toast. **2.** The final toast.

grace·ful (grās′fəl) adj. Showing grace of movement, style, form, or proportion. **—grace·ful·ly** adv. **—grace·ful·ness** n.

Usage: Graceful and gracious are occasionally confused. Graceful refers to movement, style, or form: a graceful pose/gesture. Gracious refers to a state of mind, or the behavior characteristic of a state of mind, in which kindness, compassion, or warm courtesy feature.

grace·less (grās′lĭs) adj. **1.** Lacking grace; clumsy. **2.** Having no sense of propriety or decency. **—grace·less·ly** adv. **—grace·less·ness** n.

grace note n. Music. **1.** A musical note without melodic, harmonic, or time value, especially an appoggiatura, added as an embellishment. **2.** Any decorative flourish.

Grac·es (grā′sĭz) pl.n. Greek Mythology. Three sister goddesses, Aglaia, Euphrosyne, and Thalia, who dispense charm and beauty. Also called the "Three Graces."

grac·ile (grăs′ĭl) adj. **1.** Gracefully slender. **2.** Rare. Graceful. [Latin gracilis†, slim, slender.] **—gra·cil·i·ty** (grə-sĭl′ə-tē) n.

gra·ci·o·so (grä′shē-ō′sō; Spanish grä-thyō′sō) n., pl. **-sos. 1.** A clown or buffoon in Spanish comedies. **2.** Obsolete. A court favorite. [Spanish, "amusing (person)," clown, from Latin grātiōsus, GRACIOUS.]

gra·cious (grā′shəs) adj. **1.** Characterized by kindness and warm courtesy. **2.** Merciful; compassionate. **3.** Condescendingly courteous; indulgent. **4.** Leisurely; elegant: a gracious dinner. **5.** Obsolete. Fortunate; prosperous. —See Usage note at **graceful.**
~interj. Used to express surprise or wonder. [Middle English, from Old French, from Latin grātiōsus, favorable, pleasing, from Latin grātia, GRACE.] **—gra·cious·ly** adv. **—gra·cious·ness** n.

grack·le (grăk′əl) n. **1.** Any of several New World blackbirds of the family Icteridae, and especially of the genera Quiscalus or Cassidix, having iridescent blackish plumage. Also called "crow blackbird." **2.** Any of several Asian mynas of the genus Gracula, such as the Indian grackle, G. religiosa. [New Latin Gracula, from Latin grāculus, jackdaw.]

grad (grăd) n. Informal. A graduate of a school or college.

grad. 1. grade. **2.** gradient. **3.** graduate; graduated.

grad·a·ble (grād′ə-bəl) adj. **1.** Capable of or subject to being graded. **2.** Linguistics. Of, pertaining to, or designating a word such as hot, warm, or cold, which implicitly refers to a scale or standard and can be modified by very or much, for example, to indicate degree or extent.

gra·date (grā′dāt′) v. **-dated, -dating, -dates.** —intr. To pass imperceptibly from one degree, shade, or tone to another. —tr. **1.** To cause to pass imperceptibly from one degree, shade, or tone to another. **2.** To arrange according to or in grades. [Back-formation from GRADATION.]

gra·da·tion (grā-dā′shən) n. **1.** A series of gradual, successive stages; a systematic progression. **2.** Any of the degrees or stages in such a progression. **3.** Advancement by successive stages, tones, or shades, as from one color to another. **4.** The act of gradating or arranging in grades. **5.** Geology. The process of leveling land by filling in or wearing away existing features. **6.** Linguistics. An ablaut (see). [Latin gradātiō (stem gradātiōn-), from gradus, step, GRADE.] **—gra·da·tion·al** adj. **—gra·da·tion·al·ly** adv.

grade (grād) n. Abbr. **gr., grad. 1.** A stage or degree in a process. **2.** A position in a scale of size or quality, as of eggs or meat. **3.** A group of persons or things all falling within the same limits; a class. **4.** A mark indicating a student's level of accomplishment. **5.** A class at an elementary school, or the pupils in it. **6.** A military, naval, or civil-service rank. **7.** A domestic animal produced by crossbreeding one of purebred stock with one of ordinary stock. **8.** A gradient (slope or degree of slope). **9.** Abbr. **grad.** A unit of angle equal to one hundredth of a right angle. It is indicated by a superscript g: 1ᵍ = 0.9⁰. **—at grade. 1.** On the same level. **2.** At the same degree of inclination. **—make the grade.** Informal. **1.** To succeed; reach a goal. **2.** To meet a standard.
~v. **graded, grading, grades.** —tr. **1.** To arrange in steps or degrees; rank; sort. **2.** To arrange in a series or according to a scale. **3. a.** To determine the quality of (academic work, for example); evaluate. **b.** To give a grade to (a student, for example). **4.** To level or smooth to a desired or horizontal gradient. **5.** To gradate. **6.** To improve the quality of (livestock) by crossbreeding with purebred

stock. Often used with *up.* **7.** To effect a gradual change of shading in (colors or a colored area). —*intr.* To change or progress gradually. [French, from Latin *gradus,* step.]

–grade *suffix.* Indicates progression or movement; for example, **plantigrade, retrograde.** [French, from Latin *-gradus,* stepping, going, from *gradī,* to step, go.]

grade crossing *n.* An intersection of roads, railroad tracks, or a road and a railroad track at the same level. Also *British* "level crossing."

grade point or **grade index** *n.* A point assigned to a course credit, as in a university, that corresponds to the letter grade made in a course.

grade point average or **grade point index** *n.* The average grade earned, as by a student, figured by dividing the grade points earned by the number of credits attempted.

grad·er (grād′ər) *n.* **1.** One that grades. **2.** A machine that smooths a surface to the desired gradient and flatness, especially in road building. **3.** A student in a grade school: *a third grader.*

grade school *n.* An **elementary school** *(see).*

gra·di·ent (grā′dē-ənt) *n. Abbr.* **grad. 1.** An ascending or descending part of a road, railway, or the like; an incline. **2.** The degree of slope measured by the vertical change in height per horizontal distance traveled. **3.** *Physics.* The maximum rate at which a variable physical quantity changes in value per unit change in position. **4.** *Mathematics.* **a.** The slope of the tangent to a curve at a given point. **b.** A vector having coordinate components that are the partial derivatives of a function with respect to its variables. The gradient of a function f is written grad f. or ∇f. ~*adj.* Of a consistent slope. [Perhaps from GRADE.]

gra·din (grā′dĭn; *French* grá-dăn′) *n.* Also **gra·dine** (grə-dēn′). **1.** Any of a series of steps or tiered seats, as in an amphitheater. **2.** A shelf next to an altar, for holding candles or ornaments. [French, from Italian *gradino,* diminutive of *grado,* step, GRADE.]

grad·u·al (grăj′o͞o-əl) *adj.* **1.** Occurring in small stages or degrees or by even, continuous change. **2.** Moderate and regular: *a gradual slope.* ~*n. Roman Catholic Church.* **1.** A book containing liturgical antiphons. **2.** An antiphon sung between the Epistle and the Gospel of the Tridentine Mass. [Middle English, from Medieval Latin *graduālis,* step by step, from Latin *gradus,* step, GRADE.] —**grad·u·al·ly** *adv.* —**grad·u·al·ness** *n.*

grad·u·al·ism (grăj′o͞o-ə-lĭz′əm) *n.* The belief in or policy of advancing toward a goal, especially a political goal, by gradual, often slow stages. —**grad·u·al·ist** *n.* —**grad·u·al·is·tic** *adj.*

grad·u·and (grăj′ə-wănd′) *n. Chiefly British.* A student who is on the point of receiving a degree. [Medieval Latin *graduandus,* gerundive of *graduāre,* to GRADUATE.]

grad·u·ate (grăj′o͞o-āt′) *v.* **-ated, -ating, -ates.** *Abbr.* **grad.** —*intr.* **1.** To be granted an academic degree or diploma. **2.** To change gradually, or by degrees. **3.** To progress to something more advanced: *From being stage manager, she graduated to directing.* —*tr.* **1.** To arrange or divide into categories, steps, or grades. **2.** To divide into marked intervals, especially for use in measurement. **3.** To grant a diploma or degree to. —See Usage note below. ~*n.* (grăj′o͞o-ĭt). *Abbr.* **grad.** **1.** One who has received an academic degree. **2.** A graduated container, such as a beaker or flask. ~*adj.* (grăj′o͞o-ĭt). **1.** Possessing an academic degree or diploma. **2.** Of, pertaining to, or designating studies beyond a bachelor's degree: *graduate courses.* [Middle English *graduaten,* from Medieval Latin *graduāre,* from Latin *gradus,* degree, step, GRADE.] —**grad·u·a·tor** *n.*

Usage: A strict traditionalist would insist that *she was graduated from college* is the only correct usage. But the usage *she graduated from college* is by now entirely acceptable, and the variant without a preposition, as in *she graduated college,* is rapidly gaining ground.

graduate school *n.* A school that offers studies beyond the bachelor's degree.

graduate student *n.* A student at a graduate school, especially one matriculated in a specific department and studying for a specific degree.

grad·u·a·tion (grăj′o͞o-ā′shən) *n.* **1.** The conferring or receipt of an academic degree or diploma marking completion of studies. **2.** A ceremony at which degrees or diplomas are conferred. **3. a.** A division or interval on a graduated scale. **b.** A mark indicating the boundary of such an interval. **4.** An arrangement in or division into stages, intervals, or degrees.

grad·us (grā′dəs) *n., pl.* **-duses. 1.** A dictionary of prosody used as an aid in writing Latin or Greek poetry. **2.** A manual for developing a student's ability, especially a book of musical exercises. [Short for *Gradus ad Parnassum,* "step to Parnassus," dictionary of prosody formerly used in English public schools, from Latin *gradus,* step, GRADE.]

Grae·ae, Grai·ae (grē′ē′) *pl.n. Greek Mythology.* Three female deities personifying old age, who, with only one eye and one tooth among them, guarded their sisters, the Gorgons.

Graecism. Variant of **Grecism.**
Graecize. Variant of **Grecize.**
Graeco-. Variant of **Greco-.**
Graeco-Roman. Variant of **Greco-Roman.**

Graf (gräf) *n., pl.* **Grafen** (gräf′ən). A count. Used as a title of German, Austrian, or Swedish nobility corresponding to the English earl. [German, from Old High German *grāvo.*]

graf·fi·to (grə-fē′tō) *n., pl.* **-ti** (-tē). **1.** *Archaeology.* A crude drawing or inscription scratched on stone, plaster, or some other hard surface. **2.** *Usually* **graffiti.** Any scrawling written or drawn so as to be seen by the public, as on a wall or lavatory door, and often obscene or humorous. [Italian, diminutive of *graffio,* a scratching, from *graffiare,* to scratch, perhaps from *grafio,* a pencil, stylus, from Latin *graphium,* from Greek *graphion,* from *graphein,* to write.]

graft¹ (grăft, gräft) *tr.v.* **grafted, grafting, grafts. 1.** In horticulture: **a.** To unite (a shoot or bud) with a growing plant by insertion or placing in close contact. **b.** To join (a plant or plants) by such union. **2.** *Medicine.* To transplant or implant (tissue, for example) into a bodily part to replace a damaged part or compensate for a defect. **3.** To attach or incorporate, especially in an artificial way. ~*n.* **1.** In horticulture: **a.** A detached shoot or bud united or to be united with a growing plant. **b.** The union or point of union of a detached shoot or bud with a growing plant by insertion or attachment. **c.** A plant produced by such union. **2.** *Medicine.* **a.** Material, especially tissue or an organ, surgically attached to or inserted into a bodily part to replace a damaged part or compensate for a defect. **b.** The procedure of transplanting such material. **c.** The configuration or condition resulting from such a procedure. **c.** Any act or product of attaching or incorporating. [Middle English *grafte, graff,* from Old French *grafe, grefe,* pencil, shoot for grafting (from its pencillike shape), from Latin *graphium.* See **graffito.**] —**graft·er** *n.*

graft² *n.* **1.** The unscrupulous use of one's position to derive profit or advantages; extortion. **2.** Money or an advantage gained or yielded under such circumstances. ~*v.* **grafted, grafting, grafts.** —*tr.* To gain by graft. —*intr.* To practice graft. [Perhaps extended use of GRAFT (insertion, hence "additional activity").] —**graft·er** *n.*

graft·age (grăf′tĭj, gräf′-) *n.* The process and principles of making a horticultural graft.

graft copolymer *n. Chemistry.* A copolymer that has main chains of one type of monomer with side chains of the other monomer.

graft hybrid *n.* A plant produced by grafting in which the tissue of the scion mingles with that of the stock. It is a type of **chimera** *(see).*

gra·ham (grā′əm) *adj.* Made from or consisting of whole-wheat flour. [After Sylvester *Graham* (1794–1851), U.S. vegetarian who urged dietary reform.]

Gra·ham (grā′əm), **Martha** (1894–1991). U.S. ballet dancer, teacher, and choreographer. She made her debut as a dancer in 1920 in Los Angeles and in 1930 founded the Dance Repertory Theatre in New York. Her full-length works include *Appalachian Spring* (1944) and *Clytemnestra* (1958).

Graham, Thomas (1805–69). British chemist. His investigation of gases and liquids led to the formulation of Graham's law. His work on colloids and crystalloids led to his discovery of dialysis.

Graham, William Franklin, known as "Billy" (1918–). U.S. evangelist. Ordained a minister in the Southern Baptist Church in 1939, he conducted his first intensive evangelical campaign in Los Angeles. Since then his evangelical tours have taken him throughout the world.

graham cracker *n.* A slightly sweet, usually rectangular cracker, made of whole-wheat flour.

Gra·hame (grā′əm), **Kenneth** (1859–1932). English writer. He wrote two volumes of autobiography, *The Golden Age* (1895) and *Dream Days* (1898) but is best known for his children's book *The Wind in the Willows* (1908).

Gra·ham Land (grā′əm). A part of the Antarctic Peninsula in Antarctica, bordering the Weddell Sea. Consisting chiefly of icebound rock, it was formerly a dependency of the Falkland Islands and now forms part of the British Antarctic Territory.

Graham's law *n. Physics.* The principle that the rates of diffusion of gases are inversely proportional to the square roots of their densities. Also called "Graham's law of diffusion." [Formulated by Thomas GRAHAM.]

Gra·hams·town (grā′əmz-toun′). Town and naval base in Cape Province in southern South Africa. Founded in 1820, it has two cathedrals and is the site of Rhodes University (established 1904).

Graiae. Variant of **Graeae.**

grail (grāl) *n. Often* **Grail. 1.** The cup or chalice in medieval legend used by Christ at the Last Supper and subsequently the object of many chivalrous quests. Also called "Holy Grail." **2.** The object of a prolonged endeavor. [Middle English *graal,* from Old French, from Medieval Latin *gradālis†,* dish.]

grain (grān) *n.* **1.** A small, hard seed or fruit, especially that produced by a cereal grass such as wheat, barley, rice, or oats. **2.** The seeds of such plants collectively, especially after having been harvested. **3.** Cereal grasses collectively: *a field of grain.* **4.** A relatively small discrete particle or crystalline mass: *a grain of sand.* **5.** *Aerospace.* A mass of solid propellant formed from a number of smaller pieces. **6.** The very smallest amount; a tiny quantity: *a grain of truth.* **7. a.** A unit of weight, one seven-thousandth of a pound in the avoirdupois, Troy, and apothecaries' systems. It is equal to 0.0648 gram. **b.** A metric unit of weight equal to 50 milligrams. It is used in weighing precious stones. In this sense, also called "metric grain." **8. a.** The arrangement, direction, or pattern of the fibrous tissue in wood. **b.** The arrangement, direction, or pattern of muscle fibers or meat. **9. a.** The outer side of a hide or piece of leather from which the hair or fur is removed. **b.** The pattern or markings on this side of leather. **10.** The pattern or markings on the skin. **11.** The pattern produced, as in stone, by the arrangement of

particulate constituents. **12.** The relative size of the particles composing a substance or pattern: *a coarse grain.* **13.** Any painted, stamped, or printed design that imitates the pattern found in wood, leather, or stone. **14.** The direction or texture of fibers in a woven fabric. **15.** *Chemistry.* **a.** A state of fine crystallization. **b.** A small crystalline region in a polycrystalline solid. **16.** Temperament; nature; character. **17.** Any of the particles in a photographic emulsion that determine by their size the degree of the image's resolution. **18.** *Archaic.* Color; tint; hue. **19. a.** Cochineal or kermes. **b.** Red dye made from cochineal or kermes. **c.** Any fast dye. Not in current technical usage. **—against the grain.** In contradiction to one's natural disposition or character.
    ~*v.* **grained, graining, grains.** —*tr.* **1.** To form or cause to form into grains; granulate; crystallize. **2.** To paint, stamp, or print with a design imitating the grain of wood, leather, or stone. **3.** To give a granular or rough texture to. **4.** To remove the hair or fur from (hides) in preparation for tanning. —*intr.* To form into or become grains. [Middle English, from Old French, from Latin *grānum,* seed.] **—grain·er** *n.*
grain alcohol *n.* **Alcohol** *(see).*
grain elevator *n.* **1.** A building equipped with mechanical lifting devices, used for storing grain. **2.** The machine used for lifting grain, typically having an endless belt carrying a number of scoops.
grain·ing (grān'ĭng) *n.* **1.** The pattern of the grain in wood or leather. **2.** The application of an artificial grain or design to a surface, by painting, stamping, or printing. **3.** A fabric or surface patterned in this way. **4.** An artificially produced grainlike pattern.
grains (grānz) *n.* *Usually used with a singular verb.* An iron harpoon with two or more barbed prongs used for spearing fish. [Middle English *grein,* fork, from Old Norse *grein*† branch, twig.]
grains of paradise *pl.n.* **1.** The pungent, aromatic seeds of either of two tropical African plants, *Aframomum melegueta* or *A. granumparadisi,* used medicinally. **2.** The seeds of **cardamom** *(see).*
grain·y (grā'nē) *adj.* **-ier, -iest. 1.** Made of, full of, or resembling grain; granular. **2.** Resembling the grain of wood. **3.** In photography, speckled or poor in definition, as a result of large grains in the emulsion. Said of a photograph or photographic image.
gram¹, gramme (grăm) *n. Abbr.* **g, gm., gr.** A metric unit of mass and weight, equal to one thousandth (10^{-3}) of a kilogram (0.002205 pound). [French *gramme,* from Late Latin *gramma,* a small unit, from Greek, small weight, letter of the alphabet.]
gram² *n.* **1.** Any of several plants, such as a bean, *Phaseolus mungo,* or the chickpea, bearing seeds widely used as food in tropical Asia. **2.** The seeds of such a plant. [Portuguese *grão,* from Latin *grānum,* seed, GRAIN.]
–gram¹ *suffix.* Indicates something written or drawn; for example, **diagram, telegram.** [Latin *-gramma,* something written, from Greek, *-gramma, -grammos,* respectively from *gramma,* letter and *grammē,* line.]
–gram² *suffix.* Indicates a gram, as used in the metric system; for example, **kilogram.** [From GRAM (unit).]
gram. grammar; grammatical.
gra·ma (grā'mə) *n.* Any of various grasses of the genus *Bouteloua,* of western North America and South America, forming dense tufts or mats, and often used as pasturage. Also called "grama grass." [Spanish *grama,* from Latin *grāmina,* plural of *grāmen,* grass.]
gram·a·rye (grăm'ə-rē) *n. Archaic.* Occult learning; magic; necromancy. [Middle English *gramarie,* from Old French *gramaire,* GRAMMAR.]
gram-at·om (grăm'ăt'əm) *n.* The mass in grams of an element numerically equal to the atomic weight.
gram calorie *n.* A **calorie** *(see).*
gra·mer·cy (grə-mûr'sē, grăm'ər-sē) *interj. Archaic.* Used to express surprise or gratitude. [Middle English *gramercye, grand mercy,* great thanks, from Old French *grand merci : grand,* GRAND + *merci,* thanks, MERCY.]
gram flour *n.* Flour made from gram seeds.
gram·i·cid·in (grăm'ə-sīd'n) *n.* An antibiotic produced by a bacterium, *Bacillus brevis,* and used against most Gram-positive pathogenic bacteria. [GRAM-(POSITIVE) + -CID(E) + -IN.]
gra·min·e·ous (grə-mĭn'ē-əs) *adj.* **1.** Of, pertaining to, or characteristic of grasses. **2.** Of or belonging to the family Gramineae, which includes the grasses. [Latin *grāmineus,* grassy, from *grāmen* (stem *grāmin-*), grass.]
gram·i·niv·or·ous (grăm'ə-nĭv'ər-əs) *adj.* Feeding on grasses, grain, or seeds. [Latin *grāmen* (stem *grāmin-*), grass + -VOROUS.]
gram·mar (grăm'ər) *n. Abbr.* **gram. 1.** The study of language as a systematically composed body of words that exhibit discernible regularity of structure (morphology), and their arrangement into sentences (syntax), sometimes including such aspects of language as the pronunciation of words (phonology), the meanings of words (semantics), and the history of words (etymology). **2. a.** The phenomena with which this study deals, as exhibited by a specific language at a specific time. **b.** The system of rules implicit in a language, viewed as a mechanism for generating all sentences possible in that language. **c.** A systematic description or listing of such rules. **3. a.** A normative or prescriptive system of rules setting forth the current standard of usage for teaching or reference purposes. **b.** A book containing such rules: *old-fashioned school grammars.* **4.** Writing or speech judged with regard to the rules or practice of grammar, especially syntax: *bad grammar.* **5. a.** The basic principles of any area of knowledge: *the grammar of music.* **b.** A book dealing with such principles. [Middle English, from Norman

French *gramere,* from Old French *gramaire,* from Latin *grammatica,* from Greek *grammatikē (tekhnē),* "(art) of the letters," from *grammatikos,* pertaining to letters, from *gramma,* letter.]
gram·mar·i·an (grə-mâr'ē-ən) *n.* A specialist in grammar.
grammar school *n.* **1.** An **elementary school** *(see).* **2.** *British.* A secondary preparatory school. **3.** A school stressing the study of classical languages.
gram·mat·i·cal (grə-măt'ĭ-kəl) *adj. Abbr.* **gram. 1.** Of or relating to grammar. **2.** Conforming to the rules of grammar. [Late Latin *grammaticālis,* from Latin *grammaticus,* from Greek *grammatikos,* pertaining to letters. See **grammar.**] **—gram·mat·i·cal·i·ty** (grə-măt'ĭ-kăl'ĭ-tē) *n.* **—gram·mat·i·cal·ly** *adv.*
grammatical gender *n.* The gender assigned to a word in the grammar of a language, as distinct from natural gender or sex. Compare **common gender, natural gender.**
gram·ma·tol·o·gy (grăm'ə-tŏl'ə-jē) *n.* The study and science of systems of graphic script. [French *grammatologie* : Greek *gramma* (stem *grammat-*), written character + -LOGY.] **—gram·ma·to·log·ic** (grăm'ə-tə-lŏj'ĭk), **gram·ma·to·log·i·cal** *adj.* **—gram·ma·tol·o·gist** *n.*
gramme. Variant of **gram** (metric unit).
gram-mo·lec·u·lar weight (grăm'mə-lěk'yə-lər) *n. Chemistry.* A **mole** *(see).* Also called "gram molecule."
Gram-neg·a·tive (grăm'něg'ə-tĭv) *adj. Sometimes* **gram-negative.** Of, pertaining to, or designating a microorganism that does not retain the purple dye used in Gram's method.
gram·o·phone (grăm'ə-fōn') *n.* A record player; phonograph. [Originally a trademark from earlier *graphophone,* inversion of PHONOGRAPH.]
Gram·pi·an Region (grăm'pē-ən). Since 1975 an administrative region of Scotland, bordering the North Sea in the northeast of the country. It incorporates the former counties of Aberdeen, Banff, Kincardine, and Moray. The southwest of the region is mountainous, lying in the Grampians. The terrain descends to arable lowlands in the northeast. Aberdeen is the administrative center.
Gram·pi·ans¹ (grăm'pē-ənz). Also **Grampian Mountains.** Mountain range extending across central Scotland, bounded to the north by the Great Glen and to the south by the central Lowlands. Its highest peak is Ben Nevis (1,344 meters; 4,406 feet), the highest mountain in Britain, and it also includes the peaks of the Cairngorms.
Grampians². A small range of mountains in Victoria state, southeast Australia. It forms the southwesterly extremity of the Great Dividing Range, its highest peak being Mt. William (1,166 meters; 3,827 feet).
Gram-pos·i·tive (grăm'pŏz'ə-tĭv) *adj. Often* **gram-positive.** Of, pertaining to, or designating a microorganism that retains the purple dye used in Gram's method.
gram·pus (grăm'pəs) *n.* **1.** A marine mammal, *Grampus griseus,* related to and resembling the dolphins but lacking a beaklike snout. **2.** Any of several similar cetaceans, such as the **killer whale** *(see).* **3.** *Informal.* A person who is short-winded and breathes heavily. [Middle English *graspeis,* from Old French *graspois, craspois,* from Medieval Latin *craspiscis : cras,* fat, from Latin *crassus* (see **crass**) + *piscis,* fish.]
Gram's method (grămz) *n.* A differential staining technique using the retention or lack of retention of a purple dye to classify bacteria. [After Hans Christian Joachim *Gram* (1855–1938), Danish physician.]
gran (grăn) *n. Informal.* A grandmother.
Gra·na·da (grə-nä'də). A historic city in southern Spain, the capital of Granada province. It has many fine examples of Moorish architecture, including the Alhambra. The city was the capital of the Muslim state of Granada, which, under the Nasrid dynasty (1238–1492), was the last Moorish stronghold in Spain.
gran·a·dil·la (grăn'ə-dĭl'ə) *n.* **1.** Any of various tropical American passionflowers; especially, *Passiflora quadrangularis,* bearing edible fruit. **2.** The egg-shaped, fleshy fruit of such a plant. In this sense, also called "passion fruit." [Spanish, diminutive of *granada,* pomegranate, from Vulgar Latin *granāta* (unattested), from Latin *grānātum,* seedy, from *grānum,* GRAIN.]
Gra·na·dos (grə-nä'dōs), **Enrique** (1867–1916). Spanish composer whose most important compositions were for the piano. Among them was the set called *Goyescas* (1912–14), inspired by paintings of Goya.
gran·a·ry (grăn'ə-rē, grā'nə-) *n., pl.* **-ries. 1.** A building for storing threshed grain. **2.** A region yielding a copious quantity of grain. [Latin *grānārium : grānum,* GRAIN + -ARY.]
granary meal *n.* A mixture of malted wheat and rye, and sometimes wholemeal kernels, used in making *granary bread.* Also called "granary flour."
gran cas·sa (grän'käs'ə) *n., pl.* **gran casse** (käs'ē). *Music.* A bass drum. [Italian, "great drum."]
grand (grănd) *adj.* **grander, grandest. 1.** Large and impressive in size, scope, or extent. **2. a.** Magnificent; splendid. **b.** *Chiefly British Regional.* Wonderful; outstanding; very good. **3.** Rich and sumptuous: *grand furnishings.* **4.** Having higher rank than others of the same specified category: *grand duke.* **5.** The most important; principal; main: *grand ballroom.* **6.** Illustrious; outstanding: *a grand assemblage.* **7. a.** Pretentious. **b.** Calculated to impress: *a grand manner.* **8.** Dignified and admirable: *a grand old man.* **9.** Stately; regal. **10.** Lofty; noble: *a grand purpose.* **11.** *Music.* **a.** Written for a large ensemble. **b.** Complete in form; containing all the movements. **12.** Inclusive; complete: *grand total.*
    ~*n.* **1.** A **grand piano** *(see).* **2.** *Abbr.* **G** *Slang.* A thousand dollars.

[French, from Old French, from Latin *grandis†*, grand, full-grown.] —**grand·ly** *adv.* —**grand·ness** *n.*
    Synonyms: *august, grandiose, imposing, magnificent, majestic, stately.*

grand– *prefix.* Indicates a family relationship or relative one generation removed from the relative specified; for example, **grandson.** [French, rendering Latin *magnus* in kinship terms of ascent (for example, *amita magna, grand-tante*), later extended in English to terms of descent as well (for example, *grandson,* but French *petit-fils*).]

gran·dam (grăn′dăm, -dəm) *n.* Also **gran·dame** (-dām′, -dəm). **1.** A grandmother. **2.** An old woman. [Middle English *graundam,* from Norman French *graund dame.* See **grand, dame.**]

grand-aunt (grănd′ănt′, -änt′) *n.* A **great-aunt** (*see*).

Grand Banks. A submerged plateau, rising from the continental shelf, off southeastern Newfoundland, Canada. It is *c.* 480 kilometers (300 miles) long and 640 kilometers (400 miles) wide.

Grand Canal. 1. Canal in China, longest in the world, extending *c.* 1,610 kilometers (1,000 miles) from Beijing to Hangzhou. It was begun in the 6th century B.C., and construction continued for 2,000 years. **2.** The principal canal of Venice, Italy, a waterway in the shape of an *S* that passes through the heart of the city.

Grand Canyon. A vast ravine of the Colorado River in northwestern Arizona. The river's course has cut a canyon 451 kilometers (280 miles) long, exposing multicolored tiers of rock that have been spectacularly eroded by the weather. The canyon is at some points over 1.6 kilometers (1 mile) deep. The Grand Canyon, set aside by the U.S. government in 1908 as a national monument, was expanded in 1919 and designated **Grand Canyon National Park** (272,798 hectares; 673,575 acres). The park contains the most spectacular part of the canyon. **Grand Canyon National Monument** (80,303 hectares; 198,280 acres) is a primitive area adjoining the park on the west.

grand·child (grănd′chīld′) *n., pl.* **-children** (-chĭl′drən). A child of a son or daughter.

Grand Cou·lee Dam (kōō′lē). A major dam on the Columbia River, in north-central Washington State. The reservoir has a capacity of 11,600 million cubic meters (15,080 million cubic yards) and is used for irrigation, hydroelectricity, and flood control.

grand·dad (grăn′dăd) *n. Informal.* A grandfather.

grand·dad·dy (grăn′dăd′ē) *n., pl.* **-dies.** *Informal.* **1.** A grandfather. **2.** An originator or pre-eminent figure: *the granddaddy of them all.*

grand·daugh·ter (grăn′dô′tər) *n.* The daughter of a son or daughter.

grand duchess *n. Abbr.* **G.D. 1.** The wife or widow of a grand duke. **2.** A woman who is sovereign of a grand duchy. **3.** The daughter of a czar or of one of his male descendants.

grand duchy *n. Abbr.* **G.D.** A territory ruled by a grand duke or a grand duchess.

grand duke *n. Abbr.* **G.D. 1.** A nobleman who is below a king in rank and is sovereign of a grand duchy. **2.** A son or grandson of a czar.

grande dame (grän′dăm, gränd-dăm′) *n., pl.* **grandes dames** (*pronounced as singular*). *French.* A woman revered as an authority or leading figure in her group or profession.

gran·dee (grăn-dē′) *n.* **1.** A nobleman of the highest rank in Spain or Portugal. **2.** A person of eminence or high rank. [Spanish and Portuguese *grande,* "great (one)," from Latin *grandis,* GRAND.]

gran·deur (grăn′jər, -jŏŏr) *n.* **1.** Greatness; splendor: *"The world is charged with the grandeur of God"* (Gerard Manley Hopkins). **2.** Personal dignity or proud bearing, often of an unwarranted, self-important kind. [Middle English, from Old French, from *grand,* GRAND.]

grand·fa·ther (grănd′fä′thər) *n.* **1.** The father of a mother or father. **2.** A forefather; ancestor.

grandfather clause *n.* A clause in the constitutions of several Southern states prior to 1915, exempting from poll taxes and property and literacy requirements lineal descendants of persons who were registered voters before 1867.

grandfather clock *n.* A pendulum clock enclosed in a tall, narrow cabinet. Also called **"longcase clock."**

grand·fa·ther·ly (grănd′fä′thər-lē) *adj.* **1.** Characteristic of or befitting a grandfather. **2.** Having the qualities of a grandfather; kindly; indulgent; benevolent.

Grand Gui·gnol (grän′gēn-yōl′) *n.* **1.** A short, horrifying stage play. **2.** A style typical of or resembling such a play in being sensational, violent, or macabre, often in a deliberately stylized way. [After *Le Grand Guignol,* a theater in Montmartre, Paris, that specialized in such plays.] —**Grand-Gui·gnol** *adj.*

gran·dil·o·quence (grăn-dĭl′ə-kwəns) *n.* Pompous or bombastic speech or expression. [Latin *grandiloquus,* speaking loftily : *grandis,* GRAND + *loquī,* to speak.] —**gran·dil·o·quent** *adj.* —**gran·dil·o·quent·ly** *adv.*

gran·di·ose (grăn′dē-ōs′, grăn′dē-ōs′) *adj.* **1.** Characterized by greatness of scope or intent; grand. **2.** Characterized by feigned or affected grandeur; pompous. —See Synonyms at **grand.** [French, from Italian *grandioso,* from *grande,* great, grand, from Latin *grandis,* GRAND.] —**gran·di·ose·ly** *adv.* —**gran·di·os·i·ty** (grăn′dē-ŏs′ə-tē), **gran·di·ose·ness** *n.*

gran·di·o·so (grän′dē-ō′sō) *adv. Music.* In a grand and noble style. Used as a direction. [Italian, GRANDIOSE.] —**gran·di·o·so** *adj.*

grand jury *n. Law.* A jury of 12 to 23 persons convened in private session to evaluate accusations against persons charged with crime and to determine whether the evidence warrants bringing an indictment. Compare **petit jury.**

Grand Lama *n.* Either of two senior lamas, the **Dalai Lama** or the **Panchen Lama** (*both of which see*).

grand larceny *n.* The theft of property of a value exceeding the amount constituting **petit larceny** (*see*).

grand·ma (grănd′mä′, grăn′mä′, grăm′mä′, grăm′ə) *n.* Also **grand·ma·ma** (grănd′mə-mä′, -mä′mə). *Informal.* A grandmother.

grand mal (grän mäl′) *n.* A form of epilepsy characterized by severe seizures involving spasms and loss of consciousness. Compare **petit mal.** [French, "great illness" : GRAND + *mal,* illness, from Old French, bad, ill, from Latin *malus.*]

Grandma Moses. See Anna Mary Robertson **Moses.**

grand master *n.* **1.** Often **Grand Master.** In chess, an **International Grand Master** (*see*). **2.** Often **Grand Master.** A title of or form of address for the head of any of various private and usually secret organizations, such as the Freemasons or Templars.

grand·moth·er (grănd′mŭth-ər) *n.* **1.** The mother of a father or mother. **2.** A female ancestor.

grand·moth·er·ly (grănd′mŭth′ər-lē) *adj.* **1.** Characteristic of or befitting a grandmother. **2.** Having the qualities of a grandmother; solicitous; indulgent.

grand·neph·ew (grănd′něf′yōō, -něv′yōō, grăn′-) *n.* A **great-nephew** (*see*).

grand·niece (grănd′nēs, grăn′-) *n.* A **great-niece** (*see*).

Grand Old Man *n. Abbr.* **G.O.M.** A man revered as a figure of long-standing eminence in his field.

Grand Old Party *n. Abbr.* **G.O.P.** The Republican Party.

grand opera *n.* A serious or melodramatic drama having the entire text set to music.

grand·pa (grănd′pä′, grăm′pä′, grăm′pə) *n.* Also **grand·pa·pa** (grănd′pə-pä′, -pä′pə). *Informal.* A grandfather.

grand·par·ent (grănd′pâr′ənt, grăn′-) *n.* A parent of a mother or father; a grandmother or grandfather.

grand piano *n.* A piano having the strings strung in a horizontal harp-shaped frame supported usually on three legs and ranging in size from the baby grand to the concert grand. Compare **upright piano.**

Grand Prix (grän prē′, grän prē′) *n., pl.* **Grands Prix** or **Grand Prixes** (prēz′, prē′) *Abbr.* **G.P. 1.** Any of a series of international competitive races for sports cars of specific engine size over an exacting course, and counting toward the award of the driver's world championship each year. **2.** Any of various other major races, as in cycling or horseracing, held annually. [French, big prize.]

Grand Rap·ids (răp′ĭdz). A city of southwest-central Michigan, on the Grand River. Founded in 1826, it developed as a lumber center and became famous for the manufacture of high-quality furniture, still a major industry.

grand sherif *n.* See **sherif** (sense 2).

grand siè·cle (grän sē-ěk′lə) *n. French.* The 17th century in France with reference to the arts, especially the classical period during the reign of Louis XIV. [Literally, "great age."]

grand·sire (grănd′sĭr′, -sər) *n. Archaic.* **1.** A grandfather. **2.** A male ancestor; forefather. **3.** An old man.

grand slam *n.* **1.** In bridge and other card games, the winning of all the tricks during the play of one hand. **2.** In various sports, especially tennis and golf, the winning of all major events in a particular series or season. **3.** *Baseball.* A home run hit when three runners are on base.

grand·son (grănd′sŭn′, grăn′-) *n.* The son of a son or daughter.

grand·stand (grănd′stănd′, grăn′-) *n.* **1.** A roofed stand for spectators at a sports ground or race course, usually offering the best view and having the most expensive seats. **2.** The spectators seated in such a stand.

  ~*intr.v.* **-standed, -standing, -stands.** To perform ostentatiously so as to impress an audience. —**grand·stand·er** *n.*

grandstand play *n.* A sports play or other action performed ostentatiously to impress onlookers.

grandstand view *n.* An unobstructed view.

Grand Te·ton National Park (tē′tŏn′, tēt′n). Park, *c.* 125,800 hectares (310,440 acres), in northwestern Wyoming. It encompasses the most scenic portion of the snow-covered Teton Range, including its highest elevation, Grand Teton (*c.* 5,000 meters; 13,770 feet). The park has lakes, several glaciers, and a great variety of wildlife.

grand tour *n.* **1.** Formerly, an extended tour of continental Europe considered as a part of the education of young men of the English upper class. **2.** *Informal.* A comprehensive tour or inspection.

grand·un·cle (grănd′ŭng′kəl) *n.* A **great-uncle** (*see*).

grange (grānj) *n.* **1. Grange. a.** The Patrons of Husbandry, an association of farmers founded in the United States in 1867. **b.** One of its branch lodges. **2.** *British.* A farm; especially, the residence and attached farm buildings of the farmer. **3.** A feudal farm building used for storing grain paid as tithes. **4.** *Archaic.* A granary. [Middle English, from Old French, from Medieval Latin *grānica,* from Latin *grānum,* GRAIN.]

grang·er (grān′jər) *n.* A member of a grange.

grang·er·ize (grān′jə-rīz′) *tr.v.* **-ized, -izing, -izes. 1.** To illustrate (a book) with drawings, prints, or engravings taken from other books. **2.** To mutilate (a book) by clipping out its illustrative material for such use. [After J. *Granger* (1723–1776), English biographer who published (1769) his *Biographical History of England* with blank pages where the reader could insert such illustrations.] —**grang·er·ism, grang·er·i·za·tion** *n.* —**grang·er·iz·er** *n.*

Grand Canyon *The great gorge of the Colorado River, in Arizona, has been formed by the river cutting its way down through the rock as the land around it rose.*

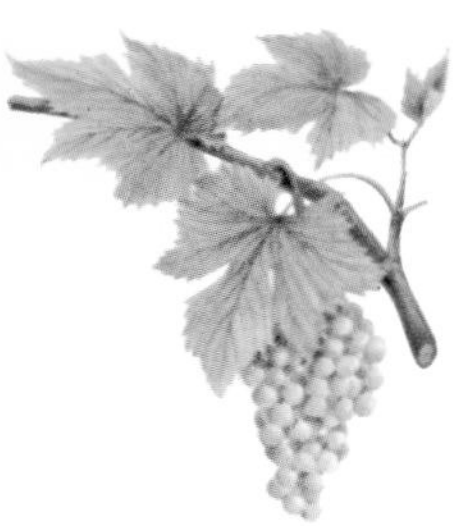

grape *Vines today are associated with warm and sunny climates, but in the Middle Ages, grapes were grown outdoors as far north as Yorkshire, England; and exploring Vikings found them on the North American coast somewhere between New England and Nova Scotia.*

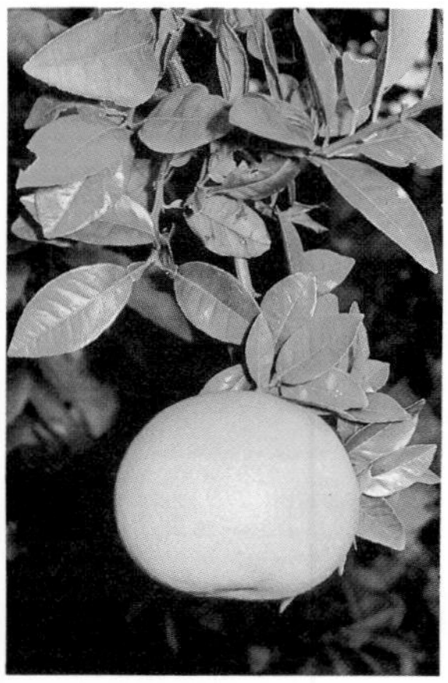

grapefruit *A segmented fruit originally from the Caribbean. As a source of vitamin C it is surpassed only by the orange and lemon.*

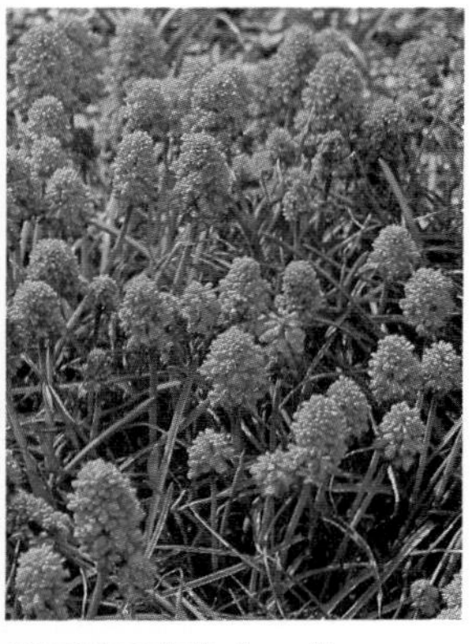

grape hyacinth *A small spring-blooming plant of the lily family.*

grani– *prefix.* Indicates grain; for example, **granivorous, graniform.** [Latin *grāni-*, from *grānum,* GRAIN.]

gra·nif·er·ous (grə-nĭf′ər-əs) *adj.* Bearing grain. [Latin *grānifer* : GRANI- + -FER.]

gran·i·form (grăn′ə-fôrm′) *adj.* Resembling a grain in form. [GRANI- + -FORM.]

gra·ni·ta (grə-nē′tə) *n.* A coarse-textured water ice. [Italian, "grained (ice)."]

gran·ite (grăn′ĭt) *n.* **1.** A common, coarse-grained, hard, and igneous rock consisting chiefly of quartz, orthoclase or microcline, and often mica, used in monuments and for building. **2.** Unyielding endurance; steadfastness; firmness. [Italian *granito,* "grained," from the past participle of *granire,* to impart a grained surface to, from *grano,* grain, from Latin *grānum,* GRAIN.] **—gra·nit·ic** (grə-nĭt′ĭk), **gran·it·oid** *adj.*

granite paper *n.* A paper containing a low proportion of colored mottling fibers.

gran·ite·ware (grăn′ĭt-wâr′) *n.* **1.** Enameled iron utensils. **2.** Earthenware with a speckled glaze resembling granite.

gra·niv·o·rous (grə-nĭv′ər-əs) *adj.* Feeding on grain and seeds. [GRANI- + -VOROUS.] **—gran·i·vore** (grăn′ə-vôr′, -vōr′) *n.*

gran·ny, gran·nie (grăn′ē) *n., pl.* **-nies. 1.** *Informal.* A grandmother. **2.** An old woman. **3.** A fussy or finicky person. **4.** *Southern U.S.* A midwife. [From obsolete *grannam,* variant of GRANDAM.]

granny glasses *pl.n.* A pair of small, round glasses with gold or steel rims.

granny knot *n.* Also **granny's knot.** A knot like a reef knot but with the second tie crossed incorrectly so that it readily comes undone. [Originally a sailor's disparaging term for such a knot.]

Granny Smith *n.* A variety of apple with a green skin and hard, crisp flesh, eaten cooked or raw.

grano– *prefix.* Indicates: **1.** Of or like granite; for example, **granolith. 2.** Granular; for example, **granophyre.** [German, from *Granit,* granite, from Italian *granito,* GRANITE.]

gran·o·di·o·rite (grăn′ō-dī′ə-rīt′) *n.* A coarse-grained acid igneous rock, intermediate between granite and diorite. It contains almost twice as much plagioclase as orthoclase.

gra·no·la (grə-nō′lə) *n.* Rolled oats mixed with various ingredients, such as dried fruit, brown sugar, and nuts, eaten especially as a breakfast cereal. [Originally a trademark.]

gran·o·lith (grăn′ə-lĭth′) *n.* A paving stone of crushed granite and cement. [GRANO- + -LITH.] **—gran·o·lith·ic** *adj.*

gran·o·phyre (grăn′ə-fīr′) *n.* A grained granite porphyry having a groundmass with irregular intergrowths of quartz and feldspar. [German *Granophyr* : GRANO- + *Porphyr,* porphyry, from Medieval Latin *porphyrium,* PORPHYRY.] **—gran·o·phyr·ic** (grăn′ə-fīr′ĭk) *adj.*

Gran Pa·ra·di·so (grän′ pär′ə-dē′zō). The highest mountain entirely within Italy, in the Alps near Aosta. It rises to 4,061 meters (13, 323 feet).

Gran Qui·vi·ra National Monument (grän′ kĭ-vîr′ə). Area of 180 hectares (451 acres) in central New Mexico, including ruins of a Spanish mission and Indian pueblos.

grant (grănt, gränt) *tr.v.* **granted, granting, grants. 1.** To allow to have; consent to the fulfillment of: *grant a wish.* **2.** To permit or accord, as a favor or privilege: *grant a kiss.* **3. a.** To bestow; confer: *grant aid.* **b.** To transfer (property) by a deed; convey. **4.** To concede; acknowledge. **—take for granted. 1.** To consider as true or proven. **2.** To accept as being likely or probable; anticipate correctly. **3.** To accept the benefit of without due acknowledgment. ~*n.* **1.** The act of granting. **2.** Something granted. **3.** *Law.* A transfer of property by deed. **4.** One of several tracts of land in New Hampshire, Maine, and Vermont originally granted to an individual or group. —See Synonyms at **bonus.** [Middle English *graunten,* from Old French *gr(e)anter, creanter,* to insure, guarantee, from Vulgar Latin *crēdentāre* (unattested), from Latin *crēdēns* (stem *crēdent-*), present participle of *crēdere,* to believe, trust.] **—grant·a·ble** *adj.* **—grant·er** *n.*

Grant (grănt), **Cary,** stage name of Archibald Leach (1904–87). U.S. film actor, born in England. In 1933 he played his first important role opposite Mae West in *She Done Him Wrong* and remained in films until 1969. His most famous films include *The Philadelphia Story* (1940), *Arsenic and Old Lace* (1944), *To Catch a Thief* (1955), and *North by Northwest* (1959).

Grant, Ulysses Simpson, originally Hiram Ulysses Grant (1822–85). 18th U.S. president and military commander. With the Illinois Volunteers he captured Fort Henry and Fort Donelson (1862), the first major Unionist victories in the Civil War, and after the victorious Vicksburg campaign (1862–63) he was made commander in chief of the Union army. He won the 1868 presidential election as the Republican candidate and was re-elected in 1872.

grant·ee (grăn-tē′, grän-) *n. Law.* One to whom a grant is made.

grant-in-aid (grănt′ĭn-ād′) *n., pl.* **grants-in-aid.** A grant made by a government or private organization to a lower level of government or local authority for the funding of public works, educational programs, or the like.

grant of probate *n. Law.* Authority given by a court to an executor to deal with the estate of a deceased person as provided for by the will.

gran·tor (grăn′tər, grăn′-) *n. Law.* One who makes a grant.

grants·man·ship (grănts′mən-shĭp′) *n.* The art of obtaining grants-in-aid. [GRANT + (GAME)SMANSHIP.]

gran·u·lar (grăn′yə-lər) *adj.* **1.** Composed of or appearing to be composed of granules or grains. **2.** Grainy. **—gran·u·lar·i·ty** *n.* **—gran·u·lar·ly** *adv.*

gran·u·late (grăn′yə-lāt′) *v.* **-lated, -lating, -lates.** —*tr.* **1.** To form into grains or granules. **2.** To make rough and grainy. —*intr.* **1.** To become granular or grainy. **2.** *Physiology.* To undergo granulation. **—gran·u·la·tive** *adj.* **—gran·u·la·tor, gran·u·lat·er** *n.*

gran·u·la·tion (grăn′yə-lā′shən) *n.* **1. a.** The act or process of granulating. **b.** The condition or appearance of being granulated. **2.** *Physiology.* **a.** The formation of small, fleshy, beadlike protuberances on the surface of a wound while healing. **b.** Any of these protuberances. Also called "granulation tissue."

gran·ule (grăn′yo͞ol) *n.* **1.** A small grain or pellet; a particle. **2.** *Astronomy.* Any of the smallest transient, brilliant markings visible in the photosphere of the sun. [Late Latin *grānulum,* diminutive of *grānum,* GRAIN.]

gran·u·lite (grăn′yə-līt′) *n.* A granular metamorphic rock often banded in appearance and composed chiefly of feldspar, quartz, and garnet. [GRANUL(E) + -ITE.] **—gran·u·lit·ic** (grăn′yə-lĭt′ĭk) *adj.*

gran·u·lo·cyte (grăn′yə-lō-sīt′) *n.* Any of a group of white blood cells having granules in their cytoplasm. [From GRANULE + -CYTE.] **—gran·u·lo·cyt·ic** (grăn′yə-lō-sĭt′ĭk) *adj.*

gran·u·lo·ma (grăn′yə-lō′mə) *n., pl.* **-mas** or **-mata** (-mə-tə). A mass of inflamed granulation tissue, usually associated with ulcerated infections. [New Latin : GRANUL(E) + -OMA.] **—gran·u·lom·a·tous** (grăn′yə-lŏm′ə-təs) *adj.*

gran·u·lose (grăn′yə-lōs′) *adj.* Having a surface covered with granules. [GRANUL(E) + -OSE.]

Gran·ville-Bark·er (grăn′vĭl′bär′kər), **Harley** (1877–1946). British actor, producer, dramatist, and critic. He was co-manager of the Royal Court Theatre (1904–07) and producer of a famous series of Shakespeare productions at the Savoy Theatre (1912–14). He is best remembered today for his drama criticism, especially the *Prefaces to Shakespeare* in six volumes (1927–47).

grape (grāp) *n.* **1.** Any of numerous woody vines of the genus *Vitis*; especially, *V. vinifera,* bearing clusters of edible fruit, and widely cultivated in many subspecies and varieties. Also called "grapevine." **2.** The fleshy, smooth-skinned, purple, red, or green fruit of such a vine, eaten raw or dried, and widely used in winemaking. **3.** Grapeshot. **—the grape.** Wine. [Middle English, from Old French, bunch of grapes, hook, from Germanic.] **—grap·ey, grap·y** *adj.*

grape fern *n.* Any of various ferns of the genus *Botrychium,* having a fertile frond bearing small, grapelike clusters of spore cases. One species, *B. lunaria,* is also called "moonwort."

grape·fruit (grāp′fro͞ot′) *n.* **1.** An evergreen tropical or semitropical tree, *Citrus paradisi,* cultivated for its edible fruit. **2.** The large, round fruit of this tree, having a yellow rind, or occasionally a pink and yellow rind, with a juicy, somewhat acid pulp. Also called "pomelo." [So called because the fruit grows in clusters.]

grape hyacinth *n.* Any of various plants of the genus *Muscari,* native to Eurasia, having narrow leaves and dense, spike-shaped clusters of rounded, usually blue flowers.

grape ivy *n.* An evergreen climbing shrub, *Rhoicissus rhomboidea,* native to Africa but widely grown as a house plant for its ornamental foliage.

grap·er·y (grā′pə-rē) *n., pl.* **-ies.** A building or plantation where grapes are grown.

grapes *n. Used with a singular verb.* An abnormal growth resembling a bunch of grapes on the pastern or fetlock of a horse.

grape·shot (grāp′shŏt′) *n.* A cluster of small iron balls formerly used as a cannon charge. [From its resemblance to a cluster of grapes.]

grape·stone (grāp′stōn′) *n.* A seed of a grape.

grape sugar *n.* **Dextrose** *(see).*

grape·vine (grāp′vīn′) *n.* **1.** A vine on which grapes grow. **2.** An informal, often secret means of transmitting information, gossip, or rumor from person to person: *heard it on the grapevine.* **3.** An information source.

graph (grăf, gräf) *n.* **1.** A drawing that expresses a relationship, often functional, between two sets of numbers as a set of points having coordinates that are plotted from a pair of axes and are determined by the relationship between the two sets. **2.** Any pictorial device, such as a pie chart or bar graph, used to display numerical relationships. Also called "chart." **3.** A representation of a quantity, as of a complex number, by a geometric object such as a point in a plane. **4.** A visual representation, such as a letter, of a phoneme or other speech unit.
~*tr.v.* **graphed, graphing, graphs. 1.** To represent by a graph. **2.** To plot (a function) on a graph. [Short for *graphic formula;* sense 4, from Greek *graphē,* writing.]

–graph *suffix.* Indicates: **1.** An apparatus that writes or records; for example, **telegraph, seismograph. 2.** Something drawn or written; for example, **lithograph, monograph.** [French *-graphe,* from Latin *-graphum,* from Greek *-graphon,* neuter of *-graphos,* written, from *graphein,* to write.]

graph·eme (grăf′ēm′) *n.* **1.** A letter of an alphabet. **2.** The sum of letters and letter combinations that represent a single phoneme. [Greek *graphēma,* letter, from *graphein,* to write.] **—gra·phe·mic** *adj.* **—gra·phe·mi·cal·ly** *adv.*

–grapher *suffix.* Indicates: **1.** A person who writes about or is skilled in a specified subject; for example, **geographer. 2.** One who employs a specified means to write, draw, or record; for example,

stenographer. [Late Latin *-graphus,* from Greek *-graphos,* from *graphein,* to write.]

graph·ic (grăf′ĭk) *adj.* Also **graph·i·cal** (-ĭ-kəl). **1.** Of or pertaining to written or pictorial representation. **2.** Of, pertaining to, or represented by or as if by a graph. **3.** Described in vivid detail; clearly outlined or set forth: *a graphic account.* **4.** Of or pertaining to the graphic arts. **5.** Of or pertaining to graphics. **6.** *Geology.* Having crystals resembling printed characters.
∼*n* **1.** A graphic device, such as a picture or map, used for illustration. **2.** *Computer Science.* A graphic display generated by a computer or imaging device. [Latin *graphicus,* from Greek *graphikos,* from *graphē,* a writing, from *graphein,* to write.] **—graph·i·cal·ly** *adv.* **—graph·ic·ness** *n.*

graphic arts *pl.n.* **1.** The fine or applied visual arts that involve the application of lines and strokes to a two-dimensional surface. **2.** The reproductions made from blocks, plates, or type, such as engravings, etchings, woodcuts, and lithographs.

graph·ics (grăf′ĭks) *n. Used with a singular or plural verb.* **1.** The making of drawings in accordance with the rules of mathematics, as in engineering or architecture. **2.** Calculations, as of structural stress, from such drawings. **3.** The artwork accompanying written matter. **4.** *Computer Science.* The processing and displaying of data in pictorial form.

graph·ite (grăf′īt′) *n.* The soft, steel-gray to black, hexagonally crystallized allotrope of carbon, used in lead pencils, lubricants, paints and coatings, bricks, electrodes, crucibles, and rocket nozzles. Also called "black lead." [German *Graphit* : Greek *graphein,* to write + -ITE.] **—gra·phit·ic** (gră-fĭt′ĭk) *adj.*

graph·i·tize (grăf′ə-tīz′) *tr.v.* **-tized, -tizing, -tizes.** **1.** To convert into graphite by a heating process. **2.** To coat or impregnate with graphite. **—graph·i·ti·za·tion** *n.*

graph·ol·o·gy (gră-fŏl′ə-jē) *n.* **1.** The study of handwriting, especially when employed as a means of analyzing the character of the writer. **2.** The study of writing systems. [Greek *graphē,* a writing (see **graphic**) + -LOGY.] **—graph·o·log·i·cal** (grăf′ə-lŏj′ĭ-kəl) *adj.* **—graph·ol·o·gist** *n.*

graph paper *n.* Paper ruled into small squares of equal size for use in drawing charts, graphs, or diagrams.

-graphy *suffix.* Indicates: **1.** A specified process or method of writing, recording, or describing; for example, **cacography, photography.** **2.** A descriptive science of a specified subject or field; for example, **oceanography.** [Latin *-graphia,* from Greek, from *graphein,* to write.]

grap·nel (grăp′nəl) *n.* **1.** An iron shaft with claws at one end for grasping and holding; especially, one for drawing and holding an enemy ship alongside. Also called "grappling," "grappling-hook," "grappling iron." **2.** A small anchor with three or more flukes. [Middle English *grapenel,* from Norman French *grapenel* (unattested), diminutive of Old French *grapon,* anchor, hook, from Germanic.]

grap·pa (grä′pə; *Italian* gräp′pä) *n.* An Italian brandy distilled from the residue of pressed grapes. [Italian, "grape stalk," from Germanic.]

grap·ple (grăp′əl) *n.* **1.** Any instrument, such as a grapnel, used for grasping and holding. **2.** The act of grappling. **3. a.** A contest in which the participants attempt to clutch or grip each other. **b.** A grasp or grip in such a contest.
∼*v.* **grappled, -pling, -ples.** *—tr.* **1.** To seize and hold with a grapnel. **2.** To seize firmly with the hands. *—intr.* **1.** To hold on to something with or as if with a grapnel. **2.** To attempt to resolve or overcome: *grapple with a problem; grapple with one's conscience.* [Middle English *grapel,* from Old French *grapil,* from Old Provençal, diminutive of *grapa,* hook, from Germanic.] **—grap·pler** *n.*

grap·to·lite (grăp′tə-līt′) *n.* Any of numerous extinct colonial marine animals chiefly of the orders Dendroidea and Graptoloidea, of the late Cambrian to Carboniferous periods. [Greek *graptos,* written, painted, from *graphein,* to write (see **graphic**) + -LITE (so called from the fossilized impressions resembling markings on slate).]

Gras·mere (grăs′mûr, gräs′-). A village in Cumbria in northwestern England, near Lake Grasmere. Set in the heart of the Lake District, it is famous for the beauty of its surroundings. Wordsworth lived there at Dove Cottage, which now houses a Wordsworth museum.

grasp (grăsp, gräsp) *v.* **grasped, grasping, grasps.** *—tr.* **1.** To take hold of or seize firmly with or as if with the hand. **2.** To hold firmly with or as if with the hand; clutch; clasp. **3.** To take in mentally; comprehend: *"It is this distinction between freedom and license that many parents cannot grasp"* (A.S. Neill). —See Synonyms at **apprehend.** *—intr.* **1.** To make a motion of seizing, snatching, or clutching. **2.** To show eager and prompt willingness or acceptance. Used with *at.*
∼*n.* **1.** The act of grasping. **2.** A firm hold or grip. **3.** The ability or power to seize or attain; reach: *The directorship was within his grasp.* **4.** Understanding; comprehension: *an intuitive grasp of the problem.* [Middle English *graspen,* Old English *grapsan* (unattested), from Germanic.] **—grasp·er** *n.*

grasp·ing (grăs′pĭng, gräs′-) *adj.* Eager for gain; greedy; avaricious. **—grasp·ing·ly** *adv.* **—grasp·ing·ness** *n.*

grass (grăs, gräs) *n.* **1. a.** Any of numerous plants of the family Gramineae, characteristically having narrow leaves, hollow, jointed stems, and spikes or clusters of membranous flowers borne in smaller spikelets. **b.** Such plants collectively. **2.** Any of various plants, such as knotgrass, having slender leaves like those of the true grasses. **3.** An expanse of ground, such as a meadow or lawn, covered with grass or similar plants. **4.** Grazing land; pasture. **5.** *Slang.* Marijuana. **6.** A condition or place of retirement: *put a horse out to grass.* **7.** *Electronics.* The small variations in amplitude of an oscilloscope display due to electrical noise.
∼*v.* **grassed, grassing, grasses.** *—tr.* **1.** To cover with grass; grow grass on. **2.** To feed (livestock) with grass. *—intr.* **1.** To become covered with grass. **2.** To graze. [Middle English *gras,* Old English *græs,* from Germanic.]

Grass (gräs), **Günter** (1927–). German poet, playwright, and novelist. Most of his novels are directly concerned with the social and political life of Germany. His two early novels, *The Tin Drum* (1959) and *Dog Years* (1963), are the most widely known.

grass cloth *n.* A material woven from rough natural plant fibers such as hemp or ramie.

grass court *n.* A tennis court with a cut grass surface.

grass-cut·ter (grăs′kŭt′ər, gräs′-) *n.* A West African water rat, *Thryonomis swinderianus,* with stiff, short fur.

Grasse (gräs). A town in the Alpes-Maritimes department of southern France, north of Cannes. Surrounded by extensive fields of flowers, it is famous for the manufacture of essences for perfume.

grass-finch (grăs′fĭnch′, gräs′-) *n.* Any of various Australian weaver finches of the genus *Poephila* and related genera, some species of which are kept as cage birds for their colorful plumage.

grass green *n.* A moderate yellow-green to strong or dark yellowish-green. **—grass-green** *adj.*

grass hockey *n. Canadian.* Field hockey as opposed to ice hockey.

grass·hop·per (grăs′hŏp′ər, gräs′-) *n.* **1.** Any of numerous insects of the families Locustidae (or Acrididae) (*short-horned grasshoppers*) and Tettigoniidae (*long-horned grasshoppers*), often destructive to plants and characteristically having long hind legs adapted for jumping. **2.** A cocktail consisting of crème de menthe, crème de cacao, and cream.

grass·land (grăs′lănd′, gräs′-) *n.* An area, such as a prairie or meadow, of grass or grasslike vegetation.

Gras·so (grăs′ō, grä′sō), **Ella Tambussi** (1919–81). U.S. public official. After serving as a state legislator (1952–59), Connecticut secretary of state (1959–70), and U.S. congresswoman (1970–75), she became the first American woman elected governor in her own right, filling that position from 1975 to 1980.

grass-of-Par·nas·sus (grăs′əv-pär-năs′əs, gräs′-) *n.* Any of various plants of the genus *Parnassia*; especially, *P. palustris,* having stalked basal leaves and a stem bearing a single white or yellowish flower.

grass parakeet *n.* Any of various small Australian parrots typically having a long tail and green plumage.

grass pink *n.* An orchid, *Calopogon pulchellus,* of marshy areas of eastern North America, having a single narrow leaf and a cluster of pinkish flowers.

grass·roots (grăs′ro͞ots′, -ro͝ots′, gräs′-) *pl.n.* **1.** People considered from a political viewpoint as constituting the basic voting population. **2.** The foundation or source of something; basis; origin.
∼*adj.* **1.** Originating in or emerging from the people who make up the mass of an electorate: *a grassroots candidate; a grassroots policy.* **2.** Fundamental; basic.

grass-ski·ing (grăs′skē′ĭng, gräs′-) *n.* The sport of skiing down grassy slopes on specially adapted skis.

grass skirt *n.* A skirt made from lengths of flax or other grasses strung from a waistband and worn especially by the Polynesians.

grass snake *n.* Any of several greenish, nonvenomous snakes; especially, *Natrix natrix,* of Europe, or *Opheodrys vernalis,* of eastern North America.

grass tree *n.* Any of several woody-stemmed Australian plants of the genus *Xanthorrhoea,* having stiff, grasslike leaves and a spike of small white flowers. They yield a gum used in making varnishes.

grass widow *n.* **1.** A woman whose husband is habitually or temporarily absent. **2.** A woman who is divorced or separated from her husband. **3.** A woman who has had an illegitimate child. [Earliest sense, "unwed mother," probably with an allusion to a bed of straw or grass as a symbol of illicit sexual conduct.]

grass wren *n.* Any of various small Australian songbirds of the genus *Amytormis,* typically having a brown body and tail and a whitish breast.

grass·y (grăs′ē, gräs′ē) *adj.* **-ier, -iest.** **1.** Covered with grass. **2.** Resembling or suggestive of grass, as in color or odor.

grate¹ (grāt) *v.* **grated, grating, grates.** *—tr.* **1.** To reduce to fragments, shreds, or powder by rubbing against an abrasive surface: *grate cabbage.* **2.** To cause to make a harsh grinding or rasping sound through friction. **3.** *Archaic.* To rub or wear away. *—intr.* **1.** To make a harsh rasping sound by or as if by scraping or grinding. **2.** To cause irritation or annoyance. Sometimes used with *on*: *grate on one's nerves.*
∼*n.* A harsh, rasping sound made by scraping or rubbing: *the grate of a key in a lock.* [Middle English *graten,* from Old French *grater,* to scrape, from Germanic.] **—grat·ing·ly** *adv.*

grate² *n.* **1.** A framework of parallel or latticed bars used to hold the fuel in a stove, furnace, or fireplace. **2.** A similar framework used to block an opening; a grille; a grating. **3.** A fireplace. **4.** A perforated iron plate or screen for sieving and grading crushed ore.
∼*tr.v.* **grated, grating, grates.** To equip with a grate. [Middle English, from Old French, grille, from Vulgar Latin *grata* (unattested), variant of Latin *crātis,* wickerwork, hurdle.]

grate·ful (grāt′fəl) *adj.* **1.** Appreciative of benefits received; thankful. **2.** Expressing gratitude. **3.** Affording pleasure or comfort; wel-

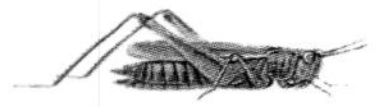

grasshopper *Around the world there are hundreds of species of grasshopper—a group that includes crickets and locusts. Most feed on plants and have long hind legs adapted for jumping. They are difficult to see in the grass where they live, but they can often be heard, since each species has a characteristic song, produced by rubbing the wings or legs together. The song is used by males to attract females and, less frequently, by females to attract males. The species shown here is* Omacestus viridulus.

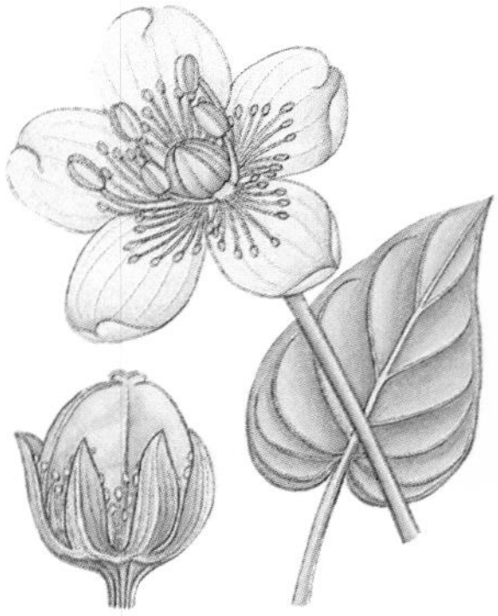

grass-of-Parnassus *This Northern Hemisphere wildflower is neither a grass nor grasslike; it is a marsh plant that takes its name from Mount Parnassus in Greece, the legendary home of the Muses. The species shown here is* Parnassia palustris.

PRONUNCIATION KEY

ă, pat; ā, pay; âr, care;
ä, father, are; b, bib;
ch, church; d, deed; ĕ, pet;
ē, be; f, fife; g, gag; h, hat;
hw, which; ĭ, pit; ī, pie;
îr, pier; j, judge; k, kick;
l, lid, needle; m, mum;
n, no, sudden; ng, thing;
ŏ, pot; ō, toe; ô, paw, for;
oi, noise; ou, out; o͝o, book;
o͞o, boot; p, pop; r, roar;
s, sauce; sh, ship, dish;
t, tight; th, thin, path;
th, this, bathe; ŭ, cut; ûr, fur;
v, valve; w, with; y, yes;
z, zebra, size; zh, vision;
ə, about, item, edible,
gallop, circus, peaceful

IN FOREIGN WORDS:

à, *Fr.* ami; œ, *Fr.* feu, *Ger.* schön; ü, *Fr.* tu, *Ger.* über;
KH, *Ger.* ich, *Scot.* loch;
N, *Fr.* bon; y′, *Fr.* Compiègne

STRESS MARKS:

Primary stress: ′
in·cite′ (ĭn-sīt′)
Secondary stress: ′
in′sight′ (ĭn′sīt′)

come: *"he left his home to enjoy the grateful air"* (Ronald Firbank). [From obsolete *grate*, agreeable, thankful, from Latin *grātus*, pleasing, favorable.] —**grate·ful·ly** *adv.* —**grate·ful·ness** *n.*

grat·er (grā′tər) *n.* **1.** One that grates. **2.** An implement with rough or sharp-edged slits and perforations on which to shred or grate foods.

grat·i·cule (grăt′ĭ-kyōōl′) *n.* **1.** A grid of meridians and parallels derived from a particular projection, used in drawing a map. **2.** *Optics.* A grid or pattern used to establish scale or position, placed in the eyepiece of an optical instrument. Also called "reticle," "reticule." [French, from Latin *crāticula*, gridiron, diminutive of *crātis*, wickerwork, hurdle.]

grat·i·fi·ca·tion (grăt′ə-fĭ-kā′shən) *n.* **1.** The act of gratifying. **2.** The condition of being gratified; satisfaction; pleasure. **3.** An instance or cause of gratification. **4.** *Archaic.* A reward; gratuity; bonus.

grat·i·fy (grăt′ə-fī′) *tr.v.* **-fied, -fy·ing, -fies. 1.** To please or satisfy: *His achievement gratified his father.* **2.** To indulge; give in to (a desire, for example). **3.** *Archaic.* To requite; reward. [Middle English *gratifien*, to favor, from Old French, from Latin *grātificārī*, to reward, do favor to, from *grātus*, favorable, pleasurable.] —**grat·i·fi·er** *n.*

grat·i·fy·ing (grăt′ə-fī′ĭng) *adj.* Causing pleasure and satisfaction, as to the self-esteem: *a most gratifying sense of accomplishment.* —**grat·i·fy·ing·ly** *adv.*

gra·tin (grăt′n, grät′n; *French* grȧ-tăN′) *n.* A rich baked crust on dishes that have been topped with grated cheese or buttered crumbs. [French, from Old French, from *grater*, to GRATE (scrape).]

grat·ing[1] (grā′tĭng) *n.* **1.** A grille or network of bars set in a window or door or used as a partition; lattice; grate. **2.** *Physics.* **Diffraction grating** (*see*).

grat·ing[2] *adj.* **1.** Rasping or scraping in sound. **2.** Nerve-racking; irritating. —**grat·ing·ly** *adv.*

gra·tis (grăt′ĭs, grā′tĭs) *adv.* Freely; for nothing; without charge. ~*adj.* Free; gratuitous. [Middle English, from Latin *grātīs*, reduced form of *grātiīs*, without reward, as a favor, from *grātia*, favor, from *grātus*, favorable.]

grat·i·tude (grăt′ə-tōōd′, -tyōōd′) *n.* An appreciative awareness and thankfulness, as for kindness shown or a gift received. [Middle English, from Old French, from Medieval Latin *grātitūdō*, from *grātus*, favorable.]

gra·tu·i·tous (grə-tōō′ə-təs, -tyōō′-) *adj.* **1.** *Law.* Given or granted without return or recompense. **2.** Given or received without cost or obligation; free; gratis. **3.** Unnecessary or unwarranted; unjustified: *gratuitous criticism.* [Latin *grātuītus*, given as a favor, from *grātus*, favorable, pleasing.] —**gra·tu·i·tous·ly** *adv.* —**gra·tu·i·tous·ness** *n.*

gra·tu·i·ty (grə-tōō′ə-tē, -tyōō′-) *n., pl.* **-ties.** A material favor or gift, usually in the form of money, given in return for service; a tip. —See Synonyms at **bonus.** [Old French *gratuite*, from Medieval Latin *grātuitās* (stem *grātuitāt*-), present, gift, from Latin *grātuītus*, given free, GRATUITOUS.]

grat·u·lant (grăch′ōō-lənt) *adj. Archaic.* Congratulatory.

grat·u·late (grăch′ōō-lāt′) *tr.v.* **-lated, -lating, -lates.** *Archaic.* **1.** To greet with pleasure; welcome. **2.** To congratulate. [Latin *grātulārī*, to greet, salute, from *grātus*, pleasing, GRATEFUL.] —**grat·u·la·tion** *n.* —**grat·u·la·to·ry** (grăch′ōō-lə-tôr′ē, -tōr′ē) *adj.*

Gratz. See **Graz.**

grau·pel (grou′pəl) *n.* Precipitation consisting of pellets of snow. Also called "snow pellets," "soft hail." [German *Graupel*, diminutive of *Graupe*, hulled grain, groats, probably from Serbo-Croatian *krupa.*]

grav (grăv) *n.* A unit of acceleration equal to the acceleration of free fall or 9.807 meters per second per second. [Shortened from *gravity.*]

gra·va·men (grə-vā′mən) *n., pl.* **-vamina** (-văm′ə-nə). **1.** *Law.* **a.** The part of a charge or accusation that weighs most substantially against the accused. **b.** The essential part of a complaint. **2.** A grievance. [Late Latin *gravāmen*, grievance, from *grāvāre*, to weigh down, burden, from *gravis*, heavy, GRAVE.]

grave[1] (grāv) *n.* **1. a.** A hole dug in the ground to receive a corpse. **b.** A tombstone, mound, or other marker indicating such a burial place. **2.** Any place of burial or final laying to rest: *The sea was his grave.* **3.** The sign or marker of a burial place. **4.** *Poetic.* Death or extinction. —**dig one's own grave.** To be the cause of one's own failure or downfall. —**turn in one's grave.** To feel shock or disapproval at some modern event or action that runs counter to one's beliefs or ideas. Used of a dead person. [Middle English *grave*, Old English *græf*, from Germanic.]

grave[2] *adj.* **graver, gravest. 1.** Extremely serious; important; weighty: *a grave decision in a time of crisis.* **2.** Fraught with danger; critical: *in grave difficulties.* **3.** Grievous; dire: *a grave sin.* **4.** Dignified in conduct; sedate: *a grave procession.* **5.** Somber or worried: *a grave expression.* **6.** (*also* grȧv). *Linguistics.* **a.** Written with or modified by the mark (`), as the è in *Sèvres.* **b.** Articulated toward the back of the oral cavity. —See Synonyms at **serious.** ~*n.* (*also* grȧv). A grave accent (`), as one indicating a pronounced *e* for the sake of meter in the usually nonsyllabic ending *-ed* in English poetry. [Old French, from Latin *gravis*, heavy, weighty.] —**grave·ly** *adv.* —**grave·ness** *n.*

grave[3] *tr.v.* **graved, graven** (grā′vən), **graving, graves. 1.** To stamp or impress deeply; fix (words or ideas, for example) permanently. **2.** *Archaic.* To sculpt or carve; engrave: *"I wish I could grave my*

sonnets on an ivory tablet" (Oscar Wilde). [Grave, graven; Middle English *graven, graven*, Old English *grafan* (dig, engrave), *grafen*, from Germanic; akin to GRAVE (place of burial).]

grave[4] *tr.v.* **graved, graving, graves.** To clean (the bottom of a wooden ship) by removing barnacles and other accretions, and coating with pitch. [Middle English *graven*, probably from Old French *greve, grave*, sand, GRAVEL.]

gra·ve[5] (grä′vā) *adv. Music.* Slowly and solemnly. Used as a direction. [Italian, from Latin *gravis*, heavy, weighty, GRAVE.] —**gra·ve** *adj.*

grave·clothes (grāv′klōz′, -klōthz′) *pl.n.* The clothes or shroud in which a body is interred.

grave·dig·ger (grāv′dĭg′ər) *n.* A person whose occupation is digging graves.

grav·el (grăv′əl) *n.* **1.** Any unconsolidated mixture of rock fragments or pebbles. **2.** *Pathology.* Sandlike granular material occurring in the kidneys or bladder. ~*tr.v.* **graveled** or **-velled, -veling** or **-velling, -vels. 1.** To apply a surface of gravel to: *gravel a drive.* **2.** *Rare.* To confuse; perplex: *His inconsistencies gravel the reader.* **3.** *Informal.* To irritate. [Middle English, from Old French *gravele, gravelle*, diminutive of *grave, greve*, gravel, sand, pebbly shore, from Celtic.]

grav·el-blind (grăv′əl-blīnd′) *adj. Literary.* Having minimal vision; purblind. [GRAVEL + BLIND (by analogy with SANDBLIND).]

grav·el·ly (grăv′ə-lē) *adj.* **1.** Of, full of, or covered with gravel. **2.** Having a harsh rasping sound: *a gravelly voice.*

graven image *n.* An idol or fetish carved in wood or stone.

grav·er (grā′vər) *n.* **1.** A person who carves or engraves; a stone-carver. **2.** An engraver's cutting tool; a burin.

grave robber *n.* A person who plunders valuables from tombs or graves or who steals corpses, as for illicit dissection.

Graves (grāvz; *French* grȧv) *n.* A dry, usually white wine produced near Bordeaux, in southwestern France. [After *Graves*, district in southwestern France.]

Graves (grāvz), **Robert Ranke** (1895–1985). British poet, novelist, and critic. As a war poet, he published *Over the Brazier* (1916) and *Fairies and Fusiliers* (1917) while serving in World War I. His novels include *I, Claudius* (1934) and a semiautobiographical work on the postwar generation, *Goodbye to All That* (1929). His major work of criticism was *The White Goddess* (1948).

Graves' disease (grāvz) *n. Pathology.* **Exophthalmic goiter** (*see*). [After Robert James *Graves* (1796–1853), Irish physician.]

grave·stone (grāv′stōn′) *n.* A stone placed over a grave as a marker; a tombstone.

grave·yard (grāv′yärd′) *n.* **1.** An area set aside as a burial ground, especially a small area around a church. **2.** An event or circumstance leading to the final ruin or failure of someone or something: *the graveyard of all our hopes.* **3.** A place for storing discarded or worn-out things, especially old automobiles.

graveyard shift *n.* **1.** A work shift that runs during the early morning hours, as from midnight to 8:00 A.M. **2.** The workers on an early-morning shift.

grav·id (grăv′ĭd) *adj.* **1.** Pregnant. **2.** Full of ripe eggs or distended by such fullness: *a fish gravid with roe.* [Latin *gravidus*, pregnant, from *gravis*, heavy.] —**gra·vid·i·ty** (grə-vĭd′ə-tē), **grav·id·ness** *n.* —**grav·id·ly** *adv.*

gra·vim·e·ter (grə-vĭm′ə-tər) *n.* **1.** Any instrument used to determine specific gravity. **2.** Any instrument used to measure the earth's gravitational field at a given point on its surface. [French *gravimètre* : Latin *gravis*, heavy, GRAVE + -METER.]

grav·i·met·ric (grăv′ə-mĕt′rĭk) *adj.* Also **grav·i·met·ri·cal** (-rĭ-kəl). Of or pertaining to measurement by weight: *gravimetric analysis.* Compare **volumetric.** [Latin *gravis*, heavy, GRAVE + METRIC.] —**grav·i·met·ri·cal·ly** *adv.* —**gra·vim·e·try** (grə-vĭm′ə-trē) *n.*

graving dock *n.* A dry dock in which ships are repaired and their bottoms are graved.

grav·i·tate (grăv′ə-tāt′) *intr.v.* **-tated, -tating, -tates. 1.** To move in response to the force of gravity. **2.** To move downward. **3.** To be attracted by or as if by an irresistible force: *"My excuse must be that all Celts gravitate towards each other"* (Oscar Wilde). [New Latin *gravitare*, from Latin *gravitās*, GRAVITY.] —**grav·i·tat·er** *n.*

grav·i·ta·tion (grăv′ə-tā′shən) *n.* **1.** *Physics.* **a.** The natural phenomenon of attraction between massive bodies. **b.** The action or process of moving under the influence of this attraction. **c.** The degree of such attraction. **2.** Any movement toward a source of attraction or place of settlement: *the gravitation of the middle classes to the suburbs.* —**grav·i·ta·tion·al, grav·i·ta·tive** (grăv′ə-tā′tĭv) *adj.* —**grav·i·ta·tion·al·ly** *adv.*

gravitational constant *n.* Symbol **G** The universal constant used in Newton's law of gravitation. It is equal to Fd^2/m_1m_2, where F is the gravitational force between two masses, m_1 and m_2, separated by a distance of d. It has the value 6.670×10^{-11} N m² kg⁻².

gravitational field *n.* The region of space in which one massive body exerts a force of attraction on another massive body. The force is inversely proportional to the square of the distance between the bodies and directly proportional to the product of their masses.

gravitational interaction *n.* The interaction that occurs between bodies as a result of their mass. It is the weakest of all forms of interaction. Compare **strong interaction, weak interaction, electromagnetic interaction.**

gravitational mass *n.* The mass of a body as determined by its response to a gravitational field, especially to the force of gravity. Compare **inertial mass.**

gravitational red shift *n.* See **red shift** (sense 2).
grav·i·ton (grăv′ə-tŏn′) *n.* A particle postulated to be the quantum of gravitational interaction, and presumed to have zero electric charge, zero rest mass, and spin 2. [GRAVIT(ATION) + -ON.]
grav·i·ty (grăv′ə-tē) *n.* **1.** *Physics.* **a.** The force of gravitation, being, for any two sufficiently massive bodies, directly proportional to the product of their masses and inversely proportional to the square of the distance between them; especially, the attractive gravitational force exerted by a celestial body, such as the earth on bodies on or near its surface. **b.** Loosely, gravitation. **c.** *Rare.* Weight. **2.** Grave nature or seriousness: *the gravity of their problem.* **3.** Solemnity or dignity of manner: *"With stern and austere gravity he persevered in his task"* (Sir Walter Scott). [Old French *gravite,* from Latin *gravitās* (stem *gravitāt-*), from *gravis,* heavy, serious, GRAVE.]
gravity cell *n.* An electrolytic cell with the electrodes in two different electrolytes, which are separated into two vertical layers as a result of differences in their relative densities.
gravity feed *n.* **1.** A method of supplying a fuel, lubricant, or other liquid to an engine, boiler, or plant, that relies on gravity rather than a pump. **2.** A system for providing a continuous supply of a powder or granular solid by allowing it to trickle from the base of a container, as, for example, the system used to supply fuel to a boiler.
gra·vure (grə-vyŏŏr′) *n.* **1.** A method of printing with etched plates or cylinders; intaglio printing. **2.** A tonal reproduction process using photomechanically prepared plates or cylinders to reproduce photographs on newsprint; photogravure. **3.** A plate or reproduction produced by gravure or used in the process. [French, from *graver,* to engrave, dig into, from Old French, from Frankish *graban* (unattested).]
gra·vy (grā′vē) *n., pl.* **-vies. 1. a.** The juices that drip from cooking meat. **b.** A sauce made by thickening and seasoning these juices. **2.** *Slang.* Money or profit easily or unexpectedly gained; especially, money in excess of that required for necessities. [Middle English *gravey,* perhaps a misreading of Old French *grané,* "(dish) seasoned with grains (of spice)," from *grain,* spice, GRAIN.]
gravy boat *n.* An elongated vessel with a lip, used for serving gravy.
gravy train *n. Slang.* An occupation or job that requires little effort while yielding considerable profit.
gray[1], grey (grā) *adj.* **1.** Of or pertaining to an achromatic color of any lightness between the extremes of black and white. **2. a.** Dull or dark, as from lack of light: *a gray, rainy day.* **b.** Lacking in cheer; gloomy. **3. a.** Having gray hair; hoary. **b.** Old, venerable, or ancient. **4.** Intermediate in character or position, especially in the area of morality or propriety.
~n. **1.** An achromatic color of any lightness between the extremes of black and white. **2.** An object or animal of the color gray. **3.** *Sometimes* **Gray. a.** A member of the Confederate Army in the Civil War. **b.** The Confederate Army itself. Compare **blue.**
gray[2] *n. Abbr.* **Gy.** The SI unit of absorbed dose of ionizing radiation equal to the energy in joules absorbed by one kilogram of irradiated material. [After L.H. *Gray* (died 1965), British radiobiologist.]
Gray (grā), **Thomas** (1716–71). English poet. He was educated at Cambridge, where he spent most of his life as a scholar and professor of history and modern languages. His most famous poem, *Elegy Written in a Country Churchyard* (1751), won him the offer of the poet laureateship in 1757, which he declined.
gray·beard (grā′bîrd′) *n.* An old man.
gray eminence *n.* An **eminence grise** *(see).*
Gray Friar *n.* A **Franciscan** *(see).*
gray hen. Variant of **greyhen.**
gray·ish (grā′ĭsh) *adj.* Having a perceptible quality of grayness.
gray·lag goose (grā′lăg′) *n.* A gray goose, *Anser anser,* of marshy areas of the Old World. [Possibly GRAY + dialectal *lag,* last.]
gray·ling (grā′lĭng) *n., pl.* **-lings** or collectively **grayling. 1.** Any of several freshwater food fishes of the genus *Thymallus,* of the Northern Hemisphere, having a small mouth and a large dorsal fin. **2.** Any of several grayish or brownish butterflies of the family Satyridae, especially the European species *Eumenis semele.*
gray matter *n.* **1.** The brownish-gray nerve tissue of the brain and spinal cord, composed of nerve cells and fibers and some supportive tissue. **2.** *Informal.* Brains; intellect.
gray mullet *n.* A fish, the **mullet** *(see).*
Gray's Inn (grāz) *n.* One of the four legal societies forming the **Inns of Court** *(see)* in England.
gray squirrel *n.* A common squirrel, *Sciurus carolinensis,* of eastern North America, having gray or blackish fur and a very bushy tail.
gray·wacke (grā′wăk′, -wăk′ə) *n.* Any of various shale-containing dark-gray sandstones. [Partial translation of German *grauwacke* : *grau,* gray + *Wacke,* boulder.]
gray whale *n.* A whalebone whale, *Eschrichtius glaucus,* of Pacific waters, having grayish coloring with white blotches.
gray wolf *n.* The **timber wolf** *(see).*
Graz (gräts). Formerly **Gratz.** The second-largest city in Austria, on the Mur River in the southeast of the country. It is the capital of Styria province.
graze[1] *v.* **grazed, grazing, grazes.** *—intr.* **1.** To feed on growing grasses and herbage. **2.** To pasture livestock. *—tr.* **1.** To put (livestock) out to feed. **2.** To tend (feeding livestock) in a pasture. **3.** To feed on (pasture). [Middle English *grasen,* to feed on grass, Old English *grasian,* from *græs,* GRASS.] **—graz·er** *n.*
graze[2] *v.* **grazed, grazing, grazes.** *—tr.* **1.** To touch lightly in passing; skim; brush. **2.** To scrape or scratch slightly; abrade. *—intr.* To scrape or touch something lightly in passing.
~n. **1.** A brushing or scraping along a surface. **2.** A scratch or abrasion resulting from such contact. [Perhaps from GRAZE (remove grass close to the ground).]
gra·zier (grā′zhər) *n.* A person who grazes and fattens cattle.
graz·ing (grā′zĭng) *n.* Land used for feeding; pasturage.
gra·zio·so (grä-tsyō′sō) *adv. Music.* Gracefully; smoothly. Used as a direction. [Italian, from Latin *grātiōsus,* GRACIOUS.] **—gra·zio·so** *adj.*
grease (grēs) *n.* **1.** Animal fat when melted or soft. **2.** Any thick oil or viscous lubricant. **3. a.** The oily substance present in raw wool; suint. **b.** Raw wool that has not been cleansed of this. In this sense, also called "grease wool," "wool in the grease."
~tr.v. (grēs, grēz) **greased, greasing, greases. 1.** To coat, smear, lubricate, or soil with grease. **2.** To smear (a muffin tin, frying pan, or the like) with cooking fat. **—grease someone's palm.** *Slang.* To bribe. [Middle English *grese,* from Old French *graisse,* from Vulgar Latin *crassia* (unattested), from Latin *crassus,* fat.]
grease monkey *n. Informal.* A mechanic.
grease paint *n.* Theatrical make-up. Also called "paint."
grease·wood (grēs′wŏŏd′) *n.* **1.** A spiny shrub, *Sarcobatus vermiculatus,* of western North America, the oil from which has been used as fuel. **2.** Any of various similar or related plants, such as the **creosote bush** *(see).*
greas·y (grē′sē, -zē) *adj.* **-ier, -iest. 1.** Coated or soiled with grease. **2.** Containing grease, especially too much grease. **3.** Suggestive of or resembling something greased; slick; unctuous: *a greasy character.* **—greas·i·ly** *adv.* **—greas·i·ness** *n.*
greasy spoon *n. Informal.* A small, usually unsanitary restaurant that sells cheap food.
great (grāt) *adj.* **greater, greatest.** *Abbr.* **gt. 1.** Extremely large; bulky; big. **2.** Larger than others of the same kind: *the great auk.* **3.** Large in quantity or number: *A great throng awaited him.* **4.** Of considerable duration; extensive in time or distance. **5.** Extreme in magnitude, degree, or extent: *a great mistake.* **6.** Significant; important; meaningful: *A great work of art.* **7.** Chief or principal: *the great house on the estate.* **8.** Superior in quality or character; noble; excellent. **9.** Powerful; influential: *"Seek to be good, but aim not to be great"* (George Lyttelton). **10.** Eminent; distinguished: *a great leader.* **11.** Grand; aristocratic. **12.** *Archaic.* Pregnant. Used with *with*: *great with child.* **13.** *Informal.* Enthusiastic: *a great boxing fan.* **14.** *Informal.* Skillful: *She is great at algebra.* **15.** *Informal.* First-rate; very good: *a great book.* **16.** Used as an intensive, especially in exclamations: *great balls of fire!* **17.** *Archaic.* Capital; upper-case. Said of letters: *a great A.* **18.** Designating a family relationship or relative one generation removed from the relative specified. Used in combination: *a great-grandfather.*
~n. **greats.** Outstanding individuals: *Many of the sport's greats were there.*
~adv. Informal. Very well. [Middle English *grete,* Old English *great,* thick, coarse, from Germanic.] **—great·ness** *n.*
great ape *n.* Any large anthropoid ape, such as a gorilla or orangutan.
Great Ar·te·sian Basin (är-tē′zhən). Largest artesian area in the world. It lies in eastern Australia, between the Great Dividing Range and the Western Plateau and stretches northward to the Gulf of Carpentaria. The basin covers *c.* 1,750,000 square kilometers (676,250 square miles). It derives its water from the Eastern Highlands.
great auk *n.* A large, flightless sea bird, *Pinguinus impennis,* formerly common on northern Atlantic coasts but extinct since the middle of the 19th century.
great-aunt (grāt′ănt′, -änt′) *n.* A sister of one's grandparent. Also called "grand-aunt."
Great Au·stra·lian Bight (ô-strāl′yən bīt). A broad bay in the coast of southern Australia. It extends from West Cape in Western Australia to South West Cape in Tasmania.
Great Bar·ri·er Reef (băr′ē-ər). Largest coral reef in the world, in the Coral Sea off the coast of northeastern Australia. It extends from Torres Strait along the coast of Queensland almost to southern New Guinea, a distance of *c.* 2,012 kilometers (1,250 miles). Its banks of vividly colored corals teem with exotic fish and crustaceans, and there are coral islets overgrown with mangroves, palms, and flowering plants.
Great Basin. Region of the western United States, between the Wasatch Mts. and the Sierra Nevada. Covering an area of *c.* 518,000 square kilometers (200,000 square miles), it consists of steep-sided block mountains with broad plains between. Though not entirely arid, it includes Death Valley and the Mojave and Great Salt Lake deserts.
Great Bear *n. Astronomy.* A constellation, **Ursa Major** *(see).*
Great Bear Lake. Lake in north-central Mackenzie district in Northwest Territories, Canada. It is 31,800 square kilometers (12,275 square miles) in area, the largest lake in Canada.
Great Brit·ain (brĭt′n). *Abbr.* **G.B.** The largest island in Europe, in the northwest of the continent and separated from the mainland by the English Channel. The name has been used since 1707 to denote the political union of England, Scotland, and Wales. Great Britain includes the Isle of Man and Channel Islands, as well as the province of Northern Ireland. It is often loosely referred to as "Britain." See also **United Kingdom.**
great circle *n.* A circle that is the intersection of the surface of a

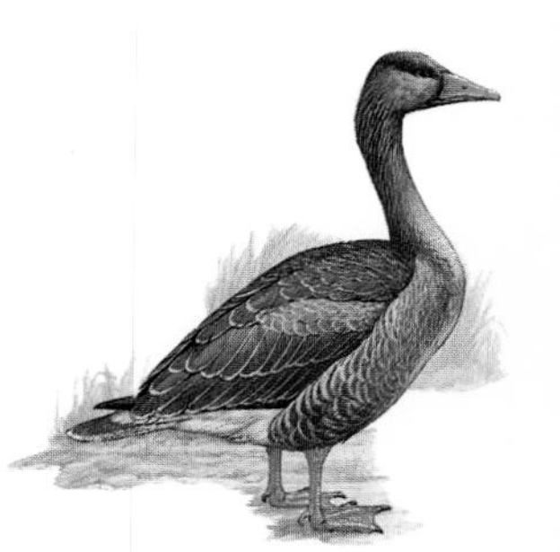

graylag goose *This European ancestor of the farmyard goose may have got its name from the fact that it lagged behind when other birds migrated. Graylags mate for life and repeat their courtship ritual whenever they meet after being separated for any length of time.*

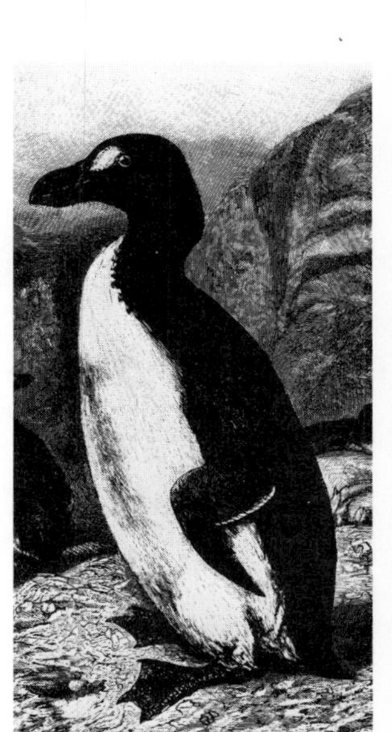

great auk *Ungainly and defenseless on land, the great auk was a fast, strong swimmer and lived on the fish that is caught around the shores of the North Atlantic. It was about 75 centimeters (2 1/2 feet) tall, black and white like a penguin, and had very small wings that were useless for flying. It was hunted to extinction in the 19th century.*

sphere with a plane passing through the center of the sphere. Compare **small circle**.

great·coat (grāt'kōt') *n.* A heavy overcoat.

Great Dane *n.* A very large and powerful dog of a breed developed in Germany, having a smooth, short coat and a narrow head.

Great Divide *n.* **1.** See **Continental Divide** (sense 2). **2.** The **Great Dividing Range**.

Great Dividing Range. Also **Great Divide.** Belt of highlands and plateaus in eastern Australia, extending roughly parallel to the coast, from the base of Cape York Peninsula to the Grampians. Acting as the watershed of the eastern seaboard, it is only partially mountainous but includes the Australian Alps, which rise to 2,228 meters (7,310 feet) at Mt. Kosciusko.

great·en (grāt'n) *v.* **-ened, -ening, -ens.** *Archaic.* —*tr.* To make great or greater; enlarge. —*intr.* To become great or greater.

Great·er, great·er (grā'tər) *adj.* Designating a city and its immediate suburbs: *Greater Los Angeles*.

Greater An·til·les (ăn-tĭl'ēz). Northern part of the chain of islands that separates the Caribbean Sea from the main body of the Atlantic Ocean. It includes Cuba, Jamaica, Hispaniola (Haiti and the Dominican Republic), and Puerto Rico, the four largest islands in the West Indies. See also **Lesser Antilles.** See map at **Latin America**.

greater doxology *n.* The **Gloria in excelsis Deo** (see).

Greater Man·ches·ter (măn'chĕs-tər, -chĭs-tər). Since 1974, a metropolitan county in northwestern England. It includes the cities of Manchester and Salford and the surrounding towns of Wigan, Bolton, Bury, Rochdale, Oldham, Ashton-Under-Lyne, and Stockport.

great·est (grāt'əst). Superlative of **great.**
~*n.* *Informal.* A wonderful or admirable person or thing. Preceded by *the: When I was a child I thought this book was just the greatest.*

Great Falls. City of north-central Montana, at the confluence of the Missouri and Sun rivers and near the falls that give the city its name. The city as oil and copper refineries and flour mills. It is often called "Electric City" because of the hydroelectric power plants in the vicinity.

Great Glen. Valley in northwest Scotland. It stretches for *c.* 97 kilometers (60 miles) from the Moray Firth to Loch Linnhe. The valley was formed by a fault in the earth's crust, and the glacial lakes that developed along the fault line, including Loch Ness, have a depth hundreds of feet below sea level.

great-grand·child (grāt'grănd'chīld') *n., pl.* **-children** (-chĭl'drən). Any of the children of a grandchild.

great-grand·daugh·ter (grāt'grăn'dô'tər, -grănd'dô'tər) *n.* Any daughter of a grandchild.

great-grand·fa·ther (grāt'grănd'fä'thər) *n.* The father of any grandparent.

great-grand·moth·er (grāt'grănd'mŭth'ər) *n.* The mother of any grandparent.

great-grand·par·ent (grāt'grănd'pâr'ənt) *n.* Either of the parents of any grandparent.

great-grand·son (grāt'grănd'sŭn') *n.* Any of the sons of a grandchild.

Great Grimsby. See **Grimsby.**

great gross *n.* *Abbr.* **g.gr.** A dozen gross.

great-heart·ed (grāt'här'tĭd) *adj.* **1.** Noble or courageous in spirit; stouthearted. **2.** Great in generosity; unselfish; magnanimous. —**great·heart·ed·ly** *adv.* —**great·heart·ed·ness** *n.*

great horned owl *n.* A large North American owl, *Bubo virginianus,* having brownish plumage and prominent ear tufts.

Great Lake. The largest natural freshwater lake in Australia, lying in the central uplands of Tasmania. It has a surface area of 142 square kilometers (54 square miles) but an average depth of only 13 meters (43 feet). It is used as a hydroelectric reservoir.

Great Lakes. Five freshwater lakes in central North America, forming part of the boundary between Canada and the United States. From east to west they are Lake Ontario, Lake Erie, Lake Huron, Lake Michigan, and Lake Superior, and together they form the world's largest area of fresh water. Only Lake Michigan is wholly in the United States. They were formed at the end of the last Ice Age, when their glacier-carved basins filled with water. The largest of the lakes, and the largest freshwater lake in the world, is Lake Superior; the smallest is Lake Erie, which is also the only one of the five whose depth does not extend below sea level.

great·ly (grāt'lē) *adv.* **1.** In a style or manner befitting greatness; nobly. **2.** To a great degree; very much; exceedingly.

great-neph·ew (grāt'nĕf'yōō, -nĕv'yōō) *n.* A son of a nephew or niece. Also called "grand-nephew."

great-niece (grāt'nēs') *n.* A daughter of a nephew or niece. Also called "grand-niece."

great organ *n.* The principal manual, together with its pipes, of an organ that has more than one manual.

Great Ouse (ōōz). River in southern England, sometimes referred to simply as the Ouse. It rises in Northamptonshire and flows northeast for *c.* 250 kilometers (155 miles) until it empties into The Wash near King's Lynn, Norfolk.

Great Plains. Vast area of grassland in North America, stretching from the Mackenzie River delta in the north to southern Texas. The plains slope generally eastward from the foot of the Rocky Mts. at *c.* 100° W, where they merge with the wetter prairies. Most of the area is given over to ranches for cattle and sheep. Wheat is grown in the east where there is sufficient water, but soil erosion can be a problem, as in the Dust Bowl, created in the 1930's. The Great Plains have vast mineral resources, including oil, gas, coal, and gold.

Great Power *n.* A nation that has great military strength and economic influence; a superpower.

great primer *n.* *Printing.* Formerly, a size of type, 18-point.

Great Rebellion *n.* The **English Civil War** (see). Preceded by *the.*

Great Red Spot *n.* *Astronomy.* A feature of Jupiter, the **Red Spot** (see).

Great Rift Valley (rĭft). An extended geologic fault system, stretching for *c.* 6,400 kilometers (4,000 miles) from northern Syria, through the trough of the Red Sea and south as far as central Mozambique. For much of its length its traces have been lost by erosion, but in some parts, most spectacularly in southern Kenya, its cliffs rise thousands of feet. In Africa the valley has a western and eastern branch, with lakes and volcanoes.

Great Russian *n.* **1.** A member of the main ethnic group of Russian-speaking people, inhabiting central and northeastern Russia. **2.** The language of these people that is the official Russian language.
~ *adj.* Of or pertaining to this people or their language.

Great Salt Lake. A shallow saltwater lake in northeastern Utah. It is the largest saltwater lake in North America, with a surface area of *c.* 2,600 square kilometers (1,000 square miles). Its size and depth vary from year to year according to climatic conditions, but its average depth is *c.* 4 meters (13 feet).

Great Salt Lake Desert. A flat, arid region of northwestern Utah, southwest of Great Salt Lake. It is *c.* 177 kilometers (110 miles) long, barren of vegetation, and virtually uninhabitable.

Great Sand Dunes National Monument. Area in southern Colorado set aside to preserve large, high sand dunes in the Sangre de Christo Mts.

Great Sanhedrin *n.* The **Sanhedrin** (see).

Great Schism *n.* The division in the Roman Catholic Church from 1378 to 1417, when rival popes ruled at Rome and Avignon.

great seal *n.* *Often* **Great Seal.** The principal seal of a government, sovereign, or state, used to stamp very important official documents.

Great Slave Lake. Canada's second-largest lake, in southern Mackenzie district, Northwest Territories. It is the deepest lake in North America, reaching a depth of 615 meters (2,015 feet).

Great Smoky Mountains. Also **Great Smokies.** Part of the Appalachians on the North Carolina–Tennessee border, named for the smokelike haze that envelops them. They include many streams and waterfalls, hiking trails, luxuriant vegetation, and numerous recreation areas.

Great Spirit *n.* The principal deity in the religion of many North American Indian tribes.

Great St. Bernard Pass. See **St. Bernard Pass.**

Great Trek *n.* In South Africa, the migration, from the mid-1830's to the mid-1840's, of Boer farmers northward away from the Cape in order to find lands free from British rule. Preceded by *the.*

Great Dane *Bred originally for boar hunting in Germany about 400 years ago, this large dog is now bred as a domestic pet and for showing. A full-grown Great Dane may stand 75 centimeters (30 inches) tall at the shoulder and weigh 54 kilograms (120 pounds).*

great-un·cle (grāt′ŭng′kəl) *n.* The uncle of one's father or mother. Also called "grand-uncle."

Great Vic·to·ri·a Desert (vĭk-tôr′ē-ə). Region, *c.* 725 kilometers (450 miles) wide, in southeastern Western Australia and western South Australia. It is bordered on the north by Gibson Desert and on the south by Nullarbor Plain.

Great Wall of Chi·na (chī′nə). A fortification, consisting of walls, watchtowers, and guard stations, extending 2,400 kilometers (1,500 miles) in a winding course across northern China from Gansu province to Hebei province. For most of its length it runs along the southern border of the Mongolian plain. It was built originally to keep out nomadic invaders from the north, and the first continuous wall was built in the 3rd century B.C. Most of the present wall was built during the Ming dynasty (1368–1644). The average height of the wall is 7.5 meters (25 feet) and the average thickness at the base is *c.* 7 meters (23 feet), although at most points it tapers to *c.* 3.5 meters (11 feet) at the top.

Great War *n.* **World War I** *(see).* Preceded by *the.*

great white shark *n.* A **white shark** *(see).*

Great Yar·mouth (yär′məth). Port and tourist resort in Norfolk, England. Built on a spit at the mouth of the Yare River, its fine harbor is one of the world's largest herring ports.

great year *n.* A period of 25,800 years that is one complete cycle of the equinoxes.

greave (grēv) *n.* Leg armor worn below the knee. [Middle English, from Old French *grevet*, shin.]

greaves (grēvz) *pl.n.* The unmelted residue left after animal fat or tallow has been rendered. [Low German *greven.*]

grebe (grēb) *n.* Any of various diving birds of the family Podicipedidae, that have lobed, fleshy membranes along each toe and a pointed bill. [French *grèbe*†.]

Gre·cian (grē′shən) *adj.* **1.** Conforming to the styles and tastes of classical Greece. Said especially of architecture. **2.** Greek.
—*n.* A native of Greece. [Latin *Graecia,* Greece, from *Graecus,* GREEK.]

Grecian bend *n.* A posture in which the upper torso is thrust forward and the pelvis and buttocks backward, assumed by women of fashion in the late 19th century and often emphasized by wearing a bustle.

Grecian nose *n.* A long, straight nose extending in an unbroken line from the forehead.

Gre·cism, Grae·cism (grē′sĭz′əm) *n.* **1.** The style or spirit of Greek culture, art, or thought. **2.** Anything done in imitation of such style or spirit. **3.** An idiom of the Greek language.

Gre·cize, Grae·cize (grē′sīz′) *v.* **-cized, -cizing, -cizes.** —*tr.* To provide with or convert into a Greek form or style; Hellenize. —*intr.* To follow or adopt Greek culture, art, or thought. [French *gréciser,* from Latin *Graecizāre,* from Greek *Graekizein,* to speak Greek, from *Graikos,* GREEK.]

Greco, El. See **El Greco.**

Greco–, Graeco– *prefix.* Indicates Greek; for example, **Greco-Roman.** [From Latin *Graecus.*]

Gre·co-Ro·man, Grae·co-Ro·man (grē′kō-rō′mən, grĕk′ō-) *adj.* Of, relating to, or pertaining to both Greece and Rome: *Greco-Roman mythology.* [GRECO- + ROMAN.]

gree[1] (grē) *n. Scottish.* **1.** Superiority or victory. **2.** The prize or reward for victory. [Middle English, rank, from Old French *gre,* from Latin *gradus,* GRADE.]

gree[2] *intr.v.* **greed, greeing, grees.** *Northern British.* To be in harmony or agreement. [Aphetic variant of AGREE.]

gree[3] *n. Obsolete.* Good will; favor. [Middle English, from Old French *gre,* from Late Latin *grātum,* from Latin *grātus,* pleasing, thankful.]

Greece (grēs). *Ancient Greek* **Hel·las** (hĕl′əs) *Modern Greek* **El·las** (ĕ-läs′). *Abbr.* **Gr.** Republic at the southern tip of the Balkan Peninsula. It comprises an indented, mountainous mainland whose ranges continue in numerous islands that make up a fifth of the country. Cereals, olives, and vines are the chief crops, and large numbers of sheep and goats are kept. Greece relies mainly on imported fuels, but oil has been discovered beneath the Aegean Sea. Tourism is a major industry, and the country has large merchant and fishing fleets. The Minoan civilization, Europe's first, flourished in Crete (*c.* 3000–1400 B.C.). Trade (*c.* 1100 B.C.) brought prosperity and heralded the Classical Age. Intercity strife allowed Philip II of Macedon to conquer most of Greece (338 B.C.), and his son Alexander (356–323 B.C.) ruled both Macedon and Greece and built a short-lived empire that was to spread Greek culture from Macedon and Egypt to India. The Romans conquered Greece (168–146 B.C.), and it was later part of the Byzantine Empire. It was conquered by the Ottoman Turks in the 15th century, but finally gained independence (1832) and a king (1833) after the Greek War of Independence. The army usurped power and deposed the king (1967) but was removed in 1974. Greece became a republic in 1975. The country became a full member of the European Economic Community (1981). It is also a strategic member of NATO but has strained relations with fellow member Turkey over its claims in the Aegean and Cyprus. Area, 131,944 square kilometers (50,944 square miles). Population, 10,000,000. Capital, Athens.

greed (grēd) *n.* A rapacious desire for more than one needs or deserves, as of food, wealth, or power; avarice. [Back-formation from GREEDY.]

greed·y (grē′dē) *adj.* **-ier, -iest. 1.** Excessively eager to acquire or possess something, especially in quantity; covetous; avaricious. **2.** Wanting to eat or drink more than one can reasonably consume; gluttonous; voracious. [Middle English *gredy,* Old English *grǣdig,* from Germanic *grǣdhuz* (unattested), hunger.] **—greed·i·ly** *adv.* **—greed·i·ness** *n.*

greegree. Variant of **grigri.**

Greek (grēk) *n.* **1.** *Abbr.* **Gk., Gr.** The language of the Hellenes, constituting the Hellenic group of Indo-European, chronologically divided into **Proto-Greek, Ancient Greek** with the **Koine, Late Greek, Medieval Greek,** and **Modern Greek** *(all of which see).* ***Note:*** Most frequently *Greek* is used to mean *Ancient Greek* or *Classical Greek,* as in the etymologies of this dictionary. **2.** *Abbr.* **Gk., Gr.** A native or inhabitant of Greece, or a descendant of such a person. **3.** *Informal.* Something unintelligible. Used chiefly in the phrase *It's Greek to me.* **4.** A member of the Greek Orthodox Church.
—*adj.* **1.** *Abbr.* **Gk., Gr.** Of, pertaining to, or designating Greece, the Hellenes, their language, or their culture. **2.** Of, pertaining to, or designating the Greek Orthodox Church. [Middle English *Grek,* Old English *Grēcas, Crēcas* (plural), from Germanic *Krēkaz* (unattested), from Latin *Graecus* (singular), from Greek *Graikos, Graikoi,* the name of a prehistoric tribe of Epirus, probably from Illyria.]

Greek Catholic *n.* **1.** A member of the Eastern Orthodox Church. **2.** A member of a Uniat Church.

Greek Church *n.* **1.** See **Eastern Church** (sense 1). **2.** The **Eastern Orthodox Church** *(see).* **3.** The **Greek Orthodox Church** *(see).*

Greek cross *n.* A cross formed by two bars of equal length crossing at the middle at right angles to each other.

Greek fire *n.* An incendiary chemical substance used in ancient and medieval times to set fire to enemy ships; specifically, the substance used by the Byzantine Greeks in the seventh century.

Greek god *n.* A handsome man, especially one whose looks seem to approach the Greek ideal of male beauty.

Greek Orthodox Church *n.* The established self-governing church of Greece, a part of the Eastern Orthodox Church, with its own chief bishop but recognizing the Patriarch of Constantinople as head. Also called "Greek Church."

Gree·ley (grē′lē), **Horace** (1811–72). U.S. journalist and politician. He founded and edited the *New Yorker* (1834–41), the *Log Cabin* (1840), and the *New York Tribune* (1841–72), a daily paper of high quality, through which he expressed his antislavery and moralistic views. In 1872 he unsuccessfully ran for president.

green (grēn) *n.* **1.** Any of a group of colors that may vary in lightness and saturation, whose hue is that of the emerald, or somewhat less yellow than that of growing grass; the hue of that portion of the spectrum lying between yellow and blue; one of the additive or light primaries; one of the psychological primary hues, evoked in the normal observer by radiant energy having a wavelength of approximately 530 nanometers. See **primary color. 2. a.** Something green in color. **b.** Green clothing. **3. greens.** Leafy plants or plant parts eaten as vegetables or in salads. **4. a.** A grassy area or lawn; especially, one used for a specified purpose: *a putting green; a bowling green.* **b.** A grass-covered area in the middle of a village. **5.** A green traffic light that signals that drivers may proceed.
—*adj.* **1.** Of the color green. **2.** Covered with green vegetation or foliage. **3.** Made with green or leafy vegetables: *a green salad.* **4.** Mild or temperate in climate. **5.** Fresh; youthful; vigorous. **6.** Not mature or ripe; young: *green bananas.* **7.** Pale and sickly in appearance; wan. **8.** Not yet fully processed, as: **a.** Not aged: *green wood.* **b.** Not cured or tanned: *green pelts.* **9.** Designating one of three quark colors, the others being red and blue. **10.** Lacking training, conditioning, or experience. **11.** Easily duped or deceived; gullible. **12.** *Informal.* Envious; jealous.
—*v.* **greened, greening, greens.** —*tr.* To make green. —*intr.* To become green. [Middle English *grene,* Old English *grēne,* from Germanic.] **—green·ish** *adj.* **—green·ly** *adv.* **—green·ness** *n.* **—green·y** *adj.*

green algae *pl.n.* Algae of the division Chlorophyta, which includes spirogyra, sea lettuce, and others having pronounced green coloring due to predominance of the pigment chlorophyll.

Green·a·way (grēn′ə-wā′), **Kate,** original name Catherine (1846–1901). English water colorist and illustrator. She excelled as an illustrator of her own children's books, such as *Under the Window* (1879), *A Day in a Child's Life* (1881), and *Kate Greenaway's Birthday Album* (1885).

green·back (grēn′băk′) *n. Informal.* **1.** A legal-tender note of U.S. currency. **2.** A dollar bill.

Greenback Party *n.* A former U.S. political party, organized in 1874, that advocated the use of inconvertible paper money.

green ban *n. Australian.* A refusal by a trade union to do work that may harm the environment.

green bean *n.* The **string bean** *(see).*

green belt *n.* An area of parks, farmland, or uncultivated land surrounding a town or city.

Green Beret *n.* A member of the U.S. Army Special Forces. [From the green beret that is part of the uniform.]

green·bot·tle (grēn′bŏt′l) *n.* A common insect, *Lucilia caesar,* related to the blowflies, that has a green metallic coloring and lays its eggs in decaying flesh.

green·bri·er (grēn′brī′ər) *n.* A plant, the **catbrier** *(see).*

green card *n.* **1.** A U.S. permit for aliens allowing unconditional residence and employment. **2.** An international insurance document for motorists.

green corn *n.* Young, tender ears of sweet corn.

green currency *n.* Formerly, any artificial currency unit, such as

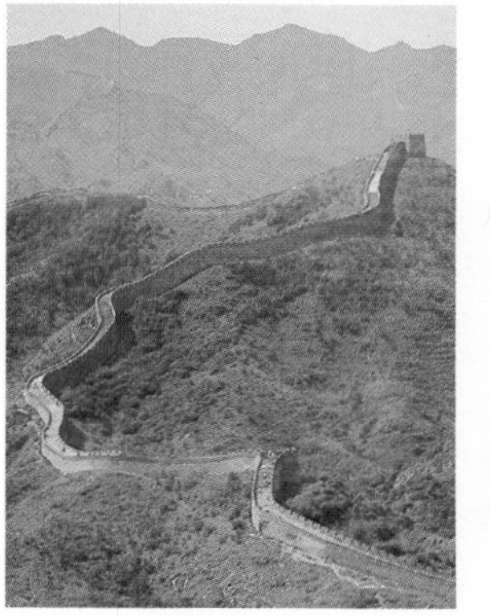

Great Wall of China *The Chinese emperor, Shih Huang Ti (259–210 B.C.), joined together several defensive wall sections to create the enormous barrier known as the Great Wall of China. This section of the present-day wall is near the Chinese capital, Beijing.*

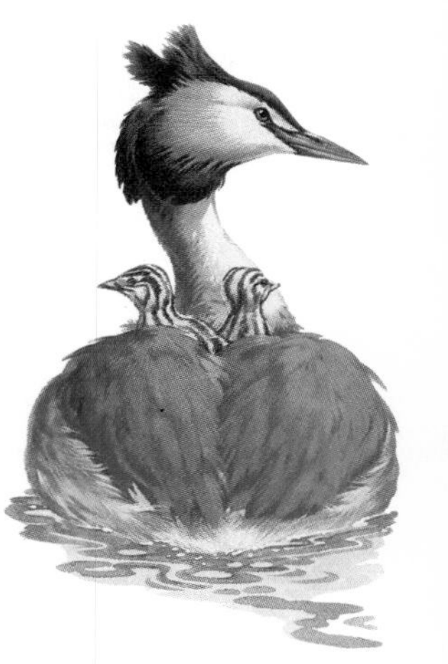

grebe *Species of grebe are found in all the world's continents except Antarctica. Most build floating nests of weeds, anchored to reeds in freshwater lakes and slow-flowing rivers, and young chicks are often carried on the parents' backs. This is the great crested grebe,* Podiceps cristatus.

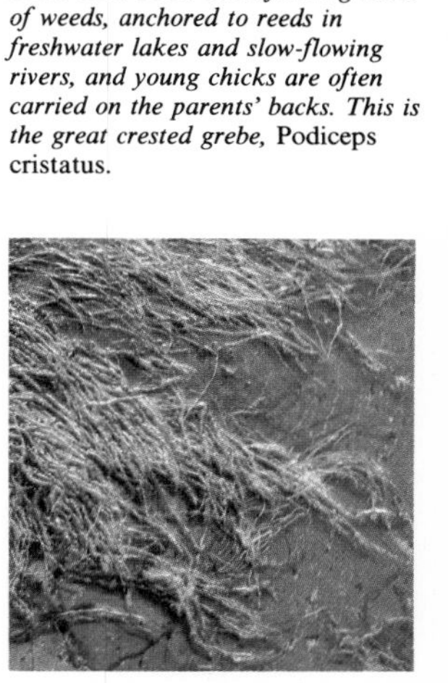

green algae *Found in water or wet places, algae are usually green, red, or brown. They include large seaweeds and the green bloom that appears on damp plant pots. Some species combine with fungi to form lichens.*

greenfinch *A farmland and garden bird of Europe and western Asia. It feeds on seeds that it cracks open with its short, stout beak.*

greenshank *The breeding grounds of the greenshank are found all through northern Europe and Asia. In winter the birds fly south to the Mediterranean and Africa. Greenshanks wade in fairly deep water, feeding on insects and small fish.*

the green pound, used for agricultural transactions within the European Economic Community in order to protect Community prices from the currency fluctuations of the member nations. See **ECU.**

green dragon *n.* A plant, *Arisaema dracontium,* of eastern North America, having minute flowers at the base of a long stalk projecting from a narrow green bract. Also called "dragonroot."

Greene (grēn). **(Henry) Grahame** (1904–91). British novelist and playwright. He wrote both serious and light novels, the former marked by questions of morality and redemption (Greene was a convert to Roman Catholicism). Among his major works are *Brighton Rock* (1938) and *The End of the Affair* (1951). Other novels displayed Greene's interest in political and social troubles; for example, *The Quiet American* (1955) and *The Human Factor* (1978). He also wrote short stories, plays, and film scripts, such as *The Third Man* (1949).

green·er·y (grē´nə-rē) *n., pl.* **-ies. 1. a.** Green foliage; verdure. **b.** Such foliage used for decoration. **2.** A place where plants are grown.

green-eyed (grēn´īd´) *adj.* **1.** Having green eyes. **2.** Jealous.

green·finch (grēn´fĭnch´) *n.* A Eurasian bird, *Carduelis chloris* (or *Chloris chloris*), having green and yellow plumage.

green fingers *pl.n. Chiefly British Informal.* A **green thumb** *(see).*

green·fly (grēn´flī´) *n., pl.* **-flies** or collectively **greenfly.** A green aphid commonly occurring as a parasite on cultivated plants.

green·gage (grēn´gāj´) *n.* **1.** A variety of plum, *Prunus domestica italica,* whose fruit has yellowish-green skin and sweet flesh. **2.** The fruit of this tree. [GREEN + *gage,* after Sir William *Gage* (1777–1864), English botanist, who introduced it into England from France.]

green gland *n.* Either of a pair of excretory organs in certain crustaceans that discharges waste matter through an opening at the base of the antennae.

green·gro·cer (grēn´grō´sər) *n. Chiefly British.* A retailer of fresh fruit and vegetables. **—green·gro·cer·y** *n.*

green·head (grēn´hĕd´) *n.* **1.** A male mallard duck. **2.** Any of various green-headed Australian ants of the genus *Chalcopnera,* having a powerful sting.

green·heart (grēn´härt´) *n.* **1.** A tropical American tree, *Ocotea rodioei* (or *Nectandra rodioei*), having dark, greenish, durable wood. **2.** Any of various similar or related trees. **3.** The wood of such a tree.

green·horn (grēn´hôrn´) *n. Informal.* **1.** An inexperienced or immature person. **2.** A newcomer, especially to a country, who is unfamiliar with local ways. **3.** A gullible person. [Originally, a young animal with immature horns.]

green·house (grēn´hous´) *n.* **1.** A usually glass-enclosed structure used for cultivating plants that require controlled temperature and humidity. **2.** *Informal.* A part of an aircraft covered with a clear plastic bubble or shell.

greenhouse effect *n.* **1.** A heating effect that occurs in greenhouses as a result of solar radiation passing through the glass and heating the contents, which emit infrared radiation that cannot escape through the glass. **2.** The analogous effect that results from the absorption of solar radiation by the earth, its conversion and re-emission in the infrared, the absorption of the infrared radiation by atmospheric ozone, water vapor, and carbon dioxide, and the consequent gradual rise in the temperature of the atmosphere.

green·ing (grē´nĭng) *n.* An apple of any of several varieties having green-skinned fruit, used chiefly in cooking.

green·keep·er (grēn´kēp´ər) *n.* A person who looks after the greens of golf courses.

Green·land (grēn´lənd, -lănd´). *Danish* **Grøn·land** (grœn´län´). Island belonging to Denmark, lying mostly within the Arctic Circle. It is the largest island in the world. Most of the island is permanently ice-covered and uninhabited. The bulk of the population, which is of mixed Eskimo and European descent, is concentrated on the west coast. Fishing and fish processing are the principal industries and there is some mining. Greenland was discovered by Eric the Red in *c.* 960, but modern settlement of the island dates from the early 18th century, when it came under Danish control. It became an integral part of Denmark (1953), but gained internal home rule in 1979. It has great strategic importance, and there are U.S. air bases on it. Area, 2,175,000 square kilometers (840,000 square miles). Capital, Nuuk (formerly Godthåb). See map at **Arctic Ocean. —Green·land·er** *n.*

Greenland Sea. Arm of the Arctic Ocean, lying off the northeast coast of Greenland. It is the principal outlet of the Arctic Ocean into the Atlantic. Drifting ice floes make the northern part of the sea virtually unnavigable.

Greenland spar *n.* A mineral, **cryolite** *(see).*

Greenland whale *n.* An arctic whale, *Balaena mysticetus,* having a black body with a pale throat.

green leek *n.* Any of various green or mostly green Australian parrots.

green·let (grēn´lĭt) *n.* Any of various greenish birds of the genus *Hylophilus,* of Central and South America, related to the vireos.

green light *n.* **1.** The green-colored traffic light, meaning "go." **2.** Permission to proceed with a project or course of action.

green·ling (grēn´lĭng) *n.* Any of various food fishes of the family Hexagrammidae, of the northern Pacific.

green manure *n.* A growing crop, such as a clover or grass, that is plowed into soil to improve fertility.

green monkey *n.* Any of several African monkeys of the genus *Cercopithecus;* especially, *C. aethiops sabaeus,* having yellowish-gray fur with a greenish tinge.

green monkey disease *n.* **Marburg disease** *(see).*

Green Mountains. Range of the Appalachian Mts. extending 402 kilometers (250 miles) from southern Quebec through Vermont to western Massachusetts. Mt. Mansfield in Vermont is the highest peak (1,340 meters; 4,393 feet). It is one of the oldest ranges in North America.

Green·ock (grē´nək, grĭn´ək, grĕn´-). Burgh in Strathclyde Region in western Scotland, on the Firth of Clyde. It is a port, and shipping and shipbuilding are the chief industries.

green·ock·ite (grĕn´ə-kīt´) *n.* A yellow to brown or red mineral, essentially cadmium sulfide (CdS), used as a cadmium ore. [After Charles Cathcart, Lord *Greenock* (died 1859), British soldier.]

green onion *n.* See **scallion** (sense 1).

green pepper *n.* The unripened green fruit of various pepper plants, especially the sweet pepper, eaten raw or cooked.

green plover *n.* A bird, the **lapwing** *(see).*

green pound *n.* See **green currency.**

green revolution *n.* The increased agricultural production in developing countries resulting from the introduction of new high-yielding crop varieties and modern farming techniques.

green·room (grēn´rōōm´, -rŏŏm´) *n.* A waiting room in a theater, concert hall, television studio, or the like for the use of performers when off-stage. [From its being typically painted green.]

green·sand (grēn´sănd´) *n.* A sand or sediment given a dark greenish color by grains of glauconite.

green·shank (grēn´shăngk´) *n.* An Old World wading bird, *Tringa nebularia,* having greenish legs and a long bill.

green·sick·ness (grēn´sĭk´nĭs) *n. Pathology.* See **chlorosis** (sense 2). **—green·sick** *adj.*

green snake *n.* Any of several nonvenomous North American snakes of the genus *Opheodrys,* having a slender yellow-green body.

green soap *n.* A translucent, yellowish-green, soft or liquid soap made chiefly from vegetable oils, potassium hydroxide, oleic acid, glycerine, and purified water, used medicinally as a stimulant in chronic skin disorders. Also called "soft soap."

green·stick fracture (grēn´stĭk´) *n.* A fracture in a long bone of a child or young animal in which the bone is bent and splintered but not completely broken.

green·stone (grēn´stōn´) *n.* **1.** Any of various altered basic igneous rocks colored green by chlorite, hornblende, or epidote. **2.** The most common variety of jade, found in New Zealand and used for making tikis, ornaments, tools, or the like.

green·stuff (grēn´stŭf´) *n.* Green vegetables.

green·sward (grēn´swôrd´) *n. Poetic.* Turf on which the grass is green.

green tea *n.* Tea made from leaves that are not fermented before being dried. Compare **black tea.**

green thumb *n.* The ability to grow plants successfully. Also *chiefly British* "green fingers."

green turtle *n.* A large marine turtle, *Chelonia mydas,* having greenish flesh prized as food, used especially in turtle soup.

green vitriol *n.* A chemical compound, **ferrous sulfate** *(see).*

green·weed (grēn´wēd´) *n.* See **dyer's greenweed.**

Green·wich (grĭn´ĭj, grĕn´-). An ancient village, now a borough of Greater London in England. It is the site of the original Royal Observatory, designed by Sir Christopher Wren, through which passes the prime meridian, or longitude 0°. The Royal Naval College and the National Maritime Museum are also in the borough.

Greenwich mean time *n. Abbr.* **GMT, G.m.t.** Mean solar time for the meridian at Greenwich, England, used as a basis for calculating time throughout most of the world. Also called "Greenwich time," "universal time."

Greenwich meridian *n.* The **prime meridian** *(see)* that passes through Greenwich in England.

Greenwich Village. Village dating from colonial times, now a residential quarter of Lower Manhattan in New York City. Since the early 20th century it has been famous as an artists' quarter. It is also renowned for its cafés, restaurants, and nightclubs.

green·wood (grēn´wŏŏd´) *n. Literary.* A wood or forest when the foliage is green.

greet¹ (grēt) *tr.v.* **greeted, greeting, greets. 1.** To address in a friendly and proper way. **2.** To receive or welcome in a friendly manner. **3.** To receive with a specified reaction: *greet a joke with laughter.* **4.** To present itself to; be perceived by: *A din greeted our ears.* [Middle English *greten,* Old English *grētan,* from Germanic.] **—greet·er** *n.*

greet² *intr.v.* **greeted, greeting, greets.** *Archaic & Scottish.* To cry; weep.

greet·ing (grē´tĭng) *n.* **1.** An act or instance of greeting a person. **2.** *Usually* **greetings.** A gesture or word of welcome or salutation: *season's greetings.*

greg·a·rine (grĕg´ə-rīn´, -rĭn) *n.* Any of various sporozoan protozoans of the order Gregarinida, that are parasitic within invertebrates such as arthropods and annelids. ~*adj.* Of or belonging to the Gregarinida. [New Latin *Gregarina* (genus name), from Latin *gregārius,* GREGARIOUS.]

gre·gar·i·ous (grĭ-gâr´ē-əs) *adj.* **1.** Tending to move in or form a group with others of the same kind, in a herd, pack, or flock. **2.** Seeking and enjoying the company of others of one's kind; sociable. **3.** *Botany.* Growing in groups that are close together but not densely clustered or matted. [Latin *gregārius,* belonging to a flock, from *grex* (stem *greg-*), herd, flock.] —**gre·gar·i·ous·ly** *adv.* —**gre·gar·i·ous·ness** *n.*

grège, greige (grāzh) *n.* Light grayish-brown.

Gre·go·ri·an (grĭ-gôr′ē-ən, grĭ-gōr′-) *adj.* Pertaining to, associated with, or introduced by Pope Gregory I or Pope Gregory XIII.

Gregorian calendar *n.* The calendar now in use, introduced in 1582 by Pope Gregory XIII (1502-85), as a corrected form of the earlier **Julian calendar**, (*see*). The Gregorian calendar stipulates that each ordinary year consists of 365 days and each leap year, or year whose number is divisible by four, of 366 days except for centenary years whose numbers are not divisible by 400.

Gregorian chant *n.* The monodic liturgical plainsong of the Roman Catholic Church, systematized during the papacy of Gregory I. Also called "plainsong."

Greg·o·ry I (grĕg′ə-rē), **Saint**, known as "the Great" (c. 540-604). Roman Doctor of the Church. As Pope Gregory I (590-604), he did much to increase papal authority and to establish the temporal independence of the papacy. He sent St. Augustine on a missionary expedition to Britain in 596.

grei·sen (grī′zən) *n.* A granitic rock composed chiefly of quartz and mica. [German *Greisen, Greissen*, from *greissen*†, to split.]

gre·mi·al (grē′mē-əl) *n.* In the Roman Catholic church, a silk cloth formerly placed on the lap of a bishop during Mass. [Medieval Latin *gremiāle*, from Latin *gremium*, lap.]

grem·lin (grĕm′lən) *n.* **1.** An imaginary gnomelike creature to whom mechanical problems in military aircraft were frequently attributed during World War II. **2.** Any source of trouble or mischief. [20th century : origin obscure, but influenced by GOBLIN.]

Gre·na·da (grə-nā′də). Independent island republic within the Commonwealth, in the southeastern Caribbean Sea. It was a British colony until 1974. It consists of the volcanic island of Grenada, the southernmost of the Windward Islands, and the smaller islands of the southern Grenadines. The economy is almost entirely agricultural. Area, 344 square kilometers (133 square miles). Population, 85,000. Capital, St. George's.

gre·nade (grə-nād′) *n.* **1.** A missile containing priming and bursting charges, designed to be thrown by hand or fired from a launcher-equipped rifle. **2.** A glass container filled with a volatile chemical or a liquid that is dispersed when the glass is thrown and smashed. [French, from Old French *pome grenate*, POMEGRANATE (from its shape).]

gren·a·dier (grĕn′ə-dîr′) *n.* **1. a.** A member of the British Grenadier Guards, the first regiment of the royal household infantry. **b.** Formerly, a soldier who threw grenades. **2.** Any of various deep-sea fishes of the family Macrouridae, having a long tapering tail and lacking a tail fin. In this sense, also called "rat-tail." **3.** Any of several African weaverbirds of the genus **Estrilda**, having a brightly colored plumage and bill. [French, "grenade thrower," from *grenade*, GRENADE.]

gren·a·dine¹ (grĕn′ə-dēn′, grĕn′ə-dēn′) *n.* A thin, openwork fabric of silk, wool, cotton, or synthetic material. [French *grenadine*, perhaps from *Granada*, in Spain.]

grenadine² *n.* A thick, sweet syrup made from pomegranates or red currants and used as flavoring, especially in mixed drinks. [French, from Old French *pome grenate*, POMEGRANATE.]

Gren·a·dines (grĕn′ə-dēnz′, grĕn′ə-dēnz′). Group of some 600 small islands and islets in the Windward Islands, which lie between the Caribbean Sea and the main body of the Atlantic Ocean. The southern Grenadines, including Carriacou, the largest island, are part of Grenada, while the northern islands are part of St. Vincent and the Grenadines.

Gre·no·ble (grə-nō′bəl). City lying in the foothills of the Alps, on the Isère River, in southeastern France. It is the capital of Isère department and a marketing and industrial center. Grenoble is the principal hydroelectric center of France and an important center for nuclear research.

Gresh·am (grĕsh′əm), **Sir Thomas** (c. 1519-79). English banker, merchant, and financier. He made a fortune as a banker and was one of the founders of the Royal Exchange (completed in 1570).

Gresh·am's law (grĕsh′əmz) *n. Economics.* The theory that if two kinds of money in circulation have the same denominational value but different intrinsic values, the money with higher intrinsic value (called *good*) will be hoarded and eventually driven out of circulation by the money with lesser intrinsic value (called *bad*). [After Sir Thomas GRESHAM.]

gres·so·ri·al (grĕ-sôr′ē-əl, grĕ-sōr′-) *adj. Zoology.* Adapted for walking or having legs adapted for walking. Said of the ostrich and other flightless birds. [New Latin *gressōrius*, from *gressor*, one that walks, from Latin *gradī* (past participle *gressus*), to step, go.]

Gret·na Green (grĕt′nə grēn′). Village in Dumfries and Galloway in Scotland, c. 2 kilometers (1.25 miles) from the English border. It was famous as a place where eloping lovers were married without residential qualifications or the consent of parents (1754-1856). After 1856 one of the parties had to have resided in Scotland for at least 21 days before the marriage. The services were usually performed by the local blacksmith, until such marriages were made illegal in 1940.

grew. Past tense of **grow.**

grey. Variant of **gray.**

Grey (grā), **Charles, 2nd Earl** (1764-1845). British politician. He became the acknowledged leader of the Whigs on the death of Charles James Fox in 1806. In 1830 he became prime minister and presided over the passing of the Great Reform Act (1832) and the

abolition of slavery throughout the British Empire (1833).

Grey, Lady Jane (1537-54). Queen of England for nine days. She was the great-granddaughter of Henry VII. On Edward VI's death (July 10, 1553) she was proclaimed queen, but the country rallied to Mary Tudor (Mary I), and after nine days Lady Jane was imprisoned. She was subsequently beheaded.

Grey, Zane (1872-1939). U.S. author. He wrote more than 60 books, which sold millions of copies during his lifetime. Most of his books were Westerns, such as *Riders of the Purple Sage* (1912), filled with self-reliant, righteous heroes, naive heroines, and ruthless villains. Many motion pictures were made from his books.

grey·hen (grā′hĕn′) *n.* The female of the **black grouse** (see).

grey·hound (grā′hound′) *n.* A large, slender dog of an ancient breed, having a smooth coat, a narrow head, and long legs, and capable of running swiftly. [Middle English *grehound*, Old English *grīghund* : *grieg* (unattested), bitch + *hund*, dog, HOUND.]

grey·lag (grā′lăg′) *n.* The **graylag goose** (see).

Grey of Fal·lo·don (făl′ə-dən), **Edward Grey, 1st Viscount** (1862-1933). British politician. As foreign secretary (1905-16), he was directly responsible for the Anglo-Russian entente (1907) and the secret Treaty of London (1915) that brought Italy into World War I.

grib·ble (grĭb′əl) *n.* Any of several small, wood-boring marine crustaceans of the genus *Limnoria*; especially, *L. lignorum*, which often damages underwater wooden structures. [Perhaps a diminutive of GRUB.]

grid (grĭd) *n.* **1.** A framework of parallel or crisscrossed bars; gridiron. **2.** A pattern of horizontal and vertical lines forming squares of uniform size on a map, chart, aerial photograph, or the like, used as a reference for locating points. **3.** *Electricity.* **a.** An interconnected system of electric cables and power stations that distributes electricity over a large area. **b.** A corrugated or perforated conducting plate in a storage battery. **c.** A network or coil of fine wires located between the anode and the cathode of a vacuum tube. **4.** A football field. [Short for GRIDIRON.]

grid bias *n.* The fixed voltage applied between the cathode and the grid of a vacuum tube.

grid·dle (grĭd′l) *n.* A thick, flat iron pan or other flat metal surface used for cooking by dry heat. —*tr.v.* **griddled, -dling, -dles.** To cook on a griddle. [Middle English *gredil*, from Old French, from Vulgar Latin *crāticulum* (unattested), small grid, from Latin *crāticula*, diminutive of *crātis*, wickerwork.]

grid·dle·cake (grĭd′l-kāk′) *n.* A pancake (see).

grid·i·ron (grĭd′ī′ərn) *n.* **1.** A flat framework of parallel metal bars used for grilling meat or fish. **2.** Any framework or network suggestive of a gridiron. **3.** A football field. **4.** A metal structure high above the stage of a theater, from which ropes or cables are strung to scenery and lights. [Middle English *gredire*, variant (influenced by *iren*, IRON) of *gredile, gredil*, GRIDDLE.]

grid·lock (grĭd′lŏk′) *n.* A traffic jam in which no traffic can move in any direction because the vehicles have formed into intersecting crisscrossed lines. —**grid·locked** *adj.*

grief (grēf) *n.* **1.** Intense mental anguish; deep remorse, acute sorrow, or the like. **2.** A source of deep remorse or acute sorrow. —See Synonyms at **regret.** —**come to grief.** To meet with disaster; fail. [Middle English *gref*, from Old French *grief, gref*, from *grever*, GRIEVE.]

Grieg (grēg), **Edvard Hagerup** (1843-1907). Norwegian composer. He was inspired by Norwegian folk music, and many of its idioms occur in his music. His most famous works are the incidental music for *Peer Gynt* (1875) and a piano concerto (1868).

griev·ance (grē′vəns) *n.* **1. a.** An actual or supposed circumstance regarded as just cause for complaint or protest. **b.** A complaint or protestation based on such a circumstance. **2.** Indignation or resentment stemming from a feeling of having been wronged. —See Synonyms at **injustice.** [Middle English *grievaunce*, from Old French *grevance*, from *grever*, GRIEVE.]

grieve (grēv) *v.* **grieved, grieving, grieves.** —*tr.* **1.** To cause to be sorrowful or anguished; distress. **2.** *Archaic.* To hurt or harm. —*intr.* To be sorrowful; lament; mourn. [Middle English *greven*, from Old French *grever*, from Latin *gravāre*, to oppress, weigh upon, from *gravis*, heavy, weighty.] —**griev·ing·ly** *adv.*

griev·ous (grē′vəs) *adj.* **1. a.** Causing grief, pain, or anguish. **b.** Expressing grief; mourning. **2.** Serious or dire; grave. —**griev·ous·ly** *adv.* —**griev·ous·ness** *n.*

grievous bodily harm *n. Abbr.* **G.B.H.** In criminal law, serious physical harm inflicted by one person on another.

grif·fin, grif·fon, gry·phon (grĭf′ən) *n. Greek Mythology.* A fabulous beast with the head and wings of an eagle and the body of a lion. [Middle English *griffon*, from Old French *grifoun*, from Late Latin *grȳphus*, from Latin, from Greek *grups*.]

Grif·fith (grĭf′ĭth), **Arthur** (1872-1922). Irish nationalist leader. In 1905 he founded the Sinn Fein movement for Irish independence, and in 1918 he was elected to the British Parliament. With the other Sinn Fein members, he withdrew and established the Irish Dáil. He headed the Irish group that negotiated the 1921 treaty establishing the Irish Free State.

Griffith, D(avid) W(ark) (1875-1948). U.S. film director and producer. His revolutionary film *The Birth of a Nation* (1915) used the innovative techniques for which he is famous: the fade-in and fade-out, close-ups, moving-camera shots, flashbacks, and montage effects.

gridiron *A metal frame placed over a fire's glowing embers for cooking.*

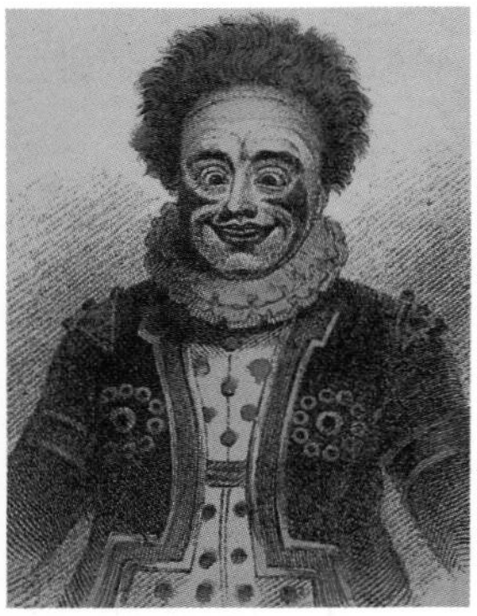

Grimaldi, Joseph *A portrait of Joseph Grimaldi (1779–1837), who was the first modern clown. He was the son of a Genoese harlequin who played in Italian commedia dell'arte.*

PRONUNCIATION KEY

ă, pat; ā, pay; âr, care;
ä, father, are; b, **bib**;
ch, **church**; d, **deed**; ĕ, pet;
ē, be; f, **fife**; g, **gag**; h, **hat**;
hw, **which**; ĭ, pit; ī, pie;
îr, **pier**; j, **judge**; k, **kick**;
l, **lid**, nee**dl**e; m, **mum**;
n, **no**, sudden; ng, **thing**;
ŏ, pot; ō, **toe**; ô, **paw**, for;
oi, **noise**; ou, **out**; o͝o, **book**;
o͞o, **boot**; p, **pop**; r, **roar**;
s, **sauce**; sh, **ship**, **dish**;
t, **tight**; th, **thin**, **path**;
th, **this**, **bathe**; ŭ, **cut**; ûr, **fur**;
v, **valve**; w, **with**; y, **yes**;
z, **zebra**, **size**; zh, **vision**;
ə, **a**bout, it**e**m, ed**i**ble, gall**o**p, circ**u**s, peaceful

IN FOREIGN WORDS:

à, *Fr.* **ami**; œ, *Fr.* **feu**, *Ger.* **schön**; ü, *Fr.* **tu**, *Ger.* **über**; KH, *Ger.* **ich**, *Scot.* **loch**; N, *Fr.* **bon**; y', *Fr.* **Compiègne**

STRESS MARKS:

Primary stress: ′
in·cite′ (ĭn-sīt′)
Secondary stress: ′
in′sight′ (ĭn′sīt′)

grif·fon (grĭf′ən) *n.* **1.** Any of several breeds of dog having a wiry coat; especially, a small dog of a breed originating in Belgium, having a short, bearded muzzle. **2.** Any of several Old World vultures of the genus *Gyps*, especially *G. fulvus*, having black wings and a grayish body. **3.** Variant of **griffin.** [From *griffon*, variant of GRIFFIN.]

grift (grĭft) *n. Slang.* **1.** Money made dishonestly, as by a swindle. **2.** A swindle or confidence game.
∼*intr.v.* **grifted, grifting, grifts.** *Slang.* To practice swindling or cheating. [Variant of GRAFT (money).] **—grift·er** *n.*

grig (grĭg) *n. Regional.* **1.** A grasshopper or cricket. **2.** A small eel. **3.** A lively merry person. [Middle English (originally "dwarf") : origin obscure.]

Gri·gnard reagent (grē-nyär′) *n. Chemistry.* Any of a group of reagents with the general formula RMgX, where R is an organic group and X is a halogen atom. They are used in the synthesis of organic compounds. [After Victor *Grignard* (1871–1935), French chemist.]

gri·gri, gree·gree, gris-gris (grē′grē) *n.* An African charm, fetish, or amulet. [17th century : of African origin.]

grill (grĭl) *v.* **grilled, grilling, grills.** —*tr.* **1.** To toast or fry on a gridiron or broil under a grill. **2.** To torture as if by subjecting to great heat. **3.** *Informal.* To question relentlessly; cross-examine. **4.** To mark or emboss with a gridiron. —*intr.* To undergo broiling.
∼*n.* **1.** A part of a cooker that gives out intense downward heat, under which food may be cooked; a gridiron. **2.** Food cooked by grilling or broiling. **3.** A grillroom. **4.** Variant of **grille.** [French *griller*, from *gril, grille*, a grating, gridiron, from Old French *grille, grail*, from Vulgar Latin *grāticula* (unattested), variant of Latin *crāticula*. See **griddle.**]

gril·lage (grĭl′ĭj) *n.* A network or frame of crossed timbers serving as a foundation, usually on treacherous soil. [French, from *grille*, grating, GRILL.]

grille, grill (grĭl) *n.* **1.** A metal grating used as a screen, divider, barrier, or decorative element, as: **a.** In a window or gateway for observing callers. **b.** In a convent or prison for separating visitors. **c.** On a motor vehicle to protect the radiator. **2.** A square opening at the back of the hazard side of a tennis court. [French, grating, GRILL.]

grilled (grĭld) *adj.* **1.** Broiled under a grill. **2.** Having a grille.

Grill·par·zer (grĭl′pär′tsər), **Franz** (1791–1872). Austrian author. Often condemned by censors and rejected by the public, he wrote several tragic poems and plays, including *The Ancestress* (1817) and *The Waves of Sea and Love* (1831). Although unheralded at first, his plays were later considered among Austria's greatest dramas.

grill·room (grĭl′ro͞om′, -ro͝om′) *n.* A restaurant or room in a restaurant where grilled foods are served. Also called "grill."

grilse (grĭls) *n., pl.* **grilse.** A young salmon on its first return from the sea to fresh or brackish waters. [Middle English *grilles*, variant of *girsil*, perhaps from Old French *grisel*, gray. See **grizzle.**]

grim (grĭm) *adj.* **grimmer, grimmest. 1.** Unrelenting; rigid; stern. **2.** Uninviting or unnerving in aspect. **3. a.** Ghastly; sinister. **b.** Savagely ironic: *a grim jest.* **4.** *Archaic.* Ferocious; savage. **5.** *Informal.* Unpleasant; repellent: *a grim prospect.* **—**See Synonyms at **ghastly.** [Middle English *grim*, Old English *grim*, fierce, severe, from Germanic.] **—grim·ly** *adv.* **—grim·ness** *n.*

grim·ace (grĭm′ĭs, grĭ-mās′) *n.* A sharp contortion of the face expressive of pain, contempt, or disgust.
∼*intr.v.* **grimaced, -macing, -maces.** To contort the facial features. [French *grimace*, earlier *grimache*, from Spanish *grimazo*, caricature, from *grima*, fright, from Germanic; akin to GRIM.]

Gri·mal·di (grĭ-mäl′dē), **Joseph** (1779–1837). English clown, one of the most famous clowns in history.

gri·mal·kin (grĭ-măl′kən, grĭ-môl′-) *n.* **1.** A cat; especially, an old female cat. **2.** A shrewish old woman. [Variant of *graymalkin* : GRAY + dialectal *malkin*, lewd woman, hussy, Middle English *Malkyn*, diminutive of *Mald*, pet form for *Matilda.*]

grime (grīm) *n.* Black dirt or soot; especially, such dirt clinging to or ingrained in a surface.
∼*tr.v.* **grimed, griming, grimes.** To cover with dirt; begrime. [Middle English *grim(e)*, from Middle Dutch *grīme.*]

Grimm (grĭm), **Jakob** (1785–1863) and his brother **Wilhelm** (1786–1859). German writers and philologists. They are famous for their collections of fairy tales (1812–14).

Grimm's Law *n. Phonetics.* A formula describing the regular changes undergone by Indo-European stop consonants represented in Germanic. It states that Indo-European *p, t,* and *k* become Germanic *f, th,* and *h*; Indo-European *b, d,* and *g* become Germanic *p, t,* and *k*; and Indo-European *bh, dh,* and *gh* become Germanic *b, d,* and *g.* [After Jakob GRIMM.]

grim reaper *n.* Death, viewed as an untimely destroyer of life, and based on the notion of Father Time wielding his scythe.

Grims·by (grĭmz′bē). Official name **Great Grims·by.** A town in the nonmetropolitan county of Humberside, at the mouth of the Humber River, in east-central England. It is one of the largest fishing ports in the world and supports a major frozen-food industry.

grim·y (grī′mē) *adj.* **-ier, -iest.** Covered or ingrained with grime. **—**See Synonyms at **dirty.** **—grim·i·ly** *adv.* **—grim·i·ness** *n.*

grin (grĭn) *v.* **grinned, grinning, grins.** —*intr.* To draw back the lips and bare the teeth, especially in a wide smile. —*tr.* To express with a grin. **—grin and bear it.** To put up with stoically; accept one's lot.
∼*n.* **1.** The act of grinning. **2.** The expression on the face produced by grinning. [Middle English *grinnen*, Old English *grennian*, to grimace (in pleasure or displeasure); akin to *grānian*, to GROAN.] **—grin·ner** *n.* **—grin·ning·ly** *adv.*

grind (grīnd) *v.* **ground** (ground), **grinding, grinds.** —*tr.* **1. a.** To crush, pulverize, or powder with friction, especially by rubbing between two hard surfaces: *grind wheat into flour.* **b.** To shape, sharpen, or refine with friction: *grind a lens.* **2.** To rub (two surfaces) together; gnash: *grind the teeth.* **3.** To bear down on harshly; oppress. Often used with *down.* **4. a.** To operate by turning a crank: *grind an organ.* **b.** To produce (a tune, for example) by turning a crank. Used with *out.* **5.** To produce mechanically or without inspiration. Used with *out*: *publishers grinding out the same old stuff year after year.* **6.** To instill or teach by persistent repetition. Used with *into*: *grind the truth into their heads.* —*intr.* **1.** To perform the operation of grinding something. **2.** To be ground. **3.** To move with noisy friction; grate. **4.** *Informal.* To devote oneself to study or work. **5.** *Slang.* To rotate the pelvis in the manner of a striptease artist. Used chiefly in the phrase *bump and grind.*
∼*n.* **1.** The act of grinding. **2.** A crunching or grinding noise. **3.** A specific grade or degree of pulverization, as of coffee beans: *coarse grind.* **4.** *Informal.* **a.** A laborious task, routine, or study: *tired of the daily grind of work and commuting.* **b.** One who works or studies excessively. [Grind, ground, ground; Middle English *grinden, grond, ygrounden;* Old English *grindan*†, *grond* (plural *grundon*), *gegrunden.*] **—grind·ing·ly** *adv.*

grin·de·li·a (grĭn-dē′lē-ə) *n.* **1.** Any plant of the genus *Grindelia*, having yellow, asterlike flowers, sometimes cultivated for ornament. **2.** The dried plants of certain species of grindelia, used medicinally in tonics, for example. [New Latin, after D.H. *Grindel* (1777–1836), Russian botanist.]

grind·er (grīn′dər) *n.* **1.** One that grinds; especially, a person who sharpens cutting edges. **2.** A grinding machine: *a coffee grinder; a meat grinder.* **3. a.** A molar. **b. grinders.** *Informal.* The teeth. **4.** See **hero** (sense 5).

grind·ing wheel (grīn′dĭng) *n.* An abrasive wheel usually consisting of a composite of hard particles, such as emery, bonded by a resin and used for grinding and sharpening tools.

grind·stone (grīnd′stōn′) *n.* **1.** A stone disk turned on an axle for grinding, polishing, or sharpening tools. **2.** A millstone. **—keep** (or **have**) **one's nose to the grindstone.** To work diligently and continuously.

grin·go (grĭng′gō) *n., pl.* **-gos.** In Latin America, a foreigner, especially an American or Englishman. Used contemptuously. [Spanish *gringo*†, unknown tongue, gibberish.]

grip[1] (grĭp) *n.* **1.** A tight hold; a firm grasp. **2.** The pressure or strength of such a grasp. **3. a.** A manner of grasping and holding something, such as a racket or golf club. **b.** A part for holding or grasping. **4.** A handshake. **5.** Mastery; command; understanding: *he has a good grip on French grammar.* **6.** A spasm or seizure, as of pain. **7. a.** A mechanical device that grasps and holds. **b.** A part designed to be grasped and held; handle. **8.** A small suitcase or valise. **9. a.** A stagehand who helps in shifting scenery. **b.** A member of a film production crew who adjusts sets and props and sometimes assists the cameraman. **10.** The degree of hold a tire has on the road. **—come to grips. 1.** To fight in hand-to-hand combat. **2.** To deal actively and conclusively, as with a problem. **—get a grip on oneself.** To be mentally in control of oneself. **—lose one's grip.** *Informal.* To lose control or mastery, especially of oneself.
∼*v.* **gripped, gripping, grips.** —*tr.* **1.** To secure and maintain a tight hold on; seize firmly. **2.** To take hold of the mind or emotions of: *The audience was gripped by suspense.* —*intr.* To hold securely. [Middle English *grip*, partly Old English *gripa*, grasp, and partly Old English *gripa*, handful.]

grip[2]. Variant of **grippe.**

gripe (grīp) *v.* **griped, griping, gripes.** —*tr.* **1.** To cause sharp pain in the bowels of. **2.** *Archaic.* To grasp; seize. **3.** *Archaic.* To oppress or afflict. —*intr.* **1.** To have sharp pains in the bowels. **2.** *Informal.* To complain naggingly or petulantly; grumble. **3.** *Nautical.* To tend to turn into the wind. Used of a boat.
∼*n.* **1. gripes.** Sharp, repeated pains in the bowels. **2.** *Informal.* A complaint. **3.** *Rare.* A grip; grasp. **4. gripes.** Ropes used to tie up a boat. **5.** *Archaic.* A handle. [Middle English *gripen*, Old English *grīpan*, from Germanic.] **—grip·er** *n.* **—grip·ing·ly** *adv.*

grippe, grip (grĭp) *n. Pathology.* **Influenza** *(see).* [French, from *gripper*, to seize, from Old French, from Frankish *grīpan* (unattested).]

grip·ping (grĭp′ĭng) *adj.* Holding one's undivided attention; riveting. **—grip·ping·ly** *adv.*

grip·sack (grĭp′săk′) *n.* A small suitcase.

Gris (grēs), **Juan,** born José Victoriano Gonzáles (1887–1927). Spanish cubist painter. He settled in Paris in 1906 and contributed especially to the development of synthetic cubism.

gri·saille (grĭ-zāl′; *French* grē-zä′y′) *n.* **1.** A style of monochromatic painting in shades of gray. **2.** A painting or design in this style. [French, from *gris*, gray, from Old French, from Frankish *gris* (unattested).]

gris·e·o·ful·vin (grĭz′ē-ō-fo͝ol′vən) *n.* An antibiotic used to treat ringworm and other fungal infections of the hair, skin, and nails. [New Latin, from *Penicillium griseofulvum dierckx*, fungus from which it was isolated : Medieval Latin *griseus*, gray + Latin *fulvus*, (reddish) yellow.]

gris·e·ous (grĭs′ē-əs, grĭz′-) *adj.* Mottled or grizzled with gray. [Medieval Latin *griseus*, from Germanic.]

gri·sette (grĭ-zĕt′) *n.* A French working girl, such as a shop assistant, for example. [French, an inexpensive gray fabric for dresses, a woman wearing such a dress, from *gris,* gray. See **grisaille.**]

gris-gris. Variant of **grigri.**

gris·ly (grĭz′lē) *adj.* **-lier, -liest.** Horrifying; repugnant; gruesome. —See Synonyms at **ghastly.** [Middle English *grisly,* Old English *grislīc.*]

gri·son (grī′sən, grīz′ən) *n.* Either of two carnivorous mammals, *Grison vittatus* or *G. cuja,* of Central and South America, having grizzled fur, a slender body, and short legs. [French, from Old French, gray animal, from *gris,* gray. See **grisaille.**]

gris·sin·i (grĭ-sē′nē) *pl.n.* Singular **grissine.** *Italian.* Long, slender, crisp sticks of bread.

grist (grĭst) *n.* **1.** Grain or a quantity of grain for grinding. **2.** Ground grain. **—grist for** (or **to**) **one's mill.** Something that can be used or turned to one's advantage. [Middle English *grist,* Old English *grīst.*]

gris·tle (grĭs′əl) *n.* Cartilage (*see*), especially when present in meat. [Middle English *gristil,* Old English *gristle,* from Germanic *gristil-* (unattested).]

gris·tly (grĭs′lē) *adj.* **-tlier, -tliest. 1.** Composed of or containing gristle. **2.** Resembling gristle. **—gris·tli·ness** *n.*

grist·mill (grĭst′mĭl′) *n.* A mill for grinding grain.

grit (grĭt) *n.* **1.** Minute rough granules, as of sand or stone. **2.** The texture or structure of stone to be used in grinding. **3.** A coarse hard sandstone, used for making grindstones and millstones. Also called "gritstone." **4.** *Informal.* Indomitable spirit; pluck. *—v.* **gritted, gritting, grits.** *—tr.* **1.** To clamp (the teeth) together, especially through anger or frustration. **2.** To cover or treat with grit. *—intr.* To make a grinding noise. [Middle English *grete,* Old English *grēot,* from Germanic.]

grith (grĭth) *n.* **1.** Protection or sanctuary provided by Old English law in certain circumstances, as when in a church or traveling on the king's highway. **2.** *Archaic.* Mercy or protection given in battle. [Middle English *grith,* Old English *grith,* from Old Norse *gridht.*]

grits (grĭts) *pl.n.* **1.** Coarsely ground grain, especially oats or corn. **2. Hominy grits** (*see*). [Middle English *gryt,* bran, Old English *grytt,* from Germanic.]

grit·ty (grĭt′ē) *adj.* **-tier, -tiest. 1.** Containing or resembling grit. **2.** Showing resolution and fortitude; plucky. —See Synonyms at **brave. —grit·ti·ness** *n.*

Gri·vas (grē′väs′), **Georgios** (1898–1974). Cypriot soldier and politician, one of the principal advocates of Enosis (Cypriot union with Greece). He formed a guerrilla army, EOKA (National Organization for the Cyprus Struggle), to fight against British rule. He opposed the 1959 agreements that gave Cyprus independence and after 1964, as commander of the Cypriot National Guard, led the Greek Cypriots in the fighting against the Turkish Cypriots.

griv·et (grĭv′ĭt) *n.* A long-tailed African monkey, *Cercopithecus aethiops,* having a greenish-gray coat and tufts of white hair on the face. [French *grivet†.*]

griz·zle¹ (grĭz′əl) *v.* **-zled, -zling, -zles.** *—tr.* To make gray. *—intr.* To become gray. *—n.* **1.** The color gray. **2.** *Archaic.* Gray hair. **3. a.** The color of a roan animal. **b.** A roan animal. [Middle English *grisel,* gray, from Old French, diminutive of *gris,* gray, from Frankish *grīs* (unattested).]

grizzle² *intr.v.* **-zled, -zling, -zles.** *Chiefly British.* **1.** To whimper; whine. **2.** To complain; grumble. [18th century (originally, to grin) : perhaps an ironic allusion to *patient Grizel* (Griselda), character in tales who exemplified the patient and uncomplaining wife.] **—griz·zler** *n.*

griz·zled (grĭz′əld) *adj.* **1.** Streaked with or partly gray. **2.** Having gray or graying hair.

griz·zly (grĭz′lē) *adj.* **-zlier, -zliest.** Grizzled. *—n., pl.* **grizzlies.** A grizzly bear.

grizzly bear *n.* The grayish form of the brown bear, *Ursus arctos,* of northwestern North America, sometimes considered a separate species, *U. horribilis.* Also called "grizzly."

gro. gross.

groan (grōn) *v.* **groaned, groaning, groans.** *—intr.* **1.** To voice a deep, wordless, prolonged sound expressive of pain, grief, annoyance, or disapproval. **2.** To produce a similar sound expressive of stress or strain: *The house groaned in the wind.* **3.** *Informal.* To complain or grumble, especially continually. **4.** To suffer oppression. *—tr.* To utter or convey with groaning. *—n.* The sound made in groaning; a moan. [Middle English *gronen,* Old English *grānian,* akin to *grennian,* to GRIN.] **—groan·er** *n.* **—groan·ing·ly** *adv.*

groat (grōt) *n.* A British silver fourpence piece used from the 14th to the 17th century. [Middle English *grote,* from Middle Dutch *groot,* "great" (referring to the thickness of the coin).]

groats (grōts) *pl.n.* **1.** Hulled, usually crushed grain, especially oats. **2.** Ground oat kernels boiled to a paste in water and used as food. [Middle English *grotes,* Old English *grotan.*]

gro·cer (grō′sər) *n.* A shopkeeper who sells foodstuffs and sundry household supplies. [Middle English, from Old French *grossier,* wholesale dealer, from Medieval Latin *grossārius,* from Latin *grossus,* thick, GROSS.]

gro·cer·y (grō′sə-rē) *n., pl.* **-ies. 1.** A store selling foodstuffs and household supplies. **2.** The occupation of a grocer. **3. groceries.** Goods sold by a grocer.

grog (grŏg) *n.* Alcoholic drinks; especially, rum diluted with water. [After Admiral Edward Vernon (1684–1757), nicknamed Old Grog because of his habit of wearing a GROGRAM coat. He ordered that diluted rather than neat rum be served to his sailors.]

grog·gy (grŏg′ē) *adj.* **-gier, -giest.** Unsteady and dazed, as from sleep or drugs. [From GROG.] **—grog·gi·ly** *adv.* **—grog·gi·ness** *n.*

grog·ram (grŏg′rəm) *n.* **1.** A coarse, often stiffened fabric of silk, mohair, or wool, or a blend of these. **2.** A garment of this fabric. [Alteration of GROSGRAIN.]

groin (groin) *n.* **1. a.** *Anatomy.* The crease at the junction of the thighs with the trunk, together with the adjacent region. **b.** The external genital organs. **2.** *Architecture.* The curved edge at the junction of two intersecting vaults. **3.** A low wall built out into the sea to prevent erosion of the shore. *~tr.v.* **groined, groining, groins.** To provide or build with groins. [Earlier *gryne,* Middle English *grynde,* perhaps from Old English *grynde,* abyss, depression, from Germanic *grundja-* (unattested), from Common Germanic *grunduz* (unattested), GROUND.]

grom·met (grŏm′ĭt) *n.* **1. a.** A reinforced eyelet in cloth, leather, or the like, through which a fastener may be passed. **b.** A rubber or plastic ring set in a hole through metal, especially in the chassis of an electronic device, through which wires can be passed without chafing. **2.** *Nautical.* A rope or metal ring used for securing the edge of a sail. Also called "grummet." [Obsolete French *grom-(m)ette, gourmette,* bridle ring, from Old French *gourmel,* perhaps from Frankish *worm* (unattested), worm.]

grom·well (grŏm′wəl) *n.* **1.** Any of several plants of the genus *Lithospermum,* such as *L. officinale,* having small yellow or white flowers. **2.** Any of several similar or related plants. [Middle English *gromil,* from Old French, perhaps from Vulgar Latin *gruīnum milium* (unattested), "crane's millet" : Latin *gruīnus,* of a crane, from *grūs,* crane + *milium,* MILLET.]

Gro·my·ko (grə-mē′kō), **Andrey Andreyevich** (1909–89). Soviet statesman. After joining the Communist Party in 1931, he was appointed ambassador to the United States (1943) and ambassador to the United Nations (1946–48). He served as foreign minister from 1957 until appointed Soviet premier in 1985.

Gro·ning·en (grō′nĭng-ən). A province in the northeastern Netherlands. It is largely an agricultural region, but it acquired new industrial importance when vast reserves of natural gas were discovered in 1961. The provincial capital is the city of Groningen.

Grønland. See Greenland.

groom (grōom, grŏom) *n.* **1.** A man or boy employed to take care of horses. **2.** A bridegroom. **3.** Any of several officers in an English royal household. **4.** *Archaic.* **a.** A man. **b.** A manservant. *~tr.v.* **groomed, grooming, grooms. 1.** To make (clothes, hair, or the like) neat and clean. **2.** To clean and brush (an animal). **3.** To train, as for a specified position: *groom a candidate for Congress.* [As "bridegroom," shortening of BRIDEGROOM; as "man," "servant," Middle English *gromt.*]

grooms·man (grōomz′mən, grŏomz′-) *n., pl.* **-men** (-mĭn). The best man or an usher at a wedding.

groove (grōov) *n.* **1.** A long, narrow furrow or channel, such as the spiral cut in a phonograph record. **2. a.** A situation or activity to which one is especially well suited; niche. **b.** A settled, humdrum routine; rut. **3.** *Slang.* Something that is very pleasing or satisfying. *~v.* **grooved, grooving, grooves.** *—intr. Slang.* **1.** To relax or let oneself move freely to the rhythm or beat of music, especially jazz. **2.** To settle easily or harmoniously into a situation, relationship, or the like. *—tr.* To cut a groove in. [Middle English *grofe,* from Middle Dutch *groeve,* ditch, from Germanic; akin to GRAVE.]

groov·er (grōo′vər) *n. Slang.* A person who grooves or is groovy.

groov·y (grōo′vē) *adj.* **-ier, -iest.** *Slang.* Pleasing; deeply satisfying. [From slang expression *in the groove,* playing (jazz) fluently, hence exciting, satisfying.]

grope (grōp) *v.* **groped, groping, gropes.** *—intr.* **1.** To reach about uncertainly; feel one's way. **2.** To search blindly or uncertainly: *rope for an answer.* *—tr.* **1.** To make (one's way) by groping. **2.** *Informal.* To touch or fondle sexually, usually in a clumsy manner. *~n.* The act or an instance of groping. [Middle English *gropen,* Old English *grāpian,* from Germanic.] **—grop·er** *n.* **—grop·ing·ly** *adv.*

Gro·pi·us (grō′pē-əs), **Walter** (1883-1969). German architect, founder of the Bauhaus school of architecture and one of the leading figures in the modern movement. He fled from Nazi Germany in 1934 and became professor of architecture at Harvard in 1938.

gros·beak (grōs′bēk′) *n.* Any of various finches of the genera *Hesperiphona, Pinicola,* and related genera, of Europe and America, having a thick, rounded bill. [Partial translation of French *grosbec* : Old French *gros,* thick, GROSS + *bec,* beak.]

gro·schen (grō′shən) *n., pl.* **groschen.** A coin equal to ¹/₁₀₀ of the schilling of Austria. See feature at **currency.** [German *Groschen,* from Middle High German *gros(se), grosche,* from Czech *grosh,* from Medieval Latin (*denārius*) *grossus,* "thick (penny)," from Latin *grossus,* thick, GROSS.]

gros·grain (grō′grān′) *n.* **1.** A heavy silk or rayon fabric with narrow ribs. **2.** A ribbon made of this. [French *gros grain,* "coarse grain" : Old French *gros,* thick, GROSS + GRAIN.]

gros point (grō) *n.* **1.** A large needlepoint stitch covering two vertical and two horizontal threads used, for example, in upholstery. **2.** Work done in this stitch. Compare **petit point.** [French, "large point."]

gross (grōs) *adj.* **grosser, grossest. 1. a.** Exclusive of deductions; total; entire. Compare **net. b.** Unmitigated in any way; utter.

grizzly bear *This variety of brown bear lives in western North America. Like other brown bears it has poor vision, but its sense of smell is acute.*

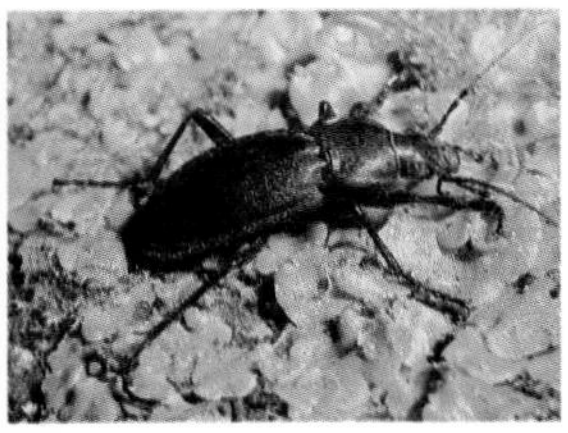

ground beetle *There are about 25,000 species of these fierce and worldwide predators. All hunt insects, including other beetles. Even the larvae are carnivorous, snapping up prey with clawlike jaws. The violet ground beetle, shown here, is so called because of the violet sheen on its wing cases.*

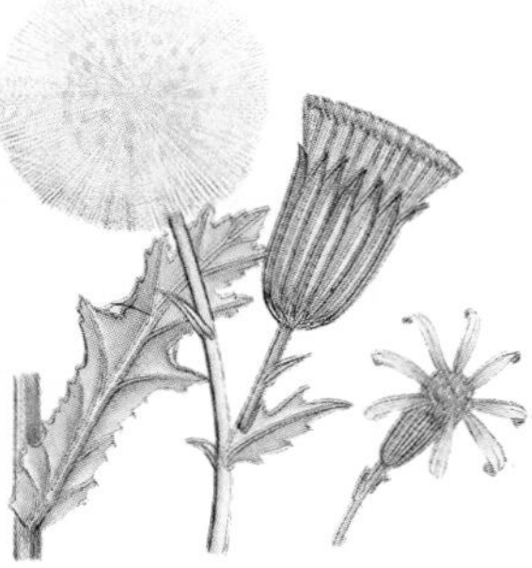

groundsel *In Anglo-Saxon times, this common weed was used in poultices—and its name comes from the Old English term* gundæswelgæ, *meaning "pus absorber." Groundsel seeds, carried on fine hairs, are spread by the wind.*

PRONUNCIATION KEY

ă, pat; ā, pay; âr, care;
ä, father, are; b, **bib**;
ch, **church**; d, **deed**; ĕ, pet;
ē, be; f, **fife**; g, **gag**; h, **hat**;
hw, **which**; ĭ, pit; ī, pie;
îr, pier; j, **judge**; k, **kick**;
l, lid, needle; m, **mum**;
n, no, sudden; ng, thing;
ŏ, pot; ō, toe; ô, paw, for;
oi, noise; ou, out; ŏŏ, book;
ōō, boot; p, **pop**; r, roar;
s, sauce; sh, ship, dish;
t, tight; th, thin, path;
th, this, bathe; ŭ, cut; ûr, fur;
v, valve; w, with; y, yes;
z, zebra, size; zh, vision;
ə, about, item, edible, gallop, circus, peaceful

IN FOREIGN WORDS:

à, *Fr.* ami; œ, *Fr.* feu, *Ger.* schön; ü, *Fr.* tu, *Ger.* über; KH, *Ger.* ich, *Scot.* loch; N, *Fr.* bon; y', *Fr.* Compiègne

STRESS MARKS:

Primary stress: ′
in·cite′ (ĭn-sīt′)
Secondary stress: ′
in′sight′ (ĭn′sīt′)

2. Glaringly obvious; flagrant: *gross injustice.* **3. a.** Coarse; vulgar; obscene. **b.** Lacking sensitivity or discernment; unrefined. **c.** *Informal.* Offensive; distasteful. **4. a.** Overweight or corpulent, especially disgustingly so. **b.** Dense; profuse. **c.** Impenetrable; thick. Said especially of vegetation. **5.** *Pathology.* Visible to the naked eye: *a gross lesion.* —See Synonyms at **coarse, flagrant.**
∼*n., pl.* **grosses** (for sense 1) or **gross** (for sense 2). **1.** The entire body or amount; total. **2.** *Abbr.* **gr., gro. a.** Twelve dozen, used as a unit of measurement. **b.** A group of 144 or 12 dozen items. **—in the gross. 1.** Taken as a whole; in bulk. **2.** Wholesale.
∼*tr.v.* **grossed, grossing, grosses.** To earn as a total income or profit before deductions. **—gross out.** *Slang.* To fill with disgust. **—gross up.** To increase a net amount to its gross value before deductions. [Middle English, from Old French *gros,* thick, large, from Latin *grossus.*] **—gross·ly** *adv.* **—gross·ness** *n.*

gross domestic product *n. Abbr.* **GDP** The total market value of the goods and services produced within a country during a given period, excluding income derived from investments abroad.

gross national product *n Abbr.* **GNP** The total market value of all the goods and services produced by a nation during a given period, including income derived from investments abroad. Compare **national income.**

gros·su·lar·ite (grŏs′yə-lə-rīt′) *n.* A light-green, pink, gray, or brown garnet with composition $Ca_3Al_2(SiO_4)_3$, found alone or as a constituent part of the common garnet. [German *Grossularit,* "gooseberry stone" (from the color of certain kinds of garnet), from New Latin *Grossularia,* former genus of gooseberry, from Old French *groiselle, grosele,* gooseberry, from Middle Dutch *croesel,* "curly berry" (from its beard), diminutive of *kroes,* curled.]

grosz (grôsh) *n., pl.* **groszy** (grô′shē). A coin equal to 1/100 of the zloty of Poland. See feature at **currency.** [Polish, from Czech *grosh.* See **groschen.**]

Grosz (grōs), **George** (1893–1959). German painter, illustrator, and caricaturist. A leading member of the Berlin Dada movement, his reputation rests on the biting wit of his antibourgeois and antimilitarist drawings of the 1920's, executed with grotesque distortions. He became a U.S. citizen (1938).

grot (grŏt) *n. Poetic.* A grotto.

gro·tesque (grō-tĕsk′) *adj.* **1.** Characterized by ludicrous or incongruous distortion. **2.** Extravagant; outlandish; bizarre. **3.** Of or designating the grotesque in art or a work executed in this style. —See Synonyms at **fantastic.**
∼*n.* **1.** Anything thought to resemble the grotesque style in art. **2. a.** An artistic and decorative style developed in 16th-century Italy, characterized by incongruous combinations of monstrous human, animal, or natural forms. **b.** A work of art executed in this style. **3.** *Printing.* The family of 19th-century sans serif typefaces. [Earlier *crotesque,* from Old French *crotesque, grotesque,* from Old Italian *(pittura) grottesca,* "grottolike (painting)," from *grottesco,* of a grotto, from *grotta,* GROTTO.] **—gro·tesque·ly** *adv.* **—gro·tesque·ness** *n.*

gro·tes·que·rie, gro·tes·que·ry (grō-tĕs′kə-rē) *n., pl.* **-ries. 1.** The state of being grotesque; grotesqueness. **2.** Something grotesque.

Gro·ti·us (grō′shē-əs), **Hugo,** originally Huig de Groot (1583–1645). Dutch lawyer and writer. He wrote on politics, theology, and law. His *Of the Law of War and Peace* (1625) is generally considered to be the first comprehensive treatise on international law.

grot·to (grŏt′ō) *n., pl.* **-toes** or **-tos. 1.** A small cave or cavern. **2.** An artificial structure or excavation, as in a garden, resembling a cave or cavern. [Italian *grotta, grotto,* from Old Italian, from Vulgar Latin *grupta* (unattested), variant of Latin *crypta,* vault, CRYPT.]

grot·ty (grŏt′ē) *adj.* **-tier, -tiest.** *Chiefly British Informal.* Unpleasant, grubby, or squalid. [From GROTESQUE.]

grouch (grouch) *intr.v.* **grouched, grouching, grouches.** To grumble or sulk.
∼*n.* **1.** A grumbling or sulky mood. **2.** A complaint; grudge. **3.** A habitually complaining or irritable person. [Middle English *grutchen,* to GRUDGE.]

grouch·y (grou′chē) *adj.* **-ier, -iest.** Inclined to grumbling and complaining; ill-humored; peevish; grumpy. **—grouch·i·ly** *adv.* **—grouch·i·ness** *n.*

ground¹ (ground) *n.* **1. a.** The solid surface of the earth. **b.** The floor of a body of water, especially the sea. **2. a.** Soil; earth: *level the ground for a lawn.* **b.** Land or earth having a specified characteristic: *high ground.* **3.** *Sometimes* **grounds.** An area of land designated for a specified purpose: *burial grounds.* **4. grounds.** The land surrounding or forming part of a house or other building: *The embassy has beautiful grounds.* **5.** *Often* **grounds.** The foundation for an argument, belief, or action; basis; premise. **6.** *Usually* **grounds.** The underlying condition prompting some action; cause; reason. Used with *for*: *grounds for suspicion.* **7.** An area of reference; a subject. **8. a.** A surrounding area; a background. **b.** The undecorated part of something. **9.** The preparatory coat of paint on which a picture is to be painted. **10. grounds.** The sediment at the bottom of a liquid, especially coffee. **11.** *Music.* A ground bass. **12.** *Electricity.* **a.** The position or portion of an electric current that is at zero potential with respect to the earth. **b.** A conducting connection to such a position or to the earth. **c.** A large conducting body, such as the earth, used as a return for electric currents and as an arbitrary zero of potential. **13.** Headway, progress, or advantage, as in a competition. —See Synonyms at **base. —cover ground. 1.** To travel a considerable distance. **2. a.** To make headway; accomplish a great deal. **b.** To deal with a subject fully. **—down to the ground.** *Chiefly British Informal.* Completely, absolutely: *His holiday plans suit me down to the ground.* **—from the ground up.** Leaving out nothing; completely; thoroughly. **—gain ground. 1.** To make progress. **2.** To gain favor or popularity. **—get off the ground. 1.** To get properly under way; have a successful beginning. Used of a project, idea, or the like. **2.** To cause to get off the ground. **—give ground.** To yield an advantage; give way. **—hold** (or **stand**) **one's ground.** To maintain one's position; not yield or retreat. **—on home ground.** In a familiar area or on a familiar subject. **—run into the ground. 1.** To work or push until exhausted. **2.** To overdo to the point of being tedious.
∼*adj.* **1.** Of, on, or near the ground. **2.** Living or used in or on the ground.
∼*v.* **grounded, grounding, grounds.** —*tr.* **1.** To place or set on the ground. **2.** To provide a basis for (an argument, theory, or the like); substantiate; justify. **3.** To supply with basic and essential information; instruct in fundamentals; school. **4.** To prevent (an aircraft or pilot) from flying. **5.** *Electricity.* To connect (an electric circuit) to a ground. **6.** *Nautical.* To run (a vessel) aground. **7.** To cover (a canvas or other surface) with a preparatory coat of paint. —*intr.* **1.** To hit or reach the ground. **2.** *Nautical.* To run aground. [Middle English *ground,* Old English *grund,* from Common Germanic *grunduz* (unattested).]

ground². Past tense and past participle of **grind.**

ground ball *n. Baseball.* A batted ball that rolls or bounces along the ground. Also called "grounder."

ground bass *n.* A short musical bass passage or motif that is continually repeated under the changing harmonies and melodies of the upper range. Also called "basso ostinato," "ground."

ground beetle *n.* **1.** Any of numerous chiefly black or brown beetles of the family Carabidae, that often crawl under stones, logs, or debris. **2.** Any of various other beetles that live near the ground, such as any member of the family Tenebrionidae.

ground cherry *n.* Any of various chiefly New World plants of the genus *Physalis,* having round, fleshy fruit enclosed in a papery, bladderlike husk.

ground cover *n.* Low-growing plants that form a dense, extensive growth and tend to prevent soil erosion and discourage weeds.

ground crew *n.* A team of mechanics and technicians who maintain and service aircraft on the ground.

ground-ef·fect machine (ground′ĭ-fĕkt′) *n.* A vehicle designed for traveling over land or water by means of an air cushion.

ground elder *n.* A perennial herbaceous Eurasian plant, *Aegopodium podagraria,* widespread as a weed and on waste ground, having clusters of small white flowers and leaves composed of three leaflets. Also called "bishop's weed," "goutweed," "herb Gerard."

ground·er (groun′dər) *n. Baseball.* A ground ball.

ground floor *n.* The floor of a building at or nearly at ground level. **—get in on the ground floor.** To work with a project or business from its inception.

ground glass *n.* Glass that has been subjected to grinding or etching to diffuse light.

ground hemlock *n.* A low-growing yew, *Taxus canadensis,* of northeastern North America.

ground hog *n.* A rodent, the **woodchuck** *(see).*

Ground Hog Day *n.* February 2, traditionally the point that indicates an early or late spring. [From the legend that the ground hog emerges from hibernation on this day and returns to its burrow if it sees its shadow, presaging prolonged winter weather.]

ground·ing (groun′dĭng) *n.* A thorough knowledge of or training in the rudiments of a subject: *has a good grounding in math.*

ground ivy *n.* A creeping or trailing aromatic plant, *Glechoma hederacea,* native to Eurasia, having rounded, scalloped leaves and small purplish flowers. Also called "gill-over-the-ground."

ground·less (ground′lĭs) *adj.* Having no grounds or reasons; unjustified; unsubstantiated: *groundless optimism.* **—ground·less·ly** *adv.* **—ground·less·ness** *n.*

ground·ling (ground′lĭng) *n.* **1. a.** A plant or animal living on or close to the ground. **b.** A fish that lives at the bottom of the water. **2.** A person with uncultivated tastes. **3.** A spectator in the cheapest part of an Elizabethan theater.

ground loop *n.* A sharp, uncontrollable turn of an aircraft while taxiing, landing, or taking off.

ground·mass (ground′măs′) *n.* The fine-grained crystalline base of porphyritic rock, in which phenocrysts are embedded.

ground·nut (ground′nŭt′) *n.* **1.** A climbing vine, *Apios tuberosa,* of eastern North America, having compound leaves, clusters of fragrant brownish flowers, and small, edible tubers. **2.** Any of several other plants having underground tubers or nutlike parts. **3.** The tuber or nutlike part of such a plant. **4.** *Chiefly British.* The **peanut** *(see).*

ground pine *n.* **1.** A low-growing plant, *Ajuga chamaepitys,* native to the Old World, having narrow leaves, yellow flowers, and a resinous odor. **2.** A North American **club moss** *(see);* especially, *Lycopodium obscurum* or any similar species.

ground pink *n.* A plant, the **moss pink** *(see).*

ground plan *n.* **1.** A plan of a floor of a building as if seen from overhead. **2.** A preliminary or basic plan.

ground plum *n.* **1.** A plant, *Astragalus crassicarpus,* of the central and western United States, having purple or white flowers and green, plumlike, edible fruit. **2.** The fruit of this plant.

ground·print (ground′prĭnt′) *n.* In telecommunications, a **footprint** *(see).*

ground rent *n. Chiefly British.* **1.** Rent reserved on land by a lessor, usually for a stipulated lengthy term, to be used chiefly for building. **2.** Rent paid by the lessee of a flat to the freeholder, over a specified period of time.

ground rule *n.* Any basic rule of procedure modified or amended to fit a particular situation or event.

ground·sel[1] (ground'səl) *n.* Any of various plants of the genus *Senecio,* especially the Eurasian species *S. vulgaris,* having rayed, usually yellow flowers. [Middle English *groundeswele,* Old English *grundeswylige,* variant (influenced by *grund,* GROUND) of *gundæswelgæ,* "pus-absorber" (from its use to reduce abscesses) : *gund,* pus + *swelgan,* to swallow.]

groundsel[2]. Variant of **groundsill.**

groundsel tree *n.* A shrub, *Baccharis halimifoliar,* of coastal areas of the eastern United States, having white, plumelike fruiting clusters.

ground sheet *n.* **1.** A waterproof cover used to protect an area of ground, such as a football field. **2.** A waterproof sheet placed in a tent or under camp bedding as a protection against damp.

ground·sill (ground'sĭl') *n.* Also **ground·sel** (ground'səl). The horizontal timber nearest the ground in the frame of a building. Also called "ground plate."

ground·speed, ground speed (ground'spēd') *n. Aeronautics.* The speed of an airborne aircraft calculated in terms of the ground distance traversed in a given period of time. Compare **air speed.**

ground squirrel *n.* Any of various squirrellike rodents of the genus *Citellus* (or *Spermophilus*) and related genera, which live in underground burrows. Also called "gopher."

ground state *n. Physics.* The stationary state of least energy in a physical system.

ground stroke *n.* In tennis, a stroke played to a ball that has bounced.

ground substance *n. Anatomy.* The matrix of connective tissue, containing various cells and fibers.

ground swell *n.* **1.** An undulation of the ocean with deep rolling waves, often caused by a distant storm or earthquake. **2.** A sudden gathering of force, as of public opinion.

ground tissues *pl.n. Botany.* Plant tissues, such as pith and cortex, that are not specialized for a particular function.

ground water, ground·wa·ter (ground'wô'tər, -wŏt'ər) *n.* **1.** Any water beneath the earth's surface. **2.** A region of subsurface water beneath the water table, including underground streams. It forms the saturation zone in which all pore spaces are filled with water.

ground wave *n.* A radio wave that travels along the earth's surface. Compare **sky wave.**

ground·work (ground'wûrk') *n.* A foundation or basis; preliminary work.

ground zero *n.* The point on the surface of the earth immediately below a nuclear explosion. Also called "hypocenter."

group (gro͞op) *n. Abbr.* **gr. 1.** An assemblage of persons or objects considered together: *a group of dinner guests; a group of Chinese porcelains.* **2.** Two or more figures that make up a unit or a design, as in sculpture or painting. **3.** A number of individuals or things considered together because of certain similarities. **4.** *Linguistics.* A subdivision of a linguistic family, less inclusive than a branch. **5.** A unit of two or more squadrons in an air force, smaller than a wing. **6.** Any class or collection of related objects or entities, as: **a.** Two or more atoms behaving or regarded as behaving as a single chemical unit. **b.** A vertical column in the periodic table of elements. Compare **period. c.** A geological stratigraphic unit, especially a unit consisting of two or more formations. **7.** *Mathematics.* A set together with a binary operation under which the set is closed and associative, and for which the set contains an identity element and an inverse for every element in the set. **8.** A small number of players, usually including a singer or singers, that perform popular or modern music.
~*v.* **grouped, grouping, groups.** —*tr.* To place or arrange in a group or groups. —*intr.* To form or be part of a group. [French *groupe,* from Italian *gruppo,* "knot," from Germanic.]
Usage: *Group,* as a collective noun, can be construed as singular or plural in determining the number of the verb it governs. A singular verb occurs when the persons or things in question are considered as one or as acting as one, or when they are related by membership in a class or category. A plural verb is possible when group refers to persons thought of as acting individually. The grammatical number of related pronouns and pronominal adjectives in turn agrees with that of the verb: *The group* (of persons) *is determined to retain its identity despite the merger. The group* (of persons) *were divided in their sympathies. This group* (of plants) *shows variation in coloring.*

group captain *n.* A commissioned officer in the Royal and Australian Air Forces, ranking between an air commodore and a wing commander, equivalent in rank to a colonel in the army and a captain in the navy.

group·er (gro͞o'pər) *n., pl.* **groupers** or collectively **grouper.** Any of various often large food and game fishes of the genera *Epinephelus, Mycteroperca,* and related genera, of warm seas. [Portuguese *garupa,* probably from a native South American name.]

group·ie (gro͞o'pē) *n. Informal.* **1.** A fan, usually female, of a rock or pop group who follows the group around on tours, usually in the hope of having personal contact with them. **2.** A sycophant or hanger-on.

group·ing (gro͞o'pĭng) *n.* **1.** The act or process of arranging in groups. **2.** A collection of objects arranged in a group.

group insurance *n.* Insurance covering members of a group under a single contract or under individual contracts, usually at reduced cost.

group·oid (gro͞o'poid') *n. Algebra.* A nonempty set *G* together with a binary operation that associates with every pair of elements *x, y* in *G* a third element *z* in *G* denoted by *xy* or *x·y.*

group practice *n.* A medical or dental practice run by a group of associated physicians or dentists who share premises, secretarial help, and other resources.

group theory *n.* The branch of mathematics concerned with the properties of groups.

group therapy *n.* Psychotherapy involving more than one patient at a time, in which the changing interaction among the patients is part of the therapeutic process. Also called "group psychotherapy."

group·think (gro͞op'thĭngk') *n.* **1.** Decision- and policy-making by a group, as a board of directors or a research team. **2.** The practice of conforming to group values or ethical standards.

grouse[1] (grous) *n., pl.* **grouse.** Any of various game birds of the family Tetraonidae, chiefly of the Northern Hemisphere, having mottled brown or grayish plumage. See **black grouse, red grouse.** [16th century : earlier *grewes,* perhaps plural of *grue* (unattested), perhaps from medieval Latin *grūtat.*]

grouse[2] *intr.v.* **groused, grousing, grouses.** *Informal.* To complain; carp; grumble.
~*n.* A complaint; grievance. [19th century : origin obscure.] **—grous·er** *n.*

grout (grout) *n.* **1. a.** A thin mortar used to fill cracks and crevices between masonry and around tiles. **b.** A finishing plaster. **2.** *Usually* **grouts.** *Chiefly British.* Sediment; lees. **3. a. grouts.** Groats. **b.** Wholemeal porridge.
~*tr.v.* **grouted, grouting, grouts.** To fill or finish with grout. Often used with *in*: *grout in tiles.* [Middle English *grout,* Old English *grūt,* akin to GRITS, GROATS.] **—grout·er** *n.*

grove (grōv) *n.* A small wood or group of trees lacking dense undergrowth. [Middle English *grove,* Old English *grāf*†.]

Grove (grōv), **Sir George** (1820–1900). British civil engineer and musicologist. His *Dictionary of Music and Musicians,* now a standard work, first appeared in four volumes between 1879 and 1889.

grov·el (grŭv'əl, grŏv'-) *intr.v.* **-eled, -eling, -els.** Also *chiefly British* **-elled, -elling. 1.** To humble oneself in a servile or demeaning manner; cringe. **2.** To lie or crawl in a prostrate position, often as a token of subservience or humility. **3.** To give oneself over to base pleasures. [Back-formation from obsolete *groveling,* prone, Middle English *gruflinge,* in prostrate position, from phrase *on grufe,* on the face, from Old Norse *ā grūfu* : *ā,* on + *grūfa*†, proneness.] **—grov·el·er** *n.* **—grov·el·ing·ly** *adv.*

grow (grō) *v.* **grew** (gro͞o), **grown** (grōn), **growing, grows.** —*intr.* **1. a.** To increase naturally in size or length, often in a specified direction. **b.** To increase in size by the addition of material through assimilation or accretion. **2. a.** To expand; gain: *The business grew under new management.* **b.** To increase in amount or degree: *membership is growing.* **c.** To become extended or intensified: *Her anxiety grew.* **3.** To develop and reach maturity. **4.** To be capable of growth; thrive; flourish: *plants that will grow in deep shade.* **5.** To become in a specified position in relation to something else or to each other, by or as if by the process of growth: *the edges of the wound grew together; we've grown apart recently.* **6.** To follow as a result of; originate. Usually used with *out*: *Their love grew out of friendship.* **7.** To develop by a gradual process or by degrees; become: *grow angry; grow cold; grow rich.* **8.** To come into existence; spring up: *Hostility grew between the two groups.* —*tr.* **1.** To cause to grow; cultivate: *grow tulips.* **2.** To let grow: *grow a beard.* **3.** To develop; put forth: *The plant has not grown any leaves yet.* —See Synonyms at **increase. —grow on** (or **upon**). To become more pleasurable, acceptable, or essential to: *a style that grows on one.* **—grow out of.** To outgrow. **—grow over.** To cover with growth: *a path grown over with moss.* **—grow up. 1.** To reach maturity; become an adult. **2.** To come into being; develop. [Grow, grew, grown; Middle English *growen, grewe, growen,* Old English *grōwan, grēow, grōwen,* from Germanic.] **—grow·er** *n.*

grow·ing (grō'ĭng) *adj.* **1.** Increasing in number or degree: *a growing desire to confess.* **2.** Of or associated with growth: *during the growing season.* **—grow·ing·ly** *adv.*

growing pains *pl.n.* **1.** Pains in the limbs and joints of children, often mistakenly attributed to rapid growth. **2.** Problems arising in the initial stages of an enterprise.

growing season *n.* The period of the year during which temperatures are high enough for the growth of a particular crop, usually regarded as the period between the last severe frost of spring and the first in the following autumn.

growl (groul) *v.* **growled, growling, growls.** —*intr.* **1.** To utter a growl. **2.** To speak in an angry or surly manner. —*tr.* To utter with a growl: *growl orders.*
~*n.* **1.** The low, guttural, menacing sound made by a dog or other animal, usually in anger. **2.** A sound suggestive of this. **3.** A gruff, surly utterance. [Perhaps imitative.]

growl·er (grou'lər) *n.* **1.** One that growls. **2.** A small iceberg or area of floe ice, large enough to be a danger to ships. **3.** *Electricity.* An electromagnetic device with two poles, used for magnetizing, demagnetizing, and finding short-circuited coils.

grown (grōn). Past participle of **grow.**
~*adj.* **1.** Having attained full growth; mature; adult. **2.** Produced

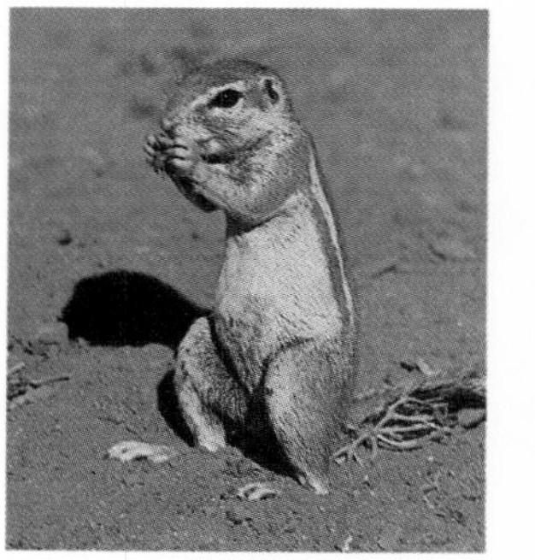

ground squirrel *Relatives of the tree-climbing squirrels, ground squirrels live in burrows in Eurasia, North America, and Africa. Those that store their food in cheek pouches are known as chipmunks in North America.*

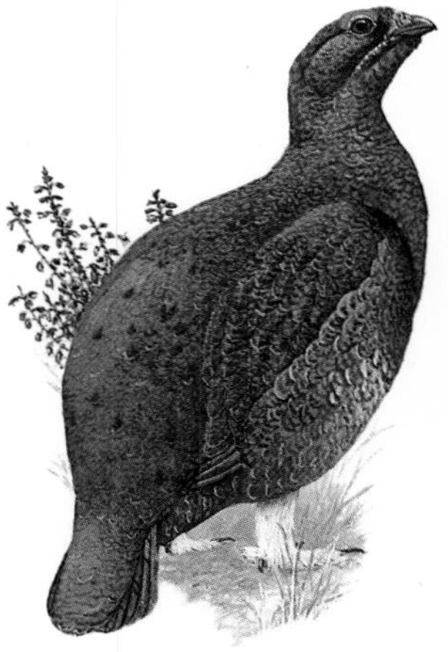

grouse *The red grouse, shown here, is the bird hunted on British moors during the grouse-shooting season. It is related to the willow grouse of Europe, Asia, and North America.*

or cultivated in a specified way or place. Used in combination: *home-grown vegetables.*

grown-up (grōn'ŭp') *adj.* **1.** Characteristic of or suitable for an adult. **2.** Being mature, fully-developed, or older than one's years in outlook, attitudes, or appearance. —*n.* An adult.

growth (grōth) *n.* **1. a.** The process of growing. **b.** A stage in the process of growing; size. **c.** Full development; maturity. **2.** Development from a lower or simpler to a higher or more complex form; evolution. **3.** An increase, as in size, number, value, or strength; extension or expansion: *population growth.* **4.** Something that grows or has grown: *a new growth of grass.* **5.** Broadly, an abnormal tissue formation, such as a tumor. **6.** The result of growth; production; cultivation.

growth company *n.* A company whose rate of growth significantly exceeds that of the average in its field or the overall rate of economic growth.

growth fund *n.* A mutual fund whose goal is capital appreciation.

growth hormone *n.* A hormone, secreted by the pituitary gland, that stimulates tissue growth, especially of the bones. Also called "somatotrophin." Compare **growth substance.**

growth ring *n.* An **annual ring** (see).

growth stock *n. Economics.* Shares that tend to increase in capital value rather than providing a high-interest income.

growth substance *n.* A substance produced by a plant that, in very small quantities, controls growth and development; a plant hormone. Also called "phytohormone." Compare **growth hormone.**

groyne. Variant of **groin** (sense 3).

grub (grŭb) *v.* **grubbed, grubbing, grubs.** —*tr.* **1.** To clear of roots and stumps by digging. **2.** To dig up by the roots. Often used with *up* or *out.* —*intr.* **1.** To dig in the earth; dig underground. **2. a.** To search laboriously; rummage. **b.** To toil arduously; drudge: *grub for a living.* —*n.* **1.** The thick, wormlike larva of certain beetles and other insects. **2.** *Informal.* Food. **3.** A dirty or unkempt person. **4.** A drudge. [Middle English *grubben,* Old English *grybban* (unattested).]

grub·ber (grŭb'ər) *n.* **1.** A person who grubs: *"The archaeologist is the last grubber among things mortal"* (Loren Eiseley). **2.** A grub hoe.

grub·by (grŭb'ē) *adj.* **-bier, -biest. 1.** Dirty; unkempt. **2.** Infested with grubs. **3.** Contemptible; beggarly. —**grub·bi·ly** *adv.* —**grub·bi·ness** *n.*

grub hoe *n.* A heavy hoe for grubbing up roots. Also called "grubbing hoe," "grubber."

grub screw *n.* A small headless screw used to secure a collar or other similar part to a shaft.

grub·stake (grŭb'stāk') *n.* Supplies or funds advanced to a mining prospector or a person starting a business, in return for a promised share of the profits. Also informally called "stake." —*tr.v.* **grubstaked, -staking, -stakes.** To supply with a grubstake. [GRUB (food) + STAKE (bet).] —**grub·stak·er** *n.*

Grub Street (grŭb) *n.* The world of impoverished writers and literary hacks. [From *Grub Street,* London, now Milton Street, formerly inhabited by such writers.]

grub·street (grŭb'strēt') *adj.* Turned out by hacks; poor; inferior: *a shelf of grubstreet novels.*

grudge (grŭj) *tr.v.* **grudged, grudging, grudges. 1.** To be reluctant to allow or grant. **2.** To show or feel reluctance about: *"His nature grudged thinking, for it crippled his speed in action"* (T.E. Lawrence). —*n.* **1.** A deep-seated feeling of resentment or rancor provoked by some incident or situation. **2.** The grounds for such a feeling. [Middle English *gruggen,* variant of *grutchen,* from Old French *grouchier†,* to murmur.] —**grudg·er** *n.*

grudg·ing (grŭj'ĭng) *adj.* Not offered willingly or spontaneously: *grudging praise.* —**grudg·ing·ly** *adv.*

gru·el (grōō'əl) *n.* **1.** A thin, watery porridge. **2.** *Chiefly British.* Severe punishment. [Middle English *gruel,* from Old French *gruel,* diminutive of *gru,* groats, oatmeal, from Frankish *grūt* (unattested).]

gru·el·ing, gru·el·ling (grōō'ə-lĭng) *adj.* Demanding and exhausting. —*n.* A grueling experience, especially punishment.

grue·some (grōō'səm) *adj.* Causing horror and repugnance; frightful and shocking: *the gruesome sight of the dismembered corpse.* —See Synonyms at **ghastly.** [From obsolete Scottish *grue,* to shiver, from Scandinavian.] —**grue·some·ly** *adv.* —**grue·some·ness** *n.*

gruff (grŭf) *adj.* **gruffer, gruffest.** Rough and stern in manner, voice, or appearance; harsh. [Dutch *grof,* from Middle Dutch, from Germanic.] —**gruff·ly** *adv.* —**gruff·ness** *n.*
  Synonyms: bluff, blunt, brusque, crusty, curt.

grum (grŭm) *adj.* **grummer, grummest.** Morose; sullen; glum. [Perhaps blend of GRIM and GLUM.]

grum·ble (grŭm'bəl) *v.* **-bled, -bling, -bles.** —*intr.* **1.** To mumble in discontent: *Bosses will always find something to grumble about.* **2.** To rumble or growl. —*tr.* To express in a grumbling, discontented manner. —*n.* **1. a.** A grumbling utterance. **b.** Grounds for grumbling. **2.** A rumble. [Frequentative of Middle English *grummen,* to grumble, perhaps from Middle Dutch *grommen.*] —**grum·bler** *n.* —**grum·bling·ly** *adv.* —**grum·bly** *adv.*

grum·met (grŭm'ĭt) *n. Nautical.* A **grommet** (see).

gru·mous (grōō'məs) *adj.* Also **gru·mose** (-mōs'). *Botany.* Formed of or consisting of granular tissue, as certain roots are. [Latin *grūmus†,* little heap of earth.]

grump (grŭmp) *n. Informal.* **1. grumps.** A fit of ill temper. **2.** A surly, complaining person. [Imitative.]

grump·y (grŭm'pē) *adj.* **-ier, -iest.** Fretful and peevish; irritable; bad-tempered. [From dialectal *grump,* ill-tempered (imitative).] —**grump·i·ly** *adv.* —**grump·i·ness** *n.*

Grund·y·ism (grŭn'dē-ĭz'əm) *n.* Narrow-minded criticism of the morals of others. [After Mrs. *Grundy,* character in *Speed the Plough* (1798), a play by Thomas Morton (*c.* 1764–1838).]

Grü·ne·wald (grōō'nə-wôld', -vält'), **Matthias,** born Mathis Gothart Neithart (*c.*1475–1528). One of the great early German masters of northern European painting. He painted chiefly religious subjects, especially the Crucifixion of Christ.

grun·gy (grŭn'jē) *adj.* **-gier, -giest.** *Slang.* Being in a dirty, run-down, or inferior condition: *grungy old jeans.* [Origin unknown.]

grun·ion (grŭn'yən) *n.* A small fish, *Leuresthes tenuis,* of coastal waters of California and Mexico, that spawns along beaches during high spring tides. [Perhaps from Spanish *gruñón,* grumbler, from *gruñir,* to grumble, grunt, from Latin *grunnīre.*]

grunt (grŭnt) *v.* **grunted, grunting, grunts.** —*intr.* **1.** To utter a grunt. **2.** To make a deep, guttural sound. —*tr.* To utter or express (a reaction, for example) with a grunt: *he grunted approval.* —*n.* **1.** The deep, guttural sound characteristic of a pig. **2.** Any of various chiefly tropical marine fishes of the genus *Haemulon* and related genera, that produce grunting sounds. Also called "grunter." **3.** *Slang.* One who performs routine or mundane tasks. [Middle English *grunten,* Old English *grunnettan,* probably frequentative of *grunnian.*] —**grunt·ing·ly** *adv.*

grunt·er (grŭn'tər) *n.* **1.** One that grunts. **2.** *Informal.* A pig. **3.** A fish, the grunt.

grun·tled (grŭnt'əld) *adj.* Extremely pleased; in a good mood. [Back-formation from DISGRUNTLED.]

Grus (grŭs) *n.* A constellation in the Southern Hemisphere near the constellations Indus and Phoenix. [New Latin, from Latin *grūs,* crane.]

Gru·yère (grōō-yâr', grē-; *French* grü-yâr') *n.* A pale yellow, firm-textured cheese with holes, made from whole milk. [Originally made in *Gruyère,* a district in Switzerland.]

gr. wt. gross weight.

gryphon. Variant of **griffin.**

grys·bok (grīs'bŏk') *n.* Either of two small African antelopes, *Raphicerus melanotis* or *R. sharpei,* having small, straight horns. [Afrikaans, "gray buck."]

GS, G.S. general staff.

G-string (jē'strĭng') *n.* **1.** A narrow strip of cloth passing between the legs and supported by a waistband, worn especially by strip-tease dancers. **2.** A string tuned to G on a musical instrument.

G-suit (jē'sōōt') *n.* A flight garment designed to counteract the effects of high acceleration by exerting pressure on parts of the body below the chest. Also called "anti-G suit." Compare **pressure suit.** [G, short for GRAVITY.]

gt. 1. gilt. **2.** great. **3.** *Medicine.* gutta.

gtd. guaranteed.

GTS gas turbine ship.

gua·ca·mo·le (gwä'kə-mō'lē) *n.* **1.** Any of a variety of Mexican or South American salads featuring avocado. **2.** A dip or spread of mashed avocado, tomato pulp, mayonnaise, and seasoning. [Mexican Spanish, from Nahuatl *ahuacamolli,* "avocado sauce" : *ahuacatl,* AVOCADO + *molli,* sauce.]

gua·cha·ro (gwä'chä-rō') *n., pl.* **-ros.** The oilbird (see). [American Spanish *guácharo,* from *guacho,* orphan, little bird, from Quechua *wáhcha,* diminutive of *wah,* strange.]

gua·co (gwä'kō) *n., pl.* **-cos.** Any of several tropical American plants used as an antidote against snakebites; especially, *Mikania guaco* or *Aristolochia serpentina.* [American Spanish, from a native word in South America.]

Gua·da·la·ja·ra (gwä'də-lə-här'ə). City and capital of Jalisco state, southwestern Mexico. It is the commercial center of a mining, industrial, and agricultural region. Situated at a height of more than 1,525 meters (5,000 feet) and surrounded by mountains, the city has a mild, dry climate and is a popular health resort.

Gua·dal·ca·nal (gwŏd'l-kə-năl'). Largest island in the Solomon Islands in the southwest Pacific Ocean. Its origin is volcanic; its dominant peak, Mt. Popomanasiu, which rises to a height of 2,331 meters (7,647 feet), is surrounded by jungle. Most of the population works on coastal coconut plantations. See map at **Pacific Ocean.**

Gua·de·loupe (gwä'də-lōōp'). An overseas department of France, one of the Leeward Islands in the Caribbean. It consists of two large islands, Basse Terre and Grande Terre, and several smaller islands. The capital is Basse-Terre. It was a French colony until 1946, when it was granted department status. See map at **Latin America.**

guai·a·col (gwī'ə-kôl', -kōl') *n.* A yellowish, oily, aromatic liquid, $C_7H_8O_2$, used chiefly as an expectorant and a local anesthetic. [GUAIAC(UM) + -OL.]

guai·a·cum (gwī'ə-kəm) *n.* **1.** A tree of the genus *Guaiacum;* especially, the **lignum vitae** (see). **2.** The wood of such a tree. **3.** A greenish-brown resin obtained from the lignum vitae, and used medicinally and in varnishes. [New Latin, from Spanish *guayacan,* from Taino.]

Guam (gwŏm). Unincorporated territory of the United States, the largest and most southerly of the Marianas Islands, in the North

Pacific Ocean. It has a mountainous interior and is fringed by coral reefs. Since 1954 it has been the site of the Pacific headquarters of the U.S. Strategic Air Command. Capital, Agana. See map at **Pacific Ocean.**

guan (gwän) *n.* Any of several birds of the genus *Penelope* and related genera, of the jungles of tropical America, related to and resembling the curassows. [American Spanish, from a native name in South America.]

gua·na·co (gwə-nä′kō) *n., pl.* **-cos.** A brownish South American mammal, *Lama guanicoe,* related to and resembling the domesticated llama. [Spanish, from Quechua *huanaco.*]

gua·nase (gwä′nāz′) *n.* An enzyme in the liver and spleen that catalyzes the removal of an amino group from guanine, which is thereby converted to xanthine. [GUAN(INE) + -ASE.]

guan·eth·i·dine (gwä-nĕth′ĭ-dēn′) *n.* A drug administered in the form of pills to reduce high blood pressure. [Blend of GUANIDINE + ETHYL.]

Guang·dong, Kuang·tung, or **Kwang·tung** (gwäng′dŏong′). Province of southeast China. It is hilly, and has more than 700 offshore islands. The province is a major producer of sugar cane, rice, silk, hemp, tea, tobacco, tropical and subtropical fruits, forest products, fish, and salt. It has reserves of tungsten, iron, uranium, and oil. Most of the people are Cantonese, and some 50 percent of overseas Chinese originated in the province, part of China since *c.* 200 B.C. Guangzhou (Canton) is the capital.

Guang·zhou, Kuang·chou, or **Kwang·chow** (gwäng′jō′). Also **Can·ton** (kăn-tŏn′). Port in southern China and the capital of Guangdong province. Situated on the Zhujiang (Pearl River) delta, it is the commercial and industrial center of southern China. The Portuguese, in the 16th century, and the British, in the 17th century, regularly used the port. The Opium War between Britain and China resulted in Guangzhou's becoming one of the first treaty ports (1842).

gua·ni·dine (gwä′nĭ-dēn′) *n.* A strong crystalline base, CH_5N_3, found in plant and animal tissues and used for organic syntheses. [GUAN(INE) + -ID(E) + -INE.]

gua·nine (gwä′nēn′) *n.* A purine, $C_5H_5N_5O$, that is a constituent of the nucleic acids DNA and RNA. [From GUANO, in which it is found.]

gua·no (gwä′nō) *n.* **1.** A substance composed chiefly of the dung of sea birds or bats, accumulated along certain coastal areas or in caves, and used as fertilizer. **2.** A similar artificially produced substance. [Spanish, from Quechua *huanu,* dung.]

gua·no·sine (gwä′nə-sēn′) *n.* A nucleoside consisting of guanine and the sugar ribose. [Blend of GUANINE + RIBOSE.]

Guan·tá·na·mo Bay (gwän-tä′nə-mō′). An inlet of the Caribbean on the southeastern coast of Cuba. U.S. Navy troops landed here (June 1898) in the Spanish-American War. In 1903 the United States leased a naval station on the bay.

guar (gwär) *n.* A legume, *Cyamopsis tetragonoloba,* adapted to semiarid regions and grown for its seeds and as forage. [Hindi *guār.*]

guar. guaranteed.

gua·ra·ni (gwär′ə-nē′) *n., pl.* **-nis** or **guarani. 1.** The basic monetary unit of Paraguay, equal to 100 céntimos. See feature at **currency. 2.** A note worth one guarani. [Spanish *guaraní,* GUARANI.]

Gua·ra·ni (gwär′ə-nē′) *n., pl.* **-nis** or collectively **Guarani. 1.** A member of a Tupi-Guaranian group of South American Indians of Paraguay, Bolivia, and southern Brazil. **2.** The Tupian language spoken by these peoples. [Spanish *guaraní,* a native tribal name.]

guar·an·tee (găr′ən-tē′) *n.* **1.** *Law.* **a.** A contract whereby a person undertakes to answer for the debt, default, or miscarriage of another. **b.** *Rare.* A person making or receiving such an undertaking. **2.** A formal undertaking whereby something is ensured; specifically, an undertaking by a manufacturer or vendor that his goods or services meet a certain standard. **3.** Something given or held as security. **4.** That which secures or ensures something: *Their name is a guarantee of quality.*
~*tr.v.* **guaranteed, -teeing, -tees. 1.** To assume responsibility for the debt, default, or miscarriage of; vouch for. **2.** To assume responsibility for the quality or execution of. **3.** To undertake to accomplish or secure: *He guaranteed to free the captives.* **4.** To ensure (a desired outcome, for example). **5.** To furnish security for. **6.** To express or declare with conviction. [Earlier *garante,* perhaps from Spanish, warrant. See **guaranty.**]

guar·an·tor (găr′ən-tər, -tôr′) *n.* **1.** A person who makes or gives a guarantee. **2.** A person who makes or gives a guaranty.

guar·an·ty (găr′ən-tē) *n., pl.* **-ties. 1.** An agreement by which one person assumes the responsibility of assuring payment or fulfillment of another's debts or obligations. **2.** That which guarantees something: *His record is a guaranty of his honesty.* **3.** Anything held or provided as security for the execution, completion, or existence of something. **4.** The provision of such security. **5.** A guarantor.
~*tr.v.* **guarantied, -tying, -ties.** To guarantee. [Old French *garantie,* from *garant,* warrant, from Frankish *wārjan* (unattested), to vouch for the truth of.]

guard (gärd) *v.* **guarded, guarding, guards.** —*tr.* **1.** To protect from harm; watch over; defend. **2. a.** To watch over to prevent escape or violence. **b.** To watch over to prevent mistakes, indiscretions, or the like: *guard one's words.* **3.** To keep watch at (a door or gate, for example) to supervise entries and exits. **4.** To supply with proper controls and checks; safeguard. **5.** To furnish (a device or object) with a protective piece. **6.** *Archaic.* To escort. —*intr.* To take precautions; secure. Used with *against: guard against infection.* —See Synonyms at **defend.**
~*n.* **1.** One that guards, keeps watch over, or protects. **2.** An individual or a group that stands watch or acts as a sentinel. **3.** One who supervises prisoners. **4.** A body of persons who form an escort or perform drill exhibitions on ceremonial occasions: *an honor guard.* **5. Guard.** *British.* A member of any of various regiments whose official duties include the ceremonial protection of the sovereign. **6.** *British.* A railway employee in charge of a train. **7.** *Football.* One of the two players on either side of the center. **8.** *Basketball.* A team member who plays the backcourt. **9.** A defensive position or stance in certain sports such as boxing or fencing. **10.** The act, condition, or duty of guarding: *"Have you had quiet guard?"* (Shakespeare). **11.** Something that gives protection; a safeguard: *a guard against tooth decay.* **12.** Any device or apparatus that prevents injury, damage, or loss. **13.** An attachment or covering put on a machine to protect the operator. **14.** A chain or band used to help safeguard a thing, such as a watch or bracelet, from loss. **15.** A guard ring. **16.** The portion of the hilt of a sword or of the handle of a knife or fork that protects the hand. **17.** The metal apparatus that encircles and guards the trigger of a firearm. —**mount guard.** To go on duty. Said of a sentinel. —**off one's guard.** Unprepared; not alert. —**on one's guard.** Alert and watchful; cautious. —**stand guard. 1.** To act as a sentinel. **2.** To keep watch over someone or something.
~*adj.* Of, relating to, or acting as a guard: *guard duty.* [As verb, Middle English *garden,* from Old French *garder, guarder,* from Germanic. As noun, Middle English, from Old French *garde,* from *garder,* to guard.] —**guard·a·ble** *adj.* —**guard·er** *n.*

guar·dant, gar·dant (gär′dənt) *adj. Heraldry.* Designating an animal shown with its face turned toward the viewer. [Old French *gardant,* present participle of *garder,* to GUARD.]

guard cell *n. Botany.* Either of the paired epidermal cells that control the opening and closing of a stoma in plant tissue.

guard·ed (gär′dĭd) *adj.* Cautious; restrained; prudent: *guarded behavior.* —**guard·ed·ly** *adv.* —**guard·ed·ness** *n.*

guard hair *n.* Any of the coarse hairs that form a layer covering the underfur of certain mammals.

guard·house (gärd′hous′) *n.* **1.** A building that accommodates a military guard. **2.** A building used as a prison for military personnel guilty of minor offenses.

guard·i·an (gär′dē-ən) *n.* **1.** One who guards, protects, or defends. **2.** *Law.* A person who is legally responsible for the care and management of the person or property of one who is considered by law to be incompetent to manage his own affairs, such as a child during its minority. **3.** A superior in a Franciscan convent. [Middle English from Norman French, variant of Old French *gardien,* from *garder,* to GUARD.] —**guard·i·an·ship** *n.*

guardian angel *n. Roman Catholic Church.* An angel appointed to watch over a person.

guard·rail (gärd′rāl′) *n.* **1.** A protective rail, as on a staircase or next to a highway. **2.** An inner rail placed along the main rail of a railroad track at curves and crossings to prevent a train from jumping the tracks.

guard ring *n.* **1.** A ring used to prevent a more valuable ring from sliding off the finger. Also called "guard." **2.** An electrode in a computer or electron lens that counteracts distortion of the electric field at the edges of other electrodes.

guard·room (gärd′rōōm′, -rŏŏm′) *n.* **1.** A room used by guards on duty. **2.** A room in which prisoners are confined.

guards·man (gärdz′mən) *n., pl.* **-men** (-mĭn). **1.** One who acts as a guard. **2.** A member of the U.S. National Guard. **3.** *British.* A soldier in a regiment of household guards.

Guar·ne·ri (gwär-nâr′ē). Also **Guar·nie·ri** (-nyâr′ē). Italian family of violinmakers, whose workshops were in Cremona. The first member of the family to make violins was **Andrea** (*c.* 1626–98). The craft was carried on by each generation down to **Giuseppe** (*c.* 1687–1744), who is considered second only to the Stradivari family for the quality of his instruments.

Guar·ne·ri·us (gwär-nâr′ē-əs, -nîr′ē-əs) *n.* Any of the violins of superlative tone made by members of the Guarneri family in the 17th and 18th centuries.

Gua·te·ma·la (gwä′tə-mä′lə). Independent republic of Central America. It was the home of the Mayan civilization for 1,000 years before the Spanish conquest of 1524. It declared its independence from Spain in 1821. The country is chiefly agricultural, and coffee, cotton, beef, timber, and chicle are the chief exports. Nickel and petroleum are mined. An earthquake in 1976 killed more than 24,000 people. Area, 108,889 square kilometers (42,042 square miles). Population, 9,200,000. Capital, Guatemala City. See map at **Central American States.** —**Gua·te·ma·lan** *adj. & n.*

Guatemala City. Capital city of Guatemala, in a broad fertile plain in the southwestern part of the country. It is the largest city in Central America. It was founded in 1776 to replace Antigua as the capital, because its site was believed to be free of the danger of an earthquake. In 1917, however, an earthquake destroyed the city and it had to be rebuilt.

gua·va (gwä′və) *n.* **1.** Any of various tropical American and Asian shrubs and trees of the genus *Psidium;* especially, *P. guajava,* having white flowers and edible fruit. **2.** The pear-shaped fruit of this tree, having a yellow rind and pink flesh, and eaten fresh or preserved. [Spanish *guava, guayaba,* of South American Indian origin.]

Guayana. See Guiana.

guelder rose *A shrub that is found both in the wild and in gardens. Its clusters of white flowers appear in June.*

Guernsey *This breed of dairy cattle originated on the island of Guernsey in the English Channel and is the only breed permitted there. Guernsey cows produce very rich, yellowish milk.*

Gua·ya·quil (gwī'ə-kēl'). City and chief port of Ecuador and capital of Guayas province. Its industries include tanning, sugar refining, and iron founding.

gua·yu·le (gwī-ōō'lē) *n.* A woody plant or shrub, *Parthenium argentatum,* of the southwestern United States and Mexico, having sap sometimes used as a source of rubber. [American Spanish, from Nahuatl *cuauhuli* : *cuahuitl,* tree + *uli,* gum.]

gu·ber·nac·u·lum (gōō'bər-năk'yōō-ləm) *n., pl.* **-la** (-lə). *Anatomy.* Either of two ligaments in the fetus that are attached to the gonads. In males they guide the testes into the scrotum. [New Latin, from Latin, rudder : *gubernāre,* to steer + *-culum,* diminutive suffix.]

gu·ber·na·to·ri·al (gōō'bər-nə-tôr'ē-əl, -tōr'-, gyōō'-) *adj.* Of or relating to a governor. [Late Latin *gubernātorius,* from Latin *gubernātor,* GOVERNOR.]

gu·ber·ni·ya (gōō-bĕr'nē-ə) *n.* 1. An administrative subdivision of a soviet in the U.S.S.R. 2. An administrative division equivalent to a province in Russia prior to 1917. [Russian, province, perhaps from Polish *gubernja,* from Latin *gubernāre,* GOVERN.]

guck (gŭk, gōōk) *n. Slang.* A messy substance, such as sludge. [Perhaps GOO + MUCK.]

gudg·eon[1] (gŭj'ən) *n.* 1. A small Eurasian freshwater fish, *Gobio gobio,* related to the carp and used as food and bait. 2. Any of various similar fishes. 3. An enticement; a bait. 4. *Slang.* Someone who is easily duped; a gullible person.
—*tr.v.* **gudgeoned, -eoning, -eons.** *Slang.* To dupe; cheat. [Middle English *gojoun,* from Old French *goujon,* from Latin *gōbiō, gōbius,* GOBY.]

gudg·eon[2] *n.* 1. A metal pivot or journal at the end of a shaft or axle, around which a wheel or other device turns. 2. The part of a hinge into which the pin fits. 3. *Nautical.* The socket for the pintle of a rudder. 4. A metal pin that joins two pieces of stone. [Middle English *gudyon,* from Old French *goujon,* diminutive of *gouge,* GOUGE (chisel).]

gudgeon pin *n.* See **wrist pin** (sense 2).

Gud·run (gōōd'rōōn'). Also **Guth·run** (gōōth'-), **Kud·run** (kōōd'-). The daughter of the king of the Nibelungs and wife of Sigurd in the *Volsunga Saga.*

guel·der rose (gĕl'dər) *n.* A shrub, *Viburnum opulus,* native to Eurasia, having clusters of white flowers and small red fruit. [Originally grown in *Gelderland* (or *Guelderland*), a province of the east-central Netherlands.]

Guelph, Guelf (gwĕlf) *n.* A member of a strong faction in medieval Italy that supported the power of the pope and the city-states in a struggle against the German emperors and the Ghibellines.
—**Guelph'ic** *adj.* —**Guelph'ism** *n.*

Guenevere. Variant of **Guinevere.**

gue·non (gə-nôn'; *French* gə-nôN') *n.* Any of various African monkeys of the genus *Cercopithecus,* having long hind legs and a long tail. [French *guenon*†.]

guer·don (gûrd'n) *n. Poetic.* A reward; recompense.
—*tr.v.* **guerdoned, -doning, -dons.** *Poetic.* To reward. [Middle English, from Old French, from Medieval Latin *widerdōnum,* alteration (influenced by Latin *dōnum,* gift) of Old High German *widarlōn* : *widar,* again + *lōn,* reward, payment.]

Gue·ric·ke (gā'rĭ-kə), **Otto von** (1602–86). German physicist. His fame rests on his experiments in pneumatics, especially the invention of an air pump (*c.* 1650). He also invented a primitive machine to generate electricity.

Guer·ni·ca (gwâr'nĭ-kə). Historic town in the Basque region of northern Spain, in the province of Vizcaya. The severe air bombing of the town by German aircraft supporting the Nationalists in April 1937 provoked Picasso to paint the famous work *Guernica.*

guern·sey (gûrn'zē) *n., pl.* **-seys.** 1. A knitted woolen sweater with a distinctive ribbed pattern across the shoulder, originally worn by seamen. 2. *Australian.* A football jersey. [First worn by seamen on the island of Guernsey.]

Guern·sey[1] (gûrn'zē). An island and bailiwick in the English Channel. Guernsey Island itself is the second largest of the Channel Islands. The bailiwick includes all the Channel Islands except the largest, Jersey. The capital is St. Peter Port. Market gardening, dairy farming, and tourism are the chief industries.

Guernsey[2] *n., pl.* **-seys.** Any of a breed of brown and white dairy cattle originally developed on the Isle of Guernsey.

guer·ril·la, gue·ril·la (gə-rĭl'ə) *n.* A member of an irregular military unit, usually associated with a revolutionary movement, that seeks to overthrow a government or an occupying enemy by means of sudden acts of harassment.
—*adj.* Of or relating to guerrillas or their methods of fighting: *guerrilla warfare.* [Spanish *guerrilla,* diminutive of *guerra,* war, from Germanic.]

guess (gĕs) *v.* **guessed, guessing, guesses.** —*tr.* 1. a. To predict (a result or event) with incomplete information. b. To assume, presume, or assert (a fact) without sufficient information. 2. To estimate correctly on the basis of incomplete information. 3. To suppose; judge. —*intr.* 1. To make a conjecture. Often used with *at: We could only guess at his motives.* 2. To make a correct guess. 3. To suppose. —See Synonyms at **conjecture.**
—*n.* 1. An act or instance of guessing. 2. A conjecture arrived at by guessing. [Middle English *gessen,* perhaps from Scandinavian; akin to Old Swedish and Danish *gisse.*] —**guess'er** *n.*

guess·ti·mate, gues·ti·mate (gĕs'tə-mĭt) *n.* An estimate based more on intuition than on strict calculation. [GUESS + ESTIMATE.]
—**guess·ti·mate** (gĕs'tə-māt') *v.*

guess·work (gĕs'wûrk') *n.* 1. The process of making guesses. 2. An estimate or judgment made by this process.

guest (gĕst) *n.* 1. One who receives hospitality at the home or table of another. 2. One to whom some entertainment or service is offered. 3. A visitor, such as a foreign dignitary, to whom the hospitality of an institution, municipality, or government has been extended. 4. The patron of a restaurant, hotel, boarding house, or the like. 5. A contestant, performer, speaker, or other person appearing in a concert, television program, or the like. 6. *Zoology.* A commensal organism; especially, an insect that lives in the nest or burrow of another species.
—*adj.* Of, for, or being a guest: *a guest conductor; a guest room.*
—*v.* **guested, guesting, guests.** —*tr.* To entertain as one's guest. —*intr.* To appear as a guest, especially on a television show. [Middle English *gest,* from Old Norse *gestr.*]

guest rope *n. Nautical.* 1. An extra line used with the towline to steady a ship being towed. 2. A rope dropped over the side of a ship for steadying or securing a smaller boat coming alongside. Also called "guess rope."

Gue·va·ra (gə-vär'ə), **Ernesto,** known as "Che" (1928–67). Latin-American revolutionary leader, born in Argentina. When Castro took power in Cuba (1959), Guevara was appointed president of the national bank, and was then minister of industry (1961–65). He later assisted revolutionary movements in other countries, but was captured by the Bolivian army and executed (1967). He wrote several books, among them a manual for revolutionaries, *Guerrilla Warfare* (1961).

guff (gŭf) *n. Slang.* Foolish talk; nonsense. [Originally, "puff," imitative.]

guf·faw (gə-fô') *n.* A hearty or coarse burst of laughter.
—*intr.v.* **guffawed, -fawing, -faws.** To laugh explosively. [Imitative.]

Gug·gen·heim (gōōg'ən-hīm'). Family of U.S. industrialists and philanthropists. **Solomon** (1861–1949) established (1937) the foundation that built the Guggenheim Museum of Modern Art in New York in 1959.

Gui·a·na or **Gua·ya·na** (gē-ăn'ə, -ä'nə). Region on the north coast of South America, bounded by the Orinoco, Amazon, and Negro rivers. It consists of eastern Venezuela, Guyana, Surinam, French Guiana, and northern Brazil.

guid·ance (gī'dəns) *n.* 1. An act or instance of guiding. 2. Counseling, as on vocational, educational, or marital problems. 3. Any of various processes or techniques by which missiles carrying sensing or information-processing equipment are guided in flight.

guide (gīd) *n. Abbr.* **g.** 1. One who shows the way by leading, directing, or advising, usually by reason of greater experience with the course to be pursued. 2. A person employed to guide a tour, group, or the like. 3. a. Any sign or mark that serves to direct. b. An example, model, or criterion of accuracy to be followed. 4. a. A guidebook. b. A book or manual that serves to instruct or to direct one's thinking. 5. Any device, such as a ruler, line, ring, tab, or bar, that acts as an indicator or that regulates the motion of one's hand, a tool, or a machine part. 6. a. A soldier stationed at the right or left of a column to control the alignment of the marchers, show the direction, or mark the point of pivot. b. A ship or vehicle on which other members of a convoy may align themselves.
—*v.* **guided, guiding, guides.** —*tr.* 1. To show the way to; lead; direct. 2. To direct the course of; steer: *guide a ship through a channel.* 3. To manage the affairs of; govern. 4. a. To influence the conduct or opinions of. b. To be a criterion for or motive of (an action, for example). —*intr.* To serve as a guide. [Middle English *g(u)ide,* from Old French, from Frankish *wītan.*] —**guid·a·ble** *adj.* —**guid·er** *n.*

guide·book (gīd'bŏŏk') *n.* A handbook of information for travelers, tourists, students, or the like.

guided missile *n.* A missile capable of being guided while it is in flight. Compare **ballistic missile.**

guide dog *n.* A dog that has been specially trained to guide a blind person.

guide·line (gīd'līn') *n.* 1. *Printing.* A mark used to orient lettering, a drawing, or the like. 2. *Usually* **guidelines.** A statement of policy or principles by a person or group having authority over an activity. 3. Something serving as an example or source of instruction.

guide·post (gīd'pōst') *n.* A post with a sign giving directions placed at an intersection or fork in a road; signpost.

guide rope *n.* 1. A rope fastened to another rope that is lifting a load, to guide the rope and steady the load. 2. A rope used to steady or moor an airship or balloon.

guide·word (gīd'wûrd') *n.* A word or term that appears at the top of the page of a reference book, such as a dictionary, to indicate the first or last entry on the page.

gui·don (gī'dŏn', gīd'n) *n. Military.* 1. A small flag or pennant, often with a forked end, carried as a standard by a regiment or other military unit. 2. The soldier bearing this standard. [French, from Italian *guidone,* from *guida,* GUIDE.]

guild, gild (gĭld) *n.* 1. An association or corporation of persons of the same trade, pursuits, or interests formed for their mutual aid and protection, the maintenance of standards, or the furtherance of some purpose; especially, in medieval times, a society of merchants or artisans. 2. *Ecology.* A group of plants having a characteristic mode of existence that involves some dependence upon other plant life, such as the lianas and epiphytes. [Middle English *gilde,* from Old Norse *gildi,* payment, fraternity, contribution.]

guil·der, gil·der (gĭl′dər) *n. Abbr.* **gld. 1.** The basic monetary unit of the Netherlands, Surinam, and the Netherlands Antilles, equal to 100 cents. See feature at **currency. 2.** A coin worth one guilder. Also called "gulden," "florin." [Middle English, alteration of Dutch *gulden*, GULDEN.]

guild·hall (gĭld′hôl′) *n.* **1.** The meeting hall of a guild or corporation, especially in medieval times. **2. a.** A town hall. **b. Guildhall.** The meeting hall of the Corporation of the City of London.

guilds·man (gĭldz′mən) *n., pl.* **-men** (-mĭn). A member of a guild.

guild socialism *n.* A type of socialism formerly advocated in England in which industry would be owned by the state but managed by a council of workers.

guilds·wom·an (gĭldz′wo͝om′ən) *n., pl.* **-women** (-wĭm′ĭn). A woman member of a guild.

guile (gīl) *n.* **1.** Cunning; craftiness. **2.** *Obsolete.* A trick; ruse. —See Synonyms at **artifice.**

~*tr.v.* **guiled, guiling, guiles.** *Archaic.* To beguile; deceive. [Middle English *gile*, from Old French *guile*, from Germanic; akin to Old English *wigle*, divination, sorcery.]

guile·ful (gīl′fəl) *adj.* Full of guile; artfully deceitful; crafty. **—guile·ful·ly** *adv.* **—guile·ful·ness** *n.*

guile·less (gīl′lĭs) *adj.* Free of guile; simple; artless. —See Synonyms at **naive. —guile·less·ly** *adv.* **—guile·less·ness** *n.*

Guil·laume (gē-yōm′), **Charles Edouard** (1861–1938). Swiss physicist. For his discovery of the steel-nickel alloy called Invar he was awarded the Nobel Prize for physics (1920).

guil·le·mot (gĭl′ə-mŏt′) *n.* Any of several small sea birds of the genera *Uria* and *Cepphus*, of northern regions, having dark plumage with white markings. [French, diminutive of *Guillaume*, William.]

guil·loche (gĭ-lōsh′, gē-yōsh′) *n. Architecture.* An ornamental border formed of two or more bands interlaced in such a way as to repeat a design. [French *guillochis*, from *guillocher*, to decorate with guilloche, perhaps from Italian *ghiocciare*, dialectal variant of *gocciare*, to drip, trickle, from *goccia*, drop, from Latin *gutta*. See **gout.**]

guil·lo·tine (gĭl′ə-tēn′, gē′ə-) *n.* **1. a.** A machine with a heavy blade that falls freely between upright guides to behead a condemned prisoner. **b.** Any of various other machines used for execution by beheading. **c.** Execution by such a machine. Preceded by *the.* **2.** Any of various more or less similar cutting instruments, such as a surgical device used to remove tonsils. **3.** A device consisting of a long blade that is brought down onto a sheet of paper, metal, or the like to cut or trim it. **4.** *British.* A method of cutting off debate on a bill in Parliament by fixing beforehand a time for voting on successive stages. Compare **kangaroo closure.**

~*tr.v.* **guillotined, -tining, -tines. 1.** To behead with a guillotine. **2.** To cut or trim with a guillotine. [After Joseph Ignace *Guillotin* (1738–1814), French doctor who proposed its use.] **—guil·lo·tin·er** *n.*

guilt (gĭlt) *n.* **1.** The fact of being responsible for an offense or wrongdoing. **2.** *Law.* Culpability for a crime or breach of regulations that carries a legal punishment or penalty. **3. a.** Remorseful awareness of having done something wrong. **b.** Feelings of remorse arising from a sense of inadequacy or imagined wrongdoing. **4.** *Rare.* Guilty behavior. [Middle English *gult, gilt*, Old English *gylt*†.]

guilt complex *n. Psychology.* An obsession with the idea of being to blame for something.

guilt·less (gĭlt′lĭs) *adj.* **1.** Free from guilt; blameless; innocent. **2.** Without knowledge or experience of something. **—guilt·less·ly** *adv.* **—guilt·less·ness** *n.*

guilt·y (gĭl′tē) *adj.* **-ier, -iest. 1.** Responsible for or chargeable with some reprehensible act. Often used with *of*: *guilty of cheating.* **2.** *Law.* Having committed a crime or a breach of regulations or having been adjudged to have done so: *plead guilty.* **3.** At fault; culpable: *the guilty party.* **4.** Suffering from or showing a sense of guilt: *a guilty conscience.* **—guilt·i·ly** *adv.* **—guilt·i·ness** *n.*

guimpe (gĭmp, gămp) *n.* **1.** A short-sleeved blouse worn under a jumper. **2.** A yoke insert for a low-necked dress. **3.** A starched cloth covering the neck and shoulders as part of a nun's habit. **4.** A trimming, **gimp** *(see).*

Guin. Guinea.

guin·ea (gĭn′ē) *n. Abbr.* **G., g. 1.** A former British gold coin worth one pound and one shilling. **2.** The sum of one pound and one shilling. [Originally made of gold from the *Guinea* coast of Africa.]

Guin·ea (gĭn′ē). *Abbr.* **Guin.** Formerly **French Guinea.** Independent republic on the west coast of Africa. The interior consists chiefly of highlands, although in the northeast the land descends to the Niger plains. The bulk of the labor force is employed in agriculture, but the major exports are bauxite and alumina. Guinea was a French colony from 1891 until 1958, when it gained its independence. Area, 245,856 square kilometers (94,925 square miles). Population, 5,700,000. Capital, Conakry. See map at **West African States.**

Guinea, Gulf of. Broad bay of the Atlantic Ocean formed by the large bend of the coast of west-central Africa. It extends, roughly, from the west coast of Ivory Coast to the Gabon estuary and includes the bights of Benin and Biafra.

Guin·ea-Bis·sau (gĭn′ē-bĭ-sou′). Formerly **Por·tu·guese Guinea** (pôr′chə-gēz′). Independent republic on the west coast of Africa. Except for the highlands on the border with Guinea, the land is low-lying. The chief exports are peanuts and peanut products, palm products, and copra. The country was a Portuguese colony from 1879 until 1974, when it gained its independence under the African Party for the Independence of Guinea and Cape Verde. There were plans to unite the two countries. Area, 36,125 square kilometers (13,948 square miles). Population, 1,000,000. Capital, Bissau. See map at **West African States.**

Guinea corn *n.* **Durra** *(see).*

guinea fowl *n.* Any of several pheasantlike birds of the family Numididae, native to Africa; especially, a widely domesticated species, *Numida meleagris*, having blackish plumage marked with many small white spots. Also called "guinea hen." [From the *Guinea* coast of Africa.]

guinea hen *n.* **1.** A female guinea fowl. **2.** The guinea fowl.

Guinea pepper *n.* **1.** A variety of the plant, *Capsicum frutescens*, from which cayenne pepper is made. **2.** The spicy fruit of an African tree, *Xylopia aethiopica*, which is made into a condiment.

guinea pig *n.* **1.** A domesticated rodent descended from the Brazilian or Peruvian cavy, *Cavia procellus*, having variously colored hair and no visible tail, and widely kept as pets and as experimental animals. **2.** Any person who is used as a subject for experimentation. [Probably from a confusion of GUIANA with the *Guinea* coast of Africa.]

guinea worm *n.* A long, threadlike nematode worm, *Dracunculus medinensis*, of tropical Asia and Africa, that is a subcutaneous parasite of man and other animals, causing ulcers on the arms, legs, and feet. [Probably from the *Guinea* coast of Africa.]

Guin·e·vere (gwĭn′ə-vîr′). Also **Guen·e·vere** (gwĕn′-). In Arthurian legend, the wife of King Arthur and the mistress of Lancelot. [Welsh *Gwenhwyvar*, perhaps "white phantom" : *gwyn*, white + *-hwyvar*†, phantom.]

Guin·ness (gĭn′ĭs), **Sir Alec** (1914–). English actor. He has played memorable roles in such films as *Kind Hearts and Coronets* (1949) in which he played eight parts, *The Lavender Hill Mob* (1951), *The Horse's Mouth* (1958), and *Lawrence of Arabia* (1962).

gui·pure (gĭ-pyo͝or′; *French* gē-pür′) *n.* **1.** A kind of coarse, large-patterned lace without a supporting net mesh. **2.** A trimming, **gimp** *(see).* [French, from Old French, from *guiper*, to cover with silk, wool, or the like, from Frankish *wīpan.*]

gui·ro (gwîr′ō) *n.* A percussion instrument consisting of a dried gourd with parallel grooves cut across it. It produces a rattling sound when a stick is drawn across it. [Spanish, gourd.]

guise (gīz) *n.* **1.** Outward appearance; aspect. **2.** False appearance; pretense. **3.** Mode of dress; garb: *in the guise of a beggar.* **4.** *Obsolete.* Custom; habit.

~*v.* **guised, guising, guises.** —*tr. Archaic.* To costume. —*intr. Chiefly Scottish.* To go in disguise; masquerade. [Middle English, fashion, manner, from Old French, from Germanic.]

Guise (gēz). A powerful French ducal line of the 16th and 17th centuries.

guis·er (gī′zər) *n. Chiefly Scottish.* One who goes from door to door wearing mask and fancy dress at Halloween, performing for money, sweets, or the like. [From dialectal *guise*, to masquerade, from GUISE (noun).]

gui·tar (gĭ-tär′) *n.* A musical instrument similar to the lute, having a large flat-backed sound box generally in the shape of a violin, a long fretted neck, and usually six strings, played by strumming or plucking. [French *guitare*, from Old French, from Spanish *guitarra*, from Arabic *qītār*, from Greek *kithara*, lyre.] **—gui·tar·ist** *n.*

gui·tar·fish (gĭ-tär′fĭsh′) *n., pl.* **-fishes** or collectively **guitarfish.** Any of several bottom-dwelling marine fishes of the family Rhinobatidae having a guitar-shaped body.

Gui·try (gē-trē′), **Sacha** (1885–1957). French playwright, actor, and film director. The best known of the films he directed are *The Story of a Cheat* (1935) and *Pearls of the Crown* (1937).

Gu·ja·rat (go͝oj′ə-rät′). State in western India, lying on the Arabian Sea and including almost all of the Kathiawar peninsula. It was created in 1960 from the Gujarati-speaking parts of the former state of Bombay. The capital is Ahmadabad. Gujarat is the center of India's cotton-textile industry.

Gu·ja·ra·ti (go͝oj′ə-rä′tē) *n., pl.* **Gujarati. 1.** The Indic language spoken in Gujarat. **2.** A native or inhabitant of Gujarat or speaker of Gujarati.

gul (go͞ol) *n.* A motif in oriental carpets, typically a stylized compact device that is repeated at regular intervals in the central field. [Persian *gul*†, rose, flower.]

gu·lag (go͞o′läg′) *n. Often* **Gulag.** A forced labor camp or prison, used especially for political prisoners. [Russian *G*lavnoye *U*pravleniye Trudovykh *Lag*erei, Main Administration for Corrective Labor Camps.]

gu·lar (go͞o′lər, gyo͞o′-) *adj.* Of, pertaining to, or located on the throat. [Latin *gula*, throat.]

gulch (gŭlch) *n.* A small ravine, especially one cut by a torrent. [Origin obscure.]

gul·den (go͞ol′dən) *n., pl.* **guldens** or **gulden.** A monetary unit, the **guilder** *(see).* [Dutch *gulden (florijn)*, golden (florin), from Middle Dutch.]

gules (gyo͞olz) *n. Heraldry.* The color red, indicated on a blazon by engraved vertical lines.

~*adj. Heraldry.* Red. Usually used after the noun: *a lion gules.* [Middle English *goules*, from Old French *go(u)les*, red, red fur neckpiece, from the plural of *gole*, throat, from Latin *gula*, throat.]

gulf (gŭlf) *n.* **1.** *Abbr.* **G.** A large area of a sea or ocean partially enclosed by land; especially, a long landlocked portion of sea opening through a strait. **2.** A deep, wide chasm; abyss. **3.** A separating

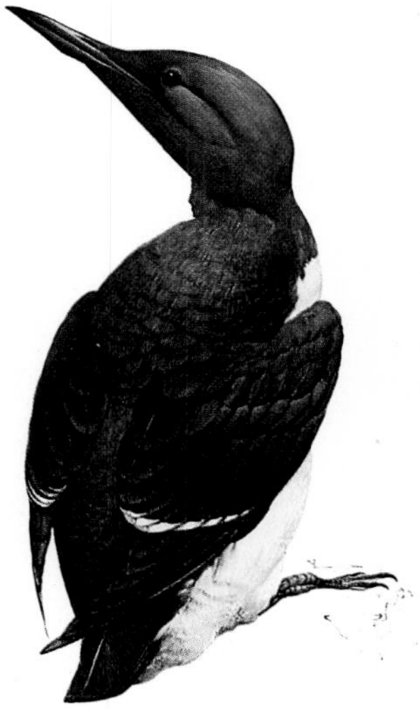

guillemot *Uria aalge, the guillemot, spends most of each year at sea, coming ashore in February to breed on cliff ledges. The birds, which breed on coasts across much of the Northern Hemisphere, do not build nests. Instead, the pear-shaped eggs are laid on bare rock.*

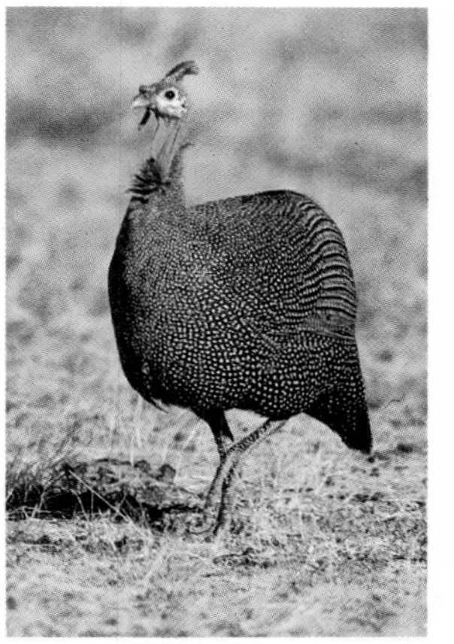

guinea fowl *Relatives of the domestic chicken, guinea fowls are native to Africa. This crowned guinea fowl—one of eight species of the bird—is in Etosha National Park in Namibia.*

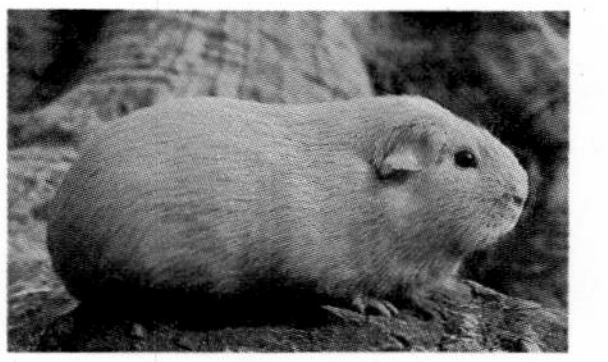

guinea pig *A tailless rodent introduced to Europe from Peru by the Spaniards soon after the discovery of America.*

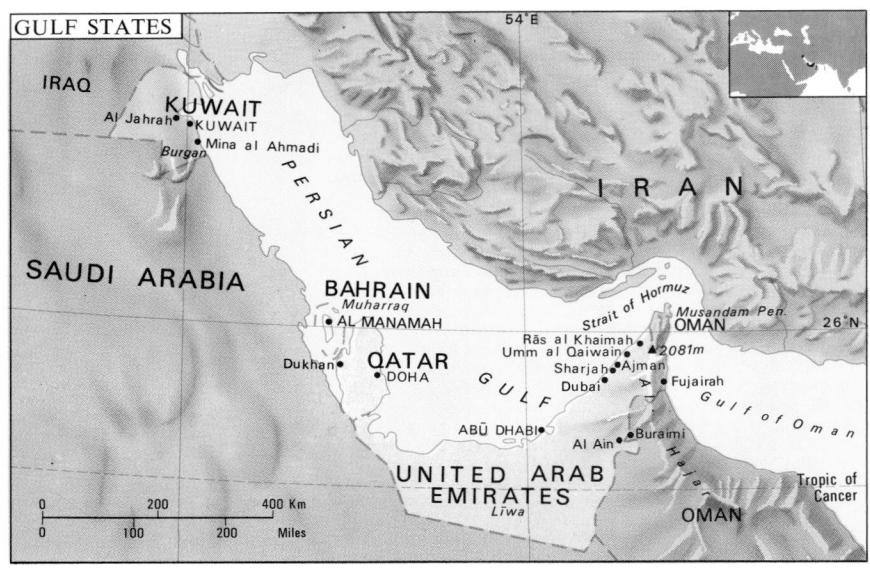

GULF STATES

IRAQ

KUWAIT
Al Jahrah• •KUWAIT
Burgan• •Mina al Ahmadi

SAUDI ARABIA

PERSIAN

IRAN

BAHRAIN
Muharraq•
•AL MANAMAH

Strait of Hormuz

Musandam Pen.

OMAN 26°N

QATAR
Dukhan• •DOHA

Rās al Khaimah•
Umm al Qaiwain• ▲2081m
Sharjah• •Ajman
Dubai• •Fujairah

GULF

Gulf of Oman

ABŪ DHABI•
Al Ain• •Buraimi

UNITED ARAB
EMIRATES
Līwa

Tropic of
Cancer

OMAN

0   200   400 Km
0 100 200 Miles

distance or wide gap caused especially by a lack of understanding or communication. **4.** A whirlpool; eddy.
~*tr.v.* **gulfed, gulfing, gulfs.** To swallow; engulf. [Middle English *golf, goulf,* from Old French *golfe,* from Old Italian *golfo,* from Vulgar Latin *colp(h)us* (unattested), from Greek *kolpos, kolphos,* bosom, fold, bay.]

Gulf, the. See Persian Gulf.

Gulf States[1]. The small, oil-rich Arab states on the Persian Gulf: Bahrain, Kuwait, Qatar, and the United Arab Emirates.

Gulf States[2]. The five southern U.S. states that have coastlines on the Gulf of Mexico: Florida, Alabama, Mississippi, Louisiana, and Texas.

Gulf Stream *n.* A warm ocean current of the North Atlantic, issuing from the Gulf of Mexico and flowing east through the Straits of Florida, northeast along the southeastern coast of the United States, then east to merge with the North Atlantic Current.

gulf·weed (gŭlf'wēd') *n.* Any of several brownish seaweeds of the genus *Sargassum,* especially *S. natans,* of tropical Atlantic waters, having rounded air bladders and often forming dense, floating masses. Also called "sargasso." [After the Gulf of Mexico, where it is found.]

gull[1] (gŭl) *n.* Any of various chiefly coastal aquatic birds of the subfamily Larinae, having long wings, webbed feet, and usually gray and white plumage. [Middle English *gull,* probably from Welsh *gwylan,* from Celtic *voilenno-* (unattested).]

gull[2] *n.* A gullible person; dupe; simpleton.
~*tr.v.* **gulled, gulling, gulls.** To deceive; cheat; dupe. [Probably from dialectal *gull,* unfledged bird, Middle English *golle, gulle,* probably from *gul,* yellow, pale, from Old Norse *gulr.*]

Gul·lah (gŭl'ə) *n.* **1.** Any of a group of Blacks inhabiting the Sea Islands and coastal area of South Carolina, Georgia, and northern Florida. **2.** The creolized English spoken by these people.

gul·let (gŭl'ĭt) *n.* **1.** *Anatomy.* The esophagus. **2.** The throat. **3.** A gully or ravine, especially one that serves as a water channel. **4.** A cut in the earth preliminary to mining or excavating. [Middle English *golet,* from Old French *goulet,* diminutive of *gole, goule,* throat, from Latin *gula.*]

gul·li·ble (gŭl'ə-bəl) *adj.* Able to be taken in; easily deceived or duped; credulous. [From GULL (dupe).] —**gul·li·bil·i·ty** *n.* —**gul·li·bly** *adv.*

Gull·strand (gŭl'strănd'), **Allvar** (1862-1930). Swedish ophthalmologist. For his experiments on the refraction of light in the eye he was awarded the Nobel Prize in 1911.

gul·ly[1] (gŭl'ē) *n., pl.* **-lies. 1.** A deep ditch or channel cut in the earth by running water, usually after a downpour. **2.** A gutter or channel.
~*tr.v.* **gullied, -lying, -lies.** To make a gully in. [Alteration of GULLET.]

gully[2] *n., pl.* **-lies.** *Chiefly Scottish.* A large knife. [Short for *gully knife* : *gully,* probably alteration of GULLET + KNIFE.]

gu·los·i·ty (gōo-lŏs'ə-tē, gyŏo-) *n. Literary.* Gluttony. [Late Latin *gulōsitās* (stem *gulōsitāt-*), from Latin *gulōsus,* greedy, from *gula,* gullet.]

gulp (gŭlp) *v.* **gulped, gulping, gulps.** —*tr.* **1.** To swallow greedily or rapidly in large amounts. Usually used with *down: gulp down coffee.* **2.** To stifle by or as if by swallowing. —*intr.* **1.** To choke or gasp; swallow hard, as in nervousness. **2.** To swallow food or drink in gulps. **3.** To make a noise in the throat when swallowing.
~*n.* **1.** The act of gulping. **2.** A large mouthful. **3.** A convulsive attempt to swallow; a catching of air in the throat. [Middle English *gulpen,* from Middle Dutch *gulpen* (imitative).] —**gulp·er** *n.* —**gulp·ing·ly** *adv.*

gulp·er eel (gŭl'pər) *n.* Any of various eellike fishes of the genera

Eurypharynx and *Saccopharynx,* which live on the sea bottom and can swallow prey much larger than themselves.

gum[1] (gŭm) *n.* **1. a.** Any of various viscous substances that are exuded by certain plants and trees and that dry into water-soluble, noncrystalline, brittle solids. **b.** Loosely, a similar plant exudate, such as a resin. **2.** Any of various adhesives made from such exudates or from some other sticky substance. **3. a.** Any of various trees, such as one of the genera *Eucalyptus, Liquidambar,* or *Nyssa,* that are a source of gum. Also called "gum tree." **b.** The wood of such a tree. Also called "gumwood." **4.** Chewing gum.
~*v.* **gummed, gumming, gums.** —*tr.* To cover, smear, seal, fill, or fix in place with gum. —*intr.* **1.** To exude or form gum. **2.** To become sticky or clogged with gum or a similar substance. —**gum up. 1.** To become clogged, as with gum. **2.** *Slang.* To ruin; bungle; spoil: *gum up the works.* [Middle English *gumme, gomme,* from Old French *gomme,* from Vulgar Latin *gumma* (unattested), from Latin *gummi, cummi,* from Greek *kommi,* from Egyptian *kemai.*]

gum[2] *n.* The firm connective tissue that is covered by mucous membrane and that envelops the bones of the jaw containing the tooth sockets and surrounds the bases of the teeth. Also called "gingiva." [Middle English *gome,* Old English *gōma,* palate, jaw.]

gum ac·croi·des (ə-kroi'dēz) *n.* A gum resin, **acaroid resin** *(see).* [New Latin *accroides,* from ACAROID.]

gum ammoniac *n.* A gum resin, **ammoniac** *(see).*

gum arabic *n.* A gum exuded by various African trees of the genus *Acacia,* especially *A. senegal,* and used in the preparation of pills and emulsions, the manufacture of mucilage and sweets, and in general as a thickener and colloidal stabilizer. Also called "acacia."

gum benzoin *n.* A gum resin, **benzoin** *(see).*

gum·bo, gom·bo (gŭm'bō) *n., pl.* **-bos. 1. a.** The mucilaginous pods of okra. **b. Okra** *(see).* **2.** A soup or stew thickened with okra and eaten especially in Africa, the Caribbean, and the southern United States. **3.** A fine silty soil, common in the southern and western United States, that forms an unusually sticky mud when wet. **4.** *Often* **Gumbo.** A patois spoken by some Blacks and Creoles in Louisiana and the French West Indies. [Louisiana French *gombo,* from Bantu.]

gum-boil (gŭm'boil') *n.* A small boil or abscess on the gum, usually opening from the root of a tooth.

gum-bo-lim-bo (gŭm'bō-lĭm'bō) *n., pl.* **-bos.** An aromatic tree, *Bursera simaruba,* of Florida and the West Indies, having compound leaves and small white flowers. [Possibly GUMBO + -*limbo,* birdlime (from its resin), from Bantu.]

gum-boot (gŭm'bōot') *n.* A **Wellington boot** *(see).*

gum-drop (gŭm'drŏp') *n.* A small candy made of flavored gum arabic or gelatin and coated with coarse granulated sugar.

gum-ma (gŭm'ə) *n., pl.* **-mas** or **gummata** (gŭm'ə-tə). A small, rubbery tumor formed in an advanced stage of syphilis. [New Latin, from Latin *gummi,* GUM.] —**gum-ma-tous** *adj.*

gum-mite (gŭm'īt') *n.* A yellow to orange amorphous mineral consisting of hydrated uranium oxides. [German *Gummi,* GUM (referring to the gummy appearance of some types) + -ITE.]

gum-mo-sis (gŭ-mō'sĭs) *n.* The pathological formation of patches of gum on certain plants, such as sugar cane and certain fruit trees, resulting from attack by insects, microorganisms, or adverse weather conditions. [New Latin : Latin *gummi,* GUM + -OSIS.]

gum-mous (gŭm'əs) *adj.* Also **gum-mose** (-ōs'). **1.** Gumlike or composed of gum. **2.** Gummy.

gum-my (gŭm'ē) *adj.* **-mier, -miest. 1.** Consisting of or containing gum. **2.** Suffused with or yielding gum. **3.** Sticky; viscid. **4.** Coated with gum or something gumlike.

gum plant *n.* Any of several North American plants of the genus *Grindelia,* especially *G. squarosa,* having sticky leaves and bracts and yellow, rayed flowers.

gump-tion (gŭmp'shən) *n. Informal.* **1.** Basic common sense; practicality. **2.** Enterprise or initiative, especially when requiring courage or nerve. [18th century (Scottish) : origin obscure.]

gum resin *n.* A mixture of gum and resin that exudes from some trees and other plants.

gum-shoe (gŭm'shōo') *n.* **1.** A rubber shoe or overshoe. **2.** A sneaker. **3.** *Slang.* A detective.
~*intr.v.* **gumshoed, -shoeing, -shoes.** *Slang.* To investigate stealthily; pry.

gum tree *n.* A tree, the **gum** *(see).*

gum-wood (gŭm'wŏod') *n.* The wood of a gum tree. See **gum.**

gun (gŭn) *n.* **1.** A weapon consisting essentially of a metal tube from which a projectile is fired at high velocity. **2.** A cannon, as distinguished from a small firearm. **3.** A portable firearm. **4.** A device that shoots a projectile. **5.** A discharge of a gun as a signal or salute. **6.** One who carries or uses a gun, such as a member of a shooting party. **7.** A device that projects something under pressure or at great speed: *a grease gun; an electron gun.* —**go great guns.** *Informal.* To proceed with vigor or success. —**jump the gun. 1.** To begin a race before the starting signal. **2.** *Informal.* To act before the appropriate moment. —**stick to one's guns.** To hold fast to an opinion or appointed course of action.
~*v.* **gunned, gunning, guns.** —*tr.* **1.** To fire upon; shoot. Often used with *down.* **2.** *Informal.* To open the throttle of so as to accelerate: *gun an engine.* —*intr.* To hunt or shoot with a gun. —**gun for. 1.** To seek to catch, overcome, or destroy. **2.** To go after in earnest; set out to obtain: *gun for the best deal available.* [Middle English *gunne, gonne,* probably from *Gunna* (unattested), pet form of feminine name *Gunhild* (sometimes applied to a war engine),

from Old Norse *Gunnhildr* : *gunnr,* battle + *hildr,* war.]

gun·boat (gŭn′bōt′) *n.* A small armed vessel.

gunboat diplomacy *n.* Diplomacy that makes use of the threat of military intervention in order to achieve its purpose.

gun carriage *n.* A frame or structure upon which a gun is mounted for firing or maneuvering.

gun·cot·ton (gŭn′kŏt′n) *n.* An explosive, **nitrocellulose** *(see).*

gun dog *n.* A dog trained or bred to assist hunters, as in flushing or retrieving game.

gun·fight (gŭn′fīt′) *n.* Also **gun·fight·ing** (-ĭng). A duel or battle with firearms. **—gun·fight·er** *n.*

gun·fire (gŭn′fīr′) *n.* The firing of guns.

gun·flint (gŭn′flĭnt′) *n.* The piece of flint used to strike the igniting spark in a flintlock.

gung ho (gŭng′ hō′) *adj. Slang.* **1.** Unswervingly dedicated and loyal. **2.** Foolishly enthusiastic. [Pidgin English : probably Mandarin Chinese *gōng,* work + *hé,* together.]

gunk (gŭngk) *n. Informal.* A filthy, slimy, or greasy substance. [Originally a trade name for a degreasing compound, later extended to apply to any viscous substance.]

gun·lock (gŭn′lŏk′) *n.* A device for igniting the charge of a firearm.

gun·man (gŭn′mən) *n., pl.* **-men** (-mĭn). **1.** One armed with a gun. **2.** A desperado; an outlaw. **3.** A professional killer.

gun·met·al (gŭn′mĕt′l) *n.* **1.** An alloy of copper with ten percent tin and sometimes a few percent of zinc. **2.** Metal used for guns. **3.** Dark gray. **—gun·met·al** *adj.*

gun moll *n. Slang.* A girlfriend or woman accomplice of a gangster.

Gunn (gŭn), **Thomson William** (1929–). British poet. His work, which includes *My Sad Captains* (1961) and *Jack Straw's Castle* (1976), is marked by strictness of form, powerful imagery, and philosophical themes. He now lives chiefly in the United States.

Gun·nar (gōōn′är′). *Norse Mythology.* The husband of Brynhild, the brother-in-law of Sigurd, and the brother of Gudrun.

Gunn effect (gŭn) *n. Electronics.* The production of high-speed current fluctuations when voltage in excess of a critical level is applied to a semiconductor device, resulting in microwave generation. [After J.B. *Gunn* (b. 1928).]

gun·nel[1] (gŭn′əl) *n.* Any of various long, eellike fishes of the family Pholidae, of northern seas. [17th century : origin obscure.]

gunnel[2]. Variant of **gunwale.**

gun·ner (gŭn′ər) *n.* **1.** A serviceman, especially a member of an aircraft crew, who aims or fires a gun. **2.** One who hunts with a gun. **3.** *British.* An artillery soldier, especially a private. **4.** A warrant officer in the navy having charge of ordnance.

gun·ner·y (gŭn′ə-rē) *n.* **1.** The art and science of constructing and operating guns. **2.** The use of guns.

gun·ny (gŭn′ē) *n.* **1.** A coarse fabric made of jute or hemp. **2.** Burlap. [Hindi *gōnī,* from Sanskrit *gonī,* sack.]

gunny sack *n.* A sack made of burlap or gunny.

gun·point (gŭn′point′) *n.* The business end of a gun. **—at gun·point.** Under the threat of being shot at.

gun·pow·der (gŭn′pou′dər) *n.* Any of various explosive powders used in blasting and to propel projectiles from guns; especially, a black explosive mixture of potassium nitrate, charcoal, and sulfur.

Gunpowder Plot *n.* A plot organized by Guy Fawkes to blow up Parliament and kill James I on November 5, 1605, in protest against the increasing repression of Roman Catholics in England. See **Guy Fawkes Day.**

gunpowder tea *n.* A type of green tea the leaves of which are rolled into pellets.

gun·room (gŭn′rōōm′, -rŏōm′) *n.* The quarters of midshipmen and junior officers on a British warship.

gun·run·ner (gŭn′rŭn′ər) *n.* One that smuggles firearms and ammunition. **—gun·run·ning** *n. & adj.*

gun·ship (gŭn′shĭp′) *n.* An armed helicopter or other aircraft used to support troops and cover transport helicopters.

gun·shot (gŭn′shŏt′) *n.* **1.** Shot fired from a gun. **2.** A shooting of a gun. **3.** The range of a gun: *within gunshot.*

gun·shy (gŭn′shī′) *adj.* Afraid of gunfire. Said especially of gun dogs.

gun·sling·er (gŭn′slĭng′ər) *n. Slang.* A gunman. **—gun·sling·ing** *n. & adj.*

gun·smith (gŭn′smĭth′) *n.* One who makes or repairs firearms.

gun·stock (gŭn′stŏk′) *n.* See **stock** (sense 14.a).

Gun·ter's chain (gŭn′tərz) *n.* See **chain** (sense 9b). [After Edmund *Gunter* (1581–1626), English mathematician.]

Gun·ther (gōōn′tər). In the *Nibelungenlied,* a king of Burgundy whose wife Brunhild is won for him by Siegfried, who in return receives Kriemhild, Gunther's sister, as his wife. Identified with Gunnar.

gun·wale, gun·nel (gŭn′əl) *n.* The upper edge of a ship's side. [Middle English *gonnewale* : GUN + WALE (so called because it served formerly as a prop for the ship's guns).]

Guo·yü, Kuo·yü (kōō′yōō′) *n.* **Mandarin Chinese** *(see).* [Mandarin Chinese *guyó* or *guó,* national, national + *yü,* language.]

gup·py (gŭp′ē) *n., pl.* **-pies.** A small, brightly colored freshwater fish, *Poecilia reticulata* (or *Lebistes reticulatus*), of northern South America and adjacent islands of the West Indies, that is popular in home aquariums. [After R.J.L. *Guppy,* 19th-century clergyman of Trinidad who supplied the British Museum with the first specimen.]

Gur (gōōr) *n.* A group of languages of the Niger-Congo family spoken chiefly in Ghana and Upper Volta.

gur·gi·ta·tion (gûr′jə-tā′shən) *n.* A whirling motion, as of water;

ebullition. [Late Latin *gurgitāre,* to engulf, from Latin *gurges* (stem *gurgit-*), whirlpool, gulf.]

gur·gle (gûr′gəl) *v.* **-gled, -gling, -gles.** *—intr.* **1.** To flow in a broken, uneven current making intermittent low sounds. **2.** To make such sounds: *the baby gurgled with pleasure.* *—tr.* To express or pronounce with a gurgling sound.
~*n.* The act or sound of gurgling. [Probably from Medieval Latin *gurgulāre,* from Latin *gurguliō,* gullet.] **—gur·gling·ly** *adv.*

Gur·kha (gōōr′kə) *n., pl.* **-khas** or collectively **Gurkha. 1.** A member of a Rajput ethnic group that was driven out of India by the Muslims and is now predominant in Nepal. **2.** A soldier from Nepal serving in the British or Indian armies.

gur·nard (gûr′nərd) *n., pl.* **gurnards** or collectively **gurnard.** Also **gur·net** (gûr′nĭt). Any of various marine fishes of the family Triglidae, and especially of the Old World genus *Trigla,* having large, fingerlike, pectoral fins and a large, armored head. Compare **flying gurnard.** [Middle English, from Old French *gornart,* from Latin *grundīre, grunnīre,* to grunt (because it grunts when caught).]

gur·ney (gûr′nē) *n., pl.* **-neys.** A cot or stretcher on wheels. [Probably from the name *Gurney.*]

gur·ry (gûr′ē) *n.* Fish offal. [Origin unknown.]

gu·ru (gōōr′ōō, gōō-rōō′) *n. Often* **Guru.** A spiritual teacher or leader, as in the Hindu or Sikh religions. [Hindi *gurū,* "the venerable one," from Sanskrit *guruh,* heavy, venerable.]

gush (gŭsh) *v.* **gushed, gushing, gushes.** *—intr.* **1.** To flow forth suddenly and violently. **2.** To issue or emanate abundantly. **3.** To make an excessively demonstrative or affected display of sentiment or enthusiasm. *—tr.* To emit abundantly.
~*n.* **1.** A sudden, violent, or copious outflow: *a gush of tears.* **2.** An excessive, usually insincere, display of emotion. [Middle English *guschen, gosshen,* perhaps from Scandinavian, akin to Icelandic *gusa.*]

gush·er (gŭsh′ər) *n.* **1.** One that gushes. **2.** A gas or oil well with an abundant natural flow.

gush·y (gŭsh′ē) *adj.* **-ier, -iest.** Characterized by excessive, affected displays of sentiment or enthusiasm.

gus·set (gŭs′ĭt) *n.* **1.** A triangular insert, as in a garment, for strengthening or enlarging. **2.** A triangular metal bracket used to strengthen a joist. [Middle English, from Old French *gousset,* armpit, piece of armor under the armpit, diminutive of *gousse†,* pod, shell.] **—gus·set·ed** *adj.*

gus·sy (gŭs′ē) *tr.v.* **-sied, -sying, -sies.** *Slang.* To dress smartly. Used with *up: all gussied up in her Sunday best.* [Origin obscure.]

gust[1] (gŭst) *n.* **1.** A violent, abrupt rush of wind, smoke, or the like. **2.** An abrupt outburst of emotion, as of rage. —See Synonyms at **wind.** [Old Norse *gustr.*]

gust[2] *n.* **1.** *Archaic.* Relish; gusto. **2.** *Obsolete.* Personal taste or inclination; liking. [Middle English *guste,* taste, from Latin *gustus.*]

gus·ta·tion (gŭs-tā′shən) *n.* The act or faculty of tasting; taste. [Latin *gustātiō* (stem *gustātiōn-*), from *gustāre,* to taste, from *gustus,* taste.]

gus·ta·to·ry (gŭs′tə-tôr′ē, -tōr′ē) *adj.* Also **gus·ta·tive** (-tĭv). Of or pertaining to the sense of taste.

Gus·ta·vus II (gŭs-tā′vəs), known as "Gustavus Adolphus" (1594–1632). King of Sweden (1611–32). As a general he fought successfully against Denmark, Russia, and Poland. He was drawn into the Thirty Years' War by his desire to assure Swedish control of the Baltic. He met his death at the Battle of Lützen (1632).

gus·to (gŭs′tō) *n.* **1.** Vigorous enjoyment; relish; zest. **2.** *Archaic.* Artistic style of execution. [Italian, from Latin *gustus,* taste.]

gus·ty (gŭs′tē) *adj.* **-tier, -tiest. 1.** Blowing in or characterized by gusts. **2.** Marked by sudden outbursts: *a gusty temperament.* **—gus·ti·ly** *adv.* **—gus·ti·ness** *n.*

gut (gŭt) *n.* **1.** The alimentary canal or a portion thereof; especially, the intestine or stomach. **2. guts.** The bowels; entrails; viscera. **3. guts.** The essential contents or part of something: *the guts of an old television set.* **4.** The intestines of some animals prepared as strings for musical instruments or as surgical sutures; catgut. **5. guts.** *Informal.* Courage; nerve. **6.** A narrow passage or channel. **7.** Fibrous material taken from the silk gland of a silkworm before it spins a cocoon, used for fishing tackle. **—hate someone's guts.** *Informal.* To detest or feel very hostile toward someone.
~*tr.v.* **gutted, gutting, guts. 1.** To remove the intestines or entrails of. **2.** To destroy the interior of: *fire gutted the house.* **3.** To extract the essential points of (a book, article, or the like).
~*adj. Slang.* Arousing or aroused by basic emotions; visceral; instinctive: *a gut response.* [Middle English *gut,* Old English *guttas* (plural).]

gut·buck·et (gŭt′bŭk′ət) *n.* **1.** An early style of jazz, with a strong beat. Also called "barrelhouse." **2.** A homemade instrument, resembling a double bass, on which this music was originally played.

Gu·ten·berg (gōōt′n-bûrg′), **Johann** (*c.* 1397–1468). German printer. He was the first European to print with movable type set in molds. His Mazarin Bible of *c.* 1455 is believed to be the first book printed with movable type.

Guth·rie test (gŭth′rē) *n.* A blood test to determine the presence of the metabolic disease phenylketonuria in young children. [After Samuel *Guthrie* (1782–1848), U.S. chemist.]

Guthrun. Variant of **Gudrun.**

gut·less (gŭt′lĭs) *adj. Informal.* **1.** Lacking courage or drive. **2.** Insubstantial; weak. **—gut·less·ness** *n.*

guts·y (gŭt′sē) *adj.* **-ier, -iest.** *Informal.* **1.** Full of courage; daring;

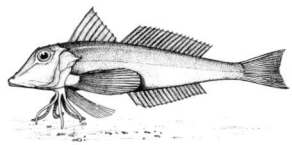

gurnard *A widely distributed inshore coastal fish. The gurnard uses its fingerlike pectoral rays to probe the seabed for the fish, small crabs, shrimp, and other shellfish on which it feeds.*

plucky. **2.** Earthy and uninhibited; raunchy: *a gutsy singing voice.* —**guts·i·ness** *n.*

gut·ta (gŭt′ə) *n., pl.* **guttae** (gŭt′ē) **1.** *Architecture.* One of a group of small, droplike ornaments on a Doric entablature. **2.** *Abbr.* **gt.** *Medicine.* A drop. [Latin, drop.]

gut·ta-per·cha (gŭt′ə-pûr′chə) *n.* **1.** Any of several tropical trees of the genera *Palaquium* and *Payena,* having sap in the form of milky latex. **2.** A rubbery substance derived from the latex of these trees, used as electrical insulation and for waterproofing. [Malay *gĕtah percha* : *gĕtah,* sap + *percha,* strip of cloth.]

gut·tate (gŭt′āt′) *adj.* Also **gut·tat·ed** (-ā′tĭd). **1.** In the form of drops or having drops. **2.** *Biology.* Spotted as if by drops. [Latin *guttatus,* from *gutta,* drop.]

gut·ta·tion (gə-tā′shən) *n.* Loss of water from the surface of a plant in the form of liquid drops rather than vapor. [Latin *gutta,* drop.]

gut·ter (gŭt′ər) *n.* **1.** A channel for draining off water at the edge of a street or road. **2.** A pipe or trough for draining off water, fitted to the edge of a roof. **3.** A furrow or groove formed by running water. **4.** The trough on either side of a bowling alley. **5. a.** The space left for perforation, between stamps on a sheet. **b.** *Printing.* The white space between the facing pages of a book. **6.** An environment of poverty, vulgarity, or criminal activities; a slum. ~*v.* **guttered, -tering, -ters.** —*tr.* To form gutters or furrows in. —*intr.* **1.** To flow in channels or rivulets. **2.** To melt away through the channel formed by a burning wick. Said of candles. **3.** To burn with a low flame; flicker. [Middle English *guter, goter,* sewer, trough, drain, from Norman French *gotere,* from Vulgar Latin *guttāria* (unattested), from Latin *gutta,* drop.]

gut·ter·ing (gŭt′ər-ĭng) *n.* The drainpipes, gutters, and the like, fitted to the outside of a building to drain off rainwater.

gutter press *n.* The section of the popular press that seeks to reveal facts about people's personal lives in a sordid way.

gut·ter·snipe (gŭt′ər-snīp′) *n.* A street urchin.

gut·tur·al (gŭt′ər-əl) *adj.* **1.** Of or pertaining to the throat. **2.** Produced in the throat. **3.** *Phonetics.* Produced in or near the throat; velar or uvular. Not in technical usage. ~*n.* A guttural sound, such as a **velar** (see). [Old French, from Latin *guttur,* throat.] —**gut·tur·al·ism, gut·tur·al·i·ty, gut·tur·al·ness** *n.* —**gut·tur·al·ly** *adv.*

gut·tur·al·ize (gŭt′ər-ə-līz′) *tr.v.* **-ized, -izing, -izes.** *Phonetics.* To make guttural; velarize. —**gut·tur·al·i·za·tion** *n.*

guy¹ (gī) *n.* A rope, cord, or cable used for steadying, guiding, or holding something. ~*tr.v.* **guyed, guying, guys.** To fasten, guide, or hold with a guy. [Probably from Low German, akin to Dutch *gei†,* brail.]

guy² *n.* **1.** *Informal.* A man; fellow. **2.** *British.* One who is odd or grotesque in appearance or dress. **3.** *Chiefly British.* An effigy of Guy Fawkes burned on Guy Fawkes Day. [After Guy FAWKES.] ~*tr.v.* **guyed, guying, guys.** To make fun of; mock.

Guy·an·a (gī-ăn′ə). Formerly **Brit·ish Gui·an·a** (brĭt′ĭsh gē-ăn′ə, -ä′nə). Independent republic within the Commonwealth, lying in northeastern South America. It was a British colony from 1814 until 1966, when it gained its independence. It became a republic in 1970. Bauxite has now overtaken sugar as its major export. Rice, gold, and diamonds are also exported. Some 51 percent of the population are of Asian origin (descendants of indentured laborers), and 33 percent are descendants of African slaves. Area, 214,969 square kilometers (83,000 square miles). Population, 800,000. Capital, Georgetown.

Guy Fawkes Day (gī′ fôks′) *n.* November 5, celebrated in England in commemoration of the **Gunpowder Plot** (see).

guy·ot (gē′ō′) *n.* A flat-topped submarine mountain. [After Arnold *Guyot* (1807–84), Swiss geographer and geologist.]

GUYANA

guz·zle (gŭz′əl) *v.* **-zled, -zling, -zles.** —*tr.* To eat or drink greedily or inordinately. —*intr.* To drink, especially alcoholic beverages, greedily or habitually. [Perhaps from Old French *gosiller,* vomit, from *gosier†,* throat.] —**guz·zler** *n.*

Gwent (gwĕnt). From 1974 a county of southeast Wales. It comprises the county of Monmouth excluding the Rhymney Valley, plus Brynmawr, formerly part of Brecknockshire. West Gwent with its chief towns (Newport, Pontypool, Ebbw Vale, and Cwmbran) is part of the South Wales industrial region. The east is fertile country crossed by the Usk and Wye rivers. The administrative center is Cwmbran.

Gwyn or **Gwynne** (gwĭn), **Eleanor,** known as "Nell" (1650–87). English actress, the mistress of Charles II. She bore Charles two sons, of whom the elder was made Duke of St. Albans.

Gwyn·edd (gwĭn′ĕth). From 1974 a county of northwest Wales. Created by the merger of the counties of Anglesey, Caernarvon, Merioneth, and that part of the Conwy Valley then in Denbighshire. Most of the land is within the Snowdonia National Park, and tourism is a major industry. The chief towns are the resorts of Llandudno, Bangor, and Conwy. The administrative center is Caenarvon.

gwyn·i·ad (gwĭn′ē-ăd) *n.* A freshwater fish, *Coregonus pennantii,* found in Lake Bala, Wales. It is a variety of whitefish. [Welsh, from *gwyn,* white.]

gybe. Variant of **jibe** (to swing).

gym (jĭm) *n.* **1.** A gymnasium. **2.** Gymnastics. **3.** A frame supporting structures used in outdoor play.

gym·kha·na (jĭm-kä′nə) *n.* **1.** An event at which various competitions are held to test the speed and skill of horses or ponies and their riders. **2.** An athletic competition or display. **3.** The place where such an event or competition is held. [Blend of GYM(NASIUM) + Hindi *(gend)-khānā,* "(ball) house," racket court, from *khāna,* house, from Persian *khāna†.*]

gym·na·si·um (jĭm-nā′zē-əm) *n., pl.* **-ums** or **-sia** (-zē-ə). **1.** A room or building equipped with ropes, mats, bars, and the like for gymnastics and sports. **2.** (gĭm-nä′zē-ōōm′). An academic high school in various central European countries, especially Germany. [Latin, *gymnasium,* school, from Greek *gumnasion,* from *gumnazein,* to train naked," practice gymnastics, from *gumnos,* naked.]

gym·nast (jĭm′năst) *n.* One skilled in gymnastic exercises. [Greek *gumnastēs,* from *gumnazein,* to practice gymnastics. See **gymnasium.**]

gym·nas·tic (jĭm-năs′tĭk) *adj.* Of, pertaining to, or involving gymnastics. —**gym·nas·ti·cal·ly** *adv.*

gym·nas·tics (jĭm-năs′tĭks) *n.* **1.** *Used with a singular verb.* The practice of performing exercises that increase strength, suppleness, or agility, especially those performed with special apparatus in a gymnasium. **2.** *Used with a plural verb.* **a.** The exercises performed. **b.** Complex intellectual or artistic exercises: *mental gymnastics.*

gymno- *prefix.* Indicates bare or naked; for example, **gymnosperm.** [Greek *gumnos,* naked.]

gym·nos·o·phist (jĭm-nŏs′ə-fĭst′) *n.* Any of an ancient sect of Hindu ascetics who went naked or nearly naked. [French *gymnosophiste,* from Latin *gymnosophistae* (plural) from Greek *gumnosophistai* : *gumnos,* naked + *sophistēs,* SOPHIST.]

gym·no·sperm (jĭm′nə-spûrm′) *n.* Any plant of the class Gymnospermae, which includes the coniferous trees and other plants having seeds not enclosed within an ovary. [New Latin *Gymnospermae* : Greek *gumnos,* naked + -SPERM.] —**gym·no·sperm·ous** *adj.*

gym·nure (jĭm′nŏŏr′) *n.* An insectivorous mammal of the family Erinaceidae, of southeast Asia. Also called "hairy hedgehog." [New Latin *gymnura* : GYMNO- + -URA (tail).]

gy·nae·ce·um (jĭn′ə-sē′əm, gī′nə-) *n., pl.* **-cea** (-sē′ə). Also **gy·nae·ci·um** *pl.* **-cia** (-sē-ə). **1.** The women's quarters in an ancient Greek or Roman household. **2.** Variant of **gynoecium.** [Latin, from Greek *gunaikeion,* from *gunaikeios,* of women, from *gunē* (stem *gunaik-*), woman.]

gy·nan·dro·morph (jī-năn′drə-môrf′, gī-) *n.* An individual having male and female characteristics; especially, an insect with such characteristics resulting from an abnormality in the sex chromosomes. [GYNO- + ANDRO- + -MORPH.] —**gy·nan·dro·morph·ic, gy·nan·dro·morph·ous** *adj.* —**gy·nan·dro·morph·ism, gy·nan·dro·mor·phy** *n.*

gy·nan·drous (jī-năn′drəs, gī-) *n. Botany.* Having the stamens and pistil united to form a column. Said of such flowers as the orchid. [Greek *gunandros,* of doubtful sex : *gunē,* woman + *anēr* (stem *andr-*), man.]

gyn·ar·chy (jĭn′är′kē, jī′när′-, gī′-) *n., pl.* **-chies.** Gynecocracy. [GYNO- + -ARCHY.] —**gy·nar·chic** *adj.*

-gyne *suffix.* Indicates female reproductive organ: *trichogyne.*

gyneco-, gynec- or **gynaeco-, gynaec-** *prefix.* Indicates woman or women; for example, **gynecology.** [Greek, from *gunē* (stem *gunaik-*), woman.]

gy·ne·coc·ra·cy (jĭn′ĭ-kŏk′rə-sē, gī′nĭ-) *n., pl.* **-cies.** Government by women. [GYNECO- + -CRACY.]

gynecol. gynecological; gynecology.

gy·ne·col·o·gy (gī′nĭ-kŏl′ə-jē, jī′-, jĭn′ə-) *n. Abbr.* **gyn., gynecol.** The medical study of disease in women, especially those diseases affecting the female reproductive organs and adjacent organs, such as the urinary tract. [GYNECO- + -LOGY.] —**gy·ne·co·log·i·cal** (gī′nĭ-kə-lŏj′ĭ-kəl), **gy·ne·co·log·ic** *adj.* —**gy·ne·col·o·gist** *n.*

gy·ne·co·mas·ti·a (gī′nĭ-kō-măs′tē-ə, jī′-, jĭn′ə-) *n.* Abnormal enlargement of the breasts in a man, due to hormone imbalance or hormone therapy. [New Latin : GYNECO- + Greek *mastis*, breast.]

gyn·e·cop·a·thy (jĭn′ĭ-kŏp′ə-thē, gī′nĭ-) *n. Pathology.* Any of various diseases peculiar to women.

gyn·i·at·rics (jĭn′ē-ăt′rĭks, gī′nē-) *n. Used with singular verb.* The treatment of diseases peculiar to women.

gyno-, gyn– *prefix.* Indicates: **1.** Woman or female; for example, **gynarchy, gynandromorph. 2.** Female reproductive organ; for example, **gynophore.** [Greek *guno-,* from *gunē,* woman.]

gy·noc·ra·cy (gī-nŏk′rə-sē) *n., pl.* **-cies.** Gynecocracy.

gy·no·di·oe·cious (gī′nō-dī-ē′shəs, jī′nō-) *adj. Botany.* Designating a species of plant in which female and hermaphrodite flowers are borne on separate plants. [GYNO- + DIOECIOUS.]

gy·noe·ci·um, gy·nae·ce·um (jī-nē′sē-əm, jī-) *n., pl.* **-cia** (-sē-ə). *Botany.* The female reproductive organs of a flower; the pistil or pistils collectively. [New Latin, alteration of GYNAECEUM.]

gy·no·mon·oe·cious (gī′nō-mŏn-ē′shəs, jī′nō-) *adj. Botany.* Designating a species of plant on which female and hermaphrodite flowers are borne on the same plant. [GYNO- + MONOECIOUS.]

gy·no·phore (jĭn′ə-fôr′, -fōr′, gī′nə-) *n. Botany.* A stalk in some plants that bears the pistil. [GYNO- + -PHORE.] —**gy·no·phor·ic** (jĭn′ə-fôr′ĭk, -fōr′-, jī′nə-, gī′-) *adj.*

–gynous *suffix.* Indicates: **1.** Women or females; for example, **monogynous. 2.** Female organs such as pistils; for example, **perigynous.** [New Latin *-gynus,* having pistils, from Greek *-gunos,* having a wife or wives, from *gunē,* woman.]

–gyny *suffix.* Indicates: **1.** The condition of having a specified number or kind of women or females; for example, **monogyny. 2.** The condition of having female organs or pistils; for example, **epigyny.** [Greek *gunē,* woman.]

gyp[1]**, gip** (jĭp) *tr.v.* **gypped** or **gipped, gypping** or **gipping, gyps** or **gips.** *Informal.* To swindle, cheat, or defraud. —*n.* **1.** The act or an instance of cheating; swindle. **2.** One who cheats; swindler. [Perhaps from GYP (servant).] —**gyp·per** *n.*

gyp[2] *n. British.* A servant who cleans students' rooms, especially at Cambridge University. [Perhaps from obsolete *gippo,* kitchen servant, short tunic, from obsolete French *jupeau;* akin to French *jupe,* skirt.]

gyp joint *n. Slang.* An establishment that makes a practice of overcharging or defrauding its clientele.

gyp·soph·i·la (jĭp-sŏf′ə-lə) *n.* Any of various plants of the genus *Gypsophila,* having small white or pink flowers, and including the baby's-breath. [New Latin *Gypsophila* : GYPSUM + -PHILA.]

gyp·sum (jĭp′səm) *n.* A white mineral, $CaSO_4 \cdot 2H_2O$, used in the manufacture of cements and plasters, especially plaster of Paris, and also in some fertilizers. [Latin, from Greek *gupsos,* from Semitic; akin to Hebrew *gephes,* plaster.] —**gyp·se·ous** (jĭp′sē-əs), **gyp·sif·er·ous** (jĭp-sĭf′ər-əs) *adj.*

Gyp·sy, Gip·sy (jĭp′sē) *n., pl.* **-sies. 1.** *Sometimes* **gypsy.** One of a nomadic Caucasoid people originally migrating from the border region between Iran and India to Europe in the 14th or 15th century and now living principally in Europe and the United States. **2.** The Indic language spoken by this people; Romany. **3.** *Often* **gypsy.** One that resembles a Gypsy in appearance or behavior, especially in having a wandering or carefree lifestyle. —*adj. Often* **gypsy.** Of, pertaining to, or resembling Gypsies. [Shortening of EGYPTIAN, because they were believed to have come from Egypt.]

gypsy moth *n.* A moth, *Porthetria dispar,* native to the Old World, having hairy caterpillars that feed on foliage and are very destructive to trees.

gyp·sy·wort (jĭp′sē-wûrt′, -wôrt′) *n.* A Eurasian plant, *Lycopus eura-*

paeus, with hairy stems and leaves and white two-lipped flowers marked with purple dots.

gy·ral (jī′rəl) *adj.* **1.** Moving in a circular or spiral path; gyratory. **2.** Pertaining to a gyrus. —**gy·ral·ly** *adv.*

gy·rate (jī′rāt′) *v.* **-rated, -rating, -rates.** —*intr.* **1.** To revolve on or around a center or axis. **2.** To circle or spiral. —*tr.* To move in circles around a center: *gyrate your hips in time with the beat.* —See Synonyms at **turn.**
~*adj. Biology.* In rings; coiled. [Latin *gȳrāre,* from *gȳrus,* circle, from Greek *guros,* GYRE.] —**gy·ra·tion** *n.* —**gy·ra·tor** *n.* —**gy·ra·tor·y** (jī′rə-tôr′ē, -tōr′ē) *adj.*

gyre (jīr) *n.* **1.** The circular flow of water that occurs in each of the great ocean basins of the world, produced by the combined effects of prevailing winds and the earth's rotation. **2.** *Chiefly Poetic.* **a.** A ring or circle; vortex; spiral. **b.** A circular or spiral motion. —*intr.v.* **gyred, gyring, gyres.** *Chiefly Poetic.* To gyrate. [Latin *gyrus,* from Greek *guros,* circle.]

gyr·fal·con, ger·fal·con (jûr′fāl′kən, -fôl′kən, -fô′kən) *n.* A large falcon, *Falco rusticolus,* of northern regions, having various color phases ranging from black to white. [Middle English *gerfaucoun,* from Old French *gerfaucon,* from Old Norse *geirfalki.*]

gy·ro (jī′rō) *n., pl.* **-ros.** A gyroscope.

gyro– *prefix.* Indicates: **1.** Gyrating; for example, **gyroplane. 2.** Spiral; for example, **gyroscope. 3.** Gyroscope; for example, **gyrocompass.** [Latin, from Greek *guro-,* from *guros,* circle.]

gy·ro·com·pass (jī′rō-kŭm′pəs, -kŏm′pəs) *n.* A nonmagnetic navigational device in which the interaction of a gyroscope's angular momentum with the force produced by the earth's rotation is used to maintain a north-south orientation of the gyroscopic spin axis, thereby providing a stable directional reference.

gy·ro·mag·net·ic (jī′rō-măg-nĕt′ĭk) *adj.* Of, pertaining to, or resulting from the magnetic properties of a spinning, electrically charged particle.

gyromagnetic ratio *n.* The ratio of the magnetic moment to the intrinsic angular momentum of a spinning particle.

gyro pilot *n.* An automatic pilot incorporating a gyroscope to maintain a preset course and altitude.

gy·ro·plane (jī′rə-plān′) *n.* An aircraft such as a helicopter or autogyro with wings that rotate about a vertical axis.

gy·ro·scope (jī′rə-skōp′) *n.* **1.** A device consisting essentially of a spinning mass, typically a disk or wheel, the spin axis of which turns between two low-friction supports and maintains its angular orientation with respect to inertial coordinates when not subjected to external torques. **2.** Broadly, any spinning mass. Also called "gyro." [French : GYRO- + -SCOPE.] —**gy·ro·scop·ic** (jī′rə-skŏp′ĭk) *adj.* —**gy·ro·scop·i·cal·ly** *adv.*

gy·ro·sta·bi·liz·er (jī′rō-stā′bə-lī′zər) *n.* A device having a heavy gyroscope whose axis spins in a vertical plane to reduce the side-to-side rolling of a ship or aircraft.

gy·ro·stat (jī′rə-stăt′) *n.* A gyrostabilizer.

gy·ro·stat·ic (jī′rō-stăt′ĭk) *adj.* Of, pertaining to, or designating a gyroscope or gyrostatics. [GYRO- + -STAT + -IC.] —**gy·ro·stat·i·cal·ly** *adv.*

gy·ro·stat·ics (jī′rō-stăt′ĭks) *n. Used with a singular verb.* The study of rotating bodies.

gy·rus (jī′rəs) *n., pl.* **gyri** (jī′rī′). Any of the prominent, rounded, elevated convolutions on the surfaces of the cerebral hemispheres. [New Latin, from Latin, circle, GYRE.]

gyve (jīv) *n. Archaic.* A shackle or fetter, especially for the leg. —*tr.v.* **gyved, gyving, gyves.** To shackle or fetter. [Middle English *gyve†.*]

gyroscope *A spinning flywheel that will hold itself in a stable plane regardless of how its frame is moved.*

Flywheel

Gimbals

Support

Pivot

H

hackle *The young bantam rooster raises its hackles—the long, narrow feathers on its neck—as part of its aggressive display, designed to make the bird appear larger than it really is. Dogs have hackles as well—special erectile hairs on the backs of their necks—that rise involuntarily if the animals are angry or frightened.*

Hackney *An English show horse, once used as a carriage horse and valued for its high-stepping trot. Developed in the 18th century, it was crossed with the Welsh pony to make a Hackney pony.*

haddock *A codlike fish found in the North Atlantic. It lives close to the sea bottom, feeding on mollusks and small fish.*

h, H (āch) *n., pl.* **h's** or **H's. 1.** The eighth letter of the modern English alphabet. See feature at **alphabet. 2.** Any of the speech sounds represented by this letter. **3.** The eighth in a series. **4.** Something shaped like the letter H.

h, H, h., H. *Note:* As an abbreviation or symbol, *h* may be a small or a capital letter, with or without a period. Established forms or those generally preferred precede the definition. When no form is given, all four forms are in general use in that sense. **1.** H *Physics.* Hamiltonian. **2.** h., H. harbor. **3.** h., H. hard; hardness. **4.** h hecto-. **5.** h, H. height. **6.** H henry. **7.** h., H. high (gear). **8.** h, H. hit. **9.** h., H. *Music.* horn. **10.** h hour. **11.** h. hundred. **12.** h., H. husband. **13.** H The symbol for the element hydrogen. **14.** h The symbol for Planck's constant.

H *adj.* Designating a pencil or pencil lead that is hard. A number sometimes precedes *H* to indicate the degree of hardness, the hardest pencil being 6H. See **B, HB.**
~*n.* An H pencil.

ha, hah (hä) *interj.* Used to express surprise, wonder, triumph, puzzlement, or pique. [Middle English.]

ha hectare.

Haa·kon VII (hô′kən, -kŏn′) (1872–1957). King of Norway (1905–57).

haar (här) *n. British Regional.* A cold fog or mist off the east coast of England or Scotland. [Probably from Old Norse *hárr*, HOAR.]

Haar·lem (här′ləm). City in the western Netherlands, the capital of North Holland province, on the Spaarne River near the North Sea. It was a major center of the golden age of Dutch painting in the 16th and 17th centuries. It is now famous for the culture and export of flowers and bulbs, especially tulips.

Hab. Habakkuk (Old Testament).

Ha·bak·kuk¹ (hə-băk′ək, hăb′ə-kŭk). Hebrew prophet of the late 7th century B.C.

Habakkuk² *n. Abbr.* **Hab.** A book of prophecies by Habakkuk in the Old Testament.

Habana. See Havana.

ha·ba·ne·ra (hä′bə-nâr′ə, ä′bə-) *n.* **1.** A slow Cuban dance. **2.** The music for this dance, in duple time, with a repetitive rhythmic pattern of a dotted eighth and sixteenth note pair followed by a pair of eighth notes. [Spanish *(danza) habanera,* "Havanan (dance)," from feminine of *habanero,* HABANERO.]

Ha·ba·ne·ro (hä′bə-nâr′ō, ä′bə-) *n., pl.* **-ros.** A native or inhabitant of Havana. [Spanish, from *La Habana,* HAVANA.]

hab. corp. habeas corpus.

hab·da·lah (hăv′dä-lä′) *n. Often* **Habdalah.** A Jewish religious ceremony observed at or marking the end of a Sabbath or holy day. [Hebrew *habdālāh,* separation.]

ha·be·as cor·pus (hā′bē-əs kôr′pəs) *n. Abbr.* **hab. corp.** *Law.* **1.** Any of a variety of writs that may be issued to bring a party before a court or judge, having as its function the release of a party from unlawful restraint. **2.** The right to demand such a writ. [Latin, "you shall have the body."]

hab·er·dash·er (hăb′ər-dăsh′ər) *n.* **1.** A dealer in men's furnishings such as shirts, hats, and socks. **2.** *British.* A dealer in sewing accessories and dressmaking materials. [Middle English *haberdassher,* probably from Norman French *haberdasser, hapertasser* (both unattested), from *hapertas†,* perhaps the name of a kind of cloth.]

hab·er·dash·er·y (hăb′ər-dăsh′ə-rē) *n., pl.* **-ies. 1.** The goods sold by a haberdasher. **2.** A shop or department selling these goods.

hab·er·geon (hăb′ər-jən) *n. Also* **hau·ber·geon** (hô′bər-jən). **1.** A short, sleeveless coat of mail. **2.** A hauberk. [Middle English *haubergeon,* from Old French *haubergeon,* from *hauberc,* HAUBERK.]

Ha·ber process (hä′bər) *n.* An industrial process, first developed in 1908, for producing ammonia from hydrogen and atmospheric nitrogen by reacting the two gases together at a temperature of about 5000°C and a pressure of 20–50 megapascals. In the later **Haber-Bosch process** a method of making the hydrogen from water gas and steam was added. [After Fritz **Haber** (1868–1934), German chemist.]

hab·ile (hăb′ĭl) *adj. Rare.* Adroit; deft. [French, from Old French, from Latin *habilis,* able, easily handled, from *habēre,* to hold, have.]

ha·bil·i·ment (hə-bĭl′ə-mənt) *n.* **1.** *Often* **habiliments. a.** The dress or garb associated with an office or occasion: *"shrouded from head to foot in the habiliments of the grave"* (Edgar Allan Poe). **b.** Clothes. **2.** *Rare.* Outfit; attire. [Middle English, from Old French *(h)abillement,* from *habiller,* to make fit, fit out, from HABILE.]

ha·bil·i·tate (hə-bĭl′ə-tāt′) *v.* **-tated, -tating, -tates.** —*tr.* **1.** To supply with the means; especially, to back (a mining operation) with working capital. **2.** *Rare.* To clothe. —*intr.* To qualify oneself for an office, especially as a teacher in a German university. [Late Latin *habilitāre* (past participle *habilitātus*), to qualify, from Latin *habilitās,* ability, from HABILE.] —**ha·bil·i·ta·tion** *n.*

hab·it (hăb′ĭt) *n.* **1. a.** A constant, often unconscious inclination to act in a particular way, acquired through frequent repetition over a long period. **b.** An established trend of the mind or character. **c.** *Psychology.* An automatic or mechanical reaction to a particular situation, acquired through frequently encountering it. **2.** *Often* **habits.** Customary manner or practice: *a man of ascetic habits.* **3.** An addiction, especially to a hard drug. **4.** *Rare.* Physical constitution. **5.** Characteristic appearance, form, or manner of growth, especially of a plant or crystal. Also called "habitus." **6. a.** A distinctive dress or costume, especially of a religious order. **b.** A riding habit.
~*tr.v.* **habited, -iting, -its. 1.** To clothe; dress. **2.** *Archaic.* To habituate. **3.** *Archaic.* To inhabit. [Middle English *(h)abit,* from Old French, from Latin *habitus,* from the past participle of *habēre,* to hold, have.]
Synonyms: *custom, fashion, practice, usage, use.*

hab·it·a·ble (hăb′ə-tə-bəl) *adj.* Suitable to live in; inhabitable. [Middle English *abitable,* from Old French *(h)abitable,* from Latin *habitābilis,* from *habitāre,* to inhabit, reside, to have frequently, from *habēre* (past participle *habitus*), to have, hold.] —**hab·i·ta·bil·i·ty, hab·it·a·ble·ness** *n.* —**hab·it·a·bly** *adv.*

hab·i·tant (hăb′ə-tənt; ä′bē-tän′ *for sense 2*) *n. Also* **ha·bi·tan** (ä′bē-tän′) (for sense 2). **1.** An inhabitant. **2.** An inhabitant of French descent in Canada or Louisiana belonging to the small farmer class. [Old French, from the present participle of *habiter,* to inhabit, from Latin *habitāre.* See **habitable.**]

hab·i·tat (hăb′ə-tăt′) *n.* **1.** The area or type of environment in which an organism or biological population normally lives or occurs. **2.** The place where a person or thing is most likely to be found. [Latin, "it dwells" (the first word in Latin descriptions of plant and animal species in old natural histories), third person singular present indicative of *habitāre,* to inhabit. See **habitable.**]

hab·i·ta·tion (hăb′ə-tā′shən) *n.* **1.** The act of inhabiting. **2.** The state of being inhabited. **3. a.** A natural environment or locality. **b.** A place of abode. [Middle English *habitacioun,* from Old French *habitation,* from Latin *habitātiō* (stem *habitātiōn-*), from *habitātus,* past participle of *habitāre,* to inhabit. See **habitable.**]

hab·it·ed (hăb′ə-tĭd) *adj.* **1. a.** Dressed. **b.** Attired in a habit. **2.** *Archaic.* Inhabited.

hab·it-form·ing (hăb′ĭt-fôr′mĭng) *adj.* **1.** Leading to psychological or physiological addiction: *a habit-forming drug.* **2.** Tending to become habitual.

ha·bit·u·al (hə-bĭch′ōō-əl) *adj.* **1. a.** Of the nature of a habit; done constantly or repeatedly. **b.** Being so by force of habit: *a habitual smoker.* **2.** Customary; constant; inveterate: *habitual rudeness.* **3.** Established by long use; usual. —See Synonyms at **usual.** —**ha·bit·u·al·ly** *adv.* —**ha·bit·u·al·ness** *n.*

ha·bit·u·ate (hə-bĭch′ōō-āt′) *tr.v.* **-ated, -ating, -ates. 1.** To accustom by frequent repetition or prolonged exposure. Often used reflexively. **2.** To cause to become psychologically dependent on a drug. [Late Latin *habituāre,* from Latin *habitus,* HABIT.] —**ha·bit·u·a·tion** *n.*

hab·i·tude (hăb′ə-tōōd′, -tyōōd′) *n.* A customary manner or way of behaving; a habit. [Middle English *(h)abitude,* from Old French *habitude,* from Latin *habitūdō,* condition, habit, from *habitus,* HABIT.]

ha·bit·u·é (hə-bĭch'o͞o-ā', hə-bĭch'o͞o-ā') *n.* A frequent visitor of a particular place, especially a place of entertainment. [French, from the past participle of *habituer,* to frequent, from Late Latin *habituāre,* to HABITUATE.]
hab·i·tus (hăb'ə-təs) *n., pl.* **habitus. 1.** Physical and constitutional characteristics, especially as related to susceptibility to a disease. **2.** The habit of a plant or animal. See **habit** (sense 5). [New Latin, from Latin, appearance, HABIT.]
Habsburg. See **Hapsburg.**
ha·bu (hä'bo͞o) *n.* A large, venomous Japanese snake, *Trimeresurus flavoviridis,* found in the Ryukyu Islands. [Japanese.]
ha·ček (hä'chĕk') *n.* A diacritical mark (ˇ) that resembles an inverted circumflex and is used over certain letters, as *č,* to indicate quality of pronunciation. [Czech, *háček.*]
ha·chure (hă-sho͝or', hăsh'o͝or) *n.* Any of the short lines used to shade or to indicate slopes on relief maps and also to show their degree and direction.
~tr.v. (hă-sho͝or') **hachured, -churing, -chures.** To make hachures on (a map). [French, from *hacher,* to engrave lines on, chop up. See **hash.**]
ha·ci·en·da (hä'sē-ĕn'də, ä'sē-) *n.* **1.** In Spanish-speaking countries or areas influenced by Spain, a large estate; a plantation or large ranch. **2.** The house of the owner of a hacienda; especially, in the southwestern United States, a low, sprawling house with a projecting roof and wide porches. [Spanish, domestic work, landed property, from Latin *facienda,* things to be done, neuter plural gerundive of *facere,* to do.]
hack[1] (hăk) *v.* **hacked, hacking, hacks.** —*tr.* **1. a.** To cut (branches or undergrowth, for example) with irregular and heavy blows or in a random manner. **b.** To chip, notch, chop off, or chop up roughly with a pick, knife, ax, or other tool. **c.** To make by cutting or chopping in such a way: *hacked a hole in the wood.* **2.** To break up (earth) into clods or ridges. **3. a.** To kick the shin of (an opponent), especially in field sports. **b.** To strike the arm of (an opponent) in basketball. **4.** To destroy the quality of (a story or article, for example) by excessive cutting or bad editing. **5.** *Informal.* To deal with successfully; cope with: *She tried living on her own but simply couldn't hack it.* —*intr.* **1.** To chop or chip away at something. **2.** To cough in short, dry-throated spasms.
~n. **1.** A rough irregular cut or notch made by hacking. **2.** A tool, such as a hoe or mattock, used for chopping or breaking up something. **3. a.** A kick or chopping blow. **b.** A wound from this. **4.** A rough, dry cough. [Middle English *hacken,* from Old English *haccian,* to cut to pieces, from Germanic, of imitative origin.] —**hack·er** *n.*
hack[2] *n.* **1.** A horse used for riding or driving; a hackney. **2.** A broken-down horse for hire; a jade. **3.** *Chiefly British.* A leisurely ride in the country on horseback. **4.** A political hireling. **5.** A person who hires himself out to do mediocre or routine work, especially writing or journalism. **6.** A carriage or hackney for hire. **7.** *Informal.* **a.** A taxicab. **b.** A taxicab driver.
~v. **hacked, hacking, hacks.** —*tr.* **1.** To let (a horse) out for hire. **2.** *Informal.* To write as a hack or in the manner of a hack. **3.** To make banal or hackneyed with indiscriminate use. —*intr.* **1.** *Informal.* To work as a hack, especially as a taxicab driver or a writer. **2.** *Chiefly British.* To ride on horseback in the country at a leisurely pace.
~adj. **1.** Working as a literary or journalistic hack: *a hack writer.* **2.** Produced by or characteristic of a hack; banal; routine; commercial. [Short for HACKNEY.]
hack[3] *n.* **1.** A drying frame or rack, as for cheese, fish, or bricks. **2.** A row of unfired bricks laid out to dry. **3.** A feeding rack, especially for hawks.
~tr.v. **hacked, hacking, hacks. 1.** To set out on a rack to dry. **2.** To keep (hawks) at partial liberty. [Variant, influenced by HECK (frame), of HATCH (door).]
hack·a·more (hăk'ə-môr', -mōr') *n.* A rope or rawhide halter with a wide band that can be lowered over a horse's eyes, used to break in horses. [Alteration (influenced by HACK) of Spanish *jaquima,* headstall of a halter, from Old Spanish *xaquima,* from Arabic *shakīmah,* bit of a bridle, restraint.]
hack·ber·ry (hăk'bĕr'ē) *n., pl.* **-ries. 1.** Any of various North American trees or shrubs of the genus *Celtis,* having inconspicuous flowers and berrylike, often edible fruit. **2.** The fruit of a hackberry. **3.** The soft, yellowish wood of a hackberry. Also called "sugarberry." [Variant of earlier *hagberry* : *hag-,* from Scandinavian, akin to Old Norse *heggr,* hackberry + BERRY.]
hack·but (hăk'bŭt') *n.* Also **hag·but** (hăg'-). An obsolete type of gun, a **harquebus** *(see).* [Old French *haguebute, hacquebute,* from Middle Dutch *hakebusse,* HARQUEBUS.] —**hack·but·eer** (hăk'bə-tîr'), **hack·but·ter** (hăk'bŭt'ər) *n.*
hack·er (hăk'ər) *n.* **1.** One that hacks. **2.** An amateur computer enthusiast. **3.** Such an enthusiast who gains unauthorized access to other people's computer programs. [From HACK (to work as a hack) + -ER.]
hack·ie (hăk'ē) *n. Slang.* A taxicab driver. [From HACK (taxicab).]
hack·ing (hăk'ĭng) *adj.* Designating a cough or laughter that is rough, dry, and usually spasmodic.
hacking jacket *n.* A riding jacket with slits at the sides or back.
hack·le[1] (hăk'əl) *n.* **1.** Any of the long, slender, often glossy feathers on the neck of a bird, especially a male domestic fowl. **2. hackles.** The erectile hairs at the back of the neck, especially of a dog or similar animal. **3. a.** A tuft of cock feathers trimming an artificial fishing fly. **b.** A **hackle fly** *(see).* **4.** A steel comb used for combing flax. —**get one's hackles up.** To make or be angry or ready to fight. —**make the hackles rise. 1.** To put in a fighting mood. **2.** To cause a dog to bristle belligerently.
~tr.v. **hackled, -ling, -les. 1.** To trim (a fly) with a hackle. **2.** To comb (flax) with a hackle. [Middle English *hakell, hekele, hechele,* HATCHEL.]
hackle[2] *v.* **-led, -ling, -les.** *Rare.* —*tr.* To chop roughly; mangle by hacking. —*intr.* To hack. [Frequentative of HACK (to cut).]
hackle fly *n.* An artificial fishing fly trimmed with hackles and usually without wings. Also called "hackle."
hack·ly (hăk'lē) *adj.* Nicked or notched; jagged; rough. [From HACKLE (to hack).]
hack·man (hăk'mən) *n., pl.* **-men** (-mĭn). The driver of a hack or hired carriage.
hack·ma·tack (hăk'mə-tăk') *n.* A tree, the **tamarack** *(see).* [From Algonquian, akin to Abnaki *akemantak,* snowshoe wood.]
hack·ney (hăk'nē) *n., pl.* **-neys. 1. Hackney.** A horse of a trotting breed developed in England, having a gait characterized by pronounced flexion of the knee. **2.** A horse suited for routine riding or driving; a hack. **3.** A coach or carriage for hire.
~tr.v. **hackneyed, -neying, -neys. 1.** To overuse and cause to become banal and trite; cheapen. **2.** To hire out; let.
~adj. **1.** Banal; trite: *a hackney phrase.* **2.** Hired: *a hackney carriage.* [Middle English *hakenei,* probably after *Hakenei,* HACKNEY, where such horses were raised.]
Hack·ney (hăk'nē). Borough in the northeast of Greater London, England.
hack·neyed (hăk'nēd) *adj.* Overused so as to become stale or meaningless; trite; banal. —See Synonyms at **trite.**
hack·saw (hăk'sô') *n.* A saw consisting of a tough, fine-toothed blade stretched taut in a frame, used for cutting metal.
hack·work (hăk'wûrk') *n.* Commissioned work, as writing, done usually by formula and in conformance with commercial standards.
had. Past tense and past participle of **have.**
ha·dal (hăd'l) *adj.* Of or designating the deepest parts of the oceans, especially those parts below about 6,000 meters (19,680 feet). [HADES (the nether world) + -AL.]
had·dock (hăd'ək) *n., pl.* **-docks** or collectively **haddock.** A food fish, *Melanogrammus aeglefinus,* of northern Atlantic waters, related to and resembling the cod. [Middle English *haddok,* from Norman French *hadoc,* variant of Old French *(h)adot*†.]
hade (hād) *n. Geology.* The angle of inclination from the vertical of a vein, fault, or lode.
~intr.v. **haded, hading, hades.** To incline from the vertical. Used of a vein, fault, or lode. [Origin unknown.]
Ha·des[1] (hā'dēz). *Greek Mythology.* The god of the netherworld and dispenser of earthly riches; a brother of Zeus and husband of Persephone; identified with the Roman god Pluto.
Hades[2] *n.* **1.** *Greek Mythology.* The netherworld kingdom of Hades, the abode of the shades of the dead. **2.** *Often* **hades.** Hell. [Greek *Haidēs.*] —**Ha·de·an** *adj.*
Ha·dith (hə-dēth') *n., pl.* **Hadith** or **-diths.** The body of traditions arising from or relating to Muhammad. [Arabic, "tradition."]
hadj, haj, hajj (hăj) *n.* A pilgrimage to Mecca made during Ramadan as an objective of the religious life of a Muslim. [Arabic *ḥajj,* pilgrimage.]
hadj·i, haj·i, haj·ji (hăj'ē) *n.* **1. a.** A Muslim who has made a pilgrimage to Mecca. **b.** A title used before the name of a Muslim who has made this pilgrimage. **2.** A Christian of the Near East or Orient who has visited the Holy Sepulcher in Jerusalem. [Arabic *ḥājjī,* from *ḥajj,* HADJ.]
had·n't (hăd'ənt). Contraction of *had not.*
Ha·dri·an (hā'drē-ən) (A.D. 76–138). Roman emperor (117–138). As emperor he initiated plans to end distinctions between Rome and the provinces. He visited Britain (122), where he ordered the building of Hadrian's Wall.
Hadrian IV. See **Adrian IV.**
Hadrian's Wall. Roman wall built by the emperor Hadrian between *c.* 122 and 126, and extended by Severus a century later, to fortify the northern boundary of Roman Britain. It stretched for *c.* 120 kilometers (75 miles) from Wallsend on the Tyne River to Bowness at the head of Solway Firth. Fragments of the wall and several stone blockhouses, or mile stations, remain.
had·ron (hăd'rŏn') *n. Physics.* An elementary particle that can take part in a strong interaction. The elementary nature of hadrons is controversial; they are believed to consist of arrangements of quarks. [Greek *hadros,* thick + -ON.] —**had·ron·ic** (hă-drŏn'ĭk) *adj.*
had·ro·saur (hăd'rə-sôr') *n.* Any of various amphibious dinosaurs of the genus *Anatosaurus* and related genera, which had webbed feet and a ducklike bill. [Greek *hadros,* thick, heavy + -SAUR.]
hadst. *Archaic.* Second person singular past indicative of **have.** Used with *thou.*
hae (hā, hă) *tr.v.* **haed, haen** (hān, hăn), **haeing, haes.** *Scottish.* To have.
ha·e·re mai, ha·e·re·mai (hä'ā-rā' mä'ē) *interj. Australian & New Zealand.* Used to express welcome or a greeting. [Maori, "come hither."]
Ha-erh-pin. See **Harbin.**
haet (hāt) *n. Scottish.* A minute amount; a whit; a jot. [Contraction of *hae it!* take it!]
ha·fiz (hä'fĭz) *n.* **1.** A Muslim who has memorized the Koran. **2.** A

Hadrian *The Roman emperor who directed the building of Hadrian's Wall in Britain and the Pantheon in Rome was also an accomplished poet and musician.*

Hadrian's Wall *Designed to defend Roman Britain against attack from the north, Hadrian's Wall was constructed by the Roman legionaries who were later to patrol it. The ruins now average 1.8 meters (6 feet) in height, but the wall was originally as much as 4.5 meters (15 feet) high.*

PRONUNCIATION KEY

ă, pat; ā, pay; âr, care;
ä, father, are; b, **bib;**
ch, **church;** d, **deed;** ĕ, pet;
ē, be; f, **fife;** g, **gag;** h, **hat;**
hw, **which;** ĭ, pit; ī, pie;
îr, pier; j, **judge;** k, **kick;**
l, lid, needle; m, **mum;**
n, no, sudden; ng, thing;
ŏ, pot; ō, toe; ô, paw, for;
oi, noise; ou, **out;** o͝o, **book;**
o͞o, **boot;** p, **pop;** r, roar;
s, **sauce;** sh, **ship, dish;**
t, **tight;** th, **thin, path;**
th, **this,** bathe; ŭ, cut; ûr, **fur;**
v, valve; w, **with;** y, yes;
z, zebra, size; zh, vision;
ə, about, item, edible, gallop, circus, peaceful

IN FOREIGN WORDS:

à, *Fr.* ami; œ, *Fr.* **feu,** *Ger.* schön; ü, *Fr.* **tu,** *Ger.* **über;**
KH, *Ger.* **ich,** *Scot.* **loch;**
N, *Fr.* bon; y', *Fr.* Compiègne

STRESS MARKS:

Primary stress: '
in·cite' (ĭn-sīt')
Secondary stress: '
in'sight' (ĭn'sīt')

title of respect used with the name of a Muslim who has accomplished this memorization. [Persian, from Arabic *hāfiz,* guard, watch, one who knows the Koran by heart, from *hafiza,* to watch, protect, memorize.]

Ha·fiz, Ha·fez (hä-fĭz′, -fēz′) (*fl.* 14th century). Persian lyric poet. Educated in the classic Islamic tradition, he served as court poet to several Persian leaders. His innovative style revived the traditional Persian themes of love and wine. *The Divan,* a collection of about 700 of his poems, was first published in English in 1891.

haf·ni·um (hăf′nē-əm) *n. Symbol* **Hf** A brilliant, silvery, metallic element separated from ores of zirconium and used in nuclear reactor control rods, as a getter for oxygen and nitrogen, and in the manufacture of tungsten filaments. Atomic number 72, atomic weight 178.49, melting point 2,150°C, boiling point 5,400°C, specific gravity 13.29, valence 4. [New Latin, from *Hafnia,* Latin name for Copenhagen, from Danish *(København).*]

haft (hăft, häft) *n.* A handle or hilt; especially, a handle of a bladed instrument, such as a sword, knife, or sickle.
~*tr.v.* **hafted, hafting, hafts.** To fit or equip with a hilt or handle; set into a handle. [Middle English *haft,* Old English *hæft.*]

Haftarah. Variant of **Haphtarah.**

hag¹ (hăg) *n.* **1.** An old woman who is repulsive in appearance or manner; a crone. **2.** A witch; a sorceress. **3.** *Obsolete.* A female demon. **4.** A **hagfish** (*see*). [Middle English *hagge,* probably short for Old English *hægtesse†,* witch.] —**hag·gish** *adj.* —**hag·gish·ly** *adv.* —**hag·gish·ness** *n.*

hag² *n. Scottish & British Regional.* **1.** A boggy area on a moor. **2.** A piece of firmer ground in boggy land. **3.** A place where peat has been dug from a bog. [Middle English *hag,* gap, chasm, probably from Old Norse *högg,* gap, cutting blow.]

Hag. Haggai (Old Testament).

Ha·gar (hā′gər). The concubine of Abraham, mother of his son Ishmael and handmaiden to his wife Sarah, who, through jealousy for her own son Isaac, turned Hagar and Ishmael out of Abraham's household. Genesis 16–19.

hagbut. Variant of **hackbut.**

Ha·gen (hä′gən). In the *Nibelungenlied,* the murderer of Siegfried.

Ha·gen (hä′gən), **Walter Charles** (1892–1969). U.S. golfer. He won the U.S. Open championship twice (1914 and 1919), the British Open four times from 1922 to 1929, and the U.S. Professional Golfers' Association championship five times from 1921 to 1927.

hag·fish (hăg′fĭsh′) *n., pl.* **-fishes** or collectively **hagfish.** Any of various primitive, eel-shaped marine fishes of the family Myxinidae, having a jawless sucking mouth with rasping teeth with which they bore into and feed on other fishes. Also called "hag." [HAG (witch) + FISH.]

Hag·ga·dah, Hag·ga·da (hə-gä′də, -gô′də) *n., pl.* **-doth** (-dōt′, -dōth′). **1.** Traditional Jewish literature; especially, the nonlegal part of the Talmud. Compare **Halakah.** **2.** The book containing the story of the Exodus and the ritual of the Seder, read at the Passover Seder. [Hebrew *haggādāh,* narration, telling, from *hagged,* to narrate, tell, from the Semitic root *ngd,* to rise, become conspicuous.] —**hag·gad·ic, Hag·gad·ic** (hə-găd′ĭk, -gä′dĭk, -gô′dĭk) *adj.*

hag·ga·dist (hə-gä′dĭst, -gô′dĭst) *n.* **1.** A haggadic writer. **2.** A student of haggadic literature. —**hag·ga·dis·tic** (hăg′ə-dĭs′tĭk) *adj.*

Hag·ga·i¹ (hăg′ē-ī′, hăg′ī′). A Hebrew prophet of the 6th century B.C.

Haggai² *n. Abbr.* **Hag.** A book of the Old Testament attributed to Haggai.

hag·gard (hăg′ərd) *adj.* **1. a.** Appearing worn and exhausted from or as if from suffering, anxiety, or deprivation; gaunt: *"he looked as haggard as an actor by daylight"* (Henry James). **b.** Wild and unruly; uncontrolled. **2.** Wild and intractable. Said of a hawk used in falconry.
~*n.* An adult hawk captured for training. [French *hagard,* untamed hawk, wild hawk, perhaps from Germanic.] —**hag·gard·ly** *adv.* —**hag·gard·ness** *n.*
Synonyms: *careworn, wasted, worn.*

Hag·gard (hăg′ərd), **Sir (Henry) Rider** (1856–1925). British novelist. He served as a government official in the Transvaal (1875–81). His novels include *King Solomon's Mines* (1885), *She* (1887), and *Allan Quatermain* (1887).

hag·gis (hăg′ĭs) *n., pl.* **-gises** or **haggis.** A Scottish dish consisting of a mixture of the minced heart, lungs, and liver of a sheep or calf mixed with suet, onions, oatmeal, and seasonings, and traditionally boiled in the stomach of the animal. [Middle English *haggeset†.*]

hag·gle (hăg′əl) *v.* **-gled, -gling, -gles.** —*intr.* **1.** To bargain, as over the price of something; wrangle: *"he preferred to be overcharged than to haggle"* (Somerset Maugham). **2.** To argue in an attempt to come to terms. —*tr.* **1.** To cut in a crude, unskillful manner; hack; mangle. **2.** *Archaic.* To harass or worry by wrangling. —See Synonyms at **argue.**
~*n.* An instance of haggling. [Frequentative of dialectal *hag,* to cut, from Middle English *haggen,* from Old Norse *höggva.*] —**hag·gler** *n.*

hag·i·ar·chy (hăg′ē-är′kē, hā′jē-) *n., pl.* **-chies.** Also **hag·i·oc·ra·cy** (hăg′ē-ŏk′rə-sē, hā′jē-) *pl.* **-cies** (for sense 1). **1.** Government by holy men, such as clerics. **2.** A hierarchy of saints. [HAGI(O)- + -ARCHY.]

hagio-, hagi- *prefix.* Indicates: **1.** A saint or body of saints; for example, **hagiology, hagiarchy. 2.** A sacred or holy place; for example, **hagioscope.** [Late Latin, from Greek, from *hagios,* holy.]

Hag·i·og·ra·pha (hăg′ē-ŏg′rə-fə, hā′jē-) *n. Used with a singular or plural verb.* The third of the three ancient Jewish divisions of the Old Testament, containing those books not in the Law (Torah) or the Prophets, and comprising usually the Psalms, Proverbs, Job, the Song of Solomon, Ruth, Lamentations, Ecclesiastes, Esther, Daniel, Ezra, Nehemiah, and Chronicles. Also called "Writings." [Late Latin, from Greek : *hagio-,* sacred + *-graphos,* written.]

hag·i·og·ra·phy (hăg′ē-ŏg′rə-fē, hā′jē-) *n., pl.* **-phies. 1.** Biography of saints. **2.** Any idealizing or worshipful biography. [HAGIO- + -GRAPHY.] —**hag·i·og·ra·pher** *n.* —**hag·i·o·graph·ic** (hăg′ē-ə-grăf′ĭk, hā′jē-), **hag·i·o·graph·i·cal** *adj.*

hag·i·ol·a·try (hăg′ē-ŏl′ə-trē, hā′jē-) *n. Theology.* Worship of the saints in a manner appropriate only to God. [HAGIO- + -LATRY.] —**hag·i·ol·a·ter** *n.* —**hag·i·ol·a·trous** *adj.*

hag·i·ol·o·gy (hăg′ē-ŏl′ə-jē, hā′jē-) *n., pl.* **-gies. 1.** Literature dealing with the lives of saints. **2.** A history of sacred writings. **3.** An authoritative list of saints. [HAGIO- + -LOGY.] —**hag·i·o·log·ic** (hăg′ē-ə-lŏj′ĭk, hā′jē-), **hag·i·o·log·i·cal** *adj.* —**hag·i·ol·o·gist** *n.*

hag·i·o·scope (hăg′ē-ə-skōp′, hā′jē-) *n.* A small opening provided in an interior wall of a church to enable those in the transept to have a view of the main altar. Also called "squint." [HAGIO- + -SCOPE.] —**hag·i·o·scop·ic** (hăg′ē-ə-skŏp′ĭk, hā′jē-) *adj.*

hag·rid·den (hăg′rĭd′n) *adj.* **1.** Harassed or pursued by or as if by a witch. **2.** Tormented or harassed, as by nightmares or unreasoning fears.

Hague, The (hāg). *Dutch* **'s Gra·ven·ha·ge** (sкнrä′vən-hä′кнə). City in the western Netherlands, the capital of South Holland province, lying on the North Sea. Most of the Netherlands government's administrative offices are located here, as are the national legislature, the supreme court, and foreign embassies. It is also the site of the International Court of Justice.

Hague Tribunal *n.* Officially, the Permanent Court of Arbitration. A tribunal established at The Hague in 1899 for the peaceful settlement of international disputes.

hah. Variant of **ha.**

ha-ha¹ (hä′hä′) *n.* A sound made in imitation of laughter.
~*interj.* Also **haw-haw** (hô′hô′). Used to express amusement or scorn. [Middle English *ha ha,* from Old English.]

ha-ha² (hä′hä′) *n.* Also **haw-haw** (hô′hô′). A moat, walled ditch, or hedge sunk in the ground to serve as a fence without impairing the view. Also called "sunk fence." [French, apparently expressing surprise at finding such an unexpected obstacle.]

Hahn (hän), **Otto** (1879–1968). German chemist and physicist who discovered the process of nuclear fission. In 1938 he found that uranium atoms could be split in two when bombarded with neutrons, releasing atomic energy. Hahn received the Nobel Prize for chemistry (1944).

Hah·ne·mann (hä′nə-mən, -män′), **(Christian Friedrich) Samuel** (1755–1843). German physician; founder of homeopathy. He postulated that a disease should be treated with minute doses of a drug that induces comparable symptoms in a healthy subject. His *Organon of the Rational Art of Healing* (1810) set forth his views.

Hai·da (hī′də) *n., pl.* **-das** or collectively **Haida. 1.** Any of the North American Indian peoples inhabiting the Queen Charlotte Islands, British Columbia, and Prince of Wales Island, Alaska. **2.** A member of these peoples. **3.** The language of these peoples, the sole survivor of the Haida family of languages. **4.** A language family of the Na-Dene phylum. —**Hai·dan** *adj.*

Hai·fa (hī′fə). The chief city of northern Israel, on the Mediterranean Sea at the foot of Mt. Carmel. The old city was destroyed by Saladin in 1191; the prosperity of the modern city dates from the early 19th century. It is an industrial center and one of Israel's chief ports.

Haig (hāg), **Douglas, 1st Earl** (1861–1928). British commander in chief on the Western Front (1915–18). He went to France as commander of the First Army Corps and then became commander in chief. He was responsible for the costly assault at the Somme (1916). In 1918 he directed the counterattack that broke the Hindenburg Line.

haik, haick (hīk, hāk) *n.* A large piece of cotton, silk, or wool cloth, draped over the head and about the body, worn as an outer garment by Arabs. [Arabic *ḥā′ik,* from *ḥāka,* to weave.]

hai·ku (hī′kōō) *n., pl.* **haiku.** A Japanese lyric poem of a fixed, 17-syllable form that often simply points to a thing or pairing of things in nature that has moved the poet. Also called "hokku." [Japanese : *hai,* amusement + *ku,* sentence, verse.]

hail¹ (hāl) *n.* **1. a.** Precipitation in the form of pellets of ice and hard snow. **b.** A hailstone. **c.** *Archaic.* A hailstorm. **2.** Something suggestive of a shower of hail, as in force and quantity: *a hail of criticism; a hail of bullets.*
~*v.* **hailed, hailing, hails.** —*intr.* **1.** To precipitate as hail: *It's hailing outside.* **2.** To fall like hail. —*tr.* To pour down or forth: *hail oaths at someone.* [Middle English *hail, hagel,* Old English *hagol, hagalian.*]

hail² *v.* **hailed, hailing, hails.** —*tr.* **1. a.** To salute or greet; welcome. **b.** To greet or acclaim enthusiastically. **2.** To call out to in order to catch the attention of: *hail a cab.* —*intr.* To signal or call to a passing ship in greeting or to identify oneself. —**hail from.** To come or originate from: *He hails from Bombay.*
~*n.* **1.** The act of hailing. **2.** A shout made to greet or catch the attention of someone. **3.** The range within which a hail will be heard: *within hail.*
~*interj.* Used to express a greeting or tribute. [Middle English *hailen, haeilen,* from *(wæs)haeil,* "(be) healthy," hail, from Old

Norse *heill,* HALE, whole, healthy.] **—hail·er** *n.*

Hai·le Se·las·sie I (hī'lē sə-lăs'ē, -lä'sē), born Ras Tafari (or Taffari) Makonnen (1891–1975). Emperor of Ethiopia (1930–36, 1941–74). After resisting the Italian invasion of his country (1936), he fled to England, returning with the Allies in 1941. His autocratic leadership brought opposition, and he was deposed in a military coup of 1974. He is revered as "the Lion of Judah, the Elect of God," by the Rastafarian cult of West Indians.

hail·fel·low (hāl'fĕl'ō) *adj.* Also **hail·fel·low·well·met** (hāl'fĕl'ō-wĕl'-mĕt'). Heartily friendly and congenial. [From the archaic greetings *Hail, fellow!* and *Hail, fellow! well met!*]

Hail Mary *n.* The Ave Maria *(see).*

hail·stone (hāl'stōn') *n.* A hard pellet of snow and ice.

hail·storm (hāl'stôrm') *n.* A storm with hail.

Hai·nan (hī'nän'). An island off the southern China coast, belonging to China and administratively part of Guangdong province. After Taiwan, it is the largest island off the China coast. The largest city and chief port is Haikou. The island is rich in minerals and the site of valuable rubber plantations.

Hai·naut (ā-nō'). *Flemish* **He·ne·gou·wen** (hā'nə-gou'wən). Low-lying province of southern Belgium, bordering on France. The capital is Mons, and the population is predominantly French-speaking.

Hai·phong (hī'fŏng', -fông'). City in northeastern Vietnam, on the delta of the Song Hong (Red River) *c.* 16 kilometers (10 miles) inland from the Gulf of Tonkin. One of Southeast Asia's leading ports, it was severely damaged by bombing during the Vietnam War.

hair (hâr) *n.* **1. a.** Any of the cylindrical, often pigmented filaments characteristically growing from the epidermis of a mammal. **b.** A growth of such filaments, such as that forming the coat of an animal or covering the scalp of a human being. **2.** Any similar filamentous projection or bristle, such as a seta of an arthropod or an epidermal process of a plant. **3.** Fabric made from the hair of certain animals: *a coat of camel's hair.* **4.** A minute distance or narrow margin: *win by a hair.* **5.** A precise or exact degree: *calibrated to a hair.* **—get in someone's hair.** To upset or annoy someone. **—let one's hair down.** To drop one's reserve or inhibitions. **—split hairs.** To make petty and fine distinctions. **—turn a hair.** To reveal discomfiture or distress. Used in negative constructions: *accepted the challenge without turning a hair.*
~*adj.* **1.** Made of or with hair. **2.** For the hair: *a hair dryer.* [Middle English *haire, hare,* Old English *hǣr,* from Germanic *hǣram* (unattested).] See feature, next page.

hair·ball (hâr'bôl') *n.* A small mass of hair swallowed by an animal, often causing indigestion or convulsions.

hair·breadth (hâr'brĕdth') *adj.* Extremely close: *a hairbreadth escape.*
~*n.* Variant of **hairsbreadth.**

hair·brush (hâr'brŭsh') *n.* A brush for grooming the hair.

hair clip *n.* A hinged clip that snaps together, used to hold the hair in place.

hair·cloth (hâr'klôth', -klŏth') *n.* A wiry fabric having usually a cotton or linen warp with a horsehair filler, used for upholstering and for stiffening and interlining garments.

hair·cut (hâr'kŭt') *n.* **1.** A cutting of the hair. **2.** The style in which hair is cut.

hair·do (hâr'dōō') *n., pl.* **-dos. 1.** A cutting or arranging of the hair, especially a woman's hair. **2.** The style in which the hair is arranged; coiffure.

hair·dress·er (hâr'drĕs'ər) *n.* A person who cuts or arranges people's hair, especially women's hair. **—hair·dress·ing** *n.*

haired (hârd) *adj.* Having hair, especially of a specified kind. Used chiefly in combination: *short-haired.*

hair follicle *n.* A tubular infolding of the epidermis that contains the root of a hair.

hair grass *n.* Any of various grasses having long, narrow stems and leaves, such as the tufted hair grass, *Deschampsia cespitosa.*

hair·grip (hâr'grĭp') *n. Chiefly British.* A **bobby pin** *(see).*

hair·less (hâr'lĭs) *adj.* Having little or no hair.

hair·line (hâr'līn') *n.* **1.** The outline of the growth of hair on the head, especially across the front. **2.** A very slender line. **3.** *Printing.* **a.** A very fine line on a typeface. **b.** A style of type using such lines. **4. a.** A textile design having thin, threadlike stripes. **b.** A fabric, usually a worsted, with such stripes. **—hair·line** *adj.*

hair·net (hâr'nĕt') *n.* A very fine net worn to hold the hair in place.

hair piece *n.* A covering or bunch of human or artificial hair used to cover baldness or give shape to a hairstyle.

hair·pin (hâr'pĭn') *n.* A thin, cylindrical strip of metal bent in a long U shape, used by women to secure a hairdo or a headdress.
~*adj.* Doubled back in a deep U: *a hairpin bend in the road.*

hair·rais·er (hâr'rā'zər) *n.* Something that causes wild excitement, terror, or thrills: *The ride in that sports car was a real hair-raiser.*

hair·rais·ing (hâr'rā'zĭng) *adj.* Horrifying; terrifying.

hairs·breadth, hair's·breadth (hârz'brĕdth') *n.* Also **hair·breadth** (hâr'brĕdth'). A small space or distance; a narrow margin: *win by a hairsbreadth.*

hair seal *n.* Any of various seals of the family Phocidae, having a stiff, hairlike coat in the adult and ears visible only as small indentations.

hair sheep *n.* Any sheep of a breed having hair rather than wool and yielding a fine-grained hide.

hair shirt *n.* A coarse haircloth garment worn next to the skin by religious ascetics to mortify the flesh.

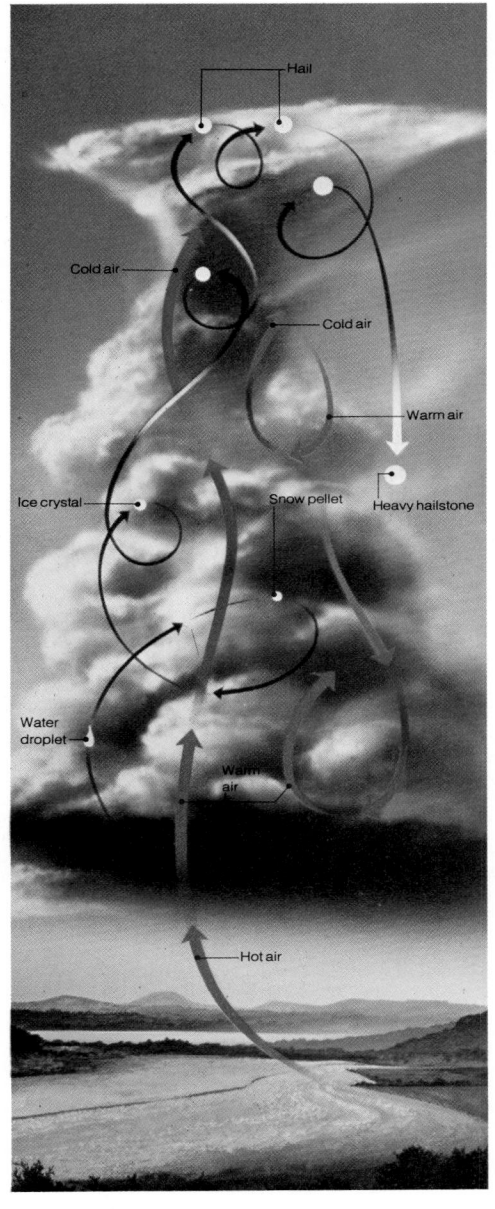

hail

RAIN THAT FALLS AS ICE
How warm air builds bigger hailstones

In the topmost layer of a thundercloud—about 9 kilometers (6 miles) above the ground—the cold altitude means that the liquid cloud droplets turn to ice. But the warm, moist air at lower levels bubbles up in strong convection currents that keep the hailstones from falling until they are much larger and are heavier than air. In a turbulent cloud current small hailstones can be tossed up and down between the layers of moisture and ice many times, growing all the time. Very warm, moist air sets up a very strong updraft that helps to create the heaviest hailstones.

Hail
Cold air
Cold air
Warm air
Ice crystal
Snow pellet
Heavy hailstone
Water droplet
Warm air
Hot air

hairstreak *Hairstreak butterflies are so called because of the fine line across the undersides of their wings (upper illustration). This is the black hairstreak, which is widespread throughout the world.*

hair space *n. Printing.* The narrowest of the spaces used for separating words or letters.

hair·split·ting (hâr'splĭt'ĭng) *n.* The making of unreasonably fine distinctions; quibbling.
~*adj.* Concerned with subtle but petty distinctions. **—hair·split·ter** *n.*

hair·spring (hâr'sprĭng') *n.* A fine coiled spring that regulates the movement of the balance wheel in a watch or clock.

hair·streak (hâr'strēk') *n.* Any of numerous butterflies of the sub-

hair

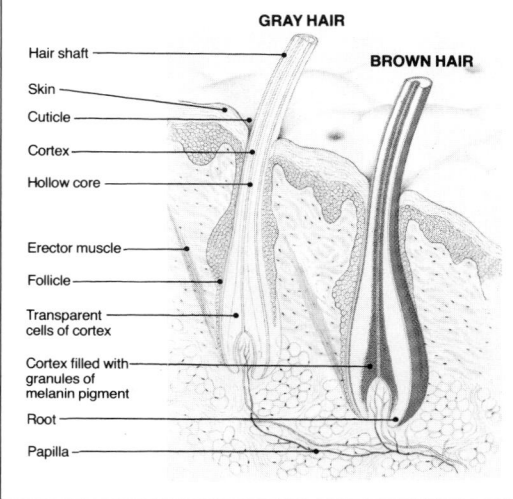

WHY HAIR TURNS WHITE
What hair is and how it gets its color

A hair is a structure of dead tissue growing from a follicle buried deep in the skin. Its hollow core is surrounded by a cortex strengthened by a sheath of keratin, a protein, and an outer cuticle of scales. The bulbous root is attached to the papillae, a layer of live cells supplied with blood vessels and nerves, from which the hair grows. Each hair follicle has oil glands and a muscle that, when it contracts, makes the hair stand on end. After growing 3 millimeters (.117 inch) a week for about three years, the hair falls out and is replaced.

Hair texture, abundance, rate of growth, and color are all hereditary. Melanin pigments in different forms and concentrations give human hair a range of colors varying from pale yellows through reds to blacks. Pigment is injected into the hair cortex from melanin cells in the papillae.

At a time preordained by genetic coding the papillae cease to inject melanin granules into the hair's cortex. Instead, there are minute air bubbles in the spaces between the transparent cells of the cortex. Light scattered by them makes the hair appear white.

GRAY HAIR

BROWN HAIR

Hair shaft
Skin
Cuticle
Cortex
Hollow core
Erector muscle
Follicle
Transparent cells of cortex
Cortex filled with granules of melanin pigment
Root
Papilla

family Theclinae, having transverse streaks on the underwings and fine, hairlike projections on the hind wings.

hair stroke *n.* A very fine line in writing or printing, as a serif.

hair style *n.* The design or style in which hair is cut, set, or arranged. —**hair stylist** *n.*

hair transplant *n.* The grafting of strands of one's own hair onto a bald area of the scalp.

hair trigger *n.* A gun trigger adjusted to respond to a very slight pressure.

hair-trig·ger (hâr′trĭg′ər) *adj.* Responding to the slightest provocation: *a hair-trigger temper.*

hair·worm (hâr′wûrm′) *n.* **1.** Any of various slender, parasitic nematode worms of the genus *Trichostrongylus*, which infest the stomach and small intestine of cattle, sheep, and related animals. **2.** A **horsehair worm** *(see).*

hair·y (hâr′ē) *adj.* **-i·er, -i·est. 1.** Covered with hair or hairlike growths; hirsute: *a hairy arm.* **2.** Of or like hair: *a hairy coat.* **3.** *Slang.* Fraught with difficulties; hazardous: *a hairy escape.* —**hair·i·ness** *n.*

hairy frog *n.* A frog, *Astylosternus robustus*, of western Africa, the males of which grow hairlike filaments on the thighs during the breeding season.

hairy hedgehog *n.* A **gymnure** *(see).*

Hai·ti (hā′tē). Republic in the Caribbean, comprising the western third of the island of Hispaniola and the two small islands of Tortuga and Gonâve. A slave rebellion against French rule won the islanders their independence in 1804, and Haiti is thus the oldest independent black republic in the world. Political instability led to U.S. occupation (1915–34) and the repressive dictatorship (1957–71) of François Duvalier, "Papa Doc." His son, Jean Claude ("Baby Doc"), ruled from 1971 to 1986, when he fled the country after widespread civil unrest. Haiti is the poorest country in Latin America. Coffee is the mainstay of the economy, and bauxite and sugar are also exported. Area, 27,713 square kilometers (10,700 square miles). Population, 6,500,000. Capital, Port-au-Prince. See map at **Dominican Republic.**

Hai·tian (hā′shən, -tē-ən) *adj.* Of or pertaining to Haiti, its people, or its dialect.
~*n.* **1.** A native or inhabitant of Haiti. **2.** The French patois spoken by most Haitians. Also called "Haitian Creole."

haj, hajj. Variants of **hadj.**

haji, hajji. Variants of **hadji.**

ha·ka (hä′kä) *n. New Zealand.* A Maori war dance accompanied by chanting. [Maori.]

hake¹ (hāk) *n., pl.* **hakes** or collectively **hake. 1.** Any of various marine food fishes of the genus *Merluccius*, such as *M. merluccius*, related to and resembling the cod. **2.** Any of various other fishes, such as species of the American genus *Urophycis* or the Australian *Thyrsites atun.* [Middle English *hake*, perhaps from *hakefish*, from dialectal *hake*, Old Norse *haki*, hook (from the shape of its underjaw).]

hake² *n.* A wooden rack or frame for drying cheese, bricks, or fish. [Variant of HECK (frame).]

ha·ke·a (hä′kē-ə, hä′-) *n.* Any Australian tree of the genus *Hakea*, some species of which produce useful wood. [After C.L. von *Hake* (died 1818), German horticulturist.]

Ha·ken·kreuz (hä′kən-kroits′) *n.* The swastika used as a symbol of Nazi Germany or of anti-Semitism. [German, "hooked cross."]

ha·kim¹, ha·keem (hä′kēm′) *n.* A Muslim physician. [Arabic *ḥakīm*, wise, learned, philosopher, from *ḥakama*, to be wise, exercise authority.]

hakim² *n. pl.* **hakim** or **-kims.** A Muslim ruler, provincial governor, or judge. [Arabic *ḥākim*, governor, from *ḥakama*, to exercise authority.]

Hak·ka (hăk′ə) *n., pl.* **-ka. 1.** A member of a Chinese people generally thought to have originated in central northern China, but now mostly scattered throughout southern China. **2.** A dialect of Chinese spoken by the Hakkas. [From dialectal pronunciation of Mandarin Chinese *kè jiā*, guest people, more recent migrants to a settled area.]

Hak·luyt (hăk′lōōt′), **Richard** (*c.* 1552–1616). English geographer. He collected accounts of English voyages of exploration and published them in *Principal Navigations, Voyages, and Discoveries of the English Nation* (1589, 1598–1600).

Ha·la·fi·an (hə-lä′fē-ən) *adj.* Of, pertaining to, or designating a culture that flourished in parts of Syria and Iraq before 3500 B.C., characterized especially by its polychrome pottery. [After Tell *Halaf*, a site near the present village of Ras el 'Ain, in northeastern Syria near the Turkish border.]

Ha·la·kah, Hal·la·cha (hä′lä-ᴋʜä′, hä-lä′ᴋʜə) *n. Judaism.* The legal part of Talmudic literature, an interpretation of the laws of the Scriptures. Compare **Haggadah.** [Mishnaic Hebrew *halākhāh*, rule, tradition, from *hālakh*, to go.] —**Ha·lak·ic** (hə-läk′ĭk) *adj.*

ha·la·kist, ha·la·chist (hä′lə-kĭst, hə-lä′kĭst) *n. Often* **Halakist. 1.** A Hebrew judge or scholar who has written parts of the Halakah. **2.** A student or scholar of the Halakah.

ha·lal, hal·lal (hə-läl′) *tr.v.* **-lalled, -lalling, -lals** or **-lalls.** To slaughter (animals) in the prescribed Muslim manner.
~*n.* Meat killed in this manner. Also used adjectivally: *halal meat; a halal butcher.* [Arabic, "lawful."]

ha·la·la (hə-lä′lə) *n., pl.* **halala** or **-las.** A monetary unit of Saudi Arabia that is equal to ¹⁄₁₀₀ of the rial. See feature at **currency.** [Arabic.]

ha·la·tion (hä-lä′shən) *n.* **1.** A blurring or spreading of light around bright objects or areas on a photographic negative or print. **2.** A ring of light appearing around a bright object on a television screen. [HAL(O) + -ATION.]

halavah. Variant of **halvah.**

hal·berd (hăl′bərd) *n.* Also **hal·bert** (-bərt). A weapon of the 15th and 16th centuries having an axelike blade and a steel spike mounted on the end of a long shaft. [Middle English *halberd*, from Old French *hallebarde*, from Middle High German *helmbarde*, "handle axe" : *helm*, handle + *barte*, axe, hatchet, from Old High German *barta*.]

hal·ber·dier (hăl′bər-dîr′) *n.* A soldier, attendant, or guard armed with a halberd.

hal·cy·on (hăl′sē-ən) *n.* **1.** A fabled bird, identified with the kingfisher, that was supposed to have had the power to calm the wind and the waves during the winter solstice while it nested on the sea. **2.** *Poetic.* A kingfisher.
~*adj.* **1.** Calm and peaceful; tranquil. **2.** Prosperous; golden: *halcyon years.* [Middle English *alceon*, from Latin *(h)alcyon*, from Greek *(h)alkuōn†*, a mythical bird, perhaps the kingfisher.]

halcyon days *pl.n.* **1.** Days of fine weather occurring near the winter solstice, especially the seven days before and the seven after, attributed by legend to the magical powers of the halcyon. **2.** A happy period of peace and tranquillity.

hale¹ (hāl) *adj.* **haler, halest.** Sound in health; not infirm; vigorous; robust. Used especially in the phrase *hale and hearty.* —See Synonyms at **healthy.** [Middle English *hal(e)*, Old English *hāl*, WHOLE.] —**hale·ness** *n.*

hale² *tr.v.* **haled, haling, hales. 1.** To compel to go; force: *hale a man into court.* **2.** *Archaic.* To pull, drag, draw, or hoist: *"The rope that haled the buckets from the well"* (Tennyson). [Middle English *halen*, from Old French *haler*, from Old Norse *hala*, from Middle Low German *halen*, to pull.]

Hale (hāl), **Edward Everett** (1822–1909). U.S. author and clergyman. A powerful preacher and prolific writer, he produced 150 literary works, many of which reflected his liberal Christian values.

Perhaps best known for his story "The Man Without a Country" (1863), he also served as the U.S. Senate chaplain from 1903 until his death.

Hale, Nathan (1755–76). U.S. soldier. A Connecticut schoolteacher turned Revolutionary War officer, he was captured by the British and sentenced to death for espionage. According to legend, his final words were "I only regret that I have but one life to lose for my country."

Haleb. See **Aleppo.**

ha·ler (hä'lər, -lĕr') *n., pl.* **-lers** or **-leru** (-lə-rōō'). A monetary unit equal to ¹/₁₀₀ of the koruna of Czechoslovakia. See feature at **currency.** [Czech, from Middle High German *haller,* an early German silver coin, from *Hall,* town in Swabia where halers were once minted.]

half (hăf, häf) *n., pl.* **halves** (hăvz, hävz). **1. a.** Either of two equal parts that together constitute a whole. **b.** A part of something approximately equal to the remainder: *Half her life is spent dreaming.* **2.** *Informal.* A fifty-cent piece. **3.** *Sports.* **a.** Either of two playing periods into which a game is divided. **b.** The turn of one baseball team at bat. **4.** Either of two periods into which an event, such as a concert or play, may be divided. **5.** *Sports.* A halfback. **6.** *Golf.* A score equal to the opponent's score on a hole or a round. **7.** *Sports.* Either of the two sections of a playing field, considered as belonging to the team defending the goal in that section. **8.** Half an hour. Used in expressing time: *half past one.* **9.** *Chiefly British.* A school term; semester. **—and a half.** *Informal.* Of an exceptional kind: *a fight and a half.* **—by half.** By a considerable and often excessive amount. **—by halves. 1.** Partially; imperfectly. **2.** Reluctantly; unenthusiastically. **—go halves.** To share equally. **—in half.** Into halves.

~*adj.* **1.** Being a half, as in size, quantity, or the like: *a half smile.* **2.** Being approximately a half. **3.** Partial; incomplete. **4.** Having only one parent in common with another person.

~*adv.* **1.** To the extent of exactly or nearly 50 percent: *a half-empty tank.* **2.** Not completely or sufficiently; partly: *only half-prepared.* **3.** To some extent; somewhat: *I was half afraid she'd leave.* **4.** *Informal.* Tolerably; reasonably: *wanting a café with half-decent food.* **—not half. 1.** Not nearly: *not half as bad as I'd expected.* **2.** *British Informal.* Really. Used as an intensive: *He didn't half get angry.* [Middle English *half,* Old English *healf,* from Germanic.]

Usage: The phrases *a half, half of,* and *half a* are all correct, though they may differ slightly in meaning. For example, *a half day* is used when *day* has the special sense "a working day," and the phrase then means "four hours." *Half of a day* and *half a day* are not restricted in this way and can mean either four or twelve hours. When the accompanying word is a pronoun, however, the phrase with *of* must be used: *half of them.* The phrase *a half a,* though frequently heard, is held by some to be unacceptable.

half-a-crown. Variant of **half-crown.**

half-and-half (hăf'ənd-hăf', häf'ənd-häf') *adj.* Being half one thing and half another.

~*adv.* In equal portions.

~*n.* **1.** A mixture of two things in equal portions; especially, a mixture of equal parts of milk and cream. **2.** *British.* A blend of light ale and bitter.

half·back (hăf'băk', häf'-) *n. Abbr.* **hb, hb. 1.** *Football.* One of the two players positioned near the flanks behind the line of scrimmage. **2.** One of several players in various sports stationed behind the forward line. **3.** The position played by a halfback.

half-baked (hăf'bākt', häf'-) *adj.* **1.** Only partly baked; not cooked through. **2.** *Informal.* Not sufficiently thought out; ill-conceived; foolish: *a half-baked scheme.* **3.** *Informal.* Lacking good judgment or common sense: *a half-baked idiot.*

half-ball (hăf'bôl', häf'-) *adj.* In billiards and snooker, designating a stroke aimed so as to make the cue ball hit the side of another ball.

half·beak (hăf'bēk', häf'-) *n.* Any of various marine and freshwater fishes of the family Hemiramphidae, related to the flying fishes, and having the lower jaw extended beyond the upper jaw.

half binding *n.* A bookbinding in which the back and often the corners of the volume are bound in a material differing from the rest of the cover: *a half binding of leather.*

half blood, half-blood (hăf'blŭd', häf'-) *n.* **1.** The relationship existing between persons having only one parent in common. **2.** A person existing in such a relationship. **3.** A half-breed. **4.** A half-blooded domestic animal.

half-blood·ed (hăf'blŭd'ĭd, häf'-) *adj.* **1.** Having only one parent in common. **2.** Having parents of different ethnic types. **3.** Having one parent of pedigreed stock and the other of unknown or mixed ancestry. Said of an animal.

half board *n.* A **demi-pension** (see).

half boot *n.* A low boot extending just above the ankle.

half-bound (hăf'bound', häf'-) *adj.* Having a half binding. Said of a book.

half-bred (hăf'brĕd', häf'-) *adj.* Having only one parent that is purebred; half-blooded.

half-breed (hăf'brēd', häf'-) *n. Offensive Slang.* A person having parents of different ethnic types.

~*adj.* Half-blooded; hybrid.

half brother *n.* A brother related through one parent only.

half-butt (hăf'bŭt', häf'-) *n.* In billiards and snooker, a cue that is shorter than a long butt though longer than an ordinary cue.

half-caste (hăf'kăst', häf'kăst') *n.* A person of mixed racial descent;

especially, a Eurasian or a person of mixed white and black descent. **—half-caste** *adj.*

half cock *n.* The position of the hammer of a firearm when it is raised halfway and locked by a catch so that the trigger cannot be pulled. **—at half cock.** At a premature stage; before proper preparations are made.

half-cocked (hăf'kŏkt', häf'-) *adj.* **1.** At the position of half cock. **2.** *Informal.* Inadequately prepared or conceived; not fully thought out.

~*adv. Informal.* Prematurely; hastily; carelessly: *fall halfcocked into an argument.*

half-crown (hăf'kroun', häf'-) *n.* Also **half-a-crown** (hăf'ə-kroun', hä'fə-). **1.** A British coin worth two shillings and sixpence, now no longer in circulation. **2.** The sum of two shillings and sixpence.

half-dead (hăf'dĕd', häf'-) *adj. Chiefly British Informal.* Exhausted; very tired.

half dollar *n.* A U.S. or Canadian coin worth 50 cents.

half gainer *n.* A dive in which the diver springs from the board facing forward, rotates backward in the air in a half backward somersault, and enters the water headfirst, facing the board.

half-har·dy (hăf'här'dē, häf'-) *adj.* Designating a cultivated plant that can survive outside during winter except during a severe frost.

half-heart·ed (hăf'här'tĭd, häf'-) *adj.* Done with or possessing little interest or enthusiasm; uninspired: *a halfhearted attempt at painting.* **—half-heart·ed·ly** *adv.* **—half-heart·ed·ness** *n.*

half hitch *n.* A hitch made by looping a rope or strap around an object, and then back around itself, bringing the end of the rope through the loop.

half-hour (hăf'our', häf'-) *n.* **1.** A period of 30 minutes. **2.** The point that marks 30 minutes after a given hour.

~*adj.* **1.** Lasting 30 minutes. **2.** Occurring on or indicating the half-hour: *a half-hour chime.* **—half-hour·ly** *adj. & adv.*

half hunter *n.* A pocket watch with a metal cover over all but the center part of the glass. Compare **hunter.**

half-in·te·gral (hăf'ĭn'tə-grəl, häf'-) *adj.* Having an integer as a numerator and 2 as a denominator. Said of a fraction.

half-jack (hăf'jăk', häf'-) *n. South African Informal.* A flat half-bottle of alcohol.

half landing *n.* A landing that is halfway up a staircase.

half-length (hăf'lĕngkth', -lĕngth', häf'-) *n.* A portrait that shows only the upper half and hands of a person.

~*adj.* **1.** Of or denoting such a portrait. **2.** Of half the full length.

half-life (hăf'līf', häf'-) *n., pl.* **-lives** (-līvz'). **1.** *Physics.* The time required for half the nuclei in a sample of a specific isotopic species to undergo **radioactive decay** (see). **2.** *Biology.* **a.** The time required by living tissue, an organ, or an organism to eliminate by biological processes half the quantity of a radioactive substance taken in. **b.** The time required for the radioactivity of material taken in by a living organism to be reduced to half its initial value by a combination of biological elimination processes and radioactive decay.

half-light (hăf'līt', häf'-) *n.* The soft, subdued light found at dusk or dawn or in dimly lit interiors.

half-line (hăf'līn', häf'-) *n.* A straight line extending in just one direction from a given point.

half-mast (hăf'măst', häf'mäst') *n.* The position about halfway up a mast or pole at which a flag is flown as a symbol of mourning for the dead or as a signal of distress.

~*tr.v.* **half-masted, -masting, -masts.** To place (a flag) at this position.

half measure *n.* An inadequate or halfhearted course of action.

half-moon (hăf'mōōn', häf'-) *n.* **1.** The moon when only half its disk is illuminated. **2.** Something shaped like a half-moon, as the lunula of the fingernail.

~*adj.* (hăf'mōōn', häf'-). Shaped like a half-moon: *half-moon spectacles.*

half nelson *n.* A wrestling hold in which one arm is passed under the opponent's arm from behind to the back of his neck. Compare **full nelson.**

half note *n. Music.* A note having one half of the value of a whole note. Also called "minim."

half-pen·ny (hā'pə-nē, hăp'nē) *n., pl.* **-nies** (for senses 1, 2); **half-pence** (hā'pəns) (for sense 3). Also **ha'pen·ny. 1.** A British coin worth half of a new penny. **2.** A British coin worth half an old penny, now no longer in circulation. **3.** The sum of half of a penny. **4.** A small or negligible amount.

half pint *n. Slang.* A small person or animal.

half-plate (hăf'plāt', häf'-) *n.* A photographic plate measuring 6½ inches (16.5 centimeters) by 4¼ inches (10.8 centimeters).

half-price (hăf'prīs', häf'-) *adv.* At a reduced price, usually half the full price. **—half-price** *adj.*

half relief *n.* **Mezzo-relievo** (see).

half sister *n.* A sister related through one parent only.

half-slip (hăf'slĭp', häf'-) *n.* A woman's slip that extends from the waist to the hem of the outer garment.

half sole *n.* A shoe sole extending from the shank to the toe.

half-sole (hăf'sōl', häf'-) *tr.v.* **-soled, -soling, -soles.** To fit or repair with a half sole.

half sovereign *n.* An obsolete British gold coin worth ten shillings.

half step *n.* **1.** *Music.* A **semitone** (see). **2.** A marching step of 15 inches at quick time and 18 at double time.

half tide *n.* **1.** The condition of the tide at a time halfway between high tide and low tide. **2.** The period during which this condition exists.

halo *A faint ring around the sun or moon, caused by refraction of light by particles in the upper atmosphere. Here the sun has been photographed on a hazy day.*

half-tim·bered (hăf'tĭm'bərd, häf'-) *adj.* Also **half-tim·ber** (-bər). *Architecture.* Having a wooden framework with plaster, brick, stone, or other masonry filling the spaces.

half-time (hăf'tīm', häf'-) *n.* The interval between two halves in certain games. Also used adjectivally: *the half-time score.*

half title *n.* **1.** The title of a book printed at the top of the first page of the text or on a full page preceding the main title page. **2.** The title of a section of a book, consisting of only one line and printed on the leaf preceding the text of that section.

half tone *n. Music.* A semitone *(see).*

half·tone (hăf'tōn', häf'-) *n.* **1.** *Art.* A tone or value halfway between a highlight and a dark shadow. **2.** *Photoengraving.* **a.** A picture in which the gradations of light are obtained by the relative darkness and density of tiny dots produced by photographing the subject through a fine screen. **b.** The technique or process that produces such pictures. **c.** The metal plate obtained by such a process. **d.** A picture made from such a plate.
~*adj.* Relating to, used in, or made by halftone.

half-track (hăf'trăk', häf'-) *n.* A military motor vehicle, often lightly armored, with caterpillar treads in place of rear wheels. —**half-track, half-tracked** *adj.*

half-truth (hăf'tro͞oth', häf'-) *n.* A statement, especially one intended to deceive, that omits some of the facts necessary for a truthful description or account.

half volley *n.* **1.** A stroke, as in tennis, cricket, or similar games, in which the ball is hit immediately after it bounces off the ground. **2.** The position of the ball immediately after it bounces: *hit it on the half volley.*

half·way (hăf'wā', häf'-) *adj.* **1.** Midway between two points or conditions; in the middle. **2.** Reaching or including only half or a portion; partial: *halfway measures.* —**half·way** *adv.*

halfway house *n.* **1.** An inn or other stopping place that marks the midpoint of a journey. **2.** A rehabilitation center where people who have left an institution, such as a mental hospital or prison, are helped to readjust to the outside world.

half-wit (hăf'wĭt', häf'-) *n.* A stupid, foolish, or frivolous person; a simpleton. —**half-wit·ted** (hăf'wĭt'ĭd, häf'-) *adj.* —**half-wit·ted·ly** *adv.* —**half-wit·ted·ness** *n.*

hal·i·but (hăl'ə-bət, hŏl'-) *n., pl.* **-buts** or collectively **halibut.** Any of several large, edible flatfishes of the genus *Hippoglossus* and related genera, of northern Atlantic or Pacific waters. [Middle English *halybutte*: *hali, holi,* HOLY (it was eaten on holy days) + *butte,* flatfish, from Middle Dutch.]

Haliç. See **Golden Horn.**

Hal·i·car·nas·sus (hăl'ə-kär-năs'əs). Ancient Greek city of Caria, in southwestern Asia Minor. It was the site of the Mausoleum, a magnificent tomb constructed by the wife of Mausolus, the satrap of Caria (377–353 B.C.). The tomb was one of the Seven Wonders of the World.

Halicz. See **Galicia** (Central Europe).

hal·ide (hăl'īd', -ĭd, hā'līd', -lĭd) *n.* A binary chemical compound of a halogen with a more electropositive element or group. Also called "haloid." [HAL(O)- + -IDE.]

hal·i·dom (hăl'ə-dəm) *n. Obsolete.* **1.** Holiness; sanctity. **2.** A holy relic. **3.** A sanctuary. [Middle English *halidom,* Old English *hāligdōm*: *hālig,* HOLY + -DOM.]

Hal·i·fax¹ (hăl'ə-făks'). Town in the metropolitan county of West Yorkshire, in northern England. Since the Industrial Revolution it has been a center for the manufacture of carpets, textiles, and, more recently, machine tools.

Halifax². Capital city of Nova Scotia, in eastern Canada. It is Canada's leading ice-free Atlantic port and the eastern terminus of the country's railroad network. It was founded in 1749 and named after George Montagu Dunk, 2nd Earl of Halifax (1716–71).

hal·ite (hăl'īt', hā'līt') *n.* Rock salt *(see).* [New Latin *halites*: HAL(O)- + -ITE.]

hal·i·to·sis (hăl'ə-tō'sĭs) *n.* Stale or foul-smelling breath. [New Latin : Latin *hālitus,* breath, from *hālāre†,* to breathe + -OSIS.]

hall (hôl) *n.* **1.** A large entrance room or vestibule in a building; a lobby; a foyer **2.** A corridor or passageway leading from an entrance in a house, hotel, or other building. **3. a.** A building for public gatherings or entertainments, such as concerts, lectures, or plays. **b.** The large room in which such events are held. **4. a.** A large building belonging to a school used for assembly, entertainments, or the like. **b.** A large room in a college or university where meals are served and lectures or concerts occasionally held. **c.** *British.* A meal served in such a building. **d.** *British.* A sitting of such a meal: *second hall.* **5.** The main house on a landed estate; especially, the house of a nobleman. **6. a.** The house or castle of a medieval king, chieftain, or nobleman. **b.** The large principal room in such a house or castle, used for dining, entertaining, and sleeping. [Middle English *hall(e),* Old English *h(e)all.*]

hallah. Variant of **challah.**

hallal. Variant of **halal.**

Hall effect *n. Electronics.* An effect in which an electric potential difference is produced between two faces of a conductor carrying a current when a magnetic field is applied at right angles to the current. [After E.H. *Hall* (1855–1938), American physicist.]

Hal·lel (hä-lāl', hä'lĕl') *n. Judaism.* A chant of praise consisting of Psalms 113 to 118, used during Passover and on certain other Jewish holidays. [Hebrew *hallēl,* song of praise, praise, from *həllēl,* to praise.]

hal·le·lu·jah (hăl'ə-lo͞o'yə) *interj.* Used, especially in religious contexts, to express praise or joy.
~*n.* **1.** The exclamation of "hallelujah." **2.** A musical composition expressing praise and based on the word "hallelujah." See **alleluia.** [Hebrew *hallelūyāh,* praise the Lord : *hallelū,* plural imperative of *hallēl,* to praise + *yāh,* short for YAHWEH.]

Hal·ley (hăl'ē), **Edmund** (1656–1742). British astronomer. He applied Newton's laws of motion to a particular comet of 1682, and in 1705 he correctly predicted its return in 1758.

Halley's comet *n.* A comet with a period of approximately 76 years, the first comet for which a return was successfully predicted. It appeared in 1910 and again in 1986. [After Edmund HALLEY.]

halliard. Variant of **halyard.**

hall·mark (hôl'märk') *n.* **1.** A mark used in the United Kingdom to stamp gold, silver, or platinum articles that meet established standards of purity. Also called "platemark." **2.** Any mark indicating quality or excellence. **3.** Any conspicuous indication of the character or quality of something: *A sense of humor is the hallmark of humanity.*
~*tr.v.* **hallmarked, -marking, -marks.** To mark with a hallmark. [After Goldsmith's *Hall* in London, England, where gold and silver articles were appraised and stamped.]

hall of fame *n.* **1.** A room or building housing busts, plaques, or the like, honoring illustrious persons. **2.** A group of persons judged to be outstanding in a sport, profession, or other category.

hal·loo (hə-lo͞o') *interj.* Also **hal·loa** (hə-lō'). **1.** Used to gain someone's attention. **2.** Used to urge on hounds in a hunt.
~*n.* Also **halloa.** A shout or call of "halloo."
~*v.* **hallooed, -looing, -loos.** Also **hal·loa, -loaed, -loaing, -loas.** —*intr.* To shout "halloo"; call out. —*tr.* **1.** To urge on or pursue by calling "halloo" or shouting. **2.** To call out to. **3.** To utter with a loud shout. [Perhaps variant of earlier *hallow,* to shout so as to incite hounds, from Middle English *halowen,* from Old French *halloer* (imitative).]

hal·low (hăl'ō) *tr.v.* **-lowed, -lowing, -lows.** **1.** To make or set apart as holy; sanctify; consecrate. **2.** To honor as being holy; revere; adore. [Middle English *halowen,* Old English *hālgian,* from Germanic *hailag-* (unattested), HOLY.]

hal·lowed (hăl'ōd) *adj.* **1.** Made or set apart as being holy; sanctified; consecrated. **2.** Highly venerated; unassailable; sacrosanct.

Hal·low·een, Hal·low·e'en (hăl'ō-ēn') *n.* The eve of All Saints' Day, falling on October 31 and celebrated by children who go in costume from door to door begging treats or playing pranks. [Short for *All Hallows Even.*]

Hal·low·mas, Hal·low·mass (hăl'ō-məs, -măs') *n. Archaic.* The feast of All Saints' Day or Allhallowmas on November 1. [Short for ALLHALLOWMAS.]

hall porter *n. Chiefly British.* A porter in the lobby of a hotel or office building who looks after keys, takes messages, arranges porters to carry luggage, and the like.

Hall process *n.* The electrolytic reduction process by which aluminum is recovered from aluminum oxide. [After Charles Martin *Hall* (1863–1914), American chemist, who invented it.]

Hall·statt (hôl'stät', häl'shtät') *adj.* Of, designating, or pertaining to a dominant late Bronze Age and early Iron Age culture of central and western Europe, probably chiefly Celtic, that flourished from the 9th century B.C. to the 4th century B.C. [After *Hallstatt,* Austria, site of remains typical of the culture.]

hal·lu·ci·nate (hə-lo͞o'sə-nāt') *v.* **-nated, -nating, -nates.** —*intr.* To undergo hallucinations. —*tr. Rare.* To cause to have hallucinations. [Latin *hallūcinārī, alūcinārī,* to wander in mind, from Greek *aluein,* to wander, be distraught.]

hal·lu·ci·na·tion (hə-lo͞o'sə-nā'shən) *n.* **1.** False perception with a characteristically compelling sense of the reality of something not really present, as occurring in some psychological and neurological disorders and under the influence of certain drugs. **2.** The hallucinatory material so perceived. **3.** Any false or mistaken idea; a delusion.

hal·lu·ci·na·to·ry (hə-lo͞o'sə-nə-tôr'ē, -tōr'ē) *adj.* **1.** Characterizing or characterized by hallucination. **2.** Inducing hallucination.

hal·lu·cin·o·gen (hə-lo͞o'sə-nə-jən) *n.* A drug, such as mescaline or LSD, that induces hallucination. [HALLUCIN(ATION) + -GEN.] —**hal·lu·cin·o·gen·ic** (hə-lo͞o'sə-nə-jĕn'ĭk) *adj.*

hal·lu·ci·no·sis (hə-lo͞o'sə-nō'sĭs) *n.* Any abnormal condition or mental state characterized by hallucination. [New Latin : HALLUCIN(ATION) + -OSIS.]

hal·lux (hăl'əks) *n., pl.* **halluces** (hăl'yə-sēz', hăl'ə-). **1.** The inner or first digit on the hind foot of a mammal; in man, the big toe. **2.** The homologous digit of a bird, reptile, or amphibian. In birds it is often directed backward. [New Latin, from Latin *hallux, (h)allus†,* big toe.]

hall·way (hôl'wā') *n.* **1.** A corridor, passageway, or hall in a house or building. **2.** An entrance hall; a foyer; a vestibule.

halm. Variant of **haulm.**

ha·lo (hā'lō) *n., pl.* **-los** or **-loes.** **1.** A luminous ring or disk of light surrounding the heads or bodies of sacred figures, as of saints in religious paintings; a nimbus. **2.** The aura of majesty or glory surrounding a person, thing, or event regarded with reverence, awe, or a similar sentiment. **3.** *Meteorology.* A circular band of light, sometimes colored, around the sun or moon, caused by the refraction and reflection of light by ice particles or water drops suspended in the intervening atmosphere. **4.** *Pathology.* Any of the colored rings seen around a light source by people with glaucoma or cataract.

~*v.* **haloed, -loing, -los** or **-loes.** —*tr.* To adorn or invest with a halo. —*intr.* To form a halo. [Medieval Latin *halō,* from Latin *halōs,* from Greek *halōs*†, threshing floor, halo, disk of the sun or moon.]

halo–, hal– *prefix.* Indicates salt or the sea; for example, **halophyte, halite.** [French, from Greek, from *hals,* salt, sea.]

hal·o·bi·ont (hăl′ō-bī′ŏnt′) *n.* An organism that lives or grows in a saline environment. [HALO- + BIONT.]

hal·o·gen (hăl′ə-jən) *n.* Any of a group of five chemically related nonmetallic elements that includes fluorine, chlorine, bromine, iodine, and astatine. [Swedish : HALO- + -GEN.] **—ha·log·e·nous** (hə-lŏj′ə-nəs) *adj.*

hal·o·gen·ate (hăl′ə-jə-nāt′) *tr.v.* **-ated, -ating, -ates.** To treat or cause to combine with a halogen. **—hal·o·gen·a·tion** *n.*

hal·oid (hăl′oid′) *adj.* Derived from or resembling a halogen.
~*n.* A **halide** *(see).* [HAL(O)- + -OID.]

hal·o·per·i·dol (hăl′ō-pĕr′ə-dôl′, -dōl′) *n.* A tranquilizer used in the treatment of psychiatric disorders, including schizophrenia. [HALO- + (PI)PERID(INE) + -OL.]

hal·o·phil·ic (hăl′ə-fĭl′ĭk) *adj.* Designating organisms, especially bacteria, that grow best in a salty environment. [HALO- + -PHILIC.] **—hal·o·phile** (hăl′ə-fīl′) *n.*

hal·o·phyte (hăl′ə-fīt′) *n.* A plant that grows in saline soil, such as that of a salt marsh. [HALO- + -PHYTE.] **—hal·o·phyt·ic** (hăl′ə-fĭt′ĭk) *adj.*

hal·o·thane (hăl′ə-thān′) *n.* A general anesthetic administered by inhalation for inducing and maintaining anesthesia during surgery. [HALO- + (E)THANE.]

Hals (häls), **Frans** (*c.* 1580–1666). Dutch painter, noted for fine portraits, including *The Laughing Cavalier* (1624).

Hal·sey (hôl′zē, -sē), **William Frederick** (1882–1959). U.S. naval officer. During World War II he led American naval forces to several pivotal victories in the Pacific, including the battles of Guadalcanal (1942–43) and Leyte Gulf (1944). On September 2, 1945, the Japanese formally surrendered aboard the *Missouri,* his flagship.

halt[1] (hôlt) *n.* **1.** A suspension or cessation of movement or progress, particularly of marching; a stop or pause. **2.** *British.* A stopping place, without station facilities, used by trains on minor routes. **—call a halt to.** To put a stop to; end.
~*v.* **halted, halting, halts.** —*tr.* To cause to stop; arrest. —*intr.* To stop; pause.
~*interj.* Used as a command to stop, especially to marching troops. [German *Halt,* from Middle High German *halt,* from the imperative of *halten,* to stop, hold, from Old High German *haltan.*]

halt[2] *intr.v.* **halted, halting, halts. 1.** To be defective or to proceed poorly, as in the development of an argument in logic or in the rhythmical structure of a verse. **2.** To proceed or act with uncertainty or indecision; waver. **3.** *Archaic.* To limp or hobble, as a cripple.
~*n. Archaic.* The act of limping; lameness.
~*adj. Archaic.* Having a limp; lame; crippled. [Middle English *halten,* to be lame, Old English *healtian,* from Germanic.]

hal·ter[1] (hôl′tər) *n.* **1.** A device made of rope or leather straps that fits around the head or neck of an animal, particularly a horse or cow, and can be used to lead or secure it. **2.** A rope with a noose used for execution by hanging. **3.** Death or execution by hanging. **4.** A bodice for women that ties behind the neck and across the back, leaving the arms, shoulders, and back bare. Also used adjectivally or in combination: *a halter-necked dress.* **5.** Variant of **haltere.**
~*tr.v.* **haltered, -tering, -ters. 1.** To put a halter on; tie up with a halter. **2.** To put to death by hanging. [Middle English *halter,* Old English *hælftre.*]

hal·ter[2] (hôl′tər, hăl′-) *n., pl.* **halteres** (hôl-tîr′ēz, hăl-). Also **hal·tere** (-tîr′). Either of the small, clublike balancing organs that are the rudimentary hind wings of dipterous insects such as flies or mosquitoes. Also called "balancer." [New Latin, from Latin *haltēr,* leaden weights used in leaping exercises, from Greek, from *hallesthai,* to jump.]

halt·ing (hôl′tĭng) *adj.* **1.** Limping; lame. **2.** Imperfect; defective: *a halting argument.* **3.** Hesitant or wavering: *a halting voice; a halting translation.* **4.** Uneven; jerky: *halting rhythm.* **—halt·ing·ly** *adv.*

hal·vah, hal·va (häl-vä′, häl′vä) *n.* Also **ha·la·vah** (hä′lə-vä′). A confection of Turkish origin consisting of crushed sesame seeds and honey. [Yiddish *halva,* from Turkish *helva,* from Arabic *ḥalwā.*]

halve (hăv, häv) *tr.v.* **halved, halving, halves. 1.** To separate or divide into two equal portions or parts. **2.** To lessen or reduce by half; remove half of. **3.** *Informal.* To share equally; divide up. **4.** *Carpentry.* To join (two pieces of wood) by cutting off half of each at the joint so they will fit together smoothly. **5.** *Golf.* To play (a game or hole) using the same number of strokes as one's opponent. —*intr.* To divide into or form two equal parts.
~*n. Carpentry.* A joint made by halving. [Middle English *halven, halfen,* from *half,* HALF.]

halves. Plural of **half.**

hal·yard, hal·liard (hăl′yərd) *n.* A rope used to raise or lower a sail, flag, or yard. [Variant (influenced by YARD) of Middle English *halier,* from *halen,* to pull, HALE.]

ham (hăm) *n.* **1.** The thigh of the hind leg of certain animals, especially a hog. **2.** The meat of this part of a hog, often preserved by smoking or drying. **3.** The back of the knee. **4.** The back of the thigh. **5. hams.** The buttocks. **6.** *Slang.* **a.** An actor who overacts or a performer who exaggerates dramatic gestures, comic effects, or the like. Sometimes used adjectivally: *a ham actress.* **b.** Any person who, liking attention or acclaim, makes himself ridiculous or obnoxious. **7.** *Informal.* A licensed amateur radio operator.
~*v.* **hammed, hamming, hams.** —*intr.* To overact. —*tr.* To exaggerate or overdo (a role, line, or the like). Often used with *up.* [Middle English *ham(me),* Old English *ham(m).*]

Ham (hăm). The second of the three sons of Noah, considered in some traditions the ancestor of the Egyptians. Genesis 5:32.

ham·a·dry·ad (hăm′ə-drī′əd) *n., pl.* **-ads** or **-ades** (-ə-dēz′). **1.** *Greek & Roman Mythology.* A wood nymph living only as long as the tree of which she is the spirit and in which she lives. **2.** A snake, the **king cobra** *(see).* [Latin *Hamādryas* (stem *Hamādryad-*), from Greek *Hamadruas,* "one together with a tree" : *hama,* together with + *druas,* dryad, from *drus,* tree.]

ha·ma·dry·as (hăm′ə-drī′əs) *n.* A baboon, *Comopithecus* (or *Papio*) *hamadryas,* of northern Africa and Arabia, the adult male of which has a heavy mane. [New Latin, from Latin, HAMADRYAD.]

ha·mal, ham·mal (hə-mäl′, -môl′) *n.* A porter or bearer in certain Muslim countries. [Arabic *ḥammāl,* porter, from *ḥamala,* to carry.]

Ha·man (hā′mən). A chief minister of the Persian king Ahasuerus, who was hanged from his own gallows when his plot against the Jews was revealed by Esther. Esther 8:7.

ha·mate (hā′māt′) *adj.* Hooked at the tip. [Latin *hāmātus,* from *hāmus*†, hook.]

hamate bone *n.* A small hook-shaped bone in the wrist. Also called "unciform bone."

ham·ba (hăm′bə, hŭm′-) *interj. South African Slang.* Used as an expletive to scare or chase away a person or animal. Often considered offensive. [Nguni, imperative of *ukuhamba,* to go.]

Ham·ble·to·ni·an (hăm′bəl-tō′nē-ən) *n.* One of a strain of American trotting horses. [Named after the stallion *Hambletonian* (1849–76), from which the strain descended.]

Ham·burg (hâm′bûrg′, häm′bŏŏrg′). City in northern Germany, capital of and coextensive with the state of Hamburg. Situated on the Elbe River near its mouth on the North Sea, it is Germany's chief port.

ham·burg·er (hăm′bûr′gər) *n.* **1. a.** A patty of chopped beef, cooked by frying or broiling. **b.** A sandwich consisting of a hamburger patty in a roll or bun. **2.** Chopped meat, especially beef. [Short for *Hamburger steak,* after HAMBURG.]

hame (hām) *n.* Either of the two curved wooden or metal pieces of a harness that fit around the neck of a draft animal and to which the traces are attached. [Middle English, probably from Middle Dutch.]

Hame·lin (hăm′lən, -ə-lən). *German* **Ha·meln** (hä′məln). Town in Lower Saxony, Germany, on the Weser River. It is the site of the legendary tale of the Pied Piper of Hamelin.

ham-fist·ed (hăm′fĭs′tĭd) *adj.* Ham-handed.

ham-hand·ed (hăm′hăn′dĭd) *adj. Informal.* **1.** Clumsy; maladroit. **2.** Having very large hands.

Ha·mil·car Bar·ca (hə-mĭl′kär′ bär′kə, hăm′əl-) (*c.* 270–228 B.C.). Carthaginian general and father of Hannibal. He led the Carthaginian forces during the final six years of the First Punic War (264–241). After signing a treaty with the Romans, he returned to Carthage and quelled a rebellion among his mercenary troops.

Ham·il·ton[1] (hăm′əl-tən). A burgh in Strathclyde Region, south-central Scotland, at the confluence of the Avon and Clyde rivers. It was near Hamilton that Rudolf Hess landed on his supposed peace mission flight from Germany in May 1941.

Hamilton[2]. Industrial city in Ontario, Canada, at the western end of Lake Ontario. It was originally settled by United Empire Loyalists in 1778 and has grown into one of Canada's largest cities and the country's leading producer of steel and iron.

Hamilton[3]. Capital of Bermuda, founded in 1790. Lying on Bermuda Island, it is a free port and tourist center.

Hamilton, Alexander (1755–1804). U.S. statesman. As the first secretary of the treasury (1789–95) he established the national bank and public credit system. He was mortally wounded in a duel with Aaron Burr.

Hamilton, Lady Emma, born Emma Lyon (*c.* 1761–1815). Mistress of Horatio Nelson. The daughter of a Cheshire blacksmith, she became the mistress of Charles Greville (1749–1809) and later married his uncle Sir William Hamilton (1730–1803), the British envoy to Naples. She met Nelson in 1793 and bore him a daughter in 1801. After her husband's death she lived with Nelson.

Ham·il·to·ni·an (hăm′əl-tō′nē-ən) *n. Symbol* **H 1.** *Physics.* A mathematical function that can be used systematically and with great generality to generate the equations of motion of a dynamic system, equal for many such systems to the sum of the kinetic and potential energies of the system expressed in terms of the system's coordinates and momenta treated as independent variables. **2.** A mathematical operator that generates such a function. [After William Rowan *Hamilton* (1805–65), Irish mathematician who formulated it.] **—Ham·il·to·ni·an** *adj.*

Ham·ite (hăm′īt′) *n.* **1.** One said to be descended from Ham. **2.** A member of a group of related peoples inhabiting northern and northeastern Africa, including the Berbers and the descendants of the ancient Egyptians.

Ha·mit·ic (hă-mĭt′ĭk) *adj.* Of or relating to Ham, the Hamites, or the language of the Hamites.
~*n.* A group of North African languages related to Semitic, including the Berber dialects, ancient Egyptian and its descendant, Coptic, and the Cushitic dialects spoken in Ethiopia.

Ham·i·to-Se·mit·ic (hăm′ə-tō-sə-mĭt′ĭk) *n.* A family of languages,

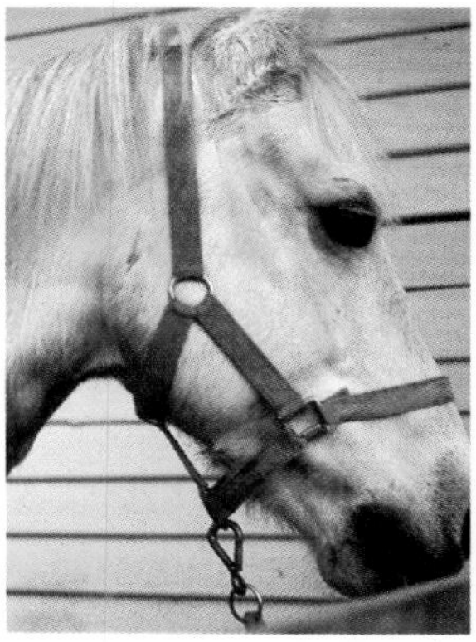

halter *An arrangement of leather straps for leading or restraining a horse or a pack animal.*

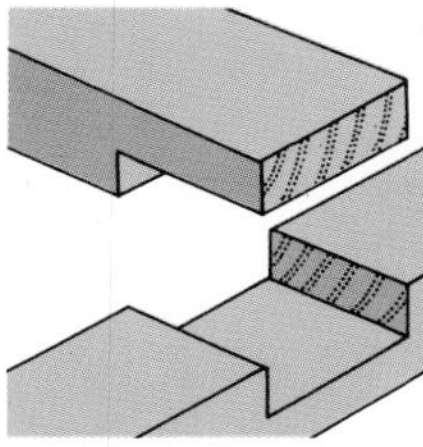

halve *A carpentry joint in which two pieces of wood—each chiseled out to half its thickness—are fitted together to form a union of the same thickness as the original pieces.*

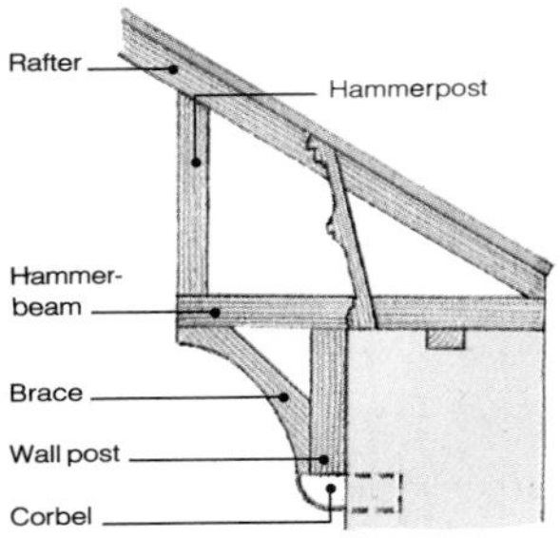

hammerbeam roof *The hammerbeam roof, using braced struts projecting from the walls to support the rafters, was common in England in the 15th century.*

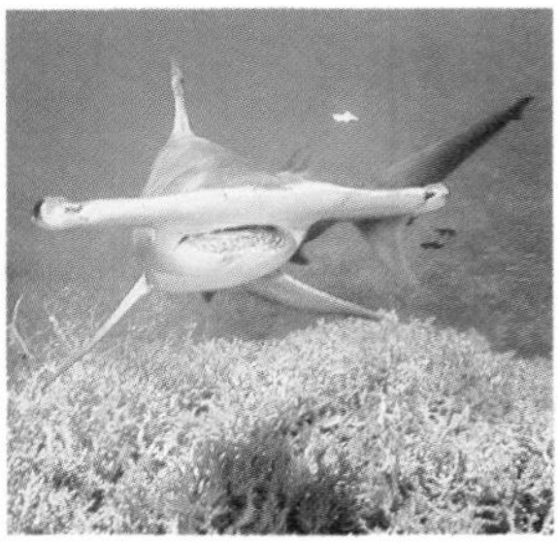

hammerhead *The broad head that gives this shark its name carries its eyes and nostrils. The shape of the head is believed to give it better vision and a directional sense of smell. There are nine species found all over the world, and all are considered dangerous.*

Afro-Asiatic *(see).* [HAMIT(IC) + SEMITIC.] **—Ham·i·to-Se·mit·ic** *adj.*

ham·let (hăm′lĭt) *n.* A small village. [Middle English, from Old French *hamelet,* diminutive of *hamel,* diminutive of *ham,* from Germanic.]

Ham·let (hăm′lĭt) *n.* An indecisive person. [After *Hamlet,* prince of Denmark, hero of Shakespeare's tragedy (1604).]

hammal. Variant of **hamal.**

Ham·mar·skjöld (hăm′ər-shōld′, -sho͝old′), **Dag Hjalmar Agne Carl** (1905–61). Swedish secretary-general of the United Nations (1953–61). During the Congo crisis he was killed in a plane crash over Zambia. He was posthumously awarded the Nobel Peace Prize in 1961.

ham·mer (hăm′ər) *n.* **1.** A hand tool used to exert an impulsive force by striking; especially, such a tool consisting of a handle with a perpendicularly attached head of a relatively heavy, rigid material, such as iron or hard rubber, used to drive nails or shape construction materials. **2.** Any tool or device of analogous function or action, as: **a.** The part of a gunlock that hits the primer or firing pin or explodes the percussion cap causing the gun to go off. **b.** One of the padded wooden pieces of a piano that strike the strings. **c.** Any part of an apparatus that strikes a gong or bell, as in a clock. **d.** A power tool that delivers blows with a weight. **3.** *Anatomy.* A bone, the **malleus** *(see).* **4.** *Sports.* A metal ball weighing 16 pounds and having a long wire or wooden handle by which it is thrown in track and field competition. **5.** A small mallet used by auctioneers. **—go (or come) under the hammer.** To be put up for auction. **—hammer and tongs.** With tremendous energy or effort; vigorously.
~v. **hammered, -mering, -mers.** *—tr.* **1. a.** To hit once or repeatedly with or as if with a hammer; strike; pound. **b.** To drive by hammering. **2.** To beat into a shape or flatten with a hammer. Often used with *out: He hammered the metal flat. The mechanic hammered out the dents.* **3.** To put together, fasten, or seal, particularly with nails, by hammering. **4.** To defeat (an opponent or enemy). **5.** To cause (ideas or information) to be absorbed by constant repetition: *She hammered the highway code into her pupils.* **6.** To subject to harsh criticism or relentless questioning. **7.** *British.* On the stock exchange, to declare (a broker) defaulted. *—intr.* **1.** To deal repeated blows with or as if with a hammer; pound; pummel: *branches hammering at the windows.* **2.** To beat in the manner of a hammer: *His pulse hammered.* **3.** To subject to repeated questioning or testing. Used with *away: hammered away at the examination candidates.* **4.** *Informal.* To work diligently; keep at something continuously. Often used with *away: He hammered away at his homework.* **—hammer out. 1.** To make by hammering. **2.** To settle or arrive at (a policy or agreement, for example) by vigorous discussion. [Middle English *hamer,* Old English *hamor.*] **—ham·mer·er** *n.*

hammer and sickle *n. Used with a singular verb.* **1.** An emblem of the Communist movement, consisting of a crossed hammer and sickle signifying the alliance of workers and peasants. **2.** *Informal.* Communism.

ham·mer·beam (hăm′ər-bēm′) *n.* A bracket projecting horizontally from the top of a wall and bearing the weight of the roof through the vertical hammerpost.

hammerbeam roof *n.* A roof whose weight is supported through a system of hammerbeams and hammerposts.

hammer drill *n.* A pneumatically operated drill for boring holes in stone in which the drilling bit is given a reciprocating motion.

ham·mered (hăm′ərd) *adj.* Created, shaped, or worked with or as if with a metalworker's hammer and often having indentations on the surface: *hammered gold.*

Ham·mer·fest (hä′mər-fĕst′). A town in northern Norway, on Kvaløy Island. Although it is the most northerly town in Europe, its harbor is ice-free the year round.

ham·mer·head (hăm′ər-hĕd′) *n.* **1.** The head of a hammer. **2.** Any of several large, predatory sharks of the genus *Sphyrna,* having the sides of the head elongated into large, fleshy extensions with the eyes at the ends. **3.** A wading bird, *Scopus umbretta,* of Africa and southwestern Asia, having brown plumage, a large, bladelike bill, and a long, backward-pointing crest. Also called "hammerkop." **4.** An African fruit bat, *Hypsignathus monstrosus,* with a hammer-shaped nose. **—ham·mer·head·ed** *adj.*

hammer lock *n.* A wrestling hold in which the opponent's arm is pulled behind his back and twisted upward.

ham·mer·post (hăm′ər-pōst′) *n.* A vertical post between a purlin and a hammerbeam.

ham·mer·smith (hăm′ər-smĭth′) *n.* One who works metals by hand with a hammer.

Ham·mer·stein (hăm′ər-stīn′), **Oscar II** (1895–1960). U.S. songwriter who collaborated with Richard Rodgers on a series of musicals. Their successes include *Oklahoma!* (1943), *South Pacific* (1949), *The King and I* (1951), and *The Sound of Music* (1959).

ham·mer·toe (hăm′ər-tō′) *n. Pathology.* A toe, usually the second, that is permanently bent downward.

Ham·mett (hăm′ĭt), **Dashiell** (1894–1961). U.S. author. He drew on his years at the Pinkerton detective agency in his highly acclaimed detective stories and novels, including *The Maltese Falcon* (1930). He later wrote several movies and also a radio serial about the tough, witty, and urbane Nick Charles, the hero of *The Thin Man* (1934).

ham·mock¹ (hăm′ək) *n.* A length of canvas, netting, or the like, hung between two supports, used for relaxation and formerly as a bed for sailors. [Spanish *hamaca,* from Taino.]

hammock². Variant of **hummock** (sense 2).

Ham·mu·ra·bi (hăm′ə-rä′bē) (died 1750 B.C.). King of Babylon (1792–1750 B.C.). He made Babylon the chief Mesopotamian kingdom and collated the laws of his people and of the Sumerians.

ham·my (hăm′ē) *adj.* **-mier, -miest. 1.** *Informal.* Characterized by exaggerated acting. **2.** Tasting or smelling of ham.

ham·per¹ (hăm′pər) *tr.v.* **-pered, -pering, -pers.** To prevent the free movement, action, or progress of; impede. —See Synonyms at **hinder.**
~n. Nautical. Necessary but encumbering equipment on a ship. [Middle English *hamperen*†.]

hamper² *n.* **1.** A large basket, typically of wickerwork, that usually has a cover. **2.** Such a basket or any other container packed with food and drink: *a Christmas hamper.* [Middle English *hampere,* variant of HANAPER.]

Hamp·shire (hămp′shîr′, -shər). Also **Hants** (hănts). County on the southern coast of England. It is crossed by chalk downs and is noted for sheep and dairy farming. Winchester, the ancient capital of Wessex, is the county town.

Hamp·stead (hămp′stĕd′, -stĭd). Residential district of northern London, noted for its heathland and intellectual community.

Hamp·ton (hămp′tən), **Lionel** (1913–). U.S. jazz musician. He was the first to popularize the vibraphone as a virtuoso solo instrument. He formed his own orchestra in 1940.

Hampton Roads. A channel of southeastern Virginia, connecting the James and Elizabeth rivers with Chesapeake Bay. One of the finest natural harbors in the world, it has been a major port since colonial times. It was the site of the Civil War battle (March 1862) between the ironclad ships *Monitor* and *Merrimack.*

ham·shack·le (hăm′shăk′əl) *tr.v.* **-led, -ling, -les. 1.** To hobble (an animal) by tying a rope or strap between one of the legs and the head. **2.** To hold back; hinder. [Perhaps from HAMPER (verb) + SHACKLE.]

ham·ster (hăm′stər) *n.* Any of several Eurasian rodents of the family Cricetidae; especially, *Mesocricetus auratus,* the golden hamster, having large cheek pouches and a short tail, popular as a pet and used in laboratory research. [German *Hamster,* from Old High German *hamustro,* from Slavic; akin to Old Slavic *chomĕstorŭ*†.]

ham·string (hăm′strĭng′) *n.* **1.** Either of two tendons at the rear hollow of the human knee. **2.** The large sinew in the back of the hock of a quadruped, such as a horse.
~tr.v. **hamstrung** (-strŭng′), **-stringing, -strings. 1.** To cut the hamstring of (an animal or person) and thereby cripple. **2.** To destroy or hinder the efficiency of (somebody or something); frustrate. [HAM (thigh) + STRING.]

Ham·sun (häm′sən), **Knut,** pen name of Knut Pedersen (1859–1952). Norwegian novelist. He wrote of individuals facing struggles of existence in works including *Hunger* (1890) and *The Growth of the Soil* (1917). In 1920 he won the Nobel Prize for literature.

ham·u·lus (hăm′yə-ləs) *n., pl.* **-li** (-lī′). A small hooklike projection or process, as at the end of a bone. [New Latin, from Latin *hāmulus,* little hook, diminutive of *hāmus*†, hook.]

ham·za, ham·zah (hăm′zə) *n.* A sign in Arabic orthography used to represent the sound of a glottal stop, transliterated in English as an apostrophe. [Arabic *hamza,* compression (of the windpipe), from *hamaza,* to press on, spur, goad.]

Han¹ (hän). A Chinese dynasty (206 B.C.–A.D. 220) noted for the unification and expansion of the national territory and for the promotion of literature and the arts.

Han² *n.* The Chinese as distinguished from other ethnic groups in China, such as the Manchus and the Mongols. **—Han** *adj.*

han·a·per (hăn′ə-pər) *n.* A wicker container or hamper used for storing documents. [Middle English *hanaper,* from Old French *hanapier,* case for holding goblets, from *hanap,* goblet, akin to Old English *hnæpp,* bowl, from Germanic *hnap* (unattested).]

hance (hăns) *n.* **1.** *Architecture.* **a.** The half arch that joins a lintel to a jamb. **b.** A **haunch** *(see).* **2.** *Nautical.* A curved rise or contour on a ship, as of the bulwarks. [Obsolete *ha(u)nce,* lintel, from *ha(u)nce,* to raise, from Middle English *hauncen,* probably short for *enhauncen,* to ENHANCE.]

Han·cock (hăn′kŏk′), **John** (1737–93). U.S. merchant, politician, and Revolutionary leader. A wealthy Bostonian, he protested against British rule, served in the Continental Congress (1775–80), and as its president was the first signer of the Declaration of Independence. He later served nine terms as governor of Massachusetts (1780–93).

hand (hănd) *n. Abbr.* **hd. 1.** The terminal part of the human arm below the wrist, consisting of the palm, four fingers, and an opposable thumb, used for grasping and holding. **2.** A homologous or similar part in other animals. **3.** A unit of length equal to four inches (10.16 centimeters), used especially to specify the height of a horse. **4.** Something suggesting the shape or function of the human hand. **5. a.** Any of the rotating pointers on the face of a mechanical clock. **b.** A pointer on any of various similar instruments, as a gauge or meter; a needle. **6.** A printer's mark, **index** *(see).* **7.** Lateral direction indicated according to the way in which one is facing: *at my right hand.* **8.** A style or individual sample of writing; handwriting; penmanship. **9.** A round of applause to signify approval; clapping. **10.** An act of physical assistance; help: *Give me a hand with these trunks.* **11.** *Card Games.* **a.** The cards held by a given player at any time: *a winning hand.* **b.** The number of cards dealt each player; a deal. **c.** A player or participant: *a fourth hand for bridge.* **d.** A portion or section of a game during which all the cards dealt out are played: *a hand of poker.* **12.** A person who performs manual labor: *a factory hand.* **13.** A person who is part of a group or crew. **14.** Any participant in an activity. **15.** A person regarded in terms of a specialized skill or trait: *an old hand at drawing.* **16.** A source of information considered in terms of its immediacy or degree of reliability: *at first hand.* **17. a.** *Usually* **hands.** Possession, ownership, or keeping: *The books should be in her hands by noon.* **b.** *Often* **hands.** Power; jurisdiction; care: *out of my hands.* **c.** Doing or involvement; participation: *The hand of the Russians is evident here.* **d.** An influence or effect; a share: *I detect the professor's hand in your decision.* **18.** Permission or a promise, especially: **a.** A pledge to marry. **b.** A business agreement sealed by a clasp or handshake; one's word: *You have my hand on that.* **19.** Capacity for doing something that requires skill: *try one's hand at painting.* **20.** A manner or way of performing something; an emphasis; an approach: *a light hand with make-up.* **21.** The lower part of a pork shoulder. **22.** A large bunch of bananas. **—at hand. 1.** Close by; near; easily accessible. **2.** Near in time; imminent. **—at the hand (or hands) of.** Through the agency of. **—by hand. 1.** Using the hands as opposed to mechanical means: *sorted by hand.* **2.** Individually delivered, rather than handled by the Post Office. **—by one's own hand.** By one's own act or agency: *die by one's own hand.* **—change hands.** To pass into different ownership. **—come to hand.** To be or become available. **—eat out of someone's hand.** To accept someone's views, wishes, or orders meekly and without protest. **—force someone's hand.** To force someone to act prematurely or against his own wishes. **—from hand to hand.** From one person successively to another person. **—from hand to mouth. 1.** In dire poverty. **2.** On an unplanned, day-to-day basis. **—hand and foot. 1.** So as to prevent movement or escape: *tied up hand and foot.* **2.** With slavish devotion: *He waited on his master hand and foot.* **—hand in glove.** In close association or collusion. **—hand in hand. 1.** Holding each other's hand. **2.** In cooperation; jointly. **—hand over fist.** At a tremendous rate: *making money hand over fist.* **—hands down.** With no trouble; easily. **—hands off.** Do not touch. Keep away. **—have one's hands full.** To be unable to take on more duties or responsibilities because one is fully occupied. **—hold (or stay) one's hand.** To restrain oneself from proceeding with a planned punishment or action. **—in hand. 1.** Under control. **2.** Presently accessible. **3.** In preparation or being processed. **—keep one's hand in.** To practice or keep in practice. **—lay hands on.** To bless, ordain, or consecrate by touching. **—on hand.** Available. **—on (or upon) one's hands.** In one's possession, often as an imposed responsibility or burden. **—on the one hand.** As one point of view or side of an issue; in one respect. **—on the other hand.** As another or opposite point of view; from another standpoint. **—out of hand. 1.** Out of control. **2.** Abruptly and without proper consideration. **—play into the hands of.** To act or behave so as to give an advantage to (an opponent). **—show one's hand.** To reveal something previously hidden, such as one's motives or intentions. **—take in hand. 1.** To put under control or care. **2.** To deal with; treat. **—throw up one's hands.** To give up in despair; concede. **—to hand. 1.** Nearby. **2.** In one's possession. **—turn (or put) one's hand to.** To take up as an activity; work at. **—wash one's hands of.** To relinquish involvement in or responsibility for. **—with a heavy hand. 1.** In a clumsy or awkward manner. **2.** With great severity or emphasis. **—with a high hand.** In a presumptuous or cavalier fashion; overbearingly.

~adj. **1.** Of or pertaining to the hand. **2.** Made to be transported by hand: *hand luggage.* **3.** Performed or operated by hand; manual. **4.** Created by hand.

~tr.v. **handed, handing, hands. 1.** To give or pass with or as if with the hands; present: *Hand me your keys.* **2.** To aid, direct, or conduct with the hands: *The usher handed the patron to her seat.* **3.** *Nautical.* To roll up and secure (a sail); furl. **—hand down. 1.** To bequeath as an inheritance to or as if to one's heirs. **2.** To release or pronounce a court decision or verdict. **—hand in.** To turn in; submit: *hand in one's work.* **—hand it to.** *Informal.* To give credit to. **—hand on. 1.** To give to a successor. **2.** To pass on (a tradition, heirloom, or the like). **—hand over. 1.** To release into the possession of another; relinquish. **2.** To transfer one's responsibility, task, or the like to another. [Middle English *hand,* Old English *hand, hond,* from Germanic *handuz* (unattested).]

Hand (hănd), **(Billings) Learned** (1872–1961). U.S. jurist. As a district judge (1909–24) and federal judge (1924–51) he earned the respect of his peers, rendering decisions in nearly all fields of law. Although he was never a Supreme Court justice, his influence was such that he was sometimes called the tenth man of the high court.

hand·bag (hănd′băg′) *n.* **1.** A bag, usually a woman's, for carrying articles such as money, keys, and personal items; pocketbook; purse. **2.** A piece of small hand luggage.

hand·ball (hănd′bôl′) *n.* **1.** A game played by two or more players batting a ball against a wall with their hands, usually with a special glove. **2.** The small rubber ball used in this game.

hand·bar·row (hănd′băr′ō) *n.* A flat framework or litter having carrying poles at each end.

hand·bell (hănd′bĕl′) *n.* A bell to be rung by hand, especially one of a set tuned in a scale.

hand·bill (hănd′bĭl′) *n.* A printed sheet or pamphlet distributed by hand; a leaflet; a notice or advertisement.

hand·book (hănd′bo͝ok′) *n. Abbr.* **hdbk.** A manual or small reference book providing specific information or instruction about a subject, activity, place, or the like; a guide; a directory.

hand·brake (hănd′brāk′) *n.* **1.** A brake on a vehicle that is operated by a hand lever. **2.** The hand lever that operates such a brake.

hand·breadth (hănd′brĕdth′) *n.* Also **hand's-breadth** (hăndz′-), **hand's breadth.** A linear measurement approximating the width of the palm of the hand, from 2½ to 4 inches, or 6.25 to 10 centimeters.

hand·cart (hănd′kärt′) *n.* A small, usually two-wheeled cart pulled or pushed by hand.

hand·clap (hănd′klăp′) *n.* A beating together of the palms of one's hands, usually repeatedly, used to indicate applause, attract attention, or provide a rhythmic accompaniment to music.

hand·clasp (hănd′klăsp′, -kläsp′) *n.* An act of clasping the hand of another person, especially to show warmth or friendship.

hand·craft (hănd′krăft′, -kräft′) *n.* Variant of **handicraft.**

~tr.v. **handcrafted, -crafting, -crafts.** To make by hand.

hand·cuff (hănd′kŭf′) *n.* *Usually* **handcuffs.** A restraining device consisting of a pair of strong, connected hoops that can be tightened and locked about the wrists and used on one or both arms of a person in custody; a manacle. Also informally "cuff."

~tr.v. **handcuffed, -cuffing, -cuffs.** To restrain with handcuffs.

hand·ed (hăn′dĭd) *adj.* **1.** Having a hand or hands. **2.** Having a specified number or kind of hands, or a specified preference as regards a hand or hands. Used in combination: *one-handed; left-handed.* **3.** Involving a specified number of people. Used in combination: *a four-handed card game.*

hand·ed·ness (hăn′dĭd-nĭs) *n. Chemistry.* **Chirality** *(see).*

Han·del (hănd′l), **George Frederick** (1685–1759). German-born composer (naturalized British subject, 1726). Handel wrote many Italianate operas, including *Rinaldo* (1711). With *Saul* (1738) he moved from opera to Biblical oratorio, a medium he brought to perfection in *Messiah* (1742). Other works include the orchestral *Water Music* (1717). **—Han·del·i·an** (hăn-dē′lē-ən, -dĕl′yən, -dĕl′ē-ən) *adj.*

hand·fast (hănd′făst′, -fäst′) *n. Archaic.* **1.** A secure grasp or grip. **2.** A handclasp used to signify a pledge, as a contract or a marriage.

~tr.v. **handfasted, -fasting, -fasts.** *Archaic.* **1.** To grip securely with the hand. **2.** To betroth or marry by joining the hands.

hand·feed (hănd′fēd′) *tr.v.* **-fed** (-fĕd′), **-feeding, -feeds. 1.** To feed (a person or animal) by hand. **2.** To feed (an animal) with regulated amounts of food at scheduled times.

hand·ful (hănd′fo͝ol′) *n., pl.* **-fuls. 1.** The quantity or number that can be held in the hand. **2.** A small but undefined quantity or number: *a handful of requests.* **3.** *Informal.* A person or thing too difficult to control or handle easily.

hand glass *n.* **1.** A small magnifying glass held in the hand. **2.** A mirror with a handle. **3.** A time glass used in timing the running out of a line used with a nautical log.

hand grenade *n.* A small grenade to be thrown by hand.

hand·grip (hănd′grĭp′) *n.* **1.** A grip by the hand or hands. **2.** Something suited to or facilitating a grip by the hand, as a handle or indentation. **3. handgrips.** Hand-to-hand fighting. **4.** A traveling bag; a holdall. In this sense, also called "grip."

hand·gun (hănd′gŭn′) *n.* A firearm that can be used with one hand; a pistol.

hand·held (hănd′hĕld′) *adj.* Designating a film camera that is carried rather than mounted.

hand·hold (hănd′hōld′) *n.* **1.** A grip by the hand or hands. **2.** Something that one can hold by the hand or hands for support, such as a branch or indentation on a rock surface.

hand·i·cap (hăn′dē-kăp′) *n.* **1.** A race or contest in which advantages or compensations are given to different contestants, according to their varied abilities or experience, to equalize the chances of winning. **2.** Such an advantage or penalty; especially, a handicap assigned to a golfer showing the number of strokes by which he is expected to exceed par for a given course. **3. a.** A deficiency, especially an anatomical, physiological, or mental deficiency, that prevents or restricts normal achievement. **b.** Any disadvantage, hindrance, or disability: *I find not being able to drive a handicap.*

~tr.v. **handicapped, -capping, -caps. 1.** To assign a handicap or handicaps to (a contestant). **2.** To put at a disadvantage; impede. [From the phrase *hand i' cap* ("hand in cap"), originally a lottery game in which players held forfeits in a cap.]

hand·i·cap·per (hăn′dē-kăp′ər) *n.* **1.** One who assigns handicaps. **2.** One who predicts the winners in a horse race, especially one who publishes such predictions as a guide for bettors.

hand·i·craft (hăn′dē-krăft′, -kräft′) *n.* Also **hand·craft** (hănd′krăft′, -kräft′). **1.** Skill and facility with the hands; workmanship. **2.** A particular trade or craft requiring skilled use of the hands, such as basketry. **3.** The work produced by such a trade or craft. [Middle English *handie-craft,* variant of *handcraft* : HAND + CRAFT.]

hand·i·crafts·man (hăn′dē-krăfts′mən, -kräfts′mən) *n., pl.* **-men** (-mĭn). A person skilled in handicraft; a craftsman.

hand·i·ly (hăn′dĭ-lē) *adv.* **1.** In a handy or easy manner; dexterously. **2.** Conveniently.

hand·i·ness (hăn′dē-nĭs) *n.* **1.** The quality of being handy; facility; expertise. **2.** The quality of being easy to use or readily accessible; convenience.

hand·i·work (hăn′dē-wûrk′) *n.* **1.** Work performed by hand or the objects produced by hand. **2.** That which is accomplished by a single person's efforts. **3.** The results of a person's actions. [Middle

PRONUNCIATION KEY

ă, pat; ā, pay; âr, care;
ä, father, are; b, bib;
ch, church; d, deed; ĕ, pet;
ē, be; f, fife; g, gag; h, hat;
hw, which; ĭ, pit; ī, pie;
îr, pier; j, judge; k, kick;
l, lid, needle; m, mum;
n, no, sudden; ng, thing;
ŏ, pot; ō, toe; ô, paw, for;
oi, noise; ou, out; o͝o, book;
o͞o, boot; p, pop; r, roar;
s, sauce; sh, ship, dish;
t, tight; th, thin, path;
th, this, bathe; ŭ, cut; ûr, fur;
v, valve; w, with; y, yes;
z, zebra, size; zh, vision;
ə, about, item, edible,
gallop, circus, peaceful

IN FOREIGN WORDS:

à, *Fr.* ami; œ, *Fr.* feu, *Ger.* schön; ü, *Fr.* tu, *Ger.* über; KH, *Ger.* ich, *Scot.* loch; N, *Fr.* bon; y′, *Fr.* Compiègne

STRESS MARKS:

Primary stress: ′
in·cite′ (ĭn-sīt′)
Secondary stress: ′
in′sight′ (ĭn′sīt′)

English *handiwork,* Old English *handgeweorc* : HAND + *geweorc,* work : *ge-,* collective prefix + *weorc,* WORK.]

hand·ker·chief (hăng′kər-chĭf) *n.* **1.** A small square of cotton, linen, or silk carried by a person for use in wiping the nose, mouth, or the like. **2.** A slightly larger piece of cloth worn as a decorative article; a kerchief; a scarf. [HAND + KERCHIEF.]

hand-knit (hănd′nĭt′) *adj.* Also **hand-knit·ted** (-nĭt′ĭd). Knit by hand. —*tr.v.* **hand-knitted, -knitting, -knits.** To knit by hand.

han·dle (hănd′l) *v.* **-dled, -dling, -dles.** —*tr.* **1.** To touch, lift, or turn with the hands. **2.** To operate with the hands; manipulate. **3.** To specialize in or have responsibility for; take charge of: *My colleague handles financial matters.* **4.** To deal with; process: *handle an application.* **5.** To manage, administer to, or represent: *handle a boxer.* **6.** To behave or act toward; treat. **7.** To confront or cope with, especially: **a.** To control or command: *handle a crowd.* **b.** To discuss or approach: *handle a problem.* —*intr.* To respond or react to control or manipulation; function under operation: *This bicycle handles well at high speed.* —*n.* **1.** A part by means of which something such as a tool, object, or door is held or manipulated with the hand. **2.** An opportunity that may serve as an advantage for someone; a means; an opening. **3.** *Slang.* A person's name or title. —**fly off the handle.** *Informal.* To fly into a rage; become very angry suddenly. [Old English *handle* (noun), *handlian* (verb), from HAND.]
   Usage: handle, manipulate, wield, ply. These verbs mean to use, operate, or manage things or, less often, persons. *Handle* can refer to management or control of tools, implements, persons, or non-physical things such as problems and situations. In every case, unless it is qualified by an adverb, the term suggests competence in gaining an end or objective. *Manipulate* connotes skillful or artful management of physical things such as tools or instruments or of persons or personal affairs, in which case it often implies use of improper influence or fraud in gaining an end. *Wield* implies that one has full command of what is used, principally tools and implements, weapons, means of expression such as the pen, or intangibles such as authority and influence. The term likewise suggests that the means are used effectively. *Ply* refers principally to use of tools and to the regular and diligent pursuit of a given trade.

han·dle·bar (hănd′l-bär′) *n.* Usually **handlebars.** A curved metal steering bar, as on a bicycle.

handlebar mustache *n.* A thick mustache that curls upward at the side of the lips.

han·dler (hănd′lər) *n.* **1.** One that handles. **2. a.** A person who trains or exhibits an animal, such as a dog. **b.** A person who acts as the trainer or second of a boxer.

han·dling (hănd′lĭng) *n.* **1.** A touching, feeling, or manipulating with the hands. **2.** The way in which a matter, especially a delicate one, is taken care of or treated; management. **3.** The way in which a subject is approached or discussed. **4.** The process of packing and distributing merchandise. **5.** *Law.* The act of receiving or selling stolen property.

hand·made (hănd′mād′) *adj.* Made or prepared by hand rather than by machine.

hand·maid (hănd′mād′) *n.* A female servant or attendant; a personal maid.

hand·maid·en (hănd′mād′n) *n.* **1.** A handmaid. **2.** That which serves or assists a higher cause: *Language is the handmaiden of thought.*

hand-me-down (hănd′mē-doun′) *adj.* **1.** Handed down to one person after being used and discarded by another; secondhand. **2.** Of inferior quality; shabby. —*n.* Something passed on from one person to another; especially, an item of clothing.

hand-off (hănd′ôf′, -ŏf′) *n.* A football play in which one player hands the ball to another.

hand organ *n.* A barrel organ operated by turning a crank.

hand out *tr.v.* To distribute (food, samples, or leaflets, for example); disseminate; proffer.

hand·out (hănd′out′) *n.* **1.** Food, clothing, or money donated to a beggar or destitute person. **2.** A folder or leaflet distributed, especially as an accompaniment to a talk or lecture. **3.** A prepared news or publicity release.

hand-pick (hănd′pĭk′) *tr.v.* **-picked, -picking, -picks. 1.** To gather or pick by hand. **2.** To select carefully, especially for a particular task or purpose.

hand·rail (hănd′rāl′) *n.* A rail, as along a staircase, to be grasped with the hand for support.

hand·saw (hănd′sô′) *n.* A saw that can be used with one hand.

hand's-breadth, hand's breadth. Variants of **handbreadth.**

hand·sel, han·sel (hăn′səl) *n. Chiefly British.* A gift to express good wishes at the beginning of a new year or enterprise. —*tr.v.* **handseled** or **handselled, -seling** or **-selling, -sels.** *Chiefly British.* **1.** To give a handsel to. **2.** To inaugurate or initiate. [Middle English *hansele,* Old English *handselen,* a giving into someone's hands, from Old Norse *handsal,* a giving of the hand : HAND + *sal,* a giving, payment.]

hand·set (hănd′sĕt′) *n.* A portable telephone transmitter and receiver module.

hand·shake (hănd′shāk′) *n.* **1.** The grasping of hands by two people as a gesture of greeting, leave-taking, congratulation, agreement, or the like. **2.** *Computer Science.* A dialogue between parts of a com-

puter system in which information is exchanged regarding the transmission and reception of data.

hands-off (hăndz′ôf′, -ŏf′) *adj.* Designating, pertaining to, or characterized by a policy of nonintervention.

hand·some (hăn′səm) *adj.* **1.** Having an attractive, pleasing, and dignified appearance: *a handsome man.* **2.** Impressively well made: *a handsome building.* **3. a.** Generous or liberal: *a handsome offer.* **b.** Considerable; plentiful: *a handsome reward.* **4.** Gracious; magnanimous: *a handsome gesture.* **5.** Marked by or requiring great skill or accomplishment: *a handsome piece of work.* —See Synonyms at **beautiful.** [Middle English *handsom,* easy to handle, handy : HAND + -SOME.] —**hand·some·ly** *adv.* —**hand·some·ness** *n.*

hands-on (hăndz′ŏn′) *adj.* Of, pertaining to, or providing direct experience, especially of the manual operation of a computer system.

hand·spike (hănd′spīk′) *n.* A heavy bar used as a lever.

hand·spring (hănd′sprĭng′) *n.* A gymnastic feat in which the body is flipped completely forward or backward from an upright position, landing first on the hands, then on the feet.

hand·stand (hănd′stănd′) *n.* The act of balancing on the hands with one's feet in the air.

hand-to-hand (hănd′tə-hănd′) *adj.* At close quarters. —**hand-to-hand** *adv.*

hand-to-mouth (hănd′tə-mouth′) *adj.* Characterized by constant financial difficulties. —**hand-to-mouth** *adv.*

hand-wash (hănd′wŏsh′, -wôsh′) *tr.v.* **-washed, -washing, -washes.** To wash (clothing or fabrics) by hand rather than in a machine.

hand·work (hănd′wûrk′) *n.* Work done by hand rather than machine.

hand·writ·ing (hănd′rī′tĭng) *n.* **1.** Writing done with the hand rather than typed or printed. **2.** The writing characteristic of a particular person.

hand·writ·ten (hănd′rĭt′n) *adj.* Written by hand: *a handwritten invitation.*

hand·y (hăn′dē) *adj.* **-ier, -iest. 1.** Manually adroit. **2.** Readily accessible. **3.** Conveniently situated. **4.** Easy to use or handle. **5.** Supplying a need; useful: *The extra cash will be handy.* —See Synonyms at **dexterous.** [From HAND.]

Han·dy (hăn′dē), **William Christopher,** known as "W.C. Handy" (1873–1958). U.S. jazz composer and publisher. He wrote *St. Louis Blues* (1914).

hand·y·man (hăn′dē-măn′) *n., pl.* **-men** (-mĕn′). **1.** A do-it-yourself enthusiast. **2.** One who does odd jobs or various small tasks; especially, one employed to do them.

hang (hăng) *v.* **hung** (hŭng) or **hanged** (for transitive sense 3 and intransitive sense 2), **hanging, hangs.** —*tr.* **1.** To fasten from above with no support from below; suspend. **2.** To suspend or fasten so as to allow free movement at or about the point of suspension: *hang a door.* **3.** To execute by suspending by the neck. **4.** To fix or attach at an appropriate angle: *hang a scythe to its handle.* **5.** To alter the hem of (a garment) so as to fall evenly at an appropriate height. **6.** To furnish, decorate, or appoint by suspending objects around or about: *hang a room with tapestries.* **7.** To hold or incline downward; let droop: *hang one's head in sorrow.* **8.** To attach to a wall: *hang wallpaper.* **9.** To deadlock (a jury) by failing to render a unanimous verdict. **10.** To leave (venison or other game) exposed to the air for some time to improve its flavor. **11. a.** To exhibit (pictures, as paintings) in an art gallery or museum. **b.** To exhibit the work of (a painter) in an art gallery or museum. **12.** *Baseball.* To throw (a pitch) so that it fails to break. —*intr.* **1.** To be attached from above with no support from below. **2.** To suffer death by hanging. **3. a.** To remain suspended or poised over a place or object; hover. **b.** To be suspended from a pivot and able to move freely. **4.** To attach oneself as an impediment or dependent; cling. Usually used with *on.* **5.** To incline downward; droop. **6.** To depend: *Everything hangs on your decision.* **7.** To pay strict or devoted attention: *hang on every word.* **8.** To remain unresolved or uncertain: *hang in the balance.* **9.** To fit or drape from the body in loose lines: *Her dress hangs awkwardly.* **10.** To be imminent; loom: *the threat hanging over us.* **11.** To be burdensome: *Time hung heavily on her hands.* —**hang around** (or **about**). *Informal.* **1.** To spend time in idleness; loiter. **2.** To remain; wait. —**hang back. 1.** To lag. **2.** To be averse; hold back. —**hang fire. 1.** To be slow in firing, as a gun. **2.** To delay. —**hang in.** *Informal.* To persevere. —**hang loose.** *Slang.* To remain calm; relax. —**hang on. 1.** To continue persistently or resolutely; persevere. **2.** To wait a while; be patient. **3.** To keep a telephone connection open; hold the line. —**hang one on. 1.** *Informal.* To strike (a person). **2.** *Slang.* To become drunk. —**hang together. 1.** To stand united; stick together. **2.** To constitute a coherent totality. —**hang tough.** *Informal.* To remain firmly resolved. —*n.* **1.** The way in which something hangs. **2.** A downward inclination or slope. —**get the hang of.** *Informal.* **1.** To come to understand a process, argument, or the like. **2.** To develop the correct technique for doing something. —**not give** (or **care**) **a hang.** To be totally unconcerned or indifferent. [Hang, hung, hung; partly Middle English *hon, hong, hongen,* Old English *hōn* (transitive verb), to hang, suspend, *heng, hangen;* partly Middle English *hangen, hong, hanged,* Old English *hangian* (transitive and intransitive verb), to hang, be hung, suspend, *hangode, hanged;* partly Middle English *hingen,* from Old Norse *hanga* (transitive verb), to cause to hang.]
   Usage: The usual past tense and past participle form of this

verb is **hung**, but in the context of capital punishment the form *hanged* is preferred: *The prisoner was hanged at six o'clock.* The use of *hung* in such a context would generally be considered nonstandard.

han·gar (hăng′ər) *n.* A large structure for housing, constructing, or maintaining aircraft. [French, from Old French, probably from Medieval Latin *angarium*†, shed for shoeing horses.]

hang·bird (hăng′bûrd′) *n.* A bird, such as an oriole, that builds a hanging nest. Also called "hangnest."

Hangchow, Hang·chou. See **Hangzhou**.

hang·dog (hăng′dôg′, -dŏg′) *adj.* **1.** Shamefaced or guilty. **2.** Downcast; intimidated.
~*n.* A sneaky or shamefaced person. [Originally, despicable person who was fit only to hang a dog.]

hang·er (hăng′ər) *n.* **1.** One that hangs. **2.** A contrivance to which something hangs or by which something is hung. **3.** A device around which a garment is draped for hanging from a hook or rod. **4.** A loop or strap by which something is hung. **5.** A bracket on a motor vehicle's spring shackle designed to hold it to the chassis. **6.** A decorative strip of cloth hung on a garment or wall.

hang·er-on (hăng′ər-ŏn′, -ôn′) *n., pl.* **hangers-on** (hăng′ərz-). A person who attaches himself to another, as from hope of gain.

hang·glide (hăng′glīd′) *intr.v.* **-glided, -gliding, -glides.** To fly by means of a hang glider. —**hang·glid·ing** *n.*

hang glider *n.* **1.** A device resembling a kite from which a harnessed rider hangs while gliding from a height. **2.** The pilot of such a device.

hang·ing (hăng′ĭng) *n.* **1.** An act of killing by putting a noose around the victim's neck and allowing him to drop. **2.** A drapery hung over a wall or window.
~*adj.* **1.** Situated on a sharp declivity. **2.** Projecting downward; overhanging. **3.** Suited for holding something that hangs. **4. a.** Susceptible to or meriting death by hanging: *a hanging crime.* **b.** Disposed to inflict the sentence of death by hanging: *a hanging judge.*

hanging indention *n.* The indention of every line in a paragraph except the first.

hanging valley *n.* A tributary valley that joins a main valley where the latter has been deepened, usually by glacial erosion. There is usually a steep fall from the floor of the tributary valley to that of the main valley.

hanging wall *n.* The wall of rock on the upper side of an inclined fault plane or mineral vein. Compare **footwall**.

hang·man (hăng′mən) *n., pl.* **-men** (-mĭn). One employed to execute condemned prisoners by hanging.

hang·nail (hăng′nāl′) *n.* A small piece of dead skin at the side or the base of a fingernail that is partly detached from the rest of the skin. [By folk etymology from AGNAIL.]

hang out *intr.v.* **1.** To project downward. **2.** *Informal.* To reside or spend time. —*tr.v.* **1.** To spread out (washing, for example) to dry. **2.** To suspend for public display: *hang out a sign.* —**let it all hang out.** *Slang.* To be entirely uninhibited.

hang·out (hăng′out′) *n. Informal.* A frequently visited place.

hang·o·ver (hăng′ō′vər) *n.* **1.** Unpleasant physical effects following the heavy consumption of alcohol; especially, a severe headache. **2.** A vestige; a holdover: *hangovers from prewar legislation.*

hang up *tr.v.* **1.** To replace (a telephone receiver) on its cradle. **2.** To retard, impede, or interrupt: *hang up a project.* **3.** To halt the movement or action of. **4.** *Informal.* To be a source of anxiety or preoccupation for: *Don't let it hang you up.* See **hung up.** —*intr.v.* **1.** To end a telephone conversation by replacing the receiver. **2.** To become halted or snagged. —**be hung up on.** *Informal.* To be obsessed or fixated by.

hang-up, hang·up (hăng′ŭp′) *n. Informal.* **1. a.** A source of irritation or inhibition. **b.** An inhibition or fixation. **2.** An obstacle; an inconvenience.

Hang·zhou (hăng′jō′). Formerly **Hang·chow, Hang·chou** (hăng′chou′, häng′jō′). City in eastern China, the capital of Zhejiang province, at the head of Hangzhou Bay, an inlet of the East China Sea. Before being destroyed by Taiping rebels in 1861, it was renowned for its architecture. It is now a modern industrial city, important for its silk manufacture.

hank (hăngk) *n.* **1.** A coil or loop. **2.** *Nautical.* A ring on a stay attached to the head of a jib or staysail. **3.** A looped bundle, as of yarn. **4.** A length of yarn (768 meters; 840 yards) or fabric (512 meters; 560 yards). [Middle English, from Scandinavian; akin to Old Norse *hönk*†, hank, skein.]

han·ker (hăng′kər) *intr.v.* **-kered, -kering, -kers.** To have a longing; crave. Often followed by *after* or *for.* —See Synonyms at **yearn**. [Akin to dialectal *hank*, probably from Dutch (dialectal) *hankeren*.] —**han·ker·er** *n.*

han·ky, han·kie (hăng′kē) *n., pl.* **hankies.** *Informal.* A handkerchief (sense 1).

han·ky-pan·ky (hăng′kē-păng′kē) *n. Informal.* **1.** Devious or mischievous activity. **2.** Foolish talk or action. [Fanciful coinage, influenced by HOCUS-POCUS.]

Han·ni·bal (hăn′ə-bəl) (247–183 B.C.). Carthaginian soldier and statesman, the son of Hamilcar Barca. Hannibal crossed the Alps in 218 with about 35,000 men and 37 elephants and routed Roman armies at Trasimene and Cannae. He lacked the resources to attack Rome itself and was recalled to Africa in 203 to defend Carthage against an invasion by Scipio Africanus. Hannibal was defeated at Zama (202).

Han·no (hăn′ō), known as "the Great" (*fl.* 3rd century B.C.). Cartha-

ginian political leader. During the Second Punic War (218–201), he was opposed to Hamilcar Barca's and Hannibal's policy of foreign conquest. He eroded Hannibal's homeland support and after Hannibal's defeat negotiated a peace treaty with the Romans.

Han·no·ver (hä-nō′vər). *English* **Han·o·ver** (hăn′ō′vər). Capital city of Lower Saxony in northern Germany, on the Leine River. It is an industrial and commercial center and the site of an important annual industrial fair.

Ha·noi (hä-noi′, hă-). Capital of Vietnam, on the right bank of the Song Hong (Red River), in northern Vietnam. It is the country's major industrial city.

Han·o·ver (hăn′ō′vər). **1.** The family name of an electoral house of Germany (1692–1815). **2.** The family name of the royal family of Britain and Ireland (1714–1901).

Han·o·ve·ri·an (hăn′ō-vîr′ē-ən) *adj.* Of or pertaining to the city of Hannover or the electoral house or royal family of Hanover.
~*n.* A heavy, strong horse of a breed developed by crossing German horses with Thoroughbreds.

Han·sard (hăn′sərd) *n. British & Canadian.* **1.** The official verbatim report of the proceedings and debates of Parliament. **2.** A similar report of the proceedings of various other legislative bodies. [After its first printer, Luke *Hansard* (1752–1828).]

hanse (hăns) *n.* **1. a.** A medieval merchant guild or trade association. **b.** The entrance fee to such a guild. **2. Hanse.** A town belonging to the Hanseatic League. Also called "Hanse town." **3. Hanse.** *Rare.* The Hanseatic League. [Middle English *hans*, from Old French *hanse*, from Middle Low German *hanse*, from Old High German *hansa*, troop, company, from Germanic *khansō* (unattested).] —**han·se·at·ic** (hăn′sē-ăt′ĭk) *adj.*

Han·se·at·ic League (hăn′sē-ăt′ĭk). A protective and commercial association of free towns in northern Germany and neighboring areas, formally organized in 1358 and dissolved in the 17th century.

hansel. Variant of **handsel**.

Han·sen's disease (hăn′sənz) *n.* **Leprosy** (see). [After G.H.A. *Hansen* (1841–1912), Norwegian physician who discovered the bacillus that causes leprosy.]

han·som (hăn′səm) *n.* A two-wheeled covered carriage with the driver's seat above and behind. Also called "hansom cab." [After Joseph A. *Hansom* (1803–82), English architect who designed it.]

Hants. See **Hampshire**.

Hanukah, Hanukkah. Variants of **Chanukah**.

han·u·man (hŭn′ə-män′, hä′nə-) *n., pl.* **-mans.** A monkey, *Presbytis entellus*, of southern Asia, having bristly hairs on the crown and the sides of the face. [Hindi, from Sanskrit *hanumant*, "having jaws," from *hanu*, jaw.]

hao. Variant of **chao**. [Vietnamese.]

hap (hăp) *n. Archaic.* **1.** Fortune; chance. **2.** A happening; an occurrence.
~*intr.v.* **happed, happing, haps.** *Archaic.* To happen. [Middle English, from Old Norse *happ*, good luck, chance.]

ha·pax le·go·me·non (hă′păks′ lə-gŏm′ə-nŏn′) *n., pl.* **hapax legomena** (-ə-nə). A word or form that occurs only once in the recorded corpus of a given language. Often shortened to "hapax." [Greek, "a thing said only once."]

ha'penny. Variant of **halfpenny**.

hap·haz·ard (hăp-hăz′ərd) *adj.* **1.** Dependent upon or characterized by mere chance. **2.** Slipshod; untidy. —See Synonyms at **chance**.
~*n.* Mere chance; fortuity.
~*adv.* Casually; by chance. [HAP + HAZARD.] —**hap·haz·ard·ly** *adv.* —**hap·haz·ard·ness** *n.*

Haph·ta·rah, Haf·ta·rah (häf′tə-rä′, häf-tôr′ə) *n., pl.* **-taroth** (-tə-rōt′, -rōs′, -tôr′ōt′, -ōs′). *Judaism.* A reading selected from the Prophets, read in the synagogue service on the Sabbath. [Mishnaic Hebrew *haphṭārāh*, "conclusion," from *haphṭēr*, to conclude, discard, dismiss, from Hebrew *pāṭar*, separated, discharged.]

hap·less (hăp′lĭs) *adj.* Luckless; unfortunate.

haplite. Variant of **aplite**.

hap·log·ra·phy (hăp-lŏg′rə-fē) *n.* The shortening of the spelling of a word by the omission of a letter or syllable that should be repeated, as the spelling *deteriate* for *deteriorate*. [Greek *haplos*, single, simple (see **haploid**) + -GRAPHY.]

hap·loid (hăp′loid′) *adj. Genetics.* Having the number of chromosomes present in the normal germ cell equal to half the number in the normal somatic cell. Compare **diploid**.
~*n.* A haploid individual or cell. [Greek *haploeidēs*, single : *haplo(u)s*, single, simple : *ha-*, one + *-plo(u)s*, -fold + -OID.]

hap·loi·dy (hăp′loi′dē) *n. Genetics.* The state or condition of being haploid.

hap·lol·o·gy (hăp-lŏl′ə-jē) *n.* The shortening of a word by the omission of a sound or syllable in its pronunciation. [Greek *haplos*, single, simple (see **haploid**) + -LOGY.]

hap·lont (hăp′lŏnt′) *n. Biology.* A haploid organism representing the vegetative phase of the life cycle of certain algae in which only the zygote is diploid. [HAPL(OID) + -ONT.]

hap·lo·sis (hăp-lō′sĭs) *n. Genetics.* Reduction of the diploid number of chromosomes by one half to the haploid number by meiosis. [New Latin : Greek *haplos*, single, simple (see **haploid**) + -OSIS.]

hap·ly (hăp′lē) *adv. Archaic.* **1.** By chance or accident. **2.** Perhaps.

ha'porth (hā′pərth) *n. British Informal.* A creature. Used in phrases like *you daft ha'porth.* [From *halfpennyworth*.]

hap·pen (hăp′ən) *intr.v.* **-pened, -pening, -pens.** **1.** To come to pass; come into being; take place. **2.** To befall or affect one. Used with *to: What happened to you?* **3. a.** To be the case by chance: *It*

hang glider *The hang glider was originally called a Rogallo wing, after its designer, who worked for the National Aeronautics and Space Administration (NASA). The pilot controls the glider with his own weight, moving himself against the fixed trapeze he holds to make the wing dive, climb, or turn.*

happens that I used to live out there. **b.** To chance: *She happened to be in.* **4.** To come upon someone or something by chance. Used with *on* or *upon.* —**happen by.** To appear by chance; turn up. [Middle English *happenen,* from HAP.]
    Synonyms: *befall, betide, chance, occur, supervene.*
hap·pen·ing (hăp′ə-nĭng) *n.* **1.** An event. **2.** An improvised spectacle or performance. —See Synonyms at **occurrence.**
hap·pen·stance (hăp′ən-stăns′) *n.* Also **hap·pen·chance** (-chăns′, -chäns′). A chance circumstance. [HAPPEN + (CIRCUM)STANCE.]
hap·py (hăp′ē) *adj.* **-pier, -piest. 1.** Characterized by good luck; fortunate. **2. a.** Having, taking, or demonstrating pleasure or satisfaction; glad. **b.** Giving or causing pleasure or satisfaction: *a happy day.* **3.** Well-adapted; appropriate; felicitous: *a happy turn of phrase.* **4. a.** Characterized by a spontaneous or obsessive inclination to use something. Used in combination: *trigger-happy.* **b.** Enthusiastic about or involved with to a disproportionate degree. Used in combination: *money-happy.* —See Synonyms at **fit, glad.** [Middle English, from HAP.] —**hap·pi·ly** *adv.* —**hap·pi·ness** *n.*
hap·py-go-luck·y (hăp′ē-gō-lŭk′ē) *adj.* Taking things easily; trusting to luck; carefree.
happy hour *n.* A period of time, usually in the early evening, when drinks are served at reduced prices in bars or hotels.
happy hunting ground *n.* **1.** *Sometimes* **happy hunting grounds.** In North American Indian mythology, heaven or paradise. **2.** *Informal.* Any place or situation offering a plentiful supply of a particularly sought-after item or commodity: *Junk shops are a happy hunting ground for collectors of antiques.*
Haps·burg or **Habs·burg** (hăps′bûrg′, häps′bŏŏrg′). The dominant royal house in Europe from the late Middle Ages until the 20th century. The family name came from the castle of Hapsburg, built (1028) on the Aar River, Switzerland, by Werner I, bishop of Strasbourg. The Hapsburgs reached the height of their power in the 16th century under Charles V when Spain, with her European and American territories, was added to the family's possessions, creating a vast and unwieldy domain. Charles abdicated in 1558, dividing his empire between the two Hapsburg lines of Spain and Austria. The Spanish branch ceased to rule after 1700. In the 19th century the Napoleonic wars and Prussian and Italian nationalism weakened the Hapsburgs' grip on central Europe. The Hapsburg-ruled Austro-Hungarian Empire finally disintegrated after World War I.
hap·ten (hăp′tĕn′) *n.* Also **hap·tene** (-tēn′). *Biology.* An antigen that is incomplete and cannot by itself cause antibody formation but can neutralize specific antibodies when combined with one of the body's proteins. [German *Hapten* : Greek *haptein,* to fasten + -ENE.]
hap·ter·on (hăp′tə-rŏn′) *n., pl.* **-tera** (-tər-ə). The tissue in certain algae, especially the large seaweeds, that serves to attach the plant to a substrate. [From Greek *haptein,* to fasten.]
hap·tic (hăp′tĭk) *adj.* Of or pertaining to the sense of touch. [Greek *haptikos,* able to touch, from *haptein,* to touch, fasten.]
hap·to·nas·ty (hăp′tə-năs′tē) *n.* Movement of a plant part in response to touch, seen particularly in the leaves of insectivorous plants. [Greek *haptein,* to touch + -NASTY.]
hap·tot·ro·pism (hăp-tŏt′rə-pĭz′əm) *n.* *Biology.* Thigmotropism *(see).* [Greek *haptein,* to touch + TROPISM.]
ha·ra-ki·ri (här′ə-kîr′ē) *n.* Ritual suicide by disembowelment as formerly practiced by the Japanese upper classes when disgraced or under sentence of death, and still occasionally practiced today. Also called "seppuku." [Japanese.]
ha·rangue (hə-răng′) *n.* **1.** A long, pompous speech, especially one delivered before a gathering. **2.** A speech characterized by strong feeling or vehement expression; a tirade.
~v. **harangued, -ranguing, -rangued.** —*tr.* To deliver a harangue to. —*intr.* To deliver a harangue. [Middle English *arang,* from Old French *arenge, harangue,* from Medieval Latin *harenga,* perhaps from Germanic.] —**ha·rangu·er** *n.*
Ha·rap·pa (hə-răp′ə). Archaeological site of the Indus Valley civilization (c. 2500–1500 B.C.) in the Punjab, Pakistan. It has the remains of a well-laid-out city.
Ha·ra·re (hə-rä′rā). Formerly **Salis·bur·y** (sôlz′bĕr′ē, -brē). Capital and largest city of Zimbabwe, situated on the Mashonaland plateau in the northeast of the country. Founded in 1890, it has two cathedrals and a university (1970). Harare is an important tobacco-marketing center, and its manufactured products include processed food and tobacco, textiles and clothing, steel, chemicals, and furniture.
har·ass (hăr′əs, hə-răs′) *tr.v.* **-assed, -assing, -asses. 1.** To disturb or irritate persistently. **2.** To wear out; exhaust. **3.** To enervate (an enemy) by repeated attacks or raids. [French *harasser,* from Old French *harer,* to set a dog on, from *hare,* cry used to set a dog on, perhaps from Old High German *harên,* to call.] —**har·ass·er** *n.* —**har·ass·ment** *n.*
    Synonyms: *badger, bait, hound, pester, plague, torment.*
Har·bin (här′bĭn). Also **Ha·erh·pin** (hä′ĕr′bĭn′). *Russian* **Khar·bin** (här-bĭn′, kär-). Capital of Heilongjiang province, northeastern China. Situated on the Songhua Jiang (Sungari River), it grew with the granting of a trade concession to Russia (1896). An important port and railroad junction, it is part of the Manchurian industrial region.
har·bin·ger (här′bĭn-jər) *n.* One that signals an approach; a forerunner: *"in a few minutes would appear the train's harbinger . . . a puff of white smoke"* (Vladimir Nabokov).

~tr.v. **harbingered, -gering, -gers.** To signal the approach of; presage. [Middle English *harbergere,* from Norman French and Old French, from *herbergier,* to provide lodging for, from *herberge,* lodging, from Old Saxon *heriberga,* lodging : *heri,* army + *berg-* (unattested), to protect.]
har·bor (här′bər) *n.* Also *chiefly British* **har·bour.** *Abbr.* **h., H. 1.** A sheltered part of a body of water deep enough to provide anchorage for ships; a port. **2.** Any protected place; a shelter; a refuge.
~v. **harbored, -boring, -bors.** Also *chiefly British* **har·bour, -boured, -bouring, -bours.** —*tr.* **1.** To give shelter to; protect; keep. **2.** To entertain or nourish (a thought or feeling). —*intr.* To shelter in or as if in a harbor. [Middle English *herberge, herber,* late Old English *hereborg.* See **harbinger.**] —**har·bor·er** *n.*
har·bor·age (här′bər-ĭj) *n.* **1.** Shelter and anchorage for ships. **2.** Shelter; refuge. **3.** A place of shelter.
har·bor·mas·ter (här′bər-măs′tər, -mä′stər) *n.* An officer who oversees and enforces the regulations of a harbor.
harbor seal *n.* A hair seal, *Phoca vitulina,* of coastal waters of the Northern Hemisphere, having a spotted coat.
hard (härd) *adj.* **harder, hardest.** *Abbr.* **h., H. 1.** Resistant to pressure; not readily penetrated; firm; rigid. **2.** Physically toughened; rugged: *hard feet.* **3.** Strong-minded; not influenced by emotional considerations. **4.** Rigorous; stringent; demanding. **5.** Mentally and emotionally toughened; unfeeling. **6.** Characterized by an unwillingness to compromise or negotiate. **7.** Intense; forceful. **8.** Keen; penetrating. **9.** Assiduous; diligent; energetic: *a hard worker.* **10.** Difficult to accomplish, finish, or continue; strenuous; arduous. **11.** Difficult to understand, express, or convey; abstruse. **12.** Difficult to endure. **13.** Cruel; oppressive; unjust. **14.** Bitter; rancorous; harsh: *hard feelings.* **15.** Unpleasant because too bright, loud, or harsh: *a hard voice.* **16.** Uncompromisingly adhering to the principles of a specified political alignment: *on the hard left of the party.* **17.** Metallic, as opposed to paper. Said of money: *hard money.* **18. a.** Backed by bullion and having a stable exchange rate. Said of a currency. **b.** Being legal tender: *hard cash.* **19.** Demonstrably true: *hard facts.* **20.** Durable: *hard merchandise.* **21.** Consisting of rigid boards, usually covered with cloth, leather, or the like. Said of the binding of a book. **22.** Having a high alcoholic content; intoxicating. **23.** Containing dissolved salts, as salts, that interfere with the lathering action of soap. Said of water. **24.** *Phonetics.* **a.** Pronounced as a stop, as the *c* in *cake* and the *g* in *log.* **b.** Voiceless. Said of consonants. **c.** Not palatalized. Said of consonants in Slavic languages. **25.** *Physics.* Of relatively high energy; penetrating: *hard x-rays.* **26.** High in gluten content: *hard wheat.* **27.** Physically addictive: *hard drugs.* —**be hard on. 1.** To be unpleasant and difficult for. **2.** To deal with severely; be harsh with. —**hard up.** *Informal.* In need; poor.
~adv. **1.** Energetically; vigorously: *drink hard.* **2.** Intently; earnestly; persistently: *think hard.* **3.** With intensity or force. **4.** With difficulty; strenuously: *a fight hard won.* **5.** Close; near. Used with *by* or *upon.* **6.** Reluctantly: *die hard.* **7.** Toward or into a solid condition: *The cement will set hard within a day.* **8. a.** As much as possible: *Turn hard right.* **b.** *Nautical.* Completely; fully: *hard alee.* —**be hard put.** To have a good deal of difficulty in doing. —**go hard with.** To cause pain or distress to; gall: *This news will go hard with him.* —**hard at it.** Working busily. —**hard put.** Only just able: *She is hard put to make ends meet.*
~n. **1.** *British Slang.* Hard labor. **2.** *British.* A firm beach or foreshore. [Middle English *hard,* Old English *hard, heard.*]
    Synonyms: *arduous, difficult, intricate, troublesome.*
hard-and-fast (härd′ən-fäst′, -fäst′) *adj.* Rigidly applied; inflexible; allowing of no exceptions: *a hard-and-fast rule.*
hard·back (härd′băk′) *adj.* Having a binding or cover of rigid boards, usually covered with cloth, leather, or the like. Said of books. Also "hardbound," "hardcover."
~n. A hardback book.
hard·bake (härd′bāk′) *n.* *British.* Almond toffee.
hard·ball (härd′bôl′) *n.* **1.** Baseball. **2.** *Informal.* The use of any means, however ruthless, to attain an objective.
hard-bit·ten (härd′bĭt′n) *adj.* Toughened by experience; unsentimental.
hard·board (härd′bôrd′, -bōrd′) *n.* Thin wooden board manufactured from compressed wood pulp and sawdust.
hard-boiled (härd′boild′) *adj.* **1.** Cooked by boiling to a solid consistency. Said of an egg. **2.** *Informal.* **a.** Callous; unfeeling. **b.** Having no illusions; unromantic; cynical.
hard case *n.* **1.** A tough, unsentimental person. **2.** *British Informal.* A person who is persistently insolent or difficult to control.
hard cheese *n.* *British Informal.* Bad luck. Used interjectionally to express sympathy, sometimes ironically, at another's misfortune.
hard cider *n.* Fermented cider. Compare **sweet cider.**
hard coal *n.* Anthracite *(see).*
hard copy *n.* Material, as a computer printout, that may be read by the human eye, as distinguished from electronically stored data.
hard core *n.* **1.** The durable and resistant central part of a given entity; especially, the most intractable or die-hard nucleus of a group or organization: *the hard core of the secession movement.* **2.** A material used in constructing foundations for buildings, roads, and the like, consisting of broken bricks, stones, and other hard debris. **3.** *Informal.* Hard-core pornography.
hard-core, hard-core (härd′kôr′, -kōr′) *adj.* **1.** Stubbornly resistant or inveterate: *the hard-core criminal element.* **2.** Held to constitute an intractable social problem: *hard-core poverty.* **3.** Sexually very

explicit and often dealing with sexual practices regarded as deviant: *hard-core pornography.*

hard court *n.* A tennis court with a hard surface, such as asphalt or concrete, rather than grass.

hard·cov·er (härd′kŭv′ər) *n. & adj.* **Hardback** (see).

Har·de·ca·nute (här′də-kə-nōōt′, -nyōōt′) (*c.* 1019–42). King of England (1040–42) and of Denmark (1035–42); the legitimate son of King Canute. His English throne was seized by Canute's illegitimate son, Harold I Harefoot. In 1040 Hardecanute claimed his throne after the usurper died.

hard-edge (härd′ĕj′) *n.* A style of abstract painting characterized by the sharp delineation of brightly colored geometric forms. —**hard-edge** *adj.*

hard·en (härd′n) *v.* **-ened, -ening, -ens.** —*tr.* **1.** To make firm or firmer; make solid or hard. **2.** To toughen mentally or physically; make rugged; inure. **3.** To make unfeeling or emotionally barren. **4.** To strengthen: *It hardened their opposition to the plan.* —*intr.* **1.** To become hard or hardened; set; fix; firm; freeze. **2.** *Economics.* **a.** To rise. Used of prices. **b.** To become stable. **3.** To become inured: *"But poor boys either harden early or are destroyed"* (T.H. White). —**harden off. 1.** To make (a cultivated plant) able to withstand outdoor conditions by gradually increasing exposure to a cold atmosphere. **2.** To become accustomed to outdoor conditions in this way. Used of plants. [Middle English, from HARD.]

hard·en·er (härd′n-ər) *n.* **1.** One that hardens. **2.** A substance added to varnish or paint to give a harder surface or finish. **3.** A substance added to certain glues to cause or hasten setting.

hard·en·ing (härd′n-ĭng) *n.* **1.** The act or process of becoming hard or harder. **2.** Something that hardens, such as a substance added to iron to yield steel.

hardening of the arteries *n.* **Arteriosclerosis** (see).

hard-fea·tured (härd′fē′chərd) *adj.* Having sharp or harsh features. Also *archaic* "hard-favored."

hard-fist·ed (härd′fĭs′tĭd) *adj.* Tightfisted; stingy; niggardly. —**hard-fist·ed·ness** *n.*

hard·hack (härd′hăk′) *n.* A woody plant, *Spiraea tomentosa,* of eastern North America, having leaves with rusty down on the undersides and spirelike clusters of small, rose-pink flowers. Also called "steeplebush." [HARD + HACK (cut).]

hard-hand·ed (härd′hăn′dĭd) *adj.* **1.** Having hands calloused or hardened by work. **2.** Heavy-handed; oppressive; tyrannical. —**hard-hand·ed·ness** *n.*

hard hat *n.* **1.** A lightweight protective helmet, usually of metal or reinforced plastic, worn by construction workers. **2.** *Informal.* A construction worker. **3.** *Informal.* A person with conservative or reactionary views; an ultraconservative. **4.** *Slang.* An extremely patriotic person.

hard-hat (härd′hăt′) *adj.* **1.** Designating an area on a building site where hard hats must be worn. **2.** Characterized by conservative or reactionary views. **3.** *Slang.* Extremely conservative.

hard·head (härd′hĕd′) *n., pl.* **-heads** or collectively **hardhead** (for sense 3). **1.** A shrewd and tough person. **2.** A stubborn, unmovable person. **3.** Any of several fishes having a bony head, especially a common croaker, *Micropogon undulatus,* of Atlantic waters.

hard·head·ed (härd′hĕd′ĭd) *adj.* **1.** Realistic; concerned with practical matters. **2.** Stubborn; willful. —**hard·head·ed·ly** *adv.* —**hard·head·ed·ness** *n.*

hard·heads (härd′hĕdz′) *n. Used with a singular verb.* A European plant, *Centaurea nigra,* with reddish-purple, thistlelike flowers.

hard-heart·ed (härd′här′tĭd) *adj.* Lacking in feeling, compassion, or sympathy; cold; pitiless. —**hard-heart·ed·ly** *adv.* —**hard-heart·ed·ness** *n.*

hard-hit (härd′hĭt′) *adj.* Badly or adversely affected.

hard-hit·ting (härd′hĭt′ĭng) *adj.* Effective; forceful.

har·di·hood (här′dē-hōōd′) *n.* **1.** Boldness and daring; audacity. **2.** Self-assured impudence or insolence.

Har·ding (här′dĭng), **Warren Gamaliel** (1865–1923). 29th U.S. president. An Ohio newspaperman turned politician, he moved from state politics to the U.S. Senate in 1914. Elected president in 1920, he made several misguided appointments that led to a corrupt administration. He died in San Francisco while on a national tour.

hard labor *n.* Compulsory physical labor imposed on convicted criminals.

hard landing *n.* The landing by impact of a spacecraft lacking devices such as retrorockets to slow it down.

hard line *n.* A firm, uncompromising policy, position, or stance.

hard-line (härd′līn′) *adj.* Characterized by a firm, uncompromising position or stance: *a hard-line foreign policy.* —**hard-lin·er** *n.*

hard·ly (härd′lē) *adv.* **1.** Barely; scarcely; just. **2.** To an almost negligible degree; almost not: *He could hardly make himself heard.* **3.** Probably not or almost surely not. **4.** Not in the prevailing circumstances: *I could hardly refuse.* **5.** Harshly. **6.** With difficulty. [Middle English *hardli,* boldly, hardily, Old English *h(e)ardlīce :* HARD + -LY.]

Usage: Hardly has the force of a negative; therefore it is not used with another negative in standard English: *I could hardly see. I had hardly left.* Constructions such as *I couldn't hardly see* or *without hardly seeing* are often heard in colloquial speech but are not acceptable in formal speech or writing. Following clauses are introduced by *when* or *before: He had hardly left when/before the fire broke out.* The use of *than* or *until* in such constructions is not acceptable in standard English.

hard maple *n.* A tree, the **sugar maple** (see).

hard-mouthed (härd′mouthd′, -mou*th*d′) *adj.* **1.** Not easily controlled by the bit. Said of a horse. **2.** Obstinate.

hard·ness (härd′nĭs) *n. Abbr.* **h., H. 1.** The quality or condition of being hard. **2.** The relative resistance of a mineral to scratching, as measured by the **Mohs scale** (see). **3.** The relative resistance of a metal to denting, scratching, or bending.

hard news *n.* News, as in a newspaper or television report, that deals with formal or serious topics and events.

hard-nosed (härd′nōzd′) *adj. Informal.* Hard-headed; tough-minded; practical: *a hard-nosed politician.*

hard of hearing *adj.* Deaf or slightly deaf.

hard pad *n.* A form of distemper in dogs.

hard palate *n.* The relatively hard, bony front part of the **palate** (see).

hard·pan (härd′păn′) *n.* **1.** A layer of hard subsoil or clay. **2.** Hard, unbroken ground. See **caliche. 3.** A foundation; bedrock.

hard-pressed (härd′prĕst′) *adj.* **1.** Closely pursued. **2.** Constantly troubled by harassment, economic difficulties, or the like. **3.** Barely able: *We'd be hard-pressed to find the time.*

hard rock *n.* A style of rock music characterized by an insistent beat and high volume.

hard rubber *n.* A relatively inelastic rubber made by vulcanization with 30 to 50 percent sulfur and usually some lime or magnesia as a filler.

hards (härdz) *n. Used with a singular verb.* The coarse refuse of flax or similar fiber. [Middle English *herdes, hurdes,* Old English *heordan* (plural).]

hard sauce *n.* A creamy sauce of butter and sugar with rum, brandy, or vanilla flavoring, served chilled with puddings, gingerbread, or fruitcakes.

hard·scrab·ble (härd′skrăb′əl) *adj.* Earning a bare subsistence, as on the land: *the sharecropper's hardscrabble life.* ~*n.* Barren or marginal farmland.

hard sell *n. Informal.* Aggressive, high-pressure selling or promotion. Compare **soft sell.**

hard-shell (härd′shĕl′) *adj.* Also **hard-shelled** (-shĕld′). **1.** Having a thick, heavy, or hardened shell. **2.** Unyieldingly orthodox; uncompromising; confirmed. ~*n.* A hard-shell clam or crab.

hard-shell clam *n.* The **quahog** (see).

hard-shell crab *n.* A marine crab with a fully hardened shell; especially, the edible species, *Cancer pagurus,* in this stage.

hard·ship (härd′shĭp′) *n.* **1.** Suffering or difficulty; adversity. **2.** A source or cause of privation or difficulty.

hard shoulder *n. British.* A reinforced or concreted strip at the side of a roadway on which vehicles may drive and stop only in emergencies.

hard-spun (härd′spŭn′) *adj.* Twisted tightly in spinning, often to the point of curling and looping. Said of yarn.

hard·stand (härd′stănd′) *n.* A hard-surfaced area, usually adjacent to an airstrip, for parking aircraft or ground vehicles.

hard·tack (härd′tăk′) *n.* A hard biscuit or bread made only with flour and water and formerly eaten by sailors. Also called "pilot bread," "sea biscuit," "sea bread," "ship's biscuit." [HARD + TACK (food).]

hard·top (härd′tŏp′) *n.* A car, often designed to resemble a convertible, having a fixed or detachable hard roof. —**hard·top** *adj.*

hard·ware (härd′wâr′) *n.* **1.** Metal goods and utensils such as locks, tools, and cutlery. **2. a.** A computer and the associated physical equipment directly involved in the performance of communications or data-processing functions. Compare **software, firmware. b.** Broadly, machines and other physical equipment directly involved in performing an industrial, technological, or military function. **3.** *Informal.* Heavy military weapons and equipment. **4.** *Informal.* Firearms; weapons.

hard water *n.* Water containing dissolved salts of calcium and magnesium; especially, water containing more than 85.5 parts per million of calcium carbonate. Compare **soft water.**

hard-wired (härd′wīrd′) *adj. Computer Science.* Designating or employing permanently wired circuits or components that are capable of logical decisions: *a hard-wired terminal.*

hard·wood (härd′wōōd′) *n.* **1.** The wood of a broad-leaved flowering tree as distinguished from that of a conifer. **2.** A broad-leaved flowering tree. Compare **softwood.**

har·dy¹ (här′dē) *adj.* **-dier, -diest. 1.** Robust; rugged; strong: *"a rude and hardy race, that lived mostly out of doors"* (Henry Thoreau). **2.** Courageous; intrepid; stouthearted. **3.** Brazenly daring; audacious; hotheaded. **4.** Capable of surviving unfavorable conditions such as cold weather or lack of moisture. Said chiefly of cultivated plants. —See Synonyms at **healthy.** [Middle English *hardy, hardi,* from Old French *hardi,* from the past participle of *hardir,* to become bold, make hard, from Germanic.] —**har·di·ly** *adv.* —**har·di·ness** *n.*

hardy² *n., pl.* **-dies.** A square-shanked chisel that fits into a square hole in an anvil. [Probably from HARD.]

Hardy, Oliver. See **Laurel and Hardy.**

Har·dy (här′dē), **Thomas** (1840–1928). British novelist and poet. A builder's son, he started his career as an architect and published his first short story in 1865. His Wessex novels, set in the southwest of England, include *Far from the Madding Crowd* (1874), *The Mayor of Casterbridge* (1886), *Tess of the d'Urbervilles* (1891), and *Jude the Obscure* (1896).

hardy hole *n.* The square hole in an anvil for inserting a hardy.

hardheads *Named for its knobby flower heads, this plant was formerly used by herbalists as an astringent. Its genus name,* Centaurea, *comes from the belief that Chiron, a centaur in Greek mythology, used the plant to heal wounds. Pictured above is* Centaurea nigra, *or black knapweed.*

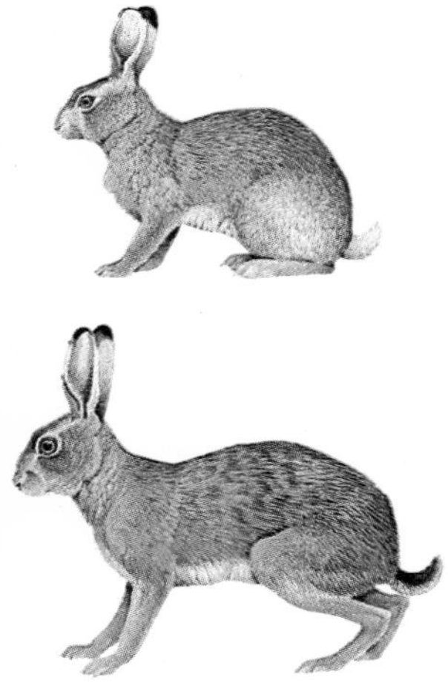

hare *The mad hares of March are male hares that stand on their hind legs and box each other to impress females during the mating season. The hare,* Lepus timidus *(above), is found in parts of northern Europe, Asia, and North America. The larger brown hare,* Lepus capensis *(bottom), is common in many parts of Africa and Asia.*

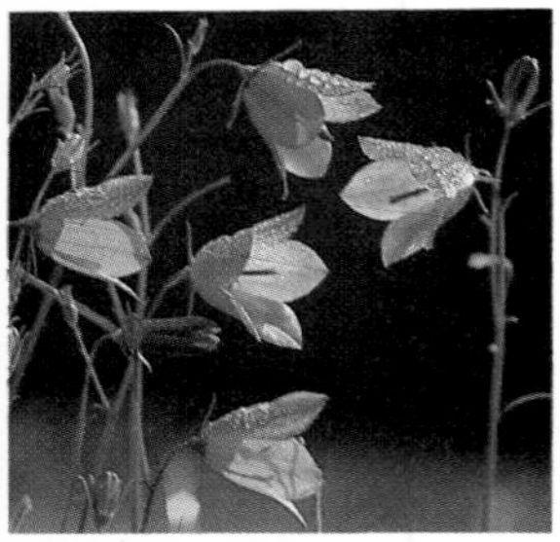

harebell *A member of the Campanulaceae family of bluebells and bellflowers, the harebell grows in dry, grassy places.*

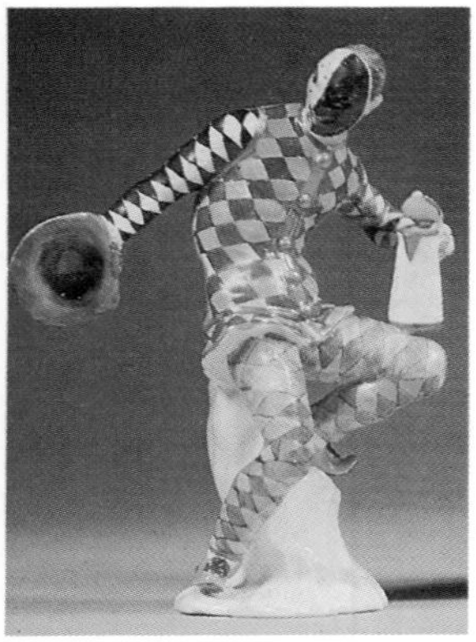

harlequin *A Meissen ceramic from about 1738. Harlequin began as a clownish peasant servant in the early Italian commedia dell'arte and survives in English pantomime today. He is amorous, yet faithful; he is clever, but credulous, because he is without guile. He gets out of trouble by means of his wit and his feline physical grace.*

hare (hâr) *n.* Any of various mammals of the family Leporidae, and especially of the genus *Lepus,* related to and resembling the rabbits but having longer ears, large hind feet, and long legs adapted for jumping. **—start** (or **raise**) **a hare.** *British.* To raise a matter for discussion.
∼intr.v. **hared, haring, hares.** To run quickly: *He hared down the corridor.* [Middle English *hare,* Old English *hara,* from Germanic.]

hare and hounds *n.* A game in which one group of players leaves a trail of paper scraps for a pursuing group to follow.

hare·bell (hâr′bĕl′) *n.* A plant, *Campanula rotundifolia,* having slender stems and leaves and bell-shaped blue flowers. Also called "bluebell." [Middle English : HARE (perhaps because it grows in places frequented by hares) + BELL.]

hare·brained (hâr′brānd′) *adj.* Foolish; ill-considered: *harebrained schemes.*

Ha·re Krish·na (hä′rē krĭsh′nə, hăr′ē) *n.* A member of the International Society for Krishna Consciousness, a sect practicing a form of Hinduism dedicated to Krishna. [Hindi *hare,* invocation of God + *Krishna,* Krishna.]

hare·lip (hâr′lĭp′) *n.* A congenital fissure or pair of fissures in the upper lip, often associated with a cleft palate. **—hare·lipped** *adj.*

har·em (hâr′əm, hăr′-) *n.* **1.** A house or a section of a house reserved for women members of a Muslim household. **2.** The women occupying a harem; the wives, concubines, female relatives, and servants of a Muslim household. **3.** The wives and concubines collectively of a Muslim man, especially a wealthy one. **4.** A number of female animals, such as seals, that are the mates of a single male. [Arabic *ḥarīm,* sacred, forbidden place, from *ḥarama,* he prohibited.]

hare's-foot (hârz′fo͝ot′) *n.* A Eurasian plant, *Trifolium arvense,* having white or pink downy cloverlike flowers. Also called "hare's-foot clover."

Har·greaves (här′grēvz′), **James** (died 1778). British inventor of the spinning jenny (*c.* 1764). A weaver in Blackburn, Lancashire, Hargreaves developed his device to allow one operator to spin several threads at once.

har·i·cot (hăr′ĭ-kō′) *n.* **1.** The edible pod or seed of any of several beans, especially the string bean. **2.** A highly seasoned mutton or lamb stew with vegetables. [French, perhaps from Aztec *ayacotl* or Nahuatl *ayecotli.*]

har·i·jan (hăr′ə-jän′) *n.* A Hindu of the lowest caste; an **untouchable** *(see).* [Sanskrit, one devoted to Vishnu : *Hari,* Vishnu + *jana,* person. The use of the term in its present sense was introduced by Mahatma Gandhi.]

Ha·ri Rud (här′ē ro͞od′). River, *c.* 1,125 kilometers (700 miles) long, rising in central Afghanistan and flowing west and then north into the steppes south of the Kara Kum desert in Turkmenistan. Its lower course forms part of the Afghanistan-Turkmenistan border.

hark (härk) *v.* **harked, harking, harks.** *—intr.* To listen attentively; hearken. Often used with *to.* *—tr. Archaic.* To listen to; hear. **—hark back. 1.** To recall or return to an earlier time or point, as in a narrative or in reminiscing: *always harking back to his childhood.* **2.** To originate in or survive from: *This custom harks back to the Middle Ages.* [Middle English *herk(i)en,* Old English *heorcian* (unattested).]

harken. Variant of **hearken.**

harl[1] (härl) *n.* Filaments or fibers, as of hemp or flax. [Middle English *herle,* fiber, perhaps from Middle Low German *herle, harle*†.]

harl[2] *tr.v.* **harled, harling, harls.** *Scottish.* To roughcast. [Middle English, of obscure origin.]

Har·lem (här′ləm). A residential and business district of New York City, in Upper Manhattan. Though economically depressed, it is an important social and cultural center for black Americans.

har·le·quin (här′lə-kwən, -kən) *n.* **1. Harlequin.** A conventional buffoon of the commedia dell'arte, traditionally presented in a mask and parti-colored tights. **2.** A clown; a buffoon. **3.** A small duck, *Histrionicus histrionicus,* having a short bill and distinctive patterned plumage. In this sense, also called "harlequin duck."
∼adj. Having a pattern of brightly colored diamond shapes like the costume of Harlequin. [Variant (influenced by obsolete French *harlequin*) of earlier *Harlicken, Harlaken,* from Old French *Herlequin, Hellequin,* leader of a troop of demon horsemen riding at night, probably from Old English *Herla cyning,* King *Herla,* a mythical figure who has been identified with Woden.]

har·le·quin·ade (här′lə-kwə-nād′) *n.* **1.** A comedy or pantomime in which Harlequin is the main attraction. **2.** A succession of farcical clownings; buffoonery.

harlequin bug *n.* A flat-bodied, brightly colored insect, *Murgantia histrionica,* that has a fetid odor, and is destructive to cabbage and other plants. Also called "calicoback," "fire bug."

Har·ley Street (här′lē). The London street in or around which many medical specialists have their private offices.

har·lot (här′lət) *n.* A promiscuous woman, especially a prostitute. [Middle English *harlot, herlot,* vagabond, itinerant jester, male servant, prostitute, from Old French *(h)arlot, herlot*†, young fellow, vagabond.] **—har·lot·ry** *n.*

Har·low (här′lō), **Jean,** stage name of Harlean Carpentier (1911–37). U.S. film actress. She won stardom with *Hell's Angels* (1930), in which she appeared as a wise-cracking sex symbol. Her other films include *Platinum Blonde* (1931) and *Bombshell* (1933).

harm (härm) *n.* **1.** Injury or damage, whether physical, psychological, or moral. **2.** Wrong; evil. **—in harm's way.** In danger; in a risky position. **—out of harm's reach** (or **way**). Out of danger; in a safe place.
∼tr.v. **harmed, harming, harms.** To damage; injure; impair. —See Synonyms at **injure.** [Middle English *harm,* Old English *hearm,* from Germanic.]

har·mat·tan (här′mə-tăn′, här-măt′n) *n.* A dry, dusty wind that blows from the Sahara across western Africa. In the humid lands along the Gulf of Guinea its dryness is refreshing. Also called "the Doctor." [Twi *haramata,* probably from Arabic *ḥarām,* a forbidden or accursed thing, from the stem of *ḥarama,* to forbid, akin to *ḥaruma,* to be forbidden. See **harem.**]

harm·ful (härm′fəl) *adj.* Causing or capable of causing harm; damaging; injurious. **—harm·ful·ly** *adv.* **—harm·ful·ness** *n.*

harm·less (härm′lĭs) *adj.* **1.** Not harmful; not capable of harming. **2.** Inoffensive. **—harm·less·ly** *adv.* **—harm·less·ness** *n.*

har·mon·ic (här-mŏn′ĭk) *adj.* **1. a.** Of or pertaining to musical harmony as distinguished from melody or rhythm. **b.** Of or pertaining to harmonics. **2.** Characterized by harmony; concordant. **3. a.** *Mathematics.* Designating a function or series that can be expressed in terms of sines or cosines. **b.** Designating a function that appears in a harmonic series.
∼n. **1.** *Acoustics.* A tone in the harmonic series of overtones produced by a fundamental tone. Also called "overtone," "partial," "partial tone." **2.** A tone produced on a stringed instrument by lightly touching an open or stopped vibrating string at a given fraction of its length so that both segments vibrate. **3.** *Physics.* A wave whose frequency is a whole-number multiple of that of another. [Latin *harmonicus,* from Greek *harmonikos,* from *harmonia,* HARMONY.] **—har·mon·i·cal·ly** *adv.*

har·mon·i·ca (här-mŏn′ĭ-kə) *n.* **1.** A small, rectangular musical instrument consisting of a row of free reeds set back in air holes, played by exhaling or inhaling. Also called "mouth organ." **2.** A **glass harmonica** *(see).* **3.** A musical instrument consisting of tuned strips of metal or glass fixed to a frame and struck with a hammer. [Variant (influenced by HARMONIC) of earlier *armonica,* from Italian, from *armonico,* harmonious, from Latin *harmonicus,* HARMONIC.]

harmonic analysis *n.* The representation of mathematical functions by means of linear operations, such as summation or integration, on characteristic sets of functions; especially, such representation by Fourier series.

harmonic mean *n.* The reciprocal of the arithmetic mean of the reciprocals of a given set of numbers.

harmonic minor scale *n. Music.* A minor scale with the seventh tone raised so that it lies only a semitone below the tonic. Compare **melodic minor scale.**

harmonic motion *n. Physics.* A form of periodic motion in which the displacement is symmetrical about a central point. See **simple harmonic motion.**

harmonic progression *n.* A sequence of quantities the reciprocals of which form an arithmetic progression; for example, $1, 1/3, 1/5, 1/7, \ldots$

har·mon·ics (här-mŏn′ĭks) *n. Used with a singular verb.* The theory or study of the physical properties and characteristics of musical sound.

harmonic series *n.* **1.** *Mathematics.* A series whose terms are in harmonic progression; for example, $1 + 1/3 + 1/5 + 1/7 + \ldots$ **2.** *Acoustics.* A series of tones consisting of a fundamental tone and the overtones produced by it, whose frequencies are consecutive integral multiples of the frequency of the fundamental.

har·mo·ni·ous (här-mō′nē-əs) *adj.* **1.** Exhibiting accord in feeling or action; sympathetic: *a harmonious relationship.* **2.** Having component elements pleasingly or appropriately combined: *a harmonious structure.* **3.** Characterized by harmony of sound; melodious. **—har·mo·ni·ous·ly** *adv.* **—har·mo·ni·ous·ness** *n.*

har·mo·nist (här′mə-nĭst) *n.* **1.** A scholar who collates and seeks to harmonize the discrepancies in parallel passages of text, especially of the Gospels. **2. a.** One skilled in musical harmony. **b.** A composer or performer of music: *"The Ocean is a mighty harmonist"* (William Wordsworth). **3.** One of a school of ancient Greek musical theorists whose principles were based on the subjective effects of notes rather than on the mathematical relations between them. **4.** One who brings into consonance or accord; a harmonizer.

har·mo·nis·tic (här′mə-nĭs′tĭk) *adj.* **1.** Of or relating to harmony. **2.** Of or relating to the harmonizing of parallel passages of text. **—har·mo·nis·ti·cal·ly** *adv.*

har·mo·ni·um (här-mō′nē-əm) *n.* An organlike keyboard instrument that produces notes with free metal reeds vibrated by air forced from a bellows. [French, from *harmonie,* harmony, from Old French *armonie,* HARMONY.]

har·mo·nize (här′mə-nīz′) *v.* **-nized, -nizing, -nizes.** *—tr.* **1.** To bring into agreement or harmony; make harmonious. **2.** To provide harmony for (a melody). *—intr.* **1.** To be in agreement; be harmonious. **2.** To sing or play in harmony. —See Synonyms at **agree.** **—har·mo·niz·er** *n.*

har·mo·ny (här′mə-nē) *n., pl.* **-nies. 1.** Agreement in feeling, approach, action, disposition, or the like; sympathy; accord. **2.** The pleasing interaction or appropriate combination of the elements in a whole. **3.** *Music.* **a.** The study of the structure, progression, and relation of chords. **b.** The simultaneous combination of tones in a chord. **c.** A chord or chords added when writing or playing a melody to provide musical emphasis, background, or substance. **d.** The structure of a musical work or passage as considered from the point of view of its chordal characteristics and relationships. **4.** A combination of musical sounds considered to be pleasing; euphony. **5.** A collation of parallel passages from a text, especially the Gospels, with a commentary demonstrating their consonance and explaining their discrepancies. —See Synonyms at **proportion.** [Middle English *armonie,* from Old French *(h)armonie,* from Latin *harmonia,* from Greek, agreement, harmony, means of joining, from *harmos,* joint.]

har·ness (härʹnĭs) *n.* **1.** The equipment, consisting of straps and sometimes buckles, used by a draft animal to pull a vehicle or implement. **2.** Anything resembling a harness, such as the arrangement of straps used to hold a parachute to the body. **3.** A device that raises and lowers the warp threads on a loom. **4.** *Archaic.* Armor for a man or a horse. —**in harness.** On duty; at work. ~*tr.v.* **harnessed, -nessing, -nesses. 1. a.** To put a harness on (a draft animal). **b.** To attach (a draft animal) to a vehicle or implement by means of a harness. **2.** To bring under control and direct the force of: *If he can harness his energy, he will accomplish a great deal.* **3.** *Archaic.* To fit with armor; arm or equip for battle. [Middle English *harness, harnais,* baggage, equipment, trappings of a horse, from Old French *harneis,* military equipment, from Old Norse *hernest* (unattested), provisions for an army : *herr,* army + *nest,* provisions.] —**harʹness·er** *n.*

harnessed antelope *n.* Any of several African antelopes with markings resembling harness straps, such as the **bushbuck** *(see).*
harness hitch *n.* A type of knot forming a fixed loop in a rope.
harness race *n.* A horse race between pacers or trotters harnessed to sulkies.

Har·old I Hare·foot (härʹəld; hârʹfŏŏt′) (died 1040). Danish king of England (1037–40). He was the illegitimate son of King Canute and became king while Hardecanute, Canute's legitimate son, was preoccupied in Denmark. He died as Hardecanute was preparing to invade England and claim his throne.
Harold II (*c.* 1022–66). King of England (1066), the last of the Anglo-Saxon monarchs. He was the son of Godwin, Earl of Essex, and brother-in-law of Edward the Confessor. Shipwrecked in France (*c.* 1064), he was forced by the Normans to swear to support William of Normandy (William the Conqueror) in any claim on the English Crown. When Edward died in 1066, Harold succeeded him. He defeated the forces of his brother Tostig and Harold III Hardraade at Stamford Bridge, Yorkshire. He then rode south to meet William's Norman invasion and died at the Battle of Hastings (1066).
Harold III Hard·raa·de or **Haard·raa·de** (hôr′rôʹdə) (1015–66). King of Norway (1046–66). In 1066 Hardraade invaded England, supporting Tostig against Harold II, and was killed at the Battle of Stamford Bridge.

harp (härp) *n.* **1.** A musical instrument consisting of an upright open triangular frame with 46 strings of graded lengths that are played by plucking with the fingers. **2.** Something similar to a harp in shape or sound. ~*v.* **harped, harping, harps.** —*intr.* To play a harp. —*tr. Archaic.* To give expression to; utter; refer to. —**harp on** (or **upon**). To talk or write about to an excessive and tedious degree; dwell upon. [Middle English *harp(e),* Old English *hearpe,* from Germanic *harpōn-* (unattested).] —**harpʹer** *n.*
Har·pers Ferry (härʹpərz). A town in eastern West Virginia, at the confluence of the Shenandoah and Potomac rivers. John Brown seized the U.S. arsenal here on October 16, 1859. The town is now a tourist center, with a national historic park and the John Brown Museum.
har·pins (härʹpĭnz) *pl.n.* Also **har·pings** (-pĭngz). **1.** *Nautical.* The wooden supports of a ship under construction. **2.** The timbers used for strengthening the bow of a ship. [Perhaps from HARP.]
harp·ist (härʹpĭst) *n.* A person who plays the harp.
har·poon (här-pōōnʹ) *n.* A spearlike implement having a barbed head and attached rope that is hurled by hand or shot from a gun in hunting whales and large fish. ~*tr.v.* **harpooned, -pooning, -poons.** To strike, kill, or capture with or as if with a harpoon. [French *harpon,* from *harpe,* clamp, dog's claw, from Latin *harpē, harpa,* sickle, from Greek *harpē.*] —**har·poonʹer, har·poon·eer** (här′pōō-nîrʹ) *n.*
harpoon gun *n.* A small cannonlike apparatus used to fire harpoons.
harp seal *n.* An earless seal, *Pagophilus groenlandicus,* found in the North Atlantic and Arctic oceans. [From the harp-shaped marking on its back.]
harp·si·chord (härpʹsĭ-kôrd′, -kōrd′) *n.* A keyboard instrument whose strings are plucked with quill or leather plectrums rather than being struck by hammers. [Obsolete French *harpechorde,* from Italian *arpicordo* : *arpi,* harp, from Late Latin *harpa,* from Germanic *harpōn-* (unattested), HARP + *corda,* string, from Latin *chorda,* from Greek *khordē.*] —**harp·si·chordʹist** *n.*
har·py (härʹpē) *n., pl.* **-pies. 1.** A predatory person. **2.** A shrewish woman. [From HARPY.]
Harpy *n., pl.* **-pies.** *Greek Mythology.* Any of several loathsome, voracious monsters having a woman's head and trunk and a bird's tail, wings, and talons. [French *harpie,* from Latin *harpyia,* from Greek *harpuiai*†, "snatchers."]
harpy eagle *n.* A large eagle of South and Central America, *Harpia harpyja,* with an erectile head crest and mottled gray plumage. [From HARPY.]
har·que·bus (härʹkə-bəs, -kwə-bəs) *n.* Also **ar·que·bus** (är′-). A heavy, portable matchlock gun invented during the 15th century.

Also called "hackbut." [Old French *(h)arquebuse,* from Middle Dutch *hakebusse* : *hake,* hook + *busse,* gun, from Late Latin *buxis,* BOX.]
har·ri·dan (härʹə-dən) *n.* A malicious, scolding woman. [Possibly from French *haridelle*†, gaunt woman.]
har·ri·er¹ (härʹē-ər) *n.* **1.** One that harries. **2.** Any of various slender, narrow-winged hawks of the genus *Circus,* such as *C. pygargus,* Montagu's harrier, that prey on small animals.
harrier² *n.* **1.** A small hound of a breed originally used in hunting hares. **2.** A cross-country runner. [From HARE.]
Har·ri·man (härʹə-mən), **(William) Averell** (1891–1986). U.S. diplomat. He was the son of a rail magnate and became ambassador to the Soviet Union (1943–46) and secretary of commerce (1946–48). He failed in 1956 to win the Democratic presidential nomination. He was governor of New York (1955–59).
Harris. See **Lewis with Harris.**
Har·ris (härʹĭs), **Joel Chandler** (1848–1908). U.S. author and journalist. While working for various Southern newspapers he developed a transcription of black plantation speech that he incorporated into *Uncle Remus: His Songs and His Sayings* (1880) and its many sequels.
Har·ris·burg (härʹĭs-bûrg′, hârʹ-). Capital of Pennsylvania, in the southeastern part of the state, on the Susquehanna River. It is an important railway junction and industrial center.
Har·ri·son (härʹĭ-sən), **Benjamin** (1833–1901). 23rd U.S. President (1889–93). A local politician and Civil War officer, he served in the U.S. Senate (1881–88) and then defeated the incumbent, Grover Cleveland, for the presidency. The Sherman Antitrust Act, the Sherman Silver Purchase Act, and the McKinley Tariff Act (all 1890) were important domestic developments during his administration.
Harrison, George (1943–). British pop musician, formerly lead guitarist with the Beatles. His best-known compositions include *Here Comes the Sun* and *My Sweet Lord.*
Harrison, Rex (1908–90). English actor. A stage and motion-picture performer, he is perhaps best remembered for his portrayal of Professor Henry Higgins in the Broadway musical and film versions of *My Fair Lady,* for which he was awarded a Tony (1956) and an Academy Award (1964).
Harrison, William Henry (1773–1841). Ninth U.S. president (1841). After winning military fame in the Battle of Tippecanoe (1811) and the War of 1812, he served as a U.S. congressman (1816–18) and senator (1819–28) before unsuccessfully running for president in 1836. Four years later he was elected president and during his inaugural address caught a cold, which proved to be fatal thirty days later.
Harris tweed *n.* A trademark for a rough tweed fabric. [After *Harris* in the Outer Hebrides, where it is woven.]
Har·ro·gate (härʹō-gĭt, -gāt′). A residential town in North Yorkshire, England. It has been a spa since 1596 and is a popular vacation resort and retirement area.
har·row¹ (härʹō) *n.* A farm instrument consisting of a heavy frame with teeth or upright disks, used to break up and level plowed ground. ~*tr.v.* **harrowed, -rowing, -rows. 1.** To break up and level (soil or land) with a harrow. **2.** To inflict great distress or torment on the mind of; torment. [Middle English, from Old Norse *herri.*]
harrow² *tr.v.* **-rowed, -rowing, -rows.** *Archaic.* To plunder or harry. [Middle English *harwen,* variant of *harien,* to HARRY.]
Har·row (härʹō). A residential borough of northwest Greater London. It is noted for one of England's most famous public schools, founded in 1571, whose former pupils include Byron, Lord Palmerston, and Sir Winston Churchill.
har·row·ing (härʹō-ĭng) *adj.* Extremely distressing.
har·rumph (hə-rŭmfʹ) *interj.* Used to express skepticism, disapproval, or discontent. ~*v.* **-rumphed, -rumphing, -rumphs.** —*intr.* To express skepticism, disapproval, or discontent by uttering "harrumph." —*tr.* To give vent to or express (skepticism or disapproval, for example) by uttering "harrumph." [Imitative.]
har·ry (härʹē) *tr.v.* **-ried, -rying, -ries. 1.** To raid, as in a war; sack; pillage. **2.** To disturb or annoy by constant attacks; harass. [Middle English *harien, herien,* Old English *hergian,* from Germanic.]
harsh (härsh) *adj.* **harsher, harshest. 1.** Producing an unpleasant sensory response, as: **a.** Coarse in texture; rough: *harsh wool.* **b.** Disagreeable to the ear; grating: *a harsh voice.* **c.** Having a bitter or astringent taste: *cheap, harsh rum.* **d.** Visually jarring: *harsh colors.* **2.** Extremely severe or exacting; stern. —See Synonyms at **burdensome.** [Middle Low German *harsch,* "hairy," rough. See **hair, -ish.**] —**harshʹly** *adv.* —**harshʹness** *n.*
harsh·en (härʹshən) *v.* **-ened, -ening, -ens.** —*tr.* To make harsh. —*intr.* To become harsh.
harslet. Variant of **haslet.**
hart (härt) *n., pl.* **harts** or collectively **hart.** A male deer; especially, a male red deer over five years old. [Middle English *hert,* Old English *heor(o)t,* from Germanic.]
Hart (härt), **Lorenz Milton** (1895–1943). U.S. lyricist. He began collaborating with Richard Rodgers in 1919, and together they produced such memorable hits as "Manhattan," "Blue Moon," and "The Lady is a Tramp" and popular musicals that included *A Connecticut Yankee* (1927), *The Boys from Syracuse* (1938), and *Pal Joey* (1940).
Hart, Moss (1904–61). U.S. dramatist and librettist. He wrote Broadway hit comedies with George S. Kaufman, including *Once in*

harpy eagle *The harpy eagle of South and Central America eats monkeys, sloths, and peccaries (wild pigs).*

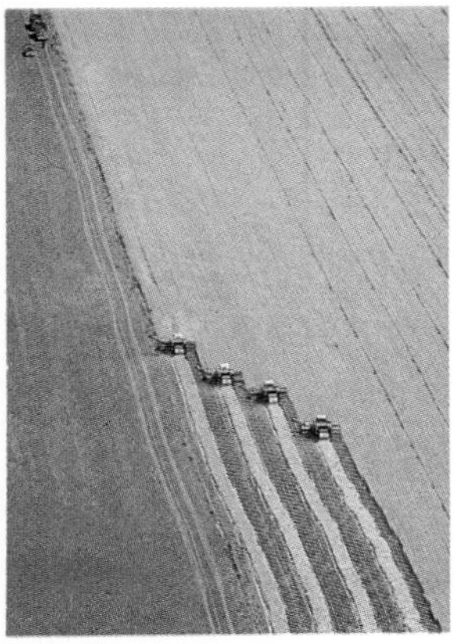

harvester *Modern harvesters on the vast wheat fields of the Middle West. The first horse-powered reaping machine was invented in 1826 by Patrick Bell, a Scottish clergyman.*

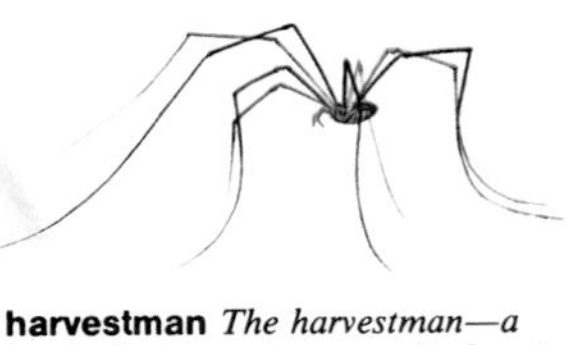

harvestman *The harvestman—a kind of spider—is commonly found in damp, shady woods of the Northern Hemisphere. It is also called daddy longlegs.*

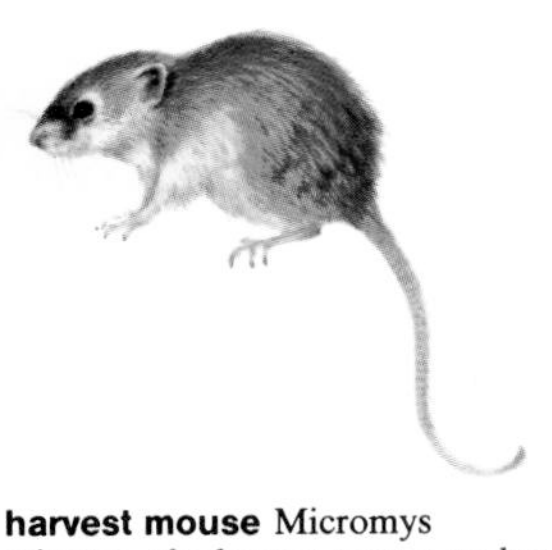

harvest mouse Micromys minutus, *the harvest mouse, makes its home in fields and hedgerows, climbing through and up tall grasses with the aid of its tail, which it uses as a fifth limb. As its scientific name suggests, it is one of the world's tiniest mammals. Fully grown, it is only about 60 millimeters (2½ inches) long and weighs a mere 5 grams (⅕ of an ounce).*

a Lifetime (1930) and *The Man Who Came to Dinner* (1939).

har·tal (här-täl′) *n.* A halting of work and business in India, usually as a political protest; a strike or boycott. [Hindi *haṛtāl,* from *haṭṭāl,* "locking of shops" : *hāṭ,* shop, from Sanskrit *haṭṭa,* shop, perhaps from *haṭika,* gold, from *hari,* yellow + *tālā,* lock, bolt, from Sanskrit *tālā, tāḍā,* latch, probably from Dravidian.]

Harte (härt), **(Francis) Bret(t)** (1836–1902). U.S. author. As editor of *Overland Monthly* (1868–71) he contributed many tales about Californian mining towns. *The Luck of Roaring Camp and Other Sketches* (1870) is his best-known collection.

har·te·beest (här′tə-bēst′, härt′bēst′) *n., pl.* **-beests** or collectively **hartebeest.** Also **hart·beest** (härt′-). Either of two African antelopes, *Alcelaphus bucelaphus* or *A. lichtensteini,* having a brownish coat and ridged, outward-curving horns. [Obsolete Afrikaans, from Dutch *hartebeest, hertebeest : hert,* HART + *beest,* BEAST.]

Hart·ford (härt′fərd). Capital of Connecticut, in the central part of the state, on the Connecticut River. Traditionally a center for commerce and finance, it is of international importance in the field of insurance.

Hart·le·pool (härt′lē-po͞ol′, här′təl-). An industrial and fishing port in northeastern England. Situated on the Tees estuary, it is the main port of the Durham coal fields; its industries include shipbuilding, heavy engineering, clothing, and tourism.

Hart·nell (härt′nəl), **Sir Norman** (1901–79). British fashion designer. He designed utility wear during World War II and later became official dressmaker to Queen Elizabeth II. He was knighted in 1977.

har·tree (här′trē′) *n.* A unit of energy used in atomic physics equal to the ratio of the square of the charge on an electron (atomic unit of charge) to the radius of the first Bohr orbit of an atom (atomic unit of length). It has the value 4.850×10^{-18} joule. [After Douglas Rayner *Hartree* (1897–1958), British mathematician and physicist.]

harts·horn (härts′hôrn′) *n. Archaic.* **Sal volatile** *(see).* [Old English *heortes horn,* hart's horn.]

hart's-tongue (härts′tŭng′) *n.* An evergreen fern, *Phyllitis scolopendrium,* having narrow, undivided fronds. [So called from the shape of its fronds.]

har·um-scar·um (hâr′əm-skâr′əm) *adj.* Lacking a sense of responsibility; rash; reckless.
~*adv.* With abandon; recklessly.
~*n. Informal.* **1.** One who acts recklessly. **2.** Reckless behavior. [Perhaps from HARE + SCARE.]

Ha·run al-Ra·shid (hä-ro͞on′ äl′rä-shēd′) (A.D. *c.* 766–809). The fifth caliph of Baghdad (786–809) of the Abbassid dynasty. He figures in many tales of the *Arabian Nights* and symbolizes the golden age of Islamic rulers.

ha·rus·pex (hə-rŭs′pĕks′, hăr′ə-spĕks′) *n., pl.* **haruspices** (hə-rŭs′pə-sēz′). Also **a·rus·pex** (ə-rŭs′pĕks′). A priest in ancient Rome who practiced divination by the inspection of the entrails of animals. [Latin.]

Har·vard classification (här′vərd) *n.* A method of classifying stars that originally used the letters *A* to *P* to indicate the strength of the hydrogen absorption lines in their spectra but was later modified so that most stars could be classified, according to decreasing surface temperature, into seven groups known by the letters *O, B, A, F, G, K, M.* [After Harvard University, where it was developed.]

har·vest (här′vĭst) *n.* **1.** The act or process of gathering a crop, especially a grain crop. **2.** The crop thus gathered. **3.** The amount or measure of such a crop. **4.** The time or season of such gathering. **5.** The result or consequence of any action.
~*v.* **harvested, -vesting, -vests.** —*tr.* **1.** To gather (a crop). **2.** To gather a crop from (a field or orchard, for example). **3.** To store; lay up. **4.** To receive (the benefits or consequences of an action). —*intr.* To gather a crop.
~*adj.* Of or relating to a harvest: *a harvest supper.* [Middle English *hervest,* autumn, Old English *hærfest,* from Germanic.]

harvest bug *n.* The **chigger** *(see).*

har·vest·er (här′vĭ-stər) *n.* **1.** A person who harvests. **2.** A machine that harvests, especially a combine harvester.

harvest festival *n.* A service of thanksgiving on the completion of the harvest, held in a church or other building decorated with flowers, fruit, and vegetables.

harvest fly *n.* Any of several cicadas of the genus *Tibicen* that produce a shrill sound heard late in summer.

harvest home *n.* **1.** The completion of a harvest. **2. a.** The time of completing a harvest. **b.** A festival held at this time, especially a harvest supper. **c.** A song sung at this time.

har·vest·man (här′vĭst-mən) *n., pl.* **-men** (-mĭn). **1.** One who harvests. **2.** An arachnid, the **daddy longlegs** *(see).*

harvest mite *n.* An insect, the **chigger** *(see).*

harvest moon *n.* The full moon that occurs nearest to the autumnal equinox.

harvest mouse *n.* A very small Eurasian mouse, *Micromys minutus,* with reddish-brown fur and a prehensile tail, found in cornfields and hedgerows.

Har·vey (här′vē), **William** (1578–1657). English physician and anatomist who discovered the circulation of the blood. He became physician to James I and Charles I. His treatise *On the Motion of the Heart and the Blood* (1628) accurately described the circulation through the heart, lungs, arteries, and veins.

Har·well (här′wĕl′, -wəl). A village in Oxfordshire, England. An atomic research station was established here in 1947.

Har·wich (hăr′ĭj, -ĭch). A port in Essex, eastern England. Situated on the Stour estuary, it is an important passenger and commercial sea link with Denmark and the Netherlands.

Harz Mountains (härts). A mountain range in Central Germany. Extending from the Weser River in the west to the Elbe River in the east, it is the northernmost range of the European mountain system. Home of legends, its forested slopes, mineral springs, and large canary population attract tourists.

has (hăz). Third person singular present indicative of **have.**

has-been (hăz′bĭn′) *n. Informal.* One that is no longer famous, popular, successful, or useful.

Has·dru·bal (hăz′dro͞o′bəl, hăz-dro͞o′-) (died 207 B.C.). Carthaginian general. Son of Hamilcar Barca and brother of Hannibal, he attempted to establish military dominance on the Iberian Peninsula during the Second Punic War. After a series of battles he retreated from present-day Spain and was ultimately defeated by Roman forces in 207 B.C.

Ha·šek (hä′shĕk′), **Jaroslav** (1883–1923). Czech novelist. He is best remembered for the novel *The Good Soldier Schweik* (1920–23).

hash[1] (hăsh) *n.* **1.** A dish of chopped or diced meat, especially meat that has been previously cooked, with potatoes and sometimes vegetables, usually browned and often baked. **2.** A jumble, hodgepodge, or mess. **3.** A reworking or restatement of material already familiar. **—make a hash of.** To make a mess of; botch. **—settle someone's hash.** *Informal.* To silence or subdue.
~*tr.v.* **hashed, hashing, hashes. 1.** To chop into pieces; mince. **2.** *Informal.* To make a mess of; mangle. **3.** *Informal.* To discuss carefully; review. Often used with *over*: *hash over future plans.* [French *hachis,* from *hacher,* to chop up, from Old French *hachier,* from *hache,* ax, HATCHET.]

hash[2] *n. Slang.* **Hashish** *(see).*

hash house *n. Slang.* A cheap restaurant.

Hash·i·mo·to's disease (hăsh′ə-mō′tōz) *n.* An autoimmune disease resulting in chronic inflammation of the thyroid gland, with partial or total suppression of thyroid-hormone secretion. [After Hakaru *Hashimoto* (1881–1934), Japanese surgeon.]

hash·ish, hash·eesh (hăsh′ēsh′, -ĭsh) *n.* A purified resin prepared from the dried flowers of the hemp plant, smoked or chewed as a narcotic and hallucinogen. Also *slang* "hash." [Arabic *ḥashīsh,* hemp, dried grass.]

hash mark *n. Slang.* A service stripe on the sleeve of an enlisted person's uniform.

Hasidim. Variant of **Chassidim.**

has·let (hăs′lĭt, hăz′-) *n.* Also **hars·let** (här′slĭt). The heart, liver, and other edible viscera of an animal, especially hog viscera. [Middle English *hastelet, hastlet,* from Old French *hastelet,* diminutive of *haste,* spit, roast meat, perhaps from Latin *hasta,* spear.]

has·n't (hăz′ənt). Contraction of *has not.*

hasp (hăsp, häsp) *n.* A metal fastener having a hinged, slotted part that fits over a staple and may be secured by a pin, bolt, or padlock.
~*tr.v.* **hasped, hasping, hasps.** To fasten or lock with a hasp. [Middle English *hasp,* Old English *hæsp(e), hæpse,* fastening, hinge, from Germanic *hasp-* (unattested).]

Has·sam (hăs′əm), **(Frederick) Childe** (1859–1935). U.S. painter. The leading American impressionist of his day, he used brilliant colors and bold brushwork to depict city street scenes and natural landscapes, including *Rainy Day in Boston* (1885) and *Allies Day, Fifth Avenue* (1917).

Has·san II (hä-săn′, hä-sän′) (1929–). King of Morocco (1961–). He succeeded his father, Muhammad V (reigned 1957–61).

Hassidim. Variant of **Chassidim.**

has·sle (hăs′əl) *n. Informal.* **1.** An argument or fight. **2.** Trouble; bother.
~*v.* **hassled, -sling, -sles.** *Informal.* —*intr.* To argue or fight. —*tr.* To bother or harass: *street gangs hassling passers-by.* [Perhaps a blend of HAGGLE + TUSSLE.]

has·sock (hăs′ək) *n.* **1.** A thick cushion used as a footstool or for kneeling upon. **2.** A dense clump of grass; a tussock. [Middle English *hassok,* Old English *hassuc*†, clump of matted vegetation.]

hast (hăst). *Archaic.* Second person singular present indicative of **have.** Used with *thou.*

has·tate (hăs′tāt′) *adj.* Shaped like the head of an arrow or spear: *a hastate leaf.* [New Latin *hastatus,* from Latin *hasta,* spear.]

haste (hāst) *n.* **1.** Swiftness; rapidity. **2.** Eagerness or necessity to move swiftly; urgency. **3.** Careless or headlong hurrying; precipitateness. **—make haste.** To move or act swiftly; hurry.
~*v.* **hasted, hasting, hastes.** —*intr.* To hasten. —*tr.* To cause to hurry; hasten. [Middle English, from Old French, from West Germanic *haisti-* (unattested), violence.]

has·ten (hā′sən) *v.* **-tened, -tening, -tens.** —*intr.* **1.** To move or act swiftly. **2.** To be eager or anxious. Used with an infinitive: *I hasten to point out that I was not actually present.* —*tr.* **1.** To cause to hurry; urge on. **2.** To bring about more quickly; accelerate: *events that hastened the downfall of the government.* —See Synonyms at **speed.**

Has·tings (hā′stĭngz). A coastal town in East Sussex, England. It was the most important of the Cinque Ports, with a long history of commercial and naval importance. Today it is a popular resort and residential town. William the Conqueror's victory at the Battle of Hastings (1066), fought nearby, ended Saxon rule in England and installed a Norman-French dynasty.

Hastings, Warren (1732–1818). The first governor-general of India (1774–85). He carried out land and legal reforms, facing the hostility of Sir Philip Francis (1740–1818), who tried to have him impeached for corruption. At the end of a long trial (1788–95) the House of Lords found Hastings not guilty.

hast·y (hā′stē) *adj.* **-ier, -iest. 1.** Characterized by speed; swift; rapid. **2.** Done, made, or acting too quickly to be accurate or wise; rash: *Don't make a hasty decision.* **3.** Easily angered; irritable. —See Synonyms at **fast** and Usage note at **impetuous.** **—hast·i·ly** *adv.* **—hast·i·ness** *n.*

hasty pudding *n.* **1.** Cornmeal mush served with maple syrup, brown sugar, or other sweetening. **2.** *British.* A sweetened milk pudding made with flour, semolina, or tapioca.

hat (hăt) *n.* **1.** A covering for the head; especially, one having a shaped crown and brim. **2. a.** A hat of distinctive color and shape worn as a symbol of office. **b.** A role or office symbolized by or as if by the wearing of such a hat: *wore different hats as executive and homemaker.* **—at the drop of a hat.** At the slightest pretext or provocation. **—hat in hand.** In a servile or apologetic way. **—my hat!** Used to express surprise, disbelief, or rejection, as of a claim or report. **—pass the hat.** To take up a monetary collection. **—take one's hat off to.** To respect, admire, or congratulate. **—talk through one's hat. 1.** To talk nonsense. **2.** To bluff. **—throw** (or **toss) one's hat into the ring.** To enter a political race as a candidate for office. **—under one's hat.** Confidential; secret.
~*tr.v.* **hatted, hatting, hats.** To supply or cover with a hat. [Middle English *hat,* Old English *hæt(t),* from Germanic.]

hat·band (hăt′bănd′) *n.* A band of ribbon or cloth around the crown of a hat just above the brim.

hat·box (hăt′bŏks′) *n.* An often round box or case for a hat.

hatch[1] (hăch) *n.* **1. a.** An opening, as in the deck of a ship, in the floor or roof of a building, or in an airplane. **b.** The cover for such an opening. **c.** A hatchway. **d.** A ship's compartment. **2. a.** A Dutch door. **b.** The lower half of a Dutch door. **3.** A floodgate. **—down the hatch.** *Slang.* Down the throat; drink up. Used as a toast. **—under hatches.** *Chiefly British.* **1.** Below decks. **2.** Concealed. **3.** *Slang.* Dead. [Middle English *hacche, hecche,* Old English *hæc(c),* hatch, from Germanic *khak-* (unattested).]

hatch[2] *v.* **hatched, hatching, hatches.** —*intr.* **1.** To emerge from or break out of an egg. **2.** To crack open and release a young animal. Used of an egg. —*tr.* **1.** To produce (young) from an egg. **2.** To cause (an egg or eggs) to produce young. **3.** To originate or formulate; especially, to devise (a plot, for example) in secret.
~*n.* **1.** The act or an instance of hatching. **2.** The young hatched at one time; a brood. [Middle English *hacchen,* Old English *hæccan* (unattested).] **—hatch·er** *n.*

hatch[3] *tr.v.* **hatched, hatching, hatches.** To shade by drawing or etching fine parallel or crossed lines on.
~*n.* Such a line. [Middle English *hachen,* from Old French *hach(i)er,* from *hache,* ax. See **hatchet.**]

hatch·back (hăch′băk′) *n.* **1.** An automobile with a sloping rear consisting of a door that opens upward. **2.** A door of this kind.

hatch·el (hăch′əl) *n.* A comb for separating flax fibers.
~*tr.v.* **hatcheled, -eling, -els.** Also *chiefly British* **-elled, -elling.** To separate (flax fibers) with a hatchel. [Middle English *hechele,* flax-comb. See **heckle.**]

hatch·er·y (hăch′ə-rē) *n., pl.* **-ies.** A place where eggs, especially those of fish or domestic fowl, are hatched.

hatch·et (hăch′ĭt) *n.* **1.** A small, short-handled ax for use in one hand. **2.** A tomahawk. **—bury the hatchet.** To stop fighting; make peace. **—dig up the hatchet.** To resume hostilities. [Middle English *hachet, hatchet,* small ax, from Old French *hachette,* diminutive of *hache,* ax, from Germanic.]

hatchet face *n.* A long, gaunt face with sharp features. **—hatch·et-faced** (hăch′ĭt-fāst′) *adj.*

hatchet job *n. Slang.* A malicious verbal attack, either spoken or written, intended to destroy the reputation of another.

hatchet man *n. Slang.* **1.** Someone who carries out unpleasant duties on behalf of another. **2.** A hired assassin. **3.** A harsh or malicious critic.

hatch·ing (hăch′ĭng) *n.* **1.** The fine lines used in graphic arts to show shading. **2.** The process of decorating with such lines.

hatch·ling (hăch′lĭng) *n.* A newly hatched bird, reptile, amphibian, or fish.

hatch·ment (hăch′mənt) *n. Heraldry.* A panel, usually diamond-shaped, bearing the coat of arms of a dead person. Also called "achievement." [Earlier *(h)achement, achiment,* perhaps short for ACHIEVEMENT.]

hatch·way (hăch′wā′) *n.* **1.** An opening, as in the deck of a ship, leading to a hold, compartment, or cellar. **2.** A ladder or stairway within a hatchway.

hate (hāt) *v.* **hated, hating, hates.** —*tr.* **1.** To feel hatred toward; loathe; detest. **2.** To find deeply distasteful or disagreeable; dislike: *hated having to borrow money.* —*intr.* To feel hatred.
~*n.* **1.** Strong dislike; animosity; hatred. **2.** An object of detestation or hatred: *a pet hate.* [Middle English, Old English *hatian,* (verb), from Germanic.] **—hate·a·ble, hat·a·ble** *adj.* **—hat·er** *n.*

hate·ful (hāt′fəl) *adj.* **1.** Inspiring hatred; detestable; despicable. **2.** Feeling or expressing hatred; malevolent. **—hate·ful·ly** *adv.* **—hate·ful·ness** *n.*
Synonyms: *abhorrent, detestable, obnoxious, odious, offensive, repellent.*

hath (hăth). *Archaic.* Third person singular present indicative of **have.**

Hath·a·way (hăth′ə-wā′), **Anne** (*c.* 1556–1623). Wife of William Shakespeare. She was born at Shottery, England, near Stratford, and married Shakespeare in 1582. She bore him three children: a daughter, Susanna, and the twins Hamnet and Judith. The farmhouse where she lived is preserved as a museum.

ha·tha yoga (hăth′ə, hŭt′ə) *n.* **1. Yoga** *(see).* **2.** A form of yoga concentrating on breathing exercises. [Sanskrit : *hatha,* force + YOGA.]

Hath·or (hăth′ôr′). The ancient Egyptian goddess of love, creation, happiness, and beauty, represented as having a cow's horns or head. [Greek *Hathōr,* from Egyptian *ḥt-ḥr.*]

Ha·thor·ic (hə-thôr′ĭk, -thŏr′ĭk) *adj.* **1.** Of or pertaining to the goddess Hathor. **2.** *Architecture.* Designating a column with a head of Hathor as its capital.

hat·pin (hăt′pĭn′) *n.* A long thick pin, usually with a decorative head, for securing a woman's hat to her hair.

ha·tred (hā′trĭd) *n.* Violent dislike or animosity; abhorrence. [Middle English *hatred, hatereden* : *hate, hete,* hate, Old English *hete* + *-reden,* Old English *rǣden,* condition.]

Hat·shep·sut (hăt-shĕp′so͞ot′). Also **Hat·shep·set** (-sĕt′). Queen of Egypt, reigned 1503–1482 B.C. On the death of her husband, King Thutmose II (*c.* 1512), she became regent for his son Thutmose III. In 1503 B.C. she bestowed the title pharaoh on herself and followed all the pharaonic customs, including the wearing of a false beard.

hat·ter (hăt′ər) *n.* One whose occupation is the manufacture, selling, or repair of hats. **—mad as a hatter.** Completely insane. [Idiom, referring to the symptoms, resembling insanity, caused by mercury poisoning, formerly a common disease of hatters, who used the metal in making hats.]

Hat·ter·as, Cape (hăt′ər-əs). Promontory on Hatteras Island, a low, sandy barrier bar in eastern North Carolina between the Atlantic Ocean and Pamlico Sound. Frequent storms drive ships landward, and the area around the cape is known as the Graveyard of the Atlantic.

hat trick *n.* **1.** The taking of three wickets in cricket by a bowler in three consecutive balls. **2.** Three consecutive wins, hits, or goals made by one player in one game, as in ice hockey. **3.** Any set of three victories or other notable achievements, especially when consecutive, in any field of endeavor. [The feat was once rewarded by the gift of a hat.]

haubergeon. Variant of **habergeon.**

hau·berk (hô′bûrk) *n.* A long tunic made of chain mail. [Middle English *hauberk,* from Old French *hauberc,* from Frankish *halsberg* (unattested), "neck protector": *hals,* neck + *berg-* (unattested), to protect.]

haugh (hôKH, hôf) *n. Scottish.* A low-lying meadow that is part of a river valley. [Middle English (Scottish) *holch, hawch,* Old English *healh,* corner of land.]

haugh·ty (hô′tē) *adj.* **-tier, -tiest.** Proud and vain to the point of arrogance; scornful and self-satisfied. —See Synonyms at **proud.** [From archaic *haught,* haughty, Middle English *haute,* from Old French *haut,* from Latin *altus,* high.] **—haugh·ti·ly** *adv.* **—haugh·ti·ness** *n.*

haul (hôl) *v.* **hauled, hauling, hauls.** —*tr.* **1.** To pull or drag forcibly; tug. **2.** To transport, as with a truck or wagon; cart. **3.** To change the course of (a ship); especially, to sail (a ship) closer into the wind. Often used with *up.* **4.** To bring before a court or other authority, especially for a reprimand. Often used with *up*: *hauled up before the directors.* —*intr.* **1.** To pull; tug. **2.** To provide transport for heavy goods; cart. **3. a.** To change compass bearing in a clockwise direction. Used of the wind. **b.** To blow from a direction nearer the bow of a ship. Used of the wind. Compare **veer. 4. a.** To sail, as on a certain course. **b.** To change the course of a ship. **—haul off. 1.** To steer a ship away from an object. **2.** To pull the arm back in order to deliver a blow.
~*n.* **1.** The act of pulling or dragging. **2.** The act of transporting or carting. **3.** The distance covered or time taken in traveling or transporting or in achieving something involving sustained effort: *the long haul to the South Pole.* **4.** Something that is pulled or transported; a load. **5.** Everything collected or acquired by a single effort; a take: *a haul of fish.* [Middle English *halen,* to pull, draw, from Old French *haler,* from Germanic.]

haul·age (hô′lĭj) *n.* **1.** The act, process, or business of hauling. **2.** The force required to haul something. **3.** The charge made for hauling something.

haul·er (hô′lər) *n.* Also *chiefly British* **haul·i·er** (hô′lē-ər). **1.** One that hauls. **2.** A company dealing in the transportation of goods by road.

haulm, halm (hôm) *n. Chiefly British.* **1.** The stems or stalks of peas, beans, potatoes, or grasses, used as litter for animals or for thatching. **2.** A single stalk of this kind. [Middle English *halm,* Old English *h(e)alm,* straw, stem.]

haulyard. Variant of **halyard.**

haunch (hônch, hŏnch) *n.* **1.** The hip, buttock, and upper thigh in humans and animals. **2.** The loin and leg of an animal, especially as used for food: *a haunch of venison.* **3.** *Architecture.* Either of the sides of an arch curving down from the apex to an impost. In this sense, also called "hance." **—sit on one's haunches.** To crouch down with the knees bent and the buttocks resting on the heels. [Middle English *ha(u)nche,* from Old French *hanche,* from Medieval Latin *hancha,* from Germanic *hanka* (unattested).]

haunt (hônt, hŏnt) *v.* **haunted, haunting, haunts.** —*tr.* **1.** To visit or appear to in the form of a ghost or other supernatural being. **2.** To visit often; frequent. **3.** To be frequently in the company of. **4.** To recur to continually; obsess: *The riddle continued to haunt her.* **5.** To linger or remain in; pervade. —*intr.* To recur or visit often; espe-

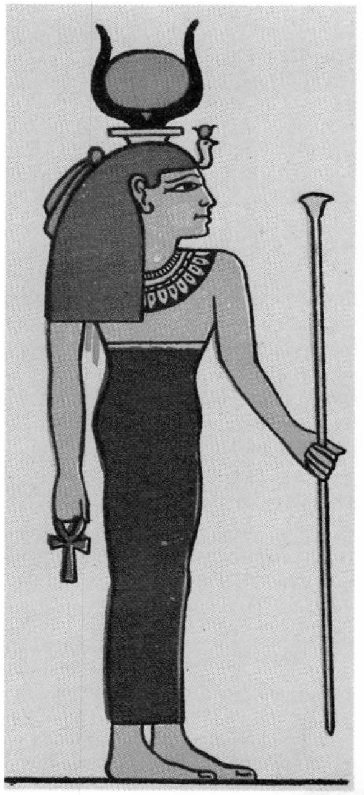

Hathor *At different times in ancient Egypt, Hathor was the wife of Horus and a goddess of love, associated with the sun god Ra and called the Lady of the West, or Underworld.*

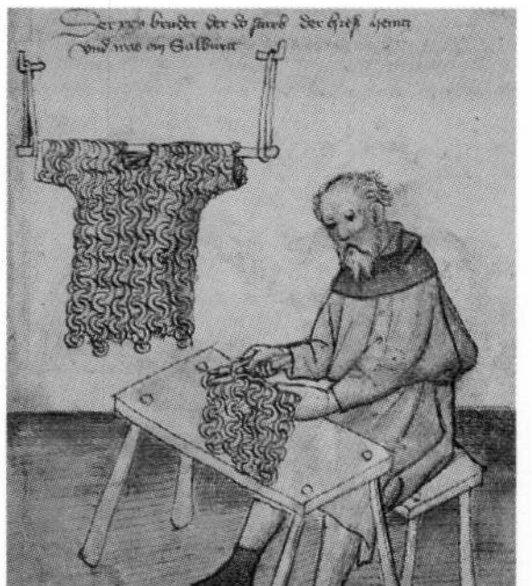

hauberk *An armorer making one of these chain mail tunics. Hauberks, which were worn by knights during the Hundred Years War (1338–1453) between England and France, were replaced by plate armor.*

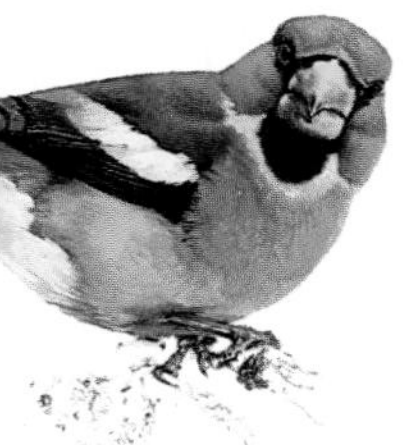

hawfinch *The thick beak of the hawfinch is operated by powerful muscles that enable it to crack open and eat large seeds and the hard stones of tree fruit such as cherries, sloes, and damsons. The birds, which also feed on holly berries and haws, are found in temperate latitudes across Europe and Asia.*

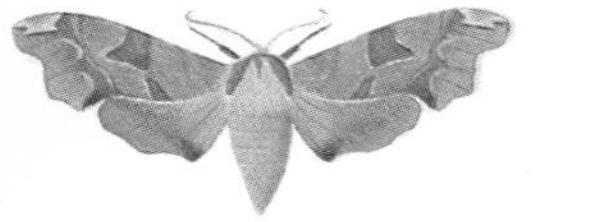

hawk moth *These powerful night fliers—some can fly at more than 50 kilometers (30 miles) per hour —get their name from the ability of some species to hover like a hawk while they suck nectar from flowers. The moths' wingspans range from 50 to 112 millimeters (2–4½ inches). This is the lime hawk moth, native to Britain, which feeds on the leaves of lime trees and elms.*

PRONUNCIATION KEY

ă, pat; ā, pay; âr, care; ä, father, are; b, bib; ch, church; d, deed; ĕ, pet; ē, be; f, fife; g, gag; h, hat; hw, which; ĭ, pit; ī, pie; îr, pier; j, judge; k, kick; l, lid, needle; m, mum; n, no, sudden; ng, thing; ŏ, pot; ō, toe; ô, paw, for; oi, noise; ou, out; ŏŏ, book; ōō, boot; p, pop; r, roar; s, sauce; sh, ship, dish; t, tight; th, thin, path; *th*, this, bathe; ŭ, cut; ûr, fur; v, valve; w, with; y, yes; z, zebra, size; zh, vision; ə, about, item, edible, gallop, circus, peaceful

IN FOREIGN WORDS:

à, *Fr.* ami; œ, *Fr.* feu, *Ger.* schön; ü, *Fr.* tu, *Ger.* über; KH, *Ger.* ich, *Scot.* loch; N, *Fr.* bon; y', *Fr.* Compiègne

STRESS MARKS:

Primary stress: ′ **in·cite′** (ĭn-sīt′)
Secondary stress: ′ **in′sight′** (ĭn′sīt′)

cially, to appear habitually as a ghost or other supernatural being. *~n.* (*also* hănt *for sense 2*). **1. a.** A place much frequented. **b.** A place where animals usually gather to feed. **2.** *Regional.* A ghost or other supernatural being. [Middle English *haunten,* from Old French *hanter,* from Germanic.]

haunt·ed (hôn′tĭd, hŏn′-) *adj.* **1.** Supposedly frequented by ghosts or other spectral beings: *a haunted house.* **2.** Obsessed by a constantly recurring memory or thought.

haunt·ing (hôn′tĭng, hŏn′-) *adj.* Continually recurring to the mind, especially in a poignant way; unforgettable. **—haunt·ing·ly** *adv.*

Haupt·mann (houpt′män′), **Gerhart Johann Robert** (1862–1946). German author. A prolific poet, playwright, and novelist, he wrote in several literary styles, although he was primarily known as a naturalist. His many works include *The Weavers* (1892), *Before Dawn* (1889), *Till Eulenspiegel* (1928), and *Atridentetralogie* (1941). In 1912 he was awarded a Nobel Prize for literature.

Hau·sa (hou′sə, -zə) *n., pl.* **Hausa. 1.** A member of a Negroid people of Niger and northern Nigeria. **2.** The language of this people, used widely as a trade language in Africa. **—Hau·sa** *adj.*

haus·frau (hous′frou′) *n.* A housewife, especially one who is houseproud. [German *Hausfrau.*]

Hauss·mann (hous′mən, ōs-män′), **Georges Eugène, Baron** (1809–91). French politician and town planner. He was responsible for rebuilding Paris during the time of Napoleon III.

haus·tel·lum (hô-stĕl′əm) *n., pl.* **haustella** (hô-stĕl′ə). The distal portion of the proboscis adapted as a sucking organ, seen in many insects, such as the bluebottle. [New Latin, from Latin *haustus,* past participle of *haurīre,* to draw, draw up.] **—haus·tel·late** (hô-stĕl′ĭt, hô′stə-lāt′) *adj.*

haus·to·ri·um (hô-stôr′ē-əm, -stōr′ē-əm) *n., pl.* **haustoria** (hô-stôr′ē-ə, -stōr′ē-ə). *Botany.* A specialized organ by which parasitic plants such as fungi obtain food from a host plant. [New Latin, from Latin *haustus,* past participle of *haurīre,* to draw, draw up.]

haut·boy (hō′boi′, ō′boi′) *n., pl.* **-boys.** Also **haut·bois** *pl.* **hautbois.** An oboe. [French *hautbois,* "high wood" (from its pitch) : *haut,* high, from Latin *altus* + *bois,* wood, from Germanic.]

haute cou·ture (ōt′ kōō-tŏŏr′) *n.* **1.** Exclusive fashions for women; high fashion. **2. a.** Leading clothes designers and dressmakers collectively. **b.** The clothes designed and made by these people. [French, "high sewing."]

haute cui·sine (ōt′ kwĭ-zēn′) *n.* Elaborate or skillful cooking; especially, that in the French tradition. [French, "high cooking."]

haute é·cole (ōt′ ā-kôl′) *n.* The art, techniques, or practice of expert horsemanship. [French, "high school."]

hau·teur (hō-tûr′) *n.* Haughtiness in bearing and attitude; arrogance. [French, from *haut,* high, pious, from Old French, from Latin *altus.*]

haut monde (ō mōNd′, ō mŏnd′) *n.* Fashionable society. [French, "high world."]

Ha·van·a (hə-văn′ə). *Spanish* **La Ha·ba·na** (lä′ ä-vä′nä). Capital city of Cuba. Situated on the northwest coast, it has an excellent natural harbor and is one of the largest cities in the West Indies. It was founded in 1519 by the Spanish and has been prominent since 1552, when it became the country's capital. Since the revolution (1959) it has been extensively modernized, and an oil refinery has been built on the outskirts. The chief exports include tobacco (especially Havana cigars), sugar, rum, and clothing.

Havana cigar *n.* Any of several high-quality cigars made in Cuba, especially in Havana.

have (hăv) *v.* **had** (hăd) or *archaic* **hadst** (hădst), **having, has** (hăz). Present tense first person **have;** second person **have** or *archaic* **hast** (for singular); third person singular **has** or *archaic* **hath**; third person plural **have.** Used as an auxiliary verb before a past participle to form the past, present, and future perfect tenses, indicating completed or virtually completed action: *We had left before dawn. They have done it. I shall have finished by then.* —*tr.* **1. a.** To be in possession of as one's property; own: *have a big house.* **b.** To possess as a physical attribute: *have red hair.* **2. a.** To be related to: *have three aunts.* **b.** To be in a particular specified or implied relationship to: *has friends in high places; has a staff of 25.* **3.** To be in a position to make use of or enjoy: *have time to play.* **4.** To hold in one's mind; entertain: *have doubts.* **5.** To hold by law or entitlement. **6.** To bribe or buy off. **7.** To engage the attention of; captivate. **8.** To win a victory or advantage over: *He has you on that point.* **9.** *Informal.* To cheat, deceive, or trick. Often used in the passive: *I've been had.* **10.** To keep or put in a specified place, position, or condition: *have the carpet in the hall; had them eating out of his hand.* **11.** To accept or take: *I'll have the gray jacket.* **12.** To partake of; consume, as by eating or drinking. **13.** To obtain or receive. **14.** To be made of, consist of, or contain. **15.** To feel as an emotion: *has great love for her parents.* **16.** To exercise or bring into play. Used with *on*: *have mercy on me.* **17.** To allow; permit. Usually used in the negative: *I will not have the children out after dark.* **18. a.** To cause or arrange for (something to be done): *have the car fixed.* **b.** To order, invite, or compel: *have him go home; want to have you over for a drink.* **19.** To perform (an action) or take part in (an activity): *have a look at this; have the next dance.* **20.** To engage in. **21.** To carry out or stage: *have a party.* **22.** To be the subject of: *have a large funeral.* **23. a.** To experience; undergo. **b.** To enjoy: *have a good summer.* **24.** To suffer from (a disease or physical disability, for example): *She has multiple sclerosis.* **25.** To give birth to; bear: *She's going to have twins.* **26.** To be compelled: *have to go now.* **27.** To be scheduled for: *have an appointment at noon.* **28.** To be able to use; be in command of or competent in: *have the necessary technique; has no Latin.* **29.** To come to know; be informed about: *have it on good authority.* **30.** To receive as a guest: *She has her mother-in-law for a week.* **—had better** (or **best**). Ought to: *You had better go now.* **—had just as well.** Might as well. **—have at.** To attack. **—have done with.** To be through with; finish. **—have had it.** *Informal.* **1.** To have done everything that is possible or that will be permitted. **2.** To have endured all that one can. **3.** To be in a state beyond remedy, repair, or salvage. **—have it. 1.** To imply or state: *Talk has it they're getting a divorce.* **2.** To find or stumble on the answer or solution. **—have it in for.** To wish to harm, especially because of a grudge. **—have it out.** To settle decisively, especially by a full discussion or by a fight. **—have on. 1.** To be wearing. **2.** *Informal.* To be scheduled for or committed to. **—have someone on.** To deceive in a teasing, lighthearted way. **—have something coming.** *Informal.* To deserve whatever one receives: *He had that rebuke coming.* **—have something on someone.** To have well-supported suspicions or incriminating evidence regarding someone. **—let someone have it.** *Informal.* To attack (someone). **—not have any.** *Informal.* **1.** To refuse to tolerate. **2.** To refuse to become interested or involved. —See Usage note at **get.**
~n. A person or class enjoying material comforts as opposed to those who are poor: *The haves and the have-nots often have different political philosophies.* [Have, had, had, has; Middle English *haven* or *habben, hadde, had, has,* Old English *habban, hæfde, (ge)hæfd, hæbbe,* from Germanic *habēn* (attested).]

have·lock (hăv′lŏk′, -lək) *n.* A cloth covering for a cap, having a flap to protect the back of the neck. [After Sir Henry *Havelock* (died 1857), British general in India.]

ha·ven (hā′vən) *n.* **1.** A harbor or anchorage; a port. **2.** A place of refuge; a sanctuary. —See Synonyms at **shelter.**
~tr.v. **havened, -vening, -vens.** *Rare.* To put into a haven. [Middle English, Old English *hæfen,* from Old Norse *höfn.*]

have-not (hăv′nŏt′) *n.* A person or class enjoying few or no material comforts. Used chiefly in the plural.

have·n't (hăv′ənt). Contraction of *have not.*

ha·ver (hā′vər) *intr.v.* **-vered, -vering, -vers. 1.** *British.* To dither; vacillate. **2.** *British Regional & Scottish.* To indulge in idle chatter; babble.
~n. British Regional & Scottish. Foolish or inconsequential talk; chitchat or nonsense. [18th century : origin obscure.]

hav·er·sack (hăv′ər-săk′) *n.* A canvas bag with straps worn over a shoulder or on the back to carry supplies on a hike or march. [French *havresac,* from German *Habersack,* originally bag for oats : *Haber,* oats + *Sack,* SACK.]

Ha·ver·sian canal (hə-vûr′zhən) *n. Anatomy.* Any of the fine interconnecting channels that carry the blood and nerve supply in bones. [After Clopton *Havers* (died 1702), English anatomist who discovered the channels.]

hav·er·sine (hăv′ər-sīn′) *n. Mathematics.* Half the value of a versed sine. [Blend of *half* + *versed* + *sine.*]

hav·il·dar (hăv′əl-där′) *n.* A noncommissioned officer in the Indian army corresponding to a sergeant. [Hindi, from Persian *hawāldār,* one having charge.]

hav·oc (hăv′ək) *n.* **1.** Destruction, as caused by a natural calamity or war; devastation. **2.** Confusion; disorder; muddle. **—cry havoc. 1.** *Archaic.* To signal an army to begin pillaging or collecting spoils. **2.** To sound an alarm. **—play havoc with.** To destroy, ruin, or make a mess of.
~v. **havocked, -ocking, -ocs.** *Poetic.* —*tr.* To destroy; devastate. —*intr.* To cause havoc. [Middle English *havok,* from Norman French, variant of Old French *havot*†, plunder, cry used to begin plunder.]

haw¹ (hô) *n.* A vocalized pause in speech.
~intr.v. **hawed, hawing, haws.** To pause in speaking. Used in the phrase *hem and haw.* See **hem** (short cough). [Imitative.]

haw² *n.* **1.** The fruit of a hawthorn. **2.** A hawthorn or similar tree or shrub. [Middle English *haw(e),* Old English *haga,* hawthorn, hedge, from Germanic.]

haw³ *n.* The nictitating membrane, especially of a domesticated animal. [16th century : origin obscure.]

haw⁴ *interj.* Used to command an animal to turn left. Compare **gee.**
~intr.v. **hawed, hawing, haws.** To turn to the left. [Origin unknown.]

Ha·wai·i (hə-wä′ē, -wä′yə, -wī′ə). Formerly **Sand·wich Islands** (sănd′wĭch, săn′-). A group of islands in the North Pacific; in 1959 it became the 50th state of the Union. Hawaii comprises more than 20 volcanic islands, including Maui, Kauai, Oahu (on which Honolulu, the state capital, is situated), and Hawaii, the principal and southernmost island of the group. Its economy depends on sugarcane and pineapple cultivation and on tourism. Since Capt. James Cook's discovery of the islands (1778), the population and culture have become a mix of European, Oriental, and Polynesian.

Ha·wai·ian (hə-wä′yən) *n.* **1.** A native or resident of Hawaii. **2.** The Polynesian language spoken by the inhabitants of Hawaii. **—Ha·wai·ian** *adj.*

Hawaiian guitar *n.* An electric guitar consisting of a long sounding board and six to eight steel strings that are plucked while being pressed with a steel bar.

haw·finch (hô′fĭnch′) *n.* A Eurasian bird, *Coccothraustes cocco-*

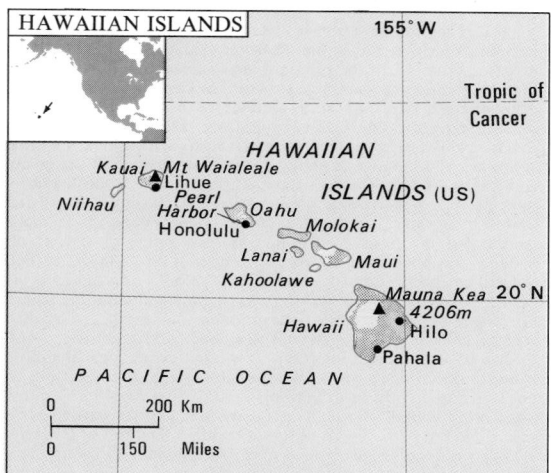

HAWAIIAN ISLANDS

155° W

Tropic of Cancer

HAWAIIAN ISLANDS (US)

Kauai · Mt Waialeale · Lihue
Niihau · Pearl Harbor · Oahu · Molokai
Honolulu · Lanai · Maui
Kahoolawe
Mauna Kea 20° N · 4206m
Hawaii · Hilo · Pahala

PACIFIC OCEAN

0 · 200 Km
0 · 150 Miles

thraustes, having a thick bill, brown, white, and black plumage, and a short tail. [HAW (fruit) + FINCH.]

haw-haw¹. Variant of **ha-ha** (laughter).

haw-haw². Variant of **ha-ha** (a ditch).

Haw-Haw, Lord. See William **Joyce.**

hawk¹ (hôk) *n.* **1.** Any of various birds of prey of the order Falconiformes, and especially of the genera *Accipiter* and *Buteo,* characteristically having a short, hooked bill and strong claws adapted for seizing. **2.** Any of various similar birds. **3.** A grasping, rapacious, or ruthless person who preys on others; a shark. **4. a.** One who favors an aggressive foreign policy. **b.** Broadly, one who takes a vigorous, uncompromising line on any matter of policy: *The hawks in the cabinet voted for further cuts in the education budget.* In this sense, compare **dove.**
  ~*v.* **hawked, hawking, hawks.** —*intr.* **1.** To hunt with trained hawks. **2.** To swoop and strike in the manner of a hawk. —*tr.* To hunt on the wing. Used of a bird. [Middle English *hauk,* Old English *h(e)afoc,* from Germanic.] —**hawk-er** *n.* —**hawk-ish** *adj.* —**hawk-ish-ly** *adv.* —**hawk-ish-ness** *n.*

hawk² *v.* **hawked, hawking, hawks.** —*intr.* To peddle; especially, to peddle wares by crying them in the streets. —*tr.* **1.** To carry (goods) about in the streets and offer them for sale by calling out; peddle. **2.** To spread (gossip, one's opinions, and the like). [Back-formation from HAWKER.]

hawk³ *v.* **hawked, hawking, hawks.** —*intr.* To clear or attempt to clear the throat by coughing up phlegm. —*tr.* To clear the throat by coughing up (phlegm).
  ~*n.* An audible effort to clear the throat by expelling phlegm. [Imitative.]

hawk⁴ *n.* A small board with a handle on the underside, used to hold mortar or plaster. [17th century : origin obscure.]

hawk-er (hô'kər) *n.* A peddler, typically one who solicits business by calling at private houses. [Probably from Low German *höker,* from Middle Low German *höker,* from *höken,* to peddle, bend.]

hawk-eyed (hôk'īd') *adj.* Having very sharp eyesight.

Haw-kins, Haw-kyns (hô'kĭnz), **Sir John** (1532–95). English naval administrator and officer. One of the most important seamen of his time, he directed the rebuilding of the royal fleet, which resulted in faster, better-armed ships that rebuffed the Spanish Armada (1588) and helped establish England as a major naval power.

hawk moth *n.* Any of various moths of the family Sphingidae, having a large body and long, narrow forewings and characteristically feeding while in flight on nectar from flowers. Also called "hummingbird moth," "sphinx moth."

Hawks (hôks), **Howard** (1896–1977). U.S. film director. His films include the thrillers *Scarface* (1932) and *The Big Sleep* (1946), the western *Red River* (1948), war films such as *The Dawn Patrol* (1930), and comedies, including *Bringing Up Baby* (1938).

hawk's-beard (hôks'bîrd') *n.* Any of various plants of the genus *Crepis,* resembling the dandelion. [After its large bristly pappus.]

hawks-bill (hôks'bĭl') *n.* A tropical sea turtle, *Eretmochelys imbricata,* valued as a source of tortoiseshell.

hawk-weed (hôk'wēd') *n.* Any of various plants of the genus *Hieracium,* having yellow or orange dandelionlike flowers.

Ha-worth (hou'ərth). Village in West Yorkshire, England. It was here that the Brontë sisters lived and wrote; some of their novels, including *Wuthering Heights,* are set in the surrounding countryside. The parsonage that was their home has been preserved as a museum.

hawse (hôz) *n. Nautical.* **1.** The part of a ship where the hawseholes are located. **2.** A hawsehole or hawsepipe. **3.** The space between the bows of an anchored ship and her anchors. **4.** The arrangement of a ship's anchor cables when both starboard and port anchors are secured. [Middle English *halse,* probably from Old Norse *hals,* neck, ship's bow.]

hawse-hole (hôz'hōl') *n. Nautical.* An opening in the bow of a ship through which a cable or hawser is passed.

hawse-pipe (hôz'pīp') *n. Nautical.* A metal pipe running through a hawsehole through which a cable or hawser is passed.

haw-ser (hô'zər) *n. Nautical.* A cable or rope used in mooring or towing a ship. [Middle English *hauceour, hawser,* from Norman French *hauceour,* from Old French *haucier,* to lift, hoist, from Vulgar Latin *altiāre* (unattested), from Latin *altus,* high.]

haw-thorn (hô'thôrn') *n.* Any of various thorny trees or shrubs of the genus *Crataegus,* especially *C. monogyna,* having white or pinkish flowers and reddish fruit. Also called "haw," "may," "may tree," "mayflower." [Middle English *haw(e)thorn,* Old English *hagathorn : haga,* HAW (fruit) + THORN.]

Haw-thorne (hô'thôrn'), **Nathaniel** (1804–64). U.S. novelist and short-story writer. He was born at Salem in Massachusetts and won fame with the novels *The Scarlet Letter* (1850) and *The House of the Seven Gables* (1851).

hay (hā) *n.* **1.** Grass or other plants such as clover or alfalfa, cut and dried for fodder. **2.** *Slang.* A trifling amount of money. Used only in negative phrases, especially in *that ain't hay.* —**hit the hay.** *Slang.* To go to bed. —**make hay while the sun shines.** To take full advantage of an opportunity.
  ~*v.* **hayed, haying, hays.** —*intr.* To convert grass into hay. —*tr.* **1.** To make (grass) into hay. **2.** To feed with hay. **3.** To put (land) under hay. [Middle English *hei, hay,* Old English *hīeg,* from Germanic.]

hay-box (hā'bŏks') *n. Chiefly British.* A box filled with hay in which heated food can be left to continue cooking by retained heat.

hay-cock (hā'kŏk') *n. Chiefly British.* A conical mound of hay in a field.

Hay-dn (hīd'n), **Franz Joseph** (1732–1809). Austrian composer. He wrote 104 symphonies and 84 string quartets, as well as operas and concertos. Among his works are the oratorios *The Creation* (1798) and *The Seasons* (1801). Mozart and Beethoven studied with him.

Hayes (hāz), **Helen** (1900–). U.S. actress. She has displayed her versatility and durability as an actress in a 50-year career encompassing stage, film, radio, and television performances, including her acclaimed portrayal of Queen Victoria in *Victoria Regina* (1933–34) and Oscar-winning performances in *The Sin of Madelon Claudet* (1935) and *Airport* (1970).

Hayes, Rutherford Birchard (1822–93). 19th U.S. president (1877–81). Winning the controversial election of 1876 by one electoral vote, he pacified the South by removing federal troops (1877), vetoed a bill restricting Chinese immigration (1879), and stemmed Congress' attempts to usurp presidential power.

hay fever *n.* An allergic condition of the upper respiratory tract and the eyes, characterized by a running nose, watering eyes, and sneezing due to histamine release caused by an abnormal sensitivity to certain airborne particles, notably pollen and dust.

hay-fork (hā'fôrk') *n.* **1.** A long-handled pronged tool for moving hay; a pitchfork. **2.** A machine-operated fork for moving hay.

hay-loft (hā'lôft', -lŏft') *n.* A loft for storing hay.

hay-mak-er (hā'mā'kər) *n.* **1.** One who makes grass into hay. **2.** A machine that makes hay; especially, one that processes it so that it dries evenly and quickly. **3.** *Slang.* A powerful blow with the fist.

hay-mow (hā'mou') *n.* **1.** A hayloft or haystack. **2.** The hay stored in a hayloft or haystack.

hay-rack (hā'răk') *n.* **1.** A rack from which livestock eat hay. **2. a.** A rack fitted to a wagon for carrying hay. **b.** A wagon so fitted.

hay-rick (hā'rĭk') *n.* A haystack.

hay-seed (hā'sēd') *n.* **1.** Grass seed shaken out of hay. **2.** Pieces of chaff or straw that fall out of hay. **3.** *Slang.* A country bumpkin.

hay-stack (hā'stăk') *n.* A large stack of hay, usually built up into a cuboid shape with a ridged top.

hay-ward (hā'wôrd') *n.* An officer formerly charged with the repair of fences and enclosures, and especially with the retention of cattle on the town common. [Middle English *hayward, heiward : obsolete heie,* hedge, fence, Old English *hege* + WARD.]

hay-wire (hā'wīr') *n.* Wire used in baling hay.
  ~*adj. Informal.* **1.** Put together in a makeshift way. **2.** Not functioning properly; broken or in a state of disorder. **3.** Mentally confused or erratic; crazy. —**go haywire. 1.** To function improperly or fall into disorder. **2.** To break down mentally and act erratically. [Baling wire is often used for makeshift repair jobs.]

haz-ard (hăz'ərd) *n.* **1. a.** A source of potential loss or danger; a peril; a risk: *an occupational hazard.* **b.** Vulnerability to loss or danger: *at hazard.* **2.** A chance or accident. **3.** *Obsolete.* A gamble; a stake. **4.** A dice game resembling craps. **5.** Any of the openings in a court-tennis court through which the ball may be hit for points. **6.** A bunker or other obstacle on a golf course. —See Synonyms at **danger.**
  ~*tr.v.* **hazarded, -arding, -ards. 1.** To imperil; jeopardize. **2.** To run the risk of; expose oneself to. **3.** To venture (something); dare: *hazard a guess.* [Middle English *hasard, hazard,* from Old French *hasard,* from Spanish *azar,* throw of the dice, accident, from Arabic *al-zahr,* luck, chance.]

haz-ard-ous (hăz'ər-dəs) *adj.* **1.** Marked by danger; perilous. **2.** Depending on chance; risky.

hazard warning signal *n.* The simultaneous flashing of all the directional indicators on a motor vehicle, used as a warning to other road users when the vehicle has broken down or is otherwise obstructing traffic.

haze¹ (hāz) *n.* **1. a.** Atmospheric moisture, dust, smoke, and vapor suspended to form a partially opaque condition. **b.** *Meteorology.* The atmospheric condition so formed when visibility is less than

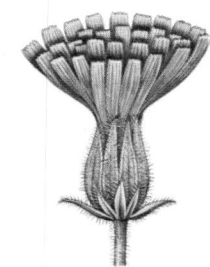

hawk's-beard *A European wildflower that is often confused with the dandelion because their blooms are so similar. Unlike the dandelion, the hawk's-beard holds its flowers on branching stems.*

hawksbill *Of about 230 species of turtle and tortoise, the hawksbill turtle is one of five marine varieties. These turtles rarely leave the water except to lay eggs in the sand on tropical beaches. The hatched young must find their own way to the water.*

hawkweed *A wildflower that grows in limestone cliffs and rocks, the hawkweed can produce ripe seed without fertilization. This leads to many mutations, making it difficult to identify different types.*

hawthorn *Hawthorns, or may trees, are widely used in Europe to form prickly, livestockproof hedges. The trees bear fleshy berries, or haws.*

1.24 miles (2 kilometers) but not less than 0.62 miles (1 kilometer). **c.** Indistinct visibility caused by rising heat: *a heat haze.* **2.** A vague or confused state of mind.
∼*v.* **hazed, hazing, hazes.** —*intr.* To become misty or hazy; blur. —*tr.* To make hazy. [Back-formation from HAZY.]

haze[2] *tr.v.* **hazed, hazing, hazes. 1.** *Nautical.* To persecute or punish with meaningless, difficult, or humiliating tasks. **2.** To initiate, as into a college fraternity, by exacting humiliating performances from or playing rough practical jokes upon. **3.** *Regional.* To drive (cattle or horses) with saddle horses. [Perhaps akin to Old French *haser*†, to insult, harass.] **—haz·er** *n.*

ha·zel (hā′zəl) *n.* **1.** Any of various shrubs or small trees of the genus *Corylus;* especially, *C. avellana,* of Europe, or *C. americana,* of North America, bearing edible nuts enclosed in a leafy husk. **2.** The nut of such a tree or shrub; a hazelnut. **3.** Light to strong brown or yellowish brown. [Middle English *hasel,* Old English *hæsel,* from Germanic.] **—ha·zel** *adj.*

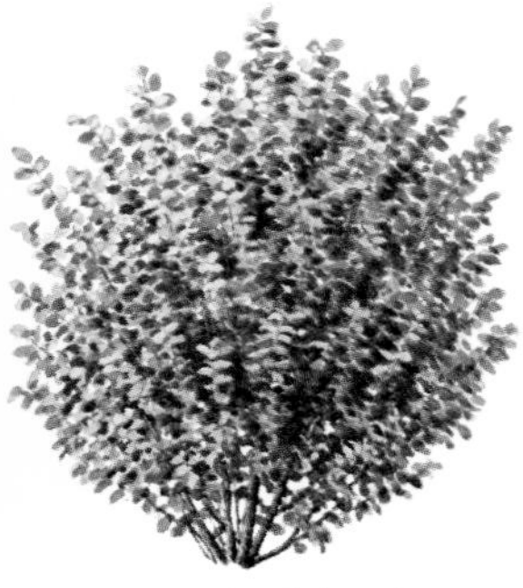

hazel *Mature hazels have been grown for centuries for their edible nuts. Young branches are also harvested because their straightness and flexibility make them ideal for fences and stakes.*

hazel hen *n.* A Eurasian grouse, *Tetrastes bonasia,* having brownish-red plumage with gray and white markings. Also called "hazel grouse."

ha·zel·nut (hā′zəl-nŭt′) *n.* The edible nut of a hazel, having a smooth, hard brown shell. Also called "cob," "cobnut," "filbert."

Haz·litt (hăz′lĭt), **William** (1778–1830). British essayist and critic. He was a friend of Coleridge and Wordsworth. His works include *Characters of Shakespeare* (1817) and *The Spirit of the Age* (1825).

haz·y (hā′zē) *adj.* **-ier, -iest. 1.** Marked by the presence of haze; misty. **2.** Not clearly defined; vague; confused. [17th century (nautical) : origin obscure.] **—haz·i·ly** *adv.* **—haz·i·ness** *n.*

hazzan. Variant of **chazan.**

hb, hb. halfback.

Hb hemoglobin.

HB (āch′bē′) *adj.* Designating a pencil or pencil lead that is medium hard.
∼*n.* An HB pencil. [Abbreviation for *hard black.*]

H-beam (āch′bēm′) *n.* A steel joist or girder with an H-shaped cross section. Also called "H-girder."

H-bomb (āch′bŏm′) *n.* A **hydrogen bomb** *(see).*

H.C. 1. Holy Communion. **2.** House of Commons.

hd. 1. hand. **2.** head.

hdbk. handbook.

hdqrs. headquarters.

he[1] (hē) *pron.* The third person singular pronoun in the nominative case, masculine gender. **1.** Used to represent the male person, animal, or other being last mentioned or implied. **2.** Used to represent any person whose sex is not specified: *Everyone knows he is mortal.* —See Usage note at **me.**
∼*n.* A male animal or person: *Is the cat a he?* Often used in combination: *a he-cat.* [Middle English *he,* Old English *hē.*]

he[2] (hā) *n.* The fifth letter of the Hebrew alphabet. See feature at **alphabet.** [Hebrew *hē,* possibly "lattice window."]

he[3] (hē) *interj.* Also **he-he** (hē′hē′). Used to express amusement or derision.

he[4] (hē) *n.* A children's game, **tag** *(see).* [From HE (pronoun).]

He The symbol for the element helium.

HE, H.E. 1. high explosive. **2.** *Ecclesiastical.* His Eminence. **3.** His (or Her) Excellency.

head (hĕd) *n., pl.* **heads** or **head** (for sense 7b). *Abbr.* **hd. 1. a.** The upper or anterior vertebrate extremity, containing the brain and the eyes, ears, nose, mouth, and jaws. **b.** The analogous part of an invertebrate. **2.** The seat of the faculty of reason; intelligence, intellect, or mind. **3. a.** A mental facility or aptitude: *a head for mathematics.* **b.** A natural ability to deal with a specified thing or situation without losing one's self-control: *no head for drink; a good head for heights.* **4. a.** Poise; wits; composure: *Keep your head in a crisis.* **b.** Freedom to move or act without restraint. **5.** A portrait or representation of a head. **6.** Life: *a crime that cost him his head.* **7. a.** An individual considered as a unit: *a head count; The cost is $25 per head.* **b.** A single animal within a herd: *20 head of cattle.* **8.** The hair on the human head. **9. a.** One who occupies the foremost position; a leader, chief, or director: *the head of a big engineering company.* **b.** A headmaster or headmistress. **c.** The foremost or leading position: *at the head of the parade.* **10. a.** The difference in depth of a liquid at two given points. **b.** The measure of pressure at the lower point expressed in terms of this difference. **c.** Pressure, as of a liquid or vapor: *a head of steam.* **11.** The foam on an effervescent liquid. **12.** The breaking point or tip of a suppurating abscess, boil, or pimple. **13.** A turning point; a crisis: *bring matters to a head.* **14.** A projection, weight, or fixture at one end of an elongated object: *the head of a pin.* **15.** The operating part of a tool, machine, or other device, as: **a.** The working end of a hammer or ax. **b.** The operative part of a tape recorder or other device for recording and detecting stored information on magnetic tape or disks. **c.** The explosive part of a bomb, missile, or the like; a warhead. **16.** A rounded, compact mass of leaves, buds, or flowers, as of cabbage, lettuce, or cauliflower. **17.** *Botany.* A dense, compact cluster of flowers, as of composite plants or clover. **18.** The end of an object whose two ends are interchangeable, such as a drum. **19.** *Nautical.* **a.** The forepart of a vessel. **b.** The latrine of a vessel. **c.** The top part or upper edge of a sail. **20.** The source of a stream; a headwater. **21.** The upper end or extremity of something, as: **a.** The top of a staircase. **b.** The top of a page. **c.** The end of a bed where one's head lies. **d.** The end associated with a real or figurative head: *sitting at the head of the table.* **e.** The upper, landward end of a bay or lake. **22.** A high promontory, cape, or cliff rising above a body of water. **23.** A passage or gallery in a mine. **24.** *Astronomy.* The coma and nucleus of a comet. **25.** *Grammar.* The word in a construction that determines the syntactic character of the construction; for example, in the phrase *a lazy young boy, boy* is the head that determines that the whole structure functions as a noun. **26.** A **cylinder head** *(see).* **27. a.** A headline or heading. **b.** A distinct topic or category. **28.** Headway; progress. **29.** The head used as a rough unit of measure: *taller by a head; lost by a head.* **30.** *Informal.* A headache. **31.** *Slang.* A habitual user of drugs such as marijuana and LSD. **—bite someone's head off.** *Informal.* To speak angrily to someone. **—down by the head.** *Nautical.* With the bow lying lower in the water than the stern. **—go to one's head. 1.** To make lightheaded or drunk. **2.** To increase the pride or conceit of. **—head and shoulders above.** Far superior to. **—head or tail.** Something clear or unmistakable: *I couldn't make head or tail of the lecture.* **—in one's head.** In one's mind; internally: *did the sum in her head.* **—keep one's head above water.** To keep out of trouble, such as debt or poverty. **—off one's head.** Crazy; insane. **—off the top of one's head.** Impromptu; without careful consideration. **—on (or upon) one's head.** Within one's own responsibility, or at one's own risk: *"My deeds upon my head!"* (Shakespeare). **—one's head off.** *Informal.* Immoderately; inordinately; to extreme: *He snored his head off.* **—out of one's head. 1.** Delirious. **2.** Crazy. **3.** High on drugs or alcohol. **—over one's head. 1.** Beyond one's ability to understand or deal with: *a subject that is over his head.* **2.** To one higher in command: *go over the sergeant's head.* **3.** Notwithstanding the claims of others: *promoted over the heads of several senior managers.* **—put (or lay) heads together.** To combine forces or abilities. **—take it into one's head.** To make a sudden decision to do something, especially something unusual or irrational. **—turn someone's head. 1.** To infatuate someone, especially if the passion inspired is groundless or rash. **2.** To make someone conceited.
∼*adj.* **1.** Foremost in rank or importance: *the head librarian.* **2.** Placed at the top or front: *the head name on the list.* **3.** Coming from ahead or from the front: *head winds.*
∼*v.* **headed, heading, heads.** —*tr.* **1.** To be director or chief of; command: *head the committee.* **2.** To assume or be placed in the first or foremost position of: *head the line of march.* **3.** To aim or direct: *head the horse for home.* **4.** To remove the top of (a plant or tree). Often used with *down.* **5.** *Soccer.* To drive (the ball) by hitting it with the head. **6.** To place a head or heading on: *headed each column with a number.* **—head off. 1.** To block the progress of and force to change direction; intercept. **2.** To forestall or deflect (criticism, for example). —*intr.* **1.** To proceed or set out in a specified direction: *head for town.* **2.** To proceed toward or be destined for a specified, often undesirable condition: *headed for bankruptcy.* **3.** To form a head, as lettuce or cabbage. **4.** To originate; rise. Used of a stream or river. [Middle English *heved, he(f)d,* Old English *hēafod,* from Germanic.]

Head (hĕd), **Edith** (1898–1981). U.S. costume designer. Her first solo credit for designing motion-picture costumes was for *She Done Him Wrong* (1933). During her years as head designer for Paramount and Universal studios, she received 34 Academy Award nominations and won a record 8 Oscars for such movies as *All About Eve* (1950), *Sabrina* (1954), and *The Sting* (1973).

head·ache (hĕd′āk′) *n.* **1.** A pain in the head caused by mental or emotional stress, fatigue, or illness. **2.** *Informal.* Someone or something that annoys or bothers. **—head·ach·y** *adj.*

head·band (hĕd′bănd′) *n.* **1.** A band worn around the head. **2.** A cloth band attached to the top of the spine of a book.

head-bang (hĕd′băng′) *intr.v.* **-banged, -banging, -bangs.** To shake the head in a wild, frenzied manner while dancing to heavy-metal music. **—head-bang·ing** *n. & adj.*

head·board (hĕd′bôrd′, -bōrd′) *n.* A board, panel, or the like that forms the head, as of a bed.

head·case (hĕd′kās′) *n. British Slang.* A very stupid person; a dolt.

head·cheese (hĕd′chēz′) *n.* **1.** A jellied loaf or sausage containing chopped and boiled parts of the feet, head, and sometimes the tongue and heart of an animal, usually a hog. **2.** *Chiefly British.* **Brawn** *(see).*

head cold *n.* **Coryza** *(see).*

head·dress (hĕd′drĕs′) *n.* Anything worn on the head, as a covering or ornament.

head·ed (hĕd′ĭd) *adj.* **1.** Growing or grown into a head. **2.** Having a head or heads of the specified type or number. Used in combination: *three-headed.* **3.** Having a mental make-up of the specified type. Used in combination: *level-headed.*

head·er (hĕd′ər) *n.* **1.** One that fits a head on an object. **2.** One that removes a head from an object; especially, a machine that reaps the heads of grain and passes them into a wagon or receptacle. **3.** A pipe that serves as a central connection for two or more smaller pipes. **4.** A wooden beam in a floor or roof placed between two long beams and supporting the ends of one or more tailpieces. **5.** A brick laid across rather than parallel with a wall. Compare **stretcher. 6.** *Informal.* A headlong dive or fall. **7.** A raised tank or hopper that maintains a constant pressure or supply to some system, especially the small tank supplying water to a central-heating system. In this sense, also called "header tank."

head·fast (hĕd′făst′, -fäst′) *n.* A mooring rope or chain that secures the bow of a ship to the wharf.

head·first (hĕd′fûrst′) *adv.* Also **head·fore·most** (hĕd′fôr′mōst′, -məst, hĕd′fōr′-). **1.** With the head leading; headlong: *go headfirst down the stairs.* **2.** Impetuously; brashly. **—head·first** *adj.*

PRONUNCIATION KEY

ă, pat; ā, pay; âr, care;
ä, father, are; b, bib;
ch, church; d, deed; ĕ, pet;
ē, be; f, fife; g, gag; h, hat;
hw, which; ĭ, pit; ī, pie;
îr, pier; j, judge; k, kick;
l, lid, needle; m, mum;
n, no, sudden; ng, thing;
ŏ, pot; ō, toe; ô, paw, for;
oi, noise; ou, out; o͝o, book;
o͞o, boot; p, pop; r, roar;
s, sauce; sh, ship, dish;
t, tight; th, thin, path;
th, this, bathe; ŭ, cut; ûr, fur;
v, valve; w, with; y, yes;
z, zebra, size; zh, vision;
ə, about, item, edible,
gallop, circus, peaceful

IN FOREIGN WORDS:

à, *Fr.* ami; œ, *Fr.* feu, *Ger.* schön; ü, *Fr.* tu, *Ger.* über; KH, *Ger.* ich, *Scot.* loch; N, *Fr.* bon; y′, *Fr.* Compiègne

STRESS MARKS:

Primary stress: ′
in·cite′ (ĭn-sīt′)
Secondary stress: ′
in′sight′ (ĭn′sīt′)

head gate *n.* A control gate upstream of a lock or canal.

head·gear (hĕd'gîr') *n.* **1.** A covering, such as a hat or helmet, for the head. **2.** The part of a harness that fits about a horse's head. **3.** The rigging for hauling or lifting located at the head of a mine shaft. **4.** *Nautical.* The rigging on the forward sails.

head·hunt·ing (hĕd'hŭn'tĭng) *n.* **1.** The taking of human heads as trophies, practiced for religious purposes in some primitive societies. **2.** *Slang.* The attempt to recruit personnel, especially executive personnel. **3.** *Slang.* The process of eliminating or neutralizing political rivals. —**head·hunt·er** *n.*

head·ing (hĕd'ĭng) *n.* **1. a.** A word or words at the head of a chapter, paragraph, letter, or the like. **b.** A division or category. **2.** *Navigation.* The course or direction of movement of a ship or aircraft. **3.** *Mining.* **a.** A gallery or drift. **b.** The end of a gallery or drift.

head·lamp (hĕd'lămp') *n.* A headlight.

head·land (hĕd'lənd, -lănd') *n.* **1.** A point of land, usually high and with a sheer drop, extending out into a body of water; a promontory. **2.** The unplowed land at the end of a plowed furrow.

head·less (hĕd'lĭs) *adj.* **1. a.** Formed without a head. **b.** Decapitated. **2.** Without a leader or director. **3.** Witless; foolish.

head·light (hĕd'līt') *n.* A powerful lamp, usually one of a pair, mounted on the front of a vehicle.

head·line (hĕd'līn') *n.* **1.** The title or caption of a newspaper article, set in large type, the size denoting the importance of the article. **2.** A line at the head of a page giving the title, author, page number, or the like. **3. headlines.** A brief résumé of the main items of interest at the beginning or end of a radio or television news bulletin. ~*tr.v.* **headlined, -lining, -lines. 1.** To supply (an article or page) with a headline. **2.** To serve as the headliner of: *He headlines the bill.*

head·lin·er (hĕd'lī'nər) *n.* A performer who receives prominent billing; a star.

head·lock (hĕd'lŏk') *n.* A wrestling hold in which the head of one wrestler is locked under the arm of the other.

head·long (hĕd'lông', -lŏng') *adv.* **1.** With the head leading; headfirst. **2.** Impetuously; rashly. **3.** At breakneck speed or with uncontrolled force. ~*adj.* **1.** Headfirst; done with the head leading: *a headlong fall.* **2.** Impetuous; rash. **3.** Uncontrollably forceful or fast. **4.** *Archaic.* Steep; sheer. —See Usage note at **impetuous.** [Middle English *hedlong,* variant of *hedling* : *hed,* HEAD + -LING.]

head·man (hĕd'măn', -mən) *n., pl.* **-men** (-měn', -mĭn). A chief or leader of a tribe or village.

head·mas·ter, head master (hĕd'măs'tər, -mä'stər) *n. Abbr.* **H.M.** A male school principal.

head·mis·tress, head mistress (hĕd'mĭs'trĭs) *n.* A female school principal.

head money *n.* **1.** A reward paid for the capture and delivery of a fugitive; a bounty. **2.** A poll tax.

head·most (hĕd'mōst', -məst) *adj.* Leading; foremost. Said especially of a ship.

head note *n.* A note at the beginning of a page or document; especially, one prefixed to a report of a legal case that summarizes its contents.

head of state *n.* One, typically a monarch or president, who acts as the formal and ceremonial head of a nation as opposed to the head of the government. The head of state may either be a figurehead or have executive power, depending on the state's constitution.

head of the river *n. British.* **1.** Any of various rowing regattas; especially, one at which bumping races are held. **2.** The boat or crew holding the leading position in such a regatta.

head-on (hĕd'ŏn', -ôn') *adj.* **1.** Facing forward; frontal. **2.** With the front end exposed and receiving the impact: *a head-on collision.* **3.** Direct and uncompromising. —**head-on** *adv.*

head over heels *adv.* **1.** Rolling, as in a somersault. **2.** To the point of abandon; hopelessly: *head over heels in love.*

head·phone (hĕd'fōn') *n.* A receiver, as for a telephone, radio, or record player, held to the ears by a band that fits over the head.

head·piece (hĕd'pēs') *n.* **1.** A helmet, hat, or other headgear. **2.** A set of headphones; a headset. **3.** *Printing.* An ornamental design at the top of a page. **4.** *Archaic.* The head as the seat of intellect.

head·quar·ter (hĕd'kwôr'tər) *v.* **-tered, -tering, -ters.** *Informal.* —*intr.* To establish headquarters. —*tr.* To provide with headquarters. [Back-formation from HEADQUARTERS.]

Usage: The verb *headquarter* is used informally in both transitive and intransitive senses: *The European correspondent will headquarter in Paris. The magazine has headquartered him in a building that houses many foreign journalists.* Neither of these examples is considered acceptable in formal writing.

head·quar·ters (hĕd'kwôr'tərz) *pl.n. Abbr.* **hdqrs., h.q., HQ, H.Q.** Sometimes used with a singular verb. **1.** The offices of a commander, as of a military unit, from which official orders are issued. **2.** Any center of operations: *Father makes the study his headquarters.*

Usage: The noun *headquarters* is used with either a singular or plural verb. The plural is more common: *The headquarters are in New York.* But the singular is sometimes preferred when reference is to authority rather than to physical location: *Battalion headquarters has approved the retreat.*

head·race (hĕd'rās') *n.* A watercourse that feeds water into a mill, water wheel, or turbine. Compare **tailrace.**

head·rest (hĕd'rĕst') *n.* A support for the head, as at the back of a chair or car seat.

head·room (hĕd'rōōm', -rŏŏm') *n.* The vertical space in a room or under a bridge, doorway, or the like; clearance.

heads (hĕdz) *n. Used with a singular verb.* The obverse side of a coin, often carrying a representation of a head. Compare **tails.**

head·sail (hĕd'səl, -sāl') *n.* A sail, such as a jib, set forward of a foremast.

head·scarf (hĕd'skärf') *n.* A scarf worn over the head, usually folded in a triangle and tied under the chin.

head sea *n.* Waves running directly against the course of a ship.

head·set (hĕd'sĕt') *n.* A pair of headphones.

head·ship (hĕd'shĭp') *n.* **1.** The position or office of the head or leader; primacy; command. **2.** *British.* The position of a headmaster or headmistress.

head shrinker *n.* **1.** *Slang.* A psychiatrist. **2.** A head-hunter who shrinks the heads of his victims.

heads·man (hĕdz'mən) *n., pl.* **-men** (-mĭn). Formerly, a public executioner who beheaded condemned prisoners.

head·spring (hĕd'sprĭng') *n.* A fountainhead; a source.

head·stall (hĕd'stôl') *n.* The section of a bridle that fits over the horse's head.

head·stand (hĕd'stănd') *n.* An act of balancing on the head, usually supported by the hands, with one's feet in the air.

head start *n.* A start before other contestants in a race, or any comparable advantage.

head·stock (hĕd'stŏk') *n.* A nonmoving part of a machine or powered tool that supports a revolving part, such as the spindle of a lathe.

head·stone (hĕd'stōn') *n.* **1.** A memorial stone set at the head of a grave. **2.** *Architecture.* A keystone *(see).*

head·strong (hĕd'strông', -strŏng') *adj.* **1.** Inclined to insist on having one's own way; willful; obstinate. **2.** Resulting from willfulness or obstinacy. —See Synonyms at **obstinate, unruly.**

head·wait·er (hĕd'wā'tər) *n.* A waiter in charge of the other waiters in a restaurant, who often seats guests and generally serves as host. Also called "maître d'hôtel."

head·wa·ter (hĕd'wô'tər, -wŏt'ər) *n. Often* **headwaters.** The water from which a river rises; source.

head·way (hĕd'wā') *n.* **1.** Forward movement or rate of forward movement, especially of a ship. **2.** Progress; advance. **3.** *Architecture.* Headroom; clearance. **4.** The distance in time or space between two vehicles traveling the same route.

head wind *n.* A wind blowing directly against the course of an aircraft or ship. Compare **tail wind.**

head·word (hĕd'wûrd') *n.* A word placed at the beginning of a paragraph or forming a heading; especially, a word entered and defined in a dictionary or encyclopedia.

head·work (hĕd'wûrk') *n.* Mental activity or work.

head·y (hĕd'ē) *adj.* **-ier, -iest. 1.** Tending to upset the balance of the senses or mental faculties; intoxicating. **2.** Exciting; exhilarating. **3.** Headstrong; obstinate. —**head·i·ly** *adv.* —**head·i·ness** *n.*

heal (hēl) *v.* **healed, healing, heals.** —*tr.* **1.** To restore to health; cure. **2.** To set right; repair: *healed the rift between us.* **3.** To rid of sin, anxiety, or the like; restore. —*intr.* **1.** To become whole and sound; return to health. **2.** To repair by natural processes, as by forming scar tissue. Used of cuts, wounds, and burns. [Middle English *helen,* Old English *hǣlen;* akin to WHOLE.] —**heal·a·ble** *adj.*

heal-all (hēl'ôl') *n.* A plant, the self-heal *(see).*

heal·er (hē'lər) *n.* **1.** One that heals; especially, a physician. **2.** A person who aims to cure by spiritual, magical, or other nonmedical means.

health (hĕlth) *n.* **1.** The state of an organism with respect to functioning, disease, and abnormality at any given time. **2.** The state of an organism functioning normally without disease or abnormality. **3.** Broadly, any state of optimal functioning, well-being, or progress. **4.** A wish for someone's good health, expressed as a toast. [Middle English *helthe,* Old English *hǣlth.* See **whole, -th.**]

health farm *n.* A residential center where people go to improve their health and fitness by following diets, taking exercise, undergoing massage, and the like. Also called "health spa."

health food *n.* Food considered to be highly beneficial to the health; especially, food that has been organically grown and has not been overrefined or processed.

health·ful (hĕlth'fəl) *adj.* **1.** Conducive to good health; salutary. **2.** *Rare.* Healthy. —**health·ful·ly** *adv.* —**health·ful·ness** *n.*

health physics *n. Used with a singular verb.* The branch of medical physics concerned with protection from radiation.

health visitor *n. Chiefly British.* A nurse who visits old and sick people and those with young children in their homes.

health·y (hĕl'thē) *adj.* **-ier, -iest. 1.** Possessing good health. **2.** Conducive to good health; healthful: *healthy air.* **3.** Indicative of a rational or constructive frame of mind; sound: *a healthy attitude.* **4.** Indicative of or being in a sound and prosperous condition: *The firm's overseas operations are particularly healthy.* **5.** Sizable; considerable: *a healthy portion.* —**health·i·ly** *adv.* —**health·i·ness** *n.*

Synonyms: hale, hardy, robust, sound, vigorous, well, well-preserved, wholesome.

Hea·ney (hē'nē), **Seamus Justin** (1939–). Irish poet born in Ulster. His poetry is typified by dense, earthy imagery and, increasingly, has shown a concern for the political crisis in Ulster. His books include *North* (1975) and *Field Work* (1979).

heap (hēp) *n.* **1.** A group of things haphazardly gathered or in disorder; a pile. **2.** *Often* **heaps.** *Informal.* A great deal; a lot. **3.** *Slang.* An old or run-down car; a jalopy. ~*tr.v.* **heaped, heaping, heaps. 1.** To put or throw in a heap; pile

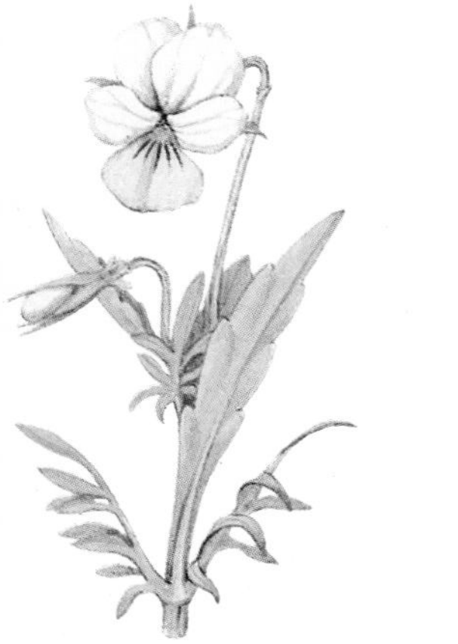

heartsease *In Shakespeare's play,* A Midsummer Night's Dream, *the fairy queen Titania falls in love with Bottom, the weaver, after the juice of heartsease is sprinkled onto her eyes. In North America this flower is more commonly known as Johnny-jump-up, or wild pansy.*

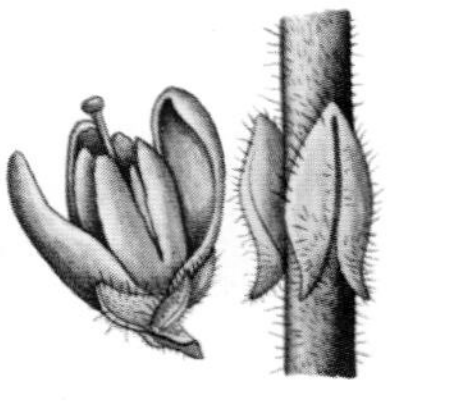

heather *Of the several species of heather, the true heather, or ling, is the most common. It grows on open moors and its young shoots are the main food of red grouse.*

PRONUNCIATION KEY

ă, pat; ā, pay; âr, care;
ä, father, are; b, bib;
ch, church; d, deed; ĕ, pet;
ē, be; f, fife; g, gag; h, hat;
hw, which; ĭ, pit; ī, pie;
îr, pier; j, judge; k, kick;
l, lid, needle; m, mum;
n, no, sudden; ng, thing;
ŏ, pot; ō, toe; ô, paw, for;
oi, noise; ou, out; o͝o, book;
o͞o, boot; p, pop; r, roar;
s, sauce; sh, ship, dish;
t, tight; th, thin, path;
th, this, bathe; ŭ, cut; ûr, fur;
v, valve; w, with; y, yes;
z, zebra, size; zh, vision;
ə, about, item, edible,
gallop, circus, peaceful

IN FOREIGN WORDS:

à, *Fr.* ami; œ, *Fr.* feu, *Ger.* schön; ü, *Fr.* tu, *Ger.* über;
KH, *Ger.* ich, *Scot.* loch;
N, *Fr.* bon; y', *Fr.* Compiègne

STRESS MARKS:

Primary stress: ′
in·cite′ (ĭn-sīt′)
Secondary stress: ′
in′sight′ (ĭn′sīt′)

up. **2.** To fill to overflowing: *heap a plate with vegetables; a heaping tablespoonful.* **3.** To bestow (praise, for example) in abundance; lavish. [Middle English *heap, hep(e),* Old English *hēap,* from Germanic.]

hear (hîr) *v.* **heard** (hûrd), **hearing, hears.** —*tr.* **1.** To perceive (sound) by the ear: *heard the siren of the fire engine.* **2.** To listen to attentively: *Hear me out.* **3.** To learn by the speech of others; be told: *I hear that you're sick.* **4.** To listen to in an official, professional, or formal capacity: *hear someone's confession; The fourth witness was heard in the afternoon.* **5.** To listen to with favor; give consideration to: *Lord, hear my plea.* **6.** To be present at and listen to: *heard an interesting lecture.* —*intr.* **1.** To be capable of perceiving sound: *The profoundly deaf cannot hear at all.* **2.** To receive a communication: *heard from them last week.* **3.** To be informed; learn: *I heard about your accident. I've never heard of him.* —**hear hear!** Used to express agreement with a speaker. —**not hear of.** To forbid mention or consideration of: *I won't hear of your going!* [Middle English *heren,* Old English *hīeran,* from Germanic.] —**hear·er** *n.*

hear·ing (hîr′ĭng) *n.* **1.** The sense by which sound is perceived; the capacity to hear. **2.** The range of audibility; earshot. **3.** An opportunity to be heard. **4.** *Law.* An opportunity for a person to put forward arguments or evidence to a judge or tribunal concerning a matter under investigation; especially, a preliminary examination, a trial, or an appeal.

hearing aid *n.* A small electronic apparatus that amplifies sound and is worn in or behind the ear to compensate for poor hearing. Also *British* "deaf-aid."

heark·en, hark·en (här′kən) *v.* **-ened, -ening, -ens.** —*intr.* To listen attentively; give heed. —*tr. Archaic.* To listen to; hear. [Middle English *herk(n)en,* Old English *he(o)rcnian,* from *he(o)rcian,* to HARK.]

hear·say (hîr′sā′) *n.* **1.** Information heard from another. **2.** *Law.* Evidence based on the reports of others rather than on a witness' own knowledge, and therefore generally not admissible as testimony. In this sense, also called "hearsay evidence."

hearse (hûrs) *n.* **1.** A vehicle for conveying a coffin. **2.** *Archaic.* A framelike structure over a coffin or tomb on which to hang epitaphs. [Middle English *herse,* harrow-shaped triangular frame for holding candles placed over a bier, from Old French, from Latin *hirpex* (stem *hirpic-*), harrow, rake, probably from Oscan (Samnite) *hirpus,* wolf (alluding to its teeth).]

Hearst (hûrst), **William Randolph** (1863–1951). U.S. newspaper and magazine publisher. Beginning with the San Francisco *Examiner* in 1887, he built the world's largest publishing empire, including 28 major newspapers, and pioneered popular journalism. Throughout his life he displayed a passion for collecting, buying everything from Egyptian mummies and Etruscan tombs to paintings, armor, entire rooms, and even a Spanish monastery. San Simeon, his "ranch" in western California, is now a popular tourist attraction.

heart (härt) *n.* **1. a.** *Anatomy.* The hollow, muscular organ in vertebrates that pumps blood through the circulatory system. It is divided vertically into two halves, each having an upper atrium and a lower ventricle. **b.** A similarly functioning structure in invertebrates. **2.** The approximate location of this organ in or on the body; the breast; the bosom. **3. a.** The heart thought of as the vital center of one's being, emotions, and sensibilities; the seat or repository of emotions: *decided with his heart rather than his head.* **b.** The heart thought of as the repository of one's deepest and sincerest feelings and beliefs: *an appeal from the heart; a subject near to his heart.* **4. a.** Character, disposition, or emotional constitution: *a man after my own heart.* **b.** One's prevailing mood or inclination: *a heavy heart; a change of heart. My heart wasn't in it.* **c.** Capacity for sympathy or generosity; compassion: *He has no heart.* **d.** Love; affection: *The child won her heart.* **5. a.** Courage; resolution; determination: *Don't lose heart.* **b.** The firmness of will or lack of feeling required for an unpleasant task or responsibility: *didn't have the heart to tell him.* **6.** A person esteemed as lovable, loyal, or courageous: *a dear heart.* **7. a.** The central or innermost part: *the heart of the financial district.* **b.** The compact central part of a cabbage, artichoke, or the like. **c.** The essential feature; the most vital part: *get to the heart of the problem.* **8.** *Chiefly British.* The condition of land with respect to fertility. Used chiefly in the phrase *in good heart.* **9.** A conventionalized two-lobed representation of the heart, usually colored red or pink. **10. a.** The red, heart-shaped symbol appearing on one of the four suits of playing cards. **b.** A card bearing this symbol. **c. hearts.** *Used with a singular or plural verb.* The suit of cards identified by this symbol. **11. hearts.** *Used with a singular verb.* A card game in which the objective is either to avoid hearts when taking tricks or to take all the hearts. —**at heart.** Essentially; fundamentally. —**break someone's heart.** To cause someone disappointment, sorrow, or grief. —**by heart.** By memory or rote. —**eat one's heart out. 1.** To undergo bitter, hopeless anguish or longing. **2.** To be consumed with envy. —**have one's heart in one's mouth.** To be anxious or apprehensive to an extreme. —**have one's heart in the right place. 1.** To mean well; have good intentions. **2.** To be an admirable and worthy person. —**in one's heart of hearts.** In one's truest feelings. —**take to heart.** To take seriously and be affected or troubled by. —**to one's heart's content.** To one's entire satisfaction, without limitation. —**wear one's heart on one's sleeve.** To show one's feelings clearly by one's behavior. [From Iago's comment "But I will wear my heart upon my sleeve / For daws to peck at . . ." in Shakespeare's *Othello* (1604), Act I, scene 1.] —**with all one's heart. 1.** With great willingness or pleasure. **2.** With the deepest feeling or devotion.
∼*v.* **hearted, hearting, hearts.** —*tr. Archaic.* To encourage; hearten. —*intr.* To form a heart. Used of a cabbage, lettuce, or similar vegetable. [Middle English *he(o)rt, hart,* Old English *heorte.*]

heart·ache (härt′āk′) *n.* Emotional anguish; deep sorrow. —See Synonyms at **regret.**

heart attack *n.* **1.** An acute medical condition marked by a sudden severe pain in the chest, and sometimes also the arms and throat, resulting from abnormal functioning of the heart; especially, **coronary thrombosis** *(see).* See **myocardial infarction. 2.** An instance or episode of such a condition.

heart·beat (härt′bēt′) *n.* A single complete pulsation of the heart.

heart block *n.* Reduction or complete lack of coordination in the beating of the atria and ventricles of the heart.

heart·break (härt′brāk′) *n.* Intense sorrow or grief; crushing disappointment.

heart·break·ing (härt′brā′kĭng) *adj.* Causing heartbreak; acutely saddening or pitiful. —**heart·break·ing·ly** *adv.*

heart·bro·ken (härt′brō′kən) *adj.* Suffering from crushing grief or despair; having a broken heart. —**heart·bro·ken·ly** *adv.* —**heart·bro·ken·ness** *n.*

heart·burn (härt′bûrn′) *n.* A burning sensation in the stomach and esophagus, often accompanied by the eructation of small quantities of a highly acid fluid, caused by the regurgitation of stomach fluids; pyrosis. Also called "cardialgia."

heart disease *n.* Any organic or functional abnormality of the heart.

heart·ed (här′tĭd) *adj.* Having or showing a specified kind of disposition or emotional make-up. Used in combination: *heavy-hearted; false-hearted.*

heart·en (härt′n) *tr.v.* **-ened, -ening, -ens.** To give strength or hope to; encourage; cheer. —**heart·en·ing·ly** *adv.*

heart failure *n.* The partial mechanical failure of the heart as a pump, resulting in congestion of the lungs and liver, shortness and wheezing of breath, and edema in the legs.

heart·felt (härt′fĕlt′) *adj.* Deeply or sincerely felt; earnest. —See Synonyms at **sincere.**

hearth (härth) *n.* **1.** The floor of a fireplace, usually extending into a room and paved with brick, flagstone, or the like. **2.** The hearth thought of as the center of family life; the fireside; the home. **3.** *Metallurgy.* **a.** The lowest part of a blast furnace or cupola, from which the molten metal flows. **b.** The bottom of a reverberatory furnace where ore is exposed to the flame. **4.** The fireplace or brazier used by a blacksmith. [Middle English *herth,* Old English *heorth,* from Germanic.]

hearth·rug (härth′rŭg′) *n.* A rug laid on the floor in front of a fireplace.

hearth·stone (härth′stōn′) *n.* **1.** Stone used in the construction of a hearth. **2.** The fireside; home. **3.** A soft stone or powder used for scouring and whitening a hearth, steps, or the like.

heart·i·ly (härt′l-ē) *adv.* **1.** In a hearty manner; with warmth, enthusiasm, or good appetite. **2.** Thoroughly; completely: *heartily sick of all the complaining.*

heart·land (härt′lănd′) *n.* A central region; especially, one considered to be strategically, economically, or politically vital.

heart·less (härt′lĭs) *adj.* **1.** Without compassion; pitiless; cruel. **2.** *Archaic.* Without enthusiasm; spiritless. —**heart·less·ly** *adv.* —**heart·less·ness** *n.*

heart-lung machine (härt′lŭng′) *n.* A machine used during heart surgery that bypasses the heart and lungs and circulates oxygenated blood through the body.

heart murmur *n.* A sound, audible through a stethoscope placed over the heart, produced by turbulent blood flow and typically indicating some structural abnormality. Also called "bruit," "murmur."

heart-rend·ing (härt′rĕn′dĭng) *adj.* Causing anguish or deep sympathy; acutely moving.

heart-search·ing (härt′sûr′chĭng) *n.* An examination of one's innermost feelings.

hearts·ease, heart's-ease (härts′ēz′) *n.* **1.** Peace of mind. **2.** A plant, *Viola tricolor,* native to Eurasia, having small, spurred violet, yellow, or violet and yellow flowers. Also called "Johnny-jump-up," "love-in-idleness," "wild pansy." [Middle English *herts ease* : *herts,* genitive of *hert,* HEART + EASE.]

heart·sick (härt′sĭk′) *adj.* Sick at heart; profoundly disappointed; despondent. —**heart·sick·ness** *n.*

heart·some (härt′səm) *adj. British Regional.* **1.** Giving heart or spirit; encouraging. **2.** Cheerful; blithe.

heart-start·er (härt′stär′tər) *n. Australian Slang.* The first drink of the day, especially the first alcoholic drink.

heart-strick·en (härt′strĭk′ən) *adj.* Also **heart-struck** (-strŭk′). Overwhelmed with grief, dismay, or remorse.

heart·strings (härt′strĭngz′) *pl.n.* **1.** The deepest feelings or affections. Often used facetiously: *a performance geared to tug at the heartstrings.* **2.** In notions of anatomy held before the 17th century, sinews and tendons bracing and sustaining the heart.

heart·throb (härt′thrŏb′) *n.* **1.** A beat of the heart. **2.** An object of infatuation; an idol or sweetheart.

heart-to-heart (härt′tə-härt′) *adj.* Personal and candid; frank.
∼*n.* A frank and intimate conversation.

heart-warm·ing (härt′wôr′mĭng) *adj.* **1.** Gratifying; encouraging. **2.** Moving.

heart·wood (härt'wŏŏd') *n.* The older, inactive central wood of a tree or woody plant, usually darker and harder than the sapwood. Also called "duramen."

heart·worm (härt'wûrm') *n.* A nematode worm, *Dirofilaria immitis,* parasitic in the heart and bloodstream of dogs and other mammals.

heart·y (här'tē) *adj.* **-ier, -iest. 1.** Expressed with warmth of feeling; exuberant and unrestrained: *a hearty welcome.* **2.** Complete or thorough; unequivocal: *hearty support.* **3. a.** Enjoying or requiring much food: *a hearty appetite.* **b.** Providing abundant nourishment; substantial: *a hearty bowl of soup.* ~*n., pl.* **hearties.** A good fellow; a comrade; especially, a sailor.

heat (hēt) *n.* **1.** A form of energy associated with the motion of atoms or molecules. It is energy transferred as a result of a temperature difference, and is transmitted through solid and fluid media by conduction, through fluid media by convection, and through empty space by radiation. **2.** The perceptible, sensible, or measurable effect of such energy so transmitted; especially, a physiological sensation of being hot. **3.** An intense or pathological manifestation of such a perception or sensation; excessive warmth. **4.** The condition of being warm or hot. **5.** A hot season; hot weather. **6. a.** Intensity, as of color, appearance, emotion, or effect. **b.** The point or moment of greatest intensity: *in the heat of the argument.* **7.** A period or condition of sexual excitement in female mammals, **estrus** *(see).* **8. a.** A single course in a race or competition made up of several. **b.** A preliminary race or contest to determine finalists. **9.** *Slang.* **a.** Entanglement with or pursuit by the police. **b.** The police. **10.** *Informal.* Pressure or stress: *have to work harder when the heat is on.* **11.** *Slang.* Adverse reaction or comments: *took a lot of heat for his mistake.* ~*v.* **heated, heating, heats.** —*tr.* **1.** To make warm or hot. **2.** To excite the feelings of; inflame. —*intr.* **1.** To become warm or hot. **2.** To become excited emotionally or intellectually. [Middle English *he(e)te,* Old English *hētu,* from Germanic.]

heat barrier *n.* **Thermal barrier** *(see).*

heat capacity *n.* The amount of heat required to raise the temperature of a body by one degree, either at constant pressure or at constant volume and without inducing chemical changes or change of phase. See **specific heat capacity.**

heat content *n.* A thermodynamic function, **enthalpy** *(see).*

heat death *n.* A state of maximum entropy in a closed system; especially, the hypothetical fate of the universe when it degenerates into a state in which no energy is available to do work.

heat·ed (hē'tĭd) *adj.* Marked by anger and emotion; impassioned: *a heated exchange.* —**heat·ed·ly** *adv.*

heat engine *n. Physics.* A device for obtaining mechanical work from heat, as by the expansion of a gas.

heat·er (hē'tər) *n.* **1.** An apparatus that heats or provides heat. **2.** Someone who heats something or tends a heating apparatus. **3.** *Electronics.* An electrically heated filament that indirectly heats the cathode in a valve. **4.** *Slang.* A pistol.

heat exchanger *n.* A device used to transfer heat from a fluid flowing on one side of a barrier to a fluid or fluids flowing on the other.

heat exhaustion *n.* A reaction to excessive heat, marked by prostration, weakness, and collapse resulting from dehydration. Also called "heat prostration." Compare **heat stroke.**

heath (hēth) *n.* **1.** Any of various usually low-growing shrubs of the genus *Erica* and related genera, native to the Old World, having small, evergreen leaves and small, urn-shaped pink or purplish flowers. Many species are also called "heather." **2.** An extensive tract of open, uncultivated land, often on sandy soil, covered with shrubby plants, especially heaths; a moor. **3.** Any of various butterflies of the genus *Coenonympha* in the family Satyridae. [Middle English *he(e)th, heath,* Old English *hēth,* from Germanic.]

Heath (hēth), **Edward Richard George** (1916–). British politician. As leader of the Conservative Party he was prime minister from 1970 to 1974, when he lost support after calling for a mandate on his tough policy against unions. His administration was marked by Britain's entry into the Common Market (January 1973).

hea·then (hē'thən) *n., pl.* **heathens** or collectively **heathen. 1.** One who does not acknowledge the God of Judaism, Christianity, or Islam; especially, one who adheres to the polytheistic or animistic beliefs of a primitive people. **2.** One who is regarded as irreligious, uncivilized, or unenlightened. [Middle English *hethen,* Old English *hēthen,* from Germanic, heath-dwelling, savage, from *haith-* (untested), HEATH.] —**hea·then** *adj.* —**hea·then·dom** (hē'thən-dəm), **hea·then·ism, hea·then·ry** *n.*

hea·then·ish (hē'thə-nĭsh) *adj.* **1.** Of or pertaining to heathens. **2.** Uncouth or barbarous in the manner ascribed to heathens. —**hea·then·ish·ly** *adv.* —**hea·then·ish·ness** *n.*

heath·er (hĕth'ər) *n.* **1.** A low-growing shrub, *Calluna vulgaris,* native to Eurasia, growing in dense masses and having small evergreen leaves and clusters of small, urn-shaped pinkish-purple flowers. Also called "ling." **2.** Any of several similar, related plants of the genus *Erica* or other genera; heath. **3.** Grayish purple to purplish red. [Middle English (Scottish) *hadder, hathir†,* assimilated to *he(e)th, heath,* HEATH.] —**heath·er** *adj.*

heath·er·y (hĕth'ə-rē) *adj.* **1.** Of or like heather. **2.** Covered with heather: *heathery hills.*

heath hen *n.* A form of the prairie chicken, *Tympanuchus cupido,* that became extinct in eastern North America during the first part of the 20th century.

Heath Rob·in·son (rŏb'ĭn-sən) *adj. British.* Ludicrously ingenious

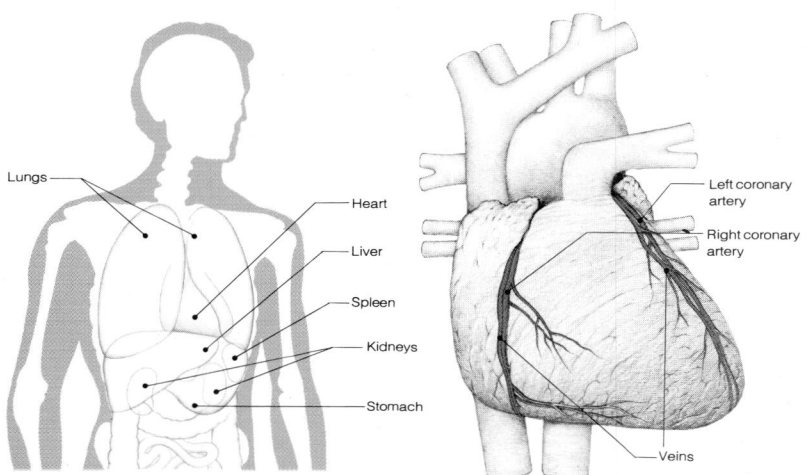

heart

THE BODY'S STRONGEST MUSCLE
How the four-chambered heart pumps blood to every cell in the human body

Although it is only the size of a man's fist, the heart is the strongest of all the muscles. As it pumps blood around the body, it works twice as hard as the leg muscles of a sprinter or the arm muscles of a heavyweight boxing champion. It pumps through 4.5 liters (8 pints) of blood a minute and can increase the amount by at least five times during exertion. The heart consists of two pumps lying side by side. Each has an upper chamber, or atrium, and a lower chamber, or ventricle. The halves are separated by a wall of muscle called the septum.

Lungs — Heart — Liver — Spleen — Kidneys — Stomach

Left coronary artery — Right coronary artery — Veins

THE HEART'S ROLE *The heart has to work nonstop to provide the body with a continuous supply of blood. The right side receives "used" blood from the veins and pumps it to the lungs to be oxygenated; oxygen-rich blood is then returned to the left side, which pumps it through the arteries.*

BLOOD SUPPLY *The heart needs its own supply of blood to keep it beating. Oxygen-rich blood is pumped to the chambers of the heart through the coronary arteries; once it has been used, the blood is returned to the right side of the heart through a network of veins.*

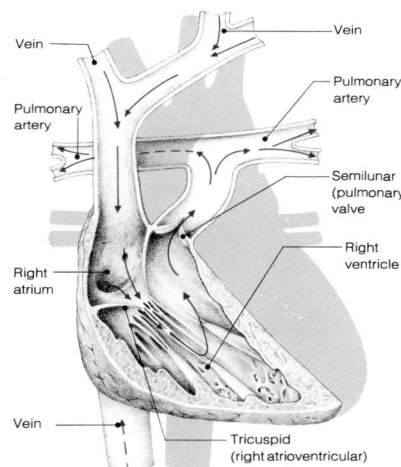

Vein — Pulmonary artery — Right atrium — Vein

Vein — Pulmonary artery — Semilunar (pulmonary) valve — Right ventricle — Tricuspid (right atrioventricular) valve

INCOMING BLOOD *Deoxygenated blood flows from the veins into the atrium on the right side of the heart. It then flows through the one-way tricuspid valve into the lower chamber, or ventricle. Contraction of the muscle surrounding the ventricle pumps the blood through the semilunar valve and along the pulmonary arteries to the lungs, where it receives oxygen.*

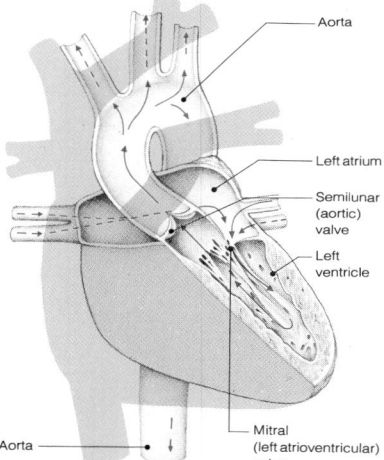

Aorta

Aorta — Left atrium — Semilunar (aortic) valve — Left ventricle — Mitral (left atrioventricular) valve

OUTGOING BLOOD *Oxygenated blood flows from the lungs into the left atrium before passing through the mitral valve into the ventricle below. Muscle surrounding the ventricle contracts and pumps the blood through the semilunar valve into the aorta. It is then circulated through the body's arteries and ultimately returned as deoxygenated blood to the right side of the heart.*

and complicated in design and construction. Said of a mechanical contrivance. [After Edward *Heath Robinson* (1872–1944), English cartoonist and book illustrator noted for his drawings of complicated contrivances.]

Heath·row (hēth'rō'). Site of London Airport. The principal air terminal of the United Kingdom, it is situated 24 kilometers (15 miles) west of central London.

heat lightning *n.* Intermittent flashes of light across the horizon on a hot summer evening, unaccompanied by thunder and thought to

FINAL DESTINATIONS FOR THE ELECT AND THE DAMNED

How different religions envisage life after death

Christian notions of heaven and hell grew out of the ancient Hebrew faith of Judaism. In Old Testament times, the Jews thought of heaven as the home of Yahweh, the God of Israel; only highly virtuous individuals, such as the prophet Elijah, were taken there. The rest of mankind, good and evil, slept in a gloomy underworld known as Sheol, where there was neither pleasure nor pain. Later Sheol—which resembled the classical Greek underworld of Hades—became in Jewish belief a place of rigorous punishment. Similarly, the Gehenna of the New Testament was a place for the wicked, while heaven became the destination of the righteous as well as the home of God.

The medieval church devised a fiery and detailed catalogue of torments for the damned, and some of these beliefs are still accepted by many Christians. Heaven, on the other hand, has usually been described only in vague terms as the place where believers are reunited for eternity with God. Most modern theologians prefer to speak of both heaven and hell as states or conditions of the soul, rather than places in any literal sense.

Other faiths have had more precise visions of paradise. For the Vikings of Scandinavia, for instance, heaven was Valhalla, the hall of the slain. Dead warriors, who were brought to Valhalla by the Valkyries, spent the day fighting. But their wounds were always healed in time for an evening of feasting with the god Odin. For devout Muslims, the Koran—the Islamic "Bible"—promises endless pleasure in heaven: shady gardens, cool fountains, beautiful women, and the wine that believers are forbidden on earth. Early Hindus also thought of paradise as earthly pleasures on an eternal scale; Vedic texts describe a realm of light with "music, sexual fulfillment, no pain and no care." Modern Hindus also believe in paradise, but it is reached only by the saintly and only after innumerable reincarnations.

Some faiths believe in multiple heavens. The largest branch of Buddhism, known as Mahayana Buddhism, teaches that there is a graded series of heavens. Buddhism also teaches, however, that man's ultimate goal is not paradise at all, but deliverance from the pain of life—the state of total blessedness called Nirvana, meaning extinction or, literally, "blowing out."

EASTERN TORMENT *The king of the underworld oversees the fate of sinners in a Japanese Buddhist view of hell. Beside him, a sinner sits in the scales of judgment; below, a liar has his tongue torn out.*

HEAVEN ON HIGH *Angels surround a dove symbolizing the Holy Spirit in an 18th-century painting on the ceiling of a German church.*

be cloud reflections of distant lightning. Also called "summer lightning."

heat of fusion *n.* The quantity of heat required to melt a given mass of a solid at a given temperature. See **latent heat.**

heat of vaporization *n.* The amount of heat required to convert a given mass of liquid into vapor at a given temperature. See **latent heat.**

heat pipe *n.* A device for conducting heat, consisting of a metal tube closed at both ends and containing volatile liquid at low pressure. Heat is carried down the tube by vaporized molecules of liquid and returns by capillary action through a wire-mesh coating inside the tube.

heat prostration *n.* Heat exhaustion (see).

heat pump *n.* An engine that transfers heat from a relatively low-temperature reservoir to one at a higher temperature, used for domestic heating.

heat rash *n. Pathology.* Miliaria (see).

heat-seal (hēt'sēl') *tr.v.* **-sealed, -sealing, -seals.** To seal by heating: *heat-sealed blood vessels.*

heat-seek·ing (hēt'sē'kĭng) *adj.* Designating or pertaining to missiles that home on a target by sensing the radiant heat emitted. **—heat-seek·er** *n.*

heat shield *n.* A barrier that prevents the heating of a space by absorbing, reflecting, or dissipating external heat; especially, a protective structure on a spacecraft or missile that dissipates heat on atmospheric re-entry by melting and vaporizing. Also called "ablator."

heat sink *n.* **1.** An environment having a much greater heat capacity and at a lower temperature than an object with which it is in thermal contact. **2.** Any device by means of which heat is absorbed or stored in or removed from a thermal system.

heat stroke *n.* A severe illness caused by exposure to excessively high temperatures and characterized by severe headache, high fever with a dry, hot skin, and, in serious cases, collapse and coma. Also called "sunstroke." Compare **heat exhaustion.**

heat-treat (hēt'trēt') *tr.v.* **-treated, -treating, -treats.** To subject (a material, especially a metal or alloy) to controlled changes of temperature in order to modify its properties.

heat wave *n.* A spell of unusually hot weather.

heave (hēv) *v.* **heaved** or *chiefly nautical* **hove** (hōv), **heaving, heaves.** —*tr.* **1.** To raise or lift with strenuous effort; hoist. **2. a.** To throw (a heavy object, for example) with great effort; hurl. **b.** To throw. **3.** To breathe or emit painfully or unhappily: *heaved a sigh.* **4.** *Nautical.* To raise (an anchor or net, for example). **b.** To pull on or haul (a rope or cable, for example). **5.** *Geology.* To cause (rock strata) to move in a horizontal direction. —*intr.* **1.** To rise up or swell, especially from turbulence; bulge; billow. **2.** *Informal.* To vomit or try to vomit. **3.** *Nautical.* **a.** To come to be in a specified position. Used of ships: *hove alongside; hove into view.* **b.** To pull on or haul a rope, cable, or the like: *heave around on the anchor.* **c.** To push or pull on a capstan bar or the like. —See Synonyms at **lift, throw. —heave to.** *Nautical.* **1.** To come to a stop. **2.** To bring (a ship) to a stop.
~*n.* **1.** The act or strain of heaving. **2.** *Geology.* The horizontal movement of rock strata displaced by a fault. **3.** *Informal.* A throw, especially one made with considerable effort. **4.** Dismissal; the heave ho. Preceded by *the.* [Heave, hove, hove; Middle English *hebben* or *heven, hove, hove,* Old English *hebban, hōf, hafen,* from Germanic.]

heave ho *interj. Nautical.* Used as a command to give a hard push or pull together.
~*n.* Also **heave-ho** (hēv'hō'). *Slang.* Dismissal, especially from a job. Preceded by *the.* [Originally used for heaving up an anchor.]

heav·en (hĕv'ən) *n.* **1.** *Often* **heavens.** The sky or universe as seen from the earth; the firmament. **2.** *Often* **Heaven. a.** In the Christian tradition, the abode of God, the angels, and the souls of those who are granted salvation. **b.** In a number of other religions and mythologies, a place of bliss where the souls of the blessed go after death. **3. a. Heaven.** Divine Providence: *May Heaven help you.* **b.** *Often* **heavens.** A euphemism for God, used in exclamations: *Good heavens!* **4. heavens.** The celestial powers; the gods: *The heavens favored the young ruler.* **5. a.** Supreme happiness; a state of bliss. **b.** A thing or place that is wonderful or enchantingly perfect; a sheer delight: *The lake was heaven.* **—move heaven and earth.** To do everything possible to bring something about. [Middle English *heven, hefen,* Old English *heofon, hefen.*]

heav·en·ly (hĕv'ən-lē) *adj.* **1.** Sublime; enchanting; lovely. **2.** Of or having to do with Heaven or the heavens; celestial. **—heav·en·li·ness** *n.*

heav·en·sent (hĕv'ən-sĕnt') *adj.* Occurring at an opportune time; providential.

heav·en·ward (hĕv'ən-wərd) *adv.* Also **heav·en·wards** (-wərdz). Toward heaven. **—heav·en·ward** *adj.*

heav·er (hē'vər) *n.* **1.** One that lifts or heaves. **2.** *Nautical.* A short bar used as a lever for twisting rope.

heaves (hēvz) *pl.n. Used with a singular or plural verb.* **1.** A pulmonary disease of horses, characterized by coughing and other serious respiratory irregularities. Also called "broken wind." **2.** *Slang.* A seizure of vomiting. Usually preceding by *the.*

heav·i·er-than-air (hĕv'ē-ər-thən-âr') *adj.* **1.** Denser than air. Said of a gas. **2.** Obtaining lift from aerodynamic forces rather than buoyancy. Said of an aircraft.

heav·i·ly (hĕv'ə-lē) *adv.* **1.** In a heavy manner. **2.** Very slowly and

with difficulty; laboriously: *walked heavily.* **3.** Greatly or severely: *heavily in debt.*

heav·i·ness (hĕv'ē-nĭs) *n.* The state or quality of being heavy.

Heav·i·side layer (hĕv'ē-sīd') *n.* A layer of the earth's atmosphere, the **E layer** *(see).* [After Oliver *Heaviside* (1850–1925), English physicist.]

heav·y (hĕv'ē) *adj.* **-ier, -iest. 1.** Having relatively great weight: *a heavy load.* **2.** Having relatively high density: *a heavy metal.* **3. a.** Of greater than average amount, volume, output, or the like; substantial: *heavy rainfall; a heavy turnout; heavy losses.* **b.** Of greater than average intensity, violence, or extent: *heavy fighting; heavy seas.* **4.** Dense or thick: *heavy fog.* **5. a.** Indulging to a great or habitual degree; chronic: *a heavy drinker.* **b.** Involved or participating on a large scale; prodigious: *a heavy investor.* **c.** Requiring or consuming relatively large quantities: *The car is heavy on oil.* **6. a.** Of great import or seriousness; grave: *heavy matters of state.* **b.** Ponderous; requiring effort to assimilate: *The report makes heavy reading.* **c.** Sad or painful: *heavy news.* **7. a.** Laborious; arduous: *a heavy day at work.* **b.** Burdensome; oppressive: *heavy taxes.* **8. a.** Copious: *a heavy breakfast.* **b.** Not easily or quickly digested: *an unusually heavy fruitcake.* **9.** Marked by a lack of fineness or gracefulness; coarse; inelegant: *heavy features; a heavy style of architecture.* **10.** Overcast: *heavy skies.* **11.** Dull and deep, suggesting great weight. Said of a sound: *fell with a heavy thump.* **12. a.** Clayey and tending to retain water. Said of soil. **b.** Spongy and tending to retard progress. Said of the going on a racecourse. **13.** Weighed with concern or sadness; despondent: *a heavy heart.* **14.** Lumbering; clumsy. **15.** Strong and pervasive; pungent: *a heavy odor.* **16. a.** Weighed down, as from being full; laden: *trees heavy with plums.* **b.** Showing weariness; listless: *heavy eyes.* **17.** Involving the large-scale extraction of raw materials or the manufacture of large commodities such as aircraft, motor vehicles, or armaments: *heavy industry.* **18.** *Archaic.* Gravid; in an advanced state of pregnancy. **19.** *Theater.* **a.** Of or pertaining to a serious or tragic dramatic role. **b.** Of or pertaining to the role of a villain. **20.** *Physics.* **a.** Designating an isotope with a mass greater than that of others found in the same element. **b.** Designating an atomic particle having a mass between that of pi mesons and protons. **21.** Bearing heavy arms or armor: *heavy cavalry.* **22.** *Slang.* **a.** Unpleasant or threatening: *a heavy scene.* **b.** Too intimate or demanding: *Don't get heavy with me.*
~*adv.* Heavily. **—hang heavy.** To pass slowly or tediously: *Time hung heavy on his hands.*
~*n., pl.* **heavies. 1.** A villain in a story or play. **2.** *Informal.* A ruffian; a tough: *a gang of heavies.* **3.** *Informal.* An important or influential person; a heavyweight. **4. a.** A serious or tragic role in a play. **b.** An actor playing such a role. **5.** *Scottish.* Heavy bitter beer. [Middle English *hevi,* Old English *hefig,* from Germanic.]

> *Synonyms:* cumbersome, hefty, massive, ponderous, unwieldy, weighty.

heav·y-dut·y (hĕv'ē-dōō'tē, -dyōō'tē) *adj.* Made to withstand hard use or wear.

heav·y-foot·ed (hĕv'ē-fŏŏt'ĭd) *adj.* Having a heavy, lumbering gait. **—heav·y-foot·ed·ness** *n.*

heav·y-hand·ed (hĕv'ē-hăn'dĭd) *adj.* **1.** Clumsy. **2.** Tactless. **3.** Oppressive. **—heav·y-hand·ed·ly** *adv.* **—heav·y-hand·ed·ness** *n.*

heav·y-heart·ed (hĕv'ē-här'tĭd) *adj.* Melancholy; sad; depressed. **—heav·y-heart·ed·ly** *adv.* **—heav·y-heart·ed·ness** *n.*

heavy hydrogen *n.* An isotope of hydrogen with mass number greater than 1; deuterium *(see).*

heav·y-lad·en (hĕv'ē-lād'n) *adj.* **1.** Laden with a heavy load. **2.** Burdened with cares; troubled.

heavy metal *n.* A style of rock music characterized by a heavy bass beat and the use of powerful amplification. **—heav·y-met·al** (hĕv'ē-mĕt'l) *adj.*

heav·y-set (hĕv'ē-sĕt') *adj.* Having a heavy, compact build.

heavy spar *n.* A mineral, **barite** *(see).*

heavy water *n.* Any of several isotopic varieties of water, especially **deuterium oxide** *(see),* consisting chiefly or exclusively of molecules containing hydrogen with mass number greater than 1 and used as a moderator in certain nuclear reactors.

heav·y-weight (hĕv'ē-wāt') *n.* **1.** One of above average weight. **2.** One that competes in the heaviest class; specifically, a boxer weighing more than 175 pounds (81 kilograms). **3.** *Informal.* A person of great importance or influence.

Heb. **1.** Hebrew. **2.** Hebrews (New Testament).

heb·do·mad (hĕb'də-măd') *n.* **1.** A group of seven. **2.** A period of seven days; a week. [Latin *hebdomas* (stem *hebdomad-*), the number seven, seven days, from Greek, from *hepta,* seven.]

heb·dom·a·dal (hĕb-dŏm'ə-dəl) *adj.* Weekly. **—heb·dom·a·dal·ly** *adv.*

he·be (hē'bē) *n.* Any plant of the genus *Hebe,* which contains small evergreen shrubs with spikes of variously colored flowers, widely grown as garden ornamentals. Also called "shrubby veronica." [New Latin, after **HEBE.**]

He·be (hē'bē). *Greek Mythology.* The goddess of youth and spring, the cupbearer of Zeus. [Greek *Hēbē,* personification of *hēbē,* youth, youthful vigor.]

He·bei (hŭ'bā'). Also **Ho·pei, Ho·peh** (hō'bā'). Province of northeastern China, the oldest continuously civilized area in the world. Tianjin (Tientsin) is the capital.

he·be·phre·ni·a (hē'bə-frē'nə-ə, -frĕn'ē-ə) *n.* A schizophrenia, typically starting at puberty, characterized by foolish mannerisms, apa-

hebe *These evergreen shrubs, once known as veronicas, are popular garden plants in coastal regions because of their ability to withstand salt-laden winds. The species shown here is* Hebe gauntleptii.

hedgehog *When frightened, the hedgehog rolls up into a spiky ball. It feeds mostly on insects, worms, and occasionally snakes.*

hedge sparrow *Properly called the dunnock, this songbird is not related to the sparrow and can be distinguished from it by its insect-eater's bill, which is thin and pointed, whereas the seed-eating sparrow's bill is short and blunt.*

thy, delusions, hallucinations, senseless laughter, and regressive behavior. [Greek *hēbē,* youth + -PHRENIA.] **—he·be·phren·ic** (hē′bə-frĕn′ĭk, -frē′nĭk) *adj.*

heb·e·tate (hĕb′ə-tāt′) *tr.v.* **-tated, -tating, -tates.** To make blunt or dull. [Latin *hebetāre,* from *hebes*† (stem *hebet-*), blunt, dull.] **—heb·e·ta·tion** *n.* **—heb·e·ta·tive** *adj.*

heb·e·tude (hĕb′ə-to͞od′, -tyo͞od′) *n.* Dullness of mind; mental lethargy. [Late Latin *hebetūdo* : Latin *hebes* (stem *hebet-*), blunt, dull + -TUDE.] **—heb·e·tu·di·nous** (hĕb′ə-to͞od′n-əs, -tyo͞od′n-əs) *adj.*

Hebr. Hebrew.

He·bra·ic (hĭ-brā′ĭk) *adj.* Also **He·bra·i·cal** (-ĭ-kəl). Of, pertaining to, or characteristic of the Hebrews or their language or culture. [Middle English *Ebrayke,* from Late Latin *Hebraicus,* from Greek *Hebraikos,* from *Hebraios,* HEBREW.] **—He·bra·i·cal·ly** *adv.*

He·bra·ism (hē′brā-ĭz′əm, hē′brə-) *n.* **1.** A manner or custom characteristic of the Hebrews; especially, a Hebrew expression or idiom. **2.** The culture, spirit, or character of the Hebrew people. [From HEBRAIC.]

He·bra·ist (hē′brā′ĭst) *n.* A scholar of Hebrew. **—He·bra·is·tic** (hē′brā-ĭs′tĭk), **He·bra·is·ti·cal** *adj.* **—He·bra·is·ti·cal·ly** *adv.*

He·bra·ize (hē′brā-īz′) *v.* **-ized, -izing, -izes.** *—tr.* To make Hebraic in form or idiom. *—intr.* To use or adopt Hebraisms.

He·brew (hē′bro͞o) *n. Abbr.* **Heb., Hebr. 1.** A member of the Semitic people claiming descent from Abraham, Isaac, and Jacob; an Israelite; a Jew. **2. a.** The Semitic language of the ancient Hebrews, used in most of the Old Testament. **b.** Any of various later forms of this language, especially the form now spoken by the people of Israel.
~adj. Of or having to do with the Hebrews. [Middle English *Ebreu, Hebrewe,* from Old French *Ebreu,* from Latin *Hebraeus,* Hebraic, from Greek *Hebraios,* from Aramaic *'ibhray, 'ebhray,* from Hebrew *'ibhrī,* "he who came from across (the river)," from *'ēbher,* region across, from *ābhar,* to pass across or over.]

Hebrew calendar *n.* The **Jewish calendar** *(see).*

He·brews (hē′bro͞oz) *n. Abbr.* **Heb.** *Used with a singular verb.* A book of the New Testament; the Epistle to the Hebrews.

Hebrew Scriptures *pl.n.* The Pentateuch, the Prophets, and the Hagiographa, forming the covenant between God and the Jewish people that is the foundation and Bible of Judaism while constituting for Christians the **Old Testament** *(see).*

Heb·ri·des (hĕb′rə-dēz′). Also **Western Isles.** An archipelago of about 500 islands off the western coast of Scotland. It is divided into the Outer Hebrides, including Lewis, Harris, and the Uists; and the Inner Hebrides, including Skye, Mull, and Islay. **—Heb·ri·de·an** (hĕb′rə-dē′ən) *n. & adj.*

He·bron (hē′brən). *Arabic* **Al Kha·lil** (ăl′ KHä-lēl′). Town on the Israeli-occupied West Bank of Jordan. It is one of the oldest inhabited cities in the world and is the traditional site of the tomb of Abraham.

Hec·a·te, Hek·a·te (hĕk′ə-tē). *Greek Mythology.* An ancient fertility goddess who later became identified with Persephone as queen of Hades and protectress of witches.

hec·a·tomb (hĕk′ə-tōm′, -to͞om′) *n.* **1.** In ancient Greece, a large-scale public offering to the gods, originally of 100 oxen. **2.** Any large-scale sacrifice. [Latin *hecatombē,* from Greek *hekatombē* : *hekaton,* hundred + *-bē,* from *bous,* ox.]

heck[1] (hĕk) *n.* Used as an intensive, as a euphemism for **hell** (sense 8): *ran like heck.*
~interj. Used as a euphemism for **hell.**

heck[2] *n. British Regional.* A frame or grating that obstructs the passage of fish in a river. [Middle English (northern dialect), variant of HATCH.]

heck·el·phone (hĕk′əl-fōn′) *n. Music.* A woodwind instrument of the oboe family having a pitch between that of the English horn and the bassoon. [German *Heckelphon,* after Wilhelm *Heckel* (1856–1909), German instrument maker.]

heck·le (hĕk′əl) *v.* **-led, -ling, -les.** *—tr.* **1.** To harass (a speaker or performer) persistently, as with questions, gibes, or objections; badger publicly. **2.** To comb (flax or hemp) with a hatchel. *—intr.* To engage in heckling a speaker or interrupting a public meeting. [Middle English *hekelen,* to comb flax, from *hekell, hechele,* flax-comb, hatchel, Old English *hæcel* (unattested).] **—heck·ler** *n.*

hec·tare (hĕk′târ′) *n. Abbr.* **ha** A metric unit of area equal to 100 ares or 2.471 acres. [French : HECT(O)- + ARE.]

hec·tic (hĕk′tĭk) *adj.* **1.** Characterized by feverish activity, confusion, or haste. See Usage note below. **2.** Of, relating to, or designating an undulating fever, as in diseases such as tuberculosis or septicemia. **3.** Consumptive; feverish. **4.** Flushed.
~n. **1.** A hectic fever. **2.** A person suffering from a hectic fever. [Middle English *etik,* from Old French *etique,* from Late Latin *hecticus,* from Greek *hektikos,* formed by habit, consumptive, hectic, from *hexis,* condition, habit, from *ekhein,* to have, hold, be in a certain condition.]

Usage: *Hectic* is well established in its general sense related to feverish activity, confusion, or haste. In earlier usage, that sense was sometimes deprecated as a loose extension of the term's meaning in medicine.

hecto-, hect- *prefix. Symbol* **h** Indicates 100; for example, **hectocotylus, hectare.** [French, from Greek *hekaton,* hundred.]

hec·to·cot·y·lus (hĕk′tō-kŏt′l-əs) *n., pl.* **-li** (-lī′). A modified arm of the male of certain cephalopods, such as the octopus, containing sperm and functioning as a reproductive organ. Also called "hectocotylus arm." [New Latin *Hectocotylus,* name given by G.L. Cuvier to the detached arm, which he thought was a parasitic worm : HECTO- + Greek *kotulē,* cup, hollow object (see **cotyledon**).]

hec·to·gram, hec·to·gramme (hĕk′tə-grăm′) *n. Abbr.* **hg** A metric unit of mass equal to 100 grams or 3.527 avoirdupois ounces. [French *hectogramme* : HECTO- + GRAM.]

hec·to·graph (hĕk′tə-grăf′, -gräf′) *n.* A machine using a glycerin-coated layer of gelatin to make copies of typed or written material. Also called "copygraph."
~tr.v. **hectographed, -graphing, -graphs.** To copy by means of a hectograph. [German *Hektograph* : HECTO- + -GRAPH.] **—hec·to·graph·ic** (hĕk′tə-grăf′ĭk) *adj.* **—hec·to·graph·i·cal·ly** *adv.*

hec·to·li·ter, hec·to·li·tre (hĕk′tə-lē′tər) *n. Abbr.* **hl 1.** A unit of capacity or volume, used in liquid measure, equal to 100 liters or 105.7 liquid quarts. **2.** A metric measure of capacity or volume, used in dry measure, equal to 100 liters or 90.8 dry quarts.

hec·to·me·ter, hec·to·me·tre (hĕk′tə-mē′tər) *n. Abbr.* **hm** A metric unit of length equal to 100 meters (about 328 feet).

hec·tor (hĕk′tər) *v.* **-tored, -toring, -tors.** *—tr.* To intimidate in a blustering way. *—intr.* To behave like a bully; swagger.
~n. A bully. [After HECTOR.]

Hec·tor (hĕk′tər). *Greek Legend.* A Trojan prince who led the forces of Troy in the Trojan War and was killed by Achilles. [Greek *Hektōr.*]

Hec·u·ba (hĕk′yo͞o-bə). *Greek Legend.* The wife of Priam and mother of Hector, Paris, and Cassandra.

he'd (hēd). **1.** Contraction of *he had.* **2.** Contraction of *he would.*

hed·dle (hĕd′l) *n.* One of a set of parallel cords or wires in a loom used to separate and guide the warp threads and make a path for the shuttle. [Probably altered from Middle English *helde,* heddle, Old English *hefeld,* from Germanic *hafjan* (unattested), to raise.]

hedge (hĕj) *n.* **1.** A row of closely planted shrubs or low-growing trees forming a fence or boundary. **2. a.** A line of objects or people forming a barrier. **b.** A means of protection or defense, especially against financial loss.
~v. **hedged, hedging, hedges.** *—tr.* **1.** To enclose or bound with or as if with a hedge or hedges. **2.** To restrict; hem in; confine. Often used with *in* or *about.* **3.** To counterbalance (a bet, for example) with other transactions so as to limit the risk of loss. *—intr.* **1.** To plant or cultivate a hedge or hedges. **2.** To take compensatory measures against possible loss. **3.** To avoid committing oneself, as by making cautious or ambiguous statements. [Middle English *hegge,* Old English *hegg, hecg* (unattested), from Germanic.] **—hedg·er** *n.* **—hedg·y** *adj.*

hedge garlic *n.* A plant, the **garlic mustard** *(see).*

hedge·hog (hĕj′hôg′, -hŏg′) *n.* **1.** Any of several small Old World mammals of the family Erinaceidae, and especially of the genus *Erinaceus,* having the back covered with dense, erectile spines and characteristically rolling into a ball for protection. **2.** Any of several similar spiny animals, as a porcupine. **3.** The spiny, burlike fruit of any of several plants. **4.** *Military.* An emplacement bristling with fortifications. [From Middle English *hedge hogge.*]

hedge·hop (hĕj′hŏp′) *intr.v.* **-hopped, -hopping, -hops.** To fly an aircraft close to the ground, rising above objects as they appear, as for spraying crops. **—hedge·hop·per** *n.*

hedge hyssop *n.* Any of various plants of the genus *Gratiola,* growing in damp places and having small yellow or whitish flowers.

hedge·row (hĕj′rō′) *n.* A row of bushes, shrubs, or trees forming a hedge.

hedge sparrow *n.* A European bird, *Prunella modularis,* of the family Prunellidae, having brownish plumage streaked with black. Also called "dunnock."

he·don·ic (hĭ-dŏn′ĭk) *adj.* **1.** Of, pertaining to, or marked by pleasure. **2.** Of or pertaining to hedonism or hedonics. [Greek *hēdonikos,* from *hēdonē,* pleasure.] **—he·don·i·cal·ly** *adv.*

he·don·ics (hĭ-dŏn′ĭks) *n. Used with a singular verb.* **1.** *Psychology.* The study of pleasant and unpleasant sensations. **2.** *Philosophy.* A branch of ethics that deals with the relation of pleasure to duty.

he·don·ism (hēd′n-ĭz′əm) *n.* **1.** Pursuit of or devotion to pleasure, especially the pleasures of the senses. **2.** The ethical doctrine that only that which is pleasant is intrinsically good. **3.** *Psychology.* The doctrine that behavior is motivated by the desire for pleasure and the avoidance of pain. [Greek *hēdonē,* pleasure (see **hedonic**) + -ISM.] **—he·don·ist** *n.* **—he·don·is·tic** (hēd′n-ĭs′tĭk) *adj.* **—he·don·is·ti·cal·ly** *adv.*

-hedral *suffix.* Indicates surfaces or faces of a given number; for example, **dihedral, polyhedral.** [From -HEDRON.]

-hedron *suffix.* Indicates a geometric figure having a given number of faces or surfaces; for example, **pentahedron, polyhedron.** [Greek *-edron,* from *hedra,* base, seat.]

hee·bie-jee·bies (hē′bē-jē′bēz) *pl.n. Slang.* A feeling of uneasiness or nervousness; the jitters. [Coined by Billy DeBeck (1890–1942), U.S. cartoonist, in his comic strip *Barney Google.*]

heed (hēd) *v.* **heeded, heeding, heeds.** *—tr.* To pay attention to; listen to and consider. *—intr.* To pay attention.
~n. Close attention or consideration. [Middle English *heden,* Old English *hēdan,* from Germanic.]

heed·ful (hēd′fəl) *adj.* Paying close attention; taking heed; mindful. **—heed·ful·ly** *adv.* **—heed·ful·ness** *n.*

heed·less (hēd′lĭs) *adj.* Paying little or no attention; not taking heed; unmindful. —See Synonyms at **careless, forgetful.** —See Usage note at **impetuous. —heed·less·ly** *adv.* **—heed·less·ness** *n.*

hee·haw (hē′hô′) *n.* **1.** The braying sound made by a donkey. **2.** A noisy laugh; a guffaw.

~*intr.v.* **heehawed, -hawing, -haws. 1.** To bray. **2.** To laugh noisily; guffaw. [Imitative.]

heel¹ (hēl) *n.* **1.** The rounded posterior portion of the human foot under and behind the ankle. **2.** A corresponding part in other vertebrates. **3.** That part of footwear, such as a sock, shoe, or stocking, that covers the heel. **4.** The built-up portion of a shoe or boot, supporting the heel. **5.** Either of the crusty ends of a loaf of bread. **6.** Something resembling the heel in position or shape; a lower, rearward surface, such as: **a.** The cushion of muscle on the palm of the hand below the thumb. **b.** The head of a golf club where it joins the shaft. **c.** The handle end of a violin bow. **d.** The lower end of a mast. **e.** The aft end of a ship's keel. **7.** *Horticulture.* The basal end of a cutting, tuber, or other plant part used in propagation. **8.** *Slang.* A callous or dishonorable man; a cad. **—cool one's heels.** To be kept waiting for a long time, especially out of deliberate rudeness. **—dig one's heels in.** To refuse to compromise or change one's position. **—down at (the) heel. 1.** Having one's shoe heels worn down. **2.** Shabby; run-down. **—lay by the heels.** To put in fetters or shackles; imprison or confine: *"If the king blames me for 't, I'll lay ye all/By the heels"* (Shakespeare). **—on** (or **upon**) **the heels of. 1.** Directly behind. **2.** Immediately following. **—show a clean pair of heels.** To run away. **—take to one's heels.** To flee; run away. **—to heel. 1.** Close behind; at one's heel. **2.** Under control; disciplined: *brought the rebellious prisoners to heel.* **—under the heel of.** Dominated or subjugated by.

~*interj.* Used when ordering a dog to keep close to the heel.

~*v.* **heeled, heeling, heels.** —*tr.* **1. a.** To furnish with a heel. **b.** To repair or replace the heels of (a shoe, for example). **2.** To follow upon the heels of; follow closely behind. **3. a.** In Rugby football, to kick (the ball) backward using the heel. **b.** In golf, to strike (the ball) with the heel of the club. —*intr.* **1.** To follow at one's heels: *taught the dog to heel.* **2.** To perform a dance step or movement with the heels. [Middle English *heel, he(e)le,* Old English *hēla,* from Germanic.] **—heel·less** *adj.*

heel² *v.* **heeled, heeling, heels.** —*intr.* To tip to one side; tilt; list. Used especially of ships. —*tr.* To cause (a ship) to list. ~*n.* A tilting or inclining to one side; a cant; a list. [Probably from obsolete *heeld,* to incline, Middle English *he(e)lden,* Old English *hieldan,* from Germanic.]

heel-and-toe (hēl'ən-tō') *adj.* Characterized by a stride in which the heel of one foot touches ground before the toe of the other foot is lifted, as in walking races.

~*intr.v.* **heel-and-toed, -toeing, -toes.** To operate the brake and accelerator of a car with the heel and toes of the same foot.

heel ball *n.* A colored wax used to stain and polish the edges of the soles and heels of shoes or to take brass rubbings.

heel bar *n. Chiefly British.* A small shop or a counter in a large shop where shoes are repaired while the customer waits.

heel bone *n.* The **calcaneus** (see).

heeled (hēld) *adj.* **1.** Having or fitted with heels. **2.** *Slang.* Provided with money. Used in combination: *well-heeled.*

heel·er (hē'lər) *n.* **1.** One who heels shoes. **2.** *Informal.* A **ward heeler** (see).

heel·post (hēl'pōst') *n.* The post to which a door or gate is hinged.

heel·tap (hēl'tăp') *n.* **1.** A layer of material added to the heel of a shoe; a lift. **2.** A small amount of alcoholic drink remaining in a container or drinking vessel.

heft (hĕft) *n.* Weight; heaviness; bulk.

~*tr.v.* **hefted, hefting, hefts. 1.** To determine or estimate the weight of by lifting. **2.** To hoist up; heave. [From HEAVE (by analogy with such pairs as *cleave, cleft.*)]

heft·y (hĕf'tē) *adj.* **-ier, -iest. 1.** Weighty; heavy. **2.** Large and powerful; bulky; muscular. **3.** Large in amount: *a hefty fine.* —See Synonyms at **heavy.** **—heft·i·ness** *n.*

He·gel (hā'gəl), **Georg Wilhelm Friedrich** (1770–1831). German philosopher. His main works, including *Encyclopedia of the Philosophical Sciences* (1817) and the *Philosophy of Right* (1821), proposed that truth is reached by a continuing dialectic: an initial *thesis,* when found unsatisfactory, generates an *antithesis;* these interact to form a *synthesis,* which may itself constitute a new thesis. Marx and Engels adapted the theory.

He·ge·li·an·ism (hā-gā'lē-ə-nĭz'əm) *n.* The monist, idealist philosophy of Hegel and his followers; especially, Hegel's doctrine of the "phenomenology of the mind," whereby all that exists must be mental, and therefore thought is reality; history, and especially the history of thought, represents the search for truth through **dialectic** (see). **—He·ge·li·an** *adj. & n.*

he·gem·o·ny (hĭ-jĕm'ə-nē, hĕj'ə-mō'nē) *n., pl.* **-nies.** Predominance; especially, the predominant influence of one state over others. [Greek *hēgemonia,* authority, rule, from *hēgemōn,* leader, from *hēgeisthai,* to lead.] **—heg·e·mon·ic** (hĕj'ə-mŏn'ĭk) *adj.*

He·gi·ra, He·ji·ra (hĭ-jī'rə, hĕj'ə-rə) *n.* **1.** The flight of Muhammad from Mecca to Medina in A.D. 622. **2.** The Muslim era, which is reckoned from this date. **3.** **hegira.** Any flight, as from danger. [Arabic *(al)hijrah,* emigration, flight, departure, from *hajara,* to leave, depart.]

he·gu·men (hĭ-gyōō'mən) *n.* Also **he·gu·me·nos** (-mə-nŏs') *n.* The head of a religious community in the Greek Orthodox Church. [Late Latin *hēgūmenus,* from Late Greek *hēgoumenos,* from Greek, leader, from *hēgeisthai,* to lead.]

heh (hā, hĕ) *interj.* **1.** Used to express surprise or inquiry, or to attract attention. **2.** Used to express malicious glee.

Hei·deg·ger (hī'dĕg'ər, -dī-gər), **Martin** (1889–1976). German phi-

losopher. His discussions on the "sense of being," which is the subject of *Being and Time* (1927), influenced Sartre and other existentialists.

Hei·del·berg (hīd'l-bûrg'). A city in Germany, on the Neckar River, in the state of Baden-Württemberg. It was once the capital of the Palatinate. It has a spectacular ruined castle dating from the 13th century, and its university (1386) is the oldest in Germany.

Heidelberg man *n.* An extinct early member of the human species, suggested as being intermediate between *Homo erectus* and Neanderthal man, known primarily from a fossil jawbone found near Heidelberg, Germany, in 1907.

heif·er (hĕf'ər) *n.* A young cow, especially one that has not yet given birth to a calf. [Middle English *heyfre, hayfre,* Old English *hēah-fore†,* young ox.]

Hei·fetz (hī'fĭts), **Jascha** (1901–87). U.S. violinist, born in Russia. Introduced to the violin at the age of three, he was considered the greatest living violinist just ten years later. After his American debut (1917) he moved to the United States and became a citizen (1925). He performed around the world, and recordings of his masterful technique and interpretation abound.

heigh (hā, hī) *interj. Archaic.* Used to express encouragement or to call attention.

heigh-ho (hī'hō', hā'-) *interj.* Used to express fatigue, melancholy, mild surprise, or disappointment.

height (hīt) *n.* Also *archaic* **heighth,** *obsolete* **highth** (hīth, hītth). *Abbr.* **h., H., hgt., ht 1. a.** The distance from the base to the top of something. **b.** The elevation of something above a given level; altitude. **2.** The condition or attribute of being sufficiently or relatively high or tall. **3.** The highest or uppermost point; the summit; the apex. **4. a.** The highest or most advanced stage or degree: *the height of stupidity; at the height of his fame.* **b.** The point of highest intensity; the climax: *the height of a storm.* **5.** *Often* **heights.** An eminence or area of high ground: *the Golan Heights.* **6.** *Obsolete.* High rank, estate, or degree. **7. a.** *Archaic.* Loftiness of mind. **b.** *Obsolete.* Arrogance; hauteur. [Middle English *he(i)ghth,* Old English *hēhthu, hīehthu.* See **high, -th.**]

height·en (hīt'n) *v.* **-ened, -ening, -ens.** —*tr.* **1.** To increase the quantity or degree of; intensify. **2.** To make high or higher; raise. —*intr.* **1.** To rise in degree or quantity; intensify. **2.** To become high or higher. **—height·en·er** *n.*

height-to-pa·per (hīt'tə-pā'pər) *n. Printing.* The height of type from foot to face, standardized at 0.9186 inch or 2.296 centimeters.

heil (hīl) *interj.* Hail! Used as a greeting, especially in the Nazi greeting *Heil Hitler!* [German.]

Hei·long·ji·ang (hā'lōong'jē-äng'). Northernmost province of China, formerly the northern part of Manchuria. Agriculture and forestry have been expanded since 1949, and its industries include oil refining, coal mining, and manufacturing. Its capital is Harbin.

Heilong Jiang. See **Amur.**

Hei·ne (hī'nə), **Heinrich** (1797–1856). German romantic poet. Heine lived after 1831 in Paris, where he supported a revolutionary literary movement known as Young Germany. He published several volumes of lyric poems, including *The Book of Songs* (1827).

hei·nous (hā'nəs) *adj.* Grossly wicked or reprehensible; abominable; odious; vile. [Middle English *heynous,* hateful, from Old French *haïneus,* from *haïne,* hate, from *haïr,* to hate, from Frankish *hatjan* (unattested).] **—hei·nous·ly** *adv.* **—hei·nous·ness** *n.*

heir (âr) *n.* **1.** *Law.* A person who inherits or is entitled by law or by the terms of a will to inherit the estate of another. **2.** A person who succeeds or is in line to succeed to a hereditary rank, title, or office. **3.** One who is entitled or regarded as entitled to receive a heritage, as of ideas, from a predecessor; a successor. [Middle English *(h)eir, (h)air,* from Old French *(h)eir,* from Latin *hērēs.*] **—heir·dom** *n.* **—heir·ship** *n.*

heir apparent *n., pl.* **heirs apparent.** *Law.* An heir whose right to inheritance is indefeasible by law provided he survives his ancestor.

heir·ess (âr'ĭs) *n.* A female heir, especially one who inherits or is due to inherit great wealth.

heir·loom (âr'lōōm') *n.* **1.** A valued possession passed down in a family through succeeding generations. **2.** *Law.* An article of personal property included in an inherited estate. [Middle English *heir lome* : HEIR + *lome,* utensil, tool, LOOM.]

heir presumptive *n., pl.* **heirs presumptive.** *Law.* An heir whose claim can be defeated by the birth of a closer relative before the death of the ancestor.

Hei·sen·berg (hī'zən-bûrg'), **Werner Karl** (1901–76). German physicist, one of the founders of quantum theory. For his **uncertainty principle** (see), which had a profound effect on physics, he was awarded the Nobel Prize in 1932.

Heisenberg uncertainty principle *n. Physics.* The **uncertainty principle** (see).

heist (hīst) *tr.v.* **heisted, heisting, heists.** *Slang.* To rob; steal. ~*n. Slang.* A robbery; a burglary. [Alteration of HOIST.]

hei·ti·ki (hā'tē'kē) *n. New Zealand.* A neck ornament of greenstone worn by Maoris. [Maori : *hei,* to hang + TIKI, amulet.]

Hejira. Variant of **Hegira.**

Hekate. Variant of **Hecate.**

Hel (hĕl). *Norse Mythology.* **1.** The daughter of Loki and the goddess of death. **2.** The underworld for the dead not killed in battle. [Old Norse *Hel.*]

He·La cell (hĕl'ə) *n.* Any of the cells of the first continuously cultured human carcinoma strain that are often used in the study of

helicopter *The rotor acts as a helicopter's wings as well as its propeller. The pilot controls the degree of lift by altering the angle of the blades to the air.*

hellebore *This highly poisonous evergreen, which flowers worldwide in woods in spring, is a relative of the popular garden Christmas rose.*

PRONUNCIATION KEY

ă, pat; ā, pay; âr, care;
ä, father, are; b, bib;
ch, church; d, deed; ĕ, pet;
ē, be; f, fife; g, gag; h, hat;
hw, which; ĭ, pit; ī, pie;
îr, pier; j, judge; k, kick;
l, lid, needle; m, mum;
n, no, sudden; ng, thing;
ŏ, pot; ō, toe; ô, paw, for;
oi, noise; ou, out; o͝o, book;
o͞o, boot; p, pop; r, roar;
s, sauce; sh, ship, dish;
t, tight; th, thin, path;
th, this, bathe; ŭ, cut; ûr, fur;
v, valve; w, with; y, yes;
z, zebra, size; zh, vision;
ə, about, item, edible, gallop, circus, peaceful

IN FOREIGN WORDS:

à, *Fr.* ami; œ, *Fr.* feu, *Ger.* schön; ü, *Fr.* tu, *Ger.* über; KH, *Ger.* ich, *Scot.* loch; N, *Fr.* bon; y', *Fr.* Compiègne

STRESS MARKS:

Primary stress: ′
in·cite′ (ĭn-sīt′)
Secondary stress: ′
in′sight′ (ĭn′sīt′)

cellular processes. [After *He*nrietta *La*cks, who donated such cells in 1951.]

held. Past tense and past participle of **hold** (to have in one's grasp).

hel·den·te·nor, Hel·den·te·nor (hĕl′dən-tə-nôr′, -nōr′) *n.* A singer with a powerful tenor voice suitable for heroic operatic parts. Also called "heroic tenor." [German : *Held,* hero, + *Tenor,* tenor.]

Hel·en (hĕl′ən). *Greek Legend.* The daughter of Zeus and Leda and wife of Menelaus. Her abduction by Paris led to the Trojan War.

Hel·e·na (hĕl′ə-nə). Capital of Montana, in the west-central part of the state. The city was founded after the discovery of gold (1864) at Last Chance Gulch. Today it is the commercial and shipping center of a mining and ranching area.

Helgoland. See **Heligoland.**

he·li·a·cal (hĭ-lī′ə-kəl) *adj.* Of or pertaining to the sun; especially, rising and setting with the sun. [From Late Latin *hēliacus,* from Greek *hēliakos,* from *hēlios,* the sun.]

he·li·an·thus (hē′lē-ăn′thəs) *n., pl.* **-thuses.** Any of various plants of the genus *Helianthus,* such as the sunflower and the Jerusalem artichoke, having large, yellow, daisylike flowers. [New Latin, from Greek *hēlios,* the sun + *anthos,* flower.]

hel·i·cal (hĕl′ĭ-kəl) *adj.* Of, pertaining to, or shaped like a helix. [Greek *helix* (stem *helik-*), HELIX.] **—hel·i·cal·ly** *adv.*

helical gear *n.* A gear in which the teeth are set in a helix around the axis.

he·li·ces. Alternate plural of **helix.**

hel·i·chrys·um (hĕl′ĭ-krĭs′əm) *n.* A plant of the genus *Helichrysum,* whose papery, daisylike flowers retain their form and color on drying. [New Latin, from Greek *helikhrusos* : *heli-,* spiral, HELIX + *khrusos,* gold.]

he·lic·i·ty (hē-lĭs′ə-tē, hĕ-) *n. Physics.* The component of the spin of a particle along its direction of motion. [Greek *helix* (stem *helik-*), HELIX + -ITY.]

hel·i·coid (hĕl′ĭ-koid′) *adj.* Arranged in or having the approximate shape of a flattened spiral.
∼*n. Geometry.* A surface generated by a plane curve or a twisted curve that is rotated about a linear axis and at the same time is translated in the direction of the axis so that the two rates have a constant ratio. [Greek *helikoeidēs* : HELIX + -OID (shaped).]

hel·i·con (hĕl′ĭ-kŏn′, -kən) *n.* A large spiral brass tuba that fits around the player's shoulder. [After *Helicon,* a mountain in Boeotia sacred to the Muses.]

hel·i·cop·ter (hĕl′ĭ-kŏp′tər) *n.* An aircraft that derives its lift from blades that rotate about an approximately vertical central axis. [French *hélicoptère,* "spiral wing" : Greek *helix* (stem *helik-*), HELIX + -PTER.]

Hel·i·go·land (hĕl′ĭ-gō-lănd′). *German* **Hel·go·land** (hĕl′gō-lănd′, -länt′). A small island, belonging to Germany, in the North Sea off the mouth of the Elbe River.

helio- *prefix.* Indicates the sun or of or by the sun; for example, **heliograph, heliotrope.** [Greek *hēlios,* the sun.]

he·li·o·cen·tric (hē′lē-ō-sĕn′trĭk) *adj.* **1.** Referred or relative to the sun. **2.** Having the sun as a center: *a heliocentric model of the universe.* **—he·li·o·cen·tric·i·ty** (hē′lē-ō-sĕn-trĭs′ə-tē) *n.*

heliocentric parallax *n. Astronomy.* **Annual parallax** *(see).*

He·li·o·gab·a·lus (hē′lē-ə-găb′ə-ləs, hē′lē-ō-), also **El·a·gab·a·lus** (ĕl′ə-găb′ə-ləs) (A.D. 204–22). Roman emperor (218–22). A priest of the pagan god Baal, he became emperor after the murder of his cousin Caracalla (217). His scandalous eccentricities and excesses and imposition of his religious beliefs caused unrest in Rome and led to a mutiny in which he was killed.

he·li·o·gram (hē′lē-ə-grăm′) *n.* A message sent by heliograph. [HELIO- + -GRAM.]

he·li·o·graph (hē′lē-ə-grăf′, -gräf′) *n.* **1.** An apparatus formerly used to photograph the sun. **2.** A signaling apparatus that reflects sunlight with a movable mirror to flash coded messages.
∼*tr.v.* **heliographed, -graphing, -graphs.** To transmit (messages) by heliograph. [HELIO- + -GRAPH.] **—he·li·og·ra·pher** (hē′lē-ŏg′rə-fər) *n.* **—he·li·o·graph·ic** (hē′lē-ə-grăf′ĭk) *adj.* **—he·li·og·ra·phy** (hē′lē-ŏg′rə-fē) *n.*

he·li·o·gra·vure (hē′lē-ō-grə-vyo͝or′) *n.* **Photogravure** *(see).*

he·li·o·lith·ic (hē′lē-ə-lĭth′ĭk) *adj.* Of or designating a civilization characterized by sun worship and the erection of megaliths. [HELIO- + -LITHIC.]

he·li·om·e·ter (hē′lē-ŏm′ə-tər) *n.* A telescope equipped to measure small angular distances between celestial bodies. [French *héliomètre* : HELIO- + -METER.] **—he·li·o·met·ric** (hē′lē-ə-mĕt′rĭk), **he·li·o·met·ri·cal** *adj.* **—he·li·om·e·try** *n.*

He·li·os (hē′lē-ŏs′). *Greek Mythology.* The sun god, son of Hyperion, depicted as driving his four-horse chariot across the sky from east to west daily. [Greek *Hēlios,* from *hēlios,* the sun.]

he·li·o·stat (hē′lē-ə-stăt′) *n.* An instrument in which a mirror is automatically moved so that it reflects sunlight in a constant direction. [New Latin *heliostata* : HELIO- + -STAT.]

he·li·o·tax·is (hē′lē-ə-tăk′sĭs) *n. Biology.* The movement of an organism in response to the light of the sun. [New Latin : HELIO- + -TAXIS.] **—he·li·o·tac·tic** (hē′lē-ə-tăk′tĭk) *adj.*

he·li·o·ther·a·py (hē′lē-ə-thĕr′ə-pē) *n.* Medical therapy involving exposure to sunlight.

he·li·o·trope (hē′lē-ə-trōp′, hēl′yə-trōp′) *n.* **1.** Any of several plants of the genus *Heliotropium*; especially, *H. arborescens,* native to South America, having small, fragrant, purplish flowers. **2.** The **garden heliotrope** *(see).* **3.** Any of various plants that turn toward the sun. **4. Bloodstone** *(see).* **5.** Moderate, light, or brilliant violet to moderate or deep reddish purple. [New Latin *Heliotropium,* from Latin *hēliotropium,* from Greek *hēliotropion,* sundial, bloodstone, heliotrope : HELIO- + *tropos,* a turning (see **trope**).] **—he·li·o·trope** *adj.*

he·li·o·tro·pin (hē′lē-ə-trō′pĭn, -ŏt′rə-pĭn) *n. Chemistry.* **Piperonal** *(see).* [New Latin *Heliotropium,* HELIOTROPE + -IN.]

he·li·ot·ro·pism (hē′lē-ŏt′rə-pĭz′əm) *n. Biology.* Growth of a plant part toward or away from the light of the sun. [HELIO- + -TROPISM.] **—he·li·o·trop·ic** (hē′lē-ə-trŏp′ĭk) *adj.* **—he·li·o·trop·i·cal·ly** *adv.*

he·li·o·type (hē′lē-ə-tīp′) *n. Printing.* **1.** A photomechanically produced plate for pictures or type made by exposing a gelatin film under a negative, hardening it with chrome alum, and printing directly from it. **2.** The process of producing such a plate. **—he·li·o·type** *v.* **—he·li·o·typ·ic** (hē′lē-ə-tĭp′ĭk) *adj.*

he·li·o·zo·an (hē′lē-ə-zō′ən) *n.* Any of various aquatic protozoans of the order Heliozoa, having numerous stiff, radiating pseudopodia. [New Latin *Heliozoa* : HELIO- + -ZOAN.] **—he·li·o·zo·an** *adj.*

hel·i·port (hĕl′ə-pôrt′, -pōrt′) *n.* An airport for helicopters. [HELI(COPTER) + -PORT.]

he·li·um (hē′lē-əm) *n. Symbol* **He** A colorless, odorless, tasteless, inert gaseous element. It is used to inflate and so provide lift for balloons, as an inert component of various artificial atmospheres, in gaseous laser media, and as a superfluid in the form of helium II for extensive cryogenic research. Atomic number 2, atomic weight 4.0026, boiling point –268.6°C, liquid density at boiling point 7.62 pounds per cubic foot. [New Latin, from Greek *hēlios,* the sun (the element was first discovered in an examination of the solar spectrum).]

helium I *n. Symbol* **He I** Liquid helium existing as a normal fluid between the superfluid transition point of approximately 2.178° K at 1 atmosphere pressure and its boiling point of 4.2° K.

helium II *n. Symbol* **He II** Liquid helium existing as a superfluid below the transition point of approximately 2.178° K at 1 atmosphere and having extremely low viscosity and extremely high thermal conductivity.

he·lix (hē′lĭks) *n., pl.* **-lixes** or **helices** (hĕl′ə-sēz′, hē′lə-). **1.** A three-dimensional curve that lies on a cylinder or cone and cuts the elements at a constant angle. **2.** Any spiral form or structure. **3.** *Anatomy.* The folded rim of skin and cartilage around the outer ear. **4.** *Architecture.* A volute on a Corinthian or Ionic capital. **5.** Any terrestrial mollusk of the genus *Helix,* such as the garden snail, *H. aspersa.* [Latin, from Greek, spiral, spiral object.]

hell (hĕl) *n.* **1.** *Sometimes* **Hell.** The abode of the dead; the underworld where departed souls were believed to dwell; specifically, Sheol in the Hebrew Scriptures and Hades in the Greco-Roman tradition. **2.** *Sometimes* **Hell.** In the Christian tradition, the abode of condemned souls and devils; the place or state of eternal torture and punishment for the wicked after death, presided over by Satan and conventionally depicted as a place of everlasting fire. **3.** The infernal powers of evil and darkness. **4. a.** A place or state of great wickedness, torment, misery, or destruction. **b.** Torment; anguish. **c.** A cause or source of great misery or agony. **5. Hell.** *Christian Science.* Mortal belief; sin or error. **6.** *Archaic.* A gambling house. **7. a.** A tailor's receptacle for discarded material. **b.** A hellbox. **8. a.** A severe punishment or reprimand: *The boss gave me hell.* **b.** Turmoil; havoc; pandemonium: *All hell was let loose.* **9.** Used to express annoyance or surprise or as an intensive: *a hell of a good book. It hurts like hell.* **—for the hell of it.** Purely for the sake of amusement. **—hell and (**or **or) high water.** *Informal.* The ultimate ordeal, suffering, or deprivation: *I followed her through hell and high water. We're staying, come hell or high water.* **—hell to pay.** *Informal.* Bad trouble to be faced: *If we're caught doing this, there'll be hell to pay.* **—like hell.** *Informal.* Most assuredly not; never. Used for emphasis, especially in rejecting a possibility. **—raise (**or **kick up) hell.** *Slang.* To make a great fuss. **—the hell in.** *South African.* Extremely angry; furious. **—what the hell.** *Informal.* Used to express indifference or resignation.
∼*intr.v.* **helled, helling, hells.** *Informal.* To behave riotously; carouse: *out all night helling around.*
∼*interj. Slang.* Used to express acute anger, disgust, or impatience. [Middle English *hel(l),* Old English *hel(l),* from Germanic.]

he'll (hēl). **1.** Contraction of *he will.* **2.** Contraction of *he shall.*

Hel·lad·ic (hĕ-lăd′ĭk) *adj.* Of or pertaining to the Bronze Age culture on the mainland of Greece prior to 1100 B.C. [Latin *Helladicus,* from Greek *Helladikos,* from *Hellas* (stem *Hellad-*), HELLAS.]

Hel·las (hĕl′əs). The Greek name for Greece. [Greek, from *Hellēn*†, eponymous ancestor of the Greeks.]

hell·bend·er (hĕl′bĕn′dər) *n.* A large aquatic salamander, *Cryptobranchus alleganiensis,* of eastern and central North America.

hell-bent (hĕl′bĕnt′) *adj.* Impetuously or recklessly bent on doing, reaching, or achieving something. Used with *on* or *for.*

hell·box (hĕl′bŏks′) *n.* A printer's receptacle for broken or discarded type. Also called "hell."

hell·cat (hĕl′kăt′) *n.* **1.** A furious and evil woman; a witch. **2.** A fiendish person.

Hel·le (hĕl′ē). *Greek Mythology.* The daughter of a Greek king who, while fleeing with her brother from their stepmother, drowned in the Hellespont, thereafter named for her.

hel·le·bore (hĕl′ə-bôr′, -bōr′) *n.* **1.** Any of various plants of the genus *Helleborus,* native to Eurasia, most species of which are poisonous. See **Christmas rose.** **2.** Any of various plants of the genus *Veratrum*; especially, *V. viride,* of North America, having large leaves and greenish flowers and yielding a toxic alkaloid used medicinally. In this sense, also called "false hellebore," "Indian poke." [Middle English *ellebre*, from Old French, from Latin *elleborus*, from Greek *(h)elleboros*, perhaps "eaten by fawns" : *(h)ellos*, fawn + *-boros*, eaten, from *bibrōskein*, to eat, devour.]

hel·le·bor·in (hĕl'ə-bôr'ĭn, -bŏr'ĭn) *n.* A poisonous compound, $C_{28}H_{36}O_6$, extracted from a species of hellebore, *Helleborus viridis*. [HELLEBOR(E) + -IN.]

Hel·lene (hĕl'ēn') *n.* A Greek. [Greek *Hellēn.* See **Hellas.**]

Hel·len·ic (hĕ-lĕn'ĭk) *adj.* Of or relating to the ancient Greeks or their language; Greek.
~*n.* The branch of the Indo-European language family that consists solely of Greek.

Hel·le·nism (hĕl'ə-nĭz'əm) *n.* **1.** An idiom, custom, or the like peculiar to the Greeks. **2.** The civilization and culture of ancient Greece. **3.** Admiration for or adoption of Greek ideas, style, or culture.

Hel·le·nist (hĕl'ə-nĭst) *n.* **1.** One in classical times who adopted the Greek language and culture, particularly a Jew of the Diaspora. **2.** A devotee or student of Greek civilization, language, or literature.

Hel·le·nis·tic (hĕl'ə-nĭs'tĭk) *adj.* **1.** Of or relating to Greek civilization, art, and culture from the death of Alexander the Great in 323 B.C. to the accession of Augustus (27 B.C.). **2.** Relating to the Hellenists.

Hel·le·nize (hĕl'ə-nīz') *v.* **-nized, -nizing, -nizes.** —*intr.* To adopt Greek ways and speech; become Greek. —*tr.* To make Greek in character or culture. —**Hel·le·ni·za·tion** *n.* —**Hel·le·niz·er** *n.*

hel·ler[1] (hĕl'ər) *n., pl.* **heller.** One of several coins of small denomination formerly used in Austria and Germany. [German *Heller*, from Middle High German *heller, haller*, HALER.]

hell·er[2] (hĕl'ər) *n. Regional.* A person who behaves recklessly or wildly. [From HELL.]

Hellespont. See **Dardanelles.**

hell·fire (hĕl'fīr') *n.* The fires, torment, or punishment of hell.
~*adj.* Preaching or zealously believing in the torments of hell: *an old-fashioned hellfire preacher.*

hell-fired (hĕl'fīrd') *adj. Regional & Informal.* Extremely; very.

hell-for-leath·er (hĕl'fər-lĕth'ər) *adv.* At breakneck speed.

hell-gram·mite (hĕl'grə-mīt') *n.* The large, brownish aquatic larva of the dobson fly, often used as fishing bait. Sometimes called "dobson." [Origin unknown.]

hell·hole (hĕl'hōl') *n.* A hellish place, especially one of extreme wretchedness, squalor, or lewdness.

hell·hound (hĕl'hound') *n.* **1.** A hound of hell; especially, Cerberus, watchdog of Hades. **2.** A devilish person; a fiend.

hel·lion (hĕl'yən) *n. Informal.* A mischievous, unrestrainable person, especially a young person or child. [Probably altered by assimilation to HELL from dialectal *hallion†*, scurvy person.]

hell·ish (hĕl'ĭsh) *adj.* **1.** Of, relating to, or worthy of hell; devilish. **2.** *Informal.* Awful; unpleasant; terrible: *hellish weather.* —**hell·ish·ly** *adv.* —**hell·ish·ness** *n.*

Hell·man (hĕl'mən), **Lillian** (1905–84). U.S. playwright. Her first play, *The Children's Hour* (1934), treated the then taboo subject of lesbianism. She also wrote *The Little Foxes* (1939) and *Watch on the Rhine* (1941). The first volume of her autobiography, *An Unfinished Woman*, won the National Book Award (1969).

hel·lo (hĕ-lō', hə-) *interj.* **1.** Used to greet another, to answer the telephone, or to attract attention. **2.** Used to express surprise.
~*n., pl.* **helloes.** Also **hullo.** A calling or greeting of "hello."
~*v.* **helloed, -loing, -loes.** Also **hullo.** —*tr.* To say or call "hello" to. —*intr.* To call "hello." [Variant of earlier *hallo, hollo, holla,* stop!, from French *holà*, "ho there!"]

Hell's Angel *n.* One who belongs to a motorcycle gang of a type that originated in the United States, whose members wear denim, black leather, and various items of antisocial ornamentation and regalia, and are generally believed to behave in a violent and lawless manner.

Hell's Canyon. Greatest of the Snake River's many gorges, on the Idaho-Oregon border. It extends for *c.* 200 kilometers (125 miles) and reaches a maximum depth of *c.* 2,410 meters (7,900 feet).

helm[1] (hĕlm) *n.* **1.** *Nautical.* The tiller or wheel or the whole steering gear of a ship. **2.** A position of leadership or control: *at the helm.* —**ease the helm.** *Nautical.* To bring the helm somewhat toward midships in order to reduce strain on the rudder.
~*tr.v.* **helmed, helming, helms.** To be at the helm of; steer; guide. [Middle English *helme*, Old English *helma*.]

helm[2] *n. Archaic.* A helmet.
~*tr.v.* **helmed, helming, helms.** *Archaic.* To cover or furnish with a helmet. [Middle English *helm(e), healm*, Old English *helm*.]

hel·met (hĕl'mĭt) *n.* **1.** A piece of ancient, medieval, or modern armor, usually of metal, designed to protect the head. **2. a.** A head covering of hard material, such as leather, metal, or plastic, worn by policemen, firemen, cyclists, and others to protect the head. **b.** The headgear with a glass mask worn by deep-sea divers. **c.** A pith helmet; a topi. **d.** Any hat or headgear resembling a helmet, such as a balaclava. **3.** *Botany.* The hood-shaped sepal or corolla of some flowers. [Middle English, from Old French, diminutive of *helme, heaume*, helmet, from Frankish *helm* (unattested).] —**hel·met·ed** *adj.*

Helm·holtz (hĕlm'hōlts'), **Hermann Ludwig Ferdinand von** (1821–94). German physicist and physiologist. He formulated the mathematical law of the conservation of energy in 1847.

Helmholtz coils *pl.n. Physics.* Two identical flat coils carrying the same electric current in the same direction, mounted parallel at a distance apart equal to their radii. The arrangement produces a uniform magnetic field between the coils of known field strength. [Invented by H.L.F. von HELMHOLTZ.]

Helmholtz function *n. Symbol* **A** A measure of the thermodynamic free energy of a system, equal to the internal energy minus the product of thermodynamic temperature and entropy. Also called "Helmholtz free energy." [Devised by H.L.F. von HELMHOLTZ.]

hel·minth (hĕl'mĭnth') *n.* A worm; especially, a parasitic intestinal nematode fluke, or tapeworm. [Greek *helmi(n)s* (stem *helminth-*), parasitic worm.]

hel·min·thi·a·sis (hĕl'mĭn-thī'ə-sĭs) *n.* A disease resulting from infestation with parasitic worms. [New Latin : HELMINTH + -IASIS.]

hel·min·thic (hĕl-mĭn'thĭk) *adj.* **1.** Of or pertaining to worms, especially parasitic intestinal worms. **2.** Tending to expel worms; anthelmintic.
~*n.* A vermifuge or anthelmintic.

hel·min·thol·o·gy (hĕl'mĭn-thŏl'ə-jē) *n.* The scientific study of worms, especially parasitic worms. [HELMINTH + -LOGY.] —**hel·min·thol·o·gist** *n.*

helms·man (hĕlmz'mən) *n., pl.* **-men** (-mĭn). One who steers a ship.

Hé·lo·ïse (ĕl'ō-ēz', ā'lō-ēz') (*c.* 1098–1164). A young Frenchwoman who fell in love with her tutor, Peter Abelard. After she bore his child and secretly married him, her incensed family arranged to have him attacked and castrated. Their marriage ended; she became a nun, and he became a monk. Their story is a classic love tragedy.

hel·o·phyte (hĕl'ə-fīt') *n.* A marsh plant. [Greek *helos*, marsh + -PHYTE.]

hel·ot (hĕl'ət, hē'lət) *n.* **1.** Helot. One of a class of serfs in ancient Sparta, neither a slave nor a free citizen. **2.** A serf; a bondsman. [Latin *Hēlōtes*, serfs, helots, from Greek *Heilōtes*, plural of *Heilōs†.*]

hel·ot·ism (hĕl'ə-tĭz'əm, hē'lə-) *n.* **1.** A system under which a particular section of the community, such as a religious or racial minority, is permanently oppressed and degraded. **2.** *Zoology.* **Dulosis** (see).

hel·ot·ry (hĕl'ə-trē, hē'lə-) *n.* **1.** The condition of serfdom. **2.** Helots as a class.

help (hĕlp) *v.* **helped** or *archaic* **holp** (hōlp), **helped** or *archaic* **holpen** (hōl'pən), **helping, helps.** —*tr.* **1. a.** To do something or provide something that will be of use to (someone) in achieving a purpose; give assistance to; aid: *I helped her to find the book.* **b.** To give assistance so as to enable (someone) to carry out an action more easily. Used elliptically with a preposition or an adverb: *He helped her into her coat. Help me down—I'm stuck.* **2.** To further the advancement or promote the interests of: *The party's disunity will only help its enemies.* **3.** To give relief to (one in difficulty or distress); succor. **4.** To alleviate or cure. **5.** To improve; benefit. **6.** To prevent, change, or rectify. Used with *can* or *cannot*: *I cannot help her laziness.* **7.** To refrain from; avoid. Used with *can* or *cannot*: *He cannot help laughing.* **8.** To serve in a shop or at table. —*intr.* To be of use or service; give assistance; aid. —See Synonyms at **improve.** —**cannot help but.** To be compelled to; be unable to avoid or resist: *He cannot help but do what they ask.* —**help oneself to.** To take (something) without asking permission. —**help out.** To help with a problem or difficulty. —**so help me God.** Used as an oath in solemn affirmation of what one has declared.
~*n.* **1.** The act of helping; aid; assistance. **2.** Someone or something that helps: *You've been a great help.* **3.** Relief; remedy. **4.** Succor. **5. a.** A person employed to assist; especially, a farm worker or a domestic servant. **b.** Such employees collectively. **6.** *Rare.* A helping.
~*interj.* Used to express an urgent need for assistance. [Middle English *helpen*, Old English *helpan*, from Germanic.] —**help·er** *n.*
    Synonyms: aid, assist, succor.

help·ful (hĕlp'fəl) *adj.* Providing help; useful; beneficial. —**help·ful·ly** *adv.* —**help·ful·ness** *n.*

help·ing (hĕl'pĭng) *n.* A portion of food for one person.

helping hand *n.* Assistance; aid.

help·less (hĕlp'lĭs) *adj.* **1.** Unable to manage by oneself; defenseless; dependent. **2.** Lacking power or strength; impotent; ineffectual. **3.** Incapable of being remedied; hopeless: *a helpless situation.* **4.** Incapable of being controlled; involuntary: *helpless laughter.* —**help·less·ly** *adv.* —**help·less·ness** *n.*

help·mate (hĕlp'māt') *n.* A helper or helpful companion, especially a spouse. [HELP + MATE (influenced by HELPMEET).]

help·meet (hĕlp'mēt') *n.* A helpmate. [From *I will make an help meet for him* (Genesis 2:18, 20), "I will make a help suitable for him" : HELP + MEET (suitable).]

Hel·sin·ki (hĕl'sĭng'kē, hĕl-sĭng'-). *Swedish* **Hel·sing·fors** (hĕl'sĭng-fôrs'). Capital of Finland. Built on a promontory and several islands in the Gulf of Finland, it has two harbors, kept open by icebreakers during winter months. Its industries include paper, textiles, and shipbuilding.

hel·ter-skel·ter (hĕl'tər-skĕl'tər) *adv.* **1.** In disorderly haste; pell-mell. **2.** In confusion; haphazardly.
~*adj.* **1.** Characterized by disorderly haste. **2.** Haphazard.
~*n.* Chaos; confusion. [16th century : perhaps based on Middle English *skelte*.]

helve (hĕlv) *n.* A handle of a tool, such as an ax, chisel, or hammer. [Middle English *helve, hilf*, Old English *hielf(e).*]

Helvetia. See **Switzerland.**

Hel·ve·tian (hĕl-vē'shən) *adj.* **1.** Of or relating to the Helvetii.

helmet *A Greek bronze helmet from Olympia, now in the British Museum, London. It dates from about 460 B.C.*

2. Swiss. [Latin *Helvētius*, of the HELVETII.] —**Hel·ve·tian** *n.*

Hel·vet·ic (hĕl-vĕt′ĭk) *adj.* Helvetian; Swiss.
~*n.* A Swiss Protestant; a Zwinglian.

Hel·ve·ti·i (hĕl-vē′shē-ī′) *pl.n.* A Celtic people inhabiting Switzerland during the time of Julius Caesar. [Latin.]

hem¹ (hĕm) *n.* **1.** An edge or border of a piece of cloth; especially, a finished edge for a garment, curtain, or the like, made by folding the selvage or raw edge under and stitching it down. **2.** The level of a hem; a hemline.
~*tr.v.* **hemmed, hemming, hems. 1.** To fold back and stitch down the edge of. **2.** To encircle and confine; enclose or restrict. Used with *in, about,* or *around: hemmed in by mountains.* [Middle English *hem(m),* Old English *hem(m).*] —**hem′mer** *n.*

hem². A short cough or clearing of the throat made to gain attention, warn, fill a pause in speech, hide embarrassment, or the like. Often used as an interjection.
~*intr.v.* **hemmed, hemming, hems. 1.** To utter this sound. **2.** To hesitate in speaking. —**hem and haw.** To be hesitant and indecisive; equivocate. [Imitative.]

hem–¹, hema–. Variant of **hemo–.**

hem–². Variant of **hemi–.**

he·ma·cy·tom·e·ter (hē′mə-sī-tŏm′ə-tər, hĕm′ə-) *n.* An instrument for estimating the number of blood cells in a measured volume of blood. [HEMA- + CYTO- + -METER.]

he·mag·glu·tin·ate (hē′mə-glōōt′n-āt′, hĕm′ə-) *tr.v.* **-ated, -ating, -ates.** To cause agglutination of (red blood cells). —**he·mag·glu·ti·na·tion** *n.*

he·mag·glu·ti·nin (hē′mə-glōōt′n-ĭn, hĕm′ə-) *n.* An antibody that causes agglutination of red blood cells containing or coated with the corresponding antigen. [HEM(O)- + AGGLUTININ.]

he·ma·gogue, he·ma·gog (hē′mə-gôg′, -gŏg′, hĕm′ə-) *n.* A drug or other agent that promotes the flow of blood, as in menstruation. [HEM(O)- + -AGOG(UE).]

he·mal (hē′məl) *adj.* **1.** Of or pertaining to the blood or blood vessels. **2.** Relating to or designating the side of the body that contains the heart. [HEM(O)- + -AL.]

he·man (hē′măn′) *n., pl.* **-men** (-mĕn′). *Informal.* A strong, muscular, virile man.

he·man·gi·o·ma (hĭ-măn′jē-ō′mə) *n., pl.* **-mas** or **-mata** (-mə-tə). A nonmalignant tumor of blood vessels, often seen on the skin as a type of birthmark. [HEM(O)- + ANGIOMA.]

hemat–. Variant of **hemato–.**

he·ma·te·in (hē′mə-tē′ĭn, hĕm′ə-, hē′mə-tēn′, hĕm′ə-) *n.* A dark-purple crystalline compound, $C_{16}H_{12}O_6$, used as an indicator and as a biological stain. [HEMAT(O)- + *-ein,* variant of -IN.]

he·ma·tem·e·sis (hē′mə-tĕm′ə-sĭs, hĕm′ə-) *n.* The vomiting of blood, often due to a bleeding gastric or duodenal ulcer. [HEMAT(O)- + Greek *emesis,* vomiting.]

he·mat·ic (hĭ-măt′ĭk) *adj.* Of, pertaining to, resembling, containing, or acting on blood.
~*n.* A remedy for anemia and other blood diseases. [Greek *haimatikos,* from *haima*† (stem *haimat-*), blood.]

he·ma·tin (hē′mə-tĭn, hĕm′ə-) *n.* A blue to blackish-brown powder, $C_{34}H_{32}N_4O_4FeOH$, that is the hydroxide of heme, containing ferric iron. [HEMAT(O)- + -IN.]

he·ma·tin·ic (hē′mə-tĭn′ĭk, hĕm′ə-) *adj.* Acting to increase the amount of hemoglobin in the blood.
~*n.* A hematinic drug used to treat iron-deficiency anemia. [HEMATIN + -IC.]

he·ma·tite (hē′mə-tīt′, hĕm′ə-) A blackish-red to brick-red mineral, essentially Fe_2O_3, the chief ore of iron. Also called "iron glance." [Latin *haematītēs,* from Greek *(lithos) haimatitēs,* "bloodlike (stone)," red iron ore, from *haima*† (stem *haimat-*), blood.]

hemato–, hemat– *prefix.* Indicates blood; for example, **hematology, hematin, hematic.** [Greek *haimato-,* from *haima*† (stem *haimat-*), blood.]

hem·a·to·blast (hĕm′ə-tō-blăst′, -blăst′, -hē′mə-, hĭ-măt′ə-) *n.* **1.** A platelet of the blood. **2.** An immature blood cell. [HEMATO- + -BLAST.] —**hem·a·to·blas·tic** (hĕm′ə-tə-blăs′tĭk, hē′mə-, hĭ-măt′ə-) *adj.*

hem·a·to·cele (hĕm′ə-tō-sēl′, hē′mə-, hĭ-măt′ə-) *n.* A hemorrhage contained within a membranous cavity, especially in the testicle. [HEMATO- + -CELE.]

hem·a·to·crit (hĕm′ə-tō-krĭt′, hē′mə-, hĭ-măt′ə-) *n.* **1.** A centrifuge used to separate the cellular and other particulate matter of blood from the plasma. **2.** Packed cell volume *(see).* [HEMATO- + Greek *kritēs,* judge, from *krinein,* to decide, judge.]

hem·a·to·gen·e·sis (hĕm′ə-tō-jĕn′ə-sĭs, hē′mə-, hĭ-măt′ə-) *n.* **Hematopoiesis.** [HEMATO- + -GENESIS.] —**hem·a·to·gen·ic** (hĕm′ə-tō-jĕn′ĭk, hē′mə-, hĭ-măt′ə-) *adj.* —**hem·a·to·ge·net·ic** (hĕm′ə-tō-jə-nĕt′ĭk, hē′mə-, hĭ-măt′ə-) *adj.*

he·ma·tog·e·nous (hē′mə-tŏj′ə-nəs, hĕm′ə-) *adj.* **1.** Producing blood. **2.** Originating or carried in the blood. [HEMATO- + -GENOUS.]

he·ma·toid (hē′mə-toid′, hĕm′ə-) *adj.* **1.** Bloody. **2.** Like blood. [Greek *haimatoeides*: HEMATO- + -OID.]

he·ma·tol·o·gy (hē′mə-tŏl′ə-jē, hĕm′ə-) *n.* The science encompassing the generation, anatomy, physiology, pathology, and therapeutics of blood. [HEMATO- + -LOGY.] —**he·ma·to·log·i·cal** (hē′mə-tə-lŏj′ĭ-kəl, hĕm′ə-) *adj.* —**he·ma·to·log·i·cal·ly** *adv.* —**he·ma·tol·o·gist** (hē′mə-tŏl′ə-jĭst, hĕm′ə-) *n.*

he·ma·tol·y·sis (hē′mə-tŏl′ə-sĭs, hĕm′ə-) *n. Biology.* **Hemolysis** *(see).* [HEMATO- + -LYSIS.]

he·ma·to·ma (hē′mə-tō′mə, hĕm′ə-) *n., pl.* **-mas** or **-mata** (-mə-tə). *Pathology.* A localized swelling filled with blood. [HEMAT(O)- + -OMA.]

hem·a·to·poi·e·sis (hĕm′ə-tō-poi-ē′sĭs, hē′mə-, hĭ-măt′ə-) *n.* The formation of blood in the body. Also called "hematogenesis," "hemopoiesis." [HEMATO- + -POIESIS.] —**hem·a·to·poi·et·ic** (hĕm′ə-tō-poi-ĕt′ĭk, hē′mə-, hĭ-măt′ə-) *adj.*

he·ma·to·sis (hē′mə-tō′sĭs, hĕm′ə-) *n.* Oxygenation of venous blood in the lungs. [HEMAT(O)- + -OSIS.]

hem·a·tox·y·lin (hĕm′ə-tŏk′sə-lĭn, hē′mə-) *n.* A yellow or red crystalline compound, $C_{16}H_{14}O_6·3H_2O$, the coloring principle of logwood, used in dyes, inks, and stains. [New Latin *Haematoxyl(on)* (plant genus) : *haemato-,* variant of HEMATO- + XYL(O)- + -IN.]

hem·a·to·zo·on (hĕm′ə-tō-zō′ŏn′, hē′mə-, hĭ-măt′ə-) *n., pl.* **-zoa** (-zō′ə). A parasitic protozoan or similar organism that lives in the blood. [HEMATO- + -ZOON.] —**hem·a·to·zo·ic** *adj.*

hem·a·tu·ri·a (hĕm′ə-tōōr′ē-ə, -tyōōr′ē-ə, hē′mə-) *n.* A condition in which blood or red blood cells are present in the urine. [HEMAT(O)- + -URIA.] —**hem·a·tu·ric** *adj.*

heme (hēm) *n.* The nonprotein, ferrous-iron-containing component of hemoglobin, having composition $C_{34}H_{32}FeN_4O_4$. [From HEMATIN.]

he·mel·y·tron (hē-mĕl′ə-trŏn′) *n., pl.* **-tra** (-trə). Also **hem·i·el·y·tron** (hĕm′ē-ĕl′ə-trŏn′). An insect forewing that is thickened at the base and membranous at the apex, characteristic of the true bugs. [HEM(I)- + ELYTRON.]

hem·er·a·lo·pi·a (hĕm′ər-ə-lō′pē-ə) *n.* A visual defect manifested as the inability to see as clearly in bright light as in dim light. Also called "day blindness." Compare **nyctalopia.** [New Latin, from Greek *hēmeralōps,* "day blind" : *hēmera,* day + *alaos*†, blind + -OPIA.]

hem·er·o·cal·lis (hĕm′ə-rō-kăl′ĭs) *n.* The **day lily** *(see).* [New Latin, from Latin, from Greek *hēmerokalles,* name of a kind of lily : *hēmera,* day + *kallos,* beauty.]

hemi–, hem– *prefix.* Indicates half; for example, **hemichordate, hemelytron.** Compare **demi-, semi-.** [Latin *hēmi-,* from Greek.]

–hemia. Variant of **-emia.**

hem·i·al·gi·a (hĕm′ē-ăl′jē-ə) *n.* Pain affecting one half of the body. [New Latin : HEMI- + -ALGIA.]

he·mic (hē′mĭk, hĕm′ĭk) *adj.* Of blood. [HEM(O) + -IC.]

hem·i·cel·lu·lose (hĕm′ĭ-sĕl′yə-lōs′, -lōz′) *n.* Any of several polysaccharides that are more complex than a sugar and less complex than cellulose, derived from plants and produced commercially from various seeds and other plant tissues.

hem·i·chor·date (hĕm′ĭ-kôr′dāt′) *n.* Any of various wormlike marine animals of the phylum or subphylum Hemichordata, having a primitive notochord and gill slits.
~*adj.* Of or belonging to the Hemichordata. [New Latin *Hemichordata* : HEMI- + CHORDATE.]

hem·i·cy·cle (hĕm′ĭ-sī′kəl) *n.* A semicircular structure or arrangement. [French *hémicycle,* from Latin *hēmicyclium,* from Greek *hēmikuklion* : HEMI- + *kuklos,* circle, CYCLE.]

hem·i·dem·i·sem·i·qua·ver (hĕm′ē-dĕm′ē-sĕm′ē-kwā′vər) *n. Chiefly British. Music.* A **sixty-fourth note** *(see).* [HEMI- + DEMISEMIQUAVER.]

hem·i·he·dral (hĕm′ĭ-hē′drəl) *adj.* Exhibiting only half the faces required for complete symmetry. Said of a crystal. [HEMI- + -HEDR(ON) + -AL.]

hem·i·hy·drate (hĕm′ĭ-hī′drāt′) *n.* A hydrate in which the molecular ratio of water molecules to anhydrous compound is 1:2. [HEMI- + HYDRATE.] —**hem·i·hy·drat·ed** *adj.*

hem·i·mor·phic (hĕm′ĭ-môr′fĭk) *adj.* Asymmetric at the axial ends. Said of a crystal. [HEMI- + -MORPHIC.]

hem·i·mor·phite (hĕm′ĭ-môr′fīt′) *n.* A mineral, **smithsonite.** [HEMIMORPH(IC) + -ITE.]

he·min (hē′mĭn) *n.* A brown or blue crystalline compound, $C_{34}H_{32}N_4O_4FeCl$, that is the chloride of heme and is used in identifying blood stains. [HEM(O)- + -IN.]

Hem·ing·way (hĕm′ĭng-wā′), **Ernest Miller** (1899–1961). U.S. novelist. He served in World War I with the Red Cross, then was a newspaper reporter in Toronto before settling in Paris with a group of expatriate U.S. writers, including Ezra Pound and Gertrude Stein. The novel *The Torrents of Spring* (1926) first revealed his clipped style. His major works are *The Sun Also Rises* (1926), *A Farewell to Arms* (1929), *For Whom the Bell Tolls* (1940), and *The Old Man and the Sea* (1952). He was awarded the Nobel Prize for literature in 1954.

hem·i·par·a·site (hĕm′ĭ-păr′ə-sīt′) *n.* **1.** An organism, such as mistletoe, that obtains some food from its host but also photosynthesizes. Also called "semiparasite." **2.** An organism that can live both parasitically and independently; a facultative parasite.

hem·i·ple·gi·a (hĕm′ĭ-plē′jē-ə) *n.* Paralysis of one side of the body only. Compare **paraplegia, quadriplegia.** [New Latin, from Middle Greek *hēmiplēgia* : HEMI- + -PLEGIA.] —**hem·i·ple·gic** *adj. & n.*

hem·ip·ter·an (hĭ-mĭp′tər-ən) *n.* Also **he·mip·ter·on** (-tə-rŏn′). A hemipterous insect.
~*adj.* Of or belonging to the Hemiptera; hemipterous. [New Latin *Hemiptera* : HEMI- + -PTER.]

he·mip·ter·ous (hĭ-mĭp′tər-əs) *adj.* Of or belonging to the Hemiptera, a large group of insects characterized by piercing or sucking mouth parts in the form of a beak or rostrum. The group includes the **heteropterous** and **homopterous** bugs *(both of which see).*

hem·i·sphere (hĕm′ə-sfîr′) *n.* **1. a.** A half of a sphere bounded by a great circle. **b.** A half of a symmetric, approximately spherical object as divided by a plane of symmetry: *cerebral hemisphere.* **2.** Either half of the celestial sphere as divided by the ecliptic, the celestial equator, or the horizon. **3.** Either the northern or southern half of the earth as divided by the equator or the eastern or western half as divided by a meridian. [Middle English *(h)emisper(i)e,* from Latin *hēmisphaerium,* from Greek *hēmisphairion* : HEMI- + *sphairion,* diminutive of *sphaira,* SPHERE.] **—hem·i·spher·ic** (hĕm′ə-sfîr′ĭk, -sfĕr′ĭk), **hem·i·spher·i·cal** *adj.* **—hem·i·spher·i·cal·ly** *adv.*

hem·i·stich (hĕm′ĭ-stĭk′) *n. Prosody.* **1.** Half a line of verse, especially when separated rhythmically from the rest of the line by a caesura. **2.** An incomplete or imperfect line of verse. [Latin *hēmistichium,* from Greek *hēmistikhion* : HEMI- + *stikhos,* line.]

hem·i·ter·pene (hĕm′ĭ-tûr′pēn′) *n.* Any of a group of hydrocarbons that have the formula C_5H_8. See **terpene.**

hem·line (hĕm′līn′) *n.* The height or level of the hem of a skirt, dress, or coat.

hem·lock (hĕm′lŏk′) *n.* **1. a.** A type of spruce tree of the genus *Tsuga,* native to North America, having small cones and short, flat needles. **b.** The wood of such a tree. **2. a.** Any of several poisonous plants of the genera *Conium* and *Cicuta,* such as the **poison hemlock** and **water hemlock** *(both of which see).* **b.** The poisonous alkaloid **coniine** *(see),* derived from the poison hemlock. [Old English *hymlic(e)*†.]

hemo–, hem–, hema– *prefix.* Indicates blood; for example, **hemocyte, hemin, hemacytometer.** [From Greek *haima*†, blood.]

he·mo·chro·ma·to·sis (hē′mə-krō′mə-tō′sĭs, hĕm′ə-) *n.* A hereditary disease in which excessive amounts of iron are absorbed by and stored in the body. Symptoms include diabetes, a bronze pigmentation of the skin, and severe damage to the liver and pancreas. Also called "bronze diabetes." [HEMO- + CHROMAT(O)- + -OSIS.]

he·mo·coel (hē′mə-sēl′, hĕm′ə-) *n.* The body cavity of arthropods and mollusks, consisting of a blood-filled expanded portion of the circulatory system. [HEMO- + Greek *koilos,* hollow.]

he·mo·cy·a·nin (hē′mə-sī′ə-nĭn, hĕm′ə-) *n.* A bluish, oxygen-bearing, copper-containing substance similar to hemoglobin, present in the blood of certain insects, crustaceans, and other invertebrates. [HEMO- + -CYAN(O) + -IN.]

he·mo·cyte (hē′mə-sīt′, hĕm′ə-) *n.* A cell in the blood. [HEMO- + -CYTE.]

he·mo·di·al·y·sis (hē′mō-dī-ăl′ə-sĭs, hĕm′ō-) *n.* A technique for removing waste products in the circulating blood of patients with kidney failure using the principle of **dialysis** *(see).* Blood is passed through a dialyzer (kidney machine) and the waste products filter through a semipermeable membrane.

he·mo·dy·nam·ics (hē′mō-dī-năm′ĭks, hĕm′ō-) *n.* The study of the circulation of the blood.

he·mo·flag·el·late (hē′mə-flăj′ə-lāt′, -lĭt, -flə-jĕl′ĭt, hĕm′ə-) *n.* A flagellate protozoan, as a trypanosome, that is parasitic in the blood.

he·mo·glo·bin (hē′mə-glō′bĭn, hĕm′ə-) *n. Abbr.* **Hb** The oxygen-bearing, iron-containing conjugated protein in vertebrate red blood cells, consisting of about 6 percent heme and 94 percent globin, and having as a typical formula $(C_{738}H_{1166}FeN_{203}O_{208}S_2)_4$. [Shortening of earlier *hematoglobulin* : HEMATIN + GLOBULIN.]

he·mo·glo·bi·nu·ri·a (hē′mə-glō′bə-no͝or′ē-ə, -nyo͝or′ē-ə, hĕm′ə-) *n.* The presence of hemoglobin in the urine. **—he·mo·glo·bi·nu·ric** *adj.*

he·mo·leu·ko·cyte (hē′mə-lo͞o′kə-sīt′, hĕm′ə-) *n.* A **leukocyte** *(see).*

he·mo·ly·sin (hē′mə-lī′sĭn, hĕm′ə-, hĭ-mŏl′ə-sĭn) *n.* An agent or substance, such as an antibody or bacterial toxin, that initiates destruction of red blood cells, thereby liberating hemoglobin. [HEMO- + LYSIN.]

he·mol·y·sis (hĭ-mŏl′ə-sĭs) *n.* The destruction of red blood cells, either in the body or in a blood sample. Also called "hematolysis." [HEM(O)- + -LYSIS.] **—he·mo·lyt·ic** (hē′mə-lĭt′ĭk) *adj.*

hemolytic disease of the newborn *n.* A condition in newborn babies resulting from destruction of the red blood cells of the fetus by antibodies from the mother's blood. It usually occurs because of incompatibility of maternal and fetal blood groups.

he·mo·phil·i·a (hē′mə-fĭl′ē-ə, hĕm′ə-) *n.* A hereditary blood coagulation disorder, principally affecting males but transmitted by females, characterized by excessive, sometimes spontaneous bleeding. [HEMO- + -PHILIA.]

he·mo·phil·i·ac (hē′mə-fĭl′ē-ăk′, hĕm′ə-) *n.* A person who suffers from hemophilia. Also called "bleeder."

he·mo·phil·ic (hē′mə-fĭl′ĭk, hĕm′ə-) *adj.* **1.** Pertaining to hemophilia. **2.** Growing well in blood, or in a culture containing blood, as do certain bacteria.

he·mo·pho·bi·a (hē′mə-fō′bē-ə, hĕm′ə-) *n.* A morbid fear of blood. [HEMO- + -PHOBIA.] **—he·mo·pho·bic** *adj.*

he·mo·poi·e·sis (hē′mə-poi-ē′sĭs, hĕm′ə-) *n. Physiology.* **Hematopoiesis** *(see).* [HEMO- + -POIESIS.]

he·mo·pro·tein (hē′mə-prō′tēn′) *n.* Any protein containing heme, such as hemoglobin, myoglobin, and cytochrome.

he·mop·ty·sis (hĭ-mŏp′tə-sĭs) *n.* The spitting up of blood from the lungs or bronchial tubes. [HEMO- + Greek *ptusis,* a spitting, from *ptuein,* to spit.]

hem·or·rhage (hĕm′ər-ĭj) *n.* Bleeding; especially, copious discharge of blood from the blood vessels.
~*intr.v.* **hemorrhaged, -rhaging, -rhages.** To bleed copiously in or as if in a hemorrhage. [Earlier *hemorrhagy,* from Old French *hemorragie,* from Latin *haemorrhagia,* from Greek *haimorrhagia* : HEMO- + -RRHAGIA.] **—hem·or·rhag·ic** (hĕm′ə-răj′ĭk) *adj.*

hem·or·rhoid (hĕm′ə-roid′) *n.* **1.** An itching or painful mass of dilated veins in swollen anal tissue. **2. hemorrhoids.** The pathological condition in which such swollen masses occur. In this sense, also called "piles." [Middle English *emeroudis,* from Old French *emeroyde,* from Latin *haemorrhoida,* from Greek *(phlebes) haimorrhoides,* bleeding (veins), from *haimorrhoos,* flowing with blood : HEMO- + *-rrhoos,* from *rhein,* to flow.]

hem·or·rhoid·al (hĕm′ə-roid′l) *adj.* **1.** Of or pertaining to hemorrhoids. **2.** *Anatomy.* Supplying the region of the rectum and anus. Said of certain arteries.

hem·or·rhoid·ec·to·my (hĕm′ə-roi-dĕk′tə-mē) *n., pl.* **-mies.** The removal of hemorrhoids by surgery.

he·mo·sid·er·in (hē′mō-sĭd′ər-ĭn) *n.* An iron-containing protein serving to store iron in the body. Excessive amounts are formed in certain disorders, such as hemochromatosis. [HEMO- + Greek *sideros,* iron + -IN.]

he·mo·sta·sis (hē′mə-stā′sĭs, hĕm′ə-) *n.* Also **he·mo·sta·sia** (-zhə, -zhē-ə, -zē-ə). The stopping of the flow or circulation of blood. [HEMO- + STASIS.]

he·mo·stat (hē′mə-stăt′) *n.* **1.** Any agent, such as a chemical, that stops bleeding. **2.** A clamplike instrument used in surgery to reduce or prevent bleeding. [HEMO- + -STAT.]

he·mo·stat·ic (hē′mə-stăt′ĭk) *adj.* Acting to stop the flow of blood or profuse bleeding.
~*n.* A hemostatic agent. [Late Greek *haimostatikos* : HEMO- + -STATIC.]

hemp (hĕmp) *n.* **1.** A tall plant, *Cannabis sativa,* native to Asia, having small greenish flowers and stems that yield a coarse fiber used in cordage. Also called "cannabis," "Indian hemp," "marijuana." **2.** The fiber of this plant. **3.** Any of various narcotic drugs, such as hashish, derived from this plant. **4. a.** Any of various similar or related plants, especially one yielding a fiber similar to that of *Cannabis sativa.* **b.** The fiber of such a plant. [Middle English *hemp(e),* Old English *hænep, henep,* from Germanic *hanipiz* (unattested); akin to Greek *kannabis.*]

hemp agrimony *n.* A Eurasian plant, *Eupatorium cannabinum,* having clusters of small reddish-purple flowers.

hemp·en (hĕm′pən) *adj.* Made of or resembling hemp.

hemp nettle *n.* Any of various Eurasian plants of the genus *Galeopsis;* especially, *G. tetrahit,* having white or reddish flowers.

hem·stitch (hĕm′stĭch′) *n.* **1.** A decorative stitch usually bordering a hem, as on a handkerchief, made by drawing out several parallel threads and catching together the cross threads in uniform groups, thus creating an open design. **2.** Needlework using this stitch. **—hem·stitch** *v.* **—hem·stitch·er** *n.*

hen (hĕn) *n.* **1.** A female bird; especially, the adult female of the domestic fowl. **2.** The female of certain aquatic animals, such as an octopus or a lobster. [Middle English *hen,* Old English *hen(n).*]

He·nan (hŭ′nän′). Also **Ho·nan, Ho-nan** (hō′-). Province of northeastern and central China. Traversed by the Huang He (Yellow River) and Huai He, which irrigate its densely populated and fertile central plain, it produces cereals and anthracite. The capital, Zhengzhou (Chengchow), is in the northwest of the province.

hen-and-chick·ens (hĕn′ən-chĭk′ənz) *n., pl.* **hens-and-chickens** (hĕnz′-). Any of several plants having many runners or offshoots; especially, the **houseleek** *(see).*

hen·bane (hĕn′bān′) *n.* A poisonous plant, *Hyoscyamus niger,* native to the Mediterranean region, having an unpleasant odor, hairy leaves, and funnel-shaped dull-yellow flowers. Several drugs used medicinally are derived from the weed. [Middle English, from HEN (fowl) + BANE (alluding to its poison).]

hen·bit (hĕn′bĭt′) *n.* A plant, *Lamium amplexicaule,* native to Europe, having toothed leaves and small purplish-pink flowers. Also called "henbit dead nettle." [HEN + BIT (morsel).]

hence (hĕns) *adv.* **1. a.** For this reason; as a result; therefore: *handmade and hence expensive.* **b.** From this source: *She grew up in the Sudan, hence her interest in Nubian art.* **2. a.** From this time; from now: *A year hence he will have forgotten.* **b.** *Rare.* Henceforth: *Hence I'll trust no one.* **3. a.** Forth from this place; away from here. Usually used with an imperative: *Get thee hence!* **b.** Distant from here: *an inn two miles hence.* **c.** From this life: *depart hence.* **—from hence.** *Archaic.* From this place.
~*interj. Archaic.* Go; get out: *"Hence, loathed Melancholy"* (Milton). **—hence with!** Away with! [Middle English *hennes,* extended form of *henne,* hence, Old English *heonane,* from here, away.]

hence·forth (hĕns′fôrth′) *adv.* Also **hence·for·ward** (hĕns-fôr′wərd). From this time forth; from now on.

hench·man (hĕnch′mən) *n., pl.* **-men** (-mĭn). **1. a.** A loyal and trusted follower or subordinate. **b.** A person who supports a political figure chiefly out of self-interest. **2.** A member of a criminal gang. **3.** *Obsolete.* A page of honor to a prince or other person of high rank. [Middle English *hengestman, henx(st)man,* probably groom, squire : *hengest,* horse, stallion, from Old English, from Germanic *hangista-* (unattested) + MAN.]

hen·coop (hĕn′ko͝op′) *n.* A coop or cage for poultry.

hendeca– *prefix.* Indicates eleven; for example, **hendecahedron.** [Greek *hendeka,* eleven : *hen,* neuter of *heis,* one + *deka,* ten.]

hen·dec·a·gon (hĕn-dĕk′ə-gŏn′) *n.* A polygon with 11 sides. [HENDECA- + -GON.] **—hen·de·cag·o·nal** (hĕn′dĭ-kăg′ə-nəl) *adj.*

hen·dec·a·he·dron (hĕn-dĕk′ə-hē′drən) *n., pl.* **-drons** or **-dra** (-drə). A polyhedron with 11 plane surfaces. [HENDECA- + -HEDRON.] **—hen·dec·a·he·dral** *adj.*

hemp agrimony *This tall riverside plant was used in medieval times as a purgative and a cure for jaundice.*

henbane *Even the yellowish purple-veined summer flowers of this wildflower have a nasty smell. The plant is very poisonous, but it is the source of the narcotic alkaloids hyoscyamine; scopolamine; and atropine, used for dilating the pupils of the eyes.*

hen·dec·a·syl·lab·ic (hĕn-dĕk′ə-sĭ-lăb′ĭk) *adj.* Containing eleven syllables.
~*n.* Also **hen·dec·a·syl·la·ble** (hĕn-dĕk′ə-sĭl′ə-bəl). A line of verse containing eleven syllables. [Latin *hendecasyllabus,* a hendecasyllable : Greek *hendeka,* eleven : *hen,* neuter of *heis,* one + *deka,* ten + *sullabē,* SYLLABLE.]

Hen·der·son (hĕn′dər-sən), **Arthur** (1863-1935). British Labour politician. He was an ironworker and trade union leader and was first elected to parliament in 1903. From 1932 until his death he was president of the World Disarmament Conference. He was awarded the Nobel Peace Prize in 1934.

hen·di·a·dys (hĕn-dī′ə-dĭs) *n.* A figure of speech in which two distinct words connected by a conjunction are used to express a single complex notion that would normally be expressed by an adjective and a noun; for example, in *He struck with steel and sword,* the phrase *steel and sword* is a hendiadys, used instead of *a steel sword.* [Medieval Latin, from Greek *hen dia duoin,* one by means of two : *hen,* neuter of *heis,* one + *dia,* through (see **dia-**) + *duoin,* genitive of *duō,* two.]

Hen·drix (hĕn′drĭks), **Jimi,** born James Marshall Hendrix (1942-70). U.S. rock musician. His innovative style of electric guitar playing changed the course of rock music. With his first major group, the Jimi Hendrix Experience, he recorded hits such as *Purple Haze* and *Foxy Lady,* which were his own compositions.

Henegouwen. See **Hainaut.**

hen·e·quen, hen·e·quin, hen·i·quen (hĕn′ə-kwən) *n.* **1.** A tropical American plant, *Agave fourcroydes,* having large, thick leaves that yield a coarse reddish fiber used in making rope and twine. **2.** The fiber obtained from this plant. [Spanish *henequén, jeniquén,* perhaps from Taino.]

henge (hĕnj) *n.* A structure of ritual significance belonging to the Neolithic or Bronze Age, circular in form and sometimes having stone or wooden posts. [Back-formation from STONEHENGE.]

Hen·gist (hĕn′gĭst) (died *c.* 488). Germanic chieftain. With his brother **Hor·sa** (hôr′sə), he led (A.D. 449) the Jutes who invaded southern Britain. They landed in the Isle of Thant, but were defeated at Aylesford, where Horsa was slain (*c.* 455). Hengist then conquered Kent, where he ruled from *c.* 455 to *c.* 488.

hen harrier *n.* The **marsh hawk** (see).

hen·house (hĕn′hous′) *n.* A chicken coop.

Hen·ie (hĕn′ē), **Sonja** (1913-69). Norwegian ice-skater. She was largely responsible for making ice-skating a popular, competitive sport. She was Norwegian champion at age 10, won Olympic gold medals in 1928, 1932, and 1936, and won 10 consecutive world championships between 1927 and 1936. In 1936 she settled in the United States, where she starred in ice shows and films.

Hen·ley (hĕn′lē), **William Ernest** (1849-1903). English editor and author. The editor of the *Scots Observer* (from 1889) and its successor, the *National Observer,* he published the early works of many aspiring English writers, including George Bernard Shaw, Thomas Hardy, and Rudyard Kipling.

Hen·ley-on-Thames (hĕn′lē-ŏn-tĕmz′). Town in Oxfordshire, in south-central England, on the Thames River. It is best known for its annual royal regatta, first held in 1839.

hen·na (hĕn′ə) *n.* **1.** A tree or shrub, *Lawsonia inermis,* of Asia and northern Africa, having fragrant white or reddish flowers. **2.** A reddish powder obtained from the leaves of this plant, used as a hair coloring and for dyeing leather. **3.** Moderate or strong reddish brown to strong brown.
~*tr.v.* **hennaed, -naing, -nas.** To dye (hair, for example) with henna. [Arabic *ḥinnā′.*] —**hen·na** *adj.*

henna wax *n.* A wax preparation derived from the henna plant and used as a noncolorant hair conditioner.

hen·ner·y (hĕn′ə-rē) *n., pl.* **-ies. 1.** A poultry farm. **2.** A coop or cage for poultry.

hen·o·the·ism (hĕn′ə-thē-ĭz′əm) *n.* Belief in one god, such as a special clan or tribal god, without denying the existence of others. Compare **monotheism.** [German *Henotheismus* : Greek *heno-,* from *hen,* neuter of *heis,* one + THEISM.] —**hen·o·the·ist** *n.* —**hen·o·the·is·tic** (hĕn′ə-thē-ĭs′tĭk) *adj.*

hen party *n. Informal.* A party or outing exclusively for women. Compare **stag party.**

hen·peck (hĕn′pĕk′) *tr.v.* **-pecked, -pecking, -pecks.** *Informal.* To dominate or harass (one's husband) with persistent nagging. [Back-formation from *henpecked,* alluding to a hen that attacks and dominates a rooster.]

Hen·ri (hĕn′rē), **Robert** (1865-1929). U.S. painter. After studying in Paris, he joined with a group of young painters, dubbed the Eight—or the Ashcan School by their detractors—who decried the artificiality and sentiment of traditional schools of art. Henri was also a well-known teacher, whose students included Edward Hopper.

Hen·ri·et·ta Ma·ri·a (hĕn′rē-ĕt′ə mə-rē′ə) (1609-69). Queen consort of Charles I of England, the daughter of Henry IV of France. She married Charles in 1625 and by remaining a Roman Catholic increased Charles's unpopularity with the Puritans.

hen·ry (hĕn′rē) *n., pl.* **-ries** or **-rys.** *Abbr.* **H** The unit of inductance in which an induced electromotive force of one volt is produced when the current is varied at the rate of one ampere per second. [After Joseph HENRY.]

Henry I (hĕn′rē), also known as "Henry Beauclerc" (1068-1135). King of England (1100-35). He was the youngest son of William the Conqueror and succeeded his brother, William II.

Henry II¹ (1133-89). King of England (1154-89), son of Queen Ma-

henge These prehistoric circles of free-standing stones or wooden uprights are thought to have been ceremonial centers in ancient Britain and France. The best-known example is Stonehenge, on Britain's Salisbury Plain. This one, dating from about 1800 B.C., is at Avebury in Wiltshire, England.

tilda, and founder (through his father, Geoffrey, Count of Anjou) of the Angevin, or Plantagenet, royal line. Henry appointed Thomas Becket archbishop of Canterbury in 1162 but quarreled with him over the issue of the Crown's authority over the Church. This led to the murder of Becket in 1170.

Henry II² (1519-59). King of France (1547-59), the son of Francis I. He regained Calais from the English in 1558.

Henry III (1207-72). King of England (1216-72). He succeeded his father, King John. His reign was troubled by baronial opposition led by Simon de Montfort, whose representative parliament, called in 1265, is regarded as the first full English parliament.

Henry IV¹, also known as "Henry Bolingbroke" (1367-1413). King of England (1399-1413), eldest son of John of Gaunt and grandson of Edward III. He was banished from England by Richard II in 1398. The following year John of Gaunt died, and Richard confiscated his estates, to which Henry was heir. Henry returned, raised a military force, and compelled Richard to abdicate. Parliament confirmed his claim, and the Lancastrian dynasty was founded.

Henry IV², also known as "Henry of Navarre" (1553-1610). King of France (1589-1610), the son of Antoine de Bourbon and founder of the Bourbon royal line. He rid France of Spanish influence by his successful war against Spain (1595-98) and gave political rights to French Protestants in the Edict of Nantes (1598).

Henry V (1387-1422). King of England (1413-22), son of Henry IV. In the first years of his reign he suppressed the Lollards, executing their leader, Sir John Oldcastle, in 1417. He also reopened the Hundred Years' War, defeating the French at Agincourt (1415). By 1419 all of Normandy was once again in English hands.

Henry VI (1421-71). King of England (1422-61, 1470-71), only son of Henry V. He succeeded to the throne as a baby and for most of his reign exercised little control over the royal administration. The Yorkist victory at Northampton in 1460 left Henry a prisoner of his enemies. The following year Edward IV was proclaimed king. Henry, rescued from captivity, regained the throne in 1470. He was recaptured at the Battle of Barnet and murdered in the Tower of London in 1471.

Henry VII, also known as "Henry Tudor" (1457-1509). King of England (1485-1509), son of Edmund Tudor and founder of the Tudor line. He was head of the house of Lancaster after the death of Henry VI in 1471 and led the opposition to Richard III. In 1485 he defeated Richard at Bosworth Field and was acclaimed king. He married Elizabeth, daughter of Edward IV, and united the houses of York and Lancaster.

Henry VIII (1491-1547). King of England (1509-47), second son and successor of Henry VII. He married the first of his six wives, Catherine of Aragon, shortly after his accession in 1509. Her failure to deliver a male heir led to the divorce that compelled Henry to break with Rome by the Act of Supremacy in 1536. That same year he began the dissolution of the monasteries.

Henry, Joseph (1797-1878). U.S. physicist. He was the first director of the Smithsonian Institution, founded in 1846. He invented the electromagnetic telegraph and, independently of Michael Faraday, discovered electromagnetic induction, the principle on which the transformer and the dynamo are based.

Henry, O. See William Sydney **Porter.**

Henry, Patrick (1739-99). U.S. Revolutionary leader and orator. A member of the House of Burgesses (1765) and the Continental Congress (1774-76), he spurred the creation of the Virginia militia with the words "Give me liberty, or give me death" (1775). He also served as governor of Virginia and in the state legislature (1776-90).

Henry's law *n. Chemistry.* The principle that at equilibrium the amount of gas dissolved in a liquid is proportional to the gas pressure. [After *William Henry* (1774-1836), English chemist.]

Henry the Navigator (1394-1460). Prince of Portugal. In 1416 he established a headquarters for overseas exploration that laid the foundations of Portugal's overseas empire.

hep·a·rin (hĕp′ər-ĭn) *n.* A complex organic acid found especially in lung and liver tissue and having the ability in certain circumstances to prevent the clotting of blood. [New Latin *hepar,* liver, from Late Latin *hēpar,* from Greek + -IN.]

he·pat·ic (hĭ-păt′ĭk) *adj.* **1.** Of, pertaining to, or resembling the liver. **2.** Liver-colored. **3.** Of or belonging to the Hepaticae, a class of mosslike plants including the liverworts.
~*n.* **1.** A drug used to treat liver diseases. **2.** A plant of the class Hepaticae, a **liverwort** (see). [Middle English *epatik,* from Latin *hēpaticus,* of liver, from Greek *hēpatikos,* from *hēpar* (stem *hēpat-*), liver.]

he·pat·i·ca (hĭ-păt′ĭ-kə) *n.* Any of several woodland plants of the genus *Hepatica;* especially, *H. americana,* of eastern North America, having three-lobed leaves and white or lavender flowers. [New Latin *Hepatica,* from Medieval Latin *hēpatica,* liverwort, from Latin, feminine of *hēpaticus,* HEPATIC.]

hep·a·ti·tis (hĕp′ə-tī′tĭs) *n.* Inflammation of the liver due to infection or toxins, characterized by fever, weakness, and jaundice. [New Latin : Greek *hēpar* (stem *hēpat-*), liver + -ITIS.]

Hep·burn (hĕp′bûrn′, -bərn), **Katharine** (1909-). U.S. actress. She made her stage debut in 1928 and became a popular Hollywood film star. She has won an Oscar as best actress four times, for *Morning Glory* (1933), *Guess Who's Coming to Dinner* (1967), *The Lion in Winter* (1968), and *On Golden Pond* (1981).

hep·cat (hĕp′kăt′) *n. Slang.* A performer or devotee of swing and jazz during the 1940's.

He·phaes·tus (hĭ-fĕs′təs). *Greek Mythology.* The lame god of fire

HOW KNIGHTS WERE IDENTIFIED IN THE MIDDLE AGES

The symbol of gentility that grew from a simple means of identification

The use of pictures and emblems on shields, flags, and coats of arms was introduced into England from western Europe during the 12th century. But the exact date and place of origin of the heraldic system in western Europe is not known.

The earliest use was on the battlefield and in tournaments, or mock battles, as a means of identification for otherwise unrecognizable armor-clad knights. Bold symbols depicting a knight's name were embroidered on his surcoat, the garment worn over his armor, which became known as the coat of arms. Since few people could read or write at that time, this means of identification spread to the seals that were used to authenticate official documents. Heralds, the messengers

of royal and noble households, whose duty it was to identify the knights, became interested in the colorful means of identification, and heraldry as it is known today began. Heraldic systems are similar throughout Europe, and a system akin to heraldry can be found in Japan.

In 1484 Richard III of England granted the heralds a charter incorporating them as a body within the Royal Household, now known as the College of Arms, or Heralds' College. The Kings of Arms (the senior heralds) grant arms on behalf of the Crown, and they also draw up the regulations regarding arms. Blazon, the language of heraldry, was invented by the early heralds and is still used to describe all coats of arms.

Originally arms were granted only to knights and nobles and were regarded as an honor. But during the 15th century the rich and powerful middle class that emerged from the crumbling feudal system were granted arms in recognition of their new "gentle" status, and since then a coat of arms has been regarded as the insignia of gentility. Arms are still granted to those who satisfy the Earl Marshal that they are eligible. Honorary arms can be granted to American citizens of English or British descent in the male line. Corporate bodies such as companies, banks, and local government authorities are also granted arms. The Kings of Arms' jurisdiction extends throughout the British Commonwealth.

HOW A COAT OF ARMS EVOLVES

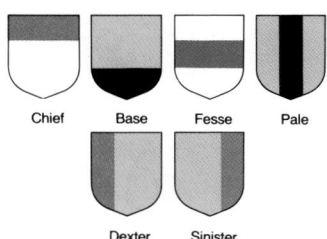

Chief | Base | Fesse | Pale

Dexter | Sinister

POSITIONS *In heraldic language, each area of the shield has its own name. The top is called the chief, the bottom is the base, the horizontal center is the fesse, the vertical center is the pale, the right side from the bearer's view is the dexter, and the left side is the sinister.*

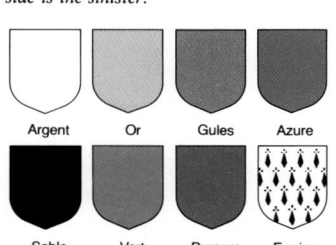

Argent | Or | Gules | Azure

Sable | Vert | Purpure | Ermine

TINCTURES *The colors, metals, and furs are called tinctures. The metals are argent (silver) and or (gold). Colors are gules (red), azure (blue), sable (black), vert (green), and purpure (purple). The furs are ermine and vair (squirrel).*

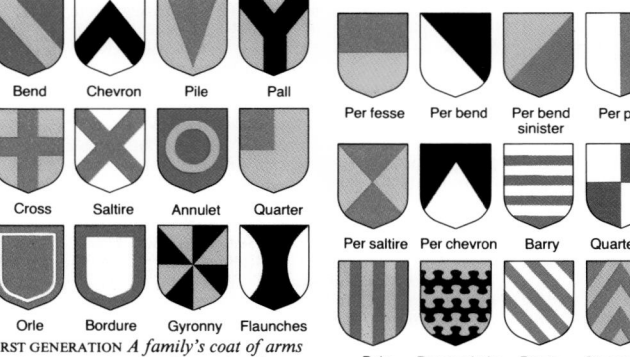

Bend | Chevron | Pile | Pall

Cross | Saltire | Annulet | Quarter

Orle | Bordure | Gyronny | Flaunches

FIRST GENERATION *A family's coat of arms can begin very simply, often with only one charge (the device on a shield) such as a chevron, cross, animal, or bird. The prominent geometric charges are called the ordinaries, and the less prominent geometric charges are called the subordi-*

naries. *If an ordinary is repeated on a shield, it must be a smaller form and is called a diminutive. Other charges are classified by the figures they depict, such as beasts, birds, or fish.*

Lion rampant | Lion passant reguardant | Leopard passant guardant | Boar passant

Talbot sejant | Stag's head cabossed | Unicorn statant | Eagle displayed

BEASTS AND BIRDS *In early heraldry few beasts were used other than the rampant or passant lion. Today various beasts and birds are used, and a variety of positions have been contrived for them.*

Bowes | Shakespeare | Cockburn | Trumpington

CANTING ARMS *Sometimes a family chooses a charge that is a pun on its surname. The Bowes Lyons, for instance, are represented by bows and lions, the Trumpingtons by trumpets. These are known as canting, or punning, arms.*

Per fesse | Per bend | Per bend sinister | Per pale

Per saltire | Per chevron | Barry | Quarterly

Paly | Barry nebuly | Bendy | Chevronny

PARTITION LINES *Some coats bear no charges and consist of a field divided by partition lines only. These lines run in the direction of almost any ordinary, which will often carry the word* per *before it.*

Label Eldest son | Crescent Second son | Mullet Third son | Martlet Fourth son

Annulet Fifth son | Fleur-de-lis Sixth son | Rose Seventh son | Cross moline Eighth son

INHERITING ARMS *Family arms are hereditary and pass from father to son. No two people can bear the same coat of arms, so the arms of sons must be differenced according to regulations laid down by the Kings of Arms. The eldest son has a label, the second a crescent, the third a mullet, the fourth a martlet, the fifth an annulet, and so on. The label is removed when the father dies and the eldest son inherits the coat. The differencing marks of younger sons are not removed. A younger son's eldest son differences the coat with a label until he inherits.*

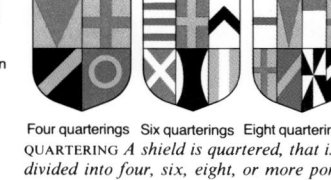

Four quarterings | Six quarterings | Eight quarterings

QUARTERING *A shield is quartered, that is, divided into four, six, eight, or more portions, to accommodate coats of arms in-*

herited from an heiress. *The quarterings read from dexter chief (top left when looking at the shield). The first quarter is the family coat, the next is the first acquired coat, the third quarter is the second acquired coat, and so on. If there is a blank at the end of the shield, then the family coat is repeated.*

THE ARMS OF A WOMAN

Lozenge | Impaling | Escutcheon of pretense

Daughters bear the same arms as their fathers, undifferenced, on a diamond-shaped figure known as a lozenge. But as a woman may not have a helmet, she cannot exhibit a crest. If a man has no sons, his daughters are his heraldic heiresses and may transmit their arms as a quartering to their descendants.

When a heraldic heiress marries, she places her arms on a small shield, known as an escutcheon of pretense, in the middle of her husband's shield. When a daughter who is not an heiress marries, she places her arms beside her husband's on a shield. This is known as impaling. If a woman is widowed, she bears her marital arms on a lozenge.

AN ACHIEVEMENT OF ARMS

Mantling Essential if a helmet is used. Probably originally protection against sun or sword blows

Supporters Granted only to peers of the realm and their heirs, and certain knights

The Field The surface of the shield on which charges are placed

Compartment The base on which supporters rest. It may be granted with supporters

Crest A hereditary device fixed to the top of the helm, or helmet

Helmet A means of displaying the crest. Shape and position vary with rank

Shield The principal vehicle for displaying arms

Charge Any figure or emblem used in the shield or crest

Motto A guiding principle for those who bear the arms

SOLA·BONA·QUAE·HONESTA

Strictly, a coat of arms refers only to the shield and the devices (known as charges) borne on it, but in common usage the expression is used to refer to an achievement of arms, which is a representation of all the armorial devices to which the bearer is entitled.

herbs

PLANTS THAT CAN FLAVOR FOOD AND IMPROVE HEALTH
Nature's supply of seasonings and remedies

There are more than 50 herbs that are commonly used by cooks to add a special flavor to their dishes, and a well-stocked herb garden is indispensable to the master chef. Herbs are aromatic plants that can add flavor to bland food or disguise an unpleasant tang.

The use of herbs as medicine has an ancient history and is still common throughout the world—even in countries with sophisticated medical services. It is freely admitted that some herbs are medically useful; digitalis, for example, is obtained from foxgloves and

used in treating heart disease. Indeed many modern drugs are derived from herbs, and the value of herbalism is seldom dismissed outright; but there is not sufficient laboratory-tested proof of its claims for it to be accepted as a science.

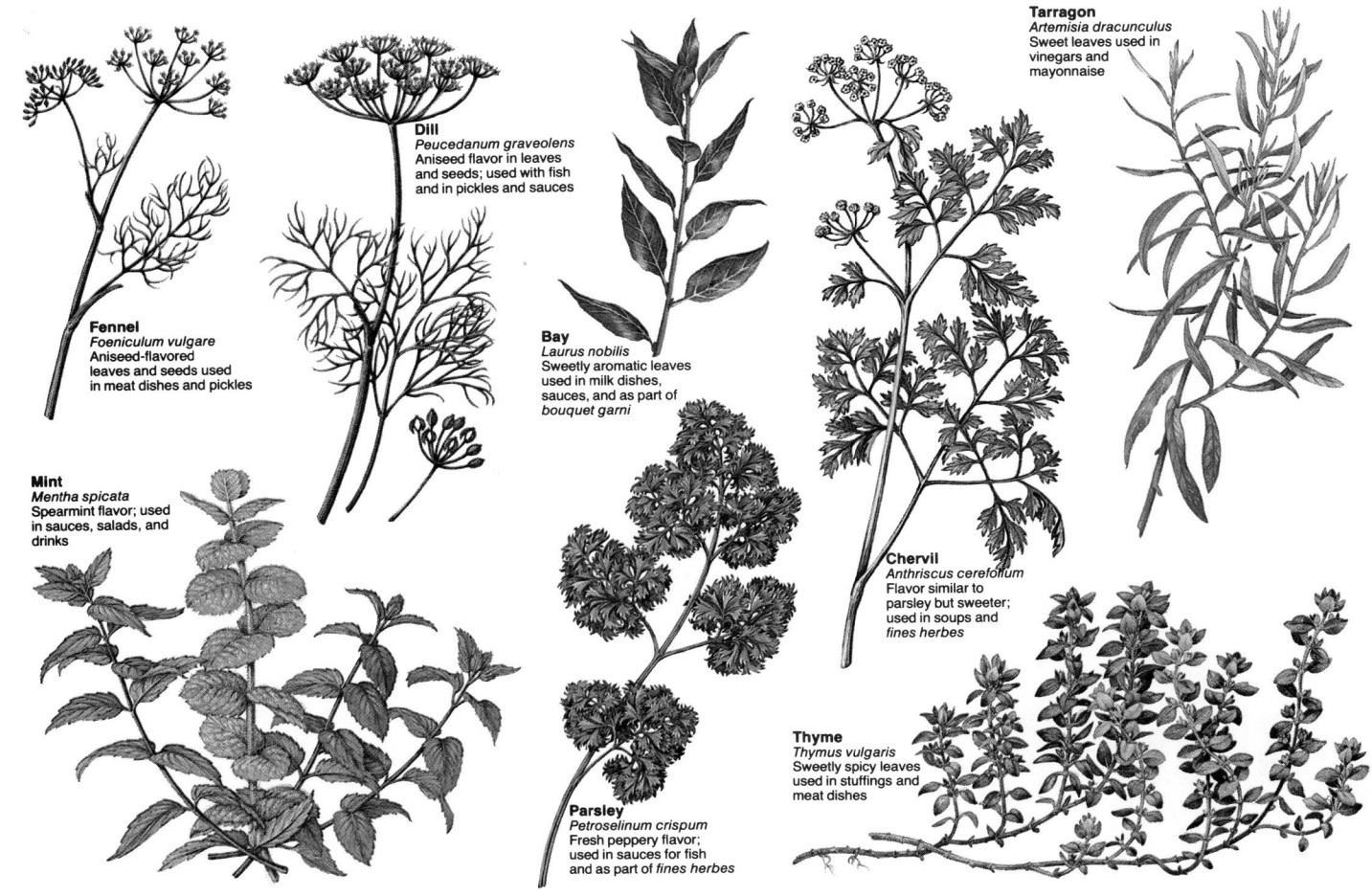

Fennel
Foeniculum vulgare
Aniseed-flavored leaves and seeds used in meat dishes and pickles

Mint
Mentha spicata
Spearmint flavor; used in sauces, salads, and drinks

Dill
Peucedanum graveolens
Aniseed flavor in leaves and seeds; used with fish and in pickles and sauces

Bay
Laurus nobilis
Sweetly aromatic leaves used in milk dishes, sauces, and as part of *bouquet garni*

Parsley
Petroselinum crispum
Fresh peppery flavor; used in sauces for fish and as part of *fines herbes*

Tarragon
Artemisia dracunculus
Sweet leaves used in vinegars and mayonnaise

Chervil
Anthriscus cerefolium
Flavor similar to parsley but sweeter; used in soups and *fines herbes*

Thyme
Thymus vulgaris
Sweetly spicy leaves used in stuffings and meat dishes

and metalworking; identified with the Roman god Vulcan.

Hep·ple·white (hĕp'əl-hwīt') *adj.* Designating an English style of furniture of the late 18th century, noted for its light, graceful lines, its use of concave curves, and the shield or heart backs of its chairs. [After George HEPPLEWHITE.]

Hepplewhite, George (died 1786). English cabinetmaker. His elegant style, now much admired, was unfashionable in his day. His reputation rests on the designs in his *Cabinet-Maker and Upholsterer's Guide* (published in 1788).

hepta–, hept– *prefix.* Indicates seven; for example, **heptahedron, heptane.** [Greek *hepta,* seven.]

hep·tad (hĕp'tăd') *n.* A group or series of seven. [Greek *heptas* (stem *heptad-*), the number seven, period of seven years, from *hepta,* seven.]

hep·ta·dec·a·no·ic acid (hĕp'tə-dĕk'ə-nō'ĭk) *n.* An organic acid, **margaric acid** (see).

hep·ta·gon (hĕp'tə-gŏn') *n.* A polygon with seven sides and seven angles. [Greek *heptagonos,* having seven angles : HEPTA- + -GON.]

hep·tag·o·nal (hĕp-tăg'ə-nəl) *adj.* **1.** Having seven sides and seven angles. **2.** Of, pertaining to, or formed in heptagons. **—hep·tag·o·nal·ly** *adv.*

hep·ta·he·dral (hĕp'tə-hē'drəl) *adj.* **1.** Having seven plane surfaces. **2.** Of, pertaining to, or formed in heptahedrons. **—hep·ta·he·dral·ly** *adv.*

hep·ta·he·dron (hĕp'tə-hē'drən) *n., pl.* **-drons** or **-dra** (-drə). A polyhedron with seven plane surfaces. [HEPTA- + -HEDRON.]

hep·ta·hy·drate (hĕp'tə-hī'drāt') *n. Chemistry.* A hydrate in which the ratio of water molecules to anhydrous compound is 7:1.

hep·tam·er·ous (hĕp-tăm'ər-əs) *adj.* Having seven parts or ar-

ranged in groups of seven. Said especially of plant parts. [HEPTA- + -MEROUS.]

hep·tam·e·ter (hĕp-tăm'ə-tər) *n.* **1.** A metrical unit consisting of seven feet. **2.** A line of verse written in such meter. [HEPTA- + -METER.]

hep·tane (hĕp'tān') *n.* A volatile, colorless, highly flammable liquid hydrocarbon, $CH_3(CH_2)_5CH_3$, obtained in the fractional distillation of petroleum, and used as a standard in determining octane ratings, as an anesthetic, and as a solvent. [HEPT(A)- (from the number of carbon atoms it possesses) + -ANE.]

hep·tan·gu·lar (hĕp-tăng'gyə-lər) *adj.* Having seven angles.

hep·tar·chy (hĕp'tär'kē) *n., pl.* **-chies. 1. a.** Government by seven persons. **b.** A state so governed. **2.** A state divided into seven units, each with its own ruler. **3.** *Often* **Heptarchy. a.** The informal confederation of the Anglo-Saxon kingdoms from the 5th to the 9th century, consisting of Kent, Sussex, Wessex, Essex, Northumbria, East Anglia, and Mercia. **b.** The historical period covering the existence of this confederation. [HEPT(A)- + -ARCHY.]

hep·ta·stich (hĕp'tə-stĭk') *n.* A poem, stanza, or strophe consisting of seven lines. [HEPTA- + Greek *stikhos,* line of verse.]

Hep·ta·teuch (hĕp'tə-tōōk', -tyōōk') *n.* The first seven books of the Old Testament. [Greek *heptateukhos (biblos),* "(book) in seven volumes" : HEPTA- + *teukhos,* tool, case holding writing material, volume.]

hep·ta·va·lent (hĕp'tə-vā'lənt) *adj. Chemistry.* Having a valence of 7; septivalent.

hep·tode (hĕp'tōd') *n.* A type of thermionic valve with seven electrodes: an anode, a cathode, and five grids. [HEPTA- + -ODE.]

Hep·worth (hĕp'wûrth', -wərth), **Dame Barbara** (1903–75). English

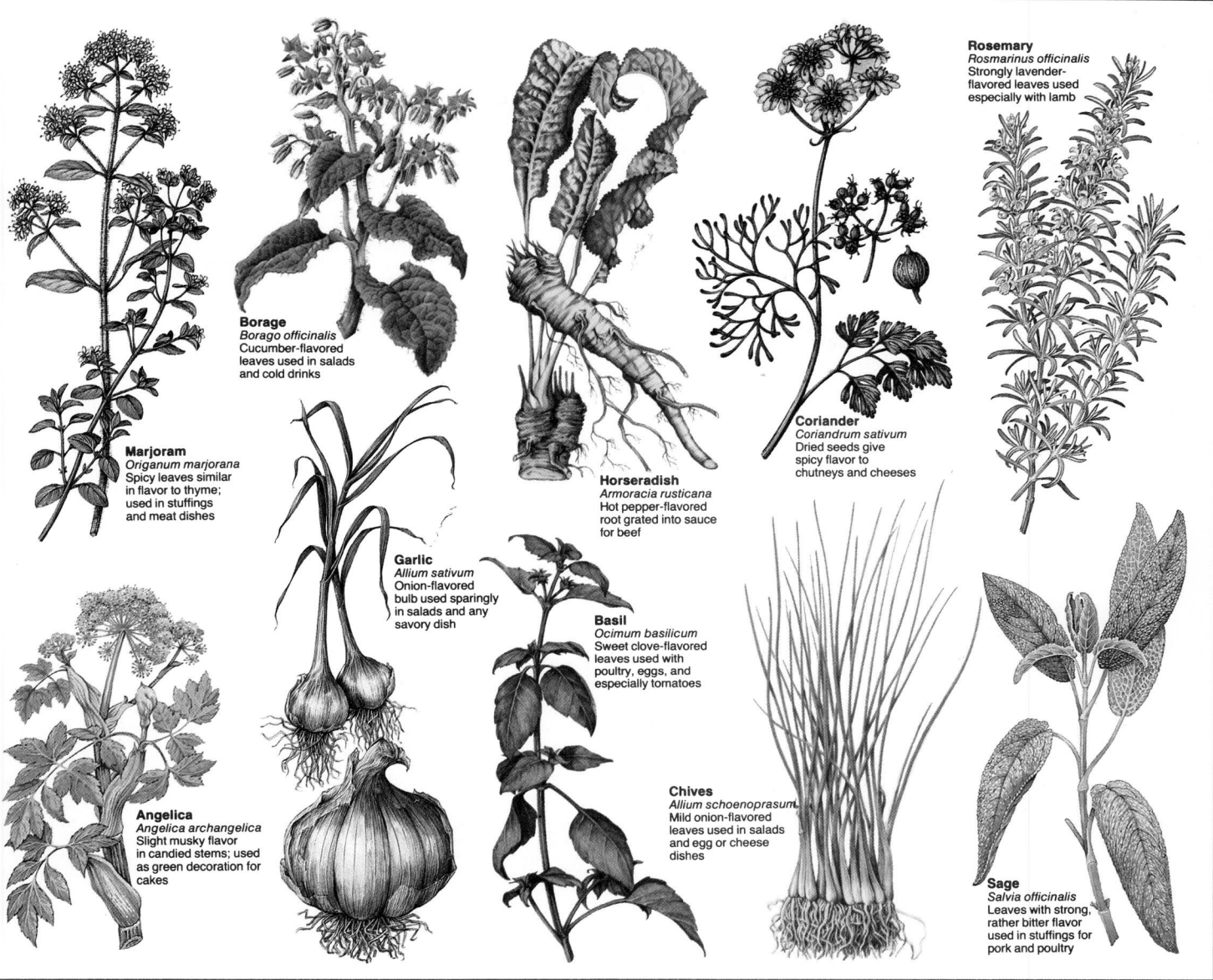

Borage
Borago officinalis
Cucumber-flavored
leaves used in salads
and cold drinks

Marjoram
Origanum marjorana
Spicy leaves similar
in flavor to thyme;
used in stuffings
and meat dishes

Garlic
Allium sativum
Onion-flavored
bulb used sparingly
in salads and any
savory dish

Horseradish
Armoracia rusticana
Hot pepper-flavored
root grated into sauce
for beef

Basil
Ocimum basilicum
Sweet clove-flavored
leaves used with
poultry, eggs, and
especially tomatoes

Coriander
Coriandrum sativum
Dried seeds give
spicy flavor to
chutneys and cheeses

Rosemary
Rosmarinus officinalis
Strongly lavender-
flavored leaves used
especially with lamb

Angelica
Angelica archangelica
Slight musky flavor
in candied stems; used
as green decoration for
cakes

Chives
Allium schoenoprasum
Mild onion-flavored
leaves used in salads
and egg or cheese
dishes

Sage
Salvia officinalis
Leaves with strong,
rather bitter flavor
used in stuffings for
pork and poultry

sculptor. Her works, like those of Henry Moore, explore the relationship between space and large rounded forms. She was made a dame in 1965.

her (hûr; *unstressed* hər, ər) *pron.* The objective case of the third person pronoun *she.* It is used: **1.** As the direct object of a verb: *They assisted her.* **2.** As the indirect object of a verb: *They offered her a lift.* **3.** As the object of a preposition: *This letter is addressed to her.* **4.** After *than* or *as* in comparisons in which the first term is in the objective case: *The judges praised him more than her.* **5.** *Informal.* In place of the reflexive pronoun *herself* as the indirect object of a verb: *She went to buy her a car.* **6.** In a certain informal style to refer to things not usually personified: *The engine's all right, so start her up.* **7.** In various elliptical, absolute, or interjectional phrases in which it is neither subject nor object: *Her and her fancy airs!*
~The possessive form of the pronoun *she.* Used attributively to indicate possession, agency, or reception of an action by the feminine person or entity spoken of: *her purse; pursuing her tasks; suffered her first rebuff.* —See Usage note at **me.** [Middle English *hire, her(e),* Old English *hire.*]

her. heraldry.

He·ra (hîr′ə). Also **He·re** (hîr′ē). *Greek Mythology.* The sister and consort of Zeus; identified with the Roman goddess Juno.

Heracles, Herakles. Variants of **Hercules.**

Her·a·cli·tus (hĕr′ə-klī′təs) (6th–5th century B.C.). Greek philosopher. He argued that strife and change are natural conditions of the universe. One of his most famous of his aphorisms is "All things are flowing."

Heraklion. See **Iráklion.**

her·ald (hĕr′əld) *n.* **1.** A person who proclaims important news; a messenger; an envoy. **2.** A person or thing that announces or gives indication of something to come; a harbinger; a precursor. **3.** *British.* An official responsible for regulating all matters and settling all questions relating to heraldry; an officer of arms. **4. a.** An official formerly charged with making royal proclamations and with bearing messages of state between sovereigns. **b.** An official who formerly made proclamations and conveyed challenges at a tournament.
~*tr.v.* **heralded, -alding, -alds. 1.** To proclaim; announce: *"the cocks that herald dawn all night"* (Malcolm Lowry). **2.** To usher in; inaugurate. [Middle English *herau(l)d,* from Old French *herau(l)t,* from Germanic.]

he·ral·dic (hə-răl′dĭk) *adj.* Of or pertaining to heralds or heraldry. —**he·ral·di·cal·ly** *adv.*

heraldic achievement *n. Heraldry.* A coat of arms, or representation of a coat of arms, complete with crest, motto, and supporters.

her·ald·ist (hĕr′əl-dĭst) *n.* One who practices or studies heraldry.

her·ald·ry (hĕr′əl-drē) *n., pl.* **-ries. 1.** *Abbr.* **her. a.** The profession of devising, granting, and blazoning arms, of tracing pedigrees, and of ruling on questions of precedence, as exercised by an officer of arms. **b.** A branch of knowledge dealing with the history and description in proper terms of armorial bearings and their accessories; armory. **2.** Armorial ensigns or similar insignia. **3.** Pomp and ceremony, especially as attended with armorial trappings; pageantry: *the heraldry of a royal progress.* See feature, page 785.

Heralds' College *n.* The **College of Arms** *(see).*

herb (ûrb, hûrb) *n.* **1.** An angiosperm plant that has a fleshy stem as distinguished from the woody tissue of shrubs and trees and that generally dies back at the end of each growing season; a herbaceous

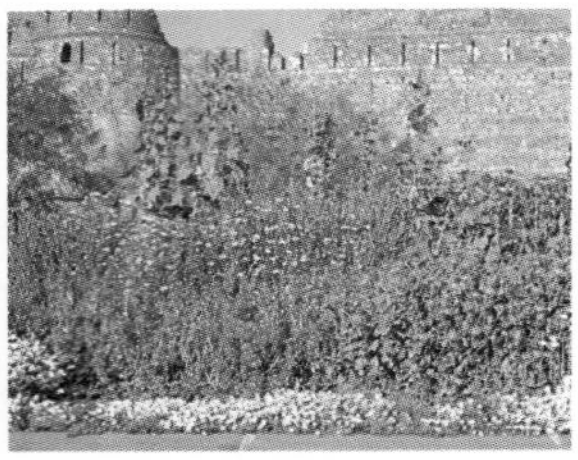

herbaceous border *A herbaceous border at Delhi Zoo in India. The English landscape gardener Gertrude Jekyll (1843–1932) was the great modern exponent of herbaceous gardens, in which perennial plants are arranged with taller species at the back, while colors and shapes are arranged to give changing patterns to the garden through the seasons.*

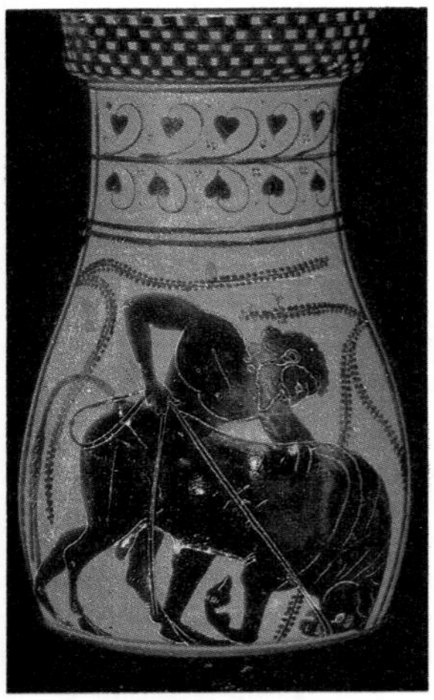

Hercules *One of the legendary 12 labors of Hercules, or Herakles, was capturing the mad bull of Crete. The episode is recalled on this Greek vase of about 500* B.C.

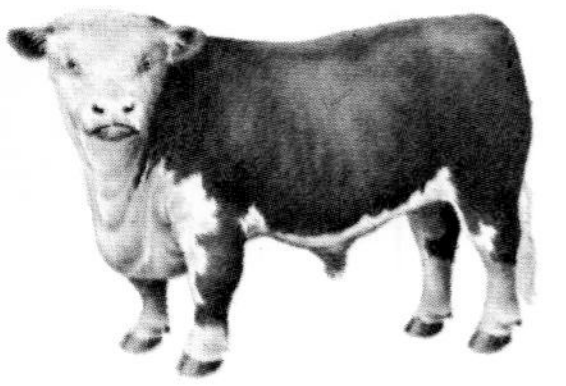

Hereford *Purebred Hereford cattle are always red and white. Cattle of other colors with white faces are crossbreeds. Herefords were originally developed in the Welsh border counties, including the former county of Herefordshire, but are now reared all over the world for beef.*

plant. **2.** Any of various often aromatic plants used especially in medicine or as seasoning. —See Note at **plant.** [Middle English *(h)erbe,* from Old French, from Latin *herba*†.]

her·ba·ceous (hûr-bā′shəs, ûr-) *adj.* **1.** Of, pertaining to, or characteristic of an herb as distinguished from a woody plant. **2.** Green and leaflike in appearance or texture. [Latin *herbāceus* : *herba,* HERB + -ACEOUS.]

herbaceous border *n.* A flower bed that contains herbaceous perennial plants rather than annuals or woody plants.

herb·age (ûr′bĭj, hûr′-) *n.* **1.** Herbaceous plant growth, especially grass or similar vegetation used for pasturage. **2.** The fleshy, often edible parts of plants. [Middle English *(h)erbage,* from Old French, from *(h)erbe,* HERB.]

herb·al (hûr′bəl, ûr′-) *adj.* Of, relating to, or containing herbs.
∼*n.* A book about plants, especially those that are useful to man.

herb·al·ist (hûr′bə-lĭst, ûr′-) *n.* One who grows, collects, sells, or specializes in the use of herbs, especially medicinal herbs.

her·bar·i·um (hûr-bâr′ē-əm, ûr-) *n., pl.* **-iums** or **-ia** (-ē-ə). **1.** A collection of dried plants mounted and labeled for use in scientific study. **2.** A place or institution where such a collection is kept. [Late Latin *herbārium,* from Latin *herba,* HERB.]

herb bennet *n.* A hairy Eurasian plant, *Geum urbanum,* having small yellow flowers and an astringent root formerly used medicinally. Also called "bennet." [Middle English *herb beneit,* from Old French *herbe beneite* (or *benoite*), from Medieval Latin *herba benedicta,* "blessed herb" (from its medicinal properties) : Latin *herba,* HERB + *benedicta,* feminine past participle of *benedīcere,* to bless (see **benediction**).]

Her·bert (hûr′bərt), **George** (1593–1633). English poet, one of the metaphysical poets. None of his poems was published in his lifetime. They were collected in *The Temple* (1633).

herb Ge·rard (jə-rärd′) *n., pl.* **herbs Gerard.** A plant, **ground elder** *(see).* [After St. *Gerard,* whose name was invoked by those suffering from gout, for which the plant was formerly prescribed.]

her·bi·cide (hûr′bĭ-sīd′, ûr′-) *n.* A substance used to destroy plants, especially weeds. [HERB + -CIDE.] —**her·bi·cid·al** (hûr′bĭ-sīd′l, ûr′-) *adj.*

her·bi·vore (hûr′bə-vôr′, -vōr′, ûr′-) *n.* A herbivorous animal. [New Latin *Herbivora* (former designation of herbivores), from the neuter plural of *herbivorus,* HERBIVOROUS.]

her·biv·o·rous (hûr-bĭv′ər-əs, ûr-) *adj.* Feeding on plants; plant-eating. [New Latin *herbivorus* : HERB + -VOROUS.]

Herblock. See Herbert **Block.**

herb-of-grace (ûrb′əv-grās′, hûrb′-) *n., pl.* **herbs-of-grace.** *Archaic.* A plant, **rue** *(see).* [Probably from the association of rue (the plant) with rue (repentance).]

herb Paris *n., pl.* **herbs Paris.** A European plant, *Paris quadrifolia,* having a whorl of four leaves and a solitary yellow or greenish flower. [Probably Medieval Latin *herba paris,* "herb of a pair" (perhaps a reference to the two pairs of leaves on the whorl), assimilated to *Paris* : Latin *herba,* HERB + *paris,* genitive of *par,* equal.]

herb Robert *n., pl.* **herbs Robert.** A low-growing plant, *Geranium robertianum,* having divided leaves and small reddish-purple flowers. [Middle English *herbe Robert,* from Medieval Latin *herba Robertī,* "herb of Robert," variously supposed to be named after *Robert,* Duke of Normandy, Saint *Robert* (died 1067), French churchman, or Saint *Rupert,* 7th-century Bavarian ecclesiastic.]

Hercegovina. See **Bosnia and Hercegovina.**

Her·cu·la·ne·um (hûr′kyə-lā′nē-əm). Ancient town of southern Italy. Situated 8 kilometers (5 miles) southeast of Naples, on the slopes of Vesuvius, it was completely buried in the volcano's eruption (A.D. 79) and remained undiscovered until 1709.

her·cu·le·an (hûr′kyə-lē′ən, hər-kyōō′lē-ən) *adj.* **1.** Tremendously difficult or demanding: *a herculean task.* **2.** *Often* **Herculean.** Resembling Hercules in size, power, or courage: *Herculean strength.* **3. Herculean.** Of or relating to Hercules.

Her·cu·les[1] (hûr′kyə-lēz′). Also **Her·a·cles, Her·a·kles** (hĕr′ə-klēz′). *Greek & Roman Mythology.* The son of Zeus and Alcmene, a hero of extraordinary strength who won immortality by performing the 12 labors demanded by Hera.

Hercules[2] *n.* **1.** *Sometimes* **hercules.** A man of enormous strength. **2.** *Astronomy.* A constellation in the Northern Hemisphere near Lyra and Corona Borealis that contains the star Ras Algethi and the globular cluster M13. [After HERCULES.]

Her·cu·les′-club (hûr′kyə-lēz-klŭb′) *n.* A tree or shrub, *Aralia spinosa,* of the southeastern United States, having prickly compound leaves and large clusters of small white flowers. Also called "devil's walking stick."

Her·cyn·i·an (hûr-sĭn′ē-ən) *adj. Geology.* Designating or belonging to a phase in the late Paleozoic era (Carboniferous and Permian periods) characterized by mountain building. Also called "Variscan," "Armorican."

herd (hûrd) *n.* **1. a.** A group of cattle or other domestic animals of a single kind kept together. **b.** A number of wild animals of one species that remain together as a group: *a herd of elephants.* **2.** A number of people grouped together by some common factor: *a herd of stranded passengers.* **3.** *Archaic.* One who tends a herd; a herdsman. Now used chiefly in combination: *a goatherd.* —**the herd.** The multitude of common people regarded as undistinguished and easily led or influenced.
∼*v.* **herded, herding, herds.** —*intr.* **1.** To congregate in a herd or group. **2.** To keep company; associate. —*tr.* **1. a.** To gather, tend, or drive (animals) in a herd. **b.** To gather or drive (people) as if in a herd. **2.** To place in a group. [Middle English *herd(e),* Old English *heord.*] —**herd·er** *n.*

her·dic (hûr′dĭk) *n.* A small horse-drawn cab having two wheels, side seats, and an entrance at the back. [After Peter *Herdic* (1824–1888), American carriage maker.]

herd instinct *n.* An instinct that impels people to come together in groups and to conform to the prevailing modes of thought and behavior of such groups.

herds·man (hûrdz′mən) *n., pl.* **-men** (-mĭn). A person who owns, breeds, or tends livestock.

here (hîr) *adv.* **1.** At or in this place: *Stop here.* **2.** At this time; now: *Let's adjourn the meeting here and resume after lunch.* **3.** At or on this point, detail, or item: *There is great disagreement here.* **4.** In the present life or condition. **5.** To this place; hither: *Come here.* **6.** Used for emphasis after an imperative: *Look here! Now you see here.* —**here and there.** In various places. —**neither here nor there.** Of no relevance or significance.
∼*adj.* **1.** Existing in this place. Used for emphasis after a noun modified by a demonstrative pronoun: *Look at this word here. I'll have this one here.* **2.** *Nonstandard.* Used for emphasis between a demonstrative pronoun and a noun: *this here word.*
∼*n.* This place: *He lives a mile from here. I left it near here.*
∼*interj.* Used as a response to a roll call, as a command to an animal, as a way of calling attention, or as a rebuke or admonishment. —**here's to.** Used to propose a toast to a specified person or thing. [Middle English *her(e),* Old English *hēr.*]

Here. Variant of **Hera.**

here·a·bout (hîr′ə-bout′) *adv.* Also **here·a·bouts** (-ə-bouts′). In this general vicinity; around here.

here·af·ter (hîr-ăf′tər, -äf′tər) *adv.* **1.** Immediately following this in time, order, or place; after this. **2.** In a world to come; in the afterlife: *win salvation hereafter.*
∼*n.* **1.** The future. **2.** The world to come; life after death: *belief in a hereafter.*

here·at (hîr-ăt′) *adv.* Because of this; at this.

here·by (hîr-bī′) *adv.* By virtue of this act, decree, bulletin, or document; by this means.

he·re·des. Plural of **heres.**

he·red·i·ta·ble (hə-rĕd′ə-tə-bəl) *adj.* Heritable.

her·e·dit·a·ment (hĕr′ə-dĭt′ə-mənt) *n. Law.* Any kind of property that can be inherited. [Medieval Latin *hērēditāmentum,* from Late Latin *hērēditāre,* to inherit, from Latin *hērēs* (stem *hērēd-*), heir.]

he·red·i·tar·i·an·ism (hə-rĕd′ə-târ′ē-ə-nĭz′əm) *n. Psychology.* The doctrine or school that regards heredity as the major factor in determining intelligence and behavior. Compare **environmentalism.** —**he·red·i·tar·i·an** *n. & adj.*

he·red·i·tar·y (hə-rĕd′ə-tĕr′ē) *adj.* **1.** *Law.* **a.** Descending from an ancestor to a legal heir; passing down by inheritance. **b.** Having title or possession through inheritance. **2.** Genetically transmitted or transmissible. **3. a.** Appearing in or characteristic of successive generations. **b.** Derived from or fostered by one's ancestors: *a hereditary prejudice.* **4.** Ancestral; traditional: *their hereditary home.* **5.** Of or pertaining to heredity or inheritance. —See Synonyms at **innate.** [Latin *hērēditārius,* from *hērēditās,* HEREDITY.] —**he·red·i·tar·i·ly** (hə-rĕd′ə-târ′ə-lē) *adv.* —**he·red·i·tar·i·ness** *n.*

he·red·i·tist (hə-rĕd′ə-tĭst) *n.* One who supports the theory that heredity rather than environment determines behavior.

he·red·i·ty (hə-rĕd′ə-tē) *n., pl.* **-ties. 1.** The genetic transmission of characteristics from parents to offspring. **2.** The totality of characteristics and associated potentialities so transmitted to an individual organism. In this sense, compare **environment.** [Old French *heredite,* from Latin *hērēditās* (stem *hērēditāt-*), inheritance, from *hērēs* (stem *hērēd-*), heir.]

Her·e·ford (hĕr′ə-fərd, hûr′fərd) *n.* Any of a breed of beef cattle developed in Herefordshire, England, having a reddish coat with white markings.

Hereford and Worces·ter (wŏŏs′tər). A county in west-central England, bordering Wales. It is traversed by the Wye, Avon, and Severn rivers, with the Malvern Hills in the center, and is mainly agricultural. The city of Worcester serves as the county town.

Her·e·ford·shire (hĕr′ə-fərd-shîr′, -shər). A former county of west-central England, now incorporated into Hereford and Worcester.

here·in (hîr-ĭn′) *adv.* In or into this; especially, in this book, document, or the like.

here·in·af·ter (hîr′ĭn-ăf′tər, -äf′tər) *adv.* In a following part of this document, statement, or book; after this.

here·in·be·fore (hîr′ĭn-bĭ-fôr′, -fōr′) *adv.* In a preceding part of this document, statement, or book; before this.

here·in·to (hîr-ĭn′tōō) *adv.* Into this matter, circumstance, situation, or place; into this.

here·of (hîr-ŭv′, -ŏv′) *adv.* Pertaining to or concerning this.

here·on (hîr-ŏn′, -ôn′) *adv.* Hereupon.

He·re·ro (hə-râr′ō, hĕr′ə-rō′) *n., pl.* **Hereros** or collectively **Herero. 1.** A member of a Negroid people living mainly in central Namibia. **2.** The Bantu language of this people.

he·res (hā′rās′) *n., pl.* **heredes** (hā-rā′dās′). *Law.* An heir. [Latin *hērēs.*]

here's (hîrz). Contraction of *here is.*

he·re·si·arch (hə-rē′zē-ärk′, hĕr′ə-sē-) *n.* The founder or chief proponent of a heresy or heretical movement. [Late Latin *haeresiarcha,* from Late Greek *hairesiarkhēs* : Greek *hairesis,* sect (see **heresy**) + -ARCH.]

her·e·sy (hĕr′ə-sē) *n., pl.* **-sies. 1. a.** A belief or doctrine at variance with the orthodox doctrine of a religious system; especially, a belief or doctrine involving dissension from or denial of Christian dogma by a professed believer: *the Pelagian heresy.* **b.** Adherence to such dissenting belief or doctrine. **2. a.** A controversial or unorthodox opinion or doctrine in politics, philosophy, science, or other fields. **b.** Adherence to such unorthodox opinion. [Middle English *(h)eresie,* from Old French, from Late Latin *haeresis,* from Late Greek *hairesis,* from Greek, "a taking," school of thought, faction, from *hairein†,* to take, grasp, choose.]

her·e·tic (hĕr′ə-tĭk) *n.* A person who holds controversial or unorthodox opinions in any area; especially, one who publicly dissents from the officially accepted dogma of a religion. [Middle English *(h)eretik,* from Old French *(h)eretique,* from Late Latin *haereticus,* from Greek *hairetikos,* able to choose, factious, from *hairetos,* from *hairein,* to take, choose. See **heresy.**] —**he·ret·i·cal** (hə-rĕt′ĭ-kəl) *adj.* —**he·ret·i·cal·ly** *adv.*

here·to (hîr-tōō′) *adv.* To this place, document, matter, or proposition; to this: *Attached hereto is my voucher.*

here·to·fore (hîr′tə-fôr′, -fōr′) *adv.* Up to the present time; before this: *The discovery disproved all that we had heretofore believed.* [Middle English : HERE + *tofore, toforn,* before, Old English *tōforan* : TO + *foran,* before, from *fore,* FORE (in front).]

here·un·der (hîr-ŭn′dər) *adv.* **1.** In a following part of this document, statement, or book; after this. **2.** By the authority or under the powers of this decree, document, or the like.

here·un·to (hîr-ŭn′tōō) *adv.* Hereto.

here·up·on (hûr′ə-pŏn′, -pôn′) *adv.* Following instantly upon this; immediately after this; at this.

Here·ward the Wake (hĕr′ə-wərd thə wāk′) (*fl.* 1070). Anglo-Saxon folk hero. He led an English uprising against William the Conqueror in 1070, establishing himself and his followers on the Isle of Ely. William took control of the island in 1071, but Hereward escaped and is believed to have been pardoned later by William.

here·with (hîr-wĭth′, -wĭth′) *adv.* **1.** Along with this. **2.** By this means; hereby.

her·i·ot (hĕr′ē-ət) *n. Feudal law.* A death duty and later a tax on the expiry or abandoning of a holding paid by a tenant to his lord. It consisted commonly of the tenant's best beast and later of a money payment. [Middle English *heriet, heriot,* Old English *heregeatwe,* military equipment, "army-trappings" : *here,* army + *geatwa,* equipment, trappings.]

her·i·ta·ble (hĕr′ə-tə-bəl) *adj.* **1.** Capable of being inherited; passing by inheritance. **2.** Transmitted from one generation to another; hereditary. **3.** Capable of inheriting or of taking by inheritance. [Middle English *heretable,* from Old French *heritable,* from *heriter,* to inherit. See **heritage.**]

her·i·tage (hĕr′ə-tĭj) *n.* **1.** Property that is or can be inherited; an inheritance. **2.** Something other than property passed down from preceding generations; a legacy; a tradition. **3.** A condition or lot accruing to one through the circumstances of one's birth; a birthright: *a heritage of affluence and position.* [Middle English *(h)eritage,* from Old French, from *heriter,* to inherit, from Late Latin *hērēditāre,* from Latin *hērēs* (stem *hērēd-),* heir.]

her·i·tor (hĕr′ə-tər) *n.* An inheritor. [Middle English *heriter,* from Norman French, variant of Old French *heritier,* from Latin *hērēditārius,* HEREDITARY.]

her·i·tress (hĕr′ə-trĭs) *n.* Also **her·i·trix** (-trĭks). A female inheritor.

herl (hûrl) *n.* **1.** The barb of a feather used in trimming an artificial fly for angling. **2.** A fishing fly made with this. [Middle English *herle,* probably from Middle Low German *herle, harle†.*]

her·ma (hûr′mə) *n., pl.* **-mae** (-mē′, -mī′). Also **herm** (hûrm). In ancient Greece, a statue consisting of the head of the god Hermes mounted on a square stone post. [Latin, from Greek *hermēs,* from *Hermēs,* HERMES.]

her·maph·ro·dite (hər-măf′rə-dīt′) *n.* **1.** One having the sex organs and many of the secondary sex characteristics of both male and female. **2.** *Biology.* An organism, such as an earthworm, or a structure, such as a monoclinous flower, having both male and female reproductive organs. **3.** Anything consisting of a combination of diverse or contradictory elements. [Middle English *hermofrodite,* from Latin *hermaphroditus,* from Greek *hermaphroditos,* after *Hermaphroditos,* Hermaphroditus, son of Hermes and Aphrodite who became united in one body with the nymph Salmacis.] —**her·maph·ro·dit·ic** (hər-măf′rə-dĭt′ĭk) *adj.* —**her·maph·ro·dit·i·cal·ly** *adv.*

hermaphrodite brig *n.* A two-masted vessel having a square-rigged foremast and a schooner-rigged mainmast. [It combines the characteristics of a brig and a schooner.]

hermaphrodite rig *n.* A jackass rig (see).

her·maph·ro·dit·ism (hər-măf′rə-dī′tĭz′əm) *n.* Also **her·maph·ro·dism** (-rə-dĭz′əm). The condition of being a hermaphrodite.

her·me·neu·tics (hûr′mə-nōō′tĭks, -nyōō′tĭks) *n. Used with a singular verb.* The science and methodology of interpretation, especially of Scriptural text. Compare **exegetics.** [New Latin *hermeneutica,* from Greek *hermēneutikē (tekhnē),* (art) of interpretation, from the feminine of *hermēneutikos,* from *hermēneutēs,* interpreter, from *hermēneuein,* to interpret, from *hermēneus†,* interpreter.] —**her·me·neu·tic, her·me·neu·ti·cal** *adj.* —**her·me·neu·ti·cal·ly** *adv.*

Her·mes (hûr′mēz′). *Greek Mythology.* The god of commerce, invention, cunning, and theft, who also served as messenger and herald for the other gods, as the patron of travelers and rogues, and as the conductor of the dead to Hades; identified with the Roman god Mercury.

CHEMICAL CHAINS THAT GOVERN HEREDITY
Mingling characteristics down through the generations

Every living thing that results from sexual reproduction resembles its parents to some extent but is never an exact replica of either of them. A kitten looks like a cat and a nestling is recognizable as a bird because of genetic information contained in their chromosomes.

Chromosomes are microscopic structures in living cells. Each chromosome contains two chains of DNA (deoxyribonucleic acid) twisted around each other in a shape known as a "double helix." The varying chemical patterns along these chains are called genes, and it is through them that characteristics are passed on from one generation to another.

Chromosomes always occur in pairs (46 pairs in humans), but since one chromosome is inherited from the male parent and one from the female, the two members of a pair do not necessarily carry the same forms of genes. When preparing to produce a new generation, the chromosomes in the reproductive cells untwist and separate, only one from each pair going into each egg or sperm. So each new organism inherits an equal number of chromosomes from each parent, and they join to provide the full complement of new pairs.

If identical genes for one characteristic are inherited from each parent, then the offspring will have that characteristic. If the genes are not identical, the characteristic will be a blend of each or a "recessive" gene will give way to a "dominant" one. If one human parent's chromosome carries a gene for blue eyes and the other contributes a chromosome with the gene for brown eyes, the child will have brown eyes because brown is dominant. The recessive characteristic is suppressed but not lost, for it may reappear in subsequent generations. For example, a blue-eyed child may be born to two brown-eyed parents, each of whom has contributed a recessive gene for blue eyes.

Genes also "mutate" or alter—as a result of either external factors or internal chemical changes. Mutation is thought to be part of the mechanism of evolution by which species change and develop over thousands of years during which each generation may alter only slightly from its predecessor.

POSSIBLE COMBINATIONS OF GENES *A dominant gene causes fruit flies to inherit normal wings, but a recessive gene giving vestigial wings may be inher-* *ited. Recessive genes from two flies with normal wings sometimes combine and produce offspring with vestigial wings.*

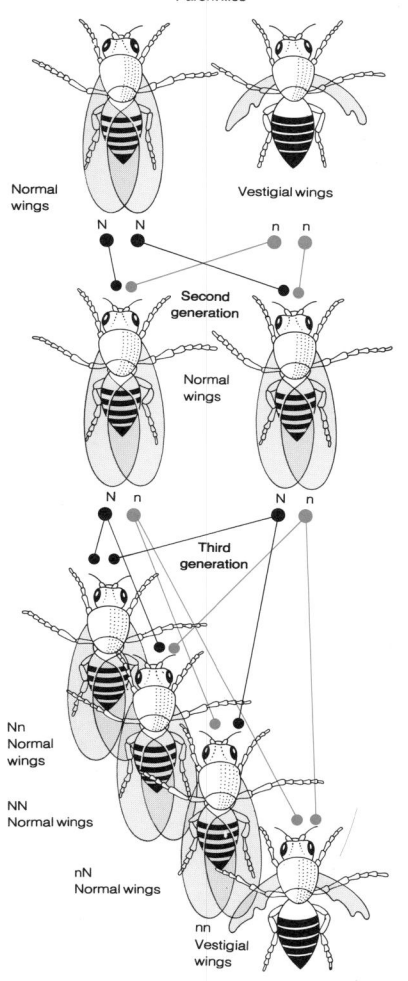

Parent flies

Normal wings

Vestigial wings

N   N   n   n

Second generation

Normal wings

N   n   N   n

Third generation

Nn Normal wings

NN Normal wings

nN Normal wings

nn Vestigial wings

Hermes Tris·me·gis·tus (trĭs′mə-jĭs′təs). The Greek name for the Egyptian god Thoth, the supposed author of works on alchemy, astrology, and magic. [Latin, from Greek *Hermēs trismegistos,* "Hermes the thrice greatest."]

her·met·ic (hər-mĕt′ĭk) *adj.* Also **her·met·i·cal** (-ĭ-kəl). **1. a.** Completely sealed; especially, sealed against the escape or entry of air. **b.** Impervious to outside interference or influence; insulated; cloistered: *retreated to the hermetic confines of his room.* **2. Hermetic.** Of or relating to Hermes Trismegistus or to the works ascribed to him. **3.** Of or pertaining to the occult sciences, especially alchemy; magical; recondite. [New Latin *hermeticus,* from Latin *Hermes* (stem *Hermet-*) *Trismegistus,* HERMES TRISMEGISTUS. He is said to have invented a magic seal to make vessels airtight.] —**her·met·i·cal·ly** *adv.*

her·mit (hûr′mĭt) *n.* A person who has withdrawn from society and lives a solitary existence, especially for religious reasons; a recluse. [Middle English *(h)ermite,* from Old French, from Late Latin *erēmīta,* from Greek *erēmitēs,* "(one) of the desert," from *erēmia,* desert, solitude, from *erēmos,* deserted, solitary.] —**her·mit·ic** (hər-mĭt′ĭk), **her·mit·i·cal** (hər-mĭt′ĭ-kəl) *adj.* —**her·mit·i·cal·ly** *adv.*

her·mit·age (hûr′mə-tĭj) *n.* **1.** The habitation of a hermit or group of hermits. **2.** A place where one can live in seclusion; a retreat; a hideaway.

hermit crab *n.* Any of various crustaceans of the section Anomura within the order Decapoda, having a soft, unarmored abdomen, and occupying and carrying about the empty shell of a snail or other univalve mollusk.

hermit thrush *n.* A North American bird, *Hylocichla guttata,* having

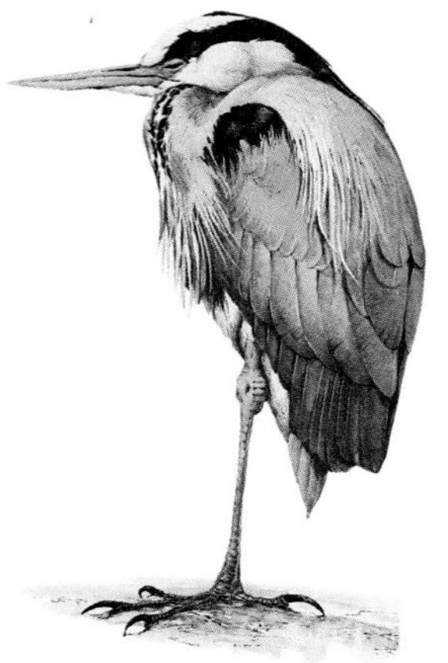

heron *These wading birds are native to Europe, Asia, and parts of Africa. They feed largely on fish, frogs, and rodents, waiting hunched on one leg for prey, then wading forward and stabbing downward with their long bills. This is* Ardea cinerea, *a species that is found in much of Europe, Asia, and the United States.*

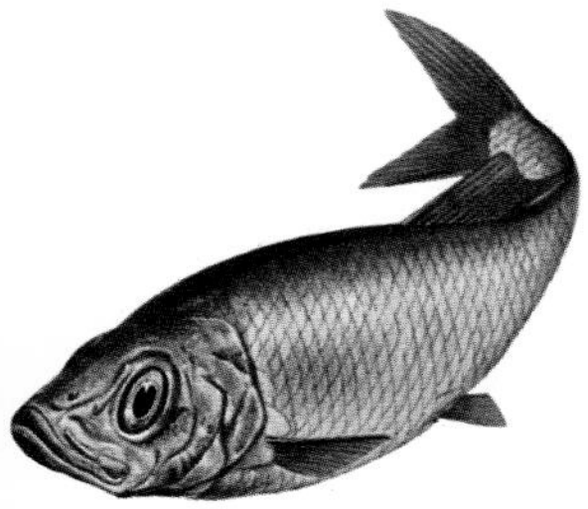

herring *The prime catch for fishing fleets in the Atlantic and Pacific oceans, herring live in large shoals that may contain up to 150 million fish. Overfishing has depleted stocks of herring in some areas.*

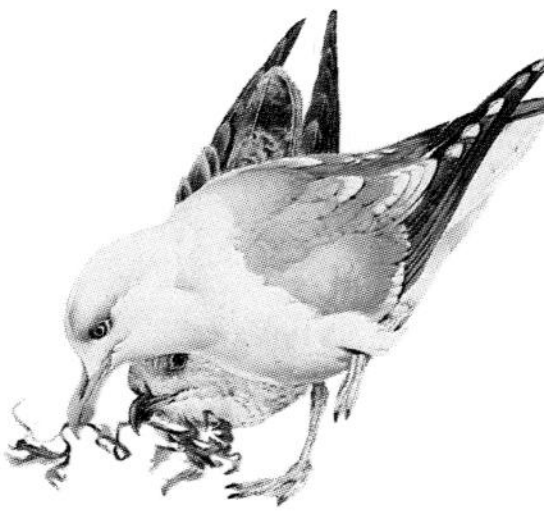

herring gull *This gull is found on coasts and inland waters in northern Europe and North America. It scavenges for food on garbage heaps and around fishing ports and harbors; it will also occasionally catch crabs and other shellfish, cracking them open by dropping them from the air.*

brownish plumage, a spotted breast, and a distinctive, melodious song.

hern (hûrn) *n. Archaic & Regional.* A heron. [Variant of HERON.]

her·ni·a (hûr′nē-ə) *n., pl.* **-as** or **-niae** (-nē-ē′). The protrusion of an organ, organic part, or any bodily structure through the wall that normally contains it. Hernia usually requires surgical treatment. Also called "rupture." [Middle English *hernia, hirnia,* from Latin *hernia.*] **—her·ni·al** *adj.*

her·ni·ate (hûr′nē-āt′) *intr.v.* **-ated, -ating, -ates.** To protrude through an abnormal bodily opening. [HERNI(A) + -ATE.] **—her·ni·a·tion** *n.*

he·ro (hîr′ō) *n., pl.* **-roes. 1.** In mythology and legend, a man, often born of one mortal and one divine parent, who is endowed with great courage and strength, celebrated for his bold exploits, and favored by the gods. **2.** Any man noted for feats of courage or nobility of purpose; especially, one who has risked or sacrificed his life: *heroes of forgotten wars.* **3.** A person who is greatly admired because of his special achievements or contributions in some event, field, or period: *The schoolboys discussed their football heroes.* **4.** The principal male character in a novel, poem, play, or the like. **5.** A very large sandwich made with a small loaf of crusty bread split lengthwise, containing lettuce, condiments, and a variety of meats and cheeses. In this sense, also called "grinder," "hero sandwich," "hoagie," "sub," "submarine." [Back-formation from Middle English *heroes* (plural), from Latin *hērōs* (plural *hērōēs*), a hero, from Greek *hērōs* (plural *hērōes*).]

Hero. *Greek Mythology.* A priestess of Aphrodite loved by Leander, who nightly swam the Hellespont to visit her; upon finding him drowned, Hero drowned herself.

Her·od (hĕr′əd), known as "Herod the Great" (*c.* 73–4 B.C.). King of Judea (37–4), son of Antipater II. He was named king of Judea by the Roman senate. He is said by St. Matthew to have ordered the killing of all children under the age of two in Bethlehem in order to destroy the infant Jesus.

Herod An·ti·pas (ăn′tĭ-păs′, -pəs) (died *c.* A.D. 40). Tetrarch of Galilee (4 B.C.–A.D. 39). Herod's marriage to his niece Herodias brought the disapproval of John the Baptist. The aggrieved Herodias persuaded her daughter, Salome, to ask for the Baptist's head as payment for dancing at Antipas' birthday celebration. Antipas complied, and the Baptist was executed.

He·rod·o·tus (hĭ-rŏd′ə-təs) (*c.* 484–425 B.C.). Greek historian, commonly known as the Father of History. His writing, chiefly concerning the Persian Wars, is the earliest known attempt at secular narrative history.

he·ro·ic (hĭ-rō′ĭk) *adj.* Also **he·ro·i·cal** (-ĭ-kəl). **1.** Of, relating to, or resembling the heroes of legend, especially of Greek and Roman legend. **2.** Having or displaying the qualities of a hero; courageous; noble: *heroic deeds.* **3.** Bold and daring, especially in the face of insurmountable odds; gallant: *a heroic attempt to halt the enemy's advance.* **4. a.** Impressive in size or scope; grand; grandiose: *a heroic undertaking.* **b.** *Fine arts.* Of a size somewhat larger than life: *heroic sculpture.* **5.** High-flown; ostentatious: *heroic language.* **6.** Of, pertaining to, or resembling heroic verse.
~*n.* **1.** A heroic verse or poem. **2. heroics.** Melodramatic behavior or language. **—he·ro·i·cal·ly** *adv.* **—he·ro·i·cal·ness** *n.*

heroic age *n.* The period in a nation's history, especially that of ancient Greece and Rome, when its legendary heroes are supposed to have lived.

heroic couplet *n.* A verse unit consisting of two rhymed lines in iambic pentameter.

heroic play *n.* A type of Restoration tragedy written in rhymed couplets and generally characterized by extravagant declamatory rhetoric.

heroic stanza *n.* An iambic pentameter quatrain rhymed *abab.* Also called "heroic quatrain."

heroic tenor *n.* A **Heldentenor** *(see).*

heroic verse *n.* Any of several verse forms suitable for and traditionally used in epic and dramatic poetry; especially, the dactylic hexameter in Greek and Latin and the iambic pentameter in English. Also called "heroic meter."

her·o·in (hĕr′ō-ĭn) *n.* A white, odorless, bitter crystalline compound, $C_{17}H_{17}NO(C_2H_3O_2)_2$, that is derived from morphine and is a highly addictive narcotic. Also called "diacetylmorphine." [From a trademark.]

her·o·ine (hĕr′ō-ĭn) *n.* **1.** A woman having or regarded as having heroic characteristics. **2.** The principal female character in a novel, poem, play, or the like. [Latin *hērōīna,* from Greek *hērōinē,* feminine of *hērōs,* HERO.]

her·o·ism (hĕr′ō-ĭz′əm) *n.* **1.** The condition or quality of being a hero. **2.** Heroic characteristics or conduct; courage; gallantry. —See Synonyms at **courage.**

he·ron (hĕr′ən) *n.* Any of various wading birds of the family Ardeidae, having a long neck, long legs, a long, pointed bill, and usually white or gray plumage. [Middle English *he(i)roun, hern(e),* from Old French *hairon,* from Frankish *haigro* (unattested).]

her·on·ry (hĕr′ən-rē) *n., pl.* **-ries. 1.** A place where herons nest and breed. **2.** A colony of herons or their nests.

hero worship *n.* **1.** Profound or excessive admiration for popular heroes or for other persons revered as ideals. **2.** Worship of the heroes of one's culture. **— he·ro-wor·ship** (hîr′ō-wûr′shĭp) *v.* **—he·ro-wor·ship·er** *n.*

herp. herpetology.

her·pes (hûr′pēz′) *n.* Any of several viral diseases causing eruptions of the skin or mucous membrane; especially, herpes simplex or herpes zoster. [Latin *herpēs,* from Greek, shingles, "a creeping," from *herpein,* to creep.] **—her·pet·ic** (hûr-pĕt′ĭk) *adj.*

herpes sim·plex (sĭm′plĕks′) *n.* A viral infection causing inflammation at junctions of the skin and mucous membrane, especially on the face. Also called "cold sore." See **genital herpes.** [New Latin, "simple herpes."]

her·pes·vi·rus (hûr′pēz-vī′rəs) *n.* Any of various DNA-containing animal viruses that produce herpes.

herpes zos·ter (zŏs′tər, zō′stər) *n.* A viral infection, **shingles** *(see).* [New Latin, "girdle herpes."]

herpetol. herpetology.

her·pe·tol·o·gist (hûr′pə-tŏl′ə-jĭst) *n.* A zoologist specializing in the study of reptiles and amphibians.

her·pe·tol·o·gy (hûr′pə-tŏl′ə-jē) *n. Abbr.* **herp., herpetol.** The scientific study of reptiles and amphibians as a branch of zoology. [Greek *herpeton,* "creeping thing," reptile, from *herpetos,* creeping, from *herpein,* to creep + -LOGY.] **—her·pe·to·log·ic** (hûr′pə-tə-lŏj′ĭk), **her·pe·to·log·i·cal** *adj.* **—her·pe·to·log·i·cal·ly** *adv.*

Herr (hĕr) *n., pl.* **Herren** (hĕr′ən). *Abbr.* **Hr.** A title of courtesy prefixed to the name or professional title of a German man, equivalent to the English *Mister.* [German, "Lord."]

Her·ren·volk (hĕr′ən-fōk′, -fôlk′) *n.* The **master race** *(see).* [German, "master race."]

Her·rick (hĕr′ĭk), **Robert** (1591–1674). English poet. Most of his work appeared in the collection *Hesperides* (1648).

her·ring (hĕr′ĭng) *n., pl.* **-rings** or collectively **herring.** Any of various fishes of the family Clupeidae; especially, a commercially important food fish, *Clupea harengus,* of Atlantic and Pacific waters. [Middle English *hering, heirreng,* Old English *hæring,* from West Germanic *hēringaz* (unattested).]

her·ring·bone (hĕr′ĭng-bōn′) *n.* **1.** A pattern consisting of rows of short, slanted parallel lines, with the direction of the slant alternating row by row, used in masonry, parquetry, and weaving. Also used adjectivally: *a herringbone brick pathway.* **2.** A twilled fabric woven in this pattern. Also used adjectivally: *a herringbone suit.* **3.** An embroidery stitch of one row of slanted parallel lines crossing another slanted in the opposite direction, so that each line is crossed symmetrically at top and bottom only. **4.** *Skiing.* A method of climbing a slope with the skis pointed outward.
~*v.* **herringboned, -boning, -bones.** —*tr.* To arrange in or decorate with a herringbone pattern. —*intr.* **1.** To produce this pattern. **2.** *Skiing.* To ascend a slope using the herringbone method. [From its resemblance to the skeletal structure of a herring.]

herringbone gear *n. Engineering.* A type of gearwheel in which two sets of teeth are cut on the rim, one set being at an angle to the other so that the teeth are V-shaped.

herring gull *n.* A common, widely distributed gull, *Larus argentatus,* having gray and white plumage with black wing tips. [From its habit of preying on herrings.]

hers (hûrz). Possessive pronoun, absolute form of *her.* **1.** Belonging to her; her own. Used predicatively: *The red boots are hers.* **2.** The one or ones belonging to her. Used substantively: *If you can't find your hat, take hers.* **—of hers.** Belonging or pertaining to her: *a friend of hers.* [Middle English *hirs, hires,* a double possessive from *hire,* HER.]

Her·schel (hûr′shəl), **Sir John Frederick William** (1792–1871). English mathematician and astronomer, son of Sir William. He extended his father's catalogue of double stars and nebulae.

Herschel, Sir William, born Friedrich Wilhelm Herschel (1738–1822). English astronomer, born in Germany. He settled in England in 1757, working as a music teacher and studying the sky in his spare time. In 1781 he discovered Uranus and was appointed astronomer to King George III. He also catalogued more than 800 double stars and some 2,500 nebulae.

her·self (hûr-sĕlf′) *pron.* A specialized form of the third person singular feminine pronoun. It is used: **1.** As a reflexive pronoun, forming the direct or indirect object of a verb or the object of a preposition: *hurt herself; gives herself the benefit of the doubt; talks to herself.* **2.** For emphasis after *she: She herself wasn't certain.* **3.** As an emphasizing substitute: *Herself in debt, she couldn't help us. It was addressed to her brother and herself.* **4.** As an indication of her real, normal, or healthy condition or identity: *She hasn't been herself lately.* **5.** *Chiefly Irish & Scottish.* An important or prominent woman, such as the mistress of a household. Sometimes used humorously.

Her·sey (hûr′sē), **John Richard** (1914–). U.S. author, born in China of missionary parents. He was a war correspondent during World War II, and his best-known works, such as *Hiroshima* (1946) and *A Bell for Adano* (Pulitzer Prize winner in 1945), reflect his feelings about man's inhumanity to man during that war.

Her·shey (hûr′shē), **Milton Snavely** (1857–1945). U.S. industrialist and philanthropist. In 1903 he acquired a site of 480 hectares (1,200 acres) near Lancaster, Pennsylvania, and formed his chocolate company. Later, as his personal fortune and the town of Hershey grew, he founded a home and school for orphan boys. The town is still populated mainly by the company's employees and is a popular tourist attraction.

Herst·mon·ceux, Hurst·mon·ceux (hûrst′mən-so͞o′). Village in East Sussex, southeastern England. Its heavily restored castle (1440), one of the finest medieval brick buildings, has housed the Royal Observatory since its transfer from Greenwich in 1950.

Hert·ford·shire (här′fərd-shîr′, -shər, härt′-). Also **Herts** (härts, hûrts). County of southeastern England. Mainly low-lying but rising to the Chiltern Hills in the northwest, it is largely agricultural. Hertford is its county town.

hertz (hûrts) *n., pl.* **hertz.** *Symbol* **Hz** A unit of frequency equal to one cycle per second. [After Heinrich HERTZ.]

Hertz (hĕrtz), **Gustav** (1887–1975). German physicist. In 1925 he was awarded the Nobel Prize in physics for his work on the impact of electrons on atoms.

Hertz, Heinrich Rudolf (1857–94). German physicist. He succeeded in producing the first radio waves artificially.

Hertz·i·an wave (hûrt′sē-ən, hĕrt′-) *n.* A **radio wave** *(see)*. [After Heinrich HERTZ.]

Hert·zog (hûrt′sŏg′, -sôg′, hĕrt′-), **James Barry Munnik** (1866–1942). South African general in the Boer War. In 1924 he became South Africa's first National Party prime minister in an election pact with the Labour Party. He steered South Africa to greater independence from Britain until 1939.

Hertz·sprung-Rus·sell diagram (hĕrts′sprŭng-rŭs′əl) *n.* A graph of the logarithms of the luminosities of stars plotted against the logarithms of their surface temperatures. Points on the diagram fall into groups corresponding to different types of star. Also called "Russell diagram." See **main sequence.** [Developed by Ejnar *Hertzsprung* (1873–1967), Danish astronomer, and Henry N. *Russell* (1877–1957), American astronomer.]

Her·zl (hĕrt′səl), **Theodor** (1860–1904). Hungarian-born founder of the Zionist movement. He reported the Dreyfus affair in Paris for a Vienna newspaper and decided that Jewish assimilation in European society was impossible. In 1896 he advocated the establishment of a Jewish national state in his pamphlet *Der Judenstaat.* In 1897 he founded the Zionist World Congress and was its president until his death.

he's (hēz). 1. Contraction of *he is.* 2. Contraction of *he has.*

Hesh·van, Hesh·wan (KHĕsh′vən, hĕsh′-) *n.* The second month of the Hebrew calendar. Also called "Marcheshvan." See feature at **calendar.** [Hebrew *ḥeshwān,* short for *marḥeshwān.*]

He·si·od (hē′sē-əd, hĕs′ē-) *(fl. c.* 8th century B.C.). Greek poet. He wrote a long didactic poem on agriculture, *Works and Days,* and may have written the *Theogony,* a genealogy of the gods, and *The Shield of Heracles.*

hes·i·tan·cy (hĕz′ə-tən-sē) *n., pl.* **-cies.** 1. The state or quality of being hesitant; indecision. 2. An instance of hesitating.

hes·i·tant (hĕz′ə-tənt) *adj.* Inclined or tending to hesitate; irresolute. —**hes′i·tant·ly** *adv.*

hes·i·tate (hĕz′ə-tāt′) *intr.v.* **-tated, -tating, -tates.** 1. a. To be slow to act or decide; hold back in uncertainty; waver. b. To be reluctant, especially out of propriety, scruples, or concern for others; have qualms; demur: *"Do you think she will hesitate to sacrifice you?"* (G.B. Shaw). 2. To pause briefly in or as if in uncertainty: *hesitate on the way upstairs.* 3. To speak haltingly; falter. [Latin *haesitāre,* to stick fast, be undecided, hesitate, frequentative of *haerēre* (past participle *haesum*), to hold or hang fast, stick.] —**hes·i·tat·er** *n.* —**hes′i·tat·ing·ly** *adv.*

Synonyms: falter, vacillate, waver.

hes·i·ta·tion (hĕz′ə-tā′shən) *n.* 1. The act or an instance of hesitating. 2. A pause or faltering in speech. —**hes·i·ta·tive** *adj.* —**hes′i·ta·tive·ly** *adv.*

Hes·pe·ri·a (hĕ-spîr′ē-ə). *Poetic.* The Western Land. A name applied by the Greeks to Italy and by the Romans to Spain or regions beyond. [Latin, from Greek, from *hesperos, hesperios,* of evening, western, from *hesperos,* evening.]

Hes·pe·ri·an (hĕ-spîr′ē-ən) *adj. Poetic.* 1. Of or pertaining to Hesperia or the west. 2. Of or relating to the Hesperides.

Hes·per·i·des (hĕ-spĕr′ə-dēz′) *pl.n. Greek Mythology.* 1. Three sisters who together with a dragon watched over the garden of the golden apples in the Islands of the Blest. 2. *Used with a singular verb.* The garden of the golden apples. 3. The Islands of the Blest, situated at the western end of the earth. [Latin *Hesperidēs,* from Greek *Hesperides,* plural of *Hesperis,* "western," daughter of the west, from *hesperos, hesperios,* of evening, western. See **Hesperia.**] —**Hes·per·id·i·an, Hes·per·id·e·an** (hĕs′pə-rĭd′ē-ən) *adj.*

hes·per·i·din (hĕ-spĕr′ə-dĭn) *n.* A white or colorless crystalline compound, $C_{28}H_{34}O_{15}$, occurring in citrus fruits, as oranges. [HESPERID(IUM) + -IN.]

hes·per·id·i·um (hĕs′pə-rĭd′ē-əm) *n., pl.* **-ia** (-ē-ə). *Botany.* A form of berry having a thickened, leathery rind and juicy pulp divided into segments, such as an orange, lemon, or other citrus fruit. [New Latin, after the golden apples in the garden of HESPERIDES.]

Hes·per·us (hĕs′pər-əs) *n.* 1. The planet Venus in its appearance as the evening star. 2. Any of various other stars or planets prominently visible in the early evening. [Latin, from Greek *hesperos,* western.]

Hess (hĕs), **Dame Myra** (1890–1965). British pianist. During World War II she organized daily lunchtime concerts at the National Gallery, London. She was made a dame in 1941.

Hess, Rudolf (1894–1987). German politician, born in Egypt. He joined Hitler in 1920 and took part in the Munich putsch, for which he was jailed. When Hitler became chancellor in 1933, he named Hess deputy führer. In 1939 Hess was named second in succession after Goering to the Nazi leadership. Hess flew to Scotland in May 1941, apparently in a bid to start peace talks with the British government. At the Nuremberg trials of 1946 he was sentenced to life imprisonment in Spandau Prison, Berlin, for war crimes.

Hess, Victor Franz (1883–1964). U.S. physicist, born in Austria.

He discovered cosmic rays, and shared the Nobel Prize for physics with Carl D. Anderson in 1936.

Hess, Walter Rudolf (1881–1973). Swiss physiologist. He shared the Nobel Prize in physiology and medicine with Moniz Antonio Egas (1874–1955) in 1949 for work on the separate control over body organs by different areas of the brain.

Hesse (hĕs). *German* **Hes·sen** (hĕs′ən). A state of Germany. In the west-central part of the country, it consists mainly of forested uplands; there is some cattle raising, and potatoes, beets, and wheat are grown. The capital is Wiesbaden.

Hes·se (hĕs′ə), **Hermann** (1877–1962). German novelist and poet. He was a pacifist and, in 1914, moved to Switzerland, becoming a Swiss citizen in 1923. His novels, which explore psychological alienation, include *Steppenwolf* (1927) and *The Glass Bead Game* (1943). He was awarded the Nobel Prize for literature in 1946.

Hes·sian (hĕsh′ən) *n.* 1. A native or inhabitant of Hesse. 2. a. A Hessian mercenary in the British army in the Revolutionary War. b. Any mercenary. 3. **hessian.** A coarse fabric; burlap. —*adj.* Of or relating to Hesse or its people.

Hessian boot *n.* A high, tasseled man's boot introduced into England from Hesse in the early 19th century.

Hessian fly *n.* A small fly, *Mayetiola destructor,* having larvae that infest and destroy wheat and other grain plants. [Supposed to have been introduced to America by Hessian troops during the Revolutionary War.]

hes·site (hĕs′īt′) *n.* A black or gray mineral form of silver telluride, Ag_2Te. [German *Hessit,* after Henry *Hess,* 19th-century Swiss chemist.]

hessonite. Variant of **essonite.**

Hes·ti·a (hĕs′tē-ə). *Greek Mythology.* The goddess of the hearth, daughter of Cronus and Rhea; identified with the Roman goddess Vesta.

he·tae·ra (hĭ-tîr′ə) *n., pl.* **-ras** or **-taerae** (-tîr′ē′). Also **he·tai·ra** (-tîr′ə) *pl.* **-ras** or **-tairai** (-tîr′ī′). A courtesan or concubine; especially, in ancient Greece, one of a special class of cultivated female companions. [Greek *hetaira,* feminine of *hetairos,* companion.]

he·tae·rism (hĭ-tîr′ĭz′əm) *n.* Also **he·tai·rism** (-tîr′ĭz′əm) 1. Concubinage. 2. *Anthropology.* The practice of communal marriage supposed to have been characteristic of primitive societies. —**he·tae·rist** *n.*

hetero-, heter- *prefix.* Indicates other, another, or different; for example, **heterogamy, heterosexual.** [Greek *heteros,* other.]

het·er·o·cer·cal (hĕt′ə-rō-sûr′kəl) *adj. Zoology.* Pertaining to, designating, or characterized by a tail fin having two unequal lobes, with the vertebral column extending into the upper, usually larger lobe, as in sharks. Compare **homocercal.** [HETERO- + Greek *kerkos,* tail.]

het·er·o·chro·mat·ic (hĕt′ə-rō-krō-măt′ĭk) *adj.* 1. Of or pertaining to different colors; varicolored. 2. Consisting of different wavelengths or frequencies. 3. Of or pertaining to heterochromatin. —**het·er·o·chro·ma·tism** (hĕt′ə-rō-krō′mə-tĭz′əm) *n.*

het·er·o·chro·ma·tin (hĕt′ə-rō-krō′mə-tĭn) *n. Genetics.* Chromosomal material exhibiting maximal staining in the nuclear meiotic interphase and lacking specific genetic activity. Compare **euchromatin.**

het·er·o·chro·mo·some (hĕt′ə-rō-krō′mə-sōm′) *n. Genetics.* 1. An atypical chromosome, such as a sex chromosome. 2. A chromosome composed primarily of heterochromatin.

het·er·o·clite (hĕt′ə-rō-klīt′) *n.* 1. A word formed or inflected in an unusual way. 2. Anything or anyone that departs from the normal or usual. [Late Latin, from Greek *heteroklitos,* irregularly inflected : HETERO- + Greek *klitos,* from *klinein,* to bend, inflect.] —**het·er·o·clit·ic** (hĕt′ə-rō-klĭt′ĭk) *adj.*

het·er·o·cy·clic (hĕt′ə-rō-sī′klĭk, -sīk′lĭk) *adj. Chemistry.* Of, pertaining to, or designating a chemical compound having a ring of atoms in its molecules that contains at least one atom of an element other than carbon. Compare **homocyclic.** —*n. Chemistry.* A heterocyclic compound.

het·er·o·dac·tyl (hĕt′ə-rō-dăk′təl) *adj.* Designating a bird's foot on which the first and second toes point backward and the third and fourth forward. —*n.* A bird having heterodactyl feet.

het·er·o·dont (hĕt′ə-rō-dŏnt′) *adj.* Having teeth of various different kinds. Said of most mammals. [HETER(O)- + -ODONT.]

het·er·o·dox (hĕt′ə-rə-dŏks′) *adj.* 1. Not in agreement with accepted beliefs; especially, departing from an established religious doctrine or dogma. Compare **orthodox.** 2. Holding unorthodox opinions. [Late Latin *heterodoxus,* from Greek *heterodoxos,* differing in opinion : HETERO- + *doxa,* opinion, notion, from *dokein,* to expect, think.]

het·er·o·dox·y (hĕt′ər-ə-dŏk′sē) *n., pl.* **-ies.** 1. The condition or quality of being heterodox. 2. A heterodox opinion or doctrine.

het·er·o·dyne (hĕt′ər-ə-dīn′) *adj.* Having alternating currents of two different frequencies that are combined to generate a current that has sum and difference frequencies, either of which may be used in radio or television receivers by proper tuning or filtering. —*tr.v.* **heterodyned, -dyning, -dynes.** To combine (a radio-frequency wave) with a locally generated wave of different frequency in order to produce a new frequency equal to the sum or difference of the two. [HETERO- + DYNE.]

het·er·oe·cious (hĕt′ə-rē′shəs) *adj.* Spending alternate stages of a life cycle on different, unrelated hosts. Said of parasites such as rusts and tapeworms. [HETERO- + Greek *oikia,* house.] —**het·er·oe·cism** (hĕt'ə-rē'sĭz'əm) *n.*

het·er·o·gam·ete (hĕt'ə-rō-găm'ēt', -gə-mēt') *n.* Either of two conjugating gametes, such as the small, motile male spermatozoon and the larger, nonmotile female ovum, that differ in size, form, or behavior.

het·er·o·ga·met·ic (hĕt'ə-rō-gə-mĕt'ĭk) *adj.* Having a dissimilar pair of sex chromosomes, as in human males, or one unpaired sex chromosome, as in some male insects. Compare **homogametic.**

het·er·og·a·mous (hĕt'ə-rŏg'ə-məs) *adj.* **1.** *Biology.* Characterized by the fusion of unlike gametes in the reproductive process. **2.** *Botany.* Bearing flowers of different kinds, especially both male and female flowers, on one plant. [HETERO- + -GAMOUS.]

het·er·og·a·my (hĕt'ə-rŏg'ə-mē) *n.* **1.** Alternation of generations, one sexual, the other parthenogenetic, as in some aphids. **2.** A state in which uniting gametes are dissimilar in structure and size as well as in function. [HETERO- + -GAMY.] —**het·er·o·gam·ic** (hĕt'-ə-rō-găm'ĭk) *adj.*

het·er·o·ge·ne·i·ty (hĕt'ə-rō-jə-nē'ə-tē) *n.* The quality or state of being heterogeneous; nonuniformity; dissimilarity.

het·er·o·ge·ne·ous (hĕt'ər-ə-jē'nē-əs, -jēn'yəs) *adj.* Also **het·er·og·e·nous** (hĕt'ə-rŏj'ə-nəs). **1.** Consisting of or involving parts that are unlike or without interrelation; having dissimilar constituents or elements; not homogeneous: *a heterogeneous collection of people.* **2.** Completely different; incongruous. **3.** *Physics & Chemistry.* Of, involving, or designating a system of two or more different phases: *a heterogeneous mixture; heterogeneous catalysis.* Compare **homogeneous.** —See Synonyms at **miscellaneous.** [Medieval Latin *heterogeneus,* from Greek *heterogenēs* : HETERO- + *genos,* kind.] —**het·er·o·ge·ne·ous·ly** *adv.* —**het·er·o·ge·ne·ous·ness** *n.*

het·er·o·gen·e·sis (hĕt'ə-rō-jĕn'ə-sĭs) *n.* **Alternation of generations** *(see).* —**het·er·o·ge·net·ic** (hĕt'ə-rō-jə-nĕt'ĭk) *adj.*

het·er·og·e·nous[1] (hĕt'ə-rŏj'ə-nəs) *adj.* Also **het·er·o·gen·ic** (hĕt'-ə-rō-jĕn'ĭk). Originating outside the body. [HETERO- + -GENOUS.] —**het·er·og·e·ny** *n.*

heterogenous[2]. Variant of **heterogeneous.**

het·er·og·o·nous (hĕt'ə-rŏg'ə-nəs) *adj.* **1.** *Biology.* Characterized by the alternation of sexual and asexual generations. **2.** *Botany.* Designating plants in which the flowers differ from each other in the lengths of the stamens and styles. [HETERO- + -GON(Y) + -OUS.] —**het·er·og·o·ny** *n.*

het·er·o·graft (hĕt'ə-rō-grăft', -gräft') *n.* A type of tissue graft in which the donor and recipient are of different species. Also called "xenograft."

het·er·og·ra·phy (hĕt'ə-rŏg'rə-fē) *n., pl.* **-phies. 1.** Spelling that is inconsistent in respect of single sounds, as the spelling of modern English is; for example, the *-uf* sound is rendered very differently in the words *cuff* and *tough.* **2.** Spelling that departs from conventional usage. [HETERO- + -GRAPHY.]

het·er·og·y·nous (hĕt'ə-rŏj'ə-nəs) *adj. Zoology.* Having two types of female, one able to reproduce sexually, the other infertile, as in ants. [HETERO- + -GYNOUS.]

het·er·o·junc·tion (hĕt'ə-rō-jŭngk'shən) *n. Electronics.* A junction between two semiconductors with different types of conductivity.

het·er·o·kar·y·on (hĕt'ə-rō-kăr'ē-ŏn') *n.* A cell containing two or more nuclei of different types, or an organism made up of such cells. —**het·er·o·kar·y·ot·ic** (hĕt'ə-rō-kăr'ē-ŏt'ĭk) *adj.*

het·er·o·kar·y·o·sis (hĕt'ə-rō-kăr'ē-ō'sĭs) *n. Biology.* The presence of more than one type of nucleus in a single cell, as occurs in certain fungi. [HETERO- + KARY(O)- + -OSIS (condition).]

het·er·o·lec·i·thal (hĕt'ə-rō-lĕs'ə-thəl) *adj.* Having nonhomogeneous distribution of yolk in an ovum. Said of birds' eggs. Compare **isolecithal.** [HETERO- + Greek *lekithos,* yolk (see **lecithin**) + -AL.]

het·er·ol·o·gous (hĕt'ə-rŏl'ə-gəs) *adj.* **1.** Derived from a different species: *a heterologous graft.* **2.** Of or pertaining to cytological or histological elements not normally occurring in a designated part of the body. [HETERO- + -LOG(Y) + -OUS.]

het·er·ol·o·gy (hĕt'ə-rŏl'ə-jē) *n.* Lack of correspondence between bodily parts, as in structure, arrangement, or development, arising from differences in origin. [HETERO- + -LOGY.]

het·er·ol·y·sis (hĕt'ə-rŏl'ə-sĭs) *n., pl.* **-ses** (-sēz'). **1.** *Biology.* Dissolution of cells or protein components in one species by lytic agents of another. Compare **autolysis. 2.** *Chemistry.* A reaction in which the breaking of a chemical bond leads to the formation of a pair of ions with opposite charges. Also called "heterolytic fission." Compare **homolysis.** [New Latin : HETERO- + -LYSIS.] —**het·er·o·lyt·ic** (hĕt'ə-rō-lĭt'ĭk) *adj.*

het·er·om·er·ous (hĕt'ə-rŏm'ər-əs) *adj. Biology.* Having unequal or differing parts within the same structure or similar structures. [HETERO- + -MEROUS.]

het·er·o·mor·phic (hĕt'ə-rō-môr'fĭk) *adj.* Also **het·er·o·mor·phous** (-môr'fəs). **1.** Having a different shape, size, or function from the normal; atypical. **2.** Designating homologous chromosome pairs in which one differs from the other in size or shape. **3.** *Biology.* Having differing forms, as in different stages of an insect's life cycle. In this sense, compare **polymorphic.** [HETERO- + -MORPHIC.] —**het·er·o·mor·phism** *n.*

het·er·on·o·mous (hĕt'ə-rŏn'ə-məs) *adj.* **1.** Subject to external or foreign laws or domination; not autonomous. **2.** Differing in development or manner of specialization, as the dissimilar segments of certain arthropods. [HETERO- + Greek *nomos,* law + -OUS.] —**het·er·on·o·mous·ly** *adv.*

het·er·o·nym (hĕt'ər-ə-nĭm') *n.* One of two or more words that have

identical spelling but different meanings and pronunciations, as *row* (a line) and *row* (a fight). [Back-formation from HETERONYMOUS.]

het·er·on·y·mous (hĕt'ə-rŏn'ə-məs) *adj.* **1.** Of or pertaining to a heteronym. **2.** Designating names or terms that are different but have correspondence or interrelationship, as *master* and *mistress.* [Late Greek *heterōnumos* : HETERO- + Greek *onoma,* name.]

Het·er·o·ou·si·an (hĕt'ə-rō-ōō'sē-ən, -ou'sē-ən) *n.* Also **Het·er·ou·si·an** (hĕt'ə-rōō'sē-ən, -rou'sē-ən). A Christian holding that the substance and nature of God the Father and God the Son are different; an Arian. Compare **Homoiousian, Homoousian.**

~*adj.* Designating or pertaining to the Heteroousians or their beliefs. [Late Greek *hetero(o)usios,* of different substance : HETERO- + Greek *ousia,* substance, essence, from *ōn* (stem *ous-*), present participle of *einai,* to be.]

het·er·oph·o·ny (hĕt'ə-rŏf'ə-nē) *n. Music.* The simultaneous playing or singing of a single melody by two or more different instruments or singers. [HETERO- + -PHONY.]

het·er·o·pho·ri·a (hĕt'ər-ə-fôr'ē-ə, -fōr'ē-ə) *n.* A tendency to squint. [HETERO- + *-phoria,* tendency, act of bearing, from Greek *pherein,* to carry, bear.]

het·er·o·phyl·lous (hĕt'ə-rō-fĭl'əs) *adj. Botany.* Having unlike leaves on one plant. [HETERO- + -PHYLLOUS.] —**het·er·o·phyl·ly** (hĕt'-ə-rō-fĭl'ē) *n.*

het·er·o·phyte (hĕt'ər-ə-fīt') *n.* A plant, such as a parasite, that can obtain its nourishment from living or dead organic sources. [HETERO- + -PHYTE.]

het·er·o·plas·ty (hĕt'ər-ə-plăs'tē) *n., pl.* **-ties.** The surgical grafting of tissue obtained from another person or from a lower animal. [HETERO- + -PLASTY.]

het·er·op·ter·ous (hĕt'ə-rŏp'tər-əs) *adj.* Of or belonging to the insect order Heteroptera, which includes the true bugs, characterized by forewings and hind wings that differ from one another. [New Latin *Heteroptera* : HETERO- + -PTEROUS.]

het·er·o·sce·das·tic (hĕt'ə-rō-sĭ-dăs'tĭk) *adj. Statistics.* Pertaining to or designating variables for which all possible values do not have constant variance. [HETERO- + *scedastic,* from Greek *skedasis,* dispersion, scattering.]

het·er·o·sex·u·al (hĕt'ə-rō-sĕk'shōō-əl) *adj.* **1.** Characterized by attraction to the opposite sex. **2.** Of or pertaining to different sexes or to sexual relations between persons of the opposite sex.

~*n.* A heterosexual person. —**het·er·o·sex·u·al·i·ty** (hĕt'ə-rō-sĕk'-shōō-ăl'ə-tē) *n.* —**het·er·o·sex·u·al·ly** *adv.*

het·er·o·sis (hĕt'ə-rō'sĭs) *n. Biology.* Increased vigor or other superior qualities arising from the crossbreeding of genetically different plants or animals. Also called "hybrid vigor." [New Latin, from Greek *heter(oi)ōsis,* alteration, transformation, from *heteroioun,* to alter, from *heteroios,* different in kind, from *heteros,* one of two, the other.]

het·er·os·po·rous (hĕt'ə-rŏs'pər-əs, -ər-ə-spôr'əs, -spōr'əs) *adj. Botany.* Producing microspores and megaspores. Said of seed plants and some ferns. [HETERO- + -SPOROUS.] —**het·er·os·po·ry** *n.*

het·er·o·tax·is (hĕt'ə-rō-tăk'sĭs) *n.* Also **het·er·o·tax·y** (hĕt'ər-ə-tăk'-sē), **het·er·o·tax·i·a** (-tăk'sē-ə). Abnormal structural arrangement, as of organs of the body. [HETERO- + -TAXIS.] —**het·er·o·tac·tic** (hĕt'ə-rō-tăk'tĭk), **het·er·o·tac·tous** (hĕt'ə-rō-tăk'təs) *adj.*

het·er·o·thal·lic (hĕt'ə-rō-thăl'ĭk) *adj. Botany.* Producing male gametangia in one structure or plant and female gametangia in a different structure or plant, as in some algae and fungi. [HETERO- + Greek *thallos,* young shoot, THALLUS.] —**het·er·o·thal·lism** *n.*

het·er·o·to·pi·a (hĕt'ə-rō-tō'pē-ə) *n.* Also **het·er·ot·o·py** (-ə-rŏt'ə-pē). *Pathology.* Displacement of an organ or other part of the body from its normal position. —**het·er·o·top·ic** (hĕt'ə-rō-tŏp'ĭk) *adj.*

het·er·o·troph·ic (hĕt'ər-ə-trŏf'ĭk, -trō'fĭk) *adj.* Obtaining nourishment from organic substances, as do all animals and some plants. Compare **autotrophic.** [HETERO- + -TROPHIC.] —**het·er·o·troph·i·cal·ly** *adv.* —**het·er·o·troph·ism, het·er·ot·ro·phy** (hĕt'ə-rŏt'rə-fē) *n.*

het·er·o·typ·ic (hĕt'ə-rō-tĭp'ĭk) *adj.* **1.** *Biology.* Relating to or designating the first reduction division of meiosis. **2.** Of a different type or form. Compare **homeotypic.** [HETERO- + TYPIC(AL).]

het·er·o·zy·go·sis (hĕt'ə-rō-zī-gō'sĭs) *n.* **1.** Derivation from or union between genetically different gametes. **2.** The condition of being a heterozygote.

het·er·o·zy·gote (hĕt'ə-rō-zī'gōt') *n.* An organism that has inherited different alleles for one or more genes; a hybrid. —**het·er·o·zy·gous** *adj.*

heth (KHăt, KHäth, KHĕt, KHĕth) *n.* The eighth letter of the Hebrew alphabet. See feature at **alphabet.** [Hebrew *hēth.*]

het·man (hĕt'mən) *n., pl.* **-mans.** A Cossack military leader. [Polish, probably from German *Hauptmann,* captain.]

het up (hĕt) *adj. Informal.* Angry or flustered; worked up. [Dialectal *het,* past participle of HEAT.]

heu·land·ite (hyōō'lən-dīt') *n.* A white, red, or yellow zeolite mineral with composition $(Ca,Na,K)_6Al_{10}(Al,Si)Si_{29}O_{80} \cdot 25H_2O$. [After Henry *Heuland,* 19th-century English mineral collector.]

heu·ris·tic (hyōō-rĭs'tĭk) *adj.* **1.** Assisting the process of learning or discovery; guiding or furthering investigation: *I propose this theory purely as a heuristic device.* **2.** Designating an educational method in which the student is allowed or encouraged to learn independently through his own investigation. **3.** *Mathematics.* Designating a method of problem solving that relies on inductive reasoning from past experience in the absence of a relevant algorithm.

~*n.* A heuristic method or process. [From Greek *heuriskein,* to discover, find.] —**heu·ris·ti·cal·ly** *adv.*

heu·ris·tics (hyŏō-rĭs′tĭks) *n. Used with a singular verb.* The science or study of heuristic methods and practices.

Heus·ler alloy (hoiz′lər, hyŏōs′-) *n.* Any of a class of alloys of manganese, aluminum, zinc, and copper that are ferromagnetic even though their components are not. [After Conrad *Heusler,* 19th-century German chemist and mining engineer.]

He·ve·sy (hĕv′ə-shē), **Georg von** (1885–1966). Hungarian physicist and chemist. He used isotopes as tracers to investigate chemical processes and discovered the element hafnium. He was awarded the Nobel Prize for chemistry in 1943.

hew (hyŏō) *v.* **hewed, hewn** (hyŏōn) or **hewed, hewing, hews.** —*tr.* **1. a.** To make or shape with an ax, knife, or other cutting tool. Often used with *out: hew out a small canoe.* **b.** To form (a fissure, channel, or the like) by natural means, as by the action of lightning or dripping water. **2.** To cut down with an ax; fell. Used with *away, down, from,* or *off: hew down an oak.* **3.** To strike or cut; cleave; chop: *hewed in pieces.* —*intr.* **1.** To cut by repeated blows of an ax, sword, or the like. **2.** To adhere or conform: *hew to the line.* [Hew, hewn; Middle English *hewen, hewen,* Old English *hēawan, hēawen,* from Germanic.] —**hew·er** *n.*

hex (hĕks) *n.* **1.** An evil spell; a curse. **2.** A person or thing that exercises an evil or dominating influence. **3.** A witch. ~*tr.v.* **hexed, hexing, hexes. 1.** To work evil on; bewitch. **2.** To wish or bring bad luck to, especially through superstitious means. [Pennsylvania Dutch, from German *Hexe,* witch, from Middle High German *hecse, häxe,* probably from Old High German *hagazussa, hagzissa.*]

hex. hexagon; hexagonal.

hexa-, hex- *prefix.* Indicates six; for example, **hexagram, hexane.** [Greek, from *hex,* six.]

hex·a·canth (hĕk′sə-kănth′) *n. Zoology.* An oncosphere *(see).* [HEXA + Greek *akantha,* thorn, spine.]

hex·a·chlo·ro·eth·ane (hĕk′sə-klôr′ō-ĕth′ăn′, -klōr′ō-ĕth′ăn′) *n.* Also **hex·a·chlor·eth·ane** (-klôr-ĕth′ăn′, -klōr-ĕth′ăn′). A colorless crystalline compound, Cl₃CCCl₃, that is used as a camphor substitute and in pyrotechnics, explosives, and veterinary medicine.

hex·a·chlo·ro·phene (hĕk′sə-klôr′ə-fēn′, -klōr′ə-fēn′) *n.* A white powder, (C₆HCl₃OH)₂CH₂, formerly used as a bactericidal agent in soaps, cosmetics, and skin medications.

hex·a·chord (hĕk′sə-kôrd′) *n.* In medieval music, any of three diatonic sequences of six tones, the central interval being a semitone, and the others whole tones. [HEXA- + -CHORD.]

hex·ad (hĕk′săd′) *n.* A group or series of six. [Late Latin *hexas* (stem *hexad-*), the number six, from Greek, from *hex,* six.] —**hex·ad·ic** (hĕk-săd′ĭk) *adj.*

hex·a·dec·a·nol (hĕk′sə-dĕk′ə-nôl′, -nōl′, -nŏl′) *n.* **Cetyl alcohol** *(see).*

hex·a·dec·i·mal (hĕk′sə-dĕs′ə-məl) *adj.* Designating or pertaining to a number system with base 16, used in computer programming to represent groups of 4 bits. ~*n.* **1.** A hexadecimal number. **2.** A hexadecimal notation.

hex·a·gon (hĕk′sə-gŏn′) *n. Abbr.* **hex.** A polygon having six sides and six angles. [Late Latin *hexagōnum,* from Greek *hexagōnon,* from *hexagōnos,* six-angled : HEXA- + -GON.]

hex·ag·o·nal (hĕk-săg′ə-nəl) *adj. Abbr.* **hex. 1.** Having six sides and six angles. **2.** Of, pertaining to, or formed in hexagons. **3.** *Chemistry & Geology.* Having three equal axes intersecting at 60° in one plane and one axis of variable length that is at right angles to the others. Said of crystals or crystal structures. —**hex·ag·o·nal·ly** *adv.*

hex·a·gram (hĕk′sə-grăm′) *n.* **1.** A six-pointed star consisting of a regular hexagon with each of the sides extended to form equilateral triangles. **2.** A figure of six lines or strokes. [HEXA- + -GRAM.]

hex·a·he·dral (hĕk′sə-hē′drəl) *adj.* **1.** Having six plane surfaces. **2.** Of, pertaining to, or formed in hexahedrons. [HEXAHEDR(ON) + -AL.] —**hex·a·he·dral·ly** *adv.*

hex·a·he·dron (hĕk′sə-hē′drən) *n., pl.* **-drons** or **-dra** (-drə). A polyhedron with six plane surfaces. [Greek *hexaedron,* from *hexaedros,* six-sided : HEXA- + -HEDRON.]

hex·a·hy·drate (hĕk′sə-hī′drāt′) *n. Chemistry.* A crystalline substance that has six molecules of water of crystallization per molecule of the compound.

hex·am·er·ous (hĕk-săm′ər-əs) *adj.* **1.** Having six similar parts or divisions. **2.** *Botany.* Having flower parts, such as petals, sepals, and stamens, in sets of six. Also written *6-merous.* [HEXA- + -MEROUS.] —**hex·am·er·ism** *n.*

hex·am·e·ter (hĕk-săm′ə-tər) *n.* A line of verse consisting of six metrical feet. [Latin, from Greek *hexametron,* from *hexametros,* having six metrical feet : HEXA- + -METER.] —**hex·a·met·ric** (hĕk′sə-mĕt′rĭk), **hex·a·met·ri·cal** *adj.*

hex·a·mine (hĕk′sə-mēn′) *n.* A colorless crystalline compound, C₆H₁₂N₄, used in solution as an antiseptic, especially for infections of the urinary tract. Also called "hexamethylenetetramine," "methenamine." [HEXA- + AMINE.]

hex·ane (hĕk′sān′) *n.* **1.** A colorless, flammable liquid, CH₃(CH₂)₄CH₃, derived from the fractional distillation of petroleum and used as a solvent and as the working fluid in low-temperature thermometers. **2.** Any of a group of isomeric alkane hydrocarbons with the formula C₆H₁₄. [HEX(A)- + -ANE.]

hex·an·gu·lar (hĕk-săng′gyə-lər) *adj.* Having six angles.

hex·a·pla (hĕk′sə-plə) *n.* An edition of the Old Testament, compiled by Origen, having six versions of the text in separate columns. [Greek, neuter plural of *hexaplous,* sixfold : HEXA- + *plous,* -fold.]

hex·a·pod (hĕk′sə-pŏd′) *n.* Any member of the class Insecta (or Hexapoda); an insect. ~*adj.* Also **hex·ap·o·dous** (hĕk-săp′ə-dəs). **1.** Of or belonging to the Hexapoda. **2.** Having six legs or feet. [New Latin *Hexapoda* : HEXA- + -POD.]

hex·ap·o·dy (hĕk-săp′ə-dē) *n.* A line of verse consisting of six metrical feet. [HEXA + -*pody,* from Greek -*podia,* condition of having a certain number of feet, from *pous* (stem *pod-*), foot.]

hex·a·stich (hĕk′sə-stĭk′) *n.* A poem, stanza, or strophe consisting of six lines. [HEXA- + Greek *stikhos,* line of verse.]

Hex·a·teuch (hĕk′sə-tōōk′, -tyŏōk′) *n.* The first six books of the Old Testament. [HEXA- + Greek *teukhos,* tool, case holding writing material, roll of papyrus, volume.]

hex·a·va·lent (hĕk′sə-vā′lənt) *adj. Chemistry.* Having a valence of 6; sexivalent.

hex·o·san (hĕk′sə-săn) *n.* Any of several polysaccharides that form a hexose on hydrolysis. [HEXOS(E) + -AN.]

hex·ose (hĕk′sōs′) *n.* Any of various simple sugars, such as glucose, that have six carbon atoms per molecule. [HEX(A)- + -OSE.]

hex·yl (hĕk′səl) *n.* The hydrocarbon radical C₆H₁₃, having a valence of 1, especially the radical derived from normal hexane, CH₃(CH₂)₅. [HEX(A)- + -YL.]

hex·yl·re·sor·ci·nol (hĕk′səl-rə-zôr′sə-nôl′, -nŏl′) *n.* A yellowish-white crystalline phenol, C₁₂H₁₈O₂, used as an antiseptic and anthelmintic.

hey (hā) *interj.* **1.** Used to express surprise, appreciation, wonder, or the like: *Hey, that's nice!* **2.** Used to attract attention: *Hey, you!* [Middle English *hei, hay.*]

hey·day (hā′dā′) *n.* The period of greatest popularity, success, fashion, power, or the like; the prime. [Earlier *heyda,* probably an extension of HEY; akin to Low German *heida,* hurrah!]

Hey·er·dahl (hā′ər-däl′, hī′-), **Thor** (1914–). Norwegian anthropologist and explorer. He led the Kon Tiki expedition on a raft across the Pacific Ocean from Peru to the Tuamotu Islands in 1947 to demonstrate that Polynesians might be of South American origin. In 1970 he crossed the Atlantic Ocean from Morocco to Barbados in a papyrus boat to show that the ancient Egyptians may have sailed to America.

hf high frequency.

Hf The symbol for the element hafnium.

hg hectogram.

Hg The symbol for the element mercury. [Latin *hydrargyrum.*]

HG, H.G. High German.

H-gird·er (āch′gûr′dər) *n.* An H-beam *(see).*

hgt. height.

H.H. **1.** His (or Her) Highness. **2.** His Holiness.

H-hour (āch′our′) *n. Military.* Zero hour *(see).* [H, abbreviation for HOUR.]

hi (hī) *interj.* **1.** *Informal.* Used as a greeting. **2.** Used to attract attention. [Middle English *hy,* parallel form to HEY.]

HI Hawaii (used with a Zip Code).

hi·a·tus (hī-ā′təs) *n., pl.* **hiatuses** or **hiatus. 1.** A gap or missing section; a lacuna. **2.** Any loss or interruption in time or continuity; a break. **3.** *Phonetics.* The immediate sequence of two vowel sounds each of which constitutes or belongs to a separate syllable. **4.** *Anatomy.* A separation, aperture, or fissure. [Latin *hiātus,* a gaping, gap, from the past participle of *hiāre,* to gape.]

hiatus hernia *n.* A hernia in which part of the stomach protrudes through the esophageal opening (hiatus) of the diaphragm.

Hi·a·wath·a (hī′ə-wŏth′ə, -wô′thə) (*fl.* 1570). An Onondagan chief who is credited with the organization of the Iroquois Confederacy. His name was also given to the hero of Longfellow's poem *The Song of Hiawatha* (1855).

hi·ba·chi (hī-bä′chē) *n., pl.* **-chis.** A portable charcoal-burning brazier with a grill, often used for cooking at table. [Japanese : *hi,* fire + *bachi,* bowl.]

hi·ber·nac·u·lum (hī′bər-năk′yə-ləm) *n., pl.* **-la** (-lə). Also **hi·ber·na·cle** (hī′bər-năk′əl). **1.** *Biology.* A case, covering, or structure in which an organism remains dormant for the winter. **2.** The shelter of a hibernating animal. [Latin *hībernāculum,* winter residence, from *hībernus,* winter.]

hi·ber·nal (hī-bûr′nəl) *adj.* Occurring in or pertaining to winter. [Latin *hībernālis,* from *hībernus,* winter.]

hi·ber·nate (hī′bər-nāt′) *intr.v.* **-nated, -nating, -nates. 1.** *Zoology.* To pass the winter in a dormant or torpid state. **2.** To be in an inactive or dormant state or period. [Latin *hībernāre,* to winter, from *hībernus,* winter.] —**hi·ber·na·tor** *n.*

hi·ber·na·tion (hī′bər-nā′shən) *n.* **1.** The action of hibernating. **2.** The state of torpidity or inactivity in which some organisms pass the winter. Compare estivation. **3.** Any state or period of inactivity likened to that of a wintering animal: "*Stirring suddenly from long hibernation I knew myself once more a poet*" (Robert Graves).

Hi·ber·ni·a (hī-bûr′nē-ə). *Poetic.* Ireland. [Latin, variant (influenced by *hībernus,* winter) of *I(u)verna, Juberna,* from Greek *Iernē.*] —**Hi·ber·ni·an** *adj.*

Hi·ber·ni·cism (hī-bûr′nə-sĭz′əm) *n.* Also **Hi·ber·ni·an·ism** (-nē-ə-nĭz′əm). An Irish idiom, trait, or custom.

hi·bis·cus (hī-bĭs′kəs) *n.* Any of various chiefly tropical plants, shrubs, or trees of the genus *Hibiscus,* having large, showy, variously colored flowers, several species of which are cultivated for ornament. [New Latin *Hibiscus,* from Latin, from Greek *hibiskos*†, marshmallow.]

hic (hĭk) *n.* The sound of a hiccup.

hibiscus *The hibiscus, the flower of Hawaii, is a genus of about 300 species of flowers, shrubs, and trees. This is* Hibiscus syriacus, *a shrub that flowers in late summer.*

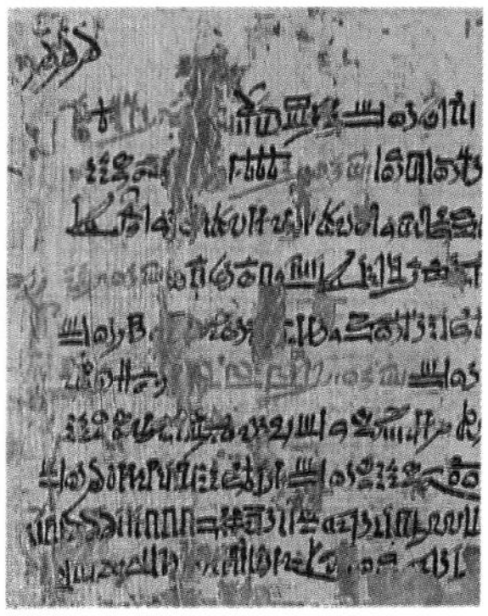

hieratic *Hieratic script used in a calendar dating from 1230 B.C. The Egyptian papyrus shows the days of the year as lucky (in black) or unlucky (in red).*

hieroglyphic *Pictographic Egyptian writing from a temple of Horus built between the third and first centuries B.C. at Edfu.*

PRONUNCIATION KEY

ă, pat; ā, pay; âr, care;
ä, father, are; b, **bib**;
ch, **church**; d, **deed**; ĕ, pet;
ē, be; f, **fife**; g, **gag**; h, **hat**;
hw, **which**; ĭ, pit; ī, pie;
îr, **pier**; j, **judge**; k, **kick**;
l, lid, needle; m, **mum**;
n, no, sudden; ng, **thing**;
ŏ, pot; ō, **toe**; ô, **paw**, **for**;
oi, noise; ou, **out**; o͝o, **book**;
o͞o, boot; p, **pop**; r, **roar**;
s, sauce; sh, **ship**, **dish**;
t, tight; th, **thin**, **path**;
th, **this**, **bathe**; ŭ, **cut**; ûr, **fur**;
v, valve; w, **with**; y, yes;
z, zebra, size; zh, vision;
ə, about, item, edible,
gallop, circus, peaceful

IN FOREIGN WORDS:

à, *Fr.* ami; œ, *Fr.* **feu**, *Ger.* schön; ü, *Fr.* **tu**, *Ger.* **über**; KH, *Ger.* **ich**, *Scot.* loch; N, *Fr.* bon; y', *Fr.* **Compiègne**

STRESS MARKS:

Primary stress: ′
in·cite′ (ĭn-sīt′)
Secondary stress: ′
in′sight′ (ĭn′sīt′)

hic·cup, hic·cough (hĭk′əp) *n.* **1.** A spasm of the diaphragm resulting in a sudden, abortive inhalation that is stopped by a spasmodic closure of the glottis. In technical usage, also called "singultus." **2. hiccups.** An attack of hiccups. **3.** *Informal.* A slight difficulty or delay.
~*v.* **hiccupped, -cupping, -cups.** Also **hic·cough, -coughed, -coughing, -coughs.** —*intr.* **1.** To make a sound resembling that of a hiccup. **2.** To have an attack of hiccups. —*tr.* To say or express while hiccupping. [Earlier *hicket, hickop* (imitative).]

hic ja·cet (hĭk jā′sĭt, hēk yä′kĭt) *Abbr.* **H.J.** Here lies. Used in epitaphs on gravestones. [Latin.]

hick (hĭk) *n. Informal.* A gullible, provincial person; a yokel; a bumpkin.
~*adj. Informal.* Backward or unsophisticated: *a hick town.* [From *Hick,* an obsolete nickname for *Richard.*]

hick·ey (hĭk′ē) *n., pl.* **-eys.** *Informal.* **1.** Any device or contrivance; a gadget. **2.** A pimple, scar, or other mark on the skin. [20th century : origin obscure.]

Hick·ok (hĭk′ŏk′), **James Butler,** known as "Wild Bill Hickok" (1837–76). U.S. marshal and gunfighter.

hick·o·ry (hĭk′ə-rē) *n., pl.* **-ries. 1.** Any of several chiefly North American deciduous trees of the genus *Carya,* having hard, smooth nuts with an edible kernel. **2.** The hard, tough, heavy wood of any of these trees. **3.** The nut of any of these trees. **4.** A walking stick or switch made from hickory wood. [Shortening of earlier *pohickery,* from Virginian native name *pawcohiccora,* food prepared from crushed hickory nuts.]

Hicks (hĭks), **Edward** (1780–1849). U.S. primitive painter. A member of the Society of Friends, he became a noted back-country preacher, supporting himself by his paintings. His best-known work is *The Peaceable Kingdom,* of which nearly 100 versions exist.

hid. Past tense and alternate past participle of **hide** (to put out of sight).

hi·dal·go (hĭ-dăl′gō) *n., pl.* **-gos.** A member of the minor nobility in Spain. [Spanish, from Old Spanish *hijo dalgo,* "son of something (that is to say, property)" : *hijo,* son + *de,* of + *algo,* something.]

hid·den (hĭd′n). Past participle of **hide** (to put out of sight).
~*adj.* Not immediately apparent; having its true nature disguised: *hidden unemployment.*

hid·den·ite (hĭd′n-īt′) *n.* A transparent emerald-green variety of spodumene, used as a gemstone. [After William E. *Hidden* (1853–1918), American mineralogist.]

hide[1] (hīd) *v.* **hid** (hĭd), **hidden** (hĭd′n) or **hid, hiding, hides.** —*tr.* **1.** To put or keep out of sight; secrete. **2.** To prevent the disclosure or recognition of; conceal. **3.** To cut off or obstruct from sight; cover up. **4.** To avert (one's gaze) in shame or grief. —*intr.* **1.** To keep oneself out of sight. **2.** To seek refuge.
~*n. British.* A hunting **blind** *(see).* [Hide, hid, hidden or hid; Middle English *hiden, hid, hidden* (formed by analogy with RIDE, RIDDEN) or *hidd,* Old English *hȳdan, hȳdde, hīdd.*] **—hid·er** *n.*
Synonyms: *bury, cache, cloak, conceal, screen, secrete.*

hide[2] *n.* **1.** The skin of an animal; especially, the comparatively thick, tough skin or pelt of a large animal. **2.** *Informal.* The human skin.
~*tr.v.* **hided, hiding, hides.** *Informal.* To beat severely; flog. [Middle English *hyde, hide,* Old English *hȳd.*]

hide[3] *n.* An old English measure of land, usually the amount held to be adequate for one free family and its dependents, and varying from 60 to 120 acres. [Middle English *hide, hyde,* Old English *hīgid, hīd.*]

hide-and-seek (hīd′n-sēk′) *n.* Also **hide-and-go-seek** (-gō-sēk′). **1.** A children's game in which one player tries to find and catch others who are hiding. **2.** Any game or action involving evasion. **—hide-and-seek** *adj.*

hide·a·way (hīd′ə-wā′) *n.* **1.** A place of concealment; a hide-out. **2.** A secluded or isolated place.

hide·bound (hīd′bound′) *adj.* **1.** Having abnormally dry, stiff skin that adheres closely to the underlying flesh. Said of undernourished domestic animals such as cattle. **2.** Having the bark so contracted and unyielding as to hinder growth. Said of trees. **3.** Unduly adhering to the rules or to one's own opinions or prejudices; narrow-minded and inflexible.

hid·e·ous (hĭd′ē-əs) *adj.* **1.** Physically repulsive; revolting; ugly. **2.** Horrifying; appalling; terrifying. **3.** Repugnant to the moral sense; despicable; odious. [Middle English, from Norman French *hidous,* from Old French *hidous, hideus,* from *hi(s)de,* fear, horror, perhaps from Latin *hispidus,* rough, shaggy.] **—hid·e·ous·ly** *adv.* **—hid·e·ous·ness** *n.*

hide-out (hīd′out′) *n.* A place of shelter or concealment, especially for a person on the run.

hid·ey-hole, hid·y-hole (hī′dē-hōl′) *n.* A hiding place; hideaway.

hid·ing[1] (hī′dĭng) *n.* A state or place of concealment: *stayed in hiding until the coast was clear.*

hiding[2] *n. Informal.* **1.** A spanking or beating. **2.** A crushing defeat.

hi·dro·sis (hĭ-drō′sĭs) *n.* Perspiration, especially in excessive or abnormal amounts. [New Latin, from Greek *hidrōsis,* sweating, from *hidrōs,* sweat.]

hi·drot·ic (hĭ-drŏt′ĭk) *n.* Any drug or other agent that promotes sweating.
~*adj.* **1.** Stimulating sweating. **2.** Pertaining to sweating.

hie (hī) *intr.v.* **hied, hieing** or **hying, hies.** To go quickly; hasten; hurry. [Middle English *hien, hyghen,* Old English *hīgian,* to strive, exert oneself, hurry.]

hi·e·mal (hī′ə-məl) *adj.* Occurring in or pertaining to winter; hibernal. [Latin *hiemālis,* from *hiems,* winter.]

hi·er·arch (hī′ə-rärk′, hī′rärk′) *n.* **1.** One who occupies a position of authority in an ecclesiastical hierarchy. **2.** One who occupies a high position in a hierarchy. [Old French *hierarche,* from Medieval Latin *hierarcha,* from Greek *hierarkhēs,* president of sacred rites, high priest : HIER(O)- + -ARCH.]

hi·er·ar·chism (hī′ə-rär′kĭz′əm, hī′rär′-) *n.* Hierarchical practice or principles. **—hi·er·ar·chist** *n.*

hi·er·ar·chy (hī′ə-rär′kē, hī′rär′-) *n., pl.* **-chies. 1. a.** A body of persons organized or classified according to rank, capacity, or authority. **b.** A body of entities arranged in a graded series. **2.** Hierocracy. **3.** The body of clergy in a country or area, especially the bishops. [Middle English *ierarchie,* from Old French, from Medieval Latin *(h)ierarchia,* rule of a priest, from Greek *hierarkhia,* from *hierarkhēs,* HIERARCH.] **—hi·er·ar·chi·cal** (hī′ə-rär′kĭ-kəl, hī-rär′-), **hi·er·ar·chic** (-kĭk) *adj.* **—hi·er·ar·chi·cal·ly** *adv.*

hi·er·at·ic (hī′ə-răt′ĭk, hī-răt′-) *adj.* Also **hi·er·at·i·cal** (-ĭ-kəl) (for sense 1). **1.** Of or associated with sacred persons or offices; sacerdotal: *a hieratic gesture.* **2.** Designating or pertaining to a simplified cursive style of Egyptian hieroglyphics that was developed and chiefly used by the priestly class. Compare **demotic. 3.** Designating or pertaining to various styles of art that follow rules or conventions established by religious tradition, especially in ancient Egypt.
~*n.* **hieratic.** The hieratic script of ancient Egypt. [Latin *hierāticus,* from Greek *hieratikos,* from *hieratos* (unattested), from *hierasthai,* to be a priest, from *hiereus,* priest, from *hieros,* sacred, supernatural.] **—hi·er·at·i·cal·ly** *adv.*

hiero–, hier– *prefix.* Indicates sacred or holy; for example, **hierocracy, hierogram.** [Greek, from *hieros,* holy, sacred.]

hi·er·oc·ra·cy (hī′ə-rŏk′rə-sē, hī-rŏk′-) *n., pl.* **-cies.** Government by the clergy; ecclesiastical rule: *"Vermont will emerge next, because least . . . under the yoke of hierocracy"* (Thomas Jefferson). [HIERO- + -CRACY.] **—hi·er·o·crat·ic** (hī′ər-ə-krăt′ĭk, hī′rə-), **hi·er·o·crat·i·cal** (-ĭ-kəl) *adj.*

hi·er·o·dule (hī′ər-ə-do͞ol′, -dyo͞ol′, hī′rə-) *n.* A temple slave in the service of a particular deity. Used especially with reference to the ritual prostitution at the temple of Aphrodite in Corinth. [Late Latin *hierodūlus,* from Greek *hierodoulos* : HIERO- + *doulos*†, slave.] **—hi·er·o·du·lic** (hī′ər-ə-do͞o′lĭk, -dyo͞o′lĭk, hī′rə-) *adj.*

hi·er·o·glyph·ic (hī′ər-ə-glĭf′ĭk, hī′rə-) *adj.* Also **hi·er·o·glyph·i·cal** (-ĭ-kəl). **1.** Written in or pertaining to a system of writing used in ancient Egypt, in which figures or objects are used to represent words or sounds. **2.** Containing or inscribed with hieroglyphic pictures or symbols. **3.** Hard to read or decipher; illegible.
~*n.* **hieroglyphic.** Also **hi·er·o·glyph** (hī′ər-ə-glĭf′, hī′rə-). **1.** A picture or symbol used in hieroglyphic writing. **2. hieroglyphics.** Hieroglyphic writing. **3.** A picture or symbol with a hidden meaning; an emblem. **4. hieroglyphics.** Illegible or undecipherable writing. [Old French *hieroglyphique,* from Late Latin *hieroglyphicus,* from Greek *hieroglyphikos,* written in hieroglyphics : HIERO- + *gluphē,* carving, engraving, from *gluphein,* to carve.] **—hi·er·o·glyph·i·cal·ly** *adv.* **—hi·er·o·glyph·ist** *n.*

hi·er·o·gram (hī′ər-ə-grăm′, hī′rə-) *n.* A sacred symbol. [HIERO- + -GRAM.]

hi·er·ol·o·gy (hī′ə-rŏl′ə-jē, hī-rŏl′-) *n., pl.* **-gies.** The sacred literature of a given people. [HIERO- + -LOGY.]

hi·er·o·phant (hī′ər-ə-fănt′, hī′rə-, hī-ĕr′ə-) *n.* **1.** In ancient Greece, an expounder of sacred mysteries, especially of the Eleusinian mysteries. **2.** An interpreter of esoteric or arcane knowledge: *"What did even the hierophants of science know of . . . evil?"* (Malcolm Lowry). [Late Latin *hierophanta, hierophantēs,* from Greek *hierophantēs,* interpreter of sacred mysteries : HIERO- + *phainein,* to reveal, show.] **—hi·er·o·phan·tic** (hī′ər-ə-făn′tĭk, hī′rə-) *adj.*

hifalutin. Variant of **highfalutin.**

hi-fi (hī′fī′) *n.* **1. High fidelity** *(see).* **2.** An electronic system or equipment for reproducing high-fidelity sound from radio, records, or magnetic tape. [*High fi*delity.] **—hi-fi** *adj.*

hig·gle (hĭg′əl) *intr.v.* **-gled, -gling, -gles.** To haggle; bargain. [Variant of HAGGLE.]

hig·gle·dy-pig·gle·dy (hĭg′əl-dē-pĭg′əl-dē) *adv.* In utter disorder or confusion.
~*n., pl.* **-dies.** A jumble; a muddle.
~*adj.* Topsy-turvy; jumbled. [Rhyming and jingling formation probably based on PIG (presumably from the manner in which pigs huddle together).]

high (hī) *adj.* **higher, highest. 1. a.** Extending, projecting, or placed far upward; tall; elevated. **b.** Extending farther upward than is usual: *a high forehead.* **2. a.** Having a specified elevation: *ten feet high.* **b.** Being at a specified level: *waist-high.* **3.** Being at or near its peak or culmination: *high noon.* **4.** Beginning to decompose, as meat; excessively gamy. **5.** Far removed in time; remote: *high antiquity.* **6.** Designating a sound produced by a relatively great frequency of vibrations: *a high note.* **7.** Situated far from the equator: *a high latitude.* **8.** Of great moment or importance, as: **a.** Preeminent in rank or standing: *the high priest; the high command.* **b.** Serious; weighty; grave: *high treason.* **9.** Lofty or exalted in quality, character, or style: *high moral standards; high culture.* **10. a.** Of relatively great quantity, magnitude, value, or degree: *a high temperature; high wage demands; a high vitamin content.* **b.** Of great force or violence: *high winds.* **11.** Luxurious: *high living.* **12.** Showing pride, arrogance, or disdain. **13.** Characterized by a state of excitement or euphoria; elated: *high spirits.* **14.** *Informal.* Intoxi-

cated by or as if by alcohol or a narcotic. **15.** At an advanced stage of development or complexity: *high finance.* **16. a.** Favorable: *a high opinion.* **b.** Well-regarded: *high standing.* **17.** *Phonetics.* Pronounced with part of the tongue close to the palate: *a high vowel.* **18.** *Usually* **High.** Of or pertaining to the High Church. **19.** Of, pertaining to, or being the gear in an automotive vehicle that produces the maximum speed.
~*adv.* **1.** At or to a high level: *rise very high.* **2.** In a high manner: *riding high; sing high; priced high.* **3.** *Nautical.* With full sails, sailing close to the wind.
~*n.* **1. a.** A high place, region, or level. **b.** A highest point: *The stock market reached a new high.* **2.** *Abbr.* **h., H.** The transmission gear of an automotive vehicle producing maximum speed. **3.** A center of high atmospheric pressure; anticyclone. **4.** *Informal.* Intoxication or euphoria induced by or as if by a stimulant or a narcotic. —**on high. 1.** At a high level or position. **2.** In heaven. [Middle English *hei, high,* Old English *hēah,* from Germanic.]
     Synonyms: *elevated, lofty, tall, towering.*
high altar *n.* The principal altar in a church.
high and dry *adv.* **1.** In a helpless or destitute state. **2.** Out of water. Said of ships.
high and low *adv.* Here and there; everywhere: *searched high and low.*
high and mighty *adj.* Arrogant; domineering; disdainful.
high·ball (hī'bôl') *n.* **1.** An iced drink consisting of alcoholic liquor and water, soda water, or the like, served in a tall glass. **2.** A railroad signal indicating full speed ahead.
~*intr.v.* **highballed, -balling, -balls.** To move ahead at full speed.
high·bind·er (hī'bīn'dər) *n.* **1.** A member of a former Chinese-American secret society of paid assassins and blackmailers. **2.** A gangster. **3.** A corrupt politician. [From the *High-binders,* a New York City gang (c. 1806).]
high blood pressure *n.* Hypertension.
high·born (hī'bôrn') *adj.* Of noble birth.
high·boy (hī'boi') *n.* A tall chest of drawers divided into two sections and supported on four legs. Compare **tallboy.**
high·brow (hī'brou') *n.* *Informal.* One who has or affects superior learning or culture. Compare **middlebrow, lowbrow.** [Referring to a lofty forehead as a conventional sign of intellectual superiority.] —**high·brow, high·browed** *adj.*
high-bush cranberry (hī'bŏŏsh') *n.* A North American shrub, *Viburnum trilobum,* having broad clusters of white flowers and scarlet fruit. Also called "cranberry bush."
high·chair (hī'châr') *n.* A baby's feeding chair, usually with a detachable tray and mounted on tall legs.
High Church *n.* The branch of the Anglican Church that stresses the value of an episcopal hierarchy and sacramental ritual. Compare **Anglo-Catholic, Broad Church, Low Church.** —**High-Church** (hī'chûrch') *adj.* —**High-Church·man** *n.*
high-class (hī'klăs', -kläs') *adj.* First-class; first-rate.
high-col·ored (hī'kŭl'ərd) *adj.* Extremely pink; florid. Said of the complexion.
high comedy *n.* Comedy marked by sophisticated characterizations and clever dialogue.
high court *n.* Supreme Court *(see).*
high day *n.* A holy day; a feast day.
high-def·i·ni·tion (hī'dĕf'ə-nĭsh'ən) *adj.* Designating a televized image with a high degree of clarity.
high-en·er·gy (hī'ĕn'ər-jē) *adj.* **1.** Of or relating to elementary particles with energies exceeding hundreds of thousands of electron volts. **2.** Yielding a large amount of energy upon undergoing chemical reaction. **3.** Vigorous; dynamic.
higher algebra *n.* The algebra of sets, groups, propositions, vectors, matrices, tensors, or the like, as opposed to the simple algebra of numbers.
higher criticism *n.* Critical study of Biblical texts with regard to such matters as their authorship, composition, editing, and compilation. Compare **lower criticism.**
higher education *n.* Education that takes place after attendance at secondary school, as at a college or university.
higher learning *n.* Education or scholastic attainment at the college or university level.
higher mathematics *n.* Mathematics involving advanced abstract ideas, including such topics as number theory, non-Euclidean geometry, topology, and analysis, as distinguished from simple arithmetic, algebra, geometry, and trigonometry.
high·er-up (hī'ər-ŭp') *n. Informal.* One who has a higher rank, position, or status.
high explosive *n. Abbr.* **HE** A powerful, fast-acting explosive.
high-fa·lu·tin, hi·fa·lu·tin (hī'fə-lōōt'n) *adj.* Also **high-fa·lu·ting** (-lōōt'n, -lōō'tĭng). *Informal.* Pompous or pretentious, especially in the use of language. [HIGH + *falutin,* perhaps variant of *fluting,* present participle of FLUTE.]
high fashion *n.* Haute couture *(see).*
high fidelity *n.* The electronic reproduction of sound, especially sound from broadcast, recorded, or taped sources, with minimal distortion. Also called "hi-fi." —**high-fi·del·i·ty** (hī'fī-dĕl'ə-tē, hī'fī-) *adj.*
high finance *n.* Complex financial dealings involving large sums of money.
high five *n.* A friendly or congratulatory slap with the open palm and the arm raised exchanged by two people.
high-fli·er, high-fly·er (hī'flī'ər) *n.* **1.** One that flies high. **2. a.** A

person of great ambition. **b.** A person expected by his superiors to go far. **3.** A very successful person, especially one who has a high status for his age.
high-flown (hī'flōn') *adj.* **1.** Lofty; exalted. **2.** Pretentious.
high-fly·ing (hī'flī'ĭng) *adj.* **1.** Rising to a great height. **2.** Lofty in form or ambitions.
high frequency *n. Abbr.* **hf** A radio frequency *(see)* in the range between 3 and 30 megahertz.
High·gate (hī'gət, -gāt'). A residential district of northern London. In its cemetery are the graves of several famous people, including Karl Marx and George Eliot.
high gear *n.* **1.** See **high** (sense 2). **2.** A state of maximum activity, energy, or force.
High German *n.* **1.** *Abbr.* **HG, H.G.** The German language as spoken and written in southern Germany. See **Low German, Old High German, Middle High German. 2.** Any of various German dialects. [Translation of German *Hochdeutsch.*]
high-grade (hī'grād') *adj.* Of superior quality.
high-hand·ed (hī'hăn'dĭd) *adj.* Arrogant or arbitrary in manner. —**high-hand·ed·ly** *adv.* —**high-hand·ed·ness** *n.*
high-hat (hī'hăt') *n. Slang.* A snobbish or patronizing person.
~*tr.v.* (hī'hăt') **high-hatted, -hatting, -hats.** *Slang.* To be condescending or supercilious toward. —**high-hat** *adj.*
High Holiday *n.* **1.** Rosh Hashanah. **2.** Yom Kippur.
highjack. Variant of **hijack.**
high jinks *pl.n.* Mischievous merriment; lively sport.
high jump *n.* **1.** An athletic event in which individual athletes compete to jump highest over an adjustable horizontal bar. **2.** Any of the jumps performed in such a competition.
high-keyed (hī'kēd') *adj.* **1.** Excitable; nervous; high-strung. **2.** Bright in color; intense. **3.** Having a high pitch; shrill.
high·land (hī'lənd) *n.* **1.** Elevated land. **2. highlands.** A mountainous or hilly region or part of a country.
~*adj.* **1.** Of, relating to, or characteristic of such a region. **2. Highland.** Of or relating to the Highlands.

Highland cattle *A hardy, shaggy-haired breed from the rugged uplands of Scotland. Highlands produce good beef even on poor pasture.*

Highland cattle *n. Used with a plural verb.* A breed of long-horned cattle having shaggy, usually reddish-brown hair.
high·land·er (hī'lən-dər) *n.* **1.** One who lives in a highland area. **2. Highlander.** An inhabitant of the Highlands.
Highland fling *n.* An energetic reel or folk dance of the Highlands.
Highland pony *n.* A pony of a breed originating in the Scottish Highlands.
Highland Region. An administrative region of northern Scotland, formed from the former counties of Caithness, Sutherland, Ross and Cromarty, Inverness, Nairn, and parts of Argyll. Its administrative center is Inverness.
Highlands, the. That part of Scotland lying north of a line drawn from Dumbarton in the west northeastward to Stonehaven.
high-lev·el (hī'lĕv'əl) *adj.* **1.** Occurring, carried out, or situated at a high level. **2.** Being at a high level of importance: *a high-level official.*
high-level language *n. Computer Science.* A programming language that uses words and common mathematical symbols. Compare **low-level language.**
high life *n.* Also **high·life** (hī'līf') (for sense 2). **1.** A fashionable or luxurious style of living. **2.** A style of West African music combining traditional African and American jazz elements. —**high·life** *adj.*
high·light (hī'līt') *n.* **1.** In painting or photography, a brilliantly lighted area of the subject appearing as a luminous spot. **2.** An outstanding event or detail. **3.** *Usually* **highlights.** A bleached or light dyed streak in the hair.
~*tr.v.* **highlighted, -lighting, -lights. 1.** To give prominence to; focus attention upon. **2.** To add highlights to, as in painting. **3.** To dye or bleach (the hair) to produce highlights. **4.** To be the highlight of.
high-light·er (hī'lī'tər) *n.* **1.** A cosmetic in powder or cream form used to create highlights on the face. **2.** A felt-tipped pen with fluorescent ink used to pick out a word or passage in a text.
high·ly (hī'lē) *adv.* **1. a.** Extremely; very. Used as an intensive: *highly indignant.* **b.** To a greater than average degree: *highly paid.* **2.** Approvingly; favorably: *I think highly of his results.*
High Mass *n. Roman Catholic Church.* A sung Mass celebrated by a priest or prelate, sometimes assisted by a deacon and a subdeacon, and with full ceremonial.
high-mind·ed (hī'mīn'dĭd) *adj.* **1.** Characterized by morally lofty ideals or conduct; principled. **2.** *Archaic.* Disdainfully proud; arrogant; haughty. —**high-mind·ed·ly** *adv.* —**high-mind·ed·ness** *n.*
high muckamuck *n. Slang.* A muckamuck *(see).*
high·ness (hī'nĭs) *n.* **1.** The quality of being high, especially: **a.** Tallness; height. **b.** Greatness, as of degree or amount. **2.** A title of honor or form of address for any of various members of a royal family. Used with *His, Her, Your,* or *Their: Their Highnesses the Prince and Princess.*
high noon *n.* **1.** Exactly noon. **2.** The highest or most advanced stage or period: *was at the high noon of her creativity.*
high-oc·tane (hī'ŏk'tān') *adj.* Having a high octane number.
high-pass filter (hī'păs', -päs') *n. Electronics.* A circuit that allows transmission of signals with frequencies above a given value, rejecting frequencies below this value.
high-pitched (hī'pĭcht') *adj.* **1. a.** Having a high pitch to the ear. **b.** Tuned to a high pitch. **2.** Lofty; exalted, as a sermon might be. **3.** Steeply sloped, as a roof might be.
high place *n.* **1.** In early Semitic religions, a place of worship on top

Highland pony *A muscular breed of horse once widely used as a pack animal in the Scottish Highlands.*

high relief *A centaur battles with a human rival in a detail from a Greek frieze sculpted in this deeply cut style.*

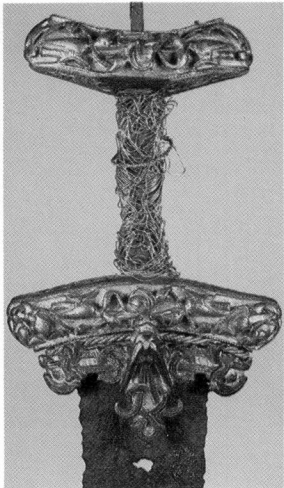

hilt *The hilt, or handle, of an 11th-century Viking sword.*

of a hill. **2. high places.** Positions of power or influence, especially in public office: *corruption in high places.*

high point *n.* The single event or moment in a period of time, project, or the like, that stands out as particularly rewarding or revealing: *The high point of the concert was the oboe concerto.*

high-pow·ered (hī´pou´ərd) *adj.* **1.** Dynamic and highly motivated: *a high-powered salesman.* **2.** Intellectually demanding or impressive: *a high-powered seminar.* **3.** Capable of very great magnification. Said of optical instruments: *a high-powered telescope.*

high-pres·sure (hī´prĕsh´ər) *adj.* **1.** Of or pertaining to pressures higher than normal; especially, much higher than atmospheric pressure. **2.** Involving great psychological stress or great dedication of energy: *a high-pressure job.* **3.** *Informal.* Using aggressive and persistent persuasion in selling.
  ~*tr.v.* **high-pressured, -suring, -sures.** *Informal.* To convince or influence by using high-pressure methods of persuasion.

high priest *n.* **1.** *Judaism.* The senior priest serving in the temple, who alone could enter the holy of holies. **2.** Any of various other senior priests in various religions or sects. **3.** The unofficial leader or most influential figure of a fashion, theory, or movement: *the high priest of monetarism.*

high priestess *n.* A woman who functions or is regarded as a high priest.

high profile *n. Informal.* A conspicuous, well-publicized presence or stance. Compare **low profile.**

high relief *n.* A sculptural relief in which the modeled forms project from the background by at least half their depth. Also called "alto-relievo." [Translation of French *haut-relief.*]

high-rise (hī´rīz´) *adj.* Designating or being a building with many stories equipped with elevators. Compare **low-rise.**
  ~*n.* A high-rise building.

high-road (hī´rōd´) *n.* **1.** *Chiefly British.* A main road; a highway. **2.** A simple, direct, or sure path: *the highroad to happiness.*

high school *n.* **1.** A secondary school that includes grades 9 or 10 through 12. **2.** A secondary school that includes junior and senior high school, consisting of grades 7 through 12.

high seas *pl.n.* The open waters of an ocean or sea beyond the limits of national territorial jurisdiction.

high season *n.* Any of the periods during a year when attendance or demand is particularly high, as at a vacation resort.

high sign *n. Informal.* A gesture or other discreet signal given especially as a secret warning.

high-sound·ing (hī´soun´dĭng) *adj.* Impressive or pompous.

high-speed (hī´spēd´) *adj.* **1.** Moving, operating, or used at a high speed. **2.** Of, pertaining to, or designating photographic film that requires only a short exposure.

high-speed steel *n.* A type of steel that remains hard when hot, used for cutting tools for lathes, milling machines, and the like.

high-spir·it·ed (hī´spîr´ə-tĭd) *adj.* **1.** Having a proud or unbroken spirit; brave. **2.** Vivacious. **—high-spir·it·ed·ly** *adv.* **—high-spir·it·ed·ness** *n.*

high spot *n.* The best or most memorable part of a particular period of time: *Dinner was the high spot of the day.*

high-street (hī´strēt´) *adj. Chiefly British.* Of, pertaining to, or designating shops or other commercial enterprises of a kind typically found on a principal street: *a high-street grocer.*

high-strung (hī´strŭng´) *adj.* Constantly nervous and tense; easily excited or upset.

hight (hīt) *adj. Archaic.* Named; called. [Middle English *highten, hihten,* from *hehte, hight,* past tense of *hoten,* to call, be called, Old English *hātan* (past tense *heht*).]

high table *n. British.* The dining table, sometimes on a raised platform, in the dining hall of an institution, such as a university, at which senior members and their guests take their meals.

high-tail (hī´tāl´) *intr.v.* **-tailed, -tailing, -tails.** *Slang.* To move or depart in a great hurry; especially, to escape. **—hightail it.** To rush; hurry. [A reference to some animals such as when startled raise their tails and flee.]

high tea *n. Chiefly British.* A substantial meal that typically includes tea, a hot course, and bread and butter, served in the late afternoon or early evening.

high tech (tĕk) *n.* **1.** A modern style of furnishings, fittings, and design in which industrial materials such as metal piping are used. **2.** High technology. **—high-tech** (hī´tĕk´) *adj.*

high technology *n.* Technology involving highly advanced or specialized systems or devices.

high-ten·sion (hī´tĕn´shən) *adj. Abbr.* **H.T.** Having or carrying a high voltage: *high-tension wires.*

high-test (hī´tĕst´) *adj.* **1.** Meeting the most exacting requirements. **2.** Of or pertaining to highly volatile, high-octane fuel.

high tide *n.* **1.** The tide at its full, when the water reaches its highest level. **2.** The time at which this occurs. **3.** A point of culmination; an acme.

high time *n.* **1.** A time almost too late; about time; fully time. **2.** *Informal.* A good time.

high-toned (hī´tōnd´) *adj.* **1.** Intellectually superior: *a high-toned lecture.* **2.** Socially superior: *a high-toned finishing school.* **3.** *Informal.* Having pretensions to elegance or slickness.

high treason *n.* Treason against one's state or sovereign.

highty-tighty. Variant of **hoity-toity.**

high-up (hī´ŭp´) *adj. Informal.* Of high position or status.
  ~*n. Informal.* A person who has a high rank or position.

High·veld (hī´vĕlt´, -fĕlt´) In South Africa, the savanna of the Afri-

can plateau above 1,500 meters (about 5,000 feet).

high water *n. Abbr.* **H.W., h.w.** **1.** High tide. **2.** The state of a body of water that has reached its highest level.

high-wa·ter mark (hī´wô´tər, -wŏt´ər) *n.* **1. a.** A mark indicating the highest level reached by a body of water. **b.** This level itself. **2.** The highest point of achievement; an apex.

high·way (hī´wā´) *n.* A main public road, especially one connecting towns and cities.

high·way·man (hī´wā´mən) *n., pl.* **-men** (-mĭn). A robber who holds up travelers on a highway.

H.I.H. His (or Her) Imperial Highness.

hi·jack, high·jack (hī´jăk´) *tr.v.* **-jacked, -jacking, -jacks.** **1.** To rob (a vehicle, such as a train or armored truck) by stopping it in transit. **2.** To steal (goods) from a vehicle by stopping it in transit. **3.** To seize or commandeer (a moving vehicle, such as an aircraft, ship, or car) by force or with threats of force, especially in an attempt to enforce political or other demands. **4.** To steal from (a person). **5.** To take control of using coercive or underhand methods: *The meeting was hijacked by a well-organized group of militants.*
  ~*n.* An act or instance of hijacking. [20th century : origin obscure.] **—hi·jack·er** *n.*

hike (hīk) *v.* **hiked, hiking, hikes.** *—intr.* **1. a.** To go on an extended walk, particularly for pleasure. **b.** To go on an extended march, especially over rough terrain; tramp. **2.** To go up, as prices. Often used with *up: The cost of living has hiked up again.* **3.** To be raised or hitched. Usually used with *up: Her coat has hiked up at the back.* *—tr.* **1.** To increase or raise in amount. Usually used with *up.* **2.** To pull, move, or raise with a sudden motion; hitch. Usually used with *up: He hiked up his pants.*
  ~*n.* **1.** A walk or march. **2.** A rise, as in prices. [19th century (dialect) : origin obscure.] **—hik·er** *n.*

hi·la. Plural of **hilum.**

hi·lar·i·ous (hĭ-lâr´ē-əs, hī-) *adj.* Boisterously funny, gay, or merry: *a hilarious joke.* [From Latin *hilarus, hilaris.* See **hilarity.**] **—hi·lar·i·ous·ly** *adv.* **—hi·lar·i·ous·ness** *n.*

hi·lar·i·ty (hĭ-lăr´ə-tē, hī-) *n.* Boisterous merriment. **—See Synonyms at mirth.** [Old French *hilarite,* from Latin *hilaritās,* from *hilaris, hilarus,* cheerful, from Greek *hilaros.*]

Hil·bert (hĭl´bərt), **David** (1862-1943). German mathematician. His work on integral equations laid the foundations of 20th-century functional analysis.

hill (hĭl) *n.* **1.** A well-defined, naturally elevated area of land smaller than a mountain. **2. hills. a.** A range or group of such elevations. **b.** *Informal.* Any remote rural area located in such elevated areas. **3.** A heap, pile, or mound, such as that formed by a living organism. Often used in combination: *anthill.* **4.** An incline, especially in a road; a slope. **—over the hill.** *Informal.* No longer young; past one's prime.
  ~*tr.v.* **hilled, hilling, hills.** **1.** To form into a hill, pile, or heap. **2.** To cover (a plant or plants) with a mound of soil. [Middle English *hill,* Old English *hyll.*] **—hill·er** *n.* **—hill·y** *adj.*

Hill (hĭl), **Archibald Vivian** (1886-1977). British physiologist and biochemist. He investigated heat production in muscles and nerves. In 1922 he shared the Nobel Prize in physiology and medicine with Otto Meyerhof.

Hil·la·ry (hĭl´ə-rē), **Sir Edmund Percival** (1919–). New Zealand mountaineer. Hillary and Tenzing Norgay became the first men to reach the summit of Mt. Everest in 1953.

hill·bil·ly (hĭl´bĭl´ē) *n., pl.* **-lies.** *Informal.* A person from the backwoods or a remote mountainous area.
  ~*adj.* Of or characteristic of the culture of such an area: *hillbilly music.* [HILL + *Billy,* a nickname for *William.*]

hill-fort (hĭl´fôrt´, -fōrt´) *n. Archaeology.* A fortified hilltop, showing traces of ramparts, ditches, and the like.

Hil·liard (hĭl´yərd), **Nicholas** (1537-1619). English miniature painter. He was appointed goldsmith, carver, and limner to Queen Elizabeth I.

hill myna *n.* A black songbird, *Gracula religiosa,* of India and the East Indies, that is kept as a cage bird for its ability to mimic human speech.

hill·ock (hĭl´ək) *n.* A small hill. [Middle English : HILL + -OCK.] **—hill·ock·y** *adj.*

hill·side (hĭl´sīd´) *n.* The side or slope of a hill.

hill station *n.* In India and various other Asian countries, a resort or settlement at a high altitude, frequented during the summer months because of its relatively cool climate.

hill·top (hĭl´tŏp´) *n.* The crest or top of a hill.

hilt (hĭlt) *n.* The handle of a weapon or tool, especially of a sword or dagger. **—to the hilt.** Completely.
  ~*tr.v.* **hilted, hilting, hilts.** To provide with a hilt. [Middle English *hilt,* Old English *hilt,* from Germanic *hilt-* (unattested).]

Hil·ton (hĭl´tən), **James** (1900-54). British novelist. He is best known for his books *Lost Horizon* (1933), set in the Tibetan lamasery of Shangri-La, and *Goodbye Mr. Chips* (1934), about an aging schoolmaster. Both were made into successful films.

hi·lum (hī´ləm) *n., pl.* **-la** (-lə). **1.** *Botany.* **a.** The scarlike mark on a seed, such as a bean, formed at the point where it was joined to the stalk connecting it to the placenta. **b.** The nucleus of a starch grain. **2.** *Anatomy.* Variant of **hilus.** [New Latin, from Latin *hīlum†,* trifle.]

hi·lus (hī´ləs) *n., pl.* **-li** (-lī´). Also **hi·lum** (hī´ləm), *pl.* **-la** (-lə). *Anatomy.* An indentation on the surface of an organ marking the point of entrance or exit of a blood vessel, nerve, or the like. [New Latin, from Latin, "a trifle."]

him (hĭm) *pron.* The objective case of the third person pronoun *he.* It is used: **1.** As the direct object of a verb: *They assisted him.* **2.** As the indirect object of a verb: *They offered him a lift.* **3.** As the object of a preposition: *This letter is addressed to him.* **4.** After *than* or *as* in comparisons in which the first term is in the objective case: *The judges praised her more than him.* **5.** *Informal.* In place of the reflexive pronoun *himself* as the indirect object of a verb: *He went to buy him a car.* **6.** In various elliptical, absolute, or interjectional phrases in which it is neither subject nor object: *Him and his sweet talk!* —See Usage note at **me.** [Middle English *him,* Old English *him.*]

H.I.M. His (or Her) Imperial Majesty.

Him·a·la·yas (hĭm′ə-lā′əz, hĭ-mäl′yəz). Also **Him·a·la·ya Mountains** (hĭm′ə-lā′ə, hĭ-mäl′yə). A mountain system of central Asia. The largest and highest chain in the world, it extends 2,415 kilometers (1,500 miles) across the northern Indian subcontinent from the Karakorum Range to the north-south section of the Brahmaputra River. Forming the southern edge of the central Asian plateau, it consists of a number of parallel ridges and is the source of the Indus, Ganges, and Brahmaputra river systems. Mt. Everest (8,848 meters; 29,028 feet), its highest peak, is the world's highest mountain. **—Him·a·la·yan** *adj.*

hi·mat·i·on (hĭ-măt′ē-ŏn′) *n., pl.* **-ia** (-ē-ə). A long loose outer garment worn by men and women in ancient Greece. [Greek, diminutive of *hima* (stem *himat-*), garment, from *hennunai,* to clothe.]

Himm·ler (hĭm′lər), **Heinrich** (1900–45). German Nazi leader. In 1929 he was given command of the SS, the party's elite corps and Hitler's bodyguard. In 1936 he became head of the Third Reich's police forces and of the secret police, the Gestapo. He was also the commandant of the concentration and extermination camps. He was captured by British troops in May, 1945, and committed suicide by taking poison.

him·self (hĭm-sĕlf′) *pron.* A specialized form of the third person singular masculine pronoun. It is used: **1.** As a reflexive pronoun, forming the direct or indirect object of a verb or the object of a preposition: *hurt himself; gives himself time; talks to himself.* **2.** For emphasis after *he*: *He himself wasn't certain.* **3.** As an emphasizing substitute: *In debt himself, he cannot help you. It was addressed to Kate and himself.* **4.** As an indication of his real, normal, or healthy condition or identity: *He hasn't been himself lately.* **5.** *Chiefly Irish & Scottish.* An important or prominent man, such as the head of a household. Sometimes used humorously. [Middle English *himself,* Old English *him selfum* : HIM + *selfum,* dative of *self,* SELF.]

Him·yar·ite (hĭm′yə-rīt′) *n.* Also **Him·yar·it·ic** (hĭm′yə-rĭt′ĭk) (for sense 2). **1.** A member of an ancient people of southwestern Arabia. **2.** The Semitic language, closely related to Ethiopian, spoken by the ancient Himyarites.
~adj. Of, relating to, or characteristic of the Himyarites, their language, or their culture. [After *Himyar,* legendary ancient king in Yemen.] **—Him·yar·it·ic** *adj.*

Hi·na·ya·na (hē′nə-yä′nə) *n.* A branch of Buddhism, **Theravada** *(see).* Compare **Mahayana.** [Sanskrit *hīnayāna,* "lesser vehicle."] **—Hi·na·ya·nist** *n.* **—Hi·na·ya·nis·tic** (hē′nə-yə-nĭs′tĭk) *adj.*
Usage: Adherents of this school of Buddhism prefer the term *Theravada,* the term *Hinayana* having originally been a disparaging term coined by Mahayana Buddhists.

hind[1] (hīnd) *adj.* Also **hind·er** (hīn′dər). Located at or forming the back or rear; posterior: *hind legs.* [Middle English *hint,* perhaps from Old English *hinder,* behind, or *hindan,* from behind.]

hind[2] *n.* **1.** A female red deer. **2.** Any of several fishes of the genus *Epinephelus,* of Atlantic waters, related to and resembling the groupers. [Middle English *hinde,* Old English *hind.*]

hind[3] *n.* **1.** *Archaic British.* A peasant or farm laborer. **2.** *Archaic.* A rustic or country bumpkin. [Middle English, from Old English *hīwan.*]

hind·brain (hīnd′brān′) *n.* The **rhombencephalon** *(see).*

Hin·de·mith (hĭn′də-mĭth, -mĭt), **Paul** (1895–1963). German violist and composer. He composed chamber music, instrumental works, and operas.

Hin·den·burg (hĭn′dən-bûrg′), **Paul Ludwig Hans Anton von** (1847–1934). German field marshal and politician, president of the Weimar Republic (1925–34). He appointed Hitler chancellor in January, 1933.

hin·der[1] (hĭn′dər) *v.* **-dered, -dering, -ders.** *—tr.* **1.** To hold back; be in the way of; hamper; delay. **2.** To obstruct or delay the progress of; prevent; stop. *—intr.* To be an obstacle or encumbrance. [Middle English *hindren,* Old English *hindrian,* from Germanic.] **—hin·der·er** *n.*
Synonyms: *balk, bar, block, dam, encumber, hamper, impede, obstruct, retard.*

hinder[2]. Variant of **hind** (rear).

hind·gut (hīnd′gŭt′) *n.* **1.** The posterior portion of the colon in vertebrates. **2.** The posterior portion of the alimentary canal in arthropods. Compare **foregut.**

Hin·di (hĭn′dē) *n.* **1.** A group of vernacular Indic dialects spoken in northern India. **2.** A literary language based upon these dialects, now an official language and usually written in the Devanagari alphabet. **3.** A member of a cultural group of northern India speaking a Hindi dialect. [Hindi *Hindī,* from *Hind,* India, from Persian, from Old Persian *Hindu,* the river Indus. See **India.**] **—Hin·di** *adj.*

hind·most (hīnd′mōst′) *adj.* Also **hind·er·most** (hīn′dər-). Farthest to the rear; most remote; last.

Hindostan. See **Hindustan.**

hind·quar·ter (hīnd′kwôr′tər) *n.* **1.** The posterior portion of a side of beef, lamb, or the like, including a hind leg and one or two ribs. **2.** *Usually* **hindquarters.** The posterior part of a quadruped, adjacent to the hind legs; the rump.

hin·drance (hĭn′drəns) *n.* **1.** The act of hindering. **2.** One that hinders; an impediment; an obstruction. —See Synonyms at **obstacle.** [Middle English *hind(e)raunce,* from *hindren,* to HINDER.]

hind·sight (hīnd′sīt′) *n.* **1.** Perception or understanding of events after they have occurred. **2.** The rear sight of a firearm.

Hin·du (hĭn′do͞o) *n.* Also *archaic* **Hin·doo. 1.** A believer in Hinduism. **2.** A native of India, especially northern India.
~adj. Also *archaic* **Hin·doo.** Of or pertaining to the Hindus or Hinduism. [Urdu, from Persian *Hindū,* from *Hind,* India. See **Hindi.**]

Hindu calendar *n.* The lunisolar calendar of the Hindus. The solar year is divided into 12 months in accordance with the successive entrances of the sun into the signs of the zodiac, the months varying in length from 29 to 32 days.

Hin·du·ism (hĭn′do͞o-ĭz′əm) *n.* Also *archaic* **Hin·doo·ism.** A diverse body of religion, philosophy, and cultural practices native to and predominant in India, characterized broadly by beliefs in reincarnation and a supreme being of many forms and natures, by the view that opposing theories are aspects of one eternal truth, by a system of **caste** *(see),* and by the view that killing animals is wrong. See feature, next page.

Hindu Kush (ko͝osh). Mountain range principally in northeastern Afghanistan. A western extension of the Himalayas, it extends 800 kilometers (500 miles) southwest from the Pamirs in Tajikistan to include the Koh i Baba range in Afghanistan. The highest peak is Tirich Mir (7,692 meters; 25,236 feet) in Chitral, Pakistan.

Hin·du·stan (hĭn′do͞o-stăn′, -stän′). Also **Hin·do·stan** (-dō-). **1.** A historical region roughly occupying the part of the Indian subcontinent that lies to the north of the Deccan Plateau, characterized by the prevalence of Indic languages. **2.** The Indian subcontinent.

Hin·du·sta·ni (hĭn′do͞o-stä′nē, -stăn′ē) *n.* **1.** A subdivision of the Indic branch of languages, including Urdu, Hindi, and other languages of northern India. **2.** A native of Hindustan.
~adj. Of or pertaining to Hindustani or Hindustan.

Hines (hīnz), **Earl Kenneth,** known as "Fatha" (1905–83). U.S. jazz musician. A leading jazz pianist for more than 50 years, he first gained national recognition through his recordings with Louis Armstrong in the 1920's. He organized and led several bands during the 1940's and continued to play until a week before his death.

hinge (hĭnj) *n.* **1.** A jointed or flexible device permitting turning or pivoting of a part, such as a door, lid, or flap, on a stationary frame. **2.** A structure or part similar to a hinge, especially: **a.** An anatomical joint between bones, such as the elbow. **b.** A joint that enables the valves of a bivalve mollusk to open and close. **3.** A small folded paper rectangle gummed on one side, used to fasten stamps, photographs, or the like in an album. **4.** A point, quality, or circumstance upon which subsequent situations or events depend.
~v. **hinged, hinging, hinges.** *—tr.* To attach by or equip with a hinge or hinges. *—intr.* **1.** To turn or hang, as on a hinge. **2.** To depend; be contingent. Usually used with *on* or *upon.* [Middle English *he(e)ng.*]

hin·ny[1] (hĭn′ē) *n., pl.* **-nies.** The hybrid offspring of a male horse and a female ass. Compare **mule.** [Latin *hinnus,* variant (influenced by *hinnīre,* to HINNY) of Greek *innos, ginnos*†.]

hinny[2] *intr.v.* **-nied, -nying, -nies.** *Rare.* To whinny; neigh. [Earlier *henny,* from Old French *hennir,* from Latin *hinnīre* (imitative).]

hint (hĭnt) *n.* **1.** A subtle suggestion or slight indication; an intimation. **2.** A statement or gesture conveying veiled information; a clue. **3.** A piece of useful advice, as on how to proceed with a task. **4.** A barely perceptible amount: *gin with a hint of vermouth.* **5.** *Obsolete.* An occasion; opportunity.
~v. **hinted, hinting, hints.** *—tr.* To make known by a hint; intimate. *—intr.* To give a hint or hints. Often used with *at*: *He hinted at the true purpose of his visit.* —See Synonyms at **suggest.** [Perhaps from obsolete *hent,* to grasp, seize, from Old English *hentan,* from Germanic.] **—hint·er** *n.*

hin·ter·land (hĭn′tər-lănd′) *n.* **1.** The land lying inland from a coast. **2.** A region served by a port city and its facilities. **3.** A region remote from urban areas; back country. **4.** Any region, period, or situation that is remote or undefined. [German : *hinter,* behind, from Old High German *hintar* + *Land,* land.]

hip[1] (hĭp) *n.* **1.** The laterally projecting prominence of the pelvis or pelvic region from the waist to the thigh. **2.** The corresponding posterior part in quadrupeds. **3.** The hip joint. **4.** *Architecture.* The external angle formed by the meeting of two adjacent sloping sides of a roof. **—shoot from the hip.** *Slang.* To act or react impulsively and without proper thought. [Middle English *hip, hupe,* Old English *hype,* from Germanic.]

hip[2] *adj.* **hipper, hippest.** *Slang.* **1.** Aware of or in accordance with fashionable tastes and attitudes. **2.** Cognizant; aware. Used with *to*: *hip to the plan.* [Origin unknown.] **—hip·ness** *n.*

hip[3] *n.* The fleshy, berrylike fruit of a rose, consisting of an enlarged receptacle containing several small, hairy achenes. Also called "rosehip." [Middle English *hepe, hipe,* Old English *heope.*]

hip[4] *interj.* Used as a cheer or a signal for a cheer: *Hip, hip, hurrah!* [19th century : origin obscure.]

hip bath *n.* A **sitz bath** *(see).*

hip·bone (hĭp′bōn′) *n.* The **innominate bone** *(see).*

hind *An adult female red deer. This hind is a European red deer,* Cervus elaphus.

Hinduism

THE OLDEST FAITH ON EARTH
About 400 million people follow a religion that has no founder and no set creed

Alone among major world religions, Hinduism, the faith commanding the loyalty of 85 percent of India, has no one founder and no one authoritative scripture such as the Christian Bible or the Muslim Koran.

Instead, Hindu beliefs grew out of the fusion of two cultures when the Aryan people of central Asia settled in northern India in about 2000 B.C. among the original inhabitants of the subcontinent. The oldest surviving Hindu texts, the *Vedas*—which are largely a collection of Aryan hymns—date from about 1500 B.C., centuries before the rise of the other great world religions. Added later were scriptures such as the 4th-century B.C. epic poem the *Mahabharata* and the hundred-odd treatises on philosophic and mystical questions, such as the nature of reality and consciousness, known as the *Upanishads,* which were written after about 800 B.C.

At the heart of all these texts is the concept of reincarnation, the philosophical basis both for the Hindu emphasis on nonviolence and for the caste system that still pervades modern Indian society.

According to this concept, the souls of all living creatures are reborn in new bodies after death. Those who act virtuously in life are reborn in higher social castes; those whose actions (or karma) are evil return as lower-caste humans or even as animals. Release from this endless cycle of death and rebirth is possible only through arduous spiritual discipline. One such discipline—which is recommended in the *Bhagavad-gita* ("Song of the Lord"), contained in the epic *Mahabharata*—is the technique of physical control and meditation known as yoga (or union).

Hinduism's emphasis on respect for all life springs directly from this belief that every creature contains an immortal soul that is working out its own sacred destiny. It is for this reason that Hindus revere cows, for example, that many are vegetarian, and that Mahatma Gandhi's policy of nonviolent resistance to British rule in the 1930's and 1940's had such a powerful appeal. The Hindu sect of Jainism takes nonviolence still further; a Jain monk sweeps his path as he walks, so as not to harm even an insect.

The same belief in reincarnation also helps to explain the tenacious hold of the caste system, despite the banning by law of discrimination against the largest and lowest caste, the harijans, or untouchables. For the doctrine leads Hindus to believe that people are born into the caste they deserve as a result of their behavior in past lives.

Hinduism's 400 million adherents worship a total of more than 30 million gods and goddesses. But most of the great Hindu temples are now devoted to one of only two: the god of creation and destruction, Shiva; and a kindly god, Vishnu, who is believed to help men in times of special need.

BRAHMA *Once the supreme god in Hindu belief, Brahma has been replaced as a focus of worship since the 7th century A.D. by Shiva and Vishnu.*

SHIVA *An 11th-century bronze shows Shiva dancing in a ring of flames. The ring symbolizes the eternal cycle of creation, destruction, and rebirth.*

TEMPLE TO THE GODS *Every Hindu home has a shrine devoted to the family's favorite god, but major religious ceremonies usually take place in one of the temples. Many ceremonies attract thousands of pilgrims. Most Hindu temples have several covered shrines linked by open courtyards and decorated with elaborate and often painted carvings in wood, plaster, and stone. The enormous temple at Khajuraho (above), about 500 kilometers (300 miles) south of the Indian capital of New Delhi, has the tiered domes typical of Hindu architecture. It also contains a huge number of stone fertility sculptures of gods and humans making love.*

VISHNU *Like other Hindu gods, Vishnu has numerous incarnations, or avatars. In this 1870 print, Vishnu, who also appears as Rama and Krishna, is reclining on a serpent that represents eternity.*

hip-flask (hĭp′flăsk′, -fläsk′) *n.* A flask, usually containing liquor, designed to fit into a hip pocket.

hip girdle *n.* The **pelvic girdle** (see).

hip joint *n.* The ball-and-socket joint between the innominate bone of the pelvis and the femur.

hip·parch (hĭp′ärk′) *n.* An ancient Greek cavalry commander. [Greek *hipparkhos,* "horse leader" : *hippos,* horse + -ARCH.]

Hip·par·chus (hĭ-pär′kəs) (*fl.* 2nd century B.C.). Greek astronomer, the first of whom there is any record. Ptolemy constructed his geocentric view of the universe from observations made by Hipparchus, chiefly on Rhodes. His chart of the skies, in which 850 stars are placed, is the first known in history.

hip·pe·as·trum (hĭp′ē-ăs′trəm) *n.* Any plant of the South American genus *Hippeastrum,* some species of which are cultivated for their large, red, funnel-shaped flowers. [New Latin, from Greek *hippeus,* horseman (referring to the appearance of the leaves, which seem to ride one another) + *astron,* star (referring to shape of the flower).]

hipped¹ (hĭpt) *adj.* **1.** Having hips of a specified kind. Used in combination: *swivel-hipped; broad-hipped.* **2.** Having the hip dislocated. **3.** *Architecture.* Having a hip or hips. Said of a roof.

hipped² *adj.* Also **hip·pish** (hĭp′ĭsh). Melancholy; depressed. [Shortened variant of HYPOCHONDRIAC.]

hipped³ *adj. Informal.* Obsessively absorbed. Used with *on: hipped on meditation.* [From HIP (aware).]

hip·pie, hip·py (hĭp′ē) *n., pl.* **-pies. 1.** A member of a loosely knit nonconformist movement of the 1960's and 1970's generally characterized by emphasis on nonviolence and universal love and a general rejection of the mores of conventional society, especially regarding dress, personal appearance, and living habits. **2.** Loosely, any young person who is exaggeratedly casual in dress, appearance, and behavior. [From HIP (aware).] **—hip·pie, hip·py** *adj.*

hip·po (hĭp′ō) *n., pl.* **-pos.** *Informal.* A hippopotamus.

hip·po·cam·pus (hĭp′ə-kăm′pəs) *n., pl.* **-pi** (-pī′, -pē′). **1.** *Anatomy.* Either of two ridges along each lateral ventricle of the brain that form part of the limbic system. **2.** *Greek & Roman Mythology.* A sea horse having the forelegs of a horse and the tail of a fish or dolphin. [Late Latin, from Greek *hippokampos : hippos,* horse + *kampos*†, sea monster.]

hip·po·cras (hĭp′ə-krăs′) *n.* A cordial made from wine and flavored with spices that was formerly used as a medicine. [Middle English *ypocras,* from Old French, from Medieval Latin *(vinum) Hippocraticum,* (wine) of Hippocrates (it was strained through a filter called Hippocrates' bag).]

Hip·poc·ra·tes (hĭ-pŏk′rə-tēz′) (*c.* 460–*c.* 370 B.C.). Greek physician, called the Father of Medicine. He played an important part in laying the foundations of scientific medicine and separating it from philosophical speculation and superstition. The Hippocratic oath, although it represented his ethical position, cannot be confidently attributed directly to him.

Hip·po·crat·ic oath (hĭp′ə-krăt′ĭk) *n.* An oath of ethical professional behavior taken by newly qualified doctors, attributed to Hippocrates.

Hip·po·crene (hĭp′ə-krēn′, hĭp′ə-krē′nē). *Greek Mythology.* A fountain on Mount Helicon, Greece, held sacred to the Muses and regarded as a source of poetic inspiration. [Latin *Hippocrēnē,* from Greek *Hippokrēnē : hippos,* horse (supposedly created by a stroke of Pegasus' hoof) + *krēnē*†, fountain.]

hip·po·drome (hĭp′ə-drōm′) *n.* **1.** An open-air stadium with an oval course for horse and chariot races in ancient Greece and Rome. **2.** An arena for horse and circus shows or similar entertainments. [Old French, from Latin *hippodromus,* from Greek *hippodromos : hippos,* horse + -DROME.]

hip·po·griff, hip·po·gryph (hĭp′ə-grĭf′) *n.* A mythological monster having the wings, claws, and head of a griffin and the body and hindquarters of a horse. [French *hippogriffe,* from Italian *ippogrifo : ippo-,* horse, from Latin *hippos,* from Greek + *grifo,* griffin, from Late Latin *grȳphus,* GRIFFIN.]

Hip·pol·y·ta (hĭ-pŏl′ə-tə). *Greek Mythology.* A queen of the Amazons, variously said to have been killed by Hercules in completion of one of his 12 labors or to have been conquered by him and given in marriage to Theseus of Athens.

Hip·pol·y·tus (hĭ-pŏl′ə-təs). *Greek Mythology.* A son of Theseus who spurned the advances of his stepmother, Phaedra, and was killed by Poseidon.

hip·po·pot·a·mus (hĭp′ə-pŏt′ə-məs) *n., pl.* **-muses** or **-mi** (-mī′). **1.** A large, chiefly aquatic African mammal, *Hippopotamus amphibius,* having dark, thick, almost hairless skin, short legs, and a broad, wide-mouthed muzzle. Also called "river horse." **2.** A similar but smaller animal, *Choeropsis liberiensis.* [Latin, from Late Greek *hippopotamos,* from Greek *hippos ho potamios,* "horse of the river" : *hippos,* horse + *potamos,* river.]

hip·py¹ (hĭp′ē) *adj.* **-pier, -piest.** Having broad or prominent hips. **—hip·pi·ness** *n.*

hippy². Variant of **hippie.**

hip roof *n.* A roof having sloping edges and sides.

hip·ster¹ (hĭp′stər) *n. Slang.* One who is in touch with contemporary ideas and fashions, especially when unconventional. [HIP + -STER.]

hipster² *adj. Chiefly British.* Worn so as to hang from the hips and not the waist. Said especially of skirts, trousers, or slacks.

hip·sters (hĭp′stərz) *pl.n. Chiefly British.* Trousers or briefs whose waistline rests at hip level.

hi·ra·ga·na (hîr′ə-gä′nə) *n.* One of two sets of Japanese syllabaries of the kana system, having a cursive form. Also called "kana." See **katakana.** [Japanese, "flat kana."]

hir·cine (hûr′sĭn′, -sīn) *adj.* Of or characteristic of a goat, especially in having a strong odor or being lustful. [Latin *hircīnus,* from *hircus*†, he-goat.]

hire (hīr) *tr.v.* **hired, hiring, hires. 1.** To engage the services of (a person) for a fee; to employ. **2.** To arrange to use (a car, for example) on a temporary basis and for a fee; rent. **3.** To grant the services or allow the use of for remuneration; rent out. Often used with *out: I hire out my cottage for the summer. He hired himself out as a laborer.*
~*n.* **1.** Payment for services or the use of something. **2.** The act of hiring. **3.** The condition or fact of being hired. **—for hire.** Available for use or services in exchange for payment. [Middle English *hiren,* Old English *hȳr(i)an,* from Germanic (Low German area) *khūrjan* (unattested), from *khūrjō* (unattested), payment.] **—hir·a·ble, hire·a·ble** *adj.* **—hir·er** *n.*

hire·ling (hīr′lĭng) *n.* One who offers his services solely for payment; especially, a person willing to perform odious or offensive tasks for a fee; a mercenary.

hire-pur·chase (hīr′pûr′chĭs) *n. Abbr.* **H.P.** *British.* The **installment plan** *(see).*

Hi·ro·hi·to (hîr′ō-hē′tō) (1901–89). Emperor of Japan (1926–89). He had little political power, but in 1945 he influenced the Japanese government to accept unconditional surrender. In 1946 he renounced his divine status.

Hi·ro·shi·ge (hîr′ō-shē′gä′), **Ando** (1797–1858). Japanese artist. A master of color wood-block printing, he captured the serenity of the Japanese landscape with his idealistic, superbly composed works, including *Fifty-three Stages on the Tokaido* (1832).

Hi·ro·shi·ma (hîr′ə-shē′mə, hĭ-rō′shĭ-). A city in southern Japan, on the coast of Honshu. On August 6, 1945, it was almost entirely destroyed by an atomic bomb, the first city to become such a target. It has since been rebuilt as an industrial center and seaport, manufacturing textiles, rubber goods, and machinery.

hir·sute (hûr′so͞ot′, hîr′-, hər-so͞ot′) *adj.* **1.** Covered or coated with hair; hairy. **2.** Of, pertaining to, or consisting of hair. **3.** *Botany.* Covered with long, soft hairs: *hirsute stems.* [Latin *hirsūtus.*] **—hir·sute·ness** *n.*

hir·u·din (hîr-o͞od′n, hîr′ə-dən, -yə-dən) *n.* A substance extracted from the salivary glands of leeches and used as an anticoagulant. [Latin *hirudo, hirudin-,* a leech.]

hi·run·dine (hĭ-rŭn′dĭn, -dīn′) *adj.* Of, pertaining to, or characteristic of a swallow or the swallow family, Hirundinidae. [Latin *hirundo*†, a swallow + -INE.]

his (hĭz). The possessive form of the pronoun *he.* Used to indicate possession, agency, or reception of an action by the masculine being or person spoken of or an unspecified person considered to be male: **1.** Used attributively: *his wallet; pursuing his tasks; suffered his first rebuff. Each child should be accompanied by his mother.* **2.** Used absolutely: **a.** As a predicate adjective: *The black boots are his.* **b.** As a substantive: *If you can't find your hat, take his.* **—of his.** Belonging or pertaining to him: *a friend of his.* [Middle English *his,* Old English *his.*]

His·pan·ic (hĭ-spăn′ĭk) *adj.* **1.** Of, pertaining to, or characteristic of the language, people, and culture of Spain or Spain and Portugal. **2.** Of or pertaining to Latin America.
~*n.* A Latin American, especially one who has emigrated to the United States. [Latin *Hispānicus,* from *Hispānia,* SPAIN.]

his·pan·i·cist (hĭ-spăn′ə-sĭst) *n.* A student of or specialist in the language, culture, or literature of Spain.

his·pan·i·cize (hĭ-spăn′ə-sīz′) *tr.v.* **-cized, -cizing, -cizes.** To give a Spanish character to.

His·pan·io·la (hĭs′pən-yō′lə). Second-largest island of the West Indies. Lying between Cuba and Puerto Rico, it is divided into French-speaking Haiti to the west and the Spanish-speaking Dominican Republic to the east.

Hispano– *prefix.* Indicates: **1.** Spanish; for example, **Hispano-Arabian. 2.** Latin-American; for example, **Hispano-American.** [From Latin *Hispānus,* Spanish.]

his·pid (hĭs′pĭd) *adj.* Covered with stiff or rough hairs; bristly: *hispid stems.* [Latin *hispidus.*]

hiss (hĭs) *n.* **1.** A sharp, sibilant sound similar to a sustained *s,* such as that produced by breathing out through closed teeth or by gas escaping through a small gap. **2.** An expression of disapproval, contempt, or dissatisfaction conveyed by a hiss. **3.** Continuous unwanted noise, as from a loudspeaker.
~*v.* **hissed, hissing, hisses.** —*intr.* To make a hiss, especially as an expression of disapproval. —*tr.* **1.** To utter (words or sounds) with a hissing sound. **2.** To express disapproval, derision, or hatred for by hissing. [Middle English *hissen* (imitative).] **—hiss·er** *n.*

Hiss (hĭs), **Alger** (1904–). U.S. public official. Charged with espionage at the height of the Communist scare, he was convicted of perjury (1950) and served a four-year jail sentence while maintaining his innocence. His conviction remains a point of emotional debate and controversy.

hist (hĭst) *interj.* Used to attract attention, enjoin silence, or the like.

hist. 1. histology. **2.** historian; historical; history.

his·tam·i·nase (hĭ-stăm′ə-nās′, -naz′, hĭs′tə-mə-) *n.* An enzyme that occurs in the digestive system and is responsible for the inactivation of histamine. [HISTAMIN(E) + -ASE.]

his·ta·mine (hĭs′tə-mēn′, -mĭn) *n.* A white crystalline compound, $C_5H_9N_3$, found in plant and animal tissue, formed from histidine by the action of putrefactive bacteria. It stimulates gastric secretion, contracts smooth muscle, and is released during allergic reactions. [HIST(O)- + -AMINE.] **—his·ta·min·ic** (hĭs′tə-mĭn′ĭk) *adj.*

his·ti·dine (hĭs′tə-dēn′, -dĭn) *n.* A colorless crystalline amino acid, $C_6H_9N_3O_2$, used as a feed additive and dietary supplement. [HIST(O)- + -ID(E) + -INE.]

his·ti·o·cyte (hĭs′tē-ə-sīt′) *n.* A **macrophage** *(see)* found in connective tissue. [Greek *histion,* diminutive of *histos,* web + -CYTE.]

histo–, hist– *prefix.* Indicates bodily tissue; for example, **histamine, histolysis.** [Greek *histos,* web, beam, mast.]

his·to·chem·is·try (hĭs′tō-kĕm′ĭ-strē) *n.* The chemistry of cells and tissues. **—his·to·chem·i·cal** *adj.*

his·to·com·pat·i·bil·i·ty (hĭs′tō-kəm-păt′ə-bĭl′ə-tē) *n.* Compatibility between the various components of tissues, especially components of cell membranes, required for survival of tissue or organ transplants.

his·to·gen (hĭs′tə-jən′) *n.* Any of the parts of a plant that give rise to the epidermis, cortex, and vascular tissue. [HISTO- + -GEN.]

his·to·gen·e·sis (hĭs′tō-jĕn′ə-sĭs) *n.* The formation and development of bodily tissues. [New Latin : HISTO- + -GENESIS.] **—his·to·ge·net·ic** (hĭs′tō-jə-nĕt′ĭk), **his·to·gen·ic** (-jĕn′ĭk) *adj.* **—his·to·ge·net·i·cal·ly, his·to·gen·i·cal·ly** *adv.*

his·to·gram (hĭs′tə-grăm′) *n. Statistics.* A graphic representation of

hippodrome *A chariot race taking place in a hippodrome. The Roman relief is probably first century* A.D.

hippopotamus *Despite its massive weight—more than three tons—and short legs, a hippo can run faster than a man. Its favorite habitat, however, is water, where it lies partly submerged with only its eyes, ears, and nostrils projecting above the surface.*

PRONUNCIATION KEY

ă, pat; ā, pay; âr, care;
ä, father, are; b, bib;
ch, church; d, deed; ĕ, pet;
ē, be; f, fife; g, gag; h, hat;
hw, which; ĭ, pit; ī, pie;
îr, pier; j, judge; k, kick;
l, lid, needle; m, mum;
n, no, sudden; ng, thing;
ŏ, pot; ō, toe; ô, paw, for;
oi, noise; ou, out; o͝o, book;
o͞o, boot; p, pop; r, roar;
s, sauce; sh, ship, dish;
t, tight; th, thin, path;
th, this, bathe; ŭ, cut; ûr, fur;
v, valve; w, with; y, yes;
z, zebra, size; zh, vision;
ə, about, item, edible, gallop, circus, peaceful

IN FOREIGN WORDS:

à, *Fr.* ami; œ, *Fr.* feu, *Ger.* schön; ü, *Fr.* tu, *Ger.* über; KH, *Ger.* ich, *Scot.* loch; N, *Fr.* bon; y′, *Fr.* Compiègne

STRESS MARKS:

Primary stress: ′
in·cite′ (ĭn-sīt′)
Secondary stress: ′
in′sight′ (ĭn′sīt′)

a frequency distribution in which the widths of contiguous vertical bars are proportional to the class widths of the variable and the heights of the bars are proportional to the class frequencies. [Greek *histos,* beam, mast + -GRAM.]

his·toid (hĭs′toid′) *adj.* **1.** Resembling normal tissue. Said of some tumors. **2.** Consisting of one particular kind of tissue. [HISTO(O)- + -OID.]

his·tol·o·gy (hĭ-stŏl′ə-jē) *n. Abbr.* **hist.** **1.** The anatomical study of the microscopic structure of animal and plant tissues. **2.** The microscopic structure of tissue. [French *histologie* : HISTO- + -LOGY.] **—his·to·log·i·cal** (hĭs′tə-lŏj′ĭ-kəl) *adj.* **—his·to·log·i·cal·ly** *adv.* **—his·tol·o·gist** *n.*

his·tol·y·sis (hĭ-stŏl′ə-sĭs) *n.* The breakdown and disintegration of organic tissue. [New Latin : HISTO- + -LYSIS.] **—his·to·lyt·ic** (hĭs′tə-lĭt′ĭk) *adj.* **—his·to·lyt·i·cal·ly** *adv.*

his·tone (hĭs′tōn′) *n.* Any of several simple, water-soluble proteins, found especially in cell nuclei associated with nucleic acids, that can release on hydrolysis a high proportion of basic amino acids. [HIST(O)- + -ONE.]

his·to·pa·thol·o·gy (hĭs′tō-pə-thŏl′ə-jē) *n.* The histology of diseased tissue. **—his·to·path·o·log·i·cal** (hĭs′tō-păth′ə-lŏj′ĭ-kəl) *adj.*

his·to·phys·i·ol·o·gy (hĭs′tō-fĭz′ē-ŏl′ə-jē) *n.* The physiology of the microscopic functioning of bodily tissues. **—his·to·phys·i·o·log·i·cal** (hĭs′tō-fĭz′ē-ə-lŏj′ĭ-kəl) *adj.*

his·to·plas·mo·sis (hĭs′tō-plăz-mō′sĭs) *n.* A disease affecting the lungs that is caused by inhalation of spores of the fungus *Histoplasma capsulatum.*

his·to·ri·an (hĭ-stôr′ē-ən, hĭ-stōr′-) *n. Abbr.* **hist.** A writer or student of history; especially, one who is an authority on history.

his·to·ri·at·ed (hĭ-stôr′ē-ā′tĭd, hĭ-stōr′-) *adj.* Decorated with artistic designs: *a historiated initial.* [Medieval Latin *historiāre* (past participle *historiātus*), to tell a story in pictures, from *historia,* HISTORY.]

his·tor·ic (hĭ-stôr′ĭk, hĭ-stŏr′-) *adj.* **1. a.** Having importance in or influence on history; renowned. **b.** Likely to become important in history; having considerable contemporary significance: *a historic meeting.* **2. a.** Historical. **b.** Associated with events in history: *historic cities.* **3.** Of or designating tenses of verbs, especially in Latin or Greek, that refer to past time.

Usage: *Historic* and *historical* are differentiated in usage, although their senses overlap. *Historic* refers to what is important in history: *the historic first voyage to outer space.* It is also used of what is famous or interesting because of its association with persons or events in history: *a historic house. Historical* refers to whatever existed in the past, whether regarded as important or not: *a historical character.* Events are *historical* if they happened, *historic* only if they are regarded as important. *Historical* refers also to anything concerned with history or the study of the past: *a historical novel; historical discoveries.* The differentiation between the words is not complete. They are often used interchangeably: *historic times* or *historical times.*

his·tor·i·cal (hĭ-stôr′ĭ-kəl, hĭ-stŏr′-) *adj. Abbr.* **hist.** **1.** Of, relating to, or of the nature of history as opposed to fiction or legend. **2. a.** Based on or concerned with events in history: *a historical novel.* **b.** Caused by events in history. **3.** Having considerable importance or influence in history; historic. **4.** *Linguistics.* **Diachronic** *(see).* —See Usage note at **historic.** **—his·tor·i·cal·ly** *adv.* **—his·tor·i·cal·ness** *n.*

historical geology *n.* The geologic study of the earth and its atmosphere from the time of its formation to the present day.

historical linguistics *pl.n.* The study of language development, especially that of a single variety, with emphasis on chronological change. Compare **comparative linguistics.**

historical materialism *n.* The Marxist theory, part of **dialectical materialism** *(see),* that states that society arises fundamentally from an economic base, and that it is characterized by a conflict of classes that will eventually result in a classless society.

historical method *n.* A method of analysis or exposition whereby a subject is considered in its origin and subsequent historical development.

historical present *n.* The present tense used as a literary device in the narration of events set in the past.

historical school *n.* A school of theorists, as in law or economics, stressing the influence of historical conditions.

his·tor·i·cism (hĭ-stôr′ə-sĭz′əm, hĭ-stŏr′-) *n.* **1.** The belief that inevitable processes are at work in history. **2.** The relativistic theory that all social and cultural phenomena are historically determined and that particular past events, cultures, or the like should be judged only in relation to other periods of history rather than in relation to one's own values. **3.** Veneration of the past or of tradition. **—his·tor·i·cist** *adj. & n.*

his·to·ric·i·ty (hĭs′tə-rĭs′ə-tē) *n.* Historical authenticity.

his·to·ri·og·ra·pher (hĭ-stôr′ē-ŏg′rə-fər, hĭ-stōr′-) *n.* **1.** One trained in or practicing historiography. **2.** A historian; especially, one officially appointed by a group or public institution.

his·to·ri·og·ra·phy (hĭ-stôr′ē-ŏg′rə-fē, hĭ-stōr′-) *n.* **1.** The principles or methodology of historical study. **2.** The writing of history. **3.** Historical literature. [Old French *historiographie,* from Greek *historiographia* : HISTORY + -GRAPHY.]

his·to·ry (hĭs′tə-rē) *n., pl.* **-ries.** **1.** *Abbr.* **hist.** The branch of knowledge that records and analyzes past events. Sometimes used adjectivally: *a history book.* **2.** A chronological record of events, as of the life or development of a people, country, or institution. **3.** *Abbr.* **hist.** A narrative of events; a story; a chronicle. **4.** The events forming the subject matter of history. **5.** An interesting past: *a house with a history.* **6.** That which is not of current concern: *My youth is now history.* **7.** A drama based on historical events. **8. a.** A study or record of what has happened to a person or thing, especially from a particular point of view: *a patient's medical history.* **b.** A past or record marked by a particular characteristic: *has a history of violence.* **—make history.** To be of historic importance, especially by being the first of one's kind. [Latin *historia,* from Greek, inquiry, observation, from *histōr,* learned man.]

his·tri·on·ic (hĭs′trē-ŏn′ĭk) *adj.* Also **his·tri·on·i·cal** (-ĭ-kəl). **1.** Overemotional or dramatic; theatrical; affected. **2.** Of or pertaining to actors or acting. [Late Latin *histriōnicus,* theatrical, from *histriō*†, actor.] **—his·tri·on·i·cal·ly** *adv.*

his·tri·on·ics (hĭs′trē-ŏn′ĭks) *n.* **1.** *Used with a singular verb.* Theatrical arts. **2.** *Used with a plural verb.* Exaggerated emotional behavior calculated for effect.

hit (hĭt) *v.* **hit, hitting, hits.** *—tr.* **1.** To come in contact with forcefully; strike. **2.** To cause to make sudden and forceful contact; knock; bump: *hit her hand against the wall.* **3.** To deal a blow to. **4.** To strike with a missile: *He fired and hit the target.* **5.** To reach and affect adversely: *hit hard by the recession.* **6.** To come upon; arrive at; reach: *hit an all-time low.* **7.** To accord with; appeal to; suit: *The idea hit his fancy.* **8.** To propel with a blow. **9. a.** To make (a shot or stroke) when striking a ball in a game: *hit a volley.* **b.** *Baseball.* To succeed in getting (a base hit): *hit a triple.* **10.** *Informal.* To set out on or toward: *hit the road.* **11.** *Informal.* To resort to excessively: *hit the bottle.* **12.** *Informal.* To request or obtain money from: *The vagrant hit me for a dime. —intr.* **1. a.** To strike or deal a blow. Often used with *out.* **b.** *Informal.* To criticize or condemn. Used with *at* or *out at.* **2.** To come in contact; bump. **3.** To achieve or find something desired or sought, often by chance. Used with *on* or *upon.* **—hit it off.** *Informal.* To get along well together. **—hit the hay** (or **sack**). *Slang.* To go to bed. **—hit the nail on the head.** To be absolutely right. **—hit the roof** (or **ceiling**). To express anger, especially vehemently. **—hit the spot.** To give total satisfaction, as food or drink.

~n. **1.** A collision or impact. **2.** A successfully executed shot, blow, thrust, or throw. **3.** A show, song, performer, or the like that has popular success. Also used adjectivally: *a hit musical.* **4.** A bit of luck. **5.** An apt or effective jest, remark, or witticism. **6.** *Abbr.* **h, h.** *Baseball.* A base hit. **7.** *Slang.* **a.** A killing by a hit man. **b.** The target of such a killing. **8.** *Slang.* A dose of a narcotic drug. [Hit (infinitive, past tense, and past participle); Middle English *hitten, hitte, hit,* from Old Norse *hitta*†, to hit.] **—hit·ter** *n.*

hit-and-run (hĭt′n-rŭn′) *adj.* **1.** Designating or involving the driver of a motor vehicle who after striking a pedestrian or another vehicle fails to stop. **2.** *Baseball.* Of or designating a play in which a man on base runs on the pitch and the batter attempts to hit the ball.

hitch (hĭch) *v.* **hitched, hitching, hitches.** *—tr.* **1.** To fasten or catch temporarily with a loop, hook, or noose; tie. **2.** To connect or attach, as to a vehicle. Often used with *up.* **3.** To move with jerks: *hitched his chair closer.* **4.** To raise by pulling or jerking. Often used with *up: hitch up one's trousers.* **5.** *Informal.* To obtain (a lift) by hitchhiking. **6.** *Slang.* To unite in marriage. Used chiefly in the phrase *get hitched. —intr.* **1.** To become entangled, snarled, or fastened. **2.** *Informal.* To hitchhike. **3.** To move haltingly, as with a limp. **4.** *Slang.* To become united in marriage.

~n. **1.** Any of various knots used for attaching a rope to a fixed object, such as a **harness hitch** or **half hitch** *(both of which see).* **2.** A short jerking motion; a tug. **3.** A hobble or limp. **4.** An impediment or delay: *a hitch in our plans for the party.* **5.** *Informal.* A lift obtained by hitchhiking. **6.** A term of service, especially of military service. [Middle English *hytchen*†.]

Hitch·cock (hĭch′kŏk′), **Alfred Joseph** (1899–1980). U.S. film director, born in London. He became a master of suspense. His first important film was *The 39 Steps* (1935). Other successes include *The Lady Vanishes* (1938), *Psycho* (1960), and *Family Plot* (1976).

hitch·hike (hĭch′hīk′) *v.* **-hiked, -hiking, -hikes.** *—intr.* To travel by soliciting free lifts along a road. *—tr.* To solicit or get (a free lift) along a road. **—hitch·hik·er** *n.*

hitching post *n.* A post for temporarily tying up a horse or other animal.

hith·er (hĭth′ər) *adv.* To or toward this place: *Come hither.*

~adj. Located toward this side; nearer. [Middle English *hither,* Old English *hider.*]

hither and thither *adv.* Toward one place and then another as if in a state of turmoil; in all directions. Also "hither and yon."

hith·er·to (hĭth′ər-tōō′) *adv.* **1.** Until this time; up to now. **2.** *Archaic.* To this place; thus far.

hith·er·ward (hĭth′ər-wərd) *adv.* Also **hith·er·wards** (-wərdz). Hither.

Hit·ler (hĭt′lər), **Adolf** (1889–1945). Austrian-born founder of the German Nazi Party and chancellor of the Third Reich (1933–45). Hitler served in the German army in World War I. He joined the German Workers' Party and by 1921 had gained the leadership of it, renaming it the National Socialist German Workers' Party. Hitler was arrested after the "beer hall putsch" in Munich in 1923 and spent some months in prison, where he wrote the major part of *Mein Kampf.* By 1930 he had built the Nazi Party into the second-largest party in Germany. He lost the 1932 presidential election to Hindenburg, but a few months later the Nazis won most seats at a general election, and in January 1933 Hitler was appointed chancellor, bringing every German institution under the totalitarian con-

PRONUNCIATION KEY

ă, pat; ā, pay; âr, care;
ä, father, are; b, bib;
ch, church; d, deed; ĕ, pet;
ē, be; f, fife; g, gag; h, hat;
hw, which; ĭ, pit; ī, pie;
îr, pier; j, judge; k, kick;
l, lid, needle; m, mum;
n, no, sudden; ng, thing;
ŏ, pot; ō, toe; ô, paw, for;
oi, noise; ou, out; ŏŏ, book;
ōō, boot; p, pop; r, roar;
s, sauce; sh, ship, dish;
t, tight; th, thin, path;
th, this, bathe; ŭ, cut; ûr, fur;
v, valve; w, with; y, yes;
z, zebra, size; zh, vision;
ə, about, item, edible,
gallop, circus, peaceful

IN FOREIGN WORDS:

à, *Fr.* ami; œ, *Fr.* feu, *Ger.* schön; ü, *Fr.* tu, *Ger.* über; KH, *Ger.* ich, *Scot.* loch; N, *Fr.* bon; y′, *Fr.* Compiègne

STRESS MARKS:

Primary stress: ′
in·cite′ (ĭn-sīt′)
Secondary stress: ′
in′sight′ (ĭn′sīt′)

trol of the Nazi Party. In September 1939 Hitler's troops invaded Poland, causing the outbreak of World War II. By the spring of 1945 Germany faced defeat. On April 29 Hitler married his mistress, Eva Braun, and the next day they committed suicide.

hit list *n. Slang.* **1.** A list of potential murder victims as drawn up by a crime syndicate. **2.** A list of people or organizations against which some punitive action is to be taken. **3.** A list of projects, enterprises, or the like, from which support is to be withdrawn.

hit man *n. Slang.* One employed to commit murder; a hired assassin.

hit parade *n.* A list of the best-selling recorded songs over a given period.

hit-or-miss (hĭt′ər-mĭs′) *adj.* Random; haphazard; only occasionally effective.

Hit·tite (hĭt′īt′) *n.* **1.** A member of an ancient people living in Asia Minor and northern Syria about 2000–1200 B.C. **2.** An extinct Indo-European language spoken by these people. [Hebrew *Ḥittī,* from Hittite *Ḥatti.*] —**Hit·tite** *adj.*

hive (hīv) *n.* **1.** A natural or artificial structure for housing bees, especially honeybees. **2.** A colony of bees living in a hive. **3.** A place swarming with active people. ~*v.* **hived, hiv·ing, hives.** —*tr.* **1.** To collect (bees) into a hive. **2.** To store (honey) in a hive. **3.** To store up; accumulate. Used with *up* or *away.* —*intr.* **1.** To enter a hive. **2.** To live together in close association. —**hive off. 1.** To leave in a large group, like bees forming a new hive. **2.** To assign or transfer (work or responsibilities, for example) elsewhere. **3.** *Chiefly British.* To dispose of (part of a nationalized company, for example) on the open market. [Middle English *hive,* Old English *hȳf.*]

hives (hīvz) *pl.n. Pathology.* **Urticaria** *(see).* [Origin unknown.]

H.J. hic jacet.

hl hectoliter.

H.L. House of Lords.

hm hectometer.

H.M. **1.** headmaster. **2.** headmistress. **3.** His (or Her) Majesty.

H.M.S. **1.** His (or Her) Majesty's Service. **2.** Her (or His) Majesty's Ship.

ho (hō) *interj.* Used to express surprise or joy, to attract attention to something sighted, or to urge onward: *Land ho! Westward ho!* [Middle English, partly from Old Norse *hō!* and partly from Old French *ho!,* halt!]

Ho The symbol for the element holmium.

HO, H.O. **1.** Head Office. **2.** *British.* Home Office.

ho. house.

hoactzin. Variant of **hoatzin.**

hoa·gie (hō′gē) *n.* See **hero** (sense 5).

hoar (hôr, hōr) *adj.* Hoary. ~*n.* **1.** Hoariness. **2.** Hoarfrost. [Middle English *ho(o)r,* Old English *hār.*]

hoard (hôrd, hōrd) *n.* **1.** A hidden or stored fund or supply guarded for future use. **2.** A cache, as of ancient coins or jewels; a treasure. **3.** An accumulated store, as of facts or ideas. ~*v.* **hoarded, hoarding, hoards.** —*intr.* **1.** To gather or accumulate a hoard. **2.** To buy an unnecessarily large stock, as of groceries, as a precaution against shortages. —*tr.* **1.** To accumulate or gather by saving or hiding. **2.** To keep an unnecessarily large stock of (goods) as a precaution against shortages. [Middle English *hord,* Old English *hord.*]

hoard·er (hôr′dər, hōr′-) *n.* One that hoards; especially, a person who never throws anything away.

hoard·ing (hôr′dĭng, hōr′-) *n. British.* **1.** A temporary wooden fence around a building or structure under construction or repair. **2.** A billboard *(see).* [Earlier *hoard,* a fence, from earlier *hourd,* from Norman French *hurdis,* from Old French *hourd,* scaffold, from Germanic.]

hoar·frost (hôr′frôst′, -frŏst′, hōr′-) *n.* Frozen dew that forms a white coating on a surface. Also called "hoar," "white frost."

hoarhound. Variant of **horehound.**

hoarse (hôrs, hōrs) *adj.* **hoarser, hoarsest. 1.** Low and grating in sound; husky; croaking. **2.** Having a husky, grating voice, often as a result of shouting or illness. [Middle English *hors,* from Old Norse *hārs* (unattested), variant of *hās,* from Germanic *hai(r)sa-* (unattested).] —**hoarse·ly** *adv.* —**hoarse·ness** *n.*

hoars·en (hôr′sən, hōr′-) *v.* **-ened, -ening, -ens.** —*tr.* To cause to be hoarse. —*intr.* To become hoarse.

hoar·y (hôr′ē, hōr′ē) *adj.* **-ier, -iest. 1.** Gray or white with or as if with age. **2.** Covered with grayish hair or down: *hoary leaves.* **3.** Very old; ancient. —**hoar·i·ness** *n.*

hoary cress *n.* A white-flowered perennial plant, *Cardaria* (or *Lepidium*) *draba,* native to the Mediterranean but widespread as a weed.

ho·at·zin (hō-ăt′sĭn, wät-sēn′) *n.* Also **ho·act·zin** (hō-ăkt′sĭn, wäkt′sēn′). A brownish, crested bird, *Opisthocomus hoazin,* of tropical South America, having claws on the wings in the young. [American Spanish, from Nahuatl *uatzin,* pheasant.]

hoax (hōks) *n.* An act intended to deceive or trick, either as a practical joke or as a serious fraud. ~*tr.v.* **hoaxed, hoaxing, hoaxes.** To deceive or trick with a hoax. [Perhaps shortened variant of HOCUS.] —**hoax·er** *n.*

hob[1] (hŏb) *n.* **1.** A shelf or projection at the back or side of the inside of a fireplace, for holding things to be kept warm. **2.** A rotating tool used for cutting machine parts, such as gear teeth. [16th century : perhaps a variant of HUB (in the sense projection, lump).]

hob[2] *n.* A hobgoblin, sprite, or elf. —**play** (or **raise**) **hob.** To make mischief or trouble. Often used with *with.* [Middle English *hob,* from *Hobbe,* a nickname for *Robert* or *Robin.*]

Ho·ba meteorite (hō′bə) *n.* The world's largest meteorite (weighing 66 tons) discovered in 1920 near Grootfontein, Namibia. [From *Hoba West* farm, site of discovery.]

Ho·ban (hō′bən), **James** (*c.* 1762–1831). U.S. architect, born in Ireland. In 1792 he won a competition for the design of "the President's House" (today the White House), which he built from 1792 to 1799 and rebuilt after it was burned by the British in 1814. He was also one of the supervising architects for the U.S. Capitol.

Ho·bart (hō′bärt′). Capital and chief seaport of Tasmania, Australia. Built on a bight approximately 19 kilometers (12 miles) from the sea, it has an excellent natural harbor. Included among its exports are agricultural produce, timber, and wool. Its principal industries are zinc refining, flour milling, and chemicals.

Hobbes (hŏbz), **Thomas** (1588–1679). English political philosopher. He wrote *Leviathan* (1651), outlining his philosophy that individuals are essentially selfish.

Hobb·ism (hŏb′ĭz′əm) *n.* A theory promulgated by Thomas Hobbes, advocating powerful, especially monarchical government as the only means of adequately controlling the problems created by competing individual needs and interests.

hob·bit (hŏb′ĭt) *n.* Any of a race of fictional creatures, half the size of human beings. [After the characters in J.R.R. Tolkien's *The Hobbit* (1937) and *The Lord of the Rings* (1954–55).]

hob·ble (hŏb′əl) *v.* **-bled, -bling, -bles.** Also **hop·ple** (hŏp′əl), **-pled, -pling, -ples.** —*intr.* **1.** To walk or move awkwardly or with difficulty; limp. **2.** To proceed haltingly or unsteadily. —*tr.* **1.** To put a hobble on (an animal or its legs). **2.** To cause to limp. **3.** To hamper the action or progress of; restrain; impede. ~*n.* Also **hop·ple. 1.** An awkward, clumsy, or irregular walk or gait. **2.** A device, such as a rope or strap, used to tie the legs of an animal together in order to restrict its movement. **3.** *Archaic.* An unfortunate or awkward situation. [Middle English *hobble,* of Low German origin, akin to Middle Dutch *hobbelen†,* to roll.]

hob·ble·bush (hŏb′əl-boosh′) *n.* A shrub, *Viburnum alnifolium,* of northeastern North America, having flat clusters of white flowers with the marginal flowers larger than the others. [From HOBBLE, because of the hindrance caused by its drooping branches.]

hob·ble·de·hoy (hŏb′əl-dē-hoi′) *n., pl.* **-hoys.** A gawky adolescent boy or girl. [16th century : origin obscure.]

hobble skirt *n.* A type of long skirt, popular between 1910 and 1914, that was so narrow below the knees that it restricted normal stride.

hob·by[1] (hŏb′ē) *n., pl.* **-bies. 1.** An occupation, activity, or interest, such as stamp collecting or gardening, engaged in primarily for pleasure; a pastime. **2.** *Regional.* A little horse; a nag. **3.** A hobbyhorse. **4.** An early kind of velocipede without pedals. [Middle English *hoby,* a hobbyhorse, something one pursues, perhaps from *Hobbin,* nickname for *Robin.*] —**hob·by·ist** *n.*

hob·by[2] *n., pl.* **-bies.** Any of several small falcons of the genus *Falco;* especially, an Old World species, *F. subbuteo,* formerly used for hawking. [Middle English *hoby,* from Old French *hobé, hobet,* diminutive of *hobet†,* a small bird of prey.]

hob·by·horse (hŏb′ē-hôrs′) *n.* **1.** A child's toy consisting of a long stick with an imitation horse's head on one end. **2.** A rocking horse. **3. a.** A figure of a horse worn around the waist of a mummer or other performer pretending to ride a horse. **b.** A person wearing such a costume. **4.** An early form of bicycle; velocipede. **5.** A pet topic or idea about which one constantly talks; a subject that obsesses one.

hob·gob·lin (hŏb′gŏb′lĭn) *n.* **1.** A goblin variously represented as being mischievous or as ugly and evil. **2.** A bugbear. [HOB (elf) + GOBLIN.]

hob·nail (hŏb′nāl′) *n.* A short nail with a thick head used to protect the soles of shoes or boots. [HOB (projection, archaic sense peg) + NAIL.]

hob·nob (hŏb′nŏb′) *intr.v.* **-nobbed, -nobbing, -nobs.** To associate familiarly; socialize. Used with *with: He hobnobs with the rich.* [Originally *hob or nob,* (drink) to one another, from earlier *hab or nab,* hit or miss : perhaps Middle English *habbe,* present subjunctive of *habben,* to HAVE + *nabbe,* from *ne habble,* not to have.]

ho·bo (hō′bō) *n., pl.* **-boes** or **-bos. 1.** A tramp; a vagrant. **2.** A migratory, usually unskilled worker. ~*intr.v.* **hoboed, -boing, -boes.** To live or wander about like a hobo. [19th century : origin obscure.] —**ho·bo·ism** *n.*

Hob·son-Job·son (hŏb′sən-jŏb′sən) *n.* The phonetic alteration of a word from another language into the sounds of an existing word in the language, as *compound,* "buildings enclosed by a barrier," from Malay *kampong.* [Anglo-Indian coinage, itself a Hobson-Jobson alteration (influenced by *Hobson* and *Jobson,* English surnames) of Arabic *yā Ḥasan, yā Ḥusayn!* O Hasan, O Husain! (ritual cry of mourning for Hasan and Husain, Muhammad's grandsons who were killed in battle).]

Hob·son's choice *n.* The option of accepting that which is offered or nothing; a choice with no real alternative. [After Thomas *Hobson* (died 1631), Cambridge, England, liveryman who required his customers to choose the next available horse.]

Ho Chi Minh (hō′ chē′ mĭn′), born Nguyen That Tanh (1890–1969). Founder and first president of North Vietnam (1954–69). After studying in Moscow, he founded the Indochinese Communist Party (1930) and returned to Vietnam to establish the Vietminh as a force

hobby *This member of the falcon family—which is found in Europe, Asia, and tropical Africa—is a spectacular flier. Capable of gliding upside-down and of looping the loop, it is fast enough to catch a dragonfly, a bat, or a swift in midair, and it will sometimes pluck and eat its kill on the wing.*

struggling for independence against French rule. In 1945, after Japan's surrender in World War II, he and his followers seized Hanoi, declaring independence. Forced to withdraw (1946), he led a jungle war that culminated in victory at Dien Bien Phu (1954). The Geneva Agreement that year established the new state of North Vietnam. Ho Chi Minh supported Vietcong guerrillas in the south, but died before the reunification of Vietnam.

Ho Chi Minh City. Formerly (until 1975) **Sai·gon** (sī-gŏn′). A port in southern Vietnam. On the Saigon River near the Mekong delta, it was successively the capital of Cochin China, French Indochina, and South Vietnam. The presence of U.S. forces during the Vietnamese War (1961–75) caused much social decay, exacerbated by their withdrawal and the republic's subsequent defeat.

hock¹ (hŏk) n. **1.** The tarsal joint of the hind leg of a horse or similar animal, corresponding to the human ankle. Also called "hough." **2.** A similar joint in the leg of a domestic fowl.
~*tr.v.* **hocked, hocking, hocks.** To disable by cutting the tendons of the hock; hamstring. [Middle English *hoch*, Old English *hōh*, heel.]

hock² n. *Chiefly British.* **1.** Any of several white wines from the Rhine valley. **2.** Any of various white wines similar to German hock. [Short for obsolete *hockamore*, from German *Hochheimer (Wein)*, wine of *Hochheim*, West Germany.]

hock³ *tr.v.* **hocked, hocking, hocks.** *Informal.* To pawn.
~*n.* *Informal.* The state of being pawned. —**in hock.** *Informal.* In debt. [From Dutch *hok†*, prison.]

hock·ey (hŏk′ē) n. **1.** A game played on a field in which two opposing teams of 11 players, using curved sticks, try to drive a ball into the opponents' goal. Also called "field hockey." **2. Ice hockey** *(see)*. [16th century : origin obscure.]

hockey stick n. A stick with one curved end, used in hockey.

Hock·ney (hŏk′nē), **David** (1937–). British artist. He developed a distinct style of fine figure drawing and also produced stage designs.

hock·shop (hŏk′shŏp′) n. *Informal.* A pawnshop.

ho·cus (hō′kəs) *tr.v.* **-cused** or **-cussed, -cusing** or **-cussing, -cuses** or **-cusses. 1.** To fool or deceive; hoax; cheat. **2.** To stupefy, as with a drug. **3.** To adulterate (food or drink) with a drug. [Short for HOCUS-POCUS.]

ho·cus-po·cus (hō′kəs-pō′kəs) n. **1.** Nonsense words or phrases used as a formula by conjurers. **2.** A trick performed by a magician

or juggler; sleight of hand. **3.** Any deception or chicanery. **4.** Any words or jargon used to mystify.
~*v.* **hocus-pocused** or **-cussed, -cusing** or **-cussing, -cuses** or **-cusses.** —*tr.* To deceive; fool; cheat. —*intr.* To be deceptive. [17th century : mock Latin.]

hod (hŏd) n. **1.** An open container carried on a pole over the shoulder for transporting loads. **2.** A coal scuttle. [Perhaps variant of earlier dialectal *hot*, from Old French *hotte*, from Germanic.]

hodge·podge (hŏj′pŏj′) n. A mixture of dissimilar ingredients; jumble. [Middle English *hochepot*, from Old French. See **hotchpot.**]

Hodg·kin (hŏj′kĭn), **Thomas** (1798–1866). British doctor. In 1832 he identified the disease of lymphatic tissues since called Hodgkin's disease.

Hodgkin's disease n. A usually chronic, progressive, malignant disease marked by enlargement of the lymph nodes, spleen, and often of the liver and kidneys and occurring approximately twice as often in adult males as females. [After Thomas HODGKIN.]

hod·o·scope (hŏd′ə-skōp′) n. *Physics.* Any of various devices for indicating the paths of high-energy particles, used especially for investigating cosmic rays. [From Greek *hodos*, path, way + -SCOPE.]

hoe (hō) n. **1.** A tool with a flat blade attached at an angle to a long handle, used for weeding and breaking up the soil. **2.** A farming tool with a blade set at right angles to a short handle, used with a hacking action for digging.
~*v.* **hoed, hoeing, hoes.** —*tr.* To weed, cultivate, or dig up with a hoe. —*intr.* To work with a hoe. [Middle English *howe*, from Old French *houe*, from Frankish *hauwa* (unattested).] —**ho·er** n.

hoe·cake (hō′kāk′) n. A thin cake made of cornmeal. [It was sometimes baked on the blade of a hoe.]

hoe·down (hō′doun′) n. **1.** A boisterous dance; especially, a square dance. **2.** The music for a hoe-down. **3.** A party at which hoe-downs are danced. [HOE + DOWN.]

Hoek Van Holland. See Hook of Holland.

Hof·fa (hôf′ə), **James Riddle,** called "Jimmy" (1913–75?). U.S. labor leader. An aggressive labor organizer, he became president of the teamsters (1957) and threatened to organize all transportation workers into one union. He was convicted of misdealings (1964) and after several appeals was jailed (1967–71). In 1975 he was abducted from a Detroit restaurant and presumably was murdered.

Hoff·man (hôf′mən, hôf′-), **Dustin** (1937–). U.S. film actor, star of *The Graduate* (1967), *Midnight Cowboy* (1969), and *Straw Dogs* (1971). His performance in *Kramer vs. Kramer* (1979) won him an Academy Award.

Hof·manns·thal (hôf′məns-täl′, hôf′-), **Hugo von** (1874–1929). Austrian author. A poet, essayist, and dramatist, he established his reputation with lyric poems and equally beautiful plays, including *Yesterday* (1891) and *Death and the Fool* (1893).

hog (hôg, hŏg) n. Also **hogg** (for sense 4). **1.** A domesticated pig; especially, a castrated male pig weighing over 120 pounds. **2.** Any of various other mammals of the family Suidae, such as the boar or the wart hog. **3.** A self-indulgent, gluttonous, or vulgar person. **4.** *British.* A young sheep before its first shearing. —**go hog wild.** To react in an excited, immoderate, or irrational manner.
~*v.* **hogged, hogging, hogs.** —*tr.* **1.** To keep or take more than one's share of. **2.** To cause (the back) to arch. **3.** To cut off (a horse's mane). —*intr.* To arch upward in the middle. Used of a ship's keel. [Middle English *hogge*, Old English *hogg*, from Celtic.]

ho·gan (hō′gän′, -gən) n. An earth-covered Navaho dwelling. [Navajo *hogan*.]

Ho·gan (hō′gən), **William Benjamin,** known as "Ben" (1912–). U.S. golfer. He won the U.S. Open championship in 1948, 1950, 1951, and 1953, the P.G.A. championship in 1948, and the British Open in 1953.

Ho·garth (hō′gärth′), **William** (1697–1764). British painter and engraver. In 1729 he started on *A Harlot's Progress*, a series of allegorical paintings. Other series included *A Rake's Progress* (1733) and *Marriage-à-la-Mode* (1745). His satirical paintings attacked the contradiction of luxury and squalor in society.

hog·back (hôg′băk′, hŏg′-) n. Also **hog's back.** A sharp ridge with steeply sloping sides, produced by the erosion of the broken edges of highly tilted strata.

hog cholera n. A highly infectious, often fatal viral disease of swine that is characterized by fever, diarrhea, and exhaustion. Also called "swine fever."

hog·fish (hôg′fĭsh′, hŏg′-) n., pl. **-fishes** or collectively **hogfish. 1.** A colorful fish, *Lachnolaimus maximus*, of warm Atlantic waters, having a long snout in the adult male. **2.** Any of several similar or related fishes, such as the **pigfish** *(see)*.

Hogg (hôg, hŏg), **James** (1770–1835). Scottish poet. Originally a shepherd, he was discovered by Sir Walter Scott. His verse included *The Queen's Wake* (1813), and his prose *The Confessions of a Justified Sinner* (1824).

hog·gish (hô′gĭsh, hŏg′ĭsh) adj. **1.** Coarsely self-indulgent or gluttonous. **2.** Filthy. —**hog·gish·ly** adv. —**hog·gish·ness** n.

Hog·ma·nay (hŏg′mə-nā′) n. *Chiefly Scottish.* New Year's Eve. [17th century (Scottish) : perhaps from Norman French *Hoguinané*, Old French *aguillanneuf†*.]

hog·nose snake (hôg′nōz′, hŏg′-) n. Also **hog·nosed snake** (-nōzd′). Any of several thick-bodied, nonvenomous North American snakes of the genus *Heterodon*, having an upturned snout.

hogs·head (hôgz′hĕd′, hŏgz′-) n. Abbr. **hhd 1.** Any of various units of volume or capacity ranging from 62.5 to 140 gallons; especially,

Hockney

a unit of capacity used in liquid measure in the United States, equal to 63 gallons (approximately 239 liters). **2.** A large barrel or cask with the capacity to hold a hogshead. [Middle English, "hog's head" (the reason for the name is obscure).]

hog-tie, hog·tie (hôg′tī′, hŏg′-) *tr.v.* **-tied, -tying** or **-tieing, -ties. 1.** To tie together the legs of. **2.** To impede or disrupt in movement or action.

hog·wash (hôg′wôsh′, hŏg′wŏsh′) *n.* **1.** Worthless, false, or ridiculous speech or writing. **2.** Garbage fed to hog; swill.

hog·weed (hôg′wēd′, hŏg′-) *n.* Any of various coarse, weedy plants.

Ho·hen·stau·fen (hō′ən-shtou′fən). Family of German rulers of the Holy Roman Empire (1138–1208, 1212–54), stemming from **Frederick** (died 1105) and his two sons, **Frederick II** (died 1147) and **Conrad** (1093–1152), who later became the German king and Holy Roman emperor (1138) and ruled until his death.

Ho·hen·zol·lern (ho′ən-zŏl′ərn, -tsô′lərn). A German royal family. It supplied the electors of Brandenburg from 1415, later extending control to Prussia (1618). Under Frederick I (reigned 1701–13) the Hohenzollerns' possessions were unified as the kingdom of Prussia. From 1871 to 1918 Hohenzollern monarchs ruled the German empire.

ho hum *interj.* Used to express a feeling of weariness, boredom, or dissatisfaction.

hoick (hoik) *tr.v.* **hoicked, hoicking, hoicks.** *Chiefly British.* To lift or bring up with a jerk. [Perhaps a variant of HIKE.]

hoi pol·loi (hoi′ pə-loi′) *n. Used with a plural verb.* The common people viewed from a position of social, economic, or intellectual advantage or privilege; the masses. Preceded by *the.* [Greek *hoi polloi,* the many, the masses : *hoi,* plural of *ho,* the + *polloi,* plural of *polus,* many.]

hoist (hoist) *tr.v.* **hoisted, hoisting, hoists.** To raise or haul up, particularly with the help of a mechanical apparatus. —See Synonyms at **lift.**

∼*n.* **1.** An apparatus for lifting heavy or cumbersome objects. **2.** An act of hoisting. **3.** *Nautical.* **a.** The height or vertical dimension of a flag or of any square sail other than a course. **b.** A group of flags raised together as a signal. **c.** The inner edge of a flag, nearest to the pole. [Variant of dialectal *hoise,* from earlier *heise;* akin to Dutch *hijsen,* Low German *hissen*†.] **—hoist·er** *n.*

hoi·ty-toi·ty (hoi′tē-toi′tē) *adj.* Also **high·ty-tigh·ty** (hī′tē-tī′tē). **1. a.** Haughtily petulant. **b.** Pretentiously snobbish. **2.** Lightheaded; flighty.

∼*n., pl.* **hoity-toities.** Also **high·ty-tigh·ty,** *pl.* **-ties 1.** Pretentious snobbery. **2.** Giddy behavior; flightiness. [Reduplication of *hoity,* from dialectal *hoit*†, to romp.]

hoke (hōk) *tr.v.* **hoked, hoking, hokes.** *Slang.* To give an artificial, false, or misleading quality to. [From HOKUM.]

hok·ey (hō′kē) *adj.* **-ier, -iest.** *Slang.* **1.** Corny; trite. **2.** Artificial; phony. **—hok·i·ly** *adv.* **—hok·i·ness** *n.*

ho·key-po·key (hō′kē-pō′kē) *n.* **1.** Hocus-pocus; chicanery. **2.** Inferior or cheap ice cream formerly sold by street venders.

Ho·kin·son (hō′kĭn-sən), **Helen Elna** (1893–1949). U.S. cartoonist. In more than 1,700 cartoons, she depicted middle-aged, usually nonplused women in stereotypical settings, such as garden-club meetings and choir practice. Published primarily in the *New Yorker,* her works were popular even among those she lampooned.

Hok·kai·do (hŏ-kī′dō). Northernmost of the four major islands that constitute Japan. It is the second largest of the islands, but the least populated. It was called Yezo until the Meiji restoration of 1868, when it was given its present name, which means "land of the northern sea." The interior of the island is largely mountainous and heavily forested and is rich in coal and iron. The northern part of the island is virtually uninhabited; the major cities, Sapporo, Hakodate, and Otaru, are all on the island's southwestern peninsula.

Hok·kien (hŏk-yĕn′) *n.* A dialect of Chinese spoken in Fujian province and also widely spoken in Taiwan and by people of Chinese origin in Southeast Asia.

hok·ku (hô′ko͞o) *n.* A Japanese poem, a **haiku** *(see).*

ho·kum (hō′kəm) *n.* **1.** Nonsense; bunk. **2.** Sentimental or clichéd material used in a play or movie as a means of obtaining a predictable audience response. [20th century : origin obscure.]

Ho·ku·sai (hō′ko͞o-sī′, hŏ′ko͞o-sī′) (1760–1849). Japanese artist. A master printmaker with unmatched technique, he captured both the serenity and the power of nature in his landscapes and historical scenes, such as *Thirty-six Views of Mt. Fuji* (1826–33).

hol–. Variant of **holo-.**

Hol·arc·tic (hō-lärk′tĭk, -lär′tĭk, hŏ-) *adj.* Of or designating the zoogeographic region that includes the northern areas of the earth and is divided into Nearctic and Palearctic regions. [HOL(O)- + ARCTIC.]

Hol·bein (hōl′bīn′), **Hans,** known as "Holbein the Younger" (*c.* 1497–1543). German painter. The son and pupil of **Hans Holbein the Elder** (*c.* 1465–1524), he worked in Basel and visited England in 1526. From *c.* 1536 he was court painter to Henry VIII. Holbein is noted for his portraits.

hold¹ (hōld) *v.* **held** (hĕld), **held** or *archaic* **holden** (hōl′dən), **holding, holds.** —*tr.* **1.** To have and keep, as in the hands, arms, or teeth; grasp; clasp. **2.** To support; keep up; bear: *This nail is too small to hold that mirror.* **3. a.** To maintain in a certain position or relationship; keep: *held his assailant at arm's length.* **b.** To maintain (oneself) in a specified posture or condition: *hold oneself erect.* **c.** To maintain in a steady or unchanged state: *hold prices down.* **4. a.** To contain; be filled by: *The jar holds one pint.* **b.** To accommodate; seat: *The church holds 500.* **5.** To keep or have (property, assets, or the like) in one's possession; own. **6. a.** To have or maintain for use; wield: *hold an advantage.* **b.** To have gained: *hold a certificate.* **7.** To maintain control over; restrain: *The dam held the flood waters. Hold your tongue!* **8. a.** To retain the attention or interest of: *She held the audience with her eyes.* **b.** To retain (a person's attention). **9. a.** To defend from attack; preserve: *hold the fort.* **b.** To keep despite a challenge: *held her seat at the last election.* **10. a.** To keep under restraint or in confinement: *held in custody.* **b.** To detain or delay: *Try to hold him until the police arrive.* **c.** To prevent from making further gains: *held to a draw.* **11.** To have the position of; occupy: *He holds the office of commander.* **12.** *Law.* **a.** To be the legal possessor of. **b.** To make (a person) fulfill the terms of a contract. Used with *to.* **c.** To adjudge or decree. **13.** To cause to fulfill an agreement or promise; bind: *They held him to his word.* **14. a.** To keep in one's mind or heart; harbor: *hold a grudge.* **b.** To regard in a specified manner: *hold her in contempt.* **15. a.** To have as an opinion or belief: *hold extreme views.* **b.** To assert; affirm: *hold that his hypotheses are incorrect.* **16.** To cause to take place; put on: *The race was held last month. Let's hold a party.* **17.** To assemble; convene: *held a meeting of the board.* **18.** To set aside; not sell or allocate: *The shop is holding the shoes until tomorrow.* **19.** To consume (alcohol) without noticeable effects: *He can't hold his liquor.* **20.** *Music.* To sustain (a note). **21.** *Computer Science.* To keep (data) on a storage device although it has been copied onto another location or another storage device. **22.** To keep (a telephone line) open. —*intr.* **1.** To maintain a grasp, clutch, or grip. **2. a.** To maintain a desired or accustomed position or condition: *Hold still!* **b.** To last; remain unchanged: *This weather won't hold.* **3.** To adhere closely; keep: *They held to a southwesterly course.* **4.** To stand up under stress, pressure, or opposition; last: *The platform will never hold under your weight.* **5.** To be valid, applicable, or true: *His theory still holds. The rule holds for all of us.* **6.** To wait while on the telephone; not hang up. —See Synonyms at **contain.** **—hold down. 1.** To keep in check; restrain; suppress. **2.** To work at and keep (a job). **—hold forth.** To talk at length; lecture. **—hold in.** To keep back, check, or suppress (an impulse or emotion, for example). **—hold it. 1.** To stop or wait. Usually used in the imperative. **2.** To maintain a position or pose; freeze. Used in the imperative. **—hold off. 1.** To prevent from reaching; keep at some distance: *hold off the enemy.* **2.** To defer or delay doing something; put off: *hold off buying a car until the spring.* **—hold on. 1.** To maintain one's grip; cling. **2.** To keep at; continue. **3.** To stop or wait for someone or something. **—hold one's own. 1.** To maintain one's ground or position; not falter. **2.** To prove oneself adequate or competent; be good enough. **—hold out. 1.** To present; offer. **2.** To last; stand up; endure. **3.** To refuse to surrender or give up; continue resisting. **—hold out for.** To insist upon or wait for, accepting no compromises. **—hold out on.** *Informal.* To refuse to give or divulge something expected or deserved. **—hold to.** To keep true or steadfast to; remain loyal or faithful to. **—hold together. 1.** To remain or cause to remain coherent or in one piece. **2.** To wear well or last a long time: *The old bike has held together well.* **—hold water.** To stand up under examination; be believable, valid, or tenable. **—hold with. 1.** To agree with. **2.** To be on the side of; support. **3.** To approve of; subscribe to.

∼*n.* **1.** The act or a means of grasping; a grip; a clasp. **2.** A means of obtaining, retaining, or controlling something. **3.** Something held onto, as for support. **4.** A device that grips something so as to keep it in place. **5.** A strong psychological influence or power: *He seems to have a hold over her.* **6.** A means of influencing the behavior of a person, as through knowing discreditable information: *Finding the letter give him a hold on me.* **7.** A prison cell. **8.** *Archaic.* A fortified place; a stronghold. **9.** *Music.* **a.** The sustaining of a note longer than its indicated time value. **b.** The symbol designating this pause; a fermata. **10.** A temporary halt or pause: *There was a hold in the countdown.* **11.** A manner of gripping an opponent in wrestling: *a neck hold.* **—get hold of. 1.** To obtain. **2.** To establish contact with. **—no holds barred.** Without any restrictions; all methods allowed, regardless of fairness. [Hold, held, held, holden; Middle English *holden, heold, haldan, holden,* Old English *healdan, hēold, healden.*]

hold² *n.* **1.** *Nautical.* The interior of a ship below decks where cargo is stored. **2.** The place in an aircraft where the cargo is put. [Variant (influenced by HOLD) of Middle English *hole,* HOLE.]

hold·all (hōld′ôl′) *n.* A case or bag for carrying miscellaneous items, as when traveling.

hold back *tr.v.* **1.** To curb; restrain. **2.** To save for future use; keep apart or aside; retain. —*intr.v.* To refrain.

hold·back (hōld′băk′) *n.* A strap or iron placed between the shaft and the harness on a drawn wagon, allowing the horse to stop or back up.

hold·en. *Archaic.* Past participle of **hold** (to grasp).

hold·er (hōl′dər) *n.* **1.** A person who holds, possesses, or occupies something. Often used in combination: *a landholder; a shareholder.* **2.** A device for holding something. **3.** *Law.* One who legally possesses and is entitled to the payment of a check, bill, or promissory note.

hold·fast (hōld′făst′, -fäst′) *n.* **1.** Any of various devices used to fasten something securely. **2.** *Biology.* An organ or structure of attachment; especially, the **hapteron** *(see)* of certain seaweeds.

hold·ing (hōl′dĭng) *n.* **1.** Land rented or leased from another. **2.** *Of-*

PRONUNCIATION KEY

ă, pat; ā, pay; âr, care;
ä, father, are; b, bib;
ch, church; d, deed; ĕ, pet;
ē, be; f, fife; g, gag; h, hat;
hw, which; ĭ, pit; ī, pie;
îr, pier; j, judge; k, kick;
l, lid, needle; m, mum;
n, no, sudden; ng, thing;
ŏ, pot; ō, toe; ô, paw, for;
oi, noise; ou, out; o͝o, book;
o͞o, boot; p, pop; r, roar;
s, sauce; sh, ship, dish;
t, tight; th, thin, path;
th, this, bathe; ŭ, cut; ûr, fur;
v, valve; w, with; y, yes;
z, zebra, size; zh, vision;
ə, about, item, edible,
gallop, circus, peaceful

IN FOREIGN WORDS:

à, *Fr.* ami; œ, *Fr.* feu, *Ger.* schön; ü, *Fr.* tu, *Ger.* über; KH, *Ger.* ich, *Scot.* loch; N, *Fr.* bon; y′, *Fr.* Compiègne

STRESS MARKS:

Primary stress: ′
in·cite′ (ĭn-sīt′)
Secondary stress: ′
in′sight′ (ĭn′sīt′)

holm oak *Oaks are among the largest and most long-lived trees of European woodlands. The giant Major Oak in England's Sherwood Forest, said to have been used as a meeting place by the legendary outlaw Robin Hood, is 1,000 years old—damaged, but still alive. Common oaks are deciduous, but the holm oak,* Quercus ilex *(above), is an evergreen.*

ten **holdings.** Legally possessed property, such as land, capital, or stocks.

holding company *n.* A company having partial or complete control of other companies.

holding operation *n.* A procedure intended only to keep a situation under control and prevent any deterioration.

holding pattern *n.* **1.** A fixed, usually circular pattern flown by an airplane awaiting clearance to land at an airport. **2.** A condition of waiting or delay.

hold over *tr.v.* **1.** To delay taking action or making a decision on. **2.** To postpone. **3.** To continue longer than expected: *hold over a movie for another week.* **4.** To use as a threat or for blackmail: *You can't hold my past over me like that.*

hold·o·ver (hōld'ō'vər) *n.* Someone or something that is held over, as an elected official kept in office after his term is over or an entertainer or entertainment continued beyond the original period of engagement.

hold up *tr.v.* **1.** To present; show: *Her work was held up as an example to all.* **2.** To hinder or interrupt; delay. **3.** To rob. *—intr.v.* To last; stand up; endure.

hold·up (hōld'up') *n.* **1.** A suspension of activity; a delay; an interruption. **2.** A robbery; especially, an armed robbery.

hole (hōl) *n.* **1.** A cavity in a solid. **2.** An opening or perforation through something; a gap; an aperture: *a hole in the clouds.* **3. a.** A deep place in water. **b.** A small, deep pond. **c.** A small bay; a cove. **4.** An animal's hollowed-out habitation, such as a burrow: *a rabbit hole.* **5.** *Informal.* An ugly, squalid, or depressing place or dwelling. **6.** A deep or isolated place of confinement; a dungeon. **7.** A fault or flaw; an error: *picked holes in the prosecution's argument.* **8.** *Informal.* A bad situation from which it seems difficult to extract oneself; a predicament. **9.** *Golf.* **a.** The small pit lined with a cup into which the ball must be hit. **b.** One of the 9 or 18 divisions of a golf course, from tee to cup. **10.** *Electronics.* A vacant electron energy state that is manifested as a charge defect in a crystalline solid, the defect behaving as a positive charge carrier with charge magnitude equal to that of the electron. **—hole in one.** *Golf.* The driving of the ball from the tee into the hole in only one stroke. **—in the hole.** *Informal.* In debt. **—make a hole in.** To use up a substantial amount of: *The trip made a big hole in my bank balance.*
~v. **holed, holing, holes.** *—tr.* **1.** To put a hole or holes in; puncture; perforate. **2.** To put, propel, or drive into a hole. *—intr.* To make a hole or holes. **—hole out.** *Golf.* To hit one's ball into the hole. **—hole up.** **1.** To hibernate in or as if in a hole. **2.** To shut oneself up, especially in cramped quarters: *They were all holed up in that tiny shack.* [Middle English *hol(e),* hole, ship's hold, Old English *hol,* hollow place.] **—hole·y** *adj.*
Synonyms: *cavity, excavation, hollow, pit, pocket.*

hole-and-cor·ner (hōl'ən-kôr'nər) *adj. Informal.* Underhand; furtive: *hole-and-corner whispering.*

hole in the heart *n.* A congenital defect in which there is an opening between the right and left sides of the heart so that a proportion of the blood is not pumped to the lungs.

hole-in-the-wall (hōl'ĭn-*thə*-wôl') *n., pl.* **holes-in-the-wall.** A small, squalid, or out-of-the-way place. **—hole-in-the-wall** *adj.*

-holic, -aholic, -oholic *suffix.* Indicates addiction to or compulsive need or desire for; for example, **workaholic.** [Back-formation from *alcoholic.*]

hol·i·day (hŏl'ə-dā') *n.* **1.** A day on which custom or the law dictates a halting of general business activity to commemorate or celebrate a particular event. **2.** A religious feast day; a holy day. **3.** A day free from work that one may spend at leisure; a day off. **4.** *Often* **holidays.** *Chiefly British.* A period of time during which one is free from work, studies, or one's usual activities; vacation. **5.** A period of time spent away from home for recreation, as in a resort.
~adj. Of, suitable for, or characteristic of a holiday: *a holiday mood.*
~intr.v. **holidayed, -daying, -days.** *Chiefly British.* To take a holiday: *holidaying in the Bahamas.* [Middle English *holiday,* Old English *hāligdæg* : *hālig,* HOLY + *dæg,* DAY.]

Hol·i·day (hŏl'ə-dā'), **Billie,** original name Eleanora, known as "Lady Day" (1915–59). U.S. singer. With no formal music training, she blended her great natural ability and her experience of economic and social hardship into a sincere, individual, and moving jazz and blues singing career. Her autobiography, *Lady Sings the Blues* (1956), was also a successful motion picture (1972).

hol·i·day·mak·er (hŏl'ə-dā'mā'kər) *n. Chiefly British.* A person who is or is about to be on holiday; vacationer.

ho·li·er-than-thou (hō'lē-ər-*thən-thou'*) *adj.* Showing an attitude of superior virtue; self-righteously pious.

ho·li·ness (hō'lē-nĭs) *n.* **1.** The state or quality of being holy; sanctity. **2. Holiness.** A title or form of address for various high ecclesiastical dignitaries, especially the pope. Preceded by *His* or *Your.*

Hol·ins·hed (hŏl'ĭnz-hĕd', -ĭn-shĕd'), **Raphael** (died *c.* 1580). Also **Hol·lings·head** (-ĭngz-hĕd'). English chronicler. His *Chronicles* (1578), a history of England, Scotland and Ireland, form a valuable source of historical information, which was extensively used by Shakespeare and other Elizabethan dramatists.

ho·lism (hō'lĭz'əm) *n.* The theory that reality is made up of organic or unified wholes that are greater than the simple sum of their parts. [HOL(O)- + -ISM.] **—ho·list** *n.*

ho·lis·tic (hō-lĭs'tĭk) *adj.* **1.** Of or pertaining to holism. **2. a.** Emphasizing the importance of the whole and the interdependence of its parts. **b.** Concerned with entire systems rather than subdivisions or specialties: *holistic medicine; holistic ecology.* **—ho·lis·ti·cal·ly** *adv.*

hol·land (hŏl'ənd) *n.* A sturdy linen fabric used especially for upholstery. [After HOLLAND, where it was made.]

Holland. See **Netherlands.**

hol·lan·daise sauce (hŏl'ən-dāz', hŏl'ən-dāz') *n.* A creamy sauce of butter, egg yolks, and lemon or vinegar, served especially with fish or vegetables. [Translation of French *sauce Hollandaise,* Dutch sauce, from *Hollandaise,* feminine of *Hollandais,* Dutch, from *Hollande,* HOLLAND.]

Hol·land·er (hŏl'ən-dər) *n.* A native or inhabitant of the Netherlands; Dutchman.

Hol·lands (hŏl'əndz) *n.* A type of gin made in the Netherlands. Also called "Holland gin." [Dutch *Hollandsch,* from *hollandsch genever,* Dutch gin.]

hol·ler (hol'ər) *v.* **-lered, -lering, -lers.** *—intr.* **1.** To yell or shout; cry out; call. **2.** *Informal.* To complain loudly. *—tr.* To yell or shout (an utterance).
~n. A yell or shout; a loud call. [Originally a dialectal variant of HOLLO.]

Hol·ler·ith (hŏl'ə-rĭth') *n.* A code used for recording alphanumeric information on punch cards. Also called "Hollerith code." [After Herman *Hollerith* (1860–1929), U.S. inventor.]

Hollingshead, Raphael. See **Holinshead.**

hol·lo, hol·loa (hŏ-lō', hə-lō') *interj.* Used as a shout to catch a person's attention.
~n., pl. **hollos.** Also **hol·loa,** *pl.* **holloas.** A cry for attention.
~intr.v. **holloed, -loing, -los.** Also **hol·loa, -loaed, -loaing, -loas.** To shout; call out. [French *holà,* "ho there!"]

hol·low (hŏl'ō) *adj.* **-lower, -lowest.** **1.** Having a cavity, gap, or space within: *a hollow wall.* **2.** Being indented or concave; having depths or inclines: *hollow land.* **3.** Deeply recessed; sunken; fallen: *hollow cheeks.* **4.** Without substance or character; empty; superficial: *a hollow person.* **5.** Not genuine or real; specious: *hollow victories.* **6.** Having a reverberating sound; echoing: *hollow footsteps.* **7.** Cynical; false: *hollow laughter.* **8.** Hungry or unsatisfied.
~n. **1.** A cavity, gap, or space within something: *the hollow behind a wall.* **2.** An indented or concave surface or area; a shallow pocket: *the hollow of one's hand.* **3.** A valley or depression. —See Synonyms at **hole.**
~adv. Outright; thoroughly: *I was beaten hollow at chess.*
~v. **hollowed, -lowing, -lows.** *—tr.* **1.** To make hollow. Used with *out*: *hollow out a pumpkin.* **2.** To scoop or form by making hollow. Used with *out*: *hollow out a nest in the sand.* *—intr.* To become hollow. [Middle English *hol(e)we,* from *holh,* hole, Old English *holh,* hole, hollow place.] **—hol·low·ly** *adv.* **—hol·low·ness** *n.*

hol·low·ware (hŏl'ō-wâr') *n.* Serving pieces, especially of silver, such as bowls, jugs, and the like. Compare **flatware.**

hol·ly (hŏl'ē) *n., pl.* **-lies.** **1. a.** Any of numerous trees or shrubs of the genus *Ilex,* such as *I. opaca,* of eastern North America, or *I. aquifolium,* of Eurasia, often having bright-red berries and glossy, evergreen leaves with spiny margins. **b.** Branches or leaves of holly, traditionally used for Christmas decoration. **2.** Any of various similar or related plants. [Middle English *holi(n),* Old English *holen,* probably of Germanic origin.]

hol·ly·hock (hŏl'ē-hŏk') *n.* A tall plant, *Althaea rosea,* native to China and widely cultivated for its showy spikes of large, variously colored flowers. [Middle English *holihoc* : *holi,* HOLY + *hoc,* a mallow, Old English *hoc*†.]

Hol·ly·wood[1] (hŏl'ē-wo͝od'). District of the city of Los Angeles, California. It has been the center of the U.S. film industry since before World War I. The Hollywood Bowl, a vast outdoor theater, is located in the foothills of the Santa Monica Mts.

Hollywood[2] *n.* The U.S. motion-picture industry or the somewhat meretriciously glamorous atmosphere often attributed to it.

Hollywood bed *n.* A mattress on a box spring supported by a metal frame or attached low legs.

holm (hōm, hōlm) *n. British.* **1.** An island in a river. **2.** Low land near a stream. [Middle English *holm,* from Old Norse *holmr,* islet, meadow.]

Holmes (hōmz, hōlmz), **Oliver Wendell** (1809–94). U.S. author. A professor of anatomy and physiology at Harvard (1847–82), he wrote humorous conversational pieces, including *The Autocrat of the Breakfast Table* (1858).

Holmes, Oliver Wendell, Jr. (1841–1935). U.S. jurist; Supreme Court justice (1902–32). One of the most influential justices in Supreme Court history, he combined his legal scholarship, philosophical mind, and fine literary style to form and express opinions that have shaped and changed the American concept of law.

hol·mic (hŏl'mĭk) *adj.* Pertaining to or containing holmium.

hol·mi·um (hŏl'mē-əm) *n. Symbol* **Ho** A relatively soft, malleable, stable rare-earth element occurring in gadolinite, monazite, and other rare-earth minerals. Atomic number 67, atomic weight 164.930, melting point 1,461°C, boiling point 2,600°C, specific gravity 8.803, valence 3. [From New Latin *Holmia,* Latinized form of Stockholm, Sweden.]

holm oak (hōm, hōlm) *n.* A tree, *Quercus ilex,* native to the Mediterranean region, having prickly evergreen leaves. Also called "holly oak," "ilex." [Middle English, variant of *holin,* HOLLY.]

holo-, hol- *prefix.* Indicates whole, entire, or entirely; for example, **holoblastic, Holarctic.** [Greek *holos,* whole, entire.]

hol·o·blas·tic (hŏl'ō-blăs'tĭk, hō'lō-) *adj.* Exhibiting or denoting cleavage in which the entire egg separates into individual blastomeres. Compare **meroblastic.** [HOLO- + -BLAST + -IC.]

hol·o·caust (hŏl′ə-kôst′, hō′lə-) n. **1.** Great or total destruction by fire; a conflagration. **2. a.** Any widespread, horrific destruction of human life. **b.** *Often* **Holocaust.** The mass killings of Jews by the Nazi regime during World War II. **3.** A sacrificial offering that is consumed entirely by flames; a burnt offering. —See Synonyms at **disaster.** [Middle English, from Old French *holocauste,* from Latin *holocaustum,* from Greek *holokauston,* from *holokaustos,* burnt whole : *holo-,* whole + *kaustos,* variant of *kautos,* burnt, from *kaein,* to burn.] —**hol·o·caus·tal** (hŏl′ə-kô′stəl, hō′lə-), **hol·o·caus·tic** (hŏl′ə-kô′stĭk, hō′lə-) *adj.*

Hol·o·cene (hŏl′ə-sēn′, hō′lə-) *adj. Geology.* Of, belonging to, or designating the geologic time or the rock system of the more recent of the two epochs of the Quaternary period, extending from the end of the Pleistocene to the present. ~*n. Geology.* The Holocene epoch or system of deposits. Preceded by *the.* Also called "Recent." [HOLO- + -CENE.]

hol·o·crine (hŏl′ə-krĭn, -krēn′, -krīn′, hō′lə-) *adj.* Pertaining to or designating a gland whose secretion is formed by the degeneration of the gland's cells, as sebaceous glands. Compare **merocrine.** [HOLO- + Greek *krinein,* to separate, divide.]

hol·o·en·zyme (hŏl′ō-ĕn′zīm′, hō′lō-) *n.* An enzyme in its active form, consisting of an apoenzyme and a coenzyme.

hol·o·gram (hŏl′ə-grăm′, hō′lə-) *n.* **1.** The pattern produced on a photosensitive medium that has been exposed by holography and then photographically developed. **2.** The photosensitive medium so exposed and so developed. Also called "holograph." [HOLO- + -GRAM.]

hol·o·graph (hŏl′ə-grăf′, -gräf′, hō′lə-) *n.* **1.** A document written wholly in the handwriting of the person whose signature it bears. **2.** A hologram. ~*tr.v.* **holographed, -graphing, -graphs. 1.** To produce an image of (a physical object) by holography. **2.** To form a hologram of (a physical object). [Late Latin *holographus,* entirely written by the signer, from Greek *holographos,* written in full : *holo-,* whole + -GRAPH.] —**hol·o·graph·ic** (hŏl′ə-grăf′ĭk, hō′lə-), **hol·o·graph·i·cal** (-ĭ-kəl) *adj.* —**hol·o·graph·i·cal·ly** *adv.*

ho·log·ra·phy (hō-lŏg′rə-fē, hə-) *n.* The technique of producing a three-dimensional image of an object by recording the wave pattern of light reflected from the object, especially by using lasers to record on a photographic plate the diffraction pattern from which a three-dimensional image can be projected. [HOLO- + -GRAPHY.] See feature, next page.

hol·o·he·dral (hŏl′ō-hē′drəl, hō′lə-) *adj.* Having as many planes as required for complete symmetry in a given crystal system. [HOLO- + -HEDRAL.]

ho·lo·me·tab·o·lism (hō′lō-mə-tăb′ə-lĭz′əm, hŏl′ō-) *n.* Complete metamorphosis of a developing insect. —**ho·lo·me·tab·o·lous** *adj.*

hol·o·phras·tic (hŏl′ə-frăs′tĭk, hō′lə-) *adj. Linguistics.* Expressing a set of ideas by means of a single word. [HOLO- + Greek *phrastikos,* indicative, expressive, from *phrazein,* to show.]

hol·o·phytic (hŏl′ō-fĭt′ĭk, hō′lō-) *adj.* Designating organisms, such as green plants, that manufacture their food by photosynthesis; autotrophic. [HOLO- + -PHYTIC.]

hol·o·plank·ton (hŏl′ō-plăngk′tən, hō′lō-) *n.* Microorganisms that are constituents of plankton for all stages of their life cycle.

hol·o·thu·ri·an (hŏl′ō-thŏŏr′ē-ən, hō′lō-) *n.* Any of various echinoderms of the class Holothuroidea, which includes the sea cucumbers. [New Latin *Holothuria* (genus), from Latin *holothūria,* water polyp, from Greek *holothourion†.*] —**hol·o·thu·ri·an** *adj.*

hol·o·type (hŏl′ə-tīp′, hō′lə-) *n.* The single specimen used as the basis of the original published description of a taxonomic species. Also called "type specimen." [HOLO- + TYPE.] —**hol·o·typ·ic** (hŏl′ə-tĭp′ĭk, hō′lə-) *adj.*

hol·o·zo·ic (hŏl′ō-zō′ĭk, hō′lō-) *adj.* Obtaining nourishment by the ingestion of organic material, as do animals. [HOLO- + -ZOIC.]

holp. *Archaic.* Past tense of **help.**

hol·pen. *Archaic.* Past participle of **help.**

Holst (hōlst, hŏlst), **Gustav Theodore** (1874–1934). British composer, of part-Swedish descent. His best-known work is the orchestral suite *The Planets* (1914–16).

Hol·stein (hōl′stīn′) *n.* Any of a breed of large black and white dairy cattle originally developed in Friesland. Also called "Friesian," "Holstein-Friesian." [After *Holstein,* Germany.]

hol·ster (hōl′stər) *n.* **1.** A leather case shaped to hold a pistol and usually designed to be attached to a belt. **2.** A belt with loops or slots for carrying equipment such as small tools. [Dutch.] —**holstered** *adj.*

holt (hōlt) *n. Archaic.* **1.** A wood or grove; a copse. Often used in place names. **2.** A wooded hill. [Middle English *holt,* wood, Old English *holt.*]

ho·lus-bo·lus (hō′ləs-bō′ləs) *adv. Informal.* All together; all at once. [Perhaps from *whole* and *bolus.*]

ho·ly (hō′lē) *adj.* **-lier, -liest. 1.** Belonging to, associated with, or consecrated to God or a divine power; sacred. **2.** Worthy of worship or high esteem; revered: *a holy book.* **3. a.** Living according to a religious or spiritual system; devout. **b.** Having great spiritual insight or wisdom; godly: *a holy man.* **c.** Morally blameless; saintly. **4.** Intended or set apart for a religious purpose: *a holy hour.* **5.** Solemnly undertaken; sacrosanct: *a holy pledge.* **6. a.** Formally associated with or pertaining to an established or organized religion. **b.** Religious in theme, depiction, or subject: *holy paintings.* **7.** Used as an intensive, especially in exclamations: *holy mackerel!* [Middle English *holy, holi, hali,* Old English *hālig,* from Germanic;

akin to WHOLE.] —**ho·li·ly** *adv.* —**ho·li·ness** *n.*

Holy Alliance *n.* An agreement that was made by Russia, Prussia, and Austria in 1815 to govern by Christian principles.

Holy Ark *n.* The cabinet in a synagogue in which the scrolls of the Torah are kept.

Holy Bible *n.* The Bible.

Holy City *n.* **1.** Any city that is held to be sacred by a particular religion, as Jerusalem by the religions of Judaism, Christianity, and Islam. **2.** Heaven. Preceded by *the.*

Holy Communion *n. Abbr.* **H.C.** The **Eucharist** (*see*).

holy day *n.* A day set aside for a religious observance.

holy day of obligation *n. Roman Catholic Church.* A day other than a Sunday on which believers are required to attend Mass, as Christmas Day.

Holy Family *n.* The child Jesus together with Mary and Joseph. Preceded by *the.*

Holy Father *n.* One of the titles of the pope.

Holy Ghost *n.* The third person of the Christian Trinity. Also called "Holy Spirit."

Holy Grail *n.* The **Grail** (*see*).

Holy Innocents' Day *n.* December 28, a day commemorating the massacre of male infants by Herod about the birth of Jesus.

Holy Island. Also **Lin·dis·farne** (lĭn′dĭs-färn′). Island off the coast of Northumberland, in northeastern England. At low tide it is connected to the mainland. Celtic Christianity found its first home in England at the church and monastery built here by St. Aidan in 635. The Lindisfarne Gospels, also known as the Book of Durham, is an illuminated manuscript made on the island in the 7th century.

Holy Joe *n. Slang.* **1.** A pious or self-righteous person. **2.** A clergyman, especially a chaplain.

Holy Land. See **Palestine.**

Holy Office *n.* Official name, Congregation of the Holy Office. A congregation of the Roman Catholic Church that deals with such matters as the protection of the faith and morals.

holy of holies *n.* **1.** The innermost shrine of a Jewish tabernacle and temple. **2.** A place held to be especially sacrosanct. Also called "sanctum sanctorum."

holy orders *pl.n. Ecclesiastical.* **1.** *Used with a singular verb.* The sacrament or rite of ordination; the ceremony of admission into the priesthood or ministry. **2.** *Used with a plural verb.* The rank of an ordained Christian minister; clerical status. **3.** *Used with a plural verb.* Any of the grades of the ordained ministry of the Christian church, especially the priesthood and the diaconate. Also called "major orders." Compare **minor orders.**

holy place *n.* **1.** The outer chamber of the sanctuary in a Jewish temple. **2.** A place to which a pilgrimage is made.

Holy Roman Empire. *Abbr.* **H.R.E.** The loosely federated political entity of European Christendom, from the coronation of Otto I as Holy Roman emperor by the pope in 962 to the dissolution of the empire by Napoleon in 1806. The last emperor was Francis II (reigned 1792–1806). The term "Holy Roman Empire" did not come into use until several centuries after Otto's accession. From the outset the rule of the emperor was bedeviled by rivalry between the papal and the secular authority and after the 13th century by the rising ambitions of the nascent nation-states of Europe. After the election of Rudolf of Hapsburg as emperor in 1273, the imperial crown remained in Hapsburg hands, and the empire came to be little more than the Hapsburg domains, chiefly Austria and Spain.

holy rood *n.* **1.** A cross or crucifix; especially, one placed over a rood screen. **2. Holy Rood.** The cross upon which Jesus was crucified.

Holy Saturday *n.* The Saturday before Easter Sunday.

Holy Scripture *n.* The Old and New Testaments of the Bible. Also called "Holy Writ," "Scripture," "Scriptures."

Holy See *n. Roman Catholic Church.* **1.** The office or jurisdiction of the pope. **2.** The administrative officials of the Vatican.

Holy Sepulcher *n.* The tomb outside Jerusalem thought to be that of Jesus and regarded as a Christian shrine.

Holy Spirit *n.* The **Holy Ghost** (*see*).

ho·ly·stone (hō′lē-stōn′) *n.* A piece of soft sandstone used for scouring the wooden decks of a ship. ~*tr.v.* **holystoned, -stoning, -stones.** To scrub or scour with a holystone. [From its being used while kneeling.]

Holy Synod *n.* The administrative or governing body of any of the Eastern Orthodox churches.

Holy Thursday *n.* **1.** *Roman Catholic Church.* **Maundy Thursday** (*see*). **2.** *Anglican Church.* Ascension Day. See **ascension.**

holy water *n.* Water blessed by a priest and used in various ceremonies.

Holy Week *n.* The week before Easter Sunday.

Holy Writ *n.* Holy Scripture.

hom·age (hŏm′ĭj, ŏm′-) *n.* **1.** Ceremonial acknowledgment under feudal law by a vassal or tenant of allegiance to his lord. **2.** Honor or respect publicly expressed to a person or idea: *pay homage to our forefathers with this hymn.* —See Synonyms at **honor.** [Middle English, acknowledgment of a man's allegiance, from Old French, from Medieval Latin *homināticum,* from Latin *homō* (stem *homin-*), man.]

hom·bre (ŏm′brā′, -brē) *n. Slang.* A man; a fellow. [Spanish, from Latin *homō.*]

hom·burg (hŏm′bûrg′) *n.* A man's felt hat having a soft, dented crown and a shallow, slightly rolled brim. [First manufactured in *Homburg,* town near Wiesbaden, Germany.]

Holstein *All over the world Holstein are used as dairy cattle. A Holstein cow may produce as much as 9,100 liters (2,000 gallons) of milk a year.*

THREE DIMENSIONS RECORDED IN TWO BY FILM AND LASERS

A technique whose full uses are still to be explored

Holography is a process that uses film and laser light to record and project three-dimensional images.

A holographic image can be produced only by laser light, which is one color and coherent—that is, all its waves are in phase. Holography was originally conceived in 1948 but did not become practicable until the invention of the laser in 1960. The first hologram was produced in the United States in 1963.

Two laser beams are used. One is bounced off an object, reflecting the shadings that give an impression of depth. The other is a reference beam. The two meet at the film, unfocused, where they interact to produce a complex pattern that holds all the information necessary to recreate the original image. This is done by reversing the process and bathing the film in laser light. The result is a pale, single-color but three-dimen-

sional image that changes as the observer moves. By using up to three lasers and plates, up to three colors can be produced.

Holography is used in scientific research and will find further uses, but its main impact on the public so far has been at exhibitions, where it is used to demonstrate how light can create images that appear to have the depth of real objects.

PRODUCING A HOLOGRAM

1. A continuous-wave gas laser directs a narrow beam of coherent light—pure light of a single wavelength—at a beam splitter

2. The beam splitter divides the beam at right angles into an object beam and a reference beam

3. Object beam

4. A mirror redirects the object beam toward the object

5. A concave lens expands the object beam passing through it

6. The object is bathed in light from the object beam and reflects light waves in all directions. The intensity of the waves varies with the shape and the surface character of the object

7. Some of the light waves travel toward the photographic plate

8. Reference beam

9. A mirror redirects the reference beam toward the photographic plate

10. A concave lens expands the reference beam passing through it

11. The converging reference beam light waves and the light waves reflected by the object overlap to set up interference (the two sets of light waves reinforce each other when the crests of the waves coincide and cancel each other out when the crests coincide with troughs)

12. The glass photographic plate with emulsion on one side records the interference as information on the depth and dimensions of the object. The object must be kept absolutely motionless while the plate is being exposed: otherwise the information provided by the interference will be obliterated

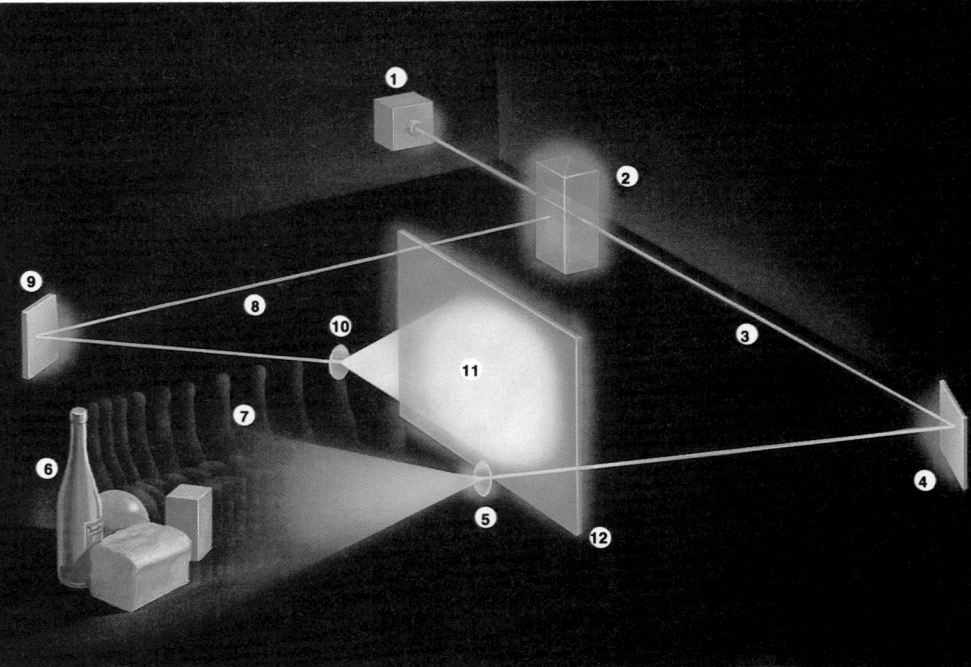

VIEWING THE IMAGE

1. After exposure, the photographic plate shows information on the recorded object as a hologram—a pattern of light and dark areas. The usual exposure time varies between one second and one minute, depending on laser power, emulsion sensitivity, and the amount of light reflected by the object

2. A source of coherent light is needed to reconstruct the hologram into an image of the object that is visible to the observer. A laser beam is directed through the plate at the same angle at which the reference beam struck it during exposure

3. A lens expands the reconstruction beam to flood the plate with light

4. An observer looking through the plate sees a three-dimensional image of the object behind it. So long as the light sources used in recording the object and in reconstructing the image are identical the image appears the same size, and at the same position and distance as the object recorded. As the observer moves from left to right around the image, its aspect alters just as that of the object would have altered

5. The three-dimensional image created by the reconstruction beam

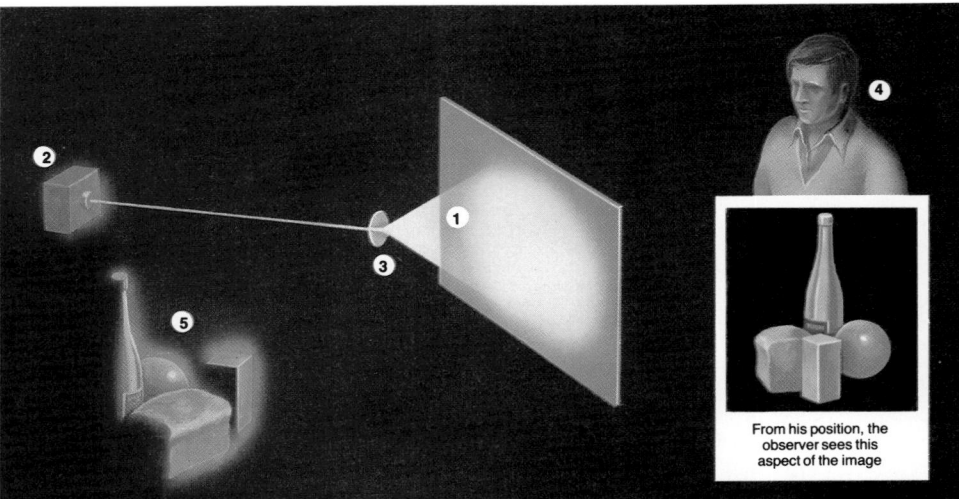

From his position, the observer sees this aspect of the image

home (hōm) *n.* **1.** A place where one lives; a residence; a habitation. **2.** The physical structure or the portion of it within which one lives, as a house or apartment. **3.** One's immediate family and its place of residence, considered as an environment to which one belongs: *house and home; didn't leave home till he was 21.* **4.** An environment or haven of shelter, happiness, or love. **5.** A place or condition valued as a refuge or place of origin. **6.** The place where one was born or spent one's early childhood, as a town, state, or country. **7.** The native habitat of a plant, animal, or the like. **8.** The place where something is discovered, founded, developed, or promoted; the source: *Boston, home of baked beans and cod.* **9.** A place where a group, such as a company or a sports team, is based or established. **10.** A goal or place of safety toward which players of a game, such as baseball, backgammon, or tag, progress. **11.** An institution providing temporary or permanent residential care, as for old people or those convalescing from illness: *a nursing home.* —**at home. 1.** In one's own house, environment, or city; not away or absent. **2.** Available to receive visitors: *a family that is home on*

Thursdays. **3.** At ease; realxed and comfortable, as if in one's own home: *a speaker who seemed completely at home on the lecture platform.* **4.** Having or feeling an easy competence and familiarity: *at home in French.* **—close to home.** So as to affect an individual or group personally: *The prime minister's speech about war economies hit close to home.*

~*adj.* **1.** Of or pertaining to a home, especially to one's household or house: *home furnishings; home cooking.* **2.** Of or pertaining to one's country, place of birth, or nation; domestic. **3.** Of or pertaining to a base of operations or headquarters: *the home office of a worldwide company.* **4.** Going straight to the point; reaching the mark directly and accurately: *a home thrust.* **5.** Taking place or based at one's own headquarters: *a home game; the home team.* ~*adv.* **1.** At, to, or toward the direction of home: *finished work and headed home.* **2.** To the point at which something is directed; on target: *The arrow struck home.* **3. a.** To the furthest possible point or extent. **b.** To the center or heart of something; deeply: *The criticism struck home.* **4.** *Nautical.* Toward a vessel. **—bring home to.** To make clear to; cause to be understood by: *cannot seem to bring it home to him how important this is.* **—come home to.** To be brought home; become clear: *The real truth finally came home to him.* **—home free.** Free of tension or stress, especially after a difficult effort: *Once we get this heavy work done, we're home free.* ~*v.* **homed, homing, homes.** —*intr.* **1.** To go or return home, especially from a distance. Used especially of birds such as pigeons. **2.** To be guided to a target automatically, as by inertial guidance or heat sensing. —*tr.* To guide (a missile or aircraft) to a target automatically. **—home in.** To move, lead, or aim toward a goal. Used with *on: home straight in on the correct answer.* [Middle English *hom(e)*, Old English *hām*, from Germanic.]

home base *n.* **1.** A base of operations; headquarters. **2.** An objective toward which players of a game progress; home. **3.** *Baseball.* The **plate** *(see).*

home·bod·y (hōm'bŏd'ē) *n., pl.* **-ies.** One who likes to stay or work at home; a domestic person.

home·bred (hōm'brĕd') *adj.* **1.** Produced, bred, or reared at home; domestic; indigenous. **2.** Not cultivated or sophisticated.

home·brew (hōm'brōō') *n.* An alcoholic beverage, especially beer, that is made at home. **—home-brewed** *adj.*

home·com·ing (hōm'kŭm'ĭng) *n.* **1.** A return to one's home or to a place where one formerly lived, worked, or studied. **2.** An annual event for visiting alumni at colleges and universities.

Home Counties. The counties of England nearest to London. Formerly the term covered Kent, Surrey, Middlesex, and Essex, but is now often used to include Buckinghamshire, Berkshire, Hertfordshire, and Sussex.

home economics *pl.n. Used with a singular verb.* The science or study of home management, including household budgets, purchase of food and clothing, child care, cooking, nutrition, and the like.

home front *n.* The civilian population of a country at war.

home·grown (hōm'grōn') *adj.* **1.** Grown or produced at home, as in one's own garden, district, or country. Said especially of fruit and vegetables. **2.** Produced or originating in one's home area: *our homegrown national hero.*

home guard *n.* **1.** A volunteer force formed to defend a homeland while the regular army is fighting elsewhere; especially, the force organized to defend Great Britain in the event of a German invasion in World War II. **2.** A member of such a force.

home·land (hōm'lănd') *n.* **1.** The land of one's allegiance; one's native land. **2.** The place of origin of a people. **3.** Any of the ten regions designated by the government of South Africa for the black population, in accordance with the policy of apartheid. Four of the homelands have already been granted self-governing status, namely, Transkei (1976), Bophuthatswana (1977), Venda (1979), and Ciskei (1980), but they have not been internationally recognized as independent states. The other homelands are Gazankulu, KaNgwane, KwaNdebele, Kwazulu, Lebowa, and Qwaqwa. In this sense, also called "Bantustan."

home·less (hōm'lĭs) *adj.* Having no home. **—home·less·ness** *n.*

home·ly (hōm'lē) *adj.* **-lier, -liest.** **1.** Of a nature associated with or suited to the home; domestic; familiar: *a homely relaxed atmosphere.* **2.** Of a simple or unpretentious nature; uncomplicated or unsophisticated; plain: *"There is a sort of homely truth and naturalness in some books"* (Thoreau). **3.** Not attractive or good-looking; plain. Said of a person. **—home·li·ness** *n.*

home·made (hōm'mād') *adj.* **1.** Made or prepared in the home or on the premises; not bought: *homemade pie; a homemade dress.* **2.** Made or assembled by oneself. **3.** Crudely or simply made: *a homemade bomb.*

home·mak·er (hōm'mā'kər) *n.* A person who manages a household or who creates a homey environment.

homeo-, homoio- *prefix.* Indicates like or similar; for example, *homeostasis, homoiotherm.* [Latin *homoeo-*, from Greek *homoio-*, from *homoios*, similar, from *homos*, same.]

Home Office *n.* A department of the British government that deals with domestic affairs, especially law and order and immigration.

Home of the Hir·sel (hyōōm; hûr'səl), **Alec Douglas-Home, Baron,** born Alexander Frederick Douglas-Home (1903–). British prime minister (1963–64). He became a Conservative M.P. in 1931. In 1951 he succeeded his father as 14th Earl of Home and subsequently became foreign secretary (1960–63). In 1963 he succeeded Harold Macmillan as prime minister, renouncing his peerage to enter the Commons. He resigned the leadership of the Conservative

Party in 1965 and again became foreign secretary (1970–74).

ho·me·o·mor·phism (hō'mē-ō-môr'fĭz'əm, hŏm'ē-) *n.* **1.** *Chemistry.* A close similarity in the crystal forms of unlike chemical compounds. **2.** *Mathematics.* A one-to-one correspondence between the points of two geometric figures that is continuous in both directions. [Greek *homoiomorph(os)*, of similar form : HOMEO- + -MORPH(OUS) + -ISM.] **—ho·me·o·mor·phous, ho·me·o·mor·phic** *adj.*

ho·me·op·a·thy (hō'mē-ŏp'ə-thē, hŏm'ē-) *n.* A system of medical treatment based on the use of minute quantities of remedies that in large doses produce effects similar to those of the disease being treated. Compare **allopathy.** [German *Homöopathie* : HOMEO- + -PATHY.] **—ho·me·o·path** (hō'mē-ə-păth', -păth', hŏm'ē-) *n.* **—ho·me·o·path·ic** (hō'mē-ə-păth'ĭk, hŏm'ē-) *adj.* **—ho·me·o·path·i·cal·ly** *adv.*

ho·me·o·sta·sis (hō'mē-ō-stā'sĭs, hŏm'ē-) *n.* A state of physiological equilibrium produced by a balance of functions and of chemical composition within an organism. [New Latin : HOMEO- + -STASIS.] **—ho·me·o·stat·ic** (hō'mē-ō-stăt'ĭk, hŏm'ē-) *adj.*

homeotherm. Variant of **homoiotherm.**

ho·me·o·typ·ic (hō'mē-ō-tĭp'ĭk, hŏm'ē-) *adj.* Relating to or designating the second nuclear division of **meiosis** *(see).* Compare **heterotypic.** [HOMEO- + TYPIC(AL).]

home plate *n.* In baseball, the **plate** *(see).*

hom·er[1] (hō'mər) *n.* **1.** A homing pigeon. **2.** *Baseball. Informal.* A home run. [From HOME.]

ho·mer[2] (hō'mər) *n.* An ancient Hebrew measure of capacity containing 10 ephahs (about 10 or 11 bushels) in dry measure or 10 baths (about 100 gallons) in liquid measure. [Hebrew *ḥomer*.]

Ho·mer (hō'mər) (8th century B.C.). Greek poet, supposed author of the epics *The Iliad* and *The Odyssey.* Both poems clearly derive from an orally transmitted tradition, describing the events of the Trojan War (*c.* 1200) and its aftermath. The epics mix fact with fantasy and embody the myths of ancient Greece.

Homer, Winslow (1836–1910). U.S. painter. Originally a magazine illustrator, he first painted rural life and Civil War battle scenes. During a trip to England (1881–82) he became fascinated with the sea, which he depicted in a series of realistic paintings such as *Eight Bells* (1886).

Ho·mer·ic (hō-mĕr'ĭk) *adj.* **1.** Of, pertaining to, or characteristic of the poet Homer, his works, or the legends and age of which he wrote. **2.** Heroic in proportion, degree, or character: *Homeric laughter.* **—Ho·mer·i·cal·ly** *adv.*

home rule *n. Abbr.* **H.R. 1.** The principle or practice of self-government in domestic matters in a dependent country or province. **2. Home Rule.** The movement in Ireland from 1870 until the 1920's to obtain self-government, the goal of the Irish Nationalists.

home run *n. Abbr.* **h.r.** *Baseball.* A hit that allows the batter to make a complete circuit of the bases and score a run.

home screen *n.* Television.

home·sick (hōm'sĭk') *adj.* Depressed by separation from one's family and home; longing for home. **—home·sick·ness** *n.*

home·spun (hōm'spŭn') *adj.* **1.** Spun or woven in the home. **2. a.** Made of a homespun fabric. **b.** Homemade. **3.** Simple and homely in character; unpretentious. ~*n.* **1.** A plain coarse woolen cloth made of homespun yarn. **2.** A similar sturdy fabric made on a power loom.

home·stead (hōm'stĕd') *n.* **1.** A house, especially a farmhouse, with adjoining buildings and land. **2.** *Law.* Property designated by a householder as his home and protected by law from forced sale to meet debts. **3.** Land claimed by a settler or a squatter, especially under the Homestead Act. **4.** The place where one's home is. **5.** *Australian & New Zealand.* The house of the owner or manager of a sheep or cattle station. ~*v.* **homesteaded, -steading, -steads.** —*intr.* To settle and farm land, especially under the Homestead Act. —*tr.* To claim and settle (land) as a homestead. **—home·stead·er** *n.*

Homestead Act *n.* An act passed by the U.S. Congress in 1862, promising ownership of a 160-acre tract of public land to a head of a family after he had cleared and improved the land and lived on it for five years.

Homestead National Monument. An area, 66 hectares (163 acres), in southeastern Nebraska, the site of the first farm claimed under the Homestead Act.

home·stretch (hōm'strĕch') *n.* **1.** The part of a racetrack from the last turn to the finish line. Also *British* "home straight." **2.** The final stages of an undertaking or journey.

home truth *n.* A fact about a person that is true but unpleasant. [From the adverbial sense of HOME, a truth that strikes home.]

home·ward (hōm'wərd) *adv.* Also **home·wards** (-wərdz). Toward home. ~*adj.* Directed toward home.

home·work (hōm'wûrk') *n.* **1.** Schoolwork that is to be done outside school hours, especially at home. **2.** Any preparatory work.

home·y, hom·y (hō'mē) *adj.* **homier, homiest.** *Informal.* Having a pleasant, homelike quality; cozy. **—hom·ey·ness** *n.*

hom·i·cid·al (hŏm'ə-sīd'l, hō'mə-) *adj.* **1.** Of or pertaining to homicide. **2.** Likely to commit homicide. **—hom·i·cid·al·ly** *adv.*

hom·i·cide (hŏm'ə-sīd', hō'mə-) *n.* **1.** The killing of one person by another. Compare **murder.** **2.** A person who kills another person. [Middle English, from Old French, from Latin *homicīda*, killer, and *homicīdium*, killing : *homō*, man + *-cīda, -cīdium*, -CIDE (killer and killing).]

hom·i·let·ic (hŏm'ə-lĕt'ĭk) *adj.* Also **hom·i·let·i·cal** (-ĭ-kəl). **1.** Per-

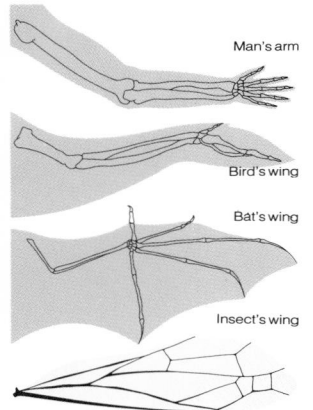

Man's arm

Bird's wing

Bat's wing

Insect's wing

homologous *The human arm is homologous with bird and bat wings because, although it serves a different function, its structure and evolutionary history are similar. Bird, bat, and insect wings are analogous because they serve the same function—flight. The insect wing, however, has a different structure from that of the bird and bat and so is not homologous with them.*

taining to or of the nature of a homily. **2.** Pertaining to homiletics. **—hom·i·let·i·cal·ly** *adv.*

hom·i·let·ics (hŏm´ə-lĕt´ĭks) *n. Used with a singular verb.* The art of preaching or writing sermons as a subject of theological study. [Greek *homilētikē*, art of conversing, from *homilētikos*, social, affable, from *homilētos*, conversation, from *homilein*, to consort with, from *homilos*, crowd. See homily.]

hom·i·ly (hŏm´ə-lē) *n., pl.* **-lies. 1.** A sermon, especially one intended to edify in a practical way rather than to expound religious doctrine. **2.** A tedious moralizing lecture or admonition. [Learned respelling of Middle English *omelie*, from Old French, from Late Latin *homīlia*, from Greek *homilia*, discourse, intercourse, association, from *homilos*, crowd : *homou*, together + *ilē†*, crowd.] **—hom·i·list** (hŏm´ə-lĭst) *n.*

hom·ing (hō´mĭng) *adj.* **1.** Of or pertaining to the ability, as of certain birds and fishes, to return home, especially from a great distance: *the homing instinct.* **2.** Assisting in guiding a missile or aircraft toward a target: *a homing guidance system.*

homing missile *n.* A missile that steers itself toward a target by means of an internal mechanism, such as a device that senses the target's heat radiation.

homing pigeon *n.* A domestic pigeon, such as one used for racing or for carrying messages, trained to return to its home roost. Also called "homer."

hom·i·nid (hŏm´ə-nĭd) *n.* Any primate of the family Hominidae, of which the human race, *Homo sapiens,* is the only extant species. ~*adj.* Of the Hominidae. [New Latin *Hominidae : Homo* (stem *homin-*), HOMO + -ID.]

hom·i·ni·za·tion (hŏm´ə-nə-zā´shən) *n.* The evolutionary development in human beings and their forebears of characteristics regarded as distinguishing humans from animals. [Latin *homō* (stem *homin-*), man + -IZ(E) + -ATION.]

hom·i·noid (hŏm´ə-noid´) *adj.* **1.** Of or belonging to the superfamily Hominoidea, which includes the apes and the human species. **2.** Resembling a human being; manlike. [New Latin *Hominoidea : Homo* (stem *homin-*), HOMO + -*oidea,* -OID.] **—hom·i·noid** *n.*

hom·i·ny (hŏm´ə-nē) *n.* Hulled and dried kernels of corn, prepared as food by boiling. [Perhaps of Algonquian origin.]

hominy grits *pl.n.* Hominy ground into a coarse white meal. Also called "grits."

ho·mo (hō´mō) *n.* Any member of the genus *Homo,* which includes one extant species, human beings. [New Latin *Homo,* from Latin *homō,* man.]

homo–, hom– *prefix.* Indicates same or like; for example, **homogamous, homodont.** [Latin, from Greek, from *homos,* same.]

   Usage: Words beginning with the prefix *homo–* are often construed by folk etymology as being derived from Latin *homo,* meaning "man." For example, *homocentric* may be felt to be synonymous with *anthropocentric.* This is an error. There is no connection between Greek *homos,* "same," and Latin *homo,* "man." If analogous words were to be formed on Latin *homo,* the form would either be *homi-,* as in *homicide,* or *homini-,* as in *hominid.*

ho·mo·cen·tric (hō´mō-sĕn´trĭk, hŏm´ō-) *adj.* Having the same center. [New Latin *homocentricus,* from Greek *homokentros : homo-,* same + *kentron,* CENTER.]

ho·mo·cer·cal (hō´mō-sûr´kəl, hŏm´ō-) *adj.* Pertaining to, designating, or characterized by a tail fin having two symmetrical lobes extending from the end of the vertebral column, as in most bony fishes. Compare **heterocercal.** [HOMO- + *-cercal,* from Greek *kerkos,* tail.]

ho·mo·chro·mat·ic (hō´mō-krō-măt´ĭk, hŏm´ō-) *adj.* Of or characterized by one color; monochromatic. **—ho·mo·chro·ma·tism** (hō´mō-krō´mə-tĭz´əm) *n.*

ho·mo·cy·clic (hō´mō-sī´klĭk, -sĭk´lĭk) *adj. Chemistry.* Of, pertaining to, or designating a chemical compound having rings in its molecules formed of only one type of atom. Compare **heterocyclic.** ~*n.* A homocyclic compound.

ho·mo·dont (hō´mə-dŏnt´, hŏm´ə-) *adj.* Having teeth that are all of the same kind. Said of most vertebrates except mammals. [HOM(O)- + -ODONT.]

ho·mo·e·rot·i·cism (hō´mō-ĭ-rŏt´ĭ-sĭz´əm) *n.* Also **ho·mo·er·o·tism** (-ĕr´ə-tĭz´əm). Sexual attraction for one's own sex; homosexuality. **—ho·mo·e·rot·ic** *adj.*

ho·mo·ga·met·ic (hō´mō-gə-mĕt´ĭk) *adj.* Having a similar pair of sex chromosomes, as in human females. Compare **heterogametic.**

ho·mog·a·mous (hō-mŏg´ə-məs) *adj. Botany.* **1.** Having flowers that are sexually alike in the same plant or inflorescence. **2.** Having stamens and pistils that mature simultaneously. [HOMO- + -GAMOUS.] **—ho·mog·a·my** (hō-mŏg´ə-mē) *n.*

ho·mo·ge·ne·i·ty (hō´mō-jə-nē´ə-tē, hŏm´ō-) *n.* The state or quality of being homogeneous.

ho·mo·ge·ne·ous (hō´mə-jē´nē-əs, -jēn´yəs, hŏm´ō-) *adj.* **1.** Like in nature or kind; similar; congruous. **2.** Uniform in structure or composition throughout. **3.** *Mathematics.* Consisting of terms of the same degree or elements of the same dimension. **4.** *Chemistry.* Having or involving only one phase. [Medieval Latin *homogeneus,* from Greek *homogenēs : homo-,* same + *-genēs,* born (see **-gen**) + -OUS.] **—ho·mo·ge·ne·ous·ly** *adv.* **—ho·mo·ge·ne·ous·ness** *n.*

ho·mog·e·nize (hō-mŏj´ə-nīz´, hə-) *tr.v.* **-nized, -nizing, -nizes. 1.** To make homogeneous. **2. a.** To reduce to particles and disperse throughout a fluid. **b.** To make uniform in consistency; especially, to render (milk) uniform in consistency by emulsifying the fat content. **—ho·mog·e·ni·za·tion** *n.* **—ho·mog·e·niz·er** *n.*

ho·mog·e·nous (hō-mŏj´ə-nəs, hə-) *adj.* **1.** *Biology.* Of or exhibiting homogeny. **2.** Homogeneous. [Medieval Latin *homogen(e)us,* HOMOGENEOUS.]

ho·mog·e·ny (hō-mŏj´ə-nē, hə-) *n. Biology.* Correspondence between organs or parts of different species, possibly of dissimilar function, due to common descent; homology. [Greek *homogeneia,* from *homogenēs,* HOMOGENEOUS.]

ho·mog·o·nous (hō-mŏg´ə-nəs, hə-) *adj.* Designating plants in which the stamens and styles are of the same length in all the flowers. [HOMO- + -GON(Y) + -OUS.] **—ho·mog·o·ny** *n.*

ho·mo·graft (hō´mə-grăft´, -gräft´, hŏm´ə-) *n.* A graft of tissue obtained from a member of the same species as the individual receiving it.

hom·o·graph (hŏm´ə-grăf´, -gräf´, hō´mə-) *n.* A word that is spelled in the same way as another word but differs in meaning and origin and may differ in pronunciation. [HOMO- + -GRAPH.] **—hom·o·graph·ic** (hŏm´ə-grăf´ĭk, hō´mə-) *adj.*

homoio–. Variant of **homeo–.**

ho·moi·o·therm (hō-moi´ə-thûrm´) *n.* Also **ho·me·o·therm** (hō-mē´ə-thûrm´). A homoiothermic organism, such as a bird or mammal. [HOMOIO- + -THERM.]

ho·moi·o·ther·mic (hō-moi´ə-thûr´mĭk) *adj.* Also **ho·moi·o·ther·mal** (-məl), **ho·me·o·ther·mic** (hō´mē-ə-thûr´mĭk). Maintaining a relatively constant and warm body temperature that is independent of environmental temperature; warm-blooded. Compare **poikilothermic.**

Ho·moi·ou·si·an (hō´moi-ōō´sē-ən, -ou´sē-ən) *n.* In the 4th century, a Christian holding a modified version of the Arian view, to the effect that God the Father and Jesus the Son were of similar but not of the same substance. Compare **Heteroousian, Homoousian.** [Greek *homoiousios,* of similar substance : HOMOIO- + *ousia,* substance, from *ōn* (stem *ous-*), present participle of *einai,* to be.]

ho·mol·o·gate (hō-mŏl´ə-gāt´, hə-) *tr.v.* **-gated, -gating, -gates.** *Chiefly Scottish Law.* To ratify, assent to, or approve (a contract, deed, or the like). [Medieval Latin *homologāre,* from Greek *homologein,* to concur, agree, from *homologos,* HOMOLOGOUS.]

ho·mo·log·i·cal (hō´mə-lŏj´ĭ-kəl, hŏm´ə-) *adj.* Also **ho·mo·log·ic** (hō´mə-lŏj´ĭk). Homologous. **—ho·mo·log·i·cal·ly** *adv.*

ho·mol·o·gize (hō-mŏl´ə-jīz´, hə-) *tr.v.* **-gized, -gizing, -gizes. 1.** To make homologous. **2.** To show to be homologous. **—ho·mol·o·giz·er** *n.*

ho·mol·o·gous (hō-mŏl´ə-gəs, hə-) *adj.* **1.** Corresponding or similar in position, value, structure, or function. **2.** *Biology.* Corresponding in structure and evolutionary origin, as the flippers of a seal and the arms of a human being. Compare **analogous. 3.** *Genetics.* Designating two chromosomes that are similar in appearance, have the same linear sequence of genes, and pair during meiosis. One is derived from the male gamete and the other from the female gamete. **4.** *Chemistry.* Belonging to or being a series of organic compounds each successive member of which differs from the preceding member by a constant increment, especially by an added CH_2 group. **5.** *Mathematics.* Having the same effect or role in different functions or figures. [Greek *homologos,* agreeing : HOMO- + *logos,* word, proportion, from *legein,* to speak.]

hom·o·lo·graph·ic (hŏm´ə-lō-grăf´ĭk) *adj.* Maintaining the ratio of parts. [Irregularly from Greek *homalos,* even, level + GRAPHIC.]

homolographic projection *n.* An equal-area projection *(see).*

ho·mo·logue, hom·o·log (hŏm´ə-lôg´, -lŏg´, hō´mə-) *n.* Something homologous; a homologous organ or part.

ho·mol·o·gy (hō-mŏl´ə-jē, hə-) *n., pl.* **-gies. 1.** The quality or condition of being homologous. **2.** A homologous relationship or correspondence. **3.** *Mathematics.* A topological classification of configurations into distinct types that imposes an algebraic structure or hierarchy on families of geometric figures. [Greek *homologia,* agreement, from *homologos,* HOMOLOGOUS.]

ho·mol·o·sine projection (hō-mŏl´ə-sīn´) *n.* An equal-area map projection in which the sinusoidal projection is used for latitudes between 40°N and 40°S and the Mollweide projection is used for higher latitudes. It is interrupted over ocean areas so that the continents appear with minimal distortion. [Irregularly from Greek *homalos,* even, flat + -INE.]

ho·mol·y·sis (hō-mŏl´ə-sĭs, hə-) *n. Chemistry.* A chemical reaction in which a bond breaks to give two electrically neutral free radicals. Also called "homolytic fission." Compare **heterolysis.** [HOMO- + -LYSIS.] **—ho·mo·lyt·ic** (hō´mə-lĭt´ĭk, hŏm´ə-) *adj.*

ho·mo·mor·phism (hō´mō-môr´fĭz´əm, hŏm´ō-) *n.* Similarity of external form, appearance, or size. [HOMO- + MORPH(O)- + -ISM.] **—ho·mo·mor·phic, ho·mo·mor·phous** *adj.*

hom·o·nym (hŏm´ə-nĭm´, hō´mə-) *n.* **1.** One of two or more words that have the same sound and often the same spelling but differ in meaning. Compare **homophone. 2. a.** A word that is used to designate several different things. **b.** A namesake. **3.** *Biology.* One of two or more identical but conflicting taxonomic designations independently proposed for members of different categories. [Latin *homōnymum,* from Greek *homōnumon,* from *homōnumos,* HOMONYMOUS.] **—hom·o·nym·ic** (hŏm´ə-nĭm´ĭk, hō´mə-) *adj.*

ho·mon·y·mous (hō-mŏn´ə-məs, hə-) *adj.* **1.** Having the same name. **2.** Of the nature of a homonym; homonymic. [Latin *homōnymus,* from Greek *homōnumos : HOMO- + onuma,* name.] **—ho·mon·y·mous·ly** *adv.*

ho·mon·y·my (hō-mŏn´ə-mē, hə-) *n.* The quality or condition of being homonymous.

Ho·mo·ou·si·an (hō´mō-ōō´sē-ən, -ou´sē-ən, hŏm´ō-) *n.* Also **Ho-**

mou·si·an (hō-mo͞o′sē-ən, hō-mou′-). A Christian supporting the Council of Nicaea's Trinitarian definition of Jesus the Son of God as consubstantial with God the Father. Compare **Heteroousian, Homoiousian.** [Late Latin *homousiānus,* from *homousius,* consubstantial, from Greek *homoousios,* of identical substance : HOMO- + *ousia,* being (see **Homoiousian**).]

ho·mo·phile (hō′mə-fīl′) *adj.* **1.** Homosexual. **2.** Actively concerned with the rights and welfare of homosexuals. **—ho·mo·phile** *n.*

ho·mo·pho·bi·a (hō′mə-fō′bē-ə) *n.* Fear of homosexuals or of homosexuality. **—ho·mo·pho·bic** *adj.*

hom·o·phone (hŏm′ə-fōn′, hō′mə-) *n.* **1.** A word having the same sound as another word but differing from it in spelling, origin, and meaning; for example, English *sum* and *some* are homophones. Compare **homonym. 2.** A symbol, such as a letter or a group of letters, that represents the same sound as another; for example, English *kn* and *n* are homophones. [HOMO- + -PHONE.]

hom·o·phon·ic (hŏm′ə-fŏn′ĭk, hō′mə-) *adj.* Also **ho·moph·o·nous** (hō-mŏf′ə-nəs, hə-). **1.** Having the same sound. **2.** *Music.* Having or characterized by parts that move in unison to a single melodic line. [Greek *homophōnos,* having the same sound : HOMO- + *phōnē,* sound (see **-phone**).]

ho·moph·o·ny (hō-mŏf′ə-nē, hə-) *n.* **1.** The quality or condition of being homophonic. **2.** Homophonic music. Compare **polyphony, monophony.**

ho·mo·phy·ly (hō′mə-fī′lē, hŏm′ə-, hō-mŏf′ə-lē) *n.* Resemblance arising from common ancestry. [HOMO- + Greek *phulē,* tribe, PHYLE.] **—ho·mo·phyl·ic** (hō′mə-fĭl′ĭk, hŏm′ə-) *adj.*

ho·mo·plas·tic (hō′mə-plăs′tĭk, hŏm′ə-) *adj.* **1.** *Biology.* Of, pertaining to, or exhibiting superficial structural similarity arising from **convergence** *(see).* **2.** Of, pertaining to, or derived from a different individual of the same species: *a homoplastic graft.* [HOMO- + -PLASTIC.] **—ho·mo·plas·ti·cal·ly** *adv.*

ho·mo·pla·sy (hō′mə-plā′sē, -plăs′ē, hŏm′ə-) *n. Biology.* Superficial structural similarity arising from convergence or parallel evolution.

ho·mo·po·lar (hō′mə-pō′lər, hŏm′ə-) *adj. Chemistry.* Not ionic or polar; having uniform charge distribution. Said of covalent bonds.

ho·mop·ter·ous (hō-mŏp′tər-əs, hə-) *adj.* Also **ho·mop·ter·an** (-ən). Of or belonging to the order Homoptera, which includes insects such as the cicadas, aphids, and scale insects. [New Latin *Homoptera* : HOMO- + -PTEROUS.]

hom·or·gan·ic (hŏm′ôr-găn′ĭk, hō′môr-) *adj. Phonetics.* Designating two or more speech sounds, such as the alveolar consonants *t, d,* and *n,* formed in the same area or with the same organs of articulation. [HOM(O)- + ORGANIC.]

Ho·mo sa·pi·ens (hō′mō sā′pē-ənz, -ĕnz′) *n.* **1.** The taxonomic designation for modern human beings, the only extant species of the genus *Homo.* **2.** The human being as a thinking creature as distinguished from other organisms. [New Latin : HOMO + Latin *sapiēns,* SAPIENT.]

ho·mo·sce·das·tic (hō′mō-sĭ-dăs′tĭk, hŏm′ō-) *adj. Statistics.* Of or being variables for which all possible values have constant variance. [HOMO- + *scedastic,* from Greek *skedasis,* dispersion, scattering.] **—ho·mo·sce·das·tic·i·ty** (hō′mō-sĭ-dă-stĭs′ə-tē, hŏm′ō-) *n.*

ho·mo·sex·u·al (hō′mō-sĕk′sho͞o-əl, hō′mə-, hŏm′ə-) *adj.* **1.** Characterized by attraction to the same sex. **2.** Of or pertaining to sexual relations between persons of the same sex.
~*n.* A homosexual person. **—ho·mo·sex·u·al·i·ty** (hō′mō-sĕk′sho͞o-ăl′ə-tē, hŏm′ō-) *n.*

ho·mos·po·rous (hō-mŏs′pər-əs, hō′mə-spôr′əs, -spōr′əs, hŏm′ə-) *adj. Botany.* Producing spores of one kind only. Said of certain ferns. [HOMO- + -SPOROUS.] **—ho·mos·po·ry** *n.*

ho·mo·tax·is (hō′mō-tăk′sĭs, hŏm′ō-) *n.* Similarity of arrangement and fossils in noncontemporaneous or widely separated geologic deposits. [New Latin : HOMO- + -TAXIS.] **—ho·mo·tax·ic** (hō′mō-tăk′sĭk, hŏm′ō-), **ho·mo·tax·i·al** (-tăk′sē-əl) *adj.*

ho·mo·thal·lic (hō′mō-thăl′ĭk, hŏm′ō-) *adj. Botany.* Having male and female reproductive structures in the same thallus, as in some fungi and algae. **—ho·mo·thal·lism** *n.*

ho·mo·zy·go·sis (hō′mō-zī-gō′sĭs, hŏm′ō-) *n.* The union of genetically identical gametes, resulting in the formation of a homozygote. **—ho·mo·zy·got·ic** (hō′mō-zī-gŏt′ĭk, hŏm′ō-) *adj.*

ho·mo·zy·gote (hō′mō-zī′gōt′, hŏm′ō-) *n.* An organism derived from the union of genetically identical gametes and having identical alleles for one or more genes. **—ho·mo·zy·gous** (hō′mō-zī′gəs, hō′mə-, hŏm′ō-, hŏm′ə-) *adj.*

ho·mun·cu·lus (hō-mŭng′kyə-ləs) *n., pl.* **-li** (-lī′). **1.** A diminutive man; a manikin. **2.** A fully formed individual believed by adherents of the early biological theory of preformation to be present in a sperm cell. [Latin, diminutive of *homō,* man.]

homy. Variant of **homey.**

hon. honorary.

Hon. 1. honorary. **2.** Honorable (title).

Honan, Ho·nan. See **Henan** (province), **Luoyang** (city).

hon·cho (hŏn′chō) *n., pl.* **-chos.** *Slang.* One who is in charge; leader or boss. [Japanese, squad leader: *han,* squad + *chō,* chief.]

Hondo. See **Honshu.**

Hon·du·ras (hŏn-do͝or′əs, -dyo͝or′əs). Republic of Central America, on the Gulf of Honduras, an inlet of the Caribbean. It gained its independence from Spain in 1821. The economy is predominantly agricultural, and the main exports are bananas, coffee, timber, and silver. Area, 112,088 square kilometers (43,266 square miles). Population, 5,100,000. Capital, Tegucigalpa. See map at **Central American States. —Hon·du·ran** *adj. & n.*

hone[1] (hōn) *n.* **1.** A fine-grained whetstone for giving a keen edge to razors and tools. **2.** A tool with a rotating abrasive tip for enlarging holes to precise dimensions.
~*tr.v.* **honed, honing, hones.** To sharpen on or as if on a hone; give an edge to. [Middle English *hone,* Old English *hān,* stone, from Germanic.]

hone[2] *intr.v.* **honed, honing, hones.** *Informal.* **1.** To whine or moan. **2.** To hanker; yearn. Often used with *for* or *after.* [Old French *hoigner,* from *hon,* cry of discontent.]

Hon·eg·ger (ŏn′ə-gər, hŏn′-, ô′nĕ-gĕr′), **Arthur** (1892–1955). Swiss composer, born in France. A prolific proponent of the modern movement in French music, he brought his bold harmonic style to chamber, orchestral, and operatic music. Among his many works are *Pastorale d'été* (1921), *Pacific 231* (1924), and *Judith* (1926).

hon·est (ŏn′ĭst) *adj.* **1.** Not given to lying, cheating, stealing, or taking unfair advantage; truthful; trustworthy. **2. a.** Not characterized by deception or fraud; genuine. **b.** Not calculated or constructed to defraud: *honest dice.* **3.** Equitable; fair: *honest wages for an honest day's work.* **4. a.** Having or manifesting integrity and truth; not false: *honest reporting.* **b.** Sincere; candid; frank: *Give me your honest opinion.* **5. a.** Of guileless or ingenuous appearance; open: *"Flushed with purple grace/He shows his honest face."* (John Dryden). **b.** Unfeigned; undisguised: *honest pleasure.* **6. a.** Of good repute; respectable; decent. **b.** Unpretentious; unaffected: *honest country folk.* **7.** *Archaic.* Free from moral stain; virtuous; chaste. Usually said of a woman. [Middle English, from Old French *honeste,* from Latin *honestus,* honorable, from *honōs,* HONOR.]

honest broker *n.* A neutral mediator.

hon·est·ly (ŏn′ĭst-lē) *adv.* **1.** In an honest manner. **2.** Really; truly. Used as an intensifier: *I honestly don't know.*

hon·es·ty (ŏn′ĭ-stē) *n.* **1.** The quality or condition of being honest; integrity; trustworthiness. **2.** Truthfulness; sincerity: *in all honesty.* **3.** *Archaic.* Chastity. **4.** A plant, *Lunaria annua,* native to Eurasia, cultivated for its fragrant purplish flowers and round, flat, papery silver-white seed pods. In this sense, also called "satinpod."
Synonyms: *honor, integrity, probity, veracity.*

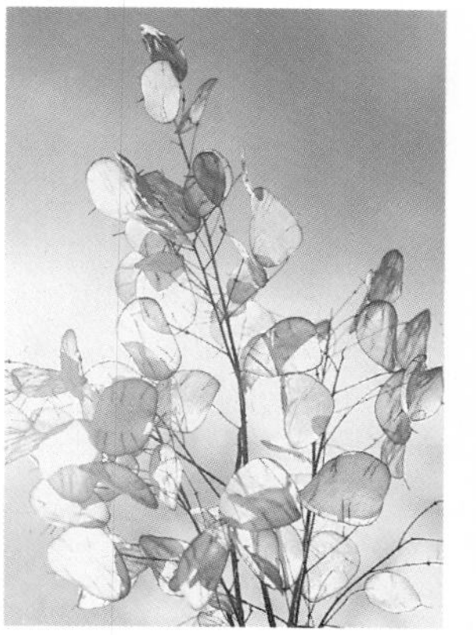

honesty Lunaria annua *has small fragrant purple flowers but is most prized for its silver, disklike seedpods (above), which are used in dried flower arrangements.*

hone·wort (hōn′wûrt′, -wôrt′) *n.* **1.** A European plant, *Trinia glauca,* having clusters of small whitish flowers. **2.** Any of several similar and related plants. [*Hone*-† (meaning unknown) + WORT.]

hon·ey (hŭn′ē) *n., pl.* **-eys. 1.** A sweet yellowish or brownish viscid fluid produced by various bees from the nectar of flowers and used as food. **2.** A similar substance made by certain other insects. **3.** A sweet substance, such as the nectar of flowers. **4.** Sweetness. **5.** *Informal.* Sweet one; dear. Used as a term of endearment. **6.** *Informal.* A remarkably fine example: *a honey of a dress.*
~*tr.v.* **honeyed** or **honied, -eying, -eys.** To sweeten with or as if with honey. [Middle English *hony,* Old English *hunig,* from Germanic.]

honey agaric *n.* The **honey mushroom** *(see).*

honey ant *n.* Any of various ants, such as one of the genus *Myrmecocystus,* that collect and store honeydew in the distensible abdomens of specialized workers.

honey badger *n.* A carnivorous mammal, *Mellivora capensis,* of Africa and Asia, having short legs and a thick coat. It feeds on honey and small animals. Also called "ratel."

honey bear *n.* A mammal, the **kinkajou** *(see).*

hon·ey·bee (hŭn′ē-bē′) *n.* Any of several social bees of the genus *Apis* that produce honey; especially, *A. mellifera,* widely domesticated as a source of honey and beeswax.

honey buzzard *n.* A European bird of prey, *Pernis apivorus,* having brown plumage with white streaks on the underparts. It feeds mainly on wasps and bee larvae.

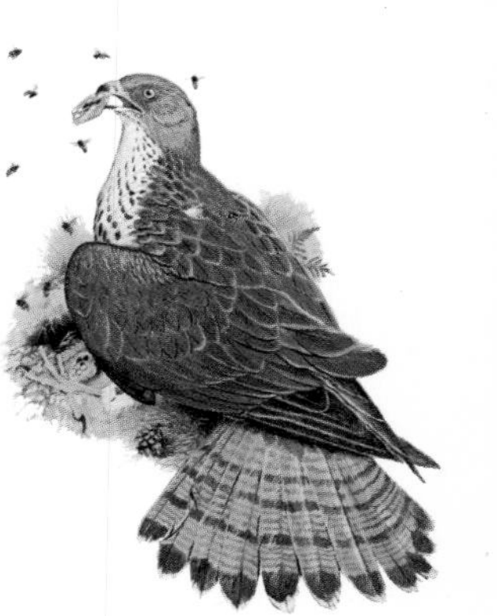

honey buzzard *Wasps and wild bees and their honey are the main diet of this bird of prey, though it also eats small frogs and lizards. Densely packed feathers on its head protect it from stings. Its breeding grounds are in Africa, Europe, and Asia.*

hon·ey·comb (hŭn′ē-kōm′) *n.* **1.** A structure of hexagonal, thin-walled cells constructed from beeswax by honeybees to hold honey and eggs. **2.** Something suggesting this in structure or pattern.
~*tr.v.* **honeycombed, -combing, -combs. 1.** To fill with cavities like a honeycomb: *castle walls honeycombed with little windows.* **2.** To penetrate thoroughly so as to weaken or undermine: *His story was honeycombed with lies.* **3.** To form in or cover with a honeycomb pattern.

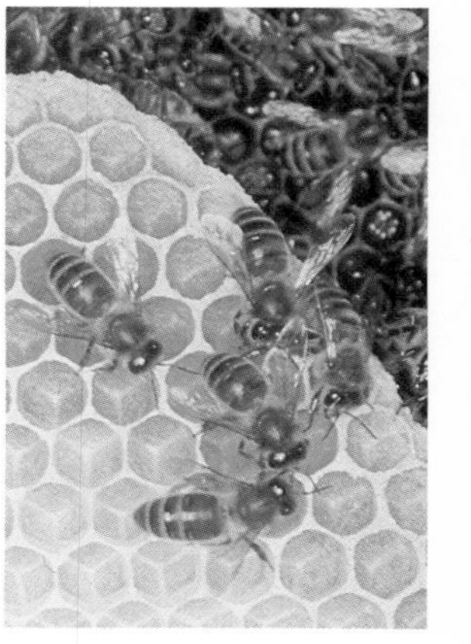

honeycomb *Worker honeybees build their hexagonal-patterned combs from beeswax secreted by their own bodies. The combs are used as nurseries for bee larvae and to store honey.*

hon·ey·creep·er (hŭn′ē-krē′pər) *n.* **1.** Any of various small, often brightly colored tropical American birds of the subfamily Dacninae, having a curved bill adapted for sucking nectar from flowers. **2.** Any of several similar birds of the family Drepanididae, of Hawaii.

hon·ey·dew (hŭn′ē-do͞o′, -dyo͞o′) *n.* **1.** A sweet, sticky substance excreted by various insects, especially aphids, on the leaves of plants. **2.** A similar sweet exudate on the leaves of plants. **3.** A honeydew melon.

honeydew melon *n.* A melon, a variety of *Cucumis melo,* having a smooth, yellow rind and greenish-white flesh.

hon·ey·eat·er (hŭn′ē-ē′tər) *n.* Any of various birds of the family Meliphagidae, of Australia and adjacent regions, having a curved bill and a long tongue adapted for sucking nectar from flowers.

hon·eyed, hon·ied (hŭn′ēd) *adj.* **1.** Containing, full of, or sweetened with honey. **2.** Ingratiating; sugary: *honeyed words.* **3.** Sweet; dulcet: *a honeyed voice.*

honey guide *n.* Any of various tropical Old World birds of the family Indicatoridae, some species of which lead animals or people to the nests of wild honeybees, where they eat the wax that remains after the honey has been removed.

honey locust *n.* **1.** A thorny tree, *Gleditsia triacanthos,* of eastern

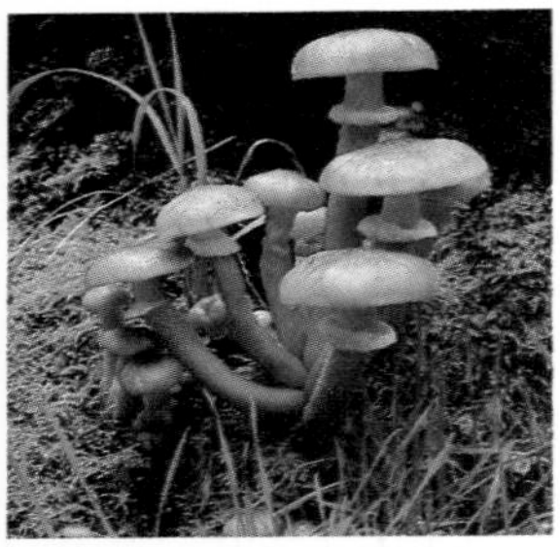

honey mushroom *Wood infected with this destructive fungus glows eerily in the dark. But its golden yellow mushrooms are safe to eat.*

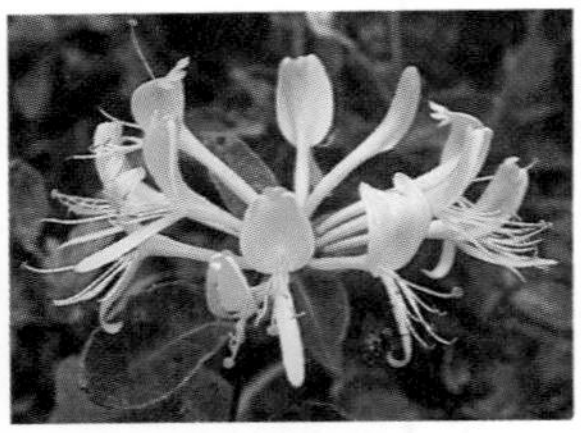

honeysuckle *A graceful and woody climber that is a popular and fragrant garden shrub. This species is* Lonicera periclymenum.

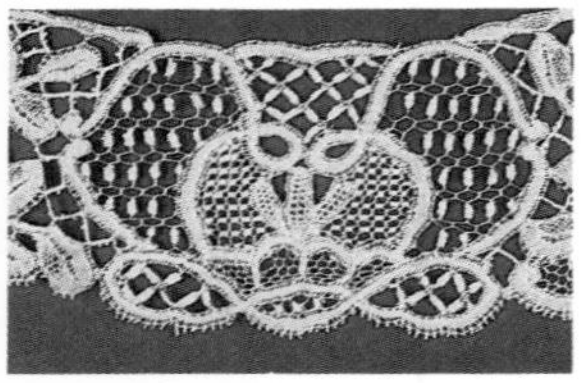

Honiton lace *One of several distinctive English styles of handmade lace. Honiton lace was employed to make the christening robe currently used by the British royal family; it was originally commissioned for one of Queen Victoria's children.*

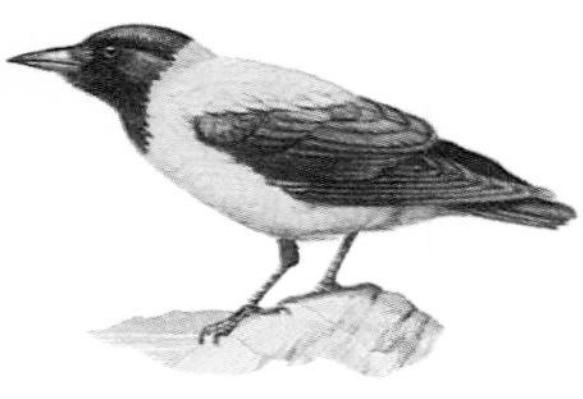

hooded crow *Like its close relative the carrion crow, with which it interbreeds, the hooded crow feeds on the flesh of dead animals. It has replaced the carrion crow in northern and eastern Europe and western Asia.*

North America, bearing long pods containing a sweet pulp. **2.** A similar tree, the **mesquite** *(see).*

hon·ey·moon (hŭn'ē-mo͞on') *n.* **1.** A holiday taken by a newly married couple. Also used adjectivally: *the honeymoon suite.* **2.** A usually short-lived period of harmony and cooperation at the beginning of any joint undertaking or working relationship: *After a brief honeymoon, relations between the new governor and the state legislature quickly deteriorated.*
—*intr.v.* **honeymooned, -mooning, -moons.** To spend a honeymoon. [HONEY + MOON (month), the first month of marriage being thought of as the sweetest.] **—hon·ey·moon·er** *n.*

honey mouse *n.* A small Australian marsupial, *Tarsipes spenserae,* having a long snout and tongue and prehensile tail. It climbs shrubs to feed on nectar. Also called "honey phalanger," "honeysucker."

honey mushroom *n.* A honey-colored mushroom, *Armillaria mellea,* that grows on tree stumps and is a serious pest of trees. Also called "honey agaric," "bootlace fungus."

hon·ey·suck·er (hŭn'ē-sŭk'ər) *n.* Any of various animals that feed on nectar, especially the honeyeater or the honey mouse.

hon·ey·suck·le (hŭn'ē-sŭk'əl) *n.* **1.** Any of various shrubs or vines of the genus *Lonicera,* having tubular, often very fragrant yellowish, white, or pink flowers. **2.** Any of various similar or related plants, such as any of certain Australian trees or shrubs of the genus *Banksia,* having dense spikes of flowers. **3.** A New Zealand tree, the **rewarewa** *(see).* [Middle English *honysoukel,* variant of *honysouke,* Old English *hunigsūce* : *hunig,* HONEY + *sūcan,* to SUCK.]

hong (hông, hŏng) *n.* A warehouse, factory, or foreign trading house in China. [Cantonese *hong,* corresponding to Mandarin Chinese *hang²,* profession, business establishment.]

Hong Kong (hŏng' kŏng', hông' kông'). British crown colony in southern China, consisting of Hong Kong Island at the mouth of the Zhujiang (Pearl River) and about 230 islets in the South China Sea, Jiulong (Kowloon Peninsula), and the New Territories on the Chinese mainland. The island was ceded to Great Britain in the Treaty of Nanking (1842); part of Jiulong was acquired (1860); and the New Territories were leased to Great Britain for 99 years in 1898. Hong Kong is a free port and a major commercial, banking, and manufacturing center. Area, 1,045 square kilometers (403 square miles). Capital, Victoria (also called Hong Kong). See map at **China.**

honied. Variant of **honeyed.**

ho·ni soit qui mal y pense (ô'nē swä' kē mäl' ē päɴs'). Shamed be he who thinks evil of it. Used as the motto of the Order of the Garter. [French.]

Hon·i·ton lace (hŏn'ĭ-tən, hŭn'-) *n.* A type of bobbin lace consisting of floral sprigs sewn on net or joined by other lace. [After *Honiton,* Devonshire, England, where it was originally made.]

honk (hôngk, hŏngk) *n.* **1.** The raucous, resonant sound characteristically uttered by a wild goose. **2.** A similar sound, such as that made by an automobile horn.
—*v.* **honked, honking, honks.** —*intr.* To emit a honk. —*tr.* To cause (a horn) to produce a honk. [Imitative.] **—honk·er** *n.*

hon·ky-tonk (hông'kē-tôngk', hŏng'kē-tŏngk') *n. Slang.* A cheap, noisy saloon or dance hall.
—*adj.* Designating a type of ragtime usually played on a tinny old piano. [20th century : origin obscure.]

Hon·o·lu·lu (hŏn'ə-lo͞o'lo͞o). Capital of the state of Hawaii, on the island of Oahu. It is a crossroads of transport across the Pacific Ocean, as well as the economic center and leading port of Hawaii.

hon·or (ŏn'ər) *n.* Also *chiefly British* **hon·our.** **1.** Esteem; respect; reverence: *the honor shown to him.* **2. a.** Reputation; good name. **b.** Credit: *It was to his honor that he refused the payment.* **3. a.** Glory; fame; distinction. **b.** A mark, token, or gesture of respect or distinction: *It is an honor to be seated next to the host.* **c.** A decoration or title conferred in recognition of distinguished conduct or achievement. **4.** Nobility of mind; probity; personal integrity. **5.** High rank; exalted position. **6.** One that imparts distinction by association: *He is an honor to our city.* **7.** Great privilege: *I have the honor to present the governor.* **8. Honor.** A title of respect used to or of mayors and judges. Preceded by *Your, His,* or *Her.* **9. a.** A code of principally male dignity, integrity, and pride maintained in some societies, as it was in feudal Europe, by force of arms. **b.** A woman's chastity or her reputation for chastity. **10. honors. a.** Special recognition for unusual academic achievement: *graduate with honors.* **b.** A course of study that is of a higher standard or more specialized or advanced than that taken by most students. Also used adjectivally: *an honors degree.* **11.** In golf, the right of teeing off first. **12. honors.** In card games, the four or five highest cards in the trump suit or in all suits. —See Synonyms at **honesty.** **—do the honors. 1.** To perform the social courtesies required of a host or hostess. **2.** To perform a particular social act such as filling glasses or carving a roast. **—(in) honor bound.** Constrained or obliged by one's moral or social standards. **—in honor of. 1.** As a sign of respect for. **2.** As a celebration of. **—on** (or **upon**) **one's honor.** With one's good name as a pledge.
—*tr.v.* **honored, -oring, -ors.** Also *chiefly British* **hon·our, -oured, -ouring, -ours. 1. a.** To esteem; hold in respect. **b.** To show respect for. **2.** To confer distinction upon: *The ambassador honored us with her presence.* **3.** To accept or pay (a credit card or check, for example) as valid. **4.** To abide by (an agreement) or fulfill (an obligation): *Both parties claim to have honored their side of the bargain.* [Middle English *hono(u)r,* from Old French *honour,* from Latin *honour, honōs*† (stem *honōr-*).] **—hon·or·er** *n.*

Synonyms: *deference, homage, reverence, veneration.*

hon·or·a·ble (ŏn'ər-ə-bəl) *adj.* Also *chiefly British* **hon·our·a·ble.** **1.** Deserving or winning honor and respect; creditable: *an honorable deed.* **2.** Bestowing honor; bringing distinction or recognition: *honorable service.* **3.** Possessing and characterized by honor: *"for Brutus is an honourable man"* (Shakespeare). **4.** Consistent with honor or good name: *the only honorable course.* **5. Honorable.** *Abbr.* **Hon. a.** Used with *the* as a title of respect for certain high officials. **b.** *British.* Used with *the* as a courtesy title for the children of barons and viscounts and the younger sons of earls. **c.** *British.* Used in the House of Commons as a title of respect when speaking of another member. **—hon·or·a·ble·ness** *n.* **—hon·or·a·bly** *adv.*

honorable discharge *n.* A discharge from the armed forces with a clean record.

honorable mention *n.* A written or spoken mention, as in a list, of one who has performed well in a competition but has not been awarded a prize.

hon·o·rar·i·um (ŏn'ə-râr'ē-əm) *n., pl.* **-ums** or **-ia** (-ē-ə). A voluntary fee paid to a person for professional services for which fees are not legally or traditionally required. [Latin, neuter of *honorārius,* HONORARY.]

hon·or·ar·y (ŏn'ə-rĕr'ē) *adj. Abbr.* **hon., Hon. 1.** Held, given, or conferred as a mark of honor without the usual prerequisites or privileges: *an honorary degree.* **2. a.** Holding an office or title given as an honor, without payment: *the honorary secretary of the association.* **b.** Voluntary; unpaid. **3.** Relying upon honor; not legally enforceable. Said of a duty or obligation.

hon·or·ee (ŏn'ə-rē') *n.* One who receives an honor.

hon·o·rif·ic (ŏn'ə-rĭf'ĭk) *adj.* Conferring or showing respect or honor.
—*n.* A title, phrase, or grammatical form conveying respect, used especially when addressing a social superior. [Latin *honorificus.* See **honor, -fic.**] **—hon·o·rif·i·cal·ly** *adv.*

ho·no·ris cau·sa (ō-nôr'ĭs kou'zə) *adv.* Conferred as a mark of honor. Said of an honorary degree. [Latin.]

honors list *n. British.* A list of persons on whom an honor, such as a peerage, is to be conferred.

honors of war *pl.n.* Certain courtesies granted a surrendering foe, such as the privilege of marching out bearing arms and colors.

honour. *Chiefly British.* Variant of **honor.**

honourable. *Chiefly British.* Variant of **honorable.**

Hon·shu (hŏn'sho͞o). Also **Hon·do** (hŏn'dō). The largest and economically most important of the four main islands that constitute Japan. It is predominantly mountainous and is the site of Japan's highest peak, Fujiyama (3,776 meters; 12,388 feet). Most of Japan's tea and silk comes from Honshu, and the island is also the industrial heartland of the country, with the Tokyo-Yokohama and Osaka-Kobe urban agglomerations.

hooch (ho͝och) *n. Slang.* Alcoholic liquor, especially when inferior or illicit. [Short for Alaskan *Hoochinoo,* a tribe that made a kind of distilled liquor.]

hood¹ (ho͝od) *n.* **1.** A loose covering for the head and neck, either attached to a cloak or jacket or separate. **2.** A draping of cloth hung from the shoulders of an academic gown that indicates the wearer's degree. **3.** A sack used to cover a falcon's head to keep it quiet. **4.** Something resembling a hood in shape or function, as: **a.** A metal cover or cowl for a hearth or stove. **b.** The hinged metal lid over an automobile engine. Also *British* "bonnet." **c.** A folding waterproof top for a carriage or baby carriage. **d.** An expanded part, crest, or marking on or near the head of an animal.
—*tr.v.* **hooded, hooding, hoods.** To supply or cover with a hood. [Middle English *ho(o)d,* Old English *hōd,* from Germanic.]

hood² *n. Slang.* **1.** A hoodlum; a thug. **2.** A tough-looking youth. [Short for HOODLUM.]

-hood *suffix.* Indicates: **1.** The state, condition, or quality of being; for example, **manhood. 2.** All the members of a grouping of a specified nature; for example, **neighborhood.** [Middle English *-hod(e),* Old English *-hād,* originally an independent noun (condition, quality), from Germanic.]

Hood, Mount (ho͝od). A peak, 3,427 meters (11,235 feet) high, in the Cascade Range in northern Oregon. A symmetrical extinct volcano with glaciers and forested lower slopes, it is a popular mountain-climbing and skiing area.

Hood, Thomas (1799–1845). British poet. He is best known for his comic and topical verse, including *The Dream of Eugene Aram* (1831). *The Song of the Shirt* (1843) exposed the miseries of industrial work.

hood·ed (ho͝od'ĭd) *adj.* **1.** Covered with or having a hood. **2.** Shaped like a hood, cowl, or similar covering. **3.** *Zoology.* Having a crest, coloration, or skin formation suggesting a hood.

hooded crow *n.* A variety of the carrion crow that has a gray back and underparts and a black head, wings, and tail.

hooded seal *n.* A seal, *Cystophora cristata,* of northern seas, having a grayish, spotted coat and an inflatable hoodlike or bladderlike pouch in the region of the nose. Also called "bladdernose."

hood·lum (ho͝od'ləm, ho͞od'ləm) *n.* **1.** A gangster; a thug. **2.** A tough, destructive youth. [19th century : origin obscure.]

hood mold *n. Architecture.* A **dripstone** *(see).*

hoo·doo (ho͞o'do͞o) *n., pl.* **-doos. 1.** Voodoo. **2. a.** Bad luck. **b.** One that brings bad luck.
—*tr.v.* **hoodooed, -dooing, -doos.** To bring bad luck to. [Perhaps variant of VOODOO.] **—hoo·doo·ism** *n.*

hood·wink (ho͝od'wĭngk') *tr.v.* **-winked, -winking, -winks. 1.** To deceive; trick; take in. **2.** *Archaic.* To blindfold. **3.** *Obsolete.* To conceal. —See Synonyms at **deceive.** [HOOD + WINK.]

hoo·ey (ho͞o′ē) *n. Slang.* Nonsense.
∼*interj. Slang.* Used as an exclamation of impatience or disbelief. [20th century : origin obscure.]

hoof (ho͝of, ho͞of) *n., pl.* **hoofs** or **hooves** (ho͝ovz, ho͞ovz). **1.** The horny sheath covering the toes or lower part of the foot of a mammal of the orders Perissodactyla and Artiodactyla, such as a horse, ox, or deer. **2.** The foot of such an animal, especially a horse. **3.** *Slang.* The human foot. **—on the hoof.** Alive; not yet slaughtered. Said especially of cattle.
∼*v.* **hoofed, hoofing, hoofs.** *—tr.* To trample or kick with the hoofs. *—intr. Slang.* **1.** To dance. **2.** To go on foot; walk. Often used with *it*: *Let's hoof it instead of taking the bus.* [Middle English *hoof,* Old English *hōf,* from Germanic.]

hoof-and-mouth disease (ho͝of′ən-mouth′, ho͞of′-) *n.* **Foot-and-mouth disease** *(see).*

hoof·bound (ho͝of′bound′, ho͞of′-) *adj.* Afflicted with drying and contraction of the hoof, resulting in lameness. Said of a horse.

hoofed (ho͝oft, ho͞oft) *adj.* Having hoofs; ungulate.

hoof·er (ho͝of′ər, ho͞o′fər) *n. Slang.* A professional dancer; especially, a tap dancer.

Hoogh·ly or **Hug·li** (ho͞og′lē). River of northeastern India. It is the most westerly arm of the Ganges delta. Leaving the mainstream near the Bangladesh border, it flows 233 kilometers (145 miles) south to the Bay of Bengal. Constantly dredged to prevent silting, the Hooghly connects Calcutta to the sea.

hoo-ha (ho͞o′hä′) *n. Informal.* A noisy fuss or uproar, especially one about nothing of importance; a hullabaloo. [Imitative.]

hook (ho͝ok) *n.* **1.** A curved or sharply bent device, usually of metal, used to catch, drag, suspend, or fasten something. **2.** A fishhook. **3.** A means of catching or ensnaring; a trap. **4.** Anything shaped like a hook, as: **a.** A curved or barbed plant or animal part. **b.** A short angled or curved line on a letter. **c.** The lip of a breaking wave. **d.** A sickle. **5. a.** A sharp bend or curve, as in a river. **b.** A spit of land with a sharply curved end. **6.** *Baseball.* A curve ball. **7.** *Boxing.* A short, swinging blow delivered with a crooked arm. **8.** *Golf.* A stroke that sends the ball to the left of a right-handed player or to the right of a left-handed player. **9.** *Basketball.* A hook shot. **10.** *Nautical.* An anchor. **11.** The part of a telephone on which the receiver sits or from which it is hung. **—by hook or (by) crook.** By whatever means possible, fair or unfair. **—get the hook.** *Slang.* To be dismissed or thrown out. **—hook, line, and sinker.** *Slang.* Without reservation; entirely; completely. **—off the hook.** *Slang.* Freed, as from blame, responsibility, or a vexatious obligation. **—on one's own hook.** *Informal.* By one's own efforts; on one's own account.
∼*v.* **hooked, hooking, hooks.** *—tr.* **1. a.** To get hold of or catch with or as if with a hook. **b.** *Informal.* To snare. **c.** *Slang.* To steal; snatch. **d.** *Informal.* To please and make a fan of. **e.** *Slang.* To cause to become addicted. **2.** To fasten or hold up with or as if with a hook. Often used with *up.* **3.** To pierce or gore with the horns. Used especially of a bull. **4.** *Baseball.* To pitch (a ball) with a curve. **5.** *Boxing.* To hit with a hook. **6.** *Golf.* To drive (a ball) with a hook. **7.** To make (a rug, for example) by looping yarn through canvas with a type of crochet hook. *—intr.* **1.** To bend like a hook. **2.** To be fastened by means of a hook or a hook and eye. Used with *on, up,* and other adverbs. **—hook it.** *Slang.* To make a getaway; escape. [Middle English *ho(o)k,* Old English *hōc.*]

hook·ah (ho͝ok′ə) *n.* An Eastern smoking pipe designed with a long tube passing through an urn of water that cools the smoke as it is drawn through. Also called "narghile," "hubble-bubble," "water pipe." [Urdu, from Arabic *ḥuqqah,* small box, casket.]

hook and eye *n.* A clothes fastener consisting of a small blunt metal hook with a corresponding loop.

hook-and-lad·der truck (ho͝ok′ən-lăd′ər) *n.* A fire engine equipped with extension ladders and hooked poles.

Hooke (ho͝ok), **Robert** (1635–1703). English physicist, mathematician, and inventor. He was curator of experiments to the Royal Society (1662–1703) and defined Hooke's law. He invented the wheel barometer, improved astronomical instruments, and formulated the theory of planetary movement.

hooked (ho͝okt) *adj.* **1.** Bent or angled like a hook. **2.** Having a hook or hooks. **3.** Made by hooking yarn. **4.** *Slang.* **a.** Addicted to a narcotic. **b.** Liking something with an intensity that suggests addiction. Often used with *on*: *He was hooked on the place and went back every year.* **—hook·ed·ness** (ho͝ok′ĭd-nĭs) *n.*

hook·er¹ (ho͝ok′ər) *n.* **1.** A single-masted fishing smack used off southwestern England and Ireland. **2.** An old worn-out or clumsy ship, especially one that uses hooks and lines rather than nets. [Dutch *hoeker,* from *hoek,* hook, fishhook (as in *hoekboot,* hookboat), from Middle Dutch *hoec.*]

hooker² *n.* **1.** One that hooks. **2.** *Slang.* A prostitute.

Hook·er (ho͝ok′ər), **Sir Joseph Dalton** (1817–1911). British botanist. He wrote *Genera Plantarum* (1862–83), a global study of the distribution of plants.

Hooker, Richard (*c.* 1554–1600). English churchman and theologian. His great work, *Laws of Ecclesiastical Polity* (1594), helped formulate the tone and direction of Anglican theology.

Hooke's law *n.* The principle that the stress applied to a solid body produces a strain proportional to it provided that the elastic limit is not reached. [After Robert HOOKE.]

hook·nose (ho͝ok′nōz′) *n.* An aquiline nose. **—hook·nosed** *adj.*

Hook of Hol·land (ho͝ok; hŏl′ənd). *Dutch* **Hoek van Hol·land** (ho͞ok′ vän hôl′änt). Outer port of Rotterdam, in the Netherlands, on the North Sea. It is on Hook of Holland Cape and is connected by canal to Rotterdam.

hook shot *n.* A basketball shot made by arcing the far hand upward while standing or moving sideways to the basket.

hook up *tr.v.* **1.** To assemble or wire (a mechanism). **2.** To connect or link (a mechanism) to another mechanism or a source of power. Often used with *to*: *hooked up to the big central computer.* **3.** To fasten together with a hook or hooks. *—intr.v. Informal.* **1.** To form a tie or connection. Often used with *with.* **2.** To marry. Often used with *with.*

hook·up (ho͝ok′ŭp′) *n.* **1.** A system of electric circuits and electrically powered equipment designed to operate together, as the linking of television or radio stations so that they can broadcast a special program together. **2.** A configuration of mechanical parts or devices acting as an integrated unit. **3.** A plan or schematic drawing of such a system. **4.** *Informal.* A connection, often between unlikely associates or factors.

hook·worm (ho͝ok′wûrm′) *n.* Any of numerous small, parasitic nematode worms of the family Ancylostomatidae, having hooked mouth parts with which they fasten themselves to the intestinal walls of various hosts, including man, causing the disease ancylostomiasis.

hookworm disease *n.* **Ancylostomiasis** *(see).*

hook·y, hook·ey (ho͝ok′ē) *n. Informal.* Absence without leave; truancy. Used in the phrase *play hooky.* [Origin unknown.]

hoo·li·gan (ho͞o′lĭ-gən) *n. Informal.* A young ruffian; a thug. [19th century : perhaps variant of the Irish surname *Houlihan.*] **—hoo·li·gan·ism** *n.*

hoop (ho͞op, ho͝op) *n.* **1.** A circular band of metal or wood put around a cask or barrel to bind the staves together. **2.** Something resembling a hoop, as: **a.** A large wooden, plastic, or metal ring used as a toy or for circus animals to jump through. **b.** One of the lightweight circular supports for a hoop skirt. **c.** One of a pair of circular wooden or metal frames used to hold material taut for embroidery or similar needlework. **3.** A croquet wicket. **4.** In basketball and other games, the metal ring to which a net is attached to form the basket. **—go** (or **be put**) **through the hoop.** To undergo or be forced to undergo an ordeal or test.
∼*tr.v.* **hooped, hooping, hoops.** To hold together or support with or as if with a hoop or hoops. [Middle English *hoop,* Old English *hōp,* from Germanic *hōpaz* (unattested).]

hoop·la (ho͞op′lä′, ho͝op′-) *n.* **1.** A game in which small rings are thrown in an attempt to encircle an object and so win it. **2.** *Slang.* Boisterous, jovial commotion or excitement. **3.** *Slang.* Talk or publicity intended to mislead or confuse; ballyhoo. [French *houp-là†.*]

hoo·poe (ho͞o′po͞o, -pō) *n.* An Old World bird, *Upupa epops,* having distinctively patterned pinkish-brown plumage, a fanlike crest, and a slender, downward-curving bill. [Variant of obsolete *hoop,* from Old French *huppe,* from Latin *upupa* (imitative).]

hoop-pet·ti·coat narcissus (ho͞op′pĕt′ĭ-kōt′, ho͝op′-) *n.* The **petticoat narcissus** *(see).*

hoop pine *n.* An Australian tree, *Araucaria cunninghamii,* having rough bark with hooplike cracks around its trunk and branches.

hoop skirt *n.* A long full skirt belled out with a series of connected hoops.

hoop snake *n.* Any of several American snakes, such as the mud snake, *Farancia abacura,* that supposedly grasp the tail in the mouth and move with a rolling, hooplike motion.

hooray. Variant of **hurrah.**

hoose·gow (ho͞os′gou′) *n. Slang.* A jail. [Spanish *juzgado,* courtroom, from the past participle of *juzgar,* to judge, from Latin *jūdicāre,* to JUDGE.]

Hoo·sier (ho͞o′zhər) *n.* A nickname for a native or resident of Indiana. [Origin unknown.]

hoot¹ (ho͞ot) *v.* **hooted, hooting, hoots.** *—intr.* **1.** To utter the characteristic cry of an owl. **2.** To make a loud derisive or contemptuous cry; jeer. **3.** To sound an automobile horn. *—tr.* **1.** To shout down or drive off with jeering cries. Used especially with *down* or *off*: *hoot a speaker off a platform.* **2.** To express or convey by hooting: *hoot one's disgust.* **3.** To cause (an automobile horn) to sound.
∼*n.* **1. a.** The characteristic cry of an owl. **b.** A sound suggesting an owl's cry; especially, the sound of an automobile horn. **2.** An inarticulate cry of contempt or derision. **3.** The least amount; a jot. Used chiefly in the phrase *not give a hoot.* **4.** *British Slang.* A very amusing person or thing. [Middle English *h(o)uten* (imitative).]

hoot² (ho͞ot, o͞ot) *interj.* Also **hoots** (ho͞ots, o͞ots). *Chiefly Scottish.* Used to express objection or annoyance. [Origin unknown.]

hoot·en·an·ny (ho͞ot′n-ăn′ē) *n., pl.* **-nies.** **1.** A gathering of folk singers, typically with participation by the audience. **2.** *Informal.* An unidentified or unidentifiable gadget. [Origin unknown.]

hoot·er (ho͞o′tər) *n. Chiefly British.* **1.** The horn of an automobile or a device that makes a similar noise. **2.** *Slang.* The nose.

hoot owl *n.* Any of various owls having a hooting cry. Compare **screech owl.**

Hoo·ver (ho͞o′vər), **Herbert Clark** (1874–1964). 31st president of the United States (1929–33). He was orphaned at the age of 10 but became a millionaire through mining. After the Wall Street crash Hoover was unwilling to finance employment through federal intervention and lost the presidency to Franklin D. Roosevelt in 1932.

Hoover, J(ohn) Edgar (1895–1972). U.S. lawyer and director of the FBI (1924–72). He led the fight against gangsterism during the

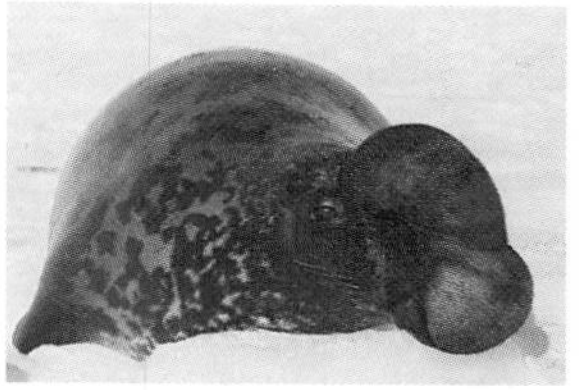

hooded seal *The male hooded seal can inflate its nose into a huge bladder (above),and is sometimes called the bladdernose. The bladder is inflated to impress rivals and cows during the mating season. Hooded seals live on arctic ice floes and grow to 3.5 meters (12 feet) long.*

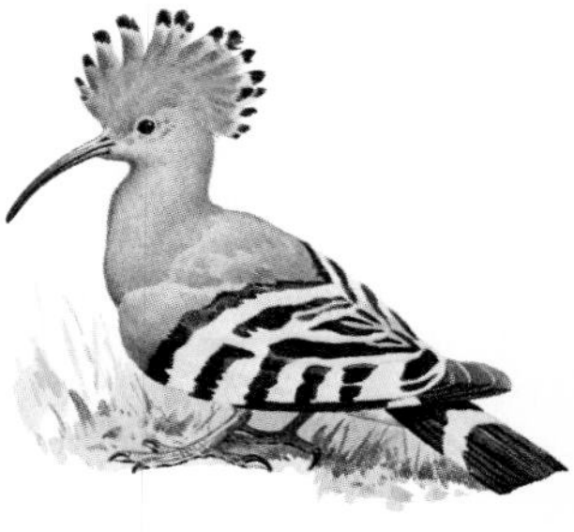

hoopoe *Widely distributed in Europe, Africa, and Asia, the hoopoe is an insect eater, related to the kingfisher.*

PRONUNCIATION KEY

ă, pat; ā, pay; âr, care;
ä, father, are; b, bib;
ch, church; d, deed; ĕ, pet;
ē, be; f, fife; g, gag; h, hat;
hw, which; ĭ, pit; ī, pie;
îr, pier; j, judge; k, kick;
l, lid, needle; m, mum;
n, no, sudden; ng, thing;
ŏ, pot; ō, toe; ô, paw, for;
oi, noise; ou, out; o͝o, book;
o͞o, boot; p, pop; r, roar;
s, sauce; sh, ship, dish;
t, tight; th, thin, path;
th, this, bathe; ŭ, cut; ûr, fur;
v, valve; w, with; y, yes;
z, zebra, size; zh, vision;
ə, about, item, edible,
gallop, circus, peaceful

IN FOREIGN WORDS:

à, *Fr.* ami; œ, *Fr.* feu, *Ger.* schön; ü, *Fr.* tu, *Ger.* über; KH, *Ger.* ich, *Scot.* loch; N, *Fr.* bon; y′, *Fr.* Compiègne

STRESS MARKS:

Primary stress: ′
in·cite′ (ĭn-sīt′)
Secondary stress: ′
in′sight′ (ĭn′sīt′)

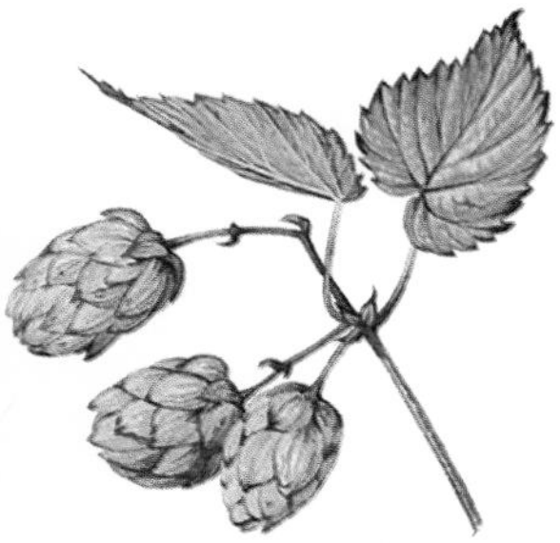

hop *Since medieval times, when French monks perfected the technique, hops have been used to clarify, preserve, and flavor beer. Their young shoots taste like asparagus when cooked.*

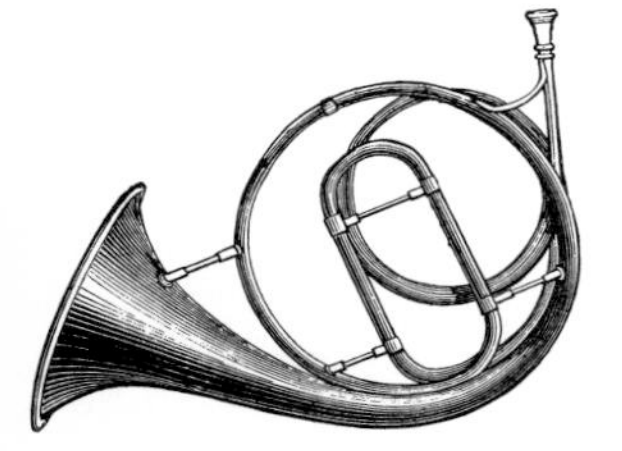

horn *A forerunner of the modern French horn, known as a "natural" horn. With this type of brass horn, changes in key are achieved by inserting extra lengths of tubing—crooks—into the center of the hoop. The development in the early 19th century of valves that automatically alter the length of tubing gave the horn a much wider range.*

PRONUNCIATION KEY

ă, pat; ā, pay; âr, care;
ä, father, are; b, bib;
ch, church; d, deed; ĕ, pet;
ē, be; f, fife; g, gag; h, hat;
hw, which; ĭ, pit; ī, pie;
îr, pier; j, judge; k, kick;
l, lid, needle; m, mum;
n, no, sudden; ng, thing;
ŏ, pot; ō, toe; ô, paw, for;
oi, noise; ou, out; o͝o, book;
o͞o, boot; p, pop; r, roar;
s, sauce; sh, ship, dish;
t, tight; th, thin, path;
th, this, bathe; ŭ, cut; ûr, fur;
v, valve; w, with; y, yes;
z, zebra, size; zh, vision;
ə, about, item, edible, gallop, circus, peaceful

IN FOREIGN WORDS:

à, *Fr.* ami; œ, *Fr.* feu, *Ger.* schön; ü, *Fr.* tu, *Ger.* über; KH, *Ger.* ich, *Scot.* loch; N, *Fr.* bon; y', *Fr.* Compiègne

STRESS MARKS:

Primary stress: ′
in·cite′ (ĭn-sīt′)
Secondary stress: ′
in′sight′ (ĭn′sīt′)

Prohibition era (1919–33). In his later years Hoover was criticized for obsessive anticommunism.

Hoover Dam. Formerly **Boul·der Dam** (bōl′dər). Dam on the Colorado River between Nevada and Arizona. Built (1931–36) for hydroelectric power, flood control, and irrigation, it is 221 meters (726 feet) high and forms Lake Mead, 640 square kilometers (247 square miles), one of the world's largest reservoirs.

Hoo·ver·ville (ho͞o′vər-vĭl′) *n.* A group of crudely built dwellings erected usually on the edge of a town to house the dispossessed and destitute during the depression of the 1930's. [(Herbert) HOOVER + *-ville,* from their prevalence during his administration.]

hooves. Alternate plural of **hoof.**

hop[1] (hŏp) *v.* **hopped, hopping, hops.** —*intr.* **1.** To move with light bounding skips or leaps: *The rabbit hopped across the field.* **2.** To jump on one foot. **3.** *Informal.* To move quickly, as: **a.** To board, get in, or mount something: *hopped on his bicycle and rode off.* **b.** To alight from, get out of, or dismount from something: *hopped out of bed and began to make breakfast.* **4.** To make a quick trip, especially by air: *hopped over to Europe on business.* **5.** *Informal.* To leave. **6.** To bounce after hitting, striking, or colliding with something: *The coin I dropped hopped around on the floor.* —*tr.* **1.** To skip or jump over: *hop the fence.* **2.** *Informal.* To jump aboard (a vehicle); get on: *hopped the train to town.*
∼*n.* **1.** A light springy jump or leap, especially on one foot. **2.** *Informal.* A dance; ball. **3.** A short distance. **4.** A short trip, especially by air. **5.** A ride; lift. **6.** A bounce taken by a batted baseball. **—on the hop.** *British Informal.* **1.** Very busy; active. **2.** Unprepared; without any warning: *caught on the hop by the unexpected snowfall.* [Middle English *hoppen,* Old English *hoppian.*]

hop[2] *n.* **1.** Any of several twining vines of the genus *Humulus;* especially, *H. lupulus,* having lobed leaves and green, conelike female flowers. **2. hops.** The dried, ripe female flowers of this plant, containing a bitter, aromatic oil and used as flavoring in brewing beer. **3. hops.** *Australian & New Zealand Slang.* Beer.
∼*v.* **hopped, hopping, hops.** —*tr.* To flavor with hops. —*intr.* To gather hops. **—hop up.** *Slang.* **1.** To increase the power or energy of. **2.** To stimulate with or as if with a narcotic. [Middle English *hoppe,* from Middle Dutch.]

hop·cal·ite (hŏp′kə-līt′) *n.* A granular mixture of the oxides of copper, cobalt, manganese, and silver, used in gas masks to convert carbon monoxide to carbon dioxide. [*(Johns) Hop(kins University + University of) Cal(ifornia)* + -ITE.]

hop clover *n.* A clover, *Trifolium agrarium,* or one of a similar closely related species, native to Eurasia, having small yellow flower heads that resemble hops when withered.

hope (hōp) *v.* **hoped, hoping, hopes.** —*intr.* To entertain a wish for something with some expectation of its fulfillment: *hoping for a favorable reply.* —*tr.* **1.** To wish for with some confidence of fulfillment: *We hope to get there by Friday, but it depends on the weather.* **2.** To expect with confidence; trust: *I hope that this apology will satisfy your client.* —See Synonyms at **expect. —hope against hope.** To persist in hoping for something against the odds.
∼*n.* **1.** A wish or desire supported by some confidence of its fulfillment. **2.** A ground for expectation, optimism, or trust. **3.** That which is desired or anticipated. **4.** That in which one places one's confidence; one on whom hopes are centered: *She was our main hope for a gold medal at the games.* [Middle English *hopen,* Old English *hopian,* akin to Old Frisian *hopia*†.]

Hope (hōp), **Anthony,** pen name of Sir Anthony Hope Hawkins (1863–1933). British novelist. The most successful of his adventure stories was *The Prisoner of Zenda* (1894). He was knighted in 1918.

Hope, Bob, born Leslie Townes Hope (1903–). U.S. comedian, born in Britain. He costarred with Bing Crosby in the popular Road films, beginning with the *Road to Singapore* (1940).

hope chest *n.* A chest used by a young woman for the gradual collection of fine linens, silver, and other small household items in anticipation of marriage. Also *British* "bottom drawer."

hope·ful (hōp′fəl) *adj.* **1.** Having or manifesting hope. **2.** Inspiring hope; promising.
∼*n.* A person who aspires to success or who shows promise of succeeding. **—hope·ful·ness** *n.*

hope·ful·ly (hōp′fə-lē) *adv.* **1.** With hope; in a hopeful manner. **2.** It is to be hoped; let us hope: *Hopefully, nuclear weapons will never be used in war again.*
Usage: The use of *hopefully* to mean "it is to be hoped," as in *Hopefully, we'll get there before dark,* is grammatically justified by analogy to the similar uses of *happily* and *mercifully.* However, this usage is by now such a bugbear to traditionalists that it is best avoided on grounds of civility, if not logic.

Hopeh, Ho-pei. See **Hebei.**

hope·less (hōp′lĭs) *adj.* **1.** Having no hope; despairing. **2.** Offering no hope; bleak. **3.** Incurable: *a hopeless case of cancer.* **4.** Insoluble; impossible: *a hopeless problem.* **5.** *Informal.* Totally lacking in competence or effectiveness: *As a comedian, he's hopeless.* **—hope·less·ly** *adv.* **—hope·less·ness** *n.*

hop garden *n.* A field in which hops are cultivated. Also called "hop yard."

hop·head (hŏp′hĕd′) *n. Slang.* **1.** A drug addict. **2.** *Australian & New Zealand.* An alcoholic. [From obsolete slang *hop,* opium, probably from HOP (plant).]

hop hornbeam *n.* Any of several trees of the genus *Ostrya;* especially, *O. virginiana,* of eastern North America, having fruit resembling hops. Also called "ironwood."

Ho·pi (hō′pē) *n., pl.* **Hopi** or **-pis. 1.** A member of a Uto-Aztecan-speaking North American Indian tribe now inhabiting a reservation in northeastern Arizona. **2.** The language of this tribe. [Hopi *hópi,* peaceful.]

Hop·kins (hŏp′kĭnz), **Sir Frederick Gowland** (1861–1947). English biochemist. He is noted for his pioneer work on vitamins. He shared (1929) the Nobel Prize for medicine with Christiaan Eijkman.

Hopkins, Gerard Manley (1844–89). British poet. He converted to Roman Catholicism (1866) and became a Jesuit priest. None of his poems was published during his lifetime, but a posthumous collection (1918) influenced the interwar poets. Among his works are "The Windhover" and the long poem "The Wreck of the Deutschland."

Hopkins, Johns (1795–1873). U.S. financier and philanthropist. He amassed a fortune in banking and the railroad business. Aware of Baltimore's lack of emergency medical facilities and of his own lack of education, he gave $7 million for the founding of a free hospital and Johns Hopkins University.

Hopkins, Mark (1802–87). U.S. educator. Renowned as a teacher and administrator, he was president of Williams College in Williamstown, Massachusetts, from 1836 to 1872 and professor of intellectual and moral philosophy from 1872 until his death.

hop·lite (hŏp′līt′) *n.* A heavily armed foot soldier of ancient Greece. [French, from Greek *hoplitēs,* from *hoplon*†, weapon.] **—hop·lit·ic** (hŏp-lĭt′ĭk) *adj.*

hop·per (hŏp′ər) *n.* **1.** One that hops; especially, a hopping insect. **2. a.** A large funnel in which materials, such as grain or fuel, are stored in readiness for dispensation and use. **b.** A freight car that is designed to discharge its load through the floor or by means of a hinged door. **c.** A barge that transports mud, silt, or the like away from a dredging operation and discharges it. **d.** A device for holding a stack of punched cards and feeding them into a computer. **3.** A receptacle in a legislature in which proposed bills are dropped.

Hop·per (hŏp′ər), **Edward** (1882–1967). U.S. painter. Sometimes called the painter of loneliness, he created calm, realistic depictions of stark city settings and lonesome roadside scenes. *Nighthawks* (1942), a haunting view of a late-night diner, is among his most famous works.

Hopper, Hedda (1890–1966). U.S. actress and columnist. After appearing on stage and in films, she began broadcasting (1936) and writing (1938) about the latest gossip from Hollywood. Known for her glittering array of exotic hats, she also carried on a celebrated feud with Louella Parsons for many years.

hop·ping (hŏp′ĭng) *adv.* Very; extremely. Used in the phrase *hopping mad.*

hopple. Variant of **hobble.**

hop·sack (hŏp′săk′) *n.* Also **hop·sack·ing** (hŏp′săk′ĭng). **1.** A loosely woven, coarse fabric of cotton or wool used in clothing. **2.** A coarse fabric of hemp, jute, or the like used to make sacks. [Used by hop growers for bags.]

hop·scotch (hŏp′skŏch′) *n.* A children's game in which players toss an object into succeeding sections of a figure such as a series of squares on the ground, then hop through the figure and back on one foot as they retrieve the object. [HOP + SCOTCH (line).]

hop, step, and jump *n.* An athletic event, the **triple jump** *(see).*

hop trefoil *n.* A Eurasian clover plant, *Trifolium campestre,* having yellow flower heads that when withered resemble the female flowers of the hop.

ho·ra, ho·rah (hôr′ə, hōr′ə) *n.* **1.** A traditional round dance of Romania and Israel. **2.** The music to which this dance is performed. [Modern Hebrew *hōrāh,* from Romanian *horă,* from Turkish *hora.*]

Hor·ace (hôr′ĭs, hŏr′-), born Quintus Horatius Flaccus (65–8 B.C.). Roman poet. His *Odes* and *Satires* express a humane philosophy.

ho·ra·ry (hôr′ə-rē, hōr′-) *adj.* **1.** Of an hour or the hours. **2.** Occurring once an hour. [Medieval Latin *hōrārius,* from Latin *hōra,* HOUR.]

Ho·ra·tian (hə-rā′shən) *adj.* Of, relating to, or characteristic of the poet Horace, as in formal rigor, succinctness, or elegance.

Horatian ode *n.* An ode in which a fixed strophic pattern is followed. [After HORACE.]

horde (hôrd, hōrd) *n.* **1.** A throng or swarm, as of people, animals, or insects. **2.** A nomadic Mongol tribe. **3.** Any nomadic group.
∼*intr.v.* **horded, hording, hords.** To form or live in a horde. [Old French, from German *Horde,* from Polish *horda,* from Turkish *ordū,* camp. See also **Urdu.**]

Ho·reb (hôr′ĕb′, hōr′-). A mountain generally identified in the Old Testament with Mt. Sinai.

hore·hound, hoar·hound (hôr′hound′, hōr′-) *n.* **1.** An aromatic plant, *Marrubium vulgare,* native to Eurasia, having leaves covered with soft whitish hairs and yielding a bitter extract used as flavoring and as a cough remedy. Also called "white horehound." **2.** Any of several similar or related plants, such as the **black horehound** *(see).* [Middle English *horhoune,* Old English *hārhūne* : *hār,* HOAR + *hūne*†, horehound.]

ho·ri·zon (hə-rī′zən) *n.* **1.** The apparent intersection of the earth and sky as seen by an observer. Also called "apparent horizon," "visible horizon." **2.** *Astronomy.* **a.** The circular intersection of a plane tangent to the earth at the observer's station with the celestial sphere. Also called "sensible horizon." **b.** The intersection with the celestial sphere of a plane through the center of the earth and perpendicular to the line connecting the zenith and the nadir. Also called "rational horizon." **c.** The great circle of the celestial sphere at the intersection of the sensible and rational horizons at infinity, its plane passing through the center of the earth. Also called "celestial horizon." **3.** *Often* **horizons.** The range or limits of knowledge, experience, observation, or interest: *broaden one's horizons.* **4.** *Geology.* **a.** A specific position in a stratigraphic column, as the location of one or more fossils, that serves to identify the stratum with a particular period. **b.** A specific layer of soil in a cross section of land. **—on the horizon.** Emerging as a possibility; becoming apparent. [Middle English *orizon(te),* from Old French, from Late Latin *horīzōn,* from Greek *horizōn,* from the present participle of *horizein,* to divide, separate, from *horos*†, boundary, limit.]

hor·i·zon·tal (hôr′ə-zŏnt′l, hŏr′-) *adj.* **1.** Of, relating to, or near the horizon. **2.** Parallel to or in the plane of the horizon; level. Compare **vertical. 3.** Of, pertaining to, or involving those at the same rank, stage, or level in a hierarchy: *a horizontal study of sixth-graders throughout the country; horizontal job mobility.* Compare **vertical. 4.** Flat.
~*n.* Anything, such as a line, plane, or object, that is horizontal or assumed to be parallel with the horizon. [From Late Latin *horīzōn* (stem *horīzont-*), HORIZON.] **—hor·i·zon·tal·ly** *adv.*

hor·mone (hôr′mōn′) *n.* **1.** A substance formed in an endocrine gland and conveyed by the bloodstream to a specific organ or tissue, whose function it modifies by means of its chemical activity. **2.** A compound produced by a plant that affects growth; a growth substance. **3.** Any of various synthetic compounds having effects similar to either of these substances. [Greek *hormōn,* from the present participle of *horman,* to urge on, from *hormē*†, impulse, onrush.] **—hor·mo·nal** (hôr-mō′nəl), **hor·mon·ic** (hôr-mŏn′ĭk) *adj.*

Hor·muz (hôr′mŭz′, hôr-mo͞oz′). Also **Or·muz** (ôr′mŭz′, ôr-mo͞oz′). An island, 44 square kilometers (17 square miles) in area, off the southern coast of Iran in the Strait of Hormuz, a strait linking the Persian Gulf with the Gulf of Oman.

horn (hôrn) *n.* **1.** Any of the hard, usually permanent structures projecting from the head of certain mammals, such as cattle, sheep, goats, or antelopes, consisting of a bony core covered with a sheath of keratinous material. **2.** A similar hard protuberance, such as an antler or a projection on the head of a giraffe or rhinoceros. **3.** A projecting structure or growth suggestive of a horn, such as the eyestalk of a snail. **4. a.** The hard, smooth, keratinous material forming the outer covering of the horns of cattle or related animals. **b.** A substance resembling this. **5.** A container made from a horn: *a powder horn.* **6.** *Archaic.* A symbol or source of strength. **7.** *Archaic.* A symbol of the cuckold. **8.** Anything resembling a horn in appearance, especially: **a.** A cornucopia. **b.** Either of the ends of a crescent moon. **c.** The point of an anvil. **d.** The pommel of a saddle. **e.** An ear trumpet. **f.** A device for projecting sound waves, as in a loudspeaker. **g.** A hollow, metallic, electromagnetic transmission antenna with a characteristically rectangular cross section. Also called "horn antenna." **9.** *Abbr.* **h., H.** *Music.* **a.** A wind instrument made of an animal horn. **b.** A wind instrument made of brass. **c.** A French horn. **d.** *Informal.* A wind instrument, especially the saxophone or trumpet. **10.** A signaling device, usually electrical, that produces a sound similar to that of a sounded animal horn: *a car horn.* **11.** *Aviation.* A short lever projecting from a control surface on an aircraft, to which is attached the cable, line, or rod by which the surface is operated. **12.** *Slang.* A telephone. **—blow** (or **toot**) **one's own horn.** To brag or boast about oneself. **—lock horns.** To become embroiled, as in argument or debate. **—on the horns of a dilemma.** Forced to choose between equally undesirable alternatives. **—pull** (or **draw**) **in one's horns. 1.** To restrain oneself; draw back. **2.** To take back a previous statement; recant. **3.** To economize.
~*tr.v.* **horned, horning, horns. 1.** To gore or wound with a horn. **2.** *Archaic.* To cuckold. **—horn in.** *Slang.* To join without being invited; intrude. [Middle English *horn,* Old English *horn,* from Germanic.] **—horn** *adj.* **—horn·less** *adj.* **—horn·like** *adj.*

Horn, Cape (hôrn). Most southerly point of South America, at Horn Island, Chile. It is also known as the Horn and is notorious for storms and heavy seas.

horn·beam (hôrn′bēm′) *n.* **1.** Any of various trees of the genus *Carpinus;* especially, the Eurasian species, *C. betulus,* having smooth, grayish bark and hard, whitish wood. **2.** The wood of such a tree. Also called "ironwood." [From its tough, close-grained wood.]

horn·bill (hôrn′bĭl′) *n.* Any of various tropical Old World birds of the family Bucerotidae, having a very large bill, often surmounted by an enlarged protuberance at the base.

horn·blende (hôrn′blĕnd′) *n.* A common, greenish-black to black amphibole mineral, essentially calcium magnesium iron sodium aluminum aluminosilicate, found in igneous and metamorphic rocks. [German *Hornblende* : HORN + BLENDE.]

horn·book (hôrn′bo͝ok′) *n.* **1.** A primer used formerly in teaching children to read, consisting of a single page protected by a transparent sheet of horn. **2.** A text that instructs in the basic skills or rudiments of a subject.

Horne (hôrn), **Lena** (1917–). U.S. singer. Noted for her versatile voice and classic beauty, she made her debut as a 16-year-old chorus dancer in Harlem and has since delighted audiences in nightclubs, Broadway musicals, motion pictures, and television productions.

Horne, Marilyn (1934–). U.S. operatic soprano. Renowned for her rich, wide-ranging voice, she became a principal performer at the Metropolitan Opera in New York City after her debut there as Adalgisa in *Norma* (1970).

horned (hôrnd) *adj.* **1.** Having a horn or horns. **2.** Having hornlike projections such as ear tufts: *a horned bird.*

horned owl *n.* Any of various owls of the genus *Bubo* that have prominent ear tufts.

horned poppy *n.* Any of various Eurasian poppies of the genera *Glaucium* and *Roemeria,* having variously colored flowers and long, curved seed capsules.

horned toad *n.* Any of several lizards of the genus *Phrynosoma,* of western North America and Central America, having hornlike projections on the head, a flattened, spiny body, and a short tail. Also called "horned lizard."

horned viper *n.* **1.** A venomous African snake, *Cerastes cornutus,* having a hornlike projection above each eye. Also called "sand viper." **2.** Any of various similar snakes of the genera *Cerastes* and *Pseudocerastes.*

hor·net (hôr′nĭt) *n.* Any of various large stinging wasps, especially *Vespa crabro,* characteristically building a large papery nest. [Middle English *hernet,* Old English *hyrnet.*]

hornet's nest *n.* A vehement or antagonistic response: *a provocative speech that stirred up a hornet's nest.*

horn·fels (hôrn′fĕlz′) *n.* A hard, compact, metamorphic rock formed by the action of heat on clay rocks. Also called "hornstone." [German, "horn rock."]

hor·ni·to (hôr-nē′tō) *n., pl.* **-tos.** A low mound of volcanic origin, sometimes emitting smoke or vapor. [Spanish, diminutive of *horno,* oven, from Latin *furnus.*]

horn-mad (hôrn′măd′) *adj.* Extremely angry; furious; enraged. [Originally "enraged enough to horn or gore someone."]

horn of plenty *n.* A **cornucopia** *(see).*

horn·pipe (hôrn′pīp′) *n.* **1.** A musical instrument with a single reed, finger holes, and a bell and mouthpiece made of horn. **2.** A spirited British folk dance originally accompanied by a hornpipe. **3.** The music for such a dance.

horn-rimmed (hôrn′rĭmd′) *adj.* Having rims or frames made of horn, tortoiseshell, or a material such as hard plastic made to resemble these. Said of eyeglasses.

horn silver *n.* A mineral, **cerargyrite** *(see).*

horn·swog·gle (hôrn′swŏg′əl) *tr.v.* **-gled, -gling, -gles.** *Regional Slang.* To deceive; bamboozle. [19th century : origin obscure.]

horn·tail (hôrn′tāl′) *n.* Any of various sawflies of the family Siricidae, the female of which has a long, stout ovipositor with which it inserts its eggs into the wood of trees.

horn·wort (hôrn′wûrt′, -wôrt′) *n.* **1.** Any of several aquatic plants of the genus *Ceratophyllum,* forming submerged branching masses in quiet water. **2.** Any of various plants of the genus *Anthoceros.*

horn·y (hôr′nē) *adj.* **-ier, -iest. 1.** Having horns or similar projections. **2.** Made of horn. **3.** Resembling horn in hardness. **4.** *Slang.* Sexually aroused; in a state of sexual excitement. **—horn·i·ness** *n.*

hor·o·loge (hôr′ə-lōj′, hŏr′-) *n.* A timepiece. [Middle English *horologe, orloge,* from Old French *orloge,* from Latin *hōrologium,* from Greek *hōrologion,* from *hōrologos,* "hour-teller" : *hōra,* HOUR + *legein,* to speak.]

Hor·o·lo·gi·um (hôr′ə-lō′jē-əm, hŏr′-) *n.* A constellation in the Southern Hemisphere near Hydrus, Eridanus, and Reticulum. [Latin *hōrologium,* HOROLOGE.]

ho·rol·o·gy (hô-rŏl′ə-jē, hō-) *n.* **1.** The science of measuring time. **2.** The art of making clocks and watches. [Middle English *horologie,* from Latin *hōrologium,* HOROLOGE.] **—ho·rol·o·gist** (hô-rŏl′ə-jĭst), **ho·rol·o·ger** (hô-rŏl′ə-jər) *n.* **—hor·o·log·ic** (hôr′ə-lŏj′ĭk, hŏr′-), **hor·o·log·i·cal** *adj.*

hor·o·scope (hôr′ə-skōp′, hŏr′-) *n. Astrology.* **1.** The configuration of the planets and stars at a given moment, such as the moment of a person's birth. **2.** A diagram of the signs of the zodiac based on such a configuration. **3.** A forecast of a person's future based on such a diagram. [Old French, from Latin *hōroscopus,* from Greek *hōroskopos,* astrologer : *hōra,* HOUR + *skopos,* observer.]

ho·ros·co·py (hô-rŏs′kə-pē, hō-) *n., pl.* **-pies.** The casting and reading of horoscopes.

Hor·o·witz (hôr′ə-wĭts′, hŏr′-), **Vladimir** (1904–89). U.S. pianist, of Russian birth. He settled in the United States in 1940. Horowitz was famed as a brilliant technician and as a leading exponent of romantic pianism.

hor·ren·dous (hô-rĕn′dəs, hō-) *adj.* **1.** Hideous; horrifying; dreadful. **2.** *Informal.* Disagreeable; unpleasant. [Latin *horrendus,* from the gerundive of *horrēre,* to tremble.] **—hor·ren·dous·ly** *adv.*

hor·rent (hôr′ənt, hŏr′-) *adj. Archaic.* **1.** Bristling. **2.** Terrified; shuddering. [Latin *horrēns* (stem *horrent-*), present participle of *horrēre,* to tremble.]

hor·ri·ble (hôr′ə-bəl, hŏr′-) *adj.* **1.** Causing horror; dreadful: *"War is beyond all words horrible"* (Winston Churchill). **2.** Unpleasant; disagreeable; offensive. [Middle English, from Old French, from Latin *horrībilis,* from *horrēre,* to tremble.] **—hor·ri·ble·ness** *n.* **—hor·ri·bly** *adv.*

hor·rid (hôr′ĭd, hŏr′-) *adj.* **1.** Unpleasant; disagreeable. **2.** Unkind; nasty: *What a horrid thing to say!* **3.** Causing horror. **4.** *Archaic.* Bristling; rough: *"horrid with fern and intricate with thorn"* (John Dryden). [Latin *horridus,* from *horrēre,* to tremble.] **—hor·rid·ly** *adv.* **—hor·rid·ness** *n.*

hor·rif·ic (hô-rĭf′ĭk, hŏ-) *adj.* **1.** Causing horror; terrifying. **2.** *Informal.* Disagreeable. [Old French *horrifique,* from Latin *horrificus* : *horrēre,* to tremble + *-ficus,* -FIC.] **—hor·rif·i·cal·ly** *adv.*

hor·ri·fy (hôr′ə-fī′, hŏr′-) *tr.v.* **-fied, -fying, -fies. 1.** To fill with horror; terrify. **2.** To cause unpleasant surprise to; shock. [Latin *horri-*

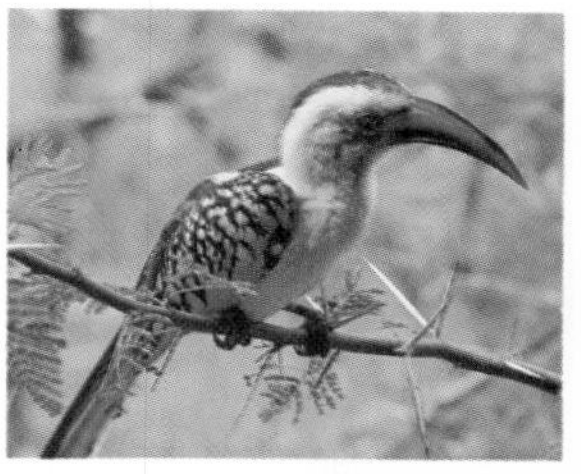

hornbill *Hornbills live in Africa and southern Asia. Unlike most birds they have long eyelashes. The huge beak is used to pick the fruit from trees.*

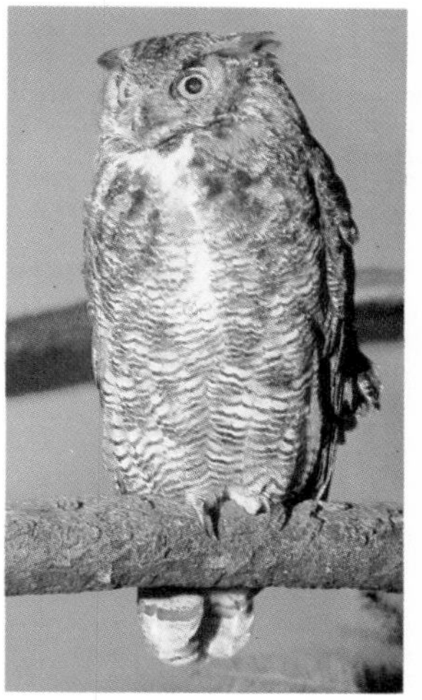

horned owl *The great horned owl,* Bubo virginianus, *can grow to nearly 60 centimeters (2 feet) tall and takes prey as large as rabbits and porcupines. It is widespread throughout North and South America.*

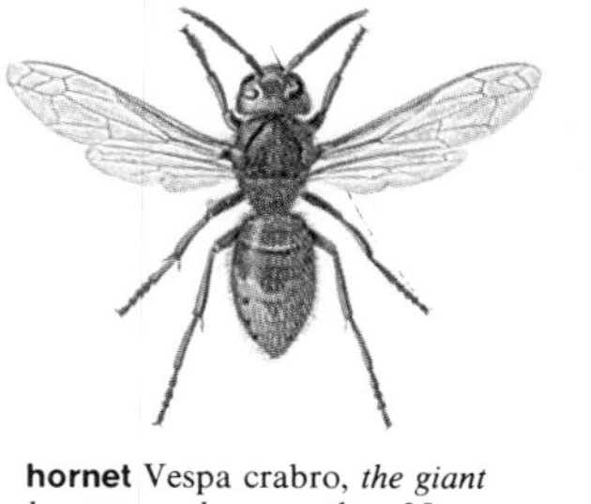

hornet Vespa crabro, *the giant hornet, can be more than 25 millimeters (1 inch) long, and even the smallest workers are larger than the queens of most other wasp species. Like common wasps, hornets live in colonies, often in hollow trees. Only the females have stings, but, despite a reputation for aggressiveness, hornets are relatively docile and rarely sting humans but the sting is a painful one.*

horse-brass *Ornaments have been used on animals since ancient times. Horse-brasses are probably of British origin, and their original purpose was to ward off evil spirits. Hundreds of different designs have been recorded.*

horsefly *Female horseflies live by sucking the blood of animals—mostly horses and cattle—though they will bite humans as well. The bite can be painful, but it is not normally dangerous. Male horseflies are harmless, feeding on flower nectar. Horsefly larvae live mostly in damp soil and feed on other small animals, commonly earthworms.*

horseradish *The horseradish originally came from central and western Asia but is now naturalized in the United States as well. Horseradish sauce is made from its grated root.*

horse

THE ANIMAL THAT WAS MAN'S MAIN POWER SOURCE
Horses bred for work, war, and sport

During most of civilized history man has used the horse as the source of greatest physical and military power and as the motive force in the most rapid means of transport. The horse was probably first domesticated during the Bronze Age by nomadic herdsmen of central Asia. Many breeds have been developed for different purposes. The breeds fall into three main types, according to their use: draft breeds, descended from the medieval warhorses and including the English Shire and the French Percheron; harness breeds such as the Hanoverian and the Hackney; and saddle breeds such as the Lipizzaner and the Thoroughbred.

The largest of all horse breeds is the English Shire, which stands about 18 hands high. A hand is equivalent to 100 millimeters (4 inches) and a horse's height is measured to the top of the shoulder. The tiny Shetland pony is never more than 10½ hands high, but it is used as both draft and saddle horse. The Thoroughbred was descended from the ancient Arabian horse; it was bred for racing and stud. The Hanoverian was crossbred with the English Thoroughbred for George I (1714–27) and, like the hardy French and Belgian Ardennes and the East Prussian Trakehner (the pride of German horse breeding), was once a cavalry horse. All three are now bred mainly for sport.

Other flourishing breeds are the Friesian, which is indigenous to the Netherlands, one of Europe's oldest breeds, and a popular circus horse; the Austrian Lipizzaner, which excels in dressage at the Spanish Riding School in Vienna; and the Australian Waler, like the American Bronco, an excellent bucking horse. The Orlov, which was bred for trotting in pre-Revolutionary Russia, has declined because the studs were destroyed during the Revolution.

Trakehner 16 hands

Lipizzaner 16 hands

Friesian 13 hands

Waler Height variable

Thoroughbred 14½ – 17 hands

Orlov 17 hands

Shetland 10½ hands

Percheron 16 hands

Shire 18 hands

Hanoverian 16 hands

Ardennes 15 hands

ficāre, from *horrificus,* HORRIFIC.] —**hor·ri·fi·ca·tion** (hôr′ə-fĭ-kā′-shən) *n.*

hor·rip·i·la·tion (hô-rĭp′ə-lā′shən, hŏ-) *n.* The bristling of the body hair, as from fear or cold; goose flesh. [Late Latin *horripilātiō,* from Latin *horripilātus,* past participle of *horripilāre,* to bristle with hairs : *horrēre,* to bristle + *pilus,* hair.]

hor·ror (hôr′ər, hŏr′-) *n.* **1.** An intense and painful feeling of repugnance and fear; terror. **2.** Intense dislike; abhorrence; loathing: *has a horror of snakes.* **3. a.** The quality of causing horror. **b.** One that excites horror; a horrifying person or thing: *the horrors of war.* **4.** An unpleasant person, especially a child: *a little horror.* **5.** *Informal.* Something unpleasant, ugly, or disagreeable: *That hat is a real horror.* **6.** *Obsolete.* A bristling or shuddering condition.

~*adj.* Calculated to terrify the reader, listener, or watcher: *a horror story.* [Middle English *(h)orrour,* from Old French, from Latin *horror,* from *horrēre,* to tremble, bristle, be in horror.]

hor·rors (hôr′ərz, hŏr′-) *pl.n. Informal.* Intense nervous depression or anxiety: *had a bad case of the horrors.*

~*interj.* Used to express dismay, often humorously.

hor·ror-strick·en (hôr′ər-strĭk′ən, hŏr′-) *adj.* Also **hor·ror-struck** (-strŭk′). Horrified; filled with sudden fear or repugnance.

Horsa. See **Hengist.**

hors de com·bat (ôr′ də kôn-bä′) *adj.* Out of action; injured or disabled. [French.] —**hors de com·bat** *adv.*

hors d'oeuvre (ôr dûrv′; *French* ôr dœ′vrə) *n., pl.* **hors d'oeuvres** (ôr dûrvz′) or **hors d'oeuvre. 1.** An appetizer served with drinks or before a meal. **2.** Any of various small dishes, such as spiced meat or specially garnished vegetables, served as a first course. [French, outside of the ordinary meal, side dish, "outside of work" : *hors,* outside, from Latin *forīs* + *de,* of + *oeuvre,* work, from Latin *opera,* from *opus* (stem *oper-*), work, OPUS.]

horse (hôrs) *n., pl.* **horses** or **horse. 1. a.** A large, hoofed mammal, *Equus caballus,* having a short-haired coat, a long mane, and a long tail and domesticated since ancient times for riding and to pull vehicles or carry loads. **b.** An adult male of this species. **2.** A horse over a certain size, usually over 14½ hands high, as opposed to a pony. **3.** Any of various other equine mammals, such as the wild Asian species, **Przewalski's horse** *(see),* or certain extinct forms

related ancestrally to the modern horse. **4.** Mounted soldiers; cavalry: *a squadron of horse.* **5.** A supportive frame or device, such as a clothes horse or sawhorse. **6.** A gymnastic device having four legs and a padded body used for vaulting and other exercises. **7.** *Slang.* Heroin. **8. horses.** *Informal.* Horse racing or horse races. Preceded by *the*: *lost a fortune on the horses.* **9.** *Often* **horses.** Horsepower. **10.** *Geology.* **a.** A block of rock interrupting a vein and containing no minerals. **b.** A large block of displaced rock that is caught along a fault. **—a horse of another (or a different) color.** Another matter entirely; something else. **—be (or get) on one's high horse.** To be or become disdainful, superior, or conceited. **—flog (or beat) a dead horse.** **1.** To continue to pursue an enterprise that has no hope of success. **2.** To dwell tiresomely on a subject that is no longer of interest. **—hold one's horses.** To check or rein one's eagerness; restrain oneself. **—the horse's mouth.** A source of information regarded as original or unimpeachable: *It's not just a rumor—I got the story straight from the horse's mouth.*
~*v.* **horsed, horsing, horses.** —*tr.* To provide with or place upon a horse. —*intr.* **1.** To mount or ride upon a horse. **2.** *Informal.* To indulge in horseplay. Usually used with *around* or *about.*
~*adj.* **1.** Of or pertaining to a horse. **2.** Mounted on a horse or horses. **3.** Drawn or operated by a horse or horses. [Middle English *hors,* Old English *hors,* from Germanic *hors-* (unattested).]

horse·back (hôrs′băk′) *n.* The back of a horse: *rode on horseback.* Also used adjectivally: *horseback riding.*
~*adv.* On horseback: *riding horseback.*

horse bean *n.* The **broad bean** *(see).*

horse·box (hôrs′bŏks′) *n.* A large van, or a trailer that can be pulled by a motor vehicle, used for transporting horses.

horse-brass, horse brass (hôrs′brăs′, -bräs′) *n.* A flat ornament made of brass and originally worn on a horse's harness to frighten away evil spirits.

horse·car (hôrs′kär′) *n.* **1.** A streetcar drawn by horses. **2.** A car for transporting horses.

horse chestnut *n.* **1.** Any of several trees of the genus *Aesculus*; especially, *A. hippocastanum,* native to Eurasia, having palmate leaves, erect clusters of pink or white flowers tinged with red, and brown, shiny nuts enclosed in a spiny bur. **2.** The nut of such a tree. In this sense, also called "conker." [Formerly used in treating ailments of horses.]

horse·flesh (hôrs′flĕsh′) *n.* **1.** Horses collectively; especially, racehorses considered in terms of their racing potential. **2.** The flesh of a horse; especially, edible horse meat.

horse·fly (hôrs′flī′) *n., pl.* **-flies.** Any of numerous large flies of the family Tabanidae, the females of which suck the blood of various mammals, including man, inflicting painful bites.

horse gentian *n.* Any of various plants of the genus *Triosteum,* having small purplish-brown flowers and leathery orange-yellow fruit. Also called "feverwort."

Horse Guards *pl.n.* **1.** A cavalry brigade of the household troops of the British royal family. **2.** The headquarters of the Horse Guards, in Whitehall, London.

horse·hair (hôrs′hâr′) *n.* **1.** The hair of a horse, especially from the mane or tail. **2.** Cloth made of horsehair, used chiefly in upholstery.
~*adj.* **1.** Made of horsehair. **2.** Covered or stuffed with horsehair.

horsehair worm *n.* Any of various slender aquatic worms of the phylum Nematomorpha, the larvae of which are parasitic within insects. Also called "hairworm." [These hairlike worms were once thought to have formed from horsehairs that dropped into drinking troughs.]

horse·hide (hôrs′hīd′) *n.* **1. a.** The hide of a horse. **b.** Leather made from this hide. **2.** *Informal.* A baseball.

horse latitudes *pl.n.* Either of two belts of latitudes located mostly over the oceans at about 30° to 35° north and south, having high barometric pressure, calms, light changeable winds, and fine weather. [18th century : perhaps alluding to the old nautical practice of throwing horses overboard to lighten becalmed ships.]

horse·laugh (hôrs′lăf′, -läf′) *n.* A loud, coarse, often mocking laugh; a guffaw.

horse·leech (hôrs′lēch′) *n.* Any of several large leeches of the genus *Haemopis.*

horse·less carriage (hôrs′lĭs) *n.* An automobile.

horse mackerel *n.* **1.** Any of several large, mackerellike marine fishes of the genus *Trachurus*; especially, *T. trachurus.* Also called "scad." **2.** Any of several tunas or related fishes.

horse·man (hôrs′mən) *n., pl.* **-men** (-mĭn). **1.** A man who rides a horse. **2.** One skilled at horsemanship.

horse·man·ship (hôrs′mən-shĭp′) *n.* The art and skill of riding a horse; equitation.

horse marine *n.* **1. a.** A marine assigned to the cavalry. **b.** A cavalryman assigned to a ship. **2.** One who is out of his element; a misfit.

horse·mint (hôrs′mĭnt′) *n.* Any of several coarse, aromatic plants such as *Mentha longifolia,* a European species of mint.

horse mushroom *n.* A large, edible mushroom, *Agaricus arvensis,* having a white cap with a grayish undersurface.

horse opera *n.* A film or other theatrical work about the American West; a Western.

horse·play (hôrs′plā′) *n.* Rowdy, rough play.

horse·pow·er (hôrs′pou′ər) *n. Abbr.* **hp** **1.** A unit of power in the U.S. Customary System equal to 745.7 watts or 550 foot-pounds per second. **2.** The power exerted by a horse in pulling.

horse·pow·er-hour (hôrs′pou′ər-our′) *n.* A unit of work or energy equal to the work done by working at 1 horsepower for 1 hour, which is equivalent to 2.686 × 10^6 joules.

horse·rad·ish (hôrs′răd′ĭsh) *n.* **1.** A coarse plant, *Armoracia rusticana* (or *A. lapathifolia*), native to Eurasia, having a thick, whitish, pungent root. **2.** The grated root of this plant, often combined with vinegar or other ingredients and used as a condiment.

horse sense *n. Informal.* Common sense.

horse·shoe (hôrs′sho͞o′, hôrsh′-) *n.* **1.** A narrow U-shaped iron plate fitted and nailed to a horse's hoof. **2.** Something having a similar shape. Also used adjectivally: *a horseshoe magnet.* **3. horseshoes.** *Used with a singular verb.* A game in which players try to toss horseshoes so that they encircle a stake.
~*tr.v.* **horseshoed, -shoeing, -shoes.** To shoe (a horse).

horseshoe bat *n.* Any of various Old World insectivorous bats of the genus *Rhinolophus* and related genera, having a fleshy, horseshoe-shaped outgrowth around the nostrils that is used in echolocation.

horseshoe crab *n.* Any of various marine arthropods of the class Merostomata; especially, *Limulus polyphemus* (or *Xiphosura polyphemus*), of eastern North America, having a large, rounded body and a stiff, pointed tail. Also called "king crab."

horse·tail (hôrs′tāl′) *n.* Any of various nonflowering pteridophytic plants of the genus *Equisetum,* having a jointed, hollow stem and narrow, sometimes much reduced leaves.

horse-trad·ing (hôrs′trā′dĭng) *n.* Negotiation characterized by shrewd and vigorous bargaining.

horse·weed (hôrs′wēd′) *n.* A weedy North American plant of the fleabane family, *Erigeron canadensis,* having narrow leaves and numerous small white or greenish flowers.

horse·whip (hôrs′hwĭp′) *n.* A whip used to control a horse.
~*tr.v.* **horsewhipped, -whipping, -whips.** To beat with or as if with a horsewhip.

horse·wom·an (hôrs′wo͝om′ən) *n., pl.* **-women** (-wĭm′ĭn). **1.** A woman who rides a horse. **2.** A woman skilled at horsemanship.

horst (hôrst) *n.* A massive block of the earth's crust that lies between two parallel faults and is higher than the surrounding land. [German *Horst,* heap.]

hors·y, hors·ey (hôr′sē) *adj.* **-ier, -iest.** **1. a.** Of, pertaining to, or characteristic of a horse. **b.** Suggestive of a horse in appearance. **2.** Devoted to horses and horsemanship: *the horsy set.*

hort. horticultural; horticulture.

hor·ta·tive (hôr′tə-tĭv) *adj.* Giving exhortation; urging strongly. [Late Latin *hortātīvus,* from Latin *hortātus,* past participle of *hortārī,* to exhort.] **—hor·ta·tive·ly** *adv.*

hor·ta·to·ry (hôr′tə-tôr′ē, -tōr′ē) *adj.* Hortative; urging strongly. [Late Latin *hortātōrius,* from *hortātus.* See **hortative.**]

hor·ti·cul·ture (hôr′tə-kŭl′chər) *n. Abbr.* **hort.** **1.** The science or art of cultivating plants, especially those for ornamental use, or fruit and vegetables for food. **2.** The cultivation of a garden. [Latin *hortus,* garden + (AGRI)CULTURE.] **—hor·ti·cul·tur·al** (hôr′tə-kŭl′chər-əl) *adj.* **—hor·ti·cul·tur·al·ly** *adv.* **—hor·ti·cul·tur·ist** (hôr′tə-kŭl′chər-ĭst) *n.*

hor·tus sic·cus (hôr′təs sĭk′əs) *n.* A collection of dried plants; a herbarium. [Latin, "dry garden."]

Ho·rus (hôr′əs, hōr′-). The ancient Egyptian god of the sun and the sky, represented as having the head of a hawk.

Hos. Hosea (Old Testament).

ho·san·na (hō-zan′ə) *interj.* Used to express praise or adoration to God or the Messiah.
~*n.* **1.** A cry of "hosanna." **2.** A shout of fervent and worshipful praise. [Middle English, from Late Latin *(h)ōsanna,* from Greek, from Hebrew *hosha'nā,* "save us!"]

hose (hōz) *n., pl.* **hose** or *archaic* **hosen** (hō′zən) (for senses 1, 2); **hoses** (for sense 3). **1.** Stockings, socks, or pantyhose. **2. a.** A man's garment that covers the legs and hips and fastens to a doublet by points. **b.** Short full breeches reaching to the knees. **3.** A flexible tube for conveying fluids under pressure.
~*tr.v.* **hosed, hosing, hoses.** To water, drench, or wash with a hose. Often used with *down.* [Middle English *hose,* a stocking, Old English *hosa,* leg covering.]

Ho·se·a[1] (hō-zē′ə, -zā′ə). Hebrew Minor Prophet of the 8th century B.C.

Hosea[2] *n. Abbr.* **Hos.** A prophetic book of the Old Testament, attributed to Hosea.

ho·sier (hō′zhər) *n.* A maker of or dealer in hose and knitted underclothing. [Middle English *hosyer,* from *hose,* HOSE.]

ho·sier·y (hō′zhə-rē) *n.* **1. a.** Stockings and socks; hose. **b.** *British.* Stockings, socks, pantyhose, and underclothing. **2.** The business of a hosier.

hosp. hospital.

hos·pice (hŏs′pĭs) *n.* **1.** A shelter or lodging for travelers, children, or the destitute, often maintained by a monastic order. **2.** An institution that specializes in the care of the terminally ill. [French, from Old French, from Latin *hospitium,* hospitality, from *hospes* (stem *hospit-*), HOST (receiver of guests).]

hos·pi·ta·ble (hŏs′pə-tə-bəl, hŏ-spĭt′ə-bəl) *adj.* **1. a.** Welcoming guests with warmth and generosity. **b.** Well disposed toward strangers. **2.** Having an open and generous mind; receptive. **3.** Promoting well-being; agreeable: *a hospitable climate.* [New Latin *hospitabilis,* from Latin *hospitārī,* to be hospitable to, from *hospes* (stem *hospit-*), HOST (receiver of guests).] **—hos·pi·ta·bly** *adv.*

hos·pi·tal (hŏs′pə-təl, -pĭt′l) *n. Abbr.* **hosp.** **1.** An institution providing medical or surgical care and treatment for people who are ill or

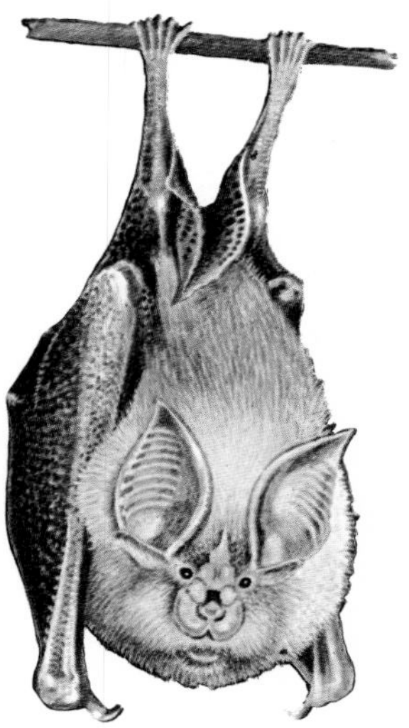

horseshoe bat *The horseshoe bat gets its name from the crescent-shaped flesh around its nose. The bat navigates in the dark by listening to the echoes of the high-pitched squeaks it emits through this fleshy area.*

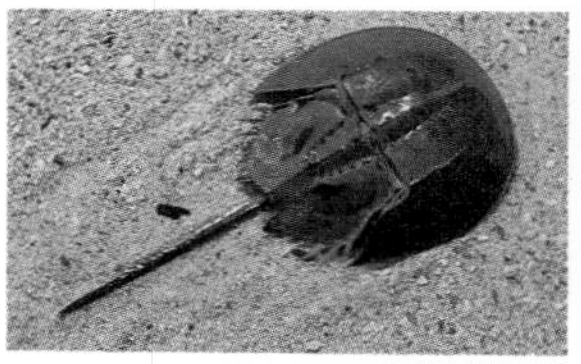

horseshoe crab *Fossil remains show that the horseshoe crab (also known as the king crab) has survived virtually unchanged for about 200 million years.*

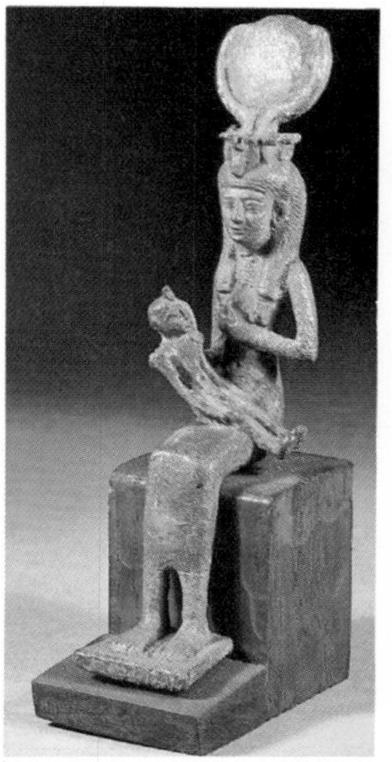

Horus *An Egyptian statue of Isis suckling Horus, the god of the sky whose eyes were the sun and the moon. In Egyptian mythology, Horus became ruler of a united Egypt and the pharaohs thought of themselves as his earthly representatives, using his name as the first of their titles.*

injured, obstetric treatment for pregnant women, psychiatric treatment for the mentally ill, and the like. See **day hospital, general hospital. 2.** *Archaic.* **a.** A hospice for travelers or pilgrims. **b.** A home, often charitable, for old people, the infirm, or foundlings. **3.** A repair shop for specified items: *a doll hospital.* [Middle English, hospice, from Old French, from Medieval Latin *hospitāle*, from Latin *hospitālis*, of a guest, from *hospes* (stem *hospit-*), HOST.]

hospital corner *n.* A method of folding sheets and blankets securely under the mattress at each corner of the foot of a bed, commonly used in making up beds in hospitals.

Hos·pi·tal·er, Hos·pi·tal·ier (hŏs′pə-tə-lər) *n.* **1.** A member of a military religious order founded among European crusaders in 11th-century Palestine. **2.** A member of any of several religious orders dedicated to the care of hospital patients. [Middle English *Hospitalier*, from Old French, from Medieval Latin *hospitāle*, hospice. See **hospital.**]

hos·pi·tal·i·ty (hŏs′pə-tăl′ə-tē) *n., pl.* **-ties. 1.** The act of being hospitable or a tendency toward being hospitable; welcoming and generous behavior toward guests or strangers. **2.** An instance of this. [Middle English *hospitalite*, from Old French, from Latin *hospitālitās* (stem *hospitālitāt-*), from *hospitālis*, from *hospitālis.* See **hospital.**]

hos·pi·tal·i·za·tion (hŏs′pə-tə-lĭ-zā′shən) *n.* **1. a.** The act of hospitalizing. **b.** The condition of being hospitalized. **2.** The length of time spent by a patient in a hospital. **3.** A form of insurance that partially or completely covers a patient's hospital expenses.

hos·pi·tal·ize (hŏs′pə-tə-līz′) *tr.v.* **-ized, -izing, -izes.** To put (a patient) into a hospital.

host[1] (hōst) *n.* **1.** One who receives or entertains guests in a social or business capacity. **2.** *Biology.* **a.** An organism that harbors and provides nourishment for a parasite. **b.** Any organism that supports another organism, as a commensal, or that supports part of another organism, as a tissue graft. **3.** The master of ceremonies of a radio or television program. **4.** A place or institution providing the venue for an organized event: *The city has been designated as host for the next Olympic Games.*
~*tr.v.* **hosted, hosting, hosts.** To serve as host for (a party or a television program, for example). [Middle English *(h)oste*, from Old French, host, guest, from Latin *hospes* (stem *hospit-*), guest, host, stranger.]

host[2] *n.* **1.** A great number: *"a host of golden daffodils"* (William Wordsworth). **2.** An army. —See Synonyms at **multitude.** [Middle English, from Old French, from Medieval Latin *hostis*, army, from Latin, stranger, enemy.]

host[3] *n.* Often **Host.** *Ecclesiastical.* The consecrated bread or wafer of the Eucharist. [Middle English *oste*, from Old French *oiste*, from Latin *hostia†*, sacrifice, victim.]

hos·ta (hō′stə) *n. Botany.* The **plantain lily** (see). [New Latin, genus name, after Nicolaus T. *Host* (d. 1834), Austrian botanist.]

hos·tage (hŏs′tĭj) *n.* **1.** A person taken, often by force, and held as a security for the fulfillment of certain terms. **2.** Anything held as a security. —**a hostage to fortune.** Something one has acquired and may lose. [Middle English *(h)ostage*, from Old French, either from *oste, hoste*, guest, HOST, or from Vulgar Latin *obsidāticum* (unattested), from Late Latin *obsidātus*, hostage (sense 2), from Latin *obses* (stem *obsid-*), a hostage : *ob-*, in the way of, in front of + *sedēre*, to sit.]

hos·tel (hŏs′təl) *n.* **1. a.** Any of various types of supervised, inexpensive lodging houses or residences for groups of people such as students, the homeless, or young travelers. **b.** A **youth hostel** (see). **2.** *Archaic.* An inn. [Middle English *(h)ostel*, from Old French, from Medieval Latin *hospitāle*, hospice. See **hospital.**]

hos·tel·er (hŏs′tə-lər) *n.* **1.** A traveler who stays at youth hostels. **2.** *Archaic.* An innkeeper.

hos·tel·ry (hŏs′təl-rē) *n., pl.* **-ries.** An inn.

host·ess (hō′stĭs) *n.* **1.** A woman who acts as a host. **2.** A woman whose occupation is greeting and assisting patrons, as in a restaurant or on an airplane.

hos·tile (hŏs′təl, -tīl′) *adj.* **1.** Of or pertaining to an enemy. **2.** Feeling or showing enmity or hatred; antagonistic. **3.** Inhospitable; unwelcoming: *a hostile environment.* [Old French, from Latin *hostīlis*, from *hostis*, HOST (enemy).] —**hos′tile·ly** *adv.*

hos·til·i·ty (hŏ-stĭl′ə-tē) *n., pl.* **-ties. 1.** The state of being hostile; antagonism; enmity. **2. a.** A hostile act or incident. **b. hostilities.** Overt warfare. —See Synonyms at **enmity.**

hostler. Variant of **ostler.**

hot (hŏt) *adj.* **hotter, hottest. 1. a.** Possessing great heat. **b.** Yielding much heat. **c.** Being at a high temperature. **2.** Warmer than is normal or desirable: *a hot forehead.* **3. a.** Causing a burning sensation because highly spiced: *a hot curry.* **b.** Heated and not having cooled down: *a hot drink.* **4. a.** Charged or energized with electricity: *a hot wire.* **b.** Radioactive, especially to a dangerous degree. **5.** Explosive; fiery: *a hot dispute; a hot temper.* **6.** Eager; excited; ardent: *in hot pursuit.* **7.** *Slang.* **a.** Recently stolen: *hot goods.* **b.** Wanted for criminal activity. **8.** Close to success or achievement: *hot on the trail.* **9.** *Informal.* Highly sensitive; dangerously controversial: *The issue proved too hot for the government to handle.* **10.** *Informal.* **a.** New; fresh: *hot off the press.* **b.** Currently popular: *one of the hottest young talents around.* **c.** Confidently expected to win: *the hot favorite.* **11.** *Slang.* Good or impressive. Usually used in the negative: *not so hot.* **12.** *Slang.* **a.** Performing with special skill or success. **b.** Lucky. **13.** *Slang.* Producing exciting emotional and physical reactions by means of strong rhythms and inspired improvisation. Said of jazz. **14.** Strong; striking; bright. Said of a

color. **15.** *Metallurgy.* At a temperature sufficiently high for metal to become soft enough to work or cast. Said of a process or a metal. —**hot under the collar.** *Informal.* Angry. —**in hot water.** *Informal.* In trouble. —**make it hot for.** *Informal.* To make things uncomfortable or dangerous for. [Middle English *hot*, Old English *hāt*, from Germanic.]

hot air *n. Informal.* Empty talk; boastful nonsense.

hot-air balloon (hŏt′âr′) *n.* A balloon consisting of a large fabric or plastic bag containing air, which is heated by a naked flame, and a passenger-carrying basket or gondola.

hot-bed (hŏt′bĕd′) *n.* **1.** A glass-covered bed of soil heated with fermenting manure or by electricity, used for the germination of seeds or for protecting tender plants. **2.** An environment conducive to rapid, excessively vigorous growth, especially of something bad: *a hotbed of intrigue.*

hot-blood·ed (hŏt′blŭd′ĭd) *adj.* **1.** Easily excited or angered. **2.** Passionate. **3.** Rash or reckless. —**hot-blood·ed·ness** *n.*

hot-box (hŏt′bŏks′) *n.* An overheated axle or journal box, as in a railway car, caused by excessive friction.

hot cake *n.* A pancake. —**go** (or **sell) like hot cakes.** To be in great demand.

hotch (hŏch) *v.* **hotched, hotching, hotches.** *Scottish.* —*tr.* To shake; jog. —*intr.* To fidget. [Perhaps from Old French *hocher, hochier*, perhaps from Frankish *hottisōn†* (unattested).]

hotch-pot (hŏch′pŏt′) *n. Law.* The gathering together of properties to secure an equal division of the total for distribution, as among the heirs of an intestate parent. [Middle English *hochepot*, from Old French : *hocher, hochier*, HOTCH + *pot*, pot, from (unattested) Vulgar Latin *pottus*.]

hotch-potch (hŏch′pŏch′) *n.* **1.** A hodgepodge. **2.** A stew made from many different ingredients. **3.** *Law.* A hotchpot. [Variant of HOTCHPOT.]

hot cross bun *n.* A sweet bun often made with raisins and marked on top with a cross of frosting traditionally eaten during Lent.

hot dipping *n.* The process of dipping metal objects in a second molten metal to give them a thin protective or decorative coating.

hot dog *n.* A frankfurter, typically served hot in a long, soft roll. ~*interj. Informal.* Used to express satisfaction or enthusiasm. [Perhaps from its fancied resemblance to a dachshund.]

hot-dog (hŏt′dôg′, -dŏg′) *intr.v.* **-dogged, -dogging, -dogs.** *Slang.* To do stunts or acrobatic feats, especially while skiing or surfing. —**hot-dog·ger** *n.*

ho·tel (hō-tĕl′) *n.* An establishment that provides accommodation and usually meals and other services for the public. [French *hôtel*, from Old French *hostel*, HOSTEL.]

ho·tel·ier (hō-tĕl′yər, ōt′l-yā′) *n.* A person who owns or manages a hotel or hotels. [French *hôtelier*, from Old French *hostelier*, innkeeper : *(h)ostel*, HOSTEL + *-ier*, -ER.]

hot flash *n.* A transient vasomotor symptom of the menopause, resulting from hormone imbalance, that involves dilation of the skin capillaries and the sensation of heat over all or part of the body. Also called "hot flush."

hot·foot (hŏt′foot′) *intr.v.* **-footed, -footing, -foots.** To go in haste. Used with *it.*
~*adv.* In haste.
~*n., pl.* **hotfoots.** A prank in which a match is stealthily inserted into the side of someone's shoe and lit. [Middle English (adverb), "with eager feet."]

hot·head (hŏt′hĕd′) *n.* One who is hotheaded.

hot·head·ed (hŏt′hĕd′ĭd) *adj.* **1.** Having a fiery temper. **2.** Impetuous; rash. —**hot·head·ed·ly** *adv.* —**hot·head·ed·ness** *n.*

hot·house (hŏt′hous′) *n., pl.* **-houses** (-hou′zĭz). A heated greenhouse or conservatory for plants requiring an even, relatively warm temperature.
~*adj.* **1.** Grown in a hothouse. **2.** Like or characteristic of a plant grown in a hothouse; delicate; sensitive.

hot line *n.* **1.** A direct communications link, as a telephone line, especially one between heads of government for use in time of crisis, as to prevent an accidental outbreak of war. **2.** A telephone facility that enables callers to talk confidentially to sympathetic listeners about personal problems.

hot·ly (hŏt′lē) *adv.* In an angry or fiery way; passionately: *answered hotly that he was innocent.*

hot-met·al printing (hŏt′mĕt′l) *n.* A method of printing using type cast from molten metal.

hot money *n.* Capital transferred from place to place at frequent intervals in order to achieve the maximum possible return.

hot pepper *n.* **1.** The pungent fruit of any of several varieties of *Capsicum frutescens.* **2.** A condiment made from such fruit.

hot plate *n.* **1.** An electrically heated plate for cooking or warming food. **2.** A table-top cooking device having one or two burners.

hot-pot (hŏt′pŏt′) *n. Chiefly British.* A stew of meat, especially lamb, with layers of potatoes, usually baked in a tight-lidded pot.

hot potato *n. Informal.* A highly controversial or sensitive issue: *The question of police accountability has become a political hot potato.*

hot-press (hŏt′prĕs′) *tr.v.* **-pressed, -pressing, -presses.** To subject (paper or cloth) to heat and pressure in order to extract oil.
~*n.* (hŏt′prĕs′). A machine for hot-pressing.

hot property *n. Informal.* A person or thing regarded as having great promise or potential.

hot rod, hot-rod (hŏt′rŏd′) *n. Slang.* A car rebuilt or remodeled for increased speed and acceleration. —**hot rodder** *n.*

hot seat *n. Slang.* **1.** A difficult or exposed position. **2.** The electric chair.

hot·shot (hŏt′shŏt′) *n. Slang.* An ostentatiously skillful person.

hot spot *n.* **1.** An area of high temperature in an engine or machine, either one that results from a malfunction or one that is used to vaporize fuel. **2.** A place full of danger, violence, or unrest. **3.** An area on the surface of the earth, away from a tectonic plate margin, that has a higher than average heat flow and that often gives rise to a volcano. **4.** An exciting, lively place, such as a nightclub.

hot spring *n.* A natural spring continuously discharging water that is above body temperature, or over 98°F (37°C).

Hot Springs. A city of west-central Arkansas, nearly coextensive with **Hot Springs National Park.** The city produces metal and electrical products and lumber. The springs were long used by Indians for medicinal purposes and were visited by Hernando de Soto in 1541. More than a million gallons of water a day, with an average temperature of 62°C (143°F), flow from 47 springs. The national park was established in 1921.

Hotspur. See **Percy, Sir Henry.**

Hot·ten·tot (hŏt′n-tŏt′) *n., pl.* **-tots** or collectively **Hottentot. 1.** A southern African people, held to be related to the Bantu and Bushmen. **2.** The language of this people. [Afrikaans.]

hot toddy *n.* A beverage, a **toddy** *(see).*

hot tub *n.* A very large, usually wooden tub in which a group of bathers can soak in hot water.

hot-wa·ter bottle (hŏt′wô′tər, -wŏt′ər) *n.* A container, usually made of rubber, designed to be filled with hot water and used to warm a part of the body or a bed.

hot-water crust *n.* A type of pie pastry made from flour, melted fat, and water.

Hou·dan (ho͞o′dăn′) *n.* A domesticated fowl having black and white plumage and a V-shaped comb. [French, developed in *Houdan,* a village near Paris, France.]

Hou·di·ni (ho͞o-dē′nē), **Harry,** born Ehrich Weiss (1874–1926). U.S. magician and showman. He was adept at escaping from chains, handcuffs, straitjackets, and padlocked containers.

Hou·don (ho͞o′dŏn′), **Jean Antoine** (1741–1828). French sculptor. He is especially noted for his statues of Washington and Voltaire and for his many portrait busts, including ones of Jefferson, Franklin, John Paul Jones, Rousseau, and Lafayette.

hough (hŏKH) *n. British.* **1.** A **hock** *(see).* **2.** A joint of meat, such as beef, from the hock or the part of the leg above it.
~*tr.v.* **houghed, houghing, houghs.** *British.* To hock or hamstring. [Middle English, from Old English *hōh,* heel, attested in *hōhsinu,* "hock-shin," hamstring.]

hound[1] (hound) *n.* **1.** A dog of any of various breeds used for hunting, characteristically having drooping ears, a short coat, and a deep, resonant voice. Also used in combination: *bloodhound; foxhound.* **2.** Any dog. **3.** A runner who pursues in the game of hare and hounds. **4.** A contemptible person; a scoundrel. **5.** One who eagerly pursues something: *a news hound.* **—follow the** (or **ride to**) **hounds.** To take part in a fox hunt.
~*tr.v.* **hounded, hounding, hounds. 1.** To pursue or harass relentlessly and tenaciously: *hounded by the press.* **2.** To incite to give chase; urge on. —See Synonyms at **harass.** [Middle English *h(o)und,* Old English *hund,* from Germanic.]

hound[2] *n.* **1.** Either of two projections at the side of a masthead that supports the trestletrees of large vessels or the rigging of smaller ones. **2.** Either of a pair of horizontal braces for reinforcing the running gear of a horse-drawn vehicle. [Middle English *hune, hownde,* probably from Old Norse *hūnn,* knob, knob at the top of a masthead.]

hound shark *n.* Any of various harmless edible sharks of the genus *Mustelus,* having flat teeth and well-developed spiracles. Also called "smooth hound," "soft-mouthed shark."

hound's-tongue (houndz′tŭng′) *n.* Any of several plants of the genus *Cynoglossum*; especially, *C. officinale,* native to Eurasia, having hairy leaves, small reddish-purple flowers, and prickly, clinging fruit. Also called "dog's tongue." [From the shape of its leaves.]

hound's-tooth check (houndz′to͞oth′) *n.* A patterned textile design consisting of small, broken checks. Also called "dog's-tooth check," "dogtooth check."

hour (our) *n. Abbr.* **h, hr 1.** The 24th part of a day. **2. a.** One of the points on a timepiece marking off 12 or 24 successive intervals of 60 minutes, from midnight to noon and noon to midnight, or from midnight to midnight. **b.** The time of day indicated by a 12-hour clock. **c. hours.** The time of day determined on a 24-hour basis: *1700 hours.* **3. a.** A customary time allotted for something: *dinner hour.* **b. hours.** A period in which a particular or specified activity takes place or is allowed to take place: *banking hours; drinking after hours.* **4. a.** The work that can be accomplished in an hour. **b.** The distance that can be traveled in an hour. **5. hours. a.** A time for daily liturgical devotion, as the canonical hours. **b.** The prayers recited during the canonical hours. **6. a.** A time of significance: *His hour had come.* **b.** The present time. Preceded by *the*: *the hero of the hour.* **7.** A time that is an exact number of hours, as one o'clock or six o'clock. Preceded by *the*: *I'll leave on the hour. The clock struck the hour.* **8. hours.** Times of rising and going to bed, working, and the like: *keeps late hours; works long hours.* **9.** An angle of 15° (a 24th part of the celestial equator), used as a measure of right ascension. **—till** (or **until**) **all hours.** Until very late at night. [Middle English *hour, (o)ure,* from Old French *(h)ore,* from Latin *hōra,* from Greek, time, season.]

hour angle *n.* The angle measured westward along the celestial equator from the celestial meridian of the observer to the hour circle passing through a celestial body.

hour circle *n.* A great circle passing through the poles of the celestial sphere and intersecting the celestial equator at right angles.

hour·glass (our′glăs′, -gläs′) *n.* An instrument for measuring time consisting of two glass chambers with a narrow connecting channel, and containing sand or mercury requiring an exact period of time, usually one hour, to trickle from one chamber to the other.
~*adj.* Shaped like an hourglass; narrow-waisted.

hour hand *n.* The indicator on a timepiece that shows the hour.

hou·ri (ho͝or′ē, ho͞or′ē) *n., pl.* **-ris. 1.** A voluptuous woman. **2.** One of the beautiful virgins of the Koranic paradise. [French, from Persian *ḥūrī,* from Arabic *ḥūr,* plural of *ḥaura',* gazellelike (dark-eyed).]

hour·ly (our′lē) *adj.* **1. a.** Occurring every hour. **b.** Frequent; continual. **2.** By the hour as a unit: *hourly pay.* **—hour·ly** *adv.*

Hou·sa·ton·ic (ho͞o′sə-tŏn′ĭk). River rising in the Berkshires in western Massachusetts and flowing *c.* 210 kilometers (130 miles) generally south through western Connecticut to Long Island Sound.

house (hous) *n., pl.* **houses** (hou′zĭz). *Abbr.* **ho. 1. a.** A structure serving as a dwelling for one or several families. **b.** A place of abode; a residence. **c.** Something that serves as an abode. **2.** A building used for shelter or storage. Often used in combination: *a warehouse; a henhouse.* **3.** A building having a particular function or providing a particular service to the public. Often used in combination: *a schoolhouse; a coffee-house.* **4.** A dwelling for a religious community. **5.** A household. **6.** *Often* **House.** A family line, including ancestors and descendants; especially, a royal or noble family: *the House of Orange.* **7.** A commercial firm: *a banking house.* Also used adjectivally: *house style; a house magazine.* **8.** A residential building for pupils at a boarding school. **9. a.** A place of entertainment, such as a theater. **b.** An audience at a theater. **10. a.** A hotel, restaurant, tavern, or club: *the specialty of the house.* Also used adjectivally: *the house wine.* **b.** *Slang.* A brothel. **11. a.** A legislative or deliberative assembly. **b.** The hall where such an assembly meets. **c.** A quorum of such an assembly. **12.** The people attending and voting in a formal debate: *spoke for the motion that this house would restore capital punishment.* **13.** *Astrology.* **a.** One of the 12 parts into which the heavens are divided. **b.** The sign of the zodiac indicating the seat or station of a planet in the heavens. Also called "mansion." **—bring the house down.** To cause wild and general applause; be an enormous popular success. **—keep house.** To look after a house and the people in it. **—like a house on fire. 1.** With great speed and effectiveness. **2.** Very well; superbly. **—on the house.** At the expense of the management or manager; free. **—put** (or **set**) **one's house in order.** To arrange one's affairs in an orderly manner.
~*v.* (houz) **housed, housing, houses.** —*tr.* **1.** To provide with a house or houses; furnish living quarters for: *The cottage housed ten boys.* **2.** To shelter, keep or store in or as if in a house. **3.** To contain; harbor. **4.** To fit into a socket or mortise. **5.** *Nautical.* To secure or stow safely. —*intr.* To lodge; dwell. [Middle English *h(o)us, house,* Old English *hūs,* from Germanic *hūsam* (unattested).]

house arrest *n.* Confinement to one's home enforced by administrative or judicial order.

house·boat (hous′bōt′) *n.* A barge or boat equipped for use as a home.

house·bound (hous′bound′) *n.* Unable to leave one's house, especially because of illness.

house·boy (hous′boi′) *n.* A male servant in a house.

house·break·ing (hous′brā′kĭng) *n.* The act of unlawfully breaking into another's house for the purpose of committing a felony. **—house·break·er** *n.*

house·bro·ken (hous′brō′kən) *adj.* **1.** Trained in habits of excretion appropriate for a house pet. **2.** Trained to be docile; compliant.

house·carl (hous′kärl′) *n.* A member of the bodyguard or household troops of a Danish or early English king or noble. [Old English *hūscarl,* from Old Norse *hūskarl* : *hūs,* house + *karl,* man.]

house·coat (hous′kōt′) *n.* A woman's garment resembling a dressing gown, used for informal wear at home.

house·craft (hous′krăft′, -kräft′) *n. Chiefly British.* Skill in the running of a household; household management.

house-dust mite (hous′dŭst′) *n.* A mite, *Dermatophagoides farinae,* that lives on shed scales of human skin and is common in the dust of mattresses and pillows. It can induce asthma or inflammation of the nasal mucous membranes in people who are allergic to it.

house·fa·ther (hous′fä′*th*ər) *n.* A male houseparent.

house finch *n.* A finch, *Carpodacus mexicanus,* native to western North America and Mexico, having a red head, throat, and breast. It is closely related to the **purple finch** *(see)* and often nests near dwellings.

house·fly (hous′flī′) *n., pl.* **-flies.** A common, widely distributed fly, *Musca domestica,* that frequents human dwellings and is a transmitter of a wide variety of diseases.

house·hold (hous′hōld′) *n.* A domestic establishment including the members of a family and others living under the same roof.
~*adj.* **1.** Of or pertaining to a household; domestic. **2.** Well-known; familiar: *has become a household name since his record-breaking run.* [Middle English HOUSE + *hold,* possession, property (from the verb).]

house·hold·er (hous′hōl′dər) *n.* One who owns or rents and occupies a house or apartment.

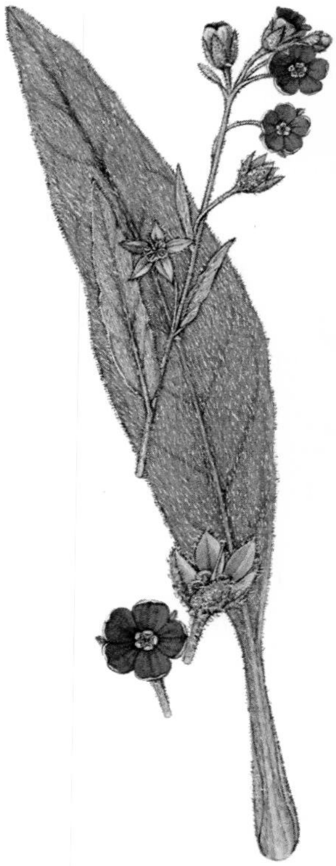

hound's-tongue *The shape and texture of the leaves of* Cynoglossum officinale *gave rise to its common English name. But the distinctive, unpleasant smell of the plant was also said to "tie the tongues of hounds"—that is, to keep them from barking. The juice of the leaves, boiled in hog lard, was once used to treat baldness.*

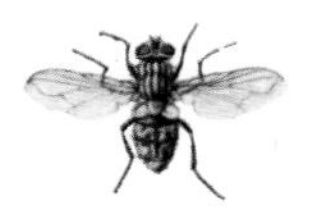

housefly *One of the most common insects in the home. Tiny suckers on the housefly's feet enable it to walk upside-down on ceilings.*

house martin *Originally house martins built their dome-shaped mud nests under overhanging cliffs or in caves, but they have adapted to the presence of man and now commonly nest under the eaves of houses— hence their name. They feed largely on flies and small beetles, catching them on the wing.*

house mouse *Mus musculus, the house mouse, is a rodent that has adapted to living in close company with man all over the world. It makes its nest in a wall near food stores and can produce as many as ten litters a year with up to seven young in each.*

house sparrow *Originally the house sparrow, Passer domesticus, was native only to Asia. But it spread westward into Europe, probably in the wake of Stone Age farmers, and now thrives near human settlements all over Europe and in much of North Africa. It has also been introduced into North America. The birds feed on seeds, insects, and—in built-up areas—on bread and scraps put out by humans.*

hovercraft

THE SHIP THAT FLIES
How a Hovercraft skims over land and sea

Hovercraft is a trademark and the popular description for an air-cushion vehicle—an amphibious craft that skims over land or sea on a bed of air created by a fan. Air is driven downward, beneath the vehicle, and is enclosed in a skirt, a rubberized fabric curtain that hangs down all around the base of the craft. The air lifts it to hover just above the surface of land or water. The craft can then be moved forward, backward, or sideways without encountering the drag that impedes a partly submerged ship.

The Hovercraft is thus swifter and more adaptable, useful for ferry work on short sea trips and ideal for work on difficult surfaces, such as swamps and ice-bound waters.

Air-cushion vehicles were pioneered in 1959 by the British Hovercraft Corporation and are now made all over the world. The technique has been applied to lawn mowers, and even to medical treatment—a severely burned patient is supported in a hover bed, which creates a cushion of sterile air under the body.

AT SEA *The most common use for the Hovercraft has been for short-distance ferry services. It is faster than conventional sea ferries and is quicker to load.*

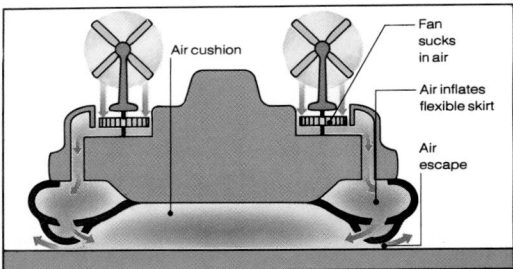

HOW IT WORKS *Powerful fans push air into the flexible skirt that surrounds the base of the craft, creating a cushion of air. This supports the craft over land or sea.*

household troops *pl.n.* The regiments of cavalry and infantry that escort and guard a sovereign and royal family.

house·hus·band (hous′hŭz′bənd) *n.* A man who stays at home and looks after the house and often the children while his wife earns the family income.

house·keep·er (hous′kē′pər) *n.* One who has charge of domestic tasks in a household.

house·keep·ing (hous′kē′pĭng) *n.* **1.** The management of a house and its occupants. **2.** Routine tasks that must be done to maintain an operation or system.

hou·sel (hou′zəl) *n. Archaic.* The Eucharist.
~*tr.v.* **houseled, -seling, -sels.** *Archaic.* To administer the Eucharist to. [Middle English *housel,* Old English *hūsl.*]

house·leek (hous′lēk′) *n.* Any of various plants of the genus *Sempervivum,* native to the Old World; especially, *S. tectorum,* having a basal rosette of fleshy leaves and a branching cluster of pinkish or purplish flowers. Also called "hen-and-chickens," "old-man-and-woman."

house·lights (hous′līts′) *pl.n.* The lights that illuminate the audience section of a concert hall, theater, or auditorium.

house·line (hous′līn′) *n. Nautical.* A small line formed of three strands, used for seizing. [From its use in housing larger ropes.]

house·maid (hous′mād′) *n.* A woman employed to do housework.

housemaid's knee *n.* A chronic, inflammatory swelling of the bursa of the knee anterior to the kneecap, caused by prolonged kneeling on hard floors.

house martin *n.* A Eurasian bird, *Delichon urbica,* having blue-black plumage with white markings and a forked tail.

house·mas·ter (hous′măs′tər, -mä′stər) *n.* A male teacher in charge of a residence hall at a boys' school.

house·mis·tress (hous′mĭs′trĭs) *n.* A female teacher in charge of a residence hall at a girls' school.

house·moth·er (hous′mŭth′ər) *n.* A female houseparent.

house mouse *n.* Any of various Old World mice of the genus *Mus,* especially *M. musculus,* that have grayish fur and are widely distributed household pests.

house name *n.* An assumed name used by a journalist, as when writing several different articles in the same newspaper.

House of Burgesses *n.* The lower house of the legislature of colonial Virginia.

House of Commons *n. Abbr.* **H.C. 1. a.** The lower house of Parliament in the United Kingdom, having the main legislative powers and an elected membership. **b.** The members of the House of Commons collectively. In both senses, also called "Commons." **2.** The lower house of the Canadian parliament.

house of correction *n.* An institution housing persons convicted of minor criminal offenses.

house of God *n.* A church or chapel.

house of ill repute *n.* A brothel. Used euphemistically. Also called "house of ill fame."

House of Lords *n. Abbr.* **H.L. 1.** The upper house of Parliament in the United Kingdom, a nonelective chamber made up of members of the nobility and high-ranking clergy. **2.** The members of the House of Lords collectively. Also called "Lords."

House of Representatives *n. Abbr.* **H.R. 1.** The lower house of the U.S. Congress and of most state legislatures. **2.** In Australia,

the lower house of Parliament. **3.** In New Zealand, the legislative assembly.

house·par·ent (hous′pâr′ənt) *n.* A person in charge of a group of children living in a residential institution, especially a school.

house party *n.* **1.** A party at which guests stay overnight or for several days in a private home or other residence. **2.** The guests at a house party.

house physician *n.* **1.** A resident physician in a hospital. **2.** A physician employed by a hotel or other establishment.

house·plant (hous′plănt, -plänt′) *n.* A plant that is grown indoors for ornament.

house·proud (hous′proud′) *adj.* Extremely fastidious about the cleaning, tidiness, and general appearance of a house.

house·rais·ing (hous′rā′zing) *n.* The construction of a house or its framework by a group of neighbors.

house·room (hous′rōōm′, -rŏŏm′) *n.* Room for lodging or storage in a house.

house·sit (hous′sĭt′) *intr.v.* **-sat** (-săt′), **-sitting, -sits.** To act as a house sitter.

house sitter *n.* A person who lives in and takes care of a house while the regular occupant is away.

house snake *n.* The **milk snake** *(see).*

Houses of Parliament *pl.n.* **1.** The British House of Commons and House of Lords collectively. **2.** The building where they meet.

house sparrow *n.* A small bird, *Passer domesticus,* native to the Old World but widely naturalized elsewhere, having brown and gray plumage, and a black throat in the male.

house·top (hous′tŏp′) *n.* The roof of a house. **—shout** (or **proclaim**) **from the housetops.** To make known publicly.

house·train (hous′trān′) *tr.v.* **-trained, -training, -trains.** To teach (a pet) to excrete outside the house or in a particular place.

house·warm·ing (hous′wôr′mĭng) *n.* A party to celebrate the occupancy of a new home. Also called "housewarming party."

house·wife (hous′wīf′ *for sense 1;* hŭz′ĭf *for sense 2*) *n., pl.* **-wives** (-wīvz′) (for sense 1); **housewifes** (hŭz′ĭfs) or **housewives** (hŭz′īvz′) (for sense 2). **1.** A married woman who supervises the affairs of a household, especially one who has no outside employment. **2.** *Chiefly British.* A pocket container for sewing equipment.

house·wife·ly (hous′wīf′lē) *adj.* Of, pertaining to, or characteristic of a housewife; domestic. **—house·wife·li·ness** *n.*

house·wif·er·y (hous′wī′fə-rē, -wīf′rē) *n.* The function or duties of a housewife; housekeeping.

house·work (hous′wûrk′) *n.* The tasks performed in housekeeping, as cleaning or cooking.

hous·ing¹ (hou′zĭng) *n.* **1.** Buildings or other shelters in which people live, considered collectively. **2.** The provision of houses or dwellings. Also used adjectivally: *housing policy.* **3. a.** Something that covers, protects, or guards. **b.** A frame, bracket, or box for holding or protecting a mechanical part: *a wheel housing.* **c.** An enclosing frame in which a shaft revolves. **4.** A hole, groove, or slot in a piece of wood for the insertion of another piece. **5.** A niche for a statue. **6.** The part of a mast that is below deck or of a bowsprit that is inside the hull.

hous·ing² *n.* **1.** An ornamental or protective covering for a saddle. **2.** *Usually* **housings.** Trappings. [Middle English, from *house,* covering, from Old French *houce,* from Medieval Latin *hultia,* from Germanic.]

housing development *n.* A group of similarly designed houses or apartment buildings, usually under a single management.

housing project *n.* A publicly funded and administered housing development, usually for low-income families.

Hous·man (hous′mən), **A(lfred) E(dward)** (1859–1936). British poet. He was professor of Latin at Cambridge University, and published two volumes of poetry, *A Shropshire Lad* (1896) and *Last Poems* (1922), and an essay, *The Name and Nature of Poetry* (1933).

Hous·ton (hyōō′stən). A city in southeastern Texas, a deep-water port on the Houston Ship Canal. It is one of the world's leading oil centers and the third-busiest port in the United States. It is also an important center for space research.

Houston, Samuel (1793–1863). U.S. general and politician. Leaving an established political career in Tennessee, he became involved in the Texan struggle for independence from Mexico. He defeated Gen. Santa Anna (1836) and became president of the Republic of Texas (1836–38; 1841–44). When Texas was admitted to the Union, he served as U.S. senator (1845–59) and as governor (1859–61).

hout·ing (hou′tĭng) *n.* A European food fish, *Coregonus oxyrhynchus,* a species of whitefish that lives in the sea but spawns in rivers and lakes. [Dutch, from Middle Dutch *houtic†.*]

hove. *Chiefly Nautical.* Past tense and past participle of **heave.**

hov·el (hŭv′əl, hŏv′-) *n.* **1.** A small, miserable dwelling. **2.** An open, low shed. **3.** A cone-shaped building housing a kiln. [Middle English *hovel†.*]

hov·er (hŭv′ər, hŏv′ər) *intr.v.* **-ered, -ering, -ers. 1.** To fly, soar, or float, remaining roughly in one place, as if suspended: *gulls hovering over the waves.* **2.** To remain or linger in close proximity; move back and forth in or near a place. **3.** To be in a state of uncertainty; waver; vacillate: *hover between skepticism and belief.* ~*n.* **1.** The condition of hovering. **2.** An act or instance of hovering. [Middle English *hoveren,* frequentative of *hoven†,* to hover, linger.] —**hov·er·er** *n.* —**hov·er·ing·ly** *adv.*

Hov·er·craft (hŭv′ər-krăft′, -krâft′, hŏv′-) *n.* A trademark for a vehicle capable of low-level flight over land or water on a cushion of air formed by the action of downward-directed fans. Also called "air-cushion vehicle."

hover fly *n.* Any fly of the family Syrphidae, having a hovering flight and typically having markings that mimic wasps or bees.

hov·er·port (hŭv′ər-pôrt′, -pōrt′, hŏv′-) *n.* A port for Hovercraft.

how¹ (hou) *adv.* **1.** In what manner or way: *He showed us how to work the machine. How did he react?* **2.** By what means; with what cause or explanation: *I don't know how you can afford it. How is it possible?* **3.** In what state or condition: *How do I look in this jacket?* **4.** To what extent, amount, or degree: *How do you like that? How much did it cost?* **5.** With what meaning: *How should I interpret this?* **6.** In what state of health or general well-being: *How are you? How is your mother?* **7.** Of what kind or quality: *How was the party?* **8.** By what name: *How is he called?* **9.** Used as an intensive: *How we laughed!* —**and how!** *Informal.* Very much so. —**how about?** What is your feeling or thought regarding? —**how come?** Why is it that? —**how is that?** or **how's that?** What? Usually used in requesting that something said be repeated: *How is that again?* —**how so?** Why is it so? ~*conj.* **1.** Of the manner or style in which: *Be careful how you address the ambassador.* **2.** The fact that: *Remember how we used to go out drinking every night?* **3.** However; in whatever way: *As long as it gets done you can do it how you like.* ~*n.* A manner or method of doing or performing: *learn the how of a procedure.* [Middle English *hou, how,* Old English *hū,* from Germanic.]

how² *interj.* Used to express greeting in presumed imitation of North American Indian speech. [From Sioux; akin to Dakota *háo* and Omaha *hau.*]

How·ard, Catherine (c. 1520–42). English Catholic noblewoman who became the fifth wife of Henry VIII (1540). Her love affairs brought charges of treason from the Protestant faction at court, and she was executed.

Howard, Leslie, born Leslie Stainer (1893–1943). British stage and screen actor. He played the lead in the film *The Scarlet Pimpernel* (1934) and Ashley Wilkes in *Gone With the Wind* (1939).

Howard, Trevor Wallace (1916–88). British actor. He made his screen debut in 1944. He starred in *Brief Encounter* (1946) and played Captain Bligh in *Mutiny on the Bounty* (1962).

how·be·it (hou-bē′ĭt) *adv. Archaic.* Be that as it may; nevertheless. ~*conj. Obsolete.* Although.

how·dah (hou′də) *n.* A seat, usually fitted with a canopy and railing, placed on the back of an elephant or camel. [Urdu, from Persian *haudah,* from Arabic *haudaj,* litter.]

how do you do *interj.* Used in greeting a person formally, especially when being introduced for the first time.

how-do-you-do (hou′də-yə-dōō′) *n.* Also **how-d'ye-do** (houd′yə-dōō′, hou′dē-). *Informal.* A difficult or embarrassing predicament. Usually used with *pretty, fine,* or *nice.*

how·dy (hou′dē) *interj. Regional.* Used to express greeting. [Short for *how do you do.*]

Howe (hou), **Elias** (1819–67). U.S. inventor. As an apprentice watchmaker he began to work at devising a sewing machine; he exhibited his first machine in 1845 and patented another in 1846. Over the next few years he brought several suits for infringement of patent, including a successful one against Isaac M. Singer.

Howe, Julia Ward (1819–1910). U.S. author, feminist, and philanthropist. Active in the woman suffrage movement, she was also concerned with peace. Her essay "Appeal to Womanhood Throughout the World" called for an international meeting of women to discuss peace. She is the author of "Battle Hymn of the Republic."

how·e·'er (hou-âr′). *Poetic.* Contraction of *however.*

How·ells (hou′əlz), **William Dean** (1837–1920). U.S. author and editor. Editor (1866–71) and editor in chief (1871–81) of the *Atlantic Monthly,* he displayed his broad-minded yet discerning taste for literature by encouraging writers ranging from Mark Twain to Henry James. He also wrote many novels, such as *The Rise of Silas Lapham* (1885), poems, and books of travel, literary criticism, and memoirs.

how·ev·er (hou-ĕv′ər) *adv.* **1. a.** By contrast; on the other hand: *The first part was easy; the second stage, however, was considerably harder.* **b.** Nevertheless; in spite of that: *The tickets are expensive; however, I still think we should go.* **2.** By whatever manner or means: *However you come, come early.* **3.** To whatever degree or extent: "*I never am bored, however familiar the scene*" (Theodore Roethke). **4.** *Informal.* How. Used to add emphasis or show surprise: *However did he manage it?* ~*conj.* **1.** In whatever way: *Dress however you like.* **2.** *Archaic.* Although; notwithstanding that. —See Usage note at **but.**

howf, howff (houf, hôf) *n. Scottish.* A popular meeting place, such as a tavern. [16th century : origin obscure.]

how·it·zer (hou′ĭt-sər) *n.* A cannon with a barrel longer than a mortar that delivers shells with medium velocities, either by a low or, more usually, by a high trajectory against targets that cannot be reached by flat trajectories. [Dutch *houwitser,* from German *Haubitze,* earlier *haufenitz,* from Czech *houfnice,* catapult.]

howl (houl) *v.* **howled, howling, howls.** —*intr.* **1.** To utter or emit a long, mournful, plaintive sound characteristic of wolves or dogs. **2.** To cry or wail loudly and uncontrollably, as in pain, sorrow, or anger. **3.** *Slang.* To laugh heartily. **4.** *Slang.* To go on a spree. —*tr.* To express or utter with a howl or howls. —**howl down.** To drown the sound of or silence (a speaker) by loud derisive calls and howls. ~*n.* **1.** The sound of one that howls. **2.** A high-pitched whine produced in a sound system by electronic feedback. **3.** *Slang.* Something uproariously funny or absurd. [Middle English *houlen, howlen,* perhaps from Middle Dutch *hūlen.*]

howl·er (hou′lər) *n.* **1.** One that howls. **2.** Any of several monkeys of the genus *Alouatta,* of tropical America, having a long, prehensile tail and a loud, howling call. Also called "howler monkey." **3.** A device that produces a loud warning noise in an incorrectly replaced telephone receiver. **4.** *Slang.* An amusing, ridiculous, or stupid blunder.

howl·et (hou′lĭt) *n. Archaic.* An owl or owlet. [Middle English *howlat,* diminutive of *(h)owle,* OWL.]

howl·ing (hou′lĭng) *adj. Informal.* Very great; tremendous: *The play is a howling success.*

how·so·ev·er (hou′sō-ĕv′ər) *adv.* **1.** To whatever degree or extent. **2.** By whatever means.

Hox·ha (hô′jə), **Enver** (1908–85). Albanian politician, the dominant figure in Albanian politics after independence (1946). He led his country's resistance forces in World War II and became prime minister (1946–54), then first secretary of the newly named (communist) Party of Labor.

hoy¹ (hoi) *n., pl.* **hoys. 1.** A small sloop-rigged coasting ship formerly used for transporting passengers or as a tender to a larger vessel. **2.** A heavy barge used for cargo. [Middle English, from Middle Dutch *hoei, hoede†.*]

hoy² *interj.* Used to attract attention or to drive or direct animals. [Middle English (expressive).]

hoy·a (hoi′ə) *n.* Any plant of the genus *Hoya;* especially, the **wax-plant** (see). [After Thomas *Hoy,* 19th-century English gardener.]

hoy·den (hoid′n) *n.* A high-spirited, often impudent girl or woman. ~*adj.* High-spirited; boisterous. [Originally, a rude youth, probably from Middle Dutch *heiden,* "heathen."]

Hoyle (hoil), **Edmond** (1672–1769). British author of the *Short Treatise on the Game of Whist* (1742), which defined the rules of the game and remained the standard authority until 1864. The expression "according to Hoyle" is used to mean "according to the rules."

Hoyle, Sir Fred (1915–). British astronomer. In 1948 he helped formulate the steady-state theory, which holds that the universe is expanding while the density of matter remains constant.

hp horsepower.

H.P. 1. hire purchase. **2.** Houses of Parliament.

HQ, h.q., H.Q. headquarters.

hr hour.

Hr. Herr.

h.r. home run.

H.R. 1. home rule. **2.** House of Representatives.

H.R.E. Holy Roman Emperor; Holy Roman Empire.

H.R.H. His (or Her) Royal Highness.

hrs hours.

Hrvatska. See **Croatia.**

H.S.H. His (or Her) Serene Highness.

Hsiamen. See **Xiamen.**

Hsi-an. See **Xi'an.**

Hsiang Chiang. See **Xiang Jiang.**

Hsi Chiang. See **Xi Jiang.**

Hsinking. See **Changchun.**

H.S.M. His (or Her) Serene Majesty.

ht height.

H.T. high tension.

hover fly *A harmless relative of the bluebottle that is commonly mistaken for a wasp or bee. The fly's maggotlike larvae feed on the sap-sucking garden pests called aphids.*

howdah *An 18th-century Mogul manuscript from India shows an English dignitary being carried in one of these seats.*

Hts. heights (in place names).

Hua Guo-feng or **Hua Kuo-feng** (hwä′ gwō′fŭng′) (1921–). Chinese prime minister (1976–80). In 1976 he succeeded Zhou En-lai as prime minister and Mao as chairman of the Communist Party. With Deng Xiao-ping, he initiated a program of modernization, increasing contacts with the West. He resigned in 1980.

Huang He, Hwang Ho (hwäng′ hē′). Also **Yellow River.** Major river of northern China, some 4,670 kilometers (2,900 miles) long. Its lower valley, a vast fertile alluvial plain, was the cradle of Chinese civilization. Since the Communists came to power (1949), the river has been much regulated, and the devastating floods that gave it the name China's Sorrow rarely occur.

hua·ra·che (wə-rä′chē, -chä, hə-) n. A flat-heeled sandal with an upper of woven leather strips. [Mexican Spanish *guarache, huarache†.*]

hub (hŭb) n. **1.** The center portion of a wheel, fan, or propeller. **2.** A center of activity or interest; a focal point. [16th century : probably a variant of HOB (lump, projection).]

Hub·ble (hŭb′əl), **Edwin Powell** (1889–1953). U.S. astronomer. In 1929, he published his discovery that the velocities of nebulae increased with distance. The Hubble constant is named after him.

hub·ble-bub·ble (hŭb′əl-bŭb′əl) n. **1.** A water pipe, the **hookah** (see). **2. a.** A bubbling sound. **b.** A confused sound, as of people talking; a hum. [Reduplication of BUBBLE.]

Hubble's constant n. The ratio of the velocity at which a distant galaxy is receding from the earth to its distance from the earth, approximately equal to about 50 to 100 kilometers per second per million parsecs. [After E.P. HUBBLE.]

hub·bub (hŭb′ŭb′) n. **1.** A confused babble of loud sounds and voices; a din; an uproar. **2.** Confusion; upheaval; tumult. —See Synonyms at **noise.** [Irish *hooboobbes,* akin to Old Irish *abú,* a war cry, from Old Irish *buide,* "victory," from Celtic *bod-io-†* (untested).]

hub·by (hŭb′ē) n., pl. **-bies.** *Informal.* A husband.

hub·cap (hŭb′kăp′) n. A round metal covering clamped over the hub of the wheel of a motor vehicle.

Hu·bei, Hu·peh, Hu·pei (hōō′bā′). Province in east-central China, consisting chiefly of an alluvial plain drained by the Chiang Jiang (Yangtze) and Han Shui. The capital is Wuhan.

hu·bris (hyōō′brĭs) n. Also **hy·bris** (hī′-). **1.** Overbearing pride or presumption; arrogance. **2.** In Greek tragedy, overbearing pride and insolence toward the gods, leading to personal downfall and ruin. [Greek *hubris,* insolence.] —**hu·bris·tic** (hyōō-brĭs′tĭk) adj.

huck (hŭk) n. Huckaback.

huck·a·back (hŭk′ə-băk′) n. A coarse absorbent cotton or linen fabric used especially for toweling. Also called "huck." [17th century : origin obscure.]

huck·le (hŭk′əl) n. The hip or haunch. [Diminutive of earlier *huck,* hip, haunch, from Middle English *huck-, huke-,* perhaps from Germanic; akin to Middle Low German *hüken,* to sit bent.]

huck·le·ber·ry (hŭk′əl-bĕr′ē) n., pl. **-ries. 1.** Any of various American shrubs of the genus *Gaylussacia,* related to the blueberries and bearing edible fruit. **2.** The glossy, blackish, many-seeded berry of such a bush. **3.** Any of various similar or related shrubs, such as the blueberry or whortleberry. [Probably variant of dialectal *hurtleberry,* WHORTLEBERRY.]

huck·ster (hŭk′stər) n. **1.** A person who sells wares in the street; a peddler; a hawker. **2.** A promoter of commercial products whose techniques are dubious or aggressive. **3.** *Slang.* A writer of advertising copy, as for television.
—v. **huckstered, -stering, -sters.** —tr. **1.** To sell; peddle. **2.** To haggle or bargain over. —intr. To haggle. [Middle English *huccstere,* perhaps from Middle Dutch *hokester.* See **hawker, -ster.**]
—**huck·ster·ism** n.

Hud·ders·field (hŭd′ərz-fēld′). Industrial town in West Yorkshire, north-central England. It is the chief woolen textile manufacturing center of the region.

hud·dle (hŭd′əl) n. **1.** A densely packed group or crowd, as of people or animals. **2.** A confused array; a jumble. **3.** A brief gathering of a football team's players behind the line of scrimmage to prepare for the next play. **4.** *Informal.* A small private conference or meeting.
—v. **huddled, -dling, -dles.** —intr. **1.** To crowd together, as from cold or fear; nestle; snuggle. **2.** To draw oneself together; curl or hunch up; crouch. Often used with *up.* **3.** To gather in a football huddle. **4.** *Informal.* To gather in order to confer secretly; meet privately. —tr. **1.** To crowd together. **2.** To draw (oneself) together; hunch; crouch. Often used with *up.* **3.** *Chiefly British.* To bring or throw together hastily or carelessly. [16th century : perhaps from Low German; akin to HIDE (to conceal).]

Hu·di·bras·tic (hyōō′də-brăs′tĭk) adj. In the mock-heroic style of Samuel Butler's satire *Hudibras* (1663–78). [From *Hudibras,* by analogy with such words as *bombastic.*]

Hud·son (hŭd′sən), **Henry** (died 1611). English navigator. In 1609 he tried to find a northwest passage and discovered the river that bears his name. While he was returning from a second attempt in which he discovered Hudson Bay (1610–11), his crew mutinied. Hudson and his son were cast adrift in a boat and never seen again.

Hudson, Rock (1925–85). U.S. actor. A ruggedly handsome and popular leading man, he starred in many movies of the 1950's, including *The Magnificent Obsession* (1954) and *Pillow Talk* (1959). At the age of 60 he died of AIDS, heightening public awareness of that devastating disease.

Hudson Bay. Large inland sea in north-central Canada, connected to the Atlantic Ocean by the Hudson Strait. It covers an area of *c.* 1,230,000 square kilometers (475,000 square miles).

Hudson River. River in New York State, rising in the Adirondack Mts. and flowing south for *c.* 510 kilometers (315 miles) to Upper New York Bay at New York City.

Hudson's Bay Company n. A British company chartered in 1670 to participate in fur trading with the North American Indians in competition with the French in Canada.

Hudson seal n. Muskrat fur that is dyed, plucked, and sheared in imitation of sealskin. [After HUDSON BAY.]

hue (hyōō) n. **1.** The dimension of color that is referred to a scale of perceptions ranging from red to yellow, green, and blue, and circularly back to red. **2.** A particular gradation of color; a tint; a shade. **3.** Color: *all the hues of the rainbow.* **4.** Character; aspect: *the somber hue of a man of the cloth.* [Middle English *hewe,* complexion, appearance, Old English *hēo, hīw,* appearance, form, color, beauty.]

hue and cry n. **1.** Formerly: **a.** The pursuit of a criminal announced by loud shouts to alert others then legally obliged to aid in the chase. **b.** The loud shout used to arouse the pursuers. **2.** A public clamor, as of protest or demand; an outcry: *a big hue and cry over the latest spending cuts.* [Middle English *hew, heu,* from Old French *heu, hu,* an outcry, from *huer,* to cry out, shout (imitative).]

Hu·é (hyōō-ā′). Also **Hue** (hwä, wä). City in central Vietnam, on the Hué River. It is one of the most ancient towns of Vietnam, dating from the 3rd century B.C., and is a former capital of Annam. It was the seat of the Nguyen dynasty from the early 19th century but lost its historic status as the capital in 1887, when Saigon became the capital of Indochina.

hued (hyōōd) adj. Having a given hue, aspect, or character. Used in combination: *rosy-hued dawn.*

huff (hŭf) n. **1.** A fit of anger or annoyance; pique: *He stormed off in a huff.* **2.** In checkers, the removal of an opponent's checker from the board for failure to make a possible capture.
—v. **huffed, huffing, huffs.** —intr. **1.** To puff; blow. **2.** To speak or act with noisy, empty threats; bluster. Now used chiefly in the phrase *huff and puff.* **3.** To act or react indignantly; take offense. —tr. **1.** To puff or blow up; inflate. **2.** *Archaic.* To treat with insolence; bully; tease. **3.** To put in a huff; anger; annoy. **4.** In checkers, to make a huff. [Imitative of the sound of puffing.]

huff·ish (hŭf′ĭsh) adj. **1.** Peevish; sulky; in a huff. **2.** Arrogant; insolent. —**huff·ish·ly** adv. —**huff·ish·ness** n.

huff·y (hŭf′ē) adj. **-ier, -iest. 1.** Easily offended; sensitive; touchy. **2.** Irritated or annoyed; indignant. **3.** Arrogant; disdainful; haughty. —**huff·i·ly** adv. —**huff·i·ness** n.

hug (hŭg) v. **hugged, hugging, hugs.** —tr. **1.** To clasp or hold closely, especially in one's arms; embrace or enfold, as in affection. **2.** To ascribe steadfastly to (a belief or opinion, for example); cherish. **3.** To keep, remain, or be situated close to: *The old footpath winds inland, hugging the foot of the hill.* **4.** To be very pleased with (oneself); congratulate (oneself). —intr. To embrace or be in physical contact; cling together closely; snuggle.
—n. **1.** An affectionate, close embrace. **2.** A crushing embrace. [Scandinavian, akin to Old Norse *hugga,* to comfort, console, from Germanic *hugjan* (unattested).] —**hug·ga·ble** adj. —**hug·ger** n.

huge (hyōōj) adj. **huger, hugest.** Of exceedingly great size, extent, degree, or quantity; tremendous. —See Synonyms at **enormous.** [Middle English *huge, hoge,* shortened from Old French *ahuge, ahoge†.*] —**huge·ly** adv. —**huge·ness** n.

huge·ous (hyōō′jəs) adj. *Informal.* Huge. Used chiefly for humorous effect. —**huge·ous·ly** adv. —**huge·ous·ness** n.

hug·ger-mug·ger, hug·ger·mug·ger (hŭg′ər-mŭg′ər) n. **1.** Disorder; confusion; muddle. **2.** Concealment; secrecy.
—adj. **1.** Disordered; jumbled: *"worry our her financial problems in her own hugger-mugger way"* (Samuel Butler). **2.** Secret; surreptitious; clandestine: *hugger-mugger political deals.*
—v. **hugger-muggered, -gering, -gers.** —tr. To keep concealed or secret. —intr. To act in a surreptitious manner. [16th century : also *hucker mucker* and earlier *hoder moder,* all perhaps akin to Middle English *hoder,* huddle, and *mokere,* to hide.] —**hug·ger·mug·ger** adv.

Hughes (hyōōz), **Charles Evans** (1862–1948). U.S. jurist and statesman. He was appointed to the U.S. Supreme Court (1910), but resigned to make an unsuccessful bid for the presidency (1916). He served as secretary of state (1920–25) and in 1930 was appointed chief justice of the Supreme Court. Hughes was instrumental in defeating Franklin D. Roosevelt's "court-packing" plan (1937).

Hughes, Howard Robard (1905–76). U.S. film producer, aviator, and multimillionaire magnate. Among his films was *Hell's Angels* (1930). He founded the Hughes Aircraft Corporation, broke the airplane speed record (1935), and flew around the world in record time (1938). From 1950 he lived as a recluse.

Hughes, (James Mercer) Langston (1902–67). U.S. author. His first poem, "The Negro Speaks of Rivers," was published in 1921. After several years of drifting, he published collections of his poems, including *The Weary Blues* (1926) and *Shakespeare in Harlem* (1942). He also wrote dramas, biographies, and a series of newspaper columns.

Hughes, Richard Arthur Warren (1900–76). British novelist. His books include *A High Wind in Jamaica* (1929) and *In Hazard* (1938).

Hughes, Thomas (1822–96). British lawyer and author. His *Tom Brown's School Days* (1857) describes public-school life at Rugby

under its famous headmaster Dr. Thomas Arnold.
Hugli. See **Hooghly.**
hug-me-tight (hŭg′mē-tīt′) *n.* A woman's close-fitting, usually knitted jacket, with or without sleeves.
Hu·go (hyōō′gō, ü-gō′), **Victor Marie** (1802–85). French poet, novelist, and dramatist. Shortly after Napoleon III seized power (1852), he went into exile in the Channel Islands, returning to France in 1870. His novels include *The Hunchback of Notre Dame* (1831), *Les Misérables* (1862), and *Toilers of the Sea* (1866).
Hu·gue·not (hyōō′gə-nŏt′, -nō′) *n.* A French Protestant of the 16th and 17th centuries. [French *huguenot,* assimilation (to *Hugues,* burgomaster of Geneva) of earlier (Genevan) French *eyguenot,* referring to those who opposed annexation by the Duke of Savoy, from Swiss German *Eidgenosse(n),* confederate(s), from Middle High German *eitgenōz* : *eit,* oath, from Old High German *eid* + *genōz,* companion, from Old High German *ginōz.*] **—Hu·gue·not, Hu·gue·not·ic** (hyōō′gə-nŏt′ĭk) *adj.* **—Hu·gue·not·ism** *n.*
huh (hŭ, hə) *interj.* Used to express surprise, interrogation, contempt, or indifference.
hu·ia (hōō′yə) *n.* An extinct New Zealand songbird, *Heteralocha acutirostris,* that had a beak that was strong and straight in the male and slender and curved in the female. [Maori.]
hu·la (hōō′lə) *n.* Also **hu·la-hu·la** (hōō′lə-hōō′lə). **1.** A Polynesian ethnic dance performed by men or women alone or together and characterized by undulating movements of the hips, arms, and hands, pantomiming a story. **2.** The music for this dance, composed typically of rhythmic drumbeats and chants. [Hawaiian.]
hula hoop *n.* A large, light hoop, often made of plastic, that is whirled around the body by the movement of the hips.
hulk (hŭlk) *n.* **1.** A heavy, unwieldy ship. **2. a.** The hull of an old, unseaworthy, or wrecked ship. **b.** An old or unseaworthy ship used as a prison or warehouse. **3. a.** A clumsy, awkward, or overweight person. **b.** A clumsy or bulky object.
∼*intr.v.* **hulked, hulking, hulks. 1.** To loom or rise in a towering or impressive fashion: *The big truck hulked out of the fog in front of our car.* **2.** *British Regional.* To move about in a lazy or clumsy manner. [Middle English *hulke,* Old English *hulc,* ship, from Medieval Latin *hulcus,* from Greek *holkas,* "ship that is towed," merchant vessel, from *helkein,* to pull, tow.]
hulk·ing (hŭl′kĭng) *adj.* Also **hulk·y** (hŭl′kē). Unwieldy, clumsy, or bulky; massive: *a hulking lumberjack.*
hull (hŭl) *n.* **1. a.** The enlarged calyx of a strawberry or similar fruit, usually green and easily detached. **b.** The dry outer covering of a fruit, seed, or nut; husk. **2.** *Nautical.* The main body of a ship, exclusive of masts, sails, yards, and rigging. **3.** The main body or frame of any of various other large vehicles, such as a tank, an airship, or a flying boat. **4.** The outer casing of a rocket, guided missile, or spaceship.
∼*tr.v.* **hulled, hulling, hulls. 1.** To remove the hull or hulls of (fruit or seeds). **2.** To pierce or break through the hull of (a ship, tank, or the like). [Middle English *hull, hole,* husk, from Old English *hulu*; akin to *helan,* to cover.]
Hull (hŭl). Also **King·ston up·on Hull** (kĭng′stən ə-pŏn hŭl′). City in Humberside, northeastern England, on the northern shore of the Humber estuary on the Hull River. It is one of Britain's largest ports and its busiest deep-sea fishing port.
hul·la·ba·loo, hul·la·bal·loo (hŭl′ə-bə-lōō′) *n., pl.* **-loos.** A great confused noise or din; an uproar. —See Synonyms at **noise.** [Earlier *hollo-ballo,* akin to the interjection HALLOO.]
hull down *adj.* **1.** So far away that the hull is below the horizon. Said of a ship. **2.** Concealed apart from the turret. Said of a tank.
hullo. Variant of **hello.**
hum¹ (hŭm) *v.* **hummed, humming, hums.** —*intr.* **1.** To utter a continuous low droning sound like that of the speech sound (m) when prolonged. **2. a.** To emit the continuous droning sound of an insect on the wing, or a similar sound. **b.** To move with such a sound. **3. a.** To give out a low, continuous drone blended of many sounds: *The avenue hummed with traffic.* **b.** To be full of activity. **4.** To produce a tune without opening the lips or forming words. —*tr.* To sing (a tune) without opening the lips or forming words.
∼*n.* **1.** A noise or tune produced by humming. **2.** A low-frequency continuous noise produced by an amplifier, usually as result of interference from the main frequency.
∼*interj.* (hŭm, hm) **1.** Uttered as a pause in speech or to indicate thought. **2.** Used to express surprise or displeasure. [Middle English *hummen* (imitative).] **—hum·mer** *n.*
hum² *tr.v.* **hummed, humming, hums.** *Australian.* To borrow; cadge. [Shortened from HUMBUG, to trick, deceive.]
hu·man (hyōō′mən) *adj.* **1.** Of, relating to, or characteristic of man or mankind: *the course of human events.* **2.** Having or manifesting the form, nature, or qualities characteristic of human beings, especially: **a.** Showing qualities characteristic of people as distinguished from machines, such as sympathy or fallibility: *human kindness. His mistake was only human.* **b.** Pertaining to or being a human being as distinguished from a lower animal; reasoning; moral. **c.** Pertaining to or being a human being as distinguished from a divine entity or infinite intelligence; mortal; earthly. **3.** Made up of people: *They formed a human bridge across the river.*
∼*n.* A human being; a person. [Middle English *humain(e), humayn(e),* from Old French *humain* (feminine *humaine*), from Latin *hūmānus,* akin to *homo* (stem *homin-*), man.] **—hu·man·ness** *n.*
Usage: *Human* (noun) is acceptable on all levels and in contexts not limited to the scientific or technical: *air not fit for humans to breathe.* In somewhat earlier usage, *human being* was often recommended as the better choice on a formal level, though *human* has a long history as a noun.
human being *n.* A member of the genus *Homo,* and especially of the species *Homo sapiens*; a person. —See Usage note at **human.**
hu·mane (hyōō-mān′) *adj.* **1.** Characterized by qualities of kindness, mercy, or compassion: *a humane judge.* **2.** Tending to evoke or promote these qualities; refining; civilizing: *a humane education.* **3.** Painless. Said especially of an agent or instrument for killing animals: *a humane drug.* [Middle English *humaine,* HUMAN.] **—hu·mane·ly** *adv.* **—hu·mane·ness** *n.*
human ecology *n.* See **ecology** (sense 2).
human engineering *n.* **1.** The industrial management of labor. **2.** The technology of efficient use of machines by human beings.
human interest *n.* The often sentimental preoccupation with the affairs or feelings of individuals, as in popular journalism. Also used adjectivally: *a human-interest story.*
hu·man·ism (hyōō′mə-nĭz′əm) *n.* **1.** Concern with the interests and needs of human beings. **2.** A philosophy or attitude that addresses itself exclusively to human as opposed to divine or supernatural concerns, often coupled with the belief that man is capable of reaching self-fulfillment without divine aid. **3.** The study of the humanities; cultured learning. **4. Humanism.** A cultural and intellectual movement of a secular character that occurred during the Renaissance following the rediscovery of the literature, art, and civilization of ancient Greece and Rome.
hu·man·ist (hyōō′mə-nĭst) *n.* **1.** A follower of the philosophy of humanism. **2.** One who is concerned with the study and welfare of human beings. **3.** One who studies the humanities; especially, a student of classical learning. **4. Humanist.** A student of the Renaissance or follower of Humanism.
∼*adj.* Also **hu·man·is·tic** (hyōō′mə-nĭs′tĭk). Of or relating to humanism or the humanities. **—hu·man·is·ti·cal·ly** *adv.*
hu·man·i·tar·i·an (hyōō-măn′ə-târ′ē-ən) *adj.* **1.** Concerned with the well-being of mankind and the alleviation of human suffering. **2.** Of or relating to humanitarianism.
∼*n.* One devoted to the promotion of human welfare and the advancement of social reforms; a philanthropist.
hu·man·i·tar·i·an·ism (hyōō-măn′ə-târ′ē-ə-nĭz′əm) *n.* **1.** The ideas, principles, or methods of humanitarians; philanthropy. **2.** *Ethics.* The belief that man's sole moral obligation is to work for the improved welfare of humanity. **3.** *Theology.* The belief or doctrine that Jesus was only human and not divine.
hu·man·i·ty (hyōō-măn′ə-tē) *n., pl.* **-ties. 1.** Human beings collectively; the human race; mankind. **2.** The condition, quality, or fact of being human; human nature; humanness. **3.** The quality of being humane; benevolence; kindness; mercy. **4.** A humane attribute or action. **5. humanities. a.** The study of the classical languages and literature of ancient Greece and Rome. **b.** Those branches of knowledge concerned with human beings and culture, as philosophy, literature, and the fine arts, as distinguished from the sciences. [Middle English *humanite,* from Old French, from Latin *hūmānitās* (stem *hūmānitāt-*), from *hūmānus,* HUMAN.]
hu·man·ize (hyōō′mə-nīz′) *v.* **-ized, -izing, -izes.** —*tr.* **1.** To make human; cause to have human characteristics or attributes. **2.** To make humane; imbue with human sympathy; civilize. —*intr.* **1.** To become human. **2.** To become humane. **—hu·man·i·za·tion** (hyōō′mə-nə-zā′shən) *n.* **—hu·man·iz·er** *n.*
hu·man·kind (hyōō′mən-kīnd′) *n.* The human race; mankind.
hu·man·ly (hyōō′mən-lē) *adv.* **1.** In a human way. **2.** By human means, capabilities, or powers. **3.** According to human experience or knowledge.
hu·man·oid (hyōō′mə-noid′) *adj.* Having human characteristics; especially, resembling a human being in appearance.
∼*n.* **1.** A humanoid being. **2.** A fictional synthetic man, an **android** *(see).*
Hum·ber (hŭm′bər). A river in Humberside, northeastern England, consisting of the estuary of the Trent and Ouse rivers and extending from their confluence for *c.* 60 kilometers (40 miles) to the North Sea. The fishing ports of Hull and Grimsby are on its northern and southern shores respectively.
Hum·ber·side (hŭm′bər-sīd′). From 1974 a nonmetropolitan county in northeastern England.
hum·ble (hŭm′bəl) *adj.* **-bler, -blest. 1.** Having or showing feelings of humility rather than of pride; aware of one's shortcomings; modest; meek. **2.** Showing deferential respect. **3. a.** Lacking high social status. **b.** Lowly; unpretentious: *a humble cottage.*
∼*tr.v.* **humbled, -bling, -bles. 1.** To curtail or destroy the pride of; humiliate. **2.** To give a lower condition or station to; abase. —See Synonyms at **degrade.** [Middle English *(h)umble,* from Old French *(h)umble,* from Latin *humilis,* low, lowly, base, from *humus,* ground, soil.] **—hum·ble·ness** *n.* **—hum·bler** *n.* **—hum·bly** *adv.*
Synonyms: *meek, modest, reserved, retiring.*
hum·ble·bee (hŭm′bəl-bē′) *n.* A **bumblebee** *(see).* [Middle English *humbylbee,* perhaps from Middle Low German *hummelbē* : *hummel,* bumblebee + *bē,* bee.]
humble pie *n.* Formerly, a pie made from the edible organs of a deer. **—eat humble pie.** To apologize for or admit one's faults abjectly in humiliating circumstances. [*Humble,* from earlier *humbles,* unexplained variant of *umbles*; see **numbles.** Phrase (influenced by HUMBLE, to humiliate) originally referred to eating the offal or least desirable part of a deer.]
Hum·boldt (hŭm′bōlt′). A river rising in northeastern Nevada and

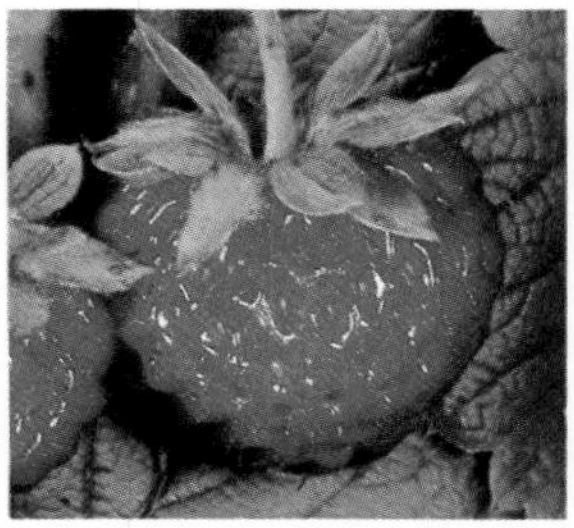

hull *The green detachable part of soft fruit such as strawberries is thought to get its name because the leaves originally form a protective outer skin —like a ship's hull— around the flower buds that produce the fruit.*

flowing *c.* 485 kilometers (300 miles) west and southwest to the Humboldt Sink in western Nevada. Its length varies with the seasons.

Humboldt, (Friedrich Wilhelm Karl Heinrich) Alexander von (1769–1859). German explorer and geographer. He originated the study of the environment, ecology. His major work, *Kosmos,* is a physical description of the universe and a history of science (1845–62). The Humboldt Current (now called the Peru Current), off Peru's Pacific coast, was named after him.

Humboldt, (Karl) Wilhelm von (1767–1835). German statesman and philologist. He explored the relationship between language and culture.

Humboldt Bay. Sheltered inlet of the Pacific Ocean, *c.* 23 kilometers (14 miles) long and from 1.6 to 8 kilometers (1 to 5 miles wide), in northwestern California.

Humboldt Current. See Peru Current.

hum·bug (hŭm′bŭg′) *n.* **1.** Something intended to deceive; a hoax; a fraud. **2.** One who tries to trick or deceive others; an impostor; a charlatan. **3. a.** Nonsense; rubbish. **b.** Pretense or hypocrisy. **4.** *British.* A usually peppermint-flavored candy. —*v.* **humbugged, -bugging, -bugs.** —*tr.* To deceive; trick; cheat. —*intr.* To practice trickery. [18th century : origin obscure.] —**hum·bug·ger** *n.* —**hum·bug·ger·y** (hŭm′bŭg′ə-rē) *n.*

hum·ding·er (hŭm′dĭng′ər) *n. Slang.* Someone or something extraordinary or superior; a marvel. [20th century : origin obscure.]

hum·drum (hŭm′drŭm′) *adj.* Without change, variety, or excitement; monotonous; ordinary. —See Synonyms at **boring.** —*n.* Something or someone dull or unexciting. [Originally also *humtrum,* probably reduplication of HUM.]

Hume (hyōōm), **David** (1711–76). Scottish philosopher and historian. He argued that the perceptions of the mind were essentially impressions from sensations, emotions, and ideas.

hu·mec·tant (hyōō-mĕk′tənt) *n.* A substance that promotes retention of moisture. —*adj.* Promoting moisture retention. [Latin *hūmectāns* (stem *hūmectant-*), present participle of *(h)ūmectāre,* to moisten, from *(h)ūmectus,* moist, from *(h)ūmēre,* to be moist.]

hu·mer·al (hyōō′mər-əl) *adj.* **1.** Pertaining to or located in the region of the humerus or the shoulder. **2.** Pertaining to or designating a body part analogous to the humerus. —**hu·mer·al** *n.*

humeral veil *n. Roman Catholic Church.* A shawllike vestment worn over the shoulders by a priest when carrying the Blessed Sacrament at benediction or in procession.

hu·mer·us (hyōō′mər-əs) *n., pl.* **-meri** (-mə-rī′). **1.** The long bone of the upper part of the arm, extending from the shoulder to the elbow. **2.** The corresponding bone in vertebrate animals. [New Latin, from Latin *umerus, humerus,* upper arm, shoulder.]

hu·mic (hyōō′mĭk) *adj.* Of, pertaining to, or derived from humus.

hu·mid (hyōō′mĭd) *adj.* Containing or marked by a high amount of moisture; oppressively damp: *humid weather.* —See Synonyms at **wet.** [Old French *humide,* from Latin *(h)ūmidus,* from *(h)ūmēre,* to be moist.] —**hu·mid·ly** *adv.*

hu·mid·i·fi·er (hyōō-mĭd′ə-fī′ər) *n.* An apparatus for increasing the humidity in a room, greenhouse, or other enclosed area.

hu·mid·i·fy (hyōō-mĭd′ə-fī′) *tr.v.* **-fied, -fying, -fies.** To make more humid; especially, to increase the amount of water vapor in (the air). —**hu·mid·i·fi·ca·tion** (hyōō-mĭd′ə-fĭ-kā′shən) *n.*

hu·mid·i·stat (hyōō-mĭd′ĭ-stăt′) *n.* An instrument designed to indicate or control the relative humidity of the air. Also called "hygrostat." [HUMIDI(TY) + -STAT.]

hu·mid·i·ty (hyōō-mĭd′ə-tē) *n.* **1.** Dampness, especially of the air. **2.** A measure of the amount of water vapor in the air. See **absolute humidity, relative humidity.** [Middle English *humidite,* from Old French, from Latin *hūmiditās* (stem *hūmiditāt-*), from *hūmidus,* HUMID.]

hu·mi·dor (hyōō′mə-dôr′) *n.* A case for the storage of cigars and other tobacco products, containing a device for keeping the humidity level constant. [From HUMID.]

hu·mil·i·ate (hyōō-mĭl′ē-āt′) *tr.v.* **-ated, -ating, -ates.** To lower the pride, dignity, or status of; humble or disgrace; degrade. —See Synonyms at **degrade.** [Late Latin *humiliāre,* from *humilis,* HUMBLE.] —**hu·mil·i·a·to·ry** (hyōō-mĭl′ē-ə-tôr′ē, -tōr′ē) *adj.*

hu·mil·i·a·tion (hyōō-mĭl′ē-ā′shən) *n.* **1.** The act of humiliating; degradation. **2.** The condition of being humiliated; disgrace; shame. **3.** A condition or circumstance that humiliates: *The child's unusual name was a humilation to her at school.*

hu·mil·i·ty (hyōō-mĭl′ə-tē) *n.* The quality or condition of being humble; lack of pride; modesty. [Middle English *humilite,* from Old French *humilite,* from Latin *humilitās* (stem *humilitāt-*), from *humilis,* HUMBLE.]

hum·ming·bird (hŭm′ĭng-bûrd′) *n.* Any of numerous chiefly tropical New World birds of the family Trochilidae, usually very small and having a long, slender bill, wings capable of beating very rapidly, and often brilliantly colored plumage. [From the humming sound produced by the rapidly vibrating wings.]

hummingbird moth *n.* A moth, the **hawk moth** (*see*), that resembles a hummingbird.

hum·mock (hŭm′ək) *n.* Also **ham·mock** (hăm′ək) (for sense 2). **1.** A low mound or ridge of earth; a knoll. **2.** In the southern United States, a tract of forested land elevated above the level of an adjacent marsh. **3.** A ridge or hill of ice in an ice field. [16th century : origin obscure.] —**hum·mock·y** *adj.*

hum·mus, hum·mous (hŭm′əs) *n.* A puree of chickpeas and oil,

often flavored with garlic, sesame seed, and lemon, eaten as a sandwich spread or dip. [Arabic *ḥummuṣ,* chickpea.]

hu·mon·gous (hyōō-mŏng′gəs, -mŭng′gəs) *adj. Slang.* Extremely large; enormous. [Perhaps a blend of HUGE and MONSTROUS.]

hu·mor (hyōō′mər) *n.* Also *British* **hu·mour.** **1.** The quality of being laughable or comical; funniness: *He saw the humor of the situation.* **2.** Something designed to induce laughter or amusement: *a story full of humor.* **3.** The ability to perceive, enjoy, or express what is comical or funny: *a sense of humor.* **4.** In medieval physiology, any of the four fluids of the body, blood, phlegm, choler (or yellow bile), and black bile, the dominance of which was thought to determine a person's character and general health. Accordingly, one's disposition might be **sanguine, phlegmatic, choleric,** or **melancholy** (*all of which see*). **5.** A state of mind; a mood: *in a bad humor.* **6.** Disposition; character; temperament: *a girl of a most sullen humor.* **7. a.** A sudden, unanticipated whim. **b.** Capricious or peculiar behavior or action. **8.** *Physiology.* Any of various body fluids; especially, the **aqueous humor** or **vitreous humor** (*both of which see*). —See Synonyms at **mood, wit.** —**out of humor.** In a bad mood; irritable. —*tr.v.* **humored, -moring, -mors.** Also *British* **hu·mour, humoured, -mouring, -mours.** **1.** To comply with the whims or wishes of (another); go along with; indulge. **2.** To adapt or accommodate oneself to. [Middle English *(h)umour,* fluid from an animal or plant, one of the four body fluids believed to affect mental disposition, from Norman French, from Latin *(h)ūmor,* liquid, fluid.]

hu·mor·al (hyōō′mər-əl) *adj.* Pertaining to or arising from any of the bodily humors.

hu·mor·esque (hyōō′mə-rĕsk′) *n.* A whimsical or playful musical composition. [German *Humoreske,* from *Humor,* humor, from English HUMOR.]

hu·mor·ist (hyōō′mər-ĭst) *n.* **1.** A person with a sharp sense of humor. **2.** A performer or writer of comedy.

hu·mor·less (hyōō′mər-lĭs) *adj.* **1.** Devoid of a sense of humor. **2.** Said or done without humor: *"She winked at me but it was humorless; a wink of warning"* (Truman Capote). —**hu·mor·less·ly** *adv.* —**hu·mor·less·ness** *n.*

hu·mor·ous (hyōō′mər-əs) *adj.* **1.** Appealing to the sense of humor; funny; laughable; comical: *a humorous sight.* **2.** Characterized by or expressing humor; comic; witty; droll: *a humorous speaker.* **3.** *Archaic.* Capricious. **4.** *Obsolete.* Damp; moist. —**hu·mor·ous·ly** *adv.* —**hu·mor·ous·ness** *n.*

hump (hŭmp) *n.* **1.** A rounded mass or protuberance, such as the fleshy structure on the back of a camel or over the shoulders of some cattle. **2.** A deformity of the back, due in human beings to an abnormal curvature of the spine. **3.** A low mound of earth; a hummock. **4.** *British Slang.* A feeling of depression or extreme annoyance. Often preceded by *the.* —**over the hump.** Past the worst or most difficult part of something. —*v.* **humped, humping, humps.** —*tr.* **1.** To make into a hump; arch; round. **2.** *Chiefly British Informal.* To carry (something large or heavy). **3.** *Slang.* To exert (oneself) strenuously. —*intr.* **1.** To bend or arch so as to become a hump. **2.** *Slang.* To exert oneself. [Shortened from earlier *humpback(ed),* possibly a blend of earlier *crumpbacked* and HUNCHBACK(ED).]

hump·back (hŭmp′băk′) *n.* **1.** A person afflicted with an abnormally curved or humped back; a hunchback. **2.** An abnormally curved or humped back. **3.** A pathological condition, **kyphosis** (*see*). **4.** A whalebone whale, *Megaptera novaeangliae,* having a rounded back and long, knobby flippers. **5.** A salmon, *Oncorhynchus gorbuscha,* of the Pacific Ocean, the male of which has a humped back and hooked jaws. —**hump·backed** *adj.*

humpback bridge *n.* Also **humpbacked bridge.** A narrow bridge forming part of a road, having a steep incline and decline.

humped (hŭmpt) *adj.* Having a hump: *humped cattle.*

Hum·per·dinck (hōōmp′pər-dĭnk′, hŭm′-), **Engelbert** (1854–1921). German composer. He wrote the fairy-tale opera *Hänsel und Gretel* (1893).

humph (hŭmf) *interj.* Used to express doubt, displeasure, or contempt.

Hum·phrey (hŭm′frē), **Hubert Horatio** (1911–78). U.S. Democratic politician. He was vice president (1965–69) under Lyndon Johnson.

hummingbird *A blue-throated hummingbird,* Lampornis clemenciae—*a native of the Americas—hovers while it extracts nectar from a flower. Its wings, frozen here by high-speed photography, flap up to 200 times a second while it hovers, causing the humming sound for which the birds are named.*

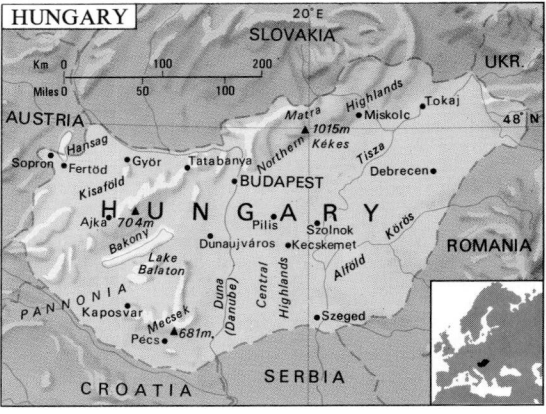

He was defeated for the presidency in 1968 by Richard Nixon and failed to win the Democratic nomination in 1972.

Hump·ty Dump·ty (hŭmp′te dŭmp′tē) *n.* **1.** An egg-shaped character in a nursery rhyme who fell off a wall and broke into pieces. **2.** *Usually* **humpty dumpty.** *Informal.* A short, fat person.

hump·y (hŭm′pē) *adj.* **-ier, -iest. 1.** Covered with or containing humps. **2.** Resembling a hump.

hu·mus (hyo͞o′məs) *n.* A brown or black organic substance consisting of decayed vegetable and animal matter that provides nutrients for plants and increases the ability of soil to retain water. [Latin *humus,* earth, ground, soil.]

Hun (hŭn) *n.* **1.** Any of a fierce barbaric race of Asiatic nomads who invaded Europe in the late 4th century A.D. and, led by Attila, overran large parts of it in the mid-5th century. **2.** Often **hun.** A savage, uncivilized, or destructive person. [Old English *Hūne* and *Hūnas* (both plural), from Late Latin *Hūnī,* from Turki *Hun-yü.*]

Hun. Hungarian; Hungary.

Hu·nan, Hu-nan (ho͞o′nän′). Province in south-central China. Rich in mineral resources and forests, the province is especially famous for its cedar. Its capital is Changsha.

hunch (hŭnch) *n.* **1.** An intuitive feeling or guess about something; a premonition. **2.** A hump. **3.** A lump or chunk.
∼*v.* **hunched, hunching, hunches.** —*tr.* To bend, arch, or draw up into a hump: *hunched his shoulders against the wind.* —*intr.* To draw oneself up closely into a crouched or cramped posture: *The scared child hunched in a corner.* [Origin unknown.]

hunch·back (hŭnch′băk′) *n.* A person afflicted with an abnormally curved or hunched back. See **humpback. —hunch·backed** *adj.*

hun·dred (hŭn′drĭd) *n., pl.* **hundred** or **-dreds** (for senses 2, 4, and 5). *Abbr.* **h. 1. a.** The cardinal number that is ten more than ninety. **b.** A symbol representing this, such as 100 or C. **2.** A currency note worth 100 dollars: *I paid with a hundred and a ten.* **3.** The number in the third position left of the decimal point in an Arabic numeral. **4. a.** An unspecified large number: *I've been there hundreds of times.* **b.** The numbers between 100 and 999: *The dress was valued in the hundreds.* **5. hundreds.** A specified era of a hundred years: *the nineteen hundreds.* **6.** A former administrative division of some English and American counties. [Middle English *hundred,* Old English *hundred, hund,* from Germanic.] **—hun·dred** *adj. & pron.* **—hun·dred·fold** (hŭn′drĭd-fōld′) *adj. & adv.*

hun·dredth (hŭn′drĭdth) *n.* **1.** The ordinal number 100 in a series. Also written 100th. **2.** One of 100 equal parts. **—hun·dredth** *adj. & adv.*

hun·dred·weight (hŭn′drĭd-wāt′) *n., pl.* **hundredweight** or **-weights.** *Abbr.* **cwt. 1.** A unit of weight in the U.S. Customary System equal to 100 pounds. Also called "short hundredweight." **2.** A unit of weight in the British Imperial System equal to 112 pounds. Also called "long hundredweight."

Hundred Years' War *n.* A series of wars between England and France that lasted from 1337 until 1453.

hung (hŭng). Past tense and past participle of **hang.**
∼*adj.* **1.** With no party having a working majority. Said of a legislative assembly: *a hung Congress.* **2.** So divided in opinion as to be unable to reach a verdict: *a hung jury.* —See Usage note at **hang.**

Hung. Hungarian; Hungary.

Hun·gar·i·an (hŭng-gâr′ē-ən) *adj. Abbr.* **Hun., Hung.** Of or relating to Hungary or its people, language, or culture.
∼*n. Abbr.* **Hun., Hung. 1.** A citizen or native of Hungary. **2.** The Finno-Ugric language spoken in Hungary; Magyar.

Hungarian goulash *n.* **Goulash** *(see).*

Hungarian puli *n.* A dog, the **puli** *(see).*

Hun·ga·ry (hŭng′gə-rē), *Abbr.* **Hun., Hung.** *Hungarian* **Ma·gyar·or·szág** (mô′dyôr-ôr′säg′). Republic of central Europe. The country consists for the most part of plains, broken by the Danube and Tisza rivers. Hungary was part of the dual kingdom of Austria-Hungary from 1867 until 1918, when a Hungarian republic was proclaimed. The Communist Party seized power in the aftermath of World War II, and a new constitution, on the Soviet model, was established (1949). A counterrevolutionary uprising in Budapest (1956) was put down by Soviet troops. The Communist Party's monopoly of power came to an end with the amendation of the constitution (1989) and multiparty national elections (1990). Area, 93,030 square kilometers (35,910 square miles). Population, 10,600,000. Capital, Budapest.

hun·ger (hŭng′gər) *n.* **1. a.** The weakness, debilitation, or pain caused by a prolonged lack of food; starvation. **b.** Mild discomfort or an uneasy sensation caused by a lack of food. **c.** A strong desire for food. **2.** A strong desire or craving for anything: *a hunger for affection.*
∼*v.* **hungered, -gering, -gers.** —*intr.* **1.** To have a need or desire for food. **2.** To have a strong desire or craving for anything. Used with *after* or *for: In exile, he hungered for his native land.*
∼*tr.* **1.** To cause to experience hunger; make hungry: *The thought of food hungered him even more.* **2.** To bring or reduce to the specified state because of hunger: *The police hungered the terrorists into submission.* —See Synonyms at **yearn.** [Middle English *hunger,* Old English *hungor, hungur,* from Germanic.]

hunger march *n.* A march or demonstration by the unemployed and poor to protest their condition. **—hunger marcher** *n.*

hunger strike *n.* A refusal to eat or a voluntary fast undertaken as a method of protest. **—hunger striker** *n.*

hung over *adj.* Suffering from a hangover.

hun·gry (hŭng′grē) *adj.* **-grier, -griest. 1.** Experiencing weakness, pain, or other discomfort from lack of food. **2.** Desiring or craving food. **3. a.** Strong desiring or craving anything: *hungry for recognition.* **b.** Using or requiring large quantities of something: *a fuel-hungry heating system.* **4.** Characterized by or expressing hunger, greed, or craving: *a hungry look.* **5.** Lacking richness or fertility: *hungry soil.* [Middle English *hungri,* Old English *hungri(g),* from *hungor,* HUNGER.] **—hun·gri·ly** *adv.* **—hun·gri·ness** *n.*

hung up *adj. Informal.* **1.** Delayed: *got hung up in rush-hour traffic.* **2.** Emotionally or psychologically disturbed or upset. **3.** Over-interested in or concerned with a subject: *hung up on punctuality.*

hunk (hŭngk) *n.* **1.** *Informal.* A large piece; a chunk: *a hunk of fresh bread.* **2.** *Slang.* A sexually appealing man, especially one with a powerful physique. [Probably akin to West Flemish *hunke*†, hunk of food.] **—hunk·y** *adj.*

hun·ker (hŭng′kər) *intr.v.* **-kered, -kering, -kers.** To squat close to the ground with the body leaning forward, the weight resting on the calves.
∼*n.* **hunkers.** *Regional.* The haunches. [Scottish, from *hunker,* to squat, perhaps from Scandinavian; akin to Old Norse *hokra,* to crouch.]

hunks (hŭngks) *n., pl.* **hunks. 1.** An irritable or disagreeable old person. **2.** A stingy, covetous man; a miser. [17th century : origin obscure.]

hun·ky-do·ry (hŭng′kē-dôr′ē, -dōr′ē) *adj. Slang.* Perfectly all right; quite satisfactory; fine. [19th century : origin obscure.]

Hun·nish (hŭn′ĭsh) *adj.* **1.** Of or pertaining to the Huns or their language. **2.** *Sometimes* **hunnish.** Barbarous.
∼*n.* The language of the Huns, variously classified as Turkic or Mongolian. **—Hun·nish·ness** *n.*

hunt (hŭnt) *v.* **hunted, hunting, hunts.** —*tr.* **1. a.** To pursue (game or other wild animals) for food or sport. See **hunting. b.** To seek out; track; search for. **c.** To search for (something deliberately hidden), as in a children's game: *hunt the thimble; hunt the slipper.* **2.** To search through (an area), as for game or prey. **3.** To make use of (hounds or horses, for example) in hunting. **4.** To drive out forcibly; chase away, especially by harassing. **5.** To harass persistently; persecute. —*intr.* **1.** To pursue game or other wild animals in order to capture or kill them. **2.** To conduct a diligent search; seek. Often used with *for.* **3.** *Aerospace.* **a.** To yaw back and forth about a flight path, as if seeking a new direction or another angle of attack. Used of aircraft, rockets, and space vehicles. **b.** To rotate up and down or back and forth without being deflected by the pilot. Used of a control surface or a rocket motor in gimbals. **4. a.** To oscillate about a selected value or setting. Used of a control system, electric motor, engine, carburetor, or the like. **b.** To swing back and forth or to oscillate. Used of an indicator on a display or measuring instrument. **—hunt down** (or **out**). To search for and locate. **—hunt up. 1.** To search for; seek. **2.** To hunt down.
∼*n.* **1.** The act or sport of hunting game; the chase. **2. a.** A hunting expedition or outing. **b.** Those taking part in a hunt with horses and hounds. **3.** A diligent search or pursuit. [Middle English *hunten,* Old English *huntian,* from Germanic *huntjan* (unattested), akin to *hanthatjan* (unattested), to HENT.]

Hunt (hŭnt), **(James Henry) Leigh** (1784–1859). British radical essayist and journalist. He edited *The Examiner* from 1808 and was jailed (1813–15) for a libel on the Prince Regent.

Hunt, Richard Morris (1827–95). U.S. architect. A prolific architect, he oversaw the addition to the Louvre in Paris and designed many important works, such as the addition to the U.S. Capitol, the base of the Statue of Liberty, numerous academic buildings, and many mansions, including The Breakers in Newport, Rhode Island.

Hunt, (William) Holman (1827–1910). British artist who with Rossetti and Millais formed the Pre-Raphaelite Brotherhood. His works include *The Light of the World* (1854), *The Scapegoat* (1856), and *The Miracle of the Sacred Fire* (1898).

Hunt, William Morris (1824–79). U.S. painter. While studying in Europe he became influenced by and interested in contemporary French paintings, particularly the works of Millet. Through his Boston and Newport art schools and his own work he brought French painting to the attention of American artists and collectors.

hunt·er (hŭn′tər) *n.* **1.** One that hunts; especially, a person who hunts game for food or sport, or who captures wild animals. **2.** A horse bred or trained for use in hunting, typically a fast, strong jumper. **3.** A dog bred or trained for use in hunting. **4.** A person who searches for or seeks something. Usually used in combination: *a house hunter.* **5.** A watch with a hinged metal covering or case protecting the face and its glass covering. Compare **half hunter.**

hunt·er-gath·er·er (hŭn′tər-găth′ər-ər) *n.* A member of a group of primitive people, such as the Bushmen of the Kalahari, whose subsistence is based on hunting and collecting fruit and other plant foods.

hunt·er-kill·er (hŭn′tər-kĭl′ər) *adj.* Designating any of a class of submarines designed to locate, chase, and destroy enemy submarines.

hunter's moon *n.* The full moon following the harvest moon.

hunt·ing (hŭn′tĭng) *n.* **1.** The sport or activity of pursuing wild animals, especially: **a.** The sport of hunting wild animals, game birds, and the like with guns. **b.** *British.* The hunting of foxes or other vermin using packs of hounds but not guns. **2.** The act of conducting a serious search for something. Often used in combination: *job hunting; house hunting.*
∼*adj.* Pertaining to or used in the sport of hunting: *a hunting horn.*

hunter *A horse bred for stamina and closely related to the Arab thoroughbreds of the racing world. Hunters are the traditional mounts for fox hunters.*

hurricane

RAGING SPIRALS OF WIND AND RAIN THAT TAKE THEIR POWER FROM HEAT AND MOISTURE

Hurricanes are born over the tropical seas near the equator

Hurricanes—or tropical cyclones or typhoons as they are also known—are powered by heat and moisture. They form near the equator over seas with a surface temperature of at least 27°C (81°F), a condition that occurs during the late summer "hurricane season." A rising column of warm, moist air forms a spiral system of clouds and strong winds. Technically, a hurricane exists when these winds reach a speed exceeding 32.7 meters a second (about 73 miles an hour).

Hurricanes drift slowly westward at about 16 kph (10 mph) with the trade winds and also veer away from the equator. When they leave the tropics or strike land, they dissipate, cut off from the warm seas that are the source of their energy. They are carefully monitored by weather satellites.

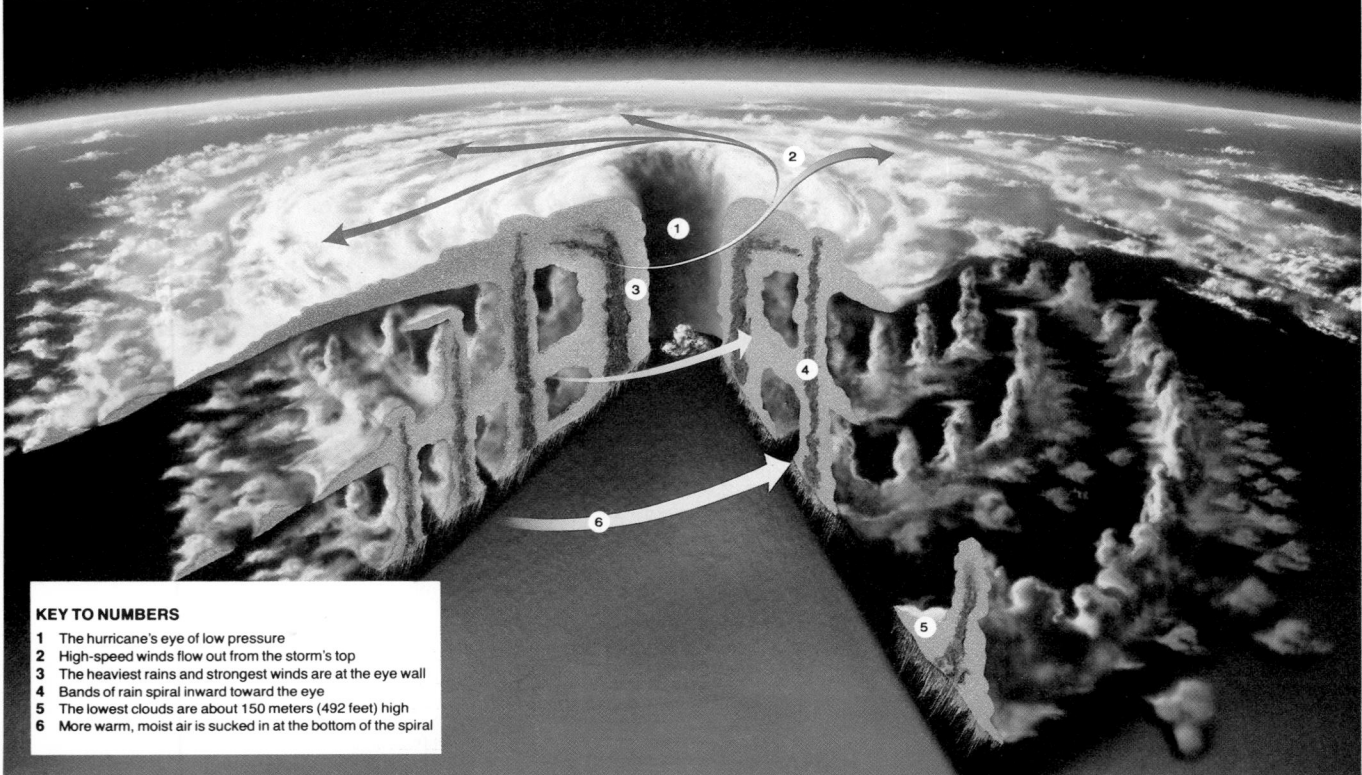

KEY TO NUMBERS
1 The hurricane's eye of low pressure
2 High-speed winds flow out from the storm's top
3 The heaviest rains and strongest winds are at the eye wall
4 Bands of rain spiral inward toward the eye
5 The lowest clouds are about 150 meters (492 feet) high
6 More warm, moist air is sucked in at the bottom of the spiral

SPIRAL OF WIND AND CLOUD *A hurricane builds up when warm, moist air begins to rise, forming cumulus clouds and allowing the prevailing trade winds to sweep in below. The system creates a spiral, twisting counterclockwise in the Northern Hemisphere and clockwise in the Southern. As the air rises, it cools and forms rain. The spiral forms an enormous catherine wheel up to 960 kilometers (600 miles) across, with winds increasing to about 320 kph (200 mph) toward the center, or eye, which is a calm area of low pressure about 32 kilometers (20 miles) across. Many hurricanes contain as much energy as 400 twenty-megaton bombs.*

Hun·ting·don and Pe·ter·bor·ough (hŭn′tĭng-dən; pē′tər-bûr′ō, -bər-ə). Former county in east-central England, created in 1965 by the merger of the counties of Huntingdonshire and the Soke of Peterborough. In 1974 it was absorbed by the nonmetropolitan county of Cambridgeshire.

hunting ground *n.* **1.** The location of a hunt. **2.** An area regarded as a potential source of a sought-after object or objective.

hunting leopard *n.* The **cheetah** *(see).*

hunting lodge *n.* A small house or lodge occupied by hunters.

hunting spider *n.* The **wolf spider** *(see).*

hunt·ress (hŭn′trĭs) *n.* **1.** A woman or female that hunts. **2.** *Rare.* A mare used for hunting.

hunts·man (hŭnts′mən) *n., pl.* **-men** (-mĭn). **1.** A person who hunts; a hunter. **2.** One who manages a pack of foxhounds or other hunting dogs and handles them when they are out hunting.

Hu·on pine (hyōō′ŏn′) *n.* A coniferous tree, *Dacrydium franklinii,* of Southeast Asia, Australia, and Chile, having scalelike leaves and berrylike fruits. [After the *Huon* River, southern Tasmania.]

Hupeh, Hupei. See **Hubei.**

hur·dies (hûr′dēz′) *pl.n. Scottish.* The buttocks or haunches. [Origin unknown.]

hur·dle (hûrd′l) *n.* **1.** A light, portable barrier, usually consisting of two uprights between which a horizontal bar can be hung at varying heights and which must be jumped by competitors in certain races. **2. hurdles.** A race for horses or human runners in which a series of such hurdles are used. **3.** Any obstacle or problem that must be overcome. **4.** *Chiefly British.* A portable section of fencing made of intertwined branches or wattle and used chiefly for fencing in sheep. **5.** *British.* A frame or sledge formerly used to carry condemned traitors to their executions.
∼*v.* **hurdled, -dling, -dles.** —*tr.* **1.** To jump over (a barrier) in or as if in a race. **2.** To enclose with hurdles. **3.** To overcome or successfully deal with (an obstacle or problem). —*intr.* To jump over barriers in or as if in a race. [Middle English *hurdel, hirdle,* Old English *hyrdel,* from Germanic.] —**hur·dler** *n.*

hur·dy-gur·dy (hûr′dē-gûr′dē) *n., pl.* **-dies.** **1.** A medieval instrument shaped like a lute, played by street musicians with a crank that causes a resin-covered wheel to scrape across the strings. **2.** Any musical instrument played by turning a crank, such as a barrel organ. [Probably imitative.]

hurl (hûrl) *v.* **hurled, hurling, hurls.** —*tr.* **1.** To throw with great force; fling; pitch. **2.** To move or impel vigorously; thrust. **3.** To exclaim vehemently; shout out: *hurl abuse.* —*intr.* **1.** To play the game of hurling. **2.** To move with great speed, force, or violence; hurtle. —See Synonyms at **throw.**
∼*n.* A forceful pitch or throw. [Middle English *h(o)urlen*†, to be driven with great force, throw, rush on.] —**hurl·er** *n.*

hurl·ey (hûr′lē) *n., pl.* **-ies.** **1.** The stick used in the game of hurling. **2.** The game of hurling. [From HURL.]

hurl·ing (hûr′lĭng) *n.* A fast Irish game resembling lacrosse and hockey, played between teams of 15 with broad-bladed netless sticks and a hard ball. [From HURL.]

hurl·y-bur·ly (hûr′lē-bûr′lē) *n., pl.* **-lies.** Turbulence; commotion; disorder.
∼*adj.* Full of noise or commotion. [Earlier *hurling and burling,* reduplication of *hurling,* tumult, from Middle English, gerund of HURL.]

Hu·ron (hyōōr′ən, -ŏn′) *n., pl.* **-rons** or collectively **Huron.** **1.** A member of a confederation of four tribes of Iroquoian-speaking North American Indians formerly inhabiting the region east of Lake Huron and the St. Lawrence Valley. **2.** The Iroquoian language spoken among these tribes. [French, "one who has disheveled hair," boor, from *hure*, disheveled head, from Old French *hure†*.] —**Hu·ron** *adj.*

Huron, Lake. One of the five Great Lakes, on the border between the United States and Canada. It is the second largest of the group of lakes. It forms part of the Great Lakes-St. Lawrence seaway system and is navigated by ocean-going vessels.

hur·rah (hŏŏ-rä′, -rô′) *interj.* Also **hoo·ray, hur·ray** (-rā′). Used as an exclamation of pleasure, approval, elation, or victory. —*n.* A shout of "hurrah." —*v.* **hurrahed, -rahing, -rahs.** Also **hoo·ray, hur·ray.** —*tr.* To applaud, cheer, or approve by shouting "hurrah." —*intr.* To shout "hurrah." [Alteration of HUZZA.]

hur·ri·cane (hûr′ə-kān′) *n.* **1. a.** A violent tropical cyclone originating in the Gulf of Mexico or Caribbean Sea, traveling north, northwest, or northeast from its point of origin, and usually involving heavy rains and thunder. **b.** A similar cyclone off the north of Australia. **2.** Wind exceeding 74 miles per hour, force 12 on the Beaufort scale. —See Synonyms at **wind.** [Earlier *furacano, haurachana,* from Spanish *huracan* and Portuguese *furacão,* both from Carib *huracan, furacan.*]

hurricane deck *n.* The upper deck on a ship such as a passenger steamer.

hurricane lamp *n.* A lamp consisting of a candle or electric bulb covered by a glass chimney.

hur·ried (hûr′ēd) *adj.* **1.** Obliged to move or act rapidly; rushed. **2.** Done in great haste: *a hurried tour.* —**hur·ried·ly** *adv.* —**hur·ried·ness** *n.*

hur·ry (hûr′ē) *v.* **-ried, -rying, -ries.** —*intr.* To move or act with haste. Often used with *up.* —*tr.* **1.** To cause to move or act rapidly or more rapidly; hasten: *hurry the children.* **2.** To cause to move or act too quickly; rush: *hurried them into marriage.* **3.** To hasten to completion; expedite: *This should hurry things along.* —See Synonyms at **speed.** —*n., pl.* **hurries. 1.** The act of hurrying; hastened progress. **2. a.** The need or wish to hurry: *There's no hurry.* **b.** A condition of urgency or eagerness: *Are you in a great hurry to leave?* [Perhaps from Middle English *horien.*]

Hurstmonceaux. See **Herstmonceux.**

Hur·ston (hûr′stən), **Zora Neale** (c. 1901-60). U.S. author. In her several books and novels, including *Jonah's Gourd Vine* (1934) and *Seraph on the Suwanee* (1948), she wrote about black life with an originality and freshness that earned her critical acclaim. Her knowledge of anthropology added to the richness of her work.

hurt (hûrt) *v.* **hurt, hurting, hurts.** —*tr.* **1. a.** To cause physical damage or pain to; injure; wound. **b.** To produce a feeling of pain in (a person or living creature): *The tight collar hurt his neck.* **2.** To cause to suffer mental or emotional anguish; distress or offend. **3.** To harm; be prejudicial to; impair: *hurt his chances.* —*intr.* **1. a.** To have a feeling of pain or discomfort: *His leg hurts.* **b.** To produce a feeling of pain: *That collar hurts.* **2.** To cause distress, hardship, or damage: *The tax bill hurts.* —See Synonyms at **injure.** —*n.* **1.** Something that hurts; a pain, injury, or wound. **2.** Mental suffering; anguish. **3.** A wrong; damage; harm. [Middle English *hurten, hirten,* to strike, harm, from Old French *hurter,* from Gallo-Roman *hūrtāre†* (unattested).]

hurt·er (hûr′tər) *n.* **1.** One that hurts. **2.** A concrete, stone, or iron block or post placed at the corner of a building to protect it from damage by passing traffic. [Middle English, shoulder of an axle against which the wheel hub strikes, from Old French *hurtoir,* from *herter,* to strike, knock against, HURT.]

hurt·ful (hûrt′fəl) *adj.* Causing hurt or injury; painful; damaging. —**hurt·ful·ly** *adv.* —**hurt·ful·ness** *n.*

hur·tle (hûrt′l) *v.* **-tled, -tling, -tles.** —*intr.* **1.** To move with or as if with great speed and often with a rushing or crashing noise: *The river hurtles over the waterfall.* **2.** To collide violently; crash. —*tr.* To throw or send forcibly or violently; hurl. [Middle English *hurtlen,* to dash one thing against another, collide, frequentative of *hurten,* to strike, HURT.]

hus·band (hŭz′bənd) *n.* **1.** *Abbr.* **h., H.** A man joined to a woman in marriage; a woman's spouse. **2.** *Archaic.* A manager or steward. **3.** A prudent and thrifty manager, as of money: *He proved a careless husband of his resources.* —*tr.v.* **husbanded, -banding, -bands. 1.** To spend or use economically; budget; conserve: *husband one's energy.* **2.** *Archaic.* **a.** To marry. **b.** *Archaic.* To find a husband for. **3.** *Archaic.* To till (land). [Middle English *housbonde, hus(e)bonde,* husband, husbandman, Old English *hūsbonda,* master of a household, husband, from Old Norse *hūsbōndi : hūs,* house, from Germanic *hūsam* (unattested), HOUSE + *bōndi,* earlier *bōandi, būandi,* present participle of *bōa, būa,* to dwell.]

hus·band·man (hŭz′bənd-mən) *n., pl.* **-men** (-mĭn). One whose occupation is husbandry; a farmer. [Middle English *housbondeman : housbonde,* husbandman, HUSBAND + MAN.]

hus·band·ry (hŭz′bən-drē) *n.* **1. a.** The cultivation of plants or the raising of livestock; farming; agriculture. **b.** The application of scientific principles to a branch of farming, especially animal breeding: *animal husbandry.* **2.** The careful management of resources; conservation. [Middle English *housbondrie : housbonde,* husbandman, HUSBAND + -(E)RY.]

hush (hŭsh) *v.* **hushed, hushing, hushes** —*tr.* **1.** To cause to be silent; to quiet. **2.** To quell or still; calm; soothe. **3.** To prevent from becoming publicly known; suppress; conceal: *tried to hush up the scandal.* —*intr.* To be or become silent or still.

—*n.* A silence; stillness; quiet.

—*interj.* Used to demand quiet or to calm a child. [Back-formation from earlier *husht* (interjection), from Middle English *huissht.*]

hush-hush (hŭsh′hŭsh′) *adj. Informal.* Secret; confidential.

hush money *n. Informal.* A bribe or payment made to keep something secret.

husk (hŭsk) *n.* **1.** The membranous or green outer envelope of many fruits and seeds. **2.** The shell or outer covering of anything, especially when worthless. —*tr.v.* **husked, husking, husks.** To remove the husk or husks from. [Middle English *husk(e),* probably from Middle Dutch *hūskijn,* diminutive of *hūs,* house, from Germanic *hūsam* (unattested), HOUSE.] —**husk·er** *n.*

husk·y¹ (hŭs′kē) *adj.* **-ier, -iest. 1.** Having a hoarse, often breathy quality, either naturally or from overuse or emotion: *"I listen to her voice which is dark, heavy, husky"* (Anaïs Nin). **2.** Like a husk. **3.** Full of husks. **4.** *Informal.* Rugged, strong, and burly. —*n., pl.* **huskies.** A husky person. [From HUSK.] —**husk·i·ly** *adv.* —**husk·i·ness** *n.*

hus·ky² (hŭs′kē) *n., pl.* **-kies. 1.** *Sometimes* **Husky.** A dog of a breed developed in Siberia for pulling sleds, having a dense, variously colored coat, small erect ears, and a bushy tail curled over the back. Also called "Siberian husky." **2.** A dog of any of several similar breeds of Arctic origin. [Probably a shortened variant of ESKIMO.]

Huss (hŭs), **John** (c. 1369-1415). Also **Jan Hus** (hŏos). Czech religious reformer. Huss attacked the corruption of the clergy and was excommunicated in 1412, when he denounced the bulls of the antipope John XXII. In exile he wrote *De Ecclesia,* which accorded the state the right to supervise the church. His death by burning made him a national hero.

hus·sar (hŏo-zär′, -sär′) *n.* **1.** A member of a light cavalry regiment having dress uniforms, typically with much frogging. **2.** A horseman of the Hungarian light cavalry that was organized during the 15th century. [Hungarian *huszár,* "freebooter," hussar, from Old Serbian *husar, gusar,* from Old Italian *corsaro,* CORSAIR.]

Hus·sein Ibn Ta·lal (hŏo-sān′ ĭb′ən tə-läl′) (1935-). King of Jordan from 1952. He succeeded his father, King Talal. Hussein suffered military defeat by Israel in 1967 and has since quelled Arab guerrilla attacks.

Hussein (hŏo-sān′), **Saddam** (1937-). President of Iraq since 1979 and chairman of the Revolutionary Command Council of the socialist, Arab nationalist Baath Party. He was instrumental in bringing his party to power in a bloodless coup (1968).

Huss·ite (hŭs′īt′, hŏos′-) *n.* A follower of John Huss. —*adj.* Of or pertaining to John Huss or his religious theories. —**Huss·it·ism** (hŭs′īt′īz′əm, hŏos′-) *n.*

hus·sy (hŭz′ē, hŭs′ē) *n., pl.* **-sies. 1.** A saucy or flippant girl. **2.** A lewd or sexually promiscuous woman. [Alteration of HOUSEWIFE.]

hust·ings (hŭs′tĭngz) *pl.n. Sometimes used with a singular verb.* **1.** *British.* A court formerly held in London. **2.** *British.* A platform from which (prior to the Ballot Act of 1872) candidates for Parliament addressed the electors. **3. a.** Any place or platform where political speeches are made. **b.** Political campaigning, especially in connection with an election: *a veteran of the hustings.* [Middle English *husting,* an assembly, Old English *hūsting,* from Old Norse *hūsthing,* "house assembly" : *hūs,* house, from Germanic *hūsam* (unattested), HOUSE + *thing,* assembly.]

hus·tle (hŭs′əl) *v.* **-tled, -tling, -tles.** —*tr.* **1.** To jostle or shove roughly. **2.** To usher hurriedly or urgently: *hustle the prisoner onto a plane.* **3.** To hurry along; cause or urge to proceed hurriedly: *hustled the board into a quick decision.* **4.** *Slang.* **a.** To sell or obtain in undignified or unethical ways: *He hustles a few dollars by peddling racetrack tips.* **b.** To gain by energetic effort. —*intr.* **1.** To jostle and push. **2.** *Informal.* To work busily and quickly. **3.** *Slang.* To use vigorous, aggressive, or questionable means in order to make money. **4.** *Slang.* To solicit customers for or as a prostitute. —*n.* **1.** The act or an instance of hustling. **2.** *Slang.* A job or business, especially one that is undignified or unethical. **3.** *Informal.* Hurried activity: *the hustle and bustle of city streets.* [Originally to shake back and forth, from Middle Dutch *husselen,* frequentative of *hutsen,* to shake, from (unattested) Germanic *khut-* (probably imitative).] —**hus·tler** *n.*

Hus·ton (hyŏo′stən), **John** (1906-87). U.S. film director. He started his film career as a scriptwriter (1938) but later made successful action films, including *The Maltese Falcon* (1941), *The African Queen* (1951), and *The Man Who Would Be King* (1975).

hut (hŭt) *n.* **1.** A makeshift or crudely constructed dwelling or shelter. **2.** *Military.* A temporary structure for sheltering troops. —*v.* **hutted, hutting, huts.** —*tr.* To shelter or store in a hut. —*intr.* To live or take shelter in a hut. [Old French *hutte,* from Middle High German *hütte* or Old High German *hutt(e)a.*]

hutch (hŭch) *n.* **1.** A box, pen, or coop, usually having a wire-mesh side, for small animals, especially rabbits. **2.** A cupboard with storage drawers. **3.** A small house or hut. [Middle English *huche,* chest, from Old French *huche, huge,* from Medieval Latin *hutica†.*]

Hutch·in·son (hŭch′ĭn-sən), **Anne** (1591-1643). U.S. colonist and religious leader, born in England. After settling in Boston (1635), she was ostracized and later excommunicated for her religious beliefs. She moved to present-day Rhode Island with her family (1638) and then to Pelham Bay, Long Island, where she was killed by Indians.

hut-cir·cle (hŭt′sûr′kəl) *n. Archaeology.* A ring or partial ring of stones or earth indicating the site of a simple prehistoric dwelling.

hut·ment (hŭt′mənt) *n.* An encampment of huts; especially, a military camp.

Hut·ter·ite (hŭt′ə-rīt′, hōō′tə-) *n.* A member of an **Anabaptist** *(see)* sect originating in Moravia and now living in parts of Canada and the United States. Hutterites are mainly farmers and hold property in common. [After J. *Hutter,* 16th-century Moravian Anabaptist.]

Hut·ton (hŭt′n), **James** (1726–97). Scottish geologist and farmer. His principle of uniformitarianism (1785), describing the igneous origins of rocks and minerals, forms the basis of modern geology.

Hux·ley (hŭk′slē), **Aldous (Leonard)** (1894–1963). British novelist and essayist. In *Brave New World* (1932) he painted a grim picture of a future utopia, a scientifically organized society in which conventional human suffering has been eliminated. His fascination with mysticism shows in *Eyeless in Gaza* (1936) and in *Time Must Have a Stop* (1944).

Huxley, Sir Julian Sorell (1887–1975). British biologist and brother of Aldous. He was professor of zoology at King's College, London (1925–27), secretary of the Zoological Society of London (1935–42), and the first director general of UNESCO (1946–48). Huxley advocated the application of scientific principles to moral, social, and political issues.

Huxley, Thomas Henry (1825–95). British biologist who championed Darwin's theory of evolution. He was the grandfather of Aldous and Julian Huxley. His works include *Zoological Evidences as to Man's Place in Nature* (1863) and *Science and Culture* (1881).

Huy·gens (hī′gənz), **Christian** (1629–95). Dutch mathematician, astronomer, and physicist. He invented the micrometer (1655), discovered Saturn's rings (1655), pioneered the use of the pendulum in clocks (1657), and formulated Huygens' principle.

Huygens' principle *n. Physics.* The principle that any point on a wave front may be regarded as the source of a secondary wave and that the position of the wave front at any time is determined by the envelope at that time of the secondary waves arising from a previous wave front. [After Christian HUYGENS.]

huz·za, huz·zah (hə-zä′) *n. Archaic.* A shout of encouragement or triumph; a cheer.
~*interj. Archaic.* Used to express joy, encouragement, appreciation, or the like.
~*v.* **huzzaed, huzzaing, huzzas.** *Archaic.* —*intr.* To shout "huzza"; cheer. —*tr.* To cheer or encourage with shouts of huzza. [16th century : perhaps of nautical origin.]

H.V. high voltage.

H.W., h.w. high water.

Hwang Ho. See **Huang He.**

hwyl (hōō′il) *n. Welsh.* Passionate poetic fervor; emotional eloquence.

hy·a·cinth (hī′ə-sĭnth) *n.* **1.** Any of several bulbous plants of the genus *Hyacinthus,* native to the Mediterranean region, having narrow leaves and a terminal cluster of variously colored, usually very fragrant flowers; especially, the widely cultivated species *H. orientalis.* **2.** Any of several similar or related plants, such as the **grape hyacinth** *(see).* **3.** A plant, perhaps a lily, gladiolus, or iris, that according to Greek mythology sprang from the blood of the slain Hyacinthus. **4.** A deep purplish blue to vivid violet. **5.** A reddish or cinnamon-colored variety of transparent zircon, used as a gemstone. Also called "jacinth." **6.** A blue semiprecious stone, perhaps aquamarine, known in antiquity. [Latin *hyacinthus,* from Greek *huakinthos,* wild hyacinth (connected by folk etymology with HYACINTHUS), of Mediterranean origin.] —**hy·a·cin·thine** (hī′ə-sĭn′thĭn, -thīn′) *adj.*

hyacinth bean *n.* A twining vine, *Dolichos lablab,* of the Old World tropics, having purple or white flowers and edible pods and seeds.

Hy·a·cin·thus (hī′ə-sĭn′thəs). *Greek Mythology.* A beautiful youth loved but accidentally killed by Apollo, from whose blood Apollo caused the hyacinth to grow.

Hy·a·des (hī′ə-dēz′) *pl.n.* **1.** *Greek Mythology.* The five daughters of Atlas and sisters of the Pleiades, placed by Zeus in the heavens. **2.** *Astronomy.* A cluster of five stars in the constellation Taurus, supposed by ancient astronomers to indicate rain when they rose with the sun. [Latin, from Greek *Huades.*]

hyaena. Variant of **hyena.**

hy·a·lin (hī′ə-lĭn) *n.* Also **hy·a·line** (hī′ə-lĭn, -līn′). **1.** *Physiology.* The uniform matrix of hyaline cartilage. **2.** *Pathology.* A transparent substance occurring in certain degenerative skin conditions. [Greek *hualos†,* glass + -IN.]

hy·a·line (hī′ə-lĭn, -līn′) *adj.* Resembling glass; glassy; translucent or transparent.
~*n.* **1.** Something having a glassy or transparent appearance, as a clear sky or a calm lake. **2.** A glassy or transparent appearance. **3.** Variant of **hyalin.** [Late Latin *hyalinus,* from Greek *hualinos,* of crystal or glass, from *hualos, huelos†,* crystalline stone, glass.]

hyaline cartilage *n.* A common type of cartilage that has a glassy, translucent appearance and a bluish color, that in the adult is composed of cells in a seemingly homogeneous, translucent matrix, as in joints, and that in the fetus forms most of the skeleton.

hyaline membrane disease *n.* **Respiratory distress syndrome** *(see).*

hy·a·lite (hī′ə-līt′) *n.* A clear, colorless opal. [German *Hyalit,* from Greek *hualos†,* glass, crystal.]

hyalo–, hyal– *prefix.* Indicates glass or glassy material; for example, **hyaloplasm.** [Greek *hualos,* glass.]

hy·a·loid (hī′ə-loid′) *adj.* Glassy or transparent in appearance; hyaline. [Greek *hualoeidēs* : *hualos,* glass (see **hyaline**) + -OID.]

hyaloid membrane *n.* The transparent membrane that separates the vitreous humor of the eye from the retina.

hy·a·lo·plasm (hī′ə-lō-plăz′əm) *n.* The clear, fluid portion of cytoplasm, as distinguished from included granular and netlike components. [German *Hyaloplasma* : Greek *hualos†,* crystal + PLASM.] —**hy·a·lo·plas·mic** (hī′ə-lō-plăz′mĭk) *adj.*

hy·al·ur·on·ic acid (hī′əl-yōō-rŏn′ĭk) *n.* A mucopolysaccharide that is present in connective tissue and in the synovial fluid around joints. [HYAL(O)- + Greek *ouron,* urine.]

hy·al·ur·on·i·dase (hī′əl-yōō-rŏn′ə-dās′, -dāz′) *n.* An enzyme that breaks down hyaluronic acid, thereby making the fluid in which it is found less viscous. [HYAL(O)- + Greek *ouron,* urine + -ID + -ASE.]

hy·brid (hī′brĭd) *n. Abbr.* **hyb.** **1.** *Genetics.* The offspring of genetically dissimilar parents or stock; especially, the offspring produced by breeding plants or animals of different varieties, species, or races. **2.** Something of mixed origin or composition. **3.** A word whose elements are derived from different languages. [Latin *hybrida, hibrida†,* hybrid, mongrel.] —**hy·brid** *adj.* —**hy·brid·ism** *n.* —**hy·brid·i·ty** *n.*

hybrid circuit *n.* An integrated electronic circuit formed from a number of distinct integrated circuits interconnected on a substrate. Compare **monolithic circuit.**

hybrid computer *n.* A computer that combines elements of both a digital and an analog computer; especially, one in which an analog input is converted to digital form for fast processing.

hy·brid·ize (hī′brĭ-dīz′) *v.* **-ized, -izing, -izes.** —*tr.* To cause to produce hybrids; crossbreed. —*intr.* To produce hybrids. —**hy·brid·i·za·tion** (hī′brĭ-də-zā′shən) *n.* —**hy·brid·iz·er** *n.*

hybrid vigor *n.* **Heterosis** *(see).*

hybris. Variant of **hubris.**

hy·da·thode (hī′də-thōd′) *n.* A microscopic epidermal structure in many plants through which water is excreted in the form of liquid drops. [Greek *hudōr* (stem *hudat-*), water + *hodos,* way.]

hy·da·tid (hī′də-tĭd) *n.* **1.** A cyst formed as a result of infestation by a tapeworm, *Echinococcus granulosus,* in a larval stage. Also called "hydatid cyst." **2.** The encysted larva of *E. granulosus.* [Greek *hudatis* (stem *hudatid-*), watery vesicle, hydatid, from *hudōr* (stem *hudat-*), water.] —**hy·da·tid** *adj.*

hydatid disease *n.* The disease caused by the presence of hydatids in the liver, lungs, or brain, characterized by malignant tumors or tissue damage. Also called "echinococcosis," "echinococciasis."

Hyde. See **Jekyll and Hyde.**

Hyde Park¹ (hīd). Ancient park in central London, England, occupying 146 hectares (360 acres). It became a royal deer park under Henry VIII. Charles I opened it to the public in 1635.

Hyde Park². A village in southeastern New York, on the Hudson River. Settled *c.* 1740, it is the site of the Roosevelt estate, where Franklin D. Roosevelt was born and is buried. The national historic site includes his house and the Roosevelt Library.

Hy·der·a·bad¹ (hī′dər-ə-băd′, -bäd′). Former state in south-central India, since 1956 partitioned among the states of Karnataka, Maharashtra, and Andhra Pradesh. It is an almost entirely agricultural region, lying within the Deccan plateau. The city of Hyderabad, formerly the capital of the state of the same name, is now the capital of Andhra Pradesh.

Hyderabad². City of the province of Sind, in southern Pakistan. It is a manufacturing center and the third-largest city in Pakistan.

hy·dra¹ (hī′drə) *n., pl.* **-dras** or **-drae** (-drē′). Any of various small, freshwater polyps of the genus *Hydra* and related genera, having a naked, cylindrical body and an oral opening surrounded by tentacles. [New Latin *Hydra,* HYDRA (so called because polyps may reproduce themselves from parts cut off).]

hydra² *n.* A multifarious source of evil, trouble, or destruction that cannot be eradicated by a single attempt. [After HYDRA.]

Hy·dra¹ (hī′drə). *Greek Mythology.* A many-headed monster that sprouted two heads for each one cut off but was finally slain by Hercules, who cauterized each neck after severing its head. [Middle English *Ydre,* from Old French, from Latin *Hydra,* from Greek *Hudra,* from *hudra,* water serpent.]

Hydra² *n.* A constellation in the equatorial region of the southern sky near Cancer, Libra, and Centaurus. Also called the "Snake." [After HYDRA.]

hy·drac·id (hī-drăs′ĭd) *n.* An acid, such as hydrocyanic acid, that contains no oxygen. [HYDR(O)- + ACID.]

hy·dran·ge·a (hī-drān′jə, -drăn′jə) *n.* Any of various shrubs or trees of the genus *Hydrangea,* cultivated for their large, flat-topped or rounded clusters of white, pink, or blue flowers. [New Latin, "water vessel" (from the cuplike shape of the seed pod) : HYDR(O)- + Greek *angos,* vessel, pitcher (see **angiology**).]

hy·drant (hī′drənt) *n.* An outlet from a water main consisting of an upright pipe with one or more nozzles or spouts. Also called "fire hydrant," "fireplug." [HYDR(O)- + -ANT.]

hy·dranth (hī′drănth′) *n. Zoology.* A polyp in a hydroid colony that is specialized for feeding. [HYDR(O)- + Greek *anthos,* flower.]

hy·drar·gy·rism (hī-drär′jə-rĭz′əm) *n.* Also **hy·drar·gy·ri·a** (hī′drär-jĭr′ē-ə). *Pathology.* **Mercurialism** *(see).* [From New Latin *hydrargyrum,* from Latin *hydrargyrus,* from Greek *hudrarguros,* "silver water" : HYDR(O)- + *aguros,* silver.]

hy·dras·tine (hī-drăs′tēn′, -tĭn) *n.* A poisonous white alkaloid, $C_{21}H_{21}NO_6$, obtained from the root of the goldenseal, *Hydrastis canadensis,* and formerly used to treat uterine hemorrhage. [From HYDRASTIS.]

hy·dras·tis (hī-drăs′tĭs) *n.* Any plant of the genus *Hydrastis,* having ornamental foliage and fruits, including the **goldenseal** *(see).* [New Latin *Hydrastis* (genus) : HYDR(O)- + -astis†.]

hy·drate (hī'drāt') *n.* A compound containing water combined in a definite ratio, the water being retained or regarded as being retained in its molecular state.
~*v.* **hydrated, -drating, -drates.** —*tr.* To combine with water; especially, to cause to form a hydrate. **2.** To become a hydrate. [HYDR(O)- + -ATE.] —**hy·dra·tion** (hī-drā'shən) *n.* —**hy·dra·tor** *n.*

hy·drat·ed (hī'drā'tĭd) *adj.* Chemically combined with water; especially, existing in the form of a hydrate.

hy·drau·lic (hī-drô'lĭk) *adj.* **1.** Of, involving, moved by, or operated by a fluid, especially water, under pressure. **2.** Of or pertaining to hydraulics. [Latin *hydraulicus,* from Greek *hudraulis,* a water organ invented by Ctesibius in the 2nd century B.C. : HYDR(O)- + *aulos,* tube, pipe.] —**hy·drau·li·cal·ly** *adv.*

hydraulic brake *n.* A brake in which the braking force is transmitted to the braking surface by a compressed fluid.

hydraulic cement *n.* A cement capable of solidifying under water. See **Portland cement.**

hydraulic press *n.* A machine in which a large force is exerted on the larger of two pistons in a pair of hydraulically coupled cylinders by means of a relatively small force applied to the smaller piston.

hydraulic ram *n.* **1.** A water pump in which the downward flow of naturally running water is intermittently halted by a valve so that the flow is forced upward through an open pipe into a reservoir. **2.** The large output piston of a hydraulic press.

hy·drau·lics (hī-drô'lĭks) *n. Used with a singular verb.* The physical science and technology of the static and dynamic behavior of fluids. Also called "fluid mechanics."

hydraulic suspension *n.* A form of motor-vehicle suspension in which springs are replaced by hydraulic devices consisting of a piston moving in a cylinder filled with fluid. See **hydroelastic suspension.**

hy·dra·zine (hī'drə-zēn', -zĭn) *n.* A colorless, fuming, corrosive hygroscopic liquid, H_2NNH_2, used in jet and rocket fuels. [HYDR(O)- + AZ(O)- + -INE.]

hy·dra·zo·ic acid (hī'drə-zō'ĭk) *n.* A colorless, highly explosive liquid, HN_3, that forms explosive salts, called azides, when combined with heavy metals. [HYDR(O)- + AZO- + -IC.]

hy·dric (hī'drĭk) *adj.* **1.** Of, containing, or pertaining to hydrogen. **2.** Pertaining to, characterized by, or requiring considerable moisture. [HYDR(O)- + -IC.]

hy·dride (hī'drīd') *n.* A compound of hydrogen with another, more electropositive element or group. [HYDR(O)- + -IDE.]

hy·dri·od·ic acid (hī'drē-ŏd'ĭk) *n.* A clear, colorless or pale-yellow aqueous solution of hydrogen iodide, HI, that is a strong acid and reducing agent. [HYDR(O)- + IODIC ACID.]

hy·dro¹ (hī'drō) *n., pl.* **hydros.** *British.* A hotel or similar establishment, especially at a spa resort, providing hydropathic treatment.

hydro² *adj. Informal.* Hydroelectric.

hydro-, hydr- *prefix.* Indicates: **1.** Water; for example, **hydrous, hydroelectric. 2.** Liquid; for example, **hydrometallurgy, hydrostatic. 3.** Composed of or combined with hydrogen; for example, **hydrochloride, hydrosulfide. 4.** Hydroid; for example, **hydrozoan.** [Greek *hudōr,* water.]

hy·dro·bro·mic acid (hī'drə-brō'mĭk) *n.* A clear, colorless or faintly yellow, highly acidic and corrosive aqueous solution of hydrogen bromide, HBr, used in the manufacture of bromides.

hy·dro·car·bon (hī'drə-kär'bən) *n.* Any of numerous organic compounds, such as benzene and methane, that contain only carbon and hydrogen.

hy·dro·cele (hī'drə-sēl') *n.* A pathological accumulation of serous fluid in a bodily cavity, especially in the testicles. [Latin *hydrocēlē,* from Greek *hudrokēlē* : HYDRO- + -CELE.]

hy·dro·cel·lu·lose (hī'drō-sĕl'yə-lōs, -lōz') *n.* A gelatinous form of hydrated cellulose made by treating cellulose with acid, alkali, or water and used in making rayon, mercerized cotton, and paper.

hy·dro·ceph·a·lus (hī'drō-sĕf'ə-ləs) *n.* Also **hy·dro·ceph·a·ly** (-lē). A usually congenital condition in which an abnormal accumulation of cerebrospinal fluid in the cerebral ventricles causes enlargement of the skull and compression of the brain. In nontechnical usage, also called "water on the brain." [Late Latin, from Greek *hudrokephalon* : HYDRO- + -CEPHALUS.] —**hy·dro·ce·phal·ic** (hī'drō-sə-făl'ĭk), **hy·dro·ceph·a·loid** (hī'drō-sĕf'ə-loid'), **hy·dro·ceph·a·lous** (hī'drō-sĕf'ə-ləs) *adj.*

hy·dro·chlo·ric acid (hī'drə-klôr'ĭk, -klōr'ĭk) *n.* A clear, colorless, fuming, poisonous, highly acidic aqueous solution of hydrogen chloride, HCl, used in petroleum production, as a chemical intermediate, and in ore reduction, food processing, pickling, and metal cleaning. Formerly called "spirits of salt."

hy·dro·chlo·ride (hī'drə-klôr'īd', -klōr'īd') *n.* A compound resulting or regarded as resulting from the reaction of hydrochloric acid with an organic base.

hy·dro·cor·al (hī'drə-kôr'əl, -kŏr'əl) *n.* Any of various colonial marine hydrozoans of the order Hydrocorallinae, having a limestone skeleton and resembling the corals.

hy·dro·cor·ti·sone (hī'drō-kôr'tə-sōn', -zōn') *n.* A bitter, crystalline hormone, $C_{21}H_{30}O_5$, derived from the adrenal cortex and having activity and medical uses similar to those of **cortisone** *(see).* Also called "cortisol."

hy·dro·cy·an·ic acid (hī'drō-sī-ăn'ĭk) *n.* A colorless, volatile, extremely toxic, flammable aqueous solution of hydrogen cyanide,

HCN, used in the manufacture of dyes, fumigants, and plastics. Also called "prussic acid," "hydrogen cyanide."

hy·dro·dy·nam·ic (hī'drō-dī-năm'ĭk) *adj.* **1.** Of or pertaining to hydrodynamics. **2.** Of, pertaining to, or operated by the force of liquid in motion. —**hy·dro·dy·nam·i·cal·ly** *adv.*

hy·dro·dy·nam·ics (hī'drō-dī-năm'ĭks) *n. Used with a singular verb.* The dynamics of fluids, especially incompressible fluids, in motion. Also called "hydromechanics."

hy·dro·e·lec·tric (hī'drō-ĭ-lĕk'trĭk) *adj.* **1.** Generating electricity by conversion of the energy of running water. **2.** Using or involving electricity so generated. —**hy·dro·e·lec·tric·i·ty** (hī'drō-ĭ-lĕk'trĭs'-ə-tē) *n.*

hy·dro·flu·or·ic acid (hī'drō-floo-ôr'ĭk, -ôr'ĭk, -floor'ĭk) *n.* A colorless, fuming, corrosive, dangerously poisonous aqueous solution of hydrogen fluoride, HF, used to etch or polish glass, pickle certain metals, and clean masonry.

hy·dro·foil (hī'drə-foil') *n.* **1.** Any of a set of blades attached to the hull of a boat and aligned in the water at a small angle to the horizontal so that when the boat is in motion the fluid striking each blade's underside creates a high-pressure region below the blade, low pressure above it, and a resultant lift that raises the craft out of the water for efficient high-speed operation. **2.** A boat equipped with hydrofoils. In this sense, also called "hydroplane."

hy·dro·gen (hī'drə-jən) *n. Symbol* **H** A colorless, highly flammable gaseous element, the lightest of all gases and the most abundant element in the universe, used in the production of synthetic ammonia and methanol, in petroleum refining, in hydrogenation of organic materials, as a reducing atmosphere, in oxyhydrogen torches, and in rocket fuels. Atomic number 1, atomic weight 1.00797, melting point −259.14°C, boiling point −252.5°C, density 0.08988 gram per liter, valence 1. [French *hydrogène,* "water generating" (it forms water when oxidized) : HYDRO- + -GEN.] —**hy·drog·e·nous** (hī-drŏj'ə-nəs) *adj.*

hy·drog·en·ase (hī-drŏj'ə-nās', -nāz') *n.* An enzyme that catalyzes reduction reactions by causing the addition of hydrogen to a compound.

hy·dro·gen·ate (hī'drə-jə-nāt', hī-drŏj'ə-) *tr.v.* **-ated, -ating, -ates.** To combine with or subject to the action of hydrogen; especially, to combine (an unsaturated compound) with hydrogen. —**hy·dro·gen·a·tion** (hī'drə-jə-nā'shən, hī-drŏj'ə-) *n.* —**hy·dro·gen·a·tor** *n.*

hydrogen bomb *n.* An explosive weapon of enormous destructive power, derived from the fusion of nuclei of various hydrogen isotopes in the formation of helium nuclei. Also called "fusion bomb," "H-bomb," "thermonuclear bomb."

hydrogen bond *n.* An essentially ionic weak chemical bond between a strongly electronegative atom and a hydrogen atom already bonded to another strongly electronegative atom.

hydrogen bromide *n.* An irritating colorless gas, HBr, used in the manufacture of barbiturates and synthetic hormones.

hydrogen chloride *n.* A colorless, fuming, corrosive, suffocating gas, HCl, used in the manufacture of plastics.

hydrogen cyanide *n.* Hydrocyanic acid *(see).*

hydrogen fluoride *n.* A colorless, fuming, mobile, corrosive liquid, or a highly soluble corrosive gas, HF, used in the manufacture of hydrofluoric acid, as a reagent, catalyst, and fluorinating agent, and in the refining of uranium and the preparation of many fluorine compounds.

hydrogen iodide *n.* A corrosive, colorless, suffocating gas, HI, used to manufacture hydriodic acid.

hydrogen ion *n.* **1.** The positively charged ion of hydrogen, H^+, formed by removal of the electron from atomic hydrogen. **2.** An ionized hydrogen molecule, H^+_2.

hy·dro·gen·ize (hī'drə-jə-nīz', hī-drŏj'ə-) *tr.v.* **-ized, -izing, -izes.** To hydrogenate. —**hy·dro·gen·i·za·tion** *n.*

hy·dro·gen·ol·y·sis (hī'drō-jə-nŏl'ĭ-sĭs) *n.* The breaking of a chemical bond in an organic molecule with the simultaneous addition of a hydrogen atom to each of the resulting molecular fragments. [HYDROGEN + -LYSIS.]

hydrogen peroxide *n.* A colorless, heavy, strongly oxidizing liquid, H_2O_2, an essentially unstable compound, capable of reacting explosively with combustibles, and used principally in aqueous solution as an antiseptic, bleaching agent, oxidizing agent, oxidizer in rocket fuels, and laboratory reagent.

hydrogen sulfide *n.* A colorless, flammable, poisonous compound, H_2S, having a characteristic rotten-egg odor and used as a precipitator, purifier, and reagent.

hy·dro·ge·o·lo·gy (hī'drō-jē-ŏl'ə-jē) *n.* The scientific study of waters below the earth's surface and the geologic aspects of the surface waters and their interaction with the solid surface of the earth.

hy·dro·graph (hī'drə-grăf', -gräf') *n.* A graph showing seasonal variations of level, flow, or velocity in a body of water. [HYDRO- + -GRAPH.]

hy·drog·ra·phy (hī-drŏg'rə-fē) *n., pl.* **-phies.** **1.** The scientific study, description, and analysis of the physical conditions, boundaries, flow, and related characteristics of oceans, seas, and coastlines, and their winds. **2. a.** The mapping of such bodies of water. **b.** Maps or charts of such bodies of water. [Old French *hydrographie* : HYDRO- + -GRAPHY.] —**hy·drog·ra·pher** *n.* —**hy·dro·graph·ic** (hī'drə-grăf'-ĭk) *adj.* —**hy·dro·graph·i·cal·ly** *adv.*

hy·droid (hī'droid') *n.* **1.** Any of numerous characteristically colonial hydrozoan coelenterates of the order Hydroida, having a polyp rather than a medusoid form as the dominant stage of the life cycle. The order includes the hydra, one of the few solitary hydroids.

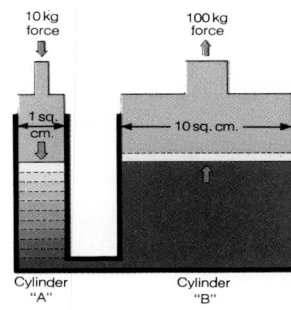
hydraulics *All hydraulic systems work on much the same principle as a lever. Moderate force exerted on a piston in a narrow liquid-filled cylinder (A) is transformed into much greater force on a broader piston in a connecting cylinder (B). If the second piston is ten times the area of the first, the force is multiplied tenfold but the second piston moves only one-tenth the distance.*

2. The asexual, hydralike polyp in the life cycle of any hydrozoan. ~*adj.* Of, pertaining to, or characteristic of a hydroid. [HYDR(A) (genus name) + -OID.]

hy·dro·ki·net·ic (hī′drō-kĭ-nĕt′ĭk, -kī-nĕt′ĭk) *adj.* **1.** Of or pertaining to hydrokinetics. **2.** Of or pertaining to the kinetic energy and motion of fluids.

hy·dro·ki·net·ics (hī′drō-kĭ-nĕt′ĭks, -kī-nĕt′ĭks) *n. Used with a singular verb.* The kinetics of fluids, especially incompressible fluids, in motion.

hy·dro·lase (hī′drə-lās′, -lāz′) *n.* Any of a group of enzymes that catalyze hydrolysis reactions by causing the addition or removal of a molecule of water. [HYDROL(YSIS) + -ASE.]

hydrologic cycle *n.* A **water cycle** (*see*).

hy·drol·o·gy (hī-drŏl′ə-jē) *n.* The scientific study of the properties, distribution, and effects of water and ice on the earth's land surface, in the soil and underlying rocks, and in the atmosphere. [New Latin *hydrologia* : HYDRO- + -LOGY.] —**hy·dro·log·ic** (hī′drə-lŏj′-ĭk), **hy·dro·log·i·cal** *adj.* —**hy·dro·log·i·cal·ly** *adv.* —**hy·drol·o·gist** (hī-drŏl′ə-jĭst) *n.*

hy·drol·y·sate (hī-drŏl′ə-sāt′, hī′drə-lī′sāt′) *n.* A product of hydrolysis. [HYDROLYS(IS) + -ATE.]

hy·drol·y·sis (hī-drŏl′ə-sĭs) *n.* Decomposition of a chemical compound by reaction with water, such as the dissociation of a dissolved salt or the catalytic conversion of glucose to starch. [HYDRO- + -LYSIS.] —**hy·dro·lyt·ic** (hī′drə-lĭt′ĭk) *adj.* —**hy·dro·lyt·i·cal·ly** *adv.*

hy·dro·lyte (hī′drə-līt′) *n.* A substance that is hydrolyzed. [HYDRO- + -LYTE.]

hy·dro·lyze (hī′drə-līz′) *v.* **-lyzed, -lyzing, -lyzes.** —*tr.* To subject to hydrolysis. —*intr.* To undergo hydrolysis. [From HYDROLYSIS.] —**hy·dro·lyz·a·ble** *adj.* —**hy·dro·ly·za·tion** (hī′drə-lə-zā′shən) *n.*

hy·dro·man·cy (hī′drə-măn′sē) *n.* Divination by means of signs appearing in water. [Middle English *ydromancy*, from Old French *hydromancie*, from Latin *hydromantīa*, from Greek *hydromanteia* (unattested) : HYDRO- + -MANCY.] —**hy·dro·man·cer** *n.* —**hy·dro·man·tic** (hī′drə-măn′tĭk) *adj.*

hy·dro·mag·net·ics (hī′drō-măg-nĕt′ĭks) *n. Used with a singular verb.* **Magnetohydrodynamics** (*see*).

hy·dro·me·chan·ics (hī′drō-mĭ-kăn′ĭks) *n. Used with a singular verb.* **Hydrodynamics** (*see*).

hy·dro·me·du·sa (hī′drō-mə-dōō′sə, -dyōō′sə) *n., pl.* **-sas** or **-sae** (-sē′). A hydrozoan in its medusan stage. See **medusa**. —**hy·dro·me·du·san** *adj.*

hy·dro·mel (hī′drə-mĕl′) *n.* A liquid composed of honey and water that after fermentation is called mead. [Middle English *ydromel*, from Old French, from Late Latin *hydromel*, from Latin *hydromeli*, from Greek *hudromeli* : HYDRO- + *meli*, honey.]

hy·dro·met·al·lur·gy (hī′drō-mĕt′l-ûr′jē) *n.* The separation of metal from ores and ore concentrates by chemical reactions in aqueous solution, such as leaching, extraction, and precipitation. —**hy·dro·met·al·lur·gi·cal** (hī′drō-mĕt′l-ûr′jĭ-kəl) *adj.*

hy·dro·me·te·or (hī′drō-mē′tē-ər, -ôr′) *n.* A precipitation body, such as rain, snow, sleet, or hail, derived from the condensation of water in the atmosphere.

hy·dro·me·te·or·ol·o·gy (hī′drō-mē′tē-ə-rŏl′ə-jē) *n.* The meteorology of the occurrence, motion, and changes of atmospheric water.

hy·drom·e·ter (hī-drŏm′ə-tər) *n.* An instrument used to determine specific gravity; especially, a sealed, graduated tube, weighted at one end, that sinks in a fluid to a depth used as a measure of the fluid's specific gravity. —**hy·dro·met·ric** (hī′drə-mĕt′rĭk), **hy·dro·met·ri·cal** *adj.* —**hy·dro·met·ri·cal·ly** *adv.* —**hy·drom·e·try** (hī-drŏm′ə-trē) *n.*

hy·dro·ni·um (hī-drō′nē-əm) *n.* A hydrated hydrogen ion, H_3O^+. Also called "hydronium ion," "hydroxonium ion." [HYDR(O)- + (AMM)ONIUM.]

hy·drop·a·thy (hī-drŏp′ə-thē) *n.* The therapeutic use of water, both internally and externally. Also called "water cure." [HYDRO- + -PATHY.] —**hy·dro·path·ic** (hī′drə-păth′ĭk), **hy·dro·path·i·cal** *adj.* —**hy·drop·a·thist** (hī-drŏp′ə-thĭst), **hy·dro·path** (hī′drə-păth′) *n.*

hy·dro·per·i·car·di·um (hī′drō-pĕr′ĭ-kär′dē-əm) *n.* Excessive serous fluid within the pericardium.

hy·dro·phane (hī′drə-fān′) *n.* An opal that is almost opaque when dry, but transparent when wet. [HYDRO- + -PHANE.]

hy·dro·phil·ic (hī′drə-fĭl′ĭk) *adj.* Having an affinity for water; absorbing, tending to combine with, or capable of dissolving in or being wetted by water. [New Latin *hydrophilus*, HYDROPHILOUS.] —**hy·dro·phile** (hī′drə-fīl′) *n.*

hy·droph·i·lous (hī-drŏf′ə-ləs) *adj. Botany.* **1.** Growing or thriving in water; hydrophytic. **2.** Having water as a pollinating agent. [New Latin *hydrophilus* : HYDRO- + -PHILOUS.]

hy·droph·i·ly (hī-drŏf′ə-lē) *n. Botany.* Pollination by water. [HYDRO- + -PHILY.]

hy·dro·pho·bi·a (hī′drə-fō′bē-ə) *n.* **1.** Fear of water; especially, an abnormal aversion to drinking water. **2. Rabies** (*see*). [Late Latin, from Greek *hudrophobia* : HYDRO- + -PHOBIA.]

hy·dro·pho·bic (hī′drə-fō′bĭk, -fŏb′ĭk) *adj.* **1.** Antagonistic to, shedding, tending not to combine with, or incapable of dissolving in water. **2.** Of or exhibiting hydrophobia.

hy·dro·phone (hī′drə-fōn′) *n.* An electrical instrument for detecting or monitoring sound under water. [HYDRO- + -PHONE.]

hy·dro·phyte (hī′drə-fīt′) *n.* A plant that grows in an aquatic or very wet environment. Compare **mesophyte, xerophyte.** [HYDRO- + -PHYTE.] —**hy·dro·phyt·ic** (hī′drə-fĭt′ĭk) *adj.*

hydroplane *The hull of a high-performance boat is designed to provide lift so that at top speed the boat "planes" across the surface.*

hy·dro·plane (hī′drə-plān′) *n.* **1.** A seaplane. **2.** A motorboat designed so that the prow and much of the hull lift out of the water and skim the surface at high speeds. **3.** A **hydrofoil** (*see*). **4.** A horizontal rudder on a submarine. —*intr.v.* **hydroplaned, -planing, -planes. 1.** To drive or ride in a hydroplane. **2. a.** To skim along on the surface of the water. **b.** To be or go out of control by skimming along the surface of a wet road. Used of an automobile.

hy·dro·pon·ics (hī′drə-pŏn′ĭks) *n. Used with a singular verb.* The cultivation of plants in gravel or other soilless substances through which water containing dissolved inorganic nutrients is pumped. Also called "aquiculture." [HYDRO- + (GEO)PONICS.] —**hy·dro·pon·i·cal·ly** *adv.*

hy·dro·qui·none (hī′drō-kwĭ-nōn′, -kwĭn′ōn′) *n.* Also **hy·dro·quin·ol** (-kwĭn′ôl′, -ōl′). A white crystalline compound, $C_6H_4(OH)_2$, used as a photographic developer, antioxidant, stabilizer, and reagent.

hy·dro·scope (hī′drə-skōp′) *n.* An optical device used for viewing objects much below the surface of water. [HYDRO- + -SCOPE.] —**hy·dro·scop·ic** (hī′drə-skŏp′ĭk) *adj.*

hy·dro·ski (hī′drō-skē′) *n.* A form of hydrofoil on some seaplanes, used to provide extra lift to assist in taking off.

hy·dro·sol (hī′drə-sôl′, -sŏl′) *n.* A sol with water as the dispersing medium. [HYDRO- + SOL(UTION).] —**hy·dro·sol·ic** (hī′drə-sŏl′ĭk) *adj.*

hy·dro·sphere (hī′drə-sfîr′) *n.* The waters of the earth distinguished from the lithosphere and the atmosphere. —**hy·dro·spher·ic** (hī′drə-sfîr′ĭk, -sfĕr′ĭk) *adj.*

hy·dro·stat (hī′drə-stăt′, hī′drō-) *n.* A device that detects the presence or absence of water, used especially in steam boilers to prevent them from boiling dry. [HYDRO- + -STAT.]

hy·dro·stat·ic (hī′drə-stăt′ĭk) *adj.* Also **hy·dro·stat·i·cal** (-ĭ-kəl). Of or pertaining to hydrostatics. —**hy·dro·stat·i·cal·ly** *adv.*

hy·dro·stat·ics (hī′drə-stăt′ĭks) *n. Used with a singular verb.* The statics of fluids, especially incompressible fluids.

hy·dro·sul·fate (hī′drə-sŭl′fāt′) *n.* A salt formed by the union of sulfuric acid with an alkaloid or other organic base.

hy·dro·sul·fide (hī′drə-sŭl′fīd′) *n.* A chemical compound derived from hydrogen sulfide by replacement of one of the hydrogen atoms with a basic radical or base.

hy·dro·sul·fite (hī′drə-sŭl′fīt′) *n.* **1.** A salt of hyposulfurous acid. **2.** A bleaching agent, **sodium hydrosulfite** (*see*).

hy·dro·sul·fu·rous acid (hī′drō-sŭl-fyŏōr′əs, -sŭl′fər-əs) *n.* **Hyposulfurous acid** (*see*).

hy·dro·tax·is (hī′drō-tăk′sĭs) *n. Biology.* Movement of an organism or cell in response to moisture. [New Latin : HYDRO- + -TAXIS.] —**hy·dro·tac·tic** (hī′drō-tăk′tĭk) *adj.*

hy·dro·ther·a·peu·tics (hī′drō-thĕr′ə-pyōō′tĭks) *n. Used with a singular verb.* Hydrotherapy. —**hy·dro·ther·a·peu·tic** *adj.*

hy·dro·ther·a·py (hī′drō-thĕr′ə-pē) *n., pl.* **-pies.** The medical use of water in the treatment of certain diseases; especially, the exercising of diseased joints and muscles in remedial swimming pools. —**hy·dro·ther·a·pist** *n.*

hy·dro·ther·mal (hī′drō-thûr′məl) *adj.* **1.** Of or pertaining to hot water. **2.** *Geology.* **a.** Of or pertaining to hot magmatic emanations rich in water. **b.** Of or pertaining to the rocks, ore deposits, and springs produced by such emanations. —**hy·dro·ther·mal·ly** *adv.*

hy·dro·tho·rax (hī′drō-thôr′ăks′, -thōr′ăks′) *n.* The presence of serous fluid from the blood in one or both pleural cavities, often associated with cardiac failure.

hy·drot·ro·pism (hī-drŏt′rə-pĭz′əm) *n. Botany.* Growth of a plant part toward or away from water. [HYDRO- + -TROPISM.] —**hy·dro·trop·ic** (hī′drə-trŏp′ĭk) *adj.* —**hy·dro·trop·i·cal·ly** *adv.*

hy·drous (hī′drəs) *adj.* Containing water, especially that of crystallization or hydration. [HYDR(O)- + -OUS.]

hy·drox·ide (hī-drŏk′sīd′) *n.* A chemical compound containing the hydroxyl group. [HYDR(O)- + OXIDE.]

hydroxide ion *n.* The ion OH⁻, characteristic of basic hydroxides. Also called "hydroxyl ion."

hy·drox·o·ni·um ion (hī′drŏk-sō′nē-əm) *n.* **Hydronium** (*see*). [HYDROX(Y)- + ONIUM (ION).]

hy·drox·y (hī-drŏk′sē) *adj.* Containing the hydroxyl group. Often used in combination: *hydroxyproline.* [From HYDROXYL.]

hy·drox·yl (hī-drŏk′sĭl) *n.* The univalent radical or group OH, characteristic of bases, certain acids, phenols, alcohols, carboxylic and sulfonic acids, and amphoteric compounds. [HYDR(O)- + OX(YGEN) + -YL.] —**hy·drox·yl·ic** (hī′drŏk-sĭl′ĭk) *adj.*

hy·drox·yl·a·mine (hī-drŏk′sə-lə-mēn′, hī′drŏk-sĭl′ə-mēn′) *n.* A colorless, crystalline compound, NH_2OH, explosive when heated above 130°C, that is used as a reducing agent and in organic synthesis.

hy·drox·y·pro·line (hī-drŏk′sĭ-prō′lēn′, -lĭn) *n.* An amino acid, $C_5H_9NO_3$, occurring in proteins, particularly collagen.

hy·drox·y·tryp·ta·mine (hī-drŏk′sĭ-trĭp′tə-mēn′, -mĭn) *n.* **Serotonin** (*see*).

hy·dro·zo·an (hī′drə-zō′ən) *n.* Any of numerous coelenterates of the class Hydrozoa, which includes the hydras, polyps, and Portuguese men-of-war. ~*adj.* Of, pertaining to, or belonging to the class Hydrozoa. [New Latin *Hydrozoa* : HYDRO- + -ZOAN.]

Hy·drus (hī′drəs) *n.* A southern constellation near Tucana and Mensa. [Latin, "water serpent," from Greek *hudros*.]

hy·e·na, hy·ae·na (hī-ē′nə) *n.* Any of several carnivorous mammals of the genera *Hyaena* or *Crocuta* of Africa and Asia, having powerful jaws and relatively short hind limbs. [Middle English *hyene*, from Latin *hyaena*, from Greek *huaina*, from *hus*, swine.]

hy·e·tal (hī′ə-təl) *adj.* Of or relating to rain or to rainy regions. [Greek *huetos*, rain, a heavy shower.]

hy·e·to·graph (hī′ə-tə-grăf′, -gräf′) *n.* **1.** A self-recording device for measuring rainfall. **2.** A rainfall chart. [Greek *huetos*, rain + -GRAPH.] —**hy·e·to·graph·ic** (hī′ə-tə-grăf′ĭk) *adj.* —**hy·e·tog·ra·phy** (hī′ə-tŏg′rə-fē) *n.*

Hy·gie·ia (hī-jē′ə). *Greek Mythology.* The goddess of health. [Greek *Hugieia*, from *hugiēs*, health, from *hugiēs*, healthy.]

hy·giene (hī′jēn′) *n.* **1.** The science of health and the prevention of disease. Also called "hygienics." **2.** Conditions and practices that serve to promote or preserve health. [French *hygiène*, earlier *hygiaine*, from New Latin *hygieina*, from Greek *hugieinē*, feminine of *hugieinos*, healthful, from *hugiēs*, healthy.]

hy·gi·en·ic (hī′jē-ĕn′ĭk, hī-jĕn′-) *adj.* **1.** Of or pertaining to hygiene. **2.** Sanitary. **3.** Tending to promote or preserve health. —**hy·gi·en·i·cal·ly** *adv.*

hy·gi·en·ics (hī′jē-ĕn′ĭks, hī-jĕn′-) *n. Used with a singular verb.* See **hygiene** (sense 1).

hy·gien·ist (hī-jē′nĭst, hī′jē′nĭst, hī-jĕn′ĭst) *n.* **1.** A specialist in hygiene. **2.** A dental hygienist (*see*).

hygro– *prefix.* Indicates wet, moist, or moisture; for example, **hygrograph.** [Greek *hugros*, wet, moist.]

hy·gro·graph (hī′grə-grăf′, -gräf′) *n.* An automatic hygrometer that records variations in atmospheric humidity. [HYGRO- + -GRAPH.]

hy·grom·e·ter (hī-grŏm′ə-tər) *n.* Any of several instruments that measure atmospheric humidity. [HYGRO- + -METER.] —**hy·gro·met·ric** (hī′grə-mĕt′rĭk) *adj.* —**hy·grom·e·try** (hī-grŏm′ə-trē) *n.*

hy·groph·i·lous (hī-grŏf′ə-ləs) *adj.* Growing in moist places. Said of certain plants. —**hy·gro·phile** (hī′grə-fīl′) *n.*

hy·gro·scope (hī′grə-skōp′) *n.* An instrument that measures changes in atmospheric moisture. [HYGRO- + -SCOPE.]

hy·gro·scop·ic (hī′grə-skŏp′ĭk) *adj.* Readily absorbing moisture, as from the atmosphere. [HYGROSCOP(E) + -IC.] —**hy·gro·scop·i·cal·ly** *adv.* —**hy·gro·sco·pic·i·ty** (hī′grə-skō-pĭs′ə-tē) *n.*

hy·gro·stat (hī′grə-stăt′) *n.* A humidistat (*see*). [HYGRO- + -STAT.]

hy·ing. Alternate present participle of **hie.**

hy·lic (hī′lĭk) *adj. Rare.* Of or pertaining to matter. [Late Latin *hylicus*, from Greek *hulikos*, from *hulē*, matter.]

hylo– *prefix.* Indicates matter; for example, **hylotheism.** [Greek *hulē*, matter, wood.]

hy·lo·mor·phism (hī′lə-môr′fĭz′əm) *n.* The philosophical doctrine that matter, as opposed to spirit, is the first cause of the universe. [HYLO- + -MORPHISM.]

hy·lo·the·ism (hī′lə-thē′ĭz′əm) *n.* The philosophical doctrine that matter and God are identical.

hy·lo·zo·ism (hī′lə-zō′ĭz′əm) *n.* The philosophical doctrine that life is a property or derivative of matter or that life and matter are inseparable. [Greek *hulē*, wood + ZO(O)- + -ISM.] —**hy·lo·zo·ic** *adj.* —**hy·lo·zo·ist** *n.* —**hy·lo·zo·is·tic** (hī′lə-zō-ĭs′tĭk) *adj.*

hy·men (hī′mən) *n.* A membranous fold of tissue partly or completely blocking the external vaginal orifice. [Latin *hymēn*, from Greek *humēn*, membrane.] —**hy·men·al** *adj.*

Hy·men (hī′mən). *Greek Mythology.* The god of marriage. [Latin, from Greek *Humēn†.*]

hy·me·ne·al (hī′mə-nē′əl) *adj.* Of or pertaining to a wedding or marriage; nuptial.
—*n.* A wedding song or poem. [Latin *hymenaeus*, from Greek *humēnaios*, bridal song, wedding, from *Humēn*, HYMEN.]

hy·me·ni·um (hī-mē′nē-əm) *n., pl.* **-nia** (-nē-ə) or **-ums.** The spore-bearing layer of the fruiting body of certain fungi, containing basidia. [New Latin, from HYMEN.]

hy·me·nop·ter·an (hī′mə-nŏp′tər-ən) *n., pl.* **-tera** (-tər-ə) or **-terans.** Also **hy·me·nop·ter·on** (-tə-rŏn′) *pl.* **-tera** or **-terons.** Any insect of the order Hymenoptera, characteristically having two pairs of membranous wings and an ovipositor modified as a sting or drill, and including the bees, wasps, and ants.
—*adj.* Also **hy·me·nop·ter·ous** (-tər-əs). Of or belonging to the Hymenoptera. [New Latin *Hymenoptera*, from Greek *humenopteros*, "membrane-wing" : *humēn*, membrane, HYMEN + -PTEROUS.]

hymn (hĭm) *n.* **1.** A song of praise or thanksgiving to God. **2.** Any song of praise or joy; a paean.
—*v.* **hymned, hymning, hymns.** —*tr.* **1.** To praise, glorify, or worship in a hymn. **2.** To express in a hymn. —*intr.* To sing hymns. [Middle English *ymne, imne*, from Old French *ymne*, from Latin *hymnus*, from Greek *humnos†*, hymn, ode of praise of gods or heroes.]

hym·nal (hĭm′nəl) *n.* A book or collection of church hymns. Also called "hymnbook."
—*adj.* Of or pertaining to a hymn or hymns. [Middle English *hymnale*, from Medieval Latin *hymnāle*, from Latin *hymnus*, HYMN.]

hym·nist (hĭm′nĭst) *n.* Also **hym·no·dist** (hĭm′nə-dĭst) A composer of hymns.

hym·no·dy (hĭm′nə-dē) *n., pl.* **-dies. 1.** The singing of hymns. **2.** The composing of hymns. **3.** The hymns of a particular period or church. [Medieval Latin *hymnōdia*, from Greek *humnōidia*, "hymn-singing" : *humnos*, HYMN + -LOGY.] —**hym·no·log·ic** (hĭm′nə-lŏj′ĭk), **hym·no·log·i·cal** *adj.* —**hym·nol·o·gist** (hĭm-nŏl′ə-jĭst) *n.*

hym·nol·o·gy (hĭm-nŏl′ə-jē) *n.* **1.** The composition of hymns. **2.** The study of hymns. [Greek *humnos*, HYMN + -LOGY.]

hy·oid bone (hī′oid′) *n.* A U-shaped bone between the mandible and the larynx at the base of the tongue. Also called "hyoid." [French *hyoïde*, from New Latin *hyoides*, from Greek *huoeides*, "in the form of an upsilon" : *hu*, name of the letter upsilon + -OID.] —**hy·oid, hy·oid·e·an** (hī-oi′dē-ən) *adj.*

hy·o·man·dib·u·lar (hī′ō-măn-dĭb′yə-lər) *n.* A U-shaped bone in fishes that attaches the jaw to the skull. [*Hyo-*, from Greek *hu*, upsilon (referring to the shape of the bone) + MANDIBULAR.]

hy·o·scine (hī′ə-sēn′) *n.* A drug, **scopolamine** (*see*). [German *Hyoscin*, from New Latin *Hyoscyamus*, genus of henbane from which it is obtained, from Greek *huoskuamus* : *huos*, genitive of *hus*, pig + *kuamos†*, bean.]

hy·o·scy·a·mine (hī′ə-sī′ə-mēn′) *n.* A poisonous white crystalline alkaloid, $C_{17}H_{23}NO_3$, isomeric with atropine and used as an antispasmodic, analgesic, and sedative. [New Latin *Hyoscyamus.* See **hyoscine.**]

hyp. **1.** hypotenuse. **2.** hypothesis.

hyp–. Variant of **hypo–.**

hyp·a·bys·sal (hĭp′ə-bĭs′əl, hī′pə-) *adj.* Solidifying chiefly as a minor intrusion, especially as a dike or sill, before reaching the earth's surface. Said of rocks. [HYP(O)- + ABYSSAL.]

hy·pae·thral (hī-pē′thrəl) *adj.* Open to the sky; roofless: *an ancient hypaethral temple.* [Latin *hypaethrus*, from Greek *hupaithros* : *hupo-*, beneath + *aithēr*, sky.]

hypesthesia. Variant of **hypoesthesia.**

hy·pan·thi·um (hī-păn′thē-əm, hĭ-) *n., pl.* **-thia** (-thē-ə). The cup-shaped or flattened floral receptacle of various plants, having the gynoecium at the center and the other flower parts around the rim. [New Latin : HYP(O)- + ANTH(O)- + -IUM.] —**hy·pan·thi·al** *adj.*

hype[1] (hīp) *n. Slang.* **1.** Deception. **2.** Deceptively inflated advertising or promotion. **3.** A promotional gimmick or campaign.
—*tr.v.* **hyped, hyping, hypes.** *Slang.* To publicize, promote, or exploit by touting and often overrating: *hyping a new film.* [20th century (originally, to shortchange, swindle) : origin obscure.]

hype[2] *n. Slang.* **1.** A hypodermic injection, syringe, or needle. **2.** A drug addict.
—*tr.v.* **hyped, hyping, hypes.** *Slang.* To stimulate with or as if with an injection of a drug. Sometimes used with *up*: *The pep talk hyped up the team.* [Short for HYPODERMIC.]

hyper– *prefix.* Indicates: **1.** Over, above, or in great amount; for example, **hypersonic. 2.** In abnormal excess; for example, **hyperacid. 3.** To an excessive degree; for example, **hypercritical.** [Greek *huper*, over, above, beyond, exceeding.]

hy·per·a·cid·i·ty (hī′pər-ə-sĭd′ə-tē) *n.* Excessive acidity, especially of the gastric juices in the stomach. —**hy·per·ac·id** (hī′pər-ăs′ĭd) *adj.*

hy·per·ac·tive (hī′pər-ăk′tĭv) *adj.* Excessively or abnormally active.

hyperaemia Variant of **hyperemia.**

hyperaesthesia Variant of **hyperesthesia.**

hy·per·bar·ic (hī′pər-băr′ĭk) *adj.* Of, pertaining to, producing, operating at, or occurring at pressures higher than normal atmospheric pressure: *a hyperbaric chamber.* [HYPER- + BAR(O)- + -IC.]

hy·per·bo·la (hī-pûr′bə-lə) *n., pl.* **-las** or **-lae** (-lē). *Geometry.* A plane curve having two branches, formed by: **1.** A conic section intersecting both halves of a right circular cone. **2.** The locus of points related to two given points such that the difference in the distances of each point from the two given points is a constant. [New Latin, from Greek *huperbolē*, "a throwing beyond," excess (when a hyperbola is formed from a conic section, the angle made by the base of the cone and the intersecting plane is greater than the angle formed by a parabola), from *huperballein*, "to throw beyond," exceed : *huper-*, beyond + *ballein*, to throw.]

hy·per·bo·le (hī-pûr′bə-le) *n.* Exaggeration or extravagant statement used as a figure of speech, as *I could sleep for a year* or *This book weighs a ton.* [Earlier *yperbola*, from Latin *hyperbolē*, from Greek *huperbolē*, excess. See **hyperbola.**]

hy·per·bol·ic (hī′pər-bŏl′ĭk) *adj.* Also **hy·per·bol·i·cal** (-ĭ-kəl). **1.** Of, pertaining to, or employing hyperbole. **2.** *Mathematics.* **a.** Of, pertaining to, or having the form of a hyperbola. **b.** Based on or having a metric that is a hyperbola: *hyperbolic geometry.* **c.** Of or pertaining to a hyperbolic function: *hyperbolic cosine.* —**hy·per·bol·i·cal·ly** *adv.*

hyperbolic function *n. Mathematics.* Any of a set of six functions that are related, for a real variable *z*, to the hyperbola in a manner analogous to the relationship of the trigonometric functions to a circle, including: **1.** *Symbol* **sinh** The *hyperbolic sine,* defined by the equation $\sinh z = 1/2(e^z - e^{-z})$. **2.** *Symbol* **cosh** The *hyperbolic cosine,* defined by the equation $\cosh z + 1/2(e^z + e^{-z})$. **3.** *Symbol* **tanh** The *hyperbolic tangent,* defined by the equation $\tanh z/\cosh z$. **4.** *Symbol* **coth** The *hyperbolic cotangent,* defined by the equation $\coth z + \cosh z/\sinh z$. **5.** *Symbol* **sech** The *hyperbolic secant,* defined by the equation $\operatorname{sech} z = 1/\cosh z$. **6.** *Symbol* **cosech** or **csch** The *hyperbolic cosecant,* defined by the equation $\operatorname{cosech} z = 1/\sinh z$.

hyperbolic paraboloid *n.* See **paraboloid.**

hy·per·bo·lism (hī-pûr′bə-lĭz′əm) *n.* **1.** The use of hyperbole. **2.** A hyperbole.

hy·per·bo·lize (hī-pûr′bə-līz′) *v.* **-lized, -lizing, -lizes.** —*intr.* To use hyperbole; exaggerate. —*tr.* To express with hyperbole; exaggerate.

hy·per·bo·loid (hī-pûr′bə-loid′) *n. Geometry.* Either of two quadric surfaces having a finite center with certain plane sections that are hyperbolas and others that are ellipses or circles.

hy·per·bo·re·an (hī′pər-bôr′ē-ən, -bōr′ē-ən, -bə-rē′ən) *adj.* **1.** Of or pertaining to the far north; arctic. **2.** Very cold; frigid. [Latin *Hyperborei*, HYPERBOREAN.]

hy·per·bo·re·an (hī′pər-bôr′ē-ən, -bōr′ē-ən, -bə-rē′ən) *n. Greek Mythology.* A member of a people known to the ancient Greeks from the earliest times, living in an unidentified country in the far north and renowned as pious and divinely favored adherents of the cult of Apollo. ~*adj.* Of or pertaining to the Hyperboreans. [Latin *Hyperborei*, from Greek *Huperboreoi* (plural) : *huper-*, beyond, extreme + *boreios*, northern, from *Boreas*, "north wind," north.]

hy·per·cap·ni·a (hī′pər-kăp′nē-ə) *n.* The presence of an abnormally high carbon dioxide concentration in the blood. Also called "hypercarbia." [HYPER- + *-capnia*, from Greek *kapnos*, smoke.]

hy·per·cat·a·lex·is (hī′pər-kăt′l-ĕk′sĭs) *n.* The addition of one or more syllables in excess of the normal number in the last foot of a line of verse. [New Latin : HYPER- + *catalexis*, omission in the last foot of a line, from Greek *katalēxis*, from *katalēgein*, to leave off (see **catalectic**.)] —**hy·per·cat·a·lec·tic** (hī′pər-kăt′l-ĕk′tĭk) *adj.*

hy·per·charge (hī′pər-chärj′) *n. Symbol* **Y** *Physics.* A quantum number numerically equal to twice the average electric charge of a particle multiplet or, equivalently, to the sum of the strangeness and the baryon number.

hy·per·cor·rec·tion (hī′pər-kə-rĕk′shən) *n.* Mispronunciation of words or use of incorrect grammatical constructions as a result of trying to avoid nonstandard speech forms. —**hy·per·cor·rect** (hī′pər-kə-rĕkt′) *adj.* —**hy·per·cor·rect·ly** *adv.*

hy·per·crit·i·cal (hī′pər-krĭt′ĭ-kəl) *adj.* Overcritical; especially, excessively critical about trivial matters. —**hy·per·crit·i·cal·ly** *adv.* —**hy·per·crit·i·cism** (hī′pər-krĭt′ə-sĭz′əm) *n.*

hy·per·du·li·a (hī′pər-dōō′lē-ə, -dyōō′lē-ə) *n.* In the Roman Catholic and Eastern Orthodox churches, the special reverence given to the Virgin Mary. Compare **dulia, latria.** [Medieval Latin : HYPER- + DULIA.] —**hy·per·du·lic** (hī′pər-dōō′lĭk, -dyōō′lĭk), **hy·per·du·li·cal** (-lĭ-kəl) *adj.*

hy·per·e·mi·a, hy·per·ae·mi·a (hī′pər-ē′mē-ə) *n.* The presence of an excessive amount of blood in the vessels supplying a particular organ of the body. [HYPER- + -EMIA.] —**hy·per·e·mic** (hī′pər-ē′mĭk) *adj.*

hy·per·es·the·sia, hy·per·aes·the·sia (hī′pər-ĕs-thē′zhə, -zhē-ə) *n. Pathology.* Abnormally high sensitivity, especially of the skin, to touch, heat, cold, or pain. [New Latin : HYPER- + ESTHESIA.] —**hy·per·es·thet·ic** (hī′pər-ĕs-thĕt′ĭk) *adj.*

hy·per·eu·tec·tic (hī′pər-yōō-tĕk′tĭk) *adj. Chemistry.* Having the minor component present in a larger amount than in the eutectic composition of the same components. Said of mixtures.

hy·per·ex·ten·sion (hī′pər-ĭk-stĕn′shən) *n.* Extension of a limb beyond normal limits, usually as part of an orthopedic exercise.

hy·per·fine structure (hī′pər-fīn′) *n. Abbr.* **hfs** *Physics.* The splitting of a spectral line into two or more components as a result of the spin or magnetic moment of the atomic nucleus.

hy·per·ga·my (hī-pûr′gə-mē) *n.* The practice or state of being married to a person of equal or superior rank, caste, or class. [HYPER- + -GAMY.] —**hy·per·ga·mous** *adj.*

hy·per·gly·ce·mi·a (hī′pər-glī-sē′mē-ə) *n.* The presence of an abnormally high concentration of glucose in the blood, as occurs in diabetes. —**hy·per·gly·ce·mic** (hī′pər-glī-sē′mĭk) *adj.*

hy·per·gol·ic (hī′pər-gŏl′ĭk) *adj.* Igniting spontaneously on contact with an oxidizer. Said of a rocket fuel. [German *Hypergol* : HYP(ER)- + Greek *ergon*, work + -OL(E) + -IC.]

hy·per·i·cum (hī-pĕr′ĭ-kəm) *n.* Any plant of the genus *Hypericum*, which includes **Saint John's wort** and **rose of Sharon** (*both of which see*). [New Latin *Hypericum* (genus), from Greek *hupereikon* : HYPER- + *ereikē*, heath.]

hy·per·in·su·lin·ism (hī′pər-ĭn′sə-lə-nĭz′əm) *n.* The presence of abnormally large quantities of insulin in the blood, resulting in hypoglycemia.

Hy·pe·ri·on[1] (hī-pîr′ē-ən). *Greek Mythology.* A Titan, the son of Gaea and Uranus and father of Helios, the sun god.

Hyperion[2] *n.* One of the smallest satellites of the planet Saturn.

hy·per·ker·a·to·sis (hī′pər-kĕr′ə-tō′sĭs) *n.* Hypertrophy of the horny, outer layer of the skin. [New Latin : HYPER- + Greek *keras* (stem *kerat-*), horn + -OSIS.] —**hy·per·ker·a·tot·ic** (hī′pər-kĕr′ə-tŏt′ĭk) *adj.*

hy·per·ki·ne·sia (hī′pər-kĭ-nē′zhə, -zhē-ə) *n.* Also **hy·per·ki·ne·sis** (-nē′sĭs). Pathologically excessive restlessness, occurring particularly in children as a symptom of certain disorders. [New Latin : HYPER- + Greek *kinēsis*, movement, from *kinein*, to move.] —**hy·per·ki·net·ic** (hī′pər-kĭ-nĕt′ĭk) *adj.*

hy·per·mar·ket (hī′pər-mär′kĭt) *n. Chiefly British.* A very large self-service store, similar to a supermarket but usually selling a wider variety of goods. [From French *hypermarché*. See **hyper-, market**.]

hy·per·me·ter (hī-pûr′mə-tər) *n.* **1.** A verse or metric line having one or more syllables in excess of the normal number. **2.** An extra syllable. —**hy·per·met·ric** (hī′pər-mĕt′rĭk), **hy·per·met·ri·cal** *adj.*

hy·per·me·tro·pi·a (hī′pər-mə-trō′pē-ə) *n. Pathology.* Hyperopia (*see*). [New Latin, from Greek *hupermetros*, beyond measure, excessive : *huper-*, beyond, excessive + *metron*, measure + -OPIA.] —**hy·per·me·trop·ic** (hī′pər-mə-trŏp′ĭk), **hy·per·me·trop·i·cal** *adj.* —**hy·per·me·tro·py** (hī′pər-mĕt′rə-pē) *n.*

hy·perm·ne·sia (hī′pərm-nē′zhə, -zhē-ə) *n.* Unusually exact or vivid memory. [New Latin : HYPER- + (A)MNESIA.]

hy·per·mo·til·i·ty (hī′pər-mō-tĭl′ə-tē) *n.* Abnormally increased movement, especially of the stomach or intestines.

hy·per·ne·phro·ma (hī′pər-nĭ-frō′mə) *n., pl.* **-mas** or **-mata** (-mə-tə). A type of malignant tumor of the kidney.

hy·per·on (hī′pə-rŏn′) *n. Physics.* A subatomic particle with mass greater than the nucleon, decaying into a nucleon or another hyperon and lighter particles and having $2I + 1$ charge states, where I is the isospin of the particle multiplet. [HYPER- + -ON.]

hy·per·o·pi·a (hī′pə-rō′pē-ə) *n.* A pathological condition of the eye in which entering light rays are focused behind the retina because of a refractive error or because of flattening of the globe of the eye, so that vision is better for distant than for near objects. Also called "hypermetropia," "farsightedness," "long-sightedness." [New Latin : HYPER- + -OPIA.] —**hy·per·ope** (hī′pə-rōp′) *n.* —**hy·per·op·ic** (hī′pə-rŏp′ĭk) *adj.*

hy·per·os·to·sis (hī′pər-ŏ-stō′sĭs) *n.* Excessive or abnormal thickening or growth of bone tissue. [New Latin : HYPER- + OST(EO)- + -OSIS.] —**hy·per·os·tot·ic** (hī′pər-ŏ-stŏt′ĭk) *adj.*

hy·per·par·a·site (hī′pər-păr′ə-sīt′) *n.* An organism that is parasitic on or in another parasite. —**hy·per·par·a·sit·ic** (hī′pər-păr′ə-sĭt′ĭk) *adj.*

hy·per·par·a·thy·roid·ism (hī′pər-păr′ə-thī′roi-dĭz′əm) *n.* An abnormal increase in the activity of the parathyroid glands.

hy·per·phys·i·cal (hī′pər-fĭz′ĭ-kəl) *adj.* Beyond the physical or material; supernatural.

hy·per·pi·tu·i·ta·rism (hī′pər-pĭ-tōō′ə-tə-rĭz′əm, -tyōō′ə-tə-rĭz′əm) *n.* Pathologically excessive production of anterior pituitary hormone, especially growth hormones, resulting in acromegaly or gigantism. —**hy·per·pi·tu·i·tar·y** (hī′pər-pĭ-tōō′ə-tĕr′ē, -tyōō′ə-tĕr′ē) *adj.*

hy·per·plane (hī′pər-plān′) *n. Mathematics.* A plane, or an analogue of a plane, with more than three dimensions.

hy·per·pla·sia (hī′pər-plā′zhə, -zhē-ə) *n.* An abnormal increase in the number of cells in an organ or tissue with consequent enlargement of the affected part. [New Latin : HYPER- + -PLASIA.] —**hy·per·plas·tic** (hī′pər-plăs′tĭk) *adj.*

hy·per·ploid (hī′pər-ploid′) *adj. Genetics.* Having a chromosome number in excess of an exact multiple of the normal haploid number. [HYPER- + -PLOID.] —**hy·per·ploid·y** *n.*

hy·perp·ne·a (hī′pərp-nē′ə, hī′pər-) *n.* Abnormally deep and rapid breathing, as after exercise. [New Latin : HYPER- + Greek *pnoia*, breath, from *pnein*, to breathe.]

hy·per·py·rex·i·a (hī′pər-pī-rĕk′sē-ə) *n.* Abnormally high fever, with a body temperature of 106°F (41.1°C) or above; hyperthermia. —**hy·per·py·rex·i·al, hy·per·py·ret·ic** (hī′pər-pī-rĕt′ĭk) *adj.*

hy·per·sen·si·tive (hī′pər-sĕn′sə-tĭv) *adj.* **1.** Abnormally sensitive; especially, oversensitive. **2.** Liable to respond abnormally to the presence of an antigen or drug. —**hy·per·sen·si·tive·ness, hy·per·sen·si·tiv·i·ty** (hī′pər-sĕn′sə-tĭv′ə-tē) *n.*

hy·per·son·ic (hī′pər-sŏn′ĭk) *adj.* Of or pertaining to speed equal to or exceeding five times the speed of sound. —**hy·per·son·i·cal·ly** *adv.* —**hy·per·son·ics** *n.*

hy·per·space (hī′pər-spās′) *n. Mathematics.* Space with more than three dimensions; especially, a four-dimensional space.

hy·per·sthene (hī′pərs-thēn′) *n.* A green, brown, or black splintery, cleavable pyroxene mineral, essentially $(Fe,Mg)_2Si_2O_6$. [French *hypersthène* : HYPER- + Greek *sthenos*, strength.] —**hy·per·sthen·ic** (hī′pərs-thĕn′ĭk) *adj.*

hy·per·ten·sion (hī′pər-tĕn′shən) *n.* **1.** Abnormally high arterial blood pressure. **2.** *Informal.* A state of high emotional tension. —**hy·per·ten·sive** (hī′pər-tĕn′sĭv) *adj. & n.*

hy·per·ther·mi·a (hī′pər-thûr′mē-ə) *n.* Unusually high fever; hyperpyrexia. [New Latin : HYPER- + THERM(O)- + -IA.] —**hy·per·therm·al** (hī′pər-thûr′məl) *adj.*

hy·per·thy·roid·ism (hī′pər-thī′roi-dĭz′əm) *n.* Overactivity of the thyroid gland, resulting in excessive production of thyroid hormones. See **thyrotoxicosis.** —**hy·per·thy·roid** *adj. & n.*

hy·per·ton·ic (hī′pər-tŏn′ĭk) *adj.* **1.** *Pathology.* Having extreme muscular or arterial tension. **2.** *Chemistry.* Having the higher osmotic pressure of two solutions. —**hy·per·to·ni·a** (hī′pər-tō′nē-ə), **hy·per·to·nic·i·ty** (hī′pər-tō-nĭs′ə-tē) *n.*

hy·per·tro·phy (hī-pûr′trə-fē) *n.* Also **hy·per·tro·phi·a** (hī′pər-trō′fē-ə). *Pathology.* Abnormal enlargement of an organ or part as a result of the enlargement without increase in number of its constituent cells. ~*v.* **hypertrophied, -phying, -phies.** —*tr.* To cause to grow abnormally large. —*intr.* To grow abnormally large. [HYPER- + -TROPHY.] —**hy·per·troph·ic** (hī′pər-trŏf′ĭk, -trō′fĭk) *adj.*

hy·per·ven·ti·la·tion (hī′pər-vĕnt′l-ā′shən) *n.* Abnormally fast or deep respiration in which excessive quantities of air are taken in, causing buzzing in the ears, tingling of extremities, and sometimes fainting. —**hy·per·ven·ti·late** (hī′pər-vĕnt′l-āt′) *v.*

hy·per·vi·ta·min·o·sis (hī′pər-vī′tə-mə-nō′sĭs) *n.* Any of various abnormal conditions resulting from excessive vitamin intake.

hy·pha (hī′fə) *n., pl.* **-phae** (-fē). Any of the threadlike filaments forming the mycelium of a fungus. [New Latin, from Greek *huphē*, web.] —**hy·phal** *adj.*

hy·phen (hī′fən) *n.* A punctuation mark (-) used to connect the parts of a compound word or name and used between syllables, especially of a word that is split over two consecutive lines. ~*tr.v.* **hyphened, -phening, -phens.** To hyphenate. [Late Latin, from Late Greek *huphen*, a sign written below two consecutive letters to show that they belong to the same word, from Greek, in the same word : *hupo-*, under + *hen*, neuter of *heis*, one.]

hy·phen·ate (hī′fə-nāt′) *tr.v.* **-at·ed, -at·ing, -ates.** To divide or connect (syllables, words, names, or word elements) with a hyphen. **—hy·phen·a·tion** (hī′fə-nā′shən) *n.*

hy·phen·at·ed (hī′fə-nā′tĭd) *adj. Informal.* Of foreign birth or mixed national origin: *German-Americans and other hyphenated Americans.*

hy·phen·ize (hī′fə-nīz′) *tr.v.* **-ized, -iz·ing, -iz·es.** To hyphenate. **—hy·phen·i·za·tion** (hī′fə-nə-zā′shən) *n.*

hyp·na·gog·ic, hyp·no·gog·ic (hĭp′nə-gŏj′ĭk, -gō′jĭk) *adj.* **1.** Inducing sleep. **2.** Of or pertaining to the state of drowsiness preceding sleep. [French *hypnagogique* : HYPN(O)- + Greek *agōgos,* leading, from *agein,* to lead.]

hypno–, hypn– *prefix.* Indicates: **1.** Sleep; for example, **hypnopompic. 2.** Hypnosis; for example, **hypnoanalysis, hypnotherapy.** [Greek *hupnos,* sleep.]

hyp·no·a·nal·y·sis (hĭp′nō-ə-năl′ə-sĭs) *n.* A psychoanalytic technique in which hypnosis is used to elicit unconscious material from a patient.

hyp·no·gen·e·sis (hĭp′nō-jĕn′ə-sĭs) *n.* The process of inducing or entering a hypnotic state or sleep. **—hyp·no·ge·net·ic** (hĭp′nō-jə-nĕt′ĭk) *adj.* **—hyp·no·ge·net·i·cal·ly** *adv.*

hyp·noid (hĭp′noid′) *adj.* Also **hyp·noid·al** (hĭp-noid′l). Of or resembling hypnosis or sleep. [HYPN(O)- + -OID.]

hyp·nol·o·gy (hĭp-nŏl′ə-jē) *n.* The scientific study of sleep. [HYPNO- + -LOGY.] **—hyp·no·log·ic** (hĭp′nə-lŏj′ĭk), **hyp·no·log·i·cal** *adj.* **—hyp·nol·o·gist** *n.*

hyp·no·pe·di·a (hĭp′nə-pē′dē-ə) *n.* A method of teaching in which information heard while the learner is asleep is supposed to be retained. [HYPNO- + Greek *paideia,* education, from *pais* (stem *paid-*), boy.] **—hyp·no·pe·dic** *adj.*

hyp·no·pho·bi·a (hĭp′nə-fō′bē-ə) *n.* Abnormal fear of sleep. [New Latin : HYPNO- + -PHOBIA.] **—hyp·no·pho·bic** *adj.*

hyp·no·pom·pic (hĭp′nə-pŏm′pĭk) *adj.* Of or pertaining to the partially conscious state preceding complete awakening. [HYPNO- + Greek *pompē,* a sending off, procession, POMP + -IC.]

Hyp·nos (hĭp′nŏs′). Also **Hyp·nus** (hĭp′nəs). *Greek Mythology.* The god of sleep. [Greek *Hupnos.*]

hyp·no·sis (hĭp-nō′sĭs) *n., pl.* **-ses** (-sēz′). **1.** An artificially induced sleeplike condition in which an individual is extremely responsive to suggestions made by the hypnotist. **2.** Hypnotism. **3.** Any sleeplike condition. [New Latin : Greek *hupnos,* sleep + -OSIS.]

hyp·no·ther·a·py (hĭp′nō-thĕr′ə-pē) *n.* Treatment for mental or physical illness based on or using hypnosis.

hyp·not·ic (hĭp-nŏt′ĭk) *adj.* **1. a.** Of, involving, or inducing hypnosis. **b.** Resembling hypnosis or inducing a state that resembles hypnosis; mesmerizing: *hypnotic music.* **c.** Of, pertaining to, or practicing hypnotism. **2.** Inducing sleep; soporific.
~*n.* **1. a.** A person who is hypnotized. **b.** A person who can be hypnotized. **2. a.** An agent that causes sleep; a soporific. **b.** An agent used to produce a hypnotic state. [French *hypnotique,* from Late Latin *hypnōticus,* from Greek *hupnōtikos,* sleepy, from *hupnoun,* to put to sleep, from *hupnos,* sleep.] **—hyp·not·i·cal·ly** *adv.*

hyp·no·tism (hĭp′nə-tĭz′əm) *n.* **1.** The theory or practice of inducing hypnosis. **2.** An act of inducing hypnosis.

hyp·no·tist (hĭp′nə-tĭst) *n.* A person who induces hypnosis.

hyp·no·tize (hĭp′nə-tīz′) *tr.v.* **-tized, -tiz·ing, -tiz·es. 1.** To put in a state of hypnosis. **2.** To fascinate; entrance. **—hyp·no·tiz·a·ble** *adj.* **—hyp·no·ti·za·tion** (hĭp′nə-tə-zā′shən) *n.* **—hyp·no·tiz·er** *n.*

hy·po¹ (hī′pō) *n.* In photography, **sodium thiosulfate** *(see).* [Short for HYPOSULFITE.]

hypo² *n., pl.* **-pos.** *Informal.* A hypodermic syringe or injection.

hypo–, hyp– *prefix.* Indicates: **1.** Below or beneath; for example, **hypodermic. 2.** At a lower point; for example, **hypogenous. 3.** Abnormally low; for example, **hypoglycemia. 4.** Deficient; for example, **hypoxia. 5.** Partial or incomplete; for example, **hypoesthesia. 6.** *Chemistry.* Designating an acid containing a low amount of oxygen; for example, **hypophosphorous acid.** [Greek *hupo-,* from *hupo,* under, from under, beneath.]

hy·po·a·cid·i·ty (hī′pō-ə-sĭd′ə-tē) *n.* **1.** *Chemistry.* Slight acidity. **2.** *Medicine.* Below normal acidity.

hy·po·bar·ic (hī′pə-băr′ĭk) *adj.* Below normal pressure. [HYPO- + BAR(O)- + -IC.] **—hy·po·bar·ism** *n.*

hy·po·blast (hī′pə-blăst′, -bläst′) *n. Embryology.* The **endoblast** *(see).* [HYPO- + -BLAST.] **—hy·po·blas·tic** (hī′pə-blăs′tĭk) *adj.*

hy·po·caust (hī′pə-kôst′, hĭp′ə-) *n.* In ancient Rome, a space under the floor where heat from a furnace was accumulated to heat a room or a bath. [Latin *hypocaustum,* from Greek *hupokauston,* from *hupokaiein,* to burn underneath : *hupo-,* under + *kaiein,* to burn.]

hy·po·cen·ter (hī′pō-sĕn′tər) *n.* **Ground zero** *(see).*

hy·po·chlo·rite (hī′pə-klôr′īt′, -klōr′īt′) *n.* A salt or ester of hypochlorous acid.

hy·po·chlo·rous acid (hī′pə-klôr′əs, -klōr′əs) A weak, unstable acid, HOCl, occurring only in solution and used as a bleach, oxidizer, deodorant, and disinfectant.

hy·po·chon·dri·a (hī′pə-kŏn′drē-ə) *n.* **1.** The persistent neurotic conviction that one is or is likely to become ill, sometimes involving experiences of real pain, when illness is neither actually present nor likely. Also called "hypochondriasis." **2.** Plural of **hypochondrium.** [Originally a region of the abdomen (formerly held to be the seat of melancholy), from Late Latin, from Greek *hupokhondria,* plural of *hupokhondrion,* belly, abdomen, from *hupokhondrios,* under the cartilage of the breastbone : *hupo-,* under + *khondros,* cartilage.]

hy·po·chon·dri·ac (hī′pə-kŏn′drē-ăk′) *n.* A person afflicted with hypochondria.
~*adj.* **1.** Pertaining to or afflicted with hypochondria. **2.** *Anatomy.* Pertaining to or located in the hypochondrium. **—hy·po·chon·dri·a·cal** (hī′pə-kən-drī′ə-kəl) *adj.* **—hy·po·chon·dri·a·cal·ly** *adv.*

hy·po·chon·dri·um (hī′pə-kŏn′drē-əm) *n., pl.* **-dria** (-drē-ə). The upper lateral region of the abdomen, below the ribs. [New Latin, from Greek *hupokhondrion,* abdomen. See **hypochondria.**]

hy·poc·o·rism (hī-pŏk′ə-rĭz′əm, hī-, hī′pə-kôr′ĭz′əm, -kōr′ĭz′əm) *n.* **1.** A name of endearment or a pet name. **2.** The use of such names. **3.** A euphemism. [Late Latin *hypocorisma,* from Greek *hupokorisma,* from *hupokorizesthai,* to call by endearing names : *hupo-,* below, beneath + *korizesthai,* to caress, from *koros,* boy, and *korē,* girl.] **—hy·po·co·ris·tic** (hī′pə-kə-rĭs′tĭk), **hy·po·co·ris·ti·cal** *adj.* **—hy·po·co·ris·ti·cal·ly** *adv.*

hy·po·cot·yl (hī′pə-kŏt′l) *n. Botany.* The part of the axis of a plant embryo or seedling plant that is below the cotyledons. [HYPO- + COTYL(EDON).] **—hy·po·cot·yl·ous** (hī′pə-kŏt′l-əs) *adj.*

hy·poc·ri·sy (hĭ-pŏk′rə-sē) *n., pl.* **-sies. 1.** The feigning of beliefs, feelings, or virtues that one does not hold or possess; gross insincerity. **2.** An instance of such insincerity. [Middle English *ipocrisie, ypocrisy,* from Old French *ypocrisie,* from Late Latin *hypocrisis,* from Greek *hupokrisis,* playing of a part on the stage, from *hupokrinein,* to separate gradually, answer, answer one's fellow actor, play a part : *hupo-,* under + *krinein,* to separate.]

hyp·o·crite (hĭp′ə-krĭt′) *n.* A person given to hypocrisy. [Middle English *ipocrite, ypocrite,* from Old French *ypocrite,* from Late Latin *hypocrita,* from Greek *hupocritēs,* actor, hypocrite, from *hupokrinein,* to play a part. See **hypocrisy.**]

hyp·o·crit·i·cal (hĭp′ə-krĭt′ĭ-kəl) *adj.* **1.** Characterized by hypocrisy; pretended or feigned: *hypocritical praise for someone she really despises.* **2.** Being a hypocrite: *a hypocritical rogue.* **—hyp·o·crit·i·cal·ly** *adv.*

hy·po·cy·cloid (hī′pō-sī′kloid′) *n. Geometry.* The plane locus of a point fixed on a circle that rolls on the inside circumference of a fixed circle.

hy·po·der·mal (hī′pə-dûr′məl) *adj.* **1.** Of or pertaining to the hypodermis. **2.** Lying below the epidermis.

hy·po·der·mic (hī′pə-dûr′mĭk) *adj.* **1.** Of or pertaining to the layer just beneath the epidermis. **2.** Pertaining to the hypodermis. **3.** Injected beneath the skin.
~*n.* **1.** A hypodermic needle or syringe. **2.** A hypodermic injection. [HYPO- + DERM(ATO)- + -IC.] **—hy·po·der·mi·cal·ly** *adv.*

hypodermic injection *n.* A subcutaneous, intramuscular, or intravenous injection by means of a hypodermic syringe and needle.

hypodermic needle *n.* **1.** A hollow needle used with a hypodermic syringe. **2.** A hypodermic syringe complete with needle.

hypodermic syringe *n.* A tubular, piston-operated syringe fitted with a hypodermic needle for hypodermic injections, withdrawing blood, and the like.

hy·po·der·mis (hī′pə-dûr′mĭs) *n.* Also **hy·po·derm** (hī′pə-dûrm′). **1.** *Zoology.* An epidermal layer of cells that secretes an overlying chitinous cuticle, as in arthropods. **2.** *Botany.* A layer of cells lying immediately below the epidermis in certain plants, usually serving to support or protect tissue beneath it. [New Latin : HYPO- + *dermis,* DERMA (skin).]

hy·po·es·the·sia (hī′pō-ĕs-thē′zhə, -zhē-ə) *n.* Also **hy·pes·the·sia** (hī′pĕs-thē′zhə, -zhē-ə). *Pathology.* Partial loss of sensation; diminished sensibility. [New Latin : HYPO- + (AN)ESTHESIA.]

hy·po·eu·tec·tic (hī′pō-yōō-tĕk′tĭk) *adj. Chemistry.* Having the minor component present in a smaller amount than in the eutectic composition of the same components. Said of mixtures, especially alloys.

hy·po·gas·tri·um (hī′pō-găs′trē-əm) *n., pl.* **-tria** (-trē-ə). The lowest of the three median regions of the abdomen. [New Latin, from Greek *hupogastrion* : HYPO- + GASTR(O)- + -IUM.] **—hy·po·gas·tric** *adj.*

hy·po·ge·al (hī′pə-jē′əl) *adj.* Also **hy·po·ge·an** (-ən), **hy·po·ge·ous** (-əs). **1.** Located under the earth's surface; underground. **2.** *Botany.* Designating germination in which the cotyledons remain below the surface of the ground. [Late Latin *hypogēus,* from Greek *hupogaios* : HYPO- + *gē, gaia,* earth.]

hyp·o·gene (hĭp′ə-jēn′) *adj.* Formed or situated below the earth's surface. Said of rocks. [HYPO- + (EPI)GENE.]

hy·pog·e·nous (hī-pŏj′ə-nəs) *adj. Botany.* Developing or growing on a lower surface, as fungi on leaves. [HYPO- + -GENOUS.]

hyp·o·ge·um (hĭp′ə-jē′əm, hī′pə-) *n., pl.* **-gea** (-jē′ə). **1.** A subterranean chamber of an ancient building. **2.** An ancient subterranean burial chamber, such as a catacomb. [Latin *hypogēum,* from Greek *hupogaion,* from *hupogaios,* HYPOGEAL.]

hy·po·glos·sal (hī′pə-glŏs′əl) *adj.* **1.** Located under the tongue. **2.** *Anatomy.* Of or pertaining to the hypoglossal nerve.
~*n.* The hypoglossal nerve. [New Latin *hypoglossus,* hypoglossal nerve : HYPO- + Greek *glōssa,* tongue.]

hypoglossal nerve *n.* The twelfth cranial nerve, which supplies motor fibers to the muscles of the tongue.

hy·po·gly·ce·mi·a (hī′pō-glī-sē′mē-ə) *n.* An abnormally low level of sugar in the blood. **—hy·po·gly·ce·mic** *adj.*

hy·pog·y·nous (hī-pŏj′ə-nəs) *adj. Botany.* Having or characterizing floral parts or organs that are below and not in contact with the ovary. [HYPO- + -GYNOUS.] **—hy·pog·y·ny** *n.*

hy·poid gear (hī′poid′) *n.* A gear in which the shapes of the teeth are hypocycloids, used for applications in which a high surface load is desirable. [Shortened from HYPOCYCLOID.]

hypocaust *The underfloor heating system used by the Romans, in which a central furnace circulated warm air through concealed sunken channels. The channels shown here, exposed in the ruins of the Roman baths at Conimbriga (now Coimbra), Portugal, date from the second century* A.D.

hyrax *Although hyraxes look like rodents, they have no close relatives. The nearest is thought to be the elephant. The animals, which grow to between 30 and 50 centimeters (12–20 inches) long, are native to Africa and southwestern Asia and have hooflike nails on most of their toes.*

PRONUNCIATION KEY

ă, pat; ā, pay; âr, care; ä, father, are; b, **bib**; ch, **church**; d, **deed**; ĕ, pet; ē, be; f, **fife**; g, **gag**; h, **hat**; hw, **which**; ĭ, pit; ī, pie; îr, pier; j, **judge**; k, **kick**; l, lid, needle; m, **mum**; n, no, sudden; ng, thing; ŏ, pot; ō, toe; ô, paw, for; oi, noise; ou, out; o͝o, book; o͞o, boot; p, **pop**; r, **roar**; s, sauce; sh, **ship**, **dish**; t, **tight**; th, **thin**, **path**; *th*, this, bathe; ŭ, cut; ûr, fur; v, valve; w, with; y, yes; z, zebra, size; zh, vision; ə, about, item, edible, gallop, circus, peaceful

IN FOREIGN WORDS:

à, *Fr.* ami; œ, *Fr.* feu, *Ger.* schön; ü, *Fr.* tu, *Ger.* über; KH, *Ger.* ich, *Scot.* loch; N, *Fr.* bon; y', *Fr.* Compiègne

STRESS MARKS:

Primary stress: ′ **in·cite′** (ĭn-sīt′)
Secondary stress: ′ **in′sight′** (ĭn′sīt′)

hy·po·lim·ni·on (hī′pō-lĭm′nē-ŏn′, -ən) *n., pl.* **-nia** (-nē-ə). The lower, colder layer of a lake or other body of water that is divided into two layers at different average temperatures. [HYPO- + Greek *limnion*, diminutive of *limnē*, lake.]

hy·po·ma·ni·a (hī′pə-mā′nē-ə, -mān′yə) *n.* A mild state of mania involving slightly abnormal elation and overactivity. —**hy·po·man·ic** (hī′pə-măn′ĭk, -mā′nĭk) *adj.*

hy·po·nas·ty (hī′pə-năs′tē) *n.* An upward bending of leaves or other plant parts, resulting from growth of the lower side. [German *Hyponastie* : HYPO- + -NASTY.] —**hy·po·nas·tic** (hī′pə-năs′tĭk) *adj.*

hy·po·ni·trite (hī′pə-nī′trīt′) *n.* A salt or ester of hyponitrous acid.

hy·po·ni·trous acid (hī′pə-nī′trəs) *n.* An unstable white crystalline acid, $H_2N_2O_2$.

hy·po·nym (hī′pə-nĭm′) *n.* A word that includes the meaning of another, more general word, such that the two can never be entirely interchangeable; for example, *cabbage* is a hyponym of *vegetable.* [HYP(O)- + -ONYM.] —**hy·pon·y·mous** (hī-pŏn′ə-məs) *adj.* —**hy·pon·y·my** (hī-pŏn′ə-mē) *n.*

hy·po·phos·phite (hī′pō-fŏs′fīt′) *n.* A salt of hypophosphorous acid.

hy·po·phos·pho·rous acid (hī′pō-fŏs′fər-əs, -fŏs-fôr′əs, -fōr′əs) *n.* A clear, colorless or slightly yellow oily liquid, H_3PO_2, used in the preparation of hypophosphites.

hy·poph·y·sis (hī-pŏf′ə-sĭs) *n., pl.* **-ses** (-sēz′). *Anatomy.* The **pituitary gland** *(see).* [New Latin, outgrowth, from Greek *hupophusis*, attachment underneath, growth, from *hupophuein*, to grow up under : *hupo-*, under + *phuein*, to bring forth, grow.] —**hy·po·phys·e·al** (hī′pə-fĭz′ē-əl, hī-pŏf′ə-sē′əl) *adj.*

hy·po·pi·tu·i·ta·rism (hī′pō-pĭ-to͞o′ə-tə-rĭz′əm, hī′pō-pĭ-tyo͞o′-) *n.* Deficient or diminished production of pituitary hormones. —**hy·po·pi·tu·i·tar·y** (hī′pō-pĭ-to͞o′ə-tĕr′ē, -tyo͞o′ə-tĕr′ē) *adj.*

hy·po·pla·sia (hī′pō-plā′zhə, -zhē-ə) *n. Pathology.* Incomplete or arrested development of an organ or part. [New Latin : HYPO- + -PLASIA.] —**hy·po·plas·tic** (hī′pō-plăs′tĭk) *adj.*

hy·po·ploid (hī′pō-ploid′) *adj. Genetics.* Having a chromosome number less by only a few chromosomes than a multiple of the normal haploid number. [HYPO- + -PLOID.] —**hy·po·ploid·y** *n.*

hy·po·pne·a (hī′pō-nē′ə) *n.* Abnormally slow and shallow breathing. [New Latin : HYPO- + Greek *pnoē*, breathing, from *pnein*, to breathe.]

hy·po·sen·si·tiv·i·ty (hī′pō-sĕn′sə-tĭv′ə-tē) *n.* Also **hy·po·sen·si·tive·ness** (-sĕn′sə-tĭv-nĭs). Less than normal sensitivity. —**hy·po·sen·si·tive** *adj.*

hy·po·sen·si·tize (hī′pō-sĕn′sə-tīz′) *tr.v.* **-tized, -tizing, -tizes.** To make less sensitive; desensitize. —**hy·po·sen·si·ti·za·tion** (hī′pō-sĕn′sə-tə-zā′shən) *n.*

hy·pos·ta·sis (hī-pŏs′tə-sĭs) *n., pl.* **-ses** (-sēz′). **1.** *Philosophy.* That which underlies something else; substance or essence as distinguished from attributes or qualities. **2.** *Theology.* **a.** Any of the persons of the Trinity as distinguished from the single nature of the godhead. **b.** The essential person of Christ in which his human and divine natures are united. **3.** *Medicine.* The accumulation of blood or fluid in a part of the body, such as the lungs, that is caused by poor circulation. **4.** *Genetics.* A condition in which the action of one gene conceals or suppresses the action of another gene that is not its allele. [Late Latin, substance, from Greek *hupostasis*, "a standing under," origin, substance, existence : *hupo-*, under + *stasis*, a standing.] —**hy·po·stat·ic** (hī′pə-stăt′ĭk), **hy·po·stat·i·cal** *adj.* —**hy·po·stat·i·cal·ly** *adv.*

hypostatic union *n. Theology.* The union of Christ's human and divine natures in one hypostasis or person. [Greek *hupostatikos*, of substance, from *hupostatos*, standing under, from *huphistasthai*, to stand under : *hupo-*, under + *histasthai*, middle voice of *histanai*, to cause to stand.]

hy·pos·ta·tize (hī-pŏs′tə-tīz′) *tr.v.* **-tized, -tizing, -tizes. 1.** To symbolize (a concept) in a concrete form. **2.** To ascribe material existence to. [Greek *hupostatos*, standing under. See **hypostatic union.**] —**hy·pos·ta·ti·za·tion** (hī-pŏs′tə-tə-zā′shən) *n.*

hy·po·sthe·ni·a (hī′pəs-thē′nē-ə) *n.* Abnormal lack of strength; extreme weakness. [New Latin : HYPO- + Greek *sthenos*, strength.] —**hy·po·sthen·ic** (hī′pəs-thĕn′ĭk) *adj.*

hyp·o·style (hĭp′ə-stīl′, hī′pə-) *n.* A building having a roof or ceiling supported by rows of columns, as in ancient Egyptian architecture. [Greek *hupostulos*, resting upon pillars set underneath : *hupo-*, under + *stulos*, pillar.] —**hyp·o·style** *adj.*

hy·po·sul·fite (hī′pō-sŭl′fīt′) *n.* **Sodium thiosulfate** *(see).*

hy·po·sul·fu·rous acid (hī′pō-sŭl-fyo͝or′əs, -sŭl′fər-əs) *n.* An unstable acid, $H_2S_2O_4$, known only in aqueous solution and used as a bleaching and reducing agent. Also called "hydrosulfurous acid."

hy·po·tax·is (hī′pə-tăk′sĭs) *n.* The subordination of one clause to another by means of a connective, as in *I shall despair if you don't come.* Compare **parataxis.** [Greek *hupotaxis*, subjection, submission, from *hupotassein*, to arrange under : *hupo-*, under + *tattein*, to arrange.] —**hy·po·tac·tic** (hī′pə-tăk′tĭk) *adj.*

hy·po·tension (hī′pō-tĕn′shən) *n.* Abnormally low arterial blood pressure. —**hy·po·ten·sive** (hī′pō-tĕn′sĭv) *adj.*

hy·pot·e·nuse (hī-pŏt′n-o͞os′, -yo͞os′)) *n. Abbr.* **hyp.** The side of a right triangle opposite the right angle. [Latin *hypotēnūsa*, from Greek *hupoteinousa*, line subtending the right angle, hypotenuse, from *hupoteinein*, to stretch under : *hupo-*, under + *teinein*, to stretch.]

hypoth. hypothesis.

hy·po·thal·a·mus (hī′pō-thăl′ə-məs) *n.* The part of the brain that lies below the thalamus and regulates bodily temperature, hunger, thirst, and other autonomic activities. —**hy·po·tha·lam·ic** (hī′pō-thə-lăm′ĭk) *adj.*

hy·poth·ec (hī-pŏth′ĭk) *n.* In Roman and Scots law, a security granted a creditor on the property of a debtor without transfer of possession or title. [French *hypothèque*, from Late Latin *hypothēca*, pledge, mortgage, from Greek *hupothēkē*, from *hupotithenai*, "to place under," put down as a deposit : *hupo-*, under + *tithenai*, to place.] —**hy·poth·e·car·y** (hī-pŏth′ĭ-kĕr′ē) *adj.*

hy·poth·e·cate (hī-pŏth′ĭ-kāt′) *tr.v.* **-cated, -cating, -cates.** *Law.* To pledge (property) as security to a creditor without transfer of title or possession; mortgage. [Medieval Latin *hypothēcāre*, from Late Latin *hypothēca*, HYPOTHEC.] —**hy·poth·e·ca·tion** (hī-pŏth′ĭ-kā′shən) *n.* —**hy·poth·e·ca·tor** *n.*

hy·po·ther·mal (hī′pō-thûr′məl) *adj.* **1.** *Geology.* Of, pertaining to, or designating high-temperature deposits derived from magmatic emanations forced under pressure into pre-existing rock openings. **2.** Of, pertaining to, or characterized by hypothermia.

hy·po·ther·mi·a (hī′pō-thûr′mē-ə) *n.* **1.** Abnormally low body temperature caused by exposure to cold. **2.** The deliberate lowering of body temperature to reduce metabolic rate during surgery. [HYPO- + Greek *thermē*, heat + -IA.]

hy·poth·e·sis (hī-pŏth′ə-sĭs) *n., pl.* **-ses** (-sēz′). *Abbr.* **hyp., hypoth. 1.** An assertion subject to verification or proof, as: **a.** A proposition stated as a basis for argument or reasoning. **b.** A premise from which a conclusion is drawn. **c.** A conjecture that accounts, within a theory or set of coherent beliefs, for a set of facts and that can be used as a basis for further investigation. **2.** An assumption used as the basis for action. [Late Latin, from Greek *hupothesis*, proposal, suggestion, supposition, from *hupotithenai*, "to place under," propose, suppose : *hupo-*, under + *tithenai*, to place.]

hy·poth·e·size (hī-pŏth′ə-sīz′) *v.* **-sized, -sizing, -sizes.** —*tr.* To assert as a hypothesis. —*intr.* To form a hypothesis or hypotheses.

hy·po·thet·i·cal (hī′pə-thĕt′ĭ-kəl) *adj.* Also **hy·po·thet·ic** (-thĕt′ĭk). **1.** Of or based on a hypothesis. **2. a.** Suppositional; conjectural; uncertain. **b.** Conditional; contingent. **3.** Existing as an idea or possibility but not actual: *That's only a hypothetical case.* [Late Latin *hypotheticus*, from Greek *hupothetikos*, from *hupothesis*, HYPOTHESIS.] —**hy·po·thet·i·cal·ly** *adv.*

hypothetical imperative *n.* In the philosophy of Immanuel Kant, a principle of conduct arising from expediency or necessity rather than from moral law. Compare **categorical imperative.**

hy·po·thy·roid (hī′pō-thī′roid′) *adj.* Affected by or manifesting hypothyroidism.
~*n.* A person affected by hypothyroidism.

hy·po·thy·roid·ism (hī′pō-thī′roi-dĭz′əm) *n.* Also **hy·po·thy·roid·e·a** (hī′pō-thī-roi′dē-ə). **1.** Insufficient production of thyroid hormones. **2.** A pathological condition resulting from severe thyroid insufficiency; especially, **myxedema** or **cretinism** *(both of which see).* [HYPO- + THYROID + -ISM.]

hy·po·ton·ic (hī′pō-tŏn′ĭk) *adj.* **1.** *Pathology.* Having less than normal muscular or arterial tone or tension. **2.** *Chemistry.* Having the lower osmotic pressure of two fluids. —**hy·po·to·nic·i·ty** (hī′pō-tə-nĭs′ə-tē) *n.*

hy·po·tro·choid (hī′pə-trō′koid′) *n. Geometry.* The locus of a point anywhere on the radius, or radius extended, of a circle that rolls inside a fixed circle. A hypotrochoid for which the moving point is on the circumference of the rolling circle is a hypocycloid.

hy·po·xan·thine (hī′pō-zăn′thēn′, -thĭn) *n.* A white powder, $C_5H_4N_4O$, that is an intermediate in the metabolism of purines.

hy·pox·i·a (hī-pŏk′sē-ə) *n.* Deficiency in the amount of oxygen reaching bodily tissues. [New Latin : HYP(O)- + OX(Y)- + -IA.] —**hy·pox·ic** *adj.*

hypso– *prefix.* Indicates height; for example, **hypsometry.** [Greek *hupsos*, height, summit.]

hyp·sog·ra·phy (hĭp-sŏg′rə-fē) *n.* **1.** The scientific study of the earth's topologic configuration above sea level, especially the measurement and mapping of land elevations. **2.** A representation or description of such features, as on a map or in an atlas. **3.** Hypsometry. [HYPSO- + -GRAPHY.] —**hyp·so·graph·ic** (hĭp′sə-grăf′ĭk), **hyp·so·graph·i·cal** *adj.*

hyp·som·e·ter (hĭp-sŏm′ə-tər) *n.* An instrument that estimates land elevations in mountainous regions from the boiling points of liquids. [HYPSO- + -METER.]

hyp·som·e·try (hĭp-sŏm′ə-trē) *n.* The measurement of elevation relative to sea level. [HYPSO- + -METRY.] —**hyp·so·met·ric** (hĭp′sə-mĕt′rĭk), **hyp·so·met·ri·cal** *adj.* —**hyp·so·met·ri·cal·ly** *adv.* —**hyp·som·e·trist** (hĭp-sŏm′ə-trĭst) *n.*

hy·rax (hī′răks′) *n., pl.* **-raxes** or **-races** (-rə-sēz′). Any of several herbivorous mammals of the family Procaviidae of Africa and adjacent Asia, resembling the rodents but more closely related to the hoofed mammals. Also called "dassie" and, especially in the Old Testament, "cony." [New Latin, from Greek *hurax*†, shrew mouse.]

hy·son (hī′sən) *n.* A type of Chinese green tea, the leaves of which are twisted or curled. [Cantonese *hei chon*, corresponding to Mandarin Chinese *xī chūn*, "bright spring," after the name of a famous tea grower, *Li Xi-chun.*]

hys·sop (hĭs′əp) *n.* **1.** A woody plant, *Hyssopus officinalis*, native to Asia, having spikes of small blue flowers and aromatic leaves used in perfumery and as a condiment. **2.** Any of several similar or related plants. **3.** An unidentified plant mentioned in the Bible as the source of twigs used for sprinkling in certain Hebraic purificatory rites. Exodus 12:22. [Middle English *ysop*, from Old English *hysope* and Old French *ysope,* both from Latin *hyssōpus,* from Greek *hussōpos,* from Semitic, akin to Hebrew *'ezōbh.*]

hys·ter·ec·to·mize (hĭs'tə-rĕk'tə-mīz') *tr.v.* **-mized, -mizing, -mizes.** To perform a hysterectomy on.

hys·ter·ec·to·my (hĭs'tə-rĕk'tə-mē) *n., pl.* **-mies.** The removal of either the whole of the uterus or the body of the uterus but not the cervix. [HYSTER(O)- + -ECTOMY.]

hys·ter·e·sis (hĭs'tə-rē'sĭs) *n., pl.* **-ses** (-sēz'). *Physics.* The failure of a property that has been changed by an external agent to return to its original value when the cause of the change is removed. See **magnetic hysteresis.** [New Latin, from Greek *husterēsis,* a shortcoming, from *husterein,* to be behind, come later, from *husteros,* later, behind.] —**hys·ter·et·ic** (hĭs'tə-rĕt'ĭk) *adj.*

hysteresis loop *n. Physics.* A closed curve obtained by plotting a graph of the magnetic induction of a ferromagnetic substance (as ordinate) against the external magnetic field. The shape of the curve is characteristic of the magnetic properties of the material and shows the ease with which it is magnetized and the ability to retain magnetization.

hys·ter·i·a (hĭ-stĕr'ē-ə, -stîr'ē-ə) *n.* **1.** A neurosis characterized by susceptibility to suggestion, emotional instability, amnesia, and other mental aberrations. **2.** Excessive or uncontrollable fear or other strong emotion. [New Latin, from Latin *hystericus,* HYSTERIC.]

hys·ter·ic (hĭ-stĕr'ĭk) *n.* A person suffering from hysteria. ~*adj.* Hysterical. [Latin *hystericus,* from Greek *husterikos,* suffering in the womb (hysteria was once thought to be caused by uterine disturbances), from *hustera,* womb.]

hys·ter·i·cal (hĭ-stĕr'ĭ-kəl) *adj.* **1.** Of, characterized by, or arising from hysteria: *hysterical paralysis.* **2.** Having or prone to having hysterics. **3.** *Informal.* Extremely funny. —**hys·ter·i·cal·ly** *adv.*

hys·ter·ics (hĭ-stĕr'ĭks) *n. Usually used with a singular verb.* **1.** An attack of hysteria. **2.** *Informal.* **a.** A fit of uncontrollable laughing. **b.** A fit of wild anger: *He'll have hysterics if he finds out.*

hystero–, hyster– *prefix.* Indicates: **1.** Womb or uterus; for example, **hysterectomy. 2.** Hysteria; for example, **hysterogenic.** [Greek *hustera,* womb.]

hys·ter·o·gen·ic (hĭs'tə-rō-jĕn'ĭk) *adj.* Causing hysteria. [HYSTERO- + -GENIC.]

hys·ter·oid (hĭs'tə-roid') *adj.* Also **hys·ter·oid·al** (hĭs'tə-roid'l). Resembling hysteria. [HYSTER(O)- + -OID.]

hys·ter·on prot·er·on (hĭs'tə-rŏn' prŏt'ə-rŏn') *n.* **1.** A figure of speech in which the natural or rational order of its terms is reversed, as *bred and born* instead of *born and bred.* **2.** *Logic.* The fallacy of assuming as a premise a proposition following something yet to be proved. [Late Latin, from Greek *husteron proteron,* "latter first" : *husteron,* neuter of *husteros,* latter + *proteron,* neuter of *proteros,* first, former.]

hys·ter·ot·o·my (hĭs'tə-rŏt'ə-mē) *n., pl.* **-mies.** Surgical incision into the uterus. [New Latin *hysterotomia* : HYSTERO- + -TOMY.]

hys·tric·o·morph (hĭ-strĭk'ə-môrf') *n.* Any rodent belonging to the suborder *Hystricomorpha,* which includes the porcupines, chinchillas, guinea pigs, and agoutis. [Greek *hustrix* (stem *hustrik*-), porcupine + -MORPH.] —**hys·tric·o·morph, hys·tric·o·morph·ic** (hĭ-strĭk'ə-môr'fĭk) *adj.*

Hz hertz (unit of frequency).

I

ibex *These wild goats live in the mountains of Europe, Asia, and North Africa. The one shown here is a male European ibex.*

i, I (ī) *n., pl.* **i's** or **I's. 1.** The ninth letter of the modern English alphabet. See feature at **alphabet. 2.** Any of the speech sounds represented by this letter. **3.** Something shaped like an I. **4.** The ninth in a series. —**dot one's i's and cross one's t's.** To pay rigorous attention to detail; be exhaustively comprehensive.

i, I, i., I. *Note:* As an abbreviation or symbol, *i* may be a small or a capital letter, with or without a period. Established forms or those generally preferred precede the definition. When no form is given, all four forms are in general use in that sense. **1. i,** *Electricity.* current. **2. i** *Mathematics.* imaginary unit; the square root of −1. **3. i.** incisor. **4. I.** independence; independent. **5. I.** institute. **6. i.** interest. **7. I.** international. **8. i.** intransitive. **9. I** The symbol for the element iodine. **10. i., I.** island; isle. **11. I** isospin. **12. i, I** The Roman numeral for one.

I (ī) *pron.* The first person singular pronoun in the nominative case. **1.** Used to represent the speaker or writer. **2.** Sometimes used in a conditional construction depending on the elliptically understood clause *if I were you,* to express advice or indirect injunction: *I wouldn't go out without a coat today.* —See Usage note at **me.**
~*n., pl.* **I's.** The self; the ego. [Middle English *i, ich,* Old English *ic,* from Germanic *eka* (unattested).]

i–¹. Variant of **y–.**

i–². Variant of **in–** (not).

–i *suffix.* Indicates a specified region, national origin, or people; for example, **Kashmiri, Pakistani, Tandoori.** [Adjective suffix in Semitic and Indo-Iranian languages.]

–i– *infix.* Used to connect the elements of a compound word, especially when they are of Latin origin; for example, **patrilineal, homicide.** [From or by analogy with French *-i-,* from Latin.]

IA Iowa (used with a Zip Code).

i.a. in absentia.

–ia¹ *suffix.* Indicates: **1.** Diseases and disorders; for example, **alexia, diphtheria. 2.** Plants or genera of plants; for example, **poinsettia, begonia. 3.** Zoological classes; for example, **Amphibia. 4.** Areas and countries; for example, **Manchuria.** [New Latin, from Latin and Greek, suffix of feminine abstract nouns.]

–ia² *suffix.* Indicates collective nouns; for example, **trivia, genitalia.** [New Latin, from Latin, neuter plural of *-ius,* and from Greek, neuter plural of *-ios.*]

I·a·coc·ca (ī'ə-kō′kə), **Lido Anthony,** known as **"Lee"** (1924–). U.S. business executive. He has served as president of the Ford Motor Company (1970–78) and as president and later chairman of the Chrysler Corporation (from 1978). As chairman of the Statue of Liberty-Ellis Island Foundation he organized the campaign to restore and refurbish the statue for its centennial in 1986.

IAEA International Atomic Energy Agency.

–ial *suffix.* Indicates of, pertaining to, or characterized by; for example, **managerial, residential.** [Middle English, from Old French *-ial, -iel,* from Latin *-iālis* : *-i-,* stem + *-ālis,* -AL.]

i·amb (ī′ămb′) *n.* **1.** A metrical foot consisting of a short syllable followed by a long (in quantitative verse), or an unstressed syllable followed by a stressed (in accentual verse). Also called "iambic," "iambus." There are four iambs in the following line: *"I-am′bics march′ from short′ to long′"* (Coleridge). **2.** A line of verse consisting of such feet. Compare **trochee.** [French *iambe,* from Latin *iambus,* IAMBUS.]

i·am·bic (ī-ăm′bĭk) *adj.* **1.** Consisting of iambs or characterized by their predominance: *iambic pentameter.* **2.** Employing this rhythm: *the iambic poets of antiquity.*
~*n.* **1.** An iamb. **2.** *Usually* **iambics.** A verse, stanza, or poem written in iambs. [Latin *iambicus,* from Greek *iambikos,* from *iambos,* IAMBUS.]

i·am·bus (ī-ăm′bəs) *n., pl.* **-buses** or **-bi** (-bī′). An iamb. [Latin, from Greek *iambos*†.]

–ian¹ *suffix.* Indicates: **1.** Of or belonging to; for example, **Bostonian. 2.** Characteristic of or resembling; for example, **Johnsonian.** [Old French *-ien,* from Latin *-iānus* : *-i-,* stem + *-ānus,* -AN.]

–ian² *suffix.* Indicates: **1.** Admirer or follower of; for example, **Chaucerian. 2.** One skilled in or a specialist, for example, **pediatri-**cian, **logistician. 3.** One belonging to a certain period of time or place; for example, **Edwardian.** [From -IAN.]

–iana. Variant of **-ana** (a collection).

IAS *Aeronautics.* indicated air speed.

–iasis *suffix.* Indicates a pathological condition; for example, **teniasis.** [New Latin, from Greek, suffix of action.]

I.A.T.A., IATA International Air Transport Association.

i·at·ric (ī-ăt′rĭk) *adj.* Also **i·at·ri·cal** (-rĭ-kəl). *Rare.* Pertaining to medicine or physicians; medical. [Greek *iatrikos,* from *iatros,* physician, healer, from *iasthai*†, to heal, cure.]

–iatric *suffix.* Indicates a specified kind of patient or medical treatment; for example, **geriatric.** [From IATRIC.]

–iatrics *suffix.* Indicates medical treatment; for example, **pediatrics.** [From IATRIC.]

i·at·ro·gen·ic (ī-ăt′rə-jĕn′ĭk) *adj.* Induced in a patient by a doctor's actions or treatment: *an iatrogenic disease.* [Greek *iatros,* physician (see **iatric**) + -GENIC.]

–iatry *suffix.* Indicates medical treatment; for example, **psychiatry.** [French *-iatrie,* from New Latin *-iatria,* from Greek *iatreia,* the art of healing, from *iatros,* physician. See **iatric.**]

ib. ibidem.

I.B.A. Independent Broadcasting Authority (in Britain).

I·ba·dan (ē-bä′dän). A city in southwestern Nigeria, *c.* 130 kilometers (80 miles) north of Lagos. It is the second-largest city in the country and one of the oldest settlements in Africa.

Ib·ár·ru·ri Gó·mez (ĭ-bär′ōōr-ē gō′mĕz), **Dolores** (1895–1989). Spanish Communist leader. Her oratory in the Spanish Civil War won her the nickname of La Pasionaria ("the passionflower"). She sought refuge in the U.S.S.R. (1939), but returned to Spain in 1977.

I-beam (ī′bēm′) *n.* A steel beam or girder with a cross section formed like the capital letter I.

I·be·ri·a (ī-bîr′ē-ə). **1.** The ancient name for the region roughly corresponding to the eastern part of modern Georgian S.S.R. **2.** An ancient name for the Iberian Peninsula.

I·be·ri·an (ī-bîr′ē-ən) *adj.* **1. a.** Of or pertaining to the ancient ethnological group or groups that inhabited the Iberian Peninsula. **b.** Of or pertaining to the language or culture of these groups. **2. a.** Of or pertaining to the Iberian Peninsula. **b.** Broadly, Spanish, or Spanish and Portuguese. **3.** Of or pertaining to ancient Iberia in the Caucasus, to its inhabitants, their language, or their culture.
~*n.* **1. a.** A member of the ancient Caucasoid people that inhabited the Iberian Peninsula. **b.** The language of this people. **2.** An inhabitant of the Iberian Peninsula. **3.** An inhabitant of ancient Iberia in the Caucasus.

Iberian Peninsula. Land mass of extreme southwestern Europe, comprising Spain and Portugal, separated from the rest of Europe by the Pyrenees and from Africa by the Strait of Gibraltar.

Ibero– *prefix.* Indicates the Iberian Peninsula or Iberian; for example, *Ibero-Celtic.*

I·ber·ville (ē-bĕr-vēl′), **Pierre Le Moyne, Sieur d'** (1661–1706). French explorer and naval officer; born in Canada. After several years of defending interests in the Hudson Bay region, he explored the Mississippi delta and founded the first permanent settlement in the Louisiana Territory (1699).

i·bex (ī′bĕks′) *n., pl.* **ibexes, ibices** (ī′bĭ-sēz′), or collectively **ibex.** Any of several wild goats of the genus *Capra,* of mountainous regions of the Old World; especially, *C. ibex,* having long, ridged, backward-curving horns. Also called "steinbok." [Latin, perhaps of Alpine origin.]

I·bib·i·o (ĭ-bĭb′ē-ō) *n., pl.* **-os** or collectively **Ibibio. 1.** A member of a people of southeastern Nigeria. **2.** The Niger-Congo language of this people. —**I·bib·i·o** *adj.*

ibid. ibidem.

i·bi·dem (ĭb′ə-dĕm′, ĭ-bī′dəm) *adv. Abbr.* **ib., ibid.** *Latin.* In the same place. Used in footnotes and bibliographies to refer to the book, chapter, article, or page cited just before.

–ibility. Variant of **–ability.**

i·bis (ī′bĭs) *n., pl.* **ibises** or collectively **ibis.** Any of various long-billed, mainly tropical, wading birds of the family Threskiornithidae, such as the sacred ibis, *Threskiornis aethiopica.* See **wood ibis.** [Latin *ībis,* from Greek *ibis,* from Egyptian *hīb.*]

I·bi·za or **I·vi·za** (ē-vē′zə). The third largest of the Balearic Islands, in the Mediterranean Sea, and the one nearest the east coast of Spain. Ibiza is also the name of the largest town. The island is a popular tourist resort.

-ible. Variant of **-able.**

ibn-Ga·bi·rol (ĭb′ən-gə-bîr′əl), **Solomon ben Yehuda,** also known as "Avicebrón" (*c.* 1021–58). Jewish philosopher and poet. He was a leading contributor to the growth of Jewish culture in Moorish Spain; his Neo-Platonist philosophy, particularly in *Fons Vitae,* had great influence on Jews and Christians.

ibn-Rushd. See **Averroës.**

ibn Saud (soud) (*c.* 1880–1953). Founder and first king of modern Saudi Arabia, which he ruled from 1932 until his death. His long struggle to gain control of central Arabia began in 1902. It continued against the Turks, with British support during World War I, and against rival Arab factions in the 1920's. The discovery of oil in 1936, which later brought great wealth, occurred in his reign.

ibn-Sina. See **Avicenna.**

I·bo (ē′bō) *n., pl.* **Ibos** or collectively **Ibo. 1.** A member of a Negroid people of Nigeria. **2.** The Kwa language spoken by this people.

Ib·sen (ĭb′sən), **Henrik** (1828–1906). Norwegian dramatist and poet, whose plays created a major scandal in his lifetime because of their realism but are now acclaimed as classics. His chief works include *A Doll's House* (1879), *Ghosts* (1881), and *An Enemy of the People* (1882). Other major plays are *Hedda Gabler* (1890) and *The Master Builder* (1892).

-ic, -ical *suffix.* Indicates: **1.** Of, pertaining to, or characteristic of; for example, **seismic, Gaelic, geological, metrical. 2.** *Chemistry.* Having or taking a valence higher than in corresponding *-ous* compounds; for example, **ferric.** Compare **-ous. —**See Usage note at **classic.** [Middle English *-ic, -ik,* from Latin *-icus.*]

IC integrated circuit.

ICA 1. Institute of Contemporary Arts. **2.** International Cooperation Administration.

ICAO International Civil Aviation Organization.

Ic·a·rus[1] (ĭk′ər-əs). *Greek Mythology.* The son of Daedalus, who, in escaping from Crete on artificial wings made for him by his father, flew so close to the sun that the wax with which his wings were fastened melted, so that he fell into the Aegean Sea and drowned.

Icarus[2] *n. Astronomy.* A small asteroid, the one that passes closest to the sun. [After ICARUS.]

ICBM intercontinental ballistic missile.

ice (īs) *n.* **1.** Water frozen solid. **2.** A surface, layer, or mass of frozen water. **3. a.** Pieces of ice, as those put in a drink, for example, to chill it. **b.** Anything resembling frozen water, such as **dry ice** *(see).* **4.** A dessert consisting of sweetened and flavored crushed ice. **5.** *Slang.* Diamonds. **6. a.** The skating surface in an ice rink. **b.** The playing field in ice hockey. **7.** *Astronomy.* A mixture of solid water, carbon dioxide, other gases, and dust, forming the nucleus of a comet. **—break the ice.** To dispel the initial mood of reserve or formality of a social situation. **—cut no ice.** *Informal.* To have no influence or effect; make no impression. **—on ice. 1.** In a refrigerator or freezer. **2.** *Informal.* **a.** In reserve or readiness. **b.** Put aside; shelved; postponed. **c.** Held incommunicado. **d.** Certain to be won. Said of games. **—on thin ice.** In a risky situation; on uncertain ground.

~*v.* **iced, icing, ices.** —*tr.* **1.** To coat with ice. **2.** To cause to become ice; freeze. **3. a.** To chill by setting in or as if in ice. **b.** To put ice in (a drink, for example). **4.** To cover or decorate (a cake) with icing. —*intr.* To turn into, or become coated with, ice; freeze. Often used with *over* or *up.* [Middle English *is,* Old English *īs,* from Germanic.]

I.C.E. Institute of Civil Engineers.

Ice. Iceland; Icelandic.

ice age *n.* **1.** A **glacial period** *(see).* **2. Ice Age.** The Pleistocene or glacial epoch.

ice ax *n.* An ax used by mountaineers for cutting steps in ice.

ice bag *n.* A small waterproof bag used as an **ice pack** *(see).*

ice barrier *n.* A section of the ice sheet covering Antarctica that extends beyond the coastline. Also called "barrier."

ice·berg (īs′bûrg′) *n.* **1.** A massive floating body of ice broken away from a glacier or ice sheet. Also called "berg." **2.** *Slang.* One who appears to be cold or aloof. [Probably partial translation of Danish and Norwegian *isberg* : *is,* ice + *berg,* mountain.]

iceberg lettuce *n.* A type of lettuce characterized by its light green coloring, crisp leaves, and compact head.

ice·blink (īs′blĭngk′) *n.* A yellowish glare in the sky over an ice field. Also called "blink."

ice-blue (īs′blo͞o′) *n.* A pale greenish blue. **—ice-blue** *adj.*

ice·boat (īs′bōt′) *n.* **1.** A boatlike vehicle set on runners that sails on ice. **2.** An icebreaker.

ice·bound (īs′bound′) *adj.* **1.** Locked in by ice: *an icebound ship.* **2.** Jammed or covered over by ice: *an icebound harbor.*

ice·box (īs′bŏks′) *n.* **1.** An insulated chest or box in which ice is put to cool and preserve food. **2.** A refrigerator.

ice·break·er (īs′brā′kər) *n.* **1.** A sturdy ship built for breaking a passage through icebound waters. Also called "iceboat." **2.** A protective pier or dock apron used as a buffer against floating ice.

ice bucket *n.* **1.** A small insulated bucket with a lid, containing ice for adding to drinks. **2.** A somewhat larger bucket of this sort, used without a lid to cool bottles placed inside it.

ice cap *n.* An extensive perennial cover of ice and snow, smaller than an ice sheet.

ice-cold (īs′kōld′) *adj.* Very cold; freezing cold.

ice cream *n.* **1.** A smooth, sweet, cold food prepared from a frozen mixture of milk products and sometimes egg yolks and flavored in a variety of ways. **2.** Such a food, but with animal fat or seaweed products used as substitutes for milk products.

ice-cream cone (īs′krēm′) *n.* **1.** A conical wafer used to hold a scoop of ice cream. **2.** This wafer with the ice cream in it.

ice-cream soda *n.* A refreshment consisting of ice cream scoops in a mixture of soda water and flavoring syrup.

iced (īst) *adj.* **1.** Covered over with ice. **2.** Chilled with ice. **3.** Decorated or coated with icing.

ice·fall (īs′fôl′) *n.* **1.** A broken, tumbled mass of ice where a glacier becomes steeper. **2.** An avalanche of ice.

ice field *n.* **1.** A large, level expanse of floating ice. **2.** A large expanse of ice on land.

ice floe *n.* A flat expanse of floating ice, smaller than an ice field.

ice foot *n.* A belt or ledge of ice that forms along the shoreline in Arctic regions.

ice hockey *n.* A game played on ice in which two opposing teams of skaters, using curved sticks, try to drive a flat disk, or puck, into the opponents' goal. Also called "hockey."

ice·house (īs′hous′) *n.* A building, often underground, formerly used for storing ice and preserving it by natural means.

Icel. Iceland; Icelandic.

Ice·land (īs′lənd). *Abbr.* **Ice., Icel.** An island republic in the North Atlantic Ocean, just south of the Arctic Circle. Much of the island is of volcanic origin and there are *c.* 200 volcanoes, several of which are still active, as well as a number of geysers and lakes of boiling mud. Less than 2 percent of the land is cultivated, and the economy is heavily dependent on the cod-fishing industry. Area, 102,819 square kilometers (39,698 square miles). Population, 253,000. Capital, Reykjavik. See map at **Western Europe.**

Ice·land·er (īs′lən-dər) *n.* A native of Iceland.

Ice·land·ic (īs-lăn′dĭk) *adj. Abbr.* **Ice., Icel.** Of or pertaining to Iceland, its inhabitants, their language, or their culture.

~*n.* The North Germanic language spoken in Iceland, specifically: **1.** This language as spoken since the 16th century. **2. Old Icelandic** *(see).*

Iceland moss *n.* A brittle, grayish-brown, edible lichen, *Cetraria islandica,* of Arctic regions and northern Europe.

Iceland poppy *n.* **1.** An Arctic poppy, *Papaver nudicaule,* widely cultivated for its white or yellow flowers. **2.** Any of several similar Arctic poppies.

Iceland spar *n.* A doubly refracting, transparent, crystalline form of calcite used in experiments on optical polarization.

ice machine *n.* A machine that freezes water into ice cubes.

ice milk *n.* A smooth, sweet, cold food prepared from a frozen mixture of milk products, usually containing less than half the butterfat of ice cream.

ice needle *n.* Any of the thin ice crystals that float high in the atmosphere in certain conditions of clear, cold weather.

ice-out (īs′out′) *n.* The thawing of ice on a body of water.

ice pack *n.* **1.** A bag or folded cloth filled with crushed ice and applied to sore or swollen parts of the body. Also called "pack." **2.** A container filled with a liquid of high thermal capacity that can be frozen, used to keep food or other materials cool.

ice pick *n.* A pointed awl for chipping or breaking ice.

ice plant *n.* A plant, *Mesembryanthemum* (or *Cryophytum*) *crystallinum,* native to southern Africa, having fleshy leaves and stems covered with glistening encrustations, and white or pink flowers.

ice point *n.* The temperature at which pure water and ice are in equilibrium in a mixture at one atmosphere of pressure; the melting point of ice, or freezing point of water, under normal atmospheric pressure. Compare **steam point.**

ice rink *n.* **1.** A building housing a level ice surface for skating. **2.** The ice surface itself. Also called "skating rink."

ice-scour·ing (īs′skour′ĭng) *n. Geology.* The erosion of rock by glacial ice. **—ice-scoured** *adj.*

ice sheet *n.* A vast, continuous expanse of land ice, such as that covering the Antarctic continent. See **glacier.**

ice shelf *n.* A thick, floating ice sheet attached to a coastline.

ice show *n.* An entertainment, such as a variety show, performed by skaters on ice.

ice skate *n.* **1.** A metal runner or blade that is fitted to the sole of a shoe for skating on ice. **2.** A shoe or light boot with such a runner permanently fixed to it.

ice-skate (īs′skāt′) *intr.v.* **-skated, -skating, -skates.** To skate on ice. **—ice-skat·er** *n.*

ice storm *n.* A storm in which rain or snow freezes on contact.

ice wall *n.* A cliff of ice forming the seaward margin of an ice sheet.

ice water *n.* **1. a.** Very cold drinking water. **b.** Such water containing ice. **2.** Melted ice.

ICFTU International Confederation of Free Trade Unions.

ich (ĭk) *n.* A contagious disease of tropical aquarium fishes, caused by a protozoan, *Ichthyophthirius multifiliis,* and characterized by small white pustules on the body. [Short for New Latin *Ichthyophthirius,* genus name : ICHTHYO- + Greek *phtheir,* louse.]

I Ching (ē′ chĭng′) *n.* A classical book of ancient China whose philosophy seeks to explain nature and human nature in terms of changing balances. As a form of fortune-telling, the book is used to explain each of 64 hexagrams, one of which is chosen at random by

iceberg *Water is less dense at its freezing point than just above it. As a result, an iceberg floats. However, only about a quarter of a berg is visible; the rest is below the sea's surface.*

I Ching *This lacquered board, bearing symbols from the* I Ching, *or "Book of Changes," was meant to be hung in a doorway to keep out devils. The central circle encloses the fishlike symbols for yin and yang, the feminine and masculine forces that shape the universe in Chinese thought. Around them are the eight trigrams, or divinatory categories, used in the* I Ching. *Each trigram is made up of three solid (masculine) or broken (feminine) bars, representing all the possible combinations of the two forces.*

ichneumon fly *Worldwide, there are about 40,000 species of this parasitic insect. The fly (seen here from above and from the side) injects its eggs into the larvae, or caterpillars, of other insects—often butterflies and moths. When the eggs hatch, the ichneumon larvae feed on the caterpillar's body from the inside, eventually killing it.*

icicle *These long spikes of ice are formed by dripping water.*

the person consulting it. [Chinese, "book of changes."]

ich·neu·mon (ĭk-no͞o′mən, -nyo͞o′mən) *n.* A mongoose of the genus *Herpestes;* especially, *H. ichneumon,* of Africa. [Latin, from Greek *ikhneumōn,* "tracker," a weasel that hunts out crocodile eggs, from *ikhneuein,* to track, from *ikhnos*†, track.]

ichneumon fly *n.* Any of various wasplike insects of the family Ichneumonidae, having larvae that are parasitic on the larvae of other insects. Also called "ichneumon wasp."

ich·nite (ĭk′nīt′) *n.* A fossilized footprint. Also called "ichnolite." [Greek *ikhnos,* footstep, track (see **ichneumon**) + -ITE.]

ich·nog·ra·phy (ĭk-nŏg′rə-fē) *n., pl.* **-phies. 1.** The art or process of drawing up ground plans. **2.** A ground plan of a building. [French *ichnographie,* from Latin, from Greek *ikhnographia* : *ikhnos,* track + *-graphia,* -GRAPHY.]

i·chor (ī′kôr′, ī′kər) *n.* **1.** *Greek Mythology.* The rarefied fluid said to run in the veins of the gods. **2.** A fluid likened to blood. **3.** *Pathology.* A watery, acrid discharge from a wound or ulcer. [Greek *ikhōr*†.] **—i·chor·ous** (ī′kər-əs) *adj.*

ich·thy·ic (ĭk′thē-ĭk) *adj.* Of, pertaining to, or characteristic of fishes. [Greek *ikhthus,* fish. See **ichthyo-**.]

ichthyo–, ichthy– *prefix.* Indicates fish; for example, **ichthyology, ichthyornis.** [Latin, from Greek *ikhthuo-,* from *ikhthus,* fish.]

ich·thy·o·fau·na (ĭk′thē-ə-fô′nə) *n.* The fish of a particular region.

ich·thy·oid (ĭk′thē-oid′) *adj.* Also **ich·thy·oid·al** (ĭk′thē-oid′l). Characteristic of or resembling a fish.
∼*n.* A fish or fishlike vertebrate. [Greek *ikhthuoeidēs* : ICHTHY(O)- + -OID.]

ich·thy·ol·o·gy (ĭk′thē-ŏl′ə-jē) *n. Abbr.* **ichthyol., ichth.** A branch of zoology specializing in the study of fishes. [ICHTHYO- + -LOGY.] **—ich·thy·o·log·ic** (ĭk′thē-ə-lŏj′ĭk), **ich·thy·o·log·i·cal** *adj.* **—ich·thy·ol·o·gist** *n.*

ich·thy·oph·a·gous (ĭk′thē-ŏf′ə-gəs) *adj.* Feeding on fish; fish-eating. [Greek *ikhthuophagos* : ICHTHYO- + -PHAGOUS.] **—ich·thy·oph·a·gy** (ĭk′thē-ŏf′ə-jē) *n.*

ich·thy·or·nis (ĭk′thē-ôr′nĭs) *n.* Any of various extinct, fish-eating birds of the genus *Ichthyornis,* that existed during the Cretaceous period. [New Latin "fish bird" : ICHTHY(O)- + Greek *ornis,* bird.]

ich·thy·o·saur (ĭk′thē-ə-sôr′) *n.* Also **ich·thy·o·saur·us** (ĭk′thē-ə-sôr′əs) *pl.* **-sauri** (-sôr′ī′), **-sauruses.** Any of various extinct fishlike marine reptiles of the order Ichthyosauria, of the Triassic to the Cretaceous periods. [New Latin *Ichthyosaurus* : ICHTHYO- + -SAUR.]

ich·thy·o·sis (ĭk′thē-ō′sĭs) *n.* A congenital skin disease, characterized by dry, thickened, scaly skin. Also called "xeroderma." [New Latin : ICHTHY(O)- + -OSIS.]

–ician *suffix.* Indicates a person who practices or is a specialist in a specified field; for example, **beautician, phonetician.**

i·ci·cle (ī′sĭ-kəl) *n.* A tapering spike of ice formed by the freezing of dripping or falling water. [Middle English *isikel* : *is,* ICE + *ikel,* icicle, Old English *gicel.*]

i·ci·ly (ī′sĭ-lē) *adv.* In an icy or chilling manner.

i·ci·ness (ī′sē-nĭs) *n.* The condition or quality of being icy.

ic·ing (ī′sĭng) *n.* **1.** A covering for cakes, cookies, and other baked goods, made from sugar, butter, water, and egg whites or milk, and often flavored and cooked. **2.** The formation of ice; especially, the formation of ice from moisture in the atmosphere, as on an aircraft or ship. **3.** The act of intentionally shooting the puck far out of defensive territory in ice hockey.

ick·y (ĭk′ē) *adj. Slang.* **1.** Sticky; cloying. **2.** Sentimental; mawkish. **3.** Nasty; unpleasant. [20th century : origin obscure.]

ICJ International Court of Justice.

Ick·nield Way (ĭk′nēld′). Prehistoric road in England. It ran southwest from the Wash, along the line of the Chiltern Hills and the Berkshire Downs, to Salisbury Plain.

i·con, i·kon (ī′kŏn′) *n.* Also **ei·kon** (for sense 2). **1.** An image; a representation. **2.** A representation or picture of a sacred Christian personage, itself regarded as sacred, especially in the tradition of the Eastern Churches. **3.** An important and enduring symbol. [Latin *īcōn,* from Greek *eikōn,* likeness, image.]

i·con·ic (ī-kŏn′ĭk) *adj.* **1.** Pertaining to or having the character of an icon. **2.** Having a conventional style. Said of certain memorial statues and busts, such as the ancient statues of victorious athletes.

Iconium. See **Konya.**

icono– or **icon–** *prefix.* Indicates likeness, image; for example, **iconolatry.** [Greek *eikono-,* from *eikōn,* image, ICON.]

i·con·o·clasm (ī-kŏn′ə-klăz′əm) *n.* The action or doctrine of an iconoclast.

i·con·o·clast (ī-kŏn′ə-klăst′) *n.* **1.** A destroyer of sacred images, specifically: **a.** Any of the opponents of the use and veneration of icons in the Eastern Churches during the 8th and 9th centuries A.D. **b.** A Protestant in the 16th and 17th centuries who opposed the veneration of sacred images and traditions. **2.** One who attacks and seeks to overthrow traditional or popular ideas or institutions. [Medieval Latin *īconoclastēs,* from Medieval Greek *eikonoklastēs,* "image breaker" : ICONO- + -CLAST.] **—i·con·o·clas·tic** (ī-kŏn′ə-klăs′tĭk) *adj.* **—i·con·o·clas·ti·cal·ly** *adv.*

i·co·nog·ra·phy (ī′kə-nŏg′rə-fē) *n., pl.* **-phies. 1. a.** Pictorial illustration of a given subject. **b.** The collected representations illustrating a subject. **2. a.** A given set of symbolic forms bearing the meaning of a stylized work of art. **b.** The conventions defining these symbolic forms and governing their interrelationship. [Greek *eikonographia,* description, sketch, "drawing of images" : ICONO- + -GRAPHY.] **—i·con·o·graph·ic** (ī-kŏn′ə-grăf′ĭk), **i·con·o·graph·i·cal** *adj.*

i·co·nol·a·try (ī′kə-nŏl′ə-trē) *n.* The worship of images or icons. [ICONO- + -LATRY.] **—i·co·nol·a·ter** *n.*

i·co·nol·o·gy (ī′kə-nŏl′ə-jē) *n., pl.* **-gies. 1.** The branch of art history dealing with the description, analysis, and interpretation of icons or iconic representations. **2.** Symbolic representation. [French *iconologie* : ICONO- + -LOGY.] **—i·con·o·log·i·cal** (ī-kŏn′ə-lŏj′ĭ-kəl) *adj.* **—i·co·nol·o·gist** *n.*

i·con·o·scope (ī-kŏn′ə-skōp′) *n.* A television-camera tube equipped for rapid scanning of an information-storing, photoactive mosaic by a beam of electrons. [Originally a trademark : ICONO- + -SCOPE.]

i·co·nos·ta·sis (ī′kə-nŏs′tə-sĭs) *n., pl.* **-ses** (-sēz′). The screen dividing the sanctuary from the main body of an Eastern Church. [Late Greek *eikonostasion,* shrine, "place where images stand" : ICONO- + Greek *stasis,* a standing.]

i·co·sa·he·dron (ī-kō′sə-hē′drən) *n., pl.* **-dra** (-drə) or **-drons.** A polyhedron having 20 faces. A regular icosahedron has faces that are equilateral triangles. [Greek *eikosaedron* : *eikosi,* twenty.] **—i·co·sa·he·dral** *adj.*

–ics *suffix.* Indicates: **1.** *Used with a singular verb.* The science or art of; for example, **graphics, poetics. 2.** *Used with a plural verb.* The act, practices, or activities of; for example, **acrobatics, athletics. 3.** *Used with a plural verb.* Characteristic properties or operations of; for example, **mechanics, dynamics.** [From -IC, originally used to render the Greek plural noun ending *-ika,* as in *mathēmatika,* MATHEMATICS.]

ICSH interstitial-cell stimulating hormone.

ic·ter·ic (ĭk-tĕr′ĭk) *adj.* **1.** Pertaining to or having jaundice. **2.** Used to treat jaundice.
∼*n.* A remedy for jaundice.

ic·ter·us (ĭk′tər-əs) *n. Pathology.* **Jaundice** *(see).* [New Latin, from Greek *ikteros*†, jaundice.]

ic·tus (ĭk′təs) *n., pl.* **-tuses** or **ictus. 1.** A metrical or rhythmical stress in verse. **2.** *Pathology.* A sudden attack; a fit; a stroke. [Latin, blow, stroke, from the past participle of *īcere*†, to strike.]

ICU intensive care unit.

i·cy (ī′sē) *adj.* **icier, iciest. 1.** Containing or covered with ice; frozen; slippery: *an icy road.* **2.** Resembling ice; cold or slippery. **3.** Bitterly cold; freezing. **4.** Chilling in manner; frigid: *an icy smile.*

id (ĭd) *n. Psychoanalysis.* That division of the psyche associated with instinctive impulses and demands for immediate satisfaction of primitive needs. See **ego, superego.** [New Latin (translation of German *es,* it), from Latin, it, neuter of *is,* he.]

ID Idaho (used with a Zip Code).

Id. Idaho.

I'd (īd). **1.** Contraction of *I had.* **2.** Contraction of *I would.* **3.** Contraction of *I should.*

–id *suffix.* Indicates: **1.** *Zoology.* A member of a family; for example, **hominid. 2.** *Chemistry.* Variant of **-ide.** [Partly from New Latin -IDAE and partly from French *-ide,* from Latin *-is* (stem *-id-*), feminine patronymic suffix.]

id. idem.

i.d. inside diameter.

I.D. 1. identification. **2.** intelligence department.

IDA International Development Association.

I·da, Mount (ī′də). Mountain in central Crete associated with the worship of Zeus. It rises to 2,456 meters (8,058 feet) and is the highest mountain on the island.

–idae *suffix.* Indicates taxonomic names of families in zoology; for example, **Hominidae.** [New Latin. See **-id.**]

I·da·ho (ī′də-hō′). State in the northwestern United States, one of the group of Rocky Mt. states. The capital and largest city is Boise. It is noted for its unspoilt natural beauty, two-fifths of the state being covered by natural forest. Hell's Canyon, also known as "Grand Canyon of the Snake," is at one point 2,401 meters (7,900 feet) below the mountain peaks and is the deepest gorge in North America. The economy is largely agricultural, beef and dairy farming being the most important activities. **—I·da·ho·an** *adj. & n.*

ID card (ī′dē′) *n.* A card that gives identifying information, such as name, age, and organizational membership, about a person, who then carries the card and uses it to establish his or her identity. Also called "identity card."

–ide, –id *suffix.* Used to form the names of chemical compounds, especially salts derived from acids that contain no oxygen; for example, **chloride.** [German *-id,* from French *-ide* (first used in *oxide,* OXIDE), from *acide,* ACID.]

i·de·a (ī-dē′ə) *n.* **1.** That which comes into existence in the mind as a product of mental activity, such as thought or knowledge; a thought; a conception: *many good ideas.* **2.** An opinion, conviction, or principle produced after thought or observation: *Upon what do you base your political ideas?* **3.** A plan, scheme, or method. **4.** The gist or significance of a specific action or situation. **5.** A notion; a fancy. **6.** *Obsolete.* A mental image of something remembered. **7.** *Music.* A theme or motif. **8.** *Philosophy.* **a.** In the philosophy of Plato, an archetype of which a corresponding being in phenomenal reality is an imperfect replica. **b.** In the philosophy of Kant, a concept of reason that is transcendent but nonempirical. **c.** In the philosophy of Hegel, absolute truth, the complete and ultimate product of reason. [Latin, from Greek, form, model, class, notion.]

Synonyms: *concept, conception, notion, thought.*

i·de·al (ī-dē′əl, ī-dēl′) *n.* **1.** A conception of something in its absolute perfection. **2.** One regarded as a standard or model of perfection.

3. An ultimate object of endeavor; a goal. **4.** A worthy principle or aim. **5.** That which exists only in the mind.
~*adj.* **1.** Conforming to an ultimate form of perfection or excellence. **2.** Considered the best of its kind. **3.** Completely or highly satisfactory. **4.** Existing only in the mind; visionary; imaginary. **5.** Of, pertaining to, or consisting of ideas or mental images. **6.** *Philosophy.* **a.** Existing as an archetype or pattern, especially as a Platonic idea. **b.** Of or pertaining to idealism. [French *idéal,* from Late Latin *ideālis,* from Latin *idea,* model, IDEA.]
Synonyms: *archetype, exemplar, model, standard.*

ideal gas *n. Physics.* A hypothetical gas that obeys the gas laws. In kinetic theory, a model of such a gas is a large number of particles of negligible size, moving randomly and making elastic collisions with the walls of the container.

ideal gas law *n. Physics.* **Gas equation** *(see).*

i·de·al·ism (ī-dē'ə-lĭz'əm) *n.* **1.** The envisaging of things in an ideal form. **2.** Pursuit of one's ideals. **3.** An idealizing treatment of a subject in literature or art. **4.** The theory that the object of external perception, in itself or as perceived, consists of ideas. In this sense, compare **materialism, realism.**

i·de·al·ist (ī-dē'ə-lĭst) *n.* **1.** One whose conduct is influenced by idealism. **2.** One who is unrealistic and impractical; a visionary. **3.** An artist or writer whose work is imbued with idealism. **4.** An adherent of any system of philosophical idealism.

i·de·al·is·tic (ī-dē'ə-lĭs'tĭk) *adj.* Pertaining to or having the nature of an idealist or idealism. **—i·de·al·is·ti·cal·ly** *adv.*

i·de·al·i·ty (ī'dē-ăl'ə-tē) *n., pl.* **-ties. 1.** The state or quality of being ideal. **2.** Existence in idea only.

i·de·al·ize (ī-dē'ə-līz') *v.* **-ized, -izing, -izes.** *—tr.* **1. a.** To regard as ideal. **b.** To treat (a person or thing) as if ideal. **2.** To depict or imagine as ideal. *—intr.* **1.** To render something as an ideal. **2.** To conceive an ideal or ideals. **—i·de·al·i·za·tion** (ī-dē'ə-lə-zā'shən) *n.* **—i·de·al·iz·er** *n.*

i·de·al·ly (ī-dē'ə-lē) *adv.* **1.** In conformity with an ideal; perfectly. **2.** In ideal conditions; theoretically.

i·de·ate (ī-dē'āt') *v.* **-ated, -ating, -ates.** *—tr.* To form an idea of; imagine; conceive. *—intr.* To conceive mental images; think. [IDEA.] **—i·de·a·tion** (ī'dē-ā'shən) *n.* **—i·de·a·tion·al** *adj.*

i·dée fixe (ē-dā fēks') *n., pl.* **idées fixes** *(pronounced as singular).* A fixed idea; an obsession.

i·dée re·çue (ē-dā rə-sü') *n., pl.* **idées reçues** *(pronounced as singular).* A received idea; an opinion that is held out of respect for convention rather than from conviction. [French.]

i·dem (ī'dĕm'). *Abbr.* **id.** The same. Used to indicate a reference previously mentioned. [Latin *īdem* (masculine), *idem* (neuter), the same, from *id,* it, neuter of *is,* he.]

i·dem·po·tent (ī'dĕm-pō'tənt, ī-dĕm'pə-tənt) *adj. Mathematics.* Unchanged by multiplication by itself. Said of matrices, functions, operators, and the like. [Latin *idem,* same + POTENT.]

i·den·tic note (ī-dĕn'tĭk) *n.* A diplomatic communication with wording that has been agreed upon by two or more governments, copies of which are dispatched simultaneously on behalf of these governments. [Medieval Latin *identicus,* IDENTICAL.]

i·den·ti·cal (ī-dĕn'tĭ-kəl) *adj.* **1.** Being the same. **2.** Being exactly alike or equal. —See Synonyms at **same.** [Medieval Latin *identicus,* from Late Latin *identitās,* IDENTITY.] **—i·den·ti·cal·ly** *adv.* **—i·den·ti·cal·ness** *n.*
Usage: Standard English recommends that the preposition following *identical* should be *with (That picture is identical with the one in my office),* but *to* is becoming increasingly common.

identical twin *n.* Either of a pair of twins of the same sex developed from a single fertilized ovum that split in half. Identical twins have identical genetic constitutions and show pronounced mutual resemblance. Also called "monozygotic twin."

i·den·ti·fi·ca·tion (ī-dĕn'tə-fĭ-kā'shən) *n.* **1.** The act of identifying. **2.** The state of being identified. **3.** *Abbr.* **I.D.** Proof of one's identity, such as a document, for example. **4.** *Psychology.* **a.** An individual's recognition of a personal or group identity. **b.** The transferal of response to an object considered identical to another. **5.** The recognition of oneself in another character, such as one in fiction or public life, with consequently strong sympathy for the character and concern for his or her fate.

identification card *n.* An **ID card** *(see).*

i·den·ti·fy (ī-dĕn'tə-fī') *v.* **-fied, -fying, -fies.** *—tr.* **1. a.** To establish the identity of. **b.** To ascertain the origin, nature, or definitive characteristics of: *His accent was difficult to identify.* **c.** To determine and select: *identify the best method.* **2.** To determine the taxonomic classification of. **3.** To consider as identical; equate. **4.** To associate with. **5.** *Psychology.* To associate or affiliate (oneself) closely with a person or group. **6.** To imagine (oneself) as another person, such as a literary character or a prominent figure. *—intr.* To establish an identification with another or others: *The reader often identifies with the hero of a novel.* [Medieval Latin *identificāre* : Late Latin *identitās,* IDENTI(TY) + -FY.] **—i·den·ti·fi·a·ble** (ī-dĕn'tə-fī'ə-bəl) *adj.* **—i·den·ti·fi·er** *n.*
Usage: When used in the sense of "to see oneself as similar or identical to," the verb *identify* may be used with or without the reflexive pronoun, as in *I identified myself with the hero* or *I identified with the hero.* Used technically, in the field of psychology, *identify* expresses close association with a person or group and lacks the reflexive pronoun, as in *He identifies with his father.*

i·den·ti·ty (ī-dĕn'tə-tē) *n., pl.* **-ties. 1.** The collective aspect of the set of characteristics by which a thing is definitively recognizable or known. **2.** The set of behavioral or personal characteristics by which an individual is recognizable as a member of a group. **3.** The name or nature of a person or thing: *reveal one's identity.* **4.** The quality or condition of being exactly the same as something else. **5.** The quality or condition of being or remaining the same. **6.** The personality of an individual regarded as a persisting entity. **7.** *Mathematics.* **a.** An equality satisfied by all values of the variables for which the expressions involved in the equality are defined. **b.** A member of a set that combines with other members and leaves them unchanged for a particular operation; for example, the integer 1 is the identity for real numbers under multiplication. Also called "identity element." [Late Latin *identitās,* from Latin *idem,* the same, IDEM.]

identity card *n.* An **ID card** *(see).*

identity crisis *n. Psychology.* A period of disorientation and anxiety resulting from difficulties experienced in resolving personal conflicts, adjusting to social demands and pressures, or the like.

identity matrix *n.* A square matrix with numeral 1's along the diagonal from upper left to lower right and 0's in all other positions.

identity sign *n.* A mathematical symbol (≡), used to denote identity rather than equality.

ideo– *prefix.* Indicates idea; for example, **ideogram.** [French *idéo-,* from Greek *idea,* form, notion.]

id·e·o·gram (ĭd'ē-ə-grăm', ī'dē-) *n.* Also **id·e·o·graph** (-grăf', -gräf'). **1.** A character or symbol representing an idea or thing without indicating pronunciation, as the characters in Chinese. **2.** A graphic symbol; for example, &, %, @. [IDEO- + -GRAM.]

id·e·og·ra·phy (ĭd'ē-ŏg'rə-fē, ī'dē-) *n.* **1.** The representation of ideas by graphic symbols. **2.** The use of ideograms to express ideas. [IDEO- + -GRAPHY.] **—id·e·o·graph·ic** (ĭd'ē-ə-grăf'ĭk) *adj.*

i·de·o·log·i·cal (ī'dē-ə-lŏj'ĭ-kəl, ĭd'ē-) *adj.* **1.** Of or relating to ideology. **2.** Of or concerned with ideas. **—i·de·o·log·i·cal·ly** *adv.*

i·de·ol·o·gist (ī'dē-ŏl'ə-jĭst, ĭd'ē-) *n.* **1.** An advocate or adherent of a given ideology. **2.** A student of ideologies. **3.** *Archaic.* A visionary; a theorist.

i·de·o·logue (ī'dē-ə-lŏg', ĭd'ē-) *n.* An advocate of a given ideology, especially one of its official exponents. [French *idéologue,* back-formation from *idéologie,* IDEOLOGY.]

i·de·ol·o·gy (ī'dē-ŏl'ə-jē, ĭd'ē-) *n., pl.* **-gies. 1.** The body of ideas reflecting the needs and aspirations of an individual, group, or culture. **2.** A set of doctrines or beliefs that form the basis of a political, economic, or other system. [French *idéologie* : IDEO- + -LOGY.]

i·de·o·mo·tor (ī'dē-ə-mō'tər, ĭd'ē-) *adj.* Of or being a motor response to an ideational rather than a sensory stimulus.

ides (īdz) *n. Used with a singular or plural verb.* In the ancient Roman calendar, the 15th day of March, May, July, or October or the 13th day of the other months. [Middle English *idus, ides,* from Old French *ides,* from Latin *īdūs*†.]

id est (ĭd ĕst'). *Abbr.* **i.e.** *Latin.* That is.

idio– *prefix.* Indicates individuality, peculiarity, isolation, or distinctness; for example, **idiolect.** [Greek, from *idios*†, personal, peculiar, separate.]

id·i·o·blast (ĭd'ē-ō-blăst') *n.* A specialized plant cell that differs from the cells around it. [IDIO- + -BLAST.] **—id·i·o·blast·ic** (ĭd'ē-ō-blăs'tĭk) *adj.*

id·i·o·cy (ĭd'ē-ə-sē) *n., pl.* **-cies. 1.** A condition of subnormal intellectual development or ability, characterized by an intelligence quotient in the range 20–50. No longer in technical usage. Compare **imbecility. 2.** Extreme folly or stupidity. **3.** A foolish or stupid utterance or deed.

id·i·o·gram (ĭd'ē-ə-grăm') *n.* A **karyotype** *(see).* [IDIO- + -GRAM.]

id·i·o·lect (ĭd'ē-ə-lĕkt') *n.* The speech of an individual, considered as a linguistic pattern unique among speakers of his language or dialect. [IDIO- + (DIA)LECT.] **—id·i·o·lect·al** (ĭd'ē-ə-lĕk'təl), **id·i·o·lect·ic** (id'ē-ə-lĕk'tĭk) *adj.*

id·i·om (ĭd'ē-əm) *n.* **1.** An expression or phrase that has a meaning of its own that is not apparent from the meanings of its individual words; for example, *to make friends,* meaning "to become acquainted," and *to do away with,* meaning "to dispose of," are English idioms. **2.** The specific grammatical, syntactical, and structural character of a given language. **3.** A regional speech or dialect. **4.** A specialized vocabulary used by a particular group of people; jargon: *legal idiom.* **5.** A style of artistic expression characteristic of a given individual, school, period, or medium. [Old French *idiome,* from Late Latin *idiōma,* from Greek, peculiarity, idiom, from *idiousthai,* to make one's own, from *idios*†, own, personal.]

id·i·o·mat·ic (ĭd'ē-ə-măt'ĭk) *adj.* **1.** Peculiar to or characteristic of a given language. **2.** Resembling or having the nature of an idiom. **3.** Using many idioms; fluent and natural: *spoke idiomatic French.* **—id·i·o·mat·i·cal·ly** *adv.*

id·i·o·mor·phic (ĭd'ē-ə-môr'fĭk) *adj.* Occurring as crystals. Said of minerals. [Greek *idiomorphos,* having one's own form : IDIO- + -MORPHOUS.] **—id·i·o·mor·phic·al·ly** *adv.* **—id·i·o·mor·phism** *n.*

id·i·op·a·thy (ĭd'ē-ŏp'ə-thē) *n. Medicine.* A disease of unknown origin or cause. [Greek *idiopathia,* disease having its own origin : IDIO- + -PATHY.] **—id·i·o·path·ic** (ĭd'ē-ō-păth'ĭk) *adj.*

id·i·o·plasm (ĭd'ē-ə-plăz'əm) *n.* A hypothetical structural unit of germ plasm. **—id·i·o·plas·mic, id·i·o·plas·mat·ic** (ĭd'ē-ō-plăz-măt'ĭk) *adj.*

id·i·o·syn·cra·sy (ĭd'ē-ō-sĭng'krə-sē) *n., pl.* **-sies. 1.** A structural or behavioral characteristic peculiar to an individual or group. **2.** A physiological or temperamental peculiarity. **3.** Unusual hypersensitivity to a drug or food. —See Synonyms at **eccentricity.** [Greek

PRONUNCIATION KEY

ă, pat; ā, pay; âr, care;
ä, father, are; b, **bib;**
ch, **church;** d, **deed;** ĕ, pet;
ē, be; f, **fife;** g, **gag;** h, **hat;**
hw, **which;** ĭ, pit; ī, pie;
îr, **pier;** j, **judge;** k, **kick;**
l, **lid,** needle; m, **mum;**
n, **no,** sudden; ng, **thing;**
ŏ, pot; ō, **toe;** ô, **paw,** for;
oi, **noise;** ou, **out;** ŏŏ, **book;**
ōō, **boot;** p, **pop;** r, roar;
s, **sauce;** sh, **ship,** dish;
t, **tight;** th, **thin,** path;
th, **this,** bathe; ŭ, **cut;** ûr, **fur;**
v, **valve;** w, **with;** y, yes;
z, **zebra,** size; zh, vision;
ə, **about,** item, edible,
gallop, circus, peaceful

IN FOREIGN WORDS:

à, *Fr.* ami; œ, *Fr.* **feu,** *Ger.* **schön;** ü, *Fr.* **tu,** *Ger.* **über;**
KH, *Ger.* **ich,** *Scot.* **loch;**
N, *Fr.* **bon;** y', *Fr.* **Compiègne**

STRESS MARKS:

Primary stress: '
in·cite' (ĭn-sīt')
Secondary stress: '
in'sight' (ĭn'sīt')

idiosunkrasia : IDIO- + *sunkrasis,* a mingling, mixture, temperament : *syn-,* together + *krasis,* mixture, CRASIS.] —**id·i·o·syn·crat·ic** (ĭd'-ē-ō-sĭn-krăt'ĭk) *adj.* —**id·i·o·syn·crat·i·cal·ly** *adv.*

id·i·ot (ĭd'ē-ət) *n.* **1.** A mentally deficient person, having an intelligence quotient in the 20 to 50 range, and classified as severely subnormal. No longer in technical usage. **2.** A very stupid person. [Middle English, from Old French *idiote,* from Latin *idiōta,* ignorant person, from Greek *idiōtēs,* private person, plebeian, layman, ignorant person, from *idiost,* peculiar, private.]

id·i·ot·ic (ĭd'ē-ŏt'ĭk) *adj.* Very stupid. —**id·i·ot·i·cal·ly** *adv.*

idiot light *n.* A light on the instrument panel of an automobile that gives forewarning, as of an overheated engine.

–idium *suffix.* Indicates a small structure or form; for example, **nephridium.** [New Latin, from Greek *-idion.*]

i·dle (ĭd'l) *adj.* **idler, idlest. 1.** Not employed; inactive: *Cancellation of the meeting left her idle.* **2.** Avoiding employment; lazy; shiftless. **3.** Not in operation or working order: *idle machinery.* **4.** Empty; pointless: *idle talk.* **5.** Unfounded; baseless: *idle rumors.* —See Synonyms at **inactive.**
~*v.* **idled, idling, idles.** —*intr.* **1.** To pass time without working or in avoiding work. **2.** To move lazily and without purpose. **3.** To run at a slow speed or out of gear. Used of a motor or a machine. —*tr.* **1.** To pass (time) without working or in avoiding work; waste. Often used with *away: idle the afternoon away.* **2.** To cause to be unemployed or inactive. **3.** To cause (a motor or machine) to idle. [Middle English *idel,* idle, void, empty, Old English *īdel,* from West Germanic *īdal* (unattested).] —**i·dle·ness** *n.* —**i·dly** *adv.*

idle character *n.* An alphanumeric or digital character that is transmitted over a communications line but does not appear in the output of the receiving terminal.

idle pulley *n.* A pulley on a shaft that rests on or presses against a drive belt to guide it or take up slack. Also called "idler," "idler pulley," "idle wheel."

i·dler (ĭd'lər) *n.* **1.** One that idles. **2.** An idle wheel or idle pulley. **3.** A sailor exempt from night watch.

idle wheel *n.* **1.** A gear, wheel, or roller interposed between two similar parts to convey motion from one to the other without change in speed or direction of motion. Also called "idler." **2.** An idle pulley.

I·do (ī'dō) *n.* An artificial language based on Esperanto. [Esperanto, offspring, from Greek *-id,* "daughter of."]

id·o·crase (ĭd'ō-krās', ī'dō-) *n.* A green, brown, yellow, or blue mineral, essentially Ca$_{10}$Al$_4$(Mg,Fe)$_2$(Si$_2$O$_4$)$_2$(SiO$_4$)$_5$(OH)$_4$. Also called "vesuvianite." [French : Greek *eidos,* form, shape + *krasis,* mixture.]

i·dol (ī'dl) *n.* **1. a.** An image used as an object of worship. **b.** A false god. **2.** One that is the object of deep love or devotion. **3.** *Archaic.* Something visible but without substance. [Middle English *idol, idel,* from Old French *idole, idele,* from Late Latin *īdōlum,* from Greek *eidōlon,* image, form, apparition, from *eidos,* form.]

i·dol·a·ter (ī-dŏl'ə-tər) *n.* **1.** One who worships idols. **2.** One who blindly admires or adores another. [Middle English *idolatrer,* from Old French *idolatre,* from Late Latin *īdōlolatrēs,* from Greek *eidōlolatreia* : *eidōlon,* IDOL + *-latrēs,* worshiper.]

i·dol·a·trize (ī-dŏl'ə-trīz') *tr.v.* **-trized, -trizing, -trizes.** To make an idol of. —See Synonyms at **revere.**

i·dol·a·trous (ī-dŏl'ə-trəs) *adj.* **1.** Given to idolatry. **2.** Constituting idolatry. —**i·dol·a·trous·ly** *adv.* —**i·dol·a·trous·ness** *n.*

i·dol·a·try (ī-dŏl'ə-trē) *n., pl.* **-tries. 1.** The worship of idols. **2.** Blind admiration of or devotion to something or someone. [Middle English, from Old French, from Medieval Latin *īdōlatrīa,* from Greek *eidōlolatreia* : *eidōlon,* IDOL + *-latreia,* LATRY.]

i·dol·ize (ī'dl-īz') *tr.v.* **-ized, -izing, -izes. 1.** To regard with blind admiration or devotion. **2.** To worship as an idol. —See Synonyms at **revere.** —**i·dol·i·za·tion** (ī'dl-ə-zā'shən) *n.* —**i·dol·iz·er** *n.*

i·do·lum (ī-dō'ləm) *n., pl.* **-la** (-lə). **1.** An image in the mind. **2.** A fallacy. [Latin, IDOL.]

Idun. Variant of **Ithunn.**

i·dyll, i·dyl (ī'dl) *n.* **1.** A short poem describing a picturesque episode or scene of rustic life. **2.** A scene or event of rural simplicity. **3.** A delightful and simple episode in life or literature. **4.** A piece of calm pastoral music. [Latin *īdyllium,* from Greek *eidullion,* diminutive of *eidos,* form, picture.]

i·dyl·lic (ī-dĭl'ĭk) *adj.* **1.** Of, pertaining to, or having the nature of an idyll. **2.** Having a natural charm and picturesqueness. —**i·dyl·li·cal·ly** *adv.*

i·dyl·list (ī'dl-ĭst) *n.* A writer of idylls.

-ie. Variant of **-y.**

i.e. id est.
Usage: The abbreviations *i.e.* and *e.g.* are not interchangeable, though they are sometimes confused. The distinction can easily be made by reference to their meanings: *i.e.* stands for the Latin *id est,* meaning "that is"; *e.g.* stands for the Latin *exempli gratia,* meaning "for example." Thus, *i.e.* always gives a fuller explanation of what precedes it: *the manager, i.e. the man in charge,* whereas *e.g.* introduces an example, or set of examples: *the people in charge, e.g. supervisors, stewards.* It is unacceptable to use such expressions as: *schoolchildren, i.e. five-year-olds and six-year-olds,* when what follows the abbreviation is an example rather than an explanation.

if (ĭf) *conj.* Used to introduce a conditional clause, meaning: **a.** In the event that: *If I were to go, I would be late.* **b.** Granting that: *Even if that's true, what should we do?* **c.** On condition that: *She will sing only if she is paid.* **d.** Whenever: *I always go if she asks me.* **e.** Although: *They are gifted, if inexperienced.* **2.** Used to introduce an indirect question, meaning whether: *Ask if he will come.* **3.** Used to introduce an exclamatory clause, indicating: **a.** A wish: *If she had only come earlier!* **b.** Surprise, anger, or a similar emotion: *If she ever does that again!* —**as if. 1.** As might be the case if: *I felt as if I was dying.* **2.** It is ridiculous to claim that: *As if you couldn't have telephoned!* —**if not. 1.** Though perhaps not: *certainly comfortable, if not rich.* **2.** And possibly even: *a millionaire, if not a billionaire.*
~*n.* A possibility, condition, or stipulation. [Middle English *(y)if,* Old English *gif.*]
Usage: Both *if* and *whether* may be used to introduce an indirect question, but *whether* is slightly more formal. It is also more likely whenever more than one condition is being expressed and linked by *or: He asked whether John would arrive on time or whether he would be late.* Sometimes it is necessary to use *whether* in order to avoid ambiguity: *Tell me if you want an answer,* for example, could mean either "Tell me whether you want an answer," or "If you expect an answer, there is something you should tell me."

IF, i.f. intermediate frequency.

IFC International Finance Corporation.

I·fe (ē'fā). City in southwestern Nigeria, a leading center for the marketing and exporting of cocoa. It is believed to be the oldest settlement of the Yoruba tribe, dating from *c.* 1300. Terra-cotta and bronze sculptures made there in that period are considered some of the finest treasures of West African art.

if·fy (ĭf'ē) *adj. Informal.* Doubtful; uncertain. [From IF.] —**if·fi·ly** *adv.* —**if·fi·ness** *n.*

I formation *n. Football.* An alignment of the offensive team in which all the backs line up in single file behind the center.

IG, I.G. inspector general.

I-gird·er (ī'gûr'dər) *n.* A girder with an I-shaped cross section.

ig·loo (ĭg'lōō) *n., pl.* **-loos.** An Eskimo house, traditionally dome-shaped and built of blocks of ice or hard snow. [Eskimo *iglu, igdlu,* house.]

ign. ignition.

Ig·na·ti·us Loy·o·la (ĭg-nā'shəs loi-ō'lə), **Saint** (1491-1556). Spanish soldier and priest who founded the Society of Jesus (the Jesuits) in 1534.

ig·ne·ous (ĭg'nē-əs) *adj.* **1.** Of, pertaining to, or characteristic of fire. **2.** *Geology.* **a.** Formed by solidification from a molten or partially molten state. Said of rocks. **b.** Of or pertaining to rock so formed; pyrogenic. [Latin *igneus,* from *ignis,* fire.]

ig·nis fat·u·us (ĭg'nĭs făch'ōō-əs) *n., pl.* **ignes fatui** (ĭg'nēz' făch'ōō-ī'). **1.** A phosphorescent light that hovers or flits over swampy ground at night, caused by spontaneous combustion of methane and other gases emitted by rotting organic matter. Also called "friar's lantern," "will-o'-the-wisp." **2.** Something that misleads or deludes; a deception. [Medieval Latin, "foolish fire."]

ig·nite (ĭg-nīt') *v.* **-nited, -niting, -nites.** —*tr.* **1. a.** To cause to burn. **b.** To set fire to. **2.** To arouse or kindle. —*intr.* To begin to burn; catch fire. [Latin *ignīre,* to set on fire, from *ignis,* fire.] —**ig·nit·a·ble, ig·nit·i·ble** *adj.* —**ig·nit·er, ig·ni·tor** *n.*

ig·ni·tion (ĭg-nĭsh'ən) *n.* **1.** The act of igniting or the point at which this occurs. **2.** *Abbr.* **ign. a.** An electrical system, typically powered by a battery or magneto, that provides the spark to ignite the fuel mixture in an internal-combustion engine. **b.** A switch or other device that activates this system.

ignition point *n.* The minimum temperature at which a substance will continue to burn without additional external heat.

ig·ni·tron (ĭg-nī'trŏn', ĭg'nə-) *n.* A single-anode, mercury-vapor rectifier in which current passes as an arc between the anode and a mercury-pool cathode, used in power rectification. [Latin *ignis,* fire + -TRON.]

ig·no·ble (ĭg-nō'bəl) *adj.* **1.** Not having an honorable character or purpose; contemptible. **2.** Not of the nobility; common. —See Synonyms at **mean** (base). [Latin *īgnōbilis* : *in-,* not + *nōbilis,* NOBLE.] —**ig·no·bil·i·ty** (ĭg'nō-bĭl'ə-tē), **ig·no·ble·ness** *n.* —**ig·no·bly** *adv.*

ig·no·min·i·ous (ĭg'nə-mĭn'ē-əs) *adj.* **1.** Characterized by shame or disgrace. **2.** Deserving disgrace or shame; despicable. **3.** Degrading; debasing. —**ig·no·min·i·ous·ly** *adv.* —**ig·no·min·i·ous·ness** *n.*

ig·no·min·y (ĭg'nə-mĭn'ē, -mə-nē) *n., pl.* **-ies. 1.** Dishonor; infamy. **2.** That which causes dishonor; a disgraceful act or disgraceful conduct. —See Synonyms at **disgrace.** [Latin *īgnōminia* : *in-,* not + *nōmen* (stem *nōmin-*), name, reputation.]

ig·no·ra·mus (ĭg'nə-rā'məs) *n., pl.* **-muses.** An ignorant person. [New Latin, from Latin, "we do not know," from *īgnōrāre,* to be ignorant, IGNORE.]

ig·no·rance (ĭg'nər-əns) *n.* The condition of being ignorant; lack of knowledge.

ig·no·rant (ĭg'nər-ənt) *adj.* **1.** Without education or knowledge. **2.** Exhibiting lack of education or knowledge. **3.** Unaware or uninformed: *ignorant of what had happened.* **4.** *Nonstandard.* Ill-mannered. [Middle English *ignoraunt,* from Old French *ignorant,* from Latin *īgnōrāns* (stem *īgnorant-*), present participle of *īgnōrāre,* to be ignorant, IGNORE.] —**ig·no·rant·ly** *adv.*
Synonyms: uneducated, unlearned, unlettered, untaught, untutored.

ig·no·ra·ti·o e·len·chi (ĭg'nə-rā'shē-ō ĭ-leng'kī) *n. Latin.* The procedure of disproving an extraneous proposition rather than one actually advanced. ["Ignoring of proof," translation of Greek *elenkhou agnoia.*]

ig·nore (ĭg-nôr′) *tr.v.* **-nored, -noring, -nores.** To refuse to pay attention to; disregard. —See Synonyms at **refuse.** [French *ignorer,* from Latin *ignōrāre,* not to know, disregard.] —**ig·nor·a·ble** *adj.* —**ig·nor·er** *n.*

ig·no·tum per ig·no·ti·us (ĭg-nō′təm pər ĭg-nō′tē-əs) *n. Latin.* An explanation that is more confusing than that which it purports to explain. ["The unknown by means of the more unknown."]

I·go·rot (ĭg′ə-rŏt′, ē′gə-), *n., pl.* **-rots** or collectively **Igorot.** Also **I·gor·ro·te** (ē′gôr-rō′tä). 1. A member of any of several related peoples of mountainous northern Luzon in the Philippines. 2. The Malayo-Polynesian language of these people.

I·gua·çu Falls (ē′gwä-sōō′). Falls in the Iguaçu River, on the Argentina-Brazil border near the Paraguay line. There are two main sections composed of hundreds of waterfalls, the highest of which is 64 meters (210 feet).

i·gua·na (ĭ-gwä′nə) *n.* Any of various large tropical American lizards of the family Iguanidae, often having spiny projections along the back. [Spanish, from Arawak *iwana.*]

i·guan·o·don (ĭ-gwä′nə-dŏn′) *n.* Any of various large dinosaurs of the genus *Iguanodontidae,* of the Jurassic and Cretaceous periods. [New Latin *Iguanodon* : IGUAN(A) + -ODON.]

IGY International Geophysical Year.

ih·ram (ē-räm′) *n.* 1. The sacred dress of Muslim pilgrims, consisting of two lengths of white cotton. 2. The sacred state in which the pilgrim exists while wearing this dress. [Arabic *iḥrām,* "prohibition," from *ḥarama,* he prohibited. See **harem.**]

IHS A graphic symbol for Jesus. [From IHΣΟΤΣ or IHSOUS, Jesus (in Greek capitals).]

Ijs·sel or **IJs·sel** or **Ys·sel** (ī′səl). River, *c.* 116 kilometers (72 miles) long, in the Netherlands, flowing from the Lower Rhine River northward to the Ijsselmeer.

Ijs·sel·meer or **IJs·sel·meer** or **Ys·sel·meer** (ī′səl-mâr′). Lake of the northwestern Netherlands. It was formed in 1932 from the Zuider Zee by the Wieringen-Friesland Barrage. A program of land reclamation has reduced its area by two thirds, increasing the land area of the Netherlands by *c.* 6 percent.

i·ke·ba·na (ē′kä-bä′nä, ĭk′ə-bä′nə) *n.* The Japanese art of formal flower arrangement with special regard to balance, harmony, and form. [Japanese, "living flowers."]

Ikhnaton. See **Akhenaton.**

ikon. Variant of **icon.**

ilang-ilang. Variant of **ylang-ylang.**

IL Illinois (used with a Zip Code).

ILA International Longshoremen's Association.

-ile *suffix.* Indicates relationship with, similarity to, or capability of; for example, **prehensile, virile.** [Middle English, from Old French, from Latin *-ilis.*]

il·e·ac (ĭl′ē-ăk′) *adj.* 1. Of or pertaining to ileus. 2. Of or pertaining to the ileum; ileal.

Île-de-France (ēl-də-fräNs′). A region and former province in north-central France, occupying the Paris basin in the Seine lowland, with Paris as its center.

Île du Diable. See **Devil's Island.**

il·e·i·tis (ĭl′ē-ī′tĭs) *n.* Inflammation of the ileum. [New Latin : IL-E(UM) + -ITIS.]

il·e·os·to·my (ĭl′ē-ŏs′tə-mē) *n., pl.* **-mies.** The surgical formation of an artificial opening through the abdominal wall into the ileum so that the intestinal contents can be discharged without passing through the colon. [ILEO- + -STOMY.]

il·e·um (ĭl′ē-əm) *n., pl.* **-ea** (-ē-ə). The lower portion of the small intestine, extending from the jejunum to the cecum. [New Latin, from Latin *īlium, īleum*†, groin, flank.] —**il·e·al** *adj.*

il·e·us (ĭl′ē-əs) *n.* Intestinal obstruction due to loss of peristalsis or to mechanical obstruction, causing colic, vomiting, and toxemia. [Latin *īleus,* from Greek *(e)ileos,* "a twisting," from *eilein, illein,* to roll, wind.]

i·lex (ī′lĕks′) *n.* 1. Any of various trees or shrubs of the genus *Ilex;* a holly. 2. The holm oak *(see).* [Latin *īlex,* holm oak, of Mediterranean origin.]

I.L.G.W.U. International Ladies' Garment Workers' Union.

Il·i·ad (ĭl′ē-əd) *n.* A Greek epic poem attributed to Homer, recounting the siege of Troy.

il·i·um (ĭl′ē-əm) *n., pl.* **-ia** (-ē-ə). The uppermost and widest of three bones constituting one of the lateral halves of the pelvis. [New Latin, from Latin *īlium, īleum*† groin, flank.] —**il·i·ac** (ĭl′ē-ăk′) *adj.*

ilk¹ (ĭlk) *n.* 1. Type or kind: *people of that ilk.* Sometimes used humorously. 2. *Scottish.* Used following a name in the phrase *of that ilk* to indicate that the one named resides on an estate bearing the same name: *Duncan of that ilk.* —See Synonyms at **type.** [Middle English *ilke, ilk,* Old English *ilca,* same.]

ilk² Variant of **ilka.**

il·ka (ĭl′kə) *adj.* Also **ilk** (ĭlk). *Scottish.* Each; every. [Middle English *ilka(n),* each one : *ilk, ech,* EACH + *a,* A.]

ill (ĭl) *adj.* **worse, worst.** 1. Not healthy; sick. 2. Not normal; unsound: *ill health.* 3. Resulting in suffering; distressing. 4. Characterized by animosity or an unpleasant disposition: *ill humor.* 5. Boding evil; unpropitious. 6. Disreputable; wicked: *a house of ill repute.* 7. *Archaic & Regional.* Difficult; hard: *He's ill to please.* —See Synonyms at **sick.**
~*adv.* **worse, worst.** 1. In an ill manner; badly. 2. Scarcely or with difficulty. *Note:* The adverb *ill* combines with many adjectives, usually derived from the participles of verbs, to form attributive modifiers before nouns: *an ill-regulated life; an ill-deserving man.* In such use, the elements are joined with a hyphen. However, when *ill* modifies an adjective coming after the noun or pronoun, the two words are written separately: *His life was ill regulated. The man is ill deserving.*
~*n.* 1. Evil; wrongdoing. 2. Disaster or harm. 3. A physical or moral trouble. [Middle English *ill(e),* from Old Norse *illr*†, bad.]

I'll (ĭl). 1. Contraction of *I will.* 2. Contraction of *I shall.*

ill. illustrated; illustration; illustrator.

Ill. Illinois (state).

ill-ad·vised (ĭl′əd-vīzd′) *adj.* Unwise; foolish. —**ill-ad·vis·ed·ly** (ĭl′-əd-vī′zĭd-lē) *adv.*

ill-as·sort·ed (ĭl′ə-sôr′tĭd) *adj.* Poorly matched: *They are an ill-assorted couple.*

ill-at-ease (ĭl′ət-ēz′) *adj.* Nervous; uncomfortable.

il·la·tion (ĭ-lā′shən) *n.* 1. The act of inferring or drawing conclusions. 2. A conclusion drawn; a deduction. [Late Latin *illātiō* (stem *illātiōn-*) from Latin, "a carrying in," deduction, from *illātus* (past participle of *inferre,* to bring in) : *in-,* in, + *-lātus,* "carried."]

il·la·tive (ĭl′ə-tĭv, ĭ-lā′-) *adj. Grammar.* 1. Expressing or preceding an inference: *"Therefore" is an illative word.* 2. Designating a case in Finnish and Hungarian that expresses movement or direction toward. —**il·la·tive** *n.*

ill-be·haved (ĭl′bĭ-hāvd′) *adj.* Ill-mannered.

ill-be·ing (ĭl′bē′ĭng) *n.* A condition of being lacking in prosperity, happiness, or health.

ill-bod·ing (ĭl′bō′dĭng) *adj.* Portending evil; inauspicious.

ill-bred (ĭl′brĕd′) *adj.* 1. Badly brought up; ill-mannered; impolite. 2. Not thoroughbred.

ill-con·sid·ered (ĭl′kən-sĭd′ərd) *adj.* Unwise; foolish.

ill-de·fined (ĭl′dĭ-fīnd′) *adj.* Not defined clearly.

ill-dis·posed (ĭl′dĭs-pōzd′) *adj.* 1. Having an unfriendly or hostile attitude. 2. Unwilling.

il·le·gal (ĭ-lē′gəl) *adj.* 1. Prohibited by law. 2. Prohibited by official rules. —**il·le·gal·ly** *adv.*

il·le·gal·i·ty (ĭl′ē-găl′ə-tē) *n., pl.* **-ties.** 1. The state or quality of being illegal. 2. An illegal act.

il·le·ga·lize (ĭ-lē′gə-līz′) *tr.v.* **-ized, -izing, -izes.** To make illegal. —**il·le·gal·i·za·tion** (ĭ-lē′gə-lə-zā′shən) *n.*

il·leg·i·ble (ĭ-lĕj′ə-bəl) *adj.* Not legible or decipherable. —**il·leg·i·bil·i·ty** (ĭ-lĕj′ə-bĭl′ə-tē), **il·leg·i·ble·ness** *n.* —**il·leg·i·bly** *adv.*

il·le·git·i·ma·cy (ĭl′ĭ-jĭt′ə-mə-sē) *n.* 1. The condition or quality of being illegitimate. 2. Bastardy.

il·le·git·i·mate (ĭl′ĭ-jĭt′ə-mĭt) *adj.* 1. Against the law; illegal. 2. Born to unmarried parents. 3. Improper; unfair. 4. Incorrectly deduced. —**il·le·git·i·mate·ly** *adv.*

ill-fat·ed (ĭl′fā′tĭd) *adj.* 1. Destined for misfortune; doomed. 2. Marked by or causing misfortune; unlucky.

ill-fa·vored (ĭl′fā′vərd) *adj.* 1. Having an ugly or unattractive face. 2. Objectionable; offensive. —**ill-fa·vored·ly** *adv.* —**ill-fa·vored·ness** *n.*

ill feeling *n.* Feelings of animosity or rancor.

ill-found·ed (ĭl′foun′dĭd) *adj.* Having no factual basis.

ill-got·ten (ĭl′gŏt′n) *adj.* Obtained in an evil manner or by dishonest means. Used chiefly in the phrase *ill-gotten gains.*

ill humor *n.* An irritable state of mind; surliness.

ill-hu·mored (ĭl′hyōō′mərd) *adj.* Irritable and surly. —**ill-hu·mored·ly** *adv.* —**ill-hu·mored·ness** *n.*

ill-judged (ĭl′jŭjd′) *adj.* Unwise; foolish.

il·lib·er·al (ĭ-lĭb′ər-əl) *adj.* 1. Narrow-minded; bigoted. 2. Ungenerous, mean, or stingy. 3. *Archaic.* a. Lacking liberal culture. b. Ill-bred; ungentlemanly; vulgar. [Latin *illīberalis* : *in-,* not + *līberalis,* LIBERAL.] —**il·lib·er·al·i·ty** (ĭ-lĭb′ə-răl′ə-tē), **il·lib·er·al·ness** *n.* —**il·lib·er·al·ly** *adv.*

il·lic·it (ĭ-lĭs′ĭt) *adj.* Not sanctioned by custom or law; illegal; unlawful. —See Usage note at **elicit.** [Latin *illicitus,* not allowed : *in-,* not + *licitus,* LICIT.] —**il·lic·it·ly** *adv.* —**il·lic·it·ness** *n.*

il·lim·it·a·ble (ĭ-lĭm′ĭ-tə-bəl) *adj.* Incapable of being limited or circumscribed; limitless. —See Synonyms at **infinite.** —**il·lim·it·a·bil·i·ty** (ĭ-lĭm′ĭ-tə-bĭl′ə-tē), **il·lim·it·a·ble·ness** *n.* —**il·lim·it·a·bly** *adv.*

Il·li·noi·an (ĭl′ə-noi′ən) *adj.* Of or pertaining to the third glacial stage in North America. [After the state of *Illinois.*]

Il·li·nois¹ (ĭl′ə-noi′, -noiz′) State in the north-central United States. The capital is Springfield; the largest city is Chicago. Its fertile prairies make it a leading agricultural state. It also has rich mineral reserves and is a leading producer of coal and fluorspar. —**Il·li·nois·an** (ĭl′ə-noi′ən) *n. & adj.*

Illinois². River, 439 kilometers (273 miles) long, formed by the confluence of the Des Plaines and Kankakee rivers in northeastern Illinois and flowing southwest to the Mississippi. It is an important commercial waterway.

Illinois³ *n., pl.* **Illinois.** 1. A member of a confederacy of Algonquian-speaking Indian peoples that inhabited Illinois and parts of Iowa, Wisconsin, and Missouri. 2. The Algonquian language of the Illinois and Miami peoples.

il·liq·uid (ĭ-lĭk′wĭd) *adj.* 1. Incapable of being readily converted into cash: *illiquid assets.* 2. Lacking in cash or liquid assets: *not bankrupt but just illiquid.* [IN-, not + LIQUID.] —**il·li·quid·i·ty** (ĭl′ĭ-kwĭd′ə-tē) *n.*

il·lit·er·ate (ĭ-lĭt′ər-ĭt) *adj.* 1. Unable to read or write. 2. a. Marked by inferiority to an expected standard of familiarity with language and literature. b. Violating prescribed standards of speech or writing. 3. Ignorant of the fundamentals of a specified art or branch of knowledge: *musically illiterate.*

iguana The iguanas are one of the biggest families of lizards, with some 700 species. They occur mainly in tropical America and many, like this common iguana, live in trees.

~n. One who is illiterate. [Latin *illiterātus* : *in-*, not + *literātus*, LITERATE.] —**il·lit·er·a·cy** (ĭ-lĭt′ər-ə-sē) n. —**il·lit·er·ate·ly** adv. —**il·lit·er·ate·ness** n.

ill-man·nered (ĭl′măn′ərd) adj. Lacking or indicating a lack of good manners; impolite; rude. —**ill-man·nered·ly** adv.

ill nature n. A disagreeable, irritable, or malevolent disposition.

ill-na·tured (ĭl′nā′chərd) adj. Disagreeable; surly. —**ill-na·tured·ly** adv. —**ill-na·tured·ness** n.

ill·ness (ĭl′nĭs) n. 1. a. Sickness of body or mind. b. A sickness; a disease. 2. Obsolete. Evil; wickedness.

il·log·ic (ĭ-lŏj′ĭk) n. The lack of logic.

il·log·i·cal (ĭ-lŏj′ĭ-kəl) adj. 1. Contradicting or disregarding the principles of logic. 2. Without logic; senseless. —**il·log·i·cal·i·ty** (ĭ-lŏj′ĭ-kăl′ə-tē), **il·log·i·cal·ness** n. —**il·log·i·cal·ly** adv.

ill-o·mened (ĭl′ō′mənd) adj. Marked by bad omens.

ill-sort·ed (ĭl′sôr′tĭd) adj. Badly matched; ill-assorted.

ill-starred (ĭl′stärd′) adj. Ill-fated; unlucky.

ill-tem·pered (ĭl′tĕm′pərd) adj. 1. Having a bad temper; irritable. 2. Archaic. Out of sorts; unwell. —**ill-tem·pered·ly** adv.

ill-timed (ĭl′tīmd′) adj. Done or occurring at an inappropriate time; untimely.

ill-treat (ĭl′trēt′) tr.v. **-treated, -treating, -treats.** To maltreat. —See Synonyms at **abuse.** —**ill-treat·ment** n.

il·lude (ĭ-lōōd′) tr.v. **-luded, -luding, -ludes.** To deceive; trick. [Latin *illūdere*, to trick, sport with, from *lūdus*, game.]

il·lume (ĭ-lōōm′) tr.v. **-lumed, -luming, -lumes.** Poetic. To illuminate. [Shortened from ILLUMINE.]

il·lu·min·ance (ĭ-lōō′mə-nəns) n. Physics. See **illumination** (sense 8).

il·lu·mi·nant (ĭ-lōō′mə-nənt) n. Something that gives off or provides light.

il·lu·mi·nate (ĭ-lōō′mə-nāt′) v. **-nated, -nating, -nates.** —tr. 1. To provide with light; turn or focus light upon. 2. To decorate or hang with lights. 3. To make understandable; clarify. 4. To enable to understand; enlighten. 5. Literary. To endow with fame or splendor; celebrate. 6. To adorn (a text, page, or initial letter) with ornamental designs, miniatures, or lettering in brilliant colors or precious metals. —intr. To become lighted; glow. ~n. (ĭ-lōō′mə-nĭt). One who has or professes to have an unusual degree of enlightenment. [Latin *illūmināre* : *in-*, in + *lūmināre*, to light up, from *lūmen*, light.]

il·lu·mi·na·ti (ĭ-lōō′mə-nä′tē) pl.n. 1. Persons claiming to be unusually enlightened with regard to some subject. 2. **Illuminati. a.** The members of a secret society of freethinkers and republicans that flourished in Germany during the late 18th century. Also called "Illuminaten." **b.** Persons regarded as atheists, libertines, or radical republicans during the 18th century (such as the French Encyclopedists, the Freemasons, or the freethinkers). 3. **Illuminati.** The members of a heretical sect of 16th-century Spain, who claimed special religious enlightenment. [Latin *illūmināti*, "enlightened ones," plural of *illūminātus*, past participle of *illūmināre*, ILLUMINATE.]

il·lu·mi·na·tion (ĭ-lōō′mə-nā′shən) n. 1. The act of illuminating. 2. The state of being illuminated. 3. A light source. 4. Often **illuminations.** Lights used as decoration. 5. Spiritual or intellectual enlightenment. 6. Clarification; elucidation. 7. a. The art or act of decorating a text, page, or initial letter with ornamental designs, miniatures, or lettering. b. An example of this art. 8. Physics. The luminous flux per unit area at any point on a surface exposed to incident light.

il·lu·mi·na·tive (ĭ-lōō′mə-nā′tĭv) adj. Causing or able to cause illumination.

il·lu·mi·na·tor (ĭ-lōō′mə-nā′tər) n. 1. One that illuminates. 2. A device for producing, concentrating, or reflecting light. 3. A person who illuminates manuscripts, texts, or the like.

il·lu·mine (ĭ-lōō′mĭn) v. **-mined, -mining, -mines.** —tr. To illuminate; give light to. —intr. To be or become illuminated. [Middle English *illuminen*, from Latin *illūmināre*, to ILLUMINATE.] —**il·lu·mi·na·ble** adj.

il·lu·mi·nism (ĭ-lōō′mə-nĭz′əm) n. 1. Belief in or proclamation of a special personal enlightenment. 2. **Illuminism.** The ideas and principles of various groups of illuminati. [ILLUMIN(ATI) + -ISM.] —**il·lu·mi·nist** n.

illus. illustrated; illustration; illustrator.

ill-use (ĭl′yōōz′) tr.v. **-used, -using, -uses.** To maltreat. ~n. (ĭl′yōōs′). Also **ill-us·age** (ĭl′yōō′sĭj). Bad or unjust treatment.

il·lu·sion (ĭ-lōō′zhən) n. 1. a. An erroneous perception of reality. b. An erroneous concept, belief, or ideal. c. Loosely, a delusion. 2. The condition of being deceived by erroneous perceptions or beliefs. 3. Something that causes an erroneous belief or perception. 4. Art. Illusionism. 5. A fine transparent silk or tulle, used for dresses or trimmings. 6. A conjuring trick. —See Usage note at **delusion.** [Middle English *illusioun*, from Old French *illusion*, from Late Latin *illūsiō* (stem *illūsiōn-*), from Latin, a mocking, jeering, from *illūdere* (past participle *illūsus*), to mock, jeer at : *in-*, against + *lūdere*, to play, from *lūdus*, game.] —**il·lu·sion·al, il·lu·sion·ar·y** (ĭ-lōō′zhə-nĕr′ē) adj.

il·lu·sion·ism (ĭ-lōō′zhə-nĭz′əm) n. 1. The doctrine that the material world is an immaterial product of the senses. 2. The use of illusionary techniques and devices in art or decoration. —**il·lu·sion·is·tic** (ĭ-lōō′zhə-nĭs′tĭk) adj.

il·lu·sion·ist (ĭ-lōō′zhə-nĭst) n. 1. An adherent of the doctrine of illusionism. 2. A conjuror or ventriloquist. 3. An artist whose work is marked by illusionism.

il·lu·sive (ĭ-lōō′sĭv) adj. Of, pertaining to, or of the nature of an illusion; lacking reality; illusory. [From ILLUSION.] —**il·lu·sive·ly** adv. —**il·lu·sive·ness** n.

il·lu·so·ry (ĭ-lōō′sə-rē, -zə-rē) adj. Tending to deceive; of the nature of an illusion; illusive.

il·lus·trate (ĭl′ə-strāt′, ĭ-lŭs′trāt′) v. **-trated, -trating, -trates.** —tr. 1. a. To clarify by use of examples, comparisons, or the like. b. To clarify by serving as an example, comparison, or the like. 2. To provide (a publication) with explanatory or decorative pictures, photographs, diagrams, or the like. 3. Obsolete. To illuminate. —intr. To present a clarification, example, or explanation. [Latin *illūstrāre* : *in-*, in + *lūstrāre*, to make bright, enlighten.] —**il·lus·tra·tor** n.

il·lus·tra·tion (ĭl′ə-strā′shən) n. Abbr. **ill., illus.** 1. a. The action of clarifying or explaining. b. The state of being clarified or explained. 2. Material used to clarify or explain. 3. a. A picture, photograph, or diagram used to clarify or to decorate a text. b. Such visual matter collectively: *a book lacking illustration.* 4. Obsolete. Illumination. —See Synonyms at **example.**

il·lus·tra·tive (ĭ-lŭs′trə-tĭv, ĭl′ə-strā′tĭv) adj. Acting as an illustration. —**il·lus·tra·tive·ly** adv.

il·lus·tri·ous (ĭ-lŭs′trē-əs) adj. Renowned; famous; celebrated. [Latin *illūstris*, shining, clear, probably back-formation from *illūstrāre*, ILLUSTRATE.] —**il·lus·tri·ous·ly** adv. —**il·lus·tri·ous·ness** n.

il·lu·vi·a·tion (ĭ-lōō′vē-ā′shən) n. The deposition in an underlying soil layer of colloids, soluble salts, and mineral particles leached out of an overlying soil layer. [IN- (in) + (AL)LUVI(UM) + -ATION.] —**il·lu·vi·al** (ĭ-lōō′vē-əl) adj.

ill will n. Unfriendly feeling; hostility; enmity.

il·ly (ĭl′lē) adv. Rare. Badly; ill.

Il·lyr·i·a (ĭ-lĭr′ē-ə). Latin **Il·lyr·i·cum** (-ĭ-kəm). Ancient region of the Balkan Peninsula, of vague extent. The name is most commonly used for the region extending from the Adriatic coast of northern Albania to the Dinaric Alps.

Il·lyr·i·an (ĭ-lĭr′ē-ən) n. 1. A member of a people inhabiting Illyria. 2. The Indo-European language of the Illyrians. ~adj. Of, pertaining to, or characteristic of the Illyrians or their language.

il·men·ite (ĭl′mə-nīt′) n. A lustrous black-to-brownish titanium ore, essentially a mixed ferrous and titanium oxide, $FeO·TiO_2$. [German *Ilmenit*; first found in *Ilmen*, range in the Ural Mountains.]

ILO International Labor Organization.

I·lo·ca·no (ē′lō-kä′nō) n., pl. **-nos** or collectively **Ilocano.** Also **I·lo·ka·no.** 1. A member of a people inhabiting northwestern Luzon in the Philippines. 2. The Austronesian language of these people. ~adj. Of, pertaining to, or characteristic of the Ilocano or their language. [Spanish, from *iloko*, native name in the Philippines.]

I.L.P. Independent Labour Party (in Great Britain).

ILS Aeronautics. instrument landing system.

ILTF, I.L.T.F. International Lawn Tennis Federation.

im-. Variant of IN-.

I.M. 1. intramuscular. 2. International Master (in chess).

I'm (īm). Contraction of *I am.*

im·age (ĭm′ĭj) n. 1. A reproduction of the appearance of someone or something; especially, a sculptured likeness. 2. A duplicate, counterpart, or other representative reproduction of an object, such as: a. An optical reproduction formed by a lens or mirror. b. A photographic reproduction, either visible or undeveloped (*latent image*). c. A reproduction of a picture on a television screen. 3. One that closely resembles another; a double: *He is the image of his uncle.* 4. a. The opinion or concept of someone or something that is held by the public. b. The character projected by someone or something to the public, especially by the mass media. 5. A personification of something specified: *He is the image of health.* 6. A mental picture of something not real or present. 7. a. A comparison or metaphor: *Plato's image of the cave.* b. A figure, usually recurrent, in art or literature that has a symbolic value: *the image of the Fool in Shakespeare.* 8. Mathematics. The function of a specific variable or the value of the function for a specific value of the variable. 9. Obsolete. An apparition. 10. Computer Science. An exact duplication of data in a file onto another medium. ~tr.v. **imaged, -aging, -ages.** 1. To make or produce a likeness of; copy or portray. 2. To mirror or reflect. 3. To symbolize or typify. 4. To picture mentally; imagine or recall. 5. To describe, especially so as to call up a mental picture. [Middle English, from Old French, from Latin *imāgō*; akin to *imitārī*, IMITATE.]

image converter n. A device for converting invisible electromagnetic radiation, such as infrared or ultraviolet radiation, into a visible optical image. Also called "image tube."

image intensifier n. A device for increasing the intensity of a faint optical image, generally using photoemission of electrons from a cathode and acceleration of these electrons onto a screen.

im·age-ma·ker (ĭm′ĭj-mā′kər) n. Informal. One who employs skillful publicity and advertising to create a favorable public image of a person or organization. —**im·age-ma·king** n.

image orthicon n. An orthicon (see).

im·age·ry (ĭm′ĭj-rē) n., pl. **-ries.** 1. The production of mental pictures or images. 2. a. The employment of comparisons or vivid descriptions in writing or speaking to produce mental images. b. Any metaphorical representation, as in literature or art. 3. a. Representative images, particularly statues or icons. b. The art of making such images. [Middle English *imagerie*, from Old French, from *image*, IMAGE.]

im·ag·i·na·ble (ĭ-măj′ə-nə-bəl) adj. Capable of being conceived of by the imagination: *chose the worst time imaginable for a vacation.* **—im·ag·i·na·bly** *adv.*

im·ag·i·nal (ĭ-măʹgə-nəl, ĭ-mäʹ-) *adj.* Of or relating to an imago. [New Latin *imago* (stem *imagin-*), IMAGO.]

im·ag·i·nar·y (ĭ-măjʹə-nĕrʹē) *adj.* **1.** Having existence only in the imagination; unreal. **2.** *Mathematics.* **a.** Of, pertaining to, or being the coefficient of the imaginary unit in a complex number. **b.** Of, pertaining to, involving, or being an imaginary number. **c.** Involving only a complex number of which the real part is zero.
~*n., pl.* **imaginaries.** *Mathematics.* An imaginary number. **—im·ag·i·nar·i·ly** *adv.* **—im·ag·i·nar·i·ness** *n.*

imaginary number *n.* A **complex number** *(see)* in which the real part is zero and the coefficient of the imaginary unit is not zero. Also called "imaginary."

imaginary unit *n. Symbol* **i** The square root of −1.

im·ag·i·na·tion (ĭ-măjʹə-nāʹshən) *n.* **1. a.** The formation of a mental image or concept of that which is not real or present. **b.** A mental image or idea. **2.** The ability or tendency to form such mental images or concepts. **3. a.** The mental faculty permitting visionary and creative thought. **b.** Visionary and creative thought. **4.** *Archaic.* **a.** An unrealistic idea or notion; a fancy. **b.** A plan or scheme. **—im·ag·i·na·tion·al** *adj.*

im·ag·i·na·tive (ĭ-măjʹə-nə-tĭv, -nāʹtĭv) *adj.* **1.** Having a strong imagination, especially a creative imagination. **2.** Tending to indulge in the fanciful or in make-believe. **3.** Created by, indicative of, or characterized by imagination or creativity. **—im·ag·i·na·tive·ly** *adv.* **—im·ag·i·na·tive·ness** *n.*

im·ag·ine (ĭ-măjʹən) *v.* **-ined, -ining, -ines.** *—tr.* **1.** To form a mental picture or image of; create in the mind. **2.** To suppose; conjecture. **3.** To believe (something that has no basis in reality): *imagines himself to be an artist.* *—intr.* **1.** To employ the imagination. **2.** To make a guess; conjecture. [Middle English *imaginen,* from Old French *imaginer,* from Latin *imāginārī,* to picture to oneself, from *imāgō,* IMAGE.] **—im·ag·in·er** *n.*

im·a·gism (ĭmʹə-jĭzʹəm) *n.* A literary movement among British and U.S. poets, launched about 1912, to promote free verse and precise imagery. **—im·a·gist** *n.* **—im·a·gis·tic** (ĭmʹə-jĭsʹtĭk) *adj.*

i·ma·go (ĭ-māʹgō) *n., pl.* **-goes** or **imagines** (ĭ-măjʹə-nēzʹ). **1.** An insect in its sexually mature adult stage after metamorphosis. **2.** *Psychoanalysis.* An often idealized image of a person, usually a parent, formed in childhood and persisting into adulthood. [New Latin, from Latin *imāgō,* IMAGE.]

i·mam (ĭ-mämʹ) *n.* Also **i·maum** (ĭ-mämʹ, ĭ-mômʹ). **1.** A prayer leader of Islam. **2.** A Muslim scholar; especially, an authority on Islamic law. **3. Imam. a.** A title accorded to Muhammad and his four immediate successors. **b.** Any of the leaders regarded by the Shiites as successors of Muhammad. **c.** Any of various religious and temporal leaders claiming descent from Muhammad. [Arabic *imām,* leader, from *amma,* he led.]

i·mam·ate (ĭ-mäʹmātʹ) *n.* **1.** The office of an imam. **2.** A country governed by an imam.

i·ma·ret (ĭ-mäʹrĕt) *n.* An inn or hostel for pilgrims in Turkey. [Turkish, from Arabic *imārah,* hospice, "cultivated land," from *amara,* he built.]

im·bal·ance (ĭm-bălʹəns) *n.* A lack of balance or proportion.

im·be·cile (ĭmʹbə-sĭl, -səl) *n.* **1.** A feeble-minded person. **2.** A dolt. **3.** A person affected by imbecility. No longer in technical usage.
~*adj.* Also **im·be·cil·ic** (ĭmʹbə-sĭlʹĭk). **1.** Deficient in mental ability. **2.** Stupid. [Old French *imbecille,* from Latin *imbēcillus,* "without support," feeble : *in-,* not + *bacillum,* diminutive of *baculum,* staff, rod.] **—im·be·cile·ly** *adv.*

im·be·cil·i·ty (ĭmʹbə-sĭlʹə-tē) *n.* A condition of moderate to severe subnormal intellectual development, characterized by an intelligence quotient in the upper range of idiocy. No longer in technical usage. Compare **idiocy.**

imbed. Variant of **embed.**

im·bibe (ĭm-bībʹ) *v.* **-bibed, -bibing, -bibes.** *—tr.* **1.** To drink (especially alcoholic drink). **2.** To absorb or take in as if by drinking: *"the whole body . . . imbibes delight through every pore"* (Thoreau). **3.** To receive and absorb into the mind. **4.** *Obsolete.* To permeate; saturate. *—intr.* To drink. [Middle English *enbiben,* to absorb, from Old French *embiber,* from Latin *imbibere,* to drink in : *in-,* in + *bibere,* to drink.] **—im·bib·er** *n.*

im·bi·bi·tion (ĭmʹbĭ-bĭshʹən) *n.* **1.** *Chemistry.* The absorption or adsorption of a liquid by a solid or a gel. **2.** In photography, the absorption of a dye by gelatin. **3.** *Rare.* The act of imbibing. [IMBIBE + -TION.]

im·bri·cate (ĭmʹbrĭ-kātʹ, -kĭt) *adj.* **1.** Having the edges overlapping in a regular pattern, as tiles on a roof, the scales of a fish, or bracts or sepals of a plant. **2.** Covered or ornamented with a pattern or design of overlapping parts or edges.
~*v.* (ĭmʹbrĭ-kātʹ) **imbricated, -cating, -cates.** *—tr.* To overlap in a regular pattern. *—intr.* To be arranged with regular overlapping edges. [Latin *imbricātus,* past participle of *imbricāre,* to cover with roof tiles, from *imbrex* (stem *imbric-*), roof tile, from *imber* (stem *imbr-*), rain.]

im·bri·ca·tion (ĭmʹbrĭ-kāʹshən) *n.* **1.** A regular overlapping of edges. **2.** A pattern or design having such overlapping.

im·bro·gli·o (ĭm-brōlʹyō) *n., pl.* **-glios. 1.** A confused or difficult situation; a predicament; an entanglement. **2.** *Rare.* A confused heap; a tangle. [Italian *imbroglio* : probably *in-,* in + *broglio,* grove, bush, from Old French *breuil,* from Late Latin *brogilus,* from Gaulish *brogilos* (unattested), from *brogos, broga*†, field.]

im·brue (ĭm-brōōʹ) *tr.v.* **-brued, -bruing, -brues.** Also **em·brue** (ĕm-). *Rare.* **1.** To stain or dye. Used of blood. **2.** To soak or saturate. [Middle English *enbrewen, enbrowen,* from Old French *embruer, embrouer,* to soak : *en-,* in + *breu,* broth, from Germanic.]

im·brute (ĭm-brōōtʹ) *v.* **-bruted, -bruting, -brutes.** *Rare.* *—tr.* To cause to become brutal. *—intr.* To become brutal.

im·bue (ĭm-byōōʹ) *tr.v.* **-bued, -buing, -bues. 1.** To inspire, permeate, or pervade. **2.** To make thoroughly wet; saturate, as with stain or dye. [Latin *imbuere,* to moisten, stain.]

IMF, I.M.F. International Monetary Fund.

Im·ho·tep (ĭm-hōʹtĕp) (*fl. c.* 2650 B.C.). Egyptian architect, astrologer, physician, and chief minister to Pharoah Djoser (*c.* 2686–2613 B.C.). He is thought to have designed the first pyramid at Saqqara.

im·id·az·ole (ĭmʹĭd-ăzʹōl, -ə-zōlʹ) *n.* Any of a group of heterocyclic nitrogen compounds, especially the white crystalline base, $C_3H_4N_2$; 1,3-diazole. Also called "glyoxaline." [IMID(E) + AZOLE.]

im·ide (ĭmʹĭdʹ, -ĭd) *n.* A compound derived from ammonia containing the divalent group —CO·NH·CO— combined with two other radicals. [Alteration of AMIDE.]

im·ine (ĭ-mēnʹ, ĭmʹĭn) *n.* A compound derived from ammonia containing the divalent NH group combined with alkyl or other radicals. [Alteration of AMINE.]

im·i·no acid (ĭ-mēʹnō) *n.* An organic compound, such as proline or hydroxyproline, similar to an amino acid and also a constituent of proteins, but containing an imino group (–NH) rather than an amino group (C–NH_2).

i·mip·ra·mine (ĭ-mĭpʹrə-mēnʹ, ĭmʹə-prăʹmēn) *n.* A water-soluble compound, $C_{19}H_{24}N_2$, used medically as an antidepressant. [IM(IDE) + PR(OPYL) + AMINE.]

im·i·tate (ĭmʹə-tātʹ) *tr.v.* **-tated, -tating, -tates. 1.** To model oneself on the behavior or actions of. **2. a.** To copy the appearance, mannerisms, or speech of; mimic. **b.** To copy the literary, artistic, or musical style of. **3.** To copy; reproduce. **4.** To resemble. [Latin *imitārī*† (past participle *imitātus*).] **—im·i·ta·tor** *n.*
Synonyms: *ape, copy, mimic, parody, simulate.*

im·i·ta·tion (ĭmʹə-tāʹshən) *n.* **1.** An act of imitating. **2.** Something derived or copied from an original. **3.** *Music.* The repetition of a phrase or sequence often with variations in key, rhythm, and voice. **—im·i·ta·tion·al** *adj.*

im·i·ta·tive (ĭmʹə-tāʹtĭv) *adj.* **1.** Of or involving imitation. **2.** Not original; derivative; copied. **3.** Tending to imitate. **4.** Onomatopoeic. **—im·i·ta·tive·ly** *adv.* **—im·i·ta·tive·ness** *n.*

im·mac·u·la·cy (ĭ-măkʹyə-lə-sē) *n.* The quality or condition of being immaculate; immaculateness.

im·mac·u·late (ĭ-măkʹyə-lĭt) *adj.* **1.** Free from stain or blemish; spotless; pure. **2.** Free from fault or error. **3.** Impeccably clean. **4.** Having no markings or spots. Said of plants and animals. [Middle English *immaculat,* from Latin *immaculātus* : *in-,* not + *maculātus,* past participle of *maculāre,* to stain, blemish, from *macula,* spot.] **—im·mac·u·late·ly** *adv.* **—im·mac·u·late·ness** *n.*

Immaculate Conception *n.* **1.** The Roman Catholic doctrine that the Virgin Mary was conceived in her mother's womb free from all stain of original sin. Compare **virgin birth. 2.** The day, December 8, on which this is celebrated.

im·ma·nent (ĭmʹə-nənt) *adj.* **1.** Existing or remaining within; inherent. **2.** Restricted entirely to the mind; subjective. Compare **transeunt. 3.** Present throughout the universe. Said of God. Compare **transcendent.** [Late Latin *immanēns* (stem *immanent-*), present participle of *immanēre,* to remain in : Latin *in-,* in + *manēre,* to remain.] **—im·ma·nence** *n.* **—im·ma·nent·ly** *adv.*

im·ma·nent·ism (ĭmʹə-nən-tĭzʹəm) *n.* Any of various religious theories postulating that a deity or abstract spirit is immanent in the world.

Im·man·u·el, Em·man·u·el (ĭ-mănʹyōō-əl) *n.* **1.** The child whose birth was prophesied by Isaiah, as a sign that Judah would not be destroyed. Isaiah 7:14. **2.** A name applied to Jesus. Matthew 1:23. [Hebrew, "God with us."]

im·ma·te·ri·al (ĭmʹə-tîrʹē-əl) *adj.* **1.** Having no material body or form. **2.** Of no importance or relevance; inconsequential. **—im·ma·te·ri·al·ly** *adv.* **—im·ma·te·ri·al·ness** *n.*

im·ma·te·ri·al·ism (ĭmʹə-tîrʹē-ə-lĭzʹəm) *n.* A metaphysical doctrine asserting that things only have an existence through perception by the mind. **—im·ma·te·ri·al·ist** *n.*

im·ma·te·ri·al·i·ty (ĭmʹə-tîrʹē-ălʹə-tē) *n., pl.* **-ties. 1.** The state or quality of being immaterial. **2.** Something immaterial.

im·ma·te·ri·al·ize (ĭmʹə-tîr-ē-ə-līzʹ) *tr.v.* **-ized, -izing, -izes.** To render immaterial.

im·ma·ture (ĭmʹə-tyŏŏrʹ, -tŏŏrʹ, -chŏŏrʹ) *adj.* **1.** Not fully grown or developed. **2.** Behaving with less than normal maturity. **3.** Not having a chance to achieve a mature state due to constant erosion. Said of soils. **4.** *Informal.* Childish; silly. [Latin *immātūrus* : *in-,* not + *mātūrus,* MATURE.] **—im·ma·ture·ly** *adv.* **—im·ma·tur·i·ty** (ĭmʹə-tyŏŏrʹə-tē), **im·ma·ture·ness** *n.*

im·meas·ur·a·ble (ĭ-mĕzhʹər-ə-bəl) *adj.* **1.** Incapable of being measured. **2.** Vast; limitless. **—im·meas·ur·a·bil·i·ty** (ĭ-mĕzhʹər-ə-bĭlʹə-tē), **im·meas·ur·a·ble·ness** *n.* **—im·meas·ur·a·bly** *adv.*

im·me·di·a·cy (ĭ-mēʹdē-ə-sē) *n., pl.* **-cies. 1.** The condition or quality of being immediate; directness. **2.** Something immediate. **3.** Immediate or direct perception; intuitiveness. **4.** *Philosophy.* Direct consciousness as opposed to that involving an intermediary such as memory.

im·me·di·ate (ĭ-mēʹdē-ĭt) *adj.* **1.** Acting or occurring without mediation or interposition; direct: *immediate consequence.* **2.** Directly ap-

imbricate *An imbricated, or overlapping, clay tile wall in Sussex, England.*

prehended or perceived; intuitive: *immediate awareness.* **3.** Next in line or relation: *the immediate successor.* **4.** Occurring without delay: *an immediate response.* **5.** Of or near the present time: *the immediate future.* **6.** Close at hand; near: *the immediate vicinity.* **7.** Of direct concern or importance. [Late Latin *immediātus* : Latin *in-*, not + *mediātus*, past participle of *mediāre*, to be in the middle, MEDIATE.] —**im·me·di·ate·ness** *n.*

immediate constituent *n. Linguistics. Abbr.* **I.C.** Any of the main grammatical divisions into which a word, phrase, or sentence can be most immediately divided; for example, the immediate constituents of *the watch has stopped* are *the watch* and *has stopped.*

im·me·di·ate·ly (ĭ-mē′dē-ĭt-lē) *adv.* **1.** Without intermediary; directly. **2.** Without delay. **3.** Nearby.
~*conj.* As soon as; directly.
    Usage: immediately, instantly, forthwith, directly, promptly, presently. These adverbs mean with little or no delay. They are arranged in approximate order of intensity. *Immediately* and *instantly* imply no delay whatever, as between request and response. *Forthwith, directly,* and *promptly* all stress readiness of response but with a brief interval prior to fulfillment of the action involved. *Presently* has the mere force of soon.

im·med·i·ca·ble (ĭ-mĕd′ĭ-kə-bəl) *adj.* Incurable.

Im·mel·mann turn (ĭm′əl-mən, -män′) *n.* A maneuver in which an airplane first completes half a loop then half a roll in order to gain altitude and change direction in flight simultaneously. [After Max Immelmann (1890–1916), German pilot.]

im·me·mo·ri·al (ĭm′ə-môr′ē-əl, -mōr′ē-əl) *adj.* Reaching beyond the limits of memory, tradition, or recorded history. Used chiefly in the phrase *from time immemorial.* [Medieval Latin *immemoriālis* : Latin *in-*, not + *memoriālis*, memorial, from *memoria*, MEMORY.] —**im·me·mo·ri·al·ly** *adv.*

im·mense (ĭ-mĕns′) *adj.* **1.** Extremely large; huge. **2.** Boundless. **3.** *Informal.* Very great: *immense pleasure.* —See Synonyms at **enormous.** [Old French, from Latin *immēnsus*, immeasurable : *in-*, not + *mēnsus*, past participle of *mētīrī*, to measure.] —**im·mense·ly** *adv.* —**im·mense·ness** *n.*

im·men·si·ty (ĭ-mĕn′sə-tē) *n., pl.* **-ties. 1.** The quality or state of being immense. **2.** Something immense. **3.** *Informal.* A very large amount.

im·men·sur·a·ble (ĭ-mĕn′shər-ə-bəl) *adj. Rare.* Immeasurable.

im·merge (ĭ-mûrj′) *v.* **-merged, -merging, -merges.** *Archaic.* —*tr.* To immerse. —*intr.* To submerge or disappear in or as if in a liquid. [Latin *immergere,* IMMERSE.] —**im·mer·gence** *n.*

im·merse (ĭ-mûrs′) *tr.v.* **-mersed, -mersing, -merses. 1.** To cover completely in a liquid; submerge. Used with *in.* **2.** To baptize by submerging in water. **3.** To involve profoundly; absorb. Used with *in: a scholar immersed in the past.* [Latin *immergere* (past participle *immersus*), to dip in : *in-*, in + *mergere,* to dip.]

im·mer·sion (ĭ-mûr′zhən, -shən) *n.* **1.** An act of immersing. **2.** The condition of being immersed. **3.** Baptism performed by totally submerging a person in water. **4.** Absorption: *her total immersion in politics.* **5.** *Astronomy.* The obscuring of a celestial body by another or by the shadow of another, as in an eclipse or occultation. Also called "ingress."

immesh. Variant of **enmesh.**

im·me·thod·i·cal (ĭm′ə-thŏd′ĭ-kəl) *adj.* Not methodical. —**im·me·thod·i·cal·ly** *adv.*

im·mi·grant (ĭm′ĭ-grənt) *n.* **1.** One who enters a country to settle permanently. Compare **emigrant. 2.** An organism living or growing in a place to which it has recently migrated. —**im·mi·grant** *adj.*

im·mi·grate (ĭm′ĭ-grāt′) *v.* **-grated, -grating, -grates.** —*intr.* To enter and settle in a country or region of which one is not a native. —*tr.* To bring in or introduce as immigrants. —See Usage note at **migrate.** [Latin *immigrāre,* to remove into, go in : *in-*, in + *migrāre,* to remove, MIGRATE.]

im·mi·gra·tion (ĭm′ĭ-grā′shən) *n.* **1.** The act, process, or an instance of immigrating. **2. a.** The area in a port or airport where passengers arriving from abroad have their passports and visas checked. **b.** The government officials in charge of this process.

im·mi·nence (ĭm′ə-nəns) *n.* Also **im·mi·nen·cy** (-nən-sē) *pl.* **-cies. 1.** The quality or condition of being imminent. **2.** Something imminent.

im·mi·nent (ĭm′ə-nənt) *adj.* **1.** About to occur; impending. **2.** *Archaic.* Jutting out; overhanging. —See Usage note at **eminent.** [Latin *imminēns* (stem *imminent-*), present participle of *imminēre,* to project over or toward, threaten : *in-*, toward + *-minēre,* to project.] —**im·mi·nent·ly** *adv.*

im·min·gle (ĭ-mĭng′gəl) *v.* **-gled, -gling, -gles.** *Archaic.* —*intr.* To intermingle; blend. —*tr.* To blend.

im·mis·ci·ble (ĭ-mĭs′ə-bəl) *adj.* Incapable of mixing or blending. Said of two or more liquids. —**im·mis·ci·bil·i·ty** (ĭ-mĭs′ə-bĭl′ə-tē) *n.* —**im·mis·ci·bly** *adv.*

im·mit·i·ga·ble (ĭ-mĭt′ĭ-gə-bəl) *adj. Rare.* Incapable of being mitigated. —**im·mit·i·ga·bly** *adv.*

im·mit·tance (ĭ-mĭt′əns) *n.* Electrical impedance or admittance. [IM(PEDANCE) + (AD)MITTANCE.]

im·mix (ĭ-mĭks′) *tr.v.* **-mixed, -mixing, -mixes.** *Rare.* To commingle; blend. [Back-formation from Middle English *immixte,* mixed in, from Latin *immixtus,* past participle of *immiscēre,* to mix in : *in-,* in + *miscēre,* to mix.] —**im·mix·ture** (ĭ-mĭks′chər) *n.*

im·mo·bile (ĭ-mō′bəl, -bēl′) *adj.* **1. a.** Unable to move. **b.** Incapable of being moved. **2.** Not moving; motionless. **3.** Not fluid; viscous. Said of liquids. [Middle English *inmobile,* from Latin *immōbilis* :

in-, not + *mōbilis,* MOBILE.] —**im·mo·bil·i·ty** (ĭm′ō-bĭl′ə-tē) *n.*

im·mo·bil·ism (ĭ-mō′bə-lĭz′əm) *n.* A highly reactionary political stance. —**im·mo·bi·list** *n. & adj.*

im·mo·bi·lize (ĭ-mō′bə-līz′) *tr.v.* **-lized, -lizing, -lizes. 1.** To render immobile. **2.** To impede movement or use of: *immobilize troops.* **3.** *Medicine.* To fix (a broken limb, for example) so that no movement is possible. **4. a.** *Finance.* To withdraw (specie) from circulation and reserve as security for other money. **b.** To convert (floating capital) into fixed capital. —**im·mo·bi·li·za·tion** (ĭ-mō′bə-lə-zā′shən) *n.* —**im·mo·bi·liz·er** *n.*

im·mod·er·ate (ĭ-mŏd′ər-ĭt) *adj.* Not moderate; extreme. —See Synonyms at **excessive.** [Middle English *immoderat,* from Latin *immoderātus* : *in-*, not + *moderātus,* MODERATE.] —**im·mod·er·ate·ly** *adv.* —**im·mod·er·ate·ness, im·mod·er·a·tion** (ĭ-mŏd′ə-rā′shən) *n.*

im·mod·est (ĭ-mŏd′ĭst) *adj.* **1.** Lacking modesty. **2. a.** Contrary to conventional standards of sexual propriety. **b.** Morally offensive. **3.** Arrogant. [Latin *immodestus* : *in-*, not + *modestus,* MODEST.] —**im·mod·est·ly** *adv.* —**im·mod·es·ty** *n.*

im·mo·late (ĭm′ə-lāt′) *tr.v.* **-lated, -lating, -lates. 1.** To kill as a sacrifice. **2.** To destroy or renounce for the sake of something else. [Latin *immolāre,* to sacrifice, originally "to sprinkle with sacrificial meal" : *in-*, on + *mola,* meal.] —**im·mo·la·tion** (ĭm′ə-lā′shən) *n.* —**im·mo·la·tor** *n.*

im·mor·al (ĭ-môr′əl, ĭ-mŏr′-) *adj.* **1.** Contrary to established morality, especially in sexual matters. **2.** Morally dissolute. **3.** Unethical or unfair. **4.** Tending to corrupt. —**im·mor·al·ly** *adv.*

im·mor·al·ist (ĭ-môr′ə-lĭst, -mŏr′-) *n.* One who advocates immorality.

im·mo·ral·i·ty (ĭm′ô-răl′ə-tē, ĭm′ə-) *n., pl.* **-ties. 1.** The quality or condition of being immoral. **2.** An immoral act. **3.** Immoral behavior; especially, sexual promiscuity.

im·mor·tal (ĭ-môrt′l) *adj.* **1.** Not subject to death. **2.** Having eternal fame; imperishable. **3.** Of or pertaining to immortality.
~*n.* **1.** One not subject to death. **2.** One whose fame is enduring. **3.** *Often* **Immortals.** The gods of ancient Greece and Rome. **4. Immortal.** A member of the French Academy. [Middle English, from Latin *immortālis* : *in-*, not + *mortālis,* MORTAL.] —**im·mor·tal·ly** *adv.*

im·mor·tal·i·ty (ĭm′ôr-tăl′ə-tē) *n.* **1.** The quality or condition of being immortal. **2.** Endless life. **3.** Enduring fame.

im·mor·tal·ize (ĭ-môrt′l-īz′) *tr.v.* **-ized, -izing, -izes. 1.** To make immortal. **2.** To give permanent fame to.

im·mor·telle (ĭ-môr-tĕl′) *n.* Any plant with flowers that retain their color when dried. [French, from the feminine of *immortel,* from Latin *immortālis,* IMMORTAL.]

im·mo·tile (ĭ-mōt′l) *adj.* Not motile. Said of living organisms. —**im·mo·til·i·ty** (ĭm′ō-tĭl′ə-tē) *n.*

im·mov·a·ble, im·move·a·ble (ĭ-mōō′və-bəl) *adj.* **1. a.** Incapable of being moved. **b.** Incapable of movement. **2.** Not capable of alteration. **3.** Unyielding in principle, purpose, or adherence; steadfast. **4.** Showing no sign of emotional stress; unimpressionable. **5.** *Law.* Not liable to be physically removed: *immovable property.* **6.** Occurring on the same date each year. Said of feast days and holidays.
~*n.* **1.** One that is incapable of movement. **2.** *Usually* **immovables.** Immovable property, such as real estate. Compare **movable.** —**im·mov·a·ble·ness, im·mov·a·bil·i·ty** (ĭ-mōō′və-bĭl′ə-tē) *n.* —**im·mov·a·bly** *adv.*

im·mune (ĭ-myōōn′) *adj.* **1.** *Biology.* **a.** Having immunity to infection. **b.** Relating to or conferring immunity. **2. a.** Exempt, as from an obligation or a duty. **b.** Not affected or responsive: *immune to tears.* **3.** Protected from danger. [Latin *immūnis.*] —**im·mune** *n.*
    Usage: In the senses of "exempt" and "protected from," *immune* is followed by *from* (*immune from tax, immune from commercial pressures*). In the senses of "resistant to a disease" and "not affected by or responsive to," *immune* is followed by *to* (*immune to diphtheria, immune to their entreaties*).

im·mu·ni·ty (ĭ-myōō′nə-tē) *n., pl.* **-ties. 1.** The quality or condition of being immune. **2.** An inherited, acquired, or induced resistance to a specific pathogen, especially by the production of antibodies or by inoculation.

im·mu·nize (ĭm′yə-nīz′) *tr.v.* **-nized, -nizing, -nizes.** To render immune. —**im·mu·ni·za·tion** (ĭm′yə-nə-zā′shən) *n.*
    Usage: Immunize is followed by *against* (*to immunize someone against a particular disease*).

immuno– *prefix.* Indicates immune response or immunity; for example, **immunogenetics, immunogenic.** [From IMMUNE.]

im·mu·no·as·say (ĭm′yə-nō-ăs′ā, ĭm-yōō′-) *n.* A method of identifying substances, particularly proteins, by studying the antibodies they induce when injected into an animal.

im·mu·no·chem·is·try (ĭm′yə-nō-kĕm′ĭ-strē) *n.* The chemistry of immunological phenomena, as of antigen stimulation of tissue or of antigen-antibody reactions.

im·mu·no·e·lec·tro·pho·re·sis (ĭm′yə-nō-ĭ-lĕk′trə-fə-rē′sĭs, ĭm-yōō′-) *n.* The separation of antigens by electrophoresis with identification through specific immunological reactions.

im·mu·no·ge·net·ics (ĭm′yə-nō-jə-nĕt′ĭks) *n. Used with a singular verb.* The study of the interrelation between immunity to disease and genetic make-up.

im·mu·no·gen·ic (ĭm′yə-nō-jĕn′ĭk) *adj.* Producing immunity.

im·mu·no·glob·u·lin (ĭm′yə-nō-glŏb′yə-lĭn) *n.* Any one of a group of structurally related proteins that show antibody activity.

im·mu·nol·o·gy (ĭm′yə-nŏl′ə-jē) *n.* The study of immunity to disease. [IMMUNO- + -LOGY.] —**im·mu·no·log·ic** (ĭm′yə-nə-lŏj′ĭk), **im·**

mu·no·log·i·cal *adj.* **—im·mu·no·log·i·cal·ly** *adv.*

im·mu·no·sup·pres·sive (ĭm′yə-nō-sə-prĕs′ĭv) *adj.* Tending to suppress a natural immune response of an organism to an antigen. *~n.* An immunosuppressive drug.

im·mu·no·ther·a·py (ĭm′yə-nō-thĕr′ə-pē, ĭm-yo͞o′-) *n.* **1.** The treatment of disease by use of antigenic preparations. **2.** The treatment of disease or infection by immunosuppressive techniques. **—im·mu·no·ther·a·pist** *n.*

im·mure (ĭ-myo͝or′) *tr.v.* **-mured, -muring, -mures. 1.** To confine within walls; imprison. **2.** To build into a wall; entomb in a wall. **3.** To shut (oneself) away in seclusion. [Medieval Latin *immūrāre* : Latin *in-*, in + *mūrus,* wall.] **—im·mure·ment** *n.*

im·mu·ta·ble (ĭ-myo͞o′tə-bəl) *adj.* Not mutable; not susceptible to change; ageless. [Middle English, from Latin *immūtābilis* : *in-*, not + *mūtābilis,* MUTABLE.] **—im·mu·ta·bil·i·ty** (ĭ-myoo′tə-bĭl′ə-tē), **im·mu·ta·ble·ness** *n.* **—im·mu·ta·bly** *adv.*

imp (ĭmp) *n.* **1.** A mischievous child. **2.** A mischievous elf. **3.** A small or young demon. **4.** *Archaic.* A descendant.
~tr.v. **imped, imping, imps. 1.** To graft (new feathers) onto the wing of a falcon to repair damage or to increase flying capacity. **2.** *Archaic.* To furnish with wings. [Middle English *impe,* scion, offspring, child, Old English *impa,* young shoot, sapling, from *impian,* to graft on, from Common Romance *impotare* (unattested), from Medieval Latin *impotus,* graft, from Greek *emphutos,* implanted, from *emphuein,* to implant : *en-*, in + *phuein,* plant.]

imp. 1. imperative. **2.** imperfect. **3.** imperial. **4.** import; imported; importer. **5.** important. **6.** imprimatur.

Imp. 1. imperator. **2.** imperatrix.

im·pact (ĭm′păkt′) *n.* **1.** The striking of one body against another; a collision. **2.** The effect of one thing upon another. **3.** The influence or force of a person, thing, or idea.
~tr.v. (ĭm-păkt′) **impacted, -pacting, -pacts.** To pack firmly together. [Latin *impactus,* past participle of *impingere,* to dash or strike against, IMPINGE.] **—im·pac·tion** (ĭm-păk′shən) *n.*

im·pact·ed (ĭm-păk′tĭd) *adj.* **1.** Wedged together at the broken ends. Said of a fractured bone. **2. a.** Placed in the alveolus in a manner prohibiting eruption into a normal position. Said of a tooth. **b.** Driven upward into the alveolar process or surrounding tissue. Said of a tooth.

im·pair (ĭm-pâr′) *tr.v.* **-paired, -pairing, -pairs.** To make worse by lessening strength, value, quantity, or quality; damage: *The accident impaired her voice. The storm impaired communications.* —See Synonyms at **injure.** [Middle English *empairen,* from Old French *empeirer,* from Vulgar Latin *impējōrāre* (unattested), to make worse : *in-* (intensive) + Late Latin *pējōrāre,* to make or become worse, from Latin *pējor,* worse.] **—im·pair·ment** *n.*

im·pa·la (ĭm-pä′lə) *n.* An African antelope, *Aepyceros melampus,* having a reddish coat, and ridged, curved horns in the male. [Zulu.]

im·pale, em·pale (ĭm-pāl′) *tr.v.* **-paled, -paling, -pales. 1. a.** To pierce with a sharp stake or point. **b.** To torture or kill by impaling. **2.** To render helpless as if by impaling. **3.** *Heraldry.* To display (arms) on either side of a vertical line on a shield. [Medieval Latin *impālāre* : Latin *in-*, in + *pālus,* stake, pole.] **—im·pale·ment** *n.* **—im·pal·er** *n.*

im·pal·pa·ble (ĭm-păl′pə-bəl) *adj.* **1. a.** Not perceptible to the touch; intangible. **b.** So fine that individual grains cannot be felt. Said of powder. **2.** Not easily perceived or grasped by the mind. **—im·pal·pa·bil·i·ty** (ĭm-păl′pə-bĭl′ə-tē) *n.* **—im·pal·pa·bly** *adv.*

im·pan·el (ĭm-păn′əl) *tr.v.* **-eled, -eling, -els** or *chiefly British* **-elled, -elling.** Also **em·pan·el** (ĕm-). To enroll (a jury) upon a panel or list. **—im·pan·el·ment** *n.*

im·par·i·syl·la·bic (ĭm-păr′ə-sĭ-lăb′ĭk) *adj.* Not having the same number of syllables in all its forms. Said of nouns or verbs in inflected languages.

im·par·i·ty (ĭm-păr′ə-tē) *n., pl.* **-ties.** Inequality; disparity; dissimilarity. [Late Latin *imparitās* (stem *imparitāt-*), from Latin *impār,* not equal : *in-*, not + *pār,* equal.]

im·park (ĭm-pärk′) *tr.v.* **-parked, -parking, -parks. 1.** To confine (deer, for example) in a park. **2.** To enclose (land) for a park. **—im·par·ka·tion** (ĭm-pär-kā′shən) *n.*

im·part (ĭm-pärt′) *tr.v.* **-parted, -parting, -parts. 1.** To grant a share of; bestow. **2.** To make known; disclose. —See Synonyms at **reveal.** [Latin *impartīre,* to cause to share in, share with : *in-*, in + *partīre,* to share, divide, from *pars* (stem *part-*), part, share.] **—im·part·a·ble** *adj.* **—im·part·er** *n.* **—im·part·ment** *n.*

im·par·tial (ĭm-pär′shəl) *adj.* Not partial; unprejudiced; fair. —See Synonyms at **fair. —im·par·ti·al·i·ty** (ĭm-pär′shē-ăl′ə-tē), **im·par·tial·ness** *n.* **—im·par·tial·ly** *adv.*

im·part·i·ble (ĭm-pär′tə-bəl) *adj. Law.* Not partible; indivisible. Said of land. [Late Latin *impartibilis* : Latin *in-*, not + *partībilis,* PARTIBLE.] **—im·part·i·bil·i·ty** (ĭm-pär′tə-bĭl′ə-tē) *n.* **—im·part·i·bly** *adv.*

im·pass·a·ble (ĭm-păs′ə-bəl) *adj.* Unable to be traversed. **—im·pass·a·bil·i·ty** (ĭm-păs′ə-bĭl′ə-tē), **im·pass·a·ble·ness** *n.* **—im·pass·a·bly** *adv.*

im·passe (ĭm′păs′) *n.* **1.** A situation where no further progress can be made; a deadlock. **2.** A road or passage having no exit; a dead end; a cul-de-sac. [French : Old French *in-*, not, in- + *passer,* to PASS.]

im·pas·si·ble (ĭm-păs′ə-bəl) *adj.* **1. a.** Not subject to suffering or pain. **b.** Incapable of being injured: *"The Godhead is impassible."* (Aldous Huxley). **2.** Impassive. [Middle English, from Old French, from Late Latin *impassibilis* : *in-*, not + *passibilis,* PASSIBLE.] **—im·pas·si·bil·i·ty** (ĭm-păs′ə-bĭl′ə-tē), **im·pas·si·ble·ness** *n.* **—im·pas·si·bly** *adv.*

im·pas·sion (ĭm-păsh′ən) *tr.v.* **-sioned, -sioning, -sions.** To arouse the passions of. [Italian *impassionare* : *in-*, in, from Latin + *passione,* passion, from Late Latin *passiō,* PASSION.]

im·pas·sioned (ĭm-păsh′ənd) *adj.* Filled with passion; ardent.

im·pas·sive (ĭm-păs′ĭv) *adj.* **1.** Devoid of or not subject to emotion; apathetic. **2.** Revealing no emotion; expressionless. **3.** Incapable of physical sensation. [IN- (not) + Latin *passīvus,* capable of feeling, PASSIVE.] **—im·pas·sive·ly** *adv.* **—im·pas·sive·ness, im·pas·siv·i·ty** (ĭm′pə-sĭv′ə-tē) *n.*

im·paste (ĭm-pāst′) *tr.v.* **-pasted, -pasting, -pastes. 1.** To make into a paste. **2.** To apply pigment thickly to. [Italian *impastare* : *in-*, in, + *pasta,* PASTE.]

im·pas·to (ĭm-păs′tō, -päs′tō) *n.* **1.** The application of thick layers of pigment. **2.** The layers of pigment thus applied. [Italian, from *impastare,* IMPASTE.]

im·pa·tience (ĭm-pā′shəns) *n.* **1.** The inability to wait patiently. **2.** The inability to endure irritation. **3.** Restive eagerness, desire, or anticipation. [Middle English *impacience,* from Old French *impatience,* from Latin *impatientia,* from *impatiēns* (stem *impatient-*), not patient : *in-*, not + *patiēns,* PATIENT.]

im·pa·ti·ens (ĭm-pā′shəns, -shənz, -shē-ənz) *n.* Any plant of the genus *Impatiens,* which includes the jewelweed. [New Latin *Impatiens,* from Latin *impatiēns,* IMPATIENT (so called because the ripe pods burst open when touched).]

im·pa·tient (ĭm-pā′shənt) *adj.* **1.** Lacking patience, as in enduring delay or imperfection. **2.** Restively eager. **—im·pa·tient·ly** *adv.*

im·peach (ĭm-pēch′) *tr.v.* **-peached, -peaching, -peaches. 1. a.** To accuse of a crime, especially a crime against the state such as treason. **b.** To charge with improper conduct in office before a proper tribunal: *President Andrew Johnson was impeached in the House, but acquitted by the Senate.* **2.** To challenge or discredit; attack. [Middle English *empeachen,* to impede, accuse, from Old French *empe(s)cher,* impede, from Late Latin *impedicāre,* to entangle, put in fetters : Latin *in-*, in + *pedica,* fetter.] **—im·peach·a·ble** *adj.* **—im·peach·er** *n.* **—im·peach·ment** *n.*

im·pearl (ĭm-pûrl′) *tr.v.* **-pearled, -pearling, -pearls.** *Archaic.* **1.** To form into pearls. **2.** To adorn with or as if with pearls.

im·pec·ca·ble (ĭm-pĕk′ə-bəl) *adj.* **1.** Without flaw; faultless. **2.** Not to be doubted: *impeccable sources.* **3.** *Rare.* Not capable of sin. [Latin *impeccābilis,* not liable to sin : *in-*, not + *peccāre,* to sin.] **—im·pec·ca·bil·i·ty** (ĭm-pĕk′ə-bĭl′ə-tē) *n.* **—im·pec·ca·bly** *adv.*

im·pe·cu·ni·ous (ĭm′pĭ-kyo͞o′nē-əs) *adj.* Lacking money; penniless. [IN- (not) + obsolete *pecunious,* rich, Middle English *pecunyous,* from Latin *pecūniōsus,* from *pecūnia,* money.] **—im·pe·cu·ni·ous·ly** *adv.* **—im·pe·cu·ni·ous·ness, im·pe·cu·ni·os·i·ty** (ĭm′pĭ-kyo͞o′nē-ŏs′ə-tē) *n.*

im·pe·dance (ĭm-pē′dəns) *n.* **1.** *Symbol* **Z** A measure of the total opposition to current flow in an alternating-current circuit, equal to the ratio of the rms electromotive force in the circuit to the rms current produced by it, and usually represented in complex notation as $Z = R + iX$, where R is the ohmic resistance and X is the reactance. **2.** An analogous measure of resistance to an alternating effect, such as the resistance to vibration of the medium in sound transmission *(acoustic impedance)* or to vibration by an applied force *(mechanical impedance).* [From IMPEDE.]

impedance matching *n.* The use of electric circuits, transmission lines, and other devices to make the impedance of a load equal to the internal impedance of the source of power, thereby making possible the most efficient transfer of power.

im·pede (ĭm-pēd′) *tr.v.* **-peded, -peding, -pedes.** To obstruct the way of; hinder the progress of; block. —See Synonyms at **hinder.** [Latin *impedīre,* to entangle, fetter.] **—im·ped·er** *n.*

im·ped·i·ment (ĭm-pĕd′ə-mənt) *n.* **1.** A hindrance; an obstruction. **2.** Something that impedes, as: **a.** An organic defect, especially one preventing clear articulation: *a speech impediment.* **b.** *Law.* Something that obstructs the making of a legal contract. —See Synonyms at **obstacle.** [Latin *impedīmentum,* from *impedīre,* IMPEDE.] **—im·ped·i·men·tal** (ĭm-pĕd′ə-mĕnt′l), **im·ped·i·men·tar·y** (ĭm-pĕd′ə-mĕn′tə-rē) *adj.*

im·ped·i·men·ta (ĭm-pĕd′ə-mĕn′tə) *pl.n.* Objects, such as provisions, baggage, or military equipment, that impede or encumber. [Latin *impedīmenta,* plural of *impedīmentum,* IMPEDIMENT.]

im·pel (ĭm-pĕl′) *tr.v.* **-pelled, -pelling, -pels. 1.** To urge to action, as through moral pressure or necessity; compel; constrain. **2.** To drive forward; propel. [Latin *impellere,* to drive on or against : *in-*, against + *pellere,* to drive.]

im·pel·lent (ĭm-pĕl′ənt) *adj.* Impelling.
~n. One that impels.

im·pel·ler (ĭm-pĕl′ər) *n.* **1.** One that impels. **2.** *Mechanics.* **a.** A rotating device used to force a gas in a given direction under pressure. **b.** A rotor or rotor blade in such a device.

im·pend (ĭm-pĕnd′) *intr.v.* **-pended, -pending, -pends. 1.** To hang or hover menacingly. **2.** To be about to take place. **3.** *Archaic.* To overhang. [Latin *impendēre* : *in-*, against + *pendēre,* to hang.]

im·pen·dent (ĭm-pĕn′dənt) *adj. Rare.* Impending.

im·pend·ing (ĭm-pĕn′dĭng) *adj.* Due to happen soon; imminent.

im·pen·e·tra·ble (ĭm-pĕn′ə-trə-bəl) *adj.* **1.** Not capable of being penetrated or entered. **2.** Incomprehensible; inscrutable; unfathomable. **3.** Impervious to argument or sentiment. **4.** *Physics.* Incapable of occupying space already occupied by matter. Said of bodies or particles. [Middle English *impenetrabel,* from Old French

impala *When alarmed, the impala takes flight in bounding leaps up to 9 meters (30 feet) long and 3 meters (10 feet) high. Impalas live in large herds in East Africa. Only the males possess horns.*

PRONUNCIATION KEY

ă, pat; ā, pay; âr, care;
ä, father, are; b, bib;
ch, church; d, deed; ĕ, pet;
ē, be; f, fife; g, gag; h, hat;
hw, which; ĭ, pit; ī, pie;
îr, pier; j, judge; k, kick;
l, lid, needle; m, mum;
n, no, sudden; ng, thing;
ŏ, pot; ō, toe; ô, paw, for;
oi, noise; ou, out; o͝o, book;
o͞o, boot; p, pop; r, roar;
s, sauce; sh, ship, dish;
t, tight; th, thin, path;
th, this, bathe; ŭ, cut; ûr, fur;
v, valve; w, with; y, yes;
z, zebra, size; zh, vision;
ə, about, item, edible,
gallop, circus, peaceful

IN FOREIGN WORDS:

à, *Fr.* ami; œ, *Fr.* feu, *Ger.* schön; ü, *Fr.* tu, *Ger.* über;
KH, *Ger.* ich, *Scot.* loch;
N, *Fr.* bon; y′, *Fr.* Compiègne

STRESS MARKS:

Primary stress: ′
in·cite′ (ĭn-sīt′)
Secondary stress: ′
in′sight′ (ĭn′sīt′)

impenetrable, from Latin *impenetrābilis* : *in-*, not + *penetrābilis*, PENETRABLE.] —**im·pen·e·tra·bil·i·ty** (ĭm-pĕn′ə-trə-bĭl′ə-tē), **im·pen·e·tra·ble·ness** *n.* —**im·pen·e·tra·bly** *adv.*

im·pen·i·tent (ĭm-pĕn′ə-tənt) *adj.* **1.** Not penitent; unrepentant. **2.** Hardened; resolute. [Late Latin *impaenitēns* (stem *impaenitent-*) : Latin *in-*, not + *paenitēns,* PENITENT.] —**im·pen·i·tence** *n.* —**im·pen·i·tent** *n.* —**im·pen·i·tent·ly** *adv.*

imper. imperative.

im·per·a·tive (ĭm-pĕr′ə-tĭv) *adj.* *Abbr.* **imp., imper. 1.** Expressing a command or plea; peremptory. **2.** Assuming the power or authority to command or control. **3.** *Grammar.* Of or designating the mood that expresses a command or request. **4.** Extremely important; essential. **5.** Obligatory; mandatory. —See Synonyms at **urgent.** ~*n.* *Abbr.* **imp., imper. 1.** *Grammar.* **a.** The imperative mood. **b.** A verb form of the imperative mood. **2. a.** A command; an order. **b.** Something that is important or essential. **c.** An obligation. [Late Latin *imperātīvus,* from Latin *imperāre,* "to prepare against (an occasion)," hence to command : *in-,* against + *parāre,* to prepare.] —**im·per·a·tive·ly** *adv.* —**im·per·a·tive·ness** *n.*

im·pe·ra·tor (ĭm′pĕ-rä′tôr′, -tôr′, -rä′tər) *n.* **1.** A title given to a victorious commander in ancient Rome. **2.** *Abbr.* **Imp.** An emperor, especially of the Roman Empire. [Latin *imperātor,* EMPEROR.]

im·pe·ra·trix (ĭm′pĕ-rä′trĭks, -rä′trĭks′) *n.* *Abbr.* **Imp.** An empress. [Latin.]

im·per·cep·ti·ble (ĭm′pər-sĕp′tə-bəl) *adj.* **1.** Not perceptible. **2.** Barely perceptible; slight or subtle. —**im·per·cep·ti·bil·i·ty** (ĭm′pər-sĕp′tə-bĭl′ə-tē), **im·per·cep·ti·ble·ness** *n.* —**im·per·cep·ti·bly** *adv.*

im·per·cep·tive (ĭm′pər-sĕp′tĭv) *adj.* Not perceptive; lacking perception. —**im·per·cep·tiv·i·ty** (ĭm′pər-sĕp-tĭv′ə-tē), **im·per·cep·tive·ness** *n.*

im·per·cip·i·ent (ĭm′pər-sĭp′ē-ənt) *adj.* Imperceptive. —**im·per·cip·i·ence** *n.*

im·per·fect (ĭm-pûr′fĭkt) *adj.* *Abbr.* **imp., imperf. 1. a.** Not perfect; having some flaw or defect. **b.** Incomplete. **2.** Of or designating the tense of a verb that shows, usually in the past, an action or condition as incomplete, continuous, or coincident with another action. **3.** *Botany.* **a.** Having either stamens or a pistil only: *imperfect flowers.* **b.** Designating fungi in which the sexual reproductive stage has not been discovered or has been lost during evolution. **4.** *Law.* Not legally enforceable because of a technical defect. **5.** *Music.* **a.** Designating a cadence ending on the dominant rather than the direct chord of the tonic. **b.** Of or designating intervals other than the fourth, fifth, and octave. ~*n.* *Abbr.* **imp., imperf. 1.** The imperfect tense. **2.** A verb in this tense. [Middle English *imparfit,* from Old French *imparfait,* from Latin *imperfectus* : *in-,* not + *perfectus,* PERFECT.] —**im·per·fect·ly** *adv.* —**im·per·fect·ness** *n.*

imperfect competition *n.* **Monopolistic competition** (see).

im·per·fec·tion (ĭm′pər-fĕk′shən) *n.* **1.** The quality or condition of being imperfect. **2.** Something imperfect; a defect; a flaw. —See Synonyms at **blemish.**

im·per·fec·tive (ĭm′pər-fĕk′tĭv) *adj.* *Grammar.* Of or designating a verb in the imperfective aspect. ~*n.* *Grammar.* **1.** The imperfective aspect. **2.** A verb in the imperfective aspect.

imperfective aspect *n.* An aspect of verbs that expresses action without regard to its beginning or completion. Compare **perfective aspect.** See **aspect.**

im·per·fo·rate (ĭm-pûr′fər-ĭt) *adj.* **1.** Not perforated. **2.** Not perforated into detachable rows. Said of stamps and sheets of stamps. **3.** *Anatomy.* Lacking a normal opening. Said of a bodily part. ~*n.* An imperforate stamp.

im·pe·ri·al¹ (ĭm-pîr′ē-əl) *adj.* *Abbr.* **imp. 1. a.** Of or pertaining to an empire or a sovereign, especially an emperor or empress. **b.** Of or pertaining to the British Empire. **2.** Designating a nation or government having sovereign rights over colonies or dependencies. **3. a.** *Obsolete.* Having supreme authority; sovereign. **b.** Regal; majestic. **4.** Outstanding in size or quality. **5.** Of or pertaining to the British Imperial system of weights and measures. ~*n.* **1.** **Imperial.** A supporter or a soldier of the Holy Roman Empire. **2.** An emperor or empress. **3.** A dome with a pointed top. **4.** Something outstanding in size or quality. **5. a.** A size of paper, usually 23 by 33 inches. **b.** A size of book; especially, *imperial octavo* (7½ by 11 inches) or *imperial quarto* (11 by 15 inches). **6.** Formerly, a Russian gold coin. [Middle English *emperial, imperial,* from Old French, from Late Latin *imperiālis,* from Latin *imperium,* command, EMPIRE.] —**im·pe·ri·al·ly** *adv.*

imperial² *n.* A pointed beard grown from the lower lip and chin. [French *impériale,* IMPERIAL (after Napoleon III, who wore one).]

im·pe·ri·al·ism (ĭm-pîr′ē-ə-lĭz′əm) *n.* **1.** The policy of extending a nation's authority by territorial acquisition or by the establishment of economic and political hegemony over other nations. **2.** The system, policies, or practices of an imperial government. **3.** The imposing of its will on others by a country or powerful organization, as in social, cultural, or other matters. Used derogatorily. —**im·pe·ri·al·ist** *n.* & *adj.* —**im·pe·ri·al·is·tic** (ĭm-pîr′ē-ə-lĭs′tĭk) *adj.* —**im·pe·ri·al·is·ti·cal·ly** *adv.*

Imperial jade *n.* A light-green jade derived from gem-quality jadeite.

imperial moth *n.* A large New World moth, *Eacles imperialis,* having yellow wings with purplish or brownish markings.

Imperial system *n.* The system of weights and measures used in Great Britain and various other countries, using units of weights such as the ounce, pound, and stone; units of length such as the inch, foot, yard, and mile; and units of volume such as the pint, quart, and gallon.

Imperial Valley. Fertile region in southeastern California, extending southward into northwestern Mexico. It has a long growing season (more than 300 days), can support two crops a year with irrigation, and is an important source of winter fruits and vegetables and cotton, grains, and dairy products.

im·per·il (ĭm-pĕr′əl) *tr.v.* **-iled, -iling, ils** or *chiefly British* **-illed, -illing.** To put in peril; endanger. —**im·per·il·ment** *n.*

im·pe·ri·ous (ĭm-pîr′ē-əs) *adj.* **1.** Domineering; overbearing. **2.** *Obsolete.* Regal; imperial. **3.** *Rare.* Urgent; pressing. —See Synonyms at **dictatorial.** [Latin *imperiōsus,* from *imperium,* IMPERIUM.] —**im·pe·ri·ous·ly** *adv.* —**im·pe·ri·ous·ness** *n.*

im·per·ish·a·ble (ĭm-pĕr′ĭ-shə-bəl) *adj.* Not perishable. —**im·per·ish·a·bil·i·ty** (ĭm-pĕr′ĭ-shə-bĭl′ə-tē), **im·per·ish·a·ble·ness** *n.* —**im·per·ish·a·bly** *adv.*

im·pe·ri·um (ĭm-pîr′ē-əm) *n., pl.* **-ria** (-ē-ə). **1.** Absolute rule; supreme power. **2.** A sphere of power or dominion; an empire. [Latin, EMPIRE.]

im·per·ma·nent (ĭm-pûr′mə-nənt) *adj.* Not permanent; not lasting or durable. —**im·per·ma·nence, im·per·ma·nen·cy** *n.*

im·per·me·a·ble (ĭm-pûr′mē-ə-bəl) *adj.* **1.** Not permeable. **2.** *Physics.* Not allowing the passage of fluids. **3.** *Geology.* Not allowing water or other fluid to pass through it easily. Said of rock. [Late Latin *impermeābilis* : *in-,* not + *permeābilis,* PERMEABLE.] —**im·per·me·a·ble·ness** *n.* —**im·per·me·a·bly** *adv.*

im·per·mis·si·ble (ĭm′pər-mĭs′ə-bəl) *adj.* Not permissible. —**im·per·mis·si·bil·i·ty** (ĭm′pər-mĭs′ə-bĭl′ə-tē) *n.* —**im·per·mis·si·bly** *adv.*

im·per·script·i·ble (ĭm′pər-skrĭp′tə-bəl) *adj.* Not supported by written authority; unrecorded.

im·per·son·al (ĭm-pûr′sə-nəl) *adj.* **1.** *Grammar.* **a.** Pertaining to or designating a verb or construction that expresses the action of an unspecified agent and is used in the third person singular without a separate subject (as *methinks*) or a purely nominal subject (as *snowed* in *it snowed*). **b.** Indefinite. Said of pronouns. **2.** Not personal; not related or connected to a person or persons: *impersonal possessions.* **3.** Exhibiting little or no individuality or personality. **4.** Lacking sympathy or human warmth. —**im·per·son·al·i·ty** (ĭm-pûr′sə-năl′ə-tē) *n.* —**im·per·son·al·ly** *adv.*

im·per·son·al·ize (ĭm-pûr′sə-nə-līz′) *tr.v.* **-ized, -izing, -izes.** To make impersonal.

im·per·son·ate (ĭm-pûr′sə-nāt′) *tr.v.* **-ated, -ating, -ates. 1.** To act the character or part of, especially in order to entertain. **2.** To assume the identity of for unlawful purposes. **3.** *Archaic.* To embody; personify. [IN- (in) + PERSON + -ATE.] —**im·per·son·ate** (ĭm-pûr′sə-nĭt) *adj.* —**im·per·son·a·tion** (ĭm-pûr′sə-nā′shən) *n.* —**im·per·son·a·tor** *n.*

im·per·ti·nence (ĭm-pûrt′n-əns) *n.* Also **im·per·ti·nen·cy** (-ən-sē) *pl.* **-cies. 1.** The quality of being impertinent; insolence. **2.** Irrelevance. **3.** An impertinent act, person, or statement.

im·per·ti·nent (ĭm-pûrt′n-ənt) *adj.* **1.** Impudent; presumptuous; rude. **2.** Not pertinent; irrelevant. [Middle English, irrelevant, from Old French, from Late Latin *impertinēns* (stem *impertinent-*) : Latin *in-,* not + *pertinēns,* PERTINENT.] —**im·per·ti·nent·ly** *adv.*

im·per·turb·a·ble (ĭm′pər-tûr′bə-bəl) *adj.* Not capable of being perturbed; calm. —See Synonyms at **cool.** —**im·per·turb·a·bil·i·ty** (ĭm′pər-tûr′bə-bĭl′ə-tē), **im·per·turb·a·ble·ness** *n.* —**im·per·turb·a·bly** *adv.*

im·per·vi·ous (ĭm-pûr′vē-əs) *adj.* **1.** Incapable of being penetrated, as by water or light. **2.** Not affected; unable to be influenced: *impervious to her charm.* [Latin *impervius* : *in-,* not + *pervius,* PERVIOUS.] —**im·per·vi·ous·ly** *adv.* —**im·per·vi·ous·ness** *n.*

im·pe·ti·go (ĭm′pə-tī′gō, -tē′gō) *n.* A contagious skin disease characterized by pustules that burst and form characteristic thick yellow crusts. [Latin *impetīgō,* "an attack," from *impetere,* to assail, attack. See **impetus.**]

im·pe·trate (ĭm′pə-trāt′) *tr.v.* **-trated, -trating, -trates.** *Theology.* **1.** To obtain by entreaty or petition. **2.** To beseech. [Latin *impetrāre,* to accomplish : *in-* (intensive) + *patrāre,* to father, achieve, accomplish, from *pater,* father.] —**im·pe·tra·tion** (ĭm′pə-trā′shən) *n.* —**im·pe·tra·tor** *n.*

im·pet·u·ous (ĭm-pĕch′ōō-əs) *adj.* **1.** Characterized or prompted by sudden energy, emotion, or the like; impulsive; brash. **2.** Having great impetus; rushing with violence: *impetuous, heaving waves.* [Middle English, from Old French *impetueux,* from Latin *impetuōsus,* from *impetus,* IMPETUS.] —**im·pet·u·os·i·ty** (ĭm-pĕch′ōō-ŏs′ə-tē), **im·pet·u·ous·ness** *n.* —**im·pet·u·ous·ly** *adv.*

Usage: *impetuous, heedless, hasty, headlong, sudden.* These adjectives describe persons and their actions and decisions when marked by abruptness or lack of deliberation. *Impetuous* suggests impulsiveness, impatience, or lack of thoughtfulness. *Heedless* implies carelessness or lack of a sense of responsibility or proper regard for the consequences of action. *Hasty* and *headlong* both stress hurried action, and the latter especially implies recklessness. *Sudden* is applied to action or to personal attributes, such as moods, that make themselves apparent abruptly or unexpectedly.

im·pe·tus (ĭm′pə-təs) *n., pl.* **-tuses. 1. a.** An impelling force; an impulse. **b.** Something that incites; a stimulus. **2.** Loosely, the force associated with a moving body. [Latin, attack, from *impetere,* to assail, attack : *in-,* against + *petere,* to go toward, seek, attack.]

im·pi·e·ty (ĭm-pī′ə-tē) n., pl. **-ties. 1.** The quality or state of being impious. **2.** An impious act. **3.** Undutifulness.

im·pinge (ĭm-pĭnj′) intr.v. **-pinged, -pinging, -pinges. 1.** To encroach; trespass. Used with on or upon. **2.** To collide; strike; dash. Used with on, upon, or against. [Latin impingere, to push against : in-, against + pangere, to fasten, drive in.] —**im·pinge·ment** n. —**im·ping·er** n.

impingement attack n. Metallurgy. Erosion of a metal surface that is in contact with a turbulent fluid containing small gas bubbles or solid particles.

im·pi·ous (ĭm′pē-əs, ĭm-pī′-) adj. **1.** Not pious; lacking reverence; profane. **2.** Lacking due respect. [Latin impius : in-, not + pius, PIOUS.] —**im·pi·ous·ly** adv. —**im·pi·ous·ness** n.

imp·ish (ĭm′pĭsh) adj. Of or like an imp; mischievous. —See Synonyms at **playful.** —**imp·ish·ly** adv. —**imp·ish·ness** n.

im·pla·ca·ble (ĭm-plăk′ə-bəl, ĭm-plā′kə-) adj. **1.** Not placable; incapable of appeasement; inexorable. **2.** Unalterable; inflexible. [Latin implācābilis : in-, not + plācābilis, PLACABLE.] —**im·pla·ca·bil·i·ty** (ĭm-plăk′ə-bĭl′ə-tē), **im·pla·ca·ble·ness** n. —**im·pla·ca·bly** adv.

im·plant (ĭm-plănt′, -plänt′) tr.v. **-planted, -planting, -plants. 1.** To entrench or set in firmly, as in the ground; infix. **2.** To establish decisively, as in the mind or consciousness; instill; ingrain. **3.** Medicine. To insert or embed surgically, as in grafting. ~n. (ĭm′plănt′, -plänt′) Something implanted; especially, an implanted drug, device, or piece of tissue.

im·plan·ta·tion (ĭm′plăn-tā′shən) n. **1.** An act or instance of implanting. **2.** The condition of being implanted. **3.** An implanted object. **4.** The attachment and embedding of the fertilized ovum in the uterine wall.

im·plau·si·ble (ĭm-plô′zə-bəl) adj. Not plausible. —**im·plau·si·bil·i·ty** (ĭm-plô′zə-bĭl′ə-tē), **im·plau·si·ble·ness** n. —**im·plau·si·bly** adv.

im·plead (ĭm-plēd′) tr.v. **-pleaded, -pleading, -pleads.** To sue or prosecute in a court of law. [Middle English impleden, from Old French empleid(i)er : en- (intensive) + pleid(i)er, PLEAD.]

im·ple·ment (ĭm′plə-mənt) n. **1.** A tool, utensil, or instrument. **2.** An article used to outfit or equip. **3.** A means employed to achieve a given end; an agent. **4.** In Scottish law, performance of a contract or an obligation. —See Synonyms at **tool.** ~tr.v. (ĭm′plə-mĕnt′) implemented, -menting, -ments. **1.** To put into practical effect; carry out: implement the new procedures. **2.** To supply with implements. [Middle English, from Late Latin implēmentum, a filling up, supplement, from Latin implēre, to fill up, fulfill : in- (intensive) + plēre, to fill.] —**im·ple·men·ta·tion** (ĭm′plə-mĕn-tā′shən) n.

im·pli·cate (ĭm′plĭ-kāt′) tr.v. **-cated, -cating, -cates. 1.** To involve intimately or incriminatingly. **2.** To imply. **3.** Archaic. To entangle; entwine. [Latin implicāre : in-, in + plicāre, to fold.]

im·pli·ca·tion (ĭm′plĭ-kā′shən) n. **1.** The act of implicating or the condition of being implicated. **2.** The act of implying or the condition of being implied. **3.** That which is implied, especially: **a.** An indirect suggestion. **b.** An inference.

im·pli·ca·tive (ĭm′plĭ-kā′tĭv) adj. Also **im·pli·ca·to·ry** (ĭm′plĭ-kə-tôr′ē, -tōr′ē) **1.** Having a tendency to implicate. **2.** Of or pertaining to implication. —**im·pli·ca·tive·ly** adv.

im·plic·it (ĭm-plĭs′ĭt) adj. **1.** Implied or understood although not directly expressed: His anger was implicit. **2.** Inherent or contained in the nature of something although not directly expressed. Used with in: Suspicion is implicit in such a tone of voice. **3.** Having no doubts or reservations; unquestioning: Her trust in him was implicit. **4.** Mathematics. Pertaining to or designating a function of two or more variables of the form f (x, y) = 0. For example, in 2xy + 1 = 0, x is an implicit function of y. [Latin implicitus, earlier implicātus, involved, entangled, from the past participle of implicāre, to involve, entangle, IMPLICATE.] —**im·plic·it·ly** adv. —**im·plic·it·ness** n.

im·plied (ĭm-plīd′) adj. Suggested, involved, or understood although not clearly or openly expressed.

im·plode (ĭm-plōd′) v. **-ploded, -ploding, -plodes.** —intr. To undergo implosion. —tr. **1.** To cause implosion in. **2.** Phonetics. To pronounce by implosion. [IN- (in) + (EX)PLODE.]

im·plore (ĭm-plôr′, -plōr′) v. **-plored, -ploring, -plores.** —tr. **1.** To appeal to in supplication; entreat; beseech: I implore you to have mercy on the defendant. **2.** To plead or beg for urgently: I implore your mercy. —intr. To make an earnest appeal. —See Synonyms at **beg.** [Latin implōrāre, to invoke with tears : in-, in + plōrāre, to weep, bewail, lament (perhaps imitative).] —**im·plo·ra·tion** (ĭm′plô-rā′shən) n. —**im·plor·er** n. —**im·plor·ing·ly** adv.

im·plo·sion (ĭm-plō′zhən) n. **1.** A more or less violent collapse inward, as of a highly evacuated glass vessel. **2.** Phonetics. The stopping of the breath while breathing in to form a stop consonant. Compare **plosion.** [IN- + (EX)PLOSION.]

im·plo·sive (ĭm-plō′sĭv) adj. Phonetics. Pronounced by implosion. ~n. Phonetics. A consonant pronounced by implosion.

im·ply (ĭm-plī′) tr.v. **-plied, -plying, -plies. 1.** To say or express indirectly; suggest: Her use of "we" implied that she was speaking for others. **2.** To involve or suggest by logical necessity; entail: His aims imply a good deal of energy. —See Synonyms at **suggest.** [Middle English implien, emplien, from Old French emplier, from Latin implicāre, infold, involve, IMPLICATE.]

Usage: It is a common mistake to confuse imply (to state or express something indirectly) with infer (to deduce, or draw a conclusion from what is stated). The speaker or writer implies: Your report implies that the mechanism was faulty. The listener or reader

infers: I infer from your report that the mechanism was faulty.

im·pol·i·cy (ĭm-pŏl′ə-sē) n., pl. **-cies. 1.** The state of or an instance of being impolitic. **2.** A bad policy.

im·po·lite (ĭm′pə-līt′) adj. Not polite; discourteous; rude. [Latin impolītus, unpolished : in-, not + polītus, polished, POLITE.] —**im·po·lite·ly** adv. —**im·po·lite·ness** n.

im·pol·i·tic (ĭm-pŏl′ə-tĭk) adj. Not wise or expedient; not politic. —**im·pol·i·tic·ly** adv. —**im·pol·i·tic·ness** n.

im·pon·der·a·ble (ĭm-pŏn′dər-ə-bəl) adj. Incapable of being weighed, measured, or evaluated with precision. ~n. Something that is imponderable; an indeterminable factor: Public support is a great imponderable. —**im·pon·der·a·ble·ness** n. —**im·pon·der·a·bly** adv.

im·po·nent (ĭm-pō′nənt) n. One who imposes a duty. [From IM-POSE, by analogy with opponent.] —**im·po·nent** adj.

im·port (ĭm-pôrt′, -pōrt′, ĭm′pôrt′, -pōrt′) v. **-ported, -porting, -ports.** —tr. **1.** To bring or carry in from an outside source; especially, to bring in (goods) from a foreign country for trade or sale. Compare **export. 2.** To mean; signify. **3.** To imply. **4.** Archaic. To have importance for. —intr. To be significant. —See Synonyms at **mean** (convey sense). ~n. (ĭm′pôrt′, -pōrt′). **1.** Abbr. **imp.** Something imported. **2. a.** The business of importing. **b.** Importation. **3.** Meaning; signification. **4.** Importance; significance. —See Synonyms at **importance, meaning.** [Middle English importen, from Latin importāre, to carry in : in-, in + portāre, to carry.] —**im·port·a·bil·i·ty** (ĭm-pôrt′ə-bĭl′ə-tē) n. —**im·port·a·ble** adj. —**im·port·er** n.

im·por·tance (ĭm-pôr′təns) n. **1.** The condition or quality of being important; significance; consequence. **2.** Personal status; standing. **3.** Obsolete. An important matter.

Synonyms: consequence, import, moment, significance, weight.

im·por·tant (ĭm-pôr′tənt) adj. Abbr. **imp. 1.** Having a great effect or being of great concern; significant: an important decision to many people. **2.** Holding or considered as holding a high position in people's estimation. **3.** Self-important. [Old French, from Old Italian importante, from Medieval Latin importāns (stem important-), present participle of importāre, to mean, be significant, from Latin, to carry in, IMPORT.] —**im·por·tant·ly** adv.

Usage: The following sentence may be written with the adjective important: The truth is evident; more important, it will prevail. It may also be written with an adverb: The truth is evident; more importantly, it will prevail. Most grammarians prescribe the adjective form, in which important stands for "what is important," but the use of importantly is now very common.

im·por·ta·tion (ĭm′pôr-tā′shən, ĭm′pōr-) n. **1.** The act, occupation, or business of importing. **2.** Something imported; an import.

im·por·tu·nate (ĭm-pôr′chə-nĭt) adj. **1.** Stubbornly or unreasonably persistent in request or demand. **2.** Urgent; pressing. —**im·por·tu·nate·ly** adv. —**im·por·tu·nate·ness** n.

im·por·tune (ĭm′pôr-tōōn′, -tyōōn′, ĭm-pôr′chən) tr.v. **-tuned, -tuning, -tunes. 1.** To beset with repeated and insistent requests. **2.** To solicit, especially for immoral purposes. **3.** Obsolete. To ask for insistently and repeatedly. **4.** Obsolete. To annoy; vex. —See Synonyms at **beg.** ~adj. Importunate. [Medieval Latin importūnārī, to be troublesome, from Latin importūnus, "without a port," difficult of access, unfit, unsuitable : in-, not + portus, port, harbor.] —**im·por·tune·ly** adv. —**im·por·tun·er** n.

im·por·tu·ni·ty (ĭm′pôr-tōō′nə-tē, -tyōō′nə-tē) n., pl. **-ties. 1. a.** The act of importuning. **b.** The state or quality of being importunate. **2. importunities.** Insistent demands or requests.

im·pose (ĭm-pōz′) v. **-posed, -posing, -poses.** —tr. **1.** To establish or apply as compulsory; levy: The amount of duties imposed now constitutes a protective tariff. **2.** To lay (something burdensome) upon another or others: impose extra duties. **3.** To obtrude or force (oneself, for example) upon another or others. **4.** Printing. To arrange (type or plates) in the correct order and lock them into a chase. **5.** To pass off (something) on others: He imposed a fraud on his company. **6.** To lay (hands) on the head of a person receiving certain sacraments. Used of a bishop or priest. —intr. **1.** To take unfair advantage of something or someone. Used with on or upon: imposed on his host by staying late. **2.** To make an impression, often fraudulently. Used with on or upon. [Old French imposer, from Latin impōnere (past participle impositus), to put on : in-, on + pōnere, to put, place.] —**im·pos·er** n.

im·pos·ing (ĭm-pō′zĭng) adj. Impressive, as in size or appearance. —See Synonyms at **grand.**

imposing stone n. Printing. A stone or metal slab on which material to be printed is arranged. Also called "imposing table."

im·po·si·tion (ĭm′pə-zĭsh′ən) n. **1.** The act of imposing. **2.** Something imposed, as a tax, undue burden, or fraud. **3.** A burdensome or unfair demand, as upon someone's time. **4.** Printing. The arrangement of printed matter to form a sequence of pages.

im·pos·si·bil·i·ty (ĭm-pŏs′ə-bĭl′ə-tē) n., pl. **-ties. 1.** The condition or quality of being impossible. **2.** Something impossible.

im·pos·si·ble (ĭm-pŏs′ə-bəl) adj. **1.** Not capable of existing or happening. **2.** Having little likelihood of happening or being accomplished. **3.** Unacceptable. **4.** Untrue or ridiculously exaggerated: an impossible claim. **5.** Not capable of being dealt with or tolerated: an impossible request; an impossible child. [Middle English, from Old French, from Latin impossibilis : in-, not + possibilis, POSSIBLE.] —**im·pos·si·bly** adv.

im·post¹ (ĭm′pōst′) n. **1.** Something imposed or levied, as a tax or duty. **2.** The weight a horse must carry in a handicap race. [Old French, from Medieval Latin *impositum,* from Latin *impositus,* past participle of *impōnere,* IMPOSE.]

impost[2] *n. Architecture.* The uppermost part of a column or pillar supporting an arch, usually projecting from a wall like a bracket. [French *imposte,* from Italian *imposta,* from Latin, feminine past participle of *impōnere,* IMPOSE.]

im·pos·tor (ĭm-pŏs′tər) *n.* A person who deceives, especially by assuming a false identity. [Old French *imposteur,* from Late Latin *impos(i)tor,* from Latin *impōnere* (past participle *impositus*), IMPOSE.]

im·pos·ture (ĭm-pŏs′chər) *n.* Deception or fraud; especially, assumption of a false identity. [Late Latin *impostura,* from Latin *impos(i)tus,* past participle of *impōnere,* IMPOSE.]

im·po·tent (ĭm′pə-tənt) *adj.* **1.** Lacking physical strength or vigor; weak. **2.** Powerless; ineffectual. **3.** Incapable of sexual intercourse. Said of males. Compare **frigid**. **4.** *Obsolete.* Lacking self-restraint. —See Synonyms at **sterile**. [Middle English, from Old French, from Latin *impotēns* : *in-,* not + *potēns,* POTENT.] **—im·po·tence, im·po·ten·cy** *n.* **—im·po·tent·ly** *adv.*

im·pound (ĭm-pound′) *tr.v.* **-pounded, -pounding, -pounds. 1.** To confine in or as if in a pound. **2.** To seize and retain, especially in legal custody. **3.** To accumulate (water) in a reservoir. **—im·pound·age, im·pound·ment** *n.* **—im·pound·er** *n.*

im·pov·er·ish (ĭm-pŏv′ər-ĭsh) *tr.v.* **-ished, -ishing, -ishes. 1.** To diminish or exhaust the wealth of; reduce to poverty. **2.** To deprive of natural richness or strength. —See Usage note at **deplete**. [Middle English *enpoverisen,* from Old French *empovrir* (present stem *empovriss-*), to make poor : *en-* (causative) + *povre,* POOR.] **—im·pov·er·ish·ment** *n.*

im·prac·ti·ca·ble (ĭm-prăk′tĭ-kə-bəl) *adj.* **1.** Not capable of being done or carried out. **2.** Unfit for use or passage, as a road may be. **3.** *Archaic.* Unmanageable; intractable. —See Usage note at **impractical**. **—im·prac·ti·ca·bil·i·ty** (ĭm-prăk′tĭ-kə-bĭl′ə-tē), **im·prac·ti·ca·ble·ness** *n.* **—im·prac·ti·ca·bly** *adv.*

im·prac·ti·cal (ĭm-prăk′tĭ-kəl) *adj.* **1.** Unwise to implement or maintain in practice. **2.** Incapable of dealing efficiently with practical matters, especially financial or mechanical matters. **3.** Not in accord with experience or common sense. Impracticable. **—im·prac·ti·cal·i·ty** (ĭm-prăk′tĭ-kăl′ə-tē), **im·prac·ti·cal·ness** *n.*

Usage: There is a certain overlap of usage between *impracticable* and *impractical,* but generally the senses are distinct. *Impracticable* applies to something that is not capable of being carried out or put into practice. *Impractical* refers to that which is not sensible or prudent. A plan may be *impractical* if it involves undue cost or effort and still not be *impracticable.* The distinction between these words is subtle, and *impractical* is often used where *impracticable* would be more precise.

im·pre·cate (ĭm′prə-kāt′) *tr.v.* **-cated, -cating, -cates.** To invoke evil or a curse upon. [Latin *imprecārī* : *in-,* on + *precārī,* to pray, entreat.] **—im·pre·ca·tor** *n.* **—im·pre·ca·to·ry** (ĭm′prə-kə-tôr′ē, -tōr′ē) *adj.*

im·pre·ca·tion (ĭm′prə-kā′shən) *n.* **1.** The act of imprecating. **2.** A curse.

im·pre·cise (ĭm′prĭ-sīs′) *adj.* Not precise; inexact. **—im·pre·cise·ly** *adv.* **—im·pre·ci·sion** (ĭm′prĭ-sĭzh′ən) *n.*

im·preg·na·ble[1] (ĭm-prĕg′nə-bəl) *adj.* **1.** Able to resist capture or entry by force: *an impregnable castle.* **2.** Unable to be shaken, refuted, or criticized: *impregnable convictions.* [Middle English *imprenable,* from Old French : *in-,* not + *prenable,* PREGNABLE.]

impregnable[2] *adj.* Able to be impregnated. [From IMPREGNATE.]

im·preg·nate (ĭm-prĕg′nāt′) *tr.v.* **-nated, -nating, -nates. 1.** To make pregnant; inseminate. **2.** To fertilize (an ovum, for example). **3.** To fill throughout or saturate. **4.** To permeate or imbue.
~*adj.* Impregnated; made pregnant. [Late Latin *impregnāre* : Latin *in-,* in + *praegnās,* PREGNANT.] **—im·preg·na·tion** *n.* **—im·preg·na·tor** *n.*

im·pre·sa (ĭm-prā′zə) *n.* Also **im·prese** (ĭm-prēz′). An emblem or device with a motto. [French *impresse,* from Italian *impresa,* undertaking, emblem. See **impresario**.]

im·pre·sa·ri·o (ĭm′prə-sär′ē-ō′, -sâr′ē-ō′) *n., pl.* **-sarios** or **-sari** (-sär′ē). **1.** One who sponsors or produces entertainments, especially theatrical and musical ones. **2.** A manager; producer. [Italian, undertaker, manager, from *impresa,* undertaking, chivalric deed, emblem, from the feminine of *impreso,* past participle of *imprendere,* to undertake, from Vulgar Latin *imprendere* (unattested). See **emprise**.]

im·pre·scrip·ti·ble (ĭm′prĭ-skrĭp′tə-bəl) *adj. Law.* Immune from prescription; inalienable. **—im·pre·scrip·ti·bly** *adv.*

im·press[1] (ĭm-prĕs′) *tr.v.* **-pressed, -pressing, -presses. 1.** To produce or apply with pressure. **2.** To mark or stamp with or as if with pressure. **3.** To produce a vivid perception or image of. **4.** To affect or influence deeply or forcibly. **5.** To emphasize; stress. **6.** To transmit a force or motion to. —See Synonyms at **affect**.
~*n.* (ĭm′prĕs′). **1.** The act of impressing. **2.** A mark or pattern produced by impressing. **3.** A stamp or seal meant to be impressed. **4.** A characteristic quality. [Middle English *impressen,* from Latin *imprimere* (past participle *impressus*) : *in-,* in + *premere,* to press.]

im·press[2] *tr.v.* **-pressed, -pressing, -presses. 1.** Formerly, to compel (a person) to serve in a military force. **2.** To confiscate (property).
~*n.* Impressment. [IN- (intensive) + PRESS (to force into service).]

im·press·i·ble (ĭm-prĕs′ə-bəl) *adj.* Susceptible to being impressed. **—im·press·i·bly** *adv.*

im·pres·sion (ĭm-prĕsh′ən) *n.* **1.** The act or process of impressing. **2.** The effect, mark, or imprint made on a surface by pressure. **3. a.** An effect, image, or feeling retained as a consequence of experience. **b.** An effect produced by an event or action. **4.** A vague notion, remembrance, or belief. **5.** An imitation or mimicking of another person or thing, especially when done by a professional entertainer. **6.** *Printing.* **a.** All the copies of a publication printed at one time from the same set of type. **b.** A single copy of this printing. **c.** A print taken from an engraving or from type. **7.** In dentistry, an imprint of the teeth and surrounding tissue in material such as wax or plaster, used as a mold in making dentures or inlays. —See Synonyms at **opinion**.

im·pres·sion·a·ble (ĭm-prĕsh′ən-ə-bəl) *adj.* Readily influenced; suggestible. **—im·pres·sion·a·bil·i·ty, im·pres·sion·a·ble·ness** *n.*

im·pres·sion·ism (ĭm-prĕsh′ə-nĭz′əm) *n. Sometimes* **Impressionism. 1.** A theory or style of painting originating and developed in France during the 1870's, characterized chiefly by concentration on the general impression produced by a scene or object and by the use of unmixed primary colors and small strokes to simulate actual reflected light. **2.** A literary style characterized generally by the use of details and mental associations to evoke subjective and sensory impressions rather than the re-creation of objective reality. **3.** A musical style of the late 19th and early 20th centuries, using unusual harmonies to evoke suggestions of mood, place, and natural phenomena. **—im·pres·sion·ist** *n.* & *adj.*

im·pres·sion·is·tic (ĭm-prĕsh′ə-nĭs′tĭk) *adj.* **1.** Of or pertaining to impressionism. **2.** Of or pertaining to a subjective, sketchy approach or attitude: *an impressionistic survey of recent history.*

im·pres·sive (ĭm-prĕs′ĭv) *adj.* Making a strong, favorable impression; awesome or stirring. **—im·pres·sive·ly** *adv.* **—im·pres·sive·ness** *n.*

im·press·ment (ĭm-prĕs′mənt) *n.* The act or policy of impressing men or property for public service or use: *army ranks swelled by impressment.*

im·pres·sure (ĭm-prĕsh′ər) *n. Archaic.* An impression.

im·prest (ĭm-prĕst′) *n.* An advance or loan of government or public funds toward the performance of some service for the government. [Probably from Italian *imprestare,* to make a loan to : *in-,* toward, from Latin + *prestare,* to lend, from Latin *praestāre,* to pay, give, from *praestō,* at hand (see **presto**).]

im·pri·ma·tur (ĭm′prə-mä′tər, -mā′tər) *n.* **1.** *Abbr.* **imp.** Official approval or license to print or publish, especially under conditions of censorship. **2.** Broadly, any official sanction. [Latin, let it be printed, from Latin *imprimere,* to print, IMPRESS.]

im·pri·mis (ĭm-prī′mĭs) *adv. Archaic.* In the first place. [Middle English, from Latin *in prīmīs,* among the first (things) : *in,* in + *prīmīs,* ablative plural of *prīmus,* first.]

im·print (ĭm-prĭnt′) *v.* **-printed, -printing, -prints.** —*tr.* **1.** To produce or impress (a mark or pattern) on a surface. **2.** To stamp or produce a mark on. **3.** To establish firmly or impress, as on the mind or memory. **4.** To subject (a young animal) to imprinting. —*intr.* To become imprinted. Used of young animals.
~*n.* (ĭm′prĭnt′). **1.** A mark or pattern produced by imprinting. **2.** A distinguishing manifestation: *the imprint of defeat.* **3. a.** The publisher's name, often with the date, address, and edition of a publication, printed at the bottom of a title page. **b.** The printer's name, usually placed on the copyright page. [Middle English *imprenten,* from Old French *empreinter,* from *empreinte,* impression, from *empreindre,* to print, from Latin *imprimere,* to IMPRESS.]

im·print·ing (ĭm′prĭnt′ĭng) *n.* A learning process occurring early in the life of certain animals, whereby the young recognize and associate with members of their own species or with a surrogate parent.

im·pris·on (ĭm-prĭz′ən) *tr.v.* To put in or as if in prison. [Middle English *inprisonen, emprisonen,* from Old French *emprisoner* : *en-* (causative) + *prison,* PRISON.] **—im·pris·on·ment** *n.*

im·prob·a·bil·i·ty (ĭm-prŏb′ə-bĭl′ə-tē) *n., pl.* **-ties. 1.** The condition of being improbable. **2.** Something improbable.

im·prob·a·ble (ĭm-prŏb′ə-bəl) *adj.* Not probable; doubtful or unlikely. [Latin *improbābilis* : *in-,* not + *probābilis,* PROBABLE.] **—im·prob·a·ble·ness** *n.* **—im·prob·a·bly** *adv.*

im·pro·bi·ty (ĭm-prō′bə-tē) *n.* Lack of probity; dishonesty. [Latin *improbitās,* from *improbus,* dishonest : *in-,* not + *probus,* honest, good.]

im·promp·tu (ĭm-prŏmp′to͞o, -tyo͞o) *adj.* Not rehearsed; improvised. —See Synonyms at **extemporaneous**.
~*adv.* In the manner of improvisation; spontaneously.
~*n.* Something made or done impromptu; specifically, a musical composition that is improvisatory in style. [French, from Latin *in promptū,* at hand : *in,* in + *promptū,* ablative of *promptus,* ready, PROMPT.]

im·prop·er (ĭm-prŏp′ər) *adj.* **1.** Not suited to the circumstances or intention. **2.** Not in keeping with propriety; indecorous: *improper conduct.* **3.** Not consistent with fact or rule; incorrect: *improper reasoning.* **4.** Irregular or abnormal. [Old French *impropre,* from Latin *improprius* : *in-,* not + *proprius,* one's own, PROPER.] **—im·prop·er·ly** *adv.* **—im·prop·er·ness** *n.*

Usage: *improper, unbecoming, unseemly, indelicate, indecent, indecorous.* These adjectives mean in violation of accepted standards of what is right or proper. *Improper* can apply to any act or statement contrary to such standards, but often refers to unethical conduct, violation of etiquette, or morally offensive behavior. *Unbecoming* suggests what is beneath the standard implied by one's character or position. What is *unseemly* or *indelicate* violates good

PRONUNCIATION KEY

ă, pat; ā, pay; âr, care;
ä, father, are; b, bib;
ch, church; d, deed; ĕ, pet;
ē, be; f, fife; g, gag; h, hat;
hw, which; ĭ, pit; ī, pie;
îr, pier; j, judge; k, kick;
l, lid, needle; m, mum;
n, no, sudden; ng, thing;
ŏ, pot; ō, toe; ô, paw, for;
oi, noise; ou, out; o͝o, book;
o͞o, boot; p, pop; r, roar;
s, sauce; sh, ship, dish;
t, tight; th, thin, path;
th, this, bathe; ŭ, cut; ûr, fur;
v, valve; w, with; y, yes;
z, zebra, size; zh, vision;
ə, about, item, edible,
gallop, circus, peaceful

IN FOREIGN WORDS:

à, *Fr.* ami; œ, *Fr.* feu, *Ger.* schön; ü, *Fr.* tu, *Ger.* über; KH, *Ger.* ich, *Scot.* loch; N, *Fr.* bon; y′, *Fr.* Compiègne

STRESS MARKS:

Primary stress: ′
in·cite′ (ĭn-sīt′)
Secondary stress: ′
in′sight′ (ĭn′sīt′)

Impressionism

THE IMPRESSIONISTS' QUEST TO CAPTURE THE FLEETING MOMENT
The style that opened the way for 20th-century art

Impressionism, the most revolutionary art movement of the second half of the 19th century, flouted the conventions of academic painting in a way that at first baffled but finally delighted the art-loving public. Inspired by Edouard Manet, the Impressionists were mainly Frenchmen, with a core consisting of Claude Monet, Auguste Renoir, Edgar Degas, Camille Pissarro, and the Englishman Alfred Sisley. They worked largely outdoors in order to avoid the contrived effects of studio work. The Impressionists developed a technique of applying dabs of color to build up an impression of what the eye sees, rather than trying to fill in every detail precisely. The "inner eye" of the painter became more important than making political or social statements. The Impressionists would represent a particular color by applying dabs of several pure colors to the canvas, allowing the eye of the beholder standing at a distance to blend them together. Compared to the work of traditional artists, the Impressionists' paintings seemed sketchlike and perhaps careless. Their aim was to capture the fleeting image and to recreate light, atmosphere, and movement in all their natural brilliance.

The group dissolved after 1886, but their influence lived on, revolutionizing European painting and preparing the way for the diverse styles of the 20th century.

IMPRESSION: SUNRISE *This painting by Claude Monet, exhibited at the Impressionists' first group show in Paris in 1874, was to give the group their name . . . and to add a word to the vocabulary of art. The name was first used mockingly by the French critic Louis Leroy.*

THE RED ROOFS *The colors seem to vibrate on the canvas in Camille Pissarro's painting, of which a part is shown above. His aim was not to define precisely but to use swift brushstrokes to give an instant impression.*

LE MOULIN DE LA GALETTE *The Moulin was a popular Montmartre entertainment spot for young Parisians and their girls. Auguste Renoir immortalized the gaiety and bustle of a Sunday afternoon dance there in the 1870's. His use of dappled light is typical of Impressionism.*

---

taste; **indelicate** suggests immodesty, coarseness, or tactlessness. **Indecent** refers to what is offensive or harmful morally. **Indecorous** implies violation of the manners of polite society.

improper fraction *n.* A fraction that is greater than or equal to one, such as $9/5$, $217/4$, $12/12$. Compare **proper fraction**.

improper integral *n.* An integral having at least one nonfinite limit or having an integrand that becomes infinite between the limits of integration.

im·pro·pri·ate (ĭm-prō′prē-āt′) *tr.v.* **-ated, -ating, -ates.** To transfer (church property, tithes, or the like) into lay hands. [Medieval Latin *impropriāre,* from *proprius,* own.] —**im·pro·pri·a·tion** *n.* —**im·pro·pri·a·tor** *n.*

im·pro·pri·e·ty (ĭm′prə-prī′ə-tē) *n., pl.* **-ties. 1.** The quality or condition of being improper. **2.** An improper act. **3.** An improper or unacceptable usage in speech or writing.

im·prove (ĭm-pro͞ov′) *v.* **-proved, -proving, -proves.** —*tr.* **1.** To advance to a better state or quality; make better. **2.** To increase the productivity or value of (property or land, for example). —*intr.* **1.** To become or get better. **2.** To make beneficial additions or changes: *improve on the translation.* [Earlier *improwe,* from Norman French *emprouer,* to turn to profit : Old French *en-* (causative) + *prou,* profit, from Late Latin *prōde,* advantageous (see **proud**).] —**im·prov·a·bil·i·ty** *n.* —**im·prov·a·ble** *adj.* —**im·prov·er** *n.*

Synonyms: ameliorate, better, enhance, help.

im·prove·ment (ĭm-pro͞ov′mənt) *n.* **1.** The act of improving. **2.** The state of being improved. **3. a.** A change or addition that improves. **b.** A person or thing that incurs a change for the better.

Usage: *Improvement* may be followed by *in* or *on,* depending on the context. To say that there is an *improvement in* something is simply to say that "something has improved." *Improvement on* is used only in the context of comparison: *That is a great improvement on yesterday's performance.*

im·prov·i·dent (ĭm-prŏv′ə-dənt) *adj.* **1.** Not providing for the future; thriftless. **2.** Rash; incautious. **—im·prov·i·dence** *n.* **—im·prov·i·dent·ly** *adv.*

im·pro·vi·sa·tion (ĭm-prŏv′ə-zā′shən, ĭm′prə-və-) *n.* **1.** The act of improvising. **2.** Something improvised, especially a dramatic skit. **—im·pro·vi·sa·tion·al** *adj.*

im·prov·i·sa·tor (ĭm-prŏv′ə-zā′tər) *n.* One who improvises; especially, one who improvises music or verse, for example. **—im·pro·vi·sa·to·ri·al** (ĭm-prŏv′ə-zə-tôr′ē-əl, -tōr′ē-əl) *adj.* **—im·pro·vi·sa·to·ry** (ĭm′prə-vī′zə-tôr′ē, -tōr′ē) *adj.*

im·pro·vise (ĭm′prə-vīz′) *v.* **-vised, -vising, -vises.** —*tr.* **1.** To invent, compose, or recite without preparation. **2.** To make or provide from available materials. —*intr.* To invent, compose, recite, or execute something spontaneously or without preparation. [French *improviser,* from Italian *improvvisare,* from *improvviso,* unforeseen, impromptu, from Latin *imprōvīsus,* : *in-,* not + *prōvīsus,* past participle of *prōvīdere,* to foresee, PROVIDE.] **—im·pro·vis·er** *n.*

im·pro·vised (ĭm′prə-vīzd′) *adj.* **1.** Invented, composed, or recited spontaneously or without preparation. **2.** Made with whatever was available at the time. —See Synonyms at **extemporaneous.**

im·pru·dence (ĭm-pro͞o′dəns) *n.* **1.** The quality or condition of being imprudent. **2.** An imprudent act.

im·pru·dent (ĭm-pro͞o′dənt) *adj.* Not prudent; unwise or injudicious; rash. [Middle English, from Latin *imprūdēns* : *in-,* not + *prūdēns,* PRUDENT.] **—im·pru·dent·ly** *adv.*

im·pu·dent (ĭm′pyə-dənt) *adj.* **1.** Impertinent; rude; disrespectful. **2.** *Obsolete.* Immodest. —See Synonyms at **shameless.** [Middle English, from Latin *impudēns* : *in-,* not + *pudēns* (stem *pudent-*), present participle of *pudēre,* to be ashamed.] **—im·pu·dence, im·pu·den·cy** *n.* **—im·pu·dent·ly** *adv.*

im·pu·dic·i·ty (ĭm′pyo͞o-dĭs′ə-tē) *n. Archaic.* Immodesty; shamelessness. [Old French *impudicite,* from Latin *impudicus,* immodest : *in-,* not + *pudicus,* modest, from *pudēre,* to be ashamed.]

im·pugn (ĭm-pyo͞on′) *tr.v.* **-pugned, -pugning, -pugns.** To oppose or attack as false; criticize; challenge. [Middle English *impugnen,* from Old French *impugner,* from Latin *impugnāre,* to fight against : *in-,* against + *pugnāre,* to fight.] **—im·pugn·a·ble** *adj.* **—im·pugn·er** *n.* **—im·pugn·ment** *n.*

im·pu·is·sance (ĭm-pyo͞o′ə-səns, ĭm-pwĭs′əns) *n.* Lack of power or effectiveness; weakness; impotence. **—im·pu·is·sant** *adj.*

im·pulse (ĭm′pŭls′) *n.* **1.** An impelling force or the motion it produces; a thrust; a push; momentum; impetus. **2.** A sudden inclination or urge; a desire; whim: *an impulse to speak up.* **3.** A motivating propensity; a drive; an instinct. **4.** *Physics.* The product of the average value of a force and the time during which it acts, equal in general to the change in momentum produced by the force in this time interval. **5.** *Physiology.* A **nerve impulse** *(see).* [Latin *impulsus,* from the past participle of *impellere,* IMPEL.]

impulse buying *n.* The purchasing of goods as a result of a sudden urge rather than deliberate planning.

impulse turbine *n.* A type of turbine that is driven by jets of fluid directed onto the blades, used especially in the generation of hydroelectricity.

im·pul·sion (ĭm-pŭl′shən) *n.* **1.** The act of impelling or the condition of being impelled. **2.** An impelling force; a thrust. **3.** Motion produced by an impelling force. **4.** An urging; compulsion.

im·pul·sive (ĭm-pŭl′sĭv) *adj.* **1.** Inclined to act on impulse rather than thought. **2.** Produced as a result of impulse; precipitate; uncalculated: *an impulsive act.* **3.** Having force or power to impel or incite; forceful. **4.** *Physics.* Acting within brief time intervals. Said especially of a force. —See Synonyms at **spontaneous.** **—im·pul·sive·ly** *adv.* **—im·pul·sive·ness** *n.*

im·pu·ni·ty (ĭm-pyo͞o′nə-tē) *n., pl.* **-ties.** **1.** Exemption from punishment or penalty. **2.** Immunity or preservation from recrimination, retribution, regret, or the like. [Latin *impūnitās* (stem *impūnitāt-*), from *impūnis,* not punished : *in-,* not + *poena,* penalty, pain, from Greek *poina, poinē,* expiation, punishment.]

im·pure (ĭm-pyo͝or′) *adj.* **1.** Not pure or clean; contaminated. **2.** Not purified by religious rite; defiled. **3.** Immoral or obscene; unchaste. **4.** Mixed with another substance; alloyed; adulterated. **5.** Being a composite of more than one color, or mixed with black or white. Said of color. **6.** Deriving from more than one source, style, or convention; bastardized. Said of the arts. **7.** Containing improper usages or foreign elements. Said of language. **—im·pure·ly** *adv.* **—im·pure·ness** *n.*

im·pu·ri·ty (ĭm-pyo͝or′ə-tē) *n., pl.* **-ties.** **1.** The quality or condition of being impure: *moral impurity.* **2. a.** Something that is impure. **b.** Something that renders something else impure; a contaminant. **3.** *Electronics.* An element added in small controlled amounts to a pure crystal of another element in order to produce or modify semiconductor properties.

im·put·a·ble (ĭm-pyo͞o′tə-bəl) *adj.* Capable of being ascribed or imputed; attributable. **—im·put·a·bil·i·ty** *n.* **—im·put·a·bly** *adv.*

im·pu·ta·tion (ĭm′pyo͞o-tā′shən) *n.* **1.** The act of imputing. **2.** Something imputed or ascribed.

im·pu·ta·tive (ĭm-pyo͞o′tə-tĭv) *adj.* Characterized by or arising from imputation. **—im·pu·ta·tive·ly** *adv.*

im·pute (ĭm-pyo͞ot′) *tr.v.* **-puted, -puting, -putes.** **1.** To ascribe (a crime or fault) to another. **2.** To attribute to a cause or source. **3.** *Theology.* To attribute (wickedness or merit) to a person. —See Synonyms at **attribute.** [Middle English *inputen,* from Old French *imputer,* from Latin *imputāre,* to bring into the reckoning : *in-,* in, into, + *putāre,* to reckon, compute, consider.]

in (ĭn) *prep.* **1. a.** Within the confines of; inside: *in the safe.* **b.** Within the area covered by: *playing in the mud; We live in Spain.* **c.** *Informal.* Into: *came in my office.* **2.** On or affecting some part of: *He was hit in the head.* **3. a.** As a part, aspect, or property of: *a delay in delivery.* **b.** Within the scope or context of: *in the story; in physics.* **c.** Included as part of: *in the first batch.* **d.** Resulting from the operations of: *in her imagination.* **4. a.** During the course of or before the expiration of: *ready in a few minutes.* **b.** At the time of: *in winter.* **5. a.** At the position of: *put in command.* **b.** Closely associated with, especially in a professional way or as an occupation: *in banking.* **6.** After the pattern or form of: *going around in circles.* **7.** To or at the condition or situation of; into: *in trouble.* **8.** As an expression of; out of; by way of: *said in anger; in answer to the question.* **9. a.** During or as part of the act or process of: *in hot pursuit.* **b.** While affected by: *in his delirium.* **10.** With the attribute of: *in silence.* **11. a.** By means of: *paid in cash.* **b.** Made with or through the medium of; using: *a text written in French.* **12.** Within the category or class of: *the latest thing in fashion.* **13.** With reference to; as regards: *in my opinion; equal in speed.* **14.** Wearing: *in pajamas.* **15.** Used to indicate ratio, rate, or number: *a one in five chance; killed in their hundreds.* **—in all.** Taking the whole sum into account: *ten dollars in all.* **—in on.** Involved or associated with: *in on the latest project.* **—in that.** Inasmuch as; since.
~*adv.* **1.** To or toward the inside or a center; inward: *He stepped in; the group closed in.* **2.** Toward a particular or appropriate destination or location: *sailed in; news is coming in.* **3.** Into a given place or position: *Let her in.* **4. a.** Present or as being present: *tell me when he's going to be in; count me in.* **b.** Indoors: *time to go in.* **5.** Into a given activity together: *joined in and sang.* **6.** Inward: *caved in.* **7.** So as to blend with or be part of something: *mix in.* **8.** So as to achieve a state of popularity or power: *skirts are coming back in; the Democrats got in.* **—all in.** *Informal.* Very tired; exhausted. **—in for.** About to experience something, usually something unpleasant: *He's in for a shock.* **—in with.** On familiar or friendly terms with: *get in with the boss.*
~*adj.* **1.** Fashionable; popular; prestigious: *the in place to go.* **2.** Exclusive or private; appealing to a clique: *a member of the in crowd; telling in jokes.* **3.** Having power; incumbent: *the in party.*
~*n.* **1.** *Often* **ins.** Those in power or having the advantage. **2.** *Informal.* A means of access or favor. **—ins and outs.** **1.** The twists and turns, as of a road. **2.** The intricacies of an activity, situation, or process. [Middle English *in,* Old English *in, inn.*]

In The symbol for the element indium.

IN Indiana (used with a Zip Code).

in-¹ *prefix.* Also **i-** (before g), **il-** (before *l*), **im-** (before *b, m, p*), **ir-** (before *r*). Indicates not, lacking, or without; for example, **inaction.** —See Usage notes at **non-, un-.** [Middle English, from Old French, from Latin.]

in-² *prefix.* Also **il-** (before *l*), **im-** (before *b, m, p*), **ir-** (before *r*). Indicates: **1.** In, into, within, or inward; for example, **incretion, intubation. 2.** Intensive action; for example, **impress, implant, inosculate. 3.** Causative function (with basic meaning "to cause to become," "to put in"); for example, **integrate, impound, imperil.** Compare **en-**¹. [Middle English, from Old French, from Latin, from *in,* in, within. In borrowed Latin compounds, *in-* indicates (in addition to the above senses): 1. On, upon, as in **inunction.** 2. Toward, to, as in **irradiate, imminent.** 3. Against, as in **impugn, infest.**]

in-³ *comb. form.* Indicates found or taking place within a specified context: for example, **in-flight, in-service.**

-in¹ *suffix.* Also **-ein** (for sense 1). Indicates: **1.** A neutral chemical compound, such as glyceride or protein, as distinguished from an alkaloid or basic substance; for example, **globulin, phthalein. 2.** Enzyme; for example, **pancreatin. 3.** Names of drugs and other pharmaceutical products; for example, **penicillin, aspirin. 4.** Certain other individual chemical compounds; for example, **glycerin.** [French *-ine,* from Latin *-īna,* feminine of *-īnus,* belonging to. See **-ine.**]

-in² *comb. form.* Indicates organized participatory activity: **phone-in; love-in.**

in. inch or inches.

-ina *suffix.* Indicates feminine names or titles: for example, **Georgina, czarina.**

in·a·bil·i·ty (ĭn′ə-bĭl′ə-tē) *n.* Lack of ability or means.

in ab·sen·ti·a (ĭn ăb-sĕn′shē-ə, -shə) *adv.* In absence; while or although not present: *The prisoner was sentenced in absentia by the judge.*

in·ac·ces·si·ble (ĭn′ăk-sĕs′ə-bəl) *adj.* **1.** Not accessible; difficult to approach or reach. **2.** Difficult to obtain. **—in·ac·ces·si·bil·i·ty** *n.* **—in·ac·ces·si·bly** *adv.*

in·ac·cu·ra·cy (ĭn-ăk′yər-ə-sē) *n., pl.* **-cies.** **1.** The quality or condition of being inaccurate. **2.** An error or mistake.

in·ac·cu·rate (ĭn-ăk′yər-ĭt) *adj.* **1.** Not accurate. **2.** Mistaken or incorrect. **—in·ac·cu·rate·ly** *adv.* **—in·ac·cu·rate·ness** *n.*

in·ac·tion (ĭn-ăk′shən) *n.* Lack or absence of action or activity.

in·ac·ti·vate (ĭn-ăk′tə-vāt′) *tr.v.* **-vated, -vating, -vates.** To render inactive. **—in·ac·ti·va·tion** *n.*

in·ac·tive (ĭn-ăk′tĭv) *adj.* **1.** Not active or not tending to be active. **2. a.** Not functioning; being out of use. **b.** Retired from or not engaged in military duty or service. **3. a.** *Chemistry.* Not readily participating in chemical reactions. **b.** *Biology.* Having no significant effect on or interaction with living organisms. **c.** *Medicine.* Quiescent. Said especially of a disease. **d.** *Physics.* Displaying little

PRONUNCIATION KEY

ă, pat; ā, pay; âr, care;
ä, father, are; b, bib;
ch, church; d, deed; ĕ, pet;
ē, be; f, fife; g, gag; h, hat;
hw, which; ĭ, pit; ī, pie;
îr, pier; j, judge; k, kick;
l, lid, needle; m, mum;
n, no, sudden; ng, thing;
ŏ, pot; ō, toe; ô, paw, for;
oi, noise; ou, out; o͝o, book;
o͞o, boot; p, pop; r, roar;
s, sauce; sh, ship, dish;
t, tight; th, thin, path;
th, this, bathe; ŭ, cut; ûr, fur;
v, valve; w, with; y, yes;
z, zebra, size; zh, vision;
ə, about, item, edible,
gallop, circus, peaceful

IN FOREIGN WORDS:

à, *Fr.* ami; œ, *Fr.* feu, *Ger.* schön; ü, *Fr.* tu, *Ger.* über; KH, *Ger.* ich, *Scot.* loch; N, *Fr.* bon; y′, *Fr.* Compiègne

STRESS MARKS:

Primary stress: ′
in·cite′ (ĭn-sīt′)
Secondary stress: ′
in′sight′ (ĭn′sīt′)

or no radioactivity. —**in·ac·tive·ly** adv. —**in·ac·tive·ness, in·ac·tiv·i·ty** n.

 Synonyms: dormant, idle, inert, passive, supine, torpid.

in·ad·e·qua·cy (ĭn-ăd′ĭ-kwə-sē) n., pl. **-cies. 1.** The quality or condition of being inadequate. **2.** A failing or lack; defect.

in·ad·e·quate (ĭn-ăd′ĭ-kwĭt) adj. **1.** Not adequate; insufficient. **2.** Not able; incapable. **3.** Socially awkward or ill-at-ease; gauche. —**in·ad·e·quate·ly** adv.

in·ad·mis·si·ble (ĭn′əd-mĭs′ə-bəl) adj. Not admissible or allowed: inadmissible evidence. —**in·ad·mis·si·bil·i·ty** n. —**in·ad·mis·si·bly** adv.

in·ad·ver·tence (ĭn′əd-vûr′təns) n. Also **in·ad·ver·ten·cy** (-tən-sē) pl. **-cies. 1.** The quality of being inadvertent. **2.** An instance of being inadvertent; a mistake; oversight. [Medieval Latin inadvertentia : Latin in-, not + advertēns, present participle of advertēre, to ADVERT.]

in·ad·ver·tent (ĭn′əd-vûr′tənt) adj. **1.** Not duly attentive; negligent. **2.** Accidental; unintentional. [Back-formation from INADVERTENCE.] —**in·ad·ver·tent·ly** adv.

in·ad·vis·a·ble (ĭn′əd-vī′zə-bəl) adj. Unwise; not recommended. —**in·ad·vis·a·bil·i·ty** n.

-inae suffix. Indicates the names of zoological subfamilies.

in ae·ter·num (ĭn ē-tûr′nəm) adv. Latin. Forever; to eternity.

in·al·ien·a·ble (ĭn-āl′yə-nə-bəl) adj. Not to be removed or transferred to another; not alienable: inalienable rights. —**in·al·ien·a·bil·i·ty** n. —**in·al·ien·a·bly** adv.

in·al·ter·a·ble (ĭn-ôl′tər-ə-bəl) adj. Not alterable; unchangeable. —**in·al·ter·a·bil·i·ty** n. —**in·al·ter·a·bly** adv.

in·am·o·ra·ta (ĭn-ăm′ə-rä′tə, ĭn′ăm-) n., pl. **-tas.** A woman with whom one is in love. [Italian, from feminine of inamorato, past participle of inam(m)orare, to inspire love in, enamor : in-, in, into + amore, love, from Latin amor, love, from amāre, to love.]

in·am·o·ra·to (ĭn-ăm′ə-rä′tō, ĭn′ăm-) n., pl. **-tos.** A man with whom one is in love. [Italian, from the past participle of inam(m)orare, enamor. See **inamorata.**]

in-and-in (ĭn′ən-ĭn′) adv. Repeatedly within the same or closely related stocks: to breed pigs in-and-in. —**in-and-in** adj.

in-and-out (ĭn′ənd-out′) adj. Involving the purchase and sale of a single security within a short period of time.

in·ane (ĭn-ān′) adj. Lacking intelligence, sense, or substance; empty; silly: an inane comment. —See Synonyms at **foolish.**
 ~n. Rare. Something that is empty; specifically, the empty void of infinite space. [Latin inānis†, empty, vain.] —**in·ane·ly** adv.

in·an·i·mate (ĭn-ăn′ə-mĭt) adj. **1.** Not animate; not having the qualities associated with active, living organisms. **2.** Not exhibiting life; appearing lifeless or dead. **3.** Not animated or energetic; listless; spiritless. —See Usage note at **dead.** —**in·an·i·mate·ly** adv. —**in·an·i·mate·ness** n. —**in·an·i·ma·tion** n.

in·a·ni·tion (ĭn′ə-nĭsh′ən) n. **1.** Exhaustion, as from lack of nourishment. **2.** The condition or quality of being spiritually or mentally empty. [Middle English, from Late Latin inānītiō (stem inānītiōn-), from inānīre, to make empty, from inānis, empty, INANE.]

in·an·i·ty (ĭn-ăn′ə-tē) n., pl. **-ties. 1.** The condition or quality of being inane. **2.** An inane or absurd act or remark.

in·ap·peas·a·ble (ĭn′ə-pē′zə-bəl) adj. Incapable of being appeased.

in·ap·pel·la·ble (ĭn′ə-pĕl′ə-bəl) adj. Law. Incapable of being appealed against: an inappellable decision. [Obsolete French inappelable, from appeler, to APPEAL.]

in·ap·pe·tence (ĭn-ăp′ə-təns) n. Also **in·ap·pe·ten·cy** (-tən-sē). Lack of appetite or desire. —**in·ap·pe·tent** adj.

in·ap·pli·ca·ble (ĭn-ăp′lĭ-kə-bəl) adj. Not applicable. —**in·ap·pli·ca·bil·i·ty** n. —**in·ap·pli·ca·bly** adv.

in·ap·po·site (ĭn-ăp′ə-zĭt) adj. Not pertinent; unsuitable. —**in·ap·po·site·ly** adv. —**in·ap·po·site·ness** n.

in·ap·pre·ci·a·ble (ĭn′ə-prē′shē-ə-bəl) adj. Not appreciable; insignificant; negligible. —**in·ap·pre·ci·a·bly** adv.

in·ap·pre·ci·a·tive (ĭn′ə-prē′shə-tĭv, -shē-ā′tĭv) adj. Feeling or showing no appreciation; unappreciative. —**in·ap·pre·ci·a·tive·ly** adv. —**in·ap·pre·ci·a·tive·ness** n.

in·ap·proach·a·ble (ĭn′ə-prō′chə-bəl) adj. Not approachable; inaccessible. —**in·ap·proach·a·bil·i·ty** n. —**in·ap·proach·a·bly** adv.

in·ap·pro·pri·ate (ĭn′ə-prō′prē-ĭt) adj. Not appropriate; unsuitable. —**in·ap·pro·pri·ate·ly** adv. —**in·ap·pro·pri·ate·ness** n.

in·apt (ĭn-ăpt′) adj. **1.** Not appropriate; unsuitable. **2.** Unskillful; inept.

 Usage: Inapt and inept are frequently interchangeable, but there is a tendency in modern English to differentiate their contexts of use. Inept generally applies to clumsiness of language or behavior: an inept remark, inept handling of the situation. Inapt tends to be used more with abstract ideas and has the sense of something inappropriate: an inapt comparison would be one which did not make its intended point. Unapt is also used in this way.

in·ap·ti·tude (ĭn-ăp′tə-tōod, -tyōod′) n. **1.** Inappropriateness. **2.** Lack of skill; ineptitude.

in·arch (ĭn-ärch′) tr.v. **-arched, -arching, -arches.** To graft by joining independently growing scions that have not been removed from the parent stock. [IN + ARCH.]

in·arm (ĭn-ärm′) tr.v. **-armed, -arming, -arms.** Rare. To embrace.

in·ar·tic·u·late (ĭn′är-tĭk′yə-lĭt) adj. **1.** Uttered without the use of normal words or syllables; incomprehensible. **2. a.** Unable to speak; speechless. **b.** Unable to speak with clarity or eloquence. **3.** Unable to be expressed in words: inarticulate sorrow. **4.** Biology.

Not having joints or segments. —**in·ar·tic·u·late·ly** adv. —**in·ar·tic·u·la·cy, in·ar·tic·u·late·ness** n.

in·ar·tis·tic (ĭn′är-tĭs′tĭk) adj. **1.** Not conforming to the principles or criteria of art. **2.** Not artistic; not appreciating or possessing skill in art. —**in·ar·tis·ti·cal·ly** adv.

in·as·much as (ĭn′əz-mŭch′) conj. **1.** Because of the fact that; since. **2.** To the extent that; insofar as. —See Usage note at **insofar.**

in·at·ten·tion (ĭn′ə-tĕn′shən) n. Lack of attention, notice, or regard; heedlessness; neglect.

in·at·ten·tive (ĭn′ə-tĕn′tĭv) adj. Showing a lack of attention; negligent. —**in·at·ten·tive·ly** adv. —**in·at·ten·tive·ness** n.

in·au·di·ble (ĭn-ô′də-bəl) adj. Incapable of being heard; not audible. —**in·au·di·bil·i·ty** n. —**in·au·di·bly** adv.

in·au·gu·ral (ĭn-ô′gyər-əl) adj. Of, pertaining to, or characteristic of an inauguration.
 ~n. A speech or address made at an inauguration.

in·au·gu·rate (ĭn-ô′gyə-rāt′) tr.v. **-rated, -rating, -rates. 1.** To admit (a president, prime minister, or the like) into office by a formal ceremony. **2.** To begin or start officially. **3.** To open or begin use of formally with a ceremony; dedicate. —See Synonyms at **begin.** [Latin inaugurāre, to take omens from the flight of birds, to consecrate, install : in, in + augurāre, to augur, from augur, soothsayer.] —**in·au·gu·ra·tor** n.

in·au·gu·ra·tion (ĭn-ô′gyə-rā′shən) n. **1.** A formal beginning or introduction. **2.** Formal introduction to an office or position of power.

Inauguration Day n. The day, January 20, on which the newly elected president of the United States is installed in office.

in·aus·pi·cious (ĭn′ô-spĭsh′əs) adj. Not auspicious; ill-omened. —**in·aus·pi·cious·ly** adv. —**in·aus·pi·cious·ness** n.

in between prep. Between two things, limits, or the like. —**in between** adv.

in-be·tween (ĭn′bĭ-twĕn′) adj. Intermediate.
 ~n. An intermediate or intermediary: conservatives, radicals, and in-betweens.

in·board (ĭn′bôrd′, -bōrd′) adj. **1.** Nautical. Within the hull or toward the center of a ship: an inboard engine. **2.** Aeronautics. Designating either of the two engines that are closest to the fuselage in an aircraft with four or more wing-mounted engines. **3.** Toward the center of a machine.
 ~n. A motor attached to the inside of the hull of a boat. Compare **outboard motor.** [IN + BOARD.] —**in·board** adv.

in·born (ĭn′bôrn′) adj. **1.** Possessed by an organism at birth. **2.** Inherited or hereditary. —See Synonyms at **innate.**

in·bound (ĭn′bound′) adj. Homeward bound or incoming.

in·bounds (ĭn′boundz′) Of or pertaining to a means of putting the ball in play by having one player standing out of bounds pass it to another player on the court.

in·breathe (ĭn′brēth′) tr.v. **-breathed, -breathing, -breathes. 1.** To breathe in; inhale. **2.** Rare. To inspire.

in·bred (ĭn′brĕd′) adj. **1.** Produced by inbreeding. **2.** Innate; deep-seated. —See Synonyms at **innate.**

in·breed (ĭn′brēd′) tr.v. **-bred** (-brĕd′), **-breeding, -breeds. 1.** To produce by the continued breeding of closely related individuals. **2.** To breed or develop within; engender. —**in·breed·ing** adj. & n.

inc. 1. income. **2.** incorporated. **3.** increase. **4.** including. **5.** inclusive.

Inc. incorporated.

In·ca (ĭng′kə) n., pl. **-cas** or collectively **Inca. 1.** A member of the group of Quechuan Indian peoples who ruled Peru before the Spanish conquest. **2.** A king or other member of the royal family of this group of peoples. [Spanish, from Quechua inka, king, prince.] See feature, next page.

in·cal·cu·la·ble (ĭn-kăl′kyə-lə-bəl) adj. **1.** Not calculable; indeterminate. **2.** Incapable of being foreseen; unpredictable; uncertain: the incalculable consequences of her actions. —**in·cal·cu·la·bil·i·ty, in·cal·cu·la·ble·ness** n. —**in·cal·cu·la·bly** adv.

in·ca·les·cent (ĭn′kə-lĕs′ənt) adj. Chemistry. Growing warm; increasing in temperature. [Latin incalescēns (stem incalescent-), present participle of incalescere : IN- + calescere, grow warm, from calēre, be warm.] —**in·ca·les·cence** n.

in camera (ĭn kăm′ər-ə) adv. **1.** In secret, private, or closed session. **2.** Law. In private with a judge rather than in open court; in the chambers of a judge. [Latin, "in the chamber."]

in·can·desce (ĭn′kən-dĕs′) v. **-desced, -descing, -desces.** —intr. To become incandescent. —tr. To cause to become incandescent. [Latin incandēscere, to become white with heat, glow : in- (intensive) + candēscere, to become white, glow, from candēre, to be white, shine.]

in·can·des·cence (ĭn′kən-dĕs′əns) n. **1.** The emission of visible light by a hot object. **2.** The light emitted by an incandescent object. **3.** A high degree of emotion, intensity, brilliance, or the like: his rhetoric reached incandescence. —See Synonyms at **blaze.**

in·can·des·cent (ĭn′kən-dĕs′ənt) adj. **1.** Emitting a visible white glow as a result of being heated. **2.** Very intense, brilliant, or bright: incandescent eyes; incandescent anger. —See Synonyms at **bright.** —**in·can·des·cent·ly** adv.

incandescent lamp n. An electric lamp in which a filament is heated to incandescence by an electric current.

in·can·ta·tion (ĭn′kăn-tā′shən) n. **1. a.** Ritual recitation or chanting of charms or spells to produce a magical effect. **b.** The casting of these spells. **2.** The formulaic words, phrases, or sounds used in this manner. [Middle English incantacioun, from Old French incanta-

Inca

EMPIRE PERCHED ON THE SPINE OF THE ANDES
State ownership and benefits 500 years ago

Most of the world's major empires have been based in valleys and lowlands, where broad rivers ease trade and communications. Uniquely, the Incas created an empire in the heights, an empire that stretched along the Andean spine of South America for nearly 5,000 kilometers (3,125 miles), from present-day Ecuador southward to Chile and Argentina.

The name Inca, which now refers to a whole culture, was originally the title given to its chief by a small tribe that settled near Cuzco in Peru in about A.D. 1000.

In about 1438, a military and administrative genius called Pachacuti became Inca. In little more than 50 years, he and his son Topa forged the mountain tribes into a tightly organized society whose ruler was worshiped as the earthly

representative of the sun god Viracocha.

The Incas made no use of the wheel for transport and they had no writing. But relay runners carrying messages in the form of knotted cords could reach anywhere in the empire within a week. Everything was owned by the state apart from a few personal possessions, and the peasants were drafted in their thousands to terrace the steep hillsides and to work on roads, irrigation schemes, and temples. In return, the state provided them with food when they grew old or were sick.

But the huge empire, of perhaps 16 million people, did not last. It fell to the Spanish in 1530 after the conquistador Francisco Pizarro, at the head of a mere 180 men, kidnapped and killed the Inca Atahualpa.

HIGH CITADEL *Machu Picchu, set on high cliffs in the Andes near Cuzco, was one of the few Inca cities never found by the Spanish. Abandoned by the Incas in the 16th century, its granite temples and terraced fields were rediscovered by U.S. explorer Hiram Bingham in July 1911.*

tion, from Late Latin *incantātiō* (stem *incantātiōn-*), enchantment, spell, from Latin *incantāre,* ENCHANT.] —**in·can·ta·tion·al** *adj.*

in·can·ta·to·ry (ĭn-kăn′tə-tôr′ē, -tōr′ē) *adj.* **1.** Of or pertaining to incantation. **2.** Of or producing a monotonously regular sound: *incantatory verse.*

in·ca·pa·ble (ĭn-kā′pə-bəl) *adj.* **1.** Not capable; lacking the requisite ability or power. **2.** Not admitting of or susceptible to: *incapable of improvement.* **3.** *Law.* Lacking legal qualifications or requirements; ineligible: *incapable of holding office.* —**in·ca·pa·bil·i·ty, in·ca·pa·ble·ness** *n.* —**in·ca·pa·bly** *adv.*

in·ca·pac·i·tate (ĭn′kə-păs′ə-tāt′) *tr.v.* **-tated, -tating, -tates. 1.** To deprive of strength or ability. **2.** To make legally ineligible; disqualify. —**in·ca·pac·i·tant** *n.* —**in·ca·pac·i·ta·tion** *n.*

in·ca·pac·i·ty (ĭn′kə-păs′ə-tē) *n., pl.* **-ties. 1.** Lack of strength or ability; disability; helplessness. **2.** *Law.* That which renders legally ineligible; a disqualification.

incapsulate. Variant of **encapsulate.**

in·car·cer·ate (ĭn-kär′sə-rāt′) *tr.v.* **-ated, -ating, -ates. 1.** To put in jail. **2.** To shut in; confine. [Latin *incarcerāre : in-,* in + *carcer,* prison, enclosed place.] —**in·car·cer·a·tion** *n.* —**in·car·cer·a·tor** *n.*

in·car·na·dine (ĭn-kär′nə-dīn′, -dēn′, -dĭn′) *adj.* **1.** Flesh-colored. **2.** Blood-red.

~*n.* A color resembling flesh or blood.

~*tr.v.* **incarnadined, -dining, -dines.** To make the color of blood or flesh. [Old French *incarnadin,* from Old Italian *incarnadino, incarnatino,* from *incarnato,* flesh-colored, from Late Latin *incarnāre,* INCARNATE.]

in·car·nate (ĭn-kär′nĭt) *adj.* **1. a.** Invested with bodily nature and form: *a god incarnate.* **b.** Embodied or personified: *wisdom incarnate.* **2.** Incarnadine.

~*tr.v.* (ĭn-kär′nāt′) **incarnated, -nating, -nates. 1.** To give bodily, especially human, form to. **2.** To embody or personify. **3.** To actu-

alize; realize. [Late Latin *incarnāre,* to make flesh : Latin *in-* (causative) + *carō* (stem *carn-*), flesh.]

in·car·na·tion (ĭn′kär-nā′shən) *n.* **1.** A manifestation or the act of making a divinity, spirit, or the like manifest in bodily form. **2. Incarnation.** *Theology.* The embodiment of God in the human form of Jesus. **3.** Any bodily manifestation of a supernatural being. **4.** One held to personify a given abstract quality or idea.

incase. Variant of **encase.**

in·cau·tious (ĭn-kô′shəs) *adj.* Not cautious; rash. —**in·cau·tious·ly** *adv.* —**in·cau·tious·ness** *n.*

in·cen·di·ar·y (ĭn-sĕn′dē-ĕr′ē) *adj.* **1. a.** Causing or capable of causing fire. **b.** Producing intense fire. Said of a military weapon. **c.** Of or involving arson. **2.** Tending to inflame or produce anger or violence; inflammatory.

~*n., pl.* **incendiaries. 1.** One who sets fire to property; an arsonist. **2.** One who stirs up violent feelings or quarrels. **3.** An incendiary bomb. [Latin *incendiārius,* from *incendium,* burning, fire, from *incendere,* to set on fire.] —**in·cen·di·a·rism** *n.*

incendiary bomb *n.* A bomb used to start a fire. Also called "fire bomb," "incendiary."

in·cense¹ (ĭn-sĕns′) *tr.v.* **-censed, -censing, -censes.** To cause to be angry or indignant; outrage. [Middle English *encensen,* from Old French *incenser,* from Latin *incendere* (past participle *incensus*), to set on fire, enrage.] —**in·cense·ment** *n.*

in·cense² (ĭn′sĕns′) *n.* **1.** An aromatic substance, as a gum or wood, that burns with a pleasant odor. **2.** The smoke or odor produced by the burning of such a substance. **3.** Broadly, any pleasant smell. **4.** Adulation; praise; admiration.

~*tr.v.* **incensed, -censing, -censes. 1.** To perfume with incense. **2.** To burn incense in front of, especially as a ritual act. [Middle English *insens, encens,* from Old French *encens,* from Late Latin *incensum,* neuter past participle of Latin *incendere,* to set on fire.]

in·cen·tive (ĭn-sĕn′tĭv) *n.* Something inciting to action or effort, such as the fear of punishment or the expectation of reward.

~*adj.* Inciting; motivating. [Middle English, from Latin *incentīvum,* from the neuter of *incentīvus,* that sets the tune, inciting, from *incinere* (past participle *incentus*), to sing, sound : *in-* (intensive) + *canere,* to sing.]

in·cept (ĭn-sĕpt′) *tr.v.* **-cepted, -cepting, -cepts. 1.** *Biology.* To take in (food); ingest. **2.** Formerly, to take the degree of master or doctor at a university. [Latin *inceptus,* begun, attempted, past participle of *incipere,* to begin : IN- + *capere,* to take.]

in·cep·tion (ĭn-sĕp′shən) *n.* The beginning of something. —See Synonyms at **origin.** [Latin *inceptiō* (stem *inceptiōn-*), from *incipere,* to take in hand, begin : *in-,* in + *capere,* to take.]

in·cep·tive (ĭn-sĕp′tĭv) *adj.* **1.** Incipient; beginning. **2.** *Grammar.* Expressing an action, state, or occurrence in its initial phase. Used of certain verbs, for example, *start* or *wake.*

~*n.* An inceptive verb.

in·cer·ti·tude (ĭn-sûr′tə-tōōd′, -tyōōd′) *n.* **1.** Uncertainty; doubt. **2.** Insecurity or instability. [Old French, from Late Latin *incertitūdō : in-,* not + *certitūdō,* CERTITUDE.]

in·ces·sant (ĭn-sĕs′ənt) *adj.* Continuing without respite or interruption; unceasing. —See Synonyms at **continual.** [Late Latin *incessāns : in-,* not + *cessāns* (stem *cessant-*), present participle of *cessāre,* CEASE.] —**in·cess·an·cy, in·cess·ant·ness** *n.* —**in·ces·sant·ly** *adv.*

in·cest (ĭn′sĕst′) *n.* **1.** Sexual union between persons who are so closely related that their marriage is illegal or contrary to custom. **2.** The crime committed by such closely related persons who marry, cohabit, or copulate illegally. [Middle English, from Latin *incestus,* "unchaste," "impure" : *in-,* not + *castus,* CHASTE.]

in·ces·tu·ous (ĭn-sĕs′chōō-əs) *adj.* **1.** Of or involving incest. **2.** Having committed incest. **3.** Resulting from incest. **4.** Excessively introspective or mutually involved: *an incestuous group of friends.* —**in·ces·tu·ous·ly** *adv.* —**in·ces·tu·ous·ness** *n.*

inch¹ (ĭnch) *n. Abbr.* **in. 1.** A unit of length in the U.S. Customary and British Imperial systems, equal to ¹/₁₂ of a foot or 25.4 millimeters. **2.** A unit of pressure equal to the pressure required to balance a column of mercury one inch high in a barometer. **3.** A depth of water or snow that would cover a surface with a layer one inch deep: *two inches of rain.* **4.** A very small amount or distance: *wouldn't budge an inch.* —**by inches.** Gradually; by small degrees. —**every inch.** In every respect: *every inch a gentleman.* —**inch by inch.** Very gradually. —**within an inch of.** Almost to the point of. —**within an inch of one's life. 1.** Close to death. **2.** Thoroughly; soundly: *beat him within an inch of his life.*

~*v.* **inched, inching, inches.** —*intr.* To move slowly or by small degrees. —*tr.* To cause to move in such a manner. [Middle English *inch(e),* Old English *ince, ynce,* from Latin *unica,* twelfth part, inch, ounce, from *ūnus,* one.]

inch² *n. Scottish.* A small island, especially one near the seacoast. Used in place names. [Middle English *inch, ynche,* from Scottish Gaelic *innis,* akin to Old Irish *inis†.*]

inch·meal (ĭnch′mēl′) *adv.* Gradually; little by little. [*inch* + *piecemeal.*]

in·cho·ate (ĭn-kō′ĭt) *adj.* **1.** In an initial or early stage; just beginning; incipient. **2.** Immature; imperfect. [Latin *inchoātus,* past participle of *inchoāre, incohāre,* to begin, originally "to harness" : *in-,* in + *cohum,* strap fastening the plough beam to the yoke.] —**in·cho·ate·ly** *adv.*

in·cho·a·tion (ĭn′kō-ā′shən) *n.* A beginning; start; origin.

in·cho·a·tive (ĭn-kō'ə-tĭv) *adj. Grammar.* Inceptive. Used of certain verbs. —**in·cho·a·tive** *n.*

In·chon (ĭn'chŏn'). City of northwestern South Korea, on the Yellow Sea. It has an ice-free harbor, and fishing is an important industry. During the Korean War U.S. troops landed at Inchon (1950) to launch the UN drive northward.

inch·worm (ĭnch'wûrm') *n.* A **measuring worm** *(see).*

in·ci·dence (ĭn'sə-dəns) *n.* **1.** An act, instance, or manner of occurring or affecting; an occurrence. **2.** The extent or frequency of the occurrence of something. **3.** *Physics.* The arrival of incident radiation or of an incident projectile at a surface.

in·ci·dent (ĭn'sə-dənt) *n.* **1.** A definite, distinct occurrence; an event. **2.** An event that is subordinate to another. **3.** Something contingent upon or related to something else. **4. a.** A relatively minor occurrence or event that precipitates a public crisis. **b.** An event involving violence or hostilities. —See Synonyms at **occurrence.**
~*adj.* **1.** Tending to arise or occur as a minor concomitant. Used with *to*: *"There is a professional melancholy . . . incident to the occupation of a tailor"* (Charles Lamb). **2.** Related to or dependent on another thing. **3.** *Law.* Contingent upon or related to something else. **4.** *Physics.* Falling upon; striking. [Middle English, from Old French, from Latin *incidēns* (stem *incident-*), present participle of *incidere,* to fall upon, happen to : *in-,* on + *cadere,* to fall.]

in·ci·den·tal (ĭn'sə-dĕnt'l) *adj.* **1.** Occurring as a fortuitous or minor concomitant: *incidental expenses.* **2.** Attending or related. Often used with *to*: *action incidental to the main plot.* **3.** Following upon incidentally. Often used with *upon.*
~*n. Usually* **incidentals.** A minor concomitant circumstance, event, expense, or the like.

in·ci·den·tal·ly (ĭn-sə-dĕnt'l-ē) *adv.* **1.** Casually; by chance. **2.** Parenthetically; by the way.

incidental music *n.* Music that accompanies the action of a play, film, or the like.

in·cin·er·ate (ĭn-sĭn'ə-rāt') *v.* **-ated, -ating, -ates.** —*tr.* To consume by burning to ashes. —*intr.* To burn or burn up. [Medieval Latin *incinerāre* : Latin *in-,* in, into + *cinis* (stem *ciner-*), ashes.] —**in·cin·er·a·tion** *n.*

in·cin·er·a·tor (ĭn-sĭn'ə-rā'tər) *n.* One that incinerates; especially, a furnace or other apparatus for burning waste.

in·cip·i·ent (ĭn-sĭp'ē-ənt) *adj.* In an initial or early stage; just beginning to exist or appear. [Latin *incipiēns* (stem *incipient-*), beginning, present participle of *incipere,* to take in hand, begin : *in-,* in + *capere,* to take.] —**in·cip·i·en·cy, in·cip·i·ence** *n.* —**in·cip·i·ent·ly** *adv.*

in·ci·pit (ĭn'sĭ-pĭt) *n.* A beginning; specifically, an introductory word of a medieval manuscript.

in·cise (ĭn-sīz') *tr.v.* **-cised, -cising, -cises. 1.** To cut into or mark with a sharp instrument. **2.** To cut (designs or writing, for example) into a surface; engrave; carve. [Old French *inciser,* from Latin *incīdere* (past participle *incīsus*) : *in-,* into, in + *caedere,* to cut.]

in·cised (ĭn-sīzd') *adj.* **1.** Cut into; engraved; carved. **2.** Made with or as if with a sharp instrument. **3.** Deeply notched.

in·ci·sion (ĭn-sĭzh'ən) *n.* **1.** The act of incising. **2.** A surgical cut into soft tissue. **3.** A notch, as in the edge of a leaf. **4.** Incisiveness.

in·ci·sive (ĭn-sī'sĭv) *adj.* **1.** Cutting; penetrating. **2.** Trenchant; marked by directness, clarity, and decisiveness: *incisive comments.* [Medieval Latin *incīsīvus,* from Latin *incisus,* past participle of *incīdere,* INCISE.] —**in·ci·sive·ly** *adv.* —**in·ci·sive·ness** *n.*
Synonyms: *biting, crisp, cutting, mordant, trenchant.*

in·ci·sor (ĭn-sī'zər) *n.* A tooth adapted for cutting, located at the front of the mouth. In man there are four incisors in each jaw.

in·cite (ĭn-sīt') *tr.v.* **-cited, -citing, -cites.** To provoke to action, stir up, or urge on. —See Synonyms at **provoke.** [Old French *inciter,* from Latin *incitāre,* to urge, set in violent motion : *in-* (intensive) + *citāre,* frequentative of *ciēre, cīre,* to set in violent motion, rouse, provoke.] —**in·ci·ta·tion** (ĭn'sī-tā'shən) *n.* —**in·cite·ment** *n.* —**in·cit·er** *n.*

in·ci·vil·i·ty (ĭn'sĭ-vĭl'ĭ-tē) *n., pl.* **-ties. 1.** Coarse or ill-mannered behavior; rudeness. **2.** An act of incivility.

incl. including; inclusive.

in·clem·ent (ĭn-klĕm'ənt) *adj.* **1.** Wild; stormy. Said of weather. **2.** *Rare.* Severe or unmerciful. [Latin *inclēmēns* : *in-,* not + *clēmēns,* CLEMENT.] —**in·clem·en·cy** *n.* —**in·clem·ent·ly** *adv.*

in·clin·a·ble (ĭn-klī'nə-bəl) *adj.* **1.** Disposed; inclined. Often used with *to.* **2.** Favorably disposed; amenable. Often used with *to.*

in·cli·na·tion (ĭn'klə-nā'shən) *n.* **1.** An attitude or disposition toward something. **2.** A trend or general tendency toward a particular aspect, condition, or character: *an inclination to be serious.* **3.** Something for which one has a preference or leaning: *an inclination to garden.* **4.** The act of inclining. **5.** The state of being inclined. **6.** A deviation from a definite direction, especially from a horizontal or vertical. **7.** The degree of deviation from a horizontal or vertical. **8.** *Mathematics.* The angle between a line on a graph and the positive limb of the *x*-axis. **9.** *Astronomy.* The angle between the plane of a planet's orbit and that of the ecliptic. **10. Magnetic dip** *(see).* —See Synonyms at **tendency.**

in·cline (ĭn-klīn') *v.* **-clined, -clining, -clines.** —*intr.* **1.** To deviate from a horizontal or vertical; lean; slant; slope. **2.** To have or express a mental tendency; be disposed: *inclines to an opposite view.* **3.** To tend toward a particular state or condition. **4.** To lower or bend the head or body, as in a nod or bow. —*tr.* **1.** To cause to lean, slant, or slope; place at an inclination. **2.** To influence (someone or something) to have a certain preference, leaning, or disposition; dispose. **3.** To bend or lower in a nod or bow.
~*n.* (ĭn'klīn'). An inclined surface; a slope or gradient. [Middle English *inclinen, enclinen,* from Old French *encliner,* from Latin *inclīnāre* : *in-,* toward + *-clīnāre,* to bend, lean.] —**in·clin·er** *n.*

in·clined (ĭn-klīnd') *adj.* **1.** Having a preference or tendency; disposed. Often used with *to.* **2.** Sloping, slanting, or leaning.

inclined plane *n.* **1.** A plane surface inclined to the horizontal. **2.** A simple machine, such as an inclined track or plank, allowing a load to be raised or lowered by rolling or sliding.

in·cli·nom·e·ter (ĭn'klə-nŏm'ə-tər) *n.* **1.** An instrument used to determine **magnetic dip** *(see);* a dip circle. **2.** An instrument for showing the inclination of an aircraft or ship relative to the horizontal. Also called "dip needle." **3.** *Machinery.* A **clinometer** *(see).*

inclose. *Rare.* Variant of **enclose.**

in·clude (ĭn-klōōd') *tr.v.* **-cluded, -cluding, -cludes. 1.** To have as a part or member; be made up of, at least in part; contain. **2.** To contain as a minor or secondary element. **3.** To cause to be a part of something; consider with or put into a group, class, or total. [Middle English *includen,* from Latin *inclūdere,* to shut in : *in-,* in + *claudere,* to close.] —**in·clud·a·ble, in·clud·i·ble** *adj.*
Synonyms: *comprehend, comprise, embrace, involve.*

in·clud·ed (ĭn-klōō'dĭd) *adj.* **1.** *Botany.* Not protruding beyond a surrounding part. Said of stamens that do not project from a corolla. **2.** *Geometry.* Formed by and between two intersecting straight lines: *an included angle.*

in·clu·sion (ĭn-klōō'zhən) *n.* **1.** The act of including or the state of being included. **2.** Something included. **3.** *Mineralogy.* Any solid, liquid, or gaseous foreign body enclosed in a mineral or rock. **4.** *Biology.* Any nonliving mass in cytoplasm. **5.** *Mathematics.* A relationship between two sets valid only when the members of one set are all members of the other. [Latin *inclūsiō* (stem *inclūsiōn-*), from *inclūdere* (past participle *inclūsus*), to INCLUDE.]

inclusion body *n.* Any of various abnormal structures in a cell nucleus or cytoplasm having characteristic staining properties and associated especially with the presence of viruses.

in·clu·sive (ĭn-klōō'sĭv) *adj. Abbr.* **incl. 1.** Taking everything into account; including everything; comprehensive. **2.** Including the specified extremes or limits as well as the area between them. Often used after the noun: *23–84 inclusive.* **3.** *Logic.* Designating a disjunction that needs only one of its elements to be true for it to be valid. [Medieval Latin *inclūsīvus,* from Latin *inclūdere* (past participial stem *inclūs-*), to INCLUDE.] —**in·clu·sive·ly** *adv.* —**in·clu·sive·ness** *n.*

inclusive of *prep.* Taking into consideration or account; including: *the whole family, inclusive of the grandparents.*

in·co·er·ci·ble (ĭn'kō-ûr'sə-bəl) *adj.* Not subject to coercion.

incog. incognito.

in·cog·i·tant (ĭn-cŏj'ə-tənt) *adj. Rare.* Thoughtless; unthinking; inconsiderate. [Latin *incōgitāns* : *in-,* not + *cōgitāns* (stem *cōgitant-*), present participle of *cōgitāre,* to think about, COGITATE.]

in·cog·ni·ta (ĭn-kŏg'nə-tə, ĭn'kŏg-nē'tə) *adv.* With one's identity disguised or concealed. Used of a woman.
~*n.* A woman who is incognito. —**in·cog·ni·ta** *adj.*

in·cog·ni·to (ĭn-kŏg'nə-tō, ĭn'kŏg-nē'tō) *adv.* With one's identity disguised or concealed: *travel incognito.*
~*n. Abbr.* **incog. 1.** One who is incognito. **2.** The anonymity or disguised appearance assumed by one who is incognito. [Italian, from Latin *incognitus,* unknown : *in-,* not + *cognitus,* past participle of *cognōscere,* to know (see **cognition**).] —**in·cog·ni·to** *adj.*

in·cog·ni·zant (ĭn-kŏg'nə-zənt) *adj.* Lacking knowledge or awareness of something; unaware. —**in·cog·ni·zance** *n.*

in·co·her·ent (ĭn'kō-hîr'ənt) *adj.* **1.** Not coherent; disordered; unconnected; inharmonious. **2.** Characterized by an inability to think or express thoughts in a clear or orderly manner: *incoherent with grief.* —**in·co·her·ence, in·co·her·en·cy** *n.* —**in·co·her·ent·ly** *adv.* —**in·co·her·ent·ness** *n.*

in·com·bus·ti·ble (ĭn'kəm-bŭs'tə-bəl) *adj.* Incapable of burning.
~*n.* An incombustible object or material. [Middle English, from Medieval Latin *incombustibilis* : Latin *in-,* not + *combūrere* (past participle *combustus*), to burn up (see **combust**).] —**in·com·bus·ti·bil·i·ty** (ĭn'kəm-bŭs'tə-bĭl'ə-tē) *n.* —**in·com·bus·ti·bly** *adv.*

in·come (ĭn'kŭm') *n. Abbr.* **inc. 1.** The amount of money or its equivalent received during a period of time, such as a year, in exchange for labor or services, from the sale of goods or property, or as profit from financial investments. **2.** *Archaic.* An influx. [Middle English, a coming in, entry : IN + *comen,* COME.]

income group *n.* A section of a population having roughly the same income.

in·com·er (ĭn'kŭm'ər) *n.* One that comes in; especially, a person who is not considered to be integrated with his new environment.

income tax *n.* A graduated tax levied on annual income.

in·com·ing (ĭn'kŭm'ĭng) *adj.* **1. a.** Coming in; entering or arriving: *incoming telephone calls.* **b.** Coming in as profits. **2.** About to come in; next in succession: *the incoming president.*
~*n.* **1.** The act of coming in; an entrance; an arrival. **2.** *Usually* **incomings.** Income; revenue.

in·com·men·su·ra·ble (ĭn'kə-mĕn'shər-ə-bəl, -sər-ə-bəl) *adj.* **1.** Having no common quality upon which to make a comparison; incapable of being measured or judged comparatively; incommensurate. **2.** *Mathematics.* **a.** Having no common measure; not having the same units. **b.** Not having a common factor other than one.
~*n.* Something that is incommensurable. —**in·com·men·su·ra·bil·i·ty** *n.* —**in·com·men·su·ra·bly** *adv.*

PRONUNCIATION KEY

ă, pat; ā, pay; âr, care; ä, father, are; b, bib; ch, church; d, deed; ĕ, pet; ē, be; f, fife; g, gag; h, hat; hw, which; ĭ, pit; ī, pie; îr, pier; j, judge; k, kick; l, lid, needle; m, mum; n, no, sudden; ng, thing; ŏ, pot; ō, toe; ô, paw, for; oi, noise; ou, out; ŏŏ, book; ōō, boot; p, pop; r, roar; s, sauce; sh, ship, dish; t, tight; th, thin, path; *th*, this, bathe; ŭ, cut; ûr, fur; v, valve; w, with; y, yes; z, zebra, size; zh, vision; ə, about, item, edible, gallop, circus, peaceful

IN FOREIGN WORDS:

à, *Fr.* ami; œ, *Fr.* feu, *Ger.* schön; ü, *Fr.* tu, *Ger.* über; KH, *Ger.* ich, *Scot.* loch; N, *Fr.* bon; y', *Fr.* Compiègne

STRESS MARKS:

Primary stress: '
in·cite' (ĭn-sīt')
Secondary stress: '
in'sight' (ĭn'sīt')

in·com·men·su·rate (ĭn′kə-mĕn′shər-ĭt, -sər-ĭt) *adj.* **1. a.** Not commensurate; unequal; disproportionate: *a reward incommensurate with his efforts.* **b.** Inadequate. **2.** Incommensurable. —**in·com·men·su·rate·ly** *adv.* —**in·com·men·su·rate·ness** *n.*

in·com·mode (ĭn′kə-mōd′) *tr.v.* **-moded, -moding, -modes.** To cause to be inconvenienced; disturb. [French *incommoder,* from Old French, from Latin *incommodāre,* from *incommodus,* inconvenient : *in-,* not + *commodus,* convenient.]

in·com·mo·di·ous (ĭn′kə-mō′dē-əs) *adj.* Inconvenient or uncomfortable, as by affording insufficient room. —**in·com·mo·di·ous·ly** *adv.* —**in·com·mo·di·ous·ness** *n.*

in·com·mod·i·ty (ĭn′kə-mŏd′ə-tē) *n., pl.* **-ties.** *Rare.* **1.** Inconvenience; discomfort. **2.** Something that is inconvenient.

in·com·mu·ni·ca·ble (ĭn′kə-myōō′nĭ-kə-bəl) *adj.* **1.** Not communicable; that cannot be told or shared. **2.** *Rare.* Incommunicative. —**in·com·mu·ni·ca·bil·i·ty** *n.* —**in·com·mu·ni·ca·bly** *adv.*

in·com·mu·ni·ca·do (ĭn′kə-myōō′nĭ-kä′dō) *adv.* Without the means or right of communicating with others, as one held in solitary confinement. [Spanish, past participle of *incomunicar,* to deny communication : *in-,* not, from Latin + *comunicar,* to communicate, from Latin *commūnicāre,* COMMUNICATE.] —**in·com·mu·ni·ca·do** *adv.*

in·com·mu·ni·ca·tive (ĭn′kə-myōō′nĭ-kā′tĭv, -kə-tĭv) *adj.* Not communicative; reticent. —**in·com·mu·ni·ca·tive·ly** *adv.* —**in·com·mu·ni·ca·tive·ness** *n.*

in·com·mut·a·ble (ĭn′kə-myōō′tə-bəl) *adj.* **1.** Incapable of being exchanged. **2.** Not changeable; unalterable. —**in·com·mut·a·bil·i·ty, in·com·mut·a·ble·ness** *n.* —**in·com·mut·a·bly** *adv.*

in·com·pa·ra·ble (ĭn-kŏm′pər-ə-bəl) *adj.* **1.** Incapable of being compared; incommensurable. **2.** Above all comparisons; unsurpassed; matchless. —**in·com·pa·ra·bil·i·ty, in·com·pa·ra·ble·ness** *n.* —**in·com·pa·ra·bly** *adv.*

in·com·pat·i·bil·i·ty (ĭn′kəm-păt′ə-bĭl′ə-tē) *n., pl.* **-ties. 1.** The state or quality of being incompatible; lack of harmony or consistency; disagreement; incongruity. **2. incompatibilities.** Mutually exclusive or antagonistic qualities or things.

in·com·pat·i·ble (ĭn′kəm-păt′ə-bəl) *adj.* **1.** Not compatible, as in being: **a.** Unable to live or work together. **b.** Not consistent with something else. **2.** Incapable of being held simultaneously by one person, as offices, ranks, or the like. **3.** *Logic.* Incapable of being simultaneously true; mutually exclusive. **4.** *Medicine.* **a.** Designating blood transfusions or tissue grafts that evoke adverse reactions in the recipient due to antibody formation. **b.** Designating drugs that in combination do not produce their desired therapeutic effects. **5.** *Botany.* **a.** Not capable of self-fertilization. **b.** Not capable of forming a viable graft union. —See Synonyms at **inconsistent.** ∼*n. Usually* **incompatibles.** An incompatible element, person, object, or the like. [Medieval Latin *incompatibilis : in-,* not + *compatibilis,* COMPATIBLE.] —**in·com·pat·i·ble·ness** *n.* —**in·com·pat·i·bly** *adv.*

in·com·pe·tent (ĭn-kŏm′pə-tənt) *adj.* **1.** Not competent; not able or not in a position to act. **2.** Lacking competence; clumsy or very inefficient. **3.** *Law.* Not qualified to act in law. ∼*n.* An incompetent person. —**in·com·pe·tence, in·com·pe·ten·cy** *n.* —**in·com·pe·tent·ly** *adv.*

in·com·plete (ĭn′kəm-plēt′) *adj.* **1.** Not complete. **2.** Not fully formed. **3.** *Football.* Not caught or not caught in bounds. Used of a forward pass. —**in·com·plete·ly** *adv.* —**in·com·plete·ness, in·com·ple·tion** *n.*

in·com·pli·ant (ĭn′kəm-plī′ənt) *adj.* Not compliant; unyielding. —**in·com·pli·ance, in·com·pli·an·cy** *n.* —**in·com·pli·ant·ly** *adv.*

in·com·pre·hen·si·ble (ĭn′kŏm-prĭ-hĕn′sə-bəl, ĭn-kŏm′-) *adj.* **1.** Incapable of being understood or comprehended, as: **a.** Unintelligible. **b.** Unknowable; unfathomable. **2.** *Archaic.* Without limits; boundless. —**in·com·pre·hen·si·bil·i·ty, in·com·pre·hen·si·ble·ness** *n.* —**in·com·pre·hen·si·bly** *adv.*

in·com·pre·hen·sion (ĭn′kŏm-prĭ-hĕn′shən, ĭn-kŏm′-) *n.* Lack of comprehension or understanding.

in·com·pre·hen·sive (ĭn′kŏm-prĭ-hĕn′sĭv, ĭn-kŏm′-) *adj.* Not comprehensive or all-inclusive; limited in range or scope. —**in·com·pre·hen·sive·ly** *adv.* —**in·com·pre·hen·sive·ness** *n.*

in·com·press·i·ble (ĭn′kəm-prĕs′ə-bəl) *adj.* Incapable of being compressed. —**in·com·press·i·bil·i·ty** *n.*

in·com·put·a·ble (ĭn′kəm-pyōō′tə-bəl) *adj.* Incapable of being computed or calculated. —**in·com·put·a·bil·i·ty** *n.*

in·con·ceiv·a·ble (ĭn′kən-sē′və-bəl) *adj.* Incapable of being conceived or thought of; unbelievable. —**in·con·ceiv·a·bil·i·ty, in·con·ceiv·a·ble·ness** *n.* —**in·con·ceiv·a·bly** *adv.*

in·con·cin·ni·ty (ĭn′kən-sĭn′ĭ-tē) *n.* Lack of congruity or harmony; unsuitability. [Latin *inconcinnitas,* awkwardness, from *inconcinnus,* awkward : *in-,* not + *concinnus,* skillfully put together.]

in·con·clu·sive (ĭn′kən-klōō′sĭv) *adj.* Not conclusive; not allowing a proper conclusion to be drawn. —**in·con·clu·sive·ly** *adv.* —**in·con·clu·sive·ness** *n.*

in·con·den·sa·ble, in·con·den·si·ble (ĭn′kən-dĕn′sə-bəl) *adj.* Incapable of being condensed; especially, that cannot be reduced to a solid or liquid. —**in·con·den·sa·bil·i·ty** (ĭn′kən-dĕn′sə-bĭl′ə-tē) *n.*

in·con·dite (ĭn-kŏn′dĭt, -dīt′) *adj. Rare.* Badly constructed; crude. Said of literary or artistic compositions. [Latin *inconditus : in-,* not + *conditus,* past participle of *condere,* to put together.] —**in·con·dite·ly** *adv.*

in·con·form·i·ty (ĭn′kən-fôr′mə-tē) *n.* Resistance to or lack of conformity; nonconformity.

in·con·gru·ent (ĭn-kŏng′grōō-ənt) *adj.* **1.** Not congruent. **2.** Incon-

gruous. —**in·con·gru·ence** *n.* —**in·con·gru·ent·ly** *adv.*

in·con·gru·i·ty (ĭn′kŏng-grōō′ə-tē, ĭn′kən-) *n., pl.* **-ties. 1.** The state or quality of being incongruous. **2.** That which is incongruous.

in·con·gru·ous (ĭn-kŏng′grōō-əs) *adj.* **1.** Inharmonious or incompatible with the surroundings; incongruent: *a plan incongruous with good sense.* **2.** Made up of disparate, inconsistent, or discordant parts or qualities. **3.** Not consistent with what is correct, appropriate, or logical; out-of-place: *an incongruous remark.* —See Synonyms at **inconsistent.** [Latin *incongruus : in-,* not + *congruus,* CONGRUOUS.] —**in·con·gru·ous·ly** *adv.* —**in·con·gru·ous·ness** *n.*

in·con·nec·tor (ĭn′kən-nĕk′tər) *n.* A flow-chart symbol that indicates continuation of a broken line of flow.

in·con·sec·u·tive (ĭn′kən-sĕk′yōō-tĭv, -sĕk′yə-) *adj.* Not consecutive; not in a logical sequence.

in·con·se·quent (ĭn-kŏn′sə-kwənt) *adj.* **1.** Not obtained as a result. **2.** Not derived from the premises or obtained by logic or reason; irrelevant. **3.** Proceeding without logical sequence; haphazard. **4.** Out of character with the nature or style of something. **5.** Unimportant; insignificant. [Late Latin *inconsequēns : * Latin *in-,* not + *consequēns,* CONSEQUENT.] —**in·con·se·quence** *n.* —**in·con·se·quent·ly** *adv.*

in·con·se·quen·tial (ĭn-kŏn′sə-kwĕn′shəl) *adj.* **1.** Without consequence; lacking importance; petty. **2.** Inconsequent. **3.** Designating the behavior of a person who disregards the consequences of his or her behavior. —**in·con·se·quen·ti·al·i·ty** (ĭn-kŏn′sə-kwĕn′shē-ăl′ə-tē), **in·con·se·quen·tial·ness** *n.* —**in·con·se·quen·tial·ly** *adv.*

in·con·sid·er·a·ble (ĭn′kən-sĭd′ər-ə-bəl) *adj.* Too small or unimportant to merit attention or consideration; trivial. —**in·con·sid·er·a·ble·ness** *n.* —**in·con·sid·er·a·bly** *adv.*

in·con·sid·er·ate (ĭn′kən-sĭd′ər-ĭt) *adj.* Not considerate; thoughtless of others. [Latin *inconsīderātus : in-,* not + *consīderātus,* CONSIDERATE.] —**in·con·sid·er·ate·ly** *adv.* —**in·con·sid·er·ate·ness, in·con·sid·er·a·tion** *n.*

in·con·sis·ten·cy (ĭn′kən-sĭs′tən-sē) *n., pl.* **-cies.** Also **in·con·sis·tence** (-təns) (for sense 1). **1.** The state or quality of being inconsistent; lack of consistency or uniformity; incongruity. **2.** Something that is inconsistent.

in·con·sis·tent (ĭn′kən-sĭs′tənt) *adj.* **1.** Not consistent, especially: **a.** Erratic. **b.** Incongruous. **c.** Contradictory. **d.** Illogical. **2.** *Mathematics.* Designating two or more equations that do not have one set of values of the variable in common. —**in·con·sis·tent·ly** *adv.*

Synonyms: *discordant, incompatible, incongruous.*

in·con·sol·a·ble (ĭn′kən-sō′lə-bəl) *adj.* Incapable of being consoled or solaced; deeply despondent. —**in·con·sol·a·bil·i·ty** (ĭn′kən-sō′lə-bĭl′ə-tē), **in·con·sol·a·ble·ness** *n.* —**in·con·sol·a·bly** *adv.*

in·con·so·nant (ĭn-kŏn′sə-nənt) *adj.* Lacking harmony, agreement, or compatibility; discordant. —**in·con·so·nance** *n.* —**in·con·so·nant·ly** *adv.*

in·con·spic·u·ous (ĭn′kən-spĭk′yōō-əs) *adj.* Not readily noticeable. —**in·con·spic·u·ous·ly** *adv.* —**in·con·spic·u·ous·ness** *n.*

in·con·stan·cy (ĭn′kən-stən-sē) *n., pl.* **-cies. 1.** Fickleness; faithlessness. **2.** Unreliability; instability. **3.** An act or instance of being inconstant.

in·con·stant (ĭn-kŏn′stənt) *adj.* **1.** Not constant. **2.** Fickle. —See Synonyms at **faithless.** —**in·con·stant·ly** *adv.*

in·con·sum·a·ble (ĭn′kən-sōō′mə-bəl) *adj.* **1.** Incapable of being consumed. **2.** Satisfying an economic requirement without being consumed, as currency. —**in·con·sum·a·bly** *adv.*

in·con·test·a·ble (ĭn′kən-tĕs′tə-bəl) *adj.* Incapable of being contested; unquestionable. —**in·con·test·a·bil·i·ty** (ĭn′kən-tĕs′tə-bĭl′ə-tē), **in·con·test·a·ble·ness** *n.* —**in·con·test·a·bly** *adv.*

in·con·ti·nent (ĭn-kŏn′tə-nənt) *adj.* **1.** Not continent; unrestrained; uncontrolled. Often said of sexual behavior. **2.** Incapable of holding back, containing, or retaining. Usually used with *of: incontinent of anger.* **3.** Incapable of controlling the passage of urine or feces. [Middle English, from Old French, from Latin *incontinēns,* unrestrained : *in-,* not + *continēns,* restrained, CONTINENT.] —**in·con·ti·nence** *n.*

in·con·ti·nent·ly (ĭn-kŏn′tə-nənt-lē) *adv.* **1.** In an incontinent manner. **2.** *Archaic.* Immediately; straightaway.

in·con·trol·la·ble (ĭn′kən-trō′lə-bəl) *adj. Rare.* Not controllable; difficult to restrain.

in·con·tro·vert·i·ble (ĭn′kŏn-trə-vûr′tə-bəl) *adj.* Not able to be contradicted; indisputable; unquestionable. —**in·con·tro·vert·i·bil·i·ty** (ĭn′kŏn′trə-vûr′tə-bĭl′ə-tē), **in·con·tro·vert·i·ble·ness** *n.* —**in·con·tro·vert·i·bly** *adv.*

in·con·ven·i·ence (ĭn′kən-vēn′yəns) *n.* **1.** The state or quality of being inconvenient; lack of ease or comfort; trouble; difficulty. **2.** Something that causes difficulty, trouble, or discomfort; an inconvenient thing or situation. ∼*tr.v.* **inconvenienced, -iencing, -iences.** To cause inconvenience to; trouble; bother.

in·con·ven·i·ent (ĭn′kən-vēn′yənt) *adj.* Not convenient, especially: **1.** Not accessible or handy. **2.** Difficult, awkward, or troublesome. [Middle English, from Old French, from Latin *inconveniēns : in-,* not + *conveniēns,* CONVENIENT.] —**in·con·ven·i·ent·ly** *adv.*

in·con·vert·i·ble (ĭn′kən-vûr′tə-bəl) *adj.* Incapable of being converted, changed, or exchanged; especially, designating currency not redeemable for another currency or for gold or silver. —**in·con·vert·i·bil·i·ty, in·con·vert·i·ble·ness** *n.* —**in·con·vert·i·bly** *adv.*

in·con·vin·ci·ble (ĭn′kən-vĭn′sə-bəl) *adj.* Incapable of being convinced.

in·co·or·di·nate (ĭn′kō-ôrd′n-ĭt, -āt′) *adj.* **1.** Not of the same order. **2.** Uncoordinated. **—in·co·or·di·nate·ly** *adv.*

in·co·or·di·na·tion (ĭn′kō-ôrd′n-ā′shən) *n.* **1.** Lack of coordination. **2.** The inability to exercise normal voluntary control of relatively complex muscular movement.

in·cor·po·rate[1] (ĭn-kôr′pə-rāt′) *v.* **-rated, -rating, -rates.** *—tr.* **1.** To unite with or blend indistinguishably into something already in existence. **2.** To cause to merge or combine together into a united whole. **3.** To admit as a member to a corporation or similar organization. **4.** To cause to form into a legal corporation. **5.** *Rare.* To give substance or material form to; embody; substantiate. *—intr.* **1.** To become united or combined into an organized body. **2.** To form a legal corporation.
~adj. (ĭn-kôr′pər-ĭt). **1.** Combined into one united body; merged. **2.** Formed into a legal corporation. [Middle English *incorporaten,* from Late Latin *incorporāre,* to form into a body : Latin *in-* (intensive) + *corporāre,* to form into a body (see **corporate**).] **—in·cor·po·ra·tion** *n.* **—in·cor·po·ra·tive** *adj.* **—in·cor·po·ra·tor** *n.*

in·cor·po·rate[2] (ĭn-kôr′pər-ĭt) *adj. Rare.* Incorporeal. [Late Latin *incorporātus,* not in the body, spiritual : Latin *in-,* not + *corporātus,* embodied, CORPORATE.]

in·cor·po·rat·ed (ĭn-kôr′pə-rā′tĭd) *adj.* **1.** United into one body; combined. **2.** *Abbr.* **Inc., inc.** Organized and maintained as a legal business corporation.

in·cor·po·ra·ting (ĭn-kôr′pə-rā′tĭng) *adj. Linguistics.* Polysynthetic.

in·cor·po·re·al (ĭn′kôr-pôr′ē-əl, -pōr′ē-əl) *adj.* **1.** Lacking material form or substance. **2.** Spiritual. **3.** *Law.* Lacking material substance but existing in the eyes of the law; intangible, such as a right or patent might be. [Latin *incorporeus* : *in-,* not + *corporeus,* CORPOREAL.] **—in·cor·po·re·al·ly** *adv.*

in·cor·po·re·i·ty (ĭn-kôr′pə-rē′ə-tē) *n.* Immateriality. [Latin *incorporeus,* INCORPOREAL.]

in·cor·rect (ĭn′kə-rĕkt′) *adj.* Not correct, especially: **1.** Erroneous. **2.** Improper; inappropriate. **—in·cor·rect·ly** *adv.* **—in·cor·rect·ness** *n.*

in·cor·ri·gi·ble (ĭn-kôr′ə-jə-bəl, ĭn-kŏr′-) *adj.* **1.** Incapable of being corrected or reformed: *an incorrigible liar.* **2.** Firmly rooted; impossible to eliminate; ineradicable: *incorrigible innocence.*
~n. A person or animal that will not be tamed or corrected. [Middle English, from Late Latin *incorrigibilis* : Latin *in-,* not + *corrigere,* to CORRECT.] **—in·cor·ri·gi·bil·i·ty, in·cor·ri·gi·ble·ness** *n.* **—in·cor·ri·gi·bly** *adv.*

in·cor·rupt (ĭn′kə-rŭpt′) *adj. Rare.* **1.** Not corrupt or immoral. **2.** Not decayed; unspoiled. **3.** Free from error or deterioration. Said of a text or manuscript. [Middle English, from Latin *incorruptus* : *in-,* not + *corruptus,* CORRUPT.] **—in·cor·rupt·ly** *adv.* **—in·cor·rupt·ness** *n.*

in·cor·rupt·i·ble (ĭn′kə-rŭp′tə-bəl) *adj.* **1.** Incapable of being morally corrupted, as by bribery; honest. **2.** Not subject to decay or decomposition. **—in·cor·rupt·i·bil·i·ty** *n.* **—in·cor·rupt·i·bly** *adv.*

in·cras·sate (ĭn-krăs′ĭt, -āt′) *adj.* Also **in·cras·sat·ed** (-ā′tĭd). *Biology.* Thickened; enlarged. Said especially of cell walls. [Late Latin *incrassāre* (past participle *incrassātus*), become thick, from *crassus,* thick.]

in·crease (ĭn-krēs′) *v.* **-creased, -creasing, -creases.** *—intr.* **1.** To become greater or larger. **2.** To multiply; reproduce. **3.** *Literary.* To advance, as in power or attainment; thrive; prosper. *—tr.* To make greater or larger.
~n. (ĭn′krēs′) *Abbr.* **inc., incr. 1.** The act of increasing; enlargement; multiplication. **2.** The amount of such increase; an increment: *a tax increase of ten percent.* **3.** *Archaic.* Crops and other produce. **—on the increase.** Increasing. [Middle English *encresen,* from Old French *encreistre* (present stem *encreiss-*), from Latin *incrēscere,* to grow in or on : *in-,* in + *crēscere,* to grow.] **—in·creas·a·ble** *adj.* **—in·creas·er** *n.* **—in·creas·ing·ly** *adv.*
Synonyms: *augment, enlarge, expand, extend, grow, magnify.*

in·cre·ate (ĭn′krē-āt′, ĭn-krē′ĭt) *adj. Archaic.* Existing without having been created. Said especially of divine beings. **—in·cre·ate·ly** *adv.*

in·cred·i·bil·i·ty (ĭn-krĕd′ə-bĭl′ə-tē) *n., pl.* **-ties. 1.** The condition or quality of being incredible. **2.** Something incredible.

in·cred·i·ble (ĭn-krĕd′ə-bəl) *adj.* **1.** Too implausible to be believed; unbelievable. **2.** Hard to believe; astonishing. **3.** *Informal.* Marvelous; wonderful. [Middle English, from Latin *incrēdibilis* : *in-,* not + *crēdibilis,* CREDIBLE.] **—in·cred·i·ble·ness** *n.* **—in·cred·i·bly** *adv.*
Usage: *Incredible* and *incredulous* are sometimes confused, but there is a clear distinction between them. *Incredible* means simply "unbelievable"; *incredulous* means "disbelieving" or "skeptical." A story may be *incredible*; the skeptical person to whom it is told is *incredulous.*

in·cre·du·li·ty (ĭn′krə-do͞o′lə-tē, -dyo͞o′lə-tē) *n.* Also **in·cred·u·lous·ness** (ĭn-krĕj′ə-ləs-nĭs). Disbelief.

in·cred·u·lous (ĭn-krĕj′ə-ləs) *adj.* **1.** Disbelieving; skeptical. **2.** Expressing disbelief: *an incredulous stare.* —See Usage note at **incredible.** [Latin *incrēdulus* : *in-,* not + *crēdulus,* CREDULOUS.] **—in·cred·u·lous·ly** *adv.*

in·cre·ment (ĭn′krə-mənt) *n.* **1.** An increase in number, size, or extent; growth; enlargement. **2.** Something added or gained; especially, an increase in salary awarded to an employee according to his progress, along a salary scale. **3.** A small increase in quantity. **4.** *Mathematics.* A small positive or negative change in a variable.
~tr.v. (-mĕnt′) **incremented, -menting, -ments.** To add a small amount to, often at regular intervals. [Middle English, from Latin *incrēmentum,* from *incrēscere,* to INCREASE.] **—in·cre·men·tal** *adj.* **—in·cre·men·tal·ly** *adv.*

in·cre·men·tal·ism (ĭn′krə-mĕn′tl-ĭz′əm) *n.* Social or political gradualism. **—in·cre·men·tal·ist** *n.*

incremental plotter *n.* A device for plotting graphs from the output of a computer.

in·cres·cent (ĭn-krĕs′ənt) *adj.* Waxing. Said of the moon. Compare **decrescent.** [Latin *incrēscēns,* present participle of *incrēscere,* to INCREASE.]

in·cre·tion (ĭn-krē′shən) *n.* **1.** Secretion directly into the bloodstream, characteristic of endocrine glands. **2.** The product of such secretion; a hormone. [IN- (in) + (SE)CRETION.]

in·crim·i·nate (ĭn-krĭm′ə-nāt′) *tr.v.* **-nated, -nating, -nates. 1.** To charge with or involve in a crime or other wrongful act. **2.** To indicate the guilt of. [Late Latin *incrīmināre* : Latin *in-,* in + *crīmen* (stem *crīmin-*), CRIME.] **—in·crim·i·na·tion** *n.* **—in·crim·i·na·to·ry** (ĭn-krĭm′ə-nə-tôr′ē, -tōr′ē) *adj.*

in·cross (ĭn′krŏs′, -krôs′) *n.* An organism produced as a result of continuous inbreeding.
~v. **incrossed, -crossing, -crosses.** *—tr.* To produce by continuous inbreeding. *—intr.* To produce an incross.

incrust. Variant of **encrust.**

in·crus·ta·tion (ĭn′krŭs-tā′shən) *n.* **1.** An encrusting; a hard coating; especially, a deposit of a fine material. **2.** A facing of marble or mosaic on a building. **3.** A scab or other concretion on a surface. [French or from Late Latin *incrustātiō,* from Latin *incrustāre,* to ENCRUST.]

in·cu·bate (ĭn′kyə-bāt, ĭng′-) *v.* **-bated, -bating, -bates.** *—tr.* **1.** To warm (eggs), as by bodily heat, so as to promote embryonic development and the hatching of young; brood. **2.** To maintain (a bacterial culture or an embryo, for example) at optimum environmental conditions for development, especially in an incubator. **3.** To cause to develop; foment. *—intr.* **1.** To brood eggs. **2.** To develop in favorable conditions. Used of eggs, embryos, bacteria, and the like. **3.** To undergo incubation. [Latin *incubāre,* to hatch, lie down upon : *in-,* on + *cubāre,* to lie down.] **—in·cu·ba·tive** *adj.*

in·cu·ba·tion (ĭn′kyə-bā′shən, ĭng′-) *n.* **1.** The act of incubating or the state of being incubated. **2.** *Medicine.* **a.** The development of an infection from the time an organism is first exposed to it up to the time of the first appearance of signs or symptoms. **b.** The time between exposure to an infection and the first appearance of signs or symptoms. In this sense, also called "incubation period." **—in·cu·ba·tion·al** *adj.*

in·cu·ba·tor (ĭn′kyə-bā′tər, ĭng′-) *n.* One that incubates, especially: **1.** A cabinet in which a uniform temperature can be maintained, used in growing bacterial cultures or hatching eggs. **2.** An apparatus for maintaining an infant, especially a premature infant, in an environment of controlled temperature, humidity, and oxygen.

in·cu·bus (ĭn′kyə-bəs, ĭng′-) *n., pl.* **-buses** or **-bi** (-bī′). **1.** An evil spirit believed to descend upon and have sexual intercourse with sleeping women. Compare **succubus. 2.** A nightmare. **3.** Something oppressively or nightmarishly burdensome. [Middle English, from Late Latin, from Latin *incubāre,* to lie down upon, INCUBATE.]

in·cu·des. Plural of **incus.**

in·cul·cate (ĭn-kŭl′kāt′) *tr.v.* **-cated, -cating, -cates.** To teach or impress by forceful urging or frequent repetition; instill: *inculcate a code of ethics.* [Latin *inculcāre,* to trample in, impress upon : *in-,* in + *calcāre,* to trample, from *calx* (stem *calc-*), heel.] **—in·cul·ca·tion** *n.* **—in·cul·ca·tor** *n.*

in·cul·pa·ble (ĭn-kŭl′pə-bəl) *adj.* Not culpable; free from guilt; blameless.

in·cul·pate (ĭn-kŭl′pāt′) *tr.v.* **-pated, -pating, -pates.** To incriminate; cause blame to be attached to. [Late Latin *inculpāre* : *in-,* on + *culpāre,* to blame, from Latin *culpa,* fault, CULPA.] **—in·cul·pa·tion** *n.* **—in·cul·pa·to·ry** (ĭn-kŭl′pə-tôr′ē, -tōr′ē) *adj.*

in·cult (ĭn-kŭlt′) *adj. Archaic.* **1.** Not cultured; uncultivated. **2.** Not tilled or cultivated. [Latin *incultus,* uncultivated : *in-,* not + *cultus,* past participle of *colere,* to till.]

in·cum·ben·cy (ĭn-kŭm′bən-sē) *n., pl.* **-cies. 1.** The condition or quality of being incumbent. **2.** Something that is incumbent. **3.** The holding and administering of an office or ecclesiastical benefice. **4.** The term of such a benefice or office.

in·cum·bent (ĭn-kŭm′bənt) *adj.* **1.** Lying, leaning, or resting upon something else. **2.** Imposed as an obligation or duty; required; obligatory. **3.** Holding a specific office or ecclesiastical benefice.
~n. A person who holds an office or ecclesiastical benefice. [Middle English, from Latin *incumbēns* (stem *incumbent-*), present participle of *incumbere,* to lean upon : *in-,* on + *cumbere,* to lean, recline.] **—in·cum·bent·ly** *adv.*

in·cu·nab·u·lum (ĭn′kyo͞o-năb′yə-ləm) *n., pl.* **-la** (-lə). **1.** A book printed from movable type before 1501. Also called "incunable." **2.** An artifact of an early period. **3. incunabula.** The earliest stages in the development of something. [Latin *incūnābula* (plural), swaddling clothes, cradle, infancy : *in-,* in + *cūnābula,* infancy, origin, cradle, from *cūnae,* cradle.] **—in·cu·nab·u·lar** *adj.*

in·cur (ĭn-kûr′) *tr.v.* **-curred, -curring, -curs. 1.** To meet with; run into. **2.** To become liable or subject to as a result of one's own actions; bring upon oneself. [Latin *incurrere,* to run into, come upon : *in-,* in + *currere,* to run.]

in·cur·a·ble (ĭn-kyo͝or′ə-bəl) *adj.* **1.** Not curable. Said of a disease. **2.** Broadly, not susceptible to modification.
~n. A person suffering from an incurable disease. **—in·cur·a·bil·i·ty, in·cur·a·ble·ness** *n.* **—in·cur·a·bly** *adv.*

incuse *The most common example of this patterned impression is a coin. This one is from Thebes in Greece and dates from the fifth century* B.C. *The outline of the stamping tool can be seen.*

PRONUNCIATION KEY

ă, pat; ā, pay; âr, care;
ä, father, are; b, bib;
ch, church; d, deed; ĕ, pet;
ē, be; f, fife; g, gag; h, hat;
hw, which; ĭ, pit; ī, pie;
îr, pier; j, judge; k, kick;
l, lid, needle; m, mum;
n, no, sudden; ng, thing;
ŏ, pot; ō, toe; ô, paw, for;
oi, noise; ou, out; o͝o, book;
o͞o, boot; p, pop; r, roar;
s, sauce; sh, ship, dish;
t, tight; th, thin, path;
th, this, bathe; ŭ, cut; ûr, fur;
v, valve; w, with; y, yes;
z, zebra, size; zh, vision;
ə, about, item, edible, gallop, circus, peaceful

IN FOREIGN WORDS:

à, *Fr.* ami; œ, *Fr.* feu, *Ger.* schön; ü, *Fr.* tu, *Ger.* über; KH, *Ger.* ich, *Scot.* loch; N, *Fr.* bon; y', *Fr.* Compiègne

STRESS MARKS:

Primary stress: ′
in·cite′ (ĭn-sīt′)
Secondary stress: ′
in′sight′ (ĭn′sīt′)

in·cu·ri·ous (ĭn-kyo͝or′ē-əs) *adj.* **1.** Not curious; uninterested. **2.** Not arousing interest; lacking novelty. **3.** Heedless; negligent. —See Synonyms at **indifferent.** [Latin *incūriōsus,* indifferent : *in-,* not + *cūriōsus,* CURIOUS.] **—in·cu·ri·os·i·ty** (ĭn-kyo͝or′ē-ŏs′ĭ-tē), **in·cu·ri·ous·ness** *n.* **—in·cu·ri·ous·ly** *adv.*

in·cur·rent (ĭn-kûr′ənt) *adj.* Affording passage to an inflowing current. Said of anatomical ducts and vessels. [Latin *incurrēns* (stem *incurrent-*), present participle of *incurrere,* to run into, INCUR.]

in·cur·sion (ĭn-kûr′zhən, -shən) *n.* **1.** A sudden attack on or invasion of hostile territory; a raid. **2.** An entering into. [Middle English, from Old French, from Latin *incursiō* (stem *incursiōn-*), from *incurrere* (past participle *incursus*), to run into, attack, INCUR.]

in·cur·vate (ĭn-kûr′vāt′) *tr.v.* **-vated, -vating, -vates.** To bend (something) into an inward curve.
~adj. (ĭn-kûr′vāt′, -vĭt). Curved, especially inward. [Latin *incurvāre* (past participle *incurvātus*) : *in-,* in + *curvāre,* to bend, from *curvus,* CURVE.] **—in·cur·va·tion** *n.* **—in·cur·va·ture** (ĭn-kûr′və-cho͝or′) *n.*

in·curve (ĭn-kûrv′) *v.* **-curved, -curving, -curves.** *—intr.* To bend into an inward curve. *—tr.* To incurvate.
~n. (ĭn′kûrv′). An inward curve. [Latin *incurvāre,* INCURVATE.]

in·cus (ĭng′kəs) *n., pl.* **incudes** (ĭng-kyo͞o′dēz). An anvil-shaped bone in the mammalian middle ear. Also called "anvil." Compare **malleus, stapes.** [Latin *incūs,* anvil, from *incūdere* (past participle *incūsus*), to forge with a hammer : *in-,* in + *cūdere,* to strike, stamp.]

in·cuse (ĭn-kyo͞oz′, -kyo͞os′) *adj.* Hammered, stamped, or pressed in. Said of a design or feature of a design on a coin.
~n. A design impressed in such a manner.
~tr.v. **incused, -cusing, -cuses. 1.** To impress (a design) on a coin. **2.** To impress (a coin) with a design. [Latin *incūsus,* past participle of *incūdere,* to beat or stamp in. See **incus.**]

Ind (ĭnd) *n.* **1.** *Archaic.* India. **2.** *Obsolete.* The Indies.

ind. 1. independence; independent. **2.** index. **3.** indicative. **4.** indigo. **5.** indirect. **6.** industrial; industry.

Ind. 1. Independent. **2.** India. **3.** Indian. **4.** Indiana. **5.** Indies.

in·da·ba (ĭn-dä′bə) *n.* **1.** A conference or meeting of indigenous tribes in southern Africa to discuss a serious issue. **2.** *South African Informal.* **a.** A discussion. **b.** A personal concern. [Zulu, "business, affair."]

in·da·mine (ĭn′də-mēn′, -mĭn) *n.* Any of a group of organic bases that form unstable bluish or greenish salts used as dyes, especially the base, $NH_2C_6H_4N{:}C_6H_4{:}NH$, used to produce the dye safranine. Also called "phenylene blue." [*ind*igo + *amine.*]

in·debt·ed (ĭn-dĕt′ĭd) *adj.* **1.** Owing gratitude or recognition for something: *indebted to her for her help.* **2.** Owing money. [Middle English *endetted,* from Old French *endette,* from the past participle of *endetter,* to involve in debt, oblige : *en-,* in + *dette,* DEBT.]

in·debt·ed·ness (ĭn-dĕt′ĭd-nĭs) *n.* **1.** The state of being indebted. **2.** That which is owed to another.

in·de·cen·cy (ĭn-dē′sən-sē) *n., pl.* **-cies. 1.** The state or quality of being indecent. **2.** Something that is indecent.

in·de·cent (ĭn-dē′sənt) *adj.* **1.** Offensive to good taste; unseemly. **2.** Offensive to public moral values; immodest. —See Synonyms at **improper. —in·de·cent·ly** *adv.*

indecent assault *n.* The act or offense of making a sexual attack other than rape on a person who has not consented.

indecent exposure *n.* The act or offense of indecently exposing one's body, especially the genitals, to public view.

in·de·ci·pher·a·ble (ĭn′dĭ-sī′fər-ə-bəl) *adj.* Incapable of being deciphered, especially by being illegible. **—in·de·ci·pher·a·bil·i·ty, in·de·ci·pher·a·ble·ness** *n.*

in·de·ci·sion (ĭn′dĭ-sĭzh′ən) *n.* Irresolution; indecisiveness.

in·de·ci·sive (ĭn′dĭ-sī′sĭv) *adj.* **1.** Not decisive; inconclusive. **2.** Prone to or characterized by indecision; vacillating; hesitant. **3.** Not clearly defined; indefinite. **—in·de·ci·sive·ly** *adv.* **—in·de·ci·sive·ness** *n.*

in·de·clin·a·ble (ĭn′dĭ-klī′nə-bəl) *adj.* Having no set of grammatical inflections; not declinable.

in·de·com·pos·a·ble (ĭn′dē-kəm-pō′zə-bəl) *adj.* Not capable of being split into component parts.

in·dec·o·rous (ĭn-dĕk′ər-əs) *adj.* Lacking propriety or good taste; unseemly. —See Usage note at **improper. —in·dec·o·rous·ly** *adv.* **—in·dec·o·rous·ness** *n.*

in·de·co·rum (ĭn′dĭ-kôr′əm, -kōr′əm) *n.* **1.** Lack of decorum; lack of propriety or good taste. **2.** An instance of indecorous behavior.

in·deed (ĭn-dēd′) *adv.* **1.** Without a doubt; certainly; truly. **2.** In fact; in reality. **3.** Admittedly; unquestionably. **4.** What is more.
~interj. Used to express surprise, skepticism, or irony. [Middle English *in dede,* in reality : *in,* IN + *dede,* DEED.]

indef. indefinite.

in·de·fat·i·ga·ble (ĭn′dĭ-făt′ĭ-gə-bəl) *adj.* **1.** Untiring; tireless. **2.** Unremitting. [Latin *indēfatīgābilis* : *in-,* not + *dēfatīgāre,* to tire out : *dē-* (intensive) + *fatīgāre,* to FATIGUE.] **—in·de·fat·i·ga·bil·i·ty, in·de·fat·i·ga·ble·ness** *n.* **—in·de·fat·i·ga·bly** *adv.*

in·de·fea·si·ble (ĭn′dĭ-fē′zə-bəl) *adj.* Not capable of being annulled or made void. **—in·de·fea·si·bil·i·ty** *n.* **—in·de·fea·si·bly** *adv.*

in·de·fec·ti·ble (ĭn′dĭ-fĕk′tə-bəl) *adj.* **1.** Having the ability to resist defect or failure; permanent; lasting. **2.** Without flaw or defect; perfect. **—in·de·fec·ti·bil·i·ty** *n.* **—in·de·fec·ti·bly** *adv.*

in·de·fen·si·ble (ĭn′dĭ-fĕn′sə-bəl) *adj.* Not capable of being defended, especially: **1.** Inexcusable. **2.** Invalid; untenable. **3.** Vulnerable to attack. **—in·de·fen·si·bil·i·ty, in·de·fen·si·ble·ness** *n.* **—in·de·fen·si·bly** *adv.*

in·de·fin·a·ble (ĭn′dĭ-fī′nə-bəl) *adj.* Not capable of being defined, described, or analyzed.
~n. A word, concept, or quality that cannot be defined. **—in·de·fin·a·ble·ness** *n.* **—in·de·fin·a·bly** *adv.*

in·def·i·nite (ĭn-dĕf′ə-nĭt) *adj. Abbr.* **indef. 1.** Not definite, especially: **a.** Unclear; vague. **b.** Lacking precise limits. **c.** Uncertain; undecided. **2.** *Grammar.* Not specifying whether an action is complete or continuous. Said of verb tenses. **3.** *Botany.* Indeterminate. [Latin *indēfīnītus* : *in-,* not + *dēfīnītus,* DEFINITE.] **—in·def·i·nite·ly** *adv.* **—in·def·i·nite·ness** *n.*

indefinite article *n. Grammar.* An article, as English *a* or *an,* that does not fix or immediately fix the identity of the noun modified. Compare **definite article.**

indefinite integral *n. Mathematics.* The set of all functions of which a given function is the derivative, usually represented by $\int f(x)dx + C$, where $\int f(x)dx$ is any member of the set and C is an arbitrary constant. Compare **definite integral.**

indefinite pronoun *n. Grammar.* A pronoun, for example *any* or *some,* that does not specify the identity of its object.

in·de·his·cent (ĭn′dĭ-hĭs′ənt) *adj.* Not splitting open at maturity: *indehiscent fruit.* Compare **dehiscent. —in·de·his·cence** *n.*

in·del·i·ble (ĭn-dĕl′ə-bəl) *adj.* **1.** Incapable of being removed, erased, or washed away. **2.** Making a mark not easily erased or washed away: *an indelible laundry pencil.* **3.** Permanent; enduring: *indelible memories.* [Latin *indēlēbilis* : *in-,* not + *dēlēbilis,* that can be obliterated, from *dēlēre,* to obliterate, DELETE.] **—in·del·i·bil·i·ty, in·del·i·ble·ness** *n.* **—in·del·i·bly** *adv.*

in·del·i·ca·cy (ĭn-dĕl′ĭ-kə-sē) *n., pl.* **-cies. 1.** The quality or condition of being indelicate. **2.** An instance of indelicate speech or behavior; a crudity.

in·del·i·cate (ĭn-dĕl′ĭ-kĭt) *adj.* **1. a.** Offensive to propriety. **b.** Coarse; tasteless. **2.** Tactless. —See Usage note at **improper. —in·del·i·cate·ly** *adv.* **—in·del·i·cate·ness** *n.*

in·dem·ni·fi·ca·tion (ĭn-dĕm′nə-fĭ-kā′shən) *n.* **1.** The act of indemnifying or the condition of being indemnified. **2.** Something that indemnifies, such as a sum paid in compensation.

in·dem·ni·fy (ĭn-dĕm′nə-fī′) *tr.v.* **-fied, -fying, -fies. 1.** To protect against possible damage, legal suit, or bodily injury; insure. **2.** To compensate for incurred damage or hurt. [Latin *indemnis,* uninjured (see **indemnity**) + -FY.] **—in·dem·ni·fi·er** *n.*

in·dem·ni·ty (ĭn-dĕm′nə-tē) *n., pl.* **-ties. 1.** Insurance or other security against possible damage, loss, or hurt. **2.** A legal exemption from prosecution or liability for damages resulting from one's actions. **3.** Compensation for damage, loss, or hurt incurred; indemnification. —See Synonyms at **reparation.** [Middle English *indempnyte,* from Old French *indemnite,* from Late Latin *indemnitās* (stem *indemnitāt-*), from Latin *indemnis,* unhurt, uninjured : *in-,* not + *damnum,* hurt, harm.]

in·de·mon·stra·ble (ĭn′dĭ-mŏn′strə-bəl) *adj.* Incapable of being proved or demonstrated. Said especially of axiomatic truths. **—in·de·mon·stra·bil·i·ty** *n.* **—in·de·mon·stra·bly** *adv.*

in·dene (ĭn′dēn′) *n.* A colorless organic liquid, C_9H_8, obtained from coal tar and used in preparing synthetic resins.

in·dent[1] (ĭn-dĕnt′) *v.* **-dented, -denting, -dents.** *—tr.* **1.** To cut or tear (a document with two or more copies) along an irregular line so that the parts can later be matched for establishing authenticity. **2.** To draw up (a deed or other document) in duplicate or triplicate. **3. a.** To notch or serrate the edge of; make jagged. **b.** To form indentations in: *a deeply indented coastline.* **4. a.** To make notches, grooves, or holes in (wood, for example) for the purpose of mortising. **b.** To fit or join together by or as if by mortising. **5.** To set in from the margin (the first line of a paragraph, for example). **6.** *Chiefly British.* To order (goods) by an indent. **7.** To bind (an apprentice) by indenture. *—intr.* **1.** To form an indentation. **2.** *Chiefly British.* To draw up or order an indent for something.
~n. (ĭn-dĕnt′, ĭn′dĕnt′). **1.** An indenture. **2.** *Chiefly British.* An official requisition or purchase order for goods. **3.** An indention. [Middle English *indenten, endenten,* to make a toothlike incision into, from Old French *endenter* : *en-,* in + *dent,* tooth, from Latin *dēns* (stem *dent-*).] **—in·dent·er, in·den·tor** *n.*

in·dent[2] *tr.v.* **-dented, -denting, -dents. 1.** To push in or press down upon so as to form a dent or impression. **2.** To make a dent in.
~n. (ĭn-dĕnt′, ĭn′dĕnt′). An indentation.

in·den·ta·tion (ĭn′dĕn-tā′shən) *n.* **1.** The act of indenting or the condition of being indented. **2. a.** A notch or jagged cut in an edge. **b.** A series of notches or jagged cuts. **3.** A deep recess in a border, coastline, or other boundary. **4.** *Printing.* An indention.

in·den·tion (ĭn-dĕn′shən) *n.* **1.** *Printing.* The blank space between a margin and the beginning of an indented line. **2.** Indentation. **3.** *Archaic.* A dint or dent.

in·den·ture (ĭn-dĕn′chər) *n.* **1.** *Law.* A deed or contract executed between two or more parties. **2.** *Usually* **indentures.** A contract binding one party into the service of another for a stipulated term. **3.** *Archaic.* A document having indented edges. **4.** An official or authenticated inventory, list, or voucher. **5.** *Archaic.* Indentation.
~tr.v. **indentured, -turing, -tures. 1.** To bind by indenture. **2.** *Archaic.* To form an indentation in. [Middle English *indenture, endenture,* from Old French *endenture,* from *endenter,* INDENT.]

in·de·pend·ence (ĭn′dĭ-pĕn′dəns) *n. Abbr.* **ind. 1.** The state or quality of being independent. **2.** The point in time at which a state attains national independence: *has made great strides since independence.* **3.** *Archaic.* Sufficient income for self-support; a sufficiency.

In·de·pend·ence (ĭn′dĭ-pĕn′dəns). City in western Missouri, a suburb of Kansas City. In the mid-19th century it was the departure point for expeditions along the Santa Fe, Oregon, and California trails.

Independence Day n. **1.** In the United States, a public holiday (July 4) celebrating the anniversary of the adoption of the Declaration of Independence in 1776. **2.** A similar holiday in other countries, celebrating the attainment of national independence.

in·de·pend·en·cy (ĭn′dĭ-pĕn′dən-sē) n., pl. **-cies. 1.** Independence. **2.** An independent territory or state. **3. Independency.** The Independent movement in England; Congregationalism.

in·de·pend·ent (ĭn′dĭ-pĕn′dənt) adj. Abbr. **ind. 1.** Politically autonomous; self-governing. **2. a.** Free from the influence, guidance, or control of another or others. **b.** Self-reliant; not seeking or relying on help or guidance from others. **3.** Not contingent upon another person or thing. **4.** Affiliated with or loyal to no one political party or organization: the independent vote. **5.** Not dependent on or affiliated with a larger or controlling group, system, or the like; separate: an independent brewery. **6.** Financially self-sufficient; self-supporting. **7.** Not having to work for a living; wealthy in one's own right. **8.** Providing a sufficient income upon which to live: independent means. **9.** Mathematics. **a.** Not dependent on other variables: independent variable. **b.** Of or pertaining to a system of equations, no one of which is necessarily satisfied by a set of values of the independent variables that satisfy all the others. **c.** Of, pertaining to, or designating an outcome of a trial of a chance experiment the probability of which does not depend on the outcome of any other trial of the chance experiment. —n. Abbr. **ind.** One that is independent; especially, a voter or politician who does not pledge allegiance to any one political party. **—in·de·pend·ent·ly** adv.

In·de·pend·ent (ĭn′dĭ-pĕn′dənt) n. **1.** A member of a movement in England in the 17th century advocating the political and religious independence of individual congregations. **2.** British. A Congregationalist. **—In·de·pend·ent** adj.

independent clause n. A main clause (see).

independent school n. A school which is not maintained or controlled by central government or a local authority, and which usually charges fees.

in-depth (ĭn′dĕpth′) adj. Detailed; thorough: an in-depth study.

in·de·scrib·a·ble (ĭn′dĭ-skrīb′ə-bəl) adj. **1.** Incapable of description; undefinable. **2.** Beyond description. **—in·de·scrib·a·bil·i·ty, in·de·scrib·a·ble·ness** n. **—in·de·scrib·a·bly** adv.

in·de·struc·ti·ble (ĭn′dĭ-strŭk′tə-bəl) adj. Not capable of being destroyed. **—in·de·struc·ti·bil·i·ty, in·de·struc·ti·ble·ness** n. **—in·de·struc·ti·bly** adv.

in·de·ter·mi·na·ble (ĭn′dĭ-tûr′mə-nə-bəl) adj. **1.** Not capable of being fixed or measured; not ascertainable. **2.** Incapable of being finally settled or decided. **—in·de·ter·mi·na·bly** adv.

in·de·ter·mi·na·cy (ĭn′dĭ-tûr′mə-nə-sē) n. The state or quality of being indeterminate. [From INDETERMINATE.]

in·de·ter·mi·nate (ĭn′dĭ-tûr′mə-nĭt) adj. **1. a.** Not precisely or quantitatively determined. **b.** Incapable of being so determined. **c.** Lacking clarity or precision. **d.** Not capable of clear interpretation; inconclusive; ambiguous. **e.** Not known in advance. **2.** Botany. **a.** Not terminating in a flower and continuing to grow at the apex: an indeterminate inflorescence. **b.** Not fixed in number, being too numerous to count: indeterminate stamens. **3.** Mathematics. **a.** Designating an equation containing more than one variable that has an unlimited number of solutions. **b.** Having no numerical meaning: 0 ÷ 0 is indeterminate. **c.** Designating a structure or framework consisting of forces that cannot be analyzed into a set of vectors. **4.** Physics. Designating an effect that appears to have no cause or does not obey a causal law. [Middle English indeterminat, from Late Latin indēterminātus : Latin in-, not + dēterminātus, DETERMINATE.] **—in·de·ter·mi·nate·ly** adv. **—in·de·ter·mi·nate·ness, in·de·ter·mi·na·tion** n.

indeterminate sentence n. A sentence whose length is determined by the prisoner's conduct while in prison.

indeterminate vowel n. Phonetics. See schwa (sense 1).

in·de·ter·min·ism (ĭn′dĭ-tûr′mə-nĭz′əm) n. The philosophical doctrine that human actions are not necessarily predetermined by physiological and psychological factors. **—in·de·ter·min·ist** n. & adj. **—in·de·ter·min·is·tic** adj.

in·dex (ĭn′dĕks′) n., pl. **-dexes** or **indices** (-də-sēz′) (for senses 5 and 6). **1.** Anything that serves to guide, point out, or otherwise facilitate reference, as: **a.** Abbr. **ind.** An alphabetized listing of names, places, and subjects included in a printed work that gives for each item the page on which it may be found. **b.** A series of notches cut into the edge of a book for easy access to chapters or other divisions; a thumb index. **c.** Any table, file, or catalogue which enables a reference to be located. **2.** Anything that reveals or indicates; a sign; token: "Her face . . . was a fair index to her disposition" (Samuel Butler). **3.** A character (☞) used in printing to call attention to a particular paragraph or section. Also called "fist," "hand." **4.** Something that serves as an indicator or pointer, as in a scientific instrument. **5.** Mathematics. **a.** A number or symbol, often written as a subscript or superscript to a mathematical expression, that indicates an operation to be performed on, an ordering relation involving, or a use of the associated expression. **b.** A number indicating a specific property of a particular material: refractive index. **6.** A formula indicating the current level of something, such as

prices, by reference to a standard, usually taken to be 100: cost-of-living index. **7.** An index finger. —tr.v. **indexed, -dexing, -dexes. 1.** To compile an index for. **2.** To enter (an item) in an index. **3.** To indicate or signal. **4.** To make index-linked. [Latin index (plural indicēs), forefinger, indicator.]

in·dex·a·tion (ĭn′dĕk-sā′shən) n. **1.** An act of indexing. **2.** The act of relating salaries, pensions, and the like to the cost-of-living index. Also called "index-linking."

index finger n. The finger next to the thumb; the forefinger.

In·dex Li·bro·rum Pro·hib·i·to·rum (ĭn′dĕks′ lĭ-brôr′əm prō-hĭb′ə-tôr′əm, lĭ-brōr′əm prō-hĭb′ə-tōr′əm) n. A list formerly published by Church authority for Roman Catholics, restricting or forbidding the reading of certain books. Also shortened to "Index." [New Latin, "index of prohibited books."]

in·dex-linked (ĭn′dĕks′lĭngkt′) adj. Directly related to the cost-of-living index. Said of salaries, pensions, and the like. **—in·dex-link·ing** n.

index number n. A number indicating change in magnitude, as of price, wage, employment, or production shifts, relative to the magnitude at some given point usually taken as 100.

index of refraction n. **Refractive index** (see).

In·di·a (ĭn′dē-ə). Abbr. **Ind.** Independent republic of southern Asia. Much of India came under British domination in the mid-18th century. Its government, initially in the hands of the East India Company, was transferred to the Crown (1858) following the Indian Mutiny (1857–58). India became independent in 1947, when the country was partitioned and the Muslim areas of the east and northwest were made into the new nation of Pakistan. India has three main natural divisions: the triangular Deccan plateau of the south, the northern plains, and the Himalayas. The whole peninsula south of the Himalayas is often referred to as the "Indian subcontinent." The northern plains, which are crossed by the Indus, Ganges, and Brahmaputra rivers, form the world's largest alluvial lowland and the most densely populated part of the country. India's population is exceeded only by that of China. Although 40 percent of the national income is derived from agriculture, especially rice and wheat, India is also rich in mineral reserves. Its iron ore is the basis of rapidly expanding steel, machinery, and transport equipment industries. India is one of the leading producers of mica, coal, manganese, and aluminum, but still relies on imported oil. Area, 3,288,000 square kilometers (1,269,496 square miles). Population, 853,100,000. Capital, Delhi (also New Delhi). See map, next page.

India ink n. **1.** A black pigment made from lampblack mixed with a binding agent and molded into cakes or sticks. **2.** A liquid ink made from this. [Formerly thought to be a product of India.]

In·di·a·man (ĭn′dē-ə-mən) n., pl. **-men** (-mĭn). A large merchant ship formerly used on trade routes to India.

In·di·an (ĭn′dē-ən) n. Abbr. **Ind. 1.** A native or inhabitant of India or of the East Indies. **2.** A member of any of the aboriginal peoples of North America, South America, or the West Indies. **3.** Loosely, any of the languages spoken by the American Indians. —adj. **1.** Of or pertaining to India or the East Indies, their culture, their languages, or their people. **2.** Of or pertaining to the aboriginal people of North America, South America, or the West Indies.

In·di·an·a (ĭn′dē-ăn′ə). Abbr. **Ind.** State in the north-central United States. The capital and largest city is Indianapolis. Arable farming and cattle raising remain important, but Indiana is now a major manufacturing state and producer of petroleum. **—In·di·an·i·an** n. & adj.

Indiana Dunes National Lakeshore. A conservation and recreation area occupying 3,488 hectares (8,720 acres) in northwestern Indiana along the southern shore of Lake Michigan.

Indian agent n. An official representing the United States government in dealings with American Indians, especially on reservations.

Indian almond n. A tree, Terminalia catappa, of tropical Asia, having fruit with edible seeds. Also called "myrobalan."

In·di·an·ap·o·lis (ĭn′dē-ə-năp′ə-lĭs). Largest city and capital of the state of Indiana, on the White River in the middle of the state. In the center of a rich agricultural region, it is a major grain and livestock market and food-processing center.

Indian bean n. A tree, the catalpa (see).

Indian club n. A bottle-shaped wooden club used in juggling or other gymnastic exercises.

Indian corn n. See corn.

Indian file n. **Single file** (see).

Indian giver n. Informal. One who gives something as a gift to another and then takes or demands it back.

Indian hemp n. **1.** A plant, hemp (see). **2.** A North American plant, Apocynum cannabinum, whose stem fibers were formerly used by Indians for making matting and ropes.

Indian licorice n. The rosary pea (see).

Indian millet n. Durra (see).

Indian mulberry n. A small tree, Morinda citrifolia, of Indonesia and Australia from which red and yellow dyes are obtained.

Indian Mutiny. A revolt by native Indian troops in 1857–58 leading to the end of the rule of the East India Company and the subsequent administration of India by the British Crown.

Indian National Congress n. One of the main political parties in India, founded in 1885, which has frequently been the governing party since India's independence.

Indian Ocean. World's third-largest ocean, occupying an area of c. 73,427,000 square kilometers (28,350,000 square miles) and having a width of c. 6,400 kilometers (4,000 miles) at the equator. It ex-

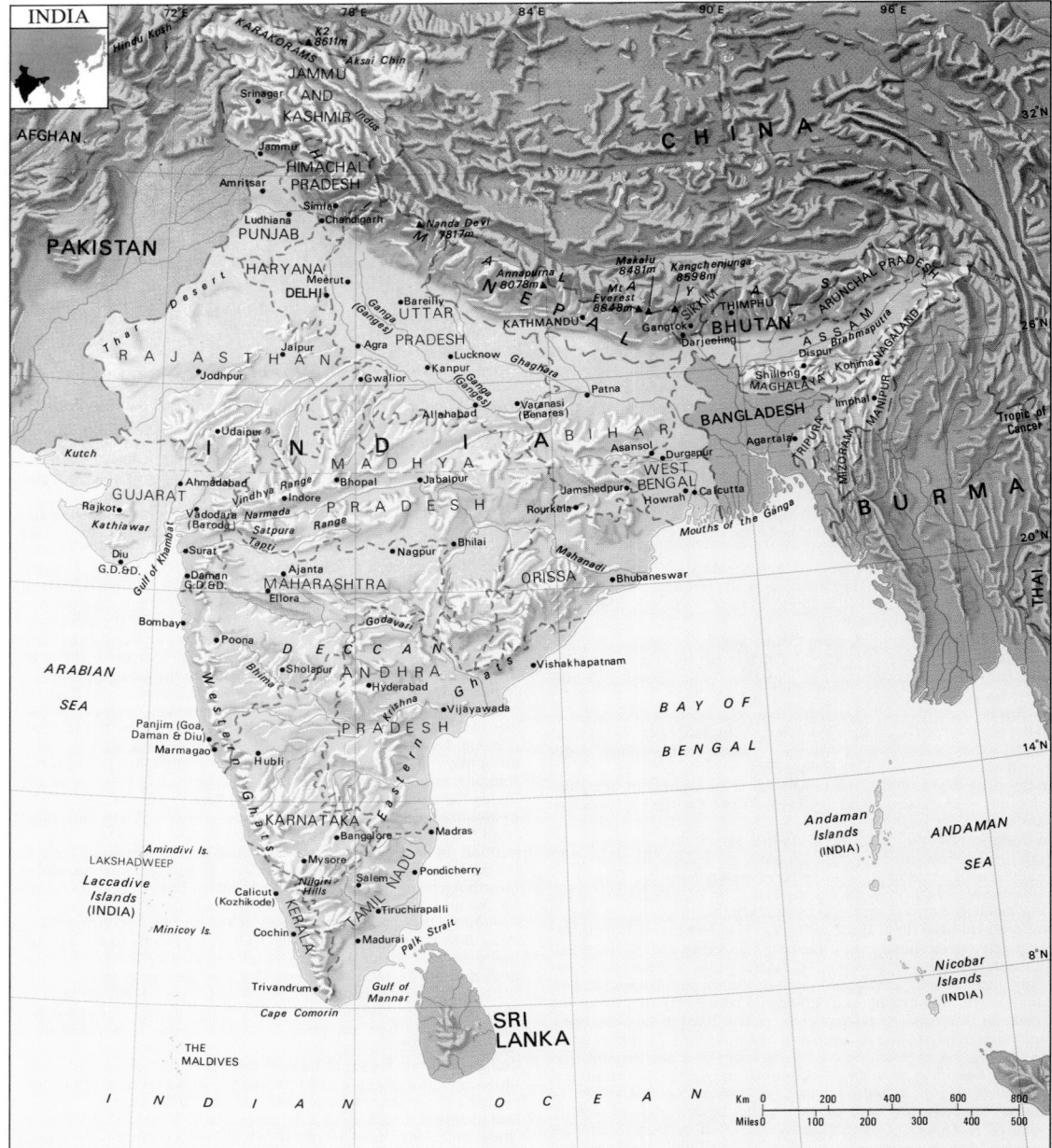

tends from southern Asia to the Antarctic and from east Africa to southeastern Australia. It is divided into eastern and western halves by the Mid-Oceanic Ridge, a few peaks of which emerge as islands. The average depth of the ocean is *c.* 3,400 meters (11,000 feet).

Indian paintbrush *n.* Any of various plants of the genus *Castilleja,* having spikes of flowers surrounded by showy, brightly colored bracts. Also called "painted cup."

Indian pipe *n.* A waxy white or sometimes pinkish saprophytic woodland plant, *Monotropa uniflora,* having scalelike leaves and a solitary, nodding flower.

Indian poke *n.* A species of **hellebore** *(see).*

Indian pudding *n.* A pudding made of cornmeal and milk and sweetened with molasses.

Indian red *n.* An iron oxide used as a paint and cosmetic pigment.

Indian rope trick *n.* The feat of climbing an unsupported rope, which some Indians are supposed to be able to perform.

Indian summer *n.* **1.** A period of mild weather occurring in late autumn or early winter. **2.** A pleasant, tranquil, or flourishing period occurring during the end of a condition or period, such as the late stage of one's life.

Indian Territory. An area occupying part of the modern state of Oklahoma. It was set aside in 1834 by the government as a homeland for five Indian tribes expelled from the east. After 1889 the land was forcibly repurchased and the surviving Indians placed on reservations.

Indian tobacco *n.* A poisonous North American plant, *Lobelia inflata,* having light-blue flowers and rounded seed pods.

Indian turnip *n.* **1.** A plant, the **jack-in-the-pulpit. 2.** The acrid tuber of this plant.

Indian wrestling *n.* A contest of strength between two people who clasp each other's hand with the elbow resting on a table, the winner being the one who forces his opponent's hand down to the table.

India paper *n.* **1.** A thin, uncoated, delicate paper made of vegetable fiber, used especially for taking impressions of engravings. **2. Bible paper** *(see).*

India rubber *n.* See **rubber** (sense 1). —**In·di·a-rub·ber** *adj.*

In·dic (ĭn′dĭk) *adj.* **1.** Of, pertaining to, or constituting the Indic languages. **2.** Of or pertaining to India, its people, or their culture. —*n.* A branch of the Indo-European languages that comprises Sanskrit and its modern descendants (including Hindi and Urdu), and Pali, Prakrit, and Dard.

in·di·can (ĭn′dĭ-kăn′) *n.* **1.** A compound, $C_8H_6NOSO_2OH$, excreted, usually in the form of its potassium salt, in the urine. **2.** A glycoside, $C_{14}H_{17}NO_6$, occurring in the indigo plant. [Latin *indicum,* IN-DIGO + -AN.]

in·di·cant (ĭn′dĭ-kənt) *n.* Something that serves to indicate. [Latin *indicāns* (stem *indicant-*), present participle of *indicāre,* to INDI-CATE.]

in·di·cate (ĭn′dĭ-kāt′) *tr.v.* **-cated, -cating, -cates. 1. a.** To demonstrate or point out with precision: *indicate a route.* **b.** To state or exhibit in complete detail. **c.** To show a reading of. Used of instruments. **2.** To serve as a sign, symptom, or token of; signify. **3.** To suggest or demonstrate the necessity, expedience, or advisability of:

The symptoms indicate immediate surgery. **4.** To state, disclose, or express briefly. [Latin *indicāre,* to show, from *index,* forefinger, indicator, INDEX.] —**in·di·ca·to·ry** (ĭn-dĭk′ə-tôr′ē, -tōr′ē) *adj.*

in·di·ca·tion (ĭn′dĭ-kā′shən) *n.* **1.** The action of indicating. **2. a.** Something that indicates; a sign, token, or symptom. **b.** Something indicated as necessary or expedient. **3.** The reading shown on a measuring instrument. —See Synonyms at **sign.**

in·dic·a·tive (ĭn-dĭk′ə-tĭv) *adj.* **1.** Serving to point out or indicate: *indicative of their cynical attitude.* **2.** *Abbr.* **ind.** *Grammar.* Pertaining to or designating a verb mood used to indicate that the denoted act or condition is an objective fact. Compare **subjunctive.** ~*n. Abbr.* **ind.** *Grammar.* **1.** The indicative mood. **2.** A verb in this mood. —**in·dic·a·tive·ly** *adv.*

in·di·ca·tor (ĭn′dĭ-kā′tər) *n.* **1. a.** A device that indicates, such as a pointer or index. **b.** A circumstance or characteristic that serves to indicate: *all the usual indicators of a weak economy.* **2.** Any of various meters, gauges, or other instruments that are used to monitor the operation or condition of an engine, furnace, electrical network, reservoir, or other physical system. **3.** The needle, dial, or other registering device on such an instrument. **4.** An indicator board. **5.** An accurate measuring instrument used to measure small linear distances or to check that a component has the correct dimensions. Also called "dial gauge." **6.** A plant species that requires special conditions of soil, temperature, and the like, and therefore indicates these conditions in places where it grows. Also called "indicator species." **7.** *Chemistry.* Any of various substances, such as litmus or phenolphthalein, that indicate the presence, absence, or concentration of a substance, or the degree of reaction between two or more substances, by means of a characteristic change, especially in color.

indicator board *n.* A board displaying information; especially, one in a railroad station or airport showing departure and arrival times. Also called "indicator."

indicator diagram *n.* A graph or oscilloscope record showing the variation of pressure and volume within the combustion chamber of an internal-combustion engine or steam engine.

in·di·ces. Alternate plural of **index.**

in·di·ci·a (ĭn-dĭsh′ē-ə, -dĭsh′ə) *pl.n.* **1.** Identifying marks or indications; signs. **2.** Markings on bulk mailings used as a substitute for stamps or cancellations. [Latin, plural of *indicium,* sign, from *indicāre,* to INDICATE.]

in·dict (ĭn-dīt′) *tr.v.* **-dicted, -dicting, -dicts.** To accuse formally of a crime or other offense; charge. [Alteration (influenced by obsolete *indict,* to proclaim) of Middle English *enditen,* to accuse, from Anglo-French *enditer,* to dictate, INDITE.] —**in·dict·ee** (ĭn′dī-tē′) *n.* —**in·dict·er, in·dict·or** *n.*

in·dict·a·ble (ĭn-dīt′ə-bəl) *adj. Law.* **1.** Liable to be indicted. **2.** Rendering a person liable to indictment. Said of a crime.

in·dic·tion (ĭn-dĭk′shən) *n.* **1.** A 15-year cycle used as a chronological unit for tax purposes in ancient Rome and incorporated in some medieval systems. **2.** *Archaic.* A proclamation. [Middle English *indiccioun,* from Late Latin *indictiō* (stem *indictiōn-*), "proclamation" (of Diocletian, fixing a 15-year assessment of property tax), from *indīcere,* to proclaim, INDITE.]

in·dict·ment (ĭn-dīt′mənt) *n.* **1.** The act of indicting or the state of being indicted. **2.** *Law.* A written statement charging a party with the commission of a crime.

Indies. See **East Indies, West Indies.**

in·dif·fer·ence (ĭn-dĭf′ər-əns) *n.* **1.** Lack of interest or concern. **2.** The quality of being indifferent.

in·dif·fer·ent (ĭn-dĭf′ər-ənt) *adj.* **1.** Having no particular interest or concern; apathetic. **2.** Unaffected; insensible: *indifferent to their pleas.* **3.** Showing no partiality, bias, or marked preference. **4.** Not mattering one way or the other; of no great importance; insignificant. **5.** Of average quality, extent, or degree. **6.** Being neither good nor bad; mediocre. **7.** Not active or involved; neutral. **8.** *Biology.* **a.** Undifferentiated, as cells or tissue. **b.** Occurring in two or more ecological communities. Said of a species. —See Synonyms at **average.** [Middle English, from Old French, from Latin *indifferēns : in-,* not + *differēns,* DIFFERENT.] —**in·dif·fer·ent·ly** *adv.*

Synonyms: *apathetic, detached, incurious, unconcerned.*

Usage: The usual preposition following this word is *to (He was indifferent to her advances)* but *as to* is sometimes used, especially in the context of abstract ideas *(He was indifferent as to the consequences of his action),* and *about* is often heard in less formal usage *(I'm indifferent about money).*

in·dif·fer·ent·ism (ĭn-dĭf′ər-ən-tĭz′əm) *n.* The belief that religions are all of like validity. —**in·dif·fer·ent·ist** *n.*

in·di·gen (ĭn′də-jən, -jēn′) *n.* Also **in·di·gene** (-jēn′). One that is native or indigenous to an area. [Latin *indigena,* native.]

in·di·gence (ĭn′də-jəns) *n.* Want or neediness.

in·dig·e·nous (ĭn-dĭj′ə-nəs) *adj.* **1.** Occurring or living naturally in an area; not introduced; native. **2.** Intrinsic; innate. [From Latin *indigena,* native.] —**in·dig·e·nous·ly** *adv.* —**in·dig·e·nous·ness** *n.*

in·di·gent (ĭn′də-jənt) *adj.* **1.** Lacking the means of subsistence; impoverished; needy. **2.** *Archaic.* Lacking or deficient in something specified. Usually used with *of.* ~*n.* A destitute or needy person. [Middle English, from Old French, from Latin *indigēns* (stem *indigent-*), present participle of *indigēre,* to lack : *indi-,* strengthened form of *in-,* in + *egēre,* to lack, want.]

in·di·gest·ed (ĭn′dĭ-jĕs′tĭd, ĭn′dī-) *adj.* **1.** Not carefully thought over or considered. **2.** Shapeless or chaotic.

in·di·gest·i·ble (ĭn′dĭ-jĕs′tə-bəl, ĭn′dī-) *adj.* **1.** Difficult or impossible

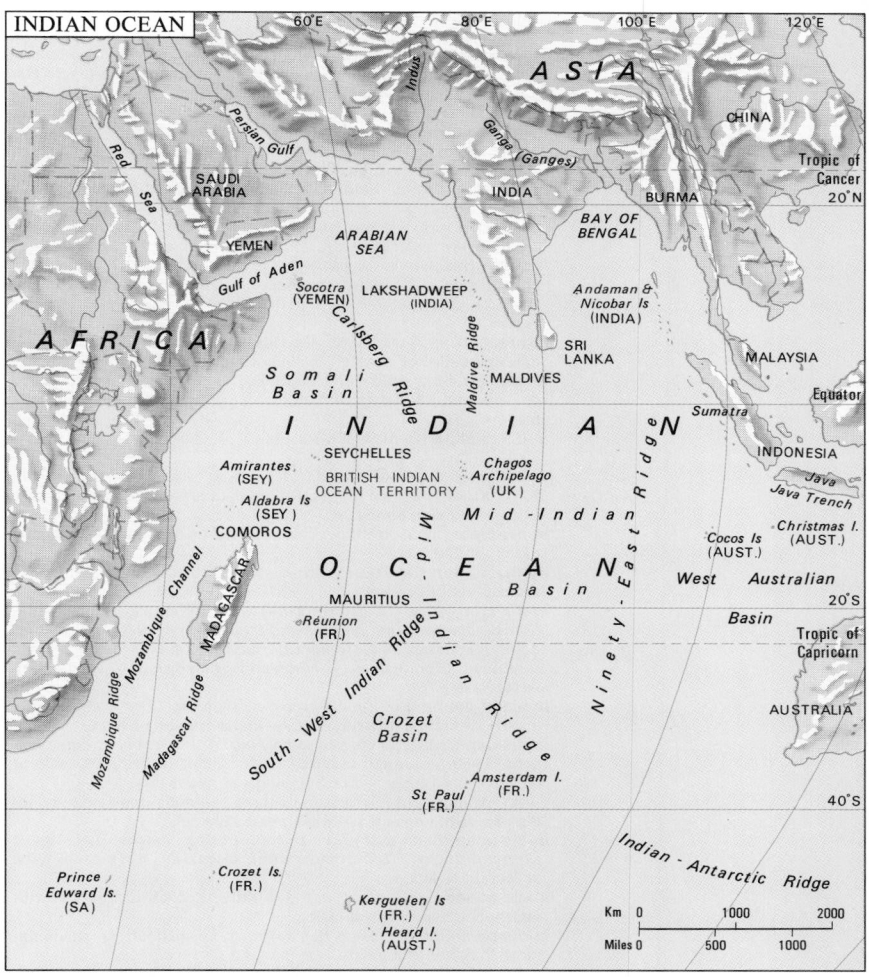

INDIAN OCEAN

to digest. **2.** Difficult for the mind to assimilate, especially because of poor expression or presentation. —**in·di·gest·i·bil·i·ty** *n.* —**in·di·gest·i·bly** *adv.*

in·di·ges·tion (ĭn′dī-jĕs′chən, ĭn′dī-) *n.* **1.** The inability to digest food. **2.** Discomfort or illness resulting from this; dyspepsia.

in·dign (ĭn-dīn′) *adj. Obsolete.* **1.** Unworthy. **2.** Shameful; disgraceful. [Middle English *indigne,* from Old French, from Latin *indignus : in-,* not + *dignus,* worthy.]

in·dig·nant (ĭn-dĭg′nənt) *adj.* Characterized by or filled with indignation; outraged. [Latin *indignāns* (stem *indignant-*), present participle of *indignārī,* to regard as unworthy, from *indignus,* unworthy, INDIGN.] —**in·dig·nant·ly** *adv.*

in·dig·na·tion (ĭn′dĭg-nā′shən) *n.* Anger aroused by something unjust, mean, or unworthy. —See Synonyms at **anger.** [Middle English *indignacioun,* from Latin *indignātiō* (stem *indignātiōn-*), from *indignārī,* to regard as unworthy. See **indignant.**]

in·dig·ni·ty (ĭn-dĭg′nə-tē) *n., pl.* **-ties. 1. a.** Humiliating, degrading, or abusive treatment of an individual. **b.** An offense to dignity; an affront. **2.** *Obsolete.* The want of dignity or honor. [Latin *indignitās* (stem *indignitāt-*), from *indignus,* unworthy, INDIGN.]

in·di·go (ĭn′dĭ-gō′) *n., pl.* **-gos** or **-goes. 1.** Any of various plants of the genus *Indigofera,* some of which yield a blue dyestuff. **2.** Any of several similar or related plants. **3.** A blue dye obtained from indigo or other plants or produced synthetically. **4.** *Abbr.* **ind.** Dark blue to grayish purplish blue. [Earlier *indico,* from Spanish, from Latin *indicum,* from Greek *indikon (pharmakon),* "Indian (dye)," from *Indikos,* Indian, from *India,* INDIA.] —**in·di·go** *adj.*

indigo bunting *n.* A small bird, *Passerina cyanea,* of North and Central America, the male of which has deep-blue plumage.

indigo snake *n.* A nonvenomous bluish-black snake, *Drymarchon corais,* of the southern United States and northern Mexico.

in·dig·o·tin (ĭn-dĭg′ə-tĭn, ĭn′dĭ-gō′-) *n.* A dark blue, crystalline compound, $C_{16}H_{10}N_2O_2$, the principal coloring matter of indigo. [INDIGO + -IN.]

in·di·rect (ĭn′-dĭ-rĕkt′, -dī-rĕkt′) *adj. Abbr.* **ind. 1. a.** Not taking a direct course; roundabout. **b.** Not proceeding or operating directly: *an indirect connection.* **2.** Not descending in a straight line of succession. Said of an inheritance or title. **3. a.** Not straight to the point; circumlocutory. **b.** Evasive; devious. **4.** Not directly planned for; secondary: *indirect benefits.* **5.** Pertaining to or characteristic of indirect speech; oblique. —**in·di·rect·ly** *adv.* —**in·di·rect·ness** *n.*

indirect discourse or **speech** *n.* A construction giving an account of a previous statement without quoting it verbatim, introduced by a verb such as *say* or *tell,* sometimes followed by *that,* and having appropriate changes in person and tense; for example, *She said that he had left.* Also called "indirect speech," "reported speech." Compare **direct speech.**

in·di·rec·tion (ĭn′dĭ-rĕk′shən, ĭn′dī-) *n.* **1.** The quality or state of being indirect. **2.** Lack of direction; aimlessness. **3.** Lack of straight-forwardness; deviousness.

indirect lighting *n.* Illumination by reflected or diffused light.

indirect object *n.* A grammatical object indirectly affected by the action of a verb; for example, *me* in *Sing me a song* and *the rabbit* in *He feeds the rabbit lettuce.* Compare **direct object.**

indirect passive *n.* A passive construction in which the subject corresponds to the indirect or prepositional object in an active construction; for example, *they* in the sentence *They were given the papers.*

indirect tax *n.* A tax levied on goods or services rather than individuals and collected through the vendor. Compare **direct tax.**

in·dis·cern·i·ble (ĭn′dĭ-sûr′nə-bəl) *adj.* **1.** Not able to be discerned or perceived. **2.** Barely discernible or perceptible. —**in·dis·cern·i·bly** *adv.*

in·dis·ci·pline (ĭn-dĭs′ə-plĭn′) *n.* Lack of discipline; unruly behavior.

in·dis·creet (ĭn′dĭs-krēt′) *adj.* **1.** Lacking discretion; injudicious. **2.** Too frank; inclined to reveal more than is wise. —**in·dis·creet·ly** *adv.* —**in·dis·creet·ness** *n.*

in·dis·crete (ĭn′dĭs-krēt′) *adj.* Not divided or divisible into separate parts; unified.

in·dis·cre·tion (ĭn′dĭs-krĕsh′ən) *n.* **1.** Lack of discretion. **2.** An indiscreet act or remark.

in·dis·crim·i·nate (ĭn′dĭs-krĭm′ə-nĭt) *adj.* **1.** Wanting in discrimination or discernment: *indiscriminate admiration of power.* **2.** Random; haphazard. **3.** Confused; motley. **4.** Not restricted or restrained; promiscuous. —**in·dis·crim·i·nate·ly** *adv.* —**in·dis·crim·i·nate·ness** *n.*

in·dis·crim·i·na·tion (ĭn′dĭs-krĭm′ə-nā′shən) *n.* The condition or quality of being indiscriminate. —**in·dis·crim·i·na·tive** *adj.*

in·dis·pen·sa·ble (ĭn′dĭs-pĕn′sə-bəl) *adj.* **1.** Incapable of being dispensed with; essential; required. **2.** Incapable of being set aside or escaped; inevitable. —See Synonyms at **necessary.** —*n.* An indispensable person or thing. —**in·dis·pen·sa·bil·i·ty, in·dis·pen·sa·ble·ness** *n.* —**in·dis·pen·sa·bly** *adv.*

in·dis·pose (ĭn′dĭs-pōz′) *tr.v.* **-posed, -posing, -poses.** **1.** To make averse; disincline. **2.** To render unfit; disqualify. **3.** To cause to be or feel ill; sicken.

in·dis·posed (ĭn′dĭs-pōzd′) *adj.* **1.** Mildly ill. **2.** Disinclined; unwilling. —See Synonyms at **sick.**

in·dis·po·si·tion (ĭn′dĭs-pə-zĭsh′ən) *n.* **1.** Disinclination; unwillingness. **2.** A minor ailment.

in·dis·put·a·ble (ĭn′dĭs-pyōō′tə-bəl) *adj.* Beyond doubt; undeniable. —**in·dis·put·a·ble·ness** *n.* —**in·dis·put·a·bly** *adv.*

in·dis·sol·u·ble (ĭn′dĭ-sŏl′yə-bəl) *adj.* **1.** Impossible to break or undo; binding: *an indissoluble contract.* **2.** Incapable of being dissolved, disintegrated, or decomposed. —**in·dis·sol·u·bil·i·ty, in·dis·sol·u·ble·ness** *n.* —**in·dis·sol·u·bly** *adv.*

in·dis·tinct (ĭn′dĭs-tĭngkt′) *adj.* **1.** Not clearly delineated; blurred. **2.** Faint; dim. **3.** Difficult to understand or make out: *indistinct speech.* —**in·dis·tinct·ly** *adv.* —**in·dis·tinct·ness** *n.*

in·dis·tinc·tive (ĭn′dĭs-tĭngk′tĭv) *adj.* Lacking distinctive qualities; not distinctive. —**in·dis·tinc·tive·ly** *adv.* —**in·dis·tinc·tive·ness** *n.*

in·dis·tin·guish·a·ble (ĭn′dĭs-tĭng′gwĭsh-ə-bəl) *adj.* Not distinguishable, especially: **1.** Difficult or impossible to perceive or make out. **2.** So similar as to be incapable of being distinguished from another

or each other. —**in·dis·tin·guish·a·bil·i·ty, in·dis·tin·guish·a·ble·ness** *n.* —**in·dis·tin·guish·a·bly** *adv.*

in·dite (ĭn-dīt′) *tr.v.* **-dited, -diting, -dites.** **1.** To write; compose. **2.** To set down in writing. **3.** *Obsolete.* To dictate. [Middle English *enditen,* to compose, write down, from Norman French *enditer,* from Vulgar Latin *indictāre* (unattested), frequentative of Latin *indīcere* (past participle *indictus*), to proclaim : *in-,* toward + *dīcere,* to pronounce.] —**in·dite·ment** *n.* —**in·dit·er** *n.*

in·di·um (ĭn′dē-əm) *n. Symbol* **In** A soft, malleable, silvery-white metallic element found primarily in ores of zinc and tin, used as a plating over silver in making mirrors, in plating aircraft bearings, and in compounds for transistors. Atomic number 49, atomic weight 114.82, melting point 156.61°C, boiling point 2,000°C, specific gravity 7.31, valencies 1, 2, 3. [New Latin, from Latin *indicum,* INDIGO (from the indigo-blue color of its spectrum).]

in·di·vert·i·ble (ĭn′dĭ-vûr′tə-bəl, -dī-) *adj.* Incapable of being diverted or turned aside. —**in·di·vert·i·bly** *adv.*

in·di·vid·u·al (ĭn′də-vĭj′ōō-əl) *adj.* **1. a.** Of or pertaining to a single human being. **b.** By or for one person: *an individual portion.* **2.** Existing as a distinct entity; single; separate. **3.** Distinguished by particular characteristics; peculiar to one person; distinctive. **4.** *Obsolete.* Indivisible; inseparable. —See Synonyms at **characteristic, single.**
~*n.* **1. a.** A single human being considered separately from his group or from society. **b.** A single organism as distinguished from a group or colony. **2.** An independent, strong-willed person. **3.** A person. [Middle English *indyvyduall,* separate, indivisible, from Medieval Latin *indīviduālis,* from Latin *indīviduus,* indivisible : *in-,* not + *dīviduus,* divisible, from *dīvidere,* to DIVIDE.] —**in·di·vid·u·al·ly** *adv.*

Usage: Individual (noun) in the sense of "a person" is fittingly used when a single human being is distinguished from a group or mass by contrast or by stress on a special quality: *the individual's right to dissent from a majority view; an individual to the core.* Careful writers and stylists avoid the use of the term *individual* as a substitute for *person: Two individuals were arrested for the crime.*

in·di·vid·u·al·ism (ĭn′dĭ-vĭj′ōō-ə-lĭz′əm) *n.* **1.** Individuality. **2.** The assertion of one's uniqueness; egoism. **3.** An individual peculiarity or foible. **4.** *Economics.* **a.** The theory that a citizen should have freedom in his economic pursuits and should succeed by his own initiative. **b.** The practice of this: *rugged individualism.* **5.** The doctrine that the interests of the individual should take precedence over the interests of the state or social group. **6.** *Philosophy.* The doctrine that reality is composed of individual entities.

in·di·vid·u·al·ist (ĭn′dĭ-vĭj′ōō-ə-lĭst) *n.* **1.** One who asserts his individuality by his independence of thought and action. **2.** One who advocates individualism. —**in·di·vid·u·al·ist, in·di·vid·u·al·is·tic** *adj.* —**in·di·vid·u·al·is·ti·cal·ly** *adv.*

in·di·vid·u·al·i·ty (ĭn′dĭ-vĭj′ōō-ăl′ə-tē) *n., pl.* **-ties.** **1.** The quality of being individual; distinctness. **2.** The aggregate of distinguishing attributes of a person or thing. **3.** A single, distinct entity. **4.** *Archaic.* Indivisibility.

in·di·vid·u·al·ize (ĭn′dĭ-vĭj′ōō-ə-līz′) *tr.v.* **-ized, -izing, -izes.** **1.** To give individuality to. **2.** To consider individually; specify; particularize. **3.** To modify to suit a particular individual. —**in·di·vid·u·al·i·za·tion** *n.*

in·di·vid·u·ate (ĭn′də-vĭj′ōō-āt′) *tr.v.* **-ated, -ating, -ates.** **1.** To individualize. **2.** To form into a separate and distinct entity.

in·di·vid·u·a·tion (ĭn′də-vĭj′ōō-ā′shən) *n.* **1.** The act or process of individuating; specifically, the process by which social individuals become differentiated one from the other. **2.** The condition of being individuated; individuality.

in·di·vis·i·ble (ĭn′də-vĭz′ə-bəl) *adj.* **1.** Incapable of being divided. **2.** *Mathematics.* Incapable of being divided exactly. —**in·di·vis·i·bil·**

INDONESIA

i·ty, in·di·vis·i·ble·ness *n.* —**in·di·vis·i·bly** *adv.*

Indo– *prefix.* Indicates India or East Indian; for example, **Indochina.**

In·do-Ar·y·an (ĭn′dō-âr′ē-ən) *adj.* **1.** Belonging to or characteristic of any of the Indo-European-speaking peoples of the Indian subcontinent. **2.** Indo-Iranian. ~*n.* **1.** Any of the Indo-Aryan peoples. **2.** An Indo-Iranian.

In·do·chi·na (ĭn′dō-chī′nə). Region of Southeast Asia. It includes Burma, Thailand, Laos, Kampuchea, Vietnam, and the Malay Peninsula. See **French Indochina.** —**In·do·chi·nese** *n. & adj.*

in·doc·ile (ĭn-dŏs′əl) *adj.* Difficult to control or instruct; not docile. —**in·do·cil·i·ty** *n.*

in·doc·tri·nate (ĭn-dŏk′trə-nāt′) *tr.v.* **-nated, -nating, -nates.** **1.** To instruct in a body of doctrine. **2.** To teach to accept a system of thought uncritically. —**in·doc·tri·na·tion** *n.*

In·do-Eu·ro·pe·an (ĭn′dō-yŏŏr′ə-pē′ən) *adj.* **1.** Belonging to or constituting a family of languages that includes the Germanic, Celtic, Italic, Baltic, Slavic, Greek, Armenian, Hittite, Tocharian, Iranian, and Indic groups. **2.** Belonging to or constituting Proto-Indo-European. **3.** Of, pertaining to, or characteristic of cultural traits appearing to be common to or widely distributed among peoples who speak Indo-European languages, and presumed to be inherited from the original speakers of Proto-Indo-European. ~*n.* **1.** The Indo-European family of languages. **2. Proto-Indo-European** *(see).* **3.** A member of any of the peoples who speak Indo-European languages. **4.** A member of the presumed prehistoric people who spoke Proto-Indo-European. [Named after the geographical extremities of the distribution of the languages : INDO- + EUROPEAN.]

In·do-Eu·ro·pe·an·ist (ĭn′dō-yŏŏr′ə-pē′ə-nĭst) *n.* A historical linguist specializing in the study of Indo-European.

In·do-Ger·man·ic (ĭn′dō-jər-măn′ĭk) *adj.* Indo-European. ~*n.* Indo-European. [Translation of German *indogermanisch.*]

In·do-Hit·tite (ĭn′dō-hĭt′īt′) *n.* Indo-European together with Hittite. Used by those who do not consider Hittite to be itself within the Indo-European family proper.

In·do-I·ra·ni·an (ĭn′dō-ĭ-rā′nē-ən, -ī-rā′nē-ən) *adj.* Belonging to or constituting the branch of Indo-European made up of the Indic and the Iranian language groups. ~*n.* The Indo-Iranian branch of Indo-European.

in·dole, in·dol (ĭn′dōl′) *n.* A white crystalline compound, C_8H_7N, obtained from coal tar and used in perfumery, medicine, and as a flavoring. [IND(IGO) + -OLE.] —**in·dol·ic** *adj.*

in·dole·a·ce·tic acid (ĭn′dō-lə-sē′tĭk) *n. Abbr.* **IAA.** An organic compound, $C_{10}H_9NO_2$, which is the most common of the group of substances that regulate plant growth (auxins).

in·dole·a·ce·to·ni·trile (ĭn′dō-lə-sē′tō-nī′trĭl) *n. Abbr.* **IAN.** A common auxin, $C_{10}H_8N_2$.

in·dole·am·ine (ĭn′dō-lăm′ēn, ĭn′dō-lə-mēn′) *n.* Any of various derivatives of indole containing an amine group.

in·do·lent (ĭn′də-lənt) *adj.* **1.** Averse to work or activity; habitually lazy. **2.** *Pathology.* **a.** Causing little or no pain: *an indolent tumor.* **b.** Slow to heal; persistent: *an indolent ulcer.* [Late Latin *indolēns,* painless : Latin *in-,* not + *dolēns* (stem *dolent-*), present participle of *dolēre,* to give pain, feel pain.] —**in·do·lence** *n.*

In·dol·o·gy (ĭn-dŏl′ə-jē) *n.* The study of Indian history, languages, and culture. [INDO- + -LOGY.] —**In·dol·o·gist** *n.*

in·do·meth·a·cin (ĭn′dō-mĕth′ə-sĭn) *n.* A drug, $C_{19}H_{16}ClNO_4$, that relieves pain and inflammation and is used particularly in the treatment of rheumatoid arthritis. [INDO(LE) + METH- + AC(ETIC ACID) + -IN.]

in·dom·i·ta·ble (ĭn-dŏm′ə-tə-bəl) *adj.* Incapable of being overcome, subdued, or vanquished; unconquerable. [Late Latin *indomitābilis,* untamable : Latin *in-,* not + *domitāre,* frequentative of *domāre* (past participle *domitus*), to tame.] —**in·dom·i·ta·bly** *adv.*

In·do·ne·si·a (ĭn′də-nē′zhə, -shə). Formerly **Dutch East Indies** (dŭch ēst ĭn′dēz). Republic in southeastern Asia, the fifth-largest nation in the world and the world's largest Muslim nation. It consists of more than 13,000 islands lying between the Indian and Pacific oceans. Despite fertile land, prolific sea fisheries, and abundant minerals, Indonesia is one of the world's poorest countries because of lack of development. The chief agricultural product is rice, and cash crops include tea, rubber, copra, coffee, and sugar. Indonesia also exports petroleum, petroleum products, and tin. It gained its independence from the Netherlands in 1949 under Ahmed Sukarno. He was removed by a bloody military coup (1965), and since then Gen. Suharto has reversed his Communist policies. Area, 1,904,345 square kilometers (735,077 square miles). Population, 184,300,000. Capital, Jakarta, on the island of Java.

In·do·ne·sian (ĭn′də-nē′zhən, -shən) *n.* **1.** A native or inhabitant of Indonesia. **2.** A member of a hypothetical non-Malay race of Indonesia, Malaysia, and the Philippines, having both Mongoloid and Polynesian characteristics. **3.** The official language of Indonesia, **Bahasa Indonesia** *(see).* ~*adj.* Of or pertaining to Indonesia, its people, or their language.

Indonesian Borneo. See **Kalimantan.**

in·door (ĭn′dôr′, -dōr′) *adj.* **1.** Of, pertaining to, or situated in the interior of a house or other building: *an indoor pool.* **2.** Carried on or used indoors: *indoor games.* [Short for earlier *within-door* : WITHIN + DOOR.]

in·doors (ĭn-dôrz′, -dōrz′) *adv.* In or into a house or other building. [Short for earlier *withindoors* : WITHIN + DOORS.]

in·do·phe·nol (ĭn′dō-fē′nôl) *n.* A green or blue organic dye, OH$C_6H_4NC_6H_4O$, or its derivatives.

indorse. Variant of **endorse.**

In·dra (ĭn′drə). *Hinduism.* A principal Vedic deity associated with rain and thunder. [Sanskrit *Indraḥ.*]

in·draft (ĭn′drăft′, -dräft′) *n.* **1.** A pulling or drawing inward. **2.** An inward flow or current: *an indraft of cold air.*

in·drawn (ĭn′drôn′) *adj.* **1.** Drawn in. **2.** Introspective; aloof.

in·dri (ĭn′drē) *n., pl.* **-dris.** A large lemur, *Indri indri,* of Madagascar, having silky fur and a short tail. [Malagasay *indry!* look! (mistakenly assumed to be the animal's name).]

in·du·bi·ta·ble (ĭn-dōō′bə-tə-bəl, ĭn-dyōō′-) *adj.* Too obvious to be doubted; unquestionable. —**in·du·bi·ta·bil·i·ty** *n.* —**in·du·bi·ta·bly** *adv.*

in·duce (ĭn-dōōs′, -dyōōs′) *tr.v.* **-duced, -ducing, -duces.** **1.** To lead or move by influence or persuasion; prevail upon: *finally induced him to give up smoking.* **2.** To stimulate the occurrence of; especially, to hasten (childbirth) artificially, as by the use of drugs. **3.** To infer by inductive reasoning. **4.** *Physics.* To produce (an electric current or magnetic effect) by induction. —See Synonyms at **persuade.** [Middle English *inducen,* from Latin *indūcere* : *in-,* in + *dūcere,* to lead.] —**in·duc·er** *n.* —**in·duc·i·ble** *adj.*

in·duce·ment (ĭn-dōōs′mənt, -dyōōs′-) *n.* **1.** The act or process of inducing: *the inducement of sleep.* **2.** That which induces; an incentive; a motive. **3.** An introductory or background statement explaining the main allegations in a legal proceeding.

in·duct (ĭn-dŭkt′) *tr.v.* **-ducted, -ducting, -ducts.** **1. a.** To place ceremoniously or formally in an office or benefice; install. **b.** To introduce, as to facts or knowledge; initiate. **c.** To admit to military service. **2.** *Physics.* To induce. [Middle English *inducten,* from Medieval Latin *indūcere* (past participle *inductus*), from Latin, to lead in, INDUCE.]

in·duc·tance (ĭn-dŭk′təns) *n.* **1.** The property of an electric circuit that enables an electromagnetic force to be generated as a result of a change of current in the same circuit *(self-inductance)* or in a nearby circuit with which it is magnetically linked *(mutual inductance).* **2.** A measure of this property in henries. **3.** A circuit element that introduces this property.

in·duc·tile (ĭn-dŭk′təl) *adj.* Unyielding; not pliant or ductile.

in·duc·tion (ĭn-dŭk′shən) *n.* **1.** The act of inducting or of being inducted. **2.** *Electricity.* **a.** The generation of electromotive force in a closed circuit by a varying magnetic flux through the circuit. **b.** The charging of an isolated conducting object by momentarily earthing it while a charged body is nearby. **3. a.** *Logic.* A principle of reasoning to a conclusion about all the members of a class from examination of only a few members of the class; broadly, reasoning from the particular to the general. Compare **deduction.** **b.** A conclusion reached by this method. **4.** *Mathematics.* A deductive method of proof in which verification of a proposition consists of proving the first case and the case immediately following an arbitrary case for which the proposition is assumed to be correct. **5.** The act of inducing. **6.** *Archaic.* A preface or preamble.

induction coil *n.* A transformer, often used in the ignition systems of gasoline engines, in which an interrupted, low-voltage direct current in the primary is converted into an intermittent, high-voltage current in the secondary.

induction hardening *n.* A method of hardening the surface of a metal component by inducing eddy currents in it to heat it rapidly, then rapidly cooling it.

induction heating *n.* A method of heating a conducting material by inducing electric currents within it as a result of applying an alternating magnetic field to it.

induction motor *n.* A brushless electric motor in which an alternating current fed to the stator induces a current in the windings of the rotor. Rotation occurs as a result of the interaction of the magnetic field of the stator with that of the rotor.

in·duc·tive (ĭn-dŭk′tĭv) *adj.* **1.** Of or utilizing induction: *inductive method.* **2.** *Electricity.* Of or arising from inductance: *inductive reactance.* **3.** Causing or influencing; inducing. —**in·duc·tive·ly** *adv.* —**in·duc·tive·ness** *n.*

inductive statistics *n.* The branch of statistics involving generalizations, predictions, estimations, and decisions from data initially presented.

in·duc·tor (ĭn-dŭk′tər) *n.* **1.** A person who inducts, as into office. **2.** *Electricity.* Symbol **L** A device that functions by or introduces inductance into a circuit.

indue. Variant of **endue.**

in·dulge (ĭn-dŭlj′) *v.* **-dulged, -dulging, -dulges.** —*tr.* **1.** To yield to the desires and whims of (oneself or another), especially to an excessive degree; humor; pamper. **2.** To gratify or yield to: *indulge a craving for chocolate.* **3.** To grant an ecclesiastical indulgence or dispensation to. —*intr.* **1.** To allow oneself some special pleasure; indulge oneself. Used with *in: indulge in an afternoon nap.* **2.** *Informal.* To consume an excessive amount of alcohol. —See Synonyms at **pamper.** [Latin *indulgēre†,* to be forbearing, grant as a favor.] —**in·dulg·er** *n.*

in·dul·gence (ĭn-dŭl′jəns) *n.* **1.** The act of indulging or the fact of being indulgent; tolerance, forbearance, or absence of restraint. **2. a.** The act of indulging in something. **b.** Something indulged in: *Sports cars are an expensive indulgence.* **3. a.** Something granted as a favor or privilege. **b.** Permission to extend the time of payment or performance, as in business. **4.** *Roman Catholic Church.* The remission of temporal punishment due for a sin after the guilt has been

Indus Valley

INDIA'S FIRST GREAT CIVILIZATION
Wealth from farming and foreign trade 4,000 years ago

As long ago as 2400 B.C. a wealthy city-based civilization flourished in the valley of the River Indus, in present-day Pakistan. At its peak it covered an area greater than that of ancient Egypt, had its own writing system, and traded with regions 2,560 kilometers (1,600 miles) away—for example, southern Mesopotamia. Its greatest centers were the capitals of Harappa and Mohenjo-Daro, excavated in the 1920's by the British archaeologist Sir John Marshall.

Its economy was based on agriculture— wheat, barley, rice, and cotton. Terra-cotta pots and models have survived, many bearing inscriptions; but the writing system has not yet been deciphered. About 1750 B.C. the cities were abandoned—possibly because the Indus River burst its banks and brought a flood; possibly because the region was under attack by light-skinned nomads from the northwest, the Aryans, whom many claim invaded India from 2000–1000 B.C. The conquered people became known as Dasyu ("dark-skinned"), and this distinction in color may have been the origin of India's caste system.

PRIESTLY RULER *One of the finds uncovered at Mohenjo-Daro in the 1920's was a soapstone bust (right) of one of the city's priest-kings.*

MOHENJO-DARO *In the foreground of the ruins stands a building that was once a granary. The city was built to a plan, with blocks of buildings laid out in a grid pattern and every house connected to main drainage.*

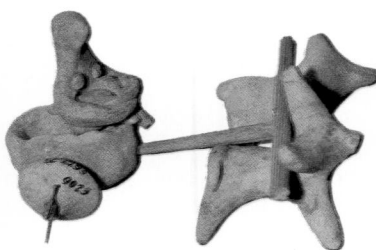

TOY FROM THE PAST *Indus Valley potters made terra-cotta models of everyday objects. This tiny bullock cart was probably used as a child's toy. Similar carts are still used in the area today.*

SACRED BULL *This soapstone seal from the Indus Valley civilization is thought to have had some religious significance. The writing on the seal has not yet been deciphered.*

---

forgiven. **5.** A royal dispensation during the reigns of Charles II and James II of England granting special religious freedom to the Nonconformists and the Roman Catholics.
 ~*tr.v.* **indulgenced, -gencing, -gences.** *Roman Catholic Church.* To grant an indulgence to.

in·dul·gent (ĭn-dŭl′jənt) *adj.* Showing, characterized by, or given to indulgence; lenient: *an indulgent employer.* —See Synonyms at **thoughtful.** —**in·dul·gent·ly** *adv.*

in·du·line (ĭn′də-lēn′) *n.* Also **in·du·lin** (-lĭn). Any of a group of blue or black synthetic azine dyestuffs used for coloring varnishes and dyeing wool.

in·dult (ĭn-dŭlt′) *n.* A temporary exemption from the common law of the Roman Catholic Church granted by the pope. [Middle English, from Medieval Latin *indultum,* from Latin *indultus,* past participle of *indulgēre†,* INDULGE.]

in·du·pli·cate (ĭn-dōō′plĭ-kĭt, ĭn-dyōō′-) *adj. Botany.* Having the edges folded or turned inward but not overlapping. Said of the parts of a bud. [IN- (in, inward) + Latin *duplicātus,* doubled up, DUPLICATE.]

in·du·rate (ĭn′dŏŏ-rāt′, ĭn′dyŏŏ-) *v.* **-rated, -rating, -rates.** —*tr.* **1.** To make hard; harden. **2.** To make callous. —*intr.* **1.** To harden. **2.** To become obdurate.
 ~*adj.* (ĭn′dŏŏ-rĭt, ĭn′dyŏŏ-). Hardened; obstinate; unfeeling. [Latin *indūrāre,* to harden : *in-* (intensive) + *dūrāre,* to harden, from *dūrus,* hard.] —**in·du·ra·tion** *n.* —**in·du·ra·tive** *adj.*

In·dus¹ (ĭn′dəs). Chief river of Pakistan, rising near Mt. Kailas. in Tibet and flowing to the Arabian Sea southeast of Karachi. It is *c.* 3,060 kilometers (1,900 miles) long. The Indus Valley is the most populous part of Pakistan. Its alluvial plains were the site of the early Indus Valley civilization that flourished from *c.* 2500 B.C. to *c.* 1500 B.C.

Indus² *n.* A constellation in the Southern Hemisphere near Tucana and Pavo.

in·du·si·um (ĭn-dōō′zē-əm, -zhē-əm, ĭn′dyōō′-) *n., pl.* **-sia** (-zē-ə, -zhē-ə). An enclosing membrane, such as that covering and protecting the sorus of a fern. [Latin, tunic, from Greek *endusis,* from *enduein,* to sink or slip into, put on : *en-,* in + *duein,* to sink.]

in·dus·tri·al (ĭn-dŭs′trē-əl) *adj. Abbr.* **ind. 1.** Of, pertaining to, or derived from industry: *an industrial exhibition.* **2.** Having highly developed industries: *an industrial nation.* **3.** Employed, required, or used in industry: *industrial diamonds.* **4.** Involving or concerning workers in industry: *industrial relations.*
 ~*n.* **industrials.** Shares in industrial companies. —**in·dus·tri·al·ly** *adv.*

industrial action *n. Chiefly British.* Any action, such as striking or boycotting, taken by workers to protest against working conditions, managerial policy, or the like.

industrial archaeology *n.* The study of machines, methods, and sites characteristic of the early history of the Industrial Revolution.

industrial arts *pl.n. Used with a singular verb.* A subject of study in schools aimed at developing the manual and technical skills required to work with tools and machinery.

industrial design *n.* The study or practice of designing manufacturable products.

industrial disease *n.* An occupational disease characteristic of workers in a particular industry, for example **asbestosis** *(see).*

in·dus·tri·al·ism (ĭn-dŭs′trē-ə-lĭz′əm) *n.* An economic system in which industries are dominant.

in·dus·tri·al·ist (ĭn-dŭs′trē-ə-lĭst) *n.* A person, such as the owner, the managing director, or a large shareholder of an industrial enterprise, who has a substantial interest in the running and profits of that enterprise.

in·dus·tri·al·ize (ĭn-dŭs′trē-ə-līz′) *v.* **-ized, -izing, -izes.** —*tr.* **1.** To develop industry in, especially on an extensive scale. **2.** To organize as an industry. —*intr.* To become industrial. —**in·dus·tri·al·i·za·tion** *n.*

industrial melanism *n.* **Melanism** *(see).*

industrial park *n.* An area usually located on the outskirts of a city and zoned for a group of industries and businesses.

industrial psychology *n.* Psychology applied to such problems of industry as personnel selection, training, and efficiency. —**industrial psychologist** *n.*

industrial relations *n.* **1.** *Used with a plural verb.* The relations that exist between the management and workers in an enterprise. **2.** *Used with a singular verb.* The art or study of managing these relations, especially from the point of view of improving them.

industrial revolution *n.* **1.** Social and economic changes brought about when extensive mechanization of production systems results in a shift from home manufacturing to large-scale factory production. **2. Industrial Revolution.** A period of such change beginning in the middle of the 18th century in England. Preceded by *the.*

industrial union *n.* A union to which all the workers of a particular industry can belong regardless of their trade. Compare **craft union.**

in·dus·tri·ous (ĭn-dŭs′trē-əs) *adj.* **1.** Diligently active; assiduous in work or study. **2.** *Obsolete.* Skillful; clever. —See Usage note at **busy.** [Latin *industriōsus,* from *industria,* skill, INDUSTRY.] —**in·dus·tri·ous·ly** *adv.* —**in·dus·tri·ous·ness** *n.*

in·dus·try (ĭn′də-strē) *n., pl.* **-tries.** *Abbr.* **ind. 1.** The commercial production and sale of goods, including the extraction and processing of raw materials and construction. **2.** A particular branch of manufacture and trade: *the textile industry.* **3. a.** Industrial management as distinguished from the work force. **b.** Manufacturing enterprises as distinguished from agriculture. **4.** Diligence; assiduity.

5. Study or interest in a specifed subject, cause, or the like, especially when considered exploitative. —See Usage note at **business**. [Middle English *industrie*, skill, diligence, from Old French, from Latin *industria*.]

in·dwell (ĭn-dwĕl′) *v.* **-dwelt** (-dwĕlt′), **-dwelling**, **-dwells**. —*intr.* **1.** To abide as a divine inner spirit, force, or principle. Usually used with *in.* **2.** To exist within permanently. Used with *in.* —*tr.* To abide within as a divine spirit, force, or principle. —**in·dwell·er** *n.*

-ine[1] *suffix.* Indicates of, pertaining to, or belonging to; for example, **Ursuline**, **elephantine**. [Middle English *-ine, -in,* from Old French *-in,* from Latin *-īnus, -inus,* from Greek *-inos.*]

-ine[2] *suffix. Chemistry.* **1.** Indicates a halogen element; for example, **chlorine, astatine. 2.** Indicates any of various nitrogen-containing compounds, such as: **a.** An amine; for example, **cadaverine. b.** An amino acid; for example, **glycine. c.** An alkaloid; for example, **strychnine. d.** An azine; for example, **induline. 3.** Variant of **-in** (sense 1). [Middle English *-ine*, -INE (pertaining to).]

-ine[3] *suffix.* Indicates made of or resembling; for example, **opaline**. [Middle English *-ine*, -INE (pertaining to).]

in·e·bri·ant (ĭn-ē′brē-ənt) *adj.* Intoxicating. ~*n.* An intoxicant.

in·e·bri·ate (ĭn-ē′brē-āt′) *tr.v.* **-ated, -ating, -ates. 1.** To make drunk; intoxicate. **2.** To exhilarate or stupefy with or as if with alcohol. ~*adj.* (ĭn-ē′brē-ĭt). Intoxicated. ~*n.* (ĭn-ē′brē-ĭt). An intoxicated person; especially, a drunkard. [Latin *inēbriāre : in-* (intensive) + *ēbriāre* (past participle *ēbriātus*), to intoxicate, from *ēbrius.*] —**in·e·bri·a·tion** *n.*

in·e·bri·at·ed (ĭn-ē′brē-ā′tĭd) *adj.* Exhilarated or confused by or as if by alcohol; intoxicated; drunk.

in·e·bri·e·ty (ĭn′ĭ-brī′ə-tē) *n.* Drunkenness; intoxication.

in·ed·i·ble (ĭn-ĕd′ə-bəl) *adj.* Not suitable for consumption; not edible. —**in·ed·i·bil·i·ty** *n.*

in·ed·it·ed (ĭn-ĕd′ĭ-tĭd) *adj.* **1.** Not edited. **2.** Not published.

in·ed·u·ca·ble (ĭn-ĕj′ə-kə-bəl) *adj.* Not able to be educated; unable to learn.

in·ef·fa·ble (ĭn-ĕf′ə-bəl) *adj.* **1.** Beyond expression; indescribable or unspeakable: *ineffable delight.* **2.** Not to be uttered; taboo: *the ineffable name of the Deity.* [Middle English, from Old French, from Latin *ineffābilis : in-*, not + *effābilis*, EFFABLE.] —**in·ef·fa·bil·i·ty, in·ef·fa·ble·ness** *n.* —**in·ef·fa·bly** *adv.*

in·ef·face·a·ble (ĭn′ĭ-fā′sə-bəl) *adj.* Not effaceable; indelible. —**in·ef·face·a·bil·i·ty** *n.* —**in·ef·face·a·bly** *adv.*

in·ef·fec·tive (ĭn′ĭ-fĕk′tĭv) *adj.* **1.** Not effective; having no effect. **2.** Incompetent; not performing to the required standard. —**in·ef·fec·tive·ly** *adv.* —**in·ef·fec·tive·ness** *n.*

in·ef·fec·tu·al (ĭn′ĭ-fĕk′chōō-əl) *adj.* **1.** Not effectual; inadequate. **2.** Powerless; lacking in force or competence: *an ineffectual king.* —**in·ef·fec·tu·al·i·ty, in·ef·fec·tu·al·ness** *n.* —**in·ef·fec·tu·al·ly** *adv.*

in·ef·fi·ca·cious (ĭn′ĕf-ĭ-kā′shəs) *adj.* Not producing a desired effect or result. —**in·ef·fi·ca·cious·ly** *adv.* —**in·ef·fi·ca·cious·ness** *n.*

in·ef·fi·ca·cy (ĭn-ĕf′ĭ-kə-sē) *n.* The state or quality of being inefficacious.

in·ef·fi·cient (ĭn′ĭ-fĭsh′ənt) *adj.* **1.** Wanting in ability; incompetent. **2.** Wasteful of time, energy, or materials. **3.** Not producing the intended result. —**in·ef·fi·cien·cy** *n.* —**in·ef·fi·cient·ly** *adv.*

in·e·las·tic (ĭn′ĭ-lăs′tĭk) *adj.* Not elastic; unyielding; unadaptable. —See Synonyms at **stiff**. —**in·e·las·tic·i·ty** (ĭn′ĭ-lă-stĭs′ə-tē) *n.*

in·el·e·gant (ĭn-ĕl′ə-gənt) *adj.* **1.** Lacking elegance or polish. **2.** Coarse; vulgar. [Old French, from Latin *inēlegāns : in-,* not + *ēlegāns,* ELEGANT.] —**in·el·e·gance** *n.* —**in·el·e·gant·ly** *adv.*

in·el·i·gi·ble (ĭn-ĕl′ə-jə-bəl) *adj.* **1.** Not qualified; not fulfilling the necessary conditions: *ineligible to enter the competition.* **2.** Not worthy of being chosen. ~*n.* A person who is not eligible. —**in·el·i·gi·bil·i·ty** *n.* —**in·el·i·gi·bly** *adv.*

in·el·o·quent (ĭn-ĕl′ə-kwənt) *adj.* Not eloquent; not fluent or vivid in expression. —**in·el·o·quence** *n.* —**in·el·o·quent·ly** *adv.*

in·e·luc·ta·ble (ĭn′ĭ-lŭk′tə-bəl) *adj.* Not to be avoided or overcome; inevitable. [Latin *inēluctābilis : in-*, not + *ēluctārī*, to struggle out : *ex-*, out + *luctārī*, to struggle.] —**in·e·luc·ta·bil·i·ty** *n.* —**in·e·luc·ta·bly** *adv.*

in·ept (ĭn-ĕpt′) *adj.* **1.** Not apt or fitting; unsuitable; inappropriate: *an inept comparison.* —See Usage note at **inapt. 2.** Not sensible; foolish: *an inept remark.* **3.** Awkward; clumsy; incompetent. —See Synonyms at **awkward**. [Latin *ineptus : in-,* not + *aptus*, APT.] —**in·ept·ly** *adv.* —**in·ept·ness** *n.*

in·ep·ti·tude (ĭn-ĕp′tə-tōōd′, -tyōōd′) *n.* **1.** The quality of being inept. **2.** An inept act or remark.

in·e·qua·ble (ĭn-ĕk′wə-bəl) *adj.* Not uniform; unevenly distributed.

in·e·qual·i·ty (ĭn′ĭ-kwŏl′ə-tē) *n., pl.* **-ties. 1.** The condition of being unequal. **2.** Lack of equality, as of opportunity, distribution of wealth, or the like. **3.** Unevenness; lack of smoothness or regularity. **4.** Variability; changeability. **5.** An instance of being unequal. **6.** *Mathematics.* An algebraic statement that a quantity is greater than another quantity or that it is less than another quantity.

in·eq·ui·ta·ble (ĭn-ĕk′wə-tə-bəl) *adj.* Not equitable; unfair; unjust. —**in·eq·ui·ta·ble·ness** *n.* —**in·eq·ui·ta·bly** *adv.*

in·eq·ui·ty (ĭn-ĕk′wə-tē) *n., pl.* **-ties. 1.** Lack of equity; injustice; unfairness. **2.** An instance of injustice or unfairness.

in·e·rad·i·ca·ble (ĭn′ĭ-răd′ĭ-kə-bəl) *adj.* That cannot be uprooted, eradicated, or erased. —**in·e·rad·i·ca·ble·ness** *n.* —**in·e·rad·i·ca·bly** *adv.*

TRANSFORMATION OF THE WORLD ECONOMY
The causes and effects of change

The complex of changes in British economic, social, and political life, which are collectively called the Industrial Revolution, had their roots in the development of overseas trade, in the founding of financial institutions, and in the formation of traditions of religious and intellectual freedom. The impetus to the transition from an agricultural to an industry-based economy came, however, from the unprecedented rise in world population that began in the 18th century. It created a reserve of labor and a steady expansion of demand for manufactured goods. A healthy foreign trade caused an increase in national wealth: more people were in paid employment and had money to save. Consequently, financial institutions accumulated funds to invest in new industries hungry for capital to manufacture industrial and consumer goods incorporating scientific or technical innovations. Textile machinery such as Crompton's "mule" (1779), which mechanized spinning, concentrated industry in factories, staffed with cheap labor often working in squalid, dangerous conditions. Whole cities of slums grew around them.

The Industrial Revolution spread from Britain to Europe and America during the 19th century, and to Asia, Australia, and Africa during the 20th. The distressing effects of social dislocation were gradually mitigated by social legislation, the development of social institutions, trade unions, and the welfare state, and an overall increase in wealth.

COALBROOKDALE *In 1703 a Shropshire ironmaster, Abraham Darby, first smelted pig iron with coke instead of costly charcoal at the Coalbrookdale ironworks (above). Iron and steel became cheaper, inventions such as the steam engine were mass-produced, and thus industrial output increased vastly.*

NIGERIA *In parts of Asia, South America, and Africa, industrialization is just beginning. Oil discoveries in Nigeria (left) are increasing national wealth.*

---

in·er·ra·ble (ĭn-ĕr′ə-bəl, -ûr′ə-bəl) *adj.* Inerrant. —**in·er·ra·bil·i·ty, in·er·ra·ble·ness** *n.* —**in·er·ra·bly** *adv.*

in·er·rant (ĭn-ĕr′ənt, ĭn-ûr′-) *adj.* Making no errors; unerring. —**in·er·ran·cy** *n.*

in·ert (ĭn-ûrt′) *adj.* **1.** Inherently unable to move or act. **2.** Resisting motion or action; sluggish. **3.** *Chemistry.* **a.** Exhibiting no chemical activity; totally unreactive. **b.** Exhibiting chemical activity under special or extreme conditions only. —See Synonyms at **inactive**. [Latin *iners* (stem *inert-*), inactive, unskilled : *in-*, not + *ars*, skill, ART.] —**in·ert·ly** *adv.* —**in·ert·ness** *n.*

inert gas *n.* Any of the elements helium, neon, argon, krypton, xenon, and radon that were formerly thought to be completely inert but which are now known to form some compounds. Also called "noble gas," "rare gas."

in·er·tia (ĭn-ûr′shə) *n.* **1.** *Physics.* **a.** The tendency of a body to resist acceleration. **b.** The tendency of a body at rest to remain at rest or of a body in motion to stay in motion in a straight line unless disturbed by an external force. **2.** Resistance or disinclination to motion, action, or change. **3.** *Medicine.* Reduction or absence of activity in certain smooth muscles: *uterine inertia.* [New Latin, from Latin, lack of skill, idleness, from *iners*, INERT.]

in·er·tial (ĭn-ûr′shəl) *adj.* **1.** Of or pertaining to inertia. **2.** Arising from or depending upon the effects of inertia. **3.** Referred to an inertial frame of reference.

inertial frame *n.* Any frame of reference relative to which the Newtonian law of motion, that a mass *m* subjected to a force *F* moves in accordance with the equation $F = ma$, where *a* is the acceleration, is valid. Also called "inertial system," "Newtonian frame."

inertial guidance *n.* Guidance of a missile in which data from a gyroscope and an accelerometer are used by a computer to maintain a predetermined course.

inertial mass *n.* The mass of a body as determined by its momentum. Compare **gravitational mass.**

inertial platform *n.* The devices used in inertial guidance and their mounting platform.

in·er·tia-reel seat belt (ĭn-ûr′shə-rēl′) *n.* A type of seat belt used in cars, in which the belt is only restrained from unwinding from a metal drum when the car is decelerating. The occupant of the seat therefore has freedom of movement except during a collision or very sharp braking.

inertia selling *n. British.* The illegal sending of unrequested goods to people in the hope that they will not be returned and payment can be demanded.

inertia welding *n.* The welding together of two metal parts caused by the heat of friction when a spinning part is pressed against a stationary part.

in·es·cap·a·ble (ĭn′ə-skā′pə-bəl) *adj.* That cannot be escaped; unavoidable; inevitable. —**in·es·cap·a·bil·i·ty** *n.* —**in·es·cap·a·bly** *adv.*

in·es·cutch·eon (ĭn′ə-skŭch′ən) *n. Heraldry.* A small escutcheon placed at the center of a larger escutcheon.

in es·se (ĭn ĕs′ē) *adj. Latin.* In actual existence. Compare **in posse.**

in·es·sen·tial (ĭn′ə-sĕn′shəl) *adj.* **1.** Not essential; unnecessary. **2.** Without essence.
~*n.* Something inessential. —**in·es·sen·ti·al·i·ty** (ĭn′ə-sĕn′shē-ăl′ə-tē) *n.*

in·es·ti·ma·ble (ĭn-ĕs′tə-mə-bəl) *adj.* **1.** Incapable of being estimated or computed; indeterminable: *inestimable damage.* **2.** Of incalculable value. —**in·es·ti·ma·bly** *adv.*

in·ev·i·ta·ble (ĭn-ĕv′ĭ-tə-bəl) *adj.* **1.** Incapable of being avoided or evaded. **2.** That cannot be prevented; certain to take place. **3.** Invariably appearing or occurring; predictable: *made the inevitable jokes about the bridegroom.*
~*n.* Something that is inevitable. Preceded by *the.* —**in·ev·i·ta·bil·i·ty, in·ev·i·ta·ble·ness** *n.* —**in·ev·i·ta·bly** *adv.*

in·ex·act (ĭn′ĭg-zăkt′) *adj.* Not exact; not quite accurate or precise. —**in·ex·act·ly** *adv.* —**in·ex·act·ness** *n.*

in·ex·act·i·tude (ĭn′ĭg-zăk′tə-tōōd′, -tyōōd′) *n.* Lack of exactness.

in·ex·cus·a·ble (ĭn′ĭk-skyōō′zə-bəl) *adj.* Not excusable; unpardonable. —**in·ex·cus·a·bil·i·ty, in·ex·cus·a·ble·ness** *n.* —**in·ex·cus·a·bly** *adv.*

in·ex·haust·i·ble (ĭn′ĭg-zô′stə-bəl) *adj.* **1.** Incapable of being exhausted or used up. **2.** Unfailing; tireless; indefatigable. —**in·ex·haust·i·bil·i·ty, in·ex·haust·i·ble·ness** *n.* —**in·ex·haust·i·bly** *adv.*

in·ex·is·tent (ĭn′ĭg-zĭs′tənt) *adj.* Not existent; nonexistent. —**in·ex·ist·ence, in·ex·ist·en·cy** *n.*

in·ex·o·ra·ble (ĭn-ĕk′sər-ə-bəl) *adj.* **1.** Not capable of being persuaded by entreaty; unyielding: *"and more inexorable far/Than empty tigers or the roaring sea"* (Shakespeare). **2.** Relentless; unremitting. [Latin *inexorabilis* : *in-*, not + *exorabilis*, from *exorāre*, to move by entreaty, from *ex-*, completely + *ōrāre*, to plead.] —**in·ex·ora·bil·i·ty, in·ex·o·ra·ble·ness** *n.* —**in·ex·o·ra·bly** *adv.*

in·ex·pe·di·ent (ĭn′ĭk-spē′dē-ənt) *adj.* Not expedient; inadvisable. —**in·ex·pe·di·ence, in·ex·pe·di·en·cy** *n.* —**in·ex·pe·di·ent·ly** *adv.*

in·ex·pen·sive (ĭn′ĭk-spĕn′sĭv) *adj.* Not expensive; fairly cheap. —**in·ex·pen·sive·ly** *adv.* —**in·ex·pen·sive·ness** *n.*

in·ex·pe·ri·ence (ĭn′ĭk-spîr′ē-əns) *n.* Lack of experience.

in·ex·pe·ri·enced (ĭn′ĭk-spîr′ē-ənst) *adj.* Lacking experience and the knowledge gained from experience.

in·ex·pert (ĭn-ĕk′spûrt′) *adj.* Not expert; not skillful or adept. —**in·ex·pert·ly** *adv.* —**in·ex·pert·ness** *n.*

in·ex·pi·a·ble (ĭn-ĕk′spē-ə-bəl) *adj.* **1.** Not capable of being expiated or atoned for: *inexpiable crimes.* **2.** *Archaic.* Implacable; unrelenting. —**in·ex·pi·a·ble·ness** *n.* —**in·ex·pi·a·bly** *adv.*

in·ex·pli·ca·ble (ĭn-ĕk′splĭ-kə-bəl, ĭn′ĭk-splĭk′ə-bəl) *adj.* Not explicable; not capable of being explained or accounted for. —**in·ex·pli·ca·bil·i·ty, in·ex·pli·ca·ble·ness** *n.* —**in·ex·pli·ca·bly** *adv.*

in·ex·plic·it (ĭn′ĭk-splĭs′ĭt) *adj.* Not explicit; indefinite; vague.

in·ex·press·i·ble (ĭn′ĭk-sprĕs′ə-bəl) *adj.* Not capable of being expressed; indescribable: *inexpressible joy.* —**in·ex·press·i·bil·i·ty, in·ex·press·i·ble·ness** *n.* —**in·ex·press·i·bly** *adv.*

in·ex·pres·sive (ĭn′ĭk-sprĕs′ĭv) *adj.* **1.** Expressing little or nothing. **2.** *Archaic.* Inexpressible. —**in·ex·pres·sive·ly** *adv.* —**in·ex·pres·sive·ness** *n.*

in·ex·pug·na·ble (ĭn′ĭk-spŭg′nə-bəl, -spyōō′nə-) *adj.* Not expugnable; impregnable. —**in·ex·pug·na·bly** *adv.*

in·ex·pung·i·ble (ĭn′ĭk-spŭn′jə-bəl) *adj.* Incapable of being expunged or obliterated.

in·ex·ten·si·ble (ĭn′ĭk-stĕn′sə-bəl) *adj.* Not extensible; unable to be extended.

in ex·ten·so (ĭn ek-stĕn′sō, ĭk-) *adv. Latin.* At full length; in full: *His article was published in extenso.*

in·ex·tin·guish·a·ble (ĭn′ĭk-stĭng′gwĭ-shə-bəl) *adj.* Not capable of

being extinguished or quenched. —**in·ex·tin·guish·a·ble·ness** *n.* —**in·ex·tin·guish·a·bly** *adv.*

in·ex·tir·pa·ble (ĭn′ĭk-stûr′pə-bəl) *adj.* Incapable of being eradicated or destroyed.

in ex·tre·mis (ĭn ek-strē′mĭs, ĭk-) *adv.* **1.** At the point of death. **2.** In grave difficulties. [Latin, "in the last (straits)."]

in·ex·tri·ca·ble (ĭn-ĕk′strĭ-kə-bəl) *adj.* **1. a.** Incapable of being disentangled or untied. **b.** Too intricate or complicated to solve. **2. a.** Firmly resisting one's attempts at escape or resolution: *an inextricable quandary.* **b.** Incapable of being freed: *The screws were rusted in and quite inextricable.* —**in·ex·tri·ca·bil·i·ty, in·ex·tri·ca·ble·ness** *n.* —**in·ex·tri·ca·bly** *adv.*

inf. 1. infantry. **2.** inferior. **3.** infinitive. **4.** influence. **5.** information.

Inf. infantry.

in·fal·li·bil·ism (ĭn-făl′ə-bə-lĭz′əm) *n. Roman Catholic Church.* The principle of the pope's infallibility. —**in·fal·li·bil·ist** *n.*

in·fal·li·ble (ĭn-făl′ə-bəl) *adj.* **1.** Incapable of erring; entirely dependable: *an infallible source of information.* **2.** Incapable of failing; certain: *an infallible antidote.* **3.** Incapable of error in expounding doctrine on faith or morals. Said especially of the pope speaking ex cathedra. [French, from Medieval Latin *infallibilis* : *in-*, not + *fallibilis*, FALLIBLE.] —**in·fal·li·bil·i·ty, in·fal·li·ble·ness** *n.* —**in·fal·li·bly** *adv.*

in·fa·mous (ĭn′fə-məs) *adj.* **1.** Having an exceedingly bad reputation; notorious. **2.** Causing or deserving infamy; loathsome; grossly shocking: *an infamous deed.* **3.** *Law.* **a.** Formerly, deprived of all or some civil rights as a result of being convicted of certain serious crimes. **b.** Designating a crime, such as treason or perjury, that entailed this deprivation. —See Synonyms at **mean** (base). [Middle English, from Medieval Latin *infamōsus*, from Latin *infāmis* : *in-*, not + *fāma*, FAME.] —**in·fa·mous·ly** *adv.* —**in·fa·mous·ness** *n.*

in·fa·my (ĭn′fə-mē) *n., pl.* **-mies. 1.** Evil fame or reputation. **2.** The condition of being infamous. **3.** An infamous act. —See Synonyms at **disgrace.** [Middle English *infamye*, from Old French *infamie, infame*, from Latin *infāmia*, from *infāmis*, INFAMOUS.]

in·fan·cy (ĭn′fən-sē) *n., pl.* **-cies. 1.** The state or period of being an infant. **2.** The earliest years or stage of something: *television in its infancy.* **3.** *Law.* The state or period of being a minor.

in·fant (ĭn′fənt) *n.* **1.** A child in the earliest period of its life; a baby. **2.** *Law.* One under the legal age of majority; a minor.
~*adj.* **1.** Of or being in infancy. **2.** Intended for infants or very young children. **3.** Young and growing: *an infant enterprise.* [Middle English *enfaunt*, from Old French *enfant*, from Latin *infāns*, "(one) unable to speak" : *in-*, not + *fāns* (stem *fant-*), present participle of *fārī*, to speak.]

in·fan·ta (ĭn-făn′tə) *n.* **1.** A daughter of a Spanish or Portuguese king. **2.** The wife of an infante. [Spanish, feminine of *infante*, INFANTE.]

in·fan·te (ĭn-făn′tā) *n.* Any son of a Spanish or Portuguese king other than the heir to the throne. [Spanish and Portuguese, "infant," from Latin *infāns*, INFANT.]

in·fan·ti·cide (ĭn-făn′tĭ-sīd′) *n.* **1. a.** The killing of an infant. **b.** *Law.* The killing by its mother of a child under one year old. **2.** A person who kills an infant. **3.** The practice of killing infants. [Late Latin *infanticidium* (killing) and *infanticida* (killer) : Latin *infāns*, INFANT + *-cidium, -cida*, -CIDE.] —**in·fan·ti·cid·al** *adj.*

in·fan·tile (ĭn′fən-tīl′, -tĭl) *adj.* **1.** Of or pertaining to infants or infancy. **2.** Lacking maturity, sophistication, or reasonableness. **3.** *Pathology.* Designating diseases occurring in adults that are recognizable in childhood: *infantile paralysis.* [French, from *infantilis*, from *infāns*, INFANT.]

infantile autism *n. Psychology.* See **autism** (sense 2).

infantile paralysis *n. Pathology.* **Poliomyelitis** (see).

in·fan·til·ism (ĭn′fən-tə-lĭz′əm) *n.* **1.** A state of arrested development in an adult, characterized by a retention of infantile mentality accompanied by stunted growth and sexual immaturity. **2.** Childish behavior or speech.

in·fan·til·ize (ĭn-făn′tə-līz′) *tr.v.* **-ized, -izing, -izes.** To treat (a person, especially an adolescent) as if still at an early stage of development.

infant mortality rate *n.* The number of deaths of infants aged under one year for every 1000 live births, occurring in any one year.

in·fan·try (ĭn′fən-trē) *n., pl.* **-tries.** *Abbr.* **Inf., inf.** The branch of an army made up of units trained to fight on foot. [French *infanterie*, from Italian *infanteria*, from *infante*, youth, foot soldier, from Latin *infāns*, INFANT.]

in·fan·try·man (ĭn′fən-trē-mən) *n., pl.* **-men** (-mĭn). A soldier serving in the infantry.

infant school *n. British.* A school for children aged between approximately five and seven years. Compare **junior school.**

in·farct (ĭn-färkt′, ĭn′färkt′) *n.* Also **in·farc·tion** (ĭn-färk′shən). A dead area of tissue resulting from failure of local blood supply. [New Latin *infarctus*, from Latin *infarctus, infartus*, past participle of *infarcīre*, to stuff in, cram : *in-*, in + *farcīre*, to stuff.] —**in·farct·ed** *adj.*

in·farc·tion (ĭn-färk′shən) *n.* **1.** Death of an organ or part of an organ that occurs when its blood supply is obstructed by a blood clot or embolus. **2.** An infarct.

in·fat·u·ate (ĭn-făch′ōō-āt′) *tr.v.* **-ated, -ating, -ates. 1.** To cause to behave foolishly. **2.** To inspire with powerful but foolish and unreasoning passion or attraction.

~*adj.* (ĭn-făch′o͞o-ĭt, -āt′). *Archaic.* Infatuated. [Latin *infatuāre* : *in-* (causative) + *fatuus,* FATUOUS.]

in·fat·u·at·ed (ĭn-făch′o͞o-ā′tĭd) *n.* Possessed by a powerful, unreasoning, often short-lived, passion or attraction. —**in·fat·u·at·ed·ly** *adv.*

in·fat·u·a·tion (ĭn-făch′o͞o-ā′shən) *n.* **1.** The state or an instance of being infatuated. **2.** An object of extravagant, short-lived passion. —See Synonyms at **love.**

in·fau·na (ĭn′fô-nə) *n., pl.* **-nas** or **-nae** (-nē). The mass of aquatic animals that live just beneath the bed of a sea, lake, or river. [Danish *ifauna* : IN- + FAUNA.]

in·fea·si·ble (ĭn-fē′zə-bəl) *adj.* Not feasible; impracticable.

in·fect (ĭn-fĕkt′) *tr.v.* **-fected, -fecting, -fects. 1.** To contaminate with pathogenic microorganisms. **2.** To communicate a disease to (another person). **3.** To invade and produce infection in. **4.** To corrupt; contaminate. **5.** To affect as if by contagion. [Middle English *infecten,* from Latin *inficere* (past participle *infectus*), to work in, dye, taint : *in-,* in + *facere,* to do.]

in·fec·tion (ĭn-fĕk′shən) *n.* **1.** Invasion of the body by pathogenic microorganisms. **2.** An instance of such invasion. **3.** The pathological state resulting from such invasion, characterized by inflammation and tissue damage due to the action of toxins produced by the microorganisms. **4.** An agent or contaminated substance responsible for such invasion. **5.** An infectious disease. **6. a.** Moral contamination or corruption, as by the communication of harmful influences. **b.** The communication or spreading from one to another of ideas, emotions, or the like, as if by contagion.

in·fec·tious (ĭn-fĕk′shəs) *adj.* **1.** Capable of causing infection. **2.** Capable of being transmitted by infection without actual contact; communicable. Said of a disease. Compare **contagious. 3.** Caused by a microorganism. Said of a disease. **4.** Tending to spread or affect others easily: *an infectious chuckle.* —**in·fec·tious·ly** *adv.* —**in·fec·tious·ness** *n.*

infectious enterohepatitis *n.* In veterinary medicine, **blackhead.**

infectious hepatitis *n.* See **hepatitis.**

infectious mononucleosis *n.* An acute, contagious, febrile disease, **mononucleosis** *(see).* Also called "glandular fever."

in·fec·tive (ĭn-fĕk′tĭv) *adj.* Capable of producing infection; infectious. —**in·fec·tive·ness, in·fec·tiv·i·ty** *n.*

in·fe·lic·i·tous (ĭn′fə-lĭs′ə-təs) *adj.* **1.** Not happy; unfortunate; sad. **2.** Inappropriate; inapt, as in style or manner of expression. —**in·fe·lic·i·tous·ly** *adv.*

in·fe·lic·i·ty (ĭn′fə-lĭs′ə-tē) *n., pl.* **-ties. 1.** The quality or condition of being infelicitous. **2.** Something inappropriate or inapt. [Middle English *infelicite,* from Latin *infēlīcitās,* from *infēlix,* unhappy : *in-,* not + *fēlix,* happy.]

in·fer (ĭn-fûr′) *v.* **-ferred, -ferring, -fers.** —*tr.* **1.** To conclude from evidence; deduce. **2.** To have as a necessary or logical consequence. —See Usage note at **imply.** —*intr.* To draw inferences. —See Synonyms at **conjecture.** [Old French *inferer,* from Latin *inferre,* to bring in, introduce, deduce : *in-,* in- + *ferre,* to bear.] —**in·fer·a·ble** *adj.* —**in·fer·a·bly** *adv.*

in·fer·ence (ĭn′fər-əns) *n.* **1.** The act or process of inferring. **2.** Something inferred; a conclusion based on a premise. **3.** *Logic.* A process of reasoning consisting of forming conclusions from premises.

in·fer·en·tial (ĭn′fə-rĕn′shəl) *adj.* Derived or capable of being derived from inference. —**in·fer·en·tial·ly** *adv.*

in·fe·ri·or (ĭn-fîr′ē-ər) *adj. Abbr.* **inf. 1. a.** Low or lower in quality, status, or estimation. **b.** Mediocre; second-rate. **2.** Low or lower in order, degree, or rank. **3.** Situated under or beneath. **4.** *Botany.* Located below the perianth and other floral parts. Said of an ovary. **5.** *Printing.* Set below the normal line. Said of type. **6.** *Astronomy.* **a.** Orbiting between the sun and the earth: *an inferior planet.* **b.** Lying below the horizon.

~*n.* **1.** A person of lesser rank or status than another. **2.** *Printing.* An inferior character. [Middle English, from Latin *īnferior,* comparative of *īnferus,* low.] —**in·fe·ri·or·i·ty** (ĭn′fîr-ē-ôr′ə-tē, -ŏr′ə-tē) *n.*

inferior court *n.* A court of law of lower rank than another, usually with a limited jurisdiction, the decisions of which are subject to appeal to a superior court.

inferiority complex *n.* A neurotic condition resulting from a persistent, unrealistic sense of inadequacy, characterized by withdrawal or by compensatory and often aggressive attempts to attract attention.

in·fer·nal (ĭn-fûr′nəl) *adj.* **1.** Of or pertaining to the world of the dead in classical mythology. **2.** Of, pertaining to, or characteristic of hell or those in it. **3.** Abominable; damnable: *Stop that infernal racket!* [Middle English, from Old French, from Late Latin *īnfernālis,* from *īnfernus,* hell, from Latin, lower.] —**in·fer·nal·ly** *adv.*

infernal machine *n. Archaic.* An explosive device maliciously designed to harm or destroy.

in·fer·no (ĭn-fûr′nō) *n., pl.* **-nos. 1.** *Often* **Inferno.** Hell. **2.** Any place or situation likened to hell; especially, a conflagration. [Italian, hell, from Late Latin *īnfernus.* See **infernal.**]

in·fer·tile (ĭn-fûrt′l) *adj.* **1.** Not fertile; unproductive; barren. **2.** Incapable of producing offspring. —See Synonyms at **sterile.** —**in·fer·til·i·ty** (ĭn′fər-tĭl′ə-tē) *n.*

in·fest (ĭn-fĕst′) *tr.v.* **-fested, -festing, -fests. 1.** To inhabit or overrun in large numbers so as to be harmful or unpleasant. **2.** To invade and live on or within (a living organism). Said of animal parasites, such as ticks and tapeworms. [Middle English *infesten,* to attack, molest, trouble, from Old French *infester,* from Latin *infestāre,* from *infestus,* hostile.] —**in·fes·ta·tion** *n.*

in·feu·da·tion (ĭn′fyo͞o-dā′shən) *n.* In feudal society: **1.** The process of granting legal possession of an estate. **2.** The deed used for this.

in·fib·u·late (ĭn-fĭb′yə-lāt′, -yo͞o-lāt′) *tr.v.* **-lated, -lating, -lates.** To enclose or fasten (especially, the female genitals) with a clasp or stitches to prevent sexual intercourse. [Latin *infībulāre* : IN- + *fībula,* clasp.] —**in·fib·u·la·tion** *n.*

in·fi·del (ĭn′fə-dəl, -dĕl′) *n.* **1.** One who has no religious beliefs. **2.** One who is an unbeliever with respect to a particular religion, especially Christianity or Islam. [Middle English *infydel,* from Old French *infidel,* from Latin *infidēlis,* unfaithful : *in-,* not + *fidēs,* faith.] —**in·fi·del** *adj.*

in·fi·del·i·ty (ĭn′fə-dĕl′ə-tē) *n., pl.* **-ties. 1.** Lack of fidelity or loyalty. **2.** Unfaithfulness to a sexual partner, especially a spouse. **3.** An act of disloyalty or sexual unfaithfulness. **4.** Lack of religious faith, especially in Christianity or Islam.

in·field (ĭn′fēld′) *n.* **1.** A field located near a farmhouse. **2.** *Baseball.* **a.** The area of the field enclosed by the foul lines and the arc of the outfield grass just beyond the bases. **b.** The defensive positions of first base, second base, third base, and shortstop. Compare **outfield. 3.** The area inside a racetrack or running track.

in·field·er (ĭn′fēl′dər) *n. Baseball.* A player who plays in the infield.

in·fight·ing (ĭn′fī′tĭng) *n.* **1.** Rivalry or competition, often bitter, between members of the same group or organization: *political infighting.* **2.** In boxing, hitting at close range, especially in order to tire out one's opponent. —**in·fight·er** *n.*

in·fil·trate (ĭn-fĭl′trāt′, ĭn′fĭl-) *v.* **-trated, -trating, -trates.** —*tr.* **1.** To pass (a liquid or gas) into something through its interstices. **2.** To permeate with a liquid or gas passed through interstices. **3.** To send (troops, for example) surreptitiously into enemy-held territory. **4.** To gain entry or cause to gain entry to (an organization or political party, for example) surreptitiously, and with subversive intent. —*intr.* To gain entrance gradually or surreptitiously.

~*n.* Any substance that accumulates gradually in bodily tissues.

in·fil·tra·tion (ĭn′fĭl-trā′shən) *n.* **1.** The act or process of infiltrating. **2.** The state of being infiltrated. **3.** Something that infiltrates. —**in·fil·tra·tive** (ĭn-fĭl′trə-tĭv) *adj.* —**in·fil·tra·tor** *n.*

infin. infinitive.

in·fi·nite (ĭn′fə-nĭt) *adj.* **1.** Having no boundaries or limits. **2.** Immeasurably or uncountably large. **3.** *Mathematics.* **a.** Existing beyond or being greater than any arbitrarily large value. **b.** Unlimited in spatial extent. **c.** Of or designating a set capable of being put into one-to-one correspondence with a proper subset of itself. **4.** Continuing endlessly in time, space, extent, or magnitude. **5.** All-encompassing; total: *God's infinite love.*

~*n.* Something infinite; infinity. Preceded by *the.* —**the Infinite (Being).** God. [Middle English *infinit,* from Old French, from Latin *infīnītus* : *in-,* not + *fīnītus,* FINITE.] —**in·fi·nite·ly** *adv.* —**in·fi·nite·ness** *n.*

Synonyms: *boundless, countless, eternal, illimitable, innumerable, limitless, measureless, numberless.*

in·fin·i·tes·i·mal (ĭn′fə-nə-tĕs′ə-məl) *adj.* **1.** Immeasurably or incalculably minute. **2.** Loosely, very small; minute. **3.** *Mathematics.* Capable of having values arbitrarily close to zero. —See Synonyms at **small.**

~*n.* **1.** An infinitesimal amount or quantity. **2.** *Mathematics.* A function having values arbitrarily close to zero. [New Latin *infinitesimus* : Latin *infīnītus,* INFINITE + *-esimus,* ordinal suffix.] —**in·fin·i·tes·i·mal·ly** *adv.*

infinitesimal calculus *n.* Differential and integral calculus.

in·fin·i·tive (ĭn-fĭn′ə-tĭv) *n. Abbr.* **inf., infin.** *Grammar.* **1.** A verb form that is not inflected to indicate person, number, or tense. **2.** Such a verb form used in English: **a.** To serve as a substantive while retaining some verbal aspects, such as modification by adverbs and connection with an object, preceded by *to*; for example, *To go willingly is to show strength.* **b.** To form verb phrases, preceded by *to*; for example, *He wished to go.* In this usage, the *to* may be dropped with certain verbs; for example, *He may go.*

~*adj.* Of, pertaining to, or using the infinitive. [Late Latin *infīnītīvus,* "unlimited" (because it has no definite numbers or persons), from Latin *infīnītus,* INFINITE.] —**in·fin·i·ti·val** (ĭn′fə-nə-tī′vəl) *adj.*

in·fin·i·tude (ĭn-fĭn′ə-to͞od′, -tyo͞od′) *n.* **1.** The state or quality of being infinite. **2.** An infinite quantity, number, or extent.

in·fin·i·ty (ĭn-fĭn′ə-tē) *n., pl.* **-ties. 1.** The quality or condition of being infinite. **2.** Unbounded space, time, or quantity. **3.** An indefinitely large number or amount. **4.** *Mathematics.* The limit that a function f is said to approach at $x = a$ when for x close to a, $f(x)$ is larger than any preassigned number. **5.** A point that is sufficiently far away from a lens or mirror for it to be assumed that light emitted by it will fall in parallel rays on the lens or mirror.

in·firm (ĭn-fûrm′) *adj.* **1.** Weak in body, especially from old age; feeble. **2.** Lacking moral firmness; irresolute. —See Synonyms at **weak.** [Middle English *infirme,* from Latin *infirmus* : *in-,* not + *firmus,* FIRM.] —**in·firm·ly** *adv.* —**in·firm·ness** *n.*

in·fir·ma·ry (ĭn-fûr′mə-rē) *n., pl.* **-ries.** A place for the care of the sick or injured; especially, a hospital or dispensary. [Medieval Latin *infirmāria,* from Latin *infirmus,* INFIRM.]

in·fir·mi·ty (ĭn-fûr′mə-tē) *n., pl.* **-ties. 1.** A disability, especially one caused by an illness or old age. **2.** Bodily weakness; frailty. **3.** Moral weakness.

in·fix (ĭn-fĭks′) *tr.v.* **-fixed, -fixing, -fixes. 1.** To fix into another.

PRONUNCIATION KEY

ă, pat; ā, pay; âr, care;
ä, father, are; b, bib;
ch, church; d, deed; ĕ, pet;
ē, be; f, fife; g, gag; h, hat;
hw, which; ĭ, pit; ī, pie;
îr, pier; j, judge; k, kick;
l, lid, needle; m, mum;
n, no, sudden; ng, thing;
ŏ, pot; ō, toe; ô, paw, for;
oi, noise; ou, out; o͝o, book;
o͞o, boot; p, pop; r, roar;
s, sauce; sh, ship, dish;
t, tight; th, thin, path;
th, this, bathe; ŭ, cut; ûr, fur;
v, valve; w, with; y, yes;
z, zebra, size; zh, vision;
ə, about, item, edible,
gallop, circus, peaceful

IN FOREIGN WORDS:

à, *Fr.* ami; œ, *Fr.* feu, *Ger.* schön; ü, *Fr.* tu, *Ger.* über; KH, *Ger.* ich, *Scot.* loch; N, *Fr.* bon; y′, *Fr.* Compiègne

STRESS MARKS:

Primary stress: ′
in·cite′ (ĭn-sīt′)
Secondary stress: ′
in′sight′ (ĭn′sīt′)

2. To fix in the mind; inculcate; instill. **3.** *Grammar.* To insert (a morphological element) as an infix.
∼*n.* (ĭn′fĭks′). *Grammar.* **1.** An inflectional or derivational element inserted into the body of a word; for example, an infix *-n-* is added to the Old Latin verb root *frag-*, "break," to form the imperfective *frang-*, "is breaking." **2.** An intermediate letter or sound, in English usually a vowel, that connects the elements of a compound word; for example, the *-o-* in *meritocracy* is an infix. [Latin *infīgere* (past participle *infixus*) : *in-*, in + *fīgere,* to FIX.]
infl. influence; influenced.
in fla·gran·te de·lic·to (ĭn flə-grän′tē də-lĭk′tō) *adv. Law.* In the actual act of committing an offense; red-handed. [Latin, with the crime still blazing.]
in·flame (ĭn-flām′) *v.* **-flamed, -flaming, -flames.** —*tr.* **1.** To set on fire; kindle. **2. a.** To arouse or excite into a state of strong emotion or passion. **b.** To arouse (strong emotion or passion) in. **3.** To intensify intolerably: *"inflamed to madness an already savage nature"* (Robert Graves). **4.** To produce inflammation in. —*intr.* **1.** To catch fire. **2.** To become excited or aroused. **3.** To be affected by inflammation. [Middle English *inflamen,* from Old French *enflammer,* from Latin *inflammāre* : *in-* (intensive) + *flammāre,* to set on fire, from *flamma,* FLAME.]
in·flam·ma·ble (ĭn-flăm′ə-bəl) *adj.* **1.** Tending to ignite easily and burn rapidly; flammable. **2.** Quickly or easily aroused to strong emotion; passionate. —See Usage note at **flammable.**
∼*n.* Something flammable. [French, from Medieval Latin *inflammābilis,* from Latin *inflammāre,* to INFLAME.] **—in·flam·ma·bil·i·ty, in·flam·ma·ble·ness** *n.* **—in·flam·ma·bly** *adv.*
in·flam·ma·tion (ĭn′flə-mā′shən) *n.* **1.** The act of inflaming or the state of being inflamed. **2.** Localized heat, redness, swelling, and pain as a result of irritation, injury, or infection.
in·flam·ma·to·ry (ĭn-flăm′ə-tôr′ē, -tōr′ē) *adj.* **1.** Arousing strong emotion, especially anger or aggression. **2.** Characterized or caused by inflammation.
in·fla·ta·ble (ĭn-flāt′ə-bəl) *adj.* Having to be inflated for use: *an inflatable rubber raft.*
∼*n.* Any object that can be inflated; especially, a large inflatable object made of sturdy material and used for children to play on.
in·flate (ĭn-flāt′) *v.* **-flated, -flating, -flates.** —*tr.* **1.** To fill and swell with a gas. **2.** To cause to increase unduly: *Success inflated his ego.* **3.** *Economics.* To raise or expand abnormally, as prices, wages, or circulating currency. —*intr.* To become inflated. [Latin *inflāre,* to blow into : *in-*, in + *flāre,* to blow.] **—in·flat·er, in·fla·tor** *n.*
in·flat·ed (ĭn-flā′tĭd) *adj.* **1.** Distended or expanded by or as if by gas or air. **2.** Unduly increased or puffed up: *inflated ideas.* **3.** Increased or raised to abnormal economic levels: *inflated wages.* **4.** Resulting from inflation. **5.** *Botany.* Hollow and enlarged: *an inflated calyx.* **—in·flat·ed·ness** *n.*
in·fla·tion (ĭn-flā′shən) *n.* **1.** The act of inflating or the state of being inflated. **2.** *Economics.* A continuing increase in available currency and credit beyond the proportion of available goods, or an increase in the costs of production, resulting in a sharp and continuing rise in price levels and a fall in the purchasing power of money. Compare **deflation.** See **cost-push, demand-pull.**
in·fla·tion·ar·y (ĭn-flā′shə-nĕr′ē) *adj. Economics.* Pertaining to or tending to cause inflation.
inflationary spiral *n. Economics.* Continually increasing inflation attributed to the mutually reinforcing effects of rising costs, wages, or the like interacting with rising prices.
in·fla·tion·ist (ĭn-flā′shə-nĭst) *n.* One who advocates inflation by increasing the supply of available currency and credit. **—in·fla·tion·ism** *n.*
in·fla·tion-proof (ĭn-flā′shən-pro͞of′) *adj.* Increasing in value at the same rate as inflation: *an inflation-proof investment.*
∼*tr.v.* **inflation-proofed, -proofing, -proofs.** To make the value of (pensions, wages, or the like) rise at the same rate as inflation.
in·flect (ĭn-flĕkt′) *v.* **-flected, -flecting, -flects.** —*tr.* **1.** To turn from a course or alignment; bend. **2.** To alter (the voice) in tone or pitch; modulate. **3.** *Grammar.* To alter (a word) as by conjugating or declining. —*intr. Grammar.* To be modified by inflection. [Middle English *inflecten,* from Latin *inflectere,* to bend, warp, change : *in-* (intensive) + *flectere,* to bend.] **—in·flec·tive** *adj.* **—in·flec·tor** *n.*
in·flec·tion (ĭn-flĕk′shən) *n.* Also *chiefly British* **in·flex·ion.** **1.** The act of inflecting or a state of being inflected. **2.** An alteration in pitch or tone of the voice. **3.** *Grammar.* **a.** An alteration of the form of a word, usually by means of affixes, to indicate different grammatical and syntactical relations, such as the declension of nouns, adjectives, and pronouns or the conjugation of verbs. **b.** An element added to a word to denote a grammatical function, such as the *s* in *apples* indicating the plural form or the *'s* in *girl's* indicating the possessive case. **c.** An inflected form of a word. **4.** *Mathematics.* A change in direction of a geometric curve, occurring at a point (the *point of inflection*) at which the curvature of the curve changes sign. **—in·flec·tion·al** *adj.* **—in·flec·tion·al·ly** *adv.*
in·flexed (ĭn-flĕkst′) *adj.* Bent or curved inward or downward, as petals or sepals. [Latin *inflexus,* past participle of *inflectere,* to bend, INFLECT.]
in·flex·i·ble (ĭn-flĕk′sə-bəl) *adj.* **1.** Not flexible; stiff; rigid. **2.** Incapable of being changed; unalterable: *inflexible rules.* **3.** Rigidly adhering to a purpose or stance; unyielding. —See Synonyms at **stiff.** **—in·flex·i·bil·i·ty, in·flex·i·ble·ness** *n.* **—in·flex·i·bly** *adv.*
Synonyms: *adamant, inexorable, obdurate, unyielding.*
in·flict (ĭn-flĭkt′) *tr.v.* **-flicted, -flicting, -flicts.** **1.** To deal or give (a blow, wound, or the like). Used with *on* or *upon.* **2.** To impose (someone or something considered unpleasant): *"malignant Nature, who reserves the right to inflict upon her children the most terrifying jests"* (Thornton Wilder). [Latin *inflīgere* (past participle *inflictus*) : *in-*, on + *flīgere,* to strike.] **—in·flict·er, in·flic·tor** *n.* **—in·flic·tive** *adj.*
in·flic·tion (ĭn-flĭk′shən) *n.* **1.** The act or process of inflicting. **2.** Something inflicted, such as blows or punishment.
in-flight (ĭn′flīt′) *adj.* **1.** Carried out or made while in flight: *in-flight refueling.* **2.** Provided for use or enjoyment while in flight: *in-flight entertainment.*
in·flo·res·cence (ĭn′flə-rĕs′əns) *n.* **1.** *Botany.* **a.** A characteristic arrangement of flowers on a single main stalk. **b.** The part of a plant consisting of the flower-bearing stalk. **2.** A flowering. [New Latin *inflorescentia,* from Late Latin *inflōrēscere,* to begin to flower : Latin *in-* (intensive) + *flōrēscere,* to begin to flower (see **florescence**).]
in·flow (ĭn′flō′) *n.* **1.** The act or process of flowing in or into. **2.** Something that flows in; an influx.
in·flu·ence (ĭn′flo͞o-əns) *n. Abbr.* **inf., infl.** **1.** A power indirectly or intangibly affecting a person or a course of events. **2.** Power to sway or affect, based on prestige, wealth, ability, character, or position. **3.** A person or thing exercising such power. **4.** An effect or change produced by such power. **5.** *Astrology.* **a.** An occult ethereal fluid believed to flow from the stars to affect the fate of humankind. **b.** The occult power emanating from the stars. **—under the influence.** *Informal.* Intoxicated, especially with alcohol.
∼*tr.v.* **influenced, -encing, -ences.** **1.** To have power over; affect. **2.** To cause a change in the nature or development of; have a modifying effect upon. —See Synonyms at **affect.** [Middle English, from Old French, from Medieval Latin *influentia,* "a flowing in," from Latin *influēns* (stem *influent-*), present participle of *influere,* to flow in : *in-*, in + *fluere,* to flow.] **—in·flu·enc·er** *n.*
in·flu·ent (ĭn′flo͞o-ənt) *adj.* Flowing in.
∼*n.* Something that flows in; especially, a tributary. [Middle English, from Latin *influēns,* flowing in. See **influence.**]
in·flu·en·tial (ĭn′flo͞o-ĕn′shəl) *adj.* Having or exercising influence. **—in·flu·en·tial·ly** *adv.*
in·flu·en·za (ĭn′flo͞o-ĕn′zə) *n.* An acute infectious viral disease characterized by inflammation of the respiratory tract, fever, muscular pain, and irritation in the intestinal tract. Also called "flu," "grippe." [Italian, influence, hence "intangible visitation," epidemic (specifically the European epidemic of influenza of 1743), from Medieval Latin *influentia,* INFLUENCE.]
in·flux (ĭn′flŭks′) *n.* **1.** A flowing in of substance. **2.** A sudden invasion or arrival of many people or things: *an influx of visitors.* **3.** The mouth of a river or stream. [Late Latin *influxus,* from Latin, past participle of *influere,* to flow in. See **influence.**]
influx control *n.* In South Africa, the legal control exercised on the movement by black people into urban areas.
in·fo (ĭn′fō′) *n. Informal.* Information.
in·fold (ĭn-fōld′) *tr.v.* **-folded, -folding, -folds.** **1.** To fold inward. **2.** Variant of **enfold.** **—in·fold·er** *n.* **—in·fold·ment** *n.*
in·form (ĭn-fôrm′) *v.* **-formed, -forming, -forms.** —*tr.* **1. a.** To impart information to. **b.** To acquaint (oneself) with knowledge of a subject. **2.** To give form or character to; be the formative principle of. **3.** To animate or inspire with a particular quality or character; imbue. **4.** *Archaic.* To form or shape (the mind or character) by teaching or training. —*intr.* To disclose or provide information, usually of an incriminating nature. Used with *on* or *against.* [Middle English *enfourmen,* from Old French *enfourmer,* from Latin *informāre,* to give form to, form an idea of : *in-* (intensive) + *formāre,* to form, from *forma,* FORM.]
in·for·mal (ĭn-fôr′məl) *adj.* **1.** Not performed or made according to prescribed regulations or forms; unofficial; irregular: *an informal truce.* **2.** Completed or performed without ceremony or formality: *an informal gathering.* **3.** Of, for, or pertaining to ordinary everyday use; casual; relaxed: *informal clothes.* **4.** Belonging to the usage of spoken or written language as used in face-to-face communication by familiar equals and considered inappropriate in certain cultural contexts, as in the standard written prose of ceremonial and official communications. **—in·for·mal·ly** *adv.*
in·for·mal·i·ty (ĭn′fôr-măl′ə-tē) *n., pl.* **-ties.** **1.** The state or quality of being informal. **2.** An informal act.
in·form·ant (ĭn-fôr′mənt) *n.* **1.** One who discloses information; an informer. **2.** A person who gives information about a subject of study; especially, a speaker of a particular language or dialect used as a source of linguistic evidence in research.
in·for·mat·ics (ĭn′fər-măt′ĭks) *n. Used with a singular verb.* Information science.
in·for·ma·tion (ĭn′fər-mā′shən) *n. Abbr.* **inf.** **1.** The act of informing or the condition of being informed; communication of knowledge. **2.** Knowledge derived from study, experience, or instruction. **3.** Knowledge of a specific event or situation; news; word. **4.** A service or agency supplying facts or news. **5.** *Law.* A formal accusation of a crime made by a public officer rather than by indictment by a grand jury. **6.** A nonaccidental signal used as an input to a computer or communications system. —See Synonyms at **knowledge.** **—in·for·ma·tion·al** *adj.*
information retrieval *n.* The branch of computer science concerned with the classification, storage, and retrieval of information by computers and associated electronic devices.
information science *n.* The science concerned with gathering, classifying, storing, retrieving, manipulating, and evaluating informa-

PRONUNCIATION KEY

ă, pat; ā, pay; âr, care;
ä, father, are; b, **bib**;
ch, **church**; d, **deed**; ĕ, pet;
ē, be; f, **fife**; g, **gag**; h, **hat**;
hw, **which**; ĭ, pit; ī, pie;
îr, pier; j, **judge**; k, **kick**;
l, lid, needle; m, **mum**;
n, no, sudden; ng, **thing**;
ŏ, pot; ō, toe; ô, paw, for;
oi, noise; ou, **out**; o͝o, **book**;
o͞o, boot; p, **pop**; r, roar;
s, sauce; sh, **ship, dish**;
t, tight; th, **thin, path**;
th, **this**, bathe; ŭ, cut; ûr, **fur**;
v, valve; w, **with**; y, yes;
z, zebra, size; zh, vision;
ə, about, item, edible,
gallop, circus, peaceful

IN FOREIGN WORDS:

à, *Fr.* ami; œ, *Fr.* **feu**, *Ger.* schön; ü, *Fr.* **tu**, *Ger.* **über**;
KH, *Ger.* **ich**, *Scot.* loch;
N, *Fr.* bon; y′, *Fr.* **Compiègne**

STRESS MARKS:

Primary stress: ′
in·cite′ (ĭn-sīt′)
Secondary stress: ′
in′sight′ (ĭn′sīt′)

tion, especially by means of computers. Also called "informatics."
information technology *n.* The technology used in information science.
information theory *n.* The theory of the probability of transmission of messages with a given degree of accuracy when the items of information constituting the messages are subject, with certain probabilities, to transmission failure, distortion, and accidental additions.
in·form·a·tive (ĭn-fôr′mə-tĭv) *adj.* Also **in·form·a·to·ry** (-tôr′ē, -tōr′ē). Providing or disclosing information; instructive.
in·formed (ĭn-fôrmd′) *adj.* **1.** Knowledgeable; educated. **2.** Reflecting or resulting from thorough knowledge of a subject: *an informed opinion.*
in·form·er (ĭn-fôr′mər) *n.* **1.** One who informs against others, often for payment. **2.** An informant.
in·fra (ĭn′frə) *adv. Latin.* Below; specifically, in a subsequent part of the text. Compare **supra.**
infra– *prefix.* Indicates: **1.** Below, beneath, inferior to; for example, **infrared, infrasonic. 2.** After, later; for example, **infralapsarianism.** [Latin *infrā,* below, beneath.]
in·fract (ĭn-frăkt′) *tr.v.* **-fracted, -fracting, -fracts.** To break (a rule, law, or agreement); infringe; violate. [Latin *infringere* (past participle *infractus*), to destroy, INFRINGE.] **—in·frac·tor** *n.*
in·frac·tion (ĭn-frăk′shən) *n.* The act or an instance of breaching or violating; infringement; violation. —See Synonyms at **breach.**
in·fra dig (ĭn′frə dĭg′) *adj. Informal.* Beneath one's dignity. [Latin *infrā dignitātem.*]
in·fra·lap·sar·i·an·ism (ĭn′frə-lăp-sâr′ē-ə-nĭz′əm) *n.* The chiefly Calvinist predestinarian doctrine that it was only after the Fall that God elected some from the fallen to be saved by a redeemer. Also called "sublapsarianism." [From INFRA- + Latin *lapsus,* to fall, LAPSE.] **—in·fra·lap·sar·i·an** *n. & adj.*
in·fran·gi·ble (ĭn-frăn′jə-bəl) *adj.* **1.** Unbreakable. **2.** Inviolable. [Old French, from Late Latin *infrangibilis* : Latin *in-,* not + *frangere,* to break.] **—in·fran·gi·bil·i·ty** *n.* **—in·fran·gi·bly** *adv.*
in·fra·or·bit·al (ĭn′frə-ôr′bĭ-təl) *adj. Anatomy.* Located or occurring beneath the orbit.
in·fra·red (ĭn′frə-rĕd′) *adj.* **1.** Of, pertaining to, or designating electromagnetic radiation having wavelengths greater than those of visible light and shorter than those of microwaves; radiation with wavelengths between 0.8 micrometer and 1 millimeter. **2.** Generating, using, or sensitive to such radiation. **—in·fra·red** *n.*
in·fra·son·ic (ĭn′frə-sŏn′ĭk) *adj.* Generating or using waves or vibrations with frequencies below that of audible sound.
in·fra·sound (ĭn′frə-sound′) *n.* A wave phenomenon having the general characteristics of sound waves except that its frequency range is below that of sound.
in·fra·struc·ture (ĭn′frə-strŭk′chər) *n.* **1.** An underlying base or supporting structure. **2.** The basic facilities, equipment, services, and installations needed for the growth and functioning of a country, community, operation, or organization.
in·fre·quent (ĭn-frē′kwənt) *adj.* **1.** Not frequent; rare. **2.** Not steady; irregular; occasional: *an infrequent guest.* **—in·fre·quence, in·fre·quen·cy** *n.* **—in·fre·quent·ly** *adv.*
in·fringe (ĭn-frĭnj′) *v.* **-fringed, -fringing, -fringes.** *—tr.* To break or ignore the terms or obligations of (an oath, agreement, law, or the like); disregard; violate. *—intr.* To go beyond the limits of something; trespass; encroach. Used with *on* or *upon.* [Latin *infringere* : *in-* (intensive) + *frangere,* to break.] **—in·fring·er** *n.*
in·fringe·ment (ĭn-frĭnj′mənt) *n.* **1.** A violation, as of a law, regulation, or agreement; a breach. **2.** An encroachment, as of a right or privilege. —See Synonyms at **breach.**
in·fun·dib·u·li·form (ĭn′fən-dĭb′yə-lə-fôrm′) *adj. Botany.* Funnel-shaped.
in·fun·dib·u·lum (ĭn′fən-dĭb′yə-ləm) *n., pl.* **-la** (-lə). Any of various funnel-shaped bodily passages or parts; especially, the conical stalk connecting the pituitary gland to the hypothalamus at the base of the brain. [Latin, funnel, from *infundere,* to pour in, INFUSE.] **—in·fun·dib·u·lar, in·fun·dib·u·late** *adj.*
in·fu·ri·ate (ĭn-fyŏŏr′ē-āt′) *tr.v.* **-ated, -ating, -ates. 1.** To make furious; enrage. **2.** To annoy or irritate intensely: *an infuriating delay.* *~adj.* (ĭn-fyŏŏr′ē-ĭt). *Archaic.* Furious. [Medieval Latin *infuriāre,* to enrage : Latin *in-* (intensive) + *furiāre,* to enrage, from *furia,* FURY.] **—in·fu·ri·at·ing·ly** *adv.*
in·fuse (ĭn-fyōōz′) *v.* **-fused, -fusing, -fuses.** *—tr.* **1.** To put in or introduce into by or as if by pouring. Used with *into.* **2.** To pervade or imbue, as with a quality or emotion. Used with *with.* **3.** To instill or inculcate (a quality). Used with *into.* **4.** To steep or soak without boiling, in order to extract soluble elements or active principles. *—intr.* To undergo infusion. [Middle English *infusen,* from Old French *infuser,* from Latin *infundere* (past participle *infūsus*), to pour in : *in-,* in + *fundere,* to pour.] **—in·fus·er** *n.*
in·fus·i·ble[1] (ĭn-fyōō′zə-bəl) *adj.* Incapable of being fused or melted; resistant to heat. **—in·fus·i·bil·i·ty, in·fus·i·ble·ness** *n.*
infusible[2] *adj.* Capable of being infused. **—in·fus·i·bil·i·ty, in·fus·i·ble·ness** *n.*
in·fu·sion (ĭn-fyōō′zhən) *n.* **1.** The act or process of infusing. **2.** A liquid product obtained by infusing. **3.** An admixture. **4.** The introduction of a solution into a vein by slow injection.
in·fu·sion·ism (ĭn-fyōō′zhə-nĭz′əm) *n. Theology.* The Christian doctrine that a pre-existing soul of divine origin is infused into the body at conception or birth. Compare **creationism. —in·fu·sion·ist** *n. & adj.*
in·fu·so·ri·al (ĭn′fyŏŏ-sôr′ē-əl, -sōr′ē-əl) *adj.* **1.** Of or pertaining to infusorians. **2.** Containing or consisting of infusorians.
in·fu·so·ri·an (ĭn′fyŏŏ-sôr′ē-ən, -sōr′ē-ən) *n.* Any of numerous microscopic organisms, especially of the phylum Protozoa or the order Rotifera, occurring in stagnant water or in infusions containing organic material. No longer in technical usage. [New Latin *Infusoria,* "found in infusions."] **—in·fu·so·ri·an** *adj.*
–ing[1] *suffix.* Indicates: **1.** The present participle of verbs; for example, **going, seeing, hoping. 2.** Participial adjectives; for example, **striking, gripping. 3.** Adjectives resembling participial adjectives but not derived from verbs; for example, **swashbuckling. 4.** Adjectives used adverbially as intensives, in the sense "to the point of"; for example, **dripping** wet. [Middle English *-inge, -ing,* variants of *-end, -ind,* Old English *-ende,* related to Latin *-āns,* -ANT.]
–ing[2] *suffix.* Indicates: **1.** The act, process, or art of performing a specified action; for example, **dancing, thinking. 2.** The thing or substance used in accomplishing such an action; for example, **coating, wadding. 3.** Something that is to undergo such an action; for example, **washing, mending. 4.** The result of such an action; for example, **peeling, opening, drawing. 5.** Something that belongs to, is connected with, used in making, or has the character of; for example, **lagging, boarding. 6.** An action upon or involving; for example, **sounding, berrying.** [Middle English *-ing,* Old English *-ung, -ing.*]
–ing[3] *suffix.* Indicates the possession of a certain quality or nature; for example, **sweeting, wilding.** [Middle English *-ing,* Old English *-ing, -ung,* of, belonging to, descended from.]
in·gath·er (ĭn-găth′ər) *tr.v.* **-ered, -ering, -ers. 1.** To reap or gather in (especially, a harvest). **2.** To collect, gather together, or gather back (dispersed people or objects). Used especially in the phrase *the ingathering of the exiles,* with reference to the founding of the state of Israel. **—in·gath·er·er** *n.*
Inge (ĭnj), **William** (1913–73). U.S. playwright. He wrote several popular and critically acclaimed dramas about the hopes and fears of small-town Midwesterners. Among his most successful works were *The Dark at the Top of the Stairs* (1957) and his Pulitzer Prize winner, *Picnic* (1953).
Inge (ĭng), **William Ralph** (1860–1954). English religious leader. His brilliant but pessimistic sermons and articles won him the nickname "the Gloomy Dean."
in·gem·i·nate (ĭn-jĕm′ĭ-nāt′) *tr.v.* **-nated, -nating, -nates.** To urge or reiterate constantly.
Ing·en·housz (ĭng′ən-hous), **Jan** (1730–99). Dutch scientist who discovered the principle of photosynthesis (1779). He demonstrated that plants absorb carbon dioxide in daylight and release oxygen at night.
in·gen·i·ous (ĭn-jēn′yəs) *adj.* **1.** Having or arising from an inventive or cunning mind; characterized by ingenuity; clever: *an ingenious idea; an ingenious gadget.* **2.** *Obsolete.* Having genius; brilliant. —See Synonyms at **clever.** [French *ingénieux,* from Latin *ingeniōsus,* from *ingenium,* inborn talent, skill.] **—in·gen·i·ous·ly** *adv.* **—in·gen·i·ous·ness** *n.*

Usage: *Ingenious* and *ingenuous* are often confused in everyday use because of the similarity of their spelling. *Ingenious* means "clever," "original" (*an ingenious plot; an ingenious solution to a problem*); *ingenuous* means "innocent," "naive" (*an ingenuous manner; his behavior was ingenuous*). The noun *ingenuity* has come to mean "ingeniousness" and not, as might have been expected, "ingenuousness."

in·gé·nue (ăn′zhə-nōō′, -nyōō′; *French* ăN-zhā-nü′) *n.* **1.** An artless, innocent girl or young woman. **2.** An actress playing an ingénue. [French, feminine of *ingénu,* guileless, artless, from Latin *ingenuus,* INGENUOUS.]
in·ge·nu·i·ty (ĭn′jə-nōō′ə-tē, -nyōō′ə-tē) *n., pl.* **-ties. 1.** Inventive skill or imagination; cleverness. **2.** The state of being ingeniously contrived. **3.** *Usually* **ingenuities.** An ingenious or imaginative device: *"sophistication in the ingenuities of language"* (T.S. Eliot). **4.** *Archaic.* Ingenuousness. [Latin *ingenuitās,* frankness, innocence (but influenced in meaning by INGENIOUS), from *ingenuus,* INGENUOUS.]
in·gen·u·ous (ĭn-jĕn′yōō-əs) *adj.* **1.** Without sophistication or worldliness; artless; innocent. **2.** Open or honest; frank; candid. —See Synonyms at **frank, naive.** —See Usage note at **ingenious.** [Latin *ingenuus,* native, free-born, noble, honest, frank.] **—in·gen·u·ous·ly** *adv.* **—in·gen·u·ous·ness** *n.*
In·ger·soll (ĭng′gər-sôl′, -sŏl′, -səl), **Robert Green** (1833–99). U.S. politician and lecturer. A Civil War officer and later attorney general of Illinois (1867–69), he is primarily known as a lecturer and adamant proponent of scientific and humanistic rationalism, a view based on the theories of Charles Darwin.
in·gest (ĭn-jĕst′) *tr.v.* **-gested, -gesting, -gests. 1.** To take (food, for example) in by or as if by swallowing. **2.** To take in (air). Used of a jet engine. [Latin *ingerere* (past participle *ingestus*), to carry in : *in-,* in + *gerere,* to bear, carry.] **—in·ges·tion** *n.* **—in·ges·tive** *adj.*
in·ges·ta (ĭn-jĕs′tə) *pl.n.* Ingested matter, especially food. [New Latin, from Latin, neuter plural of *ingestus,* past participle of *ingerere,* to INGEST.]
in·gle (ĭng′gəl) *n.* **1.** A fire upon a hearth. **2.** A fireplace.
in·gle·nook (ĭng′gəl-nŏŏk′) *n.* A space by or beside a large fireplace, often with seats inside it facing each other. [*Ingle,* Scottish, probably from Scots Gaelic *aingeal,* fire + NOOK.]
in·glo·ri·ous (ĭn-glôr′ē-əs, ĭn-glōr′-) *adj.* **1.** Ignominious; dishonorable. **2.** Obscure; unknown. [Latin *inglōrius* : *in-,* not + *glōria,* GLORY.] **—in·glo·ri·ous·ly** *adv.* **—in·glo·ri·ous·ness** *n.*

ingot *A 24-karat gold ingot weighing 1 kilogram (2.2 pounds). It was made in Chiasso, Switzerland.*

PRONUNCIATION KEY

ă, pat; ā, pay; âr, care; ä, father, are; b, **bib**; ch, **church**; d, **deed**; ĕ, pet; ē, be; f, **fife**; g, gag; h, **hat**; hw, **which**; ĭ, pit; ī, pie; îr, pier; j, **judge**; k, **kick**; l, lid, needle; m, **mum**; n, no, sudden; ng, **thing**; ŏ, pot; ō, **toe**; ô, **paw**, **for**; oi, noise; ou, **out**; o͝o, **book**; o͞o, **boot**; p, **pop**; r, **roar**; s, sauce; sh, **ship**, **dish**; t, **tight**; th, **thin**, **path**; *th*, **this**, **bathe**; ŭ, cut; ûr, **fur**; v, valve; w, **with**; y, **yes**; z, zebra, size; zh, vision; ə, about, item, edible, gallop, circus, peaceful

IN FOREIGN WORDS:

à, *Fr.* ami; œ, *Fr.* **feu**, *Ger.* schön; ü, *Fr.* **tu**, *Ger.* **über**; KH, *Ger.* **ich**, *Scot.* loch; N, *Fr.* bon; y', *Fr.* **Compiègne**

STRESS MARKS:

Primary stress: ′
in·cite′ (ĭn-sīt′)
Secondary stress: ′
in′sight′ (ĭn′sīt′)

in·go·ing (ĭn′gō′ĭng) *adj.* Entering; coming in.

in·got (ĭng′gət) *n.* **1.** A mass of metal shaped for convenient storage or transportation. **2.** A casting mold for metal. [Middle English *ingot,* mass of metal, "something poured into (the mold)" : *in,* IN + Old English *goten,* past participle of *geotan,* to pour.]

ingot iron *n.* A form of low-carbon steel containing small quantities of other elements.

ingraft. Variant of **engraft.**

in·grain, en·grain (ĭn-grān′) *tr.v.* **-grained, -graining, -grains. 1.** To impress indelibly on the mind or nature; fix; infuse. Used with *in, into,* and *on.* **2.** *Archaic.* To cause (a dye or stain) to sink indelibly into the fiber of something.
~*adj.* (ĭn′grān′) **1.** Deeply rooted; instilled. **2.** Dyed in the yarn before weaving or knitting. **3.** Made of fiber or yarn dyed before weaving. Said especially of rugs.
~*n.* **1.** Yarn or fiber dyed before manufacture. **2.** Any article made of ingrained yarns, such as a carpet. [IN- (in) + GRAIN (dye).]

in·grained (ĭn-grānd′) *adj.* **1.** Deeply infused; imbued; deep-seated: *ingrained faults.* **2.** Deeply worked into the grain, pores, or the like: *ingrained mud.* **3.** Complete; utter: *an ingrained cad.*

in·grate (ĭn′grāt′) *n.* An ungrateful person.
~*adj. Archaic.* Ungrateful. [Middle English *ingrat,* from Latin *ingrātus,* ungrateful : *in-,* not + *grātus,* pleasing, thankful.]

in·gra·ti·ate (ĭn-grā′shē-āt′) *tr.v.* **-ated, -ating, -ates.** To bring (oneself) deliberately into the good graces or favor of another. [IN- (in) + Latin *grātia,* GRACE.] **—in·gra·ti·at·ing·ly** *adv.* **—in·gra·ti·a·tion** *n.* **—in·gra·ti·a·to·ry** (ĭn-grā′shē-ə-tôr′ē, -tōr′ē) *adj.*

in·grat·i·tude (ĭn-grăt′ə-to͞od′, -tyo͞od′) *n.* Lack of gratitude; ungratefulness. [Middle English, from Old French, from Medieval Latin *ingrātitūdō* : *in-,* not + *grātitūdō,* GRATITUDE.]

in·gra·ves·cent (ĭn′grə-vĕs′ənt) *adj.* Gradually increasing in severity. Said of a disease. [Latin *ingravescēns* (stem *ingravescent-*), present participle of *ingravescere,* to become heavier, from *gravis,* heavy, GRAVE.] **—in·gra·ves·cence** *n.*

in·gre·di·ent (ĭn-grē′dē-ənt) *n.* **1.** Something added or required to form a mixture or compound: *ingredients for onion soup.* **2.** A component or constituent: *Hard work is an ingredient of success.* [Middle English, "something that enters into a mixture," from Latin *ingrediēns* (stem *ingredient-*), present participle of *ingredī,* to enter into. See **ingress.**]

In·gres (ăN′grə), **Jean Auguste Dominique** (1780–1867). French artist, who led the French classical school of painting after the death of Jacques Louis David. He is noted for his superb draftsmanship and his historical paintings, drawings, and mythological works.

in·gress (ĭn′grĕs′) *n.* Also **in·gres·sion** (ĭn-grĕsh′ən) (for sense 1). **1.** A going in or entering. **2.** The right or permission to enter. **3.** A means or place of entering. **4.** *Astronomy.* **Immersion** *(see).* [Middle English *ingresse,* from Latin *ingressus,* from the past participle of *ingredī,* to enter into : *in-,* in, into + *gradī,* to step.]

in·gres·sive (ĭn-grĕs′ĭv) *adj.* **1.** Of or pertaining to entering. **2.** Of or designating a speech sound pronounced with an inhalation of breath.
~*n.* An ingressive speech sound. **—in·gres·sive·ness** *n.*

in-group (ĭn′gro͞op′) *n.* A group united by common beliefs, attitudes, and interests, characteristically excluding outsiders.

in·grow·ing (ĭn-grō′ĭng) *adj.* Growing inward; especially, designating a toenail that grows into the surrounding flesh.

in·grown (ĭn′grōn′) *adj.* **1.** Grown abnormally into the flesh: *an ingrown toenail.* **2.** Grown within; innate: *an ingrown habit.*

in·growth (ĭn′grōth′) *n.* **1.** The act of growing inward. **2.** Something that grows inward or within.

in·gui·nal (ĭng′gwə-nəl) *adj.* Of, pertaining to, or located in the groin. [Latin *inguinālis,* from *inguen* (stem *inguin-*), groin.]

ingulf. Variant of **engulf.**

in·gur·gi·tate (ĭn-gûr′jə-tāt′) *tr.v.* **-tated, -tating, -tates.** To swallow greedily or in excessive amounts; gorge. [Latin *ingurgitāre* : *in-,* in + *gurges* (stem *gurgit-*), whirlpool, abyss.] **—in·gur·gi·ta·tion** *n.*

INH isoniazid.

in·hab·it (ĭn-hăb′ĭt) *v.* **-ited, -iting, -its.** *—tr.* To live or reside in. *—intr. Archaic.* To dwell. [Middle English *enhabiten,* from Old French *enhabiter,* from Latin *inhabitāre* : *in-,* in + *habitāre,* to dwell, frequentative of *habēre* (past participle *habitus*), to have, possess.] **—in·hab·it·a·bil·i·ty** *n.* **—in·hab·it·a·ble** *adj.* **—in·hab·i·ta·tion** *n.* **—in·hab·it·er** *n.*

in·hab·i·tan·cy (ĭn-hăb′ə-tən-sē) *n., pl.* **-cies.** Occupancy.

in·hab·i·tant (ĭn-hăb′ə-tənt) *n.* A person or animal that inhabits a place; a permanent resident.

in·hab·it·ed (ĭn-hăb′ə-tĭd) *adj.* Having inhabitants; populated.

in·ha·lant (ĭn-hā′lənt) *adj.* Used in or for inhaling.
~*n.* Something that is inhaled, such as a medicine.

in·ha·la·tion (ĭn′hə-lā′shən) *n.* **1.** The act or an instance of inhaling. **2.** A medicinal preparation that is inhaled.

in·ha·la·tor (ĭn′hə-lā′tər) *n.* A device that produces a vapor to ease breathing or to medicate the respiratory system. Also called "inhaler."

in·hale (ĭn-hāl′) *v.* **-haled, -haling, -hales.** *—tr.* To draw in by breathing. *—intr.* **1.** To breathe in. **2.** To draw cigarette smoke into the lungs. [Latin *inhālāre* : *in-,* in + *hālāre,* to breathe (see **halitosis**).]

in·hal·er (ĭn-hā′lər) *n.* **1.** One that inhales. **2.** An inhalator. **3.** A respirator.

in·har·mon·ic (ĭn′här-mŏn′ĭk) *adj.* Not harmonic; discordant.

in·har·mo·ni·ous (ĭn′här-mō′nē-əs) *adj.* **1.** Not in harmony; discordant. Said of sounds. **2.** Not in accord or agreement. **—in·har·mo·ni·ous·ly** *adv.* **—in·har·mo·ni·ous·ness** *n.*

in·haul (ĭn-hôl′) *n.* Also **in·haul·er** (ĭn-hô′lər). *Nautical.* A rope used to draw in a ship's sail.

in·here (ĭn-hîr′) *intr.v.* **-hered, -hering, -heres.** To be inherent or innate. Used with *in.* [Latin *inhaerēre* : *in-,* in + *haerēre,* to stick, remain fixed.] **—in·her·ence** (ĭn-hîr′əns, -hĕr′əns), **in·her·en·cy** *n.*

in·her·ent (ĭn-hîr′ənt, -hĕr′ənt) *adj.* Existing as an essential or characteristic constituent or attribute; intrinsic. [Latin *inhaerēns* (stem *inhaerent-*), present participle of *inhaerēre,* INHERE.] **—in·her·ent·ly** *adv.*

in·her·it (ĭn-hĕr′ĭt) *v.* **-ited, -iting, -its.** *—tr.* **1.** To receive (property, a title, or the like) from a parent, ancestor, or another person by legal succession or will. **2.** To receive or take over from a predecessor. **3.** *Biology.* To receive (a character or characteristic) genetically from a parent or ancestor. **4.** To come into possession of; possess. *—intr.* To succeed as an heir; take possession of an inheritance. [Middle English *enheriten,* from Old French *enheriter,* from Late Latin *inhērēditāre* : *in-* (intensive) + *hērēditāre,* to inherit, from *hērēs* (stem *hērēd-*), heir.] **—in·her·i·tor** *n.* **—in·her·i·trix** (ĭn-hĕr′ĭ-trĭks) *n.*

in·her·it·a·ble (ĭn-hĕr′ə-tə-bəl) *adj.* **1.** Capable of being inherited. **2.** Capable of inheriting; having the right to inherit. **3.** *Law.* Capable of being transferred by a will from one generation to a later generation. **—in·her·it·a·bil·i·ty** *n.* **—in·her·i·ta·bly** *adv.*

in·her·i·tance (ĭn-hĕr′ə-təns) *n.* **1.** The act or right of inheriting. **2.** That which is inherited or to be inherited; legacy; bequest. **3.** Anything regarded as a heritage: *the cultural inheritance of Rome.* **4.** *Biology.* **a.** The process of genetic transmission of characters or characteristics. **b.** The configuration of characters or characteristics so inherited.

inheritance tax *n.* A tax on inherited property.

in·hib·it (ĭn-hĭb′ĭt) *tr.v.* **-ited, -iting, -its. 1.** To restrain or hold back (an impulse, natural reaction, or the like). **2.** To prohibit or forbid, especially in ecclesiastical law. **3.** *Psychology.* To cause inhibition in. **4.** To act as an inhibitor. —See Synonyms at **restrain.** [Middle English *inhibiten,* from Latin *inhibēre* (past participle *inhibitus*), to restrain, hold in : *in-,* in + *habēre,* to have, hold.] **—in·hib·it·a·ble** *adj.* **—in·hib·it·ed** *adj.* **—in·hib·i·tive, in·hib·i·to·ry** (ĭn-hĭb′ĭ-tôr′ē, -tōr′ē) *adj.*

in·hi·bi·tion (ĭn′hĭ-bĭsh′ən, ĭn′ĭ-) *n.* **1.** The act of inhibiting or the state of being inhibited. **2. a.** *Psychology.* Restraint of an instinctive impulse or the condition inducing such restraint. **b.** Any emotion, idea, habit, or the like, which holds back one's impulses or desires. **3.** The prevention or reduction of the functioning of an organ or part by affecting its nerve supply.

in·hib·i·tor, in·hib·it·er (ĭn-hĭb′ə-tər) *n.* One that inhibits, as: **1.** A substance used to retard or halt a chemical reaction, such as rusting; anticatalyst. **2.** An inert substance added to another substance to inhibit some reaction. **3.** An impurity in a solid that inhibits luminescence. **4.** A substance, such as a drug, that prevents or reduces a physiological action.

in·ho·mo·ge·ne·ous (ĭn-hŏm′ə-jĕn′ē-əs, -hōm-ə-) *adj.* Not homogeneous; lacking in uniformity: *an inhomogeneous magnetic field.* **—in·ho·mo·gen·e·i·ty** (ĭn-hŏm′ə-jə-nē′ə-tē, -nā′ə-) *n.*

in·hos·pi·ta·ble (ĭn-hŏs′pĭ-tə-bəl, ĭn′hŏ-spĭt′ə-bəl) *adj.* **1.** Displaying no hospitality; unfriendly. **2.** Not affording shelter or sustenance; barren. **—in·hos·pi·ta·ble·ness** *n.* **—in·hos·pi·ta·bly** *adv.* **—in·hos·pi·tal·i·ty** (ĭn-hŏs′pĭ-tăl′ə-tē) *n.*

in-house (ĭn′hous′) *adj.* Working, originating, or produced within an organization or group: *an in-house editor, not a freelance.* **—in-house** *adv.*

in·hu·man (ĭn-hyo͞o′mən) *adj.* **1.** Not possessing desirable human qualities; lacking kindness or pity; barbarous; brutal. **2.** Not of ordinary human form or type. —See Synonyms at **cruel.** [Latin *inhūmānus* : *in-,* not + *hūmānus,* HUMAN.] **—in·hu·man·ly** *adv.* **—in·hu·man·ness** *n.*

in·hu·mane (ĭn′hyo͞o-mān′) *adj.* Not humane; lacking in pity or compassion. **—in·hu·mane·ly** *adv.*

in·hu·man·i·ty (ĭn′hyo͞o-măn′ə-tē) *n., pl.* **-ties. 1.** Lack of pity or compassion. **2.** An inhumane or cruel act.

in·hume (ĭn-hyo͞om′) *tr.v.* **-humed, -huming, -humes.** To place in a grave; bury; inter. [Latin *inhumāre* : *in-,* in + *humus,* earth, ground.] **—in·hu·ma·tion** *n.* **—in·hum·er** *n.*

in·im·i·cal (ĭn-ĭm′ĭ-kəl) *adj.* **1.** Not conducive; harmful; adverse: *habits inimical to good health.* **2.** Unfriendly; hostile; antagonistic: *"a voice apparently cold and inimical"* (Arnold Bennett). [Late Latin *inimīcālis,* from Latin *inimīcus,* enemy : *in-,* not + *amīcus,* friend.]

in·im·i·ta·ble (ĭn-ĭm′ĭ-tə-bəl) *adj.* Defying imitation; matchless; unique. **—in·im·i·ta·bil·i·ty** *n.* **—in·im·i·ta·bly** *adv.*

in·i·on (ĭn′ē-ən) *n.* The projecting point of the occipital bone at the base of the skull, used as a measuring point in craniometry. [Greek, back of the head.]

in·iq·ui·tous (ĭ-nĭk′wə-təs) *adj.* **1.** Of the nature of iniquity; wicked; sinful. **2.** *Informal.* Disgraceful; scandalous: *an iniquitous waste of money.* **—in·iq·ui·tous·ly** *adv.* **—in·iq·ui·tous·ness** *n.*

in·iq·ui·ty (ĭ-nĭk′wə-tē) *n., pl.* **-ties. 1.** Moral turpitude or sin; wickedness: *"the human mind, since the Fall, was nothing but a sink of iniquity"* (Henry Fielding). **2.** A grossly immoral act; a sin. [Middle English *iniquite,* from Old French, from Latin *inīquitās* (stem *inīquitāt-*), from *inīquus,* unjust : *in-,* not + *aequus,* just, EQUAL.]

init. initial.

in·i·tial (ĭ-nĭsh'əl) *adj. Abbr.* **init.** **1.** Occurring or existing at the beginning or outset; first. **2.** Occurring first in a word, syllable, or the like.
~*n. Abbr.* **init.** **1. a.** The first letter of a person's name, used as a shortened signature or for identification. **b. initials.** The first letters of each part of a person's full name, used as a shortened signature or for identification. **2.** The first letter of a word. **3.** A large, often highly decorated letter set at the beginning of a chapter, verse, paragraph, or the like.
~*tr.v.* **initialed, -tialing, -tials.** Also *chiefly British* **-tialled, -tialling.** To mark or sign with one's own initial or initials, especially in order to indicate approval or authorization. [Latin *initiālis,* from *initium,* beginning.] **—in·i·tial·ly** *adv.*

i·ni·tial·ism (ĭ-nĭsh'ə-lĭz'əm) *n.* An abbreviation of a phrase consisting of the initial letter of each word in the phrase; distinguishable from an acronym in that it is not pronounced as a single word; for example **C.I.A., B.B.C.**

in·i·tial·ize (ĭ-nĭsh'ə-līz') *tr.v.* **-ized, -izing, -izes.** *Computer Science.* To set to a starting position or value. **—in·i·tial·i·za·tion** *n.* **—in·i·tial·iz·er** *n.*

in·i·ti·ate (ĭ-nĭsh'ē-āt') *tr.v.* **-ated, -ating, -ates.** **1.** To begin or originate. **2.** To introduce (a person) to a new field, interest, skill, or the like. **3.** To admit into membership, as with ceremonies or ritual. —See Synonyms at **begin.**
~*adj.* (ĭ-nĭsh'ē-ĭt). Initiated.
~*n.* (ĭ-nĭsh'ē-ĭt). **1.** One who has been initiated. **2.** A novice; beginner. [Latin *initiāre,* from *initium,* beginning. See **initial.**] **—in·i·ti·a·tor** *n.*

in·i·ti·a·tion (ĭ-nĭsh'ē-ā'shən) *n.* **1.** The act of initiating or the fact of being initiated. **2.** A ceremony, ritual, test, or period of instruction by which a new member is admitted to an organization, office, or status or to knowledge.

in·i·ti·a·tive (ĭ-nĭsh'ē-ə-tĭv, -ē'ā-tĭv, -nĭsh'ə-tĭv) *n.* **1. a.** The ability or instinct to initiate and follow through a plan or task; enterprise and determination. **b.** The right or power to initiate: *has the initiative.* **2.** The first step or action; the opening move: *take the initiative; new peace initiatives.* **3. a.** The power or right to introduce a new legislative measure. **b.** The right and procedure by which citizens can propose a law by petition and ensure its submission to the electorate, as in many U.S. states and in Switzerland. **—on one's own initiative.** Without instruction or coercion; unprompted.
~*adj.* **1.** Of, pertaining to, or requiring initiative: *an initiative test.* **2.** Used to initiate; initiatory. **—in·i·ti·a·tive·ly** *adv.*

in·i·ti·a·to·ry (ĭ-nĭsh'ē-ə-tôr'ē, -tōr'ē) *adj.* **1.** Introductory; initial. **2.** Used to initiate; initiative.

inj. injection.

in·ject (ĭn-jĕkt') *tr.v.* **-jected, -jecting, -jects.** **1.** To force or drive (a fluid) into something. **2.** *Medicine.* **a.** To introduce (a fluid) into the skin, subcutaneous tissue, muscle, blood vessels, or a bodily cavity by means of a syringe. **b.** To introduce a fluid into (a part of the body) in this way. **3.** To introduce (a new element) into consideration: *inject a note of humor into the negotiations.* **4.** To place (a satellite, rocket, or the like) in an orbit, trajectory, or stream. [Latin *inicere, injicere* (past participle *injectus*), to throw or put in : *in-,* in + *jacere,* to throw.]

in·ject·a·ble (ĭn-jĕk'tə-bəl) *adj.* Able to be injected. Said of a drug.
~*n.* A drug or medicine that can be injected directly into the bloodstream.

in·jec·tion (ĭn-jĕk'shən) *n. Abbr.* **inj.** **1.** The act or an instance of injecting. **2.** A fluid that is injected. **3.** Broadly, anything injected.

injection molding *n.* **1.** A process for making molded articles by forcing a liquid under pressure into a mold. **2.** An article made by such a process.

in·jec·tor (ĭn-jĕk'tər) *n.* **1.** A device used to force water into a steam boiler. **2.** A device for spraying atomized fuel into the combustion chamber of an internal-combustion engine.

in·ju·di·cious (ĭn'jo͞o-dĭsh'əs) *adj.* Lacking judgment or discretion. **—in·ju·di·cious·ly** *adv.* **—in·ju·di·cious·ness** *n.*

In·jun (ĭn'jən) *n. Informal & Regional.* A North American Indian. [Facetious respelling of INDIAN.]

in·junc·tion (ĭn-jŭngk'shən) *n.* **1.** The act of enjoining. **2.** That which is enjoined; a command, directive, or order. **3.** *Law.* A court order enjoining or prohibiting a party from a specific course of action. [Late Latin *injunctiō,* from Latin *injungere* (past participle *injunctus*), to enjoin : *in-,* in + *jungere,* to join.] **—in·junc·tive** *adj.*

in·jure (ĭn'jər) *tr.v.* **-jured, -juring, -jures.** **1.** To cause harm or damage to; hurt. **2.** To commit an injustice or offense against; wrong. [Back-formation from INJURY.] **—in·jur·er** *n.*
Synonyms: *damage, harm, hurt, impair, mar, wound.*

in·ju·ri·ous (ĭn-jo͝or'ē-əs) *adj.* **1.** Harmful or damaging. **2.** Slanderous; libelous. **—in·ju·ri·ous·ly** *adv.* **—in·ju·ri·ous·ness** *n.*

in·ju·ry (ĭn'jə-rē) *n., pl.* **-ries.** **1.** Damage of or to a person, property, reputation, or thing. **2.** A specific damage or wound: *a leg injury.* **3.** Injustice. **4.** *Law.* Any wrong or damage done to persons, property, reputation, or rights that gives grounds for legal action. —See Synonyms at **injustice.** [Middle English *injurie,* from Norman French, from Latin *injūria,* injustice, wrong, from *injūrius,* unjust, wrongful : *in-,* not + *jūs* (stem *jūr-*), right, law.]

in·jus·tice (ĭn-jŭs'tĭs) *n.* **1.** The fact, practice, or quality of being unjust; lack of justice. **2.** An unjust act; a wrong. [Middle English, from Old French, from Latin *injūstitia,* from *injūstus,* unjust : *in-,* not + *jūstus,* JUST.]
Synonyms: *grievance, injury, wrong.*

ink (ĭngk) *n.* **1.** A pigmented liquid or paste used especially for writing or printing. **2.** A dark liquid secreted by cuttlefish and other cephalopods for protective concealment.
~*tr.v.* **inked, inking, inks.** To mark or stain with ink. **—ink in.** To retrace the pencil lines of (a drawing) in ink. **—ink up.** To put ink onto (a printing machine) to prepare for printing. [Middle English *enke,* from Old French *enke, enque,* from Late Latin *encaustum,* from Greek *enkauston,* purple ink, from *enkaiein,* to paint in encaustic.] **—ink·er** *n.*

In·ka·tha (ĭn-kä'tə) *n.* A Zulu national liberation movement founded in 1928 whose aim is a single multiracial South Africa.

ink·ber·ry (ĭngk'bĕr'ē) *n., pl.* **-ries.** **1.** A shrub, *Ilex glabra,* of eastern North America, having black, berrylike fruit. **2. Pokeweed** *(see).* **3.** The fruit of either of these plants.

ink·blot (ĭngk'blŏt') *n.* **1.** A blotted pattern of spilled ink. **2.** Such a pattern used in the Rorschach test.

ink·horn (ĭngk'hôrn') *n.* A small container made of horn or similar material, formerly used to hold writing ink.
~*adj.* Pedantic; recondite: *an inkhorn term.*

ink·ling (ĭngk'lĭng) *n.* **1.** A hint or intimation. **2.** A vague idea or notion. [Middle English *inklet*, to mutter.]

ink pad *n.* An ink-soaked cushion used to ink a rubber stamp. Also called "pad."

ink sac *n.* A gland near the anus in an octopus or other cephalopod mollusk that secretes ink.

ink·stand (ĭngk'stănd') *n.* **1.** A tray or rack for bottles of ink, pens, and other writing implements. **2.** An inkwell.

ink·well (ĭngk'wĕl') *n.* A small ink reservoir into which a pen is dipped for filling.

ink·y (ĭng'kē) *adj.* **-ier, -iest.** **1.** Of or containing ink. **2.** Dark or murky. **3.** Stained or smeared with ink. **—ink·i·ness** *n.*

inky cap *n.* Any of various mushrooms of the genus *Coprinus,* having gills that dissolve into a dark liquid on maturing.

inky cap *A group of mostly edible fungi that grow in open woodlands from spring until autumn and are easily identifiable by their dark caps. This is the shaggy inky cap,* Coprinus comatus, *which is edible and particularly tasty when young.*

inlace. Variant of **enlace.**

in·laid (ĭn'lād', ĭn-lād') *adj.* **1.** Set into a surface in a decorative pattern. **2.** Decorated with a pattern set into a surface.

in·land (ĭn'lənd) *adj.* **1.** Of, pertaining to, or located in the interior part of a land mass. **2.** Operating or applying within the borders of a country, region, or state; domestic: *inland trade.*
~*adv.* In, toward, or into the interior of a land mass.
~*n.* (-lănd', -lənd). The interior of a country, region, or state.

inland drainage *n.* **Internal drainage** *(see).*

Inland Empire. An agricultural region of the northwestern United States between the Cascade Range and the Rocky Mts., comprising portions of eastern Washington, northeastern Oregon, northern Idaho, and western Montana.

in·land·er (ĭn'lən-dər, -lăn'-) *n.* A person who lives in or near the center of a land mass, especially in a large continent such as Australia.

Inland Passage. See **Inside Passage.**

inland sea *n.* An isolated, landlocked expanse of water, with no outlet to the world's main seas.

Inland Sea. An arm of the Pacific Ocean, enclosed by the Japanese islands of Honshu, Shikoku, and Kyushu, except for a narrow channel connecting it to the Sea of Japan. Within it are *c.* 950 small islands, about two-thirds of which form the Inland Sea National Park.

in-law (ĭn'lô') *n.* Any relative by marriage. [From -IN-LAW.]

-in-law *comb. form.* Indicates relation through marriage; for example, **sister-in-law.**

in·lay (ĭn-lā', ĭn'lā') *tr.v.* **-laid, -laying, -lays.** **1.** To set (pieces of wood, ivory, or the like) into a surface, usually at the same level, to form a design. **2.** To decorate (a surface) with wood, ivory, or the like.
~*n.* (ĭn'lā'). **1.** An article, material, or substance that has been inlaid. **2.** A design, pattern, or decoration made by inlaying. **3.** *Dentistry.* A solid filling of gold, porcelain, or the like, fitted to a cavity in a tooth and cemented in place. **4.** A piece of tissue, such as bone, surgically inserted into an organ or part to repair a defect. **—in·lay·er** *n.*

in·let (ĭn'lĕt', -lĭt) *n.* **1.** A relatively narrow channel or pocket of water. **2.** A stream or bay leading inland, as from the ocean; an estuary. **3.** A narrow passage of water between two islands. **4.** An entry or drainage passage, as to a culvert. **5.** Something that is inserted, let in, or inlaid. **6.** A way or means of entering; especially, a valve or part through which a fluid enters a machine, engine, or the like. Also used adjectivally: *inlet manifold; inlet valve.*
~*tr.v.* **inletted, -letting, -lets.** To insert; let in.

in·li·er (ĭn'lī'ər) *n.* An older rock formation completely surrounded by newer strata.

in loc. cit. Variant of **loc. cit.**

in lo·co pa·ren·tis (ĭn lō'kō pə-rĕn'tĭs) *adv. Latin.* In the position or place of a parent.

in·ly (ĭn'lē) *adv. Poetic.* Inwardly.

in·ly·ing (ĭn'lī'ĭng) *adj.* Positioned within or inside.

in·mate (ĭn'māt') *n.* **1.** A resident in a building or dwelling. **2.** A person confined to an institution such as a prison or mental hospital. [Perhaps INN (influenced by IN) + MATE.]

in me·di·as res (ĭn mā'dē-äs' rās'; ĭn mē'dē-əs rēz') *adv. Latin.* Into the middle of things. Used chiefly of the classical literary or dramatic device whereby an author starts a narrative by plunging the audience into the middle of an objective sequence of events. [Taken from the passage *"in medias res . . . auditorem rapit,"* "(the poet) plunges his hearer . . . into the middle of things" (Horace, *Ars Poetica*).]

in me·mo·ri·am (ĭn mə-môr′ē-əm, mə-môr′-) *prep. Latin. Abbr.* **in mem.** In memory of; as a memorial to. Used in epitaphs.

inmesh. Variant of **enmesh.**

in·mi·grant (ĭn′mĭ′grənt) *n.* A person who moves to another area within the same country.

in·mi·gra·tion (ĭn′mĭ-grā′shən) *n.* The movement of people to another area within the same country.

in·most (ĭn′mōst′) *adj.* Innermost.

inn (ĭn) *n.* **1.** A public lodging house serving food and drink to travelers; hotel. **2.** A tavern or restaurant. **3.** *British.* Formerly, a hall of residence for students. [Middle English *inn,* Old English *inn.*]

in·nards (ĭn′ərdz) *pl.n. Informal.* **1.** Internal bodily organs; viscera. **2.** Broadly, any inner parts, as of machinery. [Variant of INWARDS.]

in·nate (ĭ-nāt′, ĭn′āt′) *adj.* **1.** Possessed at birth; inborn. **2.** Possessed as an essential characteristic; inherent. **3.** Of or produced by thought as distinguished from experience: *innate ideas.* [Middle English *innat,* from Latin *innātus,* past participle of *innāscī,* to be born in : *in-,* in + *nāscī,* to be born.] —**in·nate·ly** *adv.* —**in·nate·ness** *n.*

    Synonyms: congenital, hereditary, inborn, inbred.

in·ner (ĭn′ər) *adj.* **1.** Located further inside: *an inner room.* **2. a.** Occurring within. **b.** Closer to the center; more secret or exclusive: *inner circles of government.* **3.** Less apparent; underlying: *the inner meaning of a poem.* **4.** Pertaining to the soul or mind: *an inner struggle.* **5.** *Chemistry.* Designating a cyclic compound formed by the reaction of one functional group in a molecule with another in the same molecule. [Middle English *inner,* Old English *innera, innra.*]

inner city *n.* The older, central part of a city, especially when characterized by crowded, run-down, low-income districts. —**inner·cit·y** *adj.*

in·ner-di·rect·ed (ĭn′ər-dĭ-rĕk′tĭd, -dī-) *adj.* Guided by personal principles rather than those shared by society at large: *an inner-directed personality.* Compare **other-directed.** —**in·ner-di·rec·tion** *n.*

inner ear *n.* The **internal ear** (see).

Inner Hebrides. See **Hebrides.**

inner man *n.* The mind, soul, or spirit.

Inner Mon·go·li·an Autonomous Region (mŏng-gō′lē-ən). Autonomous region in northeast China. Since the coming of Communist rule in China in 1949 it has had limited powers of self-government within the Chinese state. Most of the Mongols in China live here, although they form less than 10 percent of the region's population. It comprises largely steppelands and arid near-desert; stock-raising is the chief economic activity. Its capital is Hohhot (Huehot).

in·ner·most (ĭn′ər-mōst′) *adj.* **1.** Situated or occurring farthest within. **2.** Most intimate: *innermost feelings.*

inner planet *n.* Any of the planets Mercury, Venus, Earth, or Mars, with orbits inside the asteroid belt. Compare **outer planet.**

inner product *n. Mathematics.* **Scalar product** (see).

inner space *n.* **1.** Space at or near the earth's surface, especially space beneath the sea. **2.** The subconscious or spiritual part of the self.

Inner Temple *n.* In England, one of the four legal societies forming the **Inns of Court** (see).

inner tube *n.* The inflatable rubber tube that fits inside the outer casing of a pneumatic tire.

in·ner·vate (ĭ-nûr′vāt′, ĭn′ər-) *tr.v.* **-vated, -vating, -vates.** **1.** To supply (a bodily part) with nerves. **2.** To stimulate (a nerve or bodily part). [IN- + NERV(E) + -ATE.] —**in·ner·va·tion** *n.*

in·nerve (ĭ-nûrv′) *tr.v.* **-nerved, -nerving, -nerves.** To give nervous energy to; stimulate.

In·ness (ĭn′ĭs), **George** (1825–94). U.S. landscape painter. He began his career as a romantic artist in the manner of the Hudson River School, but later developed a personal style that subordinated details of form and local color to a freer, more intimate atmospheric effect. His best-known work is *Peace and Plenty.*

in·ning (ĭn′ĭng) *n.* **1.** In baseball, one of nine divisions or periods of a regulation game, in which each team has a turn at bat as limited by three outs. **2.** *Archaic.* **a.** The reclamation of flooded or marshy land. **b.** *Often* **innings.** Land that has been reclaimed. [From IN.]

in·nings (ĭn′ĭngz) *n., pl.* **innings.** **1.** The period or division of a game of cricket during which one team bats. **2.** The play or the number of runs of a batsman during his turn at batting: *He had a magnificent innings.* **3.** Any period of opportunity and action: *She will get her innings soon.* [From *in* (verb), to go in.]

inn·keep·er (ĭn′kē′pər) *n.* One who owns or manages an inn.

in·no·cence (ĭn′ə-səns) *n.* **1.** The state, quality, or virtue of being innocent. **2.** A plant, **bluets** (see).

in·no·cent (ĭn′ə-sənt) *adj.* **1.** Uncorrupted by evil, malice, or wrongdoing; sinless; untainted; pure: *as innocent of evil as a babe.* **2. a.** Not guilty of a specific crime; legally blameless: *found innocent on all charges.* **b.** Not responsible for or guilty of something wrong or unethical: *innocent of negligence.* **3.** Not dangerous or harmful; not serious: *an innocent prank.* **4.** Not experienced or worldly; credulous; naive: *innocent tourists.* **5.** Not exposed to or familiar with something; devoid. Used with *of: innocent of learning.* **6.** Betraying or suggesting no deception or guile; simple; artless: *an innocent smile.* —See Synonyms at **naive.**

~*n.* **1.** A person who is free of evil or sin; one who is pure or

uncorrupted. **2.** A simple, guileless, inexperienced, or unsophisticated person; one who is vulnerable or credulous: *an innocent abroad.* **3.** A very young child. [Middle English, from Old French, from Latin *innocēns : in-,* not + *nocēns* (stem *nocent-*), present participle of *nocēre,* to harm, hurt.] —**in·no·cent·ly** *adv.*

Innocent III, Pope, born Lotario di Segni (c. 1161–1216). He became pope in 1198. Innocent III raised the papacy to new heights of power through his intervention in European politics. He also organized the Fourth Crusade and the suppression of the Albigenses. His acceptance of St. Dominic and St. Francis of Assisi sanctioned the works of these itinerant preachers.

in·noc·u·ous (ĭ-nŏk′yōo-əs) *adj.* **1.** Having no adverse effect; harmless: *an innocuous snakebite.* **2.** Inoffensive; unobjectionable: *an innocuous speech.* [Latin *innocuus : in-,* not + *nocuus,* harmful, from *nocēre,* to harm.] —**in·noc·u·ous·ly** *adv.* —**in·noc·u·ous·ness** *n.*

in·nom·i·nate (ĭ-nŏm′ə-nĭt) *adj.* **1.** Having no specific name. **2.** Anonymous. [Late Latin *innōminātus* : Latin *in-,* not + *nōminātus,* past participle of *nōmināre,* to name, NOMINATE.]

innominate artery *n.* A short artery that arises from the aortic arch and divides in the neck to form the right common carotid and right subclavian arteries.

innominate bone *n. Anatomy.* A large flat bone forming the lateral half of the pelvis, consisting of the fused ilium, ischium, and pubis. Also called "hip bone."

innominate vein *n.* Either of a pair of veins in the neck formed by the union of the internal jugular and subclavian veins. The innominate veins join to form the superior vena cava.

in·no·vate (ĭn′ə-vāt′) *v.* **-vated, -vating, -vates.** —*tr.* To begin or introduce (something new). —*intr.* To begin or introduce something new; be inventive. [Latin *innovāre,* to renew : *in-* (intensive) + *novāre,* to make new, renew, from *novus,* new.] —**in·no·va·tive,** **in·no·va·to·ry** *adj.* —**in·no·va·tor** *n.*

in·no·va·tion (ĭn′ə-vā′shən) *n.* **1.** The act of innovating. **2.** That which is newly introduced; a change. —**in·no·va·tion·al** *adj.*

Inns·bruck (ĭnz′brŏŏk′). City in western Austria, the capital of Tirol province. It is a popular summer and winter resort and was the site of the 1964 and 1976 Winter Olympics.

Inns of Court *pl.n.* **1.** The four legal societies in England founded at the beginning of the 14th century, consisting of Gray's Inn, Lincoln's Inn, the Inner Temple, and the Middle Temple, which have the exclusive right to grant law students admission to the bar as lawyers. **2.** The buildings housing these societies.

in·nu·en·do (ĭn′yōo-ĕn′dō) *n., pl.* **-does.** **1.** An indirect, oblique, or subtle implication, often derogatory in nature. **2.** *Law.* **a.** An interpretation, as in a libel suit, of allegedly libelous or slanderous material. **b.** Any explanation of a word or charge. [Latin *innuendō,* by hinting, from *innuendum,* gerund of *innuere,* to nod to, signal to : *in,* toward + *-nuere,* to nod.]

Innuit. Variant of **Inuit.**

in·nu·mer·a·ble (ĭ-nōō′mər-ə-bəl, ĭ-nyōō′-) *adj.* Also **in·nu·mer·ous** (-mər-əs). Too many to be counted or numbered. —See Synonyms at **infinite.** —**in·nu·mer·a·bil·i·ty, in·nu·mer·a·ble·ness** *n.* —**in·nu·mer·a·bly** *adv.*

in·nu·tri·tion (ĭn′nōō-trĭsh′ən, ĭn′nyōō-, ĭn′yōō-) *n.* Lack of nutrition; poor nourishment. —**in·nu·tri·tious** *adj.*

in·ob·serv·ance (ĭn′əb-zûr′vəns) *n.* **1.** Lack of heed or attention; disregard. **2.** Nonobservance, as of a law or custom. —**in·ob·serv·ant** *adj.*

in·oc·u·la·ble (ĭn-ŏk′yə-lə-bəl) *adj.* **1.** Transmissible by inoculation. **2.** Susceptible to a disease transmitted by inoculation. [From INOCULATE.] —**in·oc·u·la·bil·i·ty** *n.*

in·oc·u·late (ĭ-nŏk′yə-lāt′) *tr.v.* **-lated, -lating, -lates.** **1.** To introduce the virus of a disease or other antigenic material into the body of (a person or animal) in order to immunize, cure, or experiment: *inoculated against polio.* **2.** To communicate a disease to by transferring its virus or other causative agent. **3.** To implant (microorganisms or infectious material) into a medium suitable for their growth. **4.** To introduce nitrogen-fixing bacteria or mycorrhizal fungi into (the soil) to enhance plant growth. **5.** To influence (someone) with ideas, opinions, or the like. [Middle English, from Latin *inoculāre,* to engraft : *in-,* in + *oculus,* eye, bud.] —**in·oc·u·la·tive** *adj.* —**in·oc·u·la·tor** *n.*

in·oc·u·la·tion (ĭ-nŏk′yə-lā′shən) *n.* **1.** The act, process, or an instance of inoculating. **2.** Inoculum.

in·oc·u·lum (ĭ-nŏk′yə-ləm) *n.* **1.** The material used in an inoculation. Also called "inoculant," "inoculation." **2.** Fungal spores, bacteria, or other pathogens that initiate an outbreak of plant disease.

in·o·dor·ous (ĭn-ō′də-rəs) *adj.* Having no odor.

in·of·fen·sive (ĭn′ə-fĕn′sĭv) *adj.* Giving no offense; harmless; unobjectionable. —**in·of·fen·sive·ly** *adv.* —**in·of·fen·sive·ness** *n.*

in·of·fi·cious (ĭn′ə-fĭsh′əs) *adj. Law.* Contrary to natural affection or moral duty. Said of a will in which the testator unreasonably disinherits the rightful heirs. [Latin *inofficiōsus : in-,* not + *officiōsus,* dutiful, OFFICIOUS.] —**in·of·fi·cious·ly** *adv.*

in·op·er·a·ble (ĭn-ŏp′ər-ə-bəl) *adj.* **1.** Not operable. **2.** Not susceptible to surgery. Said especially of malignant tumors. —**in·op·er·a·bly** *adv.*

in·op·er·a·tive (ĭn-ŏp′ər-ə-tĭv) *adj.* Not working or functioning; not taking effect: *inoperative measures.*

in·op·por·tune (ĭn-ŏp′ər-tōōn′, -tyōōn′) *adj.* Not opportune; illtimed; inappropriate. —**in·op·por·tune·ly** *adv.* —**in·op·por·tune·ness** *n.*

in·or·di·nate (ĭn-ôrd′n-ĭt) *adj.* **1.** Exceeding reasonable limits; im-

---

moderate; unrestrained: *inordinate desires.* **2.** Not regulated; disorderly. —See Synonyms at **excessive.** [Middle English *inordinat,* from Latin *inordinātus* : *in-,* not + *ōrdinātus,* past participle of *ōrdināre,* to set in order, from *ōrdō* (stem *ōrdin-*), order.] —**in·or·di·na·cy, in·or·di·nate·ness** *n.* —**in·or·di·nate·ly** *adv.*

in·or·gan·ic (ĭn′ôr-găn′ĭk) *adj. Abbr.* **inorg. 1. a.** Involving neither organic life nor the products of organic life. **b.** Not composed of organic matter; especially, mineral. **2.** Of or pertaining to the chemistry of noncarbon compounds not usually classified as **organic** *(see).* **3.** Not arising in normal growth; artificial. **4.** Lacking system or structure. —**in·or·gan·i·cal·ly** *adv.*

inorganic chemistry *n.* The branch of chemistry that deals with the formation, structure, and properties of compounds of elements other than carbon, usually considered to include some simple carbon compounds such as carbon dioxide and carbonate salts. Compare **organic chemistry.**

in·os·cu·late (ĭn-ŏs′kyə-lāt′) *v.* **-lated, -lating, -lates.** —*tr.* **1.** To unite (blood vessels, nerve fibers, or ducts) by small openings. **2.** To make continuous; blend (as fibers, for example). —*intr.* **1.** To open into one another. **2.** To unite so as to be continuous; blend. **3.** To communicate by means of small channels or openings. Used of blood vessels, nerve fibers, and the like. [IN- + Latin *ōsculāre,* to provide with an opening, from *ōsculum,* little mouth, opening, diminutive of *ōs,* mouth.] —**in·os·cu·la·tion** *n.*

in·o·si·tol (ĭn-ō′sə-tōl′, -tôl′, -tŏl′) *n.* One of nine isomeric alcohols, $C_6H_6(OH)_6$; especially, one found in plant and animal tissue and classified as a member of the vitamin B complex. [Greek *īs* (genitive *īnos*), tendon, sinew, muscle + -IT(E) + -OL.]

in·o·trop·ic (ē′nə-trō′pĭk, -trŏp′ĭk, ī′nə-) *adj.* Affecting the contraction of muscles, especially heart muscle: *Digitalis is an inotropic drug.* [Greek *īs* (stem *īn-*), tendon + -TROPIC.]

in·pa·tient (ĭn′pā′shənt) *n.* A patient living or staying in a hospital. Compare **outpatient.**

in per·so·nam (ĭn pər-sō′nəm) *adv. Law.* Against a person. Said of a proceeding. Compare **in rem.** [Latin.] —**in per·so·nam** *adj.*

in pet·to (ēn pĕt′tō) *adv.* Secretly; privately. Said of appointments of cardinals by the pope undisclosed in consistory. [Italian, "in the breast."] —**in pet·to** *adj.*

in-phase (ĭn′fāz′) *adj. Physics.* Designating or pertaining to two or more waves, alternating signals, or other periodically varying quantities for which the maximum (and minimum) values of each quantity occur at the same time.

in pos·se (ĭn pŏs′ē) *adj. Latin.* Possible but not actual; potential. Compare **in esse.** [Literally, in possibility.]

in pro·pri·a per·so·na (ĭn prō′prē-ə pûr-sō′nə) *adv. Latin.* In one's own person; in one's self.

in·put (ĭn′po͝ot′) *n.* **1.** Anything put into a system or expended in its operation to achieve a result or output, especially: **a.** Energy, work, or power used to drive a machine. **b.** Current, electromotive force, or power supplied to an electric circuit, network, or device. **c.** Information put into a communications system for transmission or into a data-processing system for processing. **d.** The entirety of basic resources, including materials, equipment, and funds, required to complete a project. **2.** A position, terminal, or station at which any such input enters a system. **3.** Contribution to or participation in a common effort: *a discussion with input from all members of the group.* **4.** Information in general.
~*tr.v.* **input** or **inputted, -putting, -puts.** To insert (data) into a data-processing system.

in·put-out·put (ĭn′po͝ot-out′po͝ot′) *adj.* **1.** Designating the equipment forming part of a computer system that controls the passage of information into or out of the system. **2.** Concerned with or pertaining to the passage of information into or out of a computer. **2.** Designating an analysis of the input into a system in relation to output, especially in terms of economics.

in·quest (ĭn′kwĕst′) *n.* **1.** A judicial inquiry concerning some matter, usually before a jury; especially, an investigation into the cause of someone's death held before a jury and a coroner. **2.** A jury making such an inquiry. **3.** An investigation. [Middle English *enquest,* from Old French *enqueste,* from Vulgar Latin *inquesta* (unattested), from the feminine past participle of *inquaerere* (unattested), to INQUIRE.]

in·qui·e·tude (ĭn-kwī′ə-to͞od′, -tyo͞od′) *n.* **1.** Restlessness. **2.** Uneasiness; disquietude. [Middle English, from Late Latin *inquiētūdō,* from Latin *inquiētus,* restless : *in-,* not + *quiētus,* QUIET.]

in·qui·line (ĭn′kwə-līn′, -lĭn) *n.* An animal that characteristically lives commensally in the burrow or dwelling place of an animal of another kind. [Latin *inquilīnus,* tenant, dweller.] —**in·qui·line** *adj.* —**in·qui·lin·ism** (ĭn′kwə-lə-nĭz′əm), **in·qui·lin·i·ty** (ĭn′kwə-lĭn′ə-tē) *n.* —**in·qui·lin·ous** (ĭn′kwə-lī′nəs) *adj.*

in·quire (ĭn-kwīr′) *v.* **-quired, -quiring, -quires.** Also **en·quire** (ĕn-). —*intr.* **1. a.** To put a question. **b.** To request information. Used with *about* or *after; inquire after another's health.* **2.** To make an inquiry; look into; investigate. Used with *into.* —*tr.* **1.** To ask about. **2.** To ask: *"I am free to inquire what a work of art means to me"* (Bernard Berenson). —See Synonyms at **ask.** [Middle English *enquiren, enqueren,* from Old French *enquerrer,* from Vulgar Latin *inquaerere* (unattested), variant of Latin *inquīrere* : *in-* (intensive) + *quaerere,* to seek, ask.] —**in·quir·er** *n.* —**in·quir·ing·ly** *adv.*

in·quir·y (ĭn-kwīr′ē, ĭn′kwə-rē) *n., pl.* **-ies.** Also **en·quir·y** (ĕn-, ĕn′-). **1.** The act of inquiring. **2.** A question; query. **3.** A close examination of some matter in a quest for information or truth.

in·qui·si·tion (ĭn′kwə-zĭsh′ən) *n.* **1.** The act of inquiring into a matter; investigation. **2. a.** A judicial inquiry. **b.** The verdict of a judicial inquiry. **3. Inquisition.** A former tribunal in the Roman Catholic Church directed at the suppression and punishment of heresy. See **Spanish Inquisition. 4.** Any inquisitorial investigation or scrutiny. [Middle English *inquisicioun,* from Old French *inquisition,* from Latin *inquīsītiō* (stem *inquīsītiōn-*), from *inquīrere* (past participle *inquīsītus*), to INQUIRE.] —**in·qui·si·tion·al** *adj.*

in·quis·i·tive (ĭn-kwĭz′ə-tĭv) *adj.* **1.** Unduly curious and inquiring; prying. **2.** Eager to learn. —See Usage note at **curious.** —**in·quis·i·tive·ly** *adv.* —**in·quis·i·tive·ness** *n.*

in·quis·i·tor (ĭn-kwĭz′ə-tər) *n.* **1.** One who enquires; a questioner. **2.** One who investigates officially. **3. Inquisitor.** A member of the Inquisition.

in·quis·i·to·ri·al (ĭn-kwĭz′ə-tôr′ē-əl, -tōr′ē-əl) *adj.* **1.** Pertaining to, resembling, or having the function of an inquisitor. **2.** *Law.* Designating a form of criminal procedure, often conducted in secrecy, in which one party acts as both prosecutor and judge. Compare **accusatorial. 3.** Involving or imposing browbeating interrogation. —**in·quis·i·to·ri·al·ly** *adv.*

in re (ĭn rē′) *prep. Law.* In the matter or case of; with regard to. [Latin.]

in rem (ĭn rĕm′) *adv. Law.* Against a thing, as a property, status, or right. Compare **in personam.** [Latin.] —**in rem** *adj.*

I.N.R.I. Jesus of Nazareth, King of the Jews. Used as an inscription on a crucifix. [Latin *Iesus Nazarenus Rex Iudaeorum.*]

in·road (ĭn′rōd′) *n.* **1.** A hostile invasion; raid; incursion. **2.** *Often* **inroads.** An encroachment; an intrusion: *Her work made inroads on her free time.* [IN + ROAD (obsolete sense "raid").]

in·rush (ĭn′rŭsh′) *n.* A sudden rushing in; an irruption; influx.

ins. 1. inspector. **2.** insulated; insulation. **3.** insurance.

in·sal·i·vate (ĭn-săl′ə-vāt′) *tr.v.* **-vated, -vating, -vates.** To mix (food) with saliva in chewing. —**in·sal·i·va·tion** *n.*

in·sa·lu·bri·ous (ĭn′sə-lo͞o′brē-əs) *adj.* Not salubrious; unhealthy: *an insalubrious climate.* —**in·sa·lu·bri·ty** *n.*

in·sane (ĭn-sān′) *adj.* **1.** Of, exhibiting, or suffering from insanity. **2.** Characteristic of, used by, or for the insane. **3.** Very foolish; rash; wild. [Latin *insānus* : *in-,* not + *sānus,* SANE.] —**in·sane·ly** *adv.* —**in·sane·ness** *n.*

in·san·i·tar·y (ĭn-săn′ə-tĕr′ē) *adj.* Not sanitary; unhealthy: *insanitary conditions.*

in·san·i·ty (ĭn-săn′ə-tē) *n., pl.* **-ties. 1.** Persistent mental disorder or derangement. **2.** Unsoundness of mind sufficient to exempt a person from legal responsibility for his actions. **3. a.** Extreme foolishness; total folly. **b.** Something foolish.
***Synonyms:** dementia, lunacy, madness, mania.*

in·sa·tia·ble (ĭn-sā′shə-bəl, -shē-ə-bəl) *adj.* Incapable of being satiated or satisfied: *an insatiable lust for power.* [Middle English *insaciable,* from Old French, from Latin *insatiābilis* : *in-,* not + *satiāre,* to SATIATE.] —**in·sa·tia·bil·i·ty, in·sa·tia·ble·ness** *n.* —**in·sa·tia·bly** *adv.*

in·sa·ti·ate (ĭn-sā′shē-ĭt) *adj.* Not satisfied; never satisfied; insatiable. —**in·sa·ti·ate·ly** *adv.* —**in·sa·ti·ate·ness** *n.*

in·scribe (ĭn-skrīb′) *tr.v.* **-scribed, -scribing, -scribes. 1.** To write, print, carve, or engrave (words or letters) on or in a paper, stone, wood, or other surface. **2.** To mark or engrave (a surface) with words or letters. **3.** To enter (a name) on a list or in a register. **4.** To write an inscription, such as a message or autograph, on (a book or photograph, for example) as an informal dedication to another. **5.** *Geometry.* To enclose (a polygon or polyhedron) within a closed configuration of lines, curves, or surfaces so that every vertex of the enclosed figure is incident on the enclosing configuration. **6.** *British.* To issue (loan stocks) in the form of shares whose holders' names are registered: *inscribed securities.* [Latin *inscrībere* : *in-,* in + *scrībere,* to write.] —**in·scrib·a·ble** *adj.* —**in·scrib·er** *n.*

in·scrip·tion (ĭn-skrĭp′shən) *n.* **1.** The act or an instance of inscribing. **2.** That which is inscribed, such as the wording on a coin or monument, or a dedication of a book or work of art. [Middle English *inscripcioun,* from Latin *inscriptiō* (stem *inscriptiōn-*), a writing in or upon, from *inscrībere* (past participle *inscriptus*), to INSCRIBE.] —**in·scrip·tion·al, in·scrip·tive** *adj.* —**in·scrip·tive·ly** *adv.*

in·scru·ta·ble (ĭn-skro͞o′tə-bəl) *adj.* Not able to be fathomed or understood; impenetrable; enigmatic: *an inscrutable look.* —**in·scru·ta·bil·i·ty, in·scru·ta·ble·ness** *n.* —**in·scru·ta·bly** *adv.*

in·sect (ĭn′sĕkt′) *n.* **1.** Any of numerous usually small invertebrate animals of the class Insecta (or Hexapoda), having an adult stage characterized by three pairs of legs, a segmented body with three major divisions, and usually two pairs of wings. **2.** Loosely, any of various similar invertebrate animals such as the spider, centipede, or tick. **3.** One who is small or contemptible. [Latin *insectum (animale),* "segmented (animal)" (translation of Greek *entomon*; see **entomo-**), from *insectus,* past participle of *insecāre,* to cut into : *in-,* in + *secāre,* to cut.] See feature, next page.

in·sec·tar·i·um (ĭn′sĕk-târ′ē-əm) *n., pl.* **-ums** or **-ia** (-ē-ə). Also **in·sec·tar·y** (ĭn′sĕk-tĕr′ē) *pl.* **-ies.** A place in which living insects are kept or bred.

in·sec·ti·cide (ĭn-sĕk′tə-sīd′) *n.* A substance used to kill insects. —**in·sec·ti·ci·dal** (ĭn-sĕk′tə-sīd′l) *adj.*

in·sec·ti·vore (ĭn-sĕk′tə-vôr′, -vōr′) *n.* **1.** Any of various mammals of the order Insectivora, characteristically feeding on insects, and including the shrews, moles, and hedgehogs. **2.** An organism that feeds on insects. [New Latin *Insectivora* (order) : Latin *insectum,* INSECT + *-vorus,* -VOROUS.]

in·sec·tiv·o·rous (ĭn′sĕk-tĭv′ər-əs) *adj.* **1.** Feeding on insects.

insect

CREATURES WHOSE NUMBERS DOMINATE THE EARTH
The common features of a million diverse species

More than three-quarters of the known living species of animal are insects. Nearly a million species have so far been named throughout the world, and there may be millions more species still to be discovered, chiefly in the tropics. The name insect means "segmented." An insect's body is made up of three parts: the head, the thorax, which is composed of 3 segments, and the abdomen, which has 11 segments. On the thorax are wings and three pairs of legs.

Apart from these common features, insects are a widely varied class. They range in size from the microscopic feather-winged beetles to the Goliath beetle of West Africa, which is nearly 150 millimeters (6 inches) long. Most species are less than 6 millimeters (¼ inch) long.

Their methods of reproduction are sexual but very diverse. Their lifespan varies from as little as two hours for an adult mayfly to more than 15 years for a queen ant. Among the most familiar insects are beetles, butterflies, moths, ants, bees, wasps, grasshoppers, and flies.

Most insects use their six legs for crawling, but some use the first pair of legs to grab their prey. Some aquatic insects have legs modified for swimming, for example the flattened "oars" of water boatmen. The speed at which insect species use their wings varies widely. The gently fluttering butterfly beats its wings only ten times a second, but the mosquito's wingbeats are so rapid—about 300 a second—that they cause a high-pitched hum.

AN INSECT'S SUIT OF ARMOR

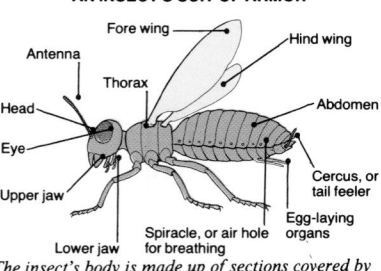

The insect's body is made up of sections covered by a hard outer skeleton, like a suit of armor. The eye is made up of thousands of lenses each of which picks up part of a scene to register on the insect's brain as an image made up of dots.

HOW AN INSECT SEES

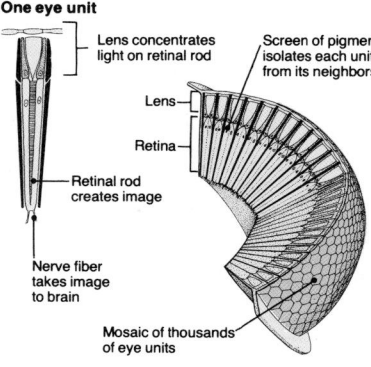

THE LIFE CYCLE OF A FLY

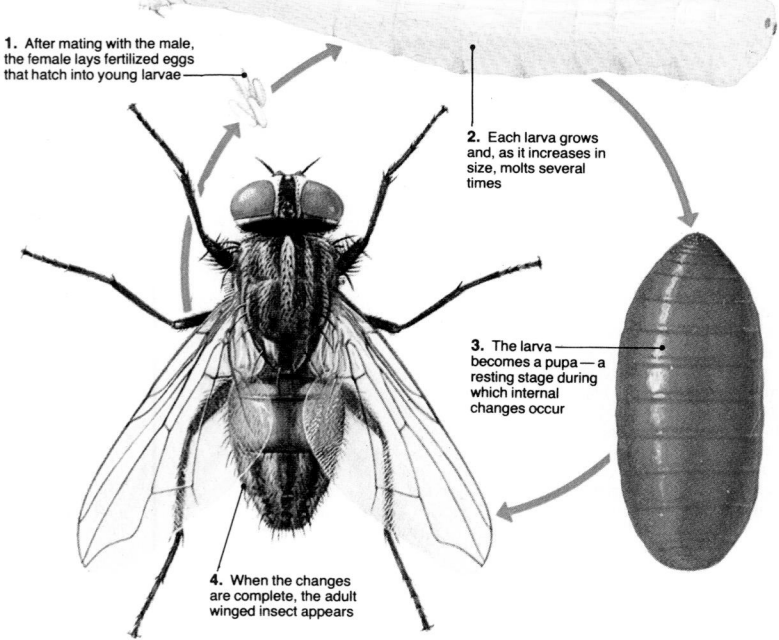

1. After mating with the male, the female lays fertilized eggs that hatch into young larvae

2. Each larva grows and, as it increases in size, molts several times

3. The larva becomes a pupa—a resting stage during which internal changes occur

4. When the changes are complete, the adult winged insect appears

A fly exists in four stages: egg, larva, pupa, and adult insect. Because its skin does not stretch, a growing larva sheds its skin several times; it emerges each time larger and with a new skin.

---

2. *Botany.* Capable of trapping and absorbing insects, as the pitcher plant or Venus's flytrap. [INSECT + -VOROUS.]
insectivorous bat *n.* Any of various bats of the suborder Microchiroptera, characteristically having large ears and feeding on insects.
in·se·cure (ĭn′sĭ-kyŏŏr′) *adj.* **1.** Not secure or safe; inadequately guarded or protected. **2.** Not firm or firmly fixed; unstable; shaky.

3. Apprehensive or lacking self-confidence: *felt insecure in company.* —**in·se·cure·ly** *adv.* —**in·se·cu·ri·ty, in·se·cure·ness** *n.*
in·sel·berg (ĭn′zəl-bûrg′) *n.* A domed hill or hard rock rising steeply from the surrounding region. [German : *Insel,* island + *Berg,* mountain.]
in·sem·i·nate (ĭn-sĕm′ə-nāt′) *tr.v.* **-nated, -nating, -nates. 1.** To sow seed in. **2.** To introduce semen into the uterus of. **3.** To introduce (ideas) into the mind of another. [Latin *insēmināre : in-,* in + *sēmināre,* to plant, from *sēmen* (stem *sēmin-*), seed, SEMEN.] —**in·sem·i·na·tion** *n.* —**in·sem·i·na·tor** *n.*
in·sen·sate (ĭn-sĕn′sāt′, -sĭt) *adj.* **1. a.** Lacking sensation; inanimate. **b.** Unconscious. **2.** Lacking sensibility; inhuman; unfeeling. **3.** Lacking sense; foolish. —**in·sen·sate·ly** *adv.*
in·sen·si·ble (ĭn-sĕn′sə-bəl) *adj.* **1.** Deprived of the power of feeling; unconscious. **2.** Imperceptible; inappreciable: *an insensible change.* **3. a.** Insusceptible; unaffected: *insensible to the cold.* **b.** Unaware; unmindful: *I am not insensible of your concern.* **c.** Not emotionally affected; unfeeling; indifferent: *insensible to their cries of pain.* **4.** *Archaic.* Lacking intelligence; irrational. —**in·sen·si·bil·i·ty** *n.* —**in·sen·si·bly** *adv.*
in·sen·si·tive (ĭn-sĕn′sə-tĭv) *adj.* **1.** Lacking sensation; not physically sensitive. **2.** Lacking sensitivity; unfeeling, unresponsive, or tactless. —**in·sen·si·tiv·i·ty, in·sen·si·tive·ness** *n.* —**in·sen·si·tive·ly** *adv.*
in·sen·ti·ent (ĭn-sĕn′shənt) *adj.* Without sensation or consciousness; inanimate. —**in·sen·ti·ence** *n.*
in·sep·a·ra·ble (ĭn-sĕp′ər-ə-bəl) *adj.* **1.** Incapable of being separated. **2.** Always together; intimate. —**in·sep·a·ra·bil·i·ty, in·sep·a·ra·ble·ness** *n.* —**in·sep·a·ra·bly** *adv.*
in·sert (ĭn-sûrt′) *tr.v.* **-serted, -serting, -serts. 1.** To put or set into, between, or among another or other things. **2.** To introduce into the body or text of something; interpolate.
~*n.* (ĭn′sûrt′). Something inserted; especially, printed material, such as a map or advertising feature, inserted in a book or magazine. [Latin *inserere* (past participle *insertus*) : *in-,* in + *serere,* to sow, plant.] —**in·sert·er** *n.*
in·sert·ed (ĭn-sûr′tĭd) *adj.* **1.** Joined to another part, as stamens to a corolla. **2.** *Anatomy.* Attached to the bone or other part that it moves. Said of a muscle.
in·ser·tion (ĭn-sûr′shən) *n.* **1.** The act of inserting. **2.** Something inserted, such as an advertisement in a newspaper. **3.** *Anatomy.* A point or mode of attachment of a muscle to a bone. **4.** A strip of lace, embroidery, or other trimming to be inserted in a garment, tablecloth, or the like. **5.** *Botany.* The point at which one part is attached to another. —**in·ser·tion·al** *adj.*
in·ser·vice (ĭn′sûr′vĭs) *adj.* Occurring while one is employed or in the context of one's work: *in-service training.*
in·ses·so·ri·al (ĭn′sə-sôr′ē-əl, -sōr′ē-əl) *adj.* *Rare.* Perching or adapted for perching: *insessorial claws.* [Late Latin *insessor,* "one that perches," from Latin *insidēre* (past participle *insessus*), to sit upon : *in-,* on + *sedēre,* to sit.]
in·set (ĭn-sĕt′) *tr.v.* **-set, -setting, -sets.** To insert; set in.
~*n.* (ĭn′sĕt′). **1.** Something set in, as: **a.** A small map or illustration set within a larger one. **b.** A leaf or group of pages inserted in a publication. **c.** A piece of material set into a dress as trimming. **2.** An inflow, as of water.
in·shore (ĭn′shôr′, -shōr′) *adj.* **1.** Situated or taking place close to the shore. **2.** Coming toward the shore. —**in·shore** *adv.*
inshrine. Variant of **enshrine.**
in·side (ĭn-sīd′, ĭn′sīd′) *n.* **1.** The inner or interior part. **2.** An inner side or surface. **3.** The middle part; the part away from the edge: *the inside of the path.* **4. insides.** *Informal.* **a.** The inner organs; the entrails. **b.** The inner parts or workings. **5.** A position affording access to exclusive or confidential information. —**inside out. 1.** With the inner surface turned out; reversed. **2.** Completely; thoroughly: *knows her subject inside out.* —**on the inside.** In a position of confidence or influence.
~*adj.* **1.** Situated within; interior. **2.** For the interior. **3.** Involving or coming from those having access to exclusive knowledge: *inside information.* **4.** *Baseball.* Passing too near the body of the batter. Said of a pitch.
~*adv.* (ĭn-sīd′). **1.** Into or in the interior; within. **2.** *British Slang.* In or into prison. **3.** In one's inner feelings or nature: *made me feel good inside.*
~*prep.* (ĭn-sīd′). **1. a.** Within: *inside an hour.* **b.** Less than: *His running time is well inside the record.* **2.** Into: *to go inside the house.* —**inside of.** Within the boundaries or limits of.
inside job *n.* A crime committed by, or with the complicity of, someone who works or lives where the crime is committed.
Inside Passage. Also **In·land Passage** (ĭn′lənd). Natural, protected waterway, *c.* 1,530 kilometers (950 miles) long, off the coast of British Columbia and southeast Alaska. Its scenic wonders include snow-capped mountains, waterfalls, glaciers, and narrow channels.
in·sid·er (ĭn-sī′dər) *n.* **1.** An accepted member of a clique. **2.** One who has access to exclusive or confidential information.
inside track *n.* **1.** In a curved race track, the path next to the inner rail. **2.** An advantageous position in a competition.
in·sid·i·ous (ĭn-sĭd′ē-əs) *adj.* **1.** Working or spreading harmfully in a subtle or stealthy manner: *insidious disease.* **2.** Intended or seeking to entrap with guile: *insidious argument.* **3.** Wily; treacherous. [Latin *insidiōsus,* "lying in wait for," from *insidiae,* ambush, from

insidēre, to sit in or on, lie in wait for. See **insessorial.**] **—in·sid·i·ous·ly** *adv.* **—in·sid·i·ous·ness** *n.*

in·sight (ĭn′sīt′) *n.* **1.** The capacity to discern the true nature of a situation; penetration. **2.** An elucidating glimpse. **3.** *Psychology.* **a.** In behavioral studies, the sudden perception by an animal of a solution to a problem or difficulty. **b.** In psychoanalysis, a patient's perception of his own mental condition.

in·sight·ful (ĭn′sīt′fəl, ĭn-sīt′-) *adj.* Showing or having insight; perceptive. **—in·sight·ful·ly** *adv.*

in·sig·ni·a (ĭn-sĭg′nē-ə) *n., pl.* **insignia** or **-as.** Also **in·sig·ne** (-nē). **1.** A badge of office, rank, membership, or nationality; an emblem. **2.** A distinguishing sign: *the insignia of success.* [Latin, plural of *insigne,* sign, mark, from *insignis,* distinguished, marked : *in-,* in + *signum,* SIGN.]

Usage: This word is now generally used as a singular, with plural forms being either *insignia* or *insignias.* The original singular, *insigne,* is rare and is restricted to technical contexts.

in·sig·nif·i·cant (ĭn′sĭg-nĭf′ĭ-kənt) *adj.* **1. a.** Trivial; unimportant. **b.** Lacking significant features or character. **c.** Contemptible. **2.** Small; trifling. **—in·sig·nif·i·cance, in·sig·nif·i·can·cy** *n.* **—in·sig·nif·i·cant·ly** *adv.*

in·sin·cere (ĭn′sĭn-sîr′) *adj.* Not sincere; hypocritical. **—in·sin·cere·ly** *adv.* **—in·sin·cer·i·ty** (ĭn′sĭn-sĕr′ə-tē) *n.*

in·sin·u·ate (ĭn-sĭn′yo͞o-āt′) *v.* **-ated, -ating, -ates.** *—tr.* **1.** To introduce gradually, subtly, artfully, or insidiously. **2.** To convey or imply with oblique hints and allusions; hint covertly: *insinuated that I wasn't telling the truth.* *—intr.* To make insinuations. —See Synonyms at **suggest.** [Latin *insinuāre,* to wind one's way into : *in-,* in + *sinuāre,* to curve, from *sinus,* curve, SINUS.] **—in·sin·u·a·tive** *adj.* **—in·sin·u·a·tor** *n.*

in·sin·u·at·ing (ĭn-sĭn′yo͞o-ā′tĭng) *adj.* **1.** Provoking gradual doubt or suspicion; suggestive: *insinuating remarks.* **2.** Ingratiating: *a silky insinuating voice.* **—in·sin·u·at·ing·ly** *adv.*

in·sin·u·a·tion (ĭn-sĭn′yo͞o-ā′shən) *n.* **1.** The act or practice of insinuating. **2.** An artfully indirect suggestion.

in·sip·id (ĭn-sĭp′ĭd) *adj.* **1.** Lacking flavor or zest; unpalatable: *insipid food.* **2.** Lacking excitement or the ability to excite; spiritless; dull; unstimulating: *an insipid character.* [Late Latin *insipidus* : Latin *in-,* not + *sapidus,* SAPID.] **—in·si·pid·i·ty** (ĭn′sĭ-pĭd′ə-tē), **in·sip·id·ness** *n.* **—in·sip·id·ly** *adv.*

in·sist (ĭn-sĭst′) *v.* **-sisted, -sisting, -sists.** *—intr.* To emphasize or keep resolutely to an assertion, demand, or course of action. Usually used with *on* or *upon*: *insisted on her rights; insisted on paying the bill.* *—tr.* To assert or demand positively and persistently: *He insisted that he was right.* [Latin *insistere,* to stand on, persist : *in-,* on + *sistere,* to cause to stand, stand firm.] **—in·sis·tence, in·sis·ten·cy** *n.*

in·sis·tent (ĭn-sĭs′tənt) *adj.* **1.** Persistent; pertinacious. **2.** Demanding notice: *insistent hunger.* **—in·sis·tent·ly** *adv.*

in si·tu (ĭn sī′to͞o, sĭt′o͞o) *adv. Latin.* In (its original) place.

insnare. Variant of **ensnare.**

in·so·bri·e·ty (ĭn′sə-brī′ə-tē) *n.* Lack of sobriety; intemperance.

in·so·far (ĭn′sō-fär′) *adv.* To such an extent.

Usage: The writing of this form as a single word, followed by *as,* is now widespread, though it is still criticized by traditionalist writers on usage, who recommend separate words: *in so far as.*

insofar as *conj.* To the extent that.

in·so·late (ĭn′sō-lāt′) *tr.v.* **-lated, -lating, -lates.** To expose to sunlight, as for bleaching. [Latin *insōlāre* : *in-,* in + *sōl,* sun.]

in·so·la·tion (ĭn′sō-lā′shən) *n.* **1.** Exposure to sunlight, as for therapeutic purposes. **2. Sunstroke** *(see).* **3. a.** The solar radiation falling on the earth or another planet. **b.** The rate of delivery of such radiation per unit surface area.

in·sole (ĭn′sōl′) *n.* **1.** The inner sole of a shoe or boot. **2.** An extra strip of material put inside a shoe for comfort or protection.

in·so·lence (ĭn′sə-ləns) *n.* **1.** The quality of being insolent. **2.** An instance of insolent behavior.

in·so·lent (ĭn′sə-lənt) *adj.* **1.** Presumptuous and insulting in manner or speech; arrogant. **2.** Audaciously impudent; impertinent. [Middle English, from Latin *insolēns,* perhaps originally "unusual," "quaint" : *in-,* not + *solēns* (stem *solent-*), present participle of *solēre,* to use (see **obsolete**).] **—in·so·lent·ly** *adv.*

in·sol·u·ble (ĭn-sŏl′yə-bəl) *adj.* **1. a.** Incapable of being dissolved in water. **b.** Incapable of being dissolved in the specified solvent. **2.** Not able to be solved or explained. [Middle English *insolible,* from Latin *insolūbilis* : *in-,* not + *solvere,* to SOLVE.] **—in·sol·u·bil·i·ty, in·sol·u·ble·ness** *n.* **—in·sol·u·bly** *adv.*

in·solv·a·ble (ĭn-sŏl′və-bəl) *adj.* Incapable of being solved. **—in·solv·a·bil·i·ty** *n.* **—in·solv·a·bly** *adv.*

in·sol·vent (ĭn-sŏl′vənt) *adj.* **1.** Unable to meet debts or discharge liabilities; bankrupt. **2.** Pertaining to bankruptcy or bankrupt persons.

~n. One who is insolvent. **—in·sol·ven·cy** *n.*

in·som·ni·a (ĭn-sŏm′nē-ə) *n.* Chronic inability to sleep. [Latin, from *insomnis,* sleepless : *in-,* not + *somnus,* sleep.] **—in·som·ni·ous** *adj.*

in·som·ni·ac (ĭn-sŏm′nē-ăk′) *n.* A person suffering from insomnia.

~adj. Causing or exhibiting insomnia.

in·so·much as (ĭn′sō-mŭch′ăz′) *conj.* **1.** To such extent or degree. **2.** Since; inasmuch. [Middle English *in so muche,* translation of Old French *en tant (que).*]

in·sou·ci·ance (ĭn-so͞o′sē-əns) *n.* Lack of concern; lighthearted indifference.

in·sou·ci·ant (ĭn-so͞o′sē-ənt) *adj.* Blithely indifferent; carefree. [French : *in-,* not + *souciant,* present participle of *soucier,* to trouble, upset (reflexively, "to care"), from Latin *sollicitāre,* to agitate, vex (see **solicit**).] **—in·sou·ci·ant·ly** *adv.*

insoul. Variant of **ensoul.**

insp. inspector.

in·span (ĭn-spăn′, ĭn′spăn′) *v.* **-spanned, -spanning, -spans.** *Chiefly South African.* *—tr.* **1.** To harness (a draft animal) as to a wagon. **2.** To prepare (a wagon, for example) for a journey. *—intr.* **1.** To inspan a draft animal. **2.** To prepare for a journey, as by making a wagon ready. [Afrikaans, from Middle Dutch *inspannen,* from *spannen,* to yoke.]

in·spect (ĭn-spĕkt′) *tr.v.* **-spected, -specting, -spects.** **1.** To examine carefully and critically, especially for flaws. **2.** To review or examine officially: *inspecting the troops.* [Latin *inspectāre,* frequentative of *inspicere* (past participle *inspectus*), to look into : *in-,* in + *specere,* to look.] **—in·spect·ive** *adj.*

in·spec·tion (ĭn-spĕk′shən) *n.* **1.** The act of inspecting. **2.** An examination, scrutiny, or review, especially one of a formal or official character: *an inspection of the troops.* **—in·spec·tion·al** *adj.*

in·spec·tor (ĭn-spĕk′tər) *n. Abbr.* **ins., insp.** **1.** One who inspects; especially, an official whose job it is to examine and supervise the running of a particular operation, institution, or organization, and to ensure that the appropriate rules and standards are maintained. **2.** A police officer of the rank next below superintendent and above sergeant. **—in·spec·to·ral, in·spec·to·ri·al** (ĭn′spĕk-tôr′ē-əl, -tōr′-ē-əl) *adj.* **—in·spec·tor·ship** *n.*

in·spec·tor·ate (ĭn-spĕk′tər-ĭt) *n.* **1.** The office or duties of an inspector. **2.** A staff of inspectors. **3.** An inspector's district.

inspector general *n., pl.* **inspectors general.** **1.** A person in charge of a staff of inspectors or a system of inspection. **2.** An officer having investigative powers in the armed forces.

insphere. Variant of **ensphere.**

in·spi·ra·tion (ĭn′spə-rā′shən) *n.* **1.** Stimulation of the mental or emotional faculties to a high level of feeling, animation, or creative activity. **2.** The condition of being so stimulated. **3.** Someone or something perceived as the source of such stimulation: *His example was an inspiration to us all.* **4.** Something that is inspired, such as an idea or action. **5.** *Theology.* Divine guidance or influence exerted directly upon the mind and soul of humankind. **6.** The act of breathing in; inhalation.

in·spi·ra·tion·al (ĭn′spə-rā′shən-əl) *adj.* **1.** Of or pertaining to inspiration. **2.** Providing or intended to convey inspiration. **3.** Resulting from inspiration. **—in·spi·ra·tion·al·ly** *adv.*

in·spi·ra·tor (ĭn′spə-rā′tər) *n.* **1.** An inhaler. **2.** A respirator.

in·spir·a·to·ry (ĭn-spīr′ə-tôr′ē, -tōr′ē) *adj.* Pertaining to or used for the drawing in of air.

in·spire (ĭn-spīr′) *v.* **-spired, -spiring, -spires.** *—tr.* **1.** To animate the mind or emotions of; serve as a source of inspiration to: *inspired by his rousing speech.* **2.** To stimulate or impel to a particular feeling or action: *inspired her to be brave.* **3. a.** To elicit; bring forth: *a woman capable of inspiring love.* **b.** To suggest or bring about; serve as a source of inspiration for: *a whole poem inspired by that fleeting smile.* **4. a.** To affect, guide, or arouse by divine influence. **b.** To communicate by divine influence: *oratory inspired by God.* **5.** To inhale (air). **6.** *Archaic.* **a.** To breathe upon. **b.** To breathe life into. *—intr.* **1.** To rouse latent energies, ideals, or reverence. **2.** To inhale. [Middle English *inspiren,* from Old French *inspirer,* from Latin *inspīrāre,* to breathe into : *in-,* into + *spīrāre,* to breathe.] **—in·spir·er** *n.* **—in·spir·ing·ly** *adv.*

in·spired (ĭn-spīrd′) *adj.* Resulting from or as if from inspiration: *an inspired guess; an inspired performance.*

in·spir·it (ĭn-spĭr′ĭt) *tr.v.* **-ited, -iting, -its.** To instill courage or life into; animate; enliven.

in·spis·sate (ĭn-spĭs′āt′, ĭn′spĭ-sāt′) *v.* **-sated, -sating, -sates.** *—tr.* To cause to thicken, as by boiling or evaporation; condense. *—intr.* To thicken. [Late Latin *inspissāre* : Latin *in-* (intensive) + *spissāre,* to thicken, from *spissus*†, thick.] **—in·spis·sa·tion** *n.* **—in·spis·sa·tor** (ĭn-spĭs′ā′tər) *n.*

inst. **1.** instance. **2.** instant. **3.** institute; institution. **4.** instrument.

Inst. institute; institution.

in·sta·bil·i·ty (ĭn′stə-bĭl′ə-tē) *n., pl.* **-ties.** Lack of stability, firmness, or steadiness: *emotional instability.*

in·stall, in·stal (ĭn-stôl′) *tr.v.* **-stalled, -stalling, -stalls** or **-stals.** **1.** To set (a machine, for example) in position and connect or adjust for use. **2.** To put in an office, rank, or position, especially with ceremonies. **3.** To settle in the place or condition specified; establish. Often used reflexively: *He installed himself by the window.* [Old French *installer,* from Medieval Latin *installāre* : *in-* (causative) + *stallum,* place, stall.] **—in·stall·er** *n.*

in·stal·la·tion (ĭn′stə-lā′shən) *n.* **1.** The act of installing or the state of being installed. **2.** A system of machinery or other apparatus set up for use. **3.** A military base or camp.

in·stall·ment[1]**, in·stal·ment** (ĭn-stôl′mənt) *n.* **1.** One of several successive payments in settlement of a debt. **2.** A portion of anything issued at intervals. **3.** A chapter, episode, or part of a work presented serially. [Variant of earlier *estallment,* from Norman French *estalement,* from *estaler,* to fix (as payments), from *estal,* place, fixed position, from Old High German *stal,* place, stall.]

installment[2]**, instalment** *n.* The act of installing (sense 2) or state of being installed.

installment plan *n.* A credit system by which payment for merchandise is made in installments over a fixed period of time.

in·stance (ĭn′stəns) *n. Abbr.* **inst.** **1.** A case or example. **2.** A legal

PRONUNCIATION KEY

ă, pat; ā, pay; âr, care;
ä, father, are; b, bib;
ch, church; d, deed; ĕ, pet;
ē, be; f, fife; g, gag; h, hat;
hw, which; ĭ, pit; ī, pie;
îr, pier; j, judge; k, kick;
l, lid, needle; m, mum;
n, no, sudden; ng, thing;
ŏ, pot; ō, toe; ô, paw, for;
oi, noise; ou, out; o͝o, book;
o͞o, boot; p, pop; r, roar;
s, sauce; sh, ship, dish;
t, tight; th, thin, path;
th, this, bathe; ŭ, cut; ûr, fur;
v, valve; w, with; y, yes;
z, zebra, size; zh, vision;
ə, about, item, edible,
gallop, circus, peaceful

IN FOREIGN WORDS:

à, *Fr.* ami; œ, *Fr.* feu, *Ger.* schön; ü, *Fr.* tu, *Ger.* über; KH, *Ger.* ich, *Scot.* loch; N, *Fr.* bon; y′, *Fr.* Compiègne

STRESS MARKS:

Primary stress: ′
in·cite′ (ĭn-sīt′)
Secondary stress: ′
in′sight′ (ĭn′sīt′)

proceeding or process; a suit: *a court of first instance.* **3.** A specified step in a procedure or list of considerations: *Apply in the first instance to the personnel manager.* **4. a.** Prompting; request: *He called at the instance of his wife.* **b.** *Archaic.* Urgent solicitation. —See Synonyms at **example.** —**for instance.** For example.
~*tr.v.* **instanced, -stancing, -stances. 1.** To offer as an example; cite. **2.** To demonstrate or show by being an example of; exemplify. [Middle English *instaunce,* from Old French *instance,* from Latin *instantia,* presence, perseverance, urgency, from *instāns,* INSTANT.]
in·stan·cy (ĭn′stən-sē) *n.* **1.** Urgency. **2.** *Rare.* Immediateness.
in·stant (ĭn′stənt) *n. Abbr.* **inst. 1.** A very brief time; a moment: *He arrived in an instant.* **2.** A particular point in time: *the instant she arrives.* —See Synonyms at **moment.**
~*adj. Abbr.* **inst. 1.** Immediate: *instant attention.* **2.** Imperative; urgent: *an instant need.* **3.** Of the current month: *my letter of the fifth instant.* Compare **proximo, ultimo. 4.** Prepared or devised so as to be made usable or accessible rapidly and with minimal effort: *instant soup; instant history.*
~*adv. Poetic.* Instantly. [Middle English, urgent, immediate, from Old French, from Latin *instāns* (stem *instant-*), present participle of *instāre,* to stand upon, be present, persist : *in-,* upon + *stāre,* to stand.]
in·stan·ta·ne·ous (ĭn′stən-tā′nē-əs) *adj.* **1.** Occurring or completed without perceptible delay. **2.** Occurring or applying at a specific instance of time. Said of changing physical quantities that are considered at a given instance: *instantaneous pressure.* [Medieval Latin *instantāneus,* from Latin *instāns,* urgent, INSTANT.] —**in·stan·ta·ne·ous·ly** *adv.* —**in·stan·ta·ne·ous·ness** *n.*
in·stan·ter (ĭn-stăn′tər) *adv.* Instantly. [Medieval Latin, from Latin, urgently, from *instāns,* urgent, INSTANT.]
in·stant·ly (ĭn′stənt-lē) *adv.* **1.** At once. **2.** *Archaic.* Urgently. —See Synonyms at **immediately.**
~*conj.* As soon as: *tell me instantly she comes.*
instant replay *n.* A recording of an event, such as a sports play, on videotape for playback, especially in slow motion, as soon as the event is completed. Also *British* "action replay."
in·star (ĭn′stär) *n.* **1.** An insect or other arthropod between molts, as during metamorphosis. **2.** This stage of development. [New Latin, from Latin *instar*†, form, likeness (referring to the successive forms of the arthropod after each molt, as *first instar, second instar,* and so on).]
in·state (ĭn-stāt′) *tr.v.* **-stated, -stating, -states.** To put in office; install. [IN- (causative) + STATE (rank).] —**in·state·ment** *n.*
in sta·tu quo (ĭn stā′cho͞o kwō′; stă′-, stăch′o͞o-) *adv. Latin.* In the same state or condition as before.
in·stau·ra·tion (ĭn′stô-rā′shən) *n. Archaic.* **1.** Renovation; restoration. **2.** Institution; establishment. [Latin *instaurātiō* (stem *instaurātiōn-*), from *instaurāre,* to restore.] —**in·stau·ra·tor** *n.*
in·stead (ĭn-stĕd′) *adv.* In the place of that previously mentioned or implied; as an alternative or substitute: *Planning to drive, he walked instead.* —**instead of.** In lieu of; rather than: *"Instead of eating monkeys/They are eating Christians"* (T.S. Eliot). [Middle English *in sted (of)* : IN + STEAD.]
in·step (ĭn′stĕp′) *n.* **1.** The arched, middle section of the human foot. **2.** The part of a shoe, stocking, or the like, covering the instep. [Probably IN + STEP.]
in·sti·gate (ĭn′stĭ-gāt′) *tr.v.* **-gated, -gating, -gates. 1.** To urge on; goad; incite, especially to wrongdoing. **2.** To foment; stir up. [Latin *instīgāre* : *in-* (intensive) + *stīgāre,* to spur on.] —**in·sti·ga·tion** *n.* —**in·sti·ga·tive** *adj.* —**in·sti·ga·tor** *n.*
in·still (ĭn-stĭl′) *tr.v.* **-stilled, -stilling, -stills.** Also *chiefly British* **in·stil, -stilled, -stilling, -stils. 1.** To introduce or impart by gradual, persistent efforts; implant. **2.** To pour in drop by drop. [Latin *instillāre,* to drip in : *in-,* in + *stillāre,* to drip, from *stilla*†, drop.] —**in·stil·la·tion** (ĭn′stə-lā′shən) *n.* —**in·still·er** *n.* —**in·still·ment, in·stil·ment** *n.*
in·stinct (ĭn′stĭngkt′) *n.* **1. a.** The innate aspect of behavior that is unlearned, complex, and normally adaptive. **b.** A powerful intuition or impulse. **2.** An innate aptitude: *an instinct for picking a winner.*
~*adj.* (ĭn-stĭngkt′). *Archaic.* Imbued or charged with something, such as energy. [Middle English, from Latin *instinctus,* instigation, from the past participle of *instinguere,* to instigate, urge on : *in-,* on + *stinguere,* to prick, incite.] —**in·stinc·tu·al** *adj.*
in·stinc·tive (ĭn-stĭngk′tĭv) *adj.* **1.** Of or pertaining to instinct. **2.** Arising from instinct. —See Synonyms at **spontaneous.** —**in·stinc·tive·ly** *adv.*
in·sti·tute (ĭn′stə-to͞ot′, -tyo͞ot′) *tr.v.* **-tuted, -tuting, -tutes. 1. a.** To establish, organize, and set in operation. **b.** To initiate; begin. **2.** To establish or invest in a position; especially, to install (a clergyman) in a position of spiritual authority.
~*n.* **1.** Something instituted, especially: **a.** An authoritative rule or precedent. **b. institutes.** A digest of the principles or rudiments of some subject, especially law. **2.** *Abbr.* **inst., Inst. a.** An organization or association set up to promote some cause. **b.** An educational institution. **c.** The building or buildings of such an organization or institution. **3.** A short, intensive workshop or seminar on one specific subject. [Middle English *instituten,* from Latin *instituere,* to establish, ordain : *in-,* in + *statuere,* to set up, from *stāre* (past participle *status*), to stand.] —**in·sti·tu·tor** *n.*
in·sti·tu·tion (ĭn′stə-to͞o′shən, -tyo͞o′shən) *n. Abbr.* **inst., Inst. 1.** The act of instituting. **2. a.** A relationship or behavioral pattern of importance in the life of a community or society: *the institution of marriage.* **b.** *Informal.* An ever-present feature; a fixture: *His corny jokes were a family institution.* **3.** An organization or establishment set up to perform a specific charitable, religious, educational, or other public service. **4.** The building or buildings housing such an organization. **5.** A place of confinement, such as a mental hospital.
in·sti·tu·tion·al (ĭn′stə-to͞o′shə-nəl, -tyo͞o′shə-nəl) *adj.* **1.** Of or pertaining to institutions. **2.** Organized through institutions or as an institution: *institutional religion.* **3.** Characteristic or suggestive of an institution, especially in being uniform, dull, or unimaginative: *institutional furniture.* **4.** Of or pertaining to the principles or institutes of a subject such as law. —**in·sti·tu·tion·al·ly** *adv.*
in·sti·tu·tion·al·ism (ĭn′stə-to͞o′shə-nə-lĭz′əm, ĭn′stə-tyo͞o′-) *n.* **1.** Belief in established forms, such as those of a religion, sometimes to the virtual exclusion of other considerations. **2.** The provision of institutional care or maintenance for those in need. —**in·sti·tu·tion·al·ist** *n. & adj.*
in·sti·tu·tion·al·ize (ĭn′stə-to͞o′shə-nə-līz′, ĭn′stə-tyo͞o′-) *tr.v.* **-ized, -izing, izes. 1.** To make into an institution; give legal or institutional status to. **2.** To confine (a person) in an institution. **3.** To expose to the harmful effects of long-term confinement in an institution, producing apathy, dependence, and boredom. —**in·sti·tu·tion·al·i·za·tion** *n.*
instr. 1. instruction; instructor. **2.** instrument; instrumental.
in·stroke (ĭn′strōk′) *n.* An inward stroke, especially a piston stroke moving away from the crankshaft.
in·struct (ĭn-strŭkt′) *v.* **-structed, -structing, -structs.** —*tr.* **1.** To furnish with knowledge; teach; educate. **2.** To provide with authoritative directions; give orders to. **3.** *Law.* To provide (a jury) with a full elucidation of the points of law in a particular case. —*intr.* To serve as an instructor. —See Synonyms at **command, teach.** [Middle English *instructen,* from Latin *instruere* (past participle *instructus*), to build, prepare, instruct : *in-,* in + *struere,* to build.]
in·struc·tion (ĭn-strŭk′shən) *n. Abbr.* **instr. 1.** The act, practice, or profession of instructing; education. **2. a.** Imparted knowledge. **b.** An imparted or acquired item of knowledge; a lesson. **3. instructions.** Directions; orders. **4.** *Computer Science.* A part of a program that causes the computer to perform a specific operation. —**in·struc·tion·al** *adj.*
in·struc·tive (ĭn-strŭk′tĭv) *adj.* Conveying knowledge or information. —**in·struc·tive·ly** *adv.* —**in·struc·tive·ness** *n.*
in·struc·tor (ĭn-strŭk′tər) *n. Abbr.* **instr. 1.** One who instructs; a teacher. **2. a.** An academic rank below that of assistant professor. **b.** One who holds such a rank. —**in·struc·tor·ship** *n.*
in·stru·ment (ĭn′strə-mənt) *n. Abbr.* **inst., instr. 1.** A means by which something is done; agency. **2.** One used to accomplish some purpose. **3.** A mechanical implement; tool. **4.** A device for recording or measuring; especially, such a device functioning as part of a control system, as in an aircraft, for example. **5.** A device for producing or playing music: *a stringed instrument.* **6.** A legal document. —See Synonyms at **tool.**
~*tr.v.* **instrumented, -menting, -ments. 1.** To provide or equip with instruments. **2.** To arrange (music) for instruments. [Middle English, from Latin *instrūmentum,* implement, equipment, tool, from *instruere,* to prepare, equip, INSTRUCT.]
in·stru·men·tal (ĭn′strə-mĕnt′l) *adj.* **1.** Serving as a means or instrument; contributing decisively to some outcome. **2.** Of, pertaining to, or accomplished with an instrument or tool. **3.** Performed on or written for a musical instrument or instruments rather than the voice. **4.** *Grammar.* Of or designating a case in Russian, Sanskrit, and certain other inflected languages, used typically to express means, agency, or accompaniment.
~*n.* **1.** The instrumental case. **2.** A form or construction in this case. —**in·stru·men·tal·ly** *adv.*
in·stru·men·tal·ism (ĭn′strə-mĕnt′l-ĭz′əm) *n.* A pragmatic theory that ideas are instruments that function as guides of action, their validity being measured by the success of the action.
in·stru·men·tal·ist (ĭn′strə-mĕnt′l-ĭst) *n.* **1.** One who plays a musical instrument. **2.** A student or advocate of instrumentalism.
in·stru·men·tal·i·ty (ĭn′strə-mĕn-tăl′ə-tē) *n., pl.* **-ties. 1.** The quality or circumstance of being instrumental. **2.** Agency; means.
in·stru·men·ta·tion (ĭn′strə-mĕn-tā′shən) *n.* **1. a.** The application or use of instruments in the performance of some work. **b.** Instruments collectively. **2.** The study and practice of arranging music for instruments. **3.** The study, development, and manufacture of instruments, as for scientific use. **4.** Instrumentality.
instrument flying *n.* The flying of an aircraft using only the recording instruments and radio instructions from the ground, without visual observation.
instrument panel *n.* A mounted array of instruments used to monitor performance. Also called "instrument board."
in·sub·or·di·nate (ĭn′sə-bôrd′n-ĭt) *adj.* Not submissive to authority; rebellious.
~*n.* An insubordinate person. —**in·sub·or·di·nate·ly** *adv.* —**in·sub·or·di·na·tion** *n.*
Usage: *insubordinate, rebellious, mutinous, factious, seditious.* These adjectives are applied to persons or their actions and mean in opposition to, and usually in defiance of, established authority. *Insubordinate* implies failure to recognize or accept the authority of a superior. *Rebellious* implies open defiance of authority to which one is subject. *Mutinous,* a still stronger term, pertains to uprising against lawful authority, especially that of a naval or military command. *Factious* describes what promotes divisiveness, dissension, or

disunity within a group or organization. *Seditious* applies principally to the stirring up of resistance against a government.

in·sub·stan·tial (ĭn′səb-stăn′shəl) *adj.* **1.** Lacking substance; imaginary. **2.** Not firm; unsubstantial. —**in·sub·stan·ti·al·i·ty** (ĭn′səb-stăn′shē-ăl′ə-tē) *n.*

in·suf·fer·a·ble (ĭn-sŭf′ər-ə-bəl) *adj.* Not endurable; intolerable. —**in·suf·fer·a·ble·ness** *n.* —**in·suf·fer·a·bly** *adv.*

in·suf·fi·cien·cy (ĭn′sə-fĭsh′ən-sē) *n., pl.* **-cies. 1.** The quality or state of being insufficient. **2.** A lack or deficiency, as of some requisite thing or quality. **3.** *Medicine.* Inability of an organ to function properly.

in·suf·fi·cient (ĭn′sə-fĭsh′ənt) *adj.* Not sufficient; inadequate: *insufficient evidence.* —**in·suf·fi·cient·ly** *adv.*

in·suf·flate (ĭn-sŭf′lāt′, ĭn′sə-flāt′) *tr.v.* **-flated, -flating, -flates. 1.** To blow or breathe into or upon. **2.** To treat medically by blowing a powder, gas, or vapor into a bodily cavity. [Late Latin *insufflāre* : Latin *in-*, into + *sufflāre*, to blow.] —**in·suf·fla·tor** *n.*

in·suf·fla·tion (ĭn′sə-flā′shən) *n.* **1.** The act or an instance of insufflating. **2.** *Ecclesiastical.* A ritual breathing upon a person or thing as a symbol of the influence of the Holy Spirit.

in·su·lar (ĭn′sə-lər, ĭns′yə-) *adj.* **1.** Of, pertaining to, or constituting an island. **2.** Characteristic or suggestive of the isolated life of an island, especially: **a.** Circumscribed and detached in outlook and experience. **b.** Narrow; prejudiced. **3.** *Anatomy.* Designating isolated tissue or an island of tissue. [Late Latin *īnsulāris*, from Latin *īnsula*, island, ISLE.] —**in·su·lar·ism, in·su·lar·i·ty** (ĭn′sə-lăr′ə-tē, ĭns′yə-) *n.* —**in·su·lar·ly** *adv.*

in·su·late (ĭn′sə-lāt′, ĭns′yə-) *tr.v.* **-lated, -lating, -lates. 1. a.** To detach; isolate. **b.** To shield (a person), as from unpleasant realities. **2.** To prevent the passage of heat, electricity, or sound into or out of (a body or region), especially by interposition of an appropriate material. [Originally "to convert into an island," from Latin *īnsula*, island, ISLE.]

in·su·la·tion (ĭn′sə-lā′shən, ĭns′yə-) *n.* **1.** The act of insulating or state of being insulated. **2.** Material used in insulating.

in·su·la·tor (ĭn′sə-lā′tər, ĭns′yə-) *n.* **1.** A material that insulates; especially, a substance that is a poor conductor of heat, electricity, or sound. **2.** A device that insulates.

in·su·lin (ĭn′sə-lən, ĭns′yə-) *n.* **1.** A polypeptide hormone secreted by the islands of Langerhans in the pancreas and functioning to regulate carbohydrate metabolism by controlling blood glucose levels. **2.** A preparation derived from the pancreas of the pig or the ox for use in the medical treatment of diabetes. [Latin *īnsula*, island.]

insulin shock *n.* **1.** Acute hypoglycemia that typically results from an overdose of insulin given to a diabetic and may lead to coma. Also called "insulin reaction." **2.** Such a condition formerly induced artificially for therapeutic purposes in schizophrenics.

in·sult (ĭn-sŭlt′) *v.* **-sulted, -sulting, -sults.** —*tr.* **1. a.** To speak to or treat in a callous or contemptuous way. **b.** To reveal a disdainful estimate of: *The paper's political analysis insults its readers' intelligence.* **2.** *Archaic.* To make an attack upon; assault. —*intr. Obsolete.* To behave arrogantly. —See Synonyms at **offend.**
—*n.* (ĭn′sŭlt). **1.** An offensive action or remark; an affront. **2.** A slur; an aspersion: *Your refusal to confide is an insult to my discretion.* **3.** *Medicine.* An injury, irritation, or trauma. [French *insulter*, to triumph over, behave arrogantly, from Latin *insultāre*, to leap on, jump over : *in-*, on, upon + *saltāre*, frequentative of *salīre*, to jump.]

in·su·per·a·ble (ĭn-so͞o′pər-ə-bəl) *adj.* Incapable of being overcome; insurmountable: *an insuperable barrier.* —**in·su·per·a·bil·i·ty, in·su·per·a·ble·ness** *n.* —**in·su·per·a·bly** *adv.*

in·sup·port·a·ble (ĭn′sə-pôr′tə-bəl, -pōr′tə-bəl) *adj.* **1.** Unbearable; intolerable. **2.** Lacking grounds or defense; unjustifiable: *an insupportable claim.* —**in·sup·port·a·ble·ness** *n.* —**in·sup·port·a·bly** *adv.*

in·sup·press·i·ble (ĭn′sə-prĕs′ə-bəl) *adj.* That cannot be suppressed; irrepressible.

in·sur·ance (ĭn-sho͝or′əns) *n. Abbr.* **ins. 1. a.** The act, business, or process of insuring persons or property. **b.** The state of being insured. **2.** A contract binding a company to indemnify an insured party against stipulated loss, damage, or injury in return for premiums paid. Also called "insurance policy." **3.** The sum for which such a contract insures something. **4.** The periodical premium paid for this indemnification. **5.** A protective measure or device: *took an umbrella as an insurance against rain.*

in·sur·ant (ĭn-sho͝or′ənt) *n.* One who is insured.

in·sure (ĭn-sho͝or′) *v.* **-sured, -suring, -sures.** —*tr.* **1.** To cover with insurance: *Am I insured if I drive your car?* **2.** To make sure or certain; ensure. **3.** To make safe or secure. Used with *from* or *against*: *Nowadays a degree doesn't insure you against unemployment.* —*intr.* To buy or sell insurance. —See Usage note at **assure.** [Middle English *insuren, ensuren*, to guarantee, from Norman French *enseurer*, perhaps variant of Old French *ass(e)urer*, to ASSURE.] —**in·sur·a·bil·i·ty** *n.* —**in·sur·a·ble** *adj.*

in·sured (ĭn-sho͝ord′) *n., pl.* **insured.** One covered by insurance.

in·sur·er (ĭn-sho͝or′ər) *n.* One who insures; an underwriter.

in·sur·gence (ĭn-sûr′jəns) *n.* **1.** Uprising. **2.** An act of revolt.

in·sur·gen·cy (ĭn-sûr′jən-sē) *n.* **1.** The quality or state of being insurgent. **2.** Insurgence.

in·sur·gent (ĭn-sûr′jənt) *adj.* Rising in revolt against civil authority or a government in power.
—*n.* **1.** One who revolts against authority. **2.** A member of a political party who rebels against its leadership. [Latin *insurgēns* (stem *insurgent-*), present participle of *insurgere*, to rise up : *in-* (intensive) + *surgere*, to rise, SURGE.]

in·sur·mount·a·ble (ĭn′sər-moun′tə-bəl) *adj.* Incapable of being surmounted; insuperable: *struggling against insurmountable difficulties.* —**in·sur·mount·a·bly** *adv.*

in·sur·rec·tion (ĭn′sə-rĕk′shən) *n.* An act or instance of open revolt against civil authority or a constituted government. —See Synonyms at **rebellion.** [Middle English *insurrecioun*, from Old French *insurrection*, from Latin *insurrectiō* (stem *insurrectiōn-*), from *insurgere* (past participle *insurrectus*), to rise up. See **insurgent.**] —**in·sur·rec·tion·al** *adj.* —**in·sur·rec·tion·ar·y** *adj. & n.* —**in·sur·rec·tion·ist** *n.*

in·sus·cep·ti·ble (ĭn′sə-sĕp′tə-bəl) *adj.* Not susceptible; unaffected.

int. 1. interest. **2.** interior. **3.** internal. **4.** international. **5.** interval.

in·tact (ĭn-tăkt′) *adj.* **1.** Not impaired in any way. **2.** Having all parts; whole. [Middle English *intacte*, untouched, from Latin *intactus* : *in-*, not + *tactus*, past participle of *tangere*, to touch.] —**in·tact·ness** *n.*

in·ta·glio (ĭn-tăl′yō; *Italian* ĭn-tä′lyō) *n., pl.* **-glios** or **-tagli** (-tăl′yē; *Italian* -tä′lyē). **1. a.** A figure or design incised into the surface of hard metal or stone. **b.** The art or process of making intaglios. **2.** Something, such as a gemstone, carved in intaglio. Compare **cameo. 3.** Printing done with a plate bearing an image in intaglio. **4.** A die incised to produce a design in relief. [Italian, from *intagliare*, to engrave : *in-*, in + *tagliare*, to cut, from (unattested) Vulgar Latin *tālliāre* (see **tailor**).] —**in·ta·glia·ted** *adj.*

in·take (ĭn′tāk′) *n.* **1.** An opening by which a fluid is admitted into a container or conduit. **2.** An airway into a mine. **3. a.** The act of taking in. **b.** A person, thing, or quantity that is taken in or received: *an intake of energy; a fresh intake of members.*

in·tan·gi·ble (ĭn-tăn′jə-bəl) *adj.* **1.** Incapable of being perceived by touch; impalpable. **2.** Imprecisely defined or identified; elusive: *intangible ideas.* —**in·tan·gi·bil·i·ty, in·tan·gi·ble·ness** *n.* —**in·tan·gi·ble** *n.* —**in·tan·gi·bly** *adv.*

in·tar·si·a (ĭn-tär′sē-ə) *n.* **1.** A mosaic worked in wood. **2.** The art or process of making such mosaics. **3. a.** A knitting technique by which large patches of different color are juxtaposed in stocking stitch to form an asymmetrical design, keeping several yarns on the needle at once and joining them by overlapping behind the work. **b.** Work produced or decorated by this method. [Perhaps IN(LAY) + *tarsia*, an inlaid mosaic, from Arabic *tarṣī*.]

intarsia *An ambitious type of inlay work developed in 15th-century Italy. A veneer is inlaid with pieces of different colors to make a pattern or elaborate picture. This example is from a cloister ceiling in the monastery of San Juan de los Reyes in Toledo, Spain.*

in·te·ger (ĭn′tə-jər) *n.* **1.** Any member of the set of positive whole numbers (1, 2, 3, . . .), negative whole numbers (−1, −2, −3, . . .), and zero (0). **2.** Any intact unit or entity. [Latin, whole, complete, perfect, virtuous.]

in·te·gra·ble (ĭn′tə-grə-bəl) *adj. Mathematics.* Capable of being integrated. Said of a function.

in·te·gral (ĭn′tə-grəl) *adj.* **1. a.** Essential for completion; necessary to the whole. **b.** Forming a constituent or intrinsic part; not separate: *a house with an integral garage.* **2.** Whole; entire; intact. **3.** *Mathematics.* **a.** Expressed or expressible as or in terms of integers. **b.** Expressed as or involving integrals.
—*n.* **1.** A complete unit; a whole. **2.** *Mathematics.* The limit of a sum of terms as the number of terms tends to infinity and the terms tend to zero. There are two types: the **definite integral** and the **indefinite integral** *(both of which see).* [Middle English, from Late Latin *integrālis*, making up a whole, from Latin *integer*, whole.] —**in·te·gral·i·ty** *n.* —**in·te·gral·ly** *adv.*

integral calculus *n.* The mathematical study of integration, the properties of integrals, and their applications.

integral domain *n. Mathematics.* A commutative ring with unity having no proper divisors of zero, that is, having no nonzero elements a, b such that $a{\cdot}b = 0$, where 0 is the additive identity.

in·te·grand (ĭn′tə-grănd′) *n.* A mathematical function or equation to be integrated. [Latin *integrandus*, from *integrāre*, to INTEGRATE.]

in·te·grant (ĭn′tə-grənt) *adj.* Integral; constituent. [Latin *integrāns* (stem *integrant-*), present participle of *integrāre*, to INTEGRATE.]

in·te·grate (ĭn′tə-grāt′) *v.* **-grated, -grating, -grates.** —*tr.* **1.** To make into a whole by bringing all parts together; unify. **2.** To unite with or incorporate into a larger body or unit; especially, to cause (members of an ethnically or culturally distinct group) to be assimilated into a society. **3.** To desegregate. **4.** *Mathematics.* To calculate the integral of (a function). **5.** To bring about the harmonious integration of (personality traits): *an integrated personality.* —*intr.* To become integrated or undergo integration. [Latin *integrāre*, to make complete, from *integer*, whole.] —**in·te·gra·tive** *adj.*

in·te·grat·ed circuit (ĭn′tə-grā′tĭd) *n. Abbr.* **IC.** An electronic circuit made of a number of components connected in a single small package, either by fixing small separate components on a ceramic wafer or by building them into the surface of a silicon chip.

in·te·gra·tion (ĭn′tə-grā′shən) *n.* **1. a.** An act or the process of integrating. **b.** The state of becoming integrated. **c.** Desegregation. **2.** The organization of the psychological or social traits and tendencies of a personality into a harmonious whole. **3.** *Physiology.* The processing of information received by the nervous system in such a way that a flexible and coordinated response is made.

in·te·gra·tor (ĭn′tə-grā′tər) *n.* **1.** One that integrates. **2.** An instrument for mechanically calculating definite integrals.

in·teg·ri·ty (ĭn-tĕg′rə-tē) *n.* **1.** Strict adherence to a code of moral values, artistic principles, or other standards; complete sincerity or honesty. **2.** The state of being unimpaired; soundness. **3.** Completeness; unity. —See Synonyms at **honesty.** [Middle English *integrite*, from Old French, from Latin *integritās* (stem *integritāt-*), completeness, purity, from *integer*, whole. See **integer.**]

in·teg·u·ment (ĭn-tĕg′yo͞o-mənt) *n.* An outer covering or coat, such

PRONUNCIATION KEY

ă, pat; ā, pay; âr, care;
ä, father, are; b, bib;
ch, church; d, deed; ĕ, pet;
ē, be; f, fife; g, gag; h, hat;
hw, which; ĭ, pit; ī, pie;
îr, pier; j, judge; k, kick;
l, lid, needle; m, mum;
n, no, sudden; ng, thing;
ŏ, pot; ō, toe; ô, paw, for;
oi, noise; ou, out; o͝o, book;
o͞o, boot; p, pop; r, roar;
s, sauce; sh, ship, dish;
t, tight; th, thin, path;
th, this, bathe; ŭ, cut; ûr, fur;
v, valve; w, with; y, yes;
z, zebra, size; zh, vision;
ə, about, item, edible,
gallop, circus, peaceful

IN FOREIGN WORDS:

à, *Fr.* ami; œ, *Fr.* feu, *Ger.* schön; ü, *Fr.* tu, *Ger.* über; KH, *Ger.* ich, *Scot.* loch; N, *Fr.* bon; y′, *Fr.* Compiègne

STRESS MARKS:

Primary stress: ′
in·cite′ (ĭn-sīt′)
Secondary stress: ′
in′sight′ (ĭn′sīt′)

as the skin of an animal, the coat of a seed, or the membrane enclosing an organ. [Latin *integumentum,* from *integere,* to cover : *in-,* on + *tegere,* to cover.] **—in·teg·u·ment·al, in·teg·u·men·ta·ry** *adj.*

in·tel·lect (ĭn′tə-lĕkt′) *n.* **1. a.** The ability to learn and reason as distinguished from the ability to feel or will; the capacity for knowledge and understanding. **b.** The ability to think abstractly or profoundly. **2. a.** A person of great intellectual ability. **b.** The intellectual members of a group. —See Synonyms at **mind.** [Middle English, from Old French, from Latin *intellectus,* perception, comprehension, from the past participle of *intellegere,* to perceive, choose between. See **intelligent.**]

in·tel·lec·tion (ĭn′tə-lĕk′shən) *n.* **1.** The act or process of exercising the intellect; mental activity. **2.** A thought or idea. [Middle English *intelleccioun,* understanding, from Latin *intellectiō* (stem *intellectiōn-*), from *intellectus,* INTELLECT.]

in·tel·lec·tive (ĭn′tə-lĕk′tĭv) *adj.* Of, pertaining to, or generated by the intellect. **—in·tel·lec·tive·ly** *adv.*

in·tel·lec·tu·al (ĭn′tə-lĕk′cho͞o-əl) *adj.* **1. a.** Of or pertaining to the intellect. **b.** Rational rather than emotional: *an intellectual debate.* **2.** Appealing to or requiring the exercise of the intellect. **3. a.** Having superior intelligence. **b.** Involved in activity requiring the use of the intellect. **c.** Given to or marked by the creative use of the intellect, as expressed in abstract thought, study, and developed artistic and literary tastes. —See Synonyms at **intelligent.**
∼*n.* **1.** An intellectual person. **2.** One belonging to an intellectual group or class, and involved in mental rather than manual labor. **—in·tel·lec·tu·al·i·ty** *n.* **—in·tel·lec·tu·al·ly** *adv.*

in·tel·lec·tu·al·ism (ĭn′tə-lĕk′cho͞o-ə-lĭz′əm) *n.* **1.** Devotion to the exercise or development of the intellect, especially to the extent of disregarding emotional or spiritual factors. **2.** The doctrine that knowledge is the product of pure reason; rationalism. **—in·tel·lec·tu·al·ist** *n.* **—in·tel·lec·tu·al·is·tic** *adj.*

in·tel·lec·tu·al·ize (ĭn′tə-lĕk′cho͞o-ə-līz′) *tr.v.* **-ized, -izing, -izes. 1.** To make rational. **2.** To treat in an intellectual way, especially at the expense of an emotional response or interpretation. **—in·tel·lec·tu·al·i·za·tion** *n.*

in·tel·li·gence (ĭn-tĕl′ə-jəns) *n.* **1. a.** The capacity to acquire and apply knowledge. **b.** The faculty of thought and reason. **c.** Superior powers of mind. **2. a.** *Often* **Intelligence.** An intelligent being, especially one that is incorporeal, such as an angel. **b. Intelligence.** *Christian Science.* "The primal and eternal quality of . . . God" (Mary Baker Eddy). **3.** Received information; news. **4. a.** Secret information, especially about an enemy. **b.** The work of gathering such information. **c.** An agency, staff, or office employed in such work. —See Synonyms at **mind.**

intelligence quotient *n. Abbr.* **IQ, I.Q.** An index of an individual's tested mental ability as compared to the rest of the population, usually arrived at by dividing an individual's mental age by his chronological age and multiplying by 100.

in·tel·li·genc·er (ĭn-tĕl′ə-jən-sər) *n. Archaic.* **1.** One who conveys news; an informant. **2.** A secret agent, informer, or spy.

intelligence test *n.* A standardized test used to establish an intelligence level rating by measuring an individual's ability to form concepts, solve problems, and perform other intellectual operations.

in·tel·li·gent (ĭn-tĕl′ə-jənt) *adj.* **1.** Having intelligence. **2.** Having a high degree of intelligence; mentally acute. **3.** Showing intelligence; perceptive and sound. **4.** Guided or motivated by the intellect; rational. **5.** Designating or pertaining to a computer terminal that can be used or programmed to perform logical operations as well as the input and output of data. [Latin *intelligēns* (stem *intelligent-*), present participle of *intellegere, intelligere,* to perceive, choose between : *inter-,* between + *legere,* to gather, choose.] **—in·tel·li·gen·tial** (ĭn-tĕl′ə-jĕn′shəl) *adj.* **—in·tel·li·gent·ly** *adv.*
Synonyms: *bright, brilliant, clever, intellectual, knowing, quick-witted, smart.*

in·tel·li·gent·si·a (ĭn-tĕl′ə-jĕnt′sē-ə, -gĕnt′sē-ə) *n. Used with a singular or plural verb.* The class within a society consisting of those who are cultured, well-educated, or intellectual. [Russian *intelligyentsia,* from Polish *inteligiencja,* from Latin *intelligentia,* intelligence, from *intelligēns,* INTELLIGENT.]

in·tel·li·gi·ble (ĭn-tĕl′ə-jə-bəl) *adj.* **1.** Comprehensible. **2.** Capable of being apprehended by the intellect alone. [Middle English, from Latin *intelligibilis,* from *intelligere,* to perceive. See **intelligent.**] **—in·tel·li·gi·bil·i·ty** *n.* **—in·tel·li·gi·bly** *adv.*

In·tel·sat (ĭn′tĕl-săt′) *n.* *In*ternational *Tel*ecommunications *Sat*ellite Consortium: an international organization formed in 1964, whose member countries cooperate in establishing and promoting nonmilitary satellite communications.

in·tem·per·ance (ĭn-tĕm′pər-əns) *n.* Lack of temperance or restraint, as in the indulgence of an appetite or passion.

in·tem·per·ate (ĭn-tĕm′pər-ĭt) *adj.* Not temperate or moderate; excessive. **—in·tem·per·ate·ly** *adv.* **—in·tem·per·ate·ness** *n.*

in·tend (ĭn-tĕnd′) *tr.v.* **-tended, -tending, -tends. 1.** To have in mind; plan: *She intended to leave.* **2.** To design for a specific purpose or destine for a particular use. **3.** To signify; mean. [Middle English *entenden,* from Old French *entendre,* from Latin *intendere,* to stretch toward, direct one's mind to : *in,* toward + *tendere,* to stretch, tend.]

in·ten·dance (ĭn-tĕn′dəns) *n.* **1.** The function of an intendant; management; superintendence. **2.** An intendancy.

in·ten·dan·cy (ĭn-tĕn′dən-sē) *n., pl.* **-cies. 1.** The position or function of an intendant. **2.** Intendants collectively. **3.** The district supervised by an intendant in Latin America.

in·ten·dant (ĭn-tĕn′dənt) *n.* **1.** Formerly, a provincial or colonial administrative official of France, Spain, or Portugal. **2.** A district administrator in some countries of Latin America. **3.** *Archaic.* A manager or superintendent. [French, from Old French, "director," administrator, from Latin *intendēns* (stem *intendent-*), present participle of *intendere,* to direct one's mind to, INTEND.]

in·tend·ed (ĭn-tĕn′dĭd) *adj.* **1.** Planned; intentional. **2.** Prospective; future.
∼*n. Informal.* A person's prospective husband or wife.

in·tend·ment (ĭn-tĕnd′mənt) *n.* The true meaning or intention of something as fixed by law.

in·ten·er·ate (ĭn-tĕn′ə-rāt′) *tr.v.* **-ated, -ating, -ates.** To make tender; soften. [IN- (causative) + Latin *tener,* TENDER + -ATE.] **—in·ten·er·a·tion** *n.*

in·tense (ĭn-tĕns′) *adj.* **1.** Of great intensity; extreme in degree, concentration, or extent. **2.** Involving or showing strain: *made an intense effort to finish on time.* **3. a.** Deeply felt; profound. **b.** Tending to feel deeply: *an intense writer.* [Middle English, from Old French, from Latin *intensus,* stretched tight, from the past participle of *intendere,* to stretch toward, INTEND.] **—in·tense·ly** *adv.* **—in·tense·ness** *n.*

in·ten·si·fi·er (ĭn-tĕn′sə-fī′ər) *n.* **1.** One that intensifies. **2.** An intensive. **3.** *Photography.* A substance added to an emulsion to increase its sensitivity.

in·ten·si·fy (ĭn-tĕn′sə-fī′) *v.* **-fied, -fying, -fies.** —*tr.* **1.** To make intense or more intense. **2.** To increase the contrast of (a photographic image). —*intr.* To become intense or more intense. [INTENSE + -FY.] **—in·ten·si·fi·ca·tion** *n.*

in·ten·sion (ĭn-tĕn′shən) *n.* **1.** *Logic.* The sum of the properties or attributes connoted by a term. Compare **extension. 2.** Intensity. [Latin *intensiō* (stem *intensiōn-*), from *intensus,* INTENSE.]

in·ten·si·ty (ĭn-tĕn′sə-tē) *n., pl.* **-ties. 1.** Exceptionally great concentration, power, or force. **2.** *Physics.* **a.** The measure of effectiveness of a force field given by the force per unit test element. **b.** The energy transferred by a wave per unit time across a unit area perpendicular to the direction of propagation.

in·ten·sive (ĭn-tĕn′sĭv) *adj.* **1.** Of, pertaining to, or characterized by intensity. **2.** Pertaining to or being a linguistic intensive. **3.** Concentrated and exhaustive: *intensive study.* **4.** Designating or pertaining to a method of land cultivation calling for large-scale employment of capital and labor and designed to increase productivity. **5.** *Physics.* Having the same value for any subdivision of a thermodynamic system. Said of pressure, for example. **6.** Having a greater than average requirement of the specified resource. Used in combination: *labor-intensive; an energy-intensive system.*
∼*n.* A linguistic element that intensifies the effect of a word or phrase but has itself little or no semantic content; for example, in the sentence *She is terribly pretty, terribly* is an intensive.

intensive care *n.* Continuous and carefully monitored medical treatment given to patients who are seriously ill, especially in a specialized section *(intensive-care unit)* of a hospital.

in·tent (ĭn-tĕnt′) *n.* **1.** That which is intended; aim; purpose. **2.** The state of mind prevailing at the time of an action: *acted with malicious intent.* **3.** Meaning; purport. —See Synonyms at **intention. —to all intents and purposes.** Practically; virtually.
∼*adj.* **1.** Firmly fixed; concentrated. **2.** Having the attention applied; engrossed. **3.** Having the mind fastened upon some purpose. [Middle English *entent,* from Old French, from Latin *intentus,* a stretching out, from the alternate past participle of *intendere,* to stretch toward, INTEND.] **—in·tent·ly** *adv.* **—in·tent·ness** *n.*

in·ten·tion (ĭn-tĕn′shən) *n.* **1.** A plan of action; a design. **2. a.** An aim that guides action; object. **b. intentions.** Purpose in regard to marriage: *honorable intentions.* **3.** *Logic.* **a.** A concept derived from an object of thought. **b.** The general connotation or concept of something. **4.** *Medicine.* The course or manner of healing of a surgical wound. **5.** *Archaic.* Import; meaning. **6.** *Archaic.* Intentness. [Middle English *entencioun,* from Old French *entention,* from Latin *intentiō* (stem *intentiōn-*), "a stretching out," from *intendere,* to stretch toward, INTEND.]
Synonyms: *aim, end, goal, intent, object, objective, purpose.*

in·ten·tion·al (ĭn-tĕn′shə-nəl) *adj.* **1.** Done deliberately; intended: *an intentional slight.* **2.** Having to do with logical intention or connotation. —See Synonyms at **voluntary. —in·ten·tion·al·i·ty** (ĭn-tĕn′shə-năl′ə-tē) *n.* **—in·ten·tion·al·ly** *adv.*

in·ter (ĭn-tûr′) *tr.v.* **-terred, -terring, -ters.** To place (a dead body) in a grave; bury. [Middle English *enteren,* from Old French *enterrer,* from Vulgar Latin *interrāre* (unattested) : Latin *in,* in + *terra,* earth, ground.]

inter– *prefix.* Indicates: **1.** Between or among; for example, **intercollegiate, international. 2.** Mutually or together; for example, **interact, intermingle. *Note:*** Many compounds other than those entered here may be formed with *inter-.* In forming compounds, *inter-* is normally joined with the following element without space or hyphen: *intercontinental.* However, if the second element begins with a capital letter, it is separated with a hyphen: *inter-American.* In Latin phrases used in English, the Latin preposition remains a separate word: *inter alia.* [Middle English *inter-, entre-,* from Old French, from Latin *inter-,* from *inter,* between, among. In borrowed Latin compounds, *inter-* indicates: 1. Between, among, as in **interregnum.** 2. Mutually, each other, as in **intersect.** 3. At intervals, as in **intermit.** 4. Preventively, destructively, as in **internecine.**]

inter. intermediate.

in·ter·act (ĭn′tər-ăkt′) *intr.v.* **-acted, -acting, -acts.** To act on each other.

in·ter·ac·tion (ĭn′tər-ăk′shən) *n.* **1.** The action, state, or result of interacting. **2.** *Physics.* Any of four fundamental ways in which elementary particles and bodies can influence each other, characterized by the strength and range of such interaction and classified as strong, weak, electromagnetic, and gravitational.

in·ter·ac·tive (ĭn′tər-ăk′tĭv) *adj.* **1.** Acting on each other. **2.** *Computer Science.* Designating or pertaining to a system in which information and instructions can be continuously transferred between computer and operator.

in·ter a·li·a (ĭn′tər ā′lē-ə) *adv. Latin.* Among other things.

in·ter a·li·os (ĭn′tər ā′lē-ōs′) *adv. Latin.* Among other persons.

in·ter·a·tom·ic (ĭn′tər-ə-tŏm′ĭk) *adj.* Occurring or operating between atoms.

in·ter·brain (ĭn′tər-brān′) *n.* A part of the brain, the **diencephalon** *(see).*

in·ter·breed (ĭn′tər-brēd′) *v.* **-bred** (-brĕd), **-breeding, -breeds.** *—intr.* **1.** To breed with another kind or species; crossbreed; hybridize. **2.** To breed within a narrow range or with closely related types or individuals; inbreed. *—tr.* To cause to interbreed.

in·ter·ca·lar·y (ĭn-tûr′kə-lĕr′ē) *adj.* **1.** Added to the calendar to make the calendar year correspond to the solar year. Said of a day or a month. **2.** Having such a day or month added. Said of a year. **3.** Interpolated; constituting an insertion. **4.** Designating nonlocalized plant growth occurring in regions other than the apical meristems, as at internodes and leaf bases. [Latin *intercalārius,* from *intercalāre,* to INTERCALATE.]

in·ter·ca·late (ĭn-tûr′kə-lāt′) *tr.v.* **-lated, -lating, -lates. 1.** To add (a day or month) to a calendar. **2.** To insert, interpose, or interpolate. [Latin *intercalāre,* to proclaim the insertion of a day : *inter-,* among, between + *calāre,* to call.] **—in·ter·ca·la·tion** *n.* **—in·ter·ca·la·tive** *adj.*

in·ter·cede (ĭn′tər-sēd′) *intr.v.* **-ceded, -ceding, -cedes. 1.** To plead on another's behalf: *interceded with the father for the child.* **2.** To act as mediator in a dispute. [Latin *intercēdere,* to come between : *inter-,* between + *cēdere,* to go.] **—in·ter·ced·er** *n.*

in·ter·cel·lu·lar (ĭn′tər-sĕl′yə-lər) *adj. Biology.* Among or between cells.

in·ter·cept (ĭn′tər-sĕpt′) *tr.v.* **-cepted, -cepting, -cepts. 1. a.** To stop, deflect, or interrupt the progress or intended course of: *intercepted a message; intercepted her at the airport.* **b.** In ball games such as football, hockey or the like, to cut off, or take possession of (a ball) by anticipating an opponent's pass. **2.** *Archaic.* **a.** To cut off from access or communication. **b.** To prevent. **3.** *Mathematics.* To cut off or bound a part of (a line, plane, surface, or solid).
—n. (ĭn′tər-sĕpt′). *Mathematics.* **1.** A point of interception. **2.** A line segment formed by an intercept; for example, the distance from the origin of coordinates along a coordinate axis to the point at which a line, curve, or surface intersects the axis. [Latin *intercipere* (past participle *interceptus*), to intercept, seize in transit : *inter,* preventively + *capere,* to take, seize.] **—in·ter·cep·tion** *n.* **—in·ter·cep·tive** *adj.*

in·ter·cep·tor, in·ter·cep·ter (ĭn′tər-sĕp′tər) *n.* One that intercepts; especially, a fast-climbing, highly maneuverable fighter plane designed to intercept enemy aircraft.

in·ter·ces·sion (ĭn′tər-sĕsh′ən) *n.* **1.** Entreaty in favor of another; especially, a prayer or petition to God on behalf of another. **2.** Mediation in a dispute. [Old French, from Latin *intercessiō* (stem *intercessiōn-*), from *intercēdere* (past participle *intercessus*), INTERCEDE.] **—in·ter·ces·sion·al** *adj.* **—in·ter·ces·sor** *n.* **—in·ter·ces·so·ry** *adj.*

in·ter·change (ĭn′tər-chānj′) *v.* **-changed, -changing, -changes.** *—tr.* **1.** To switch each of (two things) into the place of the other. **2.** To give and receive mutually; exchange. **3.** To cause to succeed each other; alternate: *interchanging wit with wisdom in the course of conversation.* *—intr.* **1.** To change places with each other. **2.** To succeed each other; alternate.
—n. (ĭn′tər-chānj′). **1.** The act or process or an instance of interchanging, especially: **a.** A switch of places. **b.** An exchange. **2.** Alternation. **3.** A highway intersection designed to permit traffic to move freely from one road to another. [Middle English *entrechaungen,* from Old French *entrechangier* : INTER- + *changier,* to CHANGE.] **—in·ter·chang·er** *n.*

in·ter·change·a·ble (ĭn′tər-chān′jə-bəl) *adj.* Capable of being interchanged; admitting transposition. **—in·ter·change·a·bil·i·ty, in·ter·change·a·ble·ness** *n.* **—in·ter·change·a·bly** *adv.*

in·ter·col·le·giate (ĭn′tər-kə-lē′jĭt, -jē-ĭt) *adj.* Involving or representing two or more colleges.

in·ter·co·lum·ni·a·tion (ĭn′tər-kə-lŭm′nē-ā′shən) *n. Architecture.* **1.** The open spaces between the columns in a colonnade. **2.** The system whereby they are spaced.

in·ter·com (ĭn′tər-kŏm′) *n. Informal.* An internal communication system, as between two rooms. [Short for INTERCOMMUNICATION.]

in·ter·com·mu·ni·cate (ĭn′tər-kə-myōō′nə-kāt′) *intr.v.* **-cated, -cating, -cates. 1.** To communicate with each other. **2.** To be connected or adjoined, as rooms. **—in·ter·com·mu·ni·ca·tion** *n.* **—in·ter·com·mu·ni·ca·tive** *adj.*

in·ter·com·mun·ion (ĭn′tər-kə-myōōn′yən) *n.* The practice by members of different Christian denominations of receiving communion at each other's eucharistic services or at a common service.

in·ter·con·nect (ĭn′tər-kə-nĕkt′) *v.* **-nected, -necting, -nects.** *—intr.* To be connected one to the other. *—tr.* To connect (one thing with another). **—in·ter·con·nec·tion** *n.*

in·ter·con·ti·nen·tal (ĭn′tər-kŏn′tə-nĕnt′l) *adj.* **1.** Extending from one continent to another: *intercontinental flight.* **2.** Carried on between continents: *intercontinental warfare.* **3.** Capable of flight from one continent to another: *intercontinental ballistic missile.*

in·ter·cos·tal (ĭn′tər-kŏst′l) *adj.* Located or occurring between the ribs. [New Latin *intercostalis* : Latin *inter-,* between + *costa,* rib.]

in·ter·course (ĭn′tər-kôrs′, -kōrs′) *n.* **1.** Interchange between persons or groups; communication. **2. Sexual intercourse** *(see).* [Middle English *intercurse,* from Old French *entrecours,* from Latin *intercursus,* past participle of *intercurrere,* to run between : *inter-,* between + *currere,* to run.]

in·ter·crop (ĭn′tər-krŏp′) *v.* **-cropped, -cropping, -crops.** *—intr.* To grow a secondary crop between the rows of a principal crop. *—tr.* To plant such a crop between (another crop).
—n. (ĭn′tər-krŏp′). A secondary crop grown between the rows of a principal crop.

in·ter·cross (ĭn′tər-krŏs′) *n.* A **crossbreed** *(see).* **—in·ter·cross** *v.*

in·ter·cur·rent (ĭn′tər-kûr′ənt) *adj.* **1.** Occurring as an interruption in a process. **2.** *Pathology.* Occurring during the course of an existing disease. [Latin *intercurrēns* (stem *intercurrent-*), present participle of *intercurrere,* to run between. See **intercourse.**]

in·ter·cut (ĭn′tər-kŭt′) *tr.v.* **-cut, -cutting, -cuts.** To insert (a scene or camera shot) into a film sequence, so as to achieve dramatic contrast or to make it appear that two or more actions are taking place simultaneously.

in·ter·de·nom·i·na·tion·al (ĭn′tər-də-nŏm′ə-nā′shən-əl) *adj.* Of or involving different religious denominations.

in·ter·den·tal (ĭn′tər-dĕnt′l) *adj.* **1.** Located between the teeth. **2.** *Phonetics.* Pronounced with the tip of the tongue protruding between the teeth, as (th) in *that* or (th) in *thumb.*
—n. Phonetics. A consonant pronounced in this manner.

in·ter·de·pen·dent (ĭn′tər-də-pĕn′dənt) *adj.* Dependent on each other. **—in·ter·de·pen·dence** *n.* **—in·ter·de·pen·dent·ly** *adv.*

in·ter·dict (ĭn′tər-dĭkt′) *tr.v.* **-dicted, -dicting, -dicts. 1.** To prohibit or place under an ecclesiastical or legal sanction. **2.** To cut or destroy (an enemy line of communication) by firepower so as to halt an enemy's advance.
—n. (ĭn′tər-dĭkt′). **1.** An authoritative prohibition or legal injunction. **2.** A Roman Catholic ecclesiastical censure whereby an offending person or district is excluded from participation in most sacraments and from Christian burial. [Learned respelling of Middle English *entrediten,* to announce ecclesiastical censure, from Old French *entredire* (past participle *entredit*), from Latin *interdīcere,* to forbid : *inter-,* preventively + *dīcere,* to say.] **—in·ter·dic·tion** *n.* **—in·ter·dic·tive, in·ter·dic·to·ry** *adj.* **—in·ter·dic·tive·ly** *adv.* **—in·ter·dic·tor** *n.*

in·ter·dis·ci·pli·nar·y (ĭn′tər-dĭs′ĭ-plĭ-nĕr′ē) *adj.* Concerned with two or more academic disciplines usually considered distinct: *an interdisciplinary degree.*

in·ter·est (ĭn′trĭst, -tər-ĭst) *n.* **1. a.** A feeling of curiosity, fascination, or absorption. **b.** The cause of any such feeling. **c.** The quality or aspect of something that enables it to cause any such feeling. **2.** *Often* **interests.** Advantage; self-interest. **3. a.** A right, claim, or legal share in something. **b.** *Usually* **interests.** Something in which such a right, claim, or share is held. **4. a.** Involvement with or participation in something. **b.** A leisure activity or pursuit: *What are your interests?* **5. a.** *Abbr.* **i., int.** A charge for a financial loan, usually a percentage of the amount loaned. **b.** An excess or bonus beyond what is expected or due: *She returned his ardor with interest.* **6.** *Usually* **interests.** A group of persons sharing an interest in an enterprise, industry, or segment of society. **—in the interest** (or **interests**) **of.** For the sake of; on behalf of.
—tr.v. **interested, -esting, -ests. 1.** To arouse the curiosity or hold the attention of. **2.** To cause to become involved or concerned. **3.** *Archaic.* To concern or affect. [Middle English, variant (influenced by Old French *interest,* damage) of *interesse,* concern, share, from Norman French, substantive use of Latin *interesse,* "to be in between," to matter, be of concern : *inter-,* between + *esse,* to be.]

in·ter·est·ed (ĭn′trĭ-stĭd, -tər-ĭ-stĭd, -tə-rĕs′tĭd) *adj.* **1.** Having or showing curiosity, fascination, or concern. **2.** Possessing a right, claim, or share; personally concerned: *the interested parties.* **3.** Influenced by considerations of personal gain; self-seeking. **—in·ter·est·ed·ly** *adv.* **—in·ter·est·ed·ness** *n.*

in·ter·est·ing (ĭn′trĭ-stĭng, -tər-ĭ-stĭng, -tə-rĕs′tĭng) *adj.* Arousing or holding attention; absorbing. **—in·ter·est·ing·ly** *adv.*

in·ter·face (ĭn′tər-fās′) *n.* **1.** A surface forming a common boundary between adjacent bodies, liquids, or regions. **2.** A link between two circuits or parts, especially in a computer. **3.** The meeting point or boundary at which two theories, systems, groups of people or the like meet and affect each other.
—v. **interfaced, -facing, faces.** *—tr.* To connect (material) with or through an interface. *—intr.* To become interfaced. **—in·ter·fa·cial** (ĭn′tər-fā′shəl) *adj.*

in·ter·fac·ing (ĭn′tər-fās′ĭng) *n.* A strip of firm fabric sewn between the layers of a garment to thicken or stiffen it.

in·ter·fas·cic·u·lar (ĭn′tər-fə-sĭk′yə-lər) *adj. Botany.* Occurring between fascicles: *interfascicular cambium.*

in·ter·fere (ĭn′tər-fîr′) *intr.v.* **-fered, -fering, -feres. 1.** To be a hindrance or obstacle. Often used with *with.* **2.** To intervene or intrude in the affairs of others; meddle. **3.** In various sports, to impede an opponent contrary to the rules of the game. **4.** To strike one hoof

PRONUNCIATION KEY

ă, pat; ā, pay; âr, care;
ä, father, are; b, bib;
ch, church; d, deed; ĕ, pet;
ē, be; f, fife; g, gag; h, hat;
hw, which; ĭ, pit; ī, pie;
îr, pier; j, judge; k, kick;
l, lid, needle; m, mum;
n, no, sudden; ng, thing;
ŏ, pot; ō, toe; ô, paw, for;
oi, noise; ou, out; ŏŏ, book;
ōō, boot; p, pop; r, roar;
s, sauce; sh, ship, dish;
t, tight; th, thin, path;
th, this, bathe; ŭ, cut; ûr, fur;
v, valve; w, with; y, yes;
z, zebra, size; zh, vision;
ə, about, item, edible, gallop, circus, peaceful

IN FOREIGN WORDS:

à, *Fr.* ami; œ, *Fr.* feu, *Ger.* schön; ü, *Fr.* tu, *Ger.* über; KH, *Ger.* ich, *Scot.* loch; N, *Fr.* bon; y′, *Fr.* Compiègne

STRESS MARKS:

Primary stress: ′
in·cite′ (ĭn-sīt′)
Secondary stress: ′
in′sight′ (ĭn′sīt′)

against the opposite hoof or leg while moving. Used of a horse. **5.** *Physics.* To produce interference with another wave. **6.** *Electronics.* To inhibit or prevent clear reception of broadcast signals. [Old French *(s')entreferir,* to strike each other : INTER- + *ferir,* to strike, from Latin *ferīre.*] —**in·ter·fer·er** *n.* —**in·ter·fer·ing·ly** *adv.*

Synonyms: *meddle, tamper, tinker.*

in·ter·fer·ence (ĭn′tər-fîr′əns) *n.* **1. a.** The act, process, or an instance of interfering. **b.** Something that interferes. **2. a.** *Football.* The blocking of defensive tacklers to protect the ball carrier. **b.** *Sports.* The illegal obstruction or hindrance of the ball or of an opposing player. **3.** *Physics.* The phenomenon of two or more waves of the same frequency combining to form a wave in which the disturbance at any point is the algebraic or vector sum of the disturbances due to the interfering waves at that point. **4.** *Electronics.* **a.** The inhibition or prevention of clear reception of broadcast signals. **b.** The distorted portion of a received signal. —**in·ter·fer·en·tial** (ĭn′tər-fə-rĕn′shəl) *adj.*

in·ter·fe·rom·e·ter (ĭn′tər-fə-rŏm′ə-tər) *n.* **1.** Any of several optical, acoustic, or radio-frequency instruments that use interference phenomena between a reference wave and an experimental wave, or between two parts of an experimental wave, to determine wavelengths, wave velocities, distances, and directions. **2.** A type of radio telescope in which the received waves are collected by two separate antennae, connected so as to combine the signals. See **aperture synthesis.** [INTERFER(E) + -METER.]

in·ter·fer·on (ĭn′tər-fîr′ŏn) *n.* A protein produced in response to, and acting to prevent replication of, an infectious viral form within a cell. [INTERFER(E) + -ON.]

in·ter·fer·tile (ĭn′tər-fûrt′l) *adj.* Able to interbreed.

in·ter·fluve (ĭn′tər-flo͞ov′) *n.* The region of higher land between two rivers that are in the same drainage system. [INTER- + Latin *fluvius,* river. See **fluvial.**] —**in·ter·flu·vi·al** *adj.*

in·ter·fuse (ĭn′tər-fyo͞oz′) *v.* **-fused, -fusing, -fuses.** —*tr.* **1.** To fuse or blend. **2.** To spread throughout; diffuse. —*intr.* **1.** To become fused or blended. **2.** To become diffused.

in·ter·ga·lac·tic (ĭn′tər-gə-lăk′tĭk) *adj.* Between galaxies.

in·ter·gla·ci·al (ĭn′tər-glā′shəl) *n.* A comparatively short period of warmth during an overall period of glaciation. —**in·ter·gla·ci·al** *adj.*

in·ter·grade (ĭn′tər-grād′) *intr.v.* **-graded, -grading, -grades.** To merge or grow into each other in a series of stages, forms, or types, Used especially of biological species.
—*n.* (ĭn′tər-grād′). A transitional step, grade, or form. —**in·ter·gra·da·tion** *n.* —**in·ter·gra·di·ent** (ĭn′tər-grā′dē-ənt) *adj.*

in·ter·im (ĭn′tər-ĭm) *n.* An interval of time between one event, process, or period and another.
—*adj.* Belonging to, made, or taking place during an interim; temporary, provisional, or partial: *interim measures; an interim payment.* [Latin, in the meantime, from *inter,* among, at intervals.]

in·te·ri·or (ĭn-tîr′ē-ər) *adj. Abbr.* **int. 1.** Of, pertaining to, or located on the inside; inner. **2.** Of or pertaining to one's mental or spiritual being. **3.** Situated away from a coast or border; inland.
—*n. Abbr.* **int. 1.** The internal portion or area of something, especially of a building; the inside. **2.** One's mental or spiritual being. **3. a.** A representation of the inside of a building or room, as in a painting. **b.** A film scene that is shot indoors. **4.** The inland part of a given political or geographical entity. **5. Interior.** The internal or domestic affairs of a country. [Latin, comparative of *inter,* in, within.] —**in·te·ri·or·i·ty** (ĭn-tîr′ē-ôr′ə-tē, -ŏr′ə-tē) *n.* —**in·te·ri·or·ly** *adv.*

interior angle *n.* **1.** Any of four angles formed between two straight lines cut by a transversal. **2.** The angle formed inside a polygon by two adjacent sides.

interior decorator *n.* One who plans and executes the layout and decoration of an architectural interior. Also called "interior designer." —**interior decoration** *n.*

interior monologue *n.* In literature, the direct representation of a character's thoughts and feelings, as opposed to a narrative description of them.

interj. interjection.

in·ter·ject (ĭn′tər-jĕkt′) *tr.v.* **-jected, -jecting, -jects.** To interpose parenthetically or by way of an interruption. [Latin *interjicere* (past participle *interjectus*), to throw between : *inter-,* between + *jacere,* to throw.] —**in·ter·jec·tor** *n.* —**in·ter·jec·to·ry** *adj.*

in·ter·jec·tion (ĭn′tər-jĕk′shən) *n.* **1.** An exclamation; an ejaculation. **2.** *Abbr.* **interj. a.** A part of speech consisting of an exclamatory word capable of standing alone; for example, *oh!* or *ahem!* **b.** A word, phrase, or other sound used exclamatorily and capable of standing alone; for example, *Heavens!* or *Shut up!* —**in·ter·jec·tion·al** *adj.* —**in·ter·jec·tion·al·ly** *adv.*

in·ter·lace (ĭn′tər-lās′) *v.* **-laced, -lacing, -laces.** —*tr.* **1.** To connect together by or as if by weaving; interweave. **2.** To intersperse. **3.** *Electronics.* To scan (a television picture, for example) in two stages, each composed of alternate lines. —*intr.* To intertwine. Used with *with.* —**in·ter·lace·ment** *n.*

In·ter·la·ken (ĭn′tər-lä′kən). Town in Switzerland on the Aar River, between Thun and Brienz lakes. It is the tourist center of the Bernese Alps.

in·ter·lam·i·nate (ĭn′tər-lăm′ə-nāt′) *tr.v.* **-nated, -nating, -nates. 1.** To insert (a layer) between other layers. **2.** To arrange in alternating layers. —**in·ter·lam·i·nar** *adj.* —**in·ter·lam·i·na·tion** *n.*

in·ter·lard (ĭn′tər-lärd′) *tr.v.* **-larded, -larding, -lards. 1.** To modify or diversify by interspersing with something different or foreign. **2.** To be interspersed through; occur in repeatedly. [Old French *entrelarder,* to alternate layers of fat and lean : INTER- + *larder,* to insert fat, cover with lard, from LARD.]

in·ter·leaf (ĭn′tər-lēf′) *n., pl.* **-leaves** (-lēvz′). A blank leaf inserted between the regular pages of a book.

in·ter·leave (ĭn′tər-lēv′) *tr.v.* **-leaved, -leaving, -leaves. 1.** To provide (a book) with an interleaf or interleaves. **2.** To insert (an interleaf) into a book. **3.** To arrange in alternating layers.

in·ter·line¹ (ĭn′tər-līn′) *tr.v.* **-lined, -lining, -lines. 1.** To insert (writing) between printed or written lines. **2.** To insert words between the lines of (a text). —**in·ter·lin·e·a·tion** (ĭn′tər-lĭn′ē-ā′shən) *n.*

interline² *tr.v.* **-lined, -lining, -lines.** To fit with an interlining.

in·ter·lin·e·ar (ĭn′tər-lĭn′ē-ər) *adj.* **1.** Inserted between the lines of a text. **2.** Written or printed with different languages or versions in alternating lines.

In·ter·lin·gua (ĭn′tər-lĭng′gwə) *n.* An artificially devised international language comprising elements of both English and the Romance languages. [Italian : INTER- + *lingua,* language.]

in·ter·lin·ing (ĭn′tər-lī′nĭng) *n.* An extra lining between the outer fabric and the ordinary lining of a garment.

in·ter·lock (ĭn′tər-lŏk′) *v.* **-locked, -locking, -locks.** —*tr.* **1.** To unite firmly or join closely, as by hooking or dovetailing. **2.** To arrange or connect (separate parts of a system) so that they cannot be operated independently. **3.** *Computer Science.* To prevent initiation of new operations until current operations are completed. —*intr.* To engage or be joined firmly.
—*n.* (ĭn′tər-lŏk′). **1.** A mechanism that ensures that a particular activity cannot take place until a prescribed sequence of operations has been carried out. **2.** A fabric knitted with interlocking stitches.

in·ter·lo·cu·tion (ĭn′tər-lō-kyo͞o′shən) *n.* Conversation. [Latin *interlocūtiō* (stem *interlocūtiōn-*) from *interloquī* (past participle *interlocūtus*), to speak between : *inter-,* between + *loquī,* to speak.]

in·ter·loc·u·tor (ĭn′tər-lŏk′yə-tər) *n.* **1.** Someone who takes part in a conversation. **2.** A partner in such a dialogue. **3.** The performer in a minstrel show who is placed midway between the end men and engages in banter with them.

in·ter·loc·u·to·ry (ĭn′tər-lŏk′yə-tôr′ē, -tōr′ē) *adj.* **1.** Made during the course of a suit, divorce trial, or the like: *an interlocutory decree.* **2.** Interspersed, as into a text or talk. **3.** Of, pertaining to, or resembling a conversation.

in·ter·lope (ĭn′tər-lōp′) *intr.v.* **-loped, -loping, -lopes. 1.** To violate the legally established trading rights of others. **2.** To interfere in the affairs of others; intrude. —See Synonyms at **intrude.** [Back-formation from *interloper* : INTER- + Dutch *loper,* running, from Middle Dutch, from *loopen,* to run.] —**in·ter·lo·per** *n.*

in·ter·lude (ĭn′tər-lo͞od′) *n.* **1.** An intervening episode, feature, or period of time. **2. a.** A short farcical entertainment performed between the acts of a medieval mystery or morality play. **b.** A 16th-century genre of comedy derived from this. **c.** An entertainment between the acts of a play. **3.** A short musical piece inserted between the parts of a longer composition. [Middle English *enterlude,* from Medieval Latin *interlūdium,* performance between acts : Latin *inter-,* between + *lūdus,* play.]

in·ter·lun·a·tion (ĭn′tər-lo͞o-nā′shən) *n.* The period during which the moon is invisible, occurring between the old and new moon. —**in·ter·lu·nar** (ĭn′tər-lo͞o′nər) *adj.*

in·ter·mar·ry (ĭn′tər-măr′ē) *intr.v.* **-ried, -rying, -ries. 1.** To marry a member of another group. **2.** To be bound together by the marriages of members. **3.** To marry within one's own family, tribe, or clan. —**in·ter·mar·riage** *n.*

in·ter·me·di·a·cy (ĭn′tər-mē′dē-ə-sē) *n.* **1.** The state of being intermediate. **2.** The act of intermediating.

in·ter·me·di·ar·y (ĭn′tər-mē′dē-ĕr′ē) *n., pl.* **-ies. 1.** One who acts as a mediator. **2.** One that acts as an agent between persons or things; a means. **3.** An intermediate state or stage.
—*adj.* **1.** Acting as a mediator. **2.** In between; intermediate.

in·ter·me·di·ate (ĭn′tər-mē′dē-ĭt) *adj. Abbr.* **inter. 1.** Lying or occurring at a point, degree, or level between two extremes; in between; in the middle. **2.** *Geology.* Designating a class of igneous rocks containing less than ten percent free quartz, some feldspar, and about 52 to 66 percent silica.
—*n. Abbr.* **inter. 1.** One that is intermediate. **2.** An intermediary. **3.** *Chemistry.* A substance formed as a necessary stage in the change from reactants to products during a chemical reaction.
—*intr.v.* (ĭn′tər-mē′dē-āt′) **intermediated, -ating, -ates.** To act as an intermediary; mediate. [Medieval Latin *intermediātus,* from Latin *intermedius* : *inter-,* between + *medius,* middle.] —**in·ter·me·di·ate·ly** *adv.* —**in·ter·me·di·ate·ness** *n.* —**in·ter·me·di·a·tion** *n.* —**in·ter·me·di·a·tor** *n.*

in·ter·ment (ĭn-tûr′mənt) *n.* The act or ritual of interring.

in·ter·mez·zo (ĭn′tər-mĕt′sō, -mĕd′zō) *n., pl.* **-zos** or **-zi** (-sē, -zē). **1.** A brief musical, theatrical, or dance performance during an interval; an entr'acte. **2. a.** A short movement separating the major sections of a symphonic work. **b.** An independent instrumental composition having the character of such a movement. [Italian, from Latin *intermedius,* INTERMEDIATE.]

in·ter·mi·na·ble (ĭn-tûr′mə-nə-bəl) *adj.* Tiresomely protracted; endless. —See Synonyms at **continual.** —**in·ter·mi·na·bly** *adv.*

in·ter·min·gle (ĭn′tər-mĭng′gəl) *v.* **-gled, -gling, -gles.** —*tr.* To mix or mingle. —*intr.* To mix or mingle with one another.

in·ter·mis·sion (ĭn′tər-mĭsh′ən) *n.* **1. a.** The act of intermitting. **b.** The state of being intermitted. **2.** A respite; a temporary cessation. **3.** The period between the separate acts or parts of a play,

PRONUNCIATION KEY

ă, pat; ā, pay; âr, care;
ä, father, are; b, bib;
ch, church; d, deed; ĕ, pet;
ē, be; f, fife; g, gag; h, hat;
hw, which; ĭ, pit; ī, pie;
îr, pier; j, judge; k, kick;
l, lid, needle; m, mum;
n, no, sudden; ng, thing;
ŏ, pot; ō, toe; ô, paw, for;
oi, noise; ou, out; o͝o, book;
o͞o, boot; p, pop; r, roar;
s, sauce; sh, ship, dish;
t, tight; th, thin, path;
th, this, bathe; ŭ, cut; ûr, fur;
v, valve; w, with; y, yes;
z, zebra, size; zh, vision;
ə, about, item, edible,
gallop, circus, peaceful

IN FOREIGN WORDS:

à, *Fr.* ami; œ, *Fr.* feu, *Ger.* schön; ü, *Fr.* tu, *Ger.* über; KH, *Ger.* ich, *Scot.* loch; N, *Fr.* bon; y′, *Fr.* Compiègne

STRESS MARKS:

Primary stress: ′
in·cite′ (ĭn-sīt′)
Secondary stress: ′
in′sight′ (ĭn′sīt′)

internal-combustion engine

THE ENGINE THAT PUT THE WORLD ON WHEELS
Rotary motion from a series of explosions

Every invention changes the world to some extent, but none has done so more than the internal-combustion engine. Gasoline-driven and diesel-powered automobiles, airplanes, modern tractors, submarines, tanks, and many other forms of transport were all made possible by it. Gas turbines and jet engines also operate by internal combustion.

Its name comes from the fact that fuel is burned inside the engine, rather than in a separate chamber—as in a steam engine, for example. The idea of burning an explosive mixture of gases to drive a piston to and fro was first put into practice in 1856 by two Italians, Eugenio Barsanti and Felice Matteucci, using a mixture of coal gas and air. Since then the idea has been steadily refined. In 1876 the German manufacturer Nikolaus August Otto built the first successful engine based on the four-stroke cycle (see below). Otto's engine was gas-fueled. It was the Ger-

man engineer Gottlieb Daimler who in 1883 made an engine that could run on gasoline. It was more powerful and, being portable, made the automobile feasible. In the diesel engine, developed in Germany in 1892 by Rudolf Diesel, the fuel-air mixture is not detonated by a spark from a spark plug but ignites because of the heat produced by compression.

All conventional engines face the problem that the reciprocating (up and down) movement of the piston has to be converted into rotary movement of a shaft to make it turn wheels or a propeller. This problem is solved by using connecting rods to link pistons and shaft. The connecting rods pump up and down like the legs of a cyclist. Several pistons operate in turn; this produces continuous rotation of the shaft, which in turn makes each piston perform its cycle of strokes before the next spark from the plug.

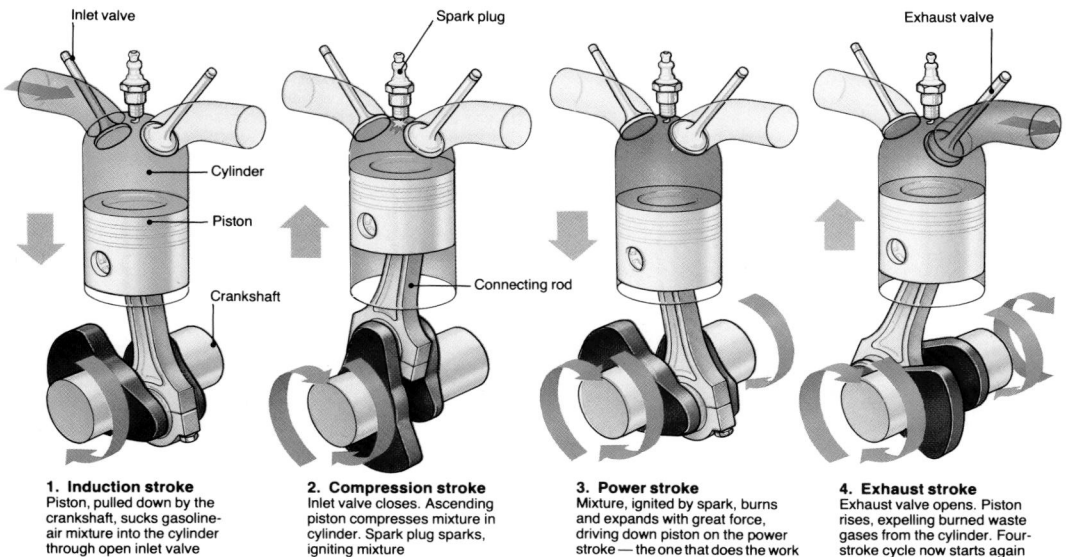

1. Induction stroke
Piston, pulled down by the crankshaft, sucks gasoline-air mixture into the cylinder through open inlet valve

2. Compression stroke
Inlet valve closes. Ascending piston compresses mixture in cylinder. Spark plug sparks, igniting mixture

3. Power stroke
Mixture, ignited by spark, burns and expands with great force, driving down piston on the power stroke — the one that does the work

4. Exhaust stroke
Exhaust valve opens. Piston rises, expelling burned waste gases from the cylinder. Four-stroke cycle now starts again

film, or other entertainment. [Latin *intermissiō* (stem *intermissiōn*-), from *intermittere,* to INTERMIT.]

in·ter·mit (ĭn'tər-mĭt') v. **-mitted, -mitting, -mits.** *—intr.* To cease activity temporarily or repeatedly. *—tr.* To suspend (activity) temporarily or repeatedly; interrupt. [Latin *intermittere,* to interrupt at intervals : *inter-,* at intervals + *mittere,* to send, let go.] **—in·ter·mit·tence** *n.*

in·ter·mit·tent (ĭn'tər-mĭt'ənt) *adj.* Stopping and starting at intervals. —See Synonyms at **periodic. —in·ter·mit·tent·ly** *adv.*

intermittent current *n.* A periodically interrupted unidirectional electric current.

intermittent fever *n.* A fever, such as malaria, in which periods of improvement alternate with periods of deterioration.

in·ter·mix (ĭn'tər-mĭks') v. **-mixed, -mixing, -mixes.** *—tr.* To mix together. *—intr.* To be or become mixed together. [Back-formation from earlier *intermixt,* from Latin *intermixtus,* past participle of *intermiscēre,* to mix together : *inter-,* mutually + *miscēre,* to mix.]

in·ter·mix·ture (ĭn'tər-mĭks'chər) *n.* **1.** The process of intermixing or the state of being intermixed. **2.** Something composed of various ingredients; a mixture. **3.** Something added to a mixture; an admixture.

in·ter·mo·lec·u·lar (ĭn'tər-mə-lĕk'yə-lər) *adj.* Occurring or operating between molecules.

in·tern, in·terne (ĭn'tûrn') *n.* An advanced student or recent graduate undergoing supervised practical training, especially medical training in a hospital. *~v.* **interned, -terning, -terns.** *—intr.* (ĭn'tûrn'). To train or serve as an intern. *—tr.* (ĭn-tûrn'). To detain or confine, especially in wartime. [French *interner,* to confine, from *interne,* inmate, resident assistant physician, from Old French, from Latin *internus,* INTERNAL.] **—in·tern·ship** *n.*

in·ter·nal (ĭn-tûr'nəl) *adj.* **1.** Of, relating to, or located within the limits or surface of something; inner; interior. **2.** Emanating from, belonging to, or dependent on the nature of something; intrinsic; inherent: *the internal contradictions of his theory.* **3.** Located, acting, or effective within the body. **4.** Pertaining to mental or spiritual life, as opposed to material things; subjective. **5.** Of or relating to

the domestic affairs of a country. **6.** Of or involving those who belong to a group or organization, as opposed to those outside it: *the party's internal squabbles; an internal appointment.* **7. a.** Designating an examination set and marked by the teaching institution itself, rather than by a public examinations board. **b.** Designating an examiner from one's own educational institution, as opposed to one brought in from outside. **8.** Designating a medical examination of the vagina or uterus. *~n. Informal.* An internal medical examination. [New Latin *internalis,* from Latin *internus,* from *inter,* in, within.] **—in·ter·nal·i·ty** *n.* **—in·ter·nal·ly** *adv.*

in·ter·nal-com·bus·tion engine (ĭn-tûr'nəl-kəm-bŭs'chən) *n.* An engine, such as a piston engine or a gas turbine, in which fuel is burned within the engine proper rather than in an external furnace as in a steam engine.

internal drainage *n.* A system of drainage with no outlet to the sea. Also called "inland drainage."

internal ear *n.* The portion of the ear that includes the semicircular canals, the vestibule, and the cochlea. Also called "inner ear," "labyrinth."

internal energy *n. Symbol* **U** A thermodynamic property of a system equal to the total kinetic and potential energies of all the molecules present. It is the quantity that changes when the system alters or suffers external work without energy transfer from or to its surroundings.

in·ter·nal·ize (ĭn-tûr'nə-līz') *tr.v.* **-ized, -izing, -izes.** **1.** To take (external conditions, values, or the like) into one's consciousness as part of one's own thinking; assimilate. **2.** To keep within oneself; repress: *internalize feelings of aggression.* **—in·ter·nal·i·za·tion** *n.*

internal medicine *n.* The medical study and treatment of nonsurgical constitutional diseases in adults.

Internal Revenue Service *n. Abbr.* **I.R.S.** The U.S. government department responsible for the collection of federal taxes.

internal rhyme *n.* Rhyme within a single line of verse, or between lines of verse, in which at least one of the rhyming syllables is not at the end of a line.

internal secretion *n. Physiology.* A secretion of an endocrine gland discharged directly into the blood.

in·ter·na·tion·al (ĭn'tər-năsh'ən-əl) *adj. Abbr.* **int., intl., internat.** **1.** Of, pertaining to, or involving two or more nations or nationalities: *an international incident.* **2.** Ordered, demanded, or controlled by a group of nations: *an international commission.* **3.** Equally accessible to all nations: *international waters.* ~*n. Sports.* **1.** A contest or match between representative teams of two or more nations. **2.** A member of any such team. —**in·ter·na·tion·al·ly** *adv.*

In·ter·na·tion·al (ĭn'tər-năsh'ən-əl) *n.* **1.** Any of several socialist organizations of international scope formed during the late 19th and early 20th centuries; especially: **a.** The *First International* (International Workingmen's Association), organized (1864) by Marx and Engels to associate the trade unions of all nations. **b.** The *Second International* (Socialist International), an association formed (1889) to promote the unity of socialist parties in various countries. **c.** The *Third International* (Communist International), organized (1919) by the Bolsheviks to coordinate the activities of communist movements throughout the world. In this sense, also called "Comintern." **d.** The *Fourth International* formed (1937) by followers of Trotsky in opposition to Stalin and the Third International. **2.** The Internationale.

International Bank for Reconstruction and Development *n.* The official name for the **World Bank** *(see).*

international candle *n. Physics.* See **candle** (sense 3a).

International Court of Justice *n. Abbr.* **ICJ** The main judicial body of the United Nations, founded in 1945 and based in The Hague. Also called "World Court."

International Criminal Police Organization *n.* See **Interpol.**

International Date Line *n.* The date line *(see).*

In·ter·na·tio·nale (ĭn-tər-năsh'ən-əl; *French* ăN-těr-nä-syô-näl') *n.* A revolutionary song adopted at different times by various syndicalist and Communist movements as an international socialist anthem. Preceded by *the.* [French, "the International."]

International Grand Master *n.* In chess, a player of the highest ranking, as certified by the World Chess Federation (F.I.D.E.). Also called "grand master."

in·ter·na·tion·al·ism (ĭn'tər-năsh'ən-ə-lĭz'əm) *n.* **1.** The state or quality of being international in character, principles, concern, or attitude. **2.** The policy or principle of cooperation among nations, especially in politics and economics. —**in·ter·na·tion·al·ist** *n.*

in·ter·na·tion·al·ize (ĭn'tər-năsh'ən-ə-līz') *tr.v.* **-ized, -izing, -izes.** **1.** To make international. **2.** To put under international control. —**in·ter·na·tion·al·i·za·tion** *n.*

International Labor Organization *n. Abbr.* **ILO** A specialized agency of the United Nations originally established in 1919 to standardize and improve international labor conditions.

international law *n.* A set of rules generally regarded and accepted as binding in relations between states and nations. Also called "law of nations."

International Master *n.* In chess, a player of the highest ranking but one, as certified by the World Chess Federation (F.I.D.E.). Also called "master."

International Monetary Fund *n. Abbr.* **IMF** An international financial organization set up (1945) by the United Nations to regulate the exchange values of currencies, and thereby promote international trade. Loans are made to member nations in difficulties with their balance of payments, often with strict conditions attached.

International Phonetic Alphabet *n. Abbr.* **IPA, I.P.A.** A phonetic alphabet sponsored by the International Phonetic Association to provide a uniform, universally comprehensible system of letters and symbols for writing the speech sounds of all languages.

international pitch *n. Music.* **Concert pitch** *(see).*

International Practical Temperature Scale *n. Abbr.* **IPTS** A temperature scale based on 11 fixed points with agreed methods of determining temperatures between these points. It ranges from 13.81 K (triple point of hydrogen) to 1337.58 K (melting point of gold).

international time zone. See **time zone.**

interne. Variant of **intern.**

in·ter·ne·cine (ĭn'tər-něs'ēn', -ən, -nē'sīn') *adj.* **1.** Mutually destructive; ruinous or fatal to both sides. **2.** Characterized by bloodshed or carnage. **3.** Carried on within a nation or organization: *internecine struggles.* [Latin *internecīnus,* from *interneciō,* massacre, from *internecāre,* to slaughter, massacre : *inter* (intensive) + *necāre,* to kill.]

in·tern·ee (ĭn'tûr-nē') *n.* One who is interned, especially during a war.

in·ter·neu·ron (ĭn'tər-noōr'ŏn', -nyoōr'-) *n. Physiology.* A neuron that acts as a link between motor neurons and sensory neurons in a reflex arc. —**in·ter·neu·ro·nal** (-noōr'ə-nəl, -nyoōr'-, -noō-rō'-, -nyoō-) *adj.*

in·tern·ist (ĭn-tûr'nĭst) *n.* A doctor who specializes in internal medicine. [INTERN(AL MEDICINE) + -IST.]

in·tern·ment (ĭn-tûrn'mənt) *n.* The act of interning or the state of being interned.

in·ter·node (ĭn'tər-nōd') *n.* A section or part between two nodes, as of a nerve or stem. —**in·ter·no·dal** (ĭn'tər-nōd'l) *adj.*

in·ter·nun·ci·o (ĭn'tər-nŭn'shē-ō', -sē-ō') *n., pl.* **-os.** A Vatican diplomatic envoy or representative ranking just beneath a nuncio. [Italian *internunzio,* from Latin *internuntius,* go-between : *inter-,* between + *nūntius,* messenger, NUNCIO.] —**in·ter·nun·cial** *adj.*

in·ter·o·cep·tor (ĭn'tə-rō-sĕp'tər) *n. Physiology.* A specialized sensory nerve receptor responding to stimuli originating in internal organs. [From INTER(IOR) + (RE)CEPTOR.] —**in·ter·o·cep·tive** *adj.*

in·ter·of·fice (ĭn'tər-ô'fĭs, -ŏf'ĭs) *adj.* Taking place between offices, especially of an organization: *an interoffice memo.*

in·ter·par·ti·cle (ĭn'tər-pär'tĭ-kəl) *adj.* Occurring or existing between particles.

in·ter·pel·late (ĭn'tər-pĕl'āt', ĭn-tûr'pə-lāt') *tr.v.* **-lated, -lating, -lates.** In some legislative bodies, to question formally about government policy or action. [Latin *interpellāre,* to interrupt by speaking.] —**in·ter·pel·lant** *n. & adj.* —**in·ter·pel·la·tion** *n.* —**in·ter·pel·la·tor** *n.*

in·ter·pen·e·trate (ĭn'tər-pĕn'ə-trāt') *v.* **-trated, -trating, -trates.** —*tr.* **1.** To penetrate thoroughly; permeate. **2.** To penetrate (each other). —*intr.* To penetrate mutually. —**in·ter·pen·e·tra·tion** *n.* —**in·ter·pen·e·tra·tive** *adj.*

in·ter·per·son·al (ĭn'tər-pûr'sə-nəl) *adj.* Occurring between or involving two or more people: *interpersonal relations.*

in·ter·phase (ĭn'tər-fāz') *n. Biology.* A period or stage between two successive mitotic divisions of a cell nucleus.

in·ter·plan·e·tar·y (ĭn'tər-plăn'ə-tĕr'ē) *adj.* Between planets.

in·ter·play (ĭn'tər-plā') *n.* Reciprocal action and reaction; interaction. ~*intr.v.* **interplayed, -playing, -plays.** To act or react on each other; interact.

in·ter·plead (ĭn'tər-plēd') *intr.v.* **-pleaded, -pleading, -pleads.** *Law.* To go to court together in order to settle a point in which a third party is involved. [Norman French *entrepleder* : INTER- + *pleder,* to plead, from Old French *plaidier, pleidier,* to PLEAD.]

in·ter·plead·er (ĭn'tər-plē'dər) *n. Law.* **1.** A legal procedure to determine which of two persons bringing the same suit against a third person is the rightful claimant. **2.** One who interpleads.

in·ter·pol (ĭn'tər-pŏl') *n.* An international police organization comprising the police forces of over 100 countries and concentrating on international crimes. The General Secretariat is in Paris. Also officially called "International Criminal Police Organization."

in·ter·po·late (ĭn-tûr'pə-lāt') *v.* **-lated, -lating, -lates.** —*tr.* **1.** To insert or introduce between other things or parts; interpose; interject. **2.** To insert (additional or false matter) in a text. **3.** To change or falsify (a text) by introducing new or false material. **4.** *Mathematics.* To determine a value of (a function) between known values by a procedure different from that specified by the function itself. —*intr.* To make insertions, additions, or interjections. [Latin *interpolāre* : *inter-,* between + *polīre,* to adorn, furbish, POLISH.] —**in·ter·po·la·tion** *n.* —**in·ter·po·la·tive** *adj.* —**in·ter·po·la·tor** *n.*

in·ter·pose (ĭn'tər-pōz') *v.* **-posed, -posing, -poses.** —*tr.* **1.** To place in an intervening position; insert or introduce between parts. **2.** To introduce or interject (a remark, question, or digression) during a conversation or speech. **3.** To exert (influence or authority) in order to interfere, obstruct, or intervene: *interpose one's veto.* —*intr.* **1.** To come between; intervene. **2.** To introduce a remark, question, or argument; interrupt. [Old French *interposer,* from Latin *interpōnere* (past participle *interpositus*), to place between : *inter-,* between + *pōnere,* to put, place.] —**in·ter·pos·er** *n.* —**in·ter·po·si·tion** (ĭn'tər-pə-zĭsh'ən) *n.*

in·ter·pret (ĭn-tûr'prĭt) *v.* **-preted, -preting, -prets.** —*tr.* **1.** To clarify the meaning of; elucidate. **2.** To explain or perceive the significance of; construe: *interpreted his grunt as a refusal.* **3.** To represent the meaning or character of (a piece of music or a dramatic role, for example). **4.** To translate. —*intr.* **1.** To offer an explanation. **2.** To act as an interpreter. —See Synonyms at **explain.** [Middle English *interpreten,* from Old French *interpreter,* from Latin *interpretārī,* from *interpres,* interpreter, negotiator.] —**in·ter·pret·a·bil·i·ty, in·ter·pret·a·ble·ness** *n.* —**in·ter·pret·a·ble** *adj.*

in·ter·pre·ta·tion (ĭn-tûr'prə-tā'shən) *n.* **1.** The act or process of interpreting; elucidation. **2.** The result of interpreting; an explanation or inference. **3.** A concept of a work of art as expressed by the character and style of its representation or performance. —**in·ter·pre·ta·tion·al** *adj.*

in·ter·pre·ta·tive (ĭn-tûr'prə-tā'tĭv) *adj.* Also **in·ter·pre·tive** (-prə-tĭv). Expository; explanatory. —**in·ter·pre·ta·tive·ly** *adv.*

in·ter·pret·er (ĭn-tûr'prə-tər) *n.* **1.** One who translates orally the words of parties communicating with each other in different languages. **2.** One who makes and expounds an interpretation: *medieval interpreters of Aristotle.* **3.** *Computer Science.* A program or circuit for changing from the language in which instructions are written into machine code for use by the computers.

in·ter·ra·cial (ĭn'tər-rā'shəl) *adj.* Involving or existing between members of different racial groups: *interracial tension.*

in·ter·reg·num (ĭn'tər-rĕg'nəm) *n., pl.* **-nums** or **-na** (-nə). **1.** The interval of time between the end of a sovereign's reign and the accession of a successor. **2.** A period of temporary suspension of the usual functions of government or control. **3.** Any gap in continuity. [Latin *interrēgnum* : *inter-,* between + *rēgnum,* REIGN.] —**in·ter·reg·nal** *adj.*

in·ter·re·late (ĭn'tər-rĭ-lāt') *v.* **-lated, -lating, -lates.** —*tr.* To place in mutual relationship. —*intr.* To come into mutual relationship. —**in·ter·re·la·tion** *n.* —**in·ter·re·la·tion·ship** *n.*

in·ter·rex (ĭn'tər-rĕks') *n., pl.* **interreges** (ĭn'tər-rē'jēz'). One who holds supreme state power during an interregnum. [Latin *interrex* : *inter-,* between + *rēx,* king.]

interrog. interrogative.

in·ter·ro·gate (ĭn-tĕr'ə-gāt') *tr.v.* **-gated, -gating, -gates.** **1.** To question closely and formally; especially, to subject to prolonged and systematic questioning, sometimes with the use of threats or force. **2.** To obtain specific information from (a computer or data store) by program. —See Synonyms at **ask.** [Latin *interrogāre,* to consult, question : *inter-,* between + *rogāre,* to ask.] —**in·ter·ro·gat·ing·ly** *adv.* —**in·ter·ro·ga·tion** *n.* —**in·ter·ro·ga·tion·al** *adj.* —**in·ter·ro·ga·tor** *n.*

interrogation point *n.* A question mark (sense 1) *(see).* Also called "interrogation mark."

in·ter·rog·a·tive (ĭn'tə-rŏg'ə-tĭv) *adj. Abbr.* **interrog.** 1. Having the form or character of a question; asking or serving to ask a question: *an interrogative raising of the eyebrows.* 2. Designating a word or form used in asking a question: *an interrogative pronoun.* Compare **demonstrative, relative.**
~*n.* 1. A word or form used in asking a question. 2. An interrogative sentence or expression. 3. A question mark. —**in·ter·rog·a·tive·ly** *adv.*

in·ter·rog·a·to·ry (ĭn'tə-rŏg'ə-tôr'ē, -tōr'ē) *adj.* Interrogative.
~*n., pl.* **-ries.** *Usually* **interrogatories.** *Law.* A formal statement of questions that one party to a civil action may require the rival party to answer under oath. —**in·ter·rog·a·tor·i·ly** *adv.*

in·ter·rupt (ĭn'tə-rŭpt') *v.* **-rupted, -rupting, -rupts.** —*tr.* 1. a. To break the continuity or uniformity of. b. To be in the way of; obstruct (a view, for example). 2. To hinder or stop the action or discourse of (someone) by breaking in. —*intr.* To break in upon an action or discourse. —See Synonyms at **intrude.**
~*n. Computer Science.* A signal or code for temporarily interrupting the processing of one computer program in order to process a different program. [Middle English *interrupten,* from Latin *interrumpere* (past participle *interruptus),* to break in : *inter,* between + *rumpere,* to break.] —**in·ter·rup·tion** *n.* —**in·ter·rup·tive** *adj.*

in·ter·rupt·ed (ĭn'tə-rŭp'tĭd) *adj.* 1. Broken in continuity; discontinuous. 2. *Botany.* Having an uneven arrangement, as of leaflets along a stem. —**in·ter·rupt·ed·ly** *adv.*

in·ter·rupt·er, in·ter·rup·tor (ĭn'tə-rŭp'tər) *n.* 1. One that interrupts. 2. A device for periodically and automatically opening or closing an electric circuit.

in·ter se (ĭn'tər sē', sā') *adv. Latin.* Between or among themselves.

in·ter·sect (ĭn'tər-sĕkt') *v.* **-sected, -secting, -sects.** —*tr.* To divide or penetrate (a line or space, for example) by cutting across or through. —*intr.* 1. To cut across or overlap each other. 2. To form an intersection. [Latin *intersecāre* (past participle *intersectus*) : *inter-,* mutually + *secāre,* to cut.]

in·ter·sec·tion (ĭn'tər-sĕk'shən) *n.* 1. a. The act or process of intersecting. b. A place where things intersect; especially, a place where two or more roads cross. 2. *Mathematics.* a. The point or locus of points common to two or more geometric figures. b. A set every member of which is an element of each of two or more given sets.

in·ter·sex (ĭn'tər-sĕks') *n.* An intersexual individual.

in·ter·sex·u·al (ĭn'tər-sĕk'shōō-əl) *adj.* 1. Existing or occurring between the sexes. 2. Having sexual characteristics intermediate between those of a typical male and a typical female. —**in·ter·sex·u·al·i·ty** *n.* —**in·ter·sex·u·al·ly** *adv.*

in·ter·space (ĭn'tər-spās') *tr.v.* **-spaced, -spacing, -spaces.** To make or occupy a space between.
~*n.* (ĭn'tər-spās'). A space between two things; an interval. —**in·ter·spa·tial** (ĭn'tər-spā'shəl) *adj.*

in·ter·sperse (ĭn'tər-spûrs') *tr.v.* **-spersed, -spersing, -sperses.** 1. To scatter or distribute among other things at irregular intervals. 2. To supply or diversify with things distributed at irregular intervals. [Latin *interspergere* (past participle *interspersus*), to scatter among : *inter-,* among + *spargere,* to scatter.] —**in·ter·spers·ed·ly** (ĭn'tər-spûr'sĭd-lē) *adv.* —**in·ter·sper·sion** (ĭn'tər-spûr'zhən, -shən) *n.*

in·ter·state (ĭn'tər-stāt') *adj.* Involving, existing between, or connecting two or more states.
~*n.* A major road running between two states.

in·ter·stel·lar (ĭn'tər-stĕl'ər) *adj.* Between the stars.

in·ter·stice (ĭn-tûr'stĭs) *n., pl.* **-stices** (-stĭ-sēz', -sĭz). A narrow or small space between things or parts; hole; crevice. [French, from Late Latin *interstitium,* from Latin *intersistere* (past participle *interstitus*), to stand in the middle of : *inter-,* in the middle of, between + *sistere,* to stand.]

in·ter·sti·tial (ĭn'tər-stĭsh'əl) *adj.* 1. Of or occurring in interstices. 2. Affecting or based on interstices.
~*n.* 1. Any of various cells occurring in the spaces between tissues or organs, especially those interspersed between the seminiferous tubules of the testis. 2. An atom or ion in a crystal, in a position between two normal lattice positions. —**in·ter·sti·tial·ly** *adv.*

in·ter·sti·tial-cell stimulating hormone (ĭn'tər-stĭsh'əl-sĕl') *n. Abbr.* **ICSH** A luteinizing hormone *(see).*

interstitial compound *n. Chemistry.* A solid compound in which atoms of a nonmetal such as carbon or boron occupy interstitial positions in a metal lattice.

in·ter·strat·i·fy (ĭn'tər-străt'ə-fī') *tr.v.* **-fied, -fying, -fies.** To alternate or vary with other strata. Used in the passive. —**in·ter·strat·i·fi·ca·tion** *n.*

in·ter·tex·ture (ĭn'tər-tĕks'chər) *n.* 1. The act of interweaving or the state of being interwoven. 2. Something interwoven.

in·ter·tid·al (ĭn'tər-tīd'l) *adj.* Of, pertaining to, or designating the region between the extremes of high and low tide.

in·ter·tri·bal (ĭn'tər-trī'bəl) *adj.* Existing or carried on between tribes.

in·ter·tri·go (ĭn'tər-trī'gō) *n.* Inflammation of two moist skin surfaces that are in contact and between which there is friction, as may occur on the inside of the thighs.

in·ter·trop·i·cal (ĭn'tər-trŏp'ĭ-kəl) *adj. Geography.* 1. Between or within the tropics. 2. Of or pertaining to the tropics.

in·ter·twine (ĭn'tər-twīn') *v.* **-twined, -twining, -twines.** —*tr.* To twist or braid together. —*intr.* To interweave with one another; become entwined. —**in·ter·twine·ment** *n.*

in·ter·ur·ban (ĭn'tər-ûr'bən) *adj.* Pertaining to or connecting urban areas: *an interurban bus.*

in·ter·val (ĭn'tər-vəl) *n. Abbr.* **int.** 1. A space between two objects, points, or units. 2. The temporal duration between two instants, events, or states. 3. *Mathematics.* a. A set consisting of all the numbers between a pair of given numbers, either including the end points *(closed interval)* or excluding the end points *(open interval).* b. A line segment representing such a set. c. A set of numbers greater than or less than a given number and including or excluding the given number. 4. *Chiefly British.* A short pause between the acts of a play, parts of a concert, and the like; an intermission. 5. *Music.* The difference in pitch between two notes on a given scale. —**at intervals.** 1. Intermittently; now and then. 2. Separated by spaces. [Middle English *intervalle,* from Latin *intervallum,* space between ramparts : *inter-,* between + *vallum,* rampart.]

in·ter·vene (ĭn'tər-vēn') *intr.v.* **-vened, -vening, -venes.** 1. To enter, appear, or have an effect as an extraneous element: *At this point fate intervened.* 2. To come, appear, or lie between two things. 3. To occur or come between two periods or points of time. 4. To come in or between so as to mediate, prevent, or otherwise affect an outcome. Often used with *between* or *in.* 5. To interfere, usually through force or threat of force, in the affairs of another nation. 6. *Law.* To enter into a suit as a third party for the protection of an alleged interest. [Latin *inter-,* between + *venīre,* to come.] —**in·ter·ven·er** *n.* —**in·ter·ven·tion** (ĭn'tər-vĕn'shən) *n.*

in·ter·ven·tion·ism (ĭn'tər-vĕn'shə-nĭz'əm) *n.* 1. The policy of intervening in the affairs of another sovereign state. 2. Government action designed to control or influence domestic economic activity, as through nationalization of industries. —**in·ter·ven·tion·ist** *adj. & n.*

in·ter·ver·te·bral disk (ĭn'tər-vûr'tə-brəl, -vûr'tē'-) *n. Anatomy.* Any of the flexible plates of fibrocartilage connecting adjacent vertebrae in the spinal column.

in·ter·view (ĭn'tər-vyōō') *n.* 1. a. A face-to-face meeting. b. Such a meeting arranged for a particular purpose, especially the assessment of a candidate for a job or award. 2. a. A conversation between a reporter and a person from whom he seeks facts or statements. b. An account or reproduction of such a conversation.
~*v.* **interviewed, -viewing, -views.** —*tr.* To have an interview with. —*intr.* To undergo an interview: *Some people don't interview well.* [Earlier *entervewe,* from Old French *entrevue,* from *entrevu,* past participle of *(s')entrevoir,* to see each other : *entre-,* INTER- + *voir,* to see, from Latin *vidēre.*] —**in·ter·view·ee** *n.* —**in·ter·view·er** *n.*

in·ter·vo·cal·ic (ĭn'tər-vō-kăl'ĭk) *adj. Phonetics.* Immediately followed and immediately preceded by a vowel.

in·ter·volve (ĭn'tər-vŏlv') *tr.v.* **-volved, -volving, -volves.** To wind or coil together.

in·ter·weave (ĭn'tər-wēv') *tr.v.* **-wove** (-wōv') or *rare* **-weaved, -woven** (-wō'vən) or *rare* **-wove, -weaving, -weaves.** 1. To weave together. 2. To intermix.

in·tes·tate (ĭn-tĕs'tāt', -tĭt) *adj.* 1. Having made no legal will: *died intestate.* 2. Not disposed of by a legal will. Said of property.
~*n.* One who dies without a legal will. [Middle English, from Latin *intestātus* : *in-,* not + *testātus,* TESTATE.] —**in·tes·ta·cy** (ĭn-tĕs'tə-sē) *n.*

intestinal flora *n.* All the harmless and beneficial bacteria that live in the intestinal tract.

intestinal fortitude *n.* Courage; endurance.

in·tes·tine[1] (ĭn-tĕs'tən) *n.* The portion of the **alimentary canal** *(see)* extending from the stomach to the anus. See **small intestine, large intestine.** [Latin *intestīnum,* from *intestīnus,* internal, from *intus,* within.] —**in·tes·ti·nal** *adj.* —**in·tes·ti·nal·ly** *adv.*

intestine[2] *adj.* Involving or restricted to the people of a country; internal; internecine: *intestine conflicts.*

in·ti·ma (ĭn'tə-mə) *n., pl.* **-mae** (-mē') or **-mas.** *Anatomy.* The innermost layer of an organ or part, especially the wall of a lymphatic vessel, artery, or vein. [New Latin, from Latin, feminine of *intimus,* innermost.]

in·ti·ma·cy (ĭn'tə-mə-sē) *n., pl.* **-cies.** 1. The condition of being intimate. 2. An instance of being intimate. 3. *Sometimes* **intimacies.** Sexual intercourse. Used formally or euphemistically. [From INTIMATE.]

in·ti·mate[1] (ĭn'tə-mĭt) *adj.* 1. Marked by close acquaintance, association, or familiarity: *an intimate friend.* 2. a. Pertaining to or indicative of one's deepest nature. b. Very personal; private; secret. 3. Essential; innermost. 4. Characterized by informality and privacy: *an intimate nightclub.* 5. Involved in a sexual relationship. —See Synonyms at **familiar.**
~*n.* A close friend or confidant. [Late Latin *intimātus,* past participle of *intimāre,* to put in, announce, INTIMATE (to hint).] —**in·ti·mate·ly** *adv.* —**in·ti·mate·ness** *n.*

in·ti·mate[2] (ĭn'tə-māt') *tr.v.* **-mated, -mating, -mates.** 1. To communicate with a hint or other indirect sign; imply subtly. 2. To announce; proclaim. —See Synonyms at **suggest.** [Late Latin *intimāre,* to make known or announce (one's inmost thoughts), from Latin *intimus,* inmost, deepest.] —**in·ti·mat·er** *n.* —**in·ti·ma·tion** *n.*

in·tim·i·date (ĭn-tĭm'ə-dāt') *tr.v.* **-dated, -dating, -dates.** 1. To make timid; frighten. 2. To discourage, silence, or inhibit by or as if by threats. —See Synonyms at **threaten.** [Medieval Latin *intimidāre* : Latin *in-* (causative) + *timidus*, TIMID.] —**in·tim·i·da·tion** *n.* —**in·tim·i·da·tor** *n.* —**in·tim·i·da·to·ry** (ĭn-tĭm′ə-də-tôr′ē, -tōr′ē) *adj.*

in·tinc·tion (ĭn-tĭngk′shən) *n. Ecclesiastical.* The administration of the Eucharist by dipping the host into the wine before offering it to the communicant. [Late Latin *intinctiō* (stem *intinctiōn-*), from Latin *intingere* (past participle *intinctus*), to dip in : *in-*, in + *tingere*, to moisten, dye.]

in·tine (ĭn′tēn′) *n.* The inner layer of the cell wall surrounding a grain of pollen. Also called "endosporium." [Latin *inti(mus)*, innermost + -INE.]

in·tit·ule (ĭn-tĭt′yo͞ol) *tr.v.* **-uled, -uling, -ules.** *British.* To give a title to (an Act of Parliament). [Old French *intituler*, from Late Latin *intitulāre* : Latin *in-*, in + *titulus*, TITLE.]

intl. international.

in·to (ĭn′to͞o) *prep.* **1.** To the inside or middle part of; to a point within. **2.** To the action or occupation of: *go into banking.* **3.** To the condition, state, or form of: *break into pieces; get into debt.* **4.** So as to be in or within: *enter into an agreement.* **5.** To a time or place in the course of: *well into the week.* **6.** Against: *ram into a tree.* **7.** Toward; in the direction of: *look into the distance.* **8.** As a divisor of: *Two into eight is four.* **9.** *Informal.* Interested in or involved with: *They are into vegetarianism.* [Middle English *into*, Old English *intō* : IN + TO.]

in·tol·er·a·ble (ĭn-tŏl′ər-ə-bəl) *adj.* **1.** Insupportable; unbearable. **2.** *Informal.* Extremely annoying; maddening. —**in·tol·er·a·bil·i·ty, in·tol·er·a·ble·ness** *n.* —**in·tol·er·a·bly** *adv.*

in·tol·er·ance (ĭn-tŏl′ər-əns) *n.* **1.** The quality or condition of being intolerant. **2.** Inability to withstand or consume: *an intolerance to certain drugs.*

in·tol·er·ant (ĭn-tŏl′ər-ənt) *adj.* **1.** Not tolerant of different characteristics or habits in others; bigoted. **2.** Irritable; short-tempered. **3.** Unable or indisposed to endure. —**in·tol·er·ant·ly** *adv.*

in·to·nate (ĭn′tō-nāt′) *tr.v.* **-nated, -nating, -nates. 1.** To intone. **2.** To utter with a particular intonation.

in·to·na·tion (ĭn′tō-nā′shən) *n.* **1. a.** The act of intoning or chanting. **b.** An intoned utterance. **2.** A manner of producing musical notes, especially with regard to accuracy of pitch. **3. a.** The use of pitch as an element of meaning in language: *a questioning intonation.* **b.** A characteristic pattern of rising and falling pitch in speaking: *a lilting intonation in his voice.* **4.** *Music.* The opening phrase of a plainsong composition, sung as a solo part.

in·tone (ĭn-tōn′) *v.* **-toned, -toning, -tones.** —*tr.* **1.** To recite in a singing voice. **2.** To utter in a monotone. —*intr.* **1.** To speak with a given intonation. **2.** To sing a plainsong intonation. [Middle English *entonen*, from Old French *entoner*, from Medieval Latin *intonāre*, to utter in a musical tone : Latin *in-*, in + *tonus*, TONE.] —**in·ton·er** *n.*

in to·to (ĭn tō′tō) *adv. Latin.* Totally; altogether.

in·tox·i·cant (ĭn-tŏk′sĭ-kənt) *n.* An agent that intoxicates; especially, an alcoholic drink. —**in·tox·i·cant** *adj.*

in·tox·i·cate (ĭn-tŏk′sĭ-kāt′) *tr.v.* **-cated, -cating, -cates. 1.** To induce, especially by the effect of ingested alcohol, any of a series of progressively deteriorating states ranging from exhilaration to stupefaction; make drunk. **2.** To stimulate or excite: *"a man whom life intoxicates, who has no need of wine"* (Anaïs Nin). **3.** To poison. [Medieval Latin *intoxicāre*, to put poison in, poison : Latin *in-*, in + *toxicum*, poison.] —**in·tox·i·ca·tion** *n.* —**in·tox·i·ca·tive** *adj.* —**in·tox·i·ca·tor** *n.*

intr. intransitive.

intra– *prefix.* Indicates in, within, or inside of; for example, **intracranial, intramuscular. Note:** Many compounds other than those entered here may be formed with *intra-*. In forming compounds, *intra-* is normally joined with the following element without space or hyphen: *intraorbital.* However, if the second element begins with a capital letter or with the letter *a*, it is separated with a hyphen: *intra-European, intra-atomic.* [Late Latin, from Latin *intrā*, within.]

in·tra·a·tom·ic (ĭn′trə-ə-tŏm′ĭk) *adj.* Within an atom.

in·tra·car·di·ac (ĭn′trə-kär′dē-ăk′) *adj.* Within the heart.

in·tra·car·ti·lag·i·nous (ĭn′trə-kär′tə-lăj′ə-nəs) *adj.* Within cartilage.

in·tra·cel·lu·lar (ĭn′trə-sĕl′yə-lər) *adj.* Occurring or situated within a cell or cells.

In·tra·coast·al Waterway (ĭn′trə-kō′stəl). A shipping passage, 3,950 kilometers (2,455 miles) long, partly manmade, partly artificial, between the U.S. Atlantic coast from Trenton, New Jersey, to Key West, Florida, and along the Gulf of Mexico to Brownsville, Texas, on the Rio Grande. The waterway, used by pleasure and commercial craft, was authorized by Congress in 1919.

in·tra·cra·ni·al (ĭn′trə-krā′nē-əl) *adj.* Within the skull.

in·trac·ta·ble (ĭn-trăk′tə-bəl) *adj.* **1.** Difficult to manage or govern; stubborn. **2.** Difficult to mold or manipulate. **3.** Difficult to deal with or solve. **4.** Difficult to alleviate, remedy, or cure. —See Synonyms at **unruly.** —**in·trac·ta·bil·i·ty, in·trac·ta·ble·ness** *n.* —**in·trac·ta·bly** *adv.*

in·tra·cu·ta·ne·ous (ĭn′trə-kyo͞o-tā′nē-əs) *adj.* Within the skin: *an intracutaneous injection.*

in·tra·der·mal (ĭn′trə-dûr′məl) *adj.* Within the skin; intracutaneous.

in·tra·dos (ĭn-trā′dŏs′, -dōs′) *n., pl.* **intrados** (-dŏz′, -dōz′) or **-doses.** *Architecture.* The inner curve of an arch. [French, "inside back" : INTRA- + *dos*, back, from Old French, from Latin *dorsum*.]

in·tra·ga·lac·tic (ĭn′trə-gə-lăk′tĭk) *adj.* Occurring or situated within one galaxy.

in·tra·mo·lec·u·lar (ĭn′trə-mə-lĕk′yə-lər) *adj.* Within a molecule.

in·tra·mu·ral (ĭn′trə-myo͝or′əl) *adj.* **1.** Existing or carried on within the bounds of an institution, especially a university. **2.** *Anatomy.* Within the wall of a cavity or organ. —**in·tra·mu·ral·ly** *adv.*

in·tra·mus·cu·lar (ĭn′trə-mŭs′kyə-lər) *adj.* Within muscle.

in·tran·si·gent (ĭn-trăn′sə-jənt) *adj.* Refusing to moderate a position; uncompromising. [French *intransigeant*, from Spanish *los intransigentes*, "the uncompromising" (name of a party of extreme republicans) : *in-*, not, from Latin + *transigente*, present participle of *transigir*, to compromise, from Latin *trānsigere*, to drive through, come to an understanding : *trāns-*, through + *agere*, to drive.] —**in·tran·si·gence, in·tran·si·gen·cy** *n.* —**in·tran·si·gent** *n.* —**in·tran·si·gent·ly** *adv.*

in·tran·si·tive (ĭn-trăn′sə-tĭv) *adj. Abbr.* **intr., i. 1.** *Grammar.* Designating a verb or verb construction that does not require a direct object to complete its meaning; for example; the verb *triumph* is always intransitive, and the verb *win* is sometimes intransitive. **2.** *Logic.* Designating or characterizing a relationship such that if A and B have the relationship, and B and C have the relationship then it is not true that A and C have the relationship; for example, if A is the uncle of B, and B is the uncle of C, it is not true to say that A is the uncle of C, and therefore "is the uncle of" is an intransitive relationship. Compare **transitive.**
~*n.* An intransitive verb. [Late Latin *intransitīvus* : *in-*, not + *transitīvus*, TRANSITIVE.] —**in·tran·si·tive·ly** *adv.* —**in·tran·si·tive·ness** *n.*

in·tra·nu·cle·ar (ĭn′trə-no͞o′klē-ər, -nyo͞o′klē-ər) *adj.* Within a nucleus.

in·tra·psy·chic (ĭn′trə-sī′kĭk) *adj.* Existing or taking place within the psyche: *intrapsychic conflict.* —**in·tra·psy·chi·cal·ly** *adv.*

in·tra·spe·cif·ic (ĭn′trə-spə-sĭf′ĭk) *adj.* Occurring within a species: *intraspecific selection.*

in·tra·state (ĭn′trə-stāt′) *adj.* Within the boundaries of a state.

in·tra·tel·lu·ric (ĭn′trə-tə-lo͝or′ĭk) *adj. Geology.* Formed or found below the earth's surface. Said of rocks.

in·tra·u·ter·ine (ĭn′trə-yo͞o′tər-ĭn, -tə-rīn′) *adj.* Within the uterus.

intrauterine device *n. Abbr.* **IUD, I.U.D.** A piece of metal or plastic, often in the shape of a loop, ring, or spiral, inserted into the uterus as a contraceptive.

in·tra·va·sa·tion (ĭn-trăv′ə-sā′shən) *n.* The entry of foreign matter into a blood vessel. [INTRA- + VAS + -ATION.]

in·tra·vas·cu·lar (ĭn′trə-văs′kyə-lər) *adj.* Within the blood vessels or lymphatics.

in·tra·ve·na·tion (ĭn′trə-vē-nā′shən) *n.* The entry of foreign matter into a vein.

in·tra·ve·nous (ĭn′trə-vē′nəs) *adj. Abbr.* **IV** Within or into a vein or veins.
~*n., pl.* **intravenouses.** An intravenous injection, drip, or transfusion. —**in·tra·ve·nous·ly** *adv.*

in-tray (ĭn′trā′) *n.* A tray, usually on an office desk, for incoming mail, documents needing attention, and the like.

intreat. Variant of **entreat.**

intrench. Variant of **entrench.**

intrenchment. Variant of **entrenchment.**

in·trep·id (ĭn-trĕp′ĭd) *adj.* Resolutely courageous; fearless; bold. —See Synonyms at **brave.** [French, *intrépide*, from Latin *intrepidus* : *in-*, not + *trepidus*, agitated, alarmed.] —**in·tre·pid·i·ty** (ĭn′-trə-pĭd′ə-tē), **in·trep·id·ness** *n.* —**in·trep·id·ly** *adv.*

in·tri·ca·cy (ĭn′trĭ-kə-sē) *n., pl.* **-cies. 1.** The condition or quality of being intricate. **2.** Something intricate.

in·tri·cate (ĭn′trĭ-kĭt) *adj.* **1.** Having many elements in a complex arrangement; convoluted. **2.** Soluble or comprehensible only with painstaking effort; complicated. —See Synonyms at **complex, hard.** [Middle English, from Latin *intrīcātus*, past participle of *intrīcāre*, to entangle : *in-*, in + *trīcae*, trifles, troubles, perplexities.] —**in·tri·cate·ly** *adv.* —**in·tri·cate·ness** *n.*

in·tri·gant, in·tri·guant (ĭn′trē-gänt′, ăn-trē-gäN′) *n.* One who intrigues; a plotter. [French, "intriguing," from Italian *intrigante*, present participle of *intrigare*, to INTRIGUE.]

in·trigue (ĭn′trēg, ĭn-trēg′) *n.* **1.** A covert maneuver to achieve an unavowed purpose; a secret or underhand scheme. **2.** The use of or involvement in such schemes. **3.** A clandestine love affair. **4. a.** The quality of exciting interest or curiosity; allurement. **b.** Mystery; suspense. —See Synonyms at **conspiracy.**
~*v.* (ĭn-trēg′) **intrigued, -triguing, -trigues.** —*intr.* To engage in covert schemes; plot. —*tr.* **1.** To insinuate (one's way, for example) by scheming. **2.** To arouse the interest or curiosity of. [French, from Italian *intrigo*, from *intrigare*, to perplex, from Latin *intrīcāre*, to entangle. See **intricate.**] —**in·tri·guer** *n.* —**in·trigu·ing·ly** *adv.*

in·trin·sic (ĭn-trĭn′sĭk) *adj.* Also *archaic* **in·trin·si·cal** (-sĭ-kəl). **1.** Belonging to the essential nature of a thing; inherent: *"the exploitive and oppressive relationships intrinsic to capitalism"* (E.P. Thompson). **2.** *Anatomy.* Situated within or belonging solely to a body part, as certain nerves and muscles are. [Old French *intrinseque*, inner, from Late Latin *intrinsecus*, inward, from Latin, inwardly, from the inside : *intrim* (unattested), inward, from *intrā*, within + *secus*, alongside.] —**in·trin·si·cal·ly** *adv.*

intrinsic factor *n. Biochemistry.* A protein secreted in the stomach that is essential for the absorption of vitamin B_{12}.

intrinsic semiconductor *n.* A semiconductor that has no dopant added, having equal numbers of current-carrying holes and electrons.

in·tro (ĭn′trō) *n. Informal.* An introduction.

intro– *prefix.* Indicates: **1.** In or into; for example, **introjection.**

2. Inward; for example, **introvert.** [Latin, from *intrō,* to the inside, inwardly.]

intro., introd. introduction; introductory.

in·tro·duce (ĭn′trə-do͞os′, -dyo͞os′) *tr.v.* **-duced, -ducing, -duces.** **1.** To identify and present; especially: **a.** To present to an audience. **b.** To make (a stranger) known to another person. Often used with *to.* **c.** To make (strangers) acquainted. **2.** To present and recommend (a plan, for example) for consideration. **3.** To bring into currency, use, or practice; institute. **4.** To bring in and establish: *introduce exotic birds.* **5.** To insert or inject. **6.** To make (a person) acquainted with something new: *introduced them to sailing.* **7.** To preface; open. [Latin *intrōdūcere,* to lead in : *intrō-,* in + *dūcere,* to lead.] **—in·tro·duc·er** *n.* **—in·tro·duc·i·ble** *adj.*

in·tro·duc·tion (ĭn′trə-dŭk′shən) *n. Abbr.* **intro., introd. 1.** An act of introducing. **2.** The state of being introduced. **3.** A means of presenting one person to another, such as a personal presentation or formal letter. **4.** Something recently introduced; an innovation. **5.** Anything spoken, written, or otherwise presented in introducing, especially: **a.** A preface, as in a book. **b.** A short preliminary movement in a musical work. **6.** A basic instructive text or course of study. [Middle English *introduccion,* from Old French *introduction,* from Latin *intrōductiō* (stem *intrōductiōn-*), from *intrōdūcere,* to INTRODUCE.]

in·tro·duc·to·ry (ĭn′trə-dŭk′tə-rē) *adj.* Also **in·tro·duc·tive** (-tĭv). *Abbr.* **intro., introd.** Serving to introduce. **—in·tro·duc·to·ri·ly** *adv.*

in·tro·gres·sion (ĭn′trə-grĕsh′ən) *n. Genetics.* The introduction of genetic material to one gene pool from another by hybridization. Also called "introgressive hybridization." [INTRO- + *-gression* (as in *digression*).]

in·tro·it, In·tro·it (ĭn-trō′ĭt) *n. Ecclesiastical.* **1.** A hymn or psalm sung at the opening of a service, especially in the Anglican Church. **2.** *Roman Catholic Church.* The beginning of the proper of the Mass, usually consisting of a psalm verse, antiphon, and the Gloria Patri followed by the repeated verse. [Middle English, "entrance," beginning, from Old French *introït,* from Latin *introitus,* from the past participle of *introīre,* to go in, enter : *intrō-,* into + *īre,* to go.]

in·tro·jec·tion (ĭn′trə-jĕk′shən) *n.* **1.** The unconscious incorporation into one's personality of the characteristics of another person or of an inanimate object. **2.** The incorporation or adoption of any attitude or belief. [INTRO- + (PRO)JECTION.] **—in·tro·ject** *v.*

in·tro·mis·sion (ĭn′trə-mĭsh′ən) *n.* **1.** Introduction; admission. **2.** *Biology.* The introduction of one organ or part into another, such as the penis into the vagina. [Medieval Latin *intrōmissiō* (stem *intrōmissiōn-*), from Latin *intrōmittere,* to INTROMIT.] **—in·tro·mis·sive** *adj.*

in·tro·mit (ĭn′trə-mĭt′) *tr.v.* **-mitted, -mitting, -mits.** To cause or permit to enter; introduce or admit. [Middle English *intromitten,* from Latin *intrōmittere,* to send or put in, introduce : *intrō-,* in + *mittere,* to send.] **—in·tro·mit·tent** *adj.* **—in·tro·mit·ter** *n.*

in·trorse (ĭn-trôrs′) *adj. Botany.* Facing inward; turned toward the axis. Said especially of anthers that shed their pollen toward the flower. [Latin *introrsus,* contracted from *intrōversus,* turned inward : *intrō-,* inward + *versus,* past participle of *vertere,* to turn.]

in·tro·spect (ĭn′trə-spĕkt′) *intr.v.* **-spected, -specting, -spects.** To turn one's thoughts inward; examine one's own feelings. [Latin *intrōspicere* (past participle *intrōspectus*), to look into : *intrō-,* into + *specere,* to look.]

in·tro·spec·tion (ĭn′trə-spĕk′shən) *n.* Contemplation of one's own thoughts and sensations; self-examination.

in·tro·spec·tive (ĭn′trə-spĕk′tĭv) *adj.* **1.** Of, pertaining, or given to introspection. **2.** Given to private thought; contemplative. **—in·tro·spec·tive·ly** *adv.* **—in·tro·spec·tive·ness** *n.*

in·tro·ver·sion (ĭn′trə-vûr′zhən, -shən) *n.* **1. a.** The directing of one's thoughts and interests inward, especially to an excessive degree, accompanied by absence of interest in or aptitude for dealing with the external world and other people. **b.** A disposition toward introversion. Compare **extroversion. 2.** *Medicine.* The turning inward of a hollow organ. **—in·tro·ver·sive** *adj.*

in·tro·vert (ĭn′trə-vûrt′) *v.* **-verted, -verting, -verts.** *—tr.* **1.** To turn or direct inward. **2.** To concentrate (one's thoughts or feelings) inward upon themselves. **3.** To turn (a tubular organ or part) inward upon itself. *—intr.* To exhibit introversion.

~n. (ĭn′trə-vûrt′). **1.** A person whose manner and behavior are characterized by introversion. Compare **extrovert. 2.** An anatomical structure, such as the intestine, that is turned inward upon itself.

~adj. Characterized by introversion; introverted. [New Latin *introvertere* : INTRO- + Latin *vertere,* to turn.]

in·trude (ĭn-tro͞od′) *v.* **-truded, -truding, -trudes.** *—tr.* **1.** To interpose (oneself or something) without invitation or permission, or quite inappropriately. **2.** *Geology.* To force (molten rock) into existing rocks. *—intr.* To come in rudely or inappropriately; enter as an improper or unwanted element: *intruding on a private conversation.* [Latin *intrūdere,* to thrust in : *in-,* in + *trūdere,* to thrust.] **—in·trud·er** *n.*

Synonyms: *interlope, interrupt, obtrude.*

in·tru·sion (ĭn-tro͞o′zhən) *n.* **1.** The act or an instance of intruding, or the state of being intruded upon. **2.** An inappropriate or unwelcome addition: *"The fields were a timid intrusion on a landscape hardly marked by man"* (Doris Lessing). **3.** *Law.* Illegal entry upon or appropriation of the property of another. **4.** *Geology.* **a.** The forcing of molten rock into existing rocks. **b.** The intrusive mass so produced.

in·tru·sive (ĭn-tro͞o′sĭv) *adj.* **1.** Intruding or tending to intrude. **2.** *Geology.* Designating igneous rock forced into existing rocks while in molten state; irruptive. **3.** *Linguistics.* Constituting an **epenthesis** *(see).* —See Usage note at **curious. —in·tru·sive·ly** *adv.* **—in·tru·sive·ness** *n.*

intrust. Variant of **entrust.**

in·tu·bate (ĭn′to͞o-bāt′, -tyo͞o-bāt′) *tr.v.* **-bated, -bating, -bates.** *Medicine.* To insert a tube into (an organ or passage); cannulate. **—in·tu·ba·tion** *n.*

in·tu·it (ĭn-to͞o′ĭt, -tyo͞o′ĭt) *v.* **-ited, -iting, -its.** *—tr.* To know or sense by intuition. *—intr.* To acquire knowledge by intuition. [Back-formation from INTUITION.]

in·tu·i·tion (ĭn′to͞o-ĭsh′ən, ĭn′tyo͞o-) *n.* **1. a.** The act or faculty of knowing without the use of rational processes; immediate cognition. **b.** Knowledge so gained; a perceptive insight. **2.** A capacity for guessing accurately; sharp insight. **3.** A sense of something not evident or deducible; impression; notion. —See Synonyms at **reason.** [Middle English *intuycion,* contemplation, from Old French *intuition,* from Late Latin, view, contemplation, from Latin *intuērī,* to look at or toward, contemplate : *in-,* on, toward + *tuērī,* to look at, watch.]

in·tu·i·tion·al (ĭn′to͞o-ĭsh′ən-əl, ĭn′tyo͞o-) *adj.* Of, pertaining to, or based on intuition. **—in·tu·i·tion·al·ly** *adv.*

in·tu·i·tion·al·ism (ĭn′to͞o-ĭsh′ən-ə-lĭz′əm, ĭn′tyo͞o-) *n. Philosophy.* Intuitionism. **—in·tu·i·tion·al·ist** *n.*

in·tu·i·tion·ism (ĭn′to͞o-ĭsh′ən-ĭz′əm, ĭn′tyo͞o-) *n.* **1.** The theory that basic truths are known by intuition rather than reason. **2.** The theory that objects of perception are known to be real by intuition. **3.** *Philosophy.* The theory that ethical principles are known to be valid and universal through intuition. **4.** The theory that mathematical statements are true or false only if they can be proved to be so. **—in·tu·i·tion·ist** *n. & adj.*

in·tu·i·tive (ĭn-to͞o′ə-tĭv, ĭn-tyo͞o′-) *adj.* **1.** Of, pertaining to, or arising from intuition; intuitional. **2.** Known or perceived through intuition. **3.** Possessing or demonstrating intuition. **—in·tu·i·tive·ly** *adv.* **—in·tu·i·tive·ness** *n.*

in·tu·i·tiv·ism (ĭn-to͞o′ə-tĭ-vĭz′əm, ĭn-tyo͞o′-) *n. Philosophy.* The theory of intuitionism in ethics. **—in·tu·i·tiv·ist** *n.*

in·tu·mesce (ĭn′to͞o-mĕs′, ĭn′tyo͞o-) *intr.v.* **-mesced, -mescing, -mesces.** To swell or expand; enlarge. [Latin *intumēscere,* to swell up : *in-* (intensive) + *tumēscere,* to begin to swell, from *tūmere,* to swell.]

in·tu·mes·cence (ĭn′to͞o-mĕs′əns, ĭn′tyo͞o-) *n.* **1.** The process or condition of swelling. **2.** A swollen organ or part. **—in·tu·mes·cent** *adj.*

in·turn (ĭn′tûrn′) *n.* A curving inward. **—in·turned** *adj.*

in·tus·sus·cept (ĭn′təs-sə-sĕpt′) *tr.v.* **-cepted, -cepting, -cepts.** *Pathology.* To fold or turn inward; invaginate. [Probably back-formation from INTUSSUSCEPTION.] **—in·tus·sus·cep·tive** *adj.*

in·tus·sus·cep·tion (ĭn′təs-sə-sĕp′shən) *n.* **1.** *Pathology.* Invagination; especially, an infolding of one part of the intestine into another. **2.** *Botany.* The deposition of molecules into a cell wall, thereby increasing the surface area. [New Latin *intussusceptio* : Latin *intus,* within + *susceptiō* (stem *susceptiōn-*), taking up, from *suscipere,* to take up : *sub-,* up from under + *capere,* to take, seize.]

intwine. Variant of **entwine.**

intwist. Variant of **entwist.**

In·u·it, In·nu·it (ĭn′yə-wət) *n., pl.* **-its** or collectively **Inuit, Innuit. 1.** An Eskimo of North America and Greenland as distinguished from one of Asia and the Aleutian Islands. **2.** The language of these Eskimos.

in·u·lin (ĭn′yə-lĭn) *n.* A fructose polysaccharide, $(C_6H_{10}O_5)_3$ or $(C_6H_{10}O_5)_4$, stored as a food reserve in the roots of many plants.

in·unc·tion (ĭn-ŭngk′shən) *n.* The process of applying and rubbing in an ointment. [Middle English, from Latin *inunctiō* (stem *inunctiōn-*), from *inunguere,* to smear oil on, anoint : *in-,* on + *unguere,* to smear, anoint.]

in·un·date (ĭn′ŭn-dāt′) *tr.v.* **-dated, -dating, -dates. 1.** To cover with water, especially flood water; overflow. **2.** To overwhelm as if with a flood; swamp: *inundated with requests.* [Latin *inundāre,* "to flow in" : *in-,* in + *undāre,* to flow, from *unda,* wave.] **—in·un·da·tion** *n.* **—in·un·da·tor** *n.* **—in·un·da·to·ry** (ĭn-ŭn′də-tôr′ē, -tōr′ē) *adj.*

in·ure, en·ure (ĭn-yo͝or′) *v.* **-ured, -uring, -ures.** *—tr.* To make used to something unpleasant by prolonged subjection. Usually used in the passive, and with *to*: *He became inured to the flies and mosquitoes.* *—intr.* To come into operation; take effect, especially in law. [Middle English *enewren* : *en-* (causative) + *ure,* use, custom, from Old French *uevre, euvre,* custom, work, from Latin *opera,* work.] **—in·ure·ment** *n.*

in·urn (ĭn-ûrn′) *tr.v.* **-urned, -urning, -urns.** *Archaic.* **1.** To put or seal (ashes of the dead, for example) in an urn. **2.** To bury or entomb.

in u·ter·o (ĭn yo͞o′tə-rō) *adj. Latin.* In the womb. **—in u·ter·o** *adv.*

in·u·tile (ĭn-yo͞ot′l, -tīl) *adj.* Useless. [Middle English, from Old French, from Latin *inūtilis* : *in-,* not + *ūtilis,* useful, from *ūtī*†, to use.] **—in·u·tile·ly** *adv.* **—in·u·til·i·ty** (ĭn′yo͞o-tĭl′ĭ-tē) *n.*

inv. 1. invented; invention; inventor. **2.** invoice.

in va·cu·o (ĭn văk′yo͞o-ō′) *adj. Latin.* **1.** In a vacuum. **2.** In isolation; considered without reference to related evidence. **—in va·cu·o** *adv.*

in·vade (ĭn-vād′) *v.* **-vaded, -vading, -vades.** *—tr.* **1.** To enter (a territory, for example) by force in order to conquer or overrun. **2.** To encroach or intrude upon; violate: *to invade someone's privacy.*

intrusion *Bands of a pale volcanic rock known as lamprophyre divide darker areas of slate near the northern coast of Cornwall, England. The markings were created when molten lamprophyre welled up from the earth's interior through cracks in the slate, then cooled and hardened, filling the cracks. Rocks that are forced into layers of other rocks in this way are said to be intrusive.*

PRONUNCIATION KEY

ă, **pat**; ā, **pay**; âr, **care**;
ä, **father, are**; b, **bib**;
ch, **church**; d, **deed**; ĕ, **pet**;
ē, **be**; f, **fife**; g, **gag**; h, **hat**;
hw, **which**; ĭ, **pit**; ī, **pie**;
îr, **pier**; j, **judge**; k, **kick**;
l, **lid, needle**; m, **mum**;
n, **no, sudden**; ng, **thing**;
ŏ, **pot**; ō, **toe**; ô, **paw, for**;
oi, **noise**; ou, **out**; o͝o, **book**;
o͞o, **boot**; p, **pop**; r, **roar**;
s, **sauce**; sh, **ship, dish**;
t, **tight**; th, **thin, path**;
th, **this, bathe**; ŭ, **cut**; ûr, **fur**;
v, **valve**; w, **with**; y, **yes**;
z, **zebra, size**; zh, **vision**;
ə, **about, item, edible, gallop, circus, peaceful**

IN FOREIGN WORDS:

à, *Fr.* **ami**; œ, *Fr.* **feu**, *Ger.* **schön**; ü, *Fr.* **tu**, *Ger.* **über**;
KH, *Ger.* **ich**, *Scot.* **loch**;
N, *Fr.* **bon**; y′, *Fr.* **Compiègne**

STRESS MARKS:

Primary stress: ′
in·cite′ (ĭn-sīt′)
Secondary stress: ′
in′sight′ (ĭn′sīt′)

3. To overrun or infest: *The kitchen was invaded by ants.* **4.** To enter and spread harm through: *Infection has invaded the membranes.* —*intr.* To make an invasion. [Middle English *invaden,* from Latin *invādere,* "to go in" : *in-,* in + *vādere,* to go.] —**in·vad·er** *n.*

in·vag·i·nate (ĭn-văj′ə-nāt′) *v.* **-nated, -nating, -nates.** —*tr.* **1.** To enclose in or as in a sheath. **2.** To turn within; introvert. —*intr.* To become enclosed or turned within itself. [Medieval Latin *invāgīnāre* : Latin *in-,* in + *vāgīna,* sheath.] —**in·vag·i·na·ble** *adj.*

in·vag·i·na·tion (ĭn-văj′ə-nā′shən) *n.* **1.** The act or process of invaginating or the condition of being invaginated. **2.** Something invaginated, as an organ or part. **3.** The infolding of an outer layer of cells to form a cavity, especially as in the embryonic development of the gastrula from the blastula.

in·va·lid¹ (ĭn′və-lĭd) *n.* A chronically ill or disabled person.
~*adj.* **1.** Disabled by illness or injury; sickly or infirm. **2.** Of, pertaining to, or for invalids.
~*v.* **invalided, -liding, -lids.** —*tr.* **1.** To make an invalid of; disable physically. **2.** *Chiefly British.* To release or exempt from duty because of ill health. —*intr.* To become invalided. [Latin *invalidus,* not strong, ineffective : *in-,* not + *validus,* strong, VALID.]

in·val·id² (ĭn-văl′ĭd) *adj.* **1.** Null; legally ineffective. **2.** Falsely based or reasoned; unjustified: *an invalid conclusion.* [Latin *invalidus,* ineffective, INVALID (infirm).] —**in·val·id·ly** *adv.*

in·val·i·date (ĭn-văl′ə-dāt′) *tr.v.* **-dated, -dating, -dates.** **1.** To make legally ineffective or void. **2.** To undermine or destroy the force or effectiveness of (an argument, for example). —See Synonyms at **nullify.** —**in·val·i·da·tion** *n.* —**in·val·i·da·tor** *n.*

in·va·lid·ism (ĭn′və-lĭd-ĭz′əm) *n.* The condition of being chronically ill or disabled.

in·val·i·di·ty¹ (ĭn′və-lĭd′ə-tē) *n.* The condition or quality of being void or unjustifiable; lack of validity.

invalidity² *n.* The condition of being ill or disabled, usually for a long period of time. Also used adjectivally: *invalidity benefit.*

in·val·u·a·ble (ĭn-văl′yo͞o-bəl) *adj.* **1.** Of inestimable use or help; indispensable; much appreciated: *an invaluable service.* **2.** Having extremely high value; priceless: *invaluable paintings.* —See Synonyms at **costly.** —**in·val·u·a·bly** *adv.*

In·var (ĭn-vär′) *n.* A trademark for an iron alloy containing 36 percent nickel, with an extremely low coefficient of expansion, and used chiefly in measuring rods and tapes, pendulums, balance wheels, tuning forks, and in temperature-regulating devices.

in·var·i·a·ble (ĭn-vâr′ē-ə-bəl) *adj.* Not changing or subject to change; constant.
~*n.* Something that does not change; especially, a mathematical expression or a physical quantity. —**in·var·i·a·bil·i·ty, in·var·i·a·ble·ness** *n.* —**in·var·i·a·bly** *adv.*

in·var·i·ant (ĭn-vâr′ē-ənt) *adj.* **1.** Not varying; constant. **2.** Unaffected by a given mathematical operation, such as a transformation of coordinates.
~*n.* An invariant quantity, function, configuration, or system. —**in·var·i·ance** *n.*

in·va·sion (ĭn-vā′zhən) *n.* **1.** The act or an instance of invading; especially, entrance by force. **2.** The onset of something injurious or harmful, as of a disease. **3.** Any intrusion or encroachment. [Middle English *invasioune,* from Old French *invasion,* from Late Latin *invāsiō* (stem *invāsiōn-*), from Latin *invādere,* to INVADE.]

in·va·sive (ĭn-vā′sĭv) *adj.* **1.** Tending to spread; especially, tending to invade healthy tissue. **2.** *Archaic.* Of, relating to, or given to armed aggression.

in·vec·tive (ĭn-vĕk′tĭv) *n.* Vehement accusation or abuse; denunciation; vituperation. [Middle English *invectiff,* abusive, vituperative, from Old French *invectif,* from Late Latin *invectīva* (*ōrātiō*), "abusive (speech)," from Latin *invehere,* to attack, INVEIGH.] —**in·vec·tive** *adj.* —**in·vec·tive·ly** *adv.* —**in·vec·tive·ness** *n.*

in·veigh (ĭn-vā′) *intr.v.* **-veighed, -veighing, -veighs.** To give vent to angry censure; protest vehemently; rail. Used with *against.* [Latin *invehī,* passive infinitive of *invehere,* to carry in, sail into, assail, attack : *in-,* in + *vehere,* to carry.] —**in·veigh·er** *n.*

in·vei·gle (ĭn-vē′gəl, ĭn-vā′-) *tr.v.* **-gled, -gling, -gles.** **1.** To lead astray or win over by deceitful flattery or persuasion: *She inveigled me into joining her plot.* **2.** To obtain by cajolery. —See Synonyms at **lure.** [Earlier *invegle,* from Norman French *envegler,* alteration of Old French *aveugler,* to blind, from *aveugle,* blind, from Medieval Latin *ab oculīs,* without eyes : Latin *ab,* out of + *oculus,* eye.] —**in·vei·gle·ment** *n.* —**in·vei·gler** *n.*

in·vent (ĭn-vĕnt′) *tr.v.* **-vented, -venting, -vents.** **1.** To conceive of or devise (something entirely new); produce (an invention). **2.** To fabricate; make up. [Middle English *inventen,* to come upon, find, from Latin *invenīre* (past participle *inventus*) : *in-,* on + *venīre,* to come.] —**in·vent·i·ble** *adj.*

in·ven·tion (ĭn-vĕn′shən) *n. Abbr.* **inv.** **1.** The act or process of inventing. **2.** A new device or process developed from study and experimentation. **3.** A mental fabrication; a falsehood or fictitious story. **4.** Skill in inventing; inventiveness. **5.** A short musical piece developing a single theme contrapuntally. **6.** *Archaic.* A discovery; a finding. —**in·ven·tion·al** *adj.*

in·ven·tive (ĭn-vĕn′tĭv) *adj.* **1.** Of or characterized by invention or imagination: *an inventive spy-story.* **2.** Adept or skillful at inventing; creative; ingenious. —**in·ven·tive·ly** *adv.* —**in·ven·tive·ness** *n.*

in·ven·tor (ĭn-vĕn′tər) *n.* Also **in·vent·er.** *Abbr.* **inv.** One who conceives or devises a previously unknown device, method, or process.

in·ven·to·ry (ĭn′vən-tôr′ē, -tōr′ē) *n., pl.* **-ries.** **1.** A detailed list of things, such as articles or goods in one's possession. **2.** The process of making such a list. **3.** The items so listed. **4.** The total quantity of goods and materials held by an organization or company. **5.** Broadly, an evaluation or survey.
~*tr.v.* **inventoried, -rying, -ries.** **1.** To make an inventory of. **2.** To include in an inventory. [Medieval Latin *inventōrium,* list, altered from Late Latin *inventārium,* "a finding out," "enumeration," from Latin *invenīre,* to come upon, find, INVENT.] —**in·ven·to·ri·al** *adj.* —**in·ven·to·ri·al·ly** *adv.*

in·ve·rac·i·ty (ĭn′və-răs′ə-tē) *n., pl.* **-ties.** **1.** Lack of veracity; untruthfulness. **2.** An untruth; a falsehood.

In·ver·car·gill (ĭn′vər-kär′gĭl). A city in New Zealand on the southeast coast of South Island. It is the center of a dairy and agricultural district and has food-processing industries.

In·ver·ness¹ (ĭn′vər-nĕs′). Royal burgh in northeast Scotland. The administrative center of the Highland Region, it supports distilling, tweed-manufacturing, sawmilling, tourism, and some coal shipping from its port at the head of the Moray Firth.

Inverness². Formerly the largest county in Scotland. It lay between the western Cairngorms and the Outer Hebrides, and was absorbed into the Highland Region in 1975.

Inverness³ *n. Often* **inverness.** **1.** A loose overcoat with a detachable cape. **2.** The cape of such a coat. Also called "Inverness cape." [First popularized in INVERNESS.]

in·verse (ĭn-vûrs′, ĭn′vûrs′) *n.* **1.** That which is opposite, as in sequence or character; the reverse. **2.** *Mathematics.* An element in a set that yields the identity element of the set when combined with another element in a binary operation; especially: **a.** The reciprocal of a designated quantity. **b.** The negative of a designated quantity.
~*adj.* **1.** Reversed in order, nature, or effect. **2.** Turned upside down; inverted. **3.** *Mathematics.* Pertaining to an inverse. Said of relationships, proportions, or functions. [Latin *inversus,* past participle of *invertere,* to INVERT.] —**in·verse·ly** *adv.*

in·ver·sion (ĭn-vûr′zhən, -shən) *n.* **1.** The act of inverting or the state of being inverted. **2.** An interchange of position, especially of adjacent objects in a sequence. **3.** A change in normal word order, such as the placing of a verb before its subject. **4.** *Music.* **a.** A rearrangement of notes in which upper and lower voices are transposed, as in counterpoint, or in which each interval in a single melody is applied in the opposite direction. **b.** An interval, chord, or melody resulting from such rearrangement. **5.** Homosexuality. **6.** *Medicine.* The turning inward or inside out of an organ or part. **7.** *Genetics.* A type of chromosome mutation in which a chromosome segment is inserted in reverse order. **8.** *Chemistry.* Conversion from the dextrorotatory to the levorotatory or from the levorotatory to the dextrorotatory form. **9.** *Meteorology.* A state in which the air temperature increases with increasing altitude, holding surface air down. [Latin *inversiō* (stem *inversiōn-*), from *invertere,* to INVERT.] —**in·ver·sive** *adj.*

in·vert (ĭn-vûrt′) *v.* **-verted, -verting, -verts.** —*tr.* **1.** To turn inside out or upside down. **2.** To reverse the position, order, or condition of. **3.** To subject to inversion. —*intr.* To be subjected to inversion.
~*n.* (ĭn′vûrt′) **1.** Something inverted. **2.** A homosexual. [Latin *invertere,* to turn inside out or upside down : *in-,* in, inward + *vertere,* to turn.] —**in·vert·i·ble** *adj.*

in·ver·tase (ĭn′vûr-tās′) *n.* A plant and animal enzyme that catalyzes the conversion of sucrose to glucose and fructose. Also called "sucrase," "saccharase."

in·ver·te·brate (ĭn-vûr′tə-brĭt, -brāt′) *adj.* **1.** Having no backbone or spinal column; not vertebrate. **2.** Lacking strength of character; spineless.
~*n.* An invertebrate animal. [New Latin *Invertebrata,* neuter plural of *invertebratus,* having no backbone : IN- (no) + VERTEBRATE.]

in·vert·ed comma (ĭn-vûr′tĭd) *n. Chiefly British.* A **quotation mark** *(see).*

inverted mordent *n. Music.* A **pralltriller** *(see).*

inverted snobbery *n.* **1.** The conscious affirmation of values, tastes, or habits characteristic of one's lower-class background, or the affectation of values, tastes, or habits supposedly characteristic of a class lower than one's own. **2.** A sense of social exclusiveness resulting from such an image of oneself.

in·vert·er (ĭn-vûr′tər) *n.* **1.** One that inverts. **2.** *Electronics.* A device used to convert direct current into alternating current. **3.** *Computer Science.* A logic component, a **NOT gate** *(see).*

invert sugar *n.* A hygroscopic mixture of equal parts of glucose and fructose resulting from the hydrolysis of sucrose and used chiefly in brewing and in medicine. [Commercially produced by inversion of sucrose.]

in·vest (ĭn-vĕst′) *v.* **-vested, -vesting, -vests.** —*tr.* **1.** To commit (money or capital) in order to gain profit or interest, as by purchasing property or shares. **2.** To spend or utilize (time, money, or effort) for future advantage or benefit. Often used with *in.* **3.** To endow with rank, authority, or power. **4.** To inaugurate with ceremony; install in office. **5.** To provide with some enveloping or pervasive quality. **6.** *Rare.* To clothe; adorn. **7.** To cover completely; envelop; shroud. **8.** *Military. Rare.* To surround with hostile troops or ships; besiege. —*intr.* **1.** To invest money; make an investment. Often used with *in.* **2.** *Informal.* To buy. Used with *in.* [Old French *investir,* from Medieval Latin *investīre,* from Latin, to clothe in, surround : *in-,* in + *vestīre,* to clothe, from *vestis,* clothes.] —**in·ves·tor** *n.*

in·ves·ti·gate (ĭn-vĕs′tĭ-gāt′) *v.* **-gated, -gating, -gates.** —*tr.* To observe or inquire into in detail; examine systematically. —*intr.* To make an investigation. [Latin *investīgāre,* to trace out, search into :

PRONUNCIATION KEY

ă, pat; ā, pay; âr, care; ä, father, are; b, bib; ch, church; d, deed; ĕ, pet; ē, be; f, fife; g, gag; h, hat; hw, which; ĭ, pit; ī, pie; îr, pier; j, judge; k, kick; l, lid, needle; m, mum; n, no, sudden; ng, thing; ŏ, pot; ō, toe; ô, paw, for; oi, noise; ou, out; o͝o, book; o͞o, boot; p, pop; r, roar; s, sauce; sh, ship, dish; t, tight; th, thin, path; *th,* this, bathe; ŭ, cut; ûr, fur; v, valve; w, with; y, yes; z, zebra, size; zh, vision; ə, about, item, edible, gallop, circus, peaceful

IN FOREIGN WORDS:

à, *Fr.* ami; œ, *Fr.* feu, *Ger.* schön; ü, *Fr.* tu, *Ger.* über; KH, *Ger.* ich, *Scot.* loch; N, *Fr.* bon; y′, *Fr.* Compiègne

STRESS MARKS:

Primary stress: ′ **in·cite′** (ĭn-sīt′)
Secondary stress: ′ **in′sight′** (ĭn′sīt′)

in-, in + *vestīgāre,* to trace, track, from *vestīgium,* trace, footprint, VESTIGE.] **—in·ves·ti·ga·ble, in·ves·ti·ga·tive, in·ves·ti·ga·to·ry** (ĭn-vĕsʹtĭ-gə-tôr′ē, -tōr′ē) *adj.* **—in·ves·ti·ga·tor** *n.*

in·ves·ti·ga·tion (ĭn-vĕs′tĭ-gāʹshən) *n.* The act, process, or an instance of investigating; an inquiry.

investigative journalism *n.* The gathering of news, especially news of crime, corruption, official mismanagement, or controversial plans, by means of investigation. **—investigative journalist** *n.*

in·ves·ti·tive (ĭn-vĕsʹtə-tĭv) *adj.* Of or pertaining to investiture.

in·ves·ti·ture (ĭn-vĕsʹtə-cho͝or′) *n.* **1.** The act or formal ceremony of conferring upon a person the authority and symbols of a high office. **2.** *Chiefly British.* An act or formal ceremony of conferring honors or awards, especially one performed by a sovereign. **3.** *Archaic.* A thing that covers or adorns, as a garment. [Middle English, from Medieval Latin *investītūra,* from *investīre,* INVEST.]

in·vest·ment (ĭn-vĕstʹmənt) *n.* **1.** The act of investing or the state of being invested. **2.** An amount invested. **3.** Property or another possession acquired or invested in for future income or benefit. **4.** Investiture. **5.** *Archaic.* A garment; vestment. **6.** An outer covering or layer. **7.** *Rare.* A siege.

investment trust *n.* Also **investment company.** *Finance.* A company that invests its capital, acquired by the issue of shares, solely in other companies.

in·vet·er·ate (ĭn-vĕtʹər-ĭt) *adj.* **1.** Firmly established by long standing; deep-rooted. **2.** Persisting in an ingrained habit; habitual: *an inveterate liar.* [Latin *inveterātus,* past participle of *inveterāre,* to render old : *in-* (causative) + *vetus* (stem *veter-*), old.] **—in·vet·er·a·cy** (ĭn-vĕtʹər-ə-sē), **in·vet·er·ate·ness** *n.* **—in·vet·er·ate·ly** *adv.*

in·vi·a·ble (ĭn-vīʹə-bəl) *adj.* Nonviable; especially, biologically incapable of growth or reproduction: *an inviable seed.*

in·vid·i·ous (ĭn-vĭdʹē-əs) *adj.* **1.** Tending to rouse ill will or animosity; offensive: *an invidious clause in the contract.* **2.** Containing or implying a slight; unfairly discriminatory. [Latin *invidiōsus,* envious, hostile, from *invidia,* ENVY.] **—in·vid·i·ous·ly** *adv.* **—in·vid·i·ous·ness** *n.*

in·vig·or·ate (ĭn-vĭgʹə-rāt′) *tr.v.* **-ated, -ating, -ates.** To impart vigor, strength, or vitality to: *"A few whiffs of the raw, strong scent of phlox invigorated her"* (D.H. Lawrence). [IN- (causative) + VIGOR + -ATE.] **—in·vig·or·at·ing·ly, in·vig·or·a·tive·ly** *adv.* **—in·vig·or·a·tion** *n.* **—in·vig·or·a·tive** *adj.* **—in·vig·or·a·tor** *n.*

in·vin·ci·ble (ĭn-vĭnʹsə-bəl) *adj.* **1.** Unconquerable; unbeatable. **2.** Incapable of being surmounted; insuperable. [Middle English, from Latin *invincibilis* : *in-,* not + *vincibilis,* VINCIBLE.] **—in·vin·ci·bil·i·ty, in·vin·ci·ble·ness** *n.* **—in·vin·ci·bly** *adv.*

in vi·no ve·ri·tas (ĭn vēʹnō vĕrʹĭ-täs′). *Latin.* When drunk, one speaks the truth. [Latin, "in wine (there is) truth."]

in·vi·o·la·ble (ĭn-vīʹə-lə-bəl) *adj.* **1.** Safe from or secured against violation or profanation; kept sacred. **2.** Impregnable to assault, trespass, or disturbance. **—in·vi·o·la·bil·i·ty, in·vi·o·la·ble·ness** *n.* **—in·vi·o·la·bly** *adv.*

in·vi·o·late (ĭn-vīʹə-lĭt) *adj.* Not violated; intact: *an inviolate shrine.* [Middle English *invyolat,* from Latin *inviolātus* : *in-,* not + *violātus,* past participle of *violāre,* VIOLATE.] **—in·vi·o·la·cy** (ĭn-vīʹə-lə-sē), **in·vi·o·late·ness** *n.* **—in·vi·o·late·ly** *adv.*

in·vis·cid (ĭn-vĭsʹĭd) *adj.* **1.** Having no viscosity. **2.** Of or pertaining to an inviscid fluid.

in·vis·i·ble (ĭn-vĭzʹə-bəl) *adj.* **1.** Incapable of being seen; not visible. **2.** Not accessible to view; hidden. **3. a.** Not easily noticed or detected; inconspicuous. **b.** Hidden from public view. **4.** *Economics.* **a.** Not published in financial statements: *an invisible asset.* **b.** Designating items of international trade consisting of services rather than goods: *invisible exports.*
~*n.* **1.** One that is invisible. **2. invisibles.** *Economics.* Imports and exports of services such as tourism, banking, or insurance, as opposed to goods. **—in·vis·i·bil·i·ty, in·vis·i·ble·ness** *n.* **—in·vis·i·bly** *adv.*

invisible ink *n.* Ink that is colorless and invisible until treated by a chemical, heat, or special light. Also called "sympathetic ink."

in·vi·ta·tion (ĭn′və-tāʹshən) *n.* **1.** The act of inviting. **2.** A spoken or written request for one's presence or participation. **3.** An allurement, enticement, or attraction.

in·vi·ta·tion·al (ĭn′və-tāʹshən-əl) *adj.* Restricted to invited participants: *an invitational golf tournament.*

in·vi·ta·to·ry (ĭn-vīʹtə-tôr′ē, -tōr′ē) *n., pl.* **-ries.** A psalm or other piece sung as an invitation to prayer in church services. [Middle English *invytatory,* from Medieval Latin *invītātōrium,* from the neuter of Late Latin *invītātōrius,* inviting, antiphonal, from Latin *invītāre,* INVITE.]

in·vite (ĭn-vītʹ) *v.* **-vited, -viting, -vites.** *—tr.* **1.** To request the presence or participation of. **2.** To request politely or formally. **3.** To tend to bring on; provoke. **4.** To lure; entice; tempt. *—intr.* To give an invitation.
~*n.* (ĭnʹvīt′). *Informal.* An invitation. [Old French *inviter,* from Latin *invītāre*†.]

in·vit·ing (ĭn-vīʹtĭng) *adj.* Attractive; tempting: *an inviting dessert.* **—in·vit·ing·ly** *adv.* **—in·vit·ing·ness** *n.*

in vi·tro (ĭn vēʹtrō) *adj.* Designating biological processes made to occur in an artificial environment outside the living organism: *in vitro fertilization.* [New Latin, "in glass."] **—in vi·tro** *adv.*

in vi·vo (ĭn vēʹvō) *adj.* Designating biological processes or experiments conducted or occurring within the living organism. [New Latin, "in a living body."] **—in vi·vo** *adv.*

in·vo·cate (ĭnʹvə-kāt′) *tr.v.* **-cated, -cating, -cates.** *Archaic.* To invoke. [Latin *invocāre,* INVOKE.] **—in·voc·a·tive** (ĭn-vŏkʹə-tĭv) *adj.* **—in·vo·ca·tor** *n.*

in·vo·ca·tion (ĭn′və-kāʹshən) *n.* **1.** The act of invoking; especially, an appeal to a higher power for assistance. **2.** A prayer or other formula used in invoking, as at the opening of a religious service. **3. a.** A conjuring or calling up of a spirit by incantation. **b.** The incantation used in conjuring. [Middle English, from Old French, from Latin *invocātiō* (stem *invocātiōn-*), from *invocāre,* INVOKE.] **—in·vo·ca·tion·al** *adj.*

in·voc·a·to·ry (ĭn-vŏkʹə-tôr′ē, -tōr′ē) *adj.* Of, pertaining to, or having the nature of an invocation.

in·voice (ĭnʹvois′) *n. Abbr.* **inv.** A detailed list of goods supplied or sent or services rendered, with an account of all costs; a bill.
~*tr.v.* **invoiced, -voicing, -voices. 1.** To list on an invoice. **2.** To present an invoice to. [Originally *invoyes,* plural of *invoy,* invoice, from Old French *envoy,* a sending, shipment of goods. See **envoi.**]

in·voke (ĭn-vōkʹ) *tr.v.* **-voked, -voking, -vokes. 1.** To call upon (a higher power) for assistance. **2.** To appeal to; petition. **3.** To call for (help, for example) earnestly; solicit. **4.** To summon (a spirit, for example) with incantations; conjure up. **5.** To cite in support or justification of one's cause. [Old French *invoquer,* from Latin *invocāre,* "to call upon" : *in-,* in, on + *vocāre,* to call.] **—in·vo·ca·ble** *adj.* **—in·vok·er** *n.*

in·vol·u·cel (ĭn-vŏlʹyo͞o-sĕl′) *n. Botany.* A secondary involucre, as at the base of an umbellule in a compound umbel. [New Latin *involucellum,* diminutive of *involucrum,* INVOLUCRE.]

in·vo·lu·crate (ĭn′və-lo͞oʹkrĭt, -krāt′) *adj. Botany.* Having an involucre.

in·vo·lu·cre (ĭnʹvə-lo͞o′kər) *n.* Also **in·vo·lu·crum** (-lo͞oʹkrəm) *pl.* **-cra** (-krə). *Botany.* A whorl or series of leaflike scales or bracts beneath or around a flower or flower cluster. [New Latin *involucrum,* from Latin, wrapper, case, envelope, from *involvere,* to enwrap, INVOLVE.] **—in·vo·lu·cral** *adj.*

in·vo·lu·crum (ĭn′və-lo͞oʹkrəm) *n., pl.* **-cra** (-krə). **1.** An enveloping sheath or envelope. **2.** *Botany.* Variant of **involucre.** [New Latin, INVOLUCRE.]

in·vol·un·tar·y (ĭn-vŏlʹən-tĕr′ē) *adj.* **1.** Not desired; enforced: *involuntary exile.* **2.** Performed without conscious willing; unintentional. **3.** *Physiology.* Not subject to conscious control: *an involuntary muscle.* —See Synonyms at **spontaneous. —in·vol·un·tar·i·ly** *adv.* **—in·vol·un·tar·i·ness** *n.*

in·vo·lute (ĭnʹvə-lo͞ot′) *adj.* Also **in·vo·lut·ed** (-lo͞oʹtĭd). **1.** Intricate; complex. **2.** *Botany.* Having the margins rolled inward. **3.** Having whorls that obscure the axis or other volutions, as the shell of a cowry.
~*n. Mathematics.* The locus of a fixed point on a tangent line as it rolls but does not slide around a fixed curve.
~*intr.v.* (ĭn′və-lo͞otʹ) **involuted, -luting, -lutes.** To become involute. [Latin *involutus,* past participle of *involvere,* to enwrap, INVOLVE.]

in·vo·lu·tion (ĭn′və-lo͞oʹshən) *n.* **1.** The act of involving or the state of being involved. **2.** Anything that is internally complex or involved. **3.** *Grammar.* A complicated construction. **4.** *Mathematics.* The multiplying of a quantity by itself a specified number of times; raising to a power. In this sense, compare **evolution. 5.** *Physiology.* The shrinking of an organ, as of the womb after childbirth, or as a result of old age. [Latin *involūtiō* (stem *involūtiōn-*), from *involvere,* INVOLVE.]

in·volve (ĭn-vŏlvʹ) *tr.v.* **-volved, -volving, -volves. 1.** To contain or include as a part. **2.** To have as a necessary feature or consequence; imply. **3.** To draw in as an associate or participant; embroil; implicate. **4.** To occupy or engross completely; absorb. **5.** To make complex or intricate; complicate. **6.** *Poetic.* To wrap; envelop: *a castle involved in mist.* **7.** *Archaic.* To wind or coil about. **8.** *Mathematics.* To raise (a number) to a specified degree. Not in technical usage. —See Synonyms at **include.** [Middle English *involven,* from Latin *involvere,* to enwrap, "roll in" : *in-,* in + *volvere,* to roll, turn.] **—in·volve·ment** *n.* **—in·volv·er** *n.*

in·volved (ĭn-vŏlvdʹ) *adj.* **1.** Complicated; intricate. **2.** Involute; twisted. **3.** Confused; tangled. **4.** Associated; implicated; concerned. Used with *in: involved in a conspiracy.* **5.** Having a romantic or sexual relationship. Used with *with.* —See Synonyms at **complex.**

in·vul·ner·a·ble (ĭn-vŭlʹnər-ə-bəl) *adj.* **1.** Immune to attack; impregnable: *an invulnerable position.* **2.** Incapable of being damaged, injured, or wounded. [Latin *invulnerābilis* : *in-,* not + *vulnerāre,* to wound (see **vulnerable**).] **—in·vul·ner·a·bil·i·ty, in·vul·ner·a·ble·ness** *n.* **—in·vul·ner·a·bly** *adv.*

in·ward (ĭnʹwərd) *adj.* **1.** Located inside; inner. **2.** Directed or moving toward the interior. **3.** Existing in thought or mind. **4.** Intimate; familiar. Used with *with.*
~*adv.* Also **in·wards** (-wərdz). **1.** Toward the inside or center. **2.** Toward the mind or the self: *thoughts turned inward.*
~*n.* **1.** An inner or central part. **2.** An inner essence or spirit. **3. inwards.** Entrails; innards. [Middle English *inward,* Old English *inweard.*]

in·ward·ly (ĭnʹwərd-lē) *adv.* **1.** On or in the inside; within. **2.** Within one's own mind or thoughts: *inwardly alarmed.* **3.** Privately; to oneself: *inwardly laughing.* **4.** *Archaic.* Intimately; closely.

in·ward·ness (ĭnʹwərd-nĭs) *n.* **1.** Intimacy; familiarity. **2. a.** Self-preoccupation; introspection. **b.** Concern with the spiritual aspect of life. **3.** Essential or fundamental nature. **4.** Internal quality or essence.

in·weave (ĭn-wēvʹ) *tr.v.* **-wove** (-wōvʹ) or **-weaved, -woven** (-wōʹvən) or *rare* **-wove, -weaving, -weaves.** To weave into a fabric or design.

in·wrought (ĭn-rôt′) *adj.* **1.** Worked or woven in, as thread might be. **2.** Having a pattern worked or woven in, as a fabric might.

in·ya·la (ĭn-yä′lə) *n.* An antelope, the **nyala** *(see).*

I·o¹ (ī′ō). *Greek Mythology.* A maiden who was loved by Zeus and transformed by him or by Hera into a heifer.

Io² *n.* The innermost of Jupiter's four large satellites, and the second nearest to the surface of the planet.

IOC International Olympic Committee.

i·o·date (ī′ə-dāt′) *tr.v.* **-dated, -dating, -dates.** To iodize. ～*n.* A salt of iodic acid. [IOD(O)- + -ATE.]

i·od·ic acid (ī-ŏd′ĭk) *n.* A colorless or white crystalline powder, HIO₃, used as an antiseptic and deodorant. [French *iodique*, from *iode*, IODINE.]

i·o·dide (ī′ə-dīd′) *n.* A binary compound of iodine with a more electropositive atom or group. [IOD(O)- + -IDE.]

i·o·dine (ī′ə-dīn′, -dīn, -dēn′) *n. Symbol* I **1.** A lustrous, grayish-black, corrosive, poisonous halogen element having radioactive isotopes, especially I-131, used as tracers and in thyroid disease diagnosis and therapy. Its compounds are used as germicides, antiseptics, and dyes. Atomic number 53, atomic weight 126.9044, melting point 113.5°C, boiling point 184.35°C, specific gravity (solid, 20°C) 4.93, valences 1, 3, 5, 7. **2.** A tincture *(see)* of iodine and sodium iodide, NaI, or potassium iodide, KI, used as an antiseptic for wounds. [French *iode*, from Greek *iōdēs, ioeidēs*, violet-colored : *ion*, violet, of Mediterranean origin + -INE.]

i·o·dism (ī′ə-dĭz′əm) *n.* Poisoning by iodine or iodine compounds. [IOD(O)- + -ISM.]

i·o·dize (ī′ə-dīz′) *tr.v.* **-dized, -dizing, -dizes.** To treat or combine with iodine or an iodide. [IOD(O)- + -IZE.]

iodo-, iod- *prefix.* Indicates iodine; for example, **iodoform, iodide.** [French *iode*, IODINE.]

i·o·do·form (ī-ō′də-fôrm′, ī-ŏd′ə-) *n.* A yellowish iodine compound, CHI₃, used as an antiseptic. [IODO- + FORM(YL).]

i·o·dom·e·try (ī′ə-dŏm′ə-trē) *n. Chemistry.* A form of volumetric analysis for the estimation of the strength of iodine solutions by titration against sodium thiosulfate, using starch as an indicator. [IODO- + -METRY.] —**i·o·do·me·tric** (ī′ə-dō-mĕt′rĭk) *adj.*

i·o·do·phor (ī-ō′də-fôr′) *n.* A substance consisting of iodine and a solubilizing agent that releases free iodine when in solution. [IODO- + -PHOR(E).]

i·o·dop·sin (ī′ə-dŏp′sĭn) *n.* A light-sensitive pigment in retinal cones of the eye.

i·o·lite (ī′ə-līt′) *n.* A blue silicate mineral, Al₃(Mg,Fe)₂AlSi₅O₁₈, occurring chiefly in metamorphic rocks. Also called "cordierite."

i·o moth (ī′ō) *n.* A large yellowish moth, *Automeris io,* of North America, having prominent eyelike spots on the hind wings. [After *Io,* who was tormented by gadflies sent by Hera as a punishment.]

i·on (ī′ən, ī′ŏn′) *n.* An atom, group of atoms, or molecule that has acquired a net electric charge by gaining electrons in or losing electrons from an initially electrically neutral configuration. [Greek *ion,* "going particle" (referring to the passage of ions to either of the electrodes in electrolysis), neuter present participle of *ienai,* to go.]

-ion *suffix.* Indicates: **1.** An act or process or the outcome of an act or process; for example, **indention. 2.** A state of being; for example, **cohesion.** [Middle English *-io(u)n,* from Old French *-ion,* from Latin *-iō* (stem *-iōn-*).]

I·o·na (ī-ō′nə). Small island of the Inner Hebrides. Of religious importance since St. Columba founded a monastery there (563), it is also the burial place of many of the monarchs of Scotland, Ireland, Norway, and Denmark. It is rich in Celtic remains.

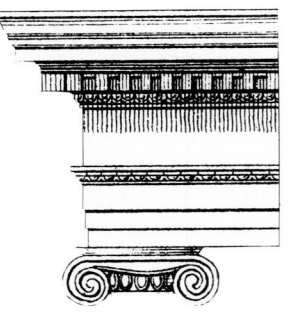

Ionic order *The scroll, or volute, of Ionic capitals has its source in natural spiral forms such as the Egyptian lotus, the nautilus shell, and rams' horns.*

IRAN AND IRAQ

ion engine *n.* A rocket engine that develops thrust by expelling ions rather than gaseous combustion products. Also called "ion rocket." See **ionic propulsion.**

I·o·nes·co (yə-nĕs′kō, ĕ′ə-), **Eugene** (1912–). Romanian-born French playwright, whose play, *The Bald Soprano* (1956), marked a new era in the Theater of the Absurd. He continued to stress his rejection of realism in plays such as *Rhinoceros* (1960) and *Exit the King* (1963).

ion exchange *n.* A reversible chemical reaction between a solid and a solution by means of which ions may be interchanged, used in water softening and separation of radioactive isotopes.

I·o·ni·a (ī-ō′nē-ə). A region on the western coast of Asia Minor. An ancient Greek settlement, it was probably colonized (*c.* 1100 B.C.) by refugees from Achaea. The Ionians became the cultural leaders of the Greek world between the 8th and 6th centuries B.C. Conquered by the Lydians (550 B.C.) and by the Persians (546 B.C.), they were eclipsed following their unsuccessful revolt (499–494 B.C.).

I·o·ni·an (ī-ō′nē-ən) *adj.* **1.** Of or pertaining to Ionia or the Ionians. **2.** *Music.* Of or designating an authentic mode represented by the scale of C on a keyboard instrument. ～*n.* A member of a Hellenic people who settled in Attica and on the northern coast of the Peloponnese in about 1100 B.C. and founded colonies in Asia Minor.

Ionian Islands. Chain of Greek islands in the Ionian Sea. They extend from Corfu, off the west coast of Greece and Albania, southward to Zante (Zákinthos), off the southwest Greek coast, and include Paxoi, Levkás, Cephalonia (Kefallinía), and Ithaca, the legendary home of Odysseus.

Ionian Sea. Area of the central Mediterranean. Bounded by Sicily and southern Italy in the west, the Strait of Otranto in the north, and Greece in the east, it includes the Ionian Islands.

i·on·ic (ī-ŏn′ĭk) *adj.* Of, containing, or involving ions.

I·on·ic (ī-ŏn′ĭk) *adj.* **1.** Ionian. **2.** Pertaining to the Ionic order. **3.** In Greek verse: **a.** Designating a metrical foot consisting of two long syllables followed by two short ones, or two short syllables followed by two long ones. **b.** Designating a verse or meter having such feet. ～*n.* **1.** The ancient Greek dialect of Ionia, belonging to Attic-Ionic, early developed as a medium for scientific and historical prose. **2.** In Greek verse, an Ionic foot, verse, or meter.

ionic bond *n.* A chemical bond characteristic of salts and formed by the complete transfer of one or more electrons from one kind of atom to another. Also called "electrovalent bond."

ionic crystal *n.* A crystal formed of an array of positive and negative ions held together by electrostatic forces.

Ionic order *n.* An order of classical Greek architecture characterized by fluted columns and two opposed volutes in the capital. Compare **Corinthian order, Doric order.**

ionic propulsion *n.* Propulsion by the reactive thrust of a high-speed beam of similarly charged ions ejected by an ion engine. Also called "ion propulsion."

ion implantation *n.* A technique for introducing controlled amounts of impurity into a material, usually into a semiconductor, by bombarding it with ions of the impurity.

i·on·i·za·tion (ī′ə-nə-zā′shən) *n.* **1.** The formation of one or more ions by the addition of electrons to or the removal of electrons from an electrically neutral atomic or molecular configuration, by heat, electrical discharge, radiation, or chemical reaction. **2.** The state or condition of being ionized.

ionization chamber *n.* A gas-filled enclosure fitted with electrodes between which electric current flows upon ionization of the gas by incident radiation, the electrodes being maintained at a potential difference just sufficient to collect ions thus produced without causing further ionization.

ionization potential *n.* The energy required to remove completely the weakest bound electron from its ground state in an atom or molecule so that the resulting ion is also in its ground state.

i·on·ize (ī′ə-nīz′) *v.* **-ized, -izing, -izes.** —*tr.* To convert totally or partially into ions. —*intr.* To become converted totally or partially into ions.

ionizing radiation *n.* Radiation capable of producing ionization, including energetic charged particles such as alpha and beta rays, and electromagnetic radiation such as x-rays, and neutrons.

i·o·none (ī′ə-nōn′) *n.* Either of two yellowish to colorless liquid isomers, C₁₃H₂₀O, having a strong odor of violets and used in perfumes. [Greek *ion,* violet (see **iodine**) + -ONE.]

i·on·o·sphere (ī-ŏn′ə-sfîr′) *n.* An electrically conducting set of layers of the earth's atmosphere, extending from altitudes of approximately 60 to 400 kilometers (35 to 250 miles) and more, caused by ionization of rarefied atmospheric gases by incident solar radiation; the D, E, and F layers. [ION + -SPHERE.]

i·on·o·spher·ic wave (ī-ŏn′ə-sfîr′ĭk) *n. Electronics.* A **sky wave** *(see).*

ion propulsion *n.* Ionic propulsion.

ion rocket *n.* **1.** A rocket using ionic propulsion. **2.** An **ion engine** *(see).*

ion trap *n.* A magnet mounted to the neck of a kinescope to prevent ions from striking the kinescope screen.

I.O.O.F. Independent Order of Oddfellows.

i·o·ta (ī-ō′tə) *n.* **1.** The ninth letter in the Greek alphabet, written I, ι. Transliterated in English as *I, i.* See feature at **alphabet. 2.** A very small amount. Often used in the phrase *not one iota.* [Greek *iōta,* of Semitic origin; akin to Hebrew *yōdh,* YOD.]

i·o·ta·cism (ī-ō′tə-sĭz′əm) *n.* The conversion of other vowel sounds in Greek to the sound of iota. [Late Latin *iotacismus,* from Greek *iotakismos,* from *iōta,* IOTA.]

IOU (ī′ō-yōō′) *n., pl.* **IOU's, IOUs.** A promise to pay a debt. [Short for *I owe you.*]

–ious *suffix.* Indicates characterized by or full of; for example, **sagacious, edacious.** [Middle English, partly from Latin *-ius,* and partly from Old French *-ieus, -ieux,* from Latin *-iōsus : -i-,* stem + *-ōsus,* -OUS.]

I·o·wa[1] (ī′ə-wə). State in the north-central United States, between the Mississippi and Missouri rivers. It was part of the Louisiana Purchase. Almost 95 percent of its gently undulating land is given over to agriculture. The capital, Des Moines, is a meat-processing center. —**I·o·wan** *adj. & n.*

Iowa[2]. River, 530 kilometers (329 miles) long, rising in the lakes of northern Iowa and flowing southeast to the Mississippi River.

Iowa[3] *n., pl.* **-was** or collectively **Iowa.** 1. A member of a Siouan-speaking North American Indian people formerly inhabiting the region of Minnesota, Iowa, and Missouri. 2. The Siouan language of this people. —**I·o·wa** *adj.*

IPA, I.P.A. 1. International Phonetic Alphabet. 2. International Phonetic Association. 3. isopropyl alcohol.

ip·e·cac (ĭp′ə-kăk′) *n.* Also **ip·e·cac·u·an·ha** (ĭp′ə-kăk′yōō-ăn′ə). 1. A low-growing South American shrub, *Cephaelis ipecacuanha.* 2. A medicinal extract from the dried roots of this shrub used as an expectorant and to induce vomiting. [Shortened from Portuguese *ipecacuanha,* from Tupi *ipekaaguéne.*]

Iph·i·ge·ni·a (ĭf′ə-jə-nī′ə, -nē′ə). *Greek Mythology.* The daughter of Clytemnestra and Agamemnon, offered as a sacrifice to Artemis to enable the Greek fleet to sail for Troy.

ip·o·moe·a (ĭp′ə-mē′ə) *n.* Any tropical or subtropical climbing plant of the genus *Ipomoea,* such as the sweet potato and morning glory, having trumpet-shaped flowers. [New Latin, from Greek *ips* (stem *ipo-*), worm + *homoios,* like.]

ip·pon (ĭp′pŏn′) *n.* In judo, a full scoring point, resulting directly in victory. [Japanese, "point."]

ip·se dix·it (ĭp′sĕ dĭk′sĭt) *n., pl.* **ipse dixits.** 1. An unsupported assertion, usually by a person of authority or standing. 2. An arbitrary statement; dictum. [Latin, he himself said (it), translation of Doric Greek *autos epha,* expression used by the Pythagoreans of sayings of Pythagoras.]

ip·si·lat·er·al (ĭp′sə-lăt′ər-əl) *adj.* On or affecting the same side of the body. [Irregularly from Latin *ipse,* self + LATERAL.]

ip·sis·si·ma ver·ba (ĭp-sĭs′ə-mə vûr′bə) *pl.n.* The very words. [Latin.]

ip·so fac·to (ĭp′sō făk′tō) *adv.* By the fact itself; by that very fact: *An alien, ipso facto, has no right to a U.S. passport.* [Latin.]

ip·so ju·re (ĭp′sō jōōr′ē) *adv.* By the law itself. [Latin.]

Ips·wich (ĭp′swĭch′). Town and port in Suffolk, eastern England, at the head of the Orwell estuary. It is the administrative center for the county and supports engineering and chemical industries.

IPTS International Practical Temperature Scale.

IQ, I.Q. intelligence quotient.

Ir The symbol for the element iridium.

Ir. Irish.

ir–[1]. Variant of **in-**[1].

ir–[2]. Variant of **in-**[2].

IRA individual retirement account.

I.R.A., IRA *n.* Irish Republican Army: a secret Irish Nationalist organization formed to oppose the partition of Ireland, active in anti-British terrorist acts in the 1930's and 1940's, and again in the 1970's and 1980's. In 1969 it split into the **Official** and **Provisional** wings *(both of which see).* See **Sinn Fein.**

i·ra·de (ĭ-rä′dĕ) *n.* A decree by a Muslim ruler. [Turkish, from Arabic *'irāda,* will.]

I·rá·kli·on (ĭ-rä′klē-ôn′). Also **He·rak·li·on** (hĭ-răk′lē-ən). *Italian* **Can·di·a** (kăn′dē-ə). Port on the north coast of the island of Crete, Greece. It is the island's chief port and exports wine, olive oil, and fruit. It is noted for its Venetian fortifications, the relics of 15th- and 16th-century Venetian rule.

I·ran (ĭ-răn′, ē-rän′). Formerly **Per·sia** (pûr′zhə, -shə). Country of western Asia. Mountainous and sparsely populated, its geographical position has made it a crossroads for trade and culture and a target for conquest. Overrun by many, including Alexander the Great (*c.* 325 B.C.) and the Arabs (7th century A.D.), who introduced Islam, Persia was always able eventually to overthrow or absorb each occupation and re-establish its own power. By the late 18th century, however, it had declined into a buffer state between Russia, Turkey, and British India. In World War II the country (known since 1935 as Iran) was occupied jointly by Russia and Britain, who installed Muhammad Reza Pahlavi as shah (1941). Despite massive U.S. aid, the shah was overthrown (1979) by a revolution led by the Muslim fundamentalist leader, Ayatollah Khomeini. Ninety percent uncultivated, the country is economically dependent on its vast oil reserves, up to 10 percent of the world's total. Area, 1,648,000 square kilometers (636,290 square miles). Population, 54,607,000. Capital, Tehran.

I·ra·ni·an (ĭ-rä′nē-ən) *adj.* Of or pertaining to Iran, its inhabitants, or their language.

~ *n.* 1. A native or inhabitant of Iran. 2. a. A group of languages including Persian, Kurdish, and Pashto, spoken principally in Iran,

IRELAND

Afghanistan, and west Pakistan, and forming a subbranch of the Indo-Iranian branch of the Indo-European language family. b. The modern Persian language as spoken in Iran; Farsi.

I·raq (ĭ-răk′, ē-räk′). Republic of western Asia. Its area includes the site of ancient Mesopotamia, between the Tigris and Euphrates rivers. Wrested from the Turkish empire and established as an independent kingdom (1921), it joined the Arab League (1945) and following the assassination of the king (1958) became a socialist republic. It began fighting an inconclusive war with Iran in 1980 and finally agreed to a truce in 1988. In 1990 it invaded Kuwait and was forced to withdraw in 1991. Iraq's oil accounts for over 90 percent of its exports. Area, 434,924 square kilometers (167,924 square miles). Population, 18,900,000. Capital, Baghdad. See map at **Iran.**

I·ra·qi (ē-rä′kē) *adj.* Of or pertaining to Iraq, its inhabitants, or their language.

~*n., pl.* **-qis** or collectively **Iraqi.** 1. A native or inhabitant of Iraq. 2. The Arabic dialect spoken in Iraq.

i·ras·ci·ble (ĭ-răs′ə-bəl, ĭ-răs′-) *adj.* 1. Prone to outbursts of temper; easily angered. 2. Characterized by or resulting from anger. [Old French, from Late Latin *īrāscibilis,* from Latin *īrāscī,* to get angry, from *īra,* anger, IRE.] —**i·ras·ci·bil·i·ty, i·ras·ci·ble·ness** *n.* —**i·ras·ci·bly** *adv.*

i·rate (ī-rāt′, ī′rāt′) *adj.* 1. Angry; enraged. 2. Characterized or occasioned by anger: *an irate phone call.* [Latin *īrātus,* from *īra,* anger, IRE.] —**i·rate·ly** *adv.*

IRBM Intermediate Range Ballistic Missile.

ire (īr) *n.* Wrath; anger. —See Synonyms at **anger.** [Middle English, from Old French, from Latin *īra,* anger.]

ire·ful (īr′fəl) *adj.* Full of ire; angry; wrathful. —**ire·ful·ly** *adv.* —**ire·ful·ness** *n.*

Ire·land (īr′lənd). *Irish* **Ei·re** (âr′ə). Second largest of the British Isles. Its fertile central lowlands contain many peat bogs and are surrounded by several low mountain ranges, including the mountains of Mourne, Wicklow, Kerry, and Ox. Once occupied by a number of Celtic kingdoms, after the 12th century it fell increasingly under English domination. Following violence and unrest during and after World War I the predominantly Roman Catholic southern 26 counties became an autonomous state, the 6 northern counties remaining within the United Kingdom as the province of Northern Ireland.

Ireland, Republic of. Country of northwestern Europe. After much bitter fighting and civil unrest the Anglo-Irish Treaty (1921) paved the way for the 26 southern counties of Ireland to become the Irish Free State (1922). In 1937 a new constitution with full sovereignty was adopted by plebiscite, and the people called their country Eire.

It left the Commonwealth in 1949 and since then has been known officially as the Republic of Ireland. Mainly agricultural, its economy rests chiefly on beef and dairy cattle, sheep, pig, and poultry farming, two-thirds of the land being used for crop or pasture. Distilling, brewing, food processing, and electronics, chemicals, and textile manufacture are also important. The republic has been a member of the European Economic Community since 1973. Area, 70,283 square kilometers (27,136 square miles). Population, 3,700,000. Capital, Dublin.

I·re·ne (ī-rē′nē). *Greek Mythology.* The goddess of peace. [From Greek *eirēnē,* peace.]

i·ren·ic, ei·ren·ic (ī-rĕn′ĭk, ī-rē′nĭk) *adj.* Also **i·ren·i·cal, ei·ren·i·cal** (ī-rĕn′ĭk-əl, ī-rē′-). Promoting peace; conciliatory; pacific. [Greek *eirēnikos,* from *eirēnē†,* peace.] —**i·ren·i·cal·ly** *adv.*

irenicon. Variant of **eirenicon.**

i·ren·ics (ī-rĕn′ĭks, ī-rē′nĭks) *n. Used with a singular verb.* The branch of theology dealing with the promotion of peace and unity among Christian churches.

Ire·ton (īr′tən), **Henry** (1611–51). English Parliamentary general during the English Civil War (1642–51). Ireton married Cromwell's daughter and later helped bring Charles I to trial, being one of the signatories of his death warrant.

Irian Jaya. See **West Irian.**

ir·i·da·ceous (ĭr′ī-dā′shəs) *adj.* Of or pertaining to the iris family. [From New Latin *Iridacea,* iris family, from *Iris,* type genus, from Latin, iris.]

ir·i·dec·to·my (ĭr′ə-dĕk′tə-mē, ī′rə-) *n., pl.* **-mies.** The surgical removal of part of the iris of the eye. [Latin *īris* (stem *īrido-*), IRIS + -ECTOMY.]

ir·i·des·cent (ĭr′ə-dĕs′ənt) *adj.* Producing a display of lustrous, rainbowlike colors. [Latin *īris* (stem *īrid-*), rainbow, IRIS + -ESCENT.] —**ir·i·des·cence** *n.*

i·rid·ic (ī-rĭd′ĭk, ī-rĭd′-) *adj.* Pertaining to the iris of the eye.

i·rid·i·um (ī-rĭd′ē-əm, ī-rĭd′-) *n. Symbol* **Ir** A very hard and brittle, exceptionally corrosion-resistant, whitish-yellow metallic element occurring in platinum ores and used principally to harden platinum and in high-temperature materials, electrical contacts, and wear-resistant bearings. Atomic number 77, atomic weight 192.2, melting point 2,410°C, boiling point 4,527°C, specific gravity 22.42 (17°C), valences 3, 4. [New Latin, from Latin *īris* (stem *īrid-*), rainbow, IRIS (from the variety of colors it gives in solutions).]

ir·i·dos·mine (ĭr′ə-dŏz′mĭn, -dŏs′mĭn, ī′rə-) *n.* An alloy, **osmiridium** *(see).* [German *Iridosmin* : IRID(IUM) + OSM(IUM) + -INE.]

i·ris (ī′rĭs) *n., pl.* **irises** or **irides** (ī′rə-dēz′, ĭr′ə-). **1.** The pigmented, round, contractile membrane of the eye, situated between the cornea and lens, and perforated by the pupil. **2.** Any of numerous plants of the genus *Iris,* having sword-shaped leaves and variously colored flowers. **3.** *Rare.* A rainbow or rainbowlike display of colors. [Middle English *iris, yris,* rainbow, kind of prismatic crystal, from Latin *īris,* from Greek *iris,* rainbow, iris of the eye.]

I·ris (ī′rĭs). *Greek Mythology.* The goddess of the rainbow and messenger of the gods.

iris diaphragm *n.* A diaphragm that can be adjusted to vary the diameter of a central aperture, commonly used on cameras to regulate the amount of light admitted to a lens.

I·rish (ī′rĭsh) *adj. Abbr.* **Ir.** Of or pertaining to Ireland, its people, or their language.
~*n. Abbr.* **Ir. 1.** *Used with a plural verb.* **a.** The inhabitants of Ireland. **b.** People of immediate Irish descent. **2.** The Celtic language spoken in Ireland; Irish Gaelic. **3.** The English spoken in Ireland. **4.** *Informal.* Fieriness of temper or passion; high spirit. [Middle English *Irisc(h),* from Old English *Īras,* the Irish.]

Irish bull *n.* An apparently consistent but actually illogical or inconsistent statement.

Irish coffee *n.* A drink of sweetened hot coffee and Irish whiskey, topped with thick cream.

Irish elk *n.* A large extinct European deer of the genus *Megaloceros,* of the Pliocene and Pleistocene epochs, having palmate antlers.

Irish English *n.* English as spoken by the Irish.

Irish Gaelic *n.* The Goidelic language of Ireland, an official language of the Republic of Ireland. Also called "Erse," "Irish."

I·rish·ism (ī′rĭsh-ĭz′əm) *n.* An Irish idiom or custom.

I·rish·man (ī′rĭsh-mən) *n., pl.* **-men** (-mĭn). A man of Irish birth, citizenship, or descent.

Irish moss *n.* An edible North Atlantic seaweed, *Chondrus crispus,* that yields a mucilaginous substance used medicinally and in preparing jellies. Also called "carrageen."

Irish Republic. 1. The free state proclaimed by Irish rebels against British rule during the abortive Easter Rebellion in Dublin (1916). **2.** The Republic of Ireland. Used erroneously.

Irish Republican Army *n.* The **I.R.A.** *(see).*

Irish Sea. An arm of the Atlantic Ocean. It separates Britain from Ireland and is connected to the Atlantic by the North Channel in the north and by St. George's Channel in the south.

Irish setter *n.* A setter having a silky reddish-brown coat. Also called "red setter."

Irish stew *n.* A stew of meat and vegetables.

Irish terrier *n.* A terrier having a wiry brown coat.

Irish water spaniel *n.* A retriever having a dark curly coat and a characteristic topknot.

Irish whiskey *n.* A whiskey made in Ireland by the distillation of barley.

Irish wolfhound *n.* A large dog of an ancient breed, having a rough, shaggy coat.

I·rish·wom·an (ī′rĭsh-wŏom′ən) *n., pl.* **-women** (-wĭm′ĭn). A woman of Irish birth, citizenship, or descent.

i·ri·tis (ī-rī′tĭs) *n.* Inflammation of the iris of the eye. [New Latin : IR(IS) + -ITIS.]

irk (ûrk) *tr.v.* **irked, irking, irks.** To vex; weary; irritate. —See Synonyms at **annoy.** [Middle English *irken, yrken,* perhaps from Old Norse *yrkja,* to work.]

irk·some (ûrk′səm) *adj.* Causing annoyance or bother; wearisome; tedious: *irksome restrictions.* —See Synonyms at **boring.** —**irk·some·ly** *adv.* —**irk·some·ness** *n.*

IRO International Refugee Organization.

i·ro·ko (ī-rō′kō) *n.* **1.** A tropical tree, *Chlorophora excelsa.* **2.** The wood of this tree, often used as a substitute for teak. [Yoruba.]

i·ron (ī′ərn) *n.* **1.** *Symbol* **Fe** A silvery-white, lustrous, malleable, ductile, magnetic or magnetizable, metallic element occurring abundantly in combined forms, notably in hematite, limonite, magnetite, and taconite, and used alloyed in a wide range of important structural materials. Atomic number 26, atomic weight 55.847, melting point 1,535°C, boiling point 3,000°C, specific gravity 7.874 (20°C), valences 2, 3, 4, 6. **2.** Great hardness or strength; firmness: *a will of iron.* **3.** An implement made of iron alloy or similar metal; especially, a bar heated for use in branding, cauterizing, or soldering. **4.** Any of various golf clubs with a metal head, numbered from one or two to nine or ten according to the degree of slant of the face of the club. **5.** A metal appliance with a handle and a weighted flat bottom, used when heated to press wrinkles from fabric. **6.** *Informal.* A harpoon. **7. irons. a.** Fetters; shackles. **b.** Stirrups. **8.** Iron taken as a dietary supplement in the form of a tonic, pill, or other medication. —**have many irons in the fire.** To be engaged in many undertakings simultaneously. —**in irons. 1.** Fettered. **2.** *Nautical.* Lying head to the wind and unable to turn either way. —**pump iron.** *Informal.* In body building, to exercise with weights. —**strike while the iron is hot.** To seize an opportunity to act.
~*adj.* **1.** Made of or containing iron. **2.** Extremely hard and strong: *an iron fist.* **3.** Hardy; robust: *an iron constitution.* **4.** Inflexible; unyielding: *an iron will.* **5.** Base; degraded.
~*v.* **ironed, ironing, irons.** —*tr.* **1. a.** To press and smooth (clothing, for example) with a heated iron. **b.** To remove (creases) by pressing. Sometimes used with *out.* **2.** *Rare.* To put in irons; fetter. **3.** To fit or clad with iron. —*intr.* **1.** To iron clothes. **2.** To be capable of being ironed: *this fabric irons well.* —**iron out.** To settle through discussion or compromise; work out: *iron out our problems.* [Middle English *yren, yron, iren,* Old English *īren,* earlier *īsern, īsen.*]

iron age *n. Classical Mythology.* The last of the ages of the history of the world, a very degenerate age, and supposedly the one we are in now. Compare **golden age, silver age.**

Iron Age *n.* The generally prehistoric period succeeding the Bronze Age, characterized by the introduction and spread of iron tools and weapons, beginning in the Middle East around the 12th century B.C., and in Europe around the 8th century B.C.

i·ron·bark (ī′ərn-bärk′) *n.* Any of several Australian trees of the genus *Eucalyptus,* often having hard, rough bark.

iron blue *n.* Any of various light- and heat-resistant, semitransparent blue pigments of powerful tinctorial strength, used chiefly in permanent industrial finishes, printing inks, and artists' colors.

i·ron·bound (ī′ərn-bound′) *adj.* **1.** Bound with iron. **2.** Rigid and unyielding. **3.** Bound with rocks and cliffs, as a coast.

i·ron·clad (ī′ərn-klăd′) *adj.* **1.** Sheathed with iron plates for protection. **2.** Rigid: *an ironclad rule.* **3.** Fully protected from attack; unshakeable: *an ironclad argument.*
~*n.* A 19th-century warship having sides armored with metal plates.

Iron Cross *n.* A medal formerly awarded to German soldiers for the highest degree of bravery.

Iron Curtain *n.* A barrier that prevents free exchange or communication; specifically, the political and ideological barrier between the Soviet bloc and western Europe after World War II. [Popularized (1946) by Winston Churchill.]

iron glance *n.* A mineral, **hematite** *(see).*

iron gray *n.* A dark gray with a slightly greenish tinge.

iron hand *n.* Rigorous or despotic control: *ruling with an iron hand.* —**i·ron·hand·ed** (ī′ərn-hăn′dĭd) *adj.*

iron horse *n. Informal.* A railroad locomotive.

i·ron·ic (ī-rŏn′ĭk) *adj.* Also **i·ron·i·cal** (ī-rŏn′ĭ-kəl). **1.** Characterized by or constituting irony. **2.** Given to the use of irony. —See Usage note at **sarcastic.** —**i·ron·i·cal·ly** *adv.* —**i·ron·i·cal·ness** *n.*

i·ron·ing (ī′ər-nĭng) *n.* **1.** The pressing of clothes with a heated iron. **2.** The clothing to be pressed or that has been pressed.

ironing board *n.* A long narrow padded board on a collapsible support, used as a working surface for ironing.

i·ron·ist (ī′rə-nĭst) *n.* A notable user of irony, especially a writer. —**i·ron·ize** *v.*

iron lung *n.* An airtight tank in which the entire body except the head is enclosed and by means of which pressure is regularly increased and decreased to provide artificial respiration. Also called "respirator."

iron maiden *n.* A medieval torture device, consisting of a coffinlike case lined with iron spikes, in which the victim was enclosed.

i·ron·mas·ter (ī′ərn-măs′tər, -mäs′tər) *n. Chiefly British.* A manufacturer of iron.

i·ron·mon·ger (ī′ərn-mŭng′gər, -mŏng′gər) *n. Chiefly British.* A hardware merchant, selling metal tools and utensils.

i·ron·mon·ger·y (ī′ərn-mŭng′gə-rē, -mŏng′gə-rē) *n., pl.* **-ies.** *Chiefly British.* **1.** Ironware. **2.** The shop or business of an ironmonger. **3.** *Slang.* Firearms.

iron oxide *n.* Any of various oxides of iron, such as ferrous oxide.

iron pyrites *n.* A mineral, **pyrite** *(see).*

iron rations *pl.n.* Emergency rations, especially those carried by a soldier.

i·ron·sides (ī′ərn-sīdz′) *n., pl.* **ironsides. 1.** A person with great stamina or powers of endurance. **2.** An ironclad ship.

i·ron·smith (ī′ərn-smĭth′) *n.* One who works in iron; a blacksmith.

i·ron·stone (ī′ərn-stōn′) *n.* **1.** Any of several kinds of iron ore with admixtures of silica and clay. **2.** A hard white pottery.

i·ron·ware (ī′ərn-wâr′) *n.* Iron utensils and other products made of iron.

i·ron·weed (ī′ərn-wēd′) *n.* Any plant of the genus *Vernonia,* having clusters of purplish flowers.

i·ron·wood (ī′ərn-wo͝od′) *n.* **1.** Any of various trees having very hard wood, such as the **hornbeam** and the **hop hornbeam** *(both of which see).* **2.** The wood of such a tree.

i·ron·work (ī′ərn-wûrk′) *n.* **1.** Iron objects, such as gratings or gates, especially when made by hand. **2.** The craft or profession of making such objects.

i·ron·work·er (ī′ərn-wûrk′ər) *n.* **1.** A person who makes ironwork. **2.** A person who works in an ironworks.

i·ron·works (ī′ərn-wûrks′) *n., pl.* **ironworks.** *Usually used with a singular verb.* A building or establishment where iron is smelted or where heavy iron products are made.

i·ro·ny[1] (ī′rə-nē) *n., pl.* **-nies. 1.** The use of words to convey the opposite of their literal meaning. **2.** An expression or utterance marked by such a deliberate contrast between apparent and intended meaning. **3.** A literary style employing such contrasts for humorous or rhetorical effect. **4.** Incongruity between what might be expected and what actually occurs: *the irony of being run over by an ambulance.* **5.** An occurrence, result, or circumstance notable for such incongruity. **6. Dramatic irony** *(see).* **7. Socratic irony** *(see).* —See Synonyms at **wit.** [Latin *īrōnia,* from Greek *eirōneia,* dissembling, feigned ignorance, from *eirōn,* dissembler, "one who says less than he thinks," from *eirein,* to say.]

i·ron·y[2] (ī′ər-nē) *adj.* Of, like, or containing iron.

Ir·o·quoi·an (ĭr′ə-kwoi′ən) *n.* **1.** A family of North American Indian languages spoken in Canada and the eastern United States by such peoples as the Iroquois, Cherokee, Conestoga, Erie, and Wyandot. **2.** A member of a people using a language of this family.
~*adj.* **1.** Of or designating this language family. **2.** Of or pertaining to the Iroquois or their culture.

Ir·o·quois (ĭr′ə-kwoi′, -kwoiz′) *n., pl.* **Iroquois. 1.** A member of any of several Iroquoian-speaking North American Indian peoples formerly inhabiting New York State, and forming the confederacy known as the *Five Nations,* including the Cayuga, Mohawk, Oneida, Onondaga, and Seneca peoples. After 1722 the confederacy was joined by the Tuscaroras to form the *Six Nations.* **2.** Any of the languages spoken among these peoples. **—Ir·o·quois** *adj.*

ir·ra·di·ance (ĭ-rā′dē-əns) *n. Symbol* **E** *Physics.* The radiant flux or radiation reaching a surface per unit area. Compare **radiance.**

ir·ra·di·ant (ĭ-rā′dē-ənt) *adj.* Sending forth radiant light. [Latin *irradiāns* (stem *irradiant-*), present participle of *irradiāre,* IRRADIATE.]

ir·ra·di·ate (ĭ-rā′dē-āt′) *v.* **-ated, -ating, -ates.** —*tr.* **1. a.** To expose to radiation. **b.** To treat with radiation. **2.** To emit in a manner analogous to the emission of light. **3.** To make intellectually interesting or spiritually radiant; clarify; illumine. —*intr. Archaic.* **1.** To send forth rays; radiate. **2.** To become radiant. [Latin *irradiāre,* to shine forth : *in-,* toward + *radiāre,* to shine, RADIATE.] **—ir·ra·di·a·tive** *adj.* **—ir·ra·di·a·tor** *n.*

ir·ra·di·a·tion (ĭ-rā′dē-ā′shən) *n.* **1.** The act of irradiating or the condition of being irradiated. **2.** *Medicine.* Therapy or treatment by exposure to radiation.

ir·rad·i·ca·ble (ĭ-răd′ĭ-kə-bəl) *adj.* Incapable of being uprooted or destroyed. [Medieval Latin *irradicabilis* : Latin *in-,* not + Latin *radix,* root.] **—ir·rad·i·ca·bly** *adv.*

ir·ra·tion·al (ĭ-răsh′ən-əl) *adj.* **1. a.** Not endowed with reason. **b.** Affected by loss of usual or normal mental clarity; incoherent, as, for example, from shock. **c.** Contrary to reason; illogical: *an irrational dislike.* **2.** In Greek and Latin verse: **a.** Designating a syllable whose length does not fit the metrical pattern. **b.** Designating a metrical foot containing such a syllable. **3.** *Mathematics.* Incapable of being expressed as an integer or a ratio or quotient of integers. **—ir·ra·tion·al·ly** *adv.* **—ir·ra·tion·al·ness** *n.*

ir·ra·tion·al·i·ty (ĭ-răsh′ə-năl′ə-tē) *n., pl.* **-ties.** Also **ir·ra·tion·al·ism** (ĭ-răsh′ən-ə-lĭz′əm). **1.** The state or quality of being irrational. **2.** An irrational idea or action.

irrational number *n. Mathematics.* A member of the set of real numbers that is not a member of the set of rational numbers; a number that cannot be expressed as an integer or an exact ratio of two integers; for example, the number π (pi).

Ir·ra·wad·dy (ĭr′ə-wä′dē). The chief river of Burma. Rising in the Patkai hills in the northeastern part of the country, it flows 2,010 kilometers (1,250 miles) south to the Bay of Bengal. Its delta, west of the Gulf of Martaban, is a major rice-growing area.

ir·re·claim·a·ble (ĭr′ĭ-klā′mə-bəl) *adj.* Incapable of being reclaimed: *irreclaimable wasteland.* **—ir·re·claim·a·bil·i·ty, ir·re·claim·a·ble·ness** *n.* **—ir·re·claim·a·bly** *adv.*

ir·rec·on·cil·a·ble (ĭ-rĕk′ən-sī′lə-bəl, ĭ-rĕk′ən-sī′-) *adj.* **1.** Not capable of being reconciled; implacably hostile. **2.** Incompatible; incongruous.
~*n.* **1.** A person who will not compromise or adjust. **2. irreconcilables.** Conflicting ideas or beliefs that cannot be brought into harmony. **—ir·rec·on·cil·a·bil·i·ty** *n.* **—ir·rec·on·cil·a·bly** *adv.*

ir·re·cov·er·a·ble (ĭr′ĭ-kŭv′ər-ə-bəl) *adj.* Incapable of being recovered; irreparable: *irrecoverable losses.* **—ir·re·cov·er·a·ble·ness** *n.* **—ir·re·cov·er·a·bly** *adv.*

ir·re·cu·sa·ble (ĭr′ĭ-kyo͞o′zə-bəl) *adj.* Not subject to challenge or objection; unexceptionable; undeniable. [French *irrécusable,* from Late Latin *irrecūsābilis* : *in-,* not + *recūsābilis,* that should be rejected, from Latin *recūsāre,* to reject.] **—ir·re·cu·sa·bly** *adv.*

ir·re·deem·a·ble (ĭr′ĭ-dē′mə-bəl) *adj.* **1.** Incapable of being bought back or paid off: *an irredeemable annuity.* **2.** Not convertible into coin: *irredeemable banknotes.* **3.** Incapable of being remedied. **4.** Incapable of being saved or reformed.
~*n.* A bond, annuity, or similar investment that cannot be redeemed before it matures. **—ir·re·deem·a·bil·i·ty** *n.* **—ir·re·deem·a·bly** *adv.*

ir·re·den·tist (ĭr′ĭ-dĕn′tĭst) *n.* One who advocates the recovery of lands of which his nation has been deprived, or of territory culturally or historically related to his nation but now subject to a foreign government. [Italian *irredentista,* from *(Italia) irredenta,* "unredeemed (Italy)" (Italian-speaking areas subject to other countries), from *irredento,* not redeemed : *in-,* not, from Latin + *redento,* redeemed, from Latin *redemptus,* past participle of *redimere,* REDEEM.] **—ir·re·den·tism** *n.* **—ir·re·den·tist** *adj.*

ir·re·duc·i·ble (ĭr′ĭ-do͞o′sə-bəl, -dyo͞o′sə-bəl) *adj.* **1.** Incapable of being reduced to a desired, simpler, or smaller form or amount. **2.** *Medicine.* Incapable of being replaced in a normal position. Said especially of a hernia. **—ir·re·duc·i·bil·i·ty, ir·re·duc·i·ble·ness** *n.* **—ir·re·duc·i·bly** *adv.*

ir·ref·ra·ga·ble (ĭ-rĕf′rə-gə-bəl) *adj.* Incapable of being refuted or controverted; indisputable. [Late Latin *irrefrāgābilis* : Latin *in-,* not + *refrāgārī,* to oppose, akin to *frangere,* to break.] **—ir·ref·ra·ga·bil·i·ty** *n.* **—ir·ref·ra·ga·bly** *adv.*

ir·re·fran·gi·ble (ĭr′ĭ-frăn′jə-bəl) *adj.* **1.** Incapable of being violated or broken; indestructible. **2.** *Physics.* Incapable of being refracted. **—ir·re·fran·gi·bil·i·ty** *n.* **—ir·re·fran·gi·bly** *adv.*

ir·ref·u·ta·ble (ĭ-rĕf′yə-tə-bəl, ĭr′ĭ-fyo͞o′tə-bəl) *adj.* Incapable of being refuted or disproved; incontrovertible: *irrefutable arguments.* **—ir·ref·u·ta·bil·i·ty** *n.* **—ir·ref·u·ta·bly** *adv.*

irreg. irregular; irregularly.

ir·re·gard·less (ĭr′ĭ-gärd′lĭs) *adv. Nonstandard.* Regardless.

ir·reg·u·lar (ĭ-rĕg′yə-lər) *adj. Abbr.* **irreg. 1.** Not according to rule, accepted order, or general practice. **2.** Not conforming to legality, moral law, or social convention: *an irregular marriage.* **3.** Not straight, uniform, or symmetrical: *a path of irregular width; irregular facial features.* **4.** Of uneven rate, occurrence, or duration: *an irregular heartbeat; irregular attendance.* **5.** Deviating from type; asymmetrically arranged or atypical. **6.** *Botany.* Having differing floral parts, especially petals. **7.** Falling below the manufacturer's standard or usual specifications; flawed; imperfect. **8.** *Grammar.* Departing from the usual set of inflectional forms; for example, the verb *be* is an irregular verb. **9.** Not belonging to a permanent, organized military force: *irregular troops.*
~*n.* **1.** A person or thing that is irregular. **2.** A soldier, such as a guerrilla, who is not a member of a regular military force. **—ir·reg·u·lar·ly** *adv.*

ir·reg·u·lar·i·ty (ĭ-rĕg′yə-lăr′ə-tē) *n., pl.* **-ties. 1.** The quality or state of being irregular. **2.** That which is irregular. **3.** Constipation.

ir·rel·a·tive (ĭ-rĕl′ə-tĭv) *adj.* **1.** Having no correlative relationship; unconnected. **2.** Irrelevant. **—ir·rel·a·tive·ly** *adv.*

ir·rel·e·vance (ĭ-rĕl′ə-vəns) *n.* Also **ir·rel·e·van·cy** (-vən-sē) *pl.* **-cies. 1.** The quality or state of being irrelevant. **2.** That which is irrelevant.

ir·rel·e·vant (ĭ-rĕl′ə-vənt) *adj.* **1.** Having no applications or effects in a specified circumstance; unrelated to the subject under discussion or the matter to be dealt with. **2.** Lacking in contemporaneity; failing to deal with current concerns. **—ir·rel·e·vant·ly** *adv.*

ir·re·lig·ion (ĭr′ĭ-lĭj′ən) *n.* Hostility or indifference to religion.

ir·re·lig·ious (ĭr′ĭ-lĭj′əs) *adj.* Indifferent or hostile to religion; ungodly. **—ir·re·lig·ious·ly** *adv.* **—ir·re·lig·ious·ness** *n.*

ir·rem·e·a·ble (ĭ-rĕm′ē-ə-bəl, ĭ-rē′mē-) *adj. Archaic.* Affording no possibility of return. [Latin *irremeābilis* : *in-,* not + *remeāre,* to return : *re-,* back + *meāre,* to go.]

ir·re·me·di·a·ble (ĭr′ĭ-mē′dē-ə-bəl) *adj.* Impossible to remedy, correct, or repair; incurable. **—ir·re·me·di·a·bly** *adv.*

ir·re·mis·si·ble (ĭr′ĭ-mĭs′ə-bəl) *adj.* **1.** Not remissible; unpardonable. **2.** In need of doing; unavoidable; obligatory. **—ir·re·mis·si·bil·i·ty** *n.* **—ir·re·mis·si·bly** *adv.*

ir·re·mov·a·ble (ĭr′ĭ-mo͞o′və-bəl) *adj.* **1.** Not physically removable. **2.** Not liable to removal from office. **—ir·re·mov·a·bil·i·ty** *n.* **—ir·re·mov·a·bly** *adv.*

ir·rep·a·ra·ble (ĭ-rĕp′ə-rə-bəl) *adj.* Incapable of being repaired, rectified, or amended; beyond repair: *irreparable harm.* **—ir·rep·a·ra·bil·i·ty, ir·rep·a·ra·ble·ness** *n.* **—ir·rep·a·ra·bly** *adv.*

ir·re·peal·a·ble (ĭr′ĭ-pē′lə-bəl) *adj.* Not capable of being repealed.

ir·re·place·a·ble (ĭr′ĭ-plā′sə-bəl) *adj.* Incapable of being replaced because so valuable.

ir·re·pres·si·ble (ĭr′ĭ-prĕs′ə-bəl) *adj.* Not capable of being repressed; impossible to control or restrain. **—ir·re·pres·si·bil·i·ty, ir·re·pres·si·ble·ness** *n.* **—ir·re·pres·si·bly** *adv.*

ironstone *A sedimentary rock rich in iron minerals. It is an important source of iron ore.*

ir·re·proach·a·ble (ĭr'ĭ-prō'chə-bəl) adj. Not meriting any reproach; beyond reproach; perfect. —ir·re·proach·a·bil·i·ty, ir·re·proach·a·ble·ness n. —ir·re·proach·a·bly adv.

ir·re·sis·ti·ble (ĭr'ĭ-zĭs'tə-bəl) adj. 1. Impossible to resist. 2. Having an overpowering appeal: an irresistible urge to dance. 3. Very attractive; alluring: an irrestible woman. —ir·re·sis·ti·bil·i·ty, ir·re·sis·ti·ble·ness n. —ir·re·sis·ti·bly adv.

ir·res·o·lu·ble (ĭ-rĕz'əl-yə-bəl, ĭr'ĭ-zŏl'-) adj. Not capable of being solved.

ir·res·o·lute (ĭ-rĕz'ə-lōot') adj. 1. Unresolved as to action or procedure. 2. Lacking in resolution; vacillating; wavering; indecisive. —ir·res·o·lute·ly adv. —ir·res·o·lute·ness, ir·res·o·lu·tion n.

ir·re·solv·a·ble (ĭr'ĭ-zŏl'və-bəl) adj. 1. Incapable of being solved or resolved. 2. Not capable of being separated into component parts; irreducible.

ir·re·spec·tive (ĭr'ĭ-spĕk'tĭv) adj. Archaic. Characterized by disregard; heedless. —irrespective of. Regardless of; without consideration of.
~adv. Informal. Regardless; without considering: We advised him against it but he carried on irrespective. —ir·re·spec·tive·ly adv.

ir·re·spir·a·ble (ĭr'ĭ-spīr'ə-bəl, ĭ-rĕs'pər-) adj. Not fit for breathing; not respirable.

ir·re·spon·si·ble (ĭr'ĭ-spŏn'sə-bəl) adj. 1. Not mentally or financially fit to assume responsibility. 2. Showing no sense of responsibility or due care; reckless; untrustworthy. 3. Archaic. Not liable to be called to account by a higher authority.
~n. An irresponsible person. —ir·re·spon·si·bil·i·ty, ir·re·spon·si·ble·ness n. —ir·re·spon·si·bly adv.

ir·re·spon·sive (ĭr'ĭ-spŏn'sĭv) adj. 1. Not responsive, as to treatment or stimuli. 2. Not responding or answering readily. —ir·re·spon·sive·ly adv. —ir·re·spon·sive·ness n.

ir·re·triev·a·ble (ĭr'ĭ-trē'və-bəl) adj. 1. Not capable of being retrieved or recovered. 2. Beyond help or repair. —ir·re·triev·a·bil·i·ty, ir·re·triev·a·ble·ness n. —ir·re·triev·a·bly adv.

ir·rev·er·ence (ĭ-rĕv'ər-əns) n. 1. Absence of reverence or due respect. 2. A disrespectful act or remark.

ir·rev·er·ent (ĭ-rĕv'ər-ənt) adj. 1. Lacking in reverence; disrespectful: an irreverent person. 2. Proceeding from irreverence: an irreverent act. —ir·rev·er·ent·ly adv.

ir·re·vers·i·ble (ĭr'ĭ-vûr'sə-bəl) adj. 1. Incapable of being reversed. 2. Chemistry. a. Designating or pertaining to a chemical reaction that takes place almost completely in one direction. b. Designating or pertaining to a change in which intermediate stages do not attain thermodynamic equilibrium. —ir·re·vers·i·bil·i·ty, ir·re·vers·i·ble·ness n. —ir·re·vers·i·bly adv.

ir·rev·o·ca·ble (ĭ-rĕv'ə-kə-bəl) adj. Incapable of being retracted or revoked; irreversible. —ir·rev·o·ca·bil·i·ty, ir·rev·o·ca·ble·ness n. —ir·rev·o·ca·bly adv.

ir·ri·ga·ble (ĭr'ĭ-gə-bəl) adj. Capable of irrigation; able to be irrigated.

ir·ri·gate (ĭr'ĭ-gāt') tr.v. -gated, -gating, -gates. 1. a. To supply (dry land) with water by means of ditches, pipes, or streams. b. To water or provide (land) with water. Used of a river, stream, or the like. 2. To wash out (a cavity or wound) with water or a medicated fluid. 3. To make fertile or vital by or as if by watering. [Latin irrigāre, to lead water to : in-, in + rigāre, to wet, water.] —ir·ri·ga·tion n. —ir·ri·ga·tion·al adj. —ir·ri·ga·tor n.

ir·ri·ta·bil·i·ty (ĭr'ə-tə-bĭl'ə-tē) n. 1. The quality or state of being irritable; testiness; petulance. 2. Medicine. Excessive sensitivity. 3. Biology. The capacity to respond to stimuli.

ir·ri·ta·ble (ĭr'ĭ-tə-bəl) adj. 1. Easily annoyed; ill-tempered. 2. Medicine. Abnormally sensitive. 3. Biology. Responsive to stimuli. [Latin irritābilis, from irritāre, IRRITATE.] —ir·ri·ta·ble·ness n. —ir·ri·ta·bly adv.

ir·ri·tant (ĭr'ə-tənt) adj. Causing physical or mental irritation.
~n. Something that causes irritation. [Latin irritāns (stem irritant-), present participle of irritāre, IRRITATE.]

ir·ri·tate (ĭr'ə-tāt') tr.v. -tated, -tating, -tates. 1. a. To annoy; vex. b. To provoke. 2. To chafe or inflame. —See Synonyms at annoy. [Latin irritāre†.] —ir·ri·tat·ing·ly adv. —ir·ri·ta·tive (ĭr'ə-tā'tĭv) adj. —ir·ri·ta·tor n.

ir·ri·ta·tion (ĭr'ə-tā'shən) n. 1. The act of irritating. 2. A source of irritation. 3. The condition of being irritated; vexation. 4. Medicine. Incipient inflammation, soreness, roughness, or irritability of a bodily part.

ir·ro·ta·tion·al (ĭr'ō-tā'shən-əl) adj. Not rotating or involving rotation.

ir·rupt (ĭ-rŭpt') intr.v. -rupted, -rupting, -rupts. 1. To break or burst in; make an incursion or invasion. 2. Ecology. To increase irregularly in number. Used of a human or animal population. [Latin irrumpere (past participle irruptus) : in-, in + rumpere, to break, burst.] —ir·rup·tion n.

ir·rup·tive (ĭ-rŭp'tĭv) adj. 1. Irrupting or tending to irrupt. 2. Geology. Intrusive. 3. Characterized by irruption.

IRS Internal Revenue Service.

Ir·tysh (ĭr'tĭsh). River in western Siberia in Russia. It rises in Xinjiang Uigur Zizhiqu in China and flows c. 4,260 kilometers (2,650 miles) to join the Ob River.

Ir·ving (ûr'vĭng), Sir Henry, born John Henry Brodribb (1838–1905). Great Shakespearean actor. His productions, particularly those at London's Lyceum Theatre, won him the first theatrical knighthood to be awarded to an Englishman (1895).

Irving, Washington (1783–1859). U.S. diplomat and writer. His best-known work is The Sketch Book (1819–20), containing the classic stories "Rip Van Winkle" and "The Legend of Sleepy Hollow."

is (ĭz). The third person singular present indicative of the verb be.

is. island; isle.

Is. 1. Isaiah (Old Testament). 2. island; isle.

is-. Variant of iso-.

Isa. Isaiah (Old Testament).

I·saac (ī'zək). A Hebrew patriarch, the son of Abraham and Sarah and the father of Jacob and Esau. Genesis 21:1–4. [Late Latin Isaacus, from Greek Isaak, from Hebrew Yiṣḥāq, "he laughs."]

I·sa·bel·la I of Castile (ĭz'ə-bĕl'ə), also called "the Catholic" (1451–1504). Queen of Castile. Her marriage to Ferdinand of Aragon (1469) led to the eventual unification of Spain. She was the patron of Christopher Columbus.

i·sa·go·gic (ī'sə-gŏj'ĭk) adj. Pertaining to or designating studies, especially Bible studies, of an introductory kind. [Latin, from Greek eisagōgikos, introductory, from eisagōgē, introduction : eis, into + agōgē, leading, from agein, to lead.]

i·sa·gog·ics (ī'sə-gŏj'ĭks) pl.n. Introductory studies, especially of the Bible.

I·sa·iah[1] (ī-zā'ə, ī-zī'ə). Also in Douay Bible I·sa·ias (ī-zā'yəs, ī-zī'əs). A Hebrew prophet of the 8th century B.C. [Hebrew Yəsha'yāh(u), "salvation of the Lord" : yēsha', yəshū'āh, salvation + yāh(u), the Lord.]

Isaiah[2] n. Abbr. Is., Isa. A book in the Old Testament attributed to Isaiah, though now considered to be the work of three writers.

i·sal·lo·bar (ī-săl'ə-bär') n. Meteorology. A line on a weather map connecting places exhibiting equal changes in barometric pressure within a given period of time. [IS(O)- + ALLO- + Greek baros, weight.]

ISBN n. International Standard Book Number; a number assigned under an international system to each newly published book, to facilitate ordering and identification.

is·che·mi·a (ĭ-skē'mē-ə) n. Pathology. A local anemia caused by mechanical obstruction of the blood supply. [New Latin ischaemia, from Greek iskhaimos, stanching, stopping blood : iskhein, to keep back, hold, restrain + haima, blood.]

is·chi·um (ĭs'kē-əm) n., pl. -chia (-kē-ə). Anatomy. The lowest of three major bones composing each half of the pelvis. [Latin, hip joint, from Greek iskhion†.]

–ise. Variant of –ize.

is·en·trop·ic (ī'sĕn-trŏp'ĭk, -trō'pĭk) adj. Without change in entropy; at constant entropy. [IS(O)- + ENTROP(Y) + -IC.]

I·seult, Y·seult (ĭ-sōolt'). Also I·sol·de (ĭ-sōl'də, ĭ-zōl'-). 1. A legendary Irish princess who married Mark, the king of Cornwall, and had a doomed love for his nephew, Tristan. 2. A legendary princess of Brittany, whom Tristan in some accounts married.

Is·fa·han (ĭs'fə-hän', -hän'). Formerly As·pa·da·na (ăs'pə-dä'nə). City in central Iran and the capital of the Isfahan province. It is noted for its carpet manufacturing and metalwork. It was the capital of Persia under Shah Abbas the Great (c. A.D. 1600).

–ish suffix. Indicates: 1. a. Having the nationality of; for example, Swedish, Finnish. b. Having the qualities or character of; for example, childish, sheepish. c. Tending to or preoccupied with; for example, bookish, selfish. d. Somewhere near or approximately. Used informally in naming hours or years: She's fortyish. 2. Somewhat or rather; for example, greenish. [Middle English -is(c)h, Old English -isc, from Common Germanic -iskaz (unattested), corresponding to Greek -iskos, diminutive noun suffix.]

Ish·er·wood (ĭsh'ər-wōod'), Christopher (1904–86). English novelist, best known for his portrayals of Berlin in the early 1930's in works such as Mr. Norris Changes Trains (1935) and Goodbye to Berlin (1939), on which the musical Cabaret is based.

Ish·ma·el[1] (ĭsh'mē-əl). The son of Abraham by Sarah's handmaid, Hagar. Genesis 16:1–16. [Late Latin Ismaēl, from Hebrew Yishmā'ēl, "God hears" : yishmā, he hears, from shāma', he heard + 'Ēl, God.]

Ishmael[2] n. An outcast. [From ISHMAEL, referring to Abraham's expulsion of Ishmael and Hagar after the birth of Isaac (Genesis 21:14).]

Ish·ma·el·ite (ĭsh'mē-ə-līt') n. 1. A member of a group of desert-dwelling people believed by the ancient Hebrews to be descended from Ishmael. 2. An outcast. —Ish·ma·el·it·ism n.

Ish·tar (ĭsh'tär'). Assyrian & Babylonian Mythology. The goddess of love, fertility, and war; identified with the Phoenician Astarte. [Akkadian Ishtar, akin to Hebrew 'Ashtoreth, ASHTORETH.]

i·sin·glass (ī'zĭng-glăs', -gläs', ī'zən-) n. 1. A transparent, almost pure gelatin prepared from the air bladder of certain fishes, such as the sturgeon. 2. A mineral, muscovite (see). [Alteration (influenced by GLASS) of obsolete Dutch huizenblas, from Middle Dutch huusblase : huus, sturgeon, from Germanic hūson- (unattested) + blase, bladder.]

I·sis[1] (ī'sĭs). Egyptian Mythology. A goddess of fertility, and sister and wife of Osiris.

Isis[2]. See Oxford.

isl. island; isle.

Is·lam (ĭs'ləm, ĭz'-, ĭs-läm') n. 1. A religion based upon the teachings of the prophet Muhammad, believing in one God (Allah) and in Paradise and Hell, and having a body of law set forth in the Koran and the Sunna; the Muslim religion. 2. a. All those nations of the world, especially in Asia and Africa, whose populations are Muslim; the Muslim world. b. Islamic civilization. 3. Muslims collectively. [Arabic islām, "submission (to God)," from aslama, he

A RELIGION BUILT ON THE DIRECT WORD OF ALLAH

Muhammad's followers observe five obligations

Islam is based on the teachings of the Koran (or Qur'an), claimed by believers to be the direct word of Allah, that is, God, and revealed to the prophet Muhammad in the 7th century A.D. It spread rapidly from Mecca in northwest Arabia across North Africa and the Middle East, and into Spain, part of Russia, and eventually India and Indonesia. Today its followers number about 600 million.

Standing in the tradition of both Christianity and Judaism, Islam promises that the faithful follower will go to Paradise and the nonbeliever to Hell. Allah is the creator of the universe and a loving but just god, and Abraham and Jesus are included in the Islamic prophets. Islam has five obligations, or pillars, that the faithful must observe—to believe in Allah and Muhammad, to pray five times daily while facing Mecca, to give money to charity, to fast between sunrise and sunset during the month of Ramadan, and to visit the holy shrine at Mecca at least once in a lifetime if circumstances permit.

The Koran also has a political message, as it details how men should live in a community and permits the waging of holy war (jihad) against nonbelievers. After the death of Muhammad, Islam split into two groups, the Sunni Muslims today numbering 536 million and the Shiite Muslims numbering 40 million.

THE KAABA SHRINE *In the Great Mosque in Mecca lies this cube-shaped building containing the Black Stone, most sacred of Islamic objects, said to have been given by Gabriel to Abraham.*

ISLAMIC ART *The Koran forbids the representation of Allah, the human form, and animals, so an abstract style developed. This tile mural is from the Jum'a Mosque, Isfahan.*

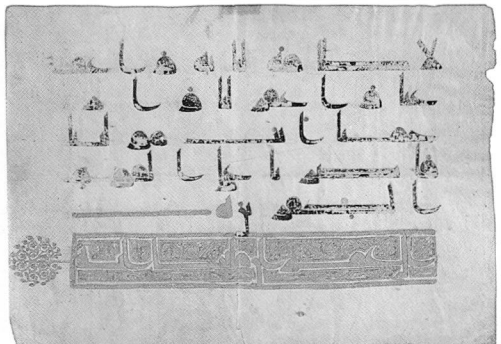

THE DIVINE WORD *After Muhammad's death, the revelations he received from God through the angel Gabriel were written down as the sacred text, the Koran. It is about as long as the New Testament in the Bible, with 114 chapters, called suras, which are placed in order according to length.*

The Koran is believed to be the direct word of God. The suras received while Muhammad was at Mecca concern spiritual truths, those he received later at Medina concern political and moral questions. The Koran teaches that there is only one God and that no intermediaries between God and man are necessary. For this reason no Islamic priesthood has developed. The text on the left is in Naskh script, the general text for Arabic manuscripts. The text above is written in Kufic.

surrendered, he resigned himself, from *salama*, he was safe.] —**Is·lam·ic** *adj.*

Is·la·ma·bad (ĭs-lä'mə-bäd', ĭz-). A new city in north Pakistan, the national capital since 1967.

Is·lam·ism (ĭs'lə-mĭz'əm, ĭz'-) *n.* The religious faith, principles, or cause of Islam. —**Is·lam·ist** *n.*

Is·lam·ize (ĭs'lə-mīz', ĭz'-) *tr.v.* **-ized, -izing, -izes.** **1.** To convert to Islam. **2.** To impose the laws and practices of Islam on. —**Is·lam·i·za·tion** *n.*

is·land (ī'lənd) *n.* **1.** *Abbr.* **i., I., is., Is., isl.** A land mass, especially one smaller than a continent, entirely surrounded by water. **2.** Anything completely isolated or regarded as resembling such an isolated land mass. **3.** A **traffic island** (*see*). **4.** *Anatomy.* A tissue or cluster of cells separated from surrounding tissue by a groove or differing from surrounding tissue in structure. ~*tr.v.* **islanded, -landing, -lands.** **1. a.** To make into or as if into an island; insulate. **b.** To place on an island. **2.** To dot or intersperse with or as if with islands. [Middle English *eland, ilond, ylond* (influenced by ISLE), Old English *ī(e)gland, īland.*]

is·land·er (ī'lən-dər) *n.* An inhabitant of an island.

is·land-hop·ping (ī'lənd-hŏp'ĭng) *n.* The making of short boat trips or short-haul flights to a number of islands in the same area.

islands of Lang·er·hans (läng'ər-häns') *pl.n.* Also **islets of Lang·er·hans.** Irregular masses of small endocrine cells that lie in the interstitial tissue of the pancreas and secrete insulin and glucagon. [After Paul *Langerhans* (1847–88), German doctor.]

Islands of the Blest *pl.n. Greek Mythology.* See **Hesperides.**

Islas Baleares. See **Baleric Islands.**

Islas Malvinas. See **Falkland Islands.**

Is·lay (ī'lā). Island lying off the west coast of Scotland, the most southerly of the Inner Hebrides. Its comparative prosperity is due chiefly to an established whiskey-distilling industry.

isle (īl) *n. Abbr.* **i., I., is., Is., isl.** An island, especially a small one. Used poetically and in place names. [Middle English *i(s)le,* from Old French, from Latin *īnsula†.*]

is·let (ī'lĭt) *n.* A little island.

ism (ĭz'əm) *n. Informal.* A distinctive doctrine, system, or theory. [From -ISM.]

–ism *suffix.* Indicates: **1.** An action, practice, or process; for example, **terrorism, favoritism.** **2.** A state or condition of being; for example, **pauperism, parallelism.** **3.** A characteristic behavior or quality; for example, **heroism, individualism.** **4.** A distinctive usage or feature, especially of language; for example, **malapropism, Latinism.** **5.** A doctrine, theory, system, or principle; for example, **Platonism, expressionism, capitalism, pacifism.** [Middle English *-isme,* from Old French, from Latin *-ismus,* from Greek *-ismos,* suffix used to form nouns of action from verbs in *-izein,* -IZE.]

Is·ma·il·i, Is·ma'i·li (ĭs'mä-īl'ē) *n.* Also **Is·ma·il·i·an** (ĭs'mä-īl'ē-ən). A Muslim of a Shiite sect. [Arabic *Isma'īlīy,* after *Isma'īl* (died A.D. 760), son of the sixth Imam Jafar.]

is·n't (ĭz'ənt). Contraction of *is not.*

ISO International Standards Organization.

iso-, is- *prefix.* Indicates: **1.** Equal, identical, or similar; for example, **isallobar, isogon.** **2.** *Chemistry.* Isomeric; for example, **isopropyl alcohol.** [Greek, from *isos†,* equal.]

i·so·ag·glu·ti·na·tion (ī'sō-ə-glōōt'n-ā'shən) *n.* The agglutination of red blood cells by the serum of another individual of the same species.

i·so·ag·glu·tin·in (ī'sō-ə-glōōt'n-ĭn) *n.* An isoantibody that causes agglutination of red blood cells.

i·so·ag·glu·tin·o·gen (ī'sō-ăg'lōō-tĭn'ə-jən) *n.* An isoantigen that on exposure to its isoantibody induces agglutination of the red blood cells to which it is attached. [ISOAGGLUTIN(IN) + -GEN.]

i·so·am·yl acetate (ī'sō-ăm'əl) *n.* A colorless compound, (CH₃)₂CHCH₂CH₂OOCCH₃, used as a solvent and a flavoring.

i·so·an·ti·bod·y (ī'sō-ăn'tē-bŏd'ē) *n., pl.* **-ies.** An antibody that occurs in only some individuals of a species and reacts specifically with the corresponding isoantigen from a different individual of the same species.

i·so·an·ti·gen (ī'sō-ăn'tĭ-jən, -jĕn') *n.* An antigen that occurs in only some individuals of a species and never in those having cells that contain the corresponding isoantibody.

i·so·bar (ī'sə-bär') *n.* **1.** A line on a map connecting points of equal atmospheric pressure. **2.** *Physics.* Any of two or more nuclides having the same mass number but different atomic numbers. [ISO- + Greek *baros,* weight.] —**i·so·bar·ic** *adj.*

i·so·bath (ī'sō-băth', -bäth') *n.* A line on a chart connecting points of equal water depth. [Greek *isobathēs,* of equal depth : ISO- + *bathēs,* depth.]

i·so·bu·tane (ī'sō-byōō'tān) *n.* An isomer of **butane** (*see*).

i·so·chor, i·so·chore (ī'sō-kôr', -kōr') *n.* A line on a graph showing how the temperature of fluid kept at constant volume varies with pressure. [ISO- + Greek *khōros,* space, place.]

i·so·chro·mat·ic (ī'sə-krō-măt'ĭk) *adj.* **1. a.** Having the same color. **b.** Of uniform color. **2.** *Photography.* Orthochromatic.

i·soch·ro·nal (ī-sŏk'rə-nəl) *adj.* Also **i·soch·ro·nous** (-nəs), **i·so·chron·ic** (ī-sō-krŏn'ĭk). **1.** Equal in duration. **2.** Characterized by or occurring at equal intervals of time. [Greek *isokhronos,* ISOCHRONOUS.] —**i·soch·ro·nal·ly** *adv.* —**i·soch·ro·nism** (ī-sŏk'rə-nĭz'əm) *n.*

i·soch·ro·nize (ī-sŏk'rə-nīz') *tr.v.* **-nized, -nizing, -nizes.** To make isochronal.

i·soch·ro·ous (ī-sŏk'rō-əs) *adj.* Having the same color throughout. [ISO- + -CHROOUS.]

i·so·cli·nal (ī'sə-klī'nəl) *adj.* Also **i·so·clin·ic** (ī'sə-klĭn'ĭk). **1.** Having the same inclination or angle of dip. **2.** *Geology.* Designating folds having limbs parallel to each other. ~*n.* Also **i·so·clin·ic.** An isoclinal line.

i·so·cline (ī'sə-klīn') *n.* An anticline or syncline with its limbs so tightly folded as to have the same dip. [ISO- + -CLINE.]

isoclinic line *n.* Also **isoclinal line.** A line on a map connecting points of equal magnetic dip.

i·soc·ra·cy (ī-sŏk'rə-sē) *n.* A form of government in which all have equal power. [ISO- + -CRACY.] —**i·soc·ra·tic** (ī'sō-krăt'ĭk, ī'sə-) *adj.*

i·so·cy·an·ide (ī'sō-sī'ə-nīd') *n. Chemistry.* **1.** An organic compound containing the group –NCO. Also called "carbylamine." **2.** A salt containing the ion NCO⁻.

i·so·di·a·met·ric (ī'sō-dī'ə-mĕt'rĭk) *adj.* **1.** Having equal diameters. **2.** Designating a crystal that has three equal axes.

i·so·di·a·phere (ī'sō-dī'ə-fîr') *n.* Any of two or more nuclides that have the same difference between their total number of constituent neutrons and constituent protons. [ISO- + *-diaphere,* from Greek *diapherein,* to differ, "carry across" : DIA- + *pherein,* to carry.]

i·so·di·mor·phism (ī'sō-dī-môr'fĭz-əm) *n.* Isomorphism between crystalline forms of two dimorphic substances.

i·so·dy·nam·ic (ī'sō-dī-năm'ĭk) *adj.* **1.** Having equal force or strength. **2.** Designating an imaginary line drawn on the earth's surface that connects points of equal horizontal magnetic intensity.

i·so·e·lec·tric (ī'sō-ĭ-lĕk'trĭk) *adj.* Having equal electric potential.

isoelectric point *n. Chemistry.* The pH value of a solution in which a given substance, especially an amino acid or protein, forms neutral zwitterions or neutral colloidal particles.

i·so·e·lec·tron·ic (ī'sō-ĭ-lĕk-trŏn'ĭk) *adj.* Having equal numbers of electrons or the same electronic configuration.

i·so·en·zyme (ī'sō-ĕn'zīm) *n.* Also **i·so·zyme** (ī'sō-zīm'). Any one of the variant forms of a given enzyme. Isoenzymes catalyze the same type of reaction but differ slightly in physical and immunological properties. —**i·so·en·zy·mic** *adj.*

i·so·gam·ete (ī'sō-găm'ēt', -gə-mēt') *n.* A gamete that is morphologically indistinguishable from one with which it unites. —**i·so·ga·met·ic** (ī'sō-gə-mĕt'ĭk) *adj.*

i·sog·a·my (ī-sŏg'ə-mē) *n.* Sexual union of isogametes, such as occurs in certain algae, fungi, and protozoans. [ISO- + -GAMY.] —**i·sog·a·mous** *adj.*

i·sog·e·nous (ī-sŏj'ə-nəs) *adj.* Also **i·so·ge·nic** (ī'sə-jĕn'ĭk) (for sense 2). *Biology.* **1.** Having a similar origin. Said, for example, of organs derived from the same embryonic tissue. **2.** Genetically identical. [ISO- + -GENOUS.] —**i·sog·e·ny** *n.*

i·so·ge·o·therm (ī'sō-jē'ō-thĕrm') *n. Geology.* An imaginary line below the earth's surface connecting points of equal temperature. [ISO- + GEO- + Greek *thermē,* heat.]

i·so·gloss (ī'sə-glôs', -glŏs') *n.* A geographical boundary line delimiting the area in which a given linguistic feature occurs. [ISO- + Greek *glōssa,* language, tongue.] —**i·so·gloss·al** *adj.*

i·so·gon (ī'sə-gŏn') *n.* An equiangular polygon. [ISO- + -GON.]

i·so·gon·ic (ī'sə-gŏn'ĭk) *adj.* Also **i·sog·o·nal** (ī-sŏg'ə-nəl). Having equal angles. ~*n.* Also **i·sog·o·nal.** An isogonic line.

isogonic line *n.* A line on a map connecting points of equal magnetic declination.

i·so·graft (ī'sə-grăft') *n.* A tissue graft in which the donor and recipient are genetically identical, as, for example, by being identical twins. Also called "syngraft."

i·so·gram (ī'sə-grăm') *n.* An **isopleth** (*see*).

i·so·hel (ī'sō-hĕl') *n.* A line drawn on a map connecting points receiving equal sunlight. [ISO- + Greek *hēlios,* sun.]

i·so·he·mo·ly·sin (ī'sō-hē'mə-lī'sən, -hĕm'ə-, -hī-mŏl'ĭ-sĭn) *n.* Hemolysin obtained from the serum of an individual injected with red blood cells from another individual of the same species.

i·so·he·mol·y·sis (ī'sō-hə-mŏl'ĭ-sĭs) *n.* Hemolysis resulting from the action of isohemolysin.

i·so·hy·et (ī'sō-hī'ət) *n.* A line drawn on a map connecting points receiving equal rainfall. [ISO- + Greek *huetos,* rain.]

i·so·la·ble (ī'sə-lə-bəl, īs'ə-) *adj.* Capable of being isolated.

i·so·late (ī'sə-lāt', īs'ə-) *tr.v.* **-lated, -lating, -lates.** **1. a.** To separate from a group or whole and set apart. **b.** To identify; pick out. **2.** To place in quarantine. **3.** *Chemistry.* To obtain (a substance) in an uncombined form. **4.** To obtain (a species or strain of bacterium or fungus, especially a pathogen) in a pure form. **5.** To render free of external influence; insulate. [Back-formation from *isolated,* from French *isolé,* from Italian *isolato,* from Late Latin *īnsulātus,* converted into an island, from Latin *īnsula,* island.] —**i·so·la·tor** *n.*

i·so·lat·ed (ī'sə-lā'tĭd, īs'ə-) *adj.* **1.** Having undergone isolation. **2.** Infrequent; sporadic: *an isolated incident.* **3.** Lacking in or having failed to maintain human contact; psychologically cut off from others.

isolated point *n.* An **acnode** (*see*).

i·so·lat·ing (ī'sə-lā'tĭng, īs'ə-) *adj.* Pertaining to or designating languages that have no inflections but convey each unit of meaning through a separate word.

isolating mechanism *n. Biology.* Any factor that prevents the breeding of one population with another. Isolating mechanisms encourage the evolution of the separated populations into new varieties and species.

i·so·la·tion (ī'sə-lā'shən, īs'ə-) *n.* **1.** The act of isolating. **2.** The condition of being isolated, especially psychologically isolated from others. **3.** Separation or quarantine imposed on a person having or suspected of having a highly infectious or contagious disease. Also used adjectivally: *isolation ward; isolation hospital.* **—in isolation.** Considered apart from context, surrounding factors, relationships, or the like. —See Synonyms at **solitude.**

i·so·la·tion·ism (ī'sə-lā'shə-nĭz'əm, ĭs'ə-) *n.* A national policy of remaining aloof from political or economic relations with other countries. **—i·so·la·tion·ist** *n. & adj.*

Isolde. Variant of **Iseult.**

i·so·lec·i·thal (ī'sə-lĕs'ə-thəl) *adj. Biology.* Having the yolk evenly distributed throughout the egg. Said of the eggs of mammals and some other vertebrates. Compare **heterolecithal.**

i·so·leu·cine (ī'sə-lōō'sēn') *n.* An essential amino acid, $C_6H_{13}NO_2$, isomeric with leucine.

i·so·line (ī'sə-līn') *n.* An **isopleth** (*see*).

i·sol·o·gous (ī-sŏl'ə-gəs) *adj.* Designating two or more organic compounds that have a similar structure but contain some different atoms of the same valence. [ISO- + (HOMO)LOGOUS.]

i·so·mag·net·ic (ī'sō-măg-nĕt'ĭk) *adj.* **1.** Designating or pertaining to points of equal magnetic induction. **2.** Designating an imaginary line on the earth's surface connecting points of equal magnetic intensity.

i·so·mer (ī'sə-mər) *n.* **1.** *Chemistry.* **a.** A compound having the same percentage composition and molecular weight as another compound but differing in chemical or physical properties. **b.** Such a compound so differing because of the manner of linkage of its constituent atoms. Also called "structural isomer." **c.** Such a compound so differing because of the manner of arrangement of its constituent atoms in space. Also called "stereoisomer." **d.** A stereoisomer manifesting one of two structures that rotate the plane of polarization of polarized light either to the left or to the right. Also called "optical isomer." **e.** A stereoisomer having no effect on polarized light but exhibiting isomerism because of a structural asymmetry about a double bond in the molecule. Also called "geometric isomer." **2.** *Physics.* An atom whose nucleus can exist in any of several bound excited states for a measurable period of time. In this sense, also called "nuclear isomer." [Greek *isomerēs,* equally divided, equal : ISO- + *meros,* part.] **—i·so·mer·ic** *adj.*

i·som·er·ase (ī-sŏm'ə-rās') *n.* Any of a group of enzymes that catalyze the conversion of one isomer into another.

i·som·er·ism (ī-sŏm'ə-rĭz'əm) *n.* **1.** The phenomenon of the existence of isomers. **2.** The complex of chemical and physical phenomena characteristic of or attributable to isomers. **3.** The state or condition of being an isomer.

i·som·er·ize (ī-sŏm'ə-rīz') *v.* **-ized, -izing, -izes.** *—tr.* To cause to change into an isomeric form. *—intr.* To become an isomeric form. **—i·som·er·i·za·tion** *n.*

i·som·er·ous (ī-sŏm'ər-əs) *adj.* **1.** Having an equal number of parts or markings. **2.** Having or designating floral whorls with equal numbers of parts. [ISO- + -MEROUS.]

i·so·met·ric (ī'sə-mĕt'rĭk) *adj.* Also **i·so·met·ri·cal** (-rĭ-kəl). **1.** Of or exhibiting equality in dimensions or measurements. **2.** *Crystallography.* Of or being a crystal system of three equal and mutually orthogonal axes. **3.** *Physiology.* Of or involving muscular contraction occurring when the ends of the muscle are fixed in place so that increase in tension occurs without appreciable decrease in length. *~n.* A line connecting isometric points. [Greek *isometros,* of equal measure : ISO- + *metron,* measure.]

i·so·met·rics (ī'sə-mĕt'rĭks) *n. Used with a singular verb.* Exercise involving isometric contraction, used to build up muscles and improve fitness. Also called "isometric exercise."

i·so·me·tro·pi·a (ī'sō-mə-trō'pē-ə) *n.* Equality of refraction in both eyes. [New Latin : Greek *isometros,* of equal measure, ISOMETRIC + -OPIA.]

i·som·e·try (ī-sŏm'ə-trē) *n.* Equality of measure. [ISO- + -METRY.]

i·so·morph (ī'sə-môrf') *n.* An object, organism, or group exhibiting isomorphism. [ISO- + -MORPH.]

i·so·mor·phism (ī'sə-môr'fĭz'əm) *n.* **1.** *Biology.* Similarity in form, as in different kinds of organisms or cells. **2.** *Mathematics.* A one-to-one correspondence between the elements of two sets such that the result of an operation on elements of one set corresponds to the result of the analogous operation on their images in the other set. **3.** *Crystallography.* The existence or an instance of the existence of two or more different substances having closely similar crystalline structure, crystalline dimensions, and chemical composition. **4.** Structural similarity due to resemblance of corresponding parts. **—i·so·mor·phic, i·so·mor·phous** *adj.*

i·so·oc·tane (ī'sō-ŏk'tān') *n.* A highly flammable liquid, $(CH_3)_3CCH_2CH(CH_3)_2$, used to determine the octane numbers of fuels.

i·so·ni·a·zid (ī'sə-nī'ə-zĭd) *n. Abbr.* **INH** A soluble, colorless, crystalline compound, $C_6H_7N_3O$, usually administered orally for the treatment of tuberculosis. [From *isoni*cotinic acid hydr*azide.*]

i·so·pi·es·tic (ī'sō-pī-ĕs'tĭk) *adj.* Marked by or indicating equal pressure; isobaric. *~n.* An isobar. [ISO- + Greek *piestos,* capable of being compressed, from *piezein,* to press tight, compress.]

i·so·pleth (ī'sə-plĕth') *n.* A line on a map connecting places at which some geographical or meteorological feature is the same. Also called "isogram," "isoline." [Greek *isoplēthēs,* of equal number : ISO- + *plēthos,* great number.]

i·so·pod (ī'sə-pŏd') *n.* Any of numerous crustaceans of the order Isopoda, which includes the woodlice and gribbles. *~adj.* Of or belonging to the Isopoda. [New Latin *Isopoda,* "those

having pairs of legs" : ISO- + *-poda,* plural of -POD.]

i·so·pren·a·line (ī'sə-prĕn'ə-lĭn) *n.* A drug that is used in the treatment of asthma and similar conditions to dilate the air passages.

i·so·prene (ī'sə-prēn') *n.* A colorless volatile liquid, CH_2:$CHC(CH_3)$:CH_2, used chiefly to make synthetic rubber. [ISO- + PR(OPYL) + -ENE.]

i·so·pro·pyl alcohol (ī'sə-prō'pəl) *n.* A clear, colorless, mobile flammable liquid, $(CH_3)_2CHOH$, used in antifreeze compounds, lotions and cosmetics, and as a solvent for gums, shellac, and essential oils. [ISO- + PROPYL.]

i·sos·ce·les (ī-sŏs'ə-lēz') *adj. Geometry.* Having two equal sides: *isosceles triangle; isosceles trapezoid.* [Late Latin *isoscelēs,* from Greek *isoskelēs,* "having equal legs" : ISO- + *skelos,* leg.]

i·so·seis·mic (ī'sō-sīz'mĭk) *adj.* Also **i·so·seis·mal** (-məl). *Geology.* Of, pertaining to, or exhibiting equal seismic intensities.

i·sos·mot·ic (ī'sŏz-mŏt'ĭk, ī'sŏs-) *adj. Chemistry.* Of or exhibiting equal osmotic pressure; isotonic. [IS(O)- + OSMOTIC.]

i·so·spin (ī'sə-spĭn') *n. Symbol* **I** A quantum number that is related to the number of charge states of a subatomic particle by the equation $2I + 1 = M$, where M is the number of such states. Also called "isotopic spin." [Short for *isotopic spin.*]

i·sos·ta·sy (ī-sŏs'tə-sē) *n. Geology.* A theoretical state of equilibrium of the earth's crust in which the crust rests on a denser underlying medium and has equal pressure at all points. [ISO- + Greek *stasis,* a standing, standstill.]

i·so·ster·ic (ī'sō-stĕr'ĭk) *adj.* Designating two molecules, such as CO_2 and N_2O, that have the same number of atoms and the same configuration of valence electrons.

i·so·tac·tic (ī'sō-tăk'tĭk) *adj. Chemistry.* Designating a polymer in which the groups attached to the main chain are not arranged regularly, although the same irregularity is repeated along the chain. Compare **syndiotactic.** [ISO- + -TACTIC.]

i·so·therm (ī'sə-thûrm') *n.* **1.** A line drawn on a weather map or chart linking all points of equal atmospheric temperature. **2.** A line on a graph connecting points of equal temperature. [French *isotherme,* having the same temperature : ISO- + -THERM.]

i·so·ther·mal (ī'sə-thûr'məl) *adj.* **1.** Of, pertaining to, or indicating equal temperatures. **2.** Of or designating changes of pressure and volume at constant temperature. **3.** Of or pertaining to an isotherm. *~n.* An isotherm.

i·so·tone (ī'sə-tōn') *n.* One of two or more atoms, the nuclei of which have the same number of neutrons but different numbers of protons. [ISO- + Greek *tonos,* stretching, TONE.]

i·so·ton·ic (ī'sə-tŏn'ĭk) *adj.* **1.** Of equal tension. Said of two or more muscles. **2.** Isosmotic. **3.** *Music.* Of equal tone; of equal intervals of the well-tempered scale. [ISO- + Greek *tonos,* tension, stretching, TONE.]

i·so·tope (ī'sə-tōp') *n.* Any of two or more atoms, the nuclei of which have the same number of protons but different numbers of neutrons. Compare **nuclide.** [ISO- + Greek *topos,* place, "position in the periodic table" (see **topic**).] **—i·so·top·ic** (ī'sə-tŏp'ĭk) *adj.* **—i·so·top·i·cal·ly** *adv.*

i·so·tron (ī'sə-trŏn') *n.* An instrument for separating small quantities of isotopes by ionizing them and applying an electric field to the ions. [ISO- + -TRON.]

i·so·trop·ic (ī'sə-trŏp'ĭk) *adj.* Also **i·so·tro·pous** (ī-sŏt'rə-pəs). **1.** Identical in all directions; invariant with respect to direction. **2.** *Biology.* Lacking predetermined axes. Said of certain ova. [ISO- + -TROPIC.] **—i·sot·ro·py** (ī-sŏt'rə-pē), **i·sot·ro·pism** (ī-sŏt'rə-pĭz'əm) *n.*

isozyme. Variant of **isoenzyme.**

I-spy (ī'spī') *n.* A game in which one player secretly chooses an object in his field of vision and specifies its initial letter, leaving the other players to guess what it is.

Is·ra·el[1] (ĭz'rē-əl). *Abbr.* **Isr.** Republic of western Asia and the world's only state with Judaism as the official religion. The country was created as a United Nations mandate (1947) from the former British League of Nations mandate of Palestine as a homeland for Jews. It declared its independence in 1948. Largely regarded as invaders by the native Palestinians, many of whom now live as refugees in neighboring countries, the Israelis have four times (1948, 1956, 1967, 1973) defeated surrounding Arab states. In the 1980's, the Sinai was returned to Egypt, but civil unrest continued in the remaining occupied territory. Israel has few natural resources, but with U.S. aid large areas of desert have been reclaimed and an industrial economy built up. The chief exports are cut diamonds, textiles, fruit, and vegetables. Area, 20,770 square kilometers (8,017 square miles). Population, 4,600,000. Capital, Jerusalem. See map, next page.

Israel[2] *n.* **1.** The descendants of Jacob. **2.** The whole Hebrew people, past, present, and future, regarded as the chosen people of Jehovah by virtue of the covenant of Jacob. **3.** Any group considered or considering itself to be God's chosen people or the inheritors of God's covenant with Jacob, especially the Christian Church or any of various Christian sects. [Latin *Isrāël,* from Greek, from Hebrew *Yisrā'ēl,* the name given to Jacob by the angel with whom he wrestled (Genesis 32:28), "he who struggles with God."]

Is·rae·li (ĭz-rā'lē) *adj.* Of or relating to the state of Israel or its people. *~n., pl.* **Israeli** or **-lis.** A native or inhabitant of the state of Israel.

Is·ra·el·ite (ĭz'rē-ə-līt') *n.* **1.** A Hebrew. **2.** A member of any of various Christian groups regarded as heirs of the covenant of Jacob.

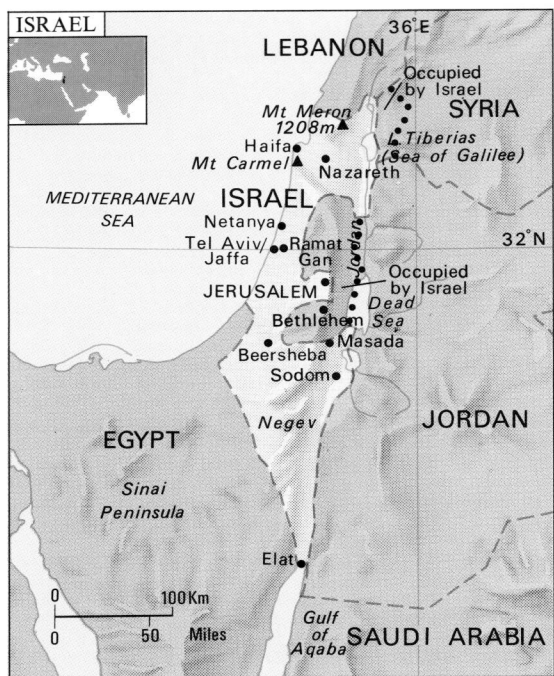

ISRAEL

LEBANON
36°E
Occupied
by Israel
SYRIA
Mt Meron
1208m▲
Tiberias
Haifa●
(Sea of Galilee)
Mt Carmel▲
Nazareth●
MEDITERRANEAN
SEA
ISRAEL
Netanya●
32°N
Tel Aviv/
Ramat
Jaffa
Gan
Occupied
JERUSALEM
by Israel
Dead
Bethlehem● Sea
Beersheba●
Masada●
Sodom●
Negev
JORDAN
EGYPT
Sinai
Peninsula
Elat●
100 Km
0
0   50   Miles
Gulf
of
Aqaba SAUDI ARABIA

~adj. Also **Is·ra·el·it·ic** (ĭz′rē-ə-lĭt′ĭk). Of or relating to Israel or the Israelites.

Is·sa·char¹ (ĭs′ə-kär′). One of the patriarchs of Israel, son of Jacob and Leah. Genesis 30:18.

Issachar² n. The tribe descended from Issachar.

Is·sei (ēs′sā′) n., pl. **-seis** or collectively **Issei.** A Japanese immigrant to the United States or Canada. [Japanese, first generation, from Chinese (Mandarin) yi¹ shi⁴ : yi¹, first + shi⁴, generation.]

is·su·a·ble (ĭsh′ōō-ə-bəl) adj. **1.** Capable of issuing or being issued. **2.** Capable of being established as an issue; open to debate or litigation. **3.** Authorized for issue.

is·su·ance (ĭsh′ōō-əns) n. An act of issuing; issue.

is·su·ant (ĭsh′ōō-ənt) adj. Archaic & Heraldry. Emerging; issuing or proceeding from.

is·sue (ĭsh′ōō) n. **1. a.** An act or instance of flowing, passing, or giving out. **b.** An act of circulating, distributing, or publishing by an office or official group: government issue of new bonds. **2.** Something produced, published, or offered, as: **a.** An item or set of items, such as stamps or coins, made available at one time by a government department or other organization. **b.** A new set of bonds, shares, or the like made available for purchase at the same time. **c.** All the copies of a periodical printed for publication at the same time. **d.** The contents of these copies: in the June issue of Reader's Digest. **3.** An allocation; that which is given out: an issue of ammunition. **4.** The result of an action or series of events. **5.** Something proceeding from a specified source: suspicions that were the issue of a deranged mind. **6. a.** A point of discussion, debate, or dispute. **b.** A matter of wide public concern. **c.** The essential point; crux: the real issue. **d.** A point of dispute in a legal action: an issue of fact; an issue of law. **e.** A culminating point leading to a decision; a result. Used chiefly in legal contexts: bring a case to an issue. **7.** A place of egress; an outlet: a lake with no issue to the sea. **8.** Children; offspring or descendants. Used chiefly in legal contexts. **9.** Pathology. **a.** A discharge, as of blood. **b.** A suppurating sore. **10.** Archaic. Termination; close. **—at issue.** **1.** In question; in dispute. **2.** At variance; in disagreement. **—force the issue.** To make decisive action unavoidable. **—join issue.** To enter into controversy. **—take issue with.** To take an opposing point of view to; disagree with.

~v. **issued, -suing, -sues.** —intr. **1.** To go or come forth; emerge. **2.** To accrue as proceeds or profit: Little money issued from the stocks. **3.** To be circulated or published. **4.** To originate or be derived. Used with from. **5.** To terminate or result. Used with in. —tr. **1.** To cause to flow out; emit. **2.** To circulate, allocate, or distribute, especially in an official capacity: The school issued uniforms to the players. **3.** To publish. **4.** To make public; announce: issue a stern warning. [Middle English, from Old French (e)issue, from Vulgar Latin exūta (unattested), "exit," altered from Latin exita, feminine of exitus, past participle of exīre, to go out : ex-, out + īre, to go.] —**is·su·er** n.

-ist suffix. Indicates: **1.** A person who does, makes, produces, operates, plays, or sells a specified thing; for example, **dramatist, lobbyist, motorist, organist, tobacconist. 2.** A person who is skilled, trained, or employed in a specified field; for example, **machinist, radiologist, industrialist. 3.** An adherent or proponent of a doctrine, system, or school of thought; for example, **anarchist, federalist, Platonist. 4.** A person characterized by a certain trait or

predilection; for example, **romanticist, sadist. 5.** A person having a disparaging or hostile attitude toward a particular social group on the basis of a specified characteristic; for example, **sexist, ageist, racist.** [Middle English -iste, from Old French, from Latin -ista, -istēs, from Greek -istēs, agential suffix for verbs in -izein, -IZE.]

Is·tan·bul (ĭs′tän-bōōl′, ĭs′tän-). Formerly (before 1930) **Con·stan·ti·no·ple** (kŏn′stăn-tə-nō′pəl). Largest city and chief port of Turkey. It is a major manufacturing, cultural, and tourist center, with many museums, including Hagia Sophia and the Seraglio (royal palace).

isth·mi·an (ĭs′mē-ən) adj. **1.** Of, pertaining to, or forming an isthmus. **2. Isthmian.** Of or pertaining to the Isthmus of Corinth, especially with regard to the biennial pan-Hellenic games held there in antiquity. **3. Isthmian.** Of or pertaining to the Isthmus of Panama.

isth·mus (ĭs′məs) n., pl. **-muses** or **-mi** (-mī′). **1.** A narrow strip of land connecting two larger masses of land. **2.** Anatomy. **a.** A narrow strip of tissue joining two larger organs or parts of an organ. **b.** A narrow passage connecting two larger cavities. [Latin, from Greek isthmos†.]

-istics suffix. Indicates study of a specified subject; for example, **statistics, cladistics.**

is·tle, ix·tle (ĭs′lē, ĭst′-) n. A plant, **pita** (see). [Mexican Spanish ixtle, from Nahuatl ichtli.]

Is·tri·a (ĭs′trē-ə). Peninsula of the northwest Yugoslavian coast. It separates the Gulf of Venice from the Bay of Kvarner in the Adriatic Sea.

it (ĭt) pron. The third person singular pronoun, neuter gender in the nominative or objective case. **1.** Used to represent the thing, non-human being, or person whose sex is unknown or disregarded, last mentioned or implied. **2.** Used without a previously understood antecedent or consequent as **a.** The formal subject of an impersonal verb: It is raining. **b.** The object, having little meaning, of various verbs: Live it up. **3.** Used to represent a word, phrase, or clause that follows: It is he. It's certain that she'll win. **4.** Used to represent a situation, topic for consideration, or any other item of discourse that the speaker assumes the hearer will comprehend without antecedent: Always try to do it right the first time. **5.** Used to represent all the experience that can be endured or desired. He'd had it; he resigned. **6.** Used to represent the crucial moment upon which an outcome depends: This is it! he thought, as the plane's engine sputtered. **7.** Used to represent a human life: The old man's eyes closed; it was all over.

~n. **1.** The player who chases the others in a game of tag. **2.** Informal. An important person. Usually used derogatorily, especially in such phrases as he thinks he's it. **3.** Informal. **a.** Sexual intercourse. **b.** Rare. Sexual attractiveness. [Middle English (h)it, (h)yt, Old English hit, hyt.]

It. Italian; Italy.

i.t.a., I.T.A. n. Initial teaching alphabet: a 44-letter phonetic alphabet used in teaching young children to read.

it·a·col·u·mite (ĭt′ə-kŏl′yə-mīt′) n. A variety of sandstone that is slightly flexible when cut into thin slabs. Also called "flexible sandstone." [Found in Itacolumi, a mountain in Brazil.]

it·a·con·ic acid (ĭt′ə-kŏn′ĭk) n. A white crystalline substance, $CH_2:C(COOH) CH_2COOH$, obtained by the fermentation of carbohydrates and used in the manufacture of synthetic resins. [Anagram of aconitic.]

ital. italic.

Ital. Italian; Italy.

Italia. See **Italy.**

I·tal·ian (ĭ-tăl′yən) adj. Abbr. **It., Ital.** Pertaining to Italy, its people, their culture, or their language.

~n. Abbr. **It., Ital.** **1.** A native or citizen of Italy, or a person of Italian descent. **2.** The Romance language of Italy and one of the three official languages of Switzerland. [Middle English, from Italian Italiano, from Italia, ITALY.]

I·tal·ian·ate (ĭ-tăl′yə-nāt′, -nĭt) adj. Italian in character. [Italian Italianato, from Italiano, ITALIAN.]

Italian East Africa. Former Italian colony in East Africa. It comprised Italian Somaliland (now part of Somalia); Eritrea (another Italian colony, now part of Ethiopia); and Abyssinia (the rest of Ethiopia, conquered by the Italians in 1935–36). The territory was captured by Allied and Ethiopian forces in 1941 and broken up.

Italian greyhound n. A dog of a breed of small greyhound having a long, narrow skull, a deep, narrow chest, and sloping hindquarters.

Italian hand n. A forward-slanting script employed by 15th-century Italian calligraphers and used as a model for modern, especially English penmanship. Also called "Italian handwriting."

I·tal·ian·ism (ĭ-tăl′yə-nĭz′əm) n. **1.** An Italian custom, trait, or expression. **2.** A quality characteristic of Italy or its people.

I·tal·ian·ize (ĭ-tăl′yə-nīz′) v. **-ized, -izing, -izes.** —tr. To give an Italian aspect to. —intr. To become Italian; adopt Italian speech, manners, or customs. —**I·tal·ian·i·za·tion** n.

Italian sandwich n. See **hero** (sense 5).

Italian Somaliland. See **Somalia.**

Italian sonnet n. A **Petrarchan sonnet** (see).

Italian vermouth n. A sweet, aromatic wine distilled and flavored with herbs.

i·tal·ic (ĭ-tăl′ĭk, ī-tăl′-) adj. Abbr. **ital.** **1.** Of, pertaining to, or being a style of printing type patterned upon a Renaissance script with the letters slanting to the right, now chiefly used to set off a word or passage within a text printed in roman type, indicating that the word or passage is emphatic, in a foreign language, or has a structurally independent function within the main text: This sentence is

ITALY

ITALY

printed in italic type. Compare **roman. 2.** Pertaining to or designating a modern style of handwriting similar to Italian hand.
~*n.* **1.** Italic handwriting. **2. a.** *Often* **italics.** Italic type or print. **b.** An italic character. [Introduced in the Aldine Virgil printed in Venice in 1501, which was dedicated to Italy.]

I·tal·ic (ĭ-tăl′ĭk) *adj.* **1.** Of or pertaining to ancient Italy or its peoples. **2.** Of or pertaining to a branch of Indo-European languages that includes the Latino-Faliscan and Osco-Umbrian groups.
~*n.* The Italic branch of the Indo-European family of languages. [Latin *Italicus,* from Greek *Italikos,* from *Italia,* Italy, from Latin.]

i·tal·i·cize (ĭ-tăl′ĭ-sīz′) *v.* **-cized, -cizing, -cizes.** —*tr.* **1.** To print in italic type. **2.** To underscore (written matter) with a single line to indicate italics. —*intr.* To print or put words in italics; use italics. —**i·tal·i·ci·za·tion** *n.*

It·a·ly (ĭt′ə-lē). *Abbr.* **It., Ital.** Italian **I·ta·li·a** (ē-tä′lyä). Republic of southern Europe. It includes Sardinia to the west. The mainland peninsula's spine is formed by the Appenines, the only lowlands of any size being the fertile Po River valley in the northeast. After the fall of the Western Roman Empire (A.D. 476), Italy was dominated by successive foreign powers until its unification (1870) under the Piedmontese royal family. A republic was declared (1946) following the country's defeat in World War II. Industries, especially textiles and motor vehicles, are concentrated in the north, with much of the south being economically depressed. Rich in cultural heritage and with many holiday resorts, much of the country is heavily depend-

ent on tourism. Italy is a founder member of the European Economic Community. Area, 301,225 square kilometers (116,303 square miles). Population, 57,000,000. Capital, Rome.

itch (ĭch) *n.***1.** An irritating or tickling skin sensation, causing a desire to scratch. **2.** Any of various contagious skin diseases, such as scabies, marked by intense irritation, eruptions, and itching. **3.** A restless desire or craving: *an itch for foreign travel.*
~*v.* **itched, itching, itches.** —*intr.* **1.** To feel, have, or produce an itch. **2.** To have a persistent, restless craving. —*tr.* To cause to itch. [Middle English *(y)icchen,* Old English *giccan,* from Germanic *juk-* (unattested).] —**itch·i·ness** *n.* —**itch·y** *adj.*

-ite¹ *suffix.* Indicates: **1.** A person who is: **a.** A native or resident of a specified place; for example, *New Jerseyite.* **b.** A member of a tribe or family; for example, **Ammonite. c.** An adherent of a doctrine, idea, way of life, or the like; for example, **socialite. d.** A supporter of someone specified, or their views; for example, **Luddite. 2.** *Biology.* A part of an organ or body; for example, **somite. 3.** A fossil; for example, **trilobite. 4.** A mineral or rock; for example, **graphite. 5. a.** An explosive; for example, **gelignite. b.** A commercial product; for example, **Lucite.** [Middle English, from Old French, from Latin *-ita, -ités,* from Greek *-ités.*]

-ite² *suffix.* Indicates a salt or ester of an acid whose adjectival denomination ends in *-ous;* for example, **sulfite.** [French, arbitrarily altered from -ATE.]

i·tem (ī′təm) *n.* **1.** A single article listed on a bill or unit included in

ivory *An ivory saltcellar with two chambers, carved in West Africa in the 16th century by a Benin craftsman. It shows two Portuguese dignitaries with their attendants, surmounted by a ship.*

ivy *The ivy genus,* Hedera, *is a group of evergreen climbers that grow throughout the temperate zones of the Northern Hemisphere. Ivy was once believed to have magical powers, and its use as a Christmas decoration stems from the belief that it would ward off goblins.*

a collection, enumeration, or series and specified separately. **2.** A separate matter for consideration, such as a topic or proposal listed on an agenda. **3.** An entry in an account. **4. a.** A bit of information; detail. **b.** A short piece in a newspaper or magazine. **5.** A member of a set of minimal units: *a lexical item.*
~*tr.v.* **itemed, iteming, items.** *Archaic.* To itemize.
~*adv.* Also; likewise. Used to introduce each article in an enumeration or list. [Middle English, also, likewise, from Latin, from *ita,* so.]

i·tem·ize (ī'tə-mīz') *tr.v.* **-ized, -izing, -izes.** To set down item by item; list. **—i·tem·i·za·tion** *n.* **—i·tem·iz·er** *n.*

it·er·ate (ĭt'ə-rāt') *tr.v.* **-ated, -ating, -ates.** To say or perform again; repeat. [Latin *iterāre,* from *iterum,* again.] **—it·er·ant** *adj.* **—it·er·a·tion, it·er·ance** *n.*

it·er·a·tive (ĭt'ə-rā'tĭv, -ər-ə-tĭv) *adj.* **1.** Repetitious. **2.** *Grammar.* Frequentative.

Ith·a·ca (ĭth'ə-kə). *Greek* **I·thá·ki** (ē-thä'kē). An island of Greece, one of the Ionian Islands. It is mountainous and has little arable land.

I·thunn, I·thun (ē'tho͝on'). Also **I·dun** (-do͝on'). *Norse Mythology.* The wife of Bragi, goddess of youth and spring. [Old Norse *Idhunn,* probably from *idh,* again, anew.]

i·tin·er·an·cy (ī-tĭn'ər-ən-sē, ĭ-tĭn'-) *n.* Also **i·tin·er·a·cy** (-ər-ə-sē). A state or system of itinerating, especially in the role or office of public speaker, minister, or judge.

i·tin·er·ant (ī-tĭn'ər-ənt, ĭ-tĭn'-) *adj.* Traveling from place to place, especially to perform some duty or work: *an itinerant preacher.*
~*n.* One who so travels. [Late Latin *itinerāns* (stem *itinerant-*), present participle of *itinerārī,* ITINERATE.]

i·tin·er·ar·y (ī-tĭn'ə-rĕr'ē, ĭ-tĭn'-) *n., pl.* **-ies. 1.** A route or proposed route of a journey. **2.** An account or record of a journey. **3.** A travelers' guidebook.
~*adj.* **1.** Of or pertaining to a journey or to a route. **2.** Traveling from place to place; itinerant. [Middle English *itinerarie,* from Late Latin *itinerārium,* course of travel, from *itinerārius,* of traveling, from Latin *iter* (stem *itiner-*), journey.]

-itis *suffix.* Indicates inflammation of or inflammatory disease; for example, **laryngitis, bronchitis.** [New Latin, from Greek *-itis,* feminine of *-itēs,* -ITE (pertaining to, native).]

it'll (ĭt'l). **1.** Contraction of *it will.* **2.** Contraction of *it shall.*

ITO International Trade Organization.

-itol *suffix. Chemistry.* Indicates an alcohol containing more than one hydroxyl group; for example, **mannitol.** [-ITE + -OL.]

its (ĭts). The possessive form of the pronoun *it.* Used to indicate possession, agency, or reception of an action by the thing, nonhuman being, or person whose sex is not known or disregarded, spoken of: *its forepaw.* [Originally *it's* : IT + *-'s,* possessive ending.]

it's (ĭts). **1.** Contraction of *it is.* **2.** Contraction of *it has.*

it·self (ĭt-sĕlf') *pron.* A specialized form of the third person singular neuter pronoun. It is used: **1.** As a reflexive pronoun, forming the direct or indirect object of a verb or the object of a preposition: *This record player turns itself off.* **2.** For emphasis, after a noun or *it*: *The trouble is in the machine itself.* **3.** As an emphasizing substitute: *Itself in difficulties, the bank could not help us.* **4.** As an indication of its real identity or normal, healthy condition: *The computer is acting itself again since the program was corrected.* **—in itself.** Considered in isolation: *in itself, quite a good idea.* [Middle English *itself,* Old English *hit self* : IT + SELF.]

it·sy-bit·sy (ĭt'sē-bĭt'sē) *adj.* Also **it·ty-bit·ty** (ĭt'ē-bĭt'ē). *Informal.* Very small; tiny. [Baby-talk reduplication of LITTLE (influenced by BIT).]

ITU International Telecommunication Union.

-ity *suffix.* Indicates a state or quality; for example, **authenticity, jollity.** [Middle English *-it(i)e,* from Old French *-ite,* from Latin *-itās* : thematic vowel *-i-* + *-tās* (stem *-tāt-*), -TY.]

IUD *n.* An **intrauterine device** *(see).*

-ium *suffix.* Indicates: **1.** *Chemistry.* **a.** A metallic chemical element; for example, **californium, unnilquadium. b.** A positive ion formed from a group or molecule; for example, **ammonium, hydroxonium. 2.** A biological or anatomical structure; for example, **pericardium.** [New Latin, from Latin, from Greek *-ion,* diminutive suffix.]

IV, i.v. intravenous; intravenously.

I·van III (ī'vən), born Ivan Vasilyevich, called "the Great" (1440–1505). Grand Prince of Muscovy (1462–1505), whose successful campaigns against the Tatars laid the foundations for eventual Russian unity. He also set up a strong central government.

Ivan IV, born Ivan Vasilyevich, called "the Terrible" (1530–84). First ruler of Russia to be proclaimed czar (1547). He greatly expanded the Russian state by war and conquest, but his later pathological fear of treachery led him to the violent suppression of suspected opposition.

I've (īv). Contraction of *I have.*

-ive *suffix.* Indicates having a tendency toward or inclination to perform some action; for example, **degenerative, disruptive.** [Middle English *-if, -ive,* from Old French *-if* (feminine *-ive*), from Latin *-īvus* (feminine *-īva,* neuter *-īvum*).]

Ives (īvz), **Charles Edward** (1874–1954). U.S. composer. Many of his works anticipated those of later 20th-century musicians in their abandonment of conventional tonality. His *Third Symphony* (1904–11) won the 1947 Pulitzer Prize.

Ives, James Merritt (1824–95). U.S. lithographer. Hired as a bookkeeper for Nathaniel Currier's lithography business (1852), he was recognized for his artistic talents, contributing many of his own drawings and directing the complicated printing process. He became a partner in the business (1857), creating the renowned American lithograph team of Currier & Ives.

IVF in vitro fertilization.

i·vied (ī'vēd) *adj.* Overgrown or covered with ivy.

Iviza. See **Ibiza.**

i·vo·ry (ī'və-rē, īv'rē) *n., pl.* **-ries. 1. a.** The hard, smooth, yellowish-white dentine forming the main part of the tusks of the elephant, and used as an ornamental material. **b.** A similar substance forming the tusks or teeth of certain other animals, such as the walrus. **2.** A tusk, especially an elephant's tusk. **3.** A substance, such as a plant product, resembling ivory. **4.** Pale or grayish yellow to yellowish white. **5.** *Often* **ivories.** An article made of ivory. **6.** *Usually* **ivories.** *Slang.* **a.** Piano keys. **b.** Dice. **c.** The teeth.
~*adj.* **1.** Made of or resembling ivory. **2.** Of the color ivory. [Middle English *ivor(ie), yvory,* from Old French *ivurie, ivoire,* from Vulgar Latin *eboreus* (unattested), from neuter of Latin *eboreus,* of ivory, from *ebur* (stem *ebor-*), ivory.]

i·vo·ry·bill (ī'və-rē-bĭl', īv'rē-) *n.* The ivory-billed woodpecker.

i·vo·ry-billed woodpecker (ī'və-rē-bĭld', īv'rē-) *n.* A large, probably extinct North American woodpecker, *Campephilus principalis,* having a white bill.

ivory black *n.* A black pigment prepared from charred ivory.

Ivory Coast. Republic in West Africa, on the Gulf of Guinea. Ceded to France (1842), it became an independent republic in 1960. It was once the center of the slave and ivory trade and is now Africa's largest exporter of timber and coffee. Area, 322,463 square kilometers (124,503 square miles). Population, 12,000,000. Capital, Abidjan. See map at **West African States.**

ivory gull *n.* An Arctic gull, *Pagophila eburnea.*

ivory nut *n.* The hard seed of the American ivory palm, *Phytelephas macrocarpa,* yielding an ivorylike substance.

ivory tower *n.* A place or attitude of retreat; especially, a preoccupation with lofty, remote, or intellectual considerations rather than with practical everyday life. [Translation of French *tour d'ivoire,* first used by C.A. Sainte-Beuve with reference to Alfred de Vigny, who was anxious to preserve the purity of his inspiration unmixed with practical matters.]

i·vy (ī'vē) *n., pl.* **ivies. 1.** Any of several woody, climbing or trailing plants of the genus *Hedera,* native to the Old World, especially *H. helix,* having lobed, evergreen leaves and berrylike black fruit. **2.** Any of various other climbing or creeping plants, such as ground ivy or poison ivy. [Middle English *ivi, ivye,* Old English *īfig,* from Germanic *ibahs* (unattested), obscurely related to Latin *ibex,* "climber," IBEX.]

Ivy League *n.* An association of eight traditional and prestigious universities in the northeastern United States, comprising Brown, Columbia, Cornell, Dartmouth, Harvard, Princeton, the University of Pennsylvania, and Yale.
~*adj.* Of or resembling the traditions of the Ivy League, especially in being conservative and restrained in style. [Referring to the ivy-covered university buildings.] **—Ivy Leaguer** *n.*

i·wis, y·wis (ī-wĭs') *adv. Archaic.* Certainly; assuredly. [Middle English *iwis(se), gewis,* Old English *gewis,* certain.]

I·wo Ji·ma (ē'wō jē'mə). The largest of the Volcano Islands. Lying in the Pacific Ocean, 1,200 kilometers (750 miles) south of Tokyo, it has been part of Japan since 1887 and was the scene of fierce fighting during World War II.

IWW, I.W.W. Industrial Workers of the World.

Ix·i·on (ĭk-sī'ən). *Greek Mythology.* A Thessalian king whom Zeus punished for his temerity in seeking Hera's love by having him bound to a perpetually revolving wheel in Hades.

ix·o·di·a·sis (ĭk'sō-dī'ə-sĭs) *n.* Any disease caused by infestation with ticks. [New Latin, from Greek *ixōdēs,* resembling birdlime, sticking, from *ixos,* birdlime + -IASIS.]

ixtle. Variant of **istle.** See **pita.**

I·yar, Iy·yar (ē-yär', ē'yär) *n.* The eighth month of the year on the Hebrew calendar. See feature at **calendar.** [Hebrew *iyyār.*]

iz·ar (ĭ-zär') *n.* A long cotton outer garment, usually white, worn by women in many Muslim countries. [Arabic *'izār, 'izr,* veil, covering.]

-ization *suffix.* Indicates action, process, or result of doing or making; for example, *colonization.* [-IZ(E) + -ATION.]

-ize *suffix.* Indicates: **1. a.** To cause to be or to become; make into; for example, **dramatize. b.** To make conform with; make like for example, **Hellenize, Anglicize. c.** To treat or regard as; for example, **idolize. 2.** To cause to acquire a specified quality; for example, **legalize, modernize, sterilize. 3.** To become or become similar to; for example, **crystallize, oxidize, materialize. 4. a.** To subject to; for example, **jeopardize, anesthetize. b.** To affect with; for example, **magnetize, galvanize. 5.** To do or follow some practice; for example, **pasteurize, bowdlerize.** [Old French *-iser,* Latin *-izāre,* Greek *-izein.*]

Iz·mir (ĭz-mîr'). Formerly **Smyr·na** (smûr'nə). City and port in western Turkey. At the head of the Gulf of Izmir, an inlet of the Aegean Sea, it is the commercial center of the Levant, with strong Greek connections.

iz·zard (ĭz'ərd) *n. Archaic.* The letter *z.* [Earlier *ezed,* probably from Old French *et zède,* "and zed."]

J

j, J (jā) *n., pl.* **j's** or **J's. 1.** The tenth letter of the modern English alphabet. See feature at **alphabet. 2.** Any of the speech sounds represented by this letter. **3.** Anything shaped like the letter J. **4.** The Roman numeral for 1, a substitute for i or I in the final position used especially in prescriptions. **5.** The tenth in a series.

j, J, j., J. *Note:* As an abbreviation or symbol, *j* may be a small or capital letter, with or without a period. Established forms or those generally preferred precede the definition. When no form is given, all four forms are in general use in that sense. **1.** J jack (playing card). **2.** J. Japan; Japanese. **3.** J current density. **4.** J joule. **5.** J. journal. **6.** J. judge; justice.

ja (yä) *interj. South African Informal.* Yes. [Afrikaans.]

J.A. judge advocate.

jaap (yäp) *n. South African.* Also **ja·pie** (yä′pē). A simple-minded, innocent person; a country bumpkin. [Afrikaans, from *Jaap,* pet form of *Jakob, Jacob.*]

jab (jăb) *v.* **jabbed, jabbing, jabs.** —*tr.* **1.** To poke abruptly, especially with something sharp. **2.** To stab or pierce. **3.** To thrust into or against something with a rough, abrupt movement. **4.** To punch with short blows. —*intr.* **1.** To make an abrupt jabbing motion. **2.** To deliver a quick punch.
~*n.* **1.** A quick stab or blow. **2.** *Boxing.* A short straight punch. [Variant of JOB.]

jab·ber (jăb′ər) *v.* **-bered, -bering, -bers.** —*intr.* To talk rapidly, unintelligibly, or idly. —*tr.* To utter rapidly or unintelligibly.
~*n.* Rapid or babbling talk. [Middle English *jaberen* (imitative).] —**jab·ber·er** *n.*

jab·ber·wock·y (jăb′ər-wŏk′ē) *n.* **1.** Nonsense verse. **2.** Unintelligible speech or writing; nonsense; gibberish. [Title of a poem in Lewis Carroll's *Through the Looking-Glass* (1871).]

jab·i·ru (jăb′ə-rōō′) *n.* **1.** A large tropical American wading bird, *Jabiru mycteria,* having white plumage and a dark, naked head and neck. **2.** A similar Australian bird, *Xenorhyncus asiaticus.* Also called "black-necked stork." **3.** Any of various other similar birds, such as the **saddlebill** *(see).* [Portuguese *jabirú,* from Tupi-Guarani.]

jab·o·ran·di (jăb′ə-răn′dē) *n., pl.* **-dis. 1.** Either of two tropical American shrubs, *Pilocarpus jaborandi* or *P. microphyllus.* **2.** The dried leaves of these shrubs, which yield **pilocarpine** *(see).* [Portuguese, from Tupi-Guarani *jaburandi.*]

jab·ot (zhă-bō′, jă-) *n.* A cascade of frills down the front of a shirt, blouse, or bodice. [French, from Auvergne or Limousin dialect, akin to Old French dialectal *gave,* throat, from a Romance root *gab-* (unattested), crop, gullet, perhaps from Gaulish.]

jac·a·mar (jăk′ə-mär′) *n.* Any of various tropical American birds of the family Galbulidae, related to the woodpeckers. [French, from Tupi-Guarani *jacamaciri.*]

ja·ca·na (zhä′sə-nä′) *n.* Any of several tropical marsh birds of the family Jacanidae, having long toes adapted for walking on floating vegetation. Also called "lily-trotter." [From Portuguese *jaçaná,* from Tupi-Guarani *jasaná.*]

jac·a·ran·da (jăk′ə-răn′də) *n.* **1.** Any of several trees of the genus *Jacaranda,* native to tropical America, having clusters of pale purple flowers. **2.** The wood of such a tree. **3.** Any similar wood, or the tree yielding it. [Portuguese *jacarandá,* from Tupi-Guarani.]

ja·cinth (jā′sĭnth, jăs′ĭnth) *n.* **1.** A reddish-orange variety of zircon, **hyacinth** *(see).* **2.** *Obsolete.* A hyacinth plant or flower. [Middle English *iacynth, iacin(c)t,* from Old French *iacinte* or Medieval Latin *jacintus,* from Latin *hyacinthus,* HYACINTH.]

jack (jăk) *n.* **1.** *Usually* **Jack.** A man; a fellow; a chap. Often used in direct address. **2. a.** *Archaic.* One who does odd jobs. **b.** One who works in the specified manual trade. Used in combination: *lumberjack; steeplejack.* **3.** A sailor; a tar. **4.** *Abbr.* **J** A playing card showing the figure of a young man or prince and ranking below a queen; a knave. **5. a.** Any of several devices or contrivances replacing human labor. Often used in combination: *bootjack.* **b.** A usually portable device for raising heavy objects, especially one for raising a motor vehicle when changing a tire, by means of force applied with a lever, screw, or hydraulic press. **c.** A wooden wedge for cleaving

rock. **d.** A support or brace; especially, the iron crosstree on a topgallant masthead. **e.** A device that turns a spit for roasting meat. **6.** The male of certain animals, especially the ass. **7.** Any of several food and game fishes chiefly of the genus *Caranx,* of Atlantic and Pacific waters. **8.** A piece of wood holding the leather or quill pluck in a harpsichord or the hammer in other keyboard instruments, such as the piano. **9.** Any of the metal pieces used in the game of **jacks** *(see).* Also called "jackstone." **10.** A socket that accepts a plug at one end and attaches to an electric circuit at the other. **11.** A jacklight. **12.** A small flag flown at the bow of a ship, usually to indicate nationality. **13.** *Slang.* Money. —**every man jack.** Every single person of a group.
~*v.* **jacked, jacking, jacks.** —*tr.* To hunt or fish for with a jacklight. —*intr.* To jacklight. —**jack up. 1.** To raise with or as if with a jack. **2.** *Informal.* To increase (prices, for example). **3.** To bolster confidence in; support. **4.** *New Zealand.* To arrange; set up; put in order. **5.** *Australian.* To refuse to cooperate; resist or rebel.
~*adj. Australian Informal.* Tired or dissatisfied. Used with *of: jack of it all.* [Transferred use of the name *Jack,* familiar form of *John,* used to represent "any man."]

jack·al (jăk′əl, -ôl′) *n.* **1.** Any of several doglike carnivorous mammals of the genus *Canis,* of Africa and Asia, that feed on carrion or prey on other animals. **2.** An accomplice or lackey characterized by the greed and baseness attributed to the jackal. [Turkish *chakāl,* from Persian *shagāl, shaghāl*†.]

jack·a·napes (jăk′ə-nāps′) *n.* **1.** A conceited, cheeky young man. **2.** A mischievous child. **3.** *Archaic.* A monkey or ape. [Earlier, "an ape," originally (c. 1450) *Jack Napes,* perhaps referring to the nickname of William de la Pole, 1st Duke of Suffolk, whose badge was a figure of a tame ape's ball and chain.]

jack·ass (jăk′ăs′) *n.* **1.** A male ass or donkey. **2.** A foolish or stupid person; a blockhead. **3.** An Australian bird, the **kookaburra** *(see).* [JACK (male) + ASS.]

jackass penguin *n.* The northernmost of penguins, *Spheniscus demersus,* found especially on the islets off the west coast of Africa, so called because of its donkeylike braying.

jackass rig *n. Nautical.* Any nonstandard combination of square rig and fore-and-aft rig on a sailing ship having two or more masts. Also called "hermaphrodite rig."

jack·boot (jăk′bōōt′) *n.* **1.** A stout military boot extending to or above the knee. **2.** Oppressive, bullying behavior. Also used adjectivally: *jackboot tactics.*

jack·daw (jăk′dô′) *n.* A Eurasian bird, *Corvus monedula,* related to and resembling the crow, having a black and gray plumage. Also called "daw."

jack·e·roo, jack·a·roo (jăk′ə-rōō′) *n., pl.* **-roos.** *Australian Informal.* An apprentice hand on a sheep or cattle ranch.
~*intr.v.* **jackerooed, -rooing, -roos.** To work as a jackeroo. [Blend of JACK (man) and KANGAROO.]

jack·et (jăk′ĭt) *n.* **1.** A short coat, usually waist- or hip-length, worn by men or women. **2.** Any of various coverings worn on the upper part of the body. Used in combination: *a straitjacket.* **3.** The coat of certain animals. **4.** An outer covering or casing, especially: **a.** The skin of a baked potato. **b.** A **dust jacket** *(see).* **c.** Insulation covering a steam pipe, wire, boiler, or the like. **d.** A paper or thin cardboard envelope for a phonograph record.
~*tr.v.* **jacketed, -eting, -ets.** To supply or cover with a jacket. [Middle English *jaket,* from Old French *jacquet, jaquet,* diminutive of *jaque,* short jacket, perhaps from the name *Jacques.*]

Jack Frost *n.* Frost or cold weather personified.

jack·fruit (jăk′frōōt′) *n.* **1.** A tree, *Artocarpus heterophyllus,* of tropical Asia, bearing large, edible fruit. **2.** The fruit of this tree, resembling breadfruit. [Portuguese *jaca,* from Malayalam *chakka* + FRUIT.]

jack·ham·mer (jăk′hăm′ər) *n.* A hand-held pneumatic machine for drilling rock.

jack-in-the-box (jăk′ĭn-thə-bŏks′) *n., pl.* **jack-in-the-boxes** or **jacks-in-the-box.** A toy consisting of a usually grotesque puppet that springs up out of a box when the lid is opened.

jackal *The common, or Indian, jackal (above) is one of several species of this doglike mammal found in the warmer parts of Asia and Africa. Jackals are mostly scavengers, feeding on the carcasses left by the larger carnivores such as lions, but also hunt in packs for birds and small animals.*

jack-in-the-box *A favorite toy of European children in the 19th century. The earliest versions, dating back to the 16th century, were modeled on Punch and Judy and known as "Punch boxes."*

jack-in-the-pul·pit (jăk′ĭn-thə-poŏol′pĭt, -poŏl′pĭt) *n., pl.* **jack-in-the-pulpits** or **jacks-in-the-pulpit.** A plant, *Arisaema triphyllum,* of eastern North America, having a leaflike spathe enclosing a clublike spadix. Also called "Indian turnip."

Jack Ketch *n. Archaic British.* A hangman. [After John KETCH.]

jack-knife (jăk′nīf′) *n., pl.* **-knives** (-nīvz) or **-knifes** (for senses 2,3). **1.** A large pocketknife. **2.** A dive executed by jumping headfirst and then bending the body at the waist and, with the legs straight, touching the feet with the hands before straightening out to enter the water, hands first. **3.** An uncontrollable maneuver of a tractor-trailer truck, in which the trailer swings round at an angle, usually of less than 90°, to the tractor or cab. —*v.* **jackknifed, -knifing, -knifes.** —*tr.* To fold or double like a jackknife. —*intr.* **1.** To bend or fold up like a jackknife. **2.** To make a jackknife dive. **3.** To go out of control by performing a jackknife. Used of a vehicle. [Probably JACK + KNIFE.]

jack-light (jăk′līt′) *n.* A light used as a lure in night hunting or fishing. —*intr.v.* **jacklighted, -lighting, -lights.** To hunt or fish with a jacklight.

jack mackerel *n.* A food and game fish, *Trachurus symmetricus,* of Pacific coastal waters. Also called "saurel."

jack-of-all-trades (jăk′əv-ôl′trādz) *n., pl.* **jacks-of-all-trades.** A person who can do many different kinds of work.

jack-o'-lan·tern (jăk′ə-lăn′tərn) *n.* **1. a.** A lantern made from a hollowed pumpkin with a carved face. **b.** A commercial imitation of this. **2.** A phosphorescent light over marshy ground or a similar phenomenon; an **ignis fatuus** *(see)* or similar phenomenon.

jack-plane (jăk′plān′) *n.* A bench plane for rough surfacing. [JACK + PLANE.]

jack plug *n.* A usually single-pronged electrical plug for use with a jack.

jack-pot (jăk′pŏt′) *n.* **1. a.** The accumulated stakes in a kind of poker that requires one to hold a pair of jacks or better in order to open the betting. **b.** Any cumulative pool or kitty in various games and competitions. **2.** A top prize or reward. —**hit the jackpot.** *Informal.* To experience great success or sudden good fortune. [JACK (playing card) + POT.]

jack rabbit *n.* Any of several large long-eared, long-legged hares of the genus *Lepus,* of western North America. [JACK(ASS) (from its long ears) + RABBIT.]

Jack Russell terrier *n.* A dog of a breed developed from the fox terrier, having a smooth, white coat with black and tan markings, short legs, and a stocky body. Also called "Jack Russell." [After John *Russell* (1795–1883), English clergyman known as the "sporting parson."]

jacks (jăks) *n. Used with a singular verb.* A game played with a set of six-pointed metal pieces and a small ball, the object being to pick up the pieces in various combinations while bouncing and catching the ball. Also called "jackstones." [Shortened from *jackstones* : JACK (man) + STONE.]

jack-screw (jăk′skroŏ′) *n.* A jack for lifting, operated by a screw. Also called "jack."

jack-shaft (jăk′shăft′, -shäft′) *n.* An auxiliary or intermediate shaft that transmits motion from a motor to a machine.

jack-snipe (jăk′snīp′) *n., pl.* **-snipes** or collectively **jacksnipe. 1.** A Eurasian wading bird, *Limnocryptes minima,* having brownish plumage and a long bill. **2.** Any of several similar birds. [JACK + SNIPE.]

Jack-son (jăk′sən). Capital of Mississippi since 1821, situated on the Pearl River. The city was the scene of bitter fighting during the Civil War and of civil rights agitation after World War II.

Jackson, Andrew (1767–1845). Seventh U.S. president. He became a national hero after his defense of New Orleans against the British in 1815 and was elected president in 1828 and 1832.

Jackson, Jesse Louis (1941–). U.S. civil rights leader and politician. A Baptist minister, he directed national antidiscrimination efforts (1966–77). In the 1980's he made controversial diplomatic missions as a private citizen, denounced U.S. ties with South Africa, and sought the 1984 Democratic presidential nomination.

Jackson, Thomas Jonathan (1824–63). U.S. Confederate general in the Civil War. He won his nickname—"Stonewall"—for his resistance to Union forces at Bull Run (1861). He was accidentally killed by his own troops at Chancellorsville (1863).

jack-stay (jăk′stā′) *n.* **1.** A stay for racing or cruising vessels used to steady the mast against the strain of the gaff. **2.** A rope, rod, or batten along the upper side of a yard, gaff, or boom to which a sail is fastened. **3.** A rope or rod running vertically on the forward side of the mast on which the yard moves.

jack-stone (jăk′stōn′) *n.* **1. jackstones.** *Used with a singular verb.* The game of **jacks** *(see).* **2.** See **jack** (sense 9).

jack-straw (jăk′strô′) *n.* **1. jackstraws.** *Used with a singular verb.* A game played with a pile of straws or thin sticks, with the players attempting in turn to remove a single stick without disturbing the others. Also called "spilikins." **2.** One of the straws or sticks used in this game. [JACK + STRAW.]

Jack Tar, Jack tar *n.* A sailor. [*Jack* (name) + TAR.]

Jack the Ripper. An unknown murderer who killed and mutilated a number of prostitutes in the East End of London in 1888.

Ja-cob (jā′kəb). Hebrew patriarch; son of Isaac and grandson of Abraham; father of 12 sons, ancestors of the 12 tribes of Israel.

Jac-o-be-an (jăk′ə-bē′ən) *adj.* **1.** Of or pertaining to the reign of James I of England or his times. **2.** Pertaining to or designating an architectural style of 17th-century England, blending late Gothic and Palladian elements. —*n.* Any prominent figure of this period. [New Latin *Jacobaeus,* from *Jacobus,* JAMES.]

Jac·o·be·than (jăk′ə-bē′thən) *adj.* Pertaining to, suggestive of, or designating a style, especially in architecture, characteristic of the reigns of Elizabeth I and James I. Often used humorously. [Blend of JACOBEAN + ELIZABETHAN, coined (1933) by Sir John Betjeman.]

Jac·o·bin (jăk′ə-bĭn) *n.* **1.** A member of the most radical republican group during the French Revolution, led by Robespierre, which overthrew the Girondins in 1793 and instituted the Reign of Terror. **2.** A leftist or extreme left-wing revolutionary. Often used derogatorily. **3.** A French Dominican friar. [French, from Late Latin *Jacobus,* after the church of *Saint-Jacques,* Paris, near which the Jacobin friars built their first convent. The French political group was founded (1789) in this convent.] —**Jac·o·bin·ic, Jac·o·bin·i·cal** *adj.* —**Jac·o·bin·ism** *n.*

Jac·o·bin·ize (jăk′ə-bĭ-nīz′) *tr.v.* **-ized, -izing, -izes.** To imbue with or convert to revolutionary ideas characteristic of the Jacobins.

Jac·o·bite (jăk′ə-bīt′) *n.* A supporter of James II of England or of the Stuart pretenders after 1688. [From New Latin *Jacobus,* JAMES.] —**Jac·o·bit·i·cal** (jăk′ə-bĭt′ĭ-kəl) *adj.* —**Jac·o·bit·ism** *n.*

Jacobite Rebellion *n.* **1.** The failed Jacobite uprising (1715–16) led by the Earl of Mar in support of James Edward Stuart, the Old Pretender. Also called the "Fifteen." **2.** The later Jacobite uprising (1745–46) led by Charles Edward Stuart, the Young Pretender, in which all hopes of restoring the Stuarts to the throne were finally crushed. Also called the "Forty-Five."

Jac·ob·sen (yăk′əb-sən), **Arne** (1902–71). Danish designer. His severely functional style, such as his three-legged stacking stool, influenced much modern design. He summed up his work in the motto "economy plus function equals style."

Jacob's ladder *n.* **1.** *Nautical.* A rope or chain ladder with rigid rungs. **2.** A widely cultivated garden plant, *Polemonium caeruleum,* having blue flowers and numerous paired leaflets. [From the ladder seen by the patriarch JACOB in a dream. Genesis 28:12.]

ja·co·bus (jə-kō′bəs) *n., pl.* **-buses.** A gold coin issued during the reign of James I. [New Latin *Jacobus,* JAMES.]

jac·o·net (jăk′ə-nĕt′) *n.* A light, cotton cloth with a soft finish used especially for bandages and poulticing. [Urdu *jagannāthī,* first made in *Jagannath* (now Puri), India.]

Jac·quard (jăk′ärd′, jə-kärd′) *adj.* Made on or pertaining to a Jacquard loom. —*n.* A fabric with an intricately woven pattern made on a Jacquard loom. Also called "Jacquard weave." [After Joseph Marie JACQUARD.]

Jac·quard (zhä-kär′), **Joseph Marie** (1752–1834). French silk weaver. His invention of the Jacquard loom (c. 1801) made it possible to weave complex patterns automatically. The silk workers of his native Lyons smashed his machines, but by 1812 some 11,000 looms were in use and they were adopted worldwide.

Jacquard loom *n.* A loom fitted with perforated cards to facilitate the weaving of a figured fabric. [After Joseph Marie JACQUARD.]

Jac·que·rie (zhä-krē′) *n.* **1.** The uprising of the French peasants against the nobility in 1358. **2.** *Often* **jacquerie.** A violent peasant revolt. [French, from Old French, from *jacques,* "peasant," from *Jacques,* James.]

jac·ta·tion (jăk-tā′shən) *n.* **1.** Bragging; boasting. **2.** *Pathology.* Jactitation. [Latin *jactātiō* (stem *jactātiōn*-), from *jactāre,* "to toss about," discuss, boast, frequentative of *jacere* (past participle *jactus*), to throw.]

jac·ti·ta·tion (jăk′tə-tā′shən) *n.* **1.** *Law.* A false boast or claim, especially of marriage, detrimental to the interests of another. **2.** *Pathology.* Extreme restlessness or tossing in bed, often associated with a high fever. In this sense, also called "jactation." [Medieval Latin *jactitātiō* (stem *jactitātiōn*-), a false assertion made to the injury of another, from *jactitāre,* frequentative of Latin *jactāre,* to boast, declare publicly. See **jactation.**]

Ja·cuz·zi (jə-koŏ′zē, jä-) *n.* A trademark for a deep bath with a device that makes the water swirl around.

jade¹ (jād) *n.* **1.** Either of two distinct minerals, **nephrite** and **jadeite** *(both of which see),* that are generally pale green or white and are used mainly as gemstones or in carved ornaments. **2.** A dull yellowish-green. [French *jade, ejade,* from Spanish *(piedra de) ijada,* "(stone of the) flank" (from the belief that it was a cure for renal colic), from Vulgar Latin *iliata* (unattested), flanks, from Latin *īlia,* plural of *īlium,* the flank, ILEUM.] —**jade** *adj.*

jade² *n.* **1.** A broken-down or useless horse; a nag. **2.** A worthless or disreputable woman. —*v.* **jaded, jading, jades.** —*tr.* To exhaust or wear out. —*intr.* To become weary or spiritless. [Middle English *jade†,* a broken-down horse.]

jad·ed (jā′dĭd) *adj.* **1.** Wearied; spiritless as through fatigue: *"My father's words had left me jaded and depressed"* (William Styron). **2.** Dulled as by surfeit; sated: *"the sickeningly sweet life of the amoral, jaded, bored upper classes"* (John Simon). —See Synonyms at **tired.** [JADE (verb).] —**jad·ed·ly** *adv.* —**jad·ed·ness** *n.*

jade·ite (jā′dīt′) *n.* A rare, emerald to light-green, white, red-brown, yellow-brown, or violet jade, $NaAlSi_2O_6$, used as a gem and for ornamental carvings. Also called "jade." [French : JADE + -ITE.]

j'a·doube (zhä-doŏb′) *interj. French.* Used in chess to express the

jack rabbit *The North American jack rabbit is, in fact, a hare. Its large ears perform two functions: they improve its ability to hear approaching predators, and they help it to lose excess body heat and so keep cool in the desert.*

intention not to move a piece that one is about to touch. [Literally "I adjust."]

jae·ger (yā'gər; *also* jā'gər *for sense 1*) *n.* **1.** Any of several sea birds of the genus *Stercorarius* that snatch food from other birds. See **skua**. **2.** A huntsman or hunting attendant. [German *Jäger*, "hunter."]

Jaf·fa (jăf'ə). *Hebrew* **Ja·fo** (yä'fô). *Arabic* **Ya·fa** (yăf'ə). Ancient city of west-central Israel. Founded by the Phoenicians, it was taken by the Israelites in the 6th century B.C. The city fell to the Arabs (A.D. 636), to the Crusaders (1126 and 1191), and to the Ottoman Turks (16th century). It became part of Tel Aviv–Jaffa in 1950.

Jaffa orange *n.* A variety of orange having a large, thick-skinned fruit. Also called "jaffa." [After JAFFA, near which it was originally grown.]

jag¹ (jăg) *n.* **1.** A sharp projection; a barb. **2. a.** A hanging flap along the edge of a garment. **b.** A slash or slit in a garment exposing material of a different color.
~*tr.v.* **jagged, jagging, jags. 1.** To cut jags in; notch. **2.** To cut unevenly; make (an edge) ragged. **3.** *Scottish.* To prick; jab sharply. [Middle English *jagge†*.]

jag² *n.* **1.** *Slang.* **a.** A bout of drinking, drug taking, or the like. **b.** Any period of indulgence in an activity: *a crying jag.* **2.** *Regional.* A small load or portion. [16th century : origin obscure.]

jag·ad·gu·ru (jŭg'əd-gŏŏ-rŏŏ', -gŏŏ'rŏŏ') *n.* A title for a revered Hindu guru. [Hindi, from Sanskrit *jagadguru*, "father of the world," title applied to Brahma, Vishnu, and Shiva : *jagat-*, world + GURU.]

Jagannath. Variant of **Juggernaut.**

jag·ged (jăg'ĭd) *adj.* **1.** Toothed or serrated; having jags. **2.** Roughly torn; having a ragged edge. —See Synonyms at **rough.** —**jag·ged·ly** *adv.* —**jag·ged·ness** *n.*

Jag·ger (jăg'ər), **Michael Philip,** known as "Mick" (1943–). English rock singer and songwriter, lead singer of the Rolling Stones. He has also appeared as a film actor.

jag·ger·y (jăg'ə-rē) *n.* Unrefined sugar made from palm sap. [From Indo-Portuguese *jagara*, from Kanarese *sharkare*, from Sanskrit *śarkarā†*, "gravel," sugar.]

jag·gy (jăg'ē) *adj.* **-gier, -giest.** Having jags; jagged.

jag·u·ar (jăg'wär', -yŏŏ-är') *n.* A large feline mammal, *Panthera onca*, of tropical America, having a tawny coat spotted with black rosettelike markings. [Spanish *jaguar, yaguar* and Portuguese *jaguar*, from Tupi-Guarani *jaguara, yaguara*.]

ja·gua·ron·di, ja·gua·run·di (jăg'wə-rŭn'dē, jə'gwə-) *n., pl.* **-dis.** A long-tailed grayish-brown wild cat, *Felis yagouaroundi*, of tropical America. [American Spanish and Portuguese, from Tupi-Guarani.]

Jah (jä) *n.* Yahweh; God. Used especially by Rastafarians. [Shortened from Hebrew, YAHWEH.]

Jahveh, Jahweh. Variants of **Yahweh.**

Jahvist, Jahwist. Variants of **Yahwist.**

jai a·lai (hī' lī', hī' ə-lī', hī' ə-lī') *n.* An extremely fast court game popular in Spain, Latin America, and the Philippines, in which players use a long hand-shaped basket strapped to the wrist to propel the ball against a wall. Also called "pelota."

jail (jāl) *n.* Also *chiefly British* **gaol.** A place for the confinement of persons in lawful detention; a prison.
~*tr.v.* **jailed, jailing, jails.** Also *chiefly British* **gaol.** To detain in custody; imprison. [*Jail* and *gaol*, respectively from Middle English *jaiole* and *gayole*, from Old French *jaiole* and Old Northern French *gaiole*, both from Vulgar Latin *gaviola* (unattested), variant of *caveola* (unattested), diminutive of Latin *cavea*, a hollow, den, coop.]

jail·bird (jāl'bûrd') *n. Informal.* A prisoner or ex-convict; especially, one who has a long record of imprisonment.

jail·break (jāl'brāk') *n.* An escape from prison. —**jail·break·er** *n.*

jail·er, jail·or (jā'lər) *n.* Also *chiefly British* **gaol·er.** A keeper of or guard in a jail.

jail fever *n.* A virulent type of typhus fever, formerly endemic in crowded and dirty prisons.

jail·house (jāl'hous') *n.* A jail.

Jain (jīn) *n.* Also **Jai·na** (jī'nə). A believer in or follower of Jainism. [Hindi *jaina*, from Sanskrit *jainas*, from *jinas*, saint, "overcomer," from *jayati*, to conquer.] —**Jain, Jai·na** *adj.*

Jain·ism (jī'nĭz'əm) *n.* An ascetic religion of India, founded in the 6th century B.C. It teaches that the soul is immortal and will be reincarnated until it reaches perfection and is liberated. The deity of Jainism consists not of a single supreme being but of the collection of these perfect liberated souls.

Jai·pur (jī'pŏŏr'). The capital of Rajasthan state, northwestern India. Founded in 1728, it was the capital of the Rajput state of Jaipur and came under British protection in 1818.

Ja·kar·ta or **Dja·kar·ta** (jə-kär'tə). Formerly **Ba·ta·vi·a** (bə-tā'vē-ə). The capital of Indonesia, situated on the northwestern coast of Java. Founded by the Dutch (*c.* 1619), it became an important center of the Dutch East India Company. Renamed Jakarta on independence in 1949, the city has fine buildings, a Roman Catholic cathedral, and a university (founded 1950). Its port, Tandjung Priok, exports oil, rubber, timber, and tea.

jake (jāk) *adj. Slang.* Fine; suitable; all right: *That's jake with me.* [Origin unknown.]

jakes (jāks) *n. Used with a singular verb. Regional.* A privy. [Perhaps from the French name *Jacques.*]

Ja·kob·son (yä'kəb-sən, jä'-), **Roman** (1896–1982). U.S. linguist. He was a principal founder (1926) of the Prague School and a major influence on contemporary linguistics. His works include *Funda-*

---

mentals of Language (with Morris Halle, 1956).

jal·ap (jăl'əp) *n.* **1.** A Mexican plant, *Exogonium purga*, having a tuberous rootstock that is dried, powdered, and used medicinally as a cathartic. **2.** Any of several similar or related plants. **3.** The dried rootstock of such a plant. [French *jalap*, from Mexican Spanish *jalapa*, short for *(purga de) Jalapa*, "(purgative of) Jalapa," capital of Veracruz state, Mexico.]

ja·lop·y (jə-lŏp'ē) *n., pl.* **-ies.** *Informal.* An old, dilapidated car. [20th century : origin obscure.]

ja·lou·sie (jăl'ŏŏ-sē; *chiefly British* zhăl'ŏŏ-zē') *n.* A blind or shutter having adjustable horizontal slats for regulating the passage of air and light. [French, "jealousy" (probably because one sees through it without being seen).]

jam¹ (jăm) *v.* **jammed, jamming, jams.** —*tr.* **1.** To drive or wedge forcibly; squeeze into a tight position. **2. a.** To force or push suddenly: *jam the lid down.* **b.** To apply (brakes) suddenly. Used with *on.* **3. a.** To cause to be stuck in a position so that movement or extrication is difficult or impossible: *Her skirt was jammed in the bicycle wheel.* **b.** To cause to lock in an unworkable position: *jam the typewriter keys.* **4.** To fill or pack to excess; cram: *He jammed the drawer with old socks.* **5.** To block, congest, or clog: *The drain was jammed by debris.* **6.** To crush or bruise between two bodies or surfaces: *jammed her finger in the door.* **7.** *Electronics.* To interfere with or prevent the clear reception of (broadcast signals) by electronic means. —*intr.* **1.** To become wedged; stick. **2.** To become inoperable because of jammed parts. **3.** To force into or through a limited space. **4.** To play in a jam session.
~*n.* **1.** The act of jamming or the condition of being jammed. **2.** A crush or congestion of people or things in a limited space: *a traffic jam.* **3.** A **jam session** (see). **4.** *Informal.* A predicament: *in a jam with the police.* [18th century : imitative.]

jam² *n.* **1.** A preserve made from whole fruit boiled to a pulp with sugar. **2.** *British.* Something that is pleasant or comes as a bonus: *always promised jam tomorrow.* [Probably from JAM (act of jamming).]

Jam. James (New Testament).

Ja·mai·ca (jə-mā'kə). An island in the Caribbean Sea. Its central uplands rise to 2,256 meters (7,402 feet) in the Blue Mts. to the east. The island was visited by Columbus (1494) and settled by the Spanish, but taken by the British in 1655. With its extensive sugar plantations, Jamaica became a major center of the slave trade. In 1962 the island became an independent Commonwealth state. In the election of 1980, the left-wing Michael Manley, in power since 1972, was replaced as prime minister by the pro-Western Edward Seaga, and much-needed foreign investment capital became available. Manley again became prime minister from 1989 until he retired in 1992. The island once depended on exports of bananas, but bauxite is now by far the main export. Tourism and sugar are also important. Area, 10,991 square kilometers (4,243 square miles). Population, 2,400,000. Capital, Kingston. —**Ja·mai·can** *n. & adj.*

jamb (jăm) *n.* A vertical post or piece forming the side of a door or window frame. [Middle English *jambe*, from Old French, "leg," from Late Latin *gamba*, hoof, from Greek *kampē*, joint.]

jam·ba·lay·a (jŭm'bə-lī'ə) *n.* A Creole dish consisting of rice with shrimp, chicken, turkey, or similar ingredients. [Louisiana French, from Provençal *jambalaia* (a stew of chicken and rice).]

jam·beau (jăm'bō) *n., pl.* **-beaux** (-bōz). A piece of armor for the leg below the knee. Also called "jambe." [Middle English, from Norman French *jambeau* (unattested), from Old French *jambe*, leg.]

jam·bo·ree (jăm'bə-rē') *n.* **1.** A lively celebration. **2.** A large assembly, often international, especially of Scouts or Guides. [19th century : origin obscure.]

James¹ (jāmz). **1.** Also **Da·ko·ta** (də-kō'tə). River rising in central North Dakota and flowing 1,142 kilometers (710 miles) generally southeast to the Missouri River in southeastern South Dakota. **2.** River rising in western Virginia and flowing 547 kilometers (340 miles) generally east to Chesapeake Bay.

James² *n. Abbr.* **Jam., Jas.** The 20th book of the New Testament, attributed to St. James the Less.

James IV of Scotland (1473–1513). King of Scotland from 1488.

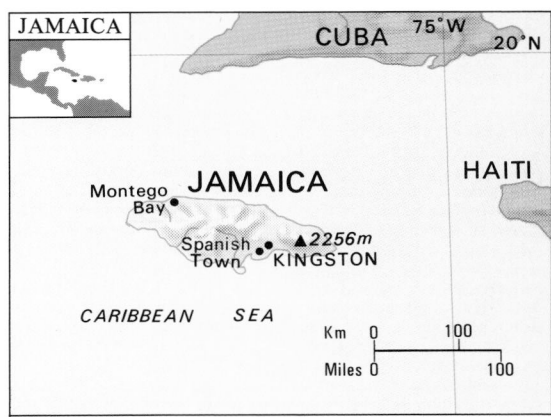

JAMAICA

CUBA 75°W 20°N

JAMAICA
Montego Bay
▲2256m
Spanish Town
KINGSTON

HAITI

CARIBBEAN SEA

Km 0 100
Miles 0 100

jaguar *The largest American cat, the jaguar is a predator like the tigers of Asia. It lives mostly in forests in South America and was revered as a god by pre-Columbian peoples from Mexico to Peru.*

He led Scotland to its greatest military defeat—at Flodden (1513) against the English, in which he died with many of his nobles.
James V of Scotland (1512–42). King of Scotland from 1513. He allied himself with the Church and people to curb the nobility, but in 1542 dissent between the king and his nobles allowed the English to overwhelm the Scottish army at Solway Moss.
James VI of Scotland and I of England (1566–1625). King of Scotland from 1567 and first Stuart king of England from 1603, when he succeeded the childless Elizabeth I. James believed in the divine right of kings and quarreled with Parliament, sowing the seeds of civil war.
James VII of Scotland and II of England (1633–1701). Last Stuart king to rule both countries (1685–88). His fervent Roman Catholicism almost denied him accession. A rebellion against him by the Duke of Monmouth (1685) was unsuccessful, but in 1688 seven leading political figures invited William of Orange to invade the country. James was deserted by his own troops and fled to France.
James, Henry (1843–1916). U.S. novelist and critic. He settled in England in 1876, and his early novels, *The American* (1877), *The Portrait of a Lady* (1881), and *The Bostonians* (1886), deal with the impact of European civilization on Americans. His other works include *The Turn of the Screw* (1898), *The Ambassadors* (1903), and *The Golden Bowl* (1904). —**James·i·an** *n. & adj.*
James, Jesse Woodson (1847–82). U.S. outlaw. He was a Confederate guerrilla during the Civil War. After the war he organized an armed band of brigands and spent the next 15 years robbing banks and trains in the West. James was murdered in St. Joseph, Missouri, by Robert Ford, a member of his own gang.
James, Saint¹, called "the Less." Described by St. Paul (Galatians 1:19) as the brother of Jesus, he is considered to be the author of the Epistle of James and 1st bishop of Jerusalem.
James, Saint², called "the Greater." One of the Twelve Apostles; son of Zebedee and brother of John; traditionally supposed to have been martyred by Herod Agrippa (*c.* A.D. 44).
James, Saint³. One of the Twelve Apostles; often identified with St. James the Less.
James, William (1842–1910). U.S. psychologist and philosopher, brother of Henry James. He developed the theory of pragmatism and is noted for his pioneering study *The Varieties of Religious Experience* (1902).
Jame·son (jām′sən), **Sir Leander Starr** (1853–1917). South African politician. His disastrous raid into the Boer Transvaal Republic (1895) led to the fall of Cecil Rhodes. Jameson later became prime minister of Cape Colony (1904–08).
James·town (jāmz′toun). Ruined village on the James River in Virginia. It was the first permanent English settlement in the New World (founded 1607).
jam·mer (jăm′ər) *n.* A device for jamming broadcast signals.
Jam·mu and Kash·mir (jŭm′ōō; kăsh-mîr′, kăsh′mîr′). A state in northern India, in the Indian part of Kashmir. The Himalayan and Karakoram ranges lie in the north and east of the state. There are two capitals: Jammu (winter) and Srinagar (summer).
jam·my (jăm′ē) *adj.* **-mier, -miest. 1.** Covered with jam. **2.** *British Informal.* **a.** Lucky. **b.** Easy or pleasant: *a jammy job.*
jam-packed (jăm′păkt′) *adj. Informal.* Full, crowded, or crammed: *an article jam-packed with new ideas.*
jam·pan (jăm′păn) *n.* A type of sedan chair, used in parts of India, that is carried by four people. [Bengali *jhāmpān.*]
jam session *n.* An informal gathering at which musicians, especially jazz musicians, play improvised music together, usually for their own enjoyment.
Jam·shid, Jam·shyd (jăm-shĕd′) *n. Persian Mythology.* A king who drank a cup of the elixir of life. He was punished for boasting that he was immortal by being made human, after which he became a great ruler for 700 years.
Jan. January.
Ja·ná·ček (yăn′ə-chĕk), **Leoš** (1854–1928). Czech composer, influenced by folk music. His works include the operas *Jenůfa* (1904), *Kátya Kabanová* (1921), and the *Glagolitic Mass* (1926).
Ja·na·ta (jŭn′ə-tä′) *n.* A political coalition that held power in India between 1977 and 1979. [Hindi, "group of the people."]
jan·gle (jăng′gəl) *n.* A harsh, discordant, metallic sound.
—*v.* **jangled, -gling, -gles.** —*intr.* **1.** To make a jangle. **2.** *Archaic.* To wrangle; dispute. —*tr.* **1.** To cause (something metallic) to jangle: *jangled the bells.* **2.** To grate on or jar (the nerves). [Middle English *janglen*, from Old French *jangler*, probably from Germanic, akin to Middle Dutch *jangelen†.*] —**jan·gler** *n.*
jan·is·sar·y (jăn′ĭ-sĕr′ē) *n., pl.* **-ies.** Also **jan·i·zar·y** (-zĕr′ē). A soldier in an elite guard of Turkish troops organized in the 14th century and abolished in 1826. [French *janissaire*, from Turkish *yeniçeri* : *yeni*, new + *çeri*, militia.]
jan·i·tor (jăn′ə-tər) *n.* **1.** One who attends to the cleaning or maintenance of a building. **2.** *Archaic.* A doorman. [Latin *jānitor*, from *jānua*, door, from *jānus*, arched passage.] —**jan·i·to·ri·al** (jăn′ə-tôr′ē-əl, -tōr′ē-əl) *adj.*
Jan·sen (jăn′sən, yän′-), **Cornelis Otto** (1585–1638). Dutch theologian. He founded a reform movement in the Roman Catholic Church known as Jansenism. In the *Augustinus* (1640) he argued against the concept of a state of grace. His movement was condemned as heretical by Pope Innocent X in 1653.
Jan·sen·ism (jăn′sə-nĭz′əm) *n.* The heretical theological principles of Cornelis Jansen, which emphasize predestination, deny free will,

and maintain that human nature is incapable of good. —**Jan·sen·ist** *n. & adj.* —**Jan·sen·is·tic** *adj.*
Jan·sky (jăn′skē), **Karl Guthe** (1905–50). U.S. engineer. He discovered in 1931 that the stars transmit radio waves, thereby laying the foundations of the science of radio astronomy.
Jan·u·ar·y (jăn′yōō-ĕr′ē) *n., pl.* **-ies.** *Abbr.* **Jan.** The first month of the year in the Gregorian calendar. January has 31 days. See feature at **calendar.** [Middle English *Januarie*, from Latin *Jānuārius (mensis)*, "(month) of Janus," from JANUS.]
Ja·nus (jā′nəs). *Mythology.* An ancient Roman god of gates and doorways, depicted with two faces looking in opposite directions, whose festival month was January.
Ja·nus-faced (jā′nəs-fāst′) *adj.* Hypocritical; two-faced.
Jap. Japan; Japanese.
ja·pan (jə-păn′) *n.* **1.** A black enamel or lacquer of a type originating in the Orient, used to produce a durable glossy finish. **2.** Any object decorated and varnished in the Japanese manner.
—*adj.* Relating to or varnished with japan.
—*tr.v.* **japanned, -panning, -pans. 1.** To enamel with japan. **2.** To coat with a glossy finish. [From JAPAN, from Malay *Japang*, from Chinese *Jih-pun* : *jih*, sun + *pun*, origin.]
Ja·pan (jə-păn′). *Japanese* **Nip·pon** (nĭp-pŏn′) or **Ni·hon** (nē-hŏn′). *Abbr.* **J., Jap.** Nation consisting of several islands in the North Pacific Ocean lying off the mainland of east Asia. The four main islands, Honshu, Shikoku, Kyushu, and Hokkaido, are mountainous. The highest peak is Fujiyama (3,776 meters; 12,388 feet). Japan has been ruled from the 5th century B.C. by emperors of the Yamato dynasty, though legends trace their origins back to the 7th century B.C. The native Shinto religion was challenged by Buddhism after the 6th century A.D. From the 12th to 19th centuries, real power lay in the hands of the shoguns, feudal warlords whose dominance ended with the accession of the emperor Meiji (Mutsuhito). During his reign (1868–1912), Japan opened its doors to Western trade and industrial technology. Victory in the Russo-Japanese war (1904–05) encouraged expansion into Asia, and Japan occupied Korea and parts of China during the first half of the 20th century. One of the Axis powers in World War II, Japan surrendered in 1945 after atomic bombs were dropped on Hiroshima and Nagasaki. In 1946 the emperor Hirohito renounced the imperial claim to divinity, remaining head of state in a constitutional monarchy. A highly industrialized country with few natural resources, Japan depends on imported oil, although nuclear power should soon provide a third of its energy. It is the world's leading fishing nation, and relies on imports of food, and exports, particularly of motor vehicles, electric and electronic products, ships, synthetic fibers, and steel. Area, 372,313 square kilometers (143,713 square miles). Population, 123,500,000. Capital, Tokyo.
Japan clover *n.* A leguminous plant, *Lespedeza striata*, native to Asia, cultivated as a forage plant and for soil improvement.
Japan current. *Japanese* **Ku·ro·shi·o** (kōō′rō-shē′ō). A warm ocean

Janus *A Roman coin portraying the double-headed deity Janus, who was the god of doorways, gates, and arches.*

current flowing northeast from the Philippine Sea past southeastern Japan to the North Pacific.

Jap·a·nese (jăp'ə-nēz', -nēs') *adj. Abbr.* **J., Jap.** Of or pertaining to Japan, or to the people, language, or culture of Japan. ~*n., pl.* **Japanese. 1.** A native or inhabitant of Japan, or a descendant of one. **2.** *Abbr.* **J., Jap.** The language of Japan, having no proven affinities to any other language.

Japanese andromeda *n.* An ornamental shrub, *Pieris japonica,* native to Japan, having small, early-blooming white flowers.

Japanese beetle *n.* A metallic-green and brownish beetle, *Popillia japonica,* native to eastern Asia, the larvae and adults of which are serious plant pests in North America.

Japanese cedar *n.* A tree, the **cryptomeria** *(see),* or its wood.

Japanese iris *n.* A plant, *Iris kaempferi,* native to Asia, and cultivated in many varieties for its large, flat, showy flowers.

Japanese ivy *n.* **Boston ivy** *(see).*

Japanese lantern *n.* A paper lantern; a Chinese lantern.

Japanese leaf *n.* A plant, the **Chinese evergreen** *(see).*

Japanese maple *n.* A shrub or small tree, *Acer palmatum,* native to eastern Asia and widely cultivated for its decorative foliage.

Japanese quince *n.* See **japonica** (sense 1).

Japanese river fever *n. Pathology.* **Scrub typhus** *(see).*

Japanese spurge *n.* A plant, **pachysandra** *(see).*

Japan paper *n.* A strong fibrous paper made in Japan, and often used for printing etchings.

Japan Trench *n.* A depression in the floor of the North Pacific off northeastern Japan, extending from the Bonin to the Kurile islands and reaching depths of over 30,000 feet.

Japan wax *n.* A pale-yellow, solid wax obtained from the berries of certain plants of the genus *Rhus* and used in wax matches, soaps, food packaging, and as a substitute for beeswax.

jape (jāp) *v.* **japed, japing, japes.** *Archaic.* —*intr.* To joke or quip. —*tr.* To joke about; make sport of. ~*n.* A joke or quip. [Middle English *japen,* to trick, joke, from Old French *japper,* to yap (imitative).] —**jap·er** *n.* —**jap·er·y** *n.*

Ja·pheth (jā'fĭth). Also **Ja·phet** (-fĭt). The second son of Noah, in some traditions considered the ancestor of the Caucasian race. Genesis 5:32.

Ja·phet·ic (jə-fĕt'ĭk) *adj.* **1.** Of or pertaining to Japheth or his descendants. **2.** Designating a discredited linguistic grouping that attempted to associate Basque, Etruscan, and sometimes Sumerian and Elamite with the Indo-European languages.

japie. Variant of **jaap.**

ja·pon·i·ca (jə-pŏn'ĭ-kə) *n.* **1.** A shrub, *Chaenomeles speciosa,* native to Japan, that has quincelike fruit and is cultivated for its red flowers. Also called "flowering quince," "Japanese quince." **2.** A shrub, the **camellia** *(see).* [New Latin, "Japanese," from *Japonia,* JAPAN.]

Jaques-Dal·croze (zhàk'dăl-krōz'), **Emile** (1865–1950). Swiss composer. He developed eurhythmics, an expression of the rhythm of music through physical movement.

jar¹ (jär) *n.* **1.** A cylindrical glass or earthenware vessel with a wide mouth and usually without handles. **2.** The contents of such a vessel; a jarful. **3.** *British Informal.* A glass of beer. [French *jarre,* from Provençal *jarra,* from Arabic *jarrah,* large earthen vase.]

jar² *v.* **jarred, jarring, jars.** —*intr.* **1.** To make or utter a harsh, discordant sound. **2.** To have an unpleasant or disturbing effect; grate: *His voice jarred on her nerves.* **3.** To shake or shiver from impact. **4.** To clash or conflict. —*tr.* **1.** To cause to make a harsh, discordant sound. **2.** To bump or cause to move or shake from impact. **3.** To startle or unsettle; shock. ~*n.* **1.** A jolt; a shock. **2.** A harsh or grating sound. [16th century : probably imitative.]

jar·di·nière (järd'n-îr'; *French* zhàr-dē-nyàr') *n.* **1.** A large, decorative stand or pot for plants. **2.** Diced, cooked vegetables served as a garnish with meat. [French, feminine of *jardinier,* gardener, from *jardin,* garden, from Old French, from Vulgar Latin *gardīnus* (unattested), GARDEN.]

jar·ful (jär'fŏŏl') *n., pl.* **-fuls. 1.** The amount a jar will hold. **2.** The contents of a jar.

jar·gon¹ (jär'gən) *n.* **1.** The specialized or technical language of a trade, profession, class, or fellowship; cant: *"She could not follow the ugly academic jargon"* (Virginia Woolf). Compare **argot, slang. 2.** A hybrid language or dialect; pidgin. **3.** Nonsensical, incoherent, or meaningless utterance; gibberish: *"Wholly a blessed time: when jargon might abate, and . . . genuine speech begin"* (Thomas Carlyle). ~*intr.v.* **jargoned, -goning, -gons.** To speak in or use jargon. [Middle English *iargoun, gargoun,* meaningless chatter, from Old French *jargon, gargon,* "twittering" (probably imitative).] —**jar·gon·ize** *v.* —**jar·gon·is·tic** *adj.*

jar·gon² (jär-gŏn') *n.* Also **jar·goon** (-gŏŏn'). A smoky, yellow, or colorless variety of zircon. [French, ZIRCON.]

jarl (yärl) *n.* A chieftain or nobleman of the medieval Scandinavians. [Old Norse, from Common Germanic *erilaz* (unattested), EARL.]

Jarls·berg (yärlz'bûrg) *n.* A mild, pale-yellow Norwegian cheese. [After *Jarlesberg,* Norway, an estate west of Oslo.]

jar·o·site (jär'ə-sīt') *n.* A yellow to brown mineral, KFe₃(SO₄)₂(OH)₆, occurring in masses or hexagonal crystals. [After *Barranco Jaroso,* Almeria, Spain, where it was first found.]

jar·rah (jär'ə) *n.* An Australian eucalyptus tree, *Eucalyptus marginata,* widely grown for its hard, red-brown timber. [From a native Australian language.]

Jar·row (jär'ō). An industrial town in Tyne and Wear, northeast England, on the Tyne River. The early historian the Venerable Bede lived at Jarrow in a 7th-century monastery, whose ruins survive. In the 20th century Jarrow developed important shipyards and steelworks, whose collapse during the 1930's Depression led to 80 percent local unemployment. The Jarrow March (1936) of the unemployed to London is famous in trade union history.

Jar·ry (zhà-rē'), **Alfred** (1873–1907). French writer. His play *Ubu Roi* (1896), which made fun of the bourgeoisie, is regarded as perhaps the earliest example of the Theater of the Absurd.

Jas. James (New Testament).

jas·mine (jăz'mən) *n.* Also **jes·sa·mine** (jĕs'ə-mĭn). **1.** Any of several shrubs of the genus *Jasminum;* especially, *J. officinalis,* native to Asia, having fragrant white flowers used in making perfume. See **winter jasmine. 2.** Any of several other plants or shrubs having fragrant flowers, such as the frangipani *(red jasmine).* **3.** Light to brilliant yellow. [French *jasmin,* from Arabic *yās(a)mīn,* from Persian *yasmīn, yāsman†.*]

Ja·son (jā'sən). *Greek Mythology.* The leader of the Argonauts in quest of the Golden Fleece; husband of Medea.

jas·pé (jăs'pā) *adj.* Being randomly colored like jasper. [French.]

jas·per (jăs'pər) *n.* **1.** An opaque variety of quartz, reddish, brown, or yellow in color. **2.** Chalcedony, especially green chalcedony. [Middle English *jaspre,* from Old French *jasp(r)e,* from Latin *jaspis,* from Greek *iaspis,* from Semitic, akin to Assyrian *ashpū,* Aramaic *yashb,* and Hebrew *yashpāh.*]

Jasper National Park. Second-largest national park in Canada, established in 1907 in the Rocky Mountains of Alberta. It has glaciers, hot springs, and game preserves.

Jas·pers (yäs'pərs), **Karl Theodor** (1883–1969). German philosopher and psychologist, advocate of existentialism. His works include *Philosophie* (1932).

jasper ware *n.* A fine stoneware invented by Josiah Wedgwood, often colored by metallic oxides with raised designs in white.

Jat (jät, jôt) *n.* A member of an Indo-Aryan people of the Punjab and Uttar Pradesh. [Hindi *jāṭ†.*]

ja·to (jā'tō) *n.* **1.** A takeoff aided by an auxiliary jet or rocket. **2.** An auxiliary unit providing thrust for such a takeoff. [From *JATO,* acronym for *jet-assisted takeoff.*]

jaun·dice (jôn'dĭs, jän'-) *n.* **1.** Yellowish discoloration of the skin and white of the eyes due to excess bile pigment in the blood. It is caused by any of several pathological conditions such as hepatitis, in which normal processing of bile is interrupted. Also called "icterus." **2.** A state of jealousy or bitterness. [Middle English *jaun-(d)is,* from Old French *jaunice,* from *jaune,* yellow, from Latin *galbinus,* greenish yellow, pale green, from *galbus†.*]

jaun·diced (jôn'dĭst, jän'-) *adj.* **1.** Affected with jaundice. **2.** Affected by envy, cynicism, prejudice, or hostility; embittered. **3.** Yellow or yellowish.

jaunt (jônt, jänt) *n.* A short trip or excursion, usually taken for pleasure; an outing. ~*intr.v.* **jaunted, jaunting, jaunts.** To make a short journey, especially for pleasure. [16th century : origin obscure.]

jaunting car *n.* A light, open cart with seats hung back to back over its two wheels, once commonly used in Ireland. Also called "jaunty car."

jaun·ty (jôn'tē, jän'-) *adj.* **-tier, -tiest. 1.** Having or expressing a buoyant or self-confident air; carefree. **2.** Crisp and dapper in appearance; smart. [Earlier *jentee, jantee,* elegant, "genteel," from French *gentil.*] —**jaun·ti·ly** *adv.* —**jaun·ti·ness** *n.*

Jau·rès (zhō-rĕs'), **Jean Léon** (1859–1914). French journalist and politician, leader of the French Socialist Party before World War I. In 1914 Jaurès argued for arbitration rather than armed conflict between the Triple Entente and the Triple Alliance. He was assassinated on July 31 by a fanatical nationalist.

Jav. Javanese.

ja·va (jăv'ə, jä'və) *n. Informal.* Brewed coffee. [From JAVA.]

Ja·va (jä'və, jăv'ə). The most populous island of Indonesia, situated between the Indian Ocean and the Java Sea. From the 1st century A.D. a distinctive Hindu-Javanese civilization flourished for 16 centuries. Java was later converted to Islam, and was colonized by the Dutch from the 17th century. The island became part of the Republic of Indonesia in 1950. It has well-irrigated soil producing rice, sugar, tea, and kapok. Java also has reserves of oil and is an important producer of textiles. The most industrialized of the Indonesian islands, Java includes the nation's three largest cities: Jakarta (the capital), Surabaya, and Bandung.

Java man *n.* A type of primitive man, **Pithecanthropus** *(see).*

Jav·a·nese (jăv'ə-nēz', -nēs') *adj. Abbr.* **Jav.** Of or pertaining to Java, or to the people, language, or culture of Java. ~*n., pl.* **Javanese.** *Abbr.* **Jav. 1.** A native or inhabitant of Java. **2.** The Indonesian language spoken in Java.

Java sparrow *n.* A small, grayish weaverbird, *Padda oryzivora,* native to tropical Asia and often kept as a cage bird.

jave·lin (jăv'lən, jăv'ə-) *n.* **1.** A light spear thrown with the hand and used as a weapon. **2.** A metal or metal-tipped spear, weighing 800 grams (1 pound 12 ounces) for men, 600 grams (1 pound 5 ounces) for women, used in contests of distance throwing. **3.** The athletic field event in which such a spear is thrown. [French *javeline,* from Old French, variant of *javelot,* from Celtic.]

Ja·velle water, Ja·vel water (zhə-vĕl') *n.* An aqueous solution of potassium or sodium hypochlorite, used as a disinfectant and bleaching agent. [From *Javel,* former French town, now part of Paris.]

jay *The harsh cry of the common jay (above) can be heard throughout much of the Northern Hemisphere. Acorns are one of the jay's main foods—it buries them in the autumn, then digs them up to eat during the winter.*

jaw (jô) *n.* **1.** Either of two bony or cartilaginous structures in most vertebrates forming the framework of the mouth and holding the teeth. See **mandible, maxilla.** **2. a.** The anatomical parts forming the wall of the mouth and serving to open and close it. **b.** The corresponding parts in insects and other invertebrate animals. **3. jaws.** A mechanical device resembling the jaws, such as the gripping parts of a vise or the hinged parts of a mechanical grab. **4. jaws.** The walls or narrow mouth of a pass, canyon, or cavern. **5. jaws.** A dangerous situation or confrontation: *the jaws of death.* **6.** *Informal.* **a.** Impudent argument or expression of opposition: *Don't give me any jaw.* **b.** Idle chatter. **c.** A moralizing lecture. —*intr.v.* **jawed, jawing, jaws.** *Informal.* To talk or chat, especially at tedious length. [Middle English *iawe, iowe,* from Old French *joe†.*]

ja·wan (jə-wän′) *n.* A soldier in the Indian Army, especially a private. [Urdu, "young man."]

jaw·bone (jô′bōn′) *n.* Any bone of the jaw; especially, the bone of the lower jaw. See **mandible.**

jaw·break·er (jô′brā′kər) *n.* **1.** *Slang.* A word that is difficult to pronounce. **2.** A kind of very hard candy.

jay (jā) *n.* **1.** Any of various often crested birds of the family Corvidae, usually having a loud, harsh call. The Eurasian jay, *Garrulus glandarius,* is brownish-pink with blue and white wings and a black and white crest. **2.** *Slang.* A noisy or talkative person; a chatterbox. **3.** *Slang.* A gullible or inexperienced person. [Middle English, from Old French, from Late Latin *gāius* and *gāia†.*]

Ja·ya Peak (jī′ə). Also **Mount Su·kar·no** (sōō-kär′nō). Highest mountain in Indonesia (5,039 meters; 16,532 feet), situated in the Maoke range of West Irian.

jay·walk (jā′wôk′) *intr.v.* **-walked, -walking, -walks.** To cross a street illegally or recklessly. [From JAY (inexperienced person).] —**jay·walk·er** *n.*

jazz (jăz) *n.* **1.** A kind of native American music first played extemporaneously by black bands in Southern towns at the turn of the century. In most styles it has syncopated rhythms with solo and ensemble improvisations on basic tunes and chord patterns, and, in more recent styles, a highly sophisticated harmonic idiom. **2.** Big-band dance music, popular especially in the 1920's and 1930's. **3.** *Slang.* Animation; enthusiasm. **4.** *Slang.* Extreme exaggeration; nonsense: *all that jazz about his big deals.* —**and all that jazz.** *Slang.* And so on; and all that sort of thing. —*v.* **jazzed, jazzing, jazzes.** —*tr.* **1.** To play in a jazz style. **2.** *Slang.* To lie or exaggerate to. —*intr.* **1.** To play or dance to jazz. **2.** *Slang.* To lie or exaggerate. —**jazz up.** *Informal.* **1.** To play or arrange (music) in a more lively or improvised way, as by a jazz arrangement. **2.** To make more interesting; enliven. [20th century : origin obscure.] —**jazz·er** *n.*

jazz ballet *n.* **1.** A choreographed dance work performed to jazz music. **2.** This style of dancing.

jazz-rock (jăz′rŏk′) *n.* Music that blends jazz elements and the heavy repetitive rhythms of rock.

jazz·y (jăz′ē) *adj.* **-ier, -iest. 1.** Resembling jazz; rhythmical. **2.** *Slang.* Showy; vivid; flashy. —**jazz·i·ly** *adv.* —**jazz·i·ness** *n.*

J.C. 1. Jesus Christ. **2.** Julius Caesar.

J.C.D. 1. Doctor of Canon Law. [Latin *Juris Canonici Doctor*] **2.** Doctor of Civil Law. [Latin *Juris Civilis Doctor*]

J.C.S. Joint Chiefs of Staff.

jct. junction.

J.D. 1. Doctor of Laws. [Latin *Jurum Doctor*] **2.** juvenile delinquent.

jeal·ous (jĕl′əs) *adj.* **1.** Fearful or wary of being supplanted; apprehensive of loss of position or affection. **2.** Resentful or bitter in rivalry; envious. Often used with *of.* **3.** Possessively watchful; vigilant. **4.** Protective; solicitous. Used with *of* or *for: jealous for his daughter's welfare.* **5.** Concerning or arising from feelings of envy, apprehension, or bitterness: *jealous thoughts.* **6.** In religious contexts, intolerant of disloyalty or infidelity: *a jealous God.* [Middle English *gelus, ielus,* jealous, zealous for, from Old French *gelos, jelous,* from Medieval Latin *zēlōsus,* from Late Latin *zēlus,* from Greek *zēlos,* zeal.] —**jeal·ous·ly** *adv.* —**jeal·ous·ness** *n.*

jeal·ous·y (jĕl′ə-sē) *n., pl.* **-ies. 1.** A jealous attitude, especially toward a rival. **2.** Close watchfulness.

jean (jēn) *n.* **1.** A heavy, strong, twilled cotton, used in making trousers, uniforms, and work clothes. **2. jeans.** Trousers made of denim, jean, or some other hard-wearing fabric. In this sense, also called "blue jeans." [Earlier *iene fustian, geane fustian,* from Middle English *Jene, Gene,* Genoa, where it was first made.] —**jean** *adj.*

Jeanne d'Arc. See Joan of Arc.

Jeans (jēnz), **Sir James Hopwood** (1877–1946). British astronomer, physicist, and mathematician. He was noted for his work on the kinetic theory of gases and his investigations into the relationships between mathematical concepts and the natural world.

Jedda. See Jiddah.

Jeep (jēp) *n.* A trademark for a small, originally military motor vehicle with four-wheel drive, suitable for use on rough terrain. [Originally *G.P.,* "general purpose."]

jeer (jîr) *v.* **jeered, jeering, jeers.** —*intr.* To speak or shout derisively; mock. Often used with *at.* —*tr.* To deride; taunt. —*n.* Often **jeers.** A scoffing or taunting remark or shout. [Middle English *geere†.*] —**jeer·er** *n.* —**jeer·ing·ly** *adv.*

Jef·fers (jĕf′ərz), **(John) Robinson** (1887–1962). U.S. poet. Most of his narrative and lyric poems have a California setting, reflecting the many years he spent living on the coast near Carmel. Among his works are *Californians* (1916), *Tamar* (1924), *Cawdor* (1928), and *Solstice* (1935).

Jef·fer·son (jĕf′ər-sən), **Thomas** (1743–1826). Third president of the United States (1801–09). In 1776 Jefferson drafted the Declaration of Independence. As president, he acquired the Louisiana Purchase from France (1803). He was also a scholar, scientist, educator, lawyer, diplomat, political philosopher, and architect. Jefferson designed his own home, Monticello, and many buildings for the University of Virginia.

Jefferson City. Capital of Missouri. It is in the central part of the state on the south bank of the Missouri River. The city was a small river village when it was chosen as the capital in 1821; today the state government is the major employer.

jehad. Variant of **jihad.**

Jehan. See Shah Jahan.

Je·ho·vah (jĭ-hō′və). God, especially in Christian translations of the Old Testament. [From the Hebrew Tetragrammaton YHWH with the addition of the vowel points of ADONAI.]

Jehovah's Witnesses *n.* A religious sect founded in the United States during the late 19th century, the followers of which practice active evangelism, preach the imminent approach of the millennium, and are strongly opposed to war and to the authority of organized government in matters of conscience.

Je·ho·vist (jĭ-hō′vĭst) *n.* The author of portions of the Hexateuch, **Yahwist** *(see).*

je·june (jə-jōōn′) *adj.* **1.** Childish; immature; unsophisticated. **2.** Lacking in substance; insipid; dull: *"and there pour forth jejune words and useless empty phrases"* (Anthony Trollope). **3.** Not nourishing; insubstantial. [From Latin *jējūnus,* hungry, fasting.] —**je·june·ly** *adv.* —**je·june·ness** *n.*

je·ju·num (jə-jōō′nəm) *n., pl.* **-na** (-nə). The section of the small intestine between the duodenum and the ileum. [Medieval Latin *jējūnum (intestīnum),* "the fasting (intestine)," translation of Greek *nēstis,* the jejunum, from *nēstis,* fasting, so named because it was always found (in dissection) empty.] —**je·ju·nal** *adj.*

Je·kyll and Hyde (jĕk′əl, jē′kəl; hīd) *n. Informal.* A person who has two distinct alternating personalities. [After *The Strange Case of Dr. Jekyll and Mr. Hyde* (1886), novel by R.L. Stevenson.] —**Je·kyll-and-Hyde** *adj.*

jell (jĕl) *v.* **jelled, jelling, jells.** —*intr.* **1.** To become firm or gelatinous; congeal. **2.** *Informal.* To take shape or fall into place; become clear and definite; crystallize: *My ideas on the subject haven't jelled yet.* —*tr.* To cause to jell. [Back-formation from JELLY.]

jel·la·ba, jel·la·bah (jĕl′ə-bə) *n.* Also **djel·la·ba.** A long, loose garment with a hood worn by men, especially in North Africa. [Arabic.]

Jel·li·coe (jĕl′ĭ-kō), **John Rushworth Jellicoe, 1st Earl,** (1859–1935). British naval officer and governor of New Zealand

---

jellyfish

THE STINGING SEA CREATURE

The primitive jellyfish stuns its prey with poison

Jellyfish are found in all the oceans of the world, mostly near the coast. About 200 species have been identified. They range in diameter from 1.5 millimeters (1/16 inch) to 2 meters (6½ feet).

The creatures are not fish but primitive animals consisting of two bell-shaped layers of cells, separated by a thick layer of jelly. The jelly is made up almost entirely of water, and jellyfish soon dry out if they are stranded on beaches in the sun.

The bell-shaped body is fringed with stinging tentacles. When a jellyfish is touched by food or an enemy, cells in the tentacles shoot needlelike threads into the victim. Through these threads the jellyfish injects a poison that stings and stuns. Inside the fringe of tentacles there are usually four longer ones, which surround the mouth and convey food to it.

Jellyfish eggs are fertilized by sperm from smaller jellyfish drawn into the creature's mouth along with the food. The earliest development of the fertilized eggs takes place in pouches at the side of the mouth. Later, larvae are released from the pouches and settle on weeds or stones. They become polyps, from which small jellyfish bud off to grow into adults.

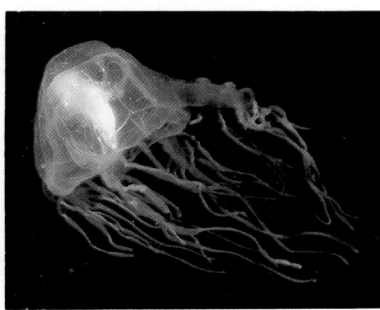

MOVEMENT *The sea wasp (Chironex fleckeri), a deadly jellyfish found off the coast of Queensland, Australia, moves itself along by contracting the two bell-shaped layers of cells.*

FEEDING *The tentacles of the lion's mane jellyfish (Cyanea capillata) wait for food—plankton, fish, or shrimp. The fringe tentacles stun the prey and the central tentacles carry it to the mouth.*

(1920–24). He was commander in chief of the fleet that fought the Germans at Jutland (1916).

jel·lied (jĕl′ēd) *adj.* **1.** Chilled or otherwise congealed into jelly. **2.** Coated with jelly. **3.** Prepared or cooked within jelly.

jel·li·fy (jĕl′ə-fī′) *v.* **-fied, -fying, -fies.** —*intr.* To become jelly. —*tr.* To make into jelly. **—jel·li·fi·ca·tion** *n.*

jel·ly[1] (jĕl′ē) *n., pl.* **-lies. 1.** A soft, semisolid food substance with a resilient consistency, made by the setting of a liquid containing pectin or gelatin, or by the addition of gelatin or a similar substance to a liquid, especially: **a.** A fruit-flavored dessert set with gelatin. **b.** A preserve made from fruit juice and sugar set with pectin and used as a jam. **c.** A savory food such as aspic or calf's-foot jelly. **2.** Any substance with the consistency of jelly, such as a petroleum ointment. **3.** Anything similar or likened to jelly.
~*v.* **jellied, -lying, -lies.** —*tr.* **1.** To make into or cause to become jelly. **2.** To set or prepare with jelly. —*intr.* To become jelly; set. [Middle English *geli, gely,* from Old French *gelee,* frost, jelly, from Vulgar Latin *gelāta* (unattested), from Latin, feminine past participle of *gelāre,* to freeze.]

jelly[2] *n. British Slang.* Gelignite.

jel·ly·bean (jĕl′ē-bēn′) *n.* A small bean-shaped candy with a hardened sugar coating over a chewy center.

jel·ly·fish (jĕl′ē-fĭsh′) *n., pl.* **-fishes** or collectively **jellyfish. 1.** Any of numerous usually free-swimming marine coelenterates of the class Scyphozoa, characteristically having a gelatinous, tentacled, often bell-shaped medusoid stage as the dominant or only phase of its life cycle. **2.** Any of various similar or related coelenterates or other organisms. **3.** *Informal.* A person who lacks force of character, resilience, or self-control.

jem·a·dar (jĕm′ə-där′) *n.* A native officer of the former British army in India with a rank corresponding to lieutenant. [Urdu *jama'dār* : Persian *jama'at,* body of men, from Arabic *jam',* collection + *dār,* holder, from Old Persian.]

jem·be (jĕm′bē) *n. East African.* A short-handled hoe with the blade set at right angles, used with a swinging, overarm motion to break up the soil. [Swahili.]

jemmy. *Chiefly British.* Variant of **jimmy.**

Je·na (yā′nə). An eastern German town situated on the Saale River. The philosophers Johann Fichte and Georg Hegel taught at its university (founded 1557–58). The town is also the headquarters of the Zeiss optical firm, founded in 1846. Napoleon defeated the Prussians at Jena (1806).

je ne sais quoi (zhə′nə-sā-kwä′, -sĕ-) *n. French.* An indefinable or unspecifiable distinctive quality. [Literally, "I don't know what."]

Jenghiz Khan. See **Genghis Khan.**

Jen·kins (jĕng′kĭnz, jĕn′-), **Roy Harris** (1920–). British politician. He was home secretary (1965), Chancellor of the Exchequer (1967–70), and president of the European Commission (1977–81). Jenkins was a founding member of the Social Democratic Party (launched 1981) and its first elected leader (1982–83).

Jen·ner (jĕn′ər), **Edward** (1749–1823). British physician and pioneer of vaccination. In 1796 he found that smallpox could be prevented by inoculation with the substance from cowpox lesions.

jen·net, gen·et (jĕn′ĭt) *n.* **1.** A small Spanish saddle horse. **2.** A female donkey or ass; a jenny. [Middle English *jennett, genett,* from Old French *genet,* from Spanish *jinete,* light horseman, from Arabic *Zenetī,* Berber tribe famed for horsemanship.]

jen·ny (jĕn′ē) *n., pl.* **-nies. 1.** A female donkey or ass. **2.** A female wren. **3.** A spinning jenny. **4.** A hand-operated machine for bending sheet metal at an angle. [From *Jenny,* pet form of *Jane.*]

je·on (jä′ôn′, jä-ôn′) *n., pl.* **jeon.** A monetary unit, the **jun** *(see).*

jeop·ard·ize (jĕp′ər-dīz′) *tr.v.* **-ized, -izing, -izes.** To expose to loss of or injury to; make vulnerable or precarious; imperil.

jeop·ard·y (jĕp′ər-dē) *n., pl.* **-ies. 1.** Danger or risk of loss or injury; peril; vulnerability. **2.** *Law.* The defendant's risk or danger of conviction when put on trial. —See Synonyms at **danger.** [Middle English *jeopartie,* even chance, from Old French *jeu parti,* "divided play, even chance" : *jeu,* game, from Latin *jocus,* jest, game + *parti,* past participle of *partir,* to divide, from Latin *partīre,* from *pars* (stem *part-*), PART.]

Jeph·thah (jĕf′thə, jĕp′-). A judge of Israel who sacrificed his daughter to fulfill a rash vow. Judges 11–12.

je·quir·i·ty bean (jĭ-kwĭr′ə-tē) *n.* The **rosary pea** *(see)* or any of its seeds. [From Tupi-Guarani *jekiritī.*]

Jer. Jeremiah (Old Testament).

jer·bo·a (jər-bō′ə) *n.* Any of various small, leaping rodents of the family Dipodidae, of desert regions of Asia and northern Africa, having long hind legs and a long, tufted tail. Also called "desert rat." [New Latin, from Medieval Latin *jerbōa,* from Arabic *yerbō', yarbu',* flesh of the loins (from the animal's highly developed thighs).]

jer·e·mi·ad (jĕr′ə-mī′əd) *n.* An elaborate and prolonged lamentation or a tale of woe. [French *jérémiade,* after *Jérémie,* JEREMIAH (the prophet who lamented the decline of morals).]

Jer·e·mi·ah[1] (jĕr′ə-mī′ə). Also in Douay Bible **Jer·e·mi·as** (-əs). A Major Prophet of the 7th and 6th centuries B.C. [Late Latin *Jeremias,* from Hebrew *Yirmayāh(ū),* "the Lord is exalted."]

Jeremiah[2] *n.* Also in Douay Bible **Jeremias.** *Abbr.* **Jer.** A book in the Old Testament containing the prophecies of Jeremiah.

Jeremiah[3] *n. Sometimes* **jeremiah.** A person given to bewailing the evils of the day or prophesying disasters to come. [After the Old Testament prophet.]

jer·e·pi·go (jĕr′ə-pē′gō) *n.* In South Africa, a sweet fortified red or white wine. [Portuguese *cheripiga.*]

Je·rez (de la Fron·te·ra) (hē-rāth′ dē lä frōn-tār′ä). A city in southwest Spain, situated on the Guadalete River in Andalusia. It is famous for the making of sherry, whose name derives from that of the city.

Jer·i·cho (jĕr′ĭ-kō′). Ancient city near the modern village of Al Ariha, just north of the Dead Sea, in the part of Jordan occupied by Israel in 1967. The earliest remains date back to before 7000 B.C. and probably represent the world's oldest known settlement. By the time the Israelites under Joshua captured Jericho (*c.* 1300 B.C.) it was a thriving Canaanite town. Herod the Great destroyed it (*c.* 30 B.C.) and later rebuilt it with a great fortress and palace in Hellenistic style.

jerk[1] (jûrk) *v.* **jerked, jerking, jerks.** —*tr.* **1.** To move (something) with a sharp, sudden, abrupt motion; give an abrupt thrust, push, pull, or twist to: *He jerked his head as a signal.* **2.** To throw or toss with a quick, abrupt motion. **3.** In weightlifting, to raise (the weight) from the height of the shoulder to above the head. **4.** To utter abruptly or sharply. Used with *out.* —*intr.* **1.** To move in sudden abrupt motions; jolt: *The train jerked ahead.* **2.** To make spasmodic motions: *His legs jerked from fatigue.*
~*n.* **1.** A sudden, abrupt motion, such as a yank, tug, or twist. **2.** A jolting or lurching motion. **3.** *Physiology.* A sudden spasmodic, muscular movement, especially a reflex movement. **4. jerks.** Violent convulsive twitching and shaking, often resulting from excitement. **5. jerks.** *Informal.* **Chorea** *(see).* **6.** *Slang.* A stupid, objectionable, or fatuous person. [16th century : perhaps imitative.] **—jerk·er** *n.*

jerk[2] *tr.v.* **jerked, jerking, jerks.** To cut (meat) into long strips and dry in the sun or cure by exposing to smoke. [Back-formation from JERKY (cured meat).]

jer·kin (jûr′kən) *n.* **1.** A man's or woman's sleeveless and collarless jacket. **2.** A short, close-fitting coat or jacket, usually of leather, worn in former times. [16th century : origin obscure.]

jerk·y[1] (jûr′kē) *adj.* **-ier, -iest.** Characterized by jerks or jerking. **—jerk·i·ly** *adv.* **—jerk·i·ness** *n.*

jerky[2] *n.* Cured meat, **charqui** *(see).* [Earlier *jerkin beef,* from CHARQUI.]

jer·o·bo·am (jĕr′ə-bō′əm) *n.* An outsize wine bottle of varying capacity, usually holding about 4/5 of a gallon. [Humorously after *Jeroboam I,* king of northern Israel, who was a "mighty man of valor" (I Kings 11:28).]

Je·rome (jə-rōm′), **Saint,** born Sophronius Eusebius Hieronymus (*c.* 340–420). Dalmatian priest, scholar, and Doctor of the Church. His *Vulgate* was the first authentic Latin translation of the Bible from Hebrew.

Jer·ry (jĕr′ē) *n., pl.* **-ries.** *Chiefly British Slang.* A German; especially, a German soldier. [Alteration of GERMAN.]

jer·ry·build (jĕr′ē-bĭld′) *tr.v.* **-built** (-bĭlt′), **-building, -builds.** To build shoddily, flimsily, and cheaply. [19th century : origin obscure.] **—jer·ry·build·er** *n.*

jerry can *n.* A flat-sided can for storing or transporting liquids, used especially for motor fuels and having a capacity of between 20 and 23 liters (4.4 and 5 gallons). [*Jerry,* perhaps short for JEROBOAM.]

jer·sey (jûr′zē) *n., pl.* **-seys. 1.** A soft, plain-knitted fabric used for clothing. **2.** A knitted pullover shirt worn as a uniform in certain sports. **3.** A close-fitting knitted garment for the upper part of the body, usually made of wool. [Originally worn by the fishermen of JERSEY.]

Jer·sey[1] (jûr′zē). The largest of the Channel Islands, situated in the English Channel to the west of Normandy. The island was annexed by the Normans in A.D. 933, and French influence has persisted since autonomy was granted in 1204. Dairy goods, potatoes, and tomatoes are important products. The capital is St. Helier.

Jersey[2] *n.* Any of a breed of fawn-colored dairy cattle developed on the island of Jersey.

Jersey City. Coastal city in New Jersey, near the mouth of the Hudson River. It is connected to Manhattan by the Hudson River tunnels. Its industries include oil refining, chemicals, and paper.

Je·ru·sa·lem (jə-ro͞o′sə-ləm, -zə-ləm). *Arabic* **Al Quds** (äl ko͝ots). The capital of Israel, situated in the east of the country. Of immense historical and religious importance, it was the royal city of King David in the 10th century B.C. and was destroyed by Nebuchadnezzar in the 6th century. Subsequently rebuilt, it was occupied by Alexander the Great (332 B.C.). Jerusalem was taken by Pompey (65 B.C.), and Jesus Christ was crucified there under the Roman procurator Pontius Pilate. The city was in Islamic hands (7th–11th centuries A.D.) and made capital of a Crusader kingdom (1099) by Godfrey of Bouillon. Reconquered by Saladin (1187), Jerusalem remained in Islamic hands, apart from brief intervals (1229–39, 1243–44), until World War I. In 1917 the city was captured from the Turks by the British. In 1948 it was divided between Israel and Jordan. Israel occupied the Jordanian sector in the Six-Day War (1967), and its status remains disputed today. Jerusalem has innumerable mosques, churches, and synagogues, as well as holy places of great historical importance, such as the Western, or Wailing, Wall, sacred to the Jews as the major surviving part of the 2nd Hebrew Temple. The Mount of Olives and 4th-century Church of the Holy Sepulcher are among the many Christian sites, while the 7th-century Dome of the Rock is sacred to Islam.

Jerusalem artichoke *n.* **1.** A North American sunflower, *Helianthus tuberosus,* having yellow, rayed flowers and widely cultivated

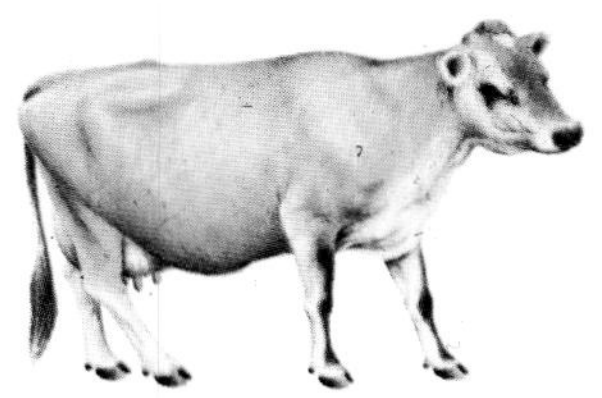

Jersey *These fine-boned dairy cattle originated on the British Channel Island of Jersey and are the only breed permitted there. They yield a rich milk high in butterfat, the oily substance from which butter is made.*

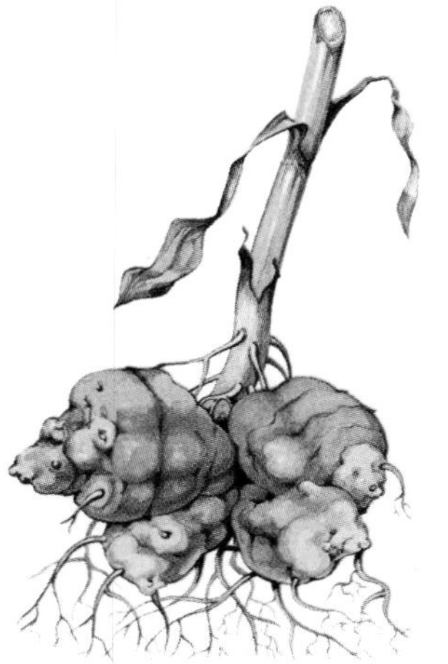

Jerusalem artichoke *The underground potatolike tubers of this plant, originally native to the United States, are eaten as a vegetable.*

PRONUNCIATION KEY

ă, pat; ā, pay; âr, care;
ä, father, are; b, bib;
ch, church; d, deed; ĕ, pet;
ē, be; f, fife; g, gag; h, hat;
hw, which; ĭ, pit; ī, pie;
îr, pier; j, judge; k, kick;
l, lid, needle; m, mum;
n, no, sudden; ng, thing;
ŏ, pot; ō, toe; ô, paw, for;
oi, noise; ou, out; o͝o, book;
o͞o, boot; p, pop; r, roar;
s, sauce; sh, ship, dish;
t, tight; th, thin, path;
th, this, bathe; ŭ, cut; ûr, fur;
v, valve; w, with; y, yes;
z, zebra, size; zh, vision;
ə, about, item, edible, gallop, circus, peaceful

IN FOREIGN WORDS:

à, *Fr.* ami; œ, *Fr.* feu, *Ger.* schön; ü, *Fr.* tu, *Ger.* über; KH, *Ger.* ich, *Scot.* loch; N, *Fr.* bon; y', *Fr.* Compiègne

STRESS MARKS:

Primary stress: ′
in·cite′ (ĭn-sīt′)
Secondary stress: ′
in′sight′ (ĭn′sīt′)

for its edible tubers. **2.** The tuber of this plant, eaten as a vegetable. Also called "artichoke." [*Jerusalem,* alteration (by folk etymology) of Italian *girasole,* sunflower, GIRASOL.]

Jerusalem Bible *n.* A translation of the Bible into various modern European languages, initiated by the Biblical School of Jerusalem and used especially in the Roman Catholic Church.

Jerusalem cherry *n.* A small shrub, *Solanum pseudo-capsicum,* native to the Old World, bearing inedible reddish fruit and used as a house plant.

Jerusalem cross *n.* A cross with four arms, each terminating in a crossbar.

jess (jĕs) *n.* A short strap fastened around the leg of a hawk or other bird used in falconry, and to which a leash may be fastened. —*tr.v.* **jessed, jessing, jesses.** To put jesses on (a hawk). [Middle English *ges(se),* from Old French *ges,* "a throwing," "something thrown around," from Vulgar Latin *jectus* (unattested), variant of Latin *jactus,* from *jacere,* to throw.]

jessamine. Variant of **jasmine.**

Jes·se (jĕs'ē). Father of King David. I Samuel 16.

Jesse tree *n.* A pictorial representation of the genealogy of Christ, proceeding from the stem of Jesse, found in church carvings and paintings, stained-glass windows, and manuscript illuminations.

[After JESSE, father of David and ancestor of Christ, whose birth, in Christian belief, is prophesied by Isaiah: "And there shall come forth a rod out of the stem of Jesse, and a branch shall grow out of his roots" (Isaiah 11:1).]

jest (jĕst) *n.* **1.** Something said or done to provoke amusement and laughter. **2.** A humorous or frivolous tone or mood: *spoken in jest.* **3.** A jeering remark; a taunt. **4.** An object of ridicule; a laughing stock. **5.** *Obsolete.* A notable exploit. —See Synonyms at **joke.** ~*v.* **jested, jesting, jests.** —*intr.* **1.** To act or speak playfully; make sport; joke. **2.** To make witty or amusing remarks. **3.** To utter scoffs or jeers; gibe. —*tr.* To make fun of; ridicule. [Middle English *geste,* deed, tale, from Old French *geste, jeste,* from Latin *gesta,* exploits, from *gerere,* to do.]

jest·er (jĕs'tər) *n.* One given to jesting; especially, a clown or buffoon employed by a king or nobleman at medieval courts.

Je·su (jē'zōō; *Latin* yā'sōō). *Poetic.* A form of the name *Jesus* used in addressing Him in hymns and prayers. [Late Latin.]

Jes·u·it (jĕzh'ōō-ĭt, jĕz'yōō-) *n.* **1.** A member of the Society of Jesus, a Roman Catholic order founded by St. Ignatius Loyola in 1534, active in missionary and other work. **2.** *Often* **jesuit.** One given to excessively subtle debating or legalistic arguments. Used derogatorily. [French *Jésuite,* from New Latin *Jesuita,* from JESUS.] —**Jes·u·it·i·cal** *adj.* —**Jes·u·it·i·cal·ly** *adv.*

Je·sus (jē'zəs), also called, in various contexts, "Jesus Christ," "Christ," "Christ Jesus," and "Jesus of Nazareth" (*c.* 4 B.C.–*c.* A.D. 29). Son of Mary; founder of Christianity; regarded by Christians as the son of God and the Messiah. ~*interj.* Also **Jesus Christ.** Used as an oath or to express outrage or surprise. [Late Latin *Jēsus,* from Greek *Iēsous,* from Hebrew *yēshūa',* from *Yəhōshūa',* JOSHUA.]

Jesus freak *n.* A member of a movement among young Christians adapting traditional evangelicalism to a pop culture.

jet[1] (jĕt) *n.* **1.** A dense, black lignite that takes a high polish and is used for jewelry. **2.** A deep, dark black. [Middle English *ge(e)t, jeet,* from Norman French *geet,* Old French *jaiet,* from Latin *gagātēs,* from Greek *gagatēs,* "stone of *Gagai*" (town in Lycia).] —**jet** *adj.*

jet[2] *n.* **1.** A high-velocity fluid stream forced under pressure out of a small-diameter opening or nozzle. **2.** Something emitted in or as if in such a stream: *a jet of sparks.* **3.** An outlet, such as a spout or nozzle, for emitting such a stream. **4. a.** A jet-propelled vehicle; especially, a jet-propelled aircraft. **b.** A jet engine. ~*v.* **jetted, jetting, jets.** —*intr.* **1.** To spurt or squirt out in a jet or jets. **2.** To travel by jet aircraft. —*tr.* To propel outward or squirt, as under pressure. [Old French, from *jeter,* to spout forth, "throw," from Vulgar Latin *jectāre* (unattested), frequentative of Latin *jacere* (past participle *jactus*), to throw.]

jet black *n.* The color of jet; a deep dark black.

je·té (zhə-tā') *n.* A ballet step executed by springing from one leg to the other, with a backward kick of the first leg. [French, from past participle of *jeter,* to throw.]

jet engine *n.* **1.** Any engine that develops thrust by ejecting a jet, especially by ejecting a jet of gaseous combustion products. **2.** Such an engine, especially a gas turbine, equipped to consume atmospheric oxygen and used mainly to propel aircraft.

jet·foil (jĕt'foil') *n.* A hydrofoil propelled by a jet engine.

jet lag *n.* The psychological dislocation and disruption of bodily rhythms caused by high-speed travel across several time zones by aircraft.

jet·lin·er (jĕt'lī'nər) *n.* A large passenger-carrying jet aircraft.

jet pipe *n.* A pipe or duct fitted to the rear end of a jet engine, through which the exhaust gases are discharged.

jet·port (jĕt'pôrt', -pōrt') *n.* An airport equipped for jet aircraft.

jet-pro·pelled (jĕt'prə-pĕld') *adj.* Propelled or powered by one or more jet engines.

jet propulsion *n.* Propulsion derived from the high-velocity expulsion of fluid or gas in a jet; especially, propulsion by jet engines.

jet·sam (jĕt'səm) *n.* **1.** Cargo or equipment thrown overboard to lighten a ship in distress. **2.** Discarded cargo or equipment found washed ashore. Used in the phrase *flotsam and jetsam.* Compare **flotsam. 3.** Discarded odds and ends. [Earlier *jetson,* from JETTISON.]

jet set *n.* A social set made up of people who are rich, sophisticated, and fashionable, and who spend much of their time traveling from one place to another. —**jet-set·ter** *n.*

jet stream *n.* **1.** A high-altitude, narrow airstream in the troposphere, generally moving from a westerly direction. It may reach speeds of more than 400 kilometers, or 250 miles per hour. **2.** A high-speed stream of emitted fluid; a jet.

jet·ti·son (jĕt'ĭ-sən, -zən) *tr.v.* **-soned, -soning, -sons. 1.** To cast off or overboard. **2.** To discard or abandon (something unwanted or burdensome). ~*n.* **1.** The act of jettisoning. **2.** Jetsam. [From Middle English *jetteson,* a throwing overboard, from Norman French *getteson,* from Latin *jactātiō* (stem *jactātiōn-*), from *jactāre,* to throw. See **jet** (to propel).]

jet·ton (jĕt'ŏn) *n.* A stamped or engraved counter used especially as a chip in casinos. [French *jeton,* from *jeter,* to throw, add up (accounts).]

jet·ty[1] (jĕt'ē) *n., pl.* **-ties. 1.** A pier, groin, mole, or other structure projecting into a body of water to influence the current or tide or to protect a harbor or shoreline. **2.** A wharf. [Middle English *jette,* from Old French *jetee,* a jutting, projection, from the feminine past

---

jet engine

POWER IN THE AIR FROM ESCAPING EXHAUST
The jet's transformation of the internal-combustion engine

The world's first jet aircraft was German—the Heinkel HE 178, test-flown in August 1939. It beat the jet plane of the English engineer Frank Whittle into the air by two years. But it is Whittle's design on which all postwar jet engines have been based. Whittle, who can therefore be regarded as the father of the jet airplane, took out his first jet engine patent in 1931 and by 1937 had built a prototype engine that was successfully tested.

The jet engine utilizes internal combustion, but in a new way. Air entering at the front has its pressure increased by about 20 times by a rotary compressor. Heated by the compression, the air passes into a combustion chamber, where it ignites injected fuel, usually kerosene. The resulting superheated gases expand rapidly and take the only way of escape open to them—through a constricting nozzle at the back. They

escape at a tremendous velocity, thrusting the aircraft forward with a force equal and opposite to the rearward thrust of the exhaust from the engine. As the gases rush toward the nozzle, they spin a turbine that drives the compressor.

World War II and the postwar boom in air travel brought great technological advances to the jet engine. The first flying prototypes developed a thrust of 450–900 kilograms (1,000–2,000 pounds). Today's turbofan bypass jets, used in jumbo jet aircraft, can deliver a thrust of 22,500 kilograms (50,000 pounds).

The jet engine has not only transformed air travel. It has also been used to power Hovercraft and ships. Most of the major car manufacturers have experimented with gas turbine (jet) engines, and since 1970 the Greyhound bus company has run over 2 million miles with experimental gas turbine buses.

TURBOFAN BYPASS JET

Combustion chamber

Fuel in

Second-stage compressor

Primary-stage compressor

Superheated gas escapes through nozzle

Turbines

Air in

Sleeve of cooler air

1. As the aircraft moves forward, air enters at the front of the engine, where it is compressed by sets of rotating and stationary vanes in the primary compressor (only one set is shown above to reveal the second-stage compressor)

2. Some of the compressed air is compressed further in the second-stage compressor. The rest bypasses the working parts of the engine. It reduces the noise level and helps to cool the casing

3. The compressed and heated air is fed into the combustion chamber, where fuel is injected and burned. The resultant superheated gases expand rapidly and rush out through the nozzle, producing forward thrust. On the way, they drive the turbines, which drive the compressors

participle of *jeter,* to throw, project. See **jet** (to propel).]

jetty² *adj.* Resembling jet, especially in color. —**jet·ti·ness** *n.*

jeu d'es·prit (zhœ dĕs-prē´) *n., pl.* **jeux d'esprit** (*pronounced as singular*). *French.* A display or stroke of wit, especially in literature.

jeu·nesse do·rée (zhœ-nĕs´ dô-rā´) *n. French. Used with a singular or plural verb.* Fashionable and wealthy young people. [Literally, "gilded youth."]

Jew (jōō) *n.* **1.** An adherent of Judaism in its religious or cultural aspects. **2.** A descendant of the Hebrew people. [Middle English *Giw, Ju,* from Old French *giu, juiu,* from Latin *Jūdaeus,* from Greek *Ioudaios,* from Aramaic *Yəhūdāy* and Hebrew *Yəhūdī,* after the tribe of *Yəhūdāh,* JUDAH.]

Jew-bait·ing (jōō´bā´tĭng) *n.* Systematic persecution of Jews. —**Jew-bait·ing** *adj.* —**Jew-bait·er** *n.*

jew·el (jōō´əl) *n.* **1.** A costly ornament of precious metal or gems used as an adornment. **2.** A precious stone; a gemstone. **3.** A small gem or gem substitute used as a bearing in a watch. **4.** A person or thing that is treasured or esteemed. **5.** A decorative glass boss in a stained glass window.
~*tr.v.* **jeweled, -eling, -els** or *chiefly British* **-elled, -elling.** **1.** To adorn with jewels. **2.** To fit (a watch, for example) with jewels. [Middle English *iuel, gewel,* from Norman French *juel,* perhaps from *jeu,* game, jest, from Latin *jocus.*]

jew·el·fish (jōō´əl-fĭsh´) *n., pl.* **-fishes** or collectively **jewelfish.** A small, brilliantly colored freshwater cichlid fish, *Hemichromis bimaculatus,* of tropical Africa, popular in home aquariums.

jew·el·er (jōō´ə-lər) *n.* Also *chiefly British* **jew·el·ler. 1.** A person who makes, repairs, or deals in jewelry. **2.** A person who is skilled in the art of cutting, polishing, and setting gemstones.

jeweler's rouge *n.* Finely powdered ferric oxide, used as a metal polish.

jew·el·ry (jōō´əl-rē) *n.* Also *chiefly British* **jew·el·ler·y. 1.** Jewels collectively. **2.** Any objects, such as bracelets, rings, necklaces, or the like, worn or used for adornment.

jew·el·weed (jōō´əl-wēd´) *n.* Any of several plants of the genus *Impatiens,* having yellowish, spurred flowers and seed pods that burst open at a touch when ripe. Also called "touch-me-not."

Jew·ess (jōō´ĭs) *n.* A Jewish woman or girl. Sometimes considered offensive. —See Usage note at **-ess.**

jew·fish (jōō´fĭsh´) *n., pl.* **-fish** or collectively **jewfish.** Any of several large, dark marine fishes of the family Serranidae, such as *Epinephelus itajara,* of tropical Atlantic waters, and the Australian **mulloway** (*see*).

Jew·ish (jōō´ĭsh) *adj.* Of, concerning, or characteristic of the Jews, their customs, or their religion.
~*n.* Yiddish. Not in technical usage. —**Jew·ish·ly** *adv.* —**Jew·ish·ness** *n.*

Jewish Autonomous Region. Also **Bi·ro·bi·dzhan** (bĭr´ō-bĭ-jän´, -jän´). Under the former Soviet regime, an autonomous region of the Russian S.F.S.R., created in 1934 as a Siberian area of settlement for Soviet Jews. Its remoteness and severe climate discouraged colonization, and Jews remained in the minority.

Jewish calendar *n.* The lunisolar calendar used by the ancient Hebrews and for religious purposes today, calculating the date from the supposed year of creation, 3761 B.C. and based on a meteoric cycle of 19 years, with the 3rd, 6th, 8th, 11th, 14th, 17th, and 19th years of each cycle designated leap years. Also called "Hebrew calendar." See feature at **calendar.**

Jew·ry (jōō´rē) *n.* **1.** Jews collectively; the Jewish people. **2.** The district of a medieval city inhabited by Jews.

jew's-ear (jōōz´îr´) *n.* An edible fungus, *Auricularia auricula,* having a brown or flesh-colored saucer-shaped fruiting body and growing on wood.

jew's-harp, jews'-harp (jōōz´härp´) *n.* A small musical instrument with a lyre-shaped metal frame that is held between the teeth when played, and a projecting steel tongue that is plucked to produce a soft, twanging sound. [Earlier *jew's trump,* perhaps alteration (influenced by JEW) of Dutch *jeugdtromp,* children's trumpet.]

jez·e·bel (jĕz´ə-bĕl´, -bəl) *n. Sometimes* **Jezebel.** A shamelessly immoral or scheming woman. [After JEZEBEL.]

Jez·e·bel (jĕz´ə-bĕl´, -bəl). Also in Douay Bible **Jez·a·bel.** Phoenician princess of the 9th century B.C. who as Ahab's wife and queen of Israel encouraged idolatry and the killing of the prophets of Israel. I Kings 16:31, 18:3.

JHVH, JHWH. Variants of YHWH.

-ji *suffix. Indian.* Used with a person's name as a sign of respect; for example, *Gandhiji.* [Hindi.]

Jiang, Jie·shi (jyäng´ jä´shə), also **Chiang Kai-shek** (chăng´ kī-shĕk´) (1887–1975). Chinese general and statesman. He joined the army and was active in the 1911 revolution. In 1918 he joined the Guomindang (Nationalist People's Party), and became its leader after the death of Sun Zhongshan (Sun Yat-sen) in 1925. In 1926 he allied his forces with the Communists against the Chinese warlords, but a year later purged left-wingers from his own forces, and the alliance broke up (1928). Later he waged war on the Communists. After World War II civil war broke out again (1946–49), and when the Guomindang was defeated Jiang withdrew to Taiwan. He was president of Taiwan until his death.

Jiang Qing (jyäng´ chĭng´), also **Chiang Ch'ing** (chăng´ chĭng´) (1914–91). Wife of Mao Ze-dong (Tse-tung). She was an actress before she married him in 1939. After his death (1976) she was arrested, expelled from the Chinese Communist Party, imprisoned, and given a suspended death sentence for plotting rebellion.

Jiang·su or **Chiang-su** or **Kiang·su** (jyäng´sōō´). Province of eastern China. It largely comprises the deltas of the Huang He and Chang Jiang, and is one of the country's smallest and most densely populated provinces. Nanjing is the capital.

Jiang·xi or **Chiang-hsi** or **Kiang·si** (jyäng´sē´). Province of central southern China. It is a major rice-growing area, with resources of coal, uranium, tin, and lead. The capital is Nanchang. The southern part of the province was held by Mao Ze-dong's Communists (1930–34) during the war against the Guomindang, and it was from here that the Long March was begun.

jiao (jou) *n., pl.* **jiao.** A monetary unit, the **fen** (*see*).

jib¹ (jĭb) *n.* **1.** A triangular sail stretching from the foretopmast head to the jib boom and in small craft to the bowsprit or the bow. **2. a.** The arm of a mechanical crane. **b.** The boom of a derrick. —**the cut of someone's jib.** *Informal.* Someone's appearance, style, or manner. [17th century : origin obscure.]

jib² *intr.v.* **jibbed, jibbing, jibs. 1.** To draw back, balk, or show reluctance. Often used with *at.* **2.** To stop short and turn restively from side to side; shy. Used of an animal.
~*n.* Also **jib·ber** (jĭb´ər). An animal that jibs. [19th century : origin obscure.]

jibbah. Variant of **jubbah.**

jib boom *n.* A spar forming a continuation of the bowsprit.

jibe¹ (jīb) *v.* **jibed, jibing, jibes.** Also **gybe.** —*intr.* To shift a foreand-aft sail from one side of a vessel to the other while sailing before the wind; to jib. —*tr.* To cause to jibe.
~*n.* The act of jibing. [From obsolete Dutch *gijben†.*]

jibe² *intr.v.* **jibed, jibing, jibes.** *Informal.* To be in accord; harmonize; agree. [19th century : origin obscure.]

jibe³. Variant of **gibe** (taunt).

Jibuti. See **Djibouti.**

Jid·dah (jĭd´ə). Also **Jed·da** (jĕd´ə) or **Jud·dah** (jŭd´ə). A Red Sea port in western Saudi Arabia. It serves Mecca, which lies about 74 kilometers (46 miles) inland.

jif·fy (jĭf´ē) *n., pl.* **-fies.** Also **jiff** (jĭf). *Informal.* A moment; no time at all: *I'll be there in a jiffy.* —See Synonyms at **moment.** [18th century : origin obscure.]

jig (jĭg) *n.* **1. a.** Any of various lively kicking or leaping dances, usually in 6/8 time. **b.** A piece of music for such a dance. Also called "gigue." **2.** A joke or trick. **3.** A fishing lure, usually made of metal and having one or more hooks, that darts or bobs about when pulled through the water. **4.** An apparatus for cleaning or separating ore by agitation in water. **5.** A device for guiding a tool or for holding machine work in place.
~*v.* **jigged, jigging, jigs.** —*intr.* **1.** To dance or play a jig. **2.** To move or bob up and down jerkily and rapidly. **3.** To operate a jig, as in fishing, machine work, or refining ore. —*tr.* **1.** To shake or jerk up and down or to and fro. **2.** To machine with the aid of a jig. **3.** To separate or clean (ore) by shaking a jig. [16th century : origin obscure.]

jig·ger¹ (jĭg´ər) *n.* **1.** A person who jigs or operates a jig. **2. a.** A small measure for alcoholic drinks, especially spirits. **b.** A small quantity of alcoholic drink. **3.** A short golf club with an iron head. **4.** In fishing, mining, or mechanics, a jig. **5.** Any device that operates with a jerking or jolting motion, such as a drill. **6.** *Nautical.* **a.** A light tackle. **b.** A small sail, set in the stern of a yawl, for example. **c.** A boat having such a sail. **d.** A jigger mast (*see*). **7.** *Informal.* Any trivial article or device whose name eludes one. **8.** A rest for a billiard cue.

jigger² *n.* **1.** A mite, the **chigger** (*see*). **2.** A flea, the **chigoe** (*see*).

jig·gered (jĭg´ərd) *adj. Slang.* **1.** Very surprised. Used as a mild oath: *I'll be jiggered.* **2.** Exhausted; tired out.

jigger mast *n. Nautical.* **1.** The short after mast from which the jigger sail is set on a ketch or yawl. Also called "mizzenmast." **2.** The fourth mast aft on a four-masted ship. Also called "jigger."

jig·ger·y-po·ker·y (jĭg´ə-rē-pō´kə-rē) *n.* Underhand scheming or behavior; trickery. [From Scottish dialect *joukery-pawkery,* based on dialect *jouk†,* to duck, dodge.]

jig·gle (jĭg´əl) *v.* **-gled, -gling, -gles.** —*intr.* To move or rock lightly up and down or to and fro in an unsteady, jerky manner. —*tr.* To cause to move in this manner.
~*n.* A jiggling motion. [Frequentative of JIG (verb).]

jig·saw (jĭg´sô´) *n.* **1.** A saw, often power-driven, with a narrow, vertical reciprocating blade, used to cut sharp curves. **2.** A jigsaw puzzle.

jigsaw puzzle *n.* A puzzle consisting of a picture pasted on cardboard or wood and cut into numerous interlocking pieces, the object being to reassemble the picture by fitting the pieces together. Also called "jigsaw," "picture puzzle."

ji·had, je·had (jĭ-häd´) *n.* **1.** A Muslim holy war against infidels. **2.** A crusade. [Arabic *jihād.*]

Ji·lin or **Ki·rin** (jē´lĭn´). Province of northeast China. It lies on the fertile Manchurian Plain and is a major cereal producer. It also has extensive coal and iron deposits, the basis of a large industrial region centered on the cities of Changchun (the capital) and Jilin.

jil·la·roo (jĭl´ə-rōō) *n., pl.* **-roos.** *Australian Informal.* A female jackeroo. [Alteration of JACKEROO, with allusion to *Jack and Jill.*]

jilt (jĭlt) *tr.v.* **jilted, jilting, jilts.** To reject or cast aside (a lover), especially after an engagement.
~*n.* A woman who discards a lover. [17th century : origin obscure.]

jim-crow, Jim-Crow (jĭm´krō´) *adj. Slang.* **1.** Favoring or promoting the segregation of blacks: *jim-crow policies.* **2.** For blacks only:

jet *This hard black stone, which has been modeled into jewelry at least since Roman times, is a type of coal. These pieces were made in Britain during the Roman occupation.*

a jim-crow waiting room. Usually considered offensive in both senses. [From JIM CROW.]

Jim Crow *n. Slang.* **1. a.** The systematic practice of segregating and suppressing black people. **b.** A black person. Used derogatorily in both senses. **2.** A device for straightening iron bars or rails. [After *Jim Crow,* a character in an act by Thomas D. Rice (1808-60), U.S. entertainer who based it on an anonymous 19th-century song called "Jim Crow."] —**Jim-Crow-ism** *n.*

Ji·mé·nez (hĕ-mĕ′nĕs), **Juan Ramón** (1881-1958). Spanish poet. His best-known work is *Platero y Yo* (1917), relating his wanderings through Andalusia with his donkey. In 1956 he received the Nobel Prize for literature.

jim-jams (jĭm′jămz′) *pl.n. Slang.* **1.** A state of extreme nervousness; the jitters. **2.** Delirium tremens. [Whimsical reduplication.]

jim·my (jĭm′ē) *n., pl.* **-mies.** Also *chiefly British* **jem·my** (jĕm′ē). A short crowbar with curved ends, especially when regarded as a burglar's tool. —*tr.v.* **jimmied, -mying, -mies.** Also *chiefly British* **jemmy.** To pry open with or as if with a jimmy. [From the pet name of *James.*]

Jimmy *n. Scottish Informal.* Used as a humorous form of address to a man whose name is not known by the speaker. [Pet form of *James,* considered as a very common Scottish name.]

jim·son·weed (jĭm′sən-wēd′) *n.* A coarse, poisonous plant, *Datura stramonium,* having large, trumpet-shaped white or purplish flowers and prickly fruit. Also called "stramonium," "thorn apple." [From archaic *Jamestown weed,* named for JAMESTOWN, Virginia.]

Ji·nan or **Chi·nan** or **Tsi·nan** (jē′nän′). Capital of Shandong province, northeast China, situated in the Huang He valley. A rail and marketing center of a rich farming area, its products include iron and steel, flour, textiles, chemicals, and agricultural machinery.

Jinghiz Khan. See **Genghiz Khan.**

jin·gle (jĭng′gəl) *v.* **-gled, -gling, -gles.** —*intr.* **1.** To make a repeated tinkling or ringing metallic sound. **2.** To have the sound of a verse jingle. —*tr.* To cause to jingle. —*n.* **1. a.** The tinkling sound produced by light bits of metal striking together: *the jingle of sleigh bells.* **b.** Something resembling or suggesting this. **2.** A simple, repetitious, catchy rhyme or song, especially one used in an advertisement. [Middle English *ginglen* (probably imitative).]

jin·go (jĭng′gō) *n., pl.* **-goes.** One who vociferously supports his country, especially one who supports a belligerent foreign policy; an uncritical patriot; a chauvinist. Also used adjectively: *jingo policies.* —**by jingo.** Used to express surprise or for emphasis. [From the refrain of a music-hall song sung in England by supporters of Benjamin Disraeli's policy against Russia in 1878: "*We don't want to fight, yet by Jingo! if we do, / We've got the ships, we've got the men, and got the money too.*" Originally used in conjuring, perhaps euphemistic for *by Jesus.*] —**jin·go·ish** *adj.* —**jin·go·ism** *n.* —**jin·go·ist** *n.* —**jin·go·is·tic** *adj.*

jink (jĭngk) *intr.v.* **jinked, jinking, jinks.** To make a quick evasive turn, especially when flying or playing Rugby football. —*n.* **1.** A sudden evasive turn. **2. jinks.** Boisterous play; frolic. Used chiefly in the phrase *high jinks.* [18th century (originally Scottish): perhaps imitative of quick movement.]

Jin·men or **Chin·men** (jĭn′měn′, chěn′mŭn′). Also **Que·moy** (kē-moi′). Island group, a possession of Taiwan, lying in the Taiwan Strait close to the mainland of China. It remained in Nationalist hands after 1949 and is still a military base. Its bombardment from the mainland (1949-58) served only to strengthen defense ties between Taiwan and the United States.

Jin·nah (jĭn′ə), **Mohammed Ali** (1876-1948). First governor-general of Pakistan. When India was about to achieve independence from Britain, Jinnah feared the Muslim minority would be kept from power by the Hindus, and he insisted on a Muslim homeland. Pakistan was established in 1947.

jin·ni, jin·ee (jĭn′ē, jĭ-nē′) *n., pl.* **jinn** (jĭn). Also **djin·ni, djin·ny,** *pl.* **djinn.** In Muslim legend, a spirit capable of assuming human or animal form and exercising supernatural influence over men. [Arabic *jinnīy.*]

jin·rick·sha (jĭn-rĭk′shô) *n.* Also **jin·rik·i·sha.** A rickshaw (*see*). [Japanese : *jin,* man + *riki,* power + *sha,* vehicle.]

jinx (jĭngks) *n. Informal.* Something or someone believed to bring bad luck or misfortune. —*tr.v.* **jinxed, jinxing, jinxes.** *Informal.* To bring bad luck to. [Perhaps from *Jynx,* genus name of the wryneck, from Greek *iunx,* wryneck (a bird used in magic), from *iuzein,* to call, cry.]

ji·pi·ja·pa (hē′pē-hä′pä) *n.* A palmlike plant, *Carludovica palmata,* of Central and South America, having long-stalked, fanlike leaves used to make Panama hats. [Spanish, after *Jipijapa,* Ecuador.]

jit·ney (jĭt′nē) *n., pl.* **-neys.** *Informal.* **1.** A small bus or automobile that transports passengers on a route for a small fare. **2.** *Archaic.* A nickel. [Origin unknown.]

jit·ter (jĭt′ər) *intr.v.* **-tered, -tering, -ters.** *Informal.* To be nervous or uneasy; fidget. [20th century : origin obscure.] —**jit·ter·y** *adj.*

jit·ter·bug (jĭt′ər-bŭg′) *n. Slang.* **1.** A fast dance performed to quick-tempo jazz or swing music and consisting of various two-step patterns embellished with twirls and throws, especially popular in the 1940's. **2.** A person who does such a dance. **3.** A highly nervous person. —*intr.v.* **jitterbugged, -bugging, -bugs.** To dance the jitterbug. [JITTER + BUG.]

jit·ters (jĭt′ərz) *pl.n. Informal.* A fit of nervousness; anxiety.

jiujitsu, jiujutsu. Variants of **jujitsu.**

Jiu·long or **Chiu·lung** (jyō′lŏng′). Also **Kow·loon** (kou′lōōn′). A port and peninsula on mainland China, forming part of the British crown colony of Hong Kong. It was ceded to Britain in 1860.

jive (jīv) *n. Slang.* **1. a.** A style of lively, fast jazz music. **b.** A fast, jerky dance, similar in style to rock'n'roll, originally performed to jive music and later to rock'n'roll music. **2. a.** Glib or deceptive talk: *Don't give me that jive.* **b.** The jargon of jazz musicians and enthusiasts. [20th century : origin obscure.] —**jive** *v.*

j.n.d. *Psychology.* just noticeable difference.

jnr., Jnr. junior.

jnt. joint.

jo, joe (jō) *n., pl.* **joes.** *Scottish.* A sweetheart. [16th century : variant of JOY.]

Joan of Arc (jōn; ärk), **Saint** (1412-31). *French* **Jeanne d'Arc** (zhän därk′). French heroine, known as the Maid of Orléans. She led the French resistance that forced the English to raise the siege of Orléans (1429). The same year, aged 17, she led an army of 12,000 to Rheims and had the dauphin crowned Charles VII. She was captured and sold to the English (1430) by the Burgundians and tried for heresy and sorcery. Joan was burned at the stake in Rouen (1431). She was beatified (1909) and canonized (1920).

job¹ (jŏb) *n.* **1.** An action requiring some exertion; a task; an undertaking. **2.** An activity performed in exchange for payment; especially, one performed regularly as one's trade, occupation, or profession. **3. a.** A specific piece of work to be done for a set fee. **b.** The object to be worked on. **c.** Anything resulting from or produced by work. **4.** A position in which one is employed. **5. a.** An assigned or assumed duty or responsibility: *It was her job to get her younger brother ready for school.* **b.** Anything that must be done: *Stitching up her cuts was a very messy job.* **6.** *Informal.* A difficult or strenuous task: *We had a job getting the piano up the stairs.* **7.** *Informal.* A thing that is notable of its kind: *driving a nice little red job.* **8.** *Chiefly British Informal.* A state of affairs: *It's a good job you called the fire brigade.* **9.** *Informal.* A criminal act, especially a robbery: *pull a bank job.* **10.** Something done ostensibly in the public interest, but actually for private gain or advantage. —See Synonyms at **task.** —**just the job.** *Chiefly British.* Precisely what is or was required. —**lie down on the job.** *Informal.* To neglect the responsibilities of one's job. —**on the job.** *Informal.* **1.** Working at one's occupation or task; at work. **2.** Paying close attention to one's work or responsibilities. —*v.* **jobbed, jobbing, jobs.** —*intr.* **1.** To do odd jobs or piecework: *a jobbing builder.* **2.** To act as a middleman or broker. **3.** To exploit a position of trust for private advantage. —*tr.* **1. a.** To purchase (merchandise) from manufacturers and sell it to retailers. **b.** *Chiefly British.* To buy and sell (stocks and shares) as a jobber. **2.** To arrange for (contracted work) to be done in portions by others; subcontract. **3.** To transact (official business) dishonestly for private profit. [Originally a piece of work, perhaps from obsolete *job†,* "piece."]

job² *v.* **jobbed, jobbing, jobs.** *Archaic.* —*tr.* To jab. —*intr.* To make a jab. —*n. Archaic.* A jab. [Middle English *jobben†.*]

Job¹ (jōb). In the Old Testament, an upright man whose faith in God survived the test of repeated calamities, and who is taken as a model of patient endurance: *the patience of Job.* [Hebrew *Iyyobh,* "hated, persecuted," from *ayabh,* to be hostile.]

Job² *n.* A book of the Old Testament, recounting the story of Job.

job·ber (jŏb′ər) *n.* **1.** One who buys merchandise from manufacturers and sells it to retailers. **2.** A person who does piecework or odd jobs. **3.** A public official who exploits his position for personal gain. **4.** *Chiefly British.* A middleman in the exchange of stocks and securities among brokers; a stockjobber.

job·ber·y (jŏb′ə-rē) *n.* Corruption among public officials. [From JOB (to seek gain).]

job·hold·er (jŏb′hōl′dər) *n.* One who has a regular job.

job·hop (jŏb′hŏp′) *intr.v.* **-hopped, -hopping, -hops.** To change jobs frequently. —**job-hop·per** *n.*

job·less (jŏb′lĭs) *adj.* Unemployed. —**job·less·ness** *n.*

job lot *n.* **1.** Miscellaneous goods sold in one lot. **2.** Any collection of unsorted and usually inferior items.

job reservation *n.* In South Africa, the practice of limiting various categories of employment to particular race groups, thereby effectively excluding blacks from many trades and professions.

Job's comforter *n.* One who discourages or saddens while seemingly offering sympathy or comfort. [From JOB, who was treated in such a way by his friends.]

job-shar·ing (jŏb′shâr′ĭng) *n.* A practice whereby the responsibility for a job is shared between two alternating part-time workers.

Job's-tears (jōbz′tîrz′) *n. Used with a singular or plural verb.* **1.** A grass, *Coix lacryma-jobi,* of tropical Asia, having edible seeds enclosed in beadlike modified leaves. **2.** The seeds of this plant. **3.** The beadlike, seed-containing structures of this plant, used for ornamentation.

Jo·cas·ta (jō-kăs′tə). *Greek Legend.* A Theban queen who unknowingly married her own son Oedipus.

jock¹ (jŏk) *n. Informal.* A jockey. [Short for JOCKEY.]

jock² *n.* **1.** A jockstrap (*see*). **2.** *Slang.* **a.** A male athlete, especially in college. **b.** A virile and promiscuous man; a playboy.

Jock (jŏk) *n. Scottish.* A Scotsman. Often used as a familiar, humorous, or derogatory form of address. [Scottish form of *Jack.*]

jock·ey (jŏk′ē) *n., pl.* **-eys.** A person who rides horses in races, especially as a profession.

~*v.* **jockeyed, -eying, -eys.** —*tr.* **1.** To ride (a horse) as jockey. **2.** To direct or maneuver by cleverness or skill. **3.** To trick; outwit. —*intr.* **1.** To ride a horse in a race. **2.** To maneuver for a certain position or advantage. Used chiefly in the phrase *jockey for position.* **3.** To employ trickery; cheat; swindle. [Originally "lad," diminutive of Scottish *Jock,* JACK (a man).]

jock·strap, jock strap (jŏk′străp′) *n.* An elastic support for the male genitals, sometimes employing a rigid metallic cup, worn especially in athletic or other strenuous activity. Also called "athletic supporter," "jock." [Slang *jock,* "penis," earlier *jockum*† + STRAP.]

jo·cose (jō-kōs′) *adj.* **1.** Given to good-humored joking; merry. **2.** Characterized by joking; humorous. [Latin *jocōsus,* from *jocus,* jest, joke.] —**jo·cose·ly** *adv.* —**jo·cos·i·ty** (jō-kŏs′ə-tē) *n.*

joc·u·lar (jŏk′yə-lər) *adj.* **1.** Given to or characterized by joking. **2.** Meant in jest; facetious. —See Synonyms at **jolly.** [Latin *joculāris,* from *joculus,* diminutive of *jocus,* jest, joke.] —**joc·u·lar·i·ty** *n.* —**joc·u·lar·ly** *adv.*

joc·und (jŏk′ənd, jō′kənd) *adj.* Having a cheerful disposition or quality; merry. [Middle English, from Old French, from Late Latin *jōcundus,* from Latin *jūcundus,* agreeable, pleasant, from *juvāre,* to entertain, delight, AID.] —**joc·und·ly** *adv.* —**jo·cund·i·ty** *n.*

Jodh·pur (jŏd′pŏor′). A city in northwestern India, in Rajasthan state. Founded in 1459, it became the capital of a large princely state and now has a university (founded 1962).

jodh·pur boots (jŏd′pər) *pl.n.* Short ankle-high leather boots worn with jodhpurs for riding.

jodh·purs (jŏd′pərz) *pl.n.* Wide-hipped riding breeches of heavy cloth, fitting tightly at the knees and ankles. [From JODHPUR.]

Jo·do (jō′dō′) *n.* **Pure Land Buddhism** (see). [Japanese.]

Joe Blow *n. Informal.* The average man; the man in the street.

Jo·el[1] (jō′əl). A Hebrew Minor Prophet.

Joel[2] *n.* A book of the Old Testament containing Joel's prophecies of the judgment of Judah.

jo·ey (jō′ē) *n., pl.* **-eys. 1.** *Australian.* **a.** A young kangaroo or other young animal. **b.** A young child. **2.** *New Zealand.* An opossum. [Native Australian name.]

jog[1] (jŏg) *v.* **jogged, jogging, jogs.** —*tr.* **1.** To jar or move by shoving, bumping, or jerking. **2.** To give a slight push or shake to; nudge. **3.** To stimulate; stir (one's memory, for example). —*intr.* **1.** To ride at a steady, slow trot. **2.** To run at a moderate pace, especially for exercise. **3.** To proceed in a leisurely, monotonous, or uneventful way.
~*n.* **1.** A slight jolt or shake. **2.** A nudge. **3.** A slow, steady pace; a trot. [Middle English (probably imitative).] —**jog·ger** *n.*

jog[2] *n.* **1.** A protruding or receding part in a surface or line. **2.** An abrupt change in direction.
~*intr.v.* **jogged, jogging, jogs.** To turn sharply; veer. [Perhaps variant of JAG.]

jog·ging (jŏg′ĭng) *n.* Exercise that consists of running at a slow, regular pace or alternately running and walking.

jog·gle[1] (jŏg′əl) *v.* **-gled, -gling, -gles.** —*tr.* To shake or jar repeatedly. —*intr.* To move with a shaking or jolting motion.
~*n.* A shaking or jolting motion. [Frequentative of JOG.]

joggle[2] *n.* **1.** A joint between two pieces of building material formed by a notch and a fitted projection. **2.** The notch or the projecting piece used in such a joint.
~*tr.v.* **joggled, -gling, -gles.** To join or attach by means of a joggle. [From JOG (protruding part).]

Jog·ja·kar·ta (jŏg′yə-kär′tə). Also **Djok·ja·kar·ta** (jŏk′-). A city in Indonesia, situated in south-central Java. Palaces and temples have been located in the surrounding area since the 8th century B.C. and include the magnificent Buddhist monument of Borobudur. Founded in 1755, Jogjakarta was the capital of the Indonesian Republic (1946–49). It has a university (founded 1949) and markets tea, tobacco, and handicrafts.

jog trot *n.* **1.** A moderate, steady, jolting pace; a jog. **2.** A regular, humdrum way of living or of doing something.

Jo·han·nes·burg (jō-hăn′ĭs-bûrg′, yō-hä′nĭs-). The largest city in South Africa, situated in the Transvaal in the northeast of the country. It lies on the Witwatersrand and was founded in 1886 when gold was discovered. Now the center of the world's largest gold field, Johannesburg is at the heart of South Africa's most highly industrialized region.

Jo·han·nine (jō-hăn′īn, -ən) *adj.* Pertaining to or designating those parts of the New Testament attributed to St. John. [From Latin *johannīnus,* from *Johannes,* JOHN.]

john (jŏn) *n. Slang.* **1.** A toilet. **2.** A prostitute's customer. [From *John* (masculine name).]

John[1] (jŏn) *n.* **1.** A book of the New Testament, the fourth Gospel, attributed to St. John. **2.** Any of three New Testament Epistles attributed to St. John.

John[2], also known as "John Lackland" (c. 1167–1216). King of England from 1199. He was the youngest son of Henry II and intrigued against his father and then his brother, Richard I. Under him, the English lost most of their possessions in France. The barons rose against John and forced him to set his seal on the Magna Carta (1215), a cornerstone of English liberty.

John, Augustus Edwin (1878–1961). British painter. He often painted gypsies, as in *Encampment on Dartmoor* (1906). He painted portraits of his wife Dorelia, of George Bernard Shaw (1914), Thomas Hardy (1923), and Dylan Thomas (c. 1936). He was elected to the Royal Academy in 1928.

John, Saint, also known as "the Evangelist," "the Divine." One of the Twelve Apostles; reputed author of the 4th Gospel, three epistles, and the Book of Revelation.

John XXIII, Pope, born Angelo Giuseppe Roncalli (1881–1963). He became pope in 1958. He called a general council of the Church, the first for almost a century, and worked for world peace and Christian unity. See **Vatican Council.**

John Bar·ley·corn (bär′lē-kôrn′) *n.* A personification of malt liquor or of alcoholic beverages in general.

John Birch Society (bûrch) *n.* An ultraconservative anticommunist organization established in the United States by Robert H.W. Welch, Jr., in 1958. [Named after *John Birch* (died 1945), U.S. intelligence officer.]

John Bull *n.* **1.** A personification of England or the English. **2.** A typical Englishman. [After *The History of John Bull* (1712), a satire by John ARBUTHNOT.]

John Doe *n.* **1.** A name formerly used in U.S. legal proceedings to designate a fictitious or unidentified person. **2.** An average citizen; the man in the street. Also called "Richard Roe."

John Do·ry (dôr′ē, dōr′ē) *n.* Any fish of the family Zeidae; especially, *Zenopsis ocellata,* of the western Atlantic, or *Zeus faber,* of the eastern Atlantic and Mediterranean, having spiny fins and a laterally compressed body.

John Han·cock (hăn′kŏk) *n. Informal.* A person's signature. [After John HANCOCK, whose signature appears prominently on the Declaration of Independence.]

Johnny Appleseed. See John **Chapman.**

john·ny·cake (jŏn′ē-kāk′) *n.* **1.** Corncake (see). **2.** *Australian.* A thin cake made with wheat meal or flour, often cooked on the embers of a campfire.

John·ny·come·late·ly (jŏn′ē-kŭm-lāt′lē) *n., pl.* **-lies.** *Informal.* A newcomer or latecomer, especially a recent adherent to a cause or fashion.

John·ny·jump·up (jŏn′ē-jŭmp′ŭp′) *n.* A plant, the **heartsease** (see). [From its quick growth.]

John·ny·on·the·spot (jŏn′ē-ŏn-thə-spŏt′, -ŏn′-) *n. Informal.* A person who is available and ready to act when necessary.

John·ny Reb (jŏn′ē rĕb′) *n. Informal.* A Confederate soldier during the Civil War.

John of Gaunt (1340–99). Duke of Lancaster, fourth son of Edward III. He effectively ruled England during his father's last years and in the first years of Richard II's reign.

John of the Cross, Saint, born Juan de Yepes y Álvarez (1542–91). Spanish monk, mystic, and poet. He tried to restore austerity to Carmelite life. Friction among the Carmelites led to his imprisonment (1577) and finally retreat to a life of solitude. He was canonized in 1726.

John o'Groats (jŏn′ ə-grōts′). Location in the extreme northeast of Scotland, named after John de Groat, a Dutchman, who built an octagonal house there in the 16th century. The northern extremity of Britain is popularly marked by John o'Groats.

John Paul II, Pope, born Karol Wojtyla (1920–). The first Polish-born pope. He was archbishop of Kraków before his election in 1978 as the first non-Italian pope since the Dutch-born Adrian VI (reigned 1522–23).

Johns (jŏnz), **Jasper** (1930–). U.S. artist. He aims to remove the boundary between art and real life, and has made bronze casts of light bulbs, toothbrushes, and beer cans.

John·son (jŏn′sən), **Amy** (1903–41). Pioneer British aviator. She was the first woman to fly solo from London to Australia (1930). She drowned after bailing out into the Thames estuary while on war service.

Johnson, Andrew (1808–75). 17th U.S. president (1865–69). A Southerner who remained loyal to the Union during the Civil War, Johnson was elected vice president in 1864 and succeeded the assassinated Abraham Lincoln. He pursued a policy of conciliation toward the defeated Confederate states to the point of readmitting them to the Union without requiring political reforms or ensuring civil rights for freed slaves.

Johnson, Lyndon Baines (1908–73). 36th U.S. president. Johnson succeeded to the office after John F. Kennedy's assassination (1963). He launched a welfare program, termed the Great Society, and overwhelmingly won the presidential election in 1964. He faced increasing criticism over the mounting involvement in Vietnam and did not stand for re-election in 1968.

Johnson, Samuel, known as "Dr. Johnson" (1709–84). British writer and lexicographer. His works include *Dictionary of the English Language* (1755) and *Lives of the Poets* (1779–81).

John·so·ni·an (jŏn-sō′nē-ən) *adj.* Of, resembling, or relating to Samuel Johnson or his writings.
~*n.* An admirer or student of Samuel Johnson or his work.

Johnson grass *n.* A coarse grass, *Sorghum halepense,* native to the Mediterranean area, cultivated for forage but often a troublesome weed. [Developed by William *Johnson,* 19th-century U.S. agriculturalist.]

John the Baptist, Saint. Son of Elizabeth and Zacharias; cousin of Jesus, whom he baptized; executed by Herod Antipas.

Jo·hore or **Jo·hor** (jō-hôr′, -hōr′). A state in Malaysia, situated in the south of the Malay Peninsula. Its extensive forests produce rubber, copra, and palm oil, and there are important reserves of tin and bauxite. The capital, Johore Baharu, is connected to Singapore by a causeway.

joie de vi·vre (zhwä′ də vē′vrə) *n.* Hearty or carefree enjoyment of life. [French, "joy of living."]

join (join) v. **joined, joining, joins.** —*tr.* **1.** To put or bring together; unite or make continuous: *The children joined hands in a circle.* **2.** To put or bring into close association or relationship: *joined in marriage.* **3.** *Geometry.* To connect (points), as with a straight line. **4.** To form a junction with; combine with. **5.** To become a part or member of (a club, society, or the like). **6.** To take a place among, in, or with; enter into the company of: *I shall join you later.* **7.** *Informal.* To adjoin. —*intr.* **1.** To come or act together; form a connection, junction, or alliance. Often used with *with.* **2.** To become a member of a group. **3.** To take part; participate. Used with *in: He joined in the singing.* —**join up.** To enlist, especially in the armed forces.

~*n.* A joint; a junction. [Middle English *joinen,* from Old French *joindre* (stem *joign-*), from Latin *jungere.*]

Synonyms: *associate, combine, connect, consolidate, link, relate, unite.*

Usage: The use of *together* following this verb is often felt to be redundant: *He joined (together) the two wires.* The longer form does have a certain value in adding emphasis, however, and it is well established in a few fixed phrases, for example: *whom God hath joined together. . . .*

---

joint

JOINTS: DESIGNED FOR DIFFERENT DEGREES OF MOVEMENT

Cartilage, ligament, and fluid to protect against wear and tear

Wherever two bones come into contact in the body there is a joint. It may be fixed, like the joints in the skull, but what most people think of as joints are movable, like the joints in the limbs.

The bone endings in joints are lined with elastic, pearly white tissue called cartilage, and between them is a smooth, thin layer of tissue called the synovial membrane. This produces a lubricant, synovial fluid, that acts like oil in a machine: the two bony surfaces never touch but are kept apart by a thin layer of fluid.

Tough, fibrous bands of tissue—ligaments—are attached to the bones on either side of a joint, giving stability and limiting the range of movement. The range of possible movement also depends on the design of the joint.

A hinged joint, as in the fingers, elbows, and knees, allows movement backward and forward and some degree of rotation. A pivot joint, as in the top of the neck, allows nodding and some rotary movement. A ball-and-socket joint, as in the shoulders, allows the maximum flexibility of movement. A sliding joint, as in the ankles and wrists, allows a range of movements similar to those of a ball-and-socket joint but more limited in flexibility.

PIVOT JOINT

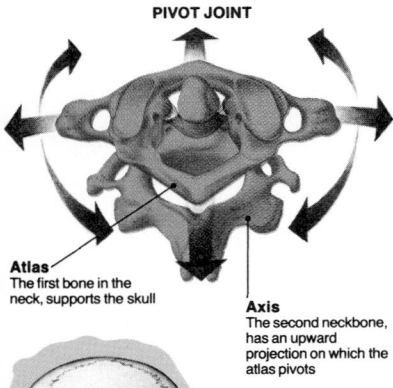

Atlas
The first bone in the neck, supports the skull

Axis
The second neckbone, has an upward projection on which the atlas pivots

Atlas

Axis

At the top of the neck, the atlas and the axis bones form between them a pivot joint, giving the head a range of movements based on the ability to nod back and forth and to rotate from side to side.

HINGED JOINT

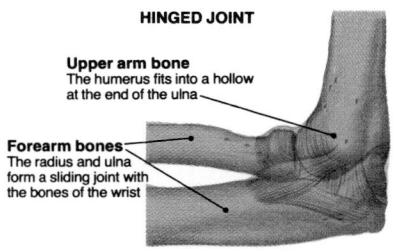

Upper arm bone
The humerus fits into a hollow at the end of the ulna

Forearm bones
The radius and ulna form a sliding joint with the bones of the wrist

In a hinged joint, the ends of the bones are connected across the joint by strong ligaments that allow bending in one plane only.

BALL-AND-SOCKET JOINT

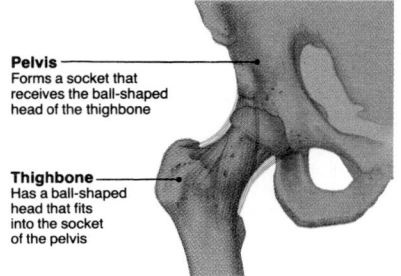

Pelvis
Forms a socket that receives the ball-shaped head of the thighbone

Thighbone
Has a ball-shaped head that fits into the socket of the pelvis

In a ball-and-socket joint, the rounded end of one bone fits into a hollow in the other, allowing swiveling movements in any plane.

SLIDING JOINT

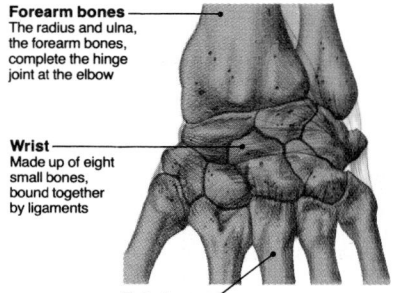

Forearm bones
The radius and ulna, the forearm bones, complete the hinge joint at the elbow

Wrist
Made up of eight small bones, bound together by ligaments

Palm bones
Have hinged and rotating joints where they meet the wristbones

Sliding joints have meeting surfaces that are almost flat, allowing the surfaces to slide over one another in a range of movements.

---

join•der (join'dər) n. **1.** The act of joining. **2.** *Law.* **a.** A joining of causes of action or defense in a suit. **b.** A joining of parties in a suit. **c.** The formal acceptance of an issue offered. [From French *joindre* (mistaken as a substantive), to JOIN.]

join•er (joi'nər) n. **1.** One that joins. **2.** *Chiefly British.* A person who makes furniture, house fittings, door frames, or the like. **3.** *Informal.* A person given to joining groups, organizations, or causes.

join•e•ry (joi'nə-rē) n. *Chiefly British.* **1.** The skill or craft of a joiner. **2.** Work done by a joiner, such as the fittings in a house.

joint (joint) n. *Abbr.* **jnt. 1. a.** A point or position at which two or more things are joined. **b.** A configuration in or by which two or more things are joined. **2.** The manner of joining. **3. a.** *Anatomy.* A point of connection or articulation between two or more bones, consisting of cartilage and connective tissue. **b.** A similar connection between segments in the body or leg of an arthropod. **4.** *Botany.* A point on a stem from which a leaf or branch may grow; a node. **5.** *Geology.* A fracture or crack in a rock mass along which no movement has occurred. **6.** A large cut of meat, such as the shoulder or leg, used for roasting. **7.** *Slang.* A cheap or disreputable gathering place, such as a nightclub or bar. **8.** *Slang.* Any dwelling or public establishment. Often used humorously. **9.** *Slang.* A marijuana cigarette. —**out of joint. 1.** Dislocated, as a bone. **2.** Not harmonious; inconsistent. **3.** Out of order; unsatisfactory.

~*adj.* **1.** Shared by or common to two or more: *a joint belief. The divorced couple received joint custody of the children.* **2.** Sharing with another or others: *joint heirs.* **3.** Formed, created, involving, or characterized by cooperation or united action: *a joint effort.* **4.** Involving both houses of a legislature: *a joint session.* **5.** *Law.* Regarded as one legal body united in identity of interest, ownership, or liability.

~*tr.v.* **jointed, jointing, joints. 1.** To combine or attach at a joint or joints. **2.** To provide or construct with joints. **3.** To cut (meat) into joints. [Middle English, from Old French, from the past participle of *joindre,* to JOIN.] —**joint•ly** adv.

Joint Chiefs of Staff *pl.n.* The principal military advisory group to the President of the United States, that is composed of the chiefs of the Army, Navy, and Air Force, and the commandant of the Marine Corps.

joint•ed (join'tĭd) adj. **1.** Having a joint or joints. **2.** Having a specified type of joint. Often used in combination: *double-jointed.*

joint•er (join'tər) n. **1.** One that joints; especially, a machine or tool used in making joints. **2.** A sharp triangular device connected to the beam of a plow to bury trash.

joint resolution n. A resolution passed by both houses of a bicameral legislature and eligible to become a law if signed by the chief executive or passed over his veto. Compare **concurrent resolution.**

joint stock n. Stock or capital funds of a company held jointly or in common by the owners.

joint-stock company (joint'stŏk') n. A business with a separate legal identity whose capital is held in shares by joint owners, each of whom enjoys limited liability.

join•ture (join'chər) n. *Law.* An estate settled on a woman by her husband, by an arrangement that takes effect in the event of her widowhood.

~*tr.v.* **jointured, -turing, -tures.** *Law.* To arrange a jointure for. [Middle English, from Old French, from Latin *junctūra,* JUNCTURE.]

joist (joist) n. Any of the parallel horizontal beams set from wall to wall to support the boards of a floor or ceiling.

~*tr.v.* **joisted, joisting, joists.** To construct with joists. [Middle English *gyste, giste,* from Old French *giste,* beam supporting a bridge, from Latin *jacitum,* from the past participle of *jacēre,* to lie down.]

jo•jo•ba (hə-hō'bə) n. A flowering shrub, *Simmondsia californica,* of southwestern North America, whose seeds contain a high proportion of liquid wax used in lubrication, polishes, pharmaceuticals, and cosmetics.

joke (jōk) n. **1.** An amusing story, especially one with a punch line. **2.** An amusing or jesting remark; a witticism, quip, or pun. **3.** A mischievous trick; a prank. **4. a.** An amusing or ludicrous incident or situation. **b.** The amusing aspect of something: *couldn't see the joke.* **5.** Something not to be taken seriously; triviality: *His accident was no joke.* **6.** An object of amusement or derision; a laughingstock.

~*v.* **joked, joking, jokes.** —*intr.* **1.** To tell or play jokes; to jest. **2.** To speak in fun; be facetious. —*tr.* To make fun of; to tease. [Latin *jocus,* jest, joke.] —**jok•ing•ly** adv.

Synonyms: *crack, gag, jest, quip, sally, wisecrack, witticism.*

jok•er (jō'kər) n. **1. a.** A person who tells or plays jokes; a clown; a prankster. **b.** An insolent person who seeks to make a show of cleverness. **2.** A playing card, usually printed with a picture of a jester, used in certain games as the highest ranking card or as a wild card. **3.** An unpredictable person or factor that may prove troublesome. Used chiefly in the phrase *joker in the pack.* **4.** *Slang.* A fellow; a man. **5.** A minor clause in a document, such as a legislative bill, that voids or changes its original purpose.

jo•lie laide (zhôl'ē lĕd') n., pl. **jolies laides.** *French.* A woman or girl whose features are not conventionally pretty but are nonetheless attractive. [Literally, "pretty ugly."]

Jo•li•et or **Jol•li•et** (jō'lē-ĕt', jō'lē-ĕt'), **Louis** (1645–1700). French-Canadian explorer of America. Traveling with six companions in birchbark canoes, he explored the Mississippi from its confluence with the Wisconsin River to its juncture with the Arkansas River (1673).

Jo·liot-Cu·rie (zhô-lyŏ′kü-rē′), **(Jean) Frédéric** (1900–58), born Jean Frédéric Joliot, and **Irène** (1897–56). French physicists. Irène Joliot-Curie was the daughter of Pierre and Marie Curie. She married Frédéric Joliot, her mother's assistant, who added Curie to his name. Together they discovered artificial radioactivity, for which they won the 1935 Nobel Prize for chemistry. Both died of cancer, after lifelong exposure to radioactivity.

jol·li·fi·ca·tion (jŏl′ə-fĭ-kā′shən) *n.* Festivity; revelry; merrymaking. [From JOLLY.]

jol·li·fy (jŏl′ə-fī′) *v.* **-fied, -fying, -fies.** —*tr.* To cause to become jolly; cheer up. —*intr.* To make merry; celebrate.

jol·li·ty (jŏl′ĭ-tē) *n.* Gaiety; merriment.

jol·ly (jŏl′ē) *adj.* **-lier, -liest. 1.** Full of merriment and good spirits; fun-loving; gay. **2.** Exhibiting or occasioning happiness or mirth; cheerful; festive. **3.** Greatly pleasing; enjoyable. ~*adv. British Informal.* Very; extremely: *a jolly good cook.* ~*tr.v.* **jollied, -lying, -lies. 1.** To keep amused or diverted for one's own purposes; humor. Often used with *up* or *along.* **2.** To poke fun at good-naturedly; tease. [Middle English *jolif, joli,* from Old French, gay, pleasant, probably from Old Norse *jōl,* name of the midwinter festival, yule, from Common Germanic *jegol* (unattested), YULE.] —**jol·li·ly** *adv.* —**jol·li·ness** *n.*
> *Synonyms:* blithe, convivial, jocular, jovial, merry.

jol·ly-boat (jŏl′ē-bōt′) *n.* A small boat kept by the stern of a larger ship. [Probably an alteration of earlier *jolywat*†.]

Jolly Rog·er *n.* A black flag bearing the emblematic white skull and crossbones of a pirate ship.

Jol·son (jōl′sən), **Al,** born Asa Yoelson (1886–1950). U.S. singer, born in Russia. He imitated black singers. His hits include "My Mammy" and "Sonny Boy." He starred in *The Jazz Singer,* the first major film with synchronized sound (1927).

jolt (jōlt) *v.* **jolted, jolting, jolts.** —*tr.* **1.** To shake or cause to move with a sudden jerk or blow. **2.** To bump into; jostle. **3.** To put into a specified condition by or as if by a jolt: *He was jolted out of his reverie by a police siren.* —*intr.* To proceed in an irregular, bumpy, or jerky fashion. ~*n.* **1.** A sudden jarring or jerking, as from a blow. **2.** An abrupt or unexpected shock or reversal: *a jolt to his complacency.* [16th century : origin obscure.] —**jolt·er** *n.* —**jolt·i·ly** *adv.* —**jolt·y** *adj.*

Jomada. Variant of **Jumada.**

Jo·nah[1] (jō′nə). An Old Testament prophet who was thrown overboard during a storm at sea caused by his disobedience to God. He was swallowed by a great fish and disgorged unharmed three days later. [Hebrew *Yōnāh,* "the moaning one," dove, pigeon, akin to *ānāh,* "moan."]

Jonah[2] *n.* A book of the Old Testament containing the story of Jonah.

Jonah[3] *n.* One thought to bring bad luck. [After JONAH.]

Jon·a·than[1] (jŏn′ə-thən). Eldest son of King Saul of Israel and friend of David. I Samuel 20.

Jonathan[2] *n.* A variety of red, late-ripening apple. [After *Jonathan* Hasbrouck (died 1846), U.S. jurist.]

Jonathan[3] *n.* **Brother Jonathan** *(see).*

Jones (jōnz), **(Alfred) Ernest** (1879–1958). British psychoanalyst, a follower of Sigmund Freud. Jones was instrumental in developing the use of psychoanalysis in Britain and North America.

Jones, (Everett) LeRoi. See Imamu Amiri Baraka.

Jones, Inigo (1573–1652). English architect. Jones studied in Italy and brought the Palladian classical style to England. Among the buildings he designed are the Queen's House, Greenwich, and the Banqueting Hall, Whitehall, London. He also introduced the use of movable scenery and the proscenium arch into England.

Jones, John Luther, known as "Casey" (1864–1900). U.S. railroad engineer. He died at the throttle while trying to stop his train from crashing into the rear of another train. All the passengers aboard Jones's train were saved. A friend wrote the well-known ballad about his heroic death.

Jones, John Paul, born John Paul (1747–92). U.S. naval hero, born in Scotland. He settled in Virginia and on the outbreak of the American Revolution gained a commission from Congress. In command of a French force he raided the British coast in 1779, destroying two British warships. Jones later became an admiral in the Russian navy. He died in Paris.

Jones, Mary Harris, known as "Mother Jones" (1830–1930). U.S. labor leader. From 1871 until shortly before her death, she traveled around the country, appearing wherever workers were striking against unfair management. She was known for her fiery speeches.

Jones, Robert Tyre, known as "Bobby" (1902–71). U.S. golfer. He was the only golfer ever to win the "Grand Slam," the British and U.S. amateur and open golf championships in the same year (1930).

jong (yŏng) *n. South African Informal.* Used as a familiar term of address to a man, woman, or child. [From Cape Dutch *jonger,* boy.]

jon·gleur (jŏng′glər; *French* zhôn-glœr′) *n.* A wandering minstrel and storyteller in medieval England and France. [French, from Old French, variant of *joglere,* JUGGLER.]

jon·quil (jŏng′kwĭl, jŏn′-) *n.* A widely cultivated plant, *Narcissus jonquilla,* having long, narrow leaves and short-tubed, fragrant yellow flowers. [New Latin *jonquilla,* from Spanish *junquillo,* diminutive of *junco,* rush, reed, from Latin *juncus*†.]

Jon·son (jŏn′sən), **Ben(jamin)** (1572–1637). English playwright and poet. His plays include *Volpone* (c. 1606), *The Alchemist* (1610), and *Bartholomew Fair* (1614).

jook. Variant of **juk.**

Jop·lin (jŏp′lĭn), **Scott** (1868–1917). U.S. pianist and composer. He developed a style of ragtime blending European musical forms and southern black rhythms. His most famous work is "Maple Leaf Rag" (1899).

Jor·dan (jôrd′n). River flowing south from Syria and Lebanon, partially marking the border between Israel and Jordan and emptying into the Dead Sea. St. John the Baptist baptized his followers in the river, which is 320 kilometers (199 miles) long.

Jordan, Hash·e·mite Kingdom of (hăsh′ə-mīt′). Formerly **Trans·jor·dan** (trăns′jôrd′n, trănz′-). A largely desert Arab state in southwest Asia. Most of its fertile land lies in the Jordan River valley and West Bank (Jordanian territory west of the Jordan, occupied by Israel since the Six-Day War of 1967). However, with foreign aid, the cultivated area is expanding. Jordan, then part of the Nabataean empire, fell to the Romans (*c.* A.D. 110), and later to the Arabs, Crusaders, and Turks (1516). After the Arab Revolt against the Turks in World War I, Transjordan, a British mandate east of the Jordan, led by the Hashemite family, was established (1923). Its independence became effective in 1948. The same year, Transjordan occupied the West Bank, adopting its present name in 1949. Resident units of the Palestine Liberation Organization provoked a civil war in 1970–71. Jordan assisted Syria in the Yom Kippur War (1973) and supported Iraq against Iran (1980–88). King Hussein, ruler since 1952, has been a mediating influence between the militant Arab states and the West. Jordan relies on exports of phosphates, vegetables, and fruit. Area, 97,740 square kilometers (37,738 square miles) including the West Bank. Population, 4,000,000. Capital, Amman. —**Jor·da·ni·an** (jôr-dā′nē-ən) *n. & adj.*

Jordan almond *n.* A large variety of almond from Málaga, Spain, used widely in confectionery. [By folk etymology from Middle English *jardin,* probably from Old French *jardin,* from Vulgar Latin *gardīnus* (unattested), GARDEN + ALMOND.]

jo·rum (jôr′əm) *n.* **1.** A large drinking bowl. **2.** The amount such a bowl contains. [Perhaps after *Joram* (II Samuel 8:10), who brought vessels of silver, gold, and brass to King David.]

jo·seph (jō′zəf) *n.* A long riding coat with a small cape, worn by women in the 18th century. [Probably after Joseph's (son of Jacob) "coat of many colors" (Genesis 37:3).]

Jo·seph[1] (jō′zəf). Son of Jacob and Rachel, sold into slavery in Egypt. Genesis 3; 37; 41; 45.

Joseph[2]. Husband of Mary the mother of Jesus. Matthew 1:16.

Joseph, Chief (c. 1840–1904). Nez Percé leader. In 1877 he led his people on a retreat to Canada to avoid relocation by the U.S. government. Chief Joseph and some 750 Nez Percé were captured by U.S. troops about 30 miles south of the Canadian border.

Jo·seph (jō′zəf, zhō′zĕf′), **Père,** born François le Clerc du Tremblay (1577–1638). French Capuchin friar and diplomat. Known as the *Eminence Grise* (Gray Eminence), he was a close friend and adviser of Cardinal Richelieu.

Jo·sé·phine (jō'zə-fēn', zhō-zā-fēn'), born Marie Joséphine Rose Tascher de la Pagerie (1763–1814). Wife of Napoleon I, Empress of France (1804–09). Born in Martinique, she married Napoleon in 1796 after the execution of her first husband, Viscount Beauharnais. Her failure to bear a child led Napoleon to repudiate their marriage in 1809, although she continued to advise him.

Joseph of Ar·i·ma·the·a (âr'ə-mə-thē'ə, är'-). An Israelite who provided a tomb for Jesus; the subject of many legends.

Joseph's coat *n.* A tropical plant, *Amaranthus tricolor,* cultivated for its variously colored foliage.

Jo·seph·son (jō'zəf-sən, -zĭf-), **Brian David** (1940–). British physicist. He predicted theoretically the Josephson effect and Josephson junction. He shared the 1973 Nobel Prize for physics with Leo Esaki and Ivar Giaever for this work.

Josephson effect *n. Physics.* Any of certain electrical phenomena observed at very low temperatures at a junction between two superconducting materials separated by a thin insulating layer. Under such conditions a direct current can flow with no applied voltage up to a critical value. A small direct voltage across the junction can cause an alternating current to flow. [Predicted theoretically by B.D. JOSEPHSON in 1962.]

Josephson junction *n. Physics.* A junction in which two superconductors at very low temperature are separated by a thin insulating layer such that Josephson effects can be observed. Josephson junctions are used in physics for accurate measurement of magnetic fields and definition of physical quantities and, in particular, for high-speed switches in advanced computers.

Josephson memory *n.* A computer memory consisting of a number of interconnected Josephson junctions, which are switched between conducting and superconducting states by variations in magnetic field.

Jo·se·phus (jō-sē'fəs), **Flavius** (A.D. 37–*c.* 100). Jewish general and historian. He was governor of Galilee and took part in the Jewish revolt against the Romans. His *History of the Jewish War* is the major source of information about the siege of Masada (72–73).

josh (jŏsh) *v.* **joshed, joshing, joshes.** *Informal.* —*tr.* To tease (someone) good-humoredly. —*intr.* To banter; joke.
~*n.* A teasing or joking remark. [19th century : origin obscure.]

Josh. Joshua (Old Testament).

Josh·u·a[1] (jŏsh'o͞o-ə) Also in Douay Bible **Jos·u·e** (-yo͞o-ē). Successor of Moses in the Exodus.

Joshua[2] *n.* Also in Douay Bible **Josue.** *Abbr.* **Josh.** An Old Testament book with the narrative of Joshua.

Joshua tree *n.* A treelike plant, *Yucca brevifolia,* of the southwestern United States, having sword-shaped leaves and greenish-white flowers. [From the greatly extended branches, recalling the outstretched arm of the prophet Joshua as he pointed with his spear to the city of Ai. Joshua 8:18.]

Joshua tree Yucca brevifolia *is the tallest and most treelike of the yuccas, growing to a height of about 10 meters (more than 30 feet). Yuccas are native to Mexico and the southern United States.*

Jo·si·ah (jō-sī'ə). Also in Douay Bible **Jo·si·as** (-əs). King of Judah (*c.* 638–*c.* 608 B.C.).

Jos·quin des Prés or **des Prez** (zhŏs-kăN' dā prā') (*c.* 1450–1521). Flemish composer. His musical style bridged the early and later Renaissance periods. He helped to introduce the northern polyphonic manner to Italy.

joss (jŏs) *n.* An image of a Chinese god. [Pidgin English, from Portuguese *deos,* god, from Latin *deus.*]

joss house *n.* A Chinese temple or shrine.

joss stick *n.* A stick of fragrant tinder mixed with clay and burned as incense.

jos·tle (jŏs'əl) *v.* **-tled, -tling, -tles.** —*intr.* **1.** To come in contact or collide repeatedly, as in a crowd; knock or push together. **2.** To make one's way by pushing or elbowing. **3.** To vie for an advantage or favorable position. **4.** To be in close proximity. —*tr.* **1. a.** To force (one's way) by pushing, shoving, and elbowing. **b.** To push or shove roughly or unceremoniously. **2.** To come into close contact or collision with. **3.** To vie with for an advantage or favorable position. **4.** To be in close proximity with: *"books written in all languages by men and women of all tempers, races, and ages jostle each other on the shelf"* (Virginia Woolf).
~*n.* A rough shove or push. [Earlier *justle,* from Middle English *justlen,* to come against in combat, frequentative of *justen,* from Old French *juster,* to JOUST.]

jot (jŏt) *n.* The smallest bit or particle; an iota.
~*tr.v.* **jotted, jotting, jots.** To write down briefly and hastily: *jot down an address.* [Earlier *iote,* from Latin *iōta,* from Greek, IOTA.]

jot·ter (jŏt'ər) *n. British.* A small pad or notebook for notes or messages.

jot·ting (jŏt'ĭng) *n. British.* A brief note or memorandum.

Jo·tun·heim (yô'to͝on-hām'). Also **Jö·tunn·heim** (yœ'-), **Jo·tunn·heim·r** (-hā'mər). *Norse Mythology.* **Utgard** *(see).*

jou·al (zho͞o-äl', zhwäl) *n. Canadian.* Uneducated, nonstandard, or dialectal Canadian French. [Respelling of French *cheval,* horse, as it would sound in nonstandard or dialectal Canadian French.]

Jou·bert (zho͞o'bâr'), **Petrus Jacobus,** known as "Piet" (1834–1900). Afrikaner statesman and commandant general of the Boer forces. Favoring political equality for British immigrants, he three times failed against Paul Kruger in bids for the presidency of the Transvaal (1883, 1893, 1898).

joule (jo͞ol) *n. Abbr.* **J** The International System unit of energy, equal to the work done when a current of 1 ampere is passed through a resistance of 1 ohm for 1 second. This is equivalent to the work done when the point of application of a force of 1 newton is displaced 1 meter in the direction of the force. [After James P. JOULE.]

Joule (jo͞ol), **James Prescott** (1818–89). British physicist who was the first to measure the mechanical equivalent of heat. A brewer by trade, he performed a number of experiments to prove that a given amount of electrical energy will always produce the same amount of heat. He provided Helmholtz with the evidence for the law of conservation of energy.

Joule's law *n.* **1.** The principle that the heat generated by an electric current passing through a wire is equal to the product of the potential difference between the ends of the wire, the current flowing through it, and the time for which it flows. **2.** The principle that the internal energy of a gas at a constant temperature is independent of the volume of the gas. This law applies only to ideal gases; in real gases the internal energy varies with volume as a result of intermolecular forces.

Joule-Thom·son effect (jo͞ol-tŏm'sən) *n.* The fall in temperature of a gas when it expands through a small hole, caused by work being done against the intermolecular forces within the gas. Also called "Joule-Kelvin effect."

jounce (jouns) *v.* **jounced, jouncing, jounces.** —*intr.* To move with bumps and jolts. —*tr.* To cause to jounce.
~*n.* A rough, jolting bounce. [Middle English *jouncen*†.]

jour. **1.** journal; journalist. **2.** journeyman.

jour·nal (jûr'nəl) *n. Abbr.* **J., jour.** **1.** A daily record of occurrences or transactions, especially: **a.** A personal record of experiences and reflections; a diary. **b.** An official record of daily proceedings, as of a legislative body. **c.** A ship's log. **2.** *Bookkeeping.* **a.** A daybook. **b.** A book of original entry in a double-entry system, listing all transactions and indicating the accounts to which they belong. **3. a.** A newspaper. **b.** A periodical presenting news or containing scholarly articles on a particular subject: *a medical journal.* **c.** Used as part of the title of certain newspapers or periodicals. **4.** The part of a shaft or axle supported by a bearing. [Middle English, from Old French *jurnal, jornal,* from *journal, jornel,* "daily," from Late Latin *diurnālis,* diurnal, from Latin *diurnus,* daily, from *diēs,* day.]

journal box *n.* A housing enclosing a journal and its bearings.

jour·nal·ese (jûr'nə-lēz', -lēs') *n.* The slick, superficial style of writing often held to be characteristic of newspapers and magazines. [JOURNAL + -ESE.]

jour·nal·ism (jûr'nə-lĭz'əm) *n.* **1. a.** The collecting, reporting, writing, photographing, editing, and publishing of news or articles for any of the media, especially for newspapers and magazines. **b.** The business or occupation of working in the news media. **2.** Material written for publication in a newspaper or magazine. **3.** A style of writing associated with newspapers and magazines, characterized by direct presentation of facts or occurrences with little attempt at analysis or interpretation. **4.** Newspapers and magazines collectively. **5.** An academic course in journalism. **6.** Written material of current interest or wide popular appeal.

jour·nal·ist (jûr'nə-lĭst) *n.* **1.** *Abbr.* **jour.** A person whose occupation is journalism. **2.** A person who keeps a journal.

jour·nal·is·tic (jûr'nə-lĭs'tĭk) *adj.* Pertaining to or characteristic of journalism or journalists. **—jour·nal·is·ti·cal·ly** *adv.*

jour·nal·ize (jûr'nə-līz') *v.* **-ized, -izing, -izes.** —*tr.* To record in a journal. —*intr.* To keep a journal. **—jour·nal·iz·er** *n.*

jour·ney (jûr'nē) *n., pl.* **-neys.** **1. a.** An act of traveling from one place to another; a trip. **b.** A long overland trip as distinguished from a voyage or a flight. **2. a.** The distance traveled on a journey. **b.** The time required for such a trip. **3.** A process of transition or progress: *our journey through life.*
~*v.* **journeyed, -neying, -neys.** —*intr.* To travel; make a trip. —*tr.* To travel over or through. [Middle English *journey, jorne,* period of travel, a day's traveling, from Old French *jornee,* from Vulgar Latin *diurnāta* (unattested), from Latin *diurnum,* daily portion, neuter of *diurnus,* daily, from *diēs,* day.] **—jour·ney·er** *n.*

jour·ney·man (jûr'nē-mən) *n., pl.* **-men** (-mĭn). **1.** *Abbr.* **jour.** One who has fully served an apprenticeship in a trade or craft and is a qualified worker in another's employ. **2.** Any competent workman. [Middle English : JOURNEY (in the dialectal sense of "a day's work") + MAN.]

jour·ney·work (jûr'nē-wûrk') *n.* **1.** The work of a journeyman. **2.** Menial or routine work.

joust (jŭst, joust, jo͞ost) *n.* Also **just** (jŭst). **1.** A combat with lances between two mounted knights or men-at-arms; a tilting match. **2.** *Usually* **jousts.** A series of these matches; a tournament. **3.** Any combat or exchange suggestive of a joust.
~*intr.v.* **jousted, jousting, jousts.** Also **just.** To engage in such combat or exchange; tilt. [Middle English, from Old French *juste, jouste,* from *juster,* to join battle, joust, from Vulgar Latin *juxtāre* (unattested), to come together, from Latin *juxtā,* close together.]

Jove (jōv) *n.* **1.** The god **Jupiter** *(see).* **2.** *Poetic.* The planet Jupiter. **—by Jove.** A mild oath used to express surprise or to give emphasis. [Middle English, from Latin *Jov-,* stem of the oblique cases of Old Latin *Jovis.*]

jo·vi·al (jō'vē-əl) *adj.* Marked by hearty conviviality. —See Synonyms at **jolly.** [Originally "born under the influence of Jupiter" (the planet, regarded as the source of happiness), from French *jovial,* from Italian *gioviale,* from *Giove,* Jove, from Latin *Jov-.*] **—jo·vi·al·i·ty** *n.* **—jo·vi·al·ly** *adv.*

Jo·vi·an (jō'vē-ən) *adj.* **1.** Of, pertaining to, or resembling the god Jove. **2.** Of, relating to, or occurring on the planet Jupiter.

Jow·ett (jou′ĕt, -ĭt), **Benjamin** (1817–93). British classical scholar and master of Balliol College, Oxford (1870–93). His work *The Interpretation of Scripture* (1860) provoked charges of heresy from orthodox Anglicans. He also published classical translations, the most notable being of Plato's *Dialogues.*

jowl[1] (joul) *n.* **1.** The jaw, especially the lower jaw. **2.** The cheek. [Middle English *chawle, chauel,* Old English *ceafl.*]

jowl[2] *n.* **1.** The flesh under the lower jaw, especially when plump or flaccid. **2.** A similar fleshy part, such as a dewlap or a wattle. [Middle English *cholle,* probably Old English *ceole, ceolu,* throat.]

joy (joi) *n.* **1.** A condition or deep feeling of pleasure or delight; happiness; gladness. **2.** The expression or manifestation of such a feeling. **3.** A source or object of pleasure or satisfaction. —See Synonyms at **pleasure.**
∼*v.* **joyed, joying, joys.** —*intr.* To take pleasure; rejoice. —*tr. Archaic.* **1.** To fill with joy. **2.** To enjoy. [Middle English *joy(e),* from Old French *joie, joye,* from Vulgar Latin *gaudia* (unattested), from Latin, plural of *gaudium,* gladness, delight, from *gaudēre,* to rejoice.]

joy·ance (joi′əns) *n.* **1.** Enjoyment; delight. **2.** Merrymaking; festivity. [JOY + -ANCE.]

Joyce (jois), **James Augustine Aloysius** (1882–1941). Irish novelist, poet, and dramatist. He lived in Europe from 1904, publishing his first collection of stories, *Dubliners,* in 1914 and his first, largely autobiographical novel, *Portrait of the Artist as a Young Man,* in 1916. He is best known for *Ulysses* (1922), a novel that minutely describes the events of a single day in Dublin and is noted for its linguistic innovation. **—Joy·ce·an** (joi′sē-ən) *adj.*

Joyce, William, also known as "Lord Haw-Haw" (1906–46). Nazi propagandist, born in the United States of Irish parentage. During World War II he made propaganda broadcasts from Germany, delivered in the upper-class accent that earned him his nickname. He was tried in Britain and executed for treason after the war.

joy·ful (joi′fəl) *adj.* Feeling, causing, or expressing joy. —See Synonyms at **glad.** **—joy·ful·ly** *adv.* **—joy·ful·ness** *n.*

joy·less (joi′lĭs) *adj.* Destitute of joy; cheerless; dismal. **—joy·less·ly** *adv.* **—joy·less·ness** *n.*

joy·ous (joi′əs) *adj.* Feeling or causing joy; joyful. —See Synonyms at **glad.** **—joy·ous·ly** *adv.* **—joy·ous·ness** *n.*

joy ride *n.* **1.** A ride taken in a car, especially a stolen car, simply for fun and often for the thrills provided by reckless driving. **2.** A hazardous, reckless, and often costly venture. **—joy-ride** (joi′rīd′) *v.*

joy·stick (joi′stĭk′) *n. Informal.* **1.** The control stick of an aircraft. **2.** A manual control device linked to a computer, used especially in making moves in a video game.

J.P. justice of the peace.

J particle, j psi particle *n.* The **psi particle** *(see).*

jr., Jr. junior.

J.S.D. Doctor of Juristic Science. [Latin *Juris Scientiae Doctor*]

Juan Car·los (hwän kär′lōs, -lōs) (1938–). King of Spain (1975–). Acceding to the throne on the death of Franco, he helped restore parliamentary democracy. His declared opposition to an attempted military coup (February 1981) contributed to its failure.

Juan de Fu·ca Strait (hwän′də fyo͞o′kə, wän′). Inlet of the Pacific Ocean, *c.* 160 kilometers (100 miles) long, between northwestern Washington State and Vancouver Island, British Columbia.

ju·ba (jo͞o′bə) *n.* A group dance, probably of West African origin, characterized by complex rhythmic clapping and body movements and practiced on plantations in the southern United States during the 18th and 19th centuries. [Probably from Zulu.]

Ju·bal (jo͞o′bəl). A descendant of Cain and the reputed inventor of musical instruments. Genesis 4:21.

jub·bah (jo͝ob′ə) *n.* Also **jib·bah** (jĭb′ə). A long, loose, open, outer garment with sleeves, worn by Muslims and Parsees. [Arabic.]

ju·be (jo͞o′bē) *n.* A loft or rood screen and gallery that separate the choir from the nave in a church. [French *jubé,* from Medieval Latin, opening word of the prayer *Jube, Domine, benedicere,* bid, Lord, a blessing : perhaps applied to the structure because the prayer was recited there by the deacon.]

ju·bi·lant (jo͞o′bə-lənt) *adj.* Filled with or expressing great joy, especially through success or triumph. [Latin *jūbilāns* (stem *jūbilant-*), present participle of *jūbilāre,* to JUBILATE.] **—ju·bi·lance, ju·bi·lan·cy** *n.* **—ju·bi·lant·ly** *adv.*

ju·bi·late (jo͞o′bə-lāt′) *intr.v.* **-lated, -lating, -lates.** To rejoice; exult. [Latin *jūbilāre,* to raise a shout of joy.]

Ju·bi·la·te (jo͞o′bə-lä′tē, -lä′-) *n.* **1.** The 100th Psalm in the King James Bible, or the 99th in the Vulgate and the Douay Bible. **2.** A musical setting of the Jubilate. **3.** The third Sunday after Easter. **4.** A song or outburst of joy and triumph. [Latin *jūbilāte!,* rejoice! (the first word in the Jubilate), imperative of *jūbilāre,* to JUBILATE.]

ju·bi·la·tion (jo͞o′bə-lā′shən) *n.* **1.** The state of being jubilant; exultation. **2.** A celebration or other expression of joy.

ju·bi·lee (jo͞o′bə-lē′) *n.* **1. a.** A special anniversary; especially, a 25th, 50th, 60th, or 75th anniversary. **b.** The celebration of such an anniversary. **2.** A season or occasion of joyful celebration. **3.** Jubilation; rejoicing. **4.** In the Old Testament, a year of rest to be observed by the Israelites every 50th year, during which slaves were to be set free, alienated property restored to its former owners, and the land left untilled. Leviticus 25:8–17. **5.** *Roman Catholic Church.* A year during which plenary indulgence may be obtained by the performance of certain pious acts. It is usually granted at intervals of 25 years. [Middle English, from Old French *jubilé,* from Late Latin *jūbilaeus (annus),* "(year) of jubilee," alteration (influenced by Latin *jūbilāre,* to JUBILATE) of Late Greek *iōbēlaios,* from *iōbēlos,* jubilee, from Hebrew *yōbhēl,* "ram's horn" (used to proclaim the jubilee), originally, "leading animal," akin to *hōbhīl,* to lead, conduct.]

Jud. **1.** Judges (Old Testament). **2.** Judith (Apocrypha).

J.U.D. Doctor of Canon and Civil Law. [Latin *Juris Utriusque Doctor,* "Doctor of either law"]

Ju·dae·a or **Ju·de·a** (jo͞o-dē′ə). The southern part of ancient Palestine. The Kingdom of Judah, located here, lay south of Israel. Under David, the two kingdoms were united, the Judaean city of Jerusalem becoming his capital. Judah became independent in *c.* 922 B.C., later falling to the Assyrians, Babylonians, Greeks, and Persians. In A.D. 135 it was absorbed into the Roman province of Syria. **—Ju·dae·an, Ju·de·an** *n. & adj.*

Ju·dah[1] (jo͞o′də). Also in Douay Bible **Ju·da.** Son of Jacob and Leah; ancestor of one of the twelve tribes of Israel. [Hebrew *Yəhūdāh,* "praised."]

Judah[2] *n.* The tribe of Israel descended from Judah.

Judah[3]. An ancient kingdom in southern Palestine, occupied by the tribes of Judah and Benjamin and governed by the descendants of Solomon. I Kings 11:31, 12:17–21. See **Judaea.**

Ju·da·ic (jo͞o-dā′ĭk) *adj.* Also **Ju·da·i·cal** (-ĭ-kəl). Of or pertaining to Jews or Judaism. [Latin *Jūdaicus,* from Greek *Ioudaikos,* from *Ioudaios,* JEW.] **—Ju·da·i·cal·ly** *adv.*

Ju·da·i·ca (jo͞o-dā′ĭ-kə) *pl.n.* Books, documents, and artifacts representing the literature, history, and culture of the Jewish people. [Latin, "Jewish matters."]

Ju·da·ism (jo͞o′dē-ĭz′əm) *n.* **1.** The monotheistic religion of the Jewish people, tracing its origins to Abraham, having its spiritual and ethical principles embodied chiefly in the Old Testament and the Talmud. **2.** Conformity to the traditional ceremonies and rites of the Jewish religion. **3.** The cultural, spiritual, and social way of life of the Jewish people. **4.** The Jewish people. [Late Latin *Jūdaismus,* from Greek *Ioudaismos,* from *Ioudaios,* JEW.] **—Ju·da·ist** *n.* **—Ju·da·is·tic** *adj.* See feature, next page.

Ju·da·ize (jo͞o′dē-īz′) *v.* **-ized, -izing, -izes.** —*tr.* To bring into conformity with or convert to Judaism. —*intr.* To adopt Jewish customs and beliefs. **—Ju·da·i·za·tion** *n.* **—Ju·da·iz·er** *n.*

Ju·das[1] (jo͞o′dəs), called "Judas Iscariot." One of the Twelve Apostles, who betrayed Jesus for 30 pieces of silver. [Late Latin *Jūdas,* from Greek *Ioudas,* from Hebrew *Yəhūdāh,* JUDAH.]

Judas[2], known as "Saint Jude" to distinguish him from Judas Iscariot. One of the Twelve Apostles.

Judas[3] *n.* **1.** One who betrays under the appearance of friendship. **2.** *Usually* **judas.** A one-way peephole in a door. [From JUDAS (Iscariot).]

Judas Maccabeus. See **Maccabeus.**

Judas tree *n.* Any of various trees of the genus *Cercis;* especially, the ornamental Eurasian species *C. siliquastrum,* having clusters of pinkish-red flowers that appear before the leaves. Also called "redbud." [From a belief that Judas Iscariot hanged himself on it.]

Juddah. See **Jiddah.**

jud·der (jŭd′ər) *intr.v.* **-dered, -dering, -ders.** *Chiefly British.* To shake, shudder, or vibrate violently.
∼*n. Chiefly British.* A juddering movement, especially in a mechanical system. [Probably from JAR + SHUDDER.]

Jude (jo͞od) *n.* The Epistle of Jude, a book of the New Testament often attributed to Saint Jude.

Judea. See **Judaea.**

Judeo–. *prefix.* Indicates Judaism; for example, *Judeo-Christian.* [From Latin *judaeus,* Jewish.]

Ju·de·o-Ger·man (jo͞o-dā′ō-jûr′mən) *n.* **Yiddish** *(see).*

Ju·de·o-Span·ish (jo͞o-dā′ō-spăn′ĭsh) *n.* **Ladino** *(see).*

Judg. Judges (Old Testament).

judge (jŭj) *v.* **judged, judging, judges.** —*tr.* **1. a.** To pass judgment upon in a court of law. **b.** To sit in judgment upon; try; hear. **2.** To determine authoritatively after deliberation, especially: **a.** To decide or settle (a controversy, for example). **b.** To appraise discriminatingly as an expert: *"You can always judge the quality of a cook or restaurant by roast chicken"* (Julia Child). **c.** To declare after deliberation: *They judged her a witch.* **d.** To choose the winners of (a competition). **3.** To form an appraisal or estimate of: *judge character; judge distances.* **4.** To criticize; censure. **5.** To consider, especially as a result of careful thought; conclude: *judged that the moment was right.* —*intr.* **1.** To act or decide as a judge; pass judgment. **2.** To form an opinion or estimation; make a critical determination or appraisal.
∼*n.* **1.** *Abbr.* **J.** A public official who hears and decides cases brought before a court of law for the purpose of administering justice; justice; magistrate. **2.** An appointed arbiter in a contest or competition. **3.** One who makes critical judgments: *He's a poor judge of character.* **4.** A leader of the Israelites during a period of about 400 years between the death of Joshua and the accession of Saul. [Middle English *jugen,* from Old French *jugier,* from Latin *jūdicāre,* from *jūdex* (stem *jūdic-*), judge.]
Synonyms: arbiter, arbitrator, referee, umpire.

judge advocate *n., pl.* **judge advocates.** *Abbr.* **J.A.** **1.** A commissioned officer in the U.S. Army assigned to the Judge Advocate General's Corps. **2.** A staff officer serving as legal adviser to a commander. **3.** An officer acting as prosecutor at a court-martial.

Judge Advocate General *n., pl.* **Judge Advocates General** or **Judge Advocate Generals.** A major general in the U.S. Army or Air Force who serves as senior legal officer.

Judg·es (jŭj′əz) *n. Used with a singular verb. Abbr.* **Jud., Judg.** A

Judas tree *Pink flowers appear on the Judas tree's bare branches in early spring. It is said to be blushing for Judas Iscariot who, according to some folk tradition, hanged himself from one of the trees, but its name may simply refer to the biblical province of Judah, now Judaea, where it grows wild.*

PRONUNCIATION KEY

ă, pat; ā, pay; âr, care;
ä, father, are; b, bib;
ch, church; d, deed; ĕ, pet;
ē, be; f, fife; g, gag; h, hat;
hw, which; ĭ, pit; ī, pie;
îr, pier; j, judge; k, kick;
l, lid, needle; m, mum;
n, no, sudden; ng, thing;
ŏ, pot; ō, toe; ô, paw, for;
oi, noise; ou, out; o͝o, book;
o͞o, boot; p, pop; r, roar;
s, sauce; sh, ship, dish;
t, tight; th, thin, path;
th, this, bathe; ŭ, cut; ûr, fur;
v, valve; w, with; y, yes;
z, zebra, size; zh, vision;
ə, about, item, edible, gallop, circus, peaceful

IN FOREIGN WORDS:

à, *Fr.* ami; œ, *Fr.* feu, *Ger.* schön; ü, *Fr.* tu, *Ger.* über;
KH, *Ger.* ich, *Scot.* loch;
N, *Fr.* bon; y', *Fr.* Compiègne

STRESS MARKS:

Primary stress: ′
in·cite′ (ĭn-sīt′)
Secondary stress: ′
in′sight′ (ĭn′sīt′)

Judaism

THE ONE GOD OF ABRAHAM
Ancient faith that binds the Jewish people

Judaism is the world's oldest surviving monotheistic religion, and from it both Christianity and Islam have arisen.

Jewish history tells that 4,000 years ago God made a covenant with Abraham, the father of the Jewish nation. He promised the land of Canaan (later called Palestine) to the Jews if Abraham would spread to all mankind the lesson that there is one God. Famine drove the Jews from Canaan to Egypt, where they became slaves. Moses was called by God to lead them back to their promised land. When they reached Mount Sinai, God (Yahweh or Jehovah) appeared to Moses, renewed the covenant made with Abraham, and revealed to Moses the Law, which included the Ten Commandments. This is regarded as the foundation of Judaism.

More formal shape was given to the religion during the latter part of the 6th century B.C., when the Jews returned to Palestine from a period of exile in Babylon. The Law and other sacred writings were studied and interpreted by rabbis, or teachers, and a detailed social code grew up.

The principles of Judaism are contained in the Torah, or Law—incorporated in the Hebrew Bible, the Old Testament, as the first five books—and in the Talmud, the ancient commentary on the Law. One God is the creator of the universe who cares for and saves the world. Obedience to the sacred teachings will win redemption. Jews hope for God to send a messiah, an ideal ruler, who will bring all mankind under just and divine rule. Christians believe that Jesus was this messiah.

Even before the Christian era, most Jews lived outside Palestine. Of today's 13 million Jews, 6 million live in the United States, 3 million in Israel, and half a million in Britain.

FOUND IN A CATACOMB *Hebrew ritual objects are portrayed on the base of a 2nd-century A.D. gold goblet found in a Jewish catacomb in Rome. The original objects are thought to have come from the Jewish Temple in Jerusalem, when it was desecrated by Antiochus IV of Syria about 170 B.C.*

THE SAVING OF THE JEWS *The story of Esther—who married Ahasuerus, a 6th century B.C. Persian king, and persuaded him to prevent a massacre of her fellow Jews—is told in this 18th-century illuminated scroll. The annual Feast of Lots, or Purim, is named after the lots drawn to choose the proposed day of slaughter. At Purim, Jews exchange gifts and make donations to the poor.*

TO THE PROMISED LAND *Throughout their bondage in Egypt the Jews never lost faith in God or in His Covenant made with Abraham that one day they would live in the Promised Land. This picture (left) in a 15th-century Jewish prayer book shows Moses leading his people across the Red Sea back to Palestine, their earlier home, that famine had forced them to leave.*

book of the Old Testament containing the history of the Israelites during the rule of the judges.

judge·ship (jŭj′shĭp) *n.* The office, duties, or jurisdiction of a judge.

judg·mat·ic (jŭj-măt′ĭk) *adj.* Also **judg·mat·i·cal** (-ĭ-kəl). *Informal.* Judicious. [From JUDGMENT.] —**judg·mat·i·cal·ly** *adv.*

judg·ment (jŭj′mənt) *n.* Also **judge·ment.** **1. a.** The capacity to appraise, discriminate, and compare, and so arrive at a sound evaluation; discernment. **b.** The capacity to make reasonable decisions, especially in regard to the practical affairs of life; good sense; wisdom. **c.** The exercise of such a capacity. **2.** A formal decision, as of an arbiter in a contest. **3.** A discriminating appraisal; an authoritative opinion. **4.** Estimation: *make a judgment of the distance.* **5.** An assertion of something believed; idea; opinion: *It's my judgment that we ought to leave soon.* **6.** Criticism; censure. **7.** *Law.* **a.** A verdict by a court of law; a judicial decision. **b.** A court act creating or affirming an obligation, such as a debt. **c.** A writ in witness of such an act. —See Synonyms at **opinion, reason.** [Middle English *jugement,* from Old French, from *jugier,* to JUDGE.]

judg·ment·al (jŭj-mĕn′tl) *adj.* **1.** Of, pertaining to, or involving a judgment. **2.** Given to making judgments, especially moral judgments.

Judgment Day *n.* **1.** In Judaism, Christianity, and Islam, the day of God's final judgment upon mankind. **2.** Any day of reckoning or final judgment. Also called "Day of Judgment."

ju·di·ca·ble (jōō′dĭ-kə-bəl) *adj.* **1.** Capable of being judged. **2.** Liable to be judged. [Late Latin *jūdicābilis,* from Latin *jūdicāre,* to JUDGE.]

ju·di·ca·tive (jōō′dĭ-kā′tĭv, -kə-tĭv) *adj.* Having the capacity to judge; judicial. [Medieval Latin *jūdicātivus,* from Latin *jūdicāre,* to JUDGE.]

ju·di·ca·tor (jōō′dĭ-kā′tər) *n.* One who acts as judge. [Late Latin *jūdicātor,* from Latin *jūdicāre,* to JUDGE.]

ju·di·ca·to·ry (jōō′dĭ-kə-tôr′ē, -tōr′ē) *n., pl.* **-ries. 1.** A court of justice; a tribunal. **2.** A system of courts of law for the administration of justice; a judiciary.
—*adj.* Of or pertaining to the administration of justice. [Medieval Latin *jūdicātōrium,* from Latin *jūdicāre,* to JUDGE.]

ju·di·ca·ture (jōō′dĭ-kə-chōōr′) *n.* **1.** The administering of justice. **2.** The position, function, or authority of a judge. **3.** A court of law. **4.** A system of law courts and their judges. [Old French, from Medieval Latin *jūdicātūra,* from Latin *jūdicāre,* to JUDGE.]

ju·di·cial (jōō-dĭsh′əl) *adj.* **1.** Of, pertaining to, or proper to courts of law or to the administration of justice: *the judicial branch of the government.* Compare **executive, legislative.** **2.** Decreed by or proceeding from a court of justice. **3.** Pertaining or appropriate to the office of a judge. **4.** Characterized by or expressing judgment. **5.** *Theology.* Proceeding from a divine judgment. [Middle English, from Old French, from Latin *jūdiciālis,* from *jūdicium,* judgment, from *jūdex* (stem *jūdic-*), JUDGE.] **—ju·di·cial·ly** *adv.*

judicial separation *n.* A court order recognizing that husband and wife are living apart and regulating their mutual rights and liabilities. Also called "legal separation."

ju·di·ci·ar·y (jo͞o-dĭsh′ē-ĕr′ē) *adj.* Of or pertaining to courts, judges, or judicial decisions.
~*n., pl.* **judiciaries.** **1.** The judicial branch of government. Compare **executive, legislature.** **2.** A system of courts of justice. **3.** Judges collectively. [Latin *jūdiciārius,* from *jūdicium,* judgment. See **judicial.**]

ju·di·cious (jo͞o-dĭsh′əs) *adj.* Having or exhibiting sound judgment. [Old French *judicieux,* from Latin *jūdicium.* See **judicial.**] **—ju·di·cious·ly** *adv.* **—ju·di·cious·ness** *n.*

Ju·dith¹ (jo͞o′dĭth). In the Apocrypha, a Jewish woman who rescued her people by slaying the Assyrian general Holofernes.

Judith² *n.* A book of the Apocrypha and the Douay Bible relating the story of Judith.

ju·do (jo͞o′dō) *n.* A modern form of jujitsu applying principles of balance and leverage, often played as a sport. [Japanese *jūdō* : *jū,* soft (see **jujitsu**) + *dō,* way.] **—ju·do·ist** *n.*

ju·do·gi (jo͞o-dō′gə) *n.* A white costume worn by judo players, consisting of loose trousers and a loose-sleeved jacket fastened by a belt. [Japanese.]

ju·do·ka (jo͞o′dō-kä) *n.* One who practices judo; judo player. [Japanese.]

Ju·dy (jo͞o′dē) *n., pl.* **-ies.** A character in a puppet show. See **Punch.**

jug (jŭg) *n.* **1.** A small pitcher. **2. a.** A vessel of earthenware, glass, or metal with a lip or spout, a handle, and sometimes a stopper or cap, made for holding and pouring liquids. **b.** The contents of a jug. **c.** The amount of liquid a jug will hold. **3.** *British Informal.* A glass for beer or some other alcoholic drink, especially one with a handle. **4.** *Slang.* Jail.
~*tr.v.* **jugged, jugging, jugs.** **1.** To stew (a hare, for example) in an earthenware vessel. **2.** *Slang.* To put in jail. [From *Jug,* pet form of *Joan* or *Judith.*]

ju·ga. A plural of **jugum.**

ju·gal (jo͞o′gəl) *adj.* Of or pertaining to the zygomatic bone.
~*n.* The zygomatic bone. Also called "jugal bone."

ju·gate (jo͞o′gāt′) *adj.* Joined in or forming a pair or pairs. Said especially of compound leaves. [From New Latin *jugum,* yoke, from Latin.]

jug band *n.* A country-and-western musical group playing improvised instruments, such as empty jugs and washboards.

JUG·FET (jŭg′fĕt) *n. Electronics.* A type of field-effect transistor in which the gate is a p-n junction with the conducting channel. [*Ju*nction-*G*ate *F*ield-*E*ffect *T*ransistor.]

jug·ger·naut (jŭg′ər-nôt′) *n.* **1.** Anything that draws blind and destructive devotion, or to which people are ruthlessly sacrificed, such as a belief or institution. **2.** *British.* A very large, heavy motor vehicle, especially a long-distance truck. [From JUGGERNAUT.]

Jug·ger·naut (jŭg′ər-nôt′) *n.* **1.** *Hinduism.* Also **Jag·an·nath** (jŭg′ə-nät′, -nôt′). A title of the deity Vishnu. **2.** A huge car or wagon on which an idol of the god Vishnu is drawn in procession; specifically, such a vehicle used in an annual procession in Puri, in the Indian state of Orissa. [From Hindi *Jagannath,* from Sanskrit *Jagannātha* : *jagat-,* world + *nāthás,* lord.]

jug·gle (jŭg′əl) *v.* **-gled, -gling, -gles.** —*tr.* **1.** To keep (two or more balls, plates, or other objects) in the air at one time by alternately tossing and catching. **2.** To keep (more than one activity) in motion or progress at one time. **3.** To attempt to balance or otherwise cope with: *juggle a handbag and glass at a cocktail party.* **4.** To manipulate, especially in order to deceive: *juggle figures in a ledger.* —*intr.* **1.** To perform the tricks of a juggler. **2.** To use trickery to deceive.
~*n.* **1.** An act of juggling. **2.** A piece of trickery for some dishonest purpose. [Middle English *jogelen,* from Old French *jogler,* from Latin *joculārī,* to jest. See **juggler.**]

jug·gler (jŭg′lər) *n.* **1.** An entertainer who performs tricks of dexterity; especially, one who juggles balls or other objects. **2.** One who uses tricks, deception, or fraud. [Middle English *iugelere, iugelour,* jester, magician, from Old French *joglere, juglere,* from Latin *joculātor,* from *joculārī,* to jest, from *joculus,* diminutive of *jocus,* jest, joke.]

jug·gler·y (jŭg′lə-rē) *n., pl.* **-ies.** **1.** The art or performance of a juggler. **2.** Trickery; deception.

Jugoslavia. See **Yugoslavia.**

jug·u·lar (jŭg′yə-lər) *adj.* **1.** Of, pertaining to, or located in the region of the neck or throat. **2.** Of, designating, or having pelvic fins in front of the pectoral fins.
~*n.* A jugular vein. [Late Latin *jugulāris,* from Latin *jugulum,* collarbone, diminutive of *jugum,* yoke.]

jugular vein *n.* Any of several veins in the neck. The *internal jugular* is a large paired vein conveying blood from the brain, face, and neck to the subclavian vein. The *external jugular* is a smaller paired vein taking blood from the face, scalp, and neck to the subclavian vein.

ju·gum (jo͞o′gəm) *n., pl.* **-ga** (-gə) or **-gums.** A paired or yokelike structure, such as a pair of opposite leaflets, a ridge or furrow connecting two parts of a bone, or a lobe joining the bases of the forewings and hind wings of certain insects. [New Latin, from Latin *jugum,* yoke.]

juice (jo͞os) *n.* **1. a.** Any fluid naturally contained in plant or animal tissue. **b.** Any bodily secretion. **c.** Any extracted fluid, especially that of a fruit. **2. a.** The essence or animating spirit of something. **b.** Vigorous life and vitality. **3.** *Slang.* **a.** Electric current. **b.** Fuel for an engine. **4.** *Slang.* Alcoholic drink. **—stew in one's own juice.** To suffer from problems of one's own making.
~*tr.v.* **juiced, juicing, juices.** **1.** To extract the juice from. **2.** *Slang.* To make lively. Used with *up.* [Middle English *iuys, jus,* from Old French *jus,* from Latin *jūs,* broth, sauce, juice.]

juic·er (jo͞o′sər) *n.* A kitchen appliance for extracting juice from fruits and vegetables.

juic·y (jo͞o′sē) *adj.* **-ier, -iest.** **1.** Full of juice; succulent. **2.** Richly interesting; suggestive; racy: *a juicy bit of gossip.* **—juic·i·ly** *adv.* **—juic·i·ness** *n.*

ju·jit·su (jo͞o-jĭt′so͞o) *n.* Also **ju·jut·su, jiu·jit·su, jiu·jut·su.** A Japanese art of self-defense or hand-to-hand combat based on maneuvers that seek to turn an opponent's weight and strength against himself. [Japanese *jūjitsu* : *jū,* soft, yielding, + *jitsu,* art.]

ju·ju (jo͞o′jo͞o′) *n.* **1.** An object used as a fetish, charm, or amulet in West Africa. **2.** The supernatural power ascribed to such an object. [Probably of West African origin.] **—ju·ju·ism** *n.*

ju·jube (jo͞o′jo͞ob′) *n.* **1. a.** Any of several spiny trees of the genus *Ziziphus;* especially, *Z. jujuba,* native to the Old World, having small yellowish flowers and dark red fruit. **b.** The fleshy, edible fruit of this tree. Also called "Chinese date." **2.** A fruit-flavored, usually chewy candy or lozenge. [Middle English *iuiube,* from Old French *jujube* or Medieval Latin *jujuba,* both from Latin *zizyphum,* from Greek *zizuphon*†.]

juk, jook (jo͝ok) *tr.v.* **juked** or **jooked, juking** or **jooking, jukes** or **jooks.** *West Indian Informal.* To prick; jab.
~*n. West Indian Informal.* A prick or jab. [West African, probably Fulani *jukka,* to spur, poke.]

juke box (jo͞ok) *n.* A coin-operated phonograph, typically encased in an illuminated and decorated cabinet and equipped with push buttons for the selection and playing of records. [From earlier *juke-house,* a brothel, from Gullah, disorderly.]

Jul. July.

ju·lep (jo͞o′lĭp) *n.* **1.** A **mint julep** *(see).* **2.** A sweet syrupy drink, especially one to which medicine may be added. [Middle English *iulep,* from Old French *julep,* from Arabic *julāb,* from Persian *gulāb,* "rose water" : *gul,* rose + *āb,* water.]

Jul·ian (jo͞ol′yən), known as "Julian the Apostate," born Flavius Claudius Julianus (A.D. 331–363). Roman emperor (361–363). He was brought up as a Christian, but on succeeding to the throne he began to take measures to restore the official dominance of the old Roman religion. He died in battle.

Ju·li·an·a (jo͞o′lē-ăn′ə), born Juliana Louise Emma Maria Wilhelmina (1909–). Queen of the Netherlands (1948–80). She married Prince Bernard (1911–) in 1937 and came to the throne after the abdication of her mother, Wilhelmina. In 1980 Juliana abdicated in favor of her daughter Beatrix.

Julian calendar *n.* The calendar introduced by Julius Caesar in Rome in 46 B.C., that fixed the length of the year at 365 days, with an extra day every fourth, or leap, year. It was eventually replaced by the Gregorian calendar. See feature at **calendar.**

ju·li·enne (jo͞o′lē-ĕn′; *French* zhü-lyĕn′) *adj.* Cut into thin strips about the size of a matchstick: *julienne potatoes.*
~*n.* Consommé or broth garnished with strips of julienne vegetables. [From French *à la julienne,* probably from the given name *Julien* or *Jules.*]

Jul·ius II (jo͞ol′yəs), born Giuliano della Rovere (1443–1513). Pope (1503–13). A soldier and statesman more than a spiritual leader, he restored papal authority in central Italy through campaigns against Venice and formed the Holy League to expel the French from Italy. He ordered the reconstruction of St. Peter's in Rome and commissioned Michelangelo to decorate the Sistine Chapel and Raphael to decorate his papal apartments.

Julius Caesar. See **Caesar.**

Ju·ly (jo͞o-lī′, jo͞o-) *n., pl.* **-lys.** *Abbr.* **Jul.** The seventh month of the year according to the Gregorian calendar. July has 31 days. See feature at **calendar.** [Middle English *Julie,* from Norman French, from Latin *Jūlius (mēnsis),* (month of) Julius Caesar.]

Ju·ma (jo͞o′mä) *n.* The Islamic Sabbath, falling on Friday.

Ju·ma·da, Jo·ma·da (jo͞o-mä′dä) *n.* **1.** The fifth month of the year in the Muslim calendar, having 30 days. **2.** The sixth month of the year in the Muslim calendar, having 29 days. See feature at **calendar.** [Arabic *Jumādā.*]

jum·ble¹ (jŭm′bəl) *v.* **-bled, -bling, -bles.** —*intr.* To move, mix, or mingle in a confused, disordered manner. —*tr.* **1.** To stir or mix in a disordered mass. **2.** To muddle; confuse.
~*n.* **1.** A confused or disordered mass: *a jumble of disconnected ideas.* **2.** A disordered state; muddle. **3.** *Chiefly British.* Goods to be sold at a jumble sale. [16th century : perhaps imitative.]

jumble² *n.* A light, thin, crisp, biscuit, variously flavored with fruit or almonds and usually tightly rolled. [17th century (originally, a cake made in rings) : perhaps from earlier *gimmal,* variant of GIMBALS.]

jumble sale *n. Chiefly British.* A rummage sale.

jum·bo (jŭm′bō) *n., pl.* **-bos.** **1.** An unusually large person, animal, or thing. **2.** *Informal.* A jumbo jet.

juggernaut *Modern British trailer trucks get their popular name from their resemblance to the huge wagon used to carry the statue of the Hindu god Jagannath in Indian festivals.*

Juggernaut *Devotees of the Hindu god Vishnu are said to have hurled themselves to death under the wheels of the huge wagon (above) used to carry the god's statue during processions. One of Vishnu's titles—Jagannath, or Juggernaut, meaning "Lord of the world"—has passed into English as the word for an overwhelming force that advances and crushes whatever is in its path.*

jumping jack *A wooden doll, suspended on twisted strings in a frame. The doll somersaults over the strings when the sides of the frame are moved apart. Toys based on the same principle have been popular for at least 200 years.*

junco *These finches are found in conifer forests throughout western North America. This is the Oregon junco.*

~*adj.* Larger than average: *a jumbo box of detergent.*
Jum·bo (jŭm′bō). A name for an elephant, as used by children and in folktales. [Probably from the second element of MUMBO JUMBO.]
jumbo jet *n.* A large jet airliner.
jum·buck (jŭm′bŭk′) *n. Australian Informal.* A sheep. [From a native Australian name.]
Jum·na (jŭm′nə). Also **Ya·mu·na** (yä′mə-nə). A river in northern India. It rises in the Himalayas of Uttar Pradesh and flows roughly south through Delhi to its confluence with the Ganges. The juncture of the two rivers is known as the Prayag, a place of pilgrimage in Hindu religion. The Jumna is 1,385 kilometers (860 miles) long.
jump (jŭmp) *v.* **jumped, jumping, jumps.** —*intr.* **1. a.** To spring off the ground or other base by a muscular effort of the legs and feet: *jumped three feet into the air.* **b.** To perform this movement repeatedly or rhythmically, as for exercise. **2. a.** To move or propel oneself, legs downward, down, off, out, or into something. **b.** To involve or commit oneself enthusiastically: *He jumped into the political fray.* **c.** To parachute from an aircraft. **3.** To spring or pounce with the intent to upbraid or censure. Used with *on* or *at*: *He jumped on me for saying such a thing.* **4.** To form judgments hastily or haphazardly. Used with *to*: *jump to conclusions.* **5.** To grab at eagerly; respond with alacrity. Used with *at*: *jump at the chance.* **6.** To start involuntarily: *You made me jump.* **7.** To rise suddenly and pronouncedly: *Prices jumped.* **8. a.** To skip over space or material, leaving a break in continuity. **b.** To be displaced vertically or laterally because of improper alignment: *The film jumped during projection.* **9.** *Computer Science.* To move from one set of instructions in a program to another farther ahead or behind rather than moving sequentially. **10.** *Checkers.* To move over an opponent's playing piece. **11.** *Bridge.* To make a jump bid. **12.** To be in agreement; coincide. **13.** *Slang.* To have a lively, pulsating quality: *a nightclub that jumps.* **14.** *Physics.* To change from one quantum state to another. —*tr.* **1.** To leap over or across: *jump a gate.* **2.** To leap aboard or jump on (a vehicle) illegally: *jump a train.* **3.** *Slang.* To spring upon in sudden attack: *The muggers jumped him.* **4.** To cause to leap: *jump a horse over a hurdle.* **5.** To cause to increase suddenly and markedly. **6.** To miss out; skip: *The typewriter jumped a space.* **7.** To drive through or move away from (traffic lights), before they change to green. **8.** *Bridge.* To raise (a partner's bid) by more than is necessary. **9.** *Checkers.* To take (an opponent's piece) by moving over it with one's own. **10.** To leave (a course or track) through mishap: *The train jumped the rails.* **11.** To leave or abandon without authorization: *jump ship; jump bail.* **—jump to it.** *Informal.* To set about a task promptly and eagerly.
~*n.* **1.** The act of jumping; leap. **2. a.** The space or distance covered by a leap: *a jump of seven feet.* **b.** A descent by parachute from an aircraft. **3.** A hurdle, fence, barrier, or span to be jumped. **4.** An athletic event featuring skill in jumping: *the high jump.* **5.** A sudden, pronounced rise, as in price or salary. **6.** A step or level: *a jump ahead of the others.* **7.** A major transition, as from one career to another. **8.** A short trip: *just a hop, skip, and a jump to the shore.* **9.** A break in continuity, as in a film. **10.** *Checkers.* A move made by jumping. **11. a.** An involuntary nervous movement, as when startled. **b. jumps.** *Informal.* The fidgets. **12.** *Physics.* A change between two quantum states. **13.** *West African.* A dance with live music. [16th century : probably imitative.]
jump bid *n. Bridge.* A bid at a higher level than that required to exceed the preceding bid.
jumped-up (jŭmpt′ŭp′) *adj. Informal.* Having risen from a humble to a significant position.
jump·er[1] (jŭm′pər) *n.* **1.** One that jumps. **2.** A type of coasting sled. **3.** *Electricity.* A short length of wire used temporarily to complete or by-pass a circuit. **4.** A bit or other boring device in a hammer drill.
jumper[2] *n.* **1.** A sleeveless dress worn over a blouse or sweater. **2.** *Chiefly British.* **a.** A jersey or sweater. **b.** Loosely, any knitted top. [Probably from British dialectal *jump, jup,* man's loose jacket, woman's underbodice, from French *juppe,* variant of *jupe,* skirt, from Arabic *jubbah,* JUBBAH.]
jumper cable *n.* A **booster cable** *(see).*
jumping bean *n.* A seed, as of certain Mexican shrubs or plants of the genera *Sebastiania* and *Sapium,* containing the larva of a moth, *Carpocapsa* (or *Enarmonia*) *saltitans,* the movements of which cause the seed to jerk or roll.
jumping jack *n.* A toy figure with jointed limbs that can be made to dance by pulling an attached string or frame.
jumping mouse *n.* Any of various small rodents of the family Zapodidae, having a long tail and long hind legs.
jump·ing-off place (jŭm′pĭng-ôf′, -ŏf′) *n.* **1.** A very remote place. **2.** A starting point for an enterprise. Also called "jumping-off point."
jump jet *n.* A fixed-wing jet aircraft in which the engine ducts can be rotated so that the aircraft can take off and land vertically.
jump lead *n. Chiefly British.* A **booster cable** *(see).*
jump-off (jŭmp′ôf′, -ŏf′) *n.* In show-jumping, a round that decides which of two or more horses previously tying for first place is the winner.
jump seat *n.* **1.** A portable or folding seat in an aircraft or in a car between the front and rear seats. **2.** A small rear seat in a sports car.
jump shot *n. Basketball.* A shot made by a player at the highest point of a jump.
jump-start (jŭmp′stärt′) *tr.v.* **-started, -starting, -starts. 1.** To start (a car engine) by pushing or rolling and suddenly releasing the clutch. **2.** To start (a car engine) using jump leads.
~*n.* The process of jump-starting.
jump suit *n.* **1.** A parachutist's uniform. **2.** Also **jump·suit** (jŭmp′sōōt′). A one-piece garment with legs, reaching from neck to ankles, and usually made of a close-fitting, stretch fabric.
jump-up (jŭmp′ŭp′) *n.* A West Indian festival dance.
jump·y (jŭm′pē) *adj.* **-ier, -iest. 1.** Characterized by fitful, jerky movements. **2.** Easily unsettled or alarmed; nervous or on edge, as with apprehension. **—jump·i·ness** *n.*
jun (jōōn) *n., pl.* **jun.** A coin equal to 1/100 of the won of North Korea. Also called "jeon." See feature at **currency.** [Korean.]
Jun. 1. June. **2.** Also **jun.** junior.
junc. junction.
jun·co (jŭng′kō) *n., pl.* **-cos.** Any of various North American finches of the genus *Junco,* having predominantly gray plumage. [Spanish, "rush," junco. See **jonquil.**]
junc·tion (jŭngk′shən) *n.* **1.** The act or process of joining or the condition of being joined. **2.** *Abbr.* **jct., junc.** The place where two things join or meet; specifically, the place where two roads or railway routes join or cross paths. **3.** A transition layer or boundary between two different materials or between physically different regions in a single material, especially: **a.** A connection between conductors or sections of a transmission line. **b.** The interface between a region of predominantly positive charge carriers and another of predominantly negative charge carriers in a semiconductor. **c.** A mechanical or alloyed contact between different metals or other materials, as in a thermocouple. [Latin *junctiō* (stem *junctiōn-*), from *junctus,* past participle of *jungere,* to join.] **—junc·tion·al** *adj.*
junction box *n.* An enclosed panel used to connect or branch electric circuits without making permanent splices.
junction transistor *n.* A common type of transistor in which contact is made between regions of different conductivity type.
junc·ture (jŭngk′chər) *n.* **1.** The act of joining, or the condition of being joined. **2.** The line or point where two things are joined; junction; joint; hinge. **3.** A point or interval in time; especially, a crisis or similar turning point. **4.** The transition or mode of transition from one sound to another in speech. [Middle English, from Latin *junctūra,* from *junctus,* past participle of *jungere,* to join.]
June (jōōn) *n. Abbr.* **Jun.** The sixth month of the year according to the Gregorian calendar. June has 30 days. See feature at **calendar.** [Middle English, from Old French *juin,* from Latin *Jūnius (mēnsis),* (month consecrated to) the goddess JUNO.]
Ju·neau (jōō′nō). The capital of Alaska, on the Gastineau Channel, in the southeastern Alaska Panhandle. The city developed as a boom town after gold was discovered nearby in 1880.
June beetle *n.* Any of various North American beetles of the subfamily Melolonthinae, having larvae that are often destructive to crops. Also called "June bug," "May beetle."
June·ber·ry (jōōn′bĕr′ē) *n., pl.* **-ries.** The **shadbush** *(see),* or its fruit.
Jung (yŏŏng), **Carl Gustav** (1875–1961). Swiss psychiatrist, a pioneer of psychoanalysis. He worked with Freud but developed his own approach to psychoanalysis, based in part on his study of schizophrenia. Jung coined the terms "introvert" and "extrovert" to define psychological types. His best-known work is *Psychology of the Unconscious* (1912). **—Jung·i·an** *n. & adj.*
Jung·frau (yŏŏng′frou′). One of the highest peaks (4,158 meters; 13,632 feet) in the Swiss Alps, situated in the Bernese Oberland overlooking Interlaken. Its summit was first scaled in 1811.
jun·gle (jŭng′gəl) *n.* **1.** Land densely overgrown with tropical vegetation and trees. **2.** Any dense thicket or growth. **3.** *Slang.* A hobo camp or place of rendezvous. **4.** A milieu characterized by intense, often ruthless competition. **5.** Any maze, entanglement, or confusion, especially one that is fruitless or leads nowhere. [Originally, "wasteland," from Hindi and Marathi *jaṅgal,* from Sanskrit *jāṅgala*†, "dry," desert.] **—jun·gly** *adj.*
jungle fever *n.* A pernicious malaria occurring in the East Indies.
jungle fowl *n.* Any of several birds of the genus *Gallus,* of southeastern Asia; especially, *G. gallus,* considered to be the ancestor of the common domestic fowl.
jungle gym *n.* A structure of poles and bars on which children can play. [Originally a trademark.]
jungle juice *n. Slang.* Alcoholic drink, especially when homemade.
jun·ior (jōōn′yər) *adj. Abbr.* **Jnr., jnr., Jr., jr., Jun., jun. 1.** Designed for or including youthful persons: *a junior tennis match; junior dress sizes.* **2.** Lower in rank or shorter in length of tenure: *the junior senator.* **3.** Younger. Used especially after a name to denote the younger of two persons who share the same name, such as a father and son: *William Jones, Jr.* **4.** Designating the third or penultimate year of a U.S. high school or college. **5.** *British.* Of or pertaining to school children between the ages of 7 and 11.
~*n.* **1.** A younger person or individual. **2.** A person lesser in rank or length of service; subordinate. **3.** An undergraduate in the third or penultimate year of a high school or college. **4.** *British.* A schoolchild between the ages of 7 and 11. [Latin *jūnior,* from preclassical *juvenior* (unattested), comparative of *juvenis,* young.]
junior college *n.* An educational institution offering a two-year course that is generally the equivalent of the first two years of a four-year undergraduate course.
junior high school *n.* A school intermediate between grammar school and high school, and generally including the seventh, eighth, and sometimes ninth grades. Also called "junior high."

junior lightweight *n.* A professional boxer who weighs between 126 and 130 pounds (57 and 59 kilograms).
junior middleweight *n.* A professional boxer who weighs between 147 and 154 pounds (66.5 and 70 kilograms).
junior school *n. British.* A school for children aged between 7 and 11. Compare **infant school.**
junior welterweight *n.* A professional boxer who weighs between 135 and 140 pounds (61 and 63.5 kilograms).
ju·ni·per (jo͞o′nə-pər) *n.* Any of various evergreen coniferous trees or shrubs of the genus *Juniperus* in the cypress family (Cupressaceae), having spine-tipped needles and aromatic, bluish-gray, berrylike cones. An oil from the berries of *J. communis* is used to flavor gin. [Middle English *junipere,* from Latin *jūniperus*†.]
junk¹ (jŭngk) *n.* **1.** Scrapped materials such as glass, rags, paper, or metals that can be converted into usable stock. **2.** *Informal.* **a.** Anything worn-out or fit to be discarded. **b.** Something of inferior quality; something cheap or shoddy. **c.** Anything meaningless, fatuous, or unbelievable; nonsense. **3.** *Slang.* A narcotic drug; especially, heroin. **4.** *Nautical.* **a.** Hard salt beef. **b.** Old cordage, reused for gaskets, oakum, and mats.
~*tr.v.* **junked, junking, junks.** To throw away or discard as useless; scrap. [Originally (until the 20th century) a nautical term meaning old, worn-out pieces of rope or cable, from Middle English *jonke*†.]
junk² *n.* A flat-bottomed ship used in China and Southeast Asia with a high poop and battened sails. [Chiefly from Portuguese *junco* and Dutch *jonk,* from Malay *jong,* sea-going ship.]
Jun·ker (yo͝ong′kər) *n.* A member of the Prussian landed aristocracy, especially of its ultrareactionary section. [German, from Old High German *junchērro* : *jung,* young + *hērro,* comparative of *hēr,* worthy, exalted.] **—Jun·ker·dom** *n.*
jun·ket (jŭng′kĭt) *n.* **1.** A sweet food made from flavored milk set with rennet. **2.** A party, banquet, or outing. **3.** A trip or excursion, especially one taken by an official and underwritten with public funds.
~*intr.v.* **junketed, -keting, -kets. 1.** To hold a party or banquet. **2.** To make an excursion using public funds. [Middle English *jonket,* a kind of egg custard served on rushes or made in a rush mat, from *junket,* rush basket, from Old Northern French *jonquette,* from *jonc,* rush, from Latin *juncus.* See **jonquil.**] **—jun·ket·er** *n.* **—jun·ket·ing** *n.*
junk food *n. Informal.* Food that has been processed so as to be easily prepared and that is often of low nutritional value.
junk·ie, junk·y (jŭng′kē) *n., pl.* **-ies.** *Slang.* A drug addict, especially one using heroin.
Ju·no (jo͞o′nō). *Roman Mythology.* The principal Roman goddess, wife and sister of Jupiter, patroness primarily of marriage and the well-being of women, identified with the Greek goddess Hera. [Latin *Jūno*†.]
Ju·no·esque (jo͞o′nō-ĕsk′) *adj.* Having the stately bearing and imposing beauty of the goddess Juno.
jun·ta (ho͝on′tə, ho͞on′-, jŭn′-) *n.* **1.** A group of military officers holding state power in a country after a coup d'état. **2.** A council or small legislative body in a government, especially in Central and South American countries. **3.** Variant of **junto.** [Spanish and Portuguese, from Vulgar Latin *juncta* (unattested), "joined," from Latin, feminine past participle of *jungere,* to join.]
jun·to (jŭn′tō) *n., pl.* **-tos.** Also **jun·ta.** A small, usually secret group or committee that gathers for some common interest or aim; cabal; clique; faction. [Variant of JUNTA.]
Ju·pi·ter¹ (jo͞o′pə-tər) *Roman Mythology.* The supreme god, patron of the Roman state, brother and husband of Juno, identified with the Greek god Zeus. Also called "Jove." [Middle English, from Latin *Jūpiter, Jūppiter,* Old Latin *Jovis Pater,* "Jove Father."]
Jupiter² *n. Astronomy.* The fifth planet from the sun, the largest and most massive in the solar system, having a diameter of approximately 142,000 kilometers (88,700 miles), a mass approximately 318 times that of earth, and a sidereal period of revolution about the sun of 11.86 years at a mean distance of 773 million kilometers (483 million miles). [After JUPITER.] See feature, next page.
ju·ra. Plural of **jus.**
Ju·ra Mountains (jo͝or′ə). A mountain range in eastern France and western Switzerland. It forms a natural boundary between the two countries. Crêt de la Neige (1,723 meters; 5,653 feet) is the highest point.
ju·ral (jo͝or′əl) *adj.* **1.** Of or pertaining to law. **2.** Of, pertaining to, or arising from rights and obligations. [From Latin *jūs* (stem *jūr-*), right, law.] **—ju·ral·ly** *adv.*
Ju·ras·sic (jo͞o-răs′ĭk) *adj. Geology.* Of, belonging to, or designating the time and deposits of the second period of the Mesozoic era, characterized by the existence of dinosaurs and primitive mammals and birds.
~*n. Geology.* The Jurassic period. Preceded by *the.* [French *jurassique,* after the JURA MOUNTAINS.]
ju·rat (jo͝or′ăt′) *n.* A certification on an affidavit declaring when, where, and before whom it was sworn. [Latin *jūrātum (est),* "(it has been) sworn," from *jūrāre,* to swear. See **jury.**]
Jur. D. Doctor of Law. [Latin *Juris Doctor*]
ju·rid·i·cal (jo͞o-rĭd′ĭ-kəl) *adj.* Also **ju·rid·ic** (-ĭk). Of or pertaining to the law and its administration. [From Latin *jūridicus* : *jūs* (stem *jūr-*), law + *dīcere,* to say.] **—ju·rid·i·cal·ly** *adv.*
juridical days *pl.n.* The days on which courts are in session. Compare **dies non.**
ju·ris·con·sult (jo͝or′əs-kŏn′sŭlt′) *n.* A person learned in law; jurist. [Latin *jūrisconsultus* : *jūris,* genitive of *jūs,* law + *consultus,* past participle of *consulere,* to CONSULT.]
ju·ris·dic·tion (jo͝or-əs-dĭk′shən) *n.* **1.** The right and power to interpret and apply the law. **2.** Authority or control. **3.** The extent of authority or control. **4.** The territorial range of authority or control. [Middle English *jurisdiccioun,* from Old French *juridiction,* from Latin *jūrisdictiō* (stem *jūrisdictiōn-*) : *jūris,* genitive of *jūs,* law + *dictiō,* declaration (see **diction**).] **—ju·ris·dic·tion·al** *adj.* **—ju·ris·dic·tion·al·ly** *adv.*
ju·ris·pru·dence (jo͝or′əs-pro͞o′dəns) *n.* **1.** The philosophy of law or the formal science of law. **2.** A division or department of law. **3.** A system or body of laws. [Originally "skill in law," from Late Latin *jūrisprūdentia* : *jūris,* genitive of *jūs,* law + *prūdentia,* foresight, knowledge, from *prūdēns,* knowing, PRUDENT.] **—ju·ris·pru·den·tial** *adj.* **—ju·ris·pru·den·tial·ly** *adv.*
ju·ris·pru·dent (jo͝or′əs-pro͞o′dənt) *n.* One who is versed in jurisprudence. **—ju·ris·pru·dent** *adj.*
ju·rist (jo͝or′əst) *n.* **1.** A person who is skilled in the law; especially, one who studies or writes about legal matters. **2. a.** A judge. **b.** A lawyer. [Old French, from Medieval Latin *jūrista,* from Latin *jūs* (stem *jūr-*), law.]
ju·ris·tic (jo͞o-rĭs′tĭk) *adj.* Also **ju·ris·ti·cal** (-tĭ-kəl). **1.** Of or pertaining to a jurist or to jurisprudence. **2.** Of or pertaining to law or legality. **—ju·ris·ti·cal·ly** *adv.*
ju·ror (jo͝or′ər, -ôr′) *n.* **1. a.** A person serving as a member of a body sworn to hear and deliver a verdict on a case. **b.** A person called or designated for jury duty. **2.** A person who serves on any body acting in a capacity analogous to that of a jury, as when judging the entries in a competition. [Middle English *juroure,* from Norman French *jurour,* from Latin *jūrātor,* "swearer," from *jūrātus,* past participle of *jūrāre,* to swear. See **jury.**]
ju·ry¹ (jo͝or′ē) *n., pl.* **-ries. 1.** A group of persons forming a body sworn to give a verdict on some matter; specifically, a body of persons summoned by law and sworn to hear and deliver a verdict upon a case presented in court. See **grand jury, petit jury. 2.** A group of persons forming a committee to judge, for example, a competition and award prizes. [Middle English *jurie,* from Norman French *juree,* from Old French *juree,* oath, inquest, from Latin *jūrāta,* "thing sworn," from the feminine past participle of *jūrāre,* to swear, from *jūs* (stem *jūr-*), law.]
jury² *adj. Nautical.* Intended or designed for emergency or temporary use; makeshift: *a jury rig.* [Perhaps ultimately from Old French *ajurie,* aid.]
jury box *n.* The enclosed area in a court where the jury sits.
ju·ry·man (jo͝or′ē-mən) *n., pl.* **-men** (-mĭn). A man serving on a jury; a male juror.
ju·ry-rigged (jo͝or′ē-rĭgd′) *adj. Nautical.* Rigged for emergency or temporary use.
ju·ry·wom·an (jo͝or′ē-wo͝om′ĭn) *n., pl.* **-women** (-wĭm′ĭn). A woman serving on a jury; a female juror.
jus (yo͞os) *n., pl.* **jura** (yo͞o′rə). *Latin.* **1.** Right; justice; law. **2.** A given right; a legal power.
jus gen·ti·um (gĕn′tē-əm) *n. Latin.* The law of nations; international law.
Jus·sieu (zhü-syœ′). A family of eminent French botanists. **Antoine de Jussieu** (1686–1758) was a director of the Jardin des Plantes in Paris, and his younger brother **Bernard de Jussieu** (*c.* 1699–1777) worked at the Jardins du Roi. **Joseph de Jussieu** (1704–79), the youngest of the brothers, lived for many years in South America and introduced the garden heliotrope into Europe. **Antoine Laurent de Jussieu** (1748–1836), their nephew, was professor of botany at the Paris Museum of Natural History, and his *Genera Plantarum* (1789) was a major work of plant classification that remains fundamental to modern botany.
jus·sive (jŭs′ĭv) *adj. Grammar.* Expressing or used to express a command.
~*n. Grammar.* A word, mood, or construction used to express command. [From Latin *jussus,* past participle of *jubēre,* to command.]
just¹ (jŭst) *adj.* **1.** Honorable and fair in one's dealings and actions. **2.** Consistent with moral right; fair; equitable. **3.** Properly due or merited: *just deserts.* **4.** Legally valid or correct; lawful: *just title.* **5.** Suitable; fitting. **6.** Well-founded; justified; legitimate: *just resentment.* **7.** Exact; accurate: *a just measure.* **8.** Upright before God; righteous. —See Synonyms at **fair.**
~*adv.* (jŭst; *unstressed* jəst, jĭst). **1.** Precisely; exactly: *That's just what I was going to say.* **2.** At the exact moment of: *Just as I was leaving, he turned up.* **3.** Only a moment ago: *He has just come.* **4.** By a narrow margin; barely: *You have just missed Tom.* **5.** But a little distance: *You'll find it just down the road.* **6.** Merely; only: *I just meant that I agree.* **7.** Conceivably; possibly: *There's just a chance she won't notice.* **8.** Simply; certainly. Used as an intensive: *It's just beautiful!* **—just about. 1.** On the point of: *I was just about to go.* **2.** Almost; very nearly: *I've just about had enough.* **—just now. 1.** At this very moment. **2.** Only a moment ago. **—just so. 1.** Carried out, arranged, or presented with due regard for neatness, accuracy, tidiness, or the like. **2.** Used to express agreement. [Middle English *just(e),* from Old French *juste,* from Latin *jūstus.*] **—just·ly** *adv.* **—just·ness** *n.*
just². Variant of **joust.**
Just (jŭst), **Ernest Everett** (1883–1941). U.S. embryologist. He researched the cellular processes of marine organisms and pioneered

juniper *The leaves and branches of this conifer were once burned with beech wood to preserve hams, and its berries are used in certain sauces and to flavor gin.*

junk *The traditional Chinese flat-bottomed boat has a large rudder that serves partly as a keel. The sails open and close like a fan.*

the study of the surface properties of cells. His major work is *Biology of the Cell Surface* (1939).

jus·tice (jŭs′tĭs) *n.* **1.** Moral rightness; equity. **2.** The quality of being just, fair, or in conformity with what is right or legal: *recognized the justice of our cause.* **3.** Good reason: *He's very angry, and with justice.* **4.** Fair handling; due reward or treatment. **5.** The administration and procedure of law. **6.** *Abbr.* **J.** A judge. **7.** A justice of the peace. **—bring to justice.** To effect the arrest and trial of (a lawbreaker). **—do justice to. 1.** To approach with proper appreciation; enjoy fully. **2.** To show to full advantage: *The picture doesn't do justice to her eyes.* [Middle English, from Old French, from Latin *jūstitia,* from *jūstus,* JUST.] **—jus·tice·ship** *n.*

Justice, Department of. The legal department of the executive branch of the U.S. government, headed by the Attorney General and having as its jurisdiction the legal representation of the government, the enforcement of antitrust and civil-rights laws, and the supervision of immigration and naturalization.

justice of the peace *n. Abbr.* **J.P.** A magistrate of the lowest level of the state court system, having authority chiefly to act upon minor offenses, commit cases to a higher court for trial, perform marriages, and administer oaths.

jus·ti·ci·a·ble (jŭ-stĭsh′ə-bəl) *adj.* Appropriate for or subject to court trial; liable to be brought before a court of law. [French, from Old French, from *justicier,* to try, from *justice,* JUSTICE.]

jus·ti·ci·ar (jŭ-stĭsh′ē-ər) *n.* Also **jus·ti·ci·a·ry** (-ē-ĕr′ē). Formerly, an English legal officer who acted for the king in his absence.

jus·ti·ci·ar·y (jŭ-stĭsh′ē-ĕr′ē) *adj.* Pertaining to the administration of the law.

~*n., pl.* **justiciaries. 1.** One who administers the law. **2.** Variant of **justiciar.** [Medieval Latin *jūstitiārius,* from Latin *jūstitia,* JUSTICE.]

jus·ti·fi·a·ble (jŭs′tə-fī′ə-bəl) *adj.* Capable of being justified. **—jus·ti·fi·a·bil·i·ty, jus·ti·fi·a·ble·ness** *n.* **—jus·ti·fi·a·bly** *adv.*

jus·ti·fi·ca·tion (jŭs′tə-fĭ-kā′shən) *n.* **1.** The act of justifying. **2.** The condition or fact of being justified. **3.** A fact, circumstance, or evidence that justifies; a ground for defense.

jus·ti·fi·ca·tive (jŭ-stĭf′ĭ-kə-tĭv) *adj.* Also **jus·ti·fi·ca·to·ry** (-tôr′ē, -tōr′ē). Serving as justification.

jus·ti·fi·er (jŭs′tə-fī′ər) *n.* **1.** One that justifies. **2.** *Printing.* A space that varies as necessary to justify a line.

Jupiter

JUPITER: THE GIANT AMONG THE PLANETS

The "space fossil" inside a swirling shroud of multicolored gases

Jupiter is much the largest of the planets, with a diameter through its equator of 142,800 kilometers (88,700 miles). It is twice as massive as the other eight planets put together. Jupiter is regarded by astronomers as a kind of space fossil, for its enormous mass and powerful gravity have retained even the lightest of the gases from which all the planets were originally formed. Jupiter is thought to resemble Earth as it was before it solidified.

Because of its great distance from the sun—at 778,300,000 kilometers (483,600,000 miles) it is five times as far as Earth is from the sun—Jupiter takes 11.86 Earth-years to make an orbit and complete its year. But its rotation on its own axis is rapid, taking less than ten hours. The speed of rotation—44,800 kilometers (28,000 miles) an hour—has caused Jupiter to become flattened at the poles.

It is believed that Jupiter has a central rocky core surrounded by layers of liquid hydrogen, which are in turn overlaid by a deep, gaseous atmosphere. Only the multicolored cloud tops can be seen from Earth. These are bitterly cold, about −130°C (−202°F), but Jupiter is certainly hot at its core, perhaps as hot as 30,000°C (about 54,000°F). It emits more heat than it can receive from the sun—perhaps as a result of slow contraction under its own gravity. Zones of intense radiation surround the planet. Jupiter has a single ring.

The gaseous surface is streaked by dark belts and bright zones; the dark belts are regions of descending gas, the bright zones regions of ascending gas. The colors are vivid and there is one remarkable feature, the Great Red Spot, whose color may be due to the presence of phosphorus. Jupiter has a family of 16 satellites—four as large as planets.

Planet location guide

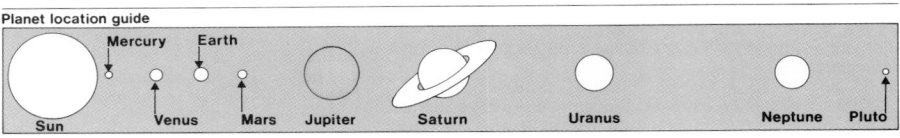

THE MOONS OF JUPITER *This composite picture shows Jupiter (upper right) and its four largest satellites. Io (upper left) is red, slightly larger than Earth's moon, and has active volcanoes. Europa (center) is a little smaller than Io and has a smooth, icy crust. Ganymede (lower left), with a diameter of 5,000 kilometers (about 3,100 miles), is larger even than the planet Mercury, and Callisto (lower right) also is much larger than Earth's moon. Ganymede and Callisto are both icy and cratered. The satellites are shown in the correct relative positions.*

GREAT RED SPOT *This dramatic view of Jupiter's Great Red Spot was taken by a U.S. Voyager spacecraft in 1979 from a distance of 9.2 million kilometers (more than 5 million miles). The oval-shaped spot on the photograph seems to be a whirling storm of colored gas. It may be phosphorus that causes the spot's red color. The spot, which stands out among the vivid clouds of gas surrounding Jupiter, is enormous. It is 48,000 kilometers (about 30,000 miles) across at its greatest dimension—so large that Earth could fall into it without touching the sides.*

jus·ti·fy (jŭs′tə-fī′) v. **-fied, -fying, -fies.** —tr. **1.** To demonstrate or prove to be just, right, or valid. **2.** To show to be well-founded; warrant. **3.** To declare free of blame; absolve. **4.** Theology. To free (man) of the guilt and penalty attached to grievous sin. Said only of God. **5.** Law. **a.** To demonstrate good reason for (an action taken). **b.** To prove to be qualified to act as a bondsman. **6.** Printing. To adjust or space (a line of type) to the proper length. —intr. Printing. To be or become properly spaced and of the correct length. Said of a line of type. [Middle English justifien, originally, to judge, punish, from Old French justifier, from Late Latin jūstificāre, to do justice toward, to forgive, pardon : jūstus, JUST + facere, to do.]

Jus·tin·i·an I (jŭs-tĭn′ē-ən), known as "the Great" (A.D. 483–565). Byzantine emperor (527–65). He held the eastern frontier of his empire against the Persians and with the brilliant generalship of Belisarius reconquered former Roman territories in Africa, Italy, and Spain. A devout if autocratic Christian, he also achieved the temporary unity of the Eastern and Western churches and built the great cathedral of St. Sophia in Constantinople. As an administrator, he revised Roman law according to a system known as the Justinian Code.

Justinian Code n. The codification of Roman law made by order of Justinian I and published in A.D. 529.

jut (jŭt) intr.v. **jutted, jutting, juts.** To project, usually sharply, beyond the limits of the main body; protrude. Often used with out: "He had a sharp crooked nose jutting out of a lean dancer's face" (Graham Greene). —n. Something that protrudes; projection. [Variant of JET (to project).] —**jut·ting·ly** adv.

jute (jōōt) n. **1.** Either of two Asian plants, Corchorus capsularis or C. olitorius, yielding a fiber used for sacking and cordage. **2.** The fiber obtained from such a plant. **3.** The coarse fabric made from the fiber of this plant. [Bengali jhōṭo, jhuṭo, from Sanskrit jūṭa†, twisted hair (of ascetics and Shiva).]

Jute (jōōt) n. A member of any of several Germanic tribes, some of whom invaded Britain and settled in Kent in the 5th century A.D. —**Jut·ish** adj.

Jut·land (jŭt′lənd). Danish **Jyl·land** (yül′län). A peninsula of northern Europe, almost entirely flat, situated between the North and Baltic seas. Mainland Denmark occupies the northern part, the southern region lying in West Germany. The Battle of Jutland (1916), fought in the North Sea off the Danish coast between the British and German fleets, was the largest naval engagement of World War I. Though the Germans inflicted the greater losses, they failed to break British control of the seas and afterward remained in the harbor until the end of the war.

juv. juvenile.

Ju·ve·nal (jōō′və-nəl), born Decimus Junius Juvenalis (c. A.D. 60–140). Roman satirical poet. He is remembered for his 16 Satires (probably written after A.D. 100), which denounce the extravagance, snobbery, and corruption of the privileged classes in Rome.

ju·ve·nes·cent (jōō′və-nĕs′ənt) adj. Becoming young or youthful. [JUVEN(AL) + -ESCENT.] —**ju·ve·nes·cence** n.

ju·ve·nile (jōō′və-nəl, -nīl′) adj. Abbr. **juv. 1.** Young; youthful. **2.** Not fully developed; not yet adult. Said of animals and plants or their parts. **3.** Characteristic of youth or children; immature: juvenile behavior. **4.** Intended for or appropriate to children or young persons: juvenile fashions. —n. Abbr. **juv. 1. a.** A young person; child. **b.** A young animal that has not reached sexual maturity. **c.** A plant bearing the juvenile form of foliage. **2.** An actor who plays roles of children or young persons. **3.** A children's book. —See Synonyms at **young.** [Latin juvenīlis, from juvenis, young, a youth.] —**ju·ve·nile·ly** adv. —**ju·ve·nile·ness** n.

juvenile court n. A court dealing with children and young offenders.

juvenile delinquent n. Abbr. **J.D.** A child or adolescent who exhibits antisocial or criminal behavior. —**juvenile delinquency** n.

juvenile hormone n. An insect hormone that prevents metamorphosis into the adult form and maintains larval characteristics.

ju·ve·nil·i·a (jōō′və-nĭl′ē-ə) pl.n. Works, particularly written or artistic works, produced in childhood or youth. [Latin juvenīlia, neuter plural of juvenīlis, JUVENILE.]

ju·ve·nil·i·ty (jōō′və-nĭl′ə-tē) n., pl. **-ties. 1.** The quality or condition of being foolishly juvenile; immaturity. **2.** The quality or condition of being young or youthful. **3.** juvenilities. Juvenile or immature acts or characteristics. **4.** Young persons collectively.

ju·ve·noc·ra·cy (jōō′və-nŏk′rə-sē) n. Rule or influence by young people. [Latin juvenis, young person + -CRACY.]

jux·ta·pose (jŭk′stə-pōz′) tr.v. **-posed, -posing, -poses.** To place or situate side by side or close together, especially so as to produce or exhibit a contrasting effect. [French juxtaposer, probably from JUXTAPOSITION.]

jux·ta·po·si·tion (jŭk′stə-pə-zĭsh′ən) n. The act of juxtaposing or the state of being juxtaposed. [French : Latin juxtā, close together + POSITION.] —**jux·ta·po·si·tion·al** adj.

Jylland. See **Jutland.**

K

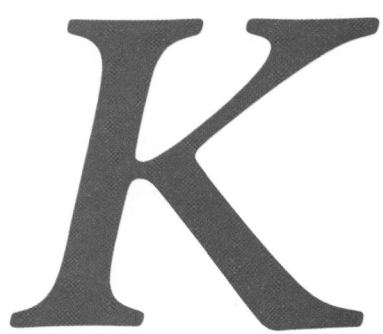

kabuki *Richly embroidered costumes are worn by the actors for historical scenes in Japanese kabuki plays. Plain costumes are worn for scenes from everyday life. The actors do not have masks as they do in No plays; instead they wear elaborate make-up.*

kale *Curled kale, shown here, is one of two types of this vegetable. The other is mossy kale. Both are related to the cabbage.*

k, K (kā) *n., pl.* **k's** or **K's. 1.** The 11th letter of the modern English alphabet. See feature at **alphabet. 2.** Any of the speech sounds represented by this letter. **3.** The 11th in a series; 10th when *J* is omitted. **4.** *Informal.* Thousand: *a job that pays $40k.* **5.** *Computer Science.* A unit of storage capacity equal to 1024 words, bytes, or bits.

k, K, k., K. *Note:* As an abbreviation or symbol, *k* may be a small or a capital letter, with or without a period. Established forms or those generally preferred precede the definition. When no form is given, all four forms are in general use in that sense. **1. K** kaon. **2. k** karat. **3. K a.** kelvin (temperature unit). **b.** Kelvin (temperature scale). **4. k** kilo-. **5. k., K.** king. **6. K** *Chess.* king. **7. K.** *Card Games.* king. **8. k., K.** knight. **9. K.** Köchel number. **10. k., K.** kopeck. **11. k., K.** koruna. **12. k., K.** krona. **13. k., K.** krone. **14. k** The symbol for the Boltzmann constant.

K The symbol for the element potassium. [New Latin *kalium.*]

K2. See **Godwin-Austen, Mount.**

ka (kä) *n.* A spirit believed by the ancient Egyptians to dwell in a man or statue. [Egyptian.]

Kaa·ba, Caa·ba (kä′bə) *n.* A Muslim shrine in Mecca that houses a sacred black stone said to have been given to Abraham by the archangel Gabriel and toward which followers of Muhammad face when praying. [Arabic *ka'bah,* "square building," from *ka'b, ka'ba,* cube.]

kab. Variant of **cab** (measure).

kabala, kabbala. Variants of **cabala.**

ka·bel·jou (kä′bəl-you′, käb′əl-) *n., pl.* **-jous** or collectively **kabeljou.** *South African.* An edible codlike fish, *Argyrosmus hololepidotus,* of the family Sciaenidae. [Afrikaans, from Dutch *kabeljauw,* from Germanic.]

ka·bob (kə-bŏb′) *n.* **Shish kebab** (see).

ka·bu·ki (kə-bōō′kē) *n.* A type of popular Japanese drama, evolved from the older No theater, in which elaborately costumed performers, usually male, enact both tragedies and comedies using stylized movements, dances, and songs. [Japanese, "art of singing and dancing" : *kabu,* singing and dancing + *ki,* art.]

Ka·bul (kä′bŏŏl). Capital of Afghanistan. It commands the northeast trade route into Pakistan and has frequently been occupied by foreign invaders during its 3,000-year history, most recently by Soviet forces. From 1504 to 1526 it was the capital of the Mogul Empire. It became Afghanistan's capital in 1773.

Ka·byle (kə-bīl′) *n., pl.* **-byles** or collectively **Kabyle. 1.** A member of one of the Berber tribes inhabiting Tunisia or Algeria. **2.** The Hamitic Berber dialect spoken by these people.

ka·chi·na (kə-chē′nə) *n.* A doll that represents one of the rain-bringing ancestral spirits of the Hopi. [Hopi *qacina,* supernatural.]

Ká·dár (kä′där), **János** (1912–89). First secretary of the Hungarian Communist Party (1956–88). He joined the invading Soviet forces during the 1956 revolution and was prime minister (1956–58, 1961–65).

Kaddafi, Muammar. See **Quaddafi.**

Kad·dish (kä′dĭsh) *n. Judaism.* A prayer in praise of God said in daily synagogue services and by mourners after the death of a close relative. [Aramaic *qaddīsh,* holy.]

kaf·fee·klatsch (kô′fē-kläch′, kä′fē-kläch′) *n.* A casual gathering for coffee and conversation. [German *Kaffee,* COFFEE + *Klatsch,* chat.]

kaf·fir, ka·fir (kăf′ər) *n.* A variety of sorghum, *Sorghum vulgare caffrorum,* of Africa, cultivated in dry regions for its grain and as fodder. Also called "kaffircorn." [From KAFFIR.]

Kaf·fir, Ka·fir (kăf′ər) *n., pl.* **-firs** or collectively **Kaffir, Kafir. 1. a.** A member of any of the Bantu-speaking tribes inhabiting South Africa. **b.** The language spoken by these people; Xhosa. **2.** A non-Muslim. Used derogatorily by Muslims. **3.** A black African, especially one living in southern Africa. Used derogatorily. **4.** Variant of **Kafir** (Iranian people). **5. Kaffirs.** On the London Stock Exchange, South African mining shares. [Arabic *kafir,* "infidel," present participle of *kafara,* to deny, be skeptical.]

kaf·fir·corn (kăf′ər-kôrn′) *n.* A variety of sorghum, **kaffir** (see).

kaffir lily *n.* A bulbous plant, *Schizostylis coccinea,* native to South Africa, that is widely cultivated as a garden plant for its showy autumn-blooming pink or red flowers.

kaf·fi·yeh (kä-fē′ə, kä-) *n.* Also **kef·fi·yeh** (kĕ-). A headdress, usually worn by Arab men, consisting of a folded triangle of material held in place with a cord. [Arabic, perhaps from Late Latin *cofea,* COIF.]

Ka·fir (kăf′ər) *n., pl.* **-firs** or collectively **Kafir. 1.** A member of a people of ancient Iranian stock living in northeastern Afghanistan. **2.** Variant of **Kaffir.**

Kaf·i·ri (käf′ə-rē) *n.* The Indic language of the Iranian Kafirs.

Kaf·ka (käf′kä), **Franz** (1883–1924). Austrian novelist, born in Prague. He wrote enigmatic stories in which individuals are constantly threatened by a nightmarishly impersonal world. Most of his work, including *The Trial* (1925) and *The Castle* (1926), was published posthumously.

Kaf·ka·esque (käf′kə-ĕsk′, käf′-) *adj.* **1.** Of, pertaining to, or characteristic of Franz Kafka or of his writings. **2.** Characterized by surreal distortion and by the evocation of a sinister impersonal force controlling human affairs.

kaftan. Variant of **caftan.**

Ka·fu·e (kä-fōō′ā). River of central Zambia. It flows 960 kilometers (600 miles) from the Zaire border to join the Zambezi. The Kafue Dam provides two thirds of Zambia's hydroelectric power.

Ka·go·shi·ma (kä′gō-shē′mä). Port and naval base on Kagoshima Bay, southern Kyushu, Japan. The first European missionary to Japan, St. Francis Xavier, landed here in 1549.

kaiak. Variant of **kayak.**

Kai·feng (kī′fŭng′). A city in northwestern Henan, China. It is a commercial, agricultural, and industrial center. The Huang He, just to the north, has frequently flooded the city. Founded in the 3rd century B.C., it was capital of the Song (Sung) dynasty (960–1127).

kail. Variant of **kale.**

Kai·las (kī-läs′). Peak and pilgrimage site in the Kailas Range of southwestern Tibet. It rises to *c.* 6,795 meters (22,280 feet).

kail·yard (kāl′yärd′) *n. Scottish.* A vegetable garden. [Scottish *kail,* kale + YARD.]

Kail·yard School (kāl′yärd′) *n.* A group of writers who make considerable use of Scots dialect in their works about Scottish life. [From KAILYARD.]

kain, kane, cain (kān) *n.* Tax or rent payments made in kind. [Middle English *cain,* from Scottish Gaelic *cāin,* rent, fine, probably from Late Latin *canōn,* tribute, decree, from Latin, rule, law, CANON.]

kai·nite (kī′nīt′, kā′-) *n.* A mineral, essentially $KCl \cdot MgSO_4 \cdot 3H_2O$, found in potash deposits and used mainly as fertilizer and as a source of potassium compounds. [German *Kainit* : Greek *kainos,* new, recently formed + -ITE.]

kai·ser, Kai·ser (kī′zər) *n.* Any of the emperors of the Holy Roman Empire (A.D. 800–1806), of Austria (1804–1918), or of Germany (1871–1918). [German *Kaiser,* from Old High German *Keisar,* from Latin *Caesar,* CAESAR.]

kai·ser·in, Kai·ser·in (kī′zər-ĭn) *n.* The wife of a kaiser; an empress. [German, feminine of *Kaiser,* KAISER.]

ka·ka (kä′kə) *n.* A brownish or greenish parrot, *Nestor meridionalis,* of New Zealand. [Maori, imitative of its cry.]

ka·ka·po (kä′kə-pō′) *n., pl.* **-pos.** A ground-dwelling owllike nocturnal parrot, *Strigops habroptilus,* of New Zealand, having greenish plumage. [Maori KAKA (parrot) + *po,* night.]

ka·ke·mo·no (kä′kə-mō′nō) *n., pl.* **-nos.** A Japanese scroll painting on silk or paper that is hung vertically. [Japanese, "hanging thing," scroll : *kake,* hanging + *mono,* thing.]

ka·la-a·zar (kä′lə-ə-zär′) *n.* A chronic, usually fatal disease that occurs in Asia, especially in India, is caused by a protozoan parasite, *Leishmania donovani,* and is characterized by irregular fever, enlargement of the spleen and liver, hemorrhages, and extreme emaciation. [Hindi *kālā-āzār,* "black disease" : *kālā,* black, from Sanskrit *kālaḥ,* blue-black, black, from Dravidian + *āzār,* disease, from Persian *āzār*†.]

Ka·la·ha·ri Desert (kä′lə-här′ē). Arid, sand-covered plateau between the Zambezi and Orange rivers in southern Africa. It occupies most of Botswana and parts of South Africa and Namibia and is inhabited by Bushmen and Hottentots.

Kal·a·ma·zoo (kăl′ə-mə-zōō′). A city of southwest Michigan, on the Kalamazoo River at its confluence with Portage Creek. It is an industrial and commercial center in a fertile farm area. The city has a large paper industry.

kal·an·cho·e (kăl′ən-kō′ē, kə-lăng′kō-ē) *n.* Any of various small tropical shrubs of the genus *Kalanchoe,* having clusters of variously colored, often red flowers on tall stems, that are cultivated as a house plant. [French, ultimately from Cantonese *goh leung choi* (Mandarin *gāo liáng cái*), tall cool plant.]

Ka·lash·ni·kov (kə-lăsh′nĭ-kôf′) *n.* A trademark for an automatic rifle, designed in the U.S.S.R., that is operated by gas, has a caliber of 7.62 millimeters, and has a high degree of accuracy over ranges of up to 300 meters. Also called "AK 47."

kale, kail (kāl) *n.* **1.** A variety of cabbage, *Brassica oleracea acephala,* eaten as a vegetable or used for livestock feed, having ruffled or crinkled leaves that do not form a tight head. Also called "borecole." **2.** *Scottish.* **a.** A cabbage. **b.** Broth containing cabbage. **3.** *Slang.* Money. [Middle English (northern dialect) *cal(e),* variant of COLE.]

ka·lei·do·scope (kə-lī′də-skōp′) *n.* **1.** A tube in which patterns of colors are optically produced and viewed for amusement; especially, one in which a pair of angled mirrors reflect light transmitted through loose bits of colored glass contained at one end, causing them to appear as symmetrical designs when viewed at the other. **2.** A constantly changing set of colors. **3.** A series of changing phases or events. [Greek *kalos,* beautiful + *eidos,* form + -SCOPE.] **—ka·lei·do·scop·ic** (kə-lī′də-skŏp′ĭk), **ka·lei·do·scop·i·cal** (-ĭ-kəl) *adj.* **—ka·lei·do·scop·i·cal·ly** *adv.*

kalends. Variant of **calends.**

ka·li (kā′lē, kăl′ē) *n.* A plant, the **saltwort** (see).

Ka·li (kä′lē). In Hindu mythology, Devi, considered as the goddess of death and destruction.

Kal·i·man·tan (kăl′ə-măn′tän′, kä′lə-). Also **Indonesian Borneo.** The Indonesian section of the island of Borneo, occupying two thirds of the island. It is densely forested and produces timber.

Ka·lim·ba (kə-lĭm′bə) *n.* An African musical instrument in the shape of a wooden box set with metal bars that are plucked with the fingers. [Of African origin.]

Ka·li·nin (kə-lē′nĭn), **Mikhail Ivanovich** (1875–1946). President of the supreme council of the U.S.S.R. (1937–46). He was born a peasant, took part in the 1917 revolution, and joined the politburo in 1926. He was a founder of *Pravda* (1912).

Ka·li·nin·grad (kə-lē′nĭn-grăd′). Also (until 1946) **Kö·nigs·berg** (kā′nĭgz-bûrg′). A port in western Russia, on the Baltic Sea. It was founded (1255) by the Teutonic Knights and eventually became the capital of East Prussia.

Ka·li·yu·ga (kä′lə-yōō′gə). *n. Hindu Mythology.* The fourth and present age of the world, characterized by moral degeneration.

kal·li·din (kăl′ə-dĭn) *n.* A type of **kinin** (see).

kal·li·kre·in (kăl′ĭ-krē′ĭn, kə-lĭk′rē-ĭn) *n.* Any of several enzymes that act on globulins in the blood to synthesize the kinins bradykinin and kallidin.

kal·mi·a (kăl′mē-ə) *n.* An evergreen shrub of the genus *Kalmia,* which includes the **mountain laurel** (see).

Kal·muck (kăl′mŭk′, käl-mŭk′) *n., pl.* **-mucks** or collectively **Kalmuck.** Also **Kal·muk** or **Kal·myk** (kăl′mĭk, käl-mĭk′) **1.** A member of one of the Buddhist Mongol peoples originally inhabiting northwestern China and later migrating westward to the lower Volga. **2.** The Mongolian language spoken by the Kalmucks.

ka·long (kä′lông, -lŏng, kə-lông′, -lŏng′) *n.* An East Indian fruit bat, *Pteropus vampyrus,* having a wingspan of over 4 feet. [Javanese.]

kalpak. Variant of **calpac.**

kalsomine. Variant of **calcimine.**

Ka·ma (kä′mə). In Hindu mythology, the god of erotic love, son of Brahma and husband of Rati.

kam·a·cite (kăm′ə-sīt′) *n.* A nickel-iron alloy found in certain meteorites. [Obsolete German *Kamacit,* from Greek *kamax* (stem *kamak-*), shaft.]

ka·ma·la (kä′mə-lə, kăm′ə-, kŭm′ə-) *n.* **1.** An Asian tree, *Mallotus philippinensis,* that bears a hairy, capsular fruit. **2.** A powder obtained from the capsules of the kamala tree that is used as a dye and was formerly used to treat tapeworm and ringworm infestations. [Sanskrit *kamala,* probably from Dravidian, akin to Kanarese *kōmaḷe.*]

Ka·ma·su·tra (kä′mə-sōō′trə) *n.* A treatise in Sanskrit (4th–7th century A.D.) setting forth rules for erotic love and marriage in accordance with Hindu law. [Sanskrit, "book on love" : *kāma,* love, desire + *sūtram,* manual.]

Kam·chat·ka Peninsula (kăm-chăt′kə). A peninsula of Far Eastern Russia, occupying 269,878 square kilometers (104,200 square miles) between the Sea of Okhotsk and the Bering Sea and Pacific Ocean.

kame (kām) *n.* A mound or long, low ridge of sand and gravel deposited during the melting of glacial ice. [Scottish, from Middle English *camb,* northern variant of COMB.]

Ka·me·ha·me·ha I (kä-mā′hä-mā′hä), called "the Great" (1753?–1819). First king of the Sandwich (now Hawaiian) Islands. He first became king of Hawaii Island and then through conquest gained control of all the islands. Kamehameha founded a dynasty that lasted until 1872.

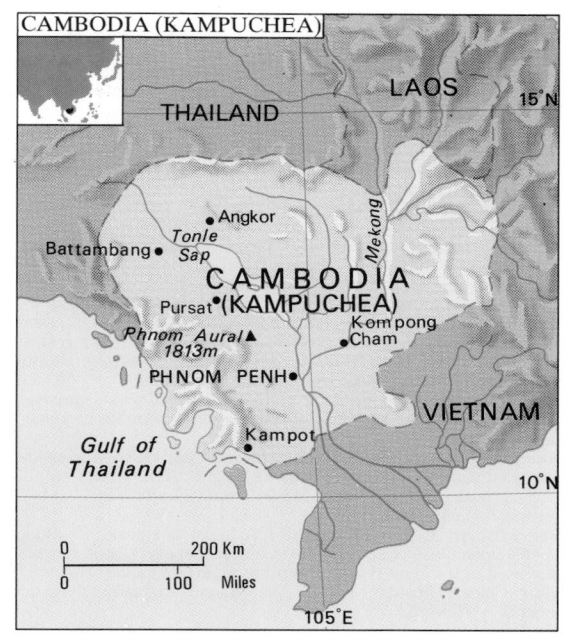

CAMBODIA (KAMPUCHEA)

ka·mi (kä′mē) *n., pl.* **kami.** A divinity or god in the Shinto religion. [Japanese, "god."]

ka·mi·ka·ze (kä′mĭ-kä′zē) *n.* **1.** During World War II, a Japanese pilot trained to make a suicidal crash attack on a target such as a naval vessel. **2.** An airplane loaded with explosives to be piloted in a suicide attack.
~*adj.* **1.** Of, pertaining to, resembling, or being a kamikaze: *enemy pilots receiving kamikaze training.* **2.** *Informal.* Courting disaster; reckless or suicidal: *a kamikaze cab driver.* [Japanese, "divine wind" : *kami,* KAMI + *kaze,* wind.]

Kam·pa·la (käm-pä′lə). The capital of Uganda, on Lake Victoria. It was founded by the British near Mengo, the seat of the kabaka (king) of Buganda. It became the country's capital in 1962.

kam·pong (käm′pông′, käm′-) *n.* A compound or village in Malaysia. [Malay.]

Kam·pu·che·a (käm′pə-chē′ə). Formerly **Cam·bo·di·a** (kăm-bō′dē-ə) and renamed the Republic of Cambodia (1989). Republic of Southeast Asia. Its fertile basin is drained by the Mekong River, and the Khmer Empire flourished here (500–1450). Cambodia became part of French Indochina in 1863 and was a battleground for foreign powers after French withdrawal (1953). From 1971 to 1975 the country was known as the Khmer Republic. During the regime of Pol Pot, leader of the successful communist Khmer Rouge (1976–79), the country was known as Democratic Kampuchea, and some 3,000,000 people are estimated to have died of starvation or to have been killed. The Vietnamese occupied Kampuchea (1978–89), and insurgency continues. Much of the country has been ruled by the pro-Vietnamese Heng Samrin since 1979. Warfare has severely disrupted Kampuchea's agriculture-based economy, and the country relies on imports of food and fuel, and foreign aid. Area, 181,035 square kilometers (69,880 square miles). Population, 8,246,000. Capital, Phnom Penh. **—Kam·pu·che·an** *n. & adj.*

kamsin. Variant of **khamsin.**

ka·na (kä′nə) *n.* Either of two Japanese syllabaries, **hiragana** or **katakana** (*both of which see*). Compare **kanji.** [Japanese, "pseudocharacters" (as distinguished from *kanji,* which are regarded as originally Chinese characters) : *ka,* false + *na,* name, character.]

Ka·na·ka (kə-nă′kə, -năk′ə) *n.* **1.** A native of the South Sea Islands. **2.** A native of Hawaii. [Hawaiian, "person."]

kan·a·my·cin (kăn′ə-mī′sĭn) *n.* An antibiotic, $C_{18}H_{36}O_{11}N_4$, obtained from the soil actinomycete bacterium *Streptomyces kanamyceticus* and used to treat a wide range of bacterial infections. [New Latin *Streptomycetes kanamyceticus* (specific epithet of the bacterium).]

Kanchenjunga. See Kangchenjunga, Mount.

Kan·da·har or **Qan·da·har** (kăn′də-här′). A city in southern Afghanistan. It is the center of a fertile region and lies on the trade route between Pakistan and the U.S.S.R.

Kan·din·sky (kăn-dĭn′skē), **Wassily** (1866–1944). Russian abstract painter, who worked in Germany. He considered form and color capable of spiritual expression. Kandinsky was appointed professor of the Bauhaus School in Weimar (1922). He was a member of the *Blaue Reiter,* a group of German expressionist painters.

Kan·dy (kăn′dē). Formerly **Can·dy.** A city in the central tea-growing district of Sri Lanka. It was the seat of the Singhalese kings until the British occupation in 1815.

kane. Variant of **kain.**

Kanea. See Canea.

kangaroo *The red kangaroo (above) is the largest species of this group of Australian marsupials. It can travel at 50 kilometers (30 miles) per hour and jump 9 meters (30 feet) in a single bound.*

kapok *The traditional stuffing for toys, cushions, and life jackets is made from silky fibers that surround the seeds of the tropical silk-cotton tree,* Ceiba pentandra.

PRONUNCIATION KEY

ă, pat; ā, pay; âr, care;
ä, father, are; b, bib;
ch, church; d, deed; ĕ, pet;
ē, be; f, fife; g, gag; h, hat;
hw, which; ĭ, pit; ī, pie;
îr, pier; j, judge; k, kick;
l, lid, needle; m, mum;
n, no, sudden; ng, thing;
ŏ, pot; ō, toe; ô, paw, for;
oi, noise; ou, out; o͝o, book;
o͞o, boot; p, pop; r, roar;
s, sauce; sh, ship, dish;
t, tight; th, thin, path;
th, this, bathe; ŭ, cut; ûr, fur;
v, valve; w, with; y, yes;
z, zebra, size; zh, vision;
ə, about, item, edible,
gallop, circus, peaceful

IN FOREIGN WORDS:

à, *Fr.* ami; œ, *Fr.* feu, *Ger.* schön; ü, *Fr.* tu, *Ger.* über; KH, *Ger.* ich, *Scot.* loch; N, *Fr.* bon; y', *Fr.* Compiègne

STRESS MARKS:

Primary stress: ′
in·cite′ (ĭn-sīt′)
Secondary stress: ′
in′sight′ (ĭn′sīt′)

kan·ga, khan·ga (kăng′gə, kăng′ə) *n.* A piece of brightly colored cloth worn as a garment by women in East Africa.

kan·ga·roo (kăng′gə-ro͞o′) *n., pl.* **-roos.** Any of various herbivorous marsupials of the family Macropodidae, of Australia and adjacent areas, characteristically having short forelimbs, large hind limbs adapted for leaping, and a long, tapered tail. [Probably from a native name in Queensland, Australia.]

kangaroo closure *n.* A form of closure in a parliamentary debate in which the speaker limits discussion to selected amendments. Compare **guillotine.**

kangaroo court *n.* **1.** A mock court set up in violation of established legal procedure. **2.** A court characterized by dishonesty or incompetence. [By allusion to its irregular procedures, suggesting the leaps of a kangaroo.]

kangaroo paw *n.* Any of various plants of the Australian genus *Anigozanthus,* having swordlike leaves and clusters of tubular flowers that when unopened resemble a kangaroo's paws.

kangaroo rat *n.* Any of various long-tailed rodents of the genera *Dipodomys* and *Microdipodops,* of arid areas of western North America, having long hind legs adapted for jumping.

kangaroo vine *n.* A climbing or trailing vine, *Cissus antarctica,* native to Australia and widely grown as a house plant for its glossy green foliage.

Kang·chen·jun·ga, Mount (kăng′chən-jŭng′gə). Also **Kan·chen·jun·ga** (kăn′-) or **Kin·chin·jun·ga** (kĭn′hĭn-). The world's third-highest peak (8,598 meters; 28,215 feet), on the India-Nepal border. It was first climbed in 1955.

kan·ji (kän′jē) *n., pl.* **kanji** or **-jis. 1.** A Japanese system of writing based upon borrowed or modified Chinese characters. **2.** A character used in the kanji system of writing. Compare **kana.** [Japanese, from Chinese (Mandarin) *hànzi* : *hàn,* Chinese (originally a dynastic name) + *zi,* word.]

Kan·na·da (kä′nə-də) *n.* A Dravidian language spoken chiefly in the state of Karnataka, in southern India. **—Kan·na·da** *adj.*

Ka·no (kä′nō). A city in northern Nigeria, capital of Kano state. It was once the terminus of a major Sahara caravan route and is still a trade center.

Kan·pur (kän′po͝or). *English* **Cawn·pore** (kôn′pōr). The largest city in Uttar Pradesh in northern India, on the Ganges River. It is a communications junction and manufacturing center. Its British garrison was massacred (1857) during the Indian Mutiny.

Kan·sas (kăn′zəs). *Abbr.* **Kans.** State of the central United States, in the Great Plains. Its main products are agricultural. It joined the Union in 1861 after a bloody fight between free staters and proslavery groups. Topeka is the capital.

Kansas City. Either of a pair of twin cities in the central United States. Kansas City, Kansas, is west of the Kansas River; the much larger Kansas City, Missouri, lies to its east.

Kansu. See **Gansu.**

Kant (kănt, känt), **Immanuel** (1724–1804). German idealist philosopher. In the *Critique of Pure Reason* (1781) Kant argued that reason was the means by which the phenomena of experience are translated into understanding. He put forward his system of ethics based on the categorical imperative in the *Critique of Practical Reason* (1788). **—Kant·i·an** *n. & adj.* **—Kant·i·an·ism** *n.*

kan·tar (kăn-tär′) *n.* Any of various units of weight used in some eastern Mediterranean countries. [Arabic *qinṭār,* ultimately from Latin *centēnārius,* of a hundred, from *centum,* hundred.]

kan·zu (kăn′zo͞o) *n.* A long, usually white garment worn by men in Africa. [Swahili.]

ka·o·lin (kā′ə-lĭn) *n.* A fine white to yellowish or grayish clay, mostly kaolinite, used as an adsorbent in medicine and in ceramics and refractories and as a filler or coating for paper and textiles. Also called "china clay," "porcelain clay," "terra alba." [French, from Mandarin Chinese *gaō lĭng,* name of a hill in Jiangxi Province where it was first obtained, "high mountain" : *gaō,* high + *lĭng,* mountain, peak.]

ka·o·lin·ite (kā′ə-lĭ-nīt′) *n.* A mineral, essentially $Al_2O_3{\cdot}2SiO_2{\cdot}2H_2O$, the principal constituent of kaolin.

ka·on (kā′ŏn′) *n. Symbol* **K** *Physics.* **1.** Either of two elementary particles in the meson family, a neutral particle, K zero, or a positively charged particle, K plus, having strangeness quantum number −1. **2.** Either of two corresponding antiparticles, K zero bar or K minus. [*ka,* the letter *k* + (MES)ON.]

ka·pell·meis·ter (kə-pĕl′mī′stər, kä-, kă-) *n., pl.* **kapellmeister.** Often **Kapellmeister.** The musical director of a choir or orchestra, especially at the court of an 18th-century German prince. [German, from *Kapelle,* choir + *Meister,* master.]

kaph, caph (käf, kôf) *n.* The 11th letter in the Hebrew alphabet. Transliterated in English as *K, k,* or *kh.* See feature at **alphabet.** [Hebrew *kāph,* "palm of the hand."]

ka·pok (kā′pŏk′) *n.* A silky fiber obtained from the fruit of the silk-cotton tree and used for insulation and as padding in pillows, mattresses, and life preservers. [Malay.]

kap·pa (kăp′ə) *n.* The tenth letter in the Greek alphabet, written Κ, κ. Transliterated in English as *K, k.* See feature at **alphabet.** [Greek, from Semitic, akin to Hebrew *kāph,* KAPH.]

ka·put (kə-po͝ot′, -po͞ot′, kä-) *adj. Informal.* **1.** Destroyed; wrecked. **2.** Not functioning; out of order. [German *kaputt,* from French *capot,* as in the expression *être capot,* to have lost all tricks at cards, "be hoodwinked," from *capot,* cloak with hood, from *cape,* CAPE (garment).]

kar·a·bi·ner (kăr′ə-bē′nər) *n.* An oblong steel ring that is snapped to the eye of a piton and through which a rope is run, used in mountaineering. [German *Karabiner(haken),* "carbine hook" (originally used to fasten carbines to a belt) : *Karabiner,* carbine, from French *carabine,* CARBINE + *Haken,* hook.]

Ka·ra·chi (kə-rä′chē). Largest city and chief port and naval base of Pakistan, on the Arabian Sea. It was the national capital from 1947 to 1959.

Ka·ra·jan (kär′ə-yän′), **Herbert von** (1908–89). Austrian conductor. He founded the Salzburg Easter Festival in 1967.

Kar·a·kal·pak (kăr′ə-kăl-păk′) *n.* **1.** A native or inhabitant of Karakalpakstan. **2.** The language spoken by the Karakalpaks. **—Kar·a·kal·pak** *adj.*

Kar·a·kal·pak·stan (kăr′ə-kăl-păk′stăn). An administrative division of the Central Asian republic of Uzbekistan. It is comprised of parts of the Kyzul Kum Desert and the Amu Darya Delta on the Aral Sea. Many of the people are Karakalpak Muslims.

Kar·a·ko·ram Range (kăr′ə-kôr′əm). Range of mountains in central Asia, stretching through Jammu and Kashmir to Tibet. It includes Mt. Godwin-Austen, which at 8,611 meters (28,250 feet) is the world's second-highest mountain.

kar·a·kul, car·a·cul (kăr′ə-kəl) *n.* **1.** Any of a breed of sheep native to central Asia, having wool that is curled and glossy in the young and wiry and coarse in the adult. Also called "broadtail." **2.** Fur made from the pelt of a karakul lamb. Compare **broadtail, Persian lamb.** [Originally bred near *Kara Kul,* "black lake," lake in eastern Tajikistan.]

Ka·ra·man·lis (kär′ə-män-lēs′), **Constantine** (1907–). Greek prime minister (1955–63, 1974–80). In 1963 he resigned and went to Paris, returning after the fall of the Greek military government (1974). He was elected president in 1980 and resigned in 1985.

Ka·ra Sea (kär′ə). Shallow section of the Arctic Ocean, off northern Russia. The ice-locked sea is an important fishing ground, but is navigable only during August and September.

kar·at, car·at (kăr′ət) *n. Abbr.* **kt.** A unit of measure for the fineness of gold, equal to 1/24 of the total amount of pure gold in an alloy. [Old French *carat,* unit of weight for precious stones, CARAT.]

ka·ra·te (kə-rä′tē) *n.* A Japanese art of self-defense in which sharp blows and kicks are struck at an opponent's body. [Japanese : *kara,* empty + *te,* hand.]

Ka·re·li·a (kə-rē′le-ə, -rēl′yə). Administrative division of northwest Russia. It lies between the White Sea and Finland and is rich in timber and mineral deposits.

Ka·re·li·an (kə-rē′lē-ən, -rēl′yən) *n.* **1.** A native or inhabitant of Karelia. **2.** The Finnish dialect spoken by the Karelians. **—Ka·re·li·an** *adj.*

Karelian Isthmus. An isthmus in Russia, between the Gulf of Finland and Lake Ladoga. From 1917 the greater part, the north, was Finnish, but this was ceded to the U.S.S.R. in 1944.

Ka·ren (kə-rĕn′) *n., pl.* **-rens** or collectively **Karen. 1.** A member of a Thai people living in south Burma. **2.** Any of the languages of this people.

Ka·ri·ba, Lake (kə-rē′bə). A reservoir on the Zambia-Zimbabwe border. It was formed on the Zambezi River after the building of the Kariba Dam (1955–59), which provides hydroelectricity for the Copper Belt in Zambia and also parts of Zimbabwe.

Kar·loff (kär′lôf′, -lŏf′), **Boris,** born William Pratt (1887–1969). British film actor. He played the monster in *Frankenstein* (1931) and starred in many horror films.

Kar·lo·vy Va·ry (kär′lō-vē vä′rē). *German* **Karls·bad** (kärlz′băd′). Famous spa in Bohemia in Czechoslovakia. Its hot medicinal springs were popular with European royalty and aristocrats before World War I.

Karls·ruh·e or **Carls·ruh·e** (kärlz′ro͞o′ə). Canal port and industrial city in western Germany. Capital of the former state of Baden.

kar·ma (kär′mə, kûr′-) *n.* **1.** *Hinduism & Buddhism.* The sum of a person's actions during the successive phases of his existence, regarded as determining his destiny in future incarnations. **2.** Fate; destiny. [Sanskrit *karman* (nominative *karma*), act, deed, work, from *karoti,* he makes, he does.] **—kar·mic** (kär′mĭk, kûr′-) *adj.*

Kar·nak (kär′năk). Village in central Egypt on the Nile River. It is the site of ancient Thebes, with its Great Temple of Amen.

Kar·na·ta·ka (kär′nə-tä′kə). Formerly **My·sore** (mī-sôr′). State of India, on the Arabian Sea coast. It produces most of the world's sandalwood. Bangalore is the capital.

Kärn·ten (kĕrn′tən). *English* **Ca·rin·thi·a** (kə-rĭn′thē-ə). State of southern Austria. It produces cereals and livestock and has deposits of magnesite, iron ore, zinc, and lead. Klagenfurt is the capital.

ka·ross (kə-rŏs′) *n.* A simple cloak made from animal skins that is worn by southern African tribesmen. [Afrikaans *karos,* perhaps from Dutch *kuras,* from French *cuirasse,* CUIRASS.]

kar·ri (kăr′ē) *n.* **1.** A eucalyptus tree, *Eucalyptus diversicolor,* of western Australia. **2.** The hard red timber of the karri. [Native Australian name.]

kar·roo, ka·roo (kə-ro͞o′) *n.* Any arid plateau of southern Africa. [Afrikaans *karo,* of Hottentot origin.]

Kar·roo or **Ka·roo** (kə-ro͞o′). Plateau of southern South Africa. It is divided by the Groot-Swartberge Range into the lower, southern Little Karroo and the higher Great Karroo. It is a grazing and fruit-growing area.

Karroo System. Vast system of rocks found in Africa south of the equator. Dating from the Permo-Carboniferous to late Triassic periods, it comprises nonmarine sediments, with coal and oil deposits, and volcanic rocks. The system is noted for its reptilian fossils. [German.]

karst (kärst) *n.* A barren limestone or dolomitic region in which erosion has produced fissures, sinkholes, underground streams, and caverns. [German.]

karyo–, caryo– *prefix.* Indicates the nucleus of a living cell; for example, **karyogamy, karyotype.** [New Latin, from Greek *karuon,* kernel, nut.]

kar·y·og·a·my (kăr′ē-ŏg′ə-mē) *n.* The coming together and fusing of two gamete nuclei. [KARYO- + -GAMY.]

kar·y·o·ki·ne·sis (kăr′ē-ō-kə-nē′sĭs) *n.* A form of cell division, **mitosis** *(see).* —**kar·y·o·ki·net·ic** (kăr′ē-ō-kə-nĕt′ĭk) *adj.*

kar·y·o·lymph (kăr′ē-ə-lĭmf′) *n.* The clear homogeneous liquid portion of nuclear protoplasm.

kar·y·o·plasm (kăr′ē-ə-plăz′əm) *n.* Nuclear protoplasm, **nucleoplasm** *(see).* [KARYO- + -PLASM.] —**kar·y·o·plas·mic** (kăr′ē-ə-plăz′-mĭk) *adj.*

kar·y·o·some (kăr′ē-ə-sōm′) *n.* **1.** An aggregation of chromatin in a resting nucleus during mitosis. **2.** A cell nucleus. [KARYO- + -SOME (body).]

kar·y·o·type (kăr′ē-ə-tīp′) *n.* A photomicrograph of metaphase chromosomes of a given species in a standard array showing their number, size, and shape. Also called "idiogram." —**kar·y·o·typ·ic** (kăr′ē-ə-tĭp′ĭk), **kar·y·o·typ·i·cal** (-ĭ-kəl) *adj.*

Kasan. See **Kazan.**

Kasbah. Variant of **Casbah.**

ka·sha (kä′shə, käsh′ə) *n.* A dish of eastern European origin consisting of buckwheat groats. [Russian *kasha,* from Old Slavonic *kāsyā* (unattested).]

Kash·mir or **Cash·mere** (kăsh′mîr, kăsh-mîr′). Former princely state on the northwestern border of India. A Hindu-led region with a largely Muslim population, it became a source of conflict between India and Pakistan after Indian independence (1947) and was partitioned in 1949, becoming Jammu and Kashmir, an Indian state, and Azad Kashmir under Pakistani control. Sporadic fighting, however, continued.

Kashmir goat. Variant of **Cashmere goat.**

Kash·mir·i (kăsh-mîr′ē, kăzh-) *n., pl.* **-miris** or collectively **Kashmiri.** **1.** A native or inhabitant of Kashmir. **2.** An Indic language spoken in Jammu and Kashmir. —**Kash·mir·i** *adj.*

kash·ruth, kash·rut (kä-shrōōth′, -shōōt′) *n.* **1.** The body of Jewish dietary laws. **2.** The state of being kosher. [Hebrew, "appropriateness."]

Kas·sel or **Cas·sel** (kä′səl). City in Hesse in central Germany. The city was chartered in 1198.

kat, khat (kät) *n.* An evergreen shrub, *Catha edulis,* native to Africa and Arabia, whose leaves have narcotic properties and are chewed or used to make a tea. [Arabic *qāt.*]

kat·a·bat·ic wind (kăt′ə-băt′ĭk) *n.* A cold flow of air traveling downward. [Greek *katabatikos,* affording a means of descent, from *katabos,* descending, steep, from *katabainein,* to go down + *-ikos,* -IC.]

ka·ta·ka·na (kä′tə-kä′nə, kăt′ə-kän′ə) *n.* A phonetic Japanese syllabary used for writing foreign words or documents, such as telegrams. Also called "kana." See **hiragana.** [Japanese : *kata,* one, one-sided + KANA.]

ka·thak (kə-täk′) *n.* A classical dance of northern India that uses complex rhythmic patterns and contains elements of mimed narrative. [Bengali, "storyteller," from Sanskrit *kathayati,* he tells.]

ka·tha·ka·li (kä′tə-kä′lē) *n.* A vigorous classical dance of Kerala in southern India that is performed by men wearing elaborate costumes and make-up and is based on episodes from Hindu literary texts. [Malayalam, drama : *katha,* story, from Sanskrit *kathā,* talk + *kali,* play.]

Ka·tha·rev·u·sa, Ka·tha·rev·ou·sa (kä′thə-rĕv′ə-sä′) *n.* The literary and official form of Modern Greek, showing many morphological and lexical features restored from Classical Greek. Compare **Dhimotiki.** [Modern Greek *kathareuousa,* from Greek, feminine present participle of *kathareuein,* to be pure, from *katharos,* pure.]

Kath·man·du or **Kat·man·du** (kăt′măn-dōō′, kät′-). Capital of Nepal. It was founded in the 8th century on the Baghmati River and became the capital when taken by the Gurkhas in 1768.

Kat·mai National Monument (kăt′mī). A nearly inaccessible region, 1,130,815 hectares (2,792,137 acres), in southern Alaska. The area includes Mt. Katmai, an active volcano, the Valley of the Ten Thousand Smokes, glacier-covered peaks, and crater lakes.

Ka·to·wi·ce (kä′tō-vēt′sĕ). City in southern Poland, producing coal, and iron and steel. It was part of Germany until the partition of Silesia (1921).

Kat·te·gat or **Cat·te·gat** (kăt′ĭ-găt′). Strait between Sweden and Jutland, Denmark, connecting with the North Sea via the Skagerrak and with the Baltic Sea via the Øresund, Store Baelt, and Lille Baelt.

ka·ty·did (kä′tē-dĭd′) *n.* Any of various green, long-horned insects of the predominantly tropical family Tettigoniidae, related to the grasshoppers and the crickets, with specialized organs on the wings of the male that produce a distinctive shrill sound when rubbed together. [Imitative.]

Kauff·mann (kouf′män′), **(Maria Anna) Angelica** (1741-1807). Swiss painter. She worked chiefly in England, often contributing small works to rooms designed by the Adam brothers.

Kauf·man (kôf′mən), **George Simon** (1889-1961). U.S. playwright and director. Working alone or collaborating with writers like Marc Connolly (1890-1980), Edna Ferber, and Moss Hart, he wrote or directed such Broadway hits as *Dulcy* (1921), *Dinner at Eight*

(1932), and the Pulitzer Prize winner *Of Thee I Sing* (1931).

Ka·un·da (kä-ōōn′də), **Kenneth David** (1924–). Zambian President (1964–91). He led his country (formerly Northern Rhodesia) to full independence under the name of Zambia (1964). He has been influential in the Organization of African Unity.

kau·ri (kou′rē) *n.* **1. a.** Any of several coniferous trees of the genus *Agathis;* especially, *A. australis,* of New Zealand, having white, close-grained, durable wood. **b.** The wood of such a tree. In both senses, also called "kauri pine." **2.** A resin obtained from a kauri or from deposits of fossilized exudations of a kauri and used in varnishes and enamels. In this sense, also called "kauri gum," "kauri resin." [Maori *kawri.*]

ka·va (kä′və) *n.* **1.** A shrub, *Piper methysticum,* of tropical Pacific islands, the dried roots of which are used to make an intoxicating drink. **2.** The beverage made from kava. [Tongan *kava,* "bitter."]

Ka·wa·sa·ki (kä′wə-sä′kē). City in Japan, part of the Tokyo Bay industrial complex. Its industries include shipbuilding, engineering, and oil refining.

kay (kā) *n.* The letter *k.*

Kay (kā), **Sir.** *Arthurian Legend.* The rude, boastful foster brother and steward of King Arthur.

kay·ak, kai·ak (kī′ăk′) *n.* **1.** A watertight Eskimo canoe made of skins stretched over a light wooden frame and having a deck covering that closes around the waist of the paddler. Compare **umiak.** **2.** A lightweight and highly maneuverable, usually canvas-covered canoe similar in construction to a kayak. [Eskimo *qajaq.*]

Kaye (kā), **Danny** (1913–87). U.S. entertainer. After several years of entertaining in upstate New York resorts, he received parts in Broadway productions such as *Lady in the Dark* (1941). He also starred in several movies, including *The Secret Life of Walter Mitty* (1947) and *Hans Christian Andersen* (1952).

kay·o (kā-ō′, kā′ō) *n., pl.* **-os.** *Slang.* A knockout in boxing. ~*tr.v.* **kayoed, -oing, -os.** *Slang.* To knock out. [Pronunciation of K.O., abbreviation of *knock out.*]

Ka·zakh (kə-zăk′, -zăk′) *n., pl.* **-zakhs** or collectively **Kazakh.** Also **Ka·zak. 1.** A member of a Turkic people dwelling in Kazakhstan and in northwestern China. **2.** The Turkic language of this people. —**Ka·zakh** *adj.*

Ka·zakh·stan (kə-zäk′stän). Republic in central Asia. A constituent republic of the U.S.S.R. from 1936, it became independent in 1991. Area, 2,727,813 square kilometers (1,049,159 square miles). Population, 16,810,000. Capital, Alma-Ata.

Ka·zan (kə-zăn′, -zän′). City in European Russia, on the Volga River. It was capital of a Tatar khanate until captured by Russia in 1552. Tolstoy and Lenin studied at its university.

Ka·zan (kə-zăn′, -zän′), **Elia,** born Elia Kazanjoglous (1909–). U.S. stage and film director, born in Turkey of Greek parents. He directed Tennessee Williams's *A Streetcar Named Desire* (1947) and the films *On the Waterfront* (1954) and *East of Eden* (1955).

Ka·zan·tza·kis (kä′zənt-sä′kēs), **Nikos** (1885-1957). Greek writer. Among his novels are *Zorba the Greek* (1946) and *Christ Recrucified* (1954).

ka·zoo (kə-zōō′) *n., pl.* **-zoos.** A toy musical instrument with a membrane that produces a sound when a player hums or sings into the mouthpiece. [Probably imitative of its sound.]

kb kilobar.

KB *Chess.* king's bishop.

K.B. 1. King's Bench. **2.** Knight Bachelor.

K.B.E. Knight (Commander of the Order) of the British Empire.

KBP *Chess.* king's bishop's pawn.

kc kilocycle.

K.C. 1. King's Counsel. **2.** Knights of Columbus.

kcal kilocalorie.

kcs, kc/s kilocycles per second.

K.D., k.d. *Finance.* knocked down.

ke·a (kē′ə) *n.* A brownish-green parrot, *Nestor notabilis,* of mountainous areas of New Zealand, that normally eats insects but sometimes kills sheep by slashing them and eating their fat and flesh. [Maori, imitative of its cry.]

Kean (kēn), **Edmund** (c. 1787-1833). British actor. He was hailed as a great tragic actor for his roles as Shylock at the Drury Lane Theatre (1814), as Richard III, and as Iago.

Kea·ton (kē′tən), **Buster,** born Joseph Francis Keaton (1895-1966). U.S. film actor. His skill as a mime artist made him a great comedian of the silent screen. His films include *The Navigator* (1924).

Keats (kēts), **John** (1795-1821). English poet. His collection *Lamia and Other Poems* (1820) includes "The Eve of St. Agnes" and the famous odes "To a Nightingale," "To Autumn," "To Psyche," and "On a Grecian Urn." He died of tuberculosis at the age of 26. —**Keats·i·an** *adj. & n.*

ke·bab, ke·bob (kə-bŏb′) *n.* **Shish kebab** *(see).*

Ke·ble (kē′bəl), **John** (1792-1866). British clergyman. He delivered a sermon in Oxford (1833) defending Catholic principles in the Church of England, so initiating the Oxford Movement.

Kechua. Variant of **Quechua.**

keck (kĕk) *intr.v.* **kecked, kecking, kecks.** To make the sound of vomiting. [Imitative.]

ked (kĕd) *n.* Any of various wingless parasitic flies; especially, the sheep ked, *Melophagus ovinus,* and the deer ked, *Liptoptena cervi.* [16th century : origin unknown.]

kedge (kĕj) *n.* A light anchor used for warping a vessel. ~*v.* **kedged, kedging, kedges.** —*tr.* To move (a ship) by pulling on a rope attached to an anchor lowered some distance away.

katydid *The katydid,* Pterophylla camellifolia, *rubs its wings together to produce its high-pitched song. The sound, which is made only by males, is designed to attract females.*

kayak *Now much used in sport, the watertight Eskimo kayak was originally developed for hunting in very cold waters.*

—intr. To move by means of a kedge. Used of a ship. [From *kedge,* earlier *cadge,* to warp a ship, perhaps from Middle English *caggen*†, to tie, bind.]

kedg·er·ee (kĕj′ə-rē′, kĕj′ə-rē′) *n.* **1.** A dish of rice, lentils, onions, eggs, and spices served in India. **2.** A dish consisting of flaked fish, boiled rice, and eggs. [Hindi *khichṛī,* from Sanskrit *khiccā*†.]

keef. Variant of **kif.**

keek (kēk) *intr.v.* **keeked, keeking, keeks.** *Scottish.* To peek; peep. *~n. Scottish.* A look, especially a quick one; peek. [Middle English *kike,* probably from Middle Dutch *kiken,* to peep.]

keel¹ (kēl) *n.* **1.** The main structural member of a ship, running lengthwise along the center line from bow to stern and forming the backbone of the vessel to which the frames are attached. **2.** A ship. **3.** A structure that resembles a ship's keel in function or shape, such as the member extending lengthwise at the bottom of an aircraft fuselage. **4.** *Biology.* A structure having a longitudinal ridge suggestive of a ship's keel, as: **a.** The anterior part of the breastbone of a flying bird. **b.** A pair of united petals in certain flowers, as those of the pea. **—on an even keel.** In an unimpaired or stable condition; steady.

~v. **keeled, keeling, keels.** *—tr.* To cause (a vessel) to capsize. *—intr.* **1.** To roll on her keel; capsize. Used of a ship. **2.** To collapse or fall in or as if in a faint: *He keeled over when he was told about the disaster.* [Middle English *ke(o)le,* from Old Norse *kjölr.*] **—keeled** *adj.*

keel² *n.* **1. a.** A barge, especially one for carrying coal on the Tyne in England. **b.** The amount carried by such a barge. **2.** A British unit of weight formerly used for coal and equal to 21.2 tons. [Middle English *kele,* from Middle Dutch *kiel,* ship.]

keel³ *tr.v.* **keeled, keeling, keels.** *Archaic & Regional.* To cool (a hot liquid, for example), especially by stirring in order to prevent boiling over. Used chiefly in the phrase *keel the pot.* [Middle English *kelen,* Old English *cēlan.*]

keel·boat (kēl′bōt′) *n.* A large, covered, flat-bottomed boat with a keel but without sails, used for river transport.

keel·haul (kēl′hôl′) *tr.v.* **-hauled, -hauling, -hauls. 1.** To punish by dragging under the keel of a ship from one side to the other or from stem to stern. **2.** To castigate; scold severely. [Dutch *kielhalen* : Middle Dutch *kiel,* keel of a ship + *halen,* to pull, haul.]

Keeling Islands. See **Cocos Islands.**

keel·son (kĕl′sən, kēl′-) *n.* Also **kel·son** (kĕl′-). *Nautical.* A timber or girder placed parallel with and bolted to the keel of a ship for additional strength. [Probably from Low German *kielswīn* : Middle Low German *kiel,* keel of a ship + *swīn,* swine, "timber."]

keen¹ (kēn) *adj.* **keener, keenest. 1.** Having a fine, sharp cutting edge or point: *a keen razor.* **2.** Intellectually acute; penetrating: *a keen mind.* **3.** Acutely sensitive: *a keen sense of hearing.* **4.** Vivid; intense: *"His entire body hungered for keen sensation, something exciting"* (Richard Wright). **5.** Bitter; piercing: *a keen wind.* **6.** Marked by sharp dispute: *a keen discussion.* **7. a.** Ardent; enthusiastic: *a keen chess player.* **b.** Eagerly desirous: *keen on going.* **8.** *Slang.* Splendid; fine: *We saw a keen movie.* —See Synonyms at **eager, sharp.** [Middle English *kene,* Old English *cēne,* wise, bold, powerful, from Common Germanic *kōnjaz* (unattested).] **—keen·ly** *adv.* **—keen·ness** *n.*

keen² *n.* A loud wailing lamentation for the dead.

~intr.v. **keened, keening, keens.** To wail or lament loudly, especially for the dead. [Irish Gaelic *caoine,* lamentation, from *caoinim,* I wail, from Old Irish *coīnim,* from Common Celtic *koinyo-* (unattested), to wail.]

keen·er (kē′nər) *n.* One who keens; especially, a professional mourner at an Irish funeral.

keep (kēp) *v.* **kept** (kĕpt), **keeping, keeps.** *—tr.* **1.** To retain possession of: *keep the change; kept his nerve.* **2.** To store; put customarily: *Where do you keep your saw?* **3.** To take in one's charge temporarily: *Keep this for me until I return.* **4. a.** To provide with the necessities of life; support: *"There's little to earn and many to keep"* (Charles Kingsley). **b.** To support (a mistress or lover) financially. Used chiefly in the past participle: *a kept woman.* **5. a.** To supply with room and board for a charge: *keep boarders.* **b.** To raise and feed: *keep chickens.* **6.** To have the resources to retain for pleasure or use: *"It is not too much for me now, in degree or cost, to keep a coach"* (Samuel Pepys). **7.** To have in ready supply: *I always keep plenty of flour and sugar on hand.* **8.** To be in charge of; manage or tend: *keeps a large garden.* **9. a.** To maintain by making regular entries in: *kept a diary.* **b.** To enter (data) in a book: *keep financial records.* **10.** To cause to continue in a specified state, condition, or course of action: *kept us all guessing; keep her away.* **11. a.** To preserve and protect; maintain: *kept up the house and grounds.* **b.** To withhold for the time being; reserve: *keep some for tomorrow.* **12.** To restrain from leaving; detain: *What kept you? The teacher kept us after school.* **13.** To cause to remain; confine: *keep in quarantine.* **14.** To prevent or deter: *used an insulated bucket to keep the ice cubes from melting.* **15. a.** To observe habitually: *keep late hours.* **b.** To observe in an appropriate or prescribed manner: *keep the Sabbath.* **16.** To adhere to; fulfill: *keep a schedule; keep one's word.* **17.** To refrain from divulging: *keep a secret; keep one's own counsel.* **18.** To associate with habitually: *She kept bad company.* *—intr.* **1.** To remain in a specified state, condition, or course of action; stay: *keep in line; keep quiet.* **2. a.** To persevere in; continue to do: *keep guessing; kept on talking.* **b.** To continue in a direction or course: *keep to the left.* **3.** To be with respect to health: *How are you keeping?* **4. a.** To remain fresh or unspoiled: *The dessert won't keep.* **b.** To continue being withheld: *I've got some interesting gossip, but it'll keep till tomorrow.* —See Synonyms at **observe.** **—keep at it.** To persevere in an action or work. **—keep back.** To refuse to tell or give; withhold. **—keep down. 1.** To maintain control over: *tried to keep costs down.* **2.** To prevent from progressing, accomplishing, or succeeding. **—keep off.** To refrain from approaching; stay away from. **—keep one's distance.** To continue in an attitude of aloofness. **—keep one's eyes open** (or **peeled**). To be alert or watchful: *keep your eyes open for danger.* **—keep one's nose clean.** To stay out of trouble: *He could have been elected if he'd kept his nose clean.* **—keep pace.** To stay even: *tried to keep pace with inflation.* **—keep to oneself. 1.** To shun the company of others. **2.** To refrain from sharing or divulging: *He's keeping the news to himself.* **—keep up. 1.** To maintain in good condition. **2.** To persevere in; carry on: *keep up traditions; can't keep this up forever.* **3.** To continue at the same level or pace: *Don't walk so fast; I can't keep up.* **4.** To remain informed or in touch: *keep up with current research.* **5.** To cause to stay up late at night. **6.** To match one's competitors, colleagues, neighbors, or associates in success or lifestyle: *unsuccessfully tried to keep up with his partners.*

~n. **1.** Care; charge: *The child is in my keep for the day.* **2.** The means by which one is supported; the necessities of life: *earn one's keep.* **3.** The main tower or donjon of a medieval castle; stronghold. —See Synonyms at **livelihood.** **—for keeps. 1.** For an indefinitely long period: *He gave it to me for keeps.* **2.** Seriously and permanently: *We're separating for keeps.* [Middle English *kepen,* Old English *cēpan*†, to seize, hold, guard.]

Synonyms: *maintain, reserve, retain, withhold.*

keep·er (kē′pər) *n.* **1.** One who keeps, especially: **a.** An attendant, guard, or warden, as in a museum or art gallery. **b.** One who has the charge or care of something, as animals in a zoo or circus. **2.** A device for keeping something in place. **3.** A small piece of iron placed across the poles of a permanent magnet when it is not in use in order to complete the magnetization.

keep·ing (kē′pĭng) *n.* **1.** Custody; care; guardianship. **2.** Harmony; conformity: *remarks out of keeping with the occasion.*

keep·net (kēp′nĕt′) *n.* A cylindrical net, open at one end and suspended in the water, into which anglers put fish to keep them alive.

keep·sake (kēp′sāk′) *n.* Something given or kept as a reminder of the giver; a memento.

kees·hond (kās′hônt′) *n., pl.* **-honden** (-hôn′dən) or **-honds.** A dog of a small breed originating in the Netherlands, having a thick grayish-black coat. [Dutch : probably *Kees,* nickname for *Cornelis,* from Latin *Cornēlius*†, name of a Roman gens + *hond,* dog.]

Kee·wa·tin (kē-wāt′n). An administrative district, 590,934 square kilometers (228,160 square miles), in the Northwest Territories, Canada, north of Manitoba and including Hudson and James bays.

kef. Variant of **kif.**

Ke·fau·ver (kē′fô′vər), **(Carey) Estes** (1903–63). U.S. legislator. A Democratic congressman (1939–49) and senator (1949–63) from Tennessee, he gained wide recognition for his investigations into organized crime (1950–51), which were the first televised Senate hearings. He was nominated as Adlai Stevenson's running mate in 1956.

keffiyeh. Variant of **kaffiyeh.**

ke·fir (kĕ-fîr′) *n.* A creamy drink made of fermented cow's milk. [Russian, of Caucasian origin.]

Kef·la·vik (kĕp′lä-vēk′). A fishing port in southwest Iceland. Its international airport, built by the United States in World War II as Meeks Field, has also been a NATO base since 1951.

keg (kĕg) *n.* **1.** A small cask or barrel, usually with a capacity of five to ten gallons. **2.** An aluminum container for transporting and storing beer. [Earlier *cag,* Middle English *kag,* from Old Norse *kaggi*†.]

keg·ler (kĕg′lər) *n.* A person who bowls; bowler. [German *Kegler,* from *kegeln,* to bowl, from *Kegel,* bowling pin, from Old High German *kegil*†, stick, peg.]

keis·ter (kē′stər) *n. Slang.* The buttocks. [Origin unknown.]

ke·ku·lé formula (kā′kə-lā′) *n. Chemistry.* A structural formula for benzene in which the six carbon atoms are positioned at the corners of a regular hexagon and linked by alternate double and single bonds. [After KEKULÉ VON STRADONITZ.]

Ke·ku·lé von Stra·do·nitz (kā′kŏŏ-lā′ fən shträ′dō-nĭts′), **(Friedrich) August** (1829–96). German chemist. He carried out important research concerning the structure and combining power of atoms and in 1865 formulated the structure of benzene.

Kel·ler (kĕl′ər), **Helen Adams** (1880–1968). U.S. writer and lecturer. She was deaf and blind from early childhood, but learned to read, write, and speak. She is noted for her work for the blind.

Kells (kĕlz). Market town in County Meath, Republic of Ireland. *The Book of the Kells,* an 8th-century illuminated Gospel, is said to have been written at a monastery founded here by St. Columba in the 6th century.

kel·ly green (kĕl′ē) *n.* A strong yellowish green. [From the Irish name *Kelly* (green being a color associated with Ireland).]

Kel·ly (kĕl′ē), **Grace Patricia** (1929–82). U.S. film actress. She starred in several films, including *High Noon* (1952), *To Catch a Thief* (1955), and *Country Girl* (1954), for which she won an Academy Award. In 1956 she gave up her career to marry Prince Rainier III of Monaco.

ke·loid, che·loid (kē′loid′) *n.* A mass of fibrous connective tissue, usually at the site of a scar. [French *kéloïde* : Greek *khēlē,* claw, CHELA + -OID.] **—ke·loid·al** (kē-loid′l) *adj.*

PRONUNCIATION KEY

ă, pat; ā, pay; âr, care; ä, father, are; b, bib; ch, church; d, deed; ĕ, pet; ē, be; f, fife; g, gag; h, hat; hw, which; ĭ, pit; ī, pie; îr, pier; j, judge; k, kick; l, lid, needle; m, mum; n, no, sudden; ng, thing; ŏ, pot; ō, toe; ô, paw, for; oi, noise; ou, out; ŏŏ, book; ōō, boot; p, pop; r, roar; s, sauce; sh, ship, dish; t, tight; th, thin, path; *th,* this, bathe; ŭ, cut; ûr, fur; v, valve; w, with; y, yes; z, zebra, size; zh, vision; ə, about, item, edible, gallop, circus, peaceful

IN FOREIGN WORDS:

à, *Fr.* ami; œ, *Fr.* feu, *Ger.* schön; ü, *Fr.* tu, *Ger.* über; KH, *Ger.* ich, *Scot.* loch; N, *Fr.* bon; y′, *Fr.* Compiègne

STRESS MARKS:

Primary stress: ′ **in·cite′** (ĭn-sīt′)
Secondary stress: ′ **in′sight′** (ĭn′sīt′)

kelp (kĕlp) *n*. **1.** Any of various brown, often very large seaweeds of the order Laminariales. Also called "oarweed." **2.** The ash of kelp, used as a source of potash and iodine. Also called "varec." [Middle English *cülpe*†.]

kel·pie[1] (kĕl′pē) *n*. A water spirit in Scottish legend, usually having the shape of a horse and causing or rejoicing in drownings. [18th century : origin obscure.]

kelpie[2] *n*. A sheep dog of a breed that originated in Australia and was developed from the Scottish collie. Also called "barb." [From *Kelpie*, the name of an early specimen of the breed.]

kelson. Variant of **keelson.**

kelt (kĕlt) *n*. A salmon that is in an exhausted condition after spawning. [Middle English : origin obscure.]

Kelt. Variant of **Celt.**

Keltic. Variant of **Celtic.**

kel·vin (kĕl′vĭn) *n*. *Symbol* **K** The unit of thermodynamic temperature, equal to 1/273.16 of the thermodynamic temperature of the triple point of water. [After Baron KELVIN.]

Kel·vin (kĕl′vĭn) *adj. Abbr.* **K** Of, pertaining to, or designating an **absolute scale** *(see)* of temperature whose zero point is approximately −273.15°C.

Kelvin, William Thomson, 1st Baron (1824–1907). British physicist and inventor. He established the Kelvin scale of temperature and supervised the laying of a cable across the Atlantic (1866). He also did important work in thermodynamics.

Kemal Atatürk. See **Atatürk.**

Kem·ble (kĕm′bəl). British theatrical family, founded by **Roger Kemble** (1722–1802). His sons, **John Philip Kemble** (1757–1823) and **Charles Kemble** (1775–1854), were both distinguished actors, and his eldest daughter was Sarah Siddons. **Frances Ann Kemble,** known as "Fanny" (1809–93), was the daughter of Charles Kemble.

kempt (kĕmpt) *adj*. Neat; tidy. [Probably back-formation from UN-KEMPT.]

ken (kĕn) *v*. **kenned** or **kent** (kĕnt), **kenning, kens.** —*tr*. **1.** *Chiefly Scottish.* To know (a person, fact, or thing). **2.** *Chiefly Scottish.* To recognize. **3.** *Archaic.* To descry; make out. —*intr. Chiefly Scottish.* To have an understanding of something.
~*n*. **1.** Range of knowledge or understanding: *beyond my ken.* **2.** Range of vision; view. [Middle English *kennen,* Old English *cennan,* to make known (probably influenced in sense by Old Norse cognate *kenna,* to know).]

Ken·dal green (kĕn′dəl) *n*. **1.** A coarse green woolen fabric similar to tweed. **2.** The color of this fabric. [Originally manufactured at *Kendal,* England.]

ken·do (kĕn′dō) *n*. A traditional Japanese martial art in which two contestants wearing protective armor fight with bamboo swords. [Japanese *kendō,* "the art of fencing," from Chinese *jiàn,* sword + *daò,* way.]

Kennedy, Cape. See **Canaveral, Cape.**

Ken·ne·dy (kĕn′ə-dē), **Edward Moore** (1932–). U.S. Democratic politician. He is the youngest of the Kennedy brothers and was elected to the Senate (1962). He campaigned unsuccessfully for the Democratic presidential nomination in 1980.

Kennedy, John Fitzgerald (1917–63). 35th president of the United States (1961–63), the youngest president ever to be elected and also the first Roman Catholic president. He studied at Harvard, where he wrote *Why England Slept,* a study of the English failure to judge adequately the Nazi threat, which became a best seller. After a distinguished war career in the navy he entered the House of Representatives (1947) and the Senate (1952). He executed (although he did not plan) the disastrous attempt by Cuban exiles to invade Cuba (1961), but caused Khrushchev to back down over his attempt to establish Soviet nuclear missiles there in 1962. A liberal in domestic policy, he established the Peace Corps, fought for slum clearance and cheap public housing, and raised the minimum wage. He agreed to a partial Test Ban Treaty with the U.S.S.R. (1963) and insisted on continued U.S. access to West Berlin. He was assassinated in Dallas, Texas on November 22, 1963.

Kennedy, Joseph Patrick (1888–1969). U.S. multimillionaire and father of the Kennedy brothers. He made a fortune from banking and the stock market and became U.S. ambassador to Britain (1937–40). He resigned because he opposed aid to the Allies.

Kennedy, Robert Francis (1925–68). U.S. Democratic politician. He was attorney general (1961) during the presidency of his brother John F. Kennedy. He was elected to the Senate (1964) and was campaigning for the Democratic nomination for the presidency when he was assassinated (June 1968).

ken·nel[1] (kĕn′əl) *n*. **1.** A shelter for a dog or cat. **2.** A pack of dogs, especially hounds. **3.** An establishment where dogs are bred, trained, or boarded. **4.** The lair of a wild animal, as a fox.
~*v*. **kenneled** or **-nelled, -neling** or **-nelling, -nels.** —*tr*. To keep or place in or as if in a kennel. —*intr*. To stay or take cover in or as if in a kennel. [Middle English *kenel,* from Old Northern French *kenil* (unattested), variant of Old French *chenil* (unattested), from Vulgar Latin *canile* (unattested), from Latin *canis,* dog.]

kennel[2] *n*. A gutter along a street. [Variant of *cannel,* Middle English *canel, canal,* CANAL.]

Ken·nel·ly (kĕn′ə-lē), **Arthur Edwin** (1861–1939). U.S. electrical engineer. At the same time as Oliver Heaviside, he correctly predicted the existence of an ionized layer in the upper atmosphere, the Kennelly-Heaviside layer.

Ken·nel·ly-Heav·i·side layer (kĕn′ə-lē-hĕv′ē-sīd′) *n*. The **E layer** *(see)* of the ionosphere.

Ken·ne·saw Mountain National Battlefield Park (kĕn′ə-sô′). Park in northwestern Georgia, site of a Civil War battle during Gen. William T. Sherman's advance on Atlanta (1864).

ken·ning (kĕn′ĭng) *n*. A metaphorical, usually compound expression used especially in Old English and Old Norse poetry; for example, *storm of swords* is a kenning for *battle.* [Old Norse *kenning,* "naming," symbol, from *kenna,* to know, name (with a kenning).]

Ken·ny (kĕn′ē), **Elizabeth** (1886–1952). Australian pioneer of polio treatment. She applied hot towels to affected limbs instead of wrapping them in plaster casts, the traditional treatment.

ke·no (kē′nō) *n*. A game of chance that is similar to lotto but uses balls rather than counters. [Probably from French *quine,* set of five (winning numbers), back-formation from Old French *quines,* five each, from Latin *quīnī* (accusative *quīnas*).]

ke·no·sis (kə-nō′sĭs) *n*. *Theology.* Christ's relinquishment of the form of God in becoming man and suffering death. Philippians 2:5–8. [Late Greek *kenōsis,* from Greek, an emptying, from *kenoun,* to empty, from *kenos,* empty.] —**ke·not·ic** (kə-nŏt′ĭk) *adj*.

Ken·sing·ton and Chel·sea (kĕn′zĭng-tən; chĕl′sē). Since 1965 a royal borough of Greater London.

ken·speck·le (kĕn′spĕk′əl) *adj. Scottish.* Easily recognized; conspicuous. [From dialectal *kenspeck,* from Scandinavian; akin to Old Norse *kennispeki,* power of recognition. See **ken.**]

kent. Alternate past tense and past participle of **ken.**

Kent (kĕnt). A county of southeast England, called "the Garden of England" for its hop and fruit crops. The Saxon kingdom of Kent was the first to be converted to Christianity (597) by St. Augustine. The administrative center is Maidstone.

Kent, Rockwell (1882–1971). U.S. artist. A world traveler, he published several collections of his stark woodcuts and other works, including *Wilderness: A Journal of Quiet Adventure in Alaska* (1920), which established his reputation as an artist and writer. He also illustrated special editions of *Moby Dick* (1930) and other classics.

ken·te (kĕn′tē, -tā′) *n*. **1.** A brightly colored cloth of Ghana, woven in strips. **2.** A large cloth made up of such strips, worn as dress in the style of a toga by Ghanaian men. [Probably from Akan.]

ken·ti·a palm (kĕn′tē-ə) *n*. A palm, *Howea belmoreana* (or *Kentia belmoreana*), often grown as a house plant. Also called "sentry palm."

Kent·ish (kĕn′tĭsh) *adj*. Of, relating to, or inhabiting Kent, England.
~*n*. The dialect originally spoken in Kent, England.

Kentish glory *n*. A large, handsome European moth, *Endromis versicolora.*

kent·ledge (kĕnt′lĭj) *n. Nautical.* Pig iron used as permanent ballast. [Old French *quintelage,* ballast, from *quintal,* hundredweight, from Medieval Latin *quintale,* from Arabic *qinṭār,* KANTAR.]

Ken·tuck·y (kən-tŭk′ē). *Abbr.* **Ky.** A state of central United States. Known as the "Bluegrass State" because of the rich pastures of bluegrass in its central area, it also has coal deposits, and heavy industry has been developed at Louisville. Frankfort is its capital.

Kentucky bluegrass *n*. See **bluegrass.**

Kentucky coffee tree *n*. A deciduous North American tree, *Gymnocladus dioica,* having flat, pulpy pods containing seeds formerly used as a coffee substitute. Also called "coffee tree."

Kentucky Derby *n*. An annual horse race for three-year-olds run since 1875 at Churchill Downs in Louisville, Kentucky.

Ken·ya (kĕn′yə). East African republic lying across the equator. The fertile southwest highlands are Africa's major source of coffee and tea, the country's main exports, along with pyrethrum and sisal. Tourism is a major industry. Kenya was proclaimed a British col-

Kerry *An Irish breed of dairy cow, moderate in size and milk yield but easy to raise. It is productive even on poor pasture.*

ony in 1920. The savage Mau Mau rebellion of the Kikuyu (1952–60) hastened independence (1963) under Jomo Kenyatta, and stability and prosperity ensued. However, the world recession of the 1970's and a disastrous drought in 1980 severely strained the economy. Area, 582,646 square kilometers (224,901 square miles). Population, 24,000,000. Capital, Nairobi. —**Ken·yan** *n. & adj.*

Kenya, Mount. Extinct volcano in Kenya. It is Africa's second-highest mountain (5,200 meters; 17,058 feet).

Ken·yat·ta (kĕn-yä′təl), **Jomo Kamau** (1894–1978). First president of independent Kenya (1964–78). In 1947 he became leader of the Kenya African Union. He was a suspected organizer of the Mau Mau rebellion (1952) and was imprisoned by the British (1952–61). Kenyatta negotiated independence and was elected prime minister.

Ke·ogh plan (kē′ō) *n.* A retirement plan for the self-employed. [After Eugene J. *Keogh* (1907–89).]

kep (kĕp) *tr.v.* **kepped, kepping, keps.** *British Regional.* To catch. [Variant of KEEP (in obsolete sense, to "seize, hold").]

ke·pi (kā′pē, kĕp′ē) *n., pl.* **-is.** A French military cap with a flat, circular top and a visor. [French *képi,* from Swiss German *käppi,* diminutive of German *Kappe,* cap.]

Kep·ler (kĕp′lər), **Johannes** (1571–1630). German astronomer, founder of modern astronomy. His three laws, based on the observations made by his teacher Tycho Brahe, made sense of the theory that the planets revolve around the sun.

Kep·ler's laws (kĕp′lərz) *pl.n.* Three laws describing planetary motion, published by Kepler between 1609 and 1619: the path of a planet is an ellipse with the sun at one focus; a line from the sun to a planet sweeps out equal areas in equal time periods; the square of the orbital period of a planet is proportional to the cube of its average distance from the sun.

kept. Past tense and past participle of **keep.**

Ker·a·la (kĕr′ə-lə). The most densely populated state in India. It lies in the southwest part of the country, between the Western Ghats and the coast. Though poor and undeveloped, Kerala has the highest literacy rate in India.

ker·a·tec·to·my (kĕr′ə-tĕk′tə-mē) *n., pl.* **-mies.** Surgical removal of all or part of the cornea.

ker·a·tin (kĕr′ə-tĭn) *n.* A tough, fibrous protein containing sulfur and forming the outer layer of epidermal structures such as hair, nails, horns, and hoofs. [Greek *keras* (stem *kerat-*), horn + -IN.] —**ke·rat·i·nous** (kə-răt′n-əs) *adj.*

ker·a·tin·ize (kĕr′ə-tĭ-nīz′) *v.* **-ized, -izing, -izes.** —*tr.* To form keratin in or on. —*intr.* To form a keratinous layer. —**ker·a·tin·i·za·tion** *n.*

ker·a·ti·tis (kĕr′ə-tī′tĭs) *n.* Inflammation of the cornea.

kerato-, kerat– *prefix. form.* Indicates: 1. Horny tissue, especially of the skin; for example, **keratin.** 2. The cornea of the eye; for example, **keratitis.**

ker·a·to·sis (kĕr′ə-tō′sĭs) *n., pl.* **-ses** (-sēz′). A horny growth or condition of the skin, as a wart.

kerb. *British.* Variant of **curb.**

ker·chief (kûr′chĭf, -chēf′) *n.* 1. A square scarf, often worn around the neck or as a head covering. 2. A handkerchief. [Middle English *c(o)urchef, kercheffe,* from Old French *couvrechef, cuerchief,* "head covering" : *co(u)vrir,* to COVER + *ch(i)ef,* head, from Latin *caput.*]

Ke·ren·sky (kə-rĕn′skē), **Aleksandr Feodorovich** (1881–1970). Russian politician. He was head of government between the two Russian revolutions in 1917, but was expelled by the Bolsheviks because of his moderate policies. He lived in the United States from 1940 until his death.

kerf (kûrf) *n.* 1. A groove or notch made by a saw, ax, or the like. 2. The cut end of a tree that has been felled. [Middle English *kyrf, kerf,* Old English *cyrf,* act of cutting.]

ker·fuf·fle (kər-fŭf′əl) *n. Chiefly British Informal.* A fuss or commotion. [20th century : origin obscure.]

Kérkyra. See **Corfu.**

ker·ma (kûr′mə) *n. Physics.* The sum of all the initial kinetic energies of particles produced in a given sample by ionizing radiation divided by the mass of the sample. [*kinetic energy released in matter.*]

ker·mes (kûr′mēz) *n.* 1. A red dyestuff prepared from the dried bodies of female scale insects of the genus *Kermes,* especially the Eurasian species *K. ilices.* 2. A small evergreen Eurasian oak, *Quercus coccifera,* on which kermes scale insects live. [French *kermès,* short form for *alkermès,* from Spanish *alkermez,* from Arabic *al-qirmiz,* "the kermes," from Sanskrit *kṛmi-ja-,* (red dye) produced by a worm : *kṛmi-,* worm + *ja-,* born, produced.]

ker·mis, ker·mess, kir·mess (kûr′mĭs) *n.* 1. An outdoor fair in the Low Countries. 2. A fund-raising fair or carnival. [Dutch *kermis(se),* from Middle Dutch *kercmisse* : *kerke, kerc,* church, from West Germanic *kirika* (unattested), from Late Greek *kurikon,* CHURCH + *misse,* Mass.]

kern[1], **kerne** (kûrn) *n.* 1. A medieval Scottish or Irish foot soldier. 2. A country bumpkin; yokel. [Middle English *kerne,* from Middle Irish *ceithern,* from Old Irish, band of foot soldiers, possibly from *cath,* battle, troop.]

kern[2] *n. Printing.* The portion of a character or typeface that projects beyond the body or shank.

~*tr.v.* **kerned, kerning, kerns.** *Printing.* To provide (a character or typeface) with a kern. [French *carne,* corner, salient angle, from Latin *cardō* (stem *cardin-*), hinge.]

kern[3] *n. Engineering.* The middle part of a wall, column, or other

kestrel *Mice, rats, and voles form the main diet of this common bird of prey. Kestrels hunt by hovering high in the air while they watch for prey, then closing in and pouncing.*

supporting structure regarded as the part subject to compressive forces. [Perhaps from German *Kern,* nucleus.]

Kern (kûrn), **Jerome David** (1885–1945). U.S. songwriter. He wrote more than 50 stage and film musicals and more than a thousand songs. His most successful musical was *Showboat* (1927), and his songs include "Ol' Man River" and "Smoke Gets in Your Eyes."

ker·nel (kûr′nəl) *n.* 1. A grain or seed, as of a cereal grass, enclosed in a hard husk. 2. The inner, usually edible part of a nut or fruit stone. 3. The most material and central part; essence or core: "*that hard kernel of gaiety that never breaks*" (Evelyn Waugh). [Middle English *kirnel, kernell,* Old English *cyrnel,* seed, kernel, diminutive of *corn,* corn, berry, seed.]

kernel sentence *n.* In generative grammar, any of a small number of basic and irreducible sentence types from which all other sentences may be formed or derived.

kern·ite (kûr′nīt′) *n.* A colorless to white crystalline mineral, $Na_2B_4O_7 \cdot 4H_2O$, that is a major source of boron. [Found in *Kern* County, California.]

ker·o·gen (kĕr′ə-jən) *n.* A bituminous material found in shale that produces hydrocarbons similar to petroleum when heated. Oil shale is rich in kerogen. [Greek *kēros,* wax + -GEN.]

ker·o·sene, ker·o·sine (kĕr′ə-sēn′, kĕr′ə-sēn′, kăr′ə-sēn′, kăr′ə-sēn′) *n.* A thin oil distilled from petroleum or shale oil and used as a fuel and alcohol denaturant. Also called "coal oil" and in British usage "paraffin." [Greek *kēros,* wax (see **ceruse**) + -ENE (from the use of paraffin in its distillation).]

Ke·rou·ac (kĕr′ōō-ăk′), **Jack** (1922–69). U.S. writer and leading figure of the beat generation. His mainly autobiographical books include *On the Road* (1957), *Dharma Bums* (1958), and *Desolation Angels* (1965).

Kerr cell (kûr) *n.* A cell consisting of a transparent liquid to which a strong electric field can be applied to stop the passage of light through the cell. The device, which depends for its action on the electrical Kerr effect, is used for producing short pulses of light for laser experiments, high speed photography, and the like. [After John *Kerr* (1824–1907), British physicist.]

Kerr effect *n. Physics.* 1. The production of double refraction in certain transparent solids or liquids by application of a strong electric field. 2. The slight elliptical polarization of light that is reflected from the surface of strongly magnetized material. [After John *Kerr* (1824–1907), British physicist.]

Ker·ry[1] (kĕr′ē). A county on the southwest coast of the Republic of Ireland. Its mountains and lakes are a tourist attraction. Its county town is Tralee.

Kerry[2] *n., pl.* **-ries.** Any of a breed of small, black dairy cattle originally raised in the county of Kerry, Ireland.

Kerry blue terrier *n.* Any of a breed of terriers of Irish origin, having a dense, wavy bluish-gray coat.

Kerry Hill *n.* A large, broad-bodied sheep of a breed originally from the Kerry Hills of Wales.

ker·sey (kûr′zē) *n., pl.* **-seys.** 1. A woolen fabric, often ribbed, formerly used for hose and trousers. 2. A twilled woolen fabric, sometimes with a cotton warp, used for coats. 3. *Often* **kerseys.** A garment, as a coat, made of kersey. [Middle English, probably after *Kersey,* a village in Suffolk, England.]

ker·sey·mere (kûr′zē-mîr′) *n.* A type of fine woolen cloth with a twill weave. Also called "cassimere." [Altered from CASSIMERE (by association with KERSEY).]

ke·ryg·ma (kə-rĭg′mə) *n., pl.* **ke·ryg·ma·ta** (-mə-tə). *Theology.* The proclamation of religious truths, especially as taught in the Gospels. [Greek, proclamation, from *kērussein,* to proclaim.] —**ker·yg·mat·ic** (kĕr′ĭg-măt′ĭk) *adj.*

Ke·sey (kē′zē), **Ken Elton** (1935–). U.S. novelist. He wrote *One Flew Over the Cuckoo's Nest* (1962, filmed 1975), set in a mental ward, and *Sometimes A Great Notion* (1964, filmed 1971).

Kes·sel·ring (kĕs′əl-rĭng′), **Albert** (1887–1960). German military commander. In World War II he led blitzkrieg operations against Poland, France, and the U.S.S.R., and Britain. He was convicted of war crimes and sentenced to death, but was reprieved and freed (1952).

kes·trel (kĕs′trəl) *n.* 1. A small Old World falcon, *Falco tinnunculus,* with brown and gray plumage, that is noted for its habit of hovering while searching for prey. Also called "windhover" in British usage. 2. Any of several small falcons. [Middle English *castrell,* alteration of Old French *cresserelle, crecelle,* "rattle," kestrel (from its cry), from Vulgar Latin *crepicella* (unattested), diminutive formation from Latin *crepitāre,* to rattle, creak, crackle, frequentative of *crepāre,* to crack.]

ketch (kĕch) *n.* A two-masted fore-and-aft-rigged sailing vessel with a mizzen or jigger mast situated aft of a taller mainmast but forward of the rudder. Compare **yawl.** [Earlier *catch,* Middle English *cache,* probably from *cachen, cacchen,* to hunt, CATCH.]

Ketch (kĕch), **John,** known as "Jack" (died 1686). English executioner, famous for his cruelty and incompetence. He bungled the execution of, among others, the Duke of Monmouth (1685). The name has passed into English folklore and is still given to the hangman in Punch and Judy puppet shows.

ketch·up (kĕch′əp, kăch′-) *n.* Also **catch·up** (kăch′əp, kĕch′-), **cat·sup** (kăt′səp, kăch′əp, kĕch′-) A condiment consisting of a thick, smooth, spicy sauce usually made from tomatoes. [Malay *kichap,* from Chinese (Amoy) *kôechiap* "brine of fish" : *kôe* (Mandarin *qui*), a kind of fish + *chiap* (Mandarin *zhī*), juice.]

ke·tene (kē′tēn′) *n.* A pungent, toxic, colorless gas, H_2CCO, used chiefly as an acetylation agent. [KET(O)- + -ENE.]

keto–, ket– *prefix.* Chemistry. Indicates a ketone or ketonic properties; for example, ketosis. [From KETONE.]

ke·to·e·nol tautomerism (kē′tō-ē′nôl′, -nōl′, -nōl′) *n.* Chemistry. A type of tautomerism involving an equilibrium between the keto and enol forms of a molecule, occurring because of migration of a hydrogen atom.

ke·to form (kē′tō) *n.* Chemistry. A structural form of an organic compound in which its molecules contain a ketone group (CO) linked to an adjacent carbon atom.

ke·to·gen·e·sis (kē′tō-jĕn′ə-sĭs) *n.* The formation of ketone bodies, as in diabetes. **—ke·to·gen·ic** (kē′tō-jĕn′ĭk) *adj.*

ke·to·hex·ose (kē′tō-hĕk′sōs′, -sōz′) *n.* A ketose sugar that has six carbon atoms in its molecules.

ke·tone (kē′tōn′) *n.* Any of a class of organic compounds having a carbonyl group linked to a carbon atom in each of two hydrocarbon radicals and having the general formula $R_1(CO)R_2$, where R_1 may be the same as R_2. [German *Keton,* from *Aketon, Azeton,* ACETONE.] **—ke·ton·ic** (kē-tŏn′ĭk) *adj.*

ketone body *n.* Any of several substances, such as acetoacetic acid, increasing in the blood during starvation and in certain diabetic and other pathological conditions. Also called "acetone body."

ketone group *n.* Chemistry. A carbonyl group (CO) linked to two carbon atoms, as in a ketone.

ke·to·nu·ri·a (kē′tō-nŏŏr′ē-ə, -nyŏŏr′ē-ə) *n.* The presence of ketone bodies in the urine.

ke·to·pen·tose (kē′tō-pĕn′tōs′, -tōz′) *n.* A ketose sugar that has five carbon atoms in its molecules.

ke·tose (kē′tōs′, -tōz′) *n.* Any of various carbohydrates containing a ketone group in each molecule. Compare **aldose.** [KET(O)- + -OSE.]

ke·to·sis (kē′tō′sĭs) *n.* A pathological accumulation of ketone bodies in the body. [New Latin : KET(O)- + -OSIS.] **—ke·tot·ic** (kē-tŏt′ĭk) *adj.*

ke·to·ste·roid (kē′tō-stîr′oid′, -stĕr′oid′) *n.* A steroid containing a steroid group.

ket·tle (kĕt′l) *n.* **1.** A metal pot, usually with a lid, for boiling or stewing. **2.** A teakettle. **3.** A kettledrum. **4.** A depression left in a mass of glacial drift, apparently formed by the melting of an isolated block of glacial ice. **5.** A pothole. **6.** Any of various large vessels used for industrial processes such as refining metals and distilling. **—kettle of fish. 1.** A troublesome, awkward, or embarrassing situation. **2.** A matter to be reckoned with: *Making money and keeping it are two quite different kettles of fish.* [Middle English *ketel,* from Old Norse *ketill,* from Common Germanic *katilaz* (unattested), from Latin *catillus,* small bowl or dish, from *catīnus†,* bowl, dish, pot.]

ket·tle·drum (kĕt′l-drŭm′) *n.* A large copper or brass hemispherical drum with a parchment head that can be tuned by adjusting the tension.

keV kiloelectron volt.

kev·el (kĕv′əl) *n.* A sturdy cleat or pin for securing the heavier cables of a ship. [Middle English *kevile,* peg, from Old North French *keville,* from Late Latin *clāvicula,* bolt, bar, from Latin, small key, from *clāvis,* key.]

Kew Gardens (kyōō). The Royal Botanic Gardens at Kew in the London borough of Richmond. Founded in 1759, they were presented to the nation in 1841.

key[1] (kē) *n., pl.* **keys. 1.** An implement designed to open a lock; especially, a usually metal notched and grooved implement that is inserted into and turned to open or close a lock. **2. a.** Something that is a means of access, control, or possession. **b.** An essential ingredient or element; requisite: *A good diet is the key to a long life.* **3. a.** A small instrument for winding a spring, as of a clock. **b.** A slotted metal strip used to open cans. **4. a.** An explanation of a set of symbols or abbreviations. **b.** A set of answers to a test or puzzle. **c.** A table, gloss, or cipher for decoding or interpreting. **d.** Something that serves to explain or interpret. **5.** A device, as a pin or wedge, inserted to lock together mechanical or structural parts. **6.** The keystone in the crown of an arch. **7. a.** A button or lever, as on a typewriter, that is pressed with the finger to operate a machine. **b.** A button or lever on a musical instrument, such as a clarinet or piano, that is pressed with the fingers to produce or modulate a sound. **8.** Music. **a.** A tonal system consisting of seven notes in fixed relationship to a tonic, having a characteristic key signature and being since the Renaissance the structural foundation of the bulk of Western music; tonality. **b.** The principal tonality of a musical work: *an étude in the key of E.* **9.** The pitch of a voice or other sound: *She spoke in a high key.* **10. a.** A characteristic tone or level of intensity, as of a speech, theatrical performance, or sales campaign. **b.** The general tone or intensity of color in a picture, as a painting. **11.** Botany. A samara (see). **12.** Biology. A list of taxonomic characters used on a presence or absence system to identify plants and animals. **13.** The roughness of a surface that provides a bond for the application of another finish, such as plaster. **14.** Slang. A kilogram of a drug, especially heroin or marijuana. **—in** (or **out of**) **key.** In (or out of) tune with other factors. **~***tr.v.* **keyed, keying, keys. 1.** To lock together with or as if with a key. **2.** To furnish (an arch) with a keystone. **3.** To supply with a key. **4. a.** To regulate the pitch of (a musical instrument). **b.** To bring into tune or harmony; coordinate: *The speech was keyed to the occasion.* **5.** To supply an explanatory key for. **6.** To roughen (a surface) so as to provide a bond for a subsequent finish. **—key up.** To raise in pitch or intensity; make tense, nervous, or excited.

~*adj.* Of crucial importance: *Mining is a key industry in many countries.* [Middle English *key(e), kay,* Old English *cǣg(e)†.*]

key[2] *n.* A low offshore island or reef, especially in the Gulf of Mexico. [Spanish *cayo,* CAY.]

Key (kē), **Francis Scott** (1799–1843). U.S. lawyer and poet. After witnessing the British attack on Baltimore on the night of September 13, 1814, and seeing the American flag still flying on the following morning, he wrote "Defense of Fort M'Henry," a patriotic poem soon after set to music and renamed "The Star-Spangled Banner." In 1931 Congress officially adopted the song as the national anthem.

key·board (kē′bôrd′, -bōrd′) *n.* A set of keys, as on a piano, an organ, or a typewriter. Also used adjectivally: *keyboard instruments.* **~***tr.v.* **keyboarded, -boarding, -boards.** To set (copy) by means of a keyed typesetting machine. **—key·board·er** *n.* See feature, next page.

Keyes (kīz, kēz), **Frances Parkinson** (1885–1970). U.S. author. Primarily remembered for her critically ill-received but highly popular novels, including *Dinner at Antoine's* (1948), that provided a glimpse into the lives of wealthy, urbane characters, she was also a magazine editor and wrote widely on religious subjects.

key fruit *n.* A **samara** *(see).* [From its shape.]

key·hole (kē′hōl′) *n.* The hole in a lock into which a key fits.

keyhole saw *n.* A narrow saw with a fine-toothed blade used for cutting small curves.

key money *n.* Payment made by a prospective tenant to a landlord to assure tenancy of an apartment or house.

Keynes (kānz), **John Maynard, 1st Baron** (1883–1946). Influential British economist who believed that high unemployment could be due to insufficient consumer spending rather than inflated wage levels and that government intervention was then necessary. At the Bretton Woods Agreement (1944) he was instrumental in establishing the International Monetary Fund and the International Bank for Reconstruction and Development.

Keynes·i·an (kān′zē-ən) *adj.* Of or pertaining to the economic theories or policies of John M. Keynes. **~***n.* A supporter of Keynes's economic theories or policies. **—Keynes·i·an·ism** *n.*

key·note (kē′nōt′) *n.* **1.** The tonic of a musical key. **2.** A prime or crucial element: *saw simplicity as the keynote of the plan.* **3.** An underlying or prevailing tone, spirit, or idea: *Pessimism was the keynote of the novel.* **~***tr.v.* **keynoted, -noting, -notes.** To give or set the keynote of.

keynote speech *n.* An opening address, as at a political convention, that outlines the issues to be considered.

key·punch (kē′pŭnch′) *n.* A keyboard machine that is used to punch holes in cards or tapes for data-processing systems. **~***tr.v.* **keypunched, -punching, -punches.** To punch holes in (cards or tape) with a keypunch. **—key·punch·er** *n.*

key signature *n.* The group of sharps or flats placed to the right of the clef on a musical staff to identify the key.

key·stone (kē′stōn′) *n.* **1.** Architecture. The central wedge-shaped stone of an arch that locks the others together. **2.** An essential part on which other parts depend.

key·stroke (kē′strōk′) *n.* A single depression of a key of a typewriter, typesetting machine, keypunch, or other keyboard device.

key·way (kē′wā′) *n., pl.* **-ways. 1.** A slot in a wheel hub or shaft for a key. **2.** The keyhole of a cylinder lock.

Key West (kē′ wĕst′). Seaport and resort at the western tip of the Florida Keys in the United States, a site of U.S. naval and air bases.

key word, key·word (kē′wûrd′) *n.* **1.** A word serving as a key to a cipher or code. **2.** A significant word or quality. **3.** A word used as an index to other words or information.

kg kilogram.

K.G. Knight of the (Order of the) Garter (in Britain).

KGB, K.G.B. (kā′jē′bē′) *n.* An intelligence agency of the Soviet Union. [Russian *Komityet Gosudarstvyennoi Byezopasnosti,* commission of state security.]

Kha·cha·tu·ri·an (kä′chä-tŏŏr′ē-ən, kåch′ə-), **Aram Ilyich** (1903–78). Russian musician. He composed concertos for piano (1936) and violin (1940), three symphonies (1934, 1943, and 1947), and the ballets *Gayaneh* (1942) and *Spartacus* (1954).

Khadafy, Muammar. See **Qaddafi.**

kha·di (kä′dē) *n.* Also **khad·dar** (kä′dər). A plain, hand-woven cotton fabric of India. [Hindi.]

khak·i (kăk′ē, kä′kē) *n., pl.* **khakis. 1.** A color ranging from light olive brown to yellowish brown. **2.** A sturdy wool or cotton cloth of the color khaki. **3.** *Often* **khakis.** A military uniform of khaki cloth. [Urdu *khākī,* dusty, dust-colored, from *khāk,* dust, from Persian *khāk†.*] **—khak·i** *adj.*

Kha·lid (kä-lēd′, KHÄ-), **Ibn Abdul Aziz** (1913–82). Fourth king of Saudi Arabia. He succeeded after the assassination of his half-brother King Faisal (1975).

khalif. Variant of **caliph.**

Khalkidhiki. See **Chalcidice.**

Khalkis. See **Chalcis.**

kham·sin, kham·seen, kam·sin (kăm-sēn′) *n.* A generally southerly hot wind from the Sahara that blows across Egypt and the southeast Mediterranean from March to early May. [Arabic *(rīḥ al-)khamsīn,* (wind of the) 50 (days), from *khamsūn,* 50.]

khan[1] (kän, kän) *n.* **1.** A ruler, an official, or an important person in India and some central Asian countries. **2.** Formerly, a title given to the rulers of Mongol, Tatar, or Turkish tribes who succeeded

THE KEYBOARD'S GROWTH FROM THE CLAVICHORD TO THE SYNTHESIZER

The device that allows a musician to play many notes at once

The piano is the best known and most popular of the keyboard instruments. When depressed, each key activates a light hammer that strikes a string, causing it to vibrate and produce the required note; the strings are of different lengths and sizes to give varied pitch. By using both hands on a keyboard, a musician can play up to ten notes at the same time.

With most keyboard instruments—from the 16th-century clavichord to the modern synthesizer—the keys are depressed with the fingers. But the organ (the largest and most complex of the group) also has a pedal keyboard that is depressed with the feet, so more than ten notes can be played at once.

Before the first piano was built in Italy at the beginning of the 18th century, the main keyboard instrument was the harpsichord. Its strings are mechanically plucked instead of struck, which means that the volume and tone cannot be varied by finger touch. Unlike the piano, it has no "loud" pedal for use in sustaining a note.

The United States has the largest keyboard instrument in the world—a 20th-century organ in Atlantic City, New Jersey. It has seven keyboards that control more than 33,000 pipes.

Clavichord
The strings of this soft-toned instrument are struck by metal tongues that stay in contact as long as the keys are depressed, so they can be used to create a vibrato

Harpsichord
A prominent solo and ensemble instrument from the 16th to the early 19th centuries, it is now used mainly for early music performances

Spinet
This wing-shaped instrument, similar to the harpsichord, has also been revived for early music

Grand Piano
The strings are horizontal. The "loud" pedal (right foot) increases note duration; the "soft" pedal (left foot) lessens the volume either by bringing the hammers nearer to the string or by causing fewer strings to be struck for each note

Electric Organ
Portable electric organs now rival pianos as family musical instruments. They have no pipes but create sounds by generating electronic signals

Upright Piano
The first successful instrument was made in London in 1811. Vertical rather than horizontal strings took less space, allowing small pianos to enter the home

Piano Accordion
Metal reeds are vibrated by bellows pushed and pulled by the player. Note selection is by studs (left hand) and keys (right hand)

Synthesizer
It can simulate all keyboard instrument sounds and a wide variety of other sounds, from rainfall to sirens

Genghis Khan, as well as to emperors of China. [Middle English *caan, c(h)an,* from Old French, from Medieval Latin *caanus,* from Turkish *khān,* contraction of *khāqān,* sovereign, ruler.]

khan[2] *n.* A caravanserai or inn in certain countries of Asia. [Middle English, from Arabic and Persian *khān,* inn.]

khan·ate (kä′nāt′, kăn′āt′) *n.* The realm or position of a khan.

khanga. Variant of **kanga.**

Khaniá. See **Canea.**

Kharbin. See **Harbin.**

kha·rif (kə-rēf′) *n.* A crop harvested at the end of autumn in India and neighboring countries. Compare **rabi.** [Urdu, from Arabic *kharafa,* to gather.]

Khar·kov (kär′kôf′, -kôv′). A city in northern Ukraine. It was the capital of Ukraine from 1919 to 1934.

Khar·toum (kär-to͞om′). *Arabic* **al-Kartum** or **Al Khartum.** Capital of Sudan. Founded as an army camp by Muhammad Ali (1821), it was destroyed by Mahdists in 1885, when Gen. Charles Gordon was killed defending it. Gen. H.H. Kitchener recaptured the city in 1898 and replanned it.

khat. Variant of **kat.**

Khayyám, Omar. See **Omar Khayyám.**

khe·dive (kə-dēv′) *n. Often* **Khedive.** A Turkish viceroy ruling Egypt between 1867 and 1914. [French *khédive,* from Turkish *hidiv,* from Persian *khidīw,* prince.]

khi. Variant of **chi.**

Khmer (kə-mâr′) *n., pl.* **Khmers** or collectively **Khmer. 1.** A member of a people of Kampuchea whose culture flourished during the Middle Ages. **2.** The Mon-Khmer language of this people.

Khmer Republic. See **Kampuchea.**

Khmer Rouge (ro͞ozh) *n.* A Communist movement in Kampuchea. Khmer Rouge guerrillas fought against the U.S.-backed government of General Lon Nol in the early 1970's. They eventually seized power in 1975 under the leadership of Pol Pot and remained in control until the end of 1978. See **Kampuchea.** [French, "red Khmer."]

Khoi·san (koi′sän′) *n.* A family of languages of southwestern Africa, including those of the Bushmen and Hottentots, that is characterized by clicks.

Kho·mei·ni (kō-mā′nē), **Ayatollah Ruholla** (*c.* 1902–1989). Iranian leader and head of the Shiite Muslims. He was arrested in 1964 and exiled for his opposition to Shah Reza Pahlavi. When the shah fled to Egypt (1979), Khomeini returned to Tehran (1979) amid wild celebrations. He established a new constitution giving himself supreme power.

Khor·ram·shahr (KHo͝or′äm-shär′). Town in Khuzestan, western Iran. It is at the confluence of the Karun River and the Shatt al Arab and is a major port and oil-refining center.

khoum (ko͞om, ko͝om) *n.* A monetary unit equal to 1/5 of the ouguiya of Mauritania. See feature at **currency.** [Native word.]

Khrush·chev (kro͞osh-chôf′, -chôv′), **Nikita Sergeyevich** (1894–1971). Soviet leader (1955–64). He was political head of the Ukraine (1938–49) under Stalin. He succeeded Georgi Malenkov as first secretary of the All Union Party (1953). He later denounced Stalin (1956). He was deposed (1964) after the Cuban missile crisis (1962) and the failure of economic reforms.

Khufu. See **Cheops.**

khur·ta, kur·ta (ko͝or′tə) *n.* A long, loose-fitting, collarless shirt worn in India. [Hindi.]

khus·khus (kŭs′kəs, ko͞os′ko͞os′) *n.* **1.** An aromatic perennial Indian grass, *Vetiveria zizanioides* (or *Andropogon squarrosus*). **2.** The root of this plant, used to make fans, mats, and the like. [Hindi.]

Khu·ze·stan (ko͞o′zĭ-stän′). Province in southwest Iran. A fertile region producing dates, citrus fruits, melons, cotton, and rice, it is also rich in petroleum and has many refineries. More than half the population is Arab.

Khy·ber Pass (kī′bər). Main mountain pass between Afghanistan and Pakistan, frequently fought over. Its gorge runs 53 kilometers (33 miles) through the Safid Koh range and for 8 kilometers (5 miles) is no more than 180 meters (*c.* 600 feet) wide.

kHz kilohertz.

ki·ang (kē-äng′) *n.* A Tibetan variety of the wild ass, *Equus hemionus kiang.* [Tibetan *rkyaṅ.*]

Kiangsi. See **Jiangxi.**

Kiangsu. See **Jiangsu.**

kib·ble[1] (kĭb′əl) *n.* An iron bucket used, as in wells or mines, for hoisting water, ore, or rubbish to the surface. [German *Kübel;* akin to Old English *cyfel,* from Medieval Latin *cupellus,* a measure for corn, diminutive of *cuppa,* CUP.]

kibble[2] *tr.v.* **-bled,-bling, -bles.** To crush or grind (grain, for example) coarsely. [18th century : origin obscure.]

kib·butz (kĭ-bo͝ots′, -bo͞ots′) *n., pl.* **kibbutzim** (kĭb′o͝ot-sēm′, kĭb′o͞ot-). A collective farm or settlement in modern Israel. [Hebrew *qibbūtz,* "gathering," from *qibbētz,* he gathered.]

kibe (kīb) *n.* An ulcerated chilblain, especially one on the heel. [Middle English *kybe,* perhaps from Welsh *cibi, cibwst*†.]

kib·itz·er (kĭb′ĭt-sər) *n. Informal.* **1.** An onlooker at a card game who gives unwanted advice to the players. **2.** A person who offers unwanted advice; a meddler. [Yiddish, from German *Kiebitz,* plover, busybody.] **—kib·itz** *v.*

kib·lah (kĭb′lə) *n.* **1.** The direction toward which Muslims face when they pray. **2.** A niche in the wall of a mosque indicating this direction. [Arabic *qiblah,* from *qābilah,* he lay opposite.]

ki·bosh (kī′bŏsh′, kĭ-bo͝osh′) *n. Informal.* Something that checks or stops: *put the kibosh on that reckless plan.* [Origin unknown.]

Kibris. See **Cyprus.**

kick (kĭk) *v.* **kicked, kicking, kicks.** *—intr.* **1.** To strike out with the foot or feet. **2.** To recoil, as a gun does when fired. **3.** *Informal.* To object vigorously; protest or rebel. **4. a.** To score or gain ground by kicking a ball. **b.** *Football.* To punt. *—tr.* **1.** To strike with the foot. **2.** To drive or move by striking with the foot. **3.** To spring back against suddenly, as a gun when fired. **4.** To score (a goal or point) by kicking a ball. **5.** *Slang.* To free oneself of (an addiction, as smoking). **—kick around.** *Informal.* **1.** To treat badly; abuse. **2.** To give consideration or thought to (an idea). **3.** To move from place to place. **4.** To lie neglected or unobserved: *There's a pen kicking around here somewhere.* **—kick in.** *Slang.* To contribute (one's share). **—kick out.** *Informal.* To throw out; dismiss. **—kick up. 1.** To cause to be propelled upward with force: *tires kicking up gravel.* **2.** To stir up (trouble): *kicking up a row.* **3.** To show signs of disorder: *His ulcer began to kick up.* **—kick up one's heels.** *Informal.* To cast off one's inhibitions and have a good time. **—kick upstairs.** To promote to a higher yet less desirable position.

∼n. **1. a.** A vigorous thrust or blow with the foot. **b.** The thrusting motion of the legs in swimming. **2.** The jolting recoil of a gun. **3.** *Slang.* Power, force, or resilience: *still a lot of kick in that engine.* **4.** *Slang.* Stimulating or intoxicating impact: *quite a kick in that martini.* **5.** *Slang.* **a.** A feeling of excitement or pleasure: *got a kick out of the show.* **b. kicks.** Fun; thrills: *just for kicks.* **6.** *Slang.* A temporary, often obsessive interest or enthusiasm: *on a health-food kick.* **7.** *Slang.* A complaint; protest. **8. a.** An act or instance of kicking a ball. **b.** A kicked ball. **c.** The distance spanned by a kicked ball: *a 47-yard kick.* **9.** A sudden momentary increase in pressure that forces drilled mud back up the bore of an oil or gas well. [Middle English *kiken, kyken*†.]

kick back *intr.v.* **1.** To recoil unexpectedly and violently. **2.** *Slang.* To pay a kickback. **3.** To suffer a sudden momentary increase in pressure. Used of an oil or gas well.

kick·back (kĭk′băk′) *n.* **1.** A sharp response or reaction; a repercussion. **2.** *Slang.* A percentage payment to a person able to influence or control a source of income, as by confidential arrangement or coercion.

kick·er (kĭk′ər) *n.* **1.** A person, animal, or thing that kicks. **2.** *Informal.* A sudden, surprising turn of events; twist. **3.** A tricky or concealed condition; pitfall. **4.** A condition that imposes an automatic increase, as in a pension plan.

kick off *intr.v.* **1.** *Sports.* To begin or resume play with a kickoff. **2.** To start; begin. **3.** *Slang.* To die.

kick·off (kĭk′ôf′, -ŏf′) *n.* **1. a.** A place kick in football or soccer with which play is begun. **b.** The time at which a game is due to begin. **2.** A beginning.

kick pleat *n.* A short pleat at the hem in a skirt that enables the wearer to walk more easily.

kick·shaw (kĭk′shô′) *n.* **1.** A trinket or trifle; gewgaw. **2.** A fancy food; delicacy. [Earlier *kickshose, quelkchose,* from French *quelque-chose,* something.]

kick sorter *n. Physics.* A device for sorting a train of pulses according to their height, used to investigate the pulses from a radiation counter to determine the energy spectrum of the incident radiation.

kick·stand (kĭk′stănd′) *n.* A swiveling metal bar on the base of a two-wheeled vehicle, as a motorcycle or bicycle, that keeps it upright when not in use.

kick-start (kĭk′stärt′) *tr.v.* **-started, -starting, -starts.** To start (an engine) by using a kick starter.

kick starter *n.* A device, as a pedal, for starting an engine, as of a motorcycle, that is activated by a downward push of the foot.

kick turn *n.* A stationary turn made in skiing by lifting one ski and positioning it in the intended direction and then lifting and positioning the other to be parallel with it.

kick·y (kĭk′ē) *adj.* **-ier, -iest.** *Slang.* Providing a kick by being unusual or unconventional. **—kick·i·ness** *n.*

kid (kĭd) *n.* **1. a.** A young goat. **b.** The young of a similar animal, such as an antelope. **2.** The flesh of a young goat. **3. a.** Leather made from the skin of a young goat. **b.** An article made of this leather. **4.** *Informal.* **a.** A child. **b.** A young person.

∼adj. **1.** Made of kid. **2.** *Informal.* Younger: *my kid brother.*

∼v. **kidded, kidding, kids.** *—tr. Informal.* **1.** To mock playfully; tease. **2.** To deceive in fun; fool. *—intr.* **1.** *Informal.* To engage in teasing or good-humored fooling. **2.** To bear young. Used of a goat or an antelope. [Middle English *kide, kyde,* from Old Norse *kidh,* young goat, from Germanic *kidhja-* (unattested).] **—kid·der** *n.*

Kidd (kĭd), **William,** known as "Captain Kidd" (1645–1701). Scottish pirate. He sailed in 1696 with a commission to defend ships of the East India Company. He was to be paid according to ships taken, so he turned pirate, attacking friendly ships. Kidd was brought from America to London, found guilty, and hanged.

Kid·der·min·ster (kĭd′ər-mĭn′stər) *n.* An ingrain carpet. [After *Kidderminster,* England, where it was originally made.]

Kid·dush (kĭd′əsh, kĭ-do͞osh′) *n. Judaism.* A traditional blessing and prayer recited over bread or a cup of wine on the eve of the Sabbath or a festival. [Hebrew *qiddūsh,* sanctification, from *qiddesh,* he sanctified.]

kid·dy, kid·die (kĭd′ē) *n., pl.* **-dies.** *Informal.* A small child.

kid glove *n.* A glove made of fine, soft leather, especially kidskin. **—handle with kid gloves.** To treat tactfully and cautiously.

kid·nap (kĭd′năp′) *tr.v.* **-napped** or **-naped, -napping** or **-naping, -naps.** To abduct and detain (a person or animal) unlawfully, often

PRONUNCIATION KEY

ă, pat; ā, pay; âr, care;
ä, father, are; b, **bib;**
ch, **church;** d, **deed;** ĕ, pet;
ē, be; f, **fife;** g, **gag;** h, **hat;**
hw, **which;** ĭ, pit; ī, pie;
îr, pier; j, **judge;** k, **kick;**
l, lid, needle; m, **mum;**
n, no, sudden; ng, **thing;**
ŏ, pot; ō, toe; ô, paw, for;
oi, noise; ou, out; o͝o, book;
o͞o, boot; p, **pop;** r, **roar;**
s, sauce; sh, **ship, dish;**
t, tight; th, **thin, path;**
th, this, bathe; ŭ, cut; ûr, fur;
v, valve; w, **with;** y, **yes;**
z, zebra, size; zh, vision;
ə, about, item, edible,
gallop, circus, peaceful

IN FOREIGN WORDS:

à, *Fr.* ami; œ, *Fr.* feu, *Ger.* schön; ü, *Fr.* tu, *Ger.* über;
KH, *Ger.* ich, *Scot.* loch;
N, *Fr.* bon; y′, *Fr.* Compiègne

STRESS MARKS:

Primary stress: ′
in·cite′ (ĭn-sīt′)
Secondary stress: ′
in′sight′ (ĭn′sīt′)

kidney

KIDNEYS: THE BODY'S "FILTER PLANT"

A system of 2¹/₂ million microscopic filters that purify the blood

The kidneys are the body's purification unit—a filtering system that cleanses the bloodstream of waste products. Nearly 70 liters (15 gallons) of blood an hour flow through the kidneys. Reddish brown organs, each about the size of a fist, they contain between them some 2¹/₂ million microscopic filter loops called nephrons. Incoming blood from the renal artery passes through the nephrons and is returned to the bloodstream, with its cargo of cells, proteins, vitamins, and other essential substances. Molecules of dissolved waste matter, however, are too large to pass through the nephrons. Along with surplus water, they are collected in the form of urine and funneled to the bladder for later expulsion from the body.

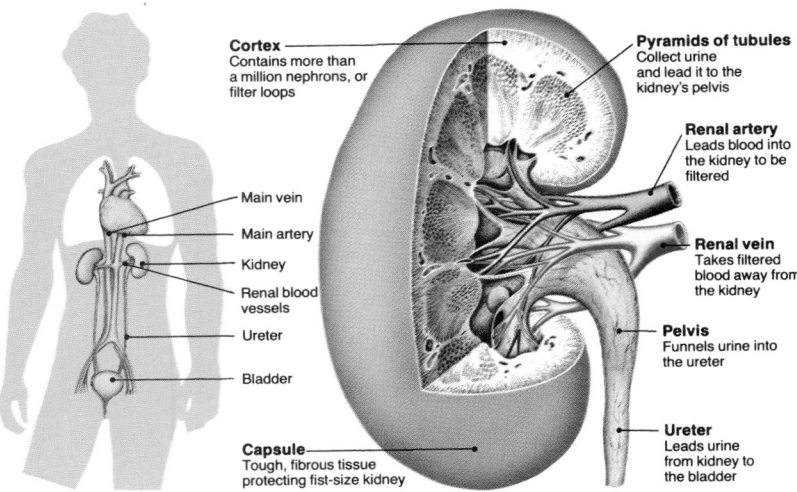

Cortex Contains more than a million nephrons, or filter loops

Pyramids of tubules Collect urine and lead it to the kidney's pelvis

Renal artery Leads blood into the kidney to be filtered

Renal vein Takes filtered blood away from the kidney

Pelvis Funnels urine into the ureter

Ureter Leads urine from kidney to the bladder

Main vein

Main artery

Kidney

Renal blood vessels

Ureter

Bladder

Capsule Tough, fibrous tissue protecting fist-size kidney

CLEANSING THE BLOODSTREAM *The kidneys lie to the back of the abdomen. Blood enters them through the renal arteries and flows to the nephrons, or filter loops; each kidney contains about 1¹/₄ million nephrons. Filtered blood is returned to the circulation through the renal veins, and waste products, such as urea, are secreted as urine and channeled along the ureter to the bladder.*

Kilauea *The lava-spouting central crater of Kilauea is called Halemaumau, or "house of everlasting fire," and is said to be the home of Hawaii's fire goddess, Pele. Kilauea, whose name means "rising smoke cloud," is one of the world's largest active volcanoes.*

for ransom. [Back-formation from *kidnapper* : KID (child) + obsolete *napper*, thief, from *nap*, to seize, probably from Scandinavian; akin to Swedish *nappa†*, to snatch.] —**kid·nap·per, kid·nap·er** *n.*

kid·ney (kĭd′nē) *n., pl.* **-neys. 1.** *Anatomy.* Either of a pair of organs in the dorsal region of the vertebrate abdominal cavity, functioning to maintain proper water balance, regulate acid-base concentration, and excrete metabolic wastes as urine. **2.** The kidney of certain animals, eaten as food. **3.** An excretory organ of certain invertebrates. **4. a.** Disposition; temperament. **b.** Kind, sort, or class. [Middle English *kidenei, kydney* : possibly *kiden-* (an obscure element) + *ei*, egg, Old English *ǣg.*]

kidney bean *n.* **1.** A bean, *Phaseolus vulgaris*, cultivated in many forms for its edible seeds. **2.** The reddish seed of the kidney bean.

kidney machine *n.* An apparatus for filtering waste products and water from the blood of a patient whose kidneys have ceased to function. Also called "artificial kidney."

kidney stone *n. Pathology.* A renal **calculus** *(see).*

kidney vetch *n.* A plant, *Anthyllis vulneraria*, native to Europe, having grayish-green leaves and small yellow flowers. [Formerly used to treat kidney disorders.]

kid·skin (kĭd′skĭn′) *n.* Soft leather made from the skin of a young goat.

kid stuff *n. Informal.* **1.** Something very easy or uncomplicated. **2.** Something suitable only for children.

kief. Variant of **kif.**

Kiel (kēl). Capital of Schleswig-Holstein, a German state. It is a Baltic seaport and was an important naval base (1871–1945).

kiel·ba·sa (kĕl-bä′sə, kĭl-, kēl-) *n.* A smoked Polish sausage. [Polish.]

Kiel Canal. Canal in western Germany. It runs 98 kilometers (61 miles) from Kiel to the Elbe estuary, connecting the Baltic with the North Sea.

kier (kîr) *n.* A vat for boiling, dyeing, or bleaching cloth or yarn. [Earlier *keare*, from Old Norse *ker*, tub, akin to Old High German *char*, Gothic *kas†*, vessel.]

Kier·ke·gaard (kîr′kə-gärd′), **Søren Aabye** (1813–55). Danish philosopher. He opposed Hegel's idea that truth was absolute and attacked the reliance on ritual and dogma in Christianity. His books include *Either-Or* (1843) and *Stages on Life's Way* (1845). —**Kier·ke·gaard·i·an** *adj. & n.*

kie·sel·guhr (kē′zəl-gŏŏr′) *n. Mineralogy.* **Diatomite** *(see).* [German : *Kiesel*, pebble + *Guhr*, earthy deposit from water.]

kie·ser·ite (kē′zə-rīt′) *n.* A whitish to yellowish hydrous magnesium sulfate mineral, used as a source of Epsom salts. [German *Kieserit*, after Dietrich G. *Kieser* (died 1862), German physicist.]

Ki·ev (kē-ĕv′). Capital and largest city of Ukraine, at the confluence of the Dnieper, Pripet, and Western Dvina rivers. Prominent since the 9th century as a commercial and industrial center, it is also the traditional center of Russian Christianity.

kif, keef, kief (kĭf, kēf) *n.* Also **kef** (kĕf, kēf, kāf). **1.** Indian hemp or other related material prepared for smoking, especially in Maghreb. **2.** The odd euphoria often associated with its use. [Arabic *kayf*, euphoria, enjoyment.]

Kikládhes. See **Cyclades.**

Ki·ku·yu (kĭ-kōō′yōō) *n., pl.* **-yus** or collectively **Kikuyu. 1. a.** A member of a Bantu people of Kenya. **b.** The Bantu language of this people. **2. kikuyu.** A hardy grass, *Pennisetum clandestinum*, used for lawns and pasture in southern Africa and central America.

Ki·lau·e·a (kē′lou-ā′ə). Volcanic crater of Hawaii. On the southeast slopes of Mauna Loa, it is one of the largest craters in the world (*c.* 3 kilometers; 2 miles across) still volcanically active.

Kil·dare (kĭl-dâr′). County of the Republic of Ireland. The Bog of Allen lies in the north. Kildare, a market town, was founded by St. Bride in A.D. 490. Naas, in the northeast, is the county town.

kil·der·kin (kĭl′dər-kĭn) *n.* **1.** A cask. **2.** An English measure of capacity that is equal to approximately 68 liters, or 18 gallons. [Middle English *kilderkyn*, earlier *kyn(d)erkyn*, from Middle Dutch *kinderkin, kinnekijn*, diminutive of *kintal*, hundredweight, from Medieval Latin *quintāle*, from Arabic *qinṭār*, KANTAR.]

ki·lim (kē-lēm′) *n.* An oriental tapestry-woven rug or other textile piece. [Turkish, from Persian *kilīm†*.]

Kil·i·man·ja·ro (kĭl′ə-mən-jär′ō). Extinct volcano in northern Tanzania. It has two peaks, Mt. Kibo (5,895 meters; 19,340 feet), Africa's highest peak, and Mt. Mawenzi (5,354 meters; 17,564 feet). The surrounding plain is a wildlife preserve.

Kil·ken·ny¹ (kĭl-kĕn′ē). County of the Republic of Ireland. In the southeast of the country in the province of Leinster, it is ringed by hills and drains toward Waterford harbor in the southeast.

Kilkenny². County town of Kilkenny, it was once the capital of the ancient kingdom of Ossory and is one of Ireland's oldest settlements.

kill (kĭl) *v.* **killed, killing, kills.** —*tr.* **1. a.** To put to death; slay. **b.** To deprive of life: *Famine killed thousands.* **2.** To put an end to; extinguish. **3.** To destroy a vitally essential quality in: *Too much garlic killed the taste of the meat.* **4.** *Informal.* To pass (time) idly or unproductively. **5.** *Informal.* To consume entirely; finish off: *kill a bottle of whiskey.* **6.** *Informal.* To cause extreme pain or discomfort to: *My shoes are killing me.* **7.** *Informal.* To mark for deletion; rule out. **8.** *Informal.* To thwart passage of; veto: *kill a congressional bill.* **9.** *Informal.* To cause to stop; turn off: *killed the engine.* **10.** *Informal.* To exhaust by overexertion. **11.** *Informal.* To destroy the effect of (a color, for example) by contrast; neutralize. **12. a.** To hit (a ball) with great force. **b.** In a racket game, as tennis, to hit (a ball) with such force as to make a return impossible. —*intr.* **1.** To be fatal; cause death or extinction: *Excessive speed kills.* **2.** To commit murder. —**kill off.** To destroy in such large numbers as to render extinct.

~*n.* **1.** The act or moment of killing. **2.** An animal killed, especially in hunting. **in at the kill.** Present at the moment of triumph. [Middle English *kullen, killen, kellen*, Old English *cyllan* (unattested).]

Kil·lar·ney (kĭ-lär′nē). Market town and tourist center in County Kerry, in the Republic of Ireland.

kill·deer (kĭl′dîr′) *n., pl.* **-deers** or collectively **killdeer.** A New World bird, *Charadrius vociferus*, of inland ponds, streams, and fields, having a distinctive cry. [Imitative of its cry.]

killed spirits *n.* A solution of zinc chloride that is used as a flux for soldering and is made by adding zinc to hydrochloric acid. [Referring to the action of zinc as killing or neutralizing hydrochloric acid.]

kill·er (kĭl′ər) *n.* **1.** One that kills; especially, a murderer. **2.** The killer whale.

killer whale *n.* A black and white predatory whale, *Orcinus orca*, of cold seas. Also called "grampus," "orc."

kil·lick (kĭl′ĭk) *n.* Also **kil·lock** (-ək). A small anchor, especially one made of a stone in a wooden frame. [Origin unknown.]

kil·li·fish (kĭl′ĭ-fĭsh′) *n., pl.* **-fishes** or collectively **killifish.** Any of numerous small fishes of the family Cyprinodontidae, chiefly of fresh and brackish waters of warm regions. [Origin unknown.]

kill·ing (kĭl′ĭng) *n.* **1. a.** Murder; homicide. **b.** A murder. **2.** An animal killed in hunting; quarry. **3.** *Informal.* A sudden large profit: *made a killing on the stock market.*

~*adj.* **1.** Designed or apt to kill; fatal. **2.** Exhausting: *a killing ordeal.* **3.** *Informal.* Hilarious. —**kill·ing·ly** *adv.*

kill·joy (kĭl′joi′) *n.* A person who spoils the enthusiasm or fun of others.

Kil·mer (kĭl′mər), **(Alfred) Joyce** (1886–1918). U.S. author. A respected journalist and lecturer, he published his first book of verse, *Summer of Love*, in 1911. His other books, including *Trees and Other Poems* (1914), were published before he volunteered to fight in World War I (1917). He was killed on a French battlefield.

kiln (kĭln, kĭl) *n.* Any of various types of ovens for hardening, burning, or drying substances such as grain, meal, or clay; especially, a brick-lined oven used to bake or fire ceramics.

~*tr.v.* **kilned, kilning, kilns.** To process in a kiln. [Middle English *kylne*, Old English *cyline, cylen*, from Latin *culīna*, kitchen, irregular variant of *coquīna,* cookery, from *coquīnus,* of cooking, from *coquere,* to cook.]

Kil·ner jar (kĭl′nər) *n.* A trademark for a glass jar having a tightly fitting lid that is used in preserving and bottling.

ki·lo (kē′lō) *n., pl.* **-los. 1.** A kilogram. **2.** A kilometer.

kilo– *prefix. Symbol* **k** Indicates 1,000 (10^3); for example, **kilowatt, kilocalorie.** [French, arbitrarily from Greek *khilioi,* thousand.]

kil·o·cal·o·rie (kĭl′ə-kăl′ə-rē) *n. Abbr.* **kcal** A kilogram calorie.

kil·o·cy·cle (kĭl′ə-sī′kəl) *n. Abbr.* **kc 1.** A unit equal to 1,000 cycles. **2.** Loosely, 1,000 cycles per second.

kil·o·gram, kil·o·gramme (kĭl′ə-grăm′) *n. Abbr.* **kg 1.** The fundamental unit of mass in the International System, equal to the mass of a prototype block of platinum–iridium kept at the International Bureau of Weights and Measures at Sèvres, France, that is equal to about 2.20462 pounds. **2.** A force equal to a kilogram weight, or the product of a kilogram mass with the acceleration of gravity.

kilogram calorie *n.* See **calorie** (sense 3).

kil·o·gram-me·ter (kĭl′ə-grăm-mē′tər) *n.* A meter-kilogram-second unit of work equal to the work performed by a one-kilogram force acting through a distance of one meter.

kil·o·hertz (kĭl′ə-hûrts′) *n. Abbr.* **kHz** One thousand hertz.

kil·o·me·ter (kĭl′ə-mē′tər, kĭ-lŏm′ə-tər) *n. Abbr.* **km** One thousand meters, approximately 0.62137 mile. **—kil·o·met·ric** (kĭl′ə-mĕt′rĭk) *adj.*

kil·o·ton (kĭl′ə-tŭn′) *n.* **1.** One thousand tons. **2.** An explosive force equivalent to that of 1,000 tons of TNT.

kil·o·volt (kĭl′ə-vōlt′) *n. Abbr.* **kV** One thousand volts.

kil·o·watt (kĭl′ə-wŏt′) *n. Abbr.* **kW** One thousand watts.

kil·o·watt-hour (kĭl′ə-wŏt′our′) *n. Abbr.* **kWh** A unit of electric power consumption indicating the total energy developed by a power of one kilowatt acting for one hour.

kilt (kĭlt) *n.* A knee-length skirt with deep pleats, usually of a tartan wool, worn especially as part of formal dress for men in the Scottish Highlands.
~*tr.v.* **kilted, kilting, kilts.** To tuck up around the body. [From the dialectal verb *kilt,* to fasten up, tuck up, Middle English (northern dialect) *kilten,* from Scandinavian, akin to Danish *kilte,* to tuck up, Old Norse *kjalta*†, shirt.] **—kilt·ed** *adj.*

kil·ter (kĭl′tər) *n.* Good condition or proper form: *The radio was out of kilter.* [17th century : origin obscure.]

Kim·ber·ley (kĭm′bər-lē). A city in central South Africa. In Cape Province, south of the Vaal River, it was founded (1871) as a diamond-mining camp and is still a major mining center.

kim·ber·lite (kĭm′bər-līt′) *n.* A type of rock that is found especially in South Africa and that often contains diamonds. [KIMBERLEY + -ITE[1].] **—kim·ber·lit·ic** (kĭm′bər-lĭt′ĭk) *adj.*

Kim il Sung (kĭm′ ĭl′ sŭng′, so͝ong′), born Kim Song Ju (1912–). North Korean political and military leader. He led the Korean People's army against Japan (1932–45) and became leader of Soviet-dominated North Korea in 1945. He proclaimed the Democratic People's Republic of Korea in 1948 and remained its premier until 1972, when he became its president.

ki·mo·no (kə-mō′nə, -nō) *n., pl.* **-nos. 1.** A long, loose, wide-sleeved Japanese robe, worn with a broad sash. **2.** A loose dressing gown that is similar to a kimono. [Japanese, "thing for wearing" : *ki,* to wear + *mono,* person, thing.]

kin (kĭn) *n.* One's relatives collectively; family; kindred; kinsfolk.
~*adj.* Related; akin. [Middle English *kin(n), kyn,* Old English *cyn(n).*]

-kin *suffix.* Indicates small or diminutive; for example, **lambkin.** [Middle English, from Middle Dutch *-kin, -kijn,* from West Germanic *-kin* (unattested).]

ki·na (kē′nə) *n., pl.* **kina** or **-nas.** The basic monetary unit of Papua New Guinea, equal to 100 toea. [Native name.]

ki·nase (kī′nās′, -nāz′) *n.* An enzyme or metal ion that activates the inactive precursor of another enzyme. [KIN(ETIC) + -ASE.]

Kin·car·dine (kĭn-kär′dən). Also **Kin·car·dine·shire** (-shîr, -shər). Former county of eastern Scotland, incorporated into Grampian Region (1975).

Kinchinjunga. See **Kangchenjunga, Mount.**

kind[1] (kīnd) *adj.* **kinder, kindest. 1.** Of a friendly, generous, and hospitable nature; warmhearted and good. **2.** Showing sympathy, generosity, or thoughtfulness: *a kind act; his kind remarks about your work.* **3.** Humane; considerate: *kind to animals.* **4.** Forbearing; tolerant: *very kind about the broken window.* **5.** Generous; liberal: *Fate has been kind to her.* **6.** Not harmful; beneficial: *a soap kind to the skin.* [Middle English *kynde, kind,* Old English *gecynde,* natural, innate.]
Synonyms: *benevolent, benign, caring, compassionate, kindhearted, kindly.*

kind[2] *n.* **1.** A class or category of similar or related individuals: *the kind of people who are cheerful in the morning.* —See Usage note at **sort. 2.** A specific type; variety: *What kind of dog is that?* **3.** A rough, often not very good approximation to the thing specified: *a kind of shelter; gave us soup of a kind.* —See Synonyms at **type. —all kinds of.** *Informal.* Plenty of; ample: *We have all kinds of time to finish the job.* **—in kind. 1.** With produce or commodities rather than with money: *pay in kind.* **2.** In the same manner or with something equivalent; accordingly: *returned the slight in kind.* **—kind of.** *Informal.* Somewhat: *I'm kind of hungry.* [Middle English *kynd(e), kind(e),* Old English *cynd, gecynd(e),* birth, nature, race.]

kin·der·gar·ten (kĭn′dər-gärt′n) *n.* A program or class for four- to six-year-old children that serves as an introduction to school. [German *Kindergarten,* "children's garden."]

kind·heart·ed (kīnd′här′tĭd) *adj.* Having or proceeding from a kind heart; sympathetic, generous, and helpful. —See Synonyms at **kind. —kind·heart·ed·ly** *adv.* **—kind·heart·ed·ness** *n.*

kin·dle (kĭnd′l) *v.* **-dled, -dling, -dles.** —*tr.* **1.** To set fire to; cause to start burning; ignite. **2.** To cause to glow; light up: *The sunset kindled the skies.* **3. a.** To inflame; excite. **b.** To arouse; inspire: *"no spark had yet kindled in him an intellectual passion"* (George Eliot). —*intr.* **1.** To catch fire; burst into flame. **2.** To become bright; glow. **3.** To become inflamed; be aroused or stirred up. [Middle English *kind(e)len,* from Old Norse *kynda,* to kindle, catch fire (but influenced in form by Old Norse *kyndill,* torch), akin to Middle High German *künden*†, to set on fire.] **—kin·dler** *n.*

kind·less (kīnd′lĭs) *adj.* **1.** Heartless. **2.** *Obsolete.* Inhuman.

kind·li·ness (kīnd′lē-nĭs) *n.* **1.** The quality of being kindly. **2.** A kindly deed; a good turn; a kindness.

kin·dling (kĭnd′lĭng) *n.* Easily ignited material, such as dry sticks of wood, used to start a fire.

kind·ly (kīnd′lē) *adj.* **-lier, -liest. 1.** Having a sympathetic, helpful, or benevolent nature; customarily showing kindness: *a kindly old soul.* **2.** Expressive of a sympathetic, helpful, or benevolent nature or impulse: *a kindly interest.* **3.** Agreeable; pleasant. **4.** *Archaic.* **a.** Lawful; legitimate. **b.** Native-born. **c.** Natural to its kind. —See Synonyms at **kind.**
~*adv.* **1.** Out of kindness: *He kindly overlooked their mistake.* **2.** In a kind manner; graciously; cordially: *She spoke kindly to him.* **3.** Pleasantly; agreeably: *The sun shone kindly.* **4.** As a matter of courtesy; please: *Would you kindly refrain from doing that?* **5.** *Obsolete.* In a way or course that is natural; fittingly. **—take kindly to. 1.** To be receptive or favorably disposed to: *doesn't take kindly to people who criticize him.* **2.** To be naturally attracted or fitted to; thrive on.

kind·ness (kīnd′nĭs) *n.* **1.** The quality or state of being kind: *We relied upon their kindness.* **2.** An instance of kind behavior: *You did him a great kindness when you hired him.*

kin·dred (kĭn′drĭd) *n.* **1.** Connection by blood or marriage; kinship. **2. a.** A group of related persons, as a family, clan, or tribe. **b.** A person's relatives; kinfolk.
~*adj.* **1.** Of the same ancestry or family: *kindred clans.* **2.** Having a similar or related origin, nature, or character: *kindred emotions; a kindred spirit.* [Middle English *kin(d)red(e), kinraden* : KIN + *-rede,* from Old English *rǣden,* condition, rule, from *rǣdan,* to advise, rule, read.] **—kin·dred·ness** *n.*

kine. *Archaic.* Plural of **cow.**

kin·e·mat·ics (kĭn′ə-măt′ĭks) *n.* *Used with a singular verb. Physics.* A branch of mechanics concerned with the study of motion exclusive of the influences of mass and force. Compare **dynamics, statics.** [Greek *kinēma* (stem *kinēmat-*), motion, from *kinein,* to move.]

kin·e·mat·ic viscosity (kĭn′ə-măt′ĭk) *n. Symbol* **ν** *Physics.* The viscosity of a fluid divided by its density.

kin·e·scope (kĭn′ə-skōp′) *n.* **1.** A cathode-ray tube in a television receiver that translates received electrical signals into a visible picture on a luminescent screen. **2.** A film of a transmitted television program.
~*tr.v.* **kinescoped, -scoping, -scopes.** To make a kinescope of (a transmitted television program). [KINE(TIC) + -SCOPE.]

ki·ne·sics (kə-nē′sĭks, -zĭks, kī-) *n.* *Used with a singular verb.* The study of nonlinguistic bodily movements, as facial expressions and gestures, as a systematic mode of communication. [Greek *kinēsis,* motion + -ICS.] **—ki·ne·sic** (kə-nē′sĭk, -zĭk, kī-) *adj.*

ki·ne·si·ol·o·gy (kə-nē′sē-ŏl′ə-jē, kə-nē′zē-) *n.* The study of locomotion in relation to the structure and working of human muscles. [Greek *kinēsis,* movement + -LOGY.] **—ki·ne·si·ol·o·gist** *n.*

-kinesis *suffix.* Indicates: **1.** Division; for example, **cytokinesis. 2.** Movement or motion; for example, **photokinesis.** [New Latin, from Greek *kinēsis,* movement, from *kinein,* to move.]

kin·es·the·sia (kĭn′ĭs-thē′zhə, kī′nĭs-) *n.* The sensation of bodily position, presence, or movement resulting chiefly from stimulation of sensory nerve endings in muscles, tendons, and joints. [New Latin, from Greek *kinein,* to move + AESTHESIA.] **—kin·es·the·tic** (kĭn′ĭs-thĕt′ĭk, kī′nĭs-) *adj.*

ki·net·ic (kĭ-nĕt′ĭk, kī-) *adj.* Of, relating to, or produced by motion. [Greek *kinētikos,* from *kinētos,* moving, from *kinein,* to move.] **—ki·net·i·cal·ly** *adv.*

kinetic art *n.* Art or art objects that move, have moving parts, or depend on a moving observer for their effect.

kinetic energy *n.* Energy associated with motion, equal for a body in pure translational motion at nonrelativistic speeds to half the product of its mass and the square of its speed. Compare **potential energy.**

ki·net·ics (kĭ-nĕt′ĭks, kī-) *n.* **1.** *Used with a singular verb. Physics.* The study of all aspects of motion, comprising both kinematics and dynamics. **2.** *Used with a singular verb. Physics.* The study of the relationship between motion and the forces affecting motion. **3.** *Used with a singular verb. Chemistry.* The study of the rates of chemical reactions. **4.** *Used with a plural verb. Physics.* The general motion of a particle or system. **5.** *Used with a plural verb. Chemistry.* The rate of a given chemical reaction, especially as affected by changes in temperature, concentration, or the like.

kinetic theory *n.* A theory of the behavior of matter, especially of pressure-volume-temperature relationships in gases, based in its simplest form on the identification of heat with the kinetic energy

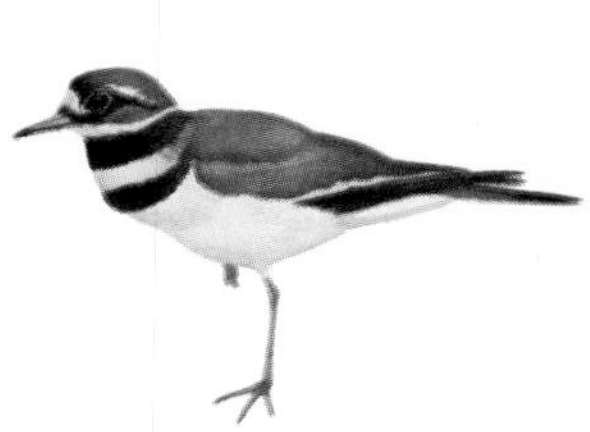

killdeer *This wader was named in imitation of its call. It is easily identified by its double breast markings. A relative of the sandpiper, the killdeer is a migratory bird of North America but is sometimes seen in Europe when high winds blow it off course.*

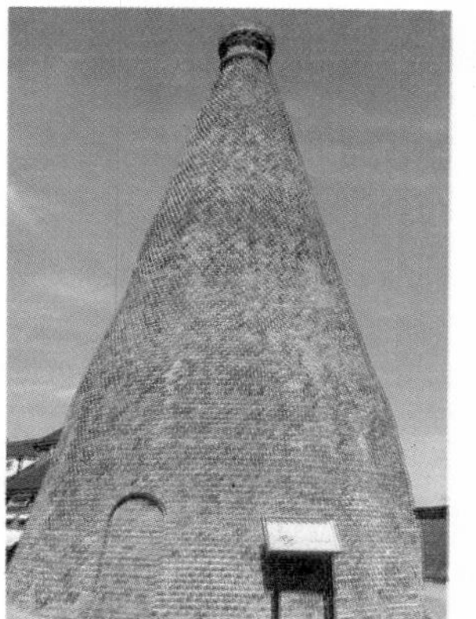

kiln *The most common type of kiln is a furnace used for firing bricks or pottery, in which the minimum working temperature is about 900° C (1650° F). The brick pottery kiln pictured is called a bottle kiln.*

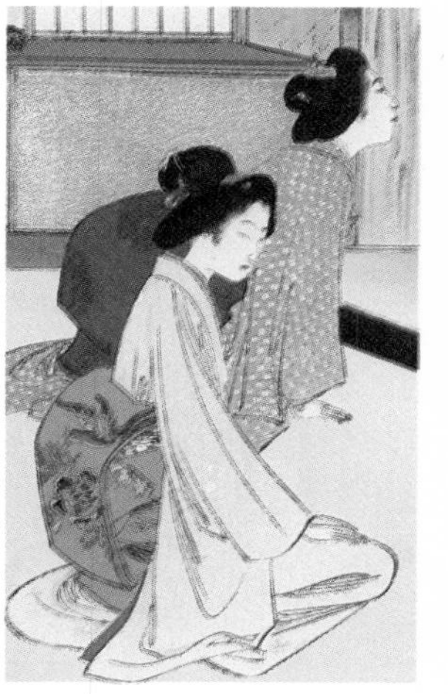

kimono *The kimono is derived from a loose robe worn by Japanese peasants in the 16th century. In the 17th century it became fashionable among wealthy townsfolk and merchants, who turned its simple shape into the backdrop for sumptuous decoration. It is fastened with a wide sash called an obi.*

of a substance's rapid, randomly moving molecules and on statistical analysis of this motion for large numbers of molecules.

ki·ne·tin (kī′nə-tĭn) *n.* An artificial cytokinin. [Greek *kinētos,* moving + -IN.]

kinfolk, kinfolks. Variants of **kinsfolk.**

king (kĭng) *n.* **1.** *Abbr.* **k., K.** A male monarch. **2.** One that is supreme or pre-eminent in a particular category, class, or sphere: *The lion is considered to be the king of the jungle.* **3. King.** God or Christ. **4.** *Abbr.* **K.** A playing card bearing a picture of a king. **5. a.** *Abbr.* **K** The principal chess piece, which can move one square in any direction and must be protected against checkmate. **b.** A piece in checkers that has reached the opponent's side of the board and been crowned and can then move both backward and forward. [Middle English *king,* Old English *cyning.*]

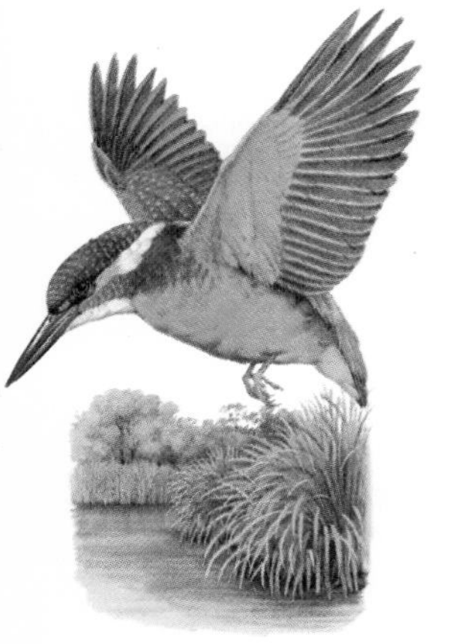

kingfisher Unlike most birds, the kingfisher nests underground, tunneling out a riverbank burrow that can be up to 1 meter (3.28 feet) long. The birds feed mainly on fish, which they snatch from the water, carry to a perch, and kill by beating them against a branch. They then swallow the fish head first so that the scales and fins lie flat.

King (kĭng), **Billie Jean,** born Billie Jean Moffitt (1943–). U.S. tennis player. She has won 20 titles at Wimbledon (6 singles, 10 women's doubles, and 4 mixed doubles). She also won the U.S. Championship in 1967, 1971, 1972, and 1974.

King, Coretta Scott (1922–). U.S. civil-rights leader. Trained as a singer, she married Martin Luther King in 1953 and first became involved in the civil-rights movement in 1955. Since her husband's death (1968), she has continued to work for peace and for nonviolent social change.

King, Martin Luther, Jr. (1929–68). U.S. clergyman and civil-rights leader. He organized the Southern Christian Leadership Council to press for black rights (1957) and led a civil-rights march on Washington (1963). King was assassinated by James Earl Ray in Memphis, Tennessee. His books include *Why We Can't Wait* (1964) and *Where Do We Go From Here: Chaos or Community?* (1967). He was awarded the Nobel Peace Prize in 1964.

King, William Lyon Mackenzie (1874–1950). Liberal politician and Canada's longest-serving prime minister (1921–26, 1926–30, and 1935–48).

king·bolt (kĭng′bōlt′) *n.* A vertical bolt used for such purposes as joining the body of a wagon to the front axle and usually serving as a pivot. Also called "kingpin."

King Charles spaniel *n.* A variety of toy spaniel having a curly black and tan coat and long ears. [After King CHARLES II of England.]

king cobra *n.* A large venomous snake, *Ophiophagus hannah,* of tropical Asia. Also called "hamadryad."

king crab *n.* **1.** A large crab, *Paralithodes camtschatica,* of coastal waters of Alaska, Japan, and Siberia, valued commercially for its edible flesh. **2.** A marine arthropod, the **horseshoe crab** *(see).*

king·craft (kĭng′krăft′, -kräft′) *n.* The art or method used by a king to rule; especially, the use of cunning in the exercise of royal power.

king·cup (kĭng′kŭp′) *n. Chiefly British.* Any of several plants having cup-shaped yellow flowers; especially, the **marsh marigold** *(see).*

king·dom (kĭng′dəm) *n.* **1.** A government, territory, state, or population that is nominally or actually ruled by a king or queen. **2. a.** The eternal spiritual sovereignty of God. **b.** The realm over which this sovereignty extends. **3.** An area, province, or realm in which one thing is dominant: *the kingdom of the imagination.* **4. a.** The broadest, most inclusive taxonomic category of organisms having certain basic characteristics: *the plant kingdom.* **b.** Any such large general category of natural forms: *the mineral kingdom.* [Middle English *kingdom,* Old English *cyningdōm* : KING + -DOM.]

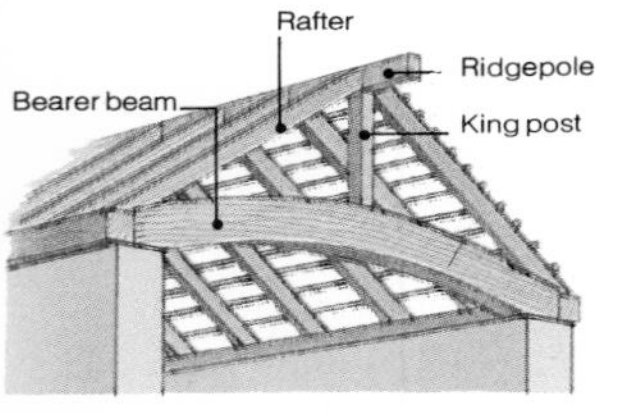

king post *The central roof beam rising from a horizontal beam to the ridge.*

kingdom come *n.* **1.** The next world: *a bomb that could blow us all to kingdom come.* **2.** The end of time; forever: *You can scream till kingdom come, but he won't take any notice.* [From the phrase *Thy kingdom come* in The Lord's Prayer.]

king·fish (kĭng′fĭsh′) *n., pl.* **-fishes** or collectively **kingfish. 1. a.** Any of several food and game fishes of the genus *Menticirrhus,* indigenous to warm Atlantic waters. **b.** Any of several similar or related fishes. **2.** *Informal.* A pre-eminent or powerful person, especially a prominent political leader.

king·fish·er (kĭng′fĭsh′ər) *n.* Any of various birds of the family Alcedinidae, characteristically having a crested head; especially, *Alcedo atthis,* which has blue-green and orange plumage. [Originally *king's fisher,* Middle English *kyngys fischare.*]

King James Bible *n.* An Anglican translation of the Bible from Hebrew and Greek into English published in 1611 under the auspices of James I. Also called "Authorized Version," "King James Version."

king·klip (kĭng′klĭp′) *n., pl.* **kingklip.** *Chiefly South African.* Either of two edible marine fishes of the Ophidiidae family, *Xiphiuris capensis* or *Hoplobrotula gnathopus.* [Afrikaans, from Dutch *koning,* KING + *klip,* stone.]

King Lear. See **Lear.**

king·let (kĭng′lĭt) *n.* **1.** Either of two small grayish North American birds, *Regulus satrapa* or *R. calendula,* with a yellowish or reddish patch on the crown of the head. **2.** A petty or insignificant king.

king·ly (kĭng′lē) *adj.* **-lier, -liest. 1.** Having the status or rank of king. **2.** Of or pertaining to a king; regal: *kingly power.* **3.** Like or suitable for a king; majestic.
∼*adv.* As a king; royally. **—king·li·ness** *n.*

king mackerel *n.* A food and game fish, *Scomberomorus cavalla,* of warm Atlantic waters. Also called "cavalla," "cero."

king·mak·er (kĭng′mā′kər) *n.* **1.** One who has control over who is king. **2.** One with sufficient political power to influence the selection of a candidate for office.

king-of-arms (kĭng′əv-ärmz′) *n., pl.* **kings-of-arms.** The title of the highest-ranking heraldic officer in the United Kingdom.

king·pin (kĭng′pĭn′) *n.* **1.** In bowling, the foremost or central pin of the arrangement of pins to be knocked down. **2.** The most important or essential person or thing in an enterprise or system. **3. a.** A hardened steel pin in the steering system of a motor vehicle that does not have independent front suspension. **b.** A **kingbolt** *(see).*

king post, king·post (kĭng′pōst′) *n.* A supporting post extending vertically from a crossbeam to the apex of a triangular truss. Compare **queen post.**

king prawn *n.* Any of various large edible prawns of the genus *Enaeus.*

Kings (kĭngz) *n. Used with a singular verb.* **1.** Either of the two Old Testament books, I Kings or II Kings, that tell the history of the kings of Israel and Judah. **2.** Any of a group of four books, I, II, III, and IV Kings, in the Douay version of the Old Testament that correspond to I Samuel, II Samuel, I Kings, and II Kings in the King James Bible.

King's Bench *n.* A division of the British superior court system that hears criminal and civil cases. Used when the monarch is a male.

King's Counsel *n. Abbr.* **K.C.** A barrister appointed as counsel to the British crown. Used when the monarch is a male.

King's English *n.* Spoken or written English that is considered a standard of good usage.

King's evil, king's evil *n.* A disease, **scrofula** *(see).* [From the belief that scrofula could be healed by the king's touch.]

king·ship (kĭng′shĭp′) *n.* **1.** The position, power, province, or prerogative of a king. **2.** The period or tenure of a king; reign. **3.** A monarchy. **4.** The domain ruled by a king; kingdom. **5.** The style of a king; majesty.

king-size (kĭng′sīz′) *adj.* Also **king-sized** (-sīzd′). Larger or longer than a standard or usual size: *king-size cigarettes; a king-size bed.*

Kings·ley (kĭngz′lē), **Charles** (1819–75). English author. He was professor of modern history at Cambridge (1860–69) and chaplain to Queen Victoria (1873). Kingsley wrote the adventure novels *Westward Ho!* (1855) and *Hereward the Wake* (1865) and the children's book *Water Babies* (1863).

king snake *n.* Any of various nonvenomous New World snakes of the genus *Lampropeltis,* having yellow or reddish markings.

King·ston[1] (kĭngz′tən). The capital and chief port of Jamaica. Founded in 1693 following the destruction of Port Royal by earthquake, it became the capital in 1872.

Kingston[2]**.** A city on Lake Ontario, Canada, connected to Ottawa by the Rideau Canal. It stands on the site of Fort Frontenac and was the capital of Canada from 1841 to 1844.

Kingston upon Hull. See **Hull.**

Kingston upon Thames (tĕmz). Royal borough in southwest Greater London. The Coronation Stone near the Guildhall is a relic of the days (901–78) when Saxon kings were crowned here.

king·wood (kĭng′wo͝od′) *n.* **1.** A South American tree, *Dalbergia cearensis,* having hard, fine-textured, purplish-brown wood used in cabinetmaking. **2.** The wood of this tree.

ki·nin (kī′nĭn) *n.* Any of a class of polypeptides found in the blood that act in the contraction of smooth muscle and the dilation of blood vessels. [Greek *kinein,* to move + -IN.]

kink (kĭngk) *n.* **1.** A tight curl or a sharp twist in a line or wirelike material that is typically caused by the tensing of a looped section. **2.** A painful muscle spasm, as in the neck or back; a crick. **3.** A quirk of personality. **4.** A clever or eccentric idea or notion. **5.** A slight difficulty or flaw, as in a plan or system. **6.** *Chiefly British.* A sexual peculiarity or deviation.
∼*v.* **kinked, kinking, kinks.** —*tr.* To cause to have a kink or kinks. —*intr.* To form kinks. [Low German *kinke,* a twist in a rope, from Middle Low German *kinke*†.]

kink·a·jou (kĭng′kə-jo͞o′) *n.* An arboreal mammal, *Potos flavus,* of tropical America, having brownish fur and a long, prehensile tail. Also called "honey bear," "potto." [French *quincajou,* from Algonquian; akin to Ojibwa *quingwâage,* wolverine.]

kink·y (kĭng′kē) *adj.* **-ier, -iest. 1.** Tightly curled; frizzy: *kinky hair.* **2.** *Informal.* **a.** Marked by or making use of a perverted eroticism. **b.** Marked by sexual perversion. **—kink·i·ly** *adv.* **—kink·i·ness** *n.*

kin·ni·kin·nick, kin·ni·kin·nic (kĭn′ĭ-kĭ-nĭk′) *n.* **1.** A tobaccolike preparation made from the dried leaves or bark of various plants and used for smoking, especially by American Indians. **2.** A plant having leaves or bark used in such a preparation, as the **bearberry** *(see).* [Algonquian; akin to Natick *kinukkinuk,* mixture.]

ki·no (kē′nō) *n., pl.* **-nos.** A reddish resin obtained from several Old World tropical trees of the genera *Pterocarpus* and *Butea* and used to treat dysentery and diarrhea. [A West African word, akin to Mandingo *keno.*]

Kin·ross (kĭn-rôs′). Also **Kin·ross-shire** (-shîr, -shər). Former county of east-central Scotland. It is now part of Tayside Region.

kin selection *n.* The theory that natural selection in animal populations may operate through the mechanism of cooperation among a group of related individuals, which ensures that the average fitness for survival of the group is increased, although one member's individual fitness may be decreased through apparently altruistic behavior.

Kin·sey (kĭn′zē), **Alfred Charles** (1894–1956). U.S. zoologist. He worked at the Institute of Sex Research, Harvard, and published *Sexual Behavior in the Human Male* (1948) and *Sexual Behavior in the Human Female* (1953), pioneer studies of their kind.

kins·folk (kĭnz′fōk′) *pl.n.* Also *informal* **kin·folk** (kĭn′fōk′), **kin·folks** (-fōks′). Members of one's family; kindred.

Kin·sha·sa (kĭn-shä'sə). Formerly **Lé·o·pold·ville** (lē'ə-pōld'vĭl', lā'-). Capital of Zaire. An ancient settlement on the Zaire River, it was founded by Henry M. Stanley (1881).

kin·ship (kĭn'shĭp') n. **1.** The state of being related by blood. **2.** The state of being related in character, origin, or the like; similarity.

kins·man (kĭnz'mən) n., pl. **-men** (-mĭn). A male relative.

kins·wom·an (kĭnz'wŏom'ən) n., pl. **-women** (-wĭm'ĭn). A female relative.

ki·osk (kē'ŏsk', kē-ŏsk') n. **1.** A small, sometimes ornamental structure used as a newsstand or refreshment booth. **2.** Chiefly British. A booth for a public telephone; a telephone booth. **3.** An open gazebo or pavilion. **4.** A cylindrical structure on which advertisements are posted. [French kiosque, from Turkish köshk, pavilion, from Persian kūshk†, palace.]

kip¹ (kĭp) n., pl. **kip.** The basic monetary unit of Laos, equal to 100 at. See feature at **currency.** [Thai.]

kip² n. The untanned hide of a small or young animal, such as a calf. [Obsolete Dutch kip, bundle (of hides), from Middle Dutch; akin to Old Norse kippi†, bundle.]

kip³ n. British Slang. **1. a.** Sleep. **b.** A period of sleep. **2.** A place to sleep, such as a room or bed. **3.** A rooming house.
~intr.v. **kipped, kipping, kips.** British Slang. To sleep or prepare to sleep: Can we kip down here? [Danish kippe†, cheap inn.]

kip⁴ n. Engineering. A 1,000-pound unit of weight, used to express loads. [KI(LO)- + P(OUND).]

Kip·ling (kĭp'lĭng), **(Joseph) Rudyard** (1865–1936). Indian-born British poet and novelist. His first volume of poetry, Departmental Ditties (1886), was followed by Plain Tales from the Hills (1888). His later works include the two Jungle Books (1894–95), Kim (1901), and the Just So Stories (1902). He received the Nobel Prize for literature (1907).

kip·per (kĭp'ər) n. **1.** A male salmon or sea trout in the spawning season. **2.** A herring that has been split, salted, and smoked.
~tr.v. **kippered, -pering, -pers.** To cure (fish) by splitting, salting, and smoking. [Middle English kypre, Old English cypera, perhaps from coper, COPPER (from the color of the fish).]

Kipp's apparatus (kĭps) n. Chemistry. A laboratory apparatus for the controlled production of a gas by the action of a liquid on a solid, used especially to prepare hydrogen sulfide by the action of sulfuric acid on iron sulfide. [After P.J. Kipp (1808–64), Dutch chemist.]

kir (kîr) n. A drink consisting of white wine flavored with cassis. [After Canon Kir, former mayor of Dijon, France, who is said to have invented the drink.]

Kir·giz¹ (kîr-gēz'). Former name of **Kyr·gyz·stan** (kîr'gə-stăn', -stän'). Mountainous republic in Central Asia. It is rich in mineral deposits, including uranium. It was annexed by Russia in 1864 and became a constituent republic of the U.S.S.R. in 1936. In 1991, with the dissolution of the Soviet Union, it joined the Commonwealth of Independent States. Area, 199,267 square kilometers (76,641 square miles). Population, 4,370,000. Capital, Bishkek.

Kirgiz² n., pl. **-gyzes** or collectively **Kirgiz.** Former term for **Kyr·gyz** (kîr-gēz'). **1.** A member of a Turkic people living principally in Kyrgyzstan. **2.** The Turkic language of this people.

Ki·ri·ba·ti (kĭr'ə-bä'tē). Formerly **Gil·bert Islands** (gĭl'bərt). Republic in the western Pacific. It includes the Phoenix Islands, the southern Line Islands, and Ocean Island (Banaba). Formerly part of the Gilbert and Ellice Islands Colony, Kiribati gained independence from the United Kingdom in 1979. The same year the phosphate deposits of Banaba became exhausted, and the country now depends on copra exports and British aid. Fishing and tourism are expanding. Area, 886 square kilometers (342 square miles). Population, 66,000. Capital, Betio (on Tarawa). See map at **Pacific Ocean.**

ki·ri·ga·mi (kĭr'ĭ-gä'mē) n. The Japanese art of making ornamental designs by cutting and folding paper. Compare **origami.** [Japanese : kiri, to cut + -gami, from kami, paper.]

Kirin. See **Jilin.**

kirk (kûrk) n. **1.** Chiefly Scottish. A church. **2.** Kirk. Chiefly British. The Presbyterian Church of Scotland. [Middle English kirk(e), from Old Norse kirkja, from Old English cir(i)ce, CHURCH.]

Kirk·cal·dy (kûr-kôl'dē). Royal burgh of east-central Scotland. In the former county of Fife, it is a port and coal-mining center on the Firth of Forth.

Kirk·cud·bright (kûr-kōō'brē). Former county of southwest Scotland, incorporated into Dumfries and Galloway Region (1975).

Kirk·wall (kûrk'wôl). Royal burgh of north Scotland. On Mainland (Pomona) Island in the Orkney Islands, it is the islands' largest town, chief port, and administrative center.

Kir·man (kər-män', kĭr-) n. A Persian rug with an elaborate border pattern and muted colors. [After Kirman, province of Iran.]

kirmess. Variant of **kermis.**

kirsch (kĭrsh) n. A colorless brandy made from the fermented juice of cherries. [German Kirsch(wasser), "cherry (water)," from Old High German kirsa, cherry, from Vulgar Latin cerasia (unattested).]

kir·tle (kûrt'l) n. **1.** A knee-length tunic or coat formerly worn by men. **2.** A woman's long dress or skirt. [Middle English ki(e)rtel, curtle, Old English cyrtel, from Germanic kurtilaz (unattested), "short coat," diminutive of kurt- (unattested), short, from Latin curtus, cut short.]

kish (kĭsh) n. Metallurgy. Graphite formed on the surface of molten iron when the iron contains large amounts of carbon. [Perhaps alteration of German Kies, gravel.]

Kish (kĭsh). A city of ancient Mesopotamia. Excavated in the 1920's, it revealed its pre-Sumerian origins when the earliest existing example of writing was discovered here—a precuneiform tablet dating from 3500 B.C.

kish·ke (kĭsh'kə) n. A food, **derma** (see). [Yiddish, probably from Russian kishka, gut.]

Kis·lev (kĭs'ləf) n. The third month of the Hebrew year. See feature at **calendar.** [Hebrew kislēw.]

kis·met (kĭz'mĕt', -mĭt) n. Fate; fortune. [Turkish kismet, from Arabic qismah, lot, from qasama, he divided, he allotted.]

kiss (kĭs) v. **kissed, kissing, kisses.** —tr. **1.** To touch or caress with the lips as a sign of sexual passion, affection, greeting, or respect. **2.** To touch lightly; brush against: The mist kissed the flowers. **3.** To touch or hit against (another billiard ball) lightly. —intr. **1.** To touch or caress each other with the lips. **2.** To meet with a light, gentle touch. —**kiss good-by.** To be forced to undergo the loss of. —**kiss off.** Informal. To get rid of; dismiss.
~n. **1.** A caress or touch with the lips. **2.** A slight or gentle touch. **3.** A gentle impact between billiard balls. **4. a.** A small piece of candy, especially of chocolate. **b.** A baked confection made of meringue. [Middle English kissen, cussen, Old English cyssan.]

kiss-curl (kĭs'kûrl') n. A small, almost circular curl of hair lying flat against the cheek, forehead, or nape of the neck.

kiss·er (kĭs'ər) n. **1.** A person who kisses. **2.** Slang. The mouth or face.

kissing bug n. An assassin bug, Melanolestes picipes, that inflicts a painful bite, often on the lips of a sleeping person.

kissing cousin n. A distant relative known well enough to be kissed when greeted.

kissing disease n. Informal. Mononucleosis.

Kis·sin·ger (kĭs'ĭn-jər), **Henry Alfred** (1923–). U.S. foreign policy adviser. He was born in Germany and fled the Nazis (1938) to live in the United States. Under presidents Richard Nixon and Gerald Ford he was executive secretary of the National Security Council (1969) and secretary of state (1973). He helped negotiate the Vietnam cease-fire (1973), for which he shared the Nobel Peace Prize (1973) with the North Vietnamese negotiator, Le Duc Tho.

kissing gate n. British. A gate that is partially enclosed in a U- or V-shaped structure on the side opposite the hinge so as to allow only one person to pass through at a time.

kiss of death n. Something that is ultimately ruinous, disastrous, or fatal: He offered to help, but assistance from an incompetent person would have been the kiss of death. [From the kiss of Judas that betrayed Jesus.]

kiss of life n. Mouth-to-mouth resuscitation.

kiss of peace n. A ceremonial gesture, as a kiss or a handshake, used as a sign of unity and brotherhood among those celebrating and attending the Eucharist.

kist¹ (kĭst) n. Chiefly Scottish & South African. A large, lidded chest. [Middle English, from Old Norse kista, CHEST.]

kist². Variant of **cist** (coffin).

kit¹ (kĭt) n. **1. a.** A set of instruments or equipment used for a specific job or purpose: a survival kit; a travel kit. **b.** A collection of clothing and other personal effects, as for travel or a sporting activity. **c.** A container, as a box, bag, or rucksack, for such a set or collection. **2.** A set of parts or materials to be assembled: a model airplane kit. **3.** A packaged set of related materials: a sales kit. **4.** British Regional. A wooden tub or barrel for holding water or foodstuffs. —**the (whole) kit and caboodle.** Informal. The entire collection or lot.
~tr.v. **kitted, kitting, kits.** Chiefly British. To equip; provide with a kit or outfit. Usually used with out or up. [Middle English kytt, kitt, wooden tub, from Middle Dutch kitte†, jug, tankard.]

kit² n. A kitten or other young fur-bearing animal. [Short for KITTEN.]

kit³ n. New Zealand. A basket, especially one woven from flax. [Maori kete, bag.]

kit⁴ n. A small three-stringed violin. [Origin unknown.]

kit bag, kit·bag (kĭt'băg') n. A traveling bag, such as a rucksack; especially, a long narrow canvas bag used by servicemen.

kitch·en (kĭch'ən) n. **1.** A room or area in which food is cooked or prepared. **2.** The facilities and equipment used in the preparation and serving of food. **3.** The staff that prepares, cooks, and serves food. [Middle English kichen, kuchene, Old English cycene, from West Germanic kocina (unattested), from Late Latin coquīna, from Latin, feminine of coquīnus, of cooking, from coquere, to cook.]

kitchen cabinet n. An unofficial but influential group of advisers to the head of a government.

Kitch·e·ner of Khar·toum and of Broome (kĭch'ə-nər; kär-tōōm'; brōōm), **Horatio Herbert, 1st Earl** (1850–1916). British soldier and statesman. As commander in chief of the Egyptian army, he won back the Sudan for Egypt at the Battle of Omdurman (1898). He brought the Boer War (1899–1902) to a conclusion. As secretary for war in World War I he recruited 3,000,000 volunteers for the armed forces. He was killed on board H.M.S. Hampshire when it was mined.

kitch·en·ette (kĭch'ə-nĕt') n. A small kitchen.

kitchen garden n. A garden in which vegetables and fruits are grown for household consumption.

kitchen midden n. A refuse heap or mound of the Mesolithic or later prehistoric periods, containing numerous artifacts, shells, and often animal bones. [Midden, Middle English myddyng, from Scandinavian; akin to Danish mødding.]

kitchen police n. Abbr. **KP** **1.** Enlisted military personnel assigned

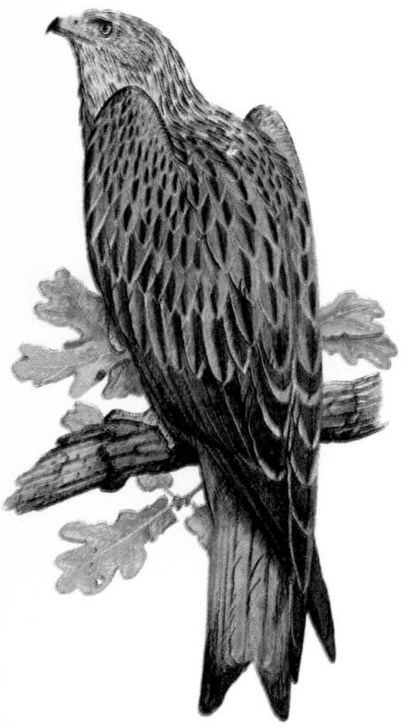

kite *The hovering, gliding flight of this hawk gave the name to the manmade kite. The red kite (above) used to scavenge the streets of Tudor London, but it has now vanished from cities and inhabits the woods and parklands of Europe and parts of the Middle East.*

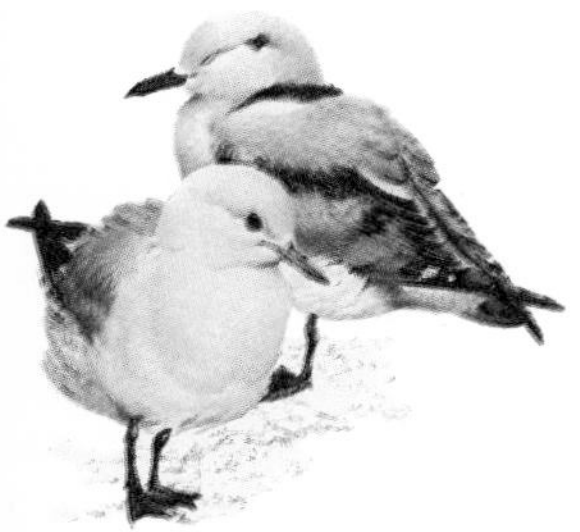

kittiwake *The kittiwake, which is a type of gull, spends most of its life at sea, following the movements of fish and ships, and rarely comes ashore except to breed. It lays its eggs in cup-shaped nests on cliff ledges around the northern coasts of Europe, Asia, and North America.*

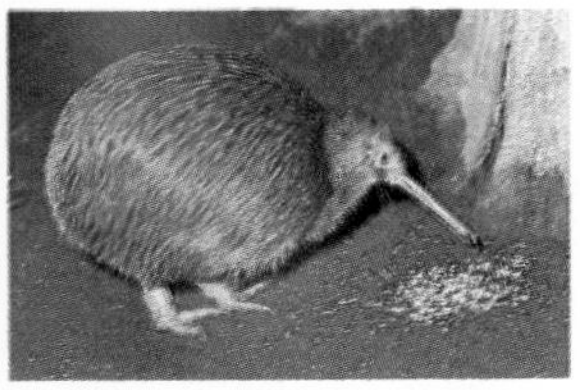

kiwi *The flightless national bird of New Zealand. The kiwi lays the largest egg in proportion to its size of any bird: the bird weighs little more than 3 kilograms (about 7 pounds), yet it produces an egg of about 500 grams (1 pound).*

to work in the kitchen. **2.** The work of the kitchen police.

kitch·en-sink (kĭch'ən-sĭngk') *adj. Chiefly British.* Portraying working-class domestic life realistically and unromantically: *kitchen-sink drama.*

kitch·en·ware (kĭch'ən-wâr') *n.* Utensils for use in the kitchen, such as pots and pans.

kite (kīt) *n.* **1.** A light framework covered with cloth, plastic, or paper that is designed to climb and hover in a steady breeze at the end of a long string. **2.** Any of the highest sails of a ship, used only in a light wind. **3.** Any of various predatory birds of the subfamilies Milvinae and Elaninae, having a long, often forked tail. **4.** A negotiable paper, as a check, that represents a fictitious financial transaction and is used temporarily to sustain credit or raise money. **5.** *Geometry.* A quadrilateral that has two pairs of equal adjacent sides. **—fly a kite.** To stop bothering or urging: *Finally I told him to go fly a kite.*
~v. **kited, kiting, kites.** *—intr.* **1.** To fly like a kite; soar or glide. **2.** To get money or credit with a kite. *—tr.* To use a kite to sustain credit or raise money. [Middle English *kyte, kete,* kite (bird), Old English *cȳta,* from Common Germanic *kūtja-* (unattested), probably imitative of its cry.]

kith and kin (kĭth' ən kĭn') *pl.n.* Friends and neighbors. [Middle English *kith, kyth,* Old English *cȳth(the), cȳththu,* "knowledge," "acquaintance," friend.]

Kithira. See **Cythera.**

kitsch (kĭch) *n.* **1.** Vulgarity, sentimentality, and pretentious bad taste, especially in the arts, sometimes achieved deliberately for effect or fun. **2.** Examples or an example of kitsch. [German, from *kitschen*†, to put together (a work of art) sloppily.] **—kitsch, kitsch·y** *adj.*

kit·ten (kĭt'n) *n.* A young cat. **—have kittens.** *Informal.* To be very angry, nervous, or upset.
~intr.v. **kittened, -tening, -tens.** To bear kittens. [Middle English *kitoun,* from Old North French *caton* (unattested), diminutive of *cat,* cat, from Late Latin *cattus,* CAT.]

kit·ten·ish (kĭt'n-ĭsh) *adj.* Playful; coy. **—kit·ten·ish·ly** *adv.*

kit·ti·wake (kĭt'ē-wāk') *n.* Either of two gulls, *Rissa tridactyla* or *R. brevirostris,* of northern regions. [Imitative of its cry.]

kit·tle (kĭt'l) *adj. Scottish.* Requiring careful handling; tricky; delicate. [Scottish *kittle,* to tickle, Middle English (Scottish) *kytyllen,* probably from Old Norse *kitla.*]

kit·ty¹ (kĭt'ē) *n., pl.* **-ties. 1.** In some card games, a sum of money contributed by each player at the start of a hand, all of which is won by the winner of that hand. **2.** A pool of money, especially one contributed to equally by a group of people and used to buy something that they all share. [Originally "small bowl," diminutive of KIT (tub).]

kitty² *n., pl.* **-ties.** *Informal.* A kitten or cat. [From *kit,* short for KITTEN.]

ki·va (kē'və) *n.* An underground or partly underground room in a Pueblo Indian village, used by the men especially for ceremonies or councils. [Hopi.]

Kivu, Lake (kē'vo͞o). Africa's highest lake. It lies at 1,459 meters (4,788 feet) on the Zaire-Rwanda border, in the western arm of the Great Rift Valley.

ki·wi (kē'wē) *n.* **1.** Any of several nocturnal flightless birds of the genus *Apteryx,* of New Zealand, having vestigial wings and a long, slender bill. **2. a.** A vine, *Actinidia chinensis,* native to Asia, bearing hairy, edible fruit. **b.** The fruit of this vine. In this sense, also called "Chinese gooseberry," "kiwi fruit." **3. Kiwi.** *Informal.* A New Zealander. [Maori.]

K.K.K. Ku Klux Klan.

Klai·pe·da (klī'pə-də). *German* **Me·mel** (mā'məl). Ice-free Baltic port and industrial city in Lithuania. A strategic fortress, it was held by the Prussians from 1635 until 1919. The city fell to the Russians in 1945.

Klam·ath (klăm'əth). River, *c.* 425 kilometers (265 miles) long, rising in the Klamath Mts. of southwestern Oregon and flowing across northwestern California to the Pacific Ocean. It is used for irrigation and is a source of hydroelectric power.

Klan (klăn) *n.* The **Ku Klux Klan** *(see).*

Klans·man (klănz'mən) *n., pl.* **-men** (-mĭn). A member of the Ku Klux Klan.

Klax·on (klăk'sən) *n.* A trademark for a loud horn formerly used on automobiles. [From Greek *klazein,* to roar.]

Klee (klā), **Paul** (1879–1940). Swiss painter. His works, mainly small abstracts, are reminiscent of doodles or children's art, as in *Twittering Machine, The Zoo,* and *Fish Magic.*

Kleen·ex (klē'nĕks') *n.* A trademark for a soft cleansing tissue.

Klein bottle (klīn) *n.* A one-sided topologic surface having no inside or outside, formed by inserting the small open end of a tapered tube through the side of the tube and making it contiguous with the larger open end. Compare **Möbius strip.** [After Felix *Klein* (1849–1925), German mathematician.]

Kleist (klīst), **Heinrich von** (1777–1811). German dramatist. In his plays, including *The Broken Pitcher* (1808) and other works, he created characters torn between reason and emotion and between heroism and cowardice. Largely unrecognized in his lifetime, he is now ranked among Germany's most profound and influential dramatists.

Klem·pe·rer (klĕm'pər-ər), **Otto** (1885–1973). German conductor. He conducted several orchestras in Germany, but left in 1933 and went on to conduct many major orchestras all over the world.

klep·to·ma·ni·a (klĕp'tə-mā'nē-ə, -mān'yə) *n.* An obsessive impulse to steal, especially in the absence of economic necessity or personal desire. [New Latin : Greek *kleptein,* to steal + -MANIA.] **—klep·to·ma·ni·ac** (klĕp'tə-mā'nē-ăk') *n.*

klieg light (klēg) *n.* A powerful carbon-arc lamp producing an intense light and used especially in making movies. [Invented by the brothers John H. *Kliegl* (1869–1959) and Anton T. *Kliegl* (1872–1927), lighting experts.]

Klimt (klĭmt), **Gustav** (1862–1918). Austrian art nouveau painter. He achieved fame as a portrait and landscape painter of great exotic and erotic sensibility. His mosaics and paintings are characterized by large predominant patterns of gold, as in *The Kiss.*

Kline (klīn), **Franz Joseph** (1919–62). U.S. painter. Establishing his particular brand of abstract expressionism after seeing his black-and-white sketches magnified by a projector, he used bold, controlled sweeps of black on a white field in most of his works. Late in his career he began using colors.

klip·spring·er (klĭp'sprĭng'ər) *n.* A small, hoofed African antelope, *Oreotragus oreotragus,* having large ears. [Afrikaans, "cliff springer" : Dutch *klip,* cliff, from Middle Dutch *klippe,* from Germanic *klibam* (unattested), CLIFF + *springer,* from *springen,* to leap, from Middle Dutch.]

Klon·dike (klŏn'dīk'). A region of the Yukon Territory, Canada. It was the scene of a famous gold rush (1897–98); the gold yield, however, has steadily declined since 1910. It takes its name from the Klondike River, a tributary of the Yukon.

kloof (klo͝of) *n.* In South Africa, a deep ravine. [Afrikaans, from Dutch, from Middle Dutch *clove,* cleft.]

klutz (klŭts) *n. Slang.* **1.** A clumsy or dull-witted person. **2.** A bungler. [German *Klotz,* clod, "block," from Middle High German *kloz,* block, lump.]

kly·stron (klī'strŏn') *n.* An electron tube used to amplify or generate radio waves of microwave range frequencies by means of velocity modulation. [Greek *klustēr,* syringe, clyster pipe, from *kluzein,* to wash out + (ELECTR)ON.]

km kilometer.

K-mes·on (kā'mĕz'ŏn', -mē'zŏn', -mĕs'ŏn', -mē'sŏn') *n. Physics.* A type of meson, a **kaon** *(see).*

km/h kilometers per hour.

kn. *Nautical.* knot.

knack (năk) *n.* **1.** A clever, expedient way of doing something. **2.** A specific skill or talent for doing something, especially one difficult to explain or teach. [Middle English *knak(ke),* probably identified with *knak,* sharp blow, from Dutch and Low German *knak.*]

knack·er (năk'ər) *n. British.* **1.** A person who buys useless or worn-out horses and slaughters them to sell their hides or meat. **2.** A person who buys up discarded structures and dismantles them to sell the materials. **3.** *Slang.* A testicle.
~tr.v. **knackered, -ering, -ers.** *British Slang.* To wear out; exhaust. [Originally "harness maker," saddler, probably from Scandinavian, akin to Old Norse *hnakkur,* saddle.] **—knack·er·y** *n.*

knack·wurst, knock·wurst (nŏk'wûrst', -wo͝orst') *n.* A short, thick sausage resembling a frankfurter. [German *Knackwurst,* "sausage whose skin cracks open when bitten" : *knacken,* to crack, from Middle High German + *Wurst,* sausage, WURST.]

knap¹ (năp) *v.* **knapped, knapping, knaps.** *—tr.* **1.** *British Regional.* To strike sharply; rap. **2.** To break or chip (flints, for example) with a sharp blow. **3.** *British Regional.* To chatter about. *—intr. British Regional.* To deliver a sharp blow. [Middle English *knappen,* probably from Low German, akin to Middle Dutch *cnappen,* Low German *knappen.*]

knap² *n. Regional.* The crest of a hill; a summit. [Middle English *knap,* Old English *cnæpp.*]

knap·sack (năp'săk') *n.* A case or bag, usually of canvas or leather, worn on the back to carry supplies and equipment, especially on a hike or march. [Low German *knappsack* : probably *knappen,* to snap, bite, eat + *sack,* bag, from Middle Low German, from Germanic, from Latin *saccus,* SACK (bag).]

knap·weed (năp'wēd') *n.* Any of various plants of the genus *Centaurea,* having purplish, thistlelike flowers. [Middle English *knopwed* : KNOP (from the knobby head of its flower) + WEED.]

knar (när) *n.* A knot or protuberance on a tree or in wood. [Middle English *knarre,* probably from Scandinavian; akin to Norwegian *knart.*]

knave (nāv) *n.* **1.** An unprincipled, crafty man. **2.** In card games, the jack. [Middle English *knave,* Old English *cnafa,* boy, lad, from Common Germanic *knabōn-* (unattested).]

knav·er·y (nā'və-rē) *n., pl.* **-ies. 1.** Dishonest or crafty dealing. **2.** A piece of mischief or trickery.

knav·ish (nā'vĭsh) *adj.* Like or characteristic of a knave; dishonest and unprincipled. **—knav·ish·ly** *adv.* **—knav·ish·ness** *n.*

knawel (nôl) *n.* A low-growing, weedy plant, *Scleranthus annuus,* native to Eurasia, having narrow leaves and inconspicuous green flowers. [German *Knäuel,* knot, knob, ball of yarn, from Middle High German *kniuwel, kliuwel(in),* from Old High German *kliuwilin,* from *kliuwa,* ball.]

knead (nēd) *tr.v.* **kneaded, kneading, kneads. 1.** To mix and work (a substance) into a uniform mass; especially, to fold, press, and stretch (dough) with the hands. **2.** To make (bread or pottery, for example) by kneading. **3.** To squeeze, press, or roll with the hands, as in massaging. **4.** To blend together or manipulate as if by kneading. [Middle English *kneden,* Old English *cnedan.*] **—knead·er** *n.*

knee (nē) *n.* **1. a.** *Anatomy.* The joint of the human leg that is the articulation for the tibia and fibula with the femur and is covered in front by the patella. **b.** The region of the leg around this joint, especially at the front. **c.** A corresponding joint of a leg of a vertebrate, as the forelimb of a hoofed animal. **2.** The part of a garment, as trousers or stockings, that covers the knee. **3.** Something resembling the knee in action, as a pivoted device, or in shape, as a bent pipe. **4.** A woody projection arising from the roots of some swamp-growing trees: *cypress knees.* **—to one's knees.** Into a state of submission or defeat.

~*tr.v.* **kneed, kneeing, knees.** To strike with the knee. [Middle English *kne(e), kn(e)ow,* Old English *cnēo.*]

knee breeches *pl.n.* Breeches extending to or just below the knee.

knee·cap (nē′kăp′) *n.* **1.** A bone, the **patella** *(see).* **2.** A kneepad.

knee-deep (nē′dēp′) *adj.* **1.** Reaching to the knees; knee-high. **2.** Submerged to the knees. **3.** Deeply occupied or engaged.

knee-high (nē′hī′) *adj.* As tall or high as the knee.

~*n.* (nē′hī′). A stocking that extends to just below the knee.

knee·hole (nē′hōl′) *n.* A space or opening for the knees, as under a desk or counter. Also used adjectivally: *a kneehole desk.*

knee jerk *n.* A sudden involuntary reflex kick forward produced by a smart tap to the tendon below the patella as the leg hangs relaxed at a right angle to the thigh.

knee-jerk (nē′jûrk′) *adj. Informal.* **1.** Automatic: *Unrest is often a knee-jerk reaction to authoritarianism.* **2.** Marked by or reacting with unthinking predictability: *knee-jerk pessimism.*

kneel (nēl) *intr.v.* **knelt** (nĕlt) or **kneeled, kneeling, kneels.** To fall or rest on bent knees. [Middle English *kne(w)len,* Old English *cnēowlian.* Knelt (past tense and past participle) is an analogous formation after FEEL, FELT.]

knee-length (nē′lĕngkth′, -lĕngth′) *adj.* Reaching the knee or just below the knee: *knee-length socks.*

kneel·er (nē′lər) *n.* **1.** One who kneels. **2.** Something, as a stool, cushion, or board, to kneel on.

knee·pad (nē′păd′) *n.* A protective covering for the knee. Also called "kneecap."

knell (nĕl) *v.* **knelled, knelling, knells.** *—intr.* **1.** To ring or sound, especially for a funeral; toll. Used of a bell. **2.** To produce a mournful or ominous sound. *—tr.* To signal, summon, or proclaim by tolling.

~*n.* **1.** The slow, solemn sounding of a bell, as at a funeral; a tolling. **2.** An omen or signal of disaster, failure, or extinction. [Middle English *knillen, knellen,* Old English *cnyllan.*]

Knel·ler (nĕl′ər), **Sir Godfrey** (1646–1723). British portrait painter, born in Germany. He moved to England in 1675 and soon acquired the patronage of the powerful Duke of Monmouth. Later patrons included Charles II, James II, William III, and Anne.

Knes·set (kə-nĕs′ĕt′) *n.* The Israeli parliament. [Hebrew (Mishnaic) *Kəneseth,* "assembly," from *kānas,* he gathered.]

knew. Past tense of **know.**

Knick·er·bock·er (nĭk′ər-bŏk′ər) *n.* **1.** A descendant of the Dutch settlers of New York. **2.** A New Yorker. **3. knickerbockers.** Full breeches gathered and banded just below the knee. Also called "knickers." [From Diedrich *Knickerbocker,* fictitious Dutch settler and pretended author of Washington Irving's *History of New York* (1809).]

knick·ers (nĭk′ərz) *pl.n.* **1.** Long bloomers formerly worn as underwear by women and girls. **2.** *British.* Underpants worn by women and girls. **3.** Knickerbockers.

knick-knack, nick-nack (nĭk′năk′) *n.* A small ornamental article; a trinket. [Reduplication of KNACK (device).]

knick·point (nĭk′point′) *n.* A place in the long or longitudinal profile of a river valley where the slope changes. [Partial translation of German *Knickpunkt.*]

knife (nīf) *n., pl.* **knives** (nīvz). **1.** A cutting instrument or weapon consisting of a sharp blade with a handle. **2.** A sharp cutting edge; blade. **—under the knife.** *Informal.* Undergoing surgery.

~*v.* **knifed, knifing, knifes.** *—tr.* **1.** To use a knife on, especially to cut, stab, or wound. **2.** *Informal.* To hurt, defeat, or betray by underhand means. *—intr.* To cut or slash a way through with or as if with a knife: *The lifeboat knifed through the surf.* [Middle English *knyf, knif,* Old English *cnīf.*]

knife-edge (nīf′ĕj′) *n.* **1.** The cutting edge of a blade. **2.** A sharp mountain ridge. **3.** A sharp, knifelike edge, such as a sharp pleat or fold. **4.** A wedge of metal used as a low-friction fulcrum for a balancing beam or lever. **5.** A position of extreme precariousness.

knife pleat *n.* One of a series of narrow, flat pleats all lying in one direction and often overlapping.

knife switch *n.* A type of electric switch in which flat, hinged metal blades are pushed between fixed contact clips.

knight (nīt) *n. Abbr.* **k., K., Knt, Kt** **1.** The holder of a nonhereditary rank conferred by a sovereign in recognition of personal merit or services rendered to the country and in Britain bearing the title *Sir* before the Christian name. **2.** A member of any of several orders or brotherhoods that call their members knights. **3.** A medieval tenant giving military service as a mounted man-at-arms to a feudal landholder. **4.** A medieval gentleman-soldier, usually of high birth, raised by a sovereign to privileged military status after training as a page and squire. **5. a.** A defender, champion, or zealous upholder of a cause or principle. **b.** The devoted champion of a lady. **6.** A chess piece usually having the shape of a horse's head that can be moved two squares horizontally and one vertically or two vertically and one horizontally.

~*tr.v.* **knighted, knighting, knights.** To give (a person) a knighthood; make a knight of. [Middle English *cniht, knyght,* Old English *cniht,* originally "boy," "lad," "servant," from West Germanic *knihtas* (unattested).]

knight bachelor *n., pl.* **knights bachelor.** One who holds a knighthood but does not belong to any special order, such as the Garter.

knight banneret *n.* A **banneret** *(see).*

knight errant *n., pl.* **knights errant.** **1.** A knight of medieval romance who wandered in search of adventure. **2.** One given to adventurous or quixotic conduct. **—knight-er·rant·ry** (nīt′ĕr′ən-trē) *n.*

knight·head (nīt′hĕd′) *n.* Either of two timbers rising from the keel of a sailing ship to support the inner end of the bowsprit. [They were sometimes adorned with a carved knight's head.]

knight·hood (nīt′ho͝od′) *n.* **1.** The rank or dignity of a knight. **2.** The behavior or qualities befitting a knight; chivalry. **3.** Knights as a body or class.

knight·ly (nīt′lē) *adj.* Of, pertaining to, or befitting a knight. **—knight·li·ness** *n.*

knight marshal *n., pl.* **knights marshal.** A royal court official, a **marshal** *(see).*

Knight of Co·lum·bus (kə-lŭm′bəs) *n.* A member of a benevolent society of Roman Catholic men.

Knight of Pyth·i·as (pĭth′ē-əs) *n.* A member of a secret fraternal order founded for philanthropic purposes.

Knights of the Round Table *pl.n. Arthurian Legend.* The knights of the court of King Arthur.

Knight Templar *n., pl.* **Knights Templars.** *Abbr.* **K.T.** A member of an order of knights founded in 1119 to protect pilgrims in the Holy Land during the second Crusade and suppressed between 1311 and 1314. Also called "Templar."

knish (kə-nĭsh′) *n.* A piece of dough stuffed with potato, cheese, or meat and baked or fried. [Yiddish, from Russian, akin to Ukrainian *knyš,* Polish *knysz*†.]

knit (nĭt) *v.* **knit** or **knitted, knitting, knits.** *—tr.* **1. a.** To make (a fabric or garment) by intertwining yarn or thread in a series of connected loops either on a machine or by hand with knitting needles: *knit a pair of mittens.* **b.** To make (yarn or thread) into a fabric or garment by knitting. **2. a.** To join closely; unite securely: *a tightly knit community.* **b.** To cause to grow together securely: *wore a cast and kept my arm immobile to knit the broken bone.* **3.** To draw (the brows) together in wrinkles; furrow. *—intr.* **1. a.** To make a fabric or garment by intertwining yarn or thread in a series of connected loops. **b.** To make a plain stitch; knit using a plain stitch. **2.** To come or grow together securely. Used especially of fractured bones. **3.** To come together in wrinkles or furrows.

~*n.* **1.** A fabric or garment made by knitting. **2.** The method, style, or way in which a garment has been knitted: *a loose knit.* [Middle English *knitten,* Old English *cnyttan,* to tie in a knot.] **—knit·ter** *n.*

knit·ting (nĭt′ĭng) *n.* **1.** The process of producing something knitted. **2.** Knitted work.

knitting needle *n.* A long, thin, pointed rod used in knitting.

knit·wear (nĭt′wâr′) *n.* Knitted clothing, especially sweaters.

knives. Plural of **knife.**

knob (nŏb) *n.* **1. a.** A rounded protuberance on a surface or extremity. **b.** A rounded handle, as on a drawer or door. **c.** A rounded control switch or dial. **2.** *Chiefly British.* A small rounded piece, as of butter. **3.** A prominent rounded hill or mountain. [Middle English *knobbe,* from Middle Low German, tree knot, knob.] **—knobbed** *adj.* **—knob·by** *adj.*

knob·bly (nŏb′lē) *adj.* **-blier, -bliest.** Having or covered with small knoblike protrusions; knobby: *knobbly knees.*

knob·ker·rie (nŏb′kĕr′ē) *n.* A short club with one knobbed end, used as a weapon by South African tribesmen. [Afrikaans *knopkierie* : *knop,* knob, from Middle Dutch *cnoppe* + *kieri,* club, from Hottentot *kīrri,* a stick.]

knock (nŏk) *v.* **knocked, knocking, knocks.** *—tr.* **1.** To strike with a hard blow; hit. **2.** To affect in a specified way by or as if by knocking: *knocked him senseless; knocked the china to bits.* **3.** To cause to collide: *knocked my head against the shelf.* **4.** To produce by hitting or striking: *She knocked a hole in the wall.* **5.** To instill with or as if with blows: *Try to knock some sense into his head.* **6.** *Slang.* To criticize adversely; disparage. **7.** *British Slang.* To astonish. *—intr.* **1.** To strike a sharp, audible blow or series of blows, as at a door when requesting admittance; rap. **2.** To collide; bump. **3. a.** To make a pounding or clanking noise, as of a laboring or defective engine. **b.** To emit a characteristic metallic sound as a result of faulty combustion. Used of a gasoline engine. **—knock around** (or **about**). *Informal.* **1.** To be rough or brutal with; maltreat. **2.** To discuss or consider. **3.** To travel around, often aimlessly. **—knock cold.** To knock out. **—knock dead.** *Slang.* To affect strongly and usually positively: *a virtuoso performance that knocked the audience dead.* **—knock for a loop.** To surprise tremendously; astonish. **—knock off. 1.** *Informal.* **a.** To take a break or rest from; stop. **b.** To cease work. **2.** *Informal.* To make, accomplish, or consume hastily or easily. **3.** *Informal.* To eliminate; deduct: *The grocer knocked off a little from the bill.* **4.** *Slang.* To kill. **5.** *Slang.* To hold up or rob. **6.** *Informal.* To copy the design or production of. **—knock out of the box.** *Baseball.* To force the removal of (an opposing pitcher) by heavy hitting. **—knock together.** To make or assemble quickly or carelessly.

~*n.* **1.** An instance of knocking; a blow. **2.** The sound of a sharp tap on a hard surface; a rap. **3. a.** A pounding, clanking noise made by an engine, especially one in poor operating condition. **b.** A characteristic metallic sound emitted by an engine as a result of faulty

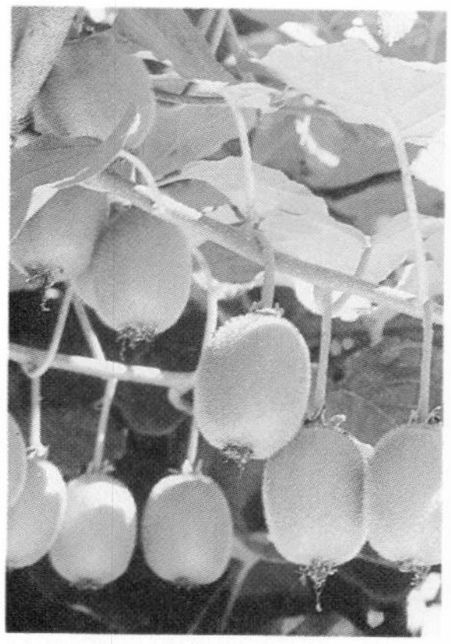

kiwi *The kiwi fruit, also called the Chinese gooseberry, is harvested from an Asian climbing bush,* Actinidia chinensis.

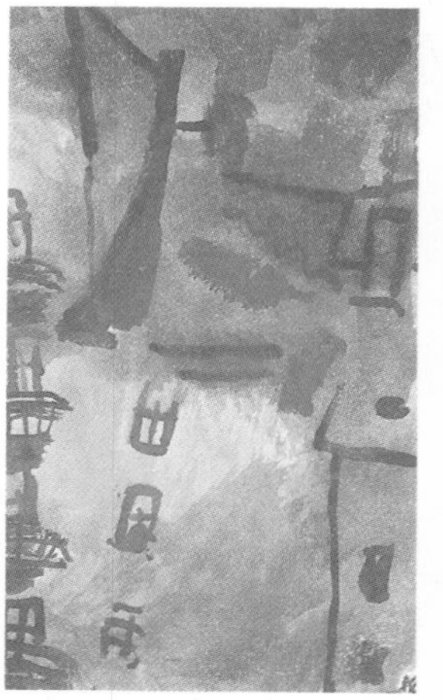

Klee painting Sun in the Courtyard. *Klee developed his own symbolic language for his childlike pictures, describing them as being like musical compositions that used colors in place of notes.*

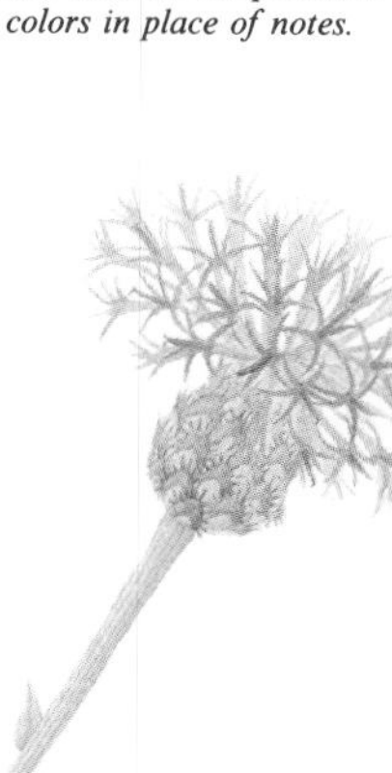

knapweed *The thistlelike knapweed is so named because its flower heads are knob-shaped. The species shown here is the common knapweed,* Centaurea scabiosa.

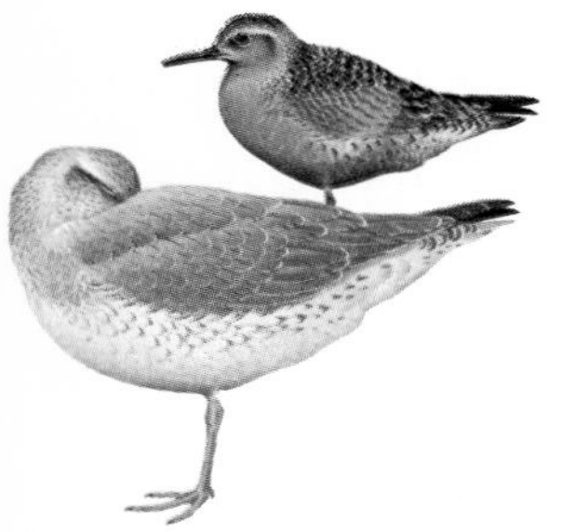

knot *A wader that breeds in the Arctic and winters along the shores of northern Europe. The adult birds have a brick-red plumage in summer and autumn, which changes to gray and white in winter.*

PRONUNCIATION KEY

ă, pat; ā, pay; âr, care; ä, father, are; b, bib; ch, church; d, deed; ĕ, pet; ē, be; f, fife; g, gag; h, hat; hw, which; ĭ, pit; ī, pie; îr, pier; j, judge; k, kick; l, lid, needle; m, mum; n, no, sudden; ng, thing; ŏ, pot; ō, toe; ô, paw, for; oi, noise; ou, out; o͝o, book; o͞o, boot; p, pop; r, roar; s, sauce; sh, ship, dish; t, tight; th, thin, path; *th*, this, bathe; ŭ, cut; ûr, fur; v, valve; w, with; y, yes; z, zebra, size; zh, vision; ə, about, item, edible, gallop, circus, peaceful

IN FOREIGN WORDS:

à, *Fr.* ami; œ, *Fr.* feu, *Ger.* schön; ü, *Fr.* tu, *Ger.* über; KH, *Ger.* ich, *Scot.* loch; N, *Fr.* bon; y', *Fr.* Compiègne

STRESS MARKS:

Primary stress: ′
in·cite′ (ĭn-sīt′)
Secondary stress: ′
in′sight′ (ĭn′sīt′)

combustion. **4.** *Slang.* A criticism or insult; a cutting remark. **5.** *Informal.* A misfortune, setback, or trouble: *has taken a few knocks over the years.* [Middle English *knokken,* Old English *cnocian.*]

knock·a·bout (nŏk′ə-bout′) *n.* A small sloop with a mainsail, a jib, and a keel but no bowsprit.
~*adj.* **1.** Rough; boisterous; rowdy. **2.** Appropriate for rough wear or use.

knock back *tr.v. Informal.* **1.** To drink (alcohol, for example) quickly or in large quantities. **2.** *British.* To cost; especially, to cost (a person) a large amount of money. **3.** *British.* To surprise and disconcert. **4.** *British.* To reject, refuse, or rebuff.

knock·back (nŏk′băk′) *n. British.* A rejection, refusal, or rebuff.

knock down *tr.v.* **1.** To disassemble into parts, as for storage or shipping. **2.** To declare as sold at an auction, as by striking a blow with a gavel. **3.** *Informal.* To reduce, as in price. **4.** *Slang.* To receive as wages; earn.

knock·down (nŏk′doun′) *adj.* **1.** Strong enough to knock down or overwhelm; powerful: *a knockdown blow.* **2.** Designed to be assembled and disassembled quickly and easily: *knockdown furniture.* **3.** *Informal.* Extremely low; cheap: *knockdown prices.*
~*n.* **1.** The act of knocking down; a toppling or overwhelming. **2.** An overwhelming blow or shock. **3.** Something designed to be assembled and disassembled quickly and easily. **4.** *Australian Informal.* An introduction to a person.

knock·down-drag·out (nŏk′doun-drăg′out′) *adj.* Marked by roughness, violence, and acrimony: *had a knockdown-dragout fight.*

knock·er (nŏk′ər) *n.* One that knocks, especially: **a.** An often decorative fixture used for knocking on a door. **b.** *Slang.* One who constantly criticizes. **—on the knocker. 1.** *British Informal.* From door to door; especially, as a door-to-door salesman: *working on the knocker.* **2.** *Australian Informal.* Punctually; promptly.

knock·er-up (nŏk′ər-ŭp′) *n., pl.* **knockers-up.** *British.* **1.** One who goes from door to door, as a salesman or a political canvasser. **2.** Formerly, one whose job was to wake people up, as for work, by going from house to house knocking on windows.

knock·ing-shop (nŏk′ĭng-shŏp′) *n. British Slang.* A brothel.

knock-knee (nŏk′nē′) *n.* An abnormal condition in which one knee is turned toward the other or in which each is turned toward the other. **—knock-kneed** *adj.*

knock·off (nŏk′ôf′, -ŏf′) *n. Informal.* A usually less expensive copy, as of a dress.

knock out *tr.v.* **1.** To render unconscious. **2.** *Boxing.* To defeat (an opponent) by knocking him to the canvas for a count of ten. **3.** To bring to an end; eliminate: *City ordinances knocked out real-estate speculation.* **4.** *Informal.* To exert or exhaust (oneself or another) to the utmost. **5.** *Informal.* To delight or amaze: *We've been really knocked out by the book's success.* **6.** *Informal.* To render useless or inoperative: *The earthquake knocked out all electricity and telephone service.*

knock·out (nŏk′out′) *n.* **1. a.** The act of knocking out. **b.** The state of being knocked out. **c.** A blow that induces unconsciousness. **d.** The knocking out of an opponent. **2.** *Slang.* Something very impressive or attractive.
~*adj.* Effecting a knockout.

knockout drops *pl.n. Slang.* A solution, as of chloral hydrate, put into a drink to render the drinker unconscious.

knock up *intr.v.* To hit a ball in practice for a period before starting to play a game, as of tennis or squash. —*tr.v.* **1.** To make or assemble quickly or carelessly. **2.** *British Informal.* To exhaust; wear out. **3.** *British.* To wake up, as by knocking at a door. **4.** *Cricket.* To score (runs) quickly. **5.** *Slang.* To make pregnant.

knock-up (nŏk′ŭp′) *n.* A practice session or warm-up period before a game, as of tennis or squash, starts.

knockwurst. Variant of **knackwurst.**

knoll (nōl) *n.* A small rounded hill or mound; a hillock. [Middle English *knol(le),* Old English *cnoll.*]

knop (nŏp) *n.* A decorative knob or boss, as on the end of the handle of a spoon. [Middle English *knoppe,* probably from Middle Low German or Middle Dutch.]

Knos·sos or **Cnos·sos** (nŏs′əs). City of ancient Crete. Just south of modern Iráklion, it was occupied from *c.* 3000 B.C. and by the time of its destruction, probably by earthquake (*c.* 1400 B.C.), it was, as the center of Minoan culture, one of the leading cities of the ancient world. The legends of the Labyrinth, the Minotaur, and Atlantis probably originated here. It was excavated and extensively restored between 1899 and 1935.

knot¹ (nŏt) *n.* **1.** A more or less complex, compact intersection of interlaced material, as cord, ribbon, or rope. **2.** A fastening made by tying together lengths of material, as rope, in a prescribed way. **3.** A decorative bow of ribbon, fabric, or braid. **4.** A unifying tie or bond, especially a marriage bond. **5.** A tight cluster of persons or things. **6.** A difficulty; a problem. **7. a.** A hard place or node on a plant, especially on a tree, at a point from which a stem or branch grows. **b.** The circular, contrastingly dark-colored cross section of such a node as it appears cross-grained on a piece of cut lumber. **8.** A growth on or enlargement of a gland, muscle, or the like. **9.** *Nautical.* **a.** A division on a log line used to measure the speed of a ship. **b.** *Abbr.* **kn., kt.** A unit of speed of ships or aircraft, one nautical mile per hour, about 1.85 kilometers or 1.15 statute miles per hour. **c.** A distance of one nautical mile. **—tie (up) in knots.** To make (a person) very tense or confused. **—tie the knot.** *Slang.* **1.** To get married. **2.** To perform a marriage ceremony.
~*v.* **knotted, knotting, knots.** —*tr.* **1.** To tie in or fasten with a knot. **2.** To snarl or entangle. **3.** To cause to form knots. —*intr.* **1.** To become snarled or entangled. **2.** To form a knot. [Middle English *knot(te),* Old English *cnotta.*]
Usage: In nautical usage *knot* is a unit of speed, not of distance, and has a built-in meaning of "per hour." Therefore, a ship would strictly be said to travel at ten knots (not ten knots per hour).

knot² *n.* A shore bird, *Calidris canutus,* related to the sandpipers, having plumage that is grayish and mottled in winter and brick-red in summer and a short, black bill. [Middle English, origin obscure.]

knot garden *n.* A formal garden having the flower beds arranged in an intricate, usually geometric pattern.

knot·grass (nŏt′grăs′, -gräs′) *n.* **1.** A low-growing, weedy plant, *Polygonum aviculare,* having very small greenish flowers. Also called "allseed." **2.** Any of several similar plants.

knot·hole (nŏt′hōl′) *n.* A hole in a piece of timber where a knot has dropped out or been removed.

knot·ted (nŏt′ĭd) *adj.* **1.** Tied or fastened in or with a knot. **2.** Intricate; knotty. **3.** Characterized by or full of knots; gnarled: *a knotted branch.*

knot·ty (nŏt′ē) *adj.* **-tier, -tiest. 1.** Tied or tangled in knots: *a knotty cord.* **2.** Covered with knots or knobs; gnarled: *knotty hands.* **3.** Difficult to understand or solve; intricate and puzzling: *a knotty problem.* —See Synonyms at **complex. —knot·ti·ness** *n.*

knot·weed (nŏt′wēd′) *n.* Any of several plants of the genus *Polygonum,* having jointed stems and inconspicuous flowers.

knout (nout) *n.* A leather scourge formerly used for flogging criminals, especially in Russia.
~*tr.v.* **knouted, knouting, knouts.** To flog with a knout. [French, from Russian *knut,* from Old Norse *knūtr,* knot.]

know (nō) *v.* **knew** (no͞o, nyo͞o), **known** (nōn), **knowing, knows.** —*tr.* **1.** To perceive directly with the senses or mind; apprehend with clarity or certainty: *didn't know the answer.* **2.** To be certain of; regard or accept as true beyond doubt: *I just know he's telling the truth.* **3.** To be capable of; have the skill to: *Do you know how to swim?* **4.** To have a thorough or practical understanding of, as through experience or study: *knows the rules of bridge.* **5. a.** To have personal experience of: *has never known real hunger.* **b.** To be subjected to or limited by: *grief that knows no bounds.* **6.** To recognize the character or quality of: *knew him for a liar.* **7.** To be able to distinguish; recognize: *Do you know him from his twin brother?* **8.** To be acquainted or familiar with: *We know them, but we wouldn't call them friends.* **9.** To see, hear, or experience: *I've never known her to lose her temper. He's known to have the habit of being late.* **10.** *Archaic.* To have sexual intercourse with: *"And Adam knew Eve his wife; and she conceived"* (Genesis 4:1). —*intr.* **1.** To possess knowledge, understanding, or information about something: *Mother knows best.* **2.** To be cognizant or aware: *We knew about what he had done.* **—in the know.** Possessing correct or exclusive information. [Know, knew, known; Middle English *knowen, knew, knowe(n),* Old English *(ge)cnāwan, (ge)cnēow, (ge)cnāwen.*] **—know·a·ble** *adj.* **—know·er** *n.*
Usage: In negative constructions, *know* may be followed by clauses introduced by *that, whether,* or *if,* but not by *as*: *I don't know that/whether/if* (not *as*) *he can come.*

know-all (nō′ôl′) *n. British Informal.* A know-it-all.

know-how (nō′hou′) *n. Informal.* The knowledge, skill, or ingenuity required to do something correctly.

know·ing (nō′ĭng) *adj.* **1.** Possessing knowledge, intelligence, or understanding. **2.** Suggestive of secret or private information: *a knowing glance.* **3.** Having or showing clever awareness and resourcefulness; shrewd. **4.** Planned; deliberate: *knowing complicity in the plot.* —See Synonyms at **intelligent. —know·ing·ly** *adv.* **—know·ing·ness** *n.*

know-it-all (nō′ĭt-ôl′) *n. Informal.* A person who believes himself to be exceptionally well-informed and displays his knowledge in an arrogant or outspoken fashion.

knowl·edge (nŏl′ĭj) *n.* **1.** The state or fact of knowing. **2.** Familiarity, awareness, or understanding gained through experience or study. **3.** That which is known, as: **a.** The sum or range of what has been perceived, discovered, or inferred. **b.** Specific information about something. **4.** Learning; erudition: *men of knowledge.* **5.** *Archaic.* Sexual intercourse; copulation. Now used only in the legal phrase *carnal knowledge.* **—to one's knowledge. 1.** So far as one knows. **2.** Known to one as a certain fact. [Middle English *knowlege, know(e)lech,* from *cnawlechen, know(e)lechen,* to confess, recognize, Old English *cnāwlǣcan* (unattested), from *cnāwan,* to KNOW.]
Synonyms: *enlightenment, erudition, information, learning, lore, scholarship, wisdom.*

knowl·edge·a·ble (nŏl′ĭ-jə-bəl) *adj.* Possessing or showing knowledge or intelligence; sharp and well informed.

known (nōn). Past participle of **know.**
~*adj.* Proved or generally recognized: *a known crook; the only known case of recovery from the disease.*
~*n.* Something that is known: *proceed from the known to the unknown.*

know-noth·ing (nō′nŭth′ĭng) *n.* **1. Know-Nothing.** A member of a mid-19th-century American political movement that was antagonistic toward immigrants and Roman Catholics. **2.** An ignoramus. **3.** An agnostic. **4.** An anti-intellectual.

Knox (nŏks), **John** (*c.* 1505–72). Leader of the Scottish Reformation. He became chaplain to Edward VI (1551), but after the accession of the Roman Catholic Mary Tudor (1553) he fled to Geneva, where he was influenced by Calvin. After Mary's death (1558),

Knox returned to Scotland (1559), and by 1560 the Confession of Faith was drawn up and Protestantism became the established religion in Scotland, despite the subsequent efforts of Mary Queen of Scots.

Knox·ville (nŏks′vĭl′) Industrial port in eastern Tennessee. On the Tennessee River, it was settled in 1786 and was twice state capital (1796–1812, 1817–19). It is the seat of the Tennessee Valley Authority.

Knt knight.

knuck·le (nŭk′əl) *n.* **1.** *Anatomy.* **a.** A joint or region around a joint of a finger, especially one of the joints connecting the fingers to the hand. **b.** Any of the rounded protuberances formed by the bones in such a joint. **2.** A cut of meat centering on the carpal joint, as of a pig. **3.** The part of a hinge through which the pin passes. **4.** A joint between two members of a structure or mechanism in which the two components are at an angle to each other. **5. knuckles.** A weapon consisting of a metal strip or chain with holes or links into which the fingers fit. **—near** (or **close to**) **the knuckle.** Approaching what is conventionally regarded as indecent.
~*tr.v.* **knuckled, -ling, -les. 1.** To press, rub, or hit with the knuckles of the fist: *"They stared gaping, and knuckling their brows"* (Mary Renault). **2.** To shoot (a marble) with the thumb over the bent forefinger. **—knuckle down.** *Informal.* To apply oneself earnestly to a task: *knuckled down to work.* **—knuckle under.** To yield to pressure; give in. [Middle English *knokel,* from Middle Low German *knökel.*]

knuck·le·bone (nŭk′əl-bōn′) *n.* **1.** A knobbed bone, as of a knuckle or joint. **2. knucklebones.** *Used with a singular verb.* A game formerly played by tossing knucklebones.

knuck·le-dust·ers (nŭk′əl-dŭs′tərz) *pl.n. Slang.* A weapon consisting of a piece of metal that fits snugly over the knuckles; knuckles.

knuck·le·head (nŭk′əl-hĕd′) *n.* A fool or idiot.

knuckle joint *n.* A hinged, flexible joint formed by the juncture of two rods or projections, one inside the other and the two locked by a pin that functions as an axle.

knuckle sandwich *n. Slang.* A punch in the mouth.

knur, knurr (nûr) *n.* A bump or knot, as on a tree trunk. [Middle English *knorre,* swelling, from Germanic, akin to Middle Low German and Middle High German *knorre,* knot, knob.]

knurl (nûrl) *n.* **1.** A knob, knot, or similar protuberance. **2.** Any of a series of small ridges or beads along the edge of a metal object, as a thumbscrew, to aid in gripping. [Probably from KNUR (influenced by GNARL).] **—knurl·y** *adj.*

KO (kā′ō′) *tr.v.* **KO'd, KO'ing, KO's.** Also **K.O., k.o.** *Slang.* To knock out, as in boxing.
~*n.* (kā-ō′, kā′ō′) *pl.* **KO's.** *Slang.* In boxing, a **knockout** *(see).*

ko·a (kō′ə) *n.* **1.** A Hawaiian tree, *Acacia koa.* **2.** The hard, reddish wood of this tree, used especially for making furniture. [Hawaiian.]

ko·a·la (kō-ä′lə) *n.* An arboreal marsupial, *Phascolarctos cinereus,* of Australia, having grayish fur and feeding chiefly on the leaves and bark of eucalyptus trees. Also called "koala bear." [Earlier *koola,* from the native Australian name *kūlla.*]

ko·an (kō′än′) *n.* In Zen Buddhism, a problem or riddle that aims to break down logical reasoning. [Japanese.]

Ko·be (kō′bē). City in south Honshu in Japan. On Osaka Bay at the eastern end of the Inland Sea, it has major shipbuilding facilities and produces sugar, rubber, and ferrous metals.

København. See **Copenhagen.**

Ko·blenz or **Co·blenz** (kō′blĕnts). A city in Germany, founded by the Romans (1st century A.D.) at the confluence of the Rhine and Moselle rivers. The center of the Moselle wine trade, it also produces pianos, furniture, clothing, and paper.

ko·bo (kō′bō) *n., pl.* **kobo.** A Nigerian coin equal to 1/100 of a naira. See feature at **currency.** [Alteration of English *copper* (penny).]

ko·bold (kō′bôld′) *n.* In German folklore: **1.** A mischievous household elf. **2.** A gnome that haunts underground places such as mines and caves. [German *Kobold,* from Middle High German *kobolt.*]

Koch (kōKH), **Robert** (1843–1910). German bacteriologist. He discovered the cholera bacillus and the bacterial origin of anthrax. He was awarded the Nobel Prize (1905) for his work on tuberculosis.

Köch·el number (kœ′KHəl) *n. Abbr.* **K.** A number that has been assigned to each of the compositions of Mozart. [After Ludwig *Köchel* (1800–77), Austrian musicologist who catalogued Mozart's compositions.]

Ko·dály (kō′dī′), **Zoltan** (1882–1967). Hungarian composer. His works include the opera *Háry János* (1926), *Te Deum* (1936), and *Missa Brevis* (1945).

Ko·di·ak (kō′dē-ăk′). An island in the Shelikof Strait off the southern coast of Alaska. It was settled by Russians (1784) as a whale- and seal-hunting center.

Kodiak bear *n.* A form of the brown bear, *Ursus arctos,* of islands and coastal areas of Alaska, sometimes considered a separate species. [After KODIAK island.]

ko·el (kō′əl) *n.* A cuckoo, *Eudynamys scolopacea,* found in India, southeast Asia, and Australia, that lays its eggs in the nests of crows. [Hindi, from Sanskrit *kokila.*]

Koest·ler (kĕst′lər, kĕs′-), **Arthur** (1905–83). Hungarian-born British author and journalist. Educated in Vienna, he became a communist, but his novel *Darkness at Noon* (1940) shows his disillusionment with communism as practiced in the U.S.S.R. While reporting the Spanish Civil War he narrowly escaped execution by Franco. In his later works, such as *The Sleepwalkers* (1959) and *The Ghost in the Machine* (1968), he explores various philosophical aspects of science and psychology.

kof·ta (kôf′tə, kŏf′-) *n.* A dish served in India in which the ingredients, usually chopped meat or vegetables together with spices, are formed into balls and served in a sauce. [Urdu.]

kohl (kōl) *n.* A preparation used chiefly in Muslim and Asian countries as a cosmetic around the eyes. [Arabic *kuḥl, koḥl,* powder of antimony. See also **alcohol.**]

Kohl (kōl), **Helmut** (1930–). West German politician. He became chancellor in 1982.

kohl·ra·bi (kōl-rä′bē, -răb′ē) *n., pl.* **-bies.** A plant, *Brassica caulorapa,* with a thickened stem that is eaten as a vegetable. Also called "turnip cabbage." [German *Kohlrabi* (influenced by *Kohl,* cabbage), from Italian *cavoli rape,* plural of *cavolo rapa* : *cavolo,* cole, cabbage, from Latin *caulis* + *rapa,* turnip, from Latin *rāpa, rāpum.*]

Koi·ne (koi-nā′, koi′nā′) *n.* **1.** A dialect of Greek that developed primarily from Attic and eventually replaced the local dialects, becoming the common language of the Hellenistic world from which the later stages of Greek are descended. **2. koine.** A language common to people speaking different languages; a lingua franca. [Greek *koinē (dialektos),* "common (language)," from *koinos,* common.]

Ko·kosch·ka (kə-kôsh′kə), **Oskar** (1886–1980). Austrian-born expressionist painter, skilled at portraits and landscapes. He left Nazi Germany and settled in England and later in Switzerland.

kok-sa·ghyz (kōk′sə-gēz′, -gĭz′, kŏk′-) *n.* A dandelion, *Taraxacum kok-saghyz,* of central Asia, having fleshy roots that yield a form of rubber. [Russian *kok-sagyz,* from Turkish *kok-sagïz* : *kok,* root + *sagïz,* rubber.]

kola. Variant of **cola** (nut-bearing tree).

kola nut. Variant of **cola nut.**

Kol·chak (kôl′chŏk′), **Alexandr Vasilyevich** (1874–1920). Russian admiral. He was commander of the Black Sea fleet during World War I, and after the 1917 October Revolution he led the White Russians against the Bolsheviks. He was recognized by the Allies as head of the provisional Russian government (1918–20), but was captured and shot by the Bolsheviks.

ko·lin·sky (kə-lĭn′skē) *n., pl.* **-skies. 1.** Any of several minks of northern Eurasia, especially *Mustela siberica.* **2.** The tawny fur of such an animal. [Russian *kolinskÿ,* "(mink) of Kola," from *Kola,* district in northwestern Russia.]

kol·khoz, kol·koz (kŏl-kôz′) *n., pl.* **-khozes** or **-khozy** (-kô′zē). A Soviet collective farm. [Russian, contraction of *kollektivnoe khozyaistvo* : *kollektivnoe,* neuter of *kollektivny,* collective + *khozyaistvo,* household, farm.]

Kol·lon·tai (kō-lōn-tī′), **Aleksandra Mikhailovna** (1872–1952). Russian revolutionary and author. Despite her privileged social position, she joined the Social-Democratic Worker's Party (1898) and after the October Revolution (1917) used her political influence to advocate social changes.

Koll·witz (kôl′vĭts′, kōl′wĭts′), **Käthe** or **Kaethe** (1867–1945). German artist. Profoundly affected by her contact with the poor, the death of her son in battle (1914), and the growing violence in the world, she used her sculptures and prints, including *The Living to the Dead* (1919), to eloquently denounce war and social injustice. During World War II, her grandson was killed in battle (1942) and her studio was bombed, destroying much of her work (1943).

Köln (kœln). *English* **Co·logne** (kə-lōn′). City and port on the west bank of the Rhine in North Rhine-Westphalia in Germany. It is a major industrial city, producing iron and steel, machinery, chemicals, textiles, and eau de cologne.

Kol Ni·dre (kōl nĭd′rā, -rə, kôl) *n. Judaism.* The opening prayer recited on the eve of Yom Kippur, containing a declaration of the annulment of all personal vows of the preceding year. [Aramaic *kol nidhrē,* "all vows," from its opening words.]

Komenský, Jan. See John Amos **Comenius.**

Ko·mo·do dragon (kə-mō′dō) *n.* A large monitor lizard, *Varanus komodoensis,* of the Indonesian islands of Komodo and Flores. It is the largest living lizard, growing up to 10 feet (3 meters) long.

kom·so·mol (kŏm′sə-môl′, -mŏl′) *n.* In the Soviet Union, a communist youth organization. [Russian, acronym of *Kommunisticheskу Soyuz Molodyozhi,* Communist Union of Youth.]

kon·fyt (kən-fīt′) *n. South African.* Crystallized or preserved fruit, often in syrup. [Afrikaans, from Dutch *konfijt,* preserves.]

Kong-fu-zi or **Kong-zi.** See **Confucius.**

Kon·go[1] (kŏng′gō). A powerful African state founded in the 14th century. It covered the area now occupied by Angola, Congo, and Zaire.

Kongo[2] *n., pl.* **Kongos** or collectively **Kongo. 1.** A member of a Bantu people of the region of the lower Congo River. **2.** The Bantu language of the Kongo.

kon·go·ni (kŏng-gō′nē) *n.* A large east African antelope, *Alcelaphus buselaphus,* that is a species of hartebeest. [Swahili.]

Königsberg. See **Kaliningrad.**

ko·ni·ol·o·gy (kō′nē-ŏl′ə-jē) *n.* The scientific study of atmospheric dust and its effects. [Greek *konia,* dust + -LOGY.]

Kon·ka·ni (kŏng′kə-nē, kông′-) *n.* An Indic language related to Marathi and spoken on the west coast of India south of Maharashtra and north of Kerala. [Marathi *koṅkaṇī,* from *Koṅkaṇ,* Konkan, region of western India.]

Kon·stanz (kôn′stänts). *English* **Con·stance** (kŏn′stəns). Port in Baden-Württemberg in Germany, on Lake Constance. Its industries include chemicals, electrical equipment, textiles, and tourism.

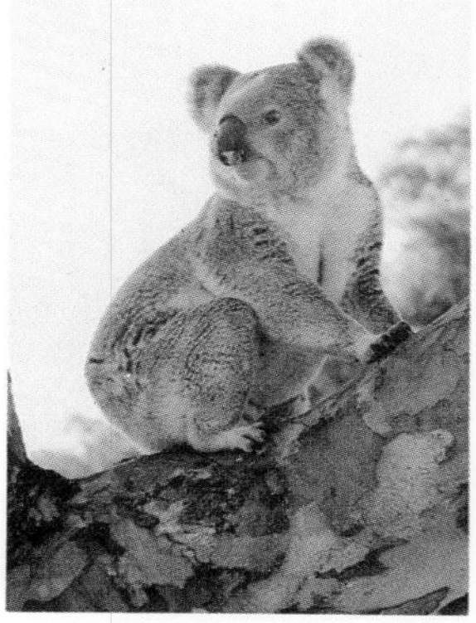

koala *These bearlike Australian marsupials feed almost exclusively on the leaves of eucalyptus trees. Their name comes from an aboriginal phrase meaning "no drink"—because the animals never take a drink, getting all the water they need from the juice of the leaves they eat.*

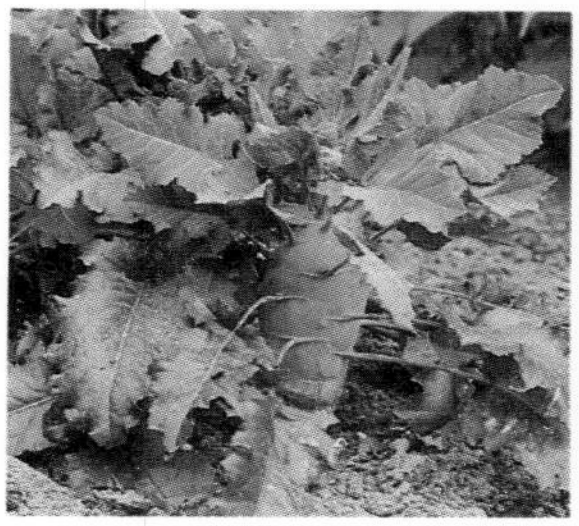

kohlrabi *This nutty-flavored vegetable is thought to have been brought to western Europe by the Crusaders. Both its turniplike stem and cabbagelike top are edible. Botanically, it is related to the cabbage, cauliflower, and Brussels sprout, though it resembles none of them.*

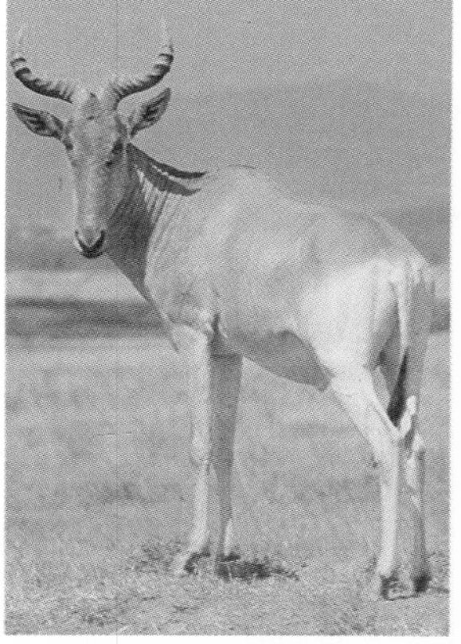

kongoni *The kongoni is one of about six species of hartebeest inhabiting the open plains of East Africa.*

kookaburra *This Australian bird is also known as the "laughing jackass." Its call starts as a low chuckle that rises sharply in volume and pitch. In a group, each bird begins its call a few notes behind its neighbor, so producing an uncanny effect of uncontrollable laughter.*

Kon·ya (kôn-yä′). *Latin* **I·co·ni·um** (ī-kō′nē-əm). Capital of Konya province in central Turkey. It markets grains, sugar, flax, fruit, and livestock and produces carpets, silk goods, and cotton. In the 13th century the order of the dancing dervishes was founded in the city.

koodoo. Variant of **kudu.**

kook (kook) *n. Slang.* An amusingly eccentric or zany person. [Perhaps from CUCKOO.] **—kook·i·ness** *n.* **—kook·y** *adj.*

kook·a·bur·ra (kook′ə-bûr′ə) *n.* A large kingfisher, *Dacelo novaeguineae* (or *D. gigas*), of Australia and adjacent areas, having a call resembling raucous laughter. Also called "jackass," "laughing jackass." [Native Australian name.]

kop (kŏp) *n. South African.* An isolated hill or peak. [Afrikaans, "head, hill."]

ko·peck, co·peck, ko·pek (kō′pĕk′) *n. Abbr.* **k., K.** A coin equal to 1/100 of the rouble of Russia. See feature at **currency.** [Russian *kopyeika*, from *kopye*, lance (from the figure of the czar with a lance in his hand originally stamped on the coin), from *kopat′*, to hack.]

Kopernik, Mikolaj. See Nicolaus **Copernicus.**

kop·pa (kŏp′ə) *n.* A letter occurring in certain early forms of the Greek alphabet, later mostly replaced by **kappa** *(see).* Transliterated in English as *q.* [Greek, from Semitic, akin to Hebrew *qōph,* KOPH.]

kop·pie, kop·je (kŏp′ē) *n. South African.* A small, isolated hill. [Afrikaans, diminutive of KOP.]

Ko·ran (kə-răn′, -rän′, kô-, kō-) *n.* The sacred text of Islam, believed to contain the revelations made by Allah to Muhammad. Also called "Alcoran." [Arabic *qur'ān,* reading, recitation, from *qara'a,* to read, recite.] **—Ko·ran·ic** (kə-răn′ĭk, kô-, kō-) *adj.*

Kor·da (kôr′də), **Sir Alexander** (1893–1956). Hungarian-born British film producer. His productions include *The Scarlet Pimpernel* and *The Third Man.*

Ko·re·a (kə-rē′ə, kō′-). *Korean* **Cho·son** (chō′sŏn′). *Japanese* **Cho·sen** (chō′sĕn′). Peninsula in northeast Asia. Extending southward between the Yellow Sea and the Sea of Japan, it is mainly mountainous. Civilized from *c.* 1200 B.C., it was united under the kingdom of Silla (A.D. 668), and despite a Mongol invasion (13th century) it survived until a Japanese occupation (1910–45). Following World War II the Soviet- and U.S.-occupied zones became separate republics; the northern, Soviet-sponsored republic invaded the south (1950), which resisted with the aid of U.N. forces. The border was established by treaty (1953), dividing the peninsula into South Korea and North Korea.

Korea, North. Officially, Democratic People's Republic of Korea. Asian republic. Lying north of the 1953 cease-fire line, it has the bulk of the peninsula's mineral resources. With Soviet aid it has built up its industries and intensified the cultivation of its limited fertile land. Its chief exports are metals. Area, 120,538 square kilometers (46,528 square miles). Population, 21,800,000. Capital, Pyongyang.

Korea, South. Officially, Republic of Korea. Asian republic. It has few natural resources apart from coal, iron ore, and graphite. Though more than a third of the population is still engaged in

agriculture, the republic has developed its industries with U.S. aid, and its growth rates in the 1970's were among the world's highest. Area, 98,484 square kilometers (38,015 square miles). Population, 42,800,000. Capital, Seoul.

Ko·re·an (kə-rē′ən, kô-, kō-) *adj.* Of or pertaining to Korea, its inhabitants, or their language.

~*n.* **1.** A native or inhabitant of Korea. **2.** The language of Korea, unclassified linguistically but containing many words of Chinese origin.

Korean War *n.* A war (1950–53) between North Korea, helped by China, and South Korea, helped by U.N. forces consisting of mainly U.S. troops.

korf·ball (kôrf′bôl′, kôrf′-) *n.* A game of Dutch origin that resembles basketball and is played by teams of both sexes. [Dutch *korfbal,* basketball.]

Kórinthos. See **Corinth.**

Kort·rijk (kôrt′rīk). *French* **Cour·trai** (koor-trā′). City of West Flanders province in Belgium, on the Leie (Lys) River. It was a major center of the medieval cloth industry of Flanders.

ko·ru·na (kôr′ə-nä′, kôr′-) *n., pl.* **-ny** (-nē) or **-nas.** *Abbr.* **k., K. 1.** The basic monetary unit of Czechoslovakia, equal to 100 halers. See feature at **currency. 2.** A coin worth one koruna. [Czech, "crown," from Latin *corōna,* CROWN.]

Kos. See **Cos.**

Kos·ci·us·ko (kŏs′ē-ŭs′kō). Australia's highest mountain (2,228 meters; 7,310 feet). Part of the Snowy Mts. of southeast New South Wales, it is a winter sports center. It is named after the Polish patriot Thaddeus Kosciusko (1746–1817).

ko·sher (kō′shər) *adj.* **1.** Conforming to or prepared in accordance with Jewish dietary laws, as: **a.** Slaughtered or prepared for eating according to rabbinic law; ritually pure: *kosher meat.* **b.** Restricted to the use of such food: *They keep a kosher house.* **c.** Specializing in the preparation or sale of such food: *a kosher delicatessen.* Compare **tref. 2.** *Slang.* **a.** Proper; correct. **b.** Genuine; legitimate. **—keep kosher.** To obey the Jewish dietary laws.

~*n.* Food prepared and served in accordance with the Jewish dietary laws.

~*tr.v.* **koshered, -shering, -shers.** To make kosher. [Yiddish, from Hebrew *kāshēr,* proper.]

Kos·suth (kŏs′ōōth′), **Lajos** (1802–94). Hungarian revolutionary leader. He aimed for Hungarian independence from Austria, declaring the Hapsburg dynasty invalid. He was appointed provisional governor of the 1849 Hungarian Republic, but after Russian intervention, he fled to Turkey.

Ko·sy·gin (kə-sē′gĭn), **Alexei Nikolayevich** (1904–80). Soviet premier (1964–80). He was deputy chairman of the Council of Ministers (1940–53), but he lost his position after Stalin's death (1953). He became premier on the fall of Khrushchev.

ko·to (kō′tō) *n., pl.* **-tos.** A Japanese musical instrument that has 13 strings stretched over an oblong box. [Japanese.]

koumis, koumiss. Variants of **kumiss.**

Kous·se·vits·ky (koo′sə-vĭt′skē), **Sergei** (1874–1951). Russian-born U.S. conductor. He left Russia in 1920 and eventually settled in the United States. He set up the Koussevitsky Music Foundation (1942) to encourage new composers.

Ko·vacs (kō′văks′), **Ernie** (1919–62). U.S. comedian. A zany and popular performer, he brought his unique brand of comedy to a series of live television shows (1950–57), a format that favored his inventive visual gags. He also played a few dramatic roles and published a novel, *Zoomar* (1957).

ko·whai (kō′wī′) *n.* A New Zealand tree, *Sophora tetraptera,* with sweet-smelling golden flowers. [Maori.]

Kowloon. See **Jiulong.**

kow·tow (kou-tou′, kou′tou′) *n.* **1.** A Chinese salutation in which the forehead is touched to the ground as an expression of respect, worship, or submission. **2.** An obsequious act.

~*intr.v.* **kowtowed, -towing, -tows. 1.** To perform a kowtow. **2.** To show servile deference; fawn: *Even the conductor kowtowed to the board of directors.* [Mandarin Chinese *ké tóu* : *ké,* to knock, bump + *tóu,* head.]

Kozhikode. See **Calicut.**

KP 1. *Chess.* king's pawn. **2.** kitchen police.

Kr The symbol for the element krypton.

KR *Chess.* king's rook.

kr. 1. krona. **2.** krone.

kraal, craal (krôl, kräl) *n.* **1.** A village of rural black people in southern Africa, typically consisting of huts surrounded by a stockade. **2.** An enclosure for livestock in southern Africa.

~*tr.v.* **kraaled, kraaling, kraals.** To put or keep (livestock) in a kraal. [Afrikaans, "enclosure for cattle," from Portuguese *curral,* possibly of Hottentot origin. See also **corral.**]

Krafft-E·bing (kräft′ĕb′ĭng, kräft′-), **Baron Richard von** (1840–1902). German neurologist and psychiatrist. He studied paranoia, epilepsy, and sexual deviance. He is best known today for his work *Psychopathia Sexualis* (1886).

kraft (kräft, kräft) *n.* A tough wrapping paper made from sulfate wood pulp. [German *Kraft,* force, strength, from Old High German, from Germanic *kraftaz* (unattested). See **craft.**]

krait (krīt) *n.* Any of several brightly colored venomous snakes of the genus *Bungarus,* of southeastern Asia. [Hindi *karait†.*]

Kra·ka·to·a (krăk′ə-tō′ə). Also **Kra·ka·tau** (-tou′). Small volcanic island, in the Strait of Sunda west of Java and east of Sumatra. It was blown apart (1883) by one of the largest volcanic eruptions ever

---

Map: **KOREA** — 126° E. RUSSIA. Chongjin. ▲ Paektusan 2744m. CHINA. NORTH KOREA. Sinuiju. Hamhung. Hungnam. Korea Bay. PYONGYANG. Chungsan. Wonsan. Kyomipo. SEA OF JAPAN. 38° N. Kaesong. SŎUL (SEOUL). Inchon. Takeshima (JAP.). SOUTH KOREA. YELLOW SEA. Taejon. Taegu. Kyongju. Kwangju. Masan. Pusan. Mokpo. JAPAN. Chejudo (S. KOREA). Km 0 ... 200. Miles 0 ... 100.

recorded, causing a tsunami that killed more than 36,000 people.

kra·ken (krä'kən) *n.* A legendary sea monster said to dwell in Norwegian waters. [Dialectal Norwegian : *krake†*, kraken + *-n*, suffix used as the definite article.]

Kra·ków or **Cra·cow** (krä'kou', krăk'ou'). City and river port in southern Poland, on the Vistula River. Founded in the 8th century, it was the national capital from 1305 to 1595 and remains an important cultural center. Its university (1364) is one of the oldest in Europe. Kraków produces metals, machinery, chemicals, clothing, and rolling stock.

Kra·mer (krä'mər), **Stanley E.** (1913–). U.S. filmmaker. He has produced and directed dramatic films that deal with emotionally charged social conflicts, such as racism, the threat of nuclear war, and religious prejudice. Among his important works are *The Defiant Ones* (1958), *On the Beach* (1959), and *Inherit the Wind* (1960).

kra·me·ri·a (krə-mîr'ē-ə) *n.* A dried root, the **rhatany** (see). [New Latin (Linnaeus), after J.G.H. *Kramer*, 18th-century Austrian botanist.]

krans (krăns, kräns) *n. South African.* An overhanging, sheer wall of rock; a precipice. [Afrikaans.]

K ration *n.* A U.S. Army emergency field ration used in World War II and consisting of a single packaged meal.

kraton. Variant of **craton.**

kraut (krout) *n.* Sauerkraut.

Krebs (krĕbz), **Sir Hans Adolf** (1900–81). British biochemist, born in Germany. He discovered the Krebs cycle. He shared the Nobel Prize for medicine (1953) with Fritz Lipmann (1899–1988).

Krebs cycle (krĕbz) *n.* A series of enzymatic reactions that constitute the second stage of respiration in aerobic organisms, involving the breakdown of acetyl units, to provide the main source of energy for cells in the form of ATP. Also called "citric acid cycle," "tricarboxylic acid cycle." [After Hans KREBS.]

Krem·lin (krĕm'lĭn) *n.* **1. a.** The citadel of an ancient Russian town or city. **b.** The citadel of Moscow. It housed the offices of the Soviet government and now houses those of the Russian government. **2.** The Soviet government. [French, from Russian *kreml'*, citadel, of Tatar origin.]

Krem·lin·ol·o·gy (krĕm'lə-nŏl'ə-jē) *n.* The study and analysis of the politics of the Soviet government. **—Krem·lin·ol·o·gist** *n.*

kreu·zer (kroit'sər) *n.* Any of several small coins of low value formerly used in Austria and Germany. [German *Kreuzer*, from Middle High German *kriuzer*, from *kriuze*, a cross (the coins were originally stamped with a cross), from Old High German *krūzi*, from Latin *crux*, CROSS.]

Kriem·hild (krēm'hĭld', -hīlt') also **Kriem·hil·de** (krēm-hĭl'də). In the Nibelungenlied, the wife of Siegfried and avenger of his murder.

krill (krĭl) *pl.n.* Small marine crustaceans of the order Euphausiacea, constituting the principal food of whalebone whales. [Norwegian *kril†*, young of fish.]

krim·mer (krĭm'ər) *n.* A gray, curly fur made from the pelts of lambs of the Crimean region. [German *Krimmer*, from *Krim*, the Crimean peninsula.]

Kri·o (krē'ō) *n., pl.* **-os. 1.** A creole language based on English and spoken in Sierra Leone. **2.** A native speaker of Krio. [Alteration of CREOLE.]

kris, creese (krēs) *n.* A sword of Malayan origin having a wavy double-edged blade. [Malay *kĕris*.]

Krish·na (krĭsh'nə) *n. Hinduism.* The eighth and principal avatar of the deity Vishnu, often depicted as a handsome young man playing a flute. [Hindi, "the black one," from Sanskrit *kṛṣṇáḥ*, black, dark blue, dark.] **—Krish·na·ism** *n.*

Kris·tian·sand (krĭs'chən-sănd'). Seaport of southern Norway. On the Skagerrak, it has shipbuilding, fishing, and timber industries.

Kriti. See **Crete.**

kro·na¹ (krō'nə) *n., pl.* **-nor** (-nôr', -nər'). *Abbr.* **k., K., kr. 1.** The basic monetary unit of Sweden, equal to 100 öre. See feature at **currency. 2.** A coin worth one krona. [Swedish, "crown," from Old Swedish *krūna, krōna*, from Latin *corōna*, wreath, CROWN.]

kro·na² *n., pl.* **-nur** (-nər). *Abbr.* **k., K., kr. 1.** The basic monetary unit of Iceland, equal to 100 aurar. See feature at **currency. 2.** A coin worth one krona. [Icelandic *krōna*, from Old Norse *krūna*, crown, from Middle Low German, from Latin *corōna*, CROWN.]

kro·ne (krō'nə) *n., pl.* **-ner** ((-nər).) *Abbr.* **k., K., kr. 1.** The basic monetary unit of Denmark and Norway, equal to 100 öre. See feature at **currency. 2.** A coin worth one krone. [Danish *krone* and Norwegian *krune*, "crown," from Old Norse *krūna*, from Latin *corōna*, CROWN.]

Kronos. Variant of **Cronos.**

Kron·shtadt (krŏn'shtät'). *German* **Kron·stadt** (krōn'stät'). Seaport and naval base of the U.S.S.R. on the island of Kotlin in the Gulf of Finland. Its importance declined in the 19th century after the construction of a deep-water canal to St. Petersburg.

Kro·pot·kin (krə-pŏt'kĭn), **Prince Pyotr Alexeyevich** (1842–1921). Russian anarchist revolutionary. He joined the anarchist movement in 1872 and was imprisoned in Russia (1874–76), but escaped. He settled in England in 1886.

KRP *Chess.* king's rook's pawn.

Kru (kroō) *n., pl.* **Krus** or collectively **Kru. 1.** A member of a Negro people living mainly on the coast of Liberia. **2.** The language of these people.

Kru·ger (kroō'gər), **(Stephanus Johannes) Paulus,** known as **"Oom Paul"** (1825–1904). Afrikaner leader of South Africa. His nationalist policies as president of the Transvaal Republic from 1883 led to the second Boer War (1899–1902). He fled the advancing British in 1900 and died in exile in Switzerland.

Kruger National Park. A wildlife preserve in northeast South Africa. Extending along the Mozambique border of the Transvaal, it occupies an area of 21,000 square kilometers (8,106 square miles). It originated as the Sabi Game Reserve, established by President Kruger in 1898 and opened to the public in 1928.

kru·ger·rand (kroō'gər-rănd', -ränd') *n.* A coin containing one troy ounce of pure gold, minted in South Africa but widely used by investors or speculators in gold. [Afrikaans, after S.J.P. KRUGER, whose portrait appears on the obverse + *rand*, rand.]

krummhorn. Variant of **crumhorn.**

Krung Thep (kroōng tĕp). *English* **Bang·kok** (băng'kŏk'). Capital and chief port of Thailand, on the Chao Phraya near the Gulf of Thailand. It is the country's main cultural, commercial, and industrial center and one of the leading cities of Southeast Asia, with an international jewelry market. Within the city are the royal palace and more than 400 Buddhist temples.

Kru·pa (kroō'pə), **Gene** (1909–73). U.S. musician. A renowned jazz drummer, he became famous with Benny Goodman's band (1935–38) for his virtuoso swing technique, flamboyant playing style, and flair for exciting solo work. He formed his own band in 1938 but continued to play with Goodman and others.

Krupp (krŭp). German family of arms manufacturers, whose factories in Essen were founded in the early 19th century and are still in production.

kryp·ton (krĭp'tŏn') *n. Symbol* **Kr** A whitish, inert gaseous element used chiefly in gas-discharge lamps, fluorescent lamps, and electronic flash tubes. Atomic number 36, atomic weight 83.80, melting point −156.6°C, boiling point −152.30°C, density 3.73 kg per m^3 (0°C). [New Latin, "hidden (element)," from Greek *krupton*, neuter of *kruptos*, hidden, from *kruptein*, to hide.]

KS Kansas (used with a Zip Code).

Ksha·tri·ya (kə-shăt'rē-ə, -chăt'rē-ə) *n.* **1.** A Hindu caste that includes the professional, governing, and military occupations. **2.** A member of the Kshatriya caste. See **caste.** [Sanskrit *kṣatriya*, "ruling, ruler," from *kṣatra*, rule, dominion, from *kṣayati*, he possesses, he rules.]

Kt knight.

kt. 1. karat. **2.** *Nautical.* knot.

K.T. Knight Templar.

Kua·la Lum·pur (kwä'lə loōm'poōr'). The capital of Malaysia, on the Kelang River. It is the commercial center of a tin-mining and rubber-growing area.

Kuang-chou. See **Guangzhou.**

Kuang-tung. See **Guangdong.**

Ku·blai Khan (koō'blī kän') (1215–94). First Mongol emperor of China. He was a grandson of Gengis Khan and became khan in 1259. He founded the Yuan dynasty (1279) and made Buddhism the state religion. Marco Polo spent 17 years at Kublai Khan's court.

Ku·brick (koō'brĭk', kyoō'-), **Stanley** (1928–). U.S. film director. His films include *Lolita* (1962), *Dr. Strangelove* (1963), *2001: A Space Odyssey* (1969), *A Clockwork Orange* (1971), and *The Shining* (1980).

ku·chen (koō'kən, -KHən) *n.* A yeast-raised coffee cake originally from Germany that contains fruits and nuts and is usually sprinkled with sugar and spices. [German *Kuchen*, from Middle High German *kuoche*, cake, from Old High German *kuocho*.]

ku·dos (kyoō'dŏs', -dōs', koō'-) *n., pl.* **kudos.** Acclaim or prestige as a result of achievement or position: *The prize gave him little material benefit but did bring kudos.* [Originally British university slang, from Greek *kudos*, glory, fame.]

Usage: *Kudos* is one of those words, like *congeries*, that look like plurals but are etymologically singular, and so it is correctly used with a singular verb: *Kudos is due her.*

ku·du, koo·doo (koō'doō) *n.* Either of two African antelopes, *Tragelaphus strepsiceros* or *T. imberbis*, having a brownish coat with narrow white vertical stripes and long, spirally curved horns in the male. [Afrikaans *koedoe*, from Xhosa *iqudu*.]

kud·zu (kŏŏd'zoō) *n.* A vine, *Pueraria lobata*, native to Japan, that has compound leaves and clusters of reddish-purple flowers and is grown for fodder and forage. [Japanese *kuzu*.]

Ku·fic, Cu·fic (koō'fĭk, kyoō'-) *adj.* Designating or pertaining to an early form of the Arabic alphabet used for making fine copies of the Koran. [Arabic *Al Kufah*, town in south-central Iraq, where such copies of the Koran were made.] **—Ku·fic** *n.*

Ku Klux Klan (koō' klŭks' klăn', kyoō') *n. Abbr.* **K.K.K. 1.** A secret society organized in the South after the Civil War to reassert white supremacy by terroristic methods. **2.** A secret fraternal organization founded in Georgia in 1915 and dedicated to maintaining legal and de facto segregation of blacks. [Said to be Greek *kuklos*, circle, CYCLE + *klan*, from CLAN.] **—Ku Klux·er** (koō klŭk'sər, kyoō) *n.* **—Ku Klux·ism** *n.*

kuk·ri (kŏŏk'rē) *n.* A large knife with a blade broadening to the point, used especially by the Gurkhas. [Hindi.]

ku·lak (koō-läk', -läk', kyoō-, koō'läk', -läk', kyoō'-) *n.* **1.** In Czarist Russia, a well-to-do or prosperous peasant. **2.** One of a class of Russian peasants who opposed the collectivization of farms during the October Revolution, a rich peasant or village usurer and landlord and regarded as an exploiter. [Russian *kulak*, fist, tight-fisted person, dated, from Turkic *kol*, their property confiscated or were themselves liquidated, akin to Turkish *kol.]

Krishna *The eighth and most important incarnation (avatar) of Vishnu, one of the principal gods of Hinduism. Krishna is a slayer of demons, a flute player, and a lover. This illustration, showing the blue-skinned god with his favorite mistress, Radha, dates from 1647.*

kudu *One of the largest antelopes, the kudu stands 1.3 meters (4¹/₂ feet) tall at the shoulder. It lives mainly in the savannah of southern and eastern Africa in small herds.*

Külek Boğazi. See Cilician Gates.

Kul·tur (kool-toor') *n.* Culture; especially, the authoritarian and chauvinistic aspects of German culture and civilization as idealized by the exponents of German imperialism during the period 1900–45. [German, from Latin *cultūra*, CULTURE.]

Kul·tur·kampf (kool-toor'kämpf') *n.* **1.** The struggle (1872–87) between the Roman Catholic Church and the German government for control over civil marriage and school and church appointments. **2.** Any conflict between secular and religious authorities. [German, "culture struggle."]

Kum. See Qom.

Ku·mas·i (koo-mä'sē). Formerly **Coo·mas·sie.** The second-largest city of Ghana. Capital of the Ashanti region west of Lake Volta, it is the country's major center for cocoa production and an important transport junction. The Golden Stool, the historical symbol of the Ashanti nation, is kept here.

ku·miss, kou·mis, kou·miss (koo-mĭs', koo'mĭs) *n.* The fermented milk of a mare or camel, drunk by certain peoples of western and central Asia. [Russian *kumys,* from Kazan Tatar *kumyz.*]

küm·mel (kĭm'əl, kü'məl) *n.* A colorless liqueur flavored with caraway seeds or cumin. [German *Kümmel,* "cumin seed," from Old High German *kumil, kumīn,* from Latin *cumīnum,* CUMIN.]

kum·quat, cum·quat (kŭm'kwŏt') *n.* **1.** Any of several trees or shrubs of the genus *Fortunella,* native to China, having small, edible, orangelike fruit. **2.** The citrus fruit of the kumquat, with an acid pulp and a thin, edible rind often used in preserves. [Cantonese *kam kwat, gam gwat,* corresponding to Mandarin Chinese *jīn jú,* "golden orange."]

Kun (koon), **Béla** (1885–c. 1939). Hungarian Communist leader. He formed the Hungarian Communist Party and became president of a coalition (1919), promising his allies Soviet support for war against Romania, but no support came. Kun fled to Vienna and then to the U.S.S.R., where he was executed in one of Stalin's purges.

Kunene. See Cunene.

kung fu (kŭng foo', koong) *n.* A martial art originating in China and resembling karate. [From Chinese *gōng fu,* skill.]

Kun·ming, K'un·ming (koon'mĭng'). Ancient walled city of southwest China. It is the capital of Yunnan province and the seat of Yunnan University.

kunz·ite (koont'sīt') *n.* A transparent lilac-colored variety of spodumene, used as a gemstone. [After George F. *Kunz* (1856–1932), gem expert.]

Kuo·yü, Guo·yü (gwô'yü', koo'yoo') *n.* **Mandarin Chinese** *(see).* [Mandarin Chinese *gúoyü* : *gúo,* nation, national + *yüh,* language.]

Kurd (kûrd, koord) *n.* A member of a formerly nomadic Muslim people living chiefly in Kurdistan.

Kurd·ish (kûr'dĭsh, koor'-) *adj.* Of or pertaining to the Kurds, their culture, or their language.
~n. The northwestern Iranian language of the Kurds.

Kurd·i·stan (kûr'dĭ-stän'). Area of western Asia. Lying west and southwest of the Caspian Sea, it was split among southeast Turkey, northern Syria, northern Iraq, northwestern Iran, and southern U.S.S.R. with the dissolution of the Ottoman Empire (1920). Its inhabitants, the Kurds, have been fighting for the establishment of an independent state.

Ku·ro·sa·wa (koor'ō-sä'wə), **Akira** (1910–). Japanese film director. His *Rashomon* won the 1951 Venice Film Festival Grand Prize and gave Japanese films international status. His work deals with traditional Japanese institutions, as in *The Seven Samurai* (1954) and *Kagemusha* (1980).

Kuroshio. See Japan Current.

kur·ra·jong (kûr'ə-jŏng', -jŏng') *n.* **1.** An Australian tree, *Brachychiton populneum,* having evergreen leaves and yellowish or reddish flowers. **2.** Any of several other Australian trees, such as the green kurrajong, *Hibiscus heterophyllus,* that have edible leaves and shoots. [Native Australian name.]

Kursk (koorsk). Industrial city in Russia. In 1943 Soviet forces routed a German army here in the world's largest tank battle.

kurta. Variant of khurta.

kur·to·sis (kər-tō'sĭs) *n. Statistics.* A deviation from the normal distribution curve in which the curve remains symmetrical but is either too sharp at the peak values *(positive kurtosis)* or too flat at the peak values *(negative kurtosis).* [Greek *kurtōsis,* convexity, curvature, from *kurtos,* convex.]

ku·ru (koor'oo) *n.* A fatal neurological disease caused by a virus, occurring in New Guinea, and characterized by tremors affecting the whole body. [New Guinea native name.]

ku·rus (kə-roosh') *n., pl.* **kurus.** A monetary unit, the Turkish piaster, equal to 1/100 of the lira (or pound) of Turkey. See feature at **currency.** [Turkish.]

Kush. See Cush.

Kushitic. Variant of Cushitic.

Ku·wait (koo-wāt'). Sheikhdom of western Asia. On the east coast of the Arabian Peninsula, it was settled in 1756 and was a British protectorate from 1899 to 1961. Oil was discovered in 1938 of Kuwait became one of the world's major oil-producing co... oil It was invaded by Iraq in 1990. Iraqi soldiers set fire to 17,818 Kuwait's oil wells upon retreat (1991). Before the 7,000,000. accounted for 80 percent of Kuwait's export *n. & adj.* square kilometers (6,878 square miles). Por Capital, Kuwait. See map at **Gulf States.**

Kuybyshev. See Samara.

Kuz·bas (kooz-bäs'). Also **Kuz·netsk Basin** (kooz-nyĕtsk'). Major industrial area of Russia, in western Siberia.

kV kilovolt.

kvass, kvas (kə-väs') *n.* A fermented Russian beverage similar to beer, made from rye or barley. [Russian *kvas.*]

kvetch (kə-vĕch') *intr.v.* **kvetched, kvetching, kvetches.** *Slang.* To complain or find fault in a persistent, querulous manner. *~ n. Slang.* A chronic and annoying complainer. [Yiddish, from German *quetschen,* to crush, squeeze, from Middle High German *quetzen.*]

kW kilowatt.

Kwa (kwä) *n.* A branch of the Niger-Congo language family that includes Ibo, Yoruba, and other languages of West Africa. **—Kwa** *adj.*

kwa·cha (kwä'chə) *n.* **1.** The basic monetary unit of Zambia, equal to 100 ngwee. **2.** The basic monetary unit of Malawi, equal to 100 tambala. See feature at **currency.** [Native word in Zambia.]

Kwangchow. See Guangzhou.

Kwangtung. See Guangdong.

kwan·za (kwän'zə) *n., pl.* **kwanza** or **-zas.** The basic monetary unit of Angola, equal to 100 lweis. See feature at **currency.** [Swahili.]

kwa·shi·or·kor (kwä'shē-ôr'kôr') *n.* Severe malnutrition caused by protein deficiency, occurring especially in African children, and characterized by anemia, edema, potbelly, depigmentation of the skin, and loss of hair or change in hair color. [Native word in Ghana.]

kWh kilowatt-hour.

KWIC (kwĭk) *n.* An index, usually generated by computer, in which key words are extracted together with the context in which the words appear. [*k*eyword *i*n *c*ontext.]

KY Kentucky (used with a Zip Code).

Ky. Kentucky.

ky·ack (kī'ăk') *n.* A packsack that hangs on either side of a packsaddle. [Origin unknown.]

ky·a·nite (kī'ə-nīt') *n.* Also **cy·a·nite** (sī'-). A bluish, greenish, or colorless mineral, essentially Al_2S_5, used as a refractory. [German *Zyanit* : *zyan(o)-,* CYANO- + -ITE.]

ky·a·nize (kī'ə-nīz') *tr.v.* **-nized, -zing, -nizes.** To treat (wood) with mercuric chloride in order to preserve it. **—ky·a·ni·za·tion** *n.*

kyat (chät) *n.* **1.** The basic monetary unit of Burma, equal to 100 pyas. See feature at **currency. 2.** A coin worth one kyat. [Burmese.]

kyle (kīl) *n.* In Scotland, a narrow strait, as between two islands. [Gaelic *caol,* narrow.]

ky·lin (kē'lĭn') *n.* A mythical animal used as a decoration on Chinese and Japanese pottery. [Mandarin Chinese *qílín* : *qí,* male + *lín,* female.]

ky·lix (kī'lĭks, kĭl'ĭks) *n., pl.* **-ikes** (kī'lĭ-kēz', kĭl'ĭ-). Also **cy·lix** (sī'lĭks, sĭl'ĭks), *pl.* **cylices** (-sēz', sĭl'ĭ-). A shallow, typically tall-stemmed drinking cup with two handles, used in ancient Greece. [Greek *kulix,* cup.]

ky·mo·graph (kī'mə-grăf', -äf') *n.* An instrument for recording variations in pressure, especially in blood pressure. [*Kymo-,* variant of *cymo-,* from CYME + -GRAPH.]

Kymric. Variant of Cymri.

Kymry. Variant of Cymry.

Kyo·to (kē-ō'tō, kyō'-). City in south-central Honshu, Japan. On the Kamo River, it is the capital of Kyoto prefecture and was Japan's capital from A.D. 794 until 1868, though its importance declined after the eclipse of the emperors by the shoguns (1192). It is the center of Buddhist Japan and has many historic palaces, temples, and shrines. Noted for craft industries, including brocades, porcelain, and lacquerware, it also manufactures chemicals, textiles, and machinery.

ky·pho·sco·li·o·sis (ō-skō'lē-ō'sĭs) *n.* Abnormal curvature of the spine both forward and sideways. [New Latin, from *kypho-,* from *kyphosis* + *scolio-*]

ky·pho·sis (kī-fō'...) ... Abnormal rearward curvature of the spine, caused by bone disease, bad posture, or congenital deformity. Also called "humpback," "hunchback." [Greek *kuphōsis,* from *kuphos,* bent, hunchbacked.] **—ky·phot·ic** (kī-fŏt'ĭk) *adj.*

Kypros. See ...

Kyr·i·e e·le·i·son (kĭr'ē-ā' ĭ-lā'ə-sŏn', sŏn, -sən) *n.* A liturgical prayer in some Christian churches beginning with or composed of the words "Lord, have mercy." [Late Latin, from Greek *Kurie eleēson,* "Lord, have mercy" : *Kurie,* vocative of *kurios,* lord, master, "powerful (one)," from *kuros,* power, supreme authority + *eleēson,* aorist imperative of *elein,* to show mercy, from *eleos,* pity, mercy (see **alms**).]

Kyrgiz. See Kirgiz².

Kyrzstan. See Kirgiz¹.

Kyu·shu (kyoo'shoo). One of the four major islands of Japan. The southerly, the third largest, and most densely populated of Japan's islands, it lies to the east of the Korea Strait and is joined to the chief Japanese island of Honshu, across the Shimonoseki Strait, by a road and rail bridge. Much of the island is mountainous, forcing a concentration of agriculture around the Chikugo River in the northwest. Its industries have developed around important coal fields in the north.

Ky·zyl Kum (kə-zĭl' koom'). Desert in central Asia, lying across the Kazakhstan-Uzbekistan border.
